# YEARBOOK OF THE
# UNITED NATIONS
# 1995

## Volume 49

# Yearbook of the United Nations, 1995

Volume 49                                    Sales No. E.96.I.1

Prepared by the Yearbook Section of the Department of Public Information, United Nations, New York. Although the *Yearbook* is based on official sources, it is not an official record.

*Chief Editor:* Elizabeth Flynn-Connors

*Senior Editors:* Christine B. Koerner, Kathryn Gordon

*Editors/Writers:* Melody C. Pfeiffer, Elizabeth Baldwin-Penn, Peter Jackson, Kikko Maeyama, Dmitri Marchenkov, Louis Germain

*Contributing Editors/Writers:* Juanita J. B. Phelan, Nancy Seufert-Barr

*Copy Editors:* Alison M. Koppelman, Janet E. Root, Bruce F. Murphy

*Copy Coordinator:* Leonard M. Simon

*Editorial Assistants:* Nidia H. Morisset, Lawri M. Moore

*Research Assistant:* Anahit Turabian

*Indexer:* Elaine Adam

*Senior Typesetter:* Sunita Chabra

*Jacket Designer:* Susan Reynolds

UN/DPI photo on p. 141 by E. Schneider
UN/DPI photo on p. 144 by G. Kinch

# YEARBOOK

## OF THE
## UNITED
## NATIONS
## 1995

Volume 49

Department of Public Information
United Nations, New York

Martinus Nijhoff Publishers
THE HAGUE / BOSTON / LONDON

Published by Martinus Nijhoff Publishers

P.O. Box 85889, 2508 CN The Hague, Netherlands

Kluwer Law International incorporates the
publishing programmes of Martinus Nijhoff Publishers

Sold and distributed in the U.S.A. and Canada
by Kluwer Law International,
101 Philip Drive, Norwell, MA 02061, U.S.A.

In all other countries, sold and distributed
by Kluwer Law International,
P.O. Box 85889, 2508 CN The Hague, Netherlands

Yearbook of the United Nations, 1995
Vol. 49
ISBN: 90-411-0376-7
ISSN: 0082-8521

| UNITED NATIONS PUBLICATION |
| --- |
| SALES NO. E.96.I.1 |

Printed in the United States of America

# *Foreword*

Signed a half century ago in San Francisco in June 1945, the United Nations Charter—the blueprint for the structure and work of the new world Organization—shaped the way for a new reality of global cooperation. For five decades, the United Nations has brought nations together to deal with challenges that no single nation could resolve on its own. Through the United Nations, the world has embraced the ideals of peace and security and has pledged itself to the goals of development and respect for human rights and international law. Within its halls, consensus can be built, sometimes on issues where Member States initially had diametrically opposed views, and strategies have been devised and implemented to realize the vision of a better world for all humanity.

The United Nations helped scores of nations to achieve independence; at the United Nations, they took their first steps as States on the international stage, and within the United Nations, they could assume their rightful place and gain recognition as equal members of the world community. Within the framework of the United Nations, the unique concept of peace-keeping was created and a strong and effective infrastructure established to protect and promote human rights. During its first fifty years of existence, the world Organization helped advance international law and promote economic and social development and cooperation. At the United Nations, disadvantaged and marginalized groups found a forum to redress long-standing injustices. In 1995, two striking examples were the World Summit for Social Development, which focused on social integration and alleviation of poverty, and the Fourth World Conference on Women in Beijing, which aimed to accelerate the process of advancing the status of women worldwide.

The Organization's celebration of its fiftieth anniversary in 1995 coincided with an era of profound worldwide change. To help harness that change for the benefit of all humanity, it has more than ever been making efforts to find ways to approach the complex new problems of the planet, helping States attain democracy vital for development and striving for solutions and progress. The new era is marked by both unprecedented levels of global cooperation in meeting common challenges, as well as by fierce conflicts centred around the assertion of national or ethnic identities, as seen most recently in the former Yugoslavia, Rwanda and Liberia.

The United Nations, as custodian of the common dream of global cooperation and an instrument of peace and justice, will endure and succeed. Its work, as recorded in the pages of the 1995 *Yearbook of the United Nations*, reflects those lofty ambitions and that common dream.

**KOFI ANNAN**
Secretary-General of the United Nations
New York, February 1997

# Contents

## Part One: *Political and security questions*

# Part Two: *Regional questions and peace-keeping*

# Part Three: *Human rights*

# Part Four: *Economic and social questions*

# Part Five: *Legal questions*

# Part Six: *Institutional, administrative and budgetary questions*

## Part Seven: *Intergovernmental organizations related to the United Nations*

# Appendices

# Indexes

# About the 1995 edition of the *Yearbook*

This volume of the *YEARBOOK OF THE UNITED NATIONS* continues the tradition of providing the most comprehensive and up-to-date coverage of the activities of the United Nations. It is an indispensable reference tool for the research community, diplomats, government officials and the general public seeking readily available information on the UN system and its related organizations.

The Department of Public Information of the United Nations remains committed to a timely annual publication of the *Yearbook* in order to ensure that the public receives detailed and current accounts of the work of the United Nations. However, the efforts to achieve timely publication have resulted in having to rely on provisional documentation and other materials to prepare the relevant articles. Largely, Security Council resolutions, presidential statements and some other texts in the present volume are provisional.

### Structure and scope of articles

The *Yearbook* is subject-oriented and divided into seven parts covering political and security questions, regional questions and peace-keeping, human rights issues, economic and social questions, legal questions, administrative and budgetary questions, and intergovernmental organizations related to the United Nations. Chapters and topical headings present summaries of pertinent UN activities, including those of intergovernmental and expert bodies, major reports, Secretariat activities and, in selected cases, the views of States in written communications. REFERENCES are listed either at the end of shorter chapters or after subchapters, linked to the text by numerical indicators.

**Activities of United Nations bodies.** All resolutions, decisions and other major activities of the principal organs and, on a selective basis, those of subsidiary bodies are either reproduced or summarized in the respective articles. The texts of all resolutions and decisions of substantive nature adopted in 1995 by the General Assembly, the Security Council and the Economic and Social Council are reproduced or summarized under the relevant topic. These texts are followed by the procedural details giving date of adoption, meeting number and vote totals (in favour-against-abstaining); information on their approval by a sessional or subsidiary body prior to final adoption, approved amendments and committee reports; and information on sponsors. Also given are the document symbols of any financial implications and relevant meeting numbers. Details are also provided of any recorded or roll-call vote on the resolution/decision as a whole.

**Major reports.** Most reports of the Secretary-General, in 1995, along with selected reports from other UN sources, such as seminars and working groups, are summarized briefly.

**Secretariat activities.** The operational activities of the United Nations for development and humanitarian assistance are described under the relevant topics. For major activities financed outside the UN regular budget, selected information is given on contributions and expenditures.

**Views of States.** Written communications sent to the United Nations by Member States and circulated as documents of the principal organs have been summarized in selected cases, under the relevant topics. Substantive actions by the Security Council have been analysed and brief reviews of the Council's deliberations given, particularly in cases where an issue was taken up but no resolution was adopted.

**Related organizations.** The *Yearbook* also briefly describes the 1995 activities of the specialized agencies and other related organizations of the UN system.

### Terminology

Formal titles of bodies, organizational units, conventions, declarations and officials are given in full on first mention in an article or sequence of articles. They are also used in resolution/decision texts, and in the SUBJECT INDEX under the key word of the title. Short titles may be used in subsequent references.

### How to find information in the *Yearbook*

The user may locate information on the United Nations activities contained in this volume by the use of the table of contents, the SUBJECT INDEX and the INDEX OF RESOLUTIONS AND DECISIONS. The volume also has five appendices: APPENDIX I comprises a roster of Member States; APPENDIX II reproduces the Charter of the United Nations, including the Statute of the International Court of Justice; APPENDIX III gives the structure of the principal organs of the United Nations; APPENDIX IV provides the agenda for each session of the principal organs in 1995; and APPENDIX V gives the addresses of the United Nations information centres and services worldwide.

*For more information on the United Nations and its activities, visit our Internet site at:*

**http://www.un.org**

# ABBREVIATIONS COMMONLY USED IN THE *YEARBOOK*

| | |
|---|---|
| ACABQ | Advisory Committee on Administrative and Budgetary Questions |
| ACC | Administrative Committee on Coordination |
| ASEAN | Association of South-East Asian Nations |
| CDP | Committee for Development Planning |
| CEDAW | Committee on the Elimination of Discrimination against Women |
| CERD | Committee on the Elimination of Racial Discrimination |
| CFA | Committee on Food Aid Policies and Programmes (WFP) |
| CILSS | Permanent Inter-State Committee on Drought Control in the Sahel |
| CPC | Committee for Programme and Coordination |
| DDSMS | Department for Development Support and Management Services |
| DESIPA | Department for Economic and Social Information and Policy Analysis |
| DHA | Department of Humanitarian Affairs |
| DPI | Department of Public Information |
| EC | European Community |
| ECA | Economic Commission for Africa |
| ECDC | economic cooperation among developing countries |
| ECE | Economic Commission for Europe |
| ECLAC | Economic Commission for Latin America and the Caribbean |
| ECOWAS | Economic Community of West African States |
| ESC | Economic and Social Council |
| ESCAP | Economic and Social Commission for Asia and the Pacific |
| ESCWA | Economic and Social Commission for Western Asia |
| EU | European Union |
| FAO | Food and Agriculture Organization of the United Nations |
| GA | General Assembly |
| GATT | General Agreement on Tariffs and Trade |
| GDP | gross domestic product |
| GNP | gross national product |
| IAEA | International Atomic Energy Agency |
| ICAO | International Civil Aviation Organization |
| ICJ | International Court of Justice |
| ICRC | International Committee of the Red Cross |
| ICSC | International Civil Service Commission |
| IDA | International Development Association |
| IFAD | International Fund for Agricultural Development |
| IFC | International Finance Corporation |
| ILC | International Law Commission |
| ILO | International Labour Organization |
| IMF | International Monetary Fund |
| IMO | International Maritime Organization |
| INCB | International Narcotics Control Board |
| INSTRAW | International Research and Training Institute for the Advancement of Women |
| IPF | indicative planning figure (UNDP) |
| ITC | International Trade Centre (UNCTAD/WTO) |
| ITU | International Telecommunication Union |
| JAG | Joint Advisory Group on the International Trade Centre |
| JIU | Joint Inspection Unit |
| LDC | least developed country |
| NATO | North Atlantic Treaty Organization |
| NGO | non-governmental organization |
| NPT | Treaty on the Non-Proliferation of Nuclear Weapons |
| NSGT | Non-Self-Governing Territory |

| | |
|---|---|
| OAS | Organization of American States |
| OAU | Organization of African Unity |
| ODA | official development assistance |
| OECD | Organisation for Economic Cooperation and Development |
| OIOS | Office of Internal Oversight Services |
| ONUMOZ | United Nations Operation in Mozambique |
| ONUSAL | United Nations Observer Mission in El Salvador |
| OPEC | Organization of Petroleum Exporting Countries |
| PLO | Palestine Liberation Organization |
| SC | Security Council |
| SDR | special drawing right |
| S-G | Secretary-General |
| TC | Trusteeship Council |
| TCDC | technical cooperation among developing countries |
| TDB | Trade and Development Board (UNCTAD) |
| TNC | transnational corporation |
| UN | United Nations |
| UNAMIR | United Nations Assistance Mission for Rwanda |
| UNAVEM | United Nations Angola Verification Mission |
| UNCDF | United Nations Capital Development Fund |
| UNCED | United Nations Conference on Environment and Development |
| UNCHS | United Nations Centre for Human Settlements (Habitat) |
| UNCITRAL | United Nations Commission on International Trade Law |
| UNCTAD | United Nations Conference on Trade and Development |
| UNDCP | United Nations International Drug Control Programme |
| UNDOF | United Nations Disengagement Observer Force (Golan Heights) |
| UNDP | United Nations Development Programme |
| UNEP | United Nations Environment Programme |
| UNESCO | United Nations Educational, Scientific and Cultural Organization |
| UNFICYP | United Nations Peace-keeping Force in Cyprus |
| UNFPA | United Nations Population Fund |
| UNHCR | Office of the United Nations High Commissioner for Refugees |
| UNIC | United Nations Information Centre |
| UNICEF | United Nations Children's Fund |
| UNIDIR | United Nations Institute for Disarmament Research |
| UNIDO | United Nations Industrial Development Organization |
| UNIFIL | United Nations Interim Force in Lebanon |
| UNIKOM | United Nations Iraq-Kuwait Observation Mission |
| UNITAR | United Nations Institute for Training and Research |
| UNOMIG | United Nations Observer Mission in Georgia |
| UNOMIL | United Nations Observer Mission in Liberia |
| UNOSOM | United Nations Operation in Somalia |
| UNPROFOR | United Nations Protection Force |
| UNRWA | United Nations Relief and Works Agency for Palestine Refugees in the Near East |
| UNSO | United Nations Sudano-Sahelian Office |
| UNU | United Nations University |
| UNV | United Nations Volunteers |
| UPU | Universal Postal Union |
| WFP | World Food Programme |
| WHO | World Health Organization |
| WIPO | World Intellectual Property Organization |
| WMO | World Meteorological Organization |
| WTO | World Trade Organization |
| YUN | *Yearbook of the United Nations* |

# EXPLANATORY NOTE ON DOCUMENTS

References at the end of each article in Parts One to Six of this volume give the symbols of the main documents issued in 1995 on the topic, arranged in the order in which they are referred to in the text. The following is a guide to the principal document symbols:

A/- refers to documents of the General Assembly, numbered in separate series by session. Thus, A/50/- refers to documents issued for consideration at the fiftieth session, beginning with A/50/1. Documents of special and emergency special sessions are identified as A/S- and A/ES-, followed by the session number.

A/C.- refers to documents of the Assembly's Main Committees, e.g. A/C.1/- is a document of the First Committee, A/C.6/-, a document of the Sixth Committee. A/BUR/- refers to documents of the General Committee. A/AC.- documents are those of the Assembly's ad hoc bodies and A/CN.-, of its commissions; e.g. A/AC.105/- identifies documents of the Assembly's Committee on the Peaceful Uses of Outer Space, A/CN.4/-, of its International Law Commission. Assembly resolutions and decisions since the thirty-first (1976) session have been identified by two arabic numerals: the first indicates the session of adoption; the second, the sequential number in the series. Resolutions are numbered consecutively from 1 at each session. Decisions of regular sessions are numbered consecutively, from 301 for those concerned with elections and appointments, and from 401 for all other decisions. Decisions of special and emergency special sessions are numbered consecutively, from 11 for those concerned with elections and appointments, and from 21 for all other decisions.

E/- refers to documents of the Economic and Social Council, numbered in separate series by year. Thus, E/1995/- refers to documents issued for consideration by the Council at its 1995 sessions, beginning with E/1995/1. E/AC.-, E/C.- and E/CN.-, followed by identifying numbers, refer to documents of the Council's subsidiary ad hoc bodies, committees and commissions. For example, E/CN.5/- refers to documents of the Council's Commission for Social Development, E/C.7/-, to documents of its Committee on Natural Resources. E/ICEF/- documents are those of the United Nations Children's Fund (UNICEF). Symbols for the Council's resolutions and decisions, since 1978, consist of two arabic numerals: the first indicates the year of adoption and the second, the sequential number in the series. There are two series: one for resolutions, beginning with 1 (resolution 1995/1); and one for decisions, beginning with 201 (decision 1995/201).

S/- refers to documents of the Security Council. Its resolutions are identified by consecutive numbers followed by the year of adoption in parentheses, beginning with resolution 1(1946).

T/- refers to documents of the Trusteeship Council. Its resolutions are numbered consecutively, with the session at which they were adopted indicated by Roman numerals, e.g. resolution 2196(LX) of the sixtieth session. The Council's decisions are not numbered.

ST/-, followed by symbols representing the issuing department or office, refers to documents of the United Nations Secretariat.

Documents of certain bodies bear special symbols, including the following:

| | |
|---|---|
| ACC/- | Administrative Committee on Coordination |
| CD/- | Conference on Disarmament |
| CERD/- | Committee on the Elimination of Racial Discrimination |
| DC/- | Disarmament Commission |
| DP/- | United Nations Development Programme |
| HS/- | Commission on Human Settlements |
| ITC/- | International Trade Centre |
| LOS/PCN/- | Preparatory Commission for the International Seabed Authority and for the International Tribunal for the Law of the Sea |
| TD/- | United Nations Conference on Trade and Development |
| UNEP/- | United Nations Environment Programme |

Many documents of the regional commissions bear special symbols. These are sometimes preceded by the following:

| | |
|---|---|
| E/ECA/- | Economic Commission for Africa |
| E/ECE/- | Economic Commission for Europe |
| E/ECLAC/- | Economic Commission for Latin America and the Caribbean |
| E/ESCAP/- | Economic and Social Commission for Asia and the Pacific |
| E/ESCWA/- | Economic and Social Commission for Western Asia |

''L'' in a symbol refers to documents of limited distribution, such as draft resolutions; ''CONF.'' to documents of a conference; ''INF.'' to those of general information. Summary records are designated by ''SR.'', verbatim records by ''PV.'', each followed by the meeting number.

United Nations sales publications each carry a sales number with the following components separated by periods: a capital letter indicating the language(s) of the publication; two arabic numerals indicating the year; a Roman numeral indicating the subject category; a capital letter indicating a subdivision of the category, if any; and an arabic numeral indicating the number of the publication within the category. Examples: E.95.II.A.2; E/F/R.95.II.E.7; E.95.X.1.

Report of the Secretary-General

# Report of the Secretary-General on the work of the Organization

*Following is the Secretary-General's report on the work of the Organization, introduced in the General Assembly on 17 October. The Assembly took note of it on 18 October* (**decision 50/405**).

## CONTENTS

## I. Introduction

1. Few events in recent history have generated as much confidence in the future and such high hopes for a better world as the fall of the Berlin Wall some five years ago, symbolizing as it did the end of the cold war. The spectre of global nuclear cataclysm, which has haunted humanity since the dawn of the nuclear age, has receded, and in its place has emerged the promise of an era

of international peace freeing the energies of nations to work together towards economic and social progress for the whole of humankind.

2. At the time, there was a widespread belief that when no longer fuelled by military assistance provided by rival major Powers, the many regional conflicts flaring in different parts of the world could be quickly extinguished. The global economy was expected to derive significant benefit from a huge ''peace dividend'' accruing as a result of the abandonment of the costly arms race. It was hoped that an important share of those resources would be invested in poor countries starved of capital and skills and thus help to accelerate economic growth and development worldwide.

3. Sadly, the record of world affairs over the past few years has largely belied those optimistic expectations. Many old conflicts continue to defy the efforts of the international community to bring about a settlement and new wars have continued to erupt, almost all of them within States. Most disappointingly, the total volume of assistance to developing countries has not only failed to show growth but has, in fact, declined.

4. The fiftieth anniversary of the United Nations is therefore not only a time to review the Organization's first half century and prepare it for its second: it is also an occasion to address ways to regain the momentum in world affairs that appeared so dramatically at the outset of this decade.

5. In the same manner as my first three annual reports to the General Assembly, my fourth report endeavours to place in focus the efforts of the Organization to respond effectively to the multitude of new demands and problems resulting from the dramatic changes engendered by the end of the cold war. Those efforts relate both to the long-term goals embodied in the Charter of the United Nations—now apparently more accessible as a result of the sea change in international relations—and to the immediate tasks arising from the outbreak of new conflicts in different parts of the world and the resulting increase in demand for the Organization's preventive, peacemaking, peace-keeping and peace-building services.

6. Addressing the implications for the Organization of the massive increase in the number and complexity of peace-keeping operations, and their profoundly changed nature, I pointed, in my previous annual report, to the widespread misperception of the United Nations as an organization dedicated primarily to peace-keeping. I underscored that, in the midst of its efforts to contain and resolve immediate conflicts by peace-keeping and other means, the United Nations remained determined to pay more attention to the foundations of peace, not least those lying in the realm of economic and social development.

7. During the past year acute armed conflicts have continued to place heavy demands on the Organization's financial and human resources and to dominate public perception of the United Nations role and effectiveness. The problems presented by conflicts such as those in the former Yugoslavia, Afghanistan, Liberia, Rwanda, Burundi and Somalia are in many ways unprecedented. More often than not the mandates and resources provided to the Organization to deal with them have proved to be inadequate to address effectively the complex tasks at hand. When journeying into uncharted territory with less-than-adequate means, set-backs are unavoidable. But these must not be allowed to become a source of disillusionment or to overshadow the successes that, notwithstanding formidable challenges, have been achieved by peace operations in various parts of the world, from Cambodia to Mozambique to El Salvador to Angola. Nor must adversity be allowed to weaken our resolve to carry forward efforts to save human lives and prevent larger conflicts, for which the United Nations remains an irreplaceable instrument. On the contrary, the set-backs suffered in the quest for peace and security must reinforce our determination to take the hard decisions required and seek continuously to develop improved approaches as a means of enhancing our capacity and effectiveness. With these objectives in mind, I issued, in January 1995, a Supplement to ''An Agenda for Peace'' (A/50/60-S/1995/1), which has been the subject of a presidential statement in the Security Council and is now being studied by the General Assembly. The experience of the past several months has given added force to the recommendations in the Supplement.

8. While the issues before the international community in this regard require careful and urgent attention, it is also extremely important that the difficulties encountered in peace-keeping operations, significant and disturbing as they may be, should not divert attention from other dimensions of the work of the Organization, which, though less visible, are equally essential and serve to lay the economic and social foundation for lasting peace.

9. In the domain of economic and social development, as in the area of peace-keeping, the international context within which the United Nations operates and the challenges that it faces have greatly changed. In the economic and social fields, as in the political, many areas of great concern remain where the United Nations has not, as yet, proved equal to the challenge. The situation of the least developed countries and of many parts of Africa remains critical. At the same time, the effort of the United Nations in support of development is vast and rich with distinct accomplish-

ments. As such, it deserves better recognition and enhanced political and public support.

10. At both the practical and the conceptual levels, the period covered by the present report has been marked by notable advances in the Organization's capacity to guide the response of the international community to global change and to the new forms of economic and social problems facing the world.

11. I attach great importance, in this regard, to the ongoing discussions within the framework of the General Assembly on "An Agenda for Development". The first report on the subject, which I presented to the Assembly in May 1994 (A/48/935), was followed by hearings and submissions by a variety of sources and was then drawn upon in a large number of statements made during the general debate at the forty-ninth session of the General Assembly. In that light, I submitted to the Assembly, in November 1994, a set of recommendations aimed at giving practical force to the emerging consensus on the priorities and dimensions of development (A/49/665). Such consensus is being further advanced through the working group that is preparing the further consideration of the matter at the fiftieth session of the General Assembly.

12. In the same context, I have been particularly encouraged by the support that the role of the United Nations in the economic and social fields and the current work on the elaboration of "An Agenda for Development" have received at the annual summit meeting of Heads of State and Government of the seven major industrialized nations. The communiqué issued at Halifax in June 1995 (A/50/254-S/1995/501, annex I) specifically declared the readiness of the Group of Seven to work with others in order to set out a fresh approach to international cooperation and to define the particular contribution expected of United Nations bodies.

13. At the same time, the ongoing series of global conferences on key issues of development was carried forward with the World Summit for Social Development, held in March 1995, at Copenhagen. On that occasion a start was made towards combined and effective action across borders to address poverty, unemployment and social disintegration. In Beijing, where the Fourth World Conference on Women will be held this September, the world will act upon the newly achieved recognition that the advancement of women is fundamentally critical to the solution of many of the world's most pressing social, economic and political problems. These conferences will be followed next year by the United Nations Conference on Human Settlements (Habitat II) and the ninth session of the United Nations Conference on Trade and Development (UNCTAD).

14. A sustained, coordinated follow-up to those conferences, together with a renewed effort in support of African development, has been the main focus of extensive consultations I have held during the year with the heads of the Bretton Woods institutions and the executive heads of the other agencies represented in the Administrative Committee on Coordination. These are covered in the section of the report dealing with the work of the Secretariat, as well as in the chapter of the report dealing with development, humanitarian action and human rights as the foundations of peace, chapter III.

15. During the period covered by the present report, I have continued to emphasize the essential linkages between the political and development missions of the United Nations and to advance a comprehensive vision of the role of the Organization where the advancement of human rights and democracy are essential elements of both of those missions.

16. In parallel with the efforts to enhance the Organization's capacity in the field of peace and security and to introduce an improved conceptual framework for pursuing the Organization's development mission, reforms in the structures and methods of work of the Organization are gaining momentum.

17. To this end, I have put forward a management plan designed to create a mission-driven and result-oriented organization. In carrying out the plan, the achievement of five objectives is fundamental:

*(a)* Better management of human resources, together with improvement in staff member capabilities and accomplishments;

*(b)* Better management of the Organization's programme, from the identification of strategic priorities, through the budgetary process by which resources are allocated to achieve those priorities and finally through a performance measurement system by which programme managers are held accountable for achieving the strategic priorities;

*(c)* Better information with which to manage, and its timely availability;

*(d)* Better management of technology and extension of its availability throughout the Organization;

*(e)* Better management of the Organization's cost structure and an enhanced programme for promoting efficiency and cost-effectiveness.

18. Reforming the United Nations into a simpler, more focused and more integrated organization, capable of pursuing the different aspects of its mission in a mutually reinforcing way and in the most efficient manner possible, has continued to be a key objective of my efforts during the past year, as it has been since I took office in January 1992. As described in the report, the past 12

months have seen further tangible progress towards streamlining operations, strengthening accountability, tightening personnel and management standards, and eliminating waste and redundancy. I am, in this context, deeply committed to continuing to reduce the budget further while improving the quality of service to Member States.

19.    In pursuing those efforts, I am keenly aware that Secretariat reform, to be truly effective, must be part of a larger restructuring effort including the intergovernmental machinery to adapt the Organization as a whole to the demands of the post-cold-war era. Such a process requires the determination and full commitment of all Member States.

20.    A crucial component of that larger reform process should be the achievement of a more dynamic relationship among the main intergovernmental organs—the General Assembly, the Security Council and the Economic and Social Council. I hope that the account of developments in the work of those organs in chapter II of the present report will prove helpful in considering what adjustments and further improvements can be introduced in this regard.

21.    Within the realm of activities covered by the Economic and Social Council, further steps to ensure more coherent management of operational activities carried out under the aegis of the various programmes and funds of the United Nations, as well as improved coordination of the humanitarian activities carried out by various parts of the Organization, are other essential elements of reform requiring renewed attention at the intergovernmental level.

22.    In the same context, I am firmly convinced that no reform effort can succeed without addressing the basic issue of providing the Organization with a more adequate and reliable financial base. This issue is developed in chapter II of the present report, where I endeavour to highlight the seriousness of the financial crisis facing the Organization. The difficult financial situation is compounded by the continuing late payment of contributions by many Governments. It is increasingly proving to be the most serious obstacle to the effective management of the Organization. I therefore particularly appreciate the serious effort under way in the High-level Open-ended Working Group on the Financial Situation of the Organization, established during the forty-ninth session of the General Assembly, to devise constructive and long-lasting solutions in this crucial area.

23.    Two other, related dimensions of the ongoing reform effort need to be highlighted and are given prominence in the present report.

24.    One relates to the expansion in the depth and coverage of the assistance provided by the Or-

ganization to Member States in the process of democratization. Requests for electoral assistance continue to grow. Beyond this type of assistance, there is a growing demand for United Nations support in preparing the social, as well as institutional, ground in which democracy can take root. I hope that the development of a comprehensive approach to the role of the United Nations in these areas will be further advanced at the fiftieth session of the General Assembly, in the light of the report on the subject I have submitted pursuant to General Assembly resolution 49/30 of 7 December 1994 (A/50/332).

25.    The past year has also deepened awareness that the efforts of States to democratize will have an increased likelihood of success when democratization extends to the international arena. The progressive opening of the United Nations to civil society is an important part of this process. Also in this respect, the global conferences held by the United Nations in recent years are making a crucial contribution. By bringing together State as well as non-State actors they are serving to create strong, worldwide, issue-based constituencies around key dimensions of development. The democratic nature of this conference series contributes immensely to the legitimacy and effectiveness of the programmes of action being adopted.

26.    Indeed, the new world environment clearly demands more systematic cooperation between the United Nations and all other actors engaged in promoting political and economic security at all levels, whether they be regional or subregional organizations (progress in cooperation with these entities is covered in chapter IV of the present report), or non-State actors such as citizen groups, grass-roots movements and nongovernmental organizations of all types. The strengthening of coordination and cooperation between these actors and the various elements of the United Nations system can serve only to enhance effectiveness in fulfilling the goals of the Charter. It also serves to reinforce democratic principles in world affairs and in the emerging international system.

27.    I have sought in this report to provide a clear and comprehensive account of the work of the Organization as it helps Member States to make the transition to a new international era. I firmly believe that success in this great task requires nothing less than the full participation of all concerned—not only the United Nations and its Member States, but individuals, the private sector, the academic community and nongovernmental, regional and international organizations. It is to inspire the widest reflection upon and assessment of the only world Organization at our disposal, and in accordance with Article 98

of the Charter of the United Nations, that I submit the present annual report.

## II. Coordinating a comprehensive strategy

### A. *Organs of the United Nations*

28. While pursuing an extremely heavy work schedule, the organs of the United Nations have consolidated reforms in their work programmes during this year, allowing for greater gains in efficiency.

#### 1. General Assembly

29. During its forty-ninth session, the General Assembly has continued to focus on issues related to the maintenance of peace and security, economic and social development and strengthening and reform of the United Nations to enhance its ability to fulfil the goals of the Charter in a world that has changed dramatically since the Charter was drafted.

30. By comparison with 20 years ago, there has been a shift of emphasis. The Assembly now devotes somewhat less attention than it did then to the main regional conflicts, several of which have fortunately been resolved during the last decade, and devotes more time to economic and social matters and to a number of generic questions of primordial importance for the effective functioning of the Organization, notably a cluster of financial issues. These arise from the failure of Member States to pay their assessed contributions in full and on time and from the enormous expansion in the cost of peace-keeping, which has risen from about $626 million per annum in 1986 to about $3.6 billion in 1995.

31. The Organization now faces a very serious financial situation. In a statement to the Assembly on 12 October 1994, I drew attention to this, emphasizing that it had become an urgent political question. I was gratified by the Assembly's subsequent decision to establish a high-level working group and to entrust to it the consideration of additional measures to ensure a sound and viable financial basis for the Organization. That working group has worked intensively during 1995. I addressed it on 22 June and sought its urgent assistance in averting a serious financial crisis. In parallel, the Assembly established another working group of experts on the principle of capacity to pay.

32. An index of the severity of the current problems is that the Organization as at January 1995 owed some $850 million to Governments who have contributed troops and equipment to peace-keeping operations. This debt represents an involuntary loan to the Organization by Member States who have in addition accepted the risk of exposing their young men and women to the perils of peace-keeping. This is manifestly unjust.

33. Another index is the number of Member States whose arrears exceed the contributions due for the last two years and who are therefore, under Article 19 of the Charter, unable to vote in the General Assembly. As at mid-August, they numbered 17, nearly 10 per cent of the membership. A number of other Member States have indicated to the President of the Assembly that they are not able to meet their obligations under Article 17 and will therefore also soon lose their right to vote.

34. As regards the financing of peace-keeping, the General Assembly reaffirmed at its forty-ninth session that the costs of peace-keeping are the collective responsibility of all Member States in accordance with Article 17 of the Charter. The Assembly also adopted procedures to strengthen the administrative and budgetary aspects of peace-keeping, including the establishment of a financial year for each peace-keeping operation starting on 1 July and a request to the Secretary-General to submit twice a year, for the Assembly's information, a table summarizing the proposed budgetary requirements of each operation.

35. Development continued to receive special attention from the General Assembly, emphasizing that the importance of this aspect of the Organization's activities should not be overshadowed by the intense public interest in its peace-keeping activities. The holding of three important United Nations conferences during a period of 12 months (on population and development in Cairo in September 1994, on social development in Copenhagen in March 1995 and on women in Beijing in September 1995) was evidence of the importance that Member States attach to the Organization's role in the economic and social fields.

36. On 6 May 1994, I published "An Agenda for Development" (A/48/935). In response the General Assembly established an ad hoc open-ended working group to elaborate further an action-oriented, comprehensive agenda that would take into account reports and recommendations presented by the Secretary-General, the work of the Economic and Social Council, views expressed in the Assembly itself and a number of other views and proposals.

37. The question of enlargement of the Security Council attracted intense interest throughout the period under review, as a possible means of making more efficient and democratic the work of the Organization in the field of peace and security. In September 1994 the General Assembly reviewed the progress report of the Open-ended Working Group on the Question of Equitable Representation on and Increase in the Membership of the Security Council and other matters related to the Security Council, and decided that the Working Group should continue its work and submit a report before the end of the forty-ninth session. The Working Group has held 21 meetings and a number of informal consultations and

has addressed two clusters of issues, the first covering the size and composition of the Council, including permanent, non-permanent and new categories of membership, and the second the Council's working methods and procedures, its efficiency and effectiveness, and its relationship with other United Nations organs.

38.   The Assembly has increasingly adopted the informal, open-ended working group as an effective instrument in seeking solutions to major problems relating to the efficient working of the Organization. These bodies, each comprising the entire membership, have been instrumental in allowing a concentrated and issue-specific exchange of views on Security Council reform, "An Agenda for Peace", "An Agenda for Development", the financial situation of the United Nations and, most recently, the strengthening of the United Nations system. The activities of these working groups, their interrelated mandates, the depth and complexity of their deliberations and the frequency of their meetings pose a challenge to the capacity of the Secretariat to provide the required substantive and technical support from within already scarce resources.

39.   The agenda for the forty-ninth session comprised 164 items, a reduction from 180 items in the previous session (*see fig. 1*). This results from the consolidation of related items and the decision to discuss some of them only every second or third year. Further rationalization seems possible. Broadly worded agenda items allow flexibility to examine several topics or aspects of a question under a single item. Areas where this possibility could be explored are disarmament (18 items on the agenda of the forty-ninth session), cooperation between the United Nations and intergovernmental organizations (5), decolonization (5) and the financing of peace-keeping operations (19). There are also 10 items that have not been considered at all for several years.

40.   An issue closely related to the number of items on the agenda is the number and periodicity of reports requested by the Assembly. In addition to the reports of principal organs and their subsidiary bodies, over 200 reports of the Secretary-General were issued at the forty-ninth session, not including several reports of special rapporteurs and of the Office of Internal Oversight Services. The difficulties and expense involved in producing so many reports in a timely manner are evident, given the frequency with which the Assembly and other principal and subsidiary organs now meet. Streamlining and cost-cutting efforts cannot ultimately succeed unless the number of reports requested is significantly reduced.

41.   During the forty-ninth session of the General Assembly, its General Committee and its Main Committees held 377 meetings, as compared with a total of 401 during the forty-eighth session and 426 during the forty-seventh session. The Main Committees held 237 informal meetings and consultations, a decrease from the 285 held during the forty-eighth session. Meetings held by working groups increased to 141 from the previous session's 86. The Assembly has so far adopted 324 resolutions during its forty-ninth session, compared with 333 during the forty-eighth session. Some 79 per cent were adopted without a vote or by consensus, as compared with 81 per cent at the previous session. The number of Heads of State and Government who participated in the general debate of the Assembly rose from 43 (23 per cent of the membership) to 45 (24 per cent) at the forty-ninth session (*see fig. 2*).

## 2.   Security Council

42.   During the period under review, the Security Council has continued to meet, on an almost daily basis, to review the issues on its agenda, to warn about the threats to peace around the world, to call on antagonists to restrain their ardour for combat, to take various types of action to control and resolve conflicts, and to muster regional and international support for those measures (*see fig. 3*). Towards these objectives, the Security Council has demonstrated a determination to unify its ranks in order to address more effectively the various complex issues that confront it today. One of the Council's greatest contributions has been its patient and deliberate search for consensus within its own ranks. This positive trend has enabled Council members to approach the issues on its agenda with a greater degree of harmony and cohesion (*see figs. 4 and 5*).

43.   The main focus of the Security Council's concern has been the former Yugoslavia and central Africa. In the former Yugoslavia the Council endeavoured to defuse the conflicts, prevent their further spread and mitigate their impact on civilian populations. To that end, it addressed many issues, including the changing peace-keeping role of the United Nations, humanitarian emergencies, mass violations of human rights and the difficult issues arising from the use of United Nations troops to protect humanitarian relief deliveries. The Council also offered active support to efforts by interested Member States, in particular those comprising the Contact Group, as well as the International Conference on the Former Yugoslavia, to bring about negotiated solutions to the conflicts in the region. The Council continued to make active use of mandatory sanctions as a means of achieving the above purposes. The Council's determination to ensure the resolution of the crises in a comprehensive way, as well as to strengthen cooperation between the United Nations and relevant regional organizations, in par-

ticular the European Union (EU) and the North Atlantic Treaty Organization (NATO), still offers the best hope of bringing to an end the human tragedy in the former Yugoslavia.

44. At the beginning of the period under review, the Security Council had authorized the deployment of six major peace-keeping operations in Africa, more than in any other continent. Four of them remain, the one in Mozambique having completed its mandate with conspicuous success and the one in Somalia having been withdrawn after it had succeeded in its humanitarian efforts but had been denied the necessary cooperation of the Somali parties with efforts to promote national reconciliation. In addition to the four remaining peace-keeping operations, in Angola, Liberia, Rwanda and Western Sahara, the Council has been concerned with peace-making efforts in other African countries, especially Burundi and Sierra Leone. During the period under review the Council dispatched an unprecedented number of missions, all of them to African destinations: Burundi (twice), Mozambique, Rwanda, Somalia and Western Sahara. The conflicts in Africa, like those in the former Yugoslavia, are primarily internal, but they have major implications for the security of the subregions concerned. As in the former Yugoslavia, they have disastrous humanitarian consequences, and the Council has had to devote as much attention to alleviating the misery of the civilian populations affected as to efforts to control and resolve the conflicts. Cooperation with the Organization of African Unity (OAU) and with subregional organizations in Africa has been an important feature of the Security Council's efforts.

45. Seven sanctions regimes remain in effect and generate much work for the Council. In order to ensure the adequate servicing of the various sanctions committees and the expeditious processing by the Secretariat of applications for humanitarian supplies, I have reinforced the unit responsible in the Department of Political Affairs. For their part, the sanctions committees, drawing on their own experience, have initiated measures to streamline their working procedures and to ensure greater transparency in the conduct of their work in conformity with a set of measures decided by the Security Council (see S/1995/234).

46. Cooperation on sanctions with regional organizations has been important, with special reference to the contributions of the Organization of American States (OAS) in Haiti and of EU and the Organization for Security and Cooperation in Europe (OSCE) in the former Yugoslavia. The temporary assignment of liaison officers from the EU/OSCE Sanctions Assistance Missions Communications Centre has provided the Secretariat and the relevant committees with customs expertise and with advice on the practical implementation

and monitoring of sanctions. Member States could further assist the efforts of the committees and the Secretariat by screening more effectively their nationals' applications to the committees and by cooperating in further streamlining of the committees' procedures.

47. In order to ensure that sanctions remain a credible instrument for promoting international peace and security, Member States will need to address a range of problems encountered in the implementation of sanctions. Recommendations in this regard were put forward in my Supplement to "An Agenda for Peace" (A/50/60-S/1995/1).

48. The Security Council's methods of work received consideration during an extensive debate on the annual report of the Council to the General Assembly at its forty-ninth session. Member States exchanged views on a broad range of issues related to the functioning of the Council. The Council made known its intention, as part of its efforts to improve the flow of information and the exchange of ideas between members of the Council and other Member States, to have increased recourse to open meetings, in particular at an early stage in its consideration of a subject, on a case-by-case basis. The Council has already initiated the holding of orientation debates. Briefings by the President of the Security Council for States non-members of the Council have become institutionalized.

49. In the face of persisting conflict in Africa, Europe and elsewhere, the Security Council has demonstrated that it remains committed to the goals of strengthening peaceful and cooperative relations between Member States and helping communities within States to live peacefully with one another, to rebuild and to work towards stable and productive societies.

50. It must be emphasized, however, that only if the decisions of the Security Council enjoy the full support of the international community, and only if the parties to the conflict carry out those decisions in full, can the Council fulfil its responsibilities under the Charter to maintain and consolidate international peace and security.

### 3. Economic and Social Council

51. The Economic and Social Council held its substantive session from 26 June to 28 July 1995 at Geneva. The Council's high-level segment dealt with one of the most pressing issues on the international agenda: the development of Africa. A spirit of partnership prevailed during the debate in the Council and conclusions were reached on conflict prevention and resolution, natural disasters, external debt, resource flows, trade, capacity-building, agriculture and food security, and other areas. The segment was attended by a large number of ministers and other high-level representatives. One day was devoted to a policy

dialogue with Mr. Michel Camdessus, Executive Director of the International Monetary Fund (IMF), Mr. James Wolfensohn, President of the World Bank, Mr. Renato Ruggiero, Director-General of the World Trade Organization, and Mr. Carlos Fortin, Officer-in-Charge of UNCTAD, on major issues in the world economy.

52.   The Council's coordination segment addressed the coordinated follow-up and implementation of the results of major recent international conferences in the economic, social and related fields. The agreed conclusions envisage the integrated consideration by the General Assembly of themes common to those conferences with a view to promoting better coherence and integrated policy guidance. This may involve measures to improve the coherence of the work of the relevant Main Committees of the Assembly. The Council, for its part, decided to carry out an annual review of cross-cutting themes common to major international conferences and to take action to ensure the necessary coordination of agendas and work programmes of the functional commissions involved in the follow-up to the various international conferences. Attention was also given to measures for the strengthening of inter-agency coordination at the regional and country levels, and to the role of the resident coordinators in facilitating national reporting on progress achieved in the follow-up to global conferences. The Council invited the Administrative Committee on Coordination to bring system-wide coordination issues to the attention of the Council and to make recommendations thereon. Implementation of the agreed conclusions will enhance complementarity and coherence between the Council and the General Assembly, including their subsidiary bodies, as well as interaction between the United Nations and the Bretton Woods institutions and the World Trade Organization. The complementary steps initiated by the Administrative Committee on Coordination to pursue conference agendas within a common framework will promote unity of purpose and action in the United Nations system as a whole.

53.   The operational activities segment began to exercise its new mandate to provide policy guidance to the United Nations funds and programmes. The guidance provided covers priorities in budget allocations, improved coherence in country programmes and improved cost-effectiveness of administrative services, including the possible use of common administrative services at the field level. The Council reaffirmed the need to increase substantially the availability of resources allocated to operational activities for development on a predictable, continuous and assured basis commensurate with the needs of developing countries.

54.   In line with these conclusions and in accordance with General Assembly resolution 47/199 of 22 December 1992, I will submit to the Assembly a range of specific recommendations, in the context of the triennial comprehensive policy review of operational activities, on further steps to strengthen the role of the Economic and Social Council in this field and on important subjects such as improved substantive operational coordination at the country level, increasing the predictability and levels of resources, strengthening the resident coordinator system and a variety of programme tools such as the country strategy note, the programme approach and national execution.

55.   The Council initiated a review of arrangements for consultations with non-governmental organizations. By its resolution 1993/80, the Council established the Open-ended Working Group on the Review of Arrangements for Consultations with Non-Governmental Organizations. A primary objective is to update and introduce coherence in the rules governing the participation of non-governmental organizations in international conferences convened by the United Nations. The Council requested the Working Group to examine ways and means of improving practical arrangements for the work of the Committee on Non-Governmental Organizations and the Non-Governmental Organizations Unit of the Secretariat.

56.   The Working Group held its first substantive session from 20 to 24 June 1994. An intersessional meeting took place on 7 and 8 November 1994. Its second substantive session was held from 8 to 12, 26 and 31 May 1995. At its substantive session, the Economic and Social Council approved the recommendation of the Working Group that its mandate be extended for one year and that its final report be presented to the Council at its substantive session of 1996.

57.   In accordance with Economic and Social Council resolution 1994/24, a Committee of Co-Sponsoring Organizations was constituted by the heads of the six co-sponsors of the joint programme on HIV/AIDS (the United Nations Children's Fund (UNICEF), the United Nations Development Programme (UNDP), the United Nations Population Fund (UNFPA), the United Nations Educational, Scientific and Cultural Organization (UNESCO), the World Health Organization (WHO) and the World Bank) known as UNAIDS. As the United Nations system's main advocate for the global response to the HIV/AIDS epidemic, UNAIDS has three mutually reinforcing roles: to provide globally relevant policy on HIV/AIDS and promote international best practice and research; to provide technical support for an expanded response to HIV/AIDS, particularly in

developing countries; and to advocate a comprehensive, multisectoral response to HIV/AIDS, well-resourced and strategically, ethically and technically sound.

58. At its second meeting, on 12 December 1994, the Committee of Co-Sponsoring Organizations unanimously recommended Dr. Peter Piot as director of the UNAIDS programme and the Secretary-General appointed Dr. Piot as Executive Director for a period of three years starting on 1 January 1995. On 5 May, the Economic and Social Council decided on the regional distribution of seats for 22 Member States to be represented on the Programme Coordinating Board of UNAIDS. It decided that each of the six co-sponsoring organizations, as well as five non-governmental organizations, would participate in the work of the Board. The Board held its first meeting on 13 and 14 July at Geneva.

59. The Commission for Social Development began its consideration of arrangements for the follow-up to the World Summit for Social Development's Copenhagen Declaration on Social Development and Programme of Action at its thirty-fourth session, held in New York from 10 to 20 April 1995. The Economic and Social Council concluded that the scope and methods of work of the Commission should be adapted to enable it to play a more effective role in promoting an integrated approach to social development in the aftermath of the World Summit. It decided that the Commission should hold a special session in 1996 to review from this perspective its mandate, terms of reference and scope of work, elaborate a multi-year programme of work and make recommendations to the Council on the frequency of the Commission's meetings.

60. During its session the Commission also heard the first report of Mr. Bengt Lindqvist, the Special Rapporteur on the Monitoring of the Standard Rules for the Equalization of Opportunities for Persons with Disabilities. The Commission also started preparations for the International Year of Older Persons, to be observed in 1999, and advanced the preparations of a world programme of action for youth, to be adopted by the General Assembly during its fiftieth session.

61. The Commission on Sustainable Development held its third session, including its high-level segment, in New York from 11 to 28 April 1995. More than 40 ministers attended, holding portfolios such as the environment, forestry, agriculture, tourism, development and finance. Fifty-five Governments submitted national reports on their activities in support of sustainable development by the twenty-first century. The session included panel discussions between senior officials from Governments, international financial institutions, United Nations agencies and pro-

grammes, the business community and non-governmental organizations. Two days were dedicated to the sharing of national experiences in implementing Agenda 21, adopted by the United Nations Conference on Environment and Development in June 1992, and a "Day of Local Authorities" examined grass-roots efforts to achieve sustainable development. These initiatives received welcome support from the large number of non-governmental organizations attending the session, who see in the Commission a transparent and participatory mechanism for addressing sustainable development concerns, including those at the national and community levels. The Commission agreed to establish an intergovernmental panel to formulate by 1997 coordinated proposals for action with regard to the management, conservation and sustainable development of all types of forest. The Commission also endorsed work programmes on consumption and production patterns, the elaboration of sustainable development indicators and the transfer of environmentally sound technology.

62. The concluding high-level segment (26-28 April) of the Commission addressed challenges on the path towards the full implementation of Agenda 21. The Chairman's summary noted that the insufficiency of the financial resources available to support national efforts, particularly in developing countries and economies in transition, remains a continuing constraint to achieving sustainable development.

63. The Committee on New and Renewable Sources of Energy and on Energy for Development, a subsidiary expert body of the Economic and Social Council, held a special session on rural development from 6 to 17 February. It proposed a strategy that would include development of national sustainable energy action programmes for agricultural and rural development; priority for rural energy development; capacity-building in rural energy development; new directions in management and institutional arrangements; new financial and investment arrangements; accelerated development and implementation of new technologies; new international actions for rural energy development; and strengthening of sustainable energy activities within the United Nations system. The Commission on Sustainable Development agreed at its April 1995 session to encourage Governments to integrate renewable forms of energy into their national strategies for sustainable and rural development. It urged Governments to support efforts of interested developing countries towards the sustainable use of an appropriate mix of fossil and renewable sources of energy for rural communities.

64. The Fourth World Conference on Women: Action for Equality, Development and

Peace is intended to coalesce reflection about the advancement of women and propose new directions into the twenty-first century. During the autumn of 1994 regional preparatory meetings were held in four regions, a number of expert group meetings on specific themes were organized and informal consultations were held with Member States on the draft of the platform for action. From 16 March to 7 April, the Commission on the Status of Women, acting as preparatory committee for the Conference, met and continued negotiations on the platform for action. Subsequent to the session, the focus shifted to promoting participation by Governments and non-governmental organizations in the Conference, ensuring public information about it and supporting the intergovernmental negotiation process. From 31 July to 4 August, informal consultations were convened by the chairperson of the Commission to continue negotiations. The Conference preparations have involved the largest number of non-governmental organizations ever accredited for a United Nations conference and a major effort has been made to facilitate their participation in the process.

65.   The Division for the Advancement of Women completed, as conference documents, two major studies, one entitled ''Women in a Changing Global Economy: The 1994 World Survey on the Role of Women in Development'', and the second a review and appraisal of the Nairobi Forward-looking Strategies for the Advancement of Women. In-depth studies of women and education and training, women in international decision-making and women in economic decision-making were also completed. Steps have been taken to ensure that the relevant human rights mechanisms of the United Nations regularly address violations of the rights of women, including gender-specific abuses, through provision of gender-based information to treaty bodies, work on the development of an optional protocol to the Convention on the Elimination of All Forms of Discrimination against Women and work on guidelines for integrating gender into human rights monitoring.

66.   The issue of how best to ensure advancement of women in the work of the Secretariat and the United Nations system as a whole is one of the major areas central to the Conference and its follow-up. The institutional mechanisms for this are being reviewed internally and by Governments of Member States.

### 4.   Trusteeship Council

67.   In 1994, with the termination of the Trusteeship Agreement for the last Trust Territory of the Pacific Islands and Palau's admission as the 185th Member of the United Nations, the Trusteeship Council completed the task entrusted to it under the Charter with respect to the 11 Territories that

had been placed under the Trusteeship System. The other 10, the majority of them in Africa and the Pacific, had already attained independence, either as separate States or by joining neighbouring States. The Trusteeship Council thereupon amended its rules of procedure and will in future meet only as and where occasion may require.

68.   In a letter dated 2 June 1995 addressed to me (A/50/142), the Permanent Representative of Malta requested, on behalf of his Government, that the General Assembly include an item entitled ''Review of the role of the Trusteeship Council'' in the provisional agenda of its fiftieth session. The Government of Malta would like the Assembly to consider transforming the Council's role so that, in addition to its role under the Charter, the Council would hold in trust for humanity its common heritage and common concerns.

69.   In my 1994 annual report on the work of the Organization, I recommended that the General Assembly proceed with steps to eliminate the organ, in accordance with Article 108 of the Charter. I regret that no decision to abolish the Trusteeship Council has been taken.

### 5.   International Court of Justice

70.   The International Court of Justice at The Hague is the principal judicial organ of the United Nations and, as such, holds important responsibilities in the settlement of disputes of a legal nature.

71.   In 1994-1995, the Court continued to have a record number of 13 cases before it. Eleven were contentious cases in which the parties were States from different parts of the world. Two were requests for an advisory opinion, one submitted by the World Health Organization (WHO) and the other by the General Assembly.

72.   In the period under review, judgments have been given in two cases, in one of which hearings were held. In a third case, hearings have been postponed. In other cases a great number of pleadings have been filed within the prescribed time-limits. One contentious case and one request for an advisory opinion were brought before the Court.

73.   The hearings in the case concerning the *Aerial Incident of 3 July 1988 (Islamic Republic of Iran v. United States of America)*, scheduled to take place in September, were postponed *sine die* at the joint request of the two parties.

74.   Written comments were filed by several States by 20 June 1995, the time-limit fixed by the President of the Court by an Order of 20 June 1994 on written statements submitted in connection with the request by WHO for an advisory opinion on the *Legality of the Use by a State of Nuclear Weapons in Armed Conflict*. The written proceedings are thus closed.

75.   In December 1994, the General Assembly laid before the Court a request for an advi-

sory opinion on the *Legality of the Threat or Use of Nuclear Weapons.* In February 1995, an Order was made fixing two time-limits, one within which written statements relating to the question might be submitted to the Court by States entitled to appear before the Court and by the United Nations, and one within which States and organizations having presented written statements might present written comments on the other written statements. Written statements have been filed by a number of States. Written comments are expected by 20 September 1995.

76. Public sittings for the purpose of hearing oral statements or comments will open on 30 October 1995. These oral proceedings will cover the requests for advisory opinion submitted by WHO and the General Assembly.

77. As each of the parties in the case concerning the *Gabcíkovo-Nagymaros Project (Hungary/Slovakia)* had filed a counter-memorial within the prescribed time-limit of December 1994, the President of the Court, also in December, made an Order fixing the time-limit for the filing of a reply by each of the parties. Each party having filed its reply within the prescribed time-limit, the written proceedings are now closed.

78. In the case concerning *Maritime Delimitation and Territorial Questions between Qatar and Bahrain (Qatar v. Bahrain),* the Court, in July 1994, had delivered a judgment in which it found that the exchange of letters of December 1987 between the King of Saudi Arabia and the Amirs of Qatar and Bahrain, and the minutes signed at Doha on 25 December 1990, were international agreements creating rights and obligations for the parties, and that, by the terms of those agreements, the parties had undertaken to submit to it the whole of the dispute. The Court fixed 30 November 1994 as the time-limit within which the parties were jointly or separately to take action to that end and reserved any other matters for subsequent decision.

79. In February 1995, the Court delivered a judgment by which it found that it had jurisdiction to adjudicate upon the dispute between Qatar and Bahrain that had been submitted to it; that it was seized of the whole of the dispute; and that the application of Qatar as formulated on 30 November 1994 was admissible. In April the Court issued an Order fixing a time-limit for the filing by each of the parties of a memorial on the merits.

80. Hearings in the case concerning *East Timor (Portugal v. Australia)* were held in January and February 1995. On 30 June, the Court delivered its judgment, by which it found that it could not, in the absence of the consent of Indonesia, adjudicate upon the dispute referred to it by Portugal concerning a treaty of December 1989 between Australia and Indonesia on exploitation of the continental shelf of the so-called "Timor Gap".

81. In the case concerning *Application of the Convention on the Prevention and Punishment of the Crime of Genocide (Bosnia and Herzegovina v. Yugoslavia (Serbia and Montenegro)),* the President of the Court, in March, made an Order extending the time-limit for the filing of the counter-memorial of Yugoslavia (Serbia and Montenegro). Yugoslavia (Serbia and Montenegro) filed preliminary objections in June 1995 relating to admissibility and jurisdiction. In July 1995, the President of the Court made an Order fixing the time-limit for the filing by Bosnia and Herzegovina of observations on the preliminary objections, proceedings on the merits having been suspended by operation of the Rules of Court.

82. In the cases concerning *Questions of Interpretation and Application of the 1971 Montreal Convention arising from the Aerial Incident at Lockerbie (Libyan Arab Jamahiriya v. United Kingdom)* and *Questions of Interpretation and Application of the 1971 Montreal Convention arising from the Aerial Incident at Lockerbie (Libyan Arab Jamahiriya v. United States of America),* the respondent States filed preliminary objections to the jurisdiction of the Court on 16 and 20 June respectively.

83. On 28 March 1995, Spain instituted proceedings against Canada with respect to a dispute relating to the Canadian Coastal Fisheries Protection Act, as amended on 12 May 1994, and to the rules of application of that Act, as well as to certain measures taken on the basis of that legislation, more particularly the boarding on the high seas, on 9 March, of a fishing boat, the *Estai,* sailing under the Spanish flag. Taking into account the agreement concerning the procedure reached between the parties at a meeting with the President of the Court, held on 27 April, the President, by an Order of 2 May, decided that the written proceedings should first be addressed to the question of the jurisdiction of the Court to entertain the dispute and fixed time-limits for the filing of the memorial of Spain and the counter-memorial of Canada.

84. By a letter dated 9 August, the Government of New Zealand gave the Court formal advance notice of its intention to bring France before the Court in connection with the French nuclear testing in the South Pacific.

85. Because of the new cases mentioned above, the Court's docket has remained well-filled. Besides the cases referred to, the following were on the Court's list during the period under review:

*(a) Maritime Delimitation between Guinea-Bissau and Senegal (Guinea-Bissau v. Senegal);*

*(b) Oil Platforms (Islamic Republic of Iran v. United States of America);*

*(c) Land and Maritime Boundary between Cameroon and Nigeria (Cameroon v. Nigeria).*

86.  Following the death, on 28 September 1994, of Mr. Nikolai K. Tarassov (Russian Federation), Mr. Vladlen S. Vereshchetin (Russian Federation) was elected to fill the resulting vacancy on 26 January 1995. The vacancy created by the death, on 24 February, of Mr. Roberto Ago (Italy) was filled by the election, on 21 June, of Mr. Luigi Ferrari Bravo (Italy). The vacancy created by the resignation, as at 10 July, of Sir Robert Yewdall Jennings (United Kingdom of Great Britain and Northern Ireland) was filled by the election, on 12 July, of Mrs. Rosalyn Higgins (United Kingdom of Great Britain and Northern Ireland).

### 6.  Secretariat

87.  The purpose of my management plan is to create a mission-driven and result-oriented Organization, with specific goals of enhanced performance, better productivity and increased cost-effectiveness. The foundation of the management plan is the new system of accountability and responsibility that I have established. The system is designed to create a new management culture, assisting and supporting programme managers in achieving the strategic objectives of the Organization and in executing legislative mandates. In effect, the new system of accountability and responsibility empowers managers with the freedom to manage—streamlining administrative procedures, introducing considerable decentralization and delegation, allowing greater flexibility in the management of resources and encouraging greater innovation and initiative.

88.  The first of the five major objectives is better management of human resources, together with improvement in staff capabilities and accomplishments. An entirely new strategy for human resources was introduced in the Organization and subsequently endorsed by the General Assembly at its forty-ninth session. The implementation of the system will modernize and reform the management of human resources. Among the components of this new system is a new work planning and performance appraisal system, which is based on staff/management-agreed work outputs and performance measurements.

89.  The strategy is based on the need to access the continuously changing and evolving role of the Organization and the requirement to respond progressively to changing needs with a breadth and depth of skills. The strategy involves a concerted effort to provide career training that meets changing staff needs. There is also the need, as a management tool, for active implementation of an attrition programme. An early separation programme for staff at various levels in both the Professional and General Service categories will contribute to an adaptable staff with a varied skills mix, leading to greater effectiveness and efficiency in the context of constantly changing demands on the Secretariat. Lastly, a total remake of the adjudication process has begun, replacing litigation of staff/management issues with an informal dispute-reconciliation process or timely and time-saving arbitral disposition.

90.  Vigorous efforts are being made by the Office of Human Resources Management to integrate goals and targets for improvement in the status of women into the overall strategy. The adoption of a proactive, more people-centred human resource strategy has been conducive to achieving this goal. The percentage of women in posts subject to geographical distribution is continually rising and at the end of July 1995 stood at 33.6 per cent, up from 32.6 per cent at the end of June 1994. During the same period 51.42 per cent of all promotions were those of women.

91.  The second objective is better management of the Organization's programme from the identification of strategic priorities, through the budgetary process by which resources are allocated to achieve those priorities and through a performance measurement system by which programme managers are held accountable for achieving the strategic priorities. Clearer lines of responsibility and greater managerial accountability characterize the new format for the medium-term plan, the Organization's basic strategic document. The new format of the medium-term plan provides for clearly defined objectives and emphasizes full congruence between the identified programmes and the departments responsible for their implementation. The process of managerial responsibility and accountability has been considerably tightened through improved linkage between programmes, budgets and performance measurement. Financial congruence has been achieved at each step in planning and execution. Member States will now be able to tell what is to be done, who is responsible for doing it and what is accomplished.

92.  Third is better information with which to manage and its timely availability. Work continued in 1994 and 1995 on the development of the Integrated Management Information System (IMIS), which aims at modernizing and enhancing the internal flow and use of management information in such areas as human resources, finance, accounts and procurement. The IMIS project represents an ambitious effort to make good, through one massive effort, 30 years of neglect in upgrading existing electronic data-processing systems. The system is a revolutionary step towards the electronic integration of all of the offices of the Organization performing administrative tasks regardless of location. The first two releases of the system, the human resource

components, were fully and successfully implemented at Headquarters. The other releases—accounts, finance and procurement—will be gradually phased in during the next year, with the whole system operational worldwide by the end of 1997.

93. Fourth is management of technology and extension of its availability throughout the Organization. Technology, with its potential for improved services and greater cost-effectiveness, will also facilitate the role of Conference Services. Technological advances in communication and networking, text-processing, desktop publishing, translation and document tracking have provided savings. Further expansion of the United Nations telecommunication network will produce additional savings for the United Nations system as a whole. The optical disk system, now being expanded to accommodate increasing user demand, offers easy, high-speed electronic access to United Nations documents. The development of remote translation and text-processing techniques has brought down the cost of holding meetings away from established headquarters by reducing the staff required on-site. As a result, the number of staff who travelled to the Cairo Conference was significantly reduced from that of previous conferences, and no translators will be going to the Beijing Conference.

94. The fifth objective is better management of the Organization's cost structure and an enhanced programme for cost-effectiveness. The budget process is being used to drive the Organization to a higher level of efficiency. The proposed 1996-1997 programme budget is smaller than the budget for the biennium 1994-1995. The proposals include the abolition of 201 posts, offset in part by the proposed creation of 66 new posts in priority areas of peace-keeping, international and regional cooperation for development, drug control, crime prevention, population, human rights and humanitarian affairs and internal oversight. The aggregate reduced spending will be achieved through more cost-effective ways of implementing mandates, rationalizing work programmes and technological innovations. The proposed reductions were achieved without curtailment of mandated activities. At the same time, efficiency gains of $35 million have been proposed throughout the Secretariat without compromising the quality of programme outputs.

95. Identifying efficiency gains is now a key component of management planning. The first phase of this programme has concentrated on the simplification of existing procedures: redefining work programmes, improving productivity, substituting lower cost alternatives, streamlining staff requirements and reducing overheads.

96. The next phase will concentrate on the elimination of duplication and overlap in programme delivery and the elimination of programmes without a mandate and programmes that do not return adequate value to Member States.

97. An Efficiency Board, chaired by the Under-Secretary-General for Administration and Management, Mr. Joseph Connor, will identify during the next biennium further significant opportunities for cost containment beyond those proposed in the 1996-1997 budget. These will include removing overregulating procedures in the personnel, finance and purchasing areas, eliminating duplicate efforts between Headquarters and other duty stations, and studying "outsourcing" alternatives.

98. Procedures are being revised for better transparency and fairness of procurement efforts. Some steps already taken, or in the initial phase, include the extension of basic professional procurement training; revised delegation of procurement authority for peace-keeping missions; institution of global system/blanket contracts; review and updating of the vendor roster; and establishment of the office of ombudsman, to which all vendors may address complaints.

99. In its first year of operations, the Office of Internal Oversight Services, headed by Under-Secretary-General Mr. Karl-Theodor Paschke, has provided the United Nations with oversight coverage, promoting effective and efficient programme management. The Office also finds and reports on instances of waste, fraud and mismanagement. I look forward to the findings and conclusions of the first annual report of the Office, to be submitted to the General Assembly in September 1995.

100. The Office of Legal Affairs, headed by Mr. Hans Corell, has been heavily involved in legal work related to the continued expansion and diversification of the activities of the Security Council, ranging from the establishment of a new international criminal tribunal to establishing new peace-keeping missions and winding down others.

101. During the period under review, the Office was involved in current operations such as those in Angola, Georgia, Guatemala, Haiti, Mozambique, Rwanda, Somalia, Tajikistan, Western Sahara and the former Yugoslavia. Legal officers from the Office have served as legal advisers in a number of those operations.

102. The Office of Legal Affairs is involved in the implementation of various aspects of Security Council decisions. It has assisted in the drafting and interpretation of status-of-forces agreements and status-of-mission agreements and given advice to operational departments. The Office has developed modalities and instruments for the procurement of necessary systems, facilities, equipment and services required for peace-keeping

and other activities. Particular attention was given to the rights of contractors and to third-party claims arising out of Chapter VII operations.

103. Novel issues of international humanitarian law have arisen during the period under review. The Office has provided advice and opinions in relation to the detention of United Nations personnel in Bosnia and the treatment of Bosnian prisoners by United Nations forces. The progress towards a referendum in Western Sahara has required legal assistance in the preparation of a code of conduct for the referendum campaign.

104. The Office of Legal Affairs advised on the question of setting up an international judicial commission to investigate the Burundi *coup d'état* of 1993 and on the proposed establishment of a commission of inquiry or truth in Burundi. The Office assisted in the drafting of the terms of reference of the International Commission of Inquiry to investigate the events at Kibeho, Rwanda.

105. The Office contributed to filling a gap in United Nations practice, highlighted following a United Nations inquiry into a 1993 massacre of civilians in Liberia, by preparing a set of guidelines for United Nations investigations into allegations of massacres. The Secretary-General has approved the guidelines for publication and circulation.

106. The establishment by the Security Council of international tribunals dealing with serious violations of international humanitarian law in the former Yugoslavia and Rwanda raises difficult and complex legal issues. The Office of Legal Affairs is providing legal and administrative support to the International Criminal Tribunal for the Former Yugoslavia. The Office played a central role in launching the International Criminal Tribunal for Rwanda by providing advice on the drafting of the statute and rules of procedure and evidence and by providing the initial budget for the administrative and financial support from Headquarters, coordinating a technical mission to the field in order to negotiate a headquarters and lease agreement for its premises and preparing reports on the seat of the Tribunal.

107. At its past session, the General Assembly established an ad hoc committee open to all States to review substantive and administrative issues arising out of the draft statute for an international criminal court elaborated by the International Law Commission. The ad hoc committee held a first series of meetings in April 1995 focusing on the following subjects: establishment and composition of the Court, applicable law and jurisdiction, exercise of jurisdiction, methods of proceedings (due process), relationship between States parties and the Court, and budget and administration. While progress has been made in the consideration of these issues, the ad hoc committee agreed to hold a second series of meetings from 14 to 25 August. Its report will be before the General Assembly at its forthcoming fiftieth session.

108. The continuation of economic sanctions and other measures against Iraq, the Federal Republic of Yugoslavia (Serbia and Montenegro) and the Libyan Arab Jamahiriya requires monitoring and assistance by the Office and advice to the various sanctions committees. In the case of Iraq, the Office advises on the scope of mandates under relevant Security Council resolutions, such as those concerning compensation to Iraqi farmers relocated from Kuwait and the return of Kuwaiti property. The Office is supporting the work of the Compensation Commission, which has been carrying out an impressive amount of work in processing claims, and will soon examine the more complex and larger claims of corporations and Governments.

109. The Office of Legal Affairs is ensuring consistency in the implementation of General Assembly decisions on the participation of the Federal Republic of Yugoslavia (Serbia and Montenegro) and its status throughout the United Nations system. The question lies at the intersection between international law and United Nations political decisions on sensitive issues.

110. The Office of Legal Affairs was responsible for the organization and agenda of the United Nations Congress on Public International Law, held from 13 to 17 March in New York, under the general theme "Towards the Twenty-First Century: International Law as a Language for International Relations". Some 571 scholars and professionals from 126 countries attended the event, which marked the mid-point of the United Nations Decade of International Law. International lawyers exchanged views on such issues as the progressive development of international law and its codification; research, education and training in international law; and the challenges expected in the twenty-first century.

111. The Office of Legal Affairs provides advice relating to the technical aspects of treaties and treaty law. The information in the *Multilateral Treaties deposited with the Secretary-General* is electronically updated daily. Outdated and disparate laws governing international trade pose an obstacle to the maintenance and expansion of trade links. The success of economic and social reforms currently under way in many States depends on the adoption of adequate laws that facilitate international trade. The Office of Legal Affairs is assisting the United Nations Commission on International Trade Law (UNCITRAL) to elaborate modern and harmonized trade laws as well as non-legislative texts aimed at facilitating international trade. Is-

sues recently addressed are the draft convention on independent bank guarantees and stand-by letters of credit, and the use of electronic data interchange in international trade.

112. The United Nations Convention on the Law of the Sea calls for the establishment of three new institutions subsequent to the entry into force of the Convention: the International Seabed Authority, the International Tribunal for the Law of the Sea and the Commission on the Limits of the Continental Shelf. The Office of Legal Affairs convened and serviced the first and second parts of the first session of the Assembly of the International Seabed Authority, held from 16 to 18 November 1994 and from 27 February to 17 March 1995, respectively, at Kingston. The third and final part of the Assembly was held also at Kingston from 7 to 18 August.

113. Pursuant to the mandate provided by the General Assembly in its resolution 49/28 of 6 December 1994, the Office of Legal Affairs convened the first part and serviced the first and second parts of the Meeting of States Parties to the United Nations Convention on the Law of the Sea, held in November 1994 and May 1995 in New York, relating to the organization of the International Tribunal for the Law of the Sea. The Meeting agreed on the approach to be taken in the establishment of the Tribunal and its initial functions. The Office is involved in the preparation of the draft budget, which will be submitted to the next Meeting of States Parties, to be held from 27 November to 1 December 1995 in New York.

114. The Office of Legal Affairs is carrying out preparatory work regarding the Commission on the Limits of the Continental Shelf. Following the 1993 findings of an ad hoc group of experts that examined the relevant provisions of the Convention on the definition of the continental shelf, the Office prepared background notes, initiated cooperative arrangements with competent international organizations and is in the process of convening a group of experts to deal with the composition and work programme of the Commission, scheduled to meet from 11 to 14 September in New York.

115. The United Nations Conference on Straddling Fish Stocks and Highly Migratory Fish Stocks concluded its substantive work on 4 August with the consensus adoption of an Agreement for the Implementation of the United Nations Convention on the Law of the Sea of 10 December 1982 relating to the Conservation and Management of Straddling Fish Stocks and Highly Migratory Fish Stocks. The Conference decided to hold a formal signature ceremony on 4 December. The Office of Legal Affairs convened and serviced the fifth and sixth sessions of the Con-

ference, from 27 March to 12 April and from 24 July to 4 August, respectively, in New York.

116. Pursuant to General Assembly resolution 49/28, the Office of Legal Affairs is strengthening the system for the collection, compilation and dissemination of information on the law of the sea and developing an integrated database on legislation and marine policy, as well as establishing a system for notifying Member States and relevant international organizations of information submitted by States and intergovernmental bodies.

117. The Department of Public Information, headed by Mr. Samir Sanbar, is seeking to surmount resource constraints by engaging in closer professional cooperation with other bodies of the United Nations system, especially UNDP, UNICEF and UNFPA.

118. A coordinated and unified public information strategy aimed at increasing public understanding and support for the United Nations has become of crucial importance for the Organization's peace-keeping and other political missions. The Department of Public Information has formed an interdepartmental working group consisting of those departments playing a leading role in such field operations with a view to developing practical proposals for informational projects.

119. To convey an accurately balanced view of United Nations activities, the Department has made a special effort to highlight economic and social development activities and issues, in particular the recent major United Nations conferences held in Cairo, Copenhagen and Beijing, and the forthcoming Habitat II Conference in Istanbul. Focal points have been established within the Department for each conference to design, in cooperation with the substantive departments concerned, public information strategies and programmes that are budgeted jointly. Assessment of post-conference feedback has shown the value of this multifaceted approach to the promotion of international conferences.

120. A major new activity of the Department's publishing programme is the Secretary-General's Blue Books Series. The Series describes the role the United Nations has played in some of the pivotal peace operations and other international issues of our time. Each volume in the Series encapsulates—in an overview provided by the Secretary-General—how the United Nations marshalled international forces, opinion or consensus to achieve objectives in such areas as the struggle against apartheid, the drive to stop the proliferation of nuclear weapons and the promotion of human rights. Blue Books on peace operations in Cambodia, El Salvador and Mozambique have been published. *The United Nations and the Advancement of Women* was published in August 1995 and made available for the Fourth World Conference

on Women in Beijing. Some 17 titles are currently planned for publication.

121.   The Department's dissemination of information to direct users and redisseminators has been enhanced by modern technology and techniques, including the use of several electronic networks. On the Internet, for example, can be found the Department's database containing important United Nations documentation and publications. These materials reach their audiences in electronic form at enormous speed and are accessed by an average of 16,000 users daily. On the occasion of the fiftieth anniversary of the signing of the Charter of the United Nations at San Francisco on 26 June 1995, the Department launched the "UN Home Page" on the World Wide Web. This pilot project provides instantaneous information to Internet users in a multimedia service format consisting of text, graphics and sound. Examples of its contents include basic information about the United Nations and its history, press releases, documents, publications and photos, as well as pictorial highlights of the guided tour of Headquarters. To make documentation accessible to a wider audience, the United Nations Bibliographic Information System (UNBIS Plus) has been produced on CD-ROM.

122.   Radio is one of the most cost-effective and penetrating media available to the Department, which is improving access by United Nations Radio to airwaves worldwide. Currently, 29 programmes in 15 languages are being sent to broadcasters in over 180 countries. The Department also operates an electronic radio news service in English, French and Spanish that facilitates access by broadcasters to news programmes updated twice daily and is accessible through regular telephone lines.

123.   The Department continues with the help of new technologies to reach its goals to explore the huge potential represented by television audiences. For instance, the Department transmitted "Year in Review" via satellite to broadcasters around the world in the six official languages. The programme was received and retransmitted by major broadcasters in over 24 countries, representing a total potential audience of over 360 million television households. This satellite transmission proved to be an extremely quick and cost-effective distribution channel and represented the largest audience ever reached by the programme.

124.   In connection with the fiftieth anniversary, the Department initiated a major campaign of television spots. A series of 40 "UN Minutes" were produced, charting the history and accomplishments of the Organization. In addition, a series of "Question and Answer" quiz announcements were made. These television spots have been aired on both domestic and international

Cable News Network channels, and by Time Warner Cable Company on many channels in the New York area. The Department thus obtained several million dollars worth of free air time donated by these two companies alone.

125.   Responsibility for the Department's global outreach activities is assumed in large part by the network of information centres and services located in 68 countries around the world. They perform both a passive information role in dealing with a mounting volume of inquiries and requests for information, and an active role in engaging in a wide variety of contacts in pursuance of their mandate. As an example of the latter role, the centres have been the catalyst for the creation of approximately 80 national committees for the observance of the fiftieth anniversary.

126.   The United Nations Office at Geneva, under its Director-General, Mr. Vladimir Petrovsky, continues to provide administrative and logistical support to Geneva-based United Nations programmes and activities in human rights, humanitarian operations, trade and development, as well as major environment, disarmament and security-related matters.

127.   There is a growing demand from Member States to visit the United Nations Office at Geneva to establish or explore further cooperation between their countries and Geneva-based specialized agencies and programmes. Seven official visits were organized for that purpose and included the Heads of State or Government of Guatemala, Italy, Kazakstan, Kyrgyzstan, Lithuania, Slovenia and Tunisia. These exchanges are a major factor in consolidating the Office's role in the region and beyond.

128.   Activities with regional organizations increased throughout the year. A number of tripartite meetings took place with the participation of the Council of Europe, OSCE and the United Nations, represented by the United Nations High Commissioner for Refugees and the Centre for Human Rights. During the course of the year, the International Committee of the Red Cross (ICRC) was also associated with the meetings, which dealt with humanitarian issues in Europe.

129.   Dialogue with Member States of the region contributed to the organizing of national committees for the United Nations fiftieth anniversary, important activities at the national level and joint projects included in the Geneva programme for the fiftieth anniversary. In that respect, cooperation with the host country and Geneva authorities, including major building projects to meet the needs of the United Nations Office at Geneva, was particularly fruitful.

130.   The United Nations Office at Geneva continues to host an increasingly large number of meetings. From September 1994 to March 1995,

1,775 meetings were serviced with interpretation (including 154 meetings outside Geneva) and 2,455 without interpretation (including 105 meetings outside Geneva). During the period from April to August 1995, 1,354 meetings were planned to be held with interpretation (including 148 meetings outside Geneva) and 1,760 without interpretation (including 68 meetings outside Geneva).

131.  In addition to servicing the Office's established bodies, the Palais des Nations hosted a number of important political or peace-keeping-related meetings, such as the International Conference on the Former Yugoslavia, the Compensation Commission, the meetings of the Georgia/Abkhazia parties and the Commission of Experts on Rwanda. The United Nations Centre on Transnational Corporations and the Centre for Science and Technology for Development were transferred to Geneva in 1993/94, and the Commission on Transnational Corporations and the Commission on Science and Technology for Development held regular sessions producing important documentation. The increasing activities of the Centre for Human Rights will give rise to new committees and/or working groups, which will meet at the United Nations Office at Geneva. These developments will require careful management of the allocation of facilities.

132.  The Office has been involved in United Nations work on the International Conference on the Former Yugoslavia; the Georgia/Abkhazia conflict; the meetings between Portugal and Indonesia concerning East Timor under the good offices of the Secretary-General; the talks on Yemen; and discussions on biological, conventional and nuclear weapons. The Office has also been involved with the Economic Commission for Europe (ECE), UNCTAD and the United Nations Compensation Commission, and has provided support for the Office of the High Commissioner for Human Rights, the United Nations Assistance Mission in Rwanda (UNAMIR), round tables organized by the Department of Humanitarian Affairs for a number of countries in Africa and Asia, and working groups of the United Nations Protection Force (UNPROFOR).

133.  During this period the round table set up by the Director-General, with the participation of senior and staff representatives of all Geneva-based organs and programmes, made recommendations aimed at strengthening and simplifying security arrangements, as well as achieving a larger degree of control over documentation, with the ultimate goal of sizeably reducing its volume.

134.  The Office has conducted two main studies aimed at identifying areas of duplication and overlap in the administrative sector within the Office, as well as between the Office and various

United Nations entities and programmes located at Geneva. The first phase of a management study led to a greater delegation of authority between Headquarters and Geneva in the personnel and budget/finance fields. Such delegation will not only sizeably reduce duplication and overlap, but will also allow for more timely processing of administrative actions at Geneva. The next phase of the management study will finalize administrative arrangements at Geneva and determine the relationship between the various entities. The second study, a work-flow analysis conducted in the context of the future introduction of IMIS at Geneva, has just been completed. By the end of the year, the reorganization will be almost completed, permitting the Office to respond more efficiently to the increasing demands placed upon it by Member States of the region and the Organization as a whole.

135.  Also located at Geneva, the United Nations Institute for Training and Research (UNITAR) has completed its restructuring process as requested by the General Assembly in its resolution 47/227 of 8 April 1993. This year UNITAR completed a training programme in international affairs management, including peacemaking and preventive diplomacy, environmental law and policy, and a fellowship in international law. In addition, the UNITAR training programme for the management of economic and social development has been reorganized. The aim of the programme now is to upgrade the professional skills of human resources in specific fields and to put the UNITAR training initiative at the service of multilateral and bilateral cooperation agencies, in particular the secretariats of organizations in charge of facilitating the implementation of international legal instruments. The coming years are likely to see a consolidation of UNITAR training and capacity-building activities, while research programmes are progressively discontinued. It is hoped that Member States will ensure the long-term continuity of the Institute.

136.  The United Nations Office at Vienna, headed by the Director-General, Mr. Giorgio Giacomelli, provides administrative support to the United Nations Fund for Drug Abuse Control and other United Nations activities based at Vienna, serves functions related to crime prevention and cooperation in space activities, and is an important meeting place and support centre for peace-keeping operations. From 1 July 1994 to 1 July 1995, a total of 2,209 meetings were planned and serviced at Vienna.

137.  Beginning 1 April 1995, after extensive negotiations, the United Nations Industrial Development Organization (UNIDO) and the United Nations Office at Vienna merged conference planning, coordinating and language and servicing

capabilities to form a Unified Conference Service under the Office's management. A number of seminars, training courses and technical cooperation projects have taken place; others are being planned or are being implemented.

138. The Crime Prevention and Criminal Justice Branch of the United Nations Office at Vienna has promoted international cooperation in crime prevention and criminal justice and provided assistance to Member States on problems of both national and transnational crime. The Office organized the International Conference on Preventing and Controlling Money Laundering and the Use of the Proceeds of Crime: A Global Approach (Courmayeur, Italy, 18-20 June 1994), the World Ministerial Conference on Organized Transnational Crime (Naples, Italy, 21-23 November 1994) and the Ninth United Nations Congress on the Prevention of Crime and the Treatment of Offenders (Cairo, 29 April–8 May 1995).

139. The World Ministerial Conference on Organized Transnational Crime adopted the Naples Political Declaration and Global Action Plan against Organized Transnational Crime, approved by the General Assembly in its resolution 49/159 of 23 December 1994. In the Declaration, Heads of State and Government, ministers responsible for criminal justice systems and other high-level representatives of Governments expressed their resolve to protect their societies from organized crime through effective legislative measures and operational instruments. The Global Action Plan emphasized that the United Nations should facilitate the provision of technical cooperation, including the systematic exchange of experience and expertise, by drafting legislation, providing special training for criminal justice officials and gathering, analysing and exchanging information.

140. The Ninth United Nations Congress on the Prevention of Crime and the Treatment of Offenders found that new forms and dimensions of crime and the links among criminal organizations threatened the security and stability of States and made global action imperative. The Congress discussed four substantive topics and held six demonstration and research workshops that permitted a more technical consideration of priority issues of direct concern to Member States. The discussion on combating corruption involving public officials attracted considerable attention and a number of recommendations were proposed. The plenary meeting on technical cooperation assessed the progress achieved and problems encountered in operational activities. Member States, in particular developing countries and countries in transition, discussed their needs for assistance from the United Nations and the international community.

141. The work of the Crime Prevention and Criminal Justice Branch was oriented towards operational activities and technical assistance, in particular for developing countries and countries in transition. The Branch focused its efforts on the promotion of effective and fair criminal justice systems based on the rule of law, taking account of United Nations norms, standards and model treaties. It provided assistance to Member States, upon request, in legislative and criminal justice reform, the elaboration and implementation of criminal codes and international treaties, the planning and formulation of national criminal justice policies and strategies, and the establishment of information networks and databases. The programme also contributed to peace-keeping and peacemaking missions of the United Nations by assisting in building legal and criminal justice infrastructures, and providing support to the missions and countries concerned. Two interregional advisers provided advisory services to various countries, carried out needs assessment missions and developed project proposals.

142. The Commission on Crime Prevention and Criminal Justice, the body responsible for policy guidance in this field, meets annually at Vienna. At its fourth session, held from 30 May to 9 June 1995, the Commission addressed the conclusions and recommendations of the Ninth United Nations Congress on the Prevention of Crime and the Treatment of Offenders, as well as of the World Ministerial Conference on Organized Transnational Crime. It recommended follow-up measures to the conclusions of the Congress and to the Naples Political Declaration and Global Action Plan adopted by the Conference. All recommendations of the Commission were approved by the Economic and Social Council during its substantive session, held at Geneva from 26 June to 28 July 1995.

143. The Crime Prevention and Criminal Justice Branch cooperated closely with the United Nations International Drug Control Programme and the Centre for Human Rights. The Branch also undertook cooperation and coordination activities with the interregional, regional and associated institutes in the field of crime prevention and criminal justice and with intergovernmental and non-governmental organizations in areas of mutual concern.

144. The Office for Outer Space Affairs, which relocated to the United Nations Office at Vienna in October 1993, implemented its multisectoral programme with political, legal, scientific and technical assistance components. Through its Programme on Space Applications, the Office organized and conducted workshops, training courses and symposia on various aspects of space science and technology and their appli-

cations for economic and social development. The Office continued its service as the substantive secretariat for the General Assembly's Committee on the Peaceful Uses of Outer Space, its Scientific and Technical Subcommittee and its Legal Subcommittee, as well as their subsidiary bodies.

145. Further progress was made on the Office's initiative to establish regional centres for space science and technology education in the developing countries. Those centres will provide individuals from developing countries with education and training in space-related disciplines and applications. In 1994, the Office decided to establish a centre, which will be co-hosted by Brazil and Mexico, for the Latin American and Caribbean region, and to establish the first node of the centre for the Asia and Pacific region in India. It is expected that 1995 will yield firm agreements on the location of the centres in the Middle East and Africa. The Office in 1994 expanded its Space Information Service to include a limited computer database capability as well as a gateway, or "home page", on the Internet. The home page provides basic data on the space-related activities of the United Nations and is the first step in the development of the broad information system mandated by the General Assembly. The Office has initiated plans to provide support for the preparatory work in intergovernmental committees concerning the convening of a third United Nations Conference on the Exploration and Peaceful Uses of Outer Space.

146. The Administrative Committee on Coordination, comprising the executive heads of the specialized agencies, including the Bretton Woods institutions, as well as all United Nations programmes under the chairmanship of the Secretary-General, provides the main instrument to establish an effective system of inter-agency cooperation and coordination within the United Nations system. In line with the objectives that have guided the recent restructuring of its machinery, the Committee's capacity to identify the main policy issues facing the international community and to promote and organize joint initiatives and responses towards common objectives has been progressively strengthened. The improvements the Secretary-General seeks to introduce within the United Nations, at both the policy and management levels, must be pursued as an integral part of a broader effort to adapt priorities and methods of work to changing requirements at the level of the system as a whole. Thus, at its past two sessions, the Committee pursued its consideration of policies that could lead to a more effective division of labour and to greater complementarity of action within the United Nations system. The Committee devoted particular attention to building and strengthening cooperative arrangements between the Bretton Woods institutions and United Nations funds, programmes and other specialized agencies. In the same context, particular attention was given by the Committee to ways and means of enhancing the capacity of the resident coordinator system to promote effective coordination among all economic and social actors at the country level in support of national development efforts. The achievement of greater complementarity between the country strategy notes, launched by the General Assembly, and the policy framework papers, under the aegis of the Bretton Woods institutions, was viewed as a key objective to those ends.

147. At the global level, the Committee's efforts to promote a coordinated follow-up to the results of major conferences on interrelated development issues are helping to promote a more effective division of labour within the system, drawing on the new policy insights, priorities and commitments generated by those conferences. The continuing discussions in the Committee on the follow-up to the United Nations Conference on Environment and Development and its consideration, at its session in February 1995, of issues relating to international drug abuse control have helped equally to promote a more effective distribution of responsibilities and mutually reinforcing activities by the organizations of the United Nations system in addressing emerging global priorities.

148. African economic recovery and development was a major focus of attention at the last two sessions of the Committee. While United Nations organizations individually and collectively have placed high priority on the development of Africa, the current level of effort does not match the scale of economic and social problems confronting the region. The Committee concluded that a much higher level of commitment and resources at all levels was necessary to overcome the crisis facing many countries of the continent. As Chairman of the Committee, the Secretary-General called for a renewed joint effort to develop further practical initiatives with clear targets. The Committee agreed to establish a high-level steering committee to present a set of concrete recommendations for approval at its next session. The broad programme areas identified for this purpose include availability and management of water; sustainable food security; human development and capacity-building; and the follow-up to the World Summit for Social Development, with special emphasis on poverty alleviation. The steering committee also focuses on the consideration of means to enhance political and financial support for African development. Its initial work was drawn upon in preparing for the high-level segment of the Economic and Social Council devoted to African development.

149.   Regarding management issues, members of the Committee reaffirmed their strong commitment to ensuring the advancement of the status of women throughout the United Nations system. It was generally agreed that management commitment at the highest levels was crucial to the achievement of gender equality. The Committee identified specific measures to increase the flexibility with which the United Nations system deals with women candidates; to remove obstacles to their recruitment, retention in service, promotion and mobility; and to create a supportive environment.

150.   The Committee also addressed issues affecting the security and safety of United Nations staff, as well as questions relating to improvements in conditions of service. A special meeting in June of the Consultative Committee on Administrative Questions, in which most senior agency officials responsible for administration and management participated, pursued ways to enhance management effectiveness throughout the system.

151.   In February 1995, all Committee members, and a number of distinguished personalities who have led independent reviews on ways to strengthen the United Nations system, met at Vienna at a Forum on the Future of the United Nations. The Forum addressed the changing requirements for global and regional governance arising from the emerging new political and economic framework and their implications for the Organization; new approaches to the financing of the United Nations system; the implications of the changing role of the system for the international civil service; and the public image of the United Nations, in particular the challenge of mobilizing and focusing the attention of the media on the Organization's economic and social work.

## B.   *Ensuring an adequate financial base*

152.   The United Nations financial crisis continues to deepen because of the delays with which Member States have paid their assessed contributions, both for the regular budget and for peace-keeping operations. As at 10 August 1995, unpaid assessed contributions totalled $3.9 billion: $858.2 million for the regular budget (of which $456.1 million relates to the current year (1995) and $402.1 million relates to prior years) and $3 billion for peace-keeping operations, current and prior shortfalls taken together (*see fig. 6*).

153.   The United Nations is able to continue its peace-keeping operations only because the payment of bills and reimbursements to troop-contributors are being delayed. By the end of the year, unpaid reimbursements to troop-contributors and payments owed for contingent-owned equipment are estimated to reach the $1 billion mark. This situation cannot continue. Troop-contributors have expressed their difficulty with continuing participation in peace-keeping operations if they are not paid on time.

154.   Many Member States have made serious efforts to expedite payment of their assessments but, without substantial additional major contributions before the end of the year, the cash balance of the United Nations will be dangerously low. This difficult financial situation, in particular when compounded by the continued unpredictability of the receipt of contributions, has a direct impact on the efficiency of the Organization and makes it more and more difficult to manage it effectively.

155.   Along with these cash difficulties, the Organization has also been facing another serious problem as a result of the growing practice on the part of the General Assembly of authorizing spending on additional or new activities without providing corresponding resources through assessments on Member States. This has further exacerbated the already difficult financial situation, since the only way to provide funding for those activities is to borrow from accounts with cash resources, without any assurance that those accounts will be replenished in order to implement activities for which Member States had initially provided resources.

156.   Unless the receipt of unpaid assessments dramatically improves, there will be no choice but to reduce spending further, focusing on those activities for which no assessments have been approved. Activities for which assessments have been approved, but have chronically not been paid by Member States, may have to be curtailed.

157.   Notwithstanding these financial problems, efforts are continuing to make the Organization more efficient and more effective in carrying out the many tasks entrusted to it. In formulating the proposed programme budget for the biennium 1996-1997, particular emphasis has been placed on management improvements, which have resulted in savings without affecting the delivery of mandated activities. On that basis, a budget has been proposed for the next biennium in the amount of $2,510 million (at current rates before re-costing) for approval by the General Assembly this year. This represents a reduction of $109 million, or 4.2 per cent less than was appropriated for 1994-1995 (*see fig. 7*). The implementation of the 1996-1997 programme budget, once approved by the General Assembly, should not suffer from the same financial uncertainties that the Organization has been experiencing.

158.   The objective of the High-level Open-ended Working Group on the Financial Situation of the Organization, which was established by the General Assembly and began meeting in January 1995, is to bring about constructive and positive

changes to provide the Organization with a long-sought-after solid financial base.

### C. *The fiftieth anniversary*

159. During the past year, much of the work of the Preparatory Committee for the Fiftieth Anniversary has focused on the preparations for the Special Commemorative Meeting of the Assembly on the occasion of the fiftieth anniversary of the entry into force of the Charter of the United Nations, to be held at United Nations Headquarters from 22 to 24 October 1995. The Committee has also continued to monitor the progress of the commemorative programme being undertaken by the Fiftieth Anniversary Secretariat. The Committee is expected to conclude its work by adopting, in early September, as part of its report to the General Assembly, a declaration in support of the Organization on its fiftieth anniversary.

160. The Fiftieth Anniversary Secretariat, headed by Ms. Gillian Martin Sorensen, has continued to develop and implement an ambitious global commemorative programme of activities and products. The goals identified for the fiftieth anniversary are to promote a more balanced image of the United Nations; to enlarge its constituency of support, especially among youth and non-traditional audiences; to improve worldwide education about the work of the Organization; and to mobilize public support in favour of the United Nations to position it to meet ever-growing demands. In line with these objectives, the Fiftieth Anniversary Secretariat has developed and implemented projects in key programme areas, among which education and communication have been given priority.

161. Educational activities include the development of educational kits for primary, intermediate and secondary schools and their distribution in all six official languages. Substantial funds have been made available for free distribution in developing countries and translation into additional languages as part of a "Global Teach-In" (a day or a week designated for teaching about the United Nations). In cooperation with UNESCO, workshops on the kits and the Global Teach-In have been conducted at several international education conferences. Other cooperative projects with specialized agencies and programmes have focused on youth and teachers. A "Passport to the Future" has been designed to sign on millions of young persons, between the ages of 7 and 14, as "global citizens". The Passport encourages them to demonstrate their concern for a better future by becoming involved in some of the world's most pressing challenges—the environment, human rights and peace—by participating in their local community.

162. Communications activities have included an international public service campaign through video, radio and print, in the six official languages. The campaign is designed to inform the public of the many achievements of the United Nations system, such as those in the areas of democratization and decolonization, women and development, environment, health, refugees, peace-keeping and food security. The videos, which were produced by directors from eight geographic regions, are appearing worldwide on television and airlines and in schools. The print and radio campaign is being distributed to broadcasters and publications in all Member States. A multimedia exhibit has been provided to Headquarters and regional offices and to headquarters of specialized agencies. Publications include a pictorial history of the United Nations, *Visions—Fifty Years of the United Nations*, and a book on the United Nations written by young people for young people, entitled *A World in Our Hands*.

163. Emphasis in all programme activity has been on achieving broad participation. As the Fiftieth Anniversary Secretariat was not in a position to implement and publicize all of the activities in each Member State, considerable efforts have been made to encourage and provide support to the fiftieth anniversary committees formed by Member States, local United Nations offices and non-governmental organizations in their implementation of these and other activities. In all, 145 countries have established national committees and are carrying out an impressive array of local commemorative events. The Fiftieth Anniversary Secretariat continues to work in close cooperation with them, providing information materials, guiding and supporting the development of activities at both the local and country levels, and recommending specific activities to complement those being implemented at the global level. Over 40 Member States are honouring the United Nations with commemorative coins and virtually every postal administration is issuing commemorative stamps honouring the Organization.

164. The Secretariat has also worked with many cities—including the cities that host our Headquarters offices—in development of appropriate commemorations, including conferences and colloquiums, concerts, art exhibits and other cultural and popular events. One among many was the myriad of activities organized at San Francisco to commemorate the fiftieth anniversary of the signing of the Charter.

165. In addition to the public service announcement campaign, the Fiftieth Anniversary Secretariat has continued to develop a wide range of information products, which are being distributed widely to national committees, United Nations information centres, United Nations field offices, permanent missions, United Nations as-

sociations, academic groups and international news media, as well as the general public. These products include the UN50 newsletter, an updated press kit, a 16-page information brochure on the fiftieth anniversary, information about the anniversary available through the computer network and a number of information brochures published jointly with the Department of Public Information, along with audio and video compilations.

166.  Overall, the funds required for developing the commemorative programme were secured from private sector support from global sponsors of the fiftieth anniversary as well as from project sponsors. Royalties from the coin programme are providing substantial revenue for educational and communications activities. Additional revenue has been derived from a commemorative watch.

167.  United Nations associations and other non-governmental organizations have supported the fiftieth anniversary effort to broaden public understanding of the work and continued relevance of the United Nations through, among other things, education programmes, conferences and activities aimed at young people, such as art projects, essay competitions and model United Nations programmes. In addition, many of these organizations, especially United Nations associations, actively participate as members of the national committees established for the fiftieth anniversary to arrange commemorative programmes within the Member States. Furthermore, in the context of the Special Commemorative Meeting of the General Assembly for the Fiftieth Anniversary, there are plans to organize a one-day non-governmental organization programme in mid-October to examine the role of non-governmental organizations in the work of the United Nations.

### D.  *United Nations University* (UNU)

168.  The Governing Council of the United Nations University (UNU) held its forty-first session from late November to early December 1994 at Accra. The Council considered proposals to further enhance the effectiveness of the University, led by Rector Heitor Gurgulino de Souza, and to strengthen the University's role and impact in United Nations research initiatives and activities. Several proposals for new academic initiatives were approved by the Council. Among them, the Council decided to establish the UNU International Leadership Academy, which will operate at Amman, with financial support from the Government of Jordan.

169.  The Director-General of UNESCO and the Secretary-General appointed new members of the Council to replace 11 members whose six-year term of office came to an end on 31 May 1995.

170.  The year 1995 marks the twentieth anniversary of the initiation of UNU academic activi-

ties. It is also the sixth and final year of the UNU research, training and dissemination activities carried out under the second medium-term perspective (1990-1995). The process of preparing the University's third medium-term perspective (1996-2001) for the next six years has accordingly been set in motion. To that end, the University prepared a mission statement as a step towards sharpening the focus of its institutional goals as an international educational institution and autonomous entity of the United Nations in a rapidly evolving global environment.

171.  At its forty-first session, the Council endorsed an institutional strategy paper setting out the programmatic development goals to take the University into the twenty-first century. In addition, the Council considered the appraisal report of an internal assessment group of the Council. The report called for the University to take a leading coordinating role in United Nations research initiatives and activities and to act to enhance the overall coherence of the University's academic programme. The assessment underlined the need for a better integration of UNU research, training and fellowship initiatives and for more effective dissemination of UNU publications. Another major recommendation of the report was the further strengthening of the UNU Centre in its key function as a coordinating mechanism of University academic programmes and research and training centres and programmes. The Council requested that the essential components of the assessment report and the institutional strategy paper and mission statement be integrated as a further step in the process of developing the University's third medium-term perspective.

172.  During the period from 1 September 1994 to 10 August 1995, 72 UNU academic meetings were held worldwide. As at 10 August 1995, 58 UNU postgraduate trainees were enrolled in training programmes at cooperating institutions around the world. The areas of training include food and nutrition, geothermal energy, remote sensing, biotechnology and micro-informatics. In 1994, 57 per cent of the training was done at institutions in developing countries and 43 per cent at institutions in industrialized countries. More than 1,340 fellows from over 100 countries have been trained by the University since 1976; an additional 2,300 persons have received training in UNU workshops and seminars. To date, more than 300 books, 5 scientific journals and numerous research papers and studies have been produced from UNU research.

173.  Research continued to be carried out within the five programme areas identified by the UNU second medium-term perspective: universal human values and global responsibilities; new directions for the world economy; sustaining

global life-support systems; advances in science and technology; and population dynamics and human welfare.

174. The University has made progress in the implementation of its programme on environmentally sustainable development (UNU Agenda 21), which places particular emphasis on human development and capacity-building in developing countries. A series of postgraduate education and capacity-building activities on environmental management has been initiated in Tokyo, together with collaborating institutions in India and Thailand.

175. The University also launched a major new long-term research effort that brings together private companies, industrial policy makers and researchers to pursue the achievement of technological breakthroughs that will facilitate manufacturing without any form of waste, the so-called Zero Emissions Research Initiative. To mobilize support and to exchange information on the design and implementation of this global multidisciplinary research programme, the University organized the first World Congress on Zero Emissions at its headquarters in Tokyo in early April 1995. The World Congress was the first multi-point Internet video conference undertaken from Japan, linking scholars and government and business leaders in Asia, Europe and North America and allowing access to an extended audience in some 100 countries.

176. To further the development of long-term initiatives related to the work of the United Nations, the Rector convened a special advisory team to assist in preparing a "UNU Agenda for Peace, Security and Global Governance". The advisory team suggested a five-year programme focusing on such topics as ethics, democracy and governance, human rights, adjudicatory tools of governance and mechanisms for peace and collective security. These mechanisms include preventive diplomacy, collective security schemes, peacekeeping, post-conflict measures and disarmament. The programme is currently being implemented.

177. The University continues to strengthen its interaction with the United Nations system and is making an intensive and concerted effort to ensure that the results of its work feed into the deliberations and operational activities of the United Nations. The University prepared policy papers for presentation at the International Conference on Population and Development and the World Summit for Social Development preparatory process. Substantive contributions are being planned or are in progress with respect to the Fourth World Conference on Women, Habitat II and the ninth session of UNCTAD. The University has also intensified its research efforts in support of the United Nations Secretariat through studies on mine-clearance technology, peacekeeping in Africa and regional security questions in Latin America.

178. The University has produced a number of policy-oriented studies, including "The Fragile Tropics of Latin America: Sustainable Management of Changing Environments"; "International Waters in the Middle East: From Euphrates-Tigris to Nile"; "Managing Water for Peace in the Middle East: Alternative Strategies"; "Hydropolitics Along the Jordan River: Scarce Water and Its Impact on the Arab-Israeli Conflict"; "Sustainable Management of Soil Resources in the Humid Tropics"; "Ocean Governance: Sustainable Development of the Seas"; "Steering Business Toward Sustainability"; "Culture, Development and Democracy: The Role of the Intellectual"; "Global Transformation: Challenges to the State System"; "State, Society and the United Nations System: Changing Perspectives on Multilateralism"; "The United Nations System: The Policies of Member States"; "Arms Reduction: Economic Implications in the Post-Cold-War Era"; "Mega-City Growth and the Future"; "Global Employment: An International Investigation into the Future of Work"; and "The Evolving New Global Environment for the Development Process".

179. From 1 September 1994 to 10 August 1995, UNU received some $19.9 million in endowment fund, operating and specific programme contributions. Nevertheless, the University faces continued resource constraints brought on by lower investment income from its endowment fund and increased competition for limited resources. Mobilization of operational contributions and of untied or unearmarked funding has become increasingly difficult in the last decade.

## III. The foundations of peace: development, humanitarian action and human rights

### A. *Implementing "An Agenda for Development"*

180. Three years ago, at its forty-seventh session, the General Assembly set in motion the process of formulating an Agenda for Development. Since then, considerable effort has been devoted both at the intergovernmental level and by the Secretariat to its elaboration.

181. In November 1994, in a report to the General Assembly (A/49/665), I presented four principal recommendations on "An Agenda for Development" for the consideration of Member States at the forty-ninth session of the General Assembly.

182. These were: *(a)* that development should be recognized as the foremost and most far-reaching task of our time; *(b)* that while it must be seen in its many dimensions—in the contexts of peace, the economy, environmental protection,

social justice and democracy—development at its core must be about improvement of human well-being, the removal of poverty, hunger, disease and ignorance, ensuring productive employment and the satisfaction of priority needs of all people in a way that can be sustained over future generations; *(c)* that the emerging consensus on the priority and dimensions of development should find expression in a new framework for international cooperation; and *(d)* that within this new framework for development cooperation, the United Nations must play a major role in both policy leadership and operations.

183. I further outlined the need for a new framework for world development cooperation that requires supporting actions at the national and international levels and a strong and effective multilateral system, at the centre of which would be the United Nations, with its unmatched global network at all levels. The United Nations can promote awareness, build consensus and inform policy in every dimension affecting development and can help rationalize and harmonize the multiplicity of public and private efforts worldwide. An important element in the new framework should be improved cooperation between the United Nations, its specialized agencies and the Bretton Woods institutions.

184. The General Assembly has primary responsibility to bring together all these aspects in an Agenda for Development. The aim should be to provide consistent policy guidance that would contribute to greater coherence and integration of the development work of the United Nations system. This implies strengthening the capacity of the Assembly to provide such harmonized policy guidance by a careful review of the working methods of its Second and Third Committees, so that the debates in those Committees could be sharply focused on key policy issues and their mutual complementarities enhanced. Secondly, a revitalized Economic and Social Council could greatly assist the Assembly by bringing to its attention recommendations leading to the adoption of harmonized and integrated policies. The relationship between those central bodies and the Bretton Woods institutions, on the one hand, and the funds and programmes and specialized agencies, on the other, could be built around shared objectives and a common purpose leading to closer cooperation and joint actions at the country level.

185. Recent pronouncements of the summit meeting of seven major industrialized countries, which was held at Halifax, Canada, in June 1995, as well as of the Ministerial Meeting of the Coordinating Bureau of the Non-Aligned Countries held at Bandung, Indonesia, in April 1995, signify a resolute willingness on the part of the international community at the political level to see a strong United Nations system working in unison for the realization of internationally agreed goals and objectives. Efforts to make United Nations operational activities more efficient and effective begin with the identification of those areas where it has special assets and strengths that can support the process of development. Given shared vision and a common purpose, coordination and integration in the Organization's operational activities can be ensured.

186. This issue was considered during the coordination segment of the Economic and Social Council in July 1995. At my request, the Administrator of UNDP, who assists the Secretary-General in ensuring policy coherence and the coordination of operational activities for development, initiated a process of consultation among senior United Nations officials on coordination mechanisms that can be instituted on conference follow-up at the inter-agency level, thus mobilizing the United Nations system as a whole through thematic inter-agency task forces at the national, regional and headquarters levels.

187. During the forty-ninth session of the General Assembly, Member States decided to establish an open-ended working group to elaborate further an action-oriented comprehensive agenda for development, taking into account the reports and recommendations presented by the Secretary-General pursuant to Assembly resolutions 47/181 of 22 December 1992 and 48/166 of 21 December 1993, the outcome of the high-level segment of the 1994 substantive session of the Economic and Social Council, the views expressed by representatives in the high-level debate held during the forty-ninth session of the Assembly, as well as the summary of the World Hearings on Development and proposals presented by Member States and other parties.

188. The Working Group was required to submit a report on the progress of its work to the General Assembly before the conclusion of its fiftieth session. A compendium containing the goals, targets and commitments of major United Nations conferences held and agreements signed since 1990, as well as an assessment of the status of their implementation, was submitted by the Secretariat to the Working Group following its first session. That document was a complement to the background information already identified in Assembly resolution 49/126 of 19 December 1994.

189. At the Working Group's second session, held from 15 to 26 May 1995, Governments presented their views on the structure and content of the Agenda for Development during the formal meetings, which were preceded and followed by inter-sessional consultations. The Working Group reached a consensus on the structure

of the Agenda and defined modalities for developing its text during the third and final session, yet to be held. A tentative comprehensive structure was adopted, consisting of three chapters, the first devoted to setting goals and objectives; the second representing the bulk of the Agenda, providing a policy framework and identifying priority actions for development, together with means of implementation; and the third dealing with institutional issues and follow-up.

### B. *Global development activities*

1.  Secretariat departments at Headquarters

190.  The Department for Policy Coordination and Sustainable Development, headed by Mr. Nitin Desai, provides support for the central coordinating and policy-making functions vested in the Economic and Social Council and its subsidiary bodies, as well as for the Second and Third Committees of the General Assembly. Ensuring the integration of economic, social and environmental concerns in policy development and implementation is a crucial objective underlying the structure and mandate of the Department.

191.  The World Summit for Social Development was convened by the General Assembly at Copenhagen from 6 to 12 March 1995 to address the urgent and universal need to eradicate poverty, expand productive employment, reduce unemployment and enhance social integration. The Summit provided an impetus for the world's Governments to give priority to the social aspects of global development and the social impact of international relations, while reaffirming their commitment to individual, family and community well-being as the fundamental concern of their policies.

192.  The Summit was the largest gathering ever of Heads of State and Government: in all, 187 countries participated in the deliberations, which produced the Copenhagen Declaration on Social Development and Programme of Action, and 117 of them were represented by Heads of State or Government. In addition, 2,315 delegates representing 811 non-governmental organizations joined the meeting, demonstrating eloquently the vitality and diversity of people's initiatives and establishing the foundation for a renewed and strengthened partnership between Governments and the actors of civil society. The preparations for the Summit and the actions initiated in pursuance of its mandate have brought into play virtually the entire spectrum of departments, agencies, programmes and offices of the United Nations system and fostered coordination between them and with Member States and non-governmental organizations.

193.  The observance of the International Year for the Eradication of Poverty (1996) will provide an excellent opportunity for the implementation of the commitments made at Copenhagen. Countries are invited to elaborate specific targets during the Year and to prepare national strategies for the struggle against poverty.

194.  The International Year of the Family (1994) has led to a remarkable evolution of the political approach to the family as an object and agent of social policy throughout the world. A greater recognition has been accorded at the global, national and individual levels to the importance of supporting families and bringing about positive changes in the family as an integral part of the efforts to achieve peace, human rights, democracy, sustainable development and social progress, as well as lasting progress on behalf of women, children and other traditionally less advantaged members of society. A large number of local, national and international activities in support of the family were arranged by Governments in more than 150 countries and by various nongovernmental, community and intergovernmental organizations in observance of the Year. Those efforts were effectively augmented by supportive action of 34 bodies and agencies of the United Nations, including the regional commissions.

195.  The International Conference on Families, held in October 1994 during the forty-ninth session of the General Assembly, marked the first occasion on which the Assembly devoted a discussion exclusively to the family. The Conference itself conveyed the growing conviction that it is in the best interests of individuals and societies to promote democratic families and family-friendly societies. I will submit to the Assembly at its fiftieth session a detailed report on the observance of the International Year of the Family, along with specific proposals on its long-term follow-up.

196.  The High-level Advisory Board on Sustainable Development, which was set up following the United Nations Conference on Environment and Development, held in June 1992, to provide independent advice to the Secretary-General on environment and development matters, held its third session from 17 to 21 October 1994. The Board examined four issues: *(a)* sustainable food security for a growing world population; *(b)* the need for mutual reinforcement between international trade and environment policies; *(c)* value-based education for sustainability; and *(d)* ways of forging new alliances for sustainable development. The Vice-Chairperson of the Board apprised the Commission on Sustainable Development, at its third session, of the conclusions reached in its deliberations and on its discussions with me. The Inter-Agency Committee on Sustainable Development of the Administrative Committee on Coordination met in February and July 1995. The Inter-Agency Committee

has received strong support from Member States, which have expressed their particular appreciation for the fact that the follow-up to the United Nations Conference on Environment and Development and the work of the Commission on Sustainable Development bring together the entire system in a coordinated and cooperative manner.

197.   Since the adoption of the Barbados Declaration and Programme of Action for the Sustainable Development of Small Island Developing States in May 1994, efforts have intensified to follow up on the work programme regarding the specific economic, social and environmental concerns of those States. There is increasing interest among the organizations of the system, including the regional commissions, as well as a number of concerned non-governmental organizations, in joint and coordinated activities in this regard. In May 1995, the Department organized a meeting of those organizations and representatives of the Alliance of Small Island States to discuss the status of implementation of the Barbados agreements. The achievement of the goals set out in those agreements, as with Agenda 21 itself, continues to be impeded by financial constraints, as well as by difficulties in the effective transfer of technology for sustainable development.

198.   The Office of the Special Coordinator for Africa and Least Developed Countries, as requested by the Secretary-General's Panel of High-level Personalities on African Development, organized a high-level brainstorming workshop on non-governmental organizations and African development on 16 and 17 January 1995. The Office prepared a pamphlet on the conclusions and recommendations of the Panel, as requested by the General Assembly in its resolution 48/214 of 23 December 1993. In addition to disseminating information to countries and organizations, the Office coordinated activities related to the United Nations New Agenda for the Development of Africa in the 1990s, adopted by the General Assembly in its resolution 46/151 of 18 December 1991, including the sixth meeting of the Working Group of the United Nations Inter-Agency Task Force on Africa's Critical Economic Situation, Recovery and Development.

199.   My report on the development of Africa, including the implementation of the United Nations New Agenda for the Development of Africa in the 1990s, prepared for the 1995 high-level segment of the Economic and Social Council, identifies key policy issues critical to African development and offers concrete recommendations on what African countries and the international community can do to improve the lives of the people of Africa. It also analyses the progress made and difficulties encountered in the implementation of the New Agenda.

200.   The Office of the Special Coordinator provided substantive assistance to donor and African countries in the negotiations on the establishment of a diversification facility in the African Development Bank, which led to General Assembly resolution 49/142 of 23 December 1994, requesting those States participating in the African Development Fund to consider making an initial adequate contribution to finance the preparatory phase of commodity diversification projects and programmes in African countries. The Office organized regular briefings on areas of concern and, together with UNDP and the Governments of Japan and Indonesia, organized the Asia-Africa Forum at Bandung, Indonesia, in December 1994, as a follow-up to the Tokyo International Conference on African Development. The Office also organized, together with the Department for Development Support and Management Services and UNDP, an international workshop on informal sector development in Africa at United Nations Headquarters. The Office participated in a number of intergovernmental and other meetings, including those of OAU.

201.   The Interim Secretariat of the Convention to Combat Desertification opened the United Nations Convention to Combat Desertification in Those Countries Experiencing Serious Drought and/or Desertification, Particularly in Africa, for signature in Paris on 14 and 15 October 1994. As at July 1995, the number of signatories had reached 106 and 2 countries had ratified the Convention. Consistent with General Assembly resolution 49/234 of 23 December 1994, the Intergovernmental Negotiating Committee for the Elaboration of an International Convention to Combat Desertification in Those Countries Experiencing Serious Drought and/or Desertification, Particularly in Africa, held its sixth session in New York, from 9 to 19 January 1995, and adopted a work programme for the interim period leading to the first session of the Conference of the Parties, which will be held within 12 months of the entry into force of the Convention. The Intergovernmental Negotiating Committee established two working groups to lay the groundwork for the first session of implementation of the resolution on urgent action for Africa, through the exchange of information and the review of progress made thereon, and through the promotion of action in other regions. It initiated this phase of its work at its seventh session, held at Nairobi from 7 to 18 August 1995.

202.   ''Awareness days'' are being held in 20 affected countries in the various subregions of Africa to sensitize key actors at the local level and to enable them to participate fully in the Convention's implementation. Seminars are also being held at the subregional level in southern, eastern

and western Africa to facilitate the preparation of relevant action programmes. A number of activities were held in various countries in observance of World Day to Combat Desertification and Drought, 17 June, pursuant to General Assembly resolution 49/115 of 19 December 1994, including seminars, exhibitions and the launching of publications.

203. The first meeting of the Conference of the Parties to the United Nations Framework Convention on Climate Change was convened from 28 March to 7 April 1995 at Berlin. The meeting aimed at setting in motion the processes needed to promote the effective implementation of the Convention—only four years after multilateral negotiations were first launched on the issue of global warming and its impact on the climate. It is to the credit of the international community that the Conference of the Parties, fully aware of the contribution that the implementation of the Convention can make towards sustainable development, has agreed by consensus to forge ahead with concrete efforts aimed at bringing emissions of greenhouse gases in the atmosphere within safe limits.

204. The Department for Economic and Social Information and Policy Analysis, headed by Mr. Jean-Claude Milleron, is the principal unit in the United Nations for the generation and elaboration of economic, demographic, social and environmental data and the analysis of national and regional development policies and trends. It also provides technical support to projects in statistics and population undertaken by developing countries.

205. A cornerstone of the Department is its wide-ranging programme of statistical publications, which continued during the year. In addition to the *Statistical Yearbook*, other annual reference volumes published included the *Demographic Yearbook, Industrial Commodity Statistics Yearbook, National Accounts Yearbook* and *Energy Statistics Yearbook*. Publications with a more frequent periodicity included the *Monthly Bulletin of Statistics, Commodity Trade Statistics* and the *Population and Vital Statistics Report*. As part of its contribution to the Fourth World Conference on Women, the Department completed the 1995 edition of *The World's Women: Trends and Statistics*. This second edition, which was a collaborative effort among 12 United Nations offices and agencies, not only presents an array of new data, but also underlines the work that still must be done to develop gender statistics that are comprehensive and of adequate quality.

206. The year has seen further progress by the Department in the development and implementation of new statistical concepts and methodologies in other areas. The 1993 System of National Accounts was the result of collaboration between the United Nations, EU, IMF, the World Bank and the Organisation for Economic Co-operation and Development (OECD). Since the adoption of the System, the Department has been working in close cooperation with the regional commissions and other international organizations on its implementation in selected developing countries. During the past year, the Department conducted seminars on the 1993 System of National Accounts in concept and practice, and on the use of the System of National Accounts for transition economy countries.

207. The Department, in cooperation with international organizations and countries, has completed a draft revision of the international concepts and definitions for international trade statistics. In addition, the Statistical Commission, at its twenty-eighth session, held in New York from 27 February to 3 March, approved an international compilation of environmental indicators that will be assembled by the Department. Close collaboration with the Commission on Sustainable Development and its secretariat will ensure comparability with its programme on indicators of sustainable development. In the area of integrated environmental and economic accounting, the framework developed by the Department is now being tested through several country projects with the support of United Nations Environment Programme (UNEP) and UNDP. The Statistical Commission also designated the period 1995-2004 as the 2000 World Population and Housing Census Decade. In this area, the Department continued its work on civil registration and vital statistics.

208. The work of the Department in the area of population was given fresh impetus towards the end of 1994 with the success of the International Conference on Population and Development, held at Cairo from 5 to 13 September 1994. The Department, in cooperation with UNFPA, undertook substantive preparations for the Conference. Following the Conference, the General Assembly decided, in its resolution 49/128 of 19 December 1994, that the revitalized Commission on Population and Development should be charged with monitoring, reviewing and assessing the implementation of the Programme of Action adopted at Cairo. The Department provides the secretariat for the Commission. At its twenty-eighth session, from 21 February to 2 March 1995, the Commission affirmed the Department as the body with competence to cover the monitoring and appraisal of the broad range of areas covered by the Programme of Action. The Department was also charged by the Secretary-General with the preparation of the report on international migration and development called for by the General Assembly in its resolution 49/127 of 19 December 1994. The report, which was submitted to the Economic and

Social Council at its 1995 substantive session, not only addressed the substantive issues involved but also included aspects related to the objectives and modalities for the convening of the United Nations Conference on Migration and Development.

209.    The Department completed its 1994 revision of *World Population Prospects*, the official United Nations population figures for all countries of the world. Reflecting the high international standing of these data, the World Bank announced that henceforth it would rely exclusively on the United Nations for population statistics. Studies in the field of population by the Department address such subjects as contraception, women's education and fertility behaviour, abortion, urbanization, population policy, international migration policies, the status of female migrants and the spread of HIV/AIDS. Much of the work undertaken in the course of these studies contributed to the deliberations on the Cairo Programme of Action.

210.    As a further dimension of its responsibility for monitoring the world economic and social situations, the Department produced the *World Economic and Social Survey 1995*. In addition to an analysis of the world economic situation and its short-term prospects and discussions of major global policy issues, the *Survey* examined some longer-term dimensions of economic and social changes in the world. As part of the continuing effort to improve the *Survey*, the 1995 edition devoted greater attention to a discussion of economic and social policies around the world. In a parallel effort to provide both the academic community and the general public with information on issues that would form the backdrop to the World Summit for Social Development, the Department published *The World Social Situation in the 1990s* prior to the Summit.

211.    The Department carried out development projections and perspective studies under Project *LINK*, an international economic research network of more than 70 country teams. During the past year, the Department convened two meetings of this network—one in Salamanca, Spain, and the other in New York—to assist in the preparation of short-term economic forecasts for the General Assembly and the Economic and Social Council. As part of its longer-term analysis, the Department prepared an update of the "Overall socio-economic perspective of the world economy beyond the year 2000" for the General Assembly at its fiftieth session. The Department has continued its work on the debt crisis, sources of finance for development, coercive economic measures and economic assistance to countries affected by sanctions imposed by the Security Council. It has produced reports on each of these subjects for the Assembly at its fiftieth session.

212.    As mandated by the General Assembly in response to the new development thinking that has evolved in recent years, the Department has been expanding its research and analysis on microeconomic issues, focusing on ways in which increased reliance on market forces can contribute to the attainment of development objectives. This work has included studies relating to employment, technology and the use of market-based mechanisms both to meet environmental objectives and to provide public services. The Department has continued to provide operational and technical assistance to developing countries and economies in transition, primarily in the areas of population and statistics and mostly with financing provided by UNDP and UNFPA. Such arrangements applied to more than 100 technical cooperation projects over the past year, with additional assistance on such matters as country strategy notes being provided through resident coordinators on a *pro bono* basis.

213.    The Department has sustained its efforts to provide information and analysis through means other than official documents and publications. In order to promote exchanges with others with shared interests, the Department convenes seminars, issues a series of working papers and continues to increase its dissemination of information by electronic means. In 1995 the *United Nations Statistical Yearbook* was again issued on CD-ROM, as well as in its traditional paper form. Version III of *Women's Indicators and Statistics Database (Wistat)* was similarly made available in CD-ROM format, while *Statbase Locator* (an inventory of international computerized databases) was released on diskette. In addition, selected information from the 1994 revisions of *World Population Prospects* and *World Urbanization Prospects* released during the year is available on-line to users of the Internet, through the Department's Population Information Network, which was used extensively during the International Conference on Population and Development. All the official documents of the Conference, as well as the statements made in the plenary, were made available on the Network, which handled more than 28,000 requests while the Conference was taking place.

214.    As part of its effort to improve the availability of economic and social information, the Department, in cooperation with the regional commissions, continues to work on a new system that will encompass the collection, processing, storage, exchange and dissemination of economic and social information. Entitled the United Nations Economic and Social Information System, phase II of the project commenced in 1995 and focuses on implementing the System's core components in selected pilot areas, such as national accounts and the development of prototype techniques.

215. The Department for Development Support and Management Services, headed by Mr. Chaozhu Ji, is responsible for providing technical assistance to developing countries and economies in transition in the broad fields of integrated development and public management, thereby assisting Governments in establishing an enabling environment for development.

216. In the planning and management of mineral resources, the Department organized international round-table conferences on foreign investment in exploration and mining in India and Pakistan in 1994. These were to familiarize foreign investors with the new mining policies and regulations in those countries, to encourage investment in development of the mineral sector, to acquaint better the Governments with the mining industry's expectations and with the elements of a successful mining investment promotion drive, and thus to arrive at mutually satisfactory and rewarding policies for mining investments. The conferences culminated in concrete joint venture investments in both countries. The Department has also prepared the Environmental Guidelines for Mining Operations in response to the need stressed in Agenda 21 for the adoption of environmental guidelines for natural resource development.

217. The water resource activities at the individual country level have been extended into subregional and regional initiatives through the use of joint programming with the regional commissions. This work has brought the added benefit of preparing the ground for several recently launched Global Environment Facility initiatives in international waters and the Okavango and Lake Chad basins. The detailed implementation experience has also provided the empirical basis for the ongoing global freshwater assessment initiated at the request of the Commission on Sustainable Development.

218. Information exchange dealing with both mineral and water resources is facilitated by the substantive services the Department provides to the Committee on Natural Resources. Dissemination of ideas is also fostered by the *Natural Resources Forum,* the quarterly technical journal produced by the Department.

219. The Department is collaborating with the African Energy Programme of the African Development Bank in a wide-ranging effort to address the serious problems within the African energy sector. In 1994 the Department undertook a study of energy institutions in 17 African countries to characterize better the strengths and weaknesses of the sector at the country, subregional and regional levels. A key recommendation that emerged from the exercise was that an African energy unit should be established, based within the African Development Bank and supported by OAU, the Economic Commission for Africa (ECA) and the Department for Development Support and Management Services. A programme of action is now being elaborated in conjunction with the African Energy Programme of the African Development Bank.

220. The Department executed a $7 million project in Zimbabwe funded by the Global Environment Facility, which provides a model for other countries with sufficient solar energy. The project addresses the issue of global warming by providing a sustainable model of solar electricity dissemination in Zimbabwe's rural areas where an expanded commercial market is being developed for affordable domestic solar electric lighting systems through the provision of low-interest financing from existing institutions to allow householders to purchase home solar systems.

221. The United Nations International Conference on Coal Methane Development and Utilization will be held in Beijing in October 1995. A primary objective of the Conference is to assist Governments in developing a legal and regulatory context for the promotion of domestic coal-bed methane resources. The Conference will review the status and potential of ongoing coal-bed methane recovery projects in China. Coal mines in that country characteristically have high seepage rates of methane gas, with consequent danger of atmospheric pollution and a grave risk to the safety of miners and the productivity of the mines. To help address this problem, the United Nations is assisting China through a $10 million programme designed for recovery of coal-bed methane prior to, during and after mining operations. Funded by the Global Environment Facility and executed by the Department for Development Support and Management Services, the programme addresses all types of gas recovery and the feasibility of various options for gas utilization. Another project is developing the geothermal resources of the Tibet region, with $3 million in trust funds contributed by the Government of Italy. This project is leading to institution-building and human resource training both in China, during the execution of the project, and overseas. The project is also oriented towards important investments to be realized in the near future.

222. Under the joint programming exercise, initiated in June 1994, pilot projects implemented by the Department together with the regional commissions include a geothermal project in conjunction with the Economic Commission for Latin America and the Caribbean (ECLAC), a capacity-building project in central Asian countries to deal with transboundary management of water resources and a small-scale mining proposal from ECA designed to train artisanal miners.

223. The Department has taken several steps to strengthen support to Governments in the area of social development policy and poverty alleviation, consistent with priorities enunciated at the World Summit for Social Development. Africa is an area of particular concern. To limit the potential for negative effects of national economic adjustment programmes on vulnerable groups and on delivery of services in social sectors like health and education, the Department has developed a system for monitoring the social effects of such programmes. This has been introduced in projects in Algeria, Cameroon, Côte d'Ivoire, Gabon, Senegal and Tunisia. In June 1995, the Department collaborated with the Department for Policy Coordination and Sustainable Development and UNDP to organize a workshop at Headquarters on the development of Africa's informal sector. Experts from Governments, the United Nations system and non-governmental organizations and academic institutions discussed experiences and perspectives.

224. In the fields of public administration and finance, the Department is assisting Governments in developing administrative and managerial systems at the central and local levels, in strengthening financial management capabilities, in undertaking public enterprise reform and encouragement of private enterprise and in improving related informational technology. For example, in Viet Nam, the Department is currently providing technical services to the Government's comprehensive public administration programme and in particular to the component on improvement of civil service management.

225. The Department has completed the establishment of a computerized information system to assist key agencies of government. This public sector planning and management information system facilitates econometric analysis, national budget preparation and modelling, the preparation of debt programmes and investment programme planning and monitoring. The system has already been demonstrated in several countries and is ready for installation upon request.

226. Laying the groundwork for a session of the General Assembly on making Governments work better was the focus of a meeting of more than 50 experts worldwide organized by the Department from 31 July to 11 August at Headquarters. The themes for the experts' discussions included policy development, administrative restructuring, civil service reform, the role of public administration in promoting social development, financial management, post-conflict rehabilitation and reconstruction of government machinery, public/private sector interaction and the role of public administration in the management of development programmes. Recommendations from the meet-

ing will be reviewed at a resumed session of the Economic and Social Council later this year.

227. The outbreak of localized conflicts throughout the world has highlighted the interdependence and interaction between peace and improvement of the human condition, as today Governments must often begin to reconstruct their human and administrative infrastructures even before conflict has ceased. The Department's work in assisting Rwanda to restore its technical, human and institutional capacities and rehabilitate its judicial system, in strengthening Yemen's water and sanitation facilities, in preparing a reconstruction and development plan for Bosnia and Herzegovina and in providing support to the rejuvenation of Haiti's public administration—these are all examples of this recognition being acted upon by the United Nations.

228. To help stimulate a better exchange of ideas on post-conflict reconstruction strategies, the Department organized a colloquium in June in Austria, with support from the Government of Austria and in cooperation with the Austrian Centre for Peace and Conflict Resolution. This informal gathering brought together representatives from several Governments, plus a number of United Nations departments and agencies, non-governmental organizations and academic institutions. The conclusions of the meeting and other documentation, including an inventory of possible post-conflict peace-building activities, have been published.

229. In the area of cartography, the Department continues to implement the recommendations presented by the Thirteenth United Nations Regional Cartographic Conference for Asia and the Pacific, which requested the United Nations to support surveying, mapping and charting activities in the Asia and Pacific region and to facilitate the participation of the least developed countries and the small island developing States of the region in the work of the Conference.

## 2. United Nations Conference on Trade and Development (UNCTAD)

230. The work of UNCTAD, under the Officer-in-Charge, Mr. Carlos Fortin, was dominated during the past year by the forty-first session of the Trade and Development Board and its subsidiary bodies, and the United Nations International Symposium on Trade Efficiency, as well as by the preparatory process for the ninth session of the United Nations Conference on Trade and Development. I have proposed for approval by the General Assembly the appointment of Mr. Rubens Ricupero as Secretary-General of UNCTAD. His appointment would be effective as at 15 September 1995.

231. During this period, the Trade and Development Board undertook a preliminary analysis

and assessment of the final act of the Uruguay Round of multilateral trade negotiations. The States members of UNCTAD recognized the important role it could play in the post–Uruguay Round period in enhancing the ability of developing countries to take maximum advantage of these new opportunities and in recommending measures to mitigate the consequences on countries that could be adversely affected. The respective roles and functions of UNCTAD and the World Trade Organization have been more clearly delineated.

232.  UNCTAD also started implementation of the decisions taken during the mid-term review of the Cartagena Commitment in May 1994. The commemoration of the thirtieth anniversary of UNCTAD at the first part of the Board's forty-first session in September was the occasion for States members to reaffirm their full support to the organization and to look to its future orientation. Finally, the preparatory process for the ninth session of the Conference, to be held in the spring of 1996, started in a spirit of cooperation and with the conviction that the Conference should address in an innovative and action-oriented way the economic issues facing the international community.

233.  The Trade and Development Board, at the first part of its forty-first session, in September 1994, adopted a declaration in which States members reaffirmed their commitment to the primary development objectives of UNCTAD and undertook to reinforce their political support for the organization and for its important role in strengthening the global Partnership for Development by addressing the economic and development problems of all countries, in particular the developing countries.

234.  The Board's discussion on interdependence was based on the *Trade and Development Report 1994*. The Board reviewed the east Asian growth and development experience and concluded that there was a wide variety of experience in east Asia: while in some fast-growing economies the policy regime had been more liberal, several Governments had successfully played active and interventionist roles.

235.  The Board concluded its policy review of technical cooperation activities of UNCTAD by noting that the agency's technical cooperation was greatly valued by developing countries and countries in transition and had also attracted increasing support in the last few years from donor countries and institutions. Accordingly, the Board emphasized the need to strengthen UNCTAD technical cooperation.

236.  At the second part of its forty-first session, in March 1995, the Board endorsed agreed conclusions on trade policies, structural adjustment and economic reform, and on the UNCTAD contribution to the implementation of the United Nations New Agenda for the Development of Africa in the 1990s. The Board also agreed on preparatory action for a high-level intergovernmental meeting to be held in September to undertake a mid-term review of the implementation of the Programme of Action for the Least Developed Countries for the 1990s. It also carried out a policy review of the work of UNCTAD on sustainable development. On trade policies, structural adjustment and economic reform, a broad convergence emerged on a number of conclusions. The Board concluded that Governments should take a positive approach to structural adjustment. A policy framework favourable to structural adjustment could facilitate the comprehensive and effective implementation of the Uruguay Round agreements, lower resistance to further liberalization and better prepare economies for future negotiations on improving market access.

237.  On preparations for the ninth session of the Conference, the Board reached agreement on the provisional agenda for the Conference. The theme of the ninth session will be promoting growth and sustainable development in a globalizing and liberalizing world economy. The Government of South Africa announced its decision to make an offer, in principle, to host the Conference. States members underlined the importance of holding the session in Africa and expressed their full support for South Africa as the host country.

238.  The United Nations International Symposium on Trade Efficiency was held at Columbus, Ohio, from 17 to 21 October 1994. More than 2,000 decision makers from both the public and private sectors participated in the Symposium and in the other parallel events: the Global Executive Trade Summit, the Global Summit for Mayors and the World Trade Efficiency and Technology Exhibition. The Symposium was chaired by the Secretary of Commerce of the United States of America. The unprecedented involvement of the private sector and of local governments made the Symposium a unique forum for bringing practical solutions to some of the problems encountered in international trade. The Symposium adopted the Columbus Ministerial Declaration and launched the Global Trade Point Network. Together, these documents constitute a blueprint for efficient international trade in the next century.

239.  The Standing Committee on Commodities held its third session from 31 October to 4 November 1994. In its agreed conclusions, the Committee requested UNCTAD to continue its analysis of ways to improve the competitiveness of natural products, giving priority to the theoretical and practical aspects of the internalization of ecological externalities. UNCTAD held a number of commodity-related meetings under its

auspices. In January 1994, the fourth session of the United Nations Conference on Tropical Timber adopted the International Tropical Timber Agreement and, as at 31 December 1994, 12 States had signed the new Agreement and one had become formally party to it, although conditions for its entry into force are not yet met. At the end of the second session of the United Nations Conference on Natural Rubber, in October 1994, 53 out of the 67 articles for a successor agreement had been cleared in principle. The Conference resumed its work, under UNCTAD auspices, at a third session, in February 1995, where 31 countries, representing nearly 90 per cent of world trade in natural rubber, adopted the 1995 International Natural Rubber Agreement aimed at stabilizing prices. The new Agreement was opened for signature at United Nations Headquarters on 1 April 1995. Other commodity-related meetings held under UNCTAD auspices dealt with iron ore and tungsten.

240.    The Standing Committee on Economic Cooperation among Developing Countries held its second session from 14 to 18 November 1994. The Committee endorsed a set of recommendations aimed at fostering economic cooperation among developing countries. Furthermore, it concluded, *inter alia*, that developing countries should adopt strategies that combine trade liberalization with other measures in the areas of production, investment, transport and communications, marketing and distribution and trade information. Special attention should be given to measures for increasing the effectiveness of trade liberalization regimes in regional integration arrangements and for increasing South-South trade.

241.    At the end of the thirteenth session of the Intergovernmental Group of Experts on Restrictive Business Practices, held from 24 to 28 October 1994, competition experts launched the preparatory process for the Third United Nations Conference to Review All Aspects of the Set of Multilaterally Agreed Equitable Principles and Rules for the Control of Restrictive Business Practices, which is scheduled to take place in November 1995. The main document prepared by the UNCTAD secretariat dealt with the role of competition policy in economic reforms in developing and other countries. The Intergovernmental Group held its fourteenth session from 6 to 10 March 1995. Anti-trust experts made a number of proposals for strengthening multilateral cooperation in the area of competition laws and policies.

242.    The three new ad hoc working groups, established in accordance with a decision of the Board taken at the resumed second part of its fortieth session, in May 1994, commenced their work. The Ad Hoc Working Group on Trade, Environment and Development held its first session from 28 November to 2 December 1994. The Working Group examined international cooperation on eco-labelling and eco-certification programmes, and market opportunities for environmentally friendly products. The session emphasized the importance of improved transparency in eco-labelling and the need for developing countries to be more closely associated with the elaboration of environmental criteria having an impact on trade and development.

243.    The Ad Hoc Working Group on the Role of Enterprises in Development held its first session from 3 to 7 April 1995, focusing upon the development of small and medium-sized enterprises. The Working Group examined the role of the State in creating an enabling environment for the promotion of entrepreneurship, as well as the viable development of enterprises, especially small and medium-sized enterprises.

244.    The Commission on International Investment and Transnational Corporations held its twenty-first session from 24 to 28 April, its first session in its new role as a subsidiary body of the Trade and Development Board. The Commission examined recent trends in foreign direct investment and exchanged experiences on ways of attracting such investment.

245.    In 1994, UNCTAD expenditure on technical cooperation amounted to some $22 million. The largest single source of funds continues to be UNDP, although the trend observed in recent years towards increased contributions by other donors has continued. As part of the programme, UNCTAD provided support to a number of countries in assessing the results of the Uruguay Round, and in preparing themselves for new issues subject to negotiations in the General Agreement on Tariffs and Trade/World Trade Organization. Continued assistance was provided in several aspects of trade policies, including competition policy, the linkage between trade and the environment, and the utilization of the generalized system of preferences. Several new packages under the UNCTAD training programme TRAINFORTRADE were developed and delivered. In the area of commodities, particular attention was devoted to the use of risk-management instruments.

246.    With the transfer to UNCTAD of the United Nations activities related to transnational corporations and to science and technology, the corresponding technical cooperation programmes, including advisory services on foreign investment, have become an integral part of UNCTAD technical cooperation. The UNCTAD software for management and analysis of debt was enhanced and installed in a number of countries. UNCTAD has also continued to provide support to countries in the areas of shipping, port management (nota-

bly in Somalia) and cargo tracking, with the training aspects being undertaken in most cases through the TRAINMAR programme. The largest single programme undertaken by UNCTAD is that on customs modernization and computerization, known as ASYCUDA. In line with the process leading to and following up after the World Symposium on Trade Efficiency, support and advice were given to a number of countries in the establishment of trade points.

247. At its tenth executive session, held on 4 May, the Trade and Development Board agreed that appropriate exploratory work should be undertaken on such new and emerging issues on the international trade agenda within the preparatory process for the ninth session of UNCTAD. Three categories of issues were identified. The first consists of issues that give rise to demands for domestic policy harmonization. Among those issues are investment and competition policies and labour standards. The second category includes issues that reflect concern about the lack of coherence among global policy objectives. The third consists of issues affecting the ability of countries, especially the least developed countries and others with weak economies, to pursue national goals effectively.

248. The Commission on Science and Technology for Development held its second session from 15 to 24 May. (The Commission, a subsidiary body of the Economic and Social Council, now meets at Geneva as a result of the designation of UNCTAD as the United Nations focal point for science and technology-related activities.) Topics considered by the Commission at that session included the use of science and technology to help meet basic needs of low-income populations, improving women's access to science and technology, and the use of science and technology towards sustainable land-management practices. The Commission decided to focus its work programme for the next two years on recent developments in information technologies and their implications for economic growth, social cohesion, cultural values and society as a whole.

249. The Standing Committee on Developing Services Sectors: Shipping held its third session from 6 to 9 June to examine progress in policy reforms for enhancing competitive services in the fields of shipping, ports and multimodal transport in developing countries and countries in transition. In particular, support was pledged by major donors for the TRAINMAR programme, through which UNCTAD enhances the management capacities of developing countries in the field of shipping, ports and multimodal transport. The role of UNCTAD in the development of the advanced cargo information system was also praised. As this was the last session of the Committee before the

ninth session of UNCTAD, the Committee reviewed work carried out since 1992. It established a set of complementary activities to be taken up by UNCTAD during the period leading up to the ninth session and suggested issues for further deliberation at that session.

250. The Ad Hoc Working Group on Trade, Environment and Development held its second session from 6 to 9 June, to examine the effects of environmental policies on market access and competitiveness. The UNCTAD secretariat was requested to outline positive measures that could be used as alternatives to trade-related measures for environmental protection for consideration at the next meeting of the Working Group, to be held in October.

251. The Standing Committee on Poverty Alleviation held its third session from 12 to 16 June to identify national and international measures to alleviate poverty through international trade and official development assistance. As this was the last session of the Committee before the ninth session of UNCTAD, the meeting reviewed the work carried out since 1992 by the Committee and suggested that the ninth session should consider whether the present form of intergovernmental machinery for addressing poverty alleviation in UNCTAD was the appropriate one or whether some alternative arrangement could be envisaged. Poverty and increased marginalization will feature high on the agenda of the ninth session.

252. In cooperation with UNDP and the United Nations regional commissions, UNCTAD organized the Symposium for Land-locked and Transit Developing Countries from 14 to 16 June, pursuant to General Assembly resolution 48/169 of 21 December 1993. The objectives of the Symposium were to analyse weaknesses in the operational, administrative, regulatory and institutional framework that is currently in place in the transit sector and to propose the future course of action at the national, bilateral, subregional and international levels. Participating countries agreed to develop a global framework for cooperation on transit transport with the support of the international community. UNCTAD has been requested to convene transit corridor-specific consultative groups that will identify priority areas for action at the national and subregional level and will establish the framework for the implementation of agreed measures. At a meeting of governmental experts from land-locked and transit developing countries, held from 19 to 22 June, the recommendations of the Symposium were widely endorsed.

253. The Standing Committee on Economic Cooperation among Developing Countries held its third session from 19 to 23 June to discuss ways to enlarge and deepen monetary, financial, investment and enterprise cooperation. The agreed con-

clusions contain suggestions for strengthening financial and monetary cooperation among developing countries, as well as at the level of investment and business.

### 3. United Nations Environment Programme (UNEP)

254.   UNEP, headed by Ms. Elizabeth Dowdeswell, is pursuing implementation of the environmental dimension of Agenda 21, adopted by the United Nations Conference on Environment and Development in June 1992.

255.   At its seventeenth session, in May 1994, the Governing Council of UNEP recognized the need for a fundamental change in the Programme's focus and priorities, and its relationship with other collaborators, in order to address the changed international environmental agenda emerging from the Conference.

256.   In addition to implementing a work programme for 1994-1995 based on a Corporate Programme Framework, UNEP held, between October 1994 and February 1995, extensive consultations with Governments and high-level advisers to develop a refocused programme, based on an integrated approach, for its biennium 1996-1997.

257.   The new integrated programme for 1996-1997 as approved by the eighteenth session of the Governing Council of UNEP addresses four principal environmental challenges: *(a)* sustainable management and use of natural resources; *(b)* sustainable production and consumption; *(c)* a better environment for environmental health and well-being; and *(d)* globalization trends and the environment.

258.   UNEP collaboration with UNDP has been advanced with the signing of two agreements, one on international information exchange and another on a new partnership for combating desertification. In March, UNEP and the International Union for Conservation of Nature and Natural Resources signed a partnership agreement to strengthen their long-standing worldwide cooperation in resource conservation and sustainable development. The agreement will facilitate collaboration at the regional level, thereby increasing the capability of UNEP and the International Union to respond to geographically diverse environmental concerns.

259.   A major recent development during the period under review has been the operationalization of the restructured Global Environment Facility, which is implemented jointly by UNDP, UNEP and the World Bank. Within the Global Environment Facility, UNEP will catalyse the development of scientific and technical analysis, and promote and implement environmental management.

260.   The Scientific and Technical Advisory Panel was constituted by the Executive Director in April. UNEP has also worked in conjunction with other major groups in the areas of chemicals, refugees, agricultural development and environmental technology.

261.   UNEP, together with the International Labour Organization (ILO), the Food and Agriculture Organization of the United Nations (FAO), WHO, UNIDO and OECD, established the Inter-Organization Programme for the Sound Management of Chemicals to increase coordination and information exchange on chemicals and chemical wastes. Additionally, UNEP, with the active collaboration of the private chemical industry sector, has issued the Code of Ethics in the International Trade in Chemicals. UNEP was asked to increase its role in managing toxic chemicals and to further the development of international environmental law. Moreover, the Governing Council of the United Nations Environment Programme authorized the Executive Director to begin negotiations, in cooperation with FAO, on the development of a prior informed consent convention relating to the international trade of certain hazardous chemicals. UNEP also participated in a regional seminar at San Salvador in May on the implementation in Central America and the Caribbean of the Basel Convention on the Control of Transboundary Movements of Hazardous Wastes and Their Disposal, which generated valuable discussion on how to incorporate cleaner production activities in the proposed subregional centres for training and technology transfer under the Basel Convention.

262.   In collaboration with the United Nations Centre for Human Settlements (Habitat), UNEP assisted Rwanda to address the issue of environmental damage caused by civil war and the massive movement of refugees.

263.   UNEP has joined the World Bank, FAO and UNDP in supporting the Consultative Group on International Agricultural Research in its efforts to confront the new challenges of sustainable agricultural development. UNEP is taking part in the development of a multilateral system on plant genetic resources. As a co-sponsor of the Consultative Group, UNEP has been requested to provide information on the negotiating process leading to the second conference of the parties to the Convention on Biological Diversity.

264.   The UNEP Environment Technology Centre became operational in September 1994. Located in Osaka and Shiga prefectures in Japan, the Centre is engaged in assisting developing countries in the transfer of technology to solve urban environmental problems and issues relating to management of freshwater lakes and reservoir basins. After the earthquake in Kobe, the Centre responded by providing staff to assist emergency medical teams.

265. The first UNEP International Seminar on Gender and Environment, held in April 1995, called for shared responsibility between women and men in achieving sustainable development and provided material for the development of a policy statement to the Fourth World Conference on Women in Beijing.

266. UNEP offered to provide the secretariat for the proposed global programme of action to protect the marine environment from land-based activities. The programme was reviewed by a meeting of government experts held in March. The meeting recognized the need to reduce and eliminate pollution by persistent organic pollutants. The final document of the draft global programme is to be presented for adoption at an intergovernmental meeting in October and November.

267. The work of UNEP with the commercial and investment banking sector since the United Nations Conference on Environment and Development in 1992 has resulted in a new alliance with major insurance companies. In March 1995, UNEP announced the forging of a new partnership at its Advisory Group Meeting on Commercial Banks and the Environment, with a view to continuing to foster responsible sustainable development policies and practices in the banking sector. UNEP signed an agreement with the International Olympic Committee to promote environmental protection in international sports competitions. Together with the Foundation for International Environmental Law and Development, UNEP convened a first meeting on liability and compensation in London, gathering experts from the United Nations, Governments and the academic community.

268. UNEP provides scientific and administrative support to the secretariats of environmental conventions. The Lusaka Agreement on Cooperative Enforcement Operations Directed at Illegal Trade in Wild Fauna and Flora, which aims to reduce and ultimately eliminate illegal international trafficking in African wildlife, was concluded in September 1994 by six eastern and southern African countries. The United Nations International Convention to Combat Desertification in Those Countries Experiencing Serious Drought and/or Desertification, Particularly in Africa, provides for a substantive role for UNEP in awareness-raising and the formulation and implementation of programmes to combat desertification. The first meeting of the Conference of the Parties to the Convention on Biological Diversity, held in November and December 1994, chose UNEP to host the permanent secretariat of the Convention. UNEP has initiated a programme to promote the safe use of biotechnology throughout the world as one of its responses to Agenda 21.

Under the auspices of the Convention on International Trade in Endangered Species of Wild Flora and Fauna, a Timber Working Group was established in March to study how the Convention should be involved in the protection of timber species.

269. The first Conference of the Parties to the United Nations Framework Convention on Climate Change was held in March and April. UNEP believes that a strong climate research base is needed to ensure the Convention's success and to this end has been playing a central role with the Intergovernmental Panel on Climate Change in collaboration with FAO, the Intergovernmental Oceanographic Commission of UNESCO, the World Meteorological Organization (WMO) and the International Council of Scientific Unions. Over 300 experts from countries that have ratified the Montreal Protocol on Substances that Deplete the Ozone Layer to the Vienna Convention for the Protection of the Ozone Layer made significant progress in proposing possible amendments and adjustments to the international treaty during a one-week session at Nairobi from 8 to 12 May. It was the second time since its inception in 1987 that the Montreal Protocol had been reviewed, demonstrating the determination of the world community to find solutions to many ozone-related issues that should be resolved by the December 1995 meeting at Vienna of the parties to the Protocol. Final recommendations will be made at a meeting at Geneva from 28 August to 1 September 1995, at which proposed amendments and adjustments to the Protocol will be considered, including advanced phase-out of methyl bromide and a revised phase-out schedule for chlorofluorocarbons and halons by the developing countries. Meanwhile, the multilateral fund for the implementation of the Montreal Protocol has disbursed $303 million to finance about 830 projects in 81 developing countries.

270. An intergovernmental agreement aimed at conserving the migratory waterbirds of Africa and Eurasia was adopted in June at The Hague at a meeting held under the auspices of the Convention on the Conservation of Migratory Species of Wild Animals. This new agreement covers more than 150 species of birds that are ecologically dependent on wetlands for at least part of their annual cycle. The coastal States of the Mediterranean Action Plan—the oldest and strongest of the UNEP regional seas programmes—adopted a cross-sectoral approach to environmental protection and development of the Mediterranean basin at the Ninth Ordinary Meeting of the Contracting Parties to the Convention, held from 9 to 10 June at Barcelona. The scope and geographical coverage of the revised Convention and Action Plan were also expanded to ensure the in-

tegration between the marine environment, the coastal areas and the associated coastal watersheds, including water resources, and soil, forest and plant coverage.

271.   The Executive Director of UNEP is chairing the Working Group on Sustainable Freshwater Resources for Africa within the Secretary-General's Special Initiative on Africa. A draft report was submitted to the meeting of the Group held in July at Geneva for the purpose of promoting dialogue and collaborative management of water resources among riparian States sharing international water resources. To that end UNEP has been implementing a series of new projects in integrated management of water resources. In June a meeting of experts was held on a diagnostic study for the Nile basin as the first phase in the development of a comprehensive management plan for the basin.

272.   At the first meeting of the Environmental Emergencies Advisory Group, held in January, experts from 24 countries commended the work of the Joint UNEP/Department of Humanitarian Affairs Environment Unit, which was established in 1994 and has since carried out a number of emergency assessments of the oil spills in Arctic Russia.

273.   UNEP efforts to link environmental and economic concerns are gaining momentum. At a workshop convened by UNEP and the World Bank in March, international experts urged the leading financial institutions to incorporate social and environmental objectives in their structural adjustment programmes. Another workshop was held in March to review the environmental impact of trade policies. UNEP has agreed to take a leading role in the development of methodologies for sustainability indicators. In a workshop hosted by the Philippines in May and June, government representatives from 33 countries, agencies, development banks and industries developed a framework for the sustainable management of reefs as outlined in the International Coral Reef Initiative: the UNEP regional seas programme was recognized as an appropriate vehicle for that effort. The implementation of Agenda 21 was reviewed in Paris in June by UNEP and 50 major international and national industry associations. This annual consultative meeting of UNEP facilitated information exchange among industries on the activities they have undertaken to promote sustainable production and consumption patterns worldwide.

274.   From May to June in Mexico City, 50 experts in urban and environmental management from Latin America analysed major problems hindering the efforts of the region's mega-cities towards sustainability. The result was a document prepared in collaboration with UNEP that will be presented at the Second United Nations Confer-

ence on Human Settlements (Habitat II), to be held at Istanbul in June 1996.

275.   The Governing Council of UNEP held its eighteenth session at Nairobi, from 15 to 26 May, adopting a record number of 64 decisions, all by consensus. A programme activity budget of $90-105 million was approved for the next biennium. UNEP celebrated World Environment Day on 5 June with the theme, "We the Peoples, United for the Global Environment", in South Africa, with the participation and support of the President of the Republic of South Africa, Mr. Nelson Mandela.

276.   The demands placed on UNEP after the United Nations Conference on Environment and Development in 1992 have not been met with any significant increase in financial resources to the Programme. The further expected reduction of the voluntary contributions to the Environment Fund of UNEP and the unpredictability of payments constitute principal constraints for the future of the Programme and its capability to provide an effective service to the international community.

### 4.   United Nations Centre for Human Settlements (Habitat)

277.   At a time when approximately one quarter of the world's population is either inadequately housed or is homeless, the growing global shelter crisis resulting from uncontrolled urbanization and rural poverty is imparting new urgency to the mandate of the United Nations Centre for Human Settlements (Habitat), under the direction of Mr. Wally N'Dow.

278.   To address these far-reaching challenges, the Centre has embarked on a number of major initiatives. Central to these are preparations now under way for the Second United Nations Conference on Human Settlements (Habitat II), also known as the "City Summit". Through its declaration of principles and commitments and its global plan of action, Habitat II is expected to reaffirm the importance of human settlements in national and international development policies and strategies.

279.   The recently concluded second session of the Preparatory Committee for the Conference mobilized those whose collaboration is essential to the forging of new partnerships for managing the urban environment: national Governments, local authorities and their international associations, private-sector enterprises, civic groups and nongovernmental and community-based organizations. Through a series of regional meetings, supported and/or organized by the regional commissions, countries are now taking stock and identifying common concerns with respect to their regions.

280.   Preparations have begun on several Habitat II–related conferences, including the In-

ternational Conference on Best Practices in Improving the Living Environment, to be convened at Dubai in November. Organizations and agencies of the United Nations system, as well as professional associations and research institutions, are collaborating with the Centre in sponsoring an extensive series of workshops, seminars, colloquiums and round tables related to the Conference's two main themes: adequate shelter for all and sustainable human settlement development in an urbanizing world.

281. The Centre continues to monitor and coordinate the implementation of the Global Strategy for Shelter to the Year 2000, which will also be reviewed by Habitat II in 1996. Technical assistance activities geared to that end were undertaken by the Centre in 91 countries over the reporting period, especially in the areas of urban management, environmental planning and management, disaster mitigation and reconstruction, housing policy and urban poverty reduction. Significant interregional programmes are currently being implemented, in urban management, sustainable cities and the housing and urban indicators programme. Among the major reconstruction projects under way in 1995 were those in Afghanistan and Rwanda.

282. Capacity-building activities were expanded in the countries in transition of eastern and central Europe and the countries of the Commonwealth of Independent States (CIS). Progress was achieved in introducing gender issues in human settlement-related training programmes. New initiatives have been launched with UNEP and WHO to promote environmental health in human settlements and work is proceeding on the second *Global Report on Human Settlements*, which will be launched at Habitat II.

283. Africa is an important focus of the Centre's activities. Over the reporting period, new responsibilities have been entrusted to the Centre by the Inter-Agency Task Force for the United Nations New Agenda for the Development of Africa in the 1990s. The Centre will be the associate lead agency responsible for urban management and human settlement programmes and policies and for the continuum from relief to development.

284. Securing adequate levels of funding to carry out its expanding mandate and role within the development agenda of the United Nations, including support for Habitat II, is one of the most important challenges facing the Centre. The urgent need for United Nations and bilateral donor emergency assistance to redress the effects of civil wars and natural disasters has resulted in continuing reductions in the level of funding available for the Centre's development cooperation activities of a longer-term nature.

C. *Operational activities for development*

1. United Nations Development Programme (UNDP)

285. As the principal arm of the United Nations for the funding and coordination of technical assistance and development, UNDP, under its Administrator, Mr. James Gustave Speth, has contributed to the development debate at both the conceptual and operational levels—internationally and in the countries it serves.

286. To strengthen its own capacity to give policy guidance and support in priority areas, UNDP restructured its Bureau for Policy and Programme Support to include four thematic divisions, on social development and poverty elimination, management development and governance, sustainable energy and environment, and science and technology.

287. Path-breaking legislation on the future of UNDP and on the successor programming arrangements for the next period was approved by the Executive Board of UNDP and UNFPA in June. The decision on the future of UNDP continued the process of redefining its role. The Board recognized poverty elimination as the overriding priority in UNDP programmes and urged concentration on areas where UNDP has demonstrable comparative advantages, in particular in capacity-building.

288. The Board's decision on successor programming arrangements constituted a major turning-point for UNDP, replacing the programming system that had been in effect since the "consensus" decision of 1970. The new system is intended to provide greater flexibility in the assignment of resources, as well as greater incentives for the formulation of focused, high-impact and high-leverage programmes to promote sustainable human development.

289. At the conceptual level, the *Human Development Report*, a report to UNDP, prepared by a team of independent development experts, has contributed to the international development debate. The 1995 *Report* focuses on gender issues and on valuing women's work as a contribution to the Fourth World Conference on Women.

290. Several Governments have requested assistance in the preparation of their own national human development reports, based on the methodologies used in the *Human Development Report*. National reports have been published in 9 countries in all regions in 1994 and 1995 and are in preparation in close to 40 more, including several in central and eastern Europe and CIS. In other countries, such as Botswana, Egypt and Bolivia, exercises based on the human development methodology for the collection of disaggregated data have been conducted. Overall, the reports and data collection exercises help to identify groups ex-

cluded from the benefits of development, whether for reasons of poverty, gender or geographic location, and to propose environmentally sound strategies for their inclusion.

291. The national long-term perspective studies programme, introduced in 1991, has helped African countries define national priorities to guide their development over a 25-year "futures" horizon. By 1994, the programme was active in 11 countries.

292. UNDP has assisted many programme countries in the preparation of their positions at global forums. Through the resident coordinator system, UNDP has contributed at the national level to preparations for the Fourth World Conference on Women. Several dozen reports on the status of women were prepared for the Conference, most of them based on gender analysis and the collection of disaggregated data. UNDP facilitated dialogue in each country among the organizations of Government, the United Nations and civil society. UNDP is now integrating the broader concept of gender in the programming process. For example, in 1993, the Government of Turkey, with support from UNDP, launched a programme for the enhancement of women's participation in the nation's development. Training was conducted on such topics as women and employment, women and entrepreneurship, and women and violence. UNDP is also cooperating with UNCHS in the preparations for Habitat II.

293. In 1994, in collaboration with the Inter-American Development Bank and Governments of the region, UNDP co-sponsored development-related preparations for the Summit of the Americas, which mapped out areas for enhanced regional cooperation and development and for movement towards greater participation in development planning and management. In the Asia and Pacific region, UNDP sponsored a regional meeting of development ministers at Kuala Lumpur to facilitate dialogue on strategies for collaboration and for development in the region. It was also heavily involved in the preparations for the International Convention to Combat Desertification and the United Nations Framework Convention on Climate Change, assisting with both the preparation of country positions and the conventions themselves.

294. UNDP experience shows that concepts can only be developed and tested against operational activities. In January 1995, in order to serve development professionals, UNDP pulled together national experience in 13 monographs in the UNDP Series on Sustainable Human Development: Country Strategies for Social Development. The series was launched during the preparatory process for the World Summit for Social Development.

295. Inter-agency cooperation has been furthered by widening the resident coordinator pool to encompass candidates from the joint consultative group on policy agencies as well as from the Office of the United Nations High Commissioner for Refugees (UNHCR) and the United Nations Secretariat. Since January 1994, a total of six resident coordinators have so far been selected from the United Nations, UNICEF, the World Food Programme (WFP), UNIDO and UNCTAD. It is hoped that this will lead to greater understanding of the priorities of different agencies and an enhanced sense of ownership of the resident coordinator system on the part of the agencies.

296. In many countries, resident coordinators have established sectoral subcommittees led by the relevant United Nations agency representative to ensure coordination at the sectoral level. Joint training of United Nations agency representatives and resident coordinators at the ILO Turin Centre has been stepped up. A total of 13 workshops had been held by April 1995, with 63 staff from UNDP and 305 staff from other United Nations agencies being trained. To give further support to inter-agency coordination, UNDP has established an Inter-Agency Coordination and External Policy Office within a restructured Bureau for Resources and External Affairs.

297. Considerable success has been achieved in increasing the clarity of respective roles within the United Nations system. A statement of principles was signed with UNEP outlining respective roles and an intention to collaborate between the two organizations. A statement of principles was also signed with FAO on food security, a central aspect of sustainable human development in many countries. The high-level task force between UNDP and the World Bank was revitalized, resulting in the negotiation of a revised statement of principles for collaboration between the two agencies, in particular in the areas of forestry and poverty alleviation. Joint programming in select countries is expected to begin in the coming year. Finally, discussions are taking place between UNDP and UNHCR on the collaborative efforts to reintegrate populations displaced by war.

298. The Administrator of UNDP established a task force under the chairmanship of the Associate Administrator for further strengthening the role of the regional economic commissions. Mechanisms are being established—with collaboration between UNDP and the commissions—for coordinating United Nations activities at the regional and subregional levels.

299. UNDP has improved its support to the round-table process in order to achieve more regular meetings and a sharper focus on policy and resource mobilization. The 1994 round table for the Gambia raised $400 million. Four others were or-

ganized in Africa in 1994 (Central African Republic, Guinea-Bissau, Mali and Seychelles). The two organized in Asia, for the Lao People's Democratic Republic and Maldives, raised $500 million and $100 million respectively. The 1995 round table for Rwanda raised $587 million.

300. UNDP is playing a more active role in consultative group meetings, focusing on capacity for sustainable human development. At the consultative group for the Philippines, the UNDP-sponsored *Philippine Human Development Report 1994* served as a principal reference for the agenda item on sustainable development.

301. In March, the Copenhagen Declaration on Social Development and Programme of Action adopted by the World Summit for Social Development called on UNDP to organize United Nations system efforts towards capacity-building at the local, national and regional levels. In April, the Administrator sent a detailed proposal for UNDP follow-up strategy to all 133 country offices. In June, the Executive Board of UNDP adopted key decisions on following up the Summit and mandated poverty elimination as its overriding priority within the framework of the goals and priority areas agreed to the previous year in support of sustainable human development. The Administrator has asked the UNDP country offices to consult with national counterparts on how the United Nations system can best assist each country in implementing the recommendations of the Summit, in particular in developing national strategies and programmes for poverty elimination. Other areas include the macroeconomic framework for a greater emphasis on poverty reduction; social sector policy and planning; systems to assist vulnerable groups; and poverty definitions, indicators and assessments. UNDP has set up a rapid response system to provide information required for Summit follow-up and to support shifts in programme emphasis.

302. Poverty elimination, as addressed by the Copenhagen Declaration and Programme of Action, requires participation and empowerment of people at all levels. This requires effective outreach mechanisms that make use of local government, institutions of civil society such as village and community groups and institutions of traditional government, national and international non-governmental organizations, United Nations Volunteer specialists and United Nations specialized agencies. Most importantly, it involves empowerment of target communities in the identification and communication of their own needs and in the management of the implementation of projects and programmes geared to eliminating critical constraints to their development. During 1994 and 1995, the United Nations Capital Development Fund provided local development funds

in addition to larger-scale infrastructure and credit facilities. These funds involve the community, whether through community groups or local government bodies, in establishing priorities and in implementing micro-scale infrastructure projects.

303. To target those who are marginalized in economic or social terms but nevertheless have the potential for productive livelihood requires pro-poor macro-policies geared to build on the productivity of the poor. Many UNDP-supported programmes and projects, as in Sri Lanka and Uganda, have demonstrated how to bring participation, employment and empowerment to poor people. In recognition of the importance of rural agriculture in the alleviation of poverty, employment creation, the preservation of the environment and bringing women into the mainstream of economic development, guidelines for UNDP, government and other development practitioners, entitled "Sustainable Human Development and Agriculture", have been produced and now serve as a basic reference for programming in UNDP.

304. UNDP took several initiatives in 1994 to promote greater participation by the potential actors and beneficiaries of development. The Conference on Peace and Development, held in Honduras in October 1994, represented the climax of effort by the countries of the region to build consensus on the issues of peace and democratization in Central America. The Conference brought together representatives of Governments, the private sector, cooperatives, trade unions, indigenous communities, universities, regional organizations and the donor community, thus institutionalizing the dialogue with civil society.

305. Employment generation requires deepening collaboration between UNDP and ILO to identify market demand systematically and to create economically viable jobs that foster sustainable livelihoods. For example, in Ethiopia, the Government has formulated a national programme on human resource development and utilization that looks at both the supply and demand for human resources. The employment and livelihoods sub-programme has set a target of creating 24,000 additional jobs per year over five years and focuses on areas such as the informal sector, promotion of small and medium-scale enterprises, agricultural wage employment and rural on- and off-farm employment.

306. Protection and regeneration of the environment has been advanced by UNDP for national capacity-building in the follow-up and implementation of Agenda 21 and the Montreal Protocol. China has developed, with UNDP support and with the involvement of over 50 government agencies, research institutes and public organizations, an Agenda 21 strategy. UNDP helped

to organize a donor conference during which the Government presented 62 high-priority projects covering such areas as sustainable agriculture; cleaner production; clean energy; conservation and sustainable use of natural resources; pollution control; population growth; and an improvement in the status of people's health, education and general welfare.

307. To meet the growing demand for national capacity to manage complex environmental concerns, a new Division for Sustainable Energy and Environment was established in August 1994 within the Bureau for Programme and Policy Support. It will further support efforts to incorporate environmental concerns at the earliest possible stages of economic decision-making and promote the full implementation of Agenda 21.

308. A new initiative for sustainable energy is being formulated to support programme formulation and to provide for greater access to improved energy technology. UNDP along with UNEP, UNIDO and the World Bank are the four implementing agencies assisting some 31 developing countries to eliminate ozone-depleting substances in a programme financed by the multilateral fund under the Montreal Protocol. As at 31 December 1994, total approved budgets amounted to $79.61 million. Eleven country programmes have been approved with UNDP as lead agency and 19 capacity-building (institution-strengthening) projects are under way. Out of a total of 97 projects completed, 20 involve technology transfer investment projects, which have phased out 1,455 tons of ozone-depleting substances.

309. The governance issues concerning the Global Environment Facility have been resolved and the Facility's Instrument has been approved, delineating the roles of UNEP, UNDP and the World Bank. By December 1994, the UNDP Global Environment Facility pilot phase portfolio consisted of 55 technical assistance projects and 28 pre-investment feasibility studies. In 1995, UNDP launched the post-pilot phase, with 20 projects. As the Programme's main effort to implement Agenda 21, Capacity 21 completed its first full year of operation in 1994, with a solid portfolio of national programmes in all regions. By August 1995, the environmental management guidelines training workshop, a major capacity-building initiative, had been held in 122 countries, involving 3,600 participants.

310. UNDP is supporting public sector reform in many countries. In Viet Nam, UNDP is helping with reform of the legal, financial and monetary systems, with particular emphasis on social adjustment concerns. It has been assigned the main responsibility for support to the Government in the coordination and management of external cooperation resources. Similar activities are under way in Lebanon, Peru and Zambia. In March, a regional meeting of Latin American and eastern European experts was held in Argentina to discuss how prudent use of regulation, competition and social safety nets can be combined to ensure that privatization contributes to sustainable human development.

311. During 1994, the United Nations Capital Development Fund began working with UNDP units dealing with governance in selected developing countries. The aim is to promote decentralization by attracting technical cooperation to the local level and providing the capital assistance necessary for newly established local authorities to gain experience in administering development programmes.

312. Collaborating closely with the Electoral Assistance Division of the Secretariat, UNDP has responded to an increasing number of country requests relating to the introduction or enhancement of the electoral process, including, in Africa, Chad, Ethiopia, Liberia, Mozambique, Togo and Uganda, and, in Latin America, Brazil and Mexico. United Nations Volunteer specialists served as electoral observers and facilitators in Mozambique and South Africa. Other UNDP-supported initiatives have aimed to ensure access to due process and acquired rights. For instance, an international ombudsman workshop was held in the Russian Federation as part of the democracy, governance and participation programme for the States of eastern Europe and the former Soviet Union.

313. UNDP is attempting to promote sustainable development even in the midst of internal conflict situations. The importance of ensuring that humanitarian relief is linked to sustainable human development is widely accepted as a prerequisite for countries to resume progress and rebuild capacity as soon as possible. A case in point is Somalia, where, despite the difficult security situation, UNDP managed to continue an active rural rehabilitation programme in some parts of the country.

314. In 1994-1995, UNDP substantively enhanced its assistance in two situations in particular. Firstly, resources for the UNDP programme of assistance to the Palestinian people doubled to $25 million between 1993 and 1994. Secondly, the Government of South Africa and UNDP concluded negotiations and signed the Basic Standard Agreement in October 1994 during the visit of President Nelson Mandela to Headquarters during the general debate of the General Assembly at its forty-ninth session.

315. In other institutional developments, UNDP has become the first United Nations organization to be accepted as a member of the Society

for Worldwide Inter-Bank Financial Telecommunications, a financial communications system using leased lines owned by banks. This has improved cash management capabilities while achieving savings of $250,000 per year in general operating expenditures and reductions in staff costs.

316. The year 1994 was the mid-point of the current fifth indicative planning figure cycle (1992-1996), and 16 mid-term reviews were completed. It was found that fifth-cycle country programmes were essentially strategic, aimed at a limited number of major national or regional development objectives. As such, they are distinctly more focused than in previous cycles. They aim to reduce the number of individual projects and, as called for in General Assembly resolution 44/211 of 22 December 1989, to move towards the programme approach under national execution, with strong emphasis on national ownership and commitment. For example, in the Lao People's Democratic Republic, individual projects have been reduced from 50 to 15 and in the regional programme for Asia and the Pacific from 350 to 80. National ownership is being reinforced, with an increase in the rate of national execution from 34 per cent of approvals in 1991 to 53 per cent in 1994.

317. In 1994, voluntary contributions by member countries to UNDP core resources amounted to $917.57 million. Contributions to non-core resources, including UNDP-administered funds, trust funds, cost-sharing arrangements and government cash counterpart contributions, raised the total funds administered by UNDP to over $1.8 billion. There has been a continued rise in funds received through cost-sharing arrangements, with cost-sharing contributions increasing by 58.7 per cent in 1994. Total field programme expenditures for technical cooperation activities in 1994 amounted to approximately $1,036.50 million.

318. It became clear in 1994 that the UNDP biennial budget would have to be reduced further to keep administrative costs in line with declining core programme resources. This is in spite of the fact that between the biennial budgets for 1992-1993 and 1994-1995 a total of $53.6 million was cut from the administrative budget. Cuts have been made primarily by reducing staff positions both at headquarters (26 per cent) and at the country level (8 per cent).

319. The stagnation of UNDP core resources since 1992 and the current uncertain outlook reflect the global situation with regard to development cooperation. It is a cause for concern that notwithstanding the substantial adjustments undertaken in response to the changed conditions of the post-cold-war era, the resource base for UNDP has been seriously eroded. The 1995 contributions to the central resources of UNDP are expected to

amount to approximately $937 million. This is much lower than the originally projected level under Governing Council decision 90/34, which, on the basis of resources of $1 billion, called for an 8 per cent annual increase during the fifth programming cycle (1992-1996). Viewed in the context of that decision, the shortfall for the cycle would amount to approximately $1.4 billion. For this reason, the Executive Board of UNDP decided to reduce national indicative planning figures by 30 per cent from their original levels.

320. Tragically, 17 UNDP staff members lost their lives in 1994 while serving the cause of development.

### 2. United Nations Children's Fund (UNICEF)

321. Ms. Carol Bellamy was appointed the fourth Executive Director of UNICEF, succeeding Mr. James P. Grant, who had led the organization for 15 years until his death in January 1995. The new Executive Director has indicated that improving the financial management and administrative and programme systems of UNICEF and ensuring more effective and efficient programme delivery will allow UNICEF to move into the next century (*see fig. 11*).

322. 1995 is the mid-point of the decade-long strategy of the World Summit for Children to meet global objectives for the welfare of children. The international community's goals and objectives for children and the broad outline of a global strategy have been set for the remainder of the decade by the World Summit for Children and by the imperatives of the Convention on the Rights of the Child. The International Conference on Population and Development and the World Summit for Social Development have reiterated the commitment of the international community to these goals. The Fourth World Conference on Women, to be held at Beijing in September 1995, can be expected to take these commitments a stage further, with a heightened emphasis on the need for gender equity and equality and for special attention to the girl-child.

323. The progress report presented to the UNICEF Executive Board on follow-up to the World Summit for Children noted that impressive progress was under way and that the majority of developing countries were on track to achieve a majority of the goals.

324. In 1994, UNICEF supported programmes in 149 countries—46 in Africa, 37 in Latin America and the Caribbean (including 10 Caribbean island countries), 34 in Asia (including 13 Pacific island countries), 14 in the Middle East and North Africa and 18 in central and eastern Europe, the Commonwealth of Independent States and the Baltic States. The total programme expenditure reached $801 million. The third issue of *The Progress of Nations*, released in June 1995,

provided up-to-date data on indicators for monitoring progress towards the goals, ranking countries according to their results.

325.   UNICEF is addressing the main causes of child mortality, with a focus on prevention, including immunization and the prevention and treatment of the major killers—acute respiratory infections, diarrhoeal diseases and malaria in areas of high endemicity. Immunization coverage was sustained globally at the 80 per cent level, but the regional average in Africa remained significantly lower, as it did in 1993. The Bamako Initiative, as a strategy for strengthening local primary health care systems, expanded to 33 countries in Africa, Asia and Latin America. Global and country-level activities continued to achieve goals for the year 2000 of universal iodization of salt and vitamin A distribution to all vulnerable people.

326.   Most countries in East Asia, Latin America and the Middle East achieved the mid-decade goal of universal access to primary education. However, more than one half of developing countries, including high-population countries in South Asia and Africa, still have to make major strides before all their children can be provided adequate opportunities for basic education. Girls' primary education was the dominant component of UNICEF support for education in South Asia, sub-Saharan Africa and the Middle East and North Africa.

327.   UNICEF assisted some 100 countries in achieving their water supply and sanitation goals and worked to refine strategies that emphasize sustainability and maximize health and socio-economic benefits. Progress was made in gaining acceptance of the women's equality and empowerment framework, as well as the life-cycle approach, as tools for promoting gender-balanced programmes for children and development.

328.   UNICEF is committed to mainstream development programming, particularly as related to activities in basic social services. While pursuing these long-term development efforts, UNICEF was also called upon to play an active role in responding to many emergencies in which women and children were the hardest-hit victims. Approximately 25 per cent of UNICEF's programme expenditure in 1994 was devoted to providing life-saving essential services for children and women in emergencies.

329.   In the former Yugoslavia, UNICEF was charged with a mandate to provide relief assistance in situations of great insecurity for its own staff. In Armenia, Azerbaijan, Georgia and Tajikistan, UNICEF helped to address the special needs of refugee populations and internally displaced people through the re-establishment of the cold chain, the provision of basic vaccines and health supplies, and support for educational systems.

330.   UNICEF continues to pay special attention to African and other least developed countries. Despite the continuing and threatening emergencies in certain parts of sub-Saharan Africa, there are many positive developments that go almost unnoticed. In the areas of special action for children, 25 of the 46 countries in sub-Saharan Africa have either increased or sustained the immunization levels of 75 per cent or higher reached in 1990; the usage rate of oral rehydration therapy has now reached 50 per cent; salt iodization measures are being implemented in 28 of the 39 countries affected by iodine deficiency disorders; and guinea worm disease is well on the way to being eliminated from most of Africa.

331.   Africa remains the continent with the greatest needs. UNICEF devotes some 38 per cent of its financial and human resources to sub-Saharan Africa. It helps to build capacities and empower communities and families. In countries emerging from disasters, programmes will aim at strengthening local capacity, solidarity and coping mechanisms, which could become the embryo of new societies. At the national level, UNICEF is strengthening its ability to support Governments in policy development affecting children and in mobilizing resources for children. At the same time, UNICEF is participating actively in a United Nations-wide initiative for Africa, working to strengthen country-level collaboration towards all the elements of sustainable human development, poverty reduction and accelerated economic growth.

332.   Unaccompanied children and internally displaced people were a major challenge for UNICEF in Rwanda, where an unprecedented relief effort was mounted to protect refugees from the rapid spread of disease and famine. In Angola, Burundi and Somalia, UNICEF continued to provide assistance in the areas of health, education and water supply and sanitation. In Mozambique, under a national plan of reconstruction, UNICEF reoriented its emergency activities towards rebuilding basic services for health, water supply and sanitation and education. In Liberia and Sierra Leone, despite facing an increasingly difficult situation, UNICEF continued to provide essential emergency services. Trauma counselling and physical rehabilitation for handicapped children were priorities, as were programmes for violently abused women and girls and vocational training for child soldiers.

333.   The Convention on the Rights of the Child has been embraced by more States than any other human rights treaty in history. By August 1995, 177 parties had ratified the Convention, with only 17 countries needed to attain the goal of universal ratification by the end of 1995.

334.   At its forty-ninth session, the General Assembly discussed for the first time the issue of chil-

dren's rights and adopted resolutions on the protection of children affected by armed conflicts; the need to adopt efficient international measures for the prevention and eradication of the sale of children, child prostitution and child pornography; implementation of the Convention on the Rights of the Child; and the plight of street children (resolutions 49/209 to 49/212, all of 23 December 1994). UNICEF was asked to play an active role in support of those resolutions. Furthermore, UNICEF, in collaboration with the Centre for Human Rights, has been assisting the Committee on the Rights of the Child in monitoring implementation of the Convention. UNICEF is supporting the comprehensive study of the impact of armed conflict on children in response to General Assembly resolution 48/157 of 20 December 1993.

335. The World Summit for Social Development has provided new impetus to the work of UNICEF on behalf of children within the United Nations system, setting that work within a wider international effort towards poverty eradication and social development. After two years of systematic mobilization and persistent technical refinement in which UNICEF played an active role along with UNDP and UNFPA, the "20/20" initiative was adopted at the World Summit for Social Development as a legitimate and useful instrument for guiding, assessing and monitoring overall official development assistance and national budgetary allocations to basic social programmes.

### 3. United Nations Population Fund (UNFPA)

336. During 1994, UNFPA, directed by Dr. Nafis Sadik, supported population programmes in 137 countries and territories. The Fund operates field offices, each headed by a country director, in 60 of those countries. The year 1994 will be remembered as the year the international community changed the way it looks at population issues. That change in perception actually evolved over two decades and culminated in the adoption of the Programme of Action of the International Conference on Population and Development, held at Cairo in September of that year.

337. The Programme of Action was the product of more than three years of intense deliberation and negotiation between Governments, non-governmental organizations, community leaders, technical experts and interested individuals. The Programme of Action goes beyond mere numbers and demographic targets and places human beings and their well-being at the centre of all population and sustainable development activities. It also sets out quantitative and qualitative goals and objectives to be reached by all countries by the year 2015: to provide universal access to reproductive health and family planning services; to reduce infant, child and maternal mortality; and to provide access to primary education for all girls and boys.

338. The Conference, and the Programme of Action it produced, spawned a series of internal and external assessments of UNFPA. For example, each UNFPA geographical division conducted internal reviews of existing policies and programmes and convened regional meetings to consider the implications of the Conference for their respective regions.

339. UNFPA held a series of joint workshops with partner agencies in the United Nations development system to examine how best to translate the recommendations of the Programme of Action into actions at the country and local levels. These workshops focused on the key areas of the Fund's programme—reproductive health and family planning (with WHO); information, education and communication (with UNESCO and WHO); and population data, policy and research (with ILO)—and involved advisers from the UNFPA technical support services/country support team system, including technical support services specialists from the respective United Nations agencies and organizations. These regional and technical consultations helped UNFPA assess the policy and programme implications of the Conference for the future work of UNFPA.

340. The programme priorities and future directions of UNFPA in the light of the Conference were considered by the UNDP/UNFPA Executive Board at its annual session in June 1995. The Executive Board, in its decision 95/15, supported the broad outline of the future programme of assistance of UNFPA, which must be implemented in full accordance with the Programme of Action of the Conference, and endorsed the Fund's core programme areas of reproductive health, including family planning and sexual health, population and development strategies, and advocacy. The Board also recommended, in its decision 95/20, that the Economic and Social Council and the General Assembly endorse the agreement between UNDP and UNFPA to designate UNFPA resident country directors as UNFPA representatives.

341. On 19 December 1994, the General Assembly adopted resolution 49/128, entitled "Report of the International Conference on Population and Development", in which it emphasized the importance of continued and enhanced cooperation and coordination by all relevant organs, organizations and programmes of the United Nations system and the specialized agencies, and requested them to take appropriate measures to ensure the full and effective implementation of the Programme of Action. In resolution 49/128, the Assembly decided that the Population Commission should be renamed the Commission on Population and Development and that it should meet on an annual basis beginning in 1996.

342.  On behalf of the Secretary-General and at the request of the Administrator of UNDP, the Executive Director of UNFPA convened in December 1994 the first meeting of the Inter-Agency Task Force on the Implementation of the Programme of Action of the International Conference on Population and Development. The meeting, attended by 12 United Nations organizations, worked to establish a common framework for follow-up to the Conference and other conferences in the social sector. The Task Force decided to use working groups to develop operational guidelines for use by resident coordinators to promote inter-agency collaboration at the country level in the following areas: *(a)* a common data system at the national level in the field of health, notably in the areas of infant, child and maternal mortality; *(b)* basic education, with special attention to gender disparities; *(c)* policy-related issues, including the drafting of a common advocacy statement on social issues; *(d)* women's empowerment; and *(e)* reproductive health.

343.  To achieve the goals of the Conference, it is necessary to mobilize resources from Governments and non-governmental organizations. At the request of the Secretary-General, the Executive Director of UNFPA convened a consultation on resource mobilization on 20 January 1995. The participants suggested using existing mechanisms at the country level, such as the resident coordinator system, the World Bank consultative groups, and UNDP round tables, for the purpose of mobilizing country-specific resources. It was agreed that global consultation on this topic should be convened periodically, preferably at the time of the annual sessions of the Commission on Population and Development.

344.  In conjunction with the International Conference on Population and Development and the World Summit for Social Development, UNFPA organized two international parliamentarian meetings, dealing specifically with population issues relevant to the themes of the conferences. Moreover, UNFPA established an NGO Advisory Committee to advise on how to make better use of and interact more effectively with non-governmental organizations and the private sector.

345.  In 1994, UNFPA organized programme review and strategy development exercises in nine countries, providing useful inputs to the formulation of the country strategy notes. By the end of 1994, UNFPA had undertaken a total of 76 such exercises.

346.  The Executive Board of UNFPA, in its decision 94/25, encouraged UNFPA, given the situation in Rwanda, to support, on an exceptional basis, in appropriate ways and in collaboration with other relief agencies, emergency assistance to the people of Rwanda from the population programme resources of the third UNFPA country pro-

gramme for Rwanda. Subsequently, UNFPA approved a project in Rwanda for emergency/rehabilitation assistance to the national maternal and child health and family planning programme, with UNICEF and UNFPA as executing agencies, and two emergency assistance projects to meet the reproductive health needs of Rwandan refugees in Burundi and the United Republic of Tanzania. The projects in Burundi and the United Republic of Tanzania, which were formulated in collaboration with UNHCR, UNICEF, the African Medical and Research Foundation and local non-governmental organizations, are progressing reasonably well. The Executive Board, in its decision 95/14, approved the continued implementation of decision 94/25, allowing for flexibility in sectoral expenditure of resources from the third UNFPA country programme for Rwanda and for overall expenditures of up to $7.8 million.

347.  At the global level, UNFPA continued to support the Special Programme of Research, Development and Research Training in Human Reproduction of WHO. UNFPA also participated in the United Nations Joint and Co-sponsored Programme on HIV/AIDS. The Fund's Global Initiative on Contraceptive Requirements and Logistics Management Needs in Developing Countries in the 1990s, co-funded by a number of multilateral and bilateral donors and non-governmental organizations, organized in-depth studies on contraceptive requirements in Brazil, Bangladesh and Egypt, generating interest by several other countries with regard to contraceptive requirements. The Global Initiative also produced technical reports and organized consultative meetings and workshops.

348.  The income of the Fund in 1994 was $265.3 million, compared to a 1993 income of $219.6 million, an increase of 20.8 per cent (*see fig. 12*). Total expenditures for projects, from regular resources, increased from $134.3 million in 1993 to $204.1 million in 1994, an increase of $67.1 million, or 50 per cent. Expenditures for reproductive health and family planning programmes increased by 46 per cent, from $68.7 million in 1993 to $100.1 million in 1994, and accounted for nearly half of all of the Fund's project expenditures. Expenditures for information, education and communication activities increased by 80 per cent, from $21.3 million in 1993 to $38.3 million in 1994, and accounted for 19 per cent of total project expenditures. The remaining expenditures were divided among basic data collection (6.6 per cent); population dynamics (5.7 per cent); formulation, implementation and evaluation of population policies (8.1 per cent); multisectoral activities (5.5 per cent); and special programmes (5.4 per cent).

349.  In 1994, the Asia and Pacific region received 31.5 per cent of UNFPA programme allo-

cations, the sub-Saharan Africa region received 31.1 per cent, the Latin America and Caribbean region 13.5 per cent and the Arab States and Europe 11.5 per cent. Support for interregional and global programmes amounted to 12.4 per cent of allocations. The Fund continued to concentrate over 71 per cent of its resources in countries most in need of assistance in the population field and notably in the poorest developing countries. In 1994, there were 58 priority countries for UNFPA assistance: 32 in sub-Saharan Africa, 17 in Asia and the Pacific, 5 in Latin America and the Caribbean and 4 in the Arab States.

### 4. World Food Programme (WFP)

350. Directed by Ms. Catherine Bertini, WFP, the food aid arm of the United Nations system, remains on the front line of the United Nations battle against hunger and poverty. WFP concentrates its efforts on the neediest people in the neediest countries of the world.

351. In 1994, food assistance provided by WFP reached 57 million poor and hungry people. Eighty-two per cent of total WFP resources went to low-income food-deficit countries; the share to least developed countries was 52 per cent. Such resources support both relief and development.

352. On the development side, WFP food aid has been an effective means of transferring income to the poor and encouraging collective action in poor communities. Currently, some 225 development projects with an aggregate commitment of $2.6 billion are being supported in over 80 developing countries (*see fig. 13*).

353. On the emergency side, WFP responds to food shortages by relying on its network of country offices and on its expertise in transport, logistics and procurement. During 1994, WFP provided relief assistance at a value of over $1 billion to the victims of man-made and natural disasters in over 40 countries.

354. In 1994, WFP managed $1.5 billion of resources—in food commodities and cash—in support of the hungry and poor throughout the developing world. Over 32 million victims of man-made and natural disasters benefited from WFP assistance in 1994. Some 16 million people participated in food-for-work projects in support of agricultural and rural development. Over 8 million people received supplementary feeding through WFP-assisted education, training, health and nutrition projects.

355. About 80 per cent of WFP relief assistance in 1994 was provided to victims of disasters coming out of civil strife or cross-border wars—some 8.5 million refugees and 16.5 million internally displaced people, representing 50 per cent of the world's population of those two groups. More than 7 million people were victims of drought and other natural disasters. Some 64 per cent of total WFP relief operations were in support of needy people in Africa. The single biggest operation was in Burundi and Rwanda, costing $242 million, or 22 per cent of total relief expenditures. This operation, associated with tragic loss of life on a massive scale, continues to be an urgent focus of attention for the United Nations today, not only in Burundi and Rwanda but also in Kenya, Tanzania, Uganda and Zaire. The Liberia regional programme, costing $96 million, provided assistance to refugees and displaced persons in Liberia and in four neighbouring countries involved in the crisis.

356. Elsewhere in the world, major emergencies faced by WFP included the former Yugoslavia, where people continued to face food shortages and real poverty as a result of unresolved conflicts. WFP operations in that region amounted to $149 million. Afghanistan represents another country that is still in a state of chronic food insecurity in the absence of peace. The WFP regional operations in support of Afghan refugees and displaced people cost $95 million in 1994.

357. The number, scale and duration of emergencies and disasters, particularly those caused by armed conflict, have escalated alarmingly in recent years. In 1994, two out of three tons of WFP-provided food aid were distributed as relief assistance, and only one ton was used in support of development projects. Five years ago it was the reverse. With fewer resources for development, "silent" emergencies, in which people live in abject poverty and chronic food insecurity, can quickly turn into acute emergencies. Relief assistance alone does not change the vulnerability of poor people to the next emergency. WFP is therefore making a deliberate effort to identify ways to increase the linkages between its relief and development assistance by integrating disaster mitigation elements into development projects, developing capacity-building elements into relief operations, and strengthening disaster preparedness through vulnerability mapping, better early warning and institutional development.

358. The Programme's approach to reducing problems associated with humanitarian emergencies is to collaborate in efforts aimed at prevention rather than cure. Wherever possible, food aid is used to support development goals. Africa and Asia continue to receive the largest shares of WFP development assistance—40 per cent and 39 per cent, respectively. However, WFP development resources continue to decline in both absolute and relative terms with respect to emergency operations. Of the target of $1.5 billion for WFP regular development resources for the biennium 1993-1994 (approved by the Economic and Social Council and the FAO Council, and endorsed by the General Assembly and the FAO Conference) only

two thirds was realized. As a result, the implementation of projects was often delayed. Moreover, WFP has been unable to support all approved projects at the level originally planned, as donors have increasingly tied and designated their development funds.

359.   Food purchases have increased significantly during the last five years. In 1994, WFP purchased a record 1.4 million tons of food, almost half of all the commodities distributed by the Programme. Sixty per cent of the food commodities were bought in developing countries, maintaining the Programme's position as the largest contributor to South-South trade in the United Nations system.

360.   WFP cooperates with other multilateral, bilateral and non-governmental organizations at all stages of its activities. In 1994, significant progress was made in ensuring greater collaboration in relief operations. Joint assessments of refugee food needs (with UNHCR) and emergency needs (with FAO) continued to be an essential part of the work of WFP. WFP-assisted development projects in 17 countries benefited from collaboration with the International Fund for Agricultural Development (IFAD). WFP signed a first memorandum of understanding on joint working arrangements for emergency relief operations with a major international non-governmental organization and will seek to conclude similar agreements with other non-governmental organizations in the future.

361.   The approach of WFP has been notably strengthened by the adoption of principles and guidelines for a country-based programme, which includes resourcing levels, and of criteria for project approval. Resource arrangements are being addressed to improve predictability, accountability and transparency, as well as actual resource levels. The General Regulations of the Programme are being amended in the light of General Assembly resolutions 47/199 of 22 December 1992 and 48/162 of 20 December 1993.

### 5.   United Nations International Drug Control Programme

362.   During the reporting period, the United Nations International Drug Control Programme, headed by Mr. Giorgio Giacomelli, continued to carry out its activities on the basis of a three-tiered strategy articulated at the country, regional and global levels.

363.   At the country level, the Programme elaborated guidelines to assist Governments in the preparation of national drug control master plans, that is, national agendas that address both illicit demand and illicit supply reduction. Support by the Programme led to the development of master plans in 14 countries and territories in the Caribbean. Master plan assistance was also provided to Algeria, Guatemala, Namibia, Pakistan, the United Arab Emirates and Viet Nam. The Programme assisted the Government of Colombia in developing drug control components within that country's 10-year National Alternative Development Plan, to become effective on 1 January 1996.

364.   In 1994, the Programme funded a comprehensive ground survey of the extent of opium poppy cultivation in Afghanistan. The results—to be confirmed in a 1995 survey—reveal a dry opium production volume substantially in excess of previous estimates of 2,000 metric tons; based on the revised estimates, Afghanistan would be the world's largest illicit producer of opium.

365.   At the regional level, the Programme held in South Africa in November 1994 a regional workshop aimed at strengthening judiciary cooperation against drug trafficking in southern Africa. Governments in the region adopted a communiqué against corruption and a plan of action comprising measures to strengthen drug trafficking interdiction in the subregion.

366.   In May 1995, at Beijing, the first ministerial meeting took place between the Lao People's Democratic Republic, Myanmar, China and Thailand, all of which are parties to the memorandum of understanding on control of illicit drugs in South-East Asia. The meeting approved the accession of Cambodia and Viet Nam to the memorandum of understanding and endorsed an Action Plan on subregional cooperation in drug control matters. In China, law enforcement capabilities in Yunnan Province were strengthened with equipment from the Programme and training needs were identified. Law enforcement officers in the border areas of China and Myanmar launched the establishment of an information exchange system. After the signing of a regional memorandum of understanding in 1994, Argentina, Bolivia, Chile, Peru and the Programme developed an action agenda for implementation in 1995-1997 emphasizing law enforcement and harmonization of demand reduction techniques.

367.   By 30 June 1995, the Baltic States, 9 central European countries and 12 countries of CIS had received legal assistance from the Programme. The central Asian republics have emerged as a high priority for the Programme, and accordingly a multisectoral subregional programme, requiring support from the international community, has been developed.

368.   In 1994-1995, the Programme continued its series of demand reduction expert forums, with technical consultations held in Brazil, the Bahamas, Cameroon, India and Morocco. In the context of the United Nations Decade against Drug Abuse, a World Forum on the Role of Non-Governmental Organizations in Drug Demand Reduction was held at Bangkok in December 1994

with participants from 115 countries. The Forum resulted in a declaration that reinforces the partnership between the United Nations and non-governmental organizations in demand reduction.

369. In April 1995, the Programme helped organize in Brazil the Second International Private Sector Conference on Drugs in the Workplace and the Community, with one result being the identification of essential elements of corporate policy needed for drug abuse prevention. In February 1995, the Programme and the International Olympic Committee signed a cooperation agreement to promote sports in the prevention of drug abuse.

370. At the global level, the Programme conducted research and synthesized the results into technical information and research papers. In order to address complex issues in drug control, the Programme prepared studies on the present status of knowledge on the illicit drug industry and the economic and social impact of drug abuse and control, as well as an interim report on the economic and social consequences of drug abuse, presented to the Commission on Narcotic Drugs at its thirty-eighth session, in March 1995.

371. The Programme's laboratory continued to expand its Quality Assurance Programme, aimed at assisting laboratories to develop effective laboratory practices in the analysis of drug-related matters. Eighty laboratories worldwide are participating in the International Proficiency Testing Scheme, which assesses the performance of laboratories and enhances output accuracy.

372. One of the major issues addressed by the Commission on Narcotic Drugs in 1994 and 1995 was the implementation of General Assembly resolution 48/12 of 28 October 1993 on measures to strengthen international cooperation against the illicit production, sale, demand, traffic and distribution of narcotic drugs and psychotropic substances and related activities. The Executive Director of the Programme convened two meetings in 1994 of an intergovernmental advisory group and produced a report which was examined by the Commission at its thirty-eighth session. That report included specific recommendations on ways to strengthen international action in drug control. The Commission, in its resolution 13(XXXVIII), invited States to consider the recommendations; it also requested the Executive Director to further refine them in the light of States' comments for submission to the General Assembly at its fifty-first session.

373. In response to General Assembly resolution 48/12, the International Narcotics Control Board, an independent treaty organ, outlined its assessment and major findings with respect to the drug control treaties in its report for 1994. The Board also issued a special supplement on the effectiveness of the treaties, highlighting areas in need of strengthening.

374. In September 1994 and February 1995, at the request of the Commission on Narcotic Drugs, the Programme convened a working group on maritime cooperation to further international cooperation in combating illicit drug traffic by sea. The recommendations and principles adopted by the working group and endorsed by the Commission represent a milestone in efforts to contain the problem of illicit drug shipments that traverse international waters.

375. Also in February 1995, the Administrative Committee on Coordination held a high-level meeting at Vienna that addressed system-wide cooperation in drug control. The meeting resulted in recognition of the need for United Nations programmes, funds and agencies to incorporate drug control components into their programmes and broad support for the leadership role of the Programme in drug control coordination.

376. The total budget of the Programme for 1994-1995 amounted to $205 million, of which approximately 93 per cent was funded from voluntary contributions. The main share of these resources, $162 million, was used for over 300 operational activities in 50 countries, aimed at countering illicit drug production, trafficking and consumption. In view of the continuous rise in drug-related problems throughout the world and the trend of dwindling resources available for drug control, I urge Member States to provide the political and financial support needed to pursue international priorities in drug control.

6. Technical cooperation programmes of the United Nations Secretariat

377. The focal point at United Nations Headquarters for technical cooperation for development efforts of developing countries and countries in transition is the Department for Development Support and Management Services. Total project expenditures for the Department in 1994 approximated $101 million for close to 1,044 projects in over a dozen sectors. Of that amount, UNDP funded about $51 million. The Department disbursed 44 per cent of its expenditures in Africa. In order to carry out its projects, over the past year the Department fielded over 900 international experts and consultants to work in collaboration with national personnel. The Department calls on a worldwide roster of over 4,330 consultants, 2,350 consulting companies and 6,330 suppliers of equipment. The Department also helps Governments to identify, select and purchase the most appropriate services and equipment for their development projects and supports capacity-building for work in those areas. Training is a vital component of such activities; in 1994, training place-

ments were made for some 2,500 persons from over 130 countries.

378. With the approval of the General Assembly, the Secretariat has proceeded with the decentralization to the regional commissions of staff and resources in the fields of natural resources and energy. These activities are managed by the Management Board of the United Nations Technical Cooperation Programme in Natural Resources and Energy, chaired by the Under-Secretary-General of the Department for Development Support and Management Services, with the participation of the regional commissions. This coordinating body has enhanced the responsiveness and effectiveness of assistance provided by the Organization in these areas.

379. Considerable progress has been made in forging closer links between the Department and UNDP. This strengthened cooperation has resulted in an increased role by the Department in "upstream" advice in development planning and management and in technical backstopping activities at the programme and project levels.

### 7. United Nations Office for Project Services

380. The United Nations Office for Project Services, formerly a part of UNDP, was established, with the approval of the General Assembly, on 1 January 1995. Consistent with my overall plan for the restructuring of the Secretariat, I proposed to separate the Office for Project Services from UNDP with the objective of strengthening the operational activities of the United Nations system for development. Within this framework, the Office for Project Services is now the principal entity in the United Nations system furnishing project management, implementation and support services.

381. The Office for Project Services is headed by the Executive Director, Mr. Reinhart Helmke, who reports to me through the Management Coordination Committee, as well as to the Executive Board of UNDP and UNFPA.

382. The Management Coordination Committee, comprising the Administrator of UNDP as chairman, the Under-Secretary-General for Administration and Management, the Under-Secretary-General for Development Support and Management Services and the Executive Director of the Office, has met twice during the reporting period to deliberate on a number of important policy and coordination issues relating to Office operations.

383. The Committee reviewed the business plan of the Office, its new financial regulations, its relationship with UNDP and the Department for Development Support and Management Services, operational follow-up activities relating to the World Summit for Social Development, held in 1994, and a set of strategic policy guidelines defin-

ing the scope of activities of the Office, including client partnerships and principal areas of concentration. Four main areas of concentration were identified for activities of the Office: executing development projects, coordinating rehabilitation and reconstruction efforts, managing environmental programmes and administering development loans. The proposed new financial regulations for the Office were approved by the Executive Board at the beginning of 1995, affording a new framework from which businesslike management practices can be instituted.

384. The portfolio of projects of the Office has grown consistently over the past 20 years, reaching more than $1 billion in 1994. Delivery in 1994 stood at $403.1 million, up 5.3 per cent from 1993. The number of projects in the portfolio also increased to nearly 1,900, as compared with roughly 1,700 during the previous year. In 1994, activities where the country portfolio was in excess of $10 million were under way in more than 20 countries.

385. In addition to implementing projects on behalf of United Nations agencies and programmes, the Office also administers management service agreements (MSAs) on behalf of multilateral development banks, bilateral donors and recipient Governments. Against a portfolio budget of $639 million, services provided under MSA arrangements totalled $142 million in 1994. Expenditures incurred by the Office during that year under the Global Environment Facility and the Montreal Protocol to the Vienna Convention for the Protection of the Ozone Layer amounted to more than $30 million.

386. In view of the experience it has acquired in managing post-conflict rehabilitation since the late 1980s, the demand for the services of the Office in designing and implementing comprehensive and integrated recovery programmes is increasing. The applicability of the lessons learned in the Horn of Africa, in Central America and in Asia are now being tested, for the first time, in eastern Europe (Ukraine) and central Asia (Tajikistan).

387. In keeping with its field orientation and in order to render its services more efficient, the Office has decentralized a number of functions. In addition to the Management Support Unit established in Central America in 1993, the Office has set up a post in Kuala Lumpur, from which it manages programmes in South-East Asia.

### D. *Regional development activities*

388. The regional commissions were established by the General Assembly to serve as the main regional centres for economic and social development. They operate at a level between global United Nations entities and country operations. As such, the regional commissions promote regional initiatives and strategies, contribute to in-depth studies of various issues and support inter-

governmental initiatives to elaborate norms, standards and legal instruments. In addition, regional commissions are a forum for dialogue for subregional groupings and help prepare regional positions to world conferences and summit meetings held by the United Nations (*see fig. 14*).

### 1. Economic Commission for Africa (ECA)

389. Assisting Member States in Africa to reinforce promising trends and overcome the obstacles to accelerated growth and socio-economic development has defined the analytical, advocacy and advisory work of ECA under its Executive Secretary, Mr. K. Y. Amoako. This provided the backdrop to the thirtieth session of the Commission, held from 24 April to 3 May 1995, the theme of which was "promoting accelerated growth and sustainable development in Africa through the building of critical capacities". At that session the Commission reviewed progress in the elaboration of the Framework Agenda for Building and Utilizing Critical Capacities in Africa and directed that the Framework Agenda be completed before the next session, in 1996.

390. The session also adopted a declaration on external debt of African countries which called for improvement in the Naples Terms, including an 80 per cent reduction in the total non-concessional debt of African countries, and urged the cancellation of concessional debt rescheduled in the Paris Club. It adopted a special memorandum on the mid-term global review of the implementation of the Programme of Action for Least Developed Countries for the 1990s scheduled for September 1995. The session noted with satisfaction the commitment of African countries to carry out necessary reforms to attract private investment, and invited all African countries and their development partners to participate in the regional forum on private investment which will be held in early 1996 at Accra.

391. At the same session the Commission strongly endorsed the need to promote food security and self-sufficiency in Africa. In this regard, the Commission called on Member States to create a macroeconomic environment conducive to the development of the food and agricultural sector and requested relevant United Nations agencies to strengthen programmes designed to promote food security and self-sufficiency in Africa.

392. With the coming into force in May 1994 of the Abuja Treaty establishing the African Economic Community, the Commission intensified its efforts in support of the implementation of the Treaty. Together with the Organization of African Unity and the African Development Bank—its partners in a Joint Secretariat—the Commission participated in setting up a committee to formulate proposals for resource mobilization in support of the African Economic Community and for-

mulating a framework for a working relationship between the subregional economic communities and the Joint Secretariat. Furthermore, the Commission undertook studies on the rationalization and harmonization of regional economic groups in West and Central Africa in the context of the establishment of the West African Economic and Monetary Union and the Central African Economic and Monetary Union.

393. The Second United Nations Transport and Communications Decade in Africa aims at facilitating development of transport and communications in Africa. A mid-term evaluation report of the Decade programme was examined by the Tenth Meeting of African Ministers of Transport and Communications held in May 1995. The main recommendations from the evaluation were that the programmes should be streamlined, resource mobilization efforts for Decade projects should be intensified and the beneficiaries of the Decade programme should assume ownership. The Commission implemented four important projects in the transport and communication sectors: human resource and institution development in transport and communications; a transport database; the reactivation of the Trans-African Highway Bureau; and the Yamoussoukro Declaration on a new air transport policy for Africa.

394. With a view to assisting Member States in formulating policies and strategies for sustainable development of natural resources, the Commission published a document entitled "Policies and strategies for the development and utilization of natural resources and energy in Africa". The Commission also organized, in collaboration with the World Meteorological Organization, an international conference entitled "Water Resources: Policy and Assessment", held at Addis Ababa from 20 to 25 March 1995. The Conference articulated a strategy to rehabilitate, build or adopt the institutional financial manpower and technological capacity of countries to assess water resources needs for socio-economic development.

395. In response to the decisions of Member States expressed at the Regional Ministerial Conference on Development and Utilization of Mineral Resources in Africa, the Commission undertook two studies on prospects for increased production and intra-African trade in copper and copper-based products and prospects for increased production and intra-African trade in aluminium commodities and metal products. The studies have been well received by Governments, private companies and entrepreneurs, as well as regional and subregional organizations.

396. The Commission continued its efforts to promote the development of scientific and technological capacities. It thus conducted studies on incentives for development and the application of

science and technology, indicators for science and technology in Africa and foreign direct investment as a vehicle for science and technology development. Furthermore, the Commission, in collaboration with OAU, organized a round table on the science and technology protocol of the African Economic Community from 21 to 27 September 1994.

397.   In the context of the implementation of the Second Industrial Development Decade for Africa, the Commission assisted Member States in the formulation of appropriate industrial policies and effective implementation of industrial programmes. The twelfth meeting of the Conference of African Ministers of Industry at Gaborone in June 1995 examined, among other things, the progress made by African countries in the implementation of their national and subregional programmes for the Decade and the role of the private sector in the implementation of the goals of the Decade.

398.   The Commission has launched a new series entitled the *Human Development in Africa Report*. The 1995 edition of the report was devoted to the themes of "Goals of the child", "Health for all" and "Basic education for all". The Commission has intensified its activities in assistance to Member States in integrating population development factors into socio-economic development programmes and policies; preparation of studies and/ or workshops on family planning and reproductive health, fertility and mortality; and the implementation of the Dakar/Ngor Declaration on Population, Family and Sustainable Development and the Programme of Action of the International Conference on Population and Development.

399.   The sixteenth meeting of the African Regional Coordinating Committee for the Integration of Women in Development was held from 20 to 22 April 1995 at Addis Ababa. It endorsed the African Platform for Action for Women adopted at the Fifth African Regional Conference on Women held at Dakar in November 1994. The African Platform for Action is the region's common position for the Fourth World Conference on Women. At the same time, the Commission continued its efforts related to the establishment of an African women's bank by convening an Ad Hoc Group Meeting in August 1994 to examine the feasibility of the creation of the bank. Entrepreneurs from some African countries have indicated their willingness to promote the bank. At its 1995 session, the Conference of Ministers requested further studies to clarify certain issues concerning the establishment of the bank. The Commission's operational role in the advancement of women was matched by the deepening of its analytical work on women's issues in Africa. For example, the Commission's *Economic and Social Survey of Africa 1995*

features a special study on gender disparities in formal education in Africa.

400.   The Commission, in collaboration with the General Agreement on Tariffs and Trade (GATT), UNCTAD and OAU, organized in Tunisia in October 1994 the International Conference to Assess the Impact of the Uruguay Round on African Economies. The aim of this Conference was to evaluate the technical requirements of African countries in adapting to the post–Uruguay Round international trade environment.

401.   During the period from December 1994 to June 1995, the Commission fielded over 65 short-term technical advisory missions. The main institutional vehicle for providing these advisory services is the ECA Multidisciplinary Regional Advisory Group. ECA rendered assistance to some Member States in the area of environmental management. It fielded advisory missions to Eritrea on protection of the marine environment and to Seychelles on water and environment. The Commission collaborated with UNEP in the preparation of studies on the contribution of the coastal/marine sector to the gross national product in the Gambia and the United Republic of Tanzania.

402.   The Commission has provided assistance to Member States in areas of public sector management, including development of indicators for public enterprise performance; strengthening of national statistical institutions; establishing information management systems; and agricultural management and policy planning. In Eritrea, for example, ECA has provided technical assistance for public enterprise reform and management, and assisted in establishing a national development information system and network linking various departments of the Government. In Angola, ECA is evaluating the development priority areas to form the basis of a policy framework for its technical assistance to the country's socio-economic development.

403.   Reflecting the diversity of requests for its support, the Multidisciplinary Regional Advisory Group also provided technical assistance to universities or institutes in some Member States. These included the Institute for Diplomacy and International Studies at the University of Nairobi, the International Relations Institute of Cameroon and the University of Ghana, Legon. Technical assistance to these institutions included short-term training and assistance in the establishment of new centres within these institutions. Advisory services were also rendered to intergovernmental, regional and subregional organizations and institutions. These included the subregional economic groupings, the ECA-sponsored institutions, the Intergovernmental Authority on Drought and Development and the Semi-Arid Food Grain Research

and Development Centre. During the period under review, the Commission had a total of 115 projects, of which 44 were terminated and 71 remained under implementation. A total amount of $5,606,603 was made available to the Commission under extrabudgetary resources for the implementation of the projects.

### 2. Economic Commission for Europe (ECE)

404. The aim of ECE is to further harmonize policies, norms and practices among the countries of the region and to strengthen their integration and cooperation.

405. Under the direction of Mr. Yves Berthelot, the Commission achieves this aim through policy analysis and dialogue on macroeconomic and sectoral issues; the elaboration of conventions, norms and standards; and a newly developed programme of assistance to the transition process.

406. ECE has continued to accord priority to the protection of the environment and the promotion of sustainable development, in particular in a transboundary context. Since 1979, ECE member countries have worked energetically to take up the environmental challenges of the region. In particular, the Commission has elaborated nine international, legally binding instruments on air pollution, environmental impact assessment, industrial accidents and transboundary waters.

407. Preparations are under way for two new protocols on persistent organic pollutants and on heavy metals to the 1979 Convention on Longrange Transboundary Air Pollution. These legal instruments constitute a unique legal framework for meeting environmental challenges. In order to make the conventions and protocols fully operational region wide, the Commission, in its decision G(50), called upon all its member States which had not already done so, to consider the earliest possible ratification of, or accession to, these instruments.

408. The Committee on Environmental Policy, with the assistance of its Working Group of Senior Governmental Officials on Environment for Europe, the central coordinating body for the Environment for Europe process, advanced in the preparations for the Sofia Ministerial Conference on Environment for Europe, to be held in October 1995. Among the main issues to be considered by the Conference are the follow-up to the 1993 Environmental Action Plan for Central and Eastern Europe, the assessment of the state of the environment for Europe and financing environmental improvements.

409. The Committee on Environmental Policy, in cooperation with OECD, has made progress in extending the OECD country environmental performance reviews to central and eastern Europe. The first two joint pilot reviews of Poland and Bulgaria have already taken place. The third

review in cooperation with OECD will take place in Belarus next year. As part of its own environmental performance review programme the Commission has undertaken a review of the situation in Estonia, to be concluded by the end of 1995 and published in early 1996.

410. During the past year, the Committee on Human Settlements continued its preparatory work for the United Nations Conference on Human Settlements (Habitat II). The Regional Preparatory Meeting for the Conference was held and a task force was established to assist the Committee in carrying out the preparatory work. An analytical report was prepared containing an overview of human settlements development in the ECE region and was submitted to the Preparatory Committee for Habitat II.

411. During the past year, the ECE Inland Transport Committee has continued to serve as a forum for cooperation in the field of transport. The Committee finalized and adopted two new legal instruments, bringing their total number to 50, and adopted amendments to a number of existing ones. Significant progress was made in the preparation of the European Agreement on Main Inland Waterways of International Importance.

412. Moreover, the Inland Transport Committee progressed in the establishment of international norms and standards for the construction of road vehicles, covering active and passive safety, environmental protection and energy consumption. The Committee has also paid special attention to activities in relation to road safety under the recently revised Vienna Convention on Road Signs and Signals and other related legal instruments. The second Road Safety Week was organized under the auspices of ECE from 27 March to 2 April 1995 and aimed at waging simultaneous campaigns addressed to young road users in each ECE member State. Substantive progress was also made in the elaboration of international norms and standards for the transport of dangerous goods by road and inland waterways and in their harmonization with those concerning the transport of such goods by rail, sea and air. The Committee acted on the basis of the recommendations developed by the Committee of Experts on the Transport of Dangerous Goods, a subsidiary committee of the Economic and Social Council.

413. The Inland Transport Committee finalized the customs container pool convention and prepared a draft convention on international customs transit procedures for the carriage of goods by rail. It was decided to undertake the revision of the Customs Convention on the International Transport of Goods under Cover of TIR Carnets (TIR Convention) in view of the current problems in its implementation. A report on the facilitation of border crossing in international rail transport

was prepared. A programme of action in the area of inland transport, aimed at assisting the countries of central and eastern Europe in their transitions to market economies, is being implemented.

414. Work has progressed as a follow-up to the decision taken by the Commission at its forty-ninth session, in April 1994, to convene a Regional Conference on Transport and the Environment in 1996. The Preparatory Committee for the Conference has thus far held five meetings and achieved agreement on a text of draft guidelines for a common strategy on transport and the environment.

415. The integrated presentation of international statistical work in the ECE region has been expanded beyond the statistical work of ECE, the European Communities and OECD to include statistical activities in the region undertaken by the Statistical Division and the Population Division of the United Nations Secretariat, the specialized agencies, the Council of Europe, CIS and other international organizations.

416. ECE supports a trade facilitation programme through its Working Party on Facilitation of International Trade Procedures. Considerable progress was made in the development of the United Nations Electronic Data Interchange for Administration, Commerce and Transport (EDIFACT) messages. Members of the Working Party and the secretariat participated in the United Nations International Symposium on Trade Efficiency held at Columbus, Ohio, in October 1994. A Compendium of Trade Facilitation Recommendations was developed. A memorandum of understanding between ECE, the International Electrotechnical Commission (IEC) and the International Organization for Standardization (ISO) was developed and approved in order to better define the division of responsibilities between these organizations.

417. *The Guide on the Adaptation of Real Property Law of Countries in Transition*, prepared under the auspices of the Working Party on International Contract Practices in Industry, was also well received. In the field of trade and investment promotion the secretariat continued to publish quarterly the *East-West Investment News* and to update its database on foreign direct investment projects and supporting legislation in countries in transition.

418. The economic analysis conducted by ECE and published in the *Economic Bulletin for Europe* and the *Economic Survey of Europe in 1994-1995* provides in-depth analysis of current economic developments in Europe, the States of the former Soviet Union, and North America. Special emphasis is given in both publications to developments in the transition economies of eastern Europe and the former Soviet Union and to their progress in creating market economies. This year's *Economic Bulletin* pays special attention to the foreign trade and payments of the transition economies and to the level of external support they have been receiving. The latest *Survey*, in addition to a detailed review of macroeconomic developments, contains an assessment of the reform process over the last five years and a review of international migration in eastern Europe and the Commonwealth of Independent States.

419. Under the second phase of the Energy Efficiency 2000 project, ECE has continued to assist countries in transition to develop their capacity to enhance energy efficiency and to implement energy efficiency standards and labelling.

420. In collaboration with national Governments, local institutions and UNDP, ECE has also formulated projects for enhancing energy efficiency in the context of programmes of conversion of military bases and manufacturing facilities to peaceful purposes in central and eastern Europe.

421. The Gas Centre was established in 1994, supported by financial contributions from major European and North American Governments and gas companies. A major regional initiative, the Gas Centre brings together almost all of the key natural gas market players in the Commission. It has already been successful in opening dialogue among the private and public gas companies and the Governments in the region.

422. The Working Party on Engineering Industries and Automation prepared and published two studies entitled "World engineering industries and automation—performance and prospects, 1993-1995" and "World industrial robots: statistics 1983-1993 and forecasts to 1997". The engineering industries continued to influence the restructuring of industry and, in particular, the process of investment and privatization. In this respect, special emphasis was given to the creation of small and medium-sized enterprises in economies in transition. At its fiftieth session, the Commission recognized the publication *Rehabilitation Engineering* as an ECE contribution to the World Summit for Social Development.

423. The Working Party on the Chemical Industry discussed the policy-oriented issues currently facing the chemical industry and stressed the importance of the work related to sustainable development and, in particular, the Chemical Industry—Sustainable Economic and Ecological Development (CHEMISEED) programme. Fifteen member countries identified 40 sites polluted by chemicals for the pilot project demonstrating environmental clean-up procedures.

424. The Working Party on Steel strengthened its regional programme on metallurgy and ecology through: the organization of a Seminar on the Steel Industry and Recycling; the addition to the

work programme of a Seminar on Processing, Utilization and Disposal of Waste in the Steel Industry; a bibliography of environmental publications in the steel sector; and activities aimed at the harmonization of regulations on environmental protection. *The Global Study on the Steel Industry in Europe* was prepared in cooperation with the European Commission, the European Bank for Reconstruction and Development (EBRD), the World Bank and the International Iron and Steel Institute. The study also served as the basis for the examination of the restructuring of steel industries in the economies in transition.

425. The Working Party on Standardization Policies reviewed developments in the fields of coordination, harmonization, conformity assessment and metrology at the international, regional and national levels and paid particular attention to assistance to the countries in transition with a view to adapting existing structures to market conditions and to assisting newly independent States to build adequate institutions. At its forty-ninth session, the Commission adopted the recommendation on the meteorological assurance of testing proposed by the Working Party as separate decision H(49).

426. In the light of the decision taken by the FAO Council in June 1994 concerning the restructuring of FAO, and in particular the increased decentralization to the regional and subregional offices, the joint ECE/FAO Agriculture and Timber Division was dismantled in 1995. In accordance with the decision of the Commission at its fiftieth session, in April 1995, interim arrangements have been made to ensure the continuation of the ECE/FAO joint activities on agriculture and the environment and on the economic analysis of the agri-food sector. The Commission will consider a proposal of the Executive Secretary to merge the ECE Committee on Agriculture with the FAO European Commission on Agriculture.

427. The ECE regional advisory services programme has elaborated a national plan of assistance to the Republic of Georgia. The first phase is scheduled to be implemented before the end of July 1995. The experience of this plan will be evaluated and applied to other cases of high priority.

### 3. Economic Commission for Latin America and the Caribbean (ECLAC)

428. The period covered by this report was marked by a certain turbulence in economic performance in Latin America and the Caribbean. This context, in turn, was reflected in the activities of ECLAC, headed by Mr. Gert Rosenthal, which tries to respond to both long-term and emerging development issues in the region.

429. In the past year, the ECLAC secretariat, which includes the Latin American and Caribbean Institute for Economic and Social Planning (ILPES) and the Latin American Demographic Centre (CELADE), focused on a number of development issues concerned with medium-term growth (macroeconomic management, innovation, enhancing savings and channelling them to productive investment) and intraregional economic cooperation. In addition, the secretariat was involved in numerous regional preparatory activities for global events, particularly the World Summit for Social Development and the Fourth World Conference on Women.

430. At the time of writing the present report, ECLAC was undertaking a major mid-decade evaluation of the strategies of adjustment, stabilization and structural reforms pursued by the region. The exercise is expected to be particularly timely in the face of recent events affecting some Latin American economies. The document is planned to be reviewed by the member Governments during the forthcoming session of the Commission to be held at San José, Costa Rica, in April 1996.

431. ECLAC continued to be a meeting place for officials. In addition to some 35 seminars held during the past 13 months, the secretariat prepared and held the sixth session of the Regional Conference on the Integration of Women into the Economic and Social Development of Latin America and the Caribbean, held at Mar del Plata, Argentina, from 25 to 29 September 1994. The secretariat played a similar role in the twenty-first meeting of Presiding Officers of the Regional Conference on the Integration of Women into the Economic and Social Development of Latin America and the Caribbean, held at Santiago, Chile, on 3 and 4 July 1995. Support was provided to the third Regional Meeting of Ministers and High-level Authorities of the Housing and Urban Development Sector in Latin America and the Caribbean, held at Quito, Ecuador, from 16 to 18 November 1994.

432. ECLAC has been actively involved in the follow-up activities to Agenda 21, most notably in those dealing with environmentally sustainable management of natural resources and various sectors of activity, and the development of statistics and environmental accounts. The extensive list of publications and research works includes a study on water resources management in Latin America and the Caribbean from the perspective of programme 21, and a study entitled "Hazardous products and wastes: impact of transboundary movements towards the Latin American and Caribbean region and possibilities for preventing and controlling it". The Commission made relevant contributions to the preparatory work of the

World Summit for Social Development through the formulation of poverty reduction strategies within the context of its major statement on changing production patterns with social equity. Among the publications most recently issued are: *Proposals for a modern social policy to foster social development* and *Educational inequalities: problems and policies.* Work is ongoing on a project that explores the relationships between this statement and the promotion of economic, social and cultural rights in the region.

433.   ECLAC has also continued to perform its established role of monitoring the economic and social performance of the region. To the Commission's list of traditional annual publications that fulfil this function—the *Preliminary Overview of the Economy of Latin America and the Caribbean*, the *Economic Survey of Latin America and the Caribbean* and the *Statistical Yearbook for Latin America and the Caribbean*— the *Social Panorama of Latin America* has now been added in keeping with the increased level of recognition that the matter is gaining in the region. Work continued on the setting up of the Short-term Indicators Database, the incorporation of new international statistical classifications and the development of a data bank on the external debt of Latin American countries. In addition, assistance was provided to Latin American countries in implementing the new System of National Accounts.

434.   The Executive Secretary participated in the Meeting of Heads of State of the Río Group (September 1994), the Hemispheric Summit of Heads of State (December 1994) and the Ibero-American Summit of Heads of State and Government (July 1995).

### 4.   Economic and Social Commission for Asia and the Pacific (ESCAP)

435.   Against the backdrop of the sustained dynamism of the Asia-Pacific region, ESCAP, headed by Mr. Adrianus Mooy, has continued to focus attention on enhancing economic growth and social development among the countries of the region.

436.   In that connection, at its fifty-first session, concluded on 1 May 1995 at Bangkok, the Commission decided to hold a ministerial conference on regional economic cooperation and directed the secretariat to initiate necessary preparations.

437.   The Commission also placed emphasis on promotion of subregional economic cooperation in various fields, including trade and investment. A second consultative meeting among executive heads of subregional organizations and ESCAP was hosted by the secretariat of the Association of South-East Asian Nations (ASEAN) at Jakarta in January 1995.

438.   The Commission emphasized the pivotal role of industrial and technological development in sustaining the growth momentum in the region.

The Commission's work in this area was guided by several mandates and directives as enshrined in the Seoul Plan of Action for Promoting and Strengthening Regional Cooperation for Technology-led Industrialization in Asia and the Pacific, the Action Programme for Regional Economic Cooperation in Investment-related Technology Transfer, the Beijing Declaration on Regional Economic Cooperation and the Delhi Declaration on Strengthening Regional Economic Cooperation in Asia and the Pacific towards the Twenty-first Century.

439.   Another important development has been the fifteenth session of the Standing Committee of the Bangkok Agreement, held at Bangkok in February 1995, which decided to launch the third round of negotiations, with a mandate to address both tariff and non-tariff barriers and to explore the possibility of including the services sector in due course.

440.   The Commission endorsed the Jakarta Declaration and Plan of Action for the Advancement of Women in Asia and the Pacific adopted at the Second Asian and Pacific Ministerial Conference on Women in Development, held at Jakarta in June 1994. The Jakarta Declaration and Plan of Action served as the regional input to the draft global platform of action for adoption by the forthcoming Fourth World Conference on Women. Following the Ministerial Conference, regional meetings of coordinating bodies of non-governmental organizations and national machineries for the advancement of women were convened to accelerate implementation of the Plan of Action.

441.   An Asian and Pacific Ministerial Conference in Preparation for the World Summit for Social Development was organized at Manila in October 1994, at which the Manila Declaration and Agenda for Action for Social Development in the ESCAP region were adopted. As part of the preparatory activities, a symposium of non-governmental organizations was convened by ESCAP prior to the Ministerial Conference.

442.   The Commission's initiatives with regard to its declaration of the Asian and Pacific Decade of Disabled Persons, 1993-2002, continued to generate significant activities at national and regional levels aimed at improving the status and participation of disabled persons. To date, 30 members and associate members have signed the Proclamation on the Full Participation and Equality of People with Disabilities in the Asian and Pacific Region.

443.   The Commission continued to support national efforts and activities to promote participatory human settlements development. Preparatory work has begun for convening an Asia-Pacific Urban Forum in 1995 which will serve as a key

preparatory activity to the second United Nations Conference on Human Settlements (Habitat II) in 1996. The Commission is also working closely with the Regional Network of Local Authorities for the Management of Human Settlements (CITYNET) and the Asian Coalition for Housing Rights to assist member countries in addressing urban poverty issues, particularly as they relate to low-income housing and settlements improvement.

444. In implementing the Bali Declaration on Population and Sustainable Development and the Programme of Action of the International Conference on Population and Development, various inter-country research projects and training courses were conducted; technical assistance was also provided relating to such areas as family planning, population ageing, migration and urbanization, the role and status of women and demographic analysis. Activities of the Asia-Pacific Population Information Network (POPIN) focused on upgrading technical skills in database development and improving population information management and sharing.

445. Under the theme of environment and sustainable development, the Commission focused attention on the preparations for the Ministerial-level Conference on Environment and Development in Asia and the Pacific, which will be organized by ESCAP at Bangkok in November 1995, and the prevention of desertification, including preparation of the Regional Implementation Annex for Asia to the United Nations Convention to Combat Desertification in Those Countries Experiencing Serious Drought and/or Desertification, particularly in Africa.

446. Under the theme of transport and communications, the Commission pursued its activities related to the implementation of the Asian Land Transport Infrastructure Development Programme, comprising the Asian Highway and Trans-Asian Railway projects. Current activities under this project include a study on developing land transport linkages of Kazakstan, Turkmenistan and Uzbekistan with seaports of the Islamic Republic of Iran and Pakistan in the south and China in the east; a study on the development of a highway network in Asian republics; a Trans-Asian Railway route requirements study; and implementation of ESCAP resolution 48/11 on road and rail transport modes in relation to facilitation measures.

447. Following the theme topic of the fiftieth session of the Commission "Infrastructure development as key to economic growth and regional economic cooperation", and Commission resolution 50/2 on the "Action plan on infrastructure development in Asia and the Pacific", the Commission at its fifty-first session adopted the New

Delhi Action Plan on Infrastructure Development in Asia and the Pacific. The Commission decided to convene a ministerial conference on infrastructure in 1996 to launch the New Delhi action plan and to review phase II (1992-1996) of the Transport and Communications Decade for Asia and the Pacific.

448. Special efforts were made to improve policies for tourism development, taking into consideration the socio-economic and environmental impact of tourism. Studies on the cultural and environmental impact of tourism provided policy recommendations for the cultural and environmental management of tourism development. ESCAP convened the first meeting of the Working Group on the Greater Mekong Subregion Tourism Sector in April 1995.

449. The statistics subprogramme of the Commission focused on promoting the improvement of capabilities of national statistical offices in the region for timely and accurate collection and dissemination of statistics needed for development planning and decision-making. Technical meetings were organized to support country work in the implementation of the 1993 System of National Accounts (SNA), in statistics on gender issues and in environment statistics and environmental and resource accounting. Assistance was also provided through advisory services, including those in population statistics, data-processing and national accounts.

450. The Commission's reaffirmation of its predominant role in promoting regional cooperation in Asia and the Pacific was manifested in the decision by the Russian Federation to seek a revision in its status in order to become a regional member. The application of the Russian Federation was unanimously endorsed by the Commission, which recommended a resolution on the matter for submission to the substantive session of 1995 of the Economic and Social Council.

451. To meet the need for an integrated and effective approach to development at the regional level, an inter-agency meeting on strengthening coordination at the regional level was convened by ESCAP in May 1994. This meeting established the Regional Inter-agency Committee for Asia and the Pacific under the chairmanship of the Executive Secretary of ESCAP. The first meeting of the Committee was concluded at Bangkok in June 1995.

## 5. Economic and Social Commission for Western Asia (ESCWA)

452. The impact of international and regional issues does not only concern the political environment, but also affects the whole economic and social fabric in ESCWA countries. Thus, ESCWA, headed by Mr. Hazem El-Beblawi, undertook multidisciplinary coverage of work programme components, combining them in a few compact

areas. The Commission's work programme was formulated around five themes featuring inter-related activities.

453.   Under the first thematic subprogramme, Management of natural resources and environ-ment, issues concerning the assessment and proper management of land, water and energy resources were addressed, as well as environmental degra-dation resulting from inadequate management of these resources.

454.   In the field of environment, ESCWA par-ticipated in several meetings and workshops such as the Technical Secretariat of the Council of Arab Ministers Responsible for Environment. A report was completed on progress made in the ESCWA plan to implement Agenda 21 in the region which was presented to the Commission at its eighteenth session, in May 1995, as well as to the Commis-sion on Sustainable Development and the Eco-nomic and Social Council. Furthermore, ESCWA, in its capacity as a member of the Executive Com-mittee of the Joint Committee on Environment and Development in the Arab Region, participated in its fifth meeting at Cairo in July 1995. The meeting discussed the implementation of the de-cisions of the second meeting of the Joint Com-mittee and preparations for a meeting on biodiver-sity in the Arab region. The meeting also included discussions on two technical reports on the estab-lishment of an integrated environmental informa-tion network in the Arab region.

455.   A report was prepared by ESCWA on ac-tivities related to the protection of the ozone layer, while issues pertaining to resource conservation were addressed through studies on wildlife con-servation for sustainable development in the Arab countries and the assessment of the fisheries sec-tor in the United Arab Emirates. In the field of water resources, ESCWA organized a meeting at Amman from 12 to 14 September 1994 of the Inter-agency Task Force on modalities of cooper-ation and coordination among United Nations specialized agencies and Arab regional agencies involved in various water-related activities. The meeting recommended that ESCWA serve as the secretariat for the Inter-agency Task Force. A long-term project on the assessment of water resources using remote-sensing techniques is under way.

456.   The second thematic subprogramme, Improvement of the quality of life, includes activi-ties to provide support for ESCWA member States in preparing, at the national and regional levels, for world conferences and meetings. Reports were submitted to the Commission at its eighteenth ses-sion on all preparatory and follow-up activities for meetings and conferences such as the International Conference on Population and Development, the International Year of the Family, the World Sum-mit for Social Development, the United Nations

Conference on Human Settlements (Habitat II) and the Fourth World Conference on Women.

457.   The Commission participated in the preparatory committee for the World Summit for Social Development and in the Summit itself. It also participated in the Ninth United Nations Congress on the Prevention of Crime and the Treatment of Offenders, held at Cairo from 29 April to 8 May 1995. Other major activities in-cluded the preparation of the Arab Declaration for Social Development, which was presented to the Council of Arab Ministers for Social Affairs, the launching of a social development database, the preparation of a project document on human de-velopment in the Arab States and a workshop on sustainable human development experiences, held at Cairo from 14 to 19 May 1995. ESCWA also un-dertook a study on the impact of the recent crisis on the social situation in the ESCWA region, which analysed the socio-economic impact of crises in the region, with particular emphasis on population migration, the quality of life and vulnerable and disadvantaged groups. ESCWA organized, in this context, a seminar entitled "The Role of the Fam-ily in Integrating Disabled Women into Society", at Amman from 16 to 18 October 1994.

458.   In the area of women and development, ESCWA organized the Arab Regional Preparatory Meeting for the Fourth World Conference on Women, which was held at Amman from 6 to 10 November 1994 and was attended by 420 par-ticipants representing all Arab countries. The meeting reviewed the implementation of the Nairobi Forward-looking Strategies for the Ad-vancement of Women and the ESCWA Strategy for Arab Women to the Year 2005. The meeting also finalized the Regional Plan of Action for the Ad-vancement of Arab Women. ESCWA also organ-ized a meeting on the Arab family in a changing society at Abu Dhabi in December 1994, in the context of preparations for the Fourth World Con-ference on Women. Other activities within this framework included national workshops in nine ESCWA countries to review the national plans of action in the light of national reports on the situ-ation of women. Information on women's issues was addressed through a publication on Arab women in ESCWA member States. This publica-tion includes statistics, indicators and trends. A database on statistics on women was also launched.

459.   In the field of rural development, two long-term rural community development projects are being implemented in Egypt and the Syrian Arab Republic. ESCWA continued to issue its an-nual publication *Agriculture and Development in West-ern Asia* (No. 16, December 1994); and it prepared a *National Farm Data Handbook for the Syrian Arab Repub-lic*. Other publications issued by the secretariat in-clude: *Land and Water Policies in the Near East Region;*

*Marketing of Agricultural Products in Lebanon; Evaluation of Agricultural Policies in the Syrian Arab Republic: Policy Analysis Matrix Approach; Prospective Development of the Agricultural Institutions in the Occupied Palestinian Territories;* and *Rehabilitation of Veterinary Services.*

460.    Information on human settlements issues was disseminated through the publication of a newsletter jointly published by ESCWA, the United Nations Centre for Human Settlements and the League of Arab States. ESCWA participated in preparatory meetings for Habitat II and convened at Amman, in March 1995, a regional preparatory meeting for the Conference.

461.    In the area of industrial development, ESCWA completed a publication entitled *Proceedings of the Expert Group Meeting on the Creation of Indigenous Entrepreneurship and Opportunities for Small and Medium-scale Industrial Investments.* In preparation for the Fourth World Conference on Women, the Commission issued a publication entitled *Participation of Women in Manufacturing: Patterns, Determinants and Analysis.* Several training-of-trainers workshops on how to start a business in war-torn areas were held in Bethlehem, Gaza, Nablus and Beirut. Moreover, a pilot workshop on upgrading entrepreneurial skills of managers of small and medium enterprises under changing conditions was held at Amman in September 1994. A study was completed entitled "Impact of the single European market on the industrial sector in the ESCWA region"; and two project documents were completed for the establishment of business incubators in the occupied Palestinian territories.

462.    The third thematic subprogramme, Economic development and cooperation, involved activities dealing with such central issues as promoting economic and technical cooperation and integration among ESCWA countries, promoting coordinated regional strategies, training officials in developing national capabilities in managerial skills, and reviewing and analysing economic performance, policies and strategies.

463.    The *Survey of Economic and Social Developments in the ESCWA Region, 1993* was issued in November 1994. The *Survey* for 1994 was completed in July 1995. Within the same context, a study was completed on "Review of developments and issues in the external trade and payments situation of countries of Western Asia", which included a chapter on the implications of the Uruguay Round on development in the region. A study was also completed entitled "Review of developments and trends in the monetary and financial sectors in the economies of the ESCWA region".

464.    The proceedings of four workshops/conferences were published, namely: the Western Asia workshop on strategies for accelerating the development of civil registration and vital statistics systems; the Second Arab Conference on Perspectives of Modern Biotechnology; the workshop on the implication of the new advanced materials technologies for the economies of the ESCWA countries; and the workshop on the integration of science and technology in the development planning and management process in the ESCWA region.

465.    In the area of transport and communications, a report was submitted to the Commission at its eighteenth session on the "Follow-up action of the implementation of the Transport and Communications Decade, second phase: 1992-1996". Furthermore, studies were completed on "Development of free zones in Western Asia"; "Development of the telecommunications sector in the ESCWA region"; and "Present status, development trends and future prospects of telecommunications in the ESCWA region"; and the ESCWA *Transport Bulletin for 1994* (No. 5) was issued. Additionally, the ESCWA secretariat conducted an expert group meeting on the Development of a Multimodal Transport Chain in Western Asia, held at Amman from 24 to 27 April 1995.

466.    In the field of statistics, ESCWA continued the development and maintenance of databases on energy and industry. A workshop on the implementation of the 1993 System of National Accounts was held at Amman from 12 to 19 December 1994 and another workshop on industrial statistics took place at Damascus from 26 November to 6 December 1994. Training was also provided on the use of statistical computer packages, geographical information systems and the application of the International Comparisons Programme.

467.    The fourth thematic subprogramme, Regional development and global changes, encompassed activities dealing with exogenous factors and global changes affecting the region. The major activity under this subprogramme is an ongoing multidisciplinary study on the impact of the single European market on different sectors in the ESCWA region.

468.    Issues concerning Palestine, the Middle East peace process and the least developed member States were the focal points for the fifth thematic subprogramme, Special programmes and issues. In its studies, the Agriculture Section covered the rehabilitation of the fisheries sector in the Gaza Strip and of veterinary services in the occupied territories. In addition, a proposed action programme for the restructuring of Palestinian agricultural public institutions was also prepared. The Industry Section undertook workshops on the development of small enterprises in the occupied Palestinian territories.

### E.   *The humanitarian imperative*

469.    This past year has seen a frightening persistence and intensity of conflicts that affect an unprecedented number of innocent civilians. The

reality of contemporary warfare is that more than 90 per cent of casualties are non-combatants who are often deliberately targeted because of their ethnic or religious affiliation. As a consequence, victims continued to flee their homes and communities in staggering numbers in 1995, reaching a global total of some 25 million refugees. A still larger number of persons have been displaced or are directly affected by warfare within their own countries.

470. Increasingly, humanitarian organizations are compelled to operate in war-torn societies where conflicting parties are often openly contemptuous of fundamental humanitarian norms. In such circumstances, a major challenge is the need to safeguard the well-being of civilians while providing assistance in a manner consistent with humanitarian principles.

471. In addition, the international community is faced with the paradox of needing ever larger resources to address the immediate survival needs of victims, while simultaneously recognizing that such action may deflect attention and support from initiatives essential to undoing the root causes of vulnerability and strife. Faced with these conflicting trends, humanitarian organizations have been reassessing the processes that shape the nature and impact of their interventions.

472. Recent experience illustrates the importance of a well-organized and adequately resourced mechanism for coordination, both within the multi-actor humanitarian arena and with other elements of the international system involved in crisis management and pre-emptive action. This is particularly evident in rapid and simultaneous mass population movements, where it is often difficult to move quickly enough to mobilize and deploy resources in a manner that will prevent avoidable deaths. However, notwithstanding the importance of support from the international community, it is the people of the country directly affected who are primarily responsible for their own recovery and that of their communities.

473. The volatile context within which humanitarian assistance is provided is a major determinant in the overall capacity of the United Nations system to pre-empt and respond to crises in a manner that minimizes avoidable suffering.

474. The scale and depth of suffering in conflict situations confronting the international community today is too often a consequence of a disregard for fundamental humanitarian principles. In many instances, the suffering endured by civilians is not an incidental element of political and military strategies but constitutes its major objective. The conflicts in Bosnia and Herzegovina and Rwanda are alarming examples of what occurs when civilians are subjected to the full brutality of contemporary warfare and gross violations

of human rights. Determination must be shown to enforce the rule of law and to hold accountable those who are responsible for heinous crimes.

475. The limited means of humanitarian organizations to provide protection is particularly glaring in conflict settings and in situations characterized by extreme violations of human rights. The Rwandan experience illustrates the way in which the capacity of the United Nations to provide protection and assistance is undermined when inputs and distribution mechanisms are used for purposes that are inimical to humanitarian objectives. Finding the means to reach those in need without entrenching the power of abusive elements is one of the most difficult challenges facing the humanitarian community in recent times.

476. The indifference of warring parties to even the most basic humanitarian principles has continued to make conditions under which relief workers must operate extremely dangerous. As the number of conflicts increases so too does the number of practitioners who have been killed or wounded, sometimes deliberately, while carrying out their humanitarian tasks. Frequent disruption and diversion of emergency relief supplies have occurred. Access has on many occasions had to be negotiated. Dependence on the agreement of armed groups often makes the provision of humanitarian assistance tenuous and subject to unacceptable conditions. If this trend continues, it could undermine the capacity of the agencies to carry out humanitarian work. Safeguarding both the concept and the reality of "humanitarian space" remains one of the most significant challenges facing the humanitarian community.

477. Another major obstacle facing humanitarian organizations is the absence of sufficient political will and support for action to address the underlying causes of crises. The provision of humanitarian assistance in a vacuum is tantamount to managing only the symptoms of a crisis. Experience shows that, in most instances, the effectiveness of humanitarian endeavour in conflict settings is predicated to a considerable extent on successful action by the international community to resolve the problems that provoked the crisis.

478. In some situations, such as in Angola and Mozambique, a determined effort has been made to stop the fighting and to consolidate the peace. In other settings, such as Haiti, assertive action has been taken to end oppression and the potential for violent conflict. This is in dramatic contrast to other settings, such as the Sudan, where conflict has smouldered for 28 of the last 39 years. In Burundi and Liberia, a volatile mix of circumstances points to the need for action to strengthen the push for peace.

479. The humanitarian agenda is often shaped by political attitudes to particular crises, strategic

interests in specific areas and the attention span of the media. Such factors, which are for the most part beyond the control of humanitarian organizations, contribute strongly to the low level of attention and support provided to victims of "silent" emergencies. Ideally, and in a more humane world, assistance would be provided according to need and the core principle of impartiality would have greater relevance when responding to emergencies.

480. Other factors that have an impact on the effectiveness of relief and protection organizations include the relationship between the level of resources and attention devoted to the prevention of, preparedness for and recovery from disasters and the amount of resources required to meet the daily needs of people in camp situations (*see fig. 15*). Rwanda is but one example of current trends. Some $1 billion was spent in the first six months of the crisis. Most of this was used for the immediate survival needs of the millions who were uprooted and displaced in 1994. Although resources were requested at an early stage for confidence-building measures to facilitate and encourage the return of those who had fled and for action focused on the problem of genocide, only a minuscule amount has been made available for activities essential to ameliorating and resolving the underlying cause of the cyclical strife that now characterizes Rwanda and other parts of the Great Lakes region.

481. However, some vital progress has been made both in responding rapidly and effectively to the needs of victims and in generating a more cohesive approach within the United Nations system. The Inter-Agency Standing Committee has played an incisive role, having on many occasions enabled consensus and decisions on pressing country-specific issues to be arrived at quickly and with immediate impact. Its uniqueness and success stem in part from the presence of, and close working relations with, certain major umbrella non-governmental organizations. In 1994, the Committee agreed on a number of measures for strengthening field coordination of humanitarian assistance in complex emergencies, in particular in the pre-emergency and initial response phases. A set of guidelines relating to the humanitarian mandate as well as the appointment of and terms of reference for humanitarian coordinators were approved and the Emergency Relief Coordinator was also designated as the focal point for internally displaced persons. Most importantly, procedures for the most expeditious agreement on the division of labour between agencies have also been approved by the Committee.

482. Within the Secretariat, the Department of Humanitarian Affairs, the Department of Political Affairs and the Department of Peace-keeping Operations have established a mechanism for the joint analysis of early warning of a looming crisis, within a broader framework for the coordination of operational planning and implementation among the three departments. Among the United Nations agencies also, agreement as to the responsibility and criteria for "sounding the alarm" in impending crises has enabled appropriate preventive and preparedness actions (such as contingency planning measures, primarily at the in-country level) to be initiated.

483. Timing is also critical in the fielding of humanitarian assistance operations. The Department of Humanitarian Affairs has established a Rapid Response Unit to field experienced personnel to work with the United Nations resident or humanitarian coordinator and to build up systematic support for field-level coordination activities. At Kigali in April 1994, the United Nations advance humanitarian team, staffed by United Nations agency representatives and Department of Humanitarian Affairs personnel, re-established a United Nations humanitarian presence during a very difficult period and was able to lay the groundwork for the expansion of humanitarian activities as the situation permitted. In Haiti, a combined Department of Humanitarian Affairs/UNDP team was deployed to support the United Nations Coordinator for Humanitarian Assistance in the immediate aftermath of the United Nations action of September 1994. During the crisis in Chechnya, Department of Humanitarian Affairs staff were dispatched to neighbouring republics, where they worked closely with UNHCR and United Nations agency representatives in addressing the needs of internally displaced persons.

484. The Central Emergency Revolving Fund has consistently proved its value in facilitating both a rapid and joint response by United Nations agencies to fast-breaking emergencies. Delays in its reimbursement have, however, offset its usefulness on a number of occasions. The past year also saw the first use of the interest on the Fund to support immediate coordination arrangements in the field, with the establishment of the United Nations Rwanda Emergency Office at Kigali.

485. With a growing number of major emergencies of all varieties requiring international assistance, the Department of Humanitarian Affairs, led by Under-Secretary-General Peter Hansen, has continued to strengthen its coordination support capacity and to act as a focal point for the development of new initiatives taken jointly by the international emergency response community towards the improved effectiveness of international relief operations. Activities since my last report include the expansion of the number of countries participating with members in the United Nations Disaster Assessment and Coordination Team, in-

cluding six disaster-prone developing countries from the Latin American region, and the development of guidelines and standards for the assessment of international relief requirements in multisectoral emergencies and for the mobilization of resources, the rapid initiation and support of field coordination, the exchange of know-how and techniques, and the development of standard operational procedures in the deployment of international response teams.

486. In this endeavour, the Department of Humanitarian Affairs has worked closely with and supported the activities of international networks of emergency teams such as the International Search and Rescue Advisory Group and the Standing Coordinating Group on the Use of Military and Civil Defence Assets in Disaster Relief. With regard to the provision of specialized human, technical and logistical resources to support the coordination of international relief operations, the Department has initiated memoranda of understanding with Governments and organizations to allow it expeditious access to their emergency relief capacities. This forward-looking, systematic approach used by the Department has proved its worth in a number of sudden-onset emergencies during the year.

487. Natural disaster reduction remains a core activity of humanitarian assistance, which tackles the root causes of disasters, and an essential ingredient of rehabilitation and reconstruction planning. The Under-Secretary-General has, therefore, brought together the Department of Humanitarian Affairs' Disaster Mitigation Branch and the secretariat for the International Decade for Natural Disaster Reduction under the umbrella of a Disaster Reduction Division. Thus the Department is able to serve all aspects of natural disaster reduction at all levels within the framework of a coherent United Nations strategy (*see table 1*).

Table 1

**Natural disasters: casualties, damage and contributions**

|  | 1992 | 1993 | 1994 |
|---|---|---|---|
| Number of disasters | 45 | 68 | 75 |
| Number of dead | 6,971 | 13,542 | 7,572 |
| Number of missing | 258 | 1,631 | 1,989 |
| Amount of damage[a] | 2.06 | 15.80 | 9.00 |
| Contributions reported to DHA[b] | 257.4 | 77.5 | 114.0 |
| Contributions channelled through DHA[b] | 3.73 | 4.23 | 7.50 |

[a]Billions of United States dollars.
[b]Millions of United States dollars.

488. Between May 1994 and July 1995, the Department of Humanitarian Affairs launched 27 appeals for international assistance on behalf of countries affected by natural, technological or environmental disasters. It coordinated international assistance following more than 85 disasters in 50 countries. Some 243 situation reports were issued on the consequences of those disasters, to which the international community reported contributions amounting to more than $115 million, $6.3 million of which were channelled through the Department. During the same period, the Department arranged 38 relief flights from its emergency stockpile at Pisa, Italy, in response to the immediate requirements of those affected by disaster.

489. However, while much vital progress has been made in augmenting the capacity of humanitarian agencies to respond quickly and coherently to the immediate needs of victims of all kinds of emergencies, the task of assisting countries to emerge from crises continues to pose significant challenges. This is particularly evident in situations of systemic breakdown when the task of rebuilding civil society is dependent on the commitment of the international community to address the underlying cause of crises. The ability of aid agencies to support a recovery process is, of course, largely determined by the extent to which affected communities engage in activities geared to making the transition from dependency on relief to sustainable development.

490. As is now widely acknowledged, the relationship between relief and development, particularly in conflict settings, is complex and needs constantly to be assessed to ensure that interventions are mutually reinforcing. In many instances, gains made by the humanitarian community in stabilizing a situation are not accompanied by the inputs necessary to nurture a recovery process. Indeed, protracted crises often experience funding shortfalls, thereby negating tenuous advances in the reduction of vulnerabilities of either a social, economic or political nature. The tragic experiences of people in Liberia, Rwanda and the Sudan illustrate the need for sustained and concerted action focused on breaking the dynamic of violence.

491. On a more positive note, the experiences of Haiti and Mozambique during this past year demonstrate the advantages of assertive action that actively nurtures the quest for peace. Likewise, the opportunity to consolidate the long-awaited peace in Angola must be fully exploited and necessary support provided for vital rehabilitation and reconstruction activities. As in other post-cease-fire situations, it is important that the international community maintain the momentum for peace; too often, critical activities, including demining and the homeward return of refugees, the dis-

placed and former combatants, are jeopardized because of insufficient support for programmes that are essential for the revitalization of community life. Aware of the challenges confronting war-torn societies, humanitarian and development staff of the United Nations system are currently reviewing mechanisms to ensure that their respective funding and operational activities are complementary and enhance peace-building initiatives.

### 1. Cooperation with regional arrangements or agencies

492.   In the field of natural disaster reduction, the primary function of the Department of Humanitarian Affairs is to promote new initiatives. This includes project activities in 28 of the more disaster-prone developing countries, including 11 new ones during the year under review.

493.   The main objectives have been to establish and apply the most effective methods for hazard and risk assessment, to promote wider interchange of knowledge and systematic application of appropriate technology, to carry out more active pooling, analysis and dissemination of early warnings, and to stimulate the development of scenario-specific disaster mitigation and preparedness plans with emphasis on maximizing the use of local resources and community involvement, while providing access to external expertise where essential. A special focus has been placed on Africa, where three subregional seminars have stimulated new national initiatives in disaster reduction. In Latin America and the Caribbean, new projects have been formulated for five countries and comprehensive programmes continue in four others. For Asia, projects are continuing or are in the process of formulation for six countries, including a new four-year programme encompassing the South Pacific island States, which has been widely sponsored and warmly welcomed by the participating countries and regional agencies. Attention is also being given to the eastern European, Middle East and CIS countries, with projects launched or in process of formulation in five States. The above activities have been carried out in close cooperation with UNDP and UNEP to promote the inclusion of development and environment issues wherever applicable. Eleven other international agencies and more than 30 non-governmental organizations have been associated.

494.   In the framework of the Department of Humanitarian Affairs' project on the use of military and civil defence assets in disaster relief, arrangements have continued for strengthening cooperation between the Department of Humanitarian Affairs and NATO, the Western European Union (WEU) and the Inter-American Defense Board. Within the provisions of the Oslo Guidelines, mechanisms for such cooperation are being

tested and improved through joint training, contingency planning and field exercises. Regional cooperation was tested in particular during an exercise hosted by the Russian Federation focusing on international assistance following a simulated major nuclear power plant accident. Standing operating procedures for the use of military and civil defence assets in disaster relief are being refined to enhance the humanitarian aspects of the NATO Partnership for Peace programme. The EU Humanitarian Office, a member of the Standing Coordinating Group, has funded the activities of the project related to relief air operations and to regional cooperation in Africa and Asia.

495.   UNDP and the Department of Humanitarian Affairs have established a Joint Environment Unit that strengthens the international capacity to respond to environmental aspects of disasters, while making the most effective use of limited resources. The Unit represents a practical synergy between the two organizations that ensures a targeted and comprehensive approach to the growing problem of environmental emergencies while at the same time avoiding duplication of effort. As such, the Joint Environment Unit is fully integrated into the Department of Humanitarian Affairs. UNEP provides staff and funding for the project, while the Department provides access to resources, expertise in disaster management and procedures for effective mobilization and coordination of relief.

496.   The Department of Humanitarian Affairs also continues to work closely with the Caribbean Disaster Emergency Response Agency, with which the Department has an agreement for early warning and exchange of information when disaster strikes.

### 2. Proactive humanitarian action

497.   Part of the Department of Humanitarian Affairs' core coordination function involves participation in the planning and execution of "proactive" humanitarian action, though this term carries different meaning when applied to the onset of complex crises, on the one hand, or natural disasters, on the other. Examples of humanitarian activities that might prevent or reduce the scale of suffering include the provision of assistance that could pre-empt mass population movements or support that facilitates the reintegration of demobilized soldiers. Prevention of natural disasters might involve the strengthening of structures against earthquakes or the resettlement of populations away from flood zones or earthquake fault lines.

498.   A functioning early warning system is critically important for the timely planning and implementation of pre-emptive action. The Humanitarian Early Warning System has been created to provide up-to-date warnings of country crisis situations through analysis of its data-

base, drawing upon the various early warning mechanisms of other United Nations agencies as well as non–United Nations information sources. The System is made up of a database that includes both statistical and other country-specific information, graphically presented trend evaluation and an analysis process that examines statistical and event information. The System completed its prototype in January 1995 and has expanded its country coverage as well as its depth of information on each country. It became fully operational in July.

499. In the field of natural disasters, activities generated by the International Decade for Natural Disaster Reduction are focused specifically on preventive measures. The momentum created by the World Conference on Natural Disaster Reduction, held at Yokohama in May 1994, has been successfully sustained by means of a participatory and continuous dialogue of traditional and new partners within the International Framework of Action. Consequently, the Yokohama Strategy for a Safer World: Guidelines for Natural Disaster Prevention, Preparedness and Mitigation, in particular its Plan of Action, has been transformed into a comprehensive and structured sequence of sectoral and cross-sectoral activities at all levels. During the second half of the International Decade for Natural Disaster Reduction, and commensurate with the proposals of the World Conference, emphasis is being shifted to concrete activities at the country and local levels. In order to maintain this broad-based inter-agency approach, the Inter-Agency Steering Committee has been extended until the end of the Decade.

500. Also in line with the Yokohama Strategy, the interdependency of natural disaster reduction, environmental protection and sustainable development is being reflected through improved cooperation between the International Framework and the major development activities inside and outside the United Nations system. Thus the Department of Humanitarian Affairs is acting, through the International Decade for Natural Disaster Relief secretariat, as task manager for natural disasters for the Commission on Sustainable Development. The process that has been outlined for the remaining years of the Decade will provide the opportunity to present its closing event with sound proposals for the full integration of disaster reduction into national planning and international development cooperation. It reflects the challenging objectives that have been laid out by the "Agenda for Development" (A/48/935).

### 3. Relief operations

501. The four major operations during the past year have taken place in Chechnya, Ukraine (Chernobyl), Kenya and the Sudan.

*Chechnya*

502. Following a request from the Russian Federation for international assistance for persons displaced from Chechnya to the neighbouring federal republics of Ingushetia, North Ossetia and Daghestan, last January I authorized a United Nations inter-agency mission to the region. This resulted in the issue of a "flash appeal" in February to mobilize immediate resources for the emergency needs of 220,000 people. Subsequently, the United Nations consolidated appeal for persons displaced as a result of the emergency situation in Chechnya, Russian Federation, covering the period from 1 January to 30 June 1995, was launched at Geneva in March. Because of the continuing crisis, the appeal was updated in June and its coverage was extended by six months to the end of 1995.

503. The extended United Nations humanitarian programme now covers the emergency needs of the 118,000 internally displaced persons identified as being the most vulnerable and seeks donor support for financial coverage of the 30 per cent shortfall of the total $25 million needed to allow relevant agencies to complete emergency assistance projects, as originally envisaged. Activities being implemented include assistance in areas such as shelter, water and sanitation, food, health and care for children in especially difficult circumstances. A high level of inter-agency cooperation has been achieved through a triangular structure among agencies operating in the field, the Humanitarian Coordinator in Moscow and the headquarters of the United Nations agencies, the International Organization for Migration (IOM) and the Department of Humanitarian Affairs. However, the situation affecting refugees and internally displaced persons in the three republics is still precarious. While the majority of those affected have sought shelter with host families, this additional burden has placed severe pressure on already meagre resources. Overcrowding has stretched the social services available to persons in the region. Food and medicines are in short supply and the onset of winter weather will result in additional hardships for the victims of the conflict unless urgent preventive action is taken. In particular, additional funding support is urgently required in order for agencies to stockpile contingency food supplies for the winter months.

504. At the end of June, peace negotiations between the Russian authorities and the Chechen delegation commenced at Grozny under the auspices of OSCE. A cease-fire came into effect on 2 July.

*Chernobyl*

505. While the tenth anniversary of the accident at the Chernobyl nuclear power plant is approaching, the extent of its impact on the popula-

tions of Belarus, the Russian Federation and Ukraine is only now being fully realized. Over 300 children now suffer from thyroid cancer, a disease practically non-existent in children before the accident, and hundreds of thousands live in constant fear of still unknown effects the accident may have on their long-term health. The fertility rate, especially in Belarus, has declined dramatically, while the morbidity and mortality rates have increased. This trend is unlikely to reach its peak until well into the next decade.

506. In September 1994, the United Nations Coordinator on International Cooperation on Chernobyl convened an expanded meeting of the quadripartite committee for coordination on Chernobyl. The meeting assessed the results of ongoing United Nations activities relating to Chernobyl and discussed the need for initiatives to commemorate the tenth anniversary of the accident in April 1986 and, in that connection, to draw attention to the continued need for funding of programmes to overcome the effects of the Chernobyl accident.

507. Members of the Inter-Agency Task Force on Chernobyl continue their efforts to bring Chernobyl projects to fruition, but the lack of funds has brought several programmes to a halt. Particularly affected is the International Programme on Health Effects of the Chernobyl Accident under the auspices of WHO. Although generous financial support by a handful of countries allowed the full and rapid implementation of the priority activities, there are now no resources to maintain the programme and initiate much-needed follow-up activities that have a direct impact on the health of the affected population.

508. In November 1994, nine community centres (three each in Belarus, the Russian Federation and Ukraine) were officially opened, marking the completion of phase I of the UNESCO programme to overcome the psychological effects of the accident. However, the implementation of phase II of the project, as well as other related projects, will depend on the possibility of raising additional funds. The FAO/International Atomic Energy Agency (IAEA) joint division completed successful projects on the use of radio-caesium binders to reduce contamination of milk and on the cultivation of rape-seed on contaminated soils. As a result of the projects, large areas that were hitherto regarded as unsafe can now be used for agricultural production. In 1995, IAEA also began, in cooperation with the French Institut de Protection et de Sûreté nucléaire, a project on environmental impact assessment.

509. Plans are now under way for events to commemorate the tenth anniversary of the Chernobyl accident. WHO will arrange a conference at Geneva in November on the health aspects of the accident, the United Nations will participate in a conference to be arranged at Minsk by the Government of Belarus and EU, while IAEA will arrange a summing-up conference at Vienna from 8 to 12 April 1996. A further meeting of the quadripartite committee will be held in the autumn of 1995 and will have as its main objective to identify those projects which remain of vital importance to the affected population and to agree on ways to ensure their funding.

*Kenya*

510. The United Nations consolidated interagency appeal for Kenya launched in February 1994 covered the period from January to December of that year, targeting a population of 1,620,000. Donor response totalled $54,860,331, an amount equal to almost 57 per cent of the total requested in the appeal. The food situation remains mixed, as agricultural conditions in some regions have improved while others remain uncertain. Aggregate production in 1994/95 is provisionally estimated at close to 3.5 million tons, almost 1 million tons above the previous year's reduced level. Good rains and high world prices for coffee are helping to maintain recovery in agriculture. Over 200,000 Somali refugees remain in Kenya, adding some strain to the food situation and increasing tension at border areas. Political tensions continue, as do both ethnic tensions in the Rift Valley and violence in Mombasa between Islamic groups.

*The Sudan*

511. The Secretary-General's report of 12 September 1994 on emergency assistance to the Sudan (A/49/376) stated that, despite progress made in the Sudan relief operation and Operation Lifeline Sudan, considerable needs still remained to be addressed, and the international community was urged to respond generously to the emergency needs and recovery of the country. In January 1995, the Department of Humanitarian Affairs issued the 1995 United Nations consolidated interagency appeal for the Sudan, in which United Nations agencies requested $101.1 million to meet the urgent humanitarian needs of 4.25 million people.

512. The donor response to the yearly United Nations consolidated appeals between 1992 and 1994 has generally been quite positive: in 1992 it was 73 per cent of the amount requested. In 1993, however, it was 64 per cent, but although there were considerable delays in the donor response to the 1994 appeal, at the close of the year approximately 85 per cent had been received. Such fluctuations have serious ramifications for programme effectiveness.

513. Regrettably, the early part of 1995 showed only limited contributions to the appeal, so that by mid-July a considerable shortfall in donor re-

sponse (less than 27 per cent of total requirements) was seriously compromising the United Nations ability to provide the urgently needed humanitarian assistance. This is all the more alarming as the shortfall occurred after increased cooperation during the previous two years with both the Government of the Sudan and the southern factions, as well as the improved cereal harvest in 1994, had permitted the United Nations to scale down its funding requirements by 45 per cent of the prior year's revised figure.

514. Since the launching of the 1995 appeal, Operation Lifeline Sudan activities have been hampered by renewed fighting, in particular in the provinces of Equatoria, Upper Nile, Junglei and northern Bahr El-Ghazal, where tens of thousands of persons have been dispossessed and dispersed. Renewed hostilities, combined with a lack of donor funding, have greatly reduced the effect of improved food production and forced people to abandon their homes and fields. In total, the United Nations estimates that there are just under 1.2 million internally displaced persons in the Sudan. The conflict has also forced the evacuation of relief workers from numerous localities, while in already three instances this year, relief workers have been kidnapped and held for periods ranging from a few days to almost two months. In another case an armed attack on a United Nations barge convoy disrupted a highly successful and cooperative logistics operation. With respect to other components of the Operation Lifeline Sudan logistics plan, operations remain dependent on air transport as the Operation has not received agreement on the use of road corridors. Moreover, both financial constraints and a recent increase in the denial of air access have cut into the Operation's effectiveness. Further affecting the United Nations and non-governmental organizations' capacity to respond were the various incidents of misuse, misappropriation and looting of food and other relief supplies, which continue despite agreements to the contrary, although improved monitoring and coordination mechanisms have reduced the overall number of incidents since last year.

515. Positive developments registered before the mid-year mark related notably to the two-month cease-fire between the Government and rebel factions mediated by the former United States President Jimmy Carter in consultation with the Intergovernmental Authority on Drought and Development, under whose aegis peace efforts have been organized since late 1993. Despite sporadic fighting, United Nations agencies were able to take advantage of opportunities for accelerating primary health-care programmes during this initial period as well as during a subsequent two-month extension. Further efforts to renew the cease-fire in late July did not meet with success.

516. Since 1989, when Operation Lifeline Sudan began as a short-term programme to deliver food and other life-saving provisions, it has developed considerably. While still providing food aid and basic health care to reduce mortality and morbidity among the affected population, the Operation now implements a much broader programme that extends to household food security, water and sanitation, basic shelter, food for work in support of agricultural production and health sector rehabilitation, primary education, support to psychologically traumatized children, capacity-building and promotion of humanitarian principles.

517. With increased access to a war-affected population of approximately 4.25 million throughout the country, Operation Lifeline Sudan reaches more people than ever before. Originally serving some 8 sites in southern Sudan, its operations have since come to include as many as 104 locations. This has been due in large part to greater flexibility shown by all the concerned parties.

518. It will be recalled from last year's report that the Intergovernmental Authority on Drought and Development had by March 1994 assumed a separate, though complementary, role in the regional peace process by facilitating negotiations on humanitarian access and related issues organized by the United Nations with the Government and the principal southern factions. Subsequent to agreements reached in March and May 1994, fixing modalities for humanitarian access across lines of conflict was identified as the priority for further negotiations. As no progress has been achieved during the intervening period, preliminary discussions intended to permit a resumption of tripartite talks were undertaken with the parties at Khartoum and Nairobi in late July and early August by the United Nations Special Envoy for Humanitarian Affairs for the Sudan, at which the question of operational modalities for international non-governmental organizations working out of Khartoum was discussed and all parties encouraged to work closely with the United Nations Special Envoy and senior Operation Lifeline Sudan personnel at Khartoum and Nairobi to secure an improved basis for progress.

519. With some exceptions, notably the suspension of an international non-governmental organization from the Operation owing to a breach of operational procedures, as well as the need to agree on guidelines for non-governmental organizations working out of Khartoum, cooperation among national, United Nations and non-governmental organizations working in the Sudan remains excellent. As in the past, the Operation provides the framework for the humanitarian efforts of 30 international non-governmental organizations working in the region. While the Nairobi office has established letters of understanding with

non-governmental organizations, which reflect the ground rules for Operation Lifeline Sudan operations, UNICEF Khartoum has sought to support government counterparts and local non-governmental organizations in relief and rehabilitation initiatives. Special efforts have been made to promote an improved framework for international non-governmental organizations to operate from Khartoum, including in the displaced person camps and the transitional zones. However, the continued strict controls on access and movement of the international non-governmental organizations in Khartoum have hampered attempts to bring to bear the comparative advantages they can offer.

520.    While the number of approximately 1.2 million beneficiaries identified as requiring emergency food aid in 1995 is a significant reduction compared with the needs of 1994, insecurity continues to plague the food delivery systems. In addition, whereas carry-over food stocks from 1994 were sufficient to cover most of the emergency food aid needs for 1995, international assistance to support monitoring, operational support costs and special transport costs had received less than 30 per cent of required donor support by July, causing the World Food Programme (WFP) to scale back monitoring activities by 50 per cent. Despite these constraints, by the end of July over half of the estimated 109,398 tons of food needs for 1995 had been transported by WFP and partner non-governmental organizations to areas in need.

521.    For Operation Lifeline Sudan non-food assistance out of Khartoum and all operations in the southern sector out of Nairobi, UNICEF has a lead responsibility. Overall 4.25 million people have been targeted for 1995, of whom 2.7 million are accessed from Khartoum and 1.7 million from Nairobi.

522.    In May 1995, the Department of Humanitarian Affairs organized a consultation of key donors and aid organizations at Geneva to review funding status and programme implementation, the status of recommendations made by donors in 1994 and the timetable for a comprehensive review of Operation Lifeline Sudan.

523.    A detailed critical review of the Operation is planned for later this year. As its main objectives, the review will analyse the Operation, its appropriateness in achieving maximum access to populations in need and in ensuring respect for fundamental humanitarian principles; assess the effectiveness of its coordination structures, in particular the relationship among the United Nations, donors, non-governmental organizations and Sudanese counterparts; and assess efficiency, identifying constraints and achievements.

524.    In the first half of 1994 alone, some 96,000 tons of emergency food aid were delivered to affected areas of the Sudan by WFP and international relief agencies, in a major initiative that benefited substantial numbers of the affected population and not least the 500,000 persons who were then on the verge of starvation. In the latter part of the year WFP continued those efforts and expanded, in particular, its surface delivery capacity in southern Sudan.

### 4.    Relief operations in the Near East (UNRWA)

525.    The activities of the United Nations Relief and Works Agency for Palestine Refugees in the Near East (UNRWA), headed by Commissioner-General Ilter Türkmen, focused during the reporting year on providing constructive support to the Middle East peace process.

526.    The Agency took immediate steps to develop an effective working relationship with the Palestinian Authority and to meet the Authority's requests for assistance to the fullest extent possible. On 24 June 1994, an exchange of letters took place between the Commissioner-General of UNRWA and the Chairman of the Palestine Liberation Organization (PLO) for the purpose of facilitating the continued provision of UNRWA services to Palestine refugees in areas under the control of the Palestinian Authority. On an ad hoc basis UNRWA provided land and buildings, temporary shelter and emergency humanitarian aid to assist the Authority in establishing its operations in the Jericho area. UNRWA actively pursued coordination of its services with those provided by the Authority, developing effective relations with it in the education, health and relief and social service sectors. The Agency also played an active role in multilateral forums established to support the peace process, such as the multilateral working group on refugees, as part of the United Nations delegation.

527.    Within the context of developments in the peace process, UNRWA began the process of relocating its headquarters from Vienna to Gaza by the end of 1995. The relocation should serve to demonstrate the commitment of the United Nations to the peace process, underline its confidence in the Palestinian Authority and contribute to the economic development of the Gaza Strip.

528.    UNRWA developed a detailed budget and action plan for the move, including the design of a new headquarters building in Gaza. The Agency was taking the necessary steps to obtain the $13.5 million in funding needed for the move and to meet the schedule for the move. As at August 1995, the Agency had received $4.07 million in pledges and contributions for the move.

529.    At my request, UNRWA undertook to administer the payment of the salaries of 9,000 members of the Palestinian Police Force from funds contributed by donors. The technical mechanism

underlying the effort was established in a memorandum of understanding signed by UNRWA and the Palestinian Police Force in September 1994. From that date until March 1995 a total of $29.8 million was disbursed in the operation, in which UNRWA worked closely with the office of the United Nations Special Coordinator in the Occupied Territories. In its resolution 49/21 O of 13 April 1995, the General Assembly requested UNRWA to continue to facilitate the payment of Palestinian Police Force salaries until the end of 1995. An additional $4.9 million was paid for the July 1995 police salaries.

530.   In September 1994, UNRWA launched the second phase of its Peace Implementation Programme with the objective of providing continuing infrastructure development and job creation to Palestine refugees throughout the Middle East. Funded projects included construction of schools, health clinics, women's programme centres and sewerage and drainage works, as well as renovation of shelters. Besides improving living conditions for refugees, related projects created an estimated 5,500 jobs over an average four-month period in Gaza alone. The programme met with a positive response on the part of donors, receiving a total of $109 million in funding as at May 1995. The Agency's project for a 232-bed general hospital in Gaza, begun in October 1993, continued during the reporting year. The hospital is due to be completed in early 1996 and recruitment of senior staff is under way.

531.   While taking on new roles and responsibilities in response to changing conditions, UNRWA continued to fulfil its basic mission of providing essential health, education and relief and social services to 3.1 million Palestine refugees located in Jordan, Lebanon, the Syrian Arab Republic and the West Bank and Gaza. Some 410,000 elementary and preparatory school pupils were enrolled in the Agency's 643 schools during the academic year 1994/95. The Agency handled nearly 6.5 million patient visits during 1994 through its network of 123 health centres and health points. More than 181,000 of the neediest Palestine refugees received special assistance from the Agency during the year, including food rations, shelter rehabilitation and subsidized medical care. Additional facilities and services provided on an ongoing basis through the Agency's core programmes included vocational training, graduate scholarships, family planning services, special infant care, community rehabilitation centres, women's programme centres and income-generation schemes.

532.   UNRWA's regular and emergency cash budget for the biennium 1994-1995 was $570 million. The Agency ended 1994 with an actual funding shortfall of $7 million. Because of the deficit the Agency was forced to carry over the austerity measures imposed in 1993 in response to an earlier deficit, which included a salary freeze, a reduction in administrative costs and cuts in the budgets for additional teacher posts, hospitalization and medical supplies. An informal meeting of UNRWA's major donors and host Governments held at Amman in March 1995 resulted in pledges that helped to reduce the projected deficit for 1995. At the Amman meeting the donors reiterated their commitment to the continued provision of UNRWA services and approved a five-year planning horizon proposed by the Agency.

### F.   *Protection and resettlement of refugees*

533.   The core functions of the Office of the United Nations High Commissioner for Refugees (UNHCR), headed by Mrs. Sadako Ogata, are those assigned by its 1950 statute: providing international protection to refugees and seeking permanent solutions to their problems. As part of its duty to ensure that voluntary repatriation schemes are sustainable, UNHCR has also become involved in assisting and protecting returnees in their home countries. In recent years, the General Assembly and the Secretary-General have called with increasing frequency on UNHCR to protect or assist particular groups of internally displaced people who have not crossed an international border but are in a refugee-like situation inside their countries of origin, as well as other populations affected by conflict.

534.   The genocide in Rwanda and the flight last year of over 2 million Rwandan nationals into neighbouring countries in the Great Lakes region of Africa was one of the darkest episodes in recent history and one that posed an unprecedented challenge for UNHCR and other humanitarian agencies. Other regions, including the former Yugoslavia, south-west Asia, the Horn of Africa and parts of western Africa, have also continued to suffer from massive population displacements, while a major new crisis erupted in the northern Caucasus in December 1994.

535.   Although the refugee population worldwide had decreased to 14.5 million by the beginning of this year because of repatriation solutions in various parts of the world, the total number of people of concern to UNHCR had risen to some 27.4 million. This included 5.4 million internally displaced persons, 3.5 million others of humanitarian concern, predominantly populations affected by conflict, and some 4 million returnees requiring assistance to re-establish sustainable reintegration in their countries of origin. In 1994, UNHCR provided material assistance to a total of 17.6 million people, as compared to 13.8 million in 1993. This included 8.9 million in Africa, 5 million in Asia, 3.5 million in Europe and 115,000 in Latin America.

536. The present period of volatility and read-justment in world affairs has been characterized by increasing levels of human displacement. In the face of this reality, UNHCR has continued to hone its emergency response capacity and to pursue preventive and solution-oriented approaches. It has aimed to assure a high level of emergency preparedness, to provide assistance and protection in such a way as to avert, where possible, the occurrence of new refugee flows and to promote concerted efforts to achieve durable solutions, notably voluntary repatriation. In so doing, it has collaborated increasingly closely with political, peace-keeping and development initiatives and organs of the United Nations, with other intergovernmental and regional bodies and with a wide range of non-governmental organizations.

### 1. Emergency response

537. As a result of its efforts since 1991, UNHCR's stand-by capacity has achieved a high level of preparedness in terms of both personnel and stockpiles of emergency relief supplies that it can deploy rapidly in an emergency. During 1994 and the first half of 1995 alone, its emergency response teams were deployed to 17 operations around the world.

538. While continuing to take the lead in the international response to refugee emergencies, UNHCR has endeavoured to ensure the effectiveness of its interventions and the durability of results by building partnerships with other United Nations agencies and by coordinating its activities in complex emergency situations with the Department of Humanitarian Affairs. In its emergency operations in the former Yugoslavia, the Great Lakes region and other parts of Africa, and the central Asian republics, UNHCR has continued to strengthen its collaboration with United Nations agencies and programmes, in particular WFP, UNICEF, WHO and the United Nations Population Fund (UNFPA), in activities such as food aid, immunization and health care, water supply and sanitation, mother and child medical care, family planning and education.

539. Faced in the Great Lakes region with the most severe refugee emergency in recent history, the Office was again obliged to innovate. With its own staff resources heavily committed in the region and elsewhere, it appealed to donor Governments to assume an operational role by providing self-contained services in a number of critical assistance sectors through the deployment of resources drawn largely from their military and civil defence establishments. The use of these so-called "service packages" in the Rwanda emergency has demonstrated how, under certain conditions, unique military skills or assets can support UNHCR emergency relief activities. The positive impact of service packages in responding to the critical conditions that characterized the massive exodus of Rwandans has led UNHCR into a process of consultation with Governments and the Department of Humanitarian Affairs on how, when necessary and appropriate, this mechanism can best be used.

### 2. The search for solutions

540. Over 2 million refugees returned to their countries of origin in 1994, most notably to Mozambique, Afghanistan and Myanmar. Return movements have continued in 1995, with prospects also opening up for the large-scale return of some 300,000 refugees to Angola. Solutions have continued to be consolidated in several other regions, especially in Central America, where the process launched by the International Conference on Central American Refugees was brought formally to a close in June 1994 and a framework agreed for the post-Conference period, and in south-east Asia with the agreement of the Steering Committee of the International Conference on Indo-Chinese Refugees to aim for the completion of activities under the comprehensive plan of action by the end of 1995.

541. Solutions to complex, refugee-producing emergencies require concerted efforts whereby humanitarian activities are complemented by both political initiatives to resolve conflict and development efforts to ensure a sustainable livelihood for the most severely affected areas and people.

542. In many areas of the world, UNHCR works increasingly closely with peace-keeping or peacemaking initiatives undertaken by the United Nations. It has continued to work with the United Nations peace-keeping operation in the former Yugoslavia where, as lead agency for the provision of humanitarian assistance, it has brought urgently needed assistance to over 2 million victims of war. Elsewhere, be it in Angola, Liberia, the Great Lakes region, the Horn of Africa, Guatemala, the Caucasus or central Asia, it has worked either within the framework of or in tandem with United Nations efforts at conflict resolution.

543. In its search for solutions to the problems of refugees and other displaced persons of concern to it, UNHCR has also placed considerable emphasis on developing closer collaboration with regional bodies. A regional conference was hosted jointly by UNHCR and OAU at Bujumbura in February this year to ensure a concerted approach to the crisis in the Great Lakes region. Working relationships have also been enhanced with other regional bodies, as, for example, in Georgia, where UNHCR and OSCE cooperate closely on efforts to resolve the Abkhazia and South Ossetia conflicts. Similar collaboration has been taking place in Nagorny Karabakh and Chechnya.

544. UNHCR continues to attach great importance not only to conflict-resolution initiatives, but

also to achieving a better interface between relief, rehabilitation and development. In the experience of the Office, the implementation of the concept of a continuum from relief to development should, on the one hand, enable humanitarian assistance to promote viable reintegration of displaced people into a process of social and economic recovery and, on the other, bring development endeavours closer to people-centred concerns and aspirations. Without this, solutions to humanitarian crises may regress into new, divisive communal problems.

545.   UNHCR has therefore continued to reinforce its community-based approach to reintegration assistance through the implementation of quick impact projects and has pursued discussions with other departments and agencies, notably the Department of Humanitarian Affairs and UNDP, on how institutional gaps can be bridged to ensure a meaningful continuum from relief to development. It has also sought to strengthen its relationship with the financial institutions, notably the World Bank. UNHCR efforts to support reconciliation and rehabilitation in post-conflict societies have been evident in the case of Mozambique, where its strategy for the reintegration of the 1.6 million refugees who have returned since the signing of the Peace Agreement aims, with the endorsement of the Government and major donors, at establishing linkages to longer-term development programmes.

### 3.   Preventing refugee crises

546.   Recognizing that, without effective preventive action, problems of human displacement will continue to spread, the Office has strengthened its institution-building and training activities in various parts of the world. In addition, UNHCR and IOM have continued their collaboration in mass information campaigns targeted, in particular, at potential migrants from the Russian Federation and other countries of CIS.

547.   The scale of actual and potential problems of displacement in the former Soviet Union has led to an important initiative, which seeks to address current problems of displacement and prevent their proliferation. Further to General Assembly resolution 49/173 of 23 December 1994, UNHCR is engaged in preparations for a conference that will establish a programme of action to address the problems of refugees, returnees and displaced persons in the CIS countries and relevant neighbouring States. It is expected that the programme of action will include measures to prevent unnecessary movements and address the consequences of past, present and future displacements.

548.   Most frequently, however, the efforts of the Office have come into play in situations where large-scale human displacement has already occurred. In such situations, UNHCR has continued to promote and participate in strategies that may help contain fragile situations. It has attempted to address or attenuate, wherever possible, the causes of refugee flows or, failing that, to reduce the necessity for affected populations or individuals to seek asylum across international borders. As part of these efforts, UNHCR has, at my request, continued or expanded its involvement in assisting and seeking solutions for groups of the internally displaced. In addition to its programme of humanitarian assistance for over 1.5 million internally displaced persons in the former Yugoslavia, UNHCR has, for example, been engaged in activities on behalf of substantial numbers of internally displaced in Angola, Ghana, Sierra Leone, Rwanda, Afghanistan, the Caucasus and the Russian Federation. These activities are frequently carried out in cooperation with other concerned United Nations bodies in the context of comprehensive approaches to displacement and conflict resolution.

### 4.   Protecting the victims

549.   The scale of recent humanitarian crises has drawn renewed attention to the protection needs of victims of persecution and conflict. Among the challenges that have come to the fore are the provision of international protection to those seeking asylum from internal conflict, the often compelling protection needs of the internally displaced, the need to ensure the security and rights of the inhabitants of refugee camps and the need to restore effective national protection for those who have returned to fragile situations in their home countries. The importance of UNHCR's protection role has thus remained primordial in all phases of its activities, be it in responding to emergencies or in pursuing and consolidating solutions.

550.   In the contemporary situation, large numbers of people in need of international protection have been forced to flee their countries because of situations of conflict. In view of political initiatives undertaken by the international community to resolve such situations, certain asylum countries have resorted with increasing frequency to providing temporary protection rather than making formal determinations of refugee status under the 1951 Convention relating to the Status of Refugees. UNHCR, together with States, has been exploring this concept, notably in relation to those who have fled the former Yugoslavia, in an effort to ensure that international protection continues to be granted to all who need it.

551.   One premise upon which temporary protection is based is the expectation of removing, within a reasonable period, the underlying cause of the outflow. UNHCR has insisted that temporary protection must not be unduly protracted before more permanent status is granted to the vic-

tims in situations where the grounds for flight have not been resolved. In addition, UNHCR has emphasized that the beneficiaries of temporary protection are, in many cases, refugees within the meaning of the 1951 Convention.

552. As the Rwanda crisis has recently demonstrated, mass flight from situations of inter-communal conflict can lead to the politicization of refugee camps and to attendant abuses of human rights. UNHCR has endeavoured to ensure that the security and human rights of refugees, including their right freely to decide to return home, are protected in such situations. In response to security problems in Rwandan refugee camps in Zaire and following close consultations with the Secretary-General, measures were taken by UNHCR to improve law and order and prevent intimidation and violence against refugees and candidates for voluntary repatriation through the deployment of Zairian forces, monitored by an international security liaison group.

553. The protection responsibilities of UNHCR also include protecting the human rights of returnees and other displaced persons of concern to the Office. UNHCR has thus continued to play a role in monitoring the situation of returnees and ensuring that national protection is restored. Recent experience in Central America has been particularly encouraging in this respect. The international colloquium held in Costa Rica in December 1994 to commemorate the tenth anniversary of the Cartagena Declaration adopted the San José Declaration on Refugees and Displaced Persons, which addresses the key issue of harmonizing legal criteria and procedures to consolidate the durable solutions of voluntary repatriation and local integration.

554. In pursuing its preventive and solution-oriented activities, UNHCR has welcomed United Nations efforts to establish a more effective operational capacity in the field of human rights, be it through intensified human rights field operations or through the establishment of international tribunals to prosecute the perpetrators of grave violations of human rights and humanitarian law. UNHCR has sought to strengthen collaboration with human rights treaty bodies and other human rights mechanisms, and has sought to establish active collaboration with the United Nations High Commissioner for Human Rights, especially at the level of field operations. Ongoing contacts with human rights working groups, rapporteurs, experts and monitors are also an integral part of the approach of UNHCR to link human rights concerns with the protection of refugees.

### G. *Protection and promotion of human rights*

555. The United Nations High Commissioner for Human Rights, Mr. José Ayala Lasso, is the United Nations official with principal responsibility for the Organization's human rights activities and, with the Centre for Human Rights, forms a unity of action. The staff of the Centre provides support for the activities of the High Commissioner and the various programmes, procedures and organs of the human rights programme.

### 1. New directions for the human rights programme

556. Over the last 12 months, the Organization's human rights work has taken action in response to the need, as seen by Governments and United Nations organs, to reach out and apply abstract human rights principles in concrete situations. A growing number of countries have requested advisory services and technical cooperation in building up national human rights infrastructures. In the last year well over 100 human rights technical cooperation projects have been implemented in some 50 countries. In order to assist in carrying out human rights technical cooperation programmes and at the request of Governments concerned, the United Nations has established human rights field presences in Burundi, Cambodia, Malawi and Rwanda. This represents a new departure in delivering human rights assistance. The human rights officers involved seek, through training, law reform, education and information, to contribute to building the structures of a society respectful of human rights and to prevent violations. Their very presence has proved to be a confidence-building measure for fragile societies.

557. The committees established by human rights treaties are also focusing their recommendations on ways the United Nations can help States live up to their human rights obligations. Further, the committees themselves are undertaking field missions to understand better the conditions in which human rights must be protected, to try to defuse situations of tension and to help develop concrete solutions to problems. They are also increasingly active in the field of early warning and preventive action.

558. Monitoring human rights violations on the ground in order to provide accurate information to the international community and to contribute to bringing serious situations to an end is another area in which our activities have grown. In 1993, the first monitors were sent to the field and today more than 120 human rights monitors are to be found in the territory of the former Yugoslavia and in Rwanda. Further, and following a resolution of the Commission on Human Rights, agreement has been reached to send two monitors to Zaire. The role of monitors is not only to report on violations, but also to be active agents of prevention.

### 2. Activities of the United Nations High Commissioner for Human Rights

559. The activities of the High Commissioner for Human Rights have opened new domains for

United Nations action to promote human rights and have given direction and provided initiative throughout the human rights programme. Strengthening international cooperation for human rights has been a main theme. In visits to over 30 States on all continents, the High Commissioner has sought to reinforce commitment to international and national protection of human rights through discussion with government officials, members of parliament and the judiciary. The High Commissioner has sought to strengthen the role of civil society in protecting human rights through contacts with non-governmental organizations, the academic community, the press and the public. These missions include appeals for ratification of treaties, for cooperation with all United Nations human rights mechanisms, inclusion of United Nations standards in national law and the establishment of national institutions to protect human rights. Human rights problems are dealt with frankly and appropriate actions suggested, including the revision of laws, release of detainees and adoption of other measures.

560. The High Commissioner's efforts to strengthen international cooperation extend also to cooperation with United Nations agencies and programmes, international and regional organizations and international and national non-governmental organizations. The High Commissioner has met with regional human rights organizations in Europe and the Americas, and he has drawn the attention of high-level international development and financial meetings to the need to support human rights activities.

561. An important aspect of the High Commissioner's activities is to help ensure that the human rights perspective is included in international conferences and that the high level of existing United Nations human rights standards is maintained. The High Commissioner took initiatives in this regard in relation to the World Summit for Social Development and the Fourth World Conference on Women. With regard to the latter, the High Commissioner has given particular attention to encouraging the inclusion of all aspects of the equal status and human rights of women and the girl-child in its deliberations.

562. The High Commissioner has also continued his activities aimed at responding to serious situations of violations and at preventing violations from developing or becoming widespread. The High Commissioner has continued to strengthen the activities of his offices in Burundi and Rwanda, has dispatched a high-level personal representative to visit the Russian Federation, including Chechnya, and has appointed a personal representative to the Office of the Special Representative of the Secretary-General in the Former Yugoslavia to deal with human rights issues.

563. Preventing violations often goes hand in hand with providing advisory services and technical cooperation in human rights. In this connection the High Commissioner has established a special programme to promote and support national human rights institutions. Other areas of activity are combating all forms of discrimination, including racism, racial discrimination, xenophobia and related forms of intolerance; promoting the equal status and rights of women; the rights of the child; and the rights of minorities and indigenous people. Of special importance is the responsibility given to the High Commissioner by the General Assembly to coordinate the implementation of the plan of action of the United Nations Decade for Human Rights Education. The High Commissioner places importance on promoting the right to development and cultural, economic and social rights. A strategy for the implementation of the right to development and protection of cultural, economic and social rights is being developed to identify, in cooperation with relevant agencies, treaty-based bodies and experts, ways of improving the implementation of those rights.

### 3. International human rights treaty system

564. Some progress has been made in ratifications within the international human rights treaty system. As at 10 August 1995, 177 States had accepted to ensure and respect the wide range of basic human rights laid down in the Convention on the Rights of the Child. This means that the rights of more than 90 per cent of the children in the world today are protected by the Convention. This is in itself a notable achievement; every effort should be made to gain universal ratification by the end of 1995. Ratification of other treaties has not progressed so rapidly: as at 10 August, 132 States were party to the International Covenant on Economic, Social and Cultural Rights; 131 to the International Covenant on Civil and Political Rights; 143 to the International Convention on the Elimination of All Forms of Racial Discrimination; and 141 to the Convention on the Elimination of All Forms of Discrimination against Women. Only 90 States had ratified the Convention against Torture and Other Cruel, Inhuman or Degrading Treatment or Punishment and only 4 had ratified the International Convention on the Protection of the Rights of All Migrant Workers and Members of Their Families.

565. In September 1994, I wrote to all Member States urging ratification of outstanding human rights treaties. In February 1995, I wrote to Heads of State or Government appealing for ratification of the Convention on the Rights of the Child. I am pleased with the numerous positive responses and I have asked the High Commissioner for Human Rights to follow up on my letters and to offer assistance where required.

Nevertheless, new efforts must be made to achieve universal ratification of these important instruments.

566. At the heart of the international human rights treaty system are the six expert committees charged with monitoring respect for human rights as laid down in the respective treaties: the Human Rights Committee; the Committee on Economic, Social and Cultural Rights; the Committee on the Rights of the Child; the Committee on the Elimination of Racial Discrimination; the Committee on the Elimination of Discrimination against Women; and the Committee against Torture. Together, they review the human rights situation in some 60 countries a year. The committees and their members represent a precious source of information and expertise.

567. The committees have been improving their methods of work, providing more focused recommendations and carrying out field missions with increasing frequency. Three objectives are shaping their work: increased interaction and participation of the specialized agencies and non-governmental organizations; the establishment of closer connections between the findings of the treaty body concerned and the programme of advisory services and technical cooperation; and the establishment by treaty bodies of procedures aimed at preventing human rights violations and preventing existing problems from escalating into conflicts.

568. In connection with situations that require special or urgent action, the committees have requested special reports on an urgent basis (former Yugoslavia, Croatia, Bosnia and Herzegovina, Haiti, Iraq, Peru, etc.), undertaken good offices missions (Belgrade, Kosovo) or carried out technical assistance missions (Croatia, Panama). Special appeals have also been issued with regard to Indonesia, concerning East Timor and Pakistan.

569. In June I met, for the first time, with the chairpersons of all six treaty-based bodies. The discussion focused on the role of those bodies in early warning and preventive action, on the greatly increased capacity of those bodies to monitor accurately the human rights situation in a wide range of countries and the assistance those bodies needed from the Secretariat to carry out those expanded responsibilities successfully. I expressed my full support for their important activities and my personal commitment to securing universal ratification of human rights treaties. I look forward to closer cooperation with the treaty bodies in the future.

4. Activities of the Commission on Human Rights and its subsidiary bodies

570. The Commission on Human Rights is a unique world forum for the public discussion of important human rights issues between Govern-ments, international organizations and non-governmental organizations. Over the years the Commission has created numerous human rights fact-finding mechanisms charged with reporting on various human rights situations or types of serious violations, dealing with individual appeals and making suggestions for action to improve respect for human rights. The human rights situation in 12 countries is under review by these procedures. In addition, 14 thematic mandates have been established dealing with particularly serious violations, wherever they may occur, running from arbitrary executions, torture, disappearances, exploitation and sale of children, to violence against women and racism, racial discrimination and xenophobia. This year saw the appointment of a special rapporteur on Burundi and one on the adverse effects on human rights of the illicit movement and dumping of toxic waste and dangerous products. Each year thousands of urgent individual cases are transmitted to Governments and some 40 field missions are carried out. In May a special meeting on these procedures took place to improve their operation, to seek ways of integrating women's human rights into their work and to decide on their contribution to the Fourth World Conference on Women.

571. The Commission on Human Rights, through various working groups, also pursued the adoption of a declaration on the rights and responsibilities of individuals, groups and organs of society to promote and protect universally recognized human rights and fundamental freedoms; a draft optional protocol to the Convention against Torture and Other Cruel, Inhuman or Degrading Treatment or Punishment concerning visits to prisons or places of detention; and a draft optional protocol to the Convention on the Rights of the Child on involvement of children in armed conflicts. Work is also under way on guidelines for a possible optional protocol to the Convention on the Rights of the Child on the sale of children, child prostitution and child pornography, as well as the basic measures needed for the prevention and eradication of those practices.

572. The Commission has given close attention to the equal status and human rights of women. The Commission's Special Rapporteur on violence against women, its causes and consequences, submitted her preliminary report to the Commission at its last session. The document deals with the different forms of violence that occur in the family and the community and are perpetrated or condoned by the State, and sets out the framework for the future work of the Special Rapporteur. The Special Rapporteur has also been actively involved in the integration of women's rights into the mainstream of United Nations activities in the field of human rights, as called for

in the Vienna Declaration and Programme of Action. The High Commissioner and the Centre for Human Rights have been helping to focus the attention of the various human rights organs and bodies on the human rights input to the Fourth World Conference on Women and on the preparation of parallel human rights activities.

573. The United Nations has continued to work for the protection of the rights of indigenous people. The Working Group on Indigenous Populations is the main forum for interaction between human rights experts, Governments and representatives of indigenous people; some 400 representatives of indigenous people take part each year. The General Assembly has proclaimed the period 1995-2004 as the International Decade of the World's Indigenous People and the Commission on Human Rights is studying the draft declaration on the rights of indigenous people. Work continues towards the establishment of a permanent forum for indigenous people, as called for by the Vienna Declaration.

574. Minorities are another especially vulnerable group often needing international action to help protect their rights. A new body, the Working Group on Minorities, has been set up with a wide mandate aimed at promoting respect for the 1992 Declaration on the Rights of Persons Belonging to National or Ethnic, Religious and Linguistic Minorities and examining possible solutions to problems involving minorities. Further, the General Assembly has asked the High Commissioner to promote the implementation of the principles contained in that Declaration.

575. The programme of action for the Third Decade to Combat Racism and Racial Discrimination is a key element in promoting equality. The General Assembly has recommended that various measures and actions be taken on the national, regional and international levels. High priority is to be given to providing assistance and relief to victims of racism and all forms of racial discrimination. The possibility of convening a world conference on the elimination of racism, racial and ethnic discrimination, xenophobia and other related contemporary forms of intolerance is being studied.

5. Advisory services and technical cooperation

576. The World Conference on Human Rights, held at Vienna in June 1993, gave heightened emphasis to the need for the international community to respond to the requests of States for technical cooperation to strengthen the institutions of human rights and human rights practices. The concrete response to this is to be found in the programme of technical cooperation in the field of human rights implemented by the Centre for Human Rights. The programme supports a wide range of projects aimed at, among other things, developing national plans of action for human rights, providing assistance in drafting constitutional provisions relating to human rights, reforming legislation, human rights aspects of elections, prison reform, developing and strengthening national institutions, strengthening the judiciary, training judges, prosecutors and lawyers in human rights, and training police and the armed forces. Technical cooperation projects also support regional human rights institutions such as the African Commission on Human and Peoples' Rights, the African Centre for Democracy and Human Rights Studies and the Arab Institute for Human Rights. Many of these activities are financed through the United Nations voluntary fund for technical cooperation in the field of human rights under the guidance of its board of trustees, composed of eminent international experts.

577. The preventive capacities of this programme have grown in importance. Contributions have been made during the past year to support the peace process in Palestine through the training of the Palestinian Police Force, to strengthening the human rights structures in the Caucasus (Armenia, Azerbaijan, Georgia), to the peacekeeping operation in Mozambique through human rights training for the ONUMOZ civilian police component and in the former Yugoslavia through training for UNPROFOR officials and the national police of the former Yugoslav Republic of Macedonia. Assistance continues in Cambodia and in Rwanda and Burundi.

6. Early warning mechanism

578. The Centre for Human Rights has increasingly brought its human rights expertise to bear on various activities dealing with early warning or with information relating to emergency situations. The Centre has participated in the Administrative Committee on Coordination Working Group on Early Warning of New Flows of Refugees and Displaced Persons and its subgroup on indicators. The Centre has also contributed to the development of the set of indicators for the Humanitarian Early Warning System led by the Department of Humanitarian Affairs and to the framework for coordination project for planning and implementation of complex operations in the field. The Centre is also an active participant in the relief net project coordinated by the Department and contributed to the May 1995 meeting on early warning activities related to the CIS region.

579. During the last year the United Nations faced a major challenge in responding to the increasingly varied demands for action made upon it by Governments and United Nations bodies. Initial difficulties encountered in fielding complex human rights missions have now been overcome

and the High Commissioner is seeking the cooperation of countries in building a solid basis for future action in the following areas: *(a)* logistical assistance capacity on a stand-by basis to provide material, communications and other support needed to contribute to emergency or preventive field missions; *(b)* the establishment and maintenance of an international roster of specialized staff to be available at short notice for human rights field missions (investigation teams, human rights field officers, legal experts etc.); and *(c)* increased contributions to the voluntary fund for technical cooperation in order to cover the financial needs of advisory service field missions and assistance.

580.    Other action must be envisaged to enable the human rights programme to respond to the new demands of the Vienna Declaration, the High Commissioner's mandate and other decisions of policy-making bodies. The structure of the programme and of the supporting secretariat is being carefully reviewed in order to rationalize the work programme and to provide the substantive and technical support needed by the programme.

## IV.    Expanding preventive diplomacy and conflict resolution

### A.    *Implementing "An Agenda for Peace"*

581.    In response to my report entitled "An Agenda for Peace", the General Assembly adopted resolutions 47/120 A and B on 18 December 1992 and 20 September 1993, respectively. In the first resolution the Assembly gave me a clear mandate to pursue preventive diplomacy and to strengthen the Secretariat's capacity in an early-warning mechanism, in particular collection and analysis of information, for situations likely to endanger international peace and security. The Security Council has also held a number of meetings to examine specific proposals made in "An Agenda for Peace", and the President of the Council has issued some 10 statements or letters as part of the review process.

582.    On 3 January 1995, I issued a position paper entitled "Supplement to 'An Agenda for Peace'" (A/50/60-S/1995/1), in which I set forth additional recommendations, highlighting the areas where unforeseen, or only partly foreseen, difficulties had arisen and where there is a need for Member States to take the "hard decisions" noted in my 1992 report (A/47/277-S/24111). I also drew conclusions with regard to the crucial distinction between peace-keeping and enforcement action, as well as to the circumstances in which military force is a useful tool of diplomacy and those in which it is counterproductive.

583.    In response to the Supplement, and after intensive discussions on 18 and 19 January 1995, the Security Council issued a presidential statement (S/PRST/1995/9) in support of that position paper. The Council welcomed and shared the priority I had given to action to prevent conflict. Furthermore, it encouraged all Member States to make the fullest possible use of instruments of preventive action, including the good offices of the Secretary-General, the dispatch of special envoys and the deployment, with the consent as appropriate of the host country or countries, of small field missions for preventive diplomacy and peace-making. Among other things, the Security Council hoped that the General Assembly, as well as other organizations and entities, would accord the Supplement a high degree of priority. It is encouraging to see that the lessons of contemporary peace-keeping have begun to appear not only in United Nations documents but in the training manuals of a number of Member States as well.

584.    In the General Assembly, the Informal Open-ended Working Group on An Agenda for Peace continued its work during 1995 on issues contained in "An Agenda for Peace" and the Supplement.

585.    Encouraged by such interest and in the belief that it is evidently better to prevent conflicts through early warning, quiet diplomacy and, in some cases, preventive deployment, than to undertake major politico-military efforts to resolve conflicts after they have broken out, I intend to redouble my efforts to perform the task entrusted to me under the Charter. If the United Nations is to play a timely and constructive role in averting or mitigating the destructive effects of complex crises, it is essential that the various elements of the Organization have an early, common view of the nature of the problem and the options for preventive action. In the Supplement, I noted that the multifunctional nature of both peace-keeping and peace-building had made it necessary to improve coordination within the Secretariat, so that the relevant departments function as an integrated whole under my authority and control.

586.    It is in this context that, following an initiative of the Department of Humanitarian Affairs, the three substantive departments of the Secretariat, the Department of Humanitarian Affairs, the Department of Political Affairs and the Department of Peace-keeping Operations, have developed a flow-chart of actions—information sharing, consultations and joint action—for the coordination of their respective activities in the planning and implementing of complex operations in the field. This mechanism, known as the "Framework for Coordination", covers the departments' activities during routine monitoring and early-warning analysis, assessment of options for preventive action where possible, fact-finding, planning and implementation of field operations, and conduct of evaluations or lessons-learned exercises.

587.   An important element of the Framework for Coordination is the provision for staff-level consultations by the three departments, as well as the United Nations Development Programme, the Commission on Human Rights, the Department of Public Information and other parts of the Organization, to undertake joint analyses of early-warning information from a variety of sources, and to formulate joint recommendations for possible preventive measures. The individual departments—particularly the Department of Political Affairs—will retain the authority to implement preventive action, under my direction.

588.   To ensure continuous consultation between the Secretary-General and the Security Council and to assist the latter in being informed about the latest developments, particularly in the area of peace-keeping operations, I have appointed one of my Special Advisers, Mr. Chinmaya Gharekhan, as my personal representative to the Council. Troop-contributing Governments are also understandably anxious to be kept fully informed. Therefore, I have endeavoured to meet their concerns by providing the Governments with regular briefings and by engaging them in dialogue about the conduct of the operation in question. Members of the Security Council have been included in such meetings, which the Council recently decided to formalize. It is important, however, that this reform should not lead to any blurring of the three distinct areas of authority, which include overall political direction that belongs to the Security Council; executive direction and command for which the Secretary-General is responsible; and command in the field, which I entrust to the chief of mission.

589.   All the efforts of the Security Council, the General Assembly and the Secretariat to control and resolve conflicts need the cooperation and support of other players on the international stage. Chapter VIII of the Charter defines the role that regional organizations can play in the maintenance of peace and security. Forms of cooperation between the United Nations and regional organizations include consultations, diplomatic support, operational support, co-deployment and joint operations. While the capacity of regional organizations for peacemaking and peace-keeping varies considerably, none has yet developed the capacity and experience the United Nations has in those fields. The United Nations is ready to help them when requested to do so and when resources are sufficient. To advance these efforts, I intend to hold another high-level meeting with regional arrangements and organizations as a follow-up to the meeting I convened on 1 August 1994.

### B.  *Preventive diplomacy and peacemaking*

590.   It has become clear that preventive diplomacy is only one of a class of actions that can be taken to prevent disputes from turning into armed conflict. Others in this class are preventive deployment of military and/or police personnel; preventive humanitarian action, for example, to manage and resolve a refugee situation in a sensitive frontier area; and preventive peace-building, which itself comprises an extensive menu of possible actions in the political, economic and social fields, applicable especially to possible internal conflicts.

591.   All these preventive actions share the following characteristics: they all depend on early warning that the risk of conflict exists; they require information about the causes and likely nature of the potential conflict so that the appropriate preventive action can be identified; and they require the consent of the party or parties within whose jurisdiction the preventive action is to take place.

592.   The element of timing is crucial. The potential conflict should be ripe for the preventive action proposed. Timing is also an important consideration in peacemaking and peace-keeping. The prevention, control and resolution of a conflict is like the prevention, control and cure of disease. If treatment is prescribed at the wrong moment in the evolution of a disease, the patient does not improve, and the credibility of both the treatment and the physician who prescribed it is compromised.

593.   The term "peacemaking", as used by the United Nations, refers to the use of diplomatic means to persuade parties in conflict to cease hostilities and negotiate a peaceful settlement of their dispute. All the types of action that can be used for preventive purposes, such as diplomatic peace-keeping, humanitarian aid and peace-building, have their role in creating conditions for successful peacemaking, and implementing and consolidating the negotiated settlement for peace.

594.   The primary responsibility for preventive action and peacemaking rests with the Department of Political Affairs, headed by Under-Secretary-General Marrack Goulding. The Department was created in 1992 to consolidate the political work of the Secretariat in a single department. There is, however, a distinction to be made between the Department's roles in these two fields. In the preventive field, its role is to identify the action required, with execution being entrusted to the specialist department or other agency concerned. In the peacemaking field, its role generally includes execution as well.

595.   The Department of Political Affairs has five main responsibilities in support of preventive action and peacemaking. First, it must monitor, analyse and assess political developments throughout the world. Next, the Department identifies potential or actual conflicts in whose control and

resolution the United Nations can play a useful role. It then prepares recommendations to the Secretary-General about appropriate actions in such cases. Fourth, the Department executes the approved policy when it is of a diplomatic nature. Finally, it assists the Secretary-General in carrying out political activities decided by him and/or mandated by the General Assembly and the Security Council in the areas of preventive diplomacy, peacemaking, peace-keeping and peace-building, including arms control and disarmament.

596. The Centre for Disarmament Affairs, an integral part of the Department of Political Affairs, provides advice, analysis and assessment on all disarmament matters and carries out the responsibilities entrusted to the Secretariat in this field. The Electoral Assistance Division, another integral part of the Department, provides services requested by Member States in the electoral field. The Department also provides secretariat services to the General Assembly, the Security Council and their various subsidiary organs.

### C. *Peace-keeping in a changing context*

597. United Nations peace-keeping is the responsibility of the Department of Peace-keeping Operations, headed by Mr. Kofi Annan. It remained a dynamic and demanding activity, responding to continuing turbulence in relations between States as well as to armed conflict within State borders. Certain peace-keeping missions were brought to a successful conclusion and new missions were established by the Security Council, while the status of existing operations ranged from relative stability to high danger. In the face of these challenges, the Organization continued to encounter grave difficulties in obtaining resources from Member States, in both specialized and properly equipped military units and adequate financing. At the end of July 1995, approximately 65,000 military personnel, 1,700 civilian police and 6,000 civilian personnel were deployed in 16 United Nations peace-keeping operations, with an aggregate annual budget of approximately $3.6 billion (*see table 2*).

598. In Haiti, the suspended United Nations Mission was redeployed after a multinational force established stable and secure conditions. Likewise, in Angola, an effectively suspended United Nations peace-keeping operation, the United Nations Angola Verification Mission, has been newly deployed after the Angolan parties, following prolonged negotiations under United Nations auspices, finalized an agreement to bring the interrupted peace process back on course. In Tajikistan, a small United Nations Mission of Observers was deployed in support of a negotiating process under United Nations auspices, with the goal of national reconciliation and the promotion of democracy. Two major missions, in Mozam-

bique and in El Salvador, were steered to a commendably successful conclusion, both culminating in elections monitored by the United Nations and the establishment of elected Governments, with the promise of the consolidation of stability in both countries. In contrast, the United Nations Operation in Somalia II, long plagued by interminable hostility between clan leaders who often turned upon the mission itself, was terminated, with a residual good offices mission being maintained to assist in the search for political compromise. Although the ambitious goal of reconstructing a stable Somali State was not achieved, the mission's principal objectives of ending the dire conditions of famine and of restoring some stability to most of the country were secured.

Table 2

**Peace-keeping troops,
military observers and civilian police
in peace-keeping operations on 31 July 1995**

|  | *Troops* | *Observers* | *Police* | *Total* |
|---|---|---|---|---|
| UNTSO | — | 220 | — | 220 |
| UNMOGIP | — | 40 | — | 40 |
| UNFICYP | 1,165 | — | 35 | 1,200 |
| UNDOF | 1,036 | — | — | 1,036 |
| UNIFIL | 4,963 | — | — | 4,963 |
| UNIKOM | 859 | 243 | — | 1,102 |
| UNAVEM | 3,014 | 333 | 207 | 3,554 |
| MINURSO | 48 | 236 | 113 | 397 |
| UNCRO | 13,683 | 347 | 435 | 14,465 |
| UNPROFOR | 27,738 | 288 | 18 | 28,044 |
| UNPREDEP | 1,107 | 25 | 26 | 1,158 |
| UNOMIG | — | 134 | — | 134 |
| UNMIH | 5,850 | — | 841 | 6,691 |
| UNOMIL | 7 | 62 | — | 69 |
| UNAMIR | 3,792 | 306 | 59 | 4,157 |
| UNMOT | — | 39 | — | 39 |
| Total | 63,262 | 2,273 | 1,734 | 67,269 |

599. In recent years, the practice of peace-keeping, developed during the cold war and based on the consent and cooperation of the parties and impartiality of United Nations forces, with resort to arms only in self-defence, has proved most effective in multidimensional operations where the parties not only entered into negotiated agreements but demonstrated the political will to achieve the goals established. However, where the climate was one of hostility and obstruction instead of cooperation and political will, peace-keeping came under heavy strains and pressures. This has been the experience in Bosnia and Herzegovina, where the United Nations itself came under armed attack. While efforts to achieve a political agreement between the parties remained futile, the determination to press for military advantage undermined laboriously negotiated cease-fires, and the

force of events on the ground drove the United Nations into situations in which mandates assigning peace-keeping tasks simultaneously with limited enforcement actions proved contradictory and ineffective. The Bosnian Serbs' use of military force to obtain their objectives demonstrated the perilous balance to be maintained by the international community between the limits of a mandate defined in response to a particular situation and the larger objective of realizing the purposes of the Charter. This has compelled renewed reflection on the instruments available to the international community in its efforts to maintain international peace and security.

600.   The limits of peace-keeping in ongoing hostilities starkly highlighted by the distressing course of events in the former Yugoslavia have become clearer, as the Organization has come to realize that a mix of peace-keeping and enforcement is not the answer to a lack of consent and cooperation by the parties to the conflict. The United Nations can be only as effective as its Member States may allow it to be. The option of withdrawal raises the question of whether the international community can simply leave the afflicted populations to their fate. The Organization has been confronted with this issue with increasing frequency, not only in Bosnia and Herzegovina, but also in Somalia, Rwanda, Liberia, Angola and elsewhere.

601.   The international community's response to these situations was varied. In some cases, it became necessary to rethink and readjust the measures taken. Such, often difficult, readjustment can be minimized if mandates given the Organization establish well-defined, achievable objectives and have the necessary political and material backing of Member States. Especially in instances where the Security Council authorizes the use of force even to a limited extent, under Chapter VII of the Charter, the composition, equipment and logistical support of such an operation must be commensurate with the task.

602.   Peace-keeping missions have multiplied in number and complexity in recent years (*see fig. 16*). United Nations personnel in much larger numbers are now involved in a wider spectrum of operations ranging from the monitoring of traditional cease-fires to the task of armed protection of humanitarian convoys, and from the control of buffer zones to assistance in the implementation of peace settlements. As expectations rise and more missions are deployed, the United Nations is finding it increasingly difficult to keep up with fast-moving situations. Delays resulting from factors such as procedures and readiness have meant that local situations could get worse while the Organization prepares forces for deployment.

603.   The Stand-by Forces Planning Team, established by the Secretary-General, developed the stand-by arrangements system in 1993, and the

process to institutionalize it in the Secretariat began in May 1994. The mandate of the Secretariat *vis-à-vis* stand-by arrangements is to maintain a system of stand-by resources, able to be deployed as a whole or in parts, anywhere in the world, at the Secretary-General's request, with agreed response times, for United Nations duties, as mandated by the Security Council. The system calls for Member States to provide the Secretariat with detailed information regarding probable contributions (military, civilian police and civilian specialists) to peace-keeping operations. The information provided by participating Member States includes such data as response times, capabilities and air and sealift volumetrics as well as indications regarding equipment requirements.

604.   The aim of the initiative is to reduce mounting times for new or expanding peace-keeping and enhancing efficiency and coordination at the Secretariat and mission levels. The stand-by arrangements system is based on conditional offers by Member States of specified resources which could be made available within agreed response times for United Nations peace-keeping operations. These resources can be military individuals or formations, civilian police, specialized personnel (civilian and military) and services, as well as material and equipment.

605.   The resources remain on "stand-by" in their home country, where training prepares them to fulfil specific tasks or functions in accordance with United Nations guidelines. Stand-by resources would be used for peace-keeping operations mandated by the Security Council and should not be confused with peace-enforcement units, which are described in "An Agenda for Peace" (A/47/277-S/24111) as forces meant to respond to "outright aggression, imminent or actual". In these arrangements, Member States retain full responsibility for stand-by resources as long as they remain in their home country. During the period of their assignment to peace-keeping operations, personnel made available by participating Member States would remain in their national service but would be under command of the United Nations.

606.   To ensure its effectiveness, the stand-by arrangements system relies on detailed volumetric information on resources specified in each of the stand-by arrangements. By maintaining a comprehensive database of the volumetrics, the Secretariat will be in a better position to assess detailed requirements. Secretariat planners will know well in advance what movement provisions are required and what items should be procured if deficiencies exist. In addition, procurement activities can be pre-planned, thereby reducing costs.

607.   So far 46 Member States have confirmed their participation in stand-by arrangements and

13 are in the process of finalizing their offers. The commitments made to date do not, however, cover the whole spectrum of resources required to mount and execute future peace-keeping operations adequately. Deficiencies still exist in critical areas such as communications, multi-role logistics, health services, supply, engineering and transportation.

608. The Stand-by Arrangements Management Team is currently manned by one United Nations–contracted military officer and three others on loan from Governments. In addition, the team is temporarily assisted by four officers from other teams within the Mission Planning Service of the Department of Peace-keeping Operations.

609. Potentially, the stand-by arrangements system will offer an effective means of rapidly deploying needed resources to new or current peace-keeping missions. If these arrangements are fully built up, the Secretariat would be in a better position to meet current challenges. The system's success is totally dependent on the support and participation of Member States, since even under the stand-by arrangements Member States will retain the right to deploy the agreed units in a particular operation.

610. The daunting experiences in United Nations peace-keeping in the turbulence following the end of the cold war also have confronted the Organization with problems on a more practical level. The difficulties in securing resources have led to unacceptable delays in deployment of peace-keeping forces in emergency situations that cannot afford delay. In the Supplement to "An Agenda for Peace", I urged that serious thought be given to the idea of a rapid reaction force to provide the Security Council with a strategic reserve for deployment in emergencies requiring the immediate presence of peace-keeping troops. The system of stand-by arrangements does not so far ensure the reliability and speed of response which is required in such emergencies. It is essential that the necessary capabilities are reliably available when they are needed and can be deployed with the speed dictated by the situation. It is evident that Member States possess such capabilities; what is needed is the will to make them available for the execution of Security Council mandates.

611. The work of peace has never been without risk, but today United Nations personnel are routinely required to face dangers to their life and health in the course of unpredictable and risky operations in hostile environments. This is demonstrated by the unfortunate fact that there have been 456 fatalities in peace-keeping missions between 1991 and 1995 as compared to 398 between 1948 and 1990. Particularly disturbing is the tendency by some to ignore the international status of United Nations personnel and to attack peace-keepers as they carry out their duties mandated by the Security Council (*see figs. 17 and 18*). The Convention on the Safety of United Nations and Associated Personnel adopted by the General Assembly at its forty-ninth session is of crucial importance, and I urge Governments to take the necessary action to ensure that the Convention enters into force as soon as possible.

612. There is an increasing awareness among Member States that public information, both internationally and in the mission area, is critical to the success of peace-keeping operations. In the planning of recent major operations, therefore, the requirements for an information capacity were examined at an early stage and the resources required were included in the proposed budget.

### D. *Current activities in preventive diplomacy, peacemaking and peace-keeping*

#### 1. Afghanistan

613. During the period under review the Special Mission established in accordance with General Assembly resolution 48/208 continued its work under the leadership of Mr. Mahmoud Mestiri. Also in January 1995, the Office of the Secretary-General in Afghanistan (OSGA) was established in Jalalabad, until conditions could permit it to return to Kabul.

614. I visited Pakistan from 6 to 8 September 1994 and was briefed by Mr. Mestiri on his intensive consultations in previous weeks about transitional arrangements which would lead to a cease-fire and the convening of a *Loya Jirga* (Grand National Assembly). I also met separately with various representatives of the party leaders and with independent Afghans. Mindful of the strong desire of the Afghan people for peace, I instructed Mr. Mestiri to continue his endeavours.

615. On Mr. Mestiri's initiative, an advisory group of recognized and respected independent Afghan personalities from within and outside the country met at Quetta for 19 days starting on 29 September 1994 to advise the United Nations in its efforts to achieve progress. Their recommendations for an early transfer of power to a fully representative Authoritative Council, a country-wide cease-fire, a security force for Kabul and the subsequent establishment of a transitional government or the convening of a *Loya Jirga* were endorsed by the Security Council in November and subsequently by the General Assembly in December. In October, President Burhanuddin Rabbani had made a conditional offer to transfer power and Afghanistan gave its support to the United Nations peace proposals in a statement issued by the Ministry for Foreign Affairs (S/1994/1227, annex).

616. Mr. Mestiri returned to the region on 29 December 1994 and focused his efforts on the early transfer of power to the Authoritative Council. During January 1995, negotiations on its membership were held with all the major leaders, including President Rabbani, who reiterated his readiness to step down on 20 February when the Council was to be set up.

617. The military successes of the Taliban, a newly established armed force, delayed the setting up of the Council in Kabul. Efforts were made to include this group in the Council but it declined to participate in the process directly. The convening of the Authoritative Council was postponed to 21 March while a committee of four personalities worked to reconcile the areas of divergence. Its proposal that the Council be composed of two representatives from each of Afghanistan's 32 provinces, plus 15 or 20 representatives nominated by the United Nations to achieve the necessary ethnic and political balance, was accepted by some, but not all, of the parties.

618. As the date for the transfer of power drew closer, changes in the political and military situation began to accelerate. On 6 March, intensive fighting erupted in Kabul and adjacent areas between the forces of General Massoud and those of Mr. Mazari (Hezb-i-Wahdat), and then between those of General Massoud and the Taliban. The renewed fighting resulted in a virtual stalemate in the peace process. No nomination for the Authoritative Council had been received by mid-April, when Mr. Mestiri departed from the area.

619. In June, I called Mr. Mestiri to New York and, after discussing the new situation with him, decided that the United Nations should immediately resume its efforts towards peace in Afghanistan. On my instructions, Mr. Mestiri visited the region between 18 July and 1 August in order to reassess the prevailing situation. During his visit, he exchanged views with key Afghan leaders and senior officials of the neighbouring countries on ways in which the United Nations could assist the peace process. His interlocutors included President Rabbani, General Dostum, Mr. Ismael Khan and leaders of the Taliban.

620. I received Mr. Mestiri's report on the latest round of his activities in early August and agreed with him that he should assume residence inside Afghanistan and pursue his efforts to obtain the agreement of all concerned to the modalities for the transition to a broad-based and widely accepted Government. I also decided to enhance the Special Mission and OSGA by stationing additional political affairs officers in the country.

621. The United Nations Office for the Coordination of Humanitarian Assistance to Afghanistan (UNOCHA) continued to coordinate the humanitarian programme throughout the country. A consolidated appeal, seeking $106 million to cover humanitarian needs for a 12-month period, was issued in October 1994. The main targets of the appeal were the emergency in Kabul, the needs of the internally displaced and support for voluntary repatriation of refugees from neighbouring countries. The total cash and in-kind contributions received during 1994 by United Nations agencies and non-governmental organizations for activities outlined in the approach are estimated at $85 million. As a result of a mid-term review that was carried out early in 1995, a general consensus has emerged among all humanitarian partners concerned over the need for a new consolidated appeal covering the period from October 1995 to September 1996. The appeal will include projects covering the provision of emergency relief to vulnerable groups in urban and rural areas, including internally displaced persons and returnees. Emergency rehabilitation projects targeting communities made vulnerable by loss of livelihood, basic services or shelter will also be incorporated.

622. When I met the leaders of all the main Afghan factions in Islamabad in September 1994, I urged them to lift the blockade of Kabul, which had prevented the delivery of humanitarian aid to the city since late June. As a result, convoys carrying over 1,500 tons of urgently needed supplies reached Kabul in December. After fighting ended in the city, regular United Nations convoys carrying relief supplies reached the city as of mid-March. Refugees and displaced people also began to return. However, much of the southern part of the city is completely devastated. Mines and unexploded ordnance present a constant danger, and little clean water is available. United Nations agencies and non-governmental organizations are working together to address these most urgent humanitarian needs, providing food, shelter, sanitation and health care.

623. Throughout 1994, internally displaced persons from Kabul continued to arrive in Jalalabad. By January 1995, almost 300,000 persons were living in camps assisted by the United Nations, the International Committee of the Red Cross (ICRC) and non-governmental organizations. As a result of coordinated efforts, the health and nutritional status of camp residents improved dramatically.

624. Joint United Nations interventions in the humanitarian field include a mass immunization campaign, organized by the World Health Organization and the United Nations Children's Fund, in collaboration with the Ministry of Public Health and non-governmental organizations. The first round took place in November 1994. Following an appeal by the United Nations, a complete cease-fire prevailed for the week of the campaign. The second and third rounds took place in April and May 1995.

## 2. Armenia and Azerbaijan

625. The conflict over the region of Nagorny Karabakh, which involves Armenia and Azerbaijan, remains unresolved, but the situation on the ground in and around Nagorny Karabakh has not deteriorated in the past 12 months. The cease-fire agreed to on 12 May 1994 through the mediation of the Russian Federation has been observed to a large extent and no additional territory has been occupied.

626. The members of the Security Council have continued to support the peacemaking efforts of OSCE, which decided at its summit meeting at Budapest on 6 December 1994 to establish a co-chairmanship for its OSCE Minsk Conference and, *inter alia*, to conduct speedy negotiations for the conclusion of a political agreement on the cessation of the armed conflict that would permit the convening of the Minsk Conference and make it possible to deploy a multinational OSCE peace-keeping force in the region.

627. In its presidential statement of 26 April 1995 (S/PRST/1995/21), the Security Council reiterated its support for the efforts of the Co-Chairmen of the OSCE Minsk Conference and, *inter alia*, strongly urged the parties to conduct negotiations constructively without preconditions or procedural obstacles and to refrain from any actions that might undermine the peace process. Furthermore, the Council stressed that the parties to the conflict themselves bore the main responsibility for reaching a peaceful settlement.

628. I remain prepared to provide my full support for the efforts of OSCE. To that end, the United Nations Secretariat has had a number of consultations with the OSCE High-level Planning Group to extend technical advice and expertise in the field of peace-keeping. I am also fully prepared, if so requested, to lend my good offices to the OSCE-led political process towards reaching a comprehensive settlement of the conflict.

629. During my visit to Baku and Yerevan in October/November last year, the first such visit of a Secretary-General to the newly independent transcaucasian nations, I was able to obtain a first-hand assessment of the very serious effects of this conflict, in particular in its humanitarian dimension, on both Armenia and Azerbaijan.

630. Active humanitarian programmes coordinated by the Department of Humanitarian Affairs are being implemented in both countries. Activities of the 1995-1996 humanitarian programmes, as presented in the United Nations consolidated inter-agency appeal for the Caucasus (1 April 1995–31 March 1996), include relief projects in the food, non-food, shelter, education and health sectors, as well as capacity-building and projects addressing the transition from emergency assistance to development. As at 31 July 1995, 37.4 per cent ($10.5 million) of funding had been received for the Armenia component of the appeal and only 37 per cent ($12.8 million) of requirements pledged for humanitarian activities in Azerbaijan. It is anticipated that the majority of refugees and internally displaced persons in both Azerbaijan and Armenia, who are among the most vulnerable members of the population, will continue to require humanitarian assistance in the foreseeable future. I requested Under-Secretary-General Aldo Ajello to undertake a mission of goodwill to Armenia and Azerbaijan.

### 3. Baltic States

631. In accordance with the agreements between the parties concerned, the Russian Federation withdrew its troops from the territory of Estonia and Latvia by 31 August 1994. In a letter addressed to me on 26 August 1994 (A/49/344-S/1994/1008), the Permanent Representative of the Russian Federation confirmed the guarantees that the Russian Federation gave to the Latvian side that the Agreement concerning the legal status of the Skrunda radar station during the period of its temporary operation and dismantling would not be used to carry out acts directed against the sovereignty and security interests of Latvia.

632. At the forty-ninth session of the General Assembly, it was generally recognized that completion of the withdrawal of foreign armed forces from the territory of the Baltic States would contribute to enhancing stability in Europe and developing better relations between the Baltic States and the Russian Federation. The General Assembly thus concluded its consideration of this item.

### 4. Bougainville

633. I welcomed the establishment of a Bougainville Transitional Government in April of this year. I am pleased to note that, following the signing of the agreement reached at the Bougainville Peace Conference at Arawa last October, and following the talks held by my Special Envoy in August 1994 and January 1995 with the leaders of Papua New Guinea and Solomon Islands, and with representatives of all Bougainvillian groups in pursuance of Commission on Human Rights resolution 1994/81 of 9 March 1994, there has been a marked improvement in the political and human rights situation on the island.

634. Convinced that reconstruction and rehabilitation are essential for the strengthening of the peace process, I dispatched a United Nations inter-agency mission to Papua New Guinea in April-May 1995. The Mission has prepared a development programme for the reconstruction and rehabilitation of Bougainville.

635. In accordance with the mandate entrusted to me by Commission on Human Rights resolution 1995/65, I will continue to lend my good offices to the peace process now under way in Bougainville.

### 5. Burundi

636. The threatening situation in Burundi has been a major preoccupation throughout the period under review. I visited the country on 16 and 17 July 1995. Since his appointment in November 1993, my Special Representative for Burundi, Mr. Ahmedou Ould-Abdallah, has actively promoted na-

tional reconciliation in the country through his contacts with all parties concerned.

637. On 10 September 1994, all the parties reached agreement on a system of power-sharing and later signed a Convention of Government, with the sole exception of the Parti pour le redressement national (PARENA), headed by former President Jean-Baptiste Bagaza. On 30 September 1994, the National Assembly elected Mr. Sylvestre Ntibantunganya, a Hutu, as the new President of the Republic of Burundi. Mr. Anatole Kanyenkiko, a Tutsi, was reconfirmed as Prime Minister on 3 October 1994, and five days later a new coalition Government, representing 7 of the 13 political parties, was sworn in.

638. In my report to the Security Council of 11 October 1994 (S/1994/1152), I noted that although the situation had stabilized somewhat with the election of a new President, it still remained precarious. The international community should therefore continue to encourage the moderate forces in Burundi.

639. Throughout the period under review, the Security Council repeatedly deplored the attempts of extremist elements to destabilize the situation further and called upon all parties to respect and implement fully the provisions of the Convention of Government. The Council dispatched a fact-finding mission, the second in six months, to Bujumbura on 10 and 11 February 1995. The mission recommended, *inter alia*, the establishment of an international commission of inquiry into the October 1993 coup attempt and the massacres that followed, a substantial increase in the number of Organization of African Unity military observers, the strengthening of the office of my Special Representative and the deployment of United Nations human rights monitors throughout the country (S/1995/163).

640. In a presidential statement of 29 March 1995 (S/PRST/1995/13), the Security Council requested me to report on the steps to be taken to establish the commission of inquiry recommended by its mission which had visited Burundi the previous month. After considering various options, I concluded that it was necessary to explore the possibility of establishing a commission on the truth for Burundi similar to the one that had worked in El Salvador. I appointed a Special Envoy, Mr. Pedro Nikken, to visit Burundi for two weeks starting 26 June 1995. His mission was to determine whether the appropriate national entities in Burundi were prepared to set up a commission on the truth. The Council also reaffirmed its support for a regional conference on peace, stability and security and called with great urgency upon the countries of the region to convene such a conference. My Special Envoy visited Bujumbura from 28 June to 9 July 1995. In his report, he concluded that neither a commission on the truth nor an international commission of

judicial inquiry would be an adequate response to the need to put an end to impunity in Burundi. However, an international commission of inquiry could be viable and useful. I reported to the Council on 28 July (S/1995/631) with recommendations for the establishment of such a commission.

641. The Conference on Assistance to Refugees, Returnees and Displaced Persons in the Great Lakes Region, organized by the Organization of African Unity and UNHCR, took place as scheduled at Bujumbura from 12 to 17 February 1995, in pursuance of General Assembly resolution 49/7 of 25 October 1994. The Conference adopted a plan of action and decided to ask UNDP to organize a round table to assist the countries affected by the Rwandan and Burundian refugees. Preparatory meetings for holding the round table are scheduled to take place from September to December 1995.

642. On 15 February, the Union pour le progrès national (UPRONA), the main opposition party, forced the resignation of Prime Minister Kanyenkiko. Five days later, Mr. Antoine Nduwayo was appointed Prime Minister. On 10 March, a new 25-member coalition Government was appointed. The security situation nevertheless remained fragile. Violence did not subside, despite a reconciliation and pacification campaign launched by the Government in April 1995, and it continued to affect parts of the country. Two problems, in particular, were potentially explosive: the sudden influx of Hutu refugees who left the Kibeho camp for displaced persons in Rwanda and crossed the northern border of Burundi (27,000 as of 12 May 1995) and the question of a shipment of small arms and ammunition ordered by Burundi from China in 1992, but blocked in Dar es Salaam by the authorities of the United Republic of Tanzania.

643. A fresh outbreak of violence in Bujumbura in June 1995 led to the announcement by President Ntibantunganya of new security measures, but they were rejected by the Parliament with the Front pour la démocratie au Burundi (FRODEBU) majority voting against them. The same month, arrest warrants were issued against two Hutu extremist leaders—former Minister of the Interior Leonard Nyagoma and his top adviser, Mr. Christian Sendegeya, who had sought refuge in Zaire. The situation was further aggravated by the unexpected resignation of the Tutsi Minister for Foreign Affairs. On 6 July 1995, Mr. Paul Munyambari, a Hutu (FRODEBU), was appointed Foreign Minister in his place. Preparations for the national debate, which is tentatively scheduled for November or December 1995, are under way.

644. During his visit to Burundi from 29 to 31 March 1995, the United Nations High Commissioner for Human Rights received support from the President of Burundi for the expansion of the office of the High Commissioner in Bujumbura,

opened since 15 June 1994. On 4 May, the Economic and Social Council appointed Mr. Paulo Pinheiro (Brazil) Special Rapporteur on the situation of human rights in Burundi. Mr. Pinheiro paid his first visit to the country from 21 June to 2 July.

645. On the humanitarian front, the violence in Burundi severely affected the northern provinces. Populations have continued to flee to the United Republic of Tanzania and Zaire. The reduction in the availability of food resources to meet regional needs has forced the World Food Programme to cease distributions among the displaced populations while continuing to serve refugees. This has led to the exacerbation of ethnic tensions within the northern regions.

646. The fact that the humanitarian needs which surfaced after the events in October 1993 in Burundi were largely met by September/October 1994 seems to account for the general consensus within the relief community in Burundi that the humanitarian crisis is past. However, although an emergency does not exist at present, there remain reasons for concern about the future. Health and educational services are continuously perturbed by ethnic turmoil, forcing the international community to set up parallel administrative structures. Dwindling international emergency resources and the absence of follow-up development assistance pose questions about the Government's capacity to take over the provision of basic services.

647. The United Nations Development Programme is actively involved in assisting the Government in its transition from a relief-assisted State to one which may lead a recovery effort. A 15-month continuum programme of close to $3.4 million was initiated to help elaborate sectoral strategies. In addition, a number of conferences attract donor support.

648. The World Health Organization is implementing a four-pronged assistance effort, totalling nearly $3.9 million. The efforts are focused on strengthening the National Epidemiological Surveillance Network, assisting in the prevention and control of communicable diseases and epidemics, supporting the provision of health services to the most affected provinces, and aiding in the prevention and control of sexually transmitted diseases.

649. The efforts of UNICEF are geared towards reinforcing the existing health network as well as the integration of preventive and curative services of health and nutrition, the provision of water supply and environmental sanitation, supporting basic education and peace education, and giving assistance to 8,000 unaccompanied children. Over $10 million has been contributed for these efforts.

650. The Food and Agriculture Organization of the United Nations has concentrated its efforts on providing displaced persons, returnees and refugees with agricultural tool kits and seeds. In addi-

tion, the organization is involved in reforestation and stockbreeding. A total of $12 million has been allocated for these tasks.

651. In addition to providing assistance to approximately 200,000 refugees, UNHCR has been assisting 220,000 returnees and displaced persons and 5,000 urban poor. UNHCR also provides secondary-school and higher education, and implements repatriation operations of former refugees from and to Rwanda. Approximately $30 million has been raised for the accomplishment of these tasks.

652. WFP continues to assist the internally displaced persons and returnees as well as 200,000 Rwandan refugees in Burundi, and 150,000 Rwandan and Burundian refugees in Zaire. The reduction in regional food availability has led WFP to implement an accelerated reintegration programme for the internally displaced.

### 6. Cambodia

653. In April 1995, the Royal Government of Cambodia agreed to my decision that the term of my Representative in Cambodia, whom I had appointed following the termination of the mandate of the United Nations Military Liaison Team in May 1994, be extended by six months and that he should be assisted during this period by one military adviser. In accordance with his mandate, my Representative has maintained close liaison with the host Government, as well as with United Nations programmes and agencies operating in the country.

654. The broad cooperation between the Government, the United Nations and the international community has brought further progress to the country during the past year. The generous pledges made at the third meeting of the International Committee on the Reconstruction of Cambodia (ICORC) are clear evidence of the sustained commitment of the international community to assist the Government in its endeavours to establish a peaceful, democratic and prosperous State.

655. Discussions in May 1995 between my Special Envoy, Under-Secretary-General Marrack Goulding, and the Cambodian Government led to an agreement to introduce measures to improve communication between the United Nations Centre for Human Rights in Phnom Penh and the Government, and for the office to continue to function with its existing mandate. At that time I issued a personal appeal to Member States for contributions to the Trust Fund for a Human Rights Education Programme in Cambodia. I repeat this appeal now.

### 7. Cyprus

656. During the past year, my mission of good offices proceeded within the overall framework set out by the Security Council in resolution 939(1994):

to continue to work for progress on both the substance of the Cyprus problem and the implementation of the package of confidence-building measures that had been the focus of efforts during the previous period.

657.    After my Special Representative, Mr. Joe Clark, visited the region in September 1994 for meetings with the Cypriot parties and the Governments of Greece and Turkey, he reported to me that matters were close to an impasse. The Greek Cypriot leader continued to insist on progress on an overall solution, while the Turkish Cypriot leader placed priority on the early implementation of the confidence-building measures. In response, I wrote to each of the community leaders on 10 October 1994, informing them that I had requested my Deputy Special Representative to invite them to join him for a number of informal consultations. These consultations were to explore, in a concrete manner, ways in which the implementation of the confidence-building measures and the long-contemplated overall settlement of the Cyprus problem might be advanced.

658.    Both leaders accepted this invitation, meeting five times between 18 and 31 October 1994. They discussed the essential elements of a federation in Cyprus as well as the implementation of the confidence-building measures, exploring a broad range of ideas pertaining to political equality, sovereignty, membership in the European Union, aspects of the federal constitutional arrangements, security and demilitarization, displaced persons, property claims and territorial adjustments, as well as modalities for the early establishment of the federation and implementation of the confidence-building measures. The ideas broached under these headings offered ways of satisfying in an equitable manner what have consistently been the most deeply held concerns and interests of each community.

659.    In November and December 1994, I met separately with each of the Cypriot leaders to hear their views on the informal meetings. I told them that given the necessary political will, the elements discussed during their meetings offered the possibility of a significant step forward both on the substance of the Cyprus question and on the confidence-building measures. I also strongly encouraged the Turkish Cypriot leader to respond in a commensurate manner to the ideas that had been broached. I instructed my Representatives to pursue their contacts with the parties in order to establish the basis for a further discussion of these issues. To this end, Mr. Clark travelled to the region in March and May 1995.

660.    The continuing support of the members of the Security Council for the efforts of my mission of good offices has been particularly encouraging. But I regret that, in spite of the presence on the negotiating table of almost all elements required for a just and lasting settlement, the negotiating process again appears to be blocked.

661.    The United Nations Peace-keeping Force in Cyprus (UNFICYP) has continued to carry out effectively its mandate despite the reduction of its strength by nearly half over the past couple of years. The two sides have generally exercised restraint in the past year. However, the continuing quiet should not obscure the fact that there is merely a cease-fire—not peace—on the island. I continue to be concerned by the excessive level of foreign troops and of armament in Cyprus, and the rate at which these are being strengthened. The two sides have not yet agreed, in accordance with the proposed package of confidence-building measures, to extend without delay the 1989 unmanning agreement to all parts of the buffer zone where their forces remain in close proximity to each other. The Security Council's repeated call for a significant reduction in the number of foreign troops and in defence spending should be heeded by all concerned. I again urge both sides to take reciprocal measures to lower the tension, including mutual commitments, through UNFICYP, not to deploy along the cease-fire lines live ammunition or weapons other than those that are hand-held and to prohibit firing of weapons within sight or hearing of the buffer zone.

### 8.    East Timor

662.    I have continued to provide my good offices in the search for a just, comprehensive and internationally acceptable solution to the question of East Timor. During the period under review, I held two more rounds of talks at Geneva, on 9 January and 8 July 1995, with the Foreign Ministers of Indonesia and Portugal. These talks identified a number of substantive issues for further discussions and explored possible avenues towards a solution.

663.    During my visit to Indonesia in April, I had very useful discussions with President Suharto. I had equally valuable meetings with President Mario Soares when I visited Portugal at the end of August. I also dispatched a mission to Portugal, Indonesia and East Timor in December 1994 to consult with the two Governments and a broad range of East Timorese personalities on a series of ideas to help move the process forward.

664.    With the support of the two Ministers, I took the initiative to facilitate and offer necessary arrangements for the convening of an all-inclusive intra–East Timorese dialogue. The dialogue does not address the political status of East Timor or represent a second negotiating track. Instead, it is intended to be a forum for free and informal discussions among the East Timorese on practical ideas aimed at creating an atmosphere conducive to the achievement of a solution to the

question. The first meeting of the dialogue was convened at Burg Schlaining, Austria, from 2 to 5 June 1995, and was attended by 30 East Timorese of all shades of political opinion. In a positive atmosphere, the delegates reached a declaration by consensus and produced a number of useful ideas that I examined in July with the Foreign Ministers of Indonesia and Portugal. The participants voiced their desire to have further meetings of this kind in the future. I share this view and intend to pursue this matter with the two parties.

665. While deep differences remain between the two sides on the core issue of the status of the Territory, I am convinced that a solution can be found through patient dialogue. I am encouraged in this belief by the willingness of the two sides to continue the dialogue and to seek a lasting solution. I am also heartened by the desire expressed by the East Timorese, recently manifested at the first session of the dialogue, to contribute to the peace process. The next ministerial meeting will take place in London in January 1996.

### 9. El Salvador

666. With the assistance of the United Nations, El Salvador continued its progress from a violent and closed society towards one in which democratic order, the rule of law and respect for human rights are being established. However, as in previous years, significant progress in the implementation of outstanding elements of the peace accords was not without problems or delay. These included the full deployment of the National Civil Police and the completion of the demobilization of the National Police; the reform of the judicial and electoral systems; the transfer of land to former combatants; and the conclusion of reintegration programmes for them. On 31 October 1994, I reported to the Security Council that I deemed it necessary to recommend that the mandate of the United Nations Observer Mission in El Salvador (ONUSAL) be extended until 30 April 1995.

667. The Government of President Armando Calderón Sol and the Frente Farabundo Martí para la Liberación Nacional (FMLN) have continued to express their determination, e.g., in a joint declaration signed on 4 October 1994, to see the peace accords promptly implemented for the benefit of all Salvadorans. Specifically in the latter part of the year, implementation of the outstanding points assumed a more rapid pace. For example, the long-delayed demobilization of the National Police was formally effected on 31 December 1994. In the early months of 1995, however, the land programme slowed and some worrisome indicators emerged.

668. In the light of these developments, I informed the President of the Security Council on 6 February 1995 of my intention to set up in El Salvador, following the expiration of the mandate of ONUSAL, a small team of United Nations officials to provide good offices and verify implementation of the outstanding provisions of the peace accords. The team, which would be established for an initial period of six months, would also provide me with a continuing flow of information, thus allowing me to keep the Council informed of further developments. On 17 February, the Council welcomed my proposal, and preparations began for the team's deployment.

669. At the beginning of April 1995, I made a visit to El Salvador, the third occasion on which I had done so as Secretary-General. Although I stressed that the primary responsibility for the process lay with Salvadorans, I assured the Government and people of El Salvador that the commitment of the United Nations remained, despite the withdrawal of ONUSAL.

670. On 27 April 1995, the parties to the Chapultepec Peace Agreement signed a programme of work for the completion of all outstanding points in the peace accords. On the following day the Security Council adopted resolution 991(1995), formally marking the end of the mandate of ONUSAL. The new United Nations Mission in El Salvador (MINUSAL), led by Mr. Enrique ter Horst, my Special Representative, began its work as planned on 1 May 1995. With its staff partly funded by voluntary contributions, MINUSAL represents a much reduced United Nations presence, but one that confirms the Organization's ongoing support for peace-building in El Salvador.

671. The Programme of Work had divided the remaining accords into six areas (public security, land transfer, human settlements, reinsertion programmes, Fund for the Protection of the Wounded and Disabled and legislative reforms) and established dates by which specific provisions in each area must be completed. Monthly updates on its progress, which I circulated informally to members of the Security Council, revealed the continuing determination of the parties to the peace accords to bring them to completion. Progress was made in all areas, with the Government's deposit of ratification of international human rights instruments with the United Nations Secretariat and the secretariat of the Organization of American States and its recognition of the jurisdiction of the Inter-American Court of Human Rights particularly to be welcomed.

672. However, by early August 1995 it was clear that significant delays had occurred in the land transfer programme (which reached the 60 per cent target set for 30 April 1995 only in the first week of July), in the design of a "special regime" for rural human settlements, in the

strengthening of the National Civil Police and in the implementation of the judicial reforms recommended by the Commission on the Truth. With a little under three months before the expiration of its term, MINUSAL continued to exercise its good offices and verification responsibilities in favour of one final effort to bring these outstanding elements of the peace accords to conclusion.

### 10. Georgia/Abkhazia

673. My Special Envoy for Georgia, Mr. Edouard Brunner, supported by the Russian Federation as facilitator and the Organization for Security and Cooperation in Europe as participant, has continued his efforts to achieve a comprehensive settlement of the conflict, particularly in identifying a political status for Abkhazia acceptable to both the Georgian and Abkhaz sides. He has visited the region and chaired several rounds of negotiations and expert talks. I visited the Republic of Georgia from 31 October to 2 November 1994 in order to explore with the Head of State, Mr. Eduard Shevardnadze, and other Georgian Government officials how the political process could be advanced. I have also offered to assist by meeting either separately or jointly with the leaders of the two sides. The Russian Federation, acting in its capacity as facilitator, made intensive efforts in 1995 to reach agreement on a draft protocol that might provide the basis for a Georgian-Abkhaz settlement. Unfortunately, all these efforts have resulted in little political progress to date.

674. A significant gap remains between the two sides regarding the political status of Abkhazia within the territorial integrity of Georgia. Abkhazia's Constitution, which was promulgated by the Supreme Soviet of Abkhazia on 26 November 1994, declares Abkhazia to be a "sovereign democratic State . . . ". Such constitutional arrangements are unacceptable to the Georgian side, which insists on preserving its territorial integrity. The Government of Georgia proposes to establish a federation for Georgia within which Abkhazia would be granted a wide degree of autonomy.

675. Assuming that it is possible to find agreement on a draft protocol now under discussion, a prolonged period of detailed negotiations will have to follow in order to agree on ways to implement a settlement. Such negotiations will require continuous attention *in situ*. I have therefore decided to appoint a deputy to my Special Envoy, who will be resident in the area and thus able to provide a continuous presence at a senior political level. Following the precedent of other operations, such as those in Cyprus and Tajikistan, the Deputy will also be the head of the United Nations Observer Mission in Georgia (UNOMIG). In carrying out the tasks of political contact and negotiation, the Deputy will divide his time between Tbilisi and Sukhumi and will travel as necessary to Moscow for direct consultations with the Russian authorities.

676. UNOMIG has been fulfilling the tasks mandated by the Security Council in resolution 937(1994) of 21 July 1994. It maintains its headquarters at Sukhumi, but because of the unavailability of suitable accommodation in that city, part of the Mission's headquarters staff is now stationed in Pitsunda. The Mission also has a liaison office in Tbilisi and three sector headquarters—at Sukhimi, Gali and Zugdidi. In addition, UNOMIG has six team site bases: three in the Gali region, two in the Zugdidi region and one in the Kodori Valley.

677. The Government of Georgia and the Abkhaz authorities have largely complied with the agreement of 14 May 1994 on a cease-fire and separation of forces. All armed forces have been withdrawn from the security zone, although a few pieces of non-operational heavy military equipment remain in the restricted weapons zone.

678. The situation in the security and restricted weapons zones, especially in the Gali region, has been tense. One of the most pressing problems in the security zone has been the presence on both sides of unauthorized weapons among the population, and among some of the Abkhaz militia, as well as the Georgian police. In addition, armed elements beyond the control of either the Government of Georgia or the Abkhaz authorities have been responsible for criminal activities in the Gali region. The situation in the Kodori Valley, which had been tense towards the end of 1994, has now calmed down. The relations on the ground between the Abkhaz and the Svan have been satisfactory, with a slow but steady build-up of mutual confidence.

679. UNOMIG has reported that the Commonwealth of Independent States (CIS) peace-keeping force has been conducting its operations within the framework of the agreement of May 1994, and any variation from the tasks set out in the agreement has been made in consultation with the parties. Cooperation between UNOMIG and the CIS peace-keeping force has been very productive. Cooperation between UNOMIG and the Government of Georgia and the Abkhaz authorities has also been satisfactory. Through its liaison office in Tbilisi, UNOMIG has been cooperating with OSCE.

680. In pursuance of paragraph 10 of Security Council resolution 937(1994), I have established a voluntary fund for contributions in support of the implementation of the agreement of 14 May 1994 for humanitarian aspects including demining, as specified by the donors, which will facilitate the implementation of UNOMIG's mandate. One pledge has been made so far.

681. At independence, the people of Georgia had one of the highest standards of living among

the republics of the former Soviet Union. Today, the country is racked by political instability, civil strife on two fronts and the displacement of some 270,000 people. Lack of foreign exchange for essential inputs, such as fuel, and hyper-inflation have devastated the economy. Agricultural production contracted in 1994 for the fourth year in succession. In the break-away region of Abkhazia, some 75 per cent of the original inhabitants have reportedly fled civil conflict into other parts of Georgia and the area remains the scene of extensive destruction. In some areas, large numbers of mines have been laid and roads are impassable.

682.    Of all the difficulties currently facing Georgia, the most immediate are the scarcity of basic foods and the critical energy supply situation. After several years of huge budget deficits, the Government lacks the resources to ensure the continued provision of basic social services. Many primary health-care units and hospitals are unable to function because of shortages of medicines and equipment. Health care is now almost entirely dependent on international humanitarian assistance.

683.    In addition, large numbers of orphans, abandoned children and people in need of special education are currently living in extremely poor circumstances because of reduced government spending. Most lack adequate food, bedding, warm clothes and learning materials. As in the neighbouring Caucasus republics, textbooks and school materials are in short supply and many school buildings urgently need rehabilitation.

684.    There has also been little progress in the return of refugees and displaced persons to Abkhazia. Though voluntary repatriation under UNHCR auspices commenced in mid-October 1994, movement as at December 1994 of a mere 311 persons out of an estimated total 250,000 refugees and displaced persons has been very disappointing. Since the end of November 1994, formal repatriation has virtually halted, and the Quadripartite Commission has not met since 16 February 1995. About 20,000 persons have returned spontaneously to the Gali district.

685.    The Abkhaz side continues to object to the large-scale and speedy return of refugees and displaced persons. Its offer of 17 April 1995 to repatriate 200 persons a week and to be more flexible with regard to those refugees and displaced persons returning spontaneously does not meet UNHCR requirements for a meaningful timetable. The continued delay in resettling internally displaced persons to Abkhazia has placed a heavy burden on the economy of Georgia, weakening its capacity to recover and exacerbating social and political tensions. The Abkhaz side continues to link progress on the question of refugees to progress on political issues. The authorities are withholding thousands of other applications and have re-fused to process further requests owing to a stalling of the peace negotiations on both sides.

686.    As part of its efforts to move from a centrally planned to a market economy, the Georgian Government is taking steps towards economic reform. The task of transferring the State-run economy into private hands is daunting and has, in itself, inflicted severe social and economic hardship. In 1994, subsidies for important staples were progressively removed, resulting in price increases. Further liberalization of prices for most commodities will be progressively instituted during 1995. Although the minimum wage and pensions have also been increased, these reforms cannot keep pace with rising inflation.

687.    In the light of these problems, the Department of Humanitarian Affairs led an inter-agency mission to Georgia in February 1995, for the second consecutive year, to assess the needs of the country and formulate an inter-agency consolidated appeal for the Caucasus, including Georgia, and covering the period from 1 April 1995 to 31 March 1996. That appeal was launched at Geneva on 23 March 1995. Activities covered in the appeal include relief projects to be undertaken by United Nations agencies/programmes and non-governmental organizations in the food, non-food, shelter and health sectors, as well as projects aimed at strengthening the country's self-reliance in a post-emergency phase.

688.    On 19 May 1995, the Quadripartite Commission convened in Moscow to explore once again the possibilities for resuming the voluntary repatriation programme under the auspices of the Office of the United Nations High Commissioner for Refugees. Representatives of UNHCR presented a concrete timetable for such returns, under which the displaced population from the Gali district would have returned before the end of 1995. Despite strenuous efforts to obtain a more flexible response, the Abkhaz side maintained its previous position of April 1995 of allowing only 200 persons per week to return. This continues to be unacceptable to the other parties.

689.    Minor improvements to security conditions in the Gali district have resulted in increased daily movements back and forth across the Inguri River by displaced persons, primarily to the lower security zone, to work in the fields, trade or repair houses. Some of these persons have decided to stay in the Gali district as long as security does not again deteriorate. The size of the semi-resident population is estimated at 25,000 to 35,000 persons. However, large numbers continue to live in difficult circumstances, placing great strain on the Georgian economy, on human relations and on local services. In these circumstances, the level of frustration and distress is very high, leading to calls for mass spontaneous repatriation.

690.   As of July 1995, $9.4 million, represent-
ing 25.7 per cent of funding requirements for
Georgia, had been contributed to the appeal, as
reported to the Department of Humanitarian Affairs by agencies making the appeal. A mid-term
review of the appeal will be launched in late August 1995, to review both the implementation of
the projects presented in the appeal and the funding situation, and to present plans for the continuation of activities until the end of the appeal
period.

### 11.   Guatemala

691.   During the reporting period, negotiations
between the Government of Guatemala and the
Unidad Revolucionaria Nacional Guatemalteca
(URNG) have continued under the auspices of the
United Nations. While advances in the process
have been uneven, the establishment of the United
Nations Mission for the Verification of Human
Rights and of Compliance with the Commitments
of the Comprehensive Agreement on Human
Rights in Guatemala (MINUGUA) and the signing
of the Agreement on Identity and Rights of In-
digenous Peoples are encouraging developments.

692.   Taking into account progress made during the first half of 1994 as well as Commission
on Human Rights resolution 1994/58, I recommended to the General Assembly in my report of
18 August 1994 (A/48/985) the earliest establishment of a human rights verification mission in
Guatemala. On 19 September 1994, by resolution
48/267, the Assembly established MINUGUA for an
initial period of six months, and I appointed Mr.
Leonardo Franco as the Mission's Director.
MINUGUA was officially inaugurated in November 1994. With eight regional offices, five subregional offices and an authorized strength of 245
international staff, the Mission represents a significant effort by the United Nations in human
rights verification and institution-building. It is
also the most tangible result so far of the talks between the Government of Guatemala and URNG.

693.   After the signing of five agreements between January and June 1994, the pace of the
negotiations slowed down during the last six
months of the year. On 28 December 1994, I expressed my concern to the General Assembly and
the Security Council and stated that the time-
frame originally foreseen for the conclusion of a
peace agreement would have to be revised. In addition, I wrote to the parties to ask them to renew
their commitment to the process and to indicate
the steps they would be prepared to take to allow
it to regain momentum.

694.   As a result of initiatives by the
Secretariat, the parties agreed in February 1995
to several proposals aimed at facilitating the continuation of the talks, including a new time-frame.
On that basis, I informed the General Assembly

and the Security Council that conditions existed
for further United Nations involvement in the
peace process. Negotiations were resumed soon
thereafter and the landmark Agreement on Identity and Rights of Indigenous Peoples was signed
at Mexico City on 31 March 1995. Immediately
afterwards, preparatory work began for the negotiation of the next item of the agenda—socio-
economic aspects and the agrarian situation.

695.   On 1 March 1995, I transmitted to the
General Assembly the first report of the Director
of MINUGUA (A/49/856 and Corr.1, annex), in
which he acknowledged the cooperation received
from the parties, the international community and
the agencies of the United Nations system. With
regard to MINUGUA's verification mandate, the
Director confirmed the existence of a pattern of
serious human rights abuses and widespread impunity in Guatemala. He also summarized
MINUGUA's institution-building activities, aimed
at strengthening those national institutions responsible for the protection of human rights. On 31
March 1995, the Assembly renewed MINUGUA's
mandate for a further six months.

696.   In April, I visited Guatemala to review
the work of MINUGUA and progress in the peace
process. I congratulated the parties on their
achievements so far, in particular the Agreement
on Identity and Rights of Indigenous Peoples, but
I stressed that their continued commitment, perseverance and political will were essential if the
process was to succeed. I emphasized that the efforts of the Guatemalans towards national reconciliation would be backed by the international
community with the United Nations as its instrument. As a follow-up to my visit, I appointed Mr.
Gilberto Schlittler as my Special Envoy for the
Guatemala Peace Process.

697.   On 29 June, I transmitted to the General
Assembly the second report of the Director of
MINUGUA on human rights (A/49/929). The
Director concluded that progress achieved since
the installation of the Mission, while insufficient,
demonstrated that with political will from the parties and commitment on the part of society as a
whole, it was possible to improve the situation of
human rights in Guatemala.

698.   Currently, the parties are negotiating on
several items, including the socio-economic aspects
and the agrarian situation. Several items remain
to be considered, namely, the strengthening of civilian power and role of the army in a democratic
society, the reintegration of URNG into political
life, a definitive cease-fire, constitutional reforms
and the electoral regime and, lastly, a schedule for
implementation, enforcement and verification.

699.   Guatemala is now in the first stages of an
electoral campaign leading to presidential elections
scheduled for November 1995. The timetable I

proposed in February 1995 partly intended to ensure that electoral considerations would not affect the negotiations. It now appears, however, that the negotiations and the electoral process will overlap in time. This complex situation notwithstanding, I hope that the parties will be able to proceed steadily towards the signing of a final peace agreement, as early as possible in 1996.

### 12. India and Pakistan

700. Since 1949, the United Nations Military Observer Group in India and Pakistan (UNMOGIP) has been deployed to monitor the cease-fire in Jammu and Kashmir. India and Pakistan have affirmed their commitment to respect the cease-fire line and to resolve the issue peacefully in accordance with the Simla Agreement of 1972. The increasing reports of incidents of violence in Jammu and Kashmir have further aggravated relations between the two countries. These developments highlight the urgency of seeking a political solution through a meaningful dialogue. In this connection, I have maintained contacts with both Governments and visited the two countries in September 1994. I reiterated to them my readiness, should they so wish, to render whatever assistance may be needed to facilitate their search for a lasting solution.

### 13. Iraq-Kuwait

701. During the past year, I have continued to stress to Iraqi representatives the importance of Iraq's cooperation in implementing all of its obligations as expressed in the resolutions of the Security Council.

702. Further significant progress was made by the United Nations Special Commission (UNSCOM), headed by Mr. Rolf Ekéus, and the International Atomic Energy Agency (IAEA) Action Team in the implementation of section C of Security Council resolution 687(1991), concerning the elimination of Iraq's weapons of mass destruction and long-range missile capabilities. They completed the process of establishing a system to monitor Iraq's dual-purpose industries (i.e., those that have non-proscribed uses but which could be used to acquire banned weapons capabilities), aimed at monitoring Iraq's compliance with its obligations not to reacquire such banned capabilities. This system became operational in April 1995.

703. Further refining of the system will continue as UNSCOM and IAEA gain experience in operating it, but all the elements of the system are now in place. Some 120 remote-controlled monitoring cameras have been installed at over 28 sites and linked in real time to the Baghdad Monitoring and Verification Centre. Twenty or so automated chemical air samplers have been installed at sites, and a highly sensitive chemical laboratory has been installed in the Centre to analyse these samples. The Centre also has a biological preparation room to prepare and package biological samples for shipment to laboratories in other countries. Communications have been upgraded to perform the new tasks associated with ongoing monitoring and verification.

704. Resident teams of inspectors in each of the weapons disciplines are now operating full-time out of the Centre. Their activities are supplemented by aerial inspection and surveys conducted using a high-altitude surveillance aircraft provided by the United States. These aerial assets remain key to the ability of UNSCOM and IAEA to fulfil their mandates as they provide the initial survey capability to identify sites which might need to be inspected and ensure the ability to conduct short-notice inspections of sites as necessary.

705. Efforts continue to elucidate and hence account for all elements of Iraq's past banned weapons capabilities. Much progress has been made in this regard but major issues remain in the biological area.

706. UNSCOM and IAEA also, in accordance with paragraph 7 of resolution 715(1991), submitted in May 1994 a proposal for an export/import monitoring mechanism which would require that all exports be notified by both Iraq and the Governments of the exporters to a joint unit to be established in New York by UNSCOM and the IAEA Action Team.

707. I wish to express my appreciation to those Governments that contributed to UNSCOM operations, and in particular to the Government of Germany, which generously provided the Special Commission with air support in the form of both C-160 transport aircraft and CH-53G helicopters.

708. In November 1994, the Government of Iraq took an important step forward by affirming its recognition of the sovereignty, territorial integrity and political independence of Kuwait. The United Nations Iraq-Kuwait Observation Mission (UNIKOM) has continued to operate within the demilitarized zone established on both sides of the border between Iraq and Kuwait. In December 1994, Iraq formally recognized the international border demarcated by the United Nations in 1993. The situation has been calm in the Mission's area of responsibility.

709. The United Nations Coordinator for the return of property from Iraq to Kuwait has continued to facilitate the hand-over of property. In September 1994, Iraq informed me that once a damaged C-130 aircraft had been dismantled and returned, it would have "nothing else whatever to return". Kuwait responded by transmitting to me what it described as "an indicative but far from exhaustive list" of Kuwaiti property that had yet to be returned. It has also stressed the importance it attaches to the return of irreplaceable archives.

710.   In January 1995, Kuwait transmitted a list of military equipment belonging to the Ministry of Defence that it claimed was still in the possession of Iraq. Arrangements were made for the hand-over, which began on 22 April 1995 and continued into July 1995. On many of the hand-over documents signed by the parties, Kuwait complained of the state of disrepair of the items returned while Iraq, for its part, noted that the vehicles had been "brought as is from Kuwait". Kuwait also noted that of 120 armoured personnel carriers handed over, only 33 were found to belong to Kuwait.

711.   Among a number of urgent humanitarian issues to which the situation between Iraq and Kuwait has given rise is the fate of over 600 Kuwaiti and third-country nationals who are still missing in Iraq. I have urged Iraq to cooperate with the International Committee of the Red Cross so that a full accounting may be achieved.

712.   The suffering of the Iraqi civilian population is also of considerable concern to me. On a number of occasions I have urged Iraqi officials to accept the Security Council's "oil for food" formula described in resolutions 706(1991) and 712(1991). I believe the Council's latest offer in resolution 986(1995) addresses the humanitarian needs of the Iraqi people while taking into account a number of concerns Iraq had previously expressed over resolutions 706(1991) and 712(1991). I can only regret that Iraq has not yet accepted this temporary humanitarian measure, which would indeed be an important step towards overcoming the crisis which exists between Iraq and the international community.

713.   I have made every effort to comply with Security Council resolution 778(1992), of 2 October 1992, in which the Council requested me to ascertain the whereabouts and amounts of assets related to Iraqi petroleum and petroleum products which could be deposited to the escrow account, as well as the existence of any Iraqi petroleum and petroleum products that could be sold. I regret to note that no further funds have been deposited into the account as a result of my effort to seek information on such assets directly from Governments with jurisdiction over relevant petroleum companies and their subsidiaries. As at 1 August 1995, $365.5 million, representing voluntary contributions and Iraqi petroleum assets, had been deposited into the escrow account since the adoption of resolution 778(1992).

714.   The United Nations recognizes Iraq's obligation to pay compensation to the victims of its aggression. The Commission established to administer the United Nations Compensation Fund, provided for in paragraph 18 of Security Council resolution 687(1991), has held four regular sessions since August 1994. During that period, its Gov-

erning Council has approved the reports and recommendations of Panels of Commissioners and issued decisions for three instalments of category "A" (departure) claims; two instalments of category "B" (serious personal injury and death) claims; and one instalment of category "C" (individual losses up to $100,000) claims. In issuing its decisions, the Governing Council awarded over $1.3 billion in compensation to 354,920 successful claimants.

715.   Unfortunately, with the exception of approximately $2.7 million paid to the first 670 successful claimants in category "B" in May 1994, and approximately $8.1 million to be paid to 2,562 category "B" claimants in 1995, depending on the availability of funds, the remaining awards of the Compensation Commission have gone unpaid owing to the lack of sufficient resources in the Compensation Fund.

716.   During 1994, the lack of adequate funding affected all sectors covered by the United Nations Inter-Agency Humanitarian Programme. In terms of food assistance, the bulk of donations was earmarked for the "Autonomous Region" (Governorates of Erbil, Dohuk and Suleimaniyah). According to reports of the World Food Programme, approximately 70 per cent of food requirements had been met in the north and only 40 per cent in the centre and south. As a result of lack of resources, a substantial amount of the food destined for the centre and south was covered by counterpart matching funds from the United Nations escrow account.

717.   Health conditions have continued to deteriorate throughout the country because of shortages of essential drugs and medical supplies. The situation is further aggravated by the inadequate supply of potable water and poor sanitation facilities, as essential equipment and spare parts are lacking to rehabilitate the water, sewage and electricity supply systems.

718.   With respect to security, since early December 1994, armed conflicts between members of the two major political parties have been reported in the northern Governorates of Erbil and Suleimaniyah. Moreover, the recent Turkish military operations on the Turkish/Iraq border, and in particular near Zakho (Dohuk Governorate), resulted in restrictions on the movements of humanitarian aid workers and relief commodities.

719.   By the end of April 1995, the strength of the United Nations Guards Contingent in Iraq had been reduced from a high of over 500 in 1991 to 50 guards, the majority deployed in the "Autonomous Region" for the protection of humanitarian personnel. As a result of recent donor contributions received in support of the Guards Contingent, arrangements are under way for the assignment of an additional 100 guards during the

summer of 1995. In a tense and volatile environment such as Northern Iraq, the continued presence of the Guards Contingent is required to protect United Nations and non-governmental organization personnel as well as assets and operations linked with the United Nations Inter-Agency Humanitarian Programme.

720.   Under the previous appeal (covering the period from 1 April 1994 to 31 March 1995), the United Nations Inter-Agency Humanitarian Programme continued to provide humanitarian assistance to vulnerable population groups throughout the country. Projects implemented by United Nations agencies and programmes and humanitarian non-governmental organizations covered all the priority sectors included in the appeal, with particular emphasis on food, health, water and sanitation, agriculture, shelter and rural integration, and education. Response to the previous appeal was inadequate, with approximately 51 per cent ($146 million) of overall Programme requirements ($288.5 million) covered by allocations of voluntary contributions, "matching" funds from the United Nations escrow account and carry-over from the previous phase. From this amount, funding for United Nations–directed humanitarian activities amounted to $92.5 million, while contributions made available to humanitarian non-governmental organizations and other direct/bilateral programmes amounted to $53.5 million.

721.   On 21 March 1995 at Geneva, during a donor consultation meeting for Iraq, the United Nations launched a consolidated inter-agency humanitarian appeal for Iraq covering the period from April 1995 to March 1996. The Programme, which calls for a total of $183.3 million, is designed to address only the most essential needs to sustain relief and rehabilitation activities as well as to prevent a further deterioration of the conditions affecting the most vulnerable population groups throughout the country. Since April 1995, approximately $27 million (representing voluntary contributions and "matching" funds from the United Nations escrow account) has been pledged/received in support of United Nations–directed activities in Iraq. In addition, a number of direct contributions have been made in support of humanitarian non-governmental organizations and bilateral programmes in northern Iraq.

722.   Under the current appeal, humanitarian needs continue to increase in practically all sectors covered by the Programme, in particular in the nutrition and health sectors. By all accounts, children are increasingly dying of ailments linked to malnutrition and lack of adequate medical care. The World Health Organization reports a rise in tuberculosis and an acute shortage of essential drugs and medical equipment in hospitals. At least 4 million people are in need of food assistance and

hunger threatens the lives of over 1 million among them. As of June 1995, because of rapidly depleted food stocks in the "Autonomous Region", the World Food Programme decided to reduce food distributions from 350,000 to only 300,000 people. In the centre and south, from a targeted 550,000 case-load, WFP was able to continue feeding only some 60,000 vulnerable people in social institutions. The support of the international community is urgently required to cover outstanding needs for the procurement and warehousing of food, medicines and shelter materials before the onset of winter.

### 14.   Korean peninsula

723.   I have continued to follow closely developments in the Korean peninsula. I am pleased to note that, in implementation of the October 1994 Framework Agreement between the Democratic People's Republic of Korea and the United States of America, the two countries reached agreement in June on the provision of two light-water reactors to the Democratic People's Republic of Korea and that discussions are in progress on the question of safe storage of the spent fuel removed from that country's reactors. In addition, trade and communications barriers between the two countries have been lowered, and liaison offices in the respective capitals are expected to open in the near future.

724.   Hopefully, progress in these areas will contribute to steady improvement of the situation on the Korean peninsula, especially through the re-establishment of the North-South dialogue. I remain ready to provide any good offices which the parties might find useful. I plan to visit the Republic of Korea in September 1995 and intend to go to the Democratic People's Republic of Korea in the first half of 1996 on a mission of goodwill.

### 15.   Liberia

725.   The United Nations Observer Mission in Liberia (UNOMIL) was established under Security Council resolution 856(1993) of 10 August 1993 to work with the Monitoring Group (ECOMOG) of the Economic Community of West African States (ECOWAS) in the implementation of the Cotonou Peace Agreement signed between the Liberian parties on 25 July 1993. However, delays and obstacles created by different Liberian factions with respect to the Agreement necessitated a range of subsequent agreements between the factions, and the work of UNOMIL had to continue far beyond the original time-frame of the Security Council resolution.

726.   Initial progress was made under the Cotonou Peace Agreement and this encouraged the Security Council, by its resolution 911(1994) of 21 April 1994, to extend the mandate of

UNOMIL until 22 October 1994, with the expectation that the Mission would be terminated in December 1994. Subsequently, the situation in Liberia took a negative turn as fighting intensified between factions and the whole peace process came to a standstill.

727. My Special Envoy, Mr. Lakhdar Brahimi, visited Liberia from 16 to 26 August 1994 in order to assist me in determining options for the United Nations in facilitating the peace process. Shortly thereafter, the Chairman of ECOWAS, President Jerry Rawlings of Ghana, convened a meeting of the factions at Akosombo, Ghana, on 7 September to review the delays in implementing the peace process. This meeting resulted in the signing at Akosombo, on 12 September, of a supplementary agreement to the Cotonou Peace Agreement.

728. The conclusion of the Akosombo Agreement coincided with an upsurge of fighting in Liberia and, on 9 September, 43 unarmed United Nations military observers and six non-governmental organization personnel were detained. By 18 September, they had all been released or otherwise found their way to safety. In September 1994, with the breakdown in the cease-fire, and the fact that the security of unarmed military observers could not be assured, I restricted UNOMIL military operations to the greater Monrovia area and reduced the Mission's military component from its authorized strength of 368 to approximately 90 observers.

729. In mid-November, I sent a high-level mission, led by the Assistant Secretary-General for Political Affairs, to the region to consult with the Chairman of ECOWAS and the heads of ECOWAS States on how best to revive the peace process. Soon thereafter, the Chairman of ECOWAS carried out further consultations with the Liberian parties and interest groups, which led to the signing of a further agreement at Accra on 21 December 1994.

730. The Accra Agreement, unlike the Akosombo Agreement, was signed by all the Liberian factions and attempted to clarify the Akosombo Agreement. Other than a new cease-fire which came into effect on 28 December 1994, the factions failed to implement all the other major elements of the Accra Agreement, including the decision to form a new Council of State. The cease-fire, while re-established on 28 December, again broke down in early February 1995.

731. On 28 December, my new Special Representative for Liberia, Mr. Anthony Nyakyi (United Republic of Tanzania), took up his office in Monrovia. Since then Mr. Nyakyi has been consulting the Liberian factions, the Chairman of ECOWAS, as well as the Heads of State of ECOWAS, with a view to facilitating the search for a peaceful solution to the continuing hostilities.

732. In its resolution 972(1995) of 13 January 1995, the Security Council expressed deep concern over the Liberian situation. It also expressed the hope that a summit of the ECOWAS States would be convened to harmonize their policies on Liberia, in particular the application of the arms embargo imposed by the Security Council in resolution 788(1992). On 11 March 1995, President Rawlings of Ghana and I agreed at a meeting in Copenhagen that, subject to the concurrence of the Nigerian Head of State, a summit of the ECOWAS Committee of Nine would be held at Abuja.

733. In my ninth progress report to the Security Council of 24 February 1995 (S/1995/158), I conveyed specific options to the Council, including the provision of necessary resources to ECOMOG if the Liberian factions would demonstrate readiness to implement the Accra Agreement. I express my appreciation to the countries contributing troops to ECOMOG; they have made enormous sacrifices since the operation was launched in 1990.

734. On 13 April 1995, the Security Council adopted resolution 985(1995) extending the mandate of UNOMIL until 30 June 1995. Following extensive consultations between the Chairman of ECOWAS and the West African Heads of State and several contacts between the Chairman and myself, the third meeting of Heads of State and Government of the ECOWAS Committee of Nine on Liberia was held at Abuja from 17 to 20 May 1995. The Heads of State of Côte d'Ivoire, the Gambia, Ghana, Liberia, Mali, Nigeria, Sierra Leone and Togo attended the meeting. Burkina Faso and Guinea were represented by their Foreign Ministers. The Senior Minister at the Presidency for Governmental Affairs and National Defence of Benin and the Minister of African Economic Integration of Senegal also attended. My Special Envoy, Mr. Vladimir Petrovsky, and my Special Representative for Liberia, Mr. Anthony Nyakyi, were also present, as were the Eminent Person for Liberia of the Organization of African Unity, Reverend Canaan Banana, and the Special Envoy for Liberia of the United States of America, Mr. Dane Smith.

735. Delegations were sent by the following Liberian parties: the Armed Forces of Liberia (AFL), the Lofa Defense Force (LDF), the Liberia National Conference (LNC), the Liberian Peace Council (LPC), the National Patriotic Front of Liberia (NPFL), the Central Revolutionary Council of the National Patriotic Front of Liberia (CRC-NPFL), Alhaji Kromah's wing of the United Liberation Movement of Liberia for Democracy (ULIMO-K) and General Roosevelt Johnson's wing of ULIMO (ULIMO-J). Mr. David Kpomakpor, the current Chairman of the Council of State, participated in the meeting. Delegations of all the

Liberian factions except NPFL were headed by their respective leaders. At the invitation of the Government of Nigeria, Mr. Charles Taylor, the leader of NPFL and the only Liberian faction leader who did not attend the ECOWAS summit, travelled to Abuja on 2 June for consultations with Nigerian officials. On 10 June 1995, I submitted my eleventh progress report on UNOMIL to the Security Council (S/1995/473). By unanimously adopting resolution 1001(1995) on 30 June 1995, the Council extended the mandate of UNOMIL until 15 September 1995 and declared that unless serious and substantial progress was made towards a peaceful settlement, the Mission would not be renewed after that date. The Council urged the Liberian parties to use the Mission's extension to implement the peace process envisaged in the Akosombo and Accra agreements of 1994, particularly their provisions on the installation of the Council of State; the re-establishment of a comprehensive and effective cease-fire; the disengagement of all forces; and the creation of a timetable for the implementation of disarmament agreements.

736. My Special Representative conveyed to the Liberian factions the contents of Security Council resolution 1001(1995) and urged them to abandon their selfish, narrow interests and agree on positive urgent steps to bring peace to their country. The Liberian factions also held a consultative meeting, with the exception of NPFL, on 19 July which was attended by my Special Representative and the representatives of OAU and ECOWAS.

737. The eighteenth summit meeting of ECOWAS was held at Accra on 28 and 29 July 1995, and was attended by the Heads of State of Benin, Côte d'Ivoire, Ghana, Guinea, Liberia and the Niger. In his report to the Committee of Nine, the Chairman of ECOWAS (the President of Ghana) pointed out that positive developments, which he characterized as confidence-building measures, had taken place since the last Abuja summit. He also referred to the recent Monrovia consultative meetings and deplored the fact that, despite all efforts made, some of the outstanding issues remained unresolved. He referred to Security Council resolution 1001(1995) and explained the final deadline set by the Council. He called on the United Nations to continue assisting the peace process.

738. The Liberian factional leaders agreed on 19 August 1995 to end hostilities and to hold elections within a year. The cease-fire in Liberia came into force on 26 August 1995.

739. In the context of Security Council resolution 1001(1995), if serious and substantial progress is achieved by 15 September, it was agreed that the Council would consider restoring UNOMIL to its full strength, with appropriate adjustment of its mandate and its relationship with ECOMOG, including matters relating to post-conflict peace-building in Liberia. In this regard, the swearing in of a Council of State for Liberia on 1 September 1995 gives rise to hopes for a new momentum for peace. The assistance of the international community will be crucial in this regard.

740. On 15 January 1995, I launched the United Nations consolidated inter-agency appeal for Liberia. The appeal sought $65 million required by United Nations agencies and programmes to meet the life-saving needs of the 1.8 million Liberians affected by the war. As at 10 August, the international donors' community had contributed 71 per cent of the funds requested.

741. United Nations humanitarian agencies and programmes, in cooperation with non-governmental organizations, have developed agreed protocols for carrying out relief work in Liberia. Guided by these principles, the humanitarian assistance community will continue to work with my Special Representative to gain access to as many war-affected civilians as possible.

## 16. The Middle East

742. In the course of the past year, significant results were achieved in the Middle East peace process, signalling the parties' continued commitment to proceed on the road to peace. An outstanding achievement was the conclusion, on 26 October 1994, of the historic Treaty of Peace between the State of Israel and the Hashemite Kingdom of Jordan. I warmly welcome this momentous agreement, which ended a decades-long state of war.

743. Israel and the Palestine Liberation Organization (PLO) continued the implementation of their Declaration of Principles on Interim Self-Government Arrangements, signed on 13 September 1993. By December 1994, the Palestinian Authority, which had been established in May in most of the Gaza Strip and the Jericho area, was given responsibility for health, education, social welfare, tourism and direct taxation in the other areas of the West Bank. Israel and the PLO are at present negotiating the redeployment of Israeli military forces in the West Bank and the holding of elections for the Palestinian Council; interim understandings on an agreement have been reached by leaders on both sides.

744. Meanwhile, multilateral negotiations on Middle East regional issues have proceeded, creating a network of common projects among countries in the region. The United Nations participates actively in the multilateral negotiations as a full extraregional participant.

745. Hope has been generated by these encouraging signs that progress can be accelerated in the Israeli-Lebanese and Israeli-Syrian negotiations leading to a comprehensive, just and last-

ing peace in the Middle East, based on Security Council resolutions 242(1967), 338(1973) and 425(1978).

746.  The Israeli-Palestinian peace talks have been complicated and set back, on more than one occasion, by terrorist attacks from enemies of peace in which dozens of civilians have been killed and wounded. I have condemned these incidents and I am encouraged by the determination of Israeli and Palestinian leaders to continue the peace process.

747.  In addition, concern in the international community has been generated by the Government of Israel's decisions to expropriate land and expand settlements in the occupied territories. The subject was taken up in deliberations in the Security Council at its formal meetings on 28 February 1995 and 12 May 1995.

748.  The peace process needs broad public support and without a visible improvement in the living conditions of the Palestinians this support will remain fragile. In this connection, I have to draw attention to the damaging effects which closures of the occupied territories by Israel have had on the nascent Palestinian economy.

749.  In its efforts to support the Arab-Israeli peace process, the United Nations has placed special emphasis on sustainable economic and social development in the occupied territories. The United Nations Special Coordinator, Mr. Terje Rod Larsen, has been active in strengthening local coordination between agencies and programmes of the United Nations system, the Bretton Woods institutions and the donor community. He works in close cooperation with the Palestinian Authority and the Palestinian Economic Council for Development and Reconstruction. The first results of the international assistance efforts are already visible, especially in institution-building and the infrastructure.

750.  In southern Lebanon hostilities have continued at a high level between Israeli forces and armed elements that have proclaimed their resistance to Israeli occupation. On several occasions civilian targets on both sides came under attack. I have called for restraint and urged the parties to refrain from attacking civilians.

751.  The United Nations Interim Force in Lebanon (UNIFIL) has sought to limit the conflict and to protect inhabitants from violence. In resolution 1006(1995) of 28 July 1995, the Security Council reaffirmed the mandate of UNIFIL as defined in its resolution 425(1978) and subsequent resolutions, to confirm the withdrawal of Israeli forces, restore international peace and security, and assist the Government of Lebanon in ensuring the return of its effective authority in the area. Although UNIFIL has not been able to make visible progress towards these objectives, it has con-

tributed to stability in the area and afforded a measure of protection to the population of southern Lebanon. On the basis of the request for my good offices regarding the detainees held in Khiam jail in the area controlled by the Israel Defence Forces in southern Lebanon, I have authorized the appropriate contacts in that regard.

752.  In July 1994, I initiated a study to determine how UNIFIL could perform its essential functions with reduced strength in view of the long-term problem of the shortfall in its assessed contributions. By its resolution 1006(1995), the Security Council approved my proposal for a streamlining, which will result in a 10 per cent reduction of the Force's strength and direct savings of $10 million a year. This will not affect UNIFIL's operational capacity.

753.  The United Nations Disengagement Observer Force (UNDOF) continued to supervise the area of separation between the Israeli and Syrian forces and the areas of limitation of armaments and forces provided for in the disengagement agreement of 1974. With the cooperation of both sides, UNDOF has discharged its tasks effectively and its area of operation has been quiet.

754.  The United Nations Truce Supervision Organization (UNTSO), which is the oldest existing peace-keeping operation, has continued to assist UNDOF and UNIFIL in carrying out their tasks and has maintained its presence in Egypt. A streamlining undertaken by UNTSO is under way and will result in a 20 per cent reduction of its strength and corresponding savings in expenditures.

### 17.  Mozambique

755.  Over a three-day period from 27 to 29 October 1994, Mozambique conducted, with the assistance and support of the United Nations, the first free and fair multi-party elections in the country's history. The elections brought together in an open democratic contest the ruling Frente de Libertação de Moçambique (FRELIMO) and the Resistência Nacional Moçambicana (RENAMO), the country's two major political parties and former foes. Immediately after the results of the election were announced, my Special Representative declared the elections free and fair, based on reports from United Nations observers. This was fully supported by the Security Council. This was a welcome change from a long-running conflict that had claimed the lives of tens of thousands of people, driven millions from their homes and destroyed much of Mozambique's economic and social infrastructure. The elections were the culmination of a major success story in United Nations peacemaking, peace-keeping, and humanitarian and electoral assistance.

756.  The mandate entrusted to the United Nations Operation in Mozambique (ONUMOZ) by

the Security Council in resolution 797(1992) of 16 December 1992 was to verify and monitor the implementation of the General Peace Agreement, signed by the Government of Mozambique and RENAMO at Rome on 4 October 1992. The peace accords required the United Nations to supervise the cease-fire between the two parties, provide security for key transport corridors, monitor a comprehensive disarmament and demobilization programme, coordinate and monitor humanitarian assistance operations throughout the country, and provide assistance and verification for national elections. ONUMOZ subsequently undertook a number of additional tasks at the request of the parties.

757.    One of the most important aspects of the operation was the emphasis it placed on peace-building. ONUMOZ's unprecedented endeavours in this regard were concentrated not only in its oversight of the electoral process but also in the channelling of special trust funds to strengthen the organizational capacity of parties contesting the election. This was particularly important in regard to RENAMO. The transformation of a guerrilla force into a political entity with a stake in the democratic process is one of the most significant legacies of the United Nations operation.

758.    The final meeting of the Supervisory and Monitoring Commission established under the Rome Agreement was held on 6 December 1994. At that meeting, final reports were submitted by the Chairmen of the Cease-fire Commission, the Commission for the Formation of the Mozambican Defence Force, the Commission for Reintegration, the National Police Affairs Commission and the National Information Commission. My Special Representative, Mr. Aldo Ajello, handed these reports over to Mr. Joaquim Alberto Chissano, the President-elect. Subsequently, the new Assembly of the Republic was installed on 8 December, and the newly elected President of Mozambique was inaugurated the next day; he appointed his Government on 16 December. In accordance with paragraph 4 of Security Council resolution 797(1992), these events marked the expiry of the political mandate of ONUMOZ, and my Special Representative left Mozambique on 13 December 1994.

759.    The withdrawal of the military, police and civilian components of the Mission proceeded according to plan, beginning on 15 November 1994. A limited force of four infantry companies and medical personnel, a skeleton headquarters staff, demining personnel and a small number of military observers were retained to assist in residual operations and the liquidation phase of the Mission. With the official closure of ONUMOZ at the end of January 1995, a small number of United Nations civilian logisticians remained in Mozambique to deal with outstanding financial, legal and logistic issues.

760.    When the last ONUMOZ contingents departed from Mozambique in January 1995, they had overseen a remarkable transformation in the country, from the ravages of civil war to the implementation of democratic government and the creation of a peaceful environment in which economic activity could once again flourish. The strong commitment of the major participants to peace, along with firm support from the international community, were important prerequisites that enabled the United Nations to help bring about this transition. In this regard, neighbouring States played a vital role; first, in bringing the major participants to the negotiating table, and then in helping to sustain the peace process under ONUMOZ.

761.    Although both the General Peace Agreement and the ONUMOZ mandate were successfully implemented, a number of concerns requiring further action remained at the time of the Mission's withdrawal. These included, on the security front, the continuing need to train and equip the new integrated armed forces and to upgrade the police in accordance with Security Council resolution 898(1994) of 23 February 1994, while attending to the collection and disposal of outstanding caches of weapons. Mozambique also needed to strengthen its democratic institutions and to promote economic and social reconstruction so that peace, democracy and development could be sustained. While the last United Nations peace-keeping forces left Mozambique in January 1995, their colleagues from the development arm of the Organization remained behind to assist Mozambique in consolidating a peaceful and stable future.

762.    I should like to express my appreciation to the international community and to those programmes and organizations whose financial and technical assistance to the Mozambican authorities made it possible to hold the elections in an exemplary manner. There is agreement among the international community that ONUMOZ was a success. Key factors that contributed to this result include: the political will of the Mozambican people and their leaders, demonstrated by their strong commitment to peace and national reconciliation; the clarity of the ONUMOZ mandate and the consistent support provided by the Security Council; and the international community's strong political, financial and technical support of the peace process.

763.    The United Nations Office for Humanitarian Assistance Coordination (UNOHAC) was made the humanitarian component of ONUMOZ by the Security Council in resolution 797(1992). In the transition from war to reconciliation to peace, UNOHAC and its humanitarian assistance

partners addressed the emergency needs of between 4 and 5 million internally displaced persons, 1.5 million returning refugees and some 90,000 demobilized soldiers. Effective and coordinated humanitarian assistance activities helped to create conditions that allowed civilians affected by the war to begin rebuilding their lives. The success of the Consolidated Humanitarian Programme, developed by UNOHAC and its partners, received tremendous support from the international community, which contributed more than 82 per cent of the approximately $775 million required for execution of the Programme.

764. As the mandate of ONUMOZ neared termination in late 1994, UNOHAC focused its activities on ensuring completion of projects where possible, and on finalizing arrangements with humanitarian assistance partners in-country for the transfer of a number of responsibilities that would continue beyond the life of the peacekeeping operation.

765. One such hand-over involved the Trust Fund for Humanitarian Activities in Mozambique, established by the Department of Humanitarian Affairs to provide financial support for the implementation of 26 projects which were to be fully implemented only after the expiration of the ONUMOZ mandate on 15 November 1994. The Trust Fund financed a variety of critical activities within the Programme, including demobilization and reintegration of demobilized soldiers, emergency supply of non-food relief items, provision of seeds for the family sector, multisectoral area-based activities, and demining. In order to ensure effective continuation of these projects, the Department has passed responsibilities for trust fund project-monitoring and coordination to the office of the United Nations Development Programme in Maputo.

766. The area of demining also required carefully planned transition arrangements. The accelerated demining programme was designed by the Department of Humanitarian Affairs and UNOHAC to ensure that Mozambique would be provided with an indigenous demining capacity. The Department and UNDP agreed that at the expiration of the ONUMOZ mandate, UNDP would assume responsibility for the financial management of resources that are or will be made available for the implementation of the programme, while policy guidance and technical support for the programme would continue to be provided by the Department of Humanitarian Affairs.

767. The accelerated demining programme has established a Mozambican demining organization of 10 platoons (450 deminers), 15 supervisors, four survey teams, an Explosive Ordnance Disposal team, demining instructors, and the headquarters and support staff to manage the in-structors and the organization. In total, 500 Mozambicans are employed by the programme. Since the commencement of demining operations in September 1994, 5,000 anti-personnel mines and some 400,000 square metres of land have been cleared. The emphasis of the programme is on training in order fully to develop local mine-clearance capability, resulting in a sustainable Mozambican entity able to address Mozambique's long-term mine-clearance problems.

## 18. Myanmar

768. In keeping with the good offices mandate I received from the General Assembly and from the Commission on Human Rights, I have established a dialogue with the Government of Myanmar in order to address various issues of concern to the international community, in particular with respect to the process of democratization and national reconciliation in that country. During the period under review, my Representatives have held several rounds of talks in New York and Yangon with Secretary 1 of the State Law and Order Restoration Council, the Minister for Foreign Affairs and other authorities of the Government. In the talks, a series of ideas were discussed, which, if implemented, would assist in moving the process forward.

769. I welcome the Government's decision to lift the restrictions imposed on Daw Aung San Suu Kyi and to release a number of other political prisoners, including several leading members of the National League for Democracy. I look forward to further steps to speed up the return of multi-party democracy in Myanmar. I will report to the General Assembly at its fiftieth session on the progress of those discussions, which are being continued on my behalf at Yangon in August by the Assistant Secretary-General for Political Affairs.

## 19. Republic of Moldova

770. I visited the Republic of Moldova on 4 November 1994 to discuss rehabilitation efforts in the aftermath of the severe droughts, hurricanes and floods that hit the country in mid-1994. At its forty-eighth session, the General Assembly, upon appeal by President Mircea Ion Snegur, adopted a resolution on 14 September calling upon the Secretary-General, in cooperation with the relevant organs and organizations of the United Nations system, to assist in the rehabilitation efforts of the Government.

771. On 21 October 1994, the Republic of Moldova and the Russian Federation signed the agreement on the withdrawal of the Russian Federation's 14th army from the Trans-Dnestr region. Both countries have agreed that the withdrawal should be synchronized with a political settlement

of the Dnestr conflict. The withdrawal is anticipated to take place within three years.

772.   Following an earlier parliamentary decision, a large majority of ethnically-mixed districts taking part in the referendum held on 5 March 1995 decided to join the Gagauz autonomous region within the Republic of Moldova.

773.   The Organization for Security and Cooperation in Europe (OSCE) has been taking the leading role on issues concerning the Republic of Moldova since the OSCE mission was established in that country on 27 April 1993.

### 20.   Sierra Leone

774.   In December 1994, in response to a formal request from Captain Valentine Strasser, Head of State of the Republic of Sierra Leone, I dispatched an exploratory mission to that country to facilitate negotiations between the Government and the forces known as the Revolutionary United Front. That mission reported to me on the serious consequences of the three-year conflict in Sierra Leone. A significant percentage of the population had taken refuge in neighbouring countries or been internally displaced and most of the country's infrastructure had been destroyed. If the conflict continued, it would further complicate the problem of bringing peace to Liberia and could have a more general destabilizing effect in the region. On the basis of the mission's findings, I decided to appoint a Special Envoy for Sierra Leone, Mr. Berhanu Dinka, to help the parties to work towards a negotiated settlement.

775.   In April and May 1995, Captain Strasser announced that to restore democracy he would set up a national reconciliation conference to prepare for a return to civilian rule in 1996 and that a three-year ban on political parties was being rescinded. He called on the Revolutionary United Front to renounce its armed struggle and to join the electoral process, declaring that the Government was ready to enter into a cease-fire in order to negotiate peace without preconditions. However, the Front spurned the offer to end the armed struggle, stressing that dialogue was conditional on the withdrawal of foreign troops fighting alongside Sierra Leonean armed forces. Notwithstanding these difficulties, my Special Envoy is continuing his efforts to help bring about a settlement of the conflict.

776.   On 26 May, I congratulated the Head of State of Sierra Leone on the democratic initiatives announced on 27 April, in particular the lifting of the ban on political parties. On 22 June, the National Provisional Ruling Council issued a decree barring for the next 10 years 57 persons, including presidents, vice-presidents, ministers, ministers of State and deputy ministers, from holding any public office or holding office in any corporation in which the State held a financial in-

terest, from being elected president of the Republic or member of parliament, or from being elected to or holding office in any local body. According to the Government, the ban was based on the findings of two commissions of inquiry.

777.   On 20 July, seven prospective political parties jointly petitioned the Head of State to repeal restrictive elements of the decree lifting the ban on political parties. Further complicating matters, on 25 July the Sierra Leone Bar Association refused to attend the National Consultative Conference on Elections (15-17 August), linking its refusal to participate to the decree banning 57 persons from holding political office and restrictions placed on political parties by the Government.

778.   It is widely recognized that the conflict in Sierra Leone cannot be resolved through military means. It is important therefore for the Revolutionary United Front to respond positively to the Government's offer to negotiate a settlement of the conflict. The sixty-second ordinary session of the Council of Ministers of OAU adopted a resolution expressing concern over the worsening conflict. I call upon the international community to support the United Nations efforts to ensure that peace and democracy prevail in Sierra Leone.

779.   Following a series of rebel attacks that began late in 1994, thousands of Sierra Leoneans were forced to leave their homes and thousands more sought asylum in neighbouring States. As a result, the total number of internally displaced persons in Sierra Leone is estimated at over 500,000 persons. They are concentrated in and around Freetown, as well as in a number of towns in eastern and central Sierra Leone, including Bo, Kenema, Makeni, Segbwema and Daru. In Freetown, it is estimated that the influx has swollen the population threefold, to 1.5 million persons. The overall result of these developments is characterized by, among other things, overcrowding in a small number of areas, acute shortages of basic survival requirements and the breakdown of overburdened infrastructure.

780.   In response to these developments, the Inter-Agency Standing Committee (IASC) took up the question of Sierra Leone at a meeting in February. The Standing Committee is composed of the executive heads of the United Nations humanitarian organizations as well as ICRC, the International Federation of Red Cross and Red Crescent Societies, the International Organization for Migration and the non-governmental consortia International Council of Voluntary Agencies, Interaction and the Steering Committee for Humanitarian Response. As a result of the discussions held, the working group of the Inter-Agency Standing Committee was charged with developing the terms of reference for an inter-agency appeal for resources required by United Nations or-

ganizations to meet emergency needs. The result was the United Nations inter-agency appeal for new refugee flows and populations affected by the humanitarian situation in Sierra Leone. From March to December 1995, the appeal sought $14.6 million to respond to the unmet needs of internally displaced persons within Sierra Leone, as well as those of the new outflow of Sierra Leonean refugees who had recently fled to the Forecariah region of Guinea. There has not yet been any response to the appeal.

781. As well as being limited by resource mobilization difficulties, humanitarian assistance efforts have been hindered by the prevailing security situation, which led to a withdrawal of United Nations international staff to Freetown in late January 1995. However, humanitarian activities continue on a smaller scale, with the involvement of national staff and the utilization of innovative implementation methods.

782. The office of the United Nations Resident Coordinator has developed an emergency information management system to ensure that United Nations organizations respond to the humanitarian crisis in Sierra Leone in a coordinated and complementary manner. The system will gather and analyse data required by the relief community to develop and target programmes for affected populations.

783. At its meeting on 2 June, the Inter-Agency Standing Committee further decided to pursue these efforts by dispatching an inter-agency mission to assess the coordination of humanitarian assistance activities in Sierra Leone. The mission, led by a representative of the Department of Humanitarian Affairs, recommended a strengthening of the capacity of the United Nations to support the Government's efforts to coordinate the emergency relief response in Sierra Leone. Actions have been taken to implement this recommendation through the placement of experienced personnel within the office of the Resident Coordinator.

### 21. Somalia

784. During the 12 months since my last report, it has become evident that the humanitarian tragedy in Somalia has been overcome, thanks to the international humanitarian assistance supported by the United Nations Operation in Somalia (UNOSOM II). This achievement contrasts sharply with the lack of tangible progress in national political reconciliation, for which the responsibility must be borne by the Somali leaders and people. Because of the deteriorating security situation in the country, including attacks and harassment directed against UNOSOM II and other international personnel, and because of the lack of cooperation from the Somali leaders concerned, the continued presence of UNOSOM II became increasingly questioned.

785. On 14 October 1994, I reported to the Security Council (S/1994/1166) that the Somali leaders still had not carried out commitments entered into under the Addis Ababa Agreement and the Nairobi Declaration. The UNOSOM goal of assisting the process of political reconciliation was becoming ever more elusive, while the burden and cost of maintaining a high level of troops were proving increasingly difficult for Member States to justify. The presence of UNOSOM II troops was having a limited impact on the peace process and on security in the face of continuing inter-clan fighting and banditry.

786. I therefore recommended that if the Security Council maintained its previous decision to end the mission in March 1995 and to withdraw all UNOSOM II forces and assets, it should extend the mission's mandate until 31 March 1995 to allow the time required to ensure a secure and orderly withdrawal. At the same time, I stressed that the withdrawal of UNOSOM II would not mean United Nations abandonment of Somalia. However, although humanitarian organizations were committed to continuing their work in Somalia, they could continue doing so only in a secure environment for which Somali leaders would bear the ultimate responsibility. The United Nations would also remain ready to assist the Somali parties in the process of national reconciliation.

787. On 26 and 27 October 1994, before taking a decision on the withdrawal of UNOSOM II, the Council sent a mission to Somalia to convey its views directly to the Somali leaders. The mission concluded that 31 March 1995 was the appropriate date for the end of the mandate of UNOSOM II. None of the Somali factions, humanitarian agencies or non-governmental organizations had requested a longer extension.

788. On 1 November, the United Somali Congress/Somali National Alliance (USC/SNA), led by General Mohamed Farah Aidid, and other factions convened a unilateral national reconciliation conference in south Mogadishu. This was against the advice and warning of the Security Council mission and my Special Representative, Mr. Victor Gbeho, who had warned that the convening of such a conference before the question of participation in it was resolved would be a recipe for continued strife.

789. On 4 November, by its resolution 954(1994), the Council extended the mandate of UNOSOM II for a final period until 31 March 1995. On 10 November, I transmitted to the Council a statement by the Inter-Agency Standing Committee reaffirming the commitment of the humanitarian agencies to continue their emergency and rehabilitation work in Somalia after the expiration of the UNOSOM mandate. The President of the Security Council, on behalf of the Council's mem-

bers, wrote to me on 7 December welcoming the commitment of the agencies. The Council also encouraged me to play a facilitating or moderating role in Somalia after March 1995 if the Somali parties were willing to cooperate.

790. Prior to the withdrawal of UNOSOM II, General Aidid and Mr. Ali Mahdi signed a peace agreement on behalf of the SNA and the Somali Salvation Alliance (SSA), respectively. In February they also signed three other agreements to manage the operations of the Mogadishu airport and seaport by a joint committee. The Mogadishu seaport was reopened to civilian traffic on 9 March. I was encouraged by the signing of these agreements, which helped to avert fighting over the facilities.

791. The withdrawal of the 15,000 United Nations troops, as well as civilian personnel, facilities and property from Somalia, began in November 1994. In response to my request, seven Member States joined forces in providing support and security for the withdrawal. To that end they established a combined task force, "United Shield", composed of France, India, Italy, Malaysia, Pakistan, the United Kingdom of Great Britain and Northern Ireland and the United States of America, under U.S. command. I announced on 2 March that the withdrawal had been completed in a safe and orderly manner, ahead of schedule and virtually without a problem. I again emphasized that the United Nations effort could continue and that the United Nations would not abandon Somalia.

792. On 28 March, I submitted to the Security Council a general assessment of the United Nations achievements in political, humanitarian, military and security matters and the police and justice programme. I recalled that, in late 1992, some 3,000 Somalis had been dying daily of starvation; that tragedy had been ended by the international relief effort. However, the endeavour to achieve political reconciliation had not succeeded because of the lack of political will among the Somali leaders. The international community could only facilitate, encourage and assist the process; it could neither impose peace nor coerce unwilling parties into accepting it.

793. In a presidential statement of 6 April (S/PRST/1995/15), the Council supported my view that Somalia should not be abandoned by the United Nations and welcomed my intention to maintain a small political mission, should the Somali parties so wish, to assist them in achieving national reconciliation. However, the SNA, then headed by General Aidid, expressed objection to a United Nations political presence and role in Somalia, although a wide range of Somali leaders representing the main factions, including a wing of the USC/SNA, had called for such a pres-

ence. In view of these divisions among the Somali parties, I have concluded that, for the time being, a political office, headed by Mr. Abdul Hamid Kabia, should monitor the situation from Nairobi. It is my intention to relocate the political office to Mogadishu when the necessary conditions exist, including adequate security. The President of the Security Council conveyed to me in his letter of 2 June (S/1995/452) the agreement of the members of the Council with my decision.

794. On 15 June, General Aidid was named "interim president" by his supporters. Following his announcement of a unilateral "government", General Aidid made an attempt to claim Somalia's seat at the OAU summit meeting, but OAU refused to recognize his "government" and decided to keep Somalia's seat open until a generally accepted government was formed. OAU urged the Somali leaders urgently to promote dialogue to ensure the formation of a broad-based national authority.

795. I remain convinced that a durable political settlement through national reconciliation is an indispensable prerequisite for the re-establishment of government, restoration of law and order, and rehabilitation and reconstruction in Somalia, and that the attainment of national reconciliation for the sake of the common good is well within the power of the Somali leaders. It is my hope that they will find the strength and the courage to pursue a more productive peace process in the coming weeks.

796. Coordination of the United Nations humanitarian assistance programme was, until December 1994, the sole responsibility of the Division for Coordination of Humanitarian Affairs of UNOSOM, which was headed by a Humanitarian Coordinator. The Division's tasks included fielding humanitarian affairs officers throughout the country, coordinating inter-agency assessment missions, providing funding for small-scale projects, assisting with emergencies, building essential structures such as schools and clinics, digging wells, facilitating the protection of humanitarian relief convoys, providing logistical support to humanitarian partners, holding security briefings and information-sharing meetings with United Nations agencies and non-governmental organizations, and providing support to local bodies such as district and regional councils.

797. In October 1994, when it became apparent that the UNOSOM mandate would not be extended and the Division would be dismantled, the agencies established a United Nations Coordination Team, chaired by the Resident Representative of UNDP (who was later appointed United Nations Humanitarian Coordinator) and composed of representatives of United Nations agencies and IOM, to manage the transition to a post-UNOSOM

period and to ensure the continued coordination of the United Nations humanitarian assistance programme. The Coordination Team works in close cooperation with both international and Somali non-governmental organization consortia. It also works to support the coordination efforts of the Somalia Aid Coordination Body, a consortium of donor Governments, United Nations agencies and organizations, and international non-governmental organizations.

798.   In 1994, no consolidated inter-agency appeal for Somalia was issued. Instead, United Nations agencies presented their requirements and plans for that year through a document prepared for the Fourth Humanitarian Coordination Meeting, held at Addis Ababa from 29 November to 1 December 1993. Consequently, in 1994 there was no systematic tracking of contributions received by various agencies for Somalia as is ordinarily done by the Department of Humanitarian Affairs under the procedures adopted for consolidated inter-agency appeals. The agencies nevertheless reported that their programmes were relatively well funded, although implementation was hindered by security conditions in the country.

799.   Despite the absence of political progress in Somalia, significant gains have been made on the humanitarian front over the past year. Agencies and organizations have focused their efforts on community-based community initiatives, providing support to capacity-building programmes while assisting local non-governmental and community-based organizations in the areas of relief and initial rehabilitation. Direct support was provided in the form of supplies, training and management services. Food-for-work schemes replaced free food distributions as the preferred mode of delivering food assistance, while agricultural assistance took the form of targeted initiatives rather than the large-scale distributions of seeds and tools undertaken in previous years.

800.   It was possible in 1994 to undertake modest rehabilitation activities in areas where relative security existed. In other areas, however, incidences of kidnapping of humanitarian aid workers occurred, while operations continued to be vulnerable to frequent labour disputes and subjected to unrealistic demands for the payment of security services. The humanitarian agencies expect that for the foreseeable future they will continue to operate against a background of uncertainty. The United Nations agencies nevertheless believe that they can, with the direct support of the Somali people and their leaders, collectively assist Somalia to progress into a new era of rehabilitation, recovery and development.

801.   In view of this, the Department of Humanitarian Affairs launched a consolidated inter-agency appeal for Somalia, covering a period of six months beginning in January 1995. The organizations participating in the appeal requested a total of $70.3 million for their activities during the first half of 1995.

802.   To date the consolidated inter-agency appeal for Somalia has received under 20 per cent of the resources requested. It is essential that funding for the humanitarian relief and rehabilitation programmes be provided to ensure that progress made by the United Nations agencies, international organizations and national and international non-governmental organizations over the past three years is not reversed.

## 22.   Tajikistan

803.   The situation in Tajikistan, particularly on its border with Afghanistan, has remained unstable during the past year. My Special Envoy, Mr. Ramiro Píriz-Ballón, continues his efforts to mediate a political dialogue between the Government of Tajikistan and the opposition to achieve progress towards national reconciliation.

804.   High-level inter-Tajik consultations, held at Tehran in September 1994, resulted in the signing of an Agreement on a Temporary Cease-fire and the Cessation of Other Hostile Acts on the Tajik-Afghan Border and within the Country. The two parties also agreed on important confidence-building measures, including the exchange of prisoners and prisoners of war. The parties also agreed to establish a joint commission consisting of representatives of the Government and the opposition. They requested the Security Council to assist the work of the Joint Commission by providing political good offices and dispatching United Nations military observers.

805.   In my report to the Security Council dated 27 September 1994 (S/1994/1102), I recommended, as a provisional measure, the strengthening of the group of United Nations officials in Tajikistan with up to 15 military observers drawn from existing peace-keeping operations, pending a decision by the Council to establish a new United Nations observer mission in Tajikistan. The cease-fire came into effect on 20 October following the deployment of 15 military observers. A technical survey mission was immediately sent to the country to assess the modalities for establishing a future observer mission.

806.   The third round of inter-Tajik talks took place at Islamabad from 20 October to 1 November. The parties succeeded in extending the Agreement for another three months, until 6 February 1995, and also signed the protocol on the Joint Commission to monitor the implementation of the 17 September cease-fire agreement. On 30 November, I submitted a report to the Security Council recommending a possible United Nations peace-keeping operation in that country (S/1994/1363). On 16 December, the Council, by its resolution

968(1994), welcomed the extension of the cease-fire agreement by the Tajik parties and decided to establish the United Nations Mission of Observers in Tajikistan (UNMOT) in accordance with the plan outlined in my report.

807. Despite the agreement reached in Islamabad to hold the fourth round of inter-Tajik talks in Moscow in December 1994, the negotiating process was at a stalemate. In order to revitalize it, my Special Envoy undertook consultations with the Government of Tajikistan, leaders of the opposition and certain Governments in the region in December. In January 1995, a United Nations team held consultations at Tehran with the Tajik opposition leaders and high-ranking officials of the Islamic Republic of Iran.

808. The fourth round of inter-Tajik talks remained blocked as a result of conditions put forward by the opposition and by the plans of the Government to hold parliamentary elections in February. However, at the end of January, President Emomali Rakhmonov and Mr. Akhbar Turajonzodah, of the Tajik opposition delegation, informed me of their decision to extend the cease-fire agreement until 6 March 1995. In a report dated 4 February (S/1995/105), I informed the Security Council that the Tajik parties had complied only in part with the provisions of Security Council resolution 968(1994).

809. At the end of February, I asked Under-Secretary-General Aldo Ajello to hold consultations with the Tajik parties and some Governments in the region in order to reach agreement on the agenda, time and venue for the fourth round of inter-Tajik talks. He obtained the agreement of the parties to extend the cease-fire agreement until 26 April 1995 and made some progress in addressing the conditions stipulated by the opposition for the resumption of inter-Tajik talks.

810. My Special Envoy held new consultations with the Tajik parties and the Governments in the region, which resulted in high-level inter-Tajik consultations in Moscow from 19 to 26 April. The two sides agreed on the agenda and dates for the fourth round of inter-Tajik talks at Almaty, the extension of the cease-fire for another month and important additions to the cease-fire agreement and the protocol on the Joint Commission.

811. The fourth round of talks took place at Almaty from 22 May to 1 June. They followed the high-level consultations at Kabul from 17 to 19 May between the President of the Republic of Tajikistan and Mr. Abdullo Nuri, leader of the opposition Islamic Revival Movement of Tajikistan, under Afghan auspices, where it was decided to extend the cease-fire agreement for a further three months, until 26 August.

812. As I reported to the Security Council on 10 June (S/1995/472), at the Almaty talks the parties for the first time held an in-depth discussion of the fundamental institutional issues and the consolidation of the statehood of Tajikistan, as set forth in the first round of talks in Moscow in April 1994; however, they were unable to reach any decisions on those issues. The parties welcomed the decision of the Kabul summit meeting to extend the Tehran cease-fire agreement until 26 August and decided to implement a number of confidence-building measures by 20 July and to request the continuation of the good offices of my Special Envoy.

813. In its resolution 999(1995), the Security Council welcomed these decisions, called for the achievement of substantive progress on the fundamental political and institutional issues, and sought the convening of a further round of talks. It encouraged the dialogue between the President of Tajikistan and the leader of the Islamic Revival Movement of Tajikistan, and urged the substantial extension of the cease-fire agreement. The Council also called for discussions with the Afghan authorities on the possible deployment of a number of United Nations personnel inside Afghanistan.

814. In accordance with this, I dispatched my Special Envoy on 31 July to hold consultations in the region with the Tajik parties and with some Governments in order to create the conditions for a second summit meeting between President Rakhmonov and Mr. Nuri. At that meeting, to be held as soon as possible, it is hoped to obtain agreement on a set of general principles for a comprehensive political solution to be negotiated during the next stage.

815. The small United Nations Mission of Observers in Tajikistan has played an important role in containing the conflict. It has provided essential support to the Joint Commission set up by the parties as the main instrument for maintaining the cease-fire and it has been instrumental in containing local conflicts.

816. The establishment of UNMOT and the extension of its mandate last June for another six months were subject to the proviso that the Tehran cease-fire agreement of 17 September 1994 remain in force and the parties continue to be committed to an effective cease-fire, national reconciliation and the promotion of democracy. The Security Council thus underlined the primary responsibility of the parties themselves for composing their differences. It is to be hoped that they will use well the goodwill and support of interested Governments and the international community as a whole in order to make decisive progress towards that goal.

817. While improvements in the overall stability of conflict-affected areas of Tajikistan in 1994 led to the return of more than 90 per cent of former

refugees and internally displaced persons and to substantial progress in their reintegration, the country continues to face critical difficulties in conditions of tremendous economic hardship, especially in the most affected communities of the Khatlon region in the south-west, Gorno-Badakshan in the east and parts of the Garm Valley. Emergency food aid is a major source of nutrition for many of the most vulnerable. Many health centres have been destroyed; functioning ones lack basic equipment and drugs are often unavailable. Schools and hospitals lack water and sanitation facilities and many schools are not operating, which threatens to erode the high levels of literacy of past decades. Shortages of fuel have severely affected the country's production capacity. Inadequate employment opportunities compound the existing deep clan and regional divisions.

818. During 1994, the humanitarian community endeavoured to address the most pressing needs. Over 60 per cent of funding requested in the Department of Humanitarian Affairs' 1994 consolidated inter-agency appeal for Tajikistan ($42.5 million) was pledged or contributed. Humanitarian assistance also included capacity- and confidence-building activities, targeting areas of return of former refugees and internally displaced people.

819. The last mission to the country led by the Department of Humanitarian Affairs took place in October 1994. The mission held extensive consultations with the United Nations and non-governmental organization community to prepare proposals for humanitarian activities in 1995. The subsequent consolidated inter-agency appeal for Tajikistan (1 January–31 December 1995) was launched on 6 December 1994 and officially presented to donors on 23 March 1995 at Geneva. The appeal seeks to meet the most urgent humanitarian needs in-country (estimated at some $37.3 million) of some 600,000 people, who have been most affected by conflict, population movements and the deterioration of the economic, health and social infrastructures. By 31 March, $9.9 million, representing 53.4 per cent of funding requirements, had been contributed, as reported to the Department of Humanitarian Affairs by agencies making the appeal.

820. The current appeal aims to provide emergency food aid, as well as assistance in the health and education sectors. This assistance, provided in consultation with the humanitarian community, national and district authorities, targets the most vulnerable, including pensioners, invalids and widows with children, and returned and displaced people. Emphasis in the 1995 humanitarian programme is also on information management and capacity-building, with programmes aiming to assist in the training of health workers, community

development, capacity- and confidence-building, and self-reliance activities. The appeal also covers a number of non-governmental organization initiatives in addition to United Nations agencies and programmes, and is the result of efforts to enhance coordination and cooperation among humanitarian partners in the field. While substantial humanitarian needs remain, support to Tajikistan will focus increasingly on rehabilitation and economic development. United Nations agencies and programmes are thus phasing down relief activities and promoting development-oriented projects.

### 23. Western Sahara

821. The referendum for the self-determination of the people of Western Sahara, to be conducted by the United Nations in cooperation with OAU, should have taken place in January 1992. However, major differences in the interpretation of the main provisions of the settlement plan resulted in delays. None the less, agreement was reached on the interpretation of the criteria for eligibility to vote, which enabled the United Nations Mission for the Referendum in Western Sahara (MINURSO) to commence the identification and registration of potential voters on 28 August 1994. Also according to the plan, the cease-fire has been in effect since 6 September 1991.

822. During my visit to the mission area in late November 1994, the parties—Morocco and the Frente Popular para la Liberación de Saguia el-Hamra y de Río de Oro (Frente POLISARIO)—assured me of their commitment to the settlement plan. The two neighbouring countries, Algeria and Mauritania, also continued to support it firmly.

823. In my report to the Security Council of 14 December (S/1994/1420), I noted that, given the large number of applications received, the only way to complete the identification and registration process within a reasonable time-frame would be through a major reinforcement of personnel and other resources. In its resolution 973(1995) of 13 January, the Council approved my recommendation to expand MINURSO and requested me to report by 31 March to confirm 1 June 1995 as the date for the start of the transitional period. The Council also decided to extend the mandate of MINURSO until 31 May 1995.

824. On 30 March, I informed the Council that, while the rate of identification and registration was increasing steadily, the progress achieved as at that date did not permit me to recommend 1 June 1995 as the start of the transitional period. I explained that problems relating, in particular, to the timely availability of tribal leaders had caused interruptions in the identification operation. At the same time, some progress had been achieved in the implementation of other aspects of the Settlement Plan. I concluded that, if the par-

ties made it possible to raise the rate of identification to 25,000 per month, and if they cooperated in resolving expeditiously the remaining issues in the Settlement Plan, it might be possible for the transitional period to begin in August 1995 and to hold the referendum in January 1996.

825. In a presidential statement of 12 April (S/PRST/1995/17), the Security Council called upon both parties to cooperate fully with the United Nations to ensure prompt and full implementation of all aspects of the Settlement Plan. The Council hoped to see continuous and rapid progress by the time of my next report, in May 1995.

826. In that report (S/1995/404), I recommended that the mandate of MINURSO be extended for a period of four months. Following my report, the Security Council decided by its resolution 995(1995) of 26 May to extend the mandate of MINURSO for only one month and to send a mission to the region in order to accelerate the implementation of the Settlement Plan. The Mission held consultations with senior government officials at Rabat, Algiers and Nouakchott and with the POLISARIO leadership at Tindouf, and visited MINURSO headquarters at Laayoune.

827. In its report presented to the Council on 20 June (S/1995/498), the Mission indicated that, given the complexity of the tasks to be performed, the continuing delays caused by the two parties and the constraints imposed by the limited resources and local conditions, there was a real risk that the identification process might be extended beyond the time previously envisaged and that the referendum might not be held in January 1996.

828. On 23 June, the Frente POLISARIO announced its decision to suspend its participation in the identification operation, because of the sentencing to 15-20 years in prison, by a Moroccan military tribunal, of eight Saharan civilians who had participated in a demonstration at Laayoune and because of the Moroccan authorities' declared intention to have 100,000 applicants residing in Morocco take part in the voter identification operation. Following POLISARIO's decision, the Prime Minister and Minister for Foreign Affairs of Morocco addressed a letter dated 26 June to the President of the Security Council. In the letter, he claimed that the Frente POLISARIO was displaying bad faith, said that its decision could have most serious consequences and requested the Security Council to take all the necessary steps to ensure the resumption of the process with a view to holding the referendum on schedule.

829. On 12 July, the Frente POLISARIO informed the President of the Security Council that it had decided to continue to participate in the identification process. In announcing its decision, POLISARIO cited efforts made by certain States

members of the Security Council to induce Morocco to reconsider the sentences imposed on the Saharan civilians, the adoption of Security Council resolution 1002(1995) and the positive discussion at the thirty-first session of the Assembly of Heads of State and Government of OAU. On 27 July, the identification process resumed in the identification centres in Western Sahara and the Tindouf area. As at mid-August 1995, some 50,000 persons had been identified by MINURSO.

830. On 30 June, the Security Council adopted resolution 1002(1995), by which it extended the mandate of MINURSO until 30 September 1995. The Council also expected, based on the report I would present by 10 September on the progress achieved, to confirm 15 November as the start of the transitional period, to allow the referendum to take place in early 1996.

## 24. Yemen

831. Over the past year, Yemen has continued its efforts to recover from the devastation of the civil war. In its resolution 931(1994), the Security Council requested me and my Special Envoy to examine appropriate ways to facilitate the aim of political dialogue directed towards the restoration of peace and stability in the country. I continue to believe that political reconciliation is an indispensable step to ensure the stability of Yemen. I thus applaud the amnesty granted by the Government to most of those who fled the country at the conclusion of the war.

832. The continued implementation of the commitments pledged by the Government—to ensure democratic order, political pluralism, freedom of opinion and the press and respect for human rights, and to develop close cooperative relations with its neighbours—will indeed contribute to the restoration of stability. Earlier this year, the Foreign Minister reiterated to me that Yemen was willing to reach a negotiated settlement of its territorial dispute with Saudi Arabia on the basis of the norms and principles of international law and in accordance with the Charter of the United Nations. Progress in this area will testify to the strength of that commitment and will add to security and stability in the area.

833. In August 1994, the Department of Humanitarian Affairs launched a consolidated interagency appeal focusing on the most urgent humanitarian requirements through February 1995, totalling some $21.7 million. The priority sectors covered in the appeal were health, water and sanitation, emergency food aid, agriculture and fisheries, education and limited mine clearance. Response from the donor community has been extremely disappointing, with only $3.3 million (15 per cent of the overall requirements) received to date, mainly for health and food supply projects.

834. Land-mines pose a continuing threat to the lives and the livelihood of civilians in the south and have hampered efforts of health rehabilitation and restoration of agricultural production in affected areas. The Department of Humanitarian Affairs, however, received limited funding ($150,000) from a mine-clearance trust fund to undertake a land-mine assistance project in the Aden region. The project began in late February 1995 and aims to provide technical advice to the government authorities. Two international land-mine specialists were recruited by the Department of Humanitarian Affairs for the purpose.

### E. *Major comprehensive efforts*

#### 1. Angola

835. During the past year, significant progress has been achieved in the search for peace in Angola. After protracted negotiations, the Lusaka Protocol was signed and the United Nations Angola Verification Mission (UNAVEM III) was established to facilitate the implementation of its provisions. A cease-fire has been generally holding throughout the country and has opened access to all regions for the delivery of humanitarian relief assistance.

836. At the Lusaka peace talks, the most contentious issue was the question of national reconciliation, which included the allocation of posts at the national, provincial and local levels to the members of the União Nacional para a Independência Total de Angola (UNITA). In May 1994, the Government accepted a set of proposals on this issue put forward by the United Nations and the three observer States to the Angolan peace process—Portugal, the Russian Federation and the United States of America. After lengthy discussions and the intervention of a number of African leaders, including President Nelson Mandela of South Africa, UNITA finally accepted the proposals in September.

837. The way was thus paved for the signing of the Lusaka Protocol in the Zambian capital on 20 November 1994 and for the cease-fire that came into force two days later. President José Eduardo dos Santos and several other Heads of State, foreign ministers and dignitaries attended the ceremony.

838. In my report to the Security Council of 1 February (S/1995/97), I recommended the establishment of a new United Nations peace-keeping operation in Angola to assist the Government and UNITA in implementing the Lusaka Protocol. In particular, I recommended that UNAVEM III be composed of political, military, police and, in future, electoral components. The Humanitarian Assistance Coordination Unit, which has been operational since March 1993, would continue to serve as a coordinating body for all humanitarian operations under the authority of my Special Representative. The main features of the new United Nations mandate would include: to assist in the implementation of the Lusaka Protocol by providing good offices and mediation to the parties; to supervise, verify and, if necessary, control the disengagement of forces and to monitor the cease-fire; to assist in the establishment of quartering areas and to verify and monitor the withdrawal, quartering and demobilization of UNITA forces; to verify the movement of the Angolan Armed Forces to barracks; to verify and monitor the completion of the formation of a new armed force and the free circulation of people and goods. Other aspects of the proposed mandate were to monitor the activities of the Angolan National Police and the quartering of the Rapid Reaction Police, and to coordinate and support humanitarian activities linked directly to the peace process.

839. Having considered my report, the Security Council adopted resolution 976(1995) on 8 February, authorizing the establishment of UNAVEM III with an initial mandate until 8 August 1995 and with an authorized strength of 7,000 military personnel, in addition to 350 military observers and 260 police observers, as well as an appropriate number of international and local staff. The Council decided that the deployment of the infantry units would take place gradually and only if the parties complied with the provisions of the Lusaka Protocol.

840. The Joint Commission, chaired by my Special Representative for Angola, Mr. Alioune Blondin Beye, and comprising the representatives of both parties and the three observer States, was established at Luanda soon after the signing of the Lusaka Protocol. It is the body responsible for the implementation of the Protocol and has met in regular and extraordinary sessions on numerous occasions at Luanda and outside the Angolan capital.

841. Owing to some initial difficulties and delays in implementation of the Protocol, I dispatched my Special Adviser, Mr. Ismat Kittani, to register my concern with the parties and to assess conditions for the deployment of peacekeepers. The peace process subsequently regained momentum in mid-April. Although a number of incidents, unauthorized movements of troops and other cease-fire violations have occurred, the general trend has been towards a progressive decrease of such violations. Two meetings between the Chiefs of General Staff from the Government and UNITA, held in January and in February, also helped to consolidate the cease-fire and strengthen the peace process. Under the supervision of UNAVEM III, progress has been achieved in the disengagement of forces. In an especially positive development, the President of the Republic of An-

gola, Mr. José Eduardo dos Santos, and Mr. Jonas Savimbi, President of UNITA, met at Lusaka on 6 May in the presence of my Special Representative. This meeting gave a new and important impetus to the peace process and the parties took further concrete steps to consolidate the progress achieved. In June and July, the parties reached agreement on several important issues and approved an accelerated timetable for the implementation of the Lusaka Protocol.

842. Following this encouraging development, I visited Angola from 14 to 16 July to give additional impetus to the peace process. I had extensive meetings with President dos Santos, and met with Mr. Savimbi in his headquarters in the central part of Angola. Both the Government and UNITA emphasized the crucial role of the United Nations in the settlement of the Angolan conflict and stressed their commitment to the implementation of the Lusaka Protocol. I also reviewed the performance of United Nations troops in several regions of Angola. Several issues were resolved following my visit. The National Assembly created two vice-presidential posts, one of which is to be filled by Mr. Savimbi. The parties have decided that the future strength of the Angolan Armed Forces would be 90,000 soldiers and they have made progress on the modalities for the incorporation of UNITA troops, 74,000 of whom would be ground troops. The national armed forces would also comprise air and naval forces of 11,000 and 5,000 personnel, respectively. President dos Santos and Mr. Savimbi held a second meeting, on 10 August in Gabon, to address outstanding questions.

843. United Nations military and police observers have been deployed to nearly 60 locations throughout the country and their presence has increased United Nations verification capabilities, as well as its ability to provide good offices on the ground.

844. The deployment of UNAVEM infantry and support units has reached an advanced stage, with some 3,500 troops present in the country, including three infantry battalions. Full deployment of the contingents is expected in September/October. The United Nations has made strenuous efforts to ensure that mine verification and clearance of major deployment routes and quartering sites is carried out in order to begin early preparations for the quartering of UNITA troops and for the withdrawal of the Angolan Rapid Reaction Police and regular troops to barracks.

845. The civilian police component of UNAVEM has proved to be indispensable in enabling the United Nations to monitor and verify the neutrality of the national police. In addition, a United Nations human rights unit has contributed to the civil education campaign and to confidence-building among the Angolan popula-

tion. The Government of Angola and the United Nations have agreed to establish an independent United Nations radio station in Angola, as recommended in my report of 1 February and endorsed by the Security Council in its resolution 976(1995), which would broadcast information programmes on the role of the United Nations in Angola and on the peace process. Equipment for the United Nations radio station is expected to arrive in Angola in September and UNAVEM is holding discussions with the Angolan authorities regarding the allocation of broadcasting frequencies. In the meantime, UNAVEM has been given access to the government radio and is broadcasting its programmes on it.

846. On 8 August, the Security Council extended the mandate of UNAVEM for an additional six months, but expressed concern at the pace of implementation of the Lusaka Protocol and strongly urged the parties to accelerate the peace process. In the meantime, the General Assembly approved some $150 million for the UNAVEM budget for 1995.

847. Improvements in the security situation and the consolidation of the cease-fire have enabled the United Nations and international and local non-governmental organizations to extend their humanitarian relief activities to all regions of the country. Since the signing of the Lusaka Protocol, humanitarian agencies have reoriented their programmes to support the peace process in three realms of activity: relief and resettlement; demobilization and reintegration of former combatants; and action related to land-mines. It is estimated that over 3 million Angolans are receiving food aid or other types of relief assistance. These activities are directed inside Angola by the Humanitarian Assistance Coordination Unit, affiliated with the Department of Humanitarian Affairs.

848. The long-term prospects for peace depend in large part on the successful demobilization and reintegration into civilian life of those combatants who are not retained in the Angolan armed forces. Preparations are under way for the quartering and disarmament of UNITA soldiers under United Nations supervision and control. Humanitarian agencies will provide basic services to the soldiers in the quartering sites and organize programmes to facilitate their return to civilian society. The Department of Humanitarian Affairs has appealed to the international community for $102 million to support the demobilization and reintegration process over a period of approximately two years.

849. The intensive mine pollution in Angola seriously hinders the movement of goods and people as well as the resumption of economic activity. The problem is being addressed through a coor-

dinated programme of mine survey and clearance, mine-awareness training for civilians and the training of Angolan technicians and managers.

850.   Despite some progress on the humanitarian front, the economic and social situation in Angola continues to be extremely precarious. As in other peace-keeping operations, I have attached particular importance to these aspects of the situation in Angola. As the peace process advances, the focus of United Nations assistance is gradually shifting from emergency relief activities to rehabilitation of the country's war-wracked economic and social infrastructure, and to development. With support from UNDP and the Secretariat, the Government of Angola has organized a round table for rehabilitation and community development to be held in September.

851.   By providing humanitarian and development assistance, the international community can ease Angola's transition from war to sustainable peace. The Angolan people and their institutions, however, remain the primary agents of the necessary social, psychological and economic transformations.

### 2.   Haiti

*Restoration of democracy*

852.   The goal of restoring democracy in Haiti was significantly advanced by the return, in October 1994, of the legally and democratically elected President of the Republic of Haiti, Reverend Jean-Bertrand Aristide, who had been forced into exile by a military coup in September 1991.

853.   Pursuant to Security Council resolution 940(1994) of 31 July 1994, the Multinational Force, led by the United States of America, started operation in Haiti on 19 September 1994. After the departure from the country of the military leadership, President Aristide returned to Port-au-Prince on 15 October. On the same day, the Security Council adopted resolution 948(1994), effectively lifting all sanctions imposed against Haiti.

854.   On 23 September, I appointed Mr. Lakhdar Brahimi as my new Special Representative for Haiti to replace Mr. Dante Caputo, whose resignation I had received with regret four days earlier. I also sent a small advance team to Haiti to assess requirements and prepare for the deployment of the United Nations Mission in Haiti (UNMIH), as well as to monitor the operations of the Multinational Force.

855.   On 25 October, President Aristide designated Mr. Smarck Michel as Prime Minister. The new Government took office on 8 November. Seven days later, I paid a visit to Haiti and assured President Aristide that the United Nations, in collaboration with OAS, would continue to assist the Government of Haiti in achieving a lasting transition to democracy.

856.   Upon my return to Headquarters on 21 November, I reported to the Security Council. Responding to my recommendation, by its resolution 964(1994) the Council authorized an expansion of the advance team to up to 500 members for the transition period.

857.   In my report to the Security Council on 17 January 1995, I noted that, following the arrival of the Multinational Force and the subsequent disintegration of the Haitian Armed Forces (FADH), politically motivated violence and human rights abuses had decreased and Haitians were enjoying fundamental rights. At the same time, however, the collapse of the FADH had created a security void that contributed to an increased level of crime in the country.

858.   The Security Council considered my report, the statement of 15 January by the commander of the Multinational Force and the accompanying recommendations of the States participating in the Force regarding the establishment of a secure and stable environment in Haiti. The Council determined that, as required by resolution 940(1994), a secure and stable environment appropriate to the deployment of UNMIH existed in Haiti and it authorized me to recruit and deploy military contingents, civilian police and other personnel sufficient to allow UNMIH to assume the full range of its functions. The full transfer of responsibility from the Multinational Force to UNMIH was to be completed by 31 March and the mandate of UNMIH was extended for a period of six months until 31 July 1995. The Council also authorized the deployment of up to 6,000 troops and 900 civilian police observers.

859.   On 13 April, I submitted a progress report on the deployment of UNMIH, informing the Council that the official ceremony of transfer of responsibilities from the Multinational Force to UNMIH had successfully taken place, as scheduled, on 31 March. My second visit to Haiti, on that occasion, provided a good opportunity to observe the beginning of the operation of UNMIH and to exchange views with the President of Haiti on the political and security situation in the country. The issue of security remained central to the entire United Nations operation, in particular at the time of elections. Legislative and local elections were held on 25 June under generally secure conditions. However, the elections were marked by organizational flaws and a partial rerun was held on 13 August. The second phase of the election is scheduled to be held in September.

860.   On 31 July, the Security Council extended the mandate of UNMIH to the end of February 1996. The Mission continues to assist the Haitian authorities in maintaining a stable and secure environment and in protecting humanitarian convoys. UNMIH also provides the Haitian Provi-

sional Electoral Council with logistical and financial assistance and its civilian police component guides the work of the Interim Public Security Force and trains the Haitian National Police on the job.

*Human rights*

861. A core group of the International Civilian Mission in Haiti (MICIVIH) had returned to Haiti on 22 October 1994. In my report to the General Assembly on the situation of democracy and human rights in Haiti of 23 November 1994 (A/49/689), I proposed that MICIVIH should also contribute to the strengthening of democratic institutions.

862. The General Assembly, in its resolution 49/27 of 5 December 1994 on the situation of democracy and human rights in Haiti, requested the speedy return of all members of MICIVIH to Haiti. At present, the United Nations component has approximately 110 members. The Mission made a major contribution to the improvement of respect for human rights in Haiti, both during the military rule and since the restoration of the constitutional order last October. On 12 July, following my report of 29 June (A/49/926) and consultations with the Government of Haiti and the Secretary-General of OAS, the General Assembly extended the mandate of the United Nations component of MICIVIH until 7 February 1996.

863. MICIVIH continued to give priority to the monitoring and promotion of respect for human rights in Haiti. During the preparation of elections, the Mission facilitated and monitored respect for the freedom of expression and association as well as investigating allegations of intimidation and violence. Both UNMIH and MICIVIH worked closely with an OAS electoral observation mission set up in May 1995. UNMIH helped to ensure that the legislative and local elections on 25 June, while marred by organizational problems, took place in a secure environment, and MICIVIH staff assisted the electoral observation mission in the performance of its tasks. In its report on the 25 June elections, released by the Secretary-General of OAS on 13 July, the observation mission concluded that the elections had established a foundation that, although shaky, provided the basis for further positive progress towards the continuing evolution of an increasingly peaceful democracy in Haiti.

*Development*

864. After the events of September 1991, United Nations agencies and the international community provided humanitarian assistance to Haiti to address the most pressing basic needs. The main sectors targeted for intervention under the humanitarian assistance programme to alleviate the situation of the poorest sectors of the population were health care, nutrition, water supply and sanitation, and agriculture. To allow for the continuation of the humanitarian programmes during the embargo, a humanitarian fuel supply programme was undertaken. A total of 3,632,277 gallons of fuel was distributed among the nongovernmental organizations and other institutions involved in humanitarian aid.

865. With the return of constitutional government in October 1994 and the restoration of democracy after years of political instability and deteriorated socio-economic conditions, reorienting Haiti towards the path of economic development will be a daunting task. After a thorough review of the ongoing humanitarian activities, it was deemed necessary to find a new approach in order gradually to phase out the emphasis on strictly humanitarian relief, while facilitating the initiation of longer-term reconstruction initiatives.

866. An appeal for a six-month transitional period was launched on 6 December 1994 simultaneously in Port-au-Prince and Washington, D.C., by the Government of Haiti, the United Nations and OAS. The activities presented in the appeal reflected urgent needs that could be implemented rapidly and be of immediate positive impact. They were also intended to be sustainable in order to facilitate a smooth transition to medium- and long-term reconstruction and development efforts. The appeal requested $78 million to meet the needs for continued humanitarian and reconstruction assistance during Haiti's critical transition periods. As at 10 August, 54.1 per cent of the appeal target, or some $50.8 million, had been either received or pledged.

867. In 1995, cooperation between the Government and its development partners has moved from emergency and ad hoc initiatives to more strategically planned public works and employment-creation projects, leading, in particular, to major agreements with EU, the United States Agency for International Development (USAID) and the World Bank in July 1995. UNDP activities centre on governance, economic growth and poverty eradication, and the Programme has also provided seed money for certain initiatives by donor countries. In order to coordinate development activities with the peace-keeping mission of UNMIH in a manner consistent with its mandate, my Deputy Special Representative has been concurrently appointed Resident Representative of UNDP.

*Natural disasters*

868. On 13 November 1994, Tropical Storm Gordon caused heavy rains and floods that devastated sections of Port-au-Prince as well as the southern part of the country. The death toll was estimated at 1,122, and some 1.5 million people were affected. Altogether, 8,600 families became

homeless and 61,500 were in need of emergency relief. Destruction of infrastructure, agricultural land and property was extensive and included 11,402 houses partially damaged and 3,905 completely destroyed.

869.   Following the appeal for international assistance by the Government of Haiti, the United Nations Humanitarian Coordinator called on the United Nations Disaster Management Team to join the relief effort undertaken in support of the affected populations. The Department of Humanitarian Affairs sent a three-person team from United Nations Disaster Assessment and Coordination to strengthen the Humanitarian Coordinator's efforts to bolster the capacity of the special task force established by the Prime Minister.

870.   In response to the emergency situation, the international community's cash contributions amounted to $8.6 million, of which United Nations contributions amounted to some $500,000. Relief items were received from the Department of Humanitarian Affairs warehouse at Pisa, Italy, as well as from the Governments of France, Japan and Mexico.

### 3.   Rwanda

871.   Since my last annual report on the work of the Organization, the situation in Rwanda has shown signs of gradual normalization, continuing a process that started with the end of the genocide and civil war and the establishment of the present Government on 19 July 1994. With the completion of the withdrawal of the French-led Operation Turquoise from south-west Rwanda on 21 August 1994, the United Nations Assistance Mission for Rwanda (UNAMIR) assumed full responsibility for the former humanitarian protection zone prior to a gradual take-over by the new Rwandan civilian administration.

872.   In my reports to the Security Council on UNAMIR, I have emphasized that while the situation in Rwanda has to some extent stabilized, a number of serious obstacles remain to be overcome. Continued problems in repatriation, reconciliation and reconstruction efforts have triggered frustration in Rwanda, which, in turn, has contributed to the deterioration of security and affected relations between UNAMIR and the Rwandan authorities. The Government of Rwanda expressed the wish that, at an appropriate time, UNAMIR's mandate and its possible phase-out from Rwanda should be discussed. However, I urged the Government to continue to extend the necessary cooperation without which the Mission could not carry out its tasks, while requesting my Special Representative, Mr. Shahryar Khan, to consider, in consultation with the Government, adjustments to UNAMIR's mandate.

873.   Following those consultations, I recommended that the mandate of UNAMIR, which was due to expire on 9 June 1995, be renewed for another period of six months and its focus shifted from a peace-keeping to a confidence-building role. In its resolution 997(1995), the Security Council extended the mandate and authorized a reduction of its force level to 2,330 troops within three months and to 1,800 troops within four months. The mandate is to end in December 1995, with all troops withdrawn. Since the adoption of UNAMIR's new mandate, relations between UNAMIR and the Rwandan authorities have improved. UNAMIR is helping them to promote national reconciliation, the return of refugees and the setting up of a national police force. It is also responsible for the protection of humanitarian organizations, human rights observers and members of the International Criminal Tribunal for Rwanda. In my report of 4 June, I described Rwanda as relatively stable and largely at peace, with some utility services back in operation, schools reopened and the economy and agriculture showing signs of revival.

874.   Three major factors have nevertheless complicated international efforts to help the Government to restore normal conditions in Rwanda. Firstly, there has been the delay in bringing to justice individuals implicated in the 1994 genocide. In October 1994, the Independent Commission of Experts concluded that acts of mass extermination against Tutsi groups had been perpetrated in a planned and systematic way by certain Hutu elements and that this constituted genocide under the United Nations Convention on Genocide.

875.   On 8 November, the Security Council, in its resolution 955(1994), decided to establish a tribunal to prosecute persons responsible for genocide and other such violations committed between 1 January and 31 December 1994. Mr. Richard J. Goldstone was appointed Prosecutor and the Prosecutor's Office, headed by the Deputy Prosecutor, Mr. Honoré Rakotomana, was to be established at Kigali. Under his supervision, the investigation of some 400 identified suspects, among them leaders of the former regime and principal planners of the genocide, who sought refuge in neighbouring countries, is being conducted in and outside Rwanda.

876.   In its resolution 977(1995), the Security Council determined that the seat of the Tribunal should be established at Arusha, United Republic of Tanzania. Since the Tribunal shares a common appeals chamber with the International Criminal Tribunal for the Former Yugoslavia, the General Assembly has appointed only six judges for the Tribunal: Mr. Lennart Aspegren (Sweden), Mr. Laïty Kama (Senegal), Mr. T. H. Khan (Bangladesh), Mr. Yakov A. Ostrovsky (Russian Federation), Ms. Navanethem Pillay (South Africa) and Mr. Willam H. Sekule (United Republic of

Tanzania). Their first plenary session was held at The Hague from 26 to 30 June 1995. During the session, the judges adopted the rules of procedure and evidence of the Tribunal and elected a President (Mr. Kama) and a Vice-President (Mr. Ostrovsky). The judges will assume their functions with the commencement of trial proceedings. The Tribunal is expected to process the first indictments in the second half of this year; however, the justice system as a whole is not yet operational and is in urgent need of support. It will be difficult to achieve national reconciliation and a meaningful political dialogue if justice in the wake of the horrific events of the summer of 1994 is not seen to be done.

877. In July 1994, an estimated 1.2 million Rwandan refugees arrived in the Kivu provinces of Zaire following the April-July civil war in Rwanda. The presence of such a large number of refugees in Zaire, and its impact on the security and economy of the country, was one of the main subjects of the discussion I held with Prime Minister Kengo Wa Dondo during his visit to Headquarters on 15 December. At that time, the Prime Minister requested me to appoint "a special representative for Rwanda in Zaire". It was agreed that a civilian UNAMIR liaison office should be established at Kinshasa to facilitate communication between my Special Representative for Rwanda and the Government of Zaire. The Prime Minister offered to provide 1,500 troops for a proposed United Nations force to ensure security in the refugee camps. The Government of Zaire cited the presence of the Rwandan refugees as one of the factors that had contributed to the postponement of the first multi-party parliamentary and presidential elections and to the extension for two more years of the transitional period in Zaire until 10 July 1997.

878. On 27 January 1995, the Government of Zaire and the United Nations High Commissioner for Refugees signed an *aide-mémoire* outlining specific measures to improve security in the camps. Under the agreement, the Government of Zaire agreed to deploy a contingent of 1,500 military and police personnel—the Zairian Camp Security Contingent—to provide security in the camps. The measures included the prevention of violence, escort of repatriation convoys and maintenance of law and order, especially at food distribution centres.

879. Some 1,513 Zairian Camp Security troops and more than 38 members of the UNHCR civilian Security Liaison Group are now deployed in refugee camps. Their deployment has greatly improved security conditions. However, rumours about military training of elements of the former Government's army have persisted in some camps. Thus, in furtherance of Security Council resolution 997(1995), I sent a Special Envoy, Mr. Aldo Ajello, to the region to discuss the issue with all countries concerned and to explore the possibility of deploying military observers, in particular in the airfield of eastern Zaire, to monitor the alleged flow of arms. From 20 to 28 June, my Envoy visited Rwanda, Burundi, Zaire, Uganda and the United Republic of Tanzania. On 9 July, I reported to the Security Council that some countries of the region were opposed to the deployment of United Nations military observers on their territory. However, Zaire reiterated that it would welcome an international commission of inquiry, under United Nations auspices, to investigate allegations of arms deliveries to the former Rwandese Government Forces. For its part, the Government of Rwanda has reiterated its determination to promote the earliest return of the refugees and has stated its readiness for dialogue with those of them who were implicated in the genocide.

880. The second complicating factor is that national reconciliation can hardly become a reality without the safe return of the refugees and internally displaced persons not implicated in acts of genocide. For that purpose, the assistance of the international community will be needed to build up structures for the resettlement of the refugees and internally displaced persons and their reintegration into society. However, efforts in this direction have been jeopardized by the continuing military activities of members of the former Rwandese Government Forces in refugee camps in neighbouring countries, including the launching of organized incursions into Rwanda. The Government is concerned that the elements abroad of the former Rwandese Government Forces receive training and arms deliveries, whereas Rwanda is still subject to an arms embargo.

881. Given the serious lack of security in the refugee camps outside Rwanda, I authorized United Nations participation in a joint working group with Zairian authorities to improve the situation. Following consultations with the Secretariat and UNHCR, I emphasized in a report to the Security Council (S/1994/1308) that any operation to achieve the repatriation of refugees and the improvement of security in the camps was futile without parallel efforts to promote national reconciliation and reconstruction. On 1 February 1995, I informed the Security Council that on 27 January UNHCR had concluded an agreement with the Government of Zaire for the deployment of 1,500 security personnel, as well as a UNHCR liaison support group, to camps in eastern Zaire to maintain law and order, to prevent intimidation of refugees by elements opposed to their repatriation and to protect returnees and relief workers. However, while the situation has improved, the problem is far from solved.

882. The Government made it clear that it wished to close down the camps of internally displaced persons for reasons of security, in particular those in Kibeho, Ndago, Kamana and Munini. At the insistence of UNAMIR, which opposed the closing of the camps by force, the Government agreed to postpone such action. However, on 18 April the Government decided to close Kibeho camp, an action that led to panic, a stampede and indiscriminate firing at displaced persons, resulting in the killing of a large number. I immediately expressed my horror at this deplorable incident and sent a Special Envoy to Kigali. In the aftermath, most displaced persons were repatriated to their communes with the help of UNAMIR and UNHCR. In its report (S/1995/411), the independent International Commission of Inquiry created to investigate the circumstances and causes of the Kibeho tragedy concluded that it was neither premeditated nor an accident that could not have been prevented. The speedy establishment of the Commission and the steps it has taken to penalize the military personnel involved have mitigated some of the tragedy's adverse effects.

883. Thirdly, there has been frustration at the slow pace of delivery of international economic and reconstruction assistance to Rwanda, including aid pledged at the UNDP round table of January 1995. Of $714 million pledged, only $69 million has been disbursed and of this $26 million has been absorbed by debt-servicing costs. With regard to the Rwanda portion of the United Nations consolidated inter-agency appeal for the Rwanda crisis, launched in February this year, out of the $219,490,162 requested for Rwanda, only 50 per cent has been funded. For the subregion, under 60 per cent of the total $586,778,007 required for programmes in the neighbouring countries has so far been received.

884. Although the international donor community made generous pledges to the Government of Rwanda's rehabilitation and reconstruction programme, the slow process in turning them into actual support has frustrated the Government. I have repeatedly invited Member States and other potential donors to contribute to the trust fund for Rwanda, which could serve as a useful channel for contributions to meet the immediate needs of the Government and people of Rwanda. To date, $6,536,911 has been contributed. I also continue to believe that the early implementation of some of the key recommendations of the OAU/UNHCR Regional Conference on Assistance to Refugees, Returnees and Displaced Persons in the Great Lakes Region, held at Bujumbura from 15 to 17 February, would ease the tremendous humanitarian crisis in the region. I appealed to all Member States to act in accordance with the Conference's recommendations.

885. In this sense, the experience of Rwanda casts a revealing light on some of the problems that a peace-keeping operation is bound to meet when operating in such difficult circumstances. A new integrated approach, enlisting and combining all the resources of the United Nations family, is urgently needed.

886. Only a small proportion of the Rwandan people who fled their country at different times have returned to Rwanda this year and of those who have the vast majority come from those living in Uganda since the early 1960s. Among the refugees who fled in 1994, enthusiasm for repatriation has waned since March, especially in the Goma area and in northern Burundi. This is a result both of intimidation in the refugee camps and of the high number of security incidents inside Rwanda, including the assassinations of the Prefect of Butare and the head of medical services in the Gisenyi area. The rate of arrests of suspected participants in genocide and strong speeches by some Rwandan authorities have also had a negative impact on repatriation. Despite these set-backs, UNHCR continues to prepare for larger-scale repatriation in the months ahead. In addition to monitoring returnees, UNHCR is trying to organize, in cooperation with the Government of Rwanda, confidence-building visits by refugee groups from camps in Burundi to their home communes.

887. The Government also has to address the social impact of large numbers of people returning to their homes. In this respect, it should not be forgotten that much of the Rwandan population is still traumatized by the events of 1994. It is thus hardly surprising that serious problems have occurred between the survivors of the genocide and those who are now returning from camps for displaced persons or refugees. Disputes concern the genocide, illegal occupancy of land and property and the settling of old scores and grudges. Since February, commune committees, comprising representatives of local authorities and human rights field officers, are being formed to address issues such as security and arrest procedures.

888. The combination of ethnic polarization in Burundi and Rwanda, massive circulation of arms, porous borders and transborder movements of refugees threaten, at best, to keep the subregion perpetually unstable and, at worst, to ignite a large-scale regional conflict. I will therefore intensify my efforts towards a broader international initiative for a long-term solution to the problems in the Great Lakes region, especially by the early convening of a regional conference on security, stability and development.

889. Food shortages within the region have also occurred and WFP and UNHCR have alerted the international community to the need to cover

the shortages, which threaten more than 3 million Rwandan and Burundian refugees and internally displaced persons. Rations in some refugee camps have had to be reduced by as much as half. Inside Rwanda itself, the United Nations and non-governmental organizations have contributed significantly to the present harvest by providing seeds, tools and seed protection programmes. A seed multiplication programme, financed by the World Bank, has been initiated and FAO has been instrumental in the establishment of a consortium of donors for the agricultural sector.

890. UNICEF has reopened a number of nutritional centres, distributed equipment to nongovernmental organizations and delivered supplementary food and material to unaccompanied children centres. With the assistance of UNICEF, ICRC, UNHCR and the Save the Children Fund—UK, 41,800 separated Rwandan children have been registered in Rwanda, Goma, Bukavu and Ngara, out of an estimated total of 95,000. Thanks to these efforts, at least 3,000 children have been reunited with their families. There is evidence that up to one fifth of all unaccompanied minors can be reunited with their families.

891. UNICEF and the Ministry of Justice have reached an agreement to move an estimated 400 children accused of genocide from prisons to a separate location. In addition, a special division for imprisoned children and women has been created within the Ministry of Justice. Five experienced lawyers have been recruited to act as defence counsels for the children. Regarding the demobilization of child soldiers, UNICEF and the Ministry of Defence have identified a location where the education and skills training of up to 4,000 child soldiers will soon begin.

892. Much progress has been made in the health conditions of the Rwandan population. WHO has assisted the Ministry of Health with training programmes to enable the national programme of diarrhoeal diseases and acute respiratory infections control to be re-launched and is supporting the Ministry in the production of the national health policy document. Training programmes have also been undertaken on the national health information system, with an emphasis on epidemiological surveillance. With the help of UNICEF and others, more than 100 of the 280 pre-war vaccination centres have reopened in Rwanda; supplies and equipment have been ordered for the remainder. A vaccination campaign against measles has also been launched in Kigali. Some progress has also been made in the rehabilitation of the country's water infrastructure and electric grid line.

893. Joint UNESCO and UNICEF efforts have continued to improve access to education. Some 1,800 teacher emergency packages, supplying basic classroom resources and an emergency curriculum to over 140,000 primary school children, were distributed inside Rwanda in February. This brings the number of such packages distributed so far to over 7,000, servicing at least 560,000 children.

894. As well as continuing its project for emergency assistance to the national maternal and child health/family planning programme, UNFPA is helping the Government to elaborate an integrated maternal and child health/family planning training programme, which incorporates maternal and child health/family planning, HIV/AIDS prevention and safe motherhood. WHO has also supported the national AIDS programme through the strengthening of managerial capabilities at central and regional levels.

895. In July, I visited Rwanda in order to observe at first hand the progress made and the challenges that remain. In my most recent report on UNAMIR, dated 8 August, I stressed that the achievement of genuine national reconciliation was an essential element in establishing lasting peace in Rwanda. The Government of Rwanda must take determined measures to that end and representatives of all sectors of Rwandan society should begin talks to reach an agreement on a constitutional and political structure necessary to achieve lasting stability. The international community also has an important role to play in the process of Rwanda's reconstruction and reconciliation. While the economic situation has marginally improved, the Government will not be able to cope with the mounting pressures from returning refugees, the rehabilitation of all sectors and tensions from neighbouring countries. The seriousness of the present situation and the growing probability that it will deteriorate further requires urgent and concerted action on the part of the international community. During my visit to the subregion, there was clear consensus among government leaders that instability in any State in the area could have a dramatic effect on all its neighbours. On 16 August, the Security Council unanimously adopted resolution 1011(1995). In that resolution, the Council, *inter alia*, lifted for the period of one year, until 1 September 1996, the restrictions on the sale or supply of arms and related *matériel* to the Government of Rwanda. Such restrictions remain in force, however, with respect to non-government forces in Rwanda and in neighbouring States. On 1 September 1996, the restrictions imposed by the Council in paragraph 13 of its resolution 918(1994) shall terminate, unless it decides otherwise after its consideration of the report of the Secretary-General on the matter.

#### 4. The former Yugoslavia

896. The Organization's continuing efforts in the former Yugoslavia remain focused on a multiplicity of mandated responsibilities that span hu-

manitarian, military and political tasks in an environment characterized by vicious cycles of cease-fire violations, human rights infringements, physical destruction and death.

897.   Unceasing conflicts, entrenched hostilities, violation of agreements and a genuine lack of commitment and good faith have become the hallmarks of this crisis. Taken together, these factors give the impression either that not enough is being done to find a peaceful resolution or that fundamental questions and issues that divide the parties are insurmountable. For too long, from the start of military confrontation in 1991 until the time of writing, all efforts aimed at reaching a negotiated and peaceful solution to the conflicts and outstanding issues have been in vain. The Organization and agencies within its common system that have programmes in the area are, however, continuing to devote the highest priority to bringing peace to the region and alleviating the suffering brought about by the conflict.

*Preventive diplomacy and preventive deployment*

898.   The presence of the United Nations Preventive Deployment Force (UNPREDEP) continues to make an important contribution to stability in the former Yugoslav Republic of Macedonia. However, as stated in my report last year, internal differences that could lead to political instability remain a cause for concern. Regarding the dispute between Greece and the former Yugoslav Republic of Macedonia, my Special Envoy, Mr. Cyrus Vance, has continued his efforts pursuant to Security Council resolution 845(1993).

899.   On 7 November 1994, Mr. Vance and I met with President Kiro Gligorov at Geneva following the elections in his country. I urged him to give favourable consideration to a number of proposals for resolving the dispute. On 6 February 1995, Mr. Vance began a series of parallel meetings with the parties with a view to convening direct negotiations. During the meetings both parties took a serious and constructive approach that could in time lead to direct talks. In a subsequent meeting with President Gligorov at Copenhagen on 10 March, I urged him to facilitate a face-to-face meeting with the other side. Between March and June, Mr. Vance continued his meetings with the two sides. When I visited Greece in July, I urged the Greek leaders to respond favourably to his proposals.

*Peacemaking and peace-keeping*

900.   The International Conference on the Former Yugoslavia continues to provide a permanent forum for the negotiation of a comprehensive political solution to the problems in the former Yugoslavia. Its Steering Committee is co-chaired by Mr. Thorvald Stoltenberg, representing the United Nations, and the former Swedish premier

Mr. Carl Bildt, who was appointed by EU on 9 June following the resignation of Lord David Owen in May. My Special Representative, Mr. Yasushi Akashi, as well as the States members of the Contact Group, have continued their efforts to advance the peace process. At an EU summit meeting at Cannes, France, in June, European leaders determined that diplomacy should be the main tool for achieving several primary objectives, including the lifting of the siege of Sarajevo; resumption of a dialogue between the parties on the basis of the Contact Group Plan; establishment of a new four-month cease-fire; re-establishment of a dialogue between the Government of Croatia and the Krajina Serbs; and mutual recognition by the former Yugoslav republics.

901.   Under the auspices of the Co-Chairmen of the International Conference on the Former Yugoslavia and the Ambassadors of the Russian Federation and the United States of America to Croatia, the Government of Croatia and the local Serb authorities in Croatia concluded, on 2 December 1994, an Economic Agreement. That Agreement was seen as a major confidence-building measure towards the restoration of normal economic activities in Croatia. With continued adherence to the cease-fire agreement of 29 March 1994, it seemed that both sides had embarked on a course of normalizing their relationship by pursuing a number of tangible and mutually beneficial economic improvements, such as the opening of the Zagreb-Belgrade highway through Sector West, opening the Adriatic oil pipeline, rehabilitating and reconnecting the electricity grid and exploring the reopening of railway connections.

902.   On 12 January 1995, I received a letter from the President of the Republic of Croatia, Dr. Franjo Tudjman, informing me of his Government's decision not to agree to a further extension of the mandate of the United Nations Protection Force (UNPROFOR) beyond 31 March. While the Government of Croatia's frustration was understandable, its decision to insist on the withdrawal of UNPROFOR from Croatia renewed mistrust and created new tensions, as a result of which cooperation on further elements of the Economic Agreement petered out.

903.   Diplomatic efforts by the international community, Mr. Stoltenberg and my Special Representative eventually won acceptance of the continuation of the United Nations peace-keeping presence in Croatia, albeit with revised tasks and a reduced troop strength of 8,750. At the end of March, the Security Council in its resolution 981(1995) established the United Nations Confidence Restoration Operation, to be known as UNCRO, which was to implement a number of core tasks that were defined in consultations between Mr. Stoltenberg and the parties. The ele-

ments of UNPROFOR stationed in Croatia were to be converted into UNCRO by the end of June 1995. At the same time separate forces were created for Bosnia and Herzegovina (retaining the name UNPROFOR) and the former Yugoslav Republic of Macedonia (UNPREDEP). Overall command and control of all these forces was to be exercised by my Special Representative and the Force Commander from United Nations Peace Forces headquarters (UNPF-HQ) at Zagreb.

904. On 1 May, the Croatian army and police undertook an offensive against Sector West from both directions on the Zagreb-Belgrade highway with some 2,500 troops, heavy equipment and air support. UNPROFOR, whose mandate was to monitor the cease-fire arrangements agreed in March 1994, was powerless to prevent an offensive on that scale. However, UNPROFOR and other international agencies were able to keep the international community at least partially informed and to discourage violence against the Serb population, though abuses undoubtedly occurred during the early stages of the conflict. More than 10,000 Serb civilians crossed into Serb-controlled areas of Bosnia and Herzegovina. Subsequently, UNPROFOR and UNHCR helped those remaining Serb civilians who so wished to leave Sector West in a protected and orderly manner. Although the Government of Croatia declared its intention to respect fully the human rights of the remaining Serb population, it was not able to create confidence among the Serbs that it was in their interests to remain in Croatia. The mistrust created by the Croatian operation against Sector West further undermined efforts to resume negotiations towards a peaceful settlement in Croatia.

905. Following the take-over of Sector West by the Croatian army, tensions in the UNCRO area of operations remained high, preventing the deployment of the Operation as originally envisaged in Security Council resolutions 981(1995), 982(1995) and 990(1995). On 19 July, the Krajina Serb army and the forces loyal to Mr. Fikaret Abdic launched offensives against the Bosnian Army V Corps in the Bihac pocket. Croatia almost immediately warned that the displacement of the population of Bihac would be considered a serious threat to its security and stability. The Presidents of Croatia and Bosnia and Herzegovina signed the Split Declaration on 22 July, which committed the Government of Croatia to assist Bosnian forces militarily in the Bihac pocket. Within Croatia, the Croatian army continued a major build-up of troops around Sectors North and South in apparent preparation for a major military offensive aimed at re-establishing Croatian control in those areas.

906. Intensive efforts to defuse the crisis and restart political negotiations were undertaken by the United Nations as well by Member States. My Special Representative met with President Tudjman to forestall a looming military confrontation. He also met with local Serb leaders at Knin. On 3 August, at Geneva, Mr. Stoltenberg chaired a meeting of the representatives of the Government of Croatia and the Croatian Serbs and presented the two sides with a paper covering seven points of contention. The Croatian Serb side was inclined to accept the paper as a useful basis for progress, subject to clearance by its political leadership, but the Government indicated that the paper did not address its fundamental concern that the Krajina Serbs should be reintegrated under the Croatian Constitution and laws. On the evening of 3 August, I telephoned President Tudjman and urged the utmost restraint.

907. On 4 August, the Croatian army launched a major offensive, which was largely completed a few days later. I immediately issued a statement expressing my regret at the outbreak of hostilities in Croatia, and urged the parties to respect international humanitarian law and the human rights of the affected population. At the start of the action, a significant number of United Nations observation posts were overrun by the Croatian army and some were deliberately fired upon. Some United Nations troops were used as human shields by Croatian army units as they conducted their attacks. Vigorous protests have been launched against these incidents by the United Nations and the troop-contributing Governments concerned. In the period following the Croatian military actions, the United Nations has concentrated on dealing with the humanitarian crisis brought about by the massive displacement of people and on maintaining contacts that would permit political negotiations to be resumed. Thus my Special Representative on 6 August concluded a nine-point agreement with the Croatian authorities allowing the United Nations, and other international organizations, to cope with the major humanitarian difficulties and to monitor the human rights situation on the ground. Mr. Stoltenberg was also in active contact with the authorities at Zagreb and Belgrade. These events had obvious implications for the future role of UNCRO in that, with the collapse of the armed forces of the Krajina Serbs, there was no longer a requirement, except in Sector East, to monitor or control the confrontation line, zone of separation, weapons storage sites and areas of limitations established by the cease-fire agreement of 29 March 1994. On 23 August, I recommended to the Security Council an immediate start to the repatriation of all UNCRO troops, except the two battalions in Sector East, with the aim of reducing troop strength to below 2,500 by mid-November 1995.

908. For the most part, developments in Bosnia and Herzegovina in the past year have been

equally discouraging. In the autumn of 1994, military activity assumed unacceptably high levels, in particular in the Bihac area and around Sarajevo. The overall situation reached a crisis point when Bosnian Serb infantry entered the designated safe area of Bihac to repulse an offensive launched from the Bihac pocket in October by the Bosnian army. Following air attacks by Krajina Serbs into the Bihac pocket on 18 and 19 November 1994 and NATO air strikes against the Udbina airfield in Sector South in Croatia and on Bosnian Serb missile sites on 21 and 23 November, respectively, the situation sharply worsened. Some 250 UNPROFOR personnel were confined to the weapon collection points around Sarajevo and 26 United Nations military observers were detained in their quarters. The situation improved when, following former United States President Jimmy Carter's visit in late December, my Special Representative was able to secure a cessation-of-hostilities agreement, which came into effect on 1 January 1995.

909.   Although the cessation of hostilities had been agreed for four months, fighting in the Bihac area never ceased, and those elements of the agreement which could have secured a more stable cease-fire, such as the creation of buffer zones and the interpositioning of UNPROFOR troops along the confrontation line, could not be implemented for lack of cooperation by the parties. In March 1995, the Government, in the first large-scale violation of the cease-fire agreement outside the Bihac area, launched offensive operations at Mount Vlasic, near Travnik, and the Majevica Hills near Tuzla. When efforts to extend the cessation-of-hostilities agreement beyond 1 May failed, the situation in and around Sarajevo began to deteriorate rapidly. The humanitarian airlift into Sarajevo airport has been blocked by the Bosnian Serbs from 8 April to the time of writing; sniping and exchanges of artillery fire have increased to levels not experienced since the establishment of the heavy weapons exclusion zone in February 1994.

910.   On 25 May, as a result of the failure of the Bosnian Serbs to respect the deadline for the return of heavy weapons, an air strike was launched against an ammunition dump near Pale, with another against the same target the following day as a result of continuing non-compliance. The Bosnian Serbs shelled all safe areas except Zepa, and 70 civilians were killed and over 130 injured as a result of a rocket attack on Tuzla. The Bosnian Serbs surrounded UNPROFOR personnel in weapon collection points and detained 199, many of them under humiliating circumstances.

911.   As the crisis heightened, NATO, on 29 June, approved a plan to send up to 60,000 troops to Bosnia and Herzegovina to cover the withdrawal of United Nations peace-keepers, should the need arise. United Nations–designated safe areas came under sustained attack from Bosnian Serb forces and Srebrenica was overrun on 11 July. The Security Council on 12 July demanded the withdrawal of the Bosnian Serb forces from Srebrenica but this demand was ignored. The Bosnian Serb army detained UNPROFOR troops from the Netherlands and by 14 July had evicted thousands of Muslim refugees from Srebrenica, while detaining Muslim men, whose fate is still unknown. The violations of international humanitarian law that appear to have been committed in the wake of the fall of Srebrenica and Zepa are a matter of utmost concern, and it is imperative that access be given to permit full international investigation of these allegations. The degrading and cruel treatment of the civilian population has been strongly, and justifiably, condemned. Zepa then came under attack and also fell to Bosnian Serb forces. In the Zepa enclave, both sides threatened to kill UNPROFOR troops from Ukraine—the Bosnian Serbs if NATO air strikes were used against them, and the Government of Bosnia and Herzegovina if NATO air assets were not used. On 20 July, the Security Council adopted a presidential statement condemning humanitarian abuses in Zepa by the Bosnian Serb army. During this period the United Nations devoted all energies to dealing with the monumental humanitarian consequences of the fall of the two enclaves. Efforts to account for the missing and gain access to the detainees are continuing.

912.   These dramatic developments and threats against the remaining safe areas were discussed at a conference in London on 21 July, which I attended along with leaders of the Contact Group and representatives of troop-contributing countries. The London conference considered measures, including air power, to deter further attacks on the safe areas. On 26 July, NATO approved plans for employing air power should Bosnian Serbs threaten or attack Gorazde. Following intensive discussions between NATO and the United Nations, appropriate procedures were agreed for this purpose, and I have delegated authority for launching air strikes in the region to the UNPF Force Commander.

913.   The crisis situation that began to develop in May once again highlighted the vulnerability of UNPROFOR as a lightly armed, widely dispersed peace-keeping force. I therefore appreciated the offer made by France, the Netherlands and the United Kingdom of Great Britain and Northern Ireland to make available to UNPROFOR some 12,500 additional troops as a rapid reaction capability in order to improve the Force's security and thus its ability to implement the mandate given to it by the Security Council. Difficulties raised by the Governments of Croatia and Bosnia and Herzegovina have delayed the entry into operation of the rapid reaction capability.

914. The five-member Contact Group continued its efforts to arrive at a political solution to the conflict in Bosnia and Herzegovina, but little progress was made in convincing the Bosnian Serb party to accept the territorial map for an overall settlement, despite the support of the Federal Republic of Yugoslavia (Serbia and Montenegro). The latter has continued to minimize its relations with the Bosnian Serb leaders, and the monitor mission of the International Conference on the Former Yugoslavia, established in September 1994, has maintained its monitoring of the closure of the 300-mile border with Bosnian Serb–controlled territory.

915. The dramatic developments that are taking place as this report is being finalized at the end of August provide, at long last, reason to hope that there may be worthwhile progress towards a political settlement. It is regrettable that in order to achieve peace the international community has had to resort to using force, but the warning that was given following the London Conference of 21 July was clear and unmistakable. After so many disappointments in past years of tragedy in Bosnia and Herzegovina, this new opportunity for political negotiation must not be wasted.

916. I am well aware that the patience, resources and will of Member States to resolve the crises in the former Yugoslavia have been sorely tested. Nevertheless, I remain convinced that only a negotiated comprehensive settlement will lead to an enduring peace. Part of that settlement must include arrangements for arms limitations and confidence-building measures that will prevent further outbreaks of conflict in the Balkans. There must also be an extensive plan for reconstruction and rehabilitation in the region as a whole. There will therefore be a continuing need for the international community to remain committed and involved.

*Human rights*

917. In August 1992, the United Nations Commission on Human Rights convened, for the first time ever in its history, in a special session to consider the human rights situation in the former Yugoslavia. The Commission requested its chairman to appoint a special rapporteur to investigate the human rights situation in the former Yugoslavia, in particular within Bosnia and Herzegovina.

918. The Special Rapporteur, Mr. Tadeusz Mazowiecki (who resigned on 27 July 1995), submitted regular reports during the past year to the Commission on Human Rights and to the General Assembly. The Commission requested the Secretary-General to make those reports available to the Security Council and to the International Conference on the Former Yugoslavia. In 17 reports, the Special Rapporteur assessed the human rights situation in Croatia, Bosnia and Herzegovina, the former Yugoslav Republic of Macedonia and the Federal Republic of Yugoslavia (Serbia and Montenegro). In each of the reports, he presented a number of recommendations for action by the international community and various parties in the region.

919. With regard to the areas under the control of the de facto Bosnian Serb authorities, the Special Rapporteur drew attention to the ongoing practice of ethnic cleansing and the widespread violation of the human rights of peoples living in those areas, including Bosnian Serbs who were perceived as disloyal by the de facto authorities. There has also been a continuation of military attacks on civilians and interference with the delivery of humanitarian aid by Bosnian Serb forces in areas throughout Bosnia and Herzegovina. The Special Rapporteur vigorously condemned all such violations of human rights and called for the prosecution of the perpetrators by the International Tribunal.

920. In addition, the Commission on Human Rights adopted resolution 1994/75, in which it requested me to report to the Commission on the situation of human rights in Bosnia and Herzegovina. In my report, I addressed the issue of the actions taken by the Special Rapporteur, the situation concerning the voluntary return of displaced persons, the problem of disappearances and actions taken by the Commission of Experts established pursuant to Security Council resolution 780(1992), the International Tribunal, the International Conference on the Former Yugoslavia, UNPROFOR and the United Nations High Commissioner for Human Rights.

921. In November 1994, the International Criminal Tribunal for the Former Yugoslavia confirmed the first indictment against a Bosnian Serb, Mr. Dragan Nikolic, on charges of gross violations of the Geneva Conventions, the laws and customs of war and crimes against humanity. Soon thereafter, a formal request was issued to the Government of Germany for the deferral of the *Tadic* case, involving charges of genocide, ethnic cleansing, rape and murder of civilians and prisoners of war. Proceedings for the transfer of the case from the German courts were completed a few months later and the first hearing of the *Tadic* case was held on 26 April 1995.

922. The Tribunal confirmed two more indictments in February 1995, bringing the total number accused to 22. Requests for their arrest and surrender to the Tribunal have been sent to the authorities of Bosnia and Herzegovina and the Serb administration at Pale. Except for Mr. Tadic, however, who was transferred to the Tribunal by Germany, the remaining 21 accused are still at large.

923. In May, the Tribunal issued a formal request to the Government of Bosnia and Herzegovina for the deferral of its investigation and criminal proceedings in respect of crimes committed against the civilian population in the Lasva river valley, where Bosnian Croat forces have allegedly committed mass killings of Bosnian civilians. The Tribunal issued another request for deferral of investigation proceedings to the Government with respect to the Bosnian Serb leadership at Pale. The latter investigation focuses on the question of possible responsibility of the Serb leaders for genocide, murder, rape, torture and forced transfer of population from large parts of Bosnia and Herzegovina. From 21 to 25 July the Tribunal handed down five indictments covering 24 people.

924. The March 1994 Washington Agreement that led to the establishment of the Federation in Bosnia and Herzegovina, the introduction of the Contact Group Plan in May 1994 and the Agreement on Cessation of Hostilities signed at the end of the year brought a period of stability to Sarajevo and improved freedom of movement. These developments, while not fundamentally changing the situation, made it possible gradually to reduce the number of beneficiaries needing international assistance to some 2.1 million persons, of whom 1.4 million were in Bosnia and Herzegovina. United Nations humanitarian agencies could then concentrate more on displaced persons and the most vulnerable groups.

925. With the exception of Bihac, overall access for humanitarian assistance was successful, at least during the period from June 1994 to March 1995, with UNHCR being able to exceed its monthly target in Sarajevo and elsewhere in central Bosnia. It was possible to bring winterization items and fuel to Sarajevo and the eastern enclaves. Arrangements were also made with FAO for the distribution of much-needed seeds and fertilizers throughout Bosnia and Herzegovina.

926. Overall security rapidly deteriorated in March 1995, making movements of humanitarian assistance increasingly difficult. The airlift to Sarajevo came to a halt on 8 April and with the escalation of the conflict from late May, land convoys became unpredictable and vulnerable. For the first time, signs of malnutrition and exhaustion were visible in Bihac and in the eastern enclaves.

927. The dramatic escalation of the conflict in June, July and August led to the displacement of hundreds of thousands of people throughout the former Yugoslavia. With the Croat authorities regaining control of western Slavonia in June, thousands of Serbs were displaced to north-west Bosnia. Following the fall of Srebrenica in mid-July, some 30,000 people were compelled to flee. At the beginning of August, thousands of men from Srebrenica still remained unaccounted for.

Some 4,350 people were evacuated from Zepa in late July. A Bosnian Croat offensive on Glamoc and Grahovo led to the displacement of some 13,000 Serbs in the Banja Luka area.

928. The retaking of the Krajina by the Croat authorities in early August led to an exodus of some 150,000 people to north-west Bosnia and to the Federal Republic of Yugoslavia. UNHCR, in cooperation with other humanitarian partners, mounted a major assistance effort to meet the needs generated by this emergency. The departing Krajina Serbs suffered widespread maltreatment, injuries and some deaths at the hands of Croatian troops and civilians, and UNCRO personnel reported much looting and burning of houses. UNHCR made efforts to monitor the situation of those Krajina Serbs remaining and to ensure the right to return of those who fled. UNHCR and other humanitarian agencies have continued to give assistance in Croatia and in western Bosnia, despite pressures for their departure, all too often through acts of violence. The practice of forced labour, often on front lines, is of great concern, and this situation has been exacerbated by renewed tensions and the recent influx of Serb refugees from western Slavonia and the Krajina, which has resulted in the Banja Luka region in worsening treatment and evictions of Muslims and Croats in retaliation.

929. In general, forced population movements, either associated with ethnic cleansing or leading to the same result, have been of great concern to UNHCR during the period. UNHCR has actively intervened against forced mobilization of refugees. The United Nations revised consolidated inter-agency appeal for the former Yugoslavia covering January-December 1995 was issued on 2 June by nine United Nations agencies, for a total of $470 million for humanitarian operations. The UNHCR component is $172 million to cover the cost of humanitarian aid for an estimated total of 2,109,500 beneficiaries in Bosnia and Herzegovina, Croatia, the former Yugoslav Republic of Macedonia, Slovenia and the Federal Republic of Yugoslavia (Serbia and Montenegro). Contributions as at 1 August 1995 were $1.36 million.

### F. *Cooperation with regional organizations*

930. Cooperation between the United Nations and regional organizations must constantly adapt to an ever-changing world situation. The Charter itself anticipated this need for flexibility by not giving a precise definition of regional arrangements and organizations, thus enabling diverse organizations and structures to contribute, together with the United Nations, to the maintenance of peace and security.

931. The growing interaction between the United Nations and regional organizations has its origins in Chapter VIII of the Charter. With this

objective in mind, the Secretary-General met in August 1994 with the heads of several regional organizations with which the United Nations had recently cooperated in peacemaking and peace-keeping efforts. In the January 1995 Supplement to "An Agenda for Peace" (A/50/60-S/1995/1), a typology of current modalities for cooperation between the United Nations and regional organizations was set forth.

932. Currently, such cooperation takes five different forms. First, there is consultation, which is practised on a regular basis and, in some cases, is governed by formal agreements. Secondly, there is diplomatic support, by which a regional organization can participate in United Nations peace-making activities through diplomatic efforts of its own. For instance, OSCE provides technical input on constitutional issues relating to Abkhazia. Conversely, the United Nations can support a regional organization in its efforts, as it does for OSCE over Nagorny Karabakh. Thirdly, the United Nations and regional organizations can engage in operational support. A recent example is the provision by NATO of air support to UNPROFOR in the former Yugoslavia. Fourthly, there is co-deployment: United Nations field missions have been deployed in conjunction with the Economic Community of West African States (ECOWAS) in Liberia and with CIS in Georgia. Finally, there can be joint operations, such as the current human rights mission of the United Nations and OAS in Haiti.

933. However, given the diversification of the forms of cooperation being established between regional organizations and the United Nations, the basic principles of the Charter should be borne in mind. Article 24 confers on the Security Council primary responsibility for the maintenance of peace and Article 52 stipulates that the action of regional organizations must in all cases remain consistent with that principle.

934. The modalities of this cooperation must be refined and adapted to the diversity of local situations. The range of procedures that can be employed is wide and varied, but they all have the same advantage: they facilitate the Security Council's work and delegate responsibility to the concerned States and organizations of the region concerned, thereby promoting the democratization of international relations.

935. In this regard the recent adoption by the General Assembly in its resolution 49/57 of 9 December 1994 of the Declaration on the Enhancement of Cooperation between the United Nations and Regional Arrangements or Agencies in the Maintenance of International Peace and Security encourages regional arrangements and agencies to consider ways and means to promote closer cooperation and coordination with the United Nations, in particular in the fields of preventive diplomacy, peacemaking and post-conflict peace-building, and, where appropriate, peace-keeping.

### 1. Cooperation with the Organization of American States

936. Relations between the United Nations and OAS have been strengthened since the adoption of resolution 49/5 on 21 October 1994. OAS Secretary-General César Gaviria visited the United Nations soon after assuming office in October 1994, and as recommended in resolution 49/5, a general meeting between representatives of the two Organizations was held in New York on 17 and 18 April 1995. OAS Secretary-General Gaviria and I opened the meeting and signed an agreement of cooperation between our two secretariats. The agreement provides for regular consultation, participation in each other's meetings when matters of common interest are on the agenda and exchange of information. The agreement also foresees appropriate measures to ensure effective cooperation and liaison between the two Organizations.

937. The general meeting adopted a set of conclusions and recommendations, mainly on economic and social issues. Reflecting new dimensions in relations between the two Organizations, the meeting adopted recommendations in the areas of preventive diplomacy, promotion of democracy and human rights, and humanitarian issues. It was agreed that the frequency of general meetings should be reviewed and that a more flexible format for consultations on cooperation between the two Organizations should be considered. The United Nations Secretariat was represented at the twenty-fifth regular session of the General Assembly of OAS, held in Haiti from 5 to 9 June 1995, at which two resolutions on cooperation between the United Nations and OAS were adopted.

938. The United Nations and OAS have continued their close cooperation in Haiti within the framework of MICIVIH. On 12 July 1995, the United Nations General Assembly adopted resolution 49/27 B, which extended the mandate of MICIVIH to 7 February 1996. The United Nations has also supported the OAS electoral observer mission in Haiti.

### 2. Cooperation with the Organization of African Unity

939. The United Nations and OAU have continued their efforts to strengthen and broaden their cooperation. In the economic and social fields, they coordinated their activities and initiatives on the preparation and outcome of international conferences, including those on population, social development and women. They also cooperated on the United Nations New Agenda for the Development of Africa in the 1990s and Agenda 21 to

harmonize positions and to facilitate the implementation of programmes on which agreement has been reached.

940.    Cooperation between the two Organizations in the areas of preventive diplomacy and peacemaking has made progress. I have maintained close contact with the Secretary-General of OAU to exchange views on how best to contribute to the prevention and resolution of conflicts in Africa. In Burundi, Liberia, Rwanda and Sierra Leone, the two Organizations continue to consult and cooperate in the search for peace and reconciliation. In Western Sahara, OAU is cooperating closely with the United Nations in the process leading to the referendum. I have also met and exchanged views with representatives of the countries that are members of the central organ of the OAU mechanism for conflict prevention, management and resolution. On 17 and 18 July 1995, I met at Addis Ababa with the current Chairman of OAU, President Meles Zenawi of Ethiopia, and the Secretary-General of OAU, Mr. Salim Ahmed Salim, and discussed with them ways and means of strengthening further the cooperation between the two Organizations.

941.    The secretariats of the United Nations system and OAU are scheduled to meet at Addis Ababa from 6 to 10 November 1995 to work out the details of the programme of cooperation between the two Organizations for 1996 and beyond. High on the agenda of the meeting is cooperation in the prevention and management of conflicts and in democratic transition in Africa.

3.    Cooperation with the Caribbean Community

942.    Since 1985, the United Nations has been represented at meetings of Heads of Government of CARICOM. In July 1994, the Heads of Government, meeting at the CARICOM Summit, requested their Secretary-General to pursue efforts to strengthen cooperation with the United Nations. In November 1994, I met in Jamaica with a number of CARICOM Heads of Government and with its Secretary-General on the situation in Haiti and on matters of regional cooperation. I expressed my appreciation for the special role the Community continues to play in the restoration of democracy in Haiti and their contribution of military and police personnel to the United Nations Mission in Haiti (UNMIH), as well as their contributions to the joint United Nations/OAS International Civilian Mission in Haiti (MICIVIH).

943.    On 20 December 1994, the General Assembly adopted resolution 49/141 on cooperation between the United Nations and CARICOM. In January 1995, the Community and ECLAC signed a Memorandum of Understanding for Cooperation. This will offer opportunities to advance cooperation between the two organizations in a number of areas of critical importance. The Secretary-General of CARICOM participated in the Intergovernmental Meeting of Experts on South-South Cooperation at United Nations Headquarters from 31 July to 4 August 1995.

4.    Cooperation in the European area

944.    During the past year, the United Nations has continued to strengthen its cooperation with European regional organizations. In December 1994, I attended the summit meeting of OSCE at Budapest. The United Nations and OSCE had previously agreed upon a practical division of labour concerning activities in the European continent and under this framework each Organization has provided support to the efforts of the other. OSCE has assisted the Special Envoy of the Secretary-General in negotiations he has arranged relating to the situation in Abkhazia, Georgia, while the United Nations has given technical advice and guidance to OSCE regarding an OSCE peace-keeping force being organized for possible deployment in Nagorny Karabakh. Cooperation between the two Organizations has also been extended to a variety of other fields, such as election monitoring. Other Europe-based organizations with which the United Nations has had substantive cooperation in the past year include EU, the Council for Europe, NATO, in the context of military operations in the former Yugoslavia, and CIS, with which the United Nations Observer Mission in Georgia (UNOMIG) works closely in Abkhazia.

5.    Cooperation with the Organization of the Islamic Conference

945.    In the context of ongoing efforts to enhance cooperation with regional organizations, the General Assembly in its resolution 49/15 of 15 November 1994 welcomed the decision of the secretariats of the United Nations and OIC to develop mechanisms of cooperation in the political field. Consultations to that end have been initiated between the two secretariats over the past year. The two Organizations have also had increased consultations during the past year with regard to a number of important regional political issues, such as Afghanistan, Tajikistan, Somalia and Bosnia and Herzegovina. The recent accordance of observer status to OIC in the United Nations-sponsored inter-Tajik talks reflects the increasing interaction between the two Organizations in the political field. The Coordination Meeting of the focal points of the United Nations system and OIC and its specialized institutions, which took place at Geneva in June, also adopted a number of important decisions to consolidate and rationalize cooperation between the two Organizations in nine mutually agreed priority areas of cooperation.

6.    Cooperation with the League of Arab States

946.    Areas of cooperation between the United Nations and LAS also continued to be consoli-

dated, pursuant to General Assembly resolution 49/14 of 15 November 1994. The general meeting on cooperation between the representatives of the secretariats of the two bodies, held at Vienna from 19 to 21 July, on the occasion of the fiftieth anniversary of the United Nations and LAS, provided an opportunity for the follow-up of multilateral proposals aimed at strengthening cooperation to promote social and economic development and the exchange of views in the fields of preventive action and mine clearance. The United Nations continued to cooperate with LAS on the question of Somalia. LAS, jointly with OAU and OIC, held a meeting on Somalia at Cairo on 22 and 23 February 1995 in which the United Nations participated as an observer. The participating organizations agreed to continue to undertake joint efforts to assist national reconciliation in Somalia.

### G. *Disarmament*

947. Since my previous report on the work of the Organization it has become increasingly evident that the proliferation of weapons of mass destruction and the availability of their basic components constitute a growing threat to international peace and security. The hypothesis that terrorists, with no territory to defend and unafraid of sacrificing themselves, could develop and use weapons of mass destruction is a frightening prospect, which is already affecting the security perceptions of many people throughout the world. Therefore, a coordinated response of the international community to those threats, and to the destabilizing effects caused by the unrestrained flow of conventional weapons, remains a high priority. Within the context of preventing the proliferation of nuclear weapons, the strengthening of the nuclear non-proliferation regime achieved in 1995 by the Review and Extension Conference of the Parties to the Treaty on the Non-Proliferation of Nuclear Weapons is an appropriate answer and should be accompanied as soon as possible by the entry into force of the Convention on the Prohibition of the Development, Production, Stockpiling and Use of Chemical Weapons, as well as by the establishment of a regime for the verification of compliance with the Convention on the Prohibition of the Development, Production and Stockpiling of Bacteriological (Biological) and Toxin Weapons and on Their Destruction.

948. While the Review and Extension Conference of the Non-Proliferation Treaty was a major focus of disarmament efforts in 1995, the international community has undertaken other disarmament initiatives to deal with the destabilizing effects and unconscionable waste of resources caused by the unrestrained flow of conventional weapons. The progress achieved, as far as the review process of the Convention on Prohibitions or Restrictions on the Use of Certain Conventional Weapons

Which May Be Deemed to Be Excessively Injurious or to Have Indiscriminate Effects is concerned, in assuring the full protection of civilians from the indiscriminate effects of anti-personnel land-mines and working towards their eventual elimination constitutes a step in the right direction. Furthermore, transparency measures, such as the Register of Conventional Arms, must be strengthened, and confidence-building and disarmament initiatives at the regional level should be developed further, in particular with reference to illicit traffic in light conventional weapons.

949. The Nuclear Non-Proliferation Treaty now has 178 States parties, commanding virtually universal adherence. The indefinite extension of the Treaty, decided upon at the 1995 Review and Extension Conference, as well as the other commitments made by the States parties reflected in the documents of the Conference, have strengthened the nuclear non-proliferation regime and will make a substantial contribution to the maintenance of international peace and security. I expressed gratification at the success of the Conference and recommended that the States parties continue to work in a spirit of cooperation and pursue the elimination of nuclear weapons as the ultimate goal of the non-proliferation process.

950. There have been advances in other areas of nuclear disarmament. The negotiations on a comprehensive test-ban treaty have made progress at the Conference on Disarmament at Geneva and strengthened determination to resolve technical issues could bring the negotiations to a successful conclusion no later than 1996. The negotiating mandate was agreed upon at the Conference on Disarmament on a treaty banning the production of fissile material and this should enable the Conference to begin the negotiations expeditiously and bring them to an early and successful conclusion. Other encouraging steps are Security Council resolution 984(1995) and the declarations by the nuclear-weapon States concerning both negative and positive security assurances. Proposals aimed at transforming these unilateral declarations into a legally binding treaty obligation would contribute considerably to further progress in this area.

951. The general strengthening of the nuclear non-proliferation regime is matched and reinforced by the remarkable results achieved so far by the United States of America, the Russian Federation and the other European countries in post-cold-war security arrangements. The elimination of intermediate-range nuclear forces in Europe under the Treaty between the United States of America and the Union of Soviet Socialist Republics on the Elimination of Their Intermediate-Range and Shorter-Range Missiles, the reduction of nuclear strategic warheads in operational deployment resulting from the START process, the

continuing successful implementation of the Treaty on Conventional Armed Forces in Europe and the ongoing security dialogue within the OSCE framework form the basis of a cooperative security system that in some measure could transcend the narrow limits of the European region. In Europe, the newly emerging cooperative security system is the product of negotiations based on consensus and cooperation. Significant initiatives for security dialogues are also being promoted in Asia, in Africa and in Latin America. Further enhancement of those initiatives would be an important step towards the strengthening of international peace and security at the regional level.

952. While progress in the dismantlement of nuclear weapons is encouraged, concerns about the safety and security of fissile material have increased. The smuggling of nuclear material is no longer only a fear but a frightening reality. Stronger global and national measures are needed to deal with illicit trafficking and to guarantee the secure disposal and storage of such material. Particularly important is universal recognition that International Atomic Energy Agency (IAEA) safeguards are an integral part of the international non-proliferation regime and that the Agency plays an indispensable role in ensuring the implementation of the Treaty on the Non-Proliferation of Nuclear Weapons.

953. The Treaty for the Prohibition of Nuclear Weapons in Latin America and the Caribbean (Treaty of Tlatelolco) and the South Pacific Nuclear Free Zone Treaty (Treaty of Rarotonga) are essential building blocks to progress towards nuclear-free regions elsewhere in the world, in particular in the Middle East and Asia, which would include in their scope all weapons of mass destruction. There has also been progress on the treaty establishing a nuclear-weapon-free zone in Africa.

954. There has been a steady increase in the number of ratifications of the Convention on the Prohibition of the Development, Production, Stockpiling and Use of Chemical Weapons, which has now reached 27 States parties. In discharging my responsibility as depositary to the Convention, I have written to all Member States urging ratification and entry into force of the Convention at the earliest possible date. In connection with the Convention on Biological Weapons, efforts of States parties are under way to strengthen the Convention by developing a legally binding verification protocol. The frightful consequences for humankind of biological warfare, or terrorism, must be avoided at all costs.

955. Measures to prevent proliferation of weapons should be fashioned to avoid any obstruction to the development process of countries. Developing countries need unimpeded access to technology and agreement is needed on appropriate controls concerning technology transfers, including transparency measures, that would be universal and non-discriminatory in nature.

956. The urgent problem of the proliferation of conventional weapons also demands the continuing attention of the international community. Unrestrained and illegal arms transfers have resulted in suffering and misery for hundreds of thousands of people, particularly in the developing world. At the global level continued support by Member States for the Register of Conventional Arms is essential. Reports to the Register indicate a degree of openness and transparency with regard to legitimate arms transfers for defensive purposes. Such openness will promote confidence and encourage responsible conduct in the transfer of major conventional weapon systems. Initiatives and ideas from regions and subregions, in particular Africa, Asia and Latin America, can enhance the global Register with complementary confidence- and security-building measures.

957. At the regional and subregional level, in particular in the developing world, direct action is needed to deal with the flourishing illicit traffic in light weapons, which is destabilizing the security of a number of countries. With the support of seven Member States in the Sahara-Sahel region, I dispatched an advisory mission with a view to assisting those States in their efforts to combat and stem the illicit flow of light weapons within and across their borders. More resources must be invested if there is to be any prospect of success.

H.  *Post-conflict peace-building*

*Strategies*

958. An International Colloquium on Post-Conflict Reconstruction Strategies was convened on 23 and 24 June at the Austrian Centre for Peace and Conflict Resolution at Stadt Schlaining, Austria. It was attended by 58 participants from United Nations political, humanitarian and development entities, specialized agencies, the Bretton Woods institutions, donor countries and non-governmental organizations as well as representatives from war-torn societies. The meeting was organized by the Department for Development Support and Management Services, in cooperation with the Austrian Centre, and supported by the Government of Austria as a contribution to the definition of the role of the United Nations in the next half century as part of the fiftieth anniversary activities. The Department for Development Support and Management Services contributed a paper setting out a strategic programme for reconstruction and development.

959. The idea for the meeting stemmed from the Supplement to the Secretary-General's "An Agenda for Peace" (A/50/60-S/1995/1), which stresses the need for integrated action between

United Nations organizations, the parties to the conflict and other institutions prepared to assist in the reconstruction of a country; its purpose was to identify the practical and institutional issues that must be addressed to bring this concept to reality.

960. The main topic of post-conflict reconstruction was addressed under four headings: strategic issues, needs and capabilities, an integrated post-conflict reconstruction framework and mobilization of resources. Because of the interrelationship between these four topics, the themes recurred throughout the deliberations and there was considerable cross-fertilization of ideas. The meeting was an example of the coming together of various organizations, within and outside the United Nations system, all with a common interest in a topic that is of increasing concern to the international community. It is hoped that the ideas and recommendations presented in the report will serve as a basis for a clear definition of the role of the United Nations in post-conflict reconstruction, and for establishing arrangements that will ensure a swift, effective and integrated response to such situations by the United Nations system.

961. Issues falling within the four categories of post-conflict peace-building discussed at the Colloquium have been addressed elsewhere in this report; here I will focus on two specific concerns: electoral assistance and mine clearance.

*Electoral assistance*

962. In the period from July 1994 to 10 August 1995, the United Nations received 19 new requests for electoral assistance, from Armenia, Azerbaijan, Bangladesh, Benin, Chad, the Congo, Côte d'Ivoire, Fiji, Gabon, the Gambia, Guinea, Haiti, Kyrgyzstan, Namibia, the Niger, Sao Tome and Principe, the former Yugoslav Republic of Macedonia, Uganda and the United Republic of Tanzania. In the case of the Congo, assistance could not be provided owing to lack of lead time. In addition to these new requests, assistance was also provided in 12 cases, to Brazil, El Salvador, Equatorial Guinea, Honduras, Lesotho, Liberia, Malawi, Mexico, Mozambique, the Netherlands Antilles, Sierra Leone and MINURSO, in response to requests received prior to July 1994 (*see fig. 19*).

963. Since July 1994, 30 States and United Nations missions have received or will soon receive some form of electoral assistance from the United Nations system. The type of electoral assistance provided has varied according to the requests received and the resources available. Following the guidelines provided to Member States (see A/49/675 and Corr.1, annex III), verification of electoral processes was conducted in Mozambique and plans for a verification mission in Liberia are currently on hold. The coordination and support approach was used in the cases of Armenia and Benin, and follow-up and report/observation was

used in Guinea, Kyrgyzstan, the former Yugoslav Republic of Macedonia and Sao Tome and Principe. Technical assistance, the most frequently provided form of electoral assistance, was given to Brazil, El Salvador, Equatorial Guinea, Haiti, Honduras, Liberia, Malawi, Mexico, Mozambique, Namibia, the Niger, Sierra Leone and Uganda. A total of 11 needs assessment missions were also conducted during this period.

964. Since the creation of the Electoral Assistance Division in 1992, the United Nations has been involved in the electoral processes of 61 Member States and some States have requested electoral assistance more than once. United Nations electoral assistance this past year in Mozambique and Armenia illustrates the process in action.

965. In Mozambique, the United Nations provided technical assistance and a verification mission for the first multi-party elections, held in October 1994. In accordance with the terms of the General Peace Agreement signed at Rome on 4 October 1992, ONUMOZ, through its electoral component, monitored the conduct of the entire electoral process. The Electoral Division of ONUMOZ fielded 148 electoral officers throughout the country to monitor voter registration, civic education, political campaigns, political party access to as well as impartiality of the media, polling, vote counting and tabulation of the vote at provincial counting centres. On the election days ONUMOZ deployed 2,300 international observers.

966. The United Nations also provided technical assistance to Mozambique through a UNDP project implemented by the Department for Development Support and Management Services. The project coordinated international financial and material support and provided technical assistance throughout the entire process in the areas of organization, training, civic education, jurisprudence, social communication and financial management. This assistance entailed management, coordination and monitoring of a $64.5 million budget made up of contributions from 17 countries and international institutions. Technical assistance included the training of 2,600 electoral officers at the national, provincial and district levels, 8,000 census agents, 1,600 civic education agents and 52,000 polling officers. In addition to a 12-person UNDP advisory team to the National Election Commission, 3 to 5 United Nations Volunteers were assigned to each of the 11 electoral constituencies and worked closely with the provincial and district electoral authorities.

967. In addition to the ONUMOZ electoral verification mandate, a United Nations trust fund for assistance to registered political parties was established to assist all political parties not signatories to the General Peace Agreement to prepare for the elections. The electoral component of

ONUMOZ also designed a programme to enhance national observation. The programme provided training, transportation and subsidies for nearly 35,000 party agents to monitor the elections. A parallel programme funded by the United Nations trust fund provided computer training to 78 representatives from all political parties to enable them to monitor the processing of the vote at the provincial and national levels.

968.    Armenia requested electoral assistance from the United Nations in January 1995 in connection with the elections to the National Assembly to be held in July 1995. In February, an officer from the Electoral Assistance Division conducted a needs assessment mission and returned in April to establish a joint operation coordinating unit together with a representative of OSCE. The purpose of the joint operation was to coordinate and support the activities of the international observers. Members of the joint operation were stationed in three regional offices for a period of six weeks in order to follow the pre-election process, including the registration of candidates, the electoral campaign, and poll preparations. On election day, 5 July, the joint operation deployed over 90 observers throughout the country to observe the conduct of the elections. Observers visited more than 300 precinct electoral committees, starting from the opening of the polls to the counting of votes at the precinct level. The group of observers represented 18 Governments and several governmental and non-governmental organizations.

*Mine clearance*

969.    The ever-growing problem of uncleared land-mines continues to pose a humanitarian crisis of enormous proportions, devastating vast amounts of territory, possibly for decades. Despite the increased efforts of the international community, more than 20 times more mines are being laid than removed. Within the United Nations system, the Department of Humanitarian Affairs has intensified its activities as focal point for the coordination of land-mine assistance programmes. Since its establishment in early 1992, the Department has been involved in the formulation and implementation of mine-assistance programmes. Pursuant to General Assembly resolutions 48/7 of 19 October 1993 and 49/215 of 23 December 1994, the Department has been convening interdepartmental/inter-agency consultations on land-mine policy to examine all aspects of United Nations involvement in mine-related activities and to develop standard United Nations policy concerning the institutional aspects that need to be addressed in an integrated United Nations land-mine operation. The United Nations approach has been to focus on the creation of a national indigenous mine-clearance capacity, including appropriate ar-

rangements to enable continuity of national mine-clearance efforts, as normalization of conditions in a country progresses.

970.    During the past year, the United Nations engaged in the implementation and/or development of demining activities in nine countries. Programmes differ in structure, size and arrangements for funding and implementation.

971.    Afghanistan is the most mature of the United Nations programmes, having been in operation for six years. There are currently almost 3,000 deminers working in the field. Over the past five years, the Programme has cleared a total of 54 square kilometres of high-priority area and destroyed over 110,000 mines and 215,000 unexploded devices. Approximately 2.5 million people received mine-awareness briefings.

972.    Angola is probably the most mine-affected country in the world and, together with the implementation of the peace-keeping operation, a mine-action programme has been launched in cooperation between the United Nations, the parties to the Lusaka Protocol and non-governmental organizations. The Central Mine Action Office has been established as part of the Humanitarian Assistance Coordination Unit in Angola and is mandated to create an indigenous mine-clearance capacity. The Office is responsible for the implementation of the mine-action plan and coordinates all mine-related activities. UNAVEM III, in conjunction with the Office, is in the process of establishing a mine-clearance training school, which will form the core of the Angolan mine-action programme.

973.    In Cambodia, the Cambodian Mine Action Centre (a governmental entity with technical advice provided through a UNDP project) has been coordinating all clearance activities. Over the past year, the Centre's 1,556 staff have continued to survey, mark and clear minefields, and teach mine awareness. Since the commencement of operations, 16,436,971 square metres of land have been cleared, with 423,708 unexploded devices and 61,787 mines destroyed.

974.    In June 1995, a United Nations demining expert undertook a mission to Chad on behalf of the Department of Humanitarian Affairs to evaluate the land-mine problem in the Tibesti region.

975.    Mine-clearance activities in Mozambique involve both the United Nations own programme, the accelerated demining programme, and non-governmental organizations and companies funded by the United Nations or by donors. The accelerated demining programme consists of 500 Mozambican deminers who were trained, equipped and deployed by the United Nations.

976.    The use of mines in the conflict in Abkhazia, Georgia, is extensive. The Department of

Humanitarian Affairs has sent an assessment mission to the area and has suggested activities to reduce the number of land-mine accidents. Approval from the Abkhaz authorities is required before a programme can be started.

977. The problem of land-mines and unexploded ordnance in Rwanda has resulted in large numbers of accidents. Both the Department of Peace-keeping Operations and the Department of Humanitarian Affairs have assessed the situation and a plan has been developed. Action is of course dependent upon the approval of the Government.

978. In Somalia, a limited demining programme implemented by local Somali entities worked well until the security situation prevented follow-up to clearance activities in the field.

979. In Yemen, the United Nations is providing expert technical assistance to the Government on mine-clearance and mapping methods.

980. The continuing conflict in the former Yugoslavia has prevented the development of a humanitarian demining programme. However, United Nations peace-keeping forces and other United Nations agencies have engaged in mine-clearance activities as part of their attempts to carry out their mandates.

981. At Headquarters, the Department of Humanitarian Affairs, pursuant to General Assembly resolution 49/215, established the Mine Clearance and Policy Unit to further strengthen support functions to demining operations. To facilitate the planning, implementation and support of mine-clearance programmes and policies, the Unit is developing a database containing information about the worldwide land-mine situation. Country-specific data, as well as general programme and financial data, are maintained in the database, which serves as a central repository of information for Member States, United Nations departments and agencies, and other interested parties.

982. On 30 November 1994, I established a voluntary trust fund for assistance in mine clearance. The fund's purpose is to provide special resources for mine-clearance programmes, including mine-awareness training and surveys, and to contract mine-clearance activities in situations where other funding is not immediately available. Some examples of the types of activities that could be funded from the trust fund include, but are not limited to, assessment missions, provision of seed money, emergency mine clearance, projects where other sources of funding are not readily available, consciousness-raising and enhancing Headquarters support for mine-clearance programmes in the field, including through the improvement of the central land-mine database.

983. In accordance with the recommendations contained in the Secretary-General's report on assistance in mine clearance (A/49/357 and Add.1),

the Mine Clearance and Policy Unit began the process of creating a United Nations demining stand-by capacity in order to expedite the provision of expert personnel, specialized equipment and facilities to United Nations mine-action programmes. These in-kind contributions have been a vital component of United Nations mine-action programmes. The establishment of a stand-by capacity is intended to institutionalize this support.

984. From 5 to 7 July 1995, I convened an international meeting on mine clearance at the Palais des Nations at Geneva. The objective of the meeting was to enhance international awareness of the land-mine problem in all its dimensions, to seek further political and financial support for United Nations mine-action activities and to increase international cooperation in this field. It consisted of three elements: a high-level segment devoted to statements by Governments and organizations, which also provided the opportunity to announce pledges to the voluntary trust fund for assistance in mine clearance and the United Nations demining stand-by capacity; nine panels of experts that discussed various aspects of the land-mine problem; and an exhibition focusing on the impact of land-mines on affected populations and international efforts to address the problem.

985. The international meeting was attended by representatives of 97 Governments and more than 60 organizations, bringing together 800 participants. Contributions in the amount of $22 million were announced towards the voluntary trust fund and 23 countries indicated contributions to the United Nations stand-by capacity totalling $7 million.

986. All delegations referred to the magnitude of the global land-mine crisis, which continues to deteriorate, and emphasized the need for urgent and effective measures to reverse the trend. Many delegations and organizations called for a total ban on land-mines; most delegations stressed the need to strengthen the provisions of the Convention on Prohibitions or Restrictions on the Use of Certain Conventional Weapons Which May Be Deemed to Be Excessively Injurious or to Have Indiscriminate Effects.

987. There are still only 49 States parties to the Convention and its protocols, which include the protocol placing prohibitions and restrictions on the use of land-mines. The Convention needs to be strengthened to make its provisions applicable to both internal and international conflicts. It is in internal conflicts that the indiscriminate use of mines has caused the most suffering and misery to civilian populations. The 1995 Review Conference provides an opportunity to strengthen the Convention and its land-mine protocol. Looking at the magnitude of the problem, States parties should seriously consider a total ban on anti-personnel land-mines.

988.   A revitalized Advisory Board on Disarmament Matters is developing ideas for the better integration of disarmament-related security measures with development in countries emerging from inter- or intra-State conflict. The Board is preparing for the Secretary-General's review a study entitled "Some thoughts on the development of the disarmament agenda at the end of the century", which should be relevant to the proposed fourth special session of the General Assembly devoted to disarmament.

## V.  Conclusion

989.   From the deep-rooted and far-reaching United Nations work for economic, social and humanitarian progress to the immediate and often urgent efforts to prevent, contain and resolve conflicts, what emerges from the pages of this report is an image of a multifaceted and ever-evolving organization—an organization responding flexibly to global change and to the changing needs of the international community.

990.   There are signs that the massive educational effort under way at all levels of national and international society in this fiftieth anniversary year is helping to create a welcome realism about the role of the United Nations in world affairs today, as well as a renewed sense of commitment to fulfil the original promise set down in the Charter 50 years ago.

991.   Major aspects of this landmark year are still to come, including the Special Commemorative Meeting of the General Assembly, to be held at Headquarters from 22 to 24 October 1995, and the commemoration in London in January 1996 of the first session of the General Assembly. None the less, it is already evident that this anniversary has created a spirit and a momentum that go well beyond the commemoration and celebration expected at such a point in time. Virtually every dimension of the United Nations has been energized. New realities are being used as the basis for reassessment and redesign. Successes are being built upon. A new spirit of cooperation at every level and on virtually every issue is within the grasp of a wider contingent of committed people than ever before.

992.   It is vital, therefore, that the spirit of the fiftieth anniversary be carried forward in all these respects. Most fundamentally, it will be important to continue the major efforts launched this year with the objective of enabling the United Nations as an institution to become more intellectually creative, more financially stable, more managerially effective and more responsive to all sectors of society.

993.   The fiftieth year has also generated criticism of the Organization, and this is serving to make the United Nations healthier and stronger. Shortcomings of the Organization itself, inadequate mandates, insufficient financial and material resources, the failure of Member States to fulfil their obligations or take on new responsibilities—all have, on occasion, been catalysts for criticism. However, the ultimate source of today's criticism can be found in the impact of globalization on the Organization and its Member States: as the United Nations is being asked to take on more duties and expand its activities, it is to be expected that the level of criticism should intensify. At the same time, globalization can work against the will to increase involvement, feeding fear and isolationism; criticisms born of these sentiments can create dangerous misperceptions.

994.   Healthy criticism is an indispensable form of participation in and support for the United Nations in its effort to revitalize the international system. This report is itself an effort at transparency, revealing both the strengths and weaknesses of the Organization to the widest possible audience. The continuing calls for reform, and the reforms already enacted and under way, testify to the recognition by far more people than ever before that the United Nations is a truly indispensable element in world affairs and that if it did not now exist, it would be impossible to create it under present conditions. Thus the legacy of 1945 must be cherished and carried forward. In parallel, techniques that have succeeded must be transformed to meet the challenges of a new era.

995.   Reflection and reform are not new to this Organization. As envisioned by the founders, the United Nations has evolved over time and adapted to new conditions, all the while in pursuit of a better life for all individuals and a better world for humanity as a whole. The fiftieth anniversary year, however, by arriving at such a critical juncture in the history of international relations, offers an unprecedented opportunity for change. As Secretary-General, I have from the outset been deeply committed to and concerned with reform. Looking back over the past three and a half years of effort for change and the substantial managerial steps taken during the period covered by this report, I believe that a continuing need exists for further, substantial reforms in the period ahead.

996.   The communiqué issued by the Heads of State and Government of seven major industrialized nations and the President of the European Commission following their twenty-first annual economic summit meeting at Halifax provided suggestions for enhancing the effectiveness and coherence of the United Nations system in the economic, social and environmental fields and in the humanitarian area. The Halifax participants expressed their intention to utilize the gathering of Heads of State and Government in New York from 22 to 24 October 1995 for the observance of the fiftieth anniversary of the United Nations as an

occasion to advance a consensus on ways to help the United Nations system to face the challenges of the next century.

997. Throughout this fiftieth anniversary year, serious consideration has been given to the future role and responsibilities of the United Nations by conferences, workshops and study programmes held at every level and in every part of the world. Two independent commissions have issued reports: "The United Nations in Its Second Half-Century", produced by an independent working group under the co-chairmanship of Mr. Richard von Weizsäcker and Mr. Moeen Qureshi, sponsored at my request by the Ford Foundation and facilitated by Yale University; and "Our Global Neighbourhood", produced by the Commission on Global Governance under the co-chairmanship of Mr. Ingvar Carlsson and Mr. Shridath Ramphal. The South Center also has been active in reviewing various aspects of reform.

998. These projects and commitments deserve appreciation and serious consideration by the international community. Discussions have taken place regarding the establishment of an open-ended high-level working group of the General Assembly that would undertake a thorough review of all relevant United Nations materials, Member States' submissions and independent studies and reports relating to the revitalization, strengthening and reform of the United Nations system.

999. The days, weeks and months covered in this report have been filled with discouraging developments. But from a larger, longer-term point of view, there are many signs that progress is being made, giving cause for confidence that, over time, success is entirely possible. Never before have so many courageous and committed people been involved in world betterment. Never before have nations recognized so clearly that their fate is bound up with each other. And never before has it been so undeniable that mutually beneficial international institutions of cooperation—with the United Nations foremost among them—are a vital global necessity.

1000. It is therefore imperative to remain focused on the reality of movement towards long-term achievement and not to permit dismay over immediate difficulties to weaken the positive momentum that has been achieved.

1001. There are three immediate problems, however, that must concern us deeply, for if they are not effectively addressed they can irreparably damage the United Nations as a mechanism for progress.

1002. First, the safety and integrity of United Nations personnel in the field must be respected. When lightly armed peace-keepers or unarmed aid workers on a humanitarian mission are threatened, taken hostage, harmed or even killed, the world must act to prevent such intolerable behaviour. The credibility of all United Nations peace operations is at stake; to preserve it, personnel must be protected as they carry out the duties the international community has sent them to accomplish.

1003. Secondly, the financial situation of the Organization must be placed on an adequate and sustainable footing. Calls for ever-greater United Nations effectiveness under conditions of financial penury make no sense. It is as though the town fire department were being dispatched to put out fires raging in several places at once while a collection was being taken to raise money for the fire-fighting equipment. The deterioration of the Organization's financial position must be reversed.

1004. And, lastly, funds for development are drying up. This is a consequence of the end of the cold-war contest, of the competing demands of peace-keeping and development for scarce resources, and of donor fatigue over the time and difficulty of creating progress on the ground. The willingness to spend money to try to contain conflicts around the world, while necessary and admirable, is not enough. Unless development is funded as well, the world can expect only the continuation of cycles marked by the alternation of terrible strife, uneasy stand-off and strife once again. To break this downward spiral, sustainable human development must be instituted everywhere. A new vision of development, and a universal commitment to it, are indispensable for the world progress all peoples seek.

1005. During the past year we have seen far too many innocent civilians, especially women and children, losing their lives or being condemned to carry on under appalling conditions. We continue to witness scenes of refugees deprived of their most basic rights and struggling desperately to survive. And hundreds of millions of people live in poverty so dire as to render them incapable of taking effective action to improve their own condition. Thus the existence of a true international community has yet to be demonstrated. Nothing could do more to bring such an instrument of human solidarity into being than a commitment undertaken now to ensure that all the poor countries of the world are set firmly on the path of development as we enter the next century. Such an achievement would bring an end to degradation and despair for a huge proportion of our fellow human beings and would represent one of history's most dramatic chapters of progress.

1006. We have before us an opportunity to combine the ongoing, incremental process of reform with a comprehensive vision of the future. The legacy of the founders at this half-century mark should be our inspiration as we step forward with pride to meet this challenge. Together we can bring the world of the Charter to the world of today.

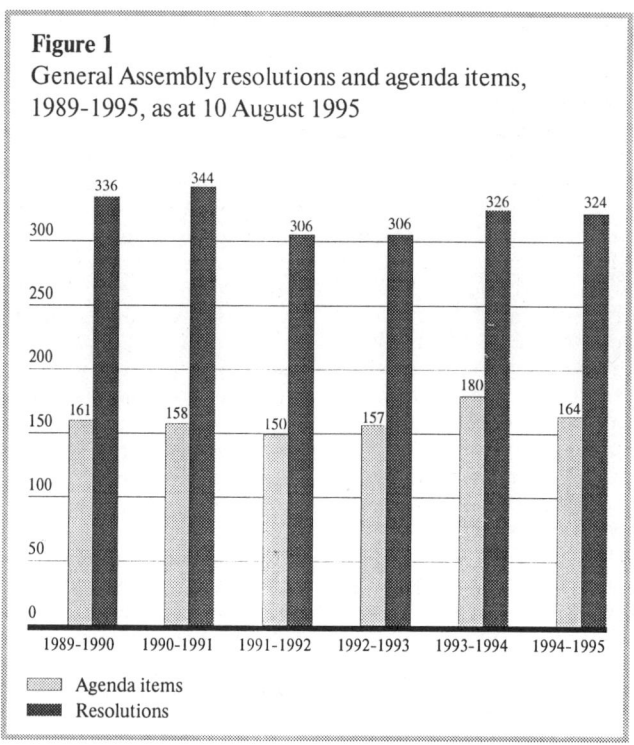

**Figure 1**
General Assembly resolutions and agenda items,
1989-1995, as at 10 August 1995

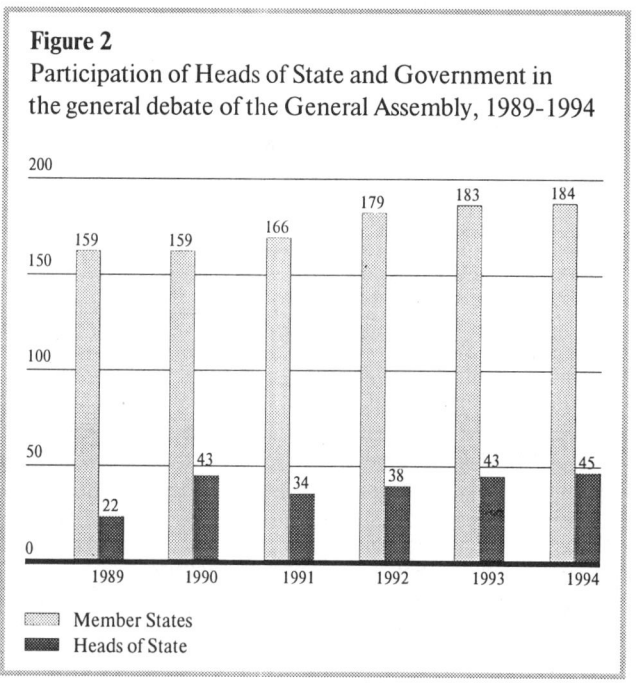

**Figure 2**
Participation of Heads of State and Government in
the general debate of the General Assembly, 1989-1994

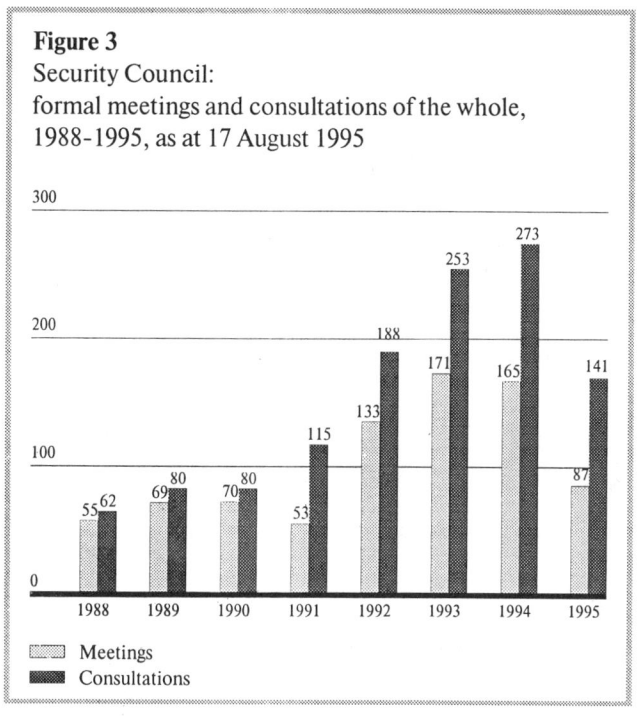

**Figure 3**
Security Council:
formal meetings and consultations of the whole,
1988-1995, as at 17 August 1995

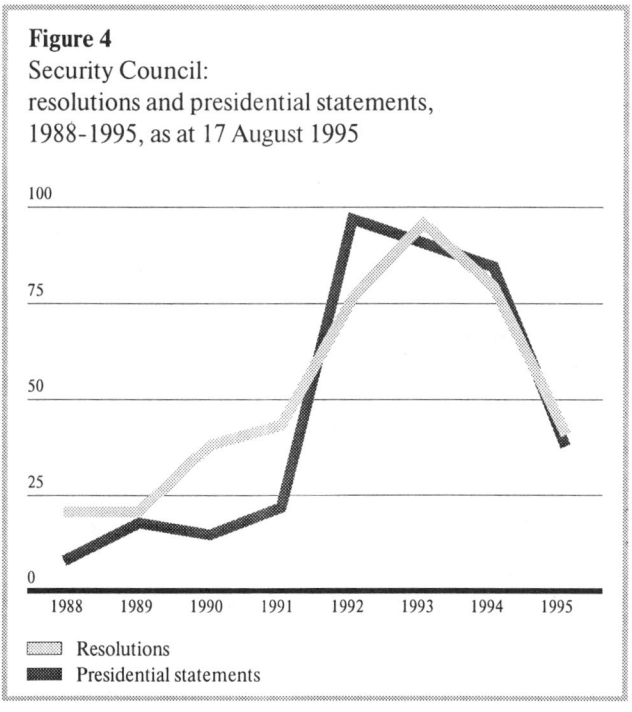

**Figure 4**
Security Council:
resolutions and presidential statements,
1988-1995, as at 17 August 1995

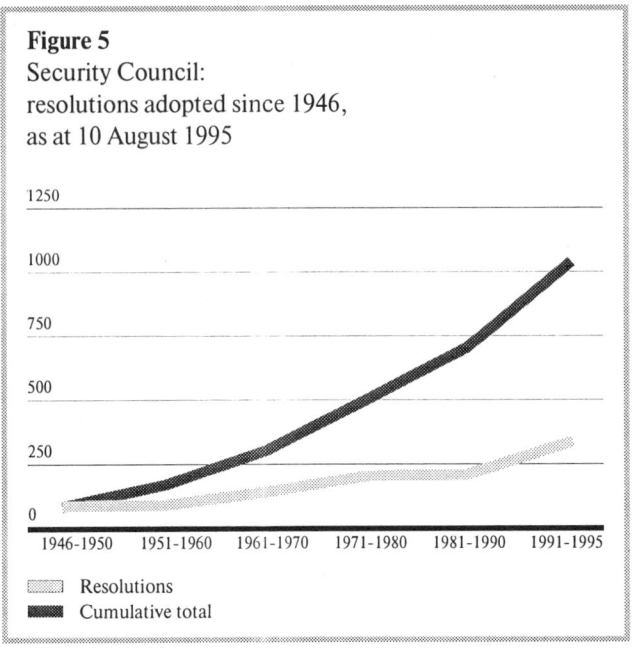

Figure 5
Security Council:
resolutions adopted since 1946,
as at 10 August 1995

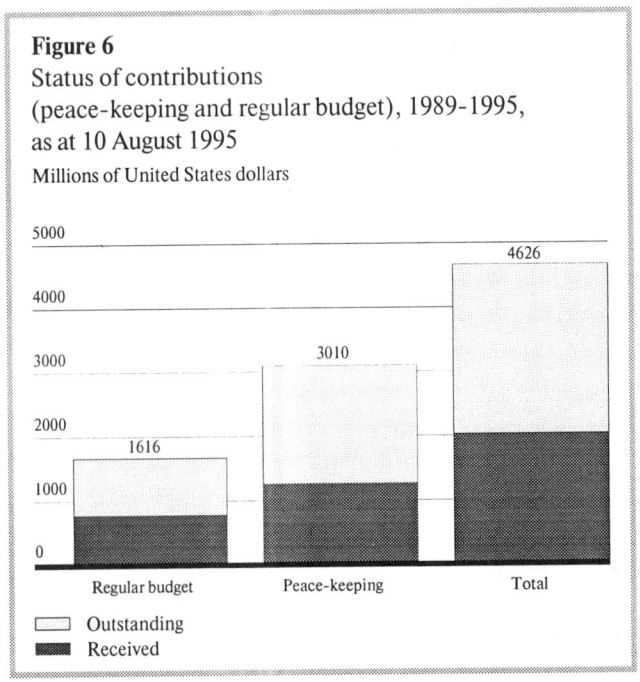

Figure 6
Status of contributions
(peace-keeping and regular budget), 1989-1995,
as at 10 August 1995
Millions of United States dollars

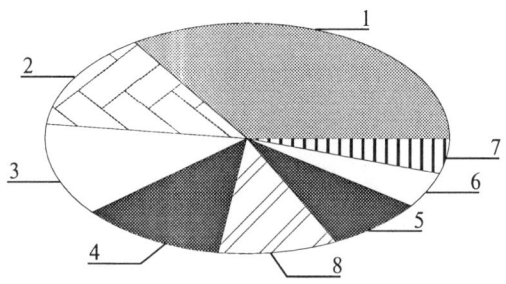

**Figure 7**

Revised appropriations for the biennium 1994-1995

Thousands of United States dollars

1 Administration and management (896,821)
2 Staff assessment (357,798)
3 Regional cooperation for development (339,333)
4 International cooperation for development (307,254)
5 Political affairs and peace-keeping operations (198,338)
6 Human rights and humanitarian affairs (132,666)
7 Public information (131,443)
8 Others (244,629)

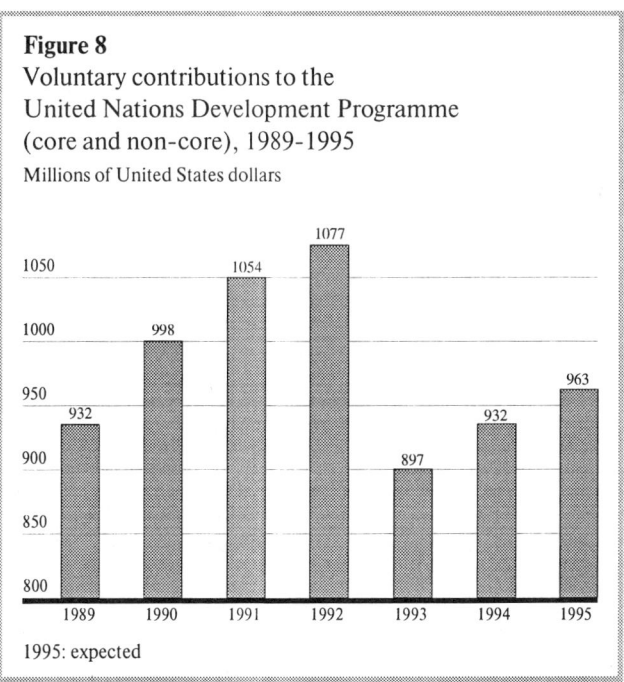

**Figure 8**

Voluntary contributions to the
United Nations Development Programme
(core and non-core), 1989-1995

Millions of United States dollars

1995: expected

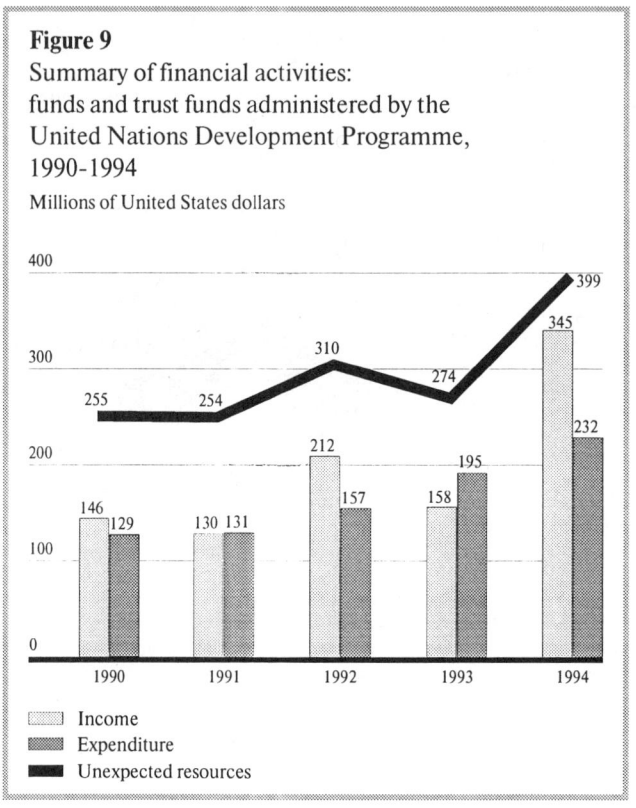

**Figure 9**
Summary of financial activities:
funds and trust funds administered by the
United Nations Development Programme,
1990-1994

Millions of United States dollars

Income
Expenditure
Unexpected resources

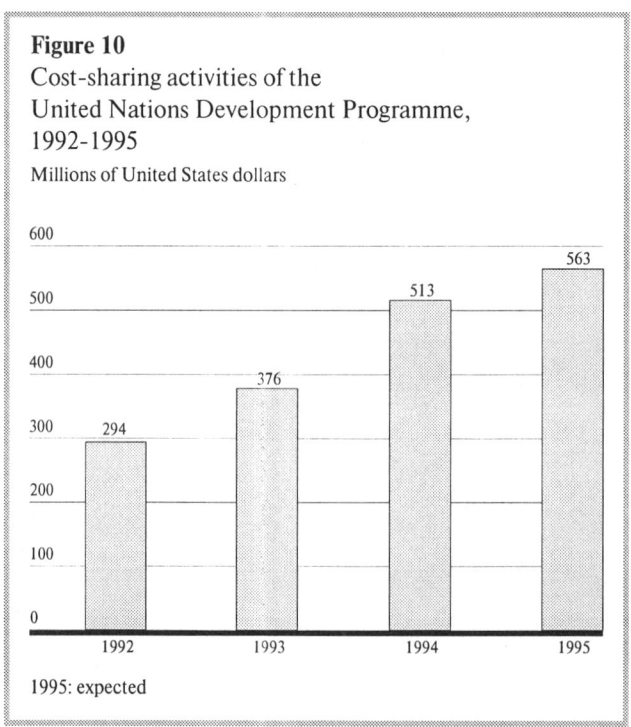

**Figure 10**
Cost-sharing activities of the
United Nations Development Programme,
1992-1995

Millions of United States dollars

1995: expected

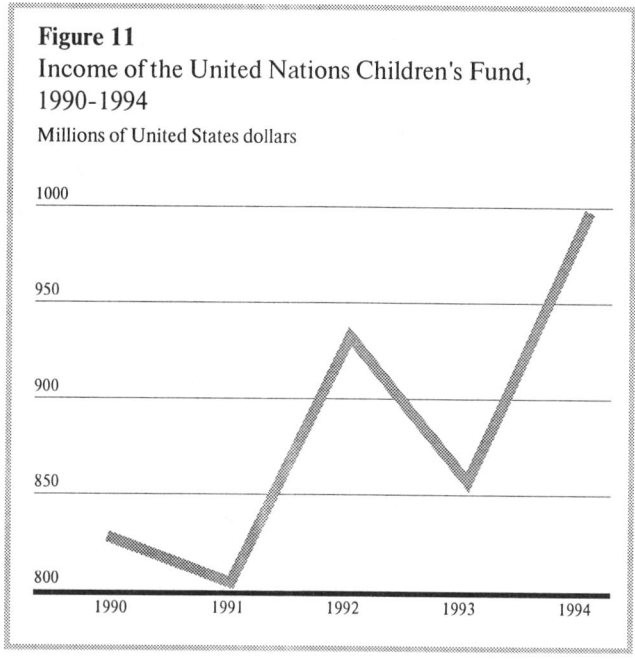

**Figure 11**

Income of the United Nations Children's Fund, 1990-1994

Millions of United States dollars

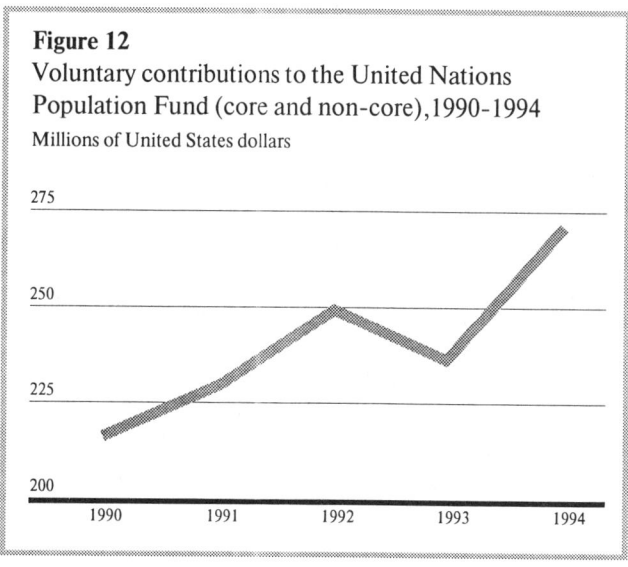

**Figure 12**

Voluntary contributions to the United Nations Population Fund (core and non-core),1990-1994

Millions of United States dollars

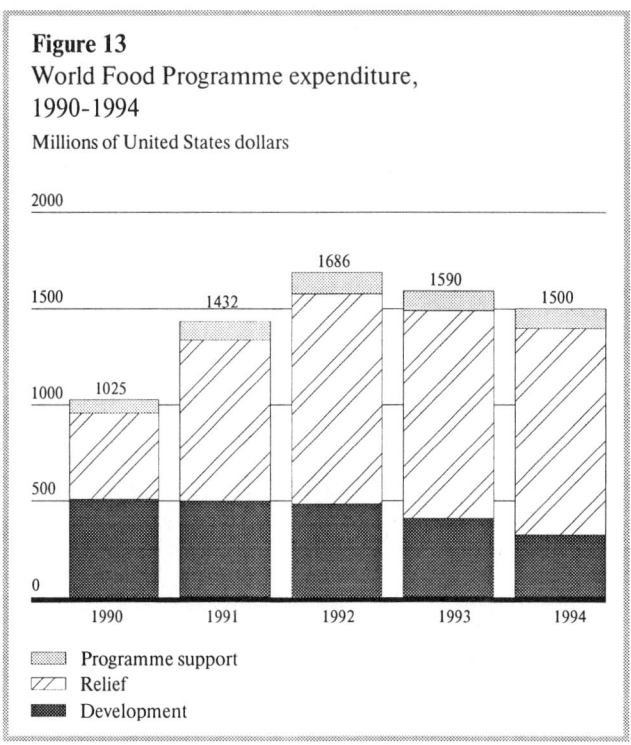

**Figure 13**
World Food Programme expenditure,
1990-1994
Millions of United States dollars

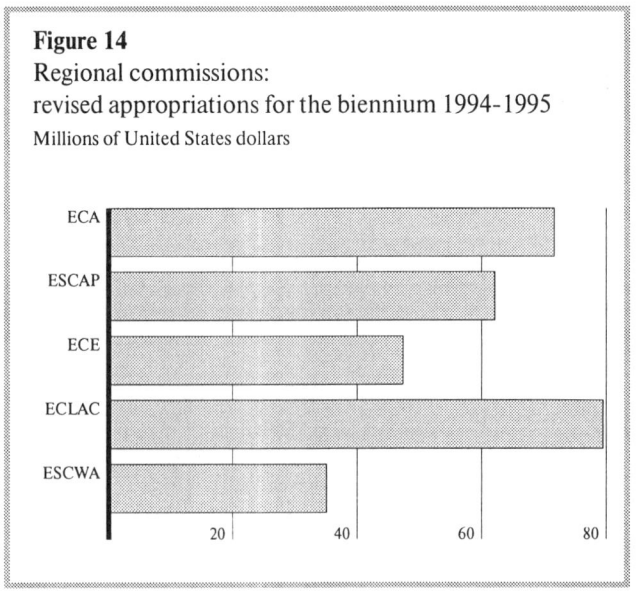

**Figure 14**
Regional commissions:
revised appropriations for the biennium 1994-1995
Millions of United States dollars

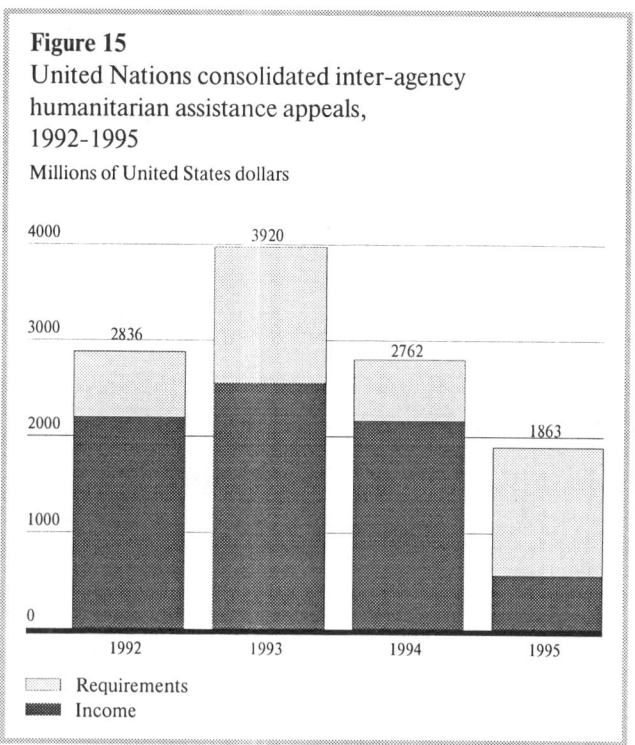

**Figure 15**
United Nations consolidated inter-agency
humanitarian assistance appeals,
1992-1995

Millions of United States dollars

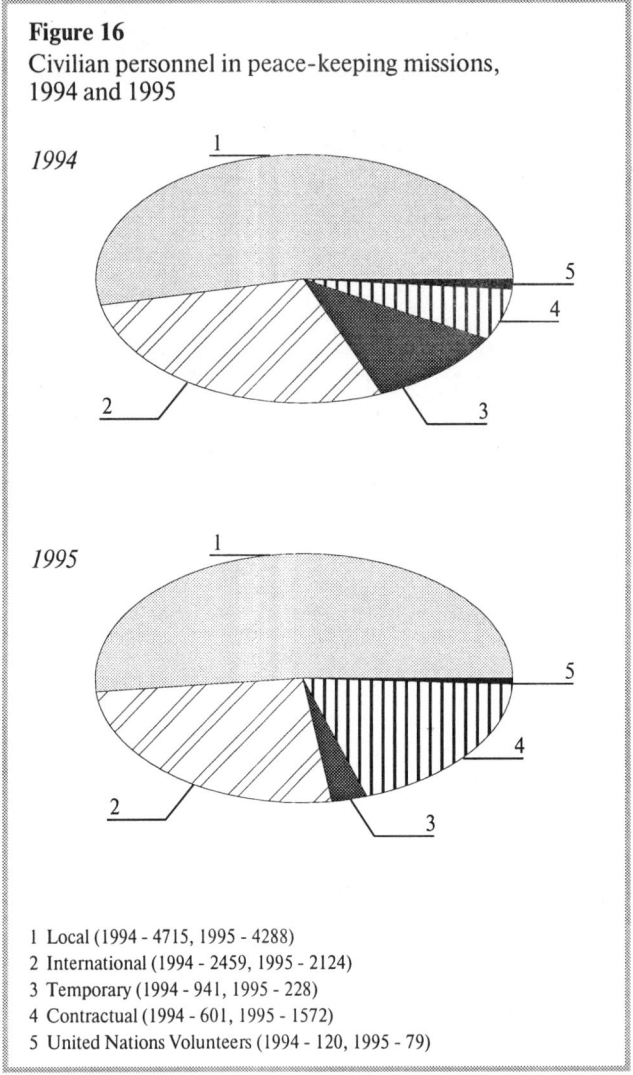

**Figure 16**
Civilian personnel in peace-keeping missions, 1994 and 1995

*1994*

*1995*

1 Local (1994 - 4715, 1995 - 4288)
2 International (1994 - 2459, 1995 - 2124)
3 Temporary (1994 - 941, 1995 - 228)
4 Contractual (1994 - 601, 1995 - 1572)
5 United Nations Volunteers (1994 - 120, 1995 - 79)

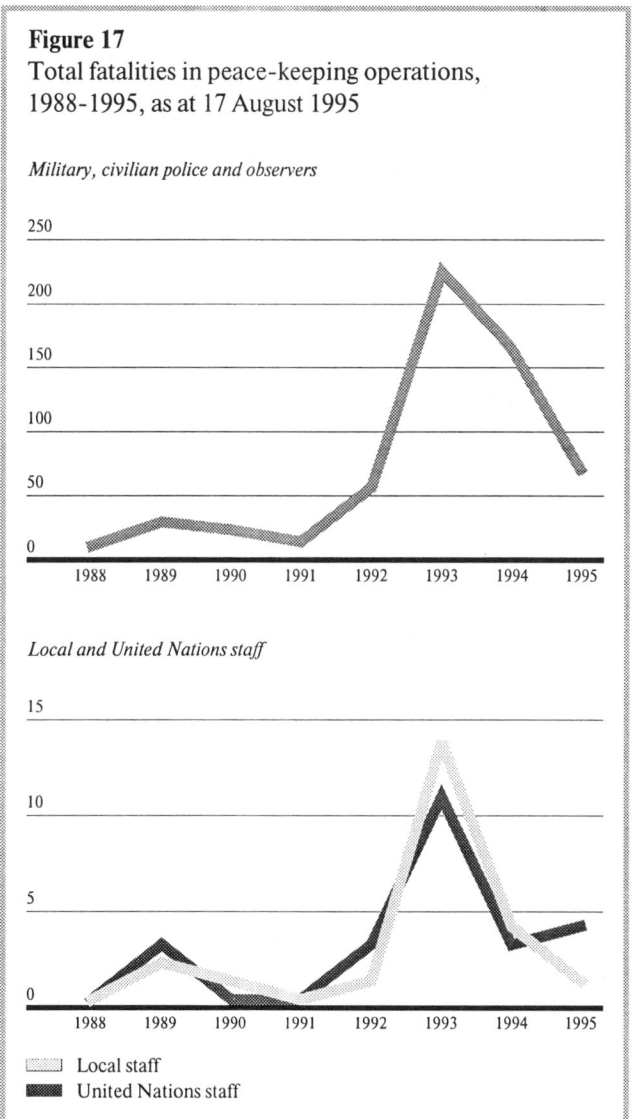

**Figure 17**
Total fatalities in peace-keeping operations,
1988-1995, as at 17 August 1995

*Military, civilian police and observers*

*Local and United Nations staff*

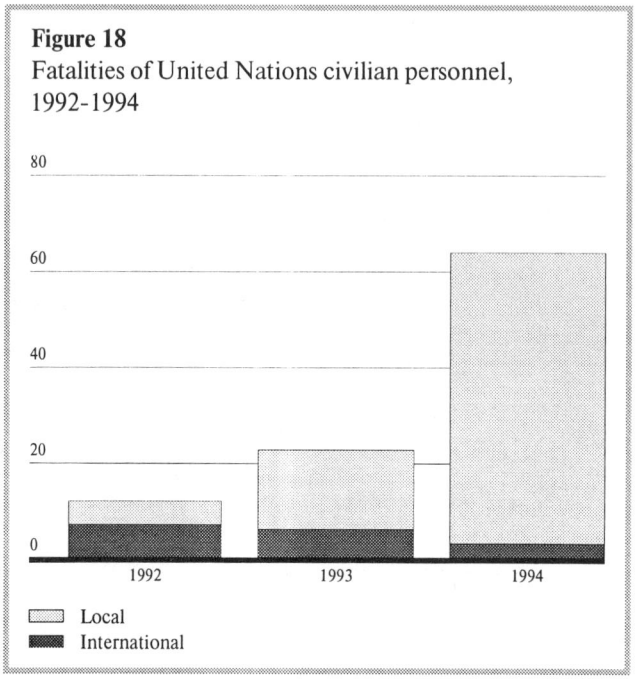

**Figure 18**
Fatalities of United Nations civilian personnel,
1992-1994

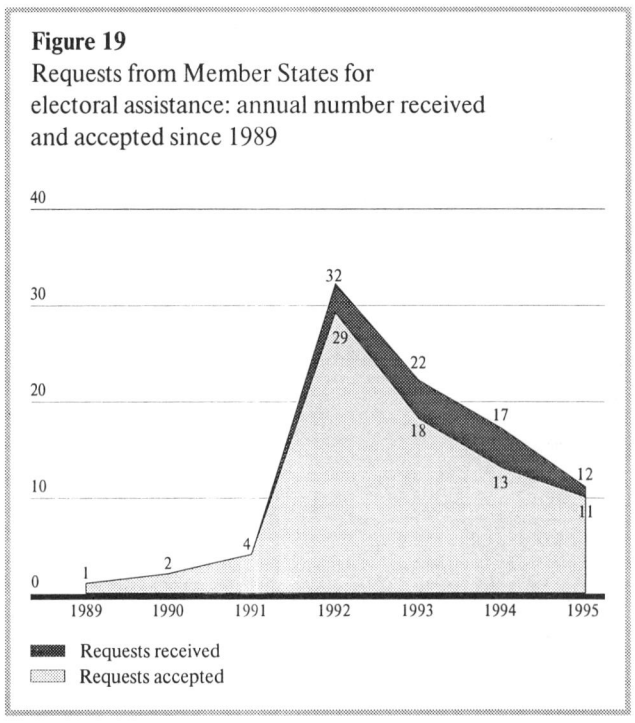

**Figure 19**
Requests from Member States for
electoral assistance: annual number received
and accepted since 1989

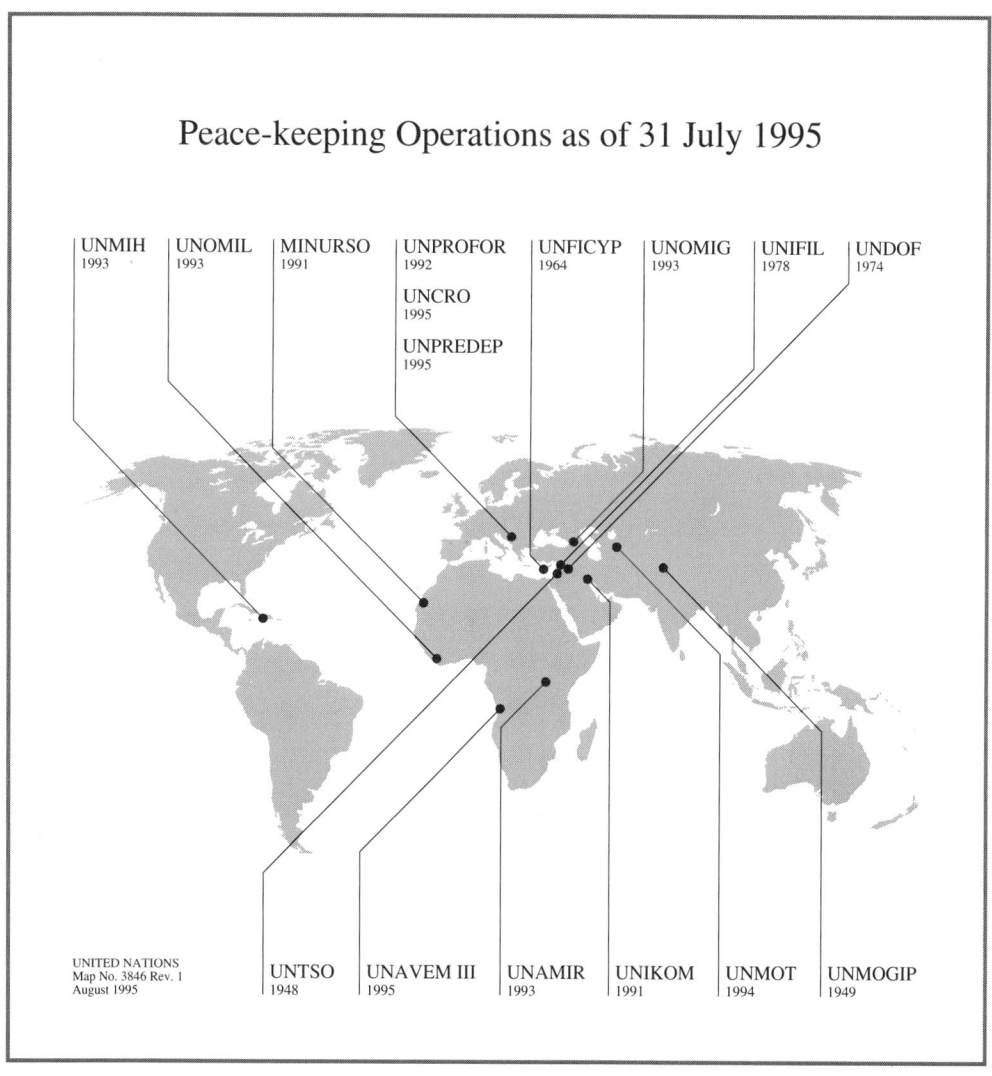

# Peace-keeping Operations as of 31 July 1995

UNMIH
1993

UNOMIL
1993

MINURSO
1991

UNPROFOR
1992

UNCRO
1995

UNPREDEP
1995

UNFICYP
1964

UNOMIG
1993

UNIFIL
1978

UNDOF
1974

UNITED NATIONS
Map No. 3846 Rev. 1
August 1995

UNTSO
1948

UNAVEM III
1995

UNAMIR
1993

UNIKOM
1991

UNMOT
1994

UNMOGIP
1949

# Special Section
## on
## Observance of the
## 50th Anniversary
## of the
## United Nations

Excerpted from Volume XXXII, 1995, Issues 3 and 4
of the UN Chronicle

# Golden anniversary of UN celebrated in city of its birth

*We the peoples of the United Nations determined to save succeeding generations from the scourge of war . . . do hereby establish an international organization to be known as the United Nations.*

–from the Preamble to the United Nations Charter

UN Secretary-General Boutros Boutros-Ghali *(left)* met with United States President William J. Clinton, following the special ceremony in San Francisco.

On 26 June 1995, half a century after United States President Harry Truman called on delegates from 50 war-weary nations to "be the architects of a better world", an array of dignitaries from around the globe gathered at the San Francisco Veterans War Memorial Building's Herbst Theatre to celebrate the golden anniversary of the United Nations.

''The blueprint for the world Organization was drawn here in San Francisco 50 years ago'', said Secretary-General Boutros Boutros-Ghali from the stage of the historic theatre where, on the same date in 1945, the UN Charter was signed and the world Organization was born. Scores of dignitaries, including United States President William Clinton, Poland's President Lech Walesa, Archbishop Desmond Tutu of South Africa, the 185 current Ambassadors to the UN, and some original members of delegations to the 1945 conference, were in the audience, as witnesses to the commemoration. ''The Charter created here is more than a document of history; it is the foundation stone of international relations'', the Secretary-General said.

## A new reality

Since 1945, a new reality of global cooperation has taken shape, based on the Charter, said Mr. Boutros-Ghali, standing before a vibrant blue backdrop adorned with the United Nations seal, which is little changed from the original symbol designed for the founding conference five decades ago. ''We are the custodians of the dream of global cooperation. We will not let it perish. As long as people seek national identities; as long as people seek protection from aggression; and as long as people yearn for a better world for their children, the United Nations will endure, and it will succeed.''

At the podium, in front of which was displayed in a lighted case the original copy of the UN Charter, United States President Clinton gave a resounding ''Yes, to the dream of the United Nations'', but also asserted: ''Today's UN must be ready to handle tomorrow's problems.''

''We must all remember that the United Nations is a reflection of the world it represents. Therefore, it will remain far from perfect. It will not be able to solve all problems, but even those it cannot solve it may well be able to limit in terms of the scope and reach of the problem, and it may well be able to limit the loss of human life until the time for solution comes'', Mr. Clinton stressed to the gathering.

''So I say especially to the opponents of the United Nations here in the United States, turning our back on the UN and going it alone will lead to far more economic, political and military burdens on our people in the future and would ignore the lessons of our own history'', said Mr. Clinton, whose speech concluded the commemoration ceremony. ''Instead, on this 50th anniversary of the Charter's signing, let us renew our vow to live together as good neighbours.''

That vow had been at the heart of the drive for collective security which resulted in the convening of the original United Nations Conference on International Organization (UNCIO) on 25 April 1945. Over the following two months, in an atmosphere shadowed by the tail-end of the Second World War and the recent death of United States President Franklin D. Roosevelt, UNCIO delegates spent hundreds of hours hammering out agreements which culminated in the unanimous approval of the United Nations Charter on 26 June 1945, including the Preamble, drafted by American poet Archibald MacLeish, among others.

## A day of hope

That day, said General Assembly President Amara Essy of Côte d'Ivoire in his address to the anniversary celebration, ''was a day of hope. The world was rising from the long night of war. The veterans of that war were gathered in this room. Today, too, is a day of hope. We ourselves are veterans of another war, the cold war. We too must be the architects of a better world. Fifty years on, the future is once again in our hands.''

The UN Charter, ''conceived at Saint James' Palace in London, nourished out on the high seas, shaped in Washington, Moscow, Tehran, Dumbarton Oaks and Yalta, and given final form in San Francisco, was designed to usher in a peaceful, just and prosperous world, a world founded no longer on force but on law'', Mr. Essy said.

''On this day 50 years ago, 51 flags floated over San Francisco. Today, 185 national emblems salute us—dazzling proof that the architects of the Charter were not mistaken. Their vision of freedom inspired the vast process of decolonization in Africa, Asia and elsewhere. And today we stand here as equal representatives of every continent on the globe.''

## Parade of Ambassadors

The commemoration opened with a procession of the 185 current UN Ambassadors, who solemnly strode to their seats, accompanied by a marching band, with the names of their nations scrolling on the big blue screen above the stage.

Amidst the speeches and musical performances by the San Francisco Opera and France's Opéra de Lyon orchestra, the blue screen behind the stage came alive with a nostalgic multi-media journey through the 50-year history of the UN, with commentary by television personality Walter Cronkite.

Archbishop Tutu gave the benediction and American poet Maya Angelou read a poem she composed especially for the event, entitled ''*A Brave and Startling Truth*''.

Following the ceremony, Secretary-General Boutros-Ghali had a 30-minute meeting with President Clinton and then attended a civic luncheon at San Francisco's Moscone Center.

''Enhancing peace, achieving progress towards development, promoting human rights, advancing international law—these were the goals of those who created the United Nations'',

> **"Fifty years ago, the world was weary of war, tired of poverty, and burdened by injustice. The United Nations was born to reject a culture of death and to create a culture of life, a culture of peace."**
> —**Secretary-General Boutros Boutros-Ghali**

said Mr. Boutros-Ghali in a keynote address to the luncheon. "They are the goals today. The United Nations helps its Member States achieve these objectives in ways that no other institution can."

Earlier the same day, the Secretary-General attended the dedication of a new United Nations Plaza at the San Francisco Civic Center. Created to serve as a permanent reminder of the history that was made in that city 50 years ago, the Plaza features granite paving-stone panels engraved with the Charter Preamble and UN seal, as well as the names of UN member nations and text from the Universal Declaration of Human Rights.

Describing the Plaza as "a composition of stones and trees and sky", Mr. Boutros-Ghali said at the ceremony: "Designed by the human mind, graced by the glory of nature, and open to the universal sphere, this place calls upon us to build upon the best that has gone before, to preserve the life which our planet provides, and never to abandon the vision of a better world which the United Nations— created in this city—is intended to achieve."

The 26 June anniversary events capped two months of festivities in San Francisco, ranging from serious debates with noted dignitaries to gala cultural performances. On 25 June, a forum of Nobel Laureates, "Visions of Peace", convened at the Herbst Theatre to offer their view of the UN role in the next 50 years.

The public forum featured such Nobel Peace Prize winners as Archbishop Tutu, who got the award in 1984; Dr. Oscar Arias Sánchez of Costa Rica in 1987; President Walesa of Poland, the recipient in 1983; and Betty Williams from Northern Ireland in 1976.

## NGO forum

The historic Herbst Theatre was also the site of a major three-day meeting (21-24 June) of non-governmental organizations (NGOs), entitled "We the People: Civil Society and the UN". A unique mix of UN personnel, early leaders and founders of the United Nations, activists and academics gathered to review the critical role that citizen groups played in the founding of the UN, their important contributions over the past 50 years and opportunities to build partnerships for the future.

An assortment of 42 citizen groups—including the American Association of University Women, American Federation of Labor, National Association for the Advancement of Colored People, League of Women Voters, and Rotary International—served as consultants to the delegates attending the 1945 conference that laid the groundwork for the UN. Today, thousands of NGOs from around the world are accredited to the UN, which is in the midst of an effort to update and deepen their integration into the daily work of the Organization.

"Today we are searching for an international system that is acceptable to all", Mr. Boutros-Ghali said in an address to the NGO gathering in San Francisco on 24 June. "In order for every woman and every man in the world to perceive their true stake in the great ideals of the world Organization, it is necessary to have many more institutions such as yours. Only thus shall we be faithful to the urgent exhortation with which the preamble to the Charter begins: We the peoples of the United Nations."

On 25 June, the Secretary-General opened the Forum on the Reform and Renewal of the UN, also at the Herbst Theatre, which drew together authors, scholars and policy leaders, to examine the strengths and weaknesses of the Organization and begin work on a "white paper" containing their findings, conclusions and recommendations to best revitalize the UN.

Calling for the colloquium to keep in mind the principles of ideas, realism, consensus, a sense of history, the contemporary political context and the nature of progress in shaping their recommendations, Mr. Boutros-Ghali said that the UN had not only evolved gradually over time, but also there had been times when Member States had summoned the will to make major changes. "Such a time may be before us again", he said. "The ongoing, incremental process may be combined with a comprehensive vision of the farther future."

The San Francisco events were a prelude to the fiftieth anniversary programme planned at UN Headquarters in New York, which culminated in a special commemorative meeting of the General Assembly from 22 to 24 October 1995. It was on 24 October 1945 that the UN Charter came into force upon ratification by the five permanent members of the Security Council and a majority of other signatory States.

# 'An age-old dream'

*UN Secretary-General Boutros Boutros-Ghali made the following statement on 26 June at the San Francisco ceremony commemorating the 50th anniversary of the signing of the United Nations Charter:*

The United Nations expresses the age-old dream of universal cooperation. We are here to renew this dream. The blueprint for the world Organization was drawn here in San Francisco 50 years ago. The Charter created here is more than a document of history; it is the foundation stone of international relations.

For five decades, the United Nations has permitted nations to join together to deal with challenges that no single nation can resolve. Universal membership offers a forum for expressing universal ideals. Through the United Nations, the world has enshrined the ideal of sovereign independence—to accommodate the emergence of new States and to secure the dignity of their peoples. Fifty-one Member States ratified the Charter of the United Nations in 1945. Since then, millions of the world's citizens won the right to determine their destiny as independent nations. Today, the United Nations comprises 185 Member States. Decolonization utterly changed the international landscape, and could have led to chaos. But through the United Nations, the framework of international relations survived—and was strengthened by—this profound transformation.

At the United Nations, peoples took their first steps as States on the international stage. Within the United Nations, they could assume their rightful place and gain recognition as legitimate members of the world community.

Through the United Nations, the world has embraced the ideals of peace and security—to preserve the integrity of States and to protect the lives of their peoples. The concept of peace-keeping is not explicit in the Charter, but the Charter proved flexible enough to respond when the need for such missions arose. Peace-keeping is a manifestation of the world's capacity to work together. For both troop-contributing countries and the lands that they serve, United Nations peace operations reinforce the ideal of international solidarity in the face of conflict. Peace-keeping operations have proven their practical importance. They can monitor compliance with the terms of an agreement. They can give combatants the time and encouragement to pursue lasting peace. They can provide humanitarian relief. And, in the context of new forms of conflict, they can help to reconstruct entire societies.

Through the United Nations, the world has pledged itself to the ideal of development—to advance the prosperity of States and the welfare of their peoples. Working through the United Nations, the world's peoples have framed a vision for global development. They have forged a consensus about the rights that belong to all humanity.

Through the United Nations, strategies have been devised to realize this vision. An understanding of the common interest between North and South has grown. The advancement of women as the key to nearly every issue of development is becoming understood. Ways to approach the complex new problems of the planet are urgently being found.

Five decades are a brief moment in history. Yet, since 1945, a new reality of global cooperation has taken shape, based on the Charter that was framed here in San Francisco. Today, the world is accepting the ideals of democracy. Democratization can balance the individual's need for identity with the need for a workable international system: it can help to prevent conflict; it is vital for development. The United Nations is helping States express the ideal of democracy, and find practical ways of attaining it. We are the custodians of the dream of global cooperation. We will not let it perish. As long as people seek national identities; as long as people seek protection from aggression; and as long as people yearn for a better world for their children, the United Nations will endure, and it will succeed.

An 'Agenda for Tomorrow'

# World leaders adopt Declaration to commemorate 50th anniversary of the United Nations

## Special Assembly session hears 200 speakers on UN past, present and future

### Three-day celebration a festive, dignified occasion

The General Assembly hall on 22 October 1995—the opening of the special commemorative session.

It was the largest gathering of world leaders in history—presidents, prime ministers, kings, princes, sultans, Heads of State and Heads of Government of all races, creeds, colour and political background. They converged on the 18-acre site of United Nations Headquarters in New York during three crisp fall days in October, their flag-bedecked limousine motorcades slowly wending their way through Manhattan streets and avenues—strangely empty due to the stricture of unprecedented security—arriving at UN Headquarters on First Avenue to pay homage to the existence for half a century of the world Organization.

"I welcome the Heads of States and Governments of the world", Boutros Boutros-Ghali, the sixth Secretary-General of the United Nations, declared in opening the special three-day commemorative session, from 22 to 24 October, which capped nine months of celebrations and observances worldwide of the UN's golden jubilee.

"Welcome to your home, the home of the world's peoples. Welcome to the forum of the United Nations—the forum of peace, understanding and development. Welcome to you all, and heartfelt greetings to the world's leaders."

General Assembly President Diogo Freitas do Amaral told the opening meeting: "Supporting the United Nations—that should be our collective pledge in this Special Commemorative Meeting. Reforming the United Nations—that should be our political commitment during these three days. We must not allow this Organization to die at the hands of its critics, nor to perish for lack of commitment of its supporters."

Over the next three days—from early Sunday morning through late Tuesday evening—some 200 speakers addressed the Assembly, including 129 Heads of State and Government, most of whom were present for the historic group photograph of debate participants (see dust-jacket) which recorded the unprecedented assemblage.

They also met, in their hotel rooms and mission offices throughout New York, to discuss ongoing political crises and problems on their everyday agendas, using the quiet, behind-the-scenes diplomacy that characterizes the real world of international politics.

And there were social gatherings for the dignitaries and their spouses: luncheons in the UN's North Lounge, at round tables decorated with colourful flowers, and at the ancient Temple of Dendur exhibit inside the Metropolitan Museum of Art; a VIP dinner at New York's World Financial Center; a special concert by the New York Philharmonic in Lincoln Center, highlighted by Beethoven's *Symphony No. 9*; and an elegant reception inside the stone-lion-guarded New York Public Library, hosted by New York City's Mayor Rudolph Giuliani.

Altogether, it was indeed at once a festive and dignified occasion—a time for praise and reflection, for plaudits and proposals.

At the end of the celebration, Secretary-General Boutros-Ghali told the assemblage: "Your presence speaks, as you have spoken, with eloquence, of confidence in the future of the United Nations." He added: "We have listened to the wisdom of these leaders. Together they have given the world an 'Agenda for Tomorrow'. An Agenda covering every aspect of human society."

Secretary-General Boutros-Ghali also lauded the participation of non-governmental organizations, some of whose representatives had addressed the Assembly, stating they had "forged a new global partnership with the United Nations", as well as that of observers from non-Member States and UN bodies throughout the world.

The UN's birthday—24 October—also marked the beginning of the World Week of Peace, which was proclaimed by the Assembly as a time for Governments and peoples of the world to pause to reflect together on the challenges before them, as the UN celebrated its 50th anniversary.

"I appeal to all warring parties, everywhere in the world, to put down their arms and to seek peaceful means to achieve their ends", said Secretary-General Boutros-Ghali in a statement at the beginning of the Week. "The World Week of Peace should be a time of dialogue and new initiatives aimed at peaceful resolution of disputes."

In conjunction with the anniversary celebration, a pledge to balance population growth and resources, signed by 75 Heads of Government, was presented to the Secretary-General by President Soeharto of Indonesia in a ceremony at UN Headquarters on 25 October. Those signing the statement represent 3.9 billion people or 68 per cent of the world's population.

Also on 25 October, a group of world leaders met for a high-level UN Forum at Headquarters to review the status of human rights and to consider the UN human rights agenda for the next 50 years, in particular, action called for by recent conferences on human rights in Vienna and on women in Beijing.

## Declaration adopted

A five-part "Declaration on the Occasion of the Fiftieth Anniversary of the United Nations", set out in resolution 50/6, was adopted by acclamation at the conclusion of the special commemorative session. It consists of an introduction and five sections on: peace, development, equality, justice, and the United Nations Organization.

In the seven-page document, the Assembly declares: "The commemoration of the fiftieth anniversary of the United Nations must be seized as an opportunity to redirect it to greater service to humankind, especially to those who are suffering and are deeply deprived. This is the practical and moral challenge of our time."

It states: "We, the Member States and observers of the United Nations, representing the peoples of the world:
● "Solemnly reaffirm the Purposes and Principles of the Charter of the United Nations and our commitments to them;
● "Express our gratitude to all men and women who have made the United Nations possible, done its work and served its ideals, particularly those who have given their lives during service to the United Nations;
● "Are determined that the United Nations of the future will work with renewed vigour and ef-

fectiveness in promoting peace, development, equality and justice and understanding among the peoples of the world;

• "Will give to the twenty-first century a United Nations equipped, financed and structured to serve effectively the peoples in whose name it was established."

The Declaration recognizes the important role of the UN in preventing another global conflict and calls for creating new opportunities for peace, development, democracy and cooperation.

Among its important provisions, the Declaration has world leaders pledge to promote the peaceful settlement of disputes, reaffirm the right to self-determination of all peoples, call for extraordinary measures by all countries to confront extreme poverty, reiterate the equal rights of men and women, and reaffirm that all human rights are universal and indivisible.

## Development, equality, justice

The Declaration calls on the UN to address more effectively and in greater measure the need for a free and equitable international economic environment as an essential condition for international peace, security and stability.

It reaffirms that "democracy, development and respect for human rights and fundamental freedoms, including the right to development, are interdependent and mutually reinforcing".

The Declaration urges the elimination of unsustainable patterns of production and consumption and the promotion of demographic policies to meet the needs of current generations without compromising the ability of future generations to meet their own needs. While national and regional particularities and historical, cultural and religious backgrounds must be borne in mind, the Declaration stresses that it is the duty of all States, "regardless of their political, economic and cultural systems, to promote and protect all human rights and fundamental freedoms".

The promotion of international law, the Declaration states, must be pursued to ensure that relations between States are based on the principles of justice and respect for the rule of law. It further states that the determination to build and maintain justice among States is in accordance with the principles of sovereign equality and territorial integrity.

## UN reform highlighted

An entire section of the Declaration is devoted to how the UN works. In order to respond effectively to future challenges, the Declaration states that: the Organization must be reformed and modernized; the General Assembly should be revitalized; the Security Council expanded; and the Economic and Social Council strengthened to carry out effectively the tasks it has been assigned with respect to the well-being and standards of life of all people. In addition, it stresses that Member States must meet, in full and on time, their obligation to bear the expenses of the Organization.

UN reform was also the dominant theme of speeches during the special meeting, with many of the 129 Heads of State and Government and 71 other high-level speakers stressing the need for greater transparency, democratization and accountability in the Security Council and other UN organs. Participants also suggested that the current financing regime of the UN be restructured, and that new and innovative sources of funding be sought. Addressing the issue of peace-keeping, many world leaders called for a greater UN role in preventive diplomacy to avert the outbreak or spread of conflict.

## Working for tomorrow

The United Nations "is the Organization that works for tomorrow", said Secretary-General Boutros-Ghali on 22 October, delivering the toast at a luncheon for Heads of State and Government. "The record of the past half century is clear. While others were called to deal with the problems of the present, the United Nations proved able to forecast—and address—the problems of the future."

The UN, he said, looked into the future and saw that decolonization must be a universal objective, that the poorest peoples of the world must have a voice, that the environment and economic development must be considered together if both were to be sustained, that the advancement of women was essential to human progress, and that the yearning of peoples for democracy must take place in the context of democratization of the international system itself.

"What is our vision of the second half century?", he asked. "It is a vision: of a world where conflicts will often be prevented before they must be countered by force of arms; of a world where material progress will go forward without excluding those now living on the margins of survival; of a world where human dignity and freedom can flourish, where no one is excluded by race, religion, class or gender; of a world where nature is allowed to renew itself, so that it may continue to provide for its human inhabitants."

The UN, concluded the Secretary-General, "cannot always be successful. But it will be essential. Of that there can be no doubt."

# "Long Live the United Nations!"

**S**ecretary-General Boutros Boutros-Ghali was both serious and optimistic as he addressed the leaders of the world during the special commemorative session of the UN's golden jubilee: "Your presence speaks, as you have spoken, with eloquence, of confidence in the future of the United Nations." A special UN photograph was taken during the October celebrations, which included 190 of the 200 participants in the session's historic debate. *(The commemorative photo is featured on the dust-jacket of the 1995 Yearbook of the United Nations.)* Among those pictured were 88 heads of State and 36 heads of Government, as well as Vice-Presidents, deputy Prime Ministers, Foreign Ministers, Permanent Representatives and heads of intergovernmental organizations. In the pages that follow are excerpts from the 200 addresses given to the General Assembly, on the occasion of the Organization's fiftieth anniversary, during six special plenary meetings of the Assembly held between 22 and 24 October. "We have listened to the wisdom of those leaders", the Secretary-General said at the end of the three-day celebration. "Together they have given the world an 'Agenda for Tomorrow'."

## AFRICA

### ALGERIA

*President Liamine Zeroual:* The fact that the United Nations has seen its membership approach universality in its 50 years of existence bears witness to the existence of a fortunate convergence between the trail that was blazed by the Charter and the course that has been followed by many of our peoples. The fact that the UN was able to foster the vast liberation movement that delivered peoples from the yoke of colonial domination holds its rightful place among the causes of satisfaction that give today's event its full meaning. The UN has woven a fabric of cooperation that spreads the benefits of man's mastery over nature.

### ANGOLA

*President José Eduardo dos Santos:* The journey has not been easy for our Organization. On the date of its foundation the world was just emerging from a devastating war, with a tragic balance of 50 million dead and profound trauma and destruction. Sooner or later, the difficulties facing the United Nations will require redefinition of its structures and mechanisms, particularly the Security Council. A permanent seat in the Council should be assigned to a country from each geographic region that can assume an effective role in preserving peace at the regional level.

### BENIN

*Désiré Vieyra, Minister of State for Coordination of Government Action:* The United Nations, as it reaches the half-century mark, must commit itself with resolve to the fight against poverty. We are pleased that at the World Summit for Social Development we finally overturned a sacrosanct principle to the effect that a country's social action must be determined by its economy. We shall now base our economies on the social sphere. Today, Benin is striving, with the help of its development partners, to reduce the rate of infant and maternal mortality and to reduce illiteracy by placing particular emphasis on health and education.

### BOTSWANA

*President Ketumile Masire:* The presence of so many world leaders in New York bears witness to the success of the United Nations during its half century of existence. For Botswana and the African continent, this is a particularly historic moment. When the Organization was born in San Francisco in 1945, only four African countries were able to adhere as independent countries to the Declaration of the United Nations. The rest of the continent was still under colonial domination. Today, the UN boasts of 53 African States among its 185 Members. The UN has served us well.

### BURKINA FASO

*Ablassé Ouédraogo, Minister for Foreign Affairs:* On the threshold of the 21st century, above and beyond the theory of States and of sovereignty, beyond the relationship of force, beyond the ambitions of domination, should we not substitute people, societies, nations, States? Should we not give new impetus to what was enshrined in the UN Charter in the words "We the peoples", and find again the human being and the humanity in each and every one of us and in each and every one of our acts? Only then will we progress with certainty towards a world of solidarity, progress, justice and peace.

## BURUNDI

*President Sylvestre Ntibantunganya:* The United Nations cannot effectively assist our countries unless it adapts to the requirements of today's world. Peace in the world is still endangered by growing poverty, which is evidently the gravest threat to peace in the years to come. Moreover, the exclusion of a major portion of humankind from the most influential bodies of the UN gives the impression of a world that is frozen in time, whereas important changes have taken place over the past 50 years. We must transform and democratize international relations as a whole.

## CAMEROON

*President Paul Biya:* Cameroon rejoices in the opportunity to take part today in the 50th anniversary ceremonies, as the United Nations played a primary role in its accession to national and international sovereignty. For us Africans, the UN is the expression of a collective will that is at the service of peace, of human dignity and solidarity among peoples. Created in the wake of one of the most harrowing conflicts in the history of mankind, in the last 50 years the UN has made an inestimable contribution to the defence of peace. In working for disarmament and encouraging negotiations, it has taken preventive action to ward off possible future conflicts.

## CAPE VERDE

*President Antonio Mascarenhas Monteiro:* Nobody would know how to define our present world without the United Nations, taking into account not only its role in promoting and facilitating the great, imperative changes, but also its specific action in the most diverse fields of human accomplishment, both individually and collectively. The current reality requires firm leadership on the part of the UN to preserve peace and security in such a way that all Member States, big and small, will focus their abilities and energy on the promotion of the well-being to which all peoples have a right.

## CENTRAL AFRICAN REPUBLIC

*President Ange-Félix Patassé:* Today, on the occasion of the jubilee of the UN, which is characterized by the density of its history and especially by its experiences, it is more than ever appropriate for the international community to draw the necessary lessons on which to base new hope, but especially, and above all, through which to fulfil the grand design of the UN, in the interests of our peoples. It appears unfair to certain nations that an

Organization that wishes to be universal and democratic excludes other nations from its decision-making bodies. The Security Council must be expanded.

## CHAD

*President Idriss Deby:* A half-century ago, immediately following the war, some 50 nations laid the foundations for a system of society turned resolutely towards freedom, peace, collective security, and economic and social well-being. While the world, over the years, has seen many upheavals and often-deadly conflicts that have resulted in sometimes severe criticism of our Organization, we must acknowledge that in many cases the United Nations has achieved substantial results and has spared humanity the worst of catastrophes.

## COMOROS

*Mouzaoir Abdallah, Minister for Foreign Affairs and Cooperation:* The celebration of the 50th anniversary of the UN is a historic occasion. We pay resounding tribute to the free nations that founded the United Nations, an Organization that has become, over the years, a global political arena that is essential to the *rapprochement* of peoples. The role of the UN in decolonization, advances in international law, respect for human rights and the identification of certain major problems such as those relating to population and the environment illustrate its growing accomplishments and progress.

## CONGO

*Destin Arsène Tsaty-Boungou, Minister for Foreign Affairs, Cooperation and Francophonie:* The 50th anniversary comes at a time when a black page in the history of mankind, the page of the cold war, has been turned. But the world continues to face other challenges. The same nations that were powerful 50 years ago are even more powerful today, thanks to their command of science and technology. The expectations of African peoples, who, like the other peoples of the planet, contributed to the liberation of mankind in the two major armed world confrontations, have not been fulfilled by a fitting display of solidarity on the part of the international community.

## CÔTE D'IVOIRE

*Prime Minister Daniel Kablan Duncan:* Certain failures notwithstanding, the Organization has achieved laudable successes. We can therefore be legitimately proud of our Organization because it is the institution that has made it possible to forge general consensus on issues of global policy. It is, moreover, the only structure capable of bringing about the implementation of and respect for the great principles of law, thanks simply to the universality of its Charter. Today, the question is how to reform the United Nations. Our Organization, a mirror on the world, must, 50 years after its creation, still be able to play the role assigned to it while adapting to the changes of our times.

## DJIBOUTI

*Roble Olhaye, Chairman of the Delegation:* Fifty years ago, a mere 51 States began the United Nations. Today, with "nation inflation", we are 185 Members. The UN must be reformed if it is to remain relevant. But it needs stable resources, reordered priorities and more relevant and representative structures. Reform must be given priority or it may soon become incapable of addressing the real global problems of disease, hunger, poverty, development, conflict, security and national breakdown. The UN is the most important vehicle we have today to forge a new international system anchored in justice and equity.

## EGYPT

*Amre Moussa, Minister for Foreign Affairs:* Today, we are gathered together here to celebrate the 50th anniversary of the United Nations. This is a unique opportunity to assess our successes and our failures. The UN has been a source of hope, a torch bearer and an element of construction. As we move closer to the beginning of the 21st century, mankind is sitting atop a volcano that is beginning to spew its lava. Let us not waste our scientific achievements by our political misconduct. Let us build up the credibility of the international order in a manner that instills confidence amongst peoples.

## EQUATORIAL GUINEA

*President Teodoro Obiang Nguema Mbasogo:* A half century of existence means a great deal for an Organization created after sufferings caused by war, injustice, discrimination, poverty, underdevelopment and the undervaluing of the individual. The creation of the UN was an act of conscience, an intention to reform by nations which decided to stop trying to take the upper hand in order to build a new world based on friendship, understanding, freedom, justice, tolerance, co-operation and love. After 50 years, it is natural that a work created by man should be examined to see if it continues to respond to the evolution of man and the times.

## GABON

*President El Hadj Omar Bongo:* Some say that the UN is merely a forum in which to make speeches. Others say that it is an ineffective Organization. Conflicts persist in Rwanda, Bosnia and Herzegovina and many other areas of the world. Underdevelopment also continues to be a problem. Many of the past inadequacies were a result of East-West confrontation. Today, the UN can take credit for ensuring respect for human rights and for democratization, although we must recognize that progress could have been considerably greater.

## GAMBIA

*Baboucarr-Blaise I. Jagne, Minister for Foreign Affairs:* The commemoration of the golden jubilee of the UN affords a unique opportunity to review past achievements and failures and to carve out a new path for our world towards a community of peoples who need each other for survival. I refer, of course, to an interdependent world, a global village, in which the achievement of socio-economic growth, peace and security in one country would depend largely on similar performance in other countries. We in the developing countries of the South need a head start, as was given to Europe in the aftermath of the Second World War through the Marshall Plan.

## GHANA

*President Jerry John Rawlings:* In congratulating the United Nations, we are applauding ourselves. The Organization is very much us. It is the collective will of the international community of sovereign States, embodying our collective weaknesses as well. For us in Africa, particularly, the next 50 years will perhaps be even more crucial than the past 50 years. We want to see in the international community and in the UN framework a reversal of our continent's marginalization. There can be no bright future for the world, no new international order that is sustainable, without Africa.

## GUINEA

*Kozo Zoumanigui, Minister for Foreign Affairs:* In attempting to take stock of the 50 years of our Organization's existence, I think it can be said that over this last half-century, the United Nations has proved irreplaceable, unique as a tool for dialogue, a concerted approach, negotiation and international cooperation. Through all these years, it has provided the ideal framework and laboured tirelessly not only for the maintenance of international peace and security, but also to mobilize the international community towards a solution of the problems of the world's economic and social development.

## GUINEA-BISSAU

*President João Bernardo Vieira:* Today, more than ever, the UN Charter is a legal, political and moral frame of reference that cannot be side-stepped in international relations. It is imperative to proceed with reforms within the Organization. The agenda of the General Assembly must be rationalized and the Security Council should be expanded on the basis of equitable geographical distribution.

Member States must forge a world organization capable of protecting future generations from the scourge of war and providing true reasons for hope.

## KENYA

*Stephen Kalonzo Musyoka, Minister for Foreign Affairs and International Cooperation:* On this occasion, we can state with confidence that the Organization has succeeded in the prevention of a third world war; that it has drastically reduced inter-State armed conflicts; that it has made much progress in the codification of international law; that it has provided a conducive climate and means for the reconstruction of Europe; that it has almost completed the mission of decolonization; and that it has withstood the cold war. Like the founders of the United Nations, we, as today's leaders, should take full cognizance of the inseparable relationship between peace and development.

## LESOTHO

*Deputy Prime Minister Bethuel Pakalitha Mosisili:* As the founder of our nation, King Moshoeshoe I, put it: ''Peace is like rain which makes the grass grow, while war is like the wind which dries it up.'' As we celebrate this historic occasion, we cannot but rejoice in the accomplishments of the United Nations in bringing the nations of the world together. Internal and international conflicts are, however, not over. We need to reflect on their causes, all of which are inimical to the UN principles. Our common resolve should be to work together to build a world devoid of them.

## LIBERIA

*Wilton S. Sankawulo, Chairman of the Council of State of the Liberian National Transitional Government:* If the spectre of war prevails in most of the countries that attained independence after the birth of the UN, it is due largely to the legacy of colonialism and the cold war. Colonial powers disregarded the traditional values and social needs of their subjects. The contest for spheres of influence during the cold war gave rise to autocratic regimes, which were insensitive to the aspirations of their peoples. The signing of the UN Charter 50 years ago was a significant milestone in the creation of a global arrangement for securing human liberty.

## LIBYAN ARAB JAMAHIRIYA

*Omar Mustafa Muntasser, Secretary of the General People's Committee for Foreign Liaison and International Cooperation:* We hope that this occasion will be a starting point for an unshackled United Nations that would continue to be revitalized and committed to the service of all peoples and not just a few States that seek to use it as a means to achieve their own ends. These few should realize that the UN has not been freed from the shackles of the cold war to find itself shackled by the fetters of major Powers. They should not forget that these small countries that helped the UN attain its universality are also capable of establishing their own organization away from the domination and hegemony of a few major Powers.

## MADAGASCAR

*President Albert Zafy:* Fifty years! We are no longer young, but neither are we old yet. This is maturity, an age replete with usefulness and reason, the result of a wealth of experience garnered over half a century. This anniversary provides us with an opportunity to take stock of the last half-century and to examine together ways and means to influence the course of the coming years to ensure that this Organization can genuinely live up to the expectations of all the peoples of the world that yearn for peace, equality, respect for human life, and peaceful technological progress.

## MALAWI

*President Bakili Muluzi:* It would have been nice if the United Nations had performed miracles these past 50 years. It would have been nice if it succeeded in preventing human beings from wantonly slaughtering each other on a regular basis. The UN failed to perform this particular miracle. Human beings all over the world continue to kill each other for political, tribal, religious and all sorts of other reasons. The world has yet to become one big happy family. And this means that the UN still has a crucial role to play in bringing about peace, stability, freedom and justice.

## MALI

*Prime Minister Ibrahim Boubacar Keita:* We hope to see the United Nations live up to the desire of 21st century man to live in peace and security, in social justice and human dignity. How can we fail here to recall the action the Organization has taken to advance the cause of the self-determination of peoples, to eradicate colonialism and to eliminate all forms of racial discrimination and oppression? The UN has thus opened new horizons for many countries and peoples, enabling them to cooperate and to live in brotherhood within a community of interests and fortunes that inspires each people to devote its resources and energy to development, progress and prosperity.

## MAURITANIA

*Mohamed Salem Ould Lekhal, Minister for Foreign Affairs and Cooperation:* The theme of today's commemoration—''We the peoples of the United Nations . . . united for a better world''—must be more than a slogan. May the wisdom and farsightedness of our forebears who wrote the UN Charter inspire us to adopt the conduct and attitudes that will enable us to avoid the misfortunes and disasters of war and insecurity. Mauritania reaffirms its commitment to work to advance the great ideals of our Organization, to consolidate international peace and security and to strengthen cooperation and solidarity amongst all nations for a world free of war, poverty and underdevelopment.

## MAURITIUS

*Prime Minister Aneerood Jugnauth:* The United Nations is at the crossroads. It has already been challenged by an unprecedented number of conflicts and humanitarian emergencies on an unprecedented scale throughout the world. The time is not for despair but for a renewal of efforts to rekindle the original aspirations of the UN. The UN must further the common objectives of the world community and promote the economic and social advancement of peoples in all countries, big and small, thus creating conditions for the peaceful development of all.

## MOROCCO

*Crown Prince Sidi Mohamed:* If it is truly our desire to have mankind reap the benefits of UN activities, in particular in the areas of health, development, education and culture, we must not waste time in making the UN capable of addressing the issues that face mankind. This must be done quickly, before there appears on the international political scene another giant harbouring unipolar aspirations who would return us, God forbid, to the era of the cold war from whose consequences humanity suffered so much and from whose influence it was deeply scarred.

## MOZAMBIQUE

*President Joaquim Alberto Chissano:* Our challenge for the next century is to further strengthen the United Nations in order to enable it to deal more efficiently and vigorously with issues related to the maintenance of international peace and security, and to promote sustainable development, human rights and fundamental freedoms. Only these can ensure a better and safer world for all. Development is the twin sister of peace. There can be no sustainable development without lasting peace, nor can there be a lasting peace without sustainable development.

## NAMIBIA

*President Sam Nujoma:* Celebration of the birth, longevity and performance of the United Nations is proper and fitting indeed. The world has been a safer place because of the UN and its continued relevance is beyond question. After 50 years, the Organization is alive and well. Its misfortunes are exaggerated. Failures are those of the Member States and not of the UN. The 50 years of the existence of the UN have brought the peoples of the world closer together than ever before. Indeed, today's world is truly a global village.

## NIGER

*President Mahamane Ousmane:* Whatever its detractors may say, and despite the many obstacles that impede its functioning, we must acknowledge that the United Nations has been at the root of striking qualitative changes on the international scene. It has been at the centre of the accession to independence of many hundreds of millions of people. In the sphere of peace-keeping, it has somehow managed to prevent the repetition of conflicts just as devastating and deadly as the war that brought it into being. It continues to be the best framework for multidirectional thought and action towards a common approach to the ills that beset mankind.

## NIGERIA

*Tom Ikimi, Minister for Foreign Affairs:* The theme of war and peace has confronted the UN since its inception. Indeed, the founding fathers of the world body expressed their determination "to save succeeding generations from the scourge of war, which . . . has brought untold sorrow to mankind". Regrettably, these wars are proliferating mostly in the developing countries and have resulted in mindless human and material waste, destruction and dislocation of social structures, tidal waves of refugees and displacement of populations.

## RWANDA

*President Pasteur Bizimungu:* Mechanisms should be worked out so that the UN can deliver on expectations. In particular, the Security Council must be reformed to make it more representative. The future of our Organization, our future, requires us to strive for unconditional solidarity and more dynamic cooperation. Mankind should never again witness the horrors of genocide that took place in Rwanda, and the current ethnic cleansing in the former Yugoslavia must be brought to an end. We count on the UN to direct and support our efforts to create a better world for humanity.

## SENEGAL

*Prime Minister Habib Thiam:* Our presence bears witness to our renewed adherence to UN ideals and our faith in its unique mission of peace and cooperation, solidarity and progress. International peace and security, economic and social development, humanitarian aid and promotion of the rule of law continue to be permanent objectives which the UN has always been striving to achieve in the constant struggle for freedom. Indeed, the UN has not only persisted in this far-reaching enterprise, it has also inspired a great number of major positive transformations with a view to finding solutions to the problems facing our human race.

## SIERRA LEONE

*Valentine E. M. Strasser, Head of State:* The dreams of those delegates in San Francisco are still shared by every single delegate here in New York. The world has changed; giant nations no longer confront each other with deadly weapons; the Iron Curtain has given way to closer cooperation; the threat of nuclear annihilation has receded. Giant economic blocs are emerging; one-time arch-enemies are now close allies. The resolution of ancient and emerging new conflicts and provision of humanitarian aid to the millions of hungry and dying peoples of the world are problems that the UN has grappled with. These are remarkable achievements.

## SOUTH AFRICA

*President Nelson R. Mandela:* When distinguished leaders came together, half a century ago, to consign to the past a war that had pitted humanity against itself, the ruins and the smoke from the dying fires were the monument to what should not have been. Fifty years after the formation of the United Nations, we meet to affirm our commitment to the founding ideal and the common desire to better the life of all human beings. What challenges us, who define ourselves as ''statespersons'', is the clarion call to dare to think that what we are about is people—the proverbial man and woman in the street. These—the poor, the hungry, the victims of petty tyrants, the objectives of policy—demand change.

## SWAZILAND

*King Mswati III, Head of State:* I believe the United Nations' founding fathers would have recognized their own goals in those of my generation. They are, after all, what every human being has a right to expect—good health, shelter, security for one's family, freedom to pursue the ideas and beliefs of choice, to be educated and employed and, above all, to be able to live in peace. In the year 2045, I wish to be able to stand and meet the gaze of my children, and my grandchildren, and say, ''We did our best.''

## TOGO

*Dahuki Péré, President of the National Assembly:* A rapid survey of UN activities over the last 50 years shows that while it has allowed the world to escape a world war of a scope comparable to the last two wars, the effects of which traumatized humanity, our Organization has not fulfilled our hopes—either

in the area of peace-keeping or in the area of economic and social development. Despite enormous means invested in safeguarding and restoring regional and international peace, this goal is far from being achieved. UN capabilities in the area of preventive diplomacy and the peaceful settlement of disputes should be strengthened.

## TUNISIA

*Al-Habib ben Yahia, Minister for Foreign Affairs:* The United Nations has done a great deal in the service of peace since its establishment in the difficult times that followed in the wake of World War II. It has saved humanity from destruction and contributed to the emergence of the national liberation movement in various parts of the world. It has championed the advocates of fraternity and equality against the forces of injustice and every form of discrimination. Notwithstanding the difficulties that faced it, the UN has shown itself to be the very embodiment of human wisdom.

## UGANDA

*President Yoweri Kaguta Museveni:* The Organization has in the last 50 years played a role in maintaining peace in the world and we salute its contribution. To properly utilize the United Nations in future, we should clearly define the circumstances under which it should assist the forces of legitimacy and democracy. Most cases which confront the UN are explosions that follow a prolonged period of the disenfranchisement of the people. The best way for the UN to handle such explosions is to seek to restore and support legitimacy.

## UNITED REPUBLIC OF TANZANIA

*Daudi N. Mwakawago, Chairman of the Delegation:* As we meet today, we look back on 50 years of illustrious history. But our main objective is to focus on the future. The Organization needs revitalization. One area is to democratize its structures, especially the Security Council, to reflect current realities. Equitable geographical representation should be the centrepiece of reforms. A second area of concern is development. The scourge of poverty and environmental degradation is the new war facing the UN. It cannot be wished away or left to the developing countries to fight. It requires the solidarity of the international community through the leadership of the UN.

## ZAIRE

*President Maréchal Mobutu Sese Seko:* For us Africans, the United Nations is first and foremost a synonym of re-found dignity and freedom. The UN flag represents the universal emblem of the decolonization of the States of our continent. Indeed, members will recall that when the UN Charter was signed in San Francisco, only a few African countries were among the first 51 States to be admitted. From 1960 to 1990, that is, from the first proclamations of independence to the independence of Namibia, all the other African States have progressively won their seat within the UN.

## ZAMBIA

*President Frederick J. T. Chiluba:* In a world of growing tensions and challenges, the UN has performed well since its inception and deserves a word of appreciation and thanks. The structures of 1945, meant to service an almost homogeneous membership of 50 countries that has since increased almost fourfold, are no longer capable of servicing the bigger and wider globe. Membership has increased in numbers as well as in regional diversity. A restructured and more representative UN will be better equipped to respond to growing demands which have become multifarious in character.

## ZIMBABWE

*President Robert G. Mugabe:* For us in Africa, the contribution of the United Nations in the decolonization and democratization processes has been an outstanding and honourable one, with the result that today southern Africa, once described by a Portuguese seafarer as a "region of storms", has finally and truly become a region of good hope where the oppressive settler regimes, apartheid and other ruthless systems of governance have succumbed to the revolutionary will of the majority, paving the way to peace, stability and regional cooperation.

# ASIA AND THE PACIFIC

## AFGHANISTAN

*Najibullah Lafraie, Minister for Foreign Affairs:* Each and every document of the UN talks about respecting the right to life, liberty and security, as well as the will of the nations. During this special commemorative meeting, world leaders have also presented speeches about the future of the world and ways and means of implementing the provisions of the UN Charter, which would remain merely beautiful expressions unless translated into practice. Let us not forget, however, that at this very moment millions of human beings go on living in poverty, hunger and deprivation.

## BAHRAIN

*Shaikh Mohamed Bin Mubarak Al-Khalifa, Minister for Foreign Affairs:* The future of the United Nations depends, now more than ever, on the extent of its ability to influence events and to mould the future, especially in an era of accelerating change and development, influenced by the dramatic communications revolution in the world. If the UN is to carry out its task of peacemaking and ensuring justice, it behooves us, peoples and Governments alike, to present the 21st century with a UN capable of promoting the causes of justice, development and equality for all.

## BANGLADESH

*Prime Minister Begum Khaleda Zia:* If we look around the world today at the numerous conflicts, big and small, at aggression perpetrated against small States, at genocidal conflicts and ethnic cleansing, and denial of the right of lower riparian countries to water of common rivers, there are many who may question the justification of this world body. Despite these drawbacks, mankind has not been able to evolve a more effective forum. The 50th anniversary offers the ideal opportunity to review its achievements and to look forward to a strengthened and reinvigorated United Nations.

## BHUTAN

*Dawa Tsering, Minister for Foreign Affairs:* The United Nations means different things to different nations around the globe. It is only natural that we should view the world through our own perspective, influenced by our historical experience, geographical setting, traditions and value system. For a small nation like Bhutan, membership of the UN enables us to participate in shaping the international agenda on numerous issues that are of importance to our people. We benefit from the activities of the UN family of organizations, whose assistance has made a real difference in the everyday lives of our people.

## BRUNEI DARUSSALAM

*Sultan Hassanal Bolkiah Mu'izzaddin Waddaulah:* The United Nations is still the best Organization to uphold a world order based on international law and the principles of sovereignty and territorial integrity. Interdependence between nations has increased, but has not displaced the sovereignty of nations as the basic principle in international relations. The UN gives all Members, big and small, an equal voice. The UN must change to meet new challenges, but I hope it will continue to give small nations an adequate voice in its deliberations.

## CAMBODIA

*First Prime Minister Samdech Krom Preah Norodom Ranariddh:* The United Nations contribution to world peace has been unique. Through its specialist bodies, it has provided both emergency assistance to people around the world in urgent need and development assistance to help raise the standard of living of millions of people. We salute the staff of these UN organizations and thank them for their noble endeavours. We, Cambodians, are particularly indebted to the Organization for helping our country and people to regain their freedom and independence. Cambodians will never forget the assistance provided to our country by the UN.

## CHINA

*President Jiang Zemin:* Over the past 50 years, the United Nations has done much useful work in mitigating regional conflicts, eradicating colonialism, expediting arms reduction and promoting peace and development in the world. However, it also has its failures and setbacks. The rivalry of certain big Powers has often left the UN in limbo. Moreover, the rights and interests of the large number of developing countries have not been fully respected. Our experience and lessons over the past half century, the Charter's purposes and principles, and epochal themes of peace and development have all placed solemn and urgent demands on us.

## CYPRUS

*President Glafcos Clerides:* The UN Charter, a great human achievement, embodying the wisdom and vision of its drafters to save succeeding generations from the scourge of war, constitutes the legal and moral foundation in international relations, and is as valid and relevant today as ever. What is really needed is to reduce the gap between principle and practice created by the failure to apply objectively and universally the Charter provisions, thus causing insecurity, frustration and bitterness. The authority of the Organization must be upheld against those who flout international opinion.

## FIJI

*Prime Minister Sitiveni Ligamamada Rabuka:* The norms of the powerful have in the past been imposed to disinherit indigenous people, and to this day in some places, to deny them the political self-determination essential for their social and economic advancement. The United Nations must guarantee that external values and forces do not continue to coerce political concessions, economic reforms and social changes not desired by indigenous peoples themselves. Not all the wrongs that history has wrought upon indigenous peoples can now be put right. The UN should not hesitate to ensure for these that remedy is expeditious.

## INDIA

*Prime Minister P. V. Narasimha Rao:* The United Nations today includes a much larger number of independent, sovereign States than when it began. In such a context, the UN cannot afford to be seen as either exclusivist or incomplete, either in appearance or in outlook. In particular, an adequate presence of developing countries is needed in the Security Council on the basis of objective criteria: nations of the world must feel that their stakes in global peace and prosperity are factored into the UN decision-making. At the 50th anniversary, we thus have the task of making the UN truly and effectively the global repository of humankind's aspirations.

## INDONESIA

*President Soeharto:* In these troubled times, we, the Governments and peoples of the world, look up to the United Nations for the sustenance of our hopes. There is no question that we need the UN. What we often forget is that the UN needs us too. We applaud its triumphs, but we often forget that its failures are ours too. Its responsibility is our responsibility. It is our hope that during the next 50 years strides can be made in achieving better harmony between the national self-interest and the legitimate rights of the less empowered people of the world.

## IRAN

*Ali Akbar Velayati, Minister for Foreign Affairs:* The UN gains its strength from its universal character, which is even more impressive in light of the diversity of its constituent elements. Faith in, and thus protection of, fundamental human rights, the dignity and worth of the human person, and equal rights of men and women cannot be divorced from respect for equality of nations, large and small. There can therefore be no justification for any attempt to impose the will or values of a few over the rest of humanity, or to enhance the perception of security of the privileged few at the expense of subjecting the rest of humanity to the nightmare of nuclear holocaust.

## IRAQ

*Vice-President Taha M. Marouf:* With the end of the cold war, all the grandiose hopes for a new era of peace have given way to an emergent unipolarism, with many armed conflicts, on both the international and the domestic levels. Within the UN, it has spawned types of behaviour characterized by selectivity, double standards and putting the UN mechanisms at the service of narrow self-interest. Now that we can diagnose the ailment, we have to be quick with the remedy. We should begin by activating the democratic process in the work of the UN.

## ISRAEL

*Prime Minister Yitzhak Rabin:* In the past 50 years, this podium has seen empires fall and borders erased. But it has also seen people awaken to their freedom and the nations of the world display their flags side by side. We are grateful to the international community for its encouragement at this historic moment which is unfolding on our little plot of land.

The road is still long. However, we are determined to continue until we have brought peace to the region, for our children and our children's children and for all the peoples of the region. This is our mission. We will fulfil it. Israel celebrates here with everyone—with all those attending here and with the entire world—50 years of the United Nations.

## JAPAN

*Prime Minister Tomiichi Murayama:* We have only five years left to the 21st century. Humankind has reached the stage at which we should all join hands and advance together so that the coming century will be one of hope, in which we can look forward to the creation and development of a new global civilization. On this occasion, I should like to re-affirm the determination that the people of Japan made 50 years ago to live in peace, trusting in the justice and faith of the peace-loving peoples of the world. As the exploration of a new vision for the United Nations continues, Japan will enhance its support for the Organization.

## JORDAN

*King Hussein Ibn Talal:* I may not be the eldest head of State among you, but God has willed that I should be the longest serving, and the one who has dealt with the United Nations for the longest period. I recall, at an early age, witnessing the endeavours of men like Trygve Lie, Count Bernadotte, Ralph Bunche, Dag Hammarskjöld, and Gunnar Jarring and many others who have served the cause of peace and stability in our region. We acknowledge our debt to the men and women of the UN who have worked over the years to preserve peace in our region and feel proud to have contributed to serve the same lofty ideals in other regions.

## KAZAKSTAN

*President Nursultan Nazarbaev:* No international structure on the eve of the 21st century will be capable of effectively resolving the issues of global security and social and political development without taking into consideration the new global balances. Today, we should be grateful to the United Nations for its effective endeavours, which have helped us all to avert potential global disasters in the second half of the 20th century. This is an undoubted accomplishment of the UN and its principal bodies and structures.

## KUWAIT

*Sheik Jaber Al-Ahmad Al-Jaber Al-Sabah, Amir of the State:* Global confidence in the United Nations system has been on the rise since it has become a beacon of hope for alleviating and redressing the human suffering caused by aggression and oppression in all their forms and manifestations. We trust that the Organization will become even more effective in confronting mankind's global problems in the coming

century. Such a contribution would indeed consolidate the lofty human values of benevolence, cooperation and interdependence for the common benefit of all human beings who yearn for a peaceful and dignified life.

## KYRGYZSTAN

*Mukar Cholponbayev, Chairman of the Legislative Chamber:* As representatives of an ancient people but a young nation, and reflecting on our own history and the half-century of efforts to create a new code of international cooperation, we express profound gratitude to the founding fathers of the UN. The world community has been successful in interrupting the tragic cycle of world wars. Today, our discussions cover not the problems of global war, but rather global development. The UN is a living body and it is needed by all of us. Let us then join efforts to make it more effective and more responsive to contemporary challenges.

## LAO PEOPLE'S DEMOCRATIC REPUBLIC

*Deputy Prime Minister Khamphoui Keoboualapha:* During the last five decades, our universal Organization has been sorely tried in many conflicts and upheavals in various parts of the world. Despite the difficulties encountered, the United Nations has survived and strengthened its role in solving world problems. While we welcome what has been achieved, we cannot but confirm the fact that today's world is entering a new era—an era of cooperation for development. Yet the world is still without true peace. The realities of the world today show us that true peace cannot prevail until the imperatives of socio-economic development have been adequately addressed.

## LEBANON

*Bahige Tabbarah, Minister of Justice:* The UN is not only a unique forum where Members can have their voices heard, and their complaints addressed. It is primarily the international institution that provides assistance and support to the developing countries so that they, in turn, can build their economies and their societies, and gradually bridge the gap between the industrial and the developing countries. World peace and understanding and respect for human rights cannot be permanent unless the economic gap between the rich and the poor countries of the world is bridged.

## MALAYSIA

*Datuk Abdullah bin Hadji Ahmad Badawi, Minister for Foreign Affairs:* We strongly believe that the UN should be the body to promote globalism and pluralism. It must stand clearly on the side of universal values in combating genocide and aggression. Peace and security cannot be built on arms reduction alone. Development focused on eradication of poverty and the removal of bottlenecks towards global prosperity must remain a UN priority. The UN should not become an instrument for disciplining developing countries, while allowing for power politics and global domination by a few powerful countries.

## MALDIVES

*President Maumoon Abdul Gayoom:* Fifty years ago, the UN was created to serve all peoples—rich and poor alike; big and small on an equal footing—based on the principle of the sovereign equality of all its Members. My question is this: has the UN been successful in the even-handed application of this principle and in ensuring the protection and security of small States? Today, the world needs an organization that will aim at a world of shared economic prosperity and national security and one in which communities can live in harmony with one another and with the environment.

## MARSHALL ISLANDS

*President Amata Kabua:* Today is an occasion to celebrate half a century of the existence of the United Nations and its accomplishments, and also to reflect over how, collectively, we may better chart our path and more clearly articulate our goals for the next 50 years or so.The current political landscape is vastly different from that of 50 years ago. This requires the UN critically to examine its performance and structures in search of practical solutions. It is imperative that those elements which are antiquated, and no longer minister to the needs of a continually changing humanity, be swept away and relegated to the currents of history.

## MICRONESIA

*President Bailey Olter:* The accomplishments of the UN as a forum for advancing world peace and security cannot be minimized. But this Organization has an even greater mission. As populations grow and make increasing demands on the planet's limited resources, even the most richly endowed must come to understand the great, futuristic vision of the Charter. It wisely calls upon peoples and Governments, large and small, rich and poor, to incorporate in their policies and actions true respect for the rights of all, including the least privileged, to live in conditions of decency and equality.

## MONGOLIA

*President Punsalmaagiin Ochirbat:* The UN, having risen from the ashes of the most devastating war in the history of mankind, is today celebrating its golden anniversary with a renewed sense of purpose and confidence in the future. From a distance of 50 years, one could reasonably argue that there were no victors nor vanquished, and that the sole winner was the entire human race. But the 50 million who perished in the war will always be a stark reminder of the imperative still fun-

damental today—to persevere in our collective efforts to achieve peace, progress and social justice.

## MYANMAR

*Maung Aye, Vice Chairman of the State Law and Order Restoration Council:* The international community has changed considerably in the past 50 years; yet the UN Charter framed in June 1945 continues to be valid. Its principles—the equality of sovereign States, territorial integrity, the political independence of States and the peaceful resolution of conflicts—must remain inviolate and be faithfully observed in international relations. Erosion of these fundamental principles will undermine the aims and purposes of the Organization. Any attempt to weaken the time-honoured and universally accepted principles of sovereignty would be cause for serious concern.

## NEPAL

*Prime Minister Sher Bahadur Deuba:* The spectre of a global nuclear catastrophe which has haunted humanity since 1945 is less threatening now with the end of the cold war. The Organization's functional approach to peace has provided economic relief to the less privileged regions of the world and restored human dignity to the neglected segments of our global society. While we are currently caught in a dilemma between our efforts to forge a new world order and face the reality of a global disorder, there is a strong need to reinforce some of its mechanisms to cope with the demanding times.

## OMAN

*Fahad Bin Mahmoud Al Said, Deputy Prime Minister for Council of Ministers:* The past epoch of United Nations history has been a period of many a positive achievement, thanks to the effectiveness of multilateral action. The fact that the UN has been able to surmount the many great difficulties that stood in its path attests to the success of the Organization and its Member States. However, the achievement of peace, security, economic prosperity and social well-being on a basis of equality and justice will not be possible unless we strengthen our collective efforts and give priority to development plans on the individual and the collective levels.

## PAKISTAN

*Prime Minister Benazir Bhutto:* Fifty years ago this day, men and women of vision assembled to create an Organization to save the world from war. For 50 years, there has been no global conflict. We applaud the United Nations humanitarian and peace-keeping interventions, to which the brave sons of Pakistan have contributed with their own blood. We welcome the UN efforts to emphasize social issues, including population, social development, women and human settlements. Let us remember the words of the philosopher Spinoza, who said: "Peace is not merely the absence of war. It is a virtue that springs from force of character."

## PALAU

*President Kuniwo Nakamura:* The UN represents the most ambitious and noble attempt humankind has ever made to craft a lens with which to transcend self-interest as individuals and as nations. With such a lens, we are able to consider issues from the vantage point of the representatives of our close-knit global family who will come here to the United Nations 50 and 100 years from now to celebrate future anniversaries of this magnificent institution. When my ancestors sailed from South-East Asia to Palau, they needed courage, knowledge and wisdom. As nations, we too will need all of these qualities in the coming years.

## PAPUA NEW GUINEA

*Ben Micah, Special Envoy of the Prime Minister:* The end of the cold war provides a rare opportunity to the international community to divert its energies and resources towards positive development directed at meeting the basic needs of our people and, thereby, ensuring long-term peace and stability. The UN no doubt remains the only global entity capable of shaping international consensus in order to instil confidence and facilitate international development cooperation. Papua New Guinea stands to salute the achievements of the UN, and will continue to support the noble cause and objectives of the Organization.

## PHILIPPINES

*President Fidel V. Ramos:* In five turbulent decades we have seen the decolonization of virtually the whole world, the rise of human rights to the forefront of world concerns, the engagement of our world community in reform for the welfare of children, women, minorities and the environment, and, most of all, the work of re-engineering development in the poor regions of the world. Now we must ensure that this Organization is adequate to meet the challenges of a new era. Let us remember that the United Nations was created—as the Charter says—"to promote better standards of life in larger freedom" all over the world.

## QATAR

*Deputy Prime Minister Sheikh Abdulla bin Khalifa Al Thani:* We ardently hope to see the birth of a new United Nations, which can firmly and effectively face up to the challenges of wars, internal conflicts, ethnic intolerance and other hurdles which hold back mankind's progress. This can happen only if the Organization can do more than

set up machinery to deal with conflicts after they erupt. Preventive measures should be taken to forestall such conflagrations through the development of societies, economically and socially, and combating poverty, sickness and all the other causes of underdevelopment.

## REPUBLIC OF KOREA

*President Kim Young Sam:* The dreams of the founders of the United Nations of a better world have already changed our planet tremendously. Riding the crest of the information age and globalization, not only is the international order undergoing an epochal change, but human civilization itself is being radically transformed. Change and reform in the UN are necessary if the Organization is to create and maintain the new world order. The UN has to be democratized and made more efficient; and every region of the world must be more equitably represented on the Security Council.

## SAMOA

*Tuiloma Neroni Slade, Chairman of the Delegation:* My own country, like so many in this Hall, came to independence through the process of decolonization made possible only through the central role played by the United Nations. That process was a historic achievement. We now have an Organization structured by a few, half-a-century ago, that has to respond to the needs of many more, and to a world which is fundamentally different and which continues to change. It needs to be reformed and assured of the financial resources it needs. Membership of the Security Council must be enlarged to reflect the realities of the present time and to enhance its effectiveness and legitimacy.

## SAUDI ARABIA

*Prince Sultan bin Abdulaziz Al Saud, Second Deputy Prime Minister:* The capabilities the UN has demonstrated over the past 50 years makes us determined to continue to support it. If the yardstick of its success lies in its effectiveness in serving the cause of international peace and security, we must underscore the importance of abiding by its Charter, and enforcing its resolutions. It is the hope of The Custodian of The Two Holy Mosques that our celebration today will make a watershed in the history of our Organization to enable it to achieve its goals and make it possible for all peoples of the world to live in security and achieve continued progress.

## SINGAPORE

*Prime Minister Goh Chok Tong:* The United Nations has been criticized, even maligned. Some of the criticisms are valid, but many of them are unfair. Let us not forget that the UN has contributed to a better world, despite its shortcomings and failures in several areas. The UN may not necessarily be the prime mover in many world events, given the increasing strength of regional and multilateral bodies. But it has a very important integrative function: that of maintaining global coherence and ensuring that no country is excluded in the march towards security, peace and prosperity.

## SOLOMON ISLANDS

*Deputy Prime Minister Danny Philip:* In the course of the last five decades, the United Nations did much to expand and strengthen the community of nations. In the Pacific, for example, the UN has been a critical factor in the emergence of independent States. The recent international recognition of the vulnerability of small island developing States to adverse economic conditions, as well as to natural and environmental disasters, is a significant example of the family of nations building mutual trust, support and respect. As the founders of this Organization understood, our problems are ultimately moral and spiritual in nature. Therefore, the very work of diplomacy can be successful only in an atmosphere of tolerance.

## SRI LANKA

*President Chandrika Bandaranaike Kumaratunga:* The effective strengthening of the United Nations system is an essential requisite for advancing its goals. The Organization has regrettably sometimes come to be seen by the more vulnerable States as primarily serving the interests of the more powerful States. The revitalizing process must enhance the capacity of the UN, rather than merely effect economies and scale down its scope. In the end, the UN will essentially be what we, the Member States, make of it—not what individual States seek to make from it.

## SYRIAN ARAB REPUBLIC

*Farouk Al Shara', Minister for Foreign Affairs:* A unanimity has crystallized among States of the world on the need to reform the UN, to render it more efficient for present and future challenges. The improvement in UN performance and the democratization of decision-making within it cannot be attained if stronger and richer States impose their selfish interests at the expense of the overwhelming majority of the world's countries. It is the tendency to do just that which lies at the source of genuine concern that has been generated by certain recent practices and experiences.

## TAJIKISTAN

*President Emomali Rakhmonov:* Designed to help States resolve disputes in a peaceful manner, the UN today faces a new challenge: to make wider

use of preventive diplomacy. The peacemaking potential of the UN can be coupled with its cooperation with regional organizations, primarily in deterring, confining and settling armed conflicts and in countering terrorism and radical manifestations of fundamentalism of various kinds. The best prospects for defending our national interests lie in cooperation with the UN, the OSCE, and other international organizations.

## THAILAND

*Prime Minister Banharn Silpa-Archa:* In this day and age, where uncertainty lurks at every turn, and where sustainable development poses a challenge, the United Nations is more important than ever. Its role in South-East Asia has shown that, with the right kind of support, it is indeed capable of promoting ''happiness in tranquility''. We should see to it that the Organization concentrates on the things which only it can do, or which it can do better than any other international body: to stop people from killing each other, to get people to treat each other fairly, and to help people live in an environment of their own choosing.

## TURKMENISTAN

*President Saparmurat Niyazov:* The 20th century ideological confrontation between blocs is gone, and mankind must choose which way to go. We stand together with those who believe in the philosophy of uniting the world while recognizing existing differences. We stand together with those who recognize the primacy of the United Nations in devising programmes of civilized partnership free from diktat and the imposition of ideas and ways of life. The new non-polar world is a community of equal partners. There should be no elite countries with special powers and prerogatives that rightfully belong to the entire world community.

## UNITED ARAB EMIRATES

*Deputy Prime Minister Sheikh Sultan bin Zayed Al-Nahayan:* Our participation in these celebrations clearly reflects our firm belief in the important and historic role of the United Nations in the establishment of a new era of international relations and in strengthening peace and security, especially in the Arab region, a region that has been ravaged, over the past few decades, by numerous wars and conflicts that have consumed its material and human energy and resources. The UN should perform a larger role in addressing those problems and in realizing the hopes and aspirations of the region's peoples.

## UZBEKISTAN

*President Islam A. Karimov:* Today, the newly independent States on the post-Soviet space are in the process of laying the foundations of their national statehood and advancing towards democratic reforms for which they need support from the world community to expedite their integration into international structures. The consistency and irreversibility of reforms, democratization and a free market economy must be maintained. This will enable us to secure the place we deserve in the world community.

## VANUATU
*Prime Minister Maxime Carlot Korman:* At a time when we are celebrating the 50th anniversary of the United Nations and, in particular, the development programmes adopted and applied for the benefit of Member States, and the means established to guarantee international peace and security, it is our duty to do more to help the Organization face the new challenges of the 21st century. Vanuatu assures the Secretary-General of its support for initiatives for reform. Let us respect peoples and guarantee life in the regions of our world. Let us effectively protect the environment in our respective regions. Let us together build a more pacific world.

## VIET NAM
*President Le Duc Anh:* Over the past 50 years, the growth of the UN has been closely linked with the struggle of peoples for the right to self-determination and for UN Charter principles. Paradoxically, just when mankind has acquired the technology to reduce the distance between the Earth and other celestial bodies, the gap between the rich and the poor has widened alarmingly. Every day, we witness the human tragedy of countless innocent people—victims of wars, conflicts, economic embargoes and epidemics. The international community should do its utmost to ensure the enjoyment of fundamental rights to a life in peace.

## YEMEN
*Vice-President Abdourabou Mansour Hadi:* Despite the challenges and difficulties facing the Organization as it discharges its functions and reaffirms its character, the last five decades have yielded important historic achievements, which have helped us to arrive at forming a collective future vision. Its greatest achievement is, perhaps, that it has spared mankind the horrors of a third world war. The Organization has also contributed to the liberation of nations, the raising of mankind's standard of living and the affirmation of the human right to a free and dignified life.

## EASTERN EUROPE

## ALBANIA
*President Sali Berisha:* The fall of the Iron Curtain—on which the United Nations had a positive influence—averted the threat of a large scale confrontation and ushered in a period of difficult transition for the countries of Eastern Europe. In this process, international institutions turned out to be not always interlocking, but interblocking. The international community, heading into the 21st century, is growing ever more aware of the need to redirect its advance towards a more reliable international order for everybody. The UN and its agencies can render a new contribution to this trend, to the benefit of present history.

## ARMENIA
*President Levon Ter-Petrossian:* In view of the situation in 1945, it was only natural that the Charter of the UN should deal primarily with the maintenance of international peace and security. The UN played a pivotal role in the reconstruction that followed the devastation of the world war, and it has so far been able to prevent the world being plunged into global conflict. Even during the cold war, the very existence of an international forum in which countries might discuss global issues prevented the outbreak of many conflicts.

## AZERBAIJAN
*President Heydar Alirza ogly Aliyev:* Great positive changes have occurred since the establishment of the United Nations involving the complete rebuilding of the world and practical implementation of the UN Charter. It was possible to avoid a new world war. Colonialism, apartheid and racial discrimination have become history. Confirmation of common human values, ideas of freedom, democracy and human rights has become widely expanded. The UN has played a special role. But problems involving international terrorism, weapons proliferation, hunger, poverty and environmental disasters require radical solutions.

## BELARUS
*President Alyaksandr Lukashenka:* The United Nations would do well today to think not so much about what has been done as about what still remains to be done. Unfortunately, on the threshold of the third millennium, the world is still burdened by many problems characteristic of the past: wars; armed conflicts in various regions; terrorism and other types of crime; environmental disasters; poverty; and hunger. Many other things threaten the future of mankind. The UN alone, this universal Organization, which reflects the interests of all peoples of the Earth, can unite the efforts of the community of nations in resolving these problems.

## BOSNIA AND HERZEGOVINA
*President Alija Izetbegovic:* The United Nations, whose anniversary we celebrate today, has always been a source of our hope, but also a constant cause

of our disappointment. Some say that it is the largest, but, on occasion, the most inefficient body in human history. The number of unimplemented resolutions is a proof of this. Being as it is, our Organization probably reflects the imperfections of our world. If the continuous improvement of the world is not work in vain, the further improvement of the UN is not only possible but very necessary. The supreme goal is the maintenance of peace.

## BULGARIA

*President Zhelyu Zhelev:* Without the principles laid down in the UN Charter and the Universal Declaration of Human Rights, the 1989 "velvet" revolutions in Eastern Europe would hardly have been able to sweep away the totalitarian regimes equipped, as they were, with the powerful tools of demagogy, propaganda and terror. The two documents proclaimed, once and for all, the universal validity of fundamental human rights. They held out the promise of social progress and a higher standard of living through individual freedom and free enterprise. Our historical experience has taught us that unity is strength.

## CROATIA

*President Franjo Tudjman:* So much power has convened today under the roof of the General Assembly Hall, and yet, so little power to provide the necessary solutions for a better common future. We are faced with a long and arduous road, but we can look back with pride on the 50 years of our common history. The UN must also be a garden of ideas related to general human values, international solidarity and an equitable international order. Our responsibility for narrowing the gap in economic development and for promoting coordinated development of all parts of our planet is equal to our responsibility for global peace.

## CZECH REPUBLIC

*President Václav Havel:* In my vision, the UN of the future would become more clearly an instrument serving all inhabitants of our planet, an instrument for pursuing their good life together. The point is not to expropriate any part of their internal identification with their own country, their people, their religious or cultural roots. The point is to forge a world in which everyone could be himself without being menaced by another. The form of a 21st century UN could be shaped precisely by this spirit, by this sense of responsibility.

## ESTONIA

*President Lennart Meri:* We, the small nations, are easily wounded; thus we are more sensitive. Because we are more sensitive, we are able to react more quickly. Because we are able to react more

quickly, we are consequently more idealistic. Small States are more idealistic, so it follows that a more active hope and a desire to remain true to our principles lives in our midst. It was this hope, it was this dedication to principles upon which, under the circumstances, this Organization was founded 50 years ago.

## GEORGIA

*Alexander Chikvaidze, Minister for Foreign Affairs:* We believe that the new philosophy of the United Nations must give priority to the strategy of "making" peace over "keeping" peace. The UN is obliged to break with neutrality in favour of mandatory implementation of Charter principles with regard to those who break the peace. There is also a need for a new method of decision-making, focusing on implementation, rather than be excessively preoccupied with procedure and self-serving adjustable wording. We must have the courage and the will to call an aggressor an aggressor, and genocide, genocide.

## HUNGARY

*President Árpád Göncz:* We should not forget that the strengths and weaknesses or the accomplishments and failures of the Organization are our common responsibility. In this respect, the vision of the founding fathers "to save succeeding generations from the scourge of war" remains to be pursued vigorously for all of us. For so many in the world, the United Nations is a beacon of hope and help. We ourselves felt this when in 1956 Hungarians in our revolution and national freedom fight, including myself, took courage from the distant but clear voice of solidarity coming from this very Hall. We remain deeply grateful for that.

## LATVIA

*President Guntis Ulmanis:* Much has been achieved during the existence of the UN. Peace and reconciliation have been made possible through preventive diplomacy and peace-keeping under UN auspices. Humanitarian assistance has been brought to crisis points around the world, ensuring survival and shelter for millions of people. The Organization has been a forum in which initiatives vitally important for humanity have been launched. The end of the cold war has given us an opportunity to fulfil the vision of the founders of the UN: the creation of a global order in which the principles of the Charter are respected and its purposes achieved.

## LITHUANIA

*President Algirdas Mykolas Brazauskas:* Fifty years of United Nations work have been crowned with tangible and laudable achievements. Most importantly, the number of democratic States has increased dramatically over those years. The global nuclear threat has decreased. Yet, the thread of life remains vulnerable. We have no other choice but to live together, seeking to better understand one another and to cooperate more closely. That is the basis of my optimism and faith in man, as well as in the future.

## POLAND

*Prime Minister Jozef Oleksy:* The world needs devoted leadership, commitment and far-sighted vision as much as it needs oxygen. It needs perseverance in the promotion of trust between States and their organizations. If we, the United Nations—united not, as 50 years ago, against someone, but driven by the desire for peaceful cooperation—show sufficient determination to give effect to our own proposals, the world stands a chance of ensuring a better and safer life in the 21st century. It stands a chance of ensuring lasting peace and sustained development for all, and ensuring respect for the rights of the citizens of this globe.

## REPUBLIC OF MOLDOVA

*President Mircea Ion Snegur:* The important international event that has brought us together has a profound historical significance. Shaken by the horrors of the Second World War and guided by the firm conviction that such apocalyptic cataclysms should never happen again, the free nations and their spiritual leaders laid the foundation of the United Nations 50 years ago. From this perspective, the first words of the Charter—''We the peoples of the United Nations''—are a natural expression of the world community's feeling of shared responsibility for the destiny of humankind.

## ROMANIA

*President Ion Iliescu:* Our most important duty now, on the 50th anniversary of the United Nations, is to make the chance of a new beginning come to fruition. Released from the fetters of bipolarity and of the cold war, the international system has regained its natural freedom of movement. Instead of ending, history is in fact starting again! We have the chance of a new beginning! The UN has a very full agenda for the 21st century. What we can do, even as of today, is to review its functional structures, mechanisms and architecture in order to render them capable of addressing those issues.

## RUSSIAN FEDERATION

*President Boris N. Yeltsin:* Half a century ago, an event occurred that paved the way to a new period in the history of mankind. Divided and bleeding, the world understood that its future was the path of mutual understanding and interaction. Only the United Nations will be able to realize the perennial dream of a world without wars and violence; of a world where controversial issues are settled through negotiation. While having won the world war, we have not yet managed to win peace. Today, the world more than ever before needs not only equality and tolerance, but also respect for the identity of each State.

## SLOVAKIA

*President Michal Kovác:* The United Nations is a living organism; it enjoys periods of success, but is aware of its weaknesses as well. On the one hand, we can appreciate the past and present role of the Organization in resolving issues related to peace and security. On the other, social issues, as well as the process of strengthening democracy and protecting human rights, will require a more sensitive and more effective approach in the future. We are currently witnessing growth in the UN role in the field of economic and social development, where a certain disproportion exists.

## SLOVENIA

*President Milan Kucan:* The United Nations has undoubtedly justified its establishment in its 50 years of existence. However, the goals defined in the UN Charter have not yet been realized. On the contrary, in the key area of its activity, the maintenance of international peace and security, the UN is burdened by an alarming lack of success. The genuine effectiveness of the UN in the maintenance of international peace and security is of crucial importance for the future of the Organization.

## THE FORMER YUGOSLAV REPUBLIC OF MACEDONIA

*Acting President Stojan Andov:* The UN Charter has survived the test of the past five decades and continues to be the basic framework on which world peace, security, cooperation, and economic and social development can successfully be built. In the past five decades, the world has changed substantially. The reforms we envisage are aimed at increasing the efficiency of the work done by the UN and its bodies, strengthening the role of the UN in preserving world peace, enhancing collective security and harmonizing global economic and social development.

## UKRAINE

*President Leonid D. Kuchma:* The peoples of the Earth in 1945 received a unique instrument for consolidating mankind as a single universal organism in its efforts to survive and build a better world. At that time, the UN might have been the only universal forum in which Ukraine could proclaim its existence as a country. The support of the UN promoted the realization of our age-old aspiration to have a State of our own. Finally, I place great hopes in the future of the UN which brings us closer to the moment when we shall be able to say, ''The United Nations means a united world''.

## WESTERN EUROPE AND OTHER STATES

### ANDORRA
*Prime Minister Marc Forné Molné:* In the face of ever-present examples of lack of tolerance and solidarity, it might seem that to speak of the ''human family'' is to speak of a desire rather than of a reality. Making facts accord with words spoken in this forum depends on us. We celebrate joyfully the establishment of the United Nations and wish it well on its first half-century of existence. Today, we all pledge to help it advance, as a standard of equality among men and women and peoples, an advocate of tolerance, an instrument for promoting peace, for defending our natural heritage and for development. Many happy returns, United Nations!

### AUSTRALIA
*Governor-General Bill Hayden:* The world is a very different place from the one which, 50 years ago, gave birth to the United Nations. As delegates in San Francisco in June 1945 prepared to sign the UN Charter, most of Europe and a great deal of Asia stood in ruins, over 48 million people had died and the survivors of the greatest conflict in human history asked themselves what could be done to stop such a catastrophe from ever happening again. Their answer was to create an organization which sought to enshrine the universal values of tolerance, social progress and respect for human dignity within international machinery.

### AUSTRIA
*Federal President Thomas Klestil:* Ever since the first moments of its existence, the United Nations has been torn between idealism and power politics, between solidarity and egoism. It has always mirrored the state of the world, but at the same time, it has been much more than the sum total of national interests. But the most fateful contradiction was already present at its creation. It was to be a community of nations, but the famous opening words of the Charter read: ''We, the peoples''. The history of the UN is the perpetual attempt to bring the world Organization closer to the people and to forge them into a genuine community of humankind.

### BELGIUM
*Prime Minister Jean-Luc Dehaene:* This 50th anniversary should be an opportunity to adapt the United Nations to new realities and to equip it to face the challenges of the next century. The best contribution of the international community to peace and security is to avoid the outbreak of conflicts by means of preventive diplomacy. The UN requires reform if it is to become more efficient and effective. But we must first give it a solid financial base. As a reflection of its Member States, the UN can do nothing unless we confirm our political commitment and comply with financial obligations.

### CANADA
*Prime Minister Jean Chrétien:* For 50 years now the United Nations has symbolized Canada's best hopes for a world at peace. Today, more than ever, we need the UN to maintain international stability and order, to tackle problems that do not respect borders—such as AIDS, drugs and terrorism. Countries should pay their dues now. Fifty years ago, in the ashes of a world war, in the shadow of 50 million dead, our predecessors found the strength to believe in a better future, and the courage and determination to build one. The result was the establishment of the UN. Surely we, the leaders of 1995, should do no less.

### DENMARK
*Prime Minister Poul Nyrup Rasmussen:* We, the political leaders, are responsible for pointing the way for the United Nations. We set the agenda. We decide the priorities. The problems of the UN are our problems and our responsibility. Reform and rationalization are needed. So is the will to provide the Organization with political support and financial resources. The UN is exactly as strong as we make it. If the Organization does not fulfil our expectations, our credibility is at stake. Instead of criticizing the UN for not doing enough, we should take a close look at ourselves to see if we are doing enough for the UN.

### FINLAND
*President Martti Ahtisaari:* The end of the cold war has provided the United Nations with new opportunities to strengthen international peace and security. It has helped the world to focus on threats to our common security which are not amenable to resolution by military means. For five decades, the UN has sought to provide security in the broadest sense of the word. The world Organization has been a source of inspiration and an obstacle to cynicism. We may not always recognize its efforts, and we may sometimes even resent them. But we cannot do without it.

## FRANCE

*President Jacques Chirac:* Fifty years after our Charter was drafted, its aims have lost none of their relevance: peace and disarmament, democracy and development, the promotion of human rights and the fight against the great scourges that threaten mankind. In these 50 years, a body of common values has gradually come to be asserted. Today, we must focus our efforts on the adaptation and renewal of our Organization, above all by giving it the resources to operate. The temptation to disengage threatens the very existence of the UN. The world needs solidarity, and yes, it needs the United Nations!

## GERMANY

*Klaus Kinkel, Vice-Chancellor and Minister for Foreign Affairs:* Unfortunately, history does not always follow the straight paths of reason, but it does give us opportunities for progress which sometimes border on the miraculous. Today, on the threshold of a new millennium, we must learn the right lessons from the experiences gained over the last 50 years. We cannot change what lies behind us, but we can do better in the future. We must influence and shape what lies ahead. What is the challenge we are facing? Nothing less than to keep the Earth habitable for our children and grandchildren; to make sure that 8 or 10 billion people can live in humane conditions.

## GREECE

*President Constantinos Stephanopoulos:* The primary objective of the UN—that of preserving new generations from the scourge of war—has been partially achieved. Thanks to what has been called the balance of terror among the Powers, but also thanks to the existence of the UN, it has been possible to avoid having the cold war transformed into a new global conflict. The UN has always been a forum for discussion and conciliation, and has been able to adopt significant resolutions which have not all remained a dead letter—quite the opposite. Strengthening the effectiveness of the UN would be to the advantage of all.

## ICELAND

*Prime Minister David Oddsson:* The fiftieth anniversary of the UN is an occasion to reaffirm our commitment to this indispensable Organization and its ideals. To ensure that the UN lives up to its full potential, the process of adapting it to a changing global agenda must be brought to a successful conclusion. Necessary reforms need to be agreed upon and implemented without delay. The composition of the Security Council should reflect new realities, and the General Assembly should become more focused on relevance and efficiency.

## IRELAND

*President Mary Robinson:* The 51 States that founded this Organization in 1945 wrought well. The United Nations has become the first universal organization of States in human history and it has shaped the whole structure of international relations through the second half of the 20th century. But our special commemorative session will be an empty ritual, quickly forgotten, if we limit ourselves to congratulation. This is a time to adapt and renew what we have inherited; a time for vision, equal now to that of half a century ago; above all a time for Member States to make a new commitment and carry it through in action.

## ITALY

*Susanna Agnelli, Minister for Foreign Affairs:* Fifty years ago the world's leaders succeeded in uniting all countries and peoples around common ideals and values. The result has been 50 years without a major war. The world has changed in the last 50 years and the United Nations has to change with it. International conflicts have been replaced by internal ones, characterized by political, economic, ethnic and religious tensions that often imply grave humanitarian crisis and human rights violations. We must seek new formulas and instruments to face the new crises. A reform of our Organization is clearly needed.

## LIECHTENSTEIN

*Prime Minister Mario Frick:* We must look forward and strengthen the capacities and the effectiveness of the United Nations, which today, more than ever, is faced with numerous, enormous tasks. New problems and new challenges call for new, creative and flexible approaches. No one can deny that the United Nations today is not always able to respond swiftly and effectively to sometimes rapidly changing situations. A comprehensive reform and restructuring of the UN system is necessary to achieve this goal. No reform, however artful, will succeed unless the UN has a sound financial base.

## LUXEMBOURG

*Deputy Prime Minister Jacques F. Poos:* Despite the paralysis engendered by the cold war, the UN was able to ensure relative stability by preventing the outbreak of a major conflagration and by limiting the scope and intensity of existing conflicts. The UN improved the living conditions of and offered sanctuary to hundreds of millions of the disinherited and homeless. It alone has the authority and legitimacy to attempt to meet such challenges as complex political, military and humanitarian crises, international terrorism, arms proliferation, drug trafficking, and environmental degradation.

## MALTA

*Deputy Prime Minister Guido de Marco:* These first 50 years have shown that the moral and political foundations of the United Nations are rooted in ideals and aspirations which go beyond a simple aggregate of membership and the search for pragmatic solutions to specific and immediate problems. The whole is more than the sum of its parts. The founding fathers of the United Nations hitched their wagon to a star in charting the course of the future. This global vision rests and depends on the recognition of and respect for the rights, freedoms and dignity of each and every human being.

## MONACO

*Prince Rainier III, Head of State:* The terrible images of the Second World War, of horrible combats, of massive destruction, of endless suffering, remind us of the dangers that brought 51 countries to San Francisco. We still see too often the tragic picture of civilians fleeing the fighting and taking the road of exodus to uncertain destinations; we see families, women and old people completely abandoned. In all circumstances, the UN has done its utmost, with the authority and means available to it, to help promote a return to peace, to protect the peoples exposed to danger and to ease the suffering of victims.

## NETHERLANDS

*Prime Minister Wim Kok:* This Commemorative Meeting is a good opportunity to reflect on both the achievements and the shortcomings of the United Nations. We have to ask ourselves why, after 50 years, so few of the original ideals laid down in the Charter have been fully realized. We also have to be aware that we, the Member States, play a crucial role in every success or failure of the UN. The main task before us is to come to grips with reality. We must determine what it is that we want from the UN and how much we are willing to pay, politically and financially, in order to let the Organization do its work.

## NEW ZEALAND

*Prime Minister James Brendan Bolger:* Those who founded this Organization had a vision of a better world. Some of that vision has been achieved. The spread of human rights and democracy and UN support for the role of women, for a fair trading system, for the protection of the environment—all these achievements must be recognized and celebrated. Today, the generation raised in the shadow of the cold war has the opportunity to direct its energy to the protection and enhancement of the planet, not its destruction. Let us put differences to one side and learn to live with diversity. There is so much we can accomplish by working together.

## NORWAY

*Prime Minister Gro Harlem Brundtland:* To millions of people, the United Nations has meant food where there was none, vaccination where epidemics raged, a school to attend, a new well in the village, and Blue Helmets who kept belligerents apart, shielding civil life. To scores of new nations, access to this rostrum meant sovereignty and self-determination. From this rostrum, for 50 years, all countries have been able to call for world attention. But let us not only commemorate the past. Let us also chart a new beginning. The ploughshare that worked for five decades is worn. Let us forge a new one.

## PORTUGAL

*President Mario Soares:* Tribute must be paid to the United Nations for its steadfast efforts to further peace, dialogue and development. In a rapidly changing world, in the face of unstoppable processes of globalization, the United Nations must do everything it can to ensure that changes occur without serious disruptions and in the service of all mankind. We must, however, have the courage to recognize that the gap that separates the poor countries from the wealthy is growing ever wider and is becoming truly explosive. Will we be capable of ensuring peace, our most precious asset?

## SAN MARINO

*Captain Regent Piero Natalino Mularoni:* No more wars! This is the strong and resolute appeal that the Captains Regent of the Republic of San Marino wish to reiterate to this Assembly. Over the years, this very Hall has witnessed the celebration of many achievements, the real sharing and resolution of peoples' problems, the condemnation of unfair treatment and dictatorships, as well as the admission of many peoples once exploited by colonial regimes and oppressed by intolerant systems. No more wars! This is the appeal of a small country which is also one of the newest UN Members.

## SPAIN

*Felipe González, President of the Government:* The birth of our Organization, so closely linked to the end of a tragic war, enshrined principles underlying the common effort to fulfil mankind's aspirations: peace, freedom, human dignity, and economic and social progress. The great sufferings caused in Europe by the wars that pitted our peoples against each other made us look upon the Charter of San Francisco for inspiration. One cannot conceive of today's world without the UN contribution to decolonization, environment, development, and to innovative concepts such as the common heritage of mankind.

## SWEDEN

*Prime Minister Ingvar Carlsson:* We live in a world where more and more services need to be provided globally, in our truly common interest. We must develop systems of financing that assure adequate, predictable and sustainable levels of funding. The mandatory contributions should continue to be the backbone of the financing of the core activities, but the dependency on one large contributor must be reduced. We need to explore the possibility of creating an international tax on foreign currency transactions. We must uphold the strictest respect for the financial commitments we all have made when accepting the UN Charter.

## TURKEY

*President Süleyman Demirel:* Fifty years ago, the United Nations was created to be a centre for harmonizing the actions of nations in achieving a better world for all. The UN Charter was to provide the road map to a new international order. However, the initial hopes and aspirations of the founders turned into disillusionment during the dark days of the cold war. Now, there is a widespread revival of the positive spirit that prevailed half a century ago. We should seize this moment to adapt the UN to the new challenges and demands of our times, and in this we must not fail.

## UNITED KINGDOM

*Prime Minister John Major:* Throughout the past 50 years, the principles of the Charter have stood the test of time. But now, we need to look ahead. The world is changing, and it is time for the United Nations to change with it. The world needs the UN, as much today as at any time in the past; a UN that works; a UN using today's methods to address tomorrow's needs; a UN that shows its worth to the taxpayer in all our countries. In that way, I believe we can capture and justify popular support for our Organization. Today, we face difficulties that we must overcome. At this commemoration, my hope is that we will find the will to do so.

## UNITED STATES

*President William J. Clinton:* The United Nations has not stopped human suffering, but it has healed the wounds and lengthened the lives of millions of human beings. The UN has not banished repression or poverty from the Earth, but it has advanced the cause of freedom and prosperity on every continent. It has been a force for good and a bulwark against evil. So at the dawn of a new century so full of promise, yet plagued by peril, we still need the UN. And so, for another 50 years and beyond, you can count the United States in.

# LATIN AMERICA & THE CARIBBEAN

## ANTIGUA AND BARBUDA

*Prime Minister Lester Bryant Bird:* I come neither to bury the United Nations nor to praise it. Today, the UN's moral authority is sorely wounded, bleeding from its wounds in Bosnia, in Rwanda and in Somalia. Rogue regimes in these places have challenged the power of the UN and found an impotent force constrained by its limited operations' mandate and weakened by the paucity of its resources. The might of the world community, which should have been an overwhelming force to end conflict, stop killing and save lives, proved to be incapable of enforcing the peace that it set out to keep—hobbled essentially by its Member States.

## ARGENTINA

*President Carlos Saúl Menem:* Fifty years have elapsed since the unspeakable pain and suffering of a terrible war gave rise to the United Nations. Today, we are celebrating much more than an anniversary. We evoke the dream, the vision, the fears and also the courage of a few men who, despite the proximity of horror, dared to imagine a space for the preservation of international peace and security, international cooperation, the promotion of human rights and fundamental freedoms and the economic and social progress of peoples. This generation—our generation—owes the founding fathers of the UN its deepest gratitude.

## BAHAMAS

*Prime Minister Hubert A. Ingraham:* It is our desire that the next five decades bear the fruit of our theme today—"We the Peoples of the United Nations . . . United for a Better World". We hope for a world freed from the scourge of illicit drug traffic, relieved of the burdens created by uncontrolled migration, protected by greater environmental consciousness, enhanced through increased literacy and health standards everywhere, strengthened by Member States that fully honour their financial obligations to this body, and liberated from poverty, disease, unemployment, racism, religious persecution, tyranny and strife.

## BARBADOS

*Prime Minister Owen S. Arthur:* Looking ahead, the United Nations of the next 50 years must embark on its unfinished journey, reformed and re-energized, to meet the challenges of a world of tumultuous global change. The reformed UN must construct a new system of security to reflect the changed nature of today's conflicts, conflicts mainly within nations, rather than between nations. It must accelerate and intensify its development mission. It must respond with dispatch to the cry and suffering of the world's poor, whose plight weighs heavily on the conscience of the world.

## BELIZE

*Prime Minister Manuel Esquivel:* The 50 original signatories could not have foreseen that 50 years later this world Organization would consist of Member States with populations ranging from 1 billion to 16,000 people. While war and the peaceful settlement of disputes was the number one priority in 1945, priority number one in 1995 is found in Article 2 of the Charter which states that the Organization is based on "the sovereign equality of all its Members". Today, as the large and powerful sit side by side with the small and vulnerable, the principle of sovereign equality is a difficult pill for some and an elusive goal for others.

## BOLIVIA

*Edgar Camacho Omiste, Chairman of the Delegation:* Lasting peace on Earth requires justice in international relations and within each country. If harmony is to prevail among nations, solutions have to be found to situations that impede fraternal relations among peoples. Someday in the not-too-distant future, there will be an end to situations of oppression and dependency, just as colonialism will come to an end, extreme poverty will disappear, friendship among peoples will flourish, and the free and sovereign presence of Bolivia on the Pacific Ocean will become possible. The power politics of yesterday will have to give way to brotherhood and cooperation as central instruments in the new international relations.

## BRAZIL

*President Fernando Henrique Cardoso:* We are living in better times than 50 years ago. By freeing the international agenda of the tensions generated by ideological confrontation, the end of the cold war created the conditions for a growing convergence of values, with democracy, economic freedom and social justice at centre stage. Human advancement is at the core of the international debate. This is a forum in which we should, within the complex context of globalization, work to overcome a persistent situation of social and economic inequalities giving rise to hopelessness and a feeling of exclusion.

## CHILE

*President Eduardo Frei Ruiz-Tagle:* Up to now, the United Nations has been the setting for intergovernmental agreement. It is now time to begin the long march towards the consolidation of ties between the peoples and groups of different societies. The exchange of cultural values in civil society can provide an important source of support for the elimination of apprehensions, racism and prejudice against human conditions of all types. The future of the UN must be marked by emphasis on human development, preservation of the environment and the consolidation of peace.

## COLOMBIA

*President Ernesto Samper Pizano:* The creation of the United Nations 50 years ago sowed the seeds of hope for mankind: hope for peace and progress, faith in the peaceful mechanisms for the settlement of conflicts and credibility in multilateralism as we confront the most wrenching issues before humankind. Today, we have to rethink what we are in order to know what we want to become. The task of the new UN system must be to regain that vision, so that we may continue to prevail as a civilization, as a democracy and as rational human beings.

## COSTA RICA

*President José María Figueres:* To remain true to the spirit of San Francisco, the UN must not remain neutral or passive in the face of major conflicts. New challenges include assuming responsibility for protecting and preserving global assets. Only an organization that represents equally all the peoples of the Earth can be successful in this undertaking. We dream of a UN that encourages forums of cooperation among all nations to reduce the greenhouse effect, to save, study and make use of the planet's biodiversity, to decontaminate the seas and thereby ensure the greater well-being of present and future generations.

## CUBA

*Fidel Castro Ruz, President of the Council of State and the Council of Ministers:* The obsolete veto privilege and the ill-use of the Security Council by the powerful are exalting a new colonialism within the United Nations. Latin America and Africa do not have a single permanent member in the Security Council. In Asia, India has a population of almost 1 billion but it does not enjoy that responsibility. How long shall we wait for the democratization of the UN and for the independence and sovereign equality of States to become a reality? How long before non-intervention in the internal affairs of States and true international cooperation take their rightful places? How long shall we have to wait before rationality, equity and justice prevail in the world?

## DOMINICA

*Prime Minister Edison C. James:* The United Nations system was designed to deal with the problems of the postwar period, mainly related to the disruption of international peace through recourse to arms. Today's threat to peace has to do primarily with development. Cost-cutting measures and streamlining should take into account the legitimate aspirations of people in small and vulnerable States. Let us always remember that every human being has a right to be clothed with dignity, and that at the very heart of the cosmos stands that same human being, that irreducible kernel of development.

## DOMINICAN REPUBLIC

*Constitutional Vice-President Jacinto Peynado Garrigosa:* United Nations achievements have been one of the most precious assets of mankind throughout this past half century. This Organization has been able to settle and avoid armed conflicts, has fostered democratic institutions by promoting free and fair elections, and has raised its voice in defence of the poor, bringing humanitarian assistance to tens of millions. It led in efforts towards reversing environmental degradation throughout the world and achieving a sustainable way of life as we approach the 21st century.

## ECUADOR

*Galo Leoro, Minister for Foreign Affairs:* To attend to the new and increasing demands being placed by the international community, our Organization needs major structural change, adopted under the obligations derived from the Charter of San Francisco. Respect for the binding nature of this fundamental universal instrument is the only way to guarantee the survival of small and weak States. We reaffirm our commitment to pursuing the ongoing quest for just and equitable solutions, arising from agreements mutually arrived at, to the conflicts that persist in the world.

## EL SALVADOR

*President Armando Calderón Sol:* The international order of the postwar period was marked by antagonism and ideological confrontation. Nonetheless, the UN attained important and substantial achievements, outstanding among which were its significant contributions to avoiding another world war with unimaginable consequences, eliminating colonialism and racial discrimination, encouraging the codification of international law, strengthening the international system of human rights and promoting improvement of political, economic and social conditions of our peoples.

## GRENADA

*Robert E. Millette, Chairman of the Delegation:* Some refer to the United Nations as the biggest debating society in the world, in which perception takes precedence over substance, rhetoric over

reality—a Tower of Babel where debates consist of grotesque rituals of recurrent irrelevancies. The truth of the matter is that the UN, as a relatively young institution, is the quintessential example of humanity's struggle for peace among nations and within nations. It bears the marks of humanity's triumphs and failures. However, in the pursuit of peace, the UN continues ''to run and not be weary, to walk and not grow faint''.

## GUATEMALA

*President Ramiro De León Carpio:* The United Nations' founding fathers, mindful of the tragedy of the two world wars, sought to create a new order based on justice for all. There can never be justice or peace if we deny the right of every human being and every nation to engage in dialogue on a footing of equality and to enjoy the identical dignity without which no member of our species can truly be free, without the shackles of poverty and without the bitterness of the hatred engendered by inequality. Universal representation should prevail at the UN, without any kind of exclusion.

## GUYANA

*President Cheddi Jagan:* A new global human order must be an adjunct to the UN Agenda for Development. A new global human order must have as its goal human development, which means meeting the basic needs of the people, attaining cultural uplift and providing a clean and safe environment. To attain a new global human order, it is necessary to establish a sound and just system of global governance based on a genuine North-South partnership and interdependence for mutual benefit; a democratic culture of representative, consultative and participatory democracy, and a lean and clean administration.

## HAITI

*President Jean-Bertrand Aristide:* Celebrating the 50th anniversary of the United Nations is especially meaningful for the world's first independent black republic. It gives us the opportunity also to celebrate the first anniversary of the return of democracy to Haiti. It came about thanks to the heroism and courage of the Haitian people, to the leadership of President Clinton, to you, Mr. Secretary-General, and to all of our dear UN friends. Gratitude is the heart's memory; let the beating of our hearts express our intense joy at having together achieved this miracle of the century.

## HONDURAS

*President Carlos Roberto Reina:* The United Nations must help us find the humanism of our times. As if in a new Renaissance, we must erect a heretofore unseen concept of man on the shoulders of science and technology, a concept by which the importance of material things is found in their relationship with the higher levels of humanitarian conscience. This road begins by vanquishing poverty, defeating illegitimate power, breaking corruption and impunity and establishing a world order loved and sustained by all. There is no better definition of a future democracy.

## JAMAICA

*Prime Minister Percival James Patterson:* We concede that the United Nations is by no means perfect. Yet, we shudder even to contemplate what kind of world would have emerged without it. It has become an indispensable instrument in the search for global dialogue in the resolution of disputes. It offers the only hope for the harmonization of global interests and for defusing the complex issues which otherwise can so easily ignite. We sometimes forget that the UN is the creature of its Members. We make it what we will. As Member States, it is our solemn obligation to build an effective system which generates lasting peace and social justice.

## MEXICO

*President Ernesto Zedillo:* In today's world, serious problems persist which are at the root of conflicts that in the past gave rise to confrontations. Globalization and interdependence coexist alongside trends towards isolationism and intolerance. Restrictive nationalism, attempts at genocide and fragmentation, environmental deterioriation and drug trafficking, economic disparities, social inequality and poverty are the current threats to peace and security. For this reason, the principles underlying and the *raison d'être* of the birth of the United Nations are today still fully valid.

## NICARAGUA

*Ernesto Leal, Minister for Foreign Affairs:* The time has come to faithfully fulfil the commitment established in the UN Charter to promote economic and social advancement of all peoples. We must begin the UN's largest peace-keeping operation—placing the human being at the centre of economic and social development. Development should be the other phase of the work of the next 50 years of the UN—a UN that looks towards the South, which is still poor and without resources, so the 21st century may also become the century of development. We face the great challenge of turning into reality the results of world conferences on children, the environment, social development, population, human rights and women.

## PANAMA

*President Ernesto Perez Balladares:* The genuinely far-reaching importance of the Organization can be measured not in quantifiable terms, but in terms of intangible but real values: wars never fought, victims that never died, children not orphaned. When we look at the record of these 50 years, many will say that the Organization has been an arena for sterile debate, but it is preferable for the world to have a forum in which conflicts can spend themselves in words rather than constantly to seek battlefields on which to resolve disputes of its own invention.

## PARAGUAY

*President Juan Carlos Wasmosy:* Paraguay has the same fervour and conviction today about the United Nations as it had when it signed the Charter, and it continues to support the Organization with a view to its pursuing peace in the world, on the basis of the harmonious and balanced development of the Member States. Our support is not shaken or destroyed by some failures which the UN may have suffered. This Organization is absolutely necessary in our world to carry out the goals the peoples of the UN undertook to accomplish after the butchery of the Second World War.

## PERU

*Vice-President César Paredes Canto:* The United Nations has had unquestionable successes in the 50 years of its existence. However, we cannot fail to stress that, during this period, we have not experienced 50 years of world peace. The conflicts that are still proliferating in many parts of the Earth mean that, at this very moment, men, women and children are falling victim to armed clashes which, far from resolving problems, aggravate them because land that is strewn with destruction and death is the most fertile ground for resentment and further sterile conflicts, even more bitter and prolonged, generating an endless spiral of violence.

## SAINT KITTS AND NEVIS

*Prime Minister Denzil Douglas:* In 50 years, the structure of the United Nations has hardly changed. Yet, its circumstances have changed beyond anything its founders would recognize. In this new era, we should endeavour to make the Security Council more representative of and responsive to its membership. The developing world should now become permanent members of the Security Council. The goal of appropriate representation should guide our efforts to ensure that all the peoples of the world, who have observed the principles of the UN Charter, are welcomed into this fraternity of nations.

## SAINT LUCIA

*Prime Minister John G. M. Compton:* In spite of developments which seem to have violated the idealism of the founding fathers, the Organization has much cause for celebration. Its many organs and agencies, which work quietly and efficiently away from the glare of the media, have many achievements to their credit. They are engaged in silent battles against man's ancient enemies of ignorance, poverty and disease. They have kept the peace in many parts of the world without the fanfare of international commendation. They have registered remarkable successes in freeing subject peoples from the yoke of colonial domination.

## SAINT VINCENT AND THE GRENADINES
*Prime Minister James Fitz-Allen Mitchell:* Over the passage of time, men with vision conceive an idea, create an institution, and one that benefits mankind for all time. Our United Nations belongs to this noble category, of which there are few that have earned 50 years' respect. The celebration of this anniversary would not have been so worthy a cause if the evils of communism had not been put to rest. We still await atonement by those who imposed such monumental waste on our civilization. I personally would wish to single out Mr. Gorbachev for his leadership in having jettisoned the awful load on our behalf, and creating the opportunities to carry us sumptuously into the 21st century.

## SURINAME
*President Runaldo Ronald Venetiaan:* There is no doubt that unless we overcome and rectify certain shortcomings of the United Nations, this Organization will not be able to play its fundamental role in the management of the new world order; neither will it be able to realize its noble principles. Thus, a most urgent task for the international community now is to reinvigorate, restructure and democratize the UN and to give it a sound financial basis for the fulfilment of old and new tasks, in order to relieve international relations of suspicion and hostility, to bring an end to violence, and to fully activate the creative potential of the UN.

## TRINIDAD AND TOBAGO
*Annette des Iles, Chairperson of the Delegation:* For Trinidad and Tobago, as for the great majority of the Member States which make up this Organization, our first responsibility is to our people: to provide an acceptable standard of living and an improved quality of life for all our citizens, including our young people and our women. It follows that in countries such as ours, this Organization will be judged largely by the extent to which it can assist in this effort. We wish to urge, therefore, that international cooperation for development be placed at the centre of the activities of the United Nations.

## URUGUAY
*Vice-President Hugo Batalla:* Today, as we commemorate the 50th anniversary of the Organiza-

tion, we are living through an anxious and uncertain present in which even human values themselves are called in question. It is our responsibility to look ahead and to build on today's anxiety a brighter tomorrow in which all people, whatever their colour, their gender, their religious creed or the place where they live, will have the right, recognized as theirs by the international community, to a life of dignity with access to all the benefits that civilization affords. The eyes of the world are on us today; we are being called on to take up this challenge.

## VENEZUELA
*President Rafael Caldera:* A new half century is beginning for the United Nations. We must prepare the Organization for a new era with a new agenda. Antagonisms of all sorts, poverty, especially abject poverty, selfishness and corruption, which eat away at our conscience and destroy institutions, all represent the most serious threat to peace. These are the greatest enemies that we must fight against in the new half century that is now dawning for the UN. It is time to stand up to those enemies, to turn our good intentions into reality.

## OTHER SPEAKERS

## HOLY SEE
*Secretary of State Angelo Cardinal Sodano:* In his address on 5 October, the Holy Father expressed the wish that the Organization might grow as a moral centre, as a family of nations. It can realize this mission only if each State feels that it is accepted and recognized for what it is and is willing to give and take, and if all share the same heritage of values whose highest expressions remain the ideals of justice, freedom, peace and solidarity.

## SWITZERLAND
*Secretary of State Jakob Kellenberger:* Fifty years ago, the founding Members of the United Nations decided to be the joint guarantors of international peace and security and to promote human rights and social and economic development in the world. In the United Nations, we have today a sound tool for global policy-making that enables us, day by day and year by year, to build our future.

## AGENCY FOR THE PROHIBITION OF NUCLEAR WEAPONS IN LATIN AMERICA AND THE CARIBBEAN
*Secretary-General Enrique Roman-Morey:* In February 1967, nearly 22 years after the signing of the Charter of the UN, Latin America and the Caribbean—at the core of the cold war without being part of it—gave mankind the example of the

Treaty of Tlatelolco for the prohibition of nuclear weapons, which established the intergovernmental organization that I represent. For a world free of nuclear tests and nuclear weapons, I congratulate the United Nations.

## ASIAN-AFRICAN LEGAL CONSULTATIVE COMMITTEE

*Secretary-General Tang Chengyuan:* Consensus-building in the codification of international law is by nature a time-consuming and complex process, but the spirit of cooperation kindled by the Organization has kept the international legislative draftsmen and lawyers totally preoccupied, in particular during the ongoing UN Decade of International Law.

## CARIBBEAN COMMUNITY

*Secretary-General Edwin Carrington:* Today, 50 years following the signing of the Charter creating the United Nations, this Organization still represents mankind's greatest hope for peace, development and international cooperation. Of particular significance to the Caribbean Community is the UN contribution to recognizing the equal sovereign status of nations, while promoting the special needs of the least developed and small nation States.

## CENTRAL AMERICAN INTEGRATION SYSTEM

*Julio Icaza Gallard, Director of Functional Integration at the General Secretariat:* The current recognition, in the United Nations, of the fact that worldwide peace, security and stability can be achieved only if the economic and social needs of peoples are met is shared by the Central American Integration System. We should tackle simultaneously the economic, social, cultural, political and environmental spheres.

## COMMONWEALTH SECRETARIAT

*Secretary-General Emeka Anyaoku:* The United Nations is the globe's only truly universal Organization. The effectiveness of the Organization is directly linked to the commitment and support of its constituents. The commitment of all Member States—including those of the Commonwealth—to the UN should reflect their determination to strengthen it and make it a dynamic and strong Organization.

## ECONOMIC COOPERATION ORGANIZATION

*Secretary-General Shamshad Ahmad:* We certainly need a just, fair and equitable economic order free of discriminatory and protectionist walls. It is in this direction that the United Nations should focus its attention in the coming years. The international community must develop new patterns of collaboration on the basis of equality, partnership, interdependence and mutuality of benefit.

## EUROPEAN COMMISSION

*Hans van den Broek, on behalf of the European Community:* The present agenda of the United Nations has become more complex and more demanding than at any other time in its history. Instability has entrenched itself in many parts of the world. We have been witnessing the revival of nationalism, of ethnic cleansing, of unprecedented humanitarian crises, of gross violations of human rights, and even of genocide. The world, therefore, needs the UN today more than ever.

## INTERNATIONAL COMMITTEE OF THE RED CROSS

*President Cornelio Sommaruga:* Abounding in symbolism, the commemoration of the 50th anniversary of the United Nations invites us to ponder history. The International Committee of the Red Cross is therefore pleased to join in this celebration, which enables it to reaffirm its faith in mankind by paying tribute to an institution moulded in its image: imperfect, unique, yet irreplaceable.

## INTERNATIONAL FEDERATION OF RED CROSS AND RED CRESCENT SOCIETIES

*President Mario Enrique Villarroel Lander:* Both the UN and our institution were founded by idealists who sought to bring works of enduring peace to the world. In our missions—yours aimed at constructing a better world with peace, full justice and freedom; ours aimed at the improvement of life for the world's vulnerable people—we have likewise brought together the world's States and their peoples.

## INTERNATIONAL ORGANIZATION FOR MIGRATION

*Director-General James N. Purcell:* How the world responds to migratory pressures is of critical importance to global stability and well-being. Once considered primarily as a positive force in nation-building, migrants are now, more often than not, seen as the visible messengers of society's failures. IOM can be a key resource in exploring comprehensive solutions, only in close partnership with the United Nations.

## LATIN AMERICAN ECONOMIC SYSTEM

*Permanent Secretary Carlos Moneta:* Clearly, the balance sheet for these 50 years of United Nations activities is positive in connection with the objective of the maintenance of international peace and security. But there still exist serious areas of tension and conflict which require more resolute action by the system. Moreover, there must be greater democratization in the decision-making process within the Security Council.

## LATIN AMERICAN PARLIAMENT

*President Humberto Celli Gerbasi:* At the close of the 20th century, the prospects for the developing countries are not very encouraging. We feel that there should be an ethical obligation to allow for the economic growth and social development of all nations, one in which there are no exploiters and no exploited, and in which freedom, peace, harmony and social justice prevail.

## LEAGUE OF ARAB STATES

*Mahmoud Aboul-Nasr, Chairman of the Delegation:* The Arab States participated in the drafting of the United Nations Charter and have taken part in the work of the Organization for the past 50 years. Today, the Arab States, like all other Member States, look forward to a new phase, a phase in which, we hope, peace and justice will prevail and in which human rights and man's fundamental freedoms will be respected all over the world.

## ORGANIZATION FOR SECURITY AND COOPERATION IN EUROPE

*Secretary-General Wilhelm Höynck:* The situation in the world today requires an ever more closely interlocking network of international organizations, in which the United Nations must have a special place. Only with such a network will we be able to cope with the challenges confronting us. We should give further thought to how we can integrate non-governmental organizations more effectively into such a network.

## ORGANIZATION OF AFRICAN UNITY

*Secretary-General Salim Ahmed Salim:* Fifty years ago, a free Africa, liberated from colonialism and racial bigotry, was only a concept of many and a distant dream even to the optimistic internationalists among those who met in San Francisco to draw up the UN Charter. To the Organization of African Unity and Africa as a whole, therefore, the United Nations has been an instrument of liberation. Today, Africa is free, thanks to a great extent to the joint struggle coming from within the United Nations.

## ORGANIZATION OF AMERICAN STATES

*Secretary-General César Gaviria:* Our continent, which is today united by the values of democracy and freedom, regards the United Nations as the most appropriate and effective instrument to further the collective aspirations of mankind. During these three days, many have mentioned the successes of the past. We should like to join this recognition of half a century of activity and success.

## ORGANIZATION OF THE ISLAMIC CONFERENCE

*Secretary-General Hamid Algabid:* The imperative need to preserve peace and save succeeding generations from the scourge of war demands adherence to universally recognized principles and a firm determination to defend law and legality wherever they are under threat. Here, the United Nations has done remarkable work. Similarly, inspiring work has been done by the entire UN system in the areas of development, culture, health, and social and humanitarian affairs in all regions, including in the Islamic world.

## PALESTINE LIBERATION ORGANIZATION

*Yasser Arafat, Chairman of the Executive Committee:* I came to this Assembly 21 years ago as a fighter for freedom, liberation and independence, carrying with me the torments of my struggling people. Today, however, I come to you with a heart filled with love and peace, now that the olive branch has been raised over the peace of the brave. The winds of change are blowing on our world.

## PERMANENT COUNCIL OF FRANCOPHONIE

*President Emile-Derlin Zinsou:* The francophone community sees itself above all as a place of solidarity. It finds unity in the diversity of its membership, which extends to every continent. In this United Nations, a lofty forum for dialogue, and especially for North-South dialogue, my presence attests to one of the fundamental dimensions of that community, most of whose members are from the South.

## SOUTH PACIFIC FORUM

*Deputy Secretary-General Nikenike Vurobaravu:* The vision on which the United Nations was built—peace, human dignity, justice, economic and social progress—will be as valid in the next 50 years as it was in the last 50. In an increasingly complex, interdependent world, the UN's role in pursuing that vision is more and more important to small countries, such as those of the South Pacific Forum.

## SOVEREIGN MILITARY ORDER OF MALTA

*Count Carlo Marullo di Condojanni, Member of the Sovereign Council:* The inception of the United Nations 50 years ago heralded the hope for a new era of peace and well-being around the world. The aim was to leave behind us a war in which the atrocities were on a scale previously unknown to mankind, a war that, with the introduction of nuclear weapons, had convinced peoples and Governments that they had to seek peace at any price.

PART ONE

Political and security questions

Chapter I

# International peace and security

During 1995, the General Assembly and the Security Council continued debate on measures to strengthen United Nations functions relating to the maintenance of international peace and security.

In January, the Secretary-General issued a supplement to his 1992 report, "An Agenda for Peace", setting forth additional recommendations for improving the Organization's peacemaking, peacekeeping and post-conflict peace-building capacity. On behalf of the Security Council, its President made a statement on the supplement, supporting the Secretary-General's conclusions and proposals and inviting Member States to submit further reflections on the subject.

The General Assembly called on States to promote the objectives of the 1986 declaration of the zone of peace and cooperation of the South Atlantic, considered that greater efforts were required to develop a focused discussion on implementing the 1971 Declaration of the Indian Ocean as a Zone of Peace, and decided to continue to review implementation of the 1970 Declaration on the Strengthening of International Security.

The Ministers expressed their appreciation for the UN efforts in maintaining world peace and security and stressed the primary responsibility of the Security Council in that respect. They further exchanged views concerning the situation in different regions as well as sanctions application, disarmament, sustainable development, and the United Nations financial situation and restructuring (see also PART ONE, Chapter III).

In a 23 October press communiqué,[3] the heads of State or Government of the non-aligned countries members of the Security Council emphasized the importance of preventive diplomacy, peace-making, peace-keeping and post-conflict peace-building in the post-cold-war era, and underscored the need to devise a more stable system of collective security and recast the concept of collective action for peace and security so as to render the United Nations more capable of carrying out its functions. They called for broader coordination between the General Assembly and the Security Council in maintaining international peace and security and for constructive use by parties to a conflict of the Secretary-General's good offices and mediation efforts.

## General aspects of international security

### Fiftieth anniversary statements

On 26 September, the Security Council, meeting at the level of Foreign Ministers to commemorate the fiftieth anniversary of the United Nations, authorized its President to make a statement[1] on its behalf, in which Council members, *inter alia*, reaffirmed their commitment to the collective security system of the United Nations Charter and to the maintenance of international peace and security, for which the Council had primary responsibility and in which it had played a crucial role since its establishment. The Council believed that effective use should be made of instruments for preventive action and that the Organization's peace-keeping capacity should continue to be improved. (For the full text of the statement, see PART ONE, Chapter III.)

On 27 September, the Foreign Ministers of the Security Council's five permanent members issued a statement[2] following their meeting with the Secretary-General to review the world situation.

### Supplement to an Agenda for Peace

Further to his 1992 report, "An Agenda for Peace",[4] the Secretary-General in January 1995 issued a position paper entitled "Supplement to an Agenda for Peace",[5] in which he set forth additional recommendations on the development of UN activities related to international peace and security and highlighted areas that required what in 1992 he had called "hard decisions" by Member States.

The Secretary-General pointed out that since the end of the cold war, there had been a dramatic increase in UN activities related to the maintenance of peace and security. Many conflicts were now within States rather than between States. There had been a rash of wars within newly independent States, often of a religious or ethnic character and often involving unusual violence and cruelty. They were often guerrilla wars accompanied by the collapse of State institutions and a breakdown of law and order, which made peace-keeping far more complex and more expensive and also necessitated the use of UN forces to protect humanitarian operations. In addition, the nature of UN operations in the field had changed, as the Organization was asked to undertake an unprecedented variety of functions in helping the parties to a conflict implement a negotiated settlement. Such multifunctional operations also highlighted the need for long-term coordinated programmes in various fields, to ensure that the original causes of war were eradicated.

The Secretary-General further examined instruments for peace and security developed by the United Nations. Stressing the importance of conflict prevention through early warning, quiet diplomacy and preventive deployment, he noted that the greatest obstacle in that area was the reluctance of individual Member States to accept UN help when they were a party to a conflict. Other problems were finding individuals having diplomatic skills and willing to serve as the Secretary-General's special representatives, and the establishment and financing of small field missions for preventive diplomacy and peacemaking to assist such representatives. The Secretary-General proposed to create a norm within the international community for Member States to accept an offer of UN good offices; to enlarge the existing provision for unforeseen and extraordinary activities and make it available for all preventive and peacemaking activities, not just those related to international peace and security strictly defined; and to include in the regular budget a contingency provision for such activities, in the range of $25 million per biennium.

Preventive diplomacy could also be supported by measures used for post-conflict peace-building, such as demilitarization, control of small arms, institutional reform, improved police and judicial systems, the monitoring of human rights, electoral reform, and social and economic development programmes. As most peace-building activities fell within the mandates of various entities of the UN system, resumption of such activities could initially be entrusted to, or coordinated by, a multifunctional peace-keeping operation. In such cases, it might also be necessary to transfer the decision-making responsibility from the Security Council to the General Assembly or other intergovernmental bodies responsible for civilian peace-building activities. In situations where no peace-keeping operation existed, the early-warning responsibility had to lie with UN Headquarters, and the Secretary-General could take the initiative of sending a mission to a country of impending crisis, with its Government's agreement.

The Secretary-General also noted the progress made in the area of disarmament, which was of paramount importance to both the security of humankind and the release of economic, scientific and technological resources for peace and human progress. He pointed to the role played by micro-disarmament in peace-keeping and post-conflict peace-building activities, giving special attention to small arms and anti-personnel mines (see next chapter). Speaking of the increased use of sanctions as another instrument for peace and security, the Secretary-General emphasized the need to ensure that provisions were made to facilitate the work of humanitarian agencies when sanctions were imposed and that the costs of applying sanctions were borne equitably by all Member States. He suggested establishing a mechanism to assess, at the Security Council's request and before the imposition of sanctions, their potential impact on the target country and on third countries; to monitor their application; to measure their effects and tailor them for maximum political impact and minimum collateral damages; to ensure the delivery of humanitarian assistance to vulnerable groups; and to explore ways of assisting affected third States and evaluate their claims submitted under Article 50 of the Charter.

The Secretary-General expressed the belief that the United Nations should, in the long term, develop a capacity for enforcement action against those responsible for threats to or breaches of the peace or acts of aggression, but advised against doing so at the current time due to the lack of resources and increased volume of peace-keeping and peacemaking activities. Noting that the Security Council could currently exercise such action by entrusting enforcement tasks to groups of Member States, he cautioned nevertheless that that arrangement could have a negative impact on the Organization's stature and credibility. He also considered various aspects of UN peace-keeping operations and made suggestions in that regard (see PART TWO, Chapter I).

The Secretary-General underscored the need for coordination of efforts in applying those instruments by the Security Council, the General Assembly and the Secretary-General, as well as by Governments, regional and non-governmental organizations (NGOs) and various entities of the UN system. A new trend in that regard was the establishment of informal groups of Member States, created on an ad hoc basis to support implementation of the Secretary-General's peacemaking and peace-keeping mandates and referred to as "Friends of the Secretary-General". While that arrangement was of value as a diplomatic instrument for bringing influence to bear on the parties to a conflict, there was a risk of duplication or overlapping of efforts if members of such groups were to take initiatives not requested by the Secretary-General.

In the UN Secretariat, the main responsibility for coordinating inputs from various departments was entrusted to the Task Force on United Nations Operations and to interdepartmental groups on each major conflict involving the Organization. At the same time, improved coordination between Headquarters and head offices of other entities of the UN system had to date proved difficult to achieve, as each of the agencies concerned had its own intergovernmental legislative body and its own mandate. The Secretary-General therefore recommended that Governments instruct their representatives in those bodies to recognize proper coordination as an essential condition for the Organization's success and that it not be made hostage to inter-institutional rivalry and competition. He further noted increasing cooperation with NGOs in providing humanitarian relief and mobilizing public support and funds for such activities, and discussed coordination of efforts with regional organizations (see below, under "Regional aspects of international peace and security").

On the subject of financing, the Secretary-General pointed out that peace-building was critically dependent on Member States' readiness to make the necessary resources available and that it could be a long-term process and expensive—except in comparison with the cost of peacemaking and peace-keeping if the conflict should recur. He suggested that in putting together peace-building elements of a comprehensive settlement plan, the UN should consult international financial institutions in good time to ensure that implementation costs were taken into account when designing economic plans of the Government concerned. The problems in that area, however, were aggravated by many donors' reluctance to finance crucial peace-building elements, such as the conversion of guerrilla movements into political parties, creation of new police forces or "arms-for-land" programmes. He concluded that overcoming crises in the post-cold-war world required a deeper commitment to cooperation and true multilateralism than humanity had ever achieved before.

In his report on the work of the Organization,[6] issued on 22 August, the Secretary-General stated that the UN Departments of Humanitarian Affairs, of Political Affairs and of Peace-keeping Operations had developed a framework for coordination of their actions—information sharing, consultations and joint action—needed to plan and implement complex operations in the field. These included routine monitoring and early-warning analysis, assessment of options for preventive action, where possible, fact-finding, planning and implementation of field operations, and conducting evaluations or "lessons-learned" exercises. He also noted that the Department of Political Affairs—created in response to the 31 January 1992 declaration by heads of State and Government at the Security Council summit,[7] which had mandated him to give priority to preventive and peacemaking activities—had completed its restructuring and was now organized to follow political developments world-

wide, so that it could provide early warning of impending conflicts and analyse possibilities for preventive action by the UN, as well as for action to help resolve existing conflicts.

With regard to post-conflict peace-building, the report stated that the United Nations had received 19 new requests for electoral assistance between July 1994 and August 1995. Also, since July 1994, 30 States and UN missions had received or would soon receive some form of electoral assistance from the UN system. Modalities for integrated action in a country's reconstruction were discussed at an international colloquium on post-conflict reconstruction strategies (Schlaining, Austria, 23 and 24 June), attended by representatives of UN political, humanitarian and development entities, specialized agencies, donor countries, NGOs and war-torn societies.

By a 22 December note,[8] the Secretary-General transmitted to the General Assembly a report of the Joint Inspection Unit on strengthening the UN-system capacity for conflict prevention.

### SECURITY COUNCIL ACTION

The Security Council met on 18 and 19 January and 22 February to discuss the supplement to "An Agenda for Peace".

On 22 February, the Council President made the following statement[9] on behalf of the Council:

The Security Council welcomes the Secretary-General's position paper entitled "Supplement to an Agenda for Peace" as an important contribution to the debate on the development of the United Nations activities related to international peace and security in all its aspects at the beginning of the year in which the Organization celebrates its fiftieth anniversary. The Council notes that the paper contains a wide range of conclusions and recommendations with regard to instruments for resolving conflict. The Council is of the view that in the light of recent developments and experience gained, efforts should be made to further enhance the Organization's ability to perform the tasks laid down for it under the Charter. The Council reiterates that, in performing the above-mentioned tasks, the purposes and principles of the Charter should always be strictly observed.

The Security Council welcomes and shares the priority given by the Secretary-General to action to prevent conflict. It encourages all Member States to make the fullest possible use of instruments of preventive action, including the Secretary-General's good offices, the dispatch of special envoys of the Secretary-General and the deployment, with the consent as appropriate of the host country or countries, of small field missions for preventive diplomacy and peacemaking. The Council believes that adequate resources must be made available within the United Nations system for these actions. It notes the problem identified by the Secretary-General in finding senior persons to act as his special representative or special envoy and encourages Member States which have not yet done so to provide the Secretary-General with the names of persons who might be considered by him for such posts, together with other resources both human and material which might be useful to such missions. It encourages the Secretary-General to make full use of resources thus put at his disposal.

The Security Council endorses the view expressed by the Secretary-General concerning the crucial importance of economic and social development as a secure basis for lasting peace. Social and economic development can be as valuable in preventing conflicts as in healing the wounds after conflicts have occurred. The Council urges States to support the efforts of the United Nations system with regard to preventive and post-conflict peace-building activities and, in this context, to provide necessary assistance for the economic and social development of countries, especially those which have suffered or are suffering from conflicts.

The Security Council welcomes the Secretary-General's analysis regarding peace-keeping operations. It recalls the statement made by its President on 3 May 1994 which, *inter alia*, listed factors to be taken into account in establishing peace-keeping operations. It notes that in resolving conflicts, primary emphasis should continue to be placed on the use of peaceful means rather than force. Without prejudice to its ability to respond to situations on a case-by-case basis, and rapidly and flexibly as the circumstances require, it reiterates the principles of consent of the parties, impartiality and the non-use of force except in self-defence. It underlines the need to conduct peace-keeping operations with a clearly defined mandate, command structure, time-frame and secure financing, in support of efforts to achieve a peaceful solution to a conflict: it stresses the importance of the consistent application of these principles to the establishment and conduct of all peace-keeping operations. It stresses the importance it attaches to the provision of the fullest possible information to the Council to assist it in making decisions regarding the mandate, duration and termination of current operations. It also emphasizes the importance of providing troop contributors with the fullest possible information.

The Security Council shares the Secretary-General's concern regarding the availability of troops and equipment for peace-keeping operations. It recalls earlier statements by the President of the Council on the subject and reiterates the importance of improving the capacity of the United Nations for rapid deployment and reinforcement of operations. To that end, it encourages the Secretary-General to continue his study of options aimed at improving the capacity for such rapid deployment and reinforcement. The Council believes that the first priority in improving the capacity for rapid deployment should be the further enhancement of the existing stand-by arrangements, covering the full spectrum of resources, including arrangements for lift and headquarters capabilities, required to mount and execute peace-keeping operations. It strongly encourages the Secretary-General to take further steps in this regard, including the establishment of a comprehensive database to cover civilian as well as military resources. In this context, it considers that particular attention

should be given to the greatest possible interoperability between elements identified in such arrangements. The Council reiterates its call to Member States not already doing so to participate in the stand-by arrangements. While affirming the principle that contributing Governments should ensure that their troops arrive with all the equipment needed to be fully operational, the Council also encourages the Secretary-General and Member States to continue to consider means, whether in the context of stand-by arrangements or more broadly, to address the requirements of contingents which may need additional equipment or training.

The Security Council strongly supports the Secretary-General's conclusion that peace-keeping operations need an effective information capacity, and his intention to address this requirement in future peace-keeping operations from the planning stage.

The Security Council welcomes the Secretary-General's ideas regarding post-conflict peace-building. It agrees that an appropriately strong overall United Nations contribution needs to be sustained after the successful conclusion of a peace-keeping operation, and encourages the Secretary-General to study ways and means of ensuring effective coordination between the United Nations and other agencies involved in post-conflict peace-building, and to take active steps to ensure that such coordination takes place in the immediate aftermath of a peace-keeping operation. The measures described by the Secretary-General may also be required, with the consent of the State or States concerned, after successful preventive action and in other cases where an actual peace-keeping deployment does not take place.

The Security Council shares the Secretary-General's assessment of the paramount importance of preventing the proliferation of weapons of mass destruction. Such proliferation is a threat to international peace and security. Appropriate measures will be taken in this respect in particular where international treaties provide for recourse to the Council when their provisions are violated. The Council underlines the need for all States to fulfil their obligations in respect of arms control and disarmament, in particular in regard to weapons of mass destruction.

The Security Council takes note of the assessment of the Secretary-General of the importance of "micro-disarmament", as described in his paper, in the solution of conflicts with which the United Nations is currently dealing and of his view that small arms are probably responsible for most of the deaths in these conflicts. It shares the concern of the Secretary-General at the negative consequences for international peace and security which often arise from the illicit traffic in conventional weapons, including small arms, and takes note of his view that the search for effective solutions to this problem should begin now. In this context the Council stresses the vital importance of the strict implementation of existing arms embargo regimes. It welcomes and supports efforts with regard to international measures to curb the spread of anti-personnel land-mines and to deal with the land-mines already laid, and in this regard welcomes General Assembly resolutions 49/75 D of 15 December 1994 and 49/215 of 23 December 1994. It reaffirms its deep concern over the tremendous humanitarian problems caused by the presence of mines and other unexploded devices to the populations of mine-infested countries and emphasizes the need for an increase in mine-clearing efforts by the countries concerned and with the assistance of the international community.

The Security Council stresses the importance it attaches to the effective implementation of all measures taken by it to maintain or restore international peace and security including economic sanctions. It agrees that the object of economic sanctions is not to punish but to modify the behaviour of the country or party which represents a threat to international peace and security. The steps demanded of that country or party should be clearly defined in Council resolutions, and the sanctions regime in question should be subject to periodic review and it should be lifted when the objectives of the appropriate provisions of the relevant Security Council resolutions are achieved. The Council remains concerned that, within this framework, appropriate measures are taken to ensure that humanitarian supplies reach affected populations and appropriate consideration is given to submissions received from neighbouring or other States affected by special economic problems as a result of the imposition of sanctions. The Council urges the Secretary-General, when considering the allocation of resources available to him within the Secretariat, to take appropriate steps to reinforce those sections of the Secretariat dealing directly with sanctions and their various aspects so as to ensure that all these matters are addressed in as effective, consistent and timely a manner as possible. It welcomes the Secretary-General's efforts to study ways and means of addressing the various aspects related to sanctions in his report.

The Security Council reaffirms the importance it attaches to the role that regional organizations and arrangements can play in helping to maintain international peace and security. It underlines the need for effective coordination between their efforts and those of the United Nations in accordance with Chapter VIII of the Charter. It recognizes that the responsibilities and capacities of different regional organizations and arrangements vary, as well as the readiness and competence of regional organizations and arrangements, as reflected in their charters and other relevant documents, to participate in efforts to maintain international peace and security. It welcomes the Secretary-General's willingness to assist regional organizations and arrangements as appropriate in developing a capacity for preventive action, peacemaking and, where appropriate, peace-keeping. It draws particular attention in this regard to the needs of Africa. It encourages the Secretary-General and Member States to continue to consider ways and means of improving practical cooperation and coordination between the United Nations and regional organizations and arrangements in these areas. The Council encourages the Secretary-General to continue the practice of meetings on cooperation between the United Nations and regional and other organizations.

The Security Council recognizes the crucial importance of the availability of the necessary financial resources both for preventive action and operations undertaken to sustain international peace and security. It therefore urges Member States to honour their financial obligations to the United Nations. At the same time, the Council emphasizes the continuing necessity for careful control of peace-keeping costs and for the most efficient possible use of peace-keeping funds and other financial resources.

The Security Council will keep the Secretary-General's paper under consideration. The Council invites all interested Member States to present further reflections on United Nations peace-keeping operations, and in particular on ways and means to improve the capacity of the United Nations for rapid deployment. It invites the Secretary-General to keep it closely informed of the action he takes in follow-up to the paper and to the present statement. It hopes that the General Assembly, as well as other organizations and entities, will give consideration of the paper a high degree of priority and will take decisions on those matters which fall within their direct responsibility.

*Meeting numbers.* SC 3492 & resumptions 1 & 2, 3503.

**GENERAL ASSEMBLY ACTION**

On 10 March, the General Assembly decided to reconvene the informal open-ended working group on "An Agenda for Peace" to consider the new supplement. The working group established subgroups on sanctions, coordination, preventive diplomacy and peacemaking, and post-conflict peace-building, which held discussions between 28 March and 14 September. On 18 September, the Assembly recommended that the working group continue its work.

By **resolution 50/41** of 8 December, the Assembly, noting that the University for Peace—a specialized international centre for research, training and education for peace located in Costa Rica—placed special emphasis on conflict prevention, peace-keeping and peace-building and the peaceful settlement of disputes in the context of "An Agenda for Peace", requested the Secretary-General to consider ways of strengthening cooperation between the UN and the University.

## Implementation of the 1970 Declaration

In response to a 1993 General Assembly request,[10] the Secretary-General on 28 July 1995 reported[11] on the implementation of the 1970 Declaration on the Strengthening of International Security.[12] The document contained replies from three Member States to the Secretary-General's 20 March request for views on the subject.

**GENERAL ASSEMBLY ACTION**

In December, the General Assembly adopted **decision 50/418.**

### Review of the implementation of the Declaration on the Strengthening of International Security

At its 90th plenary meeting, on 12 December 1995, the General Assembly, on the recommendation of the First Committee, decided to include in the provisional agenda of its fifty-first session the item entitled "Review of the implementation of the Declaration on the Strengthening of International Security".

**General Assembly decision 50/418**

109-0-54 (recorded vote)

Approved by First Committee (A/50/580) by recorded vote (102-0-52), 15 November (meeting 22); draft by Colombia, for Non-Aligned Movement (A/C.1/50/L.30); agenda item 60.

*Meeting numbers.* GA 50th session: 1st Committee 3-11, 16, 22; plenary 90.

Recorded vote in Assembly as follows:

*In favour:* Afghanistan, Algeria, Bahamas, Bahrain, Bangladesh, Barbados, Belize, Benin, Bhutan, Bolivia, Botswana, Brazil, Brunei Darussalam, Burkina Faso, Burundi, Cambodia, Cameroon, Cape Verde, Chad, Chile, China, Colombia, Congo, Costa Rica, Côte d'Ivoire, Croatia, Cuba, Cyprus, Democratic People's Republic of Korea, Djibouti, Ecuador, Egypt, El Salvador, Eritrea, Ethiopia, Fiji, Gabon, Ghana, Guatemala, Guinea, Guinea-Bissau, Guyana, Haiti, Honduras, India, Indonesia, Jamaica, Jordan, Kenya, Kuwait, Kyrgyzstan, Lao People's Democratic Republic, Lebanon, Lesotho, Libyan Arab Jamahiriya, Madagascar, Malawi, Malaysia, Maldives, Mali, Mauritania, Mauritius, Mexico, Mongolia, Morocco, Mozambique, Myanmar, Namibia, Nepal, Nicaragua, Niger, Nigeria, Oman, Pakistan, Panama, Papua New Guinea, Paraguay, Peru, Philippines, Qatar, Rwanda, Samoa, Saudi Arabia, Senegal, Sierra Leone, Singapore, Solomon Islands, South Africa, Sri Lanka, Sudan, Suriname, Swaziland, Syrian Arab Republic, Thailand, Togo, Trinidad and Tobago, Tunisia, Uganda, Ukraine, United Arab Emirates, United Republic of Tanzania, Uruguay, Vanuatu, Venezuela, Viet Nam, Yemen, Zaire, Zambia, Zimbabwe.

*Against:* None.

*Abstaining:* Albania, Andorra, Antigua and Barbuda, Argentina, Armenia, Australia, Austria, Azerbaijan, Belarus, Belgium, Bulgaria, Canada, Czech Republic, Denmark, Equatorial Guinea, Estonia, Finland, France, Georgia, Germany, Greece, Hungary, Iceland, Ireland, Israel, Italy, Japan, Kazakstan, Latvia, Liechtenstein, Lithuania, Luxembourg, Malta, Marshall Islands, Micronesia, Monaco, Netherlands, New Zealand, Norway, Poland, Portugal, Republic of Korea, Republic of Moldova, Romania, Russian Federation, Slovakia, Slovenia, Spain, Sweden, Tajikistan, the former Yugoslav Republic of Macedonia, Turkey, United Kingdom, United States.

*REFERENCES*

[1]S/PRST/1995/48. [2]S/1995/827. [3]A/50/702-S/1995/900. [4]YUN 1992, p. 35. [5]A/50/60-S/1995/1. [6]A/50/1. [7]YUN 1992, p. 33. [8]A/50/853. [9]S/PRST/1995/9. [10]YUN 1993, p. 83, GA res. 48/83, 16 Dec. 1993. [11]A/50/310. [12]YUN 1970, p. 105, GA res. 2734(XXV), 16 Dec. 1970.

# Regional aspects of international peace and security

## Cooperation between the United Nations and regional arrangements

In his supplement to "An Agenda for Peace" (see above),[1] the Secretary-General noted that regional organizations had much to contribute to maintaining international peace and security. Cooperation between the UN and regional organizations in that area took a number of forms, he said, such as consultation, diplomatic support, operational support, co-deployment and joint operations. While forms of cooperation and the peacemaking and peace-keeping capacity of regional organizations varied considerably, it was possible to identify certain principles on which their relationship with the UN should be based, he went on. They included the establishment of agreed, but not necessarily formal, mechanisms for consultation; respect for the primacy of

the United Nations, particularly the need to submit regional arrangements that assumed a level of UN support for approval by Member States; a clearly defined and agreed division of labour; and consistency by members of regional organizations, which were also UN Member States, in dealing with a common problem of interest to both organizations.

The Security Council, in a 22 February statement by its President[2] on the supplement, reaffirmed the importance it attached to the role of regional organizations and arrangements in maintaining international peace and security, underlined the need for effective coordination between their efforts and those of the UN and encouraged the Secretary-General and Member States to continue considering ways of improving such coordination and cooperation. The Council welcomed the Secretary-General's willingness to assist regional organizations and arrangements in developing a capacity for preventive action, peacemaking and, where appropriate, peace-keeping, and drew particular attention in that regard to the needs of Africa.

The General Assembly's Special Committee on Peace-keeping Operations in 1995[3] stressed the importance of the 1994 Declaration on the Enhancement of Cooperation between the United Nations and Regional Arrangements or Agencies in the Maintenance of International Peace and Security,[4] and invited the Secretary-General to develop proposals for improving the capacity to respond to emergency situations in Africa, in particular through cooperation with the Organization of African Unity (OAU) and subregional organizations in conflict prevention and peace-keeping. (For further information on the Special Committee's deliberations, see PART TWO, Chapter I.)

In a 27 September statement,[5] the Foreign Ministers of the Security Council's five permanent members underscored the importance of reinforcing cooperation between the United Nations and regional organizations and arrangements in building stability and security and in preventing and managing conflicts. In a 23 October press communiqué,[6] the heads of State or Government of the non-aligned countries members of the Security Council emphasized the need to take fully into account the special commitments and concerns of a region when joint efforts for conflict resolution were undertaken by the UN and regional organizations.

**Report of the Secretary-General.** In response to requests from the Security Council and the Special Committee, the Secretary-General on 1 November reported[7] on improving preparedness for conflict prevention and peace-keeping in Africa. He noted that the UN and OAU had held regular consultations on key African questions to coordinate initiatives and actions on a broad spectrum of issues, including conflict prevention, management and resolution. Agreement was reached on establishing a staff exchange programme to assist OAU in strengthening its Mechanism on Conflict Prevention and Management and Resolution and to reinforce collaboration between the two organizations.

The Secretary-General considered that a structured and constant exchange of information on emerging crises at an early stage was the key to closer cooperation and coordination in preventive diplomacy. In that regard, he proposed to post a UN liaison officer at OAU headquarters in Addis Ababa, Ethiopia, to ensure effective coordination of efforts in conflict prevention, management and resolution; and to send a technical team to assist in organizing an OAU situation room to monitor ongoing efforts in those areas, receive and disseminate information, and stay abreast of political developments in Africa. The UN and OAU also could: explore possibilities for engaging in regular joint peacemaking activities in Africa; co-sponsor national and regional seminars to facilitate dialogue among contending parties; and contribute to agreements and arrangements for conflict prevention, control or resolution. In addition, OAU could benefit from UN programmes concerned with good governance, peace-building and participatory democracy. (For further information on cooperation between the UN and OAU, see PART TWO, Chapter II.)

The General Assembly, by **resolution 50/158** of 21 December, commended the UN and OAU for their ongoing cooperative activities in conflict resolution in Africa and invited the UN to assist OAU in strengthening its institutional and operational capacity in the prevention, management and resolution of conflicts.

## Zones of peace

### South Atlantic

The General Assembly in 1986[8] had declared the South Atlantic a zone of peace and cooperation and, in subsequent years, reaffirmed the determination of States of the zone to enhance and accelerate their cooperation in political, economic, scientific, technical, cultural and other spheres.

In October 1995, in response to a 1994 Assembly request,[9] the Secretary-General submitted a report on implementation of the 1986 declaration,[10] containing the views of six Governments and five UN bodies.

GENERAL ASSEMBLY ACTION

On 27 November, the General Assembly adopted **resolution 50/18.**

### Zone of peace and cooperation of the South Atlantic

*The General Assembly,*

*Recalling* its resolution 41/11 of 27 October 1986, in which it solemnly declared the Atlantic Ocean, in the region between Africa and South America, the "Zone of peace and cooperation of the South Atlantic",

*Recalling also* its subsequent resolutions on the matter, including resolution 45/36 of 27 November 1990, in which it reaffirmed the determination of the States of the zone to enhance and accelerate their cooperation in the political, economic, scientific, cultural and other spheres,

*Reaffirming* that the questions of peace and security and those of development are interrelated and inseparable, and that cooperation for peace and development among States of the region will promote the objectives of the zone of peace and cooperation of the South Atlantic,

*Aware* of the importance that the States of the zone attach to the region's environment, and recognizing the threat that pollution from any source poses to the marine and coastal environment, its ecological balance and its resources,

1. *Reaffirms* the importance of the purposes and objectives of the zone of peace and cooperation of the South Atlantic as a basis for the promotion of cooperation among the countries of the region;

2. *Calls upon* all States to cooperate in the promotion of the objectives established in the declaration of the zone of peace and cooperation of the South Atlantic and to refrain from any action inconsistent with those objectives and with the Charter of the United Nations and relevant resolutions of the Organization, particularly action which may create or aggravate situations of tension and potential conflict in the region;

3. *Takes note* of the report of the Secretary-General of 24 October 1995, submitted in accordance with its resolution 49/26 of 2 December 1994;

4. *Recalls* the agreement reached at the third meeting of the States members of the zone, held at Brasilia in 1994, to encourage democracy and political pluralism and, in accordance with the Vienna Declaration and Programme of Action adopted by the World Conference on Human Rights on 25 June 1993, to promote and defend all human rights and fundamental freedoms and to cooperate towards the achievement of those goals;

5. *Welcomes* the progress towards the full entry into force of the Treaty for the Prohibition of Nuclear Weapons in Latin America and the Caribbean (Treaty of Tlatelolco), and the conclusion of a treaty on a nuclear-weapon-free zone in Africa;

6. *Expresses its appreciation* for the efforts of the international community, in accordance with Security Council resolution 976(1995) of 8 February 1995, aimed at contributing to an effective and lasting peace in Angola on the basis of the "Acordos de Bicesse" and the Lusaka Protocol;

7. *Also welcomes* recent positive developments in the situation of Liberia, including progress towards peace and national reconciliation in accordance with the Abuja Agreement to supplement the Cotonou and Akosombo Agreements as subsequently clarified by the Accra Agreement;

8. *Commends* the efforts of Member States and humanitarian organizations to render humanitarian assistance to Angola and Liberia, and urges them to continue to provide and to increase such assistance;

9. *Affirms* the importance of the South Atlantic to global maritime and commercial transactions and its determination to preserve the region for all activities

protected by international law, as reflected in the United Nations Convention on the Law of the Sea;

10.   *Further welcomes* the offer by South Africa to host at Cape Town, on 1 and 2 April 1996, the fourth meeting of the States members of the zone;

11.   *Requests* the relevant organizations, organs and bodies of the United Nations system to render all appropriate assistance which States of the zone may seek in their joint efforts to implement the declaration of the zone of peace and cooperation of the South Atlantic;

12.   *Requests* the, Secretary-General to keep the implementation of resolution 41/11 and subsequent resolutions on the matter under review and to submit a report to the General Assembly at its fifty-first session, taking into account, *inter alia*, the views expressed by Member States;

13.   *Decides* to include in the provisional agenda of its fifty-first session the item entitled "Zone of peace and cooperation of the South Atlantic".

General Assembly resolution 50/18

27 November 1995     Meeting 69     124-0-1 (recorded vote)

25-nation draft (A/50/L.25 & Add.1); agenda item 37.

Recorded vote in Assembly as follows:

   *In favour:* Algeria, Andorra, Angola, Argentina, Armenia, Australia, Austria, Azerbaijan, Barbados, Belarus, Belgium, Benin, Bhutan, Bolivia, Botswana, Brazil, Brunei Darussalam, Bulgaria, Burkina Faso, Cambodia, Cameroon, Canada, Chad, Chile, China, Colombia, Côte d'Ivoire, Croatia, Cuba, Cyprus, Czech Republic, Democratic People's Republic of Korea, Denmark, Djibouti, Ecuador, Equatorial Guinea, Estonia, Ethiopia, Finland, France, Gabon, Gambia, Georgia, Germany, Ghana, Greece, Guinea, Guinea-Bissau, Guyana, Honduras, Hungary, Iceland, India, Indonesia, Iran, Ireland, Italy, Jamaica, Japan, Jordan, Kazakstan, Kenya, Lebanon, Libyan Arab Jamahiriya, Liechtenstein, Lithuania, Luxembourg, Madagascar, Malawi, Malaysia, Maldives, Mali, Malta, Marshall Islands, Mauritius, Mexico, Micronesia, Mongolia, Mozambique, Myanmar, Namibia, Netherlands, New Zealand, Nicaragua, Nigeria, Norway, Oman, Pakistan, Panama, Papua New Guinea, Paraguay, Peru, Philippines, Poland, Portugal, Qatar, Republic of Korea, Russian Federation, Saint Lucia, San Marino, Saudi Arabia, Senegal, Singapore, Slovakia, South Africa, Spain, Sri Lanka, Suriname, Swaziland, Sweden, Thailand, the former Yugoslav Republic of Macedonia, Togo, Trinidad and Tobago, Tunisia, Turkey, Uganda, Ukraine, United Arab Emirates, United Kingdom, Uruguay, Viet Nam, Zaire, Zambia.
   *Against:* None.
   *Abstaining:* United States.

## Indian Ocean

As requested by the General Assembly in 1994,[11] the Ad Hoc Committee on the Indian Ocean (New York, 30 March and 27-30 June 1995)[12] continued to consider alternative approaches to achieving the goals contained in the 1971 Declaration of the Indian Ocean as a Zone of Peace.[13]

The Committee focused on the implementation of a 1994 Assembly resolution,[11] with a view to giving new impetus to strengthening cooperation and ensuring peace, security and stability. It noted that greater efforts and more time were needed to develop a focused discussion on practical measures to ensure those conditions in the region. Statements were made relating to initiatives taken by countries in the region to promote cooperation, particularly economic cooperation.

The Chairman of the Committee reported on his consultations with France, the United Kingdom and the United States—the three permanent members of the Security Council that had withdrawn from the Committee in 1990. The Committee stated that it remained convinced that the participation in its work of all permanent members of the Council and the major maritime users of the Indian Ocean would assist the progress of a mutually beneficial dialogue to develop conditions of peace, security and stability. The Committee encouraged those States concerned to resume their participation in its work and urged its Chairman to pursue his dialogue with their Governments and to report back at its next session. The Committee recommended that the Chairman inform it of the results of his consultations and other relevant developments at a meeting to be held in 1996 for that purpose.

GENERAL ASSEMBLY ACTION

On 12 December, the General Assembly adopted **resolution 50/76**.

### Implementation of the Declaration of the Indian Ocean as a Zone of Peace

*The General Assembly*,

*Recalling* the Declaration of the Indian Ocean as a Zone of Peace, contained in its resolution 2832(XXVI) of 16 December 1971, and recalling also its resolution 49/82 of 15 December 1994 and other relevant resolutions,

*Recalling also* the report of the Meeting of the Littoral and Hinterland States of the Indian Ocean held in July 1979,

*Having considered* the conclusions and recommendations reached by the Ad Hoc Committee on the Indian Ocean during its session in 1995,

*Emphasizing* the need to foster consensual approaches, in particular given the prevailing international climate, which is conducive to the pursuit of such endeavours,

*Noting* the initiatives taken by countries in the region to promote cooperation, in particular economic cooperation, in the Indian Ocean area and the possible contribution of such initiatives to overall objectives of a zone of peace,

*Convinced* that the participation of all the permanent members of the Security Council and the major maritime users of the Indian Ocean in the work of the Ad Hoc Committee is important and would assist the progress of mutually beneficial dialogue to develop conditions of peace, security and stability in the Indian Ocean region,

1.   *Takes note* of the report of the Ad Hoc Committee on the Indian Ocean;

2.   *Considers* that greater efforts and more time are required to develop a focused discussion on practical measures to ensure conditions of peace, security and stability in the Indian Ocean region;

3.   *Reiterates its conviction* that the participation of all the permanent members of the Security Council and the major maritime users of the Indian Ocean in the work of the Ad Hoc Committee is important and would greatly facilitate development of a mutually beneficial dialogue to advance peace, security and stability in the Indian Ocean region;

4.   *Requests* the Chairman of the Ad Hoc Committee to pursue his dialogue on the work of the Committee with the permanent members of the Security Council

and major maritime users of the Indian Ocean and to apprise the Ad Hoc Committee of his consultations and other relevant developments at a meeting to be held in 1996 for that specific purpose, to take place before the 1997 regular session of the Committee;

5. *Requests* the Ad Hoc Committee to submit to the General Assembly at its fifty-first session a report on the consultations held;

6. *Requests* the Secretary-General to continue to render all necessary assistance to the Ad Hoc Committee, including the provision of summary records;

7. *Decides* to include in the provisional agenda of its fifty-first session the item entitled ''Implementation of the Declaration of the Indian Ocean as a Zone of Peace''.

General Assembly resolution 50/76

12 December 1995     Meeting 90     123-3-39 (recorded vote)

Approved by First Committee (A/50/596) by recorded vote (115-3-38), 15 November (meeting 21); draft by Sri Lanka, for Non-Aligned Movement (A/C.1/50/L.27); agenda item 76.

*Meeting numbers.* GA 50th session: 1st Committee 3-11, 17, 21; plenary 90.

Recorded vote in Assembly as follows:

*In favour:* Afghanistan, Algeria, Angola, Antigua and Barbuda, Argentina, Australia, Azerbaijan, Bahamas, Bahrain, Bangladesh, Barbados, Belarus, Belize, Benin, Bhutan, Bolivia, Botswana, Brazil, Brunei Darussalam, Burkina Faso, Burundi, Cambodia, Cameroon, Cape Verde, Chad, Chile, China, Colombia, Congo, Costa Rica, Côte d'Ivoire, Cuba, Cyprus, Democratic People's Republic of Korea, Djibouti, Ecuador, Egypt, El Sal-vador, Equatorial Guinea, Eritrea, Ethiopia, Fiji, Gabon, Ghana, Guatemala, Guinea, Guinea-Bissau, Guyana, Haiti, Honduras, India, Indonesia, Iran, Jamaica, Japan, Jordan, Kazakstan, Kenya, Kuwait, Kyrgyzstan, Lao People's Democratic Republic, Lebanon, Lesotho, Libyan Arab Jamahiriya, Madagascar, Malawi, Malaysia, Maldives, Mali, Marshall Islands, Mauritania, Mauritius, Mexico, Micronesia, Mongolia, Morocco, Mozambique, Myanmar, Namibia, Nepal, New Zealand, Nicaragua, Niger, Nigeria, Oman, Pakistan, Panama, Papua New Guinea, Paraguay, Peru, Philippines, Qatar, Republic of Korea, Russian Federation, Rwanda, Samoa, Saudi Arabia, Senegal, Sierra Leone, Singapore, Solomon Islands, South Africa, Sri Lanka, Sudan, Suriname, Swaziland, Syrian Arab Republic, Thailand, Togo, Trinidad and Tobago, Tunisia, Uganda, Ukraine, United Arab Emirates, United Republic of Tanzania, Uruguay, Vanuatu, Venezuela, Viet Nam, Yemen, Zaire, Zambia, Zimbabwe.

*Against:* France, United Kingdom, United States.

*Abstaining:* Albania, Andorra, Armenia, Austria, Belgium, Bosnia and Herzegovina, Bulgaria, Canada, Croatia, Czech Republic, Denmark, Estonia, Finland, Georgia, Germany, Greece, Hungary, Iceland, Ireland, Israel, Italy, Latvia, Liechtenstein, Lithuania, Luxembourg, Malta, Netherlands, Norway, Poland, Portugal, Republic of Moldova, Romania, Slovakia, Slovenia, Spain, Sweden, the former Yugoslav Republic of Macedonia, Turkey, Uzbekistan.

*REFERENCES*

[1]A/50/60-S/1995/1. [2]S/PRST/1995/9. [3]A/50/230. [4]YUN 1994, p. 125, GA res. 49/57, annex, 9 Dec. 1994. [5]S/1995/827. [6]A/50/702-S/1995/900. [7]A/50/711-S/1995/911. [8]YUN 1986, p. 369, GA res. 41/11, 27 Oct. 1986. [9]YUN 1994, p. 126, GA res. 49/26, 2 Dec. 1994. [10]A/50/671 & Add.1. [11]YUN 1994, p. 155, GA res. 49/82, 15 Dec. 1994. [12]A/50/29. [13]YUN 1971, p. 34, GA res. 2832(XXVI), 16 Dec. 1971.

Chapter II

# Disarmament

The 1995 Review and Extension Conference of the Parties to the Treaty on the Non-Proliferation of Nuclear Weapons took place at UN Headquarters in New York from 17 April to 12 May, and was considered the most important event in the area of arms limitation and disarmament during the year. By agreeing to extend the duration of the 1968 Treaty indefinitely, States parties gave permanence to the only existing international legal barrier against nuclear proliferation. The decisions adopted at the Conference strengthened the existing non-proliferation regime and opened the road for further progress towards nuclear disarmament, it was widely felt.

Another important disarmament-related event occurred in 1995—the conclusion of the Treaty of Pelindaba—by which the entire continent of Africa would become a nuclear-weapon-free zone. It marked the culmination of more than three decades of effort, which began in 1960, when the proposal for a nuclear-weapon-free zone was put forward in the United Nations as a response by a group of African States to French nuclear testing in the Sahara Desert. It was the first such regional arrangement negotiated under United Nations auspices.

Negotiations on a comprehensive test-ban treaty intensified throughout the 1995 session of the Conference on Disarmament and during intersessional meetings. The measure of the progress achieved could be seen in the recording of agreed language in the rolling text of the draft treaty.

The Group of Governmental Experts to Prepare the Review Conference of the States Parties to the 1981 Convention on Prohibitions or Restrictions on the Use of Certain Conventional Weapons Which May Be Deemed to Be Excessively Injurious or to Have Indiscriminate Effects, at its fourth and final session (Geneva, 9-20 January), elaborated an integrated draft text of amendments to Protocol II. It also adopted a text of the Protocol on Blinding Laser Weapons (Protocol IV).

The world's only multilateral negotiating body on disarmament issues—the Conference on Disarmament—met in a three-part session in 1995 (30 January–7 April, 29 May–7 July and 31 July–22 September). Its agenda included items relating to: a nuclear test ban; cessation of the nuclear arms race and nuclear disarmament; prevention of nuclear war; prevention of an arms race in outer space; effective international arrangements to as-

sure non-nuclear-weapon States against the use or threat of use of nuclear weapons; new types of weapons of mass destruction and new systems of such weapons; radiological weapons; a comprehensive programme of disarmament; and transparency in armaments. Conference proceedings were marked by serious organizational difficulties arising from differences of view concerning its agenda and membership.

The Disarmament Commission, comprising all UN Member States, held four plenary meetings at its 1995 session (15-30 May). The Commission's 1995 agenda contained items on nuclear disarmament in the framework of international peace and security, with the objective of the elimination of nuclear weapons; international arms transfers, with particular reference to a 1991 General Assembly resolution; and a review of the Declaration of the 1990s as the Third Disarmament Decade.

The General Assembly decided to convene in 1997, if possible, a fourth special session devoted to disarmament.

## UN role in disarmament

### UN machinery

In 1995, UN disarmament efforts continued, mainly through the General Assembly and its First (Disarmament and International Security) Committee, the Disarmament Commission (a deliberative body) and the Conference on Disarmament (the multilateral negotiating forum which meets in Geneva).

#### Rationalization of the work of the First Committee

On 12 December, by **decision 50/421**, the General Assembly requested the Chairman of the First Committee to continue consultations on the further rationalization of the work of the Committee and decided to defer until 1997 consideration of the item entitled ''Rationalization of the work and reform of the agenda of the First Committee''.

#### Fourth special session devoted to disarmament

On 12 December, the General Assembly adopted **resolution 50/70 F**.

## Convening of the fourth special session of the General Assembly devoted to disarmament

*The General Assembly*,

*Recalling* its resolution 49/75 I of 15 December 1994,

*Recalling also* that three special sessions of the General Assembly devoted to disarmament were held in 1978, 1982 and 1988,

*Bearing in mind* the Final Document of the Tenth Special Session of the General Assembly, the first special session devoted to disarmament, and the final objective of general and complete disarmament under effective international control,

*Welcoming* the recent positive changes in the international landscape, characterized by the end of the cold war, the relaxation of tensions at the global level and the emergence of a new spirit governing relations among nations,

*Taking note* of paragraph 108 of the Final Declaration of the Eleventh Conference of Heads of State or Government of the Non-Aligned Countries, held at Cartagena de Indias, Colombia, from 18 to 20 October 1995,[a] which supported the convening of the fourth special session of the General Assembly devoted to disarmament in 1997, which would offer an opportunity to review, from a perspective more in tune with the current international situation, the most critical aspects of the process of disarmament and to mobilize the international community and public opinion in favour of the elimination of weapons of mass destruction and of the control and reduction of conventional weapons,

*Expecting* that, since negotiations and action on important disarmament issues will be completed by the end of 1996, the year 1997 would be an opportune time to review the progress in the entire field of disarmament in the post-cold-war era,

1. *Decides* to convene its fourth special session on disarmament in 1997, if possible, the exact date and agenda to be decided upon before the end of the current session of the General Assembly through consultations;

2. *Also decides* to establish a Preparatory Committee to prepare a draft agenda for the special session, to examine all relevant questions relating to that session and to submit its recommendations thereon to the General Assembly at its fifty-first session;

3. *Invites* all Member States to communicate to the Secretary-General, no later than 1 April 1996, their views on the draft agenda and other relevant questions relating to the fourth special session on disarmament;

4. *Requests* the Preparatory Committee to meet for a short organizational session before the end of the fifty-first session of the General Assembly in order, *inter alia*, to set the date for its substantive session;

5. *Also requests* the Preparatory Committee to submit its progress report to the General Assembly at its fifty-first session;

6. *Decides* to include in the provisional agenda of its fifty-first session an item entitled ''Convening of the fourth special session of the General Assembly devoted to disarmament: report of the Preparatory Committee for the Fourth Special Session of the General Assembly Devoted to Disarmament''.

---

[a]A/50/752-S/1995/1035.

General Assembly resolution 50/70 F

12 December 1995     Meeting 90     111-2-49 (recorded vote)

Approved by First Committee (A/50/590) by recorded vote (98-2-46), 21 November (meeting 29); draft by Colombia, for Non-Aligned Movement (A/C.1/50/L.25/Rev.1); agenda item 70 *(g)*.

*Meeting numbers.* GA 50th session: 1st Committee 3-11, 16, 29; plenary 90.

Recorded vote in Assembly as follows:

*In favour:* Afghanistan, Algeria, Antigua and Barbuda, Australia, Bahamas, Bahrain, Bangladesh, Barbados, Belize, Benin, Bhutan, Bolivia, Botswana, Brazil, Brunei Darussalam, Burkina Faso, Burundi, Cambodia, Cameroon, Cape Verde, Chad, Chile, China, Colombia, Congo, Costa Rica, Côte d'Ivoire, Cuba, Cyprus, Democratic People's Republic of Korea, Djibouti, Ecuador, Egypt, El Salvador, Eritrea, Ethiopia, Fiji, Gabon, Ghana, Guatemala, Guinea, Guinea-Bissau, Guyana, Haiti, Honduras, India, Indonesia, Iran, Jamaica, Jordan, Kenya, Kuwait, Lao People's Democratic Republic, Lebanon, Lesotho, Libyan Arab Jamahiriya, Madagascar, Malawi, Malaysia, Maldives, Mali, Marshall Islands, Mauritania, Mauritius, Mexico, Micronesia, Mongolia, Morocco, Mozambique, Myanmar, Namibia, Nepal, New Zealand, Nicaragua, Niger, Nigeria, Oman, Pakistan, Panama, Papua New Guinea, Peru, Philippines, Qatar, Rwanda, Samoa, Saudi Arabia, Senegal, Sierra Leone, Singapore, Solomon Islands, South Africa, Sri Lanka, Sudan, Suriname, Swaziland, Syrian Arab Republic, Thailand, Togo, Trinidad and Tobago, Tunisia, Uganda, United Arab Emirates, United Republic of Tanzania, Uruguay, Vanuatu, Venezuela, Viet Nam, Yemen, Zaire, Zambia, Zimbabwe.

*Against:* Israel, United States.

*Abstaining:* Albania, Andorra, Argentina, Armenia, Austria, Azerbaijan, Belarus, Belgium, Bulgaria, Canada, Croatia, Czech Republic, Denmark, Equatorial Guinea, Estonia, Finland, France, Georgia, Germany, Greece, Hungary, Iceland, Ireland, Italy, Japan, Kazakstan, Latvia, Liechtenstein, Lithuania, Luxembourg, Malta, Monaco, Netherlands, Norway, Paraguay, Poland, Portugal, Republic of Korea, Republic of Moldova, Romania, Russian Federation, Slovakia, Slovenia, Spain, Sweden, the former Yugoslav Republic of Macedonia, Turkey, Ukraine, United Kingdom.

Before approving the draft text as a whole, the First Committee adopted paragraphs 1, 2, 4 and 5 by recorded votes of 96 to 39, with 10 abstentions; 96 to 39, with 9 abstentions; 95 to 39, with 11 abstentions; and 95 to 39, with 11 abstentions, respectively.

The General Assembly retained the same paragraphs by recorded votes of 109 to 40, with 12 abstentions; 109 to 41, with 10 abstentions; 107 to 40, with 11 abstentions; and 107 to 40, with 11 abstentions.

## Disarmament Commission

The Disarmament Commission, comprising all UN Member States, held four plenary meetings at its 1995 session (New York, 15-30 May).[1] It also held organizational meetings on 13 April and 11 December.

The Commission's 1995 agenda contained items on nuclear disarmament in the framework of international peace and security, with the objective of the elimination of nuclear weapons; international arms transfers, with particular reference to a 1991 General Assembly resolution;[2] and a review of the Declaration of the 1990s as the Third Disarmament Decade, which was adopted by the Assembly in 1990.[3] The first two items were carried over from the Commission's 1994 session.[4] In 1995, three working groups were established, one for each item.

The Commission concluded its consideration of the items on nuclear disarmament and on the question of the Third Disarmament Decade, although without reaching agreement on relevant texts.

Working Group III, established to carry out a review and appraisal of the implementation of the Declaration of the 1990s as the Third Disarmament Decade, met between 18 and 26 May. However, in spite of intensive efforts, the Group was unable to reach consensus on a text.

(For information on the work of the Working Group on arms transfers, see below, under "Conventional weapons and advanced technologies".)

### GENERAL ASSEMBLY ACTION

On 12 December, the General Assembly adopted **resolution 50/72 D**.

### Report of the Disarmament Commission

*The General Assembly,*

*Having considered* the report of the Disarmament Commission,

*Recalling* its resolutions 47/54 A of 9 December 1992, 47/54 G of 8 April 1993, 48/77 A of 16 December 1993 and 49/77 A of 15 December 1994,

*Considering* the role that the Disarmament Commission has been called upon to play and the contribution that it should make in examining and submitting recommendations on various problems in the field of disarmament and in the promotion of the implementation of the relevant decisions adopted by the General Assembly at its tenth special session,

1. *Takes note* of the report of the Disarmament Commission;

2. *Notes with regret* that the Disarmament Commission was unable to achieve agreement on guidelines and recommendations under its agenda item entitled "Process of nuclear disarmament in the framework of international peace and security, with the objective of the elimination of nuclear weapons" and on recommendations under its agenda item entitled "Review of the Declaration of the 1990s as the Third Disarmament Decade", both of which were concluded in 1995;

3. *Notes* the progress made and continuing consideration by the Disarmament Commission of its agenda item entitled "International arms transfers, with particular reference to General Assembly resolution 46/36 H of 6 December 1991", which is to be concluded in 1996;

4. *Reaffirms* the importance of further enhancing the dialogue and cooperation among the First Committee, the Disarmament Commission and the Conference on Disarmament;

5. *Also reaffirms* the role of the Disarmament Commission as the specialized, deliberative body within the United Nations multilateral disarmament machinery that allows for in-depth deliberations on specific disarmament issues, leading to the submission of concrete recommendations on those issues;

6. *Encourages* the Disarmament Commission to continue to make every effort to enhance its working methods so as to enable it to give focused consideration to a limited number of priority issues in the field of disarmament, bearing in mind the decision it has taken

to move its agenda towards a three-item phased approach;

7. *Requests* the Disarmament Commission to continue its work in accordance with its mandate, as set forth in paragraph 118 of the Final Document of the Tenth Special Session of the General Assembly, and with paragraph 3 of Assembly resolution 37/78 H of 9 December 1982, and to that end to make every effort to achieve specific recommendations on the items on its agenda, taking into account the adopted "Ways and means to enhance the functioning of the Disarmament Commission";

8. *Recommends* that, pursuant to the adopted three-item phased approach, the Disarmament Commission, at its 1995 organizational session, adopt the following items for consideration at its 1996 substantive session:

(*a*) International arms transfers, with particular reference to General Assembly resolution 46/36 H of 6 December 1991;

(*b*) [to be added];[a]

(*c*) [to be added];[a]

9. *Requests* the Disarmament Commission to meet for a period not exceeding four weeks during 1996 and to submit a substantive report to the General Assembly at its fifty-first session;

10. *Requests* the Secretary-General to transmit to the Disarmament Commission the annual report of the Conference on Disarmament, together with all the official records of the fiftieth session of the General Assembly relating to disarmament matters, and to render all assistance that the Commission may require for implementing the present resolution;

11. *Also requests* the Secretary-General to ensure full provision to the Commission and its subsidiary bodies of interpretation and translation facilities in the official languages and to assign, as a matter of priority, all the necessary resources and services, including verbatim records, to that end;

12. *Further requests* the Secretary-General to prepare a compilation, in the format of a note by the Secretary-General, of all texts of principles, guidelines or recommendations on subject items that have been unanimously adopted by the Disarmament Commission since its inception in 1978;

13. *Decides* to include in the provisional agenda of its fifty-first session the item entitled "Report of the Disarmament Commission".

---

[a]The new item will be decided by the Disarmament Commission at its 1995 organizational session. [On 24 April 1996, the Disarmament Commission adopted the agenda for its 1996 substantive session, including, as a second substantive item, the item entitled "Exchange of views on the fourth special session of the General Assembly devoted to disarmament". The Commission did not reach a consensus on a third substantive item.]

General Assembly resolution 50/72 D

12 December 1995     Meeting 90     Adopted without vote

Approved by First Committee (A/50/592) without vote, 17 November (meeting 26); draft by Mongolia (for Disarmament Commission) and 14 other States (A/C.1/50/L.28/Rev.1); agenda item 72 *(b)*.

*Meeting numbers.* GA 50th session: 1st Committee 3-11, 26; plenary 90.

In the Committee, paragraph 12 was retained by a recorded vote of 147 to none, with 3 abstentions. Similarly, the Assembly adopted the paragraph by a recorded vote of 162 to none, with 4 abstentions.

## Conference on Disarmament

The Conference on Disarmament, a multilateral negotiating body, in 1995 held a three-part session in Geneva (30 January–7 April, 29 May–7 July and 31 July–22 September).[5] In addition to the 37 States members of the Conference (see APPENDIX III for list of members), 52 additional States, not members of the Conference, were invited to participate at their request.

During 28 formal plenary meetings and six informal meetings, the Conference considered a nuclear test ban; cessation of the nuclear arms race and nuclear disarmament; prevention of nuclear war; prevention of an arms race in outer space; effective international arrangements to assure non-nuclear-weapon States against the use or threat of use of nuclear weapons; new types of weapons of mass destruction and new systems of such weapons; radiological weapons; a comprehensive programme of disarmament; and transparency in armaments.

The proceedings of the Conference were marked by serious organizational difficulties arising from differences of view concerning its agenda and membership. Although it re-established two ad hoc committees—the first on a nuclear test ban and the second on a cut-off in fissile material—only the Ad Hoc Committee on a Nuclear Test Ban carried out its work. The committee to deal with a cut-off in fissile material could not proceed until agreement could be reached on the re-establishment of ad hoc committees on negative security assurances, prevention of an arms race in outer space, and transparency in armaments, and on the commencement of substantive consideration of nuclear disarmament. As no such agreement was reached, those questions were dealt with only in plenary meetings.

Some progress, however, was made with respect to the expansion of the Conference membership. On 21 September, the Conference adopted a decision[6] to admit 23 more States (Austria, Bangladesh, Belarus, Cameroon, Chile, Colombia, Democratic People's Republic of Korea, Finland, Iraq, Israel, New Zealand, Norway, Republic of Korea, Senegal, Slovakia, South Africa, Spain, Switzerland, Syrian Arab Republic, Turkey, Ukraine, Viet Nam, Zimbabwe) to membership at the earliest date, to be decided by the Conference. The list had originally been proposed in 1993.[7] Twelve other States had requested membership but were not included in the decision. Conference rules of procedure provide for a review of membership at regular intervals.

GENERAL ASSEMBLY ACTION

On 12 December, the General Assembly adopted **resolution 50/72 A**.

### Report of the Conference on Disarmament

*The General Assembly,*

*Having considered* the report of the Conference on Disarmament,

*Convinced* that the Conference on Disarmament, as the single multilateral disarmament negotiating forum of the international community, has the primary role in substantive negotiations on priority questions of disarmament,

*Noting with satisfaction* the results achieved so far on the subject of a comprehensive test ban, as well as the commitment to complete the negotiations on the issue as soon as possible and not later than 1996,

1. *Reaffirms* the role of the Conference on Disarmament as the single multilateral disarmament negotiating forum of the international community;

2. *Welcomes* the determination of the Conference on Disarmament to fulfil that role in the light of the evolving international situation, with a view to making early substantive progress on priority items of its agenda;

3. *Urges* the Conference on Disarmament to continue as the highest-priority task its negotiations to conclude a comprehensive nuclear-test-ban treaty;

4. *Acknowledges* decision CD/1356 taken by the Conference on Disarmament on 21 September 1995 regarding its composition and the commitment to implement that decision at the earliest possible date;

5. *Encourages* the review of the agenda and methods of work of the Conference on Disarmament;

6. *Urges* the Conference on Disarmament to make every effort to reach a consensus on its programme of work at the beginning of its 1996 session;

7. *Requests* the Secretary-General to continue to ensure the provision to the Conference on Disarmament of adequate administrative, substantive and conference support services;

8. *Requests* the Conference on Disarmament to submit a report on its work to the General Assembly at its fifty-first session;

9. *Decides* to include in the provisional agenda of its fifty-first session the item entitled ''Report of the Conference on Disarmament''.

General Assembly resolution 50/72 A

12 December 1995     Meeting 90     Adopted without vote

Approved by First Committee (A/50/592) without vote, 10 November (meeting 18); draft by Morocco, for Conference on Disarmament (A/C.1/50/L.4); agenda item 72 (b).

*Meeting numbers.* GA 50th session: 1st Committee 3-11, 18; plenary 90.

On the same date, the Assembly adopted **resolution 50/72 C.**

### Expansion of the membership of the Conference on Disarmament

*The General Assembly,*

*Having considered* the report of the Conference on Disarmament, and in particular the part concerning expansion of the membership of the Conference,

*Stressing* the role of the Conference on Disarmament as the sole multilateral global negotiating body on disarmament,

*Emphasizing* the fact that, notwithstanding dramatic changes in the international situation and continuous consultations, there has been no expansion of the membership of the Conference during the last seventeen years,

*Fully convinced* that an enlarged membership is desirable in order to take advantage of the current propitious international climate to negotiate and conclude, on the solid basis of a more representative participation, a comprehensive nuclear-test-ban treaty and other important agreements requiring universal adherence,

*Recognizing* the legitimate aspirations of all candidate countries to participate fully in the work of the Conference on Disarmament, and recalling relevant decisions taken to review the composition of the Conference, including the agreement reached among Member States during the first special session of the General Assembly devoted to disarmament on a further expansion and on the wish to review the membership of the then Committee on Disarmament[a] at regular intervals,

*Noting* that the Conference on Disarmament, which is funded from the regular budget, was granted, pursuant to General Assembly resolution 48/77 B of 16 December 1993, supplementary administrative, substantive and conference support services, *inter alia*, in anticipation of its expansion,

*Recalling in particular* its resolution 49/77 B of 15 December 1994, adopted without a vote, urging the Conference on Disarmament to make every effort to reach a solution resulting, by the beginning of 1995, in a significant expansion of its composition, which would then include at least sixty countries,

*Strongly regretting*, nevertheless, that the decision of the Conference on Disarmament to adopt the report of the then Special Coordinator for Membership, and the recommended composition attached to it, taken at the end of the 1995 session did not result in the immediate expansion of its membership,

1. *Recalls* the report of 12 August 1993 of the Special Coordinator for Membership designated by the Conference on Disarmament and the subsequent statement made by the Special Coordinator on 26 August 1993, recommending a dynamic solution to the question of membership;

2. *Recognizes* the legitimate aspirations of all countries that have applied for membership to participate fully in the work of the Conference on Disarmament;

3. *Acknowledges* decision CD/1356, taken at the 719th plenary meeting of the Conference on Disarmament on 21 September 1995, including the commitment to implement the decision at the earliest possible date;

4. *Calls for* the implementation of decision CD/1356 on the expansion of membership of the Conference on Disarmament on an urgent basis;

5. *Strongly urges* that the new members should, in pursuance of decision CD/1356 and with particular reference to the provisions contained in the second paragraph of that decision, all assume together membership of the Conference at the start of the 1996 session of the Conference;

6. *Calls on* the Conference on Disarmament, in accordance with its decision CD/1356, to review the situation following the presentation of progress reports by the President of the Conference on ongoing consultations at the end of each part of its annual session;

7. *Urges* that, following the presentation of progress reports by the President of the Conference, the other

candidatures to date be further considered by the Conference at its 1996 session.

---

[a]Redesignated the Conference on Disarmament as from 7 February 1984.

General Assembly resolution 50/72 C

12 December 1995    Meeting 90    Adopted without vote

Approved by First Committee (A/50/592) without vote, 15 November (meeting 21); 23-nation draft (A/C.1/50/L.21/Rev.1); agenda item 72 *(b)*.
*Meeting numbers.* GA 50th session: 1st Committee 3-11, 16, 21; plenary 90.

## Multilateral disarmament agreements

### Parties and signatories

As at 31 December 1995, the following numbers of States had become parties to the multilateral agreements listed below (listed in chronological order, with the years in which they were initially signed or opened for signature).[8]

(Geneva) Protocol for the Prohibition of the Use in War of Asphyxiating, Poisonous or Other Gases, and of Bacteriological Methods of Warfare (1925): 130 parties

The Antarctic Treaty (1959): 42 parties

Treaty Banning Nuclear Weapon Tests in the Atmosphere, in Outer Space and under Water (1963): 124 parties

Treaty on Principles Governing the Activities of States in the Exploration and Use of Outer Space, including the Moon and Other Celestial Bodies (1967):[9] 93 parties

Treaty for the Prohibition of Nuclear Weapons in Latin America and the Caribbean (Treaty of Tlatelolco) (1967): 38 parties

Treaty on the Non-Proliferation of Nuclear Weapons (1968):[10] 182 parties

Treaty on the Prohibition of the Emplacement of Nuclear Weapons and Other Weapons of Mass Destruction on the Seabed and the Ocean Floor and in the Subsoil Thereof (1971):[11] 90 parties

Convention on the Prohibition of the Development, Production and Stockpiling of Bacteriological (Biological) and Toxin Weapons and on Their Destruction (1972):[12] 132 parties

Convention on the Prohibition of Military or Any Other Hostile Use of Environmental Modification Techniques (1977):[13] 63 parties

Agreement Governing the Activities of States on the Moon and Other Celestial Bodies (1979):[14] 9 parties

Convention on Prohibitions or Restrictions on the Use of Certain Conventional Weapons Which May Be Deemed to Be Excessively Injurious or to Have Indiscriminate Effects (1981): 57 parties

South Pacific Nuclear Free Zone Treaty (Treaty of Rarotonga) (1985): 13 parties

Treaty on Conventional Armed Forces in Europe (1990): 30 parties

Treaty on Open Skies (1992): 22 parties

Convention on the Prohibition of the Development, Production, Stockpiling and Use of Chemical Weapons and on Their Destruction (1993): 47 parties

*REFERENCES*

[1]A/50/42. [2]YUN 1991, p. 56, GA res. 46/36 H, 6 Dec. 1991. [3]GA res. 45/62 A, 4 Dec. 1990. [4]YUN 1994,

p. 131. (5)A/50/27. (6)CD/1356. (7)YUN 1993, p. 108. (8)*The United Nations Disarmament Yearbook*, vol. 20, *1995*, Sales No. E.96.IX.1. (9)YUN 1966, p. 41, GA res. 2222(XXI), annex, 19 Dec. 1966. (10)YUN 1968, p. 17, GA res. 2373(XXII), annex, 12 June 1968. (11)YUN 1970, p. 18, GA res. 2660(XXV), annex, 7 Dec. 1970. (12)YUN 1971, p. 19, GA res. 2826(XXVI), annex, 16 Dec. 1971. (13)YUN 1976, p. 45, GA res. 31/72, annex, 10 Dec. 1976. (14)YUN 1979, p. 111, GA res. 34/68, annex, 5 Dec. 1979.

# Nuclear arms and other weapons of mass destruction

## Non-proliferation

### Non-proliferation Treaty

*New parties to the Treaty*

In 1995, Algeria, Argentina, Chile, the Comoros, Eritrea, the Marshall Islands, Micronesia, Monaco, Palau, the United Arab Emirates and Vanuatu acceded to the 1968 Treaty on the Non-Proliferation of Nuclear Weapons (NPT)[1] and the former Yugoslav Republic of Macedonia succeeded to it, bringing the number of States parties to 182 at year's end.[2] The Treaty entered into force on 5 March 1970.

### NPT Review and Extension Conference

The 1995 Review and Extension Conference of the Parties to the Treaty on the Non-Proliferation of Nuclear Weapons (New York, 17 April–12 May)[3] was held to review the Treaty's operation and to decide on its extension. The Treaty called for holding a conference 25 years after its entry into force to decide whether it should continue in force indefinitely or be extended for an additional fixed period or periods. Previous quinquennial review conferences had been held in 1975,[4] 1980,[5] 1985[6] and 1990,[7] as called for under article VIII, paragraph 3, of the Treaty.

The Preparatory Committee for the Conference held its fourth and final session (New York, 23-27 January) in 1995 to discuss substantive and organizational matters.[8] Previous sessions were held in 1993[9] and 1994.[10] The States parties to NPT had formed the Committee in 1992.[11]

States parties participating in the Conference numbered 175. Representatives of the United Nations and the International Atomic Energy Agency (IAEA) also participated, as well as a number of States non-parties, intergovernmental organizations and agencies, research institutes and non-governmental organizations (NGOs).

The Conference adopted a decision to extend the Treaty indefinitely, and two other decisions concerning strengthening the review process for the Treaty, and principles and objectives for nuclear non-proliferation and disarmament. The Conference adopted a Final Document containing the three decisions, all of which were adopted without a vote. It also adopted a resolution on the Middle East which called on all States in that region to accede to the Treaty.

The Conference established three Main Committees, the reports of which constituted part of the Final Document, and a Drafting Committee. The Main Committees reviewed the operation of the provisions of the Treaty allocated to them and were to work out language for inclusion in a final document. Discussions focused on: nuclear non-proliferation and disarmament; security assurances; nuclear-weapon-free zones; the implementation of safeguards; and the peaceful uses of nuclear energy. However, the Conference was unable to agree on a final declaration on the review of the operation of the Treaty because of insufficient time to deal with a number of issues on which positions were highly divergent.

**Report of the Secretary-General.** In response to a 1994 General Assembly request,[12] the Secretary-General, in a March report with a later addendum,[13] transmitted the replies of 11 Governments, as well as France on behalf of the European Union (EU), providing their legal interpretations of article X, paragraph 2, of NPT concerning the extension of the Treaty, and their views on the different options and actions available.

GENERAL ASSEMBLY ACTION

On 12 December, the General Assembly adopted **resolution 50/70 Q**.

**1995 Review and Extension Conference of the Parties to the Treaty on the Non-Proliferation of Nuclear Weapons**

*The General Assembly*,

*Recalling* its resolution 47/52 A of 9 December 1992, in which it, *inter alia*, took note of the decision of the parties to the Treaty on the Non-Proliferation of Nuclear Weapons, following appropriate consultations, to form a preparatory committee for a conference to review the operation of the Treaty and to decide on its extension, as provided for in article VIII, paragraph 3, and also called for in article X, paragraph 2, of the Treaty,

*Recalling also* that the parties to the Treaty on the Non-Proliferation of Nuclear Weapons convened in New York from 17 April to 12 May 1995 in accordance with article VIII, paragraph 3, and article X, paragraph 2, of the Treaty,

*Noting* that, at the time of the 1995 Review and Extension Conference of the Parties to the Treaty on the Non-Proliferation of Nuclear Weapons, there were one hundred and seventy-five of the one hundred and seventy-eight States parties to the Treaty present,

1. *Notes* that on 11 May 1995 the 1995 Review and Extension Conference of the Parties to the Treaty on the Non-Proliferation of Nuclear Weapons adopted three decisions on strengthening the review process for the Treaty, principles and objectives for nuclear non-proliferation and disarmament, and extension of the Treaty on the Non-Proliferation of Nuclear Weapons;

2.   *Takes note* of the resolution on the Middle East adopted on 11 May 1995 by the parties to the Treaty;

3.   *Notes* that the States parties to the Treaty participating in the Review Conference:

(*a*)   Agreed to strengthen the review process for the operation of the Treaty with a view to assuring that the purposes of the preamble and the provisions of the Treaty were being realized, and decided that, in accordance with article VIII, paragraph 3, the Review Conferences should continue to be held every five years, and that, accordingly, the next Review Conference should be held in the year 2000, and that the first meeting of the Preparatory Committee should be held in 1997;

(*b*)   Affirmed the need to continue to move with determination towards the full realization and effective implementation of the provisions of the Treaty, and accordingly adopted a set of principles and objectives;

(*c*)   Decided that, as a majority existed among States parties to the Treaty for its indefinite extension, in accordance with its article X, paragraph 2, the Treaty should continue in force indefinitely;

4.   *Notes* that the three decisions and the resolution were adopted without a vote.

General Assembly resolution 50/70 Q

12 December 1995      Meeting 90      161-0-2 (recorded vote)

Approved by First Committee (A/50/590) by recorded vote (155-0-3), 17 November (meeting 26); 3-nation draft (A/C.1/50/L.49/Rev.1); agenda item 70.
*Sponsors:* Bangladesh, South Africa, Sri Lanka.
*Meeting numbers.* GA 50th session: 1st Committee 3-11, 25, 26; plenary 90.

Recorded vote in Assembly as follows:

*In favour:* Afghanistan, Albania, Algeria, Andorra, Antigua and Barbuda, Argentina, Armenia, Australia, Austria, Azerbaijan, Bahamas, Bahrain, Bangladesh, Barbados, Belarus, Belgium, Belize, Benin, Bhutan, Bolivia, Bosnia and Herzegovina, Botswana, Brunei Darussalam, Bulgaria, Burkina Faso, Burundi, Cambodia, Cameroon, Canada, Cape Verde, Chad, Chile, China, Colombia, Congo, Costa Rica, Côte d'Ivoire, Croatia, Cuba, Cyprus, Czech Republic, Denmark, Djibouti, Ecuador, Egypt, El Salvador, Equatorial Guinea, Eritrea, Estonia, Ethiopia, Fiji, Finland, France, Gabon, Georgia, Germany, Ghana, Greece, Guatemala, Guinea, Guinea-Bissau, Guyana, Haiti, Honduras, Hungary, Iceland, Indonesia, Iran, Ireland, Italy, Jamaica, Japan, Jordan, Kazakstan, Kenya, Kuwait, Kyrgyzstan, Lao People's Democratic Republic, Latvia, Lebanon, Lesotho, Libyan Arab Jamahiriya, Liechtenstein, Lithuania, Luxembourg, Madagascar, Malawi, Malaysia, Maldives, Mali, Malta, Marshall Islands, Mauritania, Mauritius, Mexico, Micronesia, Monaco, Mongolia, Morocco, Mozambique, Myanmar, Namibia, Nepal, Netherlands, New Zealand, Nicaragua, Niger, Nigeria, Norway, Oman, Pakistan, Panama, Papua New Guinea, Paraguay, Peru, Philippines, Poland, Portugal, Qatar, Republic of Korea, Republic of Moldova, Romania, Russian Federation, Rwanda, Samoa, Saudi Arabia, Senegal, Sierra Leone, Singapore, Slovakia, Slovenia, Solomon Islands, South Africa, Spain, Sri Lanka, Sudan, Suriname, Swaziland, Sweden, Syrian Arab Republic, Tajikistan, Thailand, the former Yugoslav Republic of Macedonia, Togo, Trinidad and Tobago, Tunisia, Turkey, Turkmenistan, Uganda, Ukraine, United Arab Emirates, United Kingdom, United Republic of Tanzania, United States, Uruguay, Venezuela, Viet Nam, Yemen, Zaire, Zambia, Zimbabwe.

*Against:* None.

*Abstaining:* India, Israel.

## IAEA safeguards

In March, the Board of Governors of IAEA reviewed the progress made by the secretariat regarding its programme, adopted in 1993,[9] to improve the Agency's safeguards regime, and endorsed its general direction. The Board noted, however, that some Governors had reservations about the need for greater access to sites. In June, the Secretariat submitted specific proposals in a two-part document concerning measures that could be implemented under existing legal authority and measures requiring additional legal authority to be conferred by the States involved. Some of the measures foreseen in part 1 were broader access to information regarding sites and activities relevant to States' nuclear programmes, and sensitive analysis of the environment at locations to which the Agency had access. The Board approved the first part of the proposals and decided to consider the second part at a later date. In September, the IAEA General Conference requested the Director General to make arrangements to implement the first part of the measures proposed and to put before the Board of Governors clear proposals for the second part.[14] However, at its December meeting, the Board of Governors took no decision on the matter.

As at 31 December 1995, there were 100 safeguards agreements in force with 107 States with respect to NPT, 6 of which entered into force during the year (Belarus, Bolivia, Croatia, Kazakstan, Myanmar, Zimbabwe). Barbados, the Republic of Moldova and Ukraine signed safeguards agreements under the Treaty in 1995, but they had not entered into force by the end of the year. Regarding the 1967 Treaty for the Prohibition of Nuclear Weapons in Latin America and the Caribbean (Treaty of Tlatelolco), there were 20 safeguards agreements in force, 16 of which were Tlatelolco/NPT agreements; 2 of those agreements entered into force in 1995 (Bolivia, Chile). The *sui generis* safeguards agreement between Ukraine and IAEA, signed in 1994,[15] came into force on 13 January.

(For details of compliance by the Democratic People's Republic of Korea with non-proliferation and safeguards agreements, see PART TWO, Chapter IV.)

### Middle East

As requested by the General Assembly in 1994,[16] the Secretary-General submitted in October 1995 a report[17] containing the text of a 22 September resolution of the IAEA General Conference on the application of IAEA safeguards in the Middle East.

**GENERAL ASSEMBLY ACTION**

On 12 December, the General Assembly adopted **resolution 50/73**.

#### The risk of nuclear proliferation in the Middle East

*The General Assembly,*

*Bearing in mind* the relevant United Nations resolutions,

*Taking note* of the relevant resolutions adopted by the General Conference of the International Atomic Energy Agency, the latest of which is GC(39)/RES/24, adopted on 22 September 1995, and noting the danger of nuclear proliferation, especially in areas of tension,

*Cognizant* that the proliferation of nuclear weapons in the region of the Middle East would pose a serious threat to international peace and security,

*Aware* of the importance that all nuclear facilities in the region be placed under full-scope safeguards of the International Atomic Energy Agency,

*Recalling* the resolution on the Middle East adopted by the 1995 Review and Extension Conference of the Parties to the Treaty on the Non-Proliferation of Nuclear Weapons on 11 May 1995, in which the Conference noted with concern the continued existence in the Middle East of unsafeguarded nuclear facilities, reaffirmed the importance of the early realization of universal adherence to the Treaty and called upon all States in the Middle East that had not yet done so, without exception, to accede to the Treaty as soon as possible and to place all their nuclear facilities under full-scope International Atomic Energy Agency safeguards,

*Recalling also* the decision on principles and objectives for nuclear non-proliferation and disarmament adopted by the 1995 Review and Extension Conference of the Parties to the Treaty on the Non-Proliferation of Nuclear Weapons on 11 May 1995, in which the Conference urged universal adherence to the Treaty as an urgent priority and called upon all States not yet party to the Treaty to accede to it at the earliest date, particularly those States that operate unsafeguarded nuclear facilities,

*Encouraged* by the recent positive developments in the Middle East peace process, which would be further strengthened by States of the region undertaking practical confidence-building measures in order to consolidate the non-proliferation regime,

1. *Welcomes* the accession of the United Arab Emirates on 26 September 1995 to the Treaty on the Non-Proliferation of Nuclear Weapons;

2. *Calls upon* Israel and all other States of the region that are not yet party to the Treaty on the Non-Proliferation of Nuclear Weapons not to develop, produce, test or otherwise acquire nuclear weapons, to renounce possession of nuclear weapons and to accede to the Treaty at the earliest date;

3. *Calls upon* the States of the region that have not yet done so to place all unsafeguarded nuclear facilities under full-scope International Atomic Energy Agency safeguards as an important confidence-building measure among all States of the region and as a step towards enhancing peace and security;

4. *Requests* the Secretary-General to report to the General Assembly at its fifty-first session on the implementation of the present resolution;

5. *Decides* to include in the provisional agenda of its fifty-first session the item entitled ''The risk of nuclear proliferation in the Middle East''.

General Assembly resolution 50/73

12 December 1995    Meeting 90    56-2-100 (recorded vote)

Approved by First Committee (A/50/593) by recorded vote (51-4-88), 17 November (meeting 26); 3-nation draft (A/C.1/50/L.19/Rev.1); agenda item 73.
Sponsors: Afghanistan, Egypt (as Chairman of Arab Group), Malaysia.
Meeting numbers. GA 50th session: 1st Committee 3-11, 16, 26; plenary 90.

Recorded vote in Assembly as follows:

*In favour:* Afghanistan, Algeria, Australia, Azerbaijan, Bahrain, Bangladesh, Botswana, Brunei Darussalam, Burkina Faso, Burundi, Chad, China, Colombia, Costa Rica, Cuba, Democratic Republic of Korea, Djibouti, Egypt, Ghana, Guinea, Indonesia, Iran, Jordan, Kuwait, Lebanon, Libyan Arab Jamahiriya, Malawi, Malaysia, Maldives, Mali, Mauritania, Mexico, Morocco, Namibia, New Zealand, Niger, Oman, Pakistan, Papua New Guinea, Philippines, Qatar, Republic of Korea, Samoa, Saudi Arabia, Senegal, Solomon Islands, Sri Lanka, Sudan, Syrian Arab Republic, Thailand, Togo, Tunisia, United Arab Emirates, Vanuatu, Viet Nam, Yemen.

*Against:* Israel, United States.

*Abstaining:* Albania, Andorra, Angola, Antigua and Barbuda, Argentina, Armenia, Austria, Bahamas, Barbados, Belarus, Belgium, Belize, Benin, Bhutan, Bolivia, Bosnia and Herzegovina, Brazil, Bulgaria, Cambodia, Cameroon, Canada, Chile, Congo, Côte d'Ivoire, Croatia, Cyprus, Czech Republic, Denmark, Ecuador, El Salvador, Equatorial Guinea, Eritrea, Estonia, Ethiopia, Finland, France, Gabon, Georgia, Germany, Greece, Guatemala, Guinea-Bissau, Guyana, Haiti, Honduras, Hungary, Iceland, India, Ireland, Italy, Jamaica, Japan, Kazakstan, Kenya, Kyrgyzstan, Latvia, Lesotho, Liechtenstein, Lithuania, Luxembourg, Malta, Marshall Islands, Mauritius, Micronesia, Monaco, Mongolia, Myanmar, Nepal, Netherlands, Nicaragua, Nigeria, Norway, Panama, Paraguay, Peru, Poland, Portugal, Republic of Moldova, Romania, Russian Federation, Rwanda, Singapore, Slovakia, Slovenia, South Africa, Spain, Suriname, Swaziland, Sweden, the former Yugoslav Republic of Macedonia, Trinidad and Tobago, Turkey, Uganda, Ukraine, United Kingdom, Uruguay, Uzbekistan, Venezuela, Zaire, Zambia.

In the Committee, the sixth preambular paragraph was adopted by a recorded vote of 109 to 3, with 27 abstentions. The Assembly adopted it by a recorded vote of 122 to 2, with 27 abstentions.

## Strengthening the security of non-nuclear-weapon States

In April, in response to concerns expressed by the non-nuclear-weapon States, the five nuclear-weapon States (China, France, Russian Federation, United Kingdom, United States) updated their previous unilateral declarations,[18] containing both positive and negative assurances, in the course of their preparations for the 1995 NPT Review and Extension Conference (China,[19] France,[20] Russian Federation,[21] United Kingdom,[22] United States).[23] Only the assurance of China was considered unconditional.

Positive assurances meant that certain States would provide or support immediate assistance, in accordance with the UN Charter, to any non-nuclear-weapon State party to NPT that was a victim of an act or an object of a threat of aggression in which nuclear weapons were used. Negative assurances provided a commitment by the nuclear-weapon States not to use nuclear weapons against countries not possessing such weapons.

The negative security assurances of four of the nuclear-weapon States (France, Russian Federation, United Kingdom, United States) were harmonized in the light of efforts being made to draft a new Security Council resolution on assurances. The Council had adopted a resolution on the issue in 1968.[24]

Recognizing that these measures did not, however, fully meet the hopes of those States that sought legally binding commitments, the parties to NPT agreed, in their decision on principles and objectives adopted at the review Conference (see above), to consider further steps that could take the form of a multilateral, legally binding instrument.

**Communications.** On 28 February, referring to its long-standing unconditional undertaking not to use or threaten to use nuclear weapons against non-nuclear-weapon States or nuclear-weapon-free zones, China stated[25] that its position also applied to Kazakstan and assured that State that it would respect its independence, sovereignty and territorial integrity. It had made similar assurances to Ukraine in 1994.[10]

Following the adoption of Security Council **resolution 984(1995)**, Bulgaria[26] and Kazakstan[27] welcomed the granting of security guarantees by the nuclear-weapon States.

SECURITY COUNCIL ACTION

The Security Council adopted **resolution 984(1995)** on 11 April 1995.

*The Security Council,*

*Convinced* that every effort must be made to avoid and avert the danger of nuclear war, to prevent the spread of nuclear weapons, to facilitate international cooperation in the peaceful uses of nuclear energy with particular emphasis on the needs of developing countries, and reaffirming the crucial importance of the Treaty on the Non-Proliferation of Nuclear Weapons to these efforts,

*Recognizing* the legitimate interest of non-nuclear-weapon States parties to the Treaty on the Non-Proliferation of Nuclear Weapons to receive security assurances,

*Welcoming* the fact that more than 170 States have become parties to the Treaty on the Non-Proliferation of Nuclear Weapons and stressing the desirability of universal adherence to it,

*Reaffirming* the need for all States parties to the Treaty on the Non-Proliferation of Nuclear Weapons to comply fully with all their obligations,

*Taking into consideration* the legitimate concern of non-nuclear-weapon States that, in conjunction with their adherence to the Treaty on the Non-Proliferation of Nuclear Weapons, further appropriate measures be undertaken to safeguard their security,

*Considering* that the present resolution constitutes a step in this direction,

*Considering further* that, in accordance with the relevant provisions of the Charter of the United Nations, any aggression with the use of nuclear weapons would endanger international peace and security,

1. *Takes note* with appreciation of the statements made by each of the nuclear-weapon States, in which they give security assurances against the use of nuclear weapons to non-nuclear-weapon States that are parties to the Treaty on the Non-Proliferation of Nuclear Weapons;

2. *Recognizes* the legitimate interest of non-nuclear-weapon States parties to the Treaty on the Non-Proliferation of Nuclear Weapons to receive assurances that the Security Council, and above all its nuclear-weapon State permanent members, will act immediately in accordance with the relevant provisions of the Charter of the United Nations, in the event that such States are the victim of an act of, or object of a threat of, aggression in which nuclear weapons are used;

3. *Recognizes further* that, in case of aggression with nuclear weapons or the threat of such aggression against a non-nuclear-weapon State party to the Treaty on the Non-Proliferation of Nuclear Weapons, any State may

bring the matter immediately to the attention of the Security Council to enable the Council to take urgent action to provide assistance, in accordance with the Charter, to the State victim of an act of, or object of a threat of, such aggression; and recognizes also that the nuclear-weapon State permanent members of the Security Council will bring the matter immediately to the attention of the Council and seek Council action to provide, in accordance with the Charter, the necessary assistance to the State victim;

4. *Notes* the means available to it for assisting such a non-nuclear-weapon State party to the Treaty on the Non-Proliferation of Nuclear Weapons, including an investigation into the situation and appropriate measures to settle the dispute and restore international peace and security;

5. *Invites* Member States, individually or collectively, if any non-nuclear-weapon State party to the Treaty on the Non-Proliferation of Nuclear Weapons is a victim of an act of aggression with nuclear weapons, to take appropriate measures in response to a request from the victim for technical, medical, scientific or humanitarian assistance, and affirms its readiness to consider what measures are needed in this regard in the event of such an act of aggression;

6. *Expresses* its intention to recommend appropriate procedures, in response to any request from a non-nuclear-weapon State party to the Treaty on the Non-Proliferation of Nuclear Weapons that is the victim of such an act of aggression, regarding compensation under international law from the aggressor for loss, damage or injury sustained as a result of the aggression;

7. *Welcomes* the intention expressed by certain States that they will provide or support immediate assistance, in accordance with the Charter, to any non-nuclear-weapon State party to the Treaty on the Non-Proliferation of Nuclear Weapons that is a victim of an act of, or an object of a threat of, aggression in which nuclear weapons are used;

8. *Urges* all States, as provided for in article VI of the Treaty on the Non-Proliferation of Nuclear Weapons, to pursue negotiations in good faith on effective measures relating to nuclear disarmament and on a treaty on general and complete disarmament under strict and effective international control which remains a universal goal;

9. *Reaffirms* the inherent right, recognized under Article 51 of the Charter, of individual and collective self-defence if an armed attack occurs against a Member of the United Nations, until the Security Council has taken measures necessary to maintain international peace and security;

10. *Underlines* that the issues raised in this resolution remain of continuing concern to the Council.

Security Council resolution 984(1995)

11 April 1995          Meeting 3514          Adopted unanimously

5-nation draft (S/1995/275).
*Sponsors:* China, France, Russian Federation, United Kingdom, United States.

**Conference on Disarmament consideration.** At its 1995 session,[28] the Conference on Disarmament was unable to establish an ad hoc committee on assurances because that action was linked to the establishment of ad hoc bodies on some other agenda items.

The five nuclear-weapon States updated their unilateral declarations on assurances in a 6 April plenary meeting (see above). At the same meeting, France, the Russian Federation, the United Kingdom and the United States made a joint declaration.[29] A number of delegations welcomed the unilateral declarations, expressing the view that they were consistent with the commitments that the non-nuclear-weapon States had entered into in the context of NPT. However, the Group of 21 neutral and non-aligned States (Algeria, Argentina, Brazil, Cuba, Egypt, Ethiopia, India, Indonesia, Iran, Kenya, Mexico, Morocco, Myanmar, Nigeria, Pakistan, Peru, Sri Lanka, Sweden, Venezuela, Yugoslavia (Serbia and Montenegro), Zaire), in a joint statement,[30] noted that neither the Conference on Disarmament nor any members of the Group were associated with the drafting of the Security Council resolution and stressed that the text did not take into account any of the formal objections made in the past by non-nuclear-weapon States on what they called the restrictive, restrained, uncertain, conditional and discriminatory character of the guarantees already provided. The Group considered that the terms of its 31 March 1994 declaration on the subject remained valid.[31]

By the end of the session, all groups in the Conference had confirmed their readiness to address the issue in the framework of the ad hoc committee, and many recommended its re-establishment at the beginning of the 1996 session.

**GENERAL ASSEMBLY ACTION**

On 12 December, the General Assembly adopted **resolution 50/68**.

**Conclusion of effective international arrangements to assure non-nuclear-weapon States against the use or threat of use of nuclear weapons**

*The General Assembly*,

*Bearing in mind* the need to allay the legitimate concern of the States of the world with regard to ensuring lasting security for their peoples,

*Convinced* that nuclear weapons pose the greatest threat to mankind and to the survival of civilization,

*Welcoming* the progress achieved in recent years in both nuclear and conventional disarmament,

*Noting* that, despite recent progress in the field of nuclear disarmament, further efforts are necessary towards the achievement of the goal of general and complete disarmament under effective international control,

*Also convinced* that nuclear disarmament and the complete elimination of nuclear weapons are essential to remove the danger of nuclear war,

*Determined* strictly to abide by the relevant provisions of the Charter of the United Nations on the non-use of force or threat of force,

*Recognizing* that the independence, territorial integrity and sovereignty of non-nuclear-weapon States need to be safeguarded against the use or threat of use of force, including the use or threat of use of nuclear weapons,

*Considering* that, until nuclear disarmament is achieved on a universal basis, it is imperative for the international community to develop effective measures and arrangements to ensure the security of non-nuclear-weapon States against the use or threat of use of nuclear weapons from any quarter,

*Recognizing also* that effective measures and arrangements to assure the non-nuclear-weapon States against the use or threat of use of nuclear weapons can contribute positively to the prevention of the spread of nuclear weapons,

*Bearing in mind* paragraph 59 of the Final Document of the Tenth Special Session of the General Assembly, the first special session devoted to disarmament, in which it urged the nuclear-weapon States to pursue efforts to conclude, as appropriate, effective arrangements to assure non-nuclear-weapon States against the use or threat of use of nuclear weapons, and desirous of promoting the implementation of the relevant provisions of the Final Document,

*Recalling* the relevant parts of the special report of the Committee on Disarmament,[a] submitted to the General Assembly at its twelfth special session, the second special session devoted to disarmament, and of the special report of the Conference on Disarmament submitted to the Assembly at its fifteenth special session, the third special session devoted to disarmament, as well as of the report of the Conference on its 1992 session,

*Recalling also* paragraph 12 of the Declaration of the 1980s as the Second Disarmament Decade, contained in the annex to its resolution 35/46 of 3 December 1980, which states, *inter alia*, that all efforts should be exerted by the Committee on Disarmament urgently to negotiate with a view to reaching agreement on effective international arrangements to assure non-nuclear-weapon States against the use or threat of use of nuclear weapons,

*Noting* the in-depth negotiations undertaken in the Conference on Disarmament and its Ad Hoc Committee on Effective International Arrangements to Assure Non-Nuclear-Weapon States against the Use or Threat of Use of Nuclear Weapons, with a view to reaching agreement on this item,

*Taking note* of the proposals submitted under that item in the Conference on Disarmament, including the drafts of an international convention,

*Taking note also* of the relevant decision of the Eleventh Conference of Heads of State or Government of Non-Aligned Countries, held at Cartagena de Indias, Colombia, from 18 to 20 October 1995,[b] and also of the decision adopted by the Tenth Conference of Heads of State or Government of Non-Aligned Countries, held at Jakarta from 1 to 6 September 1992, as well as the relevant recommendations of the Organization of the Islamic Conference reiterated in the Final Communiqué of the Twentieth Islamic Conference of Foreign Ministers, held at Istanbul from 4 to 8 August 1991, calling upon the Conference on Disarmament to reach an urgent agreement on an international convention to assure non-nuclear-weapon States against the use or threat of use of nuclear weapons,

---

[a]Redesignated the Conference on Disarmament as from 7 February 1984.

[b]A/50/752-S/1995/1035.

*Taking note further* of the unilateral declarations made by all nuclear-weapon States on their policies of non-use or non-threat of use of nuclear weapons against non-nuclear-weapon States,

*Noting* the support expressed in the Conference on Disarmament and in the General Assembly for the elaboration of an international convention to assure non-nuclear-weapon States against the use or threat of use of nuclear weapons, as well as the difficulties pointed out in evolving a common approach acceptable to all,

*Noting also* the greater willingness to overcome the difficulties encountered in previous years,

*Noting further* Security Council resolution 984(1995) of 11 April 1995 and the views expressed on it,

*Recalling* its relevant resolutions adopted in previous years, in particular resolutions 45/54 of 4 December 1990, 46/32 of 6 December 1991, 47/50 of 9 December 1992, 48/73 of 16 December 1993 and 49/73 of 15 December 1994,

1. *Reaffirms* the urgent need to reach an early agreement on effective international arrangements to assure non-nuclear-weapon States against the use or threat of use of nuclear weapons;

2. *Notes with satisfaction* that in the Conference on Disarmament there is no objection, in principle, to the idea of an international convention to assure non-nuclear-weapon States against the use or threat of use of nuclear weapons, although the difficulties as regards evolving a common approach acceptable to all have also been pointed out;

3. *Appeals* to all States, especially the nuclear-weapon States, to work actively towards an early agreement on a common approach and, in particular, on a common formula that could be included in an international instrument of a legally binding character;

4. *Recommends* that further intensive efforts should be devoted to the search for such a common approach or common formula and that the various alternative approaches, including, in particular, those considered in the Conference on Disarmament, should be further explored in order to overcome the difficulties;

5. *Also recommends* that the Conference on Disarmament should actively continue intensive negotiations with a view to reaching early agreement and concluding effective international arrangements to assure non-nuclear-weapon States against the use or threat of use of nuclear weapons, taking into account the widespread support for the conclusion of an international convention and giving consideration to any other proposals designed to secure the same objective;

6. *Decides* to include in the provisional agenda of its fifty-first session the item entitled "Conclusion of effective international arrangements to assure non-nuclear-weapon States against the use or threat of use of nuclear weapons".

General Assembly resolution 50/68

12 December 1995     Meeting 90     122-0-44 (recorded vote)

Approved by First Committee (A/50/588) by recorded vote (113-1-42), 14 November (meeting 20); 17-nation draft (A/C.1/50/L.39/Rev.1); agenda item 68.

*Meeting numbers.* GA 50th session: 1st Committee 3-11, 15, 20; plenary 90.

Recorded vote in Assembly as follows:

*In favour:* Afghanistan, Algeria, Angola, Antigua and Barbuda, Australia, Azerbaijan, Bahamas, Bahrain, Bangladesh, Barbados, Belarus, Belize, Benin, Bhutan, Bolivia, Botswana, Brazil, Brunei Darussalam, Burkina Faso, Burundi, Cambodia, Cameroon, Cape Verde, Chad, Chile, China, Colom-

bia, Congo, Costa Rica, Côte d'Ivoire, Cuba, Cyprus, Democratic People's Republic of Korea, Djibouti, Ecuador, Egypt, El Salvador, Equatorial Guinea, Eritrea, Ethiopia, Gabon, Georgia, Ghana, Guatemala, Guinea, Guinea-Bissau, Guyana, Haiti, Honduras, India, Indonesia, Iran, Jamaica, Japan, Jordan, Kazakstan, Kenya, Kuwait, Kyrgyzstan, Lao People's Democratic Republic, Lebanon, Lesotho, Libyan Arab Jamahiriya, Madagascar, Malawi, Malaysia, Maldives, Mali, Marshall Islands, Mauritania, Mauritius, Mexico, Micronesia, Mongolia, Morocco, Mozambique, Myanmar, Namibia, Nepal, New Zealand, Nicaragua, Niger, Nigeria, Oman, Pakistan, Panama, Papua New Guinea, Paraguay, Peru, Philippines, Qatar, Republic of Korea, Rwanda, Samoa, Saudi Arabia, Senegal, Sierra Leone, Singapore, Solomon Islands, South Africa, Sri Lanka, Sudan, Suriname, Swaziland, Syrian Arab Republic, Thailand, the former Yugoslav Republic of Macedonia, Togo, Trinidad and Tobago, Tunisia, Uganda, Ukraine, United Arab Emirates, United Republic of Tanzania, Uruguay, Vanuatu, Venezuela, Viet Nam, Yemen, Zaire, Zambia, Zimbabwe.

*Against:* None.

*Abstaining:* Albania, Andorra, Argentina, Armenia, Austria, Belgium, Bulgaria, Canada, Croatia, Czech Republic, Denmark, Estonia, Fiji, Finland, France, Germany, Greece, Grenada, Hungary, Iceland, Ireland, Israel, Italy, Latvia, Liechtenstein, Lithuania, Luxembourg, Malta, Monaco, Netherlands, Norway, Poland, Portugal, Republic of Moldova, Romania, Russian Federation, Slovakia, Slovenia, Spain, Sweden, Turkey, United Kingdom, United States, Uzbekistan.

## Nuclear-arms limitation and disarmament

### Comprehensive test-ban treaty

In 1995, three treaties on nuclear testing were in effect, one multilateral—the 1963 Treaty Banning Nuclear Weapon Tests in the Atmosphere, in Outer Space and under Water[32]—and two bilateral—the Treaty on Limitation of Underground Nuclear Weapon Tests and the Treaty on Underground Nuclear Explosions for Peaceful Purposes, both of which entered into force in 1990. None of them was comprehensive.

Negotiations on a comprehensive test-ban treaty continued throughout the 1995 session of the Conference on Disarmament and during intersessional meetings. The measure of the progress achieved was in the recording of agreed language in the rolling text of the draft treaty.

**Conference on Disarmament consideration.** The Ad Hoc Committee on a Nuclear Test Ban was re-established in 1995[28] and charged with the same mandate as in 1994,[33] namely, to negotiate a comprehensive test-ban treaty.

The Committee held 28 meetings between 30 January and 19 September, during which it set up two Working Groups. Working Group 1 dealt with verification and Working Group 2 with legal and institutional issues. In addition, 10 Friends of the Chair and two Convenors were appointed to deal with specific issues in private and open-ended consultations.

Working Group 1 made intensive efforts towards structuring and revising treaty language on the verification regime in the rolling text. The rolling text was composed of two main parts: part 1 comprised draft treaty provisions that commanded a certain degree of consensus at the time of the adoption of the report; part 2 contained provisions that needed more extensive negotiation. An expert meeting was held relating to the overall structure of the International Monitoring System (IMS) to be established to verify compliance with the treaty. Later in the session, the Working Group, with the participation of experts, continued to narrow options and to specify the number and location of monitoring stations. As a result, revised draft language on provisions on verification issues was included in part 2 of the rolling text.

Working Group 2 elaborated revised draft language on legal and institutional aspects of the draft treaty, which was included in part 1 or 2 of the rolling text, depending on their respective stages of development. Thus, part 1 comprised measures to redress a situation and to ensure compliance, including sanctions; settlement of disputes; privileges and immunities; signature; ratification; accession; depositary; status of protocols and annexes; authentic texts; national implementation measures; and amendments.

The Ad Hoc Committee recommended that: the rolling text be used for further negotiation and drafting of the treaty; other documents considered by it be used in future negotiation and development of the treaty; expert work on IMS continue during the period from 4 to 15 December 1995; its work be continued during the period from 8 to 19 January 1996; and that it be re-established at the outset of the 1996 session of the Conference, with its current mandate, with a view to completing the negotiations as soon as possible and not later than in 1996.

The report[34] of the Committee containing the rolling text of the treaty was adopted by the Conference on Disarmament on 6 September.

The Ad Hoc Group of Scientific Experts to Consider International Cooperative Measures to Detect and Identify Seismic Events held its fortieth (20 February–3 March),[35] forty-first (7-18 August)[36] and forty-second (27 November–1 December)[37] sessions in 1995, all in Geneva.

At its fortieth session, the Ad Hoc Group discussed the planning, operation and evaluation of the Group of Scientific Experts Technical Test Three (GSETT-3), which was an experimental seismic IMS. In August, it reviewed results from GSETT-3, which had begun full-scale operations on 1 January 1995. The Group noted that the concepts for an experimental seismic monitoring system to be tested during GSETT-3 included a single centralized International Data Centre (IDC), a specifically designed high-quality seismographic network consisting of some 50 primary (Alpha) stations and 100 to 150 auxiliary (Beta) stations, National Data Centres in participating countries, and a modern communications system to support exchange among those elements. IDC had been in operation since 1 January 1995 and currently 37 primary and 75 auxiliary stations were participating in the experiment. The remaining tasks envisaged for the completion and evaluation of GSETT-3 monitoring system dealt with network development, communications, evaluation and completion and the transition of GSETT-3 to IMS operations. The main topic of discussion at the Group's forty-second session was consideration of an auxiliary network of seismic stations for IMS. It also reviewed progress on its GSETT-3 experiment, noting that four new primary stations and six new auxiliary stations had been added since August. The Group reviewed a preliminary report on the evaluation of GSETT-3 and asked the Evaluation Group to present a draft of a final report for its next session in February 1996.

As the final evaluation of GSETT-3 would not be done until 1996, the Group could draw only preliminary conclusions; among them, it appeared that a single IDC would be capable of acquiring and archiving not only the volume of seismic data anticipated, but also the radionuclide, hydroacoustic and infrasound data to be exchanged. It was projected that, taken together, the primary and auxiliary seismic networks should be capable of locating seismic events in continental areas of magnitude four and above with an uncertainty in location of not more than 1,000 square kilometres. GSETT-3 also confirmed that the investment costs for its stations, communications links and IDC would be some $180 million, and yearly operational and maintenance costs would be about $30 million. The Ad Hoc Group recommended that the development and testing of its experimental system be continued to provide for a seamless transition into IMS under a future treaty.

As recommended by the Ad Hoc Committee on a Nuclear Test Ban, inter-sessional meetings of the IMS Expert Group were held from 4 to 15 December.[40] The Group, which had met several times during the annual session of the Ad Hoc Committee to elaborate the networks for the four agreed monitoring systems, agreed on the number and location of the stations to be incorporated in the four monitoring networks, and based, in principle, the number and placement of the auxiliary seismic stations for IMS on the recommendation of the Ad Hoc Group of Scientific Experts.

**Note by the Secretary-General.** In response to General Assembly requests of 1986[38] and 1987,[39] the Secretary-General in June transmitted two quarterly reports (July-September and October-December 1994) from Australia, which indicated that China had detonated an underground nuclear device in Lop Nor on 7 October 1994.[40]

*Unilateral moratoriums*

In 1995, the Russian Federation, the United Kingdom and the United States continued to observe their unilateral moratoriums.

On 15 May, China conducted an underground nuclear test at Lop Nor, and two further tests at the same site on 10 June and 17 August, but reiterated that it was committed to cease nuclear testing forever upon the entry into force of a comprehensive nuclear-test-ban treaty. Ecuador, by a letter of 1 June,[41] condemned the May test. Australia on 17 August,[42] Mongolia on 18 August[43] and the Philippines on 18 August,[44] in protest to the August test, urged China to cease nuclear testing.

France carried out five nuclear-test explosions in 1995 in French Polynesia: on 5 September, 1 and 27 October, 21 November and 27 December. Before the resumed testing, France had not conducted a nuclear test since 15 July 1991. Letters condemning France's decision to resume nuclear testing in the Pacific were transmitted by: Australia,[45] Australia, as current Chair of the South Pacific Forum,[46] Ecuador,[47] Malaysia,[48] and the Philippines.[49] Belarus,[50] Peru[51] and Ukraine[52] transmitted letters of protest.

Indonesia, on behalf of the Movement of Non-Aligned Countries, on 26 July[53] condemned the recent tests conducted by a nuclear-weapon State, as well as the decision by another State to suspend its moratorium and to resume testing soon.

**GENERAL ASSEMBLY ACTION**

On 12 December, the General Assembly adopted **resolution 50/65**.

### Comprehensive nuclear-test-ban treaty
*The General Assembly,*

*Recalling* its resolutions 48/70 of 16 December 1993 and 49/70 of 15 December 1994, in which the entire international community supported the multilateral negotiations on a comprehensive nuclear-test-ban treaty,

*Reaffirming* that a comprehensive nuclear-test ban is one of the highest-priority objectives of the international community in the field of disarmament and non-proliferation,

*Convinced* that the most effective way to achieve an end to nuclear testing is through the conclusion of a universal and internationally and effectively verifiable comprehensive nuclear-test-ban treaty that will attract the adherence of all States and will contribute to the prevention of the proliferation of nuclear weapons in all its aspects, to the process of nuclear disarmament and therefore to the enhancement of international peace and security,

*Noting* the aspirations expressed by the parties to the 1963 Treaty Banning Nuclear Weapon Tests in the Atmosphere, in Outer Space and under Water to seek to achieve the discontinuance of all test explosions of nuclear weapons for all time, which are recalled in the preamble to the 1968 Treaty on the Non-Proliferation of Nuclear Weapons,

*Welcoming* the further elaboration of the rolling text in the Ad Hoc Committee on a Nuclear Test Ban of the Conference on Disarmament, as reflected in the report of the Conference and its appendix, and the decision of the Conference to continue its work in inter-sessional meetings,

1. *Welcomes* the continuing efforts in the multilateral negotiations on a comprehensive nuclear-test-ban treaty in the Ad Hoc Committee on a Nuclear Test Ban of the Conference on Disarmament, the significant contributions to the rolling text made by States participating in those negotiations and progress in key areas;

2. *Calls upon* all States participating in the Conference on Disarmament, in particular the nuclear-weapon States, to conclude, as a task of the highest priority, a universal and multilaterally and effectively verifiable comprehensive nuclear-test-ban treaty which contributes to nuclear disarmament and the prevention of the proliferation of nuclear weapons in all its aspects, so as to enable its signature by the outset of the fifty-first session of the General Assembly;

3. *Also calls upon* participants in the Conference on Disarmament to advance work on the basis of the rolling text during the inter-sessional negotiating period so as to proceed to the final phase of the negotiations at the beginning of 1996;

4. *Further calls upon* the Conference on Disarmament to re-establish the Ad Hoc Committee at the commencement of its 1996 session, and to renew its mandate in order to complete the final text of the treaty as soon as possible in 1996;

5. *Urges* all States to support the multilateral negotiations in the Conference on Disarmament for a comprehensive nuclear-test-ban treaty and their prompt conclusion;

6. *Declares* its readiness to resume consideration of this item, as necessary, before its fifty-first session in order to endorse the text of a comprehensive nuclear-test-ban treaty;

7. *Requests* the Secretary-General to ensure the provision to the Conference on Disarmament of adequate administrative, substantive and conference support services for these negotiations;

8. *Decides* to include in the provisional agenda of its fifty-first session an item entitled "Implementation of the comprehensive nuclear-test-ban treaty".

General Assembly resolution 50/65

12 December 1995　　Meeting 90　　Adopted without vote

Approved by First Committee (A/50/585 & Corr.1) without vote, 17 November (meeting 25); 91-nation draft (A/C.1/50/L.8/Rev.1); agenda item 65.
*Meeting numbers.* GA 50th session: 1st Committee 3-11, 16, 25; plenary 90.

In the Committee, a separate recorded vote was taken on paragraph 2, which was retained by 161 to none, with 1 abstention. The Assembly adopted the paragraph by a recorded vote of 166 to none, with 1 abstention.

Also on 12 December, the Assembly adopted **resolution 50/70 A**.

### Nuclear testing
*The General Assembly,*

*Welcoming* the easing of international tension and the strengthening of trust between States that have prevailed following the end of the cold war,

*Reaffirming* that the cessation of all nuclear testing will contribute to the non-proliferation of nuclear weapons in all its aspects, to the process of nuclear disarmament leading to the ultimate objective of the complete elimination of nuclear weapons and therefore to the further enhancement of international peace and security,

*Convinced* that the cessation of all nuclear testing will provide a favourable climate for the conclusion of negotiations on a comprehensive nuclear-test-ban treaty,

*Considering* that nuclear testing is not consistent with undertakings by the nuclear-weapon States at the 1995 Review and Extension Conference of the Parties to the Treaty on the Non-Proliferation of Nuclear Weapons,

*Deeply concerned* about the potential negative effects of underground nuclear testing on health and the environment,

*Sharing alarm* expressed internationally, regionally and nationally at recent nuclear tests,

1. *Commends* those nuclear-weapon States observing nuclear testing moratoria, and urges them to continue those moratoria pending the entry into force of a comprehensive nuclear-test-ban treaty;

2. *Strongly deplores* all current nuclear testing;

3. *Strongly urges* the immediate cessation of all nuclear testing.

General Assembly resolution 50/70 A

12 December 1995     Meeting 90     85-18-43 (recorded vote)

Approved by First Committee (A/50/590) by recorded vote (95-12-45), 16 November (meeting 24); 41-nation draft (A/C.1/50/L.3); agenda item 70 (a). *Meeting numbers.* GA 50th session: 1st Committee 3-11, 14, 24; plenary 90.

Recorded vote in Assembly as follows:

*In favour:* Algeria, Argentina, Australia, Austria, Bahamas, Bangladesh, Barbados, Belarus, Belgium, Belize, Bhutan, Botswana, Brazil, Brunei Darussalam, Canada, Chile, Colombia, Costa Rica, Cuba, Denmark, Ecuador, Eritrea, Ethiopia, Fiji, Finland, Ghana, Guatemala, Guyana, Iceland, India, Indonesia, Ireland, Italy, Jamaica, Japan, Kazakstan, Kyrgyzstan, Lesotho, Liechtenstein, Luxembourg, Malawi, Malaysia, Maldives, Malta, Marshall Islands, Mauritius, Mexico, Micronesia, Mongolia, Mozambique, Myanmar, Nepal, Netherlands, New Zealand, Nicaragua, Nigeria, Norway, Palau, Panama, Papua New Guinea, Paraguay, Peru, Philippines, Portugal, Republic of Korea, Rwanda, Samoa, Sierra Leone, Singapore, Solomon Islands, South Africa, Sri Lanka, Suriname, Swaziland, Sweden, Thailand, Trinidad and Tobago, Uganda, Ukraine, United Republic of Tanzania, Uruguay, Venezuela, Viet Nam, Zambia, Zimbabwe.

*Against:* Benin, Cameroon, Chad, China, Congo, Côte d'Ivoire, Djibouti, Equatorial Guinea, France, Gabon, Madagascar, Mali, Mauritania, Monaco, Niger, Senegal, Togo, United Kingdom.

*Abstaining:* Afghanistan, Albania, Andorra, Angola, Armenia, Bulgaria, Burundi, Cambodia, Croatia, Cyprus, Czech Republic, Democratic People's Republic of Korea, El Salvador, Estonia, Georgia, Germany, Greece, Guinea, Guinea-Bissau, Hungary, Israel, Kenya, Latvia, Lebanon, Libyan Arab Jamahiriya, Lithuania, Morocco, Namibia, Pakistan, Poland, Republic of Moldova, Romania, Russian Federation, Slovakia, Slovenia, Spain, Sudan, Syrian Arab Republic, the former Yugoslav Republic of Macedonia, Tunisia, Turkey, United States, Zaire.

On the same date, the Assembly adopted **resolution 50/64**.

### Amendment of the Treaty Banning Nuclear Weapon Tests in the Atmosphere, in Outer Space and under Water

*The General Assembly*,

*Recalling* its resolution 46/28 of 6 December 1991, in which it noted the convening of the Amendment Conference of the States Parties to the Treaty Banning Nuclear Weapon Tests in the Atmosphere, in Outer Space and under Water from 7 to 18 January 1991, its resolution 48/69 of 16 December 1993, in which it noted the convening of a special meeting of the States parties to that Treaty on 10 August 1993, and its resolution 49/69 of 15 December 1994, in which it noted with satisfaction the commencement of multilateral negotiations for a comprehensive nuclear-test-ban treaty in the Conference on Disarmament on 1 February 1994,

*Reiterating its conviction* that a comprehensive nuclear-test-ban treaty is the highest-priority measure for the cessation of the nuclear-arms race and for the achievement of the objective of nuclear disarmament,

*Recalling* the central role of the United Nations in the field of nuclear disarmament and in particular in the cessation of all nuclear-test explosions, as well as the persistent efforts of non-governmental organizations in the achievement of a comprehensive nuclear-test-ban treaty,

*Convinced* that the Amendment Conference will facilitate the attainment of the objectives set forth in the Treaty and thus serve to strengthen it,

*Recalling* its recommendation that arrangements be made to ensure that intensive efforts continue, under the auspices of the Amendment Conference, until a comprehensive nuclear-test-ban treaty is achieved, and its call that all parties participate in, and contribute effectively to the success of, the Amendment Conference,

1. *Urges* all States that have not already done so to adhere to the Treaty Banning Nuclear Weapon Tests in the Atmosphere, in Outer Space and under Water at the earliest possible date;

2. *Urges* all States parties to the Treaty to contribute to the conclusion of a comprehensive nuclear-test-ban treaty as soon as possible and no later than 1996 and to its expeditious entry into force;

3. *Requests* the President of the Amendment Conference to conduct consultations to those ends;

4. *Decides* to include in the provisional agenda of its fifty-first session the item entitled ''Amendment of the Treaty Banning Nuclear Weapon Tests in the Atmosphere, in Outer Space and under Water''.

General Assembly resolution 50/64

12 December 1995     Meeting 90     110-4-45 (recorded vote)

Approved by First Committee (A/50/584) by recorded vote (95-4-44), 10 November (meeting 18); 25-nation draft (A/C.1/50/L.32); agenda item 64. *Meeting numbers.* GA 50th session: 1st Committee 3-11, 15, 18; plenary 90.

Recorded vote in Assembly as follows:

*In favour:* Afghanistan, Algeria, Angola, Antigua and Barbuda, Bahamas, Bahrain, Bangladesh, Barbados, Belize, Benin, Bhutan, Bolivia, Botswana, Brazil, Brunei Darussalam, Burkina Faso, Burundi, Cambodia, Cameroon, Cape Verde, Chad, Chile, Colombia, Congo, Costa Rica, Côte d'Ivoire, Cuba, Cyprus, Democratic People's Republic of Korea, Djibouti, Ecuador, Egypt, El Salvador, Equatorial Guinea, Ethiopia, Fiji, Gabon, Ghana, Guatemala, Guinea, Guinea-Bissau, Guyana, Haiti, Honduras, India, Indonesia, Iran, Jamaica, Jordan, Kazakstan, Kenya, Kuwait, Lao People's Democratic Republic, Lebanon, Lesotho, Libyan Arab Jamahiriya, Madagascar, Malawi, Malaysia, Maldives, Mali, Mauritania, Mauritius, Mexico, Micronesia, Mongolia, Morocco, Mozambique, Myanmar, Namibia, Nepal, Nicaragua, Niger, Nigeria, Oman, Pakistan, Panama, Papua New Guinea, Paraguay, Peru, Philippines, Qatar, Rwanda, Samoa, Saudi Arabia, Senegal, Sierra Leone, Singapore, Solomon Islands, South Africa, Sri Lanka, Suriname, Swaziland, Syrian Arab Republic, Thailand, Togo, Trinidad and Tobago, Tunisia, Uganda, United Arab Emirates, United Republic of Tanzania, Uruguay, Vanuatu, Venezuela, Viet Nam, Yemen, Zaire, Zambia, Zimbabwe.

*Against:* Israel, Russian Federation, United Kingdom, United States.

*Abstaining:* Albania, Andorra, Argentina, Armenia, Australia, Austria, Azerbaijan, Belarus, Belgium, Bulgaria, Canada, Croatia, Czech Republic, Denmark, Estonia, Finland, Georgia, Germany, Greece, Hungary, Iceland, Ireland, Italy, Japan, Latvia, Liechtenstein, Lithuania, Luxembourg, Malta, Marshall Islands, Netherlands, New Zealand, Norway, Poland, Portugal, Republic of Korea, Republic of Moldova, Romania, Slovakia, Slovenia, Spain, Sweden, the former Yugoslav Republic of Macedonia, Turkey, Ukraine.

## Issues related to START

The 1991 Treaty on the Reduction and Limitation of Strategic Offensive Arms (START I)[54] and its 1992 Protocol, known as the Lisbon Protocol,[55] entered into force on 5 December 1994, as a result of Ukraine's accession to NPT.[56] Even before its entry into force, the Russian Federation and the United States had begun to dismantle and destroy close to 2,000 warheads a year, which they continued to do. The other parties to the Treaty—Belarus, Kazakstan and Ukraine—began transferring Soviet-era nuclear warheads on their territory to the Russian Federation for dismantlement.

On 24 May, Kazakstan stated that all nuclear weapons on its territory had been removed.[57] On 26 May, it further stated that the last nuclear explosive device, located at the former Semipalatinsk test site, would be destroyed at the end of May or during the first part of June.[58]

With respect to ratification of the 1993 START II Treaty,[59] the United States Senate Foreign Relations Committee's approval of the Treaty, which was required for ratification, did not take place until 12 December 1995. Ratification in the Russian Federation was delayed mainly because of concerns over proposals in the United States Congress to develop and deploy theatre missile defence (TMD)—actions that, in the opinion of the Russian Federation, might be in violation of the 1972 Anti-Ballistic Missile (ABM) Treaty.[60] On 10 May, Russian President Boris Yeltsin and United States President William J. Clinton issued a joint statement[61] in which they set out principles to serve as a basis for discussions on demarcation between ABM systems and TMD systems, but the two Governments had not come to an agreement by the end of the year.

**GENERAL ASSEMBLY ACTION**

On 12 December, the General Assembly adopted **resolution 50/70 C**.

### Nuclear disarmament with a view to the ultimate elimination of nuclear weapons

*The General Assembly*,

*Recalling* its resolution 49/75 H of 15 December 1994,

*Recognizing* that the end of the cold war has increased the possibility of freeing the world from the fear of nuclear war,

*Appreciating* the entry into force of the Treaty on the Reduction and Limitation of Strategic Offensive Arms, to which Belarus, Kazakstan, the Russian Federation, Ukraine and the United States of America are party, and looking forward to the early entry into force of the Treaty on Further Reduction and Limitation of Strategic Offensive Arms,

*Welcoming* the reductions in the nuclear arsenals of other nuclear-weapon States,

*Welcoming also* the decision of the 1995 Review and Extension Conference of the Parties to the Treaty on the Non-Proliferation of Nuclear Weapons to extend the Treaty indefinitely, taken without a vote, as well as the decisions on strengthening the review process for the Treaty and on the principles and objectives for nuclear non-proliferation and disarmament,

*Noting* the reference in the decision on the principles and objectives for nuclear non-proliferation and disarmament to the importance of the following measures for the full realization and effective implementation of article VI of the Treaty on the Non-Proliferation of Nuclear Weapons, including the programme of action as reflected below:

(*a*) The completion by the Conference on Disarmament of the negotiations on a universal and internationally and effectively verifiable comprehensive nuclear-test-ban treaty no later than 1996, and the utmost restraint that should be exercised by the nuclear-weapon States pending the entry into force of that treaty;

(*b*) The immediate commencement and early conclusion of negotiations on a non-discriminatory and universally applicable convention banning the production of fissile material for nuclear weapons or other nuclear explosive devices in accordance with the statement of the Special Coordinator of the Conference on Disarmament and the mandate contained therein;

(*c*) The determined pursuit by the nuclear-weapon States of systematic and progressive efforts to reduce nuclear weapons globally, with the ultimate goal of eliminating those weapons, and by all States of general and complete disarmament under strict and effective international control,

*Welcoming* positive developments as well as the efforts being made by the States members of the Conference on Disarmament in the negotiations on a comprehensive nuclear-test-ban treaty at the Conference on Disarmament at Geneva,

*Recalling* that nuclear non-proliferation and the promotion of nuclear disarmament are key elements in the maintenance of international peace and security, which is one of the most important purposes of the United Nations,

1. *Urges* States not parties to the Treaty on the Non-Proliferation of Nuclear Weapons to accede to it at the earliest possible date, recognizing the importance of universal adherence to the Treaty;

2. *Calls for* the determined pursuit by the nuclear-weapon States of systematic and progressive efforts to reduce nuclear weapons globally, with the ultimate goal of eliminating those weapons, and by all States of general and complete disarmament under strict and effective international control, and invites them to keep States Members of the United Nations duly informed of the progress and efforts made;

3. *Calls upon* all States to implement fully their commitments in the field of disarmament and non-proliferation of weapons of mass destruction.

General Assembly resolution 50/70 C

12 December 1995     Meeting 90     154-0-10 (recorded vote)

Approved by First Committee (A/50/590 & Corr.1) by recorded vote (144-0-13), 17 November (meeting 26); 19-nation draft (A/C.1/50/L.17/Rev.2); agenda item 70.

*Meeting numbers.* GA 50th session: 1st Committee 3-11, 15, 26; plenary 90.

Recorded vote in Assembly as follows:

*In favour:* Albania, Andorra, Antigua and Barbuda, Argentina, Armenia, Australia, Austria, Azerbaijan, Bahamas, Bahrain, Bangladesh, Barbados, Belarus, Belgium, Belize, Benin, Bhutan, Bolivia, Bosnia and Herzegovina, Botswana, Brunei Darussalam, Bulgaria, Burkina Faso, Burundi, Cambodia, Cameroon, Canada, Cape Verde, Chad, Chile, Colombia, Congo, Costa Rica, Côte d'Ivoire, Croatia, Cyprus, Czech Republic, Denmark, Djibouti, Ecuador, Egypt, El Salvador, Equatorial Guinea, Eritrea, Estonia, Ethiopia,

Fiji, Finland, France, Gabon, Georgia, Germany, Ghana, Greece, Guatemala, Guinea, Guinea-Bissau, Guyana, Haiti, Honduras, Hungary, Iceland, Indonesia, Ireland, Italy, Jamaica, Japan, Jordan, Kazakstan, Kenya, Kuwait, Kyrgyzstan, Lao People's Democratic Republic, Latvia, Lebanon,* Lesotho, Libyan Arab Jamahiriya, Liechtenstein, Lithuania, Luxembourg, Madagascar, Malawi, Malaysia, Maldives, Mali, Malta, Marshall Islands, Mauritania, Mauritius, Mexico, Micronesia, Monaco, Mongolia, Morocco, Mozambique, Namibia, Nepal, Netherlands, New Zealand, Nicaragua, Niger, Norway, Oman, Panama, Papua New Guinea, Paraguay, Peru, Philippines, Poland, Portugal, Qatar, Republic of Korea, Republic of Moldova, Romania, Russian Federation, Rwanda, Samoa, Saudi Arabia, Senegal, Sierra Leone, Singapore, Slovakia, Slovenia, Solomon Islands, South Africa, Spain, Sri Lanka, Sudan, Suriname, Swaziland, Sweden, Syrian Arab Republic, Tajikistan, Thailand, the former Yugoslav Republic of Macedonia, Togo, Trinidad and Tobago, Tunisia, Turkey, Turkmenistan, Uganda, Ukraine, United Arab Emirates, United Kingdom, United Republic of Tanzania, United States, Uruguay, Vanuatu, Venezuela, Viet Nam, Yemen, Zaire, Zambia, Zimbabwe.

*Against:* None.

*Abstaining:* Algeria, Brazil, China, Cuba, Democratic People's Republic of Korea, India, Iran, Israel, Myanmar, Pakistan.

*Later advised the Secretariat it had intended to abstain.

In the Committee, the fifth preambular paragraph and paragraph 1 were adopted by separate recorded votes of 135 to none, with 19 abstentions, and 146 to 2, with 7 abstentions, respectively.

The Assembly retained the same paragraphs by recorded votes of 143 to none, with 17 abstentions, and 156 to 2, with 4 abstentions, respectively.

Also on 12 December, the Assembly adopted **resolution 50/70 I**.

### Bilateral nuclear-arms negotiations and nuclear disarmament

*The General Assembly,*

*Recalling* its previous relevant resolutions,

*Recognizing* the fundamental changes that have taken place with respect to international security, which have permitted agreements on deep reductions in the nuclear armaments of the States possessing the largest inventories of such weapons,

*Mindful* that it is the responsibility and obligation of all States to contribute to the process of the relaxation of international tension and to the strengthening of international peace and security,

*Stressing* the importance of strengthening international peace and security through general and complete disarmament, under strict and effective international control,

*Stressing also* that it is the responsibility of all States to adopt and implement measures towards the attainment of general and complete disarmament under strict and effective international control,

*Appreciating* a number of positive developments in the field of nuclear disarmament, in particular the Treaty between the United States of America and the Union of Soviet Socialist Republics on the Elimination of Their Intermediate-Range and Shorter-Range Missiles, and the treaties on the reduction and limitation of strategic offensive arms,

*Appreciating also* the indefinite extension of the Treaty on the Non-Proliferation of Nuclear Weapons and acknowledging the importance of the determined pursuit by the nuclear-weapon States of systematic and progressive efforts to reduce nuclear weapons globally, with the ultimate goal of eliminating those weapons, and by all States of general and complete disarmament under strict and effective international control,

*Welcoming* the steps that have already been taken by the Russian Federation and the United States of America to begin the process of reducing the number of nuclear weapons and removing such weapons from a deployed status, and bilateral agreements on the issue of de-targeting strategic nuclear missiles,

*Noting* the new climate of relations between the United States of America and the States of the former Union of Soviet Socialist Republics, which permits them to intensify their cooperative efforts to ensure the safety, security and environmentally sound destruction of nuclear weapons,

*Noting also* that the Russian Federation and the United States of America concurred that, once the Treaty between them on Further Reduction and Limitation of Strategic Offensive Arms was ratified, they would proceed to deactivate all nuclear delivery systems to be reduced under the Treaty by removing their nuclear warheads or taking other steps to remove them from alert status,

*Noting further* the commitment between the Russian Federation and the United States of America to intensify their dialogue to compare conceptual approaches and to develop concrete steps to adapt the nuclear forces and practices on both sides to the changed international security situation, including the possibility, after ratification of the Treaty on Further Reduction and Limitation of Strategic Offensive Arms, of further reductions of and limitations on remaining nuclear forces,

*Taking note* of the joint statement of 10 May 1995 by the Russian Federation and the United States of America on the Treaty on the Limitation of Anti-Ballistic Missile Systems,

*Urging* the early ratification of the Treaty on Further Reduction and Limitation of Strategic Offensive Arms and further intensification of such efforts to accelerate the implementation of agreements and unilateral decisions relating to nuclear-arms reduction,

*Welcoming* the significant reductions made by other nuclear-weapon States, and encouraging all nuclear-weapon States to consider appropriate measures relating to nuclear disarmament,

1. *Welcomes* the entry into force of the Treaty on the Reduction and Limitation of Strategic Offensive Arms, signed in Moscow on 31 July 1991 by the former Union of Soviet Socialist Republics and the United States of America, including the Protocol to that Treaty signed at Lisbon on 23 May 1992 by the parties thereto, and the exchange of documents of ratification between the United States of America, Belarus, Kazakstan, the Russian Federation and Ukraine on 5 December 1994 at Budapest;

2. *Also welcomes* the signing of the Treaty between the United States of America and the Russian Federation on Further Reduction and Limitation of Strategic Offensive Arms in Moscow on 3 January 1993, and urges the parties to take the steps necessary to bring that Treaty into force at the earliest possible date;

3. *Expresses its satisfaction* at the fact that the entry into force of the 1991 Treaty on the Reduction and Limitation of Strategic Offensive Arms clears the way for prompt ratification by the Russian Federation and the United States of America of the 1993 Treaty;

4. *Also expresses its satisfaction* at the continuing implementation of the Treaty between the United States of America and the Union of Soviet Socialist Republics

on the Elimination of Their Intermediate-Range and Shorter-Range Missiles, in particular at the completion by the parties of the destruction of all their declared missiles subject to elimination under the Treaty;

5. *Encourages* the United States of America, the Russian Federation, Belarus, Kazakstan and Ukraine·to continue their cooperative efforts aimed at eliminating nuclear weapons and strategic offensive arms on the basis of existing agreements, and welcomes the contributions that other States are making to such cooperation as well;

6. *Welcomes* the accession to the Treaty on the Non-Proliferation of Nuclear Weapons of Belarus, Kazakstan and Ukraine as non-nuclear-weapon States, which thereby provided a notable enhancement to the non-proliferation regime;

7. *Encourages and supports* the Russian Federation and the United States of America in their efforts to reduce their nuclear weapons and to continue to give those efforts the highest priority in order to contribute to the ultimate goal of eliminating those weapons;

8. *Invites* the Russian Federation and the United States of America to keep other States Members of the United Nations duly informed of progress in their discussions and in the implementation of their strategic offensive arms agreements and unilateral decisions.

General Assembly resolution 50/70 I

12 December 1995     Meeting 90     150-0-14 (recorded vote)

Approved by First Committee (A/50/590) by recorded vote (139-0-17), 14 November (meeting 20); 26-nation draft (A/C.1/50/L.35/Rev.1); agenda item 70.

*Meeting numbers.* GA 50th session: 1st Committee 3-11, 20; plenary 90.

Recorded vote in Assembly as follows:

*In favour:* Afghanistan, Albania, Algeria, Andorra, Angola, Antigua and Barbuda, Argentina, Armenia, Australia, Austria, Azerbaijan, Bahamas, Bahrain, Bangladesh, Barbados, Belarus, Belgium, Belize, Benin, Bhutan, Bolivia, Bosnia and Herzegovina, Botswana, Brazil, Brunei Darussalam, Bulgaria, Burkina Faso, Burundi, Cambodia, Cameroon, Canada, Cape Verde, Chad, Chile, China, Colombia, Congo, Côte d'Ivoire, Croatia, Cyprus, Czech Republic, Denmark, Djibouti, Ecuador, Egypt, El Salvador, Equatorial Guinea, Eritrea, Estonia, Ethiopia, Fiji, Finland, France, Gabon, Georgia, Germany, Ghana, Greece, Guatemala, Guinea, Guinea-Bissau, Guyana, Haiti, Honduras, Hungary, Iceland, Ireland, Israel, Italy, Jamaica, Japan, Jordan, Kazakstan, Kenya, Kuwait, Kyrgyzstan, Lao People's Democratic Republic, Latvia, Lesotho, Liechtenstein, Lithuania, Luxembourg, Madagascar, Malawi, Malaysia, Maldives, Mali, Malta, Marshall Islands, Mauritania, Mauritius, Mexico, Micronesia, Monaco, Mongolia, Morocco, Mozambique, Namibia, Nepal, Netherlands, New Zealand, Nicaragua, Niger, Nigeria, Norway, Oman, Panama, Papua New Guinea, Paraguay, Peru, Philippines, Poland, Portugal, Qatar, Republic of Korea, Republic of Moldova, Romania, Russian Federation, Rwanda, Samoa, Saudi Arabia, Senegal, Sierra Leone, Singapore, Slovakia, Slovenia, Solomon Islands, South Africa, Spain, Suriname, Swaziland, Sweden, Syrian Arab Republic, the former Yugoslav Republic of Macedonia, Trinidad and Tobago, Tunisia, Turkey, Turkmenistan, Ukraine, United Arab Emirates, United Kingdom, United States, Uruguay, Vanuatu, Venezuela, Viet Nam, Yemen, Zaire, Zambia, Zimbabwe.

*Against:* None.

*Abstaining:* Cuba, Democratic People's Republic of Korea, India, Indonesia, Iran, Lebanon,* Libyan Arab Jamahiriya, Myanmar, Pakistan, Sri Lanka, Sudan, Thailand, Togo, United Republic of Tanzania.

*Later advised the Secretariat it had intended to vote in favour.

In the Committee, a separate recorded vote was taken on the seventh preambular paragraph, which was retained by 116 to none, with 29 abstentions. The Assembly retained the paragraph by a recorded vote of 128 to none, with 27 abstentions.

On the same date, the Assembly adopted **resolution 50/70 N**.

## Bilateral nuclear-arms negotiations and nuclear disarmament

*The General Assembly,*

*Recalling* its previous relevant resolutions,

*Recognizing* the fundamental changes that have taken place with respect to international security, which have permitted agreements on deep reductions in the nuclear armaments of the States possessing the largest inventories of such weapons,

*Mindful* that it is the responsibility and obligation of all States to contribute to the process of the relaxation of international tension and to the strengthening of international peace and security,

*Stressing* the importance of strengthening international peace and security through disarmament,

*Emphasizing* that nuclear disarmament remains one of the principal tasks of our times,

*Appreciating* a number of positive developments in the field of nuclear disarmament, in particular the Treaty between the United States of America and the Union of Soviet Socialist Republics on the Elimination of Their Intermediate-Range and Shorter-Range Missiles, concluded on 8 December 1987, and the treaties on the reduction and limitation of strategic offensive arms,

*Noting* that there are still significant nuclear arsenals and that the primary responsibility for nuclear disarmament, with the objective of the elimination of nuclear weapons, rests with the nuclear-weapon States, in particular those which possess the largest stockpiles,

*Noting also* the expressed determination of the nuclear-weapon States to pursue systematic and progressive efforts to reduce nuclear weapons globally, with the ultimate goal of eliminating those weapons within a time-bound framework,

*Welcoming* the steps that have already been taken by those States to begin the process of reducing the number of nuclear weapons and removing such weapons from a deployed status, and bilateral agreements on the issue of de-targeting strategic nuclear missiles,

*Noting* the new climate of relations between the United States of America and the States of the former Soviet Union, which permits them to intensify their cooperative efforts to ensure the safety, security and environmentally sound destruction of nuclear weapons,

*Noting also* that the Russian Federation and the United States of America concurred that, once the Treaty on Further Reduction and Limitation of Strategic Offensive Arms was ratified, they would proceed to deactivate all nuclear delivery systems to be reduced under the Treaty by removing their nuclear warheads or taking other steps to remove them from alert status,

*Noting further* the agreement between the Russian Federation and the United States of America to intensify their dialogue to compare conceptual approaches and to develop concrete steps to adapt the nuclear forces and practices on both sides to the changed international security situation, including the possibility, after ratification of the Treaty on Further Reduction and Limitation of Strategic Offensive Arms, of further reductions of and limitations on remaining nuclear forces,

*Taking note* of the joint statement of 10 May 1995 by the Russian Federation and the United States of America on the Treaty on the Limitation of Anti-Ballistic Missile Systems,

*Urging* the early ratification of the Treaty on the Further Reduction and Limitation of Strategic Offensive Arms and further intensification of such efforts to accelerate the implementation of agreements and unilateral decisions relating to nuclear-arms reduction,

*Welcoming* the reduction made by other nuclear-weapon States in some of their nuclear-weapon programmes, and encouraging all nuclear-weapon States to consider appropriate measures relating to nuclear disarmament,

*Affirming* that bilateral and multilateral negotiations on nuclear disarmament should facilitate and complement each other,

1. *Welcomes* the entry into force of the Treaty on the Reduction and Limitation of Strategic Offensive Arms, signed in Moscow on 31 July 1991 by the former Union of Soviet Socialist Republics and the United States of America, including the Protocol to that Treaty signed at Lisbon on 23 May 1992 by the parties thereto, and the exchange of documents of ratification between the United States of America, Belarus, Kazakstan, the Russian Federation and Ukraine on 5 December 1994 at Budapest;

2. *Also welcomes* the signing of the Treaty between the United States of America and the Russian Federation on Further Reduction and Limitation of Strategic Offensive Arms in Moscow on 3 January 1993, and urges the parties to take the steps necessary to bring that Treaty into force at the earliest possible date;

3. *Expresses its satisfaction* at the fact that the entry into force of the 1991 Treaty on the Reduction and Limitation of Strategic Offensive Arms clears the way to prompt ratification by the Russian Federation and the United States of America of the 1993 Treaty;

4. *Also expresses its satisfaction* at the continuing implementation of the Treaty between the United States of America and the Union of Soviet Socialist Republics on the Elimination of Their Intermediate-Range and Shorter-Range Missiles, in particular at the completion by the parties of the destruction of all their declared missiles subject to elimination under the Treaty;

5. *Encourages* the United States of America, the Russian Federation, Belarus, Kazakstan and Ukraine to continue their cooperative efforts aimed at eliminating nuclear weapons and strategic offensive arms on the basis of existing agreements, and welcomes the contributions that other States are making to such cooperation as well;

6. *Encourages and supports* the Russian Federation and the United States of America in their efforts to reduce their nuclear armaments and to continue to give those efforts the highest priority in order to contribute to the objective of the elimination of nuclear weapons within a time-bound framework;

7. *Invites* the Russian Federation and the United States of America to keep other States Members of the United Nations and the Conference on Disarmament duly informed of progress in their discussions and in the implementation of their strategic offensive arms agreements and unilateral decisions;

8. *Calls on* the Conference on Disarmament to take this information into account in the negotiations to be held on nuclear disarmament and for the ultimate elimination of nuclear weapons within a time-bound framework.

General Assembly resolution 50/70 N

12 December 1995    Meeting 90    105-37-20 (recorded vote)

Approved by First Committee (A/50/590) by recorded vote (95-37-22), 15 November (meeting 21); draft by Colombia, for Non-Aligned Movement (A/C.1/50/L.44/Rev.1); agenda item 70.

*Meeting numbers.* GA 50th session: 1st Committee 3-11, 16, 21; plenary 90.

Recorded vote in Assembly as follows:

*In favour:* Afghanistan, Algeria, Angola, Bahrain, Bangladesh, Belize, Benin, Bhutan, Bolivia, Botswana, Brazil, Brunei Darussalam, Burkina Faso, Burundi, Cambodia, Cameroon, Cape Verde, Chad, Chile, China, Colombia, Congo, Costa Rica, Côte d'Ivoire, Croatia, Cuba, Cyprus, Democratic People's Republic of Korea, Djibouti, Ecuador, Egypt, El Salvador, Eritrea, Ethiopia, Gabon, Ghana, Guatemala, Guinea, Guinea-Bissau, Guyana, Haiti, Honduras, India, Indonesia, Iran, Jamaica, Jordan, Kenya, Kuwait, Lao People's Democratic Republic, Lebanon, Lesotho, Libyan Arab Jamahiriya, Madagascar, Malawi, Malaysia, Maldives, Mali, Mauritania, Mauritius, Mexico, Mongolia, Morocco, Mozambique, Myanmar, Namibia, Nepal, Nicaragua, Niger, Nigeria, Oman, Pakistan, Panama, Papua New Guinea, Peru, Philippines, Qatar, Rwanda, Samoa, Saudi Arabia, Senegal, Sierra Leone, Singapore, Solomon Islands, South Africa, Sri Lanka, Sudan, Suriname, Swaziland, Syrian Arab Republic, Thailand, Togo, Trinidad and Tobago, Tunisia, Uganda, United Arab Emirates, United Republic of Tanzania, Uruguay, Vanuatu, Venezuela, Viet Nam, Yemen, Zaire, Zambia, Zimbabwe.

*Against:* Andorra, Argentina, Armenia, Belgium, Bulgaria, Canada, Czech Republic, Denmark, Estonia, Finland, France, Georgia, Germany, Greece, Hungary, Iceland, Israel, Italy, Latvia, Lithuania, Luxembourg, Marshall Islands, Monaco, Netherlands, Norway, Poland, Portugal, Republic of Moldova, Romania, Russian Federation, Slovakia, Slovenia, Spain, the former Yugoslav Republic of Macedonia, Turkey, United Kingdom, United States.

*Abstaining:* Antigua and Barbuda, Australia, Austria, Azerbaijan, Bahamas, Belarus, Equatorial Guinea, Fiji, Ireland, Japan, Kazakstan, Liechtenstein, Malta, Micronesia, New Zealand, Paraguay, Republic of Korea, Sweden, Tajikistan, Ukraine.

On the same date, the General Assembly adopted **resolution 50/70 R.**

### Contribution to nuclear disarmament

*The General Assembly,*

*Recalling* its resolutions 49/75 H, L and P of 15 December 1994,

*Noting with satisfaction* a number of positive developments in the field of nuclear disarmament, in particular, the entry into force of the Treaty on the Reduction and Limitation of Strategic Offensive Arms,

*Noting also with satisfaction* the conclusion of the Treaty on Further Reduction and Limitation of Strategic Offensive Arms,

*Realizing* the vital importance of further nuclear disarmament with the ultimate goals of the complete elimination of nuclear weapons and a treaty on general and complete disarmament under strict and effective international control,

*Bearing in mind* the results of the 1995 Review and Extension Conference of the Parties to the Treaty on the Non-Proliferation of Nuclear Weapons,

*Noting* that the vast majority of States Members of the United Nations are now parties to the Treaty on the Non-Proliferation of Nuclear Weapons,

1. *Welcomes* the accession to the Treaty on the Non-Proliferation of Nuclear Weapons of the following States: Algeria, Argentina, Chile, Comoros, Eritrea, Marshall Islands, Micronesia (Federated States of), Monaco, Palau, Ukraine, United Arab Emirates and Vanuatu;

2. *Also welcomes* the accession on 5 December 1994 to the Treaty on the Non-Proliferation of Nuclear Weapons of Ukraine as a non-nuclear-weapon State, and in this regard acknowledges that this decision, as well as relevant decisions previously taken by Belarus and Kazakstan, contributed to the entry into force of the Treaty on the Reduction and Limitation of Strategic

Offensive Arms, which is a major landmark in the process of nuclear disarmament;

3. *Acknowledges* the progress in the process of implementation of the Treaty on the Reduction and Limitation of Strategic Offensive Arms to date by the parties to the Treaty;

4. *Welcomes* the signing of the Treaty on Further Reduction and Limitation of Strategic Offensive Arms by the Russian Federation and the United States of America, and urges the parties to take the steps necessary to bring that Treaty into force at the earliest possible date;

5. *Also welcomes* the fact that South Africa has voluntarily given up its nuclear-weapon programme as well as the voluntary renunciation of nuclear weapons by Belarus, Kazakstan and Ukraine, and recognizes the significant contribution of those States to nuclear disarmament and the strengthening of regional and global security.

General Assembly resolution 50/70 R

12 December 1995     Meeting 90     Adopted without vote

Approved by First Committee (A/50/590) without vote, 16 November (meeting 23); 6-nation draft (A/C.1/50/L.50/Rev.2); agenda item 70.
*Sponsors:* Australia, Bangladesh, Belarus, Marshall Islands, Monaco, Ukraine.
*Meeting numbers.* GA 50th session: 1st Committee 3-11, 21, 23; plenary 90.

## Prohibition of the production of fissile material and related issues

Although the Conference on Disarmament established in 1995 an Ad Hoc Committee to negotiate a treaty banning the production of fissile material for nuclear weapons or other nuclear explosive devices, it was unable to begin work, since the appointment of a chairman for the Committee was linked to the establishment of other ad hoc committees. Further discussion on the issue was carried out in plenary meetings, during which many States reiterated their divergent positions on the scope of the future treaty. At the unilateral level, the United Kingdom announced at the 1995 NPT Review and Extension Conference that it had ceased production of fissile material for explosive purposes. In May, Russian President Yeltsin and United States President Clinton issued a joint statement[61] on the transparency and irreversibility of the process of reducing nuclear weapons, in which they agreed that fissile materials removed from nuclear weapons being eliminated and excess to national security requirements would not be used to manufacture nuclear weapons; no newly produced fissile materials would be used in nuclear weapons; and fissile materials from or within civil nuclear programmes would not be used to manufacture nuclear weapons.

### Illicit trafficking in nuclear materials

In response to the Secretary-General's request of 11 July,[62] the Security Council President responded[63] on 19 July, stating that Council members supported efforts by IAEA and other organizations regarding the illicit trafficking in nuclear materials. The Council also noted the initiative by Russian President Yeltsin to host a summit in 1996 to discuss nuclear safety, including the issue of illicit trafficking.

GENERAL ASSEMBLY ACTION

On 12 December, the General Assembly adopted **resolution 50/70 P**.

### Nuclear disarmament

*The General Assembly,*

*Reaffirming* the commitment of the international community to the goal of the total elimination of nuclear weapons and the creation of a nuclear-weapon-free world,

*Determined* to achieve the objective of prohibiting the development, production, stockpiling and use of nuclear weapons and their destruction, and to conclude such an international treaty or treaties at an early date,

*Bearing in mind* paragraph 50 of the Final Document of the Tenth Special Session of the General Assembly, the first special session devoted to disarmament, calling for the urgent negotiation of agreements for the cessation of the qualitative improvement and development of nuclear-weapon systems, and for a comprehensive and phased programme with agreed time-frames, wherever feasible, for progressive and balanced reduction of nuclear weapons and their means of delivery, leading to their ultimate and complete elimination at the earliest possible time,

*Recognizing* that a comprehensive nuclear-test-ban treaty, the proposed treaty on fissile material for nuclear weapons or other nuclear explosive devices and a convention prohibiting the use of nuclear weapons constitute important steps towards the elimination of the nuclear threat, and will contribute to the achievement of the goal of nuclear disarmament within a time-bound framework,

*Recognizing also* that the end of the cold war has brought about favourable conditions for creating a world free of nuclear weapons,

*Welcoming* the entry into force of the Treaty on the Reduction and Limitation of Strategic Offensive Arms, to which Belarus, Kazakstan, the Russian Federation, Ukraine and the United States of America are States parties, as well as the conclusion of the Treaty on Further Reduction and Limitation of Strategic Offensive Arms by the Russian Federation and the United States of America, and looking forward to full implementation of these treaties and to further concrete steps for nuclear disarmament by all nuclear-weapon States,

*Noting with appreciation* the unilateral measures of nuclear-weapon States for nuclear-arms limitation,

*Recognizing* the complementarity of bilateral and multilateral negotiations on nuclear disarmament and that bilateral negotiations can never replace multilateral negotiations in this respect,

*Recognizing also* that a comprehensive nuclear-test-ban treaty and the proposed treaty on fissile material for nuclear weapons or other explosive devices must both constitute disarmament measures and not only non-proliferation measures, and that they must be important steps leading to the total elimination of nuclear weapons within a time-bound framework,

*Noting* the support expressed in the Conference on Disarmament and in the General Assembly for the elaboration of an international convention to assure non-nuclear-weapon States against the use or threat of use of nuclear weapons, and the multilateral efforts in the Conference on Disarmament to reach agreement on such an international convention at an early date,

*Recalling* its resolution 49/75 E of 15 December 1994 on a step-by-step reduction of the nuclear threat,

*Taking note* of paragraph 84 and other relevant recommendations in the Final Document of the Eleventh Conference of Heads of State or Government of the Non-Aligned Countries, held at Cartagena de Indias, Colombia, from 18 to 20 October 1995,[a] calling on the Conference on Disarmament to establish, on a priority basis, an ad hoc committee to commence negotiations early in 1996 on a phased programme of nuclear disarmament and for the eventual elimination of nuclear weapons within a time-bound framework,

1. *Recognizes* that, in view of the end of the cold war and recent political developments, the time is now opportune for all nuclear-weapon States to undertake effective nuclear disarmament measures with a view to the total elimination of these weapons within a time-bound framework;

2. *Also recognizes* that there is a genuine need to de-emphasize the role of nuclear weapons, and to review and revise nuclear doctrines accordingly;

3. *Urges* the nuclear-weapon States to stop immediately the qualitative improvement, development, stockpiling and production of nuclear warheads and their delivery systems;

4. *Calls upon* the nuclear-weapon States to undertake step-by-step reduction of the nuclear threat and a phased programme of progressive and balanced deep reductions of nuclear weapons, and to carry out effective nuclear disarmament measures with a view to the total elimination of these weapons within a time-bound framework;

5. *Calls upon* the Conference on Disarmament to establish, on a priority basis, an ad hoc committee on nuclear disarmament to commence negotiations early in 1996 on a phased programme of nuclear disarmament and for the eventual elimination of nuclear weapons within a time-bound framework;

6. *Expresses its support* for the efforts of the Member States of the Conference on Disarmament to this end;

7. *Requests* the Secretary-General to submit to the General Assembly at its fifty-first session a report on the implementation of the present resolution;

8. *Decides* to include in the provisional agenda of its fifty-first session the item entitled ''Nuclear disarmament''.

---

[a]A/50/752-S/1995/1035.

General Assembly resolution 50/70 P

12 December 1995    Meeting 90    106-39-17 (recorded vote)

Approved by First Committee (A/50/590) by recorded vote (99-39-15), 16 November (meeting 23); 33-nation draft (A/C.1/50/L.46/Rev.1); agenda item 70.

*Meeting numbers.* GA 50th session: 1st Committee 3-11, 18, 23; plenary 90.

Recorded vote in Assembly as follows:

*In favour:* Afghanistan, Algeria, Bahrain, Bangladesh, Barbados, Belize, Bhutan, Bolivia, Botswana, Brazil, Brunei Darussalam, Burkina Faso, Burundi, Cambodia, Cameroon, Cape Verde, Chad, Chile, China, Colombia, Congo, Costa Rica, Côte d'Ivoire, Cuba, Democratic People's Republic of Korea, Djibouti, Ecuador, Egypt, El Salvador, Eritrea, Ethiopia, Fiji,

Ghana, Guatemala, Guinea, Guinea-Bissau, Guyana, Haiti, Honduras, India, Indonesia, Iran, Jamaica, Jordan, Kenya, Kuwait, Kyrgyzstan, Lao People's Democratic Republic, Lebanon, Lesotho, Libyan Arab Jamahiriya, Madagascar, Malawi, Malaysia, Maldives, Mali, Marshall Islands, Mauritania, Mauritius, Mexico, Micronesia, Mongolia, Morocco, Mozambique, Myanmar, Namibia, Nepal, Nicaragua, Niger, Nigeria, Oman, Pakistan, Panama, Papua New Guinea, Paraguay, Peru, Philippines, Qatar, Rwanda, Samoa, Saudi Arabia, Senegal, Sierra Leone, Singapore, Solomon Islands, South Africa, Sri Lanka, Sudan, Suriname, Swaziland, Syrian Arab Republic, Thailand, Togo, Trinidad and Tobago, Tunisia, Uganda, United Arab Emirates, United Republic of Tanzania, Uruguay, Vanuatu, Venezuela, Viet Nam, Yemen, Zaire, Zambia, Zimbabwe.

*Against:* Albania, Andorra, Argentina, Austria, Belgium, Bulgaria, Canada, Czech Republic, Denmark, Estonia, Finland, France, Germany, Greece, Hungary, Iceland, Ireland, Israel, Italy, Latvia, Liechtenstein, Lithuania, Luxembourg, Malta, Monaco, Netherlands, Norway, Poland, Portugal, Republic of Moldova, Romania, Slovakia, Slovenia, Spain, Sweden, the former Yugoslav Republic of Macedonia, Turkey, United Kingdom, United States.

*Abstaining:* Antigua and Barbuda, Armenia, Australia, Azerbaijan, Bahamas, Belarus, Benin, Croatia, Cyprus, Equatorial Guinea, Georgia, Japan, Kazakstan, New Zealand, Republic of Korea, Russian Federation, Ukraine.

## Nuclear-weapon-free zones

### Africa

In accordance with a 1994 General Assembly request,[64], the Secretary-General in September transmitted the final text of the African Nuclear-Weapon-Free Zone Treaty,[65] known as the Treaty of Pelindaba, which was finalized at a Joint Meeting of the Organization of African Unity (OAU)/United Nations Group of Experts to Prepare a Draft Treaty on an African Nuclear-Weapon-Free Zone and the Intergovernmental Group of Experts of OAU (Johannesburg, 29 May–1 June; Pelindaba, 2 June). The OAU/United Nations Group of Experts previously held meetings in 1991,[66] 1992,[67] 1993[68] and 1994.[69] Subsequently, the text was amended by the OAU Council of Ministers (Addis Ababa, Ethiopia, 21-23 June) and approved by the OAU Assembly of Heads of State and Government (Addis Ababa, 26-28 June).[70]

The Treaty aimed at preventing the proliferation of nuclear weapons and promoting the peaceful use of nuclear energy, and incorporated a prohibition on the dumping of radioactive wastes. A special agency—the African Commission on Nuclear Energy (AFCONE)—provided by the Treaty to supervise its implementation, was to be established with headquarters in South Africa.

Four annexes formed an integral part of the Treaty, consisting of a map illustrating the application of the Treaty (annex I), and dealing with IAEA safeguards (annex II), AFCONE (annex III) and complaints procedure and settlement of disputes (annex IV). Two of the three protocols were addressed to the nuclear-weapon States. Protocol I incorporated the undertaking not to use or threaten to use a nuclear explosive device against any party to the Treaty or territory within the zone; Protocol II incorporated the undertaking not to test a nuclear explosive device within the zone; Protocol III, addressed to France and Spain as States which were, *de jure* or de facto, responsible for territories within the zone, incorporated the undertaking to apply the relevant provisions of the Treaty to those territories.

The Treaty was to enter into force on the deposit of the twenty-eighth instrument of ratification, which meant on the ratification of a simple majority of OAU members. The OAU Secretary-General was designated depositary of the Treaty.

**GENERAL ASSEMBLY ACTION**

On 12 December, the General Assembly adopted **resolution 50/78**.

### Final text of the African Nuclear-Weapon-Free Zone Treaty (the Treaty of Pelindaba)

*The General Assembly,*

*Bearing in mind* the Declaration on the Denuclearization of Africa adopted by the Assembly of Heads of State and Government of the Organization of African Unity at its first ordinary session, held at Cairo from 17 to 21 July 1964, in which they solemnly declare their readiness to undertake, through an international agreement to be concluded under United Nations auspices, not to manufacture or acquire control of atomic weapons,

*Recalling* its resolution 2033(XX) of 3 December 1965, in which it endorsed the above-mentioned Declaration and expressed the hope that the African States would initiate studies, as they deemed appropriate, with a view to implementing the denuclearization of Africa, and take the necessary measures, through the Organization of African Unity, to achieve that end,

*Recalling also* article VII of the Treaty on the Non-Proliferation of Nuclear Weapons, which acknowledges the right of any group of States to conclude regional treaties in order to ensure the total absence of nuclear weapons in their respective territories,

*Bearing in mind* paragraph 60 of the Final Document of the Tenth Special Session of the General Assembly, the first special session devoted to disarmament, which states that the establishment of nuclear-weapon-free zones on the basis of arrangements freely arrived at among the States of the region concerned constitutes an important disarmament measure,

*Bearing in mind also* the provisions of resolution CM/Res.1592(LXII)/Rev.1 on the implementation of the Treaty declaring Africa a nuclear-weapon-free zone, adopted by the Council of Ministers of the Organization of African Unity at its sixty-second ordinary session, held at Addis Ababa from 21 to 23 June 1995,

*Noting* the adoption by the Assembly of Heads of State and Government of the Organization of African Unity at its thirty-first ordinary session, held at Addis Ababa from 26 to 28 June 1995, of the African Nuclear-Weapon-Free Zone Treaty (the Treaty of Pelindaba),

*Noting also* that the Treaty contains three Protocols open to the signature of States that, *de jure* or de facto, are internationally responsible for territories that lie within the limits of the geographical zone established in the Treaty of Pelindaba and to the signature of States possessing nuclear weapons, and convinced that the cooperation of such States is necessary for the greater effectiveness of the Treaty,

*Recognizing* that the establishment of nuclear-weapon-free zones contributes to the strengthening of the international non-proliferation regime,

*Considering* that the establishment of nuclear-weapon-free zones, especially in the Middle East, would enhance the security of Africa and the viability of the African nuclear-weapon-free zone,

1. *Welcomes with special satisfaction* the adoption by the African leaders of the final text of the African Nuclear-Weapon-Free Zone Treaty (the Treaty of Pelindaba), which constitutes an event of historic significance in the efforts to prevent the proliferation of nuclear weapons and to promote international peace and security and which, at the same time, recognizes the right of African countries to use nuclear energy for peaceful purposes in order to accelerate the economic and social development of their peoples;

2. *Invites* the African States to sign and ratify the Treaty of Pelindaba as soon as possible;

3. *Calls upon* all States to respect the continent of Africa as a nuclear-weapon-free zone;

4. *Calls upon* the States contemplated in Protocol III to the Treaty of Pelindaba to take all necessary measures to ensure the speedy application of the Treaty to territories for which they are, *de jure* or de facto, internationally responsible and which lie within the limits of the geographical zone established in the Treaty;

5. *Calls upon* the nuclear-weapon States to bring the necessary support to the Treaty of Pelindaba by signing the Protocols that concern them as soon as the Treaty becomes available for signature;

6. *Expresses its profound gratitude* to the Secretary-General for the diligence with which he has rendered effective technical advice and financial assistance to the Organization of African Unity towards the six meetings of the Group of Experts to Prepare a Draft Treaty on an African Nuclear-Weapon-Free Zone, set up jointly by the Organization of African Unity and the United Nations;

7. *Also expresses its gratitude* to the Secretary-General of the Organization of African Unity and the Director General of the International Atomic Energy Agency for the diligence with which they assisted the Group of Experts to Prepare a Draft Treaty on an African Nuclear-Weapon-Free Zone;

8. *Requests* the Secretary-General, within existing resources, to extend assistance to the African States in 1996 in order to achieve the aims of the present resolution;

9. *Decides* to include in the provisional agenda of its fifty-first session an item entitled "African Nuclear-Weapon-Free Zone Treaty".

General Assembly resolution 50/78

12 December 1995     Meeting 90     Adopted without vote

Approved by First Committee (A/50/598) without vote, 20 November (meeting 28); draft by Marshall Islands and South Africa, for African Group (A/C.1/50/L.23/Rev.1); revised in Assembly by South Africa (A/50/L.55); agenda item 78.
*Meeting numbers.* GA 50th session: 1st Committee 3-11, 16, 28; plenary 90.

### Latin America and the Caribbean

The process of consolidation of the nuclear-weapon-free zone established by the 1967 Treaty for the Prohibition of Nuclear Weapons in Latin America and the Caribbean (Treaty of Tlatelolco) continued throughout the year. By year's end, Guyana, Saint Kitts and Nevis, and Saint Lucia had ratified the Treaty, bringing the total number of parties to 38.

GENERAL ASSEMBLY ACTION

On 12 December, the General Assembly adopted **resolution 50/77**.

**Consolidation of the regime established by the Treaty for the Prohibition of Nuclear Weapons in Latin America and the Caribbean (Treaty of Tlatelolco)**

*The General Assembly,*

*Recalling* that in its resolution 1911(XVIII) of 27 November 1963 it expressed the hope that the States of Latin America would take appropriate measures to conclude a treaty that would prohibit nuclear weapons in Latin America,

*Recalling also* that in the same resolution it voiced its confidence that, once such a treaty was concluded, all States, and in particular the nuclear-weapon States, would lend it their full cooperation for the effective realization of its peaceful aims,

*Considering* that in its resolution 2028(XX) of 19 November 1965 it established the principle of an acceptable balance of mutual responsibilities and obligations between nuclear-weapon States and those which do not possess such weapons,

*Recalling* that the Treaty for the Prohibition of Nuclear Weapons in Latin America and the Caribbean (Treaty of Tlatelolco) was opened for signature at Mexico City on 14 February 1967,

*Recalling also* that in its preamble the Treaty of Tlatelolco states that military denuclearized zones are not an end in themselves but rather a means for achieving general and complete disarmament at a later stage,

*Recalling further* that in its resolution 2286(XXII) of 5 December 1967 it welcomed with special satisfaction the Treaty of Tlatelolco as an event of historic significance in the efforts to prevent the proliferation of nuclear weapons and to promote international peace and security,

*Recalling* that in 1990, 1991 and 1992 the General Conference of the Agency for the Prohibition of Nuclear Weapons in Latin America and the Caribbean approved and opened for signature a set of amendments to the Treaty of Tlatelolco, with the aim of enabling the full entry into force of that instrument,

*Bearing in mind* that, with the full adherence in 1995 of Saint Lucia, the Treaty of Tlatelolco is in force for thirty sovereign States of the region,

*Noting with satisfaction* that the Government of Saint Kitts and Nevis ratified the Treaty of Tlatelolco on 18 April 1995,

*Also noting with satisfaction* that the Government of Cuba subscribed to the Treaty of Tlatelolco on 25 March 1995, thus contributing to a greater integration among the peoples of Latin America and the Caribbean for the attainment of the aims of the Treaty,

*Further noting with satisfaction* that the amended Treaty of Tlatelolco is fully in force for Argentina, Brazil, Chile, Jamaica, Mexico, Peru, Suriname and Uruguay,

1. *Welcomes* the concrete steps taken by several countries of the region during the past year for the consolidation of the regime of military denuclearization established by the Treaty for the Prohibition of Nuclear Weapons in Latin America and the Caribbean (Treaty of Tlatelolco);

2. *Notes with satisfaction* the full adherence of Saint Lucia to the Treaty of Tlatelolco;

3. *Urges* the countries of the region that have not yet done so to deposit their instruments of ratification of the amendments to the Treaty of Tlatelolco approved by the General Conference of the Agency for the Prohibition of Nuclear Weapons in Latin America and the Caribbean in its resolutions 267(E-V) of 3 July 1990, 268(XII) of 10 May 1991 and 290(VII) of 26 August 1992;

4. *Decides* to include in the provisional agenda of its fifty-first session the item entitled "Consolidation of the regime established by the Treaty for the Prohibition of Nuclear Weapons in Latin America and the Caribbean (Treaty of Tlatelolco)".

General Assembly resolution 50/77

12 December 1995     Meeting 90     Adopted without vote

Approved by First Committee (A/50/597) without vote, 10 November (meeting 18); 29-nation draft (A/C.1/50/L.5/Rev.1); agenda item 77.
*Meeting numbers.* GA 50th session: 1st Committee 3-11, 16, 18; plenary 90.

### Middle East

In 1995, the issue of a nuclear-weapon-free zone in the Middle East figured prominently in the NPT Review and Extension Conference. At the Conference, States adopted a decision encouraging, as a matter of priority, the development of nuclear-weapon-free zones, especially in regions of tension such as the Middle East. (See above, under "Non-proliferation".)

**Report of the Secretary-General.** Pursuant to a 1994 request of the General Assembly,[71] ·the Secretary-General transmitted, in an August report with a later addendum,[72] the views of two Member States on measures outlined in a 1990 study,[73] or other relevant measures, in order to move towards the establishment of a nuclear-weapon-free zone in the Middle East.

**Communication.** The Council of the League of Arab States, meeting in Cairo, Egypt, adopted on 21 September a resolution on the establishment of a nuclear-weapon-free zone in the Middle East, by which it invited the Security Council to ensure the universal implementation, without double standards, of all provisions concerning the non-proliferation of nuclear weapons, to take the requisite steps to achieve that aim, and to provide non-nuclear-weapon States with effective and comprehensive security guarantees against the use or threat of use of such weapons.[74]

GENERAL ASSEMBLY ACTION

On 12 December, the General Assembly adopted **resolution 50/66**.

**Establishment of a nuclear-weapon-free zone in the region of the Middle East**

*The General Assembly,*

*Recalling* its resolutions 3263(XXIX) of 9 December 1974, 3474(XXX) of 11 December 1975, 31/71 of 10 December 1976, 32/82 of 12 December 1977, 33/64 of 14 December 1978, 34/77 of 11 December 1979, 35/147 of 12 December 1980, 36/87 A and B of 9 December 1981, 37/75 of 9 December 1982, 38/64 of 15 December 1983, 39/54 of 12 December 1984, 40/82 of 12 December 1985, 41/48 of 3 December 1986, 42/28 of 30 November 1987, 43/65 of 7 December 1988, 44/108 of 15 December 1989, 45/52 of 4 December 1990, 46/30 of 6 December 1991, 47/48 of 9 December 1992, 48/71 of 16 December 1993 and 49/71 of 15 December 1994 on the establishment of a nuclear-weapon-free zone in the region of the Middle East,

*Recalling also* the recommendations for the establishment of such a zone in the Middle East consistent with paragraphs 60 to 63, and in particular paragraph 63 *(d)*, of the Final Document of the Tenth Special Session of the General Assembly,

*Emphasizing* the basic provisions of the above-mentioned resolutions, which call upon all parties directly concerned to consider taking the practical and urgent steps required for the implementation of the proposal to establish a nuclear-weapon-free zone in the region of the Middle East and, pending and during the establishment of such a zone, to declare solemnly that they will refrain, on a reciprocal basis, from producing, acquiring or in any other way possessing nuclear weapons and nuclear explosive devices and from permitting the stationing of nuclear weapons on their territory by any third party, to agree to place all their nuclear facilities under International Atomic Energy Agency safeguards and to declare their support for the establishment of the zone and to deposit such declarations with the Security Council for consideration, as appropriate,

*Reaffirming* the inalienable right of all States to acquire and develop nuclear energy for peaceful purposes,

*Emphasizing* the need for appropriate measures on the question of the prohibition of military attacks on nuclear facilities,

*Bearing in mind* the consensus reached by the General Assembly at its thirty-fifth session that the establishment of a nuclear-weapon-free zone in the region of the Middle East would greatly enhance international peace and security,

*Desirous* of building on that consensus so that substantial progress can be made towards establishing a nuclear-weapon-free zone in the region of the Middle East,

*Welcoming* all initiatives leading to general and complete disarmament, including in the region of the Middle East, and in particular on the establishment therein of a zone free of weapons of mass destruction, including nuclear weapons,

*Noting* the peace negotiations in the Middle East, which should be of a comprehensive nature and represent an appropriate framework for the peaceful settlement of contentious issues in the region,

*Recognizing* the importance of credible regional security, including the establishment of a mutually verifiable nuclear-weapon-free zone,

*Emphasizing* the essential role of the United Nations in the establishment of a nuclear-weapon-free zone in the region of the Middle East,

*Having examined* the report of the Secretary-General on the implementation of resolution 49/71,

1. *Urges* all parties directly concerned to consider seriously taking the practical and urgent steps required for the implementation of the proposal to establish a nuclear-

weapon-free zone in the region of the Middle East in accordance with the relevant resolutions of the General Assembly, and, as a means of promoting this objective, invites the countries concerned to adhere to the Treaty on the Non-Proliferation of Nuclear Weapons;

2. *Calls upon* all countries of the region that have not done so, pending the establishment of the zone, to agree to place all their nuclear activities under International Atomic Energy Agency safeguards;

3. *Takes note* of resolution GC(39)/RES/24, adopted on 22 September 1995 by the General Conference of the International Atomic Energy Agency at its thirty-ninth regular session, concerning the application of Agency safeguards in the Middle East;

4. *Notes* the importance of the ongoing bilateral Middle East peace negotiations and the activities of the multilateral working group on arms control and regional security in promoting mutual confidence and security in the Middle East, including the establishment of a nuclear-weapon-free zone;

5. *Invites* all countries of the region, pending the establishment of a nuclear-weapon-free zone in the region of the Middle East, to declare their support for establishing such a zone, consistent with paragraph 63 *(d)* of the Final Document of the Tenth Special Session of the General Assembly, and to deposit those declarations with the Security Council;

6. *Also invites* those countries, pending the establishment of the zone, not to develop, produce, test or otherwise acquire nuclear weapons or permit the stationing on their territories, or territories under their control, of nuclear weapons or nuclear explosive devices;

7. *Invites* the nuclear-weapon States and all other States to render their assistance in the establishment of the zone and at the same time to refrain from any action that runs counter to both the letter and the spirit of the present resolution;

8. *Takes note* of the report of the Secretary-General;

9. *Invites* all parties to consider the appropriate means that may contribute towards the goal of general and complete disarmament and the establishment of a zone free of weapons of mass destruction in the region of the Middle East;

10. *Requests* the Secretary-General to continue to pursue consultations with the States of the region and other concerned States, in accordance with paragraph 7 of resolution 46/30 and taking into account the evolving situation in the region, and to seek from those States their views on the measures outlined in chapters III and IV of the study annexed to his report or other relevant measures, in order to move towards the establishment of a nuclear-weapon-free zone in the region of the Middle East;

11. *Also requests* the Secretary-General to submit to the General Assembly at its fifty-first session a report on the implementation of the present resolution;

12. *Decides* to include in the provisional agenda of its fifty-first session the item entitled ''Establishment of a nuclear-weapon-free zone in the region of the Middle East''.

**General Assembly resolution 50/66**

12 December 1995     Meeting 90     Adopted without vote

Approved by First Committee (A/50/586) without vote, 13 November (meeting 19); 2-nation draft (A/C.1/50/L.10); agenda item 66.
*Sponsors:* Afghanistan, Egypt.
*Meeting numbers.* GA 50th session: 1st Committee 3-11, 15, 19; plenary 90.

## South Asia

As requested by the General Assembly in 1994,[75] the Secretary-General transmitted in July the views of one Member State on the establishment of a nuclear-weapon-free zone in South Asia.[76]

**GENERAL ASSEMBLY ACTION**

On 12 December, the General Assembly adopted **resolution 50/67**.

### Establishment of a nuclear-weapon-free zone in South Asia

*The General Assembly*,

*Recalling* its resolutions 3265 B (XXIX) of 9 December 1974, 3476 B (XXX) of 11 December 1975, 31/73 of 10 December 1976, 32/83 of 12 December 1977, 33/65 of 14 December 1978, 34/78 of 11 December 1979, 35/148 of 12 December 1980, 36/88 of 9 December 1981, 37/76 of 9 December 1982, 38/65 of 15 December 1983, 39/55 of 12 December 1984, 40/83 of 12 December 1985, 41/49 of 3 December 1986, 42/29 of 30 November 1987, 43/66 of 7 December 1988, 44/109 of 15 December 1989, 45/53 of 4 December 1990, 46/31 of 6 December 1991, 47/49 of 9 December 1992, 48/72 of 16 December 1993 and 49/72 of 15 December 1994 concerning the establishment of a nuclear-weapon-free zone in South Asia,

*Reiterating its conviction* that the establishment of nuclear-weapon-free zones in various regions of the world is one of the measures that can contribute effectively to the objectives of non-proliferation of nuclear weapons and general and complete disarmament,

*Believing* that the establishment of a nuclear-weapon-free zone in South Asia, as in other regions, will assist in the strengthening of the security of the States of the region against the use or threat of use of nuclear weapons,

*Taking note with appreciation* of the declarations issued at the highest level by the Governments of South Asian States that are developing their peaceful nuclear programmes, reaffirming their undertaking not to acquire or manufacture nuclear weapons and to devote their nuclear programmes exclusively to the economic and social advancement of their peoples,

*Welcoming* the recent proposal for the conclusion of a bilateral or regional nuclear-test-ban agreement in South Asia,

*Noting* the proposal to convene, under the auspices of the United Nations, a conference on nuclear non-proliferation in South Asia as soon as possible, with the participation of the regional and other concerned States,

*Noting also* the proposal to hold consultations among five nations with a view to ensuring nuclear non-proliferation in the region,

*Considering* that the eventual participation of other States, as appropriate, in this process could be useful,

*Bearing in mind* the provisions of paragraphs 60 to 63 of the Final Document of the Tenth Special Session of the General Assembly regarding the establishment of nuclear-weapon-free zones, including in the region of South Asia,

*Taking note* of the report of the Secretary-General,

1. *Reaffirms its endorsement*, in principle, of the concept of a nuclear-weapon-free zone in South Asia;

2. *Urges once again* the States of South Asia to continue to make all possible efforts to establish a nuclear-weapon-free zone in South Asia and to refrain, in the meantime, from any action contrary to that objective;

3. *Welcomes* the support of all the five nuclear-weapon States for this proposal, and calls upon them to extend the necessary cooperation in the efforts to establish a nuclear-weapon-free zone in South Asia;

4. *Requests* the Secretary-General to communicate with the States of the region and other concerned States in order to ascertain their views on the issue and to promote consultations among them with a view to exploring the best possibilities of furthering the efforts for the establishment of a nuclear-weapon-free zone in South Asia;

5. *Also requests* the Secretary-General to report on the subject to the General Assembly at its fifty-first session;

6. *Decides* to include in the provisional agenda of its fifty-first session the item entitled "Establishment of a nuclear-weapon-free zone in South Asia".

General Assembly resolution 50/67

12 December 1995     Meeting 90     154-3-9 (recorded vote)

Approved by First Committee (A/50/587) by recorded vote (133-3-11), 10 November (meeting 18); 2-nation draft (A/C.1/50/L.6); agenda item 67.
*Sponsors*: Bangladesh, Pakistan.
*Meeting numbers*. GA 50th session: 1st Committee 3-11, 14, 18; plenary 90.

Recorded vote in Assembly as follows:

*In favour*: Afghanistan, Albania, Andorra, Angola, Antigua and Barbuda, Argentina, Armenia, Australia, Austria, Azerbaijan, Bahamas, Bahrain, Bangladesh, Barbados, Belarus, Belgium, Belize, Benin, Bolivia, Bosnia and Herzegovina, Botswana, Brazil, Brunei Darussalam, Bulgaria, Burkina Faso, Burundi, Cambodia, Cameroon, Canada, Cape Verde, Chad, Chile, China, Colombia, Congo, Costa Rica, Côte d'Ivoire, Croatia, Czech Republic, Denmark, Djibouti, Ecuador, Egypt, El Salvador, Equatorial Guinea, Eritrea, Estonia, Ethiopia, Fiji, Finland, France, Gabon, Georgia, Germany, Ghana, Greece, Grenada, Guatemala, Guinea, Guinea-Bissau, Guyana, Haiti, Honduras, Hungary, Iceland, Iran, Ireland, Italy, Jamaica, Japan, Jordan, Kazakstan, Kenya, Kuwait, Kyrgyzstan, Latvia, Lesotho, Libyan Arab Jamahiriya, Liechtenstein, Lithuania, Luxembourg, Malawi, Malaysia, Maldives, Mali, Malta, Marshall Islands, Mauritania, Mexico, Micronesia, Monaco, Mongolia, Morocco, Mozambique, Namibia, Nepal, Netherlands, New Zealand, Nicaragua, Niger, Nigeria, Norway, Oman, Pakistan, Panama, Papua New Guinea, Paraguay, Peru, Philippines, Poland, Portugal, Qatar, Republic of Korea, Republic of Moldova, Romania, Russian Federation, Rwanda, Samoa, Saudi Arabia, Senegal, Sierra Leone, Singapore, Slovakia, Slovenia, Solomon Islands, South Africa, Spain, Sri Lanka, Sudan, Suriname, Swaziland, Sweden, Tajikistan, Thailand, the former Yugoslav Republic of Macedonia, Togo, Trinidad and Tobago, Tunisia, Turkey, Turkmenistan, Uganda, Ukraine, United Arab Emirates, United Kingdom, United Republic of Tanzania, United States, Uruguay, Uzbekistan, Vanuatu, Venezuela, Yemen, Zaire, Zambia, Zimbabwe.

*Against*: Bhutan, India, Mauritius.

*Abstaining*: Algeria, Cuba, Cyprus, Indonesia, Israel, Lao People's Democratic Republic, Madagascar, Myanmar, Viet Nam.

## South-East Asia Treaty

On 15 December, the members of the Association of South-East Asian Nations (ASEAN)—Brunei Darussalam, Indonesia, Malaysia, Philippines, Singapore, Thailand, Viet Nam—together with three neighbouring countries (Cambodia, Lao People's Democratic Republic, Myanmar), signed the South-East Asia Nuclear-Weapon-Free Zone Treaty at the fifth ASEAN Summit, held in Bangkok, Thailand.

The main objectives of the Treaty included the reaffirmation by the 10 signatory States of obligations assumed under NPT, the right to use nuclear energy for peaceful purposes, and the protection of the environment from nuclear waste. The Treaty defined the zone as the area comprising, in addition to the territories of all States parties, their respective continental shelves and exclusive economic zones.

Thailand was designated as the depositary of the Treaty, which was to enter into force upon ratification by seven States parties.

As at the end of 1995, the protocol to the Treaty, addressed to the nuclear-weapon States, was still the subject of negotiations.

### South Pacific

On 20 October, France, the United Kingdom and the United States stated[77] their intention to sign during the first half of 1996 the protocols to the 1985 South Pacific Nuclear Free Zone Treaty (Treaty of Rarotonga).[78] By Protocol 1, the States internationally responsible for territories situated within the zone would undertake to apply the relevant prohibitions of the Treaty to those territories; by Protocol 2, the five nuclear-weapon States would provide security assurances to parties or to territories within the zone; and by Protocol 3, the five would undertake not to carry out nuclear tests in the zone.

(For information on zones of peace, see preceding chapter.)

### Other nuclear and related issues

**Disarmament Commission.** The Commission continued to consider the item "Process of nuclear disarmament in the framework of international peace and security, with the objective of the elimination of nuclear weapons",[79] which it had begun in 1991.[54] It established Working Group I to deal with the item, which held 10 meetings between 15 and 26 May 1995. Despite its efforts, the Working Group was unable to achieve a consensus document on the item.

**Conference on Disarmament.** Concerning nuclear-related issues, the Conference on Disarmament re-established two ad hoc committees, the first on a nuclear test ban and the second on a cut-off in fissile material, but only the Ad Hoc Committee on a Nuclear Test Ban carried out its work.[28] The Committee to deal with a cut-off in fissile material could not proceed until agreement could be reached on the re-establishment of ad hoc committees on negative security assurances, prevention of an arms race in outer space and transparency in armaments, and on the commencement of substantive consideration of nuclear disarmament. As no such agreement was reached, those questions were dealt with only in plenary meetings.

GENERAL ASSEMBLY ACTION

On 12 December, the General Assembly adopted **resolution 50/71 E.**

### Convention on the Prohibition of the Use of Nuclear Weapons

*The General Assembly,*

*Convinced* that the use of nuclear weapons poses the most serious threat to the survival of mankind,

*Convinced also* that a multilateral agreement prohibiting the use or threat of use of nuclear weapons would strengthen international security and contribute to the climate for negotiations leading to the ultimate elimination of nuclear weapons,

*Conscious* that some steps taken by the Russian Federation and the United States of America towards a reduction of their nuclear weapons and the improvement in the international climate can contribute towards the goal of complete elimination of nuclear weapons,

*Recalling* that, in paragraph 58 of the Final Document of the Tenth Special Session of the General Assembly, it is stated that all States should actively participate in efforts to bring about conditions in international relations among States in which a code of peaceful conduct of nations in international affairs could be agreed upon and that would preclude the use or threat of use of nuclear weapons,

*Reaffirming* that any use of nuclear weapons would be a violation of the Charter of the United Nations and a crime against humanity, as declared in its resolutions 1653(XVI) of 24 November 1961, 33/71 B of 14 December 1978, 34/83 G of 11 December 1979, 35/152 D of 12 December 1980 and 36/92 I of 9 December 1981,

*Stressing* that an international convention would be an important step in a phased programme towards the complete elimination of nuclear weapons within a time-bound framework,

*Noting with regret* that the Conference on Disarmament, during its 1995 session, was unable to undertake negotiations on this subject,

1. *Reiterates its request* to the Conference on Disarmament to commence negotiations, in order to reach agreement on an international convention prohibiting the use or threat of use of nuclear weapons under any circumstances, taking as a possible basis the draft Convention on the Prohibition of the Use of Nuclear Weapons annexed to the present resolution;

2. *Requests* the Conference on Disarmament to report to the General Assembly on the results of those negotiations.

### ANNEX
#### Draft Convention on the Prohibition of the Use of Nuclear Weapons

*The States Parties to the present Convention,*

*Alarmed* by the threat to the very survival of mankind posed by the existence of nuclear weapons,

*Convinced* that any use of nuclear weapons constitutes a violation of the Charter of the United Nations and a crime against humanity,

*Convinced also* that the present Convention would be an important step in a phased programme towards the complete elimination of nuclear weapons within a time-bound framework,

*Determined* to continue negotiations for the achievement of this goal,

*Have agreed* as follows:

## Article 1

The States Parties to the present Convention solemnly undertake not to use or threaten to use nuclear weapons under any circumstances.

## Article 2

The present Convention shall be of unlimited duration.

## Article 3

1. The present Convention shall be open to all States for signature. Any State that does not sign the Convention before its entry into force in accordance with paragraph 3 of the present article may accede to it at any time.

2. The present Convention shall be subject to ratification by signatory States. Instruments of ratification or accession shall be deposited with the Secretary-General of the United Nations.

3. The present Convention shall enter into force on the deposit of instruments of ratification by twenty-five Governments, including the Governments of the five nuclear-weapon States, in accordance with paragraph 2 of the present article.

4. For States whose instruments of ratification or accession are deposited after the entry into force of the Convention, it shall enter into force on the date of the deposit of their instruments of ratification or accession.

5. The depositary shall promptly inform all signatory and acceding States of the date of each signature, the date of deposit of each instrument of ratification or accession and the date of entry into force of the present Convention, as well as of the receipt of other notices.

6. The present Convention shall be registered by the depositary in accordance with Article 102 of the Charter of the United Nations.

## Article 4

The present Convention, of which the Arabic, Chinese, English, French, Russian and Spanish texts are equally authentic, shall be deposited with the Secretary-General of the United Nations, who shall send duly certified copies thereof to the Governments of the signatory and acceding States.

IN WITNESS WHEREOF, the undersigned, being duly authorized thereto by their respective Governments, have signed the present Convention, opened for signature at _____ on the _____ day of _____ one thousand nine hundred and _____ .

General Assembly resolution 50/71 E

12 December 1995    Meeting 90    108-27-28 (recorded vote)

Approved by First Committee (A/50/591) by recorded vote (95-26-26), 10 November (meeting 18); 28-nation draft (A/C.1/50/L.47); agenda item 71 *(d)*.

*Meeting numbers.* GA 50th session: 1st Committee 3-11, 16, 18; plenary 90.

Recorded vote in Assembly as follows:

*In favour:* Algeria, Angola, Bahrain, Bangladesh, Belize, Benin, Bhutan, Bolivia, Botswana, Brazil, Brunei Darussalam, Burkina Faso, Burundi, Cambodia, Cameroon, Cape Verde, Chad, Chile, China, Colombia, Congo, Costa Rica, Côte d'Ivoire, Cuba, Cyprus, Democratic People's Republic of Korea, Djibouti, Ecuador, Egypt, El Salvador, Ethiopia, Fiji, Gabon, Ghana, Guatemala, Guinea, Guinea-Bissau, Guyana, Haiti, Honduras, India, Indonesia, Iran, Jamaica, Jordan, Kazakstan, Kenya, Kuwait, Kyrgyzstan, Lao People's Democratic Republic, Lebanon, Lesotho, Libyan Arab Jamahiriya, Madagascar, Malawi, Malaysia, Maldives, Mali, Marshall Islands, Mauritania, Mauritius, Mexico, Micronesia, Mongolia, Morocco, Mozambique, Myanmar, Namibia, Nepal, Nicaragua, Niger, Nigeria, Oman, Pakistan, Panama, Papua New Guinea, Paraguay, Peru, Philippines, Qatar, Rwanda, Samoa, Saudi Arabia, Senegal, Sierra Leone, Singapore, Solo-

mon Islands, South Africa, Sri Lanka, Sudan, Suriname, Swaziland, Syrian Arab Republic, Thailand, Togo, Trinidad and Tobago, Tunisia, Uganda, United Arab Emirates, United Republic of Tanzania, Uruguay, Vanuatu, Venezuela, Viet Nam, Yemen, Zaire, Zambia, Zimbabwe.

*Against:* Andorra, Belgium, Bulgaria, Canada, Czech Republic, Denmark, Finland, France, Germany, Greece, Hungary, Iceland, Italy, Latvia, Lithuania, Luxembourg, Monaco, Netherlands, Norway, Poland, Portugal, Romania, Slovakia, Spain, Turkey, United Kingdom, United States.

*Abstaining:* Afghanistan, Albania, Antigua and Barbuda, Argentina, Armenia, Australia, Austria, Bahamas, Barbados, Belarus, Croatia, Equatorial Guinea, Estonia, Georgia, Ireland, Israel, Japan, Liechtenstein, Malta, New Zealand, Republic of Korea, Republic of Moldova, Russian Federation, Slovenia, Sweden, the former Yugoslav Republic of Macedonia, Ukraine, Uzbekistan.

On the same date, the Assembly adopted **resolution 50/70 E.**

### Prohibition of the dumping of radioactive wastes

*The General Assembly,*

*Bearing in mind* resolutions CM/Res.1153(XLVIII) of 1988 and CM/Res.1225(L) of 1989, adopted by the Council of Ministers of the Organization of African Unity, concerning the dumping of nuclear and industrial wastes in Africa,

*Welcoming* resolution GC(XXXIV)/RES/530 establishing a Code of Practice on the International Transboundary Movement of Radioactive Waste, adopted on 21 September 1990 by the General Conference of the International Atomic Energy Agency at its thirty-fourth regular session,

*Welcoming also* resolution GC(XXXVIII)/RES/6, adopted on 23 September 1994 by the General Conference of the International Atomic Energy Agency at its thirty-eighth regular session, inviting the Board of Governors and the Director General of the Agency to commence preparations for a convention on the safety of radioactive waste management,

*Considering* its resolution 2602 C (XXIV) of 16 December 1969, in which it requested the Conference of the Committee on Disarmament,[a] *inter alia,* to consider effective methods of control against the use of radiological methods of warfare,

*Recalling* resolution CM/Res.1356(LIV) of 1991, adopted by the Council of Ministers of the Organization of African Unity, on the Bamako Convention on the Ban on the Import of Hazardous Wastes into Africa and on the Control of Their Transboundary Movements within Africa,

*Aware* of the potential hazards underlying any use of radioactive wastes that would constitute radiological warfare and its implications for regional and international security, in particular for the security of developing countries,

*Recalling* its resolutions 43/75 Q of 7 December 1988, 44/116 R of 15 December 1989, 45/58 K of 4 December 1990, 46/36 K of 6 December 1991, 47/52 D of 9 December 1992, 48/75 D of 16 December 1993 and 49/75 A of 15 December 1994,

*Desirous* of promoting the implementation of paragraph 76 of the Final Document of the Tenth Special Session of the General Assembly, the first special session devoted to disarmament,

1. *Takes note* of the part of the report of the Conference on Disarmament relating to a future convention on the prohibition of radiological weapons;

---

[a] Redesignated the Conference on Disarmament as from 7 February 1984.

2. *Expresses grave concern* regarding any use of nuclear wastes that would constitute radiological warfare and have grave implications for the national security of all States;

3. *Calls upon* all States to take appropriate measures with a view to preventing any dumping of nuclear or radioactive wastes that would infringe upon the sovereignty of States;

4. *Requests* the Conference on Disarmament to take into account, in the negotiations for a convention on the prohibition of radiological weapons, radioactive wastes as part of the scope of such a convention;

5. *Also requests* the Conference on Disarmament to intensify efforts towards an early conclusion of such a convention and to include in its report to the General Assembly at its fifty-first session the progress recorded in the negotiations on this subject;

6. *Takes note* of resolution CM/Res.1356(LIV) of 1991, adopted by the Council of Ministers of the Organization of African Unity, on the Bamako Convention on the Ban on the Import of Hazardous Wastes into Africa and on the Control of Their Transboundary Movements within Africa;

7. *Expresses the hope* that the effective implementation of the International Atomic Energy Agency Code of Practice on the International Transboundary Movement of Radioactive Waste will enhance the protection of all States from the dumping of radioactive wastes on their territories;

8. *Welcomes* current efforts of the International Atomic Energy Agency in the preparation of a draft convention on the safe management of radioactive waste;

9. *Decides* to include in the provisional agenda of its fifty-first session the item entitled "Prohibition of the dumping of radioactive wastes".

General Assembly resolution 50/70 E

12 December 1995     Meeting 90     Adopted without vote

Approved by First Committee (A/50/590) without vote, 10 November (meeting 18); draft by South Africa, for African Group (A/C.1/50/L.22); agenda item 70 *(c)*.
*Meeting numbers.* GA 50th session: 1st Committee 3-11, 16, 18; plenary 90.

On the same date, the General Assembly adopted **decision 50/420**.

### Non-proliferation of weapons of mass destruction and of vehicles for their delivery in all its aspects

At its 90th plenary meeting, on 12 December 1995, the General Assembly, on the recommendation of the First Committee, recalling its decision 49/427 of 15 December 1994, decided to include in the provisional agenda of its fifty-first session the item entitled "Non-profileration of weapons of mass destruction and of vehicles for their delivery in all its aspects".

General Assembly decision 50/420

114-1-49 (recorded vote)

Approved by First Committee (A/50/590) by recorded vote (102-1-45), 10 November (meeting 18); draft by Mexico (A/C.1/50/L.2); agenda item 70.
*Meeting numbers.* GA 50th session: 1st Committee 3-11, 15, 18; plenary 90.

Recorded vote in Assembly as follows:

*In favour:* Afghanistan, Algeria, Angola, Antigua and Barbuda, Australia, Bahamas, Bahrain, Bangladesh, Barbados, Belize, Benin, Bhutan, Bolivia, Botswana, Brazil, Brunei Darussalam, Burkina Faso, Burundi, Cambodia, Cameroon, Cape Verde, Chad, Chile, China, Colombia, Congo, Costa Rica, Côte d'Ivoire, Cuba, Cyprus, Democratic People's Republic of Korea, Djibouti, Ecuador, Egypt, El Salvador, Eritrea, Ethiopia, Fiji, Gabon, Ghana, Guatemala, Guinea, Guinea-Bissau, Guyana, Haiti, Honduras, India,

Indonesia, Iran, Jamaica, Jordan, Kazakstan, Kenya, Kuwait, Kyrgyzstan, Lao People's Democratic Republic, Lebanon, Lesotho, Libyan Arab Jamahiriya, Madagascar, Malawi, Malaysia, Maldives, Marshall Islands, Mauritania, Mauritius, Mexico, Micronesia, Mongolia, Morocco, Mozambique, Myanmar, Namibia, Nepal, New Zealand, Nicaragua, Niger, Nigeria, Oman, Pakistan, Panama, Papua New Guinea, Paraguay, Peru, Philippines, Qatar, Rwanda, Samoa, Saudi Arabia, Senegal, Sierra Leone, Singapore, Solomon Islands, South Africa, Sri Lanka, Sudan, Suriname, Swaziland, Syrian Arab Republic, Thailand, Togo, Trinidad and Tobago, Tunisia, Uganda, United Arab Emirates, United Republic of Tanzania, Uruguay, Vanuatu, Venezuela, Viet Nam, Yemen, Zaire, Zambia, Zimbabwe.

*Against:* United States.

*Abstaining:* Albania, Andorra, Argentina, Armenia, Austria, Azerbaijan, Belarus, Belgium, Bosnia and Herzegovina, Bulgaria, Canada, Croatia, Czech Republic, Denmark, Equatorial Guinea, Estonia, Finland, France, Georgia, Germany, Greece, Hungary, Iceland, Ireland, Israel, Italy, Japan, Latvia, Liechtenstein, Lithuania, Luxembourg, Malta, Monaco, Netherlands, Norway, Poland, Portugal, Republic of Korea, Republic of Moldova, Romania, Russian Federation, Slovakia, Slovenia, Spain, Sweden, the former Yugoslav Republic of Macedonia, Turkey, Ukraine, United Kingdom.

## Other weapons of mass destruction

### Chemical weapons

The Convention on the Prohibition of the Development, Production, Stockpiling and Use of Chemical Weapons and on Their Destruction, adopted by the Conference on Disarmament in 1992[80] and opened for signature in 1993,[81] had 160 signatories by the end of 1995.[2] Forty-seven States had ratified the Convention, which required 65 ratifications to enter into force.

Concerning the work of the Preparatory Commission for the future Organization for the Prohibition of Chemical Weapons (OPCW), set up in 1992 to prepare for the Convention's implementation,[80] little progress was made in resolving outstanding issues. In the area of verification-related activities—the keystone of the treaty—it was possible only to adopt the draft OPCW confidentiality policy and to agree on technical specifications for inspection equipment. Other issues still showed no sign of early resolution, among them: technical issues related to declarations in the chemical industry and chemical weapons facilities; detailed procedures related to verification of old and abandoned chemical weapons; the timing of harmonizing national export control legislation with the provisions of article XI, on economic and technological development; the ultimate scope of the analytical database; and technical aspects of challenge inspection.

The Provisional Technical Secretariat made progress in selecting inspectors who were to be recruited and trained before the Convention entered into force. The Secretariat currently employed 116 staff members, representing 45 nationalities. At year's end, the Secretariat stated that it considered late 1996 or early 1997 as a possible time-frame for the Convention's entry into force.

Issues under discussion at the end of the year included preparation for the first Conference of States Parties; the transition between the Preparatory Commission and OPCW; and the status of OPCW regarding the United Nations system.

## Bacteriological (biological) weapons

Efforts continued towards strengthening the 1972 Convention on the Prohibition of the Development, Production and Stockpiling of Bacteriological (Biological) and Toxin Weapons and on Their Destruction,[82] through the Ad Hoc Group of the States Parties to the Convention, established in 1994[83] to consider measures, including verification measures, and draft proposals to strengthen the Convention, for inclusion in a legally binding instrument.

The Ad Hoc Group held three sessions in 1995 (4-6 January; 10-21 July; 27 November–8 December), all in Geneva.[84]

In January, the Group adopted its agenda and rules of procedure and elected its officers. It decided that for each session a report of a procedural nature would be prepared, to which the results of the Group's deliberations would be annexed on the understanding that they would not prejudice the positions of delegations and would not imply agreement on scope or content. Following an exchange of views at the second session, the Friends of the Chair circulated informal papers that were annexed to the Group's report and formed the basis for the discussions at the third session. At that session, the Group decided to hold two more sessions in 1996, from 15 to 26 July and from 16 to 27 September, and the Chairman appointed Friends of the Chair to assist in consultations and negotiations concerning measures related to article X (transfer of technology); measures to promote compliance; confidence-building and transparency measures; and definitions of terms and objective criteria.

### Fourth Review Conference (1996)

At the request of the States parties, a Fourth Review Conference of the Parties to the Convention, which entered into force on 26 March 1975, was scheduled to be held in Geneva from 25 November to 13 December 1996. A Preparatory Committee was formed, open to all parties, which planned to meet in Geneva from 9 to 12 April 1996. Previous review conferences were held in 1980,[85] 1986[86] and 1991.[87]

GENERAL ASSEMBLY ACTION

On 12 December, the General Assembly adopted **resolution 50/79**.

**Convention on the Prohibition of the Development, Production and Stockpiling of Bacteriological (Biological) and Toxin Weapons and on Their Destruction**

*The General Assembly,*

*Recalling* its previous resolutions relating to the complete and effective prohibition of bacteriological (biological) and toxin weapons and to their destruction,

*Noting with satisfaction* that there are more than one hundred and thirty States parties to the Convention on the Prohibition of the Development, Production and Stockpiling of Bacteriological (Biological) and Toxin Weapons and on Their Destruction, including all the permanent members of the Security Council,

*Bearing in mind* its call upon all States parties to the Convention to participate in the implementation of the recommendations of the Third Review Conference of the Parties to the Convention on the Prohibition of the Development, Production and Stockpiling of Bacteriological (Biological) and Toxin Weapons and on Their Destruction, including the exchange of information and data agreed to in the Final Declaration of the Third Review Conference, and to provide such information and data in conformity with standardized procedure to the Secretary-General on an annual basis and no later than 15 April,

*Recalling* its resolution 46/35 A, adopted without a vote on 6 December 1991, in which it welcomed, *inter alia*, the establishment, proceeding from the recommendations of the Third Review Conference, of an ad hoc group of governmental experts open to all States parties to identify and examine potential verification measures from a scientific and technical standpoint,

*Recalling also* its resolution 48/65, adopted without a vote on 16 December 1993, in which it commended the final report of the Ad Hoc Group of Governmental Experts to Identify and Examine Potential Verification Measures from a Scientific and Technical Standpoint, agreed to by consensus at the last meeting of the Ad Hoc Group at Geneva on 24 September 1993,

*Recalling further* its resolution 49/86, adopted without a vote on 15 December 1994, in which it welcomed the final report of the Special Conference of the States Parties to the Convention on the Prohibition of the Development, Production and Stockpiling of Bacteriological (Biological) and Toxin Weapons and on Their Destruction, adopted by consensus on 30 September 1994, in which the States parties agreed to establish an ad hoc group, open to all States parties, whose objective should be to consider appropriate measures, including possible verification measures, and draft proposals to strengthen the Convention, to be included, as appropriate, in a legally binding instrument to be submitted for the consideration of the States parties,

*Recalling* the provisions of the Convention related to scientific and technological cooperation and the related provisions of the Final Document of the Third Review Conference, the final report of the Ad Hoc Group of Governmental Experts and the final report of the Special Conference of the States Parties to the Convention, held from 19 to 30 September 1994,

1. *Welcomes* the information and data provided to date, and reiterates its call upon all States parties to the Convention on the Prohibition of the Development, Production and Stockpiling of Bacteriological (Biological) and Toxin Weapons and on Their Destruction to participate in the exchange of information and data agreed to in the Final Declaration of the Third Review Conference of the Parties to the Convention;

2. *Also welcomes* the work begun by the Ad Hoc Group in pursuing the mandate established by the Special Conference of the States Parties to the Convention on 30 September 1994 and urges the Ad Hoc Group, in ac-

cordance with its mandate, to complete its work as soon as possible and submit its report, which shall be adopted by consensus, to the States parties to be considered at the Fourth Review Conference or later at a Special Conference;

3. *Requests* the Secretary-General to continue to render the necessary assistance to the depository Governments of the Convention and to provide such services as may be required for the implementation of the decisions and recommendations of the Third Review Conference, as well as the decisions contained in the final report of the Special Conference, including all necessary assistance to the Ad Hoc Group;

4. *Notes* that, at the request of the States parties, a Fourth Review Conference of the Parties to the Convention will be held at Geneva from 25 November to 13 December 1996, that, following appropriate consultations, a Preparatory Committee for that Conference has been formed, open to all parties to the Convention, and that the Committee will meet at Geneva from 9 to 12 April 1996;

5. *Requests* the Secretary-General to render the necessary assistance and to provide such services as may be required for the Fourth Review Conference and its preparations;

6. *Calls upon* all signatory States that have not yet ratified the Convention to do so without delay, and also calls upon those States that have not signed the Convention to become parties thereto at an early date, thus contributing to the achievement of universal adherence to the Convention;

7. *Decides* to include in the provisional agenda of its fifty-first session the item entitled "Convention on the Prohibition of the Development, Production and Stockpiling of Bacteriological (Biological) and Toxin Weapons and on Their Destruction".

General Assembly resolution 50/79

12 December 1995　　Meeting 90　　Adopted without vote

Approved by First Committee (A/50/600 & Corr.1) without vote, 15 November (meeting 22); 55-nation draft (A/C.1/50/L.1/Rev.1); agenda item 80.
*Financial implications.* S-G, A/C.1/50/L.59.
*Meeting numbers.* GA 50th session: 1st Committee 3-11, 22; plenary 90.

*REFERENCES*

[1]YUN 1968, p. 17, GA res. 2373(XXII), annex, 12 June 1968. [2]*The United Nations Disarmament Yearbook*, vol. 20, *1995*, Sales No. E.96.IX.1. [3]NPT/CONF.1995/32 & Corr.1. [4]YUN 1975, p. 27. [5]YUN 1980, p. 51. [6]YUN 1985, p. 56. [7]NPT/CONF.IV/45/I. [8]NPT/CONF.1995/1. [9]YUN 1993, p. 110. [10]YUN 1994, p. 136. [11]YUN 1992, p. 67. [12]YUN 1994, p. 137, GA res. 49/75 F, 15 Dec. 1994. [13]A/50/115 & Add.1. [14]GC(39)/RES/DEC/(1995) (GC(39)/RES/17). [15]YUN 1994, p. 137. [16]Ibid., GA res. 49/78, 15 Dec. 1994. [17]A/50/513. [18]NPT/CONF.1995/6. [19]A/50/155-S/1995/265. [20]A/50/154-S/1995/264. [21]A/50/151-S/1995/261. [22]A/50/152-S/1995/262. [23]A/50/153-S/1995/263. [24]YUN 1968, p. 22, SC res. 255(1968), 19 June 1968. [25]A/50/86. [26]A/50/161-S/1995/317. [27]A/50/134-S/1995/298. [28]A/50/27. [29]CD/1308. [30]CD/1312. [31]YUN 1994, p. 140. [32]*Status of Multilateral Arms Regulation and Disarmament Agreements*, 4th edition: 1992, vol. 1, Sales No. E.93.IX.11. [33]YUN 1994, p. 142. [34]CD/1346 & Add.1. [35]CD/1296. [36]CD/1341. [37]CD/1372. [38]YUN 1986, p. 48, GA res. 41/59 N, 3 Dec. 1986. [39]YUN 1987, p. 54, GA res. 42/38 C, 30 Nov. 1987. [40]A/50/261. [41]A/50/210. [42]A/50/362. [43]A/50/392. [44]A/50/430. [45]A/50/415. [46]A/50/224 & A/50/225. [47]A/50/258. [48]A/50/445, A/C.1/50/6 & A/50/768-S/1995/969. [49]A/50/273 & A/50/431. [50]A/50/524. [51]A/50/223. [52]A/50/470. [53]A/50/317-S/1995/627. [54]YUN 1991, p. 34. [55]YUN 1992, p. 79. [56]YUN 1994, p. 145. [57]A/50/205-S/1995/435. [58]A/50/206-S/1995/439. [59]YUN 1993, p. 117. [60]YUN 1972, p. 5. [61]CD/1327. [62]S/1995/599. [63]S/1995/600. [64]YUN 1994, p. 150, GA res. 49/138, 19 Dec. 1994. [65]A/50/426. [66]YUN 1991, p. 43. [67]YUN 1992, p. 88. [68]YUN 1993, p. 119. [69]YUN 1994, p. 150. [70]A/50/647. [71]YUN 1994, p. 152, GA res. 49/71, 15 Dec. 1994. [72]A/50/325 & Add.1. [73]A/45/435. [74]S/1995/873. [75]YUN 1994, p. 153, GA res. 49/72, 15 Dec. 1994. [76]A/50/299. [77]A/50/665-S/1995/877. [78]YUN 1985, p. 58. [79]A/50/42. [80]YUN 1992, p. 65. [81]YUN 1993, p. 111. [82]YUN 1971, p. 19, GA res. 2826(XXVI), annex, 16 Dec. 1971. [83]YUN 1994, p. 139. [84]BWC/AD HOC GROUP/3, BWC/AD HOC GROUP/28 & BWC/AD HOC GROUP/29. [85]YUN 1980, p. 70. [86]YUN 1986, p. 64. [87]YUN 1991, p. 52.

# Conventional weapons and related issues

## Transparency, confidence-building and the arms register

In his 1995 report on the work of the Organization,[1] the Secretary-General stressed that transparency measures, such as the UN Register of Conventional Arms, established pursuant to a 1991 General Assembly request,[2] must be strengthened, and confidence-building and disarmament initiatives at the regional level should be developed further.

**Conference on Disarmament.** Despite general agreement that the item on transparency in armaments was an important matter for the Conference on Disarmament to consider in 1995,[3] divergent views persisted as to what subjects the item should cover and whether to continue deliberations within the same framework as in 1994.[4] Consequently, there was no consensus on the re-establishment of the Ad Hoc Committee on Transparency in Armaments during the 1995 session of the Conference. Moreover, the question of its re-establishment became linked to the re-establishment of other Conference committees.

### UN Register of Conventional Arms

**Reports of the Secretary-General.** In a July report with a later addendum,[5] the Secretary-General transmitted the views of six Governments and of France on behalf of EU on the continuing operation of the Register, as requested by the General Assembly in 1994.[6]

Also pursuant to a 1994 Assembly request,[6] the Secretary-General submitted in an October report, with later addenda,[7] information provided by 93 Member States for the calendar year 1994 on imports and exports of conventional arms in the seven categories (battle tanks, armoured combat vehicles, large-calibre artillery systems, combat aircraft, attack helicopters, warships, missiles and missile launchers) covered under the Register and/or background information on their military holdings, procurement through national production, legislation and policies. Of those States, 41 provided data on imports and 22 on exports, and 33 gave background information (24 reported on military holdings and 17 on procurement through national production). The level of consistency between exports and imports reported for the categories of large-calibre artillery systems, attack helicopters or warships remained very high in 1994. Greater discrepancies appeared to exist in the categories of armoured combat vehicles and missiles and missile launchers. Non-participation of one side in the reporting of a transaction—because of national security concerns, difficulties in compiling national statistics, legal obstacles, and conflicting interpretations of what constituted a transfer or of the definitions of the categories—were factors that could account for the mismatches or discrepancies, it was stated.

The Secretary-General's Advisory Board on Disarmament Matters (New York, 19-23 June) recommended that States currently participating in the Register should encourage others to do so through a partnership approach, and should offer to assist them in the political and technical aspects of reporting. The Secretary-General commended that suggestion.[8]

Not all importers participated in the Register. The number of transfers reported on export forms was 155, and the number of transfers reported on import forms was 116. Most import transactions were none the less reflected in the submissions by major exporters. In 1994, 20 States that were identified by exporting States as recipients of arms covered by the Register, as compared to 22 in 1993 and 28 in 1992, either did not report on those imports or did not participate in the information exchange.

Participation among regions continued to vary widely but fairly consistently. The submissions for 1994 again revealed high participation by Western European nations and a continuing rise in participation by States in Asia and Latin America and the Caribbean. Participation by countries of Africa and the Middle East was still low.

**GENERAL ASSEMBLY ACTION**

On 12 December, the General Assembly adopted **resolution 50/70 D**.

### Transparency in armaments

*The General Assembly,*

*Recalling* its resolutions 46/36 L of 9 December 1991, 47/52 L of 15 December 1992, 48/75 E of 16 December 1993 and 49/75 C of 15 December 1994,

*Continuing to take the view* that an enhanced level of transparency in armaments contributes greatly to confidence-building and security among States and that the estab-

lishment of the United Nations Register of Conventional Arms constitutes an important step forward in the promotion of transparency in military matters,

*Welcoming* the consolidated report of the Secretary-General on the Register, which includes the returns of Member States for 1994,

*Welcoming also* the response of Member States to the requests contained in paragraphs 9 and 10 of resolution 46/36 L to provide data on their imports and exports of arms, as well as available background information regarding their military holdings, procurement through national production and relevant policies,

*Stressing* that the continuing operation of the Register and its further development should be reviewed in order to secure a Register that is capable of attracting the widest possible participation,

1. *Reaffirms its determination* to ensure the effective operation of the United Nations Register of Conventional Arms as provided for in paragraphs 7, 8, 9 and 10 of resolution 46/36 L;

2. *Calls upon* Member States to provide the requested data and information for the Register, on the basis of resolutions 46/36 L and 47/52 L and the annex and appendices to the report of the Secretary-General on the continuing operation of the Register and its further development, to the Secretary-General by 30 April annually;

3. *Reaffirms* its decision, with a view to further development of the Register, to keep the scope of and participation in the Register under review, and, to that end:

*(a)* Recalls its request to Member States to provide the Secretary-General with their views on the continuing operation of the Register and its further development and on transparency measures related to weapons of mass destruction;

*(b)* Recalls its request to the Secretary-General, with the assistance of a group of governmental experts to be convened in 1997, on the basis of equitable geographical representation, to prepare a report on the continuing operation of the Register and its further development, taking into account the work of the Conference on Disarmament, the views expressed by Member States and the report of the Secretary-General on the continuing operation of the Register and its further development, with a view to a decision at its fifty-second session;

4. *Requests* the Secretary-General to ensure that sufficient resources are made available for the Secretariat to operate and maintain the Register;

5. *Invites* the Conference on Disarmament to consider continuing its work undertaken in the field of transparency in armaments;

6. *Reiterates its call upon* all Member States to cooperate at the regional and subregional levels, taking fully into account the specific conditions prevailing in the region or subregion, with a view to enhancing and coordinating international efforts aimed at increased openness and transparency in armaments;

7. *Also requests* the Secretary-General to report to the General Assembly at its fifty-first session on the progress made in implementing the present resolution;

8. *Decides* to include in the provisional agenda of its fifty-first session the item entitled ''Transparency in armaments''.

General Assembly resolution 50/70 D

12 December 1995　　Meeting 90　　149-0-15 (recorded vote)

Approved by First Committee (A/50/590) by recorded vote (137-0-15), 15 November (meeting 22); 83-nation draft (A/C.1/50/L.18); agenda item 70 (e).

*Meeting numbers.* GA 50th session: 1st Committee 3-11, 14, 22; plenary 90.

Recorded vote in Assembly as follows:

*In favour:* Afghanistan, Albania, Andorra, Angola, Antigua and Barbuda, Argentina, Armenia, Australia, Austria, Azerbaijan, Bahamas, Bahrain, Bangladesh, Barbados, Belarus, Belgium, Belize, Benin, Bhutan, Bolivia, Bosnia and Herzegovina, Botswana, Brazil, Brunei Darussalam, Bulgaria, Burkina Faso, Burundi, Cambodia, Cameroon, Canada, Cape Verde, Chad, Chile, China, Colombia, Congo, Costa Rica, Côte d'Ivoire, Croatia, Cyprus, Czech Republic, Denmark, Ecuador, El Salvador, Equatorial Guinea, Eritrea, Estonia, Ethiopia, Fiji, Finland, France, Gabon, Georgia, Germany, Ghana, Greece, Guatemala, Guinea, Guinea-Bissau, Guyana, Haiti, Honduras, Hungary, Iceland, Ireland, Israel, Italy, Jamaica, Japan, Jordan, Kazakstan, Kenya, Kuwait, Kyrgyzstan, Latvia, Lesotho, Liechtenstein, Lithuania, Luxembourg, Madagascar, Malawi, Malaysia, Maldives, Mali, Malta, Marshall Islands, Mauritania, Mauritius, Micronesia, Monaco, Mongolia, Morocco, Mozambique, Namibia, Nepal, Netherlands, New Zealand, Nicaragua, Niger, Nigeria, Norway, Oman, Pakistan, Panama, Papua New Guinea, Paraguay, Peru, Philippines, Poland, Portugal, Qatar, Republic of Korea, Republic of Moldova, Romania, Russian Federation, Rwanda, Samoa, Senegal, Sierra Leone, Singapore, Slovakia, Slovenia, Solomon Islands, South Africa, Spain, Suriname, Swaziland, Sweden, Tajikistan, Thailand, the former Yugoslav Republic of Macedonia, Togo, Trinidad and Tobago, Tunisia, Turkey, Turkmenistan, Uganda, Ukraine, United Arab Emirates, United Kingdom, United Republic of Tanzania, United States, Uruguay, Vanuatu, Venezuela, Yemen, Zaire, Zambia, Zimbabwe.

*Against:* None.

*Abstaining:* Algeria, Cuba, Democratic People's Republic of Korea, Egypt, India, Indonesia, Iran, Lebanon, Libyan Arab Jamahiriya, Mexico, Myanmar, Saudi Arabia, Sri Lanka, Sudan, Syrian Arab Republic.

In the First Committee, paragraphs 3 (*b*) and 5 were adopted by recorded votes of 133 to none, with 12 abstentions, and 133 to none, with 15 abstentions, respectively.

The Assembly retained the paragraphs by recorded votes of 142 to none, with 13 abstentions, and 143 to none, with 17 abstentions, respectively.

### Transparency of military budgets

In a July report with later addenda,[9] the Secretary-General presented information received from 35 Member States on their military expenditures, as requested by the General Assembly in 1985.[10]

On 12 December, the Assembly, by **decision 50/419**, took note of the report[11] of the First Committee on the reduction of military budgets.

### Regional approaches to disarmament

Throughout 1995, Member States continued to make determined efforts, within their respective regional contexts, to devise and strengthen appropriate approaches to prevent nuclear proliferation, to curb the flow of light arms, to introduce and promote confidence-building and transparency measures, and to adjust security structures to respond effectively to threats to the peace and to resolve conflict, increasingly of an intra-State nature. The United Nations was involved in many of those endeavours.

### Regional developments

#### Africa

In 1995, Africa achieved a long-sought objective, which was the conclusion of a nuclear-weapon-free zone treaty for the continent (see above, under "Nuclear-weapon-free zones", for Treaty of Pelindaba). Regarding conventional weapons, disarmament efforts focused on the regulation of the flow of small arms, especially on measures to curb illicit trade, and arrangements to facilitate the restoration of peace in societies torn by conflict. On 1 September, the UN Standing Advisory Committee on Security Questions in Central Africa (Brazzaville, Congo, 20-24 March and 28 August-1 September)[12] issued the Brazzaville Declaration on Cooperation for Peace and Security in Central Africa, which noted, among other things, that the proliferation of arms, including among civilians, was the main factor in the violence and insecurity prevailing in the subregion. The members of the Committee were Angola, Burundi, Cameroon, the Central African Republic, Chad, the Congo, Equatorial Guinea, Gabon, Rwanda, Sao Tome and Principe, and Zaire.

The Advisory Mission on the Control and Collection of Light Weapons in the Sahelo-Saharan Subregion visited six countries (Burkina Faso, Chad, Côte d'Ivoire, Mauritania, Niger, Senegal) in February and March, concluding that the subregion as a whole was suffering from severe socio-economic deprivation and intra-State conflict, aggravated by and contributing to the presence of large numbers of illicit light weapons. The Mission recommended that the United Nations work with the States and the donor community to develop support for a proportional and integrated approach to security and development, including identification of appropriate assistance for internal security forces. Practical measures of disarmament, including demobilization, were recognized as being crucial to furthering the peace processes in Angola, Liberia, Rwanda and Sierra Leone (see PART TWO, Chapter II).

#### Latin America and the Caribbean

Regional efforts to promote peace and security in Latin America and the Caribbean continued. Following the outbreak in January of a border conflict between Ecuador and Peru, the parties agreed to establish a demilitarized zone in the area of dispute. During the Regional Conference on Confidence- and Security-building Measures in the Region (Santiago, Chile, November),[13] Ecuador and Peru jointly announced the adoption of a declaration on confidence-building measures. The Conference also adopted a declaration[14] outlining specific measures for the Latin American and Caribbean region, including prior notification of military exercises; exchange of information and participation in the UN Arms Register; exchange of military observers; strengthening of civilian-military communications; and consultations to enhance the limitation and control of conventional weapons. On 15 December, the Governments of Costa Rica, El Salvador, Guatemala, Honduras, Nicaragua and Panama signed the Framework Treaty on Democratic Security in Central America, which included provisions for the establishment of confidence-building measures and cooperation in combating the illegal trafficking of arms and other military equipment.[15] (See also PART TWO, Chapter III.)

### Asia and the Pacific

On 20 October, France, the United Kingdom and the United States announced their intention to sign during the first half of 1996 the protocols of the 1985 South Pacific Nuclear Free Zone Treaty.[16]

On 15 December, in Bangkok, the South-East Asia Nuclear-Weapon-Free Zone Treaty was signed. Although none of the world's declared nuclear Powers had endorsed the Treaty as of the end of the year, the creation of the zone reflected a concerted effort by countries of the subregion to promote and strengthen regional security through nuclear non-proliferation. The 19-member ASEAN Regional Forum (ARF), composed of Asian, European and North American countries (Brunei Darussalam, 31 July–3 August), agreed that the ARF process would take place in three stages: the promotion of confidence-building measures; the development of preventive diplomacy; and the elaboration of approaches to conflict resolution. They also agreed to further institutionalize the process through the establishment of inter-sessional support groups. On the bilateral side, Australia and Indonesia signed a security agreement on 18 December. Both sides stressed, however, that the agreement was not a defence treaty or alliance; instead, it called for broad cooperation in areas such as joint military exercises and regular consultations on common security-related issues.

### Europe

During the year, there were major steps in arms control and disarmament in Europe. The dismantlement and destruction of the nuclear weapons of the Russian Federation and the United States, mandated by START I, continued. In addition, because they did not have warhead dismantlement facilities, Belarus, Kazakstan and Ukraine transferred to the Russian Federation the weapons deployed on their territories that were scheduled for dismantlement under the Treaty. The parties to the 1990 Treaty on Conventional Armed Forces in Europe (CFE)[17] completed the destruction of

more than 50,000 tanks and other heavy weapons. However, some problems persisted after the 16 November deadline for full implementation had passed. As at the end of the year, agreement had yet to be reached on the level of equipment that the Russian Federation would maintain in the Treaty's flank areas (the flank includes the area around St. Petersburg in the north and the Caucasus Mountains region in the south). A CFE review conference was scheduled to be convened in May 1996.

**GENERAL ASSEMBLY ACTION**

On 12 December, the General Assembly adopted **resolution 50/70 K**.

#### Regional disarmament

*The General Assembly,*

*Recalling* its resolutions 45/58 P of 4 December 1990, 46/36 I of 6 December 1991, 47/52 J of 9 December 1992, 48/75 I of 16 December 1993 and 49/75 N of 15 December 1994 on regional disarmament,

*Believing* that the efforts of the international community to move towards the ideal of general and complete disarmament are guided by the inherent human desire for genuine peace and security, the elimination of the danger of war and the release of economic, intellectual and other resources for peaceful pursuits,

*Affirming* the abiding commitment of all States to the purposes and principles enshrined in the Charter of the United Nations in the conduct of their international relations,

*Noting* that essential guidelines for progress towards general and complete disarmament were adopted at the tenth special session of the General Assembly, the first special session devoted to disarmament,

*Taking note* of the guidelines and recommendations for regional approaches to disarmament within the context of global security adopted by the Disarmament Commission at its 1993 substantive session,

*Welcoming* the prospects of genuine progress in the field of disarmament engendered in recent years as a result of negotiations between the two super-Powers,

*Taking note* of the recent proposals for disarmament and nuclear non-proliferation at the regional and subregional levels,

*Recognizing* the importance of confidence-building measures for regional and international peace and security,

*Convinced* that endeavours by countries to promote regional disarmament, taking into account the specific characteristics of each region and in accordance with the principle of undiminished security at the lowest level of armaments, would enhance the security of smaller States and would thus contribute to international peace and security by reducing the risk of regional conflicts,

1. *Stresses* that sustained efforts are needed, within the framework of the Conference on Disarmament and under the umbrella of the United Nations, to make progress on the entire range of disarmament issues;

2. *Affirms* that global and regional approaches to disarmament complement each other and should therefore be pursued simultaneously to promote regional and international peace and security;

3. *Calls upon* States to conclude agreements, wherever possible, for nuclear non-proliferation, disarmament and confidence-building measures at the regional and subregional levels;

4. *Welcomes* the initiatives towards disarmament, nuclear non-proliferation and security undertaken by some countries at the regional and subregional levels;

5. *Supports and encourages* efforts aimed at promoting confidence-building measures at the regional and subregional levels in order to ease regional tensions and to further disarmament and nuclear non-proliferation measures at the regional and subregional levels;

6. *Decides* to include in the provisional agenda of its fifty-first session the item entitled "Regional disarmament".

General Assembly resolution 50/70 K

12 December 1995     Meeting 90     165-0-1 (recorded vote)

Approved by First Committee (A/50/590) by recorded vote (156-0-1), 15 November (meeting 22); 35-nation draft (A/C.1/50/L.38); agenda item 70 *(j)*.

*Meeting numbers.* GA 50th session: 1st Committee 3-11, 16, 22; plenary 90.

Recorded vote in Assembly as follows:

*In favour:* Afghanistan, Albania, Algeria, Andorra, Angola, Antigua and Barbuda, Argentina, Armenia, Australia, Austria, Azerbaijan, Bahamas, Bahrain, Bangladesh, Barbados, Belarus, Belgium, Belize, Benin, Bhutan, Bolivia, Bosnia and Herzegovina, Botswana, Brazil, Brunei Darussalam, Bulgaria, Burkina Faso, Burundi, Cambodia, Cameroon, Canada, Cape Verde, Chad, Chile, China, Colombia, Congo, Costa Rica, Côte d'Ivoire, Croatia, Cuba, Cyprus, Czech Republic, Democratic People's Republic of Korea, Denmark, Djibouti, Ecuador, Egypt, El Salvador, Equatorial Guinea, Eritrea, Estonia, Ethiopia, Fiji, Finland, France, Gabon, Georgia, Germany, Ghana, Greece, Guatemala, Guinea, Guinea-Bissau, Guyana, Haiti, Honduras, Hungary, Iceland, Iran, Ireland, Israel, Italy, Jamaica, Japan, Jordan, Kazakstan, Kenya, Kuwait, Kyrgyzstan, Lao People's Democratic Republic, Latvia, Lebanon, Lesotho, Libyan Arab Jamahiriya, Liechtenstein, Lithuania, Luxembourg, Madagascar, Malawi, Malaysia, Maldives, Mali, Malta, Marshall Islands, Mauritania, Mauritius, Mexico, Micronesia, Monaco, Mongolia, Morocco, Mozambique, Myanmar, Namibia, Nepal, Netherlands, New Zealand, Nicaragua, Niger, Nigeria, Norway, Oman, Pakistan, Panama, Papua New Guinea, Paraguay, Peru, Philippines, Poland, Portugal, Qatar, Republic of Korea, Republic of Moldova, Romania, Russian Federation, Rwanda, Samoa, Saudi Arabia, Senegal, Sierra Leone, Singapore, Slovakia, Slovenia, Solomon Islands, South Africa, Spain, Sri Lanka, Sudan, Suriname, Swaziland, Sweden, Syrian Arab Republic, Tajikistan, Thailand, the former Yugoslav Republic of Macedonia, Togo, Trinidad and Tobago, Tunisia, Turkey, Uganda, Ukraine, United Arab Emirates, United Kingdom, United Republic of Tanzania, United States, Uruguay, Vanuatu, Venezuela, Viet Nam, Yemen, Zaire, Zambia, Zimbabwe.

*Against:* None.

*Abstaining:* India.

Also on 12 December, the Assembly adopted **resolution 50/70 L**.

### Conventional arms control at the regional and subregional levels

*The General Assembly,*

*Recalling* its resolutions 48/75 J of 16 December 1993 and 49/75 O of 15 December 1994,

*Recognizing* the crucial role of conventional arms control in promoting regional and international peace and security,

*Convinced* that conventional arms control needs to be pursued primarily in the regional and subregional contexts since most threats to peace and security in the post-cold-war era arise mainly among States located in the same region or subregion,

*Aware* that the preservation of a balance in the defence capabilities of States at the lowest level of armaments would contribute to peace and stability and should be a prime objective of conventional arms control,

*Desirous* of promoting agreements to strengthen regional peace and security at the lowest possible level of armaments and military forces,

*Believing* that militarily significant States, and States with larger military capabilities, have a special responsibility in promoting such agreements for regional security,

*Believing also* that two of the principal objectives of conventional arms control should be to prevent the possibility of military attack launched by surprise and to avoid aggression,

1. *Decides* to give urgent consideration to the issues involved in conventional arms control at the regional and subregional levels;

2. *Requests* the Conference on Disarmament, as a first step, to consider the formulation of principles that can serve as a framework for regional agreements on conventional arms control, and looks forward to a report of the Conference on this subject;

3. *Decides* to include in the provisional agenda of its fifty-first session the item entitled "Conventional arms control at the regional and subregional levels".

General Assembly resolution 50/70 L

12 December 1995     Meeting 90     158-0-7 (recorded vote)

Approved by First Committee (A/50/590) by recorded vote (150-0-7), 15 November (meeting 22); 8-nation draft (A/C.1/50/L.40); agenda item 70 *(k)*.

*Sponsors:* Bangladesh, Benin, Czech Republic, Djibouti, Haiti, Nepal, Pakistan, the former Yugoslav Republic of Macedonia.

*Meeting numbers.* GA 50th session: 1st Committee 3-11, 16, 22; plenary 90.

Recorded vote in Assembly as follows:

*In favour:* Afghanistan, Albania, Algeria, Andorra, Angola, Antigua and Barbuda, Argentina, Armenia, Australia, Austria, Azerbaijan, Bahamas, Bahrain, Bangladesh, Barbados, Belarus, Belgium, Belize, Benin, Bhutan, Bolivia, Bosnia and Herzegovina, Botswana, Brunei Darussalam, Bulgaria, Burkina Faso, Burundi, Cambodia, Cameroon, Canada, Cape Verde, Chad, Chile, China, Colombia, Congo, Costa Rica, Côte d'Ivoire, Croatia, Cyprus, Czech Republic, Democratic People's Republic of Korea, Denmark, Djibouti, Ecuador, Egypt, El Salvador, Equatorial Guinea, Eritrea, Estonia, Ethiopia, Fiji, Finland, France, Gabon, Georgia, Germany, Ghana, Greece, Guatemala, Guinea, Guinea-Bissau, Guyana, Haiti, Honduras, Hungary, Iceland, Indonesia, Iran, Ireland, Israel, Italy, Jamaica, Japan, Jordan, Kazakstan, Kenya, Kuwait, Lao People's Democratic Republic, Latvia, Lebanon, Lesotho, Liechtenstein, Lithuania, Luxembourg, Madagascar, Malawi, Malaysia, Maldives, Mali, Malta, Marshall Islands, Mauritania, Mauritius, Micronesia, Monaco, Mongolia, Morocco, Mozambique, Myanmar, Namibia, Nepal, Netherlands, New Zealand, Nicaragua, Niger, Norway, Oman, Pakistan, Panama, Papua New Guinea, Paraguay, Peru, Philippines, Poland, Portugal, Qatar, Republic of Korea, Republic of Moldova, Romania, Russian Federation, Rwanda, Samoa, Saudi Arabia, Senegal, Sierra Leone, Singapore, Slovakia, Slovenia, Solomon Islands, South Africa, Spain, Sri Lanka, Sudan, Suriname, Swaziland, Sweden, Syrian Arab Republic, Tajikistan, Thailand, the former Yugoslav Republic of Macedonia, Togo, Trinidad and Tobago, Tunisia, Turkey, Turkmenistan, Uganda, Ukraine, United Arab Emirates, United Kingdom, United Republic of Tanzania, United States, Uruguay, Vanuatu, Yemen, Zaire, Zambia, Zimbabwe.

*Against:* None.

*Abstaining:* Brazil, Cuba, India, Libya Arab Jamahiriya, Mexico, Nigeria, Venezuela.

On the same date, the General Assembly adopted **resolution 50/71 B**.

### Regional confidence-building measures

*The General Assembly,*

*Recalling* the purposes and principles of the United Nations and its primary responsibility for the maintenance of international peace and security in accordance with the Charter of the United Nations,

*Bearing in mind* the guidelines for general and complete disarmament adopted at its tenth special session, the first special session devoted to disarmament,

*Recalling* its resolutions 43/78 H and 43/85 of 7 December 1988, 44/21 of 15 November 1989, 45/58 M of 4 December 1990, 46/37 B of 6 December 1991, 47/53 F of 15 December 1992, 48/76 A of 16 December 1993 and 49/76 C of 15 December 1994,

*Considering* the importance and effectiveness of confidence-building measures taken at the initiative and with the participation of all States concerned and taking into account the specific characteristics of each region, in that they can contribute to regional disarmament and to international security, in accordance with the principles of the Charter,

*Convinced* that the resources released by disarmament, including regional disarmament, can be devoted to economic and social development and to the protection of the environment for the benefit of all peoples, in particular those of the developing countries,

*Bearing in mind* the establishment by the Secretary-General on 28 May 1992 of the Standing Advisory Committee on Security Questions in Central Africa, the purpose of which is to encourage arms limitation, disarmament, non-proliferation and development in the subregion,

1. *Takes note* of the report of the Secretary-General on regional confidence-building measures, which deals with the sixth and seventh meetings of the Standing Advisory Committee on Security Questions in Central Africa, held at Brazzaville in March and August 1995;

2. *Reaffirms its support* for efforts aimed at promoting confidence-building measures at regional and subregional levels in order to ease tensions and conflicts in the subregion and to further disarmament, non-proliferation and the peaceful settlement of disputes in Central Africa;

3. *Also reaffirms its support* for the programme of work of the Standing Advisory Committee adopted at the organizational meeting of the Committee held at Yaoundé in July 1992;

4. *Takes note* of the Brazzaville Declaration on Cooperation for Peace and Security in Central Africa and urges the States members of the Standing Advisory Committee to implement it promptly;

5. *Notes* the readiness of the States members of the Standing Advisory Committee to reduce the military forces, equipment and budgets in the subregion and to continue reviewing the studies carried out on the subject with a view to reaching agreements to that end;

6. *Welcomes* the initialling of the Non-Aggression Pact between the States members of the Standing Advisory Committee, which is likely to contribute to the prevention of conflicts and to confidence-building in the subregion, and encourages those States to sign the Pact as soon as possible;

7. *Welcomes with satisfaction* the decision by the States members of the Standing Advisory Committee to participate in peace operations of the United Nations and the Organization of African Unity and, to that end, to establish units specializing in peace operations within their respective armed forces;

8. *Also welcomes with satisfaction* the participation of some of the States members of the Standing Advisory Committee in the peace operations deployed in the subregion;

9. *Requests* Member States and governmental and non-governmental organizations to promote and to facilitate the holding of a training programme on peace operations in the subregion with a view to strengthening the capacity of the units specializing in peace operations in the armed forces of the States members of the Standing Advisory Committee;

10. *Requests* the Secretary-General to continue to provide assistance to the States members of the Standing Advisory Committee and to establish a trust fund to which Member States and governmental and non-governmental organizations may make additional voluntary contributions for the implementation of the programme of work of the Committee;

11. *Also requests* the Secretary-General to submit to the General Assembly at its fifty-first session a report on the implementation of the present resolution;

12. *Decides* to include in the provisional agenda of its fifty-first session the item entitled "Regional confidence-building measures".

General Assembly resolution 50/71 B

12 December 1995     Meeting 90     Adopted without vote

Approved by First Committee (A/50/591) without vote, 20 November (meeting 28); draft by Cape Verde and Congo, for Standing Advisory Committee on Security Questions in Central Africa (A/C.1/50/L.20/Rev.1); agenda item 71 *(b)*.
*Financial implications.* S-G, A/C.1/50/L.61.
*Meeting numbers.* GA 50th session: 1st Committee 3-11, 16, 28; plenary 90.

## Conventional weapons and advanced technologies

### Micro-disarmament

In his "Supplement to an Agenda for Peace",[18] issued in January, the Secretary-General used the term micro-disarmament to describe disarmament in the context of weapons used in conflicts on an everyday basis. In subsequent statements, however, he cast micro-disarmament in operational terms, as action to control and reduce the massive production, transfer and stockpiling of light weapons around the world. In the area of post-conflict peace-building, the Secretary-General had drawn the attention of Member States to the land-mines crisis and had often referred to the issue in the context of micro-disarmament.

### Small and light arms

Also in the "Supplement to an Agenda for Peace", the Secretary-General described two categories of light arms: small arms, which he stated were probably responsible for most of the deaths in current conflicts; and anti-personnel mines, a problem which the international community had begun to address. He noted that it would take a long time to find effective solutions.

**GENERAL ASSEMBLY ACTION**

On 12 December, the General Assembly adopted **resolution 50/70 B**.

#### Small arms

*The General Assembly,*

*Reaffirming* the role of the United Nations in the field of disarmament and the commitment of Member

States to take concrete steps in order to strengthen that role,

*Realizing* the urgent need to resolve underlying conflicts, to diminish tensions and to accelerate efforts towards general and complete disarmament under strict and effective international control with a view to maintaining regional and international peace and security in a world free from the scourge of war and the burden of armaments,

*Reaffirming* the inherent right to individual or collective self-defence recognized in Article 51 of the Charter of the United Nations, which implies that States also have the right to acquire arms with which to defend themselves,

*Reaffirming also* the right of self-determination of all peoples, in particular peoples under colonial or other forms of alien domination or foreign occupation, and the importance of the effective realization of this right, as enunciated, *inter alia*, in the Vienna Declaration and Programme of Action, adopted by the World Conference on Human Rights on 25 June 1993,

*Realizing* that arms obtained through the illicit arms trade are most likely to be used for violent purposes and that even small arms when so obtained, directly or indirectly, by terrorist groups, drug traffickers or underground organizations can pose a danger to regional and international security, and certainly to the security and political stability of the countries affected,

*Taking note* of the report of the Secretary-General to the Security Council entitled "Supplement to an Agenda for Peace", which stressed the urgent need for "practical disarmament in the context of the conflicts the United Nations is actually dealing with and of the weapons, most of them light weapons, that are actually killing people in the hundreds of thousands", and which identified light weapons as including, *inter alia*, small arms and anti-personnel land-mines,

*Recalling* its resolution 49/75 G of 15 December 1994, in which it welcomed the initiative taken by Mali concerning the question of the illicit circulation of small arms and their collection in the affected States of the Saharo-Sahelian subregion, as well as the action taken by the Secretary-General in implementation of this initiative,

*Noting* the work of the Disarmament Commission on international arms transfers,

1. *Requests* the Secretary-General, within the existing resources, to prepare a report, with the assistance of a panel group of qualified governmental experts to be nominated by him on the basis of equitable geographical representation, on:

   *(a)* The types of small arms and light weapons actually being used in conflicts being dealt with by the United Nations;

   *(b)* The nature and causes of the excessive and destabilizing accumulation and transfer of small arms and light weapons, including their illicit production and trade;

   *(c)* The ways and means to prevent and reduce the excessive and destabilizing accumulation and transfer of small arms and light weapons, in particular as they cause or exacerbate conflict;

with particular attention to the role of the United Nations in this field and to the complementary role of regional organizations, and taking into account views and proposals of Member States and all other relevant information, for submission to the General Assembly at its fifty-second session;

2. *Also requests* the Secretary-General to seek the views and proposals of Member States on the matters mentioned in paragraph 1 above, to collect all other relevant information and to make them available for consideration by the panel of governmental experts referred to in paragraph 1 above;

3. *Decides* to include in the provisional agenda of its fifty-second session an item entitled "Small arms".

**General Assembly resolution 50/70 B**

12 December 1995      Meeting 90      140-0-19 (recorded vote)

Approved by First Committee (A/50/590) by recorded vote (134-0-16), 20 November (meeting 28); 20-nation draft (A/C.1/50/L.7), orally amended by Colombia; agenda item 70.
*Financial implications.* S-G, A/C.1/50/L.60.
*Meeting numbers.* GA 50th session: 1st Committee 3-11, 16, 27, 28; plenary 90.

Recorded vote in Assembly as follows:

*In favour:* Afghanistan, Albania, Algeria, Andorra, Angola, Argentina, Armenia, Australia, Austria, Bahamas, Bangladesh, Barbados, Belarus, Belgium, Belize, Benin, Bhutan, Bolivia, Botswana, Brazil, Brunei Darussalam, Bulgaria, Burkina Faso, Burundi, Cambodia, Cameroon, Canada, Cape Verde, Chad, Chile, Colombia, Congo, Costa Rica, Côte d'Ivoire, Croatia, Cyprus, Czech Republic, Denmark, Ecuador, El Salvador, Equatorial Guinea, Eritrea, Estonia, Ethiopia, Finland, France, Gabon, Georgia, Germany, Ghana, Greece, Guatemala, Guinea, Guinea-Bissau, Guyana, Haiti, Honduras, Hungary, Iceland, Indonesia,* Iran, Ireland, Italy, Jamaica, Japan, Jordan, Kazakstan, Kenya, Kuwait, Lao People's Democratic Republic, Latvia, Lebanon,† Lesotho, Libyan Arab Jamahiriya, Liechtenstein, Luxembourg, Madagascar, Malawi, Malaysia, Maldives, Mali, Malta, Marshall Islands, Mauritania, Mauritius, Mexico, Micronesia, Monaco, Mongolia, Morocco, Mozambique, Myanmar, Namibia, Nepal, Netherlands, New Zealand, Nicaragua, Niger, Norway, Panama, Papua New Guinea, Paraguay, Peru, Philippines, Poland, Portugal, Republic of Korea, Republic of Moldova, Romania, Rwanda, Senegal, Singapore, Slovakia, Slovenia, Solomon Islands, South Africa, Spain, Sri Lanka, Suriname, Swaziland, Sweden, Tajikistan, Thailand, the former Yugoslav Republic of Macedonia, Togo, Trinidad and Tobago, Tunisia, Turkey, Uganda, Ukraine, United Kingdom, United Republic of Tanzania, United States, Uruguay, Vanuatu, Venezuela, Yemen, Zaire, Zambia, Zimbabwe.

*Against:* None.

*Abstaining:* Azerbaijan,‡ Bahrain, Cuba, Democratic People's Republic of Korea, Djibouti, Egypt, Fiji, India, Israel, Lithuania,‡ Nigeria, Oman, Pakistan, Qatar, Russian Federation, Samoa, Saudi Arabia, Sudan, United Arab Emirates.

*Later advised the Secretariat it had intended to abstain.
†Later advised the Secretariat it had intended not to participate.
‡Later advised the Secretariat it had intended to vote in favour.

### International arms transfers

**Disarmament Commission.** In May,[19] the Disarmament Commission again considered the item "International arms transfers, with particular reference to General Assembly resolution 46/36 H of 6 December 1991".[20] It first discussed the item in 1994.[21] By resolution 46/36 H, the Assembly had called on all States to give high priority to eradicating illicit trade in all kinds of weapons and military equipment.

Working Group II, established to deal with the item, agreed that the guidelines to be elaborated, while pertaining to the broad subject area of international arms transfers, would focus on the illicit arms trade, as had resolution 46/36 H. The Group Chairman proposed a structure for the guidelines, and the Group decided to use a paper submitted by him as a basis for its work. In the course of deliberations, many delegations put forward views and proposals, which were taken into account in revisions of the working paper. Annexed to the report of the Disarmament Commission[19] was the latest revision of the working paper as a basis for future work, without prejudice to the position of any delegation.

**Reports of the Secretary-General.** In response to a 1994 General Assembly request,[22] the Secretary-General in September described action taken or planned regarding assistance to States for curbing the illicit traffic in small arms and collecting them.[23] He stated that in February an advisory mission had been sent to the Saharo-Sahelian region at the request of States in the region. He was studying a report on that mission and it was expected that its conclusions and recommendations would result in practical steps to alleviate the problem of illicit trafficking. The Ninth United Nations Congress on the Prevention of Crime and the Treatment of Offenders adopted a resolution on trafficking in firearms, and the Commission on Crime Prevention and Criminal Justice made recommendations to the Economic and Social Council to improve international efforts to promote regulation of the trade in firearms (see PART FOUR, Chapter IX). No reports had been received from individual States on action they had taken to implement national control measures to check the illicit circulation of small arms. As to future action, the Secretary-General stated that he was encouraged by the increasing recognition of the serious problems caused by illegal arms trafficking. He urged States to increase their momentum of effort to take practical steps to deal with the problem.

Pursuant to a 1994 Assembly request,[24] the Secretary-General, in September, presented the replies of six Governments regarding measures they had taken to curb the illicit transfer and use of conventional arms.[25] He noted that as at 10 September no request had been received from concerned Member States to study the possibilities of the collection of weapons illicitly transferred in the light of the experience gained by the United Nations and the views expressed by Member States.

**GENERAL ASSEMBLY ACTION**

On 12 December, the General Assembly adopted **resolution 50/70 J**.

### Measures to curb the illicit transfer and use of conventional arms

*The General Assembly,*

*Recalling* its resolution 46/36 H of 6 December 1991 and its decision 47/419 of 9 December 1992 on international arms transfers,

*Recalling also* its resolutions 48/75 F and H of 16 December 1993 and 49/75 M of 15 December 1994 on measures to curb the illicit transfer and use of conventional arms,

*Recognizing* that the availability of massive quantities of conventional weapons and especially their illicit transfer, often associated with destabilizing activities, are most disturbing and dangerous phenomena, in particular for the internal situation of affected States and the violation of human rights,

*Bearing in mind* that in certain situations mercenaries, terrorists and child soldiers are supplied with weapons acquired from illicit transfers of conventional arms,

*Convinced* that peace and security are inextricably interlinked with and in some cases imperative for economic development and reconstruction, including in war-stricken countries,

*Realizing* the urgent need to resolve conflicts and to diminish tension, and to accelerate efforts towards general and complete disarmament with a view to maintaining regional and international peace and security,

*Recognizing* the curbing of the illicit transfer of arms as an important contribution to the relaxation of tension and peaceful reconciliation processes,

*Stressing* the need for effective national control measures on the transfer of conventional weapons,

*Convinced* that effective measures to curb the illicit transfer and use of conventional arms will help enhance regional and international peace, security and economic development,

1. *Invites* Member States:

(*a*) To take appropriate and effective enforcement measures to seek to ensure that illicit transfers of arms are immediately discontinued;

(*b*) To provide the Secretary-General promptly with relevant information on national control measures on arms transfers with a view to preventing illicit arms transfers;

2. *Requests* the Disarmament Commission:

(*a*) To expedite its consideration of the agenda item on international arms transfers, with special emphasis on the adverse consequences of the illicit transfer of arms and ammunition;

(*b*) To study and report on measures to curb the illicit transfer and use of conventional arms, bearing in mind concrete problems in various regions of the world;

3. *Requests* the Secretary-General:

(*a*) To seek the views of Member States on effective ways and means of collecting weapons transferred illicitly, in particular in the light of experience gained by the United Nations;

(*b*) To seek the views of Member States on concrete proposals concerning measures at the national, regional and international levels to curb the illicit transfer and use of conventional arms;

(*c*) To submit to the General Assembly at its fifty-first session a report containing the views expressed by Member States;

4. *Also requests* the Secretary-General to report to the General Assembly at its fifty-first session on the effective implementation of the present resolution;

5. *Decides* to include in the provisional agenda of its fifty-first session the item entitled "Measures to curb the illicit transfer and use of conventional arms".

General Assembly resolution 50/70 J

12 December 1995     Meeting 90     Adopted without vote

Approved by First Committee (A/50/590) without vote, 15 November (meeting 21); 18-nation draft (A/C.1/50/L.37/Rev.1); agenda item 70 *(i)*.
*Meeting numbers.* GA 50th session: 1st Committee 3-11, 16, 21; plenary 90.

On the same date, the General Assembly adopted **resolution 50/70 H**.

### Assistance to States for curbing the illicit traffic in small arms and collecting them

*The General Assembly,*

*Recalling* its resolutions 46/36 H of 6 December 1991, 47/52 G and J of 9 December 1992, 48/75 H and J of 16 December 1993 and 49/75 G of 15 December 1994,

*Considering* that the circulation of massive quantities of small arms throughout the world impedes development and is a source of increased insecurity,

*Considering also* that the illicit international transfer of small arms and their accumulation in many countries constitute a threat to the populations and to national and regional security and are a factor contributing to the destabilization of States,

*Basing itself* on the statement of the Secretary-General relating to the request of Mali concerning United Nations assistance for the collection of small arms,

*Gravely concerned* at the extent of the insecurity and banditry linked to the illicit circulation of small arms in Mali and the other affected States of the Saharo-Sahelian subregion,

*Taking note* of the first conclusions of the United Nations advisory missions sent to the affected countries of the subregion by the Secretary-General to study the best way of curbing the illicit circulation of small arms and ensuring their collection,

*Taking note also* of the interest shown by other States of the subregion in receiving the United Nations Advisory Mission,

*Noting* the actions taken and those recommended at the meetings of the States of the subregion held at Banjul, Algiers and Bamako to establish close regional cooperation with a view to strengthening security,

1. *Welcomes* the initiative taken by Mali concerning the question of the illicit circulation of small arms and their collection in the affected States of the Saharo-Sahelian subregion;

2. *Also welcomes* the action taken by the Secretary-General in implementation of this initiative in the context of General Assembly resolution 40/151 H of 16 December 1985;

3. *Thanks* the Governments concerned in the subregion for the substantial support that they have given to the United Nations advisory missions and welcomes the declared readiness of other States to receive the United Nations Advisory Mission;

4. *Encourages* the Secretary-General to continue his efforts in the context of the implementation of resolution 49/75 G and of the recommendations of the United Nations advisory missions, to curb the illicit circulation of small arms and to collect such arms in the affected States that so request, with the support of the United Nations Regional Centre for Peace and Disarmament in Africa and in close cooperation with the Organization of African Unity;

5. *Invites* Member States to implement national control measures in order to check the illicit circulation of small arms, in particular by curbing the illegal export of such arms;

6. *Invites* the international community to give appropriate support to the efforts made by the affected countries to suppress the illicit circulation of small arms, which is likely to hamper their development;

7. *Requests* the Secretary-General to continue to examine the issue and to report to the General Assembly at its fifty-first session.

General Assembly resolution 50/70 H

12 December 1995     Meeting 90     Adopted without vote

Approved by First Committee (A/50/590) without vote, 17 November (meeting 26); 24-nation draft (A/C.1/50/L.29/Rev.2); agenda item 70 *(i)*.
Meeting numbers. GA 50th session: 1st Committee 3-11, 15, 26; plenary 90.

## Convention on excessively injurious conventional weapons and its Protocol

### Status of the Convention

Pursuant to a 1994 General Assembly request,[26] the Secretary-General submitted in August a report[27] concerning actions in respect of the 1980 Convention on Prohibitions or Restrictions on the Use of Certain Conventional Weapons Which May Be Deemed to Be Excessively Injurious or to Have Indiscriminate Effects[28] and its three Protocols (dealing with non-detectable fragments; mines, booby traps and other devices; and incendiary weapons) between 1 September 1994 and 30 June 1995.

As at 31 December 1995, 57 States were parties to the Convention.[29] During the year, Argentina, Belgium, Brazil, Ireland, Israel, Italy, Jordan, Malta, Romania, South Africa, Togo, Uganda, the United Kingdom and the United States became parties to the Convention and its Protocols, which had entered into force in 1983.[30]

### Review Conference

The Group of Governmental Experts to Prepare the Review Conference of the States Parties to the Convention, at its fourth and final session (Geneva, 9-20 January),[31] continued to concentrate on the preparation of amendments to Protocol II on the basis of the revised rolling text submitted by the Chairman in 1994.[32]

Agreement was reached in principle for provisions on certain prohibitions and restrictions on the use of anti-personnel mines that were not self-destructing or did not comply with the Protocol's provisions on detectability. But the proposal to ban the use, development, manufacture, stockpiling and transfer of all anti-personnel mines without self-destructing or self-deactivating mechanisms and all booby traps was not supported by a majority of delegations. Although three different proposals were put forward on all aspects of a possible verification system, fact-finding missions and measures of compliance, there was no consensus.

With respect to the scope of application of the Protocol, it seemed possible to reach agreement to extend it to all armed conflicts, including conflicts not of an international character, and two alternative provisions were proposed.

The Group elaborated an integrated draft text of the amendments to Protocol II, which was eventually contained in the Chairman's rolling text annexed to the final report of the Group.[31] It also dealt with other proposals relating to the Convention, among them, wording for a protocol on blinding weapons. As a result of extensive consultations, agreement was reached to transmit to the Review Conference a draft protocol on the subject. In addition, the Group considered how to pursue further discussions on naval mines and small-calibre weapon systems. As to organizational matters, the Group decided that the Conference would be held in Vienna from 25 September to 13 October and approved a draft provisional agenda.

The Review Conference met with 44 States parties in attendance.[33] Also participating as observers were representatives of the UN Children's Fund, the UN Department of Humanitarian Affairs, the UN Development Programme, the UN High Commissioner for Refugees, the European Community, the League of Arab States, the International Committee of the Red Cross, the International Federation of Red Cross and Red Crescent Societies and the Sovereign Order of Malta. In addition, a number of NGOs attended public meetings of the Conference and its Main Committees. The main task of the Review Conference was to prepare amendments to Protocol II. As it was not possible to bridge the wide divergence of views in the time allotted, it was decided that resumed sessions of the Conference would take place in 1996, with the 1995 session constituting the first phase.

The Conference established three Main Committees: Main Committee I, to review the scope and operation of the Convention and its Protocols, consider proposals relating to the Convention, and prepare a final declaration for the Conference; Main Committee II, to consider proposals relating to the Protocols; and Main Committee III, to consider proposals for additional protocols. A Drafting Committee and a Credentials Committee were also established.

In the general exchange of views on Protocol II, delegations discussed the extension of the scope of application to non-international armed conflicts; measures to strengthen restrictions or prohibitions on mines and their export; provision for technical assistance; and verification. There was wide agreement that the scope of application of the Protocol should be extended to domestic armed conflicts.

All States parties were in favour of strengthening the prohibitions and restrictions on anti-personnel mines to some degree, particularly the aspect of export, but expressed a range of views with regard to the extent.

Discussions continued concerning the criteria for detectability and for self-destructing mecha-nisms and the modalities for their implementation, which the Group of Governmental Experts had agreed in principle should be provided for in the amended Protocol.

An overwhelming majority of parties supported the proposed ban on blinding laser weapons, to be incorporated into the Convention as Protocol IV.

As to the work of the Committees, Main Committee I discussed a proposal for eliminating the "waiting period" for States to become full parties. It also considered amending the Convention to provide for a structured process of periodic review conferences. Its task of preparing a final declaration for the Conference depended to a considerable degree on the conclusion of the work of Main Committee II, charged with preparing amendments to Protocol II. Main Committee II did not, however, complete its work as planned.

To assist itself in preparing amendments to Protocol II, Main Committee II established a Technical Military Experts Group to deal with proposals for article 2, on definitions, and proposals for specifications of the Technical Annex. In the course of its deliberations and negotiations, the Committee considered a large number of proposals. Divergent views of parties persisted, however, on various issues, in particular on criteria for detectability and for self-destructing and self-deactivating mechanisms, and a transitional period for achieving compliance with such technical requirements; a verification system and compliance mechanism; and arrangements for technical cooperation and assistance in mine clearance. As for the scope of application, no consensus could be reached on the exact wording of article 1, although there was agreement in principle on the substance. In the end, the Committee was unable to reach consensus on an amended text.

Main Committee III concentrated on the question of blinding laser weapons. On 6 October, it adopted by consensus its report, which contained a draft text entitled "Protocol on Blinding Laser Weapons (Protocol IV)".[34] During the deliberations, proposals were made and views expressed on various aspects: the scope of application, the prohibition itself (use, production, stockpiling and transfer), compliance and other pertinent issues such as the definition of "permanent blindness". The Committee did not elaborate extensively on the scope of application, but decided to leave the issue, referred to in article 1 of its draft protocol, to be decided by the Drafting Committee, pending agreement on the text on scope being negotiated in Main Committee II with respect to Protocol II. In view of the fact that production and stockpiling would entail questions of verification and compliance, the Committee finally decided to include only the prohibition of use and transfer. Also, as a result of intensive consultations among delegations as well as with the World Health Organization, the Committee adopted a compromise definition of the term ''permanent blindness'', referred to in article 5 of its draft. The report of Main Committee III was subsequently transmitted through the Conference to the Drafting Committee for its consideration. The Drafting Committee decided to delete article 1 and to maintain the remaining articles as provisions of the new Protocol IV.

At its final meeting, on 13 October, the Review Conference adopted by consensus the text of the Protocol on Blinding Laser Weapons and the interim report on the organization and work of the first phase of the Conference.[35] It decided to continue its work at resumed sessions, to be held in Geneva from 15 to 19 January and from 22 April to 3 May 1996.

**GENERAL ASSEMBLY ACTION**

On 12 December, the General Assembly adopted **resolution 50/74**.

**Convention on Prohibitions or Restrictions on the Use of Certain Conventional Weapons Which May Be Deemed to Be Excessively Injurious or to Have Indiscriminate Effects**

*The General Assembly,*

*Recalling* its resolution 49/79 of 15 December 1994 and previous resolutions referring to the Convention on Prohibitions or Restrictions on the Use of Certain Conventional Weapons Which May Be Deemed to Be Excessively Injurious or to Have Indiscriminate Effects,

*Recalling with satisfaction* the adoption, on 10 October 1980, of the Convention, together with the Protocol on Non-Detectable Fragments (Protocol I), the Protocol on Prohibitions or Restrictions on the Use of Mines, Booby Traps and Other Devices (Protocol II) and the Protocol on Prohibitions or Restrictions on the Use of Incendiary Weapons (Protocol III), which entered into force on 2 December 1983,

*Recalling* the commitment by the States that are parties to the Convention and the Protocols annexed thereto to respect the objectives and the provisions thereof,

*Reaffirming its conviction* that a general and verifiable agreement on prohibitions or restrictions on the use of certain conventional weapons would significantly reduce the suffering of civilians and combatants,

*Noting* that, in conformity with article 8 of the Convention, conferences may be convened to examine amendments to the Convention or to any of the Protocols thereto, to examine additional protocols concerning other categories of conventional weapons not covered by the existing Protocols or to review the scope and application of the Convention and the Protocols annexed thereto and to examine any proposed amendments or additional protocols,

*Noting with satisfaction* that the group of governmental experts established to prepare a conference to review the Convention and the Protocols annexed thereto held

four meetings and completed its work by submitting a final report,

*Welcoming* the fact that the Review Conference of the States Parties to the Convention on Prohibitions or Restrictions on the Use of Certain Conventional Weapons Which May Be Deemed to Be Excessively Injurious or to Have Indiscriminate Effects met at Vienna from 25 September to 13 October 1995, in accordance with article 8, paragraph 3, of the Convention, and that, in addition to the States parties, forty other States attended and took an active part in the Conference,

*Particularly welcoming* the adoption on 13 October 1995 of the Protocol on Blinding Laser Weapons (Protocol IV) annexed to the Convention,

*Noting* that the Review Conference was not able to complete its work in reviewing the Protocol on Prohibitions or Restrictions on the Use of Mines, Booby Traps and Other Devices (Protocol II), and the decision of the Conference therefore to continue its work,

*Recalling* the role played by the International Committee of the Red Cross in the elaboration of the Convention and the Protocols annexed thereto,

*Noting with satisfaction* the convening by the Secretary-General of the International Meeting on Mine Clearance at Geneva from 5 to 7 July 1995, and that substantial contributions to the Voluntary Trust Fund for Assistance in Mine Clearance were pledged at the Review Conference,

*Welcoming* the national measures adopted by Member States relating to the transfer, the production or the reduction of existing stockpiles of anti-personnel land-mines,

*Desirous* of reinforcing international cooperation in the area of prohibitions or restrictions on the use of certain conventional weapons, in particular for the removal of minefields, mines and booby traps,

*Recalling* in this respect its resolutions 48/7 of 19 October 1993 and 49/215 of 23 December 1994 on assistance in mine clearance,

1. *Registers its satisfaction* with the report of the Secretary-General;

2. *Welcomes* the fact that additional States have ratified or accepted the Convention on Prohibitions or Restrictions on the Use of Certain Conventional Weapons Which May Be Deemed to Be Excessively Injurious or to Have Indiscriminate Effects, which was opened for signature in New York on 10 April 1981, or have acceded to the Convention;

3. *Urgently calls upon* all States that have not yet done so to take all measures to become parties, as soon as possible, to the Convention and its Protocols and upon successor States to take appropriate measures so that ultimately access to these instruments will be universal;

4. *Calls upon* the Secretary-General, in his capacity as depositary of the Convention and the Protocols annexed thereto, to continue to inform it periodically of accessions to the Convention and the Protocols;

5. *Takes note* of the interim report of the Review Conference of the States Parties to the Convention on Prohibitions or Restrictions on the Use of Certain Conventional Weapons Which May Be Deemed to Be Excessively Injurious or to Have Indiscriminate Effects, held at Vienna from 25 September to 13 October 1995;

6. *Commends* the Protocol on Blinding Laser Weapons (Protocol IV) to all States, with a view to achieving the

widest possible adherence to this instrument at an early date;

7. *Calls upon* the States parties to intensify their efforts in order to conclude negotiations on a strengthened Protocol II;

8. *Also takes note* of the decision of the Review Conference to continue its work at resumed sessions at Geneva from 15 to 19 January and 22 April to 3 May 1996;

9. *Requests* the Secretary-General to continue furnishing needed assistance to the Review Conference;

10. *Again calls upon* the maximum number of States to attend the Review Conference;

11. *Decides* to include in the provisional agenda of its fifty-first session the item entitled "Convention on Prohibitions or Restrictions on the Use of Certain Conventional Weapons Which May Be Deemed to Be Excessively Injurious or to Have Indiscriminate Effects".

General Assembly resolution 50/74

12 December 1995     Meeting 90     Adopted without vote

Approved by First Committee (A/50/594) without vote, 16 November (meeting 23); 49-nation draft (A/C.1/50/L.34); agenda item 74.
*Meeting numbers.* GA 50th session: 1st Committee 3-11, 16, 23; plenary 90.

### Land-mines

As requested by the General Assembly in 1994,[36] the Secretary-General submitted a September report[37] covering the activities of the United Nations on assistance in mine clearance over the past year and on the operation of the Voluntary Trust Fund for Assistance in Mine Clearance. He noted that, in response to the Assembly's call in 1994,[36] the International Meeting on Mine Clearance had been convened (Geneva, 5-7 July 1995). Ninety-seven Governments, 11 intergovernmental organizations, 16 UN bodies and 31 NGOs participated in the Meeting, which aimed at enhancing international awareness of the different dimensions of the land-mine problem, seeking further political and financial support for UN activities and promoting greater international cooperation. The Secretary-General stated that with some $22 million pledged at the Meeting, the Voluntary Trust Fund for Assistance in Mine Clearance, established in 1994,[38] would become fully operational. Mine clearance and/or mine-awareness programmes were under way in Afghanistan, Angola, Cambodia, El Salvador, the former Yugoslavia, Guatemala, Mozambique, Rwanda, Somalia and Yemen. Assessment missions were undertaken in Chad and Georgia.

In response to a 1994 General Assembly request,[39] the Secretary-General submitted, in November, a report containing information received from 16 Governments and EU on steps taken to implement moratoriums declared on the export of anti-personnel mines.[40] The Secretary-General described unilateral, regional and global initiatives to limit their export.

On 12 December, the General Assembly adopted **resolution 50/70 O**.

### Moratorium on the export of anti-personnel land-mines

*The General Assembly,*

*Recalling with satisfaction* its resolutions 48/75 K of 16 December 1993 and 49/75 D of 15 December 1994, in which it, *inter alia*, called upon States to agree to a moratorium on the export of anti-personnel land-mines that pose grave dangers to civilian populations, and urged States to implement moratoria on the export of anti-personnel land-mines,

*Also recalling with satisfaction* its resolution 49/75 D, in which it, *inter alia*, established as a goal of the international community the eventual elimination of anti-personnel land-mines,

*Noting* that, according to the 1994 report of the Secretary-General entitled "Assistance in mine clearance", it is estimated that there are more than one hundred and ten million land-mines in the ground in more than sixty countries throughout the world,

*Noting also* that, according to the same report, the global land-mine crisis continues to worsen as an estimated two to five million new land-mines are laid each year, while only an estimated one hundred thousand were cleared in 1994,

*Expressing deep concern* that anti-personnel land-mines kill or maim hundreds of people every week, mostly innocent and defenceless civilians, obstruct economic development and reconstruction, and have other severe consequences for years after emplacement, which include inhibiting the repatriation of refugees and the return of internally displaced persons,

*Gravely concerned* over the suffering and casualties caused to non-combatants as a result of the proliferation, as well as the indiscriminate and irresponsible use, of anti-personnel land-mines,

*Recalling with satisfaction* its resolutions 48/7 of 19 October 1993 and 49/215 A of 23 December 1994 calling for assistance in mine clearance,

*Welcoming* the programmes of assistance that exist for demining and humanitarian support for the victims of anti-personnel land-mines,

*Welcoming also* the International Meeting on Mine Clearance, held at Geneva from 5 to 7 July 1995, and noting the statement of the Secretary-General at the meeting that the international community must take specific and tangible steps to address the intolerable situation caused by the proliferation of anti-personnel land-mines throughout the world,

*Recalling with satisfaction* the report of the Secretary-General concerning progress on the initiative in resolution 49/75 D,

*Convinced* that moratoria by States on the export of anti-personnel land-mines that pose grave dangers to civilian populations are important measures in helping to reduce substantially the human and economic costs resulting from the proliferation, as well as the indiscriminate and irresponsible use, of such devices,

*Noting with satisfaction* that more than twenty-five States already have declared moratoria on the export, transfer or sale of anti-personnel land-mines, with many of these moratoria being declared as a result of the afore-mentioned resolutions,

*Believing* that ongoing efforts to strengthen the Convention on Prohibitions or Restrictions on the Use of Certain Conventional Weapons Which May Be Deemed to Be Excessively Injurious or to Have Indiscriminate Effects, in particular Protocol II thereto, are an essential part of the overall effort to address problems caused by the proliferation, as well as the indiscriminate and irresponsible use, of anti-personnel land-mines,

*Noting* the efforts that were made at the Review Conference of the States Parties to the Convention, held at Vienna from 25 September to 13 October 1995, to strengthen prohibitions and restrictions in Protocol II governing land-mine use and transfer, and urging parties to build consensus towards agreement on such prohibitions and restrictions when the Review Conference reconvenes in January and April 1996,

*Believing also* that, in addition to Protocol II, other measures to control the production, stockpiling and transfer of anti-personnel land-mines are also necessary to address problems caused by anti-personnel land-mines, especially the indiscriminate or illegal use of anti-personnel land-mines that continue to inflict harm on civilian populations long after emplacement,

*Recognizing* that States can move most effectively towards the goal of the eventual elimination of anti-personnel land-mines as viable alternatives are developed that significantly reduce the risk to the civilian population, and emphasizing the need for States to work on developing such alternatives on an urgent basis,

1. *Welcomes* the moratoria already declared by certain States on the export of anti-personnel land-mines;

2. *Urges* States that have not yet done so to declare such moratoria at the earliest possible date;

3. *Requests* the Secretary-General to prepare a report on steps taken by Member States to implement such moratoria, and to submit it to the General Assembly at its fifty-first session under the item entitled "General and complete disarmament";

4. *Emphasizes* the importance of the Convention on Prohibitions or Restrictions on the Use of Certain Conventional Weapons Which May Be Deemed to Be Excessively Injurious or to Have Indiscriminate Effects and Protocol II thereto as the authoritative international instrument governing the responsible use of anti-personnel land-mines and related devices, and urges parties to build consensus towards an agreement when the Review Conference reconvenes;

5. *Encourages* the widest possible accession to the Convention and to Protocol II thereto, and further urges all States to comply immediately and fully with the applicable rules of Protocol II;

6. *Also encourages* further immediate international efforts to seek solutions to the problems caused by anti-personnel land-mines, with a view to the eventual elimination of anti-personnel land-mines.

General Assembly resolution 50/70 O

12 December 1995     Meeting 90     Adopted without vote

Approved by First Committee (A/50/590) without vote, 17 November (meeting 26); 111-nation draft (A/C.1/50/L.45); agenda item 70.
*Meeting numbers.* GA 50th session: 1st Committee 3-11, 13, 26; plenary 90.

*REFERENCES*

[1]A/50/1. [2]YUN 1991, p. 58, GA res. 46/36 L, annex, 9 Dec. 1991. [3]A/50/27. [4]YUN 1994, p. 159. [5]A/50/276 & Add.1. [6]YUN 1994, p. 160, GA res. 49/75 C, 15 Dec. 1994. [7]A/50/547 & Corr.1 & Add.1-4. [8]A/50/391. [9]A/50/277 & Add.1,2. [10]YUN 1985, p. 84, GA res. 40/91 B, 12 Dec. 1985. [11]A/50/581. [12]A/50/474. [13]A/50/783-S/1995/983. [14]CD/1371. [15]A/51/67. [16]A/50/665-S/1995/877. [17]*Status of Multilateral Arms Regulation and Disarmament Agreements*, 4th edition: 1992, vol. 1, Sales No. E.93.IX.11. [18]A/50/60-S/1995/1. [19]A/50/42. [20]YUN 1991, p. 56, GA res. 46/36 H, 6 Dec. 1991. [21]YUN 1994, p. 165. [22]Ibid., p. 167, GA res. 49/75 G, 15 Dec. 1994. [23]A/50/405. [24]YUN 1994, p. 166, GA res. 49/75 M, 15 Dec. 1994. [25]A/50/465. [26]YUN 1994, p. 170, GA res. 49/79, 15 Dec. 1994. [27]A/50/326. [28]YUN 1980, p. 76. [29]*Multilateral Treaties Deposited with the Secretary-General: Status as at 31 December 1995* (ST/LEG/SER.E/14), Sales No. E.96.V.5. [30]YUN 1983, p. 66. [31]CCW/CONF.I/GE/23. [32]YUN 1994, p. 170. [33]CCW/CONF.I/16. [34]CCW/CONF.I/4. [35]CCW/CONF.I/8/Rev.1. [36]YUN 1994, p. 173, GA res. 49/215, 23 Dec. 1994. [37]A/50/408. [38]YUN 1994, p. 172. [39]Ibid., GA res. 49/75 D, 15 Dec. 1994. [40]A/50/701.

# Other disarmament issues

In 1995, there were a number of disarmament issues that had, in most instances, been before the international community for some time, but that, for a variety of reasons, were not directly addressed to any great extent in the various disarmament forums.

## Prevention of an arms race in outer space

In 1995, the Conference on Disarmament[1] did not succeed in re-establishing during the session the ad hoc committee on the prevention of an arms race in outer space, despite general agreement among member States on the need to do so. This was partly due to the lack of agreement on the re-establishment of other ad hoc committees, including those for transparency and negative security assurances. Consequently, the subject was discussed only in plenary meetings.

**GENERAL ASSEMBLY ACTION**

On 12 December, the General Assembly adopted **resolution 50/69**.

**Prevention of an arms race in outer space**
*The General Assembly,*

*Recognizing* the common interest of all mankind in the exploration and use of outer space for peaceful purposes,

*Reaffirming* the will of all States that the exploration and use of outer space, including the Moon and other celestial bodies, shall be for peaceful purposes, shall be carried out for the benefit and in the interest of all countries, irrespective of their degree of economic or scientific development, and shall be the province of all mankind,

*Reaffirming also* provisions of articles III and IV of the Treaty on Principles Governing the Activities of States in the Exploration and Use of Outer Space, including the Moon and Other Celestial Bodies,

*Recalling* the obligation of all States to observe the provisions of the Charter of the United Nations regarding the use or threat of use of force in their international relations, including in their space activities,

*Reaffirming further* paragraph 80 of the Final Document of the Tenth Special Session of the General Assembly, in which it is stated that in order to prevent an arms race in outer space further measures should be taken and appropriate international negotiations held in accordance with the spirit of the Treaty,

*Recalling also* its previous resolutions on this issue and taking note of the proposals submitted to the General Assembly at its tenth special session and at its regular sessions, and of the recommendations made to the competent organs of the United Nations and to the Conference on Disarmament,

*Recognizing* the grave danger for international peace and security of an arms race in outer space and of developments contributing to it,

*Emphasizing* the paramount importance of strict compliance with existing arms limitation and disarmament agreements relevant to outer space, including bilateral agreements, and with the existing legal regime concerning the use of outer space,

*Considering* that wide participation in the legal regime applicable to outer space could contribute to enhancing its effectiveness,

*Noting* that bilateral negotiations, begun in 1985 between the Union of Soviet Socialist Republics and the United States of America, were conducted with the declared objective of working out effective agreements aimed, *inter alia*, at preventing an arms race in outer space,

*Welcoming* the re-establishment of the Ad Hoc Committee on the Prevention of an Arms Race in Outer Space at the 1994 session of the Conference on Disarmament, in the exercise of the negotiating responsibilities of this sole multilateral body on disarmament, to continue to examine and identify, through substantive and general consideration, issues relevant to the prevention of an arms race in outer space,

*Noting* that the Ad Hoc Committee on the Prevention of an Arms Race in Outer Space, taking into account its previous efforts since its establishment in 1985 and seeking to enhance its functioning in qualitative terms, continued the examination and identification of various issues, existing agreements and existing proposals, as well as future initiatives relevant to the prevention of an arms race in outer space, and that this contributed to a better understanding of a number of problems and to a clearer perception of the various positions,

*Regretting* the inability of the Conference on Disarmament to re-establish the Ad Hoc Committee on the Prevention of an Arms Race in Outer Space in 1995,

*Emphasizing* the mutually complementary nature of bilateral and multilateral efforts in the field of preventing an arms race in outer space, and hoping that concrete results will emerge from those efforts as soon as possible,

*Convinced* that further measures should be examined in the search for effective and verifiable bilateral and multilateral agreements in order to prevent an arms race in outer space,

*Stressing* that the growing use of outer space increases the need for greater transparency and better information on the part of the international community,

*Recalling* in this context its previous resolutions, in particular resolutions 45/55 B of 4 December 1990, 47/51 of 9 December 1992 and 48/74 A of 16 December 1993, in which, *inter alia*, it reaffirmed the importance of confidence-building measures as means conducive to ensuring the attainment of the objective of the prevention of an arms race in outer space,

*Conscious* of the benefits of confidence- and security-building measures in the military field,

*Recognizing* that there has been agreement in the Ad Hoc Committee that the conclusion of an international agreement or agreements to prevent an arms race in outer space remained the fundamental task of the Committee and that the concrete proposals on confidence-building measures could form an integral part of such agreements,

1. *Reaffirms* the importance and urgency of preventing an arms race in outer space and the readiness of all States to contribute to that common objective, in conformity with the provisions of the Treaty on Principles Governing the Activities of States in the Exploration and Use of Outer Space, including the Moon and Other Celestial Bodies;

2. *Reaffirms its recognition*, as stated in the report of the Ad Hoc Committee on the Prevention of an Arms Race in Outer Space, that the legal regime applicable to outer space by itself does not guarantee the prevention of an arms race in outer space, that this legal regime plays a significant role in the prevention of an arms race in that environment, that there is a need to consolidate and reinforce that regime and enhance its effectiveness, and that it is important strictly to comply with existing agreements, both bilateral and multilateral;

3. *Emphasizes* the necessity of further measures with appropriate and effective provisions for verification to prevent an arms race in outer space;

4. *Calls upon* all States, in particular those with major space capabilities, to contribute actively to the objective of the peaceful use of outer space and of the prevention of an arms race in outer space and to refrain from actions contrary to that objective and to the relevant existing treaties in the interest of maintaining international peace and security and promoting international cooperation;

5. *Reiterates* that the Conference on Disarmament, as the single multilateral disarmament negotiating forum, has the primary role in the negotiation of a multilateral agreement or agreements, as appropriate, on the prevention of an arms race in outer space in all its aspects;

6. *Requests* the Conference on Disarmament to re-establish the Ad Hoc Committee on the Prevention of an Arms Race in Outer Space in 1996 and to consider the question of preventing an arms race in outer space;

7. *Also requests* the Conference on Disarmament to intensify its consideration of the question of the prevention of an arms race in outer space in all its aspects, building upon areas of convergence and taking into account relevant proposals and initiatives, including those presented in the Ad Hoc Committee at the 1994 session of the Conference and at the forty-ninth and fiftieth sessions of the General Assembly;

8. *Further requests* the Conference on Disarmament to re-establish an ad hoc committee with an adequate mandate at the beginning of its 1996 session and to continue building upon areas of convergence, taking into account the work undertaken since 1985, with a view to undertaking negotiations for the conclusion of an agreement or agreements, as appropriate, to prevent an arms race in outer space in all its aspects;

9. *Recognizes*, in this respect, the growing convergence of views on the elaboration of measures designed to strengthen transparency, confidence and security in the peaceful uses of outer space;

10. *Urges* the Russian Federation and the United States of America to resume their bilateral negotiations with a view to reaching early agreement for preventing an arms race in outer space and to advise the Conference on Disarmament periodically of the progress of their bilateral sessions so as to facilitate its work;

11. *Decides* to include in the provisional agenda of its fifty-first session the item entitled "Prevention of an arms race in outer space".

General Assembly resolution 50/69

12 December 1995     Meeting 90     121-0-46 (recorded vote)

Approved by First Committee (A/50/589) by recorded vote (113-0-46), 15 November (meeting 21); 22-nation draft (A/C.1/50/L.33); agenda item 69.
*Meeting numbers.* GA 50th session: 1st Committee 3-11, 17, 21; plenary 90.

Recorded vote in Assembly as follows:

*In favour:* Afghanistan, Algeria, Angola, Argentina, Armenia, Australia, Azerbaijan, Bahrain, Bangladesh, Belarus, Benin, Bhutan, Bolivia, Botswana, Brazil, Brunei Darussalam, Burkina Faso, Burundi, Cambodia, Cameroon, Cape Verde, Chad, Chile, China, Colombia, Congo, Costa Rica, Côte d'Ivoire, Cuba, Cyprus, Democratic People's Republic of Korea, Djibouti, Ecuador, Egypt, El Salvador, Equatorial Guinea, Eritrea, Ethiopia, Fiji, Gabon, Georgia, Ghana, Guatemala, Guinea, Guinea-Bissau, Guyana, Haiti, Honduras, India, Indonesia, Iran, Jamaica, Japan, Jordan, Kazakstan, Kenya, Kuwait, Kyrgyzstan, Lao People's Democratic Republic, Lebanon, Lesotho, Libyan Arab Jamahiriya, Madagascar, Malawi, Malaysia, Maldives, Mali, Marshall Islands, Mauritania, Mauritius, Mexico, Mongolia, Morocco, Mozambique, Myanmar, Namibia, Nepal, New Zealand, Nicaragua, Niger, Nigeria, Oman, Pakistan, Panama, Papua New Guinea, Paraguay, Peru, Philippines, Qatar, Republic of Korea, Russian Federation, Rwanda, Samoa, Saudi Arabia, Senegal, Sierra Leone, Singapore, Solomon Islands, South Africa, Sri Lanka, Sudan, Suriname, Swaziland, Syrian Arab Republic, Thailand, Togo, Trinidad and Tobago, Tunisia, Turkmenistan, Uganda, Ukraine, United Arab Emirates, United Republic of Tanzania, Uruguay, Vanuatu, Venezuela, Viet Nam, Yemen, Zaire, Zambia, Zimbabwe.

*Against:* None.

*Abstaining:* Albania, Andorra, Antigua and Barbuda, Austria, Bahamas, Barbados, Belgium, Belize, Bosnia and Herzegovina, Bulgaria, Canada, Croatia, Czech Republic, Denmark, Estonia, Finland, Germany, Greece, Hungary, Iceland, Ireland, Israel, Italy, Latvia, Liechtenstein, Lithuania, Luxembourg, Malta, Micronesia, Monaco, Netherlands, Norway, Poland, Portugal, Republic of Moldova, Romania, Slovakia, Slovenia, Spain, Sweden, Tajikistan, the former Yugoslav Republic of Macedonia, Turkey, United Kingdom, United States, Uzbekistan.

In the First Committee, paragraphs 8 and 10 and the last preambular paragraph were adopted by recorded votes of 100 to 1, with 55 abstentions, 91 to 1, with 63 abstentions, and 99 to 1, with 55 abstentions, respectively.

The Assembly retained those paragraphs by recorded votes of 108 to 1, with 57 abstentions, 99 to 1, with 64 abstentions, and 106 to 1, with 57 abstentions, respectively.

## Disarmament and development

Pursuant to a 1994 General Assembly request,[2] the Secretary-General reported[3] in August on the

relationship between disarmament and development. He recalled that, in his 1994 report[4] on the subject, he had urged Member States, in the light of the changed international situation, to carry out a critical review of the action programme adopted at the 1987 International Conference on the Relationship between Disarmament and Development[5] and then to provide further guidance for Secretariat activity in that area. However, no such evaluation was made in 1995.

GENERAL ASSEMBLY ACTION

On 12 December, the General Assembly adopted **resolution 50/70 G**.

**Relationship between disarmament and development**

*The General Assembly,*

*Recalling* the provisions of the Final Document of the Tenth Special Session of the General Assembly, the first special session devoted to disarmament, concerning the relationship between disarmament and development,

*Recalling also* the adoption on 11 September 1987 of the Final Document of the International Conference on the Relationship between Disarmament and Development,

*Recalling further* its resolution 49/75 J of 15 December 1994,

*Bearing in mind* the final documents of the Eleventh Conference of Heads of State or Government of the Non-Aligned Countries, held at Cartagena de Indias, Colombia, from 18 to 20 October 1995,

*Stressing* the growing importance of the symbiotic relationship between disarmament and development in current international relations,

1. *Takes note* of the note by the Secretary-General and of actions taken in accordance with the Final Document of the International Conference on the Relationship between Disarmament and Development;

2. *Urges* the international community to devote part of the resources made available by the implementation of disarmament and arms limitation agreements to economic and social development, with a view to reducing the ever-widening gap between developed and developing countries;

3. *Requests* the Secretary-General to continue to take action, through appropriate organs and within available resources, for the implementation of the action programme adopted at the International Conference;

4. *Also requests* the Secretary-General to submit a report to the General Assembly at its fifty-first session;

5. *Decides* to include in the provisional agenda of its fifty-first session the item entitled "Relationship between disarmament and development".

General Assembly resolution 50/70 G

12 December 1995     Meeting 90     Adopted without vote

Approved by First Committee (A/50/590) without vote, 10 November (meeting 18); draft by Colombia, for Non-Aligned Movement (A/C.1/50/L.26); agenda item 70 *(h)*.
*Meeting numbers.* GA 50th session: 1st Committee 3-11, 16, 18; plenary 90.

## Science and technology

As requested by the General Assembly in 1994,[6] the Secretary-General continued to follow and assess scientific and technological developments and develop a database of research institutions and experts in order to promote transparency and international cooperation in the application of such knowledge to disarmament objectives. In a September report,[7] he noted that the Centre for Disarmament Affairs was in the process of expanding its database to provide information of the kind requested, and presented the views of two States regarding the impact of scientific and technological developments on international security.

In response to a 1989 Assembly request,[8] the Secretary-General, in August, conveyed information received from Poland relevant to the 1971 Treaty on the Prohibition of the Emplacement of Nuclear Weapons and Other Weapons of Mass Destruction on the Seabed and the Ocean Floor and in the Subsoil Thereof,[9] and to verification of compliance with its provisions.[10]

**GENERAL ASSEMBLY ACTION**

On 12 December, the General Assembly adopted **resolution 50/62**.

**The role of science and technology in the context of international security and disarmament**

*The General Assembly,*

*Recognizing* that scientific and technological developments can have both civilian and military applications and that progress in science and technology for civilian applications needs to be maintained and encouraged,

*Stressing* the interests of the international community in the subject and the need to follow closely the scientific and technological developments that may have a negative impact on the security environment and on the process of arms limitation and disarmament, and to channel scientific and technological developments for beneficial purposes,

*Cognizant* that the international transfer of high-technology products, services and know-how for peaceful purposes is important for the economic and social development of States,

*Recalling* that the Final Declaration of the Eleventh Conference of Heads of State or Government of Non-Aligned Countries, held at Cartagena de Indias, Colombia, from 18 to 20 October 1995,[a] noted that restrictions being placed on access to technology through the imposition of non-transparent ad hoc export control regimes with exclusive membership tended to impede the economic and social development of developing countries,

*Emphasizing* that the internationally negotiated guidelines for the transfer of high technology with military applications should take into account the legitimate defence requirements of all States, while ensuring that access to high-technology products and services and know-how for peaceful purposes is not denied,

1. *Affirms* that scientific and technological achievements should be used for the benefit of all mankind to promote the sustainable economic and social development of all States and to safeguard international security, and that international cooperation in the use of science and technology through the transfer and exchange of technological know-how for peaceful purposes should be promoted;

2. *Invites* Member States to undertake additional ef-

forts to apply science and technology for disarmament-related purposes and to make disarmament-related technologies available to interested States;

3. *Urges* Member States to undertake multilateral negotiations with the participation of all interested States in order to establish universally acceptable, non-discriminatory guidelines for international transfers of high technology with military applications;

4. *Requests* the Secretary-General to develop a database of concerned research institutions and experts with a view to promoting transparency and international cooperation in the applications of the scientific and technological developments for pursuing disarmament objectives such as disposal of weapons, conversion and verification, among others;

5. *Encourages* the United Nations to contribute, within existing mandates, to promoting the application of science and technology for peaceful purposes;

6. *Invites* all Member States to communicate to the Secretary-General their views and assessment;

7. *Decides* to include in the provisional agenda of its fifty-first session an item entitled "The role of science and technology in the context of international security and disarmament".

---

[a]A/50/752-S/1995/1035.

General Assembly resolution 50/62

12 December 1995    Meeting 90    104-6-53 (recorded vote)

Approved by First Committee (A/50/582) by recorded vote (98-6-51), 16 November (meeting 24); 16-nation draft (A/C.1/50/L.48); agenda item 62.
*Meeting numbers.* GA 50th session: 1st Committee 3-11, 16, 24; plenary 90.

Recorded vote in Assembly as follows:

*In favour:* Afghanistan, Algeria, Bahamas, Bahrain, Bangladesh, Barbados, Belize, Benin, Bhutan, Bolivia, Botswana, Brunei Darussalam, Burkina Faso, Burundi, Cambodia, Cameroon, Cape Verde, Chad, Chile, China, Colombia, Congo, Costa Rica, Côte d'Ivoire, Cuba, Cyprus, Democratic People's Republic of Korea, Djibouti, Ecuador, Egypt, El Salvador, Equatorial Guinea, Eritrea, Ethiopia, Gabon, Ghana, Guatemala, Guinea, Guinea-Bissau, Guyana, Haiti, Honduras, India, Indonesia, Jamaica, Jordan, Kenya, Kuwait, Lao People's Democratic Republic, Lebanon, Lesotho, Libyan Arab Jamahiriya, Madagascar, Malawi, Malaysia, Maldives, Mali, Marshall Islands, Mauritania, Mauritius, Mexico, Micronesia, Mongolia, Morocco, Mozambique, Myanmar, Namibia, Nepal, Nicaragua, Niger, Nigeria, Oman, Pakistan, Panama, Papua New Guinea, Paraguay, Peru, Philippines, Qatar, Rwanda, Saudi Arabia, Senegal, Singapore, Sri Lanka, Sudan, Suriname, Swaziland, Syrian Arab Republic, Thailand, Togo, Trinidad and Tobago, Tunisia, Turkmenistan, Uganda, United Arab Emirates, United Republic of Tanzania, Uruguay, Vanuatu, Venezuela, Viet Nam, Yemen, Zaire, Zambia, Zimbabwe.

*Against:* France, Israel, Luxembourg, Netherlands, United Kingdom, United States.

*Abstaining:* Albania, Andorra, Antigua and Barbuda, Argentina, Armenia, Australia, Austria, Azerbaijan, Belarus, Belgium, Bosnia and Herzegovina, Brazil, Bulgaria, Canada, Croatia, Czech Republic, Denmark, Estonia, Fiji, Finland, Georgia, Germany, Greece, Hungary, Iceland, Ireland, Italy, Japan, Kazakstan, Latvia, Liechtenstein, Lithuania, Malta, Monaco, New Zealand, Norway, Poland, Portugal, Republic of Korea, Republic of Moldova, Romania, Russian Federation, Samoa, Slovakia, Slovenia, Solomon Islands, South Africa, Spain, Sweden, Tajikistan, the former Yugoslav Republic of Macedonia, Turkey, Ukraine.

On the same date, the Assembly adopted **resolution 50/63**.

**The role of science and technology in the context of international security, disarmament and other related fields**

*The General Assembly,*

*Recalling* its previous resolutions on the subject of the role of science and technology in the context of international security, disarmament and other related fields, in which, *inter alia*, it recognized that scientific and technological developments could have both civilian and military applications and that progress in science and technology for civilian applications needed to be maintained and encouraged,

1. *Invites* Member States to enhance bilateral and multilateral dialogue on the role of science and technology in the context of international security, disarmament and other related fields, with a view to:

   (*a*) Ensuring implementation of relevant commitments already undertaken under international legal instruments;

   (*b*) Exploring ways and means of further developing international legal rules on transfers of high technology with military applications;

2. *Decides* to include in the provisional agenda of its fifty-first session the item entitled ''The role of science and technology in the context of international security, disarmament and other related fields''.

General Assembly resolution 50/63

12 December 1995     Meeting 90     157-0-9 (recorded vote)

Approved by First Committee (A/50/583) by recorded vote (148-0-9), 16 November (meeting 24); 33-nation draft (A/C.1/50/L.13), orally revised; agenda item 63.
*Meeting numbers.* GA 50th session: 1st Committee 3-11, 15, 24; plenary 90.

Recorded vote in Assembly as follows:

*In favour:* Afghanistan, Albania, Algeria, Andorra, Angola, Antigua and Barbuda, Argentina, Armenia, Australia, Austria, Azerbaijan, Bahamas, Bahrain, Bangladesh, Barbados, Belarus, Belgium, Belize, Benin, Bhutan, Bolivia, Bosnia and Herzegovina, Botswana, Brazil, Brunei Darussalam, Bulgaria, Burkina Faso, Burundi, Cambodia, Cameroon, Canada, Cape Verde, Chad, Chile, China, Colombia, Congo, Costa Rica, Côte d'Ivoire, Croatia, Cyprus, Czech Republic, Denmark, Djibouti, Ecuador, Egypt, El Salvador, Equatorial Guinea, Eritrea, Estonia, Ethiopia, Fiji, Finland, Gabon, Georgia, Germany, Ghana, Greece, Grenada, Guatemala, Guinea, Guinea-Bissau, Guyana, Haiti, Honduras, Hungary, Iceland, Ireland, Israel, Italy, Jamaica, Jordan, Kazakstan, Kenya, Kuwait, Kyrgyzstan, Lao People's Democratic Republic, Latvia, Lebanon, Lesotho, Libyan Arab Jamahiriya, Liechtenstein, Lithuania, Luxembourg, Madagascar, Malawi, Malaysia, Mali, Malta, Marshall Islands, Mauritania, Mauritius, Mexico, Micronesia, Monaco, Mongolia, Morocco, Mozambique, Myanmar, Namibia, Nepal, Netherlands, New Zealand, Nicaragua, Niger, Nigeria, Norway, Oman, Panama, Papua New Guinea, Paraguay, Peru, Philippines, Poland, Portugal, Qatar, Republic of Korea, Republic of Moldova, Romania, Russian Federation, Rwanda, Samoa, Saudi Arabia, Sierra Leone, Singapore, Slovakia, Slovenia, Solomon Islands, South Africa, Spain, Sri Lanka, Sudan, Suriname, Swaziland, Sweden, Syrian Arab Republic, Tajikistan, Thailand, the former Yugoslav Republic of Macedonia, Togo, Trinidad and Tobago, Tunisia, Turkey, Turkmenistan, Uganda, Ukraine, United Arab Emirates, United Republic of Tanzania, Uruguay, Vanuatu, Venezuela, Viet Nam, Yemen, Zaire, Zambia, Zimbabwe.

*Against:* None.

*Abstaining:* Cuba, Democratic People's Republic of Korea, France, India, Iran, Japan, Pakistan, United Kingdom, United States.

## Arms limitation and disarmament agreements

### Environment and disarmament and arms control agreements

On 12 December, the General Assembly adopted **resolution 50/70 M**.

**Observance of environmental norms in the drafting and implementation of agreements on disarmament and arms control**

*The General Assembly,*

*Recognizing* the importance of the observance of environmental norms in the drafting and implementation of agreements on disarmament and arms limitation,

*Taking note* of the relevant provisions of the Convention on the Prohibition of the Development, Production, Stockpiling and Use of Chemical Weapons and on Their Destruction regarding the environment,

*Convinced* of the importance of the environmentally sound implementation of the Convention on the Prohibition of the Development, Production and Stockpiling of Bacteriological (Biological) and Toxin Weapons and on Their Destruction,

*Mindful* of the detrimental environmental effects of the use of nuclear weapons,

*Conscious* of the positive potential implications for the environment of a future comprehensive nuclear-test-ban treaty,

*Desirous* of banning effectively military or any other hostile use of environment modification techniques, with a view to removing the dangers for mankind that might arise from such uses,

1. *Invites* the Conference on Disarmament to take every necessary measure to include in negotiating treaties and agreements on disarmament and arms limitation the corresponding environmental norms, with a view to ensuring that the process of implementation of such treaties and agreements is environmentally sound, in particular the destruction of weapons covered by them;

2. *Emphasizes* the importance of the compliance of all States parties to the Convention on the Prohibition of the Development, Production, Stockpiling and Use of Chemical Weapons and on Their Destruction, and calls upon them to cooperate and ensure that the process of implementation of the Convention in all relevant aspects is environmentally sound;

3. *Urges* all States parties to consider all relevant norms related to the protection of the environment in implementing the Convention on the Prohibition of the Development, Production and Stockpiling of Bacteriological (Biological) and Toxin Weapons and on Their Destruction;

4. *Calls upon* the Conference on Disarmament to conclude, as a task of the highest priority, a comprehensive nuclear-test-ban treaty as soon as possible in 1996;

5. *Urges* the States that are not yet party to the Convention on the Prohibition of Military or Any Other Hostile Use of Environmental Modification Techniques to consider adhering to it as soon as possible, in order to assure the universality of the Convention.

General Assembly resolution 50/70 M

12 December 1995     Meeting 90     157-4-2 (recorded vote)

Approved by First Committee (A/50/590) by recorded vote (149-4-4), 20 November (meeting 27); draft by Colombia, for Non-Aligned Movement (A/C.1/50/L.41/Rev.2); agenda item 70.
*Meeting numbers.* GA 50th session: 1st Committee 3-11, 16, 27; plenary 90.

Recorded vote in Assembly as follows:

*In favour:* Afghanistan, Albania, Algeria, Andorra, Angola, Antigua and Barbuda, Argentina, Armenia, Australia, Austria, Azerbaijan, Bahamas, Bahrain, Bangladesh, Barbados, Belarus, Belgium, Belize, Benin, Bhutan, Bolivia, Bosnia and Herzegovina, Botswana, Brazil, Brunei Darussalam, Bulgaria, Burkina Faso, Burundi, Cambodia, Cameroon, Cape Verde, Chad, Chile, China, Colombia, Congo, Costa Rica, Côte d'Ivoire, Croatia, Cuba, Cyprus, Czech Republic, Democratic People's Republic of Korea, Denmark, Djibouti, Ecuador, Egypt, Equatorial Guinea, Eritrea, Estonia, Ethiopia, Fiji, Finland, Gabon, Georgia, Germany, Ghana, Greece, Guatemala, Guinea, Guinea-Bissau, Guyana, Haiti, Honduras, Hungary, Iceland, India, Indonesia, Iran, Ireland, Italy, Jamaica, Jordan, Kazakstan, Kenya, Kuwait, Kyrgyzstan, Lao People's Democratic Republic, Latvia, Lebanon, Lesotho, Libyan Arab Jamahiriya, Liechtenstein, Lithuania, Luxembourg, Madagascar, Malawi, Malaysia, Maldives, Mali, Malta, Marshall Islands, Mauritania, Mauritius, Mexico, Micronesia, Mongolia, Morocco, Mozambique, Myanmar, Namibia, Nepal, Netherlands, New Zealand, Nicaragua, Niger, Nigeria, Norway, Oman, Pakistan, Panama, Papua New Guinea, Paraguay, Peru, Philippines, Poland, Portugal, Qatar, Republic of Moldova, Romania, Russian Federation, Rwanda, Samoa, Saudi Arabia, Senegal, Sierra Leone, Singapore, Slovakia, Slovenia, Solomon Islands, South Africa, Spain, Sri Lanka, Sudan, Suriname, Swaziland, Sweden, Syrian Arab Republic, Tajikistan, Thailand, the former Yugoslav Republic of Macedonia, Togo, Trinidad and Tobago, Tunisia, Turkey, Uganda, Ukraine, United Arab Emirates, United Republic of Tanzania, Uruguay, Vanuatu, Venezuela, Viet Nam, Yemen, Zaire, Zambia, Zimbabwe.

*Against:* France, Israel, United Kingdom, United States.

*Abstaining:* Canada, Japan.

## Compliance

On 12 December, the General Assembly adopted **resolution 50/60**.

### Compliance with arms limitation and disarmament agreements

*The General Assembly,*

*Recalling* its resolution 48/63 of 16 December 1993 and other relevant resolutions on the question,

*Recognizing* the abiding concern of all Member States for maintaining respect for rights and obligations arising from treaties and other sources of international law,

*Convinced* that observance of the Charter of the United Nations, relevant treaties and other sources of international law is essential for the strengthening of international security,

*Mindful,* in particular, of the fundamental importance of full implementation and strict observance of agreements and other obligations on arms limitation and disarmament if individual nations and the international community are to derive enhanced security from them,

*Stressing* that any violation of such agreements and other obligations not only adversely affects the security of States parties but can also create security risks for other States relying on the constraints and commitments stipulated in those agreements and other obligations,

*Stressing also* that any weakening of confidence in such agreements and other obligations diminishes their contribution to global or regional stability and to further disarmament and arms limitation efforts and undermines the credibility and effectiveness of the international legal system,

*Recognizing,* in this context, that full compliance by parties with all provisions of existing agreements and the resolving of compliance concerns effectively by means consistent with such agreements and international law can, *inter alia,* facilitate the conclusion of additional arms limitation and disarmament agreements, and thereby contribute to better relations among States and the strengthening of world peace and security,

*Believing* that compliance with all provisions of arms limitation and disarmament agreements by States parties is a matter of interest and concern to all members of the international community, and noting the role that the United Nations has played and should continue to play in that regard,

*Welcoming* the universal recognition of the critical importance of the question of compliance with and verification of arms limitation and disarmament agreements and other obligations,

1. *Urges* all States parties to arms limitation and disarmament agreements to implement and comply with the entirety of the spirit and all provisions of such agreements;

2. *Calls upon* all Member States to give serious consideration to the implications that non-compliance with any provisions of arms limitation and disarmament obligations has for international security and stability, as well as for the prospects for further progress in the field of disarmament;

3. *Also calls upon* all Member States to support efforts aimed at the resolution of compliance questions by means consistent with such agreements and international law, with a view to encouraging strict observance by all parties of the provisions of arms limitation and disarmament agreements and maintaining or restoring the integrity of such agreements;

4. *Welcomes* the role that the United Nations has played in restoring the integrity of, and fostering negotiations on, certain arms limitation and disarmament agreements and in the removal of threats to peace;

5. *Requests* the Secretary-General to continue to provide assistance that may be necessary in restoring and protecting the integrity of arms limitation and disarmament agreements;

6. *Encourages* efforts by States parties to develop additional cooperative measures, as appropriate, that can increase confidence in compliance with existing arms limitation and disarmament obligations and reduce the possibility of misinterpretation and misunderstanding;

7. *Notes* the contribution that verification experiments and research can make and already have made in confirming and improving verification procedures for arms limitation and disarmament agreements under study or negotiation, thereby providing an opportunity, from the time that such agreements enter into force, for enhancing confidence in the effectiveness of verification procedures as a basis for determining compliance;

8. *Decides* to include in the provisional agenda of its fifty-second session the item entitled "Compliance with arms limitation and disarmament obligations".

General Assembly resolution 50/60

12 December 1995     Meeting 90     Adopted without vote

Approved by First Committee (A/50/577) without vote, 20 November (meeting 27); 65-nation draft (A/C.1/50/L.42/Rev.1), orally revised; agenda item 57.

*Meeting numbers.* GA 50th session: 1st Committee 3-11, 27; plenary 90.

*REFERENCES*

[1]A/50/27. [2]YUN 1994, p. 174, GA res. 49/75 J, 15 Dec. 1994. [3]A/50/388. [4]YUN 1994, p. 174. [5]YUN 1987, p. 82. [6]YUN 1994, p. 168, GA res. 49/67, 15 Dec. 1994. [7]A/50/409. [8]GA res. 44/116 O, 15 Dec. 1989. [9]YUN 1970, p. 18, GA res. 2660(XXV), annex, 7 Dec. 1970. [10]A/50/383.

# Information and studies

## Disarmament Information Programme

In carrying out its mandated information and education activities, the UN Centre for Disarmament Affairs gave increasing attention to the most topical issues of global concern in the field, such as non-proliferation in all its aspects, achievement of a comprehensive test-ban treaty, and ways and means of promoting regional approaches to disarmament and confidence-building measures, including greater openness and transparency in military matters.

## Disarmament Week

The Centre for Disarmament Affairs worked closely with the NGO Committee on Disarmament, especially during the celebration of Disarmament Week. The Week, beginning 24 October, was observed by a special meeting of the First Committee. On 26 and 30 October and on 9 November, the NGO Committee, the Centre and the UN Department of Public Information sponsored panel discussions focusing on nuclear-test-ban negotiations, a fissile material cut-off, reduction of military budgets and land-mines.

**Report of the Secretary-General.** Pursuant to a 1992 General Assembly request,[1] the Secretary-General submitted a July report[2] containing information on activities carried out by three Governments and by the United Nations to promote Disarmament Week from 1992 to 1994.

GENERAL ASSEMBLY ACTION

On 12 December, the General Assembly adopted **resolution 50/72 B**.

### Disarmament Week

*The General Assembly,*

*Noting* the fundamental change that has been brought about by the end of the cold war and bipolar confrontation, and welcoming the important achievements of late in the areas of arms limitation and disarmament,

*Noting with satisfaction* that this year's observance of Disarmament Week coincides with the fiftieth anniversary of the United Nations,

*Stressing* the increasing role and prestige of the United Nations as a focal point for coordinating and harmonizing the efforts of States,

*Emphasizing anew* the need for and the importance of world public opinion in support of disarmament efforts in all their aspects,

*Noting with satisfaction* the broad and active support by Governments and international and national organizations of the decision taken by the General Assembly at its tenth special session, the first special session devoted to disarmament, regarding the proclamation of the week starting 24 October, the day of the founding of the United Nations, as a week devoted to fostering the objectives of disarmament,

*Recalling* the recommendations concerning the World Disarmament Campaign contained in annex V to the Concluding Document of the Twelfth Special Session of the General Assembly, the second special session devoted to disarmament, in particular the recommendation that Disarmament Week should continue to be widely observed,

*Noting* the support for the further observance of Disarmament Week expressed by Member States at the fifteenth special session of the General Assembly, the third special session devoted to disarmament,

*Recognizing* the significance of the annual observance of Disarmament Week, including by the United Nations,

1. *Takes note* of the report of the Secretary-General on the observance of Disarmament Week;

2. *Commends* all States, international and national governmental and non-governmental organizations for their active support for and participation in Disarmament Week;

3. *Invites* all States that so desire, in carrying out appropriate measures at the local level on the occasion of Disarmament Week, to take into account the elements of the model programme for Disarmament Week prepared by the Secretary-General;

4. *Invites* Governments and international and national non-governmental organizations to continue to take an active part in Disarmament Week;

5. *Invites* the Secretary-General to continue to use the United Nations informational organs as widely as possible to promote better understanding among the world public of disarmament problems and the objectives of Disarmament Week;

6. *Decides* to include in the provisional agenda of its fifty-fifth session the item entitled "Disarmament Week".

General Assembly resolution 50/72 B

12 December 1995      Meeting 90      Adopted without vote

Approved by First Committee (A/50/592) without vote, 10 November (meeting 18); 30-nation draft (A/C.1/50/L.16); agenda item 72 *(e).*
*Meeting numbers.* GA 50th session: 1st Committee 3-12, 14, 18; plenary 90.

## Pledging Conference

The Thirteenth Pledging Conference for the UN Disarmament Information Programme was held on 27 October in New York.[3] Fourteen countries pledged $279,755 at the Conference, with various amounts earmarked for the trust funds of the Disarmament Information Programme and the UN regional centres for peace and disarmament and for the UN Institute for Disarmament Research (UNIDIR), compared with $654,972 in 1994. In accordance with the Final Act of the Conference, the list of pledges was to remain open in order to incorporate any additional contributions up until 31 March 1996. The list of pledges made at the Thirteenth Pledging Conference in October 1995 and thereafter, up to 31 March 1996, was contained in a document of the Conference.[4]

## Regional centres for peace and disarmament

Pursuant to a 1994 General Assembly request,[5] the Secretary-General in an August report[6] described the activities of the three regional centres for peace and disarmament—in Africa, Asia and the Pacific, and Latin America and the Caribbean—during the period August 1994 to July 1995. He stated that the centres were unable to function in the manner intended by the Assembly because of a steady fall in voluntary contributions, in particular from Member States within the regions concerned. He warned that unless Member States took early and effective action, the centres would have to be closed and regional disarmament activities would have to be carried out only by staff members based in New York or Geneva.

The activities of the Regional Centre for Peace and Disarmament in Africa, established in Lomé, Togo, in 1986,[7] were curtailed owing to severe financial constraints, which entailed some cuts in staff. Nevertheless, the Centre held monthly informal meetings on topical issues, and it widened the distribution of its quarterly bilingual publication, *The African Peace Bulletin/Bulletin Africain de la Paix*. Centre staff provided substantive and administrative support to the UN Standing Advisory Committee on Security Questions in Central Africa and to the Secretary-General's Advisory Mission.

The Regional Centre for Peace, Disarmament and Development in Latin America and the Caribbean, established in Lima, Peru, in 1987,[8] was operating under extreme financial constraints. Its activities were largely directed towards maintaining contacts and cooperation with governmental and non-governmental organizations, research centres, academic institutions and other UN bodies and agencies interested in disarmament and international security issues. In February, the Centre hosted a round-table discussion on the 1995 Review and Extension Conference of the Treaty on the Non-Proliferation of Nuclear Weapons. It continued to publish its quarterly newsletter, *Boletín*, to disseminate information and promote awareness of disarmament-related issues in the region.

The Regional Centre for Peace and Disarmament in Asia and the Pacific, established in Kathmandu, Nepal, in 1989, organized major regional meetings on openness, assurance of security and disarmament (Kathmandu, 13-15 February), on disarmament in the past half century and its future prospects (Nagasaki, Japan, 12-16 June) and on multifaceted cooperation in north-east Asia (Kanazawa, Japan, 22-23 June).

**GENERAL ASSEMBLY ACTION**

On 12 December, the General Assembly adopted **resolution 50/71 C**.

**United Nations Regional Centre for Peace and Disarmament in Africa and United Nations Regional Centre for Peace, Disarmament and Development in Latin America and the Caribbean**

*The General Assembly,*

*Recalling* its resolutions 40/151 G of 16 December 1985, 41/60 D of 3 December 1986, 42/39 J of 30 November 1987 and 43/76 D of 7 December 1988 on the United Nations Regional Centre for Peace and Disarmament in Africa, its resolutions 41/60 J of 3 December 1986, 42/39 K of 30 November 1987 and 43/76 H of 7 December 1988 on the United Nations Regional Centre for Peace, Disarmament and Development in Latin America and the Caribbean, and its resolutions 45/59 E of 4 December 1990 and 46/37 F of 9 December 1991 on the United Nations Regional Centre for Peace and

Disarmament in Africa, the United Nations Regional Centre for Peace and Disarmament in Asia and the Pacific and the United Nations Regional Centre for Peace, Disarmament and Development in Latin America and the Caribbean,

*Reaffirming* its resolutions 46/36 F of 6 December 1991 and 47/52 G of 9 December 1992 on regional disarmament, including confidence-building measures,

*Recalling also* its resolutions 48/76 E of 16 December 1993 and 49/76 D of 15 December 1994 on the regional disarmament centres,

*Mindful* of the provisions of Article 11, paragraph 1, of the Charter of the United Nations stipulating that a function of the General Assembly is to consider the general principles of cooperation in the maintenance of international peace and security, including the principles governing disarmament and arms limitation,

*Bearing in mind* that the changed international environment has created new opportunities for the pursuit of disarmament, as well as posed new challenges,

*Convinced* that the initiatives and activities mutually agreed upon by Member States of the respective regions aimed at fostering mutual confidence and security, as well as the implementation and coordination of regional activities under the United Nations Disarmament Information Programme, would encourage and facilitate the development of effective measures of confidence-building, arms limitation and disarmament in these regions,

*Welcoming* the programme of activities carried out by the regional centres, which have contributed substantially to understanding and cooperation among the States in each particular region and have thereby strengthened the role assigned to each regional centre in the areas of peace, disarmament and development,

*Bearing in mind* the importance of education for peace, disarmament and development for understanding and cooperation among States and for the promotion of international peace and security,

*Recognizing with concern* the financial situation of the regional centres as described in the 1994 report of the Secretary-General on the activities of the regional centres,

*Underlining*, therefore, the need to provide the centres with financial viability and stability so as to facilitate the effective planning and implementation of their respective programmes of activities,

*Expressing its gratitude* to the Member States, international governmental and non-governmental organizations and foundations that have, so far, contributed to the trust funds of the regional centres in Africa and Latin America and the Caribbean,

1. *Commends* the activities being carried out by the regional centres in identifying and broadening the understanding of pressing disarmament and security issues and exploring optimum solutions under given specific conditions prevailing in each region, in accordance with their mandates;

2. *Reaffirms its strong support* for the further operation and strengthening of the two regional centres and encourages them to continue intensifying their efforts in promoting cooperation with subregional and regional organizations and among the States in their respective regions to facilitate the development of effective measures of confidence-building, arms limitation and disarmament, with a view to promoting peace and security;

3. *Encourages* further use of the potential of the regional centres to maintain the increased interest in and momentum for revitalization of the Organization to meet the challenges of a new phase of international relations in order to fulfil the purposes and principles of the Charter of the United Nations related to peace, disarmament and development, taking into account the guidelines and recommendations for regional approaches to disarmament within the context of global security as adopted by the Disarmament Commission at its 1993 substantive session;

4. *Requests* the Secretary-General, in consultation with the Director-General of the United Nations Educational, Scientific and Cultural Organization, to promote the development of activities within the programmes of the United Nations regional disarmament centres related to education for disarmament;

5. *Strongly appeals once again* to Member States, as well as to international governmental and non-governmental organizations and foundations, to make more substantial voluntary contributions in order to revitalize the two centres, strengthen their programmes of activities and facilitate the effective implementation of those programmes;

6. *Requests* the Secretary-General, in the light of the current financial situation of the two centres, to explore alternative financial resources and to continue to provide all necessary support to the regional centres in fulfilling their mandates;

7. *Also requests* the Secretary-General to ensure that the directors of the two regional centres are, as far as possible, locally based in order to revitalize the activities in the centres;

8. *Further requests* the Secretary-General to report to the General Assembly at its fifty-first session on his efforts to seek new alternative sources of financing for the two regional centres and on the implementation of the present resolution;

9. *Decides* to include in the provisional agenda of its fifty-first session the item entitled "United Nations Regional Centre for Peace and Disarmament in Africa, United Nations Regional Centre for Peace and Disarmament in Asia and the Pacific and United Nations Regional Centre for Peace, Disarmament and Development in Latin America and the Caribbean".

General Assembly resolution 50/71 C

12 December 1995     Meeting 90     Adopted without vote

Approved by First Committee (A/50/591) without vote, 17 November (meeting 26); draft by South Africa (for African Group) and 25 other States (A/C.1/50/L.24); agenda item 71 *(c)*.

*Meeting numbers.* GA 50th session: 1st Committee 3-11, 16, 26; plenary 90.

On the same date, the General Assembly adopted **resolution 50/71 D**.

### United Nations Regional Centre for Peace and Disarmament in Asia and the Pacific

*The General Assembly,*

*Recalling* its resolution 39/63 J of 12 December 1984, in which it requested the Secretary-General to provide assistance to such Member States in the regions concerned as might request it with a view to establishing regional and institutional arrangements for the implementation of the World Disarmament Campaign, on the basis of existing resources and of voluntary contributions that Member States might make to that end,

*Recalling also* its resolution 42/39 D of 30 November 1987, by which it established the United Nations Regional Centre for Peace and Disarmament in Asia, with headquarters at Kathmandu and with the mandate of providing, on request, substantive support for the initiatives and other activities mutually agreed upon by the Member States of the Asian region for the implementation of measures for peace and disarmament, through appropriate utilization of available resources,

*Mindful* of its resolution 44/117 F of 15 December 1989, in which it decided to rename the United Nations Regional Centre for Peace and Disarmament in Asia as the United Nations Regional Centre for Peace and Disarmament in Asia and the Pacific,

*Commending* the useful activities carried out by the Regional Centre in encouraging regional and subregional dialogue for the enhancement of openness, transparency and confidence-building, as well as the promotion of disarmament and security through the organization of regional meetings, which has come to be widely known within the Asia-Pacific region as the "Kathmandu process",

*Noting* that trends in the post-cold-war era have emphasized the function of the Regional Centre in assisting Member States as they deal with new security concerns and disarmament issues emerging in the region,

*Noting also* the efforts of the Member States to respond to these concerns and issues through the formulation of a common approach,

*Appreciating highly* the important role Nepal has played as the host nation of the headquarters of the Regional Centre,

*Recognizing* the need for the Regional Centre to pursue effectively its above-mentioned expanded function,

*Expressing its appreciation* to the Regional Centre for its organization of substantive regional meetings at Kathmandu and at Nagasaki and Kanazawa, Japan, in 1995,

1. *Commends* the important work carried out by the United Nations Regional Centre for Peace and Disarmament in Asia and the Pacific, with its headquarters at Kathmandu;

2. *Reaffirms its strong support* for the continued operation and further strengthening of the Regional Centre as an essential promoter of the regional peace and disarmament dialogue in the Asia-Pacific region known as the "Kathmandu process";

3. *Decides* that the Director of the Regional Centre at Kathmandu should operate as before until a reliable means can be found to finance the operational needs of the Regional Centre;

4. *Recommends* that the Regional Centre organize the scheduled regional meetings at Kathmandu, Hiroshima, Japan, and other cities in 1996, within the available resources voluntarily contributed by Member States and organizations for that purpose;

5. *Expresses its appreciation* for the contributions received by the Regional Centre;

6. *Appeals* to Member States, in particular those within the Asia-Pacific region, as well as to international governmental and non-governmental organizations and foundations, to make voluntary contributions in order to strengthen the programme of activities of the Regional Centre and its implementation;

7. *Requests* the Secretary-General to provide all necessary support, within existing resources, to the Regional Centre in carrying out its programme of activities;

8. *Also requests* the Secretary-General to report to the General Assembly at its fifty-first session on the implementation of the present resolution;

9. *Decides* to include in the provisional agenda of its fifty-first session the item entitled ''United Nations Regional Centre for Peace and Disarmament in Africa, United Nations Regional Centre for Peace and Disarmament in Asia and the Pacific and United Nations Regional Centre for Peace, Disarmament and Development in Latin America and the Caribbean''.

General Assembly resolution 50/71 D

12 December 1995     Meeting 90     Adopted without vote

Approved by First Committee (A/50/591) without vote, 17 November (meeting 26); 19-nation draft (A/C.1/50/L.31/Rev.1); agenda item 71 *(c)*.
*Meeting numbers.* GA 50th session: 1st Committee 3-11, 14, 26; plenary 90.

In the Committee, a separate recorded vote was taken on paragraph 4, which was retained by 143 to none, with 3 abstentions. The Assembly adopted the paragraph by a recorded vote of 161 to none, with 3 abstentions.

## Disarmament studies and research

### Advisory Board on Disarmament Matters

The Advisory Board on Disarmament Matters, which advised the Secretary-General on the disarmament studies programme and implementation of the Disarmament Information Programme and served as the Board of Trustees of UNIDIR, held two sessions in 1995 (Geneva, 10-12 January; New York, 19-23 June).[9]

The main issues discussed by the Board included nuclear issues and other weapons of mass destruction, micro-disarmament, the special session of the General Assembly on disarmament planned for 1997, the Register of Conventional Arms, the Conference on Disarmament and regional organizations in collective security.

In its capacity as the Board of Trustees of UNIDIR, the Board reviewed the Director's report for 1994 and approved the work programme for 1996.

By **resolution 49/237, section I**, of 31 March, the General Assembly, taking note of a note[10] by the Secretary-General concerning a request for a subvention in 1995 to UNIDIR, based on recommendations of its Board in 1994,[11] decided to keep under review the level of support costs charged to UNIDIR.

By **resolution 50/216, section V**, of 23 December, the Assembly approved a subvention of $220,000 for 1996, as recommended by the Board.[12]

### UN Institute for Disarmament Research

In September, the Secretary-General transmitted to the General Assembly the UNIDIR Director's report covering Institute activities from July 1994 to June 1995, and the report of the Board

of Trustees concerning the 1996 work programme.[12] During the period under review, the research programme focused on non-proliferation with respect to nuclear weapons, other weapons of mass destruction and dual-use technology transfers; disarmament and conflict resolution, in particular the utility and modalities of disarming warring parties as an element of efforts to resolve intra-State conflicts; and regional security issues, devoted to confidence-building and arms control in the Middle East.

### Disarmament studies programme

As requested by the General Assembly in 1993,[13] the Secretary-General transmitted, in a September report,[14] an in-depth study reviewing the conclusions of the 1990 study on verification,[15] prepared with the assistance of a group of qualified governmental experts. The Secretary-General concurred with the concluding observation of the group that modest steps, within the constraints facing the Organization (see PART SIX, Chapter II), to enhance its verification role would have a positive impact on implementing disarmament treaties, developing effective early-warning mechanisms for impending conflicts, and responding with appropriate strategies to manage and resolve conflicts that had occurred.

GENERAL ASSEMBLY ACTION

On 12 December, the General Assembly adopted **resolution 50/61**.

**Verification in all its aspects, including the role of the United Nations in the field of verification**

*The General Assembly,*

*Affirming* its continued support for the sixteen principles of verification drawn up by the Disarmament Commission,

*Stressing* that the critical importance of verification of and compliance with arms limitation and disarmament agreements is universally recognized and that the issue of verification is a matter of concern to all nations,

*Recalling* its resolution 48/68 of 16 December 1993, in which it requested the Secretary-General, as a further follow-up to the 1990 study on the role of the United Nations in the field of verification and in view of significant developments in international relations since that study, to undertake, with the assistance of a group of qualified governmental experts, an in-depth study on verification issues identified in that resolution,

*Also recalling* that, in its resolution 48/68, it requested the Secretary-General to submit a report on the subject to the General Assembly at its fiftieth session,

1. *Takes note* of the report of the Secretary-General, which was unanimously approved by the Group of Governmental Experts on Verification in All Its Aspects, including the Role of the United Nations in the Field of Verification, and commends the report to the attention of Member States;

2. *Requests* the Secretary-General to give the report the widest possible circulation and to seek the views of Member States on the report;

3. *Encourages* Member States to consider the recommendations contained in the report and to assist the Secretary-General in their implementation where they consider it appropriate;

4. *Also requests* the Secretary-General to report to the General Assembly at its fifty-second session on the views received from Member States on the report and on actions taken by Member States and by the Secretariat with respect to the recommendations contained in the report;

5. *Decides* to include in the provisional agenda of its fifty-second session the item entitled "Verification in all its aspects, including the role of the United Nations in the field of verification".

General Assembly resolution 50/61

12 December 1995     Meeting 90     157-1-6 (recorded vote)

Approved by First Committee (A/50/579) by recorded vote (140-1-7), 7 November (meeting 15); 18-nation draft (A/C.1/50/L.12); agenda item 59.
*Meeting numbers.* GA 50th session: 1st Committee 3-11, 15; plenary 90.

Recorded vote in Assembly as follows:

*In favour:* Afghanistan, Albania, Algeria, Andorra, Antigua and Barbuda, Argentina, Armenia, Australia, Austria, Azerbaijan, Bahamas, Bahrain, Bangladesh, Barbados, Belarus, Belgium, Belize, Benin, Bhutan, Bolivia, Bosnia and Herzegovina, Botswana, Brazil, Brunei Darussalam, Bulgaria, Burkina Faso, Burundi, Cambodia, Cameroon, Canada, Cape Verde, Chad, Chile, Colombia, Congo, Costa Rica, Côte d'Ivoire, Croatia, Cuba, Cyprus, Czech Republic, Denmark, Djibouti, Ecuador, Egypt, El Salvador, Eritrea, Estonia, Ethiopia, Fiji, Finland, Gabon, Germany, Ghana, Greece, Grenada, Guatemala, Guinea, Guinea-Bissau, Guyana, Haiti, Honduras, Hungary, Iceland, India, Indonesia, Ireland, Italy, Jamaica, Japan, Jordan, Kazakstan, Kenya, Kuwait, Kyrgyzstan, Lao People's Democratic Republic, Latvia, Lebanon, Lesotho, Libyan Arab Jamahiriya, Liechtenstein, Lithuania, Luxembourg, Madagascar, Malawi, Malaysia, Maldives, Mali, Malta, Marshall Islands, Mauritania, Mauritius, Mexico, Micronesia, Mongolia, Morocco, Mozambique, Myanmar, Namibia, Nepal, Netherlands, New Zealand, Nicaragua, Niger, Nigeria, Norway, Oman, Pakistan, Panama, Papua New Guinea, Paraguay, Peru, Philippines, Poland, Portugal, Qatar, Republic of Korea, Republic of Moldova, Romania, Russian Federation, Rwanda, Samoa, Saudi Arabia, Senegal, Sierra Leone, Singapore, Slovakia, Slovenia, Solomon Islands, South Africa, Spain, Sri Lanka, Sudan, Suriname, Swaziland, Sweden, Syrian Arab Republic, Tajikistan, Thailand, the former Yugoslav Republic of Macedonia, Togo, Trinidad and Tobago, Tunisia, Turkey, Turkmenistan, Uganda, Ukraine, United Arab Emirates, United Republic of Tanzania, Uruguay, Vanuatu, Venezuela, Viet Nam, Yemen, Zaire, Zambia, Zimbabwe.

*Against:* United States.

*Abstaining:* Democratic People's Republic of Korea, France, Georgia, Israel, Monaco, United Kingdom.

## Disarmament fellowship, training and advisory services

In 1995, 30 fellows participated in the UN disarmament fellowship, training and advisory services programme, which began on 16 August in Geneva and ended on 28 October in New York. It included a series of lectures; speaking, drafting and simulation exercises; preparation of individual research papers on various disarmament and security issues; attendance at meetings of the Conference on Disarmament and the First Committee; and study visits to Germany and Japan. The fellows visited The Hague, Netherlands, where they attended lectures dealing with the verification regime, national implementation measures and assistance to Member States with respect to the 1993 Convention on the Prohibition of the Development, Production, Stockpiling and Use of Chemical Weapons and on Their Destruction. They also visited IAEA in Vienna, where they were briefed on safeguards activities and the nuclear non-proliferation regime.

GENERAL ASSEMBLY ACTION

On 12 December, the General Assembly adopted **resolution 50/71 A**.

### United Nations disarmament fellowship, training and advisory services
*The General Assembly,*

*Recalling* its decision, contained in paragraph 108 of the Final Document of the Tenth Special Session of the General Assembly, the first special session devoted to disarmament, to establish a programme of fellowships on disarmament, as well as its decisions contained in annex IV to the Concluding Document of the Twelfth Special Session of the General Assembly, the second special session devoted to disarmament, in which it decided, *inter alia*, to continue the programme,

*Noting with satisfaction* that the programme has already trained an appreciable number of public officials selected from geographical regions represented in the United Nations system, most of whom are now in positions of responsibility in the field of disarmament affairs in their respective countries or Governments,

*Recalling* all the annual resolutions on the matter since the thirty-seventh session of the General Assembly, in 1982, including resolution 49/76 B of 15 December 1994,

*Noting also with satisfaction* that the programme, as designed, continues to enable an increased number of public officials, particularly from the developing countries, to acquire more expertise in the sphere of disarmament,

*Believing* that the forms of assistance available to Member States, particularly to developing countries, under the programme will enhance the capabilities of their officials to follow ongoing deliberations and negotiations on disarmament, both bilateral and multilateral,

1. *Reaffirms* its decisions contained in annex IV to the Concluding Document of the Twelfth Special Session of the General Assembly and the report of the Secretary-General approved by the Assembly in its resolution 33/71 E of 14 December 1978;

2. *Expresses its appreciation* to the Governments of Germany and Japan for inviting the 1995 fellows to study selected activities in the field of disarmament, thereby contributing to the fulfilment of the overall objectives of the programme;

3. *Commends* the Secretary-General for the diligence with which the programme has continued to be carried out;

4. *Requests* the Secretary-General to continue the implementation of the Geneva-based programme within existing resources and to report thereon to the General Assembly at its fifty-first session;

5. *Decides* to include in the provisional agenda of its fifty-first session the item entitled "United Nations disarmament fellowship, training and advisory services".

General Assembly resolution 50/71 A

12 December 1995      Meeting 90      Adopted without vote

Approved by First Committee (A/50/591) without vote, 10 November (meeting 18); 44-nation draft (A/C.1/50/L.11); agenda item 71 *(a)*.
*Meeting numbers.* GA 50th session: 1st Committee 3-11, 17, 18; plenary 90.

### Education and information

As requested by the General Assembly in 1993,[16] the Secretary-General presented, in July, the replies of three Member States and one UN specialized agency to his request for information on their activities regarding disarmament education.[17]

On 12 December, the Assembly, by **decision 50/417**, took note of the report[18] of the First Committee on education and information for disarmament.

*REFERENCES*

[1]YUN 1992, p. 106, GA res. 47/54 C, 9 Dec. 1992. [2]A/50/291. [3]A/CONF.179/2. [4]A/CONF.179/3. [5]YUN 1994, p. 179, GA res. 49/76 D, 15 Dec. 1994. [6]A/50/380. [7]YUN 1986, p. 85. [8]YUN 1987, p. 88. [9]A/50/391. [10]A/C.5/49/57. [11]YUN 1994, p. 180. [12]A/50/416. [13]YUN 1993, p. 129, GA res. 48/68, 16 Dec. 1993. [14]A/50/377 & Corr.1. [15]A/45/372 & *The Role of the United Nations in the Field of Verification*, Sales No. E.91.IX.11. [16]YUN 1993, p. 150, GA res. 48/64, 16 Dec. 1993. [17]A/50/309. [18]A/50/578.

Chapter III

# Other political questions

During 1995, the United Nations continued to address issues relating to the eradication of colonialism, information, international cooperation in the peaceful uses of outer space and atomic radiation effects.

In December, the General Assembly acted on the recommendations of its Special Committee on the Situation with regard to the Implementation of the Declaration on the Granting of Independence to Colonial Countries and Peoples, adopting a series of resolutions concerning decolonization issues. The Assembly also invited Member States to provide their comments on the future of the Trusteeship Council.

As recommended by its Committee on Information, the General Assembly adopted resolutions on the promotion of the establishment of a more just and more effective world information and communication order and on UN public information policies and activities. It also endorsed recommendations of the Committee on the Peaceful Uses of Outer Space and the UN Programme on Space Applications for 1996. The UN Scientific Committee on the Effects of Atomic Radiation was asked to continue reviewing problems in that field.

The year 1995 was marked by activities to commemorate the fiftieth anniversary of the birth of the United Nations as well as of the end of the Second World War. The General Assembly proclaimed a World Week of Peace in connection with the UN fiftieth anniversary and adopted a Declaration in Commemoration of the Fiftieth Anniversary of the End of the Second World War. In October, the Assembly held a special commemorative meeting and adopted a Declaration on the Occasion of the Fiftieth Anniversary of the United Nations. The Security Council held meetings to commemorate the fiftieth anniversary of the United Nations and of the end of the Second World War in Europe and in the Asia-Pacific region. The Council President made a statement on each occasion.

In December, the Assembly again recognized the important role of the United Nations in supporting government efforts to achieve democratization.

## Trusteeship and decolonization

In 1995, the United Nations continued its efforts to eliminate colonialism. The General Assembly's Special Committee on the Situation with regard to the Implementation of the Declaration on the Granting of Independence to Colonial Countries and Peoples (Special Committee on decolonization) held its annual session in New York in two parts, on 27 February and from 10 July to 16 August, with a total of 13 meetings.[1] The Committee considered various aspects of the implementation of the 1960 Declaration,[2] including decolonization issues in general and the situation of individual Non-Self-Governing Territories (NSGTs). It considered reports of its Working Group[3] and of the Subcommittee on Small Territories, Petitions, Information and Assistance.[4]

As at 1 January 1995, the Committee was composed of 24 members (see APPENDIX III). On 20 July, Bulgaria informed[5] the Chairman of its decision to withdraw from Committee membership as of 1 August 1995. On 13 July, the Committee acceded to Mexico's request for participation in its proceedings.

On 27 February, the Committee established an open-ended working group on improving the efficiency of its work, which held informal meetings and consultations during the year. On 14 July, the Committee opened its Working Group to all members.

### Decade for the Eradication of Colonialism

In accordance with a 1994 General Assembly resolution,[6] the Special Committee on decolonization carried out in 1995 a mid-term review of the 1991 plan of action[7] for the International Decade for the Eradication of Colonialism (1990-2000), which had been declared by the Assembly in 1988.[8]

The Committee organized a Caribbean Regional Seminar on the Mid-term Review of the Plan of Action (Port-of-Spain, Trinidad and Tobago, 3-5 July) to assess political, social and economic conditions in the small island NSGTs, particularly with a view to evaluating their evolution towards self-determination. The Seminar, which brought together representatives of the peoples and the administering Powers of NSGTs in the Caribbean region, examined available options for self-determination, such as independence, free association or integration with an independent State, association with an organization of independent

States or economically sustainable autonomy, as well as other possible options. A broad range of economic and social questions and environmental issues were considered, including the socio-economic advancement of NSGTs and its impact on self-determination; tourism development; drug trafficking and money laundering; human resources development; the role of specialized agencies and international and regional organizations in economic and social advancement; access to UN programmes and activities; implications of global warming, sealevel rise and other ecological hazards; disaster preparedness and relief; and questions relating to the law of the sea. The Seminar also discussed regional cooperation in the preservation and protection of marine and other natural resources from over-exploitation; transport and communications; higher education; research and development; public health care; disaster mitigation; and regional pooling arrangements for sharing special skills and expertise. On 5 July, the Seminar adopted a number of conclusions and recommendations.[9] The guidelines and rules of procedure for the Seminar were contained in a separate report.[10]

On 10 July, the Special Committee's Working Group recommended[3] that the Committee invite UN organs, agencies and institutions to apprise the Secretary-General of actions taken to implement the 1991 Assembly resolution[7] relating to the plan of action, and report to the Assembly in 1996. Noting that the action plan provided for seminars in the Caribbean and Pacific regions alternately, the Working Group recommended that the Committee organize in 1996 a seminar in the Pacific for that region's NSGTs.

The Committee[1] approved those recommendations on 14 July. On 18 July, it noted the Caribbean Seminar's report,[9] on the understanding that reservations expressed by its members would be reflected in that meeting's record.[11]

## Implementation of the 1960 Declaration

On 6 December, the General Assembly adopted **resolution 50/39**.

### Implementation of the Declaration on the Granting of Independence to Colonial Countries and Peoples

*The General Assembly,*

*Having examined* the report of the Special Committee on the Situation with regard to the Implementation of the Declaration on the Granting of Independence to Colonial Countries and Peoples,

*Recalling* its resolution 1514(XV) of 14 December 1960, containing the Declaration on the Granting of Independence to Colonial Countries and Peoples, and all its subsequent resolutions concerning the implementation of the Declaration, most recently resolution 49/89 of 16 December 1994, as well as the relevant resolutions of the Security Council,

*Recognizing* that the eradication of colonialism is one of the priorities of the Organization for the decade that began in 1990,

*Deeply conscious* of the need to take, speedily, measures to eliminate the last vestiges of colonialism by the year 2000, as called for in its resolution 43/47 of 22 November 1988,

*Reiterating its conviction* of the need for the elimination of colonialism, as well as of the need for the total eradication of racial discrimination and violations of basic human rights,

*Noting with satisfaction* the achievements of the Special Committee in contributing to the effective and complete implementation of the Declaration and other relevant resolutions of the United Nations on decolonization,

*Stressing* the importance of the participation of the administering Powers in the work of the Special Committee,

*Also noting with satisfaction* the cooperation and active participation of some administering Powers in the work of the Special Committee, as well as their continued readiness to receive United Nations visiting missions in the Territories under their administration,

*Noting with concern* the negative impact which the non-participation of certain administering Powers has had on the work of the Special Committee, depriving it of an important source of information on the Territories under their administration,

*Aware* of the pressing need of newly independent and emerging States for assistance from the United Nations and its system of organizations in the economic, social and other fields,

*Aware also* of the pressing need of the remaining Non-Self-Governing Territories, including particularly the small island Territories, for economic, social and other assistance from the United Nations and the organizations within its system,

*Taking special note* of the fact that, during its 1995 session, the Special Committee carried out a mid-term review of the Plan of Action for the International Decade for the Eradication of Colonialism in the context of the commemoration of the fiftieth anniversary of the United Nations, in which further options for self-determination were explored,

1. *Reaffirms* its resolution 1514(XV) and all other resolutions on decolonization, including its resolution 43/47, in which it declared the decade that began in 1990 as the International Decade for the Eradication of Colonialism, and calls upon the administering Powers, in accordance with those resolutions, to take all necessary steps to enable the peoples of the Territories concerned to exercise fully as soon as possible their right to self-determination, including independence;

2. *Affirms once again* that the continuation of colonialism in any form or manifestation—including economic exploitation—is incompatible with the Charter of the United Nations, the Universal Declaration of Human Rights and the Declaration on the Granting of Independence to Colonial Countries and Peoples;

3. *Reaffirms its determination* to continue to take all steps necessary to bring about the complete and speedy eradication of colonialism and the faithful observance by all States of the relevant provisions of the Charter, the Declaration on the Granting of Independence to Colonial Countries and Peoples and the Universal Declaration of Human Rights;

4. *Affirms once again* its support for the aspirations of the peoples under colonial rule to exercise their right to self-determination, including independence;

5. *Approves* the report of the Special Committee on the Situation with regard to the Implementation of the Declaration on the Granting of Independence to Colonial Countries and Peoples covering its work during 1995, including the programme of work envisaged for 1996;

6. *Calls upon* all States, in particular the administering Powers, as well as the specialized agencies and other organizations of the United Nations system, to give effect within their respective spheres of competence to the recommendations of the Special Committee for the implementation of the Declaration and other relevant resolutions of the United Nations;

7. *Calls upon* the administering Powers to ensure that no activity of foreign economic and other interests in the Non-Self-Governing Territories under their administration hinders the peoples of those Territories from exercising their right to self-determination, including independence;

8. *Takes note* of the decision of some of the administering Powers to close or downsize some of the military bases in the Non-Self-Governing Territories;

9. *Calls upon* the administering Powers to eliminate the remaining military bases in the Non-Self-Governing Territories in compliance with the relevant resolutions of the General Assembly, and urges them not to involve those Territories in any offensive acts or interference against other States;

10. *Urges* all States, directly and through their action in the specialized agencies and other organizations of the United Nations system, to provide moral and material assistance to the peoples of colonial Territories, and requests that the administering Powers, in consultation with the Governments of the Territories under their administration, take steps to enlist and make effective use of all possible assistance, on both a bilateral and a multilateral basis, in the strengthening of the economies of those Territories;

11. *Requests* the Special Committee to continue to seek suitable means for the immediate and full implementation of the Declaration and to carry out those actions approved by the General Assembly regarding the International Decade for the Eradication of Colonialism in all Territories that have not yet exercised their right to self-determination, including independence, and in particular:

   *(a)* To formulate specific proposals for the elimination of the remaining manifestations of colonialism and to report thereon to the General Assembly at its fifty-first session;

   *(b)* To continue to examine the implementation by Member States of resolution 1514(XV) and other relevant resolutions on decolonization;

   *(c)* To continue to pay special attention to the small Territories, in particular through the dispatch of regular visiting missions, and to recommend to the General Assembly the most suitable steps to be taken to enable the populations of those Territories to exercise their right to self-determination and independence;

   *(d)* To take all necessary steps to enlist worldwide support among Governments, as well as national and international organizations, for the achievement of the objectives of the Declaration and the implementation of the relevant resolutions of the United Nations;

12. *Calls upon* the administering Powers to continue to cooperate with the Special Committee in the discharge of its mandate and to receive visiting missions to the Territories to secure first-hand information and ascertain the wishes and aspirations of their inhabitants;

13. *Also calls upon* the administering Powers that have not participated in the work of the Special Committee to do so at its 1996 session;

14. *Requests* the Secretary-General, the specialized agencies and other organizations of the United Nations system to provide economic, social and other assistance to the Non-Self-Governing Territories and to continue to do so, as appropriate, after they exercise their right to self-determination, including independence;

15. *Requests* the Secretary-General to provide the Special Committee with the facilities and services required for the implementation of the present resolution, as well as of the other resolutions and decisions on decolonization adopted by the General Assembly and the Special Committee.

General Assembly resolution 50/39

6 December 1995     Meeting 82     130-4-26 (recorded vote)

9-nation draft (A/50/L.45 & Add.1); agenda item 18.
*Sponsors:* Algeria, Chile, Cuba, India, Papua New Guinea, Sierra Leone, Syrian Arab Republic, Trinidad and Tobago, Zimbabwe.
*Meeting numbers.* GA 50th session: plenary 59, 82.

Recorded vote in Assembly as follows:

*In favour:* Afghanistan, Albania, Algeria, Andorra, Antigua and Barbuda, Argentina, Armenia, Australia, Austria, Bahamas, Bahrain, Bangladesh, Barbados, Belize, Benin, Bhutan, Bolivia, Bosnia and Herzegovina, Botswana, Brazil, Brunei Darussalam, Burkina Faso, Burundi, Cambodia, Cameroon, Canada, Cape Verde, Chad, Chile, China, Colombia, Congo, Costa Rica, Côte d'Ivoire, Cuba, Cyprus, Denmark, Djibouti, Dominica, Democratic People's Republic of Korea, Ecuador, Egypt, El Salvador, Eritrea, Ethiopia, Fiji, Gabon, Ghana, Greece, Grenada, Guatemala, Guinea, Guinea-Bissau, Guyana, Haiti, Honduras, Iceland, India, Indonesia, Iran, Ireland, Jamaica, Japan, Jordan, Kazakstan, Kenya, Kuwait, Lao People's Democratic Republic, Lebanon, Lesotho, Libyan Arab Jamahiriya, Liechtenstein, Madagascar, Malawi, Malaysia, Maldives, Mali, Malta, Marshall Islands, Mauritania, Mauritius, Mexico, Micronesia, Mongolia, Mozambique, Myanmar, Nepal, New Zealand, Nicaragua, Niger, Nigeria, Norway, Oman, Pakistan, Panama, Papua New Guinea, Peru, Philippines, Portugal, Qatar, Republic of Korea, Saint Lucia, Samoa, Saudi Arabia, Senegal, Sierra Leone, Singapore, Solomon Islands, South Africa, Spain, Sri Lanka, Sudan, Suriname, Swaziland, Sweden, Syrian Arab Republic, Thailand, Togo, Trinidad and Tobago, Tunisia, United Arab Emirates, Uganda, United Republic of Tanzania, Uruguay, Vanuatu, Venezuela, Viet Nam, Yemen, Zambia, Zimbabwe.

*Against:* Israel, Russian Federation, United Kingdom, United States.

*Abstaining:* Belarus, Belgium, Bulgaria, Croatia, Czech Republic, Estonia, Finland, France, Georgia, Germany, Hungary, Italy, Latvia, Lithuania, Luxembourg, Monaco, Morocco, Netherlands, Poland, Republic of Moldova, Romania, Slovakia, Slovenia, the former Yugoslav Republic of Macedonia, Turkey, Ukraine.

## Implementation by international organizations

**Report of the Secretary-General.** As requested by the General Assembly in 1994,[12] the Secretary-General submitted in June 1995 a report with a later addendum,[13] containing summaries of information provided by two specialized agencies and an international institution forming part of or associated with the United Nations on action taken to implement the 1960 Declaration.[2]

**Report of the President of the Economic and Social Council.** In accordance with 1994 resolutions of the Economic and Social Council[14] and the General Assembly,[12] the Council President reported[15] in June on ongoing consultations with the Special Committee Chairman concerning implementation of the Declaration by international organizations. During the period under review, the UN Development Programme (UNDP) remained the primary provider of assistance to NSGTs. In close collaboration with other UN organizations and, where appropriate, the Caribbean Community, UNDP continued to fund projects covering primary economic sectors such as tourism, agriculture, fisheries industry, transportation, communication and power generation, as well as the social and educational sectors. Its recalculated indicative planning figures for 1992-1996, including estimated cost sharing, were $983,000 for St. Helena, $838,000 for Tokelau, $747,000 for Anguilla, $680,000 for the Turks and Caicos Islands, $543,000 for the British Virgin Islands, $337,000 for Montserrat and $270,000 for the Cayman Islands.

In addition to executing projects funded by UNDP, a number of specialized agencies and organizations extended assistance to NSGTs from within their own budgetary resources. The report described programmes by the Food and Agriculture Organization of the United Nations, the UN Educational, Scientific and Cultural Organization, the World Health Organization and the UN Conference on Trade and Development.

**ECONOMIC AND SOCIAL COUNCIL ACTION**

On 28 July, the Economic and Social Council adopted **resolution 1995/58**.

**Implementation of the Declaration on the Granting of Independence to Colonial Countries and Peoples by the specialized agencies and the international institutions associated with the United Nations**

*The Economic and Social Council*,

*Having examined* the report of the Secretary-General and the report of the President of the Economic and Social Council on consultations held with the Chairman of the Special Committee on the Situation with regard to the Implementation of the Declaration on the Granting of Independence to Colonial Countries and Peoples,

*Having heard* the statement by the Acting Chairman of the Special Committee,

*Recalling* General Assembly resolutions 1514(XV) of 14 December 1960 and 1541(XV) of 15 December 1960 and resolutions of the Special Committee, as well as other relevant resolutions and decisions, including in particular its resolution 1994/37 of 29 July 1994,

*Bearing in mind* the relevant provisions of the final documents of the successive Conferences of Heads of State or Government of Non-Aligned Countries and of the resolutions adopted by the Assembly of Heads of State and Government of the Organization of African Unity, the South Pacific Forum and the Caribbean Community,

*Conscious* of the need to facilitate the implementation of the Declaration on the Granting of Independence to Colonial Countries and Peoples,

*Noting* that the large majority of the remaining Non-Self-Governing Territories are small island Territories,

*Welcoming* the assistance extended to Non-Self-Governing Territories by certain specialized agencies and other organizations of the United Nations system, in particular the United Nations Development Programme,

*Stressing* that, because the development options of small island Non-Self-Governing Territories are limited, there are special challenges to planning for and implementing sustainable development and that those Territories will be constrained in meeting the challenges without the continued cooperation and assistance of the specialized agencies and other organizations of the United Nations system,

*Stressing also* the importance of securing necessary resources for funding expanded assistance programmes for the peoples concerned and the need to enlist the support of all major funding institutions within the United Nations system in that regard,

*Reaffirming* the mandates of the specialized agencies and other organizations of the United Nations system to take all the appropriate measures, within their respective spheres of competence, to ensure the full implementation of resolution 1514(XV) and other relevant resolutions,

*Expressing its appreciation* to the Organization of African Unity, the South Pacific Forum and the Caribbean Community, as well as other regional organizations, for the continued cooperation and assistance they have extended to the specialized agencies and other organizations of the United Nations system in this regard,

*Expressing its conviction* that closer contacts and consultations between and among the specialized agencies and other organizations of the United Nations system and regional organizations help to facilitate the effective formulation of assistance programmes for the peoples concerned,

*Mindful* of the imperative need to keep under continuous review the activities of the specialized agencies and other organizations of the United Nations system in the implementation of the various United Nations decisions relating to decolonization,

*Bearing in mind* the extremely fragile economies of the small island Non-Self-Governing Territories and their vulnerability to natural disasters, such as hurricanes, cyclones and sealevel rise, and recalling other relevant General Assembly resolutions,

*Recalling* General Assembly resolution 49/41 of 9 December 1994 on cooperation and coordination of the specialized agencies and the international institutions associated with the United Nations in their assistance to Non-Self-Governing Territories,

1. *Takes note* of the report of the President of the Economic and Social Council on his consultations with the Chairman of the Special Committee on the Situation with regard to the Implementation of the Declaration on the Granting of Independence to Colonial Countries and Peoples, and endorses the observations and suggestions arising therefrom;

2. *Takes note also* of the report of the Secretary-General;

3. *Recommends* that all States intensify their efforts in the specialized agencies and other organizations of the United Nations system to ensure implementation of the

Declaration on the Granting of Independence to Colonial Countries and Peoples and other relevant resolutions of the United Nations;

4. *Reaffirms* that the specialized agencies and other organizations and institutions of the United Nations system should continue to be guided by the relevant resolutions of the United Nations in their efforts to contribute to the implementation of the Declaration and all other relevant General Assembly resolutions;

5. *Reaffirms also* that the recognition by the General Assembly, the Security Council and other United Nations organs of the legitimacy of the aspirations of the peoples of Non-Self-Governing Territories to exercise their right to self-determination entails, as a corollary, the extension of all appropriate assistance to those peoples;

6. *Expresses its appreciation* to those specialized agencies and other organizations of the United Nations system that have continued to cooperate with the United Nations and the regional and subregional organizations in the implementation of General Assembly resolution 1514(XV) and other relevant resolutions of the United Nations, and requests all the specialized agencies and other organizations of the United Nations system to implement the relevant provisions of those resolutions;

7. *Requests* the specialized agencies and other organizations of the United Nations system, as well as international and regional organizations, to examine and review conditions in each Territory so as to take appropriate measures to accelerate progress in the economic and social sectors of the Territories;

8. *Requests* the specialized agencies and the international institutions associated with the United Nations, as well as regional organizations, to strengthen existing measures of support and formulate appropriate programmes of assistance to the remaining Non-Self-Governing Territories, within the framework of their respective mandates, in order to accelerate progress in the economic and social sectors of those Territories;

9. *Recommends* that the executive heads of the specialized agencies and other organizations of the United Nations system formulate, with the active cooperation of the regional organizations concerned, concrete proposals for the full implementation of the relevant resolutions of the United Nations and submit the proposals to their governing and legislative organs;

10. *Also recommends* that the specialized agencies and other organizations of the United Nations system continue to review at the regular meetings of their governing bodies the implementation of resolution 1514(XV) and other relevant resolutions of the United Nations;

11. *Welcomes* the continued initiative exercised by the United Nations Development Programme in maintaining close liaison among the specialized agencies and other organizations of the United Nations and in providing assistance to the peoples of Non-Self-Governing Territories;

12. *Encourages* Non-Self-Governing Territories to take steps to establish and/or strengthen disaster preparedness and management institutions and policies;

13. *Requests* the administering Powers concerned to facilitate the participation of appointed and elected representatives of Non-Self-Governing Territories in the relevant meetings and conferences of the agencies and organizations so that the Territories may benefit from the related activities of the specialized agencies and other organizations of the United Nations system;

14. *Recommends* that all Governments intensify their efforts in the specialized agencies and other organizations of the United Nations system of which they are members to ensure the full and effective implementation of resolution 1514(XV) and other relevant resolutions of the United Nations and, in that connection, accord priority to the question of providing assistance to the peoples of the Non-Self-Governing Territories;

15. *Draws the attention* of the Special Committee on the Situation with regard to the Implementation of the Declaration on the Granting of Independence to Colonial Countries and Peoples to the present resolution and to the discussion held on the subject at the substantive session of 1995 of the Economic and Social Council;

16. *Requests* the President of the Economic and Social Council to continue to maintain close contact on these matters with the Chairman of the Special Committee and to report thereon to the Council;

17. *Requests* the Secretary-General to follow the implementation of the present resolution, paying particular attention to cooperation and integration arrangements for maximizing the efficiency of the assistance activities undertaken by various organizations of the United Nations system, and to report thereon to the Council at its substantive session of 1996;

18. *Decides* to keep these questions under continuous review.

Economic and Social Council resolution 1995/58

28 July 1995          Meeting 57          31-0-20 (roll-call vote)

12-nation draft (E/1995/L.53/Rev.1); agenda item 5 *(c)*.
*Meeting numbers.* ESC 51, 56, 57.

Roll-call vote in Council as follows:

*In favour:* Bahamas, Bhutan, Brazil, Chile, China, Colombia, Costa Rica, Côte d'Ivoire, Cuba, Egypt, Gabon, Ghana, India, Indonesia, Jamaica, Libyan Arab Jamahiriya, Malaysia, Mexico, Nigeria, Pakistan, Philippines, Russian Federation, Senegal, South Africa, Sri Lanka, Sudan, Thailand, Uganda, United Republic of Tanzania, Venezuela, Zimbabwe.

*Against:* None.

*Abstaining:* Australia, Belarus, Bulgaria, Canada, Denmark, France, Germany, Greece, Ireland, Japan, Luxembourg, Netherlands, Norway, Poland, Portugal, Republic of Korea, Romania, Ukraine, United Kingdom, United States.

Speaking in explanation of vote, the United States said it abstained because the text had unnecessarily and inappropriately linked the work of the specialized agencies and other organizations to the 1960 Declaration whereas the time for such a link had long since passed. The Russian Federation, which voted in favour, believed nevertheless that such matters should be dealt with in the General Assembly, and stated that it might vote differently if a similar resolution were introduced in the Council in the future.

**GENERAL ASSEMBLY ACTION**

On 6 December, the General Assembly adopted **resolution 50/34.**

## Implementation of the Declaration on the Granting of Independence to Colonial Countries and Peoples by the specialized agencies and the international institutions associated with the United Nations

*The General Assembly,*

*Having considered* the item entitled "Implementation of the Declaration on the Granting of Independence to Colonial Countries and Peoples by the specialized agencies and the international institutions associated with the United Nations",

*Having also considered* the reports submitted on the item by the Secretary-General and the Chairman of the Special Committee on the Situation with regard to the Implementation of the Declaration on the Granting of Independence to Colonial Countries and Peoples,

*Having examined* the chapter of the report of the Special Committee on the Situation with regard to the Implementation of the Declaration on the Granting of Independence to Colonial Countries and Peoples relating to the item,

*Recalling* its resolutions 1514(XV) of 14 December 1960 and 1541(XV) of 15 December 1960, and resolutions of the Special Committee, as well as other relevant resolutions and decisions of the United Nations,

*Bearing in mind* the relevant provisions of the final documents of the successive Conferences of Heads of State or Government of Non-Aligned Countries and of the resolutions adopted by the Assembly of Heads of State and Government of the Organization of African Unity, the South Pacific Forum and the Caribbean Community,

*Conscious* of the need to facilitate the implementation of the Declaration on the Granting of Independence to Colonial Countries and Peoples, contained in its resolution 1514(XV),

*Noting* that the large majority of the remaining Non-Self-Governing Territories are small island Territories,

*Welcoming* the assistance extended to Non-Self-Governing Territories by certain specialized agencies and other organizations of the United Nations system, in particular the United Nations Development Programme,

*Stressing* that, because the development options of small island Non-Self-Governing Territories are limited, there are special challenges to planning for and implementing sustainable development and that those Territories will be constrained in meeting the challenges without the continuing cooperation and assistance of the specialized agencies and other organizations of the United Nations system,

*Stressing also* the importance of securing necessary resources for funding expanded assistance programmes for the peoples concerned and the need to enlist the support of all major funding institutions within the United Nations system in that regard,

*Reaffirming* the mandates of the specialized agencies and other organizations of the United Nations system to take all the appropriate measures, within their respective spheres of competence, to ensure the full implementation of resolution 1514(XV) and other relevant resolutions,

*Expressing its appreciation* to the Organization of African Unity, the South Pacific Forum and the Caribbean Community, as well as other regional organizations, for the continuing cooperation and assistance they have extended to the specialized agencies and other organizations of the United Nations system in this regard,

*Expressing its conviction* that closer contacts and consultations between and among the specialized agencies and other organizations of the United Nations system and regional organizations help to facilitate the effective formulation of assistance programmes for the peoples concerned,

*Mindful* of the imperative need to keep under continuous review the activities of the specialized agencies and other organizations of the United Nations system in the implementation of the various United Nations decisions relating to decolonization,

*Bearing in mind* the extremely fragile economies of the Non-Self-Governing small island Territories and their vulnerability to natural disasters, such as hurricanes, cyclones and sealevel rise, and recalling its relevant resolutions,

*Recalling* its resolution 49/41 of 9 December 1994 on the implementation of the Declaration by the specialized agencies and the international institutions associated with the United Nations,

1. *Takes note* of the report of the Chairman of the Special Committee on the Situation with regard to the Implementation of the Declaration on the Granting of Independence to Colonial Countries and Peoples on his consultations with the President of the Economic and Social Council and endorses the observations and suggestions arising therefrom;

2. *Recommends* that all States intensify their efforts in the specialized agencies and other organizations of the United Nations system to ensure implementation of the Declaration on the Granting of Independence to Colonial Countries and Peoples and other relevant resolutions of the United Nations;

3. *Reaffirms* that the specialized agencies and other organizations and institutions of the United Nations system should continue to be guided by the relevant resolutions of the United Nations in their efforts to contribute to the implementation of the Declaration and other relevant General Assembly resolutions;

4. *Reaffirms also* that the recognition by the General Assembly and other United Nations organs of the legitimacy of the aspiration of the peoples of Non-Self-Governing Territories to exercise their right to self-determination entails, as a corollary, the extension of all appropriate assistance to those peoples;

5. *Expresses its appreciation* to those specialized agencies and other organizations of the United Nations system that have continued to cooperate with the United Nations and the regional and subregional organizations in the implementation of resolution 1514(XV) and other relevant resolutions of the United Nations;

6. *Requests* the specialized agencies and the international institutions associated with the United Nations, as well as regional organizations, to examine and review conditions in each Territory so as to take appropriate measures to accelerate progress in the economic and social sectors of the Territories and strengthen existing measures of support, and, in that regard, to formulate appropriate programmes of assistance to the remaining Non-Self-Governing Territories, within the framework of their respective mandates;

7. *Recommends* that the executive heads of the specialized agencies and other organizations of the United Nations system formulate, with the active cooperation of the regional organizations concerned, concrete proposals for the full implementation of the relevant resolutions

of the United Nations and submit the proposals to their governing and legislative organs;

8. *Also recommends* that the specialized agencies and other organizations of the United Nations system continue to review at the regular meetings of their governing bodies the implementation of resolution 1514(XV) and other relevant resolutions of the United Nations;

9. *Welcomes* the continuing initiative exercised by the United Nations Development Programme in maintaining close liaison among the specialized agencies and other organizations of the United Nations system and in providing assistance to the peoples of Non-Self-Governing Territories;

10. *Encourages* Non-Self-Governing Territories to take steps to establish and/or strengthen disaster preparedness and management institutions and policies;

11. *Requests* the administering Powers concerned to facilitate the participation of appointed and elected representatives of Non-Self-Governing Territories in the relevant meetings and conferences of the specialized agencies and other organizations of the United Nations system so that the Territories may benefit from the related activities of those agencies and other organizations;

12. *Recommends* that all Governments intensify their efforts in the specialized agencies and other organizations of the United Nations system of which they are members to ensure the full and effective implementation of resolution 1514(XV) and other relevant resolutions of the United Nations and, in that connection, accord priority to the question of providing assistance to the peoples of the Non-Self-Governing Territories;

13. *Requests* the Secretary-General to continue to assist the specialized agencies and other organizations of the United Nations system in working out appropriate measures for implementing the relevant resolutions of the United Nations and to prepare for submission to the relevant bodies, with the assistance of those agencies and organizations, a report on the action taken in implementation of the relevant resolutions, including the present resolution, since the circulation of his previous report;

14. *Commends* the Economic and Social Council for its debate and its resolution 1995/58 of 28 July 1995 on this issue, and requests it to continue to consider, in consultation with the Special Committee, appropriate measures for coordination of the policies and activities of the specialized agencies and other organizations of the United Nations system in implementing the relevant resolutions of the General Assembly;

15. *Requests* the specialized agencies to report periodically to the Secretary-General on the implementation of the present resolution;

16. *Requests* the Secretary-General to transmit the present resolution to the governing bodies of the appropriate specialized agencies and international institutions associated with the United Nations so that those bodies may take the necessary measures to implement the resolution, and also requests the Secretary-General to report to the General Assembly at its fifty-first session on the implementation of the present resolution;

17. *Requests* the Special Committee to continue to examine the question and to report thereon to the General Assembly at its fifty-first session.

**General Assembly resolution 50/34**

6 December 1995    Meeting 82    107-0-50 (recorded vote)

Approved by Fourth Committee (A/50/611) by recorded vote (91-0-43), 3 November (meeting 14); draft by Committee on decolonization (A/50/23); agenda items 90 & 12.
*Meeting numbers.* GA 50th session: 4th Committee 2, 5-7, 14; plenary 82.

Recorded vote in Assembly as follows:

*In favour:* Afghanistan, Algeria, Antigua and Barbuda, Australia, Bahamas, Bahrain, Bangladesh, Barbados, Belize, Benin, Bolivia, Botswana, Brazil, Brunei Darussalam, Burkina Faso, Burundi, Cambodia, Cameroon, Cape Verde, Chad, Chile, China, Colombia, Congo, Côte d'Ivoire, Cuba, Cyprus, Democratic People's Republic of Korea, Djibouti, Dominica, Ecuador, Egypt, El Salvador, Ethiopia, Fiji, Gabon, Ghana, Guatemala, Guinea, Guinea-Bissau, Guyana, Haiti, Honduras, India, Indonesia, Iran, Jamaica, Jordan, Kenya, Kuwait, Lao People's Democratic Republic, Lebanon, Lesotho, Libyan Arab Jamahiriya, Madagascar, Malawi, Malaysia, Maldives, Mali, Marshall Islands, Mauritania, Mauritius, Mexico, Micronesia, Mongolia, Myanmar, Nepal, New Zealand, Nicaragua, Niger, Nigeria, Oman, Pakistan, Panama, Papua New Guinea, Paraguay, Peru, Philippines, Qatar, Republic of Korea, Saint Lucia, Samoa, Saudi Arabia, Senegal, Sierra Leone, Singapore, Solomon Islands, South Africa, Sri Lanka, Sudan, Suriname, Swaziland, Syrian Arab Republic, Thailand, Togo, Trinidad and Tobago, Tunisia, Uganda, United Arab Emirates, United Republic of Tanzania, Uruguay, Vanuatu, Venezuela, Viet Nam, Yemen, Zambia, Zimbabwe.

*Against:* None.

*Abstaining:* Albania, Andorra, Argentina, Armenia, Austria, Azerbaijan, Belarus, Belgium, Bosnia and Herzegovina, Bulgaria, Canada, Croatia, Czech Republic, Denmark, Estonia, Finland, France, Georgia, Germany, Greece, Hungary, Iceland, Ireland, Israel, Italy, Japan, Kazakstan, Latvia, Liechtenstein, Lithuania, Luxembourg, Malta, Monaco, Morocco, Netherlands, Norway, Poland, Portugal, Republic of Moldova, Romania, Russian Federation, Slovakia, Slovenia, Spain, Sweden, the former Yugoslav Republic of Macedonia, Turkey, Ukraine, United Kingdom, United States.

## Foreign interests impeding implementation of the Declaration

The Special Committee on decolonization in 1995 again considered foreign economic and other interests impeding implementation of the 1960 Declaration. It had before it working papers by the Secretariat describing economic conditions and foreign activities in Anguilla,[16] Bermuda,[17] the Cayman Islands,[18] Montserrat,[19] the Turks and Caicos Islands[20] and the United States Virgin Islands.[21]

**GENERAL ASSEMBLY ACTION**

On 6 December, the General Assembly adopted **resolution 50/33**.

**Activities of foreign economic and other interests which impede the implementation of the Declaration on the Granting of Independence to Colonial Countries and Peoples in Territories under colonial domination**

*The General Assembly,*

*Having considered* the item entitled "Activities of foreign economic and other interests which impede the implementation of the Declaration on the Granting of Independence to Colonial Countries and Peoples in Territories under colonial domination",

*Having examined* the chapter of the report of the Special Committee on the Situation with regard to the Implementation of the Declaration on the Granting of Independence to Colonial Countries and Peoples relating to the item,

*Recalling* its resolution 1514(XV) of 14 December 1960, as well as all its other relevant resolutions, including, in particular, resolution 46/181 of 19 December 1991, endorsing the plan of action for the International Decade for the Eradication of Colonialism,

*Reaffirming* the solemn obligation of the administering Powers under the Charter of the United Nations to promote the political, economic, social and educational advancement of the inhabitants of the Territories under their administration and to protect the human and natural resources of those Territories against abuses,

*Reaffirming also* that any economic or other activity that constitutes an obstacle to the implementation of the Declaration on the Granting of Independence to Colonial Countries and Peoples and obstructs efforts aimed at the elimination of colonialism is a direct violation of the rights of the inhabitants and of the principles of the Charter and all relevant resolutions of the United Nations,

*Reaffirming further* that the natural resources are the heritage of the indigenous populations of the colonial and Non-Self-Governing Territories,

*Aware* of the special circumstances of the geographical location, size and economic conditions of each Territory and bearing in mind the need to promote the stability, diversification and strengthening of the respective economy of each Territory,

*Conscious* of the particular vulnerability of the small Territories to natural disasters and environmental degradation,

*Conscious also* that foreign economic investment, when done in collaboration with the peoples of the Non-Self-Governing Territories and in accordance with their wishes, could make a valid contribution to the socioeconomic development of the Territories and could also make a valid contribution to the exercise of their right to self-determination,

*Concerned* about the activities of those foreign economic, financial and other interests which exploit the natural and human resources of the Non-Self-Governing Territories to the detriment of the interests of the inhabitants of those Territories and deprive them of their right to control the wealth of their countries,

*Bearing in mind* the relevant provisions of the final documents of the successive Conferences of Heads of State or Government of Non-Aligned Countries and of the resolutions adopted by the Assembly of Heads of State and Government of the Organization of African Unity, the South Pacific Forum and the Caribbean Community,

1. *Reaffirms* the inalienable right of the peoples of colonial and Non-Self-Governing Territories to self-determination and independence and to the enjoyment of the natural resources of their Territories, as well as their right to dispose of those resources in their best interests;

2. *Affirms* the value of foreign economic investment undertaken in collaboration with the peoples of the Non-Self-Governing Territories and in accordance with their wishes in order to make a valid contribution to the socioeconomic development of the Territories;

3. *Reiterates* that any administering Power that deprives the colonial peoples of Non-Self-Governing Territories of the exercise of their legitimate rights over their natural resources, or subordinates the rights and interests of those peoples to foreign economic and financial interests, violates the solemn obligations it has assumed under the Charter of the United Nations;

4. *Reaffirms its concern* about the activities of those foreign economic, financial and other interests which continue to exploit the natural resources that are the heritage of the indigenous populations of the colonial and Non-Self-Governing Territories in the Caribbean, the Pacific and other regions, as well as their human resources, to the detriment of their interests, thus depriving them of their right to control the resources of their Territories and impeding the realization by those peoples of their legitimate aspirations for self-determination and independence;

5. *Reiterates its deep concern* about those activities of foreign economic and other interests in the colonial and Non-Self-Governing Territories which are impeding the implementation of the Declaration on the Granting of Independence to Colonial Countries and Peoples, contained in its resolution 1514(XV), and the efforts to eliminate colonialism;

6. *Calls once again upon* all Governments that have not yet done so to take, in accordance with the relevant provisions of its resolution 2621(XXV) of 12 October 1970, legislative, administrative or other measures in respect of their nationals and the bodies corporate under their jurisdiction, if any, that own and operate enterprises in colonial and Non-Self-Governing Territories that are detrimental to the interests of the inhabitants of those Territories, in order to put an end to such practices and to prevent new investments that run counter to the interests of the inhabitants of those Territories;

7. *Reiterates* that the damaging exploitation and plundering of the marine and other natural resources of colonial and Non-Self-Governing Territories by foreign economic interests, in violation of the relevant resolutions of the United Nations, is a threat to the integrity and prosperity of those Territories;

8. *Invites* all Governments and organizations of the United Nations system to ensure that the permanent sovereignty of the peoples of colonial and Non-Self-Governing Territories over their natural resources is fully respected and safeguarded;

9. *Urges* the administering Powers concerned to continue to take effective measures to safeguard and guarantee the inalienable right of the peoples of the colonial and Non-Self-Governing Territories to their natural resources and to establish and maintain control over the future development of those resources, and requests the administering Powers to continue to take all necessary steps to protect the property rights of the peoples of those Territories;

10. *Calls upon* the administering Powers concerned to ensure that no discriminatory working conditions prevail in the Territories under their administration and to promote in each Territory a fair system of wages applicable to all the inhabitants without any discrimination;

11. *Requests* the Secretary-General to continue, through all means at his disposal, to inform world public opinion of those activities of foreign economic and other interests which impede the implementation of the Declaration;

12. *Appeals* to the mass media, trade unions and non-governmental organizations, as well as individuals, to continue their efforts for the full implementation of the Declaration;

13. *Decides* to continue to follow the situation in the colonial and Non-Self-Governing Territories so as to ensure that all economic activities in those Territories are aimed at strengthening and diversifying their economies in the interest of the indigenous peoples and at promoting the economic and financial viability of those Terri-

tories, in order to facilitate and accelerate the exercise by the peoples of those Territories of their right to self-determination and independence;

14.   *Requests* the Special Committee on the Situation with regard to the Implementation of the Declaration on the Granting of Independence to Colonial Countries and Peoples to continue to examine this question and to report thereon to the General Assembly at its fifty-first session.

**General Assembly resolution 50/33**

6 December 1995      Meeting 82      93-51-3 (recorded vote)

Approved by Fourth Committee (A/50/610) by recorded vote (70-41-4), 3 November (meeting 14); draft by Committee on decolonization (A/50/23), amended by Spain for EU (A/C.4/50/L.7); agenda items 89 & 18.
*Meeting numbers.* GA 50th session: 4th Committee 2, 5-7, 14; plenary 82.

Recorded vote in Assembly as follows:

*In favour:* Afghanistan, Algeria, Antigua and Barbuda, Bahamas, Bahrain, Bangladesh, Barbados, Belize, Benin, Bolivia, Botswana, Brazil, Brunei Darussalam, Burkina Faso, Burundi, Cameroon, Cape Verde, Chad, Chile, China, Colombia, Cuba, Cyprus, Djibouti, Dominica, Democratic People's Republic of Korea, Ecuador, Egypt, El Salvador, Ethiopia, Fiji, Gabon, Ghana, Guinea-Bissau, Guyana, Haiti, Honduras, India, Indonesia, Iran, Jamaica, Jordan, Kuwait, Lao People's Democratic Republic, Lebanon, Libyan Arab Jamahiriya, Madagascar, Malawi, Malaysia, Maldives, Mali, Mauritania, Mauritius, Mexico, Mongolia, Myanmar, Nicaragua, Niger, Nigeria, Oman, Pakistan, Panama, Papua New Guinea, Paraguay, Peru, Philippines, Qatar, Republic of Korea, Saint Lucia, Samoa, Saudi Arabia, Senegal, Sierra Leone, Singapore, Solomon Islands, South Africa, Sri Lanka, Sudan, Suriname, Swaziland, Syrian Arab Republic, Thailand, Togo, Trinidad and Tobago, Tunisia, Uganda, United Republic of Tanzania, Uruguay, Vanuatu, Venezuela, Viet Nam, Zambia, Zimbabwe.

*Against:* Armenia, Australia, Austria, Belarus, Belgium, Bulgaria, Canada, Congo, Côte d'Ivoire, Czech Republic, Denmark, Estonia, Finland, France, Georgia, Germany, Greece, Guinea, Hungary, Iceland, Ireland, Israel, Italy, Japan, Kazakstan, Kenya, Latvia, Liechtenstein, Lithuania, Luxembourg, Malta, Monaco, Nepal, Netherlands, New Zealand, Norway, Poland, Portugal, Republic of Moldova, Romania, Russian Federation, Slovakia, Slovenia, Spain, Sweden, the former Yugoslav Republic of Macedonia, Turkey, Ukraine, United Kingdom, United States, Yemen.*

*Abstaining:* Argentina, Marshall Islands, Micronesia.

*Later advised the Secretariat it had intended to vote in favour.

## Military activities and arrangements in colonial countries

The Special Committee on decolonization also considered military activities and arrangements by colonial Powers in Territories under their administration which might impede implementation of the 1960 Declaration. It had before it working papers by the Secretariat on military activities and arrangements in Bermuda,[17] Guam[22] and the United States Virgin Islands.[21]

**GENERAL ASSEMBLY ACTION**

In December, the General Assembly adopted **decision 50/412**.

**Military activities and arrangements by colonial Powers in Territories under their administration**

At its 82nd plenary meeting, on 6 December 1995, the General Assembly, on the recommendation of the Special Political and Decolonization Committee (Fourth Committee), adopted the following text:

"1.   The General Assembly, having considered the chapter of the report of the Special Committee on the Situation with regard to the Implementation of the Declaration on the Granting of Independence to Colonial Countries and Peoples relating to an item on the agenda of the Special Committee entitled 'Mili-

tary activities and arrangements by colonial Powers in Territories under their administration', and recalling its resolution 1514(XV) of 14 December 1960 and all other relevant resolutions and decisions of the United Nations relating to military activities in colonial and Non-Self-Governing Territories, reaffirms its strong conviction that military bases and installations in the Territories concerned could constitute an obstacle to the exercise by the people of those Territories of their right to self-determination, and reiterates its strong views that existing bases and installations, which are impeding the implementation of the Declaration on the Granting of Independence to Colonial Countries and Peoples, should be withdrawn.

"2.   Aware of the presence of such bases and installations in some of those Territories, the General Assembly urges the administering Powers concerned to continue to take all necessary measures not to involve those Territories in any offensive acts or interference against other States.

"3.   The General Assembly reiterates its concern that military activities and arrangements by colonial Powers in Territories under their administration might run counter to the rights and interests of the colonial peoples concerned, especially their right to self-determination and independence. The Assembly once again calls upon the administering Powers concerned to terminate such activities and to eliminate such military bases in compliance with its relevant resolutions.

"4.   The General Assembly reiterates that the colonial and Non-Self-Governing Territories and areas adjacent thereto should not be used for nuclear testing, dumping of nuclear wastes or deployment of nuclear and other weapons of mass destruction.

"5.   The General Assembly deplores the continued alienation of land in colonial and Non-Self-Governing Territories, particularly in the small island Territories of the Pacific and Caribbean regions, for military installations. The large-scale utilization of the local resources for this purpose could adversely affect the economic development of the Territories concerned.

"6.   The General Assembly takes note of the decision of some of the administering Powers to close or downsize some of those military bases in the Non-Self-Governing Territories.

"7.   The General Assembly requests the Secretary-General to continue to inform world public opinion of those military activities and arrangements in colonial and Non-Self-Governing Territories which constitute an obstacle to the implementation of the Declaration on the Granting of Independence to Colonial Countries and Peoples.

"8.   The General Assembly requests the Special Committee on the Situation with regard to the Implementation of the Declaration on the Granting of Independence to Colonial Countries and Peoples to continue to examine this question and to report thereon to the Assembly at its fifty-first session."

**General Assembly decision 50/412**

95-48-4 (recorded vote)

Approved by Fourth Committee (A/50/610) by recorded vote (76-40-3), 3 November (meeting 14); draft by Committee on decolonization (A/50/23); agenda items 89 & 18.
*Meeting numbers.* GA 50th session: 4th Committee 2, 5-7, 14; plenary 82.

Recorded vote in Assembly as follows:

*In favour:* Afghanistan, Algeria, Antigua and Barbuda, Bahamas, Bahrain, Bangladesh, Barbados, Benin, Bolivia, Botswana, Brazil, Brunei Darussalam, Burkina Faso, Burundi, Cameroon, Cape Verde, Chad, Chile, China, Colombia, Côte d'Ivoire, Cuba, Cyprus, Democratic People's Republic of Korea, Djibouti, Dominica, Ecuador, Egypt, El Salvador, Ethiopia, Fiji, Gabon, Ghana, Guinea-Bissau, Guyana, Haiti, Honduras, India, Indonesia, Iran, Jamaica, Jordan, Kenya, Kuwait, Lao People's Democratic Republic, Lebanon, Lesotho, Libyan Arab Jamahiriya, Madagascar, Malawi, Malaysia, Maldives, Mali, Mauritania, Mauritius, Mexico, Mongolia, Myanmar, Nicaragua, Niger, Nigeria, Oman, Pakistan, Panama, Papua New Guinea, Paraguay, Peru, Philippines, Qatar, Republic of Korea, Saint Lucia, Samoa, Saudi Arabia, Senegal, Sierra Leone, Singapore, Solomon Islands, South Africa, Sri Lanka, Sudan, Suriname, Syrian Arab Republic, Thailand, Togo, Tunisia, Uganda, United Arab Emirates, United Republic of Tanzania, Uruguay, Vanuatu, Venezuela, Viet Nam, Yemen, Zambia, Zimbabwe.

*Against:* Armenia, Australia, Austria, Belarus, Belgium, Bulgaria, Canada, Czech Republic, Denmark, Estonia, Finland, France, Georgia, Germany, Greece, Guinea, Hungary, Iceland, Ireland, Israel, Italy, Japan, Kazakstan, Latvia, Liechtenstein, Lithuania, Luxembourg, Malta, Monaco, Nepal, Netherlands, New Zealand, Norway, Poland, Portugal, Republic of Moldova, Romania, Russian Federation, Slovakia, Slovenia, Spain, Swaziland, Sweden, the former Yugoslav Republic of Macedonia, Turkey, Ukraine, United Kingdom, United States.

*Abstaining:* Argentina, Belize, Marshall Islands, Micronesia.

## Information dissemination

In 1995, the Subcommittee on Small Territories, Petitions, Information and Assistance held consultations with representatives of the Secretariat's Department of Public Information and Department of Political Affairs concerning dissemination of information on decolonization. The representatives described activities of their Departments in that respect, including regular contacts with intergovernmental and non-governmental organizations (NGOs), academic circles and institutions of higher education; replies to individual requests for information and distribution of relevant UN documents, as well as contacts with local media and communities through the worldwide network of 68 UN information centres and services; and coverage of decolonization issues in publications, television and radio programmes and press releases.

In a statement made on the occasion of the Week of Solidarity with the Peoples of All Colonial Territories Fighting for Freedom, Independence and Human Rights (22-26 May), the Subcommittee Chairman underscored that, despite the universally recognized success in the field of decolonization, the task in that area remained unfinished and required further concerted and determined action. He appealed for strengthened and continued support from the administering Powers to ensure the progress of NSGTs towards self-determination.

In July, the Special Committee on decolonization approved the Subcommittee's report,[4] including its Chairman's statement and recommendations on dissemination of information.

**GENERAL ASSEMBLY ACTION**

On 6 December, the Assembly adopted **resolution 50/40.**

### Dissemination of information on decolonization

*The General Assembly,*

*Having examined* the chapter of the report of the Special Committee on the Situation with regard to the Implementation of the Declaration on the Granting of Independence to Colonial Countries and Peoples relating to the dissemination of information on decolonization and publicity for the work of the United Nations in the field of decolonization,

*Recalling* its resolution 1514(XV) of 14 December 1960, containing the Declaration on the Granting of Independence to Colonial Countries and Peoples, and other resolutions and decisions of the United Nations concerning the dissemination of information on decolonization, in particular General Assembly resolution 49/90 of 16 December 1994,

*Recognizing* the need for flexible, practical and innovative approaches towards reviewing the options of self-determination for the peoples of Non-Self-Governing Territories with a view to achieving complete decolonization by the year 2000,

*Reiterating* the importance of dissemination of information as an instrument for furthering the aims of the Declaration, and mindful of the role of world public opinion in effectively assisting the peoples of Non-Self-Governing Territories to achieve self-determination,

*Aware* of the role of non-governmental organizations in the dissemination of information on decolonization,

1. *Approves* the chapter of the report of the Special Committee on the Situation with regard to the Implementation of the Declaration on the Granting of Independence to Colonial Countries and Peoples relating to the dissemination of information on decolonization and publicity for the work of the United Nations in the field of decolonization;

2. *Considers it important* to continue its efforts to ensure the widest possible dissemination of information on decolonization, with particular emphasis on the options of self-determination available for the peoples of Non-Self-Governing Territories;

3. *Requests* the Department of Political Affairs and the Department of Public Information of the Secretariat to take into account the suggestions of the Special Committee to continue their efforts to take measures through all the media available, including publications, radio and television, as well as the Internet, to give publicity to the work of the United Nations in the field of decolonization and, *inter alia:*

*(a)* To continue to collect, prepare and disseminate basic material on the issue of self-determination of the peoples of Non-Self-Governing Territories;

*(b)* To seek the full cooperation of the administering Powers in the discharge of the tasks referred to above;

*(c)* To maintain a working relationship with the appropriate regional and intergovernmental organizations, particularly in the Pacific and Caribbean regions, by holding periodic consultations and exchanging information;

*(d)* To encourage involvement of non-governmental organizations in the dissemination of information on decolonization;

*(e)* To report to the Special Committee on measures taken in the implementation of the present resolution;

4. *Requests* all States, including the administering Powers, to continue to extend their cooperation in the dissemination of information referred to in paragraph 2 above;

5. *Requests* the Special Committee to follow the implementation of the present resolution and to report thereon to the General Assembly at its fifty-first session.

General Assembly resolution 50/40

6 December 1995      Meeting 82      133-3-25 (recorded vote)

Draft by Committee on decolonization (A/50/23); agenda item 18.
*Meeting numbers.* GA 50th session: plenary 59, 82.

Recorded vote in Assembly as follows:

*In favour:* Afghanistan, Albania, Algeria, Andorra, Antigua and Barbuda, Argentina, Armenia, Australia, Austria, Bahamas, Bahrain, Bangladesh, Barbados, Belarus, Belize, Benin, Bhutan, Bolivia, Bosnia and Herzegovina, Botswana, Brazil, Brunei Darussalam, Burkina Faso, Burundi, Cambodia, Cameroon, Canada, Cape Verde, Chad, Chile, China, Colombia, Congo, Costa Rica, Côte d'Ivoire, Cuba, Cyprus, Democratic People's Republic of Korea, Denmark, Djibouti, Dominica, Ecuador, Egypt, El Salvador, Eritrea, Ethiopia, Fiji, Gabon, Ghana, Greece, Grenada, Guatemala, Guinea, Guinea-Bissau, Guyana, Haiti, Honduras, Iceland, India, Indonesia, Iran, Ireland, Jamaica, Japan, Jordan, Kazakstan, Kenya, Kuwait, Lao People's Democratic Republic, Lebanon, Lesotho, Libyan Arab Jamahiriya, Liechtenstein, Madagascar, Malawi, Malaysia, Maldives, Mali, Malta, Marshall Islands, Mauritania, Mauritius, Mexico, Micronesia, Mongolia, Mozambique, Myanmar, Nepal, New Zealand, Nicaragua, Niger, Nigeria, Norway, Oman, Pakistan, Panama, Papua New Guinea, Peru, Philippines, Portugal, Qatar, Republic of Korea, Saint Lucia, Samoa, Saudi Arabia, Senegal, Sierra Leone, Singapore, Solomon Islands, South Africa, Spain, Sri Lanka, Sudan, Suriname, Swaziland, Sweden, Syrian Arab Republic, Thailand, Togo, Trinidad and Tobago, Tunisia, Turkey, Uganda, Ukraine, United Arab Emirates, United Republic of Tanzania, Uruguay, Vanuatu, Venezuela, Viet Nam, Yemen, Zambia, Zimbabwe.

*Against:* Israel, United Kingdom, United States.

*Abstaining:* Azerbaijan, Belgium, Bulgaria, Croatia, Czech Republic, Estonia, Finland, France, Georgia, Germany, Hungary, Italy, Latvia, Lithuania, Luxembourg, Monaco, Morocco, Netherlands, Poland, Republic of Moldova, Romania, Russian Federation, Slovakia, Slovenia, the former Yugoslav Republic of Macedonia.

## Puerto Rico

In July 1995, the Special Committee on decolonization postponed for another year, until 1996, consideration of its decision of 15 August 1991,[23] by which it deplored the fact that the United States Congress had not adopted a legal framework for holding a referendum to enable the people of Puerto Rico to determine their political future. The Committee agreed, on the basis of its usual practice, to give due consideration to requests for hearings and heard six representatives of Puerto Rican organizations.

## Other general questions

### Scholarships

In response to a 1994 General Assembly request,[24] the Secretary-General reported in September 1995 on offers made by Member States of study and training facilities for inhabitants of NSGTs.[25] Three States informed him of scholarships between 1 October 1994 and 30 September 1995. Austria regularly provided vocational training and capacity-building assistance in the infrastructure and education sectors, as well as the training of kindergarten teachers, for inhabitants of Western Sahara. New Zealand reported that 20 students from New Caledonia and 33 students from Tokelau were studying in that country in 1995 on government scholarships. During the financial year 1994/95, the United Kingdom offered 55 scholarships to students from the British NSGTs.

**GENERAL ASSEMBLY ACTION**

On 6 December, the General Assembly adopted **resolution 50/35**.

## Offers by Member States of study and training facilities for inhabitants of Non-Self-Governing Territories

*The General Assembly,*

*Recalling* its resolution 49/42 of 9 December 1994,

*Having examined* the report of the Secretary-General on offers by Member States of study and training facilities for inhabitants of Non-Self-Governing Territories, prepared pursuant to its resolution 845(IX) of 22 November 1954,

*Conscious* of the importance of promoting the educational advancement of the inhabitants of Non-Self-Governing Territories,

*Strongly convinced* that the continuation and expansion of offers of scholarships is essential in order to meet the increasing need of students from Non-Self-Governing Territories for educational and training assistance, and considering that students in those Territories should be encouraged to avail themselves of such offers,

1. *Takes note* of the report of the Secretary-General;

2. *Expresses its appreciation* to those Member States that have made scholarships available to the inhabitants of Non-Self-Governing Territories;

3. *Invites* all States to make or continue to make generous offers of study and training facilities to the inhabitants of those Territories that have not yet attained self-government or independence and, wherever possible, to provide travel funds to prospective students;

4. *Urges* the administering Powers to take effective measures to ensure the widespread and continuous dissemination in the Territories under their administration of information relating to offers of study and training facilities made by States and to provide all the necessary facilities to enable students to avail themselves of such offers;

5. *Requests* the Secretary-General to report to the General Assembly at its fifty-first session on the implementation of the present resolution;

6. *Draws the attention* of the Special Committee on the Situation with regard to the Implementation of the Declaration on the Granting of Independence to Colonial Countries and Peoples to the present resolution.

General Assembly resolution 50/35

6 December 1995      Meeting 82      Adopted without vote

Approved by Fourth Committee (A/50/612) without vote, 3 November (meeting 14); 22-nation draft (A/C.4/50/L.4); agenda item 91.
*Meeting numbers.* GA 50th session: 4th Committee 2, 5-7, 14; plenary 82.

## Information to the United Nations

States responsible for the administration of NSGTs continued to inform the Secretary-General of the economic, social and educational conditions in the Territories, under the terms of Article 73 *e* of the UN Charter. In September, the Secretary-General reported[26] that he received information with respect to Tokelau (administered by New Zealand), and Anguilla, Bermuda and Gibraltar (administered by the United Kingdom).

**GENERAL ASSEMBLY ACTION**

On 6 December, the General Assembly adopted **resolution 50/32**.

## Information from Non-Self-Governing Territories transmitted under Article 73 *e* of the Charter of the United Nations

*The General Assembly,*

*Having examined* the chapter of the report of the Special Committee on the Situation with regard to the Implementation of the Declaration on the Granting of Independence to Colonial Countries and Peoples relating to the information from Non-Self-Governing Territories transmitted under Article 73 *e* of the Charter of the United Nations and the action taken by the Special Committee in respect of that information,

*Having also examined* the report of the Secretary-General on the item,

*Recalling* its resolution 1970(XVIII) of 16 December 1963, in which it requested the Special Committee to study the information transmitted to the Secretary-General in accordance with Article 73 *e* of the Charter and to take such information fully into account in examining the situation with regard to the implementation of the Declaration on the Granting of Independence to Colonial Countries and Peoples, contained in its resolution 1514(XV) of 14 December 1960,

*Recalling also* its resolution 49/39 of 9 December 1994, in which it requested the Special Committee to continue to discharge the functions entrusted to it under resolution 1970(XVIII),

*Stressing* the importance of timely transmission by the administering Powers of adequate information under Article 73 *e* of the Charter, in particular in relation to the preparation by the Secretariat of the working papers on the Territories concerned,

1. *Approves* the chapter of the report of the Special Committee on the Situation with regard to the Implementation of the Declaration on the Granting of Independence to Colonial Countries and Peoples relating to the information from Non-Self-Governing Territories transmitted under Article 73 *e* of the Charter of the United Nations;

2. *Reaffirms* that, in the absence of a decision by the General Assembly itself that a Non-Self-Governing Territory has attained a full measure of self-government in terms of Chapter XI of the Charter, the administering Power concerned should continue to transmit information under Article 73 *e* of the Charter with respect to that Territory;

3. *Requests* the administering Powers concerned to transmit or continue to transmit to the Secretary-General the information prescribed in Article 73 *e* of the Charter, as well as the fullest possible information on political and constitutional developments in the Territories concerned, within a maximum period of six months following the expiration of the administrative year in those Territories;

4. *Requests* the Secretary-General to continue to ensure that adequate information is drawn from all available published sources in connection with the preparation of the working papers relating to the Territories concerned;

5. *Requests* the Special Committee to continue to discharge the functions entrusted to it under resolution 1970(XVIII), in accordance with established procedures, and to report thereon to the General Assembly at its fifty-first session.

General Assembly resolution 50/32

6 December 1995    Meeting 82    153-0-4 (recorded vote)

Approved by Fourth Committee (A/50/609) by recorded vote (121-0-3), 3 November (meeting 14); draft by Committee on decolonization (A/50/23); agenda item 88.

*Meeting numbers.* GA 50th session: 4th Committee 2, 5-7, 14; plenary 82.

Recorded vote in Assembly as follows:

*In favour:* Afghanistan, Albania, Algeria, Antigua and Barbuda, Argentina, Armenia, Australia, Austria, Azerbaijan, Bahamas, Bahrain, Bangladesh, Barbados, Belarus, Belgium, Belize, Benin, Bolivia, Bosnia and Herzegovina, Botswana, Brazil, Brunei Darussalam, Bulgaria, Burkina Faso, Burundi, Cambodia, Cameroon, Canada, Cape Verde, Chad, Chile, China, Colombia, Congo, Côte d'Ivoire, Croatia, Cuba, Cyprus, Czech Republic, Denmark, Djibouti, Dominica, Democratic People's Republic of Korea, Ecuador, Egypt, El Salvador, Eritrea, Estonia, Ethiopia, Fiji, Finland, Gabon, Georgia, Germany, Ghana, Greece, Grenada, Guatemala, Guinea, Guyana, Haiti, Honduras, Hungary, Iceland, India, Indonesia, Iran, Ireland, Israel, Italy, Jamaica, Japan, Jordan, Kazakstan, Kenya, Kuwait, Kyrgyzstan, Lao People's Democratic Republic, Latvia, Lebanon, Libyan Arab Jamahiriya, Liechtenstein, Lithuania, Luxembourg, Madagascar, Malawi, Malaysia, Maldives, Mali, Malta, Marshall Islands, Mauritania, Mauritius, Mexico, Micronesia, Mongolia, Morocco, Myanmar, Nepal, Netherlands, New Zealand, Nicaragua, Niger, Nigeria, Norway, Oman, Pakistan, Panama, Papua New Guinea, Paraguay, Peru, Philippines, Poland, Portugal, Qatar, Republic of Korea, Republic of Moldova, Romania, Russian Federation, Saint Lucia, Samoa, Saudi Arabia, Senegal, Sierra Leone, Singapore, Slovakia, Slovenia, Solomon Islands, South Africa, Spain, Sri Lanka, Sudan, Suriname, Swaziland, Sweden, Syrian Arab Republic, Thailand, the former Yugoslav Republic of Macedonia, Togo, Trinidad and Tobago, Tunisia, Turkey, Uganda, Ukraine, United Arab Emirates, United Republic of Tanzania, Uruguay, Vanuatu, Venezuela, Viet Nam, Yemen, Zambia, Zimbabwe.

*Against:* None.

*Abstaining:* France, Guinea-Bissau, United Kingdom, United States.

## Visiting missions

The Chairman of the Special Committee on decolonization, as requested by the Committee in 1994,[27] held consultations with representatives of the administering Powers on the question of sending visiting missions to NSGTs. In July 1995, he reported[28] that some NSGTs had expressed their willingness to receive UN missions and that he had again appealed to the administering Powers for cooperation in sending such missions, which were essential for the successful implementation of the 1991 plan of action[7] for the International Decade for the Eradication of Colonialism (see above).

One administering Power said that those territorial Governments willing to receive visiting missions should first consult with the administering Power concerned. Two others declared themselves open to any suggestions by local Governments in the Territories regarding their readiness to receive such missions. Another administering Power found it difficult to facilitate access to the Territory concerned and hoped that the Secretary-General would succeed in his efforts to bring the parties together and make possible the dispatch of a visiting mission. A number of the administering Powers reiterated their willingness to continue providing information on NSGTs under their administration (see above).

On 10 July, the Committee adopted a resolution[29] stressing the need to dispatch periodic missions to NSGTs to facilitate full implementation of the 1960 Declaration,[2] calling on the administering Powers to continue to cooperate by receiving UN visiting missions in Territories under their administration and requesting them to consider new approaches in the Committee's work. The Committee requested its Chairman to continue consulting with those Powers and to report as appropriate.

## Other colonial Territories

### East Timor

The Special Committee on decolonization considered a working paper[30] by the Secretariat on political developments, the human rights situation, and economic, social and educational conditions in East Timor. The paper also described UN consideration of the situation. The Committee acceded to the request by Sao Tome and Principe to participate in the deliberations. It heard statements, among others, by Indonesia, Portugal and 33 petitioners. On 13 July, the Committee decided, on the proposal of its Acting Chairman, to continue consideration of the question in 1996, subject to any directives by the General Assembly and on the understanding that Indonesia's objection would be reflected in that meeting's record.[31]

By a 5 June note verbale,[32] Portugal informed the Secretary-General that it continued to be prevented from exercising its responsibilities for the administration of East Timor and remained unable to provide information concerning the Territory under Article 73 *e* of the Charter, owing to East Timor's illegal occupation by a third country which prevented its people from exercising freely their right to self-determination. Portugal further described the human rights situation in the Territory, based on reports of the Special Rapporteur on Extrajudicial, Summary or Arbitrary Executions[33] of the Commission on Human Rights, international media, NGOs and official UN documents; developments in the talks on the question of East Timor; and proceedings in the case concerning East Timor, brought by Portugal against Australia before the International Court of Justice (see PART FIVE, Chapter I).

On 10 July, Indonesia responded[34] that Portugal had relinquished its responsibility as the administering Power of East Timor when it abandoned the Territory in 1975, which resulted in civil war, and that the people of East Timor had exercised their right to self-determination by deciding in 1976 to be integrated with Indonesia. Portugal's note, it said, contained invalid information based on secondary and unreliable sources. Indonesia further described steps it had taken to improve the situation in East Timor.

In September,[35] the Secretary-General updated his 1994 progress report[36] on efforts to find a just, comprehensive and internationally acceptable solution to the question of East Timor. At a fifth round of talks (Geneva, 9 January 1995)

under the Secretary-General's auspices, the Foreign Ministers of Indonesia and Portugal noted positively his intention to facilitate and offer necessary arrangements for convening an all-inclusive, intra-East-Timorese dialogue to exchange views and explore practical ideas for improving the situation. It was understood that the dialogue would not address the Territory's political status and would not constitute a parallel negotiating track. The Ministers further agreed to consider at subsequent rounds of talks possible avenues towards a solution to the question and reaffirmed the need to improve the human rights situation in East Timor, including access to the Territory and the early release of the East Timorese imprisoned, and full accounting for the persons dead or missing, as a result of the 1991 incident in Dili[37] (see also PART THREE, Chapter III).

At the first meeting of the All-Inclusive Intra-East-Timorese Dialogue (Burg Schlaining, Austria, 2-5 June), a declaration was adopted which proposed holding further Dialogue meetings; called for measures to improve the human rights situation and to promote peace, stability, justice and social harmony; reaffirmed the necessity of East Timor's sociocultural development based on the preservation of its cultural identity; and expressed the need to involve all East Timorese in the Territory's development.

At the sixth round of talks (Geneva, 8 July), the Foreign Ministers welcomed the results of the first Dialogue meeting and the Secretary-General's intention to continue that process, and began discussions of possible avenues for a comprehensive solution, including an eventual framework for achieving such a solution, the preservation and promotion of East Timor's cultural identity, and bilateral relations.

### Falkland Islands (Malvinas)

On 10 and 13 July, the Special Committee on decolonization considered the question of the Falkland Islands (Malvinas); the United Kingdom, the administering Power, did not participate. The Committee acceded to Argentina's request for participation in the deliberations.

It had before it a working paper[38] by the Secretariat outlining political developments, arrangements for a mine-clearing operation and economic, social and educational conditions on the islands, and describing the Territory's Constitution and Government, its participation in international organizations and consideration of its future status by the UN and other intergovernmental organizations.

The Committee adopted a resolution[39] requesting Argentina and the United Kingdom to consolidate the current process of dialogue and cooperation through the resumption of negotiations to find a peaceful solution to the sovereignty dispute relating to the islands, and reiterating its firm support for the mission of good offices of the Secretary-General in assisting the parties.

**GENERAL ASSEMBLY ACTION**

On 31 October, the General Assembly, by **decision 50/406**, deferred consideration of the question of the Falkland Islands (Malvinas) and included it on the provisional agenda of its 1996 session.

## Gibraltar

The Special Committee on decolonization considered the question of Gibraltar on 10 and 11 July. It had before it a working paper[40] describing political developments and economic, social and educational conditions in Gibraltar, as well as UN consideration of the question and discussions of the Territory's future status. The Committee acceded to Spain's request for participation in the deliberations. It heard statements by Spain, the Chief Minister of Gibraltar and one petitioner representing an NGO.

The Committee decided to continue its consideration of Gibraltar in 1996, and to transmit relevant documentation to the Assembly to facilitate consideration by the Fourth (Special Political and Decolonization) Committee.

**GENERAL ASSEMBLY ACTION**

In December, the General Assembly adopted **decision 50/415**.

### Question of Gibraltar

At its 82nd plenary meeting, on 6 December 1995, the General Assembly, on the recommendation of the Special Political and Decolonization Committee (Fourth Committee), adopted the following text as representing the consensus of the members of the Assembly:

"The General Assembly, recalling its decision 49/420 of 9 December 1994 and recalling at the same time that the statement agreed to by the Governments of Spain and the United Kingdom of Great Britain and Northern Ireland at Brussels on 27 November 1984 stipulates, *inter alia*, the following:

'The establishment of a negotiating process aimed at overcoming all the differences between them over Gibraltar and at promoting cooperation on a mutually beneficial basis on economic, cultural, touristic, aviation, military and environmental matters. Both sides accept that the issues of sovereignty will be discussed in that process. The British Government will fully maintain its commitment to honour the wishes of the people of Gibraltar as set out in the preamble of the 1969 Constitution',

takes note of the fact that, as part of that process, the Ministers for Foreign Affairs of Spain and of the United Kingdom of Great Britain and Northern Ireland hold annual meetings alternately in each capital, the most recent of which took place in London on 20 December 1994, and urges both Governments

to continue their negotiations with the object of reaching a definitive solution to the problem of Gibraltar in the light of relevant resolutions of the General Assembly and in the spirit of the Charter of the United Nations."

General Assembly decision 50/415

Adopted without vote

Approved by Fourth Committee (A/50/602) without vote, 3 November (meeting 15); draft by Chairman (A/C.4/50/L.3); agenda item 18.
*Meeting numbers.* GA 50th session: 4th Committee 2-7, 9-11, 13-15; plenary 82.

## New Caledonia

The Special Committee on decolonization had before it a working paper[41] on political and economic developments in New Caledonia and UN consideration of the question. It heard one petitioner on the issue.

The paper described recent developments within the framework of the 1988 Matignon Accords,[42] which provided for a self-determination referendum to be held in 1998, following a 10-year period of economic and social development aimed at: effecting a more equitable economic distribution among New Caledonia's three provinces, and providing education and training to enable the indigenous Melanesians, known as Kanaks, to participate equally in the economy and Government of the Territory. It noted that the Committee to Monitor the Matignon Accords had held its second intermediate meeting (Nouméa, New Caledonia, 15 September 1994), at which the parties agreed that a comprehensive medium- and long-term development plan should be elaborated for certain strategic sectors such as energy, telecommunications, the nickel industry, air transport and tourism. A proposal was made to set up a planning team to help the provinces and the Territory seek investment and to follow up development projects. That body—the Agency for the Economic Development of New Caledonia—was inaugurated in February 1995. The parties also reached consensus on making certain technical adjustments to the Referendum Act of 1988, so as to restore the principles of decentralization enshrined in the Matignon Accords. The Referendum Act was amended accordingly by the Organic Law of 20 February 1995, approved by the parties and received favourably by the Territorial Congress and the Territorial Consultative Committee.

The sixth meeting of the Committee to Monitor the Matignon Accords, scheduled for February 1995, was replaced by an informal tripartite meeting of the parties to the Accords (Nouméa, 7-8 February). The parties reaffirmed their desire not to break off the dialogue and to bring to fruition the process initiated in 1988. The Minister for Overseas Departments and Territories indicated that the State would play a full part in future discussions and proposed to work out a method leading to the establishment of a permanent operational organization.

On 6 December, the General Assembly adopted **resolution 50/37**.

### Question of New Caledonia

*The General Assembly*,

*Having considered* the question of New Caledonia,

*Having examined* the chapter of the report of the Special Committee on the Situation with regard to the Implementation of the Declaration on the Granting of Independence to Colonial Countries and Peoples relating to New Caledonia,

*Reaffirming* the right of peoples to self-determination as enshrined in the Charter of the United Nations,

*Recalling* its resolutions 1514(XV) and 1541(XV) of 14 and 15 December 1960, respectively,

*Noting* the importance of the positive measures being pursued in New Caledonia by the French authorities, in cooperation with all sectors of the population, to promote political, economic and social development in the Territory, including measures in the area of environmental protection and action with respect to drug abuse and trafficking, in order to provide a framework for its peaceful progress to self-determination,

*Noting also*, in this context, the importance of equitable economic and social development, as well as continued dialogue among the parties involved in New Caledonia in the preparation of the act of self-determination of New Caledonia,

*Welcoming* the strengthening of the process of review of the Matignon Accords through the increased frequency of coordination meetings,

*Noting with satisfaction* the intensification of contacts between New Caledonia and neighbouring countries of the South Pacific region,

1. *Urges* all the parties involved, in the interest of all the people of New Caledonia and building on the positive outcome of the mid-term review of the Matignon Accords, to maintain their dialogue in a spirit of harmony;

2. *Invites* all the parties involved to continue promoting a framework for the peaceful progress of the Territory towards an act of self-determination in which all options are open and which would safeguard the rights of all New Caledonians according to the letter and the spirit of the Matignon Accords, which are based on the principle that it is for the populations of New Caledonia to choose how to control their destiny;

3. *Welcomes* measures that have been taken to strengthen and diversify the New Caledonian economy in all fields, and encourages further such measures in accordance with the spirit of the Matignon Accords;

4. *Also welcomes* the importance attached by the parties to the Matignon Accords to greater progress in housing, employment, training, education and health care in New Caledonia;

5. *Acknowledges* the contribution of the Melanesian Cultural Centre to the protection of the indigenous culture of New Caledonia;

6. *Notes* the positive initiatives aimed at protecting New Caledonia's natural environment, notably the "Zonéco" operation designed to map and evaluate marine resources within the economic zone of New Caledonia;

7. *Also acknowledges* the close links between New Caledonia and the peoples of the South Pacific and the positive actions being taken by the French and provincial authorities to facilitate the further development of those links, including the development of closer relations with the member countries of the South Pacific Forum;

8. *Welcomes*, in this regard, continuing high-level visits to New Caledonia by delegations from countries of the Pacific region and high-level visits by delegations from New Caledonia to member countries of the South Pacific Forum;

9. *Requests* the Special Committee on the Situation with regard to the Implementation of the Declaration on the Granting of Independence to Colonial Countries and Peoples to continue the examination of this question at its next session and to report thereon to the General Assembly at its fifty-first session.

General Assembly resolution 50/37

6 December 1995     Meeting 82     Adopted without vote

Approved by Fourth Committee (A/50/602) without vote, 3 November (meeting 15); draft by Committee on decolonization (A/50/23); agenda item 18.
*Meeting numbers.* GA 50th session: 4th Committee 2-7, 9-11, 13-15; plenary 82.

## Western Sahara

In 1995, efforts continued towards organizing a UN-supervised referendum for the self-determination of the people of Western Sahara, in accordance with a settlement plan approved by the Security Council in 1991.[43] The Secretary-General continued exercising his good offices, in close cooperation with the Chairman of the Organization of African Unity (OAU), to settle the differences between the two parties concerned—the Government of Morocco and the Frente Popular para la Liberación de Saguia el-Hamra y de Río de Oro (Frente POLISARIO). During the year, major focus was on establishing the electorate eligible to participate in the referendum and removing obstacles to completing the identification of potential voters, carried out by the Identification Commission. To accelerate the process, the Secretary-General proposed modifications to the identification procedure and repeatedly called on both parties to cooperate fully with the UN Mission for the Referendum in Western Sahara (MINURSO). In September, the Security Council extended the Mission's mandate until 31 January 1996. In November, the Secretary-General announced his intention to present the Council with alternative options, including the possibility of MINURSO's withdrawal, should the identification operation fail to proceed with the necessary speed.

On 13 January 1995, the Security Council, having considered the Secretary-General's December 1994 report[44] on the situation in Western Sahara, adopted **resolution 973(1995)**.

*The Security Council,*

*Reaffirming* its resolutions 621(1988) of 20 September 1988, 658(1990) of 27 June 1990, 690(1991) of 29 April 1991, 725(1991) of 31 December 1991, 809(1993) of 2 March 1993 and 907(1994) of 29 March 1994,

*Recalling* the statements by the President of the Security Council of 29 July 1994 and 15 November 1994,

*Having considered* the Secretary-General's report of 14 December 1994,

*Welcoming* the efforts of the Secretary-General during his visit to the region from 25 to 29 November 1994,

*Committed* to reaching a just and lasting solution of the question of Western Sahara,

*Urging* the two parties to cooperate fully with the Secretary-General and the United Nations Mission for the Referendum in Western Sahara (MINURSO) to ensure prompt and full implementation of the Settlement Plan,

*Noting* the Secretary-General's judgement that the only way to complete identification and registration in a reasonable time is through a major reinforcement of personnel and other resources,

*Concerned* that the implementation of the Settlement Plan has been delayed and that in the circumstances the mandate of MINURSO, like the other United Nations operations, should be subject to periodic consideration by the Council,

1. *Welcomes* the report of the Secretary-General on the situation concerning Western Sahara of 14 December 1994;

2. *Reiterates* its commitment to holding, without further delay, a free, fair and impartial referendum for self-determination of the people of Western Sahara in accordance with the Settlement Plan which has been accepted by the two parties;

3. *Calls upon* the two parties to cooperate fully with the Secretary-General and MINURSO in their efforts to implement the Settlement Plan in accordance with the relevant Security Council resolutions and within the time-scale outlined in paragraphs 21 and 22 of the Secretary-General's report;

4. *Welcomes* the fact that voter identification has begun and is continuing albeit at a slow pace, and commends MINURSO for the progress achieved thus far;

5. *Approves* the expansion of MINURSO as proposed in paragraphs 17 to 19 of the Secretary-General's report and expresses the hope that every effort will be made to deploy the observers necessary to complete the identification process in a timely fashion in accordance with the Settlement Plan;

6. *Requests* the Secretary-General to report by 31 March 1995 to confirm the arrangements with regard to the logistic, personnel and other resources required for the deployment of MINURSO at full strength, on his final plans for implementing all elements of the Settlement Plan and on the responses of the parties to his proposals in order to fulfil the United Nations mission in Western Sahara;

7. *Encourages* the Secretary-General to continue to deploy all possible efforts in order to create a propitious atmosphere conducive to a speedy and effective implementation of the Settlement Plan;

8. *Expects* to be able, on the basis of the report requested in paragraph 6 above, to confirm 1 June 1995 as the date for the start of the transitional period, with a view to holding the referendum in October 1995 and to bringing the mission to a successful conclusion shortly thereafter, in accordance with the Settlement Plan;

9. *Decides* that the mandate of MINURSO should continue to 31 May 1995;

10. *Also decides* to consider the possible extension of the mandate of MINURSO after 31 May 1995 on the basis of a further report from the Secretary-General and in the light of progress achieved towards the holding of the referendum and the implementation of the Settlement Plan;

11. *Requests* the Secretary-General to keep the Security Council fully informed of further developments in the implementation of the Settlement Plan for Western Sahara during this period;

12. *Decides* to remain seized of the matter.

Security Council resolution 973(1995)

13 January 1995     Meeting 3490     Adopted unanimously

Draft prepared in consultations among Council members (S/1995/24).

**Report of the Secretary-General (March).** Pursuant to the Council's January resolution, the Secretary-General on 30 March provided a report[45] updating the situation concerning Western Sahara. He noted that monitoring and verifying the cease-fire as well as the identification of potential voters, begun in 1994, remained core activities of MINURSO, with more than 21,300 persons identified by mid-March 1995. That total represented 16.5 per cent of the known applicants in the Territory and 27.3 per cent of those in the camps in the Tindouf area in Algeria. In February and March, two new identification centres were opened and one was reopened, bringing the total number to seven. Also in February, the Secretary-General's Deputy Special Representative Erik Jensen addressed to the parties a detailed proposal concerning the selection of tribal leaders (sheikhs) responsible for identifying applicants and establishing whether they belonged to a particular tribal group (subfraction). The parties, meeting on 23 February in Tindouf and on 25 February in Laayoune, Western Sahara, discussed identification arrangements and exchanged lists of candidates to be considered as replacements in the absence of sheikhs.

The Secretary-General further reported on implementation of the settlement plan. The 1991 cease-fire, he said, remained in place, and Morocco had reaffirmed its readiness to reduce its troops in Western Sahara to no more than 65,000 by the beginning of the transitional period leading to the referendum. In accordance with the plan, the Secretary-General appointed Emmanuel Roucounas (Greece) as the independent jurist to ensure the release of Saharan political prisoners and detainees and their participation in the referendum. The Office of the UN High Commissioner for Refugees began preparations for the return of refugees, other Western Saharans and members of the Frente POLISARIO entitled to vote;

its technical mission visited potential repatriation sites and the refugee camps from 2 to 15 February. Efforts also continued to finalize the draft code of conduct for the referendum campaign.

MINURSO's military component, headed by Brigadier-General André van Baelen (Belgium) and comprising 240 military observers and 48 military support personnel, conducted daily patrols in all parts of the Territory, undertaking a monthly average of 600 ground and 140 aerial reconnaissance patrols. In accordance with the Security Council's January authorization for an increase in the Mission's civilian police component from 55 to 160, its strength rose to 78 personnel as at 25 March. Civilian police observers provided technical assistance to the Identification Commission and ensured the security of identification centres and universal access to them for identification purposes. On 13 March, Colonel Wolf-Dieter Krampe (Germany) replaced Colonel Jürgen Friedrich Reiman (Germany) as the Civilian Police Commissioner. MINURSO's authorized civilian personnel level stood at 251.

The report reviewed arrangements for the Mission's deployment at the full authorized military strength of 1,695 and outlined its personnel, equipment and financial requirements (see below, under "Financing of MINURSO"). In conclusion, the Secretary-General called for the Council's continued support for MINURSO and noted that, should the parties resolve expeditiously the remaining issues and make it possible to raise the identification rate to 25,000 persons per month, the transitional period could begin in August 1995, with the referendum taking place in January 1996.

**SECURITY COUNCIL ACTION (April)**

The Security Council met on 12 April to consider the situation concerning Western Sahara. The Council President made the following statement[46] on behalf of the Council:

> The Security Council notes the report of the Secretary-General dated 30 March 1995. It welcomes progress achieved so far in the identification and registration process, in particular the acceleration in the rate of identification, and emphasizes the need to continue that acceleration. It endorses the Secretary-General's goal of achieving a rate of at least 25,000 per month. However, the Council regrets that progress was not sufficient to enable the Secretary-General to recommend 1 June 1995 as the date for the commencement of the transitional period.
>
> The Security Council also notes with concern the delays resulting from the failure to ensure the continuous presence at the identification centres of the necessary subfraction representatives. It welcomes the agreement on a method for choosing alternative subfraction representatives when necessary and it expresses the hope that this will contribute to further acceleration of the process with a view to holding the

referendum in January 1996. The Council supports the Secretary-General's call upon both parties to cooperate fully with the Identification Commission in the performance of its work, in particular by abandoning their insistence on strict reciprocity in the number of centres and on the linkage of a centre on one side with a specific centre on the other.

> The Security Council expresses its concern about the slow progress on the other aspects which are relevant to the fulfilment of the Settlement Plan and must be implemented before the referendum can take place. It calls upon both parties to cooperate fully with the Secretary-General, with his Deputy Special Representative and with the United Nations Mission for the Referendum in Western Sahara (MINURSO), and to coordinate such cooperation to ensure prompt and full implementation of all aspects of the Settlement Plan.

> The Security Council hopes to see continuous and rapid progress by the time of the Secretary-General's next report in May 1995, which would enable it to consider favourably the possible extension of MINURSO's mandate.

*Meeting number.* SC 3516.

**Report of the Secretary-General (May).** The Secretary-General on 19 May reported[47] on further developments in Western Sahara. He noted that, despite increased operational capabilities with the opening of an eighth centre, the rate of identification had been uneven. The operation had been interrupted periodically when tribal leaders and party representatives were not available on time, and because of weather conditions and logistical difficulties. The identification process was resumed on 2 May, following consultations by the Deputy Special Representative from 26 to 28 April with the Frente POLISARIO, community and tribal leaders and Moroccan officials to resolve differences regarding the selection of sheikhs.

As at 15 May, 35,851 persons were identified, representing 44.4 per cent of applicants in the Tindouf camps and 28.1 per cent of those in the Territory. The report cited the parties' insistence that if the identification process stopped at a centre on one side, it should also stop at a centre on the other side, and the unnecessary delays caused by limiting the identification of a maximum of 150 persons a day at any given centre. At the same time, additional resources enabled MINURSO to identify on occasion 800 to 900 persons in one day, making the target of 1,000 persons quite feasible. The Secretary-General also noted that the operation was observed by eight OAU representatives, with two more expected to arrive in May. He further outlined planned activities to implement various components of the settlement plan and described the composition of MINURSO and its logistical and financial requirements. While the strength of the Mission's military component had not changed since March, its civilian police component had increased to 98 observers as at 5 May.

The Secretary-General proposed that certain benchmarks be achieved before confirming the beginning date of the transitional period. These included: forwarding the code of conduct for the referendum campaign to the parties in July; progress in the release of political prisoners by August; and a ruling on the confinement of the Frente POLISARIO troops and confirmation of arrangements for the reduction of Moroccan troops in Western Sahara by September. He called on the parties to work with the Mission in a spirit of genuine cooperation and recommended extending MINURSO's mandate for a further four months.

**SECURITY COUNCIL ACTION (May)**

On 26 May, the Security Council adopted **resolution 995(1995)**.

*The Security Council,*

*Reaffirming* its resolutions 621(1988) of 20 September 1988, 658(1990) of 27 June 1990, 690(1991) of 29 April 1991, 725(1991) of 31 December 1991, 809(1993) of 2 March 1993, 907(1994) of 29 March 1994 and 973(1995) of 13 January 1995,

*Recalling* the statement by the President of the Security Council of 12 April 1995,

*Noting* the Secretary-General's report of 19 May 1995,

1. *Reiterates* its commitment to holding, without further delay, a free, fair and impartial referendum for self-determination of the people of Western Sahara in accordance with the Settlement Plan which has been accepted by the two parties;

2. *Commends* the progress in identifying potential voters since the beginning of the year;

3. *Expresses concern*, however, that certain practices identified in the Secretary-General's report are hampering further progress towards the implementation of the Settlement Plan and underlines the need for the parties to heed the Secretary-General's call on them to work with the United Nations Mission for the Referendum in Western Sahara (MINURSO) in a spirit of genuine cooperation;

4. *Decides* in this context, and with a view to accelerating the implementation of the Settlement Plan, to send a mission of the Council to the region;

5. *Decides*, therefore, to extend at this stage the present mandate of the United Nations Mission for the Referendum in Western Sahara (MINURSO) until 30 June 1995;

6. *Decides* to consider the further extension of the mandate of MINURSO beyond 30 June 1995 in the light of the Secretary-General's report of 19 May 1995 and the report of the Security Council mission referred to in paragraph 4 above;

7. *Decides* to remain seized of the matter.

Security Council resolution 995(1995)

26 May 1995     Meeting 3540     Adopted unanimously

Draft prepared in consultations among Council members (S/1995/426).

**Report of the Security Council mission (June).**
On 30 May, the Security Council President issued a note[48] in reference to the Council decision to send a mission to Western Sahara. The note set out the mission's duration, composition and terms of reference as follows: to impress on the parties the necessity of cooperating fully with MINURSO in the implementation of the settlement plan and to underline that any further delay would put the whole future of the Mission at risk; to assess progress and identify problems in the identification process; and to identify problems in other areas relevant to the implementation of the settlement plan.

The Council mission, composed of Argentina, Botswana, France, Honduras, Oman and the United States, visited Morocco, Algeria and Mauritania from 3 to 9 June. Its 21 June report[49] provided an account of meetings held with officials of the Moroccan, Algerian and Mauritanian Governments, representatives of the Frente POLISARIO and OAU observers, as well as briefings by the Deputy Special Representative of the Secretary-General and by MINURSO officials. The mission was apprised of the parties' position concerning the settlement plan and the holding of the referendum, guidelines of the Identification Commission, the status of work and difficulties encountered in the identification process and in the operation of MINURSO.

Noting continuing suspicion and lack of trust between the two parties, the mission felt that there was a risk that the identification process could be extended and the referendum not held in January 1996. In that respect, it strongly recommended that both parties abandon their insistence on reciprocity in the number and operation of identification centres on each side and refrain from blaming the other side for its lack of cooperation. The mission also called on the parties to take steps to facilitate a free and fair identification process and not to inhibit access to identification centres; suggested mobilizing additional teams in temporary fixed centres; urged lifting the limit on the number of persons to be identified in one day; and recommended expediting the review of undecided cases, while ensuring full confidentiality, and speeding up the compiling of preliminary voter eligibility lists and the administrative decision-making process regarding MINURSO's human and other resources. It called on Morocco to conduct preliminary vetting of the 100,000 applicants not residing in the Territory and recommended commencing without delay the identification operation for applicants living in Mauritania. The Security Council was to be apprised biweekly of the progress made and immediately of any interruption or slow-down in the identification process.

Other recommendations dealt with the implementation of various components of the settlement plan, including the reduction and confinement of troops, the exchange of prisoners of war and release of political detainees, voluntary repatriation of refugees and maintenance of the cease-fire.

**Communications (June).** By a 23 June letter,[50] transmitted by Honduras, the Frente POLISARIO informed the Security Council of its decision to suspend participation in the identification process and recall its observers, owing to the sentencing by a Moroccan military court on 21 June of eight Saharan civilians to prison terms of 15 to 20 years for having participated in a rally for Western Saharan independence, and to Morocco's announcement to the Security Council mission of its intention to have 100,000 Moroccan settlers take part in the identification operation. To restore credibility to the process, the Frente POLISARIO demanded the immediate release of political prisoners arrested since MINURSO's deployment, particularly the eight recently sentenced civilians, as well as the halting of retaliatory acts against Western Sahara's population and termination of the operation to move foreigners into the Territory.

On 26 June, Morocco responded[51] that the other party could not decide on the identity of an applicant, whether residing in or outside the Territory, before the Identification Commission reached such a decision based on the established criteria. It accused the other side of obstructionism and called on the Security Council to ensure the resumption of the process with a view to holding the referendum on schedule and with the participation of the Saharans residing or sequestered in Tindouf.

**SECURITY COUNCIL ACTION (June)**

On 30 June, the Security Council adopted **resolution 1002(1995)**.

*The Security Council,*

*Reaffirming* its resolutions 621(1988) of 20 September 1988, 658(1990) of 27 June 1990, 690(1991) of 29 April 1991, 725(1991) of 31 December 1991, 809(1993) of 2 March 1993, 907(1994) of 29 March 1994, 973(1995) of 13 January 1995 and 995(1995) of 26 May 1995,

*Recalling* the Secretary-General's report of 19 May 1995,

*Welcoming* the work of the mission of the Council undertaken from 3 to 9 June 1995 under the terms of reference set out in the note of the President of the Council of 30 May,

*Having considered* the report of 21 June 1995 of the mission of the Security Council,

*Committed* to reaching a just and lasting solution of the question of Western Sahara,

*Concerned* that the parties' continuing suspicion and lack of trust have contributed to delays in the implementation of the Settlement Plan,

*Noting* that, for progress to be achieved, the two parties must have a vision of the post-referendum period,

*Taking note* of the letter dated 23 June 1995 from the Secretary-General of the POLISARIO Front to the President of the Security Council,

*Taking note* of the letter dated 26 June 1995 from the Prime Minister and Minister for Foreign Affairs and Cooperation of the Kingdom of Morocco to the President of the Security Council,

*Urging* the parties to cooperate fully with the Secretary-General and the United Nations Mission for the Referendum in Western Sahara (MINURSO) to ensure prompt and full implementation of the Settlement Plan,

*Noting* that, in his report of 19 May 1995, the Secretary-General has outlined benchmarks for assessing progress on certain aspects of the Settlement Plan, including the code of conduct, the release of political prisoners, the confinement of POLISARIO troops and arrangements for the reduction of Moroccan troops in the Territory in conformity with the Settlement Plan,

*Noting also* that the mission of the Council has provided recommendations for moving forward on the identification process and other aspects of the Settlement Plan and stressing the need for the identification process to be carried out in accordance with the relevant provisions set out therein, in particular in paragraphs 72 and 73 of the Settlement Plan, as well as in the relevant resolutions of the Security Council,

1. *Welcomes* the report of the Secretary-General on the situation concerning Western Sahara of 19 May 1995 and the report of the mission of the Security Council to Western Sahara of 21 June 1995;

2. *Reiterates* its commitment to holding, without further delay, a free, fair and impartial referendum for the self-determination of the people of Western Sahara in accordance with the Settlement Plan which has been accepted by the two parties cited above;

3. *Expresses its concern* that, given the complexity of the tasks to be performed and the continuing interruptions caused by the two parties, implementation of the Settlement Plan has been further delayed;

4. *Calls upon* the two parties to work with the Secretary-General and MINURSO in a spirit of genuine cooperation to implement the Settlement Plan in accordance with the relevant Council resolutions;

5. *Stresses* the need for the parties to refrain from any actions that hinder the implementation of the Settlement Plan, calls upon them to reconsider recent relevant decisions with a view to establishing confidence, and in this regard requests the Secretary-General to make every effort to persuade the two parties to resume their participation in the implementation of the Settlement Plan;

6. *Endorses* the Secretary-General's benchmarks described in paragraph 38 of his report of 19 May 1995;

7. *Endorses also* the recommendations of the mission of the Council concerning the identification process and other aspects of the Settlement Plan, described in paragraphs 41 to 53 of its report of 21 June 1995;

8. *Requests* the Secretary-General to report by 10 September 1995 on the progress achieved in accordance with paragraphs 5 and 6 above;

9. *Expects* to be able, on the basis of the report requested in paragraph 7 above, to confirm 15 November 1995 as the start of the transitional period, to allow the referendum to take place early in 1996;

10. *Decides* to extend the mandate of MINURSO until 30 September 1995 as recommended by the Secretary-General in his report of 19 May 1995;

11. *Decides also* to consider the possible extension of the mandate of MINURSO after 30 September 1995 on the basis of the Secretary-General's report requested in paragraph 7 above and in the light of progress achieved in accordance with paragraphs 5 and 6 above towards

the holding of the referendum and the implementation of the Settlement Plan;

12. *Requests* the Secretary-General, in addition to the reports called for in paragraph 48 of the report of the Security Council mission, to keep the Council fully informed of further developments in the implementation of the Settlement Plan for Western Sahara during this period, in particular of any significant delays in the pace of the identification process or other developments that would call into question the Secretary-General's ability to set the start of the transitional period on 15 November 1995;

13. *Decides* to remain seized of the matter.

Security Council resolution 1002(1995)

30 June 1995     Meeting 3550     Adopted unanimously

10-nation draft (S/1995/523).

*Sponsors:* Argentina, Botswana, Czech Republic, France, Germany, Honduras, Italy, Russian Federation, United Kingdom, United States.

**Report of the Secretary-General (September).** Pursuant to the Council's June resolution, the Secretary-General reported[52] on 8 September on developments since his May report. He noted that Erik Jensen, confirmed as his Acting Special Representative, had held a series of meetings with Moroccan officials between 26 June and 15 July to discuss the identification procedure for applicants residing outside the Territory. Following a 9 July Moroccan royal edict reducing the 21 June prison sentences of eight Saharan civilians to one year, the Frente POLISARIO on 12 July had agreed to resume its participation in the identification process, but had also reiterated its view that the 1974 Spanish census was the only basis for identification recognized in the settlement plan. It deemed unacceptable what it called the participation of a "substitute population, sought by the occupying Power, whose most recent manoeuvre was to attempt to include 100,000 of its nationals in the voters list".

The identification operation recommenced in late July and brought the number of identified persons to more than 53,000, representing over 40 per cent of persons residing in the Territory and more than 51 per cent of those in the camps near Tindouf. The substantive review of specific cases was proceeding steadily, and arrangements were discussed for the beginning of the identification process in Mauritania. The number of OAU observers stood at 10 as at the end of June. Difficulties persisted, however, due to continued insistence on strict reciprocity and differences of perception concerning the procedure for identification of certain tribal groupings. The report also described activities to implement other components of the settlement plan.

MINURSO's military component totalled 285 as at 31 August, including 237 military observers and 48 military support personnel, while the strength of its civilian police component stood at 92 as at 1 September. Lieutenant-Colonel Jan Walmann

(Norway) was serving as Acting Civilian Police Commissioner, Colonel Krampe having completed his tour of duty on 20 August. The Mission reported two cease-fire violations during the period under review, both by the Frente POLISARIO, relating to an attempt to restrict MINURSO's freedom of movement and to the conduct of live-fire exercises and movement of troops and equipment. During the same period, the Frente POLISARIO reported three overflights by Moroccan aircraft, in the vicinity of international air corridors, which the Mission was unable to confirm.

MINURSO's personnel requirement for its full deployment in the transitional period had been revised upward to 1,780 all ranks, and the concept of operations of its civilian police had also been reviewed. The Secretary-General informed the Council of his decision to link the deployment of infantry and supporting personnel to the publication of the final voter list. The benchmarks proposed in May had not been achieved, he added, as both parties maintained their positions concerning the confinement of the Frente POLISARIO troops and objected to the terms of the proposed code of conduct. Noting the parties' reluctance to compromise, the Secretary-General appealed for every effort to expeditiously implement the settlement plan. He then proposed the extension of MINURSO's mandate until 31 January 1996, with alternative options to be presented to the Security Council should the conditions necessary for the start of the transitional period not be in place by that date.

**SECURITY COUNCIL ACTION (September)**

On 22 September, the Security Council adopted **resolution 1017(1995)**.

*The Security Council,*

*Reaffirming* its resolutions 621(1988) of 20 September 1988, 658(1990) of 27 June 1990, 690(1991) of 29 April 1991, 725(1991) of 31 December 1991, 809(1993) of 2 March 1993, 907(1994) of 29 March 1994, 973(1995) of 13 January 1995, 995(1995) of 26 May 1995 and 1002(1995) of 30 June 1995,

*Reaffirming* in particular its resolutions 725(1991) and 907(1994) relating to the criteria for voter eligibility and the compromise proposal of the Secretary-General on their interpretation,

*Having considered* the report of the Secretary-General of 8 September 1995, and noting further the fact that only two out of the eight identification centres are currently functioning,

*Committed* to reaching a just and lasting solution to the question of Western Sahara,

*Reiterating* the fact that, for progress to be achieved, the two parties must have a vision of the post-referendum period,

*Expressing the hope* for a rapid resolution of the problems causing delays in the completion of the identification process,

*Expressing its regret* that the outcome of the preliminary vetting by the Government of Morocco of the 100,000 applicants not residing in the territory is contributing to the inability of MINURSO to maintain its timetable for completing the identification process,

*Expressing its regret also* that the POLISARIO Front is refusing to participate in the identification, even within the territory, of three groups within the disputed tribal groupings, thus delaying completion of the identification process,

*Taking note* of paragraph 49 of the Secretary-General's report of 8 September 1995,

*Stressing* the need for progress to be made on all other aspects of the Settlement Plan,

*Reaffirming* its endorsement in resolution 1002(1995) of the recommendations of the mission of the Security Council concerning the identification process and other aspects of the Settlement Plan as described in paragraphs 41 to 53 of the report of the mission of 21 June 1995,

1. *Reiterates* its commitment to the holding, without further delay, of a free, fair and impartial referendum for the self-determination of the people of Western Sahara in accordance with the Settlement Plan, which has been accepted by the two parties stated above;

2. *Expresses its disappointment* that, since the adoption of resolution 1002(1995), the parties have made insufficient progress towards the fulfilment of the Settlement Plan, including the identification process, the code of conduct, the release of political prisoners, the confinement of POLISARIO troops and the arrangements for the reduction of Moroccan troops in the territory;

3. *Calls upon* the two parties to work henceforth with the Secretary-General and MINURSO in a spirit of genuine cooperation to implement the Settlement Plan in accordance with the relevant resolutions, to abandon their insistence on strict reciprocity in the operation of the identification centres and to cease all other procrastinating actions which could further delay the holding of the referendum;

4. *Requests* the Secretary-General, in close consultation with the parties, to produce specific and detailed proposals to resolve the problems hindering the completion of the identification process in the framework of the relevant Security Council resolutions, in particular resolution 907(1994) relating to the compromise proposal of the Secretary-General, and resolution 1002(1995) relating to the recommendations of the Security Council mission, and to report on the outcome of his efforts in this regard by 15 November 1995;

5. *Decides* to review the arrangements for the completion of the identification process on the basis of the report requested in paragraph 4 above, and to consider at that time any further necessary measures which might need to be taken to ensure the prompt completion of that process and of all the other aspects relevant to the fulfilment of the Settlement Plan;

6. *Decides* to extend the mandate of MINURSO until 31 January 1996 as recommended by the Secretary-General in his report of 8 September 1995 and takes note of his intention, if, before then, he considers that the conditions necessary for the start of the transitional period are not in place, to present the Security Council with alternative options for consideration, including the possibility of the withdrawal of MINURSO;

7. *Requests* the Secretary-General to report by 15 January 1996 on progress achieved towards the implementation of the Settlement Plan, and to state in that report whether or not the transitional period will be able to begin by 31 May 1996;

8. *Stresses* the need to accelerate the implementation of the Settlement Plan and urges the Secretary-General to examine ways of reducing the operational costs of MINURSO;

9. *Further stresses* that the existing mechanism for the financing of MINURSO remains unchanged, supports the invitation by the General Assembly to Member States, in General Assembly resolution 49/247 of 7 August 1995, to make voluntary contributions to MINURSO, and requests the Secretary-General, without prejudice to existing procedures, to consider the establishment of a trust fund to receive such voluntary contributions for certain specific purposes to be designated by the Secretary-General;

10. *Decides* to remain seized of the matter.

Security Council resolution 1017(1995)

22 September 1995    Meeting 3582    Adopted unanimously

Draft prepared in consultations among Council members (S/1995/816).

**Communications and reports of the Secretary-General (October/November).** On 27 October, the Secretary-General informed[53] the Security Council of decisions he had taken to accelerate the identification process. Under the modified procedure, identification in the case of the 85 subfractions with established lists of sheikhs and alternates was to continue, even in the absence of a party representative, tribal leader or OAU observer, provided that the identification schedule had been duly communicated to the parties, the convocation lists had been issued and hours of work had been announced. As for the other three tribal groupings and identification outside the Territory and the Tindouf camps, an applicant's claim for inclusion in the electoral roll was to be evaluated on the basis of a birth certificate showing him or her to be a child of a father born in the Territory or as having other links with the Territory, and a document issued by competent authorities within Western Sahara's internationally recognized frontiers before 1974 substantiating the father's birth in the Territory. A comprehensive effort was also to be launched to identify applicants residing in Mauritania and Morocco. On 6 November, the Council President communicated[54] to the Secretary-General that the Council members fully supported his efforts to accelerate the process.

In a 24 November report,[55] the Secretary-General noted that the issue of certain tribal groups and persons not resident in Western Sahara remained the main obstacle to completing the process. The Government of Morocco had rejected the proposed change in the identification procedure, stating that the differing treatment of members of the 85 subfractions and other applicants amounted to discrimination and was contrary to the settlement plan, he said. The Secretary-General would submit a new proposal, under which identification, in cases when no sheikh or alternate was available, was to be based on documentary evidence only. In November, both parties communicated their objection to the new proposal: Morocco emphasized the "privileged" place of oral testimony in identification, which would be excluded entirely under the proposed change; the Frente POLISARIO considered it as a reversal of the earlier approach, which would give Morocco the opportunity to introduce 135,000 applicants with no ties with Western Sahara.

The report further stated that all 233,487 applications had been processed as of 18 November, including 176,533 in the Territory and on the Moroccan side, 42,468 in the camps and Tindouf area, and 14,486 in Mauritania. Of those, 75,794 were convoked, of which 58,947 were identified. With identification allowed to proceed as proposed and without interruption, 12 centres could complete the process within four months, at a rate of 36,000 applicants per month.

The Secretary-General underscored that the proposed new approach was the only way to carry the process forward and hoped that both parties would be persuaded to cooperate in that regard. Should the operation fail to proceed with the necessary speed, he would present for Council consideration alternative options, including the possibility of MINURSO's withdrawal.

Pursuant to a 1994 General Assembly resolution,[56] the Secretary-General, in a 4 October report,[57] provided an overview of MINURSO activities and developments in the situation in Western Sahara between 18 September 1994 and 30 September 1995.

**SECURITY COUNCIL ACTION (December)**

On 19 December, the Security Council adopted **resolution 1033(1995)**.

*The Security Council,*

*Reaffirming* all its previous resolutions on the question of Western Sahara,

*Recalling* the letter of the Secretary-General of 27 October 1995 and the reply of the President of the Security Council of 6 November 1995,

*Recalling* the reports of the Secretary-General of 18 June 1990, 19 April 1991, 19 December 1991 and 28 July 1993,

*Having considered* the report of the Secretary-General of 24 November 1995,

*Noting* the response of the Government of Morocco to the proposal of the Secretary-General, described in paragraph 10 of his report,

*Noting also* the response of the POLISARIO Front to the proposal of the Secretary-General, described in paragraph 11 of his report,

*Noting further* other communications received by the Council on this subject,

*Stressing* that the Identification Commission will be able to carry out its work only if both parties place their trust in its judgement and integrity,

*Stressing also* the need for progress to be made on all other aspects of the Settlement Plan,

*Committed* to reaching a just and lasting solution to the question of Western Sahara,

*Reiterating* the fact that, for progress to be achieved, the two parties must have a vision of the post-referendum period,

1. *Reiterates* its commitment to the holding, without further delay, of a free, fair and impartial referendum for the self-determination of the people of Western Sahara in accordance with the Settlement Plan, which has been accepted by the two parties referred to above;

2. *Welcomes* the report of the Secretary-General of 24 November 1995 as a useful framework for his ongoing efforts aimed at accelerating and completing the identification process;

3. *Welcomes further* the decision of the Secretary-General to intensify his consultations with the two parties in order to obtain their agreement to a plan to resolve differences hindering the timely completion of the identification process;

4. *Requests* the Secretary-General to report to the Council on the results of those consultations on an urgent basis and, in the event those consultations fail to reach agreement, to provide the Council with options for its consideration, including a programme for the orderly withdrawal of the United Nations Mission for the Referendum in Western Sahara (MINURSO);

5. *Calls upon* the two parties to work with the Secretary-General and MINURSO in a spirit of genuine cooperation to implement all the other aspects of the Settlement Plan, in accordance with the relevant resolutions;

6. *Decides* to remain seized of the matter.

Security Council resolution 1033(1995)

19 December 1995     Meeting 3610     Adopted unanimously

Draft prepared in consultations among Council members (S/1995/1013).

**Consideration by the Special Committee on decolonization.** The Special Committee on decolonization[1] considered the question of Western Sahara on 10 and 14 July. It granted a request for a hearing to a representative of the Frente POLISARIO and considered a working paper[58] on developments in Western Sahara, containing an overview of General Assembly consideration of the question in 1994, of the Secretary-General's good offices, and of political and other developments between September 1994 and June 1995.

**GENERAL ASSEMBLY ACTION**

On 6 December, the General Assembly adopted **resolution 50/36**.

### Question of Western Sahara

*The General Assembly,*

*Having considered in depth* the question of Western Sahara,

*Reaffirming* the inalienable right of all peoples to self-determination and independence, in accordance with the principles set forth in the Charter of the United Nations and in General Assembly resolution 1514(XV) of 14 December 1960, containing the Declaration on the Granting of Independence to Colonial Countries and Peoples,

*Recalling* its resolution 49/44 of 9 December 1994,

*Recalling also* the agreement in principle given on 30 August 1988 by the Kingdom of Morocco and the Frente Popular para la Liberación de Saguia el-Hamra y de Río de Oro to the proposals of the Secretary-General of the United Nations and the current Chairman of the Assembly of Heads of State and Government of the Organization of African Unity in the context of their joint mission of good offices,

*Recalling further* Security Council resolutions 621(1988) of 20 September 1988, 658(1990) of 27 June 1990, 690(1991) of 29 April 1991, 725(1991) of 31 December 1991, 809(1993) of 2 March 1993 and 907(1994) of 29 March 1994 relating to the question of Western Sahara,

*Recalling with satisfaction* the entry into force of the cease-fire in Western Sahara on 6 September 1991, in accordance with the proposal of the Secretary-General accepted by the two parties,

*Noting* the adoption by the Security Council of resolutions 973(1995) of 13 January 1995, 995(1995) of 26 May 1995, 1002(1995) of 30 June 1995 and 1017(1995) of 22 September 1995,

*Welcoming* the mission of the Security Council, which visited Western Sahara and the countries of the region from 3 to 9 June 1995,

*Welcoming also* the appointment of Mr. Erik Jensen as acting Special Representative of the Secretary-General for Western Sahara,

*Concerned* that the parties' continuing suspicion and lack of trust have contributed to delays in the implementation of the settlement plan,

*Noting* that, for progress to be achieved, the two parties must have a vision of the post-referendum period,

*Expressing the hope* for a rapid resolution of the problems causing delays in the completion of the identification process, as well as the code of conduct, the release of political prisoners, the confinement of troops of the Frente Popular para la Liberación de Saguia el-Hamra y de Río de Oro and the arrangements for the reduction of the Moroccan troops in the territory,

*Stressing* the importance and usefulness of the resumption of direct talks between the two parties mentioned above in order to create a propitious atmosphere conducive to a speedy and effective implementation of the settlement plan,

*Having examined* the relevant chapter of the report of the Special Committee on the Situation with regard to the Implementation of the Declaration on the Granting of Independence to Colonial Countries and Peoples,

*Having also examined* the report of the Secretary-General,

1. *Takes note with appreciation* of the report of the Secretary-General;

2. *Pays tribute* to the Secretary-General and the personnel of the United Nations Mission for the Referendum in Western Sahara for their action with a view to settling the question of Western Sahara by the implementation of the settlement plan;

3. *Reiterates its support* for further efforts of the Secretary-General for the organization and supervision by the United Nations, in cooperation with the Organization of African Unity, of a referendum for self-determination of the people of Western Sahara, in conformity with Security Council resolutions 658(1990) and 690(1991), by which the Council adopted the settlement plan for Western Sahara;

4. *Reaffirms* that the goal on which all were agreed consists of the holding of a free, fair and impartial referendum for the people of Western Sahara, organized and conducted by the United Nations in cooperation with the Organization of African Unity and without any military or administrative constraints, in conformity with the settlement plan;

5. *Notes with concern* the insufficient progress made towards the fulfilment of the settlement plan, including the identification process, the code of conduct, the release of political prisoners, the confinement of troops of the Frente Popular para la Liberación de Saguia el-Hamra y de Río de Oro and the arrangements for the reduction of the Moroccan troops in the territory;

6. *Calls upon* the Kingdom of Morocco and the Frente Popular para la Liberación de Saguia el-Hamra y de Río de Oro and the United Nations Mission for the Referendum in Western Sahara to work with the Secretary-General and the United Nations Mission for the Referendum in Western Sahara in a spirit of genuine cooperation to implement the settlement plan in accordance with the relevant Security Council resolutions;

7. *Takes note* of the decision of the Security Council to review the arrangements for the completion of the identification process on the basis of the report of the Secretary-General requested by the Council in paragraph 4 of its resolution 1017(1995) and to consider at that time any further necessary measures which might need to be taken to ensure the prompt completion of that process and of all the other aspects relevant to the fulfilment of the settlement plan;

8. *Expresses the hope* that direct talks between the two parties will soon resume in order to create a propitious atmosphere conducive to speedy and effective implementation of the settlement plan;

9. *Requests* the Special Committee on the Situation with regard to the Implementation of the Declaration on the Granting of Independence to Colonial Countries and Peoples to continue to consider the situation in Western Sahara, bearing in mind the ongoing referendum process, and to report thereon to the General Assembly at its fifty-first session;

10. *Invites* the Secretary-General to submit to the General Assembly at its fifty-first session a report on the implementation of the present resolution.

General Assembly resolution 50/36

6 December 1995      Meeting 82      Adopted without vote

Approved by Fourth Committee (A/50/602) without vote, 3 November (meeting 15); 59-nation draft (A/C.4/50/L.5/Rev.1), orally revised; agenda item 18.

*Meeting numbers.* GA 50th session: 4th Committee 2-7, 9-11, 13-15; plenary 82.

### Financing of MINURSO

**Report of the Secretary-General (March).** In a 7 March report,[59] the Secretary-General, estimating costs for MINURSO's operations from 1 December 1994 to 30 June 1995 at $36,381,000 gross ($33,473,300 net) and the monthly cost of maintaining the Mission after 30 June 1995 at $5,619,400 gross ($5,123,000 net), requested appropriation of those amounts by the General Assembly. The totals reflected the requirements for MINURSO's expanded activities authorized by the Security Council in January, and included the phasing in of an additional 105 civilian police monitors, 124 international staff, 35 local staff and 12 OAU observers, as well as additional requirements for transportation, communications, data-processing and other equipment.

Mission expenditures from the operation's inception in 1991 to 31 January 1995 were estimated at $154,270,350 gross ($148,129,550 net). As at 31 January, outstanding assessed contributions due from Member States totalled $21,098,548, while voluntary contributions from 1 October 1994 to 31 January 1995 were valued at $1,743,200. The report also noted that troop-contributing States had been reimbursed in full for the period ending 31 August 1994.

**ACABQ recommendation (March).** In March,[60] the Advisory Committee on Administrative and Budgetary Questions (ACABQ), having considered the Secretary-General's report, revised the requested amounts and recommended their appropriation and assessment by the Assembly for the period from 1 December 1994 to 31 May 1995, as well as commitment authorization for the month of June and from 1 July to 31 December 1995, subject to MINURSO's extension by the Security Council.

**GENERAL ASSEMBLY ACTION (April and July)**

In April, the General Assembly adopted **decision 49/466 B**.

#### Financing of the United Nations Mission for the Referendum in Western Sahara

At its 100th plenary meeting, on 6 April 1995, the General Assembly, on the recommendation of the Fifth Committee and pending consideration of the report of the Secretary-General on the financing of the United Nations Mission for the Referendum in Western Sahara and the related report of the Advisory Committee on Administrative and Budgetary Questions:

*(a)* Decided to authorize the Secretary-General to enter into commitments for the operation of the Mission in an amount of 28,839,700 United States dollars gross (26,556,300 dollars net) for the period from 1 December 1994 to 31 May 1995, inclusive of the amount of 6.4 million dollars gross (5,937,400 dollars net) authorized by the General Assembly in its decision 49/466 A of 23 December 1994 for the period from 1 December 1994 to 31 January 1995 and the additional commitment authority of 17,290,100 dollars gross (16,130,300 dollars net) authorized by the Advisory Committee for the period from 1 January to 31 March 1995;

*(b)* Also decided to authorize the Secretary-General to enter into commitments for the operation of the Mission in an amount of 4,806,600 dollars gross (4,426,000 dollars net) for the period from 1 to 30 June 1995, subject to the extension of the mandate of the Mission by the Security Council for the period after 31 May 1995.

General Assembly decision 49/466 B

Adopted without vote

Approved by Fifth Committee (A/49/808/Add.1) without vote, 31 March (meeting 52); draft by Chairman (A/C.5/49/L.47); agenda item 119.

On 20 July, the Assembly adopted **resolution 49/247**.

#### Financing of the United Nations Mission for the Referendum in Western Sahara

*The General Assembly,*

*Having considered* the report of the Secretary-General on the financing of the United Nations Mission for the Referendum in Western Sahara and the related report of the Advisory Committee on Administrative and Budgetary Questions,

*Recalling* Security Council resolution 690(1991) of 29 April 1991, by which the Council established the United Nations Mission for the Referendum in Western Sahara, and its subsequent resolutions, the latest of which was resolution 1002(1995) of 30 June 1995,

*Recalling also* its resolution 45/266 of 17 May 1991 and its decisions 47/451 A, B and C of 22 December 1992, 8 April and 14 September 1993, respectively, 48/467 of 23 December 1993 and 49/466 A and B of 23 December 1994 and 6 April 1995, respectively, on the financing of the Mission,

*Reaffirming* that the costs of the Mission are expenses of the Organization to be borne by Member States in accordance with Article 17, paragraph 2, of the Charter of the United Nations,

*Recalling* its previous decisions regarding the fact that, in order to meet the expenditures caused by the Mission, a different procedure is required from the one applied to meet expenditures of the regular budget of the United Nations,

*Taking into account* the fact that the economically more developed countries are in a position to make relatively larger contributions and that the economically less developed countries have a relatively limited capacity to contribute towards such an operation,

*Bearing in mind* the special responsibilities of the States permanent members of the Security Council, as indicated in General Assembly resolution 1874(S-IV) of 27 June 1963, in the financing of such operations,

*Mindful* of the fact that it is essential to provide the Mission with the necessary financial resources to enable it to fulfil its responsibilities under the relevant resolutions of the Security Council,

1. *Takes note* of the status of contributions to the United Nations Mission for the Referendum in Western Sahara as at 7 July 1995, including the contributions outstanding in the amount of 20,270,659 United States dollars, and urges all Member States concerned to make every possible effort to ensure the payment of their outstanding assessed contributions;

2. *Expresses concern* about the financial situation with regard to peace-keeping activities, particularly in regard to the reimbursement of troop- and equipment-contributing countries, resulting from overdue payments by Member States of their assessments, particularly Member States in arrears;

3. *Urges* all Member States to make every possible effort to ensure payment of their assessed contributions to the Mission promptly and in full;

4. *Endorses* the observations and recommendations contained in the report of the Advisory Committee on Administrative and Budgetary Questions;

5. *Requests* the Secretary-General to take all necessary action to ensure that the Mission is administered with a maximum of efficiency and economy;

6. *Decides* to appropriate to the Special Account for the United Nations Mission for the Referendum in Western Sahara the amount of 28,839,700 dollars gross (26,556,300 dollars net) for the operation of the Mission for the period from 1 December 1994 to 31 May 1995 authorized under the provisions of General Assembly decision 49/466 B of 6 April 1995;

7. *Also decides*, as an ad hoc arrangement, to apportion the amount of 28,839,700 dollars gross (26,556,300 dollars net) for the period from 1 December 1994 to 31 May 1995 among Member States in accordance with the composition of groups set out in paragraphs 3 and 4 of General Assembly resolution 43/232 of 1 March 1989, as adjusted by the Assembly in its resolutions 44/192 B of 21 December 1989, 45/269 of 27 August 1991, 46/198 A of 20 December 1991 and 47/218 A of 23 December 1992 and its decision 48/472 A of 23 December 1993, the scale of assessments for the year 1994 to be applied against a portion thereof, that is, 4,912,257 dollars gross (4,523,326 dollars net), which is the amount pertaining on a *pro rata* basis to the period ending 31 December 1994, and the scale of assessments for the year 1995 to be applied against the balance, that is 23,927,443 dollars gross (22,032,974 dollars net), for the period from 1 January to 31 May 1995, inclusive;

8. *Further decides* that, in accordance with the provisions of its resolution 973(X) of 15 December 1955, there shall be set off against the apportionment among Member States, as provided for in paragraph 7 above, their respective share in the Tax Equalization Fund of the estimated staff assessment income of 2,283,400 dollars approved for the period from 1 December 1994 to 31 May 1995, inclusive;

9. *Decides* to appropriate to the Special Account the amount of 4,806,600 dollars gross (4,426,000 dollars net) for the operation of the Mission for the period from 1 to 30 June 1995, authorized under the provisions of its decision 49/466 B;

10. *Also decides*, as an ad hoc arrangement, to apportion the amount of 4,806,600 dollars gross (4,426,000 dollars net) among Member States for the period from 1 to 30 June 1995 in accordance with the scheme set out in the present resolution;

11. *Further decides* that, in accordance with the provisions of resolution 973(X), there shall be set off against the apportionment among Member States, as provided for in paragraph 10 above, their respective share in the Tax Equalization Fund of the estimated staff assessment income of 380,600 dollars approved for the period from 1 to 30 June 1995, inclusive;

12. *Decides* to appropriate to the Special Account the amount of 16,777,500 dollars gross (15,288,300 dollars net) for the operation of the Mission for the period from 1 July to 30 September 1995;

13. *Also decides*, as an ad hoc arrangement, to apportion the amount of 16,777,500 dollars gross (15,288,300 dollars net) among Member States for the period from 1 July to 30 September 1995 in accordance with the scheme set out in the present resolution;

14. *Further decides* that, in accordance with the provisions of resolution 973(X), there shall be set off against the apportionment among Member States, as provided for in paragraph 13 above, their respective share in the Tax Equalization Fund of the estimated staff assessment income of 1,489,200 dollars approved for the period from 1 July to 30 September 1995, inclusive;

15. *Decides* to authorize the Secretary-General to enter into commitments for the operation of the Mission for the period after 30 September 1995 at a monthly rate not to exceed 5,592,500 dollars gross (5,096,100 dollars net), this amount to be assessed on Member States in accordance with the scheme set out in the present resolution, subject to extension of the mandate of the Mission by the Security Council beyond 30 September 1995;

16. *Invites* voluntary contributions to the Mission in cash and in the form of services and supplies acceptable to the Secretary-General, to be administered, as appropriate, in accordance with the procedures established by the General Assembly in its resolutions 43/230 of 21 December 1988 and 44/192 A of 21 December 1989;

17. *Decides* to include in the provisional agenda of its fiftieth session the item entitled "Financing of the United Nations Mission for the Referendum in Western Sahara".

General Assembly resolution 49/247

20 July 1995      Meeting 106      Adopted without vote

Approved by Fifth Committee (A/49/808/Add.2) without vote, 14 July (meeting 66); draft by Chairman (A/C.5/49/L.61), based on informal consultations; agenda item 119.

*Meeting numbers.* GA 49th session: 5th Committee 62, 66; plenary 106.

**Report of the Secretary-General (October).** In a 19 October report,[61] the Secretary-General indicated that initial cost estimates for the Mission's operation from 1 October 1994 to 30 June 1995 amounted to $43,181,000 gross ($39,713,500 net), with $39,711,500 gross ($36,582,500 net) apportioned. Expenditures for that period totalled $37,092,900 gross ($34,364,700 net), leaving an unencumbered balance of $2,618,600 gross ($2,217,800 net), mainly due to delays in the work of the Identification Commission and the resultant lower number of international and local staff in the Mission area. However, the savings were partially offset by additional requirements in the flying hours for the aircraft, the overlap time during the increased number of rotations of military observers, spare parts for transport operations and commercial freight and cartage. As at 22 September, outstanding assessed contributions due from Member States totalled $50,321,922.

The Secretary-General recommended that the General Assembly credit the unencumbered balance to Member States. In December,[62] ACABQ agreed with that recommendation.

**GENERAL ASSEMBLY ACTION (December)**

On 22 December, the General Assembly, by **decision 50/446 A**, appropriated to the MINURSO Special Account $22,370,000 gross ($20,384,400 net) already authorized and apportioned in July (see above) for the period from 1 October 1995 to January 1996, and set off against the future apportionment or outstanding financial obligations of Member States their respective share in the unencumbered balance of $2,618,600 gross ($2,217,800 net) for the period from 1 October 1994 to 30 June 1995.

By **decision 50/469** of 23 December, the Assembly directed the Fifth (Administrative and Budgetary) Committee to continue its consideration of MINURSO financing at the resumed fiftieth session in 1996.

## Audit of MINURSO

Pursuant to a 1994 General Assembly resolution,[63] the Secretary-General on 5 April transmitted a report[64] of the Office of Internal Oversight Services (OIOS) on an investigation of alleged irregularities and mismanagement of MINURSO. The report noted that the former Deputy Chairman of the Identification Commission in December 1994 had submitted charges of fiscal irresponsibility, serious mismanagement and "anti-Americanism" as well as lack of accountability in the Mission.

The audit and investigation were conducted at MINURSO headquarters in Laayoune between 13 and 18 February. The auditors were satisfied with explanations concerning most allegations and noted that remedial action with regard to certain irregularities had been taken as recommended during a previous internal audit in 1994. They did, however, make some further recommendations dealing with the optimal utilization of staff at identification centres, periodicity and comprehensiveness of progress reports, and avoidance of retroactive extension of staff contracts. While there were also several complaints against the Chief Administrative Officer concerning the lack of adequate administrative support and "improper behaviour", including anti-American expressions and adverse references to individual nationalities, the auditors did not sense any discrimination based on any particular nationality in the course of the investigation. On the other hand, the Chief Administrative Officer himself complained of lack of cooperation in enforcing rules and regulations.

The auditors concluded that the allegations appeared to have been triggered primarily by the former Deputy Chairman's frustration over non-extension of his contract and by personal animosity, and that the Deputy Special Representative needed better management and administrative support from, respectively, his Deputy in the Identification Commission and the Chief Administrative Officer.

By a 5 July note,[65] the Secretary-General transmitted a further report of OIOS, dealing with the follow-up on recommendations made during the 1994 audit of MINURSO. The report stated that the Mission had generally implemented corrective action recommended in prior audits and that the internal control system was adequate, although with opportunities for improvement.

By **decision 49/488** of 20 July, the General Assembly took note of the two reports.

## Island Territories

The Special Committee on decolonization had before it working papers by the Secretariat describing constitutional and political developments and economic, social and educational conditions in the following 12 island Territories: American Samoa,[66] Anguilla,[16] Bermuda,[17] British Virgin Islands,[67] Cayman Islands,[18] Guam,[23] Montserrat,[19] Pitcairn,[68] St. Helena,[69] Tokelau,[70] Turks and Caicos Islands,[20] United States Virgin Islands.[21]

The Committee allocated the item to its Subcommittee on Small Territories, Petitions, Information and Assistance and considered its report[4] between 10 and 18 July. The United Kingdom and the United States did not participate in Committee consideration of the Territories under their administration. New Zealand, as the administering Power, continued to participate in Committee work in relation to Tokelau. The Committee heard one petitioner on behalf of the UN Association of the Virgin Islands. On 18 July, it adopted a consolidated draft resolution, on the understanding that reservations expressed by its members would be reflected in that meeting's record,[11] and recommended the text for action by the General Assembly.

GENERAL ASSEMBLY ACTION

On 6 December, the General Assembly adopted **resolutions 50/38 A** and **B**.

**Questions of American Samoa, Anguilla, Bermuda, the British Virgin Islands, the Cayman Islands, Guam, Montserrat, Pitcairn, St. Helena, Tokelau, the Turks and Caicos Islands and the United States Virgin Islands**

**A**

**General**

*The General Assembly,*

*Having considered* the questions of the Non-Self-Governing Territories of American Samoa, Anguilla, Bermuda, the British Virgin Islands, the Cayman Islands, Guam, Montserrat, Pitcairn, St. Helena, Tokelau, the Turks and Caicos Islands and the United States Virgin Islands, hereinafter "the Territories",

*Having examined* the relevant chapter of the report of the Special Committee on the Situation with regard to the Implementation of the Declaration on the Granting of Independence to Colonial Countries and Peoples,

*Recognizing* that 1995 is the fiftieth anniversary of the United Nations and that decolonization is one of the proudest achievements of the Organization,

*Recalling* its resolution 1514(XV) of 14 December 1960, containing the Declaration on the Granting of Independence to Colonial Countries and Peoples, and all resolutions and decisions of the United Nations relating to those Territories, including, in particular, the resolutions adopted by the General Assembly at its forty-ninth session on the individual Territories covered by the present resolution,

*Recognizing* that the specific characteristics and the sentiments of the people of the Territories require flexible, practical and innovative approaches to the options of self-determination, without any prejudice to territorial size, geographical location, size of population or natural resources,

*Recalling* its resolution 1541(XV) of 15 December 1960, containing the principles that should guide Member States in determining whether or not an obligation exists to transmit the information called for under Article 73 *e* of the Charter of the United Nations,

*Conscious* of the need to ensure the full and speedy implementation of the Declaration in respect of the Territories, in view of the target set by the United Nations to eradicate colonialism by the year 2000,

*Noting with appreciation* the continuing exemplary cooperation of New Zealand, as administering Power, in the work of the Special Committee, and welcoming its statement that it will abide by the wishes of the population of Tokelau in determining their future political status,

*Welcoming* the stated position of the Government of the United Kingdom of Great Britain and Northern Ireland that it continues to take seriously its obligations under the Charter of the United Nations to develop self-government in the dependent Territories and, in cooperation with the locally elected Governments, to ensure that their constitutional frameworks continue to meet the wishes of the people, and the emphasis that it is ultimately for the peoples of the Territories to decide their future status,

*Aware* of the special circumstances of the geographical location and economic conditions of each Territory, and bearing in mind the necessity of promoting economic stability and diversifying and strengthening further the economies of the respective Territories as a matter of priority,

*Conscious* of the particular vulnerability of the small Territories to natural disasters and environmental degradation,

*Aware* of the usefulness both to the Territories and to the Special Committee of the participation of appointed and elected representatives of the Territories in the work of the Special Committee,

*Expressing its conviction* that referendums and other forms of popular consultation on the future status of the Non-Self-Governing Territories are an appropriate means of ascertaining the wishes of the peoples in those Territories with regard to their future political status,

*Mindful* that United Nations visiting missions provide one effective means of ascertaining the situation in the Territories, and considering that the possibility of sending further visiting missions to the Territories at an appropriate time and in consultation with the administering Powers should be kept under review,

*Mindful also* that some Territories have not had any United Nations visiting mission for a long period of time,

*Noting with appreciation* the contribution to the development of some Territories by specialized agencies and other organizations of the United Nations system, in particular the United Nations Development Programme, as well as regional institutions such as the Caribbean Development Bank,

1. *Approves* the chapter of the report of the Special Committee on the Situation with regard to the Implementation of the Declaration on the Granting of Independence to Colonial Countries and Peoples relating to the Non-Self-Governing Territories of American Samoa, Anguilla, Bermuda, the British Virgin Islands, the Cayman Islands, Guam, Montserrat, Pitcairn, St. Helena, Tokelau, the Turks and Caicos Islands and the United States Virgin Islands, hereinafter ''the Territories'';

2. *Reaffirms* the inalienable right of the people of the Territories to self-determination, including independence, in conformity with the Charter of the United Nations and General Assembly resolution 1514(XV), containing the Declaration on the Granting of Independence to Colonial Countries and Peoples;

3. *Reaffirms also* that it is ultimately for the people of the Territories themselves to determine freely their future political status in accordance with the relevant provisions of the Charter, the Declaration and the relevant resolutions of the General Assembly, and in that connection calls upon the administering Powers, in cooperation with the territorial Governments, to facilitate programmes of political education in the Territories in order to foster an awareness among the people of the possibilities open to them in the exercise of their right to self-determination, in conformity with the legitimate political status options clearly defined in resolution 1541(XV);

4. *Requests* the administering Powers to ascertain expeditiously, by means of popular consultations, the wishes and aspirations of the peoples of Non-Self-Governing Territories regarding their future political status so that the Special Committee can review the status of the Territories in accordance with the expressed wishes of the peoples of the Territories;

5. *Also requests* the administering Powers to facilitate the dispatch of the United Nations visiting missions to the Non-Self-Governing Territories regarding their future political status so that the Special Committee can review the status of the Territories in accordance with the expressed wishes of the peoples of the Territory;

6. *Reaffirms* the responsibility of the administering Powers under the Charter to promote the economic and social development and to preserve the cultural identity of the Territories, and recommends that priority continue to be given, in consultation with the territorial Governments concerned, to the strengthening and diversification of their respective economies;

7. *Further requests* the administering Powers to take all necessary measures to protect and conserve the environment of the Territories under their administration against any environmental degradation, and requests the specialized agencies concerned to continue to monitor environmental conditions in those Territories;

8. *Calls upon* the administering Powers, in cooperation with the respective territorial Governments, to continue to take all necessary measures to counter problems related to drug trafficking, money laundering and other offences;

9. *Stresses* that the achievement of the declared goal of eradication of colonialism by the year 2000 requires full and constructive cooperation by all parties concerned, and appeals to the administering Powers to continue to give their full support to the Special Committee;

10. *Urges* Member States to contribute to the efforts of the United Nations to usher in the twenty-first century in a world free of colonialism, and calls upon them to continue to give their full support to the Special Committee in its endeavours towards that noble goal;

11. *Invites* the specialized agencies and other organizations of the United Nations system to initiate or to continue to take all necessary measures to accelerate progress in the social and economic life of the Territories;

12. *Requests* the Special Committee to continue the examination of the question of the small Territories and to recommend to the General Assembly the most suitable steps to be taken to enable the populations of those Territories to exercise their right to self-determination, and to report thereon to the Assembly at its fifty-first session.

## B
## Individual Territories

### I. *American Samoa*

*The General Assembly,*

*Referring* to resolution A above,

*Noting* the fact that a large number of American Samoans have emigrated to the United States of America and are residing there,

*Noting also* the constitutional developments in the Territory,

*Noting further* that the Territory, similar to isolated communities with limited funds, continues to experience lack of adequate medical facilities and other infrastructural requirements,

*Recalling* the dispatch in 1981 of a United Nations visiting mission to the Territory,

1. *Requests* the administering Power to carry out, at the earliest possible date, a democratic exercise to ascertain the wishes of the people of American Samoa regarding the future status of the Territory;

2. *Calls upon* the administering Power to continue to assist the territorial Government in the economic and social development of the Territory and the development of manpower resources.

### II. *Anguilla*

*The General Assembly,*

*Referring* to resolution A above,

*Noting* that general elections were held in March 1994,

*Conscious* of the commitment of both the Government of Anguilla and the administering Power to a new and closer policy of dialogue and partnership through the Country Policy Plan for 1993-1997,

*Aware* that the exploitation of deep-sea resources would help reduce the risk of depleting the Territory's own fishing resources as a result of overfishing,

*Noting also* the need for continued cooperation between the administering Power and the territorial Government in tackling the problems of drug trafficking and money laundering,

*Recalling* the dispatch in 1984 of a United Nations visiting mission to the Territory,

1. *Requests* the administering Power to carry out, at the earliest possible date, an exercise to ascertain the wishes of the people of Anguilla regarding the future status of the Territory;

2. *Requests* all countries, organizations and United Nations agencies with deep-sea fishing experience to assist the Territory in improving its capacity in exploiting deep-sea fishing.

### III. *Bermuda*

*The General Assembly,*

*Referring* to resolution A above,

*Noting* the results of the independence referendum held on 16 August 1995,

*Conscious* of the different viewpoints of the political parties of the Territory on the future status of the Territory,

*Noting also* the measures taken by the Government to combat racism and the plan to set up a Commission for Unity and Racial Equality,

*Noting further* the closure of the Canadian base in 1994 and the announced plans of the United Kingdom of Great Britain and Northern Ireland and the United States of America to close their respective air and naval bases in Bermuda in 1995,

*Calls upon* the administering Power to continue its programmes of socio-economic development.

### IV. *British Virgin Islands*

*The General Assembly,*

*Referring* to resolution A above,

*Noting* the completion of the constitutional review in the Territory and the coming into force of the amended Constitution, and noting also the results of the general elections held on 20 February 1995,

*Noting also* the results of the constitutional review of 1993-1994, which made it clear that a prerequisite to independence must be a constitutionally expressed wish by the people as a result of a referendum,

*Taking note* of the statement by the Chief Minister of the British Virgin Islands that the Territory was ready for constitutional and political advancement towards full internal self-government and that the administering Power should assist through gradual transfer of power to elected territorial representatives,

*Noting* that the Territory is emerging as one of the world's leading offshore financial centres,

*Noting also* the need for continued cooperation between the administering Power and the territorial Government in countering drug trafficking and money laundering,

1. *Requests* the administering Power to continue the process for facilitating the expression of the will of the people regarding the future status of the Territory;

2. *Also requests* the administering Power, specialized agencies and other organizations of the United Nations system and all financial institutions to continue to provide assistance to the Territory for socio-economic development and development of human resources, bearing in mind the vulnerability of the Territory to external factors.

### V. *Cayman Islands*

*The General Assembly,*

*Referring* to resolution A above,

*Noting* the constitutional review of 1992-1993, according to which the population expressed the sentiment that the existing relations with the United Kingdom of Great Britain and Northern Ireland should be maintained and that the current status of the Territory should not be altered,

*Noting also* the actions taken by the territorial Government to implement its localization programme to promote increased participation of the local population in the decision-making process in the Cayman Islands,

*Noting with concern* the vulnerability of the Territory to drug trafficking and related activities, as well as the measures taken by the authorities to deal with those problems,

*Noting further* that the Territory has emerged as one of the world's leading offshore financial centres,

*Recalling* the dispatch in 1977 of a United Nations visiting mission to the Territory,

1. *Requests* the administering Power to continue to provide the territorial Government with all required expertise to enable it to achieve its socio-economic aims;

2. *Also requests* the administering Power, in consultation with the territorial Government, to continue to facilitate the expansion of the current programme of securing employment for the local population, in particular at the decision-making level;

3. *Requests* the specialized agencies and other organizations of the United Nations system to continue and increase their programmes of assistance to the Territory with a view to strengthening, developing and diversifying its economy;

4. *Calls upon* the administering Power and the territorial Government to continue to cooperate to counter problems related to money laundering, smuggling of funds and other related crimes, as well as drug trafficking.

## VI. *Guam*

*The General Assembly*,

*Referring* to resolution A above,

*Noting* the results of the general elections held in November 1994,

*Recalling* that, in a referendum held in 1987, the people of Guam endorsed a draft Guam Commonwealth Act that would establish a new framework for relations between the Territory and the administering Power, providing internal self-government for Guam and recognition of the right of the people of Guam to self-determination for the Territory,

*Aware* of the continued negotiations between the administering Power and the territorial Government on the draft Guam Commonwealth Act and on the future status of the Territory, with particular emphasis on the question of the evolution of the relationship between the United States of America and Guam,

*Recalling* the statement by the Special Representative of the United States of America for Guam Commonwealth Issues on 12 December 1993 that the Administration hoped to have comments on the Commonwealth Bill before Congress by the end of 1994,

*Cognizant* that the administering Power continues to implement its programme of transferring surplus federal land to the Government of Guam,

*Noting* that the people of the Territory have called for reform in the programme of the administering Power with respect to the thorough and expeditious transfer of land property to the people of Guam,

*Conscious* that immigration into Guam has resulted in the indigenous Chamorros becoming a minority in their homeland,

*Aware* of the potential for diversifying and developing the economy of Guam through commercial fishing and agriculture and other viable activities,

*Recalling* the dispatch in 1979 of a United Nations visiting mission to the Territory,

1. *Calls upon* the administering Power and the territorial Government to expedite the early conclusion of the negotiations on the draft Guam Commonwealth Act and on the future status of the Territory;

2. *Requests* the administering Power to continue to assist the elected territorial Government in achieving its political, economic and social goals;

3. *Also requests* the administering Power, in cooperation with the territorial Government, to continue the transfer of land to the people of the Territory and to take the necessary steps to safeguard their property rights;

4. *Further requests* the administering Power to continue to recognize and respect the political rights and the cultural and ethnic identity of the Chamorro people and to take all necessary measures to respond to the concerns of the territorial Government with regard to the immigration issue;

5. *Requests* the administering Power to continue to support appropriate measures by the territorial Government aimed at promoting growth in commercial fishing and agriculture and other viable activities.

## VII. *Montserrat*

*The General Assembly*,

*Referring* to resolution A above,

*Noting* the functioning of a democratic process in Montserrat,

*Taking note* of the reported statement of the Chief Minister that his preference was for independence within a political union with the Organization of Eastern Caribbean States and that self-reliance was more of a priority than independence,

*Recalling* the dispatch in 1982 of a United Nations visiting mission to the Territory,

1. *Requests* the administering Power to conduct an appropriate exercise, at the earliest possible date, to ascertain the will of the people regarding the future status of the Territory;

2. *Requests* the specialized agencies and other organizations of the United Nations system, as well as regional and other multilateral financial institutions, to continue their assistance to the Territory in the strengthening, development and diversification of the economy of Montserrat in accordance with its medium- and long-term development plans.

## VIII. *Pitcairn*

*The General Assembly*,

*Referring* to resolution A above,

*Taking into account* the unique nature of the Territory in terms of population and area,

*Expressing its satisfaction* with the continued economic and social advancement of the Territory, as well as with the improvement of its communications with the outside world and its management plan to address conservation issues,

*Requests* the administering Power to continue its assistance for improvement of the economic, social, educational and other conditions of the population of the Territory.

## IX. *St. Helena*

*The General Assembly*,

*Referring* to resolution A above,

*Aware* of the request by the Legislative Council of St. Helena that the administering Power conduct a constitutional review in the Territory,

*Taking into account* the unique character of the Territory, its population and its natural resources,

*Aware* of the efforts of the administering Power and the territorial authorities to improve the socio-economic conditions of the population of St. Helena, in particular in the sphere of food production,

1. *Requests* the administering Power to conduct the constitutional review in the Territory, taking into account the wishes of its population;

2. *Also requests* the administering Power and relevant regional and international organizations to continue to support the efforts of the territorial Government to address the socio-economic development of the Territory.

### X.  *Tokelau*

*The General Assembly,*

*Referring* to resolution A above,

*Having heard* the statements of the representative of New Zealand, the administering Power, and the Special Representative of Tokelau, who conveyed a message from the Council of *Faipule* (joint chairmen of the General *Fono* (Council)) to the Special Committee on the Situation with regard to the Implementation of the Declaration on the Granting of Independence to Colonial Countries and Peoples,

*Recalling* the solemn declaration on the future status of Tokelau delivered by the *Ulu-o-Tokelau* (highest authority of Tokelau) on 30 July 1994, that an act of self-determination in Tokelau is now under active consideration, together with the constitution of a self-governing Tokelau, and that the present preference of Tokelau is for a status of free association with New Zealand,

*Noting* the emphasis placed in the solemn declaration on the terms of Tokelau's intended free association relationship with New Zealand, including the expectation that the form of help Tokelau could continue to expect from New Zealand in promoting the well-being of its people, besides its external interests, would be clearly established in the framework of that relationship,

*Noting also* the Territory's concentrated focus in 1995 on strengthening its national institutions and creating a structure of government to meet modern needs, preparatory to the exercise by the people of Tokelau of their right to self-determination,

*Acknowledging* the endeavours of Tokelau to be self-reliant to the greatest extent possible,

*Noting with appreciation* the continuing exemplary cooperation of the administering Power with regard to the work of the Special Committee on the Situation with regard to the Implementation of the Declaration on the Granting of Independence to Colonial Countries and Peoples relating to Tokelau and its readiness to permit access by United Nations visiting missions to the Territory,

*Recalling* the dispatch in 1994 of a United Nations visiting mission to Tokelau,

1. *Notes*, on the basis of statements made by representatives of the administering Power and Tokelau subsequent to the 1994 United Nations visiting mission, that Tokelau is working towards an act of self-determination that would result in Tokelau assuming a status in accordance with the options on future status for Non-Self-Governing Territories contained in Principle VI of the annex to General Assembly resolution 1541(XV) of 15 December 1960;

2. *Also notes* the expressed wishes of the people of the Territory indicating a strong preference for a status of free association with New Zealand;

3. *Further notes* the readiness of the people of Tokelau to assume full governmental responsibility and to conduct their own affairs within the framework of a constitution, which is currently being developed;

4. *Welcomes* the assurances of the Government of New Zealand that it will meet its obligations to the United Nations with respect to Tokelau and abide by the freely expressed wishes of the people of Tokelau with regard to their future status;

5. *Invites* the administering Power and United Nations agencies to continue their assistance to the social and economic development of Tokelau.

### XI.  *Turks and Caicos Islands*

*The General Assembly,*

*Referring* to resolution A above,

*Noting* recent changes to the Constitution of the Territory and the intention of the territorial Government to continue to campaign for further constitutional changes,

*Noting also* that general elections took place in the Territory on 31 January 1995,

*Noting further* the policy of the authorities of maintaining a balance between creating a more liberal investment environment and preserving access by the population to economic benefits,

*Noting* the increase in aid, in particular financial assistance, granted to the territorial Government by the Government of the United Kingdom of Great Britain and Northern Ireland,

1. *Requests* the administering Power to conduct, at the earliest possible date, an appropriate exercise to ascertain the will of the people regarding the future status of the Territory;

2. *Calls upon* the administering Power and the relevant regional and international organizations to continue to support the efforts of the territorial Government to address the socio-economic development of the Territory.

### XII.  *United States Virgin Islands*

*The General Assembly,*

*Referring* to resolution A above,

*Noting* that general elections were held in November 1994,

*Noting also* that a majority of those who voted in the referendum on the political status of the Territory on 11 October 1993 supported the existing territorial status arrangement with the United States of America,

*Noting further* the continuing interest of the territorial Government in seeking associate membership in the Organization of Eastern Caribbean States and observer status in the Caribbean Community,

*Noting* the necessity of further diversifying the Territory's economy,

*Noting also* that the question of Water Island is still under consideration,

*Noting further* that in 1993 the territorial Government purchased the assets of the West Indian Company, which had significant property and development interests in the Charlotte Amalie Harbour,

*Recalling* the dispatch in 1977 of a United Nations visiting mission to the Territory,

1. *Requests* the administering Power to continue to assist the elected territorial Government in achieving its political, economic and social goals;

2. *Also requests* the administering Power to facilitate the participation of the Territory, as appropriate, in various organizations, in particular the Organization of Eastern Caribbean States and the Caribbean Community;

3. *Welcomes* the negotiations between the administering Power and the territorial Government on the question of Water Island.

General Assembly resolutions 50/38 A and B

6 December 1995     Meeting 82     146-4-3 (recorded vote)

Approved by Fourth Committee (A/50/602) by recorded vote (124-4-6), 3 November (meeting 15); draft by Committee on decolonization (A/50/23), amended by United Kingdom and United States (A/C.4/50/L.6); agenda item 18.
*Meeting numbers.* GA 50th session: 4th Committee 2-7, 9-11, 13-15; plenary 82.

Recorded vote in Assembly as follows:

*In favour:* Afghanistan, Albania, Algeria, Andorra, Antigua and Barbuda, Armenia, Australia, Austria, Azerbaijan, Bahamas, Bahrain, Bangladesh, Barbados, Belarus, Belize, Benin, Bolivia, Bosnia and Herzegovina, Botswana, Brazil, Brunei Darussalam, Bulgaria, Burkina Faso, Burundi, Cameroon, Canada, Cape Verde, Chad, Chile, China, Colombia, Côte d'Ivoire, Croatia, Cuba, Cyprus, Czech Republic, Democratic People's Republic of Korea, Denmark, Djibouti, Dominica, Ecuador, Egypt, El Salvador, Estonia, Ethiopia, Fiji, Finland, Gabon, Germany, Ghana, Greece, Grenada, Guinea, Guinea-Bissau, Guyana, Haiti, Honduras, Hungary, Iceland, India, Indonesia, Iran, Ireland, Italy, Jamaica, Japan, Jordan, Kazakstan, Kenya, Kuwait, Lao People's Democratic Republic, Latvia, Lebanon, Lesotho, Libyan Arab Jamahiriya, Liechtenstein, Lithuania, Luxembourg, Madagascar, Malawi, Malaysia, Maldives, Mali, Malta, Marshall Islands, Mauritania, Mauritius, Mexico, Micronesia, Mongolia, Morocco, Myanmar, Nepal, Netherlands, New Zealand, Nicaragua, Niger, Nigeria, Norway, Oman, Pakistan, Panama, Papua New Guinea, Paraguay, Peru, Philippines, Poland, Portugal, Qatar, Republic of Korea, Republic of Moldova, Romania, Russian Federation, Saint Lucia, Samoa, Saudi Arabia, Senegal, Sierra Leone, Singapore, Slovakia, Slovenia, Solomon Islands, South Africa, Spain, Sri Lanka, Sudan, Suriname, Swaziland, Sweden, Syrian Arab Republic, Thailand, the former Yugoslav Republic of Macedonia, Togo, Trinidad and Tobago, Tunisia, Turkey, Uganda, Ukraine, United Arab Emirates, United Republic of Tanzania, Uruguay, Vanuatu, Venezuela, Viet Nam, Zambia, Zimbabwe.

*Against:* Georgia, Israel, United Kingdom, United States.

*Abstaining:* Argentina, Belgium, France.

## International Trusteeship System

During 1995, discussion continued regarding the future role of the Trusteeship Council, which in 1994 had effectively completed its work with respect to the 11 Territories placed under the International Trusteeship System. As the last remaining entity of the Trust Territory of the Pacific Islands, Palau completed the process of self-determination in November 1993, when it approved the Compact of Free Association with the United States, which had been Administering Authority for the Trust Territory. In December 1994, Palau became the 185th Member State of the United Nations.

In 1994, the Trusteeship Council had amended[71] its rules of procedure, establishing that it would henceforth meet as and where occasion might require.

On 2 June 1995,[72] Malta requested that an item on the review of the role of the Trusteeship Council be included in the provisional agenda of the General Assembly's fiftieth session in 1995. In an explanatory memorandum accompanying its request, Malta expressed the belief that the role of the Council could be enhanced to that of trustee of the common heritage of humankind, making it the focal point for coordination of endeavour in different areas related to the safeguard of common heritage and incorporated within various international conventions, thus warding the interest of current and future generations against dispersal and fragmentation of effort.

In his report on the work of the Organization,[73] the Secretary-General reiterated his 1994 recommendation[74] that the Trusteeship Council be abolished in accordance with Article 108 of the Charter.

**GENERAL ASSEMBLY ACTION**

On 11 December, the General Assembly adopted **resolution 50/55**.

### Review of the role of the Trusteeship Council

*The General Assembly,*

*Noting* the proposal made by Malta on the review of the role of the Trusteeship Council, other proposals made and different views expressed by Member States at the fiftieth session of the General Assembly on decisions relative to the future of the Trusteeship Council and the report of the Secretary-General on the work of the Organization,

*Noting also* that the General Assembly's Open-ended High-level Working Group on the Strengthening of the United Nations System will be undertaking a thorough review of studies and reports of the relevant United Nations bodies and submissions of Member States and observers, as well as studies and reports of independent commissions, non-governmental organizations, institutions, scholars and other experts on subjects relating to the revitalization, strengthening and reform of the United Nations system,

*Noting further* the role of the Special Committee on the Charter of the United Nations and on the Strengthening of the Role of the Organization,

1. *Requests* the Secretary-General to invite Member States to submit, not later than 31 May 1996, written comments on the future of the Trusteeship Council;

2. *Also requests* the Secretary-General to submit to the General Assembly, as early as possible and before the end of its fiftieth session, for appropriate consideration, a report containing comments made by Member States on the subject.

General Assembly resolution 50/55

11 December 1995     Meeting 87     Adopted by consensus

Approved by Sixth Committee (A/50/646) by consensus, 29 November (meeting 46); draft by Malta (A/C.6/50/L.6/Rev.1); agenda item 152.
*Meeting numbers.* GA 50th session: 6th Committee 44-46; plenary 68, 87.

*REFERENCES*

[1]A/50/23. [2]YUN 1960, p. 49, GA res. 1514(XV), 14 Dec. 1960. [3]A/AC.109/L.1835. [4]A/AC.109/L.1829. [5]A/AC.109/2037. [6]YUN 1994, p. 182, GA res. 49/89, 16 Dec. 1994. [7]YUN 1991, p. 777, GA res. 46/181, 19 Dec. 1991. [8]YUN 1988, p. 734, GA res. 43/47, 22 Nov. 1988. [9]A/AC.109/2030. [10]A/AC.109/2024. [11]A/AC.109/PV.1451. [12]YUN 1994, p. 186,

GA res. 49/41, 9 Dec. 1994. [13]A/50/212 & Add.1. [14]YUN 1994, p. 184, ESC res. 1994/37, 29 July 1994. [15]E/1995/85. [16]A/AC.109/2016 & Add.1. [17]A/AC.109/2020 & Add.1. [18]A/AC.109/2013 & Corr.1 & Add.1. [19]A/AC.109/2019 & Add.1. [20]A/AC.109/2015 & Add.1. [21]A/AC.109/2014. [22]A/AC.109/ 2018. [23]YUN 1991, p. 789. [24]YUN 1994, p. 192, GA res. 49/42, 9 Dec. 1994. [25]A/50/481. [26]A/50/458. [27]YUN 1994, p. 194. [28]A/AC.109/L.1831. [29]A/AC.109/2031. [30]A/AC.109/ 2026. [31]A/AC.109/PV.1446. [32]A/50/214 & Corr.1. [33]YUN 1994, p. 1022. [34]A/50/280. [35]A/50/436. [36]YUN 1994, p. 195. [37]YUN 1991, p. 798. [38]A/AC.109/2027 & Corr.1. [39]A/AC.109/ 2033. [40]A/AC.109/2025. [41]A/AC.109/2028. [42]YUN 1988, p. 742. [43]YUN 1991, p. 794, SC res. 690(1991), 29 Apr. 1991. [44]YUN 1994, p. 199. [45]S/1995/240 & Add.1. [46]S/PRST/ 1995/17. [47]S/1995/404. [48]S/1995/431. [49]S/1995/498. [50]S/1995/ 524. [51]S/1995/514. [52]S/1995/779. [53]S/1995/924. [54]S/1995/ 925. [55]S/1995/986. [56]YUN 1994, p. 200, GA res. 49/44, 9 Dec. 1994. [57]A/50/504. [58]A/AC.109/2029 & Add.1. [59]A/49/ 559/Add.1 & Corr.1. [60]A/49/771/Add.1. [61]A/50/655 & Corr.1,2. [62]A/50/802. [63]YUN 1994, p. 1362, GA res. 48/218 B, 29 July 1994. [64]A/49/884. [65]A/49/937. [66]A/AC.109/2023. [67]A/AC.109/2017 & Add.1. [68]A/AC.109/2012. [69]A/AC.109/ 2021. [70]A/AC.109/2022. [71]YUN 1994, p. 216, TC res. 2200(LXI), 25 May 1994. [72]A/50/142. [73]A/50/1. [74]YUN 1994, p. 8.

# Information

UN public information activities continued to focus on publicizing the Organization's work and goals and enhancing the information and communication capabilities of developing countries. Those activities were carried out by the Department of Public Information (DPI) of the UN secretariat, the United Nations Educational, Scientific and Cultural Organization (UNESCO) and the Joint United Nations Information Committee.

The General Assembly's Committee on Information, at its seventeenth session (New York, 1-12 May 1995), reviewed UN information policies and activities.[1] The Committee had before it a report on allocation of regular budget resources to the UN information centres (UNICs)[2] and a review of DPI publications,[3] submitted by the Secretary-General in response to a 1994 Assembly resolution.[4]

Its recommendations were considered by the Fourth Committee in November and the Assembly acted on them in December. On 6 December, the Assembly, by **decision 50/411**, increased the membership of the Committee on Information from 88 to 89, appointing the Democratic People's Republic of Korea as a new member (see APPENDIX III).

## Communication issues

At its 1995 session, the Committee discussed the establishment of a more just and more effective world information and communication order based on the free circulation and balanced dissemination of information; examined UN public information policies and activities in the light of the evolution of international relations; and evaluated efforts made

and progress achieved by the UN system in the field of information and communications.

**UNESCO activities.** In 1995, UNESCO continued to pursue its strategy for the development of communication and the free flow of information through its International Programme for the Development of Communication (IPDC) and other programmes.

In preparation for the Fourth World Conference on Women (see PART FOUR, Chapter X), UNESCO convened an international symposium on the theme "Women and the Media—Access to Expression and Decision-Making" (Toronto, Canada, 28 February–3 March). It approved the Toronto Platform for Action on women and the media, which recommended global and specific and immediate actions to increase women's participation in the media and to promote equality between men and women.

The General Conference of UNESCO, at its twenty-eighth session (Paris, 25 October–16 November 1995), adopted the Toronto Platform for Action and invited member States to implement its recommendations. In a resolution on communication, information and informatics, the Conference invited the UNESCO Director-General to: encourage women's access to expression and decision-making in communication, as well as to promote a better balanced dissemination of information, foster the cultural and educational dimension in electronic media programmes and encourage international debate on the issue of violence on the screen; study new trends in information and communication technologies and monitor new developments in the field of information; assist member States in formulating national information policies and regional strategies; and strengthen IPDC activities and intensify its interaction with the UN system and funding sources. The Director-General was also invited to: foster the development of community media in rural and disadvantaged areas and in large cities; increase audiovisual production capacities in developing countries and explore ways of improving regional and international dissemination of their products; contribute to the training of communication and information professionals, particularly women; support the establishment of an international network of schools of information studies; develop common approaches to training information specialists in the use of modern technologies; encourage the modernization of library and archival services and promote public libraries as gateways to information networks; strengthen regional informatics networks and their connection with international networks; and facilitate access to and promote the use of telematics services in developing countries.

In a resolution on promotion of independent and pluralist media, the General Conference endorsed declarations adopted by participants at a series of regional seminars in 1991,[5] 1992[6] and 1994;[7] expressed its conviction that the next UNESCO/DPI regional seminar, to be held in Yemen in 1996, would contribute to the development of pluralist media in the Arab region; and invited the Director-General to organize a similar regional seminar in Europe in 1997. In two other resolutions, the Conference called for support to cultural and educational activities undertaken by public service broadcasting, media professionals and journalists to reduce violence in the media, and invited member States to intensify cooperation on matters of information design as the basis for optimized visual communication.

IPDC sponsored activities in various regions of the world. Efforts in Africa included: a project to promote photojournalism; a seminar for women journalists from West and Central Africa on creation of newspapers, marketing and ethics; a databank for a Moroccan press agency; a computer-based documentation system in Tunisia; mobile video projection units in Zambia; assistance to a women's magazine in Ethiopia; and strengthening of a Ghanaian journalist association.

In Asia and the Pacific, projects included: a meeting of experts to discuss communications priorities in the region; publication of monographs on media laws and regulations in Asia; development of a "Women in Media" network in Central Asia; establishment of a Bengali-language news agency in Bangladesh; information programmes for Tajikistan independent television; and a fellowship programme on television programme production in the Republic of Korea.

For the Middle East, projects included a mission to study the development of Palestinian television. For countries in transition to a market economy, a seminar was held in Moscow on the ethics of journalism. For Latin America and the Caribbean, a project was executed to develop information and communications capabilities.

An international round table for broadcasters and programme managers on non-violence, tolerance and television was held in New Delhi, India. Projects aimed at education and training of journalists and other information specialists were carried out for the Arab region, Chad, China, Guatemala, Jordan, Kazakstan, the United Republic of Tanzania and Yemen. Assistance was provided to develop radio and television broadcasting in the Cook Islands, Dominica, Kyrgyzstan, Nepal, Niue, Samoa, Sao Tome and Principe and Seychelles. Other projects dealt with rural information networks and broadcasting for rural development in Egypt, Grenada, Indonesia and Trinidad and Tobago.

In September, the IPDC Intergovernmental Council Bureau examined 66 projects and selected 47 of them for submission to the Council, totalling some $7.5 million. The Council did not meet

in 1995, having deferred[7] its sixteenth session to January 1996.

GENERAL ASSEMBLY ACTION

On 6 December, the General Assembly adopted **resolution 50/31 A**.

### Information in the service of humanity

*The General Assembly,*

*Taking note* of the comprehensive and important report of the Committee on Information,

*Also taking note* of the report of the Secretary-General on questions relating to information,

*Urges* all countries, organizations of the United Nations system as a whole and all others concerned, reaffirming their commitment to the principles of the Charter of the United Nations and to the principles of freedom of the press and freedom of information, as well as to those of the independence, pluralism and diversity of the media, deeply concerned by the disparities existing between developed and developing countries and the consequences of every kind arising from those disparities that affect the capability of the public, private or other media and individuals in developing countries to disseminate information and communicate their views and their cultural and ethical values through endogenous cultural production, as well as to ensure the diversity of sources and their free access to information, and recognizing the call in this context for what in the United Nations and at various international forums has been termed "a new world information and communication order, seen as an evolving and continuous process":

*(a)* To cooperate and interact with a view to reducing existing disparities in information flows at all levels by increasing assistance for the development of communication infrastructures and capabilities in developing countries, with due regard for their needs and the priorities attached to such areas by those countries, and in order to enable them and the public, private or other media in developing countries to develop their own information and communication policies freely and independently and increase the participation of media and individuals in the communication process, and to ensure a free flow of information at all levels;

*(b)* To ensure for journalists the free and effective performance of their professional tasks and condemn resolutely all attacks against them;

*(c)* To provide support for the continuation and strengthening of practical training programmes for broadcasters and journalists from public, private and other media in developing countries;

*(d)* To enhance regional efforts and cooperation among developing countries, as well as cooperation between developed and developing countries, to strengthen communication capacities and to improve the media infrastructure and communication technology in the developing countries, especially in the areas of training and dissemination of information;

*(e)* To aim, in addition to bilateral cooperation, at providing all possible support and assistance to the developing countries and their media, public, private or other, with due regard to their interests and needs in the field of information and to action already adopted within the United Nations system, including:

(i) The development of the human and technical resources that are indispensable for the improvement of information and communication systems in developing countries and support for the continuation and strengthening of practical training programmes, such as those already operating under both public and private auspices throughout the developing world;

(ii) The creation of conditions that will enable developing countries and their media, public, private or other, to have, by using their national and regional resources, the communication technology suited to their national needs, as well as the necessary programme material, especially for radio and television broadcasting;

(iii) Assistance in establishing and promoting telecommunication links at the subregional, regional and interregional levels, especially among developing countries;

(iv) The facilitation, as appropriate, of access by the developing countries to advanced communication technology available on the open market;

*(f)* To provide full support for the International Programme for the Development of Communication of the United Nations Educational, Scientific and Cultural Organization, which should support both public and private media.

General Assembly resolution 50/31 A

6 December 1995    Meeting 82    Adopted without vote

Approved by Fourth Committee (A/50/608) without vote, 27 October (meeting 11); draft by Committee on Information (A/50/21); agenda item 87. *Meeting numbers.* GA 50th session: 4th Committee 9-11; plenary 82.

By **resolution 50/31 B**, the Assembly invited Member States that wished to do so to submit to the Secretary-General by 15 March 1996 their observations and suggestions on ways to further the development of communication infrastructures and capabilities in developing countries. The Secretary-General was asked to report on the subject in 1996 to the Committee on Information.

## UN public information

### DPI activities

In September, the Secretary-General submitted a report[8] on questions relating to information, focusing on activities of DPI, which he stated had continued in 1995 to promote an informed understanding of the work of the United Nations and to foster a positive image of the system as a whole. In an effort to strengthen and improve the public information tasks of the Organization, DPI had sought to reach public opinion within every stratum of global society, ensure a cohesive approach to the issues and their unified presentation within the UN system, and exploit the potential of electronic communications. The Office of the Spokesman for the Secretary-General organized daily briefings and an increasingly large number of one-on-one contacts with the world's media, as well as various interviews and background briefings

with senior UN officials. Contacts were also strengthened between the senior management of the Department and senior international media officials.

Services were provided to 2,900 permanently accredited and 2,500 temporarily accredited media representatives at Headquarters; in addition, more than 20,000 media representatives had been accredited since 1992 for UN conferences held away from Headquarters. The production of press releases in English and French was expanded. Radio programmes were provided in 15 languages to more than 1,800 broadcasting organizations. UN television programmes were distributed throughout the world by major international broadcasting organizations. The Department established a digital transmission system for audio recordings, laid the groundwork for a future tapeless archival system, and was introducing a compact-disc system for electronic storage, reproduction and dissemination of photographs.

The Department provided information to six publicly accessible databases and disseminated electronically more than a million pages of documents and publications during the first half of 1995. Its own database, the largest in the UN system, was accessed daily on the Internet by an average of 20,000 users; an additional 5,000 users on a daily basis accessed on the World Wide Web the UN Home Page, which had been launched during the year.

Thematically integrated information programmes on priority issues were developed. The Department conducted guided tours of UN Headquarters, organized weekly briefings for some 200 NGO representatives, and provided a wide range of information to some 1,500 NGOs worldwide. The forty-eighth annual conference of DPI for NGOs (New York, 18-20 September), centred on the theme ''The United Nations at the turn of the century: global issues; global actors; global responsibility'', was attended by more than 1,300 NGO representatives. The annual training programme for journalists took place at Headquarters from 18 September to 26 October.

The Department oversaw the comprehensive UN publications programme and provided research services through the Dag Hammarskjöld Library and its system of 347 depository libraries in 140 countries. An Integrated Library Management System for archival collection and bibliographic control of documents and publications was being launched. A variety of databases, regularly accessed by 91 Governments and 86 permanent missions, was made available in March both online and in compact-disc format. Additional steps were taken to strengthen the marketing and sales of system-wide publications through a network of agents, distributors and bookstores in more than 65 countries.

In implementing specific information programmes mandated by the General Assembly in 1994,[4] DPI pursued three thematically integrated priority areas: sustainable economic and social development in the overall context of "An Agenda for Development" (see PART FOUR, Chapter I); peacemaking, peace-keeping and peace-building (see below); and human rights and humanitarian relief activities. Economic and social issues, particularly developments with regard to "An Agenda for Development", were covered in the bimonthly *Development Update* newsletter, which provided an overview of UN activities and publications in the development sphere. The quarterly periodical *Africa Recovery* focused on issues of special concern to that continent and underscored the links between UN peace-keeping, humanitarian and developmental activities in Africa. The Department also provided information support to the Commission on Sustainable Development regarding follow-up to the 1994 Global Conference on the Sustainable Development of Small Island Developing States, the results of the UN Conference on Straddling Fish Stocks and Highly Migratory Fish Stocks and UN conventions on biodiversity, climate change and desertification (see PART FOUR, Chapter VII).

As part of its 1995 programme for human rights, DPI was organizing seminars for international journalists and prepared a series of in-depth articles on key human rights issues, including judicial independence, the right to development, violence against women, the sale of children and child prostitution, ethnic conflict and racial discrimination. Activities relating to the situation in the Middle East and the question of Palestine included a seminar on assistance to the Palestinian people in media development, a training programme for Palestinian journalists (New York, 8 October–22 November) and the production of books, pamphlets and audiovisual materials.

The Department continued to develop information campaigns for major UN conferences, in collaboration with other entities of the system. During the year, such campaigns were carried out to promote the World Summit for Social Development, the Ninth United Nations Congress on the Prevention of Crime and the Treatment of Offenders (see PART FOUR, Chapter IX) and the Fourth World Conference on Women (see PART FOUR, Chapter X). The last-mentioned campaign included a series of feature articles, *Focus on Women*, and publication of the second edition of *The World's Women: Trends and Statistics*, including new sections on women and the media and women in peace-keeping. Preparations were also under way for an information programme to promote the Second UN Conference on Human Settlements (see PART FOUR, Chapter VIII) and the International Year for the Eradication of Poverty, both in 1996.

The Department's contribution to the observance of the United Nations fiftieth anniversary (see also below, under "Other questions") included a special commemorative edition of the *Yearbook of the United Nations*; two special issues of the *UN Chronicle* (Vol. XXII, Nos. 3 and 4); the *50th Anniversary UN Minutes* television series broadcast by more than 30 major television organizations worldwide; 12 video compilations on the history of the Organization; and a catalogue of historical and thematic photographs. The Department also co-produced *A Place to Stand*—a video overview of UN history and achievements.

DPI continued to ensure the timely production and dissemination of its major publications, in particular the *Yearbook of the United Nations*, the *UN Chronicle* and *Africa Recovery*. In July, the Department and the World Bank agreed to co-produce the twice-monthly publication *Development Business* on development bank and UN procurement. By August 1995, DPI had published seven volumes of the *Blue Books Series*, comprehensive subject-oriented reference works launched in 1994 and covering major issues of concern to the international community. A new edition of *Basic Facts about the United Nations* was produced and a new publication was introduced, entitled *A Guide to Information at the United Nations*. The UN Publications Board continued to guide publications activities on issues most relevant to the Organization.

The General Assembly, by **resolution 50/31 B**, encouraged the Secretary-General to explore ways of improving the access of UN radio to airwaves worldwide and requested him to increase efforts for the early resumption of the publication *Development Forum* or an alternative system-wide publication devoted to development issues.

### Dissemination of information related to peace-keeping

By **resolution 49/233 B** of 31 March 1995, the General Assembly requested the Committee on Information to review the Secretariat's policy on dissemination of information related to peace-keeping.

The Committee's Extended Bureau subsequently submitted in May a paper on media strategies for peace-keeping and other field operations. The document noted the need for a coordinated and unified public information strategy aimed at increasing public understanding and support for the United Nations peacemaking role, and pointed out that the Secretary-General, in his "Supplement to an Agenda for Peace" (see PART ONE, Chapter I, and PART TWO, Chapter I), had underlined the vital role of an effective information capacity and the importance of establishing such a capacity at the early planning stages of every field mission.

Among measures suggested were: early consultations and coordination between DPI and the Departments of Peace-keeping Operations, Humanitarian Affairs and Political Affairs; early involvement of DPI in planning field missions to avoid fragmentation of resources and duplication of efforts with regard to public information activities; development of a joint information strategy in emergency situations; creation of DPI personnel rosters for public information duties in field operations; elaboration of draft standards for planning mission information strategies and related Headquarters activities; and dividing an integrated information programme into an internal programme within the area of the mission and an external programme for the international community at large. In addition, the paper recommended that an integrated strategy should target public opinion in countries providing support to and those hosting peace-keeping operations, in order to build support for such missions among contributing States and establish a positive environment for their functioning in countries of deployment.

The Committee on Information, at its seventeenth session,[1] took note of the review and decided to examine it further through its Extended Bureau.

In a September report,[8] the Secretary-General noted the establishment of an interdepartmental Working Group on Media Strategies for Peace-keeping and Other Field Operations as a mechanism for regular consultations among the Departments of Peace-keeping Operations, Humanitarian Affairs, Political Affairs and Public Information with regard to the information component of field operations. Consultations focused on development of information strategies and personnel rosters. DPI also continued to refine a set of standards for mission information components and to look into the development of a central UN broadcasting facility for field operations. It provided comprehensive information about UN peace-keeping and peace-making to the media, educational and research institutions, government agencies, NGOs and the general public. Other efforts resulted in the publication of a biannual collection of in-depth reviews of all current peace-keeping operations and a reference paper series on peace-keeping missions, as well as distribution of a one-hour documentary on peace-keeping, *No Place to Hide*. The third edition of *The Blue Helmets* was being prepared in 1995.

The General Assembly, by **resolution 50/31 B**, requested the Secretary-General to ensure the involvement of DPI at the planning stage of future peace-keeping and other field operations through interdepartmental consultations and coordination.

## UN information centres

In a March report[2] to the Committee on Information, the Secretary-General noted intensified efforts by UNICs—a network of information centres

in 68 countries worldwide—to reach out to key audiences, pool resources with other UN entities, adapt information material in local languages to regional needs, contribute to preparations for major international conferences, strengthen relations with local media, and explore new communications technologies for the exchange of information with Headquarters, other field offices and the media. The work of UNICs was discussed in January in Geneva at a meeting of information professionals with the Secretary-General, during which he stressed the need for an active approach towards the media, urged UNIC directors to counter erroneous reporting in the media, and emphasized that information efforts should specifically focus on the younger generation.

The Secretary-General also described ongoing efforts to integrate UNICs with UNDP field offices, as requested by the General Assembly in 1994.[4] Integrated centres would continue to carry out DPI's mandate under the immediate supervision of UNDP resident representatives. Closer cooperation was established between the UNDP field offices and UNICs in the developing world. Discussions on further integration continued on a case-by-case basis, in consultation with host Governments.

In September, the Secretary-General reported[8] further on UNIC activities, noting efforts to broaden public awareness of the issues before the United Nations and its major international conferences. Many UNICs had developed educational and youth-oriented programmes and had increased the number of model UN programmes undertaken in cooperation with local high schools and universities. The Secretary-General noted that 16 UNICs had been integrated with UNDP field offices as at September 1995.

The General Assembly, by **resolution 50/31 B**, invited the Secretary-General to continue the integration exercise and to report on the subject to the Committee on Information.

In his March report,[2] the Secretary-General discussed the ongoing efforts to strengthen UNICs within available resources. He reported that DPI continued to computerize UNIC operations, upgrade and modernize their libraries and ensure closer cooperation with field offices of other UN system entities.

In his September report,[8] he noted that UNIC libraries were fully equipped with UN bibliographic collections, including those in compact-disc format. During the year, DPI organized training workshops on technological innovations and electronic access to UN information.

## Coordination in the UN system

The Joint United Nations Information Committee (JUNIC), an inter-agency committee of UN officials to coordinate information activities within the UN system, held its twenty-first session in 1995

(Paris, 5-7 July).[9] It discussed ongoing JUNIC projects, participation in international exhibitions and special events and other issues.

The Committee endorsed the work programme of the Non-Governmental Liaison Service and agreed to discuss at its ad hoc session in early 1996 the future of the JUNIC information exchange bulletin and the feasibility of a new system-wide publication on development issues. It recommended that UNESCO be designated as the lead agency for UN participation in the Lisbon (Portugal) Exposition 1998: "The oceans, a heritage for the future"; it also considered participation in the Hannover (Germany) Exposition 2000: "Mankind, nature, technology". JUNIC reviewed proposals for inter-agency information programmes on follow-up to the 1995 World Summit for Social Development (see PART FOUR, Chapter IX) and for major UN meetings on women, least developed countries, human settlements and food. The observance of the United Nations fiftieth anniversary was also discussed, as was the International Year for the Eradication of Poverty (1996).

Also reviewed were: inter-agency cooperation in audiovisual productions; an electronic version of a new system-wide film and video catalogue; the development of a photo compact-disc and picture exchange system; and the use of computer technology in the field of public information.

The Committee considered new areas of JUNIC cooperation, including ways to facilitate UN television feeds to broadcasters from developing countries. The next Development Information Workshop was set for January/February 1996, at which communications strategies for promoting development issues, new public information technologies and possible joint projects would be discussed.

JUNIC decided to hold its twenty-second session in Nairobi, Kenya, in June/July 1996.

GENERAL ASSEMBLY ACTION

On 6 December, the General Assembly adopted **resolution 50/31 B**.

### United Nations public information policies and activities

*The General Assembly*,

*Reaffirming* its primary role in elaborating, coordinating and harmonizing United Nations policies and activities in the field of information,

*Also reaffirming* that the Secretary-General should ensure that the activities of the Department of Public Information of the Secretariat, as the focal point for the public information tasks of the United Nations, are strengthened and improved, keeping in view the purposes and principles of the Charter of the United Nations, the priority areas defined by the General Assembly and the recommendations of the Committee on Information,

*Taking note* of all the reports of the Secretary-General submitted to the Committee at its seventeenth session,

1. *Welcomes* Belize, Croatia, the Czech Republic, Kazakstan, and South Africa following the establishment of a united, non-racial and democratic Government in that country, to membership in the Committee on Information;

2. *Decides* to consolidate the role of the Committee as its main subsidiary body mandated to make recommendations relating to the work of the Department of Public Information of the Secretariat;

3. *Calls upon* the Secretary-General, in respect of the public information policies and activities of the United Nations, to implement fully the recommendations contained in paragraph 2 of its resolution 48/44 B of 10 December 1993;

4. *Requests* the Secretary-General, in order to put into practice the need for an effective public information capacity of the Department of Public Information for the formation and day-to-day functioning of the information components of peace-keeping and other field operations of the United Nations, to ensure the involvement of the Department at the planning stage of such future operations through interdepartmental consultations and coordination with the other substantive departments of the Secretariat;

5. *Takes note* of the report of the Secretary-General regarding the continuous and major publications of the Department of Public Information and urges all efforts to ensure timely production and dissemination of its major publications, in particular the *UN Chronicle*, the *Yearbook of the United Nations* and *Africa Recovery*, maintaining consistent editorial independence and accuracy, and taking the necessary measures to ensure that its output contains adequate, objective and equitable information about issues before the Organization, reflecting divergent opinions wherever they occur;

6. *Requests* the Secretary-General to increase his efforts for the early resumption of the publication *Development Forum*, or an alternative system-wide publication that meets the requirements set out for new publications by the Committee on Information;

7. *Requests* the management of the Department of Public Information to review its publications and proposals for publications to ensure that all publications fulfil an identifiable need, that they do not duplicate other publications inside or outside the United Nations system and that they are produced in a cost-effective manner, and to report thereon to the Committee at its eighteenth session;

8. *Reaffirms* the importance attached by Member States to the role of United Nations information centres in effectively and comprehensively disseminating information, particularly in developing countries and countries in transition, about United Nations activities;

9. *Takes note* of the report of the Secretary-General on the results of the trial of integrating United Nations information centres with field offices of the United Nations Development Programme, and invites the Secretary-General to continue the integration exercise whenever feasible, on a case-by-case basis, while taking into account the views of the host country, and ensuring that the information functions and autonomy of the United Nations information centres are not adversely affected, and to report thereon to the Committee;

10. *Reaffirms* the role of the General Assembly in relation to the opening of new United Nations information centres and invites the Secretary-General, as well, to make such recommendations as he may judge necessary regarding the establishment and location of these centres;

11. *Also takes note* of the report of the Secretary-General on the allocation of resources to United Nations information centres in 1994 and calls upon him to continue to study ways and means to rationalize and effect equitable disbursement of available resources to all United Nations information centres and to report thereon to the Committee at its eighteenth session;

12. *Welcomes* the action by some Member States with regard to financial and material support to United Nations information centres in their respective capitals;

13. *Welcomes also* the successful conclusion of the negotiations on the establishment of a United Nations information component at Warsaw;

14. *Notes* the progress made by the Secretary-General and the German authorities towards establishing, within existing resources of the Department of Public Information, a United Nations information centre at Bonn;

15. *Notes with appreciation* the action taken, or being taken, by the Secretary-General regarding the reactivation and enhancement of the United Nations information centres at Bujumbura, Dar es Salaam, Dhaka and Tehran;

16. *Welcomes further* the continued enhanced cooperation between the Department of Public Information and the University for Peace in Costa Rica as a focal point for promoting United Nations activities and disseminating United Nations information materials;

17. *Takes note* of the requests of Bulgaria, Gabon, Guinea, Haiti and Slovakia for information centres or information components;

18. *Expresses its full support* for the wide and prompt coverage of United Nations activities through a continuation of United Nations press releases in both working languages of the Secretariat, namely, English and French, and welcomes the improvements in the quality and speedy issue of those press releases in both working languages;

19. *Encourages* the Secretary-General to explore ways and means to improve the access of United Nations radio to airwaves worldwide, bearing in mind that radio is one of the most cost-effective and far-reaching media available to the Department of Public Information and is an important instrument in United Nations activities with regard to development and peace-keeping;

20. *Notes with appreciation* the efforts of the Department of Public Information to take advantage of recent developments in information technology in order to improve the dissemination of information on the United Nations, and encourages the Department to continue its efforts in this field;

21. *Notes* the important role the Department of Public Information will have to play in responding to the increased public interest resulting from the fiftieth anniversary of the United Nations, and requests the Department to ensure the greatest possible access to United Nations guided tours, as well as to ensure that displays in public areas are kept as informative, up to date and relevant as possible;

22. *Invites* Member States that wish to do so to submit to the Secretary-General by 15 March 1996 their observations and suggestions on ways and means of furthering the development of communication infrastructures and capabilities in developing countries, with a view to consolidating recent experience in the field of international cooperation aimed at enabling them to develop their own information and communication capacities freely and independently, and requests the Secretary-General to report thereon to the Committee on Information at its eighteenth session;

23. *Recommends,* in order to continue to facilitate contact between the Department of Public Information and the Committee on Information between sessions, that the Bureau of the Committee, together with representatives of each regional group, the Group of 77 and China, in close contact with the members of the Committee, should meet on a regular basis and consult at periodic intervals with representatives of the Department;

24. *Takes note* of the request of Belarus, the Russian Federation and Ukraine concerning information activities for the tenth anniversary in 1996 of the Chernobyl disaster and calls upon the Department of Public Information to continue cooperation with the countries concerned, and with the relevant organizations and bodies of the United Nations system, with a view to establishing and implementing such activities as appropriate, and within existing resources;

25. *Requests* the Secretary-General to report to the Committee on Information at its eighteenth session and to the General Assembly at its fifty-first session on the activities of the Department of Public Information and on the implementation of the recommendations contained in the present resolution;

26. *Decides* that the eighteenth session of the Committee should last not more than ten working days, and invites the Bureau of the Committee to explore ways and means of making optimum use of the Committee's time;

27. *Requests* the Committee to report to the General Assembly at its fifty-first session;

28. *Decides* to include in the provisional agenda of its fifty-first session the item entitled "Questions relating to information".

General Assembly resolution 50/31 B

6 December 1995     Meeting 82     Adopted without vote

Approved by Fourth Committee (A/50/608) without vote, 27 October (meeting 11); draft by Committee on Information (A/50/21); agenda item 87.
*Meeting numbers.* GA 50th session: 4th Committee 9-11; plenary 82.

*REFERENCES*

(1)A/50/21. (2)A/AC.198/1995/2. (3)A/AC.198/1995/3. (4)YUN 1994, p. 237, GA res. 49/38 B, 9 Dec. 1994. (5)YUN 1991, p. 82. (6)YUN 1992, p. 124. (7)YUN 1994, p. 233. (8)A/50/462. (9)ACC/1995/15.

# Peaceful uses of outer space

During 1995, the Committee on the Peaceful Uses of Outer Space (Committee on outer space) and its Scientific and Technical and Legal Subcommittees again considered matters relating to international cooperation in the peaceful uses of outer space, as requested by the General Assembly in 1994.[1] At its thirty-eighth session (Vienna, 12-22 June),[2] the Committee reviewed the work of its Subcommittees and discussed ways of maintaining outer space for peaceful purposes and spin-off benefits of space technology. Permanent observer status was granted to the International Academy of Astronautics and the International Astronomical Union, on the understanding that they would apply for consultative status with the Economic and Social Council.

In December, the General Assembly endorsed Committee recommendations and the 1996 UN Programme on Space Applications.

## Space science and technology

The Scientific and Technical Subcommittee of the Committee on outer space, at its thirty-second session (Vienna, 6-16 February),[3] continued to review the UN Programme on Space Applications, coordination of space activities within the UN system and implementation of the recommendations of the Second (1982) UN Conference on the Exploration and Peaceful Uses of Outer Space (UNISPACE-82).[4] The Subcommittee also considered matters relating to remote sensing of the Earth by satellites, including applications for developing countries; the use of nuclear power sources in outer space; space debris; space transportation systems and their implications for future activities in space; the physical nature and technical attributes of the geostationary orbit and its utilization for space communications; life sciences, including space medicine; national and international space activities related to the Earth environment; and issues relating to planetary exploration and astronomy.

During the session, the Committee on Space Research (COSPAR) of the International Council of Scientific Unions (ICSU) and the International Astronautical Federation (IAF) organized a symposium on the theme "Applications of space technology for education, with particular emphasis on its use in developing countries", which had been selected by the Subcommittee for special attention. The symposium considered policy issues regarding space education and applications of space technology in space education. Canada and the Russian Federation made special presentations. Member States provided specialists in space science and technology to present reports relating to Subcommittee agenda items.[5]

In June,[2] the Committee on outer space considered and acted on the Subcommittee's recommendations.

## Implementation of the recommendations of UNISPACE-82

The Subcommittee reconvened its Working Group of the Whole to Evaluate the Implementation of the Recommendations of UNISPACE-82, which held its ninth session (Vienna, 8-16 February). The Working Group's recommendations, annexed to the Subcommittee report,[3] were subsequently endorsed by the Committee on outer space and by the General Assembly in **resolution 50/27** (see below).

The Working Group reviewed international cooperation in the peaceful uses of outer space, including activities of Member States[6] and work programmes of international organizations.[7] It recommended: the continued organization of seminars and workshops on advanced applications of space science and technology and on new technological developments so as to bring recent advances in space technologies and applications for development to the attention of planners, administrators and decision makers in developing countries; periodic reporting on the resources and technological capabilities of States in space activities and in the areas of education, training, research and fellowship opportunities for the promotion of cooperation in outer space uses; annual reporting by States and international organizations to the Secretary-General on space activities subject to greater international cooperation, with particular emphasis on the needs of developing countries; and provision of expert consultants to assist in preparing integrated national plans of action for initiating, strengthening or reorienting space application programmes, in conformity with other national development programmes. The Working Group requested Member States and international organizations to support the training programme in space applications and technologies on an ongoing basis. It also made recommendations for the convening of a third UNISPACE (see below).

Four priority areas were identified to promote the applications of space science and technology for development: the stimulation of the growth of indigenous nuclei and an autonomous technological base in space technology in developing countries; a greater exchange of experiences in space applications; funding for the UN Programme on Space Applications (see below); and voluntary contributions for activities to implement UNISPACE-82 recommendations. The Working Group reiterated the UNISPACE-82 recommendation on the free exchange of scientific and technological information and transfer of technologies to promote the use and development of space technology in developing countries, as well as the recommendation that countries should not place undue restrictions on the sale of components, subsystems or systems required for peaceful space applications.

The Committee on outer space, in endorsing the recommendations, noted the Working Group's view that the Programme on Space Applications should be given full support in order to implement the UNISPACE-82 recommendations, and the disappointment expressed by developing countries at the lack of financial resources to implement those recommendations fully.

The Committee noted that the UN Secretariat continued to strengthen regional mechanisms of cooperation through regional workshops and training courses, the establishment of regional centres for space science and technology education, and technical assistance for regional activities in Africa, Asia and the Pacific and Latin America and the Caribbean.

The Committee also noted steps to augment the International Space Information Service by developing a database capability and creating a "home page" on the Internet, preparation of a feasibility study on establishing a computer-based international space information service, and contributions of other international organizations towards the implementation of UNISPACE-82 recommendations.

The Committee agreed that the Strategy for Regional Cooperation in Space Applications for Sustainable Development in Asia and the Pacific and the related Action Plan, adopted by the Ministerial Conference on Space Applications for Development in the Asia-Pacific Region in 1994,[8] and the Santiago Declaration, adopted by the Second Space Conference of the Americas in 1993,[9] were important instruments in promoting international cooperation in outer space. It recognized the contribution of the First Conference on Space Technology and Developing Countries (Tehran, Iran, May). The establishment of the Asia-Pacific Satellite Communications Council, to serve as a regional forum for information exchanges and cooperation in satellite communications and broadcasting, was also noted.

In response to a 1994 General Assembly request,[1] the Secretary-General reported in August 1995 on progress made in implementing UNISPACE-82 recommendations. The report[10] primarily reflected the work of the Committee on outer space and its subsidiary bodies in 1995. The Secretariat, responding to 1994 requests of the Working Group of the Whole, submitted to the Scientific and Technical Subcommittee studies on current projects and future perspectives for international cooperation in microsatellites and small satellites[11] and on the use of remote-sensing technologies for environmental applications.[12] It also transmitted reports of 11 Member States on their activities regarding international cooperation in the peaceful uses of outer space.[13]

## UN Programme on Space Applications

In accordance with its 1982 mandate,[14] the UN Programme on Space Applications focused on: developing indigenous capabilities in space science and technology; providing fellowships for in-depth training and technical advisory services; organizing regional and international training courses, conferences and meetings; assisting in acquiring and disseminating space-related information; and promoting greater cooperation between developed and developing countries.

In December,[15] the UN Expert on Space Applications reviewed Programme activities carried out in 1995, and those scheduled for 1996 and proposed for 1997. The Expert stated that Programme efforts to assist developing countries in building their indigenous capabilities had focused on establishing regional centres for space science and technology education in remote sensing and geographic information systems, meteorological satellite applications, satellite communications and geopositioning systems, and space and atmospheric sciences. Centre activities were aimed at developing and enhancing knowledge and skills of university educators and research and applications scientists and ensuring the use of that knowledge in pilot projects. In 1995, Morocco and Nigeria were selected to host centres for the countries of French- and English-speaking Africa, respectively, while Brazil and Mexico reached agreement on establishment of a centre for Latin America and the Caribbean. On 1 November, the Centre for Space Science and Technology Education in Asia and the Pacific was inaugurated in New Delhi, and its Governing Board held its first meeting the next day. Iran had offered to host a major node of that regional centre. Negotiations were also in progress on the establishment of a regional centre in Western Asia. Bulgaria, the Czech Republic, Greece and Romania offered to host a regional centre in Europe; Italy had proposed the establishment of a centre for Central and Eastern European countries.

The Programme received 15 long-term fellowships for 1995-96: Brazil offered 10, for research and applications in remote-sensing technology; the European Space Agency (ESA) offered five, for the study of space antennas and propagation, communications systems, remote-sensing instrumentation and remote-sensing information systems.

The Programme was expanding its technical advisory services due to increasing developmental support needs and advances in Earth observation systems technology, in communications technology and in related information systems. A feasibility study was completed on establishing a multinational Andean enterprise to facilitate operation of the Cotopaxi ground receiving station in Ecuador. An evaluation mission on user needs was planned for countries participating in the establishment of a Cooperative Information Network Linking Scientists, Educators and Professionals in Africa. The Programme and ESA continued their joint technical assistance programme to strengthen the capability of institutions in developing countries of obtaining satellite, radar and optical data for ongoing projects. Follow-up was made to a series of workshops on basic space science, and cooperation continued with the Asia-Pacific Satellite Communications Council, established in 1994, the membership of which grew to 40 in 1995, adding members in both Europe and North America.

A meeting of experts in Granada, Spain (27 February–3 March) focused on developing model curricula for the regional centres for space science and technology education. Stockholm University and the Swedish Space Corporation hosted the fifth UN training course on remote sensing in Stockholm and Kiruna (2 May–9 June).[16] A UN/ESA workshop on the applications of space techniques to prevent and combat natural disasters took place in Harare, Zimbabwe (22-26 May).[17]

Training courses were conducted on the use of data from the European Remote Sensing Satellite (ERS-1) for the mapping and inventory of natural resources in Africa (Libreville, Gabon, 15-19 May);[18] on applications of ERS-1 data (Frascati, Italy, 13-24 November);[19] and on space technology for improving life on Earth (Graz, Austria, 11-14 September),[20] reviewing use of satellite technology to enhance food security, communications infrastructure, education, health and disaster early-warning systems.

Workshops were held on space technology for health care and environmental monitoring in the developing world (Oslo, Norway, 28 September–1 October)[21] and on the applications of optics in space science and technology (Trieste, Italy, 20-24 November).[22] A Regional Conference on Space Technology for Sustainable Development and Communications (Puerto Vallarta, Mexico, 30 October–3 November)[23] reviewed the role of Earth observation satellites in the timely collection and analysis of data for sustainable development, environmental monitoring and management and global change studies, as well as the role played by communication satellites in enhancing the economic and social welfare of a country. As part of activities for disseminating space information, the seventh in a series of selected papers on remote sensing, satellite communications and space science was issued.

In 1995, the Scientific and Technical Subcommittee and the Committee on outer space had before them a report[8] of the Expert on Space Applications on the Programme's activities in 1994, as well as those scheduled for 1995 and 1996. Both the Subcommittee and the Committee were concerned over the limited financial resources available for the Programme and appealed for voluntary contributions. In that regard, the Committee noted with appreciation contributions from Aus-

tria, Spain, the United States and ESA, as well as from various organizations in and outside the UN system.

The General Assembly, in **resolution 50/27**, endorsed the Programme for 1996, as proposed by the Expert on Space Applications.[8] By **resolution 50/215 A**, the Assembly approved $4,705,500 for outer space affairs under the UN regular budget for 1996-1997, including an appropriation of $446,200 for implementing Programme activities.

**Remote sensing**

The Scientific and Technical Subcommittee continued consideration of matters relating to remote sensing of the Earth by satellites. It reviewed national and cooperative programmes in developing and developed countries, as well as international programmes based on bilateral, regional and international cooperation, including technical cooperation between developing countries and assistance by States with advanced capabilities to developing countries.

The Subcommittee noted the continuing programmes of Argentina, Australia, Brazil, China, France, Germany, India, Indonesia, Japan, Morocco, the Russian Federation, Ukraine, the United States and ESA. It noted that the launchings of ERS-1 and the Japanese Earth Resources Satellite would provide valuable microwave data to complement multispectral data from other satellites, and that Argentina, Canada, China, India, Japan, the Russian Federation and ESA were developing various remote-sensing systems for future launch. The Food and Agriculture Organization of the United Nations (FAO) continued its remote sensing of renewable natural resources, including land-cover mapping and geographic information systems, while the World Meteorological Organization (WMO) operated in the areas of weather forecasting and storm warning. The International Society for Photogrammetry and Remote Sensing continued to promote international cooperation in remote sensing and image processing.

The Subcommittee reiterated its view that remote-sensing activities should take into account the need to provide appropriate and nondiscriminatory assistance to developing countries, and emphasized the importance of making remote-sensing data and analysed information openly available to all countries at a reasonable cost and in a timely manner, while data from operational meteorological satellites should continue to be freely accessible.

The Subcommittee considered that international cooperation in the use of remote-sensing satellites should be encouraged, through both coordination of the operations of ground stations and regular meetings between satellite operators and users. It noted the need for continuity in the acquisition of data, as well as the importance of compatibility and complementarity of existing and future remote-sensing systems, sharing of experiences and technologies, cooperation through international and regional remote-sensing centres and joint work on collaborative projects. The value of remote-sensing systems for environmental monitoring was also noted; in that context, the international community should utilize fully remote-sensing data in implementing Agenda 21[25] recommendations adopted by the 1992 UN Conference on Environment and Development (UNCED).

The Committee on outer space reiterated the importance of ongoing international efforts to ensure the continuity, compatibility and complementarity of remote-sensing systems and to promote cooperation through regular meetings of satellite and ground-station operators and users. The free distribution of meteorological information, the Committee recognized, served as an example of international cooperation.

In December, the Secretariat submitted a study on the use of remote-sensing technologies for environmental applications, particularly in support of UNCED recommendations.[12] The study examined the contribution of space technology to implementing Agenda 21, reviewed remote-sensing activities for sustainable development and considered environmental challenges that could be addressed through space technology. It recommended an increased use of satellite data in projects funded by national aid agencies; improved access to inexpensive remote-sensing data in a standardized format and to low-cost hardware and software; establishment of an effective coordination policy in developing countries for implementing remote-sensing components of national development plans; increased collaboration and exchange of information between research institutions and space agencies at all levels, as well as other sectors from both developed and developing countries; expansion of the network of ground receiving stations, particularly in Africa and Latin America; improved cooperation in the assessment of user requirements in developing countries, accessibility of affordable satellite data and information services, promotion of well-designed pilot projects, increased on-site education and training, provision of infrastructures for satellite data acquisition and improved utilization of existing user interfaces; and implementation of pilot projects by space agencies to demonstrate to policy makers the usefulness of remote sensing.

### Nuclear power sources

The Scientific and Technical Subcommittee in 1995 again considered the use of nuclear power sources in outer space. After discussing a possible revision of the Principles Relevant to the Use of Nuclear Power Sources in Outer Space, adopted by the General Assembly in 1992,[26] it agreed that such revision was not warranted at the current time. Its Working Group on the Use of Nuclear Power Sources in Outer Space, however, should continue to receive contributions related to improving the scope and application of the Principles. The Subcommittee reconvened the Working Group on 13 February to enable it to resume its work.

The International Atomic Energy Agency made a statement on recent developments in nuclear safety, drawing particular attention to new international basic safety standards for protection against ionizing radiation and for the safety of radiation sources as well as to a new document on emergency planning and preparedness for nuclear-powered satellite re-entry. Mindful of the differences in the application of safety standards to space and terrestrial systems, the Subcommittee recommended further studies of those developments. It noted information provided by Member States and organizations[27] on national and international research concerning the safety of nuclear-powered satellites and the collision of nuclear power sources with space debris, and recommended that such information should continue to be provided on a regular basis and that further studies of the collision problem be conducted.

The Committee on outer space endorsed the Subcommittee's recommendations and decided to continue discussing at future sessions a possible revision of the Principles. The Committee noted a report by the Russian Federation on forecasting an emergency re-entry of a spacecraft with a nuclear power source.[28]

Legal aspects of the revision of the Principles were considered by the Legal Subcommittee (see below).

### Space debris

The Scientific and Technical Subcommittee continued consideration of space debris as a priority agenda item, focusing on the acquisition and understanding of data on the space debris environment. It noted programmes on data acquisition and understanding and on measuring, modelling and mitigating the orbital debris environment conducted by Canada, Germany, Japan, the Russian Federation, the United States and ESA, as well as the establishment by some national space agencies in 1993 of the Interagency Orbital Debris Coordination Committee to exchange information and review ongoing space debris activities, facilitate cooperation in research and identify debris mitigation options.

The Subcommittee recommended that Member States pay more attention to the issue of space debris and to the problem of collisions of space objects, including those with nuclear power sources on board (see above), with space debris. In that regard, it noted an informal working paper by the United Kingdom and national reports on the issue.[27] The Subcommittee agreed that international cooperation was needed to expand appropriate and affordable strategies for minimizing the potential impact of space debris on future space missions, and encouraged Member States and international organizations to provide information on their practices in minimizing the creation of space debris. Information should be compiled on steps taken by space agencies to reduce the growth or damage potential of space debris, and their common acceptance by the international community should be encouraged.

The Subcommittee adopted its work plan for 1996-1998, focusing on measurements of space debris, understanding of data and effects of the debris environment on space systems; modelling of that environment and risk assessment; and space debris mitigation measures. It decided to concentrate its deliberations on debris measurement techniques, mathematical modelling and characterization of the debris environment, and risk mitigation, including spacecraft design measures to protect against debris.

The Committee on outer space agreed with the Subcommittee's conclusions, endorsed its multi-year work plan and recognized the need for further research concerning space debris, data compilation and dissemination and the development of improved technology for debris monitoring. The Committee recommended that Member States continue national research on the issue and make its results available to all interested parties.

In November, the UN Secretariat reported to the Subcommittee on steps taken by space agencies to reduce the growth or damage potential of space debris,[29] including debris mitigation techniques used in launch vehicles, prevention of accidental debris creation, environmental protection of the geostationary orbit and debris protection of active spacecraft. It noted the recommendation of the International Academy of Astronautics that immediate action be taken to: stop the deliberate breakup of spacecraft producing debris in long-lived orbits; minimize mission-related debris; introduce venting procedures for rocket bodies and spacecraft remaining in orbit after completion of their mission; select transfer orbit parameters to ensure the rapid decay of transfer stages; re-orbit geostationary satellites at the end of their life; and insert separated boost motors and upper stages of geostationary satellites into a disposal orbit at least 300 kilometres above the geostationary orbit.

Also in November, the Secretariat transmitted information from four Member States regarding national research on space debris, safety of nuclear-powered satellites and the problem of collision of nuclear-powered sources with space debris.[30]

## Space transportation

The Subcommittee continued to review national and international cooperative programmes in space transportation systems, including expendable launchers, reusable space shuttles and space stations. China, India, Japan, the Russian Federation, Ukraine, the United States and ESA continued to develop their programmes; the United Kingdom cooperated with the Russian Federation and Ukraine on a reusable interim system and with ESA on its Future European Space Transportation Investigation Programme; and the United States continued to develop the International Space Station in cooperation with Canada, Japan, the Russian Federation and ESA.

The Committee on outer space noted progress achieved in the various programmes in operation or planned, as well as of developments in low-cost microsatellite technology and applications. It stressed the importance of international cooperation in space transportation to provide all countries with access to the benefits of space science and technology.

## Technical aspects of the geostationary orbit

In its examination of the physical nature and technical attributes of the geostationary orbit, the Subcommittee reviewed national and international cooperative programmes in satellite communications, including technological progress to make such communications more accessible and affordable and to increase the communications capacity of the geostationary orbit and the electromagnetic spectrum. It noted the growing use of satellite systems for telecommunications, television broadcasting, data networks, environmental data relay, mobile communications, disaster warning and relief, telemedicine and other communications functions.

As in previous years, some delegations advocated avoiding saturation of the geostationary orbit and a special regime to ensure equitable access by all States, particularly developing countries, that would also take into account the characteristics of equatorial countries. Others suggested that efforts should be made to minimize the generation of space debris by moving satellites shortly before the end of their useful lives into disposal orbits beyond the geostationary orbit. The view was also expressed that questions relating to the geostationary orbit were being addressed effectively by the International Telecommunication Union (ITU). Some delegations felt that the roles of ITU and of the Committee on outer space with regard to the geostationary orbit were complementary.

The Committee on outer space expressed appreciation to ITU for its thirty-fourth annual progress report on telecommunication and the peaceful uses of outer space.[31] Some delegations stressed the important technical scope of ITU work, while drawing attention to the Committee's competence in preparing policy decisions and the legal status of the geostationary orbit.

Legal aspects of the geostationary orbit were considered by the Legal Subcommittee (see below).

### Space and Earth environment

The Scientific and Technical Subcommittee continued consideration of national and international space activities related to the Earth environment, in particular progress in the ICSU international geosphere-biosphere (global change) programme (IGBP). It noted that joint international efforts were fundamentally important for examining the future habitability of the planet and for managing the Earth's natural resources, emphasizing the need to involve both developed and developing countries in IGBP. The Subcommittee further noted the contributions of satellite remote sensing for environmental monitoring, sustainable-development planning, water-resource development, crop-conditions monitoring and drought prediction and assessment; the contribution of meteorological and atmospheric research satellites for studying global climate change, the greenhouse effect, the degradation of the ozone layer and other global environmental processes; and the need for further space research relating to climate change, weather patterns, vegetation distribution, storm and flood risk and other environmental factors. It recommended that all States participate in international cooperation activities concerning existing and planned satellite systems for environmental monitoring.

The Committee on outer space recognized its potential for making an important contribution by promoting international cooperation in the application of space technologies for environmental monitoring and sustainable development. In particular, the UN Programme on Space Applications could play an important role in assisting developing countries in strengthening their capabilities in related space technologies and applications through education, training and technical advisory activities.

### Spin-off benefits

The Committee on outer space again reviewed spin-off benefits of space technology, which were providing new techniques for industrial measurement and control, image and data processing,

medical techniques, computer systems, robotics, power generation, special materials and chemicals, water treatment, public safety, consumer goods, manufacturing and refrigeration. The Committee noted that the conversion of military industries to productive civilian uses would facilitate the transfer and use of space technologies and their spin-off benefits, and agreed that developing countries could make important contributions in that field and that they should identify those disciplines in which their most pressing needs could be addressed by space technology. It recognized the need to strengthen and enhance international cooperation by improving access of all States to spin-off benefits, particularly those addressing the needs of developing countries, and agreed that low-cost microsatellite technologies were particularly important in that regard.

The Committee was satisfied that the Programme on Space Applications, following a 1993 Committee recommendation,[32] was planning for 1996 a workshop on challenges and opportunities of spin-off benefits. It noted with interest Ukraine's proposal to use the Evpatoria Centre of Deep Science Communication as the basis for an international centre for space research that could be used by the Programme for its activities. Some delegations reiterated the view that the UN could contribute to the development of improved procedures for disseminating spin-off benefits, with an emphasis on providing them to developing countries at a reasonable cost.

### Coordination in the UN system

Both the Scientific and Technical Subcommittee and the Committee on outer space reiterated the necessity of continuous and effective consultations and coordination of outer space activities among UN organizations and noted with satisfaction information on progress achieved in 1994 and on work programmes for 1995, 1996 and future years.[33]

The General Assembly, in **resolution 50/27**, reaffirmed its request to all UN organs, organizations and bodies, as well as other intergovernmental organizations dealing with outer space matters, to cooperate in implementing UNISPACE-82 recommendations.

### Convening of a third UNISPACE

In response to a 1994 Assembly request,[1] the Scientific and Technical Subcommittee and its Working Group of the Whole continued to discuss the possibility of holding a third UNISPACE, as well as other means for achieving the goals set for such a conference. The Working Group considered the Secretariat's 1994 suggestions for the organization, funding, logistical implications and a possible agenda of a third UNISPACE.[33] It discussed the need for such a conference and examined other means of achieving conference goals, including intensification of work in the Committee on outer space. An indicative agenda for a third conference was submitted as a framework for future discussions.

Both the Subcommittee and the Committee on outer space agreed that Working Group recommendations should be the basis for continued discussions, with the goal of submitting the matter to the General Assembly. The Committee decided to consider in 1996, within the framework to be produced by the Subcommittee, all issues regarding the possible holding of the conference, including its technical and political objectives, a detailed and sharply focused agenda, funding, timing and organizational aspects. It also decided to consider whether the conference objectives could be achieved by other means, with a view to making a final decision, and noted that the interaction between space applications and the various uses of the "information superhighway" could be reflected in the justification and agenda items of the conference. The Committee further took note of a working paper by India[34] and an informal paper by the Secretariat[35] on matters related to the convening of a third UNISPACE.

## Other questions

The Committee on outer space and its Scientific and Technical Subcommittee continued consideration of other space-related questions, including life sciences, space medicine and matters relating to planetary exploration and astronomy. The Committee noted the variety of space activities in those areas and encouraged further cooperation, particularly efforts to increase the participation of developing countries.

In the area of life sciences, the Subcommittee noted that studies of human and animal physiology under microgravity conditions had yielded important medical knowledge in such areas as blood circulation, sensory perception, immunology and the effects of cosmic radiation. Applications of space technology promised benefits for medicine and public health on Earth: satellite communications provided expert medical advice to distant areas, and products of space biotechnology, such as pharmaceutical and medical instruments, could contribute to improved health care. The Subcommittee encouraged further research and exchange of information on those applications, emphasizing that efforts should be made to promote international cooperation to enable all countries to benefit from those advances.

As for planetary exploration and astronomy, the Subcommittee noted that several missions currently under way had yielded new data, including a gravity field map of Venus and information

on its atmosphere, discovery of Jupiter's satellite Dactyl and high-resolution images of its asteroid, and investigation of solar polar regions. It took note of missions planned for future launch to investigate Mars, Saturn and its moons and near-Earth asteroids. A special presentation was made on adverse environmental effects on astronomy, emphasizing the severe impact of electromagnetic pollution on radio astronomy and the effects of space debris on astronomical observations at optical wavelengths. The Subcommittee noted that the use of spacecraft for astronomical observations had greatly advanced knowledge of the universe and that planned activities would open up further realms of the universe to detailed observation. The need to further enhance international cooperation in planetary exploration and astronomy was stressed, so that all countries could benefit from those activities.

The Subcommittee welcomed the annual reports of WMO,[36] ITU[37] and various organizations outside the UN system.[38] It expressed appreciation to COSPAR and IAF for jointly published reports on progress in space science, technology and applications, international cooperation and space law in 1994.[39]

## Space law

In accordance with a 1994 General Assembly request,[1] the Legal Subcommittee of the Committee on outer space, at its thirty-fourth session (Vienna, 27 March–7 April),[40] again considered the question of an early review and possible revision of the 1992 Principles Relevant to the Use of Nuclear Power Sources in Outer Space; matters relating to the definition and delimitation of outer space and to the character and utilization of the geostationary orbit; and legal aspects of the application of the principle that the exploration and utilization of outer space should be carried out for the benefit and in the interest of all States.

The Committee on outer space[2] took note with appreciation of the Subcommittee's report on its 1995 session.

### Nuclear power sources

The Legal Subcommittee considered the question of an early review and possible revision of the 1992 Principles Relevant to the Use of Nuclear Power Sources in Outer Space.[26] It shared the view of the Scientific and Technical Subcommittee at its 1995 session that revision of the Principles was not warranted at the current time, and suspended consideration of that item by its Working Group in 1996 for one year, pending the results of work in the Scientific and Technical Subcommittee, unless sufficient progress was made in that Subcommittee to warrant the reconvening of the

Working Group. The Legal Subcommittee, however, retained the item on its agenda.

The Committee on outer space endorsed the Subcommittee's recommendations and agreed that the Principles would remain valid until such time as they were amended, and that the Scientific and Technical Subcommittee should consider the need for their revision in the light of changing technology, before the Legal Subcommittee or the Committee undertook any actual revision.

## Geostationary orbit and definition of outer space

The Legal Subcommittee, through a Working Group, continued consideration of the definition and delimitation of outer space and the character and utilization of the geostationary orbit, on the basis of working papers submitted at previous sessions.

The Working Group undertook a general discussion of matters related to the geostationary orbit and a paragraph-by-paragraph review of a working paper introduced by Colombia in 1993.[41] Some delegations expressed the view that the Committee on outer space and its Legal Subcommittee had been mandated by the General Assembly to consider the use of the orbit with a view to elaborating legal principles on the issue, and considered their work as complementary to ITU activities. Others stated that the Subcommittee had no mandate to develop a special legal regime and that ITU had dealt successfully with various aspects of the orbit's use, and advocated avoiding any possible conflict of activities between ITU and other international bodies. The view was expressed that, as the geostationary orbit was an integral part of outer space, the legal regime established by the 1966 Treaty on Principles Governing the Activities of States in the Exploration and Use of Outer Space, including the Moon and Other Celestial Bodies,[42] adequately covered activities related to the orbit. Other delegations were of the opinion that specific characteristics and features of the orbit as a limited natural resource which could become saturated necessitated a special regime to ensure equitable access for all States, taking into account the needs of developing countries and the equatorial countries in particular, due to their special characteristics. At the close of the discussion, Colombia stated its intention to submit a revised working paper on the issue in 1996.

The Working Group also finalized the text of a questionnaire to Member States on possible legal issues with regard to aerospace objects, for the purpose of seeking their preliminary views on various matters relating to such objects. It was hoped that replies to the questionnaire would provide a basis for the Legal Subcommittee's decision on further consideration of the item.

The Committee on outer space invited its members to give their opinions on matters concerning aerospace objects, took note of Subcommittee deliberations on the question of the geostationary orbit, and recognized that space debris was a cause for concern in the geostationary and lower orbits. Some delegations suggested adding the subject of space debris to the Subcommittee's agenda.

## Exploration of outer space

The Subcommittee, through its Working Group on the item, continued to consider legal aspects related to the application of the principle that the exploration and utilization of outer space should be carried out for the benefit and in the interests of all States, taking into particular account the needs of developing countries. The Working Group based its discussion on two working papers: one containing principles regarding international cooperation in the exploration and utilization of outer space for peaceful purposes, submitted by Brazil, Chile, Colombia, Egypt, Iraq, Mexico, Nigeria, Pakistan, the Philippines, Uruguay and Venezuela;[43] the other, introduced by France and Germany, containing a declaration on international cooperation in the exploration and use of outer space for the benefit and in the interests of all States, taking into particular account the needs of developing countries.[44]

At the end of the session, the Chairman produced an informal working paper,[45] as amended, representing a merger based on the texts of the two working papers, with additional language from the Chairman, to facilitate debate on the issue in 1996. Subsequently, Cuba became a co-sponsor of the working paper on principles of international cooperation.[43]

The Committee on outer space noted the constructive work by the Subcommittee and the Working Group and the useful discussion of the working papers. It recommended that the Subcommittee continue discussing the item in 1996.

## Working methods

In accordance with a 1994 General Assembly recommendation,[1] the Chairman of the Legal Subcommittee conducted informal, open-ended consultations on the Subcommittee's working methods and agenda. The Subcommittee adopted measures concerning the utilization of conference services and agreed to apply them with the utmost flexibility. It also decided to conduct open-ended informal consultations in 1996 to identify subjects that could be considered for inclusion in its agenda.

The Committee on outer space established a Working Group of the Whole to examine the working methods of the Committee and its subsidiary bodies, based on Subcommittee recommendations. Following deliberations in the Working Group, the Committee adopted a number of procedural measures regarding organization of work, consideration of agenda items, general debate statements, its regulatory role with regard to the subsidiary bodies, technical presentations and development of a long-term work plan. It recommended that agenda items be reviewed periodically to determine the likelihood of reaching consensus and the advisability of continued consideration, and that the Working Group of the Whole be reconvened in 1996 to continue its discussions.

### GENERAL ASSEMBLY ACTION

On 6 December, the General Assembly adopted **resolution 50/27.**

#### International cooperation in the peaceful uses of outer space

*The General Assembly,*

*Recalling* its resolution 49/34 of 9 December 1994,

*Deeply convinced* of the common interest of mankind in promoting the exploration and use of outer space for peaceful purposes and in continuing efforts to extend to all States the benefits derived therefrom, and also of the importance of international cooperation in this field, for which the United Nations should continue to provide a focal point,

*Reaffirming* the importance of international cooperation in developing the rule of law, including the relevant norms of space law and their important role in international cooperation for the exploration and use of outer space for peaceful purposes,

*Concerned* about the possibility of an arms race in outer space,

*Recognizing* that all States, in particular those with major space capabilities, should contribute actively to the goal of preventing an arms race in outer space as an essential condition for the promotion of international cooperation in the exploration and use of outer space for peaceful purposes,

*Considering* that space debris is an issue of concern to all nations,

*Noting* the progress achieved in the further development of peaceful space exploration and application as well as in various national and cooperative space projects, which contribute to international cooperation, and the importance of further international cooperation in this field,

*Taking note* of the report of the Secretary-General on the implementation of the recommendations of the Second United Nations Conference on the Exploration and Peaceful Uses of Outer Space,

*Having considered* the report of the Committee on the Peaceful Uses of Outer Space on the work of its thirty-eighth session,

1. *Endorses* the report of the Committee on the Peaceful Uses of Outer Space;

2. *Invites* States that have not yet become parties to the international treaties governing the uses of outer space to give consideration to ratifying or acceding to those treaties;

3. *Notes* that, at its thirty-fourth session, the Legal Subcommittee of the Committee on the Peaceful Uses of Outer Space, in its working groups, continued its work as mandated by the General Assembly in its resolution 49/34;

4. *Endorses* the recommendations of the Committee that the Legal Subcommittee, at its thirty-fifth session, taking into account the concerns of all countries, particularly those of developing countries, should:

(*a*) Continue its consideration of the question of review and possible revision of the Principles Relevant to the Use of Nuclear Power Sources in Outer Space;

(*b*) Continue, through its working group, its consideration of matters relating to the definition and delimitation of outer space and to the character and utilization of the geostationary orbit, including consideration of ways and means to ensure the rational and equitable use of the geostationary orbit without prejudice to the role of the International Telecommunication Union;

(*c*) Continue, through its working group, its consideration of the legal aspects related to the application of the principle that the exploration and utilization of outer space should be carried out for the benefit and in the interests of all States, taking into particular account the needs of developing countries;

5. *Also endorses* the recommendation of the Committee that the Legal Subcommittee, at its thirty-fifth session, should suspend consideration in its working group of the Principles Relevant to the Use of Nuclear Power Sources in Outer Space pending the results of the work in the Scientific and Technical Subcommittee, without prejudice to the possibility of reconvening its working group on that item if in the opinion of the Legal Subcommittee sufficient progress was made in the Scientific and Technical Subcommittee at its session in 1996 to warrant the reconvening of the working group;

6. *Notes* that deliberations on the question of the geostationary orbit have been undertaken by the Legal Subcommittee as reflected in its report, on the basis of recent proposals which might provide a new and enhanced basis for future work;

7. *Endorses* the recommendations and agreements concerning the organization of work in the Legal Subcommittee;

8. *Notes* that, in accordance with its recommendation, the Chairman of the Legal Subcommittee, at its thirty-fourth session, conducted extensive, open-ended informal consultations with all members of the Subcommittee on the working methods and agenda of the Legal Subcommittee, including the consideration of possible additional items for inclusion in the agenda as outlined in the report of the Committee, and also notes that, in accordance with the recommendation of the Committee, a Working Group of the Whole was established at its thirty-eighth session to examine the working methods of the Committee and its subsidiary bodies, which took particular account of the results of the informal consultations of the Chairman of the Legal Subcommittee;

9. *Also endorses* the recommendations of the Committee as contained in the report of its thirty-eighth session with regard to its working methods and to the reconvening of the Working Group of the Whole at the thirty-ninth session of the Committee;

10. *Notes* that, in accordance with the recommendation contained in General Assembly resolutions

48/222 B of 23 December 1993 and 49/221 B of 23 December 1994, the Committee reviewed its needs for written records;

11. *Further endorses* the recommendation of the Committee that, beginning with its thirty-ninth session, the Committee would be provided with unedited transcripts of its session in lieu of verbatim records, as described in the report of the Secretariat on this matter;

12. *Requests* the Legal Subcommittee to review, at its thirty-fifth session, its requirement for summary records with a view to determining whether it may be possible to utilize unedited transcripts at its subsequent sessions and to consider under what circumstances there might be a need to revert to summary records should a decision be taken to utilize unedited transcripts;

13. *Notes* that the Scientific and Technical Subcommittee of the Committee on the Peaceful Uses of Outer Space, at its thirty-second session, continued its work as mandated by the General Assembly in its resolution 49/34;

14. *Welcomes* the decision of the Committee to consider the matter of space debris as a matter of priority on the agenda of the Scientific and Technical Subcommittee;

15. *Notes* that under that item the Scientific and Technical Subcommittee continued to consider scientific research relating to space debris, including relevant studies, mathematical modelling and other analytical work on the characterization of the space debris environment;

16. *Agrees* with the endorsement by the Committee of the multi-year plan for consideration of the agenda item on space debris adopted by the Scientific and Technical Subcommittee at its thirty-second session, and also agrees that the work plan should be implemented with flexibility;

17. *Endorses* the recommendations of the Committee that the Scientific and Technical Subcommittee, at its thirty-third session, taking into account the concerns of all countries, particularly those of developing countries, should:

(a) Consider the following items on a priority basis:
(i) United Nations Programme on Space Applications and the coordination of space activities within the United Nations system;
(ii) Implementation of the recommendations of the Second United Nations Conference on the Exploration and Peaceful Uses of Outer Space;
(iii) Matters relating to remote sensing of the Earth by satellites, including, *inter alia*, applications for developing countries;
(iv) Use of nuclear power sources in outer space;
(v) Space debris;
(b) Consider the following items:
(i) Questions relating to space transportation systems and their implications for future activities in space;
(ii) Examination of the physical nature and technical attributes of the geostationary orbit and of its utilization and applications, including, *inter alia*, in the field of space communications, as well as other questions relating to space communications developments, taking particular account of the needs and interests of developing countries;
(iii) Matters relating to life sciences, including space medicine;
(iv) Progress in national and international space activities related to the Earth's environment, in particular progress in the geosphere-biosphere (global change) programme;
(v) Matters relating to planetary exploration;
(vi) Matters relating to astronomy;
(vii) The theme fixed for special attention at the 1996 session of the Scientific and Technical Subcommittee: ''Utilization of micro- and small satellites for the expansion of low-cost space activities, taking into account the special needs of developing countries''; the Committee on Space Research and the International Astronautical Federation, in liaison with Member States, should be invited to arrange a symposium, with as wide a participation as possible, to be held during the first week of the Subcommittee's session, to complement discussions within the Subcommittee on the special theme;

18. *Considers*, in the context of paragraph 17 (a) (ii) above, that it is particularly urgent to implement the following recommendations:

(a) All countries should have the opportunity to use the techniques resulting from medical studies in space;

(b) Data banks at the national and regional levels should be strengthened and expanded and an international space information service should be established to function as a centre of coordination;

(c) The United Nations should support the creation of adequate training centres at the regional level, linked, whenever possible, to institutions implementing space programmes; necessary funding for the development of such centres should be made available through financial institutions;

(d) The United Nations should organize a fellowship programme through which selected graduates or postgraduates from developing countries should get in-depth, long-term exposure to space technology or applications; it is also desirable to encourage the availability of opportunities for such exposure on other bilateral or multilateral bases outside the United Nations system;

19. *Endorses* the recommendation of the Committee that the Scientific and Technical Subcommittee should reconvene, at its thirty-third session, the Working Group of the Whole to Evaluate the Implementation of the Recommendations of the Second United Nations Conference on the Exploration and Peaceful Uses of Outer Space, to continue its work;

20. *Also endorses* the recommendations of the Working Group of the Whole of the Scientific and Technical Subcommittee, as endorsed by the Committee and as contained in the report of the Working Group of the Whole;

21. *Decides* that, during the thirty-third session of the Scientific and Technical Subcommittee, the Working Group on the Use of Nuclear Power Sources in Outer Space should be reconvened, and invites Member States to report to the Secretary-General on a regular basis with regard to national and international research concerning the safety of nuclear-powered satellites;

22. *Endorses* the United Nations Programme on Space Applications for 1996, as proposed to the Committee by the Expert on Space Applications;

23. *Emphasizes* the urgency and importance of implementing fully the recommendations of the Second United Nations Conference on the Exploration and Peaceful Uses of Outer Space;

24. *Reaffirms its approval* of the recommendation of the Conference regarding the establishment and strengthening of regional mechanisms of cooperation and their promotion and creation through the United Nations system;

25. *Expresses its appreciation* to all Governments that have made, or expressed their intention to make, contributions towards carrying out the recommendations of the Conference;

26. *Invites* all Governments to take effective action for the implementation of the recommendations of the Conference;

27. *Requests* all organs, organizations and bodies of the United Nations system and other intergovernmental organizations working in the field of outer space or on space-related matters to cooperate in the implementation of the recommendations of the Conference;

28. *Invites* the Secretary-General to report to the General Assembly at its fifty-first session on the implementation of the recommendations of the Conference;

29. *Notes with satisfaction* that, in the context of paragraph 18 *(c)* above, significant progress has been achieved in establishing regional centres for space science and technology education in each region covered by the regional commissions;

30. *Endorses* the recommendation of the Committee that these centres be established on the basis of affiliation to the United Nations as early as possible and that such affiliation would provide the centres with the necessary recognition and would strengthen the possibilities of attracting donors and of establishing academic relationships with national and international space-related institutions;

31. *Notes* that, pursuant to its request in paragraph 27 of resolution 49/34, the Scientific and Technical Subcommittee, at its thirty-second session, continued its discussions on the possibility of holding a third United Nations Conference on the Exploration and Peaceful Uses of Outer Space and that the Committee continued these discussions at its thirty-eighth session with a view to promoting an early conclusion on the matter by the Committee;

32. *Agrees* that a third United Nations Conference on the Exploration and Peaceful Uses of Outer Space could be convened before the turn of the present century, and that, prior to recommending a date for the conference, there should be a consensus recommendation on the agenda, venue and funding of the conference;

33. *Recommends* that the Scientific and Technical Subcommittee, at its thirty-third session, continue the work it had conducted at its thirty-second session, taking into particular account the report of its Working Group of the Whole, with the aim being to complete the development and refinement of a framework that would allow an evaluation of proposals by the Committee at its thirty-ninth session, and that this framework should allow for the consideration of all possibilities of achieving the final objectives of such a conference;

34. *Also agrees* that, on the basis of the work to be conducted at the thirty-third session of the Scientific and Technical Subcommittee, the Committee, at its thirty-ninth session, should consider all issues related to the possible convening of a third United Nations Conference on the Exploration and Peaceful Uses of Outer Space, including its technical and political objectives, a detailed and sharply focused agenda, funding, timing and other organizational aspects as well as whether the objectives of the conference could be achieved by other means, with a view to making a final recommendation to the General Assembly at that session of the Committee;

35. *Notes with interest* the plans of the Government of Uruguay to host the Third Space Conference of the Americas at Punta del Este in 1996;

36. *Recommends* that more attention be paid to all aspects related to the protection and the preservation of the outer space environment, especially those potentially affecting the Earth's environment;

37. *Considers* that it is essential that Member States pay more attention to the problem of collisions of space objects, including nuclear power sources, with space debris, and other aspects of space debris, calls for the continuation of national research on this question, for the development of improved technology for the monitoring of space debris and for the compilation and dissemination of data on space debris, and also considers that, to the extent possible, information thereon should be provided to the Scientific and Technical Subcommittee;

38. *Urges* all States, in particular those with major space capabilities, to contribute actively to the goal of preventing an arms race in outer space as an essential condition for the promotion of international cooperation in the exploration and uses of outer space for peaceful purposes;

39. *Emphasizes* the need to increase the benefits of space technology and its applications and to contribute to an orderly growth of space activities favourable to the socio-economic advancement of humanity, in particular that of the people of the developing countries;

40. *Takes note* of the views expressed during the thirty-eighth session of the Committee and during the fiftieth session of the General Assembly concerning ways and means of maintaining outer space for peaceful purposes;

41. *Requests* the Committee to continue to consider, as a matter of priority, ways and means of maintaining outer space for peaceful purposes and to report thereon to the General Assembly at its fifty-first session;

42. *Also requests* the Committee to continue to consider at its thirty-ninth session its agenda item entitled "Spin-off benefits of space technology: review of current status";

43. *Requests* the specialized agencies and other international organizations to continue and, where appropriate, enhance their cooperation with the Committee and to provide it with progress reports on their work relating to the peaceful uses of outer space;

44. *Further requests* the Committee to continue its work, in accordance with the present resolution, to consider, as appropriate, new projects in outer space activities and to submit a report to the General Assembly at its fifty-first session, including its views on which subjects should be studied in the future.

General Assembly resolution 50/27

6 December 1995     Meeting 82     Adopted without vote

Approved by Fourth Committee (A/50/604) without vote, 9 November (meeting 18); draft by Austria, for Fourth Committee Working Group on International Cooperation in the Peaceful Uses of Outer Space (A/C.4/50/L.9); agenda item 83.

*Meeting numbers.* GA 50th session: 4th Committee 2, 16-18; plenary 82.

## Spacecraft launchings

During 1995, nine countries (Canada, France, India, Israel, Russian Federation, Spain, Sweden, Ukraine, United States) and ESA provided information to the United Nations on the launching of objects into orbit or beyond,[46] in accordance with a 1961 General Assembly resolution[47] and article IV of the Convention on Registration of Objects Launched into Outer Space,[48] which entered into force in 1976.

By a note verbale of 3 November,[49] Ukraine transmitted information on the launching of the first Ukrainian spacecraft on 31 August 1995.

## Convention on registration of launchings

As at 31 December 1995, 39 States were parties to the Convention on registration. Norway acceded to the Convention on 28 June. In 1979, ESA had declared its acceptance of the rights and obligations of the Convention.

*REFERENCES*

[1]YUN 1994, p. 228, GA res. 49/34, 9 Dec. 1994. [2]A/50/20. [3]A/AC.105/605. [4]YUN 1982, p. 162. [5]A/AC.105/606. [6]A/AC.105/592 & Add.1-4. [7]A/AC.105/601. [8]YUN 1994, p. 220. [9]YUN 1993, p. 183. [10]A/50/384. [11]A/AC.105/611. [12]A/AC.105/632. [13]A/AC.105/592/Add.5,6, A/AC.105/614 & Add.1. [14]YUN 1982, p. 163, GA res. 37/90, 10 Dec. 1982. [15]A/AC.105/625. [16]A/AC.105/617. [17]A/AC.105/610. [18]A/AC.105/613. [19]A/AC.105/623. [20]A/AC.105/615. [21]A/AC.105/612. [22]A/AC.105/624. [23]A/AC.105/622. [24]A/AC.105/621. [25]YUN 1992, p. 672. [26]Ibid., p. 116, GA res. 47/68, 14 Dec. 1992. [27]A/AC.105/593 & Add.1-4. [28]A/AC.105/1995/CRP.5. [29]A/AC.105/620. [30]A/AC.105/619. [31]A/AC.105/608. [32]YUN 1993, p. 187. [33]YUN 1994, p. 225. [34]A/AC.105/1995/CRP.9. [35]A/AC.105/1995/CRP.7. [36]A/AC.105/597. [37]A/AC.105/603. [38]A/AC.105/598-600, 604. [39]A/AC.105/583. [40]A/AC.105/607 & Corr.1. [41]YUN 1993, p. 190. [42]YUN 1966, p. 41, GA res. 2222(XXI), annex, 19 Dec. 1966. [43]A/AC.105/C.2/L.182/Rev.2. [44]A/AC.105/C.2/L.197. [45]A/AC.105/C.2/1995/CRP.5. [46]ST/SG/SER.E/279-296, A/AC.105/INF/399. [47]YUN 1961, p. 35, GA res. 1721 B (XVI), 20 Dec. 1961. [48]YUN 1974, p. 63, GA res. 3235(XXIX), annex, 12 Nov. 1974. [49]A/50/766.

# Effects of atomic radiation

The UN Scientific Committee on the Effects of Atomic Radiation held its forty-fourth session in Vienna from 12 to 16 June 1995.[1] In accordance with a 1994 General Assembly request,[2] the Committee continued to review important problems relating to radiation sources and effects.

It considered recent information on sources of exposure, dose assessment for radionuclides, effects of radiation on the environment, DNA repair and mutagenesis, hereditary effects of radiation, epidemiological evaluation of radiation-induced cancer, combined effects of radiation and other agents, and Chernobyl-related local doses and effects. The Committee made suggestions for fur-

ther development of those topics and expressed its intention to review critically all available information on the consequences of the 1986 nuclear power plant accident in Chernobyl, Ukraine, in particular to clarify the possible relationships of childhood thyroid cancers to radiation exposures in Belarus, Ukraine and the Russian Federation. It also decided to continue collecting data on radiation exposures to determine representative values and ranges of variations, and to review new information from radiobiological and epidemiological studies.

**GENERAL ASSEMBLY ACTION**

On 6 December, the General Assembly adopted **resolution 50/26.**

### Effects of atomic radiation

*The General Assembly,*

*Recalling* its resolution 913(X) of 3 December 1955, by which it established the United Nations Scientific Committee on the Effects of Atomic Radiation, and its subsequent resolutions on the subject, including resolution 49/32 of 9 December 1994, in which, *inter alia*, it requested the Scientific Committee to continue its work,

*Taking note with appreciation* of the report of the United Nations Scientific Committee on the Effects of Atomic Radiation,

*Reaffirming* the desirability of the Scientific Committee continuing its work,

*Concerned* about the potentially harmful effects on present and future generations resulting from the levels of radiation to which mankind and the environment are exposed,

*Conscious* of the continuing need to examine and compile information about atomic and ionizing radiation and to analyse its effects on mankind and the environment,

1. *Commends* the United Nations Scientific Committee on the Effects of Atomic Radiation for the valuable contribution it has been making in the course of the past forty years, since its inception, to wider knowledge and understanding of the levels, effects and risks of atomic radiation and for fulfilling its original mandate with scientific authority and independence of judgement;

2. *Requests* the Scientific Committee to continue its work, including its important activities to increase knowledge of the levels, effects and risks of ionizing radiation from all sources;

3. *Endorses* the intentions and plans of the Scientific Committee for its future activities of scientific review and assessment on behalf of the General Assembly;

4. *Also requests* the Scientific Committee to continue at its next session the review of the important problems in the field of radiation and to report thereon to the General Assembly at its fifty-first session;

5. *Requests* the United Nations Environment Programme to continue providing support for the effective conduct of the work of the Scientific Committee and for the dissemination of its findings to the General Assembly, the scientific community and the public;

6. *Expresses its appreciation* for the assistance rendered to the Scientific Committee by Member States, the specialized agencies, the International Atomic Energy

Agency and non-governmental organizations, and invites them to increase their cooperation in this field;

7. *Invites* Member States, the organizations of the United Nations system and non-governmental organizations concerned to provide further relevant data about doses, effects and risks from various sources of radiation, which would greatly help in the preparation of future reports of the Scientific Committee to the General Assembly.

**General Assembly resolution 50/26**

6 December 1995     Meeting 82     Adopted without vote

Approved by Fourth Committee (A/50/603) without vote, 18 October (meeting 8); 39-nation draft (A/C.4/50/L.2); agenda item 82.
*Meeting numbers.* GA 50th session: 4th Committee 7, 8; plenary 82.

*REFERENCES*
(1)A/50/46. (2)YUN 1994, p. 238, GA res. 49/32, 9 Dec. 1994.

## Other questions

### UN fiftieth anniversary

The Preparatory Committee for the Fiftieth Anniversary of the United Nations, established by the General Assembly in 1992,[1] held 14 meetings in 1995 to consider preparations for the Special Commemorative Meeting of the General Assembly, which took place in New York from 22 to 24 October (see special section, pp. 141-72), as well as other preparations for the observance of the anniversary and administrative and financial issues. The Committee concluded its work on 5 December.

In response to a 1994 General Assembly request,[2] the Preparatory Committee submitted in May 1995 its recommendations[3] concerning a list of speakers for the Special Commemorative Meeting.

**GENERAL ASSEMBLY ACTION (May and July)**

On 24 May, the General Assembly adopted **resolution 49/12 B**.

**Organization of the list of speakers for the Special Commemorative Meeting of the General Assembly on the occasion of the fiftieth anniversary of the United Nations**
*The General Assembly,*

*Recalling* its resolution 48/215 B of 26 May 1994, in which it decided to convene a special commemorative meeting on the occasion of the fiftieth anniversary of the entry into force of the Charter of the United Nations, to be held at United Nations Headquarters from 22 to 24 October 1995,

*Recalling also* paragraph 8 of the report of the Preparatory Committee for the Fiftieth Anniversary of the United Nations, in which the modalities for inviting Palestine and, if they so request, other observers to attend the Special Commemorative Meeting were agreed upon,

1. *Decides* that the Special Commemorative Meeting shall consist of a total of six meetings, on the basis of two meetings a day;

2. *Also decides* that the list of speakers for the Special Commemorative Meeting shall be organized in accordance with the procedure set forth in the annex to the present resolution.

#### ANNEX
**Organization of the list of speakers for the Special Commemorative Meeting of the General Assembly on the occasion of the fiftieth anniversary of the United Nations**

1. The list of speakers for the Special Commemorative Meeting will be established on the basis of six meetings, each meeting having 25 speaking slots, with the exception of the meeting on Tuesday, 24 October 1995, in the afternoon, which will have 60 speaking slots.

2. The first speaker in the Special Commemorative Meeting will be the head of State of the host country of the Organization.

3. The list of speakers for the Special Commemorative Meeting will be initially established as follows:

(a) The Secretary-General or his representative will draw one name from a box containing the names of all Member States, observer States and Palestine, in its capacity as observer, participating in the Special Commemorative Meeting. This procedure will be repeated until all names have been drawn from the box, thus establishing the order in which participants will be invited to choose their meetings and select their speaking slots;

(b) Six boxes will be prepared, each one representing a meeting and each one containing numbers corresponding to speaking slots at that meeting;

(c) Once the name of a Member State, observer State or Palestine, in its capacity as observer, has been drawn by the Secretary-General or his representative, that Member State, observer State or Palestine, in its capacity as observer, will be invited first to choose a meeting and then to draw from the appropriate box the number indicating the speaking slot in the meeting;

(d) A number of speaking slots at each meeting will be reserved for observers participating in the Special Commemorative Meeting. They will be invited to participate in the initial establishment of the list of speakers in the same manner as Member States, observer States and Palestine, in its capacity as observer, but from a different set of six boxes.

4. The establishment of the initial list of speakers for the Special Commemorative Meeting as outlined in paragraph 3 of the present annex will take place at a meeting of the Preparatory Committee for the Fiftieth Anniversary of the United Nations to be held on 7 June 1995.

5. Subsequently, the list of speakers for each meeting will be rearranged in accordance with the established practice of the General Assembly when organizing each category of speakers, following the order resulting from the selection process outlined in paragraph 3 of the present annex:

(a) Heads of State will thus be accorded first priority, followed by vice-presidents, crown princes/princesses, heads of Government, the highest-ranking official of the Holy See and Switzerland, as observer States, and Palestine, in its capacity as observer, ministers, permanent representatives and other observers;

(b) In the event that the level at which a statement is to be made is subsequently changed, the speaker will be moved to the next available speaking slot in the appropriate category at the same meeting;

*(c)* Participants may arrange to exchange their speaking slots in accordance with the established practice of the General Assembly;

*(d)* Speakers who are not present when their speaking turn comes will be automatically moved to the next available speaking slot within their category.

6. In order to accommodate all speakers at the Special Commemorative Meeting, statements should be limited to five minutes, on the understanding that this will not preclude the circulation of more extensive texts.

7. The full text of all speeches provided to the Special Commemorative Meeting will be subsequently published in a bound book.

General Assembly resolution 49/12 B

24 May 1995     Meeting 103     Adopted without vote

Draft by Preparatory Committee for the Fiftieth Anniversary of the UN (A/49/48/Add.1); agenda item 44.

On 12 July, Costa Rica introduced to the Assembly a draft resolution calling for a week-long cessation of hostilities in celebration of the United Nations fiftieth anniversary.

On the same date, the Assembly adopted **resolution 49/244**.

### World Week of Peace

*The General Assembly,*

*Cognizant* of the fact that the promotion of peace and the prevention of war are among the primary goals of the United Nations,

*Recognizing* that the Preamble to the Charter of the United Nations states that the peoples of the United Nations are determined to save succeeding generations from the scourge of war, which twice in our lifetime has brought untold sorrow to mankind,

*Recalling* that the United Nations was established to prevent war and seek peace through peaceful means and through negotiation, as well as to promote international cooperation,

*Recalling also* its resolution 47/120 A of 18 December 1992, in which it welcomed the report of the Secretary-General entitled "An Agenda for Peace", stressing the importance of preventive diplomacy and peace-keeping operations,

*Recalling* that 1995 has been proclaimed the United Nations Year for Tolerance,

*Recognizing* the important role that Disarmament Week, which will be observed concurrently with the World Week of Peace, is playing in promoting international peace and security,

*Recognizing also* that the United Nations is universal in nature and is the only instrument for global interdependence and cooperation that has the moral authority and the influence to promote and maintain world peace,

*Recognizing further* the importance of promoting the culture of peace,

*Concerned* that recent conflicts between States have brought with them deplorable ethnic strife, destruction and displacement of individuals and communities,

*Deeply concerned* at the large proportion of civilians, especially women and children, who have been injured or killed during the armed conflicts that have increased in recent years,

*Recognizing* that civil society organizations are now playing a more important role in promoting tolerance and understanding,

*Convinced* that a short period of peace resulting from a cease-fire or a truce can offer opportunities for building a just and lasting peace,

*Noting with satisfaction* the valuable initiative taken by the United Nations Children's Fund to facilitate "days of tranquillity" and "corridors of peace", which have been used to provide humanitarian relief, such as immunization, health care, food and clothing, to children trapped by armed conflicts,

1. *Decides* to proclaim the World Week of Peace, beginning on 24 October 1995, in solemn commemoration of the fiftieth anniversary of the United Nations;

2. *Approves* the Proclamation of the World Week of Peace, the text of which is annexed to the present resolution;

3. *Invites* all Member States to begin this task of cooperation with their own citizens and with civil society organizations, so as to give maximum publicity and assistance to the launching of the proclamation of a universal week of truce or cease-fire during the commemoration of the fiftieth anniversary of the United Nations;

4. *Requests* the Secretary-General to ensure the broadest possible dissemination of this resolution through the Department of Public Information of the Secretariat;

5. *Also requests* the Secretary-General to report on the implementation of the present resolution to the General Assembly at its fiftieth session.

#### ANNEX
#### Proclamation of the World Week of Peace

*Whereas* the General Assembly has decided unanimously to proclaim the World Week of Peace in commemoration of the fiftieth anniversary of the United Nations,

*Whereas* the promotion of peace and the prevention of war are among the primary goals of the United Nations,

*Whereas*, in welcoming "An Agenda for Peace", the United Nations has rededicated itself to the effort to establish a universal peace according to the purposes and principles of the Charter of the United Nations, signed at San Francisco,

*Whereas*, in increasing the size and scope of its peace-keeping operations, the United Nations has demonstrated its commitment to the task of peace-keeping and peacemaking,

*Whereas* the World Week of Peace offers a special opportunity for Governments, civilian organizations, local communities and individuals to take part in new initiatives for the commendable goal of conflict resolution, cease-fires and truces, and for a period of universal peace that could be used for the humanitarian relief that has become so critically necessary,

*Accordingly,*

*The General Assembly*

*Solemnly proclaims* the World Week of Peace, beginning on 24 October 1995, to coincide with the commemoration of the fiftieth anniversary of the United Nations.

General Assembly resolution 49/244

12 July 1995     Meeting 105     Adopted without vote

61-nation draft (A/49/L.66 & Corr.1 & Add.1); agenda item 44.

**Report of the Preparatory Committee (December).** In a December report,[4] the Preparatory Committee summarized its activities since its establishment, as well as anniversary programmes undertaken by Member and observer States, global projects and activities within the UN system and of NGOs.

The Committee noted that, as at 10 November, 152 Member or observer States had established national committees that had organized numerous events to celebrate the fiftieth anniversary. These included: school essay and art competitions; global teach-in programmes and other symposia and seminars on the United Nations; production of special publications, radio and television programmes and newspaper and magazine feature sections; exhibitions, national galas and concerts and sport events honouring the Organization; special "Model United Nations" exercises with student participants; and the naming of public streets, plazas and parks in honour of the United Nations. The UN Postal Administration issued three special stamp series in 1995, and throughout the world national postal administrations produced commemorative stamps depicting UN programmes and activities. More than 40 Member States minted legal tender coins, both gold and silver, honouring the anniversary, and base-metal coins for general circulation. In 1994, the General Assembly[5] had decided that States participating in the UN coin programme were to donate royalties on each special proof or uncirculated coin sold to collectors to the Trust Fund for the Fiftieth Anniversary Celebrations, to be used for education and communications activities promoting the work of the United Nations.

Major events were held during the year to commemorate the fiftieth anniversary: in San Francisco, where the UN Charter had been signed in 1945, at Headquarters in New York, and at the Geneva and Vienna Offices (see special section beginning on p. 141). A special "global citizen passport to the future" programme, initiated in connection with anniversary celebrations, involved schoolchildren and community service activities. A world youth leadership training summit took place at UN Headquarters in August. A book entitled *A World In Our Hands* was written, illustrated and edited by young people, in honour of the anniversary. A multimedia exhibit was mounted at UN Headquarters, and fiftieth anniversary information sites were created on the Internet and other on-line services. A variety of publications, including a pictorial history of the Organization entitled *Visions—Fifty Years of the United Nations*, were issued.

Within the UN system, a Forum on the Future of the United Nations was convened in conjunction with a session of the Administrative Committee on Coordination (Vienna, February). Joint projects were undertaken with UNESCO, FAO and the regional commissions. NGOs actively supported many celebratory events; a one-day NGO programme was held in November to examine the role of NGOs and the United Nations and its future in the twenty-first century.

The Trust Fund for the Fiftieth Anniversary Celebrations supported both global projects and national educational and communications initiatives about the work of the Organization. It was expected to continue receiving revenues, in particular from commemorative coins and publications.

**Security Council observances.** On 27 September,[6] the Foreign Ministers of the Security Council's five permanent members met with the UN Secretary-General to review the world situation on the occasion of the fiftieth anniversary of the end of the Second World War and the birth of the United Nations. The Ministers noted with satisfaction what had been achieved and the fact that institutions of the United Nations had been central to the pursuit of peace and security for the past 50 years in accordance with the UN Charter. They pointed out that serious challenges remained and that effective and efficient institutions within the UN system had an important role to play in confronting them. Affirming their commitment to the United Nations, they stressed the primary responsibility of the Security Council in maintaining world peace and security, and underscored the importance of reinforcing cooperation between the UN and regional organizations and arrangements in building stability and security and in preventing and managing conflicts (see also PART ONE, Chapter I, and PART TWO, Chapter I).

The Ministers also stated their position concerning the situations in different regions, and in the areas of sanctions application, disarmament, sustainable development, and the UN financial situation and restructuring. They pointed out that the Organization's proper functioning depended on the full and punctual payment by Member States of their contributions, which was crucial for the success of UN peace-keeping operations. They emphasized the importance of UN reform to make it more transparent, accountable, efficient and effective (see PART SIX, Chapter I).

Heads of State or Government of the non-aligned countries members of the Security Council, meeting on 23 October on the occasion of the UN fiftieth anniversary,[7] noted that the authority and credibility of the Council had grown substantially in recent years as its members rediscovered a sense of common purpose in confronting dangers to peace and stability. In that regard, they pointed to the need for strengthening and revitalizing the Council to adapt it to the new realities and challenges of the time, and expressed their support for ongoing efforts to increase its membership based on equitable geographic representation. The heads of State or Government also called for improving the peacemaking and peacekeeping capacity of the UN, as well as cooperation between the General Assembly and the Security Council (see also PART ONE, Chapter I).

**Communications.** During the year, the Secretary-General received a number of communications from Member States on the occasion of the fiftieth anniversary, transmitting commemorative resolutions adopted by parliaments, national assemblies and other important bodies. A statement by 16 heads of State or Government in support of global cooperation was issued in New York on 23 October.[8]

## SECURITY COUNCIL ACTION

On 26 September, the President of the Security Council made the following statement[9] on behalf of the Council members:

> The Security Council has met on 26 September 1995, at the level of Foreign Ministers, to commemorate the fiftieth anniversary of the United Nations and to exchange views on the challenges which the Security Council faces.
>
> Since its establishment the Security Council has played a crucial role in the maintenance of international peace and security on which development and cooperation among nations are based. The past few years in particular have been ones of momentous change, bringing fresh hope and new challenges. Operations mandated by the Council have assisted in the restoration of peace and stability to countries long-plagued by war. Although such operations have largely been successful, there are areas where success has not been achieved. The Council must continue to spare no effort in working for the maintenance of international peace and security, and build upon its experience of past and existing operations.
>
> The Security Council recognizes that the challenges facing the international community demand a resolute response, based on the principles and purposes of the Charter of the United Nations. The members of the Security Council consider that the United Nations must be strengthened and revitalized to help meet these challenges. They take note of the conclusions of the Working Group of the General Assembly on the Question of Equitable Representation on and Increase in the Membership of the Security Council and Other Matters Related to the Security Council, *inter alia*, that the Council should be expanded, and that its working methods should continue to be reviewed, in a way that further strengthens its capacity and effectiveness, enhances its representative character and improves its working efficiency and transparency; and that important differences on key issues continue to exist. The Council also believes that effective use should be made of instruments for preventive action, and the Organization's capacity to conduct effective peace-keeping operations should continue to be improved. The Council will continue to attach utmost importance to the safety and security of all who serve under the United Nations flag in the field.
>
> The members of the Security Council reaffirm their commitment to the collective security system of the Charter. On the solemn occasion of the fiftieth anniversary of the United Nations, the Council, along with other United Nations bodies, commemorates what has been achieved so far, but also commits itself once again to the maintenance of international peace and security for which it has primary responsibility, and to working to save succeeding generations from the scourge of war.

*Meeting number.* SC 3583.

## GENERAL ASSEMBLY ACTION (October and December)

The General Assembly, at six special plenary meetings on 22, 23 and 24 October at UN Headquarters in New York, held the Special Commemorative Meeting on the occasion of the fiftieth anniversary of the United Nations. (For details, see special section, pp. 141-72.)

On 24 October, the Assembly adopted **resolution 50/6**.

### Declaration on the Occasion of the Fiftieth Anniversary of the United Nations

*The General Assembly*

*Adopts* the following Declaration:

Declaration on the Occasion of the Fiftieth Anniversary of the United Nations

Fifty years ago the United Nations was born out of the sufferings caused by the Second World War. The determination, enshrined in the Charter of the United Nations, "to save succeeding generations from the scourge of war" is as vital today as it was fifty years ago. In this, as in other respects, the Charter gives expression to the common values and aspirations of humankind.

The United Nations has been tested by conflict, humanitarian crisis and turbulent change, yet it has survived and played an important role in preventing another global conflict and has achieved much for people all over the world. The United Nations has helped to shape the very structure of relations between nations in the modern age. Through the process of decolonization and the elimination of apartheid, hundreds of millions of human beings have been and are assured the exercise of the fundamental right of self-determination.

At this time, following the end of the cold war, and as the end of the century approaches, we must create new opportunities for peace, development, democracy and cooperation. The speed and extent of change in today's world point to a future of great complexity and challenge and to a sharp increase in the level of expectations of the United Nations.

Our resolve on this historic occasion is clear. The commemoration of the fiftieth anniversary of the United Nations must be seized as an opportunity to redirect it to greater service to humankind, especially to those who are suffering and are deeply deprived. This is the practical and moral challenge of our time. Our obligation to this end is found in the Charter. The need for it is manifest in the condition of humankind.

On the occasion of the fiftieth anniversary of the United Nations, we, the Member States and observers of the United Nations, representing the peoples of the world:

—Solemnly reaffirm the Purposes and Principles of the Charter of the United Nations and our commitments to them;

—Express our gratitude to all men and women who have made the United Nations possible, done its work and served its ideals, particularly those who have given their lives during service to the United Nations;

—Are determined that the United Nations of the future will work with renewed vigour and effectiveness in promoting peace, development, equality and justice and understanding among the peoples of the world;

—Will give to the twenty-first century a United Nations equipped, financed and structured to serve effectively the peoples in whose name it was established.

In fulfilment of these commitments we will be guided in our future cooperation by the following, with respect to peace, development, equality, justice and the United Nations Organization:

*Peace*

1. To meet these challenges, and while recognizing that action to secure global peace, security and stability will be futile unless the economic and social needs of people are addressed, we will:

—Promote methods and means for the peaceful settlement of disputes in accordance with the Charter of the United Nations and enhance the capabilities of the United Nations in conflict prevention, preventive diplomacy, peace-keeping and peace-building;

—Strongly support United Nations, regional and national efforts on arms control, limitation and disarmament and the non-proliferation of nuclear weapons, in all aspects, and other weapons of mass destruction, including biological and chemical weapons and other forms of particularly excessively injurious or indiscriminate weapons, in pursuit of our common commitment to a world free of all these weapons;

—Continue to reaffirm the right of self-determination of all peoples, taking into account the particular situation of peoples under colonial or other forms of alien domination or foreign occupation, and recognize the right of peoples to take legitimate action in accordance with the Charter of the United Nations to realize their inalienable right of self-determination. This shall not be construed as authorizing or encouraging any action that would dismember or impair, totally or in part, the territorial integrity or political unity of sovereign and independent States conducting themselves in compliance with the principle of equal rights and self-determination of peoples and thus possessed of a Government representing the whole people belonging to the territory without distinction of any kind;

—Act together to defeat the threats to States and people posed by terrorism, in all its forms and manifestations, and transnational organized crime and the il-

licit trade in arms and the production and consumption of and trafficking in illicit drugs;

—Strengthen consultation and cooperation between regional arrangements or agencies and the United Nations in the maintenance of international peace and security.

*Development*

2. A dynamic, vigorous, free and equitable international economic environment is essential to the well-being of humankind and to international peace, security and stability. This objective must be addressed, in greater measure and more effectively, by the United Nations system.

3. The United Nations has played an important role in the promotion of economic and social development and has, over the years, provided life-saving assistance to women, children and men around the world. But the pledge recorded in the Charter that all Members of the United Nations shall take joint and separate action in cooperation with the Organization for the achievement of higher standards of living, full employment and conditions of economic and social progress and development has not been adequately implemented.

4. It must be recognized that notwithstanding past efforts, the gap between the developed and developing countries remains unacceptably wide. The specific problems of countries with economies in transition with respect to their twofold transition to democracy and a market economy should also be recognized. In addition, accelerating globalization and interdependence in the world economy call for policy measures designed to ensure the maximization of the benefits from and the minimization of the negative effects of these trends for all countries.

5. Of greatest concern is that one fifth of the world's 5.7 billion people live in extreme poverty. Extraordinary measures by all countries, including strengthened international cooperation, are needed to address this and related problems.

6. In response to these facts and circumstances, the United Nations has convened a number of specifically focused global conferences in the last five years. From these conferences, a consensus has emerged, *inter alia*, that economic development, social development and environmental protection are interdependent and mutually reinforcing components of sustainable development, which is the framework of our efforts to achieve a higher quality of life for all people. At the core of this consensus is the recognition that the human person is the central subject of development and that people must be at the centre of our actions towards and concerns for sustainable development.

7. In this context, we reaffirm that democracy, development and respect for human rights and fundamental freedoms, including the right to development, are interdependent and mutually reinforcing.

8. In order to foster sustained economic growth, social development, environmental protection and social justice in fulfilment of the commitments we have made on international cooperation for development, we will:

—Promote an open and equitable, rule-based, predictable and non-discriminatory multilateral trading system and a framework for investment, transfers of technology and knowledge, as well as en-

hanced cooperation in the areas of development, finance and debt as critical conditions for development;
—Give particular attention to national and international action to enhance the benefits of the process of globalization for all countries and to avoid the marginalization from and promote the integration of the least developed countries and countries in Africa into the world economy;
—Improve the effectiveness and efficiency of the United Nations system for development and strengthen its role in all relevant fields of international economic cooperation;
—Invigorate the dialogue and partnership between all countries in order to secure the existence of a favourable political and economic environment for the promotion of international cooperation for development based on the imperatives of mutual benefit and interest and genuine interdependence, while recognizing that each country is ultimately responsible for its own development but reaffirming that the international community must create a supportive international environment for such development;
—Promote social development through decisive national and international action aimed at the eradication of poverty as an ethical, social, political and economic imperative of humankind and the promotion of full employment and social integration;
—Recognize that the empowerment and the full and equal participation of women is central to all efforts to achieve development;
—Reduce and eliminate unsustainable patterns of production and consumption and promote appropriate demographic policies in order to meet the needs of current generations without compromising the ability of future generations to meet their own needs, recognizing that environmental sustainability constitutes an integral part of the development process;
—Intensify cooperation on natural disaster reduction and major technological and man-made disasters, disaster relief, post-disaster rehabilitation and humanitarian assistance in order to enhance the capabilities of affected countries to cope with such situations.

*Equality*

9. We reiterate the affirmation by the Charter of the dignity and worth of the human person and the equal rights of men and women and reaffirm that all human rights are universal, indivisible, interdependent and interrelated.

10. While the significance of national and regional particularities and various historical, cultural and religious backgrounds must be borne in mind, it is the duty of all States, regardless of their political, economic and cultural systems, to promote and protect all human rights and fundamental freedoms, the universal nature of which is beyond question. It is also important for all States to ensure the universality, objectivity and non-selectivity of the consideration of human rights issues.

11. We will therefore:
—Promote and protect all human rights and fundamental freedoms, which are inherent to all human beings;
—Strengthen laws, policies and programmes that would ensure the full and equal participation of women in all spheres of political, civil, economic, social and cultural life as equal partners and the full realization of all human rights and fundamental freedoms for all women;
—Promote and protect the rights of the child;
—Ensure that the rights of persons who can be particularly vulnerable to abuse or neglect, including youth, persons with disabilities, the elderly and migrant workers, are protected;
—Promote and protect the rights of indigenous people;
—Ensure the protection of the rights of refugees and of displaced persons;
—Ensure that the rights of persons belonging to national, ethnic and other minorities are protected, and that such persons are able to pursue economic and social development and live in circumstances of full respect for their identity, traditions, forms of social organization and cultural and religious values.

*Justice*

12. The Charter of the United Nations has provided a durable framework for the promotion and development of international law. The continued promotion and development of international law must be pursued with a view to ensuring that relations between States are based on the principles of justice, sovereign equality, universally recognized principles of international law and respect for the rule of law. Such action should take account of developments under way in such areas as technology, transport, information and resource-related fields and international financial markets, as well as the growing complexity of the work of the United Nations in the humanitarian and refugee assistance fields.

13. We are determined to:
—Build and maintain justice among all States in accordance with the principles of the sovereign equality and territorial integrity of States;
—Promote full respect for and implementation of international law;
—Settle international disputes by peaceful means;
—Encourage the widest possible ratification of international treaties and ensure compliance with the obligations arising from them;
—Promote respect for and the implementation of international humanitarian law;
—Promote the progressive development of international law in the field of development, including that which would foster economic and social progress;
—Promote respect for and implementation of international law in the field of human rights and fundamental freedoms and encourage ratification of or accession to international human rights instruments;
—Promote the further codification and progressive development of international law.

*United Nations Organization*

14. In order to be able to respond effectively to the challenges of the future and the expectations of the United Nations held by peoples around the world, it is essential that the United Nations itself be reformed and modernized. The work of the General Assembly, the universal organ of the States Members of the United

Nations, should be revitalized. The Security Council should, *inter alia*, be expanded and its working methods continue to be reviewed in a way that will further strengthen its capacity and effectiveness, enhance its representative character and improve its working efficiency and transparency; as important differences on key issues continue to exist, further in-depth consideration of these issues is required. The role of the Economic and Social Council should be strengthened to enable it to carry out effectively, in the modern age, the tasks it has been assigned with respect to the well-being and standards of life of all people. These and other changes, within the United Nations system, should be made if we are to ensure that the United Nations of the future serves well the peoples in whose name it was established.

15.   In order to carry out its work effectively, the United Nations must have adequate resources. Member States must meet, in full and on time, their obligation to bear the expenses of the Organization, as apportioned by the General Assembly. That apportionment should be established on the basis of criteria agreed to and considered to be fair by Member States.

16.   The secretariats of the United Nations system must improve significantly their efficiency and effectiveness in administering and managing the resources allocated to them. For their part, Member States will pursue and take responsibility for reforming that system.

17.   We recognize that our common work will be the more successful if it is supported by all concerned actors of the international community, including non-governmental organizations, multilateral financial institutions, regional organizations and all actors of civil society. We will welcome and facilitate such support, as appropriate.

General Assembly resolution 50/6

24 October 1995     Meeting 40     Adopted by acclamation

Draft by Preparatory Committee for the Fiftieth Anniversary of the UN (A/50/48); agenda item 29.
*Meeting numbers.* GA 50th session: plenary 35-40

On 12 December, the Assembly adopted **resolution 50/59**.

### Work of the Preparatory Committee for the Fiftieth Anniversary of the United Nations

*The General Assembly,*

*Having considered* the report of the Preparatory Committee for the Fiftieth Anniversary of the United Nations,

1.   *Expresses its appreciation* to the national committees and to the innumerable non-governmental and other organizations around the world that have supported the goals of the anniversary;

2.   *Also expresses its appreciation* to the secretariat of the fiftieth anniversary of the United Nations for the series of commemorative programmes and projects it has undertaken and coordinated and for its efforts to involve national committees, non-governmental organizations and the United Nations system and staff in the global commemoration of the anniversary;

3.   *Further expresses its appreciation* to those Member States, corporations and individuals that have contributed to the Trust Fund for the Fiftieth Anniversary;

4.   *Requests* the Secretary-General to ensure that the funds remaining in and which will be paid into the Trust Fund are applied to the purposes for which they were committed, and to report thereon to the General Assembly before the end of the fiftieth session;

5.   *Expresses its deep appreciation* to the host country for the arrangements it made in support of the conduct of the Special Commemorative Meeting of the General Assembly;

6.   *Approves* the report of the Preparatory Committee for the Fiftieth Anniversary of the United Nations and takes note with deep appreciation of the successful conclusion of its work.

General Assembly resolution 50/59

12 December 1995     Meeting 89     Adopted without vote

Draft by Preparatory Committee for the Fiftieth Anniversary of the UN (A/50/48/Rev.1); agenda item 29.
*Meeting numbers.* GA 50th session: plenary 35-37, 89.

## End of the Second World War anniversary

In accordance with a 1994 General Assembly appeal[10] to all States and peoples to commemorate the fiftieth anniversary of the end of the Second World War and its proclamation of the year 1995 as World Year of Peoples' Commemoration of the Victims of the Second World War, several countries transmitted to the UN in 1995 statements made on the occasion of that anniversary. Communications addressed to the Secretary-General included a joint message by the heads of States of the members of the Commonwealth of Independent States,[11] a statement by the Government of the Federal Republic of Yugoslavia (Serbia and Montenegro),[12] a memorandum by the Ministry of Foreign Affairs of the Democratic People's Republic of Korea[13] and a formal appeal by the President of Romania for historical reconciliation between Hungary and Romania, launched in Bucharest on 30 August.[14] On 15 August, Japan communicated to the President of the Security Council a statement made by its Prime Minister.[15]

#### SECURITY COUNCIL ACTION

The Security Council on 9 May met in connection with the commemoration of the end of the Second World War in Europe. In a statement made on behalf of the Council, its President said, *inter alia*, that the United Nations was created primarily to preserve future generations from the scourge of war and that its Charter had entrusted the Security Council with the principal responsibility for maintaining international peace and security. For that reason, it seemed appropriate for the Council to pay tribute, on the fiftieth anniversary of the end of the Second World War in Europe, to all the victims of that war and to recall the Council's firm desire to make every effort to help mitigate human suffering resulting from war. At the invitation of the President, the Council members observed a minute of silence in memory of the combatants and victims of the Second World War.

The Council also met on 15 August to commemorate the end of the Second World War in the Asia-Pacific region. Its President made the following statement on behalf of the Council members:

"It was fifty years ago that the Asia-Pacific region saw the end of the Second World War, a devastating war that shattered the lives of tens of millions of people in this region. On this solemn occasion, we pay tribute to those who laid down their lives and the other victims of the war.

"Having survived the catastrophe of the Second World War, mankind sought to embrace new means to prevent the recurrence of such a tragedy. To this end, the United Nations was established, with primary responsibility for the maintenance of international peace and security conferred on the Security Council by the Charter.

"Unity and harmony among nations would be the most honourable and noble way to pay tribute to those who sacrificed their lives for peace during the Second World War. For this reason, it is appropriate for the Security Council to pay homage on this anniversary to all the victims of the Second World War in the Asia-Pacific region."

The Council members then observed a minute of silence in memory of the victims of the Second World War.

*Meeting numbers.* SC 3532, 3565.

**GENERAL ASSEMBLY ACTION**

In accordance with a 1994 resolution,[10] the General Assembly held a solemn meeting on 18 October 1995 in commemoration of victims of the Second World War. On the same date, the Assembly adopted **resolution 50/5.**

**Commemoration of the fiftieth anniversary of the end of the Second World War**

*The General Assembly,*

*Recalling* its resolution 49/25 of 2 December 1994,

*Having considered* item 36 of the agenda of its fiftieth session entitled "Commemoration of the fiftieth anniversary of the end of the Second World War",

*Approves* the Declaration in Commemoration of the Fiftieth Anniversary of the End of the Second World War, the text of which is annexed to the present resolution.

**ANNEX**

**Declaration in Commemoration of the Fiftieth Anniversary of the End of the Second World War**

1. We, the representatives of the States Members of the United Nations, have gathered at a solemn meeting of the fiftieth anniversary session of the United Nations General Assembly to commemorate the fiftieth anniversary of the end of the Second World War, which brought untold suffering and ravages to humankind.

2. In this World Year of Peoples' Commemoration of the Victims of the Second World War, we bow our heads before the tens of millions who perished in their towns and villages or on the battlefields, or became victims of genocide in the death camps, and remember with gratitude those who fought against dictatorship, oppression, racism and aggression.

3. We note that one of the most remarkable results of the end of the Second World War was the establishment of a community based on new principles—the United Nations, whose task is to save succeeding generations from the scourge of war. We reaffirm the resolve of our States to adhere strictly to the purposes and principles of the Charter of the United Nations and of the Universal Declaration of Human Rights.

4. We note with satisfaction that today, now that many ideological barriers have fallen and the "cold war" has ended, new opportunities are emerging for building a non-violent world and a system of genuine global security with the United Nations as the central element.

5. We recall the tragedy of the Second World War and the unprecedented suffering it inflicted upon various peoples and upon all of humanity. We are fully aware of the vital necessity of making all possible efforts to put an end to existing armed conflicts, to avert such conflicts in the future and to overcome the remaining legacies of the Second World War as well as the manifestations of political, economic and social inequality, and we call upon the States of the world:

(*a*) To reaffirm the commitment to refrain from the use or threat of use of force against the territorial integrity or political independence of any State or in any other manner inconsistent with the principles and purposes of the Charter of the United Nations;

(*b*) To redouble their efforts to put an end to all conflicts and to save future generations from the scourge of new wars, *inter alia*, by drawing the lessons that emerge from the history of past conflicts;

(*c*) To promote democracy and human rights and to support universal access to culture;

(*d*) To focus their efforts on the objective of creating conditions for the general progress of humankind in larger freedom.

6. The fulfilment of these commitments will be the best way to pay tribute to those who fought for peace, freedom, democracy and human dignity and to honour the memory of the victims of the Second World War. Only in this way can we prevent new tragedies and ensure that all nations become a single community living in peace, stability, cooperation and prosperity.

General Assembly resolution 50/5

18 October 1995      Meeting 33      Adopted without vote

52-nation draft (A/50/L.3 & Corr.1 & Add.1); agenda item 36.

Speaking in explanation of its position, Israel stated that it could not become a sponsor of the resolution because it did not mention the Holocaust, which the State of Israel, as the Jewish National Home, had an obligation to remember; however, it had decided not to request that a vote be taken.

## Support for democracies

In response to a 1994 General Assembly request,[16] the Secretary-General in August 1995 reported[17] on ways and mechanisms in which the UN system could support the efforts of Governments to promote and consolidate new or restored democracies. He reviewed the experience gained in promoting a participatory culture and an open society through: establishment of political parties and movements, free and independent media and civic education; electoral assistance, including organization and conduct of elections, supervision, verification, coordination and support for international observers, support for national election observers, technical assistance and observation; and building institutions for democracy by creating and strengthening democratic structures of government, enhancing the rule of law, reforming the civil service and improving accountability, transparency and quality in public sector management.

The Secretary-General noted that the number of requests for electoral assistance had increased from 7 to 89 between 1992 and June 1995, 77 of which had been accepted. Elections, albeit necessary, he said, were not sufficient to ensure the durability of a democratization process; the United Nations had therefore broadened its activities to focus on the creation of independent judicial systems, establishment of armed forces respectful of the rule of law, training of police forces to safeguard public freedoms and the setting up of human rights institutions. As the breadth of democratization, governance and institution-building made it difficult for any UN entity to support the entire spectrum of programmes in that area, the Secretary-General recommended an expanding network for policy development and programme cooperation, involving UN agencies, bilateral donors and interested professional organizations. He further suggested that different components of the UN system should pay particular attention to such key areas as: strengthening of leadership skills and political institutions; linkages between government and civil society, including NGOs, the media, local authorities and professional associations; support for effective judiciaries guaranteeing the rule of law and protection of human rights; and participation in decentralization efforts. In conclusion, the Secretary-General underscored that the UN system and Governments, while remaining the principal actors in the democratization process, should work actively with a multiplicity of partners, including regional organizations, NGOs, parliamentarians, business leaders, professional associations, the academic community and ordinary citizens.

**GENERAL ASSEMBLY ACTION**

On 20 December, the General Assembly adopted **resolution 50/133**.

**Support by the United Nations system of the efforts of Governments to promote and consolidate new or restored democracies**

*The General Assembly,*

*Bearing in mind* the indissoluble links between the principles enshrined in the Universal Declaration of Human Rights and the foundations of any democratic society,

*Recalling* the Manila Declaration adopted in June 1988 by the First International Conference of New or Restored Democracies,

*Considering* the major changes taking place on the international scene and the aspirations of all the peoples for an international order based on the principles enshrined in the Charter of the United Nations, including the promotion and encouragement of respect for human rights and fundamental freedoms for all and other important principles, such as respect for the equal rights and self-determination of peoples, peace, democracy, justice, equality, the rule of law, pluralism, development, better standards of living and solidarity,

*Recalling also* its resolution 49/30 of 7 December 1994, in which it recognized the importance of the Managua Declaration and the Plan of Action adopted by the Second International Conference of New or Restored Democracies in July 1994,

*Recalling further* the view expressed in the Managua Declaration that the international community must pay closer attention to the obstacles facing the new or restored democracies,

*Taking note* of the views of Member States expressed in the debate on this item at its forty-ninth and fiftieth sessions,

*Bearing in mind* that such activities of the United Nations carried out in support of the efforts of Governments are undertaken in accordance with the Charter of the United Nations and only at the specific request of the Member States concerned,

*Bearing in mind also* that democracy, development and respect for human rights and fundamental freedoms are interdependent and mutually reinforcing and that democracy is based on the freely expressed will of the people to determine their own political, economic, social and cultural systems and on their full participation in all aspects of their lives,

*Noting* that a considerable number of societies have recently undertaken considerable efforts to achieve their social, political and economic goals through democratization and the reform of their economies, pursuits that are deserving of the support and recognition of the international community,

*Noting with satisfaction* that a Third International Conference on New or Restored Democracies will take place at Bucharest,

*Having considered* the report of the Secretary-General on assistance provided in the past by the United Nations, at the request of Member States, as well as important concepts and considerations that are pertinent to this question,

1. *Welcomes* the report of the Secretary-General;

2. *Commends* the Secretary-General and through him the United Nations system for the activities undertaken at the request of Governments to support the efforts to consolidate democracy, as reflected in his report;

3. *Recognizes* that the Organization has an important role to play in providing timely, appropriate and coherent support to the efforts of Governments to achieve democratization within the context of their development efforts;

4. *Stresses* that activities undertaken by the Organization must be in accordance with the Charter of the United Nations;

5. *Encourages* the Secretary-General to continue to improve the capacity of the Organization to respond effectively to the requests of Member States through coherent, adequate support of their efforts to achieve the goal of democratization;

6. *Encourages* Member States to promote democratization and to make additional efforts to identify possible steps to support the efforts of Governments to promote and consolidate new or restored democracies;

7. *Requests* the Secretary-General to submit to the General Assembly at its fifty-first session a report on the implementation of the present resolution, including innovative ways and means, as well as new reflections, to enable the Organization to respond effectively and in an integrated manner to requests of Member States for assistance in this field;

8. *Decides* to include in the provisional agenda of its fifty-first session the item entitled ''Support by the United Nations system of the efforts of Governments to promote and consolidate new or restored democracies''.

General Assembly resolution 50/133

20 December 1995     Meeting 96     Adopted without vote

59-nation draft (A/50/L.19/Rev.1 & Rev.1/Add.1); agenda item 41.
*Meeting numbers.* GA 50th session: plenary 55, 56, 96.

*REFERENCES*

[1]YUN 1992, p. 142, GA dec. 46/472, 13 Apr. 1992. [2]YUN 1994, p. 249, GA res. 49/12 A, 9 Nov. 1994. [3]A/49/48/Add.1. [4]A/50/48/Rev.1 & Corr.1. [5]YUN 1994, p. 1412, GA res. 49/11, 9 Nov. 1994. [6]S/1995/827. [7]A/50/702-S/1995/900. [8]A/50/679. [9]S/PRST/1995/48. [10]YUN 1994, p. 250, GA res. 49/25, 2 Dec. 1994. [11]A/50/167. [12]A/50/174. [13]A/50/376. [14]A/50/406. [15]S/1995/702. [16]YUN 1994, p. 251, GA res. 49/30, 7 Dec. 1994. [17]A/50/332 & Corr.1.

PART TWO

# Regional questions and peace-keeping

Chapter I

# General aspects of peace-keeping operations

Over the course of 1995, a total of 20 UN peace-keeping operations were deployed worldwide. Four of those were new missions; another four completed their mandates, so that by year's end, 16 UN peace-keeping missions were operating. As a result of the termination of the UN Protection Force (UNPROFOR) in Bosnia and Herzegovina and the substantial reduction in the strength of the UN Confidence Restoration Operation (UNCRO) in Croatia, the number of military and civilian peace-keeping personnel under UN command fell from almost 73,000 as at 31 July to some 26,000 by the end of 1995. The cost of UN peace-keeping operations in 1995 totalled some $3.2 billion, while unpaid assessed contributions from Member States to the peace-keeping budget amounted to $3 billion as at 10 August, which exacerbated further the severe financial situation of the Organization (see PART SIX, Chapter II).

In January, the Secretary-General set forth additional recommendations for improving the UN peace-keeping capacity in his "Supplement to an Agenda for Peace". The position paper, provided on the occasion of the Organization's fiftieth anniversary, was welcomed by the Security Council. The Special Committee on Peace-keeping Operations made recommendations on various aspects of peace-keeping, which were endorsed by the Assembly in December. Both the Council and the Special Committee called for enhancing further stand-by arrangements between the UN and Member States for resources to be used in UN operations, so as to improve the Organization's rapid reaction capability, as well as for reinforcing cooperation in peace-keeping with regional organizations. The Security Council continued to review arrangements for consultations with troop-contributing countries.

During the year, the General Assembly considered various aspects of peace-keeping financing, including reimbursement for contingent-owned equipment, management of peace-keeping assets,

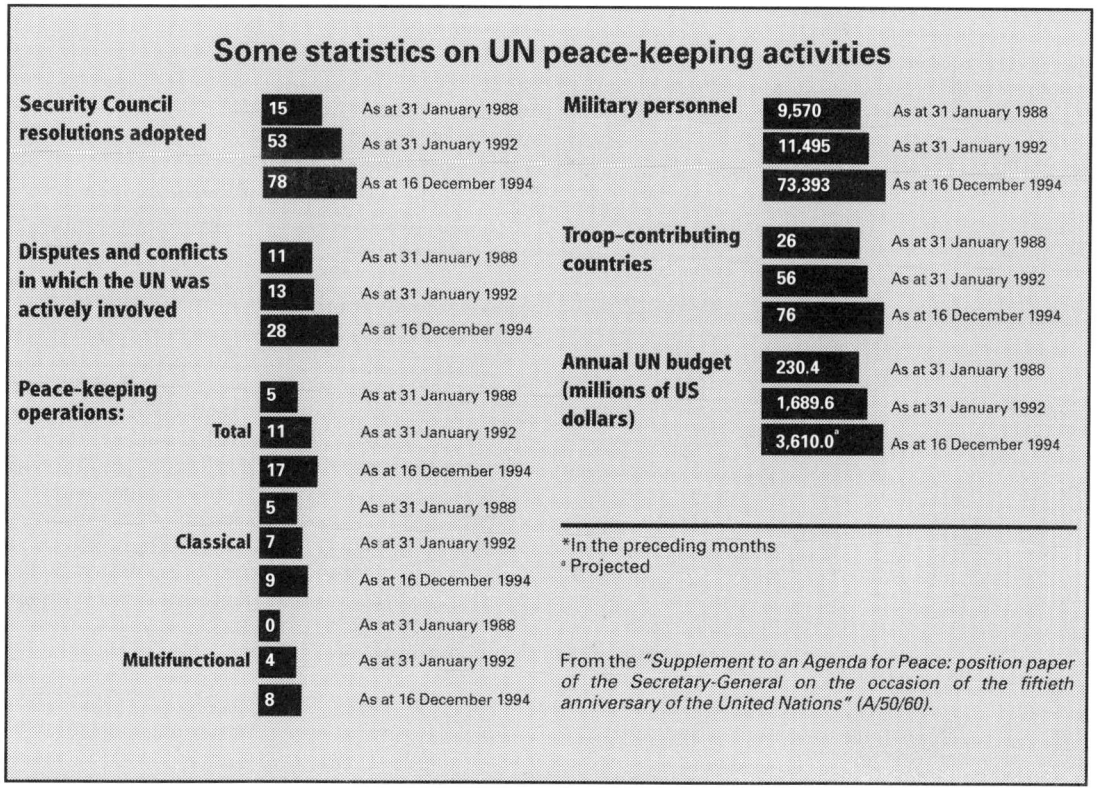

**Some statistics on UN peace-keeping activities**

| | | |
|---|---|---|
| **Security Council resolutions adopted** | 15 | As at 31 January 1988 |
| | 53 | As at 31 January 1992 |
| | 78 | As at 16 December 1994 |
| **Disputes and conflicts in which the UN was actively involved** | 11 | As at 31 January 1988 |
| | 13 | As at 31 January 1992 |
| | 28 | As at 16 December 1994 |
| **Peace-keeping operations:** Total | 5 | As at 31 January 1988 |
| | 11 | As at 31 January 1992 |
| | 17 | As at 16 December 1994 |
| Classical | 5 | As at 31 January 1988 |
| | 7 | As at 31 January 1992 |
| | 9 | As at 16 December 1994 |
| Multifunctional | 0 | As at 31 January 1988 |
| | 4 | As at 31 January 1992 |
| | 8 | As at 16 December 1994 |
| **Military personnel** | 9,570 | As at 31 January 1988 |
| | 11,495 | As at 31 January 1992 |
| | 73,393 | As at 16 December 1994 |
| **Troop-contributing countries** | 26 | As at 31 January 1988 |
| | 56 | As at 31 January 1992 |
| | 76 | As at 16 December 1994 |
| **Annual UN budget (millions of US dollars)** | 230.4 | As at 31 January 1988 |
| | 1,689.6 | As at 31 January 1992 |
| | 3,610.0* | As at 16 December 1994 |

\*In the preceding months
* Projected

From the *"Supplement to an Agenda for Peace: position paper of the Secretary-General on the occasion of the fiftieth anniversary of the United Nations" (A/50/60).*

procurement reform, entitlements of peace-keeping personnel, the support account for peace-keeping operations and the apportionment of costs among Member States.

## Review of peace-keeping operations

### Secretary-General's views

In his report on the work of the Organization,[1] issued on 22 August, the Secretary-General observed that peace-keeping remained a dynamic and demanding activity, responding to continuing turbulence in relations between States as well as to armed conflicts within State borders. As at 31 July, some 65,000 military personnel, 1,700 civilian police and 6,000 civilian staff were deployed in 16 operations, serving in conditions that ranged from relative stability to high danger. He noted that peace-keeping missions had multiplied in number and complexity in recent years and involved a wider spectrum of operations, from the monitoring of traditional cease-fires and control of buffer zones to assistance in the implementation of peace settlements and armed protection of humanitarian convoys. At the same time, where the climate was one of hostility and obstruction instead of cooperation and political will, peace-keeping came under heavy strains, making it necessary to rethink and readjust the measures taken or to terminate the mission. The Organization also continued to encounter grave difficulties in obtaining resources from Member States both in specialized and properly equipped military units and in adequate financing, which had led to delays in deployment of peace-keeping forces. Due to the shortfalls in the peace-keeping budget as a result of unpaid assessed contributions from Member States, the United Nations was able to continue peace-keeping operations only by delaying reimbursements to troop-contributing countries and payments owed for contingent-owned equipment.

The Secretary-General further described efforts to improve the Organization's peace-keeping capacity, including the establishment of a coordination framework among the UN Secretariat's Departments of Peace-keeping Operations, Political Affairs and Humanitarian Affairs (see PART ONE, Chapter I), and a system of stand-by arrangements—proposed in his 1992 report, "An Agenda for Peace''[2]—based on conditional offers by Member States of specified resources to be made available, within agreed response times, for UN peace-keeping operations. By the end of July, 46 States had confirmed their participation in stand-by arrangements and 13 were finalizing their offers. However, those commitments did not cover existing deficiencies in communications, multi-role logistics, health services, supply, engineering and transportation, nor did the system of stand-by arrangements ensure the reliability and speed of response required in emergency situations. While Member States possessed the necessary capabilities, the Secretary-General pointed out that there was a lack of will to make them available for the execution of Security Council mandates.

He also emphasized the importance of a public information component for the success of peace-keeping operations, stating that information requirements of recent missions were being examined at an early planning stage for inclusion in the proposed budget. Noting that there had been 456 fatalities among UN civilian personnel from 1991 to 1995, compared to 398 for the entire period between 1948 and 1990, the Secretary-General urged Governments to ensure the early entry into force of the Convention on the Safety of United Nations and Associated Personnel, adopted by the General Assembly in 1994.[3]

In January 1995, the Secretary-General issued a position paper entitled "Supplement to an Agenda for Peace",[4] in which he elaborated further on his 1992 proposals[2] for developing UN activities related to peace and security (see also PART ONE, Chapter I).

There had, he said, been dramatic changes in both the volume and the nature of UN activities in the field of peace and security since the end of the cold war. In January 1988, only five UN peace-keeping missions were operating; over the next seven years, another 21 were established. By 16 December 1994, 17 of them remained active.

Qualitative changes were even more significant than quantitative ones: of the five operations that existed in early 1988, all but one related to wars between States; of the 21 operations subsequently established, 13 related to conflicts within a State. Of the 11 missions between January 1992 and December 1994, all but two related to intra-State conflicts. The nature of peace-keeping also changed, in that UN operations, which had been largely military in character and confined to monitoring cease-fires and controlling buffer zones with the consent of the States involved, were increasingly mandated to undertake an unprecedented variety of functions: helping parties to a conflict implement a negotiated settlement and secure a post-conflict economic rehabilitation, as well as protecting humanitarian operations, often in a hostile environment. As a result, new and more comprehensive concepts to guide those activities, and their links with development work, were emerging and old concepts were being modified. In that regard, the Secretary-General set forth additional recommendations for improving the peace-keeping capacity of the United Nations (see below).

## Operations in 1995

On 8 February, the Security Council authorized the establishment of a UN Angola Verification Mission (UNAVEM III) with an enlarged mandate, to replace UNAVEM II, established in 1991,[5] whose mandate had expired on the same date. Under the supervision of the new Mission, progress was achieved in the disengagement of forces in Angola, and the parties to the conflict reached agreement on an accelerated timetable for the implementation of their peace accords. In August, the Mission's mandate was extended for an additional six months, until 8 February 1996.

The UN Operation in Somalia (UNOSOM II), launched in 1993,[6] officially ended on 31 March 1995, its withdrawal having been completed by 2 March. However, the situation in that country continued to be monitored by the UN from an office in Nairobi, Kenya (see next chapter).

On 31 March, the Security Council decided to establish three separate operations for the former Yugoslavia. It decided to extend the mandate of UNPROFOR within Bosnia and Herzegovina only and—for Croatia and for the former Yugoslav Republic of Macedonia—to incorporate elements of the former UNPROFOR into two new missions: the UN Confidence Restoration Operation (UNCRO) and the UN Preventive Deployment Force (UNPREDEP), respectively. In August, due to developments in Croatia, the Secretary-General recommended that the strength of UNCRO be reduced—from more than 14,000 to fewer than 2,500 troops by mid-November. In November, following the signing of the "Basic Agreement on the Region of Eastern Slavonia, Baranja and Western Sirmium" by the Croatian Government and local Serb representatives, the Security Council decided to terminate the UNCRO mandate after an interim period ending on 15 January 1996 or upon the Council's decision to deploy a transitional peace-keeping force to implement relevant provisions of the Basic Agreement. Also in November, the Council extended the mandate of UNPREDEP until 30 May 1996. On 20 December, with the transfer of authority to the multinational Implementation Force (IFOR) following the signing of a peace agreement for Bosnia and Herzegovina in Dayton, Ohio, United States, the mandate of UNPROFOR in Bosnia and Herzegovina was terminated. Also in December, the Security Council established a UN civilian police force, the International Police Task Force (IPTF), and a UN civilian office. Their purpose was to implement rele-

vant provisions of the Dayton Peace Agreement (see PART TWO, Chapter V).

The UN Mission in Haiti (UNMIH), which had been redeployed by December 1994,[7] assumed the responsibilities of the Multinational Force in Haiti (MNF) on 31 March 1995. The Mission provided a secure environment for the country's legislative and local elections held in June; on 31 July, its mandate was extended to the end of February 1996.

The UN Observer Mission in El Salvador (ONUSAL) completed its mandate at the end of April, as that country, with UN assistance, continued progressing towards establishing a democratic society based on the rule of law and respect for human rights. Following the withdrawal of ONUSAL, a small team of UN officials—the UN Mission in El Salvador (MINUSAL)—was set up to provide good offices and to verify implementation of the 1992 Peace Agreement[8] (see PART TWO, Chapter III).

In June, the Security Council renewed the mandate of the UN Assistance Mission for Rwanda (UNAMIR), established in 1993,[9] shifting its focus from a peace-keeping to a confidence-building role, and authorized a reduction of its force level. The Mission assisted Rwandan authorities in promoting national reconciliation and the return of refugees and in setting up a national police force; it was also responsible for the protection of humanitarian organizations, human rights observers and members of the International Tribunal for Rwanda. In December, UNAMIR's mandate was extended for a final period to end on 8 March 1996.

Efforts also continued to achieve a comprehensive settlement of the conflict in Liberia: the Security Council, noting the progress made, in September extended the UN Observer Mission in Liberia (UNOMIL) until 31 January 1996; in November, it adjusted the UNOMIL mandate, increasing its strength to 160 observers. As the UN Mission for the Referendum in Western Sahara (MINURSO) continued to assist in identifying and registering potential voters, the Council in September extended its mandate until 31 January 1996, but took note of the Secretary-General's intention to propose alternative options, including the possibility of the Mission's withdrawal, if before that date conditions were not in place for the start of a transitional period leading to the referendum (see PART ONE, Chapter III).

The UN Observer Mission in Georgia (UNOMIG) continued to monitor the implementation of the 1994 agreement on a cease-fire and separation of forces between the Government of Georgia and authorities of the Georgian region of Abkhazia;

in May, its mandate was extended until 12 January 1996. The UN Mission of Observers in Tajikistan (UNMOT) was extended in December until 15 June 1996; it was verifying the compliance of the parties to the conflict in that country with their 1994 cease-fire agreement (see PART TWO, Chapter IV).

The UN Iraq-Kuwait Observation Mission (UNIKOM) remained in operation during 1995 to monitor the demilitarized zone along the border between the two countries. The UN Military Observer Group in India and Pakistan (UNMOGIP), in place since 1949, continued its activities (see PART TWO, Chapter IV), as did other long-standing missions, including the UN Peace-keeping Force in Cyprus (UNFICYP) (see PART TWO, Chapter V) and three operations in the Middle East—the UN Truce Supervision Organization (UNTSO), the UN Interim Force in Lebanon (UNIFIL) and the UN Disengagement Observer Force (UNDOF) (see PART TWO, Chapter VI).

## Roster of 1995 operations

### UNTSO
*Established:* June 1948.
*Mandate:* To assist in supervising the observance of the truce in Palestine.
*Strength as at July 1995:* 220 military observers.

### UNMOGIP
*Established:* January 1949.
*Mandate:* To supervise the cease-fire between India and Pakistan in Jammu and Kashmir.
*Strength as at July 1995:* 40 military observers.

### UNFICYP
*Established:* March 1964.
*Mandate:* To prevent the recurrence of fighting between the two Cypriot communities.
*Strength as at July 1995:* 1,165 military personnel and 35 civilian police.

### UNDOF
*Established:* June 1974.
*Mandate:* To supervise the cease-fire between Israel and the Syrian Arab Republic and the disengagement of Israeli and Syrian forces in the Golan Heights.
*Strength as at July 1995:* 1,036 military personnel.

### UNIFIL
*Established:* March 1978.
*Mandate:* To confirm the withdrawal of Israeli forces from southern Lebanon, restore peace and security, and assist the Lebanese Government in ensuring the return of its effective authority in the area.
*Strength as at July 1995:* 4,963 military personnel.

### UNIKOM
*Established:* April 1991.
*Mandate:* To monitor the demilitarized zone along the border between Iraq and Kuwait.
*Strength as at July 1995:* 859 military personnel, 243 military observers.

### MINURSO
*Established:* April 1991.
*Mandate:* To monitor and verify the implementation of a settlement plan for Western Sahara and assist in the holding of a referendum in the Territory.
*Strength as at July 1995:* 48 military personnel, 236 military observers, 113 civilian police.

### UNAVEM II
*Established:* May 1991.
*Terminated:* February 1995.
*Mandate:* To verify cease-fire arrangements and assist the parties to the conflict in restoring peace in Angola.
*Strength as at January 1995:* 171 military observers, 122 civilian police.

### UNAVEM III
*Established:* February 1995.
*Mandate:* To assist in national reconciliation and restoration of peace, monitor the cease-fire and the disengagement and demobilization of forces as well as the disarming of civilians, coordinate humanitarian activities and verify the electoral process.
*Strength as at July 1995:* 3,014 military personnel, 333 military observers, 207 civilian police.

### ONUSAL
*Established:* May 1991.
*Terminated:* April 1995.
*Mandate:* To verify implementation of peace agreements between the parties to the conflict in El Salvador.
*Strength as at March 1995:* 3 military observers, 32 civilian police.

### UNPROFOR
*Established:* February 1992.
*Reconfigured:* March 1995.
*Terminated:* December 1995.
*Mandate:* To assist in efforts for a peace settlement in Bosnia and Herzegovina, secure the delivery of humanitarian assistance and support humanitarian relief, provide protection to "safe areas" and monitor the ban on military flights; to create conditions of peace and security required for negotiating an overall settlement and ensure a demilitarization process in UN Protected Areas in Croatia; and to monitor border areas in the former Yugoslav Republic of Macedonia.

(Beginning on 31 March 1995, the UNPROFOR mandate was continued for Bosnia and Herzegovina only.)
*Strength as at July 1995:* 27,738 military personnel, 288 military observers, 18 civilian police.

## UNCRO

*Established:* March 1995.
*Mandate:* To facilitate implementation of cease-fire and economic agreements between the Government of Croatia and local Serb authorities as well as the delivery of humanitarian assistance, monitor the demilitarization of the Prevlaka peninsula and assist in controlling the movement of military personnel, equipment, supplies and weapons across Croatian borders.
*Strength as at July 1995:* 13,683 military personnel, 347 military observers, 435 civilian police.

## UNPREDEP

*Established:* March 1995.
*Mandate:* To monitor border areas in the former Yugoslav Republic of Macedonia.
*Strength as at July 1995:* 1,107 military personnel, 25 military observers, 26 civilian police.

## UNOSOM II

*Established:* March 1993.
*Terminated:* March 1995.
*Mandate:* To monitor the cessation of hostilities in Somalia and prevent any resumption of violence, maintain control of heavy weapons of the Somali factions and seize small arms of unauthorized armed elements, secure the delivery of humanitarian assistance, carry out a mine-clearing programme, assist in the repatriation of refugees and protect UN and associated personnel, installations and equipment.
*Strength as at February 1995:* 7,956 military personnel.

## UNOMIG

*Established:* August 1993.
*Mandate:* To verify compliance with a cease-fire agreement between the parties to the conflict in Georgia and investigate cease-fire violations; expanded in 1994 to include monitoring the implementation of an agreement on a cease-fire and separation of forces and observing the operation of a multinational peace-keeping force.
*Strength as at July 1995:* 134 military observers.

## UNMIH

*Established:* September 1993.
*Mandate:* To provide non-combat military training to the armed forces and carry out engineering and medical assistance projects; revised in 1994 to include assistance to the Government of Haiti in sustaining a secure and stable environment, modern-izing the armed forces, creating a separate police force and organizing legislative elections.
*Strength as at July 1995:* 5,850 military personnel, 841 civilian police.

## UNOMIL

*Established:* September 1993.
*Mandate:* To investigate cease-fire violations and monitor compliance with a peace agreement between the parties to the conflict in Liberia, verify the election process, assist in coordinating humanitarian activities and develop a plan for the demobilization of combatants; revised in 1995 to include monitoring the disengagement of forces, disarmament and observance of the arms embargo and assisting with demobilization programmes.
*Strength as at July 1995:* 7 military personnel, 62 military observers.

## UNAMIR

*Established:* October 1993.
*Mandate:* To monitor observance of a cease-fire agreement between the parties to the conflict in Rwanda as well as the security situation and repatriation of refugees, and to assist with mine clearance and coordination of humanitarian activities; adjusted in 1994 to include intermediary functions in securing a cease-fire agreement, assistance in the resumption of humanitarian relief operations and monitoring of developments in the country; adjusted in 1995 to include good offices in achieving national reconciliation, assistance to the Government in facilitating the return of refugees and training a national police force, support for the provision of humanitarian aid and contribution to the security of UN activities.
*Strength as at July 1995:* 3,792 military personnel, 306 military observers, 59 civilian police.

## UNMOT

*Established:* December 1994.
*Mandate:* To assist in monitoring a temporary cease-fire agreement between the parties to the conflict in Tajikistan.
*Strength as at July 1995:* 39 military observers.

## IPTF

*Established:* December 1995.
*Mandate:* To monitor and facilitate law enforcement activities in Bosnia and Herzegovina, train and assist law enforcement personnel in carrying out their responsibilities, advise government authorities on the organization of civilian law enforcement agencies, and assess threats to public order and the agencies' capability to deal with such threats.
*Authorized strength:* 1,721 civilian police monitors.

## Improving UN peace-keeping capacity

In the "Supplement to an Agenda for Peace",[4] the Secretary-General noted that peace-keeping had become both more complex and more expensive as the UN had to deal with an increasing number of conflicts both between and within States, often accompanied by the collapse of government authority. In that regard, he emphasized that respect for certain basic principles, such as the consent of the parties, impartiality and the non-use of force except in self-defence, was essential to the success of UN operations. However, some new aspects of recent peace-keeping mandates—protection of humanitarian operations during continuing warfare, protection of civilian populations in designated safe areas, and pressure on the parties to achieve national reconciliation at a pace faster than they were ready to accept—necessitated deviation from one or another of those principles. Coupled with insufficient military capabilities, such deviation undermined the viability of the mission and endangered its personnel.

The Secretary-General further underscored the need to distinguish between three levels of authority in peace-keeping—overall political direction of the Security Council, executive direction and command by the Secretary-General, and command in the field entrusted to the chief of mission. He cautioned against an increasing tendency for the Security Council to micro-manage operations, and also warned against any attempt by troop-contributing Governments to provide guidance, let alone give orders, to their contingents on operational matters, the unity of command being another important principle of peace-keeping. To avoid such incidents, steps were being taken to improve procedures for consultations with the Council and troop-contributing States to keep them informed of developments in the field. As for the availability of troops and equipment, which had palpably declined as measured against the Organization's requirements, efforts had been made to expand and refine stand-by arrangements between the UN and Member States; however, such arrangements did not guarantee that troops would actually be provided for a specific operation.

At the same time, peace-keeping was particularly affected by the financial crisis of the United Nations (see PART SIX, Chapter II), as the shortage of funds for the start-up of missions and for the recruitment and training of personnel imposed severe constraints on the Organization's ability to deploy newly approved operations. In that regard, it was advisable to establish the availability of necessary troops and equipment before the decision to create a new mission or assign a new task to an existing one.

The Secretary-General concluded that the UN had to give serious thought to the idea of a rapid reaction force, to serve as the Security Council's strategic reserve for deployment in emergency situations. He also proposed that a reserve stock of standard peace-keeping equipment be set up, as a possible measure to address the growing problem of inadequately equipped and trained troops offered for operations. The public information capacity of missions, which had proved to be a critical factor in an operation's success, also needed to be strengthened, with a mission's information requirements to be identified at an early planning stage and included in the proposed budget.

SECURITY COUNCIL ACTION

The Security Council, in a 22 February statement[10] by its President, welcomed the Secretary-General's analysis regarding peace-keeping operations and reiterated the basic principles of peace-keeping identified in the Supplement. The Council underlined the need to conduct operations with a clearly defined mandate, command structure and time-frame and secure financing, and stressed the importance of providing the fullest possible information concerning missions to the Council and to troop contributors. The Secretary-General was encouraged to continue his study of options for improving the capacity for rapid deployment and reinforcement of UN operations and to take further steps to enhance the existing stand-by arrangements, including the establishment of a comprehensive database covering civilian and military resources, as well as to consider ways of addressing the requirements of contingents in need of additional equipment or training.

The Council called on Member States to participate in stand-by arrangements and urged them to honour their financial obligations to the UN, which was of crucial importance to peace-keeping. At the same time, it emphasized the continuing necessity for careful control of peace-keeping costs and for the most efficient use of peace-keeping funds. The Security Council then invited States to present further reflections on UN operations and on ways of improving its capacity for rapid deployment.

**Report of the Special Committee.** As requested by the General Assembly in 1994,[11] the Special Committee on Peace-keeping Operations continued a comprehensive review of the whole question of peace-keeping operations in all their aspects. In 1995, it held eight meetings in New York between 10 April and 12 May. Committee deliberations were summarized in its report[12] to the Assembly, issued on 22 June.

The Special Committee noted the qualitative and quantitative changes in peace-keeping operations and the new challenges facing them, and considered that it was time to evaluate the experiences gained and to draw appropriate lessons from both successes and setbacks. It stressed that the principles and purposes of the UN Charter should be strictly observed and that respect for the principles of sovereignty, territorial integrity and political independence of States and non-intervention in matters essentially within the domestic jurisdiction of any State was crucial to common efforts, including peace-keeping. The Committee concurred with the Secretary-General's observation in the "Supplement to an Agenda for Peace" that basic principles of peace-keeping should be respected. It welcomed the view of the Security Council expressed in its President's statement on the Supplement and underscored the importance of factors to be taken into account when considering the establishment of peace-keeping operations, listed in a 1994 statement[13] by the Council President. It also emphasized the need to ensure congruence between mandates, resources and objectives in formulating and implementing peace-keeping mandates.

The Committee welcomed the Secretary-General's 1994 report on command and control of UN operations[14] and recommended that a Special Representative of the Secretary-General be appointed for larger operations, with authority over all components, so as to coordinate their activities at all levels. The need to enhance cooperation between peace-keeping missions and other related UN activities was stressed, and the Secretary-General was requested to ensure cooperation with other agencies of the UN system. Noting the importance of the unity of command and control, the Special Committee considered it useful to reach an agreed definition of the different kinds of command relationships applicable to peace-keeping operations. It also believed it necessary to delegate to UN missions in the field the appropriate financial and administrative autonomy, while strengthening measures relating to responsibility and accountability.

The Secretariat was urged to continue to improve the safety and security environment for peace-keepers and to ensure their physical well-being, as well as to assure appropriate protection for the information utilized by peace-keeping operations, including through the training of personnel responsible for managing such information. The Secretary-General was encouraged to continue strengthening the Department of Peace-keeping Operations (DPKO) and the Secretariat's capacity for the effective planning, organization, coordination and management of UN missions. In that regard, the Special Committee welcomed the development of the capacity for operational predeployment planning of UN missions, through the dispatch of a DPKO team. It also welcomed the establishment of the UN Office of Internal Oversight Services and urged the Secretary-General to assign a qualified representative of that Office to each large operation, or a visiting representative in the case of smaller missions.

The Committee called for the widest possible participation of Member States in peace-keeping operations as well as for the early identification of potential troop contributors and their involvement in the planning process. It reiterated its request to the Secretary-General to strengthen the civilian police unit within DPKO, and made recommendations concerning the training of peace-keeping personnel, an effective public information capacity of UN missions, and the availability of financial resources. Other recommendations dealt with consultations with troop-contributing countries, rapid deployment and stand-by arrangements, cooperation with regional organizations, and evaluation of operations (see below, under relevant subject headings).

**JIU reports.**    By notes of 24 October[15] and 14 November,[16] the Secretary-General transmitted to the General Assembly reports of the Joint Inspection Unit (JIU) on the relationship between humanitarian assistance and peace-keeping operations and on the military component of peace-keeping operations. The November note contained recommendations on command and control of operations, the decision-making process and consultations concerning peace-keeping, a UN rapid reaction force and capability, stand-by arrangements, the relationship with regional organizations and arrangements, safety of personnel, and the Secretariat's planning and management capacity.

**Communication.**   On 11 September,[17] Austria transmitted recommendations adopted by the Conference on the Preparation of the Civilian Personnel of UN Peace-keeping Operations (Schlaining, Austria, 1-3 July), organized by Austria as a contribution to the observance of the UN fiftieth anniversary.

## Stand-by arrangements

In 1995, the Special Committee on Peace-keeping Operations expressed deep concern at continuing and protracted delays between the establishment of peace-keeping mandates and the deployment of missions, and reaffirmed the need to improve the UN rapid-response ability. Noting that the Secretary-General's proposal for a rapid reaction force had raised a variety of complex political, legal and financial issues, the Committee recommended that priority be given to reinforcing the system of stand-by arrangements, which should be extended to headquarters components, transport capacity and civilian police personnel. Member States were invited to identify elements capable of rapid deployment and to clarify their offers, including in terms of volume and the time needed for deployment. The Secretary-General was asked to develop a rapidly deployable head-quarters team and to examine the question of establishing additional logistics bases, possibly on a regional basis. He was also requested to consider ways of coordinating arrangements for the storage and maintenance of equipment between operations.

**Report of the Secretary-General.** In response to a 1994 Security Council request,[18] the Secretary-General on 10 November 1995 reported[19] on the current status of stand-by arrangements. Since the launch of that initiative in 1993, the Secretariat had been in regular contact with 80 Governments and its teams had visited 57 other countries. As at 31 October, 47 Member States had confirmed their willingness to provide stand-by resources totalling 55,000 personnel, up from 21 States in June 1994. Of the 47 Governments, some 30 had provided information on specific capabilities and two—Denmark and Jordan—formalized their stand-by arrangements through a memorandum of understanding. However, as the bulk of resources consisted of infantry, there was a need to complement them with necessary logistic support in such areas as communications, multi-role logistics, transport, health services, engineering, mine-clearing and transport utility aircraft. As most fully equipped troops were provided by members of the Group of Western European and Other States, the Secretariat continued to seek the broadest possible participation by Member States as well as a proper mix of troops and supporting units.

To facilitate the planning and preparation process, the Secretariat defined standard components or "building blocks" for constructing various types of operations. Those included: headquarters support units, infantry battalions, civilian police, communications units, air services, engineer support, health services, multi-role logistic units, transportation, maintenance, supply, movement control, and food and catering services. The Secretariat also sought to expand its database with detailed information from participating Governments, so it could determine in advance the requirements of peace-keeping forces and individual units. Since few Governments were able to adhere to the preferred response time for confirmed stand-by resources—defined as the period between the request for resources and when resources were ready for air/sealift to the mission area—the Secretariat had begun to register those periods according to the declared individual capacities of Member States, which varied from 7 to more than 90 days. That would facilitate plans for deployment of units with longer response times in later stages of an operation.

The Secretary-General concluded that the UN was currently far from having a rapid reaction capability, and that the issue should continue to be addressed by both Member States and the Secretariat.

SECURITY COUNCIL ACTION

On 19 December, the President of the Security Council made the following statement[20] on behalf of Council members:

The Security Council has noted with interest and appreciation the report of the Secretary-General of 10 November 1995 on stand-by arrangements for peace-keeping operations. It recalls earlier statements by the President of the Security Council on this subject and strongly supports the efforts of the Secretary-General to enhance the capacity of the United Nations for the planning, rapid deployment and reinforcement and logistical support of peace-keeping operations.

The Security Council encourages Member States not yet doing so to participate in the stand-by arrangements. It invites them, and those States already participating in the arrangements, to provide information in as detailed a manner as possible on those elements which they are ready to make available to the United Nations. It also invites them to identify components, such as logistic support elements and sea/airlift resources, presently underrepresented in the arrangement. In this context the Security Council welcomes the initiative undertaken by the Secretariat for the creation of a stand-by Headquarters component within the Mission Planning Service of the Department of Peace-keeping Operations. The Security Council also joins with the Secretary-General in suggesting the establishment of partnerships between those troop-contributing countries that need equipment for units that may be provided to the United Nations and those Governments ready to provide such equipment and other support.

The Security Council looks forward to further reports from the Secretary-General on the progress of the stand-by arrangements initiative and undertakes to keep the matter under review.

*Meeting number:* SC 3609.

## Consultations with troop contributors

The Special Committee in 1995 welcomed the new arrangements for consultation and exchanges of information with troop-contributing countries, as set out in a 1994 statement[21] by the Security Council President. The Committee stressed that consultations should be held before the Council decided on the mandate of any particular mission and sufficiently in advance of decisions affecting existing operations. It encouraged the Secretary-General to transmit regular situation reports on all peace-keeping missions to troop contributors, Council members and, where possible, other Member States.

SECURITY COUNCIL CONSIDERATION

On 8 December,[22] a number of Member States requested that the Council meet to consider further measures for enhancing arrangements for consultations with troop-contributing countries. On 20 December, the Security Council convened to hear the views of its members and of other Member States on the Council agenda item, "An agenda for peace: peace-keeping". At the meeting's conclusion, the Council President said those views would be taken into account when the Council gave further consideration to the question of consultations with troop contributors.

### Cooperation with regional organizations

The Special Committee, at its 1995 session, encouraged the strengthening of cooperation between the UN and regional organizations in order to enhance the rapid reaction capability of the international community, and stressed the importance of the 1994 Declaration on the Enhancement of Cooperation between the United Nations and Regional Arrangements or Agencies in the Maintenance of International Peace and Security.[23] The Committee invited the Secretary-General to develop proposals for improving the capacity of the Organization to respond to emergency needs for conflict prevention and peace-keeping in Africa, in particular through cooperation with the Organization of African Unity (OAU) and subregional organizations.

The Security Council, in a 22 February statement by its President[10] on the Secretary-General's Supplement to an Agenda for Peace, welcomed his willingness to assist regional organizations and arrangements in developing a capacity for preventive action, peacemaking and, where appropriate, peace-keeping, and drew particular attention in that regard to the needs of Africa.

In response to those requests, the Secretary-General on 1 November reported[24] on improving preparedness for conflict prevention and peace-keeping in Africa (see also PART ONE, Chapter I). He pointed out that the implementation of peace-keeping mandates in the region was affected by a lack of experienced personnel, insufficient material resources and the slow deployment of troops and equipment, and that any effort to strengthen the UN peace-keeping capacity should address those constraints. In that regard, he proposed to give priority to enhancing African participation in the system of stand-by arrangements; to share information on that participation with OAU, subject to the agreement of the States concerned; to compile a list of the specialized and heavy equipment needs of African participants; and to promote, on the basis of that information, bilateral "partnerships" among nations with complementary strengths, under which one country would make available the necessary troops while another would provide the required equipment. The Secretary-General noted that 10 African States had already agreed to participate in the system and

that consultations on the subject had been held with other Governments in the region.

The report further reviewed issues relating to the training of personnel and to the planning and financing of operations. Among suggested measures were: a distribution campaign of UN peace-keeping training materials; regional training workshops and seminars; and joint peace-keeping exercises for key officers and, in the longer term, units of African contingents participating in stand-by arrangements. As for the financial aspects of enhancing preparedness for peace-keeping in Africa, the Secretary-General proposed the idea of "partnerships" also in the form of bilateral assistance, with no direct cost to the UN, which could be coordinated within the framework of stand-by arrangements. He observed that the Organization could assist in planning and evaluating logistic and financial requirements of approved regional or subregional peace-keeping operations and that the UN and OAU could consider co-deployment of their operations, as in Liberia.

By a 17 October note,[25] the Secretary-General transmitted to the General Assembly a JIU report on sharing responsibilities in peace-keeping between the UN and regional organizations.

### Evaluation of peace-keeping operations

In accordance with a 1994 Assembly resolution,[26] the Secretary-General, by a 17 March note,[27] transmitted the final report of the Office of Internal Oversight Services (OIOS) on an in-depth evaluation of the start-up phase of peace-keeping operations.

The report contained findings and recommendations on the Organization's capacity to provide overall direction and coordination for the start-up of missions, carry out preparations during the negotiation phase, learn from experience, allocate responsibility for support functions, and develop and maintain a ready capacity to act. It reviewed the status of such capacity in relation to substantive elements of complex missions, including information, electoral, repatriation, human rights, civilian police and military components, as well as in relation to support functions such as planning, financing, staffing, logistics, procurement and training. The report also examined humanitarian and civil administration aspects of peace-keeping operations and provided recommendations dealing with responsibility centres, doctrine, early warning, mobilization of international emergency response, coordination of humanitarian assistance, and civil administration.

The Special Committee on Peace-keeping Operations welcomed the OIOS final report and underlined the importance of developing an institutionalized and systematic mechanism for analysis of the lessons to be drawn from each operation. In that regard, the Committee called on the Secretary-General to ensure that both his Special Representative and the mission commander report to him at the end of their tour or the mandate, and that Member States be briefed on completed operations.

The Committee for Programme and Coordination (CPC) considered the OIOS final report at its 1995 session.[28] The Committee endorsed the recommendations dealing with mission assessment and the establishment of a documentation centre by DPKO; assignment of responsibilities for support functions to various units within DPKO and the Department of Administration and Management; coordination of peace-keeping readiness activities outside DPKO; civilian police and military components; planning for stand-by arrangements; elaboration of peace-keeping planning guidelines; a strategic plan for developing a ready capacity to act within the Secretariat; standard planning procedures for the start-up phase; development of a prototype of the analytical peace-keeping budgeting system; incorporation of provisions for security requirements into mission plans and budgets and security-related training of civilian personnel; revision of manuals on field administration, operational support and procurement; and OIOS review of compliance with recommendations on logistics and procurement issues.

CPC also endorsed the recommendations to draw up training guidelines and a peace-keeping training plan for military and civilian personnel from the Secretariat, but felt that the need to prepare similar guidelines for personnel contributed by other organizations required further examination. It recognized the importance of information in peace-keeping operations and recommended that the Secretary-General take necessary measures to provide adequate support in that area. The Committee concluded that the remaining five recommendations needed to be examined further by relevant intergovernmental bodies.

By a 31 August note,[29] the Secretary-General transmitted to the General Assembly an OIOS report on the review of the DPKO Field Administration and Logistics Division.

**GENERAL ASSEMBLY ACTION**

On 6 December, the General Assembly adopted **resolution 50/30**.

**Comprehensive review of the whole question of peace-keeping operations in all their aspects**

*The General Assembly,*

*Recalling* its resolution 2006(XIX) of 18 February 1965 and all other relevant resolutions,

*Recalling in particular* its resolution 49/37 of 9 December 1994,

*Affirming,* on the occasion of the fiftieth anniversary of the United Nations, that the efforts of the United Nations in the peaceful settlement of disputes, including through its peace-keeping operations, are indispensable,

*Stressing* the important role played by peace-keeping operations in maintaining international peace and security, and recognizing the need to ensure the safety of United Nations peace-keepers,

*Taking note* of the section on peace-keeping of the position paper of the Secretary-General, "Supplement to an Agenda for Peace", and of the statement by the President of the Security Council of 22 February 1995,

*Taking note also* of the report of the Secretary-General on the work of the Organization,

*Welcoming* the report of the Secretary-General on the command and control of United Nations peace-keeping operations,

*Taking note further* of the report of the Secretary-General on improving preparedness for conflict prevention and peace-keeping in Africa and the recommendations therein, which should be considered further in consultation with the Organization of African Unity,

*Noting* the widespread interest in contributing to the work of the Special Committee on Peace-keeping Operations expressed by many Member States, including troop-contributing countries,

*Bearing in mind* the continuous necessity of strengthening the effectiveness of the work of the Committee,

*Convinced* of the need for the United Nations to continue to improve its capabilities in the field of peace-keeping and to enhance the effective and efficient deployment of its peace-keeping missions,

*Taking note* in this regard of the various proposals and views regarding United Nations peace-keeping put forward during the Special Commemorative Meeting and the general debate at the present session of the General Assembly,

1. *Welcomes* the report of the Special Committee on Peace-keeping Operations;

2. *Endorses* the proposals, recommendations and conclusions of the Committee contained in paragraphs 35 to 93 of its report;

3. *Urges* Member States, the Secretariat and relevant organs of the United Nations to take all necessary steps to implement the proposals, recommendations and conclusions of the Committee;

4. *Recommends* that, should any of the proposals contained in the present resolution result in budgetary implications for the bienniums 1994-1995 and 1996-1997, such additional costs be accommodated within the appropriation levels approved by the General Assembly for those bienniums, in accordance with the Financial Regulations and Rules of the Organization;

5. *Decides* that the Special Committee, in accordance with its mandate, should continue its efforts for a comprehensive review of the whole question of peace-keeping operations in all their aspects; the Special Committee should review the implementation of its previous proposals and consider new proposals so as to enhance the capacity of the United Nations to fulfil its responsibilities in this field;

6. *Requests* the Committee to consider the expansion of its membership, analysing all available options, invites its chairman to consult with interested States and requests the Committee to submit specific recommendations to the General Assembly at its fifty-first session;

7. *Also requests* the Special Committee to submit a report on its work to the General Assembly at its fifty-first session;

8. *Decides* to include in the provisional agenda of its fifty-first session the item entitled "Comprehensive re-

view of the whole question of peace-keeping operations in all their aspects''.

General Assembly resolution 50/30

6 December 1995    Meeting 82    Adopted without vote

Approved by Fourth Committee (A/50/607) without vote, 16 November (meeting 23); 6-nation draft (A/C.4/50/L.10), orally revised; agenda item 86.
*Sponsors:* Argentina, Canada, Egypt, Japan, Nigeria, Poland.
*Meeting numbers.* GA 50th session: 4th Committee 19-23; plenary 82.

### REFERENCES

[1]A/50/1. [2]YUN 1992, p. 35. [3]YUN 1994, p. 1289, GA res. 49/59, annex, 9 Dec. 1994. [4]A/50/60-S/1995/1. [5]YUN 1991, p. 127, SC res. 696(1991), 30 May 1991. [6]YUN 1993, p. 290, SC res. 814(1993), 26 Mar. 1993. [7]YUN 1994, p. 431, SC res. 964(1994), 29 Nov. 1994. [8]YUN 1992, p. 222. [9]YUN 1993, p. 285, SC res. 872(1993), 5 Oct. 1993. [10]S/PRST/1995/9. [11]YUN 1994, p. 113, GA res. 49/37, 9 Dec. 1994. [12]A/50/230. [13]YUN 1994, p. 117. [14]Ibid., p. 121. [15]A/50/572. [16]A/50/576. [17]A/50/437. [18]YUN 1994, p. 119. [19]S/1995/943. [20]S/PRST/1995/61. [21]YUN 1994, p. 120. [22]S/1995/1025. [23]YUN 1994, p. 125, GA res. 49/57, annex, 9 Dec. 1994. [24]A/50/711-S/1995/911. [25]A/50/571. [26]YUN 1994, p. 1362, GA res. 48/218 B, 29 July 1994. [27]E/AC.51/1995/2 & Corr.1. [28]A/50/16. [29]A/49/959.

# Financing of peace-keeping operations

In 1995, the cost of peace-keeping operations totalled an estimated $3.233 billion, of which $3.2 billion was financed from the special account and $33 million from the regular UN budget. The cost of activities funded from the support account for peace-keeping operations stood at an additional $33.3 million.

At the same time, unpaid assessed contributions from Member States to the peace-keeping budget amounted to $3 billion as at 10 August. To continue its peace-keeping operations, the Organization had to delay reimbursements to troop-contributing countries and payments owed for contingent-owned equipment, with the debt estimated to have reached the $1 billion mark by the end of the year.

During the year, the General Assembly considered various aspects of peace-keeping financing, including reimbursement for contingent-owned equipment, management of peace-keeping assets, procurement reform, entitlements of peace-keeping personnel, the support account and the apportionment of costs among Member States. The Assembly placed Palau in group D and reclassified Belarus and Portugal for the apportionment of peace-keeping expenses. Issues related to the peace-keeping scale of assessments were also discussed by the Assembly's High-level Open-ended Working Group on the Financial Situation of the United Nations (see PART SIX, Chapter II).

## Review of administrative and budgetary aspects

Further to its 1994 resolution,[1] the General Assembly, at its resumed forty-ninth session in 1995, took up the question of administrative and budgetary aspects of the financing of peace-keeping operations.

**GENERAL ASSEMBLY ACTION (March)**

On 31 March, the Assembly adopted **resolution 49/233 B**.

**Administrative and budgetary aspects of the financing of the United Nations peace-keeping operations**
*The General Assembly*

I

*Survey mission handbook*
*Endorses* the intention of the Secretariat to complete development of a survey mission handbook as described in paragraphs 8 and 9 of the report of the Secretary-General;

II

*Funding of public information activities*
*Endorses* the proposal of the Secretary-General and requests the Committee on Information to review the policy of the Secretariat on the dissemination of information related to peace-keeping;

III

*United Nations Joint Staff Pension Fund*
*Requests* the Secretary-General to submit to the General Assembly the views of the United Nations Joint Staff Pension Board on the implications for the United Nations Joint Staff Pension Fund of the participation in the Fund of the different categories of civilian staff in peace-keeping operations;

IV

*Provision of services to troops*
*Endorses* the comments of the Secretary-General with regard to the provision, through local contractors, of services to troops;

V

*Portable and temporary accommodation*
*Endorses* the comments of the Secretary-General;

VI

*Operational support manual*
*Endorses* the intention of the Secretariat to complete development of an operational support manual.

General Assembly resolution 49/233 B

31 March 1995    Meeting 99    Adopted without vote

Approved by Fifth Committee (A/49/803/Add.2) without vote, 17 March (meeting 46); draft by Chairman (A/C.5/49/L.36), based on informal consultations; agenda item 132 (a).

Also in March, the Assembly adopted **decision 49/478 A**.

**Administrative and budgetary aspects of the financing of the United Nations peace-keeping perations: financing of the United Nations peace-keeping operations**

At its 99th plenary meeting, on 31 March 1995, the General Assembly, on the recommendation of the Fifth Committee:

(a) Decided that the financial period and the budgetary cycle referred to in section I of General Assembly resolution 49/233 A of 23 December 1994 should be interpreted as indicated in the annex to the present decision, and requested the Advisory Committee on Administrative and Budgetary Questions and the Secretary-General to arrange their work programmes accordingly;

*(b)* Requested the Secretary-General to submit to the General Assembly on a semi-annual basis a report containing consolidated information on the application of section IV of resolution 49/233 A.

## ANNEX

**Preparation, presentation and consideration of peace-keeping budgets and performance reports**

*Resolution 49/233 A, section I\**
(example: 1995/1996)

*Budgets reviewed on an annual basis*

| | July | October | November | January | May | June |
|---|---|---|---|---|---|---|
| Secretariat action | Open account<br>Prepare FPR<br>(July 1994-<br>June 1995) | | Prepare budget<br>(July 1996-<br>June 1997) | Prepare LFD<br>(July-December<br>1995) | | Close account |
| Presentation | | | FPR (July 1994-<br>June 1995) | | LFD (July-<br>December<br>1995)<br><br>Budget<br>(July 1996-<br>June 1997) | |
| Consideration | | | | | FPR (July 1994-<br>June 1995)<br>LFD (July-<br>December<br>1995)<br>Budget<br>(July 1966-<br>June 1997) | |

*Budgets reviewed on a semi-annual basis*

| | July | October | November | January | May | June |
|---|---|---|---|---|---|---|
| Secretariat action | Open account<br><br>Prepare FPR<br>(July 1994-<br>June 1995) | Revise budget<br>(July 1995-<br>June 1996) | Prepare budget<br>(July 1996-<br>June 1997) | Prepare LFD<br>(July-December<br>1995) | | Close account |
| Consideration | | | FPR (July 1994-<br>June 1995)<br>Revised budget<br>(July 1995-<br>June 1996) | | LFD (July-<br>December 1995)<br>Budget<br>(July 1996-<br>June 1997) | |

\*FPR = Final performance report.

LFD = Latest financial data ("such supplementary, up-to-date . . . performance data . . . as are available" (resolution 49/233 A, sect. I, para. 6)).

**General Assembly decision 49/478 A**

**Adopted without vote**

Approved by Fifth Committee (A/49/803/Add.3) without vote, 17 March (meeting 46); draft by Chairman (A/C.5/49/L.37), based on informal consultations; agenda item 132 (a).

**Report of the Secretary-General.** In response to a 1994 Assembly request for a sample budget of a single peace-keeping operation,[1] the Secretary-General on 1 August 1995 submitted a mock-up budget[2] of the UN peace-keeping activities in the former Yugoslavia, including UNPROFOR, UNCRO, UNPREDEP and the UN Peace Forces (UNPF) headquarters that reflected the modifications proposed by the Secretary-General in 1994.[3] It included a month-by-month phasing-in of military and civilian personnel; a monthly phased budget showing the planned expenditure; a table of statistics highlighting deviations from standard interrelationships between staffing, vehicles, communications equipment and computers; and an organizational chart of all major components or divisions, functions and locations.

The mock-up budget also included a review of: the political mandate of the missions; their operational plan and requirements; status of assessed contributions, voluntary contributions and trust funds; financial administration from 12 January 1992 to 30 June 1995; cost estimates from 1 July 1995 to 30 June 1996; staffing requirements; status of reimbursement to troop-contributing Governments; observations and comments on previous recommendations of the Advisory Committee on Administrative and Budgetary Questions (ACABQ); status-of-forces agreements with host countries; and recommendations for action by the General Assembly.

**ACABQ recommendations.** The Advisory Committee, having considered the mock-up budget and additional information from the Controller and other representatives of the Secretary-General, recommended that future budgets should include: an explanation of the linkage between the political mandate of a mission and its operational requirements; a distinction between essential and support activities; full justification of resource requirements; a detailed description and cost estimates of activities financed from voluntary contributions and other sources; a comprehensive review of the cash situation, including unliquidated obligations; administrative and financial implications resulting from status-of-forces agreements; detailed information on the equipment to be transferred from UN stockpiles and from other operations; and information on budget performance for previous periods and the latest available financial data for the period in progress.

The Committee's recommendations were provided in its 1 December report[4] to the General Assembly.

GENERAL ASSEMBLY ACTION (December)

By **decision 50/451 A** of 22 December, the Assembly took note of the Secretary-General's note on the mock-up budget and endorsed ACABQ's observations and recommendations.

**JIU report.** By a 14 November note,[5] the Secretary-General transmitted to the Assembly a JIU report on the military component of UN peace-keeping operations, containing recommendations on, *inter alia*, the rotation of troops, death and disability benefits, and reimbursement for and procurement of equipment.

## Amendments to financial regulations

Pursuant to the Assembly's 1994 decision[1] that the financial period for each peace-keeping operation would be from 1 July to 30 June, the Secretary-General on 29 November submitted draft amendments[6] to the Financial Regulations to change the budget cycle of peace-keeping operations. If amended, the regulations would incorporate provisions that: the financial period would consist of two consecutive calendar years, the first of which would be an even year, except for peace-keeping operations with special accounts whose financial periods would be one year from 1 July to 30 June (Financial Regulation 2.1); and that the accounts for the financial period, except those for peace-keeping operations with special accounts, would be submitted by the Secretary-General to the Board of Auditors no later than 31 March following the end of the financial period. The annual accounts for peace-keeping operations with special accounts would be submitted by the Secretary-General to the Board of Auditors no later than 30 September each year (Financial Regulation 11.4).

By **decision 50/472** of 23 December, the General Assembly amended the Financial Regulations as proposed.

## Reimbursement for troops and contingent-owned equipment

In response to a 1994 General Assembly request,[1] the Secretary-General on 8 December reported[7] on a reform of the procedure for determining reimbursement to Member States for contingent-owned equipment. He noted that the reform—aimed at setting comprehensive standards for each category of equipment and establishing rates of reimbursement following procedures similar to those used for compensation to Member States for military contingent personnel—proceeded in accordance with the project plan and the timetable set out by the Assembly. The plan called for five phases, with phases II and III representing the critical aspects of the project.

As part of phase I, the Secretariat identified items for consideration as either major or minor contingent-owned equipment. Under phase II, a working group of technical experts from troop-contributing countries met from 27 March to 7 April to identify standards for major and minor equipment and consumables for which reimbursement would be authorized. The Phase II Working Group's recommendations were provided in its Chairman's report[8] of 2 May. Also in May, an ad hoc working group of technical and financial experts from seven troop-contributing States met with Secretariat representatives to develop rates for consideration during phase III of the project.

A working group of financial experts, meeting under phase III from 10 to 20 July, considered recommendations of the Phase II Working Group, reviewed the reimbursement rates proposed by the ad hoc working group, and made recommendations for comprehensive reimbursement standards, which were contained in its Chairman's report[9] of 20 July. Another ad hoc working group, meeting from 31 July to 4 August, concluded that the system proposed by the Phase III Working Group was less expensive to the Organization than the current methodology.

The Secretary-General therefore recommended that the General Assembly approve the following principles proposed by the Working Groups: the wet and dry lease concept and associated rates; the self-sustainment concept for reimbursement of minor equipment and consumables and services, and the associated rates; the policy concerning preparation costs; the transportation policy for deployment/redeployment, including loss and damage incurred during shipment, except inland transportation; the transportation policy concerning resupply of contingents; the identification of one or more ports of embarkation/disembarkation; the policy for reimbursement of ammunition; the proposal to include an insurance factor for loss or damage due to no-fault incidents; the proposal for a mission-approved hostility factor applicable to self-sustainment rates and the spare parts element of the wet lease; the proposal that the UN not be responsible for loss or damage incurred due to wilful misconduct or negligence; the proposal relating to loss or damage of contingent-owned equipment, except that it would not apply to special equipment; the proposed standards and verification procedures related to major equipment under the leasing concept; and the proposed standards related to minor equipment and services provided under the self-sustainment concept.

It was further recommended that the Assembly approve one environmental/operational mission-specific factor not exceeding 5 per cent of the reimbursement rates for minor equipment and of the leasing costs for major equipment.

It was recommended that the Assembly not approve the proposal for reimbursement for inland transportation, nor the proposals that, should the United Nations not meet its full liability under the lease system, total responsibility for loss or damage due to no-fault incidents to contingent-owned equipment and supplies would revert to the Organization; and that the UN be responsible for compensation for all loss and damage of major equipment due to hostile action or forced abandonment whose collective value equalled or exceeded $250,000. Should the Assembly decide to approve compensation for all loss and damage of major equipment due to hostile action or forced abandonment whose unit value equalled or exceeded $250,000, the Secretary-General recommended acceptance of such liability only if fixed and reasonable limits of the amounts compensable by the UN, per peace-keeping operation and per contributing Member State, were established.

## Management of peace-keeping assets

As requested by the Assembly in 1994,[1] the Secretary-General on 3 July submitted a report[10] on storage facilities for surplus peace-keeping assets as well as on mission start-up kits. He noted that the recent trend towards missions of short duration had made available to the Organization substantial amounts of reusable and temporarily surplus equipment and supplies, estimated at more than $100 million, which necessitated an update of the reserve stock concept. The proposed approach would provide for a modular system of mission start-up kits—preconfigured supplies—to be held in reserve. A single kit, valued at some $3.4 million, would be sufficient to sustain a mission of up to 100 persons for up to three months. The Secretariat intended to maintain five start-up kits, stocked in ways to facilitate immediate packing and shipment. That stock, once established, was to be maintained by replenishment from the budgets of the missions receiving kits. The Secretary-General further noted that the policy of transferring assets from closing operations to other missions and/or the start-up kit reserve was an efficient and cost-effective method of maintaining operational readiness, and that demobilization (formerly "liquidation") guidelines were being promulgated to ensure that UN assets were fully utilized throughout their serviceable life.

The report also reviewed the use of the UN Logistics Base in Brindisi, Italy, the principal functions of which were to receive, inspect, repair and store surplus assets; to maintain a reserve of mission start-up kits; and to serve as a "rear logistics" base for UNPF in the former Yugoslavia. The Logistics Base was intended to perform a central coordinating activity for peace-keeping assets in general and to provide a broad oversight and control function. The Secretary-General estimated the immediate requirements for managing the overall operation in Brindisi at $6.6 million for the six months until 31 December, to be covered, as an ad hoc arrangement, from the existing budgets of UNPF as well as other missions. Accordingly, he recommended that the Assembly confirm its acceptance of Italy's offer of the premises in Brindisi, approve the establishment of the UN Logistics Base and take note of the mission start-up kit concept and of the ad hoc financing arrangements for 1995.

## Procurement

In response to a 1994 General Assembly request,[11] the Secretary-General on 22 June submitted a progress report[12] on the implementation of procurement reform in the Secretariat. The report described the steps taken to date, including a training programme for procurement personnel of DPKO and on-the-job training for procurement personnel of peace-keeping operations; an increase in procurement authority granted to missions worldwide, including authority in key areas for commitments of up to 75 per cent against future allotments; as well as other issues relating to the use of system contracts, the vendor roster and database, responsibility sharing between DPKO and the Department of Administration and Management, a comprehensive review of financial regulations and rules and of standard operating procedures, staff resources, and the use of information technology. The Secretary-General pointed out that the position of a full-time Chairman of the Headquarters Committee on Contracts had been created and filled as at 1 June and that an Ombudsman's office was to be established by the end of the year to review vendors' complaints. He concluded that the work being done provided a firm foundation for further change in improving specifications, establishing a comprehensive vendor database and reviewing existing documentation to bring about greater standardization and simplification.

On 20 July, the General Assembly, having considered the Secretary-General's report, welcomed in **decision 49/486** the progress made in the implementation of procurement reform.

## Peace-keeping personnel

### Death and disability benefits

On 2 June, the Secretary-General reported[13] on death and disability benefits of UN peace-keeping personnel, as requested by the Assembly in 1994.[1] The report reviewed the current system of compensation for death or injury sustained by contingent troops while in the UN service and compared it with alternative schemes, based on the principles of: equal treatment of Member States, compensation to the beneficiary not lower than reimbursement by the UN, simplification of administrative arrangements and speedy settlement of death and disability claims.

The alternative options reviewed would provide for one of the following: replacing the current system with a uniform global insurance scheme to cover all troops; applying to contingent troops current arrangements for military observers and civilian police; introducing standardized rates of reimbursement for death and disability; establishing an amount payable to a troop-contributing country per soldier per month to enable national authorities to provide suitable compensation, in lieu of any other reimbursement by the UN for service-incurred death or disability; or adding to the current system either a reasonable minimum level of compensation or a liability ceiling.

Upon review, the Secretary-General recommended that the Assembly approve a UN-administered global insurance system of standardized awards for death and disability, as both the fairest and most practical scheme, and consider extending it to military observers and civilian police as well. The level of awards, to be determined by Member States, was suggested at $50,000 for service-incurred death.

**ACABQ recommendations.** In October,[14] ACABQ considered the Secretary-General's report and observed that a necessary prerequisite for a new system was agreement on the precise legal status of contingent personnel and the nature of their legal, administrative and operational relationship with the Organization and their Government. The Advisory Committee requested further guidance from the Assembly as to whether payments should be in the form of an allowance, a reimbursement or an award and whether they should be made to Member States or individuals directly; the amount to be paid by the United Nations; the status of the additional allowance mechanism put forward by the Secretary-General in his additional option; and whether an insurance scheme should be established. Pending the introduction of a new system, the Committee recommended improving the management of the current system so as to handle outstanding claims expeditiously.

### Entitlements of mission staff

In a 1 December report[15] on entitlements of staff assigned to peace-keeping missions, including mission subsistence allowance (MSA), the Secretary-General reviewed the entitlements applicable both to the normal movement of staff under regular rotation or assignment schemes and to special and non-family missions, and examined the purpose of MSA; the procedure for establishing and maintaining MSA rates; eligibility criteria for receipt of MSA; the relationships between MSA and daily subsistence allowance and between MSA, hazard pay and hardship allowance; and MSA in relation to the practices of the comparator civil service. He concluded that MSA, defined as the Organization's total contribution towards living expenses incurred in the field in connection with special mission assignment and applicable to international personnel assigned to peace-keeping and other UN operations in the field, was a central element in the entitlements of mission staff and one which provided a cost-effective and administratively simple mechanism to meet subsistence costs. As currently established and applied, MSA was commensurate with the exposure of staff to expenses arising from mission service, its rates being lower than either the equivalent entitlements in the comparator civil service or the daily subsistence allowance established by the International

Civil Service Commission for short-term travel purposes.

## Apportionment of costs

In 1995, the General Assembly again considered the question of placement of Member States into groups for the apportionment of peace-keeping expenses. First specified in 1973[16] and again in March 1989,[17] the groups were subsequently adjusted in December 1989[18] and in 1991.[19] The original four groups were: (A) permanent members of the Security Council; (B) specifically named economically developed Member States not permanent members of the Council; (C) economically less developed Member States; and (D) economically less developed Member States that were specifically named. In 1993,[20] Belarus and Ukraine, citing economic hardship since the breakup of the former Soviet Union, had requested reclassification from group B to group C. In 1994,[21] the Assembly had called on both countries to prepare proposals for the treatment of their arrears in the financing of peace-keeping operations.

### Belarus

On 20 July, the General Assembly, by **resolution 49/249 A**, decided to consider the request of Belarus for reclassification and to take action no later than at its fiftieth session.

On 14 August,[22] Belarus transmitted a memorandum regarding its relocation to group C. It stated that the original motives for assigning Belarus to group B had become historically obsolete, its legal status under international law had changed and its economic situation had greatly deteriorated. Belarus said it faced a serious and constant decline in its solvency, due to such factors as bearing, almost singlehandedly, the cost of mitigating the consequences of the Chernobyl disaster, and substantial expenses resulting from disarmament treaty obligations, including destroying weapons. Belarus, due to conditions beyond its control, had therefore become chronically in arrears for financing peace-keeping operations. Given the discrepancy between its rate of assessment and its capacity to pay, and taking into account the relocation of Portugal from group C to group B (see below), Belarus requested to be relocated to group C, which would have no financial implications for other Member States.

**GENERAL ASSEMBLY ACTION**

On 14 September, the General Assembly adopted **resolution 49/249 B**.

*The General Assembly,*

*Recalling* its resolution 3101(XXVIII) of 11 December 1973 and its subsequent resolutions relating to the composition of the groups for the apportionment of the expenses of peace-keeping operations, the latest of which is resolution 47/218 A of 23 December 1992, and its decision 48/472 A of 23 December 1993,

*Recalling also* its resolution 49/249 A of 20 July 1995 and its decision 49/470 A of 23 December 1994,

*Taking into account* the relevant provisions of the report of the Fifth Committee of 19 July 1995 on the administrative and budgetary aspects of the financing of the United Nations peace-keeping operations,

*Having considered* the request of Belarus for reclassification from group B to group C,

*Recognizing* that the High-level Open-ended Working Group on the Financial Situation of the United Nations is considering, *inter alia*, issues relevant to this matter and noting divergent views expressed thereon,

1. *Decides*, as a special ad hoc arrangement, to place Belarus among the Member States referred to in paragraph 3 *(c)* of General Assembly resolution 43/232 of 1 March 1989, on the understanding that the reduction in the United States dollar amounts to be assessed on Belarus beginning 1 July 1995 shall be equal to the additional United States dollar amounts assessed on Portugal in accordance with Assembly resolution 49/249 A, on the basis that this decision will be adjusted as appropriate to conform with any future relevant decisions adopted by the Assembly;

2. *Takes note* of the stated intention of Belarus concerning the treatment of its arrears.

General Assembly resolution 49/249 B

14 September 1995     Meeting 107     Adopted without vote

Approved by Fifth Committee (A/49/947/Add.1) without vote, 13 September (meeting 69); draft by Vice-Chairman (A/C.5/49/L.70), based on informal consultations; agenda item 132.

Before adoption of the resolution in the Fifth (Administrative and Budgetary) Committee, Belarus had made a statement pointing out that its Government was considering a procedure and timetable for payments of its arrears and that it would inform the Assembly during its fiftieth session of its intentions in that matter.

### Palau

By **decision 50/451 B** of 23 December, the General Assembly, as an ad hoc arrangement, included Palau in group D of Member States for the apportionment of peace-keeping appropriations.

### Portugal

On 20 July, the Assembly adopted **resolution 49/249 A**.

*The General Assembly,*

*Recalling* its resolution 3101(XXVIII) of 11 December 1973 and its subsequent resolutions relating to the composition of the existing groups, the latest of which is resolution 47/218 A of 23 December 1992, and its decision 48/472 A of 23 December 1993,

*Having received* the request of Belarus for reclassification from group B to group C,

1. *Welcomes with great satisfaction* the voluntary decision made by the Government of Portugal to reclassify Portugal from group C to group B;

2. *Decides*, as an ad hoc arrangement, to note the voluntary decision made by the Government of Portugal and to place Portugal among the Member States referred to in paragraph 3 *(b)* of its resolution 43/232 of 1 March 1989 and, in accordance with that decision, to apportion its share of the costs of peace-keeping operations financed through assessed contributions on the basis of the proportion determined by the scale of assessments in the following manner: 35 per cent beginning 1 July 1995, 50 per cent in 1996, 70 per cent in 1997, 85 per cent in 1998 and 100 per cent in 1999 and subsequent years;

3. *Also decides* to consider the request of Belarus for reclassification from group B to group C at its resumed forty-ninth session and to take action thereon no later than at its fiftieth session.

General Assembly resolution 49/249 A

20 July 1995     Meeting 106     Adopted without vote

Approved by Fifth Committee (A/49/947) without vote, 14 July (meeting 66); draft by Chairman (A/C.5/49/L.64), based on informal consultations; agenda item 132.

### Ukraine

By **decision 49/493** of 20 July, the Assembly included in the provisional agenda of its fiftieth session the sub-item on relocation of Ukraine to group C.

On 27 September,[23] Ukraine transmitted a letter from its President concerning that country's arrears. The letter pointed out that as a result of the redistribution of the assessment of the former USSR, Ukraine's rate of assessment was three times higher than its capacity to pay. The unprecedented 50 per cent increase in its contribution to the regular UN budget was not based on real economic indicators. At the same time, Ukraine's transition to a market economy required additional financial resources, and the country was incurring considerable economic losses implementing sanctions against the Federal Republic of Yugoslavia (Serbia and Montenegro). Asserting that Ukraine was not in a position to pay its outstanding contribution as a result of conditions beyond its control, its President requested that the country be placed in group C for the apportionment of peace-keeping expenses.

On 23 December, the General Assembly, by **decision 50/474**, deferred action on the relocation of Ukraine to group C until its resumed fiftieth session in 1996.

### Support account for peace-keeping operations

In 1995, the General Assembly continued to examine issues relating to the support account established in 1990 for peace-keeping operations. The account was intended to meet the needs at Headquarters for the support of ongoing operations and some of the additional workload during the pre-implementation phase of prospective missions. It was funded by including in, and setting aside from, the budgets of all operations financed outside the regular budget an amount equalling 8.5 per cent of the cost of the mission's civilian staff component (salaries, common staff costs and travel). Those moneys were to be kept in a separate account and used to fund temporary posts. The cost of activities funded during the year stood at $33.3 million, while the support account income totalled less than $33.2 million, leaving an operating deficit of some $145,000. The income comprised $25.1 million generated by applying the funding formula, $7.9 million of unencumbered balance from the prior year and some $32,000 transferred from the operating reserve.

**ACABQ recommendations.** In May,[24] ACABQ submitted to the Assembly its recommendations and observations concerning the Secretary-General's 1994 report[25] on the support account.

The Advisory Committee recommended maintaining the concept of a support account, including its method of financing, but restoring simplicity to the procedures for the approval of expenditures. It suggested that proposals for variations from previously approved levels in the number of posts financed from the special account be justified on an individual basis and be subject to procedures for classification as to grade; that specific requests for such variations be considered by ACABQ on behalf of the General Assembly; and that requests under the support account be justified not only on the basis of workload and operational need but also in the context of the totality of resources available to the particular unit or programme. The Committee stated that the requirements of the UN Financial Regulations and Rules as well as Staff Regulations and Rules must be fully respected and recommended that the Secretary-General review all previously authorized posts in the support account to ensure that they were used only for purposes approved by the Assembly, that they had been properly classified and that their vacancy announcements were handled in compliance with Staff Rules and procedures.

ACABQ further reviewed resource requirements for 1995 and recommended approval of non-post resources for the period from 1 April to 31 December 1995.

GENERAL ASSEMBLY ACTION (July)

On 12 July, the General Assembly decided to maintain the current level of resources approved under the support account for peace-keeping operations for the month of July 1995 (**decision 49/478 B**).

On 20 July, the Assembly adopted **resolution 49/250**.

**Support account for peace-keeping operations**

*The General Assembly*,

*Recalling* its resolutions 45/258 of 3 May 1991, 47/218 A of 23 December 1992, 48/226 A, B and C of 23 December 1993 and 5 April and 29 July 1994, respectively, and decisions 48/489 of 8 July 1994 and 49/469 of 23 December 1994,

*Having considered* the reports of the Secretary-General on the support account for peace-keeping operations and the related reports of the Advisory Committee on Administrative and Budgetary Questions,

*Reaffirming* the need to continue to improve the administrative and financial management of peace-keeping operations,

1. *Endorses* the observations and recommendations contained in the report of the Advisory Committee on Administrative and Budgetary Questions, subject to the provisions of the present resolution;

2. *Decides* that support account funds shall be used for the sole purpose of financing human and non-human resource requirements for backstopping and supporting peace-keeping operations at Headquarters, and that any change to this limitation will require the prior approval of the General Assembly;

3. *Decides also* to maintain the current methodology of financing the support account at the rate of 8.5 per cent of the estimated cost of the civilian staff component of each peace-keeping operation, on the understanding that this percentage shall be reviewed annually and for the first time no later than the spring of 1996, taking into account the report to be submitted by the Board of Auditors;

4. *Affirms* that upon the approval of a peace-keeping budget the amounts thus approved with regard to the support account are funds appropriated and therefore available to the Secretary-General, subject to specific use and purpose as specified by the General Assembly;

5. *Also affirms* that the level of resources is clearly a function of the income in the support account and that, therefore, it is the responsibility of the Secretary-General to ensure that, at any one time, the level of income to the support account is not exceeded;

6. *Decides* that once a year, for its consideration and approval, the Secretary-General shall submit to the General Assembly, through the Advisory Committee, a report on the use of the resources in the support account during the past calendar year and on the proposed expenditure for the following twelve-month period beginning 1 July, specifying the proposed establishment of posts and the projected expenditure for non-post requirements by category of expenditure, including, for the former, the grade structure in tabular form;

7. *Decides also*, taking into account the above-mentioned responsibility of the Secretary-General to ensure that expenditure remains within the level of income, to authorize the Secretary-General to redeploy and discontinue posts, according to functional requirements, and requests him to report thereon every six months to the General Assembly for information purposes;

8. *Decides further* that posts funded from the support account shall be filled and managed in compliance with the Charter of the United Nations, the Financial Regulations and Rules of the United Nations, the Staff Regulations and Rules of the United Nations and relevant General Assembly resolutions, including, where ap-

propriate, the classification and advertisement of posts approved for more than ninety days;

9. *Requests* the Board of Auditors to report on an interim basis to the General Assembly by 31 October 1995 on the management of the support account, including, *inter alia*, the appropriateness of the funding level in view of actual experience, taking into account actions taken by relevant intergovernmental bodies, consistency in the use of human resources for purposes authorized by the Assembly and confirmation that contractual arrangements for the employment of personnel are consistent with the temporary nature of the posts;

10. *Welcomes* the contribution by Member States, on a non-reimbursable basis, of personnel to fill back-stopping positions within the Department of Peace-keeping Operations, and reiterates its request to the Secretary-General contained in paragraph 7 of its resolution 48/226 C;

11. *Authorizes*, for the period from 1 July 1995, the continuation of the 346 posts previously authorized, and notes the redeployment of 10 posts (5 Professional and 5 General Service) from the Finance Management and Support Service of the Field Administration and Logistics Division, Department of Peace-keeping Operations, to the Accounts Division (3 Professional and 2 General Service) and the Peace-keeping Financing Division (2 Professional and 3 General Service), Department of Administration and Management;

12. *Also authorizes*, on an exceptional basis, for the period from 1 July 1995 to 31 January 1996, the conversion of the 61 positions under general temporary assistance to temporary posts exclusively for the purposes proposed by the Secretary-General in his report, including, *inter alia*, staffing of the Civilian Police Unit, on the understanding that the contracts for the staff encumbering these posts will terminate on 31 January 1996 unless the General Assembly decides otherwise;

13. *Decides* that further consideration of these staffing requirements will be subject to review during the autumn part of its fiftieth session, based on additional information provided by the Secretary-General through established procedures on, *inter alia*, the 61 posts cited in paragraph 12 above (to include, *inter alia*, an organizational chart reflecting current number, grade and function of posts), and the report by the Board of Auditors requested in paragraph 3 above;

14. *Authorizes* the resources for general temporary assistance, including the position of Special Adviser to the Secretary-General (319,600 United States dollars), overtime (157,500 dollars), travel on official business (90,000 dollars), training (372,500 dollars) and common services (4,028,200 dollars) for the period from 1 April to 31 December 1995.

General Assembly resolution 49/250

20 July 1995      Meeting 106      Adopted without vote

Approved by Fifth Committee (A/49/803/Add.5) without vote, 14 July (meeting 66); draft by Chairman (A/C.5/49/L.68), based on informal consultations and orally amended by Ireland; agenda item 132 *(a)*.
*Meeting numbers.* GA 49th session: 5th Committee 55, 61, 66; plenary 106.

**Fifth Committee consideration.** On 28 November,[26] the Fifth Committee, in considering the question of financing peace-keeping operations, heard a statement by the Controller concerning the support account. The Controller pointed to an anticipated 50 per cent decrease in support account income for 1996, as a result of the reduction in peace-keeping budgets, and to the on-going efforts to reduce support account staffing requirements. He also observed that the current formula of financing the account had not foreseen the recent expansion of the Secretariat's role and responsibilities in backstopping peace-keeping operations, noting that completed missions did not generate income for the support account but continued to require backstopping activities. In addition, a recent increase in the military component of operations changed the ratio of military to civilian personnel and significantly transformed the Secretariat's administrative backstopping requirements. In that regard, it was recommended that the current financing formula, based solely on civilian costs, be reviewed. The Controller also stated that it might be appropriate, in order to avoid wide fluctuations in the level of the support account, to establish a separate budget for backstopping requirements, to be financed according to the peace-keeping scale of assessment. He also listed staffing requirements for the beginning of 1996.

**GENERAL ASSEMBLY ACTION (December)**

On 23 December, the General Assembly, noting the Controller's statement on the support account, decided to review at its resumed fiftieth session in 1996 the current methodology for financing the account and, on an exceptional basis, to establish a temporary post of Special Adviser to the Secretary-General; extend the 61 temporary posts authorized in July 1995 for the period from 1 February to 31 March 1996; and authorize $40,000 for overtime and $900,000 for common services for the period from 1 January to 31 March 1996 (**decision 50/473**).

## Unforeseen and extraordinary expenses

In a 17 November report,[27] submitted in preparation of the UN programme budget for the biennium 1996-1997 (see PART SIX, Chapter II), the Secretary-General pointed out that, in the light of the increased demand for his good offices and peace-making activities as well as the expansion of peace-keeping operations, the level of commitment authority to meet unforeseen and extraordinary expenses, granted to him under a 1993 General Assembly resolution,[28] was proving to be inadequate. Under the current procedure, he was authorized to enter into commitments of up to $5 million per year, without prior concurrence of ACABQ, for unforeseen activities certified by him as relating to the maintenance of peace and security. That commitment had been used principally for the appointment of special envoys for peacemaking activities, fact-finding and advisory missions, as well as for the establishment of political offices upon completion

of peace-keeping missions. At the same time, financial requirements to implement Security Council decisions relating to both peace and security and peace-keeping operations, without prior concurrence of ACABQ, had to be met from the balance remaining of the $5 million per year.

The Secretary-General noted that the $5 million ceiling had been reached in October, committing him to seeking the concurrence of ACABQ for all additional unforeseen expenses. However, given the level of detail required by the Advisory Committee, that process took several weeks to complete, which created a time-lag between Security Council decisions and the granting of commitment authority by ACABQ. At the same time, those decisions often necessitated urgent action, such as the dispatch of advance teams during the start-up phase. Owing to the urgent nature of start-up requirements of new or expanded operations, the Secretary-General said he did not have the time to make a presentation and await the concurrence of the Advisory Committee.

The Secretary-General concluded that the current procedures needed to be revised so as to avoid situations whereby he was prevented from taking prompt action because of delays and/or financial constraints. He recommended that his authority to incur expenditures for the maintenance of peace and security be increased to $7 million in any one year of the biennium, and that he be granted authority to enter into commitments not exceeding $3 million in any one year, without prior concurrence of ACABQ, for the immediate requirements of the start-up phase of peace-keeping operations or for unforeseen extensions of mandates by the Security Council.

In December, the Fifth Committee, noting that ACABQ had been unable to consider the report in depth for lack of time, deferred consideration of the issue to the resumed fiftieth session. The General Assembly, by **resolution 50/216, section IX**, of 23 December, decided to consider the Secretary-General's report at its resumed session and authorized him to continue with the current arrangements until a decision on his proposal was taken.

## Liquidation of missions

By a 2 August note,[29] the Secretary-General transmitted a report of the Board of Auditors on the liquidation audit of the UN Transitional Authority in Cambodia (see PART TWO, Chapter IV), in which the Board recommended, *inter alia*, that standard procedures be developed for the transfer and acknowledgement of assets redeployed from a peace-keeping operation in liquidation to other missions or UN bodies; a physical verification of the assets and liabilities of a mission in liquidation be carried out before the assets were realized and liabilities discharged; and, pending the establishment of a policy on the valuation and transfer of costs of assets between missions, the current practice of not giving credit to operations under liquidation for assets transferred to other missions be reported in a note to the consolidated financial statements of peace-keeping operations.

**GENERAL ASSEMBLY ACTION**

On 23 December, the General Assembly adopted **resolution 50/204 C** under the item on financial reports and audited financial statements, and reports of the Board of Auditors.

*The General Assembly,*

*Recalling* its resolutions 47/211 of 23 December 1992 and 48/216 B of 23 December 1993, as well as previous relevant resolutions,

*Noting* that the responses requested in the aforementioned resolutions have not been received,

*Noting with concern* the numerous weaknesses highlighted by the Board of Auditors in its report on the liquidation of the United Nations Transitional Authority in Cambodia, especially as far as inventories are concerned,

*Deeply concerned* by the delays encountered in liquidating the Transitional Authority,

*Bearing in mind* that a number of peace-keeping operations are expected to be scaled down and liquidated during the next twelve months,

*Taking note* of the observation of the Board of Auditors in its report that there is at present no policy on the valuation and transfer of costs of assets between missions,

*Noting* the absence of standard procedures for the transfer and acknowledgement of assets between missions and United Nations entities,

*Noting also* that the Board of Auditors has recommended the establishment of appropriate policies and procedures for the valuation, transfer and disposal of assets of missions for consistent application in peace-keeping operations,

1. *Notes with regret* that the Secretary-General has not yet completed the feasibility study on procedures for the valuation and transfer of costs of assets redeployed from a peace-keeping operation in liquidation to other operations or United Nations bodies, as requested by the General Assembly in its resolution 49/233 A of 23 December 1994;

2. *Requests* the Secretary-General to proceed with all urgency to complete the study mentioned in paragraph 1 above and submit it to the General Assembly at the earliest opportunity during the first part of its resumed fiftieth session;

3. *Takes note with concern* of the findings of the Board of Auditors on the audit of the United Nations Transitional Authority in Cambodia and the need for an additional review as a consequence of the many unresolved administrative and financial issues involved and the incomplete nature of the liquidation documentation available to the Board;

4. *Requests* the Secretary-General to study the most expeditious and cost-effective ways of liquidating peace-keeping operations and to report thereon to the General Assembly at its resumed fiftieth session;

5. *Also requests* the Secretary-General to take immediate action to implement the recommendations of the Board of Auditors, keeping the Board fully informed regarding the measures being taken, and requests the Board to report thereon to the General Assembly at its fifty-first session;

6. *Regrets* the absence of a report on measures taken or proposed to be taken by the Secretariat in response to the recommendations contained in the report of the Board of Auditors;

7. *Further requests* the Secretary-General to submit such a report to the General Assembly, through the Advisory Committee on Administrative and Budgetary Questions, before the beginning of the first part of its resumed fiftieth session, containing, *inter alia*, proposals for establishing:

(a) An appropriate policy for the physical verification of all assets and liabilities of a mission in liquidation before its assets are disposed of and its liabilities discharged;

(b) Standard procedures for the transfer of assets and the acknowledgement of assets transferred to other missions and other United Nations entities;

(c) Standard procedures for the valuation of all assets of a mission in liquidation as well as an appropriate policy for the financial accounting of transfers of assets for consistent application in all peace-keeping operations;

8. *Appeals* to Member States to pay their assessed and pledged contributions as soon as possible, in order to facilitate the completion of the liquidation process.

General Assembly resolution 50/204 C

23 December 1995      Meeting 100      Adopted without vote

Approved by Fifth Committee (A/50/839) without vote, 21 December (meeting 44); draft by Vice-Chairman (A/C.5/50/L.20, part C) following informal consultations; agenda item 113.

*Meeting numbers.* GA 50th session: 5th Committee 21, 25, 27, 44; plenary 100.

*REFERENCES*

[1]YUN 1994, p. 1338, GA res. 49/233 A, 23 Dec. 1994. [2]A/50/319. [3]YUN 1994, p. 1337. [4]A/50/798. [5]A/50/576. [6]A/50/787. [7]A/50/807. [8]A/C.5/49/66. [9]A/C.5/49/70. [10]A/49/936. [11]YUN 1994, p. 1369, GA res. 49/216 C, 23 Dec. 1994. [12]A/C.5/49/67. [13]A/49/906 & Corr.1. [14]A/50/684. [15]A/50/797. [16]YUN 1973, p. 222, GA res. 3101 (XXVIII), 11 Dec. 1973. [17]GA res. 43/232, 1 Mar. 1989. [18]GA res. 44/192 B, 21 Dec. 1989. [19]YUN 1991, pp. 129 & 159, GA res. 45/269, 27 Aug. 1991 & 46/198 A, 20 Dec. 1991. [20]YUN 1993, p. 1177. [21]YUN 1994, p. 1343, GA dec. 49/470, 23 Dec. 1994. [22]A/49/956. [23]A/50/502. [24]A/49/904. [25]YUN 1994, p. 1345. [26]A/C.5/50/SR.32. [27]A/C.5/50/30. [28]YUN 1993, p. 1201, GA res. 48/229, 23 Dec. 1993. [29]A/49/943.

Chapter II

# Africa

Millions of Africans continued to suffer in 1995 as a consequence of ethnic strife, political tensions and economic difficulties, despite intense United Nations efforts to address those often-tragic situations in a variety of ways during the year. While some progress was made in creating political frameworks for dealing with ongoing crises, the prognosis for Africa remained bleak.

Civil wars persisted in Burundi, Liberia and Sierra Leone. The flow of arms into those countries was a serious problem. The consequences of other conflicts—in Angola, Mozambique, Rwanda and Somalia—continued to plague those nations.

The plight of the vast numbers of African refugees and internally displaced persons, many in overcrowded camps concentrated in the central and western parts of the continent, was the focus of activities by several UN organizations, in particular the Office of the UN High Commissioner for Human Rights. A Regional Conference on Assistance to Refugees, Returnees and Displaced Persons in the Great Lakes Region was held in February in Bujumbura, Burundi. Consultations were held with regard to convening another Great Lakes regional conference—on security, stability and development—as called for by the Security Council.

The dispatch by the United Nations of humanitarian and emergency aid for Africa (see PART FOUR, Chapter III), as well as efforts to promote rehabilitation and reconstruction, brought some relief and hope for a brighter future.

Four of the 16 United Nations peace-keeping operations active at the end of 1995 were based in Africa: a new, third UN Angola Verification Mission (UNAVEM III); the UN Observer Mission in Liberia (UNOMIL); the UN Assistance Mission for Rwanda (UNAMIR); and MINURSO, the UN Mission for the Referendum in Western Sahara (see PART ONE, Chapter III). Two others—the second UN Operation in Somalia (UNOSOM II) and the UN Operation in Mozambique (ONUMOZ)—concluded in the early part of 1995.

A Security Council mission was sent to Rwanda and Burundi in February to assess the deteriorating political and social situations in those nations. An arms embargo against Rwanda was lifted in September. A first-time Human Rights Field Operation was launched in Rwanda, and a Special Rapporteur on human rights in Burundi was appointed. Two Special Envoys were sent to Rwanda in 1995, one to consult on possible deployment of UN observers in neighbouring countries, the other on a security conference for the Great Lakes region. The International Tribunal for Rwanda began the process of bringing to justice those responsible for genocidal acts in that country.

For Liberia, against the backdrop of the continuing conflict, the Abuja Agreement was signed in August, renewing the cease-fire—broken again later in the year—and instituting the Liberian National Transitional Government. Neighbouring Sierra Leone, also victimized by the consequences of a political coup, saw 2 million internally displaced as it struggled to prepare for 1996 elections.

In Angola, implementation of the 1994 Lusaka Protocol included efforts to demobilize and integrate former combatants into a peaceful society. In Mozambique, the withdrawal of ONUMOZ signalled the full implementation of the 1992 Rome General Peace Agreement.

Another final chapter in UN peace-keeping history was written with the withdrawal of UNOSOM II from Mogadishu at the end of March 1995. The Secretary-General stressed that the United Nations was not abandoning Somalia; there were, however, important lessons to be learned from the UN experience in that country and the clear line that needed to be drawn between peace-keeping and enforcement action, he said.

The General Assembly on 15 December 1995 accepted, due to exceptional and unique circumstances, South Africa's request not to pay its contributions for the 20-year period from September 1974 to June 1994, when a democratic, non-racial Government, elected after the full elimination of the apartheid system, was inaugurated and resumed participation in the work of the Assembly.

## Angola

During 1995, the UN Security Council reported slow progress in the implementation of the Lusaka Protocol,[1] signed on 20 November 1994 by the Government of Angola and the National Union for the Total Independence of Angola (UNITA), with the goal of re-establishing peace and stability in the country and achieving national reconciliation.

In February 1995, the Security Council established the third UN Angola Verification Mission (UNAVEM III), with an authorized strength of more than 7,000, to assist the parties in implementing the Protocol. It succeeded two previous UN operations in Angola-UNAVEM I,[2] an observer group established in December 1988 to verify the withdrawal of Cuban troops from Angola, and UNAVEM II,[3] established in May 1991 to verify the Peace Accords (Acordos de Paz), signed earlier in the month to establish a cease-fire and transition period leading to elections, stability and internal security, including the formation of a single national army. The first multi-party elections in Angola were held in September 1992,[4] the results of which were, however, disputed. Fighting resumed and, despite a UN cease-fire, escalated throughout 1993. Peace negotiations culminated in the adoption of the Lusaka Protocol in 1994.

During 1995, efforts focused on the demobilization and integration of armed forces, demining, restoring Angola's infrastructure, including roads, providing humanitarian assistance and return of refugees. Meetings were held between Angolan President José Eduardo dos Santos and Jonas Savimbi, President of UNITA, to reach agreement on outstanding issues. Despite a 13 November joint statement declaring that all issues had been resolved, by the end of the year the Security Council noted that certain tasks required for full implementation of the Protocol had not been completed, including exchange of detailed military information, release of all prisoners, demobilization, disarming and quartering of troops, and final resolution of the issue of mercenaries.

## Implementation of Lusaka Protocol

On 10 January, the Chiefs of Staff of the Angolan Armed Forces (FAA) and the military forces of UNITA met in Chipipa to consolidate the cease-fire and promote the military elements of the Lusaka Protocol. By a joint statement[5] on the same day, they agreed to ensure the immediate cessation of hostilities throughout the country; to proceed with demobilization of troops in sensitive areas, starting in Huambo and Uige, Moxico, Lunda Norte and Lunda Sul, Malange, and Bailundo and Andulo, in order of priority; to enable surveying of all the areas proposed for the deployment of UN troops and to provide operational support; to permit the movement of people and goods within the whole national territory; to form joint work teams for the land-mine deactivation operations and assist UNAVEM, including providing information on land-mines, surveying operations and mine deactivation; to cooperate with UNAVEM to enable it to establish monitoring and verification teams and

permit access to all areas in the country; to ensure the cessation of all hostile propaganda between the parties; to establish three-way communications, effective 12 January; and to release all military prisoners and supply a list of their names to the International Committee of the Red Cross (ICRC).

### Third UN peace-keeping operation (UNAVEM III)

**Communication.** In a 24 January message[6] to the Secretary-General, the President of Angola stated that the Government was deeply committed to the 1994 Lusaka Protocol and had taken initiatives which had contributed to the *détente* of the internal political climate and were conducive to establishing a basis for mutual trust between the Angolan authorities and UNITA, so that the implementation of the understandings reached in Lusaka might proceed normally. It was crucial that the mechanisms in the Protocol be immediately established, not only to speed the process significantly, but also to strengthen peace. The Government believed that UN efforts would have a more effective impact on the peace process if the Security Council approved UNAVEM III at its next meeting on 8 February. That would demonstrate the determination with which the international community viewed the maintenance of peace in Angola and help eliminate a certain ambiguity and hesitation that still seemed to persist within UNITA.

**Report of the Secretary-General (February).** On 1 February, the Secretary-General reported[7] that as at 25 January the number of UN military observers in Angola had increased from 50 to 171, and civilian police observers, from 18 to 122. Before the expiry of the UNAVEM II mandate on 8 February, the combined total of military and police personnel was expected to be 400. They were deployed to 22 sites throughout the country, in addition to headquarters in Luanda and recently established regional headquarters in Huambo, Lubango, Luena, Menongue, Saurimo and Uige. Thirty outstations were expected to be established soon in the most critical areas.

As mandated by the Security Council in 1994,[8] the Secretary-General had continued contingency planning for an enlarged UN operation in Angola and intensified contact with potential contributors, who had indicated their willingness to contribute a significant number of units and military and police personnel.

The Secretary-General recommended that a new UN operation—UNAVEM III—immediately take over from UNAVEM II. The main features of its new mandate would be (1) *political:* to assist in the implementation of the Lusaka Protocol by providing good offices and mediation to the parties and taking appropriate initiatives to give impetus to the peace process; (2) *military:* to supervise, control and verify the disengagement of forces and to monitor the cease-fire, verify information received from the Government and UNITA regarding their forces, verify and monitor all troop movements, assist in the establishment of quartering areas, verify and monitor the withdrawal, quartering and demobilization of UNITA forces, supervise the collection and storage of UNITA armaments, verify the movement of FAA to barracks and monitor the completion of its formation and other tasks, and verify the free circulation of persons and goods; (3) *police:* to verify and monitor the neutrality of the Angolan National Police, the disarming of civilians, the quartering of the rapid reaction police, and security arrangements for UNITA leaders; (4) *humanitarian:* to coordinate, facilitate and support humanitarian activities directly linked to the peace process, in particular those relating to the quartering and demobilization of troops and their integration into civilian life, as well as participating in mine-clearing activities; (5) *electoral:* to declare formally that all requirements for holding the second round of presidential elections had been fulfilled and to support, verify and monitor the entire electoral process. The new operation would be authorized to use force in self-defence, including against forcible attempts to impede the discharge of its mandate.

The Mission, with headquarters remaining in Luanda, would be led by the Secretary-General's Special Representative, Alioune Blondin Beye (Mali); its political affairs component would be headed by a senior political affairs officer, with officers at each of the six regional headquarters, and would include a public information section, with staff available to establish a UNAVEM radio station. The military component would be headed by a force commander and would include military observers and formed units. There would also be a demobilization and reintegration office to assist in quartering and demobilization. The police observer component would be headed by a chief police observer in Luanda and would have six regional headquarters. There would also be an administrative component. The Special Representative would have authority over all activities in support of the peace process and would oversee coordination efforts. All components would rely on integrated logistic, air support, communication and medical evacuation systems. A main logistic base would be established in the port city of Lobito, supplemented by one or two hub stations in the countryside, to avoid the serious bottlenecks being experienced at the port and airport of Luanda. The Secretary-General had instructed his Special Representative to pursue with the Government the provision of adequate material support to all elements of UNAVEM. At the same time, UNAVEM was discussing with the authorities the need for the Government to demine, repair and open as soon as possible major supply routes and airfields, as well as prepare accommodation and storage facilities throughout the country.

The Secretary-General observed that the cease-fire, which entered into force on 22 November 1994, was generally holding. However, despite steps announced on 10 January 1995 at the meeting of the Chiefs of Staff of FAA and UNITA (see above), expeditious measures were needed to facilitate further the effective application of the free movement of persons and goods, the functioning of the triangular communications system, the start of mine-clearing, and the disengagement of troops in areas of tension.

The Joint Commission, the principal body in charge of the implementation of the Lusaka Protocol, in which the two parties and the three observer countries (Portugal, the Russian Federation and the United States) participated, had met several times since the return of the UNITA delegation to Luanda in December 1994. Other high-level contacts between the Government and UNITA officials had contributed to improved relations between the two parties. Conditions for the delivery of humanitarian assistance had also improved considerably.

**SECURITY COUNCIL ACTION (February)**

The Security Council on 8 February adopted **resolution 976(1995).**

*The Security Council,*

*Reaffirming* its resolution 696(1991) of 30 May 1991 and all subsequent relevant resolutions,

*Having considered* the report of the Secretary-General dated 1 February 1995,

*Reaffirming* its commitment to preserve the unity and territorial integrity of Angola,

*Welcoming* the signing of the Lusaka Protocol of 20 November 1994 as a major step towards the establishment of peace and stability in Angola,

*Reiterating* the importance it attaches to the full implementation of the "Acordos de Paz", the Lusaka Protocol and relevant Security Council resolutions,

*Noting* the schedule for implementation set forth in the Lusaka Protocol, in particular the need for the Government of Angola and UNITA to provide all relevant military data to the United Nations, to allow freedom of movement and free circulation of goods, and to begin limited disengagement where forces are in contact,

*Welcoming* the maintenance of a cease-fire which has been generally holding,

*Welcoming also* the progress made in meetings of the Angolan Armed Forces and UNITA Chiefs of Staff on 10 January 1995 in Chipipa and on 2 to 3 February 1995 in Waco Kungo,

*Further welcoming* the deployment of United Nations Angola Verification Mission (UNAVEM II) observer forces, and the contributions of Member States to this mission,

*Welcoming* the offer from the Government of Angola to provide substantial contributions in kind to United Nations peace-keeping operations in Angola as set out in "Costs of the Implementation of the Lusaka Protocol",

*Deeply concerned* that the implementation of the Lusaka Protocol has fallen behind schedule,

*Stressing* the need for the President of Angola, Mr. José Eduardo dos Santos, and the leader of UNITA, Dr. Jonas Savimbi, to meet without delay with a view to building the necessary political momentum for the successful implementation of the Lusaka Protocol,

*Welcoming* the ministerial delegation of the Organization of African Unity (OAU) to the Security Council to participate in its consideration of the situation in Angola,

1. *Authorizes* the establishment of a peace-keeping operation, UNAVEM III, to assist the parties in restoring peace and achieving national reconciliation in Angola on the basis of the "Acordos de Paz", the Lusaka Protocol and relevant Security Council resolutions, as outlined in part IV of the report of the Secretary-General dated 1 February 1995, with an initial mandate until 8 August 1995 and with a maximum deployment of 7,000 military personnel, in addition to the 350 military observers and 260 police observers mentioned in the Secretary-General's report, with an appropriate number of international and local staff;

2. *Urges* the expeditious deployment of the military and police observers to monitor the cease-fire;

3. *Authorizes* the immediate deployment of such planning and support elements as are needed to prepare for the deployment of peace-keeping forces provided that the Secretary-General remains satisfied that an effective cease-fire and effective joint cease-fire monitoring mechanisms are in place, and that both parties are allowing the free and safe flow of humanitarian assistance throughout the country, and authorizes the subsequent deployment of such additional elements as are necessary to establish operational quartering areas for UNITA forces;

4. *Decides* that the deployment of infantry units will take place on the basis of a report from the Secretary-General to the Security Council that the conditions contained in paragraph 32 of the Secretary-General's report, *inter alia*, effective cessation of hostilities, provision of all relevant military data, and designation of all quartering areas, have been met, provided the Council does not decide otherwise;

5. *Stresses* the importance it attaches to the expeditious establishment of a well-coordinated and comprehensive mine-clearance programme in Angola as set out in the Secretary-General's report dated 1 February 1995, and requests him to inform the Council of progress in its implementation;

6. *Endorses* the Secretary-General's view set out in his report as to the need for UNAVEM III to have an effective information capability, including a United Nations radio station to be established in consultation with the Government of Angola;

7. *Requests* the Secretary-General to inform the Council monthly of progress in the deployment of UNAVEM III and in implementation of the Lusaka Protocol, including the maintenance of an effective cease-fire, free access by UNAVEM III to all areas of Angola, free flow of humanitarian assistance throughout Angola and compliance by both the Government of Angola and

by UNITA with their obligations under the Lusaka Protocol, and further requests the Secretary-General to submit to the Council a complete report by 15 July 1995;

8. *Welcomes* the Secretary-General's intention to include human rights specialists in the political component of UNAVEM III to observe the implementation of the provisions related to national reconciliation;

9. *Expresses* its intention to review the role of the United Nations in Angola should the Secretary-General report that the cooperation required from the parties is substantially delayed or not forthcoming;

10. *Declares* its intention to conclude the mission of UNAVEM III when the objectives of the Lusaka Protocol have been achieved in accordance with the schedule attached to the Lusaka Protocol and with the expectation of its completion by February 1997;

11. *Welcomes* the substantial contributions of the Member States, United Nations agencies and non-governmental organizations to meet the humanitarian needs of the Angolan people and encourages additional substantial contributions;

12. *Reaffirms* the obligation of all States to implement fully the provisions of paragraph 19 of resolution 864(1993), and calls upon the Government of Angola and UNITA during UNAVEM III's presence in Angola to cease any acquisition of arms and war *matériel*, as agreed upon in the "Acordos de Paz", and to devote their resources instead to priority humanitarian and social needs;

13. *Calls upon* the Government of Angola to conclude no later than 20 March 1995 an agreement with the United Nations on the status of forces;

14. *Encourages* the Secretary-General to pursue urgently the offer of direct assistance by the Government of Angola to UNAVEM III, to reflect this as appropriate in the Status-of-Forces Agreement referred to in paragraph 13 above, and to explore with the Government of Angola and UNITA possibilities for substantial additional assistance related to peace-keeping and to report to the Council on the results of these explorations;

15. *Urges* Member States to respond positively to the request made to them by the Secretary-General to contribute personnel, equipment and other resources to UNAVEM III in order to facilitate its early deployment;

16. *Demands* that all concerned in Angola take the necessary measures to ensure the safety and freedom of movement of United Nations and other personnel deployed under UNAVEM III;

17. *Welcomes* the presence of the OAU ministerial delegation and notes, in this connection, the need for continued cooperation between the United Nations and OAU in the promotion of peace and security in Angola and the contribution which regional organizations can make to crisis management and conflict resolution;

18. *Decides* to remain actively seized of the matter.

Security Council resolution 976(1995)

8 February 1995      Meeting 3499      Adopted unanimously

Draft prepared in consultations among Council members (S/1995/117).

On 14 February, the President of Angola informed[9] the Secretary-General that while Angola welcomed the decision to deploy UN peace-keeping forces, it was concerned about the Council call in paragraph 12 of resolution 976(1995) for the cessation of the acquisition of arms and war *matériel*. That was not in conformity with the right to exercise fully its sovereignty and defend its territorial integrity, as well as to have the means to achieve that objective, he said. It constituted a departure from and was incompatible with the Lusaka Protocol, whose spirit and letter recognized the rights and competences of the Government on the issue of national defence. Angola reaffirmed its willingness to continue collaborating with the United Nations so that UNAVEM III could accomplish its mission of peace. It wished that the United Nations would also obtain the necessary cooperation from UNITA.

In a further letter,[10] on 3 March, Angola provided details of UNITA actions which, it alleged, related to intense preparations for war. Those included impeding the free movement of people and goods; attacks against UN and government aircraft; forced recruitment and training of young people by foreign instructors; lack of compliance with the decisions regarding the disengagement of forces; reactivation and enlargement of airfields, in locations such as Andulo and Nagage, to permit the landing of large transport aircraft with war *matériel;* and attacks against humanitarian assistance convoys.

Angola believed that there was still time to halt the military adventure that UNITA intended to launch again. It proposed setting a time-period for UNITA to fulfil provisions of the Lusaka Protocol not implemented to date; if, at the end of that period, UNITA maintained the same attitude, the application of a second package of sanctions should be considered. In addition, the Sanctions Committee should establish an effective monitoring programme for Zaire, in view of that country's non-observance of Security Council resolution 864(1993).[11] Angola added that it had also verified outside the country worrisome signs of UNITA's preparation for war.

**Report of the Secretary-General (March).** In his first progress report on UNAVEM III,[12] dated 5 March, the Secretary-General said that its establishment had bolstered the hopes of the Angolan people for genuine peace and national reconciliation. His Special Representative, in continuing efforts to facilitate the implementation of the Lusaka Protocol, had met with the President of UNITA and later with the President of Angola. Mr. Savimbi assured the Special Representative of his readiness to participate in the proposed meeting with President dos Santos and to begin discussions with the Government on the modalities for it, with the participation of UNAVEM. Moreover, the UNITA leader agreed to consider, in the context of political consultations between the two parties, or at the meeting with President dos Santos, the incorporation of UNITA members into the Government. An understanding was reached that the issue of mercenaries and the early release of prisoners would be considered by the Joint Commission. The Secretary-General said that President dos Santos had confirmed his readiness to meet with Mr. Savimbi. The Secretary-General hoped that both sides would move expeditiously to organize and hold the meeting, so as to signal to the Angolans and the international community that the national reconciliation process had effectively begun.

The Joint Commission, chaired by the Special Representative, held an extraordinary session on 20 February to discuss a 13 February incident in which a UN helicopter was shot at in Quibaxe, Cuanza Sul province. The Commission noted that UNITA had recognized its responsibility for the incident. At a Commission session on 1 March, following a similar incident in Licua, UNITA agreed to issue orders to all its personnel to avoid such incidents and promised to use various channels of communication, including its radio ''Vorgan'', and to facilitate liaison procedures. The Joint Commission established an ad hoc working group to expedite resolution of those issues.

The Secretary-General reported that the ceasefire continued in general to hold and in many areas tension had decreased markedly, although in other areas the situation remained volatile, particularly in the north. Progress was achieved in the disengagement of troops in the central region, but agreements reached by the government and UNITA Chiefs of Staff concerning the areas of Uige and Negage proved difficult to implement. However, UNITA confirmed to the Special Representative that, as at 2 March, it would commence disengagement in areas where it had not yet done so, in particular in Uige and Negage, and would ensure the safety of UN flights. It pledged to cooperate in the full integration of its troops into the national army.

In the meantime, UNAVEM III continued to expand. As at 1 March, 418 UN military and police observers were deployed to 38 sites outside Luanda. Deployment to the countryside was slowed because of shooting incidents by UNITA, lack of security clearances to visit certain areas and restriction on freedom of movement, in particular by UNITA, but also by FAA. In general, UN access to UNITA-controlled areas was limited.

UN humanitarian agencies and non-governmental organizations (NGOs) had stepped up their efforts to assess needs in newly accessible areas and to extend the geographic reach of their assistance programmes. Inter-agency teams visited localities in many provinces, identifying major health and nutritional problems.

The mine-awareness campaign continued throughout the country. A UN mine-action office, together with UNAVEM, established a working group with the participation of NGOs to identify areas requiring urgent action. International NGOs were training Angolan instructors and technicians in such towns as Kuito and Luena, where a number of mine-clearance operations had begun. A committee was formed on quartering areas to establish criteria for site selection, infrastructure and provision of services.

The Secretary-General stated that deployment of UNAVEM III infantry units by 9 May could be achieved only if the parties had substantially complied by 25 March with paragraph 4 of resolution 976(1995), requiring a cessation of hostilities and quartering of troops. If not, deployment of those units would have to be deferred.

**SECURITY COUNCIL ACTION (March)**

At a 10 March meeting, after consultations among Security Council members, the President made the following statement[13] on behalf of the Council:

The Security Council has considered the Secretary-General's report of 5 March 1995 on the United Nations Angola Verification Mission (UNAVEM III).

The Security Council welcomes the assessment by the Secretary-General that the cease-fire is generally holding. It also welcomes the continued deployment of United Nations military and police observers to sites outside Luanda. It notes, however, that this deployment has been complicated by a lack of full cooperation by the parties, in particular UNITA. In the month since the adoption of its resolution 976(1995), a number of developments have taken place which give rise to serious concern. These include the lack of progress in disengagement around Uige and Negage, the escalation of tensions in the last few weeks, especially in the northern region, the lack of security clearances to visit certain areas and restrictions on movement of UNAVEM III personnel, attacks on villages, mine-laying, unauthorized movement of troops and military air activity, and attacks on United Nations aircraft, in particular that by UNITA in Quibaxe on 13 February 1995. The Council calls upon the parties, particularly UNITA, to refrain from such activities, to end negative propaganda, to improve their cooperation with each other and the United Nations through the Joint Commission and to cooperate fully with humanitarian operations.

The Security Council reiterates its call upon President dos Santos and Dr. Savimbi to meet without delay as a sign of their joint commitment to the peace process and urges the Government of Angola and UNITA to finalize arrangements towards this end immediately, with a view to ensuring the necessary political momentum for the successful implementation of the Lusaka Protocol. It also encourages the observer States to the peace process, the Organization of African Unity and the neighbouring countries involved to continue their efforts aimed at the full implementation of the peace process.

The Security Council reaffirms the obligations of all States to implement fully the provisions of paragraph 19 of resolution 864(1993) and reiterates its call upon the Government of Angola and UNITA to cease the acquisition of arms and war *matériel* as agreed in the "Acordos de Paz".

The Security Council notes that the United Nations is currently pursuing with the Government of Angola the provision of critical services and access to key facilities such as ports and airports for UNAVEM III. Early and positive responses from the Government of Angola to the United Nations requirements in this respect are essential to UNAVEM III's deployment. It calls on both parties to expedite the completion of the initial tasks in order to ensure the prompt deployment of UNAVEM III units. The Council reiterates the importance it attaches to the Government of Angola and the United Nations agreeing on a Status-of-Forces Agreement by 20 March 1995 as called for in paragraph 13 of its resolution 976(1995). It will continue to monitor closely developments in these areas.

The Security Council commends the United Nations agencies and non-governmental organizations for their continuing efforts to distribute humanitarian relief throughout Angola. It reiterates the importance it attaches to a well-coordinated and comprehensive mine-clearance programme which will, *inter alia*, improve the logistics of humanitarian operations. It calls upon both parties to cooperate with the United Nations and with the non-governmental organizations to put this in place. It deplores the killing on 2 March of three Angolans and one German, all members of the "Cap Anamur" non-governmental organization involved in demining activities, as well as attacks in the last month on ICRC aircraft and road transport, and reminds the parties of its repeated demands that they refrain from all actions which could jeopardize the safety of humanitarian personnel in Angola.

The Security Council endorses the Secretary-General's conclusions that the Government of Angola and UNITA must provide more concrete signs of cooperation and goodwill in the implementation of the peace process. It reminds the parties that the deployment of the units of UNAVEM III will not take place unless the conditions contained in paragraph 32 of his report of 1 February 1995 have been met. It has taken careful note of the Secretary-General's statement that, unless he can report by 25 March 1995 that the parties have complied with these conditions, it will not be possible to ensure that deployment begins on 9 May 1995. Time is short if the opportunity created by the Lusaka Protocol and the Council's resolution 976(1995) is not to be lost. The Council joins the Secretary-General in calling upon the parties to take the necessary steps now to ensure that deployment of these units can begin as planned on 9 May 1995. It requests the Secretary-General to keep it closely informed of developments in this regard.

*Meeting number.* SC 3508.

**Communications (March).** On 25 March, the Secretary-General informed[14] the Security Council President that on 16 March he had briefed the Council of his intention to send his Special Adviser, Ismat Kittani, to Angola to deliver letters to President dos Santos and Mr. Savimbi and discuss with the Angolan parties measures to bring the military situation under control and facilitate preparations for the deployment of UNAVEM III.

The Special Adviser visited Angola from 17 to 22 March. In discussions with the Government and UNITA, in which the Secretary-General's Special Representative also participated, he conveyed the Secretary-General's concern regarding the status of the cease-fire and the parties' failure to cooperate fully with UNAVEM. He stressed that Council members needed convincing evidence that both the Government and UNITA had renounced the military option and were genuinely committed to the peace process. President dos Santos and Mr. Savimbi assured the Special Adviser that they were fully committed to implementing the Lusaka Protocol and favoured accelerated deployment of all UN troops. The two leaders undertook to create the political, military and logistic conditions conducive to such deployment.

The Special Adviser reported that, while the conditions stipulated in Council resolution 976 (1995) had not been fully met, some progress had been made with regard to the cessation of hostilities, disengagement of troops, establishment of verification mechanisms, modalities for integration of military forces and other essential tasks. It was necessary to assist the parties in overcoming their mutual mistrust and create additional impetus to the peace process. In the circumstances, the Secretary-General decided that it would be in the best interest of the peace process to proceed with preparations for deploying UN infantry to Angola, although he realized that there were certain risks involved. However, unless the parties complied without delay with their commitments under the Lusaka Protocol and provided logistic support to UNAVEM, it would not be possible to ensure that deployment would begin in May. UN efforts, he stressed, had to be matched by an unambiguous political will and concrete action by the parties.

The three observer countries, in a 24 March statement,[15] said that complete cooperation with UNAVEM personnel was required from the Government and UNITA and would continue to be the standard by which their compliance with the Lusaka Protocol would be measured. They urged both sides to accelerate preparations for a meeting between the President and Mr. Savimbi, as it would send a strong message to the Angolan people and the international community of their commitment to peace and national reconciliation. Angola's leaders had to recognize their responsibility not to lose that opportunity for peace. The observer States also reaffirmed their commitment to ensure that the Protocol was implemented fairly and rigorously and expressed the hope that sufficient funding and means, including aerial surveillance, would be available to enable UNAVEM to meet critical monitoring objectives.

**Report of the Secretary-General (April).** In a 7 April report,[16] the Secretary-General said cease-fire violations remained at a relatively low level. Not all reported cases could be verified and confirmed by UNAVEM, since its movements were still restricted by poor road conditions, unidentified mines and other factors. Complaints involved attacks on villages, ambushes, raids, looting, abduction of civilians, mine-laying and other violations. At the same time, unauthorized troop movements, extensive military preparations and heavy air activity continued. In some instances, tensions still rose dangerously high. On 29 March, a military aircraft attacked a UNITA-controlled airport in Andulo and, on 25 March, the UNAVEM team site in Chongoroi (southern region) was subjected to a deliberate, apparently planned attack by unidentified armed military elements. The team site was temporarily evacuated.

With regard to mechanisms for the verification of the cease-fire, improved access to UNITA-controlled areas made it possible to establish 47 of the 52 team sites and six regional headquarters outside Luanda. As at 1 April, UNAVEM strength was 527 military and police personnel. Despite the improved military situation, several logistic obstacles remained to the deployment of UNAVEM troops, including the provision of essential services and access to key facilities, air and vehicular transport, and the repair of roads, railways and airfields. Although the Government had made some accommodation and transport available to UNAVEM, more direct assistance was required. In addition, the Government had not indicated its readiness to sign the agreement with the United Nations on the status of UNAVEM forces.

Progress was made in the disengagement of troops in the central and northern regions. The two parties committed themselves to maintaining disengagement positions and agreed to complete the second phase of disengagement by 10 April. In the meantime, the Joint Commission held its twelfth regular session in Luanda on 28 March. It noted that the first phase of the disengagement of forces had been completed and took measures to ensure that the second phase, which involved Lunda Norte, Lunda Sul and Moxico provinces, would be completed as scheduled. The demobilization and reintegration process was reviewed in the light of the agreement on the incorporation of UNITA troops into FAA prior to any demobilization. The UN Unit for the Coordination of Humanitarian Assistance (UCAH) and UNAVEM finalized mechanisms for coordinating responsibilities in establishing and managing the quartering areas for UNITA troops.

Overall progress was made in the humanitarian sphere, despite the continuing tension in many parts of the country. Relief programmes were launched, while new evaluation missions were planned for isolated communities. Because of logistical constraints and insecure conditions, possibilities for transportation by road continued to be severely limited. Relief activities continued to rely heavily on airlift operations. With respect to the comprehensive mine-action programme, the Government established the National Mine Action Institute, and the Mine Advisory Group in Luena resumed clearance activities. The Central Mine Action Office of UCAH and UNAVEM began collecting information on the location of mines throughout the country. Several NGOs continued to remove mines in the provinces of Bié, Cunene, Kwanza Norte and Malange, but suspended their activities in Benguela province following an attack on relief workers on 2 March.

By a 12 April communiqué,[17] Angola, responding to the Secretary-General's report,[16] clarified that there had been substantial progress with respect to the cessation of hostilities. It said the replenishment of logistical supplies for UNITA continued to be verified; the deployment of military observers and police had been concluded, as had the disengagement of forces. The Government had provided all information requested by the United Nations concerning the bilateral cease-fire, and had notified the United Nations that it had allocated 800 demining troops and was waiting for UNAVEM to present its action plan. Angola said it had already been agreed at a military meeting between the Government and UNITA that identification of quartering areas was a UNAVEM responsibility. The Government had put at UNAVEM's disposition all it had been asked to provide for its installation. The status-of-forces agreement between the United Nations and Angola was to be signed before 15 April, Angola concluded.

**SECURITY COUNCIL ACTION (April)**

At its meeting on 13 April, the Council President, following consultations among Council members, made a statement on behalf of the Council:[18]

> The Security Council has considered the Secretary-General's progress report of 7 April 1995 on the United Nations Angola Verification Mission (UNAVEM III).
> The Security Council welcomes the confirmation by the Secretary-General that the cease-fire is generally holding and that the level of cease-fire violations has remained relatively low. It also welcomes the continued deployment of UNAVEM III military and police observers to team sites and regional headquarters outside Luanda, and the progress reported by him in a number of important areas, including liaison with UNITA, the completion of the first phase of disengagement and discussions of the modalities for the incorporation of UNITA into the national army. It commends the parties for their efforts in this regard.

> The Security Council notes that a number of developments give cause for concern. These include reports of continuing military actions and preparations, in particular the attack on the airstrip at Andulo by the Angolan air force, the failure to complete the second phase of disengagement by 10 April 1995, some restrictions on UNAVEM III's access to government military facilities, and recent attacks on the personnel of UNAVEM III and non-governmental organizations (NGOs). It welcomes the improved access by UNAVEM III to UNITA-controlled areas but notes that some local UNITA commanders continue to impose restrictions on the movement of UNAVEM III personnel and calls upon UNITA to ensure unrestricted access.

> The Security Council calls on the parties to co-operate fully with the United Nations, in particular through the Joint Commission, and to ensure the safety of the personnel of UNAVEM III and the NGOs. It notes with satisfaction that the members of the Joint Commission, including representatives of the Government of Angola, met Dr. Savimbi in Bailundo on 7 April and that at that meeting he publicly confirmed his commitment to the Lusaka Protocol. It reiterates its call for a meeting between President dos Santos and Dr. Savimbi as a matter of urgency because such a meeting may help to improve the climate of trust and give new impetus to the peace process in Angola.

> The Security Council welcomes the Secretary-General's decision to proceed with preparations for the deployment of UNAVEM III's infantry units. It notes that he has reminded the Angolan parties that they must implement without delay the requirements of the Lusaka Protocol, provide UNAVEM III with the indispensable logistic support, and undertake essential tasks such as mine-clearance, the repair of major transport routes, and the designation of quartering areas, to make it possible for United Nations infantry battalions to deploy to Angola in May 1995. The Council fully supports the Secretary-General in this regard and emphasizes the need for full implementation of the Lusaka Protocol. It welcomes his intention to deploy the infantry battalions in stages. It stresses the importance it attaches to the Government of Angola providing the logistic support envisaged for UNAVEM III. In this context it welcomes the Government of Angola's agreement to allow the United Nations full operational access to Catumbela airfield and calls upon the Government of Angola to ensure that this arrangement is extended for as long as required by UNAVEM III. It also welcomes the Government of Angola's intention to conclude, by 15 April 1995, a Status-of-Forces Agreement with the United Nations.

> The Security Council reaffirms the obligation of all States to implement fully the provisions of paragraph 19 of resolution 864(1993) and states that the continuing flow of arms into Angola contrary to the provisions of the "Acordos de Paz" and resolution 976 (1995) contributes to the country's instability and undermines efforts at confidence-building.

> The Security Council is encouraged that the Secretary-General has been able to report overall progress in the humanitarian situation in the month since his last report to the Council. It calls upon the parties to continue to facilitate access to all areas of the country for the delivery of humanitarian assistance.

It also calls once again upon the parties to respect the safety and security of all humanitarian personnel in Angola. It endorses the call on the parties by the three observer States to the Angolan peace process to co-operate fully in releasing all war-related detainees through the International Committee of the Red Cross, as well as all captured foreign citizens or to provide information about their fate.

While the Security Council takes note of the progress made in the implementation of the comprehensive mine-action programme, it also notes the statement in the Secretary-General's report that the mine situation in Angola remains critical. The Council therefore urges both parties to support and facilitate mine-clearance and to comply fully with the relevant provisions of the Lusaka Protocol. In this context, it welcomes the statement by the Special Representative of the Secretary-General following the 13th meeting of the Joint Commission that the Government of Angola and UNITA have pledged to put 800 and 400 personnel respectively at the disposal of UNAVEM III for mine-clearance activities.

The Security Council will continue to monitor the situation in Angola closely. It looks forward to the next monthly report of the Secretary-General and requests him, in the meantime, to ensure that it is kept informed of developments in Angola and on prospects for the prompt deployment of the infantry battalions of UNAVEM III.

*Meeting number.* SC 3518.

**Report of the Secretary-General (May).** On 3 May, the Secretary-General reported[19] that preparations for the meeting between President dos Santos and Mr. Savimbi were at an advanced stage. Agreement had been reached on the agenda and on practical details. His Special Representative had travelled to Lusaka, Zambia, on 21 April to discuss final arrangements. He also reported that on 3 May the status-of-forces agreement for UNAVEM III was signed. The cease-fire continued to hold generally and there had been a further reduction in the number of violations reported. However, the situation in several areas remained tense, as both sides continued to occupy forward positions, sporadically attacking the local population and conducting troop movements. Despite some problems, the second phase of disengagement was almost complete. A number of difficulties persisted in the area of communication links; contact with government troops was established in all regions, but effective communication with UNITA existed only in the regions of Huambo and Uige. Deployment of military observers to all 53 team sites was completed. The civilian police component of UNAVEM III was fully operational. As at 26 April, 185 civilian police observers from 17 countries were deployed to all 29 team sites, including the six regional headquarters.

No additional military data had been provided to the United Nations by the Government or UNITA since November 1994. However, at a Joint Commission meeting on 20 April, the parties agreed on the principle of "global incorporation" of UNITA soldiers into the national army, to be followed by gradual demobilization, until FAA reached the level of 90,000 troops, a figure accepted by both parties.

UNAVEM continued to accelerate the start of country-wide demining. Although the Government and UNITA had pledged to put 800 and 400 personnel, respectively, at the disposal of UNAVEM mine-clearance activities, both parties had yet to release funds or equipment for the programme to become operational. In the meantime, UNAVEM recommended to the parties that they begin mine-sweeping operations on major roads under their control to make the deployment of UN troops possible. A substantial increase was registered in the number of mine incidents involving civilians. The Government and UNITA agreed to provide the United Nations with information on the location of mines.

Efforts to intensify the distribution of humanitarian aid by road had begun to show results. Several overland convoys had been successfully organized. Although some progress was made in opening the three main road corridors—Luanda/Malanje, Benguela/Kuito and Namibe/Menongue—much reconstruction and mine-clearing work remained to be done. The same factors were hindering the return of displaced people to their places of origin. The UN Demobilization and Reintegration Office visited UNITA headquarters in Bailundo to discuss the humanitarian assistance component of the demobilization and reintegration programme. The second phase of the survey on the social and economic needs of demobilized soldiers from UNITA and FAA was launched; the results of that survey would be used in the design of training and social integration programmes.

The Secretary-General later reported[20] that President dos Santos and Mr. Savimbi met in Lusaka on 6 May. They had discussed all aspects of the peace process and pledged their cooperation to consolidate peace in Angola and to implement the Lusaka Protocol, he said. In preparation for their next meeting, which they agreed would take place in Luanda, senior government officials visited Mr. Savimbi on 25 May in Bailundo.

**SECURITY COUNCIL ACTION (May)**

The Security Council met on 11 May to consider the Secretary-General's report. Following consultations among its members, the President made a statement on behalf of the Council:[21]

The Security Council has considered the Secretary-General's third progress report of 3 May 1995 on the United Nations Angola Verification Mission (UNAVEM III) and the oral briefing from the Secretariat.

The Security Council welcomes the positive developments in Angola. It welcomes in particular the meeting in Lusaka on 6 May 1995 between President dos Santos and Dr. Savimbi which took place in a positive atmosphere and gave new impetus to the consolidation of the peace process and the furthering of national reconciliation in Angola. The Council commends the efforts of the Special Representative of the Secretary-General, of the observer States to the Angola peace process, of States of the region and, in particular, of the President of Zambia which assisted in bringing about this meeting. It expresses the hope that the meeting will mark the beginning of a regular and constructive dialogue between the President of Angola and the leader of UNITA.

The Security Council notes with satisfaction the progress in the implementation of the Lusaka Protocol concerning, *inter alia*, reduction of cease-fire violations, the disengagement of forces, the cooperation among the parties and UNAVEM III, the signing of the status-of-forces agreement and the providing of logistic facilities for the mission. The Council welcomes the ongoing deployment of UNAVEM III support units and stresses the importance of a timely deployment of the infantry battalions of UNAVEM III.

The Security Council is however concerned by the slow progress in other areas. It stresses the necessity for the increased cooperation of the Government and UNITA with the United Nations in carrying out all major provisions of the Lusaka Protocol and relevant Security Council resolutions. While welcoming the release of the first group of prisoners, the Council urges the parties to expedite this process. Urgent attention should be given to the quartering of UNITA soldiers by the parties as well as the United Nations and the withdrawal of government troops to their barracks in order to permit the incorporation of UNITA troops within the national army and police in accordance with the Lusaka Protocol. The Council stresses also the importance of the completion of the disengagement process and the improvement of communication links with UNITA in all regions. It recalls the conditions set forth in Security Council resolution 976(1995) for the deployment of infantry units and calls upon the parties in Angola to take all necessary steps to ensure that these conditions are met promptly for the timely deployment of sustainable infantry units throughout Angola capable of fully discharging their mandated tasks.

The Security Council particularly underlines the urgency of a mine-clearance programme and calls upon the parties to provide, as promised, the funds and equipment necessary in order for the programme to become operational, and to begin mine-sweeping operations on major roads under their control. The demining, the opening of major roads and repair of airfields and other infrastructure are of crucial importance for the expeditious deployment of UNAVEM infantry units, the distribution of humanitarian aid, and the return of displaced persons to their places of origin. The Council invites the donors as well as the United Nations, its agencies and non-governmental organizations to support actively demining actions.

The Security Council notes with satisfaction the amelioration of the humanitarian situation in Angola and calls upon the parties to cooperate without restriction with the United Nations and other humanitarian international organizations to facilitate the distribution of aid in all the regions and to intensify their efforts to guarantee the security of humanitarian transports and of UNAVEM personnel. It requests Member States to continue to support the ongoing humanitarian activities in Angola and to disburse as soon as possible the contributions pledged during the donors' meeting in February 1995.

The Security Council will continue to monitor the situation in Angola closely and looks forward to the next monthly report of the Secretary-General.

*Meeting number.* SC 3534.

**Report of the Secretary-General (June).** On 4 June, the Secretary-General reported[20] that he had written to President dos Santos and Mr. Savimbi on 10 May to express the hope that some of the issues raised at their 6 May meeting would be resolved at the next meeting so that the peace process could be accelerated, and to assure them of UN support. In other positive developments, the Joint Commission travelled to and from Lobito by road for its special meeting on 18 May to demonstrate that a major road was now safe for travel; the Government had released through ICRC more than 200 UNITA prisoners; and, pending the establishment of an independent UN radio station, UNAVEM had started broadcasting an information programme over radio and television facilities made available by the Government.

Nevertheless, the second phase of disengagement was not fully completed. Agreement was reached in the Joint Commission that, after the demobilization of troops, 74,000 of the 90,000 FAA soldiers would be ground troops, provided in equal numbers by the two parties. The national defence force would also comprise air and naval forces of 11,000 and 5,000 troops, respectively. In that regard, UNITA provided the Special Representative with additional details of the strength of its forces. The Secretary-General considered it important to initiate as soon as possible an exchange of information between the parties on their military equipment and installations.

The Secretary-General said that he intended to strengthen the military component of UNAVEM by adding two specialized engineering companies, within the Mission's authorized strength of 7,000. The further dispatch of UN infantry would depend on progress in opening major access roads and in mine clearance. The number of civilian police observers stood at 210 as at 30 May. Although support from the Angolan police was encouraging in most areas, there was still room for improvement in others. There had been little progress in quartering the Government's rapid reaction police, due mainly to delays in making adequate barracks available.

There had been an increase in banditry against the civilian population, including international staff, the Secretary-General went on; on 15 May, a senior UNAVEM police observer had been killed in Luanda, an apparent act of banditry. The Government promised to investigate the incident and would take additional measures to enhance the security of UN and other international personnel.

A plan was finalized to address mine-clearance requirements for the deployment of UNAVEM infantry troops and other essential functions of the Mission. Demining operations were initiated in several parts of the country, and the Government pledged $3 million for mine-clearance activities. That effort was to be supplemented by the Central Mine Action Training School, to be established by the United Nations.

Progress had been made in opening cost-efficient overland routes for the delivery of humanitarian assistance. NGOs continued to clear mines in and around major towns, and the Norwegian People's Aid had initiated a mine survey in the northern provinces. The UN Children's Fund and the Office of the UN High Commissioner for Refugees (UNHCR) had launched mine-awareness and -avoidance programmes for internally displaced persons and refugees. Humanitarian agencies reported improved nutritional conditions in a few areas, allowing suspension of general food distribution there. However, overall food aid requirements were still considerable. Only 15 per cent of resources solicited in the 1995 humanitarian appeal for Angola had been received. The Secretary-General appealed to the international community to replenish the humanitarian stocks for Angola as a matter of urgency.

By a 15 June letter,[22] the Security Council President informed the Secretary-General that the Council members welcomed the positive developments, supported the ongoing dialogue between the two parties and encouraged a further meeting between President dos Santos and Mr. Savimbi. They noted with concern that the peace process was still behind schedule and remained concerned about the problem of mines. They endorsed the Secretary-General's call that the parties reinforce their recent actions in mine clearance and road and bridge repair, and they agreed that the international community should support those vital tasks. They also supported the Secretary-General's appeal to the parties to work out modalities for the quartering of UNITA troops and the withdrawal of the rapid reaction police to barracks.

Expressing distress over the loss of life of a UN police observer and the wounding of a military observer, the Council members recalled the parties' responsibility for the safety and security of all UN personnel in Angola.

**Report of the Secretary-General (July).** On 17 July, the Secretary-General reported[23] that since the 6 May meeting between President dos Santos and Mr. Savimbi, high-level contacts between the Government and UNITA had intensified. In addition, the two leaders were in regular telephone contact. On 16 June, the Central Committee of the ruling Movimento Popular para a Libertacão de Angola (MPLA) offered Mr. Savimbi one of two positions of Vice-President, with the other to be held by a senior member of MPLA. In late June, the two parties signed a comprehensive working document following a review of modalities for accelerating the implementation of the Lusaka Protocol. The Secretary-General visited Angola from 14 to 16 July to review progress made and assess the situation on the ground.

UNITA insisted that no further disengagement of troops should take place until the Government withdrew from areas it had reoccupied in Huambo and Uige provinces. However, agreement was reached that both parties would keep their troops *in situ* until UNITA troops moved to quartering areas and government troops moved to barracks. Both sides had begun essential demining activities throughout the country, with the cooperation of UNAVEM, UCAH and NGOs. That notwithstanding, the pace of mine clearance remained slow and there were allegations about renewed laying of mines in some parts of the country. UNAVEM called on the parties to end that practice. An effort was under way to establish 4 of the planned 14 sites in the northern and central regions for the quartering and demobilization of UNITA troops. High-level government and UNITA delegations met from 19 June to 1 July and agreed on almost all quartering locations and the sequence of the quartering process; on basic conditions for assembly areas; on the modalities of FAA withdrawal to barracks; and on the need to eliminate checkpoints and organize additional humanitarian convoys to formerly inaccessible areas. However, certain aspects, such as the incorporation of UNITA troops with FAA, required further consideration, and the delegations were to meet again in Luanda.

As at 4 July, in addition to the six regional headquarters, 337 military observers had been deployed at 55 sites throughout Angola. Deployment of UN-formed units, whose total strength was 1,970, proceeded in accordance with the adjusted timeframe. Civilian police observers (CIVPOL) numbered 209.

CIVPOL reported that the situation in most of the country was fairly calm and complaints about the conduct of the national police were relatively few. The Angolan parties registered complaints about human rights violations with the Special Representative and the Joint Commission. In response, UNAVEM established a small sub-unit to deal with human rights issues and to observe implementation of the relevant provisions of the Lusaka Protocol. Five human rights specialists had been put at UNAVEM's disposal by the European Union. The Secretary-General intended, with the agreement of the Security Council, to strengthen that unit by up to 11, so that human rights monitors could be stationed in all 18 provinces. He noted that the Lusaka Protocol provided for the disarmament of the civilian population; with the proliferation of weapons and the increase in banditry, he said, the disarmament programme must begin without further delay.

An important step towards building confidence and facilitating humanitarian aid was the 14 June meeting in Bailundo of the Humanitarian Coordination Group, the first to be held outside Luanda, with strong UNITA representation. Another significant development was the initiation of plans to resettle some 40,000 displaced persons residing in Jamba, whom UNITA had requested the Angolan Government and the United Nations to help return to their places of origin. Progress was made in launching joint humanitarian initiatives in areas under the control of both parties, in which government agencies, UNITA and the United Nations were working together. There had been significant spontaneous movement of internally displaced persons to their places of origin in the provinces of Bengo, Benguela and Kwanza Norte. A workshop for representatives of the Government, UNITA, UN agencies and NGOs had been held (Luanda, 22-24 June) to develop a standard strategy for providing assistance to internally displaced persons. In June, UNHCR appealed for $44 million to fund the repatriation of 300,000 Angolan refugees residing in neighbouring countries (see PART FOUR, Chapter XII).

Economic and social conditions continued to be extremely precarious. The enormous difficulties facing Angola during the transition period were reflected in the fact that up to 70 per cent of the basic health system was destroyed, only 18 per cent of the population had access to sanitation and 34 per cent to safe water, the infant mortality rate was 195 per 1,000, the food deficit for 1995 was expected to be 360,000 tons, some 70,000 people were mutilated by weapons or mines, and 1.2 million internally displaced persons, 300,000 refugees and 3.2 million other people were in need of emergency humanitarian assistance. The country's debt/export ratio had reached 365 per cent, and the estimated gross domestic product per capita had fallen to $410, half that of 1990. The inflation rate was 1,838 per cent in 1993 and 972 per cent in 1994, while military spending in 1994 was estimated to be 39 per cent of the State budget.

The World Bank had developed plans to support Angola's reconstruction efforts. In addition, with the participation of UN agencies, a debt strategy for Angola had been prepared, as had pro-grammes for divesting public companies and streamlining public services. The Government, with support from the UN Development Programme (UNDP) and the Special Representative, organized a round table on rehabilitation and community development in September (see PART FOUR, Chapter III). UN agencies were prepared to assist in strengthening national capacity for coordinating assistance and intended to accelerate discussions with the Government concerning joint programming.

The Secretary-General recommended that the UNAVEM mandate be extended until 8 February 1996, the beneficial effects of UN involvement in the settlement of the Angolan conflict having become evident.

**SECURITY COUNCIL ACTION (August)**

Following consideration of the Secretary-General's report, the Security Council on 7 August adopted **resolution 1008(1995)**.

*The Security Council,*

*Reaffirming* its resolution 696(1991) of 30 May 1991 and all subsequent relevant resolutions,

*Having considered* the report of the Secretary-General dated 17 July 1995,

*Welcoming* the briefing by the Secretary-General on 25 July 1995 on his recent visit to Angola,

*Reaffirming* its commitment to preserve the unity and territorial integrity of Angola,

*Reiterating* the importance it attaches to the full implementation by the Government of Angola and União Nacional para a Independência Total de Angola (UNITA) of the "Acordos de Paz", the Lusaka Protocol and relevant Security Council resolutions,

*Noting* the agreement reached between the Government of Angola and UNITA on the adjusted and accelerated timetable for the implementation of the Lusaka Protocol,

*Commending* the continued efforts of the Secretary-General, his Special Representative, the three observer States to the Angolan peace process and the personnel of the United Nations Angola Verification Mission (UNAVEM III) to facilitate the implementation of the Lusaka Protocol and to consolidate the cease-fire and the peace process which has entered a new and promising phase,

*Noting also* that the situation in most of the country is fairly calm, but concerned at the number of cease-fire violations,

*Welcoming* the meeting in Lusaka on 6 May 1995 between the President of Angola, Mr. José Eduardo dos Santos, and the leader of UNITA, Mr. Jonas Savimbi, which led to the diminishing atmosphere of mistrust and intensification of high-level contacts between the Government of Angola and UNITA,

*Recognizing* that the progressive deployment of United Nations military and police observers and troops has significantly contributed to consolidation of the cease-fire,

*Welcoming* the commitment of the international community to assist and support the economic, social and reconstruction efforts of Angola and recognizing the importance of such assistance in sustaining a secure and stable environment,

*Expressing concern* at reports of human rights violations and recognizing the contribution that human rights monitors can make in building confidence in the peace process,

1. *Welcomes* the report of the Secretary-General dated 17 July 1995;

2. *Decides* to extend the mandate of UNAVEM III until 8 February 1996;

3. *Commends* the Government of Angola and UNITA for their commitment to the peace process and notes the progress made thus far in the implementation of the Lusaka Protocol;

4. *Expresses concern* at the slow pace in the implementation of the Lusaka Protocol, in particular troop disengagement, demining and the establishment of quartering areas, and expects the Government of Angola and UNITA, in cooperation with UNAVEM III, to finalize arrangements for establishment of quartering areas, complete troop disengagement, and to expedite the conduct of demining;

5. *Urges* the Government of Angola and UNITA to adhere strictly to the revised timetable on the implementation of the Lusaka Protocol and make concerted efforts to accelerate that process;

6. *Stresses* the importance of the completion of the electoral process, as provided for in the Lusaka Protocol;

7. *Calls upon* the Government of Angola and UNITA to adopt without further delay a comprehensive and workable programme for the formation of the new armed forces, and accelerate the exchange of prisoners and the repatriation of mercenaries with a view to reinforcing the freedom of movement of people throughout the country;

8. *Takes note* of the progress noted by the Secretary-General in the establishment of triangular communications between the Angolan parties and UNAVEM III and requests the Government of Angola and UNITA to assign urgently liaison officers to UNAVEM III regional headquarters;

9. *Urges* the two parties to put an immediate and definitive end to the renewed laying of mines and to reported unauthorized movement of troops;

10. *Requests* the Secretary-General to continue the deployment of UNAVEM III infantry units and accelerate it as conditions for sustaining and employing troops improve, with the objective of reaching full strength as soon as possible;

11. *Urges* the Government of Angola and UNITA to provide UNAVEM III with the necessary information and ensure the freedom of movement of UNAVEM III, including full unimpeded access to all military facilities, to enable it effectively to discharge its mandate;

12. *Requests* that the Secretary-General report on his analysis on the completion of the objectives of the Lusaka Protocol and of the mandate of UNAVEM III, in the light of the alterations in the timetable for deployment of UNAVEM III;

13. *Stresses* the need for dissemination of objective information through radio UNAVEM and for the Government of Angola to provide all facilities for the prompt functioning of the radio;

14. *Stresses* the importance it attaches to the disarmament of the civilian population, and urges that it begin without further delay;

15. *Notes with concern* increasing levels of violence perpetrated by unaffiliated groups, and calls on all parties to seek to control and disarm these threats to the peace process;

16. *Authorizes* the Secretary-General to increase as appropriate the strength of UNAVEM III's human rights unit;

17. *Commends* Member States, United Nations agencies and non-governmental organizations for their substantial contributions to meet the humanitarian needs of the Angolan people;

18. *Demands* that the Government of Angola and UNITA take necessary measures to ensure the safe passage of humanitarian supplies throughout the country;

19. *Requests* the Government of Angola to continue providing substantial contributions to the United Nations peace-keeping operations and call upon UNITA to make every effort to contribute proportionally in order to assist with the United Nations peace-keeping operation in Angola;

20. *Endorses* the Secretary-General's appeal and encourages donors to respond with generous and timely financial contributions to the humanitarian effort and provision of mine clearance, bridging and road repair equipment and materials and other supplies necessary for setting up the quartering areas;

21. *Endorses also* the Secretary-General's intention to submit a comprehensive report to the Council every two months;

22. *Decides* to remain actively seized of the matter.

Security Council resolution 1008(1995)

7 August 1995     Meeting 3562     Adopted unanimously

Draft prepared in consultations among Council members (S/1995/646).

**Report of the Secretary-General (October).** In October, the Secretary-General reported[24] that President dos Santos and Mr. Savimbi had met in Franceville, Gabon, on 10 August and in Brussels, Belgium, on 25 September. During their August meeting, they agreed on modalities to continue bilateral discussions on the completion of the formation of FAA, including the global incorporation of UNITA troops in FAA. General understandings were reached on ways to define the powers and responsibilities of the two Vice-Presidents and on the holding of legislative and presidential elections. In Brussels, the two leaders agreed on consolidating the peace process and the progress achieved so far. Following a special session of the Joint Commission, held in Uige—headquarters of the northern region—on 19 August, the Government and UNITA issued a joint statement on 25 August reaffirming their intention to guarantee free movement of persons and goods throughout the territory, with certain controls at border posts and access points to cities.

Reports of cease-fire violations showed a steady decline, to their lowest level to date. The situation in most regions remained relatively calm and stable, except for numerous acts of banditry. Troops from both sides remained generally *in situ*, but tensions persisted, particularly in the diamond-rich area of Lucapa in the north-east, where both sides were seeking to consolidate and enlarge the areas they controlled. Reinforcements and sporadic shelling by both sides were reported in the northern region, and there was some tension in the southern region. UNAVEM reconnoitred all 15 proposed quartering areas, 11 of which were approved by the parties. The establishing of quartering areas began and work at Vila Nova and Londiumbali, in the province of Huambo, was practically completed. The Demobilization and Reintegration Office of the UCAH finalized preparations for the humanitarian assistance programme in the quartering areas. Equipment for registering UNITA soldiers had been received and UN Volunteers, who were to carry out the registration process in the quartering areas, arrived in the country. A coordination group, chaired by the Special Representative's Deputy, was set up to enhance coordination and decision-making during the pre-quartering and quartering phases.

Modalities for the formation of FAA were entrusted to the Joint General Staff, which established a standing committee of high-ranking officers under the direct supervision of President dos Santos and Mr. Savimbi. A high-ranking UNITA military delegation arrived in Luanda on 18 September to begin discussions with the Government on the issue.

During August, roads in the northern and south-eastern regions were successfully demined. However, UNAVEM continued to investigate allegations about renewed laying of mines. The United Nations contracted a commercial company from South Africa to undertake mine clearance and verification on approximately 7,000 kilometres of roads, while international NGOs were active in mine-awareness training and demining in some provinces.

Several meetings were held with officials of the Angolan national police to discuss the quartering of the rapid reaction police and the disarming of the civilian population. It was agreed that those two operations were to be undertaken simultaneously with the quartering of UNITA soldiers. The issue of special security for UNITA leaders had yet to be resolved. In addition to the special security arrangements in the Lusaka Protocol, UNITA asked for special protection and accommodation for its officials in all provincial headquarters, while the Government insisted on the letter of the Protocol, which provided only for members of the political committee and the national provincial secretaries.

Frequent violations of human rights continued, particularly by elements of the armed forces and police of both sides. The Joint Commission requested UNAVEM to report periodically on the human rights situation and on violations. In Au-gust, 10 more prisoners were released by the Government and UNITA, bringing the total released to 230. Another 213 detainees on both sides were visited by ICRC, but were yet to be released.

A priority for UN agencies and NGOs was to support internally displaced persons returning to their home areas. With the gradual consolidation of the peace process and the reopening of roads, displaced persons began to return, particularly in the provinces of Benguela, Huambo, Bié and Bengo. On the other hand, in Uige some 3,000 new displacements occurred as a result of hostilities between government and UNITA forces. In July, the Government, UNITA and UNHCR held talks with Zambian authorities on a repatriation and reintegration programme for 26,000 Angolan refugees living in Zambia. Meanwhile, some spontaneous repatriation took place from the Republic of Zaire to the provinces of Uige and Zaire.

With the planting season starting and with the coordination of the Food and Agriculture Organization of the United Nations and the Ministry of Agriculture, UN agencies and NGOs were distributing 7,000 tons of seeds and more than 1.2 million agricultural tools. Increased road access reduced the need for costly airlifts. By mid-September, the World Food Programme was able to deliver 70 per cent of its humanitarian assistance by road. With the assistance of UNDP and other agencies, the Government mapped out a strategy to bring the country out of its humanitarian crisis and guide it to economic revival and sustained development. A programme of community rehabilitation and national reconciliation was presented to the first Round-Table Conference of donors (Brussels, September) (see PART FOUR, Chapter III). The International Monetary Fund collaborated in the implementation of the Government's new economic and social programme for 1995 and 1996. The World Bank planned a substantially increased programme, working with the Government to prepare projects dealing with emergency reconstruction, agricultural rehabilitation and manpower training. With funding from Japan and the Bank, preparations for a community-based rehabilitation programme were completed and a Social Support Fund established.

**SECURITY COUNCIL ACTION**

The Security Council met on 12 October. After consultations among Council members, the President made the following statement on behalf of the Council:[25]

The Security Council welcomes the Secretary-General's report of 4 October 1995 on the United Nations Angola Verification Mission (UNAVEM III) pursuant to paragraph 21 of Security Council resolution 1008(1995) of 7 August 1995.

The Security Council has noted the positive developments in Angola since the Secretary-General's report of 17 July 1995. The Council is encouraged by the meetings in Franceville and Brussels between President dos Santos and Dr. Savimbi which provided the opportunity to discuss the critical issues and reach agreement on consolidation of the peace process. These meetings, particularly the round table in Brussels, provided important reassurance to the international community. The Council welcomes the continued commitment of both parties to the process of dialogue. The Council commends the efforts of the Secretary-General and his Special Representative, of the observer States to the Angola peace process and of States in the region to help in carrying forward the process.

The Security Council notes with satisfaction the progress in the implementation of the Lusaka Protocol, including the reduction of cease-fire violations, the disengagement of forces, the enhanced cooperation between the parties and UNAVEM III, the signing of the status-of-forces agreement, the provision of logistic facilities for the mission and the conclusion of the joint declaration on the free circulation of persons and goods. The Council also welcomes the ongoing deployment of UNAVEM III support units and stresses the importance of a timely deployment of the infantry battalions of UNAVEM III. The Council stresses the importance of an independent UNAVEM radio and urges the Government of Angola to provide, without delay, the facilities to allow it to operate.

The Security Council none the less remains concerned at delays in the peace process, in particular in respect of quartering of UNITA and the rapid reaction police, demining, disarmament, the return of the FAA to barracks and the formation of the new armed forces as well as the repatriation of mercenaries. The Council underscores the peril that may result from further delays. The Council is also deeply concerned at allegations of renewed laying of mines and demands that all parties refrain from such actions.

The Security Council emphasizes that continuing cooperation between the parties is essential if a sustained cessation of hostilities is to take hold. In this regard, the Council calls on the parties to refrain from troop movements or military activities that might create tension or lead to renewed hostilities.

The Security Council is concerned about the continuing complaints of human rights violations, and endorses the decision of the Joint Commission to inscribe human rights in the agenda of all its regular sessions.

The Security Council wishes to emphasize that post-peace-keeping elements can make an important contribution to a viable long-term peace. The Council notes the linkage between political and economic well-being and the need to ensure that displaced people and refugees are able to return to their places of origin. The Council reaffirms the Secretary-General's call for a comprehensive coordinated and integrated effort on the part of all relevant international organizations to help rebuild the Angolan economic infrastructure. The Council requests Member States to continue to support the ongoing humanitarian activities in Angola. It welcomes the commitments made at the Round-Table Conference, held in Brussels in September 1995, and urges those that have made pledges to fulfil their commitments as soon as possible.

The Security Council will continue to monitor closely the situation in Angola and looks forward to future reports of the Secretary-General.

*Meeting number.* SC 3586.

**Communication.** On 13 November, the Government and UNITA issued a joint communiqué,[26] noting that, following various problems which had created difficulties in re-establishing confidence between them, discussions were held on 9 and 13 November during which all issues were resolved. The Government and UNITA reaffirmed their good faith and good will to cooperate in carrying out the provisions of the Lusaka Protocol to a successful conclusion. They undertook to continue working on all aspects connected with the security of all citizens, including the security of the leader of UNITA; to carry on the work of the UNITA military group with the General Staff of FAA, on the overall incorporation and completion of formation of the Angolan armed forces and gradual demobilization; and to work with UNAVEM III and within the framework of the Joint Commission in order to initiate quickly and efficiently the movement of forces and means, particularly the quartering of UNITA military forces and subsequent actions, the quartering of the rapid reaction police and the return of FAA to the nearest quarters.

**SECURITY COUNCIL ACTION (November)**

The Security Council met on 28 November to consider the situation in Angola. Following consultations, the President made a statement on behalf of the Council members:[27]

The Security Council welcomes the joint communiqué issued by the Government of Angola and UNITA on 13 November 1995 in which they reaffirmed their commitment to the peace process. The Council is pleased to note that some of the steps necessary to carry out the provisions of the Lusaka Protocol have been taken recently, including the resumption of the military talks in Luanda, and the movement of the first UNITA combatants to quartering areas on 20 November 1995, the first anniversary of the signing of the Lusaka Protocol. The Council underlines the need for the quartering process to be completed as soon as possible.

The Security Council, however, notes that despite these positive steps there continue to be cease-fire violations, importation of weapons, restrictions on freedom of movement, and the presence of mercenaries. The Council stresses that much remains to be done urgently to implement fully the Lusaka Protocol, including strict observance of the cease-fire, the continuation of the quartering process, the quartering of the rapid reaction police, the return of the Forças Armadas Angolanas (FAA) to defensive positions, and the resolution of questions regarding the modalities of military integration. The Council calls upon the

Government of Angola and UNITA to continue to cooperate with UNAVEM III and to respect fully the status and security of international personnel.

The Security Council will follow developments in Angola closely and looks forward to receiving the comprehensive report of the Secretary-General on the situation in Angola by 8 December 1995.

*Meeting number.* SC 3598.

### Report of the Secretary-General (December).

In December, the Secretary-General reported[28] that full deployment of the UNAVEM military component was close to completion. As at 30 November, there were 6,184 military personnel all ranks, including 331 military observers. Their presence had already had a positive impact on the overall military situation in the country, despite the delays in the quartering process, the Secretary-General stated. Deployment of UN troops to the eastern parts of the country was hindered by mined roads and damaged bridges, as well as difficulties in sustaining UNAVEM III sites by air, given financial constraints.

UNAVEM continued to monitor the military situation and defuse individual incidents. In many areas, government and UNITA troops were still in close proximity and their aggressive patrolling undermined attempts to create the atmosphere of trust necessary for the quartering of troops. Tensions were most acute in Uige, Cabinda, Lunda Norte and Lunda Sul, where large troop movements had taken place. A propaganda campaign was launched against UNAVEM III in Uige and Benguela. Hostile demonstrations were held and, in a Government-controlled radio programme, the population of the province had been urged to "prepare for war" against UNAVEM III. In separate incidents on 24 and 25 October, UNAVEM and UCAH convoys were detained and subjected to harassment by UNITA. Increased acts of banditry also posed a threat to the peace process, as well as to the security of UN and other international staff.

Negotiations on the completion of the formation of FAA had resumed on 17 November. In the meantime, reconnaissance of 15 quartering areas for UNITA troops was completed and all sites but one were approved by the parties. A phased approach to quartering was adopted and construction of six additional cantonment areas began. The quartering of UNITA forces was finally launched in Vila Nova, Huambo province, on 20 November, the date of the first anniversary of the signing of the Lusaka Protocol. On 1 December, 363 individuals reported for cantonment there. The Government complained that they were "boy soldiers" with unserviceable weapons. The target of quartering an average of 150 soldiers daily was far from being realized. The Government finally provided UNAVEM with information on locations,

in Huambo and Uige provinces, to which FAA forces would withdraw.

The presence of large numbers of unexploded mines still seriously affected UN operations. However, joint demining activities in the province of Cuando Cubango had already resulted in the opening of several important roads. Germany was providing the services of experts to assist in quality control of the contract with a South African demining firm working in Angola, while the United States was to supply bridging equipment in December. The demining school established by the Central Mine Action Office of UCAH began training of a first group of 112 Angolan students. The Office also cooperated with the Angolan National Institute for the Removal of Explosive Devices in the joint training of some 250 local deminers, recruited from the ranks of former Angolan soldiers.

Human rights continued to be of special concern. At the request of the parties, UNAVEM III intended to launch a nationwide programme to disseminate basic information on human rights. The Special Representative held a series of training workshops and seminars for government officers, in the capital and in the regions. Additional human rights monitors were to be deployed to the regions to generate support from local government and UNITA officials for better respect for human rights.

The spontaneous, as well as organized, return of internally displaced persons continued. However, the return movement still involved less than 10 per cent of the displaced population, estimated at 1.2 million, and was expected to slow down even further because of transport difficulties during the rainy season and because people would not be able to return in time for the agricultural season. Progress continued in the expansion of overland humanitarian access. Several main roads from the coast to major towns in the hinterland were opened, as were some secondary roads in the interior. The opening of the Lobito-Huambo road and other routes facilitated the assistance programme to UNITA quartering areas in the provinces of Huambo and Bié and in the central highlands.

The Secretary-General observed that much had been achieved since the signing of the Lusaka Protocol, but many factors that prevented implementation of the earlier peace accords were still very much in evidence. He appealed to the Government and UNITA to demonstrate through concrete action that they were indeed committed to peace and ready to correct those negative factors.

**SECURITY COUNCIL ACTION (December)**

The Security Council met on 21 December to consider the report of the Secretary-General. Following consultations among its members, the President made a statement on behalf of the Council:[29]

The Security Council has considered the Secretary-General's report of 7 December 1995 on the United Nations Angola Verification Mission (UNAVEM III) pursuant to paragraph 21 of Security Council resolution 1008(1995) of 7 August 1995.

The Security Council reiterates its concern at the slow progress in implementation of the provisions of the Lusaka Protocol. The Council stresses the importance of full implementation of the political and all other aspects of the peace process. It underlines that several important tasks that were to have been resolved in the early stages of the peace process remain incomplete, including the exchange of detailed military information, the release of all prisoners, the redeployment of those government troops near UNITA quartering areas, and the final resolution of the issue of mercenaries. In this respect, the Council welcomes the recent announcement by the Government of Angola that it will terminate the contract and repatriate the personnel of the firm involved and will release all remaining prisoners.

The Security Council notes that the deployment of UNAVEM III troops is nearly complete and that four quartering areas are prepared to receive troops. The Council expresses its disappointment at the slow pace at which the quartering process has proceeded. It calls upon UNITA and the Government of Angola to fulfil their commitments regarding the expeditious quartering and demobilization of former combatants, the quartering of the rapid reaction police, and the return of the Forças Armadas Angolanas (FAA) to the nearest barracks.

The Security Council expresses deep concern at the delays in establishing modalities for the integration of the armed forces which is vital for the process of national reconciliation. The Council notes with dismay the series of disruptions in the military talks between the parties. It urges the parties to continue the military talks without interruption and to conclude an equitable and practicable agreement without further delay. The Council underlines that such an agreement should give particular attention to the expeditious completion of the demobilization and integration of former combatants. It recognizes that the prompt and complete exchange of military information is vital to the success of these talks and urges the parties to provide the information required by the Lusaka Protocol without further delay.

The Security Council is gravely concerned by continued violations of the cease-fire and military offensives, in particular events in the north-west. The Council calls on both parties to refrain from military activities or troop movements which lead to increased tensions and resumed hostilities and to implement without delay the disengagement plan being prepared by UNAVEM.

The Security Council deplores the recent threat to the safety of UNAVEM III personnel. The Council reminds the parties, in particular UNITA, that they must take the steps necessary to ensure the safety and security of all UNAVEM III and other international personnel.

The Security Council expresses regret that UNAVEM radio is not yet operational. The Council calls upon the Government of Angola to facilitate its immediate establishment. It also calls upon both parties to cease the dissemination of hostile propaganda.

The Security Council is concerned at delays in implementing mine-clearance programmes planned by the United Nations and by Member States, and calls upon the Government of Angola to facilitate issuance of necessary authorizations to relevant personnel. The Council calls upon the Government of Angola and UNITA to intensify their individual and joint demining efforts. It underlines that the opening of roads within Angola, including the clearance of mines and the restoration of bridges, is vital not only to the peace process and the complete deployment of UNAVEM III but also to the effective delivery of humanitarian assistance and future peace-building efforts. The Council is gravely concerned at the reports of remining in violation of the Lusaka Protocol.

The Security Council emphasizes that Angolans themselves bear ultimate responsibility for restoring peace and stability in their country. The Council stresses that concrete actions are urgently needed from the parties to put the peace process on an irreversible course. It notes that continued support for UNAVEM III will depend on the extent to which the parties demonstrate their political will to achieve a lasting peace.

The Security Council notes the important role played by the Special Representative of the Secretary-General and by the three observer countries in the promotion of the peace process in Angola and calls upon them to further contribute appropriately to the implementation of the Lusaka Protocol within the agreed time framework and to assist UNAVEM III in the successful fulfilment of its tasks.

The Security Council requests the Secretary-General to update it on the progress of the Angolan peace process and the deployment and activities of UNAVEM III at least on a monthly basis.

*Meeting number.* SC 3614.

Before the statement was approved, Angola, in a 21 December letter[30] to the Council President, said the text did not reflect the reality of the situation of the peace process on the ground, and did not point out the perpetrator of the violations, UNITA. The statement did not mention the recent information provided by UNAVEM's military chief and did not take into account the important decisions regarding the return of the rapid reaction police, which was a gesture of the Government's good intentions regarding full implementation of the Lusaka Protocol. As to the so-called South African mercenaries, the Government had terminated the contract of the South African company "Executive Outcomes". Angola reiterated its denial that the South African military officials contracted to train Angola's national army were mercenaries, while it was well known that mercenaries had been used by UNITA. The Government had also sent a delegation to UNITA headquarters in Bailundo to discuss with Mr. Savimbi matters related to the proposal by President dos Santos to hold a meeting soon, within Angolan territory. Angola recommended reformulation of some of the statement's paragraphs, taking into account its comments.

**Further report of the Secretary-General.** In a later report,[31] the Secretary-General informed the Security Council that the peace process had suffered a serious set-back towards the end of 1995, when FAA took control of several locations in the oil-producing region of Soyo, in the province of Zaire. Citing that offensive, UNITA suspended the quartering of its troops, withdrew its assistance to UNAVEM in the construction of quartering areas and, in some areas under its control, imposed restrictions on the movement of UNAVEM and other international personnel, including those of NGOs. In late December, FAA withdrew from the positions concerned and, as a confidence-building measure, a platoon of UN troops was deployed to the area. On 21 December, a government delegation met with UNITA leaders in their Bailundo headquarters to review implementation of the Lusaka Protocol. The two parties undertook once again to start fulfilling their obligations, including the definitive cessation of all military activities, the conclusion of military talks, the release of prisoners, an end to hostile propaganda, the resumption of the quartering of UNITA troops, the quartering of the rapid reaction police and withdrawal of FAA to the nearest barracks. However, UNITA failed to take the necessary steps to move the peace process forward, citing military threats to its forces in several parts of the country.

Since the beginning of December, security for humanitarian assistance activities had deteriorated in many parts of the country, especially those controlled by UNITA. As a result, one international NGO suspended its activities in UNITA-held areas and several that had previously expressed willingness to expand their humanitarian activities to those areas were increasingly reluctant to do so.

### Mission composition

On 6 January, the Secretary-General reported[32] that the military component of UNAVEM II was composed of personnel from Argentina, Brazil, the Congo, Guinea-Bissau, Hungary, India, Jordan, Malaysia, the Netherlands, New Zealand, Nigeria, Norway, Slovakia, Sweden and Zimbabwe. He proposed the addition of Algeria, Bangladesh, Bulgaria, Egypt, Kenya, Mali, Pakistan, Poland, Portugal, the Russian Federation, Senegal, Uruguay and Zambia to the list of countries contributing to UNAVEM II, which the Council approved on 13 January.[33]

Following the establishment of UNAVEM III on 8 February, he further proposed adding France, Namibia, the Republic of Korea, Romania, Ukraine

and the United Kingdom.[34] The Council agreed with those proposals in letters dated 17 March,[35] 4 August[36] and 1 November.[37] On 29 December, the Secretary-General also proposed adding Fiji and Italy to the list.[38]

On 8 August, the Council agreed[39] with his 4 August proposal[40] to appoint Major-General Phillip Valerio Sibanda (Zimbabwe) to succeed Major-General Chris Abutu Garuba (Nigeria) as Force Commander of UNAVEM III.

As at 27 January 1995, UNAVEM II's military and civilian police personnel numbered 304 all ranks, including 171 military observers and 122 civilian police officers. As at 30 November, UNAVEM III's total military and civilian police personnel stood at 6,184, including 331 military observers and 253 civilian police officers.

The Council, by **resolution 976(1995)** of 8 February, had authorized a maximum of 7,000 military personnel, in addition to 350 military observers and 260 police observers.

### Financing

**Reports of the Secretary-General and ACABQ (June).** In June 1995, the Secretary-General presented[41] a proposed budget for UNAVEM III totalling $305,191,900 gross ($300,004,800 net) for the period from 9 February to 31 December 1995, consisting of $187,541,000 gross ($185,269,900 net) for the mandate period from 9 February to 8 August and $117,650,900 gross ($114,734,900 net) from 9 August to 31 December.

The Advisory Committee on Administrative and Budgetary Questions (ACABQ), also in June, recommended[42] that detailed consideration of the Secretary-General's report be deferred until the General Assembly's fiftieth session. It believed that the total resources requested would not be required before it had reviewed the estimates in detail. In the meantime, it recommended that the Assembly initially approve an amount of $215.7 million gross ($211.2 million net) for the period from 9 February to 31 December 1995, with an initial assessment of $150 million gross ($148 million net) from 9 February to 8 August. Should UNAVEM III's mandate be extended beyond the latter date, the Secretary-General should be authorized to enter into commitments not exceeding $13.9 million gross ($13.3 million net) per month.

**GENERAL ASSEMBLY ACTION (July)**

On 20 July, the General Assembly adopted **resolution 49/227 B**.

### Financing of the United Nations Angola Verification Mission

*The General Assembly*,

*Having considered* the report of the Secretary-General on the financing of the United Nations Angola Verification

Mission and the related report of the Advisory Committee on Administrative and Budgetary Questions,

*Recalling* Security Council resolution 626(1988) of 20 December 1988, by which the Council established the United Nations Angola Verification Mission, and Council resolution 696(1991) of 30 May 1991, by which the Council decided to entrust a new mandate to the United Nations Angola Verification Mission (thenceforth called the United Nations Angola Verification Mission II), and its subsequent resolutions, the most recent of which was resolution 976(1995) of 8 February 1995, by which the Council authorized the establishment of a peace-keeping operation, the United Nations Angola Verification Mission III, to assist the parties in restoring peace and achieving national reconciliation in Angola on the basis of the Peace Accords for Angola, the Lusaka Protocol and the relevant Security Council resolutions, with an initial mandate period of six months until 8 August 1995 and with a maximum deployment of 7,000 military personnel, in addition to the 350 military observers and 260 police observers and appropriate international and local staff,

*Recalling also* its resolution 43/231 of 16 February 1989 on the financing of the Verification Mission, and its subsequent resolutions and decisions thereon, the most recent of which was resolution 49/227 A of 23 December 1994,

*Reaffirming* that the costs of the Verification Mission are expenses of the Organization to be borne by Member States in accordance with Article 17, paragraph 2, of the Charter of the United Nations,

*Recalling* its previous decisions regarding the fact that, in order to meet the expenditures caused by the Verification Mission, a different procedure is required from that applied to meet expenditures of the regular budget of the United Nations,

*Taking into account* the fact that the economically more developed countries are in a position to make relatively larger contributions and that the economically less developed countries have a relatively limited capacity to contribute towards such operations,

*Bearing in mind* the special responsibilities of the States permanent members of the Security Council, as indicated in General Assembly resolution 1874(S-IV) of 27 June 1963, in the financing of such operations,

*Mindful* of the fact that it is essential to provide the Verification Mission with the necessary financial resources to enable it to fulfil its responsibilities under the relevant resolutions of the Security Council,

1. *Takes note* of the status of contributions to the United Nations Angola Verification Mission as at 6 July 1995, including the contributions outstanding in the amount of 7,162,443 United States dollars, and urges all Member States concerned to ensure the payment of their outstanding assessed contributions;

2. *Expresses concern* about the financial situation with regard to peace-keeping activities, due to overdue payments by Member States of their assessments, particularly Member States in arrears;

3. *Urges* all Member States to make every possible effort to ensure payment of their assessed contributions to the Verification Mission promptly and in full;

4. *Endorses* the observations and recommendations contained in the report of the Advisory Committee on Administrative and Budgetary Questions;

5. *Decides*, as an interim measure, pending the submission by the Secretary-General of updated budget information by September 1995 and a detailed report of the Advisory Committee thereon, to appropriate initially to the Special Account for the United Nations Angola Verification Mission the amount of 150 million dollars gross (148 million dollars net), for the financing of the Verification Mission for the period from 9 February to 8 August 1995, inclusive of the amount of 10.5 million dollars gross (9.9 million dollars net) already authorized and apportioned under the terms of General Assembly resolution 49/227 A, and the amount of 50 million dollars gross (49,604,200 dollars net) authorized by the Advisory Committee under the terms of Assembly resolution 49/233 A of 23 December 1994;

6. *Decides also*, as an ad hoc arrangement, and taking into account the amount of 10.5 million dollars gross (9.9 million dollars net) already apportioned in accordance with resolution 49/227 A, to apportion the additional amount of 139.5 million dollars gross (138.1 million dollars net) for the period from 9 February to 8 August 1995 among Member States in accordance with the composition of groups set out by the General Assembly in paragraphs 3 and 4 of its resolution 43/232 of 1 March 1989, as adjusted by the Assembly in its resolutions 44/192 B of 21 December 1989, 45/269 of 27 August 1991, 46/198 A of 20 December 1991 and 47/218 A of 23 December 1992 and its decision 48/472 A of 23 December 1993, and taking into account the scale of assessments for the year 1995 as set out by the Assembly in its resolution 49/19 B of 23 December 1994;

7. *Decides further* that, in accordance with the provisions of its resolution 973(X) of 15 December 1955, there shall be set off against the apportionment among Member States, as provided for in paragraph 6 above, their respective share in the Tax Equalization Fund of the estimated staff assessment income of 1.4 million dollars approved for the period from 9 February to 8 August 1995;

8. *Decides*, with regard to the period beyond 8 August 1995, to authorize the Secretary-General to enter into commitments at a rate not to exceed 13.9 million dollars gross (13.3 million dollars net) per month until 31 December 1995, and that this amount shall be assessed on Member States, in accordance with the scheme set out in the present resolution, subject to the decision of the Security Council to extend the mandate of the Verification Mission beyond 8 August 1995;

9. *Invites* voluntary contributions to the Verification Mission in cash and in the form of services and supplies acceptable to the Secretary-General, to be administered, as appropriate, in accordance with the procedure established by the General Assembly in its resolutions 43/230 of 21 December 1988, 44/192 A of 21 December 1989 and 45/258 of 3 May 1991;

10. *Requests* the Secretary-General to take all necessary action to ensure that the Verification Mission is administered with a maximum of efficiency and economy;

11. *Decides* to include in the provisional agenda of its fiftieth session the item entitled ''Financing of the United Nations Angola Verification Mission''.

General Assembly resolution 49/227 B

20 July 1995      Meeting 106      Adopted without vote

Approved by Fifth Committee (A/49/816/Add.1) without vote, 14 July (meeting 66); draft by Chairman (A/C.5/49/L.62), based on informal consultations; agenda item 117.

*Meeting numbers.* GA 49th session: 5th Committee 62, 66; plenary 106.

**Reports of the Secretary-General and ACABQ (October-December).** In October, the Secretary-General submitted to the General Assembly a performance report of UNAVEM II for the periods from 1 October to 8 December 1994 and from 9 December 1994 to 8 February 1995.[43] In November, he presented[44] revised estimates for UNAVEM III amounting to $268,072,500 gross ($264,592,000 net) from 9 February to 31 December 1995, including $93,099,000 in start-up costs and $174,973,500 gross ($171,493,000 net) in recurrent costs. Later in the same month, he submitted[45] cost estimates for maintaining the Mission from 1 January to 30 June 1996 of $171,879,800 gross ($168,728,400 net), consisting of $37,241,000 gross ($36,558,200 net) from 1 January to 8 February and $134,638,800 gross ($132,170,200 net) from 9 February to 30 June.

ACABQ, in a December report,[46] recommended that $250,764,400 gross be appropriated for the period from 9 February to 31 December 1995, inclusive of the amount of $150 million gross for the period from 9 February to 8 August and $65,912,903 gross for the period from 9 August to 31 December, authorized and assessed in accordance with General Assembly **resolution 49/227 B** of 20 July (see above).

For the period from 1 January to 30 June 1996, ACABQ recommended that $169,376,000 gross be appropriated, and that $36,698,400 gross be assessed for the period from 1 January to 8 February. In addition, it recommended that, should the Security Council extend the mandate of UNAVEM III beyond that latter date, the Assembly authorize the Secretary-General, with ACABQ's prior concurrence, to enter into commitments and to assess, for the period from 9 February to 30 June 1996, at a monthly rate not to exceed $28,229,100 gross.

**GENERAL ASSEMBLY ACTION (December)**

On 23 December, the General Assembly adopted **resolution 50/209 A**.

### Financing of the United Nations Angola Verification Mission

*The General Assembly,*

*Having considered* the reports of the Secretary-General on the financing of the United Nations Angola Verification Mission and the related report of the Advisory Committee on Administrative and Budgetary Questions,

*Bearing in mind* Security Council resolution 626(1988) of 20 December 1988, by which the Council established the United Nations Angola Verification Mission, resolution 696(1991) of 30 May 1991, by which the Council decided to entrust a new mandate to the United Nations Angola Verification Mission (thenceforth called the United Nations Angola Verification Mission II), resolution 976(1995) of 8 February 1995, by which the Council authorized the establishment of a peace-keeping operation in Angola (thenceforth called the United Nations

Angola Verification Mission III), and resolution 1008(1995) of 7 August 1995, in which the Council extended the mandate of the Verification Mission until 8 February 1996,

*Recalling* its resolution 43/231 of 16 February 1989 on the financing of the Verification Mission, and its subsequent resolutions and decisions thereon, the latest of which was resolution 49/227 B of 20 July 1995,

*Reaffirming* that the costs of the Verification Mission are expenses of the Organization to be borne by Member States in accordance with Article 17, paragraph 2, of the Charter of the United Nations,

*Recalling also* its previous decisions regarding the fact that, in order to meet the expenditures caused by the Verification Mission, a different procedure is required from the one applied to meet expenditures of the regular budget of the United Nations,

*Taking into account* the fact that the economically more developed countries are in a position to make relatively larger contributions and that the economically less developed countries have a relatively limited capacity to contribute towards such an operation,

*Bearing in mind* the special responsibilities of the States permanent members of the Security Council, as indicated in General Assembly resolution 1874(S-IV) of 27 June 1963, in the financing of such operations,

*Mindful* of the fact that it is essential to provide the Verification Mission with the necessary financial resources to enable it to fulfil its responsibilities under the relevant resolutions of the Security Council,

*Concerned* that the Secretary-General continues to face difficulties in meeting the obligations of the Verification Mission on a current basis, including reimbursement to current and former troop-contributing States,

1. *Takes note* of the status of contributions to the United Nations Angola Verification Mission as at 19 December 1995, including the contributions outstanding in the amount of 38,878,476 United States dollars, representing 10 per cent of the total assessed contributions from the inception of the Verification Mission to the period ending 31 December 1995, notes that some 21 per cent of the Member States have paid their assessed contributions in full, and urges all other Member States concerned, particularly those in arrears, to ensure the payment of their outstanding assessed contributions;

2. *Expresses concern* about the financial situation with regard to peace-keeping activities, particularly as regards the reimbursement of troop contributors, notably those troop-contributing Member States that have paid their assessed contributions in full, which bear an additional burden owing to overdue payments by Member States of their assessments;

3. *Urges* all Member States to make every possible effort to ensure the payment of their assessed contributions to the Verification Mission promptly and in full;

4. *Endorses* the observations and recommendations contained in the report of the Advisory Committee on Administrative and Budgetary Questions;

5. *Requests* the Secretary-General to take all necessary action to ensure that the Verification Mission is administered with a maximum of efficiency and economy;

6. *Decides* to appropriate to the Special Account for the United Nations Angola Verification Mission the additional amount of 34,851,497 dollars gross (36,216,158 dollars net) for the financing of the Verification Mission for the period from 9 February to 31 December

1995, in addition to the appropriation of 150,000,000 dollars gross (148,000,000 dollars net) and the commitment authority of 65,912,903 dollars gross (63,067,742 dollars net) already apportioned under the terms of Assembly resolution 49/227 B;

7. *Decides also*, as an ad hoc arrangement, and taking into account the amounts already apportioned, as provided for in paragraph 6 above, to apportion the additional amount of 34,851,497 dollars gross (36,216,158 dollars net) for the period from 9 February to 31 December 1995 among Member States in accordance with the composition of groups set out in paragraphs 3 and 4 of Assembly resolution 43/232 of 1 March 1989, as adjusted by the Assembly in its resolutions 44/192 B of 21 December 1989, 45/269 of 27 August 1991, 46/198 A of 20 December 1991 and 47/218 A of 23 December 1992 and its decisions 48/472 A of 23 December 1993 and 50/451 B of 23 December 1995, and taking into account the scale of assessments for the year 1995;

8. *Decides further* that, in accordance with the provisions of its resolution 973(X) of 15 December 1955, the apportionment among Member States, as provided for in paragraph 7 above, shall take into consideration the decrease in their respective share in the Tax Equalization Fund of the estimated staff assessment income of 1,364,661 dollars approved for the Verification Mission for the period from 9 February to 31 December 1995, inclusive;

9. *Decides* that, for Member States that have fulfilled their financial obligations to the Mission, there shall be set off against the apportionment, as provided for in paragraph 7 above, their respective share in the unencumbered balance of 537,900 dollars gross (502,400 dollars net) for the period from 1 October 1994 to 8 February 1995;

10. *Decides also* that, for Member States that have not fulfilled their financial obligations to the Verification Mission, their share of the unencumbered balance of 537,900 dollars gross (502,400 dollars net) for the period from 1 October 1994 to 8 February 1995 shall be set off against their outstanding obligations;

11. *Decides further* to appropriate to the Special Account the amount of 36,698,400 dollars gross (36,049,700 dollars net) for the maintenance of the Verification Mission for the period from 1 January to 8 February 1996;

12. *Decides*, as an ad hoc arrangement, to apportion the amount of 36,698,400 dollars gross (36,049,700 dollars net) for the period from 1 January to 8 February 1996 among Member States in accordance with the composition of groups set out in paragraphs 3 and 4 of Assembly resolution 43/232, as adjusted by the Assembly in its resolutions 44/192 B, 45/269, 46/198 A and 47/218 A and its decisions 48/472 A and 50/451 B, and taking into account the scale of assessments for the year 1996;

13. *Decides also* that, in accordance with the provisions of its resolution 973(X) there shall be set off against the apportionment among Member States, as provided for in paragraph 12 above, their respective share in the Tax Equalization Fund of the estimated staff assessment income of 648,700 dollars approved for the Verification Mission for the period from 1 January to 8 February 1996, inclusive;

14. *Authorizes* the Secretary-General to enter into commitments for the maintenance of the Verification Mission at a rate not to exceed 28,229,100 dollars gross (27,730,100 dollars net) per month until 30 June 1996 and to assess the amount of 76,218,600 dollars gross (74,871,300 dollars net) for the period from 9 February to 30 April 1996 on Member States in accordance with the scheme set out in the present resolution, subject to the decision of the Security Council to extend the mandate of the Verification Mission beyond 8 February 1996;

15. *Notes with appreciation* the voluntary contributions made by Germany, South Africa, the United Kingdom of Great Britain and Northern Ireland and the United States of America, and invites voluntary contributions to the Verification Mission in cash and in the form of services and supplies acceptable to the Secretary-General, to be administered, as appropriate, in accordance with the procedure established by the Assembly in its resolutions 43/230 of 21 December 1988, 44/192 A of 21 December 1989 and 45/258 of 3 May 1991;

16. *Decides* to keep the agenda item entitled "Financing of the United Nations Angola Verification Mission" under review during its fiftieth session.

General Assembly resolution 50/209 A

23 December 1995     Meeting 100     Adopted without vote

Approved by Fifth Committee (A/50/845) without vote, 21 December (meeting 44); draft by Chairman (A/C.5/50/L.25), based on informal consultations; agenda item 123.
*Meeting numbers.* GA 50th session: 5th Committee 41, 44; plenary 100.

On the same date, by **decision 50/469**, the Assembly decided that the Fifth (Administrative and Budgetary) Committee should continue consideration of the item on the financing of UNAVEM at the resumed fiftieth session.

*REFERENCES*
[1]YUN 1994, p. 348. [2]YUN 1988, p. 159. [3]YUN 1991, p. 127. [4]YUN 1992, p. 178. [5]S/1995/51. [6]S/1995/94. [7]S/1995/97 & Corr.1. [8]YUN 1994, p. 349, SC res. 966(1994), 8 Dec. 1994. [9]S/1995/142. [10]S/1995/192. [11]YUN 1993, p. 256, SC res. 864(1993), 15 Sep. 1993. [12]S/1995/177. [13]S/PRST/1995/11. [14]S/1995/230. [15]S/1995/239. [16]S/1995/274. [17]S/1995/296. [18]S/PRST/1995/18. [19]S/1995/350. [20]S/1995/458. [21]S/PRST/1995/27. [22]S/1995/487. [23]S/1995/588. [24]S/1995/842. [25]S/PRST/1995/51. [26]S/1995/991. [27]S/PRST/1995/58. [28]S/1995/1012. [29]S/PRST/1995/62. [30]S/1995/1052. [31]S/1996/75. [32]S/1995/36. [33]S/1995/37. [34]S/1995/204, S/1995/648, S/1995/912. [35]S/1995/205. [36]S/1995/649. [37]S/1995/913. [38]S/1996/6. [39]S/1995/669. [40]S/1995/668. [41]A/49/433/Add.1. [42]A/49/927. [43]A/50/651. [44]A/50/651/Add.1. [45]A/50/651/Add.2. [46]A/50/814.

# Burundi

In 1995, the United Nations continued its efforts to help end the political and humanitarian crises in Burundi, resulting from the October 1993 *coup d'état*[1] and subsequent massacres, and the deaths of the Presidents of Burundi and Rwanda, who were killed in a plane crash in April 1994.[2] Following intense consultations mediated by the Secretary-General's Special Representative, Burundi's political parties had signed on 10 September 1994 the Convention on Governance—a power-sharing mechanism for a four-year transitional period.[3]

Nevertheless, the year 1995 saw a continuation of ethnic and political tensions and an atmosphere of crisis. The Secretary-General's Special Representative reported some hope for optimism, following a Security Council mission in February to Burundi and Rwanda, which recommended the creation of an international commission of inquiry into the events that had triggered the crisis, which would seek ways to identify those responsible for the violence and prevent future incidents. With violence escalating and thousands fleeing the brutality of the conflict, the Commission on Human Rights decided to appoint a special rapporteur on the situation of human rights in Burundi. In August, the Security Council asked for the establishment of the international commission, and, in September, the Secretary-General appointed five members to it.

Meanwhile, the refugee situation in the region worsened, with half a million Burundians internally displaced and thousands more seeking refuge in neighbouring countries. More than 240,000 Rwandans fleeing violence in their country had become refugees in Burundi, and hundreds of thousands more were in other countries. A Regional Conference on Assistance to Refugees, Returnees and Displaced Persons in the Great Lakes Region was held in February, and international assistance was sought during the year to alleviate the widespread human suffering resulting from the political upheavals and violence.

### Tensions and crises

**Communication.** On 25 January, Burundi informed[4] the Security Council President that, despite some problems of insecurity, relative stability and a delicate balance had prevailed since the signing of the Convention on Governance. The Special Representative of the Secretary-General, Ahmedou Ould Abdallah (Mauritania), had noted also that Burundi's problems were very sensitive and highly complex and could be properly treated only in a global manner. Burundi said it firmly denounced ''manoeuvres which are designed to sabotage the fragile work of national reconciliation'' and affirmed that it had never requested an embargo or military intervention. It stressed the urgent need to avoid taking fixed positions on delicate matters in Burundi at a time when the political parties and civil society had agreed to hold a national debate.

SECURITY COUNCIL ACTION

The Security Council President, following consultations, made the following statement on behalf of the Council at a meeting on 31 January:[5]

The Security Council, which has been following closely developments in Burundi, has learned with

concern that the situation in the country has deteriorated considerably over the last few days.

In this context, the Security Council deeply deplores the pronouncements made by the leadership of one political party which calls for the withdrawal of the Prime Minister and the overthrow of his Government by all means available.

The Security Council denounces such attempts to threaten by way of intimidation the coalition Government which was established in line with the Convention on Governance of 10 September 1994. It further condemns the extremist groups that continue to undermine the national reconciliation process.

The Security Council calls upon all parties and others concerned, in particular the national security forces, to refrain from committing acts of violence and to give support to the Government institutions established in line with the above-mentioned Convention.

The Security Council requests the Secretary-General to continue to keep it fully informed of developments in Burundi. The Council will remain actively seized of the matter.

*Meeting number.* SC 3497.

**Communication.** On 9 February, Burundi informed[6] the Security Council President that its leaders had the political will and resources to solve any problem so as to maintain the momentum of national reconciliation and the institutional normalization currently under way. At the invitation of Burundi's President, Sylvestre Ntibantunganya, it said, a meeting of the Conciliation Framework and all political partners had been held in Bujumbura on 7 February. Participants in the meeting agreed on the need for the Convention on Governance to be applied scrupulously in respect of the structure and the settlement mechanisms relating to the formation of the Government; President Ntibantunganya emphasized that all conflicts and disputes as to the interpretation and application of that Convention should be settled by the mechanisms and frameworks provided in it. Should the current Prime Minister no longer be the subject of political consensus, he said, opposition parties would be invited to nominate another candidate for the post, and a new Prime Minister would then be responsible for forming a new Government.

### Missions to Burundi

*February mission*

In a 6 February note,[7] the Security Council President said that Council members had decided to send a mission to Burundi and Rwanda, departing on 8 February and comprising representatives of China, the Czech Republic, Germany, Honduras, Indonesia, Nigeria and the United States. The mission's terms of reference for Burundi would be to hold consultations with the Special Representative on political and security developments in Burundi, his efforts in that regard, and additional ways in which the United Nations might further underpin those efforts; hold talks with the President, the Prime Minister and the leadership of the security forces and of the opposition parties, as well as UN agencies, the diplomatic corps, NGOs, the Office of the Organization of African Unity (OAU) and other interested parties; convey to them the serious concerns of the Council over the recent political developments in Burundi; and stress to all parties the strong support of the Council for the Convention on Governance and the Government constituted on the basis of it and for the process of national reconciliation, and the Council's rejection of all attempts to undermine them or to destabilize the region.

**Mission report.** In its report[8] to the Security Council, the mission, having visited Burundi on 10 and 11 February, observed that the political and security situation remained precarious and potentially explosive.

The root cause of the continuing political instability, it stated, was the unwillingness of the Tutsi and Hutu extremist elements, both within the coalition Government and outside it, to accept the power-sharing arrangements contained in the Convention on Governance. They had usurped the political initiative at the expense of the moderate elements who constituted the majority of the population and had been silenced through threat and intimidation. They were systematically undermining the coalition Government, particularly those among the ranks of the Union pour le progrès national (UPRONA), through inflammatory statements, calls for ''dead city'' strikes, street demonstrations, intimidation and incitement to violence.

Further aggravating the situation was the fact that the mainly Tutsi security forces constituted an independent power centre, and their support of the coalition Government could not be taken for granted.

The mission stated that the survival of the coalition Government, the Convention and peace and security in Burundi was jeopardized by the persistence of impunity, since there had been no accountability, political or judicial, on the part of those involved in the October 1993 coup attempt and subsequent massacres. In addition, the judicial system, which had largely collapsed, was often perceived as being partial, and the effectiveness of OAU military observers was limited by the restraints imposed on them by the Burundi security forces and the inadequacy of their numbers.

The mission recommended creation of an international commission of inquiry into the 1993 coup attempt and subsequent massacres, as proposed by the Government, as soon as possible, and augmentation of the UN presence in Burundi to assist capacity-building by the Government in the areas of building an impartial judicial system; civilian police training, impartial investigations and support services, especially in urban centres; and establishment of an effective administrative presence in the provinces. The number of OAU observers should be substantially increased and restrictions on their movement removed. Also, the UN High Commissioner for Human Rights should deploy human rights monitors throughout the country, as requested by Burundi.

The mission supported the holding of a national debate, with the participation of all segments of society, as a means of fostering political dialogue in the country. Also recommended was the continuation of visits to Burundi of high-level international delegations to underscore international concern and help diffuse tension. Some mission members believed that to promote political stability and national reconciliation, the Council should explore the possibility of imposing selective sanctions against individuals believed to belong to extremist groups in Burundi.

**Communications.** Burundi on 6 March informed[9] the Security Council President that, since the February mission, the situation in the country had developed in a positive direction. The tension observed during the mission's stay was linked to the opposition demand for the ousting of Prime Minister Anatole Kanyenkiko. A new Prime Minister and a new Government had been appointed by consensus, as provided for in the Convention on Governance. There were, however, problems of insecurity in certain parts of the country and acts of criminality in both rural and urban areas. The disarmament of armed population groups had provoked confrontations between the forces of law and order and groups in possession of firearms. Burundi refuted the statement that the security forces constituted an independent power centre and that their support of the coalition Government could not be taken for granted. Those forces obeyed the policy laid down by the Government, and those that did commit excesses were subject to military regulations. Neither the Government nor its security forces had restricted the movement of the OAU military observer group. However, any increase in those observers should be determined by Burundi. As for strengthening the United Nations presence in the country, Burundi said it needed support for the existing judicial system and called on the United Nations to join with other partners in that area. The establishment of a civilian police force was unnecessary in Burundi's view, as it was in the process of creating, with the assistance of external partners, a specialized anti-terrorism squad and a specialized disarmament squad. The Government was already experiencing difficulties in coordinating the activities of various existing police forces.

With regard to an effective administrative presence in the provinces, Burundi said it had already assigned territorial administration officials, as provided for in the Convention on Governance. It wanted the international community to assist in providing the logistical means to guide the population more effectively in the direction of peace and reconciliation.

Concerning the imposition of selective sanctions against individuals believed to belong to extremist groups, Burundi said that the hard core of extremists was relatively small. On the other hand, it would be wise to attack the "declared warmongers", especially the "Forces for the Defence of Democracy", who had mobilized a parallel army and were "provoking attacks and deadly confrontations" from both outside and inside the country. The international community should also support the Government's pursuit of a return to peace and security and provide positive and reassuring encouragement. Burundi offered its full cooperation to the United Nations to prevent further conflicts.

On 8 March, Burundi transmitted to the Secretary-General a copy of the Agreement embodying the Convention on Governance.[10]

### SECURITY COUNCIL ACTION

On 9 March, the Security Council considered the report of the February mission to Burundi. It also had before it the report[11] of the March 1994 preparatory fact-finding mission to Burundi (see below). Following consultations, the President made the following statement on behalf of the Council:[12]

The Security Council has considered the reports of its Mission to Burundi which visited Bujumbura on 10 and 11 February 1995 and welcomes the observations and recommendations contained in the report of the Mission. It expresses its appreciation to the Mission members for their efforts.

The Security Council recalls its earlier statements on the situation in Burundi, in particular that of 31 January 1995. It remains deeply concerned that a climate of insecurity continues to prevail in Burundi. It condemns the activities of those, both within and outside the country, who seek to nullify the agreed power-sharing arrangements contained in the Convention on Governance of 10 September 1994 by resorting to undemocratic methods such as intimidation and incitement to violence, as well as guerrilla activities and subversive political activity. Such actions have threatened peace, stability and national reconciliation.

The Security Council reaffirms its support for the Convention on Governance and for the coalition Government established under it. In this connection, it notes the appointment of the Prime Minister and his Cabinet and urges all parties in Burundi to work together to ensure stability in the country.

The Security Council reaffirms the view that impunity is a fundamental problem in Burundi, one which seriously endangers security in the country, and

stresses the importance it attaches to assistance being given to help strengthen the national judicial system. In this context, it underlines the role that could be played by an international commission of inquiry into the 1993 coup attempt and into the massacres that followed, established in accordance with the Convention on Governance.

The Security Council strongly reaffirms its support for the implementation of the provisions of the Convention on Governance calling for the holding of a national debate with the participation of all segments of the society in Burundi, as a means of fostering political dialogue.

The Security Council underlines the importance of assisting the Government of Burundi in its efforts to restore stability and promote national reconciliation. In this context, it encourages the Secretary-General, in consultation with the Government of Burundi, to augment the United Nations presence in the country, in order to assist the Government of Burundi in strengthening the national judicial system, training civilian police forces and establishing an effective administrative presence in the provinces. It commends the important role played by the Special Representative of the Secretary-General.

The Security Council reiterates that improving the security situation in Burundi must be given high priority. It encourages the High Commissioner for Human Rights, in consultation with the Government of Burundi and in close coordination with the Special Representative of the Secretary-General, to reinforce the office he has established in Burundi. Consideration could also be given to the role human rights monitors could play.

The Security Council also recognizes the significant contribution made by the Organization of African Unity (OAU) military observers. It encourages the OAU, in consultation with the Government of Burundi, to further increase their number and calls upon the international community to assist the OAU in this regard.

The Security Council further calls on all parties in Burundi to cooperate with international observers and other personnel by ensuring unimpeded access to all parts of the country.

The Security Council requests the Secretary-General to continue to keep it fully informed of developments in Burundi. The Security Council will remain actively seized of the matter.

*Meeting number.* SC 3506.

The Council met again on 29 March to consider the situation in Burundi. Following consultations, the President made the following statement on behalf of the Council:[13]

The Security Council is deeply concerned about the escalation of violence in Burundi. It condemns the murders of the Minister of Energy and Mines and of the former Mayor of Bujumbura by extremists, and deplores the ensuing ethnic killings of many people that have caused thousands to flee their homes. It stresses the futility of resorting to violence and condemns the activities of the extremist elements who try to destabilize the country and threaten the whole region. It encourages all States to take the measures deemed necessary to prevent them from travelling abroad and receiving any kind of support. It reaffirms its determination to support the Convention on Governance of 10 September 1994, the provisions of which constitute the institutional framework for the necessary national reconciliation. The Council calls on all political parties, military forces and all elements of civil society fully to respect and implement it in a spirit of dialogue, moderation and compromise.

The Security Council urges all parties to work together to further the dialogue. It underlines the urgency of organizing, in accordance with the Convention on Governance, a national debate with the participation of all elements of the nation with a view to consolidating national reconciliation and restoring democracy. It invites the Secretary-General to help the various political parties and elements of civil society to initiate this comprehensive consultation.

The Security Council warns that those who commit crimes against humanity are individually responsible for their crimes, and will be brought to justice. The Council specifically warns that if acts of genocide are committed in Burundi, it will consider taking appropriate measures to bring to justice under international law any who may have committed such acts.

The Security Council reaffirms its view that the perception of impunity is a fundamental problem in Burundi, one which seriously endangers security in the country. The Council expresses once again its grave concern at reports indicating that systematic, widespread and flagrant violations of international humanitarian law have been committed in Burundi.

The Security Council recalls the statement by the President of the Security Council of 9 March 1995 in which the Security Council, *inter alia*, underlined the role that could be played in Burundi by an international commission of inquiry into the October 1993 coup attempt and into the massacres that followed. It requests the Secretary-General to report to the Council on an urgent basis on what steps should be taken to establish such an impartial commission of inquiry.

The Security Council favours measures to restore a state of law and improve the functioning of the judicial system. It also favours the organization of a round table of donors. It urges States to provide for these projects financial contributions directly or through a trust fund to be created for this purpose.

The Security Council supports the reinforcement of the action decided by the United Nations High Commissioner for Human Rights and welcomes the dispatching of experts.

The Security Council pays tribute to the actions taken by the Organization of African Unity (OAU). It calls upon the OAU and its members in the subregion to continue to use their influence to help stabilize the situation in Burundi. It further calls upon all States, in particular neighbouring States, to refrain from supplying or allowing the transit of arms and to deny sanctuary and any other assistance to those extremist elements which seek to destabilize the situation in Burundi.

Aware of the close interconnection between various humanitarian and political problems in the region and of the risk of subsequent destabilization, the Security Council reaffirms its support for a regional conference on peace, stability and security and calls upon the countries of the region to convene such a conference as a matter of urgency.

The Security Council remains seized of the matter. The Council will consider taking action as the situation demands.

*Meeting number.* SC 3511.

### Preparatory fact-finding mission

On 23 February 1995, the Secretary-General forwarded to the Security Council President the report of his March 1994 preparatory fact-finding mission to Burundi,[11] dispatched in response to a 1993 Council request.[14] The mission, comprising Siméon Aké (Côte d'Ivoire), Martin Huslid (Norway) and a political affairs officer of the UN Secretariat, was sent to investigate the *coup d'état* of 21 October 1993, to consider the assassination of President Melchior Ndadaye and subsequent massacres and to consider, with the Government and the Special Representative, what activities future missions or an expanded UN political presence could undertake to encourage a return to civil peace.

The mission observed that the tragic events of October 1993 should be considered in the light of the historical, political and economic and social situation which prevailed in Burundi, especially since its accession to independence in 1962, in which the ethnic factor played a decisive role. The Hutu majority had been practically excluded from power during that period. The victory of the Front pour la démocratie au Burundi in both presidential and legislative elections in June 1993 gave the Hutu majority an opportunity to take over the running of the country. That led to the rejection, in some opposition circles, of the new political majority and refusal to accept the democratic change-over of power. The October 1993 *coup d'état* was planned by army units, led by certain officers, non-commissioned officers and senior officers, including those who had carried out the 3 July 1993 coup. There was indication that individuals belonging to political, civil and military circles were also involved. The Hutu majority saw the *coup d'état* of 21 October 1993, and especially the assassination of the President, as a rejection by the Tutsi minority, UPRONA and other opposition parties of the new Hutu-led Government, and as a challenge to the democratic system. Those events triggered inter-ethnic massacres. The Hutu reacted with a violent and bloody attack on the Tutsi, prompting the latter to react in similar fashion. In some cases, army units engaged in acts of reprisal, which were often directed selectively at the Hutu population. The mission believed that those massacres were not premeditated, but were the consequences of the October 1993 *coup d'état* and political assassinations. The mission considered that some moral responsibility had to be borne by those political leaders who gave insufficient consideration to the effect their statements were having on the supporters of their respective parties.

The mission proposed that the United Nations, OAU and the world community should continue and strengthen the actions of UN agencies and organs already present in Burundi, the special assistance from the UN Educational, Scientific and Cultural Organization in education, aid from traditional or potential donors and emergency UN aid. They should also: reinforce the Office of the Special Representative, who had played a particularly useful role, especially in getting government institutions to function again; send an international judicial mission, in consultation with the Burundi authorities, to investigate the crimes committed in October 1993 and to identify those responsible so that they could be brought to justice, or make available a number of experts to act as advisers to help Burundi's competent authorities carry out the same task; support, through a proposed trust fund, the presence of 47 military observers and a small number of civilians from OAU; continue support from the international community for the democratic process and the promotion of human rights in Burundi; and organize an international conference on Burundi and Rwanda, under UN auspices, focusing on regional issues, to strengthen security, stability and cooperative links among the countries of the region.

### Escalation of crisis

On 7 April,[15] Burundi informed the Secretary-General that the decline in the situation in the country during March was a consequence of repeated provocations and attacks by Hutu militia and gangs against the forces of law and order and the Tutsi civilian population. It was also a logical consequence of the illegal distribution of arms to young Hutu by political leaders. The crisis had generated distrust among the various elements of the Burundi nation, with the Tutsi afraid of being wiped out altogether and the Hutu believing that the Tutsi, helped by the Tutsi-dominated army, were going to avenge their kin massacred in 1993 and seek to destabilize the national army.

In the face of this situation, the Government of Burundi had made a return to peace and security the top priority. The President and the Prime Minister had proposed that, for three years, the priority objective should be peace, national reconciliation and the reconstruction of the country. Parallel with that public awareness campaign, senior government authorities had decided to pursue systematically the disarmament of those holding weapons illegally; take action against those attempting to destabilize the nation; protect Burundians against any attack on their security,

regardless of the origin or perpetrator; create conditions conducive to the reintegration of displaced persons and the return of refugees; and resume national economic and social development efforts, particularly in the areas of education, health and agriculture.

Burundi called on the international community to denounce the destabilizers on all sides who were undermining the process of national reconciliation, and to propose specific assistance activities in those areas agreed by the General Assembly in 1994.[16]

The OAU Central Organ of the Mechanism for the Prevention, Management and Resolution of Conflicts in Africa (Tunis, Tunisia, 20 April)[17] expressed deep concern at the resurgence of political and institutional crises in Burundi, particularly the recent outbreak of violence, political assassinations and ethnic cleansing, and condemned the continuing militarization of Burundi society. It also appealed for regional action to deal with the instability and insecurity caused by the introduction of weapons into Burundi, and for concerted international action to isolate and neutralize the extremists and disarm and dismantle the militias and armed gangs. It urged all parties concerned to ensure the fulfilment of the commitments made at the February 1995 conference on refugees and displaced persons in the Great Lakes region (see below) and emphasized the need for the international community to increase humanitarian assistance and every other form of assistance to countries of asylum and displaced persons. The Central Organ urged the States members of OAU and the international community to encourage and support the forces of moderation in Burundi, and emphasized the importance for OAU to be fully involved in any action that the Security Council might take concerning the situation in Burundi.

The Economic and Social Council, by **decision 1995/219** of 4 May and **decision 1995/291** of 25 July, approved the request of the Commission on Human Rights to appoint a special rapporteur to report on the situation of human rights in Burundi (see PART THREE, Chapter III).

On 8 May,[18] Burundi transmitted to the Secretary-General the views on the Burundi situation of the Ministerial Meeting of the Coordinating Bureau of the Movement of Non-Aligned Countries (Bandung, Indonesia, 25-27 April), which had expressed concern over the escalation of violence and immense human suffering in Burundi. Burundi said that the Security Council might wish to translate the views of the Non-Aligned Movement into action by helping Burundi to disarm and disband the militias and other illegally armed organizations. The coalition Government was determined to put an end to the militarization of Burundi society, but its efforts would be successful only if accompanied by concerted international action. The United Nations should devise a strategy to stem the illegal supply of weapons into the region, which resulted in arming of extremist elements.

The Ministers of Defence and Security of the States members of the Economic Community of the Great Lakes Countries (CEPGL), meeting in Bujumbura on 10 June, decided[19] to establish a Tripartite Subcommission on Security to: conduct reconnaissance, verification, monitoring and other activities to counter the circulation of instruments of war and subversion as well as elements not currently subject to control on both sides of common borders; receive and respond to security-related complaints from States members; implement security-related decisions of CEPGL Ministers of Defence and of the summit of heads of State of CEPGL; and propose appropriate measures for strengthening peace and security along common borders in the event of non-compliance with decisions taken. In particular, the Subcommission would have to introduce measures to solve issues such as the permeability of borders, the organization of joint patrols along common borders, the abuse of CEPGL passes, and efforts to combat subversive activities along common borders, as well as other acts creating insecurity.

### International commission of inquiry

The 1994 Convention on Governance[10] provided for the formation of an international judicial fact-finding mission composed of competent, impartial persons to investigate the October 1993 coup and what the political partners had agreed to call genocide, without prejudice to the outcome of independent national and international investigations, as well as the various political crimes committed since October 1993. The Security Council on 9 March[12] underlined the role that could be played by an international commission of inquiry established in accordance with the Convention and on 29 March[13] requested the Secretary-General to report on what steps should be taken to establish such a commission.

On 28 July, the Secretary-General reported[20] to the Security Council President that he had studied various options for establishing such a commission, which had given rise to considerable difficulties. He had therefore decided to investigate the alternative of proposing to Burundi the establishment of a commission on the truth, similar to the one that had been established for El Salvador.[21] In that regard, he had sent Pedro Nikken, who played a central role in designing the El Salvador commission, to Burundi to discuss that option. After visiting Burundi from 28 June to 9 July, Mr. Nikken recommended that neither a commission on the truth on the Salvadoran model nor an international commission of judicial inquiry, whose mandate would be limited to purely judicial matters, would be an adequate response to the need to put an end to impunity in Burundi. However, an international judicial commission of inquiry could be viable and useful if its mandate guaranteed that its conclusions and recommendations would be put into effect and achieve the objective of prosecuting and punishing those responsible for the assassination of the President of Burundi on 21 October 1993, for the subsequent massacres, and for other serious acts of violence and political crimes committed since then. The international commission should not only undertake a judicial inquiry but also make recommendations of an institutional nature in the legal, political and/or administrative fields.

On that basis, the Secretary-General recommended that the Security Council set up such a commission with a threefold mandate: to establish the facts relating to the assassination of 21 October 1993, the massacres that followed and other serious acts of violence and political crimes committed between that date and the date on which the resolution of the Council was adopted; to recommend modalities for the trial and punishment of persons identified by the commission as being responsible for offences investigated by it; and to recommend measures of a legal, political or administrative nature, including measures requiring legislative or constitutional reform, to prevent any repetition of deeds similar to those investigated by the commission and, in general, to eradicate impunity in Burundi.

The Secretary-General recommended that the commission have three members appointed by him. The full cooperation of the Burundian authorities would be needed for the success of the commission's work, the Secretary-General stipulated, including free access to official archives; freedom to collect information it considered relevant, to use useful and reliable sources of information, to interview, in private, any person it judged necessary, and to visit any establishment or place without prior notice; and a guarantee of full respect for the integrity, security and freedom of witnesses, experts and any other persons who helped the commission in its work. The Secretary-General believed that seeking such a commitment from the Government in advance would further delay the commission's establishment. He proposed instead that the Security Council invite the commission to submit an interim report, at its convenience, to address in particular the question of how persons identified by it as being responsible for massacres and other political crimes should be brought to trial and in particular whether their trial should be entrusted to the Burundian judicial system or to an international tribunal.

**Communications.** On 8 August, Burundi reported[22] that it had set up a national interministerial technical commission to draw up the terms of reference of the international judicial fact-finding commission to be established. The Council, it felt, should adopt only a resolution establishing the commission, whose terms of reference would be finalized in consultation with Burundi. Burundi also wished to be consulted on the appointment of the three members of the commission. The Council must bear in mind that Burundi would at the final stage exercise its sovereign right to try persons presumed guilty at the conclusion of the inquiry.

On 23 August, Burundi submitted to the Security Council President its terms of reference for an international commission of judicial inquiry.[23] It also requested that, because of the extreme importance and sensitivity of the mission assigned to the international commission, the Council postpone its vote on the draft resolution before it to allow Burundi time to scrutinize the draft.

SECURITY COUNCIL ACTION

The Security Council on 28 August adopted **resolution 1012(1995)**.

*The Security Council,*

*Having considered* the report of the preparatory fact-finding mission to Burundi dated 20 May 1994,

*Having further considered* the report of the Security Council's mission to Burundi dated 9 March 1995,

*Recalling* the statement by the President of the Council of 29 March 1995, in which the Council, *inter alia*, underlined the role that could be played in Burundi by an international commission of inquiry into the 1993 coup attempt and into the massacres that followed,

*Welcoming* the letter of the Secretary-General to the President of the Council dated 28 July 1995 recommending that such a commission of inquiry should be created by resolution of the Council,

*Taking into account* the initiative of the Government of Burundi in calling for the establishment of an international judicial commission of inquiry as referred to in the Convention on Governance,

*Recalling also* the letter of the Permanent Representative of Burundi dated 8 August 1995 noting with interest the letter of the Secretary-General of 28 July 1995,

*Taking note* that the parties in Burundi, in the Convention on Governance, agreed, without prejudice to the outcome of the independent national and international investigations, to call the massacres which followed the assassination of the President of Burundi on 21 October 1993 genocide,

*Deeply concerned* that impunity creates contempt for law and leads to violations of international humanitarian law,

*Expressing once again* its grave concern at reports indicating that systematic, widespread and flagrant violations of international humanitarian law have been committed in Burundi,

*Stressing* the importance of strengthening, in cooperation with the Government of Burundi, the Burundi judicial system,

*Reiterating* its profound concern over the resumption of radio broadcasts inciting ethnic hatred and violence and recognizing the need for ending such broadcasts,

*Recalling* that all persons who commit or authorize the commission of serious violations of international humanitarian law are individually responsible for these violations and should be held accountable,

1. *Requests* the Secretary-General to establish, as a matter of urgency, an international commission of inquiry, with the following mandate:

*(a)* To establish the facts relating to the assassination of the President of Burundi on 21 October 1993, the massacres and other related serious acts of violence which followed;

*(b)* To recommend measures of a legal, political or administrative nature, as appropriate, after consultation with the Government of Burundi, and measures with regard to the bringing to justice of persons responsible for those acts, to prevent any repetition of deeds similar to those investigated by the commission and, in general, to eradicate impunity and promote national reconciliation in Burundi;

2. *Recommends* that the international commission of inquiry be composed of five impartial and internationally respected, experienced jurists who shall be selected by the Secretary-General and shall be furnished with adequate expert staff, and that the Government of Burundi be duly informed;

3. *Calls upon* States, relevant United Nations bodies and, as appropriate, international humanitarian organizations to collate substantiated information in their possession relating to acts covered in paragraph 1 *(a)* above, to make such information available as soon as possible and to provide appropriate assistance to the commission of inquiry;

4. *Requests* the Secretary-General to report to the Council on the establishment of the commission of inquiry, and further requests the Secretary-General, within three months from the establishment of the commission of inquiry, to submit an interim report to the Council on the work of the commission and to submit a final report when the commission completes its work;

5. *Calls upon* the Burundi authorities and institutions, including all Burundi political parties, to fully cooperate with the international commission of inquiry in the accomplishment of its mandate, including responding positively to requests from the commission for security, assistance and access in pursuing investigations, including:

*(a)* Adoption by the Government of Burundi of any measures needed for the commission and its personnel to carry out their functions throughout the national territory with full freedom, independence and security;

*(b)* Provision by the Government of Burundi of all information in its possession which the commission requests or is otherwise needed to carry out its mandate and free access for the commission and its staff to any official archives related to its mandate;

*(c)* Freedom for the commission to obtain any information the commission considers relevant and to use all sources of information which the commission considers useful and reliable;

*(d)* Freedom for the commission to interview, in private, any persons the commission judges necessary;

*(e)* Freedom for the commission to visit any establishment or place at any time;

*(f)* Guarantee by the Government of Burundi of full respect for the integrity, security and freedom of witnesses, experts and any other persons who help the commission in its work;

6. *Calls upon* all States to cooperate with the commission in facilitating its investigations;

7. *Requests* the Secretary-General to provide adequate security for the commission in cooperation with the Government of Burundi;

8. *Requests* the Secretary-General to establish, as a supplement to financing as an expense of the Organization, a trust fund to receive voluntary contributions to finance the commission of inquiry;

9. *Urges* States and intergovernmental and non-governmental organizations to contribute funds, equipment and services to the commission of inquiry including the offer of expert personnel in support of the implementation of this resolution;

10. *Decides* to remain actively seized of the matter.

Security Council resolution 1012(1995)

28 August 1995     Meeting 3571     Adopted unanimously

10-nation draft (S/1995/724).

*Sponsors:* Argentina, Czech Republic, France, Germany, Honduras, Italy, Russian Federation, Rwanda, United Kingdom, United States.

On 22 September, the Secretary-General informed[24] the Security Council President that he had appointed to the commission Edilbert Razafindralambo (Madagascar) as Chairman, and Abde El Ali El Moumni (Morocco), Mehmet Güney (Turkey), Luis Herrera Marcano (Venezuela) and Michel Maurice (Canada) as members.

**Refugee situation**

**Communications.** In a 31 March statement,[25] the United Republic of Tanzania reported on the situation in Burundi, particularly in the capital, Bujumbura, citing a marked deterioration in the country's security, with violence and politically motivated killings. It was concerned that those developments could plunge Burundi into another bloodbath. Tanzania appealed to Rwanda to receive Rwandese refugees fleeing Burundi. The deterioration in the situation had caused more than 40,000 refugees from Burundi to cross into Tanzania; also, 100,000 Rwandese refugees from camps in northern Burundi were fleeing towards Tanzania. This had seriously increased the burden of caring for the large number of refugees in the country, numbering over 700,000. In view of the gravity of the situation, Tanzania had decided to close its borders with Burundi and had so advised the Governments of Rwanda and Burundi and relevant UN agencies.

In April, the Secretary-General reported[26] some 240,000 refugees in Burundi, mostly from southern Rwanda. The deteriorating situation in Burundi had affected the refugees both inside and outside the camps.

In their 10 June communiqué,[19] the Ministers of Defence and Security of the States members of

CEPGL agreed that a lasting solution to the question of peace in the subregion would have to involve the voluntary return of refugees to their countries of origin. They undertook to adopt the following measures: identification and internment of activists; prohibition of their activities in the territory of the other countries; their expulsion from the national territory; denial of entry visas to them; revocation of political refugee status, in accordance with international law; and population monitoring of refugee sites, so as to prevent refugees from being recruited and from taking part in activities against the security and sovereignty of Burundi, Rwanda and Zaire.

The United Republic of Tanzania, in a 19 June press statement,[27] reported that it was hosting more than 1.4 million refugees, over half of which were from Burundi and Rwanda. In Burundi, a new exodus of refugees was prompted by ethnic unrest and increased violence at the end of March. Rwandan refugees who had settled in Burundi had been forced out of their designated camps. Mass migration, it said, was threatening the very survival of Tanzania. Owing to the prevailing political instability in Burundi, Tanzania would continue to deploy its troops along the border area to protect the Tanzanian local population, and to avoid further Burundi/Rwanda refugee influxes into the country. The continued presence of refugees in Tanzania was a cause of insecurity and a potential cause of conflict with its neighbours. The onus of responsibility was on Burundi to create conditions conducive to the safe return of refugees. Tanzania remained committed to the Convention Governing the Specific Aspects of Refugee Problems in Africa, adopted by OAU in 1969.[28]

On 17 August,[29] Zaire stated that, in the light of the adoption of **resolution 1011(1995)** by the Security Council lifting the arms embargo imposed on Rwanda in 1994,[30] it had no choice but to ask that the Secretary-General indicate the arrangements made by the United Nations in relation to the new country or countries to which the Burundi refugees should be evacuated. In the absence of any clear indication, Zaire intended to evacuate them to their countries of origin.

Responding on 18 August, the Secretary-General[31] said that he noted Zaire's difficulties but was appealing to Zaire to continue to assist the Burundi refugees, pending a Council review of its position.

On 23 August, the Council President[32] stated that the Council viewed with deep concern the forcible repatriation of Burundian refugees by Zaire and the increasingly tense situation in the region. It called on Zaire to stand by its humanitarian obligations regarding refugees and to reconsider and halt the forcible repatriation of refugees to Burundi. It supported the decision of the

Secretary-General to send the UN High Commissioner for Refugees to the region to engage in urgent discussions with Zaire with a view to resolving the situation.

**Report of the Secretary-General.** In October, the Secretary-General reported[33] on the most recent political developments in Burundi, as well as international efforts to normalize the situation there.

Although the situation in Burundi remained precarious and continued to be of great concern to the international community, the political instability since mid-1994 had not led to a full-scale armed confrontation, in large part because of the international presence there. Despite increasing attempts by extremists to disrupt life throughout the country, governmental institutions, the agricultural sector, schools, banks, telephone communications and public transport continued to function. Extremists on both sides, inside and outside Burundi, continued to attempt to destabilize the Government in order to implement their own agenda. A fresh outbreak of violence in Bujumbura in June had led to new security measures, which were subsequently rejected by the Parliament.

The Secretary-General's Special Representative was actively promoting national reconciliation and a permanent dialogue among the various political actors and others in civil society, which had helped to lessen tensions in the country. During a visit to Bujumbura on 16 and 17 July, the Secretary-General held discussions with Burundi leaders and addressed the Parliament. He stressed adherence to the principles of the 1992 Constitution and the 1994 Convention on Governance and emphasized that all parties should work jointly towards the convening of a national debate to put an end to the confrontation that had devastated the country. On 15 March, an office of the UN High Commissioner for Human Rights opened in Bujumbura, providing technical assistance and advisory services in the field of human rights. OAU continued to pursue political and diplomatic efforts to prevent further instability and civil strife in Burundi. It had increased the military component of its mission in Burundi from 47 to 67, as well as funds for the mission's civilian component for the deployment of constitutional legal experts, human rights monitors and mediators. The presence in northern Burundi of some 200,000 Rwandese refugees had added to the complexity of the situation. There had been a number of armed incursions into Burundi from Rwandan refugee camps located in eastern Zaire. In addition, there were about 500,000 internally displaced persons, mostly Hutus, within Burundi.

A Regional Conference on Assistance to Refugees, Returnees and Displaced Persons in the Great Lakes Region, coordinated by the UNHCR

and OAU, was held in Bujumbura from 15 to 17 February. The Conference adopted a Plan of Action outlining a strategy for the peaceful resolution of the problem of displacement in the Great Lakes region, including the voluntary return and reintegration of refugees and internally displaced persons (see PART FOUR, Chapter XII).

In conclusion, the Secretary-General said that the international community should continue to coordinate its efforts so that the message to the political leaders of Burundi was consistent and unanimous. It was hoped that the planned national debate later in 1995 would help the parties move from confrontation and violence towards peace and reconciliation, while discouraging and deploring the actions of extremist elements.

On 22 December, the Security Council agreed[34] with the Secretary-General's decision[35] of 20 December to appoint Marc Faguy (Canada) as his Special Representative in Burundi, to replace Mr. Ould Abdallah. On 7 November, the Council had noted[36] his previous decision[37] to appoint Aziz Hasbi (Morocco) to that position. The Secretary-General confirmed that his Special Representative left for Bujumbura on 28 December and would assume functions upon his arrival on 30 December.

**GENERAL ASSEMBLY ACTION**

On 22 December, the General Assembly adopted **resolution 50/159**.

### The situation in Burundi

*The General Assembly,*

*Taking into account* the report of the Secretary-General of 11 October 1995,

*Noting with satisfaction* the beneficial role played by the Secretary-General, and welcoming the mission carried out by his Special Representative for Burundi,

*Noting also* the praiseworthy efforts made by the Secretary-General of the Organization of African Unity and his Special Representative,

*Welcoming* the holding at Bujumbura from 15 to 17 February 1995 of the Regional Conference on Assistance to Refugees, Returnees and Displaced Persons in the Great Lakes Region, pursuant to resolution CM/Res. 1527(LX) of the Council of Ministers of the Organization of African Unity,

*Reaffirming* its resolution 48/118 of 20 December 1993, which stresses the necessity of mobilizing assistance to refugees, returnees and displaced persons in Africa,

*Recognizing* the importance of the missions carried out in August 1994 and February 1995 by representatives of the Security Council and of the statements by the President of the Security Council of 9 March 1995 and 29 March 1995 on the situation in Burundi,

*Recognizing also* the efforts being made by the Organization of African Unity and by its current Chairman to assist Burundi in regaining peace, confidence and stability,

*Recognizing further* the important role played by the Organization of African Unity Mission in Burundi, and stressing the need for the United Nations and the Organization of African Unity to coordinate their efforts in dealing with the situation in Burundi,

*Welcoming* the agreement signed on 22 September 1994 by the United Nations High Commissioner for Human Rights and the Government of Burundi on the implementation of a major programme of technical assistance and advisory services in the field of human rights, the various components of which form part of preventive action supported by the international community,

*Appreciating* the efforts of the United Nations High Commissioner for Human Rights to promote and protect human rights in Burundi, in particular by setting up an office of the Centre for Human Rights of the Secretariat and by mobilizing international cooperation in the quest for peace and security in Burundi,

*Reiterating* the special importance of the Convention on Governance signed on 10 September 1994,

*Welcoming* the constructive negotiations between the parties signatories to the Convention on Governance, which resulted in the formation of a coalition Government on 1 March 1995,

*Expressing great regret* at the subversive acts, acts of violence and looting perpetrated by armed terrorist groups and armed militias against innocent populations which seriously jeopardize civil peace,

*Welcoming* the joint message of the President and the Prime Minister of Burundi addressed to the Secretary-General, and condemning the inflammatory broadcasts transmitted by the radio station "La voix de la démocratie—Ijwi Ry'abanyagihugu", as well as those transmitted by other radio stations which incite ethnic hatred in Burundi,

*Stressing* the importance of cooperation between all parties in Burundi in order to achieve national reconciliation and respect for human rights,

*Taking note* of the declaration on Burundi adopted by the Eleventh Conference of Heads of State or Government of Non-Aligned Countries, held at Cartagena de Indias, Colombia, from 18 to 20 October 1995,

*Welcoming* the establishment, by Security Council resolution 1012(1995) of 28 August 1995, of the International Commission of Inquiry in Burundi, as mandated in paragraph 1 of that resolution,

*Welcoming also* the Declaration adopted at Cairo on 29 November 1995 by the heads of State of the Great Lakes region with the assistance of President Jimmy Carter, President Julius Nyerere and Archbishop Desmond Tutu,

1. *Congratulates* the political parties of the Mouvance présidentielle and of the Burundian opposition on the outcome of their dialogue and their concerted action, which led to the formation of a coalition Government representing the different shades of opinion;

2. *Calls upon* all the guarantors of the Convention on Governance to ensure its full and impartial implementation for the benefit of all;

3. *Again encourages* all the parties to that Convention and its additional protocols to abide strictly by them;

4. *Urges* all political parties, military leaders, the media and civil society to dissociate themselves from extremist forces, to reject all extremism and all ethnic or political fanaticism, to settle disputes through negotiation and dialogue and to unite in order to bring about national reconciliation and respect for human rights;

5. *Expresses its conviction* concerning the need to increase preventive action in Burundi without delay, in particular through the presence of human rights experts and through human rights training programmes, in full cooperation with the Government of Burundi;

6. *Strongly urges* all the people of Burundi to cooperate with the coalition Government and with the security forces to promote national reconciliation and to fight all forms of extremism, in particular by armed terrorist groups and armed militias;

7. *Condemns* all those from within or outside the country who are attacking innocent populations, arming extremists, heedlessly violating human rights and seriously undermining national peace and security;

8. *Calls upon* all parties to create the conditions for the return of refugees and internally displaced persons;

9. *Also condemns* the militia attack on the Organization of African Unity Mission in Burundi which took place on 14 June 1995 in the province of Cibitoke and resulted in the death of a military observer of that organization;

10. *Endorses* resolution CM/Res.1582(LXII) on Burundi, adopted by the Council of Ministers of the Organization of African Unity at its sixty-second ordinary session, held at Addis Ababa from 21 to 23 June 1995;

11. *Endorses also* the declaration on Burundi adopted at Cartagena de Indias, Colombia, on 20 October 1995 by the heads of State or Government of non-aligned countries;

12. *Requests* the States Members of the United Nations and international organizations to cooperate with the Government of Burundi and other Governments of the region in the identification and dismantling of radio stations which incite hatred and encourage acts of genocide;

13. *Invites* all political partners to organize, in accordance with the Convention on Governance, a national debate on the country's basic problems with a view to the conclusion of a national covenant and the adoption of a constitution adapted to the current socio-political requirements;

14. *Supports* the role assigned to the International Commission of Inquiry in Burundi, as mandated by Security Council resolution 1012(1995), as an important step towards the eradication of impunity;

15. *Encourages* the international community and the Government of Burundi to implement the various recommendations of the Plan of Action adopted by the Regional Conference on Assistance to Refugees, Returnees and Displaced Persons in the Great Lakes Region, held at Bujumbura from 15 to 17 February 1995;

16. *Appeals earnestly* to the States that signed the Cairo Declaration on the Great Lakes Region of 29 November 1995 to abide faithfully by the commitments embodied in that declaration and designed to provide appropriate solutions in order to eliminate the socio-political conflicts currently taking place in that part of Africa;

17. *Encourages* the Secretary-General to continue his contacts with a view to an early convening of the Regional Conference on Security, Stability and Development in the Great Lakes Region of Central Africa, under the auspices of the United Nations, with the collaboration of the Organization of African Unity and with the participation of all the countries of the region;

18. *Reiterates its urgent appeal* to the international community to continue its efforts to mobilize political, diplomatic, human, economic, financial and material resources with a view to assisting Burundi in definitively overcoming the crisis which it has been facing for more than two years;

19. *Invites* the Secretary-General of the United Nations and the Secretary-General of the Organization of African Unity to continue their respective and complementary missions aimed at securing effective national reconciliation in Burundi, and welcomes in particular the positive role played by the Organization of African Unity Mission observers;

20. *Expresses the hope* that the Secretary-General of the United Nations will undertake consultations, following the usual procedure, with the Government of Burundi for the appointment as soon as possible of a special representative possessing all the qualifications, particularly an in-depth knowledge of the socio-political situation in Burundi;

21. *Decides* to include in the provisional agenda of its fifty-first session the item entitled ''The situation in Burundi''.

General Assembly resolution 50/159

22 December 1995      Meeting 98      Adopted without vote

12-nation draft (A/50/L.59/Rev.1), orally revised; agenda item 26.
*Financial implications.* 5th Committee, A/50/836; S-G, A/C.5/50/48.
*Meeting numbers.* GA 50th session: 5th Committee 43; plenary 95, 98.

**Further developments.** In a report on the situation in Burundi,[38] the Secretary-General stated that December 1995 had been characterized by widespread violence and by attempts by members of the opposition, with support from among the military, to remove from office President Ntibantunganya. Violence was also directed against the international humanitarian community.

The Secretary-General, in a 29 December letter[39] to the Security Council President, shared his deep concern over the persistence of violence and further escalation of human rights violations in Burundi. The Special Rapporteur of the Commission on Human Rights had reported that the country was a scene of smouldering civil war. The situation had continued to deteriorate since May and was characterized by daily killings, massacres, torture and arbitrary detention. The situation revealed an increasingly marked genocidal trend of a socio-ethnic nature and perpetrators were still enjoying impunity. The Special Rapporteur made a number of recommendations ranging from the consolidation of democratic institutions and the reform of the judicial system to the establishment of a national police force accepted by both communities and the deployment of human rights observers.

The deteriorating situation was underscored by recent decisions of international organizations, including ICRC, the World Food Programme and many NGOs, to curtail or suspend activities in Burundi following violent attacks against their personnel and assets. Burundi's borders with Zaire and the United Republic of Tanzania had remained closed recently. The Secretary-General felt there was a real danger of the situation degenerating to the point where it might explode into ethnic violence on a massive scale. In view of the worsening situation, the Security Council might wish to reconsider his 1994 proposals[40] for preventive deployment of military personnel and guards.

*REFERENCES*

[1]YUN 1993, p. 262. [2]YUN 1994, p. 276. [3]Ibid., p. 278. [4]S/1995/76. [5]S/PRST/1995/5. [6]S/1995/129. [7]S/1995/112. [8]S/1995/163. [9]S/1995/185. [10]A/50/94-S/1995/190. [11]S/1995/157. [12]S/PRST/1995/10. [13]S/PRST/1995/13. [14]YUN 1993, p. 264. [15]A/50/158-S/1995/278. [16]YUN 1994, p. 829, GA res. 49/21 C, 2 Dec. 1994. [17]S/1995/362. [18]A/50/177-S/1995/380. [19]A/50/222-S/1995/491. [20]S/1995/631. [21]YUN 1992, p. 231. [22]S/1995/673. [23]S/1995/731. [24]S/1995/825. [25]S/1995/266. [26]S/1995/304. [27]A/50/275-S/1995/555. [28]YUN 1969, p. 471. [29]S/1995/722. [30]YUN 1994, p. 285, SC res. 918(1994), 17 May 1994. [31]S/1995/723. [32]S/PRST/1995/41. [33]A/50/541 & Add.1. [34]S/1995/1057. [35]S/1995/1056. [36]S/1995/932. [37]S/1995/931. [38]S/1996/116. [39]S/1995/1068. [40]YUN 1994, p. 279.

# Liberia

In 1995, the Liberian conflict was exacerbated by deteriorating security and humanitarian situations, bordering at times on chaos. Despite the 28 December 1994 cease-fire, the ongoing civil war resulted in many deaths and hundreds of thousands of internally displaced persons, and widespread destruction of the country's infrastructure burgeoned. Arms continued to flow across Liberian borders despite the 1992 Security Council embargo.

In January, a high-level UN mission was dispatched to visit members of the Economic Community of West African States (ECOWAS), which since January 1994 had provided a Monitoring Group (ECOMOG) to act as regional peace-keepers in Liberia. Both ECOMOG and the UN Observer Mission in Liberia (UNOMIL), in place since late 1993, threatened to withdraw or reduce their presence in Liberia unless factions to the conflict demonstrated the will to achieve reconciliation.

On the positive side, after months of political wrangling and military skirmishes, the Abuja Agreement was signed in September 1995, renewing a cease-fire and instituting the Liberian National Transitional Government. A six-member Council of State was inaugurated on 1 September. The Abuja Agreement, which followed two ECOWAS summits, was the fifth major agreement reached during the search for peace in Liberia, building on the 1991 Yamoussoukro Accord, the 1993 Cotonou Peace Agreement, and the

Akosombo Agreement and Accra Agreement, both concluded in 1994.

At year's end, the peace process suffered another serious set-back when one faction attacked ECOMOG troops and widespread fighting again broke out among various factions.

During the year, a $65 million UN Consolidated Appeal was launched to provide humanitarian assistance to victims of the Liberian conflict.

## Peace process developments

### The Accra Agreement

The Accra Agreement was transmitted to the Security Council President by a 5 January 1995 letter[1] from Ghana, as Chairman of ECOWAS. Negotiated and signed on 21 December 1994 by eight factions then involved in the Liberian civil war, the Agreement consisted of texts of an acceptance and accession agreement and an agreement on clarification of the September 1994 Akosombo Agreement,[2] which had not been signed by all parties. Under the Accra Agreement, parties committed themselves to the terms and conditions of the Akosombo Agreement, as expanded, and the clarification agreement, which stipulated that a cease-fire would come into effect by midnight 28 December 1994. A new five-member Council of State was to be installed within 14 days thereafter, composed of one member each appointed by the Central Revolutionary Council of the National Patriotic Front of Liberia (CRC-NPFL), the United Liberation Movement of Liberia (ULIMO), the Armed Forces of Liberia (AFL/Coalition) and the Liberia National Conference (LNC) and a traditional chief selected by NPFL and ULIMO, Mr. Tamba Tailor. Elections were to be held on 14 November 1995 and a new Government installed on 1 January 1996. The signatories further agreed to facilitate the establishment of safe havens and buffer zones throughout Liberia.

According to the Agreement, the Liberian National Transitional Government was to be put in place immediately internal security arrangements, including police, customs and immigration, and begin formation of an appropriate national security structure, including the restructuring of AFL so that it could assume its character as a national army. The Transitional Government was to conclude a status-of-forces agreement with ECOWAS, and the Council of State was to set up committees to determine the criteria for recruitment of combatants and non-combatants into a restructured national army, as well as police and immigration units. Under the Agreement, the factions committed themselves to the regrouping of combatants to encampment sites and to maintain command and control over them at those sites. They also called on the Transitional Government,

the United Nations, the Organization of African Unity (OAU), ECOWAS, other international organizations and donors to design a programme of financial assistance for the process of demobilization, retraining, rehabilitation and the reintegration of former combatants into civilian life.

**Report of the Secretary-General (January).** On 6 January, the Secretary-General reported[3] on a high-level mission to six African nations led by Lansana Kouyaté, UN Assistant Secretary-General for Political Affairs, to discuss with ECOWAS member States the deterioration of the situation in Liberia; to consult on how best to revive the peace process and achieve reconciliation; to explore means of implementing the 1992 arms embargo imposed on Liberia;[4] to assess the future role of ECOMOG in Liberia; and to examine ways in which the UN and the international community could assist ECOMOG in carrying out its mandate.

The mission visited Côte d'Ivoire, Ghana, Guinea, Liberia, Nigeria and Sierra Leone. It concluded that, notwithstanding the efforts of the ECOWAS Chairman, Liberian political and factional leaders were not yet committed to a sustainable peace. It recommended that those leaders be brought to understand that, in the absence of political accommodation and reconciliation, continued support from the international community would not be forthcoming. ECOWAS member States, especially the six directly involved with Liberia (Burkina Faso, Côte d'Ivoire, Ghana, Guinea, Nigeria and Sierra Leone), should urgently organize an extraordinary meeting of Heads of State to resolve their differences and harmonize their policies on Liberia. Further, ECOWAS should strengthen and restructure ECOMOG in order to achieve a better balance of troops, including contributions from other African countries. It also recommended that international support—including financial support, logistics and equipment—be sought to enable ECOMOG to carry out its mandate, particularly with respect to deployment, encampment and disarmament. A planning and logistics team from the UN Department of Peacekeeping Operations could offer ECOMOG technical assistance in preparing the necessary proposal, the mission suggested. UNOMIL's future should depend on the successful implementation of those steps; meanwhile, its mandate should be extended for a limited period of three months, beginning on 13 January 1995.

In the Secretary-General's view, it was too early to assess to what extent the Liberian factions would adhere to the terms and conditions of the 1994 Accra Agreement. However, the cease-fire, which came into effect as stipulated, was holding. The AFL/Coalition members were experiencing some difficulties in agreeing on their nominee for the

Council of State, and Ghana was assisting them to reach a compromise. No similar difficulties appeared to be facing the larger factions. The next step under the Accra Agreement was the installation of a new Council of State. President Jerry Rawlings of Ghana was to convene a meeting of all Liberian factions on 9 January to finalize measures in that regard.

The military situation remained highly charged and unstable, the Secretary-General went on. The hostilities, which had resumed in September 1994, had spread to more than 80 per cent of the country. The fighting had caused massive population displacement. Humanitarian assistance outside the capital city of Monrovia had been suspended, and there were reports of human rights violations by all factions. The security situation in Monrovia had deteriorated significantly. UN military observers were withdrawn from most UNOMIL-team sites and their number reduced to approximately 90, compared to the authorized strength of 368. UNOMIL operations were restricted to areas under ECOMOG control—Monrovia, Kakata and Buchanan—and were limited to monitoring the cease-fire and assisting in the delivery of humanitarian support.

Fighting between factions mainly took the form of low-level skirmishes accompanied by looting and destruction of infrastructure. The northern and eastern regions, control of which had been contested by NPFL and Coalition forces, were the worst affected. All factions experienced serious problems of command and control. In some instances, ground commanders seemed to have wrestled the initiative from faction leaders, thus marginalizing the influence of some political leaderships.

The inability of ECOMOG to deploy troops at major points along the borders of Liberia, in accordance with the 1993 Cotonou Agreement,[(5)] was a factor in the continuing breach of the 1992 arms embargo, the Secretary-General said. Due to insecurity and logistical difficulties, ECOMOG was now deployed in less than 15 per cent of the country. Factions continued to acquire arms across the borders and from sources within Liberia. Some ECOMOG troop-contributing countries, frustrated over the failure of Liberian leaders to agree on a political solution and experiencing financial hardships in maintaining their troops, had indicated their intention to withdraw their troops unless there was significant progress in the peace process or financial assistance was provided. Some had already reduced their contingents and other forms of support.

The condition of the civilian population continued to deteriorate, the Secretary-General reported. An estimated 1.8 million Liberians now required humanitarian assistance. A constant influx of displaced persons to Monrovia had raised its population to 1.3 million, nearly three times the level before the civil war. In seeking to respond to humanitarian needs in that volatile environment, relief organizations were functioning under even more difficult circumstances than before. The loss of command and control by the leaders of warring factions and the complete disregard for human suffering by their fighters limited humanitarian activities to ECOMOG-controlled areas, the Secretary-General said. Relief assets and supplies had been looted by factions, and humanitarian staff had been displaced. Some organizations had redeployed some professional staff to other countries. Donors continued to support efforts to resume delivering humanitarian assistance throughout the country, and UNOMIL also used its limited assets to advance the cause of humanitarian relief. A consolidated UN inter-agency appeal of almost $65 million was prepared for Liberia to meet emergency, life-saving needs for the first six months of 1995 (see PART FOUR, Chapter III).

The Secretary-General recommended that the Security Council extend the UNOMIL mandate for three months. During that time, his Special Representative, Anthony Nyakyi (United Republic of Tanzania), would make an in-depth assessment of the role that UN military observers could play in the peace process and recommend adjustments in their strength. The Special Representative would also work out, in consultation with ECOMOG, its financial and logistic needs so an appropriate appeal to Member States could be made to maintain ECOMOG troops in Liberia.

The Secretary-General expressed concern that should the conflict in Liberia continue, the displacement of people and flow of arms over its borders would have serious consequences for stability in the subregion. All ECOWAS members were called on to adhere strictly to the arms embargo; he hoped ECOWAS leaders would convene a summit at the earliest possible date, to harmonize their policies on Liberia and promote implementation of the Accra Agreement, including tightening the arms embargo.

**SECURITY COUNCIL ACTION**

The Security Council on 13 January adopted **resolution 972 (1995)**.

*The Security Council,*

*Recalling* its resolutions 788(1992) of 19 November 1992, 813(1993) of 26 March 1993, 856(1993) of 10 August 1993, 866(1993) of 22 September 1993 and 911(1994) of 21 April 1994 and 950(1994) of 21 October 1994,

*Having considered* the reports of the Secretary-General dated 18 May 1994, 24 June 1994, 26 August 1994, 14 October 1994 and 6 January 1995 on the United Nations Observer Mission in Liberia (UNOMIL),

*Viewing with appreciation* the diplomatic achievement of the current chairman of the Economic Community of West African States (ECOWAS), President Jerry Rawlings of Ghana, in bringing together the factions leaders of Liberia to sign the Accra Agreement, on 21 December 1994, which builds upon the Yamoussoukro, Cotonou and Akosombo agreements and includes a timetable for the implementation of its provisions,

*Commending* once again the efforts of the Economic Community of West African States (ECOWAS), which has played a crucial role in the search for a peaceful solution to the Liberian conflict,

*Commending* also those African States that have contributed troops to the ECOWAS Monitoring Group (ECOMOG), and those Member States that have provided assistance in support of the peace negotiations and the peace-keeping forces, including contributions to the Trust Fund for Liberia,

*Expressing the hope* that a summit of the ECOWAS States will be convened at the earliest possible date to harmonize their policies on Liberia and promote implementation of the Accra Agreement, including tightening the application of the arms embargo,

*Taking note* with concern that there has been a continuing inflow of arms in Liberia in violation of the existing arms embargo, which has further destabilized the situation in Liberia,

*Deeply concerned* that the humanitarian situation in Liberia has worsened due to the lack of security in the country and the resulting inability of national and international relief organizations to function effectively,

*Calling* on the Liberian leaders and factions to demonstrate their commitment to the peace process by maintaining the cease-fire, which came into effect on 28 December 1994, recommitting themselves to the disarmament process and implementing without delay all provisions of the Accra Agreement,

1. *Welcomes* the report of the Secretary-General dated 6 January 1995;

2. *Decides* to extend the mandate of UNOMIL until 13 April 1995;

3. *Expresses* deep concern at the failure of the Liberian parties so far to reach agreement on the composition of the Council of State as stipulated in the Accra Agreement at the recent talks in Accra and calls upon them to work together to implement the Accra Agreement by upholding the cease-fire, resuming disarmament and demobilization of combatants and implementing the other relevant aspects of the Agreement in accordance with the timetable, including the prompt installation of the New Council of State;

4. *Requests* that the Secretary-General base any decision to return UNOMIL and its civilian staff to the level authorized under resolution 866(1993) on the existence of an effective cease-fire and on the ability of UNOMIL to carry out its mandate;

5. *Further requests* that the Secretary-General report to the Security Council on the situation in Liberia, on the role of UNOMIL and of ECOMOG, including on the needs of ECOWAS States to maintain their troops in ECOMOG, on or before 1 March 1995;

6. *Reminds* all Member States of their obligation strictly to abide by and comply with the embargo on all deliveries of weapons and military equipment to Liberia imposed by resolution 788(1992);

7. *Demands* once more, that all factions in Liberia strictly respect the status of ECOMOG and UNOMIL personnel, and those of organizations and personnel delivering humanitarian assistance throughout Liberia and further demands that these factions facilitate such deliveries and that they strictly abide by applicable rules of international humanitarian law;

8. *Urges* Member States to provide support for the peace process in Liberia by contributing to the United Nations Trust Fund for Liberia, and by providing financial, logistical and other assistance in support of the troops participating in ECOMOG in order to enable ECOMOG to deploy fully and to carry out its mandate, particularly with respect to encampment and disarmament of the Liberian factions;

9. *Requests*, in this regard, the Secretary-General to continue his efforts to obtain financial and logistical resources from Member States;

10. *Commends* the efforts made by Member States and humanitarian organizations to provide emergency humanitarian assistance and especially the efforts of neighbouring countries to assist Liberian refugees;

11. *Commends* also the ongoing efforts of ECOWAS to further the Liberian peace process and the commitment of ECOMOG to ensure the safety of UNOMIL military observers and civilian staff;

12. *Welcomes* the tireless efforts by the Secretary-General and his Special Representative to promote the cause of peace in Liberia;

13. *Decides* to remain actively seized of the matter.

Security Council resolution 972(1995)

13 January 1995     Meeting 3489     Adopted unanimously

Draft prepared in consultations among Council members (S/1995/22).

**Report of the Secretary-General (February).** On 24 February, the Secretary-General reported[6] to the Security Council that, in accordance with the Accra Agreement,[1] the Liberian parties had met in Accra on 9 January under ECOWAS auspices to consult on the new Council of State, with a view to its installation by 11 January. However, they were not able to reach agreement on its composition and chairmanship, and the failure to install a new Council of State had led to massive demonstrations in Monrovia on 14 January, resulting in injuries to civilians and party members, as well as destruction of property. Further proposals were made, which were also not agreed upon and, on 30 January, the Chairman of ECOWAS informed the parties they should return to Liberia to continue their negotiations. At the time of the February report, through ECOMOG efforts, the security situation in Monrovia had improved.

In response to the request in Security Council **resolution 972(1995)** (see above) for information on the needs of ECOWAS troops in ECOMOG, the Secretary-General dispatched a technical team to Monrovia from 6 to 10 February. ECOMOG indicated that it required some 12,000 troops all ranks, an increase of 4,250 over its current strength, and detailed logistical and other requirements to fulfil its tasks under the Accra Agreement, including accommodation, transport, communications and other equipment. The estimated cost would be about $90 million for a 12-month period.

The team found that ECOMOG resources and logistic assets were clearly insufficient for effective execution of its tasks. It concluded that while estimates of logistic support requirements were justified, they were not convinced that 4,250 additional troops were needed to implement the ECOMOG operation.

The Secretary-General believed it unlikely that estimated resources for ECOMOG could be provided through voluntary contributions. He therefore asked ECOWAS to indicate which budget areas troop-contributing countries would be prepared to continue financing and those that were critical for external financing on a voluntary basis.

Because of the delay in installing the Council of State, the Secretary-General said, none of the military disengagement and restructuring provided for under the Accra Agreement had yet taken place. In addition, certain aspects of the peace process needed greater coordination, including those relating to the demobilization process, including transportation of combatants to encampment sites and to home communities, provision to them and their families of food and supplies at assembly and encampment sites, construction of those sites and coordination and financing of reintegration of combatants, as well as war-affected civilians, into Liberian society. He proposed the establishment of a joint ECOMOG-UNOMIL Liaison and Coordination Cell at ECOMOG headquarters to enable more effective coordination of their respective mandates.

The Secretary-General observed, in his 24 February report, that two months after the signing of the Accra Agreement, the Liberian factions and political leaders had yet to show that they were genuinely committed to the fulfilment of their obligations. With their failure to implement yet another agreement, he said, the time had come to consider how the international community could assist in the search for peace and stability in Liberia and what form that assistance could take. If the parties were willing to implement that agreement, one option before the Council for future UN political and military involvement in Liberia was the maintainance of UNOMIL as mandated under resolution 866(1993).[7] However, that option's viability depended on providing ECOMOG with adequate resources to support its responsibilities in Liberia, a restructuring of ECOMOG, effective enforcement of the 1992 arms embargo, and more effective harmonization of ECOWAS member States policies regarding Liberia. Another option was to establish, in cooperation with ECOWAS, a UN peace-keeping force to help the parties implement all aspects of the Accra Agreement. If the current political stalemate continued, however, the Council could either further reduce UNOMIL's military component and limit the Mission's mandate to the provision of good offices, until the parties clearly demonstrated the political will to activate the peace process; or the Council could decide to withdraw UNOMIL.

**Report of Secretary-General (April).** On 10 April the Secretary-General reported[8] increased fighting in various parts of the country, which resulted in a large influx of displaced persons in areas controlled by ECOMOG. The Special Representative had attempted to re-establish the Cease-fire Violations Committee, but some factions still had not designated representatives. In the meantime, Uganda and the United Republic of Tanzania informed the Secretary-General of their intention to withdraw from ECOMOG, dropping the group's strength by almost 2,000 to about 6,800 of all ranks.

The Secretary-General reported he had discussed with Ghana's President Rawlings the convening of an ECOWAS summit in Abuja, Nigeria, as soon as possible, bringing together the Heads of State of the ECOWAS Committee of Nine on Liberia and also involving the leaders of the Liberian factions. The summit was set for May 1995.

Given frequent reports of human rights violations, the Secretary-General appointed a legal/ human rights officer to UNOMIL to investigate them.

Humanitarian assistance continued to be severely hampered by the security situation in areas controlled by the factions. Since January, 67,000 persons had sought refuge in Buchanan, bringing its population to 180,000—more than four times its pre-civil war size. Some 90,000 persons were living in shelters, and the UN Humanitarian Coordinator in Liberia had set up a special task force to address their needs. In addition to implementing immediate emergency programmes concerning food, shelter, water and sanitation, the task force was planning income-generating, quick-impact projects and trauma counselling.

As at 22 March, only 41 per cent of the $65 million sought by the UN Consolidated Inter-Agency Appeal had been pledged or contributed by the international community.

The Secretary-General then recommended that the Security Council extend UNOMIL's mandate until 30 June, with the provision that its military strength be reduced by about 20 observers given the Mission's limited ability to carry out its mandate. The military component would be strengthened as soon as the security situation improved. He urged parties to use that period to install the Council of State, re-establish an effective cease-fire, and implement other provisions of the Accra Agreement.

SECURITY COUNCIL ACTION

The Security Council on 13 April, following consideration of the Secretary-General's reports, adopted **resolution 985(1995)**.

*The Security Council,*

*Recalling* its resolutions 813(1993) of 26 March 1993, 856(1993) of 10 August 1993, 866(1993) of 22 September 1993, 911(1994) of 21 April 1994, 950(1994) of 21 October 1994 and 972(1995) of 13 January 1995,

*Recalling also* its resolution 788(1992) of 19 November 1992, in which it decided, under Chapter VII of the Charter of the United Nations, that all States shall, for the purpose of establishing peace and stability in Liberia, immediately implement a general and complete embargo on all deliveries of weapons and military equipment to Liberia until the Security Council decides otherwise, and in which it decided also that the embargo shall not apply to weapons and military equipment destined for the sole use of the peace-keeping forces of the Economic Community of West African States (ECOWAS) in Liberia, subject to any review that may be required in conformity with the report of the Secretary-General,

*Having considered* the reports of the Secretary-General dated 24 February 1995 and 10 April 1995 on the United Nations Observer Mission in Liberia (UNOMIL),

*Deeply concerned* that the cease-fire in Liberia has broken down, precluding the full deployment of UNOMIL and preventing UNOMIL from fully carrying out its mandate,

*Noting with deep concern* that in violation of resolution 788(1992) arms continue to be imported into Liberia, exacerbating the conflict,

*Welcoming* the decision of ECOWAS to hold a summit of Heads of State in May 1995,

1. *Decides* to extend the mandate of UNOMIL until 30 June 1995;

2. *Urges* all Liberian parties to implement the Akosombo Agreement and the Accra Agreement by re-establishing an effective cease-fire, promptly installing the Council of State, and taking concrete steps towards the implementation of the other provisions of the Agreements;

3. *Encourages* the ECOWAS States to promote implementation of the Akosombo and Accra Agreements, and to continue to do all in their power to facilitate a political settlement in Liberia;

4. *Urges* all States, and in particular all neighbouring States, to comply fully with the embargo on all deliveries of weapons and military equipment to Liberia imposed by resolution 788(1992), and to that end decides to establish, in accordance with rule 28 of its provisional rules of procedure, a Committee of the Security Council, consisting of all the members of the Council, to undertake the following tasks and to report on its work to the Council with its observations and recommendations:

*(a)* To seek from all States information regarding the action taken by them concerning the effective implementation of the embargo imposed by paragraph 8 of resolution 788(1992);

*(b)* To consider any information brought to its attention by States concerning violations of the embargo, and in that context to make recommendations to the Council on ways of increasing the effectiveness of the embargo;

*(c)* To recommend appropriate measures in response to violations of the embargo imposed by paragraph 8 of resolution 788(1992) and provide information on a regular basis to the Secretary-General for general distribution to Member States;

5. *Expresses* its appreciation to the Chairman of ECOWAS for his initiative in organizing a regional summit on Liberia and to the Government of Nigeria for agreeing to host it, and urges all parties to participate;

6. *Demands* once more that all factions in Liberia strictly respect the status of personnel of the ECOWAS Monitoring Group (ECOMOG) and UNOMIL, and those of organizations and personnel delivering humanitarian assistance throughout Liberia and further demands that these factions facilitate such deliveries and that they strictly abide by applicable rules of international humanitarian law;

7. *Requests* the Secretary-General to report to the Security Council by 15 June 1995 on the situation in Liberia, including whether there is an effective cease-fire and whether UNOMIL can carry out its mandate, and on the status of contributions of financial and logistical resources from the international community in support of the troops participating in ECOMOG, and notes that the Council will consider the future of UNOMIL in the light of the Secretary-General's report;

8. *Decides* to remain actively seized of the matter.

Security Council resolution 985(1995)

13 April 1995     Meeting 3517     Adopted unanimously

Draft prepared in consultations among Council members (S/1995/291).

## Sanctions Committee

The Security Council Committee, established under resolution 985(1995) to supervise implementation of the mandatory arms embargo imposed by the Council regarding Liberia, held its first meeting on 28 April. Pursuant to a decision taken at its second meeting on 25 May, the Committee on 7 June appealed to governmental or non-governmental organizations and individuals to provide information on suspected violators of that mandatory arms embargo.

In reporting on its activities up to 31 December 1995,[9] the Committee stated that it had received no reports from Member States on alleged violations of the arms embargo.

**Report of the Secretary-General (June).** The Secretary-General reported[10] on 10 June that, following extensive consultations, the Third Meeting of Heads of State and Government of the ECOWAS Committee of Nine on Liberia was held in Abuja from 17 to 20 May. It had been preceded, on 15 May, by a meeting of ECOWAS Foreign Ministers, who recommended that the Liberian Council of State should be made up of six members, with Chief Tamba Tailor as its Chairman, and that each group should designate its own representative to the Council. Consensus was not reached on the designation of Vice-Chairmen. The Foreign Ministers agreed on the need to strengthen the arms embargo, undertake peace-enforcement measures and increase financial resources for implementing the peace process.

The Abuja meeting was attended by eight Heads of State—of Côte d'Ivoire, the Gambia, Ghana, Liberia, Mali, Nigeria, Sierra Leone and Togo—as well as the Foreign Ministers of Burkina Faso and Guinea, and senior Ministers from Benin and Senegal. Delegations of all the Liberian factions present were headed, except for the NPFL, by their respective leaders.

While the Liberian parties did not reach final agreement on the composition of the Council of State, the Heads of State and Government observed that in building on gains made during the Accra consultations in January 1995, a substantial measure of agreement had emerged on nearly all outstanding issues. They emphasized the need to preserve and consolidate those gains and requested the leaders of the Liberian parties to consult towards a definite solution. The Heads of State entrusted the Ministers of the Committee of Nine with responsibility for reconvening a meeting of Liberian parties to resolve the outstanding issues.

The ECOWAS leaders noted that, if and when agreement was secured, it would be imperative that the United Nations fully support the implementation of the peace process by restoring UNOMIL to full strength and securing resources for ECOMOG. They expressed concern over the continued flow of arms into Liberia and called on Member States to bring all embargo violations to the attention of the sanctions committee. They requested ECOMOG and UNOMIL to improve monitoring mechanisms and appealed to the international community to provide logistical support to ECOWAS to facilitate the effective patrolling of Liberia's borders and stem the flow of arms into the country. They stressed that the provision of adequate resources for ECOMOG would enhance its capacity to compel the armed factions to conform to ECOWAS decisions.

At the invitation of Nigeria, NPFL President Charles Taylor, the only Liberian faction leader who did not attend the summit, travelled to Abuja on 2 June for consultations with Nigerian officials.

In March and April 1995, ambushes and skirmishes continued, as a result of which UNOMIL had to suspend its patrolling in certain areas. Efforts by UNOMIL to bring all relevant faction representatives to participate in the Cease-fire Violations Committee remained unsuccessful, the Secretary-General stated.

In late April, concerns relating to food security led to a demonstration by Sierra Leonean refugees and internally displaced persons in Monrovia and an attack on offices and vehicles of the Office of the UN High Commissioner for Refugees (UNHCR). The Special Representative convened a task force to formulate a comprehensive programme of disarmament, demobilization and long-term reintegration of ex-combatants. The office of the Humanitarian Coordinator developed a strategy for the delivery of humanitarian assistance that took those developments into account and formed the basis of a resource mobilization campaign for humanitarian activities in Liberia.

The Secretary-General recommended that the Security Council extend UNOMIL's mandate until 30 September. In the event that the political stalemate continued, UNOMIL would be terminated on that date and converted into a good offices mission, including a small military cell, which would maintain liaison with ECOMOG. Those military observers who, in the absence of a cease-fire and the resumption of disarmament, might be unable to perform their monitoring functions effectively would also be withdrawn. The Secretary-General would consult with ECOWAS on the modalities of the good offices role of the United Nations and make recommendations to the Council. If, on the other hand, there were significant progress over the next three months, he would recommend that the Council restore UNOMIL to its full strength. It was evident, however, that UNOMIL's role in Liberia and its relationship with ECOMOG would have to be adjusted and he intended to consult with ECOWAS with a view to enhancing cooperation between UNOMIL and ECOMOG and defining a joint concept of operations.

**SECURITY COUNCIL ACTION**

On 30 June, the Security Council adopted **resolution 1001(1995)**.

*The Security Council,*

*Recalling* its resolutions 788(1992) of 19 November 1992, 813(1993) of 26 March 1993, 856(1993) of 10 August 1993, 866(1993) of 22 September 1993, 911(1994) of 21 April 1994, 950(1994) of 21 October 1994, 972(1995) of 13 January 1995, and 985(1995) of 13 April 1995,

*Having considered* the report of the Secretary-General dated 10 June, on the United Nations Observer Mission in Liberia (UNOMIL),

*Emphasizing* that the people of Liberia bear the ultimate responsibility for achieving peace and national reconciliation,

*Commending* the positive role of the Economic Community of West African States (ECOWAS) in its continuing efforts to restore peace, security and stability in Liberia,

*Welcoming* the recent summit meeting of Heads of State and Government of the Committee of Nine on Liberia of the Economic Community of West African States, in Abuja, Nigeria, from 17 to 20 May 1995,

*Noting* that a further concerted and harmonized effort by all concerned, including the ECOWAS States, would be helpful to advance the peace process,

*Concerned* that the Liberian parties have so far failed to install the Council of State, re-establish an effective cease-fire and take concrete steps towards the implementation of the other provisions of the Accra Agreement,

*Deeply concerned also* at the continuing inter- and intra-factional fighting in parts of Liberia, which has further worsened the plight of the civilian population, particularly in rural areas, as well as affected the ability of humanitarian agencies to provide relief,

*Calling on* the Liberian factions, especially the combatants, to respect the human rights of the civilian population and to respect international humanitarian law,

*Expressing great concern* over the continued flow of arms into Liberia in violation of Security Council resolution 788(1992),

*Commending also* those African States that have contributed troops to the ECOWAS Monitoring Group (ECOMOG), and those Member States that have provided assistance in support of the peace negotiations and the peace-keeping forces, including contributions to the Trust Fund for Liberia,

1. *Welcomes* the report of the Secretary-General dated 10 June 1995;

2. *Stresses* that continued international community support for the peace process in Liberia, including the continued presence of UNOMIL, is contingent on immediate actions by the Liberian parties to peacefully resolve their differences and achieve national reconciliation;

3. *Decides* to extend the mandate of UNOMIL until 15 September 1995;

4. *Urges* that the Liberian parties use this period to make serious and substantial progress towards implementation of the Akosombo and Accra Agreements and specifically to accomplish the following steps:

   *(a)* Installation of the Council of State;

   *(b)* Re-establishment of a comprehensive and effective cease-fire;

   *(c)* Disengagement of all forces;

   *(d)* Creation of an agreed timetable and schedule for the implementation of all other aspects of the Agreements, in particular the disarmament process;

5. *Declares* its intention, after consideration of the report of the Secretary-General, that UNOMIL's mandate would not be renewed by the Security Council on 15 September 1995, unless the steps in paragraph 4 above are complied with by that date;

6. *Declares* its readiness if significant progress in the peace process in Liberia regarding the steps in paragraph 4 above is achieved by 15 September 1995 to consider restoring UNOMIL to its full strength with appropriate adjustment of its mandate and the relationship with ECOMOG to enable these two operations to carry out their respective functions more effectively as well as to consider other aspects of post-conflict peace-building in Liberia;

7. *Urges* the ECOWAS Ministers of the Committee of Nine as authorized by their Heads of State and Governments at the Abuja Summit of 17 to 20 May 1995, to reconvene a meeting of the Liberian parties and political leaders as soon as possible in order to finally resolve the outstanding issues of political settlement;

8. *Urges* Member States in the meantime to provide additional support for the peace process in Liberia by contributing to the United Nations Trust Fund for Liberia, and by providing financial, logistical and other assistance in support of the troops participating in ECOMOG in order to enable it to deploy fully and to carry out its mandate, particularly with respect to encampment and disarmament of the Liberian factions;

9. *Requests* the Secretary-General in this regard, to continue his efforts to obtain financial and logistical resources from Member States and urges those States that have pledged assistance to fulfil their commitments;

10. *Reminds* all States of their obligations to comply strictly with the embargo on all deliveries of weapons and military equipment to Liberia imposed by resolution 788(1992) and to bring all instances of violations of the arms embargo before the Committee established pursuant to resolution 985(1995);

11. *Reaffirms* the continued necessity for ECOMOG and UNOMIL to cooperate in fulfilling their respective mandates and to this end urges ECOMOG to enhance its cooperation with UNOMIL at all levels to enable the mission to discharge its mandate;

12. *Urges* ECOMOG, in accordance with the agreement regarding the respective roles and responsibilities of UNOMIL and ECOMOG in the implementation of the Cotonou Agreement, to take necessary action to provide security for UNOMIL observers and civilian staff;

13. *Demands* once more, that all factions in Liberia strictly respect the status of ECOMOG and UNOMIL personnel, as well as organizations and agencies delivering humanitarian assistance throughout Liberia, and further demands that these factions facilitate such deliveries and that they strictly abide by applicable rules of international humanitarian law;

14. *Commends* the efforts made by Member States and humanitarian organizations in providing emergency humanitarian assistance and especially those of neighbouring countries in assisting Liberian refugees;

15. *Urges* the Organization of African Unity to continue its collaboration with ECOWAS in promoting the cause of peace in Liberia;

16. *Expresses its appreciation* to the Secretary-General and his Special Representative for their tireless efforts to bring peace and reconciliation to Liberia;

17. *Requests* the Secretary-General to continue, as described in his report, to review the level of personnel of UNOMIL, to adapt the practical implementation of the mandate and to report as appropriate;

18. *Requests* the Secretary-General to report to the Security Council before 15 September 1995 on the situation in Liberia;

19. *Decides* to remain seized of the matter.

Security Council resolution 1001(1995)

30 June 1995     Meeting 3549     Adopted unanimously

Draft prepared in consultations among Council members (S/1995/521).

**July summit statement.** The Authority of Heads of State and Government of ECOWAS, at its summit meeting (Accra, Ghana, 28 and 29 July), adopted a resolution,[11] later transmitted to the Security Council, stating that it was convinced that withdrawal of UNOMIL would irreparably compromise all efforts made so far by ECOMOG and would be catastrophic for all States of the sub-region. It appealed to the Security Council to reconsider the situation in Liberia, taking into account recent initiatives and ongoing actions and to reconsider its decision, irrespective of the stage the Liberian peace process had reached by 15 September. The Heads of State renewed their appeal to the international community to provide adequate financial resources to ECOWAS and logistic support to ECOMOG for the restoration of peace in Liberia.

### The Abuja Agreement

At the Consultative Meeting of Liberian parties, facilitated by ECOWAS (Monrovia, 19-23 July), factions attending a meeting of the Women's Groups of Liberia, also held in July, endorsed some recommendations made there. Subsequently, Charles Taylor discussed in Accra with the Chairman of ECOWAS and the OAU Eminent Person for Liberia, Reverend Canaan Banana, modalities for convening an all-inclusive meeting of Liberian factions. Following further consultations with some ECOWAS leaders and Liberian parties, the Chairman of ECOWAS convened a meeting of the factions at Abuja (16-19 August) attended by leaders of all parties, as well as Chief Tamba Tailor, representing the traditional chiefs.

The Abuja talks culminated on 19 August in the signing of the Abuja Agreement[12] to Supplement the Cotonou and Akosombo Agreements, as subsequently clarified by the Accra Agreement. The Abuja Agreement provided for the establishment of a cease-fire and cessation of hostilities on 26 August at midnight; a six-member Council of State composed of: Wilton Sankawolo as Chairman; Dr. George Boley, representing the coalition of Liberia Peace Council (LPC), CRC-NPFL, and Lola Defence Force (LDF); Alhaji Kromah of ULIMO; Oscar Quiah of LNC; Chief Tamba Tailor; and Charles Taylor of NPFL. All other members of the Council would be Vice-Chairmen of equal status. The new Council would remain in power for one year, until the elections scheduled for 20 August 1996.

On 28 August 1995, the Minister of Foreign Affairs of Ghana, on behalf of President Rawlings, Chairman of ECOWAS, informed[13] the Secretary-General of the successful outcome of the negotiations and the conclusion of the Abuja Agreement, whose successful implementation called for additional resources in terms of troops, guns, ammunition and money. Progress was also linked to the percentage of guns that could be taken away from the current fighters in Liberia by ECOMOG and the Council of State.

### Council of State inauguration

**Report of the Secretary-General (September).** On 9 September, the Secretary-General reported[14] that the new Council of State was inaugurated on 1 September in Monrovia and held its first session immediately after its installation. Reports indicated that the new transitional Government enjoyed the full support of all key political leaders of Liberia and was warmly welcomed by the population at large. It had already announced new appointments to the Cabinet and assigned oversight responsibilities of Ministries, autonomous agencies and public corporations to Council members. Nominations to the Supreme Court had also been made and consultations took place to fill the remaining posts in the Transitional Legislative Assembly and the Electoral Commission.

A cease-fire had been established on 26 August, the Secretary-General reported. An ECOWAS delegation, visiting Liberia from 25 to 27 August, confirmed that the factions had instructed their respective forces to observe the cease-fire. The Cease-fire Violations Committee, chaired by UNOMIL and consisting of ECOMOG and representatives of the Liberian National Transitional Government (LNTG) and the factions, met on 4 September to review plans for monitoring the cease-fire and implementing the other provisions of the peace agreement, including disarmament and demobilization. A Disarmament Committee, chaired by ECOMOG and comprising UNOMIL, LNTG and representatives of the armed factions, with the participation of the International Committee of the Red Cross, was also established to draw up plans for the disengagement of forces, disarmament and the exchange of prisoners of war. The Council of State, taking advantage of ECO-MOG's extended presence in the interior, established local administrations and appointed superintendents for certain counties.

### UN operations in Liberia

The Secretary-General observed in his September report that prospects for peace in Liberia were perhaps better now than they had been at any time since the outbreak of the civil war. The ECOWAS States had harmonized their policies towards Liberia and a new spirit of cooperation seemed to have emerged between the Liberian parties and ECOWAS. He recommended that the Security Council extend UNOMIL's mandate until 31 January 1996, during which time the parties should make every effort to complete the disengagement, assembly, disarmament and demobilization of their forces. In his view, effective reintegration of ex-combatants into civilian life would be an essential element in the peace process; UNOMIL, in consultation with the transitional Government, ECOMOG, UNDP and other United Nations agencies, as well as non-governmental organizations (NGOs), had established a task force on disarmament, demobilization and reintegration, to develop a framework in which those issues could be addressed in an integrated manner. Technical and logistic assistance should also be provided so that the national police could effectively carry out its duties and progressively assume a greater share in the maintenance of law and order.

In accordance with his earlier decision to reduce the number of military observers in Liberia, the Secretary-General reported that, in July, 17 UNOMIL military observers had been redeployed to the UN Assistance Mission for Rwanda. UNOMIL's current military strength consisted of 45 observers and 7 medical personnel. However, in the light of the developments in the peace process, he intended to increase immediately the military component by some 42 observers. That would enable the Mission to re-establish a presence at Tubmanburg and, subsequently, at Gbarnga and Tapeta, subject to the security situation and to the deployment of ECOMOG at those locations. Plans for the further expansion of UNOMIL, to carry out its responsibilities under the Abuja Agreement, were being prepared and UNOMIL was discussing with ECOMOG a joint concept of operations.

There was also a significant expansion planned in humanitarian assistance, the Secretary-General reported. Major humanitarian aid organizations had agreed to a set of operating principles, designed to maintain a common approach to working in the Liberian context. Also, major UN agencies, NGOs and other donor representatives in Liberia had adopted a joint mission statement, emphasizing the importance of neutral, impartial and need-driven humanitarian assistance, the promotion of self-reliance among those populations receiving assistance, and the efficient use of resources. That statement was to form the basis of an inter-agency consolidated appeal for Liberia. United Nations agencies, NGOs and their partners developed means of assuring the smooth and permanent reabsorption of demobilized fighters into civilian society, and programmes for the reintegration of internally displaced persons and refugees.

The Secretary-General said he would consult with the ECOWAS Chairman on holding a pledging conference to raise resources for ECOMOG and for other critical needs to advance the peace process in Liberia. He would send a mission to Liberia to consult with Liberian leaders and other interested parties to assess the requirements for implementing the Abuja Agreement. He also intended to present to the Council, by the end of October, UNOMIL's new concept of operations, which would include aspects of disarmament and demobilization.

**SECURITY COUNCIL ACTION**

Meeting on 15 September, the Security Council adopted **resolution 1014(1995)**.

*The Security Council,*

*Recalling* all its previous resolutions concerning the situation in Liberia, in particular resolution 1001(1995) of 30 June 1995,

*Having considered* the report of the Secretary-General dated 9 September 1995 on the United Nations Observer Mission in Liberia (UNOMIL),

*Welcoming* the recent Abuja Agreement signed by the Liberian parties on 19 August 1995 which amends and supplements the Cotonou and Akosombo Agreements as subsequently clarified by the Accra Agreement,

*Welcoming* the installation of a new Council of State, the re-establishment of a comprehensive and effective cease-fire, the beginning of the disengagement of forces and the agreement on a new timetable and schedule for the implementation of all other aspects of the Agreement,

*Commending* the positive role of the Economic Community of West African States (ECOWAS), in its continuing efforts to restore peace, security and stability in Liberia,

*Commending* in particular the efforts of the Governments of Nigeria and Ghana as host and Chairman respectively of the Abuja meeting, which have significantly contributed to the conclusion of the Abuja Agreement by the Liberian parties,

*Noting* that with these positive developments the Liberian parties have made appreciable progress towards the peaceful resolution of the conflict,

*Emphasizing* the need for all the Liberian parties to respect and implement fully all the agreements and commitments they have entered into, in particular with regard to maintenance of the cease-fire, disarmament and demobilization of combatants, and national reconciliation,

*Emphasizing also* once again that the people of Liberia bear the ultimate responsibility for achieving peace and national reconciliation,

*Expressing its appreciation* to those African States that have contributed and are contributing troops to the ECOWAS Monitoring Group (ECOMOG),

*Commending* also those Member States that have provided assistance in support of the peace process, including contributions to the Trust Fund for Liberia,

*Noting also* that with the signing of the Abuja Agreement, additional resources in terms of troops, equipment and logistic support would be required by ECOMOG if it is to be able to deploy throughout the country to oversee the implementation of the various aspects of the Agreement, in particular the disarmament and demobilization process,

1. *Welcomes* the report of the Secretary-General dated 9 September 1995;

2. *Decides* to extend the mandate of UNOMIL until 31 January 1996;

3. *Welcomes* the Secretary-General's intention to increase immediately by 42 the number of military observers to monitor the cease-fire and the disengagement of forces, and considers that any increase beyond that should be based on progress on the ground in implementing the peace agreement;

4. *Welcomes* also the intention of the Secretary-General to submit by the end of October 1995, for the Council's consideration, recommendations concerning the new concept of operations of UNOMIL which should address, *inter alia*, measures to enhance the relationship between UNOMIL and ECOMOG, aspects of disarmament and demobilization, and the resources which UNOMIL will require to carry out its tasks effectively; and expresses its intention to review and respond to the Secretary-General's recommendations in an expeditious manner;

5.  *Urges* Member States to provide additional support for the peace process in Liberia by contributing to the United Nations Trust Fund for Liberia, and in this regard calls on those States that have pledged assistance to fulfil their commitments;

6.  *Urges also* all Member States to provide financial, logistical and other assistance in support of ECOMOG to enable it to carry out its mandate, particularly with respect to encampment and disarmament of the Liberian factions;

7.  *Requests* the Secretary-General in this regard to continue his efforts to obtain financial and logistical resources from Member States and welcomes his intention to organize, in consultation with the Chairman of ECOWAS, the holding of a pledging conference for Liberia as soon as possible to raise the resources needed by ECOMOG and for other needs critical to the advancement of the peace process in Liberia;

8.  *Welcomes* further the Secretary-General's intention to dispatch a mission to Liberia to consult with the Liberian leaders and other interested parties on the requirements in the evolving implementation of the Abuja Agreement and looks forward to his report on the mission's results and recommendations;

9.  *Encourages* Member States, in particular African countries, to consider providing troops to the expanded ECOMOG;

10.  *Stresses* that continued support by the international community for the peace process in Liberia including the continued participation of UNOMIL is contingent on the continued commitment by the Liberian parties to resolve their differences peacefully and to achieve national reconciliation;

11.  *Reminds* all States of their obligations to comply strictly with the embargo on all deliveries of weapons and military equipment to Liberia imposed by resolution 788(1992) and to bring all instances of violations of the arms embargo before the Committee established pursuant to resolution 985(1995);

12.  *Calls* on ECOMOG, in accordance with the agreement regarding the respective roles and responsibilities of UNOMIL and ECOMOG in the implementation of the Cotonou Agreement, to take necessary action to provide security for UNOMIL observers and civilian staff;

13.  *Demands,* once more, that all factions in Liberia strictly respect the status of ECOMOG and UNOMIL personnel, as well as organizations and agencies delivering humanitarian assistance throughout Liberia, and further demands that these factions facilitate such deliveries and that they strictly abide by applicable rules of international humanitarian law;

14.  *Commends* the efforts made by Member States, including those of neighbouring countries, and humanitarian organizations in providing emergency humanitarian assistance to Liberian refugees and calls upon them to increase the efforts already made to handle the voluntary and rapid return of refugees in their country and other aspects of humanitarian assistance;

15.  *Encourages* the Organization of African Unity to continue its post-conflict peace-building collaboration with ECOWAS in promoting the cause of peace in Liberia;

16.  *Expresses its appreciation* to the Secretary-General, his Special Representative and all UNOMIL personnel

for their tireless efforts to bring peace and reconciliation to Liberia;

17.  *Decides* to remain seized of the matter.

Security Council resolution 1014(1995)

15 September 1995      Meeting 3577      Adopted unanimously

Draft prepared in consultations among Council members (S/1995/790).

## Transitional Government progress

**Report of the Secretary-General (October).** Since its installation on 1 September, the new Council of State had shown strong determination to make the Liberian National Transition Government an effective one, the Secretary-General stated in a 23 October report to the Security Council.[15] Appointments to the Cabinet were completed and new Ministers had been sworn into office on 26 September. Appointments to the Supreme Court were also completed and the Ad Hoc Elections Commission reconstituted. The distribution of positions in Government, public corporations and autonomous agencies had been carried out in accordance with the Abuja Agreement, he said.

The Council of State directed all government departments and agencies to prepare plans to expand the authority of LNTG into the interior of the country and had declared its intention to reopen all roads to ensure free and secure access into the hinterland. It envisaged that local government administrations, which had not existed in most counties during the six years of civil war, would be re-established. The Supreme Court announced its intention to re-establish the judiciary system throughout the country. Commissions were established to oversee the process of disarming and demobilization; repatriation and resettlement; national reconstruction; the restructuring of AFL; and the rehabilitation of the Liberian National Police.

As for the military situation, there had been violations of the cease-fire, including intermittent fighting between factions over a diamond-rich area. Despite an order from the Cease-fire Violations Committee to disengage, hostilities continued. All relief agencies had temporarily relocated their staff to Monrovia and reduced activities in the area. Harassment of civilians and looting of property were reported.

Disengagement of forces was occurring, but not completed, by 26 September. The ECOMOG/UNOMIL joint verification team reported that some factions said because of mutual distrust it was unlikely that significant disengagement would take place until ECOMOG deployed to those areas. The LNTG Disarmament and Demobilization Commission was to oversee the disarmament and demobilization of the 60,000 combatants into civil society. United Nations agencies, NGOs and bilateral donors planned reintegration assistance programmes, addressing the needs of ex-combatants, internally displaced persons and refugees. To provide for the ex-combatants during the time-lag between demobilization and reintegration, it was envisaged that assistance for the demobilization process would be provided under the assessed budget to help combatants for a two- or three-month period. UNICEF and its traditional partners established programmes to address the specific needs of child soldiers.

## Further developments

Outlining the main objectives and revised mandate of UNOMIL in his October report, the Secretary-General said that in accordance with the Cotonou, Akosombo, Accra and Abuja Agreements, ECOWAS would continue to play the lead role in the peace process in Liberia, while ECOMOG would retain the primary responsibility for assisting LNTG in the implementation of the military provisions of the Agreements. UNOMIL would continue to observe and monitor the implementation of the peace agreements. Its main functions would be to exercise its good offices to support ECOWAS and LNTG to: investigate allegations of cease-fire violations reported to the Cease-fire Violations Committee, recommend measures to prevent the recurrence of such violations and report to the Secretary-General; monitor compliance with the other military provisions of the peace agreements and verify their impartial application, especially the disarming and demobilization of combatants; assist in the maintenance of agreed assembly sites and the implementation of a programme for demobilization of combatants, in co-operation with LNTG, donors and NGOs; support humanitarian assistance activities; investigate and report to the Secretary-General on human rights violations and assist local human rights groups in raising voluntary assistance for training and logistic support; and observe and verify the election process, in consultation with OAU and ECOWAS.

The new concept of operations envisaged that UNOMIL would monitor and verify the implementation of the military provisions of the Abuja Agreement and deploy its military observers with the emphasis on disarmament and demobilization. Teams of UN military observers would co-deploy with ECOMOG troops at each assembly site to monitor and verify the disarming of combatants. In addition, three mobile teams would be co-located within ECOMOG brigade headquarters. They would act as sector commanders for the UNOMIL military observers stationed at assembly sites in each sector. One mobile team would be stationed in Monrovia. Teams would investigate, jointly with ECOMOG and LNTG observers or independently, reported violations of the cease-fire and arms embargo, as well as the disengagement of forces.

To implement that concept of operations, it was estimated that 160 military observers would be needed; maximum strength would be reached during the period of disarmament and demobilization, scheduled between 1 December 1995 and 31 January 1996. UNOMIL would also require additional air assets. LNTG should ensure respect for the status of UN personnel and extend full cooperation to UNOMIL. At the same time, ECOMOG must provide security for UNOMIL personnel and property. Joint coordination meetings between UNOMIL and ECOMOG would be held.

ECOMOG estimated that it needed 12,000 troops, some 4,700 more than its strength at that time. Ghana, Guinea, Nigeria and other ECOWAS countries indicated in principle their preparedness to contribute additional troops.

### Humanitarian aid

The Secretary-General, following consultations with the Chairman of ECOWAS and LNTG, also announced in his 23 October report the convening of a conference of assistance to Liberia in New York scheduled for 27 October. It would focus on support required to implement the Abuja Agreement, including humanitarian assistance, the disarmament and demobilization processes, recovery and rehabilitation needs, as well as assistance to ECOMOG.

To address the new humanitarian requirements, coordination mechanisms were to be expanded and strengthened. A UN Humanitarian Coordinator was to be appointed to support and coordinate efforts of UN operational agencies and to support efforts of the wider humanitarian community, including non-governmental, international and multilateral organizations. The Humanitarian Assistance Coordination Unit would include units on humanitarian assistance coordination and demobilization and reintegration. UNHCR was preparing for the repatriation of refugees starting in early 1996.

The Secretary-General identified a number of areas where Liberia needed assistance. Those included assistance for the holding of legislative and presidential elections, scheduled for 20 August 1996; technical assistance in the restructuring and management of the national police, financial and logistic support to obtain uniforms and communications and transportation equipment, and basic technical and financial assistance to the national police academy, including training material, training of trainers and the rehabilitation of buildings; and support for the Monrovia Central Prison.

The Secretary-General was encouraged by the progress and hoped that the Council of State and the faction leaders would abide by their commitments under the Abuja Agreement. He was, however, concerned about reports of cease-fire violations and resulting delays in the disengagement process. He urged LNTG to take action to avoid further incidents and to maintain the momentum of the peace process.

## SECURITY COUNCIL ACTION

On 10 November the Security Council adopted **resolution 1020(1995)**.

*The Security Council,*

*Recalling* all its previous resolutions concerning the situation in Liberia, in particular resolutions 866(1993) of 22 September 1993 and 1014(1995) of 15 September 1995,

*Having considered* the report of the Secretary-General dated 23 October 1995 on the United Nations Observer Mission in Liberia (UNOMIL),

*Commending* the positive role of the Economic Community of West African States (ECOWAS), in its continuing efforts to restore peace, security and stability in Liberia,

*Stressing* the importance of full cooperation and close coordination between UNOMIL and the ECOWAS Monitoring Group (ECOMOG) in the implementation of their respective mandates,

*Noting* the appreciable progress the Liberian parties have recently made towards the peaceful resolution of the conflict including the re-establishment of a cease-fire, installation of the new Council of State and an agreement on a timetable for the implementation of the peace process from cease-fire to election,

*Noting also* that the Liberian parties appear more determined than ever before to take tangible steps towards the restoration of peace and stability in their country,

*Expressing its concern* about the incidence of cease-fire violations and delays in the process of disengagement of forces,

*Expressing also* its appreciation to those African States that have contributed and are contributing troops to ECOMOG,

*Commending* also those Member States that have provided assistance in support of the peace process, including contributions to the Trust Fund for Liberia,

1. *Welcomes* the report of the Secretary-General dated 23 October 1995;

2. *Decides* to adjust the mandate of UNOMIL to be defined as follows:

(*a*) To exercise its good offices to support the efforts of ECOWAS and the Liberian National Transitional Government (LNTG) to implement the peace agreements and to cooperate with them for this purpose;

(*b*) To investigate all allegations of violations of the cease-fire reported to the Cease-fire Violations Committee, to recommend measures to prevent the recurrence of such violations and to report to the Secretary-General accordingly;

(*c*) To monitor compliance with the other military provisions of the peace agreements including disengagement of forces, disarmament and observance of the arms embargo and to verify their impartial application;

(*d*) To assist, as appropriate, in the maintenance of assembly sites agreed upon by ECOMOG, the LNTG and the factions, and in the implementation of a programme for demobilization of combatants, in cooperation with the LNTG, donor agencies and non-governmental organizations;

(*e*) To support, as appropriate, humanitarian assistance activities;

(*f*) To investigate and report to the Secretary-General on violations of human rights and to assist local human rights groups, as appropriate, in raising voluntary contributions for training and logistic support;

(*g*) To observe and verify the election process, in consultation with the Organization of African Unity and ECOWAS, including the legislative and presidential elections to be held in accordance with provisions of the peace agreements;

3. *Decides* that the number of military observers should be a maximum of 160;

4. *Welcomes also* in this context the recommendations contained in the Secretary-General's report concerning the new concept of operations for UNOMIL;

5. *Calls upon* all the Liberian parties to respect and implement fully and expeditiously all the agreements and commitments they have entered into, in particular with regard to the maintenance of the cease-fire, disarmament and demobilization of combatants, and national reconciliation, taking into account that the restoration of peace and democracy in Liberia is primarily the responsibility of those parties which signed the Abuja Agreement on 19 August 1995;

6. *Urges* Member States to provide additional support for the peace process in Liberia by contributing to the United Nations Trust Fund for Liberia, and in this regard encourages States that pledged assistance to fulfil their commitments;

7. *Urges also* all Member States to provide financial, logistical and other assistance in support of ECOMOG to enable it to carry out its mandate, particularly with respect to assembly and disarmament of the Liberian factions;

8. *Welcomes* the commitments made at the Conference on Assistance to Liberia, held in New York on 27 October 1995;

9. *Reiterates* that continued support by the international community for the peace process in Liberia is contingent on the continued commitment by the Liberian parties to achieve national reconciliation in line with the peace process;

10. *Urges* the LNTG to take the necessary action to avoid further incidents of cease-fire violations and maintain the momentum of the peace process;

11. *Reminds* all States of their obligations to comply strictly with the embargo on all deliveries of weapons and military equipment to Liberia imposed by resolution 788(1992) and to bring all instances of violations of the arms embargo before the Committee established pursuant to resolution 985(1995);

12. *Calls* on ECOMOG, in accordance with the agreement regarding the respective roles and responsibilities of UNOMIL and ECOMOG in the implementation of the Cotonou Agreement and the new concept of operations, to take necessary action to provide security for UNOMIL observers and civilian staff;

13. *Stresses* the need for close contacts and enhanced coordination between UNOMIL and ECOMOG in their operational activities at all levels;

14. *Demands* once more that all factions in Liberia strictly respect the status of ECOMOG and UNOMIL personnel, as well as organizations and agencies delivering humanitarian assistance throughout Liberia, and further demands that these factions facilitate such deliv-

eries and that they strictly abide by applicable rules of international humanitarian law;

15. *Stresses* the need for improved coordination in carrying out the repatriation of refugees and the resettlement of internally displaced persons;

16. *Stresses* also the importance of respect of human rights in Liberia as well as the necessity to rehabilitate promptly the penitentiary system in this country;

17. *Requests* the Secretary-General to submit by 15 December 1995 a progress report on the situation in Liberia including the implementation of the adjusted mandate of UNOMIL, as well as its new concept of operations;

18. *Expresses its appreciation* to the Secretary-General, his Special Representative and all UNOMIL personnel for their tireless efforts to bring peace and reconciliation to Liberia;

19. *Decides* to remain seized of the matter.

Security Council resolution 1020(1995)

10 November 1995    Meeting 3592    Adopted unanimously

Draft prepared in consultations among Council members (S/1995/923).

## Composition and financing

### Composition of UNOMIL

In January 1995, the number of UNOMIL military observers was about 90, compared with the mission's authorized strength of 368. They still numbered 86 in April but fell to 45, plus 7 medical staff, in July.

However, in September, after the signing of the Abuja Agreement, UNOMIL's military component rose by 42. In October, the Secretary-General outlined a new concept of operations for UNOMIL, requiring a strength of 160 military observers. At mid-December, including medical staff, observers numbered 71.

On 16 November, the Council agreed[16] with the Secretary-General's proposal[17] to appoint Major-General Mahmoud Talha (Egypt) as Chief Military Observer of UNOMIL, to replace Major-General Daniel I. Opande (Kenya).

### Financing of UNOMIL

In May 1995, the Secretary-General presented[18] cost estimates for the maintenance of UNOMIL, amounting to $12,222,500 gross ($11,385,500 net) from 14 April to 31 December 1995 and $8,004,900 gross ($7,408,500 net) for the period from 1 January to 30 June 1996.

The Advisory Committee on Administrative and Budgetary Questions (ACABQ) in June recommended[19] the suggested appropriations for the period from 14 April to 31 December 1995. For the later period from 1 January to 30 June 1996, it recommended that the Secretary-General submit his budget proposal to the General Assembly at its fiftieth session.

**GENERAL ASSEMBLY ACTION**

On 12 July, the General Assembly adopted **resolution 49/232 B**.

## Financing of the United Nations Observer Mission in Liberia

*The General Assembly,*

*Having considered* the report of the Secretary-General on the financing of the United Nations Observer Mission in Liberia and the related report of the Advisory Committee on Administrative and Budgetary Questions,

*Recalling* Security Council resolution 866(1993) of 22 September 1993, by which the Council established the United Nations Observer Mission in Liberia, and the subsequent resolutions by which the Council renewed the mandate of the Observer Mission, the latest of which was resolution 985(1995) of 13 April 1995,

*Recalling also* its decision 48/478 of 23 December 1993 on the financing of the Observer Mission and its subsequent resolutions thereon, the latest of which was resolution 49/232 A of 23 December 1994,

*Reaffirming* that the costs of the Observer Mission are expenses of the Organization to be borne by Member States in accordance with Article 17, paragraph 2, of the Charter of the United Nations,

*Recalling* its previous decisions regarding the fact that, in order to meet the expenditures caused by the Observer Mission, a different procedure is required from the one applied to meet expenditures of the regular budget of the United Nations,

*Taking into account* the fact that the economically more developed countries are in a position to make relatively larger contributions and that the economically less developed countries have a relatively limited capacity to contribute towards such operations,

*Bearing in mind* the special responsibilities of the States permanent members of the Security Council, as indicated in General Assembly resolution 1874(S-IV) of 27 June 1963, in the financing of such operations,

*Mindful* of the fact that it is essential to provide the Observer Mission with the necessary financial resources to enable it to fulfil its responsibilities under the relevant resolutions of the Security Council,

1. *Takes note* of the status of assessed contributions to the United Nations Observer Mission in Liberia as at 20 June 1995, including the contributions outstanding in the amount of 9,267,175 United States dollars, and urges all Member States concerned to make every possible effort to ensure the payment of their outstanding assessed contributions;

2. *Expresses concern* about the financial situation with regard to peace-keeping activities, due to overdue payments by Member States of their assessments, particularly Member States in arrears;

3. *Urges* all Member States to make every possible effort to ensure payment of their assessed contributions to the Observer Mission promptly and in full;

4. *Endorses* the observations and recommendations contained in the report of the Advisory Committee on Administrative and Budgetary Questions;

5. *Requests* the Secretary-General to take all necessary action to ensure that all United Nations activities related to the Liberian peace process are administered in a coordinated fashion with a maximum of efficiency and economy;

6. *Decides* to appropriate to the Special Account for the United Nations Observer Mission in Liberia an amount of 4,781,400 dollars gross (4,533,300 dollars net), authorized and apportioned in accordance with General Assembly resolution 49/232 A for the maintenance of

the Observer Mission for the period from 14 January to 13 April 1995;

7. *Decides also* to appropriate to the Special Account the amount of 3,695,200 dollars gross (3,442,200 dollars net), authorized and apportioned in accordance with resolution 49/232 A, for the maintenance of the Observer Mission for the period from 14 April to 30 June 1995;

8. *Decides further,* with regard to the period from 1 July to 31 December 1995, to appropriate to the Special Account the amount of 8,527,300 dollars gross (7,943,300 dollars net) for the maintenance of the Observer Mission and to apportion this amount among Member States at the rate of 1,421,200 dollars gross (1,323,900 dollars net) per month in accordance with the scheme set out in resolution 49/232 A, and taking into account the scale of assessments for the years 1995, 1996 and 1997, as set out in General Assembly resolution 49/19 B of 23 December 1994, subject to the extension of the mandate of the Observer Mission by the Security Council;

9. *Decides* that, in accordance with the provisions of its resolution 973(X) of 15 December 1955, there shall be set off against the apportionment among Member States, as provided for in paragraph 8 above, their respective share in the Tax Equalization Fund of the estimated staff assessment income of 584,000 dollars, which is equivalent to a monthly rate of 97,300 dollars, approved for the Observer Mission for the period from 1 July to 31 December 1995;

10. *Decides also* that there shall be set off against the apportionment among Member States, as provided for in paragraph 8 above, their respective share in the amount of 395,553 dollars gross (436,290 dollars net) remaining from the assessment for the period from 14 April to 30 June 1995, which represents the balance remaining between the commitment authority approved in resolution 49/232 A and the appropriation provided for in paragraph 7 above;

11. *Invites* voluntary contributions to the Observer Mission in cash and in the form of services and supplies acceptable to the Secretary-General, to be administered, as appropriate, in accordance with the procedure established by the General Assembly in its resolutions 43/230 of 21 December 1988, 44/192 A of 21 December 1989 and 45/258 of 3 May 1991.

General Assembly resolution 49/232 B

12 July 1995      Meeting 105      Adopted without vote

Approved by Fifth Committee (A/49/812/Add.1) without vote, 23 June (meeting 58); draft by Chairman (A/C.5/49/L.57), based on informal consultations and orally corrected; agenda item 129.
*Meeting numbers.* GA 49th session: 5th Committee 56, 58; plenary 105.

## Report of the Secretary-General (October).

On 18 October, the Secretary-General presented to the General Assembly a performance report on UNOMIL financing for the period from 23 October 1994 to 13 January 1995.[20]

In November, following the Security Council's decision, in **resolution 1020(1995)** to adjust the mandate and concept of operations of UNOMIL, including an increase in the number of military observers to 160, he submitted revised cost estimates[21] for a six-month period from 1 July to 31

December 1995, totalling $22,233,600 gross ($21,653,900 net), and $17,481,600 gross ($16,489,200 net) for the six-month period from 1 January to 30 June 1996.

ACABQ, in an oral report to the Fifth (Administrative and Budgetary) Committee in December, said that the initial plan for the period from 1 July to 31 December 1995 could not be fully implemented owing to delays in deployment of personnel and in military demobilization. Revised estimates amounted to $8,100,093 gross ($7,730,800 net). As the Assembly in July had appropriated $8.5 million for UNOMIL, no additional appropriation would be needed.

However, revised estimates for the second six-month period beginning 1 January 1996 represented an increase of $2.3 million over the amount requested in November, and included recurrent costs related to demobilization and information activities. ACABQ thus recommended that $21,943,200 gross ($21,447,000 net) be approved to maintain UNOMIL through 31 March 1996.

**GENERAL ASSEMBLY ACTION**

On 23 December, the General Assembly adopted **resolution 50/210**.

### Financing of the United Nations Observer Mission in Liberia

*The General Assembly,*

*Having considered* the reports of the Secretary-General on the financing of the United Nations Observer Mission in Liberia and the related oral report of the Chairman of the Advisory Committee on Administrative and Budgetary Questions,

*Recalling* Security Council resolution 866(1993) of 22 September 1993, by which the Council established the United Nations Observer Mission in Liberia, and subsequent resolutions by which the Council extended the mandate of the Observer Mission, the latest of which was resolution 1014(1995) of 15 September 1995, and resolution 1020(1995) of 10 November 1995, by which the Council adjusted the mandate of the Observer Mission,

*Recalling also* its decision 48/478 of 23 December 1993 on the financing of the Observer Mission and its subsequent resolutions thereon, the latest of which was resolution 49/232 B of 12 July 1995,

*Reaffirming* that the costs of the Observer Mission are expenses of the Organization to be borne by Member States in accordance with Article 17, paragraph 2, of the Charter of the United Nations,

*Recalling further* its previous decision regarding the fact that, in order to meet the expenditures caused by the Observer Mission, a different procedure is required from that applied to meet expenditures of the regular budget of the United Nations,

*Taking into account* the fact that the economically more developed countries are in a position to make relatively larger contributions and that the economically less developed countries have a relatively limited capacity to contribute towards such an operation,

*Bearing in mind* the special responsibilities of the States permanent members of the Security Council, as indicated in General Assembly resolution 1874(S-IV) of 27 June 1963, in the financing of such operations,

*Mindful* of the fact that it is essential to provide the Observer Mission with the necessary financial resources to enable it to fulfil its responsibilities under the relevant resolutions of the Security Council,

1. *Takes note* of the status of contributions to the United Nations Observer Mission in Liberia as at 19 December 1995, including the contributions outstanding in the amount of 8,684,042 United States dollars, representing 15 per cent of the total assessed contributions from the inception of the Observer Mission to the period ending 31 December 1995, notes that some 22 per cent of the Member States have paid their assessed contributions in full, and urges all other Member States concerned, particularly those in arrears, to ensure the payment of their outstanding assessed contributions;

2. *Expresses concern* about the financial situation with regard to peace-keeping activities, particularly as regards the reimbursement of troop contributors, notably those troop-contributing Member States that have paid their assessed contributions, which bear an additional burden owing to overdue payments by Member States of their assessments;

3. *Urges* all Member States to make every possible effort to ensure payment of their assessed contributions to the Observer Mission promptly and in full;

4. *Endorses*, on an exceptional basis in the absence of a written report, the oral observations and recommendations presented by the Chairman of the Advisory Committee on Administrative and Budgetary Questions;

5. *Notes with concern* the exchange of posts between the Observer Mission and the United Nations Protection Force, which is not properly reflected in the report of the Secretary-General;

6. *Requests* the Secretary-General to take all necessary action to ensure that all United Nations activities related to the Liberian peace process are administered in a coordinated fashion with a maximum of efficiency and economy;

7. *Approves*, on an exceptional basis, the special arrangements for the Observer Mission with regard to the application of article IV of the Financial Regulations of the United Nations, whereby appropriations required in respect of obligations owed to Governments providing contingents and/or logistic support for the Observer Mission shall be retained beyond the period stipulated under financial regulations 4.3 and 4.4, as set out in the annex to the present resolution;

8. *Decides* to appropriate to the Special Account for the United Nations Observer Mission in Liberia the amount of 9,773,600 dollars gross (9,608,200 dollars net), for the maintenance of the Observer Mission for the period from 1 January to 31 January 1996;

9. *Decides also*, as an ad hoc arrangement, to apportion among Member States the amount of 9,773,600 dollars gross (9,608,200 dollars net) in accordance with the composition of groups set out in paragraphs 3 and 4 of General Assembly resolution 43/232 of 1 March 1989, as adjusted by the Assembly in its resolutions 44/192 B of 21 December 1989, 45/269 of 27 August 1991, 46/198 A of 20 December 1991 and 47/218 A of 23 December 1992 and its decisions 48/472 A of 23 December 1993 and 50/451 B of 23 December 1995, and tak-

ing into account the scale of assessments for the years 1995 and 1996;

10. *Decides further* that, in accordance with the provisions of its resolution 973(X) of 15 December 1955, there shall be set off against the apportionment among Member States, as provided for in paragraph 9 above, their respective share in the Tax Equalization Fund of the estimated staff assessment income of 165,400 dollars approved for the Observer Mission for the period from 1 January to 31 January 1996;

11. *Decides* that, for Member States that have fulfilled their financial obligations to the Observer Mission, there shall be set off against the apportionment, as provided for in paragraph 9 above, their respective share in the unencumbered balance of 226,890 dollars gross (224,900 dollars net) for the period from 23 October 1994 to 30 June 1995;

12. *Decides also* that, for Member States that have not fulfilled their financial obligations to the Observer Mission, their share of the unencumbered balance of 226,890 dollars gross (224,900 dollars net) for the period from 23 October 1994 to 30 June 1995 shall be set off against their outstanding obligations;

13. *Authorizes* the Secretary-General to enter into commitments in the amount of 12,169,600 dollars gross (11,838,800 dollars net) for the maintenance of the Observer Mission for the period from 1 February to 31 March 1996, subject to the extension of the mandate of the Observer Mission by the Security Council, this amount to be apportioned among Member States in accordance with the scheme set out in the present resolution;

14. *Invites* voluntary contributions to the Observer Mission in cash and in the form of services and supplies acceptable to the Secretary-General, to be administered, as appropriate, in accordance with the procedure established by the General Assembly in its resolutions 43/230 of 21 December 1988, 44/192 A of 21 December 1989 and 45/258 of 3 May 1991;

15. *Decides* to keep the agenda item entitled ''Financing of the United Nations Observer Mission in Liberia'' under review during the fiftieth session.

## ANNEX
### Special arrangements with regard to the application of article IV of the Financial Regulations of the United Nations

1. At the end of the twelve-month period provided for in financial regulation 4.3, any unliquidated obligations of the financial period in question relating to goods supplied and services rendered by Governments for which claims have been received or which are covered by established reimbursement rates shall be transferred to accounts payable; such accounts payable shall remain recorded in the Special Account for the United Nations Observer Mission in Liberia until payment is effected.

2. *(a)* Any other unliquidated obligations of the financial period in question owed to Governments for goods supplied and services rendered, as well as other obligations owed to Governments, for which required claims have not yet been received, shall remain valid for an additional period of four years following the end of the twelve-month period provided for in financial regulation 4.3;

*(b)* Claims received during this four-year period shall be treated as provided for under paragraph 1 of the present annex, if appropriate;

(c)   At the end of the additional four-year period, any unliquidated obligations shall be cancelled and the then remaining balance of any appropriations retained therefor shall be surrendered.

**General Assembly resolution 50/210**

23 December 1995      Meeting 100      Adopted without vote

Approved by Fifth Committee (A/50/846) without vote, 21 December (meeting 44); draft by Chairman (A/C.5/50/L.24), based on informal consultations; agenda item 134.
*Meeting numbers.* GA 50th session: 5th Committee 42, 44; plenary 100.

On the same date, the Assembly, by **decision 50/469**, decided that the Fifth Committee should continue consideration of the agenda item on the financing of UNOMIL at the resumed fiftieth session.

## End-of-year developments

### Humanitarian appeal

At the 27 October Conference on Assistance to Liberia, co-chaired by the Secretary-General with the Chairman of ECOWAS and the Chairman of the Liberian Council of State, a total of $145.7 million was pledged for humanitarian assistance, demobilization and for ECOMOG. To sustain the momentum of the peace process, the Secretary-General visited Ghana from 26 to 29 November for consultations with the Chairman of ECOWAS, then proceeded to Monrovia on 29 November where he met with members of the Council of State. He told them of the need to demonstrate their full commitment to the peace process by ensuring respect for the cease-fire and timely implementation of the Abuja Agreement, especially the disarmament and demobilization provisions. He stressed that such action would encourage the international community to disburse funds pledged at the Conference. The members of the Council of State assured him of their commitment to the peace process and that, while some skirmishes were unavoidable, they would not allow the peace process to be derailed and were determined to hold presidential and national elections on schedule in August 1996. They regretted the lack of support for ECOMOG from the international community which, they felt, could delay and even jeopardize the peace process.

### UNOMIL situation

**Report of the Secretary-General (December).** The Liberian peace process remained generally on course, observed the Secretary-General in an 18 December report to the Security Council on UNOMIL.[22] LNTG continued to fill appointments in the various governmental bodies. To date, 12 of the 13 members of the Transitional Legislative Assembly had been inducted. However, implementation of the military aspects of the Abuja Agreement had fallen behind schedule. Little pro-

gress was made in the disengagement of forces, which was to have been completed by 26 September. Although the cease-fire generally held, violations and recurrent skirmishes were reported. In November, some Liberian faction fighters harassed ECOMOG soldiers, and reports were received of harassment of civilians. The factions continued to maintain that they would disengage and dismantle their checkpoints only when ECOMOG deployed to their areas of control. The deployment of ECOMOG and UNOMIL had been set for completion by 14 December, in accordance with the implementation schedule of the Abuja Agreement. Owing to a lack of logistic resources, however, ECOMOG troops could not be deployed on schedule, the Secretary-General stated.

ECOWAS and the Secretary-General's Special Representative had encouraged LNTG and faction leaders to contain the skirmishes that emerged during the first two months after the August cease-fire. In that connection, the Council of State designated George Boley, leader of LPC, to mediate between the contending forces. On 30 November, Charles Taylor (NPFL) and Alhaji Kromah (ULIMO-K wing) signed a Memorandum of Understanding agreeing to cease all hostilities, to create a buffer zone between their forces in Lofa County, to guarantee the free movement of civilians and commercial activity in the areas under their control, and to cooperate fully with relief organizations. They called on ECOMOG to deploy immediately to the buffer zone. That agreement prompted other factions to withdraw their allegations of cease-fire violations and to reaffirm their commitment to resolve their differences peacefully. It also prompted the faction leaders to open major roads to inaccessible areas of the country, including those linking Monrovia to Lofa, Nimba and Grand Gedeh counties through Bong County. Some forces worked together to facilitate the delivery of humanitarian assistance to the newly accessible areas.

Since the 30 November Memorandum of Understanding, hostilities between the factions were reported to have ended. On 14 December, with the provision of initial assistance, ECOMOG began to deploy to critical areas, including assembly sites and brigade headquarters, to facilitate disarmament and demobilization. UNOMIL and ECOMOG finalized a draft plan for disengagement and demobilization, which was forwarded to the Council of State. While the final requirements for rehabilitation of facilities at the assembly sites were near completion, actual work had not begun.

A number of NGOs had been forced to suspend their activities in early October for security reasons although some 1.5 million persons still needed emergency relief. With an improved security situation toward the end of the year, humanitarian organizations planned to expand operations to previously inaccessible areas, especially in the northern and eastern sections of the country which had been cut off from aid for up to three years. The return from neighbouring countries of the more than 750,000 Liberian refugees remained slow. An influx of refugees continued from Sierra Leone into Grand Cape Mount and Lofa counties, with 3,000 refugees registered since early September. The humanitarian assistance community was planning a coordination framework in anticipation of an eventual large-scale return of refugees, internally displaced persons and demobilized combatants.

In a later report,[23] the Secretary-General indicated that after 14 December, when ECOMOG began deploying its troops to several regions of Liberia, the Chairman and Vice-Chairman of the Council of State travelled extensively throughout the country to explain the peace process and prepare combatants for disarmament and demobilization. The faction leaders issued directives to their combatants to cooperate with ECOMOG and UNOMIL in the implementation of the Abuja Agreement.

However, the peace process suffered a setback when the ULIMO-J wing attacked and overran ECOMOG positions in Tubmanburg and elsewhere on 28 December. Some LDF fighters were also reportedly involved in the attacks against ECOMOG. All UNOMIL personnel deployed to Tubmanburg were evacuated by 30 December. ECOMOG reported that it suffered 94 casualties (16 dead, 78 wounded), with an additional 10 soldiers missing in action. ECOMOG arms, ammunition and equipment were also seized. Some skirmishes between factions were also reported prior to the Tubmanburg incident. ECOMOG forces were attacked on 24 and 25 December, and on 27 December a humanitarian convoy was seized. The Cease-fire Violations Committee dispatched a team to investigate the Tubmanburg incident.

The fighting in Tubmanburg had serious human rights implications, the Secretary-General said, as estimated civilian casualties were significant. UNOMIL confirmed that on 30 December civilians had been forced out of a government hospital, where they had taken refuge, and used as human shields. Other civilians had been prevented from fleeing the town.

Although the peace process had seen some increase in economic activity, full recovery of an economy devastated by war remained one of the principal challenges facing Liberia, the Secretary-General had noted in his December report.[22] A joint UN Development Programme/World Bank mission visited Liberia at the end of the year to prepare for a Special Consultation Meeting on Liberia in March 1996, and other UN humanita-

rian agencies and programmes were also working to link their emergency relief activities to rehabilitation.

*REFERENCES*

[1]S/1995/7. [2]YUN 1994, p. 380. [3]S/1995/9. [4]YUN 1992, p. 192, SC res. 788 (1992), 19 Nov. 1992. [5]YUN 1993, p. 268. [6]S/1995/158. [7]YUN 1993, p. 269. [8]S/1995/279. [9]S/1996/72. [10]S/1995/473. [11]S/1995/701. [12]S/1995/742. [13]S/1995/756. [14]S/1995/781. [15]S/1995/881 & Add.1. [16]S/1995/960. [17]S/1995/959. [18]A/49/571/Add.2. [19]A/49/786/Add.1. [20]A/50/650 & Add.1. [21]A/50/650/Add.1. [22]S/1995/1042. [23]S/1996/47 & Add.1.

# Mozambique

The United Nations Operation in Mozambique (ONUMOZ) formally ended on 31 January 1995, signalling the successful implementation of the 1992 Rome General Peace Agreement[1] between Mozambique and the Resistência Nacional Moçambicana (RENAMO). The Agreement dealt with monitoring the cease-fire, reintegration into society of demobilized military personnel and other military questions, formation of political parties, elections and guarantees, among other things. On 16 December 1992, the Security Council had established ONUMOZ[2] to implement the Rome Peace Agreement.

After more than three decades wracked by the turbulance of an ongoing bloody civil war—which killed, maimed and made refugees of millions—Mozambique, with UN assistance over a three-year period, saw the institution of a cease-fire, withdrawal of foreign forces, the demobilization of warring factions, elections, installation of President Joaquim Alberto Chissano, a new National Assembly and the launching with international support of a rehabilitation process for its shattered infrastructure.

**Security Council consideration.** On 27 January, the Security Council met to consider the situation in Mozambique.

In his address to the Council, the Minister for Foreign Affairs and Cooperation of Mozambique commended the Council and its members for their valuable contribution since the signing of the 1992 General Peace Agreement. He also commended the Secretary-General for his role in the consolidation of peace and security. Mozambique, he said, was now in an era in which political pluralism, national reconciliation and peaceful coexistence between Mozambicans would have to be ensured to enable lasting peace to be attained. A presidential forum, composed of distinguished political figures, would be created to enhance the national reconciliation process and consolidate democracy. The Government was preparing the national budget, whose approval by the National Assembly was scheduled to take place in March. To that end, President Chissano launched an appeal to the donor community for its continued involvement in the process of national reconstruction, stating that the Government's Economic and Social Rehabilitation Programme could register better results if it were supported by the international community. He hoped that the consultative group meeting scheduled for March 1995 in Paris would respond positively to the country's needs.

The Government attached great importance to promoting the involvement of national and foreign private sectors and had carried out a thorough review of the legislation on foreign investment in order to provide substantial incentives. Assistance was required for the reintegration of demobilized soldiers, returnees and displaced persons, as well as for eradicating poverty. Those initiatives should be complemented by actions aimed at promoting rural development and restoring primary health-care services in urban and rural areas. To consolidate the normalization of life in rural areas, the issue of land-mines had to be addressed.

The Government further attached great importance to strengthening national institutions responsible for the maintenance of peace and public order, such as the future Mozambican Defence Force, the national police and the judicial system.

Mozambique said it greatly appreciated the assurances of the UN Secretary-General that, despite the withdrawal of ONUMOZ, the United Nations would continue to assist the Government in strengthening the national reconstruction process and its new democratic institutions, as well as in its economic and social integration.

## Liquidation of ONUMOZ

As stated in the final report on ONUMOZ,[3] the Secretary-General, in a 31 January 1995 report,[4] confirmed that following the closure of the operation a small number of UN civilian logisticians would remain in Mozambique for one or two months to deal with outstanding issues, including disposition of property and equipment.

Based on inventory records as at 13 October 1994, assets were estimated to have a value of $31.5 million. The greater portion ($27.3 million) was to be transferred to other peace-keeping missions or shipped to the UN Logistics Base in Brindisi, Italy, for storage and future use; the remainder ($4.2 million) was to be sold to commercial entities, donated to the Government or transferred to the demining programme, or transferred to UNDP projects.

Final ONUMOZ costs for the period from 16 November 1994 to 31 January 1995 were estimated at $47.8 million.

GENERAL ASSEMBLY ACTION

On 10 March, the General Assembly, following consideration of the Secretary-General's report and the comments of ACABQ,[5] adopted **resolution 49/235**.

### Financing of the United Nations Operation in Mozambique

_The General Assembly,_

_Having considered_ the report of the Secretary-General on the financing of the United Nations Operation in Mozambique and the related report of the Advisory Committee on Administrative and Budgetary Questions,

_Recalling_ Security Council resolution 797(1992) of 16 December 1992, by which the Council established the United Nations Operation in Mozambique, and the subsequent resolutions by which the Council extended the mandate of the Operation, the latest of which were resolutions 957(1994) of 15 November 1994 and 960(1994) of 21 November 1994,

_Recalling also_ its resolutions 47/224 A and B of 16 March 1993 on the financing of the Operation and its subsequent resolutions and decisions thereon, the latest of which were resolution 48/240 B of 29 July 1994 and decision 49/467 of 23 December 1994,

_Reaffirming_ that the costs of the Operation are expenses of the Organization to be borne by Member States in accordance with Article 17, paragraph 2, of the Charter of the United Nations,

_Recalling_ its previous decisions regarding the fact that, in order to meet the expenditures caused by the Operation, a different procedure is required from the one applied to meet expenditures of the regular budget of the United Nations,

_Taking into account_ the fact that the economically more developed countries are in a position to make relatively larger contributions and that the economically less developed countries have a relatively limited capacity to contribute towards such an operation,

_Bearing in mind_ the special responsibilities of the States permanent members of the Security Council, as indicated in General Assembly resolution 1874(S-IV) of 27 June 1963, in the financing of such operations,

_Mindful_ of the fact that it is essential to provide the Operation with the necessary financial resources to enable it to fulfil its responsibilities under the relevant resolutions of the Security Council,

1. _Takes note_ of the status of contributions to the United Nations Operation in Mozambique as at 28 February 1995, including the contributions outstanding in the amount of 62,831,938 United States dollars, and urges all Member States concerned to make every possible effort to ensure the payment of their outstanding assessed contributions;

2. _Expresses concern_ about the financial situation with regard to peace-keeping activities, particularly in regard to the reimbursement of troop- and equipment-contributing countries, due to overdue payments by Member States of their assessments, particularly Member States in arrears;

3. _Urges_ all Member States to make every possible effort to ensure payment of their assessed contributions to the Operation promptly and in full;

4. _Expresses deep concern_ at the late submission of documentation, in particular the financial perform-

ance report for the period from 1 May to 15 November 1994;

5. *Expresses concern* at delays in the processing and settlement of claims for the reimbursement of the cost of the contingent-owned equipment provided by troop-contributing countries;

6. *Endorses* the observations and recommendations contained in the report of the Advisory Committee on Administrative and Budgetary Questions;

7. *Expresses deep concern* that the failure of Member States to pay their assessed contributions promptly and in full threatens to leave the Special Account for the United Nations Operation in Mozambique with insufficient liquid funds to meet its liabilities, in particular, to the troop-contributing countries;

8. *Requests* the Secretary-General to explore all possibilities in order to ensure prompt reimbursement to troop- and equipment-contributing countries;

9. *Decides* to appropriate to the Special Account for the United Nations Operation in Mozambique a total amount of 40 million dollars gross (39,053,300 dollars net) for the liquidation of the Operation for the period from 16 November 1994 to 31 March 1995, inclusive of the commitment authority of 25 million dollars authorized under the provisions of General Assembly resolution 48/240 B, with the prior concurrence of the Advisory Committee;

10. *Decides also,* as an ad hoc arrangement, to apportion the amount of 40 million dollars gross (39,053,300 dollars net) for the period from 16 November 1994 to 31 March 1995 among Member States in accordance with the composition of groups set out in paragraphs 3 and 4 of General Assembly resolution 43/232 of 1 March 1989, as adjusted by the Assembly in its resolutions 44/192 B of 21 December 1989, 45/269 of 27 August 1991, 46/198 A of 20 December 1991 and 47/218 A of 23 December 1992 and its decision 48/472 A of 23 December 1993, the scale of assessments for the year 1994 to be applied against a portion thereof, that is, 13,529,400 dollars gross (13,209,200 dollars net), which is the amount pertaining on a *pro rata* basis to the period ending 31 December 1994, and the scale of assessments for the year 1995 to be applied against the balance, that is, 26,470,600 dollars gross (25,844,100 dollars net), for the period from 1 January to 31 March 1995;

11. *Decides further* that, in accordance with the provisions of its resolution 973(X) of 15 December 1955, there shall be set off against the apportionment among Member States, as provided for in paragraph 10 above, their respective share in the Tax Equalization Fund of the estimated staff assessment income of 946,700 dollars approved for the period from 16 November 1994 to 31 March 1995, 320,200 dollars being the amount pertaining on a *pro rata* basis to the period ending 31 December 1994, and the balance, that is, 626,500 dollars, for the period from 1 January to 31 March 1995;

12. *Decides* that there shall be set off against the apportionment among Member States, as provided for in paragraph 10 above, their respective share in the unencumbered balance of 4,458,900 dollars gross (4,258,900 dollars net) in respect of the Operation for the period from 1 November 1993 to 30 April 1994;

13. *Decides also* that the disposition of the assets of the Operation shall proceed on the basis of the following principles and policies, listed in order of priority, and

requests the Secretary-General to proceed with the disposition accordingly:

(*a*) All equipment that meets the requirements of other United Nations operations and that it is cost-effective to move shall be redeployed to such operations or held in reserve for use by future operations;

(*b*) Other equipment shall be transferred to United Nations organizations, as well as to national and international non-governmental organizations already operating in Mozambique or in the process of establishing a presence there, upon request and against appropriate credit to the Special Account for the United Nations Operation in Mozambique;

(*c*) Any remaining material that cannot be moved shall be sold commercially on an ''as is, where is'' basis in accordance with standard United Nations procedures;

(*d*) Assets or installations that cannot be dismantled, including airfield installations, shall be donated to the Government of Mozambique;

14. *Decides further* to accept the proposal of the Secretary-General to donate certain assets to the mine-clearance programme on the understanding that it is not cost-effective to move them and that they cannot be financed through the voluntary contributions;

15. *Takes note* of the comments of the Advisory Committee in paragraph 26 of its report, and of the fact that the feasibility of procedures for valuation and transfer of costs for the assets of the Operation will be reconsidered during the discussion of the report of the Secretary-General requested by the General Assembly in its resolution 49/233 of 23 December 1994, to be submitted no later than 31 March 1995, and affirms that any decision on the methodology of the transfer of such costs of the Operation will be taken accordingly;

16. *Requests* the Secretary-General to submit to the General Assembly by 31 July 1995, in the context of the performance report related to the liquidation of the Operation, a further report on the disposal of the assets and liabilities of the Operation;

17. *Invites* voluntary contributions to the Operation in cash and in the form of services and supplies acceptable to the Secretary-General, to be administered, as appropriate, in accordance with the procedure established by the General Assembly in its resolutions 43/230 of 21 December 1988, 44/192 A of 21 December 1989 and 45/258 of 3 May 1991;

18. *Requests* the Secretary-General to take all necessary action to ensure that all United Nations activities related to the Operation are administered under the authority of his Special Representative in a coordinated fashion with a maximum of efficiency and economy and in accordance with the relevant mandate, and to include information on the arrangements made in this regard in his report on the financing of the Operation;

19. *Decides* to include in the provisional agenda of its fiftieth session an item entitled ''Financing of the liquidation of the United Nations Operation in Mozambique''.

General Assembly resolution 49/235

10 March 1995    Meeting 98    Adopted without vote

Approved by Fifth Committee (A/49/817/Add.1) without vote, 3 March (meeting 41); draft by Chairman (A/C.5/49/L.34), based on informal consultations; agenda item 124.

*Meeting numbers.* GA 49th session: 5th Committee 39, 41; plenary 98.

In July, the Secretary-General presented a financial performance report[6] of ONUMOZ for the period from 1 May to 15 November 1994 and a final report on the disposition of its assets, the value of which, as at 30 April 1995, amounted to approximately $36.9 million.

The Assembly, by **decision 50/469** of 23 December, decided that the Fifth Committee should continue consideration of the agenda item on the financing of the liquidation of ONUMOZ at the resumed fiftieth session.

*REFERENCES*

[1]YUN 1992, p. 193. [2]Ibid., p. 197, SC res. 797(1992), 16 Dec. 1992. [3]YUN 1994, p. 364. [4]A/49/649/Add.2. [5]A/49/849. [6]A/49/649/Add.3.

# Rwanda

In 1995, United Nations involvement in Rwanda continued, with the aim of achieving reconciliation, rehabilitation and reconstruction for that country, still in the throes of the devastation inflicted on it in 1994 by the consequences of bloody ethnic strife, genocidal massacres and wide-ranging refugee flows.

Civil unrest continued during the year, mainly concentrated in camps for some 2 million refugees and internally displaced persons, located in Rwanda and in the neighbouring States of Burundi, the United Republic of Tanzania and Zaire.

A Security Council mission was dispatched to Rwanda and Burundi in February to help assess the situation and chart the role of the United Nations in the area.

In 1995, progress in identifying perpetrators of the massacres was made by the International Criminal Tribunal for the Prosecution of Persons Responsible for Genocide and Other Serious Violations of International Humanitarian Law Committed in the Territory of Rwanda and Rwandan Citizens Responsible for Genocide and Other Such Violations Committed in the Territory of Neighbouring States between 1 January and 31 December 1994 (see PART FIVE, Chapter II).

The mandate of the UN Assistance Mission for Rwanda (UNAMIR)—more than 5,000 strong at the beginning of 1995—was extended and adjusted in the light of the continuing crisis. Its authorized troop level was reduced to 1,200 by the end of the year, as the Government of Rwanda expressed reservations about the scope and nature of its mission.

The arms embargo imposed in 1994 by the Security Council was terminated as of 1 September. An International Commission of Inquiry was created by the Council to investigate reports of arms supplies to Rwandan government forces.

Through the Human Rights Field Operation in Rwanda—the first such undertaking to be run by the UN High Commissioner for Human Rights—monitors were deployed throughout the country to help protect returning refugees, quell further violence and promote education programmes to prevent future incidents.

In 1995, Special Representative Shaharyar M. Khan continued his efforts to obtain a peaceful solution to the crisis. The Secretary-General also dispatched two Special Envoys during the year—Aldo Ajello, to deal with possible deployment of UN observers in neighbouring States, and José Luis Jesús, who undertook consultations on a regional conference on security, stability and development in the Great Lakes region.

## Security Council mission

In a 6 February note by its President,[1] the Security Council stated that it would send a seven-member mission to Rwanda and Burundi. Its members—from China, the Czech Republic, Germany, Honduras, Indonesia, Nigeria and the United States—visited Rwanda on 12 and 13 February (see above for information on Burundi). Its mandate in Rwanda included: holding consultations with the Government regarding national reconciliation and reconstruction and the problem of returning refugees; and consulting with the Secretary-General's Special Representative, UNAMIR, the diplomatic corps and representatives from UN agencies and NGOs.

On 28 February, the mission reported[2] to the Security Council President, stating that it had been encouraged by the progress towards returning to normalcy in Rwanda; yet the country's problems were far from over. The critical challenges of social and political accommodation, on which genuine stability and long-term healing depended, were still to be addressed. Rwandese society had to be enabled to rebuild and to continue to function. The primary responsibility in that regard rested with the Rwandese themselves, who had to determine how to come to terms with each other. As long as 2 million Rwandese remained in camps inside and outside their country, the situation in Rwanda would remain unstable, the mission predicted. It considered their return home as a matter of highest priority. Ensuring security in the camps, it agreed, was vital for the success of efforts to accelerate repatriation. The return and resettlement of internally displaced persons and refugees—a prerequisite for long-term stability and progress—was a task being undertaken through "Opération Retour", a programme coordinated by UNAMIR and UN agencies and supported by NGOs. However, fear remained the single most important factor impeding that process.

Progress towards reconciliation had so far been marginal. A number of immediate steps and measures were called for, such as active repatriation, the creation of a political and psychological climate conducive to reconciliation, and the restoration of an effective and functioning judiciary. Many accused or suspected of carrying out atrocities had so far shown no remorse or contrition, a situation seen as discouraging efforts towards reconciliation. The Government emphasized that it remained committed to the spirit of an inclusive, broad-based Government, as provided for under the 1993 Arusha Peace Agreement.[3] The Government had commenced a dialogue with representatives of Rwandese refugee communities in Burundi, but that was not feasible with respect to the refugee community in Zaire in view of the insecurity and intimidation by armed elements in their midst.

The mission stated that as the emergency phase was now over, emphasis was increasingly being placed on long-term measures to rebuild the country. The importance of setting up an effective mine-clearance programme was emphasized, in order to support resettlement efforts and to revive agriculture and other reconstruction activities.

Reinvigorating the political process, including the creation of a framework for dialogue between the Government, refugee representatives and the United Nations, was considered especially important. The mission also recommended launching civic education programmes, especially in refugee camps; an effective mechanism to protect property rights; a transparent and effective judiciary; a nationwide, trained police force; an effective civil administration throughout the country; and unimpeded access throughout the country to UNAMIR, humanitarian personnel and human rights monitors. The mission recommended that the International Tribunal, established in 1994,[4] become operational soon. A list of persons sought for questioning in connection with the violations of international humanitarian law concerning recent events in Rwanda would be established and made public (see PART FIVE, Chapter II).

### Refugee camp security and repatriation efforts

#### General situation

**Report of the Secretary-General (January).** In January, the Secretary-General reported[5] that while there had been some positive developments in creating conditions conducive to repatriation, the continuing presence of nearly 2 million Rwandese refugees in Burundi, the United Republic of Tanzania and Zaire remained a matter of serious concern.

The general security situation in the camps remained dangerous for both refugees and relief workers, and was potentially destabilizing for both the host countries and the subregion. Rwanda and UNHCR had signed tripartite agreements with Burundi and Zaire, respectively, on voluntary repatriation of refugees, defining conditions for repatriation, including returnee protection and land tenure. Rwanda and the United Republic of Tanzania were also involved in an ongoing dialogue on issues affecting refugees in the latter country and their repatriation to Rwanda.

The Secretary-General reported that only 200,000 refugees out of those who had left Rwanda after the events of 6 April 1994[6] had returned to their country. A joint technical team from the UN Department of Peace-keeping Operations and UNHCR had been dispatched to Rwanda, the United Republic of Tanzania and Zaire to review the situation in the camps, and had recommended measures to establish secure conditions in them. UNHCR's efforts to address security concerns in the camps were centred on improved monitoring of prevailing conditions, through an effective field presence and vigorous *démarches* with civilian and military authorities.

The camps in Zaire, where some 1.4 million Rwandese refugees were living, continued to be the most potentially explosive, with the most acute security situation in camps north of Lake Kivu in the Goma region, where some 850,000 refugees were located. The refugee population in Zaire tended to include more political, military and militia elements of the former Government than camps in Tanzania and Burundi. Their hostility towards the Government in Kigali was reflected in actions that had led to insecure conditions in the camps, including significant threats of civil disturbances, common crime and threats to the safety of international relief workers. There were reports of hoarding and/or sale of humanitarian assistance by some camp leaders. Zaire had taken steps in recent months to enhance the security situation in the camps, which had improved somewhat, but the potential for serious disturbances remained high.

In the United Republic of Tanzania, there were approximately 600,000 Rwandese refugees living in eight camps; the continuing influx consisted mostly of Rwandese refugees from Burundi and Burundi nationals. The camps in Tanzania were relatively more secure and better organized than those in Zaire and the refugees had created governing structures similar to those that existed in Rwanda, beginning at the prefecture level and extending down to the commune level. The structure provided a sense of organization and a security mechanism, and facilitated the delivery of relief assistance. Extremist elements, however, had considerable influence over the refugee population, though to a lesser degree than in Zaire.

The Secretary-General said that a technical mission had confirmed the feasibility of his 1994 proposal[7] for a possible peace-keeping operation to enhance camp security. But because the operation would require substantially more than the originally estimated 3,000 to 5,000 troops, and because only one of about 60 potential troop-contributing countries had, as of 23 January 1995, formally offered a unit, it was clear that that option was not feasible.

Two other alternatives were examined: the deployment of Zairian security forces, with the support of UN civilian police and military observers, to patrol, escort and guard storage and transport of humanitarian assistance and provide security for repatriation; or provision of training and monitoring support to local security forces, through contractual arrangements, for deployment to camps both north and south of Lake Kivu. Neither option appeared feasible. After consultations with the UN High Commissioner for Refugees, it was decided that UNHCR would follow up with Zaire to conclude appropriate arrangements to enhance security in the camps. UNHCR would also continue to explore means of augmenting support to Tanzania to enable it to increase the level of security in its camps. UNAMIR would continue to coordinate closely with UNHCR in facilitating the safe and voluntary repatriation of the refugees to Rwanda.

The Secretary-General said that the summit meeting of the leaders of the subregion, held in Nairobi, Kenya, on 7 January, had usefully contributed towards defining a framework for action to address security in the camps and the repatriation of refugees to Rwanda and should also facilitate the work of the OAU/UNHCR Regional Conference on Assistance to Refugees, Returnees and Displaced Persons in the Great Lakes Region (Bujumbura, Burundi, February).

**Communication.** On 1 February, the Secretary-General informed[8] the Security Council President that on 27 January Zaire and UNHCR had signed an *aide-mémoire* outlining specific measures to improve the security situation in the refugee camps. Under that agreement, Zaire would deploy 1,500 experienced military and police security personnel to the camps in the Goma, Bukavu and Uvira regions. They would assist in the maintenance of law and order; prevent violence against and intimidation of refugees; provide protection for relief workers and for the storage and delivery of humanitarian assistance; and escort to the border of Rwanda those refugees who had voluntarily chosen to return to their homes. UNAMIR would assist in escorting the repatriated refugees to their home communities and would coordinate closely with UNHCR to facilitate the repatriation process. The Secretary-General's Special Representative would continue to have overall responsibility for all matters relating to UN efforts to assist in the restoration of peace and stability.

### SECURITY COUNCIL ACTION (February)

The Security Council met on 10 February to consider the report of the Secretary-General. Following consultations among Council members, the President made the following statement on their behalf:[9]

The Security Council has considered the second report of the Secretary-General dated 25 January 1995 on the security in the Rwandese refugee camps, particularly those located in Zaire, and his letter dated 1 February 1995 on this subject.

The Security Council agrees with the Secretary-General's assessment that the present situation in many of the refugee camps remains dangerous for both refugees and relief workers and that the situation is also potentially destabilizing for the subregion as a whole. It is gravely concerned at reports of continuing intimidation and security problems in the camps, particularly in Zaire, and reaffirms its condemnation of actions of former Rwandese leaders living in the camps, and of former government forces and militias, to prevent, in some cases by force, the repatriation of the refugees. It also remains concerned at the security threat to international relief workers. It welcomes the steps taken by some of the host countries concerned to improve the security situation in the camps. The Council remains concerned at the obstacles posed by the former civil and military authorities and militias to effective local administration by the host countries and the discharge by UNHCR of its mission.

The Security Council attaches great importance to the earliest possible action to address the security problems in the camps. In this context it welcomes the decision that UNHCR, under its refugee protection and humanitarian assistance mandate, conclude appropriate arrangements with the Government of Zaire to enhance security in the camps. It welcomes the agreement between UNHCR and the Government of Zaire of 27 January 1995 to deploy 1,500 Zairian security forces and a UNHCR liaison group. It also welcomes the agreement reached between the Governments of Zaire and Rwanda on the return of refugees and property and urges its full implementation. The Security Council urges Member States to provide UNHCR with the resources needed in the context of the agreement concluded between it and the Government of Zaire. It stresses the importance of close coordination of all operations with UNAMIR. The Council endorses the efforts of UNHCR, in cooperation with the United Republic of Tanzania, to put in place security arrangements in the Tanzanian camps, and encourages UNHCR also to address the situation in Burundi. The Council requests the Secretary-General to report to it on a regular basis on the implementation of operations carried out by UNHCR.

The Security Council stresses the importance of ensuring that accurate information about the situation inside Rwanda is disseminated to the camps. In this respect, it reaffirms the importance of UNAMIR Radio commencing its broadcasts as soon as possible.

The Security Council encourages efforts to provide security in the camps and notes that they have to be accompanied by further efforts in Rwanda to ensure that refugees can return to their homes without fear of retribution or persecution. In this regard it acknowledges the achievements of the Government of Rwanda, despite the difficulty of the task and the lack of resources. It encourages the Government of Rwanda to continue to provide a framework for the action to be taken to repatriate the refugees, to promote national reconciliation and to reinvigorate the political process and calls upon the international community to continue to support the Government of Rwanda in its task. The Council reaffirms its view that such a framework should also include an appropriate mechanism for sustaining a dialogue between the Government of Rwanda, the refugee community and the United Nations. It welcomes the conclusions of the summit meeting of leaders in the subregion, held in Nairobi on 7 January 1995. The Council encourages the International Tribunal for Rwanda established in resolution 955(1994) in its work, as well as efforts to rebuild the local Rwandese judicial system to facilitate the maintenance of law and order. The Council welcomes the commitments made at the recent Round-table Conference on Rwanda and in response to the consolidated inter-agency appeal that will assist the Government of Rwanda in its efforts to rebuild the country and to promote national reconciliation.

The Security Council looks forward to the Regional Conference on Assistance to Refugees, Returnees and Displaced Persons in the Great Lakes Region, to be hosted by the Organization of African Unity (OAU) and UNHCR in Bujumbura from 15 to 17 February 1995. The Council expresses the hope that this conference will lead to further progress in creating the conditions necessary for the refugees and displaced persons to return to their homes and that it will facilitate the identification of long-term solutions to promote and ensure peace, security and development in the subregion, those issues to be the subject-matter of a further and broader conference of a political nature.

The Security Council underlines that the presence of the refugee camps should only be temporary and that the return of the refugees to their homes in Rwanda remains the ultimate goal. It requests the Secretary-General to continue his exploration of all options and to make any further recommendations necessary for ensuring security in the camps as soon as possible and to submit a further report on this subject in the light of the outcome of the conference in Bujumbura.

The Security Council will remain seized of the matter and will keep it under close review.

*Meeting number.* SC 3500.

On 27 February, in **resolution 978(1995)**, the Council urged the arrest of individuals responsible for acts within the jurisdiction of the International Tribunal for Rwanda, and condemned all attacks against persons in the refugee camps near the borders with Rwanda. It demanded that such attacks immediately cease and called on States to take appropriate steps to prevent them. It also urged States, on whose territory such serious acts of violence took place, to arrest and detain and submit to the appropriate authorities for prosecution persons against whom there was sufficient evidence that they incited or participated in such acts.

**Report of the Secretary-General (April).** In a 14 April report[10] on security in the Rwandese refugee camps, the Secretary-General said that in early April there were 240,000 refugees in Burundi, mostly from southern Rwanda. The deteriorating security situation in Burundi had affected refugees inside and outside the camps, with a constant movement of refugees to and from neighbouring countries. The strict border control by the army and the presence of uncontrolled armed groups in border areas had resulted in acts of violence and loss of life in and outside the camps. In view of the general insecurity, several thousand Rwandese refugees left for the United Republic of Tanzania. Between 17 February and 10 March, 8,000 Rwandese arrived in Tanzania from Burundi. In late March, some 70,000 more Rwandese refugees left camps in northern Burundi for Tanzania. As at 26 March, 600,000 refugees were reported in camps in Tanzania.

By early April, there were 1.1 million refugees in camps in Zaire. The number of refugees departing from the Goma camps rose from 2,000 in January to 10,000 in February. Those figures declined substantially in March, however, partly due to reports of increased arrests and detentions inside Rwanda. Food shortages and reduced rations in the camps were perceived by the refugees as a deliberate measure to force repatriation. On 31 March, the food situation in Goma was described by the World Food Programme (WFP) as critical. The militia of the former Rwandese Government exploited the shortage to incite the refugee population and reinforce their campaign against repatriation.

The Secretary-General also reported on the OAU/UNHCR Regional Conference on Assistance to Refugees, Returnees and Displaced Persons in the Great Lakes Region (Bujumbura, 15-17 February). A plan of action was adopted, with a primary focus on voluntary repatriation as the preferred durable solution to the refugee problem. The roles to be played by countries of origin, countries of asylum and the international community were stressed, and the international community was urged to assist countries of asylum and countries of origin—among the least developed—to alleviate and redress the negative impact on local communities of the presence of refugees and displaced persons. UNDP was to convene a round-table meeting of donors for the countries in the region to coordinate actions to be undertaken.

**Communication.** Rwanda, in a 6 April statement,[11] cited the return of Rwandese refugees as one of its priorities. It would continue contacts with responsible officials in the countries of refuge in order to facilitate their return; request the host countries to segregate innocent persons from those responsible for genocide and massacres; promote awareness both within and beyond its frontiers concerning the need for the return of the refugees; and promote their return.

Rwanda said it had set up an inter-ministerial commission to settle lawsuits over properties abandoned by refugees and temporarily occupied by other persons. It had also identified sites for resettlement and areas for the settlement of former refugees; integrated members of the former government forces; and continued aid for displaced persons and refugees. A commission for the repatriation of the refugees, provided under the Arusha Peace Agreement,[3] had been set up, as had a unit to coordinate humanitarian assistance. Rwanda also intended to establish, with the support of the international community, centres for the reception and transit of refugees who returned to Rwanda, including a service to register persons repatriated and their property and to distribute humanitarian assistance. Rwanda urged neighbouring countries sheltering refugees, and the international community, to note the following: innocent persons in the camps should be segregated from criminals guilty of massacres and genocide; refugees who did not wish to return should be kept at a distance from the frontiers of Rwanda; there should be collaboration with the Rwandese tribunals and the International Criminal Tribunal in the arrest and transfer of those guilty of the massacres and genocide; and humanitarian, technical and financial assistance on behalf of Rwandese refugees should be continued.

### Events at Kibeho

A serious outbreak of violence occurred on 22 April at a camp for internally displaced persons in Kibeho in south-western Rwanda, resulting in a considerable number of deaths. Divergent accounts were given of what had happened, of the number of casualties and of the alleged responsibility of various parties.

On 27 April, Rwandan President Pasteur Bizimungu announced the establishment of an Independent International Commission of Inquiry, inviting Belgium, Canada, France, Germany, the Netherlands, the United Kingdom, the United States, the United Nations and OAU to participate, together with Rwanda, in the Commission's work.

At a meeting of the Security Council on 27 April, the President made the following statement on its behalf:[12]

The Security Council has considered the Secretary-General's progress report on the United Nations Assistance Mission for Rwanda (UNAMIR) and his third report on security in the Rwandese refugee camps, as well as the oral briefings from the Secretariat on the tragic events on 22 April 1995 at the Kibeho camp for internally displaced persons.

The Security Council condemns the killing of numerous civilians in the camp and is encouraged by the decision of the Government of Rwanda to carry out a full investigation of these events without delay and to bring to justice those responsible. In this regard it welcomes the decision of the Rwandese authorities to establish an independent inquiry with United Nations and other international participation to carry out this investigation of the events. The Council also requests the Secretary-General to report to it, without delay, on these events and on the role of UNAMIR.

The Security Council is concerned by the generally deteriorating security situation in Rwanda. It underlines that the Government of Rwanda bears primary responsibility for maintaining security throughout the country and for the safety of internally displaced persons and returnees, as well as for ensuring respect for their basic human rights. In this context it reaffirms the need for coordination between the Government of Rwanda and UNAMIR and other agencies on these matters. The Council does, however, note with satisfaction that the Government of Rwanda has in previous months made considerable efforts directed at national reconciliation, rehabilitation and reconstruction, which are of crucial importance. The Council calls on the Government of Rwanda to intensify these efforts and on the international community to continue to support those efforts, in order to bring about a climate of trust and confidence which would assist in the early and safe return of refugees. In this context, it underlines the importance it attaches to demining, including the United Nations proposal.

The Security Council notes with deep concern disturbing reports of increased incursions into Rwanda from neighbouring countries and allegations of arms shipments into the Goma airport and of elements of the former Rwandese government forces being trained in a neighbouring country. It calls upon all States, especially those neighbouring Rwanda, to refrain from any action that would further exacerbate the security situation in that country and to prevent incursions into Rwanda from their own territories. The Council invites States and organizations which have information on the transport of arms into countries neighbouring Rwanda for the purpose of their use in Rwanda in contravention of resolution 918(1994) to pass that information to the Committee established under resolution 918(1994) and requests the Committee to consider that information as a matter of urgency and to report thereon to the Security Council.

The Security Council notes with satisfaction that the deployment of the Zairian Camp Security Contingent and the Civilian Security Liaison Group has had a positive effect on the security situation in refugee camps in Zaire.

The Security Council pays tribute to all members of UNAMIR. It reaffirms that UNAMIR constitutes one essential factor for creating a climate of confidence and for promoting stability and security. In this context, it underlines the responsibility of the Government of Rwanda for the safety and security of all UNAMIR personnel and other international staff serving in the country. It urges the Rwandese authorities to proceed with the exchange of letters supplementing the agreement on the status of UNAMIR and its personnel, reflecting the changes in UNAMIR's mandate following from Security Council resolution 918(1994). The Council calls for increased cooperation and collaboration between the Government of Rwanda, its neighbouring countries and UNAMIR as well as other agencies, including in the humanitarian field.

The Security Council expresses grave concern at the situation created by the overcrowded prisons in Rwanda which has resulted in the death of numerous persons in custody and requests the Secretary-General to consider urgently measures which could be taken quickly in conjunction with the Government of Rwanda and humanitarian agencies to improve the conditions of those in detention or under investigation. The Council emphasizes that the development of the Rwandese justice system continues to be an important factor in creating conditions of security, law and order, conducive to the return of refugees from abroad and of displaced persons to their homes. The Council calls on the international community to assist the Government of Rwanda in re-establishing the justice system as a contribution to confidence-building and the maintenance of law and order.

The Security Council expresses its appreciation for the action of those States which have arrested and detained persons following the adoption of resolution 978(1995). It urges States, in accordance with that resolution, to arrest and detain persons against whom there is sufficient evidence of responsibility for acts within the jurisdiction of the International Tribunal for Rwanda. It requests the Secretary-General to facilitate the rapid establishment of the Tribunal.

The Security Council requests the Government of Rwanda to facilitate the delivery and distribution of humanitarian assistance to refugees and displaced persons in need, in conformity with the principles and current practice of UNHCR. It invites States and donor agencies to deliver on their earlier commitments and to further increase their assistance. It urges all Governments in the region to keep their borders open for this purpose.

The Security Council appeals to all States to act in accordance with recommendations adopted in the Regional Conference on Assistance to Refugees, Returnees and Displaced Persons in the Great Lakes Region held in Bujumbura in February 1995, in order to contribute to facilitating the return of refugees. The Council welcomes the Dar es Salaam trilateral agreement of 12 April 1995, on the voluntary repatriation of Rwandese refugees from Tanzania.

The Security Council reaffirms the view that an international conference would contribute substantially to peace and security in the subregion. It welcomes the intention of the Secretary-General to carry out consultations with all concerned so that such a conference can be held at the earliest possible date.

The Security Council will remain seized of the matter.

*Meeting number.* SC 3526.

**Inquiry Commission report.** On 19 May, the Secretary-General forwarded to the Security Council President the report[13] of the Independent International Commission of Inquiry. The Commission posed a number of questions, including those as to: the context in which the decision was taken to close the camps and the Kibeho camp; information about militias in the camp; consultation, before proceeding with closure, by the Government with various partners involved; the intent of the closure operation, especially whether it aimed to eliminate a certain category of people, especially one ethnic group; how the operation had been carried out since 18 April and what actually had happened on 22 and 23 April; the role, limitations and behaviour of the Rwandese Army, NGOs and UNAMIR; the role of the militia; and responsibility for the deaths at Kibeho.

The Commission concluded that the tragedy of Kibeho had neither resulted from a planned action by Rwandan authorities to kill a certain group of people, nor been an accident that could not have been prevented. It recognized the legitimate interests of the Rwandan Government and the international community to have the camps closed as quickly as possible, both for reasons of national security and to remove an important obstacle to the country's efforts to recover from the devastating effects of the 1994 genocide. The Commission also recognized the efforts by the Special Representative, UNAMIR, the Government of Rwanda and various organizations to keep the situation at Kibeho under control. It regretted that UN agencies and NGOs were not able to contribute more efficiently to the speedy evacuation of internally displaced persons in the camp. There was sufficient reliable evidence to establish that, during the events at Kibeho camp between 18 and 23 April, unarmed internally displaced persons were subjected to arbitrary deprivation of life and serious bodily harm by Rwandese Patriotic Army military personnel in violation of human rights and humanitarian law, and by armed elements among the internally displaced persons themselves.

The Commission recommended an analysis by the Rwandan authorities of mistakes made in the preparation and handling of the closure of the camps, as well as a thorough, prompt and impartial investigation of individual responsibilities within the armed forces and any other factors that might have contributed to the event. In the future, high priority should be given to improving the capability of Rwandan State and local authorities to react adequately and within the internationally recognized framework of human rights and of humanitarian law to situations of social tension and emergency. The international community should continue encouraging and assisting Rwanda in its efforts to achieve justice, national reconciliation and reconstruction. The Commission called on the UN system to review its chain-of-command and operation procedures to make sure that an entire operation was not held hostage or bogged down by one or several agencies and organizations with limited mandates and responsibilities.

**Report of the Secretary-General (June).** In a 4 June report,[14] the Secretary-General stated that the Kibeho tragedy underscored the tensions and fears that remained in Rwanda. On 18 April, the Rwandan Government had cordoned off and closed eight remaining camps for internally displaced persons in the Gikongoro region, of which Kibeho was the largest. The Government considered that those camps were being used as sanctuaries by elements of the former Rwandese government forces and militia, and they were a destabilizing factor and a security threat. Negotiations were taking place between the Government and the United Nations for the voluntary closure of the camps when the decision to act was taken without notice or consultation. Seven camps were closed without serious incident. However, at Kibeho an estimated 80,000 internally displaced persons attempted to break out on 22 April, after spending five days on a single hill without adequate space, shelter, food or sanitation. A large number of deaths occurred from firing by government forces, trampling and crushing during an ensuing stampede, and machete attacks by hardliners in the camp, who assaulted and intimidated those who wished to leave.

The Secretary-General reported that when the Rwandese Patriotic Army launched the operation, UNAMIR reacted immediately and, within 24 hours, trucks had been deployed to transport the internally displaced; two casualty collection posts were established to provide emergency medical assistance; and a UNAMIR command post with communication facilities was set up. UNAMIR engineers improved the Butare-Kibeho road to facilitate movement of convoys of internally displaced persons and humanitarian assistance. The sick and injured were evacuated. The presence of UNAMIR troops at open relief centres, way stations and transit centres was increased. Patrols were intensified to facilitate the reception and evacuation of internally displaced persons from those temporary facilities to their home communes. From the establishment of the Rwandese Patriotic Army cordon on 18 April to the tragic events of 22 April, senior UNAMIR officials visited Kibeho and the surrounding areas on several occasions to assess the situation, urge restraint and help coordinate the activities of UNAMIR personnel and relief agencies. Following the tragedy, Special Envoy Aldo Ajello was dispatched to Kigali to convey the Secretary-General's concern to the Rwandan leaders and to urge them to undertake an impartial investigation.

After three weeks of persuasion, through the combined efforts of UNAMIR and the Government of Rwanda, the approximately 2,500 internally displaced persons remaining in Kibeho were returned to their communes.

**Neighbouring State concerns**

The United Republic of Tanzania, in a 19 June press statement,[15] reported that it was hosting more than 1.4 million refugees, with individuals from Burundi and Rwanda constituting over half of that number. Since 1993, refugees from those two countries had poured into Tanzania. Ethnic differences and a lack of good governance and accountability had made them refugee-generating States. Tanzania could not afford to take more than it could absorb and any move from Rwanda would be met with equal force. To avoid any future outbreak of ethnic tensions in Rwanda, Tanzania called on the Rwandan Government to create the correct political atmosphere in the country by creating a government of national unity. Efforts at implementing the Bujumbura Plan of Action (see PART FOUR, Chapter XII), particularly after the signing of the tripartite voluntary repatriation agreement with Rwanda on 12 April, had not helped much, even in restoring normalcy in the camps.

**Report of the Secretary-General.** The Secretary-General in July reported[16] on the implementation of paragraph 6 of Security Council resolution 997(1995), which called for possible deployment of UN observers in States neighbouring Rwanda. Special Envoy Aldo Ajello carried out the consultations requested by the Council from 20 to 28 June. He stressed the Council's great concern over increasing reports of military activities that threatened to destabilize Rwanda. The countries concerned reiterated their support for efforts to prevent the resumption of armed conflict in Rwanda, to ensure the return and resettlement of its refugees and to promote lasting reconciliation. The uncontrolled circulation of arms, including to civilians and refugees in the subregion, was seen as a major cause of destabilization, especially in Rwanda and Burundi. There was agreement that a broader approach, with the involvement of Rwanda and its neighbours and the support of the international community, would offer better opportunities for a lasting solution to the Rwandan crisis. The neighbouring countries expressed the wish to receive concrete assistance from the international community to help them deal with the main problems that followed the conflict in Rwanda and prevent any repetition of such conflict.

Rwanda welcomed the Council's initiative to deploy military observers in neighbouring countries as a step in the right direction. There were mixed reactions from the neighbouring countries; some questioned the utility, relevance and feasibility of the proposed deployment, arguing that it was in Rwanda that the international observers should be stationed to help create a climate of confidence that would encourage the refugees to return home and reduce the danger of destabilization from refugee camps. There was scepticism about the effectiveness of such deployment and what it could achieve. It was suggested that instead of tackling the effects of the crisis, the Council should address its causes and identify the countries that were providing support for the delivery of weapons and military training to the former Rwandan government forces. Zaire, while expressing support for any effective action that could prevent the destabilization of Rwanda, reiterated its strong denial of recent accusations that it was aiding the former Rwandan government forces with arms and training to enable them to attack Rwanda. It pointed out that it had called for an international commission of inquiry to investigate the allegations. Zaire felt that, instead of being criticized, it should be assisted by the international community to cope with the immense ecological, socio-economic, security and political burdens imposed by the refugees. The Secretary-General said that Zaire had also pointed out to him on 23 June its contribution, in response to a UNHCR request, of 1,500 troops, which had been deployed for security protection in the Rwandan refugee camps, and its unilateral action in disarming the former Rwandan government forces soldiers who had fled to Zaire. Those actions were evidence of its determination to prevent insecurity in the camps and the destabilization of Rwanda from Zairian territory.

The Secretary-General referred to the suggestion of his Special Envoy that relocation of the camps farther away from the borders with Rwanda could facilitate efforts to curb the threat of destabilization. However, the cost, logistical difficulties and fear of resistance from the population of the country of refuge had prevented concrete action. In addition, Zaire explained that such a move would be seen by its population as implying that the refugees were being resettled for a longer period and perhaps a permanent stay in Zaire. The United Republic of Tanzania, for its part, criticized any effort aimed at transferring refugees from one country of refuge to another. The Secretary-General said that he would explore further the positions of the Governments concerned while he was in the region.

SECURITY COUNCIL ACTION

The Security Council on 23 August met to consider the situation concerning Rwanda. Following consultations among Council members, the President made the following statement on behalf of the Council:[17]

> The Security Council views with deep concern the forcible repatriation of Rwandan and Burundian refugees by the Government of Zaire and the increasingly tense situation in the region.
> The Security Council takes note of the recent letter from the Government of Zaire to the Secretary-General and the Secretary-General's reply in which he urges the Government of Zaire to continue to provide assistance to Rwandan and Burundian refugees.
> The Security Council considers that Zaire and the other States which have accepted refugees from Rwanda and Burundi make an important contribution, in spite of the considerable difficulties created for them thereby, to peace and stability in the region. Their contribution is of special importance in view of the genocide which took place in Rwanda and the possibility of further bloodshed in Burundi. The Council also notes the commitment of the Government of Rwanda to take the necessary steps to facilitate the safe return of its nationals as soon as possible and encourages it to continue its efforts in order to implement its undertakings in this respect.
> The Security Council calls on the Government of Zaire to stand by its humanitarian obligations regarding refugees, including, *inter alia*, those under the Convention relating to the Status of Refugees of 1951, and to reconsider and halt its declared policy of the forcible repatriation of refugees to Rwanda and Burundi.
> The Security Council supports the decision by the Secretary-General to send the United Nations High Commissioner for Refugees to the region to engage in urgent discussions with the Government of Zaire and neighbouring States with a view to resolving the situation. It encourages all Governments in the region to cooperate with the United Nations High Commissioner for Refugees to achieve the voluntary and orderly repatriation of refugees. It also calls on the international community to provide all possible assistance to help care for the refugees.

*Meeting number.* SC 3569.

**Communications.** On 29 August, the Secretary-General informed[18] the Security Council President that he had received assurances from Zaire that it would not pursue forcible repatriation of refugees. On the same date, in Geneva, the High Commissioner for Refugees met with the Prime Minister of Zaire, who expressed the wish that the repatriation be completed by 31 December. The Prime Minister made evident the political and social pressures the refugees were imposing on Zaire. While appreciating the special needs of the host country, the High Commissioner made it clear that a policy of forcible repatriation would not solve the problem. The Secretary-General added that the enormous economic, environmental and political burden which the presence of almost 2 million refugees placed on Zaire, Tanzania and other countries in the region needed to be fully recognized.

On 11 September, Rwanda transmitted to the Security Council President a presidential statement[19] made on the occasion of the visit of the UN High Commissioner for Refugees, reiterating Rwanda's determination to enable the safe return of all Rwandan refugees, in the letter and spirit of the Bujumbura Declaration (see PART FOUR, Chapter XII). It said that the Government employed great effort to ensure that the Rwandan nationals expelled from Zaire were safely and conveniently settled.

In anticipation of further repatriation, reception centres at the border had been reinforced and were to remain open and be further strengthened to receive more returnees. Rwanda appealed to all nationals outside the country to take advantage of that momentum. International monitoring and a strengthened judiciary would guarantee that there would be no arbitrary arrests. Those who had settled on properties of other persons had been mobilized to vacate them for their legitimate owners, and disputes over property were being handled by special committees at various levels of government. All those efforts were paying off, with a rising number of persons returning voluntarily from Tanzania, Burundi and Zaire. More than 30,000 had repatriated voluntarily from Burundi; it was expected that most of the 100,000 to 150,000 still there would have repatriated by the end of 1995. The Government was developing further mechanisms, in collaboration with the UN and other members of the international community, to ensure that more people could be comfortably received in large numbers. It was soliciting the support and involvement of the international community in seeking innovative ways to expedite the healing process and national reconciliation.

### Great Lakes region conference

In response to the Security Council's request of November 1994,[20] and as reiterated in **resolution 1011(1995)** of 16 August 1995, the Secretary-General reported on efforts to convene a regional conference on security, stability and development in the Great Lakes region. He proposed to appoint José Luis Jesús (Cape Verde) as his Special Envoy to facilitate the preparations for such a conference. The Council, in a 25 August letter[21] of its President, welcomed the Secretary-General's proposal.[22]

On 29 August, the Secretary-General updated[18] the Council on recent developments in the region, stating that a lasting solution of the crisis facing the Great Lakes region lay only in the early restoration of political stability and security.

The Special Envoy would travel to the region for consultation and to donor countries for talks with multilateral institutions to facilitate longer-term activities in host communities and in areas of return.

On 7 September, in a letter[23] of its President, the Council informed the Secretary-General that it shared his concern at the continued gravity of the situation and underlined the need for a coordinated and effective response from the international community. The Council expressed its support for his initiatives and looked forward to their implementation.

On 30 October, the Secretary-General reported[24] that his Special Envoy had held high-level consultations with Burundi, Ethiopia, Kenya, Rwanda, Uganda, the United Republic of Tanzania and OAU, most of which supported the idea of a regional conference. Rwanda expressed strong opposition to the idea and Uganda indicated that it was not keen on having the United Nations actively involved in that process. The Secretary-General said that the United Nations would continue to monitor developments in the region and he would revert to the Council if conditions existed for the successful convening of a conference.

On 10 November, in a letter of its President,[25] Council members stated that they supported all efforts to reduce tension and restore stability in the Great Lakes region. They encouraged the Secretary-General to continue contacts with the aim of convening the conference.

On 30 November, the United Republic of Tanzania forwarded[26] to the Security Council President a copy of the Cairo Declaration on the Great Lakes Region, adopted by the Presidents of Burundi, Rwanda, Uganda, the United Republic of Tanzania and Zaire, following their meeting in Cairo, Egypt, on 28 and 29 November. They pledged to advance peace, justice, reconciliation, stability and development in the region. Former United States President Jimmy Carter and Archbishop Desmond Tutu of South Africa served as facilitators to that meeting.

## Arms embargo

### General aspects

In May 1994,[27] the Security Council had imposed mandatory arms sanctions against Rwanda and established a Committee to monitor the implementation of those sanctions, to consider violations of the embargo and to make recommendations for increasing its effectiveness.

In **resolution 997(1995)** of 9 June 1995 (see below), dealing with the extension and mandate adjustment of UNAMIR, the Security Council affirmed that the restrictions imposed by its 1994 embargo against Rwanda applied to the sale or supply of arms and *matériel* to persons in the States neighbouring Rwanda, if that sale or supply was for use within Rwanda. It called on States neighbouring Rwanda to take steps, with the aim of putting an end to factors contributing to the destabilization of Rwanda, to ensure that such arms and *matériel* were not transferred to Rwandan camps within their territories. The Council requested the Secretary-General to consult Governments of neighbouring countries on the possibility of deploying UN military observers, and Zaire, on the deployment of observers including in the airfields located in eastern Zaire, in order to monitor the sale or supply of arms and *matériel*. He was to report to the Council within one month.

**Communication.** On 5 July 1995, Rwanda, in a letter to the Security Council President,[28] complained that the United Nations had taken no action on reports by Human Rights Watch and Amnesty International which confirmed that the arms embargo imposed on the former regime in Rwanda was not achieving its objectives; the perpetrators were rebuilding their military infrastructure in Zaire, had spoken openly of their intention to return to Rwanda and had threatened to wage war and to complete the genocide begun in April 1994. The United Nations had been unable to prevent infiltration of Rwanda and Burundi by those elements; nor had it been able to detect the rearming of the perpetrators of genocide.

Rwanda said the arms embargo was preventing the Government from ensuring the security of its citizens. Its lifting would ensure that the country regained its full sovereignty and its capability to protect its citizens. The embargo, originally imposed against a genocidal Government, should not be extended to subsequent Governments and to the State of Rwanda. Preventive measures had to focus on the leaders, soldiers and the militia of the former Government who violated humanitarian law and on the Governments that continued to support them. Rwanda requested urgent Council action to lift the embargo.

**SECURITY COUNCIL ACTION (July)**

The Security Council met on 17 July to consider the situation concerning Rwanda and adopted **resolution 1005(1995)**.

*The Security Council*,

*Recalling* its previous resolutions 918(1994) of 17 May 1994 and 997(1995) of 9 June 1995,

*Noting with concern* that unexploded land-mines constitute a substantial hazard to the population of Rwanda and an impediment to the rapid reconstruction of the country,

*Noting also* the desire of the Government of Rwanda to address the problem of unexploded land-mines, and the interest on the part of other States to assist with the detection and destruction of these mines,

*Underlining* the importance the Council attaches to efforts to eliminate the threat posed by unexploded land-mines in a number of States, and the humanitarian nature of demining programmes,

*Recognizing* that safe and successful humanitarian demining operations in Rwanda will require the supply to Rwanda of an appropriate quantity of explosives for use in these operations,

*Acting* under Chapter VII of the Charter of the United Nations,

*Decides* that, notwithstanding the restrictions imposed in paragraph 13 of resolution 918(1994), appropriate amounts of explosives intended exclusively for use in established humanitarian demining programmes may be supplied to Rwanda upon application to and authorization by the Committee of the Security Council established by resolution 918(1994).

Security Council resolution 1005(1995)
17 July 1995     Meeting 3555     Adopted unanimously

Draft by United States (S/1995/580).

**Further developments.** On 10 August, Zaire, in transmitting to the Security Council President its position[29] on the lifting of the Council's 1994 arms embargo[27] against Rwanda, said that the massive influx of refugees into its territory threatened its security, territorial integrity and sovereignty; Rwanda was spurring a new flow of refugees while at the same time obstructing the return to Rwanda of the refugees in dignity and safety; Rwanda had not shown good faith in fulfilling its obligations under the 1994 tripartite agreement, in particular its obligation to create security and reception zones within Rwanda to receive refugees from camps in Zaire and to ensure their reintegration and safety; and Rwanda was seeking to resolve its problems of scarcity of territory, overpopulation of arable land and its inter-ethnic conflict, to the detriment of its neighbours, through violence and methods that ran counter to domestic and international law. Zaire said that the Council should deplore the proliferation of weapons in the region and take measures to end it, rather than lifting the embargo on the supply of arms and other *matériel* to Rwanda. Priority should be given to disarming the militias and other armed bands in the countries of the Great Lakes region. Zaire rejected the idea of redeploying military observers to Zaire and reiterated support for an international commission of inquiry under UN auspices to investigate the supply of weapons to the former Rwandan armed forces and to verify allegations of destabilization.

**SECURITY COUNCIL ACTION (August)**

The Security Council met on 16 August to consider the report of the Secretary-General on the implementation of resolution 997(1995). It invited Zaire to participate without the right to vote under rule 37ᵃ of its provisional rules of procedure. The Council adopted **resolution 1011(1995)**.

*The Security Council,*

*Recalling* all its previous resolutions on the situation in Rwanda, in particular its resolutions 918(1994) of 17 May 1994, 997(1995) of 9 June 1995 and 1005(1995) of 17 July 1995,

*Having considered* the report of the Secretary-General on monitoring of the restrictions on the sale or supply of arms dated 9 July 1995,

*Having also considered* the progress report of the Secretary-General on the United Nations Assistance Mission for Rwanda (UNAMIR) dated 8 August 1995,

*Emphasizing* that the uncontrolled circulation of arms, including to civilians and refugees, is a major cause of destabilization in the Great Lakes subregion,

*Welcoming* the proposal of the Government of Zaire to establish an international commission under United Nations auspices to investigate reports of arms supplies to former Rwandan government forces,

*Recognizing* that the registration and marking of weapons are of considerable assistance in monitoring and enforcing restrictions on the illicit deliveries of weapons,

*Noting with great concern* reports of military preparations and increasing incursions into Rwanda by elements of the former regime and underlining the need for effective measures to ensure that Rwandan nationals currently in neighbouring countries, including those in camps, do not undertake military activities aimed at destabilizing Rwanda or receive arms supplies, in view of the great likelihood that such arms are intended for use within Rwanda,

*Stressing* the need for representatives of all sectors of Rwandan society, excluding those political leaders suspected of planning and directing the genocide last year, to begin talks in order to reach an agreement on a constitutional and political structure to achieve lasting stability,

*Taking note* of the letter dated 5 July 1995 from the Permanent Representative of Rwanda to the United Nations addressed to the President of the Security Council, requesting urgent action to lift the restrictions on the sale or supply of arms and *matériel* to the Government of Rwanda to ensure the security of the Rwandan population,

*Welcoming* the improvement in the working relations between the Government of Rwanda and UNAMIR and recalling the mandate of UNAMIR, as adjusted in resolution 997(1995), in particular to help achieve national reconciliation,

*Recalling* that the prohibition on the delivery of arms and *matériel* to Rwanda was originally aimed at stopping the use of such arms and equipment in the massacres of innocent civilians,

*Taking note* of the Council's decision in resolution 997(1995) to reduce the force level of UNAMIR, and reaffirming that the security of that country is the primary responsibility of the Government of Rwanda,

*Deeply concerned* by the situation in Rwanda's prisons and judicial system, particularly overcrowding, the lack of judges, detention of minors and elderly prisoners, and absence of speedy judicial or administrative review of charges, and, in this respect, welcoming renewed efforts by the United Nations and donor countries, in coordi-

nation with the Government of Rwanda, to initiate, on an urgent basis, measures to improve this situation,

*Underlining* the need for increased efforts by the Government of Rwanda in the promotion of a climate of stability and trust in order to facilitate the return of Rwandan refugees in neighbouring countries,

A

1. *Commends* the efforts of the Secretary-General and his Special Envoy in pursuing regional responses to the problem of illicit arms supplies in the region and encourages the Secretary-General to continue his consultations in this regard;

2. *Requests* the Secretary-General, as proposed in paragraph 45 of his report, to make recommendations to the Security Council, as soon as possible, on the establishment of a Commission mandated to conduct a full investigation to address allegations of arms flows to former Rwandan government forces in the Great Lakes region of Central Africa;

3. *Calls upon* the Governments of Rwanda and neighbouring States to cooperate with the Commission's investigation;

4. *Encourages* the Secretary-General to continue his consultations with the Governments of neighbouring States concerning the deployment of United Nations military observers in the airfields and other transportation points in and around border crossing points and calls on the neighbouring States to cooperate with and assist these observers to ensure that arms and related *matériel* are not transferred to Rwandan camps within their territories;

5. *Requests* the Secretary-General to report to the Council within one month of the adoption of this resolution on his efforts for the preparation and convening, at the earliest possible time, of the regional Conference on Security, Stability and Development, as well as for the convening of a regional meeting to address the problems facing the repatriation of refugees;

6. *Calls upon* the Government of Rwanda to continue its efforts to create an atmosphere of trust and confidence for the safe return of refugees and take further steps to resolve the humanitarian problems in its prisons, and to expedite disposition of the charges against those detained;

B

*Acting* under Chapter VII of the Charter of the United Nations,

7. *Decides* that, with immediate effect and until 1 September 1996, the restrictions imposed by paragraph 13 of resolution 918(1994) shall not apply with regard to the sale or supply of arms and related *matériel* to the Government of Rwanda through named points of entry on a list to be supplied by that Government to the Secretary-General, who shall promptly notify all Member States of the United Nations of the list;

8. *Decides also* that on 1 September 1996 the restrictions imposed by paragraph 13 of resolution 918(1994)

---

ᵃRule 37 of the Council's provisional rules of procedure states: "Any Member of the United Nations which is not a member of the Security Council may be invited, as the result of a decision of the Security Council, to participate, without vote, in the discussion of any question brought before the Security Council when the Security Council considers that the interests of that Member are specially affected, or when a Member brings a matter to the attention of the Security Council in accordance with Article 35(1) of the Charter."

on the sale or supply of arms and related *matériel* to the Government of Rwanda shall terminate, unless the Council decides otherwise after its consideration of the second report of the Secretary-General referred to in paragraph 12 below;

9. *Further decides*, with a view to prohibiting the sale and supply of arms and related *matériel* to non-governmental forces for use in Rwanda, that all States shall continue to prevent the sale or supply, by their nationals or from their territories or using their flag vessels or aircraft, of arms and related *matériel* of all types, including weapons and ammunition, military vehicles and equipment, paramilitary police equipment and spare parts, to Rwanda, or to persons in the States neighbouring Rwanda if such sale or supply is for the purpose of the use of such arms or *matériel* within Rwanda, other than to the Government of Rwanda as specified in paragraphs 7 and 8 above;

10. *Decides also* that no arms or related *matériel* sold or supplied to the Government of Rwanda may be resold to, transferred to, or made available for use by any State neighbouring Rwanda, or person not in the service of the Government of Rwanda, either directly or indirectly;

11. *Further decides* that States shall notify all exports from their territories of arms or related *matériel* to Rwanda to the Committee established by resolution 918(1994), that the Government of Rwanda shall mark and register and notify to the Committee all imports made by it of arms and related *matériel*, and that the Committee shall report regularly to the Council on notifications so received;

12. *Requests* the Secretary-General to report to the Council within 6 months of the date of adoption of this resolution, and again within 12 months, regarding, in particular, the export of arms and related *matériel* referred to in paragraph 7 above, on the basis of the reports submitted by the Committee established by resolution 918(1994);

13. *Decides* to remain actively seized of the matter.

Security Council resolution 1011(1995)

16 August 1995     Meeting 3566     Adopted unanimously

Draft prepared in consultations among Council members (S/1995/703).

**Communications.** On 17 August, the Prime Minister of Zaire declared in a letter to the Secretary-General[30] that Zaire now had no choice but to request that the Secretary-General indicate the arrangements made by the United Nations in relation to the new country or countries to which the Rwandan and Burundi refugees in Zaire should be evacuated. Zaire intended to evacuate them to their countries of origin at the expense of UNAMIR, the United Nations and the Governments of their respective countries.

Responding on 18 August, the Secretary-General noted[31] the difficulties encountered by the Government of Zaire and said he would communicate the Prime Minister's letter to the Security Council *in extenso*. Pending the reaction of the Council, he was appealing to Zaire to continue to assist the Rwandan refugees.

## Sanctions Committee activities

In a report[32] on its activities since its establishment in May 1994[26] until 31 December 1995, the Security Council Committee to monitor sanctions on Rwanda said it had appealed to Governments, intergovernmental organizations and NGOs, as well as individuals, to provide information on violations or suspected violations of the embargo imposed against Rwanda; considered a request from the United States pursuant to resolution 1005(1995) for the supply of a quantity of explosives and related materials for use in a bilateral humanitarian demining assistance programme; and adopted new consolidated guidelines based on sections of resolution 1011(1995). On 11 October, the Committee asked Rwanda to notify it of all imports of arms and related *matériel*.

A report by Human Rights Watch, entitled "Rearming with impunity: international support for the perpetrators of the Rwandan genocide", was transmitted to China, France, South Africa and Zaire for comment. China and France denied allegations of suspected violations. The report and replies received were transmitted to the International Commission of Inquiry (see below).

## International Commission of Inquiry

On 7 September, the Security Council established an International Commission of Inquiry (see below). In August, the Secretary-General had reported[33] that, during his visit to the subregion, strong interest was expressed in establishing such a commission under UN auspices to address allegations of arms flows to former Rwandan government forces.

On 16 August, the Council, in **resolution 1011(1995)**, had asked the Secretary-General to make recommendations on the establishment of a commission and called on Rwanda and neighbouring States to cooperate with the commission's investigations.

On 25 August, in a letter[34] to the Security Council President, the Secretary-General set out the terms of reference and other details of the proposed commission. It would collect information and investigate reports relating to the sale or supply of arms and related *matériel* to former Rwandan government forces in violation of the Council's embargo and allegations that such forces were receiving military training in order to destabilize Rwanda; and attempt to identify parties aiding and abetting the illegal acquisition of arms by those forces and recommend measures to curb the illegal flow of arms in the subregion. States, international and other organizations and individuals were to provide relevant information to the commission and any other assistance that might be required. Governments in whose territories investigations would be conducted should be requested to guarantee the safety and security of commission members and to ensure the necessary freedom of movement and contacts. The commission would be composed of an eminent person, appointed by the Secretary-General, who would serve as chairman, assisted by 5 to 10 legal, military and police experts, serving in their personal capacity.

The Secretary-General recommended that the commission commence its work in Zaire and could extend its work to other countries.

SECURITY COUNCIL ACTION

The Security Council met on 7 September and adopted **resolution 1013(1995)**.

*The Security Council,*

*Recalling* all its previous resolutions on the situation in Rwanda, in particular its resolutions 918(1994) of 17 May 1994, 997(1995) of 9 June 1995 and 1011(1995) of 16 August 1995,

*Having considered* the letter of the Secretary-General to the President of the Security Council dated 25 August 1995 on the establishment of a commission of inquiry,

*Having also considered* the note verbale of 10 August 1995 from the Government of Zaire to the President of the Security Council and welcoming the proposal of the Government of Zaire contained therein for the establishment under the auspices of the United Nations of an international commission of inquiry and its offer to assist such a commission,

*Recognizing* that destabilizing influences in the Great Lakes region, including the illegal acquisition of arms, can be prevented by the cooperative efforts of all Governments concerned,

*Expressing once again* its grave concern at allegations of the sale and supply of arms and related *matériel* to former Rwandan government forces in violation of the embargo imposed under its resolutions 918(1994), 997(1995) and 1011(1995), and underlining the need for Governments to take action to ensure the effective implementation of the embargo,

*Underlining* the importance of regular consultations between the commission of inquiry and the countries concerned, as appropriate, in view of the necessity to respect the sovereignty of States in the region,

1. *Requests* the Secretary-General to establish, as a matter of urgency, an International Commission of Inquiry, with the following mandate:

*(a)* To collect information and investigate reports relating to the sale or supply of arms and related *matériel* to former Rwandan government forces in the Great Lakes region in violation of Council resolutions 918 (1994), 997(1995) and 1011(1995);

*(b)* To investigate allegations that such forces are receiving military training in order to destabilize Rwanda;

*(c)* To identify parties aiding and abetting the illegal acquisition of arms by former Rwandan government forces, contrary to the Council resolutions referred to above; and

*(d)* To recommend measures to end the illegal flow of arms in the subregion in violation of the Council resolutions referred to above;

2. *Recommends* that the Commission to be appointed by the Secretary-General be composed of five to ten impartial and internationally respected persons, including legal, military and police experts, under the Chairmanship of an eminent person, and assisted by the appropriate support staff;

3. *Calls upon* States, relevant United Nations bodies, including the Committee established by resolution 918(1994), and, as appropriate, international humanitarian organizations and non-governmental organizations to collate information in their possession relating to the mandate of the Commission, and requests them to make this information available as soon as possible;

4. *Requests* the Secretary-General to report to the Council on the establishment of the Commission, and further requests him to submit, within three months from its establishment, an interim report on the conclusions of the Commission and, as soon as possible thereafter, to submit a final report, containing its recommendations;

5. *Calls upon* the Governments of the States concerned in which the Commission will carry out its mandate to cooperate fully with the Commission in the fulfilment of its mandate, including responding positively to requests from the Commission for security, assistance and access in pursuing investigations, including:

*(a)* Adoption by them of any measures needed for the Commission and its personnel to carry out their functions throughout their respective territories with full freedom, independence and security;

*(b)* Provision by them of all information in their possession which the Commission requests, or is otherwise needed to fulfil its mandate, and free access for the Commission and its staff to any relevant archives;

*(c)* Freedom of access at any time for the Commission and its staff to any establishment or place as they deem necessary for their work, including border points, airfields and refugee camps;

*(d)* Appropriate measures to guarantee the safety and security of the members of the Commission and guarantees from the Governments of full respect for the integrity, security and freedom of witnesses, experts and any other persons working with the Commission in the fulfilment of its mandate;

*(e)* Freedom of movement for members of the Commission, including freedom to interview any person in private, at any time, as appropriate;

*(f)* The grant of relevant privileges and immunities in accordance with the General Convention on the Privileges and Immunities of the United Nations;

6. *Recommends* that the Commission begin its work as soon as possible and to this end requests the Secretary-General to pursue his consultations with the countries of the region;

7. *Calls upon* all States to cooperate with the Commission in facilitating its investigations;

8. *Encourages* States to make voluntary contributions to the Secretary-General's United Nations Trust Fund for Rwanda as a supplement to financing the work of the Commission as an expense of the organization, and to contribute through the Secretary-General equipment and services to the Commission;

9. *Decides* to remain seized of the matter.

Security Council resolution 1013(1995)

7 September 1995    Meeting 3574    Adopted unanimously

Draft prepared in consultations among Council members (S/1995/771).

On 20 October, the Council took note[35] of a 16 October letter[36] from the Secretary-General, who informed the Council that the six members of the Commission were: Mahmoud Kassem (Egypt), Chairman; Inspector Jean-Michel Hanssens (Canada); Colonel Jürgen G. H. Almeling (Germany); Lt.-Col. Jan Meijvogel (Netherlands); Brigadier Mujahid Alam (Pakistan); and Colonel Lameck Mutanda (Zimbabwe). He intended to assemble the Commission in New York on 25 October.

The Commission arrived in Nairobi, Kenya, on 4 November and in Rwanda on 8 November. During November and December, it travelled around Rwanda, returning to Kigali from time to time to meet with officials. After a two-week delay, resulting from questions raised by Zaire concerning the terms of reference and the proposed activities of the Commission while in Zaire, the Commission paid a preliminary visit to Kinshasa from 8 to 16 December.

The General Assembly, having considered the Secretary-General's proposals[37] and the comments[38] of ACABQ, approved the amount of $419,200 gross ($392,100 net) for the biennium 1994-1995 (**resolution 50/205 A**) and $742,800 gross ($688,600 net) for 1996-1997 (**resolution 50/215 A**) for the operation of the Commission from 1 November 1995 to 30 April 1996.

## Human Rights Field Operation

In a 13 November note,[39] the Secretary-General transmitted to the General Assembly the report of the UN High Commissioner for Human Rights on the UN Human Rights Field Operation in Rwanda.

The Operation was the key response of the High Commissioner to the catastrophe that had occurred in Rwanda. From April to July 1994, Rwanda had suffered the slaughter of between 500,000 and 1 million persons. The massive human rights violations had been perpetrated in a preplanned, organized and systematic manner, and the mass killings had been condemned by all principal organs of the United Nations. The ensuing civil war and atrocities perpetrated against the civilian population had exacerbated the trauma, which had been worsened further by the extensive destruction of the country's infrastructure. The new Government that had taken power in mid-1994 had been able to halt the genocide and was faced with the immense task of restoring law and order, fostering national reconciliation and reconstructing public and economic

institutions. The return of refugees to Rwanda and their resettlement, together with that of internally displaced persons, remained another major problem to be resolved. The Operation was serving Rwanda by charting with its Government the long and difficult path to national reconciliation and by ensuring that human rights were fully respected at all stages in that process. The High Commissioner observed that the Operation in Rwanda was the first human rights field operation to be run under his authority.

The Operation had carried out extensive investigations of genocide and other serious violations of human rights and humanitarian law that had taken place between April and July 1994 in Rwanda. Some 120 human rights field officers had been deployed throughout the country to monitor the human rights situation. These included experts on investigations, such as prosecutors, criminal investigators and forensic experts, as well as specialists for human rights advisory services and education. A broad-based programme of promotional activities in the field of human rights had been launched, including projects to rebuild the Rwandan administration of justice and human rights education.

The Operation had continued its genocide-related investigations until the Deputy Prosecutor's Office of the International Tribunal for Rwanda with its own investigative unit was established. Thereafter, the emphasis of the Operation's investigative work shifted to coordinating the activities of field teams with the work of the Tribunal.

As for repatriation and resettlement of refugees and internally displaced persons, the Operation tried to ensure that basic human rights were not violated during the return, resettlement or reintegration process through monitoring of conditions at principal frontier crossing points, transit centres and interim detention centres and during reintegration into home communes. It also monitored the subsequent treatment and security of resettled refugees. In cooperation with ICRC, the Operation regularly visited prisons and detention centres to monitor conditions and make proposals for improvement. It actively promoted respect for legal procedures governing arrest and detention, and urged the appropriate authorities to review promptly cases where arrests appeared not to be based on strong indications of criminal responsibility. The Operation also worked to assist in the rehabilitation of the justice system at the national and local levels. It assisted in channelling material assistance made available by UNDP and other donors to local needs and encouraged the gradual resumption of the functioning of the Rwanda justice system. In cooperation with the Ministry of Justice and UNDP, it developed a plan to deploy

50 foreign legal experts to assist the Government in restarting all essential functions of the judicial system. In September, the Government asked for the temporary suspension and re-examination of that project.

In its efforts to promote respect for Rwandan law and human rights standards, seminars were held on arrest and detention procedures and training seminars were prepared for the gendarmerie and the Rwandese Patriotic Army on the role of the armed forces and law enforcement officials in the protection and promotion of human rights. A project for the creation of centres to provide legal and other advice to women was developed with local legal associations and competent ministries. The Operation worked with Rwandan NGOs and promoted human rights standards and awareness through radio broadcasts, newsletters and a weekly human rights club.

The General Assembly, in **resolution 50/200** of 22 December, took note with concern of the findings of the Human Rights Field Operation in Rwanda that the human rights situation was exacerbated by the inadequate system for the administration of justice, characterized by the shortage of both human and material means. It requested the High Commissioner to report regularly on the activities of the Field Operation and requested the Secretary-General to ensure adequate financial and human resources and logistical support for it, taking into account the need to deploy a sufficient number of human rights field officers and the need for programmes of technical assistance and advisory services.

## UN Assistance Mission

### Work of UNAMIR

In October 1993, the Security Council established[40] the UN Assistance Mission for Rwanda to assist in implementing the 1993 Arusha Peace Agreement. In June 1993, it had established[41] the UN Observer Mission Uganda-Rwanda (UNOMUR) to monitor the border between those two Central African nations to ensure that no military assistance reached Rwanda. UNOMUR was phased out in September 1994.

In 1994, following the deaths in April in an aeroplane crash of the Presidents of both Rwanda and Burundi, widespread civil unrest ensued, resulting in large-scale massacres of civilians and massive flows of refugees and displaced persons. The mandate of UNAMIR was expanded during the year to deal with the burgeoning crisis. From June to August, a multinational force—"Operation Turquoise"—was deployed to Rwanda to serve humanitarian purposes.

In 1995, the activities of UNAMIR, under adjusted mandates set out in June and December by

the Security Council (see below), continued in the areas of: exercising good offices to help achieve national reconciliation within the Arusha Peace Agreement, facilitating the safe return of refugees and their reintegration into their home communities, supporting the provision of humanitarian aid and other forms of assistance and expertise, contributing to the security of UN personnel, including those of the International Tribunal for Rwanda and human rights officers, and assisting in the training of a national police force. During 1995, UNAMIR's strength dropped from about 5,700 to 1,200, in the light of the adjusted mandates.

The Secretary-General reported on the work of UNAMIR in 1995 in several reports (see below), which included details on situations related to security, refugee flows, human rights, food supplies and infrastructure rebuilding, among others.

**Report of the Secretary-General (February).** On 6 February, the Secretary-General reported[42] that the security situation continued to be a matter of serious concern, with reports of summary executions, secret detention, torture, banditry and other violent acts against civilians. UNAMIR was assisting the Government to establish a new police force, as Rwandese military personnel continued to perform police duties. As part of its efforts to unify the Army, some 2,200 members of the former Rwandese government forces had undergone a five-month retraining programme.

The Government continued to take steps towards national reconciliation and reconstruction but, for the most part, lacked the resources to run an effective public administration, the Secretary-General reported. Also, Rwanda's court system was not functioning, its prisons were overcrowded and thousands of suspects awaited trial.

By 30 January, Opération Retour, an integrated inter-agency initiative to facilitate the safe resettlement of internally displaced persons, launched in December 1994, had resettled some 25,000 displaced persons.

The Government had established in 1994 a commission for the repatriation and resettlement of refugees, as provided for in the Arusha Agreement. In 1995, it was planning a socio-economic survey of refugees, a pre-repatriation census and registration of returnees, and an information and sensitization campaign directed at the refugees and the local population. It also was identifying resettlement sites, supervising the distribution of plots and facilitating the rehabilitation of basic infrastructure and transport of returnees.

The Secretary-General said the dissemination of factual information was a vital tool in creating conditions for refugees and internally displaced persons to decide freely to return to their homes.

On 14 January, the Government and UNAMIR signed an agreement to establish Radio UNAMIR in Kigali.

The Human Rights Field Operation (see above) continued to monitor human rights conditions, liaise with the Government with respect to human rights education, monitor the conditions of detainees, participate in confidence-building measures aimed at the re-establishment of civic society and coordinate with other international agencies in the field.

The Secretary-General also reported that UN organizations continued to provide urgently needed assistance, in particular, food, health and children's services, to displaced persons and other vulnerable population groups. Humanitarian organizations, with the Ministries of Defence and Justice, were developing plans for the demobilization, education and retraining of some 4,000 "child soldiers" for reintegration into society. Food-for-work schemes supported at least 7,000 civil servants and 17,000 teachers. As requested in 1994,[43] a comprehensive plan for a mine-clearance programme had been proposed, including a mine survey, marking and fencing operations, and emergency mine clearance. The UN Children's Fund (UNICEF) was also conducting mine-awareness education activities in all prefectures.

On 10 February, the Security Council, in a letter from its President,[44] noted that a functioning judicial system was essential in the government recovery programme for the establishment of internal security, and also for the return of refugees. They also attached importance to the establishment of an effective mine-clearance programme on the basis of the UN plan.

**Report of the Secretary-General (April).** In a 9 April report,[45] the Secretary-General said that continued UN support was pledged to building a new Rwandese society based on tolerance, harmony and justice. In the nine months since the new Rwandese Government had assumed office, the overall situation had improved considerably. The private sector had revived, markets, shops and small businesses had sprung up, agricultural activities had started and schools had reopened. Radio UNAMIR had begun broadcasting on 16 February and was on the air seven days a week in three languages.

Over the past two months, tensions and frustrations had surfaced and the security situation in the country had deteriorated, with armed saboteurs entering the country and more and more people being detained by the Government. Those developments contributed to a decline in the repatriation of Rwandese refugees from Burundi, the United Republic of Tanzania and Zaire.

There were also reports that the armed forces of the former Rwandese Government were training and rearming; due to the tightened security, some incidents had occurred involving searches of UN vehicles and staff and a cut-off of goods and equipment at Kigali airport. Middle- and lower-level government authorities were often uncooperative.

Radio Rwanda had initiated a propaganda campaign against UNAMIR personnel, and strained relations between UNAMIR and Rwandese Army personnel persisted. The Army frequently restricted the movement of UNAMIR personnel and denied them access to certain areas, thus affecting their ability to discharge mandated tasks fully. Difficulties were also encountered during troop rotations, when UNAMIR personnel were delayed or denied entry at Kigali airport. Rwanda was reminded of its responsibility for the safety and security of all UNAMIR personnel, as well as for ensuring that their freedom of movement and access throughout the country were respected.

Human rights monitors were increased from 88 in January to 113 by 1 April. The UN High Commissioner for Human Rights launched an international appeal to assist Rwanda to re-establish the judicial systems and for funds to recruit more human rights monitors.

Some 3,000 unaccompanied minors were registered in an attempt to reunite them with their families. Psychosocial counselling and trauma recovery programmes were to be enlarged. Agreement was reached with the Ministry of Justice to permit 400 children between the ages of 11 and 17, imprisoned for alleged involvement in genocide, to be moved to a separate location for children only. Vaccination and nutritional centres had reopened. An emergency curriculum was made available for over 140,000 primary schoolchildren.

A team of United States experts visited Rwanda to discuss with UNAMIR officials a possible plan of action for mine clearing. UNAMIR explosives demolition teams continued to carry out limited mine-clearing operations.

Substantial food shortages existed within the country and the subregion, and NGOs were distributing seeds and tools. The Secretary-General urged donors to accelerate the flow of aid to Rwanda, possibly through the Trust Fund for Rwanda.

**Report of the Secretary-General (June).** On 4 June, the Secretary-General reported[14] that the country was now largely at peace. Electricity, water and communications had been partly restored, primary and secondary schools had reopened, and economic and agricultural activities had resumed. The National Assembly had begun discussions on a new Constitution to replace the 1992 Constitution.

The Kibeho tragedy, he went on, had underscored the tensions and fears that remained just beneath the surface in Rwanda. The Government continued to report military preparations and incursions by elements of the former regime. The number of arrests for alleged complicity in the genocide remained high. As a result, the sense of insecurity within the communes inhibited the repatriation of refugees. Acrimonious criticism of the international community in general, and UNAMIR in particular, continued unabated, encouraging non-cooperation, even hostility, at the middle and lower levels of the Rwandan Government and by the Army.

Because of a deteriorating security situation in Kigali and an increase in armed robberies, UNAMIR had deployed troops there. Emergency medical assistance was provided to Rwandans at UNAMIR locations and to internally displaced persons in south-western Rwanda. Transportation was made available to internally displaced persons and returning refugees.

The Secretary-General reported that under a new mandate UNAMIR would shift its focus from peace-keeping to confidence-building, undertaking tasks specifically required to sustain a UN peace-keeping presence in Rwanda, mainly in Kigali. Those would include the protection of UN premises, as well as of personnel of the International Tribunal, UN agencies and NGOs; deployment throughout the country of military/police observers, as a complement to human rights monitors; helping in the distribution of humanitarian assistance; facilitating the return and reintegration of refugees in cities and communes; providing assistance and expertise in engineering, logistics, medical care and demining; and stationing a limited reserve of formed troops in certain provinces.

However, the Government of Rwanda had taken the position that most UNAMIR peace-keeping functions had become redundant, the Secretary-General went on. Rwanda believed the concept of promoting security and confidence through the presence of UNAMIR could no longer be accepted, since it had assumed responsibility for national security throughout the country; Rwanda felt the protection of humanitarian convoys was the responsibility of the Government and UNAMIR's role should be one of monitoring. Also, there was no need for UNAMIR to play a role in border monitoring. The training programme of UNAMIR's civilian police should be replaced by bilateral arrangements. Rwanda had proposed that UNAMIR should be reduced to a maximum of 1,800 formed troops, to be deployed in Kigali and the provinces. Rwanda wanted the mandate to be extended for six months, on the understanding that there would be no further extension and that steps to reduce UNAMIR troops outside Kigali should commence immediately.

With respect to a long-term solution of the refugee and related problems in the Great Lakes region, the Secretary-General intended to appoint a special envoy to consult with the countries concerned, as well as with OAU, on the convening of a Regional Conference on Security, Stability and Development.

The Human Rights Field Operation in Rwanda continued its investigations into the genocide of 1994. Reports and extensive evidence gathered at massacre sites were made available to the Special Rapporteur of the Commission on Human Rights and the International Tribunal. The process of investigating acts of genocide and other serious violations of international humanitarian law committed in Rwanda was launched. Most activity took place in other African countries, Europe and North America, and covered 400 identified suspects, many of whom had sought refuge abroad.

Humanitarian efforts mainly dealt with the consequences of the forced closure of internally displaced persons camps in south-west Rwanda. The rapid and coordinated response of UNAMIR, the UN Rwanda Emergency Office, UN agencies, international organizations and NGOs prevented greater casualties and suffering. The massive return of internally displaced persons, many of whom were forced to leave their possessions in the camps or were robbed on their way home, placed heavy demands on the communes. The closure of camps resulted in an increased number of unaccompanied minors; UNICEF reported nearly 2,000, some 70 per cent of whom were under the age of five.

Health facilities throughout the country needed urgent rehabilitation and additional staff. The World Health Organization had conducted training programmes in epidemiological surveillance and epidemic control. UNICEF supported the rehabilitation of the water-supply system in the north-eastern part of the country. Food shipments to refugee camps were affected, and many people lacked the means to produce food until the next agricultural season, from September 1995 to January 1996.

**SECURITY COUNCIL ACTION (June)**

The Security Council met on 9 June to consider the Secretary-General's June report. It invited Zaire to participate in the discussion under rule 37[a] of the Council's rules of procedure. The Council adopted **resolution 997(1995)**.

*The Security Council,*

*Recalling* all its previous resolutions on the situation in Rwanda, in particular its resolution 872(1993) of 5 October 1993 by which it established the United Nations Assistance Mission for Rwanda (UNAMIR), and its resolutions 912(1994) of 21 April 1994, 918(1994) of 17 May 1994, 925(1994) of 8 June 1994, and 965(1994) of 30 November 1994, which set out the mandate of UNAMIR,

*Having considered* the report of the Secretary-General on UNAMIR dated 4 June 1995,

*Recalling also* its resolution 955(1994) of 8 November 1994 establishing the International Tribunal for Rwanda, and its resolution 978(1995) of 27 February 1995, concerning the necessity for the arrest of persons suspected of certain offences in Rwanda,

*Stressing* the importance of achieving genuine reconciliation among all members of Rwandan society within the frame of reference of the Arusha Peace Agreement,

*Noting with great concern* reports of military preparations and increasing incursions into Rwanda by elements of the former regime and underlining the need for effective measures to ensure that Rwandan nationals currently in neighbouring countries, including those in camps, do not undertake military activities aimed at destabilizing Rwanda or receive arms supplies, in view of the great likelihood that such arms are intended for use within Rwanda,

*Underlining* the need for increased efforts to assist the Government of Rwanda in the promotion of a climate of stability and trust in order to facilitate the return of Rwandan refugees in neighbouring countries,

*Emphasizing* the necessity for the accelerated disbursement of international assistance for the rehabilitation and reconstruction of Rwanda,

*Calling again upon* all States to act in accordance with recommendations adopted by the Regional Conference on Assistance to Refugees, Returnees and Displaced Persons in the Great Lakes Region, held in Bujumbura in February 1995,

*Recognizing* the valuable contribution that the human rights officers deployed by the High Commissioner for Human Rights to Rwanda have made towards the improvement of the overall situation,

*Acknowledging* the responsibility of the Government of Rwanda for the safety and security of all UNAMIR personnel and other international staff serving in the country,

*Reaffirming* the need for a long-term solution to the refugee and related problems in the Great Lakes States, and welcoming, therefore, the intention of the Secretary-General to appoint a special envoy to carry out consultations on the preparation and convening, at the earliest possible time, of the regional Conference on Security, Stability and Development,

1. *Decides* to extend the mandate of UNAMIR until 8 December 1995 and authorizes a reduction of the force level to 2,330 troops within three months of the adoption of this resolution and to 1,800 troops within four months;

2. *Decides* to maintain the current level of military observers and civilian police personnel;

3. *Decides*, in the light of the current situation in Rwanda, to adjust the mandate of UNAMIR so that UNAMIR will:

(*a*) Exercise its good offices to help achieve national reconciliation within the frame of reference of the Arusha Peace Agreement;

(*b*) Assist the Government of Rwanda in facilitating the voluntary and safe return of refugees and their reintegration in their home communities, and, to that end, to support the Government of Rwanda in its ongoing efforts to promote a climate of confidence and trust through the performance of monitoring tasks throughout the country with military and police observers;

(*c*) Support the provision of humanitarian aid, and of assistance and expertise in engineering, logistics, medical care and demining;

(*d*) Assist in the training of a national police force;

(*e*) Contribute to the security in Rwanda of personnel and premises of United Nations agencies, of the International Tribunal for Rwanda, including full-time protection for the Prosecutor's Office, as well as those of human rights officers, and to contribute also to the security of humanitarian agencies in case of need;

4. *Affirms* that the restrictions imposed under Chapter VII of the Charter of the United Nations by resolution 918(1994) apply to the sale or supply of arms and *matériel* specified therein to persons in the States neighbouring Rwanda, if that sale or supply is for the purpose of the use of such arms or *matériel* within Rwanda;

5. *Calls upon* the States neighbouring Rwanda to take steps, with the aim of putting an end to factors contributing to the destabilization of Rwanda, to ensure that such arms and *matériel* are not transferred to Rwandan camps within their territories;

6. *Requests* the Secretary-General to consult the Governments of neighbouring countries on the possibility of the deployment of United Nations military observers, and to consult, as a matter of priority, the Government of Zaire on the deployment of observers including in the airfields located in eastern Zaire, in order to monitor the sale or supply of arms and *matériel* referred to above; and further requests the Secretary-General to report to the Council on the matter within one month of the adoption of this resolution;

7. *Takes note* of the cooperation existing between the Government of Rwanda and UNAMIR in the implementation of its mandate and urges the Government of Rwanda and UNAMIR to continue to implement the agreements made between them, in particular the Status-of-Mission Agreement of 5 November 1993 and any subsequent agreement concluded to replace that Agreement in order to facilitate the implementation of the new mandate;

8. *Commends* the efforts of States, United Nations agencies and non-governmental organizations which have provided humanitarian assistance to refugees and displaced persons in need, encourages them to continue such assistance, and calls upon the Government of Rwanda to continue to facilitate their delivery and distribution;

9. *Calls upon* States and donor agencies to fulfil their earlier commitments to give assistance for Rwanda's rehabilitation efforts, to increase such assistance, and in particular to support the early and effective functioning of the International Tribunal and the rehabilitation of the Rwandan judicial system;

10. *Encourages* the Secretary-General and his Special Representative to continue to coordinate the activities of the United Nations in Rwanda, including those of the organizations and agencies active in the humanitarian and developmental field, and of the human rights officers;

11. *Requests* the Secretary-General to report to the Council by 9 August 1995 and 9 October 1995 on the discharge by UNAMIR of its mandate, the humanitarian situation and progress towards repatriation of refugees;

12. *Decides* to remain actively seized of the matter.

Security Council resolution 997(1995)

9 June 1995    Meeting 3542    Adopted unanimously

Draft prepared in consultations among Council members (S/1995/465).

**Report of the Secretary-General (August).** On 8 August, the Secretary-General reported[33] that repatriation of troops had begun. As at 3 August, its troop strength had been reduced to 3,571 all ranks. Civilian police observers numbered 56.

Working relations between the Government of National Unity and UNAMIR had improved and a spirit of cooperation with UN programmes and agencies, international NGOs and bilateral donors had emerged. The Secretary-General's visit to Rwanda on 13 and 14 July was intended to help strengthen those trends. Rwanda also had taken steps to improve relations with neighbouring countries, especially Burundi, the United Republic of Tanzania and Zaire.

Although senior government officials had publicly called on the Army and security forces to respect the rights of citizens, acts of violence continued to be reported. On 20 June, the Government issued a statement that opened the possibility for contacts with refugee representatives who had not been implicated in acts of genocide. At the same time, it encouraged refugees to visit Rwanda to assess conditions personally and thus expedite the pace of repatriation. Radio UNAMIR, heard in more than 70 per cent of Rwanda, continued its confidence-building broadcasts, providing the population with factual and objective information on the situation in the country, the Secretary-General said.

Several candidates for the offices of President and five Deputy Presidents of the Supreme Court had not been acceptable to the National Assembly, and efforts were under way to identify mutually acceptable nominees. On 19 July, President Bizimungu, responding to charges that political activities of non-governmental parties were prohibited, stated that while multi-party political activities, as such, had not been banned, political competition and mutual accusing among political parties which caused instability and divisions would not be allowed.

Restrictions on UNAMIR's freedom of movement had generally ceased. In addition, incidents of banditry and theft had decreased significantly. The closure of the displaced persons camps and the subsequent return of a large number of displaced persons to their previous neighbourhoods, as well as the continued repatriation of refugees, increased the pressure for housing and land. In some areas, however, acute housing shortages and disputes over property continued to result in violence. Although numbers had decreased, cases of

arbitrary arrests and detention continued to be reported, as were attacks, disappearances and killings, mostly of new returnees. Both Rwanda and Zaire conceded that the situation in their border zone had deteriorated and accused each other of involvement. Rwanda had enhanced security measures, and requested that restrictions on its acquisition of arms be lifted.

Efforts to enhance the administration of justice, establish law and order and promote national reconciliation continued. On 17 July, the Minister of Justice inaugurated a four-month training course for future magistrates. The conditions in the prisons constituted a major humanitarian crisis, with more than 50,000 people incarcerated in 12 prisons and other places of detention. Death rates in the prisons were estimated at more than 200 per month.

The rate of repatriation of Rwandan refugees from neighbouring countries increased slightly. In June, 2,727 returned from Zaire. UNHCR estimated that, in addition to the 6,250 repatriated from Burundi in June and July under its auspices, up to 10,000 persons had returned to Rwanda on their own. Officials from the United Republic of Tanzania and Rwanda met with UNHCR in Kigali from 17 to 19 July to examine modalities for the return of the estimated 700,000 persons in Tanzania. They agreed to establish a joint commission on security and the resettlement of refugees. Since the closure of the camps for the internally displaced in south-west Rwanda, international humanitarian organizations had increased their activities at the commune level. The Government launched the first phase of its rehabilitation programme. Food-aid deliveries throughout the country had increased and there were sufficient stocks of food to cover planned distribution programmes.

By 1 August, the UN Human Rights Field Operation had established 11 field offices throughout the country. Plans were under way to establish sub-offices in additional communes. Human rights committees were being created at the provincial or prefectural level, with local participation, which would meet regularly with representatives of various government authorities. The Operation organized education seminars for civil, military and judicial representatives.

Following a bilateral agreement between the United States and Rwanda, a national demining programme was established in July, providing for the establishment of a national demining office, demining training for government soldiers and creation of a mine database.

Although a large-scale humanitarian effort was still required to meet emergency needs, Rwanda was gradually shifting towards rehabilitation and reconstruction. As a result, the UN Rwanda Emergency Office in Kigali, established in 1994, began preparing for its eventual closure. Transitional arrangements, including the establishment of a small UN disaster management team, were being made to ensure that the coordination of humanitarian assistance continued.

Donor countries and UN agencies met in Kigali on 6 and 7 July for a mid-term review of the January round-table conference. They recognized the need to expedite the disbursement of already committed funds and pledged an additional $200 million. Several programmes to facilitate the return to Rwanda of former members of the country's public service were initiated. The World Bank, the International Monetary Fund and UNDP were involved in a project designed to strengthen the Government's capacity to manage its economic, financial and human resources.

The Secretary-General concluded that in order to address the urgent problems surrounding the repatriation of refugees, it might be useful to convene, at the earliest possible date, a regional meeting to develop measures to implement the commitments embodied in the Nairobi summit declaration (see above, under ''Refugee camp security and repatriation efforts''), the Bujumbura Action Plan (see PART FOUR, Chapter XII) and the tripartite agreements signed by UNHCR, Rwanda and neighbouring countries hosting Rwandan refugees. That would be in addition to the possible holding of round-table meetings, in which all sectors of Rwandan society would participate and which had been discussed with Rwandan government officials during the Secretary-General's visit to Rwanda in July.

**Communication.** On 29 August, the Secretary-General informed[18] the Security Council President that following his July visit to Rwanda, he had asked the Under-Secretary-General for Humanitarian Affairs to initiate urgent measures to address the crisis resulting from the prison conditions in Rwanda and the inability of the justice system to process the cases of those incarcerated. Immediate action was needed to improve prison conditions and expand prison capacity by up to 21,000. Rwanda would also receive assistance to strengthen its justice system and to implement a proper arrest and detention policy.

In Rwanda, the Department of Humanitarian Affairs continued to assume responsibility for coordinating humanitarian actions. UNHCR, in collaboration with the Rwandese Ministry of Rehabilitation, oversaw the reception of returning refugees. Notwithstanding recent changes in the Rwandese Government, the Secretary-General said he was confident that work would continue in a constructive and positive spirit to enhance Rwanda's capacity for ensuring the observance of human rights, the safety of returnees and justice for all.

**Report of the Secretary-General (October).** In a 7 October report,[46] the Secretary-General said that despite the unexpected expulsion of some 13,000 Rwandese from Zaire, Rwanda, with logistical support from UNAMIR, UN agencies and NGOs, was receiving and resettling its nationals in a generally humane and orderly manner. At a meeting of the Tripartite Commission involving the United Republic of Tanzania, Rwanda and UNHCR (Arusha, Tanzania, 18-21 September), agreement was reached on measures to launch large-scale repatriation of the more than 600,000 Rwandese refugees in Tanzania. At a Tripartite Commission meeting involving Zaire, Rwanda and UNHCR (Geneva, 25 September), Rwanda agreed to strengthen reception facilities, reduce border controls and provide security and protection to returnees, in collaboration with UNHCR and other human rights organizations. Zaire agreed to reduce all forms of intimidation in the camps within its borders. In the context of a renewed regional effort to promote voluntary repatriation, UNHCR was expanding its mass information campaign to counter extremist propaganda. In anticipation of an increased rate of return of refugees to Rwanda, UNHCR was augmenting its facilities at official border entry points and expanding activities in the communes of origin, in cooperation with UNDP.

UNAMIR troops and military observers, in coordination with UNHCR and other UN agencies, supported Rwanda's efforts to resettle the refugees forced across the border from Zaire between 19 and 24 August. They also helped to improve conditions in transit camps, in anticipation of a large-scale return of refugees, and to construct and renovate detention centres to relieve the overcrowding in Rwandese jails; and assisted in the construction or repair of bridges, roads and schools and in the transport of humanitarian assistance.

The deadline of 31 December set by Zaire for the voluntary departure of all refugees from its territory intensified the humanitarian challenges facing Rwanda and the international community. The task of organizing the voluntary repatriation of the estimated 2 million refugees was a difficult one. The UN High Commissioner for Refugees believed that a more realistic target was between 500,000 and 600,000 persons by the end of the year, due in part to the limited absorption capacity of many of the home communes in Rwanda. UNCHR had undertaken a demographic survey and assessment of existing infrastructure and population groups in Rwanda's communes to identify those communes that were ready to receive returnees and those that needed infrastructure rehabilitation.

Cross-border infiltration and sabotage, leading to countermeasures by the Government, constituted the most worrying security problem in the country, the Secretary-General said. An international commission of inquiry would look into allegations of arms supplies to and training of former Rwandese government forces. Training of the Rwandan National Police Force continued; the training of the communal police had been delayed because of the rehabilitation of the Communal Police Training Centre.

Conditions in the prisons continued to constitute a major humanitarian crisis. More than 52,000 people were incarcerated, with arrests continuing to take place. A plan of action, drafted by Rwanda and UNDP for urgent action on prisons and in the justice sector, had been circulated to the international community and a team set up, under the Special Representative, to mobilize resources and to accelerate the improvement of prison conditions.

In terms of humanitarian assistance, the situation remained fragile. According to the Food and Agriculture Organization of the United Nations and WFP, some 15 per cent of Rwanda's estimated 1 million families were vulnerable. However, efforts to promote household food security and income generation for women had intensified.

There was a sizeable increase in the commitment and disbursement of funds pledged for Rwanda's Programme of National Reconciliation and Socio-Economic Rehabilitation and Recovery. WFP provided more than 100,000 individuals with food, but also assisted Rwanda's agricultural recovery, rehabilitation of destroyed infrastructure and construction of new houses, schools and water facilities.

**SECURITY COUNCIL ACTION (October)**

The Security Council met on 17 October to consider the report of the Secretary-General on UNAMIR. Following consultations among Council members, the President made the following statement on behalf of the Council:[47]

The Security Council has considered the Secretary-General's report on the United Nations Assistance Mission for Rwanda (UNAMIR) of 7 October 1995.

The Security Council welcomes progress made by the Government of Rwanda in the reconciliation process, including the integration of more than 2,000 members of former Rwandan Government Forces (RGF) troops into the Rwanda Patriotic Army (RPA). The Council calls on the Government of Rwanda to intensify its contacts with all sectors of Rwandan society, except with those directly responsible for the genocide. The Council reiterates its concern at reports about continuing cross-border infiltrations from neighbouring countries which have a destabilizing effect within Rwanda. The Council also reiterates its concern at the danger for peace and stability in the Great Lakes region which would be caused by uncontrolled arms flows and in this context reaffirms the

relevant provisions of its resolution 1013(1995). The Council condemns all acts of violence in Rwanda. The Council welcomes the fact that the Government of Rwanda has voluntarily and without delay initiated an investigation into the killing of civilians at Kanama and expects that prosecution of those responsible will follow.

The Security Council calls again upon all States to act in accordance with the conclusions of the summit meeting of the leaders in the subregion in Nairobi in January 1995 and the recommendations by the Regional Conference on Assistance to Refugees, Returnees and Displaced Persons in the Great Lakes Region, held in Bujumbura in February 1995. The Council welcomes recent efforts to improve relations among the States in the region, which should help pave the way for the proposed Regional Conference on Peace, Security and Development. In this regard, the Council supports the efforts of the Special Envoy of the Secretary-General to the Great Lakes region for the preparation and convening of such a conference. It requests the Secretary-General to submit his report on the results of the first round of consultations of the Special Envoy in the region as soon as possible.

The Security Council reaffirms the important role UNAMIR has played in Rwanda and the subregion. In this respect, the Council underlines its commitment to UNAMIR which, *inter alia*, assists the Government of Rwanda in facilitating the voluntary return and resettlement of refugees and has made available to the Rwandan authorities its engineering and logistics capacity. The Council underlines that UNAMIR can effectively implement its current mandate only if it has an adequate force level and sufficient means. The Council stands ready to study carefully any further recommendations that the Secretary-General might make on the issue of force reductions in relation to the fulfilment of the mandate of UNAMIR.

The Security Council reaffirms its view that genuine reconciliation as well as long-lasting stability in the region as a whole cannot be attained without the safe, voluntary and organized return to their country of all Rwandan refugees. In this respect, the Council welcomes the joint efforts of Rwanda, neighbouring countries and UNHCR to speed up the voluntary return of refugees through, *inter alia*, the work of the Tripartite Commissions. The Council underlines that, in order to foster the process of national reconciliation, an effective and credible national judiciary has to be established. In this respect, it welcomes the appointment of the members of the Rwandan Supreme Court. The Council further underlines that the International Tribunal for Rwanda should begin its proceedings as soon as possible. The Council calls on Member States to comply with their obligations with regard to cooperation with the Tribunal in accordance with resolution 955(1994). It urges once more all States to arrest and detain persons suspected of genocide and other serious violations of international humanitarian law in accordance with resolution 978(1995). The Council underlines the necessity for the Tribunal to be fully financed, as a matter of priority, and for continued access to the Voluntary Trust Fund established for the Tribunal. The Council continues to support the work of human rights monitors in Rwanda in cooperation with the Rwandan Government.

The Security Council reaffirms its concern at the appalling situation in the Rwandan prisons. In this respect, it welcomes measures initiated by the Department of Humanitarian Affairs, in coordination with the international community and the Government of Rwanda, to alleviate the intolerable conditions in Rwandan prisons. It calls on the international community to continue its assistance in this regard and encourages the Rwandan Government to continue its efforts to improve the situation in the prisons. The Council underlines the importance of parallel action by the Rwandan Government to restore the Rwandan judicial system and requests the international community to assist the Rwandan Government in this urgent task.

The Security Council underlines that sound economic foundations are also vital for achieving lasting stability in Rwanda. In this respect, it welcomes the increased commitments and funds pledged for the Government's Programme of National Reconciliation and Socio-Economic Rehabilitation and Recovery following the mid-term review of the Geneva Round-Table Conference, and calls on the international community to continue to support Rwanda's rehabilitation process.

The Security Council will remain seized of the matter.

*Meeting number.* SC 3588.

**Report of the Secretary-General (December).** On 1 December, the Secretary-General reported[(48)] that the humanitarian situation in Rwanda continued to improve, with steady progress in the transition from emergency relief to rehabilitation, reconstruction and development. A complex relationship existed between several critical areas: reintegration of refugees; prison overcrowding and rehabilitation of the justice system; security for returnees at the communal level; and insufficient housing and scarcity of serviceable land.

During September and October, a total of 32,190 refugees returned to Rwanda, mainly from UNHCR-organized convoys. The rate of return from Tanzania increased from 1,000 returnees in September to 2,000 in October, of whom 1,144 were new case-load refugees. Approximately 19,000 refugees had returned from Zaire. Voluntary repatriation from Burundi fell from 7,773 in September to 1,012 in October. The low number of returnees could be attributed to the continuing campaign of intimidation and misinformation in the refugee camps; fear that their suspected role in the genocide would expose them to reprisal, denunciation or imprisonment; the affirmation by Rwanda that although refugees were welcomed to return, those involved in planning or carrying out the genocide would face imprisonment; and the shortage of adequate housing. To pre-empt drastic measures by countries of asylum and avoid the chaos and probable violence that massive repatriation would trigger inside Rwanda, UNHCR was encouraging large-scale organized voluntary repatriation. It also strengthened mass information campaigns, exchange visits of officials and refugees and regular monitoring of returnees within Rwanda, together with Human Rights Field Operation officers and UNAMIR military and police observers.

Some improvement in the socio-economic sectors had occurred, and the first effective step towards the revival of the national judicial system had been taken, with the appointment by the National Assembly on 17 October of six Supreme Court judges.

The prison population continued to grow and had reached 60,000. The Rwandan Prison Commission took emergency measures to create additional space for prisoners, leading to noticeably fewer deaths and better medical facilities. Prisoners were transferred to the extensions and temporary detention centres. There was frustration both in Rwanda and within the international community over the delay in restoring the procedures of justice throughout the country. A conference on genocide held in Kigali from 2 to 5 November focused on issues that the justice system would need to address, such as special courts for those accused of genocide, degrees of culpability and plea bargaining.

Progress continued to be made within Rwanda on security and normalization, but an atmosphere of tension and instability pervaded the region. Relations between Rwanda and both Zaire and Kenya had deteriorated and conditions in Burundi also contributed to the tension. In Rwanda itself, no major incidents of violence involving civilians were reported. However, there was a noticeable increase in insurgent activities in the western prefectures. Security was markedly better in areas where formed UNAMIR troops were present than in those areas where only military observers were stationed. The International Commission of Inquiry, established to investigate reports of military training and arms transfers to former Rwandese government forces, began its work on 3 November.

UNAMIR civilian police continued to train the Rwandan National Police Force. So far, 403 new gendarmes had completed the programme, with 515 more scheduled to complete training on 20 December.

The overall food situation improved, permitting reductions in the food-aid allocations to populations at risk. However, several regions in Rwanda remained areas of concern, owing to the high concentration of former displaced persons or returnees with no assets or income.

The Secretary-General observed that a large part of the international community believed that a further six-month extension of UNAMIR's current mandate was desirable. UNAMIR's role could be only one of facilitation. The principal responsibility for providing security and material support for the return of the refugees lay with Rwanda. The continued presence of UNAMIR could help to build confidence among the refugees and encourage them to take the decision to return. However, Rwanda had officially informed him on 24 November[49] that it did not agree to an extension of the UNAMIR mandate beyond its expiration on 8 December, as it felt the Mission did not serve the real needs of Rwanda. It would be receptive to a continued UN presence, provided its purpose was to assist Rwanda in rehabilitation and reconstruction, including the provision of technical expertise, financial assistance and equipment. The Secretary-General stated that he would therefore initiate a drawdown of the operation as of 8 December. The withdrawal process would take two to three months to complete, during which time UNAMIR would ensure the smooth and peaceful departure of UN military personnel and equipment.

The Secretary-General recommended that the United Nations maintain a political presence in Rwanda after the withdrawal of UNAMIR. A UN office, headed by his Special Representative, could be established to further, in consultation with Rwanda, the search for peace and stability through justice and reconciliation. His Special Representative would have overall authority for the coordination and expansion of the assistance that the United Nations and the international community were providing in support of Rwanda's rehabilitation and reconstruction efforts. Rwanda had also requested in August that the equipment belonging to UNAMIR be left to the Government after its departure. The Secretary-General said that was clearly an issue on which only the General Assembly could decide.

**SECURITY COUNCIL ACTION (December)**

The Security Council met on 8 December to consider the situation in Rwanda. It adopted **resolution 1028(1995)**.

*The Security Council,*

*Recalling* all its previous resolutions on the situation in Rwanda, in particular its resolution 997(1995) of 9 June 1995,

*Having considered* the report of the Secretary-General on the United Nations Assistance Mission for Rwanda (UNAMIR) of 1 December 1995,

1. *Decides* to extend the mandate of UNAMIR for a period expiring on 12 December 1995;

2. *Decides* to remain actively seized of the matter.

Security Council resolution 1028(1995)

8 December 1995     Meeting 3604     Adopted unanimously

Draft prepared in consultations among Council members (S/1995/1019).

The Council met again on 12 December and adopted **resolution 1029(1995)**.

*The Security Council,*

*Recalling* all its previous resolutions on the situation in Rwanda, in particular its resolution 872(1993) of 5 October 1993 by which it established the United Nations Assistance Mission for Rwanda (UNAMIR), and its resolutions 912(1994) of 21 April 1994, 918(1994) of 17 May 1994, 925(1994) of 8 June 1994, 965(1994) of 30 November 1994 and 997(1995) of 9 June 1995, which set out the mandate of UNAMIR,

*Recalling* its resolution 955(1994) of 8 November 1994, establishing the International Tribunal for Rwanda, and its resolution 978(1995) of 27 February 1995, concerning the necessity for the arrest of persons suspected of committing genocide in Rwanda,

*Having considered* the report of the Secretary-General on UNAMIR dated 1 December 1995,

*Noting* the letters of the Foreign Minister of Rwanda to the Secretary-General of 13 August 1995 and 24 November 1995,

*Stressing* the importance of the voluntary and safe repatriation of Rwandan refugees and of genuine national reconciliation,

*Noting with great concern* continuing reports of military preparations and incursions into Rwanda by elements of the former regime, underlining the need for effective measures to ensure that Rwandan nationals currently in neighbouring countries, including those in camps, do not undertake military activities aimed at destabilizing Rwanda or receive arms supplies, in view of the great likelihood that such arms are intended for use within Rwanda, and welcoming in this context the establishment of the International Commission of Inquiry pursuant to its resolution 1013(1995) of 7 September 1995,

*Underlining* the need for increased efforts to assist the Government of Rwanda in the promotion of a climate of confidence and trust in order to facilitate the return of Rwandan refugees in neighbouring countries,

*Emphasizing* the necessity for the accelerated disbursement of international assistance for the rehabilitation and reconstruction of Rwanda,

*Welcoming* the Summit of the Heads of State of the Great Lakes Region held in Cairo on 28-29 November and the Declaration of 29 November 1995 issued by them,

*Emphasizing* the importance of all States acting in accordance with the recommendations adopted by the Regional Conference on Assistance to Refugees, Returnees and Displaced Persons in the Great Lakes Region held in Bujumbura in February 1995 and those contained in the Cairo Declaration,

*Commending* the Government of Rwanda's continuing efforts to maintain peace and security as well as to reconstruct and rehabilitate the country,

*Recognizing* the valuable contribution that the human rights officers deployed by the High Commissioner for Human Rights to Rwanda have made towards the improvement of the overall situation,

*Acknowledging* the responsibility of the Government of Rwanda for the safety and security of all UNAMIR personnel and other international staff serving in the country,

1. *Decides* to extend the mandate of UNAMIR for a final period until 8 March 1996;

2. *Decides also*, in the light of current efforts to restore peace and stability through the voluntary and safe repatriation of Rwandan refugees, to adjust the mandate of UNAMIR so that UNAMIR will:

*(a)* Exercise its good offices to assist in achieving the voluntary and safe repatriation of Rwandan refugees within the frame of reference of the recommendations of the Bujumbura Conference and the Cairo Summit of the Heads of State of the Great Lakes Region, and in promoting genuine national reconciliation;

*(b)* Assist the Government of Rwanda in facilitating the voluntary and safe return of refugees and, to this end, to support the Government of Rwanda in its ongoing efforts to promote a climate of confidence and trust through the performance of monitoring tasks;

*(c)* Assist the United Nations High Commissioner for Refugees and other international agencies in the provision of logistical support for the repatriation of refugees;

*(d)* Contribute, with the agreement of the Government of Rwanda, to the protection of the International Tribunal for Rwanda as an interim measure until alternative arrangements agreed with the Government of Rwanda can be put in place;

3. *Requests* the Secretary-General to reduce the force level of UNAMIR to 1,200 troops to carry out the mandate set out in paragraph 2 above;

4. *Requests* the Secretary-General to reduce the number of military observers and headquarters and other military support staff to 200;

5. *Requests* the Secretary-General to initiate planning for the complete withdrawal of UNAMIR after the expiry of the present mandate, that withdrawal to take place within a period of six weeks after the expiry of the mandate;

6. *Requests* the Secretary-General to withdraw the Civilian Police component of UNAMIR;

7. *Requests* the Secretary-General to examine, in the context of existing United Nations regulations, the feasibility of transferring UNAMIR non-lethal equipment, as elements of UNAMIR withdraw, for use in Rwanda;

8. *Takes note* of the cooperation existing between the Government of Rwanda and UNAMIR in the implementation of its mandate and urges the Government of Rwanda and UNAMIR to continue to implement the Status-of-Mission Agreement of 5 November 1993 and any subsequent agreement to replace that Agreement in order to facilitate the implementation of the new mandate;

9. *Calls upon* the Government of Rwanda to take all necessary measures to ensure that UNAMIR personnel and equipment that are scheduled to withdraw can do so in an orderly and safe manner;

10. *Commends* the efforts of States, United Nations agencies and non-governmental organizations which have provided humanitarian assistance to refugees and displaced persons in need, encourages them to continue such assistance, and calls upon the Government of Rwanda to continue to facilitate their delivery and distribution;

11. *Calls upon* States and donor agencies to fulfil their earlier commitments to give assistance for Rwanda's rehabilitation efforts, to increase such assistance, and in particular to support the early and effective functioning of the International Tribunal and the rehabilitation of the Rwandan justice system;

12. *Also calls upon* States to cooperate fully with the International Commission of Inquiry established pursuant to resolution 1013(1995);

13. *Encourages* the Secretary-General and his Special Representative to continue to coordinate the activities of the United Nations in Rwanda, including those of the organizations and agencies active in the humanitarian and developmental field, and of the human rights officers;

14. *Requests* the Secretary-General to report to the Council by 1 February 1996 on the discharge by UNAMIR of its mandate and progress towards repatriation of refugees;

15. *Decides* to remain actively seized of the matter.

Security Council resolution 1029(1995)

12 December 1995     Meeting 3605     Adopted unanimously

Draft prepared in consultations among Council members (S/1995/1015).

**Further developments.** In a 21 December letter to the Security Council President,[50] Rwanda responded to statements about the situation in Rwanda made by the Secretary-General during a press conference on 18 December.

On 22 December, the General Assembly, in **resolution 50/58 L**, requested the Secretary-General to consult with Rwanda and relevant UN agencies on the nature of a continued UN presence in Rwanda after 8 March 1996 and on the role such a presence might play in furthering the search for peace and stability through justice, reconciliation and refugee return and in assisting Rwanda in its pressing task of rehabilitation and reconstruction.

The Secretary-General later reported that Rwanda's relations with its neighbours, especially Tanzania and Zaire, had improved. President Bizimungu visited Tanzania on 14 December and held discussions with the newly elected President, Benjamin Mkapa. The Foreign Minister of Rwanda also visited Kinshasa, Zaire. The International Tribunal for Rwanda issued its first indictments on 12 December, so as to carry forward the process of bringing to justice persons accused of genocide and crimes against humanity. In December, the number of returnees increased slightly. More than 13,500 refugees returned to Rwanda compared to 6,700 in November. That increase was due to an influx of refugees from Burundi, when 5,499 returnees crossed the border in UNHCR-organized convoys between 19 and 23 December. At the Rwanda/Zaire/UNHCR Tripartite Commission meeting (Geneva, 20 December), the parties expressed strong concern at the recent decline in the repatriation of refugees to Rwanda. In a joint communiqué, Rwanda reaffirmed its commitment to establish the necessary conditions for the safe return of refugees and to strengthen its capacity to welcome them, while Zaire reaffirmed its commitment to rid the camps of those resorting to intimidation to block the return of refugees. The Rwanda/Tanzania/UNHCR Tripartite Commission held its third meeting in Kigali on 7 and 8 December. The "go and see" visits of refugees to Rwanda continued during December. On 15 December, UNDP and the Rwandan Ministry of Planning signed a project for the urgent urban resettlement of refugees.

A one-year, $1.5 million project, financed by the United Kingdom and to be executed by the UN Centre for Human Settlements, in cooperation with the Ministry of Rehabilitation and Social Integration, would facilitate the resettlement of returnees in urban and semi-urban areas by preparing and developing sites. On 9 December, UNDP also signed a preparatory assistance project to support the same Ministry in the implementation of the Government's accelerated plan of action for the reinstallation and reinsertion of refugees and formerly displaced persons. That would reinforce the Government and local administration capacity to plan, implement, monitor and evaluate activities at both the national and local levels. Co-financed by the Netherlands, the one-year project, costing $1,159,000, would be executed by the UN Office for Project Services.

### Financing of UNAMIR

In March, the Secretary-General presented revised cost estimates for UNAMIR[51] amounting to $158,449,600 gross ($156,371,700 net) for the period 10 December 1994 to 9 June 1995; cost estimates of $141,832,300 gross ($139,286,300 net), or the equivalent of $21,169,000 gross ($20,789,000 net) per month, for the period 10 June to 31 December 1995; and cost estimates of $126,912,900 gross ($124,634,400 net) for the period 1 January to 30 June 1996.

**GENERAL ASSEMBLY ACTION**

In April, the General Assembly, having considered the Secretary-General's proposals and the comments of ACABQ,[52] adopted **decision 49/481**.

#### Financing of the United Nations Observer Mission Uganda-Rwanda and the United Nations Assistance Mission for Rwanda

At its 100th plenary meeting, on 6 April 1995, the General Assembly, on the recommendation of the Fifth Committee, recalling its resolution 49/20 A of 29 November 1994 and pending its review of the report of the Secretary-General and of the report of the Advisory Committee on Administrative and Budgetary Questions on the financing of the United Nations Observer Mission Uganda-Rwanda and the United Nations Assistance Mission for Rwanda:

*(a)* Authorized the Secretary-General to enter into commitments up to the amount of 80 million United States dollars gross (79,502,500 dollars net) for the operation of the Assistance Mission for the period from 10 December 1994 to 9 June 1995, in addition to the com-

mitment authority in the amount of 60 million dollars gross (58,542,300 dollars net) already granted by the General Assembly in accordance with resolution 49/20 A;

*(b)* Decided, as an ad hoc arrangement, to apportion the amount of 30 million dollars gross (29,271,150 dollars net) for the period from 10 February to 9 April 1995, in addition to the amount of 30 million dollars gross (29,271,150 dollars net) already apportioned in accordance with resolution 49/20 A, among Member States in accordance with the composition of groups set out in paragraphs 3 and 4 of General Assembly resolution 43/232 of 1 March 1989, as adjusted by the Assembly in its resolutions 44/192 B of 21 December 1989, 45/269 of 27 August 1991, 46/198 A of 20 December 1991 and 47/218 A of 23 December 1992 and its decision 48/472 A of 23 December 1993, and the scale of assessments for the year 1995;

*(c)* Also decided that, in accordance with the provisions of its resolution 973(X) of 15 December 1955, there should be set off against the apportionment among Member States, as provided for in subparagraph *(b)* above, their respective share in the Tax Equalization Fund of the estimated additional staff assessment income of 728,850 dollars for the period from 10 February to 9 April 1995;

*(d)* Took note of the status of contributions to the Observer Mission and to the Assistance Mission as at 30 March 1995, including the contributions outstanding in the amount of 46,468,705 dollars to the Special Account for the United Nations Assistance Mission for Rwanda, and urged all Member States concerned to make every possible effort to ensure the payment of their outstanding assessed contributions promptly and in full;

*(e)* Authorized the Secretary-General to enter into commitments up to the amount of 19,558,000 dollars gross (19,204,000 dollars net) for the period from 10 June to 9 July 1995, should the Security Council extend the mandate of the Assistance Mission beyond 9 June 1995.

General Assembly decision 49/481

Adopted without vote

Approved by Fifth Committee (A/49/687/Add.1) without vote, 31 March (meeting 53); draft by Chairman (A/C.5/49/L.46), based on informal consultations and orally revised; agenda items 127 & 130.
*Meeting numbers.* GA 49th session: 5th Committee 52, 53; plenary 100.

On 12 July, the Assembly, having reviewed those reports and also a report by the Secretary-General on the financial performance of UNAMIR from 5 April to 9 December 1994,[53] adopted **resolution 49/20 B**.

#### Financing of the United Nations Observer Mission Uganda-Rwanda and the United Nations Assistance Mission for Rwanda

*The General Assembly,*

*Having considered* the report of the Secretary-General on the financing of the United Nations Observer Mission Uganda-Rwanda and the United Nations Assistance Mission for Rwanda and the related report of the Advisory Committee on Administrative and Budgetary Questions,

*Recalling* Security Council resolutions 846(1993) of 22 June 1993 and 872(1993) of 5 October 1993, by which the Council established, respectively, the United Nations Observer Mission Uganda-Rwanda and the United Nations Assistance Mission for Rwanda, as well as the subsequent resolutions by which the Council extended the mandate of the Assistance Mission, the most recent of which was resolution 997(1995) of 9 June 1995,

*Recalling also* its resolution 48/245 of 5 April 1994 on the financing of the Observer Mission, its resolution 48/248 of 5 April 1994 and its decisions 48/479 A of 23 December 1993 and 48/479 B of 14 September 1994 on the financing of the Assistance Mission and its resolution 49/20 A of 29 November 1994 and its decision 49/481 of 6 April 1995 on the financing of the Observer Mission and the Assistance Mission,

*Reaffirming* that the costs of the Assistance Mission are expenses of the Organization to be borne by Member States in accordance with Article 17, paragraph 2, of the Charter of the United Nations,

*Recalling* its previous decisions regarding the fact that, in order to meet the expenditures caused by the Assistance Mission, a different procedure is required from that applied to meet expenditures of the regular budget of the United Nations,

*Taking into account* the fact that the economically more developed countries are in a position to make relatively larger contributions and that the economically less developed countries have a relatively limited capacity to contribute towards such an operation,

*Bearing in mind* the special responsibilities of the States permanent members of the Security Council, as indicated in General Assembly resolution 1874(S-IV) of 27 June 1963, in the financing of such operations,

*Mindful* of the fact that it is essential to provide the Assistance Mission with the necessary financial resources to enable it to fulfil its responsibilities under the relevant resolutions of the Security Council,

1. *Takes note* of the status of contributions to the United Nations Assistance Mission for Rwanda as at 16 June 1995, including the contributions outstanding in the amount of 66,539,201 United States dollars, and urges all Member States concerned to make every possible effort to ensure the payment of their outstanding assessed contributions;

2. *Expresses concern* about the financial situation with regard to peace-keeping activities, particularly as regards the reimbursement of troop- and equipment-contributing countries, due to overdue payments by Member States of their assessments, particularly Member States in arrears;

3. *Urges* all Member States to make every possible effort to ensure payment of their assessed contributions to the Assistance Mission promptly and in full;

4. *Endorses* the observations and recommendations contained in the report of the Advisory Committee on Administrative and Budgetary Questions, subject to the provisions of the present resolution, and urges the Secretary-General to take the recommendations into account in the management of this operation and the formulation of future budget proposals;

5. *Requests* the Secretary-General to take all necessary action to ensure that the Assistance Mission is administered with a maximum of efficiency and economy;

6. *Decides* to appropriate to the Special Account for the United Nations Assistance Mission for Rwanda a total amount of 143,417,100 dollars gross (141,461,900 dollars net) for the operation of the Assistance Mission for the period from 10 December 1994 to 9 June 1995, inclusive of the commitment authority of 60 million dol-

lars gross (58,542,300 dollars net) authorized under the provisions of General Assembly resolution 49/20 A and 80 million dollars gross (79,502,500 dollars net) authorized under the provisions of Assembly decision 49/481;

7. *Decides also*, as an ad hoc arrangement, to apportion the additional amount of 83,417,100 dollars gross (82,919,600 dollars net) for the period from 10 December 1994 to 9 June 1995, taking into account the amount of 30 million dollars gross (29,271,150 dollars net) already apportioned in accordance with resolution 49/20 A and 30 million dollars gross (29,271,150 dollars net) already apportioned in accordance with General Assembly decision 49/481 among Member States in accordance with the composition of groups set out in paragraphs 3 and 4 of Assembly resolution 43/232 of 1 March 1989, as adjusted by the Assembly in its resolutions 44/192 B of 21 December 1989, 45/269 of 27 August 1991, 46/198 A of 20 December 1991 and 47/218 A of 23 December 1992, and its decision 48/472 A of 23 December 1993, the scale of assessments for the year 1994 to be applied against a portion thereof, that is, 10,083,386 dollars gross (10,023,248 dollars net), which is the amount pertaining on a *pro rata* basis to the period ending 31 December 1994, and the scale of assessments for the year 1995 to be applied against the balance, that is, 73,333,714 dollars gross (72,896,352 dollars net), for the period from 1 January to 9 June 1995;

8. *Decides further* that, in accordance with the provisions of its resolution 973(X) of 15 December 1955, there shall be set off against the apportionment among Member States, as provided for in paragraph 7 above, their respective share in the Tax Equalization Fund of the estimated additional staff assessment income of 497,500 dollars approved for the period from 10 December 1994 to 9 June 1995, 60,138 dollars being the amount pertaining on a *pro rata* basis to the period ending 31 December 1994, and the balance, that is, 437,362 dollars, for the period from 1 January to 9 June 1995;

9. *Decides*, as an interim measure, pending presentation of the revised cost estimate by the Secretary-General and the report of the Advisory Committee thereon, to appropriate to the Special Account for the United Nations Assistance Mission for Rwanda a total amount of 109,951,900 dollars gross (107,584,300 dollars net) for the operation of the Assistance Mission for the period from 10 June to 31 December 1995;

10. *Decides also*, as an ad hoc arrangement, to apportion the amount of 99,628,200 dollars gross (97,508,000 dollars net) for the maintenance of the Assistance Mission for the period from 10 June to 8 December 1995 in accordance with the scheme set out in the present resolution;

11. *Decides further* that, in accordance with the provisions of resolution 973(X), there shall be set off against the apportionment among Member States, as provided for in paragraph 10 above, their respective share in the Tax Equalization Fund of the estimated staff assessment income of 2,120,200 dollars approved for the period from 10 June to 8 December 1995;

12. *Decides* that there shall be set off against the apportionment among Member States, as provided for in paragraph 10 above, their respective share in the unencumbered balance for the period from 5 April to 9 December 1994, the exact amount to be determined by the Advisory Committee no later than 14 July 1995;

13. *Requests* the Secretary-General, in the light of Security Council resolution 997(1995), to submit to the General Assembly, no later than 31 October 1995, revised budget proposals for the periods from 10 June to 31 December 1995 and from 1 January to 30 June 1996;

14. *Invites* voluntary contributions to the Assistance Mission in cash and in the form of services and supplies acceptable to the Secretary-General, to be administered, as appropriate, in accordance with the procedure established by the General Assembly in its resolutions 43/230 of 21 December 1988, 44/192 A of 21 December 1989 and 45/258 of 3 May 1991;

15. *Decides* to include in the provisional agenda of its fiftieth session the item entitled "Financing of the United Nations Assistance Mission for Rwanda".

General Assembly resolution 49/20 B

12 July 1995     Meeting 105     Adopted without vote

Approved by Fifth Committee (A/49/687/Add.2) without vote, 7 July (meeting 62); draft by Chairman (A/C.5/49/L.59), based on informal consultations; agenda items 127 & 130.

*Meeting numbers.* GA 49th session: 5th Committee 57, 60, 62; plenary 105.

In November, the Secretary-General presented revised cost estimates[54] of $96,685,400 gross ($94,880,600 net) for UNAMIR for the period from 10 June to 31 December 1995 and $51,733,200 gross ($50,417,400 net) from 1 January to 30 June 1996.

On 23 December, the Assembly adopted **resolution 50/211 A**.

### Financing of the United Nations Assistance Mission for Rwanda

*The General Assembly,*

*Having considered* the report of the Secretary-General on the financing of the United Nations Assistance Mission for Rwanda and the related oral report of the Chairman of the Advisory Committee on Administrative and Budgetary Questions,

*Recalling* Security Council resolution 1029(1995) of 12 December 1995, by which the Council adjusted and extended the mandate of the Assistance Mission for a final period until 8 March 1996, as well as all previous Council resolutions on the Assistance Mission,

*Recalling also* its resolution 48/248 of 5 April 1994 on the financing of the Assistance Mission and its subsequent resolutions and decisions thereon, the latest of which was resolution 49/20 B of 12 July 1995,

*Reaffirming* that the costs of the Assistance Mission are expenses of the Organization to be borne by Member States in accordance with Article 17, paragraph 2, of the Charter of the United Nations,

*Recalling further* its previous decisions regarding the fact that, in order to meet the expenditures caused by the Assistance Mission, a different procedure is required from that applied to meet expenditures of the regular budget of the United Nations,

*Taking into account* the fact that the economically more developed countries are in a position to make relatively larger contributions and that the economically less developed countries have a relatively limited capacity to contribute towards such an operation,

*Bearing in mind* the special responsibilities of the States permanent members of the Security Council, as indicated in General Assembly resolution 1874(S-IV) of 27 June 1963, in the financing of such operations,

*Mindful* of the fact that it is essential to provide the Assistance Mission with the necessary financial resources to enable it to fulfil its responsibilities under the relevant resolutions of the Security Council,

1. *Takes note* of the status of contributions to the United Nations Assistance Mission for Rwanda as at 19 December 1995, including the contributions outstanding in the amount of 74,322,512 United States dollars, representing 17 per cent of the total assessed contributions from the inception of the Assistance Mission to the period ending 8 December 1995, notes that some 22 per cent of the Member States have paid their assessed contributions in full, and urges all other Member States concerned, particularly those in arrears, to ensure the payment of their outstanding assessed contributions;

2. *Expresses concern* about the financial situation with regard to peace-keeping activities, particularly as regards the reimbursement of troop contributors, notably those troop-contributing Member States that have paid their assessed contributions in full, which bear an additional burden owing to overdue payments by Member States of their assessments;

3. *Urges* all Member States to make every possible effort to ensure payment of their assessed contributions to the Assistance Mission promptly and in full;

4. *Endorses*, on an exceptional basis, in the absence of a written report, the oral observations and recommendations presented by the Chairman of the Advisory Committee on Administrative and Budgetary Questions;

5. *Requests* the Secretary-General to take all necessary action to ensure that the Assistance Mission is administered with a maximum of efficiency and economy;

6. *Decides* to appropriate to the Special Account for the United Nations Assistance Mission for Rwanda the amount of 32,324,500 dollars gross (31,828,900 dollars net) for the operation of the Assistance Mission for the period from 1 January to 8 March 1996;

7. *Decides also*, as an ad hoc arrangement, to apportion the amount of 32,324,500 dollars gross (31,828,900 dollars net) for the period from 1 January to 8 March 1996 among Member States in accordance with the composition of groups set out in paragraphs 3 and 4 of General Assembly resolution 43/232 of 1 March 1989, as adjusted by the Assembly in its resolutions 44/192 B of 21 December 1989, 45/269 of 27 August 1991, 46/198 A of 20 December 1991 and 47/218 A of 23 December 1992 and its decisions 48/472 A of 23 December 1993 and 50/451 B of 23 December 1995, and taking into account the scale of assessments for the year 1996;

8. *Decides further* that, in accordance with the provisions of its resolution 973(X) of 15 December 1955, there shall be set off against the apportionment among Member States, as provided for in paragraph 7 above, their respective share in the Tax Equalization Fund of the estimated staff assessment income of 495,600 dollars for the period from 1 January to 8 March 1996, inclusive;

9. *Invites* voluntary contributions to the Assistance Mission in cash and in the form of services and supplies acceptable to the Secretary-General, to be administered, as appropriate, in accordance with the procedure established by the General Assembly in its resolutions 43/230 of 21 December 1988, 44/192 A of 21 December 1989 and 45/258 of 3 May 1991;

10.  *Decides* to keep the agenda item entitled "Financing of the United Nations Assistance Mission for Rwanda" under review during the fiftieth session.

General Assembly resolution 50/211 A

23 December 1995    Meeting 100    Adopted without vote

Approved by Fifth Committee (A/50/848) without vote, 21 December (meeting 44); draft by Chairman (A/C.5/50/L.23), based on informal consultations; agenda item 135.
*Meeting numbers.* GA 50th session: 5th Committee 43, 44; plenary 100.

Also on 23 December, the Assembly, by **decision 50/469**, decided that the Fifth Committee should continue consideration of the agenda item on the financing of UNAMIR at its resumed fiftieth session.

*REFERENCES*

[1]S/1995/112. [2]S/1995/164. [3]YUN 1993, p. 284. [4]YUN 1994, p. 299, SC res. 955(1994), 8 Nov. 1994. [5]S/1995/65. [6]YUN 1994, p. 282. [7]Ibid., p. 295. [8]S/1995/127. [9]S/PRST/1995/7. [10]S/1995/304. [11]S/1995/310. [12]S/PRST/1995/22. [13]S/1995/411. [14]S/1995/457. [15]A/50/275-S/1995/555. [16]S/1995/552. [17]S/PRST/1995/41. [18]S/1995/762. [19]S/1995/784. [20]YUN 1994, p. 296. [21]S/1995/736. [22]S/1995/735. [23]S/1995/774. [24]S/1995/945. [25]S/1995/946. [26]S/1995/1001. [27]YUN 1994, p. 285, SC res. 918(1994), 17 May 1994. [28]S/1995/547. [29]S/1995/683. [30]S/1995/722. [31]S/1995/723. [32]S/1996/82. [33]S/1995/678. [34]S/1995/761. [35]S/1995/880. [36]S/1995/879. [37]A/C.5/50/27. [38]A/50/7/Add.4. [39]A/50/743. [40]YUN 1993, p. 285, SC res. 872(1993), 5 Oct. 1993. [41]Ibid., p. 284, SC res. 846(1993), 22 June 1993. [42]S/1995/107 & Add.1. [43]YUN 1994, p. 311, SC res. 965(1994), 30 Nov. 1994. [44]S/1995/130. [45]S/1995/297. [46]S/1995/848. [47]S/PRST/1995/53. [48]S/1995/1002. [49]S/1995/1018. [50]S/1995/1055. [51]A/49/375/Add.2. [52]A/49/501/Add.1. [53]A/49/375/Add.3. [54]A/50/712.

# Sierra Leone

In 1995, the Security Council addressed the seriously deteriorating situation in Sierra Leone, which had resulted from a civil conflict begun in 1991. The Secretary-General in February 1995 reported that about 10 per cent of the country's population were now refugees in neighbouring countries and at least 30 per cent were internally displaced. Vital infrastructure had been destroyed and three quarters of the national budget was being spent on defence. If that continued, the Secretary-General said, the conflict in Sierra Leone would further complicate the problem of bringing peace to Liberia and could have a more general destabilizing effect in the region. On 7 February, the Security Council welcomed the Secretary-General's decision to appoint Berhanu Dinka (Ethiopia) as his Special Envoy for Sierra Leone, to work with the parties towards a negotiated settlement.

The 1991 conflict had erupted when the forces of the Revolutionary United Front (RUF) launched attacks to overthrow the Government of the All People's Congress (APC). Thousands of civilians had been killed, with many thousands more internally displaced or becoming refugees in Guinea and Liberia. On 29 April 1992, the Government of President Joseph S. Momoh was overthrown by a military coup and a National Provisional Ruling Council (NPRC) was established, with Captain Valentine Strasser as Chairman and Head of State. After regaining control of areas held by RUF in the southern and eastern parts of the country, NPRC announced a unilateral cease-fire in December 1993. Nevertheless, attacks on towns, villages and major highways escalated to unprecedented levels and spread throughout the country. The Secretary-General reported[1] to the Security Council on 7 February that Chairman Strasser had formally requested in November 1994 the good offices of the UN Secretary-General to bring the Government and RUF to negotiations, with the United Nations to serve as intermediary.

A UN mission was sent to Sierra Leone from 15 to 22 December 1994 to explore the possibilities of dialogue between the Government and RUF. During that period, discussions were held with government officials, prominent citizens, religious leaders, resident diplomats and representatives of UN bodies and agencies.

**Report of the Secretary-General (November).** In a 21 November report,[2] the Secretary-General stated that over the last three years, while taking military measures against RUF, the Government of Sierra Leone had followed a two-track political approach: a negotiated settlement with RUF and democratization of the political process, including transition to an elected civilian Government within a fixed time-frame. Prior to requesting the good offices of the Secretary-General, the Government had in November 1994 dispatched a delegation of prominent Sierra Leoneans to the border with Liberia to establish contact with RUF and to pave the way for peace talks. Delegations from the two sides held meetings on 24 November and 4 and 7 December 1994.

The Secretary-General said that his Special Representative had spared no effort to establish contact with RUF. In May 1995, Foday Sankoh, leader of RUF, invited the Special Envoy to visit him at his base, but later changed his mind. Similarly, at the beginning of September, he invited, through the International Committee of the Red Cross (ICRC) in Freetown, a number of prominent Sierra Leoneans to meet with him. The Government agreed to allow those invited to proceed to the meeting. ICRC so informed RUF on 18 September, requesting it to fix a date and venue. So far, he said, no response had been received.

As to the process of democratization, Chairman Strasser on 26 November 1993 had set out a programme of transition to democratic constitutional rule, the Secretary-General stated. Registration of voters was to have been completed between March and June 1994 and presidential elections held in November 1995. However, the continued conflict and limited State resources delayed implementation of the programme by one year. On 27 April 1995, on the occasion of the thirty-fourth anniversary of independence, Chairman Strasser pledged that everything would be done to complete implementation of the transition programme by January 1996, when a democratically elected President would be sworn in.

Following that announcement, the Interim National Electoral Commission (INEC), established in 1994, intensified its activity under the chairmanship of James O. C. Jonah. Its sister organization, the National Commission for Democracy, established in the same year, promoted civic and voter education throughout the country. The UN Electoral Assistance Division had conducted a needs assessment mission from 22 November to 2 December 1994 to identify the technical requirements for organizing the electoral process, including voter registration, polling, civic education, training of electoral officers, legal issues and the electoral timetable.

On 20 June 1995, the Government lifted the ban on political activities, which it had imposed when it came to power, and authorized INEC to register political parties. Fifteen parties had so far registered and had begun campaigning. In order to build broad-based support for the electoral process, a National Consultative Conference was held (Freetown, 15-17 August) with the participation of all political parties, representatives of Government and 78 organizations representing a wide spectrum of civil society. The Conference adopted a system of elections based on proportional representation, a code of conduct for political parties and rules to govern campaign financing. It agreed to hold elections by the end of February 1996 and the date of 26 February was subsequently set. However, the process of voter registration and preparation for the elections was endangered by financial constraints. The Secretary-General planned to convene a donors' conference on electoral assistance to Sierra Leone in New York on 30 November 1995. However, there were some elements within Sierra Leone that sought to derail the electoral process, as was attested by an attempted coup on 2 October, the Secretary-General stated.

After the December 1994 offensive by RUF, the Secretary-General went on, it became clear that the military forces of Sierra Leone were inadequate to confront the challenges they faced. Given the links to the conflict in Liberia, certain regional and other countries provided military and other assistance to Sierra Leone. In addition, NPRC used non–Sierra Leonean military advisers. The military situation on the ground had not changed dramatically since 1994. RUF moved closer to Freetown and captured several villages in Kono District, an area rich in diamonds. Recently, morale and discipline within Sierra Leone's military forces appeared to have improved. The diamond fields of Kono and a number of villages were retaken by government forces in July and August, and the frequency of ambushes on the highways decreased. The Government had expressed its desire to demobilize part of its army, but would need assistance to reintegrate the soldiers into society. In the meantime, the military forces held a seminar on 16 and 17 November with civilians and representatives of political parties to discuss differences of perception and mutual suspicion between the military and the civilian population. It was hoped that the seminar would create a harmonious environment in preparation for the transition to civilian rule.

Concerning the economic situation in Sierra Leone, much of the fighting had taken place in the mineral-rich areas of the south and east and the agriculturally viable regions. As a result, gold and diamond production dropped and exports declined sharply. At the same time, government expenditures rose as a result of the war; it was estimated that some 75 per cent of total revenue was being spent on the war effort. Infrastructure damage was enormous and the humanitarian situation was critical, the Secretary-General reported. Nearly 2 million people, representing close to 50 per cent of the country's population, were internally displaced, the majority flocking to major towns. Only 1.1 million received assistance with any degree of regularity, owing to security constraints. Highways linking Freetown to key population centres were usable only sporadically and the impact on the civilian population was severe. In the eastern and south-eastern areas, which had been totally inaccessible for more than eight months, it was feared that malnutrition would soon reach life-threatening levels. Beginning in September, however, there was a relative improvement in access, allowing humanitarian organizations to deliver relief without armed escorts. Areas in the eastern portion of the country remained inaccessible.

In March 1995, a UN inter-agency consolidated appeal for $14.7 million was launched. The Department of Humanitarian Affairs (DHA) intended to establish a humanitarian assistance coordination unit in Freetown, to support the UN Humanitarian Coordinator.

The Secretary-General observed that while the situation in Sierra Leone had generally been characterized by conflict, human suffering and economic decline, some positive trends were emerging which, if assisted, would contribute to the re-establishment of peace and stability. He urged the international community to demonstrate its solidarity with the people of Sierra Leone by taking some initial steps to signal its commitment to assist the democratization process.

He had instructed DHA and the United Nations Development Programme to field a team of experts to prepare, in collaboration with the Government, a coordinated and workable action plan for the demobilization and reintegration of combatants. He had also instructed the Electoral Assistance Division to work closely with other United Nations agencies to assist INEC in coordinating international observers during the elections and in strengthening national observer groups. In his view, the time had come for the international community to urge RUF to take advantage of his good offices and initiate a process of negotiation. His Special Envoy would be retained in Sierra Leone to continue efforts to establish a dialogue between RUF and the Government and support the process of democratization. His efforts would be coordinated with OAU and the Commonwealth.

**SECURITY COUNCIL ACTION**

The Security Council met on 27 November to consider the situation in Sierra Leone. Following consultations among Council members, the President made a statement on behalf of the Council:[3]

> The Security Council has considered the Secretary-General's report of 21 November on the situation in Sierra Leone. It is deeply concerned at the conflict in that country, and at the suffering resulting from it, in particular that of the nearly two million internally displaced Sierra Leoneans. It calls for an immediate end to the fighting.
>
> The Security Council expresses its appreciation to the Secretary-General for his offer of good offices in Sierra Leone and urges the Revolutionary United Front to take advantage of that offer, thus enabling both parties to enter into negotiations. It thanks the Special Envoy of the Secretary-General for his efforts to that end, in close coordination with the Organization of African Unity, the Commonwealth, the Economic Community of West African States, and other organizations and neighbouring States supporting the negotiations and the process of democratization in Sierra Leone, and welcomes the Secretary-General's decision that his Special Envoy's mission should continue for the time being.
>
> The Security Council stresses the importance it attaches to a coordinated international effort to alleviate the humanitarian situation in Sierra Leone. It welcomes the Secretary-General's efforts in this regard and his initiative in preparing, in collaboration with the Government of Sierra Leone, an action plan for the demobilization and reintegration of combatants.
>
> The Security Council underlines the need for generous humanitarian assistance in a situation in which nearly half the population of the country have been internally displaced, and calls upon Member States

to provide such assistance. The Council commends those humanitarian agencies active in Sierra Leone. The Council deeply deplores attacks on humanitarian convoys and demands that those responsible cease such actions immediately.

> The Security Council welcomes the programme of transition to democratic constitutional rule set by the Government of Sierra Leone, which is crucial to the restoration of peace and stability in that country. It expresses its strong support for the work of the Interim National Electoral Commission (INEC) in preparing for the elections to be held on 26 February 1996. It welcomes the assistance being given by the United Nations to the INEC at the request of the Government of Sierra Leone, and calls upon Member States to provide the fullest possible material and financial support to the INEC in order to ensure the success of the elections, with the broadest possible participation.
>
> The Security Council urges the Secretary-General to continue to monitor closely the situation in Sierra Leone.

*Meeting number.* SC 3597.

*REFERENCES*

[1]S/1995/120. [2]S/1995/975. [3]S/PRST/1995/57.

# Somalia

In 1995, the social, economic and political upheavals in Somalia continued, even as the second UN Operation in Somalia (UNOSOM II) wound down and completed its withdrawal, protected by an international force, at the end of March. Thus ended three years of intense UN and international efforts to address the ongoing crises caused by famine, civil strife and political chaos in that Horn of Africa nation.

The continuing lack of progress in the peace process and in national reconciliation efforts, in particular the lack of sufficient cooperation from the Somali parties over security issues, undermined UN objectives in Somalia and prevented the continuation of the UNOSOM II mandate beyond the end of March 1995, the Security Council stated on 6 April. It reaffirmed that, based on its experience in UNOSOM II, the people of Somalia bore the ultimate responsibility for achieving national reconciliation and restoring peace to Somalia. The international community, it stressed, could only facilitate, encourage and assist the process, but not try to impose any particular solution on it.

The Secretary-General stressed that the withdrawal of UNOSOM did not mean that the United Nations was abandoning Somalia. UN humanitarian operations would continue, with the focus on rehabilitation, recovery and reconstruction in the post-UNOSOM era. There were important lessons to be learned, he added, about the theory and practice of multifunctional peace-keeping operations in conditions of civil war and chaos, and especially about the clear line that needed to be drawn between peace-keeping and enforcement action.

The Secretary-General made a number of proposals for a role for the United Nations after the UNOSOM withdrawal. Subsequently, the UN Political Office for Somalia, with headquarters in Nairobi, Kenya, was opened to maintain contact with political leaders and coordinate UN humanitarian activities throughout the country.

Despite efforts by many factions, the convening of a national reconciliation conference for Somalia did not take place in 1995.

### End of mission in Somalia

The UN Security Council, on 24 April 1992,[1] established the United Nations Operation in Somalia to facilitate and maintain a cease-fire throughout the country, to promote reconciliation and political settlement and to provide urgent humanitarian assistance. That action was taken in the wake of widespread lawlessness and starvation, which occurred throughout Somalia as a result of a clan-based civil war begun in 1991.

During 1992, the tragic conflict continued, with increased human suffering and continued chaos, and widespread banditry diverting the delivery of humanitarian assistance. The UN instituted an urgent airlift operation and continued strict monitoring of the arms embargo imposed in January 1992. On 3 December, in the face of the magnitude of the human tragedy and gravely alarmed by the deterioration of the humanitarian situation,[2] the Security Council authorized action, under Chapter VII of the Charter of the United Nations, by the Unified Task Force (UNITAF). That multinational force, led by the United States, and at its peak more than 30,000 strong, had a mandate to establish a secure environment for humanitarian relief operations in Somalia.

On 26 March 1993, the Council,[3] acknowledging the need for a smooth transition from UNITAF to an expanded UN operation, authorized the mandate for UNOSOM II. Subsequently during 1993 violent attacks took place against UN troops, which had been mandated by the Council to engage in disarmament efforts. In 1994, attacks on and harassment of UN personnel, as well as other difficulties, continued. On 4 November, the Council,[4] in extending the UNOSOM II mandate for a final period until 31 March 1995, affirmed that the mission's primary purpose until its termination was to facilitate political reconciliation in Somalia, and decided that every effort should be made to withdraw all UNOSOM II forces and as-

sets in a secure and orderly manner and as quickly as possible.

**Secretary-General's report.** In a 28 March report,[5] submitted in accordance with a 1994 Security Council request,[4] the Secretary-General made a general assessment of what had been achieved by the United Nations in Somalia with regard to political, humanitarian, military and security matters, the police and justice programme, and financial issues, and provided information on the withdrawal of UNOSOM II. The report also presented some views on the role the United Nations could play in Somalia beyond the conclusion of the UNOSOM II mandate on 31 March 1995.

The Secretary-General stated that the mission, which addressed the concerns of a people and a country caught in the throes of famine, civil war and the collapse of all institutions of government, had been a difficult one that had not attained all its objectives. Nevertheless, the Secretary-General declared, UNOSOM could claim major accomplishments, especially taking into consideration that, in late 1992, an estimated 3,000 men, women and children were dying daily of starvation, a tragedy that had been ended by the international relief effort.

In the area of national reconciliation, through the efforts of UNITAF, UNOSOM I and UNOSOM II, the international community had striven to create an environment conducive for the Somali leaders to achieve that goal, the Secretary-General said.

The most the international community could do for the Somali parties, he went on, was to afford every opportunity for them to agree among themselves on the modalities to re-establish their political and administrative structures based on a broad-based reconciliation, leading to the reconstruction of their country. If the political will to achieve a durable compromise was lacking, he said, the responsibility lay with the Somali leadership.

### Withdrawal phase

In the initial phase of UNOSOM II force withdrawal, troops were redeployed to Mogadishu from Baidoa, Baledogle, Afgoye and Kismayo, the Secretary-General reported in March.[5]

As the troops left, military support to UN agencies, human rights organizations and NGOs was greatly reduced. The final withdrawal phase was assisted by a combined task force, known as "United Shield", with units from France, India, Italy, Malaysia, Pakistan, the United Kingdom and the United States. The withdrawal, which began with the repatriation of some 1,750 Pakistani personnel from 12 to 15 February, proceeded with minimal interruption and was to have been completed by 6 March, three weeks ahead of the time-limit set by the Security Council. On 28 February, the Mogadishu seaport was handed over to the combined task force and closed to commercial traffic. The Special Representative of the Secretary-General, James Victor Gbeho (Ghana), and other UN staff, the Force Commander and remaining UNOSOM staff left Mogadishu that same day. The withdrawal of the rearguard was completed on 2 March, and the combined task force, which had landed in Mogadishu on 28 February to cover the withdrawal, departed on 3 March, bringing operation ''United Shield'' to a successful conclusion.

### Future role of UN

Following the end of operation ''United Shield'', UNOSOM II offices were temporarily relocated to Nairobi, while the Force headquarters closed in Nairobi on 8 March, the Secretary-General reported.[5] Equipment worth $235,761, which was vital for the support of local communities, was donated to Somali district councils. As of 20 March, only 30 international staff continued to operate in Somalia. As soon as the security situation permitted, the Secretary-General stated, international staff would return to Mogadishu where agencies had retained small offices run by Somali nationals. The Secretary-General affirmed that he would continue to make available his good offices to assist Somali factions to arrive at a political settlement and would maintain a political presence in the area for that purpose, the size and mandate of which would depend on whether the factions wanted the United Nations to play a facilitating or mediating role. He stated that he intended to re-establish a UN presence in Mogadishu as soon as practicable.

UNOSOM had been authorized, during its withdrawal phase, to donate essential equipment, including generators, water pumps, office equipment and furniture. UNDP agreed in principle to support institution-building in the post–UNOSOM II era and to assist in strengthening the capacity of regional and district councils for local government and administration.

#### SECURITY COUNCIL ACTION

The Security Council met on 6 April to consider the Secretary-General's report. Following consultations among its members, the President made the following statement on behalf of the Council:[6]

The Security Council has considered carefully the report of the Secretary-General on the situation in Somalia dated 28 March 1995 and notes the successful conclusion of the withdrawal of UNOSOM II forces from Somalia. It expresses its appreciation to those Governments and agencies that have provided the personnel, humanitarian assistance and other support to the peace-keeping operation in Somalia, including those Governments which participated in the multinational operation for UNOSOM's withdrawal. It pays tribute in particular to all personnel who sacrificed their lives in this service.

The Security Council underlines that the timely intervention of UNOSOM II and the humanitarian assistance given to Somalia helped to save many lives and much property, mitigate general suffering and contributed to the search for peace in Somalia. The Council notes that, over the past three years, the United Nations and the international community have made significant efforts to restore peace and stability and facilitate the re-emergence of a civil society. However, the continuing lack of progress in the peace process and in national reconciliation, in particular the lack of sufficient cooperation from the Somali parties over security issues, undermined the United Nations objectives in Somalia and prevented the continuation of the UNOSOM II mandate beyond 31 March 1995.

The Security Council believes that the Somalia operation provides important lessons for the theory and practice of peacemaking, peace-keeping and peace-building.

The Security Council remains convinced that only a genuinely representative and broad-based approach to reconciliation will bring about a lasting political settlement and allow for the re-emergence of a civil society in Somalia. The Council reaffirms, based on its experience in UNOSOM II, that the people of Somalia bear the ultimate responsibility for achieving national reconciliation and restoring peace to Somalia. The international community can only facilitate, encourage and assist the process, but not try to impose any particular solution on it. The Council, therefore, calls upon the Somali parties to pursue national reconciliation, rehabilitation and reconstruction in the interest of peace, security and development.

The Security Council notes the recent agreements reached between the factions in Mogadishu, especially on the control of sea and airport facilities. It expresses the hope that this encouraging development is indicative of a new spirit of cooperation among the factions and that it will lead to further progress in the search for a lasting peace in Somalia.

The Security Council supports the view of the Secretary-General that Somalia should not be abandoned by the United Nations, which will continue to assist the Somali people to achieve a political settlement and to provide humanitarian and other support services, provided that the Somalis themselves demonstrate a disposition to peaceful resolution of the conflict and to cooperation with the international community. It welcomes the Secretary-General's intention to continue a small political mission, should the Somali parties so wish, to assist them in coming together in national reconciliation and looks forward to the report which the Secretary-General has indicated he will forward on this matter. The Council urges close cooperation between the United Nations and regional organizations, in particular the Organization of African Unity (OAU), the League of Arab States and the Organization of the Islamic Conference (OIC), as well as the Governments of neighbouring countries in these efforts. The Council considers it essential that the Somali parties clearly express their acceptance of such assistance and their willingness to cooperate with the United Nations.

The Security Council recognizes that humanitarian assistance in Somalia is an important element in the effort to restore peace and security in the country. It is therefore important to sustain United Nations humanitarian activities in Somalia and to encourage non-governmental organizations to do likewise. However, their ability to do so will depend on the degree of cooperation and security offered by the Somali parties. The Council welcomes the willingness expressed by the international humanitarian agencies and NGOs to continue to provide rehabilitation and reconstruction assistance in areas where security is guaranteed by the Somalis. The Council stresses that the creation of a long-lasting, stable and secure environment throughout the country is vital for the resumption of large-scale activity in these fields.

The Security Council reaffirms the obligations of States to implement fully the embargo on all deliveries of weapons and military equipment to Somalia imposed by paragraph 5 of resolution 733(1992), and calls on States, especially neighbouring States, to refrain from actions capable of exacerbating the conflict in Somalia.

The Security Council requests the Secretary-General to continue to monitor the situation in Somalia and to keep it informed about further developments. The Council will remain seized of the matter.

*Meeting number.* SC 3513.

**Communication.** On 18 April, the Secretary-General brought to the attention of Council members an 11 April press release[7] issued by the Somali National Alliance (SNA), which stated that it was inappropriate to talk about the UN political return to Somalia for the time being, let alone re-establish an office there. SNA stated that the Somali people were capable of sorting out their political differences and achieving their own reconciliation and would not accept any further interference in their political affairs.

In that connection, the Secretary-General stated that he would stay in touch with the parties with a view to overcoming those reservations. He had dispatched a security assessment mission to Mogadishu to determine whether the situation there was sufficiently secure to allow for the establishment of an office. Meanwhile, he had concluded that the retention of a full-time Special Representative at the Under-Secretary-General level could not be justified in view of the limited possibilities for UN political efforts, and he had therefore decided to establish a small political office, headed by a representative at the D-2 level and assisted by two Professional officers and a limited number of support staff. Operating temporarily from Nairobi, it would monitor the situation in Somalia and keep contact with the parties concerned to the extent possible.

On 21 April, the Security Council welcomed[8] the decision of the Secretary-General.

On 31 May, the Secretary-General reported[9] to the Council that a new set of guidelines for Mogadishu had been adopted on the basis of the assessment mission's conclusions, including the provision that international UN staff members be authorized to travel to Mogadishu and stay there no longer than three days a week. However, the instability and unpredictability of security conditions had severely curtailed visits by international staff. He had tried in late April and early May to dispatch special envoys to request the views of Somali leaders concerning a possible UN political presence in their country, but they declined to meet UN envoys. Nevertheless, a wide range of leaders representing the main Somali factions, including a wing of the United Somali Congress (USC)/SNA, had welcomed the Secretary-General's intention to set up an office. He had therefore decided to keep the political office for Somalia operating out of Nairobi until the situation allowed its transfer to Mogadishu and to reduce the staff to one Director and one General Service staff member. On 2 June, the Council agreed[10] with that decision.

## Humanitarian and other aspects

As for humanitarian concerns, the Secretary-General in March reported[5] that, to meet such needs in the post-UNOSOM era, a UN Coordination Team had been established under the chairmanship of the UNDP Resident Representative, who also served as the Humanitarian Coordinator. The Coordination Team interacted with national and international NGOs and the donor community to harmonize and ensure coherence among their activities. A coordinated relationship with recognized district and regional councils was also to be formalized. To cover humanitarian relief needs, the UN Department of Humanitarian Affairs (DHA) launched a consolidated appeal for Somalia for $70 million for the first half of 1995 (see PART FOUR, Chapter III). UN agencies were to support capacity-building programmes, while assisting in relief and initial rehabilitation, focusing on agriculture, fishing and reconstruction. UNDP continued to implement integrated, community-based rehabilitation projects, including those for schools and water systems. It launched credit schemes for women and activities aimed at income generation. UNHCR's quick-impact programmes provided some stability for the more than half a million returning Somali refugees. UN agencies also considered the needs of the large numbers of unemployed, to help revitalize the economy and stimulate productive capacities.

Under a police training programme administered by UNOSOM II, 2,179 policemen had attended refresher courses. At the end of January,

Somali police were at work in 82 district stations, providing a visible presence on the roads and in various communities. Donations of equipment and uniforms were received.

UNOSOM also provided training for judicial personnel in judicial administration and ethics, juvenile justice, sentencing practices and attitudes, human rights and the rule of law. It refurbished courtrooms, and by late March, 11 appeals courts, 11 regional courts and 46 district courts were functioning. UNOSOM also provided 12 prisons with food, water and medical services, and concluded arrangements with the UN Educational, Scientific and Cultural Organization (UNESCO) to begin educational and vocational training programmes in those prisons.

### National reconciliation

In a March report,[5] the Secretary-General stated that the proposed national reconciliation conference still had not taken place. However, in November 1994, the SNA factions had convened a unilateral conference with a view to establishing an interim Government. The Somali Salvation Alliance (SSA) held a parallel meeting in anticipation of that move and to complete plans to establish its own Government. Although those efforts were not successful, discussions reportedly focused on the nature of a federal system of government, powers of the central Government *vis-à-vis* regional authorities, distribution of government posts, and drafting of a transitional charter. In December 1994, the Secretary-General's Special Representative in Somalia, Ambassador James Victor Gbeho (Ghana), met with President Meles Zenawi of Ethiopia to discuss ways of bringing together Ali Mahdi of the SSA faction and General Mohammed Farah Aidid of the SNA faction to resolve their differences over the convening of a genuine national reconciliation conference.

Acting under the authority of the Organization of African Unity (OAU) and the Intergovernmental Authority on Drought and Development, President Zenawi dispatched a fact-finding mission to Somalia at the beginning of January 1995. In March, he sent a delegation of ethnic Somali leaders from Djibouti, Ethiopia and Kenya to persuade political and traditional leaders throughout Somalia to come together to work for national reconciliation. Meanwhile, contacts continued between SSA and SNA factions throughout January and February to discuss new initiatives to break the political impasse. On 6 February, SSA formally presented its proposal for national reconciliation in Somalia, which called for the convening of a unified and all-inclusive national reconciliation conference on 25 February or any agreed date, with the United Nations playing a mediatory and

supportive role. Ali Mahdi of SSA stressed that their proposal was subject to modification and that no one political faction or alliance could form a Government of national unity. Earlier, at the urging of the Special Representative, the two factions in January had established a negotiating committee with a view to setting up joint committees to manage the operations of the Mogadishu seaport and airport. The SNA/SSA negotiating committee was later given a wider mandate to coordinate political and economic matters relating to reconciliation among the Habr Gedir and Mudulood clans; work out modalities for bringing General Aidid and Ali Mahdi together; and merge the two proposed separate meetings on national reconciliation.

On 21 February, a peace agreement was signed by General Aidid and Ali Mahdi on behalf of SNA and SSA to promote national reconciliation and a peaceful settlement. The two sides accepted the principle of power-sharing; pledged to seek the presidency not through military means but through democratic elections; agreed to resolve disputes through dialogue and peaceful means; and agreed on a common platform for tackling problems. The pact also provided for confining "technicals" (combat vehicles) to designated areas; discouraging the open carrying of arms in Mogadishu; removing roadblocks; and reopening the main city markets. Another agreement, endorsed by the two leaders on 23 February, called for the establishment of two joint committees to manage the operations of the Mogadishu airport and seaport. It also provided a basis for cooperation between the Somali parties and the UN system. A third agreement, signed on 5 March by the two leaders, reopened the Mogadishu seaport on 9 March under the administration of the SSA/SNA joint committees.

On 8 March, the two leaders agreed to establish a security committee, comprising militia and police officers from both sides, to ensure the exclusion of unauthorized "technicals" from the airport and seaport and to arrange for the police force to provide security inside those facilities, while joint militias with specially marked "technicals" secured outer perimeters and routes used to deliver commodities to the markets. The committee chairmen were invited to consult with the UN Coordination Team in Nairobi (see below) on arrangements to reactivate civilian operations at the airport and seaport.

In the meantime, the Secretary-General agreed provisionally with the International Civil Aviation Organization (ICAO) to continue to act in civil aviation matters concerning Somalia, pending further guidance from the Council and/or the reestablishment of government authority in Somalia. That agreement, the Secretary-General decided, had a salutary effect on the political process as a whole. As a result, the situation in Mogadishu had improved and both sides seemed to have settled down to serious discussions regarding convening a broad-based national reconciliation conference, establishing a regional council and appointing a governor for the Benadir region (Mogadishu). Of some 92 district councils, 58 had been established, as had 8 of 18 regional councils.

**Further developments.** In a later report,[11] the Secretary-General stated that since the establishment of the United Nations Political Office for Somalia (UNPOS), its Director had opened contacts with all major Somali political factions, except those in the north-west. In May 1995, consultations of the local clans (Digil and Mirifle) on local governance in the Bay and Bakool regions led to the establishment of a regional authority for the two regions, centring on a supreme governing council with rotating leadership among the three Somali Democratic Movement (SDM) factions that had been contending for power there. The authority became a focal point for cooperation with the international aid community. However, on 19 September, it had come to an abrupt end with the incursion of General Aidid's militia into Baidoa.

### Financial and administrative matters

#### Financing of UNOSOM II

In March 1995, the Secretary-General presented revised cost estimates[12] for the maintenance and liquidation of UNOSOM II for the period 1 October 1994 to 31 March 1995, amounting to $290,162,400 gross ($286,664,300 net), and cost estimates of $3,314,100 gross ($2,928,800 net) for the establishment of the temporary UNOSOM II administrative office in Nairobi from 1 April to 30 June. In June, he submitted a final performance report on UNOSOM II from 1 November 1993 to 31 May 1994,[13] and in July, a financial performance report for the period 1 June to 30 September 1994, including a preliminary report on the disposition of UNOSOM's assets and liabilities.[14]

By **decision 49/415 B** of 20 July, the General Assembly, on the recommendation of the Fifth Committee,[15] deferred consideration of the item on the financing of UNOSOM II to its fiftieth session.

In November, the Secretary-General presented a further financial performance report for UNOSOM II[16] indicating additional requirements of $40,540,000 gross ($39,184,800 net) for the period from 1 October 1994 to 31 March 1995, and $1,216,400 gross ($1,064,600 net) for the period from 1 April to 30 June 1995.

In an October report[17] on the activities of the Office of Internal Oversight Services (OIOS) (see PART SIX, Chapter I), the Secretary-General

stated that a resident audit team, posted to Mogadishu from June 1994 to May 1995 to provide continuous audit coverage of UNOSOM II, reviewed procurement, transport and building activities, management services, communications, and finance and accounts. It audited all major contracts and found serious internal control deficiencies, resulting in significant monetary losses to the Organization.

The Assembly, by **decision 50/469** of 23 December, decided that the Fifth Committee should continue consideration of the financing of UNOSOM II at its resumed fiftieth session.

#### UNOSOM theft

On 17 April 1994, the theft of $3.9 million in cash from UNOSOM II headquarters in Mogadishu was reported,[18] and investigations by the UN Office of Internal Oversight Services and by Scotland Yard of the United Kingdom were launched shortly thereafter. The General Assembly in December 1994[19] had asked for a progress report on the OIOS investigation and action to determine responsibility for the theft and to recover the missing funds, as well as disciplinary measures taken and controls put in place to avoid the recurrence of similar incidents in the future.

On 2 February 1995, the Secretary-General submitted that report,[20] which provided details of the circumstances surrounding the theft, including general aspects of the security situation; findings of the investigations; corrective measures taken; and recommendations for further action.

The Secretary-General reported that, despite warnings regarding the lack of security for the cashier's office, where from $1 million to $3 million in cash received weekly was stored, large amounts of cash continued to be kept in the bottom drawer of a reinforced filing cabinet.

Following the investigation, the OIOS investigation team concluded that there had been an incredible lack of concern on the part of the UNOSOM administration for security in both the handling and the safe keeping of the stolen money. The Director of Administration and the Chief Finance Officer had been grossly negligent in the performance of their duties, the team stated, particularly in regard to the institution and maintenance of adequate controls for the management and security of the cash, and that negligence had provided the opportunity for the theft. The Director of Administration resigned but was informed that that would be considered a summary dismissal; he was contesting that decision before the UN Administrative Tribunal. The Chief Finance Officer, who had left the job three weeks before the theft, was denied his repatriation grant and other financial emoluments, a decision which was not contested. A third UNOSOM official, the Chief

Cashier, was found to be generally inadequate for the job and was transferred to another position.

Following the theft, the Secretary-General reported, immediate corrective measures were taken to improve security, including installing a burglar alarm and posting a 24-hour guard at the cashier's office; changing procedures in that office; and using safes which were placed in a locked strongroom.

Other measures were also put in place, including reducing amounts of cash used by UNOSOM II to a minimum and instituting detailed policies on use and physical security of cash.

After the incident, chiefs of administration in all UN peace-keeping missions were asked to take additional precautions to safeguard and protect the Organization's assets, especially cash and blank and signed cheques awaiting collection by vendors.

*REFERENCES*

[1]YUN 1992, p. 202, SC res. 751(1992), 24 Apr. 1992. [2]Ibid., p. 209, SC res. 794(1992), 3 Dec. 1992. [3]YUN 1993, p. 290, SC res. 814(1993), 26 Mar. 1993. [4]YUN 1994, p. 325, SC res. 954(1994), 4 Nov. 1994. [5]S/1995/231. [6]S/PRST/1995/15. [7]S/1995/322. [8]S/1995/323. [9]S/1995/451. [10]S/1995/452. [11]S/1996/42. [12]A/49/563/Add.2. [13]A/49/563/Add.3. [14]A/49/563/Add.4. [15]A/49/757/Add.2. [16]A/50/741. [17]A/50/459. [18]YUN 1994, p. 330. [19]YUN 1994, p. 331, GA res. 49/229, 23 Dec. 1994. [20]A/49/843.

# Other questions

## South Africa

### Cancellation of unpaid assessments

On 14 September 1995, South Africa and Namibia requested[1] the inclusion in the agenda of the fiftieth session of the General Assembly of an item entitled "Normalization of the situation concerning South Africa".

An explanatory memorandum recalled that, following the eradication of apartheid and the establishment of a united, non-racial and democratic South Africa, the international community had invited the South African delegation to resume its participation in the work of the General Assembly on 23 June 1994.

In 1974, the General Assembly had voted not to accept the credentials of the delegation of South Africa. Recalling that South Africa continued to practise its policy of apartheid and racial discrimination against the majority of the population in South Africa, the Assembly, in resolution 3207(XXIX),[2] called on the Security Council to review the relationship between the United Nations and South Africa "in the light of the constant violation by South Africa of the principles of the Charter and the Universal Declaration of Human Rights".

Subsequently, on 30 October 1974, a draft resolution recommending the expulsion of South Africa from the Organization was not adopted by the Security Council, due to the negative votes of three permanent members.[3] On 12 November 1974, the General Assembly, by 91 votes to 22, with 19 abstentions, decided to suspend South Africa from participation in the work of the twenty-ninth session of the Assembly, upholding a ruling to that effect by its President.[4]

The 14 September memorandum explained that during the apartheid era, the Assembly had adopted numerous resolutions in which the policies of apartheid of the Government of South Africa were condemned as a crime against humanity and a negation of the UN Charter. The representatives of apartheid were thus excluded from participation in the Assembly in order to protest those apartheid policies. That step, taken by the international community to isolate the apartheid regime, had been vindicated by the liberation of South Africa. The regime had retaliated by withholding its contribution to the United Nations.

South Africa said it had paid on 3 October 1994 $11 million in respect of its UN assessments, regarding both the regular budget and various peace-keeping operations, as from 23 June 1994. It had thereby fulfilled its undertaking to meet fully and on time its financial obligations to the United Nations.

However, a substantial amount remained attributed to South Africa as so-called "arrears" that had been accumulated during the apartheid period. Therefore, South Africa now found itself confronted with an untenable situation: owing to the assistance of the United Nations, the scourge of apartheid had been eradicated and the people of South Africa liberated. Yet, South Africa continued to be held liable for the arrears accumulated during the apartheid period.

In view of the unique historical circumstances relating to South Africa, it was hoped that the Assembly, which had taken a principled and moral decision to exclude the South African delegation from participation in its work, would once again take a political decision to resolve this outstanding matter. A draft resolution was proposed for adoption by the Assembly, providing an appropriate formula that would hold South Africa responsible solely for contributions relating to the period following 23 June 1994.

On 1 December, the Assembly (**decision 50/402 A**) decided to consider the item in plenary and invited the Fifth Committee to present its technical observations regarding the implementation of any draft resolution on the matter by 12 December.

On that date, the Fifth Committee Chairman, responding[5] to the request of the Assembly President to provide technical observations, said agreement had been reached by the Committee in informal consultations on a number of proposed amendments to the draft resolution submitted on the subject. The Committee, on 12 December, endorsed those amendments.

GENERAL ASSEMBLY ACTION

On 15 December, the General Assembly adopted **resolution 50/83** without vote.

### Normalization of the situation concerning South Africa

*The General Assembly,*

*Recalling* its resolution 48/258 A, adopted by consensus on 23 June 1994, the date on which South Africa was invited to resume its participation in the work of the General Assembly,

*Noting* that South Africa has since that date commenced payment of its assessed contributions,

*Also recalling* the exceptional circumstances pertaining to the resumption of South Africa's participation in the work of the General Assembly following the elimination of apartheid and the establishment of a democratic, non-racial South Africa,

*Recognizing* that, owing to the exceptional circumstances arising from apartheid, South Africa requested not to be held liable for contributions relating to the period from 30 September 1974 to 23 June 1994,

*Recognizing also* that the General Assembly took a moral and political decision to exclude South Africa from participation in its work,

*Recognizing further* that the exclusion of South Africa from the work of the General Assembly was unprecedented,

1. *Accepts,* owing to these exceptional and unique circumstances, South Africa's request not to pay its contributions for the period from 30 September 1974 to 23 June 1994, and decides that the consequent burden for the Organization shall be borne by Member States pursuant to Article 17 of the Charter of the United Nations and the provisions of the present resolution;

2. *Welcomes and endorses* the statement of South Africa that it will waive any credits it would receive in the amount of 549,606 United States dollars, and 737,142 dollars from budgetary surpluses retained in the regular budget and the peace-keeping special accounts, respectively, for the period from 30 September 1974 to 23 June 1994;

3. *Decides* to reduce the net amount of 122,238,000 dollars available as credits to Member States, arising from the implementation of resolutions 2947 A and B (XXVII) of 8 December 1972, 36/116 B of 10 December 1981, 40/241 B of 18 December 1985 and 42/216 A of 21 December 1987, by 53,881,711 dollars, and to waive the share of the credits in the amount of 53,332,105 dollars among other Member States on the basis of the respective scale of assessments contained in resolutions 34/6 A of 25 October 1979, 37/125 A of 17 December 1982 and 40/248 of 18 December 1985, in order to account for the reduction in outstanding contributions resulting from paragraph 1 above;

4. *Also decides* to reduce the amount of 173,392,935 dollars, available as credits to Member States, arising from the implementation of resolutions 33/13 E of 14 December 1978, 34/7 D and 34/9 E of 17 December

1979, 35/45 B of 1 December 1980, 35/115 B of 10 December 1980, 36/66 B of 30 November 1981, 36/138 B of 16 December 1981, 37/38 B of 30 November 1982, 37/127 B of 17 December 1982, 38/35 B of 1 December 1983, 38/38 B of 5 December 1983, 39/28 B of 30 November 1984, 39/71 B of 13 December 1984, 40/59 B of 2 December 1985, 40/246 B of 18 December 1985, 41/44 B of 3 December 1986, 41/179 B of 5 December 1986, 42/70 B of 3 December 1987, 42/223 of 21 December 1987, 43/228 and 43/229 of 21 December 1988, 44/187 and 44/188 of 21 December 1989, 46/194 of 20 December 1991, 47/204 and 47/205 of 22 December 1992 and 49/226 of 23 December 1994, by 40,905,714 dollars and to waive the share of credits in the amount of 40,168,572 dollars among other Member States on the basis of the respective scale of assessments for the period in which the surpluses arose, in order to account for the reduction in outstanding contributions resulting from paragraph 1 above;

5. *Further decides* that, owing to the unique and exceptional circumstances arising from apartheid, the decisions set out in paragraphs 3 and 4 of the present resolution shall under no circumstances constitute a precedent.

General Assembly resolution 50/83

15 December 1995     Meeting 93     Adopted without vote

138-nation draft (A/50/L.44/Rev.1 & Rev.1/Add.1); agenda item 164.
*Meeting numbers.* GA 50th session: 5th Committee 37, 39; plenary 93.

## UN Educational and Training Programme for Southern Africa

Scholarship holders under the UN Educational and Training Programme for Southern Africa (UNETPSA) numbered 1,445 in 1994/95, compared to 2,630 in 1993/94, according to a report of the Secretary-General covering the period 1 September 1994 to 31 August 1995.[6] The Programme, administered by the Secretary-General in consultation with the Advisory Committee on UNETPSA, was financed from a trust fund made up of voluntary contributions from Member States, organizations and individuals. Scholarship assistance was granted to 1,438 students from South Africa, as well as 7 from Namibia. Of these, 766 were new awards.

During the period, $3,125,482 in contributions was received from 13 countries, with additional pledges totalling $21,408 from three countries still outstanding. The amount of $209,781.35 made to the UN Trust Fund for South Africa during 1994/95 was also available to UNETPSA.

The Advisory Committee on UNETPSA held three meetings to consider the development of the Programme in the light of the changing circumstances in South Africa. Most donors refocused their aid in favour of bilateral programmes, which had a negative effect on UNETPSA's funding situation. Several new projects were initiated in cooperation with a broad network of scholarship agencies, educational institutions, NGOs and the Government of South Africa. The

Programme continued to co-sponsor training programmes with *technikons*, teacher training institutions and other institutions involved in distance education, with a focus on teacher upgrading in South Africa to strengthen the educational infrastructure.

The training and placement of cadres for middle- and high-level management in key sectors of science and technology, viewed as a crucial requirement for sustained growth and development in South Africa, remained a priority for the Programme. Concerted efforts were made to include poverty alleviation projects geared towards supporting community economic empowerment, with an emphasis on projects that benefited rural women. Closer relations and consultations with various government ministries resulted in increased support for projects aligned with the needs identified in the Government's Reconstruction and Development Programme. Particular attention was given to enhancing institution- and capacity-building and contributing to South Africa's human resources needs during the transition period and beyond. Administrative costs of UNETPSA were maintained at a minimum through group arrangements with educational institutions in South Africa. A National Programme Officer in South Africa was recruited and deployed as soon as UNDP became operational there.

The Secretary-General appealed for continued financial and other support to the Programme and recommended its extension for three to five years beyond 1994. As with past practice and depending on donor support, full new awards should be given and the maximum three-year period allowed for most degree programmes in South Africa. UNETPSA then had a window of opportunity to sponsor first-year students, who had the hardest time finding sponsors, within the priority fields. In order to integrate the goals of the Programme with the overall multilateral development programmes for the region, the management of UNETPSA and the Trust Fund should be transferred no later than 1 May 1996 to UNDP. Consequently, the Secretary-General asked the General Assembly to transfer the decision-making authority and review of the Programme to the Executive Board of UNDP and to discontinue the Advisory Committee.

**GENERAL ASSEMBLY ACTION**

On 20 December, the General Assembly adopted **resolution 50/131**.

### United Nations Educational and Training Programme for Southern Africa

*The General Assembly,*

*Recalling* its resolutions on the United Nations Educational and Training Programme for Southern Africa, in particular resolution 49/17 of 23 November 1994,

*Also recalling* its resolution 2349(XXII) of 19 December 1967, by which it established the United Nations Educational and Training Programme for Southern Africa by integrating earlier special programmes, and resolution 2431(XXIII) of 18 December 1968, by which it established the Advisory Committee on the United Nations Educational and Training Programme for Southern Africa,

*Having considered* the report of the Secretary-General of 7 December 1995 containing an account of the work of the Advisory Committee and the administration of the Programme for the period from 1 September 1994 to 31 August 1995,

*Recognizing* the valuable assistance rendered over the years by the Programme to disadvantaged students in South Africa, its support for institution-building in that country and the measures it has taken to ensure that commitments made with regard to educational and training assistance can be met in full,

*Fully recognizing* the need for the Government of South Africa to lay a proper foundation, in particular in the field of human resources development, during the transition and post-apartheid period,

1. *Endorses* the report of the Secretary-General on the United Nations Educational and Training Programme for Southern Africa;

2. *Agrees* with the recommendation of the Advisory Committee on the United Nations Educational and Training Programme for Southern Africa that the Programme be extended for three to five years beyond April 1994;

3. *Decides*, for the purpose of integrating the goals of the Programme with the overall multilateral development programmes of the United Nations Development Programme, to transfer, no later than 1 May 1996, management of the Programme and its funds and decision-making authority to the Administrator of the United Nations Development Programme through the Executive Board of the Development Programme which will be entrusted with the following:

(a) To continue the United Nations Educational and Training Programme for Southern Africa Trust Fund as an identifiable entity for three to five years beyond April 1994;

(b) To undertake fund-raising and mobilization of resources for the Programme;

(c) To monitor and review the Programme;

4. *Also decides* to endorse the activities of the Programme, and requests the United Nations Development Programme to continue to place the primary focus of the Programme on human resources development aimed at capacity- and institution-building by contributing to South Africa's human resources during this critical period of development through:

(a) Expanding arrangements for co-sponsored training for the disadvantaged majority in sectors previously neglected;

(b) Continuing to utilize the catalyst function of the Programme by expanding the co-sponsorship and job-placement arrangements with corporations, non-governmental organizations and educational institutions;

5. *Recommends* administrative streamlining with the objective of strengthening the office of the Programme in South Africa;

6. *Endorses* the recommendation that the Advisory Committee should be discontinued;

7. *Expresses its appreciation* to the Governments that have supported the Programme and to the organizations and agencies that have cooperated with it;

8. *Expresses its gratitude* to the Secretary-General and the staff of the United Nations Educational and Training Programme for Southern Africa and to the Advisory Committee for their persistent efforts, and congratulates them for their outstanding achievements since the start of the Programme.

General Assembly resolution 50/131

20 December 1995     Meeting 96     Adopted without vote

34-nation draft (A/50/L.65 & Add.1); agenda item 34.

*REFERENCES*

[1]A/50/231 & Add.1. [2]YUN 1974, p. 118, GA res. 3207(XXIX), 30 Sep. 1974. [3]Ibid., p. 115. [4]Ibid., p. 117. [5]A/50/815. [6]A/50/750.

## Libyan Arab Jamahiriya

In spite of efforts of the Council of the League of Arab States (LAS), the Movement of Non-Aligned Countries and OAU to have the Security Council reconsider the sanctions imposed in 1992[1] and strengthened in 1993[2] against the Libyan Arab Jamahiriya, the Council upheld its measures, intended to obtain the surrender for trial of two Libyan nationals, Abdelbaset Ali Mohamed Al Megrahi and Al Amin Khalifa Fhima, suspects in the 1988 bombing of Pan Am flight 103 over Lockerbie, Scotland, and Libya's cooperation with French authorities investigating the crash in 1989 of a Union de transports aériens (UTA) flight 772 in the Niger.

The sanctions related to various aspects of air links with, supply of arms and military weapons to, reduction and restriction of the activities of the diplomatic and consular missions of, and restrictions on known or suspected terrorist nationals of Libya, and included, after adoption of the 1993 resolution, other measures such as the freezing of Libyan financial funds abroad.

**Communications.** The OAU Council of Ministers, by a resolution adopted in January 1995 and transmitted to the UN Secretary-General on 13 February by Libya[3] and on 27 March by the OAU Secretary-General,[4] reiterated its appeal to the Security Council to lift the sanctions against Libya and called for a fair trial of the two suspects in a neutral country to be agreed upon. The LAS Council, in a March resolution,[5] adhered to its 1994 proposal[6] that the two suspects should be judged equitably by Scottish judges, in conformity with Scottish law, at the seat of the International Court of Justice in The Hague. LAS called on the Security Council to conduct a new and impartial inquiry into the crash over Lockerbie and urged it to lift the sanctions pending the results of the inquiry.

On 27 March, Libya noted[7] that recent reports in the media, a debate in the British Parliament and statements by the spokesman for the victims' families had pointed to serious flaws and shortcomings in the Lockerbie investigation, and that it was no longer possible to place any reliance on indictments brought as a result of the investigation. It further underscored that despite those developments and the fact that the Libyan Government had complied in full with Security Council resolution 731(1992),[8] France, the United Kingdom and the United States maintained their intransigent attitude, deliberately linking their demand relating to terrorism with Libya and confining that universal phenomenon to the Lockerbie and UTA incidents. The question of terrorism on a wide scale had been forcibly injected into Council resolution 748(1992),[1] by which sanctions had been imposed that had done great harm to the Libyan people in all aspects of life. Since those sanctions were no longer justified in the light of recent developments, Libya said other Security Council members must urge the institution of an impartial inquiry into the Lockerbie case and suspend the application of the sanctions pending the outcome of the inquiry.

By a tripartite declaration of 30 March 1995,[9] France, the United Kingdom and the United States reaffirmed their joint declaration of 5 August 1994[10] and their common determination to bring to justice those responsible for the bombings of the Pan Am and UTA flights. They regretted that Libya had not satisfied the French judicial authorities with respect to the bombing of UTA flight 772 and expressed their commitment to full and comprehensive enforcement of the sanctions. The three States also reaffirmed that Libya must commit itself definitively to ceasing all forms of terrorist activity and all assistance to terrorist groups, and demonstrate by concrete action its renunciation of terrorism. They reiterated that Libya must ensure the appearance of the two suspects in the United Kingdom or the United States, where they would receive a fair trial, and reaffirmed that alternative proposals for trial in The Hague or elsewhere did not meet Security Council requirements and were unacceptable.

By a declaration[11] adopted at a round-table meeting of the Arab Lawyers Union, the Arab Jurists Union, the Libyan Bar Association and the General Syndicate of Libyan Attorneys (The Hague, 28-30 March), it was stated that the Security Council, by imposing sanctions against Libya, had exceeded its powers under Article 24 of the UN Charter and *ultra vires* its competence, and that the United Kingdom and the United States remained obliged to exhaust all means for the peaceful resolution of the Lockerbie dispute under Articles 2 and 33 of the Charter. The declaration called for the immediate suspension and ultimate removal of the sanctions and for a special session of the General Assembly to consider the Lockerbie case.

By a 3 May letter,[12] Libya protested its inclusion by the United States in the list of countries providing support to international terrorism, trying to obstruct peace in the Middle East and seeking to acquire weapons of mass destruction. It firmly rejected those charges, noting that no evidence existed to support them and that it had condemned terrorism on many occasions, was a party to the 1968 Treaty on the Non-Proliferation of Nuclear Weapons,[13] and was anxious for the success of peace in the region. Libya called on the Security Council to prevent the United States from undertaking any action prejudicial to its sovereignty and independence or tending to undermine its security and stability.

On 9 May, Libya communicated to the Council President a paragraph[14] from the communiqué issued by the Ministerial Meeting of the Coordinating Bureau of the Non-Aligned Countries (Bandung, Indonesia, 25-27 April), in which the Ministers expressed their deep concern over Libya's human and material losses and those of neighbouring States as a result of the sanctions and urged the Security Council to lift the air embargo and other measures it had imposed. They affirmed that the escalation of the crisis, the threatened imposition of additional sanctions and the use of force as a way for States to deal with each other constituted a violation of the UN Charter, the principles of the Non-Aligned Movement and international laws and precepts. On 9 June, Libya reported[15] on the humanitarian and economic consequences of the implementation of the Council's resolutions during the period from 15 April 1992 to 31 December 1994, describing their negative impact on the health and social welfare sector, agriculture and animal husbandry, transport and communications, the industrial and mining sector, and finance and trade. The report estimated total financial losses at some $10 billion.

By a resolution adopted in June,[16] the OAU Council of Ministers again called for a lifting of the sanctions and for a fair trial of the suspects in a neutral country. The Council of Ministers also expressed strong opposition to any move to deny Libya a seat on the Security Council on account of the Lockerbie dispute. By a tripartite declaration of 26 July,[17] France, the United Kingdom and the United States reaffirmed their position as stated on 30 March, and deplored the sanctions violations of 19 and 20 April (see below), which had been condemned by the Council members via the Committee on sanctions.

On 27 July, Libya requested[18] the Security Council to organize a committee to study the United States claim that Libyan policies and actions threatened its national security and foreign policies. Libya repeated its willingness to receive a delegation sent by the Secretary-General to ascertain that there were no camps used for training terrorists on Libyan territory, and reiterated its demand for an independent inquiry into the Lockerbie incident and for the suspension of the sanctions until the results of the investigation were published. In a 31 July reply[19] to the 26 July tripartite declaration, Libya stated that it had complied with the requests made in Security Council resolution 731(1992),[8] condemned all forms of terrorism, severed its relations with all organizations suspected of resorting to terrorism, and cooperated with France and the United Kingdom. It reiterated its request for a committee to investigate allegations regarding the presence of training camps for terrorists in Libyan territory and its acceptance of the proposal for a trial of the two suspects in the Lockerbie case in The Hague. Libya said the 1971 Montreal Convention for the Suppression of Unlawful Acts against Civil Aviation[20] accorded it the right to try the case and did not provide for extradition of the accused which, it said, would be contrary to Libyan national law, as well as to international law, given the absence of an extradition agreement between it and the United Kingdom or the United States. Libya emphasized its adherence to the sanctions, but stated that they did not apply to an airflight of Libyan pilgrims to the holy land, described in the tripartite declaration as a sanctions violation, as the performance by Libyans of their religious rites was not subject to any authorization.

On 22 August, Libya transmitted a resolution[21] adopted at the Eighteenth Conference of the Union of African Parliaments (Ouagadougou, Burkina Faso, 28-29 July), calling on the Security Council to rescind the sanctions as a matter of urgency, urging the States concerned to resolve the dispute by peaceful means, and inviting the three Western countries to respond to the proposal for a just and impartial trial of the two accused in a neutral country. The resolution called on all Governments to cease implementing the measures imposed on Libya and to participate in the search for a peaceful and just solution to the issue. The LAS Council, by a 21 September resolution,[22] upheld its March resolution,[5] expressing regret at the continuation of the sanctions. The Eleventh Conference of Heads of State or Government of the Movement of Non-Aligned Countries (Cartagena de Indias, Colombia, 18-20 October), in its Final Document,[23] restated the position expressed at the Ministerial Meeting of its Coordinating Bureau[14] and called for a positive response to the initiatives that would lead to an acceptable solution for the parties. Unless the Western countries concerned responded to the proposals for a peaceful settlement, the Conference said, non-aligned States would not be able to continue to abide by Council resolutions imposing the sanctions. Libya communicated the pertinent paragraph of the Final Document on 30 October.[24]

On 17 November, Libya acknowledged[25] receipt of a 16 November letter from the Secretary-General, informing it, within the context of its implementation of Security Council resolutions, that the United Kingdom was satisfied with answers provided by Libya regarding its relationship with the Provisional Irish Republican Army. The Secretary-General considered that response to be an important step towards implementation of the relevant resolutions and removal of the difficulties in the relations between Libya and the United Nations. By a 20 November statement,[26] the United Kingdom confirmed its satisfaction with the Libyan disclosures as a positive step towards implementation of relevant Council resolutions, in particular towards its renunciation of terrorism, but pointed to remaining gaps and omissions in the information provided and to the fact that Libya had satisfied just one in a number of demands placed on it by the Council. The United Kingdom remained committed to the sanctions until Libya complied with those demands.

**Report of the Committee on sanctions.** The Committee on sanctions against Libya, established under resolution 748(1992),[1] on 22 December 1995 adopted a report on its activities during the year.[27]

Pursuant to the 1992 resolution, the Committee consistently advised Governments against the shipment to Libya of goods and material that could be of possible dual use. It considered queries from Member States regarding the provision to Libya of items listed in the annex to its 1993 resolution expanding the sanctions,[2] including equipment designed for use in the transportation of crude oil and natural gas, or for use in crude oil export terminals, as well as refinery equipment; it also considered the permissibility of the provision of aircraft components and parts to foreign commercial airlines operating within Libya.

With regard to the transfer of funds to Libya "for legitimate commercial purposes", the Committee decided on 23 February 1995 that it was the responsibility of Member States to enforce the sanctions imposed under resolution 883(1993), in particular the freezing of assets, using mechanisms they deemed appropriate and practical.

During the reporting period, the Committee received two reports of sanction violations, both concerning humanitarian flights. The first concerned an unauthorized stopover on 30 January 1995 in direct contravention of the Committee's authorization for an emergency medical evacuation flight; the second concerned unauthorized

flights from Tripoli to Jeddah, Saudi Arabia, on 19 and 20 April (see below). Appropriate measures were taken by the Committee in response to the two reported violations.

During 1995, the Committee approved 42 emergency medical evacuation flights, as compared to 21 in 1994. On 19 April, the Committee approved, under certain conditions, Egypt's request for 45 flights on Egypt Air from Cairo to Tripoli and Benghazi and on to Jeddah, and an equal number of return flights, for the purpose of transporting 6,000 Libyan pilgrims to perform the Haj. According to verified reports, Libyan aircraft crossed Egyptian airspace and landed in Jeddah on 19 and 20 April. Those flights, which had not been authorized by the Committee, constituted a major violation of the sanctions regime, the Committee stated. The matter was discussed at informal consultations of the Security Council on 20 April. On 31 May, the Committee concluded deliberations on the violations by adopting the text of three communications to Libya, Egypt and Saudi Arabia. On 17 July, the Committee approved further procedures and arrangements concerning the authorization and monitoring procedures for emergency medical evacuation flights and the related issue of maintenance and supply of spare parts for the predesignated air ambulances.

On 17 October, the Committee considered two Libyan notes verbales requesting authorization for air transport facilities by Libyan or UN aircraft to enable over a million "illegal infiltrators, nationals of African States, to return to their countries in order to avoid the hardships and dangers of travel created by the air embargo". The intended repatriation would involve nationals from Benin, Côte d'Ivoire, Guinea, Guinea-Bissau and Senegal (10,000 nationals, 40 flights); Chad (300,000, 600 flights); Ghana (20,000, 40 flights); Mali (250,000, 500 flights); Niger (30,000, 60 flights); Nigeria (7,000, 15 flights); and Sudan (500,000, 1,000 flights). After careful consideration of the matter, the Committee was unable to accede to the Libyan request; it was of the view that the presence of foreign nationals in Libya and its desire to repatriate them did not constitute grounds for granting a humanitarian exception.

As recommended by the Security Council in a note of 29 March,[28] the Committee adopted certain measures to make its procedures more transparent. To that end, it decided to increase the practice of issuing press releases reflecting the most important matters discussed at its meetings. It would continue to make available tables indicating the status of emergency medical evacuation flights processed under the "no-objection procedure". A compilation of its decisions on other major issues would also be prepared on a regular basis and furnished to any delegation upon request.

After consultations held on 30 March, 28 July and 22 November in connection with the sanctions imposed on Libya under resolution 748(1992),[1] the President of the Security Council made three identical statements on behalf of the Council members:[29]

> The members of the Security Council held informal consultations on 30 March [28 July, 22 November] 1995 pursuant to paragraph 13 of resolution 748(1992), by which the Council decided to review every 120 days or sooner, should the situation so require, the measures imposed by paragraphs 3 to 7 against the Libyan Arab Jamahiriya.
>
> After hearing all the opinions expressed in the course of consultations, the President of the Council concluded that there was no agreement that the necessary conditions existed for modification of the measures of sanctions established in paragraphs 3 to 7 of resolution 748(1992).

*REFERENCES*

[1]YUN 1992, p. 55, SC res. 748(1992), 31 Mar. 1992. [2]YUN 1993, p. 101, SC res. 883(1993), 11 Nov. 1993. [3]S/1995/138. [4]S/1995/250. [5]S/1995/224. [6]YUN 1994, p. 129. [7]S/1995/226. [8]YUN 1992, p. 53, SC res. 731(1992), 21 Jan. 1992. [9]A/50/128-S/1995/247. [10]YUN 1994, p. 128. [11]S/1995/267. [12]S/1995/355. [13]YUN 1968, p. 17, GA res. 2373(XXII), annex, 12 June 1968. [14]S/1995/381. [15]S/1995/474. [16]S/1995/596. [17]A/50/315-S/1995/622. [18]S/1995/624. [19]S/1995/633. [20]YUN 1971, p. 739. [21]S/1995/725. [22]S/1995/834. [23]A/50/752-S/1995/1035. [24]S/1995/902. [25]S/1995/968. [26]S/1995/973. [27]S/1996/2. [28]S/1995/234. [29]S/PRST/1995/14, S/PRST/1995/36, S/PRST/1995/56.

## Egypt-Sudan

On 29 June 1995, the Sudan informed[1] the Security Council President of an exchange of fire between Egyptian and Sudanese police forces on 27 June in the Halaib area, specifically at the outer stations of Bageih and Alnus, resulting in three Sudanese policemen being killed and seven others seriously wounded. The Sudan said that those developments were part of a hostile campaign against it by Egyptian authorities and media, while the Sudan had exerted all efforts to settle the Sudanese/Egyptian dispute over the Sudanese province of Halaib by peaceful means. However, the Egyptian aggression continued, imposing a de facto occupation of the province. The Sudan reiterated that the province of Halaib was Sudanese territory under Sudanese administration and occupied by Sudanese population. It called on the Security Council to urge Egypt to withdraw its military presence and rescind administrative measures in the Halaib area south of Argin; start immediately towards resolving the dispute through negotiations based on previous agreements between the two countries; and compensate the families of Sudanese nationals, victims of its aggression.

By a letter of 6 July,[2] the Sudan informed the Council President of further incidents, which it said took place between 27 June and 1 July. It charged that Egypt was engaging in many organized military acts of aggression against Sudanese territory; Egypt's failure to respond to the Sudan's calls for a resumption of dialogue affirmed its lack of will to resolve the dispute by peaceful means; and Egypt's position remained characterized by its rejection of all efforts by the Sudan to deal with the problem in bilateral negotiation, while it insisted that Halaib was Egyptian and not subject to negotiation.

The Sudan reiterated its call to the Council to exert pressure on Egypt to accept international arbitration, non-resort to the use of force and immediate commencement of action to resolve the dispute by peaceful means; and to withdraw its military presence from the Halaib area and refrain from perpetuating and confirming its occupation of the area, with payment of compensation to the families of the victims of the attacks.

Egypt, responding on 10 July,[3] stated that since the Sudan's independence in 1956, all territory north of the 22nd parallel had been under Egyptian sovereignty; Sudanese claims disputing Egyptian sovereignty over the Halaib region were, therefore, devoid of any historical or legal foundation. The Sudan's unfriendly acts against Egypt, its President and Government had taken on a distinctly hostile tone and several Egyptian citizens in the Sudan had been arbitrarily arrested and imprisoned or subjected to other forms of detention without trial and without charges having been brought against them. Egyptian property in the Sudan, including the Egyptian diplomatic mission, had been confiscated. In addition, the Sudan had attempted to undermine the Egyptian Government as well as the relations between the two peoples and had threatened to denounce the provisions of the agreement in force on the waters of the Nile. Egypt called on the Sudan to respect rules governing relations among States, to comply with the principles and objectives of the United Nations and to cease supporting terrorism.

The Sudan on 17 July informed[4] the Security Council President that the 1899 agreement betwen the two parties, amended in 1902 and 1907, provided that the Sudan had sovereignty over the territories and region of Halaib, which had since then remained fully under Sudanese sovereignty. The inhabitants of the area had participated, as Sudanese citizens, in the first elections to the Sudanese Parliament in 1953 and in subsequent parliamentary elections; they had never taken part in an Egyptian election. The Sudan recalled its complaint to the Council in 1958[5] against the concentration of Egyptian troops on Sudanese territory in the Halaib region and drew the Council's attention to what it called unjustified and irresponsible acts of aggression perpetrated by Egypt which, it charged, was seeking to provoke the secession of a part of Sudanese territory. The Sudan declared that it was ready to accept the principle of a settlement or international arbitration or even a ruling of the International Court of Justice concerning the dispute over Halaib and requested the Council to compel Egypt to accept international arbitration.

By a further letter of 24 July,[6] the Sudan alleged that Egypt continued to escalate tension through provocative acts against Sudanese citizens belonging to the Bisharin and Amra'ar tribes, and that it attempted to establish electoral districts in Halaib with a view to its participation in Egyptian elections. The Egyptian President had threatened the Sudan and accused it of the attempt on his life in Addis Ababa, without waiting for the results of the investigation carried out by the Ethiopian authorities, which established that the assassination attempt had been carried out by Egyptian elements. Furthermore, the Egyptian security service had attacked four Sudanese diplomats in Cairo. The Sudan reiterated its earlier requests to the Council that Egypt be compelled to lift the blockade on the inhabitants of the Halaib area and authorize deliveries to them of water and food; cease forcing Sudanese citizens in the province to participate in the election campaign; and stop provoking Sudanese citizens by seizing their property, freezing their accounts in Egyptian banks and subjecting them to illegal interrogation. It also requested that the Council assume direct responsibility in order to prevent a deterioration of the situation and forestall Egyptian escalation thereof.

On 3 October, the Secretary-General informed[7] the Council of a statement by Ethiopia on 11 September at the Extraordinary Ministerial Meeting of the Central Organ of OAU, indicating that the Ethiopian authorities had concluded that the terrorist assault on President Hosni Mubarak of Egypt on 26 June in Addis Ababa, although the work of Al-Gama'a Al-Islamia, was supported, assisted and facilitated by the security organs of the Sudan. Ethiopia felt compelled to present the information it had collected, since the alternative would have been to ignore the involvement in State-sponsored terrorism in its capital by a neighbouring country against an African head of State who was its guest. The Ministerial Meeting condemned the assassination attempt, called on the Sudan to hand over the three alleged perpetrators, and requested the OAU Secretary-General to report on additional measures to deal with the dangers posed by State-sponsored terrorism. At a meeting with the Ethiopian Foreign Minister on 29 September, it was agreed that it would be appropriate to inform the Council of the Ethiopian

statement. The Minister requested that the Council be informed that Ethiopia would defer a decision on further action until it had ascertained what progress could be made at the level of OAU.

The Council members, as stated in a 12 October letter by the President,[8] noted the contents of the Secretary-General's letter and welcomed OAU efforts to resolve the issue. They also looked forward to being kept informed of developments.

Responding to the charges on 13 October, the Sudan denied[9] any direct or indirect involvement or connivance in the assassination attempt. It re-emphasized its condemnation of the incident and of all forms of terrorism and political violence, and reaffirmed that the suspects were not in its territory and that it had never allowed its territory to be used as a safe haven for criminals committing terrorist acts. It had taken steps to investigate the matter and expressed its willingness to cooperate. It had asked Ethiopia to provide any additional information that could be helpful in the search for the culprits and suspects, as well as the cooperation of the authorities concerned in both countries, and requested bilateral and joint efforts of those authorities.

### Eritrea-Sudan

On 26 June, the Sudan, in a letter[10] to the Security Council President, drew attention to a communiqué calling for the formation of a Supreme Political and Military Committee to coordinate the escalation of the struggle to overthrow the Sudanese regime. Taking part in the meeting were representatives of the self-styled Sudanese opposition factions and the rebel movement in southern Sudan, as well as the Ambassadors of the United States and Israel. The Sudan considered the gathering, sponsored by and held under the auspices of a neighbouring country and OAU member, a flagrant violation of the Charters of both the United Nations and OAU, and considered participation in it as a hostile act and a direct threat to its security, sovereignty and territorial integrity, and an interference in its internal affairs. The encouragement by Eritrea of secessionist tendencies clearly violated OAU resolutions on the retention by African States of the boundaries inherited upon independence. The Sudan asked all countries to refrain from interfering in its internal affairs and called on the international community to ensure that there was no recurrence of such conduct on Eritrea's part.

On 5 July, Eritrea charged[11] the Sudan with intensifying its subversive acts against Eritrea, forcing it to sever diplomatic ties with Khartoum. It called on the international community not to give credence to the Sudan's accusations, but to take measures to defuse its aggressive designs.

The Sudan, in an 11 July response,[12] urged the international community to enjoin Eritrea to adopt a responsible mode of conduct in its international relations, based on full respect for the UN Charter and resolutions, as well as for the principles of mutual respect and non-interference in the internal affairs of States. Failing that, Eritrea would face the consequence of its hostile conduct towards the Sudan.

### Eritrea-Yemen

By a communiqué of 18 December,[13] Yemen charged Eritrea with an attack against the island of Hanish, located in the international navigation channel in the Red Sea, after it had issued on 11 November a warning to the Yemeni citizens and the military guard stationed there to leave the island and halt work on an investment project there. Despite agreement reached in meetings between representatives of the two countries that any dispute be contained and dialogue be continued after the month of Ramadan, Eritrea launched its attack on the island on 15 December. Yemen condemned Eritrea's involvement in that premeditated aggression against Yemeni territory as a violation of Yemeni waters and affirmed its right to repulse any attack against them.

At a meeting on 20 December, according to a press release of the same date, Yemen's Permanent Representative to the United Nations informed the Secretary-General that Yemen demanded the release of all Yemeni prisoners of war, total withdrawal of Eritrean forces from the island, and that Eritrea engage in negotiations to delineate the maritime borders between the two countries. Yemen would welcome any good-offices initiative by the Secretary-General aimed at settling the conflict peacefully. The Secretary-General said he continued to follow the situation and welcomed the cease-fire. He called on the parties to exercise restraint and reiterated his willingness to offer his good offices, with a view to finding a peaceful solution.

In a press statement of 21 December,[14] Eritrea said that a lasting solution to the dispute rested solely on international mediation. The issue of captured soldiers was not acceptable as a precondition, and it undertook to hand over all prisoners to ICRC at Asmara. If both countries agreed in principle to withdraw their forces from the Hanish archipelago, a neutral mediating body acceptable to both parties should be established until such time as a lasting solution was found through international arbitration. That body would be entrusted with the task of observing and monitoring both the evacuation process and its sequel. Eritrea reiterated its proposal that an impartial and independent body should be established to investigate the incident and that Yemen should make the effort to contribute to the resumption of a constructive dialogue.

*REFERENCES*

[1]S/1995/534. [2]S/1995/544. [3]S/1995/559. [4]S/1995/587. [5]YUN 1958, p. 82. [6]S/1995/616. [7]S/1995/867. [8]S/1995/868. [9]S/1995/872. [10]S/1995/522. [11]S/1995/542. [12]S/1995/569. [13]S/1995/1044. [14]S/1995/1054.

### Mayotte

The question of the Comorian island of Mayotte—one of four islands in the Indian Ocean Comoro Archipelago—remained on the General Assembly's agenda in 1995. Following a referendum in 1974, the Islamic Federal Republic of the Comoros acceded to independence from France on 6 July 1975. France, however, continued to administer the island of Mayotte.

**Communication.** On 18 January 1995, the Council of Ministers of the Comoros issued a communiqué,[1] by which it noted the 24 November 1994 decision of the French Government to require inhabitants of the other three islands of the Comoros to possess a visa for entry to Mayotte. The Comoros strongly condemned that initiative, which, it said, reflected the deliberate intention of the French authorities to separate Mayotte from the geographical unit of which it was a natural part, and was inconsistent with French statements expressing willingness to seek a negotiated settlement and maintain the free movement of goods and persons between Mayotte and the other three islands of the Comoros. The Government of the Comoros intended to consult the nation with the aim of finding appropriate solutions. It was also seeking the support of the Federal Assembly, which would be convened in special session to consider the matter.

**Report of the Secretary-General.** In a 22 November report,[2] the Secretary-General stated that he had addressed a note verbale to the Comoros and France, drawing their attention to the General Assembly's 1994 resolution on the question of Mayotte[3] and inviting them to provide him with any pertinent information on the issue. A similar communication was sent to the Secretary-General of OAU. Under the 1994 resolution, the Assembly requested the UN Secretary-General to make available his good offices in the search for a peaceful negotiated solution.

France responded that it remained willing to promote a just and lasting solution in conformity with its Constitution and on the basis of respect for the wishes of the peoples concerned. The population had voted freely and democratically in favour of maintaining the territory of Mayotte within the French Republic. A constructive dialogue was continually taking place at the highest level with the Comoros. France was convinced that such consultation should be pursued in a spirit of accommodation, conciliation and openness.

The Comoros stated that it was again bringing to the Secretary-General's attention its proposal for a positive and constructive approach to the question of Mayotte which took into account the current realities and the need to adapt it to the human and economic imperatives of the times. It was time for the French and Comorian parties to translate into action their mutual and often expressed determination to resolve the issue. The restrictive and selective administrative measures, with which the inhabitants of the three other islands had to comply upon entering Mayotte, could only serve to entrench the feeling of separation even further. The Comoros proposed to France the establishment of a joint Franco-Comorian Commission to explore all options available and promote a *rapprochement* between the inhabitants of the four islands. The Comoros hoped that France would pursue a policy of cooperation aimed at promoting an economic realignment, with a view to reintegrating Mayotte gradually into the Comorian group as a whole, and that the elaboration of a programme of integrated development would enable the authorities of both parties to ensure a progressive *rapprochement* between Mayotte and its sister islands. The Comoros was convinced of the need to include Mayotte in the dynamics and process of regional integration in which its sister islands in the Indian Ocean were involved. The Secretary-General was asked to use his influence with the French authorities to ensure that they favoured dialogue in the search for a viable solution; to ensure that they took no action to compromise the climate of entente, understanding and mutual appreciation in Franco-Comorian relations; and to keep the question of Mayotte on the Assembly agenda until a final settlement was reached.

OAU quoted a resolution adopted by its Council of Ministers in January,[4] reaffirming Africa's solidarity with the people of the Comoros in their determination to recover their political rights and to defend the territorial integrity of the Comoros. The OAU Council appealed to its member States to condemn and disregard any action by France to force Mayotte to participate in events where a distinction could be made between the latter and the Comoros. It urged France to satisfy the legitimate claims of the Comoros in accordance with resolutions adopted by OAU, the United Nations, the Organization of the Islamic Conference, LAS and the Non-Aligned Movement. The Council condemned the introduction of entry visas into Mayotte for Comorian citizens of the other three islands and urged the OAU Ad Hoc Committee of Seven (Algeria, Cameroon, Comoros, Gabon,

Madagascar, Mozambique, Senegal) to consider ways of facilitating the resumption of a dialogue with France. On 22 June, the Committee recommended that a meeting of the heads of State of the member countries of the Ad Hoc Committee be held to study the best way of reviving the dialogue on the question. It also recommended that OAU member States submit to the General Assembly a draft resolution reiterating solidarity with the people of the Comoros in their determination to regain their rights respecting the island of Mayotte.

The OAU Assembly of Heads of State and Government in June endorsed[5] those recommendations, pursuant to which the head of State of Gabon proposed that a meeting be held in New York on 4 and 5 October to exchange views on the best way of reviving the dialogue with France. However, that meeting could not be held in view of the new situation that had arisen in the Comoro Archipelago as a result of the *coup d'état* at the end of September by mercenaries led by Bob Denard.

The Secretary-General maintained contact with all parties and informed them of his readiness to make available his good offices in the search for a peaceful solution.

The Assembly took no action on the agenda item on the question of Mayotte but, on 23 December, by **decision 50/475**, decided that it should remain on the agenda of its fiftieth session.

*REFERENCES*

[1]A/50/68. [2]A/50/779. [3]YUN 1994, p. 369, GA res. 49/18, 28 Nov. 1994. [4]A/50/116. [5]A/50/647.

## Cooperation between OAU and the UN system

In October 1995, the Secretary-General reported[1] on cooperation between the United Nations and the Organization of African Unity. In 1994,[2] the General Assembly had called on UN organs to involve OAU closely in all their activities concerning Africa and to cooperate with OAU in the context of the pacific settlement of disputes and the maintenance of international peace and security in Africa. The Secretary-General reviewed the exchange of information and cooperation between the two organizations in the field of economic and social development, which involved the Centre for Human Rights of the UN Secretariat, the UN Children's Fund, the UN Conference on Trade and Development, UNDP, the UN Environment Programme, the UN Population Fund, the UN International Drug Control Programme, the World Food Programme, the Economic Commission for Africa, the UN Centre for Human Settlements (Habitat), the International Labour Organization, the Food and Agriculture Organization of the United Nations, the UN Educational, Scientific and Cultural Organization, the World Health Organization, the World Bank, the International Finance Corporation, the International Monetary Fund, the International Fund for Agricultural Development, the UN Industrial Development Organization and UNHCR. Cooperation in other areas was extended by the Department of Political Affairs of the Secretariat, the International Civil Aviation Organization, the Universal Postal Union and the World Meteorological Organization.

The Secretary-General met on 7 April with members of the Central Organ of the OAU Mechanism for Conflict Prevention, Management and Resolution. They exchanged views on the conflict situations in Africa and discussed actions that could be considered to ameliorate them. The Secretary-General also met with the Chairman and the Secretary-General of OAU, discussing with them the importance of cooperation between the two organizations in efforts to bring about lasting peace and sustainable development in Africa.

In November, the Secretary-General reported[3] on the tenth annual meeting on cooperation between the UN system and OAU (Addis Ababa, 6-10 November), which reviewed cooperation between the two organizations, especially in the areas of peace, security and democracy, and economic and social questions.

With regard to conflict prevention and management, the meeting requested the United Nations to assist OAU in establishing an early-warning or alert system as well as a "situation centre" similar to that of the United Nations, to enhance OAU's capability to collect, analyse and disseminate information, as well as to monitor and keep abreast of political developments and potential conflict situations. A mechanism should be set up for the exchange of information between the two organizations' respective early-warning systems, with a view to preventing or minimizing duplication. Whenever the need arose, joint OAU-UN fact-finding missions should be mounted, whose tasks should include assessing existing and potential conflicts as well as mediation. A common list should be established of eminent persons who could be fielded for such assignments, as well as common guidelines and rules of engagement for joint operations in Africa. In that regard, OAU envisaged the creation of peacemaking contingents and the limited deployment of observers which would require logistical support from the United Nations. The United Nations was also requested to assist in mobilizing financial and logistical support for specific OAU peacemaking activities, and to strengthen the institutional and operational capacity of OAU's Conflict Management Division through human resources development, research activities, public awareness and sensitization campaigns. In the context of post-conflict peace-

building, the two organizations should collaborate in identifying, designing and implementing rehabilitation and reconstruction programmes, as well as programmes to address the needs of refugees, returnees, displaced persons, demobilized combatants and others affected by conflict. They should also promote education for democracy, human rights and freedom. The meeting asked the United Nations to support OAU's electoral unit in enhancing its institutional capacity for assisting countries, on request, in their electoral processes. Common criteria should be developed for verifying electoral processes and for debriefing and issuance of statements relating to those processes.

In the area of economic and social questions, UN organizations and bodies were asked to cooperate with OAU in strengthening the institutional, analytical and operational capacity of regional economic communities and in formulating specific programmes to that end; and in the preparation of protocols on various aspects of the Treaty Establishing the African Economic Community, which entered into force in 1994,[4] and the review of existing protocols (see also PART FOUR, Chapter V). The meeting also adopted recommendations in respect of the UN System-wide Special Initiative for Africa, to be launched in early 1996, the UN New Agenda for the Development of Africa in the 1990s (see PART FOUR, Chapter III) and the implementation of Agenda 21, adopted by the 1992 UN Conference on Environment and Development.[5] It identified the areas for cooperation in human resources development and training, calling on the United Nations to assist African countries in, among other areas, restructuring their educational curricula, promoting free and compulsory education for all children, as well as civic education, and fighting drug trafficking and juvenile delinquency.

The meeting agreed that OAU and UNHCR should develop a comprehensive strategy and plan of action with the following objectives: to ensure that asylum and protection of refugees continued to be granted in Africa, taking into account the interests of States and hosting communities; to emphasize durable solutions to the complex refugee crisis in Africa; to reinforce cooperation in the field of conflict prevention, particularly as far as an early-warning mechanism was concerned; to ensure that the recommendations of the 1994 Symposium on Refugees and Forced Population Displacements[6] and the Plan of Action adopted by the February 1995 Regional Conference on Assistance to Refugees, Returnees and Displaced Persons in the Great Lakes Region (see above, under "Burundi", and PART FOUR, Chapter XII) were effectively implemented; to develop a more comprehensive programme of assistance and support to the host countries and communities; and to mobilize additional resources for refugees from non-traditional donors. Other recommendations concerned women and development; the Second Industrial Development Decade for Africa; the Second Transportation and Communications Decade in Africa (see PART FOUR, Chapter V); and health, particularly the prevention of HIV/AIDS/sexually transmitted diseases, and the provision of care and support to people with HIV/AIDS.

In a 1 November report,[7] the Secretary-General outlined a number of proposals for strengthening the capabilities of OAU and institutionalizing mechanisms in the area of cooperation in conflict prevention and peace-keeping in Africa (see PART ONE, Chapter I, and PART TWO, Chapter I, for details).

**GENERAL ASSEMBLY ACTION**

On 21 December, the General Assembly adopted **resolution 50/158**.

**Cooperation between the United Nations and the Organization of African Unity**

*The General Assembly,*

*Having considered* the report of the Secretary-General of 17 October 1995 on cooperation between the United Nations and the Organization of African Unity,

*Recalling* the provisions of Chapter VIII of the Charter of the United Nations on regional arrangements or agencies, which set forth the basic principles governing their activities and establishing the legal framework for cooperation with the United Nations in the area of the maintenance of international peace and security, as well as resolution 49/57 of 9 December 1994, the annex to which contains the Declaration on the Enhancement of Cooperation between the United Nations and Regional Arrangements or Agencies in the Maintenance of International Peace and Security,

*Recalling also* the agreement of 15 November 1965 on cooperation between the United Nations and the Organization of African Unity as updated and signed on 9 October 1990 by the Secretaries-General of the two organizations,

*Recalling further* its resolutions on the enhancement of cooperation between the United Nations and the Organization of African Unity, in particular resolutions 43/12 of 25 October 1988, 43/27 of 18 November 1988, 44/17 of 1 November 1989, 45/13 of 7 November 1990, 46/20 of 26 November 1991, 47/148 of 18 December 1992, 48/25 of 29 November 1993 and 49/64 of 15 December 1994,

*Recalling* that, in its resolutions 46/20, 47/148 and 48/25, it, *inter alia*, urged the Secretary-General of the United Nations and the relevant agencies of the United Nations system to extend their support for the establishment of the African Economic Community,

*Recalling also* its resolution 48/214 of 23 December 1993 on the implementation of the United Nations New Agenda for the Development of Africa in the 1990s,

*Taking note* of the resolutions, decisions and declarations adopted by the Council of Ministers of the Organization of African Unity at its sixty-second ordinary

session, held at Addis Ababa from 21 to 23 June 1995, and by the Assembly of Heads of State and Government of the Organization of African Unity at its thirty-first ordinary session, held at Addis Ababa from 26 to 28 June 1995,

*Considering* the important statement made by the representative of the current Chairman of the Assembly of Heads of State and Government of the Organization of African Unity before the General Assembly on 27 September 1995,

*Mindful* of the need for continued and closer cooperation between the United Nations and its specialized agencies and the Organization of African Unity, in particular in the political, economic, social, technical, cultural and administrative fields,

*Noting* that the Mechanism for Conflict Prevention, Management and Resolution of the Organization of African Unity is developing its capacity in preventive diplomacy,

*Also noting* the efforts of the Organization of African Unity, and the support and assistance of the United Nations, to promote the peaceful settlement of disputes and conflicts in Africa and the harmonious continuation of the process of democratization,

*Deeply concerned* that, despite the policies of reform being implemented by most African countries, their economic situation remains critical and African recovery and development continue to be severely hindered by the persistence of lower-level commodity prices, the heavy debt burden and the paucity of funding possibilities,

*Aware* of the efforts being made by the Organization of African Unity and its member States in the area of economic integration and of the need to accelerate the process of implementation of the African Economic Community,

*Deeply concerned also* about the gravity of the situation of refugees and displaced persons in Africa and the urgent need for increased international assistance to help refugees and, subsequently, African countries of asylum,

*Acknowledging* the assistance already rendered by the international community, in particular to refugees, displaced persons and African countries of asylum,

*Recognizing* the importance of developing and maintaining a culture of peace, tolerance and harmonious relationships in order to contribute to the prevention of conflicts and wars in Africa,

1. *Takes note* of the report of the Secretary-General on cooperation between the United Nations and the Organization of African Unity and of his efforts to strengthen that cooperation and to implement the relevant resolutions;

2. *Notes with appreciation* the continued and increasing participation of the Organization of African Unity in the work of the United Nations and the specialized agencies and its constructive contribution to that work;

3. *Calls upon* the United Nations organs, in particular the Security Council and the Economic and Social Council, to continue to involve the Organization of African Unity closely in all their activities concerning Africa;

4. *Welcomes* the fact that both the United Nations and the Organization of African Unity have agreed to strengthen and broaden their cooperation in measures to prevent and resolve conflicts in Africa, and in this regard invites the United Nations to provide the Organization of African Unity with the necessary support

for the promotion of a culture of peace, tolerance and harmonious relationships in Africa;

5. *Calls upon* the United Nations to coordinate its efforts and to cooperate with the Organization of African Unity in the context of the pacific settlement of disputes and the maintenance of international peace and security in Africa, as provided for under Chapter VIII of the Charter of the United Nations;

6. *Commends* the efforts of the Organization of African Unity to strengthen its capacity in the field of conflict resolution and to operationalize its Mechanism for Conflict Prevention, Management and Resolution in Africa;

7. *Also commends* the United Nations and the Organization of African Unity for their ongoing cooperative activities in the resolution of conflicts in Africa, and stresses the need to enhance and strengthen the existing pattern of exchange of information and consultations, especially in the areas of preventive diplomacy, peacemaking and peace-keeping operations;

8. *Invites* the United Nations to assist the Organization of African Unity, within existing resources, in strengthening its institutional and operational capacity in the prevention, management and resolution of conflicts in Africa, in particular in the following areas:

(*a*) Establishment of an early-warning system;

(*b*) Technical assistance and training of personnel, including a staff exchange programme;

(*c*) Exchange and coordination of information between their respective early-warning systems;

(*d*) Logistical support;

(*e*) Mobilization of financial support;

9. *Urges* the United Nations to facilitate the participation of the Organization of African Unity in its peacemaking and peace-keeping operations and, with the consent of parties concerned, in joint fact-finding missions in Africa, by providing technical assistance and assisting in the mobilization of financial and logistical support;

10. *Notes with appreciation* the assistance provided by the United Nations and its agencies to African countries in the context of the democratization process;

11. *Urges* the United Nations to continue to support the Organization of African Unity in its efforts to manage a peaceful democratic transition in Africa, in particular in the areas of education for democracy, election observation, human rights and freedom, including technical support to the African Commission on Human and Peoples' Rights;

12. *Urges* all Member States and regional and international organizations, in particular those of the United Nations system, as well as non-governmental organizations, to provide the necessary and appropriate economic, financial and technical assistance to refugees and displaced persons, as well as to African countries of asylum, taking into account recent disquieting developments in this respect;

13. *Commends* the continued efforts of the Organization of African Unity to promote multilateral cooperation and economic integration among African States, and requests United Nations agencies to continue to support those efforts;

14. *Stresses* that the economic, technical and development assistance provided to Africa by the organizations of the United Nations system must continue, and emphasizes the current need for those organizations to accord priority to Africa in this field;

15. *Urges* the Secretary-General, Member States, regional and international organizations, in particular those of the United Nations system, and non-governmental organizations to extend their support to the operations of the African Economic Community and to assist in economic integration and cooperation in Africa;

16. *Requests* the Secretary-General to support the efforts of the Secretary-General of the Organization of African Unity, in particular in the preparation of the first meeting of the Economic and Social Commission of the African Economic Community, the strengthening of the regional economic communities, and the preparation of the protocols to the Treaty Establishing the African Economic Community, its popularization and the strengthening of its institutional support;

17. *Requests* the agencies of the United Nations system working in Africa to include in their programmes at the national and regional levels activities that will enhance regional cooperation in their respective areas and to facilitate the realization of the objectives of the Treaty Establishing the African Economic Community;

18. *Calls upon* United Nations agencies to intensify the coordination of their regional programmes in Africa in order to create interlinkages among them and to ensure the harmonization of their programmes with those of the African regional and subregional economic organizations;

19. *Emphasizes* the urgency of the need to adopt appropriate measures to ensure the effective implementation of the United Nations New Agenda for the Development of Africa in the 1990s, in particular in the areas of resource flows, debt relief and diversification of African economies;

20. *Invites* the Secretary-General to associate the Organization of African Unity closely with the follow-up and monitoring of the implementation of the United Nations New Agenda for the Development of Africa in the 1990s, including the conduct of the mid-term review of its implementation in 1996;

21. *Recalls* its resolution 48/214, in paragraph 10 of which it invited the Secretary-General to reinforce the capabilities of the Office of the Special Coordinator for Africa and the Least Developed Countries of the Department for Policy Coordination and Sustainable Development of the Secretariat to follow up and promote the responses of the United Nations system and the international community to the development concerns of Africa, as expressed in the United Nations New Agenda for the Development of Africa in the 1990s;

22. *Takes note with satisfaction* of the recommendations of the meeting between the secretariats of the Organization of African Unity and the United Nations held at Addis Ababa from 6 to 9 November 1995, and endorses the convening of a meeting in 1996, at Addis Ababa, to review and evaluate the progress made in the implementation of the recommendations agreed at the November meeting and to adopt new and effective joint action;

23. *Calls upon* the relevant organs of the United Nations system to ensure the effective, fair and equita-

ble representation of Africa at senior and policy levels at their respective headquarters and in their regional field operations;

24.   *Requests* the relevant organs of the United Nations system to assist the Organization of African Unity to strengthen its capacity for information gathering, analysis and dissemination through the training of personnel and the mobilization of technical and financial assistance;

25.   *Requests* the Secretary-General to report to the General Assembly at its fifty-first session on the implementation of the present resolution and on the de-velopment of cooperation between the Organization of African Unity and the organizations of the United Nations system.

General Assembly resolution 50/158

21 December 1995      Meeting 97      Adopted without vote

Draft by Sudan (A/50/L.51/Rev.1); agenda item 43.
*Meeting numbers.* GA 50th session: plenary 9, 88, 97.

*REFERENCES*

(1)A/50/575. (2)YUN 1994, p. 386, GA res. 49/64, 15 Dec. 1994. (3)A/50/575/Add.1. (4)YUN 1994, p. 682. (5)YUN 1992, p. 670. (6)YUN 1994, p. 1225. (7)A/50/711-S/1995/911.

Chapter III

# Americas

In 1995, the political situation in Central America and the Caribbean continued to improve, with positive developments in a number of areas. The parties to the political process in El Salvador agreed to accelerate implementation of their 1992 Peace Agreement; following the withdrawal of the UN Observer Mission in El Salvador (ONUSAL) at the end of April, the Mission of the UN in El Salvador (MINUSAL) was established to verify the Agreement's implementation. The negotiating process between the parties to the internal armed conflict in Guatemala continued throughout the year; the UN human rights verification mission in that country verified compliance with the 1994 Comprehensive Agreement on Human Rights and with human rights aspects of the Agreement on Identity and Rights of Indigenous Peoples, signed in March 1995. The process of transition to a democratic society in Nicaragua was consolidated further and continued to receive international support; in June, the executive and legislative branches in that country reached agreement on the constitutional reform, promulgated in July, which cleared the way for 1996 general elections.

The UN Mission in Haiti (UNMIH) was fully deployed in 1995 and took over responsibilities from the Multinational Force in Haiti following the establishment of a secure and stable environment. In cooperation with the International Civilian Mission to Haiti, mandated to monitor and promote the observance of human rights, UNMIH assisted in the organization and conduct of local, legislative and presidential elections. In December, René Préval was elected President of Haiti, to succeed Jean-Bertrand Aristide.

In a resolution concerning the economic embargo by the United States against Cuba, the General Assembly called for the repeal of laws which had extraterritorial effects on States' sovereignty and freedom of trade and navigation. In another resolution, the Assembly supported the initiative of Panama to convene the Universal Congress on the Panama Canal.

## Central America situation

In response to a 1994 General Assembly request,[1] the Secretary-General reported[2] on 3 October 1995 on the situation in Central America, covering the progress achieved since October 1994 by Central American countries in the areas of peace, freedom, democracy and development. The report summarized major developments in those countries and described their efforts to convert into a reality the improved prospects for peace and development, which the Secretary-General had been able to observe during his visit to Honduras, El Salvador and Guatemala from 1 to 3 April 1995.

It was pointed out that in 1995 democratically elected Governments of the region had shown themselves to be stable in the face of internal difficulties. Democratic institutions continued to be strengthened, with the consolidation of activities by national councils for human rights in El Salvador, Guatemala and Honduras as well as by non-governmental organizations (NGOs) in the region, which provided new channels for political participation. In El Salvador, the Government had committed itself to promoting development by signing the Pact of San Andrés on 31 May. The parties to the conflict in Guatemala signed on 22 August a declaration on a cease-fire during the electoral period and on the results of elections. In Nicaragua, months of dispute over constitutional reform had ended in an agreement between the country's executive and legislative branches. A conflict over a programme of reforms between the Government and the opposition in Costa Rica was defused by a pact agreed on in June.

At the same time, the pursuit of policies for macroeconomic stabilization, liberalization of the economy and modernization of the State had been accompanied by a decline in social conditions across much of Central America, which could be redressed only through increased investment in the region. To create an environment conducive to economic growth and investment, Governments had taken steps to consolidate further the Alliance for the Sustainable Development of Central America—a new regional strategy for cooperation and integration adopted in 1994.[3] In June, Costa Rica joined the Central American Integration System, which was also strengthened with the installation of its executive committee in March. Other regional institutions, such as the Central American Parliament, the Central American Bank for Economic Integration and the Central American Court of Justice, increased their activities within the framework of the Alliance. In August, the countries of the "northern triangle"—El Salvador, Guatemala and Honduras—ratified the Guatemala Protocol to the General Treaty on Central American Integration, with a view to increasing the potential of their subregional market. However, the potential for conflict between regional and individual priorities in the area of economic integration remained great, as evidenced by Costa Rica's bilateral free trade agreement with Mexico, which came into effect on 1 January in advance of any regional agreement, and by the region's response to El Salvador's proposal for lowering the existing common tariff ceiling and floor.

The elaboration of an accord on regional security issues was discussed by the Central American Security Commission. A proposed treaty sought to define a security model making use of democratic institutions to find integral and peaceable solutions to the region's problems. In the meantime, Panama joined Costa Rica in abolishing its army; Nicaragua and El Salvador continued to make progress in subordinating their armies to civilian rule; and Honduras and Guatemala began to address that issue in depth. On 29 June, the Ministers of Defence and heads of the armed forces of Honduras, El Salvador and Nicaragua signed a declaration for peace, democracy, development and integration in Central America, by which they recognized the need to define a new model for regional defence respectful of human rights, the strengthening of the rule of law and the integral development of the human person and society. Progress was also made in overcoming territorial disputes in the region, but difficulties remained with regard to border disputes between Honduras and El Salvador and between Guatemala and Belize, as well as to the demarcation of waters in the Gulf of Fonseca shared by Honduras, El Salvador and Nicaragua. Binational commissions of El Salvador and Honduras continued discussions to resolve both border demarcation and dual nationality and property issues; in September, the two countries agreed to undertake the verification of property registration, examine issues of nationality and introduce a new system of monitoring borders so as to reduce tensions in the area.

The report further described international assistance for Central American efforts to promote peace, freedom, democracy and development. It noted activities of the Group of Friends of the Guatemalan Peace Process (Colombia, Mexico, Norway, Spain, United States, Venezuela) and the support group to follow the transition process and internal consensus-building in Nicaragua (Canada, Mexico, Netherlands, Spain, Sweden), as well as political dialogue and economic cooperation with the European Union (EU) maintained

through the eleventh meeting in the "San José Process" (Panama City, 23-24 February) between the Foreign Ministers of Central America, EU and the Group of Three (Colombia, Mexico, Venezuela). The economic contribution of the international community was extended by commitments made during informal consultative group meetings of donors on Nicaragua, Guatemala and El Salvador, organized by the Inter-American Development Bank and the World Bank in Paris from 19 to 22 June. The Rio Group of countries, at their ninth summit meeting (Quito, Ecuador, 4-5 September), expressed support for integration processes in Latin America and the Caribbean and reaffirmed their commitment to establishing a hemispheric free trade zone by 2005, as agreed at the Summit of the Americas in December 1994 in Miami, Florida, United States. Cooperation also continued between Central America and the Organization of American States (OAS) in the areas of trade and mine clearance, as well as within the framework of the Alliance for Sustainable Development.

As for UN efforts in Central America, the Secretary-General noted that the peace process in El Salvador, initiated by the 1992 Peace Agreement, had maintained its impetus, although difficulties were encountered and delays had occurred in a number of areas; ONUSAL completed its mandate, and MINUSAL was set up to verify completion of the Agreement's implementation (see below, under "El Salvador situation"). Positive developments had also occurred in the peace process in Guatemala, which proceeded in accordance with the Framework Agreement and other accords concluded in 1994; in that regard, the report cited ongoing preparations for general elections in that country, scheduled for November 1995. At the same time, while compliance by the parties to the peace process with the 1994 Comprehensive Agreement on Human Rights showed some improvement, the overall human rights situation remained a source of concern, as reported by the UN human rights verification mission in Guatemala (see below, under "Guatemala situation").

The Secretary-General also outlined UN operational activities in support of processes in the region, which were described in detail in his 26 October report[4] on international assistance to and cooperation with the Alliance for Sustainable Development (see PART FOUR, Chapter III), and noted that they focused on poverty alleviation, economic reform and public sector policies and management, emergency and development assistance, strengthening of democratic institutions, environmental protection and promotion of sustainable development, population-related programmes and natural disaster prevention and rehabilitation. He urged the Central American countries and the international community to remain fully engaged in the consolidation of peace throughout the region, and expressed his readiness to continue to play the active role in that process entrusted to him by the General Assembly.

**Communications.** The Presidents of Costa Rica, El Salvador, Guatemala, Honduras, Nicaragua and Panama and the Prime Minister of Belize, at their sixteenth summit meeting (Cerro Verde, El Salvador, 29-31 March), adopted a declaration on the strengthening of peace and security in the Central American region, reiterating, *inter alia*, their commitment to the procedure for a firm and lasting peace in Central America, set out in 1987.[(5)] They also adopted a declaration of support for the establishment and operation of the Central American Radio Network and a declaration on the situation in Nicaragua, as well as a treaty on Central American social integration, a programme of immediate action for investment in human capital, and an agreement for the joint implementation of the 1992 UN Framework Convention on Climate Change (see PART FOUR, Chapter VII). The results of the meeting were transmitted to the Secretary-General on 18 April.[(6)]

On 5 April, the Secretary-General communicated[(7)] to the Presidents of the General Assembly and of the Security Council the Agreement on Identity and Rights of Indigenous Peoples, signed by the parties to the conflict in Guatemala on 31 March (see below). On 11 October, El Salvador transmitted[(8)] a declaration on the peace process in Guatemala, adopted by the Presidents of Costa Rica, El Salvador, Honduras and Nicaragua and the Vice-President of Panama at a special meeting held in Costa del Sol, El Salvador, on 5 October, as well as their position and that of the Guatemalan President concerning education as a vital element of economic and social development.

**GENERAL ASSEMBLY ACTION**

On 20 December, the General Assembly adopted **resolution 50/132**.

**The situation in Central America: procedures for the establishment of a firm and lasting peace and progress in fashioning a region of peace, freedom, democracy and development**

*The General Assembly,*

*Recalling* the relevant resolutions of the Security Council and its own resolutions, particularly resolutions 48/161 of 20 December 1993 and 49/137 of 19 December 1994, in which it recognized the importance of international support for Central America, within an appropriate global frame of reference, in order to preserve and extend the progress made in the process of consolidating peace, democracy and sustainable development and thereby to overcome the obstacles that are preventing Central America from becoming a region of peace, freedom, democracy and sustainable development,

*Recognizing* the importance and validity of the commitments made by the Central American Presidents since the Esquipulas II summit meeting of 7 August 1987 and their subsequent summit meetings, especially the fifteenth meeting, held at Guácimo, Costa Rica, from 18 to 20 August 1994, the Central American Environment Summit for Sustainable Development, held at Managua on 12 and 13 October 1994, the International Conference on Peace and Development in Central America, held at Tegucigalpa on 24 and 25 October 1994, and the sixteenth meeting of Central American Presidents, held in El Salvador in March 1995,

*Reaffirming* that there can be no peace in Central America without sustainable development or democracy, which are essential for ensuring the processes of change in the region and for implementing the integrated proposal for sustainable development agreed on at the most recent meetings of Central American Presidents, in particular the Central American Environment Summit for Sustainable Development and the International Conference on Peace and Development in Central America,

*Convinced* of the hopes that inspire the peoples of Central America to achieve peace, reconciliation, development and social justice, and the commitment to settle their differences by means of dialogue, negotiation and respect for the legitimate interests of all States, in accordance with their own decision and their own historical experience, while fully respecting the principles of self-determination and non-intervention,

*Recognizing* the validity of the Declaration of Commitments in favour of the populations affected both by uprootedness and by conflicts and extreme poverty, adopted at Mexico City on 29 June 1994, and the role of lead agency which the United Nations Development Programme has assumed in the place of the mandate formerly discharged by the Office of the United Nations High Commissioner for Refugees,

*Drawing attention* to the establishment of the Alliance for the Sustainable Development of Central America, which constitutes the new integrated development strategy at the national and regional levels and defines the political, moral, economic, social and environmental priorities, and to the signing, at the El Salvador summit meeting in March 1995, of the Treaty on Central American Social Integration, one of whose main objectives is investment in human capital, and bearing in mind that the Central American Integration System is the institutional framework which makes possible the effective, ordered and coherent promotion of integrated development,

*Emphasizing* the importance of cooperation and international solidarity in supporting the efforts being made by the peoples and Governments of Central America for the consolidation of a firm and lasting peace, and the need to strengthen the new programme of cooperation and economic, technical and financial assistance for Central America in the light of the new situation in the region,

*Noting* the efforts made by the Central American Security Commission and the importance of the ongoing negotiation of the Central American security treaty in accelerating the establishment of a new model of regional security, as provided for in the Tegucigalpa Protocol, and the agenda and programme of specific action for sustainable development adopted at the fifteenth Central American summit meeting, held at Guácimo,

*Welcoming* the role played by the peace-keeping operations of the United Nations, which carried out fully their mandate in Central America pursuant to the relevant resolutions of the Security Council, and recognizing the importance of the observer and monitoring missions planned or under way in the region in accordance with the resolutions adopted by the General Assembly,

*Stressing* the importance of the determination of the Government of Guatemala and of the Unidad Revolucionaria Nacional Guatemalteca to achieve the full exercise of human rights and to reach, as promptly as possible, an agreement to establish a firm and lasting peace, in accordance with the Framework Agreement for the Resumption of the Negotiating Process between the Government of Guatemala and the Unidad Revolucionaria Nacional Guatemalteca of 10 January 1994 and the hopes of the Guatemalan people, and the importance of full compliance by both parties with the other agreed commitments,

*Recalling* its resolutions 48/267 of 19 September 1994, 49/236 A of 31 March 1995 and 49/236 B of 14 September 1995, by which it decided to establish the United Nations Mission for the Verification of Human Rights and of Compliance with the Commitments of the Comprehensive Agreement on Human Rights in Guatemala and extended the mandate of the Mission,

*Emphasizing* the role of international cooperation in national efforts towards peace, in particular in contributing to the trust fund for the Guatemala peace process set up by the Secretary-General on 1 March 1995,

*Stressing also* the importance of the current electoral process in strengthening the democratic institutions of Guatemala,

*Noting with satisfaction* the signing of the Agreement on Identity and Rights of Indigenous Peoples on 31 March 1995, at Mexico City, in the framework of the Guatemala peace process,

*Noting with appreciation* the efforts being made by the people and Government of El Salvador to consolidate the progress made in the transition towards a society characterized by democracy, the rule of law and respect for human rights, and commending the reaffirmation by the Government of El Salvador of its political will to honour fully its commitments under the Peace Agreement, for the benefit of all Salvadorans,

*Welcoming* resolution 50/7 of 31 October 1995, in which it approved the proposal of the Secretary-General to extend the mandate of the Mission of the United Nations in El Salvador for a period of six months, with a gradual reduction of its strength and costs, in a manner consistent with the effective performance of its duties, in order to exercise his good offices and to monitor the application of pending questions related to the peace agreements,

*Welcoming also* the adoption of resolution 49/16 of 17 November 1994, in which it recognized the exceptional circumstances that still prevail in Nicaragua,

*Recognizing* that the efforts of the Government of Nicaragua to consolidate peace and democracy, repair its economy and rebuild the nation merit the urgent support of the international community and the United Nations system in order to preserve the gains made and overcome the effects of the war and natural disasters which persist in Nicaragua, and that the request of the Nicaraguan Government for United Nations observers during the elections to be held in 1996 also merits support,

*Recognizing also* the valuable and effective contribution made by the United Nations and by various governmental and non-governmental mechanisms to the gradual transformation of Central America into a region of peace, freedom, democracy and development, and the importance of the political dialogue and economic cooperation which are taking place in the ministerial conference between the European Union and the Central American countries, and the joint initiative by the industrialized countries of the Group of Twenty-four and the countries of the Group of Three as cooperating countries, under the auspices of the Association for Democracy and Development in Central America,

*Taking note* of the report of the Secretary-General of 3 October 1995 on the situation in Central America,

1. *Commends* the efforts of the peoples and Governments of the Central American countries to consolidate peace and promote sustainable development by implementing the agreements adopted at the summit meetings, especially the commitments adopted at the recent presidential meetings, and requests the Secretary-General to continue to give the fullest possible support to the initiatives and activities of the Governments of the Central American countries;

2. *Supports* the decision of the Presidents of the Central American countries to declare Central America a region of peace, freedom, democracy and development, and encourages the initiatives of the Central American countries, in the framework of the integrated strategy for sustainable development and based on the latest Central American meetings, to consolidate Governments that base their development on democracy, peace, cooperation and respect for human rights;

3. *Draws attention* to the decision of the Presidents of the Central American countries embodied in the Declaration of Guácimo, in which the national and regional strategy known as the Alliance for the Sustainable Development of Central America became an integrated initiative reflected in a programme of immediate action in the political, moral, economic, social and environmental fields, through which the Central American countries hope to become, with the support of the international community, an example of sustainable development for other regions;

4. *Welcomes* the efforts of the Central American countries to promote economic growth oriented towards human development, as well as the progress achieved in strengthening democracy and consolidating peace in the region;

5. *Emphasizes* the work accomplished by the Central American Integration System, the registry of the Tegucigalpa Protocol with the United Nations Secretariat and the granting of observer status by the General Assembly, expresses its full support for the progress achieved by the Central American countries in stimulating and broadening the process of Central American integration, and calls on Member States and international organizations to provide effective cooperation to Central America so that subregional integration is strengthened and becomes an effective mechanism for achieving sustainable development;

6. *Supports* the concern of the Central American countries to create a new model of regional security based on a reasonable balance of forces and the pre-

eminence of civil authority, urges the Central American Security Commission to pursue negotiations for the preparation of the treaty on democratic security in Central America, which constitutes one of the basic aims of the Central American Integration System, and requests the Secretary-General to provide it with the requisite support in a timely manner;

7. *Encourages* the Security Commission to pursue negotiations for the preparation of the treaty on democratic security in Central America with a view to speeding up the establishment of the new model of regional security;

8. *Stresses* the importance of intensifying the serious and resolute negotiations between the Government of Guatemala and the Unidad Revolucionaria Nacional Guatemalteca, and urges that negotiations on the remaining agenda items should be concluded without delay with a view to reaching at the earliest possible date a firm and lasting peace agreement, thus completing the peace process in Central America;

9. *Takes note with satisfaction* of the Agreement on Identity and Rights of Indigenous Peoples as an important step in the peace process in Guatemala and a milestone in the International Decade of the World's Indigenous People;

10. *Calls upon* the parties to comply fully with their commitments under the Comprehensive Agreement on Human Rights in Guatemala and their human rights commitments under the Agreement on Identity and Rights of Indigenous Peoples and to implement the corresponding recommendations of the United Nations Mission for the Verification of Human Rights and of Compliance with the Commitments of the Comprehensive Agreement on Human Rights in Guatemala;

11. *Requests* the Secretary-General, the organizations of the United Nations system and the international community to continue their support for the peace process and hence for efforts to promote national reconciliation, democracy and development in Guatemala;

12. *Reiterates its appreciation* of the peace efforts of the Secretary-General, the Group of Friends (Colombia, Mexico, Norway, Spain, the United States of America and Venezuela) and the relevant United Nations bodies, as well as its appreciation of the contribution of the Assembly of Civil Society and other Guatemalans within the constitutional framework and the peace agreements;

13. *Welcomes* the Contadora Declaration signed on 22 August 1995 by the political forces of Guatemala, in which they committed themselves to assuring that the Government that will take office on 14 January 1996 will respect the agreements already reached in the peace process and will make every effort to bring that process to an early and successful conclusion;

14. *Calls upon* the Government of El Salvador and all the political forces involved in the peace process to make all possible efforts to complete the implementation of all remaining aspects of the Peace Agreement;

15. *Notes with satisfaction* the establishment by the Secretary-General of the Trust Fund for the Mission of the United Nations in El Salvador and the extension of the Mission's mandate for a six-month period as from 31 October 1995 in order to continue to observe and monitor the implementation of the remaining commitments until they have been fully met, and emphasizes the importance of continued cooperation between the Mission of the United Nations in El Salvador and other

organizations of the United Nations system in the consolidation of the Peace Agreement;

16. *Reiterates its recognition* of the effective and timely participation of the Secretary-General and his representatives and encourages them to continue to take all necessary steps to ensure the successful implementation of all the commitments made by the parties to the El Salvador Peace Agreement, including the joint effort undertaken by the Government of El Salvador and the Frente Farabundo Martí para la Liberación Nacional to obtain resources to facilitate the full implementation of the Peace Agreement;

17. *Recognizes* the achievements made by the people and Government of Nicaragua in their efforts to consolidate peace, democracy and reconciliation among Nicaraguans, as well as the importance of reaching a national understanding in order to define a national development strategy through political dialogue and economic and social consultation among all sectors of the country, thereby strengthening grass-roots support for the country's reconstruction, and emphasizes how important it is for the Secretary-General to comply with Nicaragua's request for observers to be present during the electoral process in 1996;

18. *Supports* the treatment accorded to Nicaragua in the light of its continuing exceptional circumstances, so that the international community and financial institutions can incorporate that treatment into programmes to support the country's economic recovery and social reconstruction;

19. *Expresses its appreciation* of the work of the support group for Nicaragua (Canada, Mexico, the Netherlands, Spain and Sweden), which, under the coordination of the Secretary-General, is playing an active role in supporting the country's efforts towards economic recovery and social development, particularly with regard to solving the external debt problem and securing investments and new resources that will allow the country's economic and social reconstruction programmes to continue, and requests the Secretary-General to continue to support those efforts;

20. *Emphasizes* the importance that the political dialogue and economic cooperation taking place within the ministerial conference between the European Union and its member States and the Central American countries, with the participation of the Group of Three as cooperating countries, have for the efforts of the Central American countries to achieve peace, consolidate democracy and ensure sustainable development;

21. *Also emphasizes* the commitments on sustainable development adopted at the fifteenth meeting of Central American Presidents, held at Guácimo, Costa Rica, the sixteenth meeting of Central American Presidents, held in El Salvador in March 1995, the Central American Environment Summit for Sustainable Development, held at Managua, and the International Conference on Peace and Development in Central America, held at Tegucigalpa, and urges the international community to give them every support;

22. *Reiterates* the importance of the support of the United Nations system through its operational activities, in particular the United Nations Development Programme, aimed at facilitating the development of programmes and projects which are indispensable for strengthening peace and the development process in the region, bearing particularly in mind the new strategy

for subregional development established by the Alliance for the Sustainable Development of Central America, and urges the international community to lend its support to the achievement of the goals of the new strategy for development in Central America;

23. *Recognizes* the importance of accessions to the Treaty on Central American Social Integration and the fulfilment of the commitments made at Mexico City in June 1994 to benefit populations affected by uprooting, conflicts and extreme poverty;

24. *Reiterates its full appreciation and gratitude* to the Secretary-General for his efforts to promote the pacification process and the consolidation of peace in Central America, and to the groups of friendly countries which have made a direct contribution to attaining those ends, and requests that those efforts be continued;

25. *Requests* the Secretary-General to report to the General Assembly at its fifty-first session on the implementation of the present resolution;

26. *Decides* to include in the provisional agenda of its fifty-first session the item entitled "The situation in Central America: procedures for the establishment of a firm and lasting peace and progress in fashioning a region of peace, freedom, democracy and development".

General Assembly resolution 50/132

20 December 1995     Meeting 96     Adopted without vote

37-nation draft (A/50/L.17/Rev.1 & Rev.1/Add.1); agenda item 45.
*Financial implications.* 5th Committee, A/50/826; S-G, A/C.5/50/36.
*Meeting numbers.* GA 50th session: 5th Committee 41; plenary 54, 96.

On 12 October, the Assembly, by **resolution 50/2**, granted observer status to the Central American Integration System.

At their seventeenth summit meeting (San Pedro Sula, Honduras, 13-15 December),[9] the Central American Presidents adopted a declaration as well as a framework treaty on democratic security in Central America, containing provisions for the Central American Democratic Security Model, its constituent organs and governing principles in relation to the rule of law, security of individuals and their property, and regional security. They also adopted an agreement on an electrical interconnection system for Central America and a treaty on the recovery and return of stolen, appropriated or illicitly retained vehicles.

## El Salvador situation

Implementation of the 1992 Peace Agreement[10] between the Government of El Salvador and the Frente Farabundo Martí para la Liberación Nacional (FMLN) continued in 1995, but was hindered by lengthy delays in several important areas. In April, the Salvadoran parties agreed on a work programme to complete the Agreement's implementation. The UN Observer Mission in El Salvador (ONUSAL), established in 1991[11] to monitor all agreements between the Government and FMLN, was withdrawn by the end of April, in accordance with a 1994 Security Council resolution.[12] The termination of the Mission's man-

date, which had been enlarged in 1992[13] to include verification and monitoring of the implementation of the 1992 Peace Agreement, and in 1993[14] to include observance of the electoral process, was affirmed by the Council in April.

Following ONUSAL's withdrawal, the Mission of the UN in El Salvador (MINUSAL) was established to provide good offices and verify implementation of outstanding provisions of the peace accords. In September, Ricardo Vigil (Peru) replaced Enrique ter Horst (Venezuela) as the Secretary-General's Special Representative for El Salvador and Chief of Mission. In October, the General Assembly extended the Mission's mandate until 30 April 1996.

**Report of the Secretary-General (March).** In a 24 March report[15] on ONUSAL, the Secretary-General assessed the implementation of the peace accords in El Salvador. He noted the progress made in the reduction and transformation of the Armed Forces and readjustment of their mission, but pointed out that some complementary measures were still required to complete the process. Despite efforts to collect weapons from civilians and government institutions, a large number of unregistered arms in the country continued to pose a problem. Although the Government reported having seized some 2,000 such weapons since the beginning of the year, voluntary surrender had been negligible and prompt steps were needed to address the issue.

The long-delayed demobilization of the National Police had been formally effected on 31 December 1994, and the dissolution of the Customs Police was expected to be completed by the end of March 1995. The National Police was replaced by the National Civil Police (PNC), whose strength had reached more than 7,000 agents, in addition to 220 middle- and high-level officers, all graduates of the newly established National Public Security Academy. At the same time, PNC's functioning was still affected by legal voids and its regulatory machinery required strengthening, as did the criteria and procedures for admission to the Academy and its courses on key subjects. In addition, an increase in criminal violence prompted a decision by the authorities to use military patrols to deter crime in rural areas. Although the patrols operated together with PNC and under its command, the decision was not in compliance with the procedures established under the peace accords, which entailed undeniable risks, the Secretary-General stated.

Following implementation of several crucial judicial reforms, the National Counsel for the Defence of Human Rights and the new Supreme Court consolidated their activities against the backdrop of a marked decline in human rights violations. The Joint Group for the Investigation of Politically Motivated Illegal Armed Groups, established in 1993[16] following the assassination of several FMLN leaders, made recommendations whose implementation could reduce impunity for both political and organized crime; however, no action was taken to implement them and the assassination cases remained unresolved. At the same time, non-binding recommendations of the National Counsel were often ignored, and the rate of conviction or sentencing for crimes such as homicides, attempted homicides and death threats remained low, which explained continuing popular mistrust of or scepticism about human rights institutions in the country. In addition, basic reforms to strengthen the human rights machinery called for by the Commission on the Truth were still pending, as was implementation of the Commission's binding recommendations aimed at enabling Salvadorans to have access to the international protection system.

The report noted that the presidential, legislative and municipal elections in El Salvador, held in 1994, had revealed a need for reform of the electoral system, including introduction of a single identity document; provision for voting in the area of residence of the voter; standardization of the formula for representation in the Legislative Assembly and municipalities; and depoliticization of the Supreme Electoral Tribunal. While no measures had been implemented since the elections, those issues were expected to be included in a package of reforms for consideration by the Legislative Assembly during the year.

Addressing economic and social issues, the Secretary-General pointed out that 18,362 people had received title to land under the land-transfer programme, including 5,420 during the reporting period alone; however, that total represented only 45 per cent of the 40,648 potential beneficiaries. The programme's implementation had accelerated in November/December 1994 with the adoption of a decree facilitating the procedure for legalization and titling of land, a number of administrative measures, and decentralization of the process to the regions, but the remaining administrative and legal impediments had led to its slow-down at the beginning of 1995 and made it impossible to complete the programme by the target date of 30 April. These included problems related to coordination of activities, measurement, identification of original owners and certification of ownership, inheritance issues, the need to title a large number of properties, and a lack of land title and the need to relocate, without breaking up existing human settlements, landholders occupying properties whose owners did not wish to sell. A lack of progress in finding a solution to the human settlements issue, due to differences in positions of the Government and of FMLN, led

to repeated incidents between landowners and landholders and created a potentially explosive situation.

There was also a need to accelerate the implementation of outstanding reintegration programmes, including immediate action to remedy the delays in disbursement of agricultural credit, since only 2,500 landholders of the 22,000 potential beneficiaries had to date received access to such credit. While almost 12,000 war-disabled and some 18,000 war victims were in critical need of assistance, the operations of the Fund for the Protection of the Wounded and War-disabled as a Consequence of the Armed Conflict continued to experience delays for lack of resources and administrative capacity. On the other hand, most micro-enterprise credit had been disbursed, and the housing programme for the 600 former medium-level FMLN commanders was scheduled to begin at the end of March. As at the end of February, almost 19,000 demobilized former combatants of the Armed Forces had received compensation payments, and more than 4,300 former National Police agents had received counselling with regard to educational and training opportunities. Labour rights issues were on the agenda of the High Labour Council, established in accordance with the new labour code and inaugurated on 6 March, which replaced de facto the Forum for Economic and Social Consultation provided for under the peace accords.

The Secretary-General further described developments in the political process in El Salvador, noting that two of FMLN's five constituent groups had established separate political parties and that the National Commission for the Consolidation of Peace, supervising the implementation of the peace accords, was considering ways to extend its functions beyond 30 April, the target date for conclusion of its work. He observed that despite the evident progress achieved by the country in moving away from a violent and closed society towards a democratic order, the unfulfilled commitments pertained to aspects of the peace accords of such importance as to call into question the irreversibility of the whole process. Opposition from pressure groups and continuing institutional fragility had forestalled decisive government action regarding accession to international human rights instruments, electoral reform and, to a significant extent, the land-transfer programme, and no agreement existed on modalities for the transfer of human settlements, while the slow pace in implementing other reintegration programmes created a potential source of unrest. Those problems, the Secretary-General said, needed to be defused urgently.

**Report of ONUSAL Human Rights Division.** By an 18 April note,[17] the Secretary-General transmitted to the General Assembly and the Security Council the thirteenth and final report of the Director of the ONUSAL Human Rights Division, mandated to verify compliance of the parties with the 1990 San José Agreement on Human Rights.[18] The report, covering the period from 1 October 1994 to 31 March 1995, assessed the development of human rights protection mechanisms in El Salvador and the status of agreements concerning respect for and protection of human rights. It provided an overview of institutional developments and proposed actions to be taken so as to ensure full compliance with the human rights obligations under the peace agreements. It also confirmed the trend towards improvement in the human rights situation, which had prompted the UN Commission on Human Rights to terminate in March 1995 the mandate of its Independent Expert for El Salvador. However, an increase in ordinary crime and the persistence of organized violence highlighted the need for continuing efforts to fulfil the human rights commitments, as well as an urgent need to accelerate the modernization and purification of the judiciary and to strengthen the investigative capacity of PNC.

The report noted that the new Supreme Court had begun implementing its proposals for modernizing the judiciary, eradicating corruption, training judicial officials, avoiding delays in the administration of justice and contributing to the effectiveness of auxiliary judicial bodies. Action was taken to eliminate the backlog of administrative matters and pending cases, revitalize the Judicial Training School and solve the prison crisis; purification of the judiciary was also started, albeit at a slower pace. In March, the Legislative Assembly elected the National Counsel for the Defence of Human Rights, recognized the jurisdiction of the Inter-American Court of Human Rights and ratified the Additional Protocol to the American Convention on Human Rights in the Area of Economic, Social and Cultural Rights (the "San Salvador Protocol"), as well as the Optional Protocol to the 1966 International Covenant on Civil and Political Rights, the latter giving victims of violations access to the UN Human Rights Committee once domestic jurisdictional remedies had been exhausted. However, action remained pending with regard to ratification of International Labour Organization conventions on protection of freedom of association and the 1968 Convention on the Non-Applicability of Statutory Limitations to War Crimes and Crimes against Humanity, as well as with regard to the lifting of reservations denying competence to the Committee against Torture to conduct investigations into systematic violations of the 1984 Convention against Torture and Other Cruel, Inhuman or Degrading Treatment or Punishment. Legislative reforms were also needed in respect of the career judicial service, constitutional justice, guarantees of due process, criminal legislation and arbitrary detention for petty offences.

The report pointed to persistent deficiencies in the work of PNC—which had officially taken over command from the National Police on 12 January 1995—including weak investigation mechanisms, lack of coordination with judicial and human rights institutions, and inadequate knowledge or application of various legal procedures. The Human Rights Division confirmed a number of serious human rights violations by PNC members and reported mishandling of certain crisis situations; at other times, however, PNC had acted prudently in coping with serious breaches of peace, it was stated. The report noted that a number of public demonstrations in El Salvador in recent months had gone beyond the limits of peaceful protest and had tested the Government's ability to respond in a spirit of peace and respect for democratic legality. On 24 January, demobilized soldiers occupied several buildings in San Salvador, including the Legislative Assembly, and blocked traffic on three main roads, which resulted in one fatality and three injuries. On 27 January, during a march of some 300 demobilized members of the former security forces to the Presidential Palace, clashes between demonstrators and PNC occurred and three police officers were taken hostage. On 29 March, PNC violently dispersed a demonstration of some 1,500 war-wounded, some of whom were armed with scythes, stones and even a firearm.

Among other disturbing developments were the murder, on 10 November 1994, of the leader of one of FMLN's constituent groups—an act which appeared to be politically motivated; the Government's decision to use the armed forces in crisis situations; and its public security plan for combating crime, put into effect in March 1995, which relied heavily on the participation of the armed forces. The report noted that such reliance, although constitutional, should be resorted to only in exceptional cases, once normal means of maintaining public order had been exhausted. It underscored the importance of strengthening the Government's capacity to fight organized and politically motivated crime, but pointed out that the recommendations made in that regard by the Joint Group for the Investigation of Politically Motivated Illegal Armed Groups remained unfulfilled. The report also noted a significant increase in the incidence and extent of violence against women.

The Director of the Human Rights Division concluded that the change in the human rights situation had to be consolidated and sustained over time, one of the greatest challenges being to deal with the increasing crime while remaining strictly within the framework of the Constitution and the peace agreements and putting into practice a new doctrine of public security. Bilateral and multilateral cooperation agencies were urged to contribute to that process.

**Communication of the Secretary-General (May).** On 18 May, the Secretary-General transmitted[19] to the Security Council a programme of work to complete implementation of the peace accords, agreed to by the Salvadoran Government and other signatories to the accords on 27 April. The programme assigned responsibilities and set deadlines for implementing specific aspects of the peace agreements relating to public security, land transfer, human settlements, reintegration, protection of the war-wounded and war-disabled, and legislative reforms. Under the work programme, the parties committed themselves to completing implementation of most agreements by 31 October 1995. They also provided recommendations for the completion of programmes not subject to a timetable.

The Secretary-General noted that implementation of the work programme would be verified by a small UN team set up pursuant to his recommendation of 6 February (see below), to be known as the Mission of the United Nations in El Salvador.

## UN Observer Mission in El Salvador

In a 6 February letter[20] to the Security Council President, the Secretary-General recalled a 1994 Council decision[12] to renew the mandate of ONUSAL for a final period until 30 April 1995, but pointed to the remaining difficulties in the implementation of peace agreements concerning El Salvador, particularly with regard to land and other reintegration programmes, including the issue of human settlements, as well as related to the judiciary and electoral reform and binding recommendations of the Commission on the Truth. Accordingly, he considered it essential to put in place a mechanism to continue ONUSAL's verification and good offices functions following its withdrawal, and proposed to establish, for an initial period of six months from the end of ONUSAL's mandate, a small team of Professionals, with the necessary support staff, to carry out those responsibilities as well as to ensure continued coordination with activities of the United Nations Development Programme (UNDP) in El Salvador. On 17 February, the Council President informed[21] the Secretary-General that Council members welcomed the proposed arrangement.

On 24 March, the Secretary-General reported[15] on ONUSAL activities from 1 November 1994 to 20 March 1995, including the work carried out by its Military Division, Police Division and Human Rights Division. He noted that preparations for dismantling the Mission were under way, with the official closure to take place at the end of April, and that nearly all Mission assets not required for its current functioning had been either transferred to other operations and UN organizations or sold commercially. As at 17 March, unpaid contributions from Member States to the ONUSAL Special Account since its inception totalled $23,649,501, and $10.5 million had had to be borrowed from other peace-keeping accounts to maintain the Mission. Final reports on the liquidation of assets and on the financial aspects of ONUSAL activities were to be submitted later in the year (see below).

The Secretary-General reviewed the situation in El Salvador (see above), stating that ONUSAL's withdrawal marked the end of a presence which had provided strong support for peace and democratization. However, implementation of the peace agreements in a number of important areas could not be completed before the expiry of ONUSAL's mandate and required further verification. In that regard, he reiterated his proposal to set up a small team to verify compliance with pending aspects of the peace accords and provide good offices.

### SECURITY COUNCIL ACTION

On 28 April, the Security Council adopted **resolution 991(1995)**.

*The Security Council,*

*Recalling* all its relevant resolutions and the statements of its President on the question of El Salvador,

*Having considered* the Secretary-General's report of 24 March 1995,

*Having also considered* the report of the Director of the Human Rights Division of the United Nations Observer Mission in El Salvador (ONUSAL) of 18 April 1995,

*Recognizing* with satisfaction that El Salvador has evolved from a country riven by conflict into a democratic and peaceful nation,

*Paying tribute* to those Member States which contributed personnel to the Mission,

*Recalling* the letters of the Secretary-General of 6 February 1995 and of the President of the Security Council of 17 February 1995,

1. *Pays tribute* to the accomplishments of ONUSAL, under the authority of the Secretary-General and his Special Representatives;

2. *Welcomes* the continued commitment of the Government and people of El Salvador to reconciliation, stabilization and development of political life in El Salvador;

3. *Urges* the Government of El Salvador, the Frente Farabundo Martí para la Liberación Nacional (FMLN) and all concerned in El Salvador to accelerate the pace of implementation of the Peace Accords and to work together to achieve fulfilment of outstanding commitments in order to ensure the irreversibility of the peace process;

4. *Reiterates* its call that States and international institutions continue to provide assistance to the Govern-

ment and people of El Salvador as they consolidate the gains made in the peace process;

5. *Affirms*, in accordance with paragraph 8 of resolution 961(1994), that the mandate of ONUSAL will terminate as of 30 April 1995.

Security Council resolution 991(1995)

28 April 1995    Meeting 3528    Adopted unanimously

Draft prepared in consultations among Council members (S/1995/335).

### Financing of ONUSAL

**Reports of the Secretary-General and ACABQ (March and June).** On 22 March, the Secretary-General reported[22] that the total expenditure of ONUSAL from 1 June to 30 November 1994 amounted to $11,704,200 gross ($10,397,300 net), resulting in an unencumbered balance of $270,400 gross ($338,900 net). He estimated the cost of maintaining the Mission from 1 December 1994 to 30 April 1995 at $5,215,600 gross ($4,613,900 net), taking into account its gradual phasing out from a strength of three military observers, 46 civilian police monitors and 150 civilian staff. The cost of its liquidation, for the period from 1 to 31 May 1995, was estimated at $113,300 and comprised salaries of 8 international and 16 local staff, common staff costs, mission subsistence allowance, rental of premises and staff assessment.

The report further indicated that ONUSAL equipment and other property was to be disposed of in accordance with a 1994 General Assembly resolution on administrative and budgetary aspects of financing UN peace-keeping operations,[23] and that unpaid assessed contributions from Member States to the ONUSAL Special Account, which had been merged with the Special Account for the UN Observer Group in Central America (ONUCA) in 1992,[24] totalled $23,650,597 as at 1 March 1995, including $10,666,652 for ONUCA and $12,983,945 for ONUSAL. Also at that date, voluntary contributions to ONUSAL amounted to $78,398, while the Trust Fund for the Commission on the Truth showed an income of $2,475,322. The report also provided observations and comments of the Secretary-General on previous recommendations of the Advisory Committee on Administrative and Budgetary Questions (ACABQ).

The Secretary-General proposed the appropriation and assessment of respective amounts for the periods from 1 June to 30 November 1994 and from 1 December 1994 to 30 April 1995, as well as for the Mission's liquidation from 1 to 31 May 1995, and action concerning the unencumbered balance of $542,100 gross ($534,500 net) for the period from 1 December 1993 to 31 May 1994.

In a 1 June report,[25] ACABQ recommended acceptance of the Secretary-General's proposals concerning the unencumbered balance and appropriation of the amount expended from 1 June

to 30 November 1994 and that requested for ONUSAL's liquidation. It recommended reductions to the cost estimates from 1 December 1994 to 30 April 1995 and the appropriation of $4,634,000 gross ($4,080,500 net) for that period. It noted with concern that the $10.5 million borrowed from other peace-keeping operations remained unpaid, and was of the view that the total amount to be assessed should depend on the General Assembly's treatment of those loans. ACABQ also noted the establishment of MINUSAL and recommended that the Secretary-General make proposals to the Assembly on its financing.

Pursuant to a 1994 Assembly resolution,[26] the Secretary-General submitted a 22 June report[27] on the final disposition of ONUSAL assets. He noted that the assets, with a total inventory value of $11,458,600, were classified under 10 categories as vehicular equipment, communications equipment, electronic data-processing equipment, mobile offices, generators, photocopying equipment, furniture and fixtures, solar panels, facsimile machines and other equipment. They were placed into three groups and four subgroups by method of disposition. The assets meeting the requirements of other UN missions, valued at $10,568,100, had been transferred either to other operations or to the UN Logistics Base in Brindisi, Italy, for temporary storage. Those identified as not suitable for transfer outside El Salvador were to be either sold commercially, with estimated proceeds of $624,000 to be credited to the ONUSAL Special Account, or donated to the Government, for a total value of $5,700. Other assets were either written off ($249,200) or classified as lost ($11,600).

The Secretary-General also pointed out that measures had been initiated to settle amounts owed by the Mission, noting that its unliquidated obligations totalled some $2,966,000 as at 31 March. Outstanding contributions due from Member States amounted to $23,643,957 as at 4 June. The Secretary-General stated that the disposal of the Mission's assets and liabilities was a continuing process; he sought the General Assembly's concurrence with the disposition of assets as outlined in the report.

**GENERAL ASSEMBLY ACTION (July)**

On 12 July, the Assembly adopted **resolution 49/246**.

### Financing of the United Nations Observer Mission in El Salvador

*The General Assembly,*

*Having considered* the report of the Secretary-General on the financing of the United Nations Observer Mission in El Salvador and the related report of the Advisory Committee on Administrative and Budgetary Questions,

*Recalling* Security Council resolution 693(1991) of 20 May 1991, by which the Council established the United Nations Observer Mission in El Salvador, and Council resolution 729(1992) of 14 January 1992, by which the Council extended and enlarged the mandate of the Observer Mission, as well as the subsequent resolutions by which the Council extended the mandate of the Mission, the most recent of which was resolution 961(1994) of 23 November 1994,

*Recalling also* its resolutions 47/223 of 16 March 1993 and 47/234 of 14 September 1993 and its decisions 48/468 A of 23 December 1993 and 49/405 of 14 October 1994 on the financing of the Observer Mission,

*Reaffirming* that the costs of the Observer Mission are expenses of the Organization to be borne by Member States in accordance with Article 17, paragraph 2, of the Charter of the United Nations,

*Recalling* its previous decisions regarding the fact that, in order to meet the expenditures caused by the Observer Mission, a different procedure is required from that applied to meet expenditures of the regular budget of the United Nations,

*Taking into account* the fact that the economically more developed countries are in a position to make relatively larger contributions and that the economically less developed countries have a relatively limited capacity to contribute towards such an operation,

*Bearing in mind* the special responsibilities of the States permanent members of the Security Council, as indicated in General Assembly resolution 1874(S-IV) of 27 June 1963, in the financing of such operations,

*Mindful* of the fact that it is essential to provide the Observer Mission with the necessary financial resources to enable it to meet its outstanding liabilities,

1. *Takes note* of the status of contributions to the United Nations Observer Mission in El Salvador as at 26 June 1995, including the contributions outstanding in the amount of 23,643,957 United States dollars, and urges all Member States concerned to make every possible effort to ensure the payment of their outstanding assessed contributions;

2. *Expresses concern* about the financial situation with regard to peace-keeping activities, due to overdue payments by Member States of their assessments, particularly Member States in arrears;

3. *Urges* all Member States to make every possible effort to ensure payment of their assessed contributions to the Observer Mission promptly and in full to enable speedy completion of its liquidation period;

4. *Endorses* the observations and recommendations contained in the report of the Advisory Committee on Administrative and Budgetary Questions, in particular those contained in paragraph 5 thereof;

5. *Takes note* of the unencumbered balances of appropriations for the period from 1 December 1993 to 31 May 1994 in the amount of 542,100 dollars gross (534,500 dollars net);

6. *Decides* to appropriate to the Special Account for the United Nations Observer Mission in El Salvador the amount of 11,704,200 dollars gross (10,397,300 dollars net) for the operation of the Observer Mission for the period from 1 June to 30 November 1994, inclusive of the amount of 3,895,900 dollars gross (3,612,300 dollars net) authorized by the General Assembly in its resolution 48/243 of 5 April 1994, the amount of 5,643,700 dollars gross (5,040,800 dollars net) authorized in its de-

cision 49/405 and the reduced amount of 2,164,600 dollars gross (1,744,200 dollars net) authorized by the Advisory Committee under the terms of Assembly resolution 48/229 of 23 December 1993 on unforeseen and extraordinary expenses for the biennium 1994-1995;

7. *Decides also*, as an ad hoc arrangement, to apportion the amount of 11,704,200 dollars gross (10,397,300 dollars net) for the period from 1 June to 30 November 1994 among Member States in accordance with the composition of groups set out in paragraphs 3 and 4 of General Assembly resolution 43/232 of 1 March 1989, as adjusted by the Assembly in its resolutions 44/192 B of 21 December 1989, 45/269 of 27 August 1991, 46/198 A of 20 December 1991 and 47/218 A of 23 December 1992, and its decision 48/472 A of 23 December 1993, and taking into account the scale of assessments for the year 1994;

8. *Decides further* that, in accordance with the provisions of its resolution 973(X) of 15 December 1955, there shall be set off against the apportionment among Member States, as provided for in paragraph 7 above, their respective share in the Tax Equalization Fund of the estimated staff assessment income of 1,306,900 dollars approved for the period from 1 June to 30 November 1994;

9. *Decides* to appropriate to the Special Account the amount of 4,634,000 dollars gross (4,080,500 dollars net) for the operation of the Observer Mission for the period from 1 December 1994 to 30 April 1995;

10. *Decides also*, as an ad hoc arrangement, to apportion the amount of 4,634,000 dollars gross (4,080,500 dollars net) for the period from 1 December 1994 to 30 April 1995 among Member States in accordance with the scheme set out in paragraph 7 above, the scale of assessments for the year 1994 to be applied against a portion thereof, that is, 951,351 dollars gross (837,718 dollars net), being the amount pertaining on a *pro rata* basis to the period ending 31 December 1994, and the scale of assessments for the year 1995 to be applied against the balance, that is, 3,682,649 dollars gross (3,242,782 dollars net), for the period from 1 January to 30 April 1995;

11. *Decides further* that, in accordance with the provisions of resolution 973(X), there shall be set off against the apportionment among Member States, as provided for in paragraph 10 above, their respective share in the Tax Equalization Fund of the estimated staff assessment income of 553,500 dollars approved for the period from 1 December 1994 to 30 April 1995, 113,632 dollars, being the amount pertaining on a *pro rata* basis to the period ending 31 December 1994, and the balance, that is, 439,868 dollars, for the period from 1 January to 30 April 1995;

12. *Decides* to appropriate to the Special Account the amount of 113,300 dollars gross (95,400 dollars net) for the liquidation of the Observer Mission for the period from 1 to 31 May 1995;

13. *Decides also*, as an ad hoc arrangement, to apportion the amount of 113,300 dollars gross (95,400 dollars net) for the period from 1 to 31 May 1995 among Member States in accordance with the scheme set out in paragraph 7 above, and taking into account the scale of assessments for the year 1995;

14. *Decides further* that, in accordance with the provisions of resolution 973(X), there shall be set off against the apportionment among Member States, as provided for in paragraph 13 above, their respective share in the

Tax Equalization Fund of the estimated staff assessment income of 17,900 dollars approved for the period from 1 to 31 May 1995;

15. *Decides* that there shall be set off against the apportionment among Member States, as provided for in paragraph 7 above, their respective share in the unencumbered balances of 542,100 dollars gross (534,500 dollars net) in respect of the period from 1 December 1993 to 31 May 1994;

16. *Requests* the Secretary-General to include in his report on the disposition of the assets of the Observer Mission information on the proper accounting procedures for any transfer of equipment from peace-keeping operations to regular budget activities;

17. *Decides* that the disposition of the property of the Observer Mission shall proceed in accordance with section VII, paragraph 1, of General Assembly resolution 49/233 A of 23 December 1994;

18. *Decides also* to include in the provisional agenda of its fiftieth session the item entitled "Financing of the United Nations Observer Mission in El Salvador".

General Assembly resolution 49/246

12 July 1995      Meeting 105      Adopted without vote

Approved by Fifth Committee (A/49/503/Add.1) without vote, 7 July (meeting 62); draft by Vice-Chairman (A/C.5/49/L.56), based on informal consultations; agenda item 120.
*Meeting numbers.* GA 49th session: 5th Committee 56, 62; plenary 105.

**Reports of the Secretary-General and ACABQ (November/December).** On 8 November, the Secretary-General reported[28] that ONUSAL's expenditures from 1 December 1994 to 30 April 1995 totalled $5,460,000 gross ($4,825,800 net), resulting in an additional requirement of $826,000 gross ($745,300 net) for that period, while the cost of the liquidation phase amounted to $129,600 gross ($113,100 net), resulting in an additional requirement of $16,300 gross ($17,700 net). Those increases stemmed from the need to retain more staff than projected until the end of the Mission's mandate, and one staff member until the end of June, as well as from upward revision of local salaries and rental costs. Outstanding contributions due from Member States totalled $22,554,171 as at 31 October, and $4 million had been borrowed from another peace-keeping operation to cover the expenses. The Secretary-General proposed approval of the additional requirements and deferral of their appropriation and assessment, as well as deferral of the treatment of the unencumbered balance, to the Assembly's resumed fiftieth session.

In a 4 December report,[29] ACABQ noted that the overexpenditure was to be financed from savings from ONUSAL's prior mandate periods. It stated its intention to comment on the Mission's performance and liquidation upon consideration of the Secretary-General's November report and his final report on ONUSAL financing, to be submitted in 1996.

On 22 December, the General Assembly decided that, pending submission of the final performance report on ONUSAL, the additional requirements of $842,300 gross ($763,000 net) for the period from 1 December 1994 to 31 May 1995 would be financed from savings from prior mandate periods (**decision 50/447**). The next day, it decided that the Fifth (Administrative and Budgetary) Committee should continue consideration of the agenda item on ONUSAL financing at its resumed fiftieth session (**decision 50/469**).

### Mission of the UN in El Salvador

In a 6 October report,[30] submitted pursuant to the General Assembly's 1994 request[1] that the Secretary-General devise procedures for providing El Salvador with the necessary cooperation and assistance in the period after ONUSAL, the Secretary-General summarized the developments leading to the establishment of MINUSAL, which began its work on 1 May, and described its activities between 1 May and 30 September. The Mission comprised 11 international staff, 8 civilian police consultants and a small administrative unit, and was partly funded by voluntary contributions to the Trust Fund for MINUSAL. The report noted that, due to advances in implementing the work programme for the completion of the peace accords, agreed on in April (see above), it was possible to reduce MINUSAL's strength to 10 international staff and 4 civilian police consultants, with the necessary support staff.

In assessing the status of peace agreements verified by the Mission, the Secretary-General noted that PNC had reached a strength of 8,482 agents and assumed virtually all public security functions in the country. However, the authorities continued to argue that the deployment of joint patrols of PNC and the Armed Forces in rural areas was necessary to combat and deter delinquency. In that regard, MINUSAL suggested adoption of a secondary law regulating the constitutional provision for the use of armed forces in the public security sector. At the Government's request, the Mission carried out a second evaluation of the sector, with recommendations for action. The Government also requested MINUSAL to provide advisory services in drafting a Police Career Law, to be submitted to the Legislative Assembly before the end of November.

The Mission continued to encourage efforts by the Supreme Court in screening and vetting judges, and participated in technical discussions in the Legislative Assembly concerning legislative reforms to comply with the binding recommendations of the Commission on the Truth. While reforms relating to penal and criminal procedures codes, penitentiary law and guarantees of due process were likely to be adopted by the end of November, others were not expected to be ready for approval before mid-1996. Delays also persisted in implementing the land-transfer programme; although 74 per cent of the potential beneficiaries had received titles to land as at 19 September, only 25 per cent of them had had their titles filed with the land registry. At the same time, a special regime for the relocation of human settlements was approved in August, together with an operational plan for their transfer, and it was foreseeable that such transfer would begin in rural areas before 31 October. Reintegration programmes also registered steady advances and were expected to be completed by year's end; however, concerns were raised about their impact and sustainability, and the Government requested UNDP to prepare an evaluation of their effectiveness.

The Secretary-General urged all parties in El Salvador to ensure the timely adoption of electoral reforms and reiterated the necessity of an administrative and structural transformation of the Supreme Electoral Tribunal. He further pointed out that MINUSAL and UNDP had prepared and submitted for funding a set of 10 technical assistance projects, with a total cost of $9.8 million, covering administration of justice, public security and land and reintegration programmes; as at September, the projects had received pledges of $4.23 million. The Secretary-General concluded that the continued presence of MINUSAL was necessary to fulfil the task of verifying implementation of the peace agreements, including monitoring and assisting in the land-transfer programme and providing advisory support for the formulation of legislative reforms and improvement of the public security sector. Accordingly, he proposed extending the Mission's mandate until 30 April 1996, with a gradual reduction of its strength and costs.

### Financing of MINUSAL

In a 24 October statement[31] to the Fifth Committee, the Secretary-General estimated the requirements for maintaining MINUSAL from 1 November 1995 to 30 April 1996 at $1,366,200, including $452,500 relating to 1995 and $913,700 for 1996. Those costs provided for 10 Professionals, 4 civilian police, and 1 international and 15 local staff. Of the 1995 requirements, $70,000 could be financed from the Trust Fund.

In a 27 October report,[32] ACABQ considered that additional requirements for 1995 should not exceed $367,400, and noted that the extension of MINUSAL's mandate entailed an additional requirement of up to $886,900 under the proposed programme budget for 1996-1997.

GENERAL ASSEMBLY ACTION

On 31 October, the Assembly adopted **resolution 50/7**.

## Mission of the United Nations in El Salvador

*The General Assembly,*

*Recalling* its resolutions on the situation in Central America, in particular resolution 49/137 of 19 December 1994, in which, *inter alia*, it requested the Secretary-General to devise procedures for providing El Salvador with the necessary cooperation and assistance in the period after the United Nations Observer Mission in El Salvador, in order to safeguard peace and the strengthening and consolidation of national reconciliation, democracy and sustainable development,

*Recalling also* the letter dated 6 February 1995 from the Secretary-General addressed to the President of the Security Council and the letter dated 17 February 1995 from the President of the Security Council addressed to the Secretary-General,

*Having considered* the report of the Secretary-General of 6 October 1995 on the Mission of the United Nations in El Salvador,

*Recognizing with satisfaction* the continuing evolution of El Salvador from a country torn by conflict into a democratic and peaceful nation,

*Paying tribute* to those Member States which contributed personnel and voluntary funding to the Mission,

1. *Welcomes* the continued commitment of the Government and people of El Salvador to the consolidation of the peace process;

2. *Pays tribute* to the accomplishments of the Mission of the United Nations in El Salvador, under the authority of the Secretary-General and his Special Representative;

3. *Recognizes* the political commitment of the Government of El Salvador and the other parties to the Chapultepec Agreement to continue to work together in order to complete its implementation;

4. *Approves* the proposal by the Secretary-General to extend the Mission for a further period of six months, with a gradual reduction of its strength and costs, in a manner compatible with the efficient performance of its functions;

5. *Calls upon* Member States and international institutions to continue to provide assistance to the Government and people of El Salvador and to lend support to the efforts of the Mission for the purposes of peace-building and development;

6. *Requests* the Secretary-General to report on the implementation of the present resolution.

General Assembly resolution 50/7

31 October 1995      Meeting 45      Adopted without vote

35-nation draft (A/50/L.7/Rev.1 & Rev.1/Add.1); agenda item 45.
*Financial implications.* 5th Committee, A/50/700; SG, A/C.5/50/14.
*Meeting numbers.* GA 50th session: 5th Committee 11, 12; plenary 45.

## Guatemala situation

The peace process in Guatemala—relaunched in 1994 with the conclusion of the Framework Agreement for the Resumption of the Negotiating Process between the Government of Guatemala and the Unidad Revolucionaria Nacional Guatemalteca (URNG),[33] the Comprehensive Agreement on Human Rights and a number of other agreements—showed further positive developments during 1995. In March, the parties signed the Agreement on Identity and Rights of

Indigenous Peoples and requested the UN human rights verification mission in Guatemala to verify implementation of its human rights aspects. In April, they began negotiations on socio-economic aspects and the agrarian situation in the country. The negotiating process was assisted by UN Moderator Jean Arnault, appointed in 1994. In November and December, URNG declared a unilateral suspension of hostilities, on the occasion of presidential, congressional and municipal elections.

The Mission for the Verification of Human Rights and of Compliance with the Commitments of the Comprehensive Agreement on Human Rights in Guatemala (MINUGUA), established by the General Assembly in 1994,[34] verified complaints of human rights violations in the country and assisted in strengthening human rights institutions, promoting human rights education and securing international support for the Guatemalan peace process. The Assembly extended the Mission's mandate in March and again in September, until 18 March 1996.

**Report of the Secretary-General (March).** In a 1 March report,[35] the Secretary-General informed the General Assembly and the Security Council of having received, in January 1995, replies from the President of Guatemala and the leadership of URNG to his December 1994 request[36] to indicate further steps to enable the peace negotiations to regain momentum. Both parties recognized the need to give new dynamism to the peace process and shared the view that steps could be taken to facilitate the early conclusion of negotiations on three groups of substantive issues: economic and social issues and the agrarian situation; strengthening of civilian power and the role of the army in a democratic society; and constitutional reforms and electoral regime. However, whereas the Government proposed to transfer consideration of the first and second groups of issues to representative bodies of Guatemalan society, with joint or separate suggestions from the parties, URNG suggested signing agreements on the three groups as already prepared by the Assembly of Civil Society—a body established in May 1994 in accordance with the Framework Agreement for the Resumption of the Negotiating Process.[33]

To overcome the impasse, Marrack Goulding, UN Under-Secretary-General for Political Affairs, met with the Government and URNG in Guatemala and in Mexico City, respectively, suggesting that they agree: to present their proposals on all pending issues, with drafts on those issues to be prepared by the UN Moderator; to prepare a revised timetable aimed at completing the negotiations in May or June, before the start of the campaign for presidential elections to be held

in November; to accept an informal three-month suspension of offensive military activities, the results of the negotiations, and measures to intensify implementation of their 1994 agreements; and to inform the Guatemalan people of current benefits and future gains from the peace process. While the Government agreed to those proposals, URNG expressed serious reservations about several elements. Accordingly, a revised set of measures was prepared and conveyed to the parties on 17 February, stressing that modalities for UN participation in the Guatemalan peace process and the Secretary-General's continued "moderation" of negotiations and verification of agreements depended on their response. In February, both sides accepted the revised package.

The Secretary-General therefore considered that minimum conditions existed for continued UN involvement, and instructed the Moderator to make arrangements for an early finalization of the agreement on identity and rights of indigenous peoples, currently on the negotiating agenda. He found it difficult, however, to recommend that UN support be continued in its current form, barring a genuine effort to achieve progress by target dates under the timetable agreed on in 1994.[33] The Secretary-General hoped that the parties would negotiate on outstanding issues in the same spirit they had demonstrated in the previous year.

**Communications of the Secretary-General (March/April).** On 29 March, the Secretary-General informed[37] the Assembly and the Council that the text of an agreement on identity and rights of indigenous peoples had been finalized and was ready to be signed. On 5 April, he transmitted[7] the Agreement on Identity and Rights of Indigenous Peoples between the Government of Guatemala and URNG, signed in Mexico City on 31 March, which comprised seven parts dealing with: the identity of indigenous peoples; the struggle against discrimination; cultural rights; civil, political, social and economic rights; joint commissions; resources; and final provisions. The Agreement provided for the establishment of joint commissions on education reform, on reform and participation and on rights relating to land of the indigenous peoples, to be composed of an equal number of representatives of the Government and of indigenous organizations, as determined in consultations between the Government and the Maya sectors of the Assembly of Civil Society. The Secretary-General was requested to verify the Agreement's implementation.

Although the Agreement was to enter into force at the signing of a final peace agreement, aspects relating to the human rights recognized in Guatemala's legislation and in international instruments to which Guatemala was a party had immediate force and application, and the UN human rights verification mission in Guatemala (see below) was accordingly requested to verify their implementation. In that regard, the Secretary-General noted that he had asked the MINUGUA Director to assess whether such verification would entail additional resource requirements.

### Human rights verification mission

**First report of Mission Director (March).** By a 1 March note,[38] the Secretary-General transmitted the first report of MINUGUA Director Leonardo Franco (Argentina), describing Mission activities from 21 November 1994 to 21 February 1995. The report provided background information on the situation in Guatemala and on MINUGUA's establishment and mandate; reviewed efforts for institution-building, international technical and financial cooperation and human rights promotion and education; and focused on the verification of compliance with human rights commitments.

It was noted that the Mission had established working relations with local civilian authorities, representatives of the army and the police and auxiliary offices of the Counsel for Human Rights, as well as arrangements for regular discussion of specific human rights aspects with the President of Guatemala, the leadership of URNG and the Presidential Human Rights Committee (COPREDEH). A MINUGUA/UNDP Joint Unit was set up to promote projects to strengthen national human rights institutions and to secure the necessary technical and financial cooperation, and a number of activities were identified for immediate implementation, in support of the Office of the Public Prosecutor, the Counsel for Human Rights and the Ministry of the Interior. The Mission was engaged in consultations on the establishment of a coordinating commission for the structural reform of the administration of justice, which would include the adoption of a new criminal procedures code and a law on the Public Prosecutor's Office, institutional modernization and a comprehensive legal education plan. MINUGUA also explored possibilities of cooperation with human rights NGOs, assisted in drafting a human rights promotion and education strategy, and held regular consultations with representatives of the Group of Friends of the Guatemalan Peace Process, EU and Japan to secure their cooperation in support of those projects.

The report further provided information on specific cases of human rights violations verified by the Mission. During the reporting period, MINUGUA received some 1,000 complaints, of which 288 were admitted for verification because they affected specific commitments made or rights accorded priority under the Comprehensive Agreement on Human Rights. Complaints in relation to the general commitment regarding human rights, under which the parties undertook to guarantee and protect their full observance and to promote and perfect norms and mechanisms for their protection, included alleged violations of: the right to life, involving 22 extrajudicial executions and deaths in violation of legal guarantees, 10 attempted executions and 68 death threats; the right to integrity and security of person, accounting for some 22 per cent of all complaints and involving cases of torture and of other threats to that right; and the right to individual liberty, involving 21 cases of arbitrary or illegal detention, 5 cases of enforced disappearances and 13 cases of forcible recruitment. There were also 46 alleged violations of procedural guarantees under the right to due process and complaints relating to political rights and the freedom of expression, of movement and of association.

The Mission also verified compliance with other commitments, including those: to strengthen human rights protection institutions; against impunity; against illegal security forces and clandestine structures, as well as regulation of the bearing of arms; to guarantee freedom of association and of movement; concerning military conscription; to safeguard individuals and entities working for the protection of human rights; to compensate and/or assist the victims of human rights violations; and concerning human rights and the internal armed conflict. The report listed 31 specific recommendations by MINUGUA regarding each commitment, including 27 to the Government and 4 to URNG, and concluded that the Mission could contribute to improving the human rights situation in the country through its permanent presence on the ground, verification work and strengthening of the human rights machinery.

**Report of the Secretary-General (March).** In an 8 March report,[39] the Secretary-General noted that MINUGUA had been fully deployed since 28 February, at headquarters in Guatemala City and at eight regional offices and five sub-offices. By 21 February, it had reached a strength of 67 local staff and 211 international staff, comprising 10 military liaison officers, 30 civilian police observers, 60 administrative and logistic support staff, and 111 substantive staff, of whom 72 were UN Volunteers. The status-of-mission agreement had been approved by the Guatemalan Congress and passed into law, and agreements on security arrangements were signed with both parties.

The Secretary-General stated that the first three months of the MINUGUA operation had confirmed the need for substantial improvements in the observance of human rights; he described the role played by the Mission in that process. Noting that its presence could be an important factor both in improving the human rights situation and in enhancing the prospect for an early end to the armed confrontation, he recommended an extension of the Mission's mandate for a further six months. He also appealed for contributions to the recently established Trust Fund for the Guatemala peace process.

### GENERAL ASSEMBLY ACTION (March)

On 31 March, the General Assembly adopted **resolution 49/236 A** on MINUGUA, under the agenda item on the situation in Central America.

*The General Assembly,*

*Recalling* its resolutions 45/15 of 20 November 1990, 46/109 A of 17 December 1991, 47/118 of 18 December 1992, 48/161 of 20 December 1993 and, in particular, 48/267 of 19 September 1994, in which it decided to establish the United Nations Mission for the Verification of Human Rights and of Compliance with the Commitments of the Comprehensive Agreement on Human Rights in Guatemala in accordance with the recommendations contained in the report of the Secretary-General for an initial period of six months, and its resolution 49/137 of 19 December 1994, in which it requested the Secretary-General to continue his support for the Guatemalan peace process, through his representative, and his assistance in implementing the agreements,

*Welcoming* the inauguration and full deployment of the Mission and the support and cooperation provided to it by the Government of Guatemala and the Unidad Revolucionaria Nacional Guatemalteca,

*Also welcoming* the conclusion of the status-of-mission agreement between the Government of Guatemala and the Secretary-General and its subsequent approval by the Guatemalan Congress,

*Taking into account* the note by the Secretary-General containing the report of the Director of the Mission on the first three months of the Mission's activities,

*Taking note* of the recommendations addressed to the Government of Guatemala and the Unidad Revolucionaria Nacional Guatemalteca contained in that report, regarding the implementation of their commitments under the Comprehensive Agreement on Human Rights,

*Stressing* the importance of mobilizing national and international resources for institution-building and cooperation projects intended to strengthen the Guatemalan system for the protection of human rights,

*Recognizing* the efforts of the Secretary-General and the Group of Friends of the Guatemalan peace process in support of the peace negotiations,

*Concerned* that the peace negotiations slowed down during the second half of 1994 and that the target dates agreed by the parties for the conclusion of an agreement on a firm and lasting peace were not met,

*Emphasizing* the importance of giving new momentum to the peace negotiations with a view to reaching promptly a package of agreements that will put an end to the armed confrontation and lay the foundations for a lasting peace in Guatemala,

*Taking note with appreciation* of the report of the Secretary-General concerning steps taken since 22 December 1994 to give new dynamism to the peace negotiations,

*Having considered* the recommendation of the Secretary-General regarding the extension of the mandate of the Mission, contained in his report on the Mission,

1. *Welcomes* the report of the Secretary-General on the United Nations Mission for the Verification of Human Rights and of Compliance with the Commitments of the Comprehensive Agreement on Human Rights in Guatemala;

2. *Takes note with satisfaction* of the report of the Director of the Mission on the first three months of the Mission's activities;

3. *Decides* to authorize the renewal of the mandate of the Mission for a further period of six months, in accordance with the recommendation of the Secretary-General;

4. *Calls upon* the Government of Guatemala and the Unidad Revolucionaria Nacional Guatemalteca to follow the recommendations of the Mission and to comply fully with their commitments under the Comprehensive Agreement on Human Rights;

5. *Reiterates* the importance of the undertaking by the parties, contained in the Comprehensive Agreement on Human Rights, to provide their broadest support to the Mission and whatever cooperation it may need to carry out its functions, particularly with respect to the security of the members of the Mission;

6. *Invites* the international community to increase its support for institution-building and cooperation projects with governmental and non-governmental organizations, intended to strengthen the Guatemalan system for the protection of human rights, in particular through voluntary contributions to the trust fund for the Guatemalan peace process being established by the Secretary-General;

7. *Reiterates* the great importance it attaches to the early conclusion of the agreement on a firm and lasting peace and urges the parties to make good on their commitment to give new momentum to the negotiating process;

8. *Requests* the Secretary-General to keep the General Assembly fully informed of the implementation of the present resolution.

General Assembly resolution 49/236 A

31 March 1995			Meeting 99			Adopted without vote

34-nation draft (A/49/L.64 & Add.1); agenda item 42.
*Financial implications.* 5th Committee, A/49/871; S-G, A/C.5/49/61.
*Meeting numbers.* GA 49th session: 5th Committee 48; plenary 99.

**Second report of Mission Director (June).** By a 29 June note,[40] the Secretary-General transmitted the second report of the MINUGUA Director, describing Mission activities from 21 February to 21 May. The report noted that Mission personnel totalled 339 and comprised 112 local staff and 227 international staff, including 10 military liaison officers, 41 police human rights observers, 103 UN staff and 73 UN Volunteers. The overall situation in Guatemala was characterized by a lack of public security, land-related disputes, tensions between the Government and the business sector over tax policy, an increase in harassment of and attacks on military units, continuing public concern over the human rights situation, and the launching of the presidential elections campaign. According to National Police data, 2,053 people had been killed and 4,078 injured in Guatemala between 1 January and 15 May as a result of criminal violence. The high incidence of kidnappings prompted the Guatemalan Congress to adopt a decree extending the death penalty to such cases, the compatibility of which with international human rights law was questioned by MINUGUA. The Counsel for Human Rights expressed concern at the increase in political and social violence and the ineffectiveness of State institutions responsible for investigating and punishing human rights violations; however, no action was taken on the Counsel's non-binding recommendations. The issue of impunity also remained a national concern.

The Mission continued to hold regular consultations with the Government and URNG and maintained regular contact with human rights institutions in Guatemala. During the reporting period, it received some 1,600 complaints, 570 of which were admitted for verification. Of those, 225 dealt with violations of the right to life, including 54 extrajudicial executions and deaths in violation of legal guarantees, 25 attempted extrajudicial executions and 146 death threats; 140 related to violations of the right to integrity and security of person, involving 10 cases of torture; 50 reported violations of the right to individual liberty, including 6 enforced disappearances; and 75 alleged violations of the right to due process. Other complaints dealt with political rights and the freedom of expression, of movement and of association. The report noted that of the 858 cases admitted since MINUGUA's inception, 261 had been closed and violations confirmed in 46.5 per cent of them.

The report further described the situation in respect of the rights not accorded priority under the Comprehensive Agreement and compliance with other commitments, as well as Mission activities related to institution-building, international technical and financial cooperation and human rights promotion and education. It noted that on 24 February the MINUGUA/UNDP Joint Unit had signed an agreement with the Attorney-General of the Republic to provide support to prosecutors in carrying out their duties under the new Code of Criminal Procedure. Support and assistance were also provided to the criminal public defender, the Judicial Training School, the Ministry of the Interior and the Counsel for Human Rights, and talks had begun on areas of cooperation with COPREDEH. The Joint Unit was compiling a list of human rights and indigenous NGOs with a view to strengthening their activities; in addition, a newly established team of 11 human rights promoters had organized more than 100 encounters in communities and 45 seminars and workshops for human rights workers, community leaders,

teachers, prosecutors and police officers. MINUGUA produced a number of documents in local languages and disseminated its first report and the Agreement on Identity and Rights of Indigenous Peoples (see above) among the indigenous population. In an effort to secure international financial support for the peace process, the Government presented its Human Rights Programme, incorporating the Comprehensive Programme for Strengthening the Rule of Law, at an informal meeting of the Consultative Group of donors on Guatemala, held in Paris. The Trust Fund for the Guatemala peace process totalled $2.6 million, including a $1 million pledge from Norway.

In his conclusions and recommendations, the Mission Director stressed several positive elements, such as the parties' cooperation with MINUGUA and support for its work; the virtual cessation of forcible military conscription; the widespread exercise of freedom of expression; the readiness of senior public security authorities to promote the investigation and solving of crimes; restraint in the use of force by the police during demonstrations and evictions from rural estates; acknowledgement by the army of its responsibility in two cases of arbitrary detention and torture; and the fact that the Government had not encouraged the organization of new voluntary civil defence committees (CVDCs). The Director also noted that URNG had fulfilled its commitment to suspend the destruction of electric power pylons. He noted with concern, however, that the greatest number of complaints referred to violations of the rights to life, to integrity and security of person and to liberty, in which the State failed in its duty to provide guarantees, and pointed to activities of illicit groups and abuses committed by CVDC members and military commissioners operating in rural areas. The report also noted that URNG had committed human rights violations and failed to observe its commitment to end the suffering of the civilian population, by making threats and taking action against civilian property in collecting "war tax", by unnecessarily endangering civilians not involved in the conflict during attacks on military bases and units, by taking reprisals and by laying mines and other explosives in places where civilians worked, lived or circulated.

MINUGUA reiterated the need for the Government to have a decisive overall policy for combating impunity, as well as its recommendations concerning the need to organize specific training courses for law enforcement officials, to recognize the competence of the Committee against Torture to investigate systematic violations of the 1984 Convention against Torture and Other Cruel, Inhuman or Degrading Treatment or Punishment, and to ratify the Optional Protocol to the 1966 International Covenant on Civil and Political Rights, thus providing Guatemalans with access to the Human Rights Committee. The Mission made a number of other recommendations, both to the Government and to URNG.

**Report of the Secretary-General (August).** On 11 August, the Secretary-General reported[41] on the signing of the Agreement on Identity and Rights of Indigenous Peoples, which was endorsed by the Assembly of Civil Society, and on MINUGUA's assessment of the Agreement's human rights aspects related to new verification activities to be undertaken by the Mission and additional resource requirements for their implementation. The Secretary-General recommended that additional resources be provided to MINUGUA accordingly, should the General Assembly extend its mandate.

The report also summarized Mission activities and drew attention to ongoing efforts by the international community in Guatemala to facilitate implementation of the preparatory phase of the Agreement on Resettlement of Population Groups Uprooted by the Armed Conflict. It noted that the parties had begun consideration of the next item on the negotiating agenda, dealing with socio-economic aspects and the agrarian situation, and that an agreement on the subject could be reached soon. Accordingly, the Secretary-General remained convinced that the United Nations should continue to assist the parties in reaching the earliest conclusion of an agreement on a firm and lasting peace, and that the international community should continue its support to the Guatemalan peace process and the efforts of MINUGUA. He recommended the renewal of the Mission's mandate until 18 March 1996.

**GENERAL ASSEMBLY ACTION (September)**

On 14 September, the General Assembly adopted **resolution 49/236 B**.

*The General Assembly,*

*Recalling* its resolutions 45/15 of 20 November 1990, 46/109 A of 17 December 1991, 47/118 of 18 December 1992, 48/161 of 20 December 1993 and 48/267 of 19 September 1994, in which it decided to establish the United Nations Mission for the Verification of Human Rights and of Compliance with the Commitments of the Comprehensive Agreement on Human Rights in Guatemala, and its resolutions 49/137 of 19 December 1994 and, in particular, 49/236 A of 31 March 1995, in which it decided to authorize the renewal of the mandate of the Mission for a further period of six months,

*Welcoming* the signing by the parties on 31 March 1995 of the Agreement on Identity and Rights of Indigenous Peoples,

*Taking into account* the note by the Secretary-General containing the second report of the Director of the Mission,

*Taking note* of the recommendations addressed to the Government of Guatemala and the Unidad Revolucionaria Nacional Guatemalteca contained in the second report of the Director of the Mission, regarding the implementation of their commitments under the Comprehensive Agreement on Human Rights,

*Also taking note* of the request of the parties regarding the immediate verification by the Mission of human rights aspects of the Agreement on Identity and Rights of Indigenous Peoples and the recommendation of the Secretary-General contained in his report on the Mission on resources required to allow the Mission to continue to fulfil its mandate, including verification activities relating to human rights aspects of the Agreement,

*Stressing once again* the importance of mobilizing national and international resources to strengthen the Guatemalan system for the protection of human rights,

*Welcoming,* in that respect, the support of the donor community for the implementation of the agreements reached in the Guatemala peace process, including the Comprehensive Agreement on Human Rights, expressed in Guatemala and reiterated at the informal donors meeting on Guatemala held in Paris on 21 June 1995 under the auspices of the World Bank,

*Acknowledging* the efforts of the Secretary-General, the Group of Friends of the Guatemala peace process and the United Nations agencies and programmes concerned for their support to the Guatemala peace process,

*Emphasizing* the importance it attaches to the full observance by the parties of human rights and the other commitments they have undertaken,

*Stressing the need* to continue the existing momentum towards the early conclusion of an agreement on a firm and lasting peace,

*Having considered* the recommendation of the Secretary-General regarding the extension of the mandate of the Mission, contained in his report on the Mission,

1. *Stresses* the significance of the Agreement on Identity and Rights of Indigenous Peoples as an important step in the Guatemala peace process and a landmark in the International Decade of the World's Indigenous People;

2. *Welcomes* the report of the Secretary-General on the United Nations Mission for the Verification of Human Rights and of Compliance with the Commitments of the Comprehensive Agreement on Human Rights in Guatemala;

3. *Takes note with satisfaction* of the second report of the Director of the Mission;

4. *Decides* to authorize the renewal of the mandate of the Mission for a further period of six months, that is, until 18 March 1996, in accordance with the recommendation of the Secretary-General;

5. *Welcomes* the efforts of international and regional financial institutions aiming at mobilizing resources for the implementation of the Guatemala peace agreements, including the Comprehensive Agreement on Human Rights;

6. *Also welcomes* voluntary contributions already made to the Trust Fund for the Guatemala peace process established by the Secretary-General, and invites the international community to make further contributions to the Fund;

7. *Calls upon* the Government of Guatemala and the Unidad Revolucionaria Nacional Guatemalteca to implement the recommendations contained in the first and

second reports of the Director of the Mission and to comply fully with their commitments under the Comprehensive Agreement on Human Rights and with the human rights aspects of the Agreement on Identity and Rights of Indigenous Peoples;

8. *Reiterates* the importance of the undertaking by the parties, contained in the Comprehensive Agreement on Human Rights, to provide their broadest support to the Mission and whatever cooperation it may need to carry out its functions, particularly with respect to the security of the members of the Mission;

9. *Calls upon* the parties to reach agreement on the item entitled ''Socio-economic aspects and agrarian situation'', currently under discussion in the negotiating process, and to strive for the earliest conclusion of an agreement on a firm and lasting peace;

10. *Requests* the Secretary-General to keep the General Assembly fully informed of the implementation of the present resolution.

General Assembly resolution 49/236 B

14 September 1995     Meeting 107     Adopted without vote

36-nation draft (A/49/L.69 & Add.1); agenda item 42.

**Third report of Mission Director (October).**
By a 12 October note,[42] the Secretary-General transmitted the third report of the MINUGUA Director, covering the period from 21 May to 21 August. The report noted that the political situation in Guatemala continued to be dominated by the electoral process leading to presidential, congressional and municipal elections in November. The participation of political parties and candidates was more comprehensive than in previous elections, as evidenced by the formation of the Frente Democrático Nueva Guatemala and numerous civilian election boards at the municipal level; URNG urged the public to vote and announced a cease-fire from 1 to 13 November, while President Ramiro de León Carpio met with representatives of political parties in an effort to encourage a high turnout at the polls. At the same time, the society continued to suffer from general violence, as demonstrated by the high rate of abductions and violent deaths and by the proliferation and use of firearms, which prompted a steady rise in the number of private security companies and self-defence groups.

On 30 June, the President announced his decision to demobilize some 25,000 military commissioners effective 15 September; the commissioners had been identified by MINUGUA and human rights activists for their involvement in acts of violence, harassment and intimidation against the civilian population. The Guatemalan Congress adopted two important laws: one classifying torture as an offence under the Penal Code, the other on the removal and deactivation of mines and other explosive devices to reduce risk to the inhabitants of areas affected by the armed confrontation. On 22 August, at a conference organized by the Central American Parliament, the main Guatema-

lan parties undertook to support whatever agreements might be reached as being of vital importance to the signatory Government.

Although both parties continued to cooperate with MINUGUA, no action had been taken on the Mission's recommendations either by the Government or by URNG. In June, the Mission deplored the lack of initiative and effectiveness on the part of the authorities in dealing with acts of illegal interference with the return of refugees to Guatemala, which culminated on 28 June in the taking of five international hostages, including three UN officers. In general, despite certain positive steps, the human rights situation in the country remained a cause for concern, due to the serious lack of public security and persistent impunity. During the reporting period, MINUGUA received 2,156 complaints, 424 of which were admitted for verification. Of those, 156 dealt with violations of the right to life, including 49 extrajudicial executions and deaths in violation of legal guarantees, 18 attempted extrajudicial executions and 89 death threats; 87 related to violations of the right to integrity and security of person; 43 reported violations of the right to individual liberty, including 2 cases of enforced disappearances; and 60 alleged violations of the right to due process. Other complaints dealt with political rights and the freedom of expression, of movement and of association. The report noted that of the 1,282 cases verified since MINUGUA's inception, 511 had been closed and violations confirmed in 46 per cent of them.

Verification activities in respect of other commitments indicated that: judges and prosecutors continued to be subjected to threats, intimidation and even attacks, without any investigation or punishment to follow; deficiencies persisted in the functioning of the Public Prosecutor's Office, the judiciary and the security forces responsible for preventing and punishing crime; illegal groups of various types continued their operations with impunity; the autonomy enjoyed by the army in its counter-insurgency and anti-subversive activities facilitated certain abuses and protection of officers implicated in corruption and crime; CVDCs and military commissioners prior to their dissolution continued to exert control over rural communities and commit abuses; no new measures had been adopted to regulate the bearing of arms, and the number of firearms in individual possession had risen sharply; and no measures or programmes had been devised to assist victims of human rights violations.

In addition, complaints were received regarding safeguards of individuals and entities working for the protection of human rights, infliction of suffering on the civilian population by URNG guerrillas, threats and actions by URNG against civilian property, the treatment of wounded and captured combatants, and illegal interference with the return of refugees and displaced persons as well as the treatment of returnees. On the positive side, the amended Criminal Code, characterizing extrajudicial execution and enforced disappearances as especially serious crimes and establishing penalties for them, entered into force on 14 July; some progress continued to be noted as to the freedom of association and of movement; and no cases of forced military conscription had occurred. Following claims by the Counsel for Human Rights that the Government's failure to strengthen that institution constituted a violation of the Comprehensive Agreement, the President stated that the Counsel's criticism provided grounds for the State to revise its relevant decisions and that he had reminded his ministers to obey the Counsel's resolutions and to cooperate with him.

On 4 August, a framework agreement on technical cooperation was concluded between MINUGUA and the judiciary branch, providing for assistance to the Public Defender's Office and measures to improve the juridical information system and the Judicial Training School. A technical cooperation agreement between the Public Prosecutor's Office and the MINUGUA/UNDP Joint Unit provided for the establishment of a technical advisory unit within that Office to train prosecutors. The Mission also continued to cooperate in improving the functioning of the National Police, and organized 66 human rights training seminars and nearly 250 informal talks on various agreements, which attracted more than 18,000 participants. It launched activities to verify compliance with the human rights aspects of the Agreement on Identity and Rights of Indigenous Peoples, and negotiated with donors providing for financial assistance to human rights projects in Guatemala, including a cooperation agreement with Norway, signed on 26 June; an agreement with Denmark's Human Rights Programme for Central America; and a letter of intent with the Inter-American Institute of Human Rights. The Trust Fund for the Guatemala peace process received $1.7 million in contributions and a pledge of 10 million kronor from Sweden.

The report concluded that the human rights situation in Guatemala had deteriorated in some aspects, owing to a crisis in the administration of justice, and noted that the right to life was still the right most seriously affected, that the rights to integrity and security of person and to individual liberty were not adequately guaranteed and that the right to due process was being violated more frequently. It was stated that URNG had failed to observe its commitments under the Comprehensive Agreement, with its troops continuing to commit human rights violations, and both parties were called on to implement measures recommended by the Mission.

**Further developments.** The negotiations on socio-economic aspects and the agrarian situation in Guatemala continued until their agreed interruption by the parties on 15 December. The presidential elections, held on 12 November, failed to produce a winner, and a second round was scheduled for 7 January 1996. URNG declared a further unilateral suspension of hostilities from 24 December 1995 to 8 January 1996. On 22 November, the Guatemalan Congress gave legal confirmation to the President's decision to demobilize military commissioners as of 15 September. By late November, contributions to the Trust Fund for the Guatemala peace process totalled $3.6 million. According to the Office of the UN High Commissioner for Refugees (UNHCR), 9,524 refugees had returned to Guatemala in 1995, significantly more than in previous years.

From its inception to the end of 1995, MINUGUA received more than 7,700 complaints, 1,567 of which were admitted for verification. Of that total, 1,078 cases, or 68.7 per cent, were closed, and violations were confirmed in 43.2 per cent of them, involving 3,161 victims. Confirmed violations concerned the rights to life, integrity and security of person and individual liberty in 64.2 per cent of cases, and responsibility was attributed to National Police officers in 24.5 per cent of them, to military commissioners in 17 per cent, to members of the army in 17 per cent, to members of CVDCs in 15.1 per cent and to URNG members in 5.4 per cent. Responsibility for violations of human rights during the internal armed conflict was attributed to URNG in 92.5 per cent of confirmed cases, and to the army in 5 per cent.

The Mission organized 650 encounters to clarify its mandate, attended by some 45,000 people, and 350 training seminars on human rights issues, with more than 15,000 participants. It signed a framework agreement on technical cooperation with the Counsel for Human Rights on 11 September, and renewed the cooperation agreement with the Public Prosecutor's Office on 10 October, which was expanded to include advisory services to the Attorney-General and the Council of the Office. Starting in September, the Mission cooperated with COPREDEH in human rights education for civil servants and public schools. On 31 August, Denmark agreed to provide MINUGUA with four professionals, to help meet the need for qualified personnel.

### Financing of MINUGUA

In a 21 March statement[43] to the Fifth Committee, the Secretary-General estimated that the extension of MINUGUA's mandate until 30 September 1995 would require an additional appropriation of $10,138,800, net of staff assessment ($769,000), under the programme budget for 1994-

1995. That requirement provided for a strength of 10 military liaison officers, 60 civilian police, 113 international staff, 72 UN Volunteers and 135 local staff. He also requested commitment authority not exceeding $5,600,000 until the end of December 1995, should the mandate be extended beyond 30 September.

On 27 March, the Fifth Committee, based on the recommendations of ACABQ,[44] revised the requested amounts downward and informed[45] the General Assembly that, should it extend MINUGUA's mandate until 30 September, an additional appropriation of $9,423,100 would be required under the programme budget for 1994-1995 and that, should the mandate be extended beyond 30 September, the Secretary-General would be authorized to enter into commitments not exceeding $4,711,500 from 1 October to 31 December.

On 20 November, the Secretary-General submitted to the Fifth Committee revised estimates[46] amounting to $7,299,800 to maintain MINUGUA from 1 January to 31 March 1996, and to provide for an additional 14 international staff and 34 Volunteers to verify the Agreement on Identity and Rights of Indigenous Peoples. He requested an appropriation of that amount, net of staff assessment ($587,000), under the proposed programme budget for 1996-1997, as well as commitment authority not exceeding $2,347,000 per month, should the Assembly extend the mandate beyond 31 March 1996.

In a 12 December report,[47] ACABQ revised both staff requirements and cost estimates downward and recommended an appropriation of $7,124,800, net of staff assessment ($554,800), under the proposed programme budget for 1996-1997, as well as the granting of commitment authority not exceeding $2,329,700 per month, should the mandate be extended beyond 31 March 1996.

**GENERAL ASSEMBLY ACTION (December)**

On 23 December, the General Assembly adopted **resolution 50/216, section I**.

**United Nations Mission for the Verification of Human Rights and of Compliance with the Commitments of the Comprehensive Agreement on Human Rights in Guatemala**

[*The General Assembly*]

1. *Takes note* of the report of the Secretary-General and the recommendations of the Advisory Committee on Administrative and Budgetary Questions in its report;

2. *Approves* the estimate of 7,124,800 United States dollars for the United Nations Mission for the Verification of Human Rights and of Compliance with the Commitments of the Comprehensive Agreement on Human Rights in Guatemala for the period from 1 January to 31 March 1996, under section 3 (Peace-keeping operations and special missions) of the proposed programme budget for the biennium 1996-1997;

3. *Authorizes* the Secretary General to enter into commitments in an amount not exceeding a monthly level of 2,329,700 dollars should the mandate of the Mission be extended beyond 31 March 1996;

. . .

General Assembly resolution 50/216, section I

23 December 1995     Meeting 100     Adopted without vote

Approved by Fifth Committee (A/50/842) without vote, 20 December (meeting 43); oral proposal by Chairman; agenda item 116.
*Meeting numbers.* GA 50th session: 5th Committee 40, 43; plenary 100.

## Nicaragua

In a 10 October report[48] on international assistance for the rehabilitation and reconstruction of Nicaragua (see PART FOUR, Chapter III), the Secretary-General noted that pacification in that country had advanced significantly, with 1995 being the first year with no politically motivated armed groups there. More than 20,000 members of the Nicaraguan Resistance had been demobilized, and the army had been reduced from 92,000 combatants to 12,500, the smallest in Central America. The transformation of the Sandinista Army into a new National Army culminated in the transfer of command on 21 February 1995. On 15 June, agreement was reached between the legislative and executive branches of government on constitutional reform, which was promulgated by the President of Nicaragua on 4 July, clearing the way for presidential, parliamentary and local elections in November 1996. Significant advances were also achieved in creating and strengthening democratic institutions. Following the end of the conflict, some 350,000 displaced persons and refugees returned to the country; however, reintegration of refugees and demobilized combatants still remained outstanding goals.

In the economic field, municipal development committees were set up in 120 of Nicaragua's 143 municipalities, and a Department of Property was established in January within the Ministry of Finance to deal with complex property issues. A Conference on Property in Nicaragua, held on 4 and 5 July, produced agreements on security for occupants of small rural and urban properties, speedy and fair compensation for victims of confiscation, and payment for titles by occupants of large urban properties. The Consultative Group of donors for Nicaragua, meeting in Paris on 19 and 20 June, confirmed their support for the transition process in that country with commitments of $560 million for 1995 and $1.5 million for 1995-1997, intended to relieve Nicaragua's balance-of-payments gap.

The report noted that, while most Nicaraguans continued to support reconciliation, a number of serious challenges remained to be addressed for the establishment of lasting conditions of public security, including the recovery of output and improvement of living conditions, the finding of definitive solutions to the property issue and the problem of external debt, the conduct of a clean electoral process leading to broad participation in 1996 elections, and the management of such destabilizing factors as uncontrolled migration and trafficking of drugs, weapons and people.

*REFERENCES*

[1]YUN 1994, p. 390, GA res. 49/137, 19 Dec. 1994. [2]A/50/499. [3]YUN 1994, p. 389. [4]A/50/534. [5]YUN 1987, p. 188. [6]A/49/901-S/1995/396. [7]A/49/882-S/1995/256. [8]A/50/690. [9]A/51/67. [10]YUN 1992, p. 222. [11]YUN 1991, p. 149, SC res. 693(1991), 20 May 1991. [12]YUN 1994, p. 403, SC res. 961(1994), 23 Nov. 1994. [13]YUN 1992, p. 223, SC res. 729(1992), 14 Jan. 1992. [14]YUN 1993, p. 323, SC res. 832(1993), 27 May 1993. [15]S/1995/220. [16]YUN 1993, p. 316. [17]A/49/888-S/1995/281. [18]A/44/971-S/21541. [19]S/1995/407. [20]S/1995/143. [21]S/1995/144. [22]A/49/518/Add.1. [23]YUN 1994, p. 1338, GA res. 49/233 A, 23 Dec. 1994. [24]YUN 1992, p. 224, GA res. 46/240, 22 May 1992. [25]A/49/458/Add.1 & Add.1/Corr.1. [26]YUN 1994, p. 405, GA res. 48/243, 5 Apr. 1994. [27]A/49/518/Add.2. [28]A/50/735. [29]A/50/802. [30]A/50/517. [31]A/C.5/50/14. [32]A/50/7/Add.3. [33]YUN 1994, p. 407. [34]Ibid., p. 408, GA res. 48/267, 19 Sep. 1994. [35]A/49/857-S/1995/168. [36]YUN 1994, p. 409. [37]A/49/879-S/1995/241. [38]A/49/856 & Corr.1. [39]A/49/860. [40]A/49/929. [41]A/49/955. [42]A/50/482. [43]A/C.5/49/61. [44]A/49/7/Add.13. [45]A/49/871. [46]A/C.5/50/26. [47]A/50/7/Add.9. [48]A/50/535.

# The Caribbean

## Haiti

In 1995, the international community continued to assist Haiti in the process of restoring democracy and accelerating economic recovery, following the departure of that country's military authorities and the return of its first democratically elected President, Jean-Bertrand Aristide, in October 1994. In January, the Security Council determined that a secure and stable environment had been established and authorized the deployment of the UN Mission in Haiti (UNMIH) at full strength, in accordance with a 1994 Council resolution.[1] The Mission, created in 1993,[2] had first established its presence in Haiti in 1994, with the deployment of an advance team.[1] At its full strength, UNMIH consisted of military, civilian and civilian police components under the control of the Secretary-General's Special Representative for Haiti, Lakhdar Brahimi (Algeria). On 31 March, it took over responsibilities from the multinational force in Haiti (MNF), deployed there since September 1994. The Security Council extended the Mission's mandate in January and again in July, until the end of February 1996, with a view to completing it by that time.

UNMIH provided a secure environment as well as assistance during the country's local, legislative and presidential elections. Prior to the elections, President Aristide affirmed that he would hand over power to a newly elected President in February 1996. On 23 December, René Préval was announced President-elect of Haiti. The electoral process was also supported by the UN/OAS International Civilian Mission to Haiti (MICIVIH), established in 1993[3] to monitor and promote the observance of human rights. In July, the General Assembly extended UN participation in MICIVIH until 7 February 1996; in December, it expressed its readiness to extend the UN component beyond that date, upon receipt of a request from the Haitian Government and the Secretary-General's recommendations to that effect.

(See also PART THREE, Chapter III, for the human rights situation in Haiti.)

**Report of the Secretary-General and communication (January).** In a 17 January report,[4] the Secretary-General noted that the security situation in Haiti had improved following the arrival of MNF in September 1994 and the subsequent disintegration of the Armed Forces of Haiti (FADH). Politically motivated violence and human rights abuses had decreased, although individual acts still occurred sporadically, and Haitians could enjoy freedom of expression, association and assembly. Large numbers of displaced persons had returned to their homes. At the same time, people in a number of areas continued to be intimidated by former members of the Front révolutionnaire pour l'avancement et le progrès d'Haïti (FRAPH), while the collapse of FADH had created a security void that contributed to a marked increase in banditry and criminality throughout the country. Violent deaths were reported daily, and acts of extortion and robberies by unidentified armed groups were widespread. Land conflicts also gave rise to violence.

The report characterized the relative security currently enjoyed by Haitians as fragile, and examined existing factors that could lead to future instability, including the disaffection of former FADH members; the probable continued existence of paramilitary networks and the availability of arms; rising frustration at the inability of the justice system to address past human rights violations and current criminality; the delay in translating economic measures and development programmes into concrete improvements in daily life; and the additional tension that might be generated by forthcoming elections. The Secretary-General underscored the need to develop a clear plan for resettling demobilized personnel, carry out reform of the judicial system and improve conditions in prisons as well as their infrastructure, accelerate economic recovery, and undertake an effective civic education campaign as part of the electoral process. In that regard, he noted the establishment of the Commission for Truth and Justice in January 1995 and the inauguration of the Provisional Electoral Council in December 1994.

The report also reviewed the establishment of Haitian security forces, noting that the Interim Public Security Force (IPSF) had totalled some 3,000 personnel at the end of 1994 and was supported by some 900 newly trained police auxiliaries. The Force worked in cooperation with 800 international police monitors; it was to be gradually replaced by the National Police, expected to reach a strength of 3,000 by January 1996. In addition, President Aristide signed a decree on 6 January 1995 setting up a Committee to Restructure the Armed Forces of Haiti, which was to establish rules for the creation of a new army of 1,500 soldiers. Noting that IPSF operations were adversely affected by deficiencies in the functioning of the justice system and the lack of essential equipment, the Secretary-General urged Governments and development agencies to accelerate implementation of their aid programmes and provide the needed support as early as possible.

He further provided an overview of the UNMIH mandate, rules of engagement, structure, deployment and concept of operations, as well as of preparations for the transition from MNF to UNMIH (see below).

On 27 January, Haiti informed[5] the Security Council President that its Government supported the Secretary-General's recommendations.

## UN Mission in Haiti

On 12 January, the Security Council President informed[6] the Secretary-General that Council members agreed with his 1994 proposal[7] to appoint Major-General Joseph Kinzer (United States) as Commander of the UNMIH military component.

In his January 1995 report,[4] the Secretary-General stated that, in accordance with the mandate established by the Security Council in 1994,[1] the Mission would consist of civilian, military and civilian police components under the control of his Special Representative for Haiti. It would be deployed in such a manner as to be conducive to the protection of international personnel and key installations; to facilitate resupply, command and control and force protection; to be logistically supportable; and to support the maintenance of the quick reaction force. The Mission's rules of engagement were to be defined in accordance with its mandate. The Secretary-General pointed out that the tasks originally entrusted to UNMIH by the Council in 1993[2] and 1994,[1] especially those relating to military training and construction projects, as well as

civilian police activities, had to be adapted to the realities on the ground.

The proposed concept of operations provided for the establishment of a headquarters and five sector subheadquarters, with logistical requirements including 15 helicopters, 1,400 overland vehicles and a 24-hour communication system. The UNMIH military component was to total 6,000 personnel and to comprise five infantry battalions, including Special Forces elements and a number of support units. Some two thirds of the military and one third of the civilian police component of UNMIH was to be staffed by MNF personnel, transferred from MNF two weeks prior to the transfer of command. The Secretary-General estimated that the transition from MNF to UNMIH would be completed by 31 March, with the Mission headquarters to be set up by the end of February. He noted that the strength of the UNMIH advance team in Haiti had been increased to 110 personnel, including 18 military observers, 40 civilian police personnel, 15 military planners and 37 administrative staff, in accordance with a 1994 Security Council resolution[8] authorizing its progressive increase to 500 personnel.

The Secretary-General expressed his confidence that the Mission would be able to fulfil its mandate and to assist the Government of Haiti in sustaining a secure and stable environment, and recommended extension of its mandate for a further six months, until 31 July 1995. He estimated the cost of UNMIH for the first six months after the take-over from MNF at $178,317,000, providing for 6,000 military contingent personnel, 900 civilian police and 227 international and 193 local civilian staff, as well as 29 UN Volunteers.

**MNF reports (January).** On 9 January, the United States transmitted[9] the eighth report of MNF, covering its operations from 19 December 1994 to 9 January 1995. The report noted that MNF, at a strength of 7,412 troops and 717 international police monitors, continued its expansion into outlying areas of the country so as to establish its presence in all 133 subdistricts, and had begun to carry out additional daily patrols in high-crime areas. It characterized the security situation in Haiti as positive, except for a brief eruption of violence on 26 December 1994 as a result of tension between the Haitian armed forces and the Government over pay and retirement benefits, which led to the killings of three members of the armed forces with six more wounded. The number of weapons seized or bought under the weapons control programme since MNF's inception totalled 20,345, including 5,853 grenades and 1,736 machine-guns. The report also described activities of the international police monitors in training IPSF personnel, as well as MNF assistance to local authorities and civil action projects.

The ninth MNF report, covering the period from 8 to 22 January and transmitted[10] by the United States on 23 January, pointed to the continued security and stability in Haiti, with incidents of violence being minimal and indiscriminate in nature. On 12 January, however, one such incident resulted in a fatality in the United States contingent of MNF. The strength of MNF stood at 9,113 troops and 683 international police monitors; on 15 January, Major-General Fisher assumed command from Major-General Meade. During the reporting period, an additional 180 weapons and 173 munitions had been purchased under the weapons control programme, bringing the total number to some 21,000. The Government of Haiti continued with the reorganization of the armed forces and the creation of a new police force, as well as with preparations for elections, scheduled for May. On 17 January, the UNMIH Commander arrived in Haiti to conduct further planning for the transition from MNF to the Mission.

**Communication (January).** On 18 January, Member States participating in MNF recommended[11] that the Security Council determine it appropriate for UNMIH to begin assuming the full range of its functions. Annexed to the letter was a 15 January statement by the MNF Commander, declaring that a secure and stable environment had been established in Haiti and that one requirement for the transition to UNMIH, set out in the Council's 1994 resolution,[1] had thus been attained.

**SECURITY COUNCIL ACTION (January)**

On 30 January, the Security Council adopted **resolution 975(1995)**.

*The Security Council,*

*Recalling* the provisions of its resolutions 841(1993) of 16 June 1993, 861(1993) of 27 August 1993, 862(1993) of 31 August 1993, 867(1993) of 23 September 1993, 873(1993) of 13 October 1993, 875(1993) of 16 October 1993, 905(1994) of 23 March 1994, 917(1994) of 6 May 1994, 940(1994) of 31 July 1994, 944(1994) of 29 September 1994, 948(1994) of 15 October 1994 and 964(1994) of 29 November 1994,

*Recalling also* the terms of the Governors Island Agreement and the related Pact of New York,

*Recalling* its determination in resolution 940(1994) that the situation in Haiti constituted a threat to peace and security in the region which required the successive deployment of the Multinational Force in Haiti (MNF) and the United Nations Mission in Haiti (UNMIH),

*Having considered* the reports of the Secretary-General dated 18 October 1994, 21 November 1994 and 17 January 1995, and having considered the reports of MNF, dated 26 September 1994, 10 October 1994, 24 October 1994, 7 November 1994, 21 November 1994, 5 December 1994, 19 December 1994, 9 January 1995 and 23 January 1995,

*Noting in particular* the MNF commander's statement of 15 January 1995 and the accompanying recommendation, based on the MNF commander's report, of the

States participating in the MNF, regarding the establishment of a secure and stable environment in Haiti,

*Noting* the recognition in these reports and recommendations that a secure and stable environment has been established in Haiti,

*Taking note* of the letter dated 27 January 1995 from the Permanent Representative of Haiti to the United Nations,

*Underlining* the importance of ensuring that force levels of peace-keeping operations are suited to the tasks involved, and noting the need for the Secretary-General to keep the force levels of UNMIH under constant review,

*Recognizing* that the people of Haiti bear the ultimate responsibility for national reconciliation and reconstruction of their country,

1. *Welcomes* the positive developments in Haiti, including the departure from Haiti of the former military leadership, the return of the legitimately elected President and the restoration of the legitimate authorities, as envisaged in the Governors Island Agreement and consistent with resolution 940(1994);

2. *Commends* the efforts of the States participating in the MNF to work closely with the United Nations to assess requirements and to prepare for the deployment of UNMIH;

3. *Expresses* appreciation to all Member States who have contributed to the MNF;

4. *Expresses its appreciation* to the Organization of American States (OAS) and for the work of the International Civilian Mission (MICIVIH) and requests that the Secretary-General, bearing in mind the expertise and potential of the OAS, consult with the Secretary-General of the OAS regarding other appropriate measures which might be taken by both organizations consistent with this resolution and to report to the Council on the results of these consultations;

5. *Determines*, as required by resolution 940(1994) and based on the recommendations of the Member States participating in the MNF and in concurrence with paragraph 91 of the report of the Secretary-General of 17 January 1995, that a secure and stable environment, appropriate to the deployment of UNMIH as foreseen in the above-mentioned resolution 940(1994), now exists in Haiti;

6. *Authorizes* the Secretary-General, in order to fulfil the second condition specified in paragraph 8 of resolution 940(1994) for the termination of the mission of the MNF and the assumption by UNMIH of its functions specified in that resolution, to recruit and deploy military contingents, civilian police and other civilian personnel sufficient to allow UNMIH to assume the full range of its functions as established by resolution 867(1993) and as revised and extended by paragraphs 9 and 10 of resolution 940(1994);

7. *Further authorizes* the Secretary-General, working with the MNF commander, to take the necessary steps in order for UNMIH to assume these responsibilities as soon as possible, with the full transfer of responsibility from the MNF to UNMIH to be completed by 31 March 1995;

8. *Decides* to extend the existing mandate of UNMIH for a period of six months, that is until 31 July 1995;

9. *Authorizes* the Secretary-General to deploy in Haiti, in accordance with resolution 940(1994), up to 6,000

troops and, as recommended in paragraph 87 of his report of 17 January 1995, up to 900 civilian police officers;

10. *Recalls* the commitment of the international community to assist and support the economic, social and institutional development of Haiti and recognizes its importance for sustaining a secure and stable environment;

11. *Recognizes* that the situation in Haiti remains fragile and urges the Government of Haiti, with the assistance of UNMIH and the international community, to establish without delay an effective national police force and to improve the functioning of its justice system;

12. *Requests* the Secretary-General to establish a fund, in addition to that authorized in paragraph 10 of resolution 867(1993), through which voluntary contributions from Member States can be made available to support the international police monitoring programme and assist with the creation of an adequate police force in Haiti;

13. *Further requests* that the Secretary-General apprise the Council at an early date of the modalities of the transition from the MNF to UNMIH, and also submit to the Council no later than 15 April 1995 a progress report on the deployment of UNMIH;

14. *Decides* to remain actively seized of the matter.

Security Council resolution 975(1995)

30 January 1995     Meeting 3496     14-0-1

10-nation draft (S/1995/85).

*Sponsors:* Argentina, Canada, France, Germany, Honduras, Italy, Rwanda, United Kingdom, United States, Venezuela.

Vote in Council as follows:

*In favour:* Argentina, Botswana, Czech Republic, France, Germany, Honduras, Indonesia, Italy, Nigeria, Oman, Russian Federation, Rwanda, United Kingdom, United States.

*Against:* None.

*Abstaining:* China.

In China's view, the deployment of UNMIH would lead to changes in the security situation in Haiti, currently characterized by rampant crime in the absence of a police force, which necessitated reconsideration of the Mission's mandate and size; however, no agreement had been reached among Council members on amendments it had proposed.

**Further MNF reports (February/March).** On 6 February, the United States transmitted[12] the tenth report of MNF, summarizing its operations from 23 January to 5 February. The report indicated that the situation in Haiti remained secure and stable, due to a combination of such factors as functioning government ministries, IPSF deployments and MNF activities. A marked decrease in violence had been witnessed during the reporting period, and no incidents of politically motivated human rights abuses had been reported. MNF, at a strength of 7,758 troops and 686 international police monitors, maintained a visible presence and undertook a number of missions to outlying areas; at the same time, international police monitors conducted joint patrols and operated police stations with IPSF, which continued to improve its capabilities, reaching a strength of some 3,300 personnel. The number of weapons seized or purchased to date totalled 26,544, and it was estimated that few weapons remained in circulation. On 25

January, registration began for a job-training programme for former FADH members, while the National Police Training Academy started classes on 31 January. Measures were implemented to improve sanitary conditions in prisons, and a phased plan was initiated by the Government to assume full control of the detention facility operated jointly with MNF. In preparation for the transition to UNMIH, MNF activities were coordinated in all functional areas with the Mission staff already deployed.

The eleventh MNF report, communicated[13] by the United States on 21 February and covering the period from 6 to 19 February, stated that the force, at a strength of 7,938 troops and 677 international police monitors, had adjusted patrol routes and patterns to ensure maximum coverage during times of increased criminal activity, and initiated market patrols in daylight hours. IPSF, which had reached a strength of 3,381, conducted joint and independent patrols and made numerous arrests; it was assisted by the MNF military police, which helped improve IPSF facilities and operations, identify the required equipment and procure uniforms. Although the overall climate remained secure and stable, three significant violent incidents occurred: an IPSF officer was found dead on 11 February; an international police monitor was wounded on 14 February; and one suspect in a murder case was beaten to death by a crowd that took control of a jail on 15 February. A disarmament operation targeting police stations and the national prison concluded with 2,010 weapons collected, bringing the number of weapons and grenades taken out of circulation to 29,903, of which 12,589 had been bought back and the rest seized. Agreement was reached between MNF and MICIVIH on cooperation in prison and jail clean-up, sanitation, structure restoration and prison guard training. Of the 2,500 eligible former FADH members, 1,912 had been registered for the job-training programme. The Haitian Parliament adopted an electoral law, promulgated by the President on 17 February. A donors' conference, which ended on 31 January in Paris, approved aid packages totalling $900 million, including $660 million for a reconstruction programme and $240 million in assistance funds, to be provided over 12 to 18 months.

On 6 March, the United States transmitted[14] the twelfth report of MNF on its operations from 20 February to 5 March. The MNF strength stood at 7,892 troops and 665 international police monitors; it conducted out-of-sector missions and special missions to provide aircraft support to the Provisional Electoral Council and security for the testing of police academy candidates, as well as to conduct site surveys of proposed UNMIH base camp locations. Issues related to the transition to

UNMIH continued to be discussed in working groups composed of United States, UN and Haitian officials. In the meantime, an increase in hijackings and lootings prompted MNF to provide escort to food convoys and to a pay team of IPSF personnel. It also agreed to conduct training of the presidential palace security force, at President Aristide's request. Force engineers executed an operation to repair three bridges destroyed by a tropical storm, and work continued on the power grid system in the capital of Port-au-Prince and on two water projects. The weapons buy-back programme collected more than 800 guns and 2,700 munitions during the reporting period, bringing the total to 33,000, while the destruction of confiscated ammunition was 75 per cent complete. Between 20 and 24 February, 375 National Police candidates graduated to the second police academy class, to begin on 13 March. Following the signing by the President of the electoral law, parliamentary and local elections in Haiti were set for 4 June.

The thirteenth and final MNF report, communicated[15] on 20 March, stated that the force, the strength of which totalled 7,143 troops and 654 international police monitors, was finalizing plans for transition to UNMIH. In the meantime, it had changed patrol operations in response to sporadic increases in violence, such as a rise in the number of murders in Port-au-Prince between 12 and 14 March, and continued to provide security for humanitarian convoys, conduct missions to outlying areas, assist IPSF and train personnel for a national police force. The force worked closely with MICIVIH in analysing human rights and prison reform issues, and cooperated in conducting an assessment of Haiti's national forests, delivering construction material and developing a nation-wide vaccination programme against rabies. It also sponsored civil action projects aimed at distributing school supplies and food as well as repairing roads, prisons, the IPSF regional headquarters, and water, sewage and electricity systems. Between 6 and 19 March, 692 weapons had been collected under the buy-back programme, and registration for the job-training programme for demobilized FADH members concluded on 8 March, with a total of 2,619 registered.

**Report of the Secretary-General (April).** On 13 April, the Secretary-General reported[16] that the transfer of responsibilities from MNF to UNMIH had taken place on 31 March, at an official ceremony attended by President Aristide of Haiti, President William J. Clinton of the United States and himself, among others. The transition was made possible due to the preparatory work by the advance team in developing the concept of operations, force structure and deployment plans; early deployment of some 70 per cent of the Mis-

sion's military component, including the Quick Reaction Force and Special Forces elements, within MNF; a six-day integrated staff training exercise in early March; and two tripartite meetings of Haitian, UN and MNF officials to address questions relating to security, elections, rehabilitation of the justice and penitentiary systems, and economic recovery. Matters concerning the Haitian police and the justice system were also discussed in working groups of Haitian officials and UNMIH representatives. A status-of-forces agreement for the Mission was signed on 15 March.

On 31 March, an advance team of 24 military observers concluded its mission; 10 of them were incorporated into UNMIH. The Mission established its headquarters in Port-au-Prince, with sub-headquarters in six operational sectors (Cap Haïtien, Gonaïves, Jacmel, Les Cayes and two in Port-au-Prince). Five infantry battalions, including the Quick Reaction Force, as well as support units, a military police battalion, an engineering unit, aviation and logistics elements, a military information support team and a civil affairs unit were deployed in 10 locations, and Special Forces elements in 25 locations throughout the country. UNMIH took over four military camps built by MNF in Port-au-Prince and two of the three camps in Cap Haïtien; its engineering battalion was to complete construction of an additional eight camps by 20 June. As at 31 March, the Mission's strength was 5,906 military contingent personnel, including 4,193 transferred from MNF; 791 civilian police (CIVPOL), including 379 transferred from international police monitors within MNF; and 122 international civilian staff, 175 local staff and 12 UN Volunteers.

UNMIH began to discharge its duties in a situation characterized by wide popular support for President Aristide and few human rights violations, as well as by major institutional weaknesses and growing frustrations over the slow pace of economic recovery. Following the expiry of mandates of most elected officials on 4 February, the country was without a Parliament; on 25 February, a presidential decree authorized either extension of mandates for local officials or their replacement by new interim officials. Due to technical difficulties, the parliamentary and local elections initially scheduled for 4 and 25 June were postponed until 25 June and 16 July. At the Government's request, efforts of the Provisional Electoral Council in preparing the elections were supported by a 17-person UN Electoral Assistance Team; it was also envisaged that the election process would be supported and observed by MICIVIH, other UN agencies in Haiti and OAS. As for the judiciary, a number of judges and the Chief Prosecutor in Port-au-Prince had been replaced, and the National Commission for Truth and Justice, responsible for investigating human rights violations committed under the military authorities, was inaugurated on 30 March. The Government created, on 6 April, a commission of five interim police officers to investigate recent assassinations, and launched a campaign to encourage court testimonies in assassination cases.

The Secretary-General noted that tremendous economic challenges persisted in Haiti and that the extreme poverty and high unemployment prevailing in much of the country required sustained international attention. Recovery signals were still weak, with industrial revival hindered by electricity shortages. Private and public investments were urgently needed to stimulate the economy suffering from a lack of basic infrastructure; however, foreign investment seemed to be impeded by perceptions of the public security situation. Although multilateral agencies and donors approved substantial aid packages in January, Haiti's absorptive capacity continued to be quite modest.

The report emphasized that the issue of security was central to the entire UN operation in Haiti. While very few human rights violations had been reported in the past two months, crime remained at a high level, with an increase in vigilante killings at the beginning of March, which led to concern that UNMIH, operating without enforcement authority, would not prove as effective as MNF. In that regard, the Secretary-General pointed to assertive rules of engagement of the Mission's military component and CIVPOL's proactive operation guidelines, and emphasized that effective coordination had been established between contingents with respect to security preparations. Discussions were also under way of steps to accelerate the deployment of a functional National Police force, which was still a long way from the minimum 7,000 agents needed to maintain law and order. On 24 March, Japan pledged $3 million to the newly established UN trust fund to support the international police monitoring programme and assist with the creation of an adequate police force in Haiti. At the same time, no programmes were in place to absorb in civilian employment IPSF members replaced by Police Academy graduates.

**Communication (April).** On 7 April, a group of Member States known as the Friends of the Secretary-General for Haiti (Argentina, Canada, France, United States, Venezuela) transmitted a statement[17] welcoming the transition from MNF to UNMIH and noting with satisfaction the role of MICIVIH and UNMIH in assisting the Haitian authorities with the electoral process. The statement pointed out, however, that the security situation in Haiti remained a matter of concern and that the early deployment of a permanent and effective police force as well as the reactivation of a functioning and fair justice system were central

to long-term stability. In that regard, the Friends joined the Secretary-General's call for contributions to the UN trust fund. They also appealed for intensified national reconstruction and reconciliation efforts, and underlined the importance of immediate and sustained international assistance to Haiti and of ongoing political engagement, which was indispensable to the prospects for long-term peace and stability. The Friends reaffirmed their determination to support the Secretary-General in those efforts.

**SECURITY COUNCIL ACTION (April)**

On 24 April, the Security Council President made the following statement[18] on behalf of the Council:

> The Security Council welcomes the transfer of responsibilities from the multinational force (MNF) to UNMIH that took place on 31 March 1995 and shares the Secretary-General's view, as stated in his report of 13 April, that this transfer was a milestone in the overall efforts of the international community to bring peace and stability to Haiti. The Council commends the Secretary-General, his Special Representative, the MNF Force Commander and the other dedicated personnel of the United Nations and MNF who made the transition possible.
>
> The Security Council notes, however, that much remains to be done to institutionalize democracy in Haiti and reiterates the Secretary-General's call for the people of Haiti and their leaders to help UNMIH help them. While UNMIH's presence will assist the Haitian Government to sustain a secure and stable environment, the existence of a functioning and fair justice system and the early deployment of a permanent and effective police force by the Haitian authorities are central to Haiti's long-term stability. The Council joins the Secretary-General and Friends of Haiti in inviting Member States to make voluntary contributions to support the international police monitoring programme and assist with the creation of an adequate police force.
>
> The Government and people of Haiti bear the primary responsibility for Haiti's political, economic and social reconstruction. However, the Security Council notes that the sustained commitment of the international community is indispensable for long-term peace and stability in Haiti.
>
> The Security Council shares the opinion of the Secretary-General that the issue of security is central to the entire United Nations operation in Haiti.
>
> The Security Council underlines the crucial importance of free, fair and secure elections for the democratic future of Haiti. The Council stresses the necessity of a secure environment in Haiti, including during the June and July legislative and local election period, and underlines the importance of a functioning police force and an established judicial system. The Council urges the Government of Haiti to take all necessary steps to ensure the success of the elections, and in particular to register as many voters as possible prior to the elections and to assure, in cooperation with the international community, that

political campaigning occurs in an environment free from partisan intimidation.

The Security Council welcomes President Aristide's meetings with leaders of political parties and members of the Provisional Electoral Council and stresses the importance of dialogue with a view to achieving the political consensus needed to enhance the benefits and credibility of the electoral process. The Council also calls on the Government of Haiti to cooperate fully with the United Nations and the Organization of American States (OAS) to ensure that the preparations for elections and the elections themselves can take place in a secure and stable environment. Consistent with the objectives of Security Council resolution 940(1994), the Council emphasizes the importance for the Presidential elections to take place on schedule before UNMIH's scheduled withdrawal in February 1996.

Finally, the Security Council welcomes the Secretary-General's decision to coordinate UNMIH's peace-keeping mission with development activities carried out by others, in a manner consistent with UNMIH's mandate, to help the Government of Haiti strengthen its institutions, particularly the judicial system. The Council hopes this coordination will promote closer cooperation of all concerned in Haiti as well as improve the effectiveness of international support for rebuilding Haiti's economy.

*Meeting number.* SC 3523.

On 25 April, Haiti addressed a note verbale[19] to the Council President, containing its Government's reactions to his statement. The note stated that the Government of Haiti was deeply committed to peace and stability in the country and to the organization of free and democratic elections, and that it had taken steps to guarantee maximum participation of the electorate and to involve all parties in the electoral process. The Government counted on the success of the elections to make the process of restoring democracy irreversible, and called on international observers to join it in its efforts to ensure transparency. The elections were to be held in accordance with the timetable as planned.

**Report of the Secretary-General (July).** In a 24 July report,[20] the Secretary-General noted that by the end of June UNMIH had reached a strength of 6,065 troops, 847 civilian police, 191 international staff, 240 local staff and 19 UN Volunteers. The Mission had completed deployment to its locations; its headquarters was fully established and five additional military camps had become fully operational. It provided security throughout the country, escorted humanitarian NGOs as well as logistical and food convoys, carried out prison guard duties for more than a month in Cap Haïtien and Gonaïves, undertook harbour patrols, and executed civil projects providing assistance to improve power supply, the transportation of repatriated refugees, the development of a disaster response training programme, support

for animal immunization and nutrition management programmes, as well as for public construction activities, and the removal of wrecked vehicles off the streets of Port-au-Prince. Information campaigns were carried out on various issues, including the role of UNMIH, the electoral process, public safety and the Haitian National Police.

CIVPOL encouraged and guided the work of both IPSF and the National Police, and provided on-the-job training for the latter; its resources, however, had been strained to the limit. It also coordinated the delivery of food for prisoners, helped to provide prison security, and undertook such unanticipated tasks as firearm training for the ministerial security force and security surveys of facilities for several ministries and the National Commission for Truth and Justice. Issues related to the UNMIH mandate were reviewed at weekly meetings between the Secretary-General's Special Representative, the Mission Force and CIVPOL Commanders and President Aristide. In May, an ACABQ delegation visited UNMIH to examine its administrative, logistical and financial aspects.

Despite technical difficulties with voter registration and ballot preparation, the municipal and local elections and the first round of parliamentary elections were held as scheduled on 25 June, observed by both MICIVIH and OAS. The UN Electoral Assistance Team provided technical expertise to the Provisional Electoral Council in such areas as logistical planning, distribution of electoral materials, preparation of technical documentation, registration of candidates, and polling and counting, while UNMIH's military and CIVPOL components assisted in maintaining security throughout the election period. Nevertheless, organizational problems prevented many Haitians from voting, and election results drew strong criticism from Haitian political leaders. The Provisional Electoral Council admitted that mistakes and irregularities had occurred and that complementary elections had to be held in certain constituencies.

The security situation continued to improve and was marked by a drop in vigilante killings and a decrease in common crime, although humanitarian aid convoys and warehouses were still targeted by organized gangs. In May, CIVPOL carried out its first monthly performance evaluation of IPSF; from 29 May to 13 July, initial training in prison guard duties was provided to 288 IPSF members and 140 other participants. IPSF was gradually being replaced by the Haitian National Police, the first two groups of which, totalling 766 agents, had completed training and were deployed. Following adjustments in the programme to provide for accelerated training in the United States, the number of police officers trained and deployed was expected to reach 6,000 by the end of February 1996.

Most demobilized IPSF members enrolled in the six-month retraining programme offered to former FADH personnel. In addition, steps were taken to set up a number of specialized security units in Haiti, and the creation of other services, such as coastal and border patrols, was under consideration. The report also noted that the UN trust fund for the Haitian National Police had received $3.2 million in contributions.

Improvements were made in the judicial and penal systems, with 6 of 15 prisons rehabilitated under the penal reform programme funded by UNDP and the United States Agency for International Development (USAID), and providing for a system of registration of prisoners, establishment of a penal administration system, training of prison wardens and renovation of certain detention centres. A national penitentiary administration was created in June, and a UN project to train prosecutors, in coordination with a USAID project, was launched on 3 July at the new Justice Academy, inaugurated that same day. The National Commission for Truth and Justice began to collect information on complaints of human rights violations during the period from 29 September 1991 to 15 October 1994 and to investigate certain cases.

The report further described development assistance to Haiti, provided by the UN system, multilateral donors and international financial institutions. It noted that a meeting of multilateral agencies and donors in Port-au-Prince on 11 and 12 May had identified commitments of $1.5 billion from October 1994 to the year 2000, and that aid disbursements of some $400 million had been made since October 1994 towards balance-of-payments support, emergency imports, governance and humanitarian assistance. A $50 million loan was granted by the World Bank for job-creation activities, while UNDP-funded programmes, expected to total $15 million in 1995, focused on governance, economic growth, poverty alleviation and environmental regeneration. A number of projects were financed by contributions from Governments and dealt with agricultural development, education, job creation, women in development, reintegration of refugees and displaced persons, and establishment of regional centres for coordination between UN agencies, NGOs and local civilian authorities. Joint activities by the Pan American Health Organization/World Health Organization concentrated on health programme development, including clean water supply, control of communicable diseases, immunization against preventable diseases and maternal and child health. In cooperation with the UN Children's Fund (UNICEF), a national campaign for the eradication of measles was launched; UNICEF also assisted with a campaign against childhood diarrhoea and acute respiratory infections, as well as with nutrition programmes. Among other UN bodies and agencies, the UN Population Fund implemented reproductive, health and family planning programmes; the World Food Programme and the Food and Agriculture Organization of the United Nations assisted with agricultural development and food production; the UN Educational, Scientific and Cultural Organization carried out a literacy and women's education programme in rural areas; and the UN Capital Development Fund executed projects in the water and sanitation sector. The UN Volunteers programme for Haiti was relaunched in January 1995 and brought in more than 60 Volunteers, with a budget of some $2.6 million, focusing on community-led education projects. UNHCR assisted in the repatriation of some 20,400 Haitians from September 1994 to June 1995, with disbursements of about $500,000.

Pointing to the progress achieved by UNMIH in fulfilling its tasks, as well as to the need for sustaining a secure and stable environment in Haiti in order to promote a lasting restoration of democracy, the Secretary-General recommended extension of the Mission's mandate until the end of February 1996, with a view to completing it by that time.

### SECURITY COUNCIL ACTION (July)

On 31 July, the Security Council adopted **resolution 1007(1995)**.

*The Security Council,*

*Recalling* the provisions of its resolutions 841(1993) of 16 June 1993, 861(1993) of 27 August 1993, 862(1993) of 31 August 1993, 867(1993) of 23 September 1993, 873(1993) of 13 October 1993, 875(1993) of 16 October 1993, 905(1994) of 23 March 1994, 917(1994) of 6 May 1994, 933(1994) of 30 June 1994, 940(1994) of 31 July 1994, 944(1994) of 29 September 1994, 948(1994) of 15 October 1994, 964(1994) of 29 November 1994 and 975(1995) of 30 January 1995,

*Recalling* General Assembly resolutions 46/7 of 11 October 1991, 46/138 of 17 December 1991, 47/20 A and B of 24 November 1992 and 20 April 1993, respectively, 47/143 of 18 December 1992, 48/27 A and B of 6 December 1993 and 8 July 1994, respectively, 48/151 of 20 December 1993, 49/27 A and B of 5 December 1994 and 12 July 1995, respectively, and 49/201 of 23 December 1994,

*Having considered* the report of the Secretary-General of 24 July 1995 on the work of the United Nations Mission in Haiti (UNMIH),

*Supporting* the continuing leadership by the Secretary-General of the United Nations and the Secretary-General of the Organization of American States in the efforts of the United Nations and the Organization of American States to assist with political progress and stability in Haiti,

*Supporting also* the role of UNMIH in assisting the Government of Haiti in its efforts to maintain a secure and stable environment as called for in resolution 940(1994),

*Stressing* the importance of free and fair municipal, legislative and presidential elections in Haiti as crucial steps in the complete consolidation of democracy in Haiti,

*Welcoming* the commitment of the international community to assist and support the economic, social and institutional development of Haiti and recognizing the importance of such assistance in sustaining a secure and stable environment,

*Commending* all efforts to establish a fully functioning, national police force of adequate size and structure, necessary for the consolidation of democracy and revitalization of Haiti's system of justice and noting the key role played by the civilian police component of UNMIH in creating such a police force,

*Underlining* the need to keep under review the progress of UNMIH's fulfilment of its mandate,

1. *Commends* UNMIH on its successful efforts, as authorized in resolution 940(1994), to assist the Government of Haiti in sustaining a secure and stable environment, protecting international personnel and key installations, establishing the conditions for holding elections, and professionalizing the security forces;

2. *Expresses thanks* to UNMIH and the International Civilian Mission (MICIVIH), and to States contributing to these Missions, for their assistance with the municipal and legislative elections held on 25 June 1995 and looks forward to their continuing efforts as Haiti prepares for the completion of these elections and for subsequent presidential elections;

3. *Commends* the people of Haiti for their peaceful participation in the first round of municipal and legislative elections and calls upon the Government and political parties in Haiti to work together to ensure that the remaining municipal and legislative elections and the presidential elections to be held at the end of this year are conducted in an orderly, peaceful, free and fair manner, in accordance with the Haitian Constitution;

4. *Expresses its deep concern* with irregularities observed in the first round of municipal and legislative elections and urges all parties to the process to pursue every effort to ensure that such problems are corrected in future balloting;

5. *Welcomes* the continuing efforts of President Jean-Bertrand Aristide to work towards national reconciliation and calls upon the Secretaries-General of the United Nations and the Organization of American States, respectively, to continue to render all appropriate assistance to the Haitian electoral process;

6. *Reaffirms* the importance of a fully functioning, national police force of adequate size and structure to the consolidation of democracy and revitalization of Haiti's system of justice;

7. *Notes* the key role played by the civilian police component of UNMIH in establishing such a police force;

8. *Recalls* the commitment of the international community to assist and support the economic, social and institutional development of Haiti and stresses its importance for sustaining a secure and stable environment in Haiti;

9. *Decides*, in order to achieve the objectives established in resolution 940(1994), to extend the mandate of UNMIH for a period of seven months, and looks forward to the conclusion of UNMIH's mandate at that time and to the safe, secure and orderly assumption of office by a new, constitutionally elected government;

10. *Calls upon* States and international institutions to continue to provide assistance to the Government and the people of Haiti as they consolidate the gains made towards democracy and stability;

11. *Requests* the Secretary-General to apprise the Council of progress in the fulfilment of UNMIH's mandate and, to this end, also requests the Secretary-General to report to the Council at the mid-point of this mandate;

12. *Pays tribute* to the Special Representative of the Secretary-General and the members and staff of UNMIH and MICIVIH for their respective contributions in assisting the Haitian people in their quest for strong and lasting democracy, constitutional order, economic prosperity and national reconciliation;

13. *Decides* to remain actively seized of the matter.

Security Council resolution 1007(1995)

31 July 1995          Meeting 3559          Adopted unanimously

6-nation draft (S/1995/629).

*Sponsors:* Argentina, Canada, France, Honduras, United States, Venezuela.

**Further report of the Secretary-General (November).** On 6 November, the Secretary-General reported[21] that UNMIH's strength had reached 5,958 military personnel, 780 civilian police, 184 international staff, 240 local staff, 28 UN Volunteers and 39 local interpreters. Three new base camps were established, completing deployment of the military component in all nine departments, and the boundaries of six operational sectors were modified at the end of August, while CIVPOL personnel were deployed in 19 locations, regrouped into five divisions. The Mission continued to carry out patrols, escort humanitarian relief convoys, provide logistical and security support for elections, serve as a backup to the Haitian authorities in law and order situations, and ensure the security of UNMIH personnel and property. Mission engineers carried out bridge reconstruction projects, while its civil affairs unit assisted with emergency medical training and worked on projects ranging from repairing infrastructure and rehabilitating prisons to improving the electric power distribution, maintenance and billing systems. It also initiated a clean-up of abandoned vehicles from the streets of Saint-Marc. As at 1 October, 332 small projects had been completed and 375 were in progress. CIVPOL provided specialized and general training to the Haitian National Police, tailored to meet local requirements. Although a CIVPOL officer was seriously wounded on 31 August, the threat to UNMIH was assessed as low. Mission-related issues continued to be discussed at regular meetings between its command, the Special Representative and President Aristide.

The report noted that the internal security situation was marked by a decline in violent crime but an increase in public unrest over economic issues. Vigilante groups had disbanded in many places and no political violence was reported. At the same time, growing popular discontent with the Government's programme of economic reforms led to the creation of an anti-privatization committee, by trade unions, public organizations and political parties, to coordinate protest activities. Following the resignation of the Prime Minister and interruption of the privatization process on 10 October, the President convened a special session of the National Assembly to approve the appointment of a new Prime Minister and to consider other outstanding issues. In the wake of the first round of elections, the President of the Provisional Electoral Council admitted to serious mistakes and resigned; despite renewed efforts by the Special Representative and the Friends of the Secretary-General for Haiti to encourage the resumption of a dialogue between all parties involved, most opposition parties decided not to participate in the second round, reruns or complementary elections. Nevertheless, complementary legislative and municipal elections were held in 21 electoral districts on 13 August, and the second round of legislative elections and additional reruns took place on 17 September. Additional run-offs and complementary elections were held on 8 October. The polls resulted in a clear victory for the pro-Aristide Lavalas coalition.

Following the Government's assessment of security requirements, it was decided that the strength of the Haitian National Police would total 5,000 officers, all of whom had been recruited for training. By the beginning of October, more than 1,400 officers had been deployed and received essential equipment and supplies. The deployment of an additional 1,450 cadets was expected to be completed by November; however, considerable resources were required to provide them with the necessary equipment. Demobilization of IPSF personnel was carried out in parallel, but additional efforts were needed to ensure their reintegration into society. As for the judicial and penal systems, the programme for rehabilitation of penitentiaries continued to be implemented, with sanitary and medical services introduced in 8 of the 15 prisons, and a comprehensive assistance project for penitentiary reform was being finalized by the Government, UNDP and bilateral donors. In addition, some 420 members of the national penitentiary administration received initial training and assumed their responsibilities, while the Justice Academy trained more than 100 judges and prosecutors and 50 court security guards. The mandate of the National Commission for Truth and Justice, which had received more than 5,000 complaints of past human rights violations, was extended until 31 December 1995.

Further progress was made towards restoring macroeconomic stability, as evidenced by declining inflation, a relatively stable national currency, record-level fiscal revenues and an estimated growth of gross domestic product per capita for 1995. At the same time, serious challenges remained, highlighting the need for continuing international assistance. As at 31 August, total financial commitments for Haiti had reached $1.7 billion, of which some $650 million was expected to be disbursed by year's end. The commitments of the UN system amounted to $630 million, or 37 per cent, of total resources. The report further described specific assistance activities.

The Secretary-General noted that UNMIH had made substantial progress in fulfilling its mandate, and that it was reasonable to presume that it would be able to ensure an environment free of fear, violence and intimidation during presidential elections expected to be held in December 1995 or January 1996. Pointing to the expected completion of deployment of the Haitian National Police, he reiterated his appeal for contributions to the UN trust fund, and proposed a significant reduction in the strength of the CIVPOL component before the end of the year.

**SECURITY COUNCIL ACTION (November)**

On 16 November, the Security Council President made the following statement[22] on behalf of the Council:

The Security Council welcomes the report of the Secretary-General of 6 November 1995 on the United Nations Mission in Haiti (UNMIH), issued pursuant to resolution 1007(1995).

The Security Council commends UNMIH on the substantial progress it has made towards fulfilling its mandate, as set out in resolution 940(1994), to assist the Government of Haiti in sustaining a secure and stable environment, protecting international personnel and key installations, establishing the conditions for holding elections and creating a new professional police force. The Council commends the Secretary-General, his Special Representative, and other dedicated personnel of the United Nations who have contributed to this effort.

The Security Council also commends the Government of Haiti for holding local and legislative elections in a peaceful and non-violent environment, and notes the recent convocation of the special session of the National Assembly and its approval of the new Cabinet and plan of government. The Council notes with satisfaction the role of UNMIH and the joint United Nations/Organization of American States (OAS) International Civilian Mission (MICIVIH) in assisting the Haitian authorities with the electoral process.

The Security Council emphasizes that the continued engagement and commitment of all Haitian parties is necessary to the successful organization of free, fair and peaceful presidential elections. Consistent with the objectives of Security Council resolutions 940(1994) and 1007(1995), the Council welcomes the announcement by the provisional Electoral Council of presidential elections scheduled for 17 December

1995 that should allow a transition of power to a duly-elected successor before UNMIH's scheduled termination on 29 February 1996. The holding of presidential elections on schedule is a crucial step in consolidating long-lasting democracy in Haiti and ensuring a smooth transition of government. The Council calls on all political parties in Haiti to participate in the forthcoming elections and to contribute actively to maintain the secure and stable conditions necessary for their conduct.

The Security Council notes with concern recent instances of violence in Haiti and calls for respect for the rule of law, national reconciliation and cooperation.

The Government and people of Haiti bear the primary responsibility for Haiti's political, economic and social reconstruction. The Security Council underlines its firm support for the progress Haiti has already made in this regard. The Council emphasizes that a sustained commitment by the international community is indispensable for long-term peace and stability in Haiti. In this regard the Council encourages the Haitian Government to continue its dialogue with the international financial institutions.

The Security Council shares the view of the Secretary-General that the establishment of a professional police force capable of maintaining law and order throughout the country is central to Haiti's long-term stability. As the end of UNMIH's mandate approaches, attention should be focused on the selection and training of the Haitian National Police supervisors and on interested Member States providing the police force with the necessary equipment.

The Security Council also supports the efforts of the Secretary-General to streamline UNMIH, including the CIVPOL component.

The Security Council expresses its confidence that the Special Representative of the Secretary-General, UNMIH and UN/OAS MICIVIH will continue to assist the Government and people of Haiti. It notes in particular the useful role played by the OAS and the valuable cooperation with Haiti of interested Member States on a bilateral basis and stresses the importance of continuing such cooperation. The Council requests that the Secretary-General, in consultation with the Friends of Haiti and the Haitian authorities, report to the Council, at the appropriate time, on next steps in the areas of security, law enforcement and humanitarian assistance, including by United Nations specialized agencies and programmes, which the international community may take to help Haiti achieve a long-term future that is secure, stable and free.

*Meeting number.* SC 3594.

**Further developments.** Prior to the December presidential elections, President Aristide affirmed that he would hand over power, as provided for in the Haitian Constitution, on 7 February 1996. The election results, announced on 23 December, showed that René Préval, President Aristide's Prime Minister in 1991 and the candidate of the ruling Lavalas Movement, had won, with 87.9 per cent of all votes.

The security situation deteriorated abruptly in the wake of an attack on 7 November against two National Assembly deputies, one of whom was killed and the other seriously injured. Violent demonstrations erupted in Les Cayes, necessitating the deployment of the Quick Reaction Force and joint Haitian National Police/UNMIH patrols for several days. Agitation quickly spread to other cities; roadblocks were set up and demonstrations, acts of arson, looting, weapons searches and vigilante justice occurred in various places. Following a meeting with President Aristide, the Secretary-General's Special Representative appealed to the Haitian people on 13 November not to take the law into their own hands, and the police, with UNMIH support, re-established control. At the same time, common crime remained a serious problem throughout the country and a major concern for the population. On the other hand, as the deployment of the National Police progressed, IPSF was abolished on 6 December by presidential decree.

In November and December, Haitian authorities signed a number of agreements for multilateral and bilateral project assistance. UNDP agreed to fund projects for strengthening the national Parliament and the Office of the Prime Minister, and sponsored a seminar for newly elected mayors to assist them in their work. An agreement was signed between Haiti, France, UNDP and USAID to co-finance a $2.9 million project for the rehabilitation of jails and the training of penitentiary personnel. From 22 to 24 November, 16 Latin American and Caribbean countries met in Port-au-Prince to negotiate 144 development cooperation projects in Haiti, which led to agreement on 22 projects totally financed and 73 projects partially financed.

Activities were also initiated for the transfer of responsibilities from UNMIH, a phased reduction of which began in October, to the Government of Haiti. The Trilateral Commission, comprising the Government, the United Nations and the Friends of the Secretary-General for Haiti, held its first meeting in Port-au-Prince on 16 November and agreed to set up joint working groups on transition-related issues, such as disarmament; information; justice, prisons and human rights; presidential security; election security; airports, seaports and coastguards; fire-fighting and urban disorders; and traffic.

*Composition*

On 16 January, the Secretary-General proposed[23] that UNMIH's military component be composed of contingents from Antigua and Barbuda, Argentina, Bangladesh, Barbados, Canada, Djibouti, France, Guatemala, Guyana, Hungary, India, Ireland, Jamaica, New Zealand, Pakistan, Suriname, Trinidad and Tobago, Tunisia and the United States; on 19 January, he added[24] to that list the Bahamas, Botswana, Costa Rica, Honduras, Nepal, the Netherlands and Slovakia. The Security Council's agreement with those proposals was communicated to the Secretary-General on 19 January[25] and 23 January,[26] respectively.

## Financing

**Reports of Secretary-General and ACABQ (February/March).** On 22 February, the Secretary-General reported[27] that the budget of the UNMIH advance team from 1 August 1994 to 31 January 1995 totalled $5,902,500 gross ($5,707,100 net) and provided for up to 24 military observers, 19 contingent personnel, 40 civilian police and 51 international and 33 local civilian staff. The cost of maintaining the Mission from 1 February to 31 December 1995 was estimated at $272,966,400 gross ($268,301,000 net), providing for up to 6,000 troops, 900 civilian police, 220 international and 240 local civilian staff and 29 UN Volunteers.

Estimated expenditures from 23 September 1993 to 28 February 1995 amounted to $11,157,100 gross ($10,634,600 net), resulting in an unencumbered balance of $1,491,100 gross ($1,403,800 net). As at 31 January, outstanding contributions due from Member States totalled $2,090,369; at the same time, $2.7 million had been pledged to the trust fund for electoral assistance to Haiti.

The Secretary-General requested the appropriation of $5,946,700 gross ($5,749,600 net) and the assessment of $3,644,800 gross ($3,650,500 net) for the period from 1 July 1994 to 31 January 1995; action with regard to the unencumbered balance; the appropriation and assessment of $163,824,500 gross ($161,396,400 net) from 1 February to 31 July 1995; and commitment authority of $21,828,380 gross ($21,380,920 net) per month after 31 July, subject to UNMIH's continuation beyond that date.

In a 22 March report,[28] ACABQ recommended that the costs from 1 February to 31 December 1995 not exceed $257,556,300; it did not recommend assessment of the requested additional amount from 1 July 1994 to 31 January 1995 until review of a performance report for that period. It pointed out that its concurrence with commitments for March 1995 was being sought *ex post facto*, and reiterated its insistence that there be strict adherence to the established procedure for such concurrence, as well as to the UN financial regulations and rules. Noting that the Secretary-General's report had been submitted to it in an advance draft form and in only one language version, ACABQ trusted that the Secretary-General would, in future, ensure timely submission of comprehensive final documentation in all official UN languages.

**GENERAL ASSEMBLY ACTION (March)**

On 31 March, the General Assembly adopted **resolution 49/239**.

## Financing of the United Nations Mission in Haiti

*The General Assembly,*

*Having considered* the report of the Secretary-General on the financing of the United Nations Mission in Haiti and the related report of the Advisory Committee on Administrative and Budgetary Questions,

*Recalling* Security Council resolution 862(1993) of 31 August 1993, in which the Council approved the dispatch of an advance team of no more than thirty persons to assess requirements and prepare for the possible dispatch of both the civilian police and the military assistance components of the proposed United Nations Mission in Haiti, and decided that the mandate of the advance team would expire within one month,

*Recalling also* Security Council resolution 867(1993) of 23 September 1993, in which the Council authorized the establishment and immediate dispatch of the Mission for a period of six months subject to the proviso that it would be extended beyond seventy-five days only upon a review by the Council to be based on a report from the Secretary-General indicating whether or not substantive progress had been made towards the implementation of the Governors Island Agreement of 3 July 1993 between the President of the Republic of Haiti and the Commander-in-Chief of the Armed Forces of Haiti and the political accords contained in the New York Pact,

*Recalling further* Security Council resolution 940(1994) of 31 July 1994, in which the Council, acting under Chapter VII of the Charter of the United Nations, authorized Member States to form a multinational force under unified command and control and, in that framework, to use all necessary means to facilitate the departure from Haiti of the military leadership, consistent with the Governors Island Agreement, the prompt return of the legitimately elected President and the restoration of the legitimate authorities of the Government of Haiti, and to establish and maintain a secure and stable environment that would permit implementation of the Governors Island Agreement, and approved the establishment of an advance team of no more than sixty persons, including a group of observers, to establish the appropriate means of coordination with the multinational force, to carry out the monitoring of the operations of the force and to assess requirements and to prepare for the deployment of the United Nations Mission in Haiti upon completion of the mission of the multinational force,

*Recalling* Security Council resolution 964(1994) of 29 November 1994, in which the Council authorized the Secretary-General to strengthen progressively the advance team of the Mission up to five hundred persons in order to further facilitate the planning of the Mission, identification of conditions required for the transition from the multinational force and preparation for the actual transition, as well as to make good offices available for the achievement of the purposes approved by the Council in resolution 940(1994),

*Recalling also* Security Council resolution 975(1995) of 30 January 1995, in which the Council authorized the Secretary-General to deploy up to six thousand troops and nine hundred civilian police officers, and extended the mandate of the Mission for a period of six months, to 31 July 1995,

*Recalling further* its decision 48/477 of 23 December 1993, its resolution 48/246 of 5 April 1994 and its decision 49/468 of 23 December 1994 on the financing of the Mission,

*Reaffirming* that the costs of the Mission are expenses of the Organization to be borne by Member States in accordance with Article 17, paragraph 2, of the Charter of the United Nations,

*Recalling* its previous decisions regarding the fact that, in order to meet the expenditures caused by the Mission, a different procedure is required from the one applied to meet expenditures of the regular budget of the United Nations,

*Taking into account* the fact that the economically more developed countries are in a position to make relatively larger contributions and that the economically less developed countries have a relatively limited capacity to contribute towards such an operation,

*Bearing in mind* the special responsibilities of the States permanent members of the Security Council, as indicated in General Assembly resolution 1874(S-IV) of 27 June 1963, in the financing of such operations,

*Mindful* of the fact that it is essential to provide the Mission with the necessary financial resources to enable it to fulfil its responsibilities under the relevant resolutions of the Security Council,

1. *Expresses concern* about the financial situation with regard to peace-keeping activities, particularly as regards the reimbursement of troop contributors, because of overdue payments by Member States of their assessments, particularly Member States in arrears;

2. *Urges* all Member States to make every possible effort to ensure payment of their assessed contributions to the United Nations Mission in Haiti promptly and in full, which will contribute to the operational effectiveness of the Mission;

3. *Endorses* the observations and recommendations contained in the report of the Advisory Committee on Administrative and Budgetary Questions, subject to the provisions of the present resolution;

4. *Takes note with concern* of the relevant issues raised in the report of the Advisory Committee, and requests the Secretariat:

(a) To facilitate the work of the General Assembly and the Advisory Committee by providing adequate reports in a timely fashion, in all the official languages of the Organization, as well as by supplying expeditiously requested supporting information or clarification;

(b) To adhere strictly to the procurement rules and regulations;

(c) To seek prior concurrence of the Advisory Committee before entering into commitments under the provisions of section IV of General Assembly resolution 49/233 A of 23 December 1994;

5. *Reaffirms* resolution 49/233 A, in particular section II thereof regarding contingent-owned equipment, and takes note of the fact that the procedures used for budgeting for the reimbursement of contingent-owned equipment in the Mission do not prejudge the decision to be taken by the General Assembly on this matter in accordance with resolution 49/233 A;

6. *Stresses* the importance of the coordination between the United Nations Mission in Haiti, the International Civilian Mission in Haiti and all organizations and bodies involved in the implementation of the aid programme in Haiti, with a view to rationalizing the use of funds provided from voluntary and assessed contributions and avoiding duplication of activities and waste of resources;

7. *Requests* the Secretary-General to take all necessary action to ensure that the Mission is administered with a maximum of efficiency and economy;

8. *Decides* to appropriate to the special account referred to in its decision 48/477 an amount of 44,200 United States dollars gross (42,500 dollars net), authorized and apportioned for the period from 1 to 31 July 1994 under the provisions of its resolution 48/246;

9. *Decides also* to appropriate to the special account a total amount of 5,902,500 dollars gross (5,707,100 dollars net) for the operation of the Mission for the period from 1 August 1994 to 31 January 1995, inclusive of the amount of 221,000 dollars gross (212,500 dollars net) authorized and apportioned for the period from 1 August to 31 December 1994 under the provisions of resolution 48/246, the amount of 1,347,000 dollars gross (1,217,900 dollars net) authorized by the Advisory Committee for the period from 19 September to 18 December 1994 under the terms of General Assembly resolution 48/229 of 23 December 1993 and the reduced amount of 4,334,500 dollars gross (4,276,700 dollars net) authorized by the Advisory Committee for the period from 1 December 1994 to 31 January 1995 under the terms of resolution 48/229;

10. *Decides further* to appropriate to the special account a total amount of 151,545,100 dollars gross (149,579,700 dollars net) for the operation of the Mission for the period from 1 February to 31 July 1995, inclusive of the amount of 3,720,700 dollars gross (3,409,600 dollars net) authorized by the Advisory Committee for the period from 1 to 28 February 1995 under the terms of resolution 48/229;

11. *Decides*, as an ad hoc arrangement, to apportion the amount of 151,545,100 dollars gross (149,579,700 dollars net), for the period from 1 February to 31 July 1995, among Member States in accordance with the composition of groups set out in paragraphs 3 and 4 of General Assembly resolution 43/232 of 1 March 1989, as adjusted by the Assembly in its resolutions 44/192 B of 21 December 1989, 45/269 of 27 August 1991, 46/198 A of 20 December 1991 and 47/218 A of 23 December 1992 and its decision 48/472 A of 23 December 1993, and taking into account the scale of assessments for the years 1995, 1996 and 1997 as set out in Assembly resolution 49/19 B of 23 December 1994;

12. *Decides also* that, in accordance with the provisions of its resolution 973(X) of 15 December 1955, there shall be set off against the apportionment among Member States, as provided for in paragraph 11 above, their respective share in the Tax Equalization Fund of the estimated staff assessment income of 1,965,400 dollars approved for the Mission for the period from 1 February to 31 July 1995;

13. *Decides further* that there shall be set off against the apportionment among Member States, as provided for in paragraph 11 above, their respective share in the unencumbered balance of 37,000 dollars gross (26,700 dollars net) in respect of the period from 23 September 1993 to 31 July 1994;

14. *Decides*, with regard to the period beyond 31 July 1995, to authorize the Secretary-General, on a provisional basis, to enter into commitments at a monthly rate not to exceed 21,202,240 dollars gross (20,840,040 dollars net) for the three-month period from 1 August to 31 October 1995 in connection with the maintenance of the Mission, the amount of 21,202,240 dollars gross

(20,840,040 dollars net) to be apportioned, in accordance with the scheme set out in the present resolution, subject to the decision of the Security Council to extend the mandate of the Mission beyond 31 July 1995;

15. *Requests* the Secretary-General, to enable the General Assembly to take a decision on the definite amount of expenditure for the period beyond 31 July 1995, to submit revised budget proposals by the end of August 1995;

16. *Invites* voluntary contributions to the Mission in cash and in the form of services and supplies acceptable to the Secretary-General, to be administered, as appropriate, in accordance with the procedure established by the General Assembly in its resolutions 43/230 of 21 December 1988, 44/192 A of 21 December 1989 and 45/258 of 3 May 1991;

17. *Decides* to include in the provisional agenda of its fiftieth session the item entitled "Financing of the United Nations Mission in Haiti".

General Assembly resolution 49/239

31 March 1995     Meeting 99     Adopted without vote

Approved by Fifth Committee (A/49/818/Add.1) without vote, 29 March (meeting 50); draft by Chairman (A/C.5/49/L.43), based on informal consultations; agenda item 128.
*Meeting numbers.* GA 49th session: 5th Committee 49, 50; plenary 99.

**Reports of Secretary-General and ACABQ (August/September).** On 22 August, the Secretary-General reported[29] that UNMIH's financial performance from 1 August 1994 to 31 January 1995 had resulted in an unencumbered balance of $1,982,600 gross ($1,915,700 net), from an appropriation of $5,902,500 gross ($5,707,100 net), of which, however, only $2,257,700 gross ($2,056,600 net) had been assessed. He estimated the Mission's cost from 1 August 1995 to 29 February 1996 at $152,011,500 gross ($149,680,400 net), providing for 6,000 contingent personnel, 900 civilian police, 207 international and 379 local civilian staff and 33 UN Volunteers.

As at 31 July, outstanding contributions due from Member States totalled $59,962,047; at the same time, $9.6 million had been contributed to the trust fund for electoral assistance to Haiti and $3.3 million to the trust fund for the international police monitoring programme and other specific purposes. The report also provided observations and comments on previous recommendations of ACABQ, including additional information requested by it in March.

The Secretary-General requested the assessment of $3,644,800 gross ($3,650,500 net) for the period from 1 August 1994 to 31 January 1995; action with regard to the unencumbered balance; the appropriation of $152,011,500 gross ($149,680,400 net) for the period from 1 August 1995 to 29 February 1996 and assessment of $130,809,260 gross ($128,840,360 net) for that period; and commitment authority of $21,182,900 gross ($20,849,900 net) per month after 29 February 1996, subject to UNMIH's continuation beyond that date.

In a 29 September report,[30] ACABQ noted that the monthly cost estimate for the period beyond 29 February 1996 was indicative and would be revised before that date. It recommended approval of the Secretary-General's other requests.

GENERAL ASSEMBLY ACTION (November)

In November, the Assembly adopted **decision 50/407 A** on the financing of UNMIH.

At its 46th plenary meeting, on 1 November 1995, the General Assembly, on the recommendation of the Fifth Committee:

*(a)* Decided, as an ad hoc arrangement, and having taken into account the amount of 21,202,240 United States dollars gross (20,840,040 dollars net) already apportioned in accordance with General Assembly resolution 49/239 of 31 March 1995, to apportion the additional amount of 42,404,480 dollars gross (41,680,080 dollars net) for the period from 1 August to 31 October 1995 among Member States in accordance with the composition of groups set out in paragraphs 3 and 4 of Assembly resolution 43/232 of 1 March 1989, as adjusted by the Assembly in its resolutions 44/192 B of 21 December 1989, 45/269 of 27 August 1991, 46/198 A of 20 December 1991, 47/218 A of 23 December 1992, 49/249 A of 20 July 1995 and 49/249 B of 14 September 1995 and its decision 48/472 A of 23 December 1993, and having taken into account the scale of assessments for the year 1995;

*(b)* Also decided that, in accordance with the provisions of its resolution 973(X) of 15 December 1955, there should be set off against the apportionment among Member States, as provided for in paragraph *(a)* above, their respective share in the Tax Equalization Fund of the additional estimated staff assessment income of 724,400 dollars authorized for the United Nations Mission in Haiti for the period from 1 August to 31 October 1995;

*(c)* Authorized the Secretary-General to enter into commitments for the operation of the Mission for the period from 1 to 30 November 1995 in the amount of 21,202,240 dollars gross (20,840,040 dollars net);

*(d)* Decided, as an ad hoc arrangement, to apportion the amount of 21,202,240 dollars gross (20,840,040 dollars net), for the period from 1 to 30 November 1995, among Member States in accordance with the scheme set out in paragraph *(a)* above;

*(e)* Also decided that, in accordance with the provisions of its resolution 973(X), there should be set off against the apportionment among Member States, as provided for in paragraph *(d)* above, their respective share in the Tax Equalization Fund of the estimated staff assessment income of 362,200 dollars authorized for the Mission for the period from 1 to 30 November 1995.

General Assembly decision 50/407 A

Adopted without vote

Approved by Fifth Committee (A/50/705) without vote, 31 October (meeting 14); draft by Chairman (A/C.5/50/L.3), based on informal consultations; agenda item 133.
*Meeting numbers.* GA 50th session: 5th Committee 8, 14; plenary 46.

**Further reports of Secretary-General and ACABQ (November).** On 9 November, the Secretary-General reported[31] that the Mission's expenditures from 1 February to 31 July 1995 amounted to $133,531,900 gross ($132,305,000 net), resulting in an unencumbered balance of $18,013,200 gross ($17,274,700 net). He proposed that Member States' respective share in that balance be set off against the future assessment.

ACABQ concurred[32] with the Secretary-General's proposal.

**Fifth Committee consideration (November/December).** On 29 November, the UN Controller told the Fifth Committee that the Secretary-General's commitment authority for UNMIH was due to expire on 30 November and that urgent action by the General Assembly was required. On 1 December, the Committee recommended[33] a decision for adoption by the Assembly.

GENERAL ASSEMBLY ACTION (December)

On 4 December, the General Assembly, by **decision 50/407 B**, authorized the Secretary-General, on an exceptional basis, to enter into commitments of $10,601,120 gross ($10,420,020 net) for the period from 1 to 15 December 1995.

On 19 December, the Assembly adopted **resolution 50/90 A**.

**Financing of the United Nations Mission in Haiti**

*The General Assembly,*

*Having considered* the reports of the Secretary-General on the financing of the United Nations Mission in Haiti and the related reports of the Advisory Committee on Administrative and Budgetary Questions,

*Recalling* Security Council resolution 1007(1995) of 31 July 1995, in which the Council extended the mandate of the Mission for an additional period of seven months, to 29 February 1996, in anticipation of the conclusion of the mandate at that time, as well as all previous Security Council resolutions on the Mission,

*Recalling also* its decision 48/477 of 23 December 1993 on the financing of the Mission and its subsequent resolutions and decisions thereon, the latest of which was decision 50/407 B of 4 December 1995,

*Reaffirming* that the costs of the Mission are expenses of the Organization to be borne by Member States in accordance with Article 17, paragraph 2, of the Charter of the United Nations,

*Recalling further* its previous decisions regarding the fact that, in order to meet the expenditures caused by the Mission, a different procedure is required from the one applied to meet expenditures of the regular budget of the United Nations,

*Taking into account* the fact that the economically more developed countries are in a position to make relatively larger contributions and that the economically less developed countries have a relatively limited capacity to contribute towards such an operation,

*Bearing in mind* the special responsibilities of the States permanent members of the Security Council, as indicated in General Assembly resolution 1874(S-IV) of 27 June 1963, in the financing of such operations,

*Mindful* of the fact that it is essential to provide the Mission with the necessary financial resources to en-

able it to fulfil its responsibilities under the relevant resolutions of the Security Council,

1. *Takes note* of the status of contributions to the United Nations Mission in Haiti as at 13 December 1995, including the unpaid contributions in the amount of 78,677,550 United States dollars, representing 33 per cent of the total assessed contributions from the inception of the Mission to the period ending 30 November 1995, notes that some 8 per cent of the Member States have paid their assessed contributions in full, and urges all other Member States concerned, particularly those in arrears, to ensure the payment of their outstanding assessed contributions;

2. *Expresses concern* about the financial situation with regard to peace-keeping activities, particularly as regards the reimbursement of troop contributors, notably those troop-contributing Member States that have paid their assessed contributions in full, which bear an additional burden owing to overdue payments by Member States of their assessments;

3. *Urges* all Member States to make every possible effort to ensure payment of their assessed contributions to the Mission promptly and in full;

4. *Endorses* the observations and recommendations contained in the reports of the Advisory Committee on Administrative and Budgetary Questions;

5. *Requests* the Secretary-General to take all necessary action to ensure that the Mission is administered with a maximum of efficiency and economy;

6. *Decides*, as an ad hoc arrangement and taking into account the amount of 2,257,700 dollars gross (2,056,600 dollars net) already apportioned in accordance with General Assembly resolution 48/246 of 5 April 1994 and decision 49/468 of 23 December 1994, to apportion the additional amount of 3,644,800 dollars gross (3,650,500 dollars net) for the period from 1 August 1994 to 31 January 1995 among Member States in accordance with the composition of groups set out in paragraphs 3 and 4 of General Assembly resolution 43/232 of 1 March 1989, as adjusted by the Assembly in its resolutions 44/192 B of 21 December 1989, 45/269 of 27 August 1991, 46/198 A of 20 December 1991 and 47/218 A of 23 December 1992 and its decision 48/472 A of 23 December 1993, and taking into account the scale of assessments for the year 1994 to be applied against a portion thereof, that is, 3,030,730 dollars gross (3,035,470 dollars net), which is the amount pertaining on a *pro rata* basis to the period ending 31 December 1994, and the scale of assessments for the year 1995 to be applied against the balance, that is, 614,070 dollars gross (615,030 dollars net), for the period from 1 to 31 January 1995 inclusive;

7. *Decides also* that, in accordance with the provisions of its resolution 973(X) of 15 December 1955, the apportionment among Member States, as provided for in paragraph 6 above, shall take into consideration the decrease in their respective share in the Tax Equalization Fund of the estimated staff assessment income of 5,700 dollars approved for the Mission for the period from 1 August 1994 to 31 January 1995 inclusive, 4,740 dollars being the amount pertaining on a *pro rata* basis to the period ending 31 December 1994, and the balance, that is, 960 dollars, for the period from 1 to 31 January 1995;

8. *Decides further* that, for Member States that have fulfilled their financial obligations to the Mission, there shall be set off against the apportionment, as provided for in paragraph 6 above, their respective share in the unencumbered balance of 1,982,600 dollars gross (1,915,700 dollars net) for the period from 1 August 1994 to 31 January 1995;

9. *Decides* that, for Member States that have not fulfilled their financial obligations to the Mission, their share of the unencumbered balance of 1,982,600 dollars gross (1,915,700 dollars net) for the period from 1 August 1994 to 31 January 1995 shall be set off against their outstanding obligations;

10. *Decides* to appropriate to the Special Account for the United Nations Mission in Haiti a total amount of 152,011,500 dollars gross (149,680,400 dollars net) for the period from 1 August 1995 to 29 February 1996, inclusive of the amount of 63,606,720 dollars gross (62,520,120 dollars net) authorized under the provisions of Assembly resolution 49/239 of 31 March 1995 for the period from 1 August to 31 October 1995, the amount of 21,202,240 dollars gross (20,840,040 dollars net) authorized by the Assembly in its decision 50/407 A of 1 November 1995 for the period from 1 to 30 November 1995 and the amount of 10,601,120 dollars gross (10,420,020 dollars net) authorized by the Assembly in its decision 50/407 B for the period from 1 to 15 December 1995;

11. *Decides also*, as an ad hoc arrangement, and taking into account the amount of 21,202,240 dollars gross (20,840,040 dollars net) apportioned in accordance with General Assembly resolution 49/239 and the amount of 63,606,720 dollars gross (62,520,120 dollars net) apportioned in accordance with its decision 50/407 A, to apportion the additional amount of 67,202,540 dollars gross (66,320,240 dollars net) for the period from 1 August 1995 to 29 February 1996 among Member States in accordance with the composition of groups set out in paragraphs 3 and 4 of Assembly resolution 43/232 of 1 March 1989, as adjusted by the Assembly in its resolutions 44/192 B of 21 December 1989, 45/269 of 27 August 1991, 46/198 A of 20 December 1991, 47/218 A of 23 December 1992, 49/249 A of 20 July 1995 and 49/249 B of 14 September 1995 and its decision 48/472 A of 23 December 1993, and taking into account the scale of assessments for the year 1995 to be applied against a portion thereof, that is, 48,272,247 dollars gross (47,638,482 dollars net), which is the amount pertaining on a *pro rata* basis to the period ending 31 December 1995, and the scale of assessments for the year 1996 to be applied against the balance, that is, 18,930,293 dollars gross (18,681,758 dollars net), for the period from 1 January to 29 February 1996 inclusive;

12. *Decides further* that, in accordance with the provisions of its resolution 973(X), there shall be set off against the apportionment among Member States, as provided for in paragraph 10 above, their respective share in the Tax Equalization Fund of the additional estimated staff assessment income of 882,300 dollars approved for the Mission for the period from 1 August 1995 to 29 February 1996 inclusive, 633,765 dollars being the amount pertaining on a *pro rata* basis to the period ending 31 December 1995, and the balance, that is, 248,535 dollars, for the period from 1 January to 29 February 1996;

13. *Decides* that, for Member States that have fulfilled their financial obligations to the Mission, there shall be

set off against the apportionment, as provided for in paragraph 10 above, their respective share in the unencumbered balance of 18,013,200 dollars gross (17,274,700 dollars net) for the period from 1 February to 31 July 1995;

14. *Decides also* that, for Member States that have not fulfilled their financial obligations to the Mission, their share of the unencumbered balance of 18,013,200 dollars gross (17,274,700 dollars net) for the period from 1 February to 31 July 1995 shall be set off against their outstanding obligations;

15. *Decides further*, with regard to the period beyond 29 February 1996, to authorize the Secretary-General to enter into commitments in connection with the maintenance of the Mission for a three-month period from 1 March to 31 May 1996 at a monthly rate not to exceed 10 million dollars gross (9.5 million dollars net) and to assess the amount of 20 million dollars gross (19 million dollars net) on Member States in accordance with the scheme set out in the present resolution, subject to the decision of the Security Council to extend the mandate of the Mission beyond 29 February 1996;

16. *Invites* voluntary contributions to the Mission in cash and in the form of services and supplies acceptable to the Secretary-General, to be administered, as appropriate, in accordance with the procedure established by the General Assembly in its resolutions 43/230 of 21 December 1988, 44/192 A of 21 December 1989 and 45/258 of 3 May 1991;

17. *Decides* to keep the agenda item entitled "Financing of the United Nations Mission in Haiti" under review during its fiftieth session.

General Assembly resolution 50/90 A

19 December 1995      Meeting 95      Adopted without vote

Approved by Fifth Committee (A/50/705/Add.2) without vote, 17 December (meeting 41); draft by Chairman (A/C.5/50/L.10), based on informal consultations; agenda item 133.

On 23 December, the General Assembly decided that the Fifth Committee should continue consideration of the agenda item on financing of UNMIH at its resumed fiftieth session (**decision 50/469**).

## International Civilian Mission to Haiti

**Report of the Secretary-General (June).** In a 29 June report[34] on the situation of democracy and human rights in Haiti, submitted in response to 1994 General Assembly requests,[35] the Secretary-General noted that the UN/OAS International Civilian Mission to Haiti had opened eight additional offices in 1995, for a total of 10, while its strength had been increased to 190 observers and other substantive staff, including 84 from OAS, and nine administrative staff, two of whom were contracted by OAS, representing 50 nationalities. The Mission continued to give priority to the monitoring and promotion of the observance of human rights.

The report pointed out that the number of human rights violations had fallen substantially since the deployment of the multinational force and the restoration of President Aristide and the constitutional Government. Different sectors of society had exercised their rights to freedom of expression, association and assembly, and internally displaced persons had begun to return to their homes. As most current violence was criminal in motivation, it fell outside the MICIVIH mandate. However, the Mission continued to investigate killings and other acts that might have a political context. The report referred to intimidation of political opponents, the murders of two political figures on 3 and 28 March, and killings of former FADH members, local officials or members of popular organizations. The Mission also continued to monitor compliance with legal procedures in cases of arrest and detention, and reported that torture and ill-treatment of people in custody had almost entirely ceased. It provided assistance in the organization and observance of elections (see above) and made efforts to ensure that they took place in an atmosphere unmarred by violence.

Activities to strengthen Haiti's human rights machinery included assistance to the National Commission for Truth and Justice in such areas as its operational aspects, working methods, work programme and budget. MICIVIH undertook regular visits to prisons and places of detention, whose conditions remained of acute concern, and cooperated in implementing a multilateral penal reform project; investigated the judicial status of detainees and promoted the rapid processing of their cases; and worked closely with Haitian NGOs in fostering human rights education. The Mission continued to provide medical assistance to victims of past human rights violations, and was involved in a network to promote psychiatric treatment for severely traumatized victims of torture. Following the deployment of UNMIH, mechanisms were put in place to facilitate coordination and exchange of information between the two Missions at all levels.

Referring to his agreement with the Secretary-General of OAS, as well as to President Aristide's request of 23 June, the Secretary-General recommended that the General Assembly extend the mandate of MICIVIH's UN component until 7 February 1996.

**GENERAL ASSEMBLY ACTION (July)**

On 12 July, the Assembly adopted **resolution 49/27 B** on the situation of democracy and human rights in Haiti.

*The General Assembly,*

*Having considered further* the item entitled "The situation of democracy and human rights in Haiti",

*Recalling* its resolutions 46/7 of 11 October 1991, 46/138 of 17 December 1991, 47/20 A and B of 24 November 1992 and 20 April 1993, respectively, 47/143 of 18 December 1992, 48/27 A and B of 6 December 1993 and 8 July 1994, respectively, 48/151 of 20 December 1993, 49/27 A of 5 December 1994 and 49/201 of 23 December 1994, as well as the resolutions and decisions adopted on the question by the Economic and Social Council and the Commission on Human Rights,

*Recalling also* Security Council resolutions 841(1993) of 16 June 1993, 861(1993) of 27 August 1993, 862(1993) of 31 August 1993, 867(1993) of 23 September 1993, 873(1993) of 13 October 1993, 875(1993) of 16 October 1993, 905(1994) of 23 March 1994, 917(1994) of 6 May 1994, 933(1994) of 30 June 1994, 940(1994) of 31 July 1994, 944(1994) of 29 September 1994, 948(1994) of 15 October 1994, 964(1994) of 29 November 1994 and 975(1995) of 30 January 1995,

*Welcoming* resolutions MRE/RES.1/91, MRE/RES.2/91, MRE/RES.3/92, MRE/RES.4/92, MRE/RES.5/93 Corr.1, MRE/RES.6/94 and MRE/RES.7/95, adopted on 3 and 8 October 1991, 17 May and 13 December 1992, 5 June 1993, 8 June 1994 and 5 June 1995, respectively, by the Ministers for Foreign Affairs of the member countries of the Organization of American States, as well as resolutions CP/RES.567(870/91), CP/RES.575(885/92), CP/RES.594(923/92), CP/RES.610(968/93), CP/RES.630 (987/94) and CP/RES.633(995/94), and declarations CP/DEC.2(896/92), CP/DEC.8(927/93), CP/DEC.9 (931/93), CP/DEC.10(934/93), CP/DEC.14(960/93), CP/ DEC.15(967/93), CP/DEC.18(986/94) and CP/DEC.21 (1006/94), adopted by the Permanent Council of the Organization of American States,

*Reaffirming* that the goal of the international community remains the full observance of human rights and fundamental freedoms and the promotion of social and economic development in Haiti,

*Noting* in this context the importance of free and fair legislative elections now in progress in Haiti, and the willingness of the Government of Haiti to hold such elections as called for in the Constitution, within the framework of the full restoration of democracy in Haiti,

*Stressing* the importance of free and fair presidential elections in Haiti, and the willingness of the Government of Haiti to hold such elections in accordance with the Constitution, as a crucial step in the complete consolidation of long-lasting democracy in Haiti,

*Strongly supportive* of the continuing leadership of the Secretary-General of the United Nations and the Secretary-General of the Organization of American States in the efforts of the international community in furthering political progress in Haiti,

*Welcoming* the success of the United Nations Mission in Haiti and the contributions of the Special Representative of the Secretary-General of the United Nations and his staff to that success,

*Welcoming also* the continued efforts by States to provide humanitarian assistance and technical cooperation to the people of Haiti,

*Supporting fully* the renewed role of the International Civilian Mission to Haiti in the establishment of a climate of freedom and tolerance propitious to the full observance of human rights and the full restoration of the constitutional democracy of Haiti,

*Paying tribute* to the members and staff of the International Civilian Mission to Haiti for their contribution, undertaken in difficult and sometimes dangerous circumstances, in accompanying the Haitian people in their efforts to return to constitutional order and democracy,

*Taking note* of the report of the Secretary-General of 29 June 1995 on the situation of democracy and human rights in Haiti, and in particular its annex containing the letter dated 23 June 1995 from President Jean-Bertrand Aristide to the Secretary-General requesting the extension of the mandate of the Mission created by the General Assembly in its resolution 47/20 B,

1. *Approves* the recommendation of the Secretary-General contained in his report to renew the mandate of the joint participation of the United Nations with the Organization of American States in the International Civilian Mission to Haiti, with the task of verifying full observance by Haiti of human rights and fundamental freedoms, with a view to making recommendations thereon, in order to further the establishment of a climate of freedom and tolerance propitious to the consolidation of long-term constitutional democracy in Haiti and to contribute to the strengthening of democratic institutions;

2. *Decides* to authorize the extension of the mandate of the United Nations component of the Mission until 7 February 1996, according to the terms of reference and modalities under which the Mission is operating;

3. *Expresses its full support* for the Mission and trusts that the Government of Haiti will continue to afford it timely, complete and effective cooperation;

4. *Pays tribute* to the Haitian people in their ongoing quest for strong and lasting democracy, economic prosperity and national reconciliation;

5. *Expresses its appreciation* to those States which have assisted in the restoration of democracy to Haiti and the return of President Jean-Bertrand Aristide to office, including those participating in the United Nations Mission in Haiti and those which have accompanied the Haitian people in their efforts to return to constitutional order and democracy;

6. *Welcomes* the prospect of free and fair presidential elections and the smooth transition to a new, democratically elected government in February 1996, in accordance with the Constitution of Haiti;

7. *Reaffirms once again* the commitment of the international community to an increase in technical, economic and financial cooperation with Haiti, in support of its economic and social development efforts and in order to strengthen those institutions responsible for dispensing justice and guaranteeing democracy, political stability and economic development;

8. *Commends* the cooperation between the Secretary-General of the United Nations and the Secretary-General of the Organization of American States in their efforts to promote respect for the rights of all Haitians and to contribute to the strengthening of democratic institutions, including the support of those organizations for election monitoring;

9. *Reaffirms its request* that the Secretary-General support the Government of Haiti as it works towards the national reconstruction and development of Haiti, in order to consolidate a climate propitious to the establishment of a lasting democracy and full respect for human rights;

10. *Requests* the Secretary-General to continue coordination of the efforts of the United Nations system towards an appropriate response capable of providing humanitarian aid and of meeting the development requirements of Haiti;

11. *Also requests* the Secretary-General to submit to the General Assembly regular reports on the work of the International Civilian Mission to Haiti;

12. *Decides* to keep open its consideration of this item.

General Assembly resolution 49/27 B

12 July 1995    Meeting 105    Adopted without vote

42-nation draft (A/49/L.67/Rev.1 & Rev.1/Add.1); agenda item 34.

**Further report of the Secretary-General (October).** On 12 October, the Secretary-General reported[36] that the number of MICIVIH regional offices had increased to 12, while its strength stood at 188 staff, of which 88 were from OAS, representing 46 nationalities. He noted that the human rights situation in Haiti had improved considerably, with the number of human rights violations remaining low, although there were sporadic reports of ill-treatment of detainees and of abuse of power by State agents. However, the Mission had examined some 20 killings since January 1995, where the victims appeared to have been targeted for assassination, but was not able to determine the motives for any of them. Several cases were raised with the authorities concerning the use of excessive force by IPSF and the National Police, and several cases of abuse of power by off-duty police officers were also under investigation. The Mission continued to monitor cases of summary ''justice'' by local people, the number of which had peaked at 50 in March and subsequently dropped to less than 10 in August, as well as their possible links to vigilante groups.

While the systematic use of cruel, inhuman or degrading treatment had ceased, the Mission raised with the authorities several alleged cases of ill-treatment of detainees by IPSF officers, including three cases of beating, most of which were reported as being under investigation. The report further described Mission activities in monitoring possible violations of the rights to freedom of expression and association, and the right to justice for victims of past human rights abuses, as well as cases of arbitrary or illegal arrests and detention. It noted a gradual improvement in the administration of criminal justice but pointed to persistent problems in that area, including excessive delays in the processing of cases and extremely poor conditions of detention. Of a total 1,703 prisoners in Haiti as at the beginning of September, 1,504 were awaiting trial and only 199 had been convicted. The right to defence was not always upheld, and, having observed a number of recent jury trials, the Mission considered that criminal proceedings fell short of basic standards for a fair trial in most cases. In addition, the conduct of pre-trial investigations was impeded by a serious lack of resources.

MICIVIH continued technical cooperation activities for the reform of the judicial system, including assistance in the preparation of legal texts, improvement of the prison system and provision of training. It participated in the training of National Police cadets and penitentiary administration officials; continued regular visits to detention centres to monitor their conditions; assisted the National Commission for Truth and Justice in collecting information on past human rights abuses; monitored the conduct of elections; ensured the provision of medical assistance to victims of human rights violations, certified their medical condition during investigation and undertook a study on psychological effects of such violations; cooperated with local human rights and popular organizations; and disseminated information on human rights and its activities through, *inter alia*, the *MICIVIH News* monthly newsletter, the first issue of which had been released in September.

A series of recommendations was being prepared by the Mission for submission to the Government, aimed at strengthening the criminal justice system, improving the treatment of detainees and the conduct of law enforcement officials, as well as carrying out penal reform, and urging the Government to ratify international human rights instruments and to create an ombudsman institution for human rights protection. MICIVIH was also considering a proposal for an international conference on human rights and the administration of criminal justice in Haiti.

The Secretary-General stated that he had had consultations with the OAS Secretary-General who had expressed readiness for a continued MICIVIH presence after 7 February 1996. Accordingly, the Secretary-General intended to recommend an extension of the Mission's mandate upon receipt of a request to that effect from the Government of Haiti. Should that be the case, he recommended that the terms of reference be adjusted to place greater emphasis on technical cooperation with the Government in the area of institution-building, as well as on the promotion and protection of human rights.

### GENERAL ASSEMBLY ACTION (December)

On 15 December, the General Assembly adopted **resolution 50/86 A**.

#### The situation of democracy and human rights in Haiti

*The General Assembly,*

*Having considered further* the item entitled "The situation of democracy and human rights in Haiti",

*Recalling* all its relevant resolutions, as well as those adopted on the question by the Security Council, the Economic and Social Council and the Commission on Human Rights,

*Recalling also* the relevant resolutions adopted on the question by the Organization of American States,

*Reaffirming* that the goal of the international community remains the full observance of human rights and fundamental freedoms and the promotion of social and economic development in Haiti,

*Welcoming* the legislative and municipal elections being held in a peaceful environment and observed by the Organization of American States in close coordination with the United Nations,

*Stressing* the willingness of the Government of Haiti to hold the forthcoming presidential elections in accordance with the Constitution, as a crucial step in the complete consolidation of long-lasting democracy in Haiti,

*Strongly supportive* of the continuing leadership of the Secretary-General of the United Nations and the Secretary-General of the Organization of American States in the efforts of the international community in furthering political progress in Haiti,

*Welcoming* the success of the United Nations Mission in Haiti and the contributions of the Special Representative of the Secretary-General of the United Nations and his staff to that success,

*Welcoming also* the continued efforts by States to provide humanitarian assistance and technical cooperation to the people of Haiti,

*Supporting fully* the contribution of the International Civilian Mission to Haiti and the United Nations Mission in Haiti in the establishment of a climate of freedom and tolerance propitious to the full observance of human rights and the full restoration of the constitutional democracy of Haiti,

*Paying tribute* to the members and staff of the International Civilian Mission to Haiti for their contribution in accompanying the Haitian people in their efforts to return to constitutional order and democracy,

*Welcoming* the continuous improvement in the situation of human rights in Haiti,

*Taking note* of the report of the Secretary-General of 12 October 1995 on the situation of democracy and human rights in Haiti,

1. *Welcomes* the report of the Secretary-General, outlining the continuation until 7 February 1996 of the joint participation of the United Nations with the Organization of American States in the International Civilian Mission to Haiti, with the task of verifying full observance by Haiti of human rights and fundamental freedoms, in order to further the establishment of a climate of freedom and tolerance propitious to the consolidation of long-term constitutional democracy in Haiti and to contribute to the strengthening of democratic institutions;

2. *Stands ready*, upon consideration of a recommendation by the Secretary-General and at the request of the Haitian authorities, to extend the United Nations component of the International Civilian Mission to Haiti beyond 7 February 1996 in an appropriate resolution;

3. *Expresses its full support* for the International Civilian Mission to Haiti and trusts that the Government of Haiti will continue to afford it timely, complete and effective cooperation;

4. *Commends* the Haitian authorities on the progress accomplished in the advance of democracy, respect for human rights and the reconstruction of Haiti;

5. *Pays tribute* to the Haitian people in their ongoing quest for strong and lasting democracy, justice and economic prosperity;

6. *Expresses its appreciation* to those States participating in the United Nations Mission in Haiti and those that have accompanied the Haitian people in their efforts to return to constitutional order and democracy;

7. *Expresses its confidence* that the forthcoming presidential elections will further strengthen democracy in Haiti;

8. *Reaffirms once again* the commitment of the international community to continue its technical, economic and financial cooperation with Haiti in support of its economic and social development efforts and in order to strengthen Haitian institutions responsible for dispensing justice and guaranteeing democracy, respect for human rights, political stability and economic development;

9. *Commends* the cooperation between the Secretary-General of the United Nations and the Secretary-General of the Organization of American States in their efforts to promote respect for the rights of all Haitians and to contribute to the strengthening of democratic institutions, including through election monitoring;

10. *Requests* the Secretary-General to support the Government of Haiti as it works towards the national reconstruction and development of Haiti, in order to consolidate a climate propitious to the establishment of a lasting democracy and full respect for human rights;

11. *Also requests* the Secretary-General to continue to coordinate the efforts of the United Nations system to help provide humanitarian aid and meet the development requirements of Haiti;

12. *Further requests* the Secretary-General to submit to the General Assembly regular reports on the work of the International Civilian Mission to Haiti;

13. *Decides* to keep the item entitled "The situation of democracy and human rights in Haiti" under review at its fiftieth session.

General Assembly resolution 50/86 A

15 December 1995     Meeting 93     Adopted without vote

47-nation draft (A/50/L.53/Rev.1); agenda item 38.
*Meeting numbers.* GA 50th session: plenary 88, 93.

### Financing

In a 5 July statement[37] to the Fifth Committee, the Secretary-General estimated requirements for maintaining MICIVIH from 7 July 1995 to 7 February 1996 at $13,754,100 net of staff assessment, including $11,483,700 for the period from 8 July to 31 December 1995, while estimated expenditures from 1 January 1994 to 7 July 1995 amounted to $11,966,800. Estimated requirements for 1994-1995 totalled $23,450,500, which necessitated an additional appropriation of $19,463,400 for the biennium.

In an oral report to the Fifth Committee,[38] ACABQ stated that there was no immediate need to appropriate additional resources for the Mission. On 11 July, the Fifth Committee decided[39] to inform the General Assembly that, should it extend the Mission's mandate, total costs would not exceed $23,450,500 and no additional appropriation would be required at the current stage.

According to revised estimates[40] under the proposed programme budget for 1996-1997, submitted to the Fifth Committee on 13 November, the amount to be appropriated by the Assembly for maintaining MICIVIH until 7 February 1996 totalled $2,270,400. In a 1 December report,[41]

ACABQ recommended reductions in that amount and the appropriation of $2,042,897 net of staff assessment ($278,200).

*REFERENCES*

[1]YUN 1994, p. 426, SC res. 940(1994), 31 July 1994. [2]YUN 1993, p. 351, SC res. 867(1993), 23 Sep. 1993. [3]Ibid., p. 339, GA res. 47/20 B, 20 Apr. 1993. [4]S/1995/46 & Add.1. [5]S/1995/90. [6]S/1995/32. [7]YUN 1994, p. 432. [8]Ibid., p. 431, SC res. 964(1994), 29 Nov. 1994. [9]S/1995/15. [10]S/1995/70. [11]S/1995/55 & Add.1. [12]S/1995/108. [13]S/1995/149. [14]S/1995/183. [15]S/1995/211. [16]S/1995/305. [17]S/1995/306. [18]S/PRST/1995/20. [19]S/1995/328. [20]S/1995/614. [21]S/1995/922. [22]S/PRST/1995/55. [23]S/1995/60. [24]S/1995/67. [25]S/1995/61. [26]S/1995/68. [27]A/49/318/Add.2 & Corr.1. [28]A/49/869. [29]A/50/363 & Corr.1. [30]A/50/488. [31]A/50/363/Add.1. [32]A/50/488/Add.1. [33]A/50/705/Add.1. [34]A/49/926. [35]YUN 1994, pp. 413 & 415, GA res. 49/27 A & 48/27 B, 5 Dec. & 8 July 1994. [36]A/50/548. [37]A/C.5/49/69. [38]A/C.5/49/SR.63. [39]A/49/941. [40]A/C.5/50/25. [41]A/50/7/Add.5.

# Other questions relating to the Americas

## Cuba–United States

By a 3 May letter[1] to the Secretary-General, Cuba transmitted a memorandum by its Ministry of Foreign Affairs, containing a legal and political analysis of the implications of the so-called Cuban Liberty and Democratic Solidarity Act (the Helms/Burton bill). The proposed legislation, under consideration in the United States Congress, had the stated purpose of strengthening "international sanctions" against Cuba, when, Cuba maintained, the only existing sanctions were the United States unilateral economic, commercial and financial blockade that most other nations had opposed; the legislation in question represented a new set of coercive measures targeting third countries and aimed at disrupting their trade and investment relations with Cuba.

According to the memorandum, the bill would authorize bringing lawsuits before United States courts with regard to the property nationalized in Cuba and would require a United States administrative agency to certify restitution or compensation claims by Cuban-Americans for espousal in future dealings with Cuba. Some provisions would entail exclusion of sugar imports from countries purchasing sugar from Cuba; lawsuits in United States courts against third-country nationals and prohibition of credit to, and other retaliation measures against, third-country companies trading with or investing in Cuba; interference with international financial institutions; and attempted coercion of the independent States of the former Soviet Union.

The memorandum emphasized that United States espousal of property claims would violate international law and constituted an encroachment on Cuba's sovereignty, and underscored the willingness of the Cuban Government to negotiate the claims issue with the United States, pointing out that it had reached negotiated settlements with all other countries whose citizens' properties in Cuba had been nationalized. At the same time, the Helms/Burton bill would complicate immensely any effort to normalize relations between the two countries and its implications must be viewed with grave concern, the memorandum said.

On 26 May, Cuba communicated[2] a document entitled ''Renewed attempts to tighten the United States economic embargo against Cuba and the truth about the Cuban nationalizations''. In reference to the Helms/Burton bill, Cuba stated that nationalizations had been carried out in full compliance with principles set forth by the General Assembly in connection with the right of countries engaged in a process of social transformation to nationalize foreign property. It also listed settlement agreements between Cuba and other countries and noted that, since the Second World War, the United States had negotiated 10 lump-sum settlement agreements concerning American-owned property nationalized in other countries.

On 25 August, Cuba transmitted[3] a decision adopted on 13 July by the Council of the Latin American Economic System, which rejected the draft law entitled ''Cuban Liberty and Democratic Solidarity Act of 1995'' of the United States Congress, considering that it violated international law, and called for the lifting of the economic, commercial and financial embargo imposed by the United States against Cuba.

**Report of the Secretary-General.** As requested by the General Assembly in its 1994 resolution on the necessity of ending the United States embargo against Cuba,[4] the Secretary-General submitted a 20 September report with later addendum,[5] containing information from 48 States and six UN agencies and organs on their implementation of the resolution, by which the Assembly had called on States to refrain from unilateral application of economic and trade measures against Cuba and urged them to repeal or invalidate such measures.

GENERAL ASSEMBLY ACTION

On 2 November, the General Assembly adopted **resolution 50/10**.

**Necessity of ending the economic, commercial
and financial embargo imposed by
the United States of America against Cuba**
*The General Assembly,*
*Determined* to encourage strict compliance with the purposes and principles enshrined in the Charter of the United Nations,

*Reaffirming,* among other principles, the sovereign equality of States, non-intervention and non-interference in their internal affairs and freedom of international trade and navigation, which are also enshrined in many international legal instruments,

*Recalling* the statements of the heads of State or Government at the Ibero-American Summits concerning the need to eliminate the unilateral application of economic and trade measures by one State against another which affect the free flow of international trade,

*Taking note* of Decision 360 adopted on 13 July 1995 by the Twenty-first Council of the Latin American Economic System, held at the ministerial level at San Salvador, which urged that the economic, commercial and financial embargo against Cuba be lifted,

*Concerned* about the continued promulgation and application by Member States of laws and regulations, the extraterritorial effects of which affect the sovereignty of other States and the legitimate interests of entities or persons under their jurisdiction, as well as the freedom of trade and navigation,

*Recalling* its resolutions 47/19 of 24 November 1992, 48/16 of 3 November 1993 and 49/9 of 26 October 1994,

*Concerned* that, since the adoption of its resolutions 47/19, 48/16 and 49/9, further measures of that nature aimed at strengthening and extending the economic, commercial and financial embargo against Cuba continue to be promulgated and applied, and concerned also about the adverse effects of such measures on the Cuban people and on Cuban nationals living in other countries,

1. *Takes note* of the report of the Secretary-General of 20 September 1995 on the implementation of resolution 49/9;

2. *Reiterates its call* to all States to refrain from promulgating and applying laws and measures of the kind referred to in the preamble to the present resolution in conformity with their obligations under the Charter of the United Nations and international law which, *inter alia,* reaffirm the freedom of trade and navigation;

3. *Once again urges* States that have and continue to apply such laws and measures to take the necessary steps to repeal or invalidate them as soon as possible in accordance with their legal regime;

4. *Requests* the Secretary-General, in consultation with the appropriate organs and agencies of the United Nations system, to prepare a report on the implementation of the present resolution in the light of the purposes and principles of the Charter and international law, and to submit it to the General Assembly at its fifty-first session;

5. *Decides* to include in the provisional agenda of its fifty-first session the item entitled ''Necessity of ending the economic, commercial and financial embargo imposed by the United States of America against Cuba''.

General Assembly resolution 50/10

2 November 1995     Meeting 48     117-3-38 (recorded vote)

Draft by Cuba (A/50/L.10); agenda item 27.

Recorded vote in Assembly as follows:

*In favour:* Afghanistan, Algeria, Andorra, Antigua and Barbuda, Argentina, Australia, Austria, Bahamas, Bangladesh, Barbados, Belarus, Belgium, Belize, Benin, Bolivia, Botswana, Brazil, Brunei Darussalam, Bulgaria, Burkina Faso, Burundi, Cambodia, Cameroon, Canada, Cape Verde, Chile, China, Colombia, Congo, Costa Rica, Côte d'Ivoire, Cuba, Cyprus, Democratic People's Republic of Korea, Denmark, Dominica, Ecuador, Eritrea, Ethiopia, Finland, France, Gambia, Ghana, Greece, Grenada, Guinea, Guinea-Bissau, Guyana, Haiti, Honduras, Iceland, India, Indonesia, Iran, Ireland, Italy, Jamaica, Kazakstan, Kenya, Lao People's Democratic

Republic, Lebanon, Lesotho, Libyan Arab Jamahiriya, Liechtenstein, Luxembourg, Madagascar, Malawi, Malaysia, Mali, Mauritania, Mexico, Monaco, Mongolia, Mozambique, Myanmar, Namibia, New Zealand, Nicaragua, Nigeria, Norway, Pakistan, Panama, Papua New Guinea, Paraguay, Peru, Philippines, Portugal, Russian Federation, Saint Lucia, Saint Vincent and the Grenadines, Samoa, San Marino, Seychelles, Sierra Leone, Singapore, Solomon Islands, South Africa, Spain, Sri Lanka, Sudan, Suriname, Sweden, Syrian Arab Republic, Thailand, Togo, Trinidad and Tobago, Tunisia, Uganda, Ukraine, United Republic of Tanzania, Uruguay, Venezuela, Viet Nam, Yemen, Zaire, Zambia, Zimbabwe.
*Against:* Israel, United States, Uzbekistan.
*Abstaining:* Albania, Armenia, Bhutan, Czech Republic, Egypt, El Salvador, Estonia, Georgia, Germany, Guatemala, Hungary, Japan, Kyrgyzstan, Latvia, Lithuania, Maldives, Malta, Marshall Islands, Mauritius, Micronesia, Morocco, Netherlands, Niger, Oman, Palau, Poland, Republic of Korea, Republic of Moldova, Romania, Rwanda, Saudi Arabia, Slovakia, Slovenia, Swaziland, Tajikistan, the former Yugoslav Republic of Macedonia, Turkey, United Kingdom.

Speaking prior to the vote, Cuba pointed out that the United States–imposed embargo against it had had extraterritorial effects on third States as well, and that the embargo itself constituted an attempt by the United States to decide the system of government and social structures that should exist in Cuba. In response, the United States reiterated its position that the question of the embargo was a bilateral issue and that it had the right to determine its bilateral trading relationships; the objective of United States policy towards Cuba was a peaceful transition to a democratic system in which human rights were fully observed.

## Universal Congress on the Panama Canal

On 18 August, France, Panama and the United States requested[(6)] the inclusion in the agenda of the General Assembly's fiftieth session a supplementary item entitled "Universal Congress on the Panama Canal". An explanatory memorandum accompanying the request stated that 7 September 1997 would mark the twentieth anniversary of the signing of the Panama Canal Treaty and the Treaty concerning the Permanent Neutrality and Operation of the Panama Canal, which provided for the transfer of control over the Canal to Panama on 31 December 1999. In that context, Panama had decided to convene a Universal Congress on the Panama Canal in September 1997, to examine the Canal's role in the twenty-first century and to promote sustainable development of the uses and resources of the Atlantic and Pacific Oceans, as well as the rational exploitation and development of the Canal basin and coastal areas. Annexed to the memorandum was a draft resolution calling for support for the organization of the Universal Congress.

**GENERAL ASSEMBLY ACTION**

On 7 November, the General Assembly adopted **resolution 50/12**.

### Universal Congress on the Panama Canal

*The General Assembly,*

*Recalling* its resolutions 49/28 of 6 December 1994 on the law of the sea, 49/99 of 19 December 1994 on international trade and development and 49/131 of 19 December 1994 on the declaration of 1998 as International Year of the Ocean, and resolutions 2.5 of 16 November 1993, adopted by the General Conference of the United Nations Educational, Scientific and Cultural Organization at its twenty-seventh session, and 1994/48 of the Economic and Social Council of 29 July 1994, both on the International Year of the Ocean,

*Bearing in mind* that on 7 September 1977 Mr. Jimmy Carter, President of the United States of America, and General Omar Torrijos, Head of Government of the Republic of Panama, signed in Washington the Treaty concerning the Permanent Neutrality and Operation of the Panama Canal and the Panama Canal Treaty, known as the Torrijos-Carter treaties, which stipulate that, at noon on 31 December 1999, the Canal, including all improvements, is to come under the control of the Republic of Panama, which shall assume total responsibility for its management, operation and maintenance,

*Emphasizing* the significance of the Washington Declaration, signed on 7 September 1977 by the heads of State, heads of Government and representatives of the American republics, which recognizes "the importance for the hemisphere, for trade and for world shipping of the agreements designed to ensure the accessibility and continued neutrality of the Panama Canal",

*Welcoming* the plans of the Government of Panama to hold a Universal Congress on the Panama Canal in Panama City in September 1997, with the participation of Governments, international bodies, public and private academic institutions, maritime users and international shipping companies, to examine jointly the role which the Panama Canal should play in the twenty-first century,

*Underlining* the fact that the International Congress for Study of the Interocean Canal (Congrès international d'études du canal interocéanique) was convened by the Société de géographie de Paris, met from 15 to 29 May 1879 in the French capital, under the presidency of Count Ferdinand de Lesseps, builder of the Suez Canal, and culminated in the resolution that the canal should be built along the route traced between the Gulf of Limón on the Atlantic Ocean and the Bay of Panama on the Pacific Ocean,

*Cognizant* of the fact that, in keeping with the spirit of a new global alliance for sustainable development, it is necessary to formulate a balanced, integrated approach to environmental, trade and development issues,

*Convinced*, therefore, that the Universal Congress on the Panama Canal will promote international cooperation towards ensuring an orderly, sustainable development of the uses and resources of the Atlantic and Pacific Oceans and the rational exploitation and development of the Canal watershed and coastal areas, bearing in mind that Panama's coastline on the two oceans stretches for 2,988.3 kilometres in all, of which 1,700.6 kilometres are on the Pacific Ocean and 1,287.7 are on the Caribbean Sea,

*Noting with appreciation* the progress of the Tripartite Commission, consisting of the Republic of Panama, the United States of America and Japan, in the plans for the construction in the Isthmus of Panama of a sea-level canal or the enlargement of the present lock canal,

*Reaffirming* its resolution 31/142 of 17 December 1976, on the one hundred and fiftieth anniversary of the Amphictyonic Congress of Panama, in which it recalled that Simón Bolívar, the Liberator, referred on several occasions to the need for a possible opening of a canal in Panama, which "will shorten distances throughout the world, strengthen commercial ties" between the continents and promote the exchange of products "from the four corners of the globe",

*Noting with satisfaction* that by its resolution 49/131, 1998 was proclaimed International Year of the Ocean, during which year the Lisbon World Exposition is to be held,

*Emphasizing* that the Universal Congress on the Panama Canal has among its priority aims the promotion of international cooperation with a view to achieving an orderly, sustainable development of the uses and resources of the Atlantic and Pacific Oceans,

1. *Supports* the initiative of the Government of Panama in convening the Universal Congress on the Panama Canal, with the participation of Governments, international bodies, public and private academic institutions, maritime users and international shipping companies, to examine jointly the role which the Panama Canal should play in the twenty-first century;

2. *Requests* Member States to assist generously in this undertaking;

3. *Urges* the competent organs, programmes and specialized agencies of the United Nations system, in particular, the United Nations Development Programme, the United Nations Environment Programme and the International Maritime Organization, to study the possibility of providing assistance from within existing resources for the organization of the Universal Congress on the Panama Canal;

4. *Emphasizes* the importance of the Universal Congress on the Panama Canal and expresses the hope that its results will contribute to the growth of world trade and to sustained economic growth and sustainable development throughout the world;

5. *Requests* the Secretary-General to submit to the General Assembly at its fifty-first session a report on the implementation of the present resolution;

6. *Decides* to include in the provisional agenda of its fifty-first session the item entitled "Universal Congress on the Panama Canal".

**General Assembly resolution 50/12**

**7 November 1995      Meeting 52      Adopted without vote**

3-nation draft (A/50/L.13); agenda item 162.
*Sponsors:* France, Panama, United States.

### REFERENCES

[1]A/50/172. [2]A/50/211. [3]A/50/393. [4]YUN 1994, p. 411, GA res. 49/9, 26 Oct. 1994. [5]A/50/401 & Add.1. [6]A/50/193.

Chapter IV

# Asia and the Pacific

In 1995, UN efforts to secure peace for the vast region of Asia and the Pacific continued to be marred by continuing conflicts in Afghanistan and Tajikistan, the lingering consequences of wars between Iraq and Kuwait and between Iran and Iraq, and tensions relating to the Korean peninsula and to Jammu and Kashmir.

Ways to achieve national reconciliation in Afghanistan and in Tajikistan were sought by the UN during the year. Fighting in Afghanistan continued among three major armed factions controlling different parts of the country. The UN Special Mission to Afghanistan aimed to bring about the establishment of a representative and broad-based authoritative council and the transfer of power from the current President. A Protocol between the Tajik Government and its opposition, on fundamental principles for establishing peace and national accord in that country, was signed on 17 August 1995; its implementation was to be monitored by the UN Mission of Observers in Tajikistan.

Matters centred on Iraq were dominant among UN concerns in the region. The United Nations maintained sanctions and an oil embargo against that country, seeking its compliance with relevant Security Council resolutions. The UN Special Commission on Iraqi disarmament and the International Atomic Energy Agency (IAEA) continued to monitor Iraq's ability to develop and produce nuclear, chemical and biological weapons and means for their delivery. During the year, it was acknowledged by Iraq for the first time that it had carried out an extensive biological weapons programme and developed and tested radiological weapons. The Security Council in April authorized a limited import of oil and petroleum products from Iraq and the use of revenue resulting from those imports to meet humanitarian needs of the Iraqi people.

The Democratic People's Republic of Korea (DPRK) made attempts in 1995 to dismantle the mechanism created under the 1953 Armistice Agreement between it and the Republic of Korea. IAEA sought to ensure DPRK compliance with the safeguards agreement in implementation of the 1968 Treaty on the Non-Proliferation of Nuclear Weapons, and to implement verification measures pursuant to the Agreed Framework between the DPRK and the United States concerning the denuclearization of the Korean peninsula.

In 1995, the General Assembly acted to settle matters relating to the liquidation of the UN Transitional Authority in Cambodia and to the special account of the UN Military Liaison Team in Cambodia. The Secretary-General kept abreast of developments in the relations between India and Pakistan and offered his assistance in facilitating their search for a lasting solution to the issue of Jammu and Kashmir. The UN Military Observer Group in India and Pakistan continued to monitor observance of the cease-fire between the two countries, last agreed to in 1971.

In December, the General Assembly recognized and supported the status of permanent neutrality declared by Turkmenistan.

# East Asia

## Korean question

### Situation in 1995

In a 16 January 1995 letter[1] to the Secretary-General, the Democratic People's Republic of Korea stated, *inter alia*, that the new situation after the cold war demanded the establishment of a new peace arrangement on the Korean peninsula, and noted that the issue of such a peace mechanism should be resolved between it and the United States. The DPRK said that the United Nations should dissolve the United Nations Command (UNC), which had been established illegally and neither belonged to nor obeyed instructions from the United Nations, so that a favourable atmosphere for a new peace arrangement could be created.

On 23 February, the United States, on behalf of the Unified Command established pursuant to a 1950 Security Council resolution,[2] submitted a special report[3] of UNC on the maintenance of the 1953 Korean Armistice Agreement.[4] The report concerned the Neutral Nations Supervisory Commission (NNSC), set up under the Armistice Agreement and composed of four senior officers from neutral countries nominated by the UNC Commander-in-Chief and jointly by the Korean People's Army (KPA) Supreme Commander and the Commander of the Chinese People's Volunteers (CPV).

On 23 January, it was reported, the NNSC member from Poland—a neutral nation nominated by KPA/CPV—was informed that KPA would withdraw all support to the Polish camp in the Korean demilitarized zone (DMZ) effective 28 February, including rations, medical and dental care, transportation, utilities and physical security, which would prevent the Polish delegation from performing its duties and force it to leave the camp. On 9 February, the Polish officers were informed that transportation support to their activities would be withdrawn as of 10 February, and that they would be considered "illegal foreigners in the DMZ" after 28 February. As a result, the Polish member was unable to attend the NNSC weekly plenary session on 14 February; it was the first time in 42 years that such an incident had occurred.

UNC communicated to KPA its concern over that unilateral action, taken in violation of the Armistice Agreement, and pointed out that any changes to the Agreement had to be agreed upon by all signatories and that the UNC Commander-in-Chief had not agreed to any change regarding NNSC. UNC also requested that KPA/CPV nominate a neutral nation to replace the former Czechoslovakia, which had withdrawn its delegation from NNSC in 1993, following its division into the Czech Republic and Slovakia;[5] however, no response had been received. The report underscored the high value of NNSC's continued participation in the Korean armistice system, as it provided an alternate channel of communications between the two sides, a credible neutral perspective in the resolution of incidents, and an important moderating influence in Panmunjom, the joint security area, which served to alleviate tension.

In a 28 February statement[6] by its Ministry of Foreign Affairs, transmitted on 7 March, the DPRK, in reference to the withdrawal of the Polish delegation from NNSC, said that NNSC had lost its purpose and that Poland's withdrawal had been necessitated by the Commission's unproductive position and was indispensable for the establishment of a solid peace mechanism on the Korean peninsula. The DPRK also accused the United States of unilaterally abrogating the Armistice Agreement's provisions related to NNSC.

In a 5 June letter,[7] the DPRK called for the dissolution of UNC and the replacement of the Armistice Agreement with a peace agreement, as stipulated by a 1975 General Assembly resolution.[8] On 6 July, the DPRK communicated[9] a 29 June memorandum by its Ministry of Foreign Affairs, stating that the establishment of a new peace mechanism in place of the outdated armistice system should not be further delayed, and accusing the United States of systematic violations of the Armistice Agreement as well as of ignoring the DPRK's proposal for the establishment of a new mechanism.

## Armistice Agreement

### Violations

On 9 May, the United States submitted a report[10] on UNC activities in 1994. The report, provided annually, noted that no serious armistice violations had been observed in the DMZ during that year; nevertheless, UNC had dispatched joint observer teams to its guard posts along the DMZ on 56 occasions, while KPA continued to refuse to participate in the investigations proposed by UNC. The military demarcation line between the DPRK and the Republic of Korea had been crossed in Panmunjom several times: the incidents involved three United States delegations visiting the DPRK; the return of two KPA soldiers rescued at sea by the Republic of Korea Navy; and the return of a United States Army warrant officer and of the remains of the other crewman whose helicopter had mistakenly entered DPRK airspace and was shot down. UNC also provided administrative and security assistance to the political talks and other contacts between the two sides in Panmunjom. In addition, the decision of the Republic of Korea to lift its ban on business investment in the DPRK, announced on 7 November 1994, brought into question the issue of granting transit permission to private citizens travelling between the two countries.

The recovery and return of UNC Korean War remains proceeded on the basis of the 1993 agreement on remains-related matters,[5] which served to regularize cooperation on remains-recovery operations and establish a KPA-UNC Remains Working Group to locate, exhume, repatriate and identify the remains of UNC personnel located north of the military demarcation line. Between 30 November 1993 and 13 September 1994, KPA had returned 145 sets of remains, bringing the total so far to 208.

### Other developments

The UNC report[10] further described events related to the functioning of the armistice mechanism, particularly the Military Armistice Commission (MAC) and NNSC (see above). It recalled that in March 1991, having rejected the credentials of a UNC MAC senior member from the Republic of Korea,[11] KPA had suspended its participation in MAC plenary sessions and communications at the senior level, as well as its reports to MAC and NNSC on compliance with the non-introduction of reinforcing arms and military personnel into the Korean peninsula. On 28 April 1994, KPA decided to recall its remaining members and staff personnel from MAC, to cease participation in MAC activities and to no longer recognize the UNC MAC as a counterpart. It also announced its intention to withdraw the Polish delegation to NNSC (see also above) and to send a new team appointed by the KPA Supreme Commander to make contact with the United States military regarding pending military issues, including a new "durable peace-ensuring system" to replace MAC. Notwithstanding UNC's rejection of that unilateral attempt to dismantle MAC and NNSC, KPA maintained its decision and notified the Polish NNSC delegation to withdraw from the DPRK. It reaffirmed, however, that it would abide by the Agreement's provisions not related to MAC.

On 1 September 1994, the report said, KPA rejected the credentials of the new UNC MAC Secretary. On the same day, China announced its decision to recall the CPV delegation from MAC; the delegation left the DPRK in December. In November, the DPRK informed Poland that its nomination as an NNSC member had been terminated. In addition, UNC's continued calls on KPA to nominate a successor to the former Czechoslovakia in NNSC met with no response.

The report stated that KPA attempts to end both MAC and NNSC, thus chipping away at the basic foundation of the armistice architecture, had to be opposed by the international community, as their dissolution could lead to an increase in minor incidents, with the potential to escalate into a more serious situation. It called on both sides to preserve the existing means of communication through MAC, which was vital to maintaining the armistice until a more durable peace was attained. UNC also affirmed that it would continue its efforts to implement the Armistice Agreement and thereby contribute to sustaining a stable environment and achieving the ultimate goal of a durable peace on the peninsula.

## Compliance with non-proliferation and safeguards agreements

In 1995, the International Atomic Energy Agency (IAEA) continued its efforts to ensure full compliance by the DPRK with the agreement between that country and IAEA for the application of safeguards in connection with the Treaty on the Non-Proliferation of Nuclear Weapons (safeguards agreement), in force since 1992.[12] In accordance with a 1994 statement[13] by the Security Council President, IAEA also monitored developments related to the Agreed Framework between the United States and the DPRK, reached in 1994[13] to resolve the nuclear issue on the Korean peninsula.

**IAEA communication (May).** On 2 May, the IAEA Director General transmitted[14] his report, which had been submitted to the Agency's Board of Governors in March. The report described discussions held in the DPRK in November 1994,[15] stating that an IAEA technical team had again visited that country, between 21 and 28 January 1995, to discuss outstanding issues as well as the implementation of agreed verification measures performed at facilities subject to freeze under the Agreed Framework.

The DPRK continued to make clear that it viewed acceptance of measures for monitoring the freeze as being only in the context of the Agreed Framework, not under the safeguards agreement. While accepting containment and surveillance measures, it declined level and density measurements which IAEA considered necessary, as well as measurements relevant to assessing the total amount of plutonium in the spent fuel from the DPRK's 5-MWe Experimental Nuclear Power Plant. The report pointed out that such measurements had to be taken during the transfer of the spent fuel for storage, planned for the second quarter of 1995. The technical team also visited the manufacturing site of nuclear graphite blocks for use in the 50-MWe reactor core, and was informed that the production of reactor-related equipment and components other than some of the graphite blocks had stopped long ago.

The report clarified that issues under discussion with the DPRK concerned only verification of the freeze of activities at relevant nuclear facilities and had not yet addressed the steps deemed necessary to verify the accuracy and completeness of the DPRK's initial inventory of nuclear material subject to safeguards. Those issues were to be considered at further technical talks. In the meantime, IAEA continued its inspector presence at facilities in Nyongbyon; in January, the DPRK accepted the designation of 10 additional inspectors, bringing the total to 20.

**IAEA communication (October).** On 10 October, the IAEA Director General provided[16] further information on Agency activities in the DPRK, stating that a further round of technical discussions had taken place from 12 to 18 September, during which the DPRK agreed to measurements of irradiated fuel rods in storage at the 5-MWe experimental reactor, but declined measures to assess the total amount of plutonium in the spent fuel. No agreement was reached about the installation of additional monitoring equipment at nuclear waste tanks in the reprocessing plant, and no discussion was held on IAEA requirements for the verification of the initial DPRK inventory of nuclear material; however, the DPRK indicated its intention to study the requirements and to discuss them at a future meeting. It also agreed to proceed with implementation measures delayed since January. The Director General noted that, in the meantime, inspections had been carried out since

March at three nuclear facilities that were not subject to the freeze, and that IAEA inspectors continued their presence in the Nyongbyon area and had been able to observe the maintenance work at the 5-MWe Experimental Nuclear Power Plant.

**Further developments.** Subsequent to the September discussions, the DPRK raised new objections to implementation measures which would enable IAEA inspectors to photograph the new process line and other areas of the Radiochemical Laboratory, the DPRK's reprocessing plant. The issue of nuclear waste monitoring also remained to be resolved. In the meantime, IAEA requested the DPRK to introduce minor but essential modifications to the design of the storage racks for cans containing spent fuel, so that the cans could be effectively sealed in the racks under water.

### GENERAL ASSEMBLY ACTION

On 1 November, the General Assembly, by **resolution 50/9**, adopted in connection with its consideration of the IAEA report (see PART FOUR, Chapter VI), expressed concern over the DPRK's continuing non-compliance with the safeguards agreement and urged it to cooperate fully with IAEA in the agreement's implementation and to take all steps the Agency might deem necessary to preserve, intact, all information relevant to verifying the accuracy and completeness of the initial DPRK report on the inventory of nuclear material subject to safeguards until that country's full compliance with the agreement.

*REFERENCES*

(1)A/49/830-S/1995/44. (2)YUN 1950, p. 230, SC res. 84(1950), 7 July 1950. (3)S/1995/156. (4)YUN 1953, p. 136, GA res. 725(VIII), annex, 7 Dec. 1953. (5)YUN 1994, p. 438. (6)S/1995/187. (7)S/1995/461. (8)YUN 1975, p. 204, GA res. 3390 B (XXX), 18 Nov. 1975. (9)S/1995/541. (10)S/1995/378. (11)YUN 1991, p. 154. (12)YUN 1992, p. 73. (13)YUN 1994, p. 442. (14)S/1995/353. (15)YUN 1994, p. 443. (16)S/1995/860.

# South Asia

## India-Pakistan

In his August 1995 report on the work of the Organization,[1] the Secretary-General noted that India and Pakistan had affirmed their commitment, in accordance with the 1972 Simla Agreement,[2] to resolve peacefully a long-standing dispute over Jammu and Kashmir, which was first inscribed on the agenda of the United Nations in 1948,[3] and to respect the cease-fire line established in 1971.[4] However, increasing incidents of violence in Jammu and Kashmir had further aggravated relations between the two countries and highlighted the urgency of seeking a political solution through a meaningful dialogue. The Secretary-General noted that, during his visit to India and Pakistan in September 1994, he had reiterated to both Governments his readiness to render assistance in facilitating their search for a lasting solution.

**Communications.** On 16 May, Morocco transmitted[5] a statement adopted at a 15 May meeting in New York of the Organization of the Islamic Conference (OIC) Contact Group on Jammu and Kashmir, deploring the desecration and destruction of a Muslim shrine, an adjacent mosque and an institution of learning in Jammu and Kashmir, and urging the Secretary-General to take cognizance of the threat to regional peace and security posed by the deteriorating situation there. The Group appealed to the Security Council President to take note of the situation and to bring it to the Council's attention.

On 16 October, Morocco communicated[6] the final documents adopted at the annual coordination meeting of the Foreign Ministers of OIC member States, held in New York on 2 October. The Ministers, *inter alia*, expressed concern at the deteriorating situation in Jammu and Kashmir and reaffirmed the commitment of OIC to promote a peaceful political settlement of that dispute on the basis of UN resolutions.

### UN Military Observer Group

In 1995, the UN Military Observer Group in India and Pakistan (UNMOGIP), established in 1949 in accordance with a 1948 Security Council resolution,[7] continued to monitor the cease-fire in Jammu and Kashmir, as mandated by the Council in 1951.[8] As at 31 July, the Group comprised 40 military observers. It continued to be financed under the regular UN budget, its costs being assessed as part of each biennial programme budget.

*REFERENCES*

(1)A/50/1. (2)YUN 1972, p. 145. (3)YUN 1947-48, p. 387. (4)YUN 1971, p. 156. (5)S/1995/392. (6)A/50/723-S/1995/927. (7)YUN 1947-48, p. 396, SC res. 47(1948), 21 Apr. 1948. (8)YUN 1951, p. 343, SC res. 91(1951), 30 Mar. 1951.

# South-East Asia

## Cambodia

In his August 1995 report on the work of the Organization,[1] the Secretary-General noted that the broad cooperation between the Government of Cambodia, the United Nations and the international community had brought further progress to that country during the past year. In May, the

Secretary-General's Special Envoy, Marrack Goulding, visited Cambodia and negotiated an agreement on the continued functioning of the UN Centre for Human Rights in the capital of Phnom Penh and on measures to improve communication between the Centre and the Government. UN activities in Cambodia continued to be coordinated by the Secretary-General's Representative, Benny Widyono, whose mandate was extended during the year, with the agreement of the Security Council.

The liquidation phase of the UN Transitional Authority in Cambodia (UNTAC), which had concluded its mandate in 1993,[2] continued throughout 1995. During the year, the General Assembly took action with regard to UNTAC's liquidation, as well as to the Special Account for the UN Military Liaison Team in Cambodia, which had ceased its operations in 1994.[3]

## UN Transitional Authority in Cambodia

**Report of the Secretary-General (February).** On 23 February, the Secretary-General reported[4] on the final disposition of UNTAC assets, which was carried out in accordance with a 1993 General Assembly resolution.[5] He noted that the assets, with a total original inventory value of $232,010,300, had been either transferred to other UN missions and offices, donated to the Government of Cambodia, sold commercially, classified as stolen or written off. The total value of assets transferred stood at $154,159,600. The residual value of assets donated, estimated originally at $58,018,900, amounted to $38,249,400, while that of assets sold, valued initially at $8,113,300, totalled $6,074,600. Assets lost owing to theft amounted to $8,089,700, and those written off totalled $3,628,800.

The report provided a breakdown of the final disposition of UNTAC property by category of assets and by method of disposition, as well as a graphical presentation of its distribution and the rationale used in developing depreciation scales. The Secretary-General recommended that the Assembly note the final disposition at its resumed forty-ninth session.

**Report of ACABQ (March).** The Advisory Committee on Administrative and Budgetary Questions (ACABQ) considered in 1995 the Secretary-General's 1994 report[6] on UNTAC's financial performance for the period ending 30 June 1994, as well as his February 1995 report on the final disposition of UNTAC property.

In its 21 March report,[7] ACABQ noted that outstanding contributions due from Member States totalled $78,192,615 as at 28 February, including $4,548,398 for the UN Advance Mission in Cambodia and $73,644,217 for UNTAC, and that the outstanding loan to UNTAC from the Peace-keeping Reserve Fund amounted to $18 million. It was also informed that full and final reimbursement had been

made to troop-contributing States up to 31 December 1993, and that UNTAC's unliquidated obligations for the period from 1 November 1991 to 31 December 1995 stood at $65,535,900. It revised the requested amount to be credited as income for that period to the UNTAC Special Account from $12,969,830 to $14,462,709. ACABQ further noted that the amount requested for appropriation and assessment to meet UNTAC's additional requirements was based on preliminary projections, and that the team for the liquidation of UNTAC assets had been redeployed and continued operating from New York. In that regard, ACABQ recommended that requirements for the team be met from existing resources at Headquarters, and was of the opinion that no additional appropriation was necessary at that time. It was of the same opinion in respect of the requested assessment of the amount already appropriated by the General Assembly, pointing out that the Secretary-General could report to the Assembly as necessary prior to the final closing of accounts on the need for an additional appropriation and/or assessment.

As for the final disposition of assets, ACABQ noted that the value of stolen property was higher than previously reported, that a number of thefts had occurred during the withdrawal of UNTAC's military component in 1993, and that efforts to recover stolen assets had not been successful. It emphasized the need for full disclosure of property lost due to theft, and requested that the Secretary-General include information on all losses of peace-keeping assets over the past three years in his comprehensive report on the administration and management of UNTAC, requested by the Assembly in 1994.[8] It was also of the opinion that the Secretary-General should make recommendations on measures to improve the security and protection of UN property in all missions, and recommended that the report, due in March but not yet received, be submitted to the Assembly at its fiftieth session.

ACABQ further expressed its intention to discuss a number of problems relating to procurement during its consideration of that report, and to review the transfer of assets to other missions, including from UNTAC, when considering the Secretary-General's report on the feasibility of procedures for valuation and transfer of costs for assets to be redeployed from a peace-keeping operation during its liquidation phase to other missions or UN bodies, requested by the Assembly in its 1994 resolution on administrative and budgetary aspects of the financing of UN peace-keeping operations.[9]

**GENERAL ASSEMBLY ACTION (July)**

On 20 July, the General Assembly, by **decision 49/492**, deferred consideration of the item on financing and liquidation of UNTAC to its fiftieth session, and reiterated its request for a comprehensive evaluation of all aspects of the administration and management of the operation, to be submitted by the Secretary-General at that session.

**Report of the Board of Auditors (August).** By a 2 August note,[10] the Secretary-General transmitted a report of the Board of Auditors on the liquidation audit of UNTAC, submitted in accordance with a 1994 Assembly resolution.[8] The audit, which covered the period from 1 October 1993 to 30 June 1994, examined planning for the liquidation process, disposition of non-expendable property, establishment of fair value of other assets and liabilities, maintenance of financial records during the liquidation phase, and reporting on the liquidation results. The report provided detailed findings and recommendations for corrective actions pertaining to both UNTAC and the liquidation of peace-keeping operations in general.

The Board recommended that: a number of investigations be carried out with regard to particular aspects of UNTAC's liquidation; the review of outstanding property write-off cases be expedited so as to determine accurately the value of those assets; and consideration be given to expediting the discharge of UNTAC's outstanding obligations to avoid additional costs associated with a prolonged liquidation process. Other recommendations dealt with the establishment of standard procedures for the transfer of assets, physical verification of a mission's assets and liabilities prior to its liquidation, and reporting on the costs of assets transferred between missions (for details, see PART TWO, Chapter I). In view of the large number of unresolved issues, the Board intended to carry out a final audit of UNTAC within three months after the completion of the liquidation, scheduled for 31 December 1995.

GENERAL ASSEMBLY ACTION (December)

On 23 December, the General Assembly decided that the Fifth (Administrative and Budgetary) Committee should continue its consideration of the item on financing and liquidation of UNTAC at its resumed fiftieth session (**decision 50/469**).

By **resolution 50/204 C** of the same date, the Assembly took note with concern of the Board of Auditors' findings, noting numerous weaknesses in UNTAC's liquidation as well as the delays encountered in the process, and requested the Secretary-General to take immediate action to implement the Board's recommendations. The Board was asked to report at the Assembly's fifty-first (1996) session on measures being taken, while Member States were called on to pay their contributions as early as possible so as to facilitate the completion of the liquidation process. The Assembly also asked the Secretary-General to complete urgently the feasibility study it had requested in 1994[9] on procedures for the

valuation and transfer of costs of assets, and to submit, before the beginning of its resumed fiftieth session, proposals for such procedures as well as for a policy for the physical verification of assets and liabilities of a mission in liquidation.

## UN Military Liaison Team in Cambodia

In response to a 1994 General Assembly request,[11] the Secretary-General submitted a 14 October 1995 report[12] on the financing of the UN Military Liaison Team in Cambodia. The Team, comprising 20 military liaison officers, had been established by the Security Council in 1993[13] for a single six-month period, from 15 November 1993 to 15 May 1994.

The report noted that total expenditures for that period amounted to $616,500 gross ($590,300 net), resulting in an unencumbered balance of $293,900 gross ($281,800 net). At the same time, outstanding contributions due from Member States totalled $409,706 as at 30 September 1994. As a result, the Team's Special Account showed a deficit of $46,400. The Secretary-General proposed that the unencumbered balance be credited to Member States as appropriate.

In a 5 June report,[14] ACABQ noted that outstanding contributions amounted to $122,050 as at 31 March 1995; it recommended that credits be apportioned among Member States in the balance of $375,406, which included the unencumbered balance plus accrued interest and miscellaneous income. ACABQ also noted that no credit had been given to the Team's Special Account for the value of its equipment transferred to other operations, since such a value had not been determined. In that regard, ACABQ intended to review the issue of disposition of assets in the context of its consideration of the final disposition of UNTAC property (see above).

GENERAL ASSEMBLY ACTION

On 12 July, the General Assembly endorsed ACABQ's observations and recommendations, urged Member States to make every effort to ensure payment of their assessed contributions to the Military Liaison Team promptly and in full, and decided to apportion among Member States credits resulting from the unencumbered balance of $293,900 gross ($281,800 net) for the period from 15 November 1993 to 15 May 1994 and the accrued interest and miscellaneous income of $81,506 in the Team's Special Account (**decision 49/485**).

## Office of the Secretary-General's Representative in Cambodia

On 1 April 1995, the Secretary-General informed[15] the Security Council of his decision to extend for a further six months, as requested by the Government of Cambodia, the term of his Representative in Cambodia, Benny Widyono, appointed in 1994[16] and initially assisted by three military advisers. He was to be assisted by one military adviser during his extended term. The Council's agreement with that decision was communicated[17] to the Secretary-General on 6 April.

During the year, the Representative, in carrying out his mandate, continued to monitor the political situation in Cambodia, to maintain close liaison and dialogue with the Government and to coordinate UN assistance aimed at helping that country move towards greater prosperity and democratization, in accordance with the spirit and principles of the 1991 Paris Agreements[18] on the settlement of the conflict in Cambodia. In response to the Government's request, his term was again extended for six months, as proposed by the Secretary-General on 10 October[19] and agreed to by the Security Council on 13 October.[20]

REFERENCES

[1]A/50/1. [2]YUN 1993, p. 373, SC res. 860(1993), 27 Aug. 1993. [3]YUN 1994, p. 448. [4]A/49/714/Add.1. [5]YUN 1993, p. 376, GA res. 47/209 B, 14 Sep. 1993. [6]YUN 1994, p. 447. [7]A/49/867. [8]YUN 1994, p. 445, GA res. 48/255, 26 May 1994. [9]Ibid., p. 1338, GA res. 49/233 A, 23 Dec. 1994. [10]A/49/943. [11]YUN 1994, p. 449, GA res. 48/257, 26 May 1994. [12]A/49/521. [13]YUN 1993, p. 379, SC res. 880(1993), 4 Nov. 1993. [14]A/49/913. [15]S/1995/268. [16]YUN 1994, p. 450. [17]S/1995/269. [18]YUN 1991, p. 155. [19]S/1995/869. [20]S/1995/870.

# West Asia

## Afghanistan

In January 1995, the Office of the Secretary-General in Afghanistan (OSGA) was established in Jalalabad (to move to the capital of Kabul as soon as conditions permitted), following the discontinuation in December 1994 of the Office of the Secretary-General in Afghanistan and Pakistan and the function of the Personal Representative of the Secretary-General for Afghanistan. OSGA provided assistance to Mahmoud Mestiri (Tunisia), Head of the UN Special Mission to Afghanistan, established in 1993[1] to facilitate national reconciliation and reconstruction.

During the year, the rivalry among the nine political parties in Afghanistan concentrated into a conflict among three major armed groups: the government forces of President Burhanuddin Rabbani; the forces controlled by General Rashid Dostum and his allies in the Supreme Coordination Council, comprising four parties; and the Taliban, a new military faction. The issues in contention were the relinquishing of power by President Rabbani, whose term of office had expired in December 1994, and the establishment of a representative and broad-based authoritative council as an interim mechanism. The Head of the Special Mission visited the region three times in 1995 and secured several agreements on the date of transfer of power to the interim mechanism; each time, however, the resumption of hostilities prevented it from taking place. At the end of the year, renewed fighting highlighted the urgent need for a cease-fire, so that political negotiations could continue.

In December, the General Assembly supported the Secretary-General's decision to strengthen the Special Mission and requested him to authorize continuation of its efforts. The Assembly also urged the leaders of all Afghan parties to renounce the use of force and to settle their political differences by peaceful means, and called on all States to refrain from interfering in Afghanistan's internal affairs.

(See also PART FOUR, Chapter III, for humanitarian assistance, PART THREE, Chapter III, for the human rights situation, and PART FOUR, Chapter XII, for refugee situation.)

### UN Special Mission to Afghanistan

In response to a 1994 General Assembly request,[2] the Secretary-General submitted an 8 November 1995 report, with a later addendum,[3] which described activities of the UN Special Mission to Afghanistan and the political situation in that country, as well as UN rehabilitation and development activities and emergency humanitarian assistance (see PART FOUR, Chapter III).

The report noted that Mr. Mestiri, Head of the Special Mission, had begun another round of mediation efforts on 26 December 1994, to secure agreement on the transfer of power from the current President, whose term of office was to expire two days later, to an acceptable and broadly representative "mechanism". Mr. Mestiri met with President Rabbani; General Dostum of the National Islamic Movement of Afghanistan and other members of the Supreme Coordination Council, including the leader of the Hezb-el-Islami party, Gulbuddin Hekmatyar; and the Governors of Nangarhar and Herat provinces and leaders of the Taliban—an emerging military faction which had taken control of several provinces. Agreement was reached on the composition of an interim mechanism and the transfer of power, to take place on 20 February 1995. That plan, however, was disrupted by the rapid advance of Taliban forces, which reached the outskirts of Kabul on 11 February.

Following the Taliban's refusal to participate in the interim mechanism, a working group of four prominent Afghans was established on 22 February to negotiate an acceptable modality for the transfer of power. The group secured the agreement of both President Rabbani and the Taliban that the transfer would take place on 21 March. On 6 March, however, the negotiations were disrupted by heavy fighting, which broke out in Kabul between government forces and the Hezb-e-Wahdat party of Abdul Mazari, subsequently joined by the Taliban. At the Secretary-General's request, the Head of the Special Mission left the region on 13 April.

From mid-April to the end of August, the situation in Kabul and most parts of Afghanistan was relatively calm. The country was controlled by three major groups, including President Rabbani and his Commander, Ahmad Shah Massoud, joined by the Governor of Herat; General Dostum, mainly in the northern part; and the Taliban in the south and south-eastern provinces. On 20 June, the Head of the Special Mission briefed the Security Council on the situation and prospects for peace in Afghanistan and received the Council's support and encouragement to continue his efforts. On 19 July, following consultations with senior government officials of Saudi Arabia and with the OIC Secretary-General, Mr. Mestiri returned to the region and held a number of meetings with representatives of the Afghan political factions, both in Afghanistan and in Pakistan. He also met with the Prime Minister and the Foreign Minister of Pakistan, and reported his assessment of the situation on 1 August, concluding that an overwhelming desire existed among the Afghan people for a UN-mediated peace in their country, and that the Special Mission should continue its efforts regarding the establishment of a transfer-of-power mechanism. The Secretary-General endorsed that conclusion and requested Mr. Mestiri to resume his mission as early as possible.

On 23 August, heavy fighting began in western Afghanistan, leading to the take-over of Herat province by the Taliban on 5 September. By mid-September, fighting had spread to much of the country, except in three eastern provinces, as the rivalry among Afghanistan's nine political parties changed into a conflict among the three major armed groups (see above). The situation was exacerbated by a reported increase in external interference in support of one or another faction, through the direct or indirect supply of weapons, ammunition and other forms of military assistance.

On 16 September, Mr. Mestiri arrived in Islamabad, Pakistan. He was instructed by the Secretary-General to seek agreement on a limited cease-fire, to be followed immediately by negotiations on the transfer of power, and the establishment of a representative mechanism. Mr. Mestiri held discussions with representatives of the factions, as well as with other prominent Afghan personalities and organizations in various cities in Afghanistan; he also met with the Deputy Foreign Minister of Iran and his advisors in Tehran on 27 and 28 September, and with the Foreign Minister of Pakistan, the OIC Secretary-General, a Saudi Arabian official and a United States Assistant Secretary of State. While President Rabbani was willing to accept an unconditional and nationwide cease-fire, his opponents insisted that he relinquish power prior to a cease-fire agreement. Following several meetings with Mr. Mestiri in Kabul, the President on 6 November announced publicly his willingness to transfer power to an individual or commission, and proposed that the warring parties and neutral personalities meet under UN mediation to agree on a mechanism and the date of the transfer. As a precondition, however, he called for the cessation of hostilities and for an end to all forms of foreign interference.

In November, Mr. Mestiri held another round of meetings with the parties, to prepare a list of names recommended for membership in the transfer-of-power mechanism. That process, however, was disrupted by renewed hostilities in and around Kabul between the Taliban and government forces, often involving indiscriminate rocketing and aerial bombardment. On 26 November, the Head of the Special Mission left the region at the Secretary-General's request.

The report also noted that the Special Mission's good offices were requested to secure the release of seven Russian crew members of an aircraft forced down by the Taliban, who had been detained in Kandahar since August. The Secretary-General stated that negotiations to that effect had not been successful, and he appealed for the release of any and all non-combatants in detention in Afghanistan. He pointed out that the issue of former President Mohammed Najibullah, who had been given refuge in the UN compound in Kabul in 1992, also remained a matter of great concern, as the authorities would not allow him and his companions to leave the country.

The Secretary-General concluded that leaders of the principal factions in Afghanistan seemed to prefer the route of continued war and confrontation over peaceful negotiations, but expressed his belief that peace and stability were nevertheless attainable and that the United Nations should continue its efforts towards that goal. In that regard, he decided to strengthen the Special Mission by stationing four additional Political Affairs Officers in four major cities in Afghanistan, so as to ensure the continuity of information exchange and consultation between the Mission and political leaders based in those cities.

**Communications.** On 3 February, France transmitted[4] a 30 January statement on behalf of the European Union, calling on all Afghans to support a lasting cease-fire and to join in the efforts of the Head of the Special Mission. The Union also deemed it important to put a stop to foreign intervention, and invited countries in the region to support Mr. Mestiri's plan and to facilitate the delivery of humanitarian assistance and development aid. It further appealed for rapid and unimpeded delivery of emergency food and medical assistance to the Afghan population.

On 20 June, the Russian Federation communicated[5] a 9 June statement by its Ministry of Foreign Affairs, which reaffirmed that country's position of non-involvement in the struggle between Afghan parties and urged other States to refrain from interfering. The Russian Federation stated that Afghan territory should not be used for activities that undermined the stability and security of neighbouring countries, as was happening in connection with Tajikistan (see below), and appealed to all parties in Afghanistan to refrain from armed conflict and to initiate serious efforts to achieve national reconciliation through the formation of a broad-based leadership.

### Office of the Secretary-General in Afghanistan

The Office of the Secretary-General in Afghanistan was established in January 1995 in lieu of the Office of the Secretary-General in Afghanistan and Pakistan, which had been terminated in December 1994. OSGA was located in Jalalabad until conditions could permit it to move to Kabul. During the year, it provided assistance to the UN Special Mission to Afghanistan.

In a 13 December statement,[6] the Secretary-General said that the Mission would in future operate on a full-year basis from OSGA offices in Jalalabad and Islamabad, with four additional political officers stationed in Herat, Kabul, Kandahar and Mazar-i-Sharif, and that three more staff would be required for OSGA in addition to the 14 temporary posts and two military observers authorized for 1995. He estimated additional budget requirements for 1996 at $2,684,400, including $972,600 for the Special Mission and $1,711,800 for OSGA.

GENERAL ASSEMBLY ACTION

On 18 September, the General Assembly, by **decision 49/501**, deferred consideration of the item on the situation in Afghanistan and its implications for international peace and security, and included it in the provisional agenda of its fiftieth session.

On 19 December, the Assembly adopted **resolution 50/88 B**.

### The situation in Afghanistan and its implications for international peace and security

*The General Assembly,*

*Recalling* its resolution 49/140 of 20 December 1994 on emergency international assistance for peace, normalcy and reconstruction of war-stricken Afghanistan,

*Recalling also* the statements on Afghanistan of the President of the Security Council of 24 January, 23 March, 11 August and 30 November 1994,

*Taking note* of the report of the Secretary-General of 8 November 1995,

*Wishing* the people of Afghanistan peace and prosperity,

*Firmly committed* to national reconciliation in Afghanistan and to its sovereignty, unity and territorial integrity,

*Emphasizing* the importance of democracy and of the realization of human rights in any future political process in Afghanistan,

*Deeply concerned* about the lack of progress in reaching an agreement on the establishment of an acceptable and broadly representative "mechanism", the transfer of power and an immediate and durable cease-fire,

*Affirming* the readiness of the United Nations to assist the people of Afghanistan in their effort to resolve internal political differences, facilitating national reconciliation leading to the restoration of a fully representative, broad-based government and to the start of the process of rehabilitation and reconstruction in their country,

*Welcoming* the efforts of the United Nations Special Mission to Afghanistan headed by Mr. Mahmoud Mestiri to bring about the restoration of peace, normalcy and national reconciliation,

*Expressing its support* for the continuing efforts of the Special Mission, particularly the steps taken by the Mission to begin a political process in which all segments of Afghan society are represented,

*Expressing its appreciation* for the efforts of the Organization of the Islamic Conference in support of the Special Mission and the engagement of that organization in Afghanistan, in coordination with the United Nations, with a view to achieving a just and lasting political settlement,

*Noting with mounting concern* the prolongation, and in some regions the intensification, of armed hostilities among the parties in the country, including indiscriminate attacks on civilians and other violations of international humanitarian law which have caused significant civilian casualties, displaced populations and destruction of the economic and social infrastructure of the country, in spite of repeated calls by the Security Council and the Secretary-General for a cessation of hostilities,

*Deeply concerned* about the recurring abuses of human rights in Afghanistan,

*Reaffirming* the call of the Security Council on all States to stop the flow of weapons to the parties in Afghanistan,

*Expressing its concern* about actions undermining the security of State frontiers, including illicit traffic in arms and narcotics by criminal elements and groups from certain areas of Afghanistan which creates a threat to peace and stability in the whole region, including Afghanistan,

*Bearing in mind* the close interrelationship between ensuring peace and normalcy in Afghanistan and the ability of the country to take effective steps towards revitalizing the economy, and stressing that a cessation of armed hostilities between the warring parties in Afghanistan and political stability are indispensable if reconstruction measures are to have a lasting effect,

*Emphasizing* the continuing need for strong political support by the international community for the United Nations Special Mission, and welcoming the Secretary-General's decision to strengthen the Mission,

1. *Takes note* of the report of the Secretary-General and endorses the observations and recommendations set out therein;

2. *Expresses its support* for the decision of the Secretary-General to strengthen the United Nations Special Mission to Afghanistan by stationing four additional political counsellors in Afghanistan, and urges the Secretary-General to initiate the necessary arrangements as soon as possible;

3. *Supports* the Secretary-General in his efforts to pursue all possible means of cooperation with the Afghan parties and with the Organization of the Islamic Conference and regional States with a view to achieving national reconciliation in Afghanistan;

4. *Requests* the Secretary-General to authorize the United Nations Special Mission to Afghanistan, established under resolution 48/208 and supported by the Office of the Secretary-General in Afghanistan, to continue its efforts to facilitate national reconciliation and reconstruction in Afghanistan, in particular by ensuring transfer of power through the urgent establishment of a fully representative and broad-based authoritative council with authority, *inter alia:*

(*a*)  To negotiate and oversee an immediate and durable cease-fire;

(*b*)  To create and control a national security force to provide for security throughout the country and oversee the collection and safeguarding of all heavy weapons in the country, and to stop the flow of arms and of equipment related to arms production to the parties;

(*c*)  To form an acceptable transitional government which could, *inter alia*, control the national security force until conditions for free and fair elections are established throughout the country, possibly utilizing traditional decision-making structures, such as a grand assembly, to help establish those conditions;

5. *Reiterates its call upon* all Afghans, especially the leaders of warring parties, to cooperate fully with the broad-based authoritative council, priority being given to the implementation of the steps referred to in paragraph 4 above;

6. *Urges* the leaders of all Afghan parties to renounce the use of force and to settle their political differences by peaceful means;

7. *Urgently calls upon* all parties strictly to respect all provisions of international humanitarian law;

8. *Calls upon* all warring parties in Afghanistan to refrain from detaining foreign nationals, and urges the captors of the members of the crew of the Russian aircraft in Kandahar to release them immediately;

9. *Calls upon* all States:

(*a*)  To respect Afghanistan's sovereignty and territorial integrity, strictly to refrain from interfering in the internal affairs of Afghanistan and to respect the right of the Afghan people to determine their own destiny;

(*b*)  To take all steps necessary to promote peace in Afghanistan, to stop the flow of arms and of equipment

related to arms production to all parties and to put an end to this destructive conflict;

10. *Calls upon* the international community to promote stability in Afghanistan and, without prejudice to the provisions of paragraph 9 *(a)* above, urges all States, including Afghanistan, to strengthen cooperation against the use of the Afghan territory for international terrorism, which, if not curtailed, extends beyond the region with detrimental consequences;

11. *Supports* the intention of the Secretary-General to move the Office of the Secretary-General in Afghanistan to Kabul as soon as the situation permits;

12. *Requests* the Secretary-General to report to the General Assembly every three months during its fiftieth session on the progress of the United Nations Special Mission and to report to the Assembly at its fifty-first session on the progress made in the implementation of the present resolution;

13. *Decides* to include in the provisional agenda of its fifty-first session the item entitled "The situation in Afghanistan and its implications for international peace and security".

**General Assembly resolution 50/88 B**

19 December 1995      Meeting 95      Adopted without vote

54-nation draft (A/50/L.60 (part B) & Add.1); agenda item 54.
*Financial implications.* 5th Committee, A/50/825; S-G, A/C.5/50/42.
*Meeting numbers.* GA 50th session: 5th Committee 41; plenary 95.

### Afghanistan-Pakistan

In a 5 September letter[7] to the Secretary-General, the Foreign Minister of Afghanistan accused Pakistan of assisting the Taliban, with both equipment and personnel, to overrun the western part of the country, and stated that the level of foreign interference in Afghanistan's internal affairs, particularly by Pakistan, had thus reached a dangerous point. In its 10 September response,[8] the Foreign Minister of Pakistan refuted the accusations as unfounded and reaffirmed its policy of strict neutrality and non-interference in Afghanistan's internal affairs. It attributed the continued armed conflict in that country to the fact that the regime in Kabul had reneged on its commitment to relinquish power, and stated that Pakistan was ready to assist the Afghan parties to arrive at a peaceful and durable political solution.

In a 14 September letter,[9] Afghanistan stated that the Pakistani militia, backed by Pakistani regular air and ground forces and in collusion with the mercenaries known as Taliban, had overrun western parts of the country, including the city of Herat. It considered the Pakistani infringement on Herat and its subsequent occupation as totally intolerable, and called for the dispatch of a UN fact-finding mission to western Afghanistan. The letter also accused Pakistan of plundering Afghan national property in Herat, and called on the United Nations to take urgent steps to stop those acts. In a 19 September letter to the Head of the UN Special Mission, transmitted[10] on 26 September, Afghanistan said that with the occupation of Herat, Pakistan's interference in its internal affairs had developed into aggression, and that Pakistan could no longer act as a mediator in inter-Afghan affairs. It also requested that the UN Special Mission to Afghanistan give priority to Herat's occupation and depart from the principle of impartiality in dealing with Afghan groups. In a 30 September letter, communicated[11] on 3 October, Afghanistan proposed the establishment of a contact group, composed of States and organizations dedicated to facilitating the search for peace and mobilizing international assistance for the reconstruction of the country.

On 12 October, Afghanistan informed[12] the Secretary-General and the Security Council that on the previous day bands of mercenaries enforced by Pakistani militia had engaged in a heavy artillery and ground attack to the south-west and south of Kabul, inflicting a heavy toll on the civilian population. It requested that the Council take into consideration that recent evolution of the situation. On 25 October, Pakistan replied[13] that the Afghan allegations regarding support for the Taliban and interference in Afghanistan's internal affairs were baseless and unwarranted, and that the Taliban owed its success to the disaffection among the Afghan people with the policies of the regime in Kabul. It reaffirmed its continued neutral position towards intra-Afghan rivalries and urged the regime in Kabul to desist from blaming Pakistan for its own failures.

On 1 December, Afghanistan informed[14] the Security Council President of further attacks by the Taliban on Kabul, involving an aerial bombardment on 24 November and a rocket attack on 29 November, causing deaths and injuries among civilians. It requested an urgent meeting of the Security Council to address the situation. In a 7 December letter,[15] Afghanistan referred to several recent incidents of the transportation of weapons and ammunition by air to the Taliban, allegedly from Pakistan, which it considered a violation of its airspace and an act of aggression, and called for an end to the illicit transfer of arms.

### Afghanistan-Tajikistan

During 1995, Afghanistan and Tajikistan addressed several communications to the Secretary-General and the Security Council President with regard to the situation on the Afghan-Tajik border. Afghanistan protested the shelling and bombardment of its northern part, hosting refugees from the internal conflict in Tajikistan, from the Tajik side of the border. Tajikistan lodged protests against attacks on its border posts and infiltrations into its territory from northern Afghanistan by armed groups of the Tajik opposition, and against the opposition's use of Afghan territory to undermine the stability and security of Tajikistan (see below, under ''Tajikistan'').

*REFERENCES*

[1]YUN 1993, p. 732, GA res. 48/208, 21 Dec. 1993. [2]YUN 1994, p. 839, GA res. 49/140, 20 Dec. 1994. [3]A/50/737 & Add.1. [4]S/1995/119. [5]A/50/228-S/1995/499. [6]A/C.5/50/42. [7]S/1995/767. [8]A/49/962-S/1995/786. [9]S/1995/795. [10]S/1995/823. [11]A/50/510-S/1995/841. [12]S/1995/866. [13]A/50/693-S/1995/891. [14]S/1995/1004. [15]S/1995/1014.

### Iran-Iraq

Iran and Iraq continued throughout 1995 to address numerous communications to the Secretary-General, each charging repeated violations by the other of the 1988 cease-fire agreement[1] and the agreements reached in Tehran in 1991.[2] Those violations included, *inter alia*, engineering activities and military patrolling in the no-man's land, installation of new observation posts, reinforcement of posts, helicopter and other aircraft overflights and incursions into the other side's airspace, the firing of small arms ammunition and mortars across the border, incursions into the other side's territory, tugging of vessels in the no-man's land, seizure and searches of tugboats and fishing boats, harassment of vessel crews and abduction of fishermen.

On 15 February, Iraq alleged[3] that Iranian military forces had carried out between 11 and 13 February a wide-ranging offensive against Iraqi units in the Hawr al-Hawizah area, which involved the use of all types of light and medium weapons and was successfully repelled. Iraq stated that the attack constituted an act of aggression and was a flagrant violation of Security Council resolution 598(1987)[4] and norms of international law. It further charged that the operation had been preceded by the collusion between the so-called ''Supreme Council of the Islamic Revolution in Iraq'', which it said was supported by Iran and by Kuwaiti government officials, and was thus to be regarded as open intervention by Kuwait in Iraq's internal affairs.

On 18 February, Kuwait categorically rejected[5] the Iraqi accusation, affirmed its respect for the principles of good-neighbourliness and non-intervention in the internal affairs of other States, and asserted that the leader of the Supreme Council of the Islamic Revolution in Iraq had visited Kuwait for purely humanitarian purposes, which reflected that country's desire to assist in the supply of foodstuffs and medicines to those suffering deprivation in Iraq. In its 24 February reply,[6] Iran also rejected the allegations, stating that its armed forces had had no movement along the borders during the indicated period and the prevailing situation in border areas during that period was calm and normal. Iran reiterated its commitment to the Security Council's resolution and to the principles of respect for Iraq's sovereignty and territorial integrity and non-intervention in its internal affairs. For its part, Iran, on 9 March, claimed[7] that several Iraqis, dressed as shepherds and accompanying a herd of cattle, had penetrated its territory on 7 January and fired at the border police, causing the death of an Iranian soldier, before fleeing into Iraqi territory. It also said that a number of Iraqi smugglers had engaged in an armed confrontation with the Iranian border police on 8 January, which resulted in the death of one smuggler.

On 10 July, Iraq alleged[8] that elements of the Iranian guard had infiltrated Iraqi territory on 9 July and fired rockets at a civilian location, causing property damage. It strongly condemned the aggression and urged the Iranian Government to desist from engaging in hostile acts incompatible with the norms of international law and the UN Charter. On 29 August, Iran strongly rejected[9] the allegations.

*REFERENCES*

[1]YUN 1988, p. 188. [2]YUN 1991, p. 163. [3]S/1995/141. [4]YUN 1987, p. 223, SC res. 598(1987), 20 July 1987. [5]S/1995/150. [6]S/1995/160. [7]S/1995/194. [8]S/1995/557. [9]S/1995/754.

## Iraq-Kuwait situation

The United Nations continued in 1995 to seek Iraq's full compliance with its obligations under Security Council resolution 687(1991),[1] which set out the terms of the cease-fire that formally ended the 1991 military action—known as the Gulf War—taken by a coalition of States to bring about Iraq's withdrawal from Kuwait, and provided for other conditions essential to restore peace and security in the region. The Council had called for the destruction, removal or rendering harmless of Iraqi weapons of mass destruction and means for their delivery; proscribed to Iraq programmes and activities for the development of such weapons; and banned the sale or supply to Iraq of specific items related to such programmes. Those activities were to be monitored and verified by the UN Special Commission (UNSCOM), established[2] pursuant to the cease-fire resolution, and also by IAEA, entrusted with monitoring Iraq's nuclear capabilities.

Iraq's compliance was also sought in respect of other relevant Council resolutions, including resolution 707(1991),[3] demanding from Iraq complete disclosure of information related to its proscribed programmes and unconditional cooperation with UNSCOM and IAEA; and resolution 715(1991),[4] by which the Council approved the plans of UNSCOM and IAEA for their future ongoing monitoring and verification activities in Iraq. Pending full implementation of all relevant resolutions, the UN sanctions and oil embargo against Iraq remained in effect in 1995; in April,

however, the Council decided to authorize a limited import of oil and petroleum products from Iraq and to use revenues from it for meeting humanitarian needs of Iraqi people.

Also in April, UNSCOM began ongoing biological monitoring in Iraq, in addition to its already operational missile, chemical and nuclear monitoring systems, the latter being coordinated with IAEA. UNSCOM and IAEA finalized their proposal for an export/import monitoring mechanism, submitted for Security Council approval in December. During the year, Iraq disclosed new information on its past proscribed programmes, acknowledging for the first time an extensive biological weapons programme and radiological weapons activities, and provided UNSCOM and IAEA with a large amount of additional important documentation and materials, which revealed that its past programmes had been more advanced than previously known.

The UN Iraq-Kuwait Observation Mission (UNIKOM) continued to monitor the demilitarized zone (DMZ) along the Iraq-Kuwait boundary and to investigate its alleged violations. The Security Council reviewed UNIKOM activities in April and again in October, extending the operation until 6 April 1996. Other outstanding issues relating to the Iraq-Kuwait situation involved the return of Kuwaiti property seized during Iraq's occupation of Kuwait; accounting for Kuwaiti and third-country nationals missing in Iraq; and settlement of claims against Iraq for losses or damage as a result of its occupation of Kuwait, processed by the UN Compensation Commission. In 1995, the Commission's Governing Council held one special session and four regular sessions.

By **decision 49/503** of 18 September, the General Assembly deferred consideration of the item entitled "Consequences of the Iraqi occupation of and aggression against Kuwait" and included it in the provisional agenda of its fiftieth session. By **decision 50/445** of 21 December, the Assembly again deferred consideration of that item and included it in the provisional agenda of its fifty-first session.

(See also PART THREE, Chapter III, for the human rights situation in Iraq, and PART FOUR, Chapter III, for humanitarian assistance to Iraq.)

**Communications.** During the year, Iraq addressed numerous communications to the Secretary-General, listing tens of thousands of miscellaneous bombs, shells, rockets and other ordnance, some of the remnants of what it termed the 30-Power aggression against Iraq, that were found and disposed of in all parts of the country.

In letters of 6 January[5] and 15 May,[6] Iraq called for investigation of the information that projectiles with depleted uranium had been used by the coalition forces against Iraq during the Gulf

War, stating the the use of such weapons constituted a violation of international humanitarian law due to its serious consequences for human health and the environment and should be regarded as a war crime, and requesting examination of those violations by the international community.

In a 28 February communication,[7] Iraq quoted some statements of senior government officials in Kuwait, who it said were calling, directly or indirectly, for the removal of the political regime in Iraq and for interference in that country's internal affairs. Iraq accused Kuwait of seeking to undermine its sovereignty, territorial integrity and political independence, in violation of the norms of international law and the relevant Security Council resolutions.

### Sanctions compliance

The Committee established by Security Council resolution 661(1990)[8] (Sanctions Committee) issued four reports during 1995—one every 90 days—on the implementation of sanctions against Iraq, in accordance with the guidelines for facilitating full international implementation of resolution 687(1991), approved by the Council in resolution 700(1991).[9] The reports were transmitted to the Council on 1 March,[10] 31 May,[11] 25 August[12] and 27 November.[13]

Each report stated that, during the period under review, the Committee had received no information relating to possible violations of the arms and related sanctions against Iraq committed by other States or foreign nationals. It had not been consulted by any State or international organization on whether certain items fell within the categories of proscribed items or on dual- or multiple-use items (meant for civilian use but with potential for diversion or conversion to military use), nor had any allegations of violations in that connection been reported to it. No international organization had reported any relevant information that might have come to its attention, as requested under the guidelines.

Each report further stated that, since the last report of the Secretary-General submitted in 1991[14] pursuant to resolution 700(1991), no additional States had replied to his request for information on measures instituted by their Governments for meeting the obligations set out in resolution 687(1991). In addition, the November report described measures adopted by the Committee to make its procedures more transparent, as recommended by the Security Council in a 29 March note[15] of its President (see PART SIX, Chapter IV).

**Communication (October).** In a 5 October letter[16] to the Security Council President, Iraq affirmed that it would continue to cooperate fully with UNSCOM and IAEA in the performance of their tasks pursuant to the relevant Council resolutions; that it had kept none of the proscribed weapons or weapon components since the end of 1991, and had undertaken no activity contravening its obligations under those resolutions; and that it had participated effectively in the establishment of UNSCOM's and IAEA's monitoring system (see below, under ''Ongoing monitoring and verification''). Iraq therefore claimed to have fulfilled its essential obligations, and expressed the hope that the Council would take it into consideration during its next deliberation on the question of sanctions against Iraq.

### SECURITY COUNCIL ACTION

The Security Council met on 14 April to consider the situation between Iraq and Kuwait. Japan was invited to participate in the discussion without the right to vote, in accordance with rule 37 of the Council's provisional rules of procedure.[a]

Speaking before the Council, Japan expressed deep concern about the plight of the Iraqi people, suffering from severe medical and nutritional problems as a result of their Government's intransigence which had necessitated the application of UN sanctions. Acting out of that humanitarian concern, Japan supported the draft resolution (see below), which, in Japan's view, contained a balanced approach to alleviating those hardships. At the same time, Japan stated that the well-being of the Iraqi people could be ensured only when their Government faithfully implemented all relevant Council resolutions and made efforts to rejoin the international community.

On the same date, the Council adopted **resolution 986(1995)**.

*The Security Council,*

*Recalling* its previous relevant resolutions,

*Concerned* by the serious nutritional and health situation of the Iraqi population, and by the risk of a further deterioration in this situation,

*Convinced* of the need as a temporary measure to provide for the humanitarian needs of the Iraqi people until the fulfilment by Iraq of the relevant Security Council resolutions, including notably resolution 687(1991) of 3 April 1991, allows the Council to take further action with regard to the prohibitions referred to in resolution 661(1990) of 6 August 1990, in accordance with the provisions of those resolutions,

*Convinced also* of the need for equitable distribution of humanitarian relief to all segments of the Iraqi population throughout the country,

---

[a]Rule 37 of the Council's provisional rules of procedure states: ''Any Member of the United Nations which is not a member of the Security Council may be invited, as a result of a decision of the Security Council, to participate, without vote, in the discussion of any question brought before the Security Council when the Security Council considers that the interests of that Member are specially affected, or when a Member brings a matter to the attention of the Security Council in accordance with Article 35(1) of the Charter.''

*Reaffirming* the commitment of all Member States to the sovereignty and territorial integrity of Iraq,

*Acting* under Chapter VII of the Charter of the United Nations,

1. *Authorizes* States, notwithstanding the provisions of paragraphs 3 *(a)*, 3 *(b)* and 4 of resolution 661(1990) and subsequent relevant resolutions, to permit the import of petroleum and petroleum products originating in Iraq, including financial and other essential transactions directly relating thereto, sufficient to produce a sum not exceeding a total of one billion United States dollars every 90 days for the purposes set out in this resolution and subject to the following conditions:

*(a)* Approval by the Committee established by resolution 661(1990), in order to ensure the transparency of each transaction and its conformity with the other provisions of this resolution, after submission of an application by the State concerned, endorsed by the Government of Iraq, for each proposed purchase of Iraqi petroleum and petroleum products, including details of the purchase price at fair market value, the export route, the opening of a letter of credit payable to the escrow account to be established by the Secretary-General for the purposes of this resolution, and of any other directly related financial or other essential transaction;

*(b)* Payment of the full amount of each purchase of Iraqi petroleum and petroleum products directly by the purchaser in the State concerned into the escrow account to be established by the Secretary-General for the purposes of this resolution;

2. *Authorizes* Turkey, notwithstanding the provisions of paragraphs 3 *(a)*, 3 *(b)* and 4 of resolution 661(1990) and the provisions of paragraph 1 above, to permit the import of petroleum and petroleum products originating in Iraq sufficient, after the deduction of the percentage referred to in paragraph 8 *(c)* below for the Compensation Fund, to meet the pipeline tariff charges, verified as reasonable by the independent inspection agents referred to in paragraph 6 below, for the transport of Iraqi petroleum and petroleum products through the Kirkuk-Yumurtalik pipeline in Turkey authorized by paragraph 1 above;

3. *Decides* that paragraphs 1 and 2 of this resolution shall come into force at 00.01 Eastern Standard Time on the day after the President of the Council has informed the members of the Council that he has received the report from the Secretary-General requested in paragraph 13 below, and shall remain in force for an initial period of 180 days unless the Council takes other relevant action with regard to the provisions of resolution 661(1990);

4. *Further decides* to conduct a thorough review of all aspects of the implementation of this resolution 90 days after the entry into force of paragraph 1 above and again prior to the end of the initial 180-day period, on receipt of the reports referred to in paragraphs 11 and 12 below, and expresses its intention, prior to the end of the 180-day period, to consider favourably renewal of the provisions of this resolution, provided that the reports referred to in paragraphs 11 and 12 below indicate that those provisions are being satisfactorily implemented;

5. *Further decides* that the remaining paragraphs of this resolution shall come into force forthwith;

6. *Directs* the Committee established by resolution 661(1990) to monitor the sale of petroleum and petroleum products to be exported by Iraq via the Kirkuk-Yumurtalik pipeline from Iraq to Turkey and from the Mina al-Bakr oil terminal, with the assistance of independent inspection agents appointed by the Secretary-General, who will keep the Committee informed of the amount of petroleum and petroleum products exported from Iraq after the date of entry into force of paragraph 1 of this resolution, and will verify that the purchase price of the petroleum and petroleum products is reasonable in the light of prevailing market conditions, and that, for the purposes of the arrangements set out in this resolution, the larger share of the petroleum and petroleum products is shipped via the Kirkuk-Yumurtalik pipeline and the remainder is exported from the Mina al-Bakr oil terminal;

7. *Requests* the Secretary-General to establish an escrow account for the purposes of this resolution, to appoint independent and certified public accountants to audit it, and to keep the Government of Iraq fully informed;

8. *Decides* that the funds in the escrow account shall be used to meet the humanitarian needs of the Iraqi population and for the following other purposes, and requests the Secretary-General to use the funds deposited in the escrow account:

*(a)* To finance the export to Iraq, in accordance with the procedures of the Committee established by resolution 661(1990), of medicine, health supplies, foodstuffs, and materials and supplies for essential civilian needs, as referred to in paragraph 20 of resolution 687(1991) provided that:

(i) Each export of goods is at the request of the Government of Iraq;

(ii) Iraq effectively guarantees their equitable distribution, on the basis of a plan submitted to and approved by the Secretary-General, including a description of the goods to be purchased;

(iii) The Secretary-General receives authenticated confirmation that the exported goods concerned have arrived in Iraq;

*(b)* To complement, in view of the exceptional circumstances prevailing in the three Governorates mentioned below, the distribution by the Government of Iraq of goods imported under this resolution, in order to ensure an equitable distribution of humanitarian relief to all segments of the Iraqi population throughout the country, by providing between 130 million and 150 million United States dollars every 90 days to the United Nations Inter-Agency Humanitarian Programme operating within the sovereign territory of Iraq in the three northern Governorates of Dihouk, Arbil and Suleimaniyeh, except that if less than one billion United States dollars worth of petroleum or petroleum products is sold during any 90 day period, the Secretary-General may provide a proportionately smaller amount for this purpose;

*(c)* To transfer to the Compensation Fund the same percentage of the funds deposited in the escrow account as that decided by the Council in paragraph 2 of resolution 705(1991) of 15 August 1991;

*(d)* To meet the costs to the United Nations of the independent inspection agents and the certified public accountants and the activities associated with implementation of this resolution;

*(e)* To meet the current operating costs of the Special Commission, pending subsequent payment in full

of the costs of carrying out the tasks authorized by section C of resolution 687(1991);

*(f)* To meet any reasonable expenses, other than expenses payable in Iraq, which are determined by the Committee established by resolution 661(1990) to be directly related to the export by Iraq of petroleum and petroleum products permitted under paragraph 1 above or to the export to Iraq, and activities directly necessary therefor, of the parts and equipment permitted under paragraph 9 below;

*(g)* To make available up to 10 million United States dollars every 90 days from the funds deposited in the escrow account for the payments envisaged under paragraph 6 of resolution 778(1992) of 2 October 1992;

9. *Authorizes* States to permit, notwithstanding the provisions of paragraph 3 *(c)* of resolution 661(1990):

*(a)* The export to Iraq of the parts and equipment which are essential for the safe operation of the Kirkuk-Yumurtalik pipeline system in Iraq, subject to the prior approval by the Committee established by resolution 661(1990) of each export contract;

*(b)* Activities directly necessary for the exports authorized under subparagraph *(a)* above, including financial transactions related thereto;

10. *Decides* that, since the costs of the exports and activities authorized under paragraph 9 above are precluded by paragraph 4 of resolution 661(1990) and by paragraph 11 of resolution 778(1991) from being met from funds frozen in accordance with those provisions, the cost of such exports and activities may, until funds begin to be paid into the escrow account established for the purposes of this resolution, and following approval in each case by the Committee established by resolution 661(1990), exceptionally be financed by letters of credit, drawn against future oil sales the proceeds of which are to be deposited in the escrow account;

11. *Requests* the Secretary-General to report to the Council 90 days after the date of entry into force of paragraph 1 above, and again prior to the end of the initial 180-day period, on the basis of observation by United Nations personnel in Iraq, and on the basis of consultations with the Government of Iraq, on whether Iraq has ensured the equitable distribution of medicine, health supplies, foodstuffs, and materials and supplies for essential civilian needs, financed in accordance with paragraph 8 *(a)* above, including in his reports any observations he may have on the adequacy of the revenues to meet Iraq's humanitarian needs, and on Iraq's capacity to export sufficient quantities of petroleum and petroleum products to produce the sum referred to in paragraph 1 above;

12. *Requests* the Committee established by resolution 661(1990), in close coordination with the Secretary-General, to develop expedited procedures as necessary to implement the arrangements in paragraphs 1, 2, 6, 8, 9 and 10 of this resolution and to report to the Council 90 days after the date of entry into force of paragraph 1 above and again prior to the end of the initial 180-day period on the implementation of those arrangements;

13. *Requests* the Secretary-General to take the actions necessary to ensure the effective implementation of this resolution, authorizes him to enter into any necessary arrangements or agreements, and requests him to report to the Council when he has done so;

14. *Decides* that petroleum and petroleum products subject to this resolution shall while under Iraqi title be immune from legal proceedings and not be subject to any form of attachment, garnishment or execution, and that all States shall take any steps that may be necessary under their respective domestic legal systems to assure this protection, and to ensure that the proceeds of the sale are not diverted from the purposes laid down in this resolution;

15. *Affirms* that the escrow account established for the purposes of this resolution enjoys the privileges and immunities of the United Nations;

16. *Affirms* that all persons appointed by the Secretary-General for the purpose of implementing this resolution enjoy privileges and immunities as experts on mission for the United Nations in accordance with the Convention on the Privileges and Immunities of the United Nations, and requires the Government of Iraq to allow them full freedom of movement and all necessary facilities for the discharge of their duties in the implementation of this resolution;

17. *Affirms* that nothing in this resolution affects Iraq's duty scrupulously to adhere to all of its obligations concerning servicing and repayment of its foreign debt, in accordance with the appropriate international mechanisms;

18. *Also affirms* that nothing in this resolution should be construed as infringing the sovereignty or territorial integrity of Iraq;

19. *Decides* to remain seized of the matter.

Security Council resolution 986(1995)

14 April 1995        Meeting 3519        Adopted unanimously

5-nation draft (S/1995/292).

*Sponsors:* Argentina, Oman, Rwanda, United Kingdom, United States.

On 1 June, the Secretary-General informed[17] the Council of his 15 May meeting with Iraq's Foreign Minister, who stated that his Government would not implement resolution 986(1995) because it objected, *inter alia*, to the proportion of petroleum to be exported via the Kirkuk-Yumurtalik pipeline and to the modalities for distribution of humanitarian relief in three northern governorates. The Secretary-General expressed his regret at that decision, urged the Government to reconsider it, and stated the Secretariat's readiness to enter into discussions with Iraq on practical arrangements for implementing the resolution.

Noting that Iraqi cooperation was an essential prerequisite for the resolution's implementation, he believed it appropriate to postpone preparation of his report requested in the resolution until further progress on the subject. The Security Council endorsed that decision on 23 June.[18]

### Escrow accounts

In his August 1995 report on the work of the Organization,[19] the Secretary-General stated that he continued efforts to ascertain the existence of any Iraqi petroleum and petroleum products that could be sold, as well as the availability of funds pursuant to Security Council resolution 778(1992),[20] by which it had been decided that all States having Iraqi assets representing the proceeds of sale of Iraqi petroleum or petroleum products, paid for on or after 6 August 1990, should transfer those funds to the escrow account provided for in resolutions 706(1991)[21] and 712(1991).[22] The Secretary-General noted with regret that no further funds had been deposited into the account as a result of his effort to seek information on such assets directly from Governments with jurisdiction over relevant petroleum companies and their subsidiaries.

As at 1 August 1995, $365.5 million had been deposited into the escrow account since the adoption of resolution 778(1992), representing both voluntary contributions and Iraqi assets. At the end of the year, Kuwait transferred to the account $613,780 as revenue obtained from the sale of the cargoes of ships seized in the Persian Gulf for carrying illegal Iraqi oil exports.

By **resolution 986(1995)**, the Security Council established an escrow account for the funds resulting from the authorized import of petroleum and petroleum products from Iraq; decided that the funds in the account should be used to meet the humanitarian needs of the Iraqi population as well as for other purposes described in the resolution; and requested the Secretary-General to use those funds accordingly.

### UN Iraq-Kuwait Observation Mission

The UN Iraq-Kuwait Observation Mission, set up pursuant to Security Council resolution 687(1991), continued in 1995 to discharge its tasks in accordance with its expanded mandate: to monitor the Khawr Abd Allah waterway and the DMZ along the Iraq-Kuwait boundary established under the same resolution; to deter violations of the boundary through its presence in and surveillance of the DMZ; to observe any potentially hostile action mounted from the territory of one State into the other; and, as from 1993,[23] to take physical action to prevent or redress small-scale violations of the DMZ or the boundary.

UNIKOM maintained the three sectors—north, central and south—into which, for operational purposes, it had divided the DMZ. From its patrol and observation bases, observation points and static checkpoints, the Mission carried out ground and air patrols, as well as random checks within the DMZ; it also maintained a force mobile reserve and investigation teams at both the sector and headquarters level. The military observers performed UNIKOM's main patrol, observation, investigation and liaison activities, while the infantry battalion—the Mission's reserve—conducted armed patrols, operated checkpoints and provided security for UNIKOM's easternmost position on the shore of the Khawr Abd Allah.

The Mission continued to provide administrative and logistic support for other UN agencies in Iraq and Kuwait. It maintained headquarters in Umm Qasr, Iraq, and liaison offices in Baghdad and Kuwait City; in January, its logistic base in Doha, Kuwait, was moved to a support centre in Kuwait City.

**Reports of the Secretary-General (March and October).** During the year, the Secretary-General submitted to the Security Council two reports, on 31 March[24] and on 2 October,[25] on UNIKOM activities, in order for the Council to carry out its six-month review of the operation and to decide on its continuation or termination. The first report covered the period from 1 October 1994 to 31 March 1995, and the second, from 1 April to 30 September 1995.

The Secretary-General noted that the situation in the DMZ remained generally calm, although there had been a period of tension in October 1994 in connection with reports about the deployment of Iraqi troops north of the DMZ. The number of violations was limited and involved primarily overflights by aircraft and the carrying or firing of weapons other than sidearms. Shooting incidents had resulted in the deaths of two civilians, one on each side of the border. On the night of 28/29 December 1994, a UNIKOM patrol vehicle came under automatic fire on the Kuwaiti side of the DMZ and one military observer was wounded in the leg; the Mission, however, was not able to determine the perpetrators. Investigations on all ground violations were carried out, and the findings communicated to the parties; in addition, UNIKOM investigated 14 formal complaints, 6 from Iraq and 8 from Kuwait.

On 13 March 1995, two United States citizens mistakenly crossed the border from Kuwait into Iraq, their white vehicle having been misidentified at the checkpoint as belonging to the United Nations. They were apprehended by the Iraqi police, and subsequently released on 16 July. Checkpoint procedures were tightened in the wake of the incident. Another development involved the question of Iraqi fishing boats operating in Kuwaiti waters, which was raised by UNIKOM with Iraq. The Mission continued to act in coordination with the authorities on each side in cases of unauthorized border crossings and when responding to requests to facilitate repatriation. It exchanged information and cooperated closely on such matters with the UN High Commissioner for Refugees (UNHCR) and the International Committee of the Red Cross (ICRC). At the latter's request, UNIKOM provided the venue and support for meetings of the Technical Subcommittee on Military and Civilian Missing Prisoners of War and Mortal Remains (see also below, under ''Kuwaiti property and missing persons'') on 29 and 30 August and on 26 and 27 September.

The Secretary-General also reviewed financial aspects of the operation (see below) and organizational matters, noting that the Mission had relied on locally contracted medical services since February, following the withdrawal of medical units by Austria and Bangladesh. In that regard, he proposed to accept the offer by Germany to provide a civilian medical unit, thus becoming a new contributor to UNIKOM. The Secretary-General concluded that the Mission had contributed significantly to the reduction of tension and the maintenance of calm in its area of operation, while enjoying effective cooperation of both Iraqi and Kuwaiti authorities, and recommended that UNIKOM be maintained.

On 10 April,[26] the Security Council concurred with the recommendation to maintain the Mission for another six-month period; on 6 October,[27] it further extended the operation and decided to review the question again by 6 April 1996.

**Communications.** On 17 January, Iraq strongly protested[28] the overflight by a UNIKOM helicopter of an Iraqi port outside the DMZ, which had taken place on 11 January, regarding it as a violation of the Mission's mandate and an infringement of Iraqi national sovereignty. In a 25 January letter,[29] it made a reference to reports in the United States media that the company contracting helicopters to UNIKOM might be connected with the United States Central Intelligence Agency; it called for reconsideration of the contract to ensure continued cooperation between the Mission and the Iraqi Government. That request was renewed on 28 February.[30] On 9 October, Iraq complained[31] that a Kuwaiti military helicopter had landed inside the DMZ in violation of the DMZ regime.

In October, a helicopter unit from Bangladesh replaced the chartered helicopter.

### Composition

As at September 1995,[25] UNIKOM had a strength of 1,331 personnel, including 244 military observers from 32 Member States; an infantry battalion of 775 from Bangladesh; an engineer unit of 50 from Argentina; a logistics unit of 35 from Denmark; and 227 civilian staff, of whom 80 were recruited internationally.

On 23 October, the Secretary-General informed[32] the Security Council of his intention to appoint Major-General Gian Giuseppe Santillo (Italy) to replace Major-General Krishna N. S. Thapa (Nepal) as UNIKOM Force Commander, effective 1 December 1995. The Security Council's agreement was communicated[33] to the Secretary-General on 26 October.

### Financing

**Report of the Secretary-General.** In a 20 March report[34] on the financing of UNIKOM, the Secretary-General noted that Member State assessments for the Mission for the period from its inception on 9 April 1991 to 31 March 1995 totalled $216,092,900, while contributions received for the same period amounted to $157,932,123 as at 28 February 1995, leaving an unpaid balance of $27,892,868. Resources made available to UNIKOM by the General Assembly for the same period totalled $279,566,400 gross ($272,116,200 net), while operating costs amounted to $237,803,933 gross ($231,031,260 net). As for voluntary contributions, two thirds of the Mission's cost for the period from 1 November 1993 to 31 March 1995, in the amount of $58,273,500, had been received from Kuwait, which also contributed 35 vehicles for use by the Mission's engineering unit.

In response to a 1994 General Assembly request,[35] the Secretary-General reported that 11 international General Service and Field Service staff of UNIKOM had been replaced by local staff between 1 November 1994 and 31 March 1995, while an additional nine were expected to be replaced between 1 April 1995 and 30 June 1996. He also recalled that Kuwait had provided two camps for the infantry battalion, free of charge, which resulted in savings of $7.1 million from the allocation for the construction of UNIKOM premises.

UNIKOM expenditures from 1 November 1993 to 31 October 1994 totalled $58,830,600 gross ($56,755,600 net), resulting in an unencumbered balance of $11,169,400 gross ($10,997,700 net), of which $7,800,000 had already been credited to Member States. Troops were provided during that period by Argentina, Austria, Bangladesh, Denmark and Norway; full reimbursement of costs to troop-contributing States had been made for the period ending December 1994. The cost of maintaining UNIKOM was estimated at $43,718,300 gross ($41,997,500 net) from 1 November 1994 to 30 June 1995 and at $5,326,000 gross ($5,108,200 net) per month from 1 July 1995 to 30 June 1996, providing for 255 military observers, 910 contingent personnel and up to 259 international and local civilian staff.

The Secretary-General requested that the General Assembly approve the amounts required for maintaining UNIKOM from 1 May to 31 October 1994, from 1 November 1994 to 31 March 1995, and from 1 April to 30 June 1995; appropriate one third of each amount for the respective periods and assess it for the first two periods, with the remainder to be funded by Kuwait; and approve the amount for the Mission's maintenance from 1 July 1995 to 30 June 1996. He also proposed action with regard to the unencumbered balance for the period from 1 to 30 April 1995, and requested commitment authority of $3,916,700 gross ($3,480,900 net) from 1 May to 30 June 1995 and of $1,920,600 gross ($1,702,700 net) per month from 1 July 1995 to 30 June 1996.

GENERAL ASSEMBLY ACTION (March)

In March, the General Assembly adopted **decision 49/477**.

### Financing of the United Nations Iraq-Kuwait Observation Mission

At its 99th plenary meeting, on 31 March 1995, the General Assembly, on the recommendation of the Fifth Committee and pending consideration of the report of the Secretary-General on the United Nations Iraq-Kuwait Observation Mission and the related report of the Advisory Committee on Administrative and Budgetary Questions:

(a) Approved, provisionally, an amount of 12 million United States dollars net for the maintenance of the Mission for the period from 1 April to 30 June 1995, including the two thirds of that amount to be funded from voluntary contributions from the Government of Kuwait, should the Security Council decide to continue the Mission;

(b) Authorized the Secretary-General to enter into commitments in an amount of 4 million dollars net, representing one third of the cost of the maintenance of the Mission for the period from 1 April to 30 June 1995, in addition to the amount of 8 million dollars to be made available by the Government of Kuwait.

General Assembly decision 49/477

Adopted without vote

Approved by Fifth Committee (A/49/877) without vote, 29 March (meeting 50); oral proposal by Chairman; agenda item 118 *(a)*.

**ACABQ report.** In a 19 May report,[36] ACABQ noted that the amount of unliquidated obligations had been reduced from $6.7 million at the end of February to $4.6 million at the end of March, and that reimbursement of troop costs to Member States had been made in full up to March 1995. It had been informed that a project to consolidate facilities in a new UNIKOM support centre had been under way since January and was expected to be completed in July, and that the Mission's logistics base was being moved from Doha to Kuwait City. Having reviewed UNIKOM personnel costs as well as transport and air operations, ACABQ recommended approval of amounts for the Mission's maintenance from 1 November 1994 to 30 June 1995 and from 1 July 1995 to 30 June 1996, appropriation and assessment of one third of the amount for the former period, and commitment authorization not exceeding $1,811,900 gross ($1,594,100 net) per month for the latter.

GENERAL ASSEMBLY ACTION (July and December)

On 12 July, the General Assembly adopted **resolution 49/245**.

### Financing of the United Nations Iraq-Kuwait Observation Mission

*The General Assembly,*

*Having considered* the report of the Secretary-General on the financing of the United Nations Iraq-Kuwait Observation Mission and the related report of the Advisory Committee on Administrative and Budgetary Questions,

*Bearing in mind* Security Council resolutions 687(1991) of 3 April 1991 and 689(1991) of 9 April 1991, by which the Council decided to set up the United Nations Iraq-Kuwait Observation Mission and to review the question of its termination or continuation every six months,

*Recalling* its previous decisions regarding the fact that, in order to meet the expenditures caused by the Observation Mission, a different procedure is required from that applied to meet expenditures of the regular budget of the United Nations,

*Recalling also* its resolution 45/260 of 3 May 1991 on the financing of the Observation Mission and its subsequent resolutions thereon, the latest of which was resolution 48/242 of 5 April 1994,

*Recalling further* its decision 49/477 of 31 March 1995,

*Reaffirming* that the costs of the Observation Mission are expenses of the Organization to be borne by Member States in accordance with Article 17, paragraph 2, of the Charter of the United Nations,

*Taking into account* the fact that the economically more developed countries are in a position to make relatively larger contributions and that the economically less developed countries have a relatively limited capacity to contribute towards such an operation,

*Bearing in mind* the special responsibilities of the States permanent members of the Security Council, as indicated in General Assembly resolution 1874(S-IV) of 27 June 1963, in the financing of such operations,

*Expressing its appreciation* for the substantial voluntary contributions made to the Observation Mission by the Government of Kuwait and the contributions of other Governments,

*Mindful* of the fact that it is essential to provide the Observation Mission with the necessary financial resources to enable it to fulfil its responsibilities under the relevant resolutions of the Security Council,

1. *Takes note* of the status of contributions to the United Nations Iraq-Kuwait Observation Mission as at 12 June 1995, including the contributions outstanding in the amount of 27,668,567 United States dollars;

2. *Expresses its continued appreciation* for the decision of the Government of Kuwait to defray two thirds of the cost of the Observation Mission, effective 1 November 1993;

3. *Endorses* the observations and recommendations contained in the report of the Advisory Committee on Administrative and Budgetary Questions;

4. *Requests* the Secretary-General to take all necessary action to ensure that the Observation Mission is administered with a maximum of efficiency and economy;

5. *Urges* all Member States to make every possible effort to ensure payment of their assessed contributions to the Observation Mission promptly and in full;

6. *Approves* the amount of 33 million dollars gross (31,876,800 dollars net) for the maintenance of the Observation Mission for the period from 1 May to 31 October 1994, two thirds of this amount, equivalent to 21,251,200 dollars, to be funded from voluntary contributions from the Government of Kuwait;

7. *Decides* to appropriate to the special account referred to in General Assembly resolution 45/260 an amount of 11,748,800 dollars gross (10,625,600 dollars

net) authorized by the Assembly in paragraph 17 of its resolution 48/242 for the maintenance of the Observation Mission for the period from 1 May to 31 October 1994;

8. *Decides also*, as an ad hoc arrangement, to apportion the amount of 11,748,800 dollars gross (10,625,600 dollars net), inclusive of the amount of 11 million dollars gross (9,876,800 dollars net) already apportioned among Member States in accordance with paragraph 17 of General Assembly resolution 48/242;

9. *Decides further* that, in accordance with the provisions of its resolution 973(X) of 15 December 1955, the credits already given to Member States totalling 1,123,200 dollars against the apportionment as provided for in paragraph 8 above represent their respective share in the Tax Equalization Fund of the estimated staff assessment income for the period from 1 May to 31 October 1994 approved for the Observation Mission;

10. *Approves* the amount of 43 million dollars gross (41,279,200 dollars net) for the maintenance of the Observation Mission for the period from 1 November 1994 to 30 June 1995, two thirds of this amount, equivalent to 27,519,500 dollars, to be funded from voluntary contributions from the Government of Kuwait;

11. *Decides* to appropriate the amount of 15,480,500 dollars gross (13,759,700 dollars net), equivalent to one third of the cost of the maintenance of the Observation Mission for the period from 1 November 1994 to 30 June 1995, inclusive of the amount of 9,133,600 dollars gross (8,777,900 dollars net) authorized and apportioned, under the terms of paragraph 18 of General Assembly resolution 48/242 and decision 49/477;

12. *Decides also*, as an ad hoc arrangement, to apportion the amount of 6,346,900 dollars gross (4,981,800 dollars net) for the period from 1 November 1994 to 30 June 1995 among Member States, taking into account the amount of 9,133,600 dollars gross (8,777,900 dollars net) already apportioned among Member States in accordance with paragraph 18 of resolution 48/242, in accordance with the composition of groups set out in paragraphs 3 and 4 of General Assembly resolution 43/232 of 1 March 1989, as adjusted by the Assembly in its resolutions 44/192 B of 21 December 1989, 45/269 of 27 August 1991, 46/198 A of 20 December 1991 and 47/218 A of 23 December 1992 and its decision 48/472 A of 23 December 1993, and taking into account the scale of assessments for the years 1995, 1996 and 1997 as set out in Assembly resolution 49/19 B of 23 December 1994;

13. *Decides further* that, in accordance with the provisions of resolution 973(X) of 15 December 1955, there shall be set off against the apportionment among Member States, as provided for in paragraph 12 above, their respective share in the Tax Equalization Fund of the additional estimated staff assessment income of 1,365,100 dollars approved for the period from 1 November 1994 to 30 June 1995;

14. *Decides* to set off against the apportionment among Member States for the period from 1 November 1994 to 30 June 1995 their respective share in the remaining portion of the one-third share of the unencumbered balance for the period from 1 November 1993 to 31 October 1994, equivalent to 1,237,600 dollars gross (1,065,900 dollars net), taking into account the amount of 2.6 million dollars already credited to Member States against the amounts of their apportionment for the

period from 1 November 1994 to 31 March 1995, the remaining portion of the unencumbered balance to be credited to the Government of Kuwait;

15. *Approves* the amount of 60 million dollars gross (57,386,000 dollars net) for the maintenance of the Observation Mission from 1 July 1995 to 30 June 1996, two thirds of this amount, equivalent to 38,257,300 dollars, to be funded from voluntary contributions from the Government of Kuwait, subject to the review by the Security Council with regard to the question of termination or continuation of the Observation Mission;

16. *Authorizes* the Secretary-General to enter into commitments in the amount of 1,811,900 dollars gross (1,594,100 dollars net) per month, equivalent to one third of the cost of the maintenance of the Observation Mission, and the apportionment thereof in accordance with the scheme set out in the present resolution, in addition to the two-thirds share of 3,188,100 dollars per month to be met through voluntary contributions from the Government of Kuwait for the period from 1 July 1995 to 30 June 1996, subject to the review by the Security Council;

17. *Invites* voluntary contributions to the Observation Mission in cash and in the form of services and supplies acceptable to the Secretary-General, to be administered, as appropriate, in accordance with the procedure established by the General Assembly in its resolutions 43/230 of 21 December 1988, 44/192 A of 21 December 1989 and 45/258 of 3 May 1991;

18. *Decides* to include in the provisional agenda of its fiftieth session, under the item entitled "Financing of the activities arising from Security Council resolution 687(1991)" the sub-item entitled "United Nations Iraq-Kuwait Observation Mission".

General Assembly resolution 49/245

12 July 1995     Meeting 105     Adopted without vote

Approved by Fifth Committee (A/49/877/Add.1) without vote, 23 June (meeting 58); draft by Vice-Chairman (A/C.5/49/L.53); agenda item 118 *(a)*.
Meeting numbers. GA 49th session: 5th Committee 56, 58; plenary 105.

On 23 December, the Assembly decided that the Fifth Committee should continue consideration of the item on financing of UNIKOM at its resumed fiftieth session (**decision 50/469**).

## Ongoing monitoring and verification

During the year, IAEA and UNSCOM continued to report on their activities to monitor and verify Iraq's compliance with the provisions of the Security Council's 1991 resolutions, primarily section C of resolution 687(1991). Those activities, carried out under the respective ongoing monitoring and verification (OMV) plans approved by the Council in resolution 715(1991), pertained to Iraq's nuclear, chemical and biological weapons programmes as well as ballistic missiles; and to an export/import mechanism, called for in the same resolution, to monitor any future sale or supply to Iraq of items relevant to the implementation of resolutions 687(1991) and 707(1991) and of the OMV plans. In coordination with the Sanctions Committee, IAEA and UNSCOM in 1995 finalized the development of such a mechanism, and revised accordingly lists of items to be reported to them by exporting countries, contained in annexes to their OMV plans.

The discovery of a large amount of additional important documentation in August, coupled with Iraq's new disclosures, necessitated substantial adjustments in IAEA's and UNSCOM's understanding of and accounting for Iraq's past programmes, which were revealed to have been more extensive and advanced in every dimension than previously known. At the end of the year, Iraq also acknowledged having had a radiological weapons programme, information on which had been previously unavailable.

### IAEA activities

**Seventh IAEA report on OMV (April).** By an 11 April note,[37] the Secretary-General transmitted to the Security Council the seventh report of the IAEA Director General on the implementation of the Agency's OMV plan related to Iraq's nuclear capabilities, submitted in response to resolution 715(1991). The report noted that most Agency activities in Iraq were carried out by its Nuclear Monitoring Group (NMG), headquartered at the Baghdad Monitoring and Verification Centre (BMVC), which also was cooperating with UNSCOM resident teams as necessary.

The Director General provided background information on Iraq's past nuclear weapons programme, noting that the documents seized by IAEA inspectors in 1991 had revealed the progress made in the covert Iraqi nuclear programme, ''Petrochemical Project 3'' (PC3), in 1988-1991. Two questions, he said, had been left open; these covered the progress made by PC3 from June 1990 to January 1991, and the completeness of information regarding gas centrifuge enrichment. In that regard, Iraqi authorities asserted that the Kuwait invasion had brought all Iraqi Atomic Energy Commission activities to a virtual halt; that the sanctions imposed by the Security Council had interrupted the flow of equipment and material needed for completing the project; and that all sensitive documents had been surrendered to the Iraqi army for destruction. For its part, IAEA believed that some programme documents forcibly taken from IAEA inspectors in 1991 had been withheld by Iraq, despite its claim to the contrary, and that Iraq's assertion that all programme documents had been destroyed was not credible.

The Agency undertook independent verification of the information concerning the gas centrifuge programme, as well as materials and equipment imported by Iraq that were subject to control and monitoring under the OMV plan; to date, the investigation had entailed inquiries involving 186 companies in 28 countries. The Director General also pointed out that IAEA had recently received copies of documents alleging ongoing nuclear weapons–related studies in Iraq; however, initial analysis could not establish the documents' authenticity, while Iraqi authorities denied the existence of such a programme. The Agency continued to pursue the matter.

The report further described OMV activities, including inspections at facilities, installations and sites; environmental monitoring; verification of the use of items listed in annex 3 of the OMV plan as related to the nuclear programme; interviews with Iraqi personnel connected with the former programme; and verification of information provided by Iraq as well as acquired from Member States, from aerial surveillance and open sources and assessed to warrant further investigation. Since the establishment of NMG in 1994, more than 160 inspections had been conducted at some 70 facilities, including 23 facilities which had been inspected for the first time: 3 identified by Iraq as the recipients of monitored items for which it had requested release or change of use; 2 where previously undeclared items of dual-use equipment were located; 16 declared as having a means of power supply greater than 10 MWe; 1 where radio-isotopes were used or stored; and 1 inspected on the basis of information obtained from Member States. The inspections revealed shortcomings in the inventory of declared facilities with a power supply greater than 10 MWe, and the Iraqi National Monitoring Directorate was requested to prepare a correct inventory declaration.

Environmental monitoring involved the twice-yearly hydrological survey of the watersheds of the Tigris and Euphrates, during which samples of water, sediment and biota were collected, as well as aerial and ground-based gamma radiation surveys, the collection of airborne particulate matter and the sampling of materials deposited on surfaces. IAEA video surveillance and recording equipment installed in two major engineering establishments had been modified to enable transmission of television signals from monitored locations to BMVC; the relevant information was shared with UNSCOM. IAEA and UNSCOM also cooperated in processing requests for the release of, or for permission to relocate, equipment and material, as well as for permission to change the use of monitored buildings. Also, to confirm that critical items of equipment were at their declared locations, and to prevent the undetected use of controlled equipment, IAEA continued to attach seals with unique verifiable signatures to such items.

As previously reported, all weapons-usable nuclear material had been removed from Iraq by February 1994, and was fully accounted for and stored under IAEA safeguards in the Russian Federation. The nuclear material remaining in Iraq comprised 1.8 tonnes of low-enriched uranium, 6 tonnes of depleted uranium and 540 tonnes of natural uranium, in a variety of physical and chemical forms, in sealed storage under IAEA control. The Agency was currently seeking Iraq's cooperation in consolidating its three semi-annual declarations made since November 1993 concerning the inventories of facilities, installations and sites suitable for nuclear activities of any kind, as well as of all material, equipment and items identified in annex 3 of the OMV plan; in that regard, IAEA had received an assurance that the necessary work was in progress. The report also noted the high level of cooperation by Iraqi counterparts in facilitating IAEA field activities. Those activities continued to be supported as well by the IAEA data analysis and processing centre, which maintained a computerized system for the management, analysis and retrieval of all information relevant to Iraq.

In implementation of the OMV plan, the Agency examined the extent to which technical assistance and cooperation might be accommodated within the constraints of the relevant Security Council resolutions. It identified five technical assistance projects, approved by its Board of Governors and perceived as falling outside the proscribed conduct of nuclear activities by Iraq. Three projects related to agriculture (mutation techniques for crop protection, immunoassay techniques for rinderpest diagnosis, improvement of soil fertility) and two to nuclear medicine (rehabilitation of nuclear medicine services and of radiotherapy services for cancer); they involved the provision by IAEA of experts, equipment and fellowships, as well as the funding of visits by Iraqi scientists to foreign laboratories. At the Agency's request, the Sanctions Committee examined the issue, concurred that the assistance in question fell within the limited exceptions to the sanctions, and approved the implementation of those projects.

The report also reviewed activities pertaining to IAEA on-site inspections, development of an export/import-monitoring mechanism, and a related revision to annex 3 of the OMV plan (see below).

**Communication of the IAEA Director General (July).** In a follow-up to the Agency's seventh report, transmitted[38] on 17 July, the Director General informed the Security Council that IAEA had completed its investigation of the documents referred to in the April report (see above), alleging that Iraq's nuclear weapons programme had been reconstituted. Owing to a large number of errors and inconsistencies in the documents, the conclusion was reached that the documents were not authentic. Furthermore, no credible evidence had been found to corroborate the allegations, it was stated.

**Eighth IAEA report on OMV (October).** The eighth IAEA report on implementation of the OMV plan, transmitted[39] on 6 October, stated that an Agency delegation had visited Baghdad from 17 to 20 August at the invitation of the Iraqi Government, following the arrival in Jordan, on 8 August, of General Hussein Kamel, the former Iraqi Minister of Industry and Military Industrialization. The delegation received information concerning Iraq's past nuclear programme, previously withheld allegedly at the instruction of General Kamel. In addition to new details of the programme, Iraqi officials provided documents on a hitherto undisclosed project said to have been ordered by General Kamel and consisting of a crash programme, launched in September 1990, to extract and further enrich the already highly enriched uranium contained in safeguarded research reactor fuel at the Tuwaitha site. The programme was aimed at accelerating the availability of weapons-grade material for the fabrication of a nuclear device and was to have been carried out between the twice-yearly IAEA safeguards inspections in November 1990 and May 1991. However, while the extraction equipment had been assembled by late January 1991, the damage caused by the coalition air raids on Tuwaitha and other relevant facilities made further work on the project impossible; in May 1991, the IAEA inspection had fully accounted for the safeguarded reactor fuel.

The Agency delegation also received information on activities of PC3 in the second half of 1990, involving, *inter alia*, activities of the gas centrifuge enrichment programme. On 20 August, Iraqi authorities announced the discovery of thousands of documents, and several tons of metals and other materials, on a farm said to be owned by the family of General Kamel. The documents, totalling some 680,000 pages, were inventoried by a joint IAEA/UNSCOM team in BMVC and subsequently transferred to IAEA headquarters in Vienna for evaluation. The metals and other materials were also transported to BMVC for analysis. Following the talks in Baghdad, the Agency delegation met in Jordan with General Kamel, whose detailed description of the past nuclear programme provided useful information. The report noted that, while the sheer magnitude of the documentation made it impossible to draw definitive conclusions at the current time, nothing warranted a change in IAEA's determination that Iraq's nuclear weapons programme had for all practical purposes been destroyed, removed or rendered harmless. However, it was clear that the crash programme to extract weapons-grade material from safeguarded reactor fuel constituted an additional violation of Iraq's safeguards agreement with IAEA, while its failure to disclose information on that programme and other weapons-related activities constituted violations of Iraq's obligations under relevant Security Council resolutions.

To follow up on the new information, an ad hoc IAEA inspection mission was sent to Iraq from 9 to 20 September (see below). In the meantime, NMG resident inspectors continued their work in the field and conducted 105 inspections at some 51 sites and facilities, 11 of which were visited for the first time. The sixth radiometric survey of Iraq's main water bodies was completed in April, with samples of water, sediment and biota having been taken at 15 sites selected from the 52 locations for which baseline data had been established in 1992. Twelve additional locations along the Euphrates watercourse, close to the Al Qaim phosphate fertilizer plant, were sampled as well, to establish a baseline for future analyses. In July, Iraq submitted a semi-annual update on facilities, installations and sites suitable for nuclear activities, which provided detailed information on 29 additional facilities, thus bringing the total number of declared sites to 169. IAEA and UNSCOM approved 12 of 20 requests for the release, relocation or change of the use of equipment, materials and facilities, received since August 1994.

### On-site inspections

During 1995, IAEA conducted two on-site inspections in Iraq—the twenty-eighth and the twenty-ninth since such inspections were instituted in accordance with Security Council resolution 687(1991).

The twenty-eighth inspection (9-20 September)[40] investigated and documented the information declared by Iraq in August concerning its former crash programme to accelerate the production of a nuclear weapon. For the first time, Iraq acknowledged that activities had been carried out at the Tuwaitha and Al Atheer sites for the direct purpose of producing nuclear weapons and not, as previously asserted, merely to define the capabilities required for their production. Credible descriptions were obtained as to the purpose and utilization of the main buildings at the Al Atheer site, with particular respect to the internal explosion chamber and the gas gun laboratory, and an admission was gained regarding the processing of undeclared nuclear material in the former fuel fabrication laboratory at Tuwaitha, where some 10.3 tons of natural uranium, comprising uranium dioxide of Brazilian origin and yellowcake of indigenous origin, had been processed. Iraq also admitted that the Engineering Design Centre at Rashdiya was the headquarters of the centrifuge enrichment project; it provided a detailed explanation of its establishment, building utilization and achievements; however, no convincing rationale was offered for the prior concealment of that fact. Wide-ranging information was obtained clarifying and confirming certain aspects of the procurement system set up to support the centrifuge enrichment project.

Although there were no indications to suggest that Iraq had retained any practical indigenous capability to produce weapons-usable nuclear material, it was recognized that its intellectual capabilities and resources in that regard remained. In the light of the new information, it became evident that a further revision had to be issued to Iraq's so-called "full, final and complete" declaration made in June 1992.[41] The revision would provide a comprehensive description of all facets of the past programme, in particular the work of the 1987 nuclear weapons study group at the Ministry of Industry and Military Industrialization, and the crash programme, including programme milestones and deadlines and the military strategy. The revised declaration also had to include details of the various procurement networks; achievements of the weaponization group set up within PC3; work on other enrichment technologies; the handling, processing and use of nondeclared nuclear material; work on radiological weapons; activities since the end of 1990; and information on the current location of materials, equipment and documents removed from the Engineering Design Centre at Rashdiya after April 1991.

The twenty-ninth on-site inspection (17-24 October)[42] sought to obtain further details related to the organization, management and facilities of the centrifuge enrichment programme, centrifuge machines and cascades, procurement and foreign assistance, and weaponization activities. Discussions were held with the Iraqi counterpart at the headquarters of the Military Industrial Corporation, and inspections were conducted at the Al Shakyli store, the Engineering Design Centre and the Al Furat site, as well as at the Al Qaqaa State Establishment and at Balat Ash Shuada.

The inspectors noted a remarkable level of openness displayed by Iraqi counterparts in the discussions, but pointed to a certain remaining degree of reticence and to contradictions between verbal statements and the content of some original PC3 documents. They concluded that Iraq's original plan had had the objective of creating a small arsenal of nuclear weapons, with the first device being produced in 1991; however, the programme's main components had not progressed at the same pace to meet the initial deadline. The decision to embark upon a crash programme modified substantially the original objective and restricted the development of a delivery system to the short-term option of missile delivery. It was noted that Iraq had developed or otherwise acquired many of the technologies necessary to produce deliverable nuclear weapons, but the Gulf War had destroyed electromagnetic isotope separation facilities and halted efforts to master centrifuge technology. Subsequently, IAEA had removed from

Iraq all existing research reactor fuel, and hence any in-country source of quickly available heavy enriched uranium.

The inspection emphasized that adequate provisions were currently in place in Iraq to detect the resurgence of a capability to produce significant quantities of nuclear weapons–usable material; however, vigilance was necessary to prevent the direct acquisition of such material, in view of the low signature associated with the assembly of a nuclear device.

### Reports under resolution 699(1991)

In accordance with Security Council resolution 699(1991),[43] IAEA submitted in 1995 two progress reports on the implementation of the plan for the destruction, removal or rendering harmless of the items specified in paragraph 12 of Council resolution 687(1991).

The June report[44] stated that no development relevant to Agency activities in Iraq was to be reported for the period from 17 December 1994 to 17 June 1995, beyond what had been communicated to the Council in the April report on OMV (see above). In December,[45] information was provided on the events described in the October report on OMV, as well as on follow-up IAEA inspections (see above). It was noted that the documents obtained by the Agency during the period under review indicated the presence in Iraq of hitherto undeclared items that could fall in the categories proscribed to Iraq under resolution 687(1991). IAEA said it was in the process of locating, identifying and analysing the characteristics of such items.

### UNSCOM activities

The UN Special Commission, headed by Executive Chairman Rolf Ekéus, continued its monitoring and verification operations in Iraq, which were carried out from three offices: the Executive Office in New York, the monitoring and verification centre in Baghdad and a field office in Muharraq, Bahrain. In 1995, UNSCOM launched its biological monitoring system, augmenting systems already operational for monitoring missile, chemical and nuclear activities.

UNSCOM operations continued to be financed from frozen Iraqi assets made available through the escrow account, as established under Security Council resolution 778(1992)[20] (see also above, under "Sanctions compliance"), as well as from voluntary contributions from Kuwait, Qatar and Saudi Arabia. In addition, a number of experts, facilities, equipment and services were provided to the Commission by Governments at their own expense, including the premises of its field office in Bahrain.

The status, privileges and immunities of UNSCOM and other UN agencies involved in imple-menting resolution 687(1991) continued to be regulated by relevant Council resolutions and by agreements reached in 1993 with Iraq and Bahrain,[46] the latter being extended every six months. In a 7 March 1995 memorandum[47] to the Fifth Committee, the Secretary-General proposed that the General Assembly grant to the UNSCOM Executive Chairman, not a staff member of the UN Secretariat, the privileges and immunities referred to in articles V and VII of the 1946 Convention on the Privileges and Immunities of the United Nations.[48] By **decision 49/475** of 31 March, the Assembly approved that proposal.

During the year, the Security Council received four reports from the Special Commission: two on UNSCOM activities, submitted by its Executive Chairman; and two on the implementation of its OMV plan, submitted by the Secretary-General pursuant to Council resolution 715(1991).

**Seventh report on OMV (April).** On 10 April, the Secretary-General submitted the seventh report[49] on the implementation of the UNSCOM OMV plan. The report noted that the basic elements of the OMV system comprised regular inspections of relevant facilities, inventories of dual-purpose items (those permitted for use but which could be used for the acquisition of banned weapons), and accounting for all inventoried items until they were consumed, disposed of or no longer operable. The system was underpinned by the use of aerial surveillance with a variety of sensors, remote sensors, tags and seals, various detection technologies and the export/import control mechanism, as well as information obtained from other sources. The main areas of application of the OMV plan included Iraq's missile, chemical, biological and nuclear activities and export/import monitoring. The plan also required Iraq to adopt measures necessary to implement its obligations under resolutions 687(1991) and 707(1991), as well as the plan itself, including penal legislation forbidding any activity proscribed to Iraq from being carried out under its jurisdiction.

The report noted that the UNSCOM missile-monitoring system had become operational, with the completion of the baseline survey of Iraq's permitted missile and related dual-purpose capabilities, installation of sensors and tags for monitored missiles and production equipment and related dual-purpose items, and the inception of a resident missile-monitoring team. UNSCOM had essentially completed the accounting of facilities, equipment and materials used in the past proscribed missile programmes, but was waiting for responses to its requests for information from a number of countries from which Iraq had acquired or sought to acquire items for proscribed purposes. While the Commission believed it had a broad understanding of Iraq's achievements and its level of technological development in that area, it continued to investigate certain related programmes, such as those for the development of a supersonic parachute recovery system and production of unsymmetrical dimethyl hydrazine—a liquid fuel capable of improving the performance of liquid-propellant rocket engines.

The resident missile-monitoring team conducted 178 inspections of research, development, testing, production and modification activities and facilities, to ensure that there was no research or development into or production of missile systems exceeding the specifications of the relevant Security Council resolutions; that all declared equipment was accounted for; and that records agreed with information available from other sources. It continued regular collection and review of video coverage of missile-related activities in critical areas and key equipment, to guarantee that all produced missiles subject to monitoring were accounted for and tagged and that no production of proscribed missile systems occurred. Three inspections were also carried out of the tagged operational missiles, to ensure that none had been modified to exceed the allowed specifications. In addition, UNSCOM continued to conduct twice-yearly research and development update inspections, most recently in March 1995, to review technical details of the design, development and testing of missile systems and missile-related technologies and to confirm that current designs did not exceed the established limits.

The Commission's chemical-monitoring system was also operational, with the installation of its monitoring equipment almost complete. On 25 March, Iraq presented a new full, final and complete declaration of its past chemical warfare activities, as promised during the high-level talks in Baghdad in February. The report provided background information available to UNSCOM on Iraq's past chemical programmes, including in the areas of agent production, precursor chemical production, equipment and munitions. It noted that baseline inspections had been conducted in January and February at 17 universities, colleges and research institutions to assess their relevance for monitoring, and five military storage depots had been visited because of their potential to store munitions for chemical weapons. The Commission concluded that, except for two facilities related to pesticide formulation, none of the chemical sites currently monitored had the capability to produce banned items, while the inspected research laboratories had no potential for conducting significant chemical weapons–related research and development.

In addition to the monitoring capabilities shared across the sectors, chemical monitoring was centred around visits to monitored sites, tagging and inventorying of key materials and equipment, collection and analysis of air samples using automatic samplers located at certain sites, and monitoring of key equipment items by remote-controlled cameras. By the end of January, sensor systems had been installed at all sites of interest, 30 cameras had been mounted at six sites, and 15 air samplers had been placed at eight sites. In February, a chemical laboratory was installed at BMVC for sample analysis. The chemical-monitoring group, which began work in October 1994, had conducted 70 inspections; its capabilities were to be enhanced in May 1995 with the provision of manual-transportable air samplers and personal detection and protection equipment.

The report further pointed to difficulties encountered by UNSCOM in establishing its biological-monitoring system, owing to the nature and scope of the task as well as to the incompleteness of and inconsistencies in Iraq's declarations regarding its dual-purpose capabilities. A new full, final and complete declaration recently received by UNSCOM had not definitively accounted for all the materials and items known to have been acquired by Iraq that might have been used in a biological warfare programme; in UNSCOM's view, there was a high risk that those items had been purchased and in part used for proscribed purposes. The report stated that, given the circumstances, the Commission's biological monitoring could not be considered comprehensive in coverage and properly focused; nevertheless, it summarized the available information on Iraq's past programmes, including in the areas of complex growth media, equipment and construction of biological facilities, and noted that interim biological monitoring, begun in December 1994 with a series of intrusive inspections, sought to establish the baseline data necessary for the commencement of monitoring. For that purpose, biological audits were conducted at 10 priority sites for which information was the most disparate.

The nature of biological weapons necessitated a broader effort than in the other areas, it was stated. The OMV plan provided for the monitoring of Iraq's basic biological research potential, its stocks of micro-organisms and complex growth media, its biological production capacity, and its ability to isolate micro-organisms and create particles usable in biological warfare, as well as its ability to fill containers with biological material and to disperse such material. In all, monitoring activities covered some 80 sites, comprising biological laboratories, biological production facilities and agricultural crop sprayers. To date, 24 cameras had been installed at five key sites and locations, and monitoring of certain sites had been initiated. A total of 13 biological inspections were undertaken in the period from October 1994 to

March 1995, and interim monitoring groups conducted 51 visits to 20 sites. In addition, a biological room was installed at BMVC for the processing, packaging and onward transmission of biological samples.

UNSCOM continued to assist and cooperate with IAEA in the area of nuclear activities (see above, under "IAEA activities"). It participated in IAEA inspections and monitoring teams, provided logistic support as well as aircraft for the transport of IAEA inspectors, and commented on the Iraqi requests, considered by IAEA, to relocate nuclear-related, dual-use materials and equipment within the country. In addition to supporting the surface-water sampling programme, the Commission recently approved fitting its helicopters with air samplers to complement IAEA's investigative ability. It also shared information obtained by its U2 high-altitude surveillance aircraft and the Baghdad-based aerial inspection team, which continued to conduct regular aerial surveillance of monitored sites. The report noted that some 243 missions had been undertaken to date by the U2 aircraft and 550 missions by the aerial inspection team.

As for national implementation measures, the report stated that Iraq had consulted with UN-SCOM on draft legislation, expected to be adopted in April, to ban any activity proscribed by relevant Security Council resolutions. It further reviewed activities to establish and implement an export/import-monitoring mechanism and described organizational and financial aspects of the Commission's work (see below).

**Eighth report on OMV (October).** The eighth report,[(50)] submitted on 11 October, on the implementation of the Special Commission's OMV plan, stated that the UNSCOM Executive Chairman had made five visits to Baghdad during the period under review (29 May–1 June, 30 June–2 July, 4-6 August, 17-20 August, 29 September–1 October). Two visits were also paid to Baghdad by the Deputy Executive Chairman (14-17 May, 17-20 September) to address issues relating to Iraq's prohibited programmes. Those visits were necessitated by indications that Iraq was contemplating ceasing its cooperation with UNSCOM.

In May, Iraq required statements from the Commission that the chemical weapons and missile files were closed and the monitoring system was operational, and from IAEA that the nuclear file was closed, following which it would address the outstanding issue of its biological activities. The Executive Chairman responded that, while the bulk of requirements with regard to chemical weapons and missiles had been implemented, uncertainties remained in those areas which needed to be resolved. On 1 July, Iraq acknowledged an offensive biological weapons programme, including the production of a number of biological agents, but denied the weaponization of such agents. In early August, it submitted its "full, final and complete" disclosure of the biological weapons programme and threatened to cease cooperation with the Security Council and UNSCOM if there were no progress, by 31 August, towards lifting sanctions and the oil embargo. Upon his return to New York, the Executive Chairman informed the Council accordingly in a 10 August oral briefing. However, following the departure of General Hussein Kamel for Jordan, Iraq withdrew the ultimatum and invited the Executive Chairman, as well as the IAEA Director General, to visit Baghdad (see also above, under "IAEA activities"). During that visit, it disclosed a much more extensive programme than was described in its "full, final and complete" declaration, admitting weaponization of biological warfare agents immediately prior to the outbreak of the Gulf War, including the filling of 166 bombs and 25 "Al Hussein" missiles. Subsequently, it made further disclosures with regard to other prohibited programmes, including the indigenous production and testing of Scud-type missile engines.

On 20 August, a large cache of documents and other materials was located and taken possession of by UNSCOM and IAEA, including microfiches, computer diskettes, videotapes, photographs and prohibited hardware components. While the bulk of the cache related to the nuclear area, many concerned chemical, biological and missile activities. Following the discovery, Iraq admitted that directors of the sites involved in proscribed programmes had been ordered in 1991 to deliver production technology–related documents to special security organizations, which was contrary to Iraq's original claim that all documentation had been destroyed. Nevertheless, the Commission believed that more such documentation existed, particularly in areas such as production records, procurement networks and sources of supply; the relevant documents and archives of the Military Industrialization Corporation and the Ministry of Defence were also missing. Initial analysis of the discovered documents at BMVC revealed programmes larger or more advanced in every dimension than previously declared; in particular, Iraq acknowledged a more extensive programme for the production and storage of the chemical warfare nerve agent VX.

The new evidence necessitated re-examination of Iraq's declarations on unilateral destruction of elements related to proscribed missiles and chemical and biological programmes, it was stated. The Commission had to press for additional documentation. It was evident that the Commission had to have a complete understanding of the concept behind each stage of the development of all proscribed weapons systems, together with their intended and actual deployment plans.

The report further reviewed OMV activities in each of the Commission's mandated areas. It noted that UNSCOM continued to: conduct regular inspections of more than 30 missile-related facilities, having performed some 450 inspections since August 1994; collect, on a monthly basis, videotapes from 40 cameras installed at 16 monitored facilities; and review more than 120 tagged pieces of missile-related equipment. During the reporting period, the Commission carried out the second annual verification of Iraq's non-proscribed operational missiles (with ranges less than 150 kilometres), and established modalities requiring Iraq to present 10 per cent of its missiles, three times per year, for verification. It also investigated Iraq's resumed acquisition efforts in support of missile facilities, which involved the actual import of equipment and materials without notifications to the UN Sanctions Committee; in most cases, Iraq wrongly asserted that those items had been purchased within the country. On 2 July, UNSCOM informed the Security Council of having detected the continued operation of the equipment purchased for proscribed missile activities, in contravention of the Commission's instructions for its destruction; shortly thereafter, Iraq agreed to comply and completed the destruction by the end of July.

The report stated that, prior to mid-August 1995, Iraq had continued to mislead UNSCOM by withholding requested information, attributing cases on which information was requested to non-proscribed areas, denying activities to which it later admitted, and falsifying its accounting of missiles, warheads and supporting materials. Further to the disclosures made in August, the Commission, at the end of September, obtained new information on Iraq's testing activity, including both static and flight testing of Scud-variant missile systems; development and testing of new liquid-propellant engine designs and of a warhead separation system; an indigenous design of a 600-mm-diameter supergun system; three flight tests of chemical warheads; and several new designs of longer-range missile systems, which involved missiles with ranges of up to 3,000 km as well as a missile for delivery of a nuclear explosive device. Based on the totality of the available information, the Commission concluded that earlier declarations on unilateral destruction of proscribed operational missiles had been intentionally falsified; that a new definite accounting of weapons, equipment and materials used in the proscribed missile programme had to be provided; and that Iraq had not yet disclosed fully and completely its proscribed missile activities.

In the chemical area, four additional baseline inspections were completed and monitoring and verification protocols were prepared for one re-search institute and three chemical storage and production sites, bringing the number of inspected facilities to 62 chemical sites and 18 universities, colleges and research institutes. In addition to 19 air samplers installed at six chemical production sites, the chemical monitoring team received 10 sampling pumps and supporting calibration equipment for random air sampling at any location. Protective equipment had also been procured for operations both in the field and at BMVC. Since its inception, the team had undertaken more than 200 inspections. In June and July, it detected the unauthorized movement and use of four major items of tagged equipment at two monitored sites; upon instruction, they were returned to the original position.

As the new information obtained in August and September showed that the disclosures made in March and May had been incorrect and incomplete, Iraq in October provided UNSCOM with a number of revised chapters; however, these covered only those areas in which shortcomings had been indicated by the Commission. The additional documentation revealed the existence of the nerve agent VX production programme from May 1985 to December 1990, not from April 1987 to September 1988; the production in 1990 of choline and other precursors in an amount sufficient to produce more than 400 tonnes of VX, with no conclusive evidence to support claims of their complete disposal; the development of binary sarin-filled artillery shells, rockets and aerial bombs, as well as flight tests of long-range missiles with chemical warheads; and significant foreign assistance to the chemical weapons programme, with at least $100 million in procurement remaining undeclared. Iraq's recent declarations invalidated the accounting for chemical munitions and weaponized chemical agents, since the munitions previously declared as used for chemical weapons were now declared as used for biological agents. Under the circumstances, the Commission would require a new full, final and complete disclosure from Iraq concerning its chemical weapons programme.

Biological monitoring began in full on 4 April 1995, preceded by a four-month interim phase. It involved 79 sites, of which 9 were subject to the most intense monitoring; 3 sites were equipped with a total of 22 cameras for video monitoring. Since 10 April, some 150 inspections or visits had been made to different sites, including more than 20 inspections to the Al Hakam facility, known to have played a significant role in Iraq's biological weapons programme. During the year, Iraq made a number of declarations in the biological area, including a full, final and complete disclosure (FFCD) in March; admission in July to having had an offensive biological weapons programme from

April 1986 to September 1990; a new FFCD in August, subsequently declared invalid; and additional information disclosed in the light of August events (see above). As that information remained subject to verification, the Commission could not give assurances as to its correctness and comprehensiveness; nevertheless, the report provided a detailed account of new findings. As described, the programme comprised both lethal and incapacitating agents, anti-personnel and anti-plant weapons, a variety of weapons delivery means, and the production and actual weaponization of bacterial agents and research on a number of other biological agents. However, the new documentation appeared to represent only a fraction of all the documents generated under the programme; in addition, information obtained from other sources did not correspond in important aspects to that provided by Iraq.

The Commission continued to cooperate in nuclear-monitoring activities carried out by IAEA, including the review of Iraqi requests for relocation of materials and equipment, the management and control of machine-tool movements within Iraq, and participation in negotiations regarding the sale of nuclear materials removed from Iraq and reprocessed in the Russian Federation. Its U2 surveillance aircraft and the aerial inspection team had undertaken a total of 269 and 600 missions, respectively, while the establishment of a photo laboratory at BMVC facilitated the processing and review of the aerial imagery. No new developments were reported regarding the national implementation measures, as the adoption of the necessary legislation continued to be delayed. The report also reviewed activities related to the export/import-monitoring mechanism, as well as organizational and financial aspects of the Commission's work (see below).

**Ninth report on UNSCOM activities (June).** On 20 June, the UNSCOM Executive Chairman submitted the ninth report[51] on Commission activities, covering the period from 10 December 1994 to 16 June 1995. The report reviewed developments in the mandated areas (see above) and described high-level talks held in Baghdad during visits of the Executive Chairman and the Deputy Executive Chairman. Those visits were aimed at continuing the high-level dialogue initiated in July 1993[52] and at clarifying outstanding issues between Iraq and UNSCOM.

During the talks, Iraq sought the Commission's agreement to declare all areas except biological as closed, stating that its sole reason for cooperating with UNSCOM and IAEA was the desire for reintegration into the international community through the lifting of sanctions and the embargo. In the absence of prospects for such reintegration, Iraq would find it difficult to justify the expense

and effort involved in such cooperation. For his part, the Executive Chairman insisted that certain outstanding technical issues, relating to the level of technical expertise achieved by Iraq and to accounting for components and materials, needed to be resolved first. At the same time, he welcomed the pledge, reaffirmed by the Iraqi Deputy Prime Minister, that Iraq would cooperate with UNSCOM efforts even after any decision by the Security Council to ease or lift the sanctions.

The report concluded that Iraq's cooperation in implementing the OMV plan had been of a degree that satisfied the provisions of Council resolution 715(1991).

**Tenth report on UNSCOM activities (December).** The tenth report[53] on UNSCOM activities, submitted on 17 December and covering the period from 17 June to 17 December, reviewed developments which took place after the October report on OMV (see above). It stated that the Executive Chairman had visited the capitals of States members of the Gulf Cooperation Council (Bahrain, Kuwait, Oman, Qatar, Saudi Arabia, United Arab Emirates) to inform their Governments of UNSCOM activities and to seek their political and financial support, and held high-level talks in Baghdad from 27 to 29 November.

During that visit, he was provided with a personal diary relating to the destruction of certain chemical and biological bombs and with an inventory of chemical agents and precursors; he also received assurances from the Deputy Prime Minister that Iraq would continue its cooperation with UNSCOM without time-limits. The Executive Chairman also drew attention to the fact that Iraq's disclosure of its biological weapons programme had given rise to new issues relating to the destruction, removal or rendering harmless of weapons, stocks of agents, subsystems and components, as well as research, development, support and manufacturing facilities. The Deputy Prime Minister recognized that some destruction might be necessary, but appealed for a deferral for as long as possible. At a 12 December meeting with the Executive Chairman, the Deputy Prime Minister reiterated his August statement that all proscribed weapons in Iraq had been destroyed, and invited an expert team to Baghdad to investigate issues of concern to the Commission. The Chairman agreed to send a team of missile experts as soon as the necessary expertise and information could be assembled.

The report further noted that on 16 November Iraq had submitted a new FFCD on its missile activities, which, *inter alia*, reversed its assertion that the large radar destroyed by UNSCOM in 1994 had not been used in proscribed activities. Iraq also admitted to the production of some 80 major subsystems of Scud-type engines, all of which were claimed to have been disposed of or destroyed, and of 120 indigenous warheads, with no evidence supporting that number. A preliminary review of the declaration revealed inconsistencies with information available from other sources, as well as significant gaps in Iraq's accounting for missile guidance and control systems, liquid propellant fuels and ground support equipment. Iraq also admitted to having conducted a covert programme to develop and produce a surface-to-surface missile after the adoption of resolution 687(1991). Therefore, the Commission stated that it continued to believe that additional important documents were being withheld. In the meantime, it launched an investigation into Iraq's recent acquisition efforts, following the interception by Jordan of a large shipment of high-grade missile components destined for Iraq, and, between 9 and 15 December, carried out a regular research and development update inspection.

On 5 November, Iraq also submitted a draft FFCD of chemical weapons, acknowledging the production of 1.8 tonnes of VX agent in 1988 and 1.5 tonnes in 1990, compared with its earlier declarations that only 260 kilogrammes had been produced in 1988. It further admitted its 1988 plans to relocate the production of chemical precursors to civilian chemical factories, and agreed to supplement the draft FFCD with supporting documentation, as discussed at technical talks in Baghdad from 29 November to 2 December. Among other developments in the chemical area were the first night-time inspection of a chemical site and initial testing with temporary mobile monitoring cameras.

Along with the draft FFCD on chemical weapons, Iraq submitted a draft declaration in the biological area, largely supporting its admissions made since August. Nevertheless, the draft contained serious gaps and omissions relating to biological warfare-agent and munition production, munition filling and destruction of weaponized and bulk agents. Some information did not coincide with the Commission's current findings in a number of important aspects, and definite figures were absent on amounts of biological weapons agents and munitions produced, weaponized and destroyed. In the meantime, an UNSCOM mission identified equipment, material and facilities subject to destruction, removal or being rendered harmless in line with resolution 687(1991).

Another important development was the acknowledgement by Iraq of a programme related to radiological weapons. According to Iraq's statements, an experiment involving the explosion of several containers with irradiated zirconium oxide had been conducted in 1987 at a chemical-weapons test site, ostensibly to study the military effectiveness of using irradiated materials. Although Iraq

initially claimed that only a few kilogrammes of zirconium oxide had been irradiated in the research reactor in Tuwaitha and that no special weapons system had been created, it subsequently admitted to having modified 100 empty casings of aerial chemical bombs for the purpose of radiological weapons. Additional information obtained on 4 December revealed the production of three prototype radiological bombs with a gross weight of 1,400 kg and a radioactive content of some 2 curies, all of which had been exploded at test sites. It was also disclosed that a bomb with an alternative design had been developed to fit in the aircraft bomb bay, and 80 casings for such bombs had been prepared. Iraq stated that a comprehensive account of the programme would be included in the nuclear FFCD to IAEA.

**Communication (November).** In a 6 November letter,[54] the Foreign Minister of Iraq again raised the issue of UNSCOM's use of a U2 "spy" plane, which Iraq had been protesting since UNSCOM's 1991 decision to do so. Iraq stated that the paths followed by the aircraft during its overflights indicated that the targets chosen had been dictated by the intelligence requirements of the United States. In that regard, Iraq reiterated its request that Iraqi aircraft be used in the Commission's work, to exclude any possibility of foreign aircraft being used for purposes prejudicial to its sovereignty and security.

### Organizational and financial aspects

The seventh report on OMV[49] stated that UNSCOM was in the process of creating a customized database in New York to support the export/import mechanism. Preparations to support the mechanism had also been made at BMVC.

The Commission reported that its work was complicated by the lack of secure long-term funding. Whereas UNSCOM estimated requirements from its inception to 31 December 1995 at $104,620,704, only $91,595,500 had been made available for its operations, resulting in a deficit of $13,025,204 as at 31 March.

The eighth report on OMV[50] stated that the financial situation had become more precarious than ever, with no funds identified as at October 1995 to meet the 1996 requirements, estimated at some $20 million. Also, the office space situation in New York had worsened, with the recruitment of additional experts to cope with the growing workload and the arrival of the documents obtained in Iraq in August.

The tenth report on UNSCOM activities[53] noted that the Commission continued to receive contributions in kind, including the secondment of experts and other personnel; donation of vehicles, laboratories, computers, monitoring cameras and detection and communications equipment;

and provision of air support and ground facilities in Bahrain. Donors included all members of the European Union and Australia, New Zealand, the Russian Federation, Switzerland, the United States and some Latin American countries. The report pointed to Germany's decision to reduce the number of aircraft stationed in both Bahrain and Iraq, which, in UNSCOM's view, would deal a serious blow to its and IAEA's operations in Iraq.

### Export/import-monitoring mechanism

During 1995, UNSCOM and IAEA, in coordination with the UN Sanctions Committee, finalized the development of an export/import mechanism called for in Security Council resolution 715(1991) to monitor any future sale or supply to Iraq of items relevant to the implementation of resolutions 687(1991) and 707(1991) and of OMV plans. In December, the mechanism was submitted for Council approval.

On 17 March, the Secretary-General transmitted[55] a note from the UNSCOM Executive Chairman, stating that the development of the mechanism had necessitated revision of annexes to the OMV plan, listing items to be reported by exporting countries to UNSCOM and IAEA, for the purpose of defining precisely items subject to notification. In accordance with the procedure established under resolution 715(1991), the Executive Chairman submitted the revised annexes related to chemical, biological and missile items to the Council and said he intended to notify Iraq of the changes 30 days thereafter. The revised annex 3 to the IAEA OMV plan, listing nuclear programme-related items to be reported to the Agency,[56] was communicated to the Council by the IAEA Director General.

**Action by UNSCOM and IAEA.** A third seminar of export-control experts, held in New York in January 1995, reviewed final drafts of item lists, considered draft notification forms to be completed by Governments pursuant to the mechanism and discussed its practical implementation. On 15 February, UNSCOM and IAEA resubmitted their joint proposal concerning the mechanism to the Sanctions Committee, further to their initial proposal submitted in 1994.[57]

The mechanism envisaged the creation of an UNSCOM/IAEA Joint Unit, to be represented by customs experts and data-entry clerks in New York and at BMVC and responsible for receiving and processing notifications provided by Iraq and exporting Governments, inspecting notified items on their arrival in Iraq, and undertaking no-notice inspections at points of entry into Iraq and other sites to verify that all notifiable items were being declared. Studies indicated that the number of shipments of dual-use goods would not exceed 2,000 during a normal year.

In response to the Sanctions Committee's request, the Executive Chairman, on 17 July, set out modalities for implementing the mechanism, requesting that they be included with the tripartite proposal on the mechanism forwarded to the Security Council, once approved by the Committee. The Chairman explained that an office of export/import specialists, to be established at BMVC, would serve as an administrative clearing-house for communications from Iraq regarding notification forms, as well as conduct inspections within Iraq, in cooperation with BMVC monitoring teams. Those inspections were to take place not only at declared end-user sites where notified items would be tagged, but also anywhere else in Iraq, including points of entry, where there was reason to believe that notified items or dual-use items subject to notification could be found.

**Sanctions Committee action.** On 20 July, the Sanctions Committee approved the joint UNSCOM/IAEA proposal for the export/import mechanism, deciding that it should be accompanied by the 17 July letter from the Executive Chairman setting out implementation modalities. However, formal transmission to the Security Council was postponed, pending indications of concurrence from the Governments of all Committee members.

By a 7 December letter,[58] the Sanctions Committee Chairman transmitted to the Security Council, for its approval, the proposed provisions for the export/import-monitoring mechanism, including its objective, scope and characteristics, as well as special cases falling under the mechanism.

### Kuwaiti property and missing persons

In a 9 January letter,[59] Kuwait drew the attention of the Security Council President to Iraq's remaining obligations related to the release of Kuwaiti and third-country prisoners and detainees in Iraq, as well as the return of property seized during Iraq's invasion and occupation of Kuwait. Kuwait claimed that Iraq had not responded to some 600 individual files delivered to it through ICRC, and that it had in its possession almost 200 Kuwaiti armoured vehicles, a missile system and other equipment, in addition to official documents and property stolen from the private sector, with a value of hundreds of millions of dollars. In that regard, Kuwait urged Security Council members to continue their efforts to compel Iraq to fulfil its obligations relating to those issues.

On 13 January, Kuwait transmitted[60] a list of its military equipment that it claimed was still in Iraq's possession. Kuwait stated its non-acceptance of compensation as an alternative to the immediate return of equipment, but affirmed its right to compensation for the equipment determined on its return to be unserviceable. Kuwait, in a 6 March communication,[61] reiterated its request for the return of property, and informed the Council President that positive results had not been obtained from recent meetings on Kuwaiti and third-country prisoners and hostages, held by the tripartite committee—comprising representatives of Iraq, the coalition States (France, Kuwait, Saudi Arabia, the United Kingdom and the United States) and ICRC as Chairman—and its technical subcommittee.

On 9 March, Iraq replied[62] that Kuwait's allegations were unsubstantiated, stating that the tripartite committee had considered the question of "missing persons" rather than "prisoners and hostages". It also noted that additional information on those persons was currently pending from Kuwait, and accused the Kuwaiti side of politicizing the matter. Iraq further stated that it had already returned large amounts of Kuwaiti property and that Kuwait's most recent list of items had been subjected to careful examination.

According to the Secretary-General's August report on the work of the Organization,[19] the hand-over of property to Kuwait began on 22 April and continued into July. In many instances, however, Kuwait complained of the state of disrepair of the items returned, while Iraq contended that the vehicles had been "brought as is from Kuwait". Kuwait also noted that of the 120 armoured personnel carriers handed over, only 33 were found to belong to Kuwait. The Secretary-General further stated that he had urged Iraq to cooperate with ICRC in achieving a full accounting for more than 600 Kuwaiti and third-country nationals still missing in Iraq.

On 3 May, Kuwait alleged[63] that Iraq persisted in its refusal to allow ICRC visits to Iraqi prisons; that its replies on certain files forwarded to it by ICRC had been inadequate; and that its participation in meetings of the tripartite committee and its technical subcommittee served only the purpose of creating a false impression of cooperation, which cast doubt on the utility of holding such meetings. In a similar vein, Kuwait questioned the seriousness of Iraq in dealing with the issue of property. In its 25 May reply,[64] Iraq refuted Kuwait's allegations, claiming that some 230 files on missing Kuwaitis and third-country nationals had been processed since the beginning of investigations in June 1994, with the technical subcommittee having processed 168 dossiers since December 1994. As a result, Kuwaiti authorities had closed four cases and the remains of one Kuwaiti had been returned to his relatives. For its part, Iraq accused Kuwait of withholding technical cooperation from Iraqi authorities.

In a 6 July letter,[65] Kuwait called Iraq's statements untrue, asserting that the number of dossiers processed by Iraq did not exceed 23, and that the information provided to Kuwait had been general and imprecise. No Kuwaiti prisoner, it went on, had been released in the past four years, and the property cited in earlier communications had not been returned. On 16 July, Iraq responded[66] that the number of dossiers had been reduced from the 627 originally submitted to 605, noted that 36 files contained duplicate names and pertained to only 18 cases, and provided background information on three Kuwaiti nationals, two of whom were dead and one was living in Baghdad of her own free will. Iraq further accused Kuwait of politicizing the issue of missing persons, thwarting the work of the technical subcommittee and calling for an end to that body's operations on the grounds that it had failed to fulfil its mandate. As for return of property, Iraq listed 28 items of naval equipment handed over to Kuwait on 9 July, and noted that two additional items had been returned on 28 June and 10 July.

## UN Compensation Commission and Fund

The UN Compensation Commission, established in 1991[67] for the resolution and payment, through the UN Compensation Fund, of claims against Iraq for losses and damage resulting from its invasion and occupation of Kuwait, continued in 1995 to process claims for prompt settlement. During the year, the Commission's Governing Council held one special session on 19 January to elect its new President and Vice-President, and four regular sessions, all in Geneva: the sixteenth (20-22 March),[68] seventeenth (15-17 May),[69] eighteenth (9-11 October)[70] and nineteenth (11-13 December).[71]

In March, the Council considered recommendations of its panels of commissioners (review panels) on the second instalment of claims, and approved 162,720 category A claims (for departure from Iraq or Kuwait) and 811 category B claims (for serious personal injury or death). The number of claims approved in categories A, B and C (individual losses up to $100,000) had thus reached more than 220,000, with a value exceeding $870 million; all of the 95 Governments and 15 international organizations that had filed claims had received compensation awards in at least one category. However, compensation awards issued for those categories since October 1994 remained unpaid, owing to the lack of sufficient resources in the Compensation Fund.

The Governing Council also decided to accept a number of "late claims" under various categories, submitted after the expiration of the prescribed time-limits, and limited acceptance of claims in categories A, B, C and D (individual losses above $100,000) submitted after 1 January 1995. It further approved the appointment of a review panel on the claim submitted by Kuwait on behalf of the Kuwait Oil Company for the cost of extinguishing some 700 oil-well fires in 1991, and reviewed the progress in processing the consolidated claim by Egypt, on behalf of some 900,000 workers who had been in Iraq prior to 2 August 1990, deciding to extend the jurisdictional phase for that claim until 10 July 1995.

In May, the Governing Council approved 132,080 category A claims (third instalment) from 16 countries, totalling $517,650,500 (decision 29); decided not to accept claims in category E (corporate claims) from corporations and other entities and claims in category F (government claims) from Governments and international organizations after 1 January 1996, except as otherwise provided in its decision 12[72] or for reasons of civil disorder (decision 30); took note of reports from Governments on the distribution of payments to claimants, pursuant to its decision 18;[73] examined claims in categories A, B, C and D filed after 1 January 1995, and accepted those from Bangladesh, Canada, Jordan, the Syrian Arab Republic and Turkey as having satisfied the criteria of "strong and compelling reasons" for accepting late submission; and noted with concern that actual payment from the Compensation Fund had thus far totalled only some $8.1 million. The Council's secretariat was asked to inform Governments that claims filed late as a result of delays attributable to Governments would not be considered after 1 September 1995.

In October, the Council approved 217,513 category A claims (fourth instalment) from 67 countries and three international organizations filing on behalf of Palestinians, totalling $771,513,000; and authorized $8.2 million in payment of outstanding compensation awards issued in the second instalment of category B claims to claimants from 41 countries and three international organizations filing Palestinian claims. It also accepted 3,087 claims in categories A, B, C and D filed after 1 January 1995, rejected 130 such claims and retained 1,349 others for further consideration. The Council further reviewed the progress in processing the Kuwaiti and Egyptian claims.

In December, the Governing Council approved 719 category B claims (third instalment) and authorized payment of compensation awards for those claims in the amount of $2.5 million, thus concluding its consideration of claims in that category. The total disbursement in category B stood at $13,460,000 for more than 4,000 claimants from 40 States and three international organizations filing Palestinian claims. The only category B claims remaining unresolved pertained to some 550 missing persons, mostly Kuwaitis, whose fate was still unknown (see above, under "Kuwaiti property and missing persons"). The Council further approved 217,520 category A claims (fifth instalment) with a value of $784,076,500, submitted by 60

Governments and three international organizations filing Palestinian claims. That brought the total of paid claims, amounting to $2.8 billion, to close to 800,000. A third decision related to further procedures for the review of claims, aimed at enhancing the efficiency of review panels and expediting the processing of claims in categories D, E and F.

The Council accepted six category E claims filed after the initial deadline as well as 271 claims in categories A to D submitted after 1 January 1995, rejecting 1,326 other late claims in those categories and retaining two claims for its next session. It also asked its Executive Secretary to request Governments, international organizations and other entities submitting claims to identify any confidential or privileged information that should be removed before claims documents were provided to third parties.

At each session, the Governing Council expressed concern over the lack of resources in the Compensation Fund. In May, October and December, it appealed for efforts to locate and transfer the proceeds from the sale of Iraqi oil and petroleum products to the escrow account (see above, under "Sanctions compliance"), with 30 per cent to be deposited in the Compensation Fund. The Council also reiterated its commitment to pursue efforts for obtaining revenues due to the Fund from the sale of the ship cargoes seized in the Persian Gulf for violating the UN oil embargo. In December, the Governing Council was informed that Kuwait had transferred $613,780 to the escrow account as revenue from the sale of illegal cargoes, of which 30 per cent would be available to the Compensation Fund.

## Other matters relating to the Iraq-Kuwait situation

### Complaints of airspace and other violations

During the year, Iran and Iraq communicated numerous complaints of violations of their airspace and of other violations allegedly committed by the military forces operating the Persian Gulf region.

On 31 January, Iran transmitted information[74] on incidents involving United States warships positioned in the Sea of Oman and the Persian Gulf, which, it said, created nuisances for Iranian aircraft and ships. Iran protested what it called illegal activities by the United States Government and asked for an end to such actions. Similar protests were communicated on 9 August[75] and 25 October.[76]

On 6 October, Iran categorically rejected[77] allegations in a special warning by the United States, which declared the area of the northern Persian Gulf unsafe for commercial shipping owing to actions of Iranian flag ships. Iran said that the measures by its naval forces referred to in the warning were aimed at maintaining the security and safety of international navigation in the region, implementing sanctions against Iraq, and preventing misuse of the Iranian flag or the use of forged documents and manifests.

On 21 November[78] and 13 December,[79] Iran alleged that aircraft of the allied forces operating in Iraq had repeatedly violated its airspace, and provided information on 19 incidents.

Iraq continued throughout 1995 to address communications to the Secretary-General, recording daily violations of its airspace by United States aircraft engaged in reconnaissance and in what Iraq termed provocative activities, including the dropping of heat flares. In separate communications, it lodged[80] strong protests against violations of its airspace by aircraft of the United States and its coalition partners, flying at low altitudes and breaking the sound barrier over Iraqi townships, and condemned[81] hostile and provocative overflights by United States and other aircraft from bases in Saudi Arabia and Kuwait, holding the Governments of those countries fully responsible for their complicity in those acts of aggression and for the physical damage they caused. Following two incidents in which formations of United States military aircraft broke the sound barrier over residential quarters, causing sonic-boom damage to glass in windows of residences and government buildings, Iraq requested[82] the Secretary-General to intervene to prevent the recurrence of such unjustified acts against civilian targets.

In a 28 March letter,[83] the Foreign Minister of Iraq stated that since March 1991 his country had been the object of acts of aggression and grave violations of its sovereignty, territorial integrity and political independence, despite the stipulations of Security Council resolution 687(1991). Iraq claimed that between March 1991 and March 1995, more than 1,000 such acts or violations had been committed by Iran and 56 by Turkey, while the United States and the United Kingdom had been engaged in ongoing aggression, using their military power to impose no-fly zones that excluded Iraqi aircraft from the northern and southern parts of the country. Those aircraft, Iraq said, had violated its airspace in the north 36,362 times between 9 May 1991 and 16 March 1995, while the number of violations in the south was even greater. Iraq said the fact that the Security Council had taken no action to address or prevent those violations constituted an alarming failure on the Council's part not only to maintain international peace and security, but also to implement the provisions of its own resolutions affirming commitment to Iraq's sovereignty.

In another series of communications, Iraq protested what it called acts of provocation by American warships and helicopters against Iraqi civilian vessels in its territorial waters, including oil and water tankers and fishing boats, as well as ships bound for Iraqi ports. These incidents, Iraq said, involved obstruction of navigation, interrogation of crews and detention of crews and vessels, the towing of vessels for inspection as well as on-the-spot searches, and escorting. On 21 August, Iraq stated[84] that a patrol flying the United States flag had carried out reconnaissance activities in its territorial waters on 7 and 8 August, and that a cruiser flying the flag of the United Kingdom had arrived in the same area on 9 August. On 20 November, Iraq informed[85] the Secretary-General that members of the crew from a United Kingdom frigate had boarded a tugboat inside Iraqi territorial waters and questioned its master. Both communications contained requests that the Secretary-General intervene to prevent the repetition of such unwarranted actions.

### Iraq-Turkey

In communications addressed to the Secretary-General or the Security Council President, Iraq protested the invasion of its territory by Turkish forces, which it said was carried out on the pretext of pursuing elements that threatened the security of Turkey. On 7 April, it stated[86] that the Turkish air force had conducted 107 sorties into Iraqi airspace between 20 and 31 March 1995, and condemned those violations of its sovereignty. It further claimed that the appearance of terrorist armed bands in its northern part, as well as in southern Turkey, was a consequence of the United States and United Kingdom military intervention in northern Iraq from Turkish territory, which had prevented it from exercising its authority in that region. In a 9 May letter,[87] Iraq alleged that repression by Turkish forces had caused thousands of Turkish Kurds to seek refuge in Iraq. In a 4 July communication,[88] Iraq described activities of Turkish forces in northern Iraq, which involved the bombardment of villages, shootings, searches of civilians and their property, forced disappearances and seizure of livestock. It claimed that the approximate strength of one brigade remained in Iraq, contrary to Turkey's statement that its forces had been withdrawn on 2 May. Iraq lodged a vehement protest against the violation of its territorial integrity and the inviolability of its civilian inhabitants and their property.

On 24 July, Turkey responded[89] that, since Iraq had not been able to exercise authority over its northern part, it could not be asked to prevent the use of its territory for the staging of cross-border terrorist attacks against Turkey. Under those circumstances, the resort by Turkey to measures which were imperative to its own security could not be regarded as a violation of Iraq's sovereignty.

*REFERENCES*

[1]YUN 1991, p. 172, SC res. 687(1991), 3 Apr. 1991. [2]Ibid., p. 183. [3]Ibid., p. 188, SC res. 707(1991), 15 Aug. 1991. [4]Ibid., p. 194, SC res. 715(1991), 11 Oct. 1991. [5]S/1995/12. [6]S/1995/400. [7]S/1995/172. [8]SC res. 661(1990), 6 Aug. 1990. [9]YUN 1991, p. 198, SC res. 700(1991), 17 June 1991. [10]S/1995/169. [11]S/1995/442. [12]S/1995/744. [13]S/1995/992. [14]YUN 1991, p. 199. [15]S/1995/234. [16]S/1995/846. [17]S/1995/495. [18]S/1995/507. [19]A/50/1. [20]YUN 1992, p. 320, SC res. 778(1992), 2 Oct. 1992. [21]YUN 1991, p. 207, SC res. 706(1991), 15 Aug. 1991. [22]Ibid., p. 209, SC res. 712(1991), 19 Sep. 1991. [23]YUN 1993, p. 406, SC res. 806(1993), 5 Feb. 1993. [24]S/1995/251. [25]S/1995/836. [26]S/1995/280. [27]S/1995/847. [28]S/1995/52. [29]S/1995/77. [30]S/1995/171. [31]S/1995/854. [32]S/1995/885. [33]S/1995/886. [34]A/49/863 & Corr.1. [35]YUN 1994, p. 464, GA res. 48/242, 5 Apr. 1994. [36]A/49/902. [37]S/1995/287. [38]S/1995/604. [39]S/1995/844. [40]S/1995/1003. [41]YUN 1992, p. 303. [42]S/1996/14. [43]YUN 1991, p. 184, SC res. 699(1991), 17 June 1991. [44]S/1995/481. [45]S/1995/1040. [46]S/1995/471. [47]A/C.5/49/58. [48]YUN 1946-47, p. 100, GA res. 22 A (I), annex, 13 Feb. 1946. [49]S/1995/284. [50]S/1995/864. [51]S/1995/494. [52]YUN 1993, p. 419. [53]S/1995/1038. [54]S/1995/942. [55]S/1995/208 & Corr.1. [56]S/1995/215 & Corr.1,2. [57]YUN 1994, p. 476. [58]S/1995/1017. [59]S/1995/13. [60]S/1995/39. [61]S/1995/184. [62]S/1995/195. [63]S/1995/357. [64]S/1995/446. [65]S/1995/546. [66]S/1995/592. [67]YUN 1991, p. 196, SC res. 692(1991), 20 May 1991. [68]S/1995/285. [69]S/1995/471. [70]S/1995/903. [71]S/1995/41. [72]YUN 1992, p. 317. [73]YUN 1994, p. 478. [74]S/1995/96. [75]S/1995/680. [76]S/1995/894. [77]S/1995/852. [78]S/1995/982. [79]S/1995/1037. [80]S/1995/100. [81]S/1995/615. [82]S/1995/1061. [83]S/1995/254. [84]S/1995/719. [85]S/1995/974. [86]S/1995/272. [87]S/1995/379. [88]S/1995/540. [89]S/1995/605.

# Central Asia

## Tajikistan

United Nations efforts for a comprehensive settlement of the conflict in Tajikistan continued in 1995. The Secretary-General's Special Envoy for Tajikistan, Ramiro Píriz-Ballón (Uruguay), and other UN officials held frequent consultations with both the Tajik Government and its opposition, as well as with other Governments concerned. The negotiation process between the two sides included high-level consultations in Moscow in April, summit meetings between the leaders of the parties in Kabul, Afghanistan, in May and in Tehran, Iran, in July, the fourth round of inter-Tajik talks in Almaty, Kazakstan, in May/June, indirect talks between the two leaders in August, and the first phase of the continuous round of inter-Tajik negotiations in Ashkhabad, Turkmenistan, in November/December. In August, the two sides signed a protocol on fundamental principles for establishing peace and national accord in Tajikistan, in which they decided to begin continuous negotiations on a general peace agreement, to consist of several separate protocols.

The validity of the Agreement on a Temporary Cease-fire and the Cessation of Other Hostile Acts on the Tajik-Afghan Border and within the Country for the Duration of the Talks (the Tehran Agreement) of 17 September 1994[1] was extended several times, the last time until 26 February 1996, and its text was amended. The UN Mission of Observers in Tajikistan (UNMOT), established in 1994,[2] continued to assist the Joint Commission of the Tajik parties, set up under the Agreement to monitor its implementation, in investigating cease-fire violations and in fulfilling other tasks under its mandate. During the year, the Mission reached its full authorized strength of 40 military observers, but suffered one fatality in September. It maintained liaison with the Collective Peace-keeping Forces of the Commonwealth of Independent States (CIS) in Tajikistan, whose length of stay was extended until 31 December 1995, as well as with the office of the Organization for Security and Cooperation in Europe (OSCE), and provided coordination for humanitarian assistance to the country. Brigadier-General Hasan Abaza (Jordan) continued as Chief Military Observer, while Darko Silovic (Croatia) in March replaced Liviu Bota (Romania) as Deputy Special Envoy and Head of Mission. The Security Council extended the Mission's presence in Tajikistan on several occasions; it renewed its mandate in June and again in December, until 15 June 1996.

### Continued negotiations

**Communications (January).** The Ministry of Foreign Affairs of Afghanistan issued a 6 January note[3] concerning violations of its airspace by war-planes belonging to the Russian Federation's border forces and the bombardment of villages on the Afghan side of the Tajik-Afghan border. The Ministry conveyed its strong protest to the Tajik authorities and once again rejected allegations of the use by the Tajik opposition of Afghan territory to conduct attacks on Russian border forces stationed in Tajikistan. In the letter of transmittal, Afghanistan expressed its continuing belief that the Security Council's endorsement of the stationing of Russian armed forces in Tajikistan was not a healthy course of action, and that national reconciliation in Tajikistan could not be achieved without the creation of a favourable political atmosphere and conditions for the voluntary repatriation of Tajik refugees.

In a 3 January statement[4] concerning the latest developments on the Tajik-Afghan border, the Ministry of Foreign Affairs of Tajikistan cited what it saw as continuing attempts to cross the border illegally, incessant shelling of Russian border troops and other hostile acts perpetrated by detachments of the Tajik opposition. It described an incident that had occurred on 2 January (see below). Tajikistan stated that Russian border guards were restricted to safeguarding the Tajik-Afghan border, which did not contradict the

1994 Tehran Agreement.[(1)] It also emphasized that Afghan border troops, despite assurances that they would prohibit illegal acts perpetrated from the territory of Afghanistan, appeared not to be in control of the situation. In that regard, Tajikistan lodged a protest with the leaders of Afghanistan, drawing their attention to the continuing provocations and appealing for additional steps to safeguard the Tajik-Afghan border.

**Report of the Secretary-General (February).** On 4 February, the Secretary-General reported[(5)] that a particularly serious breach of the cease-fire had occurred on 2 January when opposition fighters, apparently coming from Afghanistan, ambushed Russian border troops, nine of whom were killed and eight wounded. There were a number of reports of attempts to infiltrate Tajikistan from Afghanistan across the Pyanj River; also, UNMOT observed shelling by Russian border forces towards Afghanistan on four occasions, and the Joint Commission carried out an investigation in northern Afghanistan in response to a complaint by the opposition. Another complaint dealt with the redeployment of some 350 government troops to join the border forces, confirmed by the Tajik authorities, in violation of the 1994 Tehran Agreement. In addition, efforts continued to reconcile the mandate of the Russian border forces, which had broad powers of search and arrest, with the spirit and provisions of the Agreement.

The Secretary-General further reported that his Special Envoy, from 12 to 21 December 1994, had held consultations with senior officials of the Russian Federation, Tajikistan and Uzbekistan, during which President Rakhmonov of Tajikistan supported the idea of an early fourth round of inter-Tajik negotiations in Moscow to extend the Tehran Agreement and to achieve further progress with the opposition in securing confidence-building measures. President Rakhmonov also indicated his willingness to postpone parliamentary elections, scheduled for 26 February, in order to amend the electoral law, as recommended by OSCE, provided that opposition leaders would participate in the electoral process and recognize the election results. However, during consultations held by a UN Secretariat team with opposition leaders and high-ranking government officials in Iran from 12 to 15 January, the Tajik opposition showed no interest in participating in elections, focusing instead on complaints against the Tajik Government and the Russian border forces, alleging violations of the Tehran Agreement. It stated that it could not accept Moscow as the venue for the next round of talks, unless the Russian Federation officially recognized the Agreement, returned to the opposition weapons and ammunition seized since the Agreement's entry into force, removed new checkpoints established be-tween Khorog and Kalaikhumb, and delegated a representative of the border forces to the Russian observer team during negotiations.

Noting that the Tehran Agreement was to expire on 6 February 1995, the Secretary-General referred to communications he had received on 25 and 27 January, respectively, from President Rakhmonov and from Akbar Turajonzodah, head of the Tajik opposition delegation and First Deputy Chairman of the Islamic Revival Movement of Tajikistan. President Rakhmonov stated that the Government of Tajikistan was prepared to extend the Agreement for any length of time without additional conditions, and was committed to the continuation of talks, while the Tajik opposition declared the Agreement's extension until 6 March and expressed the hope that inter-Tajik talks would continue and lead to significant progress in resolving fundamental issues on their agenda. In subsequent consultations in New York on 3 February, the opposition expressed its readiness to meet for the fourth round of talks at any time, in any capital of a CIS member other than Moscow.

At the end of January, UNMOT comprised 11 international civilian staff, 22 local staff and 22 military observers. The Mission maintained its headquarters in Dushanbe and field stations in Garm, Kurgan-Tyube and Pyanj. It was closely involved in the work of the Joint Commission and chaired its meetings. At UNMOT's suggestion, the Joint Commission met periodically with representatives of observer States, OSCE and ICRC. The Mission also continued to conduct patrols in the valley between Dushanbe and Garm, to maintain close liaison with the parties to the conflict, as well as with the CIS forces and the Russian border forces, on matters relating to the cease-fire, and to provide political liaison and coordination for humanitarian assistance to Tajikistan.

The Secretary-General noted that the Tajik Government had formally agreed to his proposals on the status of UNMOT, and that a trust fund to support the Joint Commission had been set up but to date had received no contributions. He concluded that the situation in Tajikistan remained tense and that the economic crisis there had had a serious negative impact on efforts to reach political stabilization and to complete the repatriation of refugees. However, activities of UNMOT were an important stabilizing factor, recognized by both parties to the conflict. Accordingly, he recommended that the Mission's presence be continued until 6 March 1995, on the understanding that every effort would be made during that period to obtain agreement on the holding of the next round of talks.

**UNMOT extension (February).** On 6 February, the Security Council President communicated[(6)] to the Secretary-General that Council members had noted his report and endorsed his recommendation to continue the presence of UNMOT in Tajikistan until 6 March. The Council urged the parties to reconfirm through concrete steps their commitment to resolve the conflict only through political means, and their commitment to national reconciliation and the promotion of democracy.

**Communications (February/March).** On 6 February, Tajikistan transmitted[7] a 30 January statement announcing the decision to hold elections to the Republic's Majlis-i Oli (Parliament) on 26 February and requesting the participation of foreign observers in the electoral process. Subsequently, Tajikistan announced the elections results[8] and transmitted a press release thereon by its Ministry of Foreign Affairs.[9]

On 8 February, the Russian Federation transmitted[10] a joint statement on Tajikistan, adopted on 26 January in Moscow at a meeting of the Foreign Ministers of Kyrgyzstan, the Russian Federation and Tajikistan and the Deputy Foreign Ministers of Kazakstan and Uzbekistan. Participants called on the Tajik opposition to resume talks in Moscow with the Government of Tajikistan without prior conditions. They welcomed the establishment of UNMOT, expressed support for a substantial increase in its personnel and called for the deployment of a full-scale UN peace-keeping operation on the basis of the CIS Collective Peace-keeping Forces in Tajikistan. They also appealed for an end to hostilities on the Tajik-Afghan border and for strict observance of the Tehran Agreement, expressed their intention to step up joint efforts to ensure the defence of the Tajik-Afghan portion of the CIS southern borders, and called on the Afghan authorities and military-political groups to prevent the use of Afghan territory for launching armed actions against Tajikistan. Participants further expressed their readiness to continue economic assistance to Tajikistan and appealed for international humanitarian assistance to the Tajik people.

On 10 February, meeting in Almaty, Kazakstan, those same States adopted a joint appeal, transmitted on 14 February,[11] requesting the Security Council to establish a full-fledged peace-keeping operation in Tajikistan, and declaring their willingness to make available their units in the CIS Collective Peace-keeping Forces to serve as UN peace-keeping forces at the initial stage of the operation.

**UNMOT extension (March).** In a 3 March letter,[12] the Secretary-General informed the Security Council that Under-Secretary-General Aldo Ajello had held consultations in Moscow, Dushanbe and Islamabad from 24 February to 4 March, and had achieved agreement on the extension of the Tehran Agreement until 26 April.

Accordingly, the Secretary-General recommended that UNMOT's presence in Tajikistan be continued until that date.

On 6 March, the Council President communicated[13] to the Secretary-General that Council members endorsed his recommendation and urged the parties to resolve the remaining differences in arranging the fourth round of inter-Tajik talks.

**Communications (April).** On 10 April,[14] Kazakstan lodged a vigorous protest with the authorities of Afghanistan in connection with the fire-power attack launched by detachments of the Tajik opposition from Afghan territory against Kazak, Russian and Tajik border troops, which resulted in fatalities and injuries. It called on the Afghan leaders to take measures to resolve the situation on the border and prevent similar acts by irregulars of the Tajik opposition.

On 9 April,[15] the Russian Federation, stating that attacks by opposition fighters had increased in frequency and had become particularly audacious and provocative, causing casualties among Kazak, Russian and Tajik border troops, strongly protested to the central and local authorities of Afghanistan, with whose evident connivance, it said, such attacks were made from Afghan territory. It called on Tajik opposition leaders to stop their dangerous provocations and to hold constructive negotiations with the Government of Tajikistan.

In a 13 April letter,[16] Afghanistan referred to repeated incursions into and bombing of Afghan territory by Russian war-planes stationed in Tajikistan, causing heavy casualties among civilians as well as property damage. It strongly protested to the Russian Federation and to Tajikistan against those attacks. Afghanistan stated that its attitude towards Tajik refugees in its northern part was characterized only by humanitarian intentions, and that the delay in their voluntary repatriation was attributable to the security situation in Tajikistan. In view of the described events, Afghanistan urgently expected the Special Envoy to visit Kabul.

SECURITY COUNCIL ACTION (April)

At a meeting of the Security Council on 12 April, the President made the following statement[17] on behalf of the Council:

> The Security Council expresses its deep concern at the escalation of military activities on the Tajik-Afghan border which resulted in grave loss of life. In this context, the Council reminds the parties of their obligations to ensure the safety of the Secretary-General's Special Envoy and all other United Nations personnel.
>
> The Council strongly believes that armed activities by the Tajik opposition in violation of the cease-fire Agreement of 17 September 1994 jeopardize the inter-Tajik dialogue and the process of national recon-

ciliation as a whole. Noting also recent violations of the 17 September 1994 Agreement by government forces, the Council calls on the Tajik opposition and the Government of Tajikistan to comply strictly with the obligations they have assumed under that Agreement and calls on the Tajik opposition in particular to extend it for a substantial period beyond 26 April 1995.

The Council fully supports the appeal of the Secretary-General to the Tajik parties and other countries concerned to exercise restraint, to do their utmost to continue the political dialogue and to hold the next round of talks as soon as possible. It welcomes the agreement by the Government of Tajikistan and the Tajik opposition to the proposal of the Secretary-General's Special Envoy to hold an urgent high-level meeting of their representatives in Moscow. It calls upon the countries of the region to discourage any activities that could complicate or hinder the peace process in Tajikistan.

Reaffirming its resolution 968(1994) of 16 December 1994, the Council once again urges the parties to reconfirm through concrete steps their commitment to resolve the conflict only through political means. The Council reiterates its call on the parties to hold the fourth round of the inter-Tajik talks without delay on the basis as agreed during the previous rounds of consultations.

*Meeting number.* SC 3515.

**Joint statement (April).** In April, the Special Envoy undertook new consultations with the Tajik parties and Governments in the region to clear the way for the next round of talks. As a result of his discussions in Moscow and Dushanbe and his conversation with Abdullo Nuri, Chairman of the Islamic Revival Movement of Tajikistan, by shortwave radio from Dushanbe, the parties agreed to hold high-level consultations in Moscow, without preconditions, to reach agreement on the agenda, time and venue for the fourth round of talks, as well as to extend the Tehran Agreement and prevent further escalation of fighting. The consultations were subsequently held in Moscow under UN auspices from 19 to 26 April, with the participation of Afghanistan, Iran, Kazakstan, Kyrgyzstan, Pakistan, the Russian Federation and Uzbekistan as observers.

In a joint statement on Tajikistan,[18] made on 20 April and transmitted on 26 April, Kazakstan, Kyrgyzstan, the Russian Federation, Tajikistan and Uzbekistan called on the Tajik parties to step up the negotiation process under UN auspices, welcomed the decision by Tajikistan not to make the Tehran Agreement subject to a time-limit and called on the opposition leaders to follow that example. They advocated making the work of the Joint Commission more effective and improving the mechanism for monitoring observance of the cease-fire; emphasized the important role of the CIS Collective Peace-keeping Forces and confirmed their commitment to establishing close

coordination between those Forces and UNMOT; stressed the importance of their joint appeal for deployment of a full-scale UN peace-keeping operation in Tajikistan (see above); and called on the Tajik Government to speed up the process of establishing its own armed forces and border troops.

**UNMOT extension (April).** On 26 April, the Secretary-General recommended[19] that, in the light of the continuing high-level consultations in Moscow, UNMOT should continue to function until the review by the Security Council of his report on the situation in Tajikistan, to be submitted upon the return of the Special Envoy to New York.

In a letter of the same date,[20] the Council President noted that Council members were deeply concerned about the insufficient progress at the Moscow talks and the continuing military activities on the Tajik-Afghan border. They called on the parties and others concerned to resolve urgently outstanding questions with regard to extending the cease-fire and arranging a fourth round of talks; stressed again that the primary responsibility for resolving their differences rested with the Tajik parties themselves; and urged them to comply strictly with the Tehran Agreement. Council members agreed that UNMOT should continue its presence in Tajikistan, pending a further Council decision.

**Communication (April).** On 27 April, the Russian Federation transmitted[21] a joint statement by the Government of Tajikistan and the Tajik opposition, adopted at the close of the consultations in Moscow on 26 April. The parties expressed their firm commitment to settling the conflict and achieving national reconciliation through exclusively peaceful, political means on the basis of mutual concessions and compromises, and agreed to: extend the validity of the Tehran Agreement until 26 May; hold the fourth round of inter-Tajik talks in Almaty, beginning on 22 May; and include in the agenda for the talks the questions of the constitutional structure and consolidation of the statehood of the Republic of Tajikistan, as set forth during the first round of talks in 1994.[22] The parties also agreed on additions to the text of the Tehran Agreement, extending its scope, *inter alia*, to military formations in the territory of Afghanistan, and decided to expand the Joint Commission to 14 members, 7 on each side. They confirmed their obligation to provide material and technical assistance to the Commission and appealed for international financial support for its activities. The parties welcomed the agreement between President Rakhmonov and Abdullo Nuri to meet before the fourth round of talks, and the statement by the Russian Federation that its border guards and servicemen with the CIS Forces, respecting and recognizing the agreements by the Tajik parties, were not violating them in carrying out their functions.

**Report of Secretary-General (May).** On 12 May, the Secretary-General described[23] the activities of his Special Envoy leading to the holding of consultations in Moscow, as well as their outcome. He noted that the situation in Tajikistan was marked by increasing tension due to attempts at infiltration by opposition fighters from Afghanistan and the continued presence of Tajik government troops in Gorno-Badakshan, in violation of the Tehran Agreement. UNMOT had carried out 32 investigations, either independently or together with the Joint Commission, and confirmed three violations of the Agreement, involving deployment of Tajik government troops and their participation in a training exercise of the CIS Peace-keeping Forces, as well as clashes between opposition fighters and government forces in the Garm district. Beginning on 7 April, a series of violent incidents occurred, including attacks against Russian border troops and their retaliation against targets within Afghan territory. Those hostilities caused numerous casualties on both sides.

Except for an investigation on 18 April, the Joint Commission had been inactive since late March, after the departure of three of the four opposition representatives. That had followed a decision by the opposition, later suspended, to withdraw from the Commission if the Government did not remove its 350 troops from Gorno-Badakshan and proceed with the participation of its troops in training exercises of the CIS Peace-keeping Forces. In addition, the report noted that logistic support for the Commission was inadequate, creating a serious impediment to its effective functioning. UNMOT, on the other hand, continued to maintain close liaison with the parties, as well as with the CIS Forces and Russian border forces, and to provide political liaison and coordination for humanitarian assistance to Tajikistan. In late March, the Mission established a radio link with the opposition headquarters in Taloqan in northern Afghanistan. As at 1 May, UNMOT personnel numbered 69, including 36 military observers and 33 civilian staff. The Mission opened three additional field stations, in Kalaikhumb, Khorog and Moskovskiy, for a total of six.

The Secretary-General observed that, although the results of the consultations in Moscow had provided ground for continuing UN efforts in Tajikistan and maintaining UNMOT, progress had yet to be achieved on the substantive issues dividing the parties. He appealed to the parties to comply strictly with the Tehran Agreement and to refrain from steps that could aggravate the situation or complicate the peace process, and underlined the need to strengthen the Joint Commission, calling for full cooperation with the Commission and UNMOT of the authorities and forces operating in the region.

President Rakhmonov and Abdullo Nuri, meeting in Kabul from 17 to 19 May, issued a joint declaration,[24] by which both sides confirmed their readiness to solve the inter-Tajik conflict, to repatriate all refugees to their places of origin and to stabilize fully the political situation in Tajikistan. They decided to extend the Tehran Agreement until 26 August and pledged to make every effort to resolve the conflict through political means at the negotiating table.

**SECURITY COUNCIL ACTION (May)**

On 19 May, the Security Council President made the following statement[25] on behalf of the Council:

> The Security Council has considered the report of the Secretary-General on the situation in Tajikistan of 12 May 1995.
>
> The Security Council welcomes the Joint Statement of the delegation of the Government of Tajikistan and the delegation of the Tajik opposition signed in Moscow on 26 April 1995 as a result of the high-level consultations through the good offices of the Secretary-General's Special Envoy with the assistance of the representatives of all countries acting as observers at the inter-Tajik talks. The Council expects the full implementation of the agreements reached in Moscow and, in particular, supports the convening of the fourth round of inter-Tajik talks on 22 May 1995 in Almaty and looks to the parties to cooperate fully in those talks.
>
> The Security Council commends the efforts of the Secretary-General's Special Envoy, the Russian Federation as a host country and all observer countries which significantly contributed to the positive outcome of the high-level inter-Tajik consultations held in Moscow from 19 to 26 April 1995.
>
> The Security Council is concerned over the actions of both sides in the past three months, which posed obstacles to the peace process, as noted in the report of the Secretary-General. The Council stresses the urgent need for the Tajik parties to resolve the conflict and to confirm, by taking concrete steps, their commitment to achieve national reconciliation in the country exclusively through peaceful political means on the basis of mutual concessions and compromises. In this context, it welcomes the agreement by the President of the Republic of Tajikistan and the leader of the Islamic Revival Movement of Tajikistan to hold a meeting, which took place in Kabul on 17-19 May 1995.
>
> The Security Council notes with concern the recent inactivity of the Joint Commission and is therefore encouraged by the parties' decision to strengthen the Commission and its mechanism for monitoring the Cease-fire Agreement of 17 September 1994. It welcomes the commitments by some Member States to the voluntary fund for contributions established by the Secretary-General in accordance with its resolution 968(1995), and reiterates its encouragement to other Member States to contribute.

The Security Council calls upon the parties to agree on a substantial extension of the Cease-fire Agreement of 17 September 1994 and to achieve substantive progress during the fourth round of inter-Tajik talks, in particular on fundamental institutional issues and consolidation of the statehood of Tajikistan as defined in the agenda agreed upon during the Moscow round in April 1994. It stresses that strict compliance by the parties with all the obligations they have assumed is a necessary condition for successful political dialogue.

The Security Council notes the observation of the Secretary-General contained in his report of 12 May 1995 that grounds exist for continuing United Nations efforts and maintaining the United Nations Mission of Observers in Tajikistan and recalls its view that extension of the cease-fire is necessary for this.

*Meeting number.* SC 3539.

**Communications and report (June).** On 2 June, the Russian Federation transmitted[26] a decision to extend until 31 December 1995 the stay of the Collective Peace-keeping Forces in Tajikistan, adopted by the CIS Council of Heads of State on 26 May in Minsk, Belarus.

On 10 June, the Secretary-General reported[27] on results of the fourth round of inter-Tajik talks, which took place under UN auspices in Almaty from 22 May to 1 June, with the participation of observers from Afghanistan, Iran, Kazakstan, Kyrgyzstan, Pakistan, the Russian Federation, Uzbekistan, OSCE and the Organization of the Islamic Conference. For the first time, parties had an in-depth discussion of fundamental institutional issues and the consolidation of the statehood of Tajikistan. The opposition suggested the establishment of a Council of National Accord as a supreme legislative and executive body for the transitional period of up to two years, on the basis of parity, responsible for drafting amendments to the current constitution and other legislative acts and for preparing and holding elections to a new parliament. The Government suggested a discussion of issues related to the permanent cessation of hostilities, repatriation of refugees and simultaneous release of detainees and prisoners of war, and stated its readiness to allow free activities of political parties and movements and the mass media, as well as to declare an amnesty for opposition supporters and to consider the integration of armed opposition units into Tajikistan's military structures and the appointment of opposition representatives to government posts.

The parties also discussed a number of compromise proposals presented by the Special Envoy, but were not able to reach mutually acceptable decisions. In a joint statement[28] on the results of the talks, transmitted on 5 June, they welcomed the decision to extend the Tehran Agreement until 26 August, agreed to exchange an equal number of detainees and prisoners of war by 20 July and to ensure unobstructed access of ICRC representatives and Joint Commission members to places of detention and incarceration, and set out measures to ensure the voluntary and safe return of refugees and displaced persons to their places of permanent residence. Tajikistan agreed that measures would be taken to suspend, for the duration of the inter-Tajik talks, the death sentences on opposition members and that those sentences would subsequently be reviewed. The parties requested the Special Envoy to continue his good offices in the search for a peaceful solution to the conflict.

The Secretary-General further reported that the situation in Tajikistan remained relatively calm, except in areas along the Tajik-Afghan border. UNMOT had carried out 17 investigations and confirmed two violent incidents, involving a helicopter attack on a village in Gorno-Badakshan by Russian border forces, as well as an attack by government troops on a village south of Garm, causing one death and two injuries, which had followed an attack against a government defence post that had resulted in five fatalities. UNMOT also confirmed a helicopter attack on a village in northern Afghanistan, causing up to 20 civilian casualties, but was unable to verify those responsible for it. At the same time, reports continued of infiltration attempts across the border in the Pyanj and Moskovskiy areas, as well as of rocket attacks against border posts from Afghan territory; Russian border troops responded to the infiltration attempts by shelling across the border.

The Joint Commission focused its activities on monitoring the cease-fire and investigating its violation, but was not able to assume the political responsibilities envisaged under the Tehran Agreement, and support to Commission activities remained inadequate. UNMOT continued to carry out the tasks under its mandate; as at 1 June, its personnel included 39 observers and 33 civilian staff. Outstanding assessed contributions from Member States to its Special Account totalled $2.2 million as at 31 May.

**UNMOT extension (June).** The Secretary-General noted that the Mission had been recognized by the Tajik parties as playing an instrumental role in containing the conflict and recommended that its mandate be extended until 16 December. He also recommended that the Security Council approve in principle a proposal for expanding the UNMOT deployment to northern Afghanistan, subject to the agreement of Afghan authorities.

**SECURITY COUNCIL ACTION (June)**

On 16 June, the Security Council adopted **resolution 999(1995)**.

*The Security Council,*

*Recalling* its resolution 968(1994) of 16 December 1994 and the statements of the President of the Security Council of 30 October 1992, of 23 August 1993, of 22

September 1994, of 8 November 1994, of 12 April 1995 and of 19 May 1995,

*Having considered* the report of the Secretary-General of 10 June 1995,

*Reaffirming* its commitment to the sovereignty and territorial integrity of the Republic of Tajikistan and to the inviolability of its borders,

*Welcoming* the positive outcome of the meeting between the President of the Republic of Tajikistan and of the leader of the Islamic Revival Movement of Tajikistan held in Kabul from 17 to 19 May 1995 and of the fourth round of the inter-Tajik talks held in Almaty from 22 May to 1 June 1995,

*Welcoming also*, in particular, the extension for the period of three months, until 26 August 1995, of the Agreement on a Temporary Cease-fire and the Cessation of Other Hostile Acts on the Tajik-Afghan Border and within the Country for the Duration of the Talks, signed in Tehran on 17 September 1994, as well as the agreements on further confidence-building measures,

*Noting with appreciation* that the parties started in-depth discussions on fundamental institutional issues and consolidation of the statehood of Tajikistan and confirmed their readiness to search for practical solutions to the above-mentioned problems,

*Commending* the efforts of the Secretary-General and his Special Envoy as well as of the countries and regional organizations acting as observers at the inter-Tajik talks which contributed to reaching these agreements,

*Emphasizing* that the primary responsibility rests with the Tajik parties themselves in resolving their differences, and that the international assistance provided by this resolution must be linked to the process of national reconciliation and the promotion of democracy,

*Recalling* that the Tajik parties have reaffirmed their commitment to resolve the conflict and to achieve national reconciliation in the country exclusively through peaceful, political means on the basis of mutual concessions and compromises, and urging them to take concrete steps to this end,

*Stressing* the urgency of the cessation of all hostile acts on the Tajik-Afghan border,

*Noting* the decision of the Council of the Heads of State of the Commonwealth of Independent States (CIS) of 26 May 1995 to extend the mandate of the CIS Collective Peace-keeping Forces in Tajikistan until 31 December 1995,

*Recalling* the joint appeal by the Presidents of the Republic of Kazakstan, the Kyrgyz Republic, the Russian Federation, the Republic of Tajikistan and the Republic of Uzbekistan of 10 February 1995 addressed to the President of the Security Council, the statements of Ministers for Foreign Affairs of these countries of 24 August and of 30 September 1993, of 13 October 1994, of 26 January and 20 April 1995 addressed to the Secretary-General,

*Taking note with appreciation* of the statement of the Ministry of Foreign Affairs of the Russian Federation of 26 April 1995 that the Russian border forces and the Russian military personnel of the CIS Collective Peace-keeping Forces stationed in Tajikistan, respecting and recognizing the agreements between the Tajik parties, do not violate them in the performance of their duties,

*Expressing its satisfaction* over the close contacts of the United Nations Mission of Observers in Tajikistan (UNMOT) with the parties to the conflict, as well as over its close liaison with the CIS Collective Peace-keeping Forces, with the border forces, and with the Mission of the Organization for Security and Cooperation in Europe (OSCE) in Tajikistan,

1. *Welcomes* the report of the Secretary-General of 10 June 1995;

2. *Decides* to extend the mandate of UNMOT until 15 December 1995 subject to the proviso that the Agreement of 17 September 1994 remains in force and the parties continue to be committed to an effective cease-fire, to national reconciliation and to the promotion of democracy and further decides that the mandate will remain in effect unless the Secretary-General reports that these conditions have not been met;

3. *Requests* the Secretary-General to continue to pursue through the good offices of his Special Envoy and with the assistance of the countries and regional organizations acting as observers at the inter-Tajik talks, efforts to speed up the progress towards national reconciliation;

4. *Requests also* the Secretary-General to report to the Council every three months on the progress towards national reconciliation and on the operations of UNMOT;

5. *Reiterates* its call upon the parties to cooperate fully with UNMOT, and to ensure safety and freedom of movement of United Nations personnel;

6. *Stresses* the urgent need for the parties to achieve a comprehensive political settlement of the conflict through the inter-Tajik dialogue and to cooperate fully with the Secretary-General's Special Envoy in this regard;

7. *Calls upon* the parties, in particular, to achieve as soon as possible substantive progress on fundamental institutional and political issues;

8. *Calls upon* the parties to agree to the early convening of a further round of inter-Tajik talks and to implement without delay all confidence-building measures agreed at the fourth round of these talks, *inter alia*, on the exchange of detainees and prisoners of war and on intensification of the efforts by the parties to ensure the voluntary return, in dignity and safety, of all refugees and displaced persons to their homes;

9. *Encourages* the continuation of direct political dialogue between the President of the Republic of Tajikistan and the leader of the Islamic Revival Movement of Tajikistan;

10. *Emphasizes* the absolute necessity for the parties to comply fully with all the obligations they have assumed and urges them, in particular, to observe strictly the Agreement of 17 September 1994 and to agree to its substantial extension;

11. *Stresses* the urgency of the cessation of all hostile acts on the Tajik-Afghan border and calls upon all States and others concerned to discourage any activities that could complicate or hinder the peace process in Tajikistan;

12. *Requests* the Secretary-General to report to the Council on his discussions with relevant Afghan authorities regarding a possible deployment of a small number of United Nations personnel in northern Afghanistan and expresses its willingness to consider a relevant recommendation of the Secretary-General in the context of the implementation of this resolution;

13. *Underlines* the need to pursue the close cooperation already existing between UNMOT and the parties to the conflict, as well as its close liaison with the CIS

Collective Peace-keeping Forces, with the border forces and with the OSCE Mission in Tajikistan;

14. *Welcomes* the obligation assumed by the Government of the Republic of Tajikistan to assist the return and the reintegration of refugees as well as the obligations by the parties to cooperate in ensuring the voluntary return, in dignity and safety, of all refugees and displaced persons to their homes, *inter alia* by stepping up the activities of the Joint Commission on problems relating to refugees and displaced persons from Tajikistan formed by the parties in accordance with the Protocol signed on 19 April 1994, and in this context notes the request by the parties addressed to international organizations and States to provide additional substantial financial and material support to the refugees and internally displaced persons and to the Joint Commission on refugees;

15. *Welcomes* the commitment of some Member States to the voluntary fund for contributions established by the Secretary-General in accordance with its resolution 968(1995) and reiterates its encouragement to other States to contribute thereto;

16. *Welcomes also* the humanitarian assistance already provided and calls for greater contributions from States for humanitarian relief efforts of the United Nations and other international organizations;

17. *Decides* to remain actively seized of the matter.

Security Council resolution 999(1995)

16 June 1995     Meeting 3544     Adopted unanimously

Draft prepared in consultations among Council members (S/1995/486).

### New Protocol signed

On 23 July, Iran informed[29] the Secretary-General of a meeting between President Rakhmonov and Abdullo Nuri in Tehran on 19 July. The two sides signed a declaration confirming their readiness to take measures for the comprehensive implementation of the agreements that had been reached before and for the continuation of peaceful negotiations. They also agreed to establish a consultative forum of Tajik people to facilitate a solution to the political and social crisis in Tajikistan, and decided that modalities of the forum would be worked out during a fifth round of talks.

Indirect talks between President Rakhmonov and Mr. Nuri were arranged from 2 to 17 August through the good offices of the Special Envoy, which required him to shuttle between Dushanbe and Kabul four times. As a result, the two sides signed a Protocol on the fundamental principles for establishing peace and national accord in Tajikistan,[30] by which they agreed to conduct a continual round of negotiations, beginning on 18 September, aimed at concluding a general agreement on the establishment of peace and national accord. The general agreement was to consist of separate protocols on political problems; military problems; repatriation and reintegration of refugees; a monitoring and verification commission; guarantees for the agreement's implementation;

and a donor conference for financing reintegration and economic reconstruction programmes. The Government assumed the obligation to refrain from carrying out any acts that would run counter to the provisions of the protocols and from adopting laws or measures that might be incompatible with those protocols, while the opposition undertook to wage a political struggle by exclusively peaceful means, in accordance with Tajik laws and in conformity with the general agreement. The two sides also decided to extend the Tehran Agreement until 26 February 1996.

**SECURITY COUNCIL ACTION (August)**

On 25 August, the Security Council President made the following statement[31] on behalf of the Council:

The Security Council welcomes the Protocol on the fundamental principles for establishing peace and national accord in Tajikistan signed by the President of the Republic of Tajikistan and the leader of the Tajik opposition on 17 August 1995. It commends the efforts of the Secretary-General's Special Envoy and all countries acting as observers at the inter-Tajik talks, which have significantly contributed to reaching the above agreement between the Tajik parties.

The Security Council calls upon the parties to implement fully the commitments contained in the Protocol. It supports the agreement of the parties to conduct the continual round of talks due to begin on 18 September 1995, with the aim of concluding a general agreement on the establishment of peace and national accord in Tajikistan and urges the parties to agree as soon as possible on the venue of the negotiations. It reiterates that the primary responsibility rests with the Tajik parties themselves in resolving their differences.

The Security Council welcomes the agreement reached by the parties to extend the Agreement on a Temporary Cease-fire and the Cessation of Other Hostile Acts on the Tajik-Afghan Border and within the Country signed in Teheran on 17 September 1994 for a period of six months until 26 February 1996, and calls upon the parties to comply strictly with the obligations assumed under this agreement, including cessation of all hostile acts on the Tajik-Afghan border and within Tajikistan. The Council calls upon all States and others concerned to discourage any activities that could complicate or hinder the peace process respecting fully the sovereignty and the territorial integrity of Tajikistan and the inviolability of the Tajik-Afghan border.

The Security Council urges the parties to implement as quickly as possible the confidence-building measures agreed upon during the fourth round of inter-Tajik talks held in Almaty.

The Security Council stresses the need to continue the existing close contacts of the United Nations Mission of Observers in Tajikistan with the parties to the conflict as well as its close liaison with the CIS Collective Peace-keeping Forces, with the Russian border forces and with the OSCE Mission in Tajikistan.

The Security Council welcomes the contributions by some Member States to the voluntary fund for contributions established by the Secretary-General in accordance with its resolution 968(1994), and reiterates its encouragement to other Member States to contribute thereto.

The Security Council expresses its readiness to consider in due course the recommendations of the Secretary-General regarding the possible role of the United Nations in the context of the present and future agreements between the Tajik parties.

*Meeting number.* SC 3570.

### Further talks

**Report of Secretary-General (September).** On 16 September, the Secretary-General reported[32] on the outcome of the indirect talks and noted that his Special Envoy was engaged in consultations with the parties and others concerned to decide on a possible venue for negotiations. He also noted that the situation in Tajikistan remained relatively stable. UNMOT and the Joint Commission had received 61 complaints of cease-fire violations, dealing mainly with cross-border infiltration of opposition fighters, as well as with the detention of persons without charge and their treatment while in detention. Credible reports were received of redeployments of military units by both the Government and the opposition. Russian border forces continued occasional shelling across the border into Afghanistan; on two occasions, a border post in the Moskovskiy district had been attacked by rocket fire from Afghan territory, resulting in casualties. Other incidents involved a series of killings and clashes between local armed groups and government security forces in the Garm district, and exchanges of fire between Russian border troops and self-defence forces and between two brigades of the Tajik army.

The Joint Commission had been expanded to 14 members, including four permanently located in Gorno-Badakshan, two in Khorog and two in Vanj; however, its activities continued to be hampered by lack of office space and logistic support. UNMOT personnel numbered 87 as at 31 August, including its full complement of 40 military observers. The Mission established an additional team site in Vanj and secured agreement of the Afghan officials for a small liaison post in Taloqan. In that regard, the Secretary-General proposed that the Security Council authorize the establishment of the liaison post, once the modalities were agreed upon with the Afghan authorities, and expressed his intention to seek the necessary budgetary authority for a small increase in UNMOT staff in the light of the establishment of posts in Vanj and Taloqan. He noted with concern the delays in implementation of the confidence-building measures agreed upon during the fourth round of talks, and appealed to the parties to take steps for their early implementation, emphasizing that further inaction could undermine the credibility of the whole negotiating process.

**Further developments (October/November).** Following consultations in Dushanbe and Taloqan in October, by Assistant Secretary-General for Peace-keeping Operations Iqbal Riza and Deputy Special Envoy Darko Silovic, and a visit by the deputy leader of the Tajik opposition to Ashkhabad (Ashgabat) between 30 October and 2 November, the parties agreed in principle on Ashkhabad as the venue of negotiations, deciding they should begin on 30 November.

#### SECURITY COUNCIL ACTION (November)

On 6 November, the Security Council President made the following statement[33] on behalf of the Council:

> The Security Council welcomes the planned convening of the continual round of inter-Tajik talks in Ashgabat. It commends the efforts of the President of Turkmenistan in this regard.
>
> The Security Council calls upon the Tajik parties to begin as a matter of urgency the continual round of talks with the aim of concluding a general agreement in accordance with the provisions of the Protocol on the fundamental principles for establishing peace and national accord in Tajikistan signed by the President of the Republic of Tajikistan and the leader of the Tajik opposition on 17 August 1995.
>
> The Security Council expresses the hope that the Secretary-General's Special Envoy will be able to resume promptly his efforts with regard to the preparation of the forthcoming round of talks. The Council reaffirms its full support for the activities of the Special Envoy.
>
> The Security Council urges the Tajik parties to comply strictly with the obligations assumed under the Agreement on a Temporary Cease-fire and the Cessation of Other Hostile Acts on the Tajik-Afghan Border and within the Country signed in Tehran on 17 September 1994. The Council expresses the hope that the convening of the talks will contribute to a lessening of tensions along the Tajik-Afghan border and inside Tajikistan.
>
> The Security Council notes that the relevant Afghan authorities have given their agreement to the establishment of a liaison post of UNMOT in Taloqan (northern Afghanistan). The Council welcomes this development and agrees with the proposal to establish such a post as suggested in paragraph 20 of the Secretary-General's report of 16 September 1995 with the privileges and immunities necessary for the security of the United Nations personnel concerned and for their ability to carry out the mandate.
>
> The Security Council also notes the Secretary-General's observations regarding the strengthening of UNMOT in paragraph 21 of his report. The Council supports a corresponding increase in the Mission's strength.

*Meeting number.* SC 3589.

**Communications and report (November/December).** On 13 November, the Secretary-General communicated[34] to the Security Council his decision to extend the mandate of the Special Envoy until 26 March 1996. On 15 November, the Council President informed[35] the Secretary-General that Council members had taken note of the decision.

In an 8 December report,[36] the Secretary-General informed the Council of the beginning of inter-Tajik negotiations, stating that, at the first working plenary session on 7 December, both parties had confirmed their commitment to the cease-fire and their determination to work to find viable solutions to the problems listed in the 17 August Protocol. He further noted that the delay in resuming the negotiations had been accompanied by an increase in hostilities in Gorno-Badakshan and in the areas of Garm and Tavildara, involving attacks against government installations and personnel, as well as against State police and internal security forces, clashes between government troops and opposition fighters, and friction between Russian border troops and the so-called "self-defence forces". In addition, the conflict between two brigades of the Tajik army in the Kurgan-Tyube area had culminated in a military confrontation, in the course of which a UN military observer was shot and killed on 18 September. The brigades had since been redeployed and the Tajik authorities assured UNMOT that the trial of those responsible for the observer's death would take place in the near future.

A serious incident also occurred on 10 October, when nine soldiers of the Russian border forces were killed and their truck burnt. On 21 October, an opposition fighter was killed at a checkpoint by Russian border troops. On a number of occasions, border forces fired into Afghanistan; they continued to report infiltration attempts and rocket attacks against their posts. UNMOT and the Joint Commission had received 79 complaints of alleged cease-fire violations, carried out 31 investigations and confirmed six violations, four by the Government and two by the opposition. As for the Tehran Agreement provisions pertaining to the security and rights of individuals, the opposition filed numerous complaints regarding abductions, arrests, unlawful detention, long and illegal imprisonment, denial of the right to defence or communication, and murder, whereas the Government submitted 33 reports of murder, rape, harassment, abuse, beatings, hostage-taking and threats.

UNMOT continued to carry out its mandated tasks, although sporadic fighting compelled it to close temporarily two of its team sites. The functioning of the Joint Commission had been adversely affected by the delay in negotiations and the rising tension between the parties, as well as by a lack of office space, logistic support and security for its opposition members; its activities included, *inter alia*, two rounds of talks under ICRC auspices on the issue of prisoners of war, an initial press conference, held on 21 November, and a special broadcast on Tajik television on 22 November. As for the humanitarian situation, the Secretary-General pointed out that most refugees and internally displaced persons in Tajikistan had been successfully resettled, and that the Office of the UN High Commissioner for Refugees was scaling down its operations and handing over certain programmes and activities to other agencies.

Noting that the parties had resumed negotiations on the basis of the 17 August Protocol, he recommended that the UNMOT mandate be extended for another six months, and estimated the cost for maintaining the Mission for that period at $4,304,400 gross. He also noted that outstanding contributions from Member States totalled $1,168,930 as at 30 November.

## SECURITY COUNCIL ACTION (December)

On 14 December, the Security Council adopted **resolution 1030(1995)**.

*The Security Council,*

*Recalling* all its previous resolutions and the statements of its President, in particular, the statement of its President of 6 November 1995,

*Having considered* the report of the Secretary-General of 8 December 1995,

*Reaffirming* its commitment to the sovereignty and territorial integrity of the Republic of Tajikistan and to the inviolability of its borders,

*Welcoming* the beginning of the continual round of talks between the Government of Tajikistan and the Tajik opposition in Ashgabat,

*Commending* the efforts of the Secretary-General and his Special Envoy as well as of the countries and regional organizations acting as observers at the inter-Tajik talks,

*Emphasizing* that the primary responsibility rests with the Tajik parties themselves in resolving their differences, and that the international assistance provided by this resolution must be linked to the process of national reconciliation and the promotion of democracy,

*Recalling* the commitments made by the Tajik parties to resolve the conflict and to achieve national reconciliation in the country exclusively through peaceful, political means on the basis of mutual concessions and compromises and stressing the inadmissibility of any hostile acts on the Tajik-Afghan border,

*Recalling* the joint appeal by the Presidents of the Republic of Kazakstan, the Kyrgyz Republic, the Russian Federation, the Republic of Tajikistan and the Republic of Uzbekistan of 10 February 1995 addressed to the President of the Security Council, the statements of Ministers of Foreign Affairs of these countries of 24 August and 30 September 1993, of 13 October 1994, of 26 January and 20 April 1995 addressed to the Secretary-General,

*Taking note with appreciation* of the statement of the Ministry of Foreign Affairs of the Russian Federation of 26 April 1995 that the Russian border forces and the Russian military personnel of the Collective Peace-keeping

Forces of the Commonwealth of Independent States (CIS) stationed in Tajikistan, respecting and recognizing the agreements between the Tajik parties, do not violate them in the performance of their duties,

*Expressing its satisfaction* over the close contacts of the United Nations Mission of Observers in Tajikistan (UNMOT) with the parties to the conflict, as well as over its liaison with the CIS Collective Peace-keeping Forces, with the border forces and with the Mission of the Organization for Security and Cooperation in Europe (OSCE) in Tajikistan,

1. *Welcomes* the report of the Secretary-General of 8 December 1995;

2. *Decides* to extend the mandate of UNMOT until 15 June 1996 subject to the proviso that the Tehran Agreement of 17 September 1994 remains in force and the parties continue to be committed to an effective cease-fire, to national reconciliation and to the promotion of democracy and further decides that the mandate will remain in effect unless the Secretary-General reports that these conditions have not been met;

3. *Requests* the Secretary-General to continue to pursue, through the good offices of his Special Envoy and with the assistance of the countries and regional organizations acting as observers at the inter-Tajik talks, efforts to speed up the progress towards the establishment of a durable peace and national accord in Tajikistan;

4. *Requests also* the Secretary-General to report to the Council every three months on the progress towards a comprehensive political settlement of the conflict and on the operations of UNMOT;

5. *Reiterates* its call upon the parties to cooperate fully with UNMOT, and to ensure the safety and freedom of movement of United Nations personnel;

6. *Regrets* the slow rate of progress towards a political solution to the conflict in Tajikistan and emphasizes the need for the Tajik parties to take the opportunity of the continual round of talks in Ashgabat to reach a general agreement which will restore peace and national accord in their country in accordance with the provisions of the Protocol on the Fundamental Principles, signed by the President of the Republic of Tajikistan and the leader of the Islamic Revival Movement of Tajikistan on 17 August 1995;

7. *Calls upon* the parties to cooperate fully with the Secretary-General's Special Envoy in order to achieve a comprehensive political settlement of the conflict through the inter-Tajik dialogue;

8. *Calls also* on the parties to implement without delay all the confidence-building measures to which they committed themselves during the fourth round of the inter-Tajik talks;

9. *Encourages* the continuation of direct political dialogue between the President of the Republic of Tajikistan and the leader of the Islamic Revival Movement of Tajikistan;

10. *Emphasizes* the absolute necessity for the parties to comply fully with all their obligations they have assumed and urges them, in particular, to observe strictly the Tehran Agreement of 17 September 1994 and to agree to its substantial extension;

11. *Stresses* the urgency of the cessation of all hostile acts on the Tajik-Afghan border and calls upon all States and others concerned to discourage any activities that could complicate or hinder the peace process in Tajikistan;

12. *Encourages* the relevant Afghan authorities to facilitate the arrangements that will permit the establishment of a liaison post at Taloqan in northern Afghanistan;

13. *Underlines* the need to develop further close cooperation between UNMOT and the parties to the conflict, as well as its close liaison with the CIS Collective Peace-keeping Forces, with the border forces and with the OSCE Mission in Tajikistan;

14. *Welcomes* the successful resettlement of the vast majority of internally displaced persons and refugees and the role played by the Office of the United Nations High Commissioner for Refugees in this effort and commends the activities of other agencies and organizations assisting the civilian population;

15. *Welcomes* the contributions to the voluntary fund established by the Secretary-General in accordance with its resolution 968(1995), reiterates its encouragement to other States to contribute thereto and also welcomes the voluntary contribution made to UNMOT;

16. *Decides* to remain actively seized of the matter.

Security Council resolution 1030(1995)

14 December 1995     Meeting 3606     Adopted unanimously

Draft prepared in consultations among Council members (S/1995/1032).

### End-of-year developments

The first phase of the Ashkhabad talks continued until 22 December. On 13 December, the parties adopted a joint declaration in connection with the continued fighting in Tajikistan, in which they condemned the serious violations of the Tehran Agreement that had been committed since 18 August 1995; entrusted the Joint Commission and UNMOT to carry out an investigation of the most recent events in the Tavildara and Shuroabad areas; undertook to respect and observe unconditionally the Agreement's provisions; and requested UNMOT to redeploy its posts to those districts. On 17 December, an UNMOT team was stationed in Tavildara. After joint efforts by the United Nations and the Russian Federation, the fighting was halted and calm restored.

Following the institution of the cease-fire, the parties considered the main political issues dealt with in the 17 August Protocol. The Government proposed a consultative forum of Tajik peoples on the basis of equal representation, to consider the further improvement of political, economic and social reforms; its recommendations were to be adopted by consensus. The Tajik opposition, however, rejected the concept of the forum, proposing a council of national reconciliation for a transitional period of up to two years, to replace the current Parliament (Majlis-i Oli) and prepare for new parliamentary and presidential elections. After the Government rejected that suggestion, the opposition presented its own proposals on the consultative forum, which were not accepted by the other side.

The second phase of the negotiations was scheduled to resume in January 1996.

## Financing of UNMOT

**Reports of Secretary-General and ACABQ (February/March).** In a 22 February report,[37] the Secretary-General estimated the cost of maintaining UNMOT from its inception on 16 December 1994 until 30 June 1995 at $4,339,700 gross ($4,138,400 net), providing for the deployment of 40 military observers and 44 civilian staff and including start-up costs of $1.2 million. Estimated costs from 1 July 1995 to 30 June 1996 amounted to $9,033,600 gross ($8,599,200 net). The report also included additional information requested by ACABQ, concerning the type of support provided by UNMOT to the Joint Commission and related budgetary implications, as well as the nature of cooperation between UNMOT and the OSCE Mission, the CIS Peace-keeping Forces and border forces and the extent of their assistance to UNMOT.

The Secretary-General recommended establishing a special account for the Mission and the appropriation and assessment of the amounts stipulated above for the period from 16 December 1994 to 30 June 1995. He also requested commitment authorization at a monthly rate of $752,800 gross ($716,600 net) after 30 June 1995 and the assessment of such amounts, subject to the extension of the Mission's mandate. The monthly cost was higher than the estimates of $442,300, provided in November 1994,[38] and of $708,500, communicated to ACABQ on 17 January 1995, due to additional requirements for helicopter operations, communications and public information.

In a 21 March report,[39] the ACABQ recommended the appropriation and assessment of $3,251,200 gross for the period from 16 December 1994 to 26 April 1995 and the appropriation of $10,044,200 gross from 27 April 1995 to 30 June 1996, to be assessed on Member States at the rate of $717,400 gross per month.

**GENERAL ASSEMBLY ACTION (March)**

On 31 March, the General Assembly adopted **resolution 49/240.**

### Financing of the United Nations Mission of Observers in Tajikistan

*The General Assembly,*

*Having considered* the report of the Secretary-General on the financing of the United Nations Mission of Observers in Tajikistan and the related report of the Advisory Committee on Administrative and Budgetary Questions,

*Bearing in mind* Security Council resolution 968(1994) of 16 December 1994, by which the Council decided to establish the United Nations Mission of Observers in Tajikistan for a period of up to six months, subject to the proviso that it would continue beyond 6 February 1995 only if the Secretary-General reported to the Council by that date that the parties had agreed to extend the Agreement on a Temporary Cease-fire and the Ces-

sation of Other Hostile Acts on the Tajik-Afghan Border and within the Country for the Duration of the Talks, signed at Tehran on 17 September 1994, and that they remained committed to an effective cease-fire, national reconciliation and the promotion of democracy,

*Recognizing* that the costs of the Mission of Observers are expenses of the Organization to be borne by Member States in accordance with Article 17, paragraph 2, of the Charter of the United Nations,

*Recognizing also* that, in order to meet the expenditures caused by the Mission of Observers, a different procedure is required from the one applied to meet expenditures of the regular budget of the United Nations,

*Taking into account* the fact that the economically more developed countries are in a position to make relatively larger contributions and that the economically less developed countries have a relatively limited capacity to contribute towards such an operation,

*Bearing in mind* the special responsibilities of the States permanent members of the Security Council, as indicated in General Assembly resolution 1874(S-IV) of 27 June 1963 in the financing of such operations,

*Mindful* of the fact that it is essential to provide the Mission of Observers with the necessary financial resources to enable it to fulfil its responsibilities under the relevant resolutions of the Security Council,

1. *Endorses* the observations and recommendations contained in the report of the Advisory Committee on Administrative and Budgetary Questions;

2. *Requests* the Secretary-General to take all necessary action to ensure that the United Nations Mission of Observers in Tajikistan is administered with a maximum of efficiency and economy;

3. *Urges* all Member States to make every possible effort to ensure payment of their assessed contributions to the Mission of Observers in full and on time;

4. *Decides* to appropriate to the Special Account for the United Nations Mission of Observers in Tajikistan an amount of 3,251,200 United States dollars gross (3,123,600 dollars net) for the operation of the Mission of Observers from 16 December 1994 to 26 April 1995, inclusive of the amount of 1,759,700 dollars gross (1,711,800 dollars net) authorized under the terms of paragraph 1 (a) of General Assembly resolution 48/229 of 23 December 1993 on unforeseen and extraordinary expenses for the biennium 1994-1995 and the amount of 651,600 dollars gross (611,600 dollars net) authorized with the concurrence of the Advisory Committee under the terms of section IV, paragraph 2, of Assembly resolution 49/233 A of 23 December 1994;

5. *Decides also,* as an ad hoc arrangement, to apportion the amount of 3,251,200 dollars gross (3,123,600 dollars net) for the period from 16 December 1994 to 26 April 1995 among Member States in accordance with the composition of groups set out in paragraphs 3 and 4 of General Assembly resolution 43/232 of 1 March 1989, as adjusted by the Assembly in its resolutions 44/192 B of 21 December 1989, 45/269 of 27 August 1991, 46/198 A of 20 December 1991 and 47/218 A of 23 December 1992 and its decision 48/472 A of 23 December 1993, the scale of assessments for the year 1994 to be applied against a portion thereof, that is, 394,100 dollars gross (378,600 dollars net), which is the amount pertaining on a *pro rata* basis to the period ending 31 December 1994, and the scale of assessments for the year 1995 to be applied against the balance, that is, 2,857,100

dollars gross (2,745,000 dollars net), for the period from 1 January to 26 April 1995, inclusive;

6. *Decides further* that, in accordance with the provisions of its resolution 973(X) of 15 December 1955, there shall be set off against the apportionment among Member States, as provided for in paragraph 5 above, their respective share in the Tax Equalization Fund of the estimated staff assessment income of 127,600 dollars approved for the period from 16 December 1994 to 26 April 1995, inclusive; 15,500 dollars being the amount pertaining on a *pro rata* basis to the period ending 31 December 1994 and the difference, that is, 112,100 dollars, being for the period from 1 January to 26 April 1995, inclusive;

7. *Decides* to appropriate the amount of 10,044,200 dollars gross (9,547,000 dollars net) for the continued operation of the Mission of Observers for the period from 27 April 1995 to 30 June 1996, to be assessed at the rate of 717,400 dollars gross (681,900 dollars net) per month in accordance with the scheme set out in the present resolution, subject to the decision of the Security Council to extend the mandate of the Mission of Observers beyond the period authorized by the Council in its resolution 968(1994);

8. *Invites* voluntary contributions to the Mission of Observers in cash and in the form of services and supplies acceptable to the Secretary-General, to be administered, as appropriate, in accordance with the procedure established by the General Assembly in its resolutions 43/230 of 21 December 1988, 44/192 A of 21 December 1989 and 45/258 of 3 May 1991;

9. *Decides* to include in the provisional agenda of its fiftieth session the item entitled "Financing of the United Nations Mission of Observers in Tajikistan".

General Assembly resolution 49/240

31 March 1995     Meeting 99     Adopted without vote

Approved by Fifth Committee (A/49/878) without vote, 29 March (meeting 50); draft by Chairman (A/C.5/49/L.42), based on informal consultations; agenda item 162.
*Meeting numbers.* GA 49th session: 5th Committee 47, 49, 50; plenary 99.

## Reports of Secretary-General and ACABQ (November/December).

On 13 November, the Secretary-General reported[40] that the Mission's financial performance from 16 December 1994 to 16 June 1995 resulted in an unencumbered balance of $378,600 gross ($373,800 net). Voluntary contributions totalling 100,000 Swiss francs and $54,200 were received, the latter to the trust fund to support the Joint Commission, and free office space for UNMOT headquarters was provided by the host Government. The Secretary-General requested the General Assembly to retain the unencumbered balance in the UNMOT Special Account, in the light of requirements from the establishment of additional posts.

In a 4 December report,[41] ACABQ recalled that under the current practice an unencumbered balance was returned to Member States unless the Assembly decided otherwise.

**GENERAL ASSEMBLY ACTION (December)**

On 22 December, the General Assembly decided that Member States' respective shares in the unencumbered balance of $378,600 gross ($373,800 net) for the period from 16 December 1994 to 16 June 1995 should be set off against their future apportionments if they had fulfilled financial obligations to UNMOT and against their outstanding obligations if they had not (**decision 50/450**).

*REFERENCES*

[1]YUN 1994, p. 594. [2]Ibid., p. 596, SC res. 968(1994), 16 Dec. 1994. [3]S/1995/20. [4]S/1995/27. [5]S/1995/105. [6]S/1995/109. [7]S/1995/113. [8]S/1995/176 & S/1995/225. [9]S/1995/237. [10]S/1995/126. [11]S/1995/136. [12]S/1995/179. [13]S/1995/180. [14]S/1995/283. [15]S/1995/303. [16]S/1995/308. [17]S/PRST/1995/16. [18]A/50/165-S/1995/336. [19]S/1995/331. [20]S/1995/332. [21]S/1995/337. [22]YUN 1994, p. 592. [23]S/1995/390. [24]S/1995/429. [25]S/PRST/1995/28. [26]S/1995/459. [27]S/1995/472 & Corr.1 & Add.1. [28]S/1995/460. [29]S/1995/639. [30]S/1995/720. [31]S/PRST/1995/42. [32]S/1995/799. [33]S/PRST/1995/54. [34]S/1995/954. [35]S/1995/955. [36]S/1995/1024. [37]A/49/854. [38]YUN 1994, p. 596. [39]A/49/868. [40]A/50/749. [41]A/50/802.

## Turkmenistan

In a 20 October statement[1] before the First (Disarmament and International Security) Committee, Turkmenistan announced its decision to make permanent neutrality the main principle of its foreign policy. That principle, enshrined in the country's Constitution, had been endorsed on 16 March by its Majlis (Assembly) and supported by the summit meeting of the Economic Cooperation Organization held in Islamabad in March and by the Eleventh Conference of Heads of State or Government of the Movement of Non-Aligned Countries (Cartagena, Colombia, 18-20 October), which also welcomed Turkmenistan as a new member of the Movement.[2] Turkmenistan stated that it was ready and willing to play an active part in the peace-keeping processes carried out under UN auspices and appealed for the General Assembly's endorsement of its new policy.

On 8 November, Turkmenistan reiterated its appeal before the First Committee[3] and expressed its conviction that, by following a policy of neutrality, good-neighbourliness and cooperation, it would ensure its national interests to the maximum extent and contribute to the strengthening of world stability and peace.

**GENERAL ASSEMBLY ACTION**

On 12 December, the General Assembly adopted **resolution 50/80 A**.

### Permanent neutrality of Turkmenistan

*The General Assembly,*

*Having considered* the question of the permanent neutrality of Turkmenistan,

*Reaffirming* the sovereign right of every State to determine independently its foreign policy in accordance with the norms and principles of international law and the Charter of the United Nations,

*Welcoming* the legislative confirmation by Turkmenistan of its status of permanent neutrality,

*Welcoming also* the desire of Turkmenistan to play an active and positive role in developing peaceful, friendly and mutually beneficial relations with the countries of the region and other States of the world,

*Expressing the hope* that the status of permanent neutrality of Turkmenistan will contribute to the strengthening of peace and security in the region,

*Taking note* of the support by the Movement of Non-Aligned Countries and by the Economic Cooperation Organization of the status of permanent neutrality of Turkmenistan,

*Recognizing* that the adoption by Turkmenistan of the status of permanent neutrality does not affect the fulfilment of its obligations under the Charter and will contribute to the achievement of the purposes of the United Nations,

1. *Recognizes and supports* the status of permanent neutrality declared by Turkmenistan;

2. *Calls upon* States Members of the United Nations to respect and support this status of Turkmenistan and also to respect its independence, sovereignty and territorial integrity.

General Assembly resolution 50/80 A

12 December 1995      Meeting 90      Adopted without vote

Approved by First Committee (A/50/601) without vote, 15 November (meeting 22); 25-nation draft (A/C.1/50/L.9); agenda item 81.
*Meeting numbers.* GA 50th session: 1st Committee 3-11, 16, 22; plenary 90.

*REFERENCES*
[1]A/C.1/50/PV.8. [2]A/50/752-S/1995/1035. [3]A/C.1/50/PV.16.

Chapter V

# Europe and the Mediterranean

The crisis in the former Yugoslavia continued to dominate the agenda of the Security Council in 1995 and to engage the peace-keeping efforts and resources of the United Nations in unprecedented proportions. The situations in Georgia and in the Nagorny Karabakh region of Azerbaijan, and the long-standing question of the Mediterranean island of Cyprus, also remained on the Organization's agenda.

Following a surge of widespread military activity in Bosnia and Herzegovina and in Croatia— between May and September—that was beyond the concerted efforts of the United Nations, the International Conference on the Former Yugoslavia, the European Union and the rest of the international community to forestall, a United States–led peace effort succeeded in making a breakthrough that culminated in the conclusion of a Peace Agreement for Bosnia and Herzegovina, initialled on 22 November by that country, Croatia and the Federal Republic of Yugoslavia (Serbia and Montenegro), and formally signed on 14 December. A Peace Implementation Council was created to replace the International Conference and administer the civilian aspects of the Peace Agreement; an international force was to oversee its military aspects.

After Croatia had militarily reintegrated a majority of its occupied territories, originally designated as UN protected areas, negotiations for the peaceful reintegration of the remainder of those territories led to the Basic Agreement on the Region of Eastern Slavonia, Baranja and Western Sirmium, concluded on 12 November between the Government of Croatia and the local Serb authorities in Eastern Slavonia.

The Secretary-General described the Basic Agreement as a landmark accomplishment and the Peace Agreement as brilliantly constructed on foundations laid during more than three years by many peacemakers, notably his Special Envoy Cyrus Vance (United States), and Thorvald Stoltenberg (Norway) and Lord David Owen (United Kingdom), who served as Co-Chairmen of the Steering Committee of the Conference on behalf of, respectively, the United Nations and the European Union. The Secretary-General welcomed the interrelated agreements as offering real hope of ending the crisis in the former Yugoslavia—if the parties would allow their implementation. At the same time, he saluted the outgoing UN peace-keepers, military and civilian alike, for having successfully discharged their mission of protecting the humanitarian effort in the former Yugoslavia, and the United Nations Protection Force for successfully negotiating and helping to implement local cease-fires and other military arrangements in order to create conditions necessary for political negotiations.

In keeping with new arrangements envisaged by the agreements, military responsibility in Bosnia and Herzegovina was transferred to a new implementation force on 20 December, and consultations were under way for the emplacement of a transitional administration and a transitional peace-keeping force in Croatia's remaining occupied territories. To allow for an orderly emplacement, the Security Council extended the United Nations Confidence Restoration Operation in Croatia for an additional period terminating on 15 January 1996. It extended the mandate of the United Nations Preventive Deployment Force in the former Yugoslav Republic of Macedonia until 30 May 1996, pending new arrangements for its functioning.

In connection with the continuing tensions between Armenia and Azerbaijan over Nagorny Karabakh, the Council reaffirmed the inviolability of international borders and the inadmissibility of the use of force for the acquisition of territory. The Council extended the mandate of the United Nations Observer Mission in Georgia for a further period, terminating on 12 January 1996.

To give the conflicting parties in Cyprus continued opportunity to arrive at a final political solution to their differences, the Council extended the mandate of the United Nations Force in Cyprus until 31 December 1995 and, subsequently, until 30 June 1996.

In other actions relating to Europe and the Mediterranean, the General Assembly called on all Balkan States to endeavour to promote good neighbourly relations among them, welcomed the intensified cooperation and coordination between the United Nations and the Organization for Security and Cooperation in Europe, and commended the continuing efforts of the Mediterranean countries to contribute actively to the elimination of all causes of tension in the region and to turn it into an area of dialogue and cooperation.

# Situation in the former Yugoslavia

## General aspects

The International Conference on the Former Yugoslavia continued throughout 1995 to serve as a framework for peacemaking and peace-building in the territory of the former Yugoslavia. The Co-Chairmen of its Steering Committee remained in constant consultations with the warring parties in Bosnia and Herzegovina and in Croatia, as well as with the Federal Republic of Yugoslavia (Serbia and Montenegro) and all other interested Governments, to help promote a negotiated settlement of the conflicts in those two countries.

The United Nations Protection Force continued to operate as a single peace-keeping force until 31 March. Thereafter, it was restructured by the Security Council: to continue as a separate operation in Bosnia and Herzegovina; its operations in Croatia to be replaced by the United Nations Confidence Restoration Operation; and, in the former Yugoslav Republic of Macedonia, to be known as the United Nations Preventive Deployment Force. The restructuring was made at the request of the host countries, to meet more effectively their respective requirements.

The Office of the United Nations High Commissioner for Refugees continued as the lead agency in operating a multifaceted humanitarian relief programme throughout the former Yugoslavia. Despite crippling war conditions that prevailed during a significant part of the year, intermittent or protracted road and airport closures, and obstructions and confiscations of humanitarian convoys, the agency managed to deliver 66,935 metric tons of humanitarian relief to beneficiaries, whose numbers rose to some 3.5 million in 1995.

With the signature on 14 December of the General Framework Agreement for Peace in Bosnia and Herzegovina (the Peace Agreement), military responsibility in that country was transferred on 20 December to a multinational force, which was to oversee implementation of the Agreement's military aspects; a Peace Implementation Council was constituted to supersede the International Conference as the new structure to administer implementation of the civilian aspects.

As early as 22 November, when the Peace Agreement was initialled, the Council, by two resolutions, suspended indefinitely all sanctions it had imposed against Yugoslavia (Serbia and Montenegro), subject to certain conditions, and provided for the phased termination of the 1991 embargo on deliveries of weapons and military equipment to the former Yugoslavia.

As a result of the military offensives of Croatia in May and August, and in view of the Basic Agreement on the Region of Eastern Slavonia, Baranja and Western Sirmium, concluded on 12 November between the Government and the local Serb authorities in Eastern Slavonia, which called for new arrangements for its implementation, the Council decided that the existing UN operation in Croatia should terminate on 15 January 1996.

(For the situation of human rights in the former Yugoslavia, see PART THREE, Chapter III.)

## International Conference on the Former Yugoslavia

The Geneva-based International Conference on the Former Yugoslavia (ICFY), organized in 1992[1] and co-chaired by the Secretary-General of the United Nations and the head of State or Government of the Presidency of the European Union (EU), maintained its Steering Committee and Arbitration Commission throughout 1995.

The Steering Committee was co-chaired by Thorvald Stoltenberg (United Nations) and Carl Bildt (EU), who replaced Lord David Owen on 13 June. Together with the Committee's six working groups[1] and ad hoc task forces, the Co-Chairmen carried out the day-to-day activities of the Conference, summarized in two biannual reports submitted to the Security Council through the Secretary-General.

The first (January-June) report[2] noted that the Committee had met on 31 January, 10 March and 13 June to consider reports by the Co-Chairmen and ICFY negotiators, and to review developments in Bosnia and Herzegovina and in Croatia, including humanitarian issues in those countries, in the former Yugoslav Republic of Macedonia, in Slovenia, and in Yugoslavia (Serbia and Montenegro). Also discussed were State succession issues and problems between ethnic and national communities in the former Yugoslav Republic of Macedonia (ethnic Albanians, Serbs, Turks, Macedonian-speaking Muslims), in Croatia (ethnic Serbs) and in Yugoslavia (Serbia and Montenegro), specifically the non-Serb ethnics in Kosovo (Albanians), Sandjak (Muslims) and Vojvodina.

The report also set out in detail the competence of the Arbitration Commission, its composition and current membership.

The second (July-December) report[3] stated that ICFY continued to provide a valuable framework for peacemaking, peace-building and humanitarian and human rights activities in the former Yugoslavia. Those mainly included collaborating with the five-member Contact Group (France, Germany, Russian Federation, United Kingdom, United States)[4] in the development of a settlement for Bosnia and Herzegovina and for Eastern Slavonia in Croatia; alerting the international community to pressing humanitarian problems and making humanitarian appeals;

promoting dialogue between national authorities and ethnic minorities regarding the latter's human rights; and operating the ICFY Mission to Yugoslavia (Serbia and Montenegro).[5] (For the Co-Chairmen's reports on the ICFY Mission, see "Border control", under "Bosnia and Herzegovina".)

To enhance the focus of the Co-Chairmen's efforts, peacemaking was spearheaded by Mr. Bildt in respect of Bosnia and Herzegovina and by Mr. Stoltenberg in respect of Croatia.

In the context of renewed hopes for the achievement of a peace agreement and for an eventual peace implementation process, the Working Group on Economic Issues met on 10 October with an open agenda. It explored such questions as the lifting of restrictions on trade and financial transactions, the conditionality that should be attached to economic reconstruction programmes, and the economic aspects of State succession. Emphasis was laid on the need to promote trade and economic relations among the successor States in order to consolidate peace, when it came, and to ensure the success of a future reconstruction process.

By a decision of the Peace Implementation Conference (see below), ICFY and its Steering Committee were to cease to exist as of 31 January 1996.

**Peace Implementation Council**

Following the initialling in November of the General Framework Agreement for Peace in Bosnia and Herzegovina and of its annexes, collectively known as the Peace Agreement, a Peace Implementation Conference was convened in early December to initiate the civilian implementation of the Peace Agreement and to establish the structures for its administration (for details, see under "Bosnia and Herzegovina" below).

Accordingly, the Conference approved the designation of Mr. Bildt as High Representative, whose mandate under the Peace Agreement was to monitor its implementation, and to mobilize and, as appropriate, to coordinate the activities of civilian organizations and agencies. Concluding that important ICFY objectives had been met and that a new structure was required, the Conference decided that a Peace Implementation Council (PIC), composed of all those States, international organizations and agencies participating in the Conference, would subsume ICFY, which should aim for dissolution by 31 January 1996. The ICFY working groups, as well as the ICFY Mission to Yugoslavia (Serbia and Montenegro), were to be kept in being for as long as necessary.

The Conference further established a PIC Steering Board composed of Canada, France, Germany, Italy, Japan, the Russian Federation, the United Kingdom and the United States, the EU Presidency, the European Commission (the administrative arm of EU) and the Organization of the Islamic Conference (OIC). The Board, to be chaired by the High Representative, would meet monthly and keep PIC informed of the progress of implementation.

Operating costs of PIC would be covered by a budget proposed by the Steering Board. All funds remaining in the ICFY accounts would, upon ICFY's dissolution, be transferred to PIC.

**UN peace forces:**
**UNCRO, UNPROFOR, UNPREDEP**

The UN Protection Force (UNPROFOR), established in 1992,[6] was restructured by the Security Council in 1995 in the light of two reports submitted to it by the Secretary-General on 14 January and 22 March, in accordance with Council resolution 947(1994).[7] The reports took account of the position of Croatia, made known the previous year, regarding its conditions for the extension of the current UNPROFOR mandate in the country.[8] Also taken account of were two follow-up communications on the subject addressed to the Secretary-General on 12 January[9] and 17 March 1995.[10]

In the 14 January report, the Secretary-General assessed UNPROFOR's performance in Croatia and the likely consequences of its withdrawal, and requested that Croatia reconsider its position.[11]

The 22 March report outlined UNPROFOR's current structure and composition, and comprehensively updated developments and the circumstances affecting implementation of the UNPROFOR mandates in the three main countries of its operation—Bosnia and Herzegovina, Croatia, and the former Yugoslav Republic of Macedonia—as well as its functions in Yugoslavia (Serbia and Montenegro).[12]

As a result of Croatia's announcement on 12 March of its agreement to the retention of a UN peace-keeping force, the Secretary-General suggested that its mandate should include support for implementing the 1994 cease-fire and economic agreements,[13] those elements of the existing UN peace-keeping plan for Croatia acceptable to the Government and the local Serb authorities, and those functions arising from various relevant Council resolutions.

The Secretary-General drew attention to the wish expressed by Croatia and by the former Yugoslav Republic of Macedonia that the UN forces in their countries should be separate from UNPROFOR, as well as to that expressed by Bosnia and Herzegovina for possible changes in existing arrangements for the UN presence there.

To respond to those wishes without compromising the cost-effectiveness and efficiency of an integrated UN peace-keeping effort in the theatre, the Secretary-General proposed that the current UNPROFOR be replaced by three separate but interlinked peace-keeping operations: United Nations Peace Force-One (UNPF-1) in Croatia, which would be smaller than the current UNPROFOR operation in that country; United Nations Peace Force-Two (UNPF-2) in Bosnia and Herzegovina; and United Nations Peace Force-Three (UNPF-3) in the former Yugoslav Republic of Macedonia. Each would be headed by a civilian Chief of Mission at the assistant secretary-general level and would have its own military commander. Given the interlinked nature of the problems in the theatre and to avoid the expense of duplicating existing structures, overall command and control of the three operations would be exercised by the Special Representative of the Secretary-General for the Former Yugoslavia; command over their military elements would be exercised by the Force Commander. The theatre headquarters, to be known as United Nations Peace Forces Headquarters (UNPF-HQ), would be located in Zagreb, Croatia, where the administrative, logistical and public information responsibilities of the three operations would be coordinated. UNPF-HQ would also be responsible for liaison with Yugoslavia (Serbia and Montenegro), with other concerned Governments and with the North Atlantic Treaty Organization (NATO).

The Secretary-General recommended approval of: (a) the restructuring of UNPROFOR as described above; (b) negotiations based on the elements and functions he had identified for inclusion in the UNPF-1 mandate—to take effect upon Council approval of his report setting forth the details of the mandate, together with the two parties' undertakings to cooperate in its implementation, and confirming the conclusion of a status-of-forces agreement with Croatia, and to extend until 30 November 1995; (c) the conversion of UNPROFOR in Bosnia and Herzegovina and the former Yugoslav Republic of Macedonia into UNPF-2 and UNPF-3, respectively, with the same responsibilities and composition as UNPROFOR currently had in those countries and with mandates also extending to 30 November 1995; (d) the Secretary-General's proposed appeals to the host Governments to conclude status-of-forces agreements with the United Nations and grant it suitable broadcasting facilities; and (e) the transfer to the three peace forces of the applicability of all relevant Council resolutions and authorities relating to the functioning of UNPROFOR in the territories of Croatia, Bosnia and Herzegovina and the former Yugoslav Republic of Macedonia.

The restructuring as recommended took effect at the end of the current UNPROFOR mandate, on 31 March, when the Council adopted three resolutions.

By **resolution 981(1995)**, the Council established the United Nations Confidence Restoration Operation in Croatia (UNCRO) for a period terminating on 30 November 1995, and defined its new mandate to include: performing fully the functions envisaged in the 1994 cease-fire and economic agreements between Croatia and the local Serb authorities; facilitating implementation of all relevant Council resolutions, including the functions identified by the Secretary-General's March report; assisting in controlling, by monitoring and reporting, the crossing of military personnel, equipment, supplies and weapons over the international borders between Croatia and Bosnia and Herzegovina and between Croatia and Yugoslavia (Serbia and Montenegro) at the border-crossing points for which UNCRO was responsible, as specified in the UN peace-keeping plan for Croatia;[14] facilitating the delivery of international humanitarian assistance to Bosnia and Herzegovina through Croatia; and monitoring the demilitarization of the Prevlaka peninsula in accordance with Council resolution 779(1992).[15]

**Resolution 982(1995)** extended UNPROFOR's mandate in Bosnia and Herzegovina for an additional period terminating on 30 November 1995 and established that all previous resolutions relating to UNPROFOR should continue to apply. UNPROFOR should continue to perform fully the functions envisaged in implementation of the two 1994 agreements (see above), including the functions identified in the Secretary-General's 22 March report, and to facilitate the delivery of international humanitarian assistance to Bosnia and Herzegovina until the effective deployment of UNCRO or 30 June 1995, whichever occurred sooner. In addition, UNPROFOR should retain its existing support structures in Croatia, including the operation of its headquarters.

By **resolution 983(1995)**, the Council decided that UNPROFOR in the former Yugoslav Republic of Macedonia should be known as the United Nations Preventive Deployment Force (UNPREDEP), for a period terminating also on 30 November, with the same responsibilities as UNPROFOR previously had in that republic.

Thus, three independent but interlinked peace-keeping forces, collectively called the United Nations Peace Forces, were created and deployed as UNPROFOR in Bosnia and Herzegovina, UNCRO in Croatia, and UNPREDEP in the former Yugoslav Republic of Macedonia, covering a total mission area of some 98,700 square miles. UNPF maintained a liaison office in Belgrade, Yugoslavia (Serbia and Montenegro). UNPF-HQ was located in Zagreb, Croatia, with two support bases, one in Pleso to the north and another in Split along the southern coast. UNPF maintained storage and warehouse facilities in Brindisi, Italy.

General Bernard Janvier (France), who succeeded General Bertrand de Sauville de la Presle (France) on 1 March as Force Commander of UNPROFOR, became Force Commander of the United Nations Peace Forces at the end of that month. His appointment by the Secretary-General was agreed to by the Council in January.[16] Under him were former UNPROFOR field commanders—Lieutenant-General Rupert Smith (United Kingdom) in Bosnia and Herzegovina, Major-General Eid Kamel Al-Rodan (Jordan) in Croatia, and Brigadier-General Juha Engstrom (Finland) in the former Yugoslav Republic of Macedonia—who became, respectively, Commanders of UNPROFOR, UNCRO and UNPREDEP. Civilian Chiefs of Mission were Antonio Pedauye (Spain) for UNPROFOR, Byung Suk Min (Republic of Korea) for UNCRO and Henryk Sokalski (Poland) for UNPREDEP.

UNPF remained under the overall direction of the Special Representative of the Secretary-General to the Former Yugoslavia, Yasushi Akashi, until 31 October. With effect from 1 November, Kofi Annan, the Under-Secretary-General for Peace-keeping Operations of the UN Secretariat, was appointed temporarily as Special Representative to the Former Yugoslavia. These changes were made through an exchange of letters between the Secretary-General and the Council in October.[17]

On 16 June, the Council welcomed the establishment of a rapid reaction capacity for UNPROFOR and, accordingly, authorized an increase in its strength of up to 12,500 troops to enable it to carry out its mandate more effectively (**resolution 998(1995)**). In November, the UNPROFOR mandate was extended for a further period ending on 31 January 1996 (**resolution 1026(1995)**).

Following the initialling in November of the Peace Agreement, the Secretary-General began to make arrangements for the transfer of military authority from UNPROFOR to a multinational Implementation Force (IFOR), as specified in the Agreement. That transfer took place on 20 December, with Admiral Leighton Smith (NATO) assuming command of IFOR. As at that date, a number of UNPROFOR troops had already left the theatre; 18,500 of the approximately 21,000 troops who remained were designated to join IFOR; repatriation of the rest began shortly thereafter.

Besides the forcible reintegration into Croatia in May and August of a majority of the territories held by the Croatian Serbs, which eliminated the need for a substantial UN presence in Croatia, the Basic Agreement on the Region of Eastern Slavonia, Baranja and Western Sirmium, concluded on

12 November between the Government of Croatia and the local Serb authorities in Eastern Slavonia, called for the establishment of new arrangements for that Agreement's implementation. The Council thus decided to terminate UNCRO's mandate on 15 January 1996 (**resolution 1025(1995)**).

In other action, the Council extended the mandate of UNPREDEP for a period terminating on 30 May 1996 (**resolution 1027(1995)**).

*Composition*

In the early part of 1995, the total authorized strength of the three UNPF operations was more than 46,000—748 UN military observers (UNMOs), 44,870 contingent personnel and 1,011 civilian police monitors. Based on Security Council **resolution 990(1995)** of 28 April, troop strength in Croatia was to be reduced to 8,750 troops by 30 June.

UNPF had a total of 6,303 civilian support staff assigned to the Office of the Special Representative of the Secretary-General, the Office of the Special Coordinator for Sarajevo, the UNPF Force Commander, the Division of Information, the Office of Civil Affairs and the Division of Management and Administration. Owing to the shortage of military support personnel, approximately 55 per cent of the civilian staff were assigned specialized technical and support functions in communications, transport, supply and property management, movement control and engineering services.

As a result of military events in Croatia in May and August and subsequent political agreements relating to that country and to Bosnia and Herzegovina, which required new arrangements for their implementation, a significant reduction of the UN presence in Croatia subsequently took place, as did withdrawal of UNPROFOR from Bosnia and Herzegovina.

As at 31 December, therefore, the military strength of the UNPF missions stood at 7,318, consisting of 6,847 troops and support units and 471 UNMOs. A breakdown of the total among the UNPF components was as follows: UNPF-HQ—184 personnel; UNCRO—3,110; UNPROFOR—2,433; and UNPREDEP—1,120.

**Communications.** On 5 May, the Secretary-General, having completed the necessary consultations regarding implementation of the Security Council resolutions creating the three new, separate operations, proposed[18]—and the Council agreed[19]—that the military contingents of UNCRO be composed of personnel already deployed in Croatia and contributed by: Argentina, Belgium, Canada, Czech Republic, Denmark, Estonia, Jordan, Lithuania, Nepal, Poland, Russian Federation. (Estonia's addition to the Member States authorized to contribute military personnel to UNPROFOR had been put forward by the Secretary-General on 3 February[20] and agreed to by the Council on 8 February.[21]) In addition, Ukraine had been invited to provide a helicopter squadron.

The current composition of UNPROFOR was to be maintained, with contingents from: Bangladesh, Belgium, Canada, Denmark, Egypt, France, Jordan, Malaysia, Netherlands, New Zealand, Norway, Pakistan, Russian Federation, Spain, Sweden, Turkey, Ukraine, United Kingdom. The current composition of UNPREDEP, whose contingents were from Denmark, Finland, Norway, Sweden and the United States, was also to be maintained.

The Secretary-General further proposed that UNPF-HQ be staffed by military personnel and support units from all those contingents as well as from Indonesia and Slovakia. He felt it desirable to maintain the existing UNMOs, contributed by: Argentina, Bangladesh, Belgium, Brazil, Canada, Colombia, Czech Republic, Denmark, Egypt, Finland, France, Ghana, Indonesia, Ireland, Jordan, Kenya, Malaysia, Nepal, Netherlands, New Zealand, Nigeria, Norway, Pakistan, Poland, Portugal, Russian Federation, Spain, Sweden, Switzerland, Ukraine, United Kingdom, Venezuela. The observers would be deployed as needed throughout the three zones of operation.

On 14 July, the Secretary-General proposed that Germany, which had offered to make a field hospital available to UNPF, be added to the list of Member States authorized to contribute troops to UNPF,[22] to which the Council agreed on 17 July.[23] This was preceded by a letter of 6 July from Yugoslavia (Serbia and Montenegro) expressing concern over Germany's decision to become a troop contributor, contending that neighbouring countries and former occupying Powers were not to be engaged in UNPF operations; Germany, it stated, had occupied the former Yugoslavia in two world wars and the presence of its troops would constitute an open provocation and a threat to the peace process, which should be unacceptable to the international community.[24]

### Status-of-forces agreements

By an exchange of letters on 13 March 1995, the Special Representative and the Minister for Foreign Relations of the former Yugoslav Republic of Macedonia reached an agreement on the status of UNPREDEP in that republic. A status-of-forces agreement in respect of UNCRO was likewise reached on 15 May between the United Nations and Croatia.

### Financing

**GENERAL ASSEMBLY ACTION (July and December)**

On 20 July, the General Assembly, having considered the Secretary-General's proposals[25] and

the related recommendations of the Advisory Committee on Administrative and Budgetary Questions (ACABQ)[26] on the financing of UNPROFOR, UNCRO, UNPREDEP and UNPF-HQ for the periods 1 April to 30 June and 1 July to 31 December 1995, adopted **resolution 49/248**.

**Financing of the United Nations Protection Force, the United Nations Confidence-Restoration Operation in Croatia, the United Nations Preventive Deployment Force and the United Nations Peace Forces headquarters**

*The General Assembly,*

*Taking note* of the reports of the Secretary-General on the financing of the United Nations Protection Force and the related reports of the Advisory Committee on Administrative and Budgetary Questions, pending a detailed consideration of these reports at the fiftieth session of the General Assembly,

*Recalling* Security Council resolutions 727(1992) of 8 January 1992 and 740(1992) of 7 February 1992, in which the Council endorsed the sending of a group of military liaison officers to Yugoslavia to promote maintenance of the cease-fire,

*Recalling also* Security Council resolution 743(1992) of 21 February 1992, by which the Council established the Force, and the subsequent resolutions by which the Council extended its mandate,

*Recalling further* Security Council resolution 981(1995) of 31 March 1995, by which the Council established the United Nations Confidence-Restoration Operation in Croatia, which is known as UNCRO, for a period terminating on 30 November 1995,

*Recalling* Security Council resolution 982(1995) of 31 March 1995, by which the Council extended the mandate of the United Nations Protection Force in Bosnia and Herzegovina for an additional period terminating on 30 November 1995,

*Recalling also* Security Council resolution 983(1995) of 31 March 1995, by which the Council decided that the United Nations Protection Force within the former Yugoslav Republic of Macedonia should be known as the United Nations Preventive Deployment Force and that its mandate would continue for a period terminating on 30 November 1995,

*Recalling further* all the Security Council resolutions providing for an increase in the authorized strength of the United Nations Protection Force, of which the latest is resolution 998(1995) of 16 June 1995, which authorized an increase in United Nations Peace Forces/United Nations Protection Force personnel by up to 12,500 additional troops to provide the Force with a rapid reaction capacity,

*Recalling* its resolution 46/233 of 19 March 1992 on the financing of the Force and its subsequent resolutions and decisions thereon, the latest of which was resolution 49/228 of 23 December 1994,

*Reaffirming* that the costs of the Force are expenses of the Organization to be borne by Member States in accordance with Article 17, paragraph 2, of the Charter of the United Nations,

*Recalling* its previous decisions regarding the fact that, in order to meet the expenditures caused by the Force, a different procedure is required from the one applied to meet expenditures of the regular budget of the United Nations,

*Taking into account* the fact that the economically more developed countries are in a position to make relatively larger contributions and that the economically less developed countries have a relatively limited capacity to contribute to such an operation,

*Bearing in mind* the special responsibilities of the States permanent members of the Security Council, as indicated in General Assembly resolution 1874(S-IV) of 27 June 1963, in the financing of such operations,

*Noting with appreciation* that voluntary contributions have been made to the Force by certain Governments,

*Mindful* of the fact that it is essential to provide the Force with the necessary financial resources to enable it to fulfil its responsibilities under the relevant resolutions of the Security Council,

1. *Takes note* of the status of contributions to the United Nations Protection Force as at 10 July 1995, including the contributions unpaid in the amount of 862.2 million United States dollars, representing 22.5 per cent of the total assessed contributions from the inception of the Force to the period ending 30 June 1995, notes that some 16 per cent of the membership has paid its assessed contributions in full, and urges all other Member States concerned, particularly those in arrears, to ensure the payment of their outstanding assessed contributions;

2. *Expresses concern* about the financial situation with regard to peace-keeping activities, particularly as regards the reimbursement of troop contributors, which is due to overdue payments by Member States of their assessments;

3. *Urges* all Member States to make every possible effort to ensure the payment of their assessed contributions to the Force promptly and in full;

4. *Endorses* the observations and recommendations contained in the reports of the Advisory Committee on Administrative and Budgetary Questions;

5. *Requests* the Secretary-General to take all necessary action to ensure that the Force is administered with a maximum of efficiency and economy;

6. *Decides* to utilize the special account established by its resolution 46/233 for the recording of income and expenditures relating to the United Nations Protection Force, the United Nations Confidence-Restoration Operation in Croatia, the United Nations Preventive Deployment Force and the United Nations Peace Forces headquarters;

7. *Also decides* to appropriate to the special account referred to in paragraph 6 above the amount of 404,194,500 dollars gross (401,106,600 dollars net) for the period from 1 April to 30 June 1995, authorized and apportioned under the terms of its resolution 49/228;

8. *Further decides* to appropriate to the special account a total amount of 673,657,500 dollars gross (668,511,000 dollars net) for the operation of the Force for the period from 1 July to 30 November 1995;

9. *Decides*, as an ad hoc arrangement, to apportion the amount of 673,657,500 dollars gross (668,511,000 dollars net) for the period from 1 July to 30 November 1995 among Member States in accordance with the composition of groups set out in paragraphs 3 and 4 of General Assembly resolution 43/232 of 1 March 1989, as adjusted by the Assembly in its resolutions 44/192 B of 21 December 1989, 45/269 of 27 August 1991, 46/198 A of 20

December 1991 and 47/218 A of 23 December 1992 and its decision 48/472 A of 23 December 1993, and taking into account the scale of assessments for the year 1995 as set out in Assembly resolution 49/19 B of 23 December 1994;

10. *Also decides* that, in accordance with the provisions of its resolution 973(X) of 15 December 1955, there shall be set off against the apportionment among Member States, as provided for in paragraph 9 above, their respective share in the Tax Equalization Fund of the estimated staff assessment income of 5,146,500 dollars approved for the Force for the period from 1 July to 30 November 1995, inclusive;

11. *Takes note* of the fact that the Secretary-General has estimated that an overall level of resources for the reinforcement of the Force with a rapid reaction capacity, not to exceed 297,112,600 dollars gross (275,290,800 dollars net), will be required for the period from 1 July to 31 December 1995 and that the General Assembly will carry out a detailed consideration of all reports of the Secretary-General at its fiftieth session;

12. *Decides*, in the context of section IV, paragraph 3, of its resolution 49/233 A of 23 December 1994, to authorize the Secretary-General to enter into commitments for the reinforcement of the Force with a rapid reaction capacity, up to the amount of 100 million dollars gross (99,569,800 dollars net) for the period from 1 July to 30 November 1995;

13. *Also decides*, as an ad hoc arrangement, to apportion the amount of 100 million dollars gross (99,569,800 dollars net) for the period from 1 July to 30 November 1995 among Member States in accordance with the composition of groups set out in paragraphs 3 and 4 of resolution 43/232, as adjusted by the General Assembly in its resolutions 44/192 B, 45/269, 46/198 A and 47/218 A and its decision 48/472 A, and taking into account the scale of assessments for the year 1995 as set out in Assembly resolution 49/19 B;

14. *Further decides* that, in accordance with the provisions of resolution 973(X), there shall be set off against the apportionment among Member States, as provided for in paragraph 13 above, their respective share in the Tax Equalization Fund of the estimated staff assessment income of 430,200 dollars approved for the Force for the period from 1 July to 30 November 1995, inclusive;

15. *Takes note* of the decision of the Secretary-General to establish a sub-account of the Special Account for the United Nations Protection Force for the purposes described in paragraph 15 *(c)* of document A/49/540/Add.4;

16. *Invites* voluntary contributions to the sub-account of the Special Account for the United Nations Protection Force in cash and in the form of services and supplies acceptable to the Secretary-General, to be administered in accordance with the Financial Regulations and Rules of the United Nations;

17. *Decides* to defer consideration of the treatment of the unencumbered balances arising in respect of the period from 1 July 1993 to 30 September 1994 until it has an opportunity at its fiftieth session to examine fully the reports contained in documents A/49/540/Add.2 and A/49/540/Add.3 and any update of document A/49/540/Add.3 and the related reports of the Advisory Committee;

18. *Invites* voluntary contributions to the Force in cash and in the form of services and supplies acceptable to

the Secretary-General, to be administered, as appropriate, in accordance with the procedure established by the General Assembly in its resolutions 43/230 of 21 December 1988, 44/192 A of 21 December 1989 and 45/258 of 3 May 1991;

19. *Decides* to include in the provisional agenda of its fiftieth session an item entitled "Financing of the United Nations Protection Force, the United Nations Confidence-Restoration Operation in Croatia, the United Nations Preventive Deployment Force and the United Nations Peace Forces headquarters".

General Assembly resolution 49/248

20 July 1995          Meeting 106          Adopted without vote

Approved by Fifth Committee (A/49/756/Add.2) without vote, 14 July (meeting 66); draft by Chairman (A/C.5/49/L.63), based on informal consultations; agenda item 122.

*Meeting numbers.* GA 49th session: 5th Committee 62, 63, 66; plenary 106.

In December, the Assembly met two more times to take the interim action necessary to meet further operational requirements relating to UNPF and other new missions in the former Yugoslavia. The estimated costs were presented by the Secretary-General in further reports on the financing of UNPROFOR for 1 October 1994 to 31 March 1995, prior to its restructuring;[27] of all UNPF components for 1 July to 31 December 1995, as revised,[28] together with their financial performance from 1 April to 30 June 1995;[29] and, for the period 1 January to 31 March 1996, of UNPREDEP, of the liquidation of UNCRO and UNPROFOR, and of the new operations expected to be authorized by the Security Council.[30]

Pending detailed consideration of those reports, the Assembly adopted **decision 50/410 A.**

At its 78th plenary meeting, on 4 December 1995, the General Assembly, on the recommendation of the Fifth Committee, authorized the Secretary-General, on an exceptional basis, to enter into commitments for the operation of the combined forces for the period from 1 to 31 December 1995 in the amount of 115,373,000 United States dollars gross (113,866,300 dollars net), subject to the decision of the Security Council to continue the forces beyond 30 November 1995.

General Assembly decision 50/410 A

                                               Adopted without vote

Approved by Fifth Committee (A/50/796) without vote, 1 December (meeting 35); draft by Chairman (A/C.5/50/L.6), based on informal consultations; agenda item 128.

*Meeting numbers.* GA 50th session: 5th Committee 33, 35; plenary 78.

Subsequently, the Assembly, having heard the 20 December oral observations of ACABQ[31] concerning the Secretary-General's last report, adopted **decision 50/410 B.**

At its 100th plenary meeting, on 23 December 1995, the General Assembly, on the recommendation of the Fifth Committee:

*(a)* Authorized the Secretary-General, on an exceptional basis, to enter into commitments for the operations in the former Yugoslavia for the period from

1 January to 31 March 1996 in the amount of 100 million United States dollars gross (98,430,700 dollars net);

*(b)* Requested the Secretary-General to submit cost estimates to the General Assembly at its resumed fiftieth session covering the new operations in Croatia and in Bosnia and Herzegovina, the maintenance of the United Nations Preventive Deployment Force and the liquidation of the United Nations Confidence Restoration Operation in Croatia and the United Nations Protection Force;

*(c)* Decided, as an ad hoc arrangement, to apportion the amount of 89,484,800 dollars gross (87,915,500 dollars net) for the period from 1 January to 31 March 1996 among Member States in accordance with the composition of groups set out in paragraphs 3 and 4 of Assembly resolution 43/232 of 1 March 1989, as adjusted by the Assembly in its resolutions 44/192 B of 21 December 1989, 45/269 of 27 August 1991, 46/198 A of 20 December 1991, 47/218 A of 23 December 1992, 49/249 A of 20 July 1995 and 49/249 B of 14 September 1995 and its decisions 48/472 A of 23 December 1993 and 50/451 B of 23 December 1995, and taking into account the scale of assessments for the year 1996;

*(d)* Also decided that, in accordance with the provisions of its resolution 973(X) of 15 December 1955, there should be set off against the apportionment among Member States, as provided for in paragraph *(c)* above, their respective share in the Tax Equalization Fund of the estimated staff assessment income of 1,569,300 dollars approved for the operations in the former Yugoslavia for the period from 1 January to 31 March 1996.

General Assembly decision 50/410 B

                                               Adopted without vote

Approved by Fifth committee (A/50/796/Add.1.) without vote, 21 December (meeting 44); draft by Chairman (A/C.1/50/L.26), based on informal consultations; agenda item 128.

*Meeging numbers.* GA 50th Committee 43, 44 plenary 100.

## *Audit of personnel pilot project*

By a note of 6 June, the Secretary-General transmitted to the General Assembly an audit report [32] on the UNPROFOR personnel pilot project, submitted in keeping with a 1994 Assembly request.[33] The project was begun in 1992 for the recruitment of international contractual personnel to provide a variety of support skills, especially in the technical and trade areas, which could not be met through traditional means of recruitment. The audit was conducted by the UN Office of Internal Oversight Services (OIOS) on the basis of an ACABQ recommendation that the project be suspended, pending an independent evauation of UNPROFOR's contracting practices.

The audit covered the procurement processes; administrative procedures for managing the project, including determination of contractual personnel requirements, post classification and selection of candidates; policies and procedures for administering the contracts, including determination of billable costs, invoice checking, and monitoring of performance and compliance with contractual requirements; and recent developments in the management of the project.

The audit's basic finding was that deployment of contractual personnel had proved to be a viable means of meeting UNPROFOR support needs and could be an alternative method of providing support staff for other peace-keeping operations. The series of recommendations that emerged from the audit included: applying the project with flexibility to ensure fulfilment of the operational requirements of UNPROFOR or of other missions; engaging contractual personnel only upon determination by a review board and on the consent of the Department of Peace-keeping Operations; and limiting the engagement of such personnel to technical and trade functions.

By **decision 49/487**, the General Assembly, on the recommendation of the Fifth Committee,[34] took note of the audit report.

### Cooperation with NATO

In his 22 March report,[12] the Secretary-General noted that NATO had continued to support the United Nations with substantial maritime and aerial operations. The joint NATO/Western European Union operation "Sharp Guard" enforced the Adriatic embargo under Security Council resolution 820(1993),[35] while operation "Deny Flight" continued to provide aerial monitoring and enforcement of the ban on military flights in the airspace of Bosnia and Herzegovina, as decided by the Security Council in 1992[36] and 1993,[37] as well as protective close air support, air strikes and enhancement of the security of the UN-designated safe areas in Bosnia and Herzegovina when requested by UNPROFOR. The availability of NATO air power had strengthened UNPROFOR's bargaining position in negotiating clearances for humanitarian convoys, it was stated.

At the Secretary-General's request, NATO had also devoted considerable resources to contingency planning and other preparations in support of a possible UNPROFOR withdrawal from Bosnia and Herzegovina and/or Croatia.

The Secretary-General emphasized that despite regular and frequent infringements of the ban on military flights by helicopters and some occasional fixed-wing activity, he was convinced that the deterrent effect of NATO operations had contributed to the effective containment of the warring factions' air activity for combat purposes. He placed a high value on the security that UNPROFOR derived from NATO's operations and contingency measures.

### International Tribunal for the Former Yugoslavia

By a letter of 31 October 1995, the President of the International Tribunal for the Prosecution of Persons Responsible for Serious Violations of International Humanitarian Law Committed in the Territory of the Former Yugoslavia since 1991[38] brought to the attention of the Security Council the Trial Chamber's decision of 20 October that there were reasonable grounds for believing that Dragan Nikolic, indicted in 1994,[39] had committed the crimes with which he had been charged.[40] Owing to the inability of Bosnia and Herzegovina to serve the indictment and warrant of arrest because the accused was residing in territory outside its control, and in the absence of a response from the Bosnian Serb administration, the decision provided for the issuance of an international warrant for Dragan Nikolic's arrest and invited the President to so advise the Council.

The Council took note of the President's letter in **resolution 1019(1995)** of 9 November.

(For the activities of the International Tribunal for the Former Yugoslavia, see PART FIVE, Chapter II).

### Sanctions

The sanctions regimes imposed by the Security Council on the former Yugoslavia between 1991 and 1993[41] and in 1994[42] included the general and complete arms embargo applicable to the whole of the former Yugoslavia and the sanctions specific to the Federal Republic of Yugoslavia (Serbia and Montenegro) and the Bosnian Serb party.

In the course of 1995, the Council, by **resolution 992(1995)**, altered the 1993 restrictions on navigation on the Danube River.[35] In addition, by **resolutions 982(1995)**, **988(1995)**, **992(1995)**, **1003(1995)** and **1015(1995)**, the Council extended the 1994 partial suspension of economic sanctions against Yugoslavia (Serbia and Montenegro)[43] for four successive periods from 12 January, the last period extending to 18 March 1996.

On 22 November, the day after Bosnia and Herzegovina, Croatia and Yugoslavia (Serbia and Montenegro) had initialled the Peace Agreement, the Council, by **resolution 1021(1995)**, provided for the phased termination of the 1991 embargo on deliveries of weapons and military equipment to the former Yugoslavia,[44] excepting those deliveries as defined in the Peace Agreement, which should continue to be prohibited until the arms control agreement referred to therein had taken effect.

By **resolution 1022(1995)**, also of 22 November, the Council suspended indefinitely and with immediate effect all sanctions against Yugoslavia (Serbia and Montenegro), the suspension to be automatically reimposed in the event of that country's failure formally to sign the Peace Agreement, or to be terminated if that country or the Bosnian Serb authorities were failing significantly to meet their obligations under the Agreement. Such suspension was not to apply to the measures imposed on the Bosnian Serb party until such time as it had withdrawn behind the separation zones established by the Agreement.

Following the formal signature of the Peace Agreement on 14 December and the Secretary-General's report to the Council on 20 December that, on that day, the transfer of military authority from UNPROFOR to IFOR had taken place, the provisions of Council resolutions 781(1992)[36] and 816(1993)[37] relating to the ban on military flights in the airspace of Bosnia and Herzegovina were terminated with immediate effect, in accordance with Council **resolution 1031(1995)**.

### Navigation on the Danube

On 8 May 1995, the Chairman of the Committee established pursuant to Security Council resolution 724(1991)[45] (Sanctions Committee) conveyed to the Council Romania's request that vessels of Yugoslavia (Serbia and Montenegro) be authorized to use the Romanian locks of the Iron Gates I system on the left bank of the Danube during the forthcoming repairs to the locks on the right bank.[46] Supported by other Danube riparian States and by the Sanctions Coordinator of the European Union/Organization for Security and Cooperation in Europe (EU/OSCE), the request was made as an exception to paragraph 16 of resolution 820(1993).[35]

Having noted the importance placed on the proper maintenance and timely repair of the Iron Gates I system for the safety of international navigation on the Danube, and taking account of Romania's readiness to ensure that the vessels in question would not engage in any activity that might contravene the relevant Council resolutions, the Sanctions Committee decided to recommend that the Council consider adopting a technical resolution granting the request.

**SECURITY COUNCIL ACTION**

In the light of the foregoing request, the Security Council convened on 11 May and adopted **resolution 992(1995)**.

*The Security Council,*

*Recalling* all its previous relevant resolutions on the former Yugoslavia, and in particular its resolution 820(1993),

*Desiring* to promote free and unhindered navigation on the Danube in accordance with those resolutions,

*Recalling* statements made by the President of the Security Council on freedom of navigation on the Danube, in particular that made on 13 October 1993 expressing concern about the imposition of illegal tolls on foreign vessels transiting the section of the Danube which passes through the territory of the Federal Republic of Yugoslavia (Serbia and Montenegro),

*Reminding* States of their obligations under paragraph 5 of resolution 757(1992) not to make available to the authorities in the Federal Republic of Yugoslavia (Ser-

bia and Montenegro) or to any commercial, industrial or public utility undertaking in the Federal Republic of Yugoslavia (Serbia and Montenegro) any funds or any other financial or economic resources and to prevent their nationals from making available to those authorities or to any such undertaking any such funds or resources, and noting that flag States may submit claims to the authorities in the Federal Republic of Yugoslavia (Serbia and Montenegro) for reimbursement of tolls illegally imposed on their vessels transiting the section of the Danube which passes through the territory of the Federal Republic of Yugoslavia (Serbia and Montenegro),

*Taking note* of the letter of the Chairman of the Committee established pursuant to resolution 724(1991) regarding use by vessels registered in, or owned or controlled by persons in, the Federal Republic of Yugoslavia (Serbia and Montenegro) of the locks of the Iron Gates I system on the left-hand bank of the Danube while repairs are carried out to the locks on the right-hand bank,

*Recognizing* that the use by vessels registered in, or owned or controlled by persons in, the Federal Republic of Yugoslavia (Serbia and Montenegro) of these locks will require an exemption from the provisions of paragraph 16 of resolution 820(1993) and acting, in this respect, under Chapter VII of the Charter of the United Nations,

1.  *Decides* that the use of the locks of the Iron Gates I system on the left-hand bank of the Danube by vessels *(a)* registered in the Federal Republic of Yugoslavia (Serbia and Montenegro) or *(b)* in which a majority or controlling interest is held by a person or undertaking in or operating from the Federal Republic of Yugoslavia (Serbia and Montenegro) shall be permitted in accordance with this resolution;

2.  *Further decides* that this resolution shall come into force on the day following the receipt by the Council from the Committee established pursuant to resolution 724(1991) of a report by the Danube Commission that they are satisfied that preparations for the repairs to the locks of the Iron Gates I system on the right-hand bank of the Danube have been completed; and that this resolution shall remain in force, subject to paragraph 6 below, for a period of 60 days from the date on which it comes into force, and, unless the Council decides otherwise, for further periods of up to 60 days if the Council is notified by the Committee established pursuant to resolution 724(1991) that each such further period is required for completion of the necessary repairs;

3.  *Requests* the Government of Romania, with the assistance of the European Union/Organization for Security and Cooperation in Europe Sanctions Assistance Missions, strictly to monitor this use including if necessary by inspections of the vessels and their cargo, to ensure that no goods are loaded or unloaded during the passage by the vessels through the locks of the Iron Gates I system;

4.  *Further requests* the Government of Romania to deny passage through the locks of the Iron Gates I system on the left-hand bank of the Danube to any vessel using the locks of the Iron Gates I system under the authority of paragraph 1 above which is identified as being a party to any suspected or substantiated violation of the relevant Council resolutions;

5.  *Requests* the Sanctions Assistance Missions Communications Centre to report to the Committee established pursuant to resolution 724(1991) and to the

Romanian authorities operating the locks of the Iron Gates I system on the left-hand bank of the Danube any suspected violation of any of the relevant Council resolutions by vessels using the locks of the Iron Gates I system under the authority of paragraph 1 above and to transmit to the Committee and to the Romanian authorities evidence that any such violation has in fact occurred; and decides that the Chairman of the Committee shall, after consulting members of the Committee, transmit to the Council any substantiated evidence of such a violation forthwith;

6. *Decides* that the exemption provided for in paragraph 1 above shall terminate on the third working day after the Council receives substantiated evidence from the Chairman of the Committee established pursuant to resolution 724(1991) of a violation of any of the relevant Council resolutions of the Council by a vessel using the locks of the Iron Gates I system under the authority of paragraph 1 above, unless the Council decides to the contrary, and that the Government of Romania shall be so informed immediately;

7. *Requests* the Executive Director of the Danube Commission to inform the Chairman of the Committee established pursuant to resolution 724(1991) of the date of completion of the repairs, or, if the repairs have not been completed within 60 days of the entry into force of this resolution, or within the subsequent periods of up to 60 days for which the provisions of this resolution may be extended, to provide the Chairman with a report on the state of the repairs 10 days before the expiry of any such period;

8. *Confirms* that, in accordance with the provisions of resolution 760(1992), the importation into the Federal Republic of Yugoslavia (Serbia and Montenegro) of supplies essential to the repair of the locks on the right-hand bank of the Danube may be approved in accordance with the procedures of the Committee established pursuant to resolution 724(1991) at a meeting or meetings of the Committee;

9. *Decides* to remain seized of the matter.

Security Council resolution 992(1995)

11 May 1995      Meeting 3533      Adopted unanimously

Draft prepared in consultations among Council members (S/1995/373).

In keeping with paragraph 2 of the resolution, the Sanctions Committee, on 21 June, transmitted the Danube Commission's communication that preparations for the repairs to the locks in question had been completed.[47] The resolution, and hence the authorization sought, entered into force on 23 June. On the basis of two letters from the Sanctions Committee, dated 16 August and 16 October, each stating that an additional 60 days were required to complete the repairs, and in the absence of a Council decision to the contrary, the resolution remained in force for a further two periods of 60 days each, from 22 August to 20 October[48] and from 21 October to 19 December.[49]

### Economic assistance to States affected by sanctions

The States bordering Yugoslavia (Serbia and Montenegro) and some Danube riparian States—

Bulgaria, Greece, Moldova, Romania and Ukraine —continued in 1995 to suffer from special economic problems as a result of the strict enforcement of the comprehensive trade and economic sanctions imposed against Yugoslavia (Serbia and Montenegro).

To alleviate their situation, those States jointly suggested a series of measures on 18 May,[50] almost all of which the General Assembly embodied in its **resolution 50/58 E** of 12 December.

### Humanitarian assistance programme

Various bodies of the UN system—including the Office of the United Nations High Commissioner for Refugees (UNHCR), the World Food Programme (WFP), the World Health Organization (WHO) and the United Nations Children's Fund (UNICEF)—continued in 1995 to operate the humanitarian assistance programme for war-affected populations in the former Yugoslavia. As the lead agency, UNHCR was responsible for logistics, transport, food monitoring, domestic needs, shelter, community services, legal assistance and other protection services. UNPROFOR continued to provide escorts and engineering support to humanitarian convoys and to determine the safest convoy routes.

The UN inter-agency effort continued to be complemented by Governments acting on a bilateral basis, by various intergovernmental and non-governmental organizations and by the International Committee of the Red Cross (ICRC).

The ICFY Working Group on Humanitarian Issues, chaired by UN High Commissioner for Refugees Sadako Ogata, met on 19 July and 10 October. It continued its efforts to generate financing for humanitarian activities, to provide protection and assistance for refugees and displaced persons, and to help uphold international norms of human rights and humanitarian law. The High Commissioner undertook a mission to the capitals of Bosnia and Herzegovina, Croatia and Yugoslavia (Serbia and Montenegro)—Sarajevo, Zagreb, Belgrade—from 4 to 6 December, to discuss humanitarian issues connected with implementation of the Peace Agreement.

On 2 June, a revised consolidated inter-agency appeal was issued by the United Nations for an estimated $470 million to cover humanitarian operations from 1 January to 31 December 1995 for some 2,109,500 beneficiaries in the whole of the former Yugoslavia. The UNHCR component was $172 million. Owing to the dramatic escalation of humanitarian needs since May, a supplement to the revised inter-agency appeal was issued on 15 September, increasing the estimate from $470 million to $514.8 million to cover tens of thousands of newly displaced persons raising the number of beneficiaries to some 3,523,500. The UNHCR component was correspondingly increased to $222.7 million.

A new UN consolidated inter-agency appeal was launched on 20 November for $179.6 million to fund humanitarian assistance to 3.3 million beneficiaries from January to April 1996, of which the UNHCR component was $70.9 million.

According to UNHCR, contributions to the programme during 1995 consisted of $166 million in cash and some $6.4 million in kind. Humanitarian assistance in metric tonnage provided to the war-affected populations in the former Yugoslavia was as follows: Bosnia and Herzegovina—213,155 metric tons; Croatia (excluding the UN protected areas (UNPAs))—521; UNPAs—5,803; the former Yugoslav Republic of Macedonia—1,139; Slovenia—18; Serbia—31,589; Montenegro—5,231. (Procurement and distribution of assistance to Croatia, excluding the UNPAs, had been executed by EU since the end of 1992.) The beneficiaries totalled 3.5 million.

(See also "Humanitarian assistance", under "Bosnia and Herzegovina"; and PART FOUR, Chapters III and XII.)

## Succession issues

As noted in its first biannual report,[2] the ICFY Working Group on Succession Issues conducted negotiations on all aspects of succession related to the former Yugoslavia. The Group's meticulous and persistent work, it was stated, had brought the parties within reach of agreement on draft treaty provisions, cast into two sections, which could constitute independent treaties or parts of a single treaty, depending on development of events.

The first section, dealing with citizenship, pensions, acquired rights, archives, treaty succession and arbitration mechanisms, contained provisions on which a large measure of agreement had been achieved. The draft text on that section had been presented to the parties for consideration.

The second section dealt with disposition of assets and liabilities, and had been the subject of consultations over the past six months with Governments and creditors, the report stated. Consultations were continuing on the question of how to distribute assets and liabilities among the successor republics.

**Communications.** On 24 January 1995, Yugoslavia (Serbia and Montenegro) communicated[51] to the Secretary-General its reply to objections raised in 1994[52] by Bosnia and Herzegovina, Croatia, Slovenia and the former Yugoslav Republic of Macedonia with regard to its request that it be allowed to pay UN budget contributions from the assets of the former Yugoslavia frozen abroad. The reply stated that, pending an agreement to regulate the effects of secession from the Yugoslav federation, which would also define the rights of

the seceded territories in respect of the former Yugoslavia's assets, Yugoslavia (Serbia and Montenegro) was the owner of those assets by virtue of continuing the federation in international relations. Accordingly, its request that a portion of the former Yugoslavia's funds in foreign banks be unfrozen so that it could meet its financial obligations was fully in compliance with the factual and legal state of affairs.

Bosnia and Herzegovina,[53] on 16 February, and Croatia[54] and Slovenia,[55] on the following day, renewed their objections, stating that Yugoslavia (Serbia and Montenegro) was one of the five equal successor States and recalling Security Council resolution 777(1992),[56] which determined that the State formerly known as the Socialist Federal Republic of Yugoslavia had ceased to exist and that the Federal Republic of Yugoslavia (Serbia and Montenegro) could not continue automatically the former Yugoslavia's membership in the United Nations.

*REFERENCES*

[1]YUN 1992, p. 327. [2]S/1995/626. [3]S/1996/4. [4]YUN 1994, p. 553. [5]Ibid., p. 558. [6]YUN 1992, p. 333, SC res. 743(1992), 21 Feb. 1992. [7]YUN 1994, p. 495, SC res. 947(1994), 30 Sep. 1994. [8]Ibid., p. 494. [9]A/50/64-S/1995/28. [10]A/50/111-S/1995/206. [11]S/1995/38. [12]S/1995/222 & Corr.1,2. [13]YUN 1994, pp. 563 & 569. [14]YUN 1992, p. 327. [15]Ibid., p. 343, SC res. 779(1992), 6 Oct. 1992. [16]S/1995/41, S/1995/42. [17]S/1995/898, S/1995/899. [18]S/1995/386. [19]S/1995/387. [20]S/1995/124. [21]S/1995/125. [22]S/1995/585. [23]S/1995/586. [24]A/50/270-S/1995/543. [25]A/49/540/Add.2-4. [26]A/49/928. [27]A/50/696. [28]A/50/696/Add.1. [29]A/50/696/Add.2. [30]A/50/696 & Add.3. [31]A/C.5/50/SR.43. [32]A/49/914. [33]YUN 1994, p. 503, GA res. 49/228, 23 Dec. 1994. [34]A/49/820/Add.1. [35]YUN 1993, p. 471, SC res. 820(1993), 17 Apr. 1993. [36]YUN 1992, p. 371, SC res. 781(1992), 9 Oct. 1992. [37]YUN 1993, p. 463, SC res. 816(1993), 31 Mar. 1993. [38]Ibid., p. 440, SC res. 827(1993), 25 May 1993. [39]YUN 1994, p. 507. [40]S/1995/910. [41]YUN 1993, p. 443. [42]YUN 1994, p. 511. [43]Ibid., p. 557, SC res. 943(1994), 23 Sep. 1994. [44]YUN 1991, p. 215, SC res. 713(1991), 25 Sep. 1991. [45]Ibid., p. 219, SC res. 724(1991), 15 Dec. 1991. [46]S/1995/372. [47]S/1995/502. [48]S/1995/705. [49]S/1995/874. [50]A/50/189-S/1995/412. [51]A/49/839-S/1995/75 & Corr.1. [52]YUN 1994, p. 1356. [53]A/49/853-S/1995/147. [54]A/49/851-S/1995/145. [55]A/49/852-S/1995/146. [56]YUN 1992, p. 138, SC res. 777(1992), 19 Sep. 1992.

## Bosnia and Herzegovina

When 1995 began, an agreement on a comprehensive cease-fire had been in effect for seven days in Bosnia and Herzegovina and an agreement on a complete cessation of hostilities had just entered into force. Both were concluded between the Government and the Bosnian Serb leadership during the second half of December 1994, and it was widely felt that they provided yet another opportunity, until their expiry on 30 April 1995, for creating stable military conditions favourable to the conduct of political negotiation. Thus, monitoring and verification of the parties' compliance with the agreements became the main focus of UNPROFOR activities during the first months of the year.

In March, it became apparent to those concerned that the parties regarded the agreements as a mere winter truce for troop rest, regroupment and reinforcement. Following the expiration of the agreements, rapidly accelerating military activities began to be unleashed country-wide, but especially in and around the UN-designated safe areas. In May, Bosnian Serb violations of the heavy-weapons exclusion zone in Sarajevo drew NATO air strikes against an ammunition depot in Pale, seat of the Bosnian Serb administration. In response, the Bosnian Serbs took more than 300 UNPROFOR personnel hostage, using some of them as human shields at strategic locations, as in Gorazde, to deter further NATO air strikes.

In July, the Bosnian Serb forces mounted a full-scale assault on Srebrenica and nearby Zepa, quickly overrunning those two northern safe areas. In the Bihac pocket, in north-west Bosnia, where the agreements had never been respected, internal fighting flared up, also in July, between the Bosnian Army and the Bosnian separatists there who were being assisted by the Croatian Serbs from Krajina and by the Bosnian Serbs, who kept up their attacks from without. In early August, the intermittent shelling of Sarajevo reached a critical point when the city's Markale market-place was targeted, taking a heavy toll in civilian deaths and injuries. To restore the heavy-weapons and safe-area regimes, NATO conducted multiple air strikes at the end of August through the beginning of September against Bosnian Serb anti-aircraft systems, heavy-weapons sites and other military facilities throughout eastern Bosnian Serb territory. During that operation, mortar and artillery of the rapid reaction force of UNPROFOR engaged Bosnian Serb targets. Soon after, joint Bosnian and Croatian forces began to advance in the western part of the country, with the Bosnian forces taking much of the Ozren salient, while the Croatian forces made sweeping advances to the south-west, capturing areas traditionally populated by Serbs.

Those offensives resulted in dramatic flows of refugees and displaced persons inside and out of Bosnia and Herzegovina, exacerbated by refugee flows into that country due to two major offensives launched by Croatia in May and August against Croatian Serb–held areas within its territory. In July, thousands of Bosnian Muslim residents of Srebrenica and Zepa were expelled, as both fell to the Bosnian Serbs. In the same month, the counter-offensive of the Krajina Serbs on the Bosnian Army in the Bihac pocket caused some 8,000 residents there to abandon their homes and flee to neighbouring Cazin. At the beginning of August, approximately 26,000 Bosnian Croats and Muslims were either expelled from or pressured into leaving Banja Luka in northern Bosnia, due to the influx there of some 14,000 Bosnian Serbs who had fled Bosansko Grahovo and Glamoc in late July in the wake of the advance of the joint Bosnian and Croatian forces into those western Bosnian towns bordering Croatia. Because of Croatia's military offensive at the end of August through the beginning of September, some 150,000 Serbs from the Krajina region of Croatia crossed into northern Bosnia and Herzegovina and thence to Yugoslavia (Serbia and Montenegro). As the Bosnian Army swept through western Bosnia in mid-September, some 127,000 Bosnian Serbs fled to Banja Luka, significantly adding to the 14,000 Bosnian Serbs already in refuge there.

Amidst the fighting and population upheavals, widespread violations of human rights and international humanitarian law persisted, particularly in Bosnian Serb–controlled territory.

Shortly after mid-August, the United States began a determined pursuit of its peace initiative, securing a cease-fire agreement on 5 October, which UNPROFOR brought into force on 12 October. Meanwhile, Bosnia and Herzegovina, Croatia, and Yugoslavia (Serbia and Montenegro)—the latter representing also the Bosnian Serb party—had committed themselves on 8 September, under the auspices of the Contact Group, to Agreed Basic Principles and, on 26 September, to Further Agreed Basic Principles, which were to govern the forthcoming difficult and intensive proximity negotiations.

Those negotiations began on 1 November in Dayton, Ohio, United States, with the United States Under-Secretary of State for European and Canadian Affairs, Richard Holbrooke, as chief United States mediator. They culminated in the initialling on 21 November of the General Framework for Peace in Bosnia and Herzegovina and all the annexes thereto, known as the Peace Agreement. A Peace Implementation Conference was convened in London on 8 and 9 December, which set in motion implementation of the civilian aspects of the Peace Agreement. With the formal signing of the Peace Agreement in Paris on 14 December 1995, the military authority in Bosnia and Herzegovina was transferred from UNPROFOR to a multinational implementation force (IFOR) authorized by the Security Council on 15 December, to operate under the authority and political control of the North Atlantic Council through the NATO chain of command.

With that transfer of authority, the Council resolutions relating to the safe areas and to the ban on military flights in the airspace of Bosnia and Herzegovina were terminated with immediate effect.

## 1994 cease-fire and cessation-of-hostilities agreements

As of 1 January 1995, UNPROFOR had begun to focus on monitoring and verifying compliance by the Bosnian Government and the Bosnian Serb leadership with the 1994 agreements[1] on a comprehensive cease-fire and on a complete cessation of hostilities, negotiated by the Special Representative of the Secretary-General for the Former Yugoslavia. The agreements were to expire on 30 April 1995, but were subject to renewal. Their texts were conveyed to the Security Council by the Secretary-General on 6 January 1995.[2]

The cease-fire agreement, which had taken effect on 24 December 1994, was for an initial period of seven days and four months. It provided for the following: a general cease-fire along all confrontation lines; a procedure for reporting any breach of the agreement to the Council through UNPROFOR and the Secretary-General; the free passage of UNPROFOR, humanitarian convoys and teams monitoring the cease-fire; the international monitoring of the human rights situation in all areas; the prompt and unconditional release of all detainees, including prisoners of war (POWs), and of all available information on missing persons, in accordance with an ICRC action plan; and immediate negotiations aimed at achieving an agreement on a comprehensive cessation of hostilities.

The cessation-of-hostilities agreement went into effect on 1 January along all confrontation lines for an initial period of four months. Under the terms of the agreement, compliance was to be monitored by UNPROFOR through regional joint commissions and a central joint commission which it would chair. UNPROFOR and the parties were to exchange liaison officers by 15 January. Cessation of hostilities was to include the separation of forces to mutually agreed positions and the inter-positioning of UNPROFOR between them, a halt to the use of all explosive munitions and of weapons to fire them, and the withdrawal of heavy weapons of 12.7-millimetre calibre or greater, to be monitored by UNPROFOR. The parties were to accord UNPROFOR and other official international agencies, particularly UNHCR, full freedom of movement and respect for their safety and security. They were to comply fully with all existing agreements relating to: Gorazde,[3] Sarajevo airport,[4] Srebrenica,[5] Srebrenica and Zepa,[6] the Mount Igman demilitarized zone, and anti-sniping.[1] They were to assist in the total restoration of utilities and engage in joint economic activities to normalize life in all territories, particularly in and around the safe areas. Under ICRC auspices, the parties were to begin, by 15 January, releasing detained persons and searching for the missing. In addition, the parties were to cooperate with UNPROFOR in monitoring the withdrawal of all foreign troops.

Having received the texts of the two agreements, the Security Council met on 6 January and, after consultations among its members, authorized the President to make the following statement[7] on the Council's behalf:

The Security Council welcomes the agreements between the Bosnian parties on a cease-fire and on a complete cessation of hostilities in the Republic of Bosnia and Herzegovina concluded on 23 December 1994 and 31 December 1994 respectively. It commends the efforts of all who worked to achieve them.

The Security Council stresses the importance it attaches to immediate and full compliance with the agreements. It attaches the highest priority at this juncture to the timely completion of the various steps envisaged in the agreement on a complete cessation of hostilities. It looks to the parties and others concerned to cooperate fully with the United Nations Protection Force (UNPROFOR) in their implementation. The Security Council calls upon all forces to cease fighting around Bihac. It supports efforts in train to strengthen UNPROFOR, and encourages Member States to make available the personnel and equipment needed for UNPROFOR to supervise and monitor the agreements.

The Security Council will continue its consideration of all aspects of the crisis in Bosnia and Herzegovina and of the Secretary-General's report of 1 December 1994.[8]

The Security Council deems it imperative to intensify efforts under the auspices of the Contact Group to achieve an overall settlement on the basis of the acceptance of the peace plan of the Contact Group as a starting point. It will give its full support to such efforts.

*Meeting number.* SC 3486.

**Report of the Secretary-General (March).** In his report of 22 March 1995,[9] intended to assist the Security Council in its consideration of the UNPROFOR mandate, the Secretary-General noted that the Bosnian Croat leaders had joined in the two agreements on 2 January.

A month into the implementation of the agreements, military activities declined significantly throughout the country, except in the Bihac region in north-western Bosnia and Herzegovina (see below, under "Bihac"), the Secretary-General reported. There had been a marked improvement in the quality of life in Sarajevo, and in freedom of movement and in the humanitarian situation in general. Compliance with certain other existing agreements (on Sarajevo, Mount Igman, Srebrenica, Gorazde), stipulated in the cessation-of-hostilities agreement, improved significantly. The roads around Sarajevo, closed since July 1994, were opened, first to a limited number of "official international humanitarian organizations" and then to civilians and other humanitarian organizations. A joint reconnaissance of the Mount Igman demilitarized zone verified the Bosnian Army's evacuation of that zone, although UNPROFOR continued to observe government troops transiting through.

The evacuation of Mount Igman made progress possible on the issue of routes: on 1 February, the airport roads were opened to the first category of humanitarian organizations; on 5 February, UNPROFOR informed the two sides that those roads would be opened the next day to civilian traffic; three days later, the Sarajevo-Visoko bus route, via Serb-controlled territory, was opened on the same basis. In February, therefore, an estimated 116,000 people crossed the airport roads, with some 88,000 people travelling between the two Bosnian Government–controlled areas and 28,000 between the two Bosnian Serb–controlled areas. Towards the end of the month, however, the bus route to Visoko was closed by the Bosnian Serbs, as were the airport roads in March, following the killing of two Serb girls by a Bosnian sniper.

Despite the general success of the cease-fire agreement and some success of the cessation-of-hostilities agreement, little was achieved in January on the provisions relating to separation of forces, interpositioning of UNPROFOR troops and heavy-weapons withdrawal. The vital mechanism of the joint commissions failed to function, for both sides refused to participate in commission meetings. Those developments, coupled with the Government's refusal to accept the posting of Bosnian Serb liaison officers at the UNPROFOR sector headquarters on Government-controlled territory and the parties' continued military preparations, gave rise to concerns about the long-term viability of the cessation-of-hostilities agreement. It increasingly appeared that the parties' objective was a winter truce, during which their forces would be able to rest, reorganize and train for a future offensive, the Secretary-General said.

The Government had already made clear to UNPROFOR that it was not interested in extending the agreement if the Bosnian Serbs were unwilling to accept the 1994 Contact Group peace proposal,[10] at least as a starting point for negotiations. Government forces had begun to restrict UNPROFOR's freedom of movement in Government-controlled territory, thus precluding UNPROFOR access to certain areas of central Bosnia and Herzegovina. Likewise, the Bosnian Serbs had begun imposing restrictions and tight controls on supplies to the enclaves, particularly fuel and medical supplies, and had threatened to renew hostilities unless the Government immediately complied with the cessation-of-hostilities agreement. The impasse led to a deterioration of the security situation in Sarajevo. Shelling incidents

increased, as did sniping at civilians and targeting of UNPROFOR and UNHCR aircraft. Those, in addition to recent government offensives in Travnik and Tuzla, the Secretary-General noted, were some of the signs of a steady deterioration in the overall situation in the country.

The continued lack of trust between the parties and their unwillingness to break out of a vicious circle of linkages had made it difficult to achieve further progress in implementation of the cessation-of-hostilities agreement and had undermined the achievements gained so far. In the absence of a real will by the parties to cooperate, UNPROFOR was unable to resolve outstanding issues among them, the Secretary-General concluded.

**SECURITY COUNCIL ACTION (3 May)**

Following the expiration on 30 April of the comprehensive cease-fire and cessation-of-hostilities agreements, and in view of the parties' failure to renew them, the Council met on 3 May and authorized the President to make the statement below[11] on the Council's behalf:

> The Security Council is deeply concerned about the failure of the Bosnian parties to agree to an extension of the agreements on a cease-fire and a complete cessation of hostilities in the Republic of Bosnia and Herzegovina and the recent deterioration of the situation there. It stresses once again the unacceptability of all attempts to resolve the conflict in the Republic of Bosnia and Herzegovina by military means.
>
> The Security Council calls upon the Bosnian parties to agree without further delay to a further cease-fire and a complete cessation of hostilities and, in this regard, fully supports the negotiating efforts of UNPROFOR and other international efforts aimed at persuading the Bosnian parties to agree to such a cease-fire and complete cessation of hostilities. The Council urges the Bosnian parties to abstain from any steps which may lead to further escalation of the conflict and reaffirms the need for a political settlement on the basis of the acceptance of the Contact Group plan as a starting point.

*Meeting number.* SC 3530.

**Report of the Secretary-General (May).** The Secretary-General on 30 May reported on developments in Bosnia and Herzegovina, both on the ground and regarding the parties' attitude affecting the UNPROFOR mandate,[12] taking account of the concerns raised by the Security Council, as well as of issues raised by the Bosnian Government on 22 March[13] regarding the mandate's implementation.

The Secretary-General stated that the continued lack of diplomatic progress and the breakdown of the 1994 cessation-of-hostilities agreement in March 1995 caused fighting to spread from the Bihac area to central Bosnia and Tuzla and thence to Sarajevo. Bosnian Serb forces increased pressure on the city by harassing convoys, hijacking UN vehicles, closing the airport to humanitarian and civilian traffic, sniping, and targeting the Mount Igman road with heavy-weapons fire. Government forces were also responsible for a number of incidents. After the agreement expired on 30 April, the fighting around Sarajevo further intensified, marked by the sustained use of heavy weapons by the two sides, increased civilian casualties and mounting calls for the stricter enforcement of the "heavy-weapons exclusion zone", i.e., the 20-kilometre radius around Sarajevo, excluding Pale.

As previous measures had failed to restore respect for the heavy-weapons agreement and as neither side appeared ready to stop fighting, UNPROFOR called for air strikes on 25 and 26 May, targeting eight bunkers within an ammunition dump near Pale. Bosnian Serb forces reacted by surrounding additional weapons collection points; shelling all safe areas, except Zepa, resulting in particularly heavy casualties in Tuzla where some 70 civilians were killed and over 130 injured; taking more than 300 UNMOs into custody, using a number of them as human shields to deter further air strikes; and cutting electricity to the city.

The Secretary-General presented a detailed analysis of the UNPROFOR mandate as it had progressively been expanded, emphasizing throughout that its effective implementation required the consent and cooperation of the parties. This was illustrated by UNPROFOR's use of its good offices, in keeping with repeated Council requests, to assist the parties to settle their differences peacefully. While it had earlier achieved considerable successes, beginning with the 1992 Sarajevo airport agreement,[14] UNPROFOR had less success in subsequently persuading the parties to honour their commitments. With the deterioration of the military situation in recent weeks, UNPROFOR, having been denied the parties' cooperation, was no longer able to fulfil its mandate of ensuring the security and functioning of Sarajevo airport or the uninterrupted continuation of humanitarian operations there.[15] The principal threat to airport security had been the frequent firings at aircraft using it, mainly by Bosnian Serbs and, on several occasions, by Bosnian government forces.

As to UNPROFOR's task to support UNHCR efforts to deliver humanitarian relief throughout Bosnia and Herzegovina, particularly through convoy protection,[16] the difficulties impeding its full implementation centred essentially on the refusal by the various parties, especially the Bosnian Serb party, to respect UNPROFOR's freedom of movement and their readiness in some areas to use humanitarian assistance to further their war aims, including denying such assistance to populations so as to make them leave their homes, or seizing a proportion of humanitarian cargoes for their own use. None the less, UNHCR and UNPROFOR had been successful in meeting humanitarian requirements in most parts of the country. It was mainly in Bihac, and more recently in Sarajevo, that the parties' non-cooperation had caused major shortfalls in delivery.

UNPROFOR's ground monitoring at selected airfields of compliance with the ban on all military flights over the airspace of Bosnia and Herzegovina[17] had been largely successful. A recent exception involved several Croatian sorties through Bosnian airspace to bomb positions in Sector West (Western Slavonia) in Croatia. The deployment of international observers to monitor the borders of Bosnia and Herzegovina[18] was never implemented, since Member States were unable to make available the number of observers required for the task, the Secretary-General said.

UNPROFOR had mixed results in carrying out its responsibilities in the safe areas.[19] When consent and cooperation of the parties had been forthcoming, it had achieved considerable success in monitoring cease-fires, stabilizing confrontation lines and improving security by resolving localized disputes or outbreaks of fighting in those areas. It had also assisted in arranging medical evacuations, delivering and reporting on humanitarian aid, brokering local agreements to improve the populations' living conditions and promoting confidence-building arrangements. However, its ability to carry out its safe-area mandate and particularly to deter deliberate attacks on the areas had been severely limited by the inherent deficiencies of the safe-area regime described by the Secretary-General in his 1994 report[8] and by the military activities of the two sides. In recent weeks those difficulties had increased as relations deteriorated between the parties and as the safe areas were drawn into the intensifying conflict throughout the country (see below).

Regarding UNPROFOR's tasks relating to the monitoring of the 1994 cease-fire agreement between the Chiefs of Staff of the Army of Bosnia and Herzegovina and the Croatian Defence Council,[20] the Secretary-General stated that the presence of UNPROFOR on both sides of the cease-fire line had greatly contributed to stabilizing the situation within the Federation of Bosnia and Herzegovina and to building confidence between the Bosnian Muslim and Bosnian Croat communities.

### Safe areas

The Secretary-General, in his account of the situation in the safe areas, as contained in his 30 May report,[12] pointed to the fact that Security Council resolution 836(1993),[19] defining UNPROFOR's mandate as to the safe areas and the parameters for the use of force in "self-defence", did not require the Government of Bosnia and Herzegovina to withdraw its military or paramilitary units from those areas. The Council had made clear in presidential statements, however, that "provocative actions by whomsoever committed" were unacceptable. He recalled emphasizing that the party defending a safe area must comply with certain obligations—especially not to launch unprovoked attacks from the area—if it was to achieve the primary objective of the safe-area regime: the protection of the civilian population.

The Secretary-General noted that the Government's forces in recent months had considerably increased their military activity in and around most safe areas; many of them, including Sarajevo, Tuzla and Bihac, had been incorporated into the Government's broader military campaigns. The headquarters and logistics installations of the Fifth Corps of the Army of Bosnia and Herzegovina were located in the town of Bihac and those of the Second Corps in the town of Tuzla. The Government also maintained a substantial number of troops in Srebrenica (in this case in violation of a demilitarization agreement[5]), Gorazde and Zepa, while Sarajevo was the site of the General Command and other military installations.

The Bosnian Serb reaction to government offensives launched from safe areas had generally been to respond against military targets within those areas, often disproportionately. Notwithstanding the provocation, such military responses were in violation of the safe-area regime and other local agreements. The Bosnian Serbs had also initiated unprovoked shelling of safe areas. In both cases, civilian casualties had occurred. UNPROFOR's mandate to deter attacks on the safe areas required it to react to Serb actions, irrespective of whether they were in response to offensives launched by the other side. This made the impartiality of UNPROFOR difficult to maintain and it was seen as a party to the conflict, with resulting risks to isolated UN personnel.

UNPROFOR's capacity to carry out its safe-area mandate had also been affected by the Bosnian Serbs' denial of freedom of movement to and from the three eastern safe areas (Gorazde, Srebrenica, Zepa) so that supplies for UNPROFOR personnel by road had become virtually impossible. The alternative to resupply convoys would be airlifting by helicopter, which involved considerable dangers, the Secretary-General stated.

### Bihac

**Report of the Secretary-General.** According to the Secretary-General's report of 22 March,[9] fighting and the blockade of humanitarian supplies continued in the Bihac pocket. In active support of the Bosnian rebel leader Fikret Abdic,[21] who maintained his stronghold in Velika Kladusa, the Krajina (or Knin) Serbs continued to launch cross-border artillery and ground attacks on the pocket and to frustrate UNPROFOR and UNHCR by insisting that humanitarian convoys destined for the pocket and UNPROFOR supplies for the Bangladeshi battalion there pass through Velika Kladusa, as well as by subjecting convoy personnel to erratic and obstructive "checking" and to the dangers of either deliberate targeting or being caught in crossfire. UNPROFOR's repeated efforts to achieve a cease-fire and attempts by the Special Representative of the Secretary-General, in coordination with UNHCR, to gain regular access to the region without traversing Velika Kladusa had not met with success.

The complexity of the situation in Bihac, where five more or less distinct parties could be identified, posed a daunting challenge for UNPROFOR, the Secretary-General continued. In the south, near Bihac town, the situation was at an impasse. The Bosnian Serbs insisted on their demand that the Government's forces return to the positions they had occupied at the signing of the 1994 cessation-of-hostilities agreement. The Government, having retaken control of the safe area and its water supply, refused, and equally insisted that the Krajina Serb forces withdraw from the pocket, as stipulated by the agreement. Fighting continued in the north, near Velika Kladusa, where the Krajina Serb forces remained actively involved. The resultant instability and the prospect of an UNPROFOR withdrawal from Croatia (upon the expiry of the mandate on 31 March) made unlikely UNHCR access to the south, where there was fear of imminent and widespread malnutrition. The Secretary-General warned that, should the situation fester, Bihac could again become a flashpoint for wider conflict in Bosnia and Herzegovina.

**Communications.** The role of the Krajina Serbs in Bihac was the subject of two communications from Bosnia and Herzegovina on 10[22] and 30 January.[23] The latter reported that the allied Bosnian Serb and Croatian Serb forces had fired more than 900 shells on the safe area proper and on other towns in the region; and, moreover, that UNMOs confirmed having observed soldiers in Bosnian Serb uniforms manning five artillery guns south of Velika Kladusa and two trucks carrying 40 such soldiers driving south through it. Bosnia and Herzegovina called on the Council to put an end to that aggression and see to the compliance with its relevant resolutions, or risk erosion of the agreements.

**SECURITY COUNCIL ACTION**

The Security Council met on 17 February and, following consultations among its members, authorized the President to make the statement below[24] on the Council's behalf:

> The Security Council is deeply concerned at the continued fighting around Bihac and deplores the serious humanitarian situation in the Bihac area. It reaffirms its support for the Special Representative of the Secretary-General and UNPROFOR.
>
> The Security Council recalls the statement of the President of the Security Council of 6 January 1995. It reiterates the importance it attaches to full compliance with the agreements between the Bosnian parties on a cease-fire and on a complete cessation of hostilities in the Republic of Bosnia and Herzegovina concluded on 23 December 1994 and 31 December 1994 respectively. All involved must now make a concerted effort to consolidate what has been achieved so far to avoid the risk of a renewed outbreak of hostilities.
>
> The Security Council demands that all forces in the Bihac area cease fighting immediately and cooperate fully with UNPROFOR in achieving an effective cease-fire. The Security Council reiterates its condemnation of the continued violations of the international border between the Republic of Croatia and the Republic of Bosnia and Herzegovina.
>
> The Security Council condemns the recent obstruction of humanitarian convoys destined for the Bihac area by the Croatian Serb and Abdic forces. It welcomes the fact that convoys are now getting through, and calls upon all parties and others concerned henceforth to facilitate the unhindered flow of humanitarian assistance and complete freedom of movement for UNPROFOR.

*Meeting number.* SC 3501.

**Further communications.** Bosnia and Herzegovina alerted the Security Council on 30 April to the sharply deteriorating situation in the Bihac region: during the weekend, the Bosnian Serbs had fired six shells on the Bihac safe area and five more on Cazin; as reported by a UN spokesman, the Knin Serbs had dispatched 70 of their troops across the border into the region and, in renewed aerial attacks, dropped two cluster bombs.[25] On 23 July, it reported that a 20,000-strong combined force of Bosnian and Croatian Serbs, and Abdic paramilitary and special Yugoslav Army units, supported by 100 tanks, had mounted an all-out assault on Bihac.[26] It further reported on 1 August that the region continued to be under assault, precipitating an alarming humanitarian situation.[27]

In the meantime, Croatia on 20 July alleged that the offensive on Bihac was being coordinated by Yugoslavia (Serbia and Montenegro) and led by two Yugoslav Army generals. It further alleged that, in support of that offensive, a major troop build-up and heavy-weapons deployment were under way in Knin and Glina. Reiterating its view that displacement of the 200,000 residents of Bihac was a serious threat to its security and stability, Croatia warned that it might be compelled to take

measures to secure the safe-area status of Bihac, should it become threatened.[28]

By identical letters of 24 July to the Secretary-General and the Security Council, Bangladesh, which had 1,200 of its troops deployed in Bihac, urged the use of air strikes and the immediate deployment of UNPROFOR's rapid reaction force to all enclaves under attack.[29]

### Gorazde

During the year, a number of communications were addressed to the Security Council and the Secretary-General regarding the safe area of Gorazde. Chief among those was a 26 July letter by the Secretary-General informing the Council of his support of the North Atlantic Council (NAC) decisions of 25 July regarding the use of NATO air power to deter Bosnian Serb attacks on Gorazde.[30] He agreed with NATO that a Bosnian Serb attack on that safe area should be met by a decisive response, including through air strikes. To streamline decision-making within the UN chain of command when the use of air power was deemed necessary, the Secretary-General on 26 July delegated his authority to make such a decision to the Special Representative, who in turn delegated it to the UNPF Force Commander and from him to the UNPROFOR Commander.

The Secretary-General noted that NAC had asked NATO, in consultation with UNPF, to formulate proposals on the possible use of air power also in connection with the ongoing attacks on Sarajevo and the Bihac pocket. He had informed the troop-contributing countries of those steps and had instructed the Special Representative to take all measures necessary to protect UN personnel in the theatre and to reduce their vulnerability to retaliation and hostage-taking.

In furtherance of United Nations–NATO cooperation, the Secretary-General instructed the Under-Secretary-General for Peace-keeping Operations, Kofi Annan, and the UNPF Force Commander to undertake consultations with NATO in Brussels, Belgium, on the operational modalities for implementing the agreed measures.

Earlier, on 21 July, Yugoslavia (Serbia and Montenegro) called on the leadership of "Republika Srpska" not to attack the enclave of Gorazde, stressing that the solution to the Bosnian crisis could be achieved only by political means.[31]

Bosnia and Herzegovina on 18 August sought clarification of press reports on new arrangements for the Gorazde safe area and its 20-kilometre military exclusion zone;[32] namely, that UNPROFOR would withdraw from the area, which would then come under NATO air protection.[33] Reporting on 21 August that the Serb shelling of Gorazde earlier that day had killed three children, Bosnia and Herzegovina asked what it would take for NATO to react to such terrorism.[34] On 24 August, it requested either the immediate suspension of UNPROFOR's withdrawal from Gorazde or the adoption of a new Council resolution providing for an efficient defence of that safe area.[35]

**Statement for the Secretary-General.** The Spokesman for the Secretary-General on 18 August issued a press statement to the effect that the Secretary-General had taken note with concern of press reports suggesting that the United Nations was in the process of abandoning the safe area of Gorazde, from which the UNPROFOR infantry presence was about to be withdrawn. The statement reaffirmed that the United Nations remained fully committed to its mandate of deterring attacks on Gorazde and other safe areas—to be achieved through a combination of a UN military presence on the ground and the threat of robust strikes from the air.

The statement explained that the UN presence in Gorazde currently consisted of some 180 British and some 90 Ukrainian troops. The latter had been disarmed by the Government's soldiers and were thus unable to function. At the request of the United Kingdom, its troops were scheduled to withdraw from Gorazde upon completion of their rotation at the end of August. UN attempts to replace them with a battalion from another country or from a combination of countries had been unsuccessful.

In the absence of a feasible infantry option to replace the British troops, the United Nations had no choice but to deploy UNMOs in Gorazde, backed up by NATO air power. Accordingly, the Secretary-General had instructed the Force Commander to draw up plans for a revised UN military deployment in Gorazde to serve as the eyes and ears of the international community, working in close cooperation with NATO. The Secretary-General remained committed to deterring attacks on Gorazde and, in particular, on its 60,000 resident civilians.

## Sarajevo

**Communications.** By several letters transmitted between 8 February and 1 May, Bosnia and Herzegovina drew attention to what it described as the strangulation of Sarajevo by the Bosnian Serbs, who, it claimed, had come to exercise de facto control of the Sarajevo airport. It alleged, on 8 February, that humanitarian deliveries to Sarajevo had remained blocked at the airport for months due to obstructions by a Bosnian Serb checkpoint at a key intersection on the access route from the airport to Sarajevo city. Bosnia and Herzegovina demanded that, in accordance with existing agreements, UN control of that route be restored and that airport local staff, other than cargo inspectors, be removed forthwith.[36] It complained on 29 March that the "blue route" to Sarajevo exclusively transecting Government-controlled territory and the few hundred metres of runway mandated to be under UNPROFOR control had been closed on demand by the Bosnian Serbs and could be reopened only with their agreement.[37] On 24 April, it reported that Contact Group members had recently been denied access to Sarajevo, that the Ambassador of the United States to Bosnia and Herzegovina had been prevented from departing Sarajevo on a UN flight, and that, on 21 April, four United States and German diplomats, on arriving at the airport, had been forbidden to proceed to the city.[38]

Germany and the United States, on 25 April, voiced their profound concern over the 21 April statement by the Bosnian Serb liaison officer at Sarajevo airport that his authorities would guarantee the safety neither of the UN aircraft, if the German and United States Contact Group members proceeded to Sarajevo to meet with the Bosnian Government, nor of the Contact Group members themselves during their transit from the airport to the city. They also voiced concern over statements by the Bosnian Serb leader, Radovan Karadzic, threatening imposition of conditions on the airport's use by diplomatic delegations. They supported UNPROFOR's position that recent Bosnian Serb actions to obstruct the airport's normal functioning were totally unacceptable.[39]

On 1 May, Bosnia and Herzegovina reported that on the morning of that day, Bosnian Serb troops had raided a weapons collection site at Ilidza, seizing all the heavy weapons; and that sniping and shelling had escalated sharply, drawing no response from UNPROFOR and but two NATO overflights of the city.[40]

### SECURITY COUNCIL ACTION

When the Security Council met on 3 May to urge the extensions of the cease-fire and cessation-of-hostilities agreements, it also considered the ongoing restrictions at Sarajevo airport. After consultations among its members on the latter, the Council authorized the President to make the following statement[41] on the Council's behalf:

> The Security Council is deeply concerned about the obstruction of the normal operation of Sarajevo airport, including the suspension of the humanitarian relief airlift, caused by Bosnian Serb threats against United Nations aircraft and humanitarian relief flights, and by their attempts to impose restrictions on the use of Sarajevo airport by official missions as foreseen in the 5 June 1992 agreement. Such obstruction is in breach of the 5 June 1992 agreement and of the Council's previous resolutions, in particular resolution 761(1992), and is unacceptable.

Obstruction of the humanitarian relief also constitutes a violation of international humanitarian law.

In that context the Security Council demands that all parties and others concerned comply fully with the 5 June 1992 agreement and create immediately the necessary conditions for unimpeded delivery of humanitarian supplies to Sarajevo and other destinations in the Republic of Bosnia and Herzegovina. It calls upon the Bosnian Serb party to guarantee the safety of all UNPROFOR supervised flights to Sarajevo, including humanitarian relief flights.

The Security Council requests the Secretary-General to keep it informed of discussions with the Bosnian Serb party on the restoration of the normal functioning of Sarajevo airport so that it might take further action as necessary.

*Meeting number.* SC 3530.

**Further communications.** Updating its reports on developments in Sarajevo on 7 May, Bosnia and Herzegovina stated that a single shell fired that day from a Bosnian Serb position within the Sarajevo exclusion zone had killed at least 10 civilians and wounded some 50 others.[42] Further stating that Sarajevo had for some time been increasingly targeted by heavy weapons, it asked whether Council resolutions 824(1993),[43] 836(1993)[19] and 900(1994),[44] as well as the 1994 NATO declaration[6] regarding heavy-weapons withdrawal from a 20-kilometre radius from the centre of Sarajevo, were still valid. Bosnia and Herzegovina reiterated this inquiry on 29 May[45] and demanded a formal reply to it on 1 June.[46]

Meanwhile, on 8 May, Bosnia and Herzegovina drew attention to the incessant shelling and deliberate targeting of Sarajevo's civilian areas, in particular the suburb of Hrasnica, located at the base of the "blue route" and Mount Igman, within the Sarajevo exclusion zone.[47] In the face of the deteriorating political and humanitarian situation in the country, it asked the Secretary-General on 11 May, as a minimum, to call for the urgent reopening of Sarajevo airport to humanitarian flights and of the Butmir-Dobrinja section of the "blue route" (in addition to calling for an immediate halt to the transfer of the Croatian Serb population from Western Slovenia into Bosnia and Herzegovina).[48] It further reported as follows: on 16 May, that the Bosnian Serbs had that day launched a multi-pronged and multifaceted assault on Sarajevo's defensive lines and population;[49] on 24 May, that, according to an UNPROFOR spokesman, some shells that had landed in Sarajevo's market-place and surrounding areas contained "white phosphorus", a substance banned by the 1949 Geneva Conventions on the protection of the victims of war;[50] on 25 May, that it welcomed NATO's limited action but did not appreciate being lectured to or threatened by a UN command, which, by its own admission, had not reacted to earlier Serb violations and murder of

civilians because its first priority was to avoid Bosnian Serb reprisals on UN personnel;[51] and, on 29 May, that the Bosnian Serbs had again deprived Sarajevo city of electricity (by disconnecting the main transformer stations), natural gas (by shutting the gas valve at Zvornik) and water (by diverting the power supply intended for the Bacevo water pumping station), and had blocked deliveries of fuel, thus making for an extremely critical situation in the city.[52]

On 31 May, following an extraordinary session of its Government held earlier that day on the critical security and humanitarian situation in Sarajevo, Bosnia and Herzegovina demanded that UNPROFOR be restored in full in Sarajevo to assume protection of the city's entire exclusion zone and of the humanitarian convoys destined for it; that UNHCR and UNPROFOR start food deliveries via the Metkovic-Tarcin-Hrasnica-Sarajevo land route and secure that route by all means necessary; and that UNPROFOR take control of the city's energy and water supply systems.[53]

Between June and August, Bosnia and Herzegovina continued to report on the unrelenting siege of Sarajevo, describing the heavy toll it was taking on the civilian population,[54] such as the deaths of 31 civilians and the wounding of 18 others due to intermittent shelling and sniping,[55] the deaths on 28 August of a further 33 civilians and the wounding of 84 others due to the shelling of the Markale market-place,[56] and the continued bombardment of civilians.[57]

Yugoslavia (Serbia and Montenegro) on 7 September expressed concern over what it said were inconsistencies in the findings of UNPROFOR's investigation into the 28 August explosion in the Markale market, which singled out the Bosnian Serbs as the party responsible for the crime.[58] It claimed that NATO's unprecedented "retaliation" against that party had resulted in serious consequences, including loss of life and extensive material damage. It drew attention to scepticism regarding the official report, heightened by a statement of UNPROFOR Chief of Staff Colonel Andrei Demourenko (Russian Federation) that the chances were one in a million that the Bosnian Serb side was responsible and by the 2 September press statement by UNPROFOR spokesman Lieutenant-Colonel Chris Vernon (United Kingdom) that "Demourenko was not the only one to have challenged the official version of the event". In its letter, Yugoslavia (Serbia and Montenegro) cited other events that, like this one and the 1994 shelling of the same market-place,[59] were, it said, usually orchestrated on the eve of crucial negotiations to resolve the crisis in Bosnia and Herzegovina.

Also on 7 September, Yugoslavia (Serbia and Montenegro) demanded an immediate halt to the continuing NATO bombardment of Serb positions and other targets in "Republika Srpska", as well as to the actions of UNPROFOR's rapid reaction force, reasoning that those represented a direct attack on the announced peace initiative that had been accepted by "Republika Srpska".[60] Yugoslavia (Serbia and Montenegro) said it was both unacceptable and incomprehensible to continue with air and other attacks and simultaneously to push for negotiations. It warned that UN and NATO military intervention against only one party encouraged the other parties to the conflict to resort to the war option, thus triggering a chain reaction of unforeseeable consequences that might be difficult to avert.

### Srebrenica

**Communications (9-12 July).** Bosnia and Herzegovina on 9 July requested an emergency session of the Security Council to address the situation in the eastern safe area of Srebrenica.[61] The area, which had sustained a shattering barrage of more than 1,000 shells the previous day, was currently under a full-scale offensive by the Bosnian Serbs, who had advanced into the town, at some points as deep as 5 kilometres. The UNPROFOR observation posts, manned by the Netherlands contingent, had also come under siege, causing some to be abandoned.

The offensive and subsequent occupation of Srebrenica on 11 July drew immediate condemnation by the President of the Federation of Bosnia and Herzegovina,[62] EU[63] and the Organization of the Islamic Conference Contact Group on Bosnia and Herzegovina (OICCG).[64]

**SECURITY COUNCIL ACTION (12 July)**

The Security Council convened on 12 July and adopted **resolution 1004(1995)**.

*The Security Council,*

*Recalling* all its earlier relevant resolutions,

*Reaffirming* its commitment to the sovereignty, territorial integrity and political independence of the Republic of Bosnia and Herzegovina,

*Gravely concerned* at the deterioration in the situation in and around the safe area of Srebrenica, Republic of Bosnia and Herzegovina, and at the plight of the civilian population there,

*Gravely concerned also* at the very serious situation which confronts personnel of the United Nations Protection Force (UNPROFOR) and a great number of displaced persons within the safe area at Potocari, especially the lack of essential food supplies and medical care,

*Paying tribute* to the personnel of UNPROFOR deployed in the safe area of Srebrenica,

*Condemning* the offensive by the Bosnian Serb forces against the safe area of Srebrenica, and in particular the detention by the Bosnian Serb forces of UNPROFOR personnel,

*Condemning also* all attacks on UNPROFOR personnel,

*Recalling* the Agreement for the demilitarization of Srebrenica of 18 April 1993 by the Government of the Republic of Bosnia and Herzegovina and the Bosnian Serb party, and regretting that it has not been implemented in full by either party,

*Stressing* the importance of renewed efforts to achieve an overall peaceful settlement, and the unacceptability of any attempt to resolve the conflict in the Republic of Bosnia and Herzegovina by military means,

*Acting* under Chapter VII of the Charter of the United Nations,

1. *Demands* that the Bosnian Serb forces cease their offensive and withdraw from the safe area of Srebrenica immediately;

2. *Demands also* that the parties respect fully the status of the safe area of Srebrenica in accordance with the Agreement of 18 April 1993;

3. *Demands further* that the parties respect fully the safety of UNPROFOR personnel and ensure their complete freedom of movement, including resupply;

4. *Demands* that the Bosnian Serb forces immediately and unconditionally release unharmed all detained UNPROFOR personnel;

5. *Demands* that all parties allow unimpeded access for the United Nations High Commissioner for Refugees and other international humanitarian agencies to the safe area of Srebrenica in order to alleviate the plight of the civilian population, and in particular that they cooperate on the restoration of utilities;

6. *Requests* the Secretary-General to use all resources available to him to restore the status as defined by the Agreement of 18 April 1993 of the safe area of Srebrenica in accordance with the mandate of UNPROFOR, and calls on the parties to cooperate to that end;

7. *Decides* to remain actively seized of the matter.

Security Council resolution 1004(1995)

12 July 1995      Meeting 3553      Adopted unanimously

5-nation draft (S/1995/560).

*Sponsors:* France, Germany, Italy, United Kingdom, United States.

**Communications (13 and 14 July).** On 13 July, Bosnia and Herzegovina conveyed reports of human rights violations in Srebrenica: males 13 years and older were being separated from their families and subjected to forced labour at the trenches and to other abuses, while females aged between 15 and 35 were being rounded up and removed, along with truckloads of males, to unknown destinations.[65] It asked the Secretary-General to dispatch UNPROFOR troops and medical units to the area to protect and assist the civilian population, to ensure the safe passage of all refugees fleeing Srebrenica for Government-held territories, emergency assistance for them, and an accounting of all persons taken by the Bosnian Serbs, as well as their immediate release. In addition, on 14 July, Bosnia and Herzegovina demanded that the Tuzla airport be opened to allow emergency airlifts of food, clothing, medical supplies and temporary shelters for the refugees.[66]

Ukraine on 13 July called for the immediate withdrawal of the Bosnian Serbs from Srebrenica,[67] as did the Group of Arab States on 14 July,[68] with Ukraine further calling for the immediate and unconditional release of all detained UN peace-keepers. Also on 14 July, the Federation of Bosnia and Herzegovina, in condemning the actions of the Bosnian Serb forces against Srebrenica, spoke of the assistance provided to those forces by the Army of Yugoslavia (Serbia and Montenegro).[69]

SECURITY COUNCIL ACTION (14 July)

The Security Council met on 14 July and, following consultations among its members, authorized the President to make the statement below[70] on the Council's behalf:

The Security Council recalls its resolution 1004(1995). The Council is deeply concerned about the ongoing forced relocation of tens of thousands of civilians from the Srebrenica safe area to the Tuzla region by the Bosnian Serb party. Such a forced relocation is a clear violation of the human rights of the civilian population. It is especially concerned about reports of grave mistreatment and killing of innocent civilians. It is equally concerned about reports that up to 4,000 men and boys have been forcibly removed by the Bosnian Serb party from the Srebrenica safe area. It demands that in conformity with internationally recognized standards of conduct and international law the Bosnian Serb party release them immediately, respect fully the rights of the civilian population of the Srebrenica safe area and other persons protected under international humanitarian law, and permit access by the International Committee of the Red Cross.

The Security Council again condemns the unacceptable practice of "ethnic cleansing" and reaffirms that those who have committed or have ordered the commission of such acts will be held individually responsible in respect of such acts.

The Security Council demands that the Bosnian Serb party immediately allow unimpeded access to the civilian population of the Srebrenica safe area by international humanitarian organizations and cooperate with any procedure established by those organizations to determine which civilians wish to depart the area of Srebrenica. It further demands that the Bosnian Serb party respect fully the rights of those civilians who wish to remain in the safe area and cooperate with efforts to ensure that civilians who wish to depart are allowed to do so with their families in an orderly, safe way in conformity with international law.

The Security Council demands that both sides allow the unhindered movement of humanitarian relief and cooperate with efforts by international organizations and agencies and concerned Governments to provide food, medicine, facilities and housing to the displaced.

The Security Council reiterates its demand that the Bosnian Serb forces immediately and unconditionally release unharmed all detained personnel of the United Nations Protection Force (UNPROFOR), and that the parties respect fully the safety of all UNPROFOR personnel and ensure their complete freedom of movement.

The Security Council pays tribute to all the personnel of UNPROFOR, and of the United Nations High Commissioner for Refugees, especially those deployed in the area of Srebrenica. It notes that the presence and bravery of the troops has undoubtedly saved the lives of many civilians in the Srebrenica area.

*Meeting number.* SC 3554.

**Further communications.** By a statement transmitted on 17 July, the OSCE Chairman-in-Office noted that, as a result of the fall of Srebrenica, 40,000 civilian lives were at risk; the Netherlands contingent of UNPROFOR had been forced to leave the area, along with thousands of civilians.[71] In addition to demanding the immediate release of the UN peace-keepers detained by the Bosnian Serbs, the Chairman-in-Office stated that the take-over of Srebrenica, the attacks on the civilian population and on the UN personnel there and in other safe areas, and the blockade of humanitarian deliveries to Sarajevo were elements of a consistent pattern of the Bosnian Serbs' repudiation of the United Nations and the international community and of all efforts to settle the Bosnian crisis peacefully.

A statement by Malaysia, transmitted also on 17 July, strongly condemned the Bosnian Serb aggression on Srebrenica and called on the Security Council and NATO to stop the Serbs, using all means available, including military action and air strikes.[72]

Yugoslavia (Serbia and Montenegro), in a 1 November statement, labelled as completely unfounded the claims that the Yugoslav Army had either directly or indirectly taken part in the "operations for the liberation of the Muslim military stronghold of Srebrenica".[73] Such falsehoods, it claimed, were part of well-known campaigns launched at crucial moments when peace in the former Yugoslavia was about to be reached.

*Tuzla*

On 26 May, Bosnia and Herzegovina reported a Bosnian Serb mortar attack on Tuzla that took the lives of 71 mostly teenaged civilians and maimed many others.[74] Calling the massacre a deliberate act of terrorism in retaliation for NATO's recent limited air strike, it demanded that the Security Council urgently meet to condemn the action and deal with it as it would any other terrorist act. It went on to say, in two subsequent letters that day, that the massacre would have caused shock and drawn resolute action against its perpetrators had it happened elsewhere in the West;[75] it voiced profound disappointment that the Council's condemnation, in a press statement, had merely referred to "shelling of the safe areas", rather than identifying the massacre for what it was: a terrorist act.[76]

Also on 26 May, OICCG joined in condemning the "barbaric attack"; it called on the Council and NATO to live up to their commitments and obligations under relevant resolutions and decisions and resolutely respond to it.[77] On 9 June, Saudi Arabia, in addition to condemning the Tuzla attack, also condemned the shooting down on 28 May of the aircraft carrying the Minister for Foreign Affairs of Bosnia and Herzegovina near Bihac.[78]

On 8 October, Bosnia and Herzegovina demanded that, consistent with the relevant Council resolutions and NATO decisions, vigorous action be taken against the Bosnian Serbs, who earlier that day had fired Orkan rockets and anti-tank missiles on the Oskova refugee camp in Zivinice, a town within the borders of the Tuzla safe area, and launched an air attack on Tesanj; in all, eight people died and 75 others were injured.[79]

## Zepa

**Communications (13 and 17 July).** Bosnia and Herzegovina notified the Security Council on 13 July that the safe area of Zepa was under the onslaught of Bosnian Serb artillery, tank and infantry; owing to a complete blockade, the humanitarian situation in the area was dire.[80] On 17 July, Bosnia and Herzegovina reported that, despite the courageous resistance of its Army, it could not halt the onslaught; therefore, to prevent a repetition of the brutality dealt the civilian population of Srebrenica, it requested an emergency meeting of the Council to consider the evacuation of Zepa.[81]

SECURITY COUNCIL ACTION (20 July)

Accordingly, the Security Council met on 20 July. Upon completion of consultations among its members, it authorized the President to make the statement below[82] on the Council's behalf:

The Security Council, recalling its previous resolutions, is deeply concerned by the situation in and around the safe area of Zepa. It condemns in the strongest possible terms the offensive by the Bosnian Serb forces against the safe area. The Security Council is also concerned in particular at the plight of the civilian population there.

The Security Council attaches the utmost importance to the safety and well-being of the civilian population in Zepa. It demands that the Bosnian Serb forces refrain from any further action that threatens the safety of that population, and that they respect fully the rights of the civilian population and other persons protected under international humanitarian law. The Council reaffirms its condemnation of all violations of international humanitarian law, and reiterates to all concerned that those who have committed or ordered the commission of such acts will be held

individually responsible in respect of such acts. It reminds the military and political leaders of the Bosnian Serb party that this responsibility extends to any such acts committed by forces under their command.

The Security Council underlines the importance it attaches to the fullest cooperation with UNHCR and other international humanitarian organizations, and demands that they be given unhindered freedom of movement and access to that area. It further demands that the Bosnian Serb authorities cooperate with all efforts, including those of UNPROFOR, to ensure the safety of the civilian population, and in particular its most vulnerable members, including evacuation as requested by the Foreign Minister of the Republic of Bosnia and Herzegovina in his letter of 17 July 1995.

The Security Council strongly condemns the recent acts of violence and intimidation which have occurred against the personnel of UNPROFOR. It demands that both parties ensure the safety and freedom of movement of UNPROFOR personnel at all times.

*Meeting number.* SC 3556.

**Communications (21-25 July).** The Presidents of Bosnia and Herzegovina and of Turkey, by a joint statement issued on 21 July, assessed the grave situation arising from recent developments in the safe areas of Srebrenica and Zepa.[83] Among other things, Turkey's President expressed solidarity with Bosnia and Herzegovina and the readiness of the Turkish Red Crescent to accommodate refugees from Srebrenica and other parts of Bosnia and Herzegovina.

Owing to the deteriorating situation in Zepa and the imminent threat to its civilian population, Bosnia and Herzegovina on 24 July reiterated its request for an UNPROFOR-escorted evacuation of the civilian population and called for another emergency meeting of the Council.[84] It reiterated that request on 25 July, stating that the incessant shelling of the town had driven the population into the neighbouring woods.[85] On the same date, it stressed that if the ongoing negotiations with the Bosnian Serb military, undertaken with UN assistance, were to produce an agreement, clear indications from the Council were crucial; otherwise the civilian population of Zepa would face the fate of Srebrenica.[86]

SECURITY COUNCIL ACTION (25 July)

The Security Council met on 25 July regarding the situation in Zepa and, after consultations among its members, authorized the President to make the following statement[87] on the Council's behalf:

The Security Council is deeply concerned about the situation in and around the safe area of Zepa in the Republic of Bosnia and Herzegovina. The Council notes the letter of 25 July 1995 from the President of the Republic of Bosnia and Herzegovina to the President of the Security Council.

The Security Council reaffirms its previous relevant resolutions and its statement of 20 July 1995. It reiterates in the strongest possible terms its condemnation of the Bosnian Serb offensive against the safe area and demands that the Bosnian Serbs comply fully with the requirements set out in that statement as well as its earlier resolutions. The Council further demands that Bosnian Serb forces withdraw from the safe areas of Srebrenica and Zepa.

The Security Council remains particularly concerned at the plight of the civilian population and other persons protected under international humanitarian law in the Zepa area. It welcomes and supports the efforts being made by UNPROFOR and the international humanitarian agencies, as requested by the President of the Republic of Bosnia and Herzegovina, to achieve a safe evacuation of those civilians who wish to leave and stresses the importance it attaches to the success of these efforts. It requests the Secretary-General to use all resources available to him to that end and calls on the parties to cooperate.

The Security Council demands that UNPROFOR and the international humanitarian agencies be provided with immediate and unhindered access to the population of the area and, in particular, that the Bosnian Serb party provide access to representatives of the International Committee of the Red Cross (ICRC) to all civilians who decide to remain and permit the ICRC to register any persons detained against their will and visit them immediately.

*Meeting number.* SC 3557.

## Bosnia and Herzegovina–Croatia

### Bilateral agreements

The Presidents of Bosnia and Herzegovina, Croatia and the Federation of Bosnia and Herzegovina adopted a declaration on 22 July in Split, Croatia. (The Federation in the Areas of the Republic of Bosnia and Herzegovina with a Majority Bosniac and Croat Population was established in accordance with the March 1994 agreements concluded in Washington, D.C., between the Bosniacs—the term preferred by Bosnia and Herzegovina to refer to citizens loyal to it irrespective of their ethnic origin—and the Bosnian Croats in central Bosnia, following the peace accord between them the month before.[88]) In the declaration, the Presidents addressed those portions of the Washington agreements on joint defence against Serb aggression and on a political solution congruent with the efforts of the international community; pursuant to their declared agreement on strengthening defence cooperation, the Republic of Bosnia and Herzegovina and the Federation of Bosnia and Herzegovina called on Croatia to extend urgent military and other assistance in the defence against aggression, especially in the Bihac area, which Croatia accepted; they also declared to continue to coordinate all aspects of mutual defence.[89]

The Presidents subsequently concluded an agreement on the establishment of a Joint Cooperation Council to promote, plan and coordinate foreign policy, economic and social endeavours and other matters of common interest.[90]

### Intervention in western Bosnia

In his account of events during the UNPROFOR mandate period from April to November,[91] the Secretary-General stated that soon after NATO had conducted multiple air strikes towards the end of August against Bosnian Serb anti-aircraft systems and heavy weapons in the vicinity of Sarajevo, as well as against ammunition supply depots and other military facilities throughout eastern Bosnian-Serb territory, Bosnian government and Croatian forces had begun advancing in the western part of the country. In the week of 10 September, the Bosnian government forces took much of the Ozren salient, while the Croatian forces simultaneously made sweeping advances in the southwest of the country, including the capture of areas traditionally populated by Bosnian Serbs.

**SECURITY COUNCIL ACTION (18 September)**

The Security Council held a meeting on 18 September to consider the military offensives in western Bosnia. After consultations among its members, the Council authorized its President to make the following statement[92] on the Council's behalf:

> The Security Council deplores the rapidly escalating military situation on the ground in the Republic of Bosnia and Herzegovina, and expresses its deep concern about the plight of the civilian population resulting therefrom.
>
> The Security Council demands that all the parties involved in offensive military activities and hostile acts in western Bosnia cease them immediately and respect fully the rights of the local population. It stresses the importance it attaches to intensified efforts to alleviate the plight of refugees and displaced persons, and to the fullest cooperation in this regard by the parties with the United Nations Protection Force (UNPROFOR) and the international humanitarian agencies. The Council reiterates that there can be no military solution to the conflict in the Republic of Bosnia and Herzegovina, and urges all parties not to take military advantage of the present situation. It once again expresses its full support for the Geneva Declaration of Principles of 8 September 1995 which provides a basis for negotiations with the aim of achieving a lasting peace throughout the region.
>
> The Security Council furthermore deplores the death of one Danish peace-keeper and injury to nine others and expresses its condolences to the Government of Denmark and to the family of the peace-keeper who lost his life.

*Meeting number.* SC 3580.

**Communications (19 and 20 September).** Bosnia and Herzegovina explained to the Security Council on 19 September that the actions of the Bosnian, HVO (Croatian Defence Council) and Croatian forces in western and central Bosnia and

Herzegovina were designed to halt the intensifying ethnic cleansing in the region, from which more than 21,000 Bosniacs and Bosnian Croats had been expelled.[93] Bosnia and Herzegovina was convinced that the actions of those allied forces would contribute more effectively to a political solution, based on the Agreed Basic Principles signed in Geneva on 8 September (see below).

Croatia informed the Security Council on 20 September that it was operating in the territory of Bosnia and Herzegovina at the express request of that country's Government, consistent with international law and within the framework of the bilateral agreement concluded between their Governments.[94] Croatia had decided, however, to desist from further action in western Bosnia and Herzegovina that could lead to confrontation in the city of Banja Luka. Croatia firmly viewed its current and previous limited operations as having contributed positively to the peace process in the region, making ever more likely a just and timely political settlement of the problems there. Its actions, Croatia asserted, were the solution, not the problem.

**SECURITY COUNCIL ACTION (21 September)**

The Security Council met again on 21 September and adopted **resolution 1016(1995)**.

*The Security Council,*

*Recalling* all its earlier relevant resolutions and the statement of its President of 18 September 1995,

*Deeply concerned* by the military situation on the ground in the Republic of Bosnia and Herzegovina, and by the plight of the civilian population there which constitutes a humanitarian crisis of significant proportions,

*Especially concerned* by the humanitarian consequences, as a result of the recent fighting, including loss of life and suffering among the civilian population, and a new flow of tens of thousands of refugees and displaced persons,

*Reiterating* its full support for the Geneva Declaration of Principles of 8 September 1995.

*Gravely concerned* about all offensives and hostile acts in the Republic of Bosnia and Herzegovina by the parties concerned, including those most recently undertaken,

1. *Notes* the assurances given by the Governments of the Republic of Bosnia and Herzegovina and the Republic of Croatia regarding offensive actions in western Bosnia and, while taking note of the reports that the offensive actions have slowed down, affirms the need for full compliance with the demands set out in the statement of its President of 18 September 1995;

2. *Deplores* the casualties suffered by the Danish peace-keepers, expresses its condolences to the Government of Denmark and to the families of the peace-keepers who lost their lives, and demands that all parties fully respect the safety of United Nations personnel;

3. *Calls upon* all parties and others concerned to refrain from violence and hostile acts and to reach immediately a cease-fire and a cessation of hostilities throughout the territory of the Republic of Bosnia and Herzegovina;

4. *Calls upon* Member States involved in promoting an overall peaceful settlement in the region to intensify their efforts to this end with the parties to ensure that they take no advantage from the current situation and show utmost restraint;

5. *Demands* that the parties negotiate in good faith on the basis of the Geneva Declaration of Principles of 8 September 1995 with the aim of achieving lasting peace throughout the region;

6. *Reiterates* that there can be no military solution to the conflict in the Republic of Bosnia and Herzegovina;

7. *Urges* all States and international humanitarian organizations to intensify their efforts to help to alleviate the plight of refugees and displaced persons;

8. *Requests* the Secretary-General to provide to the Council as soon as possible information on the humanitarian situation, including information available through the United Nations High Commissioner for Refugees and other sources;

9. *Decides* to remain actively seized of the matter.

Security Council resolution 1016(1995)

21 September 1995   Meeting 3581   Adopted unanimously

Draft prepared in consultations among Council members (S/1995/810).

**Communications (22 September–17 October).** On 22 September, Bosnia and Herzegovina reported an aerial attack north-west of the town of Bosanska Dubica (north-west of Banja Luka), which a UN spokesperson in Zagreb confirmed, and the cluster-bombing of the village of Arabus and parts of Bosanski Petrovac (south-west of Banja Luka), as well as of the city of Zenica (central Bosnia).[95] On 28 September, it further reported a rocket attack on the centre of Travnik and on Zenica, which left two civilians dead, injured some 20 others and inflicted extensive material damage.[96]

On 27 September, Yugoslavia (Serbia and Montenegro) drew attention to a Reuters news agency report, according to which Croatian regular troops who had entered 50 kilometres into "Republika Srpska" had opened fire on a convoy of Bosnian Serb refugees near the town of Bosanski Novi, killing 47 of them. The report further stated that the current Bosnian Muslim and Croat offensive, in which 60,000 regular Croatian Army troops were engaged, had resulted in the expulsion of some 150,000 Bosnian Serbs from north-western and central Bosnia. Yugoslavia (Serbia and Montenegro) asserted that this latest tragic Serb exodus, which came soon after the mass flight of Serbs from the Krajina area of Croatia, constituted an unprecedented act of genocide.[97]

On 17 October, Yugoslavia (Serbia and Montenegro) wrote that despite the 12 October cease-fire agreement, the Bosnian Muslim and Croat forces, supported by Croatia's regular Army, were pressing their offensive forward against the Bosnian Serb towns of Sanski Most, Mrkonjic Grad and Kljuc, causing heavy civilian casualties and a mass exodus of some 50,000 Bosnian Serb refugees into Banja Luka. It claimed that the offensive in north-western Bosnia, whose ultimate goal was the seizure of Prijedor and Banja Luka, had been reinforced recently by fresh units of Croatian troops armed with the most sophisticated weapons. Calling the Croatian Army's engagement in Bosnia and Herzegovina illegal and politically and morally unacceptable, Yugoslavia (Serbia and Montenegro) asked the Council urgently to take measures to put a stop to the offensive and prevent a humanitarian catastrophe that seriously threatened the entire peace process.[98]

SECURITY COUNCIL ACTION (7 December)

The Security Council met on 7 December and, following consultations among its members, authorized the President to make the statement below[99] on the Council's behalf:

> The Security Council expresses deep concern over the looting and burning of houses by the HVO forces in the area of Mrkonjic Grad and Sipovo, which have continued for some time, and it also notes with concern that similar acts have been committed by Bosnian Serb forces in other areas of Bosnia and Herzegovina. The Council is also deeply concerned by reports that the HVO is moving mine-laying equipment into the Mrkonjic Grad and Sipovo areas.
>
> The Security Council considers that such actions are dangerous and detrimental to the spirit of confidence essential for the implementation of the Peace Agreement on Bosnia and Herzegovina.
>
> The Security Council demands that all such actions be stopped immediately and stresses the need for all parties to exercise maximum restraint and to demonstrate the cooperation essential for the successful implementation of the Peace Agreement.

*Meeting number.* SC 3603.

## UN Protection Force (UNPROFOR)

In response to the wishes of the host Governments of Bosnia and Herzegovina, Croatia and the former Yugoslav Republic of Macedonia, the Secretary-General, in a report of 22 March, proposed that the UNPROFOR operations in those countries be replaced by three separate but interlinked peace-keeping operations.[100] The proposal in respect of the peace-keeping force in Bosnia and Herzegovina was approved by the Security Council resolution below.

SECURITY COUNCIL ACTION

On 31 March, the Council adopted **resolution 982(1995)**.

*The Security Council,*

*Recalling* all its previous relevant resolutions on the conflicts in the territory of the former Yugoslavia and reaffirming in this context its resolution 947(1994) of 30 September 1994 on the mandate of the United Nations

Protection Force (UNPROFOR) and subsequent relevant resolutions,

*Having considered* the report of the Secretary-General of 22 March 1995,

*Affirming* its commitment to the search for an overall negotiated settlement of the conflicts in the former Yugoslavia, ensuring the sovereignty and territorial integrity of all the States there within their internationally recognized borders, and stressing the importance it attaches to the mutual recognition thereof,

*Reaffirming* its commitment to the independence, sovereignty and territorial integrity of the Republic of Bosnia and Herzegovina,

*Welcoming* the continuing efforts of the Co-Chairmen of the Steering Committee of the International Conference on the Former Yugoslavia,

*Welcoming also* the efforts of Member States, in particular those of the Contact Group, and emphasizing the utmost importance of the work of the Contact Group in the overall peace process in the area,

*Welcoming* the acceptance by the Government of the Republic of Bosnia and Herzegovina of the Contact Group peace plan,

*Welcoming also* the agreements between the Bosnian parties on a cease-fire and on the complete cessation of hostilities in the Republic of Bosnia and Herzegovina concluded on 23 December 1994 and 31 December 1994, and the essential role UNPROFOR plays in implementation of these agreements, and stressing the importance it places thereupon,

*Wishing* to encourage UNPROFOR's efforts, as part of its activities to facilitate an overall settlement of the conflict in the Republic of Bosnia and Herzegovina, and as detailed in paragraphs 30 to 32 of the above-mentioned report of the Secretary-General, to help the parties implement the Washington agreements regarding the Federation of Bosnia and Herzegovina,

*Recognizing* the need for Member States to take appropriate steps to enhance the capacity of UNPROFOR in the Republic of Bosnia and Herzegovina to execute its mandate as set out in the relevant resolutions of the Security Council, including providing the Secretary-General with all the resources authorized by previous resolutions of the Security Council,

*Reiterating* the importance of maintaining Sarajevo, the capital of the Republic of Bosnia and Herzegovina, as a united city and a multicultural, multi-ethnic and plurireligious centre, and noting in this context the positive contribution that agreement between the parties on the demilitarization of Sarajevo could make to this end, to the restoration of normal life in Sarajevo, and to achieving an overall settlement, consistent with the Contact Group peace plan,

*Noting* that UNPROFOR plays an essential role in preventing and containing hostilities thus creating the conditions for achieving an overall political settlement, and paying tribute to all UNPROFOR personnel, especially those who have given their lives for the cause of peace,

*Noting also* that the mandate of UNPROFOR expires on 31 March 1995, in conformity with resolution 947(1994),

*Noting further* the letter of 29 March 1995 from the Permanent Representative of the Republic of Bosnia and Herzegovina,

*Noting also* the letter from the Permanent Representative of the Republic of Croatia of 17 March 1995

regarding his Government's views on the continued presence of UNPROFOR in the Republic of Croatia,

*Paying tribute* to the UNPROFOR personnel in the performance of the mandate of UNPROFOR, in particular in assisting the delivery of humanitarian assistance and monitoring the cease-fires,

*Emphasizing* that improved observance of human rights, including appropriate international monitoring thereof, is an essential step towards restoration of confidence between the parties and building a durable peace,

*Reaffirming* its determination to ensure the security of UNPROFOR and freedom of movement for all its missions, and to these ends, acting under Chapter VII of the Charter of the United Nations, as regards UNPROFOR in the Republic of Croatia and in the Republic of Bosnia and Herzegovina,

1. *Welcomes* the report of the Secretary-General of 22 March 1995, and in particular approves the arrangements contained in paragraph 84;

2. *Decides* to extend UNPROFOR's mandate in the Republic of Bosnia and Herzegovina for an additional period terminating on 30 November 1995 and further decides that all previous relevant resolutions relating to UNPROFOR shall continue to apply;

3. *Authorizes* the Secretary-General to redeploy before 30 June 1995 all UNPROFOR personnel and assets from the Republic of Croatia with the exception of those whose continued presence in the Republic of Croatia is required for UNCRO or for the functions referred to in paragraphs 4 and 5 below;

4. *Decides* that UNPROFOR shall continue to perform fully the functions envisaged in the implementation of the Cease-fire Agreement of 29 March 1994 and the Economic Agreement of 2 December 1994 between the Republic of Croatia and the local Serb authorities and all relevant Security Council resolutions, including the functions identified in paragraph 72 of the report of the Secretary-General of 22 March 1995, and to facilitate the delivery of international humanitarian assistance to the Republic of Bosnia and Herzegovina through the territory of the Republic of Croatia until the effective deployment of UNCRO or 30 June 1995, whichever is sooner;

5. *Decides* that UNPROFOR shall retain its existing support structures in the Republic of Croatia including the operation of its headquarters;

6. *Emphasizes* the responsibility of the parties and others concerned in the Republic of Croatia and the Republic of Bosnia and Herzegovina for the security and safety of UNPROFOR and in this context demands that all parties and others concerned refrain from any acts of intimidation or violence against UNPROFOR;

7. *Reiterates* the importance it attaches to full compliance with the agreements between the Bosnian parties on a cease-fire and on a complete cessation of hostilities in the Republic of Bosnia and Herzegovina; calls upon them to agree to a further extension and implementation of these agreements beyond 30 April 1995 and to use that period to negotiate an overall peaceful settlement on the basis of the acceptance of the Contact Group peace plan as a starting-point; and further calls upon the Bosnian Serb party to accept this;

8. *Calls upon* Member States to consider favourably requests by the Secretary-General for necessary assistance to UNPROFOR in the performance of its mandate;

9. *Calls on* all parties and others concerned to comply fully with all Security Council resolutions regarding the situation in the former Yugoslavia to create the conditions that would facilitate the full implementation of UNPROFOR's mandate;

10. *Notes* with satisfaction the progress made in the discussions between the Government of the Republic of Bosnia and Herzegovina and the United Nations referred to in paragraph 49 of the report of the Secretary-General of 22 March 1995, and urges the Government of the Republic of Bosnia and Herzegovina to provide suitable radio broadcasting frequencies and television broadcasting slots at no cost to the United Nations for the purposes described in paragraphs 47 to 51 of that report;

11. *Requests* the Secretary-General to keep the Council regularly informed on progress with regard to the implementation of UNPROFOR's mandate and to report, as necessary, on any developments on the ground, the attitude of the parties and other circumstances affecting the mandate of the Force, and in particular to report within eight weeks of the adoption of this resolution taking into account, *inter alia*, the concerns raised by the members of the Council and issues raised by the Government of the Republic of Bosnia and Herzegovina;

12. *Urges* the Government of the Republic of Bosnia and Herzegovina to implement fully the provisions of the status-of-forces agreement of 15 May 1993 between that Government and the United Nations;

13. *Decides* to remain seized of the matter.

Security Council resolution 982(1995)

31 March 1995     Meeting 3512     Adopted unanimously

8-nation draft (S/1995/243).

*Sponsors:* Argentina, Czech Republic, France, Germany, Italy, Russian Federation, United Kingdom, United States.

## Security and freedom of movement

As the Secretary-General indicated in his 22 March report,[100] the deterioration of the security situation beginning in March was characterized by increased shelling, sniping at civilians and targeting of UNPROFOR and UNHCR personnel, especially in and around Sarajevo.

**SECURITY COUNCIL ACTION (14 and 19 April)**

The Security Council met on 14 and 19 April to address the question of violent acts against UNPROFOR, in particular, the separate killings by sniper fire of two soldiers of the French contingent deployed in Sarajevo.

At the 14 April meeting, convened when the second shooting occurred, the Council, following completion of consultations among its members, authorized its President to make the statement below[101] on the Council's behalf:

The Security Council is gravely concerned at the recent attacks on UNPROFOR personnel in the Republic of Bosnia and Herzegovina and, in this regard, has learned with particular indignation that once again a soldier of UNPROFOR, this time a soldier of the French contingent, was deliberately targeted and shot to death by an unidentified sniper in Sarajevo today. The Council notes with similar concern that several other soldiers of the United Nations have been killed recently in similar circumstances.

The Council condemns in the strongest terms such acts directed at peace-keepers who are serving the cause of peace in the Republic of Bosnia and Herzegovina. Deliberate targeting of UNPROFOR personnel reflects the overall deterioration of the situation in the Republic of Bosnia and Herzegovina. The Council wishes to state once again that this is totally unacceptable. It reiterates that the cooperation of all parties and others concerned is indispensable for the missions of the Force to be carried out and demands that they respect fully the status of United Nations personnel.

The Security Council invites the Secretary-General to investigate the circumstances of these acts and to report to the Security Council, taking into consideration the views of troop-contributing countries, on any measures which might be necessary to prevent further similar attacks, which should not remain unpunished.

*Meeting number.* SC 3520.

Bosnia and Herzegovina on 18 April offered its condolences to the families of the two UNPROFOR soldiers who had been killed. Referring to the inconclusiveness of UNPROFOR's analysis of the incidents, which somehow rendered ''both sides'' equally blameworthy, Bosnia and Herzegovina assured the Council that there was no basis to believe that any of the Government's soldiers were involved in those tragic incidents.[102]

At its 19 April meeting, the Council, determined to obtain strict respect for the status of UN personnel, adopted **resolution 987(1995)**.

*The Security Council,*

*Recalling* all its previous relevant resolutions on the conflicts in the territory of the former Yugoslavia and reaffirming in this context its resolution 982(1995) of 31 March 1995 and in particular its paragraphs 6 and 7,

*Expressing* its grave concern at the continued fighting in the Republic of Bosnia and Herzegovina despite the agreements on a cease-fire and on the complete cessation of hostilities concluded on 23 and 31 December 1994, and deploring the violations of these agreements and of the ban imposed by its resolutions 781(1992) of 9 October 1992 and 816(1993) of 31 March 1993 by whomsoever committed,

*Stressing* the unacceptability of all attempts to resolve the conflict in the Republic of Bosnia and Herzegovina by military means,

*Noting once again* the need for resumed negotiations aimed at an overall peaceful settlement of the situation in the Republic of Bosnia and Herzegovina on the basis of the acceptance of the Contact Group peace plan as a starting-point,

*Gravely preoccupied* at the recent attacks on the United Nations Protection Force (UNPROFOR) personnel in the Republic of Bosnia and Herzegovina and at the fatalities resulting therefrom, condemning in the strongest terms such unacceptable acts directed at members of peace-keeping forces and determined to obtain a strict respect of the status of United Nations personnel in the Republic of Bosnia and Herzegovina,

*Reaffirming* its determination to ensure the security of UNPROFOR and freedom of movement for all its missions, and, to these ends, acting under Chapter VII of the Charter of the United Nations,

1. *Emphasizes* once again the responsibility of the parties and others concerned in the Republic of Bosnia and Herzegovina for the security and safety of UNPROFOR and, in this context, demands again that all parties and others concerned refrain from any act of intimidation or violence against UNPROFOR and its personnel;

2. *Recalls* its invitation to the Secretary-General, in this context, to submit proposals on any measures which could be taken to prevent attacks against UNPROFOR and its personnel and allow it to perform effectively its mission, and invites him to submit such proposals on an urgent basis;

3. *Calls upon* the Bosnian parties to agree to an extension of the agreements on a cease-fire and complete cessation of hostilities concluded on 23 and 31 December 1994 beyond 30 April 1995 and looks to all parties and all others concerned to cooperate fully with UNPROFOR in their implementation;

4. *Urges* all parties and others concerned to resume forthwith negotiations towards an overall peaceful settlement on the basis of the acceptance of the Contact Group peace plan as a starting-point;

5. *Decides* to remain seized of the matter.

Security Council resolution 987(1995)

19 April 1995     Meeting 3521     Adopted unanimously

Draft by France (S/1995/311).

In a presidential statement of 18 September, the Council deplored the death of one Danish peace-keeper and injury to nine others. By **resolution 1016(1995)** of 21 September, the Council further deplored the casualties suffered by the Danish peace-keepers and expressed its condolences to Denmark and to the bereaved families.

**Report of the Secretary-General.** In his 30 May report[12] on developments on the ground and on the parties' attitude affecting the UNPROFOR mandate, the Secretary-General, in response to Council **resolution 987(1995)** of 19 April, also proposed measures to prevent attacks against UNPROFOR and allow it to perform its mission effectively. His proposals came on the heels of the crisis brought about by the Bosnian Serb detention of more than 300 UNPROFOR personnel as hostages, some of whom were used as human shields in strategically important locations, in retaliation for the NATO air strikes near Pale.

The Secretary-General noted the repeated threats to the security of UNPROFOR and other UN personnel and the continual obstruction of their freedom of movement, which impaired the discharge of their mandated tasks. The Council decisions taken under Chapter VII of the Charter of the United Nations to limit those difficulties had created ambiguities as to how UNPROFOR should react under those circumstances, in particular as to the use of force other than in self-defence. Those ambiguities, he asserted, had adversely affected the performance of UNPROFOR and its credibility, not only with the parties but with Council members and the public at large.

In this connection, the Secretary-General analysed the use of NATO air power in defence of UNPROFOR and as a deterrent to attacks on the safe areas. Experience gained from air power use on nine occasions between March 1994 and 26 May 1995 had confirmed the difficulties involved in such actions in support of a peace-keeping operation. Moreover, the use of force against only one party had altered that party's perception of UNPROFOR's neutrality and, realizing its extreme vulnerability, that party had resorted to retaliatory action in the form of detaining large numbers of UN personnel and obstructing their movement, as well as refusing to participate in negotiations.

The Secretary-General pointed to the absence of a clear enforcement mandate in the Council resolutions on Bosnia and Herzegovina, notwithstanding their frequent references to Chapter VII of the Charter, and the Council's reluctance to authorize additional troops deemed necessary to enable UNPROFOR to perform even its peace-keeping functions. Thus, to the inevitable question as to whether UNPROFOR was a peace-keeping or enforcement mission, the Secretary-General concluded that, so far, the Council had wished it to be a peace-keeping operation.

Meanwhile, the Secretary-General continued, UNPROFOR remained deployed in a war situation where, after more than three years, there was still no peace to keep. Further complicating its position was the gradual enlargement of its original mandate to include elements of enforcement, causing it to be seen as a party to the conflict. The safe-areas mandate, for instance, required UNPROFOR to cooperate and negotiate daily with a party against whom it was also expected to call air strikes in certain circumstances. Similarly, the United Nations had imposed sanctions on one party, but at the same time had deployed a Force obliged to work with that party's consent and cooperation. Consequently, the Bosnian Serb leaders had largely withdrawn their consent and cooperation, declaring that, in response to UN sanctions against them, they were applying their own "sanctions" against the United Nations.

In conclusion, the Secretary-General presented four options as to UNPROFOR's future role: withdraw the Force, leaving only a small political mission, if the parties so wished; retain its existing tasks and methods of implementation; change the existing mandate to permit the greater use of force; or revise the mandate to include only those tasks that a peace-keeping operation could realistically be expected to perform under the circumstances prevailing in Bosnia and Herzegovina. The Secretary-General said he would not advocate the first two options and had concerns regarding the viability of the third. He believed, however, that the fourth would give UNPROFOR a realistic mandate that would enable it to help contain the situation in Bosnia and Herzegovina without creating expectations that it could either enforce an end to the war or join it to fight on the side of one of the parties.

### SECURITY COUNCIL ACTION (23 June)

The Security Council met on 23 June and, after consultations among its members, authorized the President to make the statement below[103] on the Council's behalf:

> The Security Council reiterates its condemnation of interference with humanitarian supplies and the freedom of movement of the United Nations Protection Force (UNPROFOR) by all parties within the territory of the Republic of Bosnia and Herzegovina. In this context it is deeply concerned by the blockading by Bosnian government forces of UNPROFOR personnel in the Visoko, Gorazde, Gorni Vakuf and Kladanj areas, which included on 20 June 1995 placing mines outside the UNPROFOR camp in Visoko. The Council is also deeply concerned at the deterioration in the situation in and around Sarajevo, the obstruction by the Bosnian Serb party of freedom of movement and utilities to the city and the continued obstruction of the normal operation of Sarajevo airport.
>
> The Security Council stresses that all such actions are unacceptable and demands that all parties fully respect the safety and security of UNPROFOR personnel and ensure their complete freedom of movement to enable UNPROFOR to carry out its mandate in accordance with the Council's resolutions.
>
> The Security Council calls upon the parties to enter into negotiations as provided for in its resolution 998(1995) of 16 June 1995 and to agree without further delay to a cease-fire and a complete cessation of hostilities in the Republic of Bosnia and Herzegovina. The Council emphasizes that there can be no military solution to the conflict in the Republic of Bosnia and Herzegovina. It stresses the importance it attaches to the vigorous pursuit of a political settlement, and reiterates its demand that the Bosnian Serb party accept the Contact Group peace plan as a starting-point.

*Meeting number.* SC 3548.

### Rapid reaction capability

**Communications from the Secretary-General.** The Secretary-General on 9 June informed the Security Council President that, in the light of his 30 May report on deteriorating conditions in Bosnia and Herzegovina, France, the Netherlands and the United Kingdom had offered to provide military reinforcements for UNPROFOR in order to reduce the vulnerability of its personnel and to enhance its capacity to carry out its mandate.[104]

Annexed to the letter was an agreed summary of their proposal.

The reinforcements proposed were as follows: a multinational brigade of two battalion groups totalling some 4,500 troops, one approximately 2,000 strong to be provided by France and the other, approximately 2,500 strong, to be based upon the current UNPROFOR Reserve and to consist of a British battalion group and of a mortar-locating radar group from the Netherlands; a British airmobile brigade of approximately 6,300, composed of two infantry battalions, two aviation regiments, engineers, artillery elements and logistic support, including 800 temporary personnel; and a French brigade of 4,000 troops on stand-by in France, should further reinforcements prove necessary.

The rapid reaction force (RRF) would be an integral part of UNPROFOR and would be financed through normal UN peace-keeping assessments. It would act in support of UNPROFOR within its existing mandate, and would be available to UN military commanders for the defence of UN personnel. Its purpose would be to give the commander a capacity between ''strong protest and air strikes''; it would increase tactical operational flexibility and would be intended to have a deterrent effect, but would not change the UN role to peace-enforcement.

In recommending acceptance of the proposal, the Secretary-General noted that the proposed troops numbered about 15,000, of whom 2,500 were already in the theatre. Thus, in order to incorporate those additional troops within UNPF/UNPROFOR, the Council would need to increase the authorized troop levels by 12,500, inclusive of the stand-by brigade.

In an addendum of 15 June to his letter, the Secretary-General stated that the cost of such an increase, including the corresponding increase in civilian support staff, was estimated at $414.3 million for a six-month period. The cost of deployment, excluding the 4,000 French troops on stand-by, was estimated at $304.4 million.[105]

**SECURITY COUNCIL ACTION (June)**

Having considered the foregoing report and letters of the Secretary-General, the Security Council met on 16 June and adopted **resolution 998(1995)**.

*The Security Council*,

*Recalling* all its earlier relevant resolutions,

*Reaffirming* the mandate of the United Nations Protection Force (UNPROFOR) as referred to in resolution 982(1995) of 31 March 1995 and the need for its full implementation,

*Having considered* the report of the Secretary-General of 30 May 1995,

*Having considered* also the letter of the Secretary-General of 9 June 1995 and its annex,

*Noting* that the rapid reaction force referred to in the above-mentioned letter will be an integral part of the existing United Nations peace-keeping operation, and that the status of UNPROFOR and its impartiality will be maintained,

*Deeply concerned* by the continuing armed hostilities in the territory of the Republic of Bosnia and Herzegovina,

*Expressing* its deep regret that the situation in the Republic of Bosnia and Herzegovina has continued to deteriorate and that the parties were not able to agree to a further cease-fire following the breakdown of the cease-fire agreement of 23 December 1994 and its subsequent expiration on 1 May 1995,

*Gravely concerned* that the regular obstruction of deliveries of humanitarian assistance, and the denial of the use of Sarajevo airport, by the Bosnian Serb side threaten the ability of the United Nations in Bosnia and Herzegovina to carry out its mandate,

*Condemning* in the strongest possible terms all attacks by the parties on UNPROFOR personnel,

*Condemning also* the increasing attacks on the civilian population by Bosnian Serb forces,

*Determined* to enhance the protection of UNPROFOR and to enable it to carry out its mandate,

*Noting* the letter of 14 June 1995 from the Foreign Minister of the Republic of Bosnia and Herzegovina welcoming the reinforcement of UNPROFOR,

*Stressing* the importance at this juncture of renewed efforts to achieve an overall peaceful settlement,

*Underlining once again* the urgent need for acceptance by the Bosnian Serb party of the Contact Group peace plan as a starting-point, opening the way to the negotiation of such an overall peaceful settlement,

*Reaffirming* the sovereignty, territorial integrity and political independence of the Republic of Bosnia and Herzegovina,

*Reaffirming further* that the Republic of Bosnia and Herzegovina, as a State Member of the United Nations, enjoys the rights provided for in the Charter of the United Nations,

*Determining* that the situation in the former Yugoslavia continues to be a threat to international peace and security,

*Reaffirming* its determination to ensure the security of the United Nations Peace Forces (UNPF)/UNPROFOR and its freedom of movement for the accomplishment of all its missions, and to these ends, acting under Chapter VII of the Charter of the United Nations,

1. *Demands* that the Bosnian Serb forces release immediately and unconditionally all remaining detained UNPROFOR personnel, and further demands that all parties fully respect the safety of UNPROFOR personnel, and others engaged in the delivery of humanitarian assistance, and ensure their complete freedom of movement;

2. *Emphasizes* that there can be no military solution to the conflict, stresses the importance it attaches to vigorous pursuit of a political settlement, and reiterates its demand that the Bosnian Serb party accept the Contact Group peace plan as a starting-point;

3. *Calls upon* the parties to agree without further delay to a cease-fire and a complete cessation of hostilities in the Republic of Bosnia and Herzegovina;

4. *Demands* that all parties allow unimpeded access for humanitarian assistance to all parts of the Republic of Bosnia and Herzegovina and, in particular, to the safe areas;

5. *Demands further* that the Bosnian Serb forces comply immediately with the agreement of 5 June 1992 and ensure unimpeded access by land to Sarajevo;

6. *Demands* that the parties respect fully the status of the safe areas and in particular the need to ensure the safety of the civilian population therein;

7. *Underlines* the need for a mutually agreed demilitarization of the safe areas and their immediate surroundings and the benefits this would bring to all parties, in terms of the cessation of attacks on the safe areas and of launching military attacks therefrom;

8. *Encourages*, in this context, the Secretary-General further to intensify efforts aimed at reaching agreement with the parties on the modalities for demilitarization, taking particular account of the need to ensure the safety of the civilian population, and calls upon the parties to cooperate fully with these efforts;

9. *Welcomes* the letter of the Secretary-General of 9 June 1995 on the reinforcement of UNPROFOR and the establishment of a rapid reaction capacity to enable UNPF/UNPROFOR to carry out its mandate;

10. *Decides* accordingly to authorize an increase in UNPF/UNPROFOR personnel, acting under the present mandate and on the terms set out in the above-mentioned letter, by up to 12,500 additional troops, the modalities of financing to be determined later;

11. *Authorizes* the Secretary-General to carry forward the implementation of paragraphs 9 and 10 above, maintaining close contact with the Government of the Republic of Bosnia and Herzegovina and others concerned;

12. *Requests* the Secretary-General, in taking any decisions with respect to the deployment of UNPROFOR personnel, to take full account of the need to enhance their security and minimize the dangers to which they might be exposed;

13. *Decides* to remain actively seized of the matter.

Security Council resolution 998(1995)

16 June 1995       Meeting 3543       13-0-2

7-nation draft (S/1995/478).

*Sponsors:* Czech Republic, France, Germany, Honduras, Netherlands, Oman, United Kingdom.

Vote in Council as follows:

*In favour:* Argentina, Botswana, Czech Republic, France, Germany, Honduras, Indonesia, Italy, Nigeria, Oman, Rwanda, United Kingdom, United States.

*Against:* None.

*Abstaining:* China, Russian Federation.

Before the vote, China pointed out that the establishment under Chapter VII of the Charter of a force that, once put into operation, was bound to become a party to the conflict, would de facto change the peace-keeping status of UNPROFOR. Besides leading to many political and military complications, such a force would substantially increase peace-keeping expenditures. At a time when the Organization was in a financial crisis, it was neither appropriate nor desirable to finance such a force from the peace-keeping budget. China regretted that its amendment on this issue, repeatedly put forward during informal consultations, had not been accepted.

The Russian Federation likewise stated that some of its amendments had not been taken into account. Among those were the inclusion of a reference to the inadmissible violations of the arms embargo in the former Yugoslavia, including in Bosnia and Herzegovina; and of wording to preclude the impression that the force was intended to operate against only the Bosnian Serb party and not also against the Bosnian Government, which also bore responsibility for provocations, violations of agreements and direct attacks on UNPROFOR. To illustrate, the Russian Federation cited the Government's recent demand that the Canadian contingent withdraw its two observation posts near Visoko, which it then subjected to mortar and artillery fire, as well as to the Government's ongoing attempt to mount a massive attack in the Sarajevo region. Also underscored was the lack of time for the Council to agree on reliable guarantees against the use of the force in a manner to involve UNPROFOR in a war.

**Communication from the Secretary-General.** The Secretary-General informed the Security Council on 17 August that his Special Representative and the UNPROFOR Force Commander had undertaken consultations with Bosnia and Herzegovina with a view to expediting the deployment there of RRF and facilitating its freedom of movement.[106] Consultations had also been undertaken with Croatia to facilitate the disembarkation, transit and, as required, stationing in Croatian territory of the RRF units as part of UNPROFOR.

The Secretary-General drew attention to the position taken by the two countries that the Council resolution establishing RRF was adopted subsequent to the 1993 status-of-forces agreement[107] concluded with Bosnia and Herzegovina for UNPROFOR troop deployments in the country and, hence, was not applicable to RRF, whose status therefore needed a separate agreement.

The Special Representative conveyed the UN position that the Council decision to authorize an increase in UNPROFOR's strength to include RRF could not be interpreted as excluding the expansion of UNPROFOR from the scope of the 1993 agreement. That expansion constituted neither an exceptional Council decision in the context of the UN forces and operations in the former Yugoslavia nor a new development in the general context of peace-keeping; nor did it alter the mandate of the forces and operations concerned. Croatia had been assured that the operational mandate of RRF was confined to Bosnia and Herzegovina and that what was being sought was merely the use of transit facilities already assured by the 1993 agreement.

The Secretary-General also drew attention to the demands by the local Croat authorities in Bosnia and Herzegovina, sometimes in their own capacity and sometimes on behalf of the Federation of Bosnia and Herzegovina,[88] that the United Nations sign an agreement with them governing the status of RRF. In the view of the United Nations, it was unnecessary to do so, since the 1993 agreement was applicable throughout the entire territory of Bosnia and Herzegovina. The local Croat authorities, maintaining their position, had posed substantial impediments to RRF's deployment, training and freedom of movement in areas under their control. Bosnia and Herzegovina had not ensured, in this case, that the terms of the 1993 agreement were applied throughout its territory; it had also stipulated additional financial requirements, such as compensation for "environmental damage" that RRF might cause.

As a result, the deployment of major RRF elements currently in Ploce, Croatia, could not proceed. They included the helicopters of an airmobile brigade, an artillery battery designated for Mount Igman, a transport platoon bound for Federation-controlled territory and 16 logistic convoys. Those elements already in Bosnia and Herzegovina had been encountering continuous restrictions on their movements.

To break the impasse, the Special Representative had suggested to the Bosnian authorities that supplementary arrangements, as envisaged in the 1993 status-of-forces agreement, be concluded to cover the issues in question, with a proviso that, in the event of a conflict between those arrangements and the agreement, the latter should prevail.

(The Secretary-General's communication was preceded by a letter of 3 July from the President of the Federation of Bosnia and Herzegovina asking for the particulars of RRF's mandate and deployment;[108] and by letters of 11 August from Croatia[109] and 14 August from Bosnia and Herzegovina[110] on the question of expediting separate arrangements for RRF.)

**SECURITY COUNCIL ACTION (August)**

The Security Council met on 19 August to consider the Secretary-General's communication. Following consultations among its members, the Council authorized the President to make the statement below[111] on its behalf:

> The Security Council is deeply concerned by the contents of the Secretary-General's letter of 17 August 1995 regarding the continued impediments to the functioning and deployment of the rapid reaction force (RRF) established by resolution 998(1995) of 16 June 1995.
> The Council reaffirms in this regard that the RRF is an integral part of UNPF/UNPROFOR and that its deployment is crucial for the strengthening of UNPROFOR's capacity to carry out its mandate in the Republic of Bosnia and Herzegovina. It shares the Secretary-General's view that the existing status-of-forces agreements constitute an appropriate and sufficient basis for the presence of UNPF/UNPROFOR, including the RRF.

The Security Council is deeply concerned at the implications of the continued impediments to the functioning of the RRF for the effectiveness of the United Nations mission in the Republic of Bosnia and Herzegovina. It calls upon the Governments of the Republic of Croatia and the Republic of Bosnia and Herzegovina immediately to remove all impediments and to give clear undertakings concerning the freedom of movement and provision of facilities for the RRF, in order that it may perform its tasks without further delay. It further calls upon them to resolve forthwith within the framework of the existing status-of-forces agreements any outstanding difficulties with the relevant United Nations authorities.

The Security Council supports fully the efforts of the Secretary-General in this matter and will return to this question in the light of a further report which the Security Council requests the Secretary-General to submit no later than 24 August 1995.

*Meeting number.* SC 3568.

*Mandate extension*

**Report of the Secretary-General.** On 23 November, the Secretary-General issued a report intended to assist the Security Council in its deliberations on the future of UNCRO, UNPROFOR and UNPREDEP, whose mandates were to end on 30 November.[91] The report included a summary of developments in Croatia, in Bosnia and Herzegovina, in the former Yugoslav Republic of Macedonia and in Yugoslavia (Serbia and Montenegro) since the inception of those three separate but interlinked missions on 1 April, as well as the effect of those developments on the missions' implementation of their respective mandates. (For information on UNCRO and UNPREDEP, see below, under "Croatia" and "The former Yugoslav Republic of Macedonia".)

The report noted three dominant developments in Bosnia and Herzegovina during the reporting period. First, upon the expiration of the 1994 cessation-of-hostilities agreement at the end of April 1995, an unprecedented level of military activity had ensued, including offensives by all sides, resulting in major movements of refugees and displaced persons and in widespread violations of international humanitarian law, especially by Bosnian Serb forces. Second, NATO and UNPROFOR, through the rapid reaction force, had become militarily engaged against the Bosnian Serbs in order to prevent further violations of the heavy-weapons and safe-area regimes, to reduce UNPROFOR's vulnerability to hostage-taking and to improve its untenable situation. Third, the United States–led peace process, begun in the summer, had advanced to the stage at which the General Framework Agreement for Peace in Bosnia and Herzegovina had been initialled on 21 November. Together with the country-wide cease-fire secured by the United States on 5 October and brought into force by UNPROFOR on 12 October, the

Agreement provided the first real opportunity for a political solution to the conflict in Bosnia and Herzegovina, the Secretary-General said. (For details, see below.)

Compliance with the 5 October cease-fire was noticeably better than with previous cease-fires. All parties refrained from offensive activity and constructively participated in joint military commissions. UN military observers were operating in Bosnian Serb–held areas, with UNPROFOR and humanitarian convoys, as well as escorted civilian vehicles, moving freely in and out of Sarajevo and Gorazde. Sarajevo airport was operating safely and without hindrance, and the release of POWs and detainees was under way. The cease-fire provision regarding freedom of movement for UNPROFOR patrols, however, had yet to be complied with fully, for restrictions were still being imposed by Bosnian Croat military units in north-western Bosnia.

The limited progress in the political, social and economic integration of the Bosniac-Croat Federation had resulted in difficulties for UN activities. Continuation of the Federation—the foundation for the peace process—was threatened by the failure of the Bosniacs and Bosnian Croats to agree on certain fundamental issues and to implement what they had agreed upon. The most important of those were transfers of responsibility to the Federation, accommodation in areas recently recovered from the Bosnian Serbs in western Bosnia, and the resettlement of displaced persons. The recently announced accord on those issues (see below, under "Dayton Agreement on implementing the Federation of Bosnia and Herzegovina") still had to be translated into meaningful cooperation on the ground, the Secretary-General stated. The difficult relationship between the Government of the Federation and that of the Republic of Bosnia and Herzegovina had also caused some operational problems for the United Nations, notably in connection with the deployment of the rapid reaction force of UNPROFOR.

As envisaged in the Peace Agreement, and in close consultation with NATO, UNPROFOR was to arrange for the transfer of military responsibility to a new multinational implementation force to be authorized by the Security Council. Pending finalization of that arrangement, the Secretary-General recommended that the current UNPROFOR mandate be extended for two months ending on 31 January 1996.

In keeping with the Special Representative's recommendations, which the Secretary-General had accepted, only essential forces were being retained to implement UNPROFOR's mandate. Thus, two battalions and four sub-units were being repatriated, six other battalions were being reduced to a standard strength of about 965 all ranks, and portions of the rapid reaction force were being placed on stand-by in their home countries. As a result, the strength of UNPROFOR would be reduced from about 30,500 to about 21,600 by mid-December 1995. Those contingents not joining the new multinational force would be withdrawn as soon as practicable.

**SECURITY COUNCIL ACTION**

In the light of the Secretary-General's recommendation above, on 30 November the Security Council adopted **resolution 1026(1995).**

*The Security Council,*

*Recalling* all its previous relevant resolutions and in particular its resolutions 982(1995) of 31 March 1995 and 998(1995) of 16 June 1995,

*Reaffirming* its commitment to the independence, sovereignty and territorial integrity of the Republic of Bosnia and Herzegovina,

*Welcoming again* the initialling of the General Framework Agreement for Peace in Bosnia and Herzegovina and the Annexes thereto by the Republic of Bosnia and Herzegovina, the Republic of Croatia and the Federal Republic of Yugoslavia and the other parties thereto on 21 November 1995, in Dayton, Ohio, signifying agreement between the parties to sign formally the Peace Agreement,

*Stressing* the need for all parties to comply fully with all provisions of the Peace Agreement, and, prior to the entry into force of that agreement, the need for all parties to cooperate fully with the United Nations Protection Force (UNPROFOR) and to maintain the current cease-fire agreement,

*Welcoming* the positive role played by UNPROFOR, and paying tribute to the personnel of UNPROFOR in the performance of their mandate,

*Having considered* the report of the Secretary-General of 23 November 1995,

*Reaffirming* its determination to ensure the security and freedom of movement of the personnel of United Nations peace-keeping operations in the territory of the former Yugoslavia, and, to these ends, acting under Chapter VII of the Charter of the United Nations,

1. *Welcomes* the report of the Secretary-General of 23 November 1995;

2. *Decides* to extend the mandate of UNPROFOR for a period terminating on 31 January 1996, pending further action by the Council with regard to the implementation of the Peace Agreement;

3. *Invites* the Secretary-General to keep the Council informed on developments in the peace process and to submit as soon as possible to the Council reports, containing the necessary information and recommendations, on aspects of the implementation of the Peace Agreement as they affect the United Nations in order to enable the Council to take a decision ensuring an orderly transfer of authority as envisaged in the Peace Agreement;

4. *Decides* to remain actively seized of the matter.

Security Council resolution 1026(1995)

30 November 1995     Meeting 3601     Adopted unanimously

9-nation draft (S/1995/995).

*Sponsors:* Argentina, Czech Republic, France, Germany, Honduras, Italy, Russian Federation, United Kingdom, United States.

## United States–led peace process

The United States–led peace process began on 19 August, when Under-Secretary of State for European and Canadian Affairs Richard Holbrooke undertook the first of his shuttles to the former Yugoslavia in a determined pursuit of that peace initiative. It gathered pace during the last quarter of the year, culminating in the initialling by Bosnia and Herzegovina, Croatia and Yugoslavia (Serbia and Montenegro) of the General Framework Agreement for Peace in Bosnia and Herzegovina on 21 November in Dayton, Ohio, and its formal signing on 14 December in Paris. That event was preceded by a commitment made by the signatories, under the auspices of the Contact Group, to certain basic principles that formed the basis for the peace negotiations.

### Agreed Basic Principles

On 8 September in Geneva, the five-member Contact Group convened the Ministers for Foreign Affairs of Bosnia and Herzegovina, Croatia and Yugoslavia (Serbia and Montenegro). The latter country represented the Bosnian Serbs in a joint delegation. By a statement at the meeting's conclusion, the Contact Group announced that the Foreign Ministers, speaking for their Governments, had authorized it to issue the text of three basic principles they had agreed upon—referred to as the Agreed Basic Principles—as the basis for talks on ending the war in Bosnia and Herzegovina. The text and the statement were transmitted to the Secretary-General also on 8 September.[112]

According to the statement, as important as the agreement was, significant differences existed among the parties that required continued intense negotiations. While the parties returned to their capitals for consultations, Richard Holbrooke, acting as Chief United States Mediator, and EU Special Negotiator for the Former Yugoslavia, Carl Bildt, would be returning to the region with their delegations; on 9 September, First Deputy Minister Igor Ivanov of the Russian Federation would travel to Belgrade for consultations. The Contact Group would meet again in Geneva the following week, with subsequent meetings in Moscow and, in an expanded format, in Rome.

By the Agreed Basic Principles, Bosnia and Herzegovina would continue its legal existence with its present borders and continuing international recognition. It would consist of two entities: the existing Federation of Bosnia and Herzegovina as established by the Washington agreements[88] and Republika Srpska, the territory to be divided 51 per cent for the former and 49 per cent for the latter; each entity would continue to exist under its current constitution, amended to accommodate the basic principles, and have the right to establish parallel special relationships with neighbouring countries; the two entities would enter into reciprocal commitments to hold elections under international auspices, to adhere to international human rights standards and obligations, and to engage in binding arbitration to resolve disputes between them. The entities would appoint: a Commission for Displaced Persons to enforce their obligation to enable displaced persons to repossess their homes or receive just compensation; a Human Rights Commission to enforce human rights obligations; jointly financed Bosnia and Herzegovina public corporations to own and operate transportation and other facilities; and a Commission to Preserve National Monuments.

The Security Council met on 8 September and, following consultations among its members, authorized the President to make the statement below[113] on the Council's behalf:

> The Security Council welcomes the meeting held under the auspices of the Contact Group in Geneva on 8 September 1995 between the Foreign Ministers of the Republic of Bosnia and Herzegovina, of the Republic of Croatia and of the Federal Republic of Yugoslavia (Serbia and Montenegro). It welcomes the joint statement issued at the conclusion of that meeting and in particular the agreement by the parties on the Declaration of Principles. It strongly urges the parties to negotiate in good faith and expeditiously on the basis of that Declaration with the aim of achieving a lasting peace throughout the region.

*Meeting number.* SC 3576.

**Communication from the Secretary-General.** On 18 September, the Secretary-General communicated his conclusions following an in-depth review of the situation in Bosnia and Herzegovina on 16 September with his senior advisers, the UN Co-Chairman of the ICFY Steering Committee, the Special Representative and the Deputy Force Commander of UNPROFOR.[114]

He welcomed the United States peace initiative and took note of the two positive developments in the form of the Agreed Basic Principles of 8 September and the Framework for a Cessation of Hostilities within the Sarajevo Temporary Exclusion Zone, signed by the Bosnian Serb party in Belgrade on 14 September. He pointed out that, after more than three years' experience of international efforts to control and resolve the Bosnian conflict, it would be wrong to underestimate the difficulties in negotiating the further arrangements envisaged in those two agreements.

Believing, however, that there might finally be credible prospects for a viable and lasting peace in Bosnia and Herzegovina, and having re-examined the different ways in which the international community could support implementation of a peace agreement when concluded, the Secretary-General recommended that the Council authorize an ad hoc coalition of Member States, acting as appropriate with regional organizations or arrangements, to support all aspects of implementation of the agreement, with the exception of those relating to the relief and return of refugees and displaced persons, which should continue to be entrusted to UNHCR.

Should the current peace initiative not succeed and more enforcement action be decided upon by the Council, it was the Secretary-General's intention to recommend that UNPROFOR be replaced by a multinational force authorized by the Council to carry out such action and to assume responsibility for those aspects of UNPROFOR's existing mandate which would remain valid. In either case, urgent preparations would be required for an expeditious hand-over by UNPROFOR to the multinational force. The Council would also wish to consider appropriate arrangements to ensure that it was kept duly informed about the operations of such a force, including its civilian components.

### Further Agreed Basic Principles

In New York on 26 September, Bosnia and Herzegovina, Croatia and Yugoslavia (Serbia and Montenegro) agreed on three additional basic principles, referred to as the Further Agreed Basic Principles. These were intended to govern the entities' responsibilities regarding the international obligations of Bosnia and Herzegovina; free democratic elections and related freedom of movement, rights of displaced persons, freedom of speech and of the press, and human rights protection; and the governmental institutions to be constituted following elections.

### 1995 comprehensive cease-fire agreement

On 5 October, the three parties signed an agreement by which they would implement a cease-fire throughout all territory within the borders of Bosnia and Herzegovina, effective 10 October, provided that at that time full gas and electrical utility services should have been restored in the city of Sarajevo, or effective at 0001 hours on the day following such restoration. The cease-fire would last 60 days or until completion of the proximity peace talks and a peace conference, whichever was later.

On the effective date, all parties would immediately cease all offensive operations, patrol and reconnaissance activities, offensive-weapons firings including sniper fire, laying mines and creating additional barriers. The parties would ensure the humane treatment of civilians and prisoners and the exchange of POWs under UNPROFOR supervision, cooperate with UNPROFOR's cease-fire monitoring activities, and provide free passage and unimpeded road access between Sarajevo and Gorazde along the two primary routes of Sarajevo-Rogatica-Gorazde and Belgrade-Gorazde for all non-military and UNPROFOR traffic. Further, the parties would honour their commitments to the Agreed Basic Principles, the Framework for a Cessation of Hostilities within the Sarajevo Temporary Exclusion Zone, and the Further Agreed Basic Principles, including the obligation to afford all persons freedom of movement and all displaced persons the right to return home and repossess their property.

The Further Agreed Basic Principles and the cease-fire agreement were transmitted by the Contact Group and Italy to the Secretary-General on 31 October.[115]

### SECURITY COUNCIL ACTION (6 and 12 October)

In the light of the cease-fire agreement, the Security Council met on 6 October and, after consultations among its members, authorized the President to make the statement below[116] on the Council's behalf:

> The Security Council welcomes the 5 October 1995 agreement by the Bosnian parties to a cease-fire, including by terminating all hostile military activities throughout the territory of the Republic of Bosnia and Herzegovina, as of 10 October 1995 provided that full gas and electrical utility service is restored to Sarajevo. It welcomes all efforts to restore such service and calls upon the parties to cooperate fully with such efforts. The Security Council urges the parties fully to comply with all provisions in the cease-fire agreement once they come into effect.
>
> The Security Council also welcomes the decision of the Governments of the Republic of Bosnia and Herzegovina, the Republic of Croatia, and the Federal Republic of Yugoslavia (Serbia and Montenegro) to attend proximity peace talks by the end of this month, to be followed by a peace conference. It reiterates that there can be no military solution to the conflict in the Republic of Bosnia and Herzegovina, and strongly urges the parties to negotiate in good faith on the basis of the Geneva Declarations of Principles of 8 September 1995, and the Further Agreed Principles of 26 September 1995.
>
> The Security Council also welcomes the 3 October 1995 agreement by the Government of the Republic of Croatia and the local Croatian Serb authorities in eastern Slavonia to Guiding Basic Principles for Negotiations. It strongly urges both parties to negotiate in good faith towards a peaceful final settlement to the conflict consistent with the Council's resolutions.

*Meeting number.* SC 3585.

On 12 October, when the cease-fire entered into force, the Council met again and authorized the President to make the following statement[117] on its behalf:

> The Security Council welcomes the entry into force of the cease-fire agreement between the Bosnian parties of 5 October 1995.

The Security Council takes this opportunity to express its gratitude to all those who negotiated the cease-fire agreement, and to the United Nations Protection Force and others who, often at risk to their own lives, have made possible, with the cooperation of all the parties, the restoration of gas and electricity supplies to the inhabitants of Sarajevo enabling them to live in more decent conditions.

The Security Council demands that all parties fully comply with the provisions of the cease-fire agreement and refrain from any military activity that could jeopardize the peace process. It expresses its deepest concern at any operation that provokes large-scale movements of population detrimental to the peace process and a final and fair settlement. The Council is particularly concerned about new reports related to the movements of the displaced population in the areas of Sanski Most and Mrkonjic Grad.

The Security Council reiterates its strong condemnation of all practices of ethnic cleansing wherever they occur and by whomsoever committed. It demands their immediate cessation and underlines the need to alleviate the sufferings caused by these acts. The Council urges all Bosnian parties to respect fully the rights of all communities, including their right to remain where they are or to return to their homes in safety.

The Security Council is in particular deeply concerned about new reports concerning acts of ethnic cleansing committed in the Banja Luka and Prijedor areas, especially about reports, including those by international humanitarian organizations, that non-Serb men and boys of draft age are being taken away by Bosnian Serb and other paramilitary forces. The Council demands that these persons be immediately released.

The Security Council demands that the Bosnian Serb party grants immediate and unimpeded access for United Nations personnel and the representatives of the International Committee of the Red Cross (ICRC) to all the areas of concern. It also demands that ICRC representatives be allowed to visit and register any persons detained against their will. The Council reiterates in this context the demands set out in resolution 1010(1995) and in the statement of its President of 7 September 1995 on Srebrenica and Zepa.

The Security Council reaffirms that those who have committed or have ordered the commission of violations of international humanitarian law will be held individually responsible for them. The Council recalls in this context the establishment of the International Tribunal pursuant to its resolution 827(1993) and reiterates that all States shall cooperate fully with the Tribunal and its organs.

The Security Council will remain actively seized of the matter.

*Meeting number.* SC 3587.

## General Framework Agreement for Peace in Bosnia and Herzegovina

On 21 November, following a period of intense negotiations that began on 1 November in Dayton, Ohio, under the auspices of the United States Government, the three parties—Bosnia and Herzegovina, Croatia and Yugoslavia (Serbia and Montenegro)—initialled the General Framework Agreement for Peace in Bosnia and Herzegovina, including all the annexes thereto. Collectively known as the Peace Agreement, it was scheduled to be signed formally in Paris on 14 December. Its text was transmitted to the Secretary-General by the United States on 29 November.[(118)]

By the first of the Agreement's 11 articles, the parties agreed to conduct their relations in accordance with the Charter of the United Nations, as well as with the Helsinki Final Act and other OSCE documents, to respect fully the sovereign equality of one another, to settle disputes by peaceful means and to refrain from action against the territorial integrity or political independence of Bosnia and Herzegovina or any other State (article I).

By the other articles, the parties welcomed and endorsed the arrangements made concerning the following: the military aspects of the peace settlement and aspects of regional stabilization, as set forth in annex I A and B (article II); the boundary demarcation between the Federation of Bosnia and Herzegovina and Republika Srpska (annex 2, article III); the elections programme (annex 3, article IV); the Constitution of Bosnia and Herzegovina (annex 4, article V); the arrangements on the establishment of an arbitration tribunal, a Commission on Human Rights, a Commission on Refugees and Displaced Persons, a Commission to Preserve National Monuments, and Bosnia and Herzegovina Public Corporations (annexes 5 to 9, article VI); human rights provisions (annex 6, article VII); arrangements for implementing the peace settlement, including those pertaining to non-military implementation and the international police task force (annexes 10 and 11, article VIII).

The parties further agreed to cooperate fully with all entities involved in implementing the peace settlement (article IX). Yugoslavia (Serbia and Montenegro) and Bosnia and Herzegovina agreed to recognize each other as sovereign independent States within their international borders (article X). The Agreement was to enter into force upon signature (article XI).

**SECURITY COUNCIL ACTION**

In the light of the initialling of the Peace Agreement, the Security Council convened on 22 November and adopted two resolutions, the first of which was **1021(1995)**.

*The Security Council,*

*Recalling* all its previous relevant resolutions concerning the conflicts in the former Yugoslavia, and in particular its resolutions 713(1991) and 727(1992),

*Reaffirming* its commitment to a negotiated political settlement of the conflicts in the former Yugoslavia, preserving the territorial integrity of all States there within their internationally recognized borders,

*Welcoming* the initialling of the General Framework Agreement for Peace in Bosnia and Herzegovina and the annexes thereto (collectively the Peace Agreement) by the Republic of Bosnia and Herzegovina, the Republic of Croatia and the Federal Republic of Yugoslavia and the other parties thereto on 21 November 1995, in Dayton, Ohio, signifying agreement between the parties to sign formally the Peace Agreement,

*Welcoming also* the commitments of the parties set out in annex 1 B (Agreement on Regional Stabilization) of the Peace Agreement,

*Determining* that the situation in the region continues to constitute a threat to international peace and security,

*Acting* under Chapter VII of the Charter of the United Nations,

1. *Decides* that the embargo on deliveries of weapons and military equipment imposed by resolution 713(1991) shall be terminated as follows, beginning from the day the Secretary-General submits to the Council a report stating that the Republic of Bosnia and Herzegovina, the Republic of Croatia and the Federal Republic of Yugoslavia have formally signed the Peace Agreement:

(*a*) During the first ninety days following the submission of such a report, all the provisions of the embargo shall remain in place;

(*b*) During the second ninety days following the submission of such a report, all provisions of the arms embargo shall be terminated, except that the delivery of heavy weapons (as defined in the Peace Agreement), ammunition therefor, mines, military aircraft and helicopters shall continue to be prohibited until the arms control agreement referred to in annex 1 B has taken effect; and

(*c*) After the 180th day following the submission of such a report and after the submission of a report from the Secretary-General on the implementation of annex 1 B (Agreement on Regional Stabilization) as agreed by the parties, all provisions of the arms embargo terminate unless the Council decides otherwise;

2. *Requests* the Secretary-General to prepare in a timely way and to submit to the Council the reports referred to in paragraph 1 above;

3. *Maintains* its commitment to progressive measures for regional stability and arms control and, if the situation requires, to consider further action;

4. *Requests* the Committee established pursuant to resolution 724(1991) to review and to amend its guidelines in the light of the provisions of this resolution;

5. *Decides* to remain seized of the matter.

Security Council resolution 1021(1995)

22 November 1995          Meeting 3595          14-0-1

10-nation draft (S/1995/977).

Sponsors: Argentina, France, Germany, Honduras, Indonesia, Italy, Oman, Rwanda, United Kingdom, United States.

Vote in Council as follows:
    *In favour:* Argentina, Botswana, China, Czech Republic, France, Germany, Honduras, Indonesia, Italy, Nigeria, Oman, Rwanda, United Kingdom, United States.
    *Against:* None.
    *Abstaining:* Russian Federation.

The Russian Federation stated that the resolution raised serious doubts and concerns, since neither in spirit nor in letter did it follow the logic of the political process, which was aimed at ending military confrontation in the region. Because

of its belief that the Balkans should never again pose a threat to international security and stability, the Russian Federation was in favour, not of an arms build-up in the region, but of an arms reduction. It would have preferred the resolution to provide for a more clear-cut mechanism to operate, should the peace process be derailed.

The second resolution that the Council adopted was **1022(1995)**.

*The Security Council,*

*Recalling* all its previous relevant resolutions concerning the conflicts in the former Yugoslavia,

*Reaffirming* its commitment to a negotiated political settlement of the conflicts in the former Yugoslavia, preserving the territorial integrity of all States there within their internationally recognized borders,

*Commending* the efforts of the international community, including those of the Contact Group, to assist the parties in reaching a settlement,

*Praising* the decision of the Governments of the Republic of Bosnia and Herzegovina, the Republic of Croatia and the Federal Republic of Yugoslavia to attend and participate constructively in proximity talks in the United States of America, and acknowledging with appreciation the efforts made by these Governments to reach a lasting peace settlement in Bosnia and Herzegovina,

*Welcoming* the initialling of the General Framework Agreement for Peace in Bosnia and Herzegovina and the annexes thereto (collectively the Peace Agreement) by the Republic of Bosnia and Herzegovina, the Republic of Croatia and the Federal Republic of Yugoslavia and the other parties thereto on 21 November 1995, in Dayton, Ohio, signifying agreement between the parties to sign formally the Peace Agreement,

*Noting* the Concluding Statement issued at the adjournment of the proximity talks, in which all parties undertook, *inter alia*, to assist in locating the two French pilots missing in Bosnia and Herzegovina and to ensure their immediate and safe return,

*Stressing* the need for all parties to comply fully with all provisions of the Peace Agreement,

*Noting* that compliance with the requests and orders of the International Tribunal for the former Yugoslavia constitutes an essential aspect of implementing the Peace Agreement,

*Recognizing* the interests of all States in the implementation of the suspension and subsequent termination of measures imposed by the Council, and in particular the interests of the successor States to the State formerly known as the Socialist Federal Republic of Yugoslavia, with respect to the disposition of assets affected by the fact that that State has ceased to exist, and the desirability of accelerating the process now under way under the auspices of the International Conference on the Former Yugoslavia (ICFY) to reach a consensual agreement among the successor States as to the disposition of such assets,

*Determining* that the situation in the region continues to constitute a threat to international peace and security,

*Acting* under Chapter VII of the Charter of the United Nations,

1. *Decides* that the measures imposed by or reaffirmed in resolutions 757(1992), 787(1992), 820(1993), 942(1994),

943(1994), 988(1995), 992(1995), 1003(1995) and 1015(1995) are suspended indefinitely with immediate effect subject to the provisions of paragraphs 2 to 5 below, and provided that if the Secretary-General reports to the Council that the Federal Republic of Yugoslavia has failed formally to sign the Peace Agreement on the date announced by the Contact Group for such purpose, and that the other parties thereto have expressed their readiness so to sign, the measures described above shall be automatically reimposed from the fifth day following the date of such report;

2. *Decides also* that the suspension referred to in paragraph 1 above shall not apply to the measures imposed on the Bosnian Serb party until the day after the commander of the international force to be deployed in accordance with the Peace Agreement, on the basis of a report transmitted through the appropriate political authorities, informs the Council via the Secretary-General that all Bosnian Serb forces have withdrawn behind the zones of separation established in the Peace Agreement; and urges all parties concerned to take all necessary measures to assist in locating the two French pilots mission in Bosnia and Herzegovina, and to ensure their immediate and safe return;

3. *Further decides* that if at any time, with regard to a matter within the scope of their respective mandates and after joint consultation if appropriate, either the High Representative described in the Peace Agreement, or the commander of the international force to be deployed in accordance with the Peace Agreement, on the basis of a report transmitted through the appropriate political authorities, informs the Council via the Secretary-General that the Federal Republic of Yugoslavia or the Bosnian Serb authorities are failing significantly to meet their obligations under the Peace Agreement, the suspension referred to in paragraph 1 above shall terminate on the fifth day following the Council's receipt of such a report, unless the Council decides otherwise taking into consideration the nature of the non-compliance;

4. *Further decides* that it will terminate the measures described in paragraph 1 above on the tenth day following the occurrence of the first free and fair elections provided for in annex 3 of the Peace Agreement, provided that the Bosnian Serb forces have withdrawn from, and have continued to respect, the zones of separation as provided in the Peace Agreement;

5. *Further decides* that so long as the measures referred to in paragraph 1 above remain suspended, or are terminated by a subsequent Council decision in accordance with paragraph 4 above, all funds and assets previously frozen or impounded pursuant to resolutions 757(1992) and 820(1993) may be released by States in accordance with law, provided that any such funds and assets that are subject to any claims, liens, judgements, or encumbrances, or which are the funds or assets of any person, partnership, corporation, or other entity found or deemed insolvent under law or the accounting principles prevailing in such State, shall remain frozen or impounded until released in accordance with applicable law, and decides further that obligations of States related to freezing or impounding funds and assets contained in such resolutions shall be suspended pursuant to paragraph 1 above with respect to all funds and assets not currently frozen or impounded until the measures concerned are terminated by a subsequent Council decision;

6. *Further decides* that the suspension or termination of obligations pursuant to this resolution is without prejudice to claims of successor States to the former Socialist Federal Republic of Yugoslavia with respect to funds and assets; stresses the need for the successor States to reach agreement on the distribution of funds and assets and the allocation of liabilities of the former Socialist Federal Republic of Yugoslavia; encourages all States to make provision under their national law for addressing competing claims of States, as well as claims of private parties affecting funds and assets; and further encourages States to take appropriate measures to facilitate the expeditious collection of any funds and assets by the appropriate parties and the resolution of claims related thereto;

7. *Further decides* that all States shall continue to take the necessary measures to ensure that there shall be no claim in connection with the performance of any contract or other transaction where such performance was affected by the measures imposed by the resolutions referred to in paragraph 1 above and related resolutions;

8. *Requests* the Committee established pursuant to resolution 724(1991) to review and to amend its guidelines in the light of the provisions of this resolution;

9. *Pays tribute* to the neighbouring States, the ICFY mission, the European Union/Organization for Security and Cooperation in Europe Sanctions Coordinator, the Sanctions Communications Centre and the Sanctions Assistance Missions, the Western European Union operation on the Danube and the North Atlantic Treaty Organization/Western European Union Sharp Guard operation in the Adriatic Sea for their significant contribution to the achievement of a negotiated peace;

10. *Decides* to remain seized of the matter.

Security Council resolution 1022(1995)

22 November 1995    Meeting 3595    Adopted unanimously

10-nation draft (S/1995/978).

*Sponsors:* Argentina, Czech Republic, France, Germany, Honduras, Italy, Russian Federation, Rwanda, United Kingdom, United States.

Pursuant to the Council's request in paragraph 1 of **resolution 1021(1995)**, the Secretary-General informed the Council President on 14 December that, on that date, Bosnia and Herzegovina, Croatia and Yugoslavia (Serbia and Montenegro) and other parties thereto had formally signed the Peace Agreement in Paris.[119]

### Peace Implementation Conference

Before the formal signature of the Peace Agreement, the United Kingdom convened a Peace Implementation Conference in London on 8 and 9 December, to mobilize the international community to assist in the Agreement's implementation.[120] The Conference set forth its conclusions on a series of implementation objectives, the realization of which would involve, at the initial phase, a wide range of international and regional organizations and agencies.

The Conference was briefed on implementation of the military aspects of the Agreement, to be undertaken by a multinational military Implementation Force (IFOR), whose primary tasks were to ensure the continued compliance with the 5 October cessation-of-hostilities agreement, the withdrawal of forces from the Agreed Cease-Fire Zone of Separation, and the separation of forces from the Inter-Entity Boundary Line. Its supporting tasks, to be performed within the limits of its capabilities, were to help secure the conditions necessary for the conduct by others of other tasks associated with the Agreement, prevent interference with the freedom of movement of civilian populations, including refugees and displaced persons, monitor minefield clearance, and assist UNHCR and other international organizations in their humanitarian missions.

The Conference strongly urged the parties to observe the deadlines set out in the Peace Agreement for agreeing on confidence-building and arms-control measures. It supported the commitment made by OSCE at its ministerial meeting (Budapest, Hungary, 7-8 December) to assist the parties' negotiations in this regard, and endorsed Germany's decision to convene an international meeting (Bonn, 18 December) to initiate this process.

Having been briefed also on the wide range of tasks involved in implementing the civilian aspects of the Agreement, the Conference approved the designation of Carl Bildt (Sweden) as the High Representative and invited the Security Council's agreement to that designation. As envisaged in the Agreement, a High Representative was to monitor the Agreement's implementation, and mobilize and, as appropriate, coordinate the activities of the civilian organizations and agencies involved. The Conference established a Peace Implementation Council (PIC), composed of all those States, international organizations and agencies attending the Conference, together with a Steering Board, to subsume ICFY and manage the peace implementation process (for details, see under "General aspects" above).

The Conference noted that the tasks involved in humanitarian assistance, refugee repatriation, the release of prisoners and the search for missing persons required extra effort by the international community and called for generous assistance and contributions to UNHCR, ICRC and other humanitarian agencies. It outlined urgent action required for the protection of human rights and noted that a task force would meet in Sarajevo to address that issue. It heard OSCE's presentation of its preparations for the elections, scheduled to take place six to nine months after the formal signature of the Agreement, and decided that PIC would give a lead in providing staff and resources as well as election monitors. The process of reconstructing the economic and physical infrastructure of Bosnia and Herzegovina would begin with a meeting (Brussels, 20-21 December) organized by the World Bank and the European Commission, to outline priority reconstruction proposals. The EU President, in his statement to the Conference, stressed that legitimate and effective political structures in Bosnia and Herzegovina were needed to enable the country to establish strong relations with EU.

In addition, an informal meeting was held in the margins of the Conference to discuss implementation of the Basic Agreement on the Region of Eastern Slavonia, Baranja and Western Sirmium (see under "Croatia" below).

### UN transition arrangements

**Report of the Secretary-General.** As requested by Security Council **resolution 1026(1995)**, the Secretary-General on 13 December submitted a report addressing those aspects of the Peace Agreement's implementation affecting the United Nations.[121]

Under the terms of the Agreement, the Council was to authorize Member States or regional organizations or arrangements to establish a multinational military Implementation Force, composed of ground, air and maritime units from NATO members and non-NATO States. IFOR would begin implementation of the Agreement's military aspects upon the transfer of authority for the forces deployed in Bosnia and Herzegovina from the UNPROFOR Commander to the IFOR Commander. Such transfer could occur within 96 hours of the Council's authorization; the UNPF Force Commander would become the Deputy Commander of IFOR, retaining his UNPF authority, however, over UNPROFOR units not transferring to IFOR, until their withdrawal from the theatre.

A United Nations Coordinator would be appointed by the Secretary-General to exercise authority over the Commissioner of the proposed international police task force and to coordinate other UN activities in Bosnia and Herzegovina. The Coordinator's office, comprising political and legal advisers and information staff, would be located in Sarajevo close to that of the High Representative, from whom the Coordinator would receive guidance.

UNHCR would continue as lead agency for coordinating humanitarian relief assistance and in implementing a plan for the return of refugees and displaced persons. Its aim was to reduce the scale of the first task and redirect efforts towards the second to ensure organized and phased return movements. Accurate planning in this connection was difficult because the choice to return or resettle elsewhere was left to the refugees and displaced persons, who numbered 1.2 million inside Bosnia and Herzegovina and 900,000 elsewhere.

The Secretary-General proposed temporarily maintaining the Mine Action Centre at UNPF-HQ (with one civilian and six military personnel), saying the Centre had a wealth of mine-related information and databases for both Bosnia and Herzegovina and Croatia. He further proposed the temporary retention of four military mines information officers to work under the direction of the UN Coordinator.

As to the establishment of an international police task force, the Agreement specified that it be established by the Council as a UN civilian operation charged with monitoring, observing and inspecting law enforcement activities and facilities; advising and training law enforcement personnel; facilitating the parties' law enforcement activities; advising government authorities in Bosnia and Herzegovina on the organization of effective civilian law enforcement agencies; accompanying the parties' law enforcement personnel as they discharged their responsibilities; and assisting the parties to ensure conditions for free and fair elections.

Based on the assessments of a mission recently dispatched to Bosnia and Herzegovina, and bearing in mind the tasks to be performed, the Secretary-General recommended that the proposed police task force set up its central headquarters in Sarajevo and five regional headquarters in Sarajevo, Banja Luka, Gornji Vakuf, Mostar and Tuzla, as well as 17 central police districts and 109 police stations. He further recommended that the locations of those regional headquarters, police districts and stations correspond with those of the local enforcement authorities and bodies. A total of 1,721 police monitors would be required, in addition to 45 civil affairs and public information officers to be assigned to the central headquarters.

The UN contribution in the human rights field would come from: UNHCR, whose mandate called for providing protection to newly returned refugees; the proposed police task force, whose responsibilities would include monitoring the local security forces' respect for human rights; and the Office of the UN High Commissioner for Human Rights, which had declared its readiness to develop and facilitate training for human rights personnel, to make available a limited number of experienced human rights officers to deal with human rights violations, and to continue to support the work of the Special Rapporteur and of the Expert on the special process dealing with missing persons in the former Yugoslavia.

The Secretary-General indicated that the Under-Secretary-General for Political Affairs, in his capacity as UN Focal Point for Electoral Assistance Activities, would provide technical advice to OSCE based on the extensive experience of the United Nations in that area. The UN system would play its usual role in the rehabilitation of the country's infrastructure and economic reconstruction. In addition, the Secretary-General had encouraged the High Representative to consider appointing some UNPROFOR civil affairs and public information officers, whose experience in Bosnia and Herzegovina would be of great assistance to him.

Regarding UN activities that would be discontinued, the Secretary-General accepted the recommendation of the Peace Implementation Conference that ICFY and its Steering Committee be dissolved on 31 January 1996 and, accordingly, extended the appointment of the UN Co-Chairman of the Steering Committee to that date. He recommended that the office and functions of the Special Coordinator for Sarajevo be subsumed, with effect from 30 April 1996, in the arrangements to be established by the World Bank, the European Commission and others for the rehabilitation and reconstruction of Bosnia and Herzegovina, and that the 1994 Council resolution which had created that office[44] be allowed to lapse on that date.

In view of the transfer to IFOR of UNPROFOR's military responsibilities, the Secretary-General recommended that UNPROFOR's monitoring of the ban on military flights in the airspace of Bosnia and Herzegovina[122] be discontinued and the airfield monitors repatriated, and that its responsibilities for operating Sarajevo airport,[15] as well as Tuzla airport and other airfields, be transferred to IFOR.

The Secretary-General recommended making the three UN operations in the former Yugoslavia fully independent of one another. UNPF-HQ would be restructured and its civilian and military personnel drastically reduced. The Office of the Special Representative could be phased out by the end of February 1996. However, because of the complex and time-consuming nature of the transition arrangements and the emplacement of new civilian operations in Bosnia and Herzegovina and Croatia, and in order to secure UN premises and assets during the liquidation of UNPROFOR and UNCRO, the Secretary-General recommended retaining a coordinated civilian and military capacity at UNPF-HQ in Zagreb for six months beyond the expiry of the mandates of UNPROFOR and UNCRO.

In a 15 December addendum to his report, the Secretary-General estimated the cost associated with the emplacement and maintenance of a UN international police task force at $89,952,000, to cover costs of 1,721 police monitors and 254 internationally and 811 locally recruited staff for an initial period of six months.[123] An itemized breakdown of the estimate was annexed to the addendum.

**SECURITY COUNCIL ACTION**

Following receipt of the Secretary-General's report, the Security Council met on 15 December and adopted **resolution 1031(1995)**.

*The Security Council,*

*Recalling* all its previous relevant resolutions concerning the conflicts in the former Yugoslavia,

*Reaffirming* its commitment to a negotiated political settlement of the conflicts in the former Yugoslavia, preserving the territorial integrity of all States there within their internationally recognized borders,

*Welcoming* the signing on 14 December 1995 at the Paris Peace Conference of the General Framework Agreement for Peace in Bosnia and Herzegovina and the annexes thereto by the Republic of Bosnia and Herzegovina, the Republic of Croatia and the Federal Republic of Yugoslavia and the other parties thereto,

*Welcoming also* the Dayton Agreement on implementing the Federation of Bosnia and Herzegovina of 10 November 1995,

*Welcoming further* the conclusions of the Peace Implementation Conference held in London on 8 and 9 December 1995 (the London Conference), and in particular its decision to establish a Peace Implementation Council and its Steering Board as referred to in those conclusions,

*Paying tribute* to the International Conference on the Former Yugoslavia (ICFY) for its efforts aimed at achieving a peace settlement and taking note of the decision of the London Conference that the Peace Implementation Council will subsume the ICFY,

*Having considered* the report of the Secretary-General of 13 December 1995,

*Determining* that the situation in the region continues to constitute a threat to international peace and security,

*Determined* to promote the peaceful resolution of the conflicts in accordance with the purposes and principles of the Charter of the United Nations,

*Acting* under Chapter VII of the Charter of the United Nations,

### I

1. *Welcomes and supports* the Peace Agreement and calls upon the parties to fulfil in good faith the commitments entered into in that Agreement;

2. *Expresses* its intention to keep the implementation of the Peace Agreement under review;

3. *Welcomes* the progress made towards mutual recognition among the successor States to the former Socialist Federal Republic of Yugoslavia, within their internationally recognized borders;

4. *Reaffirms* its resolutions concerning compliance with international humanitarian law in the former Yugoslavia, reaffirms also that all States shall cooperate fully with the International Tribunal for the Former Yugoslavia and its organs in accordance with the provisions of resolution 827(1993) of 25 May 1993 and the Statute of the International Tribunal, and shall comply with requests for assistance or orders issued by a Trial Chamber under article 29 of the Statute, and calls upon them to allow the establishment of offices of the Tribunal;

5. *Recognizes* that the parties shall cooperate fully with all entities involved in implementation of the peace settlement, as described in the Peace Agreement, or which are otherwise authorized by the Security Council, including the International Tribunal for the Former Yugoslavia, and that the parties have in particular authorized the multinational force referred to in paragraph 14 below to take such actions as required, including the use of necessary force, to ensure compliance with annex 1 A of the Peace Agreement;

6. *Welcomes* the agreement by the Organization for Security and Cooperation in Europe (OSCE) to adopt and put in place a programme of elections for Bosnia and Herzegovina, at the request of the parties to annex 3 of the Peace Agreement;

7. *Welcomes also* the parties' commitment, as specified in the Peace Agreement, to securing to all persons within their jurisdiction the highest level of internationally recognized human rights and fundamental freedoms, stresses that compliance with this commitment is of vital importance in achieving a lasting peace, and welcomes the invitation by the parties to the United Nations Commission on Human Rights, the OSCE, the United Nations High Commissioner for Human Rights and other intergovernmental or regional human rights missions or organizations to monitor closely the human rights situation in Bosnia and Herzegovina;

8. *Welcomes further* the parties' commitment to the right of all refugees and displaced persons freely to return to their homes of origin in safety, notes the leading humanitarian role which has been given by the Peace Agreement to the United Nations High Commissioner for Refugees, in coordination with other agencies involved and under the authority of the Secretary-General, in assisting with the repatriation and relief of refugees and displaced persons, and stresses the importance of repatriation being phased, gradual and orderly;

9. *Emphasizes* the importance of the creation of conditions conducive to the reconstruction and development of Bosnia and Herzegovina and encourages Member States to provide assistance for the programme of reconstruction in that country;

10. *Underlines* the relationship, as described in the conclusions of the London Conference, between the fulfilment by the parties of their commitments in the Peace Agreement and the readiness of the international community to commit financial resources for reconstruction and development;

11. *Welcomes* the agreement of the parties to annex 1 B of the Peace Agreement that establishment of progressive measures for regional stability and arms control is essential to creating a stable peace in the region, emphasizes the importance of all Member States supporting their efforts to this end, and supports the OSCE's commitment to assist the parties with the negotiation and implementation of such measures;

### II

12. *Welcomes* the willingness of the Member States acting through or in cooperation with the organization referred to in annex 1 A of the Peace Agreement to assist the parties to the Peace Agreement by deploying a multinational implementation force;

13. *Notes* the invitation of the parties to the international community to send to the region for a period of approximately one year a multinational implementation force to assist in implementation of the territorial and other militarily related provisions of annex 1 A of the Peace Agreement;

14. *Authorizes* the Member States acting through or in cooperation with the organization referred to in annex 1 A of the Peace Agreement to establish a multinational implementation force (IFOR) under unified command and control in order to fulfil the role specified in annex 1 A and annex 2 of the Peace Agreement;

15. *Authorizes* the Member States acting under paragraph 14 above to take all necessary measures to effect the implementation of and to ensure compliance with

annex 1 A of the Peace Agreement, stresses that the parties shall be held equally responsible for compliance with that annex, and shall be equally subject to such enforcement action by IFOR as may be necessary to ensure implementation of that annex and the protection of IFOR, and takes note that the parties have consented to IFOR's taking such measures;

16. *Authorizes* the Member States acting under paragraph 14 above, in accordance with annex 1 A of the Peace Agreement, to take all necessary measures to ensure compliance with the rules and procedures, to be established by the Commander of IFOR, governing command and control of airspace over Bosnia and Herzegovina with respect to all civilian and military air traffic;

17. *Authorizes* Member States to take all necessary measures, at the request of IFOR, either in defence of IFOR or to assist the force in carrying out its mission, and recognizes the right of the force to take all necessary measures to defend itself from attack or threat of attack;

18. *Demands* that the parties respect the security and freedom of movement of IFOR and other international personnel;

19. *Decides* that, with effect from the day on which the Secretary-General reports to the Council that the transfer of authority from the United Nations Protection Force (UNPROFOR) to IFOR has taken place, the authority to take certain measures conferred upon States by resolutions 770(1992) of 13 August 1992, 781(1992) of 9 October 1992, 816(1993) of 31 March 1993, 836(1993) of 4 June 1993, 844(1993) of 18 June 1993 and 958(1994) of 19 November 1994 shall be terminated, and that the provisions of resolution 824(1993) of 6 May 1993 and subsequent resolutions regarding safe areas shall also be terminated from the same date;

20. *Requests* the Government of Bosnia and Herzegovina to cooperate with the IFOR Commander to ensure the effective management of the airports in Bosnia and Herzegovina, in the light of the responsibilities conferred on IFOR by annex 1 A of the Peace Agreement with regard to the airspace of Bosnia and Herzegovina;

21. *Decides*, with a view to terminating the authorization granted in paragraphs 14 to 17 above one year after the transfer of authority from UNPROFOR to IFOR, to review by that date and to take a decision whether that authorization should continue, based upon the recommendations from the States participating in IFOR and from the High Representative through the Secretary-General;

22. *Decides also* that the embargo imposed by resolution 713(1991) of 25 September 1991 shall not apply to weapons and military equipment destined for the sole use of the Member States acting under paragraph 14 above, or of international police forces;

23. *Invites* all States, in particular those in the region, to provide appropriate support and facilities, including transit facilities, for the Member States acting under paragraph 14 above;

24. *Welcomes* the conclusion of the agreements concerning the status of forces as referred to in appendix B to annex 1 A of the Peace Agreement, and demands that the parties comply fully with those agreements;

25. *Requests* the Member States acting through or in cooperation with the organization referred to in annex 1 A of the Peace Agreement to report to the Council, through the appropriate channels and at least at monthly intervals, the first such report to be made not later than 10 days following the adoption of this resolution;

26. *Endorses* the establishment of a High Representative, following the request of the parties, who, in accordance with annex 10 on the civilian implementation of the Peace Agreement, will monitor the implementation of the Peace Agreement and mobilize and, as appropriate, give guidance to, and coordinate the activities of, the civilian organizations and agencies involved, and agrees to the designation of Mr. Carl Bildt as High Representative;

27. *Confirms* that the High Representative is the final authority in theatre regarding interpretation of annex 10 on the civilian implementation of the Peace Agreement;

28. *Decides* that all States concerned, and in particular those where the High Representative establishes offices, shall ensure that the High Representative enjoys such legal capacity as may be necessary for the exercise of his functions, including the capacity to contract and to acquire and dispose of real and personal property;

29. *Notes* that close cooperation between IFOR, the High Representative and the agencies will be vital to ensure successful implementation;

30. *Affirms* the need for the implementation of the Peace Agreement in its entirety and, in this context, stresses the importance it attaches to the urgent implementation of annex 11 of the Peace Agreement, decides to act expeditiously on the report of the Secretary-General recommending the establishment of a United Nations Civilian Police Force with the tasks set out in that annex, together with a civilian office with the responsibilities described in the report of the Secretary-General, and further decides that in the interim civilian police, de-mining, civil affairs and other personnel that might be required to carry out the tasks described in that report shall continue in theatre, notwithstanding the provisions of paragraphs 33 and 34 below;

31. *Stresses* the need for early action in Sarajevo to create confidence between the communities and to this end requests the Secretary-General to ensure the early redeployment of elements of United Nations civilian police from the Republic of Croatia to Sarajevo;

32. *Requests* the Secretary-General to submit to the Council reports from the High Representative, in accordance with annex 10 of the Peace Agreement and the conclusions of the London Conference, on the implementation of the Peace Agreement;

## III

33. *Decides* that the mandate of UNPROFOR shall terminate on the date on which the Secretary-General reports to the Council that the transfer of authority from UNPROFOR to IFOR has taken place;

34. *Approves* the arrangements set out in the report of the Secretary-General on the withdrawal of UNPROFOR and headquarters elements from the United Nations Peace Force (UNPF), including the arrangements for the command and control of UNPROFOR following the transfer of authority from it to IFOR;

35. *Expresses* its warmest appreciation to all UNPROFOR personnel, who have served the cause of peace in the former Yugoslavia, and pays tribute to those who have given their lives and those who have suffered serious injuries in that service;

36. *Authorizes* the Member States acting under paragraph 14 above to use all necessary means to assist in the withdrawal of UNPROFOR;

37. *Calls upon* the parties to ensure the safety and security of UNPROFOR and confirms that UNPROFOR will continue to enjoy all existing privileges and immunities, including during the period of withdrawal;

38. *Requests* the Secretary-General to report to the Council when the withdrawal of UNPROFOR is complete;

IV

39. *Recognizes* the unique, extraordinary and complex character of the present situation in Bosnia and Herzegovina, requiring an exceptional response;

40. *Decides* to remain seized of the matter.

Security Council resolution 1031(1995)

15 December 1995    Meeting 3607    Adopted unanimously

8-nation draft (S/1995/1033).

*Sponsors:* Argentina, Czech Republic, France, Germany, Italy, Russian Federation, United Kingdom, United States.

Responding to paragraph 19 of the foregoing resolution, the Secretary-General informed the Council President on 20 December that, on that date, the transfer of authority from UNPROFOR to IFOR had taken place in Sarajevo,[124] thus terminating the authority conferred upon States by Council resolutions 770(1992),[125] 781(1992),[17] 816(1993),[126] 836(1993),[19] 844(1993)[127] and 958(1994),[128] as well as the provisions of resolution 824(1993)[43] and subsequent resolutions concerning safe areas.

### International Police Task Force and UN civilian office

The Security Council, having further considered the Secretary-General's report on transition arrangements,[121] met on 21 December and adopted **resolution 1035(1995)**.

*The Security Council,*

*Recalling* its resolution 1031(1995) of 15 December 1995,

*Recalling also* the General Framework Agreement for Peace in Bosnia and Herzegovina and the annexes thereto,

*Having further considered* the report of the Secretary-General of 13 December 1995,

1. *Approves* the report of the Secretary-General and the proposals for involvement by the United Nations in the implementation of the Peace Agreement contained therein;

2. *Decides* to establish, for a period of one year from the transfer of authority from the United Nations Protection Force to the multinational implementation force (IFOR), a United Nations civilian police force to be known as the International Police Task Force (IPTF) to be entrusted with the tasks set out in annex 11 of the Peace Agreement and a United Nations civilian office with the responsibilities set out in the report of the Secretary-General, and to that end endorses the arrangements set out in the report of the Secretary-General;

3. *Notes with satisfaction* that the IPTF and the United Nations civilian office will be under the authority of the Secretary-General and subject to coordination and guidance as appropriate by the High Representative, welcomes the Secretary-General's intention to appoint a United

Nations Coordinator, and requests the Secretary-General to submit to the Council, at least every three months, reports about the work of the IPTF and of the civilian office accordingly;

4. *Decides* to remain seized of the matter.

Security Council resolution 1035(1995)

21 December 1995    Meeting 3613    Adopted unanimously

Draft prepared in consultations among Council members (S/1995/1049).

### Dayton Agreement on implementing the Federation of Bosnia and Herzegovina

During the Dayton negotiations, on 10 November, Bosnia and Herzegovina and Croatia signed the Dayton Agreement on implementing the Federation of Bosnia and Herzegovina, to which was annexed a set of Agreed Principles for the interim statute for the City of Mostar, signed by the Mayors of West and East Mostar and the EU Administrator for Mostar. The text was transmitted to the Secretary-General on 7 December.[129]

The Dayton Agreement set forth the general principles relating to the governance of the Federation and provided for the transfer of governmental functions from the Government of the Republic to the Government of the Federation, specifying the areas of responsibility for each. It further contained provisions concerning the Federation's boundaries; fiscal, customs and budgetary matters for the Federation; cantons and municipalities; ambassadors; police; defence; refugees and displaced persons; the administration of Mostar; and reporting obligations on the Agreement's implementation.

### Ban on military flights

The ban on military flights established by Security Council resolution 781(1992),[130] reaffirmed by resolution 786(1992)[122] and extended by resolution 816(1993)[126] to flights by all fixed-wing and rotary-wing aircraft, except to flights authorized by UNPROFOR, remained in force until 19 December 1995.

By notes verbales addressed to the Council President, the Secretary-General drew attention to information received by UNPROFOR and annexed to the notes regarding apparent violations of the ban on flights in the airspace of Bosnia and Herzegovina between 20 December 1994 and 16 December 1995.[131] Since the ban's imposition on 9 October 1992 until 16 December 1995, the number of flights assessed as apparent violations totalled 7,552.

In accordance with paragraph 19 of Council **resolution 1031(1995)**, the provisions of resolution 816(1993) were terminated with effect from 20 December 1995, the date on which the Secretary-General reported to the Council that the transfer of authority from UNPROFOR to IFOR had taken place.[132]

## Border control

### *ICFY Mission to Yugoslavia (Serbia and Montenegro)*

The ICFY Mission to Yugoslavia (Serbia and Montenegro), set up in 1994[133] with head-quarters in Belgrade, continued in 1995 to monitor and verify whether Yugoslavia (Serbia and Montenegro) was in compliance with that country's 1994 decision to close its border with Bosnian Serb–held areas of Bosnia and Herzegovina to all but shipments of humanitarian aid.[134] That decision, taken primarily to influence the Bosnian Serbs to accept the peace plan proposed by the five-member Contact Group,[10] resulted in the suspension by the Security Council, for an initial 100-day period, of those restrictions and other measures imposed on Yugoslavia (Serbia and Montenegro) by its resolution 943(1994).[135]

Based on the reports of the Co-Chairmen of the ICFY Steering Committee on the Mission's operations during the year, the Council, by four resolutions, successively extended the suspension period to: 22 April (**resolution 970(1995)**), 5 July (**988(1995)**), 18 September 1995 (**1003(1995)**), and 18 March 1996 (**1015(1995)**).

The border area monitored by the Mission extended 330 miles (approximately 527 kilometres) from the north of Serbia to the south of Montenegro. Besides providing static coverage at 19 border control posts on a 24-hour basis, the Mission conducted day and night mobile patrols along the border, usually in cooperation with the local army or police. The Mission was organized into five field sectors, between two and nine hours' drive from Belgrade and located as follows: Sector Belgrade, responsible for observing the loading and customs inspection of goods destined for points beyond the border with "Republika Srpska"; Sector Alpha, headquartered in Banja Koviljaca, responsible for the border area from the junction of the Drina and Sava in the north to Drlace in the south; Sector Bajina Basta, responsible for the border area from Drlace in the north to 3 kilometres north of Priboj and for checking and controlling freight trains into and out of "Republika Srpska"; Sector Bravo, headquartered in Priboj, responsible for the border area 3 kilometres north of Priboj to the Tara River in Montenegro; and Sector Charlie, headquartered in Niksic, Montenegro, responsible for the border area from the Tara River in the north to the point at which the border of Yugoslavia (Serbia and Montenegro) with Bosnia and Herzegovina abuts the border of Yugoslavia (Serbia and Montenegro) with Croatia, near the Adriatic coast.

As of 14 December, the Mission had 217 international members from 15 countries.

### 1994 activities

The Security Council met on 12 January 1995 in connection with the 1994 reports on the ICFY Mission activities[133] and adopted **resolution 970(1995)**.

*The Security Council,*

*Recalling* all its earlier relevant resolutions, and in particular resolution 943(1994) of 23 September 1994,

*Welcoming* the measures taken by the authorities of the Federal Republic of Yugoslavia (Serbia and Montenegro), in particular those detailed in the annex to the Secretary-General's letter of 4 January 1995 to the President of the Security Council, to maintain the effective closure of the international border between the Federal Republic of Yugoslavia (Serbia and Montenegro) and the Republic of Bosnia and Herzegovina with respect to all goods except foodstuffs, medical supplies and clothing for essential humanitarian needs, and noting that those measures were a necessary condition for the adoption of the present resolution,

*Stressing the importance* of the maintenance by the authorities of the Federal Republic of Yugoslavia (Serbia and Montenegro) of the effective closure of that border, and of further efforts by them to enhance the effectiveness of that closure, including by the prosecution of persons suspected of violating measures to that end and by sealing border crossing points as requested by the Mission of the International Conference on the Former Yugoslavia (ICFY),

*Expressing appreciation* for the work of the Co-Chairmen of the Steering Committee of the ICFY and of the ICFY Mission to the Federal Republic of Yugoslavia (Serbia and Montenegro), and stressing the importance it attaches to the availability of all necessary resources for the work of the Mission,

*Noting* that paragraph 9 of resolution 757(1992) of 30 May 1992 remains in force,

*Acting* under Chapter VII of the Charter of the United Nations,

1. *Decides* that the restrictions and other measures referred to in paragraph 1 of resolution 943(1994) shall be suspended for a further period of 100 days from the adoption of the present resolution;

2. *Calls upon* all States and others concerned to respect the sovereignty, territorial integrity and international borders of all States in the region;

3. *Reaffirms* that the requirements in paragraph 12 of resolution 820(1993) that import to, export from and transshipment through the United Nations Protected Areas in the Republic of Croatia and those areas of the Republic of Bosnia and Herzegovina under the control of Bosnian Serb forces, with the exception of essential humanitarian supplies including medical supplies and foodstuffs distributed by international humanitarian agencies, shall be permitted only with proper authorization from the Government of the Republic of Croatia or the Government of the Republic of Bosnia and Herzegovina respectively, apply to all shipments across the international border between the Federal Republic of Yugoslavia (Serbia and Montenegro) and the Republic of Bosnia and Herzegovina;

4. *Requests* the Committee established by resolution 724(1991) urgently to expedite its elaboration of

appropriate streamlined procedures as referred to in paragraph 2 of resolution 943(1993), and to give priority to its consideration of applications concerning legitimate humanitarian assistance, in particular applications from the International Committee of the Red Cross and from the United Nations High Commissioner for Refugees and other organizations in the United Nations system;

5. *Requests* that every thirty days the Secretary-General submit to the Security Council for its review a report as to whether the Co-Chairmen of the ICFY Steering Committee certify that the authorities of the Federal Republic of Yugoslavia (Serbia and Montenegro) are effectively implementing their decision to close the international border between the Federal Republic of Yugoslavia (Serbia and Montenegro) and the Republic of Bosnia and Herzegovina with respect to all goods except foodstuffs, medical supplies and clothing for essential humanitarian needs, and are complying with the requirements of paragraph 3 above in respect of all shipments across the international border between the Federal Republic of Yugoslavia (Serbia and Montenegro) and the Republic of Bosnia and Herzegovina, and further requests the Secretary-General to report to the Council immediately if he has evidence, including from the Co-Chairmen of the ICFY Steering Committee, that those authorities are not effectively implementing their decision to close that border;

6. *Decides* that if at any time the Secretary-General reports that the authorities of the Federal Republic of Yugoslavia (Serbia and Montenegro) are not effectively implementing their decision to close that border, the suspension of the measures referred to in paragraph 1 above shall terminate on the fifth working day following the report of the Secretary-General, unless the Security Council decides to the contrary;

7. *Decides* to keep the situation closely under review and to consider further steps with regard to measures applicable to the Federal Republic of Yugoslavia (Serbia and Montenegro) in the light of further progress in the situation;

8. *Decides* to remain actively seized of the matter.

Security Council resolution 970(1995)

12 January 1995     Meeting 3487     14-0-1

5-nation draft (S/1995/21).

*Sponsors:* Czech Republic, France, Germany, Italy, United Kingdom.

Vote in Council as follows:

*In favour:* Argentina, Botswana, China, Czech Republic, France, Germany, Honduras, Indonesia, Italy, Nigeria, Oman, Rwanda, United Kingdom, United States.
*Against:* None.
*Abstaining:* Russian Federation.

The representative of Yugoslavia (Serbia and Montenegro), who had been invited at his request, expressed disappointment at the extension for only another 100 days of what he called the very limited partial suspension of the sanctions against his country, reflecting a lack of political will to assess objectively his country's constructive role in the search for a peaceful solution to the civil war in Bosnia and Herzegovina. The Sanctions Committee, instead of streamlining procedures for expediting applications for legitimate humanitarian assistance, as called for by Council resolution

943(1994),[135] had resorted, he said, to an ever-stricter implementation of the sanctions, consistently rejecting requests for the importation of gas and raw materials for the pharmaceutical industry. The Council itself had ignored the request for a one-shot export of $70 million worth of goods, whose proceeds would have been used for the import of emergency humanitarian items. He considered unacceptable any linking of the further suspension of sanctions against his country to conditions that were not valid at the time the sanctions were imposed, or had no connection with resolving the crisis in Bosnia and Herzegovina.

The Russian Federation cited the December 1994 economic agreement concluded between Croatia and the local Serb authorities in the UNPAs[136] and the cessation-of-hostilities agreement in Bosnia and Herzegovina,[1] as well as what it called the encouraging changes in the attitude of the Bosnian Serb leadership towards the Contact Group's peace proposal, due in large measure, it said, to the Yugoslav Government's constructive role during the past 100 days. It thus regretted that the Council could not agree on a draft text that would have provided further measures of encouragement to Yugoslavia (Serbia and Montenegro)—in the form, not only of indefinitely extending suspension of the limited sanctions, but of a wider easing of the sanctions—and thereby give impetus to the peace process.

1995 activities

The 1995 activities of the ICFY Mission were covered in 30- and 10-day reports submitted by the Co-Chairmen of the ICFY Steering Committee to the Security Council, through the Secretary-General, on 2 February,[137] 1 March,[138] 30 March,[139] 11 April,[140] 17 May,[141] 23 June,[142] 2 August,[143] 6 September,[144] 9 October,[145] 8 November[146] and 7 December.[147]

In addition to providing up-to-date information on the Mission's organization and financing, staffing and logistic requirements, each report described in detail the Mission's monitoring and verification of the enforcement of national legislation to implement the 1994 Yugoslav decision, including enforcement shortcomings;[134] verification of information received from national and other sources relevant to the Mission's mandate; the status of the Mission's freedom of movement and security, noting curtailment of or threats thereto; the level of the cooperation accorded to the Mission by the national and local authorities; and the Mission's representations to those authorities for action to correct or resolve problems encountered in the course of its monitoring activities.

The main problems encountered included: smuggling operations, usually through bypass roads and tracks; lax customs checks; border police allowing military *matériel* and personnel to cross into Bosnia and Herzegovina; tampering with border barricades; and other isolated violations.

Each of the reports recorded the Co-Chairmen's consistent certification—based on the Mission's on-site observation and the Mission Coordinator's advice, and in the absence of contrary information from the air (through national technical means or NATO's airborne reconnaissance system)—that Yugoslavia (Serbia and Montenegro) was continuing to meet its 1994 commitment[133] to close the border between it and the areas of Bosnia and Herzegovina under Bosnian Serb control. The Co-Chairmen also concluded that, during the periods covered by the reports, there had been no commercial transshipments across the border between Yugoslavia (Serbia and Montenegro) and Bosnia and Herzegovina.

However, the certifications in the 30 March[139] and 11 April[140] reports noted the tracking of helicopter crossings between the two countries, as reported by UN airfield monitors working at the civilian radar screens at Surcin airport near Belgrade. Regarding 26 tracks of likely helicopter flights reported to have been observed moving from Bosnia and Herzegovina into Yugoslavia (Serbia and Montenegro) in March, the latter wrote on 11 April[148] that its extensive investigations could confirm only six helicopter flights, and that their purpose was to transport the critically wounded from the "Republic of Srpska": four were authorized by UNPROFOR; two were not, as the transportees were in a life-threatening condition.

The 25 radar contacts similarly noted between 2 and 7 April and on 29 April were the subject of an expert inquiry, whose broader aim was to attempt to resolve the issue of over 100 unexplained radar contacts reported since 9 October 1994 by UNPROFOR airfield monitors at Surcin. Inquiry findings, transmitted by the Co-Chairmen on 9 May,[149] noted that while the radar system was found to be fully serviceable and well-suited to its primary purpose, namely, air traffic control of the airspace of Yugoslavia (Serbia and Montenegro), shortcomings were observed when used for detection of difficult targets flying at the limit of the radar's operational parameters and in the difficult terrain in the area where the majority of the unexplained traces had been observed. A detailed analysis gave rise to the suspicion that some unauthorized border crossings by slow-flying objects might have taken place in the past, requiring other evidence, however, to prove or disprove each case conclusively. Apart from the unexplained trace on 29 April, which could not be reviewed by the inquiry, the flights appeared to have stopped. The conclusion was that the ICFY Mission, particularly at its staffing level, did not have the capability to monitor effectively the closure of the air border.

**SECURITY COUNCIL ACTION (21 April, 5 July, 15 September)**

The Security Council met on three other occasions in order to consider the extension or termination of the suspension of sanctions against Yugoslavia (Serbia and Montenegro), on the basis of the reports of the Co-Chairmen of the ICFY Steering Committee. With the exception of the third meeting, the representative of Yugoslavia (Serbia and Montenegro), at his request, was again invited to address the Council.

The Council met on 21 April, just before the end of the second 100-day suspension period. Before it was the report on developments during the first 10 days of April,[140] supplementing the three previous 30-day reports and indicating confiscations by the Yugoslav authorities of, among other items, significant tons of petrol and diesel fuel, construction materials, cigarettes, food and other goods. On the same date, the Council adopted **resolution 988(1995)**.

*The Security Council,*

*Recalling* all its earlier relevant resolutions, and in particular resolution 943(1994) of 23 September 1994 and resolution 970(1995) of 12 January 1995,

*Noting* the measures taken by the authorities of the Federal Republic of Yugoslavia (Serbia and Montenegro), as described in the annex to the Secretary-General's letter of 31 March 1995 and in the annex to the Secretary-General's letter of 13 April 1995, to maintain the closure of the international border between the Federal Republic of Yugoslavia (Serbia and Montenegro) and the Republic of Bosnia and Herzegovina with respect to all goods except foodstuffs, medical supplies and clothing for essential humanitarian needs, and noting that those measures were a necessary condition for the adoption of the present resolution,

*Concerned,* however, about reports suggesting that helicopter flights may have crossed the border between the Republic of Bosnia and Herzegovina and the Federal Republic of Yugoslavia (Serbia and Montenegro), and noting that an investigation of those reports is being undertaken by the Mission of the International Conference on the Former Yugoslavia (ICFY),

*Noting with satisfaction* that the cooperation of the ICFY Mission with the authorities of the Federal Republic of Yugoslavia (Serbia and Montenegro) continues to be good and stressing the importance of effective closure by the authorities of the Federal Republic of Yugoslavia (Serbia and Montenegro) of the international border between the Federal Republic of Yugoslavia (Serbia and Montenegro) and the Republic of Bosnia and Herzegovina, and of further efforts by them to enhance the effectiveness of that closure, including by the prosecution of persons suspected of violating measures to that end and by sealing border crossing points as requested by the ICFY Mission,

*Expressing appreciation* for the work of the Co-Chairmen of the Steering Committee of the ICFY and of the ICFY

Mission to the Federal Republic of Yugoslavia (Serbia and Montenegro),

*Noting* that paragraph 9 of resolution 757(1992) of 30 May 1992 remains in force,

*Acting* under Chapter VII of the Charter of the United Nations,

1. *Decides* that the restrictions and other measures referred to in paragraph 1 of resolution 943(1994) shall be suspended until 5 July 1995;

2. *Confirms* that commodities and products, including fuel beyond immediate needs for a flight or ferry voyage taking into account internationally recognized safety requirements, shall not be carried on flights and ferry services permitted in accordance with paragraph 1 above, except in accordance with the provisions of relevant resolutions and in conformity with the procedures of the Committee established by resolution 724(1991) of 15 December 1991; and that if a need is established for the supply of additional fuel for the operation of flights permitted in accordance with paragraph 1 above, the Committee established by resolution 724(1991) shall consider such applications on a case-by-case basis;

3. *Reminds* States of the importance of strict enforcement of measures imposed under Chapter VII of the Charter and calls upon all States which allow flights or ferry services permitted in accordance with paragraph 1 above from their territories or using their flag vessels or aircraft to report to the Committee established by resolution 724(1991) on the controls adopted by them to implement such measures in earlier relevant resolutions;

4. *Calls upon* all States and others concerned to respect the sovereignty, territorial integrity and international borders of all States in the region;

5. *Underlines* the importance it attaches to the work of the ICFY Mission, expresses its concern that a shortage of resources hampers the effectiveness of that work, and requests the Secretary-General to report to the Security Council within 30 days of the adoption of the present resolution on measures to increase the effectiveness of the work of the ICFY Mission, including on the question of helicopter flights;

6. *Requests* Member States to make available the necessary resources so as to strengthen the ICFY Mission's capacity to carry out its tasks, and encourages the authorities of the Federal Republic of Yugoslavia (Serbia and Montenegro) to give additional support for the operation of the ICFY Mission;

7. *Calls on* the authorities of the Federal Republic of Yugoslavia (Serbia and Montenegro) to cooperate fully with the ICFY Mission, in particular in investigating alleged breaches of the closure of the border, whether by land or by air, between the Federal Republic of Yugoslavia (Serbia and Montenegro) and the Republic of Bosnia and Herzegovina and ensuring the continued closure of that border;

8. *Stresses the importance* it attaches to a thorough investigation of reports that helicopter flights may have crossed the border between the Federal Republic of Yugoslavia (Serbia and Montenegro) and the Republic of Bosnia and Herzegovina; calls upon the authorities of the Federal Republic of Yugoslavia (Serbia and Montenegro) to comply with their commitment to cooperate fully in that investigation; and requests the Secretary-General to report to the Security Council on the outcome of the investigation;

9. *Reaffirms its decision* that import to, export from and transshipment through the United Nations Protected Areas in the Republic of Croatia and those areas of the Republic of Bosnia and Herzegovina under the control of Bosnian Serb forces, with the exception of essential humanitarian supplies including medical supplies and foodstuffs distributed by international humanitarian agencies, shall be permitted only with proper authorization from the Government of the Republic of Croatia or the Government of the Republic of Bosnia and Herzegovina respectively;

10. *Encourages* the authorities of the Federal Republic of Yugoslavia (Serbia and Montenegro) to reinstate the severance of international telecommunication links between the Federal Republic of Yugoslavia (Serbia and Montenegro) and the areas of the Republic of Bosnia and Herzegovina under the control of Bosnian Serb forces which they instituted in August 1994;

11. *Requests* the Committee established by resolution 724(1991) to conclude urgently its elaboration of appropriate streamlined procedures and invites the Chairman of that Committee to report to the Security Council as soon as possible on the matter;

12. *Also requests* the Committee established by resolution 724(1991) to continue to give priority to its consideration of applications concerning legitimate humanitarian assistance, in particular applications from the International Committee of the Red Cross and from the United Nations High Commissioner for Refugees and other organizations in the United Nations system;

13. *Requests* that every 30 days and no fewer than ten days before the expiration of the period referred to in paragraph 1 above the Secretary-General submit to the Security Council for its review a report as to whether the Co-Chairmen of the ICFY Steering Committee, on the basis of information made available to them from the ICFY Mission and all other available sources deemed relevant by the ICFY Mission, certify that the authorities of the Federal Republic of Yugoslavia (Serbia and Montenegro) are implementing their decision to close the international border, on land and in the air, between the Federal Republic of Yugoslavia (Serbia and Montenegro) and the Republic of Bosnia and Herzegovina with respect to all goods, except foodstuffs, medical supplies and clothing for essential humanitarian needs, and are complying with the requirements of paragraph 3 of resolution 970(1995) in respect of all shipments across the international border between the Federal Republic of Yugoslavia (Serbia and Montenegro) and the Republic of Bosnia and Herzegovina; and inform the Council in his report if the Co-Chairmen of the ICFY Steering Committee have received substantiated evidence, from sources deemed relevant by the ICFY Mission, of substantial transshipments of goods, except foodstuffs, medical supplies and clothing for essential humanitarian needs, from the Federal Republic of Yugoslavia (Serbia and Montenegro) through the Republic of Croatia to the areas of the Republic of Bosnia and Herzegovina under the control of Bosnian Serb forces in violation of earlier relevant resolutions;

14. *Further requests* the Secretary-General to report to the Security Council immediately if he has evidence, including from the Co-Chairmen of the ICFY Steering Committee, that the authorities of the Federal Republic of Yugoslavia (Serbia and Montenegro) are not implementing their decision to close the border between

the Federal Republic of Yugoslavia (Serbia and Montenegro) and the Republic of Bosnia and Herzegovina;

15. *Decides* that if at any time the Secretary-General reports that, from sources deemed relevant by the ICFY Mission, the authorities of the Federal Republic of Yugoslavia (Serbia and Montenegro) are not implementing their decision to close the border between the Federal Republic of Yugoslavia (Serbia and Montenegro) and the Republic of Bosnia and Herzegovina or that they are permitting substantial diversion of goods, except foodstuffs, medical supplies and clothing for essential humanitarian needs from the Federal Republic of Yugoslavia (Serbia and Montenegro) through the Republic of Croatia to the areas of the Republic of Bosnia and Herzegovina under the control of Bosnian Serb forces in violation of earlier relevant resolutions, the suspension of the measures referred to in paragraph 1 above shall terminate on the fifth working day following the report of the Secretary-General, unless the Security Council decides to the contrary;

16. *Encourages* the Co-Chairmen of the ICFY Steering Committee to ensure that the ICFY Mission keep the Government of the Republic of Bosnia and Herzegovina, the Government of the Republic of Croatia and the authorities of the Federal Republic of Yugoslavia (Serbia and Montenegro) fully informed about the findings of the ICFY Mission;

17. *Decides* to keep the situation closely under review and to consider further steps with regard to measures applicable to the Federal Republic of Yugoslavia (Serbia and Montenegro) in the light of further progress in the situation;

18. *Decides* to remain actively seized of the matter.

Security Council resolution 988(1995)

21 April 1995          Meeting 3522          13-0-2

6-nation draft (S/1995/319).

*Sponsors:* Czech Republic, France, Germany, Italy, United Kingdom, United States.

Vote in Council as follows:

*In favour:* Argentina, Botswana, Czech Republic, France, Germany, Honduras, Indonesia, Italy, Nigeria, Oman, Rwanda, United Kingdom, United States.

*Against:* None.

*Abstaining:* China, Russian Federation.

The representative of Yugoslavia (Serbia and Montenegro) reiterated that the Council, by opting to maintain the greatest part of the comprehensive sanctions imposed on his country, was continuing its policy of punishing the Serbian and Montenegrin people for things they neither bore responsibility for nor had any control over—this, despite appeals by numerous States underscoring the superfluity of the sanctions, their ineffectual nature and their devastating effect on the economy, not only of his country but also of the whole of south-eastern Europe. None the less, he assured the Council that Yugoslavia (Serbia and Montenegro) would continue to pursue the option of a peaceful and negotiated settlement of the crisis in the former Yugoslavia.

China recalled that all along it had been against the introduction of mandatory measures in con-

nection with the conflict in the former Yugoslavia, for it was a proven fact that sanctions or pressure in no way helped resolve any issue but rather complicated and perpetuated it.

The Russian Federation stated that it was beyond its understanding as to why the Council had cut back the suspension period to 75 days (paragraph 1). It characterized as puzzling the resolution's provisions making fresh demands on Yugoslavia (Serbia and Montenegro), as illustrated by the harsh fuel restrictions for that country's flights and ferry voyages (paragraph 2), by linking its commitment to close its border with Bosnia and Herzegovina to the situation on its border with Croatia (paragraph 9), and by calling on it to reinstate the severance of telecommunication links with the Bosnian Serbs (paragraph 10). The Russian Federation hoped that in the future the Council would be guided in its decisions by the interests of achieving a comprehensive and truly just settlement in the former Yugoslavia.

The Council met again on 5 July, at the end of the 75-day suspension period, to consider its extension. Before it were the Co-Chairmen's report of 23 June[(142)] and a 5 July letter[(150)] from Bosnia and Herzegovina and Croatia stressing the utmost importance they attached to the need for timely and mutual recognition between all successor States of the former Yugoslavia within their internationally recognized borders. At the same meeting, the Council adopted **resolution 1003(1995)**.

*The Security Council,*

*Recalling* all its earlier relevant resolutions, and in particular resolution 943(1994) of 23 September 1994, resolution 970(1995) of 12 January 1995 and resolution 988(1995) of 21 April 1995,

*Calling upon* all States and others concerned to respect the sovereignty, territorial integrity and international borders of all States in the region,

*Noting* the measures taken by the authorities of the Federal Republic of Yugoslavia (Serbia and Montenegro), in particular those detailed in the annex to the Secretary-General's letter of 25 June 1995 to the President of the Security Council, to maintain the effective closure of the international border between the Federal Republic of Yugoslavia (Serbia and Montenegro) and the Republic of Bosnia and Herzegovina with respect to all goods except foodstuffs, medical supplies and clothing for essential humanitarian needs and noting with satisfaction that the cooperation of the Mission of the International Conference on the Former Yugoslavia (ICFY) with the authorities of the Federal Republic of Yugoslavia (Serbia and Montenegro) continues to be good,

*Reaffirming* the importance of further efforts by the authorities of the Federal Republic of Yugoslavia (Serbia and Montenegro) to enhance the effectiveness of the closure of the international border between the Federal Republic of Yugoslavia (Serbia and Montenegro) and the Republic of Bosnia and Herzegovina with respect to all goods except foodstuffs, medical supplies and clothing for essential humanitarian needs,

*Underlining* the particular importance it attaches to there being no provision of military assistance, in terms of finance, equipment, coordination of air defences or recruitment of troops, to the Bosnian Serb forces,

*Expressing appreciation* for the work of the Co-Chairmen of the Steering Committee of the ICFY and of the ICFY Mission to the Federal Republic of Yugoslavia (Serbia and Montenegro), and underlining the importance of the necessary resources being made available so as to strengthen the ICFY Mission's capacity to carry out its tasks,

*Noting with satisfaction* that the Committee established pursuant to resolution 724(1991) of 15 December 1991 has adopted streamlined procedures for expediting its consideration of applications concerning legitimate humanitarian assistance, as well as a number of measures facilitating legitimate transshipments via the Danube River,

*Acting* under Chapter VII of the Charter of the United Nations,

1. *Decides* that the restrictions and other measures referred to in paragraph 1 of resolution 943(1994) shall be suspended until 18 September 1995;

2. *Decides also* that the arrangements referred to in paragraphs 13, 14 and 15 of resolution 988(1995) shall continue to apply;

3. *Renews* its call for early mutual recognition between the States of the former Yugoslavia within their internationally recognized borders, recognition between the Republic of Bosnia and Herzegovina and the Federal Republic of Yugoslavia (Serbia and Montenegro) being an important first step, and urges the authorities of the Federal Republic of Yugoslavia (Serbia and Montenegro) to take it;

4. *Reaffirms* its decision to keep the situation closely under review and to consider further steps with regard to measures applicable to the Federal Republic of Yugoslavia (Serbia and Montenegro) in the light of further progress in the situation;

5. *Decides* to remain actively seized of the matter.

Security Council resolution 1003(1995)

5 July 1995     Meeting 3551     14-0-1

5-nation draft (S/1995/537).

Sponsors: Czech Republic, France, Germany, United Kingdom, United States.

Vote in Council as follows:

In favour: Argentina, Botswana, China, Czech Republic, France, Germany, Honduras, Indonesia, Italy, Nigeria, Oman, Rwanda, United Kingdom, United States.

Against: None.

Abstaining: Russian Federation.

The representative of Yugoslavia (Serbia and Montenegro) stated that if the Council truly wished to open the road towards peace in the former Yugoslavia, it must make a resolute move and lift the sanctions against his country. Such a move would undermine the position of extremists in all camps who used the sanctions as a pretext to pursue the war option. He described as absolutely false the view that by lifting the sanctions against his country the international community would lose its leverage and influence on the policies of Belgrade. He reasoned that if the sanctions were lifted, Yugoslavia (Serbia and Montenegro) would become a full and equal partner in the peace process and could even more effectively contribute to the attainment of a just and lasting settlement in Bosnia and Herzegovina.

The Russian Federation disagreed with the arbitrary attachment of irrelevant elements to the resolutions on the limited sanctions relief, such as the (fifth) preambular paragraph underlining the importance of not providing military assistance in the form of finance, equipment and coordination of air defences to the Bosnian Serbs. Application of that injunction to only one party, instead of to all, inevitably led to its interpretation as application of a double standard, with all of its negative consequences. The Russian Federation also disagreed with the call for mutual recognition between the States of the former Yugoslavia, with the recognition between Bosnia and Herzegovina and Yugoslavia (Serbia and Montenegro) as a first step (paragraph 3).

On 15 September, three days before the expiry of the 75-day period of limited sanctions relief, the Council met in the light of the 6 September report of the Co-Chairmen of the ICFY Steering Committee.[144] The Council adopted **resolution 1015(1995)** extending the next suspension period to six months.

*The Security Council,*

*Recalling* all its earlier relevant resolutions, and in particular resolutions 943(1994) of 23 September 1994, 970(1995) of 12 January 1995, 988(1995) of 21 April 1995 and 1003(1995) of 5 July 1995,

*Calling upon* all States and others concerned to respect the sovereignty, territorial integrity and international borders of all States in the region,

*Noting* the measures taken by the Federal Republic of Yugoslavia (Serbia and Montenegro), in particular those detailed in the annex to the Secretary-General's letter of 6 September 1995 to the President of the Security Council, to maintain the effective closure of the international border between the Federal Republic of Yugoslavia (Serbia and Montenegro) and the Republic of Bosnia and Herzegovina with respect to all goods except foodstuffs, medical supplies and clothing for essential humanitarian needs and noting with satisfaction that the cooperation of the Mission of the International Conference on the Former Yugoslavia (ICFY) with the Federal Republic of Yugoslavia (Serbia and Montenegro) continues to be generally good,

*Reaffirming* the importance of further efforts by the Federal Republic of Yugoslavia (Serbia and Montenegro) to enhance the effectiveness of the closure of the international border between the Federal Republic of Yugoslavia (Serbia and Montenegro) and the Republic of Bosnia and Herzegovina with respect to all goods except foodstuffs, medical supplies and clothing for essential humanitarian needs,

*Expressing appreciation* for the work of the Co-Chairmen of the Steering Committee of the ICFY and of the ICFY Mission to the Federal Republic of Yugoslavia (Serbia and Montenegro) and underlining the importance of the necessary resources being made available so as to strengthen the ICFY Mission's capacity to carry out its tasks,

*Acting* under Chapter VII of the Charter of the United Nations,

1.  *Decides* that the restrictions and other measures referred to in paragraph 1 of resolution 943(1994) shall be suspended until 18 March 1996;

2.  *Decides also* that the arrangements referred to in paragraphs 13, 14 and 15 of resolution 988(1995) shall continue to apply;

3.  *Reaffirms* its decision to keep the situation closely under review and to consider further steps with regard to measures applicable to the Federal Republic of Yugoslavia (Serbia and Montenegro) in the light of further progress in the situation;

4.  *Decides* to remain actively seized of the matter.

Security Council resolution 1015(1995)

15 September 1995     Meeting 3578     Adopted unanimously

7-nation draft (S/1995/789).

*Sponsors:* Czech Republic, France, Germany, Italy, Russian Federation, United Kingdom, United States.

China and the Russian Federation restated their position for the complete lifting of the sanctions against Yugoslavia (Serbia and Montenegro).

## Violations of human rights and international humanitarian law

SECURITY COUNCIL ACTION (10 August)

The Security Council met on 10 August in connection with reports regarding the treatment of the civilian populations of Srebrenica and Zepa in the wake of the Bosnian Serb occupation in July of those two safe areas. The Council had before it communications from Kazakstan[151] and the Sudan[152] concerning recent events in those two areas in particular and in Bosnia and Herzegovina in general.

In statements before the Council, Bosnia and Herzegovina spoke of the expulsion of some 60,000 civilians from Srebrenica and Zepa. The United States estimated that, of those, about 10,000 from Srebrenica and 3,000 from Zepa were missing and unaccounted for, while Germany stated that the fate of some 7,000 to 8,000 male Bosnian Muslims was still unknown and that, so far, only 164 detainees from Srebrenica and 44 from Zepa had been registered by ICRC.

At the same meeting, the Council adopted **resolution 1010(1995)**.

*The Security Council,*

*Recalling* all its earlier relevant resolutions, and reaffirming its resolution 1004(1995) of 12 July 1995,

*Reaffirming also* the statements of its President of 20 and 25 July 1995, and deeply concerned that the demands set out therein have not been fully complied with by the Bosnian Serb party,

*Reiterating* the unacceptability of the violation of the safe areas of Srebrenica and Zepa by Bosnian Serb forces,

*Reaffirming* its commitment to the sovereignty, territorial integrity and independence of the Republic of Bosnia and Herzegovina,

*Affirming* its commitment to the search for an overall negotiated settlement of the conflicts in the former Yugoslavia ensuring the sovereignty and territorial integrity of all the States there within their internationally recognized borders, and stressing the importance it attaches to the mutual recognition thereof,

*Deeply concerned* at reports of grave violations of international humanitarian law in and around Srebrenica and at the fact that many of the former inhabitants of Srebrenica cannot be accounted for,

*Concerned also* at the plight of the civilian population and other persons protected under international humanitarian law, originating in the Zepa area,

*Expressing* its strong support for the efforts of the International Committee of the Red Cross (ICRC) in seeking access to displaced persons and condemning the failure of the Bosnian Serb party to comply with their commitments to the ICRC in respect of such access,

1.  *Demands* that the Bosnian Serb party give immediate access for representatives of the United Nations High Commissioner for Refugees, the ICRC and other international agencies to persons displaced from Srebrenica and Zepa who are within the areas of the Republic of Bosnia and Herzegovina under the control of Bosnian Serb forces, and that the Bosnian Serb party permit representatives of the ICRC to visit and register any persons detained against their will, including any members of the forces of the Republic of Bosnia and Herzegovina;

2.  *Also demands* that the Bosnian Serb party respect fully the rights of all such persons and ensure their safety, and urges that any persons detained be released;

3.  *Reiterates* that all those who commit violations of international humanitarian law will be held individually responsible in respect of such acts;

4.  *Requests* the Secretary-General to report to the Council as soon as possible, and no later than 1 September 1995, with any information available to United Nations personnel regarding compliance with this resolution and concerning violations of international humanitarian law;

5.  *Decides* to remain seized of the matter.

Security Council resolution 1010(1995)

10 August 1995     Meeting 3564     Adopted unanimously

Draft prepared in consultations among Council members (S/1995/677).

**Report of the Secretary-General.** Pursuant to the Security Council resolution above, the Secretary-General submitted a report on 30 August summarizing information gathered mainly by UNPROFOR, UNHCR and the Special Rapporteur of the Commission on Human Rights, as well as by ICRC and the United States Government.[153] It indicated that investigators for the International Tribunal for the Prosecution of Persons Responsible for Serious Violations of International Humanitarian Law Committed in the Territory of the Former Yugoslavia since 1991 had been dispatched to the field, including Tuzla, to interview refugees and relevant military personnel. The information focused on questions of access, detention and violations of international humanitarian law following the fall of Srebrenica and Zepa. (See also PART THREE, Chapter III.)

(Annexed to the report was a chronology of events, beginning with the intensive bombardment of Srebrenica on 6 July and ending with the fall of Zepa and subsequent forced evacuation, by the Bosnian Serb forces, of several thousands of its residents to collective centres in the Zenica region from 25 to 27 July.)

According to the report, a fact-finding mission of the civil affairs component of UNPF, which had spent eight days in the Tuzla area working in conjunction with the Centre for Human Rights of the UN Secretariat, had gathered substantial evidence indicating the perpetration in Srebrenica of three categories of violations of international humanitarian law: arbitrary detention, abductions and disappearances; summary executions; and cruel, inhuman and degrading treatment. The civil affairs mission to Zepa (25-30 July) identified looting and the reported demolition of a mosque, and confirmed the forced evacuation of some 4,800 Zepaljaci, mostly women and children, to the Zenica region via Kladanj (near the confrontation line north-west of Srebrenica), on the way to which 36 males of draft age had been taken off the convoys. Another 1,500 males of draft age reportedly escaped to the surrounding woods.

UNHCR presented unconfirmed reports of rape, robbery, executions, the separation of men from their families, and the shelling of civilians. From the testimony gathered, it appeared that between 6,000 and 8,000 men who began their escape from Srebrenica to Tuzla remained unaccounted for. The Special Rapporteur of the Commission on Human Rights confirmed much of the information presented by UNPROFOR; while he could not fully verify the allegations of mass executions, he provided pieces of information that appeared to be of relevance.

ICRC was granted access to the Bosnian Serb detention camps in Batkovic, where it registered 164 detained persons from Srebrenica, and in Rogatica (south of Zepa), where it registered 44 prisoners from Zepa. It evacuated 88 wounded from Bratunac and Potocari to Tuzla, but was not allowed to evacuate another 23 wounded from Bratunac. Considering the latter group to be POWs, ICRC registered their identities for follow-up purposes.

Information gathered by the United States Government indicated credible estimates of missing persons varying between 6,000 and 12,000 for Srebrenica and 3,000 for Zepa, as well as eyewitness accounts of alleged mass executions and photographs showing, *inter alia*, large groups of persons being held in fields near Nova Kasaba and patches of freshly disturbed earth in those fields taken a few days later.

Despite repeated requests by the Special Representative, UNHCR, the UN High Commissioner for Human Rights, the Special Rapporteur of the Commission on Human Rights, ICRC (which in the past had limited access) and other international agencies, the Bosnian Serb authorities refused them access to persons displaced from Srebrenica and Zepa who were within the Bosnian Serb–controlled areas of Bosnia and Herzegovina. The Special Representative's request that UNPROFOR be allowed to investigate a report on the existence of mass graves near Srebrenica had also been denied. It had thus not been possible to collect first-hand information on the extent to which the Bosnian Serbs had respected the rights of all displaced persons and ensured their safety.

The Secretary-General said there was significant *prima facie* evidence, however, of violations of international humanitarian law during and after the Bosnian Serb offensive on Srebrenica. The Council, he said, might therefore wish to reiterate its urgent call for full access to include a possible impartial international investigation to take place. However, he stressed that access weeks or months after the occurrence of the events cited could not adequately substitute for monitoring and investigation during or immediately following those events. There was little doubt that sufficient time had elapsed to permit interested parties to tidy up much of the evidence that could have been used to substantiate and expand on the findings noted in the current report. Access remained a crucial step in terms of establishing the full extent of violations of humanitarian law and human rights, and in addressing any persistent abuses, he concluded.

**SECURITY COUNCIL ACTION (7 September, 12 October, 9 November)**

In the light of the Secretary-General's report, the Security Council met on 7 September and, after consultations among its members, authorized the President to make the following statement[154] on the Council's behalf:

The Security Council has considered the report of the Secretary-General of 30 August 1995 submitted pursuant to its resolution 1010(1995) of 10 August 1995.

The Security Council strongly condemns the failure of the Bosnian Serb party to comply with the demands contained in resolution 1010(1995). The Bosnian Serb party's refusal to cooperate with the United Nations High Commissioner for Refugees (UNHCR) and the International Committee of the Red Cross (ICRC) cannot but reinforce the deep concern expressed in that resolution and in previous resolutions and statements.

The Security Council stresses its determination that the fate of persons displaced from Srebrenica and Zepa be established. It reaffirms its demands to the Bosnian Serb party to give immediate access for representatives of the UNHCR, the ICRC and other international agencies to such persons who are within the areas of the Republic of Bosnia and Herzegovina under the control of Bosnian Serb forces, and to permit representatives of the ICRC to visit and register any persons detained against their will.

The Security Council also reaffirms its demands to the Bosnian Serb party to respect fully the rights of all such persons, to ensure their safety and to release them.

The Security Council reiterates that all those who commit violations of international humanitarian law will be held individually responsible in respect of such acts.

The Security Council takes note of the investigations which are being carried out by the International Tribunal established pursuant to its resolution 827(1993). The Council reiterates in this context that all States shall cooperate fully with the Tribunal and its organs, including by providing access to sites the Tribunal deems important for its investigations.

The Security Council requests the Secretary-General to continue his efforts and to report to the Council no later than 6 October 1995 regarding compliance with resolution 1010(1995) and any further relevant information that may become available.

The Security Council will remain actively seized of the matter.

*Meeting number.* SC 3572.

In the presidential statement of 12 October,[117] welcoming the 5 October cease-fire, the Council reiterated its strong condemnation of all practices of ethnic cleansing by whomsoever committed; urged the Bosnian parties to respect fully the rights of all communities, including their right to remain where they were or to return to their homes in safety; again demanded that the Bosnian Serb party grant immediate and unimpeded access for UN personnel and ICRC to all the areas of concern; and reaffirmed that those who had committed or had ordered the commission of violations of international humanitarian law would be held individually responsible for them.

By **resolution 1019(1995)** of 9 November, the Council reaffirmed its demand that the Bosnian Serb party grant unimpeded access to persons displaced or detained or reported missing from Srebrenica and Zepa, among other places, and that it respect the rights of all such persons, ensure their safety and release them immediately. It further demanded that all detention camps throughout Bosnia and Herzegovina be closed immediately.

**Communications.** On 31 October, Bosnia and Herzegovina noted that the Netherlands had properly undertaken an inquiry into the response of its troops who were on watch when the Bosnian Serbs overran Srebrenica and Zepa.[155] It enjoined the Security Council to undertake its own review of why its resolutions had been undermined—for the sake of its own credibility, if not of the thousands of victims who had been massacred or raped or forcibly relocated in pursuit of the policy of ethnic cleansing. The Netherlands report, it said, "should raise serious questions about the conduct of United Nations–mandated officials". Bosnia and Herzegovina called on the Council to "pay special heed to glaring contradictions" in the information provided to it by some of the most senior UNPROFOR officials.

Bosnia and Herzegovina further stated on 31 October that it was essential for the Council to remind all who were investigating the various aspects of the fall of Srebrenica and Zepa that it was a violation of international humanitarian law not only to commit war crimes but also to cover up evidence of their commission.[156] In particular, "shielding perpetrators, concealing evidence or even not making relevant information available" was "acquiescing or abetting in the crimes", it stated.

**SECURITY COUNCIL ACTION (9 November)**

The Security Council met on 9 November and, ascertaining the failure of the Bosnian Serb party to comply with its demands, including those contained in the presidential statements of 7 September and 12 October (and in the light of simultaneous reports of violations of human rights and international humanitarian law in Croatia), adopted **resolution 1019(1995)**.

*The Security Council,*

*Recalling* all its earlier resolutions on the situation in the Republic of Bosnia and Herzegovina, and reaffirming its resolutions 1004(1995) of 12 July 1995 and 1010(1995) of 10 August 1995, and the statements of its President of 7 September 1995 and 12 October 1995, and deeply concerned that despite repeated calls that it should do so, the Bosnian Serb party has not complied with the demands contained therein,

*Gravely concerned* at reports, including by the representative of the Secretary-General of the United Nations, of grave violations of international humanitarian law and of human rights in and around Srebrenica, and in the areas of Banja Luka and Sanski Most, including reports of mass murder, unlawful detention and forced labour, rape, and deportation of civilians,

*Recalling also* all its earlier relevant resolutions on the situation in the Republic of Croatia, and reaffirming its resolution 1009(1995) of 10 August 1995, and the statements of its President of 7 September 1995 and of 3 October 1995,

*Deeply concerned* at reports, including by UNCRO and United Nations humanitarian agencies, of serious violations of international humanitarian law and of human rights in the former sectors West, North and South, in the Republic of Croatia, including burning of houses, looting of property, and killings of civilians,

*Reiterating* its strong support for the efforts of the International Committee of the Red Cross (ICRC) in seeking access to displaced persons and to persons detained or reported missing and condemning in the strongest possible terms the failure of the Bosnian Serb party to comply with their commitments in respect of such access,

*Commending* the efforts of the United Nations peace forces and other United Nations personnel in the former Yugoslavia, in particular in the Republic of Bosnia and Herzegovina, despite extreme difficulties,

*Taking note* of the letter to the President of the Security Council from the President of the International Criminal Tribunal for the former Yugoslavia of 31 October 1995,

*Expressing* its strong support for the work of the International Tribunal established pursuant to its resolution 827(1993) of 25 May 1993,

1. *Condemns* in the strongest possible terms all violations of international humanitarian law and of human rights in the territory of the former Yugoslavia and demands that all concerned comply fully with their obligations in this regard;

2. *Reaffirms* its demand that the Bosnian Serb party give immediate and unimpeded access to representatives of the United Nations High Commissioner for Refugees, the ICRC and other international agencies to persons displaced and to persons detained or reported missing from Srebrenica, Zepa, and the regions of Banja Luka and Sanski Most who are within the areas of the Republic of Bosnia and Herzegovina under the control of Bosnian Serb forces and that the Bosnian Serb party permit representatives of the ICRC (i) to visit and register any persons detained against their will, whether civilians or members of the forces of the Republic of Bosnia and Herzegovina, and (ii) to have access to any site it may deem important;

3. *Reaffirms also* its demand that the Bosnian Serb party respect fully the rights of all such persons, ensure their safety, and release them immediately;

4. *Reaffirms further* the obligation on all the parties to ensure the complete freedom of movement of personnel of the United Nations and other relevant international organizations throughout the territory of the Republic of Bosnia and Herzegovina at all times;

5. *Demands* that all detention camps throughout the territory of the Republic of Bosnia and Herzegovina should be immediately closed;

6. *Reaffirms* its demand that the Government of the Republic of Croatia take urgent measures to put an end to violations of international humanitarian law and of human rights, and investigate all reports of such violations so that those responsible in respect of such acts be judged and punished;

7. *Reiterates* its demand that the Government of the Republic of Croatia respect fully the rights of the local Serb population including their right to remain or return in safety and reiterates also its call upon the Government of the Republic of Croatia to lift any time-limits placed on the return of refugees to Croatia to reclaim their property;

8. *Demands* that all States, in particular those in the region of the former Yugoslavia, and all parties to the conflict in the former Yugoslavia, comply fully and in good faith with the obligations contained in paragraph 4 of resolution 827(1993) to cooperate fully with the International Tribunal established pursuant to that resolution, including by providing access to individuals and sites the Tribunal deems important for its investigations and by complying with requests for assistance or orders issued by a trial chamber under article 29 of the Statute of the Tribunal, and calls upon them to allow the establishment of offices of the Tribunal;

9. *Demands* that all parties, and in particular the Bosnian Serb party, refrain from any action intended to destroy, alter, conceal or damage any evidence of violations of international humanitarian law and that they preserve such evidence;

10. *Reaffirms* its support for the actions of the United Nations peace forces, and other United Nations personnel, including the great importance of their contribution in the humanitarian field, and demands that all parties fully ensure their safety and cooperate fully with them;

11. *Requests* the Secretary-General to submit to the Council as soon as possible a written report based on all information available to the United Nations concerning recent violations of international humanitarian law in the areas of Srebrenica, Zepa, Banja Luka and Sanski Most;

12. *Requests also* the Secretary-General to continue to inform the Council on a regular basis of measures taken by the Government of the Republic of Croatia to implement resolution 1009(1995) and the present resolution;

13. *Decides* to remain seized of the matter.

Security Council resolution 1019(1995)

9 November 1995     Meeting 3591     Adopted unanimously

8-nation draft (S/1995/940).

*Sponsors:* Argentina, Czech Republic, France, Germany, Italy, Russian Federation, United Kingdom, United States.

**Report of the Secretary-General.** Responding to the Security Council's request, the Secretary-General submitted a report on 27 November concerning recent violations of international humanitarian law in Srebrenica, Zepa, Banja Luka and Sanski Most.[157] The report gave an overview of the current state of information on the key issues of missing persons, executions and the involvement of Bosnian Serb leaders and Serbian paramilitary forces, based on information available to the United Nations, UNHCR, UNPF and UNPROFOR. It pointed out, however, that UN personnel had had very limited access to the four areas in question.

The report stated that the Bosnian Serb offensive on Srebrenica from 6 to 11 July had led to the displacement of the entire Bosnian Muslim community there. The Bosnian Serb authorities organized the forcible evacuation of some 25,000 people on a convoy of buses and trucks. Between 10,000 and 15,000 persons, mostly men, left Srebrenica on foot, but the exact number of those who had arrived safely in Bosnian Government–held territory was not known. Most estimates put the number of Srebrenica's population before the offensive at between 38,000 and 40,000, although UNHCR's estimate for food distribution purposes was 42,600. The best current estimate of the number of missing persons, derived from all available information including ICRC data, was perhaps between 3,500 and 5,500.

The report indicated the existence of substantial evidence to support the conclusion that an unknown number of Bosnian Muslim men had been executed by Bosnian Serb soldiers. Such evidence fell into four categories: statements by eyewitnesses of executions, statements by UNPROFOR's Netherlands soldiers present in Srebrenica during the Bosnian Serb offensive, eyewitness reports of indirect evidence of executions (sightings of groups of detained persons and corpses), and other corroborative evidence (photographs of alleged mass graves and material evidence found at alleged execution sites). Witnesses and others mentioned several execution sites in the Srebrenica area: Nova Kasaba-Konjevic Polje (Kaldrumica), Kravica, Rasica Gai, Zabrde, Karakaj, Bratunac and Potocari.

Evidence further pointed to the involvement in those executions of Bosnian Serb leaders, including General Ratko Mladic, and of paramilitary forces (Drina Wolves, Seselj Militia, Specialna Policia, White Eagles, Arkan Tigers, Krajina Serbs). According to UN military observers, paramilitary leader Zeljko Raznatovic ("Arkan") and his troops had been positively identified at the scene of the evacuation of refugees in Potocari on 13 July. Other reports pointed to the involvement of paramilitary forces and soldiers from Yugoslavia (Serbia and Montenegro).

ICRC reported it had had access to 793 Bosnian Muslims who had fled Zepa into Yugoslavia (Serbia and Montenegro), 10 per cent of whom, by UNHCR estimates, came from Srebrenica. As at the reporting date, 342 people were in detention in Mitrovo Polje and 450 in Slivovica, in the Uzice region. There were no reliable figures for missing persons from Zepa. UN observers in Zepa reported the presence of a large number of foreign mercenaries, including Greeks and Russians, among the Bosnian Serb forces. There were also reports that many buses used in the forcible evacuation of Zepa bore licence plates of Yugoslavia (Serbia and Montenegro).

In northern Bosnia and Herzegovina, at least 26,000 Croats and Muslims were evicted from Banja Luka in two waves. The first took place during August and September, during which some 14,000 Croats and 6,000 Muslims crossed into Croatia via Srbac-Davor on the Sava River. That wave of forced evictions was the result of the massive influx into the Banja Luka area of Bosnian Serbs in July (14,000), of Croatian Serbs in August (150,000), and of Bosnian Serbs in mid-September (127,000), who by their presence and, in some cases, their acts, exerted pressure on the Croats and Muslims to leave. The second wave of evictions occurred in October, when more than

6,000 Bosnian Muslims were expelled from their homes in the Bosnian Serb–held territories of Banja Luka, Bjeljina, Bosanska Dubica, Bosanski Novi, Doboj, Prijedor and Sanski Most, and forced to travel to Bosnian Government–held territory.

By all accounts, the persons reported as missing from those areas were males separated from their families, taken from convoys during expulsions, conscripted into forced labour, or summarily executed; others were the elderly who had died during the expulsions, most likely from exhaustion. In all, the missing numbered between 1,200 and 2,000. In meetings with United States Assistant Secretary of State John Shattuck in early November, Bosnian Serb authorities conceded that there were approximately 400 Bosnians missing from the Banja Luka area, and that another 1,000 had been conscripted for forced labour or detained or were "homeless".

The presence of Arkan paramilitary forces and, to a lesser extent, of Seselj units was observed in Sanski Most in September, where through harassment, killings and rape they provoked massive expulsions. As those forces moved to Bosanski Novi at the beginning of October, the attitude of the resident Serbs towards the Bosnian Muslims changed from friendly to hostile.

**SECURITY COUNCIL ACTION (21 December)**

In the light of the Secretary-General's report, the Security Council met on 21 December and adopted **resolution 1034(1995)**.

*The Security Council,*

*Reaffirming* all its earlier relevant resolutions on the situation in Bosnia and Herzegovina, including its resolution 1019(1995) of 9 November 1995, and condemning the Bosnian Serb party's failure, despite repeated calls that it should do so, to comply with the demands contained therein,

*Having considered* the report of the Secretary-General pursuant to resolution 1019(1995) on violations of international humanitarian law in the areas of Srebrenica, Zepa, Banja Luka and Sanski Most of 27 November 1995,

*Gravely concerned* at the information contained in the above-mentioned report that there is overwhelming evidence of a consistent pattern of summary executions, rape, mass expulsion, arbitrary detentions, forced labour and large-scale disappearances,

*Reiterating* its strong support for the work of the International Tribunal established pursuant to its resolution 827(1993) of 25 May 1993,

*Noting* that the General Framework Agreement for Peace in Bosnia and Herzegovina and the annexes thereto initialled at Dayton, Ohio, on 21 November 1995 provides that no person who is serving a sentence imposed by the International Tribunal for the former Yugoslavia, and no person who is under indictment by the Tribunal and who has failed to comply with an order to appear before the Tribunal, may stand as a candidate or hold any appointive, elective or other public office in Bosnia and Herzegovina,

*Condemning* the failure of the Bosnian Serb party to comply with their commitments in respect of giving access to displaced persons and to persons detained or reported missing,

*Reiterating* its concern expressed in the statement of its President of 7 December 1995,

*Deeply concerned* by the plight of hundreds of thousands of refugees and displaced persons as a result of hostilities in the former Yugoslavia,

1. *Strongly condemns* all violations of international humanitarian law and of human rights in the territory of the former Yugoslavia and demands that all concerned comply fully with their obligations in this regard, and reiterates that all those who commit violations of international humanitarian law will be held individually responsible in respect of such acts;

2. *Condemns* in particular in the strongest possible terms the violations of international humanitarian law and of human rights by Bosnian Serb and paramilitary forces in the areas of Srebrenica, Zepa, Banja Luka and Sanski Most as described in the report of the Secretary-General of 27 November 1995 and showing a consistent pattern of summary executions, rape, mass expulsions, arbitrary detentions, forced labour and large-scale disappearances;

3. *Notes* with the utmost concern the substantial evidence referred to in the report of the Secretary-General of 27 November 1995 that an unknown but large number of men in the area of Srebrenica, namely in Nova Kasaba-Konjevic Polje (Kaldrumica), Kravice, Rasica Gai, Zabrde and two sites in Karakaj, and possibly also in Bratunac and Potocari, have been summarily executed by Bosnian Serb and paramilitary forces and condemns in the strongest terms the commission of such acts;

4. *Reiterates* its strong support for the efforts of the International Committee of the Red Cross (ICRC) in seeking access to displaced persons and to persons detained or reported missing and calls on all parties to comply with their commitments in respect of such access;

5. *Reaffirms* its demand that the Bosnian Serb party give immediate and unimpeded access to representatives of the United Nations High Commissioner for Refugees, the ICRC and other international agencies to persons displaced and to persons detained or reported missing from Srebrenica, Zepa and the regions of Banja Luka and Sanski Most who are within the areas of Bosnia and Herzegovina under the control of Bosnian Serb forces and that the Bosnian Serb party permit representatives of the ICRC (i) to visit and register any persons detained against their will, whether civilians or members of the forces of Bosnia and Herzegovina, and (ii) to have access to any site it may deem important;

6. *Affirms* that the violations of humanitarian law and human rights in the areas of Srebrenica, Zepa, Banja Luka and Sanski Most from July to October 1995 must be fully and properly investigated by the relevant United Nations and other international organizations and institutions;

7. *Takes note* that the International Tribunal established pursuant to resolution 827(1993) of 25 May 1993 issued on 16 November 1995 indictments against the Bosnian Serb leaders Radovan Karadzic and Ratko Mladic for their direct and individual responsibilities for the atrocities committed against the Bosnian Muslim population of Srebrenica in July 1995;

8. *Reaffirms* its demand that the Bosnian Serb party give immediate and unrestricted access to the areas in question, including for the purpose of the investigation of the atrocities, to representatives of the relevant United Nations and other international organizations and institutions, including the Special Rapporteur of the Commission on Human Rights;

9. *Underlines* in particular the urgent necessity for all the parties to enable the Prosecutor of the International Tribunal to gather effectively and swiftly the evidence necessary for the Tribunal to perform its task;

10. *Stresses* the obligations of all the parties to cooperate with and provide unrestricted access to the relevant United Nations and other international organizations and institutions so as to facilitate their investigations and takes note of their commitment under the Peace Agreement in this regard;

11. *Reiterates* its demand that all parties, and in particular the Bosnian Serb party, refrain from any action intended to destroy, alter, conceal or damage any evidence of violations of international humanitarian law and that they preserve such evidence;

12. *Reiterates further* its demand that all States, in particular those in the region of the former Yugoslavia, and all parties to the conflict in the former Yugoslavia, comply fully and in good faith with the obligations contained in paragraph 4 of resolution 827(1993) to cooperate fully with the International Tribunal and calls on them to create the conditions essential for the Tribunal to perform the task for which it has been created, including the establishment of offices of the Tribunal when the latter deems it necessary;

13. *Reiterates* its demand that all detention camps throughout the territory of Bosnia and Herzegovina should be immediately closed;

14. *Urges* the parties to ensure full respect for the norms of international humanitarian law and of human rights of the civilian population, living in the areas in Bosnia and Herzegovina now under their control, which under the Peace Agreement will be transferred to another party;

15. *Condemns* the widespread looting and destruction of houses and other property, in particular by HVO forces in the area of Mrkonjic Grad and Sipovo, and demands that all sides immediately stop such action, investigate them and make sure that those who violated the law be held individually responsible in respect of such acts;

16. *Demands* that all sides refrain from laying mines, in particular in those areas now under their control, which under the Peace Agreement will be transferred to another party;

17. *Urges* Member States to continue to assist the efforts of the United Nations, humanitarian agencies and non-governmental organizations under way in the former Yugoslavia to alleviate the plight of hundreds of thousands of refugees and displaced persons;

18. *Also urges* all the parties to the conflicts in the territory of the former Yugoslavia to fully cooperate with these efforts with the view to create conditions conducive to the repatriation and return of refugees and displaced persons in safety and dignity;

19. *Requests* the Secretary-General to keep the Council regularly informed on progress reached in the

investigation of the violations of international humanitarian law referred to in the report mentioned above;

20.  *Decides* to remain actively seized of the matter.

Security Council resolution 1034(1995)

21 December 1995    Meeting 3612    Adopted unanimously

7-nation draft (S/1995/1047).

*Sponsors:* Argentina, Czech Republic, France, Germany, Italy, United Kingdom, United States.

**Communications.** Twice during the year, Yugoslavia (Serbia and Montenegro) transmitted to the Secretary-General information gathered by its Committee for the Collection of Data on Crimes Committed against Humanity and International Law. The first, dated 15 March, described in detail the forensic, medical and psychiatric aspects of the torture of Serbs in Bosniac-Croat detention camps.[158] The second, dated 23 August, concerned the genocidal practices of the Government of Bosnia and Herzegovina against the Serb population in the country.[159]

### Humanitarian assistance

In their first (January-June) biannual report of 1995,[160] the Co-Chairmen of the ICFY Steering Committee noted that, following the entry into force on 1 January 1995 of the 1994 cessation-of-hostilities agreement,[1] the Government of Bosnia and Herzegovina and the Bosnian Serb party agreed on 23 January 1995 to reopen the routes across the Sarajevo airport to civilian traffic, at the latest by 1 February. The routes were also to be used by UNHCR and other UN bodies (UNICEF, WFP, Office of the Coordinator for Sarajevo) and specialized agencies (FAO, UNESCO, WHO), ICRC and local humanitarian organizations assisting in normalizing life in Bosnia and Herzegovina. The parties also agreed to provide increased freedom of movement for Sarajevans, further POW exchanges in line with the ICRC plan, medical evacuations from Gorazde and freedom of residence.

Thus, UNHCR land convoys and airlifts regularly reached Sarajevo, Tuzla, Zenica and the eastern enclaves in quantities to permit stockpiling of contingency supplies for Sarajevo and other areas in central Bosnia. Besides food and medical supplies, assistance included seed fertilizers and pesticides for the planting season in March, as well as firewood for Sarajevo.

However, a breakdown in March of the cessation-of-hostilities agreement led to a deterioration of the security situation in the country in general and in Sarajevo in particular, causing the intermittent closure of the "blue routes" across Sarajevo airport, including the Mount Igman route, and an intermittent suspension of the humanitarian airlift. The NATO air strikes on 25 and 26 May and the retaliatory detention of UNPROFOR troops in Bosnian Serb custody led to an almost complete blockade of UNHCR operations in the Bosnian Serb-held territories and in the eastern enclaves and to a halt of full access to Sarajevo.

UNHCR reported it had encountered repeated obstructions posed by the escalating hostilities or by the Bosnian Serb party, which continually withheld convoy clearance and which, in rejecting the weekly Metkovic-Sarajevo convoy plan at the beginning of March, demanded 50 per cent of humanitarian deliveries—a significant increase from its allotted 23 per cent based on need. As to assistance to the Bihac pocket, to which virtually all supplies had been blocked since May 1994,[161] two convoys arrived separately in the southern part of the pocket on 25 May and 29 June; a third convoy for the area obtained clearance to proceed on 30 June. The last convoy to reach Gorazde in the reporting period was on 20 May; that which reached Zepa on 21 June was the first since 24 May.

Through the joint UNHCR/IOM (International Organization for Migration) medical evacuation programme for Bosnia and Herzegovina, 51 patients were evacuated to third countries for medical treatment during the period.

In cooperation with the UNPROFOR civil affairs unit, UNHCR held numerous meetings with the Bosnian Serb authorities in Banja Luka to call a halt to the continuous pressure placed on the Bosnian Muslim and Croat minorities to leave the area. That pressure took the form of evictions, house bombings, midnight shooting raids, arrests and interrogations, telephone calls, veiled threats, harassment on the streets, physical and verbal assaults of women and students, and the rounding up of males between the ages of 17 and 70 to perform civilian work, often in the first and second front lines—all of which grew worse with the influx in May of approximately 10,000 Croatian Serb refugees from Western Slavonia into Bosnian Serb-controlled territory, especially in the Banja Luka region, where some 6,000 to 7,000 such refugees were registered.

According to the ICFY Co-Chairmen's second (July-December) biannual report,[162] the humanitarian situation in Bosnia and Herzegovina reached crisis proportions during the reporting period owing to the continuous and unprecedented influx of refugees and displaced persons. The fall on 11 and 25 July of the eastern enclaves of Srebrenica and Zepa to the Bosnian Serb forces resulted in the exodus of some 36,000 persons into Tuzla and Zenica. Responding to this emergency, UNHCR formed a committee to coordinate relief action and, with the help of UNPROFOR and a number of NGOs, set up transit camps at Tuzla airbase and in Zenica, where refugees were registered and supplied with emergency items. Also assisted were an estimated 14,000 Bosnian Serbs fleeing to the northern part of the country from Glamoc and Grahovo (directly south of Banja Luka), which fell in late July to the combined forces of the Croatian Defence Council and Croatian Army.

UNHCR temporarily redeployed a number of its field staff to Banja Luka to assist the thousands of Krajina Serbs who had taken refuge there in early August. With the help of two helicopters made available by the United Kingdom, relief supplies were transported from Zagreb to Banja Luka. Humanitarian activities in Banja Luka were hampered, however, by repeated hijackings at gunpoint, harassment and banditry.

The massive influx of Serb refugees into Banja Luka led to a dramatic deterioration of the plight of the resident Bosnian Muslim and Croat minorities, driving some 22,000 of them to Croatia. UNHCR extended full support to that country in providing assistance to those refugees, including shelter for the Bosnian Muslim refugees at UNCRO bases at Pustara and Novska in Western Slavonia. In addition, UNHCR took up with Croatia the issue of keeping its doors open to both Bosnian ethnic groups and refraining from selecting any of them for forcible repatriation.

Following the recapture of the Bihac region by the Bosnian Army on 7 August, UNHCR established a permanent presence at a refugee centre in the border town of Kuplensko in Croatia, where some 20,000 refugees from Velika Kladusa and Cazin, loyal to the Bosnian Muslim rebel leader Fikret Abdic,[21] were encamped. Together with other humanitarian agencies, UNHCR provided those refugees with food, shelter, water, sanitation and medical assistance and set in motion an operation to get them through the winter. Through a bus service instituted on 30 October, UNHCR had enabled the voluntary return of more than 4,200 of those refugees to their homes by mid-December.

Humanitarian assistance to Sarajevo—which was so irregular during the summer months that only 15 per cent of the target amount was delivered in June, 30 per cent in July and 45 per cent in August—improved with the reopening of the "blue routes" and the resumption on 16 September of the airlift.

**Communications.** Bosnia and Herzegovina informed the Secretary-General on 6 August that as many as 120,000 residents of the former Serb-occupied territories of Croatia were crossing into Bosnia and Herzegovina, some with the assistance of UN authorities.[163] Whereas it supported UN action providing for the welfare of those affected by war, it could neither accept nor provide for those incoming refugees, it said, especially as Croatia had guaranteed them full security and humanitarian assistance, consistent with that country's desire to reintegrate the former Serb-occupied territories with maximum respect for human and civil rights. Bosnia and Herzegovina stressed that a new influx of Serb paramilitaries, who were among those crossing into the country, posed a threat to non-Serb communities in Serb-occupied Bosnia and thus would significantly contribute to the deterioration of the situation in those communities.

On 7 August, Bosnia and Herzegovina expressed reservations on the agreement between Croatia and UNCRO on temporary measures intended to alleviate the hardships of the Serb residents leaving northern and southern Krajina, stressing that any such agreement should be consistent with the territorial integrity and sovereignty and consent of Bosnia and Herzegovina.[164] The agreement had facilitated the influx of Serb paramilitaries, who could not proceed to Yugoslavia (Serbia and Montenegro), which had closed its borders, thus leaving them at the disposal of the Bosnian Serb authorities who would likely arm them. In the circumstances, Bosnia and Herzegovina asked that its representatives be present at all relevant centres, processing points and border crossings and demanded that UNHCR list all persons crossing into its territory, the better to facilitate their resettlement in Croatia or in other voluntarily chosen destinations.

On 11 August, Yugoslavia (Serbia and Montenegro) categorically rejected Bosnia and Herzegovina's letter, and characterized as ill-intentioned the allegation that the Yugoslav borders had been closed to male Serbs of fighting age leaving the Krajina region so that, having no choice but to seek refuge in Bosnian Serb–controlled territory, they would be integrated into and expand the army of "Republika Srpska".[165]

*REFERENCES*

[1]YUN 1994, p. 551. [2]S/1995/8. [3]YUN 1994, p. 536. [4]YUN 1992, p. 356; YUN 1994, p. 542. [5]YUN 1993, p. 455. [6]YUN 1994, p. 523. [7]S/PRST/1995/1. [8]YUN 1994, p. 525. [9]S/1995/222 & Corr.1,2. [10]YUN 1994, p. 553. [11]S/PRST/1995/24. [12]S/1995/444. [13]A/49/870-S/1995/216. [14]YUN 1992, p. 356. [15]Ibid., p. 359, SC res. 761(1992), 29 June 1992. [16]Ibid., p. 370. SC res. 776(1992), 14 Sep. 1992. [17]Ibid., p. 371, SC res. 781(1992), 9 Oct. 1992. [18]YUN 1993, p. 466, SC res. 838(1993), 10 June 1993. [19]Ibid., p. 457, SC res. 836(1993), 4 June 1993. [20]YUN 1994, p. 492, SC res 908(1994), 31 Mar. 1994. [21]Ibid., p. 522. [22]S/1995/26. [23]S/1995/91. [24]S/PRST/1995/8. [25]S/1995/344. [26]A/50/304-S/1995/607.[27]S/1995/637. [28]S/1995/601. [29]S/1995/606. [30]S/1995/623. [31]S/1995/613. [32]YUN 1994, p. 535. [33]S/1995/710. [34]S/1995/716. [35]A/50/382-S/1995/740. [36]A/49/850-S/1995/140. [37]A/49/880-S/1995/245. [38]S/1995/327. [39]S/1995/329. [40]S/1995/345. [41]S/PRST/1995/25. [42]A/49/898-S/1995/364. [43]YUN 1993, p. 455, SC res. 824(1993), 6 May 1993. [44]YUN 1994, p. 542, SC res. 900(1994), 4 Mar. 1994. [45]A/49/908-S/1995/433. [46]S/1995/443. [47]S/1995/370. [48]A/49/900-S/1995/389. [49]S/1995/391. [50]S/1995/415. [51]S/1995/420. [52]A/49/907-S/1995/432. [53]A/49/912-S/1995/447. [54]S/1995/496. [55]S/1995/513. [56]A/50/387-S/1995/743, S/1995/746. [57]S/1995/750, S/1995/751. [58]S/1995/777. [59]YUN 1994, p. 540. [60]S/1995/778.

(61)S/1995/548. (62)A/50/284-S/1995/572. (63)S/1995/574. (64)S/1995/563. (65)A/50/285-S/1995/573. (66)A/50/289-S/1995/576. (67)A/50/290-S/1995/577. (68)S/1995/581. (69)S/1995/579. (70)S/PRST/1995/32. (71)A/50/293-S/1995/583. (72)A/50/294-S/1995/584. (73)S/1995/916. (74)S/1995/423. (75)S/1995/424. (76)S/1995/425. (77)S/1995/428. (78)A/49/917. (79)S/1995/849. (80)S/1995/571. (81)S/1995/582. (82)S/PRST/1995/33. (83)A/50/314-S/1995/621. (84)S/1995/610. (85)S/1995/611. (86)S/1995/617. (87)S/PRST/1995/34. (88)YUN 1994, pp. 513 & 550. (89)A/50/306-S/1995/609. (90)A/50/835-S/1995/1046. (91)S/1995/987. (92)S/PRST/1995/47. (93)S/1995/808. (94)S/1995/812. (95)S/1995/819. (96)S/1995/829. (97)S/1995/833. (98)S/1995/875. (99)S/PRST/1995/60. (100)S/1995/222 & Corr.1,2. (101)S/PRST/1995/19. (102)S/1995/316. (103)S/PRST/1995/31. (104)S/1995/470. (105)S/1995/470/Add.1. (106)S/1995/707. (107)YUN 1994, p. 497. (108)A/49/938-S/1995/539. (109)S/1995/684. (110)S/1995/691. (111)S/PRST/1995/40. (112)A/50/419-S/1995/780. (113)S/PRST/1995/45. (114)S/1995/804. (115)A/50/718-S/1995/920. (116)S/PRST/1995/50. (117)S/PRST/1995/52. (118)A/50/790-S/1995/999. (119)S/1995/1034. (120)S/1995/1019. (121)S/1995/1031. (122)YUN 1992, p. 373, SC res. 786(1992), 10 Nov. 1992. (123)S/1995/1031/Add.1. (124)S/1995/1050. (125)YUN 1992, p. 365, SC res. 770(1992), 13 Aug. 1992. (126)YUN 1993, p. 463, SC res. 816(1993), 31 Mar. 1993. (127)Ibid., p. 459, SC res. 844(1993), 18 June 1993. (128)YUN 1994, p. 528, SC res. 958(1994), 19 Nov. 1994. (129)A/50/810-S/1995/1021. (130)YUN 1992, p. 371, SC res. 781(1992), 9 Oct. 1992. (131)S/1995/5 & Add.1-6 & Add.6/Corr.1 & Add.7-67. (132)S/1995/Add.67. (133)YUN 1994, p. 558. (134)Ibid., p. 554. (135)Ibid., p. 557, SC res. 943(1994), 23 Sep. 1994. (136)Ibid., p. 569. (137)S/1995/104. (138)S/1995/175. (139)S/1995/255. (140)S/1995/302. (141)S/1995/406. (142)S/1995/510. (143)S/1995/645. (144)S/1995/768. (145)S/1995/865. (146)S/1995/944. (147)S/1995/1027. (148)S/1995/288. (149)S/1995/385. (150)S/1995/538. (151)A/49/954-S/1995/674. (152)A/50/342-S/1995/679. (153)S/1995/755. (154)S/PRST/1995/43. (155)S/1995/904. (156)S/1995/905. (157)S/1995/988. (158)A/50/769-S/1995/970. (159)A/50/733-S/1995/936. (160)S/1995/626. (161)YUN 1994, p. 526. (162)S/1996/4. (163)A/50/335-S/1995/662. (164)A/50/337-S/1995/664. (165)A/50/349-S/1995/686.

## Croatia

Major developments occurred in Croatia during 1995 in respect of the designated UN protected areas (UNPAs)—Sectors East, West, North and South—that drastically altered the situation on the ground and, hence, the UN presence in the country.

Following the January withdrawal of Croatia's consent to the extension of the UNPROFOR mandate beyond its 31 March expiration and Croatia's subsequent intention to negotiate with the United Nations for a separate international presence under a new mandate, the Security Council, on the recommendation of the Secretary-General, restructured UNPROFOR so that its operation in Croatia was replaced by the United Nations Confidence Restoration Operation (UNCRO), entrusted with a new mandate. On the basis of a plan agreed upon by the Government and the local Serb authorities for the mandate's implementation, the Council authorized the deployment of UNCRO on 28 April.

Three days later, on 1 May, the Croatian Army launched a military offensive in Western Slavonia (Sector West), completely wresting the area from Croatian Serb control by 4 May. Notwithstanding the concerted efforts of the Special Representative of the Secretary-General for the Former Yugoslavia and the Co-Chairmen of the ICFY Steering Com-

mittee to forestall a full-scale outbreak of hostilities, the Croatian Army mounted another military offensive on 4 August, this time on the Krajina region (Sectors North and South), and declared on 7 August its complete control of the region.

The forcible reintegration into Croatia of the three Sectors of the UNPAs, or what became known in 1994 as the occupied territories of Croatia, left only one sector of operation for UNCRO: Eastern Slavonia, Baranja and Sirmium (Sector East), thus eliminating the need for a substantial UN presence in Croatia.

As a result of several weeks of shuttle diplomacy by the UN Co-Chairman of the ICFY Steering Committee, the Government and the local Serb leaders in Sector East agreed on 11 guiding basic principles. These governed the parties' subsequent negotiations in Croatia, where, on 12 November, they signed the Basic Agreement on the Region of Eastern Slavonia, Baranja and Western Sirmium, providing for the peaceful reintegration of that region into Croatia.

By the terms of the Basic Agreement, the Council was requested to establish a transitional administration and authorize deployment of an international force to implement the Agreement's relevant provisions. On 21 December, the Council indicated its readiness to consider the option that both be components of a UN operation. Meanwhile, on 30 November, the Council decided that, to allow for the orderly establishment of such an operation, the mandate of UNCRO should terminate after an interim period on 15 January 1996.

During the remainder of the year, arrangements were under way for further discussions with the parties regarding the Agreement's implementation and the practical aspects of establishing a UN operation for that purpose.

### UNPROFOR mandate in Croatia

**Communications.** Croatia's President, Franjo Tudjman, informed[1] the Secretary-General on 12 January 1995 of his Government's decision not to agree to extend UNPROFOR's current mandate in Croatia beyond its expiration on 31 March, for the reason that the condition described by the Secretary-General himself in 1994[2] remained unchanged; that is, UNPROFOR's inability to implement fully the UN peace-keeping plan for Croatia[3] and all other additional tasks authorized by subsequent Security Council resolutions. President Tudjman went on to say that although UNPROFOR had played an important role in stopping violence and major conflicts in Croatia, it was indisputable that the current character of the UNPROFOR mission did not provide conditions necessary for establishing order and lasting peace in the country.

Croatia would arrange with the Special Representative for the withdrawal of UNPROFOR on 31 March, or no later than three months thereafter. Croatia was prepared, however, to conclude with the United Nations an agreement on Croatia's continued logistic support for UNPROFOR operations in Bosnia and Herzegovina, including the uninterrupted functioning of UNPROFOR headquarters at Zagreb.

In a 12 March statement, however, President Tudjman indicated his intention to negotiate a new Council-mandated international presence in Croatia[4] that would: control its international borders with Yugoslavia (Serbia and Montenegro) and with Bosnia and Herzegovina at such principal crossing points not currently controlled by Croatia; control access and communications for UNPROFOR and other humanitarian operations to Bosnia and Herzegovina through territory not currently under Croatian control; and facilitate implementation of the 1994 cease-fire[5] and economic agreements,[6] as well as implementation of any future agreement aimed at the reintegration of Croatia. Pending the successful negotiation of the new international presence, for a limited period, the Government of Croatia agreed that UNPROFOR might continue to perform functions essential to the implementation of the 1994 agreements and to those related to its mandate in Bosnia and Herzegovina.

## SECURITY COUNCIL ACTION

The Security Council met on 17 January to consider Croatia's 12 January letter. After consultations among its members, the Council authorized the President to make the following statement[7] on the Council's behalf:

The Security Council, which has begun its consideration of the Secretary-General's report of 14 January 1995 [see below] submitted pursuant to resolution 947(1994), has learned with concern of the position adopted by the Republic of Croatia on the extension of the mandate of the United Nations Protection Force (UNPROFOR) in Croatia beyond 31 March 1995, as set out in the letter from the Permanent Representative of the Republic of Croatia to the Secretary-General of 12 January 1995. It is particularly concerned about the wider implications of this development for the peace process throughout the former Yugoslavia.

The Security Council reiterates its commitment to the sovereignty and territorial integrity of the Republic of Croatia within its internationally recognized borders. It understands the concerns of the Government about the lack of implementation of major provisions of the United Nations peace-keeping plan for Croatia. It will not accept the status quo becoming an indefinite situation. It believes, however, that UNPROFOR's continued presence in the Republic of Croatia is of vital importance for regional peace and security, and that the United Nations in general and UNPROFOR in particular have a positive role to play in achieving the further implementation of the peace-

keeping plan and bringing about a settlement which ensures full respect for the territorial integrity and sovereignty of Croatia. It recalls the important role UNPROFOR plays in helping to sustain the cease-fire in Croatia, facilitating humanitarian activities and international relief work, and supporting implementation of the Economic Agreement of 2 December 1994.

It is in that perspective that the Security Council hopes that discussions over the weeks ahead will lead to a re-examination of the position now taken in relation to the continuing role of UNPROFOR in the Republic of Croatia.

Meanwhile, the Security Council calls upon all parties and others concerned to avoid any action or statement which might lead to an increase in tension. It welcomes the conclusion, under the auspices of the Co-Chairmen of the International Conference on the Former Yugoslavia, of the Economic Agreement of 2 December 1994, and urges the parties to continue, and accelerate, its implementation; it notes the need for adequate international financial support, and encourages the international community to respond to this need. It calls for the intensification in the coming weeks of all these efforts to consolidate this achievement and to bring about a political settlement in Croatia, and it also calls upon the parties to cooperate with these efforts and to negotiate in earnest to that end.

The Security Council affirms its commitment to the search for an overall negotiated settlement of the conflicts in the former Yugoslavia ensuring the sovereignty and territorial integrity of all the States there within their internationally recognized borders, and stresses the importance it attaches to the mutual recognition thereof.

*Meeting number.* SC 3491.

The Council met again on 7 February, having received additional communications from Croatia on the subject. Among those were an 18 January letter fixing the date of UNPROFOR's withdrawal,[8] and a 27 January declaration by the House of Representatives of Croatia's Parliament rejecting all pressures on Croatia to change its decision, which, it emphasized, should not be interpreted as opening the path to the war option.[9]

Upon completion of its consultations, the Council authorized its President to make the statement below[10] on the Council's behalf.

The Security Council reiterates its support for the efforts to bring about a political settlement in the Republic of Croatia which ensures full respect for the sovereignty and territorial integrity of the Republic of Croatia and which guarantees the security and rights of all communities living in a particular area irrespective of whether they constitute in this area the majority or a minority.

The Security Council strongly supports the recent efforts of representatives of the International Conference on the Former Yugoslavia, the European Union, the Russian Federation and the United States of America aimed at achieving a political settlement in the Republic of Croatia. The Security Council calls upon the Government of the Republic of Croatia and the local Serb authorities in the United

Nations Protected Areas to enter urgently and without preconditions into negotiations on such a settlement, benefiting from proposals now made to them as part of these efforts. It calls upon all other relevant parties to support this process.

The Security Council reaffirms its commitment to the search for an overall negotiated settlement of the conflicts in the former Yugoslavia ensuring the sovereignty and territorial integrity of all the States there within their internationally recognized borders and stresses the importance it attaches to the mutual recognition thereof.

The Security Council reaffirms its view that UNPROFOR's continued and effective presence in the Republic of Croatia is of vital importance for regional peace and security and expresses its desire that discussions over the weeks ahead will lead the Government of the Republic of Croatia to re-examine its position taken on 12 January 1995 in relation to the continuing role of UNPROFOR in the Republic of Croatia.

*Meeting number.* SC 3498.

**Report of the Secretary-General.** As requested by Security Council resolution 947(1994),[11] the Secretary-General submitted an interim report on 14 January 1995 on progress towards implementation of the UN peace-keeping plan for Croatia and all relevant Council resolutions.[12]

The Secretary-General noted that effective UNPROFOR monitoring and verification of the 1994 cease-fire agreement had dramatically reduced the number of war casualties and allowed for an increasing normalization of life, an essential precondition for confidence-building and political reconciliation. Further progress had been brought about by the 1994 economic agreement, with the swift implementation of priorities identified by Croatia: opening part of the Zagreb-Belgrade highway through Sectors East and West of the UNPAs;[13] opening of the Zagreb-Lipovac and Zagreb-Split railway lines and the Adriatic oil pipeline; and restoration (repair and de-mining phase) of the water and electricity infrastructure. As passage through local Serb–held territory became part of normal experience, conditions were expected gradually to improve for increased cooperation, political dialogue and conflict resolution.

The Co-Chairmen of the ICFY Steering Committee and two ICFY negotiators, together with the Ambassadors of the Russian Federation and of the United States to Croatia, continued to work on a plan for a political settlement of the conflict between the Croatian Government and the local Serb authorities in the UNPAs. No progress had been made, however, on the deployment of international monitors on Croatia's international borders with Bosnia and Herzegovina and Serbia. For reasons outlined in his 1994 reports,[14] the Secretary-General stated that UNPROFOR would be in no position to deploy monitors on those borders unless there was a significant change in the attitude of the local Serbs and unless substantial additional resources were made available to UNPROFOR.

Thus, with the cooperation of the parties, UNPROFOR's primary tasks over the preceding four months had developed beyond maintenance of the cease-fire agreement to encompass implementing the economic agreement and facilitating the start of a cooperative dialogue between the parties.

The Secretary-General pointed out that, despite the earlier inability of UNPROFOR to fulfil important parts of its mandate under the UN peace-keeping plan for Croatia, the successful implementation of the 1994 cease-fire and economic agreements had been positive steps towards confidence-building and reconciliation. He expressed disappointment that the potential for success through the three-step approach— cessation of hostilities, economic normalization and political negotiations—had not been fully explored before Croatia's decision to withdraw its support for the continuing role of UNPROFOR.[3]

The Secretary-General hoped for a reconsideration of that position before the expiration of the current UNPROFOR mandate. Failing that, he would have to make a detailed study of the practical consequences and financial implications of UNPROFOR's withdrawal, as well as an examination of whether the headquarters and logistic base of a peace-keeping force should be maintained in the capital of a country where a mandate or a troop presence no longer existed.

The Secretary-General stressed his concern that such a withdrawal would considerably increase the likelihood of a resumption of hostilities. However much Croatia might reiterate its commitment to a "peaceful reintegration of its occupied territories" and ask that its decision not be misunderstood, UNPROFOR's withdrawal would likely lead to the resumption of a war even more destructive than that which had raged in 1991-1992. Precisely because of that concern, he had consistently rejected recommending to the Council the option of a withdrawal.

## UN Confidence Restoration Operation in Croatia (UNCRO)

**Report of the Secretary-General.** In a 22 March report, the Secretary-General, commenting on developments affecting implementation of the UNPROFOR mandate in Croatia,[15] noted that in the past two months the escalation of military activity and tension, the suspension of further cooperation in implementing the 1994 economic agreement, and the continued failure of the parties to begin serious political negotiations had brought them to the brink of a major war. He therefore welcomed the fact that President Tudjman, in his 12 March statement,[4] had recognized the grave dangers that would result from a premature departure of UNPROFOR from Croatia and had agreed to its retention for the time being. Principal among the many factors that had precipitated the current crisis had been the lingering lack of trust and confidence between the parties, and the resulting political stalemate for the past three years.

The Secretary-General reiterated that a UN peace-keeping force could operate effectively only with the consent and full cooperation of the parties, and that the three-step approach to a durable peace was the only practical one. It was clear, however, that the retention of UNPROFOR with its current form and mandate would not enjoy Croatia's consent. It was equally clear that deployment under Chapter VII of the Charter of the United Nations of a much larger force to perform the same tasks was not feasible, in either political or resource terms. At the same time, total UNPROFOR withdrawal would immediately result in a grave threat to peace and security extending beyond Croatia's borders. Renewed conflict would become highly probable, and participation of Bosnian Serb forces with support from forces belonging to Yugoslavia (Serbia and Montenegro) could not be ruled out. Nor was it clear whether the UNPROFOR operation in Bosnia and Herzegovina could be continued without substantial UN presence and support facilities in Croatia.

The Secretary-General therefore welcomed the joint announcement on 12 March by President Tudjman and United States Vice-President Albert Gore, which opened the way to a solution along the lines of maintaining a reduced force in Croatia under a new mandate. That mandate should include support for implementation of the 1994 cease-fire and economic agreements, as well as of those elements of the existing UN peace-keeping plan for Croatia accepted by both parties as having continuing relevance, namely, maintenance of a UN presence on Croatia's international borders and confidence-building and humanitarian tasks (assistance to refugees and displaced persons, protection of ethnic minorities, mine clearance, convoy assistance). In addition to this "core mandate", the new force would continue to perform functions arising from the 1992 agreement on the demilitarization of the Prevlaka peninsula[16] and from relevant Council resolutions (monitoring of the ban on military flights in the airspace of Bosnia and Herzegovina, extension of close NATO air support in Croatia).

Accordingly, and in response to the wishes of Croatia, as well as to those of Bosnia and Herzegovina and the former Yugoslav Republic of Macedonia, the Secretary-General proposed that the UNPROFOR operations in those countries be replaced by three separate but interlinked peace-keeping operations (see "UN peace forces: UNCRO, UNPROFOR, UNPREDEP" above, under "General aspects"). The proposed new peace-keeping force in Croatia was approved by the Security Council resolution below.

SECURITY COUNCIL ACTION

On 31 March, the Security Council adopted **resolution 981(1995)**.

*The Security Council,*

*Recalling* all its previous relevant resolutions on the conflicts in the territory of the former Yugoslavia,

*Having considered* the report of the Secretary-General of 22 March 1995,

*Affirming* its commitment to the search for an overall negotiated settlement of the conflicts in the former Yugoslavia ensuring the sovereignty and territorial integrity of all the States there within their internationally recognized borders, and stressing the importance it attaches to the mutual recognition thereof,

*Reaffirming* its commitment to the independence, sovereignty and territorial integrity of the Republic of Croatia, including its rights and obligations in respect of control over its international trade,

*Welcoming* also the continuing efforts of representatives of the United Nations, the European Union, the Russian Federation and the United States of America to facilitate a negotiated solution to the conflict in the Republic of Croatia, and reaffirming its call upon the Government of the Republic of Croatia and the local Serb authorities to enter into the negotiations, urgently and without preconditions, for such a settlement, making full use of the plan presented to them by those representatives,

*Recognizing* that major provisions of the United Nations peace-keeping plan for the Republic of Croatia remain to be implemented, in particular those regarding demilitarization of the areas under the control of the local Serb authorities, the return of all refugees and displaced persons to their homes, and the establishment of local police forces to carry out their duties without discrimination against persons of any nationality in order to protect the human rights of all residents, and urging the parties to agree to their implementation,

*Recognizing also* that major provisions of relevant Security Council resolutions, in particular resolutions 871(1993) and 947(1994), still remain to be implemented,

*Noting* that the mandate of the United Nations Protection Force in the Republic of Croatia expires on 31 March 1995, in conformity with resolution 947(1994),

*Noting also* the letter from the Permanent Representative of the Republic of Croatia of 17 March 1995 regarding his Government's views on the establishment of a United Nations peace-keeping operation in the Republic of Croatia,

*Emphasizing* that improved observance of human rights, including appropriate international monitoring thereof, is an essential step towards restoration of confidence between the parties and building a durable peace,

*Reaffirming* its determination to ensure the security and freedom of movement of personnel of United Nations peace-keeping operations in the territory of the former Yugoslavia, and, to these ends, acting under Chapter VII of the Charter of the United Nations,

1. *Welcomes* the report of the Secretary-General of 22 March 1995, and in particular approves the arrangements in paragraph 84;

2. *Decides* to establish under its authority the United Nations Confidence Restoration Operation in Croatia, which shall be known as UNCRO, in accordance with paragraph 84 of the above-mentioned report for a period terminating on 30 November 1995 and requests the Secretary-General to take the measures necessary to ensure its earliest possible deployment;

3. *Decides* that in accordance with the report of the Secretary-General, and based on the United Nations peace-keeping plan for the Republic of Croatia, relevant resolutions of the Security Council, the Cease-Fire Agreement of 29 March 1994 and the Economic Agreement of 2 December 1994, UNCRO's mandate shall include:

(a) Performing fully the functions envisaged in the Cease-Fire Agreement of 29 March 1994 between the Republic of Croatia and the local Serb authorities;

(b) Facilitating implementation of the Economic Agreement of 2 December 1994 concluded under the auspices of the Co-Chairmen of the International Conference on the Former Yugoslavia;

(c) Facilitating implementation of all relevant Security Council resolutions, including the functions identified in paragraph 72 of the above-mentioned report;

(d) Assisting in controlling, by monitoring and reporting, the crossing of military personnel, equipment, supplies and weapons, over the international borders between the Republic of Croatia and the Republic of Bosnia and Herzegovina, and the Republic of Croatia and the Federal Republic of Yugoslavia (Serbia and Montenegro) at the border crossings for which UNCRO is responsible, as specified in the United Nations peace-keeping plan for the Republic of Croatia;

(e) Facilitating the delivery of international humanitarian assistance to the Republic of Bosnia and Herzegovina through the territory of the Republic of Croatia;

(f) Monitoring the demilitarization of the Prevlaka peninsula in accordance with resolution 779(1992);

4. *Requests* the Secretary-General to continue his consultations with all concerned on the detailed implementation of the mandate outlined in paragraph 3 above, and to report to the Council not later than 21 April 1995 for its approval;

5. *Decides* that UNCRO shall be an interim arrangement to create the conditions that will facilitate a negotiated settlement consistent with the territorial integrity of the Republic of Croatia and which guarantees the security and rights of all communities living in a particular area of the Republic of Croatia, irrespective of whether they constitute in this area a majority or minority;

6. *Decides* that Member States, acting nationally or through regional organizations or arrangements, may take, under the authority of the Security Council and subject to close coordination with the Secretary-General and the United Nations Theatre Force Commander, using the existing procedures which have been agreed with the Secretary-General, all necessary measures to extend close air support to the territory of the Republic of Croatia in defence of UNCRO personnel in the per-

formance of UNCRO's mandate, and requests the Secretary-General to continue to report to the Council on any use of close air support;

7. *Emphasizes* the responsibility of the parties and others concerned in the Republic of Croatia for the security and safety of UNCRO and in this context demands that all parties and others concerned refrain from any acts of intimidation or violence against UNCRO;

8. *Calls upon* the Government of the Republic of Croatia and the local Serb authorities to refrain from the threat or use of force and to reaffirm their commitment to a peaceful resolution of their differences;

9. *Invites* the Secretary-General to report as appropriate and not less than every four months on progress towards a peaceful political settlement and the situation on the ground including UNCRO's ability to implement its mandate as described above, and undertakes in this connection to examine without delay any recommendations that the Secretary-General may make in his reports and adopt appropriate decisions;

10. *Calls upon* Member States to consider favourably requests by the Secretary-General for necessary assistance to UNCRO in the performance of its mandate;

11. *Stresses* the importance of the necessary arrangements, including agreements on the status of forces and other personnel, being concluded by the Republic of Croatia, calls upon it to agree to such arrangements without delay, and requests the Secretary-General to inform the Council of progress on this issue in the report mentioned in paragraph 4 above;

12. *Urges* the Government of the Republic of Croatia to provide suitable radio broadcasting frequencies and television broadcasting slots at no cost to the United Nations as described in paragraphs 47 to 51 of the report of the Secretary-General of 22 March 1995;

13. *Decides* to remain seized of the matter.

Security Council resolution 981(1995)

31 March 1995      Meeting 3512      Adopted unanimously

8-nation draft (S/1995/242).

*Sponsors:* Argentina, Czech Republic, France, Germany, Italy, Russian Federation, United Kingdom, United States.

### Deployment

**Report of the Secretary-General.** In response to the Security Council resolution above, the Secretary-General reported on 18 April on the results of consultations on implementation of the UNCRO mandate.[17] He noted that Thorvald Stoltenberg (Norway), UN Co-Chairman of the ICFY Steering Committee, acting as the Special Envoy of the Secretary-General, carried out those consultations with representatives of the Croatian Government and of the local Serb authorities, including with the military authorities of both sides. In the process, the Special Envoy kept in close contact with the Special Representative and the UNPF Force Commander.

The plan proposed by the Special Envoy set out in detail the functions and measures for implementing each of the six main tasks comprising the UNCRO mandate, as defined by **resolution 981(1995)**. Under the task calling for ''facilitating implementation of all relevant Security Council resolutions'', the plan spelt out implementation measures for humanitarian aid, human rights protection, the return of refugees and displaced persons, and confidence-building.

The Special Representative and the UNPF Force Commander, having analysed the proposed plan, determined that some 8,750 troops would be required for the mandate's implementation, on the assumption that UNCRO would enjoy the cooperation of all concerned. The UNPROFOR troops currently in Croatia could be reduced to the assessed level and deployed under UNCRO, the deployment to be completed by 30 June.

Consultations were also pursued on a status-of-forces agreement for the presence in Croatia of UNCRO, UNPF-HQ and, for a transition period, UNPROFOR, as well as for the use of Croatian territory for the support of UNPROFOR in Bosnia and Herzegovina and of UNPREDEP in the former Yugoslav Republic of Macedonia. Notwithstanding the difficulties brought to the fore in the consultations, UNPF-HQ forwarded a draft agreement to Croatia on 14 April for its consideration.

The Secretary-General recommended that the Council approve the arrangements set out in the report and authorize the deployment of UNCRO.

SECURITY COUNCIL ACTION

The Security Council met on 28 April. It had before it, in addition to the foregoing report of the Secretary-General, a letter dated that day from Croatia, assuring the Council of its full cooperation and stressing, among its other views on the implementation plan, that UNCRO's primary concern should be the control of Croatia's internationally recognized borders.[18]

On the same date, the Council adopted **resolution 990(1995)**.

*The Security Council,*

*Recalling* all its previous relevant resolutions on the conflicts in the territory of the former Yugoslavia and in particular resolutions 981(1995) and 982(1995) of 31 March 1995,

*Having considered* the report of the Secretary-General of 18 April 1995,

*Bearing in mind* the importance of any information relevant to the implementation of all its previous resolutions being made available to the Secretary-General,

*Reaffirming* its determination to ensure the security and freedom of movement of personnel of United Nations peace-keeping operations in the territory of the former Yugoslavia, and, to these ends, acting under Chapter VII of the Charter of the United Nations,

1. *Welcomes* the report of the Secretary-General, and in particular approves the arrangements in paragraphs 11 to 28 for the implementation of the mandate of the United Nations Confidence Restoration Operation in Croatia, which is known as UNCRO;

2. *Decides* to authorize the deployment of UNCRO as set out in paragraph 29 of the above-mentioned report;

3. *Calls upon* the Government of the Republic of Croatia and the local Serb authorities to cooperate fully with UNCRO in the implementation of its mandate;

4. *Expresses its concern* that an agreement on the status of forces and other personnel has not yet been signed, calls once again on the Government of the Republic of Croatia to conclude expeditiously such an agreement, and requests the Secretary-General to report to the Council no later than 15 May 1995;

5. *Decides* to remain seized of the matter.

Security Council resolution 990(1995)
28 April 1995     Meeting 3527     Adopted unanimously
Draft prepared in consultations among Council members (S/1995/334).

## Occupied territories

Since their inception in 1992,[19] the peace-keeping operations of the United Nations in Croatia were centred in the three designated UN protected areas where Croatian Serbs constituted a majority or a substantial minority of the population—divided into four sectors: Sector East (Eastern Slavonia, including Baranja and Sirmium), Sector North (northern Krajina), Sector South (southern Krajina) and Sector West (Western Slavonia).

Croatia, having defined the UNPAs in 1994 as Serb-occupied territories of the State and the pink zones outside the UNPAs as being under effective Serb occupation, requested the inclusion in the General Assembly's agenda for that year of an item entitled ''The situation in the occupied territories of Croatia'', in order to give all Member States an opportunity to contribute to finding a just solution to that situation.[20] For Croatia, that meant their eventual peaceful reintegration into the State's constitutional and legislative system. The item remained inscribed on the Assembly's 1995 agenda.

Pursuant to the Assembly's 1994 request, as contained in resolution 49/43 on the item,[21] the Secretary-General submitted a report on 18 October 1995, stating that developments in the ''occupied territories'' during the summer had dramatically altered the context in which that resolution had been adopted.[22] The report provided a detailed description of developments since then until the reporting date.

Those included the replacement of UNPROFOR in Croatia by UNCRO on 31 March; the authorized deployment of UNCRO on 28 April, on the basis of a detailed plan for the new mandate's implementation as agreed upon by the Government and the local Serb authorities in the UNPAs; the major military offensive launched by the Croatian Army on Sector West on 1 May, and another major offensive on Sectors North and South on 4 August, by which Croatia brought the first Sector under complete control on 4 May and the other two on 7 August.

Those forcible reintegrations left Sector East as the only occupied territory where UNCRO remained deployed. That Sector's proximity to Yugoslavia (Serbia and Montenegro), the Secretary-General pointed out, could increase the risk of spreading the conflict beyond the borders of Croatia, should it try to recover that Sector by force. An important, if tentative, step towards peace occurred on 3 October, however, when the parties agreed on 11 "guiding basic principles" for a settlement of their dispute.

The report noted that the recovery of the three Sectors by force constituted a defiance of the relevant Council resolutions; it ignored Assembly resolution 49/43, making its major elements irrelevant, and changed the status of most of the "occupied territories". From it a different form of crisis had resulted: large numbers of refugees and displaced persons, and reported human rights violations.

(For details on UNCRO, the four Sectors, refugees and displaced persons, and the resultant human rights situation, see below under those topics.)

GENERAL ASSEMBLY ACTION

On the basis of the Secretary-General's foregoing report and on the recommendation of the Fourth (Special Political and Decolonization) Committee,[23] the General Assembly, by **decision 50/413** of 6 December, deferred consideration of the item entitled "The situation in the occupied territories of Croatia" and included it in the agenda of its fifty-first session.

*Sector West (Western Slavonia)*

**Report of the ICFY Co-Chairmen.** The Co-Chairmen of the ICFY Steering Committee, in their report of 17 July describing their activities during the first half of the year,[24] stated that, following the conclusion of the economic agreement of 2 December 1994[6] and the opening shortly thereafter of the Zagreb-Lipovac highway (running through Sectors East and West), their immediate priority was to expedite implementation of the agreement's remaining provisions, in cooperation with the ICFY negotiators and UNPROFOR. On 9 January 1995, the electricity poles were returned to the Obrovac power plant and, on 27 January, the oil pipeline running through Sector North was opened.

On 30 January, the so-called Zagreb Four (the Ambassadors of the Russian Federation and of the United States to Croatia, the EU Special Negotiator for the Former Yugoslavia and the ICFY negotiator) presented a plan for a peaceful resolution regarding the UNPAs. It was received by the Government, but the Croatian Serb "Assembly" in Knin (seat of the Croatian Serb administration

in southern Krajina) declined to receive it. On 8 February, that "Assembly" decided to freeze all further implementation of the economic agreement because of President Tudjman's 12 January statement withdrawing consent to UNPROFOR's presence beyond 31 March.[1] Through constant consultations conducted by the ICFY Co-Chairmen and negotiators in Zagreb, Knin and Belgrade, the parties agreed on a text for a joint commercial oil company but postponed its signature until the political climate improved. Some progress was achieved towards opening the Zagreb-Okucani-Mirkovici railway and towards implementing a number of water projects. The Zagreb-Lipovac highway remained in full operation and, by mid-April, it was estimated that more than 250,000 vehicles had used it.

On 24 April, however, the Croatian Serbs closed that segment of the Zagreb-Lipovac highway running through Sector West for 24 hours. Although they reopened the highway, a series of incidents led to a rapid deterioration of the situation on the highway and around it. On 1 May, the Croatian Army mounted a military offensive in those areas of Sector West under Croatian Serb control. To avert further deterioration of the situation and in an effort to re-establish dialogue between the parties, the ICFY Co-Chairmen invited them for talks in Geneva. Their acceptance in principle notwithstanding, the level of military tension and the preconditions they posed precluded holding the meeting.

SECURITY COUNCIL ACTION (1 and 4 May)

The Security Council, having been apprised of the situation, met on 1 May and, following consultations among its members, authorized the President to make the statement below[25] on the Council's behalf:

The Security Council is deeply concerned by the resumption of hostilities in the Republic of Croatia over the last few days.

The Security Council demands that the Government of the Republic of Croatia put an end immediately to the military offensive launched by its forces in the area of Western Slavonia known as Sector West which started on the morning of 1 May 1995 in violation of the cease-fire agreement of 29 March 1994.

The Security Council also demands that the parties respect the economic agreement signed between them on 2 December 1994 and, in particular, take all necessary steps to ensure the safety and security of the Zagreb-Belgrade highway and its immediate environs.

The Security Council urges the parties to cease hostilities and comply with the existing cease-fire agreement.

The Security Council calls upon the parties to fully respect the safety and freedom of movement of all United Nations and European Community Monitoring Mission personnel in the area concerned, in the area known as Sector South and elsewhere, and therefore to remove all restrictions placed on UN personnel.

The Security Council urges the parties, in order to achieve these objectives, to accept without delay the proposals put to them by the Special Representative of the Secretary-General.

The Security Council expresses its full support to the Secretary-General and his Special Representative in their efforts. The Council further requests the Secretary-General to keep it informed of developments on the ground as well as in the ongoing talks.

*Meeting number.* SC 3529.

The Council met again on 4 May; after consultations among its members, it authorized the President to make the following statement[26] on the Council's behalf.

The Security Council is deeply concerned at the continuation of hostilities in the Republic of Croatia.

The Security Council reaffirms in this context its statement of 1 May 1995 in all its aspects, and demands that the parties comply with the requirements set out therein immediately and in full.

The Security Council condemns the incursions into the zone of separation by the forces of the Government of the Republic of Croatia in Sectors North and South, and by both sides in Sector East. It demands that the forces in question withdraw immediately.

The Security Council also condemns the bombardment of Zagreb and other centres of civilian population by the forces of the local Serb authorities and demands that they cease immediately.

The Security Council further condemns acts of harassment and intimidation against United Nations personnel and reminds the parties of their obligations to respect such personnel at all times and to ensure their safety, security and freedom of movement.

The Security Council calls on the parties to cooperate fully with UNCRO, UNHCR and the ICRC in protecting and assisting the local civilian population and any displaced persons. The Council is deeply concerned by reports that the human rights of the Serb population of Western Slavonia are being violated. It demands that the Government of the Republic of Croatia respect fully the rights of the Serb population concerned, in conformity with internationally recognized standards.

The Security Council insists that the authority of UNCRO be re-established and respected in Sector West and other areas affected by the hostilities.

The Security Council demands that the parties act in accordance with the proposals put to them by the Special Representative of the Secretary-General, that they cease all hostilities immediately, and that they cooperate fully with the Special Representative of the Secretary-General and with UNCRO.

The Security Council further calls upon the parties to enter without delay into the discussions in Geneva to which they have been invited by the Co-Chairmen of the Steering Committee of the International Conference on the Former Yugoslavia.

The Security Council will remain actively seized of the matter and will be ready to consider further steps as necessary.

*Meeting number.* SC 3531.

**Communications.** Croatia informed the Security Council President on 5 May that the situation in the formerly occupied Croatian territory of Western Slavonia (Sector West) was calm and that peace and order had been restored.[27] ICRC, UNHCR, the international media and the diplomatic corps had been allowed into the area and complete freedom of movement of UNCRO personnel, previously restricted for their own safety, had also been restored. The Zagreb-Vinkovci railway line had been reopened, the Okucani radio station had begun operating and elementary schools were continuing their educational programme. Health and social insurance had been extended to all citizens in the area. Croatia's Ministry of Social Services had appropriated a one-time financial grant to help all needy persons in the liberated territories, while the Ministry of Reconstruction was arranging grants and loans for rebuilding destroyed property.

Croatia's Abolition Act would be applied to the approximately 600 members of the disbanded paramilitary forces in Western Slavonia after they had been cleared of any allegations of war crimes. Civilians had been temporarily moved into hotels and other accommodations in Varazdin, Krapina and Novska until full normalization of living conditions in the Pakrac area was achieved. More than 3,000 Croatian Serbs had so far decided to remain in their towns and villages, but the Government would facilitate the departure of those opting to leave for another part of Croatia or for another country.

Croatia expressed dismay at the Council's acceptance of the serious accusations levelled against it by UN Under-Secretary-General Chinmaya R. Gharekhan (acting as Special Political Adviser to the Secretary-General), charging widespread violations of the human rights of the Serb populations in the liberated territory. As those had been proved unfounded by the European Community Monitoring Mission (ECMM) and the foreign media, as well as by the Special Representative, Croatia said, it demanded an apology from the Under-Secretary-General.

Also on 5 May, Yugoslavia (Serbia and Montenegro) reported having received information about systematic crimes being committed by Croatia's armed forces and police units against captured soldiers and the defenceless population of the "Republic of Serb Krajina".[28] Serb refugees were being strafed and shelled while fleeing Okucani for Bosnia and Herzegovina. There were reports of continuing mass executions, arrests, harassment and maltreatment of civilians in violation of the cease-fire agreement recently negotiated by the Special Representative between Croatia and the "Republic of Serb Krajina".

Yugoslavia (Serbia and Montenegro) demanded that the Council take steps under Chapter VII of the United Nations Charter to put an immediate stop to those crimes, to ensure the withdrawal of Croatia's forces to their positions before 1 May and to prevent renewed aggression against the "Republic of Serb Krajina".

Croatia on 8 May informed the Council President of its proposal that representatives of its Army and of the Croatian Serb paramilitary forces meet under the auspices of the Special Representative to defuse tensions in the zones of separation of Sectors South (southern Krajina), North (northern Krajina) and East (Eastern Slavonia, including Baranja and Sirmium).[(29)] While all efforts were being made to normalize life in the liberated territories, the Government had detained some 1,475 members of the Serb paramilitary who, under ECMM and ICRC supervision, had been taken to three processing centres in Varazdin, Pozega and Bjelovar. Of those, 554 had been released and the Abolition Act applied to them; a criminal investigative process had begun against 105; the processing of another 816 in Varazdin and Bjelovar was under way.

Croatia affirmed its commitment to the full and speedy implementation of the UNCRO mandate, aimed at the peaceful reintegration of the occupied territories into Croatia, and indicated its readiness to negotiate with the local Serbs in Knin to that end.

**SECURITY COUNCIL ACTION (17 May)**

The Security Council met on 17 May and adopted **resolution 994(1995)**.

*The Security Council,*

*Recalling* all its previous resolutions on the conflicts in the territory of the former Yugoslavia and in particular resolutions 981(1995) of 31 March 1995, 982(1995) of 31 March 1995 and 990(1995) of 28 April 1995,

*Deeply concerned* that the objectives set out in the statements of the President of the Security Council of 1 May 1995 and of 4 May 1995 have not been implemented in all their aspects and that the agreement reached by the parties on 7 May 1995 through the mediation of the United Nations Peace Forces Headquarters (UNPF-HQ) has been violated, in particular regarding the withdrawal of forces from the zones of separation,

*Emphasizing* the necessity for full compliance by the parties with the Cease-Fire Agreement of 29 March 1994 and stressing the importance of such compliance for the implementation of the mandate of the United Nations Confidence Restoration Operation in Croatia known as UNCRO,

*Emphasizing further* that withdrawal from the zones of separation is a condition for the implementation of the mandate of UNCRO,

*Affirming* its commitment to the search for an overall negotiated settlement of the conflicts in the former Yugoslavia ensuring the sovereignty and territorial integrity of all the States there within their internationally recognized borders and stressing the importance it attaches to the mutual recognition thereof, and in this context welcoming all international efforts to facilitate a negotiated solution to the conflict in the Republic of Croatia,

*Emphasizing* that full observance of human rights, including appropriate international monitoring thereof, in particular in the area of Western Slavonia known as Sector West, is an essential step towards restoration of confidence between the parties and building a durable peace,

*Condemning* in the strongest terms all unacceptable acts which were directed at the personnel of the United Nations peace-keeping forces and determined to obtain strict respect of the status of such personnel in the Republic of Croatia as provided for in the Agreement between the United Nations and the Government of the Republic of Croatia signed on 15 May 1995,

*Reaffirming* its determination to ensure the security and freedom of movement of the personnel of United Nations peace-keeping operations in the territory of the former Yugoslavia, and, to these ends, acting under Chapter VII of the Charter of the United Nations,

1. *Reaffirms* the statements of the President of the Security Council of 1 May 1995 and 4 May 1995 issued as a result of the military offensive launched by the forces of the Government of Croatia in the area of Western Slavonia known as Sector West on 1 May 1995 in violation of the Cease-Fire Agreement of 29 March 1994;

2. *Notes with satisfaction* the steps taken so far to meet the requirements set out in the above-mentioned statements, but demands that the parties complete without further delay the withdrawal of all their troops from the zones of separation and refrain from any further violations of those zones;

3. *Stresses* the need for the early re-establishment of the authority of UNCRO in accordance with its mandate;

4. *Requests* the Secretary-General to make the necessary arrangements in order to ensure full deployment of UNCRO, after the withdrawal of the troops of the parties, as provided for in its mandate established by resolutions 981(1995) and 990(1995);

5. *Demands* that the status and the mandate of UNCRO as well as the safety and security of its personnel be respected;

6. *Demands also* that the Government of the Republic of Croatia respect fully the rights of the Serb population including their freedom of movement and allow access to this population by international humanitarian organizations, in conformity with internationally recognized standards;

7. *Requests* the Secretary-General, in cooperation with the United Nations High Commissioner for Refugees, the United Nations High Commissioner for Human Rights, the International Committee of the Red Cross and other relevant international humanitarian institutions, to assess the humanitarian situation of the local Serb population in Sector West, including the problem of refugees, and to report thereon as soon as possible;

8. *Fully supports* the efforts of the Special Representative of the Secretary-General to achieve the objectives outlined in the statements of the President of the Security Council of 1 May 1995 and of 4 May 1995 and requests the parties to cooperate fully to this end;

9. *Calls upon* the parties to respect the Economic Agreement signed by them on 2 December 1994 and in particular to take all necessary steps to ensure the safety and security of the Zagreb-Belgrade highway and its immediate environs as provided for in that Agreement;

10. *Demands* that the parties refrain from taking any further military measures or actions that could lead to the escalation of the situation and warns that in the event of failure to comply with this demand it will consider further steps needed to ensure such compliance;

11. *Requests* the Secretary-General to report to the Council for its consideration within two weeks on the implementation of the provisions of this resolution, including on the modalities for the implementation of the mandate of UNCRO in Sector West;

12. *Decides* to remain actively seized of the matter.

Security Council resolution 994(1995)

17 May 1995    Meeting 3537    Adopted unanimously

6-nation draft (S/1995/395).

*Sponsors:* France, Germany, Italy, Russian Federation, United Kingdom, United States.

**Report of the Secretary-General.** In response to Security Council **resolution 994(1995)**, the Secretary-General submitted a report on 9 June describing developments in the UNCRO mission area since April, the resolution's implementation and modalities for implementing the UNCRO mandate, with particular reference to Sector West, and providing an initial assessment of the humanitarian situation of the local Serb population in that Sector, including the problem of refugees.[30]

The report noted that in April, following the adoption of Council **resolution 981(1995)** creating UNCRO, tension between the Croatian Government and local Serb authorities decreased slightly, except in the areas along Croatia's border with the western part of Bosnia and Herzegovina. Both sides continued to fortify their defensive positions around the zones of separation, causing the number of violations of the 1994 cease-fire agreement to rise to 250 at the end of March. Restrictions to UNCRO's freedom of movement continued, particularly in and around Sectors East, West and South. On 24 April, the Serb authorities closed the highway through Sector West for a 24-hour period in protest over the number of trucks denied passage by the EU/OSCE Sanctions Assistance Mission in Croatia at the Lipovac crossing in Sector East because their passage would have violated the sanctions regime on Yugoslavia (Serbia and Montenegro).

On 1 May, the Croatian Army and police entered Sector West from both directions on the Zagreb-Belgrade highway with some 2,500 troops, heavy equipment and air support. That operation was initially described by the Government as a police action intended only to restore security on the highway following the stabbing of a Serb by a Croatian refugee on 28 April, the subsequent retaliatory killing of three Croats by Serbs, and a further alleged attack on a Croat on 30 April. The operation cut off the Serb-controlled part of the Sector from Bosnian Serb–held areas of Bosnia and Herzegovina. Croatian military movements continued through 5 May in the central part of Sector West and in the main Serb town of Okucani, the Secretary-General said, revealing that Croatia's intention was to establish complete control over the Sector. As of 2 May, the Croatian Army had secured all militarily important positions. The Krajina Serbs responded by firing missiles on 2 and 3 May into urban areas of Zagreb and the Pleso airfield and shelling the towns of Karlovac and Sisak.

On 3 May, agreement was reached on a cessation of hostilities in all areas, including Sector West, and on arrangements to ensure the safe passage from that Sector into Bosnian Serb–controlled parts of Bosnia and Herzegovina for Serb civilians and soldiers who wished to leave under UNCRO and UNHCR surveillance. In the afternoon of 4 May, however, while UNCRO was attempting to negotiate implementation of the cessation-of-hostilities agreement with some 600 Serb soldiers in Pakrac, the Croatian Army began shelling the Serb-inhabited part of Pakrac in response to alleged attacks on Croatian police and attempts by Serb soldiers to escape. As a result, the Serbs surrendered to the Croatian Army and police, who then began to assemble the remaining Serb inhabitants, separating males and females. Males, mainly of draft age, were transported to three detention centres outside the Sector.

During the offensive on Sector West, Croatian forces advanced to improved tactical positions in the zone of separation near Osijek in Sector East, Petrinja in Sector North, and Gospic and Medak in Sector South, giving those forces considerable local tactical advantage, thereby further weakening the 1994 cease-fire agreement and threatening adjacent UN positions. The most significant Serb advance into the zone of separation in response to the Croatian action was in Sector East. Elsewhere, the Serbs removed heavy weapons from storage sites and impeded UN freedom of movement.

The Croatian Army's successes in Sector West seemed to have prompted a similar campaign in Sector South, despite assurances by the Government that it would not pursue further military objectives. On 4 June, the Croatian Army and Bosnian Croats launched a combined small-scale infantry and artillery attack in the area of Mount Dinara in Sector South, 20 kilometres south-east of Knin, shelling several villages in the environs. On 6 June, a similar attack was launched from the Mount Dinara area, resulting in several bouts of shelling, with three rounds impacting inside the Kenyan battalion camp of UNCRO at Civiljane.

Compliance with the Council's demand for all forces to withdraw from the Sector's separation zone had yet to be achieved. Croatian troops and heavy weapons had been observed inside the zone at different times and 28 heavy weapons were within the 10- and 20-kilometre zones, in violation of the terms specified for those zones in the cease-fire agreement. While Croatia had satisfied the technical demands of troop withdrawal, the current deployment of its troops in close proximity to the separation zone served neither to reduce tensions nor to allay the Serbs' apprehension of further attacks, the Secretary-General stated. Moreover, Croatia's position was that its forces would withdraw only to the positions they had held before the 1 May offensive. The Serb side maintained a major presence in the separation zone, including more than 1,700 troops and 84 heavy weapons, as well as a deployment of more than 300 heavy weapons in contravention of the 10- and 20-kilometre zones.

Attempts by the Special Representative and the Force Commander to stabilize the military situation met with difficulties. To their proposal for face-to-face negotiations between the military leaders of both sides, the Serbs placed preconditions calling for the withdrawal of all Croatian forces from the Mount Dinara area in Sector South and from Sector West, and the return of all heavy weapons confiscated during the offensive. Apart from the Serbs' refusal of ICFY's invitation to talks in Geneva, a move was afoot by the Krajina Serbs to establish a union with the Bosnian Serbs, the report stated. Croatia viewed with concern the effect such a union would have on the 1994 economic agreement and on political negotiations.

Until the 1 May offensive, the overall human rights and humanitarian condition of the Serbs in Sector West had been fragile but stable. About 5,000 of them lived among 35,000 Croats and other minorities in the northern part, but were concentrated in Pakrac, Daruvar and Grubisno Polje; between 13,500 and 17,000 lived in the formerly Serb-controlled part of the Sector, clustered around Okucani and Gavrinica. While UNCRO investigations revealed instances of serious human rights violations during the offensive, they were not indicative of a systematic or strategic design. It appeared that 1,494 persons had initially been detained, in three centres, in violation of the 3 May cessation-of-hostilities agreement. Visits to those detention centres by UNCRO and other international organizations revealed no reports of unsatisfactory conditions, but interviews of released detainees pointed to mistreatment, mostly beatings, not suggestive, however, of widespread or systematic violations.

The International Tribunal for the Former Yugoslavia and the Special Rapporteur of the UN Commission on Human Rights had begun looking into possible violations in Sector West. UNCRO had received unconfirmed reports from local residents and other sources of looting by the Croatian Army, forced eviction of families from their dwellings, the burning or blowing up of scores of abandoned houses (Covac, Gredani, Okucani, Vrbovljani), harassment and intimidation of the local Serb population, and confiscation of personal documents (vehicle registrations and drivers' licences).

About 10,000 Serb civilians and military personnel living in areas immediately affected by the fighting crossed into Bosnia and Herzegovina using the Sava bridge. At the demand of the Krajina Serb authorities, the safe departure of the remaining 4,000 Serbs from Sector West was begun on 9 May under UNCRO's "Operation Safe Passage", with UNHCR assistance. In the meantime, UNCRO and UNHCR were trying to obtain government guarantees for the safety of the ethnic Serbs who had left in haste but wished to return and for the return of their homes and assets.

In view of the fear and uncertainty voiced by most Serbs remaining in Sector West, mainly in the Gavrinica area, the Croatian Government had taken steps to normalize life for them, which included infrastructure improvements (bus line and telephone links), small family grants and assistance from the Croatian Red Cross. A registration centre in Gavrinica had begun processing citizenship applications. Of a total 1,070 applications, 675 had been approved, for which citizenship papers had been issued. Civic committees had also been formed to promote local Serb participation in normalizing life in the Sector.

In meetings with the Special Representative following the 1 May offensive, the leaders of both sides had stated their desire for UNCRO to continue and complete deployment in Sector West, but for different purposes. For Croatia, it was so that UNCRO could attest to government efforts to pursue high standards of respect for the human rights of the Serbs remaining in the Sector. For the Serb side, it was so that UNCRO could monitor the situation of the local Serbs, facilitate the departure of those voluntarily wishing to leave, investigate human rights abuses and press for the withdrawal of the Croatian Army and police forces from the Sector. The Serb side had also sought international assistance for more than 10,000 refugees and displaced persons who had fled the Sector, but had restricted UNCRO movement in the Sectors it controlled, making it impossible for UNCRO to monitor the situation of the minority Croats in those Sectors.

Further, both sides had sought UNCRO's assistance in restoring the integrity of the 1994 cease-fire agreement, starting with full troop withdrawal from the separation zone and heavy-weapons withdrawal to the 10- and 20-kilometre lines specified in the agreement. While both sides recognized that a meeting between their military commanders was essential for stabilizing the tense situation, no progress had been made to bring about such a meeting.

The Secretary-General noted that, despite their declared support for UNCRO's mandate with respect to the cease-fire agreement, both sides had exhibited a high degree of cynicism towards their cease-fire obligations. It was thus vital for them to reaffirm their commitment to the agreement and their intention to cooperate with UNCRO. An essential step for the Serb side was to take firm action to stop the hijacking of UN vehicles and the armed robbery and intimidation of UNCRO personnel and to allow UNCRO full freedom of movement within the Sectors.

Of the six principal functions constituting UNCRO's mandate, there appeared to be common ground between the parties that the mission should fulfil the tasks arising from the 1994 cease-fire and economic agreements and from its humanitarian and human rights mandates. Given the hostility engendered by the Croatian offensive, the tasks associated with border monitoring required substantially more time than originally envisaged. The functions related to the Prevlaka peninsula and the delivery of humanitarian assistance through Croatian territory to Bosnia and Herzegovina remained unchanged. However, rather than UNCRO's complete deployment being achieved by 30 June as required by **resolution 982(1995)**, it was likely to take up the major part of the mandate period.

As to the modalities for implementing the UNCRO mandate in Sector West, discussions with the Government were at an advanced stage for the comprehensive deployment throughout the Sector of UN civilian police and civilian affairs personnel. Their tasks would be to provide assistance to the needy, ensure respect for human rights, facilitate the voluntary return of refugees and displaced persons and support confidence-building measures between communities.

The Secretary-General stressed that more than words were required to justify the expensive and dangerous UNCRO mission. He would therefore closely monitor the parties' level of cooperation with UNCRO, in particular the extent of their compliance with the 1994 cease-fire agreement, and of making good their word to allow UNCRO full freedom of movement and to ensure the security of its personnel. The Secretary-General expressed grave concern over the reported joint military manoeuvres by the Croatian Army and Bosnian Croat forces in the Mount Dinara area adjacent to Sector South, including the shelling of UNCRO positions.

**Communications.** Yugoslavia (Serbia and Montenegro) continued on 13 June to report atrocities committed by the Croatian armed forces during their 1 May offensive on Western Slavonia, including the massacre of columns of Croatian Serb refugees, destruction and looting of their property in seven villages, the taking of some 380 to 1,000 prisoners and of 1,000 to 1,200 wounded to unknown destinations—for all of which compelling evidence existed.[31]

Yugoslavia (Serbia and Montenegro) further claimed on 16 June that the Croatian Army had killed more than 3,300 civilians and 1,000 soldiers of the "Republic of Serb Krajina" after they had complied with the cease-fire; more than 9,000 houses had been torn down, and the Sava River bridge had been blown up to prevent Serb refugees from returning.[32]

SECURITY COUNCIL ACTION (16 June)

The Security Council met on 16 June to consider the Secretary-General's 9 June report. After consultations among its members, the Council authorized the President to make the statement below[33] on the Council's behalf:

The Security Council has considered the report of the Secretary-General of 9 June 1995 submitted pursuant to its resolution 994(1995) of 17 May 1995. It is concerned at the situation described therein, and at the continuing failure of the parties to cooperate satisfactorily with UNCRO and to comply fully with the demands of the Council. It condemns in particular the continuation of offensive actions and the intimidation of UNCRO personnel in violation of its resolution 994(1995).

The Security Council looks to the parties to cooperate fully and unconditionally with UNCRO in the performance of its mandate and to ensure the safety, security and freedom of movement of its personnel. The Council demands that they fulfil their commitment under the cease-fire agreement of 29 March 1994, in particular in respect of the withdrawal of all forces and heavy weapons from the zones of separation, and fully implement the 2 December 1994 agreement on economic confidence-building measures. It calls upon the parties, and in particular the Government of Croatia, to cease all military action in and around Sector South. It also calls upon all parties to respect fully the international border between the Republic of Croatia and the Republic of Bosnia and Herzegovina and to stop any action which extends the conflict across this border, since this is in violation of the Council's resolutions. It reiterates its warning that in the event of failure to comply with the demand in its resolution 994(1995) that the parties refrain from taking any further military measures or actions that could lead to the escalation of the situation, it will consider further steps needed to ensure such compliance.

The Security Council requests the Committee established under resolution 724(1991) of 15 December 1991 to continue to investigate, in accordance with its mandate, reports of violations of resolution 713(1991) of 25 September 1991.

The Security Council welcomes the agreement of the Government of Croatia to a continued UNCRO presence in the area of Western Slavonia known as Sector West for the purposes of implementing its mandate, in particular in respect of human rights, to which it continues to attach great importance. It endorses the Secretary-General's view as to the necessity for reconciliation and confidence-building in that Sector. It stresses the importance it attaches to full respect for the human rights of the Serb population there. It encourages the Secretary-General to continue his coordination with the United Nations High Commissioner for Human Rights as well as other international organizations and agencies in this regard.

The Security Council notes the Secretary-General's judgement that completion of the redeployment of United Nations peace-keeping personnel in the Republic of Croatia by 30 June 1995 envisaged in its resolution 982(1995) of 31 March 1995 is no longer possible. It requests the Secretary-General to proceed as expeditiously as possible with this redeployment with the aim of fulfilling all UNCRO's tasks under its mandate. It demands that the parties cooperate with UNCRO's efforts to implement fully its mandate.

The Security Council notes the fact that both parties have stated their desire that the peace-keeping mission should continue, and are seeking UNCRO's assistance. It welcomes the Secretary-General's intention to monitor closely their cooperation with UNCRO and their compliance with the cease-fire agreement of 29 March 1994, and requests him to keep the Council fully informed. Such cooperation and compliance are essential for the implementation of UNCRO's mandate and for progress towards a negotiated settlement respecting fully the sovereignty and territorial integrity of the Republic of Croatia and which guarantees the security and rights of all communities.

The Security Council could not countenance moves by the local Serb authorities in the Republic of Croatia and the Republic of Bosnia and Herzegovina to establish a union between them, since this would be inconsistent with the Council's commitment to the sovereignty and territorial integrity of the Republic of Croatia and the Republic of Bosnia and Herzegovina.

The Security Council stresses that there can be no military solution to the conflict and calls upon the parties to reaffirm their commitment to a peaceful resolution of their differences.

The Security Council notes with distress the loss of life and casualties which have been suffered by UNCRO and extends its condolences to the families of the bereaved.

The Security Council will remain seized of the matter.

*Meeting number.* SC 3545.

**Report of the Secretary-General.** In keeping with Security Council **resolution 981(1995)**, the Secretary-General on 3 August reported[(34)] on developments in Croatia during the past four months, including their effect on UNCRO's ability to implement its mandate. He stated that given the high degree of uncertainty of developments in Croatia, which were inextricably linked with those in Bosnia and Herzegovina, it was not currently possible to make a recommendation as to the future of UNCRO.

Although there had been no further large-scale hostilities since the 1 May offensive when the Croatian Army and police had taken control of those areas of Western Slavonia previously held by the Croatian Serbs, continuous skirmishes, exchanges of fire, troop deployments within the zone of separation and increased violations of the 10- and 20-kilometre heavy-weapons exclusion zones had created a high level of tension in the three remaining Sectors. Those actions by both sides had eroded the credibility of the cease-fire agreement to the point where neither appeared committed to its key provisions. As of 30 July, there were 83 reported violations of the separation zone, 47 by the Krajina Serb side and 36 by the Croatian side, the Secretary-General stated.

Contrary to Croatia's assurances that it would not pursue military objectives before the end of the current UNCRO mandate, the attack launched on 4 June in the Mount Dinara area by the combined Croatian and Bosnian Croat forces had led to the seizure and occupation of positions in areas covered by the cease-fire agreement—indicating a possible decision by the Government to reintegrate the Serb Krajina region by force. The military situation and the constant restrictions imposed by both sides on freedom of movement had prevented UNCRO from taking any significant remedial action and, at times, even from monitoring the situation.

There were fire and shelling exchanges as the Krajina Serbs launched retaliatory attacks against Croatian positions in Sector South, using small arms, mortar and artillery, as well as air strikes from Udbina. Efforts by the Special Representative and UNCRO to defuse the situation had been thwarted. In line with its actions to the west of Sector South, the Croatian Army was conducting a series of exercises west of Sisak and south-west of Karlovac in the immediate proximity of the separation zone, further increasing tension and insecurity. The Krajina Serbs, who had also been conducting extensive military training, had placed Sectors North and South in a state of high alert and under martial law.

Croatian Defence Council (HVO) forces, apparently supported by Croatian Army (HV) elements, had also continued their attacks in the Livansko Polje area of western Bosnia and Herzegovina, adjacent to the Croatian border, capturing Bosansko Grahovo and Glamoc on 28 July, thus directly threatening Knin and cutting its main supply route to Banja Luka. Those forces had moved closer to the international border and set up a blocking position near Strmica. Between 25 June and 30 July, approximately 2,861 Croatian Army troops with vehicles and equipment had been observed crossing into Bosnia and Herzegovina at Kamensko, causing some 12,000 to 14,000 Bosnian Serbs to flee towards Banja Luka.

Sector North saw relatively little activity except in the area bordering the Bihac pocket. In response to an attack by the Bosnian Army's Fifth Corps on the Krajina Serb–controlled territory in Sector North to the pocket's east and west sides, the "Army of Serb Krajina" ("ARSK") and the separatist Bosnians under Fikret Abdic, supported by Bosnian Serb artillery along the southern confrontation line, mounted a major counter-offensive on 19 July that restored the 1994 confrontation line in the north-west and moved the western confrontation line 3 to 5 kilometres eastwards. Those operations in the Bihac pocket had caused some 8,000 civilians to abandon their homes and flee to Cazin. UNHCR humanitarian assistance to Bihac was obstructed by the Krajina Serbs, while that to the Sectors was obstructed by Croatia.

The Secretary-General noted the numerous restrictions to UNCRO's freedom of movement which impeded its monitoring of the cease-fire agreement, adding that UNCRO had received no cooperation from the Krajina Serbs in its efforts to deploy along the international border. From the 21 border checkpoints it had so far set up, it had observed a total of 7,946 soldiers with 1,212 vehicles entering and 8,610 soldiers with 1,049 vehicles leaving Croatia.

The Secretary-General also noted evidence of significant qualitative and quantitative improvements to the military capabilities of both sides. Croatia had acquired a minimum of 12 Mig-21 aircraft, and was capable of deploying six armed Mi-24 attack helicopters and new types of small arms and military vehicles. The Krajina Serbs had likewise recently displayed new arms and equipment, including small arms, night observation devices and re-engineered naval surface-to-surface missiles. After their set-back in Western Slavonia, the Krajina Serbs appointed a new military commander to professionalize the army and formulate a new military doctrine. The resultant improved army discipline had reportedly reduced robbery, hijackings and threats to UNCRO personnel and equipment.

Political trends within the area administered by the Krajina Serbs had remained volatile: differences had arisen between the regional factions in Sector East, where "separatist tendencies" favoured joining Yugoslavia (Serbia and Montenegro), and those in Sectors North and South, which favoured union between the Krajina and Bosnian Serbs.

As to the humanitarian situation, both UNHCR and UNPF had lodged strong protests with Yugoslavia (Serbia and Montenegro) in response to reports of the forced mobilization there of more than 2,500 Serb refugees for military service in Bosnia and Herzegovina and in the Krajina.

From 9 to 30 May, some 2,170 Serbs voluntarily left Western Slavonia under UNCRO's "Operation Safe Passage". UNHCR and UNCRO assisted another 130 Serbs to leave for Sector East and 16 for Banja Luka via Sector North, and were also assisting in the return to Western Slavonia of 84 Serb refugees. Of some 1,475 Serbs originally detained by Croatia after the 1 May offensive on Sector West, about 130 remained in detention. As for legal proceedings instituted against those accused of war crimes, there was concern regarding the nature of the charges and whether the right to legal counsel was being respected.

The Prevlaka peninsula remained an area of strategic interest to both Croatia and Yugoslavia (Serbia and Montenegro). Since the meeting of the Joint Inter-State Commission, convened by the Special Representative on 25 July, there had been relative stability in the area, especially since Croatia halted construction of defence works in the demilitarized zone. Ongoing local bilateral water negotiations were among the indications of the increased readiness of the parties to cooperate. However, their different interpretations of the established UN security modalities remained a potentially destabilizing factor. Furthermore, movement restrictions imposed by both parties on UN military observers inhibited investigations of violations. The Secretary-General had asked his Special Representative, in conjunction with the Co-Chairmen of the ICFY Steering Committee, to seek consensus on the modalities envisaged under Council resolutions 779(1992)[35] and **981(1995)**.

**SECURITY COUNCIL ACTION (3 August)**

The Security Council met on 3 August and, following consultations among its members, authorized the President to make the statement below[36] on the Council's behalf:

The Security Council is deeply concerned at the deterioration in the situation in and around the Republic of Croatia.

The Security Council fully supports the efforts of the Secretary-General's Special Representative and of the Co-Chairman of the Steering Committee of the International Conference on the Former Yugoslavia to defuse the situation, in line with the Council's previous resolutions.

The Security Council stresses that there can be no military solution to the conflict in Croatia and welcomes the holding of talks between the parties in

Geneva earlier today. It calls on both parties to commit themselves fully to that process, and to acceptance of the Draft Agreement drawn up by the Co-Chairman as a basis for continuing those talks.

The Security Council demands that the parties halt all military actions and exercise the utmost restraint.

*Meeting number.* SC 3560.

### Sector North (northern Krajina) and Sector South (southern Krajina)

**Communication from Croatia.** Croatia informed the Security Council on 4 August that, at 0500 hours that day, the Croatian military and police forces had begun a decisive operation aimed at restoring the rule of law, constitutional order and public safety in the occupied territories of Croatia, as defined in General Assembly resolution 49/43,[37] and helping to sustain the defence of the UN-designated safe area of Bihac.[38]

Croatia provided some major reasons for its action: the Croatian Serbs' outright rejection of the Government's proposal, at the 3 August ICFY-mediated negotiations in Geneva, for the immediate reintegration into Croatia of the territories they occupied; the continued attacks on Croatian urban centres from the UNPAs; the unrelenting siege of the Bihac safe area, regarding which Croatia recalled its warning that it would be compelled to take action to secure the safe-area status of Bihac, if threatened, in order ultimately to secure Croatia's strategic interests;[39] the failure to implement the UNCRO mandate, especially control of Croatia's international borders to prevent military interference from Yugoslavia (Serbia and Montenegro); the frustration of the Governments of the Republic and Federation of Bosnia and Herzegovina over UNPROFOR's failure to discharge its mandate, especially with respect to preventing attacks on the safe areas; Croatia's obligation to fulfil its commitments under the Split Declaration of 22 July 1995,[40] among other agreements, for the joint defence of the two Governments against Serbian aggression; and the international community's continued policy of appeasement towards Yugoslavia (Serbia and Montenegro), sponsor of the occupation of parts of Croatia and of Bosnia and Herzegovina.

Croatia said it would ensure the security of UNCRO troops, whom it considered repositioning to prevent their being taken hostage by the Serbs. It reaffirmed its intention to minimize civilian casualties and uphold all principles of international humanitarian law in the course of its operations. It referred to President Tudjman's appeal to the Serb population in the occupied territories to lay down their arms, and his assurances of amnesty for all mobilized Serb irregular forces and of guarantees for the safety and constitutional rights of the Serb community within Croatia. In the post-conflict restoration of Croatian authority, Croatia offered its cooperation to promote respect for human rights and reconciliation, and to help in the reconstruction of the occupied territories.

**SECURITY COUNCIL ACTION (4 August)**

The Council convened on 4 August and, following consultations among its members, authorized the President to make the statement below[41] on the Council's behalf:

The Security Council is deeply concerned at the resumption of hostilities in and around the Republic of Croatia. The Council recalls the statement of its President of 3 August 1995. It strongly deplores the decision by the Croatian Government to launch a broad military offensive, thereby unacceptably escalating the conflict, with the risk of further consequent attacks by whatever party, and demands that all military action cease immediately and that there be full compliance with all Council resolutions including resolution 994(1995).

The Security Council condemns any shelling of civilian targets. It demands that no military action be taken against civilians and that their human rights be fully respected. It reminds the parties of their responsibilities under international humanitarian law and reiterates that those who commit violations of international humanitarian law will be held individually responsible in respect of such acts. The Council calls on the parties to cooperate fully with UNCRO, the United Nations High Commissioner for Refugees and the International Committee of the Red Cross in ensuring access and protection to the local civilian population as appropriate.

The Security Council strongly condemns attacks by Croatian government forces on personnel of the United Nations peace-keeping forces which have resulted in casualties, including the death of one member of the peace-keeping forces. It demands that such attacks cease immediately and that all detained personnel be released. It also reminds the parties, and in particular the Croatian Government, that they have an obligation to respect United Nations personnel, to ensure their safety and freedom of movement at all times and to enable UNCRO to fulfil its mandate in accordance with the relevant Security Council resolutions. The Council expresses condolences to the Government of Denmark and to the family of the member of the United Nations peace-keeping forces who lost his life.

The Security Council deeply regrets the breakdown of the talks which began in Geneva on 3 August 1995. It calls upon the Croatian Government to return to the talks. It reiterates that there can be no military solution to the conflict in Croatia. It reaffirms its call for an unreserved commitment to the search for a negotiated settlement and to resumption of talks on the basis of the Draft Agreement drawn up by the Co-Chairman of the Steering Committee of the International Conference on the Former Yugoslavia.

The Security Council will remain seized of the matter, and will consider any further measures that may be necessary.

*Meeting number.* SC 3561.

**Other communications.** The Croatian offensive on the Krajinas was the subject of an EU declaration on 4 August, demanding an end to Croatia's military operations, suspending negotiations on a trade and cooperation agreement with that country, and condemning the Krajina Serbs' involvement in the attacks on the Bihac pocket.[42] The Russian Federation, in a letter of the same date, stated it was forced to conclude that Croatia's delivery of ultimatums to the Croatian Serbs at the Geneva talks of 3 August indicated it had already decided to seek not a political but an exclusively military solution.[43]

In four letters written between 4 and 7 August, Yugoslavia (Serbia and Montenegro) condemned the Croatian aggression against the "Republic of Serb Krajina" and demanded that the Security Council take steps to compel Croatia to withdraw from the territory of that "Republic";[44] drew attention to the continuing Croatian aggression, to violations of international humanitarian law, especially ethnic cleansing, and to the displacement of more than 100,000 Krajina Serbs;[45] requested that the Special Representative and General Peeters of UNPROFOR intervene to prevent the further massacre of officers and soldiers of the "Republic of Serb Krajina";[46] and demanded that the international community and the Council in particular take measures to put an end to Croatia's aggression, killing of innocent civilians and ethnic cleansing.[47]

**Letter from the Secretary-General.** On 7 August, the Secretary-General conveyed information to the Security Council President to the effect that tensions had remained high in the area of UNCRO operations since the Croatian Army's takeover of Western Slavonia in early May.[48] Croatian Army mobilization, troop movements and live-firing exercises had increased throughout June and July.

The pace of events gathered momentum after the Presidents of Croatia and Bosnia and Herzegovina signed the Split Declaration on 22 July,[40] which committed Croatia militarily to assist Bosnia and Herzegovina in the defence of the Bihac pocket, under siege since 19 July by the Bosnian separatists and "ARSK". Responding to the HVO/HV capture of Bosansko Grahovo and Glamoc in western Bosnia and Herzegovina on 28 July, the Krajina and Bosnian Serbs declared states of war against the Croats and mobilized their respective armies.

As the Croatian Army continued a major troop build-up around Sectors North and South, the Supreme Defence Council of the Croatian and Bosnian Serbs convened on 1 August to appeal to all Serbs and to Yugoslavia (Serbia and Montenegro) to assist in defence of Serb territory. Meanwhile, in a meeting with President Tudjman on 29 July,

the Special Representative sought Croatia's participation in political and military talks with Knin to forestall what appeared to be an imminent military confrontation. In indicating the Government's willingness to participate, the President stressed that talks must be followed by progress on the ground, failing which Croatia would do whatever it deemed necessary to redress the situation. The President specifically insisted on the reopening of the Adriatic oil pipeline within 24 hours, rapid agreement on the opening of the Zagreb-Knin-Split railway, and immediate progress on the political reintegration of the Serbs on the basis of Croatia's Constitution and Law on Minorities.

In emergency talks on 30 July with local Serb authorities, the Special Representative secured a six-point commitment[48] whereby they would: fully withdraw their forces from the Bihac pocket; desist from further cross-border interference, with the expectation that the Bosnian Army's Fifth Corps would take no further offensive action in the pocket; allow unhindered UNCRO monitoring of the border area between Krajina and the Bihac pocket; continue talks regarding setting up border monitoring posts in the Mount Dinara area; and allow the unhindered delivery of humanitarian assistance to the pocket, provided such assistance would also be allowed into the Krajina region. In addition, the "ARSK" commander would be prepared to meet with the Croatian Army commander under UNPF auspices as early as 31 July.

In a written reply,[48] President Tudjman rejected the six-point commitment on the grounds that it did not meet Croatia's terms, especially its firm request that UNCRO monitor not just the border towards the Bihac pocket and along the Mount Dinara area, but also the internationally recognized borders between Croatia and Bosnia and Herzegovina and between Croatia and Serbia, to which new Yugoslav Army formations and equipment had been transferred from across the Danube. The President stated that only under certain conditions would he propose holding negotiations with representatives of the "rebel Croatian Serbs from the occupied areas", namely: that negotiations should be with other than the "ARSK" commander, Milan Martic, among the war criminals listed by the International Tribunal for the Former Yugoslavia; and that negotiations would begin if the oil pipeline passing through the occupied areas became operational within 24 hours, if direct discussions would include opening all communication lines through those areas, particularly the Zagreb-Knin-Split railway line, and if Croatia's Constitution and Constitutional Law were immediately to be applied in the occupied areas.

At a preliminary round of talks in Geneva on 3 August, chaired by the UN Co-Chairman of the

ICFY Steering Committee, the Croatian Government was firm in its position that the local Serb leadership immediately accept reintegration under Croatia's Constitution and Laws. The local Serb leadership, on the other hand, called for a complete cessation of hostilities as a starting-point, from which discussions on other issues would proceed. Following a series of bilateral meetings, the Co-Chairman presented a list of seven points covering, *inter alia*, the reopening of the oil pipeline and railway in question, and negotiations on a final settlement on the basis of the Zagreb Four plan. The Government rejected the seven-point paper as not addressing its fundamental concern regarding reintegration of the Krajina Serbs.

Despite concerted efforts by the United Nations and various Member States to avert an outbreak of hostilities, the Croatian Army launched a major offensive against Sectors North and South (northern and southern Krajina) at 0500 hours on 4 August. A significant number of UN observation posts were overrun and some came under fire, direct and indirect. On two occasions, UN troops and Serb prisoners were used as human shields by Croatian Army units as they pursued their offensive. Notwithstanding efforts by the Special Representative and the Force Commander to seek assurances for the safety of all UN personnel from the Croatian Commission for Relations with UNCRO and from the Chief of Staff of the Croatian Army, the United Nations had suffered 18 casualties, including three dead and two seriously injured.

On 6 August, the Special Representative secured a nine-point agreement[48] with the Croatian Commission on measures to: cope with the humanitarian difficulties caused by the offensive; monitor the human rights situation; permit the safe return of displaced persons; and guarantee the inviolability of UN premises and establishments, as well as all assets and those therein.

Also on 6 August, the Co-Chairmen of the ICFY Steering Committee, along with the EU Presidency and its External Relations Commissioner, met with Croatia's Foreign Minister to discuss the political consequences of the Croatian offensive. Croatia assured them that it would investigate reported incidents of attacks on UN troops and would guarantee access by humanitarian organizations to civilians displaced by the fighting.

**Communications (8-10 August).** On 8 August, the Russian Federation stated[49] that the massive Croatian offensive negated all efforts to continue the search for a political settlement. Croatia's inclination forcibly to integrate the Serb-populated areas had been indirectly encouraged from the capitals of major States. The principles of a just settlement, it said, were being sacrificed to the philosophy of *fait accompli*. Drawing attention to the

exodus that had begun of more than 150,000 Serbs from Krajina, the Russian Federation said it expected the Secretary-General to take all measures to protect the civilian population, provide humanitarian assistance to the refugees, and exert pressure on Croatia fully to respect their human rights. It was of paramount importance to continue the UNCRO operation, Russia said, to prevent a complete humanitarian catastrophe and to ensure the objective monitoring of Croatia's actions with respect to the Serb population that had come under its control.

On 9 August, Yugoslavia (Serbia and Montenegro) expressed[50] both astonishment and disappointment that the Security Council had still not convened an emergency meeting to condemn Croatia's brutal aggression. Such inaction and lenient attitude, it claimed, directly encouraged Croatian military aggression against Krajina and even against Bosnia and Herzegovina. Yugoslavia (Serbia and Montenegro) urged the Council to condemn Croatia's aggression in the strongest terms, bring it to a halt and demand the withdrawal of the Croatian Army to its pre-offensive positions. It was moreover incumbent on the Council, Yugoslavia (Serbia and Montenegro) stressed, to initiate action to identify, bring to trial and punish those responsible for genocide and other war crimes against the Serbs, including murder, the gunning down of trapped soldiers and civilians, the shelling of refugees in flight, mistreatment of civilians and POWs alike, blockade of humanitarian supplies, and mass destruction of Serb property.

On 10 August, Yugoslavia (Serbia and Montenegro) reiterated[51] its disappointment and resentment over the Council's reluctance to condemn Croatia's aggression against the "Republic of Serb Krajina", along with what it termed as monstrous crimes committed by the Croatian Army. It appealed to the Secretary-General to use his good offices to persuade the Council to adopt a resolution embodying such condemnation, a call for an immediate stop to the aggression and for the withdrawal of the Croatian Army from the UNPAs, guaranteed protection of the Krajina Serb populations encircled by the Croatian Army, particularly in Topusko, Petrova Gora and Glina, and punitive measures against Croatia for its aggression, war crimes, ethnic cleansing and human rights violations.

Meanwhile, on 9 August, Bosnia and Herzegovina denied[52] the allegations of UN officials that the Bosnian Army's Fifth Corps had engaged in unlawful acts in Croatia during the offensive on the Krajina region; however, should evidence surface to support such allegations, it would, it said, bring to justice all those responsible for any violations of international humanitarian law.

In the light of the Secretary-General's 3 August report and 7 August letter, the Security Council met on 10 August and adopted **resolution 1009(1995)**.

*The Security Council,*

*Recalling* all its previous resolutions on the conflicts in the territory of the former Yugoslavia and in particular resolutions 981(1995) of 31 March 1995, 990(1995) of 28 April 1995 and 994(1995) of 17 May 1995,

*Reaffirming* the statements of its President of 3 and 4 August 1995 and deeply concerned that the demands set out therein have not yet been fully complied with by the Government of the Republic of Croatia,

*Having considered* the report of the Secretary-General of 3 August 1995 and his letter of 7 August 1995,

*Noting with concern* reports of violations of resolution 713(1991) of 25 September 1991 as reflected in the Secretary-General's report of 3 August 1995,

*Deeply regretting* the breakdown of the talks which began in Geneva on 3 August 1995,

*Affirming* its commitment to the search for an overall negotiated settlement of the conflicts in the former Yugoslavia ensuring the sovereignty and territorial integrity of all the States there within their internationally recognized borders, stressing the importance it attaches to the mutual recognition thereof, and in this context welcoming all international efforts to facilitate a negotiated solution to the conflict in the Republic of Croatia,

*Strongly deploring* the broad military offensive launched on 4 August 1995 by the Government of the Republic of Croatia, thereby unacceptably escalating the conflict, with the risk of further consequent attacks by whatever party,

*Condemning* the shelling of civilian targets,

*Deeply concerned* at the grave situation of persons displaced from their homes as a result of the conflict and at reports of violations of international humanitarian law,

*Stressing the need* to protect the rights of the local Serb population,

*Condemning* in the strongest terms the unacceptable acts by Croatian government forces against personnel of the United Nations peace-keeping forces, including those which have resulted in the death of a Danish member of those forces and two Czech members and expressing its condolences to the Governments concerned,

*Noting* the agreement between the Republic of Croatia and the United Nations Peace Forces signed on 6 August 1995 and stressing the need for the Government of the Republic of Croatia to adhere strictly to its provisions,

*Reaffirming* its determination to ensure the security and freedom of movement of the personnel of the United Nations peace-keeping operations in the territory of the former Yugoslavia, and, to these ends, acting under Chapter VII of the Charter of the United Nations,

1. *Demands* that the Government of the Republic of Croatia cease immediately all military actions and that there be full compliance with all Council resolutions, including resolution 994(1995);

2. *Demands further* that the Government of the Republic of Croatia, in conformity with internationally recognized standards and in compliance with the agreement of 6 August 1995 between the Republic of Croatia and the United Nations Peace Forces (a) respect fully the rights of the local Serb population including their rights to remain, leave or return in safety, (b) allow access to this population by international humanitarian organizations, and (c) create conditions conducive to the return of those persons who have left their homes;

3. *Reminds* the Government of the Republic of Croatia of its responsibility to allow access for representatives of the International Committee of the Red Cross to members of the local Serb forces who are detained by the Croatian government forces;

4. *Reiterates* that all those who commit violations of international humanitarian law will be held individually responsible in respect of such acts;

5. *Requests* the Secretary-General in cooperation with the United Nations High Commissioner for Refugees, the United Nations High Commissioner for Human Rights, the International Committee of the Red Cross and other relevant international humanitarian institutions to assess the humanitarian situation of the local Serb population including the problem of refugees and displaced persons, and to report thereon as soon as possible;

6. *Demands* that the Government of the Republic of Croatia fully respect the status of United Nations personnel, refrain from any attacks against them, bring to justice those responsible for any such attacks, and ensure the safety and freedom of movement of United Nations personnel at all times, and requests the Secretary-General to keep the Council informed of steps taken and decisions rendered in this regard;

7. *Urges* the parties and others concerned to exercise maximum restraint in and around Sector East and requests the Secretary-General to keep the situation there under review;

8. *Reminds* all parties of their obligation to comply fully with the provisions of resolution 816(1993) of 31 March 1993;

9. *Reiterates* its call for a negotiated settlement which guarantees the rights of all communities and urges the Government of the Republic of Croatia to resume talks under the auspices of the Co-Chairmen of the Steering Committee of the International Conference on the Former Yugoslavia;

10. *Requests* the Secretary-General to report to the Council within three weeks of the adoption of this resolution on the implementation of this resolution and on the implications of the situation for UNCRO and expresses its readiness to consider promptly his recommendations in relation to UNCRO;

11. *Decides* to remain actively seized of the matter and to consider further measures to achieve compliance with this resolution.

Security Council resolution 1009(1995)

10 August 1995     Meeting 3563     Adopted unanimously

Draft prepared in consultations among Council members (S/1995/676).

**Report of the Secretary-General.** Pursuant to Security Council **resolution 1009(1995)**, the Secretary-General submitted a report[53] on 23 August to assist the Council in considering the implications for the UNCRO mandate of Croatia's 4 August military offensive on Sectors North and

South. The Secretary-General reported that since his letter of 7 August neither party had ceased military actions, nor had they complied fully with relevant Council resolutions.

The offensive against Sector South, which had been preceded by intense shelling, resulted in the fall of Knin on 5 August. With the collapse of the Krajina Serb defences, 700 civilians took shelter in UNCRO's headquarters in the Sector, while large numbers fled for Bosnian Serb–held territory. Meanwhile, the Bosnian Army's Fifth Corps launched a cross-border offensive against the Krajina Serbs in the Licko Ptrovo Selo area, linking up with the Croatian Army at Rakovica.

In Sector North, where resistance was stronger, particularly around Turnaj and Petrinja, attempts to conclude an agreement for the surrender of Krajina Serb elements collapsed when the latter tried to take heavy-weapons systems with them as they withdrew. However, a cease-fire was concluded on 8 August for the Topusko and Glina areas, providing for the surrender of Serb heavy weapons, the withdrawal of Krajina Serb soldiers with side-arms only, and the safe passage of civilians from those areas. A convoy of refugees from Sector North, moving through Sisak as authorized under that agreement, was nevertheless attacked by a mob of Croatian civilians on 9 August, resulting in injuries to many, death to one and damage to a large number of vehicles. Heavy fighting took place in the Dvor area, where UNCRO's Danish battalion reported witnessing a military unit of unknown identity kill 11 disabled civilians.

In the course of the fighting, several incidents occurred in which the safety of UN troops was not sufficiently considered by the parties. A total of 98 UN observation posts were destroyed by the Croatian Army, which also arrested and temporarily disarmed UN soldiers and seized UN equipment. On 5 August, several UN soldiers and a group of Krajina Serb POWs were used as human shields by a Croatian Army unit which forced them to walk ahead of its forward lines. In all, four UN peace-keepers died—three as a result of actions by Croatian troops and one by those of Krajina Serbs; 16 others were injured. In response to a vigorous protest lodged by UNPF, Croatia's Foreign Minister promised an investigation into the incidents.

As the situation in the former Sector South stabilized, Croatia's civilian authorities asserted control over the area and displaced Croatians began returning to identify and claim their homes. On 12 August, the Zagreb-Knin-Split railway started operating.

A humanitarian crisis of significant proportions had been created by the mass exodus of Krajina Serbs, estimated at 150,000 by UNHCR, to Yugoslavia (Serbia and Montenegro) through Bosnia and Herzegovina. Only about 3,500 Krajina Serbs remained in the former Sector North and about 2,000 in the former Sector South. Another group of some 21,000 refugees, largely Bosnian Muslims from the former "Autonomous Province of Western Bosnia" under Fikret Abdic, made its way from Velika Kladusa into Croatia. Through negotiations between Croatia, Bosnia and Herzegovina and Abdic representatives, agreement was reached for the return of the group to Velika Kladusa; many were unwilling to do so, however, without guarantees for their safety.

In view of the rapidly deteriorating humanitarian situation, the Special Representative set up a humanitarian crisis cell, composed of UNPF staff, to collate information on the observance of human rights, communicate with all humanitarian affairs agencies and coordinate responses through four recently created human rights action teams. The looting and burning of abandoned houses, as well as of crops, in the two former Sectors were reported by UNCRO soldiers and civilian police, as well as by human rights action teams. Some incidents of physical violence were also reported.

ICRC, which reported favourably on its access to all detained persons, had registered more than 600 detainees, most of whom had been subsequently released.

Commenting on the impact on UNCRO of recent events in the former Sectors North and South, the Secretary-General said that with the collapse and departure of the political leadership and armed forces of the Krajina Serbs, no longer was there a requirement, except in Sector East, that UNCRO monitor or control the confrontation line, separation zone, weapons-storage sites and areas of limitation set by the 1994 cease-fire agreement. Nor did UNCRO have to assist with economic projects across former confrontation lines, as specified in the 1994 economic agreement. The Croatian Government had established full control over its territory, with the exception of Sector East, and over access to its international borders. The remaining aspects of the UNCRO mandate, including confidence-building, assisting in humanitarian activities, and the protection of refugees and displaced persons had become primarily the responsibility of the Croatian Government and could in any case be performed without the presence of UNCRO infantry battalions, the Secretary-General stated.

Croatia's reintegration of former Sectors West, North and South by force had eliminated the need for infantry battalions in those areas. The UNCRO Force Commander had therefore begun the immediate reduction of UNCRO's troop strength to within the level authorized by Council **resolution 990(1995)**, that is, 8,750 troops. The Secretary-General recommended Council approval of the further repatriation, during the remainder of the current mandate, of all remaining battalions, except two in Sector East.

In the light of the drastically changed situation on the ground, the Secretary-General had instructed his Special Representative to consult with the parties regarding a precise definition of UNCRO's mandate in Sector East (see below) and to discuss with the Government what tasks, if any, UNCRO could usefully continue to perform elsewhere in Croatia. Those could include: monitoring and good offices in relation to the Prevlaka peninsula and Dubrovnik; monitoring of Croatia's international border with Bosnia and Herzegovina; and monitoring of the Croatian police and other matters relating to human rights in those parts of Croatia where a minority Serb community remained.

The Secretary-General recommended no changes with respect to UNPF-HQ in Zagreb and the logistics bases there and elsewhere. He pointed out in this connection, however, that Croatia had yet to implement fully certain of its commitments under the status-of-forces agreement, concluded on 15 May, regulating the presence and functioning of the UNPF elements in the country, including making the necessary premises available rent-free and exempting UN forces and operations from various taxes and tolls. The amounts involved were substantial, running at about $2 million a month for taxes and fuel alone.

**SECURITY COUNCIL ACTION (29 August and 7 September)**

On 29 August, the Security Council President conveyed[54] to the Secretary-General the Council's agreement with his recommendation concerning the repatriation of remaining UNCRO battalions, with the exception of the two in Sector East. The President further conveyed the Council's support for the possible future configuration and tasks of UNCRO as described, and expressed the Council's readiness to consider further recommendations. As to the status-of-forces agreement with Croatia, the Council looked to the Croatian Government to implement fully and unconditionally the terms of the agreement in all its aspects. The Council further expressed concern over the humanitarian problems described by the Secretary-General and stressed the importance it attached to the fulfilment of the provisions of the relevant Council resolutions and to the international community's efforts to alleviate the plight of refugees and displaced persons.

On 7 September, the Council met and, after consultations among its members, authorized the President to make the following statement[55] on the Council's behalf:

The Security Council has considered the report of the Secretary-General of 23 August 1995 submitted pursuant to its resolution 1009(1995) of 10 August 1995 on Croatia and in particular the humanitarian situation and human rights violations described therein.

The Security Council expresses its deep concern at the grave situation of refugees and persons displaced during the Croatian offensive and at reports of violations of international humanitarian law as described in the report of the Secretary-General of 23 August 1995. The Council shares the view of the Secretary-General that the mass exodus of the local Serb population has created a humanitarian crisis of significant proportions. The Council is also concerned by reports of human rights violations including the burning of houses, looting of property and killings and demands that the Government of Croatia immediately investigate all such reports and take appropriate measures to put an end to such acts.

The Security Council reiterates its demand that the Government of the Republic of Croatia respect fully the rights of the local Serb population including their right to remain or return in safety.

The Security Council welcomes efforts made by the Secretary-General in coordination with international humanitarian organizations in response to this acute humanitarian situation. It calls upon all Member States to provide urgent humanitarian relief and assistance to these refugees and displaced persons.

The Security Council reiterates that all those who commit violations of international humanitarian law will be held individually responsible in respect of such acts. The Council reiterates in this context that all States shall cooperate fully with the International Tribunal established pursuant to its resolution 827(1993) and its organs.

The Security Council will remain actively seized of the matter.

*Meeting number.* SC 3573.

**Further report of the Secretary-General.** In a further report[56] of 29 September, the Secretary-General conveyed to the Security Council the results of the Special Representative's consultations with the Croatian Government and the local Serb leadership on the tasks of UNCRO, in Sector East and in other areas of Croatia, for the remainder of its current mandate under what he called the radically changed situation in the country.

The requirements arising from that situation were stipulated in the report. First, both parties asked that UNCRO remain in Sector East to continue its mandated tasks and to facilitate the development of a peaceful solution. In that regard, it had been made clear to the parties that a new spirit of cooperation with UNCRO was indispensable. Second, in view of reports of continuing human rights abuses in the former Sectors North and South, the Government needed to create conditions conducive to the return of the Serbs who had fled (90 per cent) and for the residual Serbs (10 per cent) to remain. UNCRO could play a valuable role towards realizing that objective, the Secretary-General maintained. Third, the Government had asked that UNCRO monitor its border with both Bosnia and Herzegovina and Yugoslavia (Serbia and Montenegro). Its concern included those areas of Croatia close to or contiguous with Bosnian Serb–controlled territory in Bosnia and Herzegovina, including Dubrovnik and the Prevlaka peninsula.

Accordingly, the Special Representative proposed that the UNCRO mandate, as defined in Council **resolution 981(1995)**, be modified to include performance of: those functions envisaged in the 1994 cease-fire and economic agreements only with respect to Sector East (paragraphs 3 *(a)* and *(b)*); monitoring and reporting only at the border crossings in that Sector where UNCRO remained deployed (3 *(d)*); and the new task of observing and reporting on military incidents in the vicinity of the Croatia–Bosnia and Herzegovina international border.

Withdrawal of UNCRO infantry battalions, except for the two in Sector East, was in progress, and troop strength should be reduced to about 2,500 in October. In the remaining mandate period, the tasks in Sector East could be accomplished by retaining the current numbers of infantry; those in the rest of Croatia could be performed by the existing UN military observers (UNMOs), civilian police and civilian support staff. The border crossing points in Sector East would be maintained by the battalions currently deployed there, while other border monitoring actions would be executed by UNMO mobile patrols.

In view of both sides' undertaking to improve their level of compliance with existing agreements and of their cooperation with UNCRO, the Secretary-General recommended that the Council approve the foregoing arrangements. They would apply to the remainder of UNCRO's current mandate, pending ongoing negotiations on the ultimate future of Sector East in the context of an overall political settlement of the crisis in the former Yugoslavia.

On 10 October, the Council agreed to the arrangements as recommended.[57]

### Sector East

On 11 August, Yugoslavia (Serbia and Montenegro) warned[58] of a possible imminent armed attack on Sector East (Eastern Slavonia, including Baranja and Sirmium), based on reports of a massive troop build-up by the Croatian Army in the area and provocative artillery strikes against civilian targets and ''ARSK'' positions; an all-out attack on Sector East could endanger Yugoslavia (Serbia and Montenegro) and Hungary, leading to a spillover of the conflict to the wider Balkan region.

**Reports of the Secretary-General (August, September).** As described in the Secretary-

General's report of 23 August,[53] the situation in Sector East deteriorated rapidly as events unfolded in Sectors North and South during Croatia's 4 August offensive on those areas. Local Serb forces and the Croatian Army exchanged artillery, mortar and small-arms fire, and both began deploying in the separation zone. Tension and uncertainty among the local Serbs was reflected in a breakdown of law and order that saw the hijacking of UN vehicles, harassment of UN personnel and the temporary detention of five Sector headquarters staff by Serb elements. Both sides had adopted an aggressive stance against UNCRO, firing on its positions and seizing 16 of its observations posts, 14 by the Croatian Army and 2 by the Serb forces. Fearing an imminent Croatian offensive, the Serb forces sought tactically advantageous positions within the separation zone, while the Croatian forces appeared poised to apply pressure on the Sector by forcing UNCRO to evacuate its observation posts.

Adding to the tension were reports of the presence of ''volunteers'' from Yugoslavia (Serbia and Montenegro), of some 600 to 700 Serb police seen entering Baranja by way of the Batina bridge, and of Yugoslav Army units massed on the Yugoslav side of the Danube. Severe restrictions on all UN movements imposed by both sides critically hampered UNCRO's ability, not only to implement its mandate, but also to conduct such simple tasks as resupplying observation posts.

The Secretary-General felt that UNCRO's immediate task in Sector East was to re-establish the regime created by the 1994 cease-fire agreement. If that could be achieved, there would be a continuing role for UN forces (infantry, logistics units, UNMOs) in the Sector, which he would recommend only if the parties demonstrated a new spirit of cooperation. That required, *inter alia*, according UNCRO unrestricted freedom of movement, returning all seized observation posts and putting a complete stop to the hijacking of UN vehicles. The Special Representative had been instructed to pursue consultations with the Croatian Government and the local Serb leadership in order to define in detail a possible mandate for UNCRO that the Secretary-General could recommend to the Council.

In a 29 September report,[56] the Secretary-General recommended to the Council approval of the modified mandate for UNCRO, including those arrangements applicable to Sector East. He further stated that, after intensive consultations with both parties, the Special Representative had been assured of their willingness to resolve the issue of Sector East through negotiation.

The military commanders of both sides had met nine times between 25 August and 25 September in a Joint Commission convened by the UNCRO

Commander of Sector East in pursuit of a plan to stabilize the situation, which called for troop and weapons withdrawal from the separation zone, restoration of full freedom of movement to UNCRO and the return of seized observation posts. In addition, the local Serb authorities had given their word to comply with all the requirements of Council **resolution 981(1995)**.

Reporting to the General Assembly on 18 October[22] on implementation of its request that Yugoslavia (Serbia and Montenegro) immediately cease any military and logistic support to the self-proclaimed authorities in the Serb-controlled parts of Croatia, the Secretary-General pointed to the difficulty of obtaining accurate information in that regard, but noted that the reported influx of Serb police into Baranja via the Batina bridge could be presumed to happen elsewhere, and that many roads from Serbia led into the southern part of Sector East, unmonitored by UNCRO, by which food, fuel and weapons could be brought in. Much of the Sector's infrastructure, including electricity, telephone lines, railway links and postal services, was provided by or linked with Yugoslavia (Serbia and Montenegro). The significant economic cooperation between them was thus based not only on recent circumstances but also on historic trade patterns.

The Secretary-General also spoke of persistent concern over the activities of Serb paramilitary groups, which had been operating in and from Sector East since fighting began in 1991. The so-called Arkan Tigers, whose training facility in Erdut was only a few hundred metres from the UNCRO Sector headquarters, were reported to have been responsible for recent atrocities in north-western Bosnia.

### Basic Agreement on the Region of Eastern Slavonia, Baranja and Western Sirmium

Following intensive negotiations throughout September and October, undertaken by the UN Co-Chairman of the ICFY Steering Committee, Thorvald Stoltenberg, and the United States Ambassador to Croatia, Peter Galbraith, that extended into further negotiations at the peace talks in Dayton, Ohio, a commitment was reached on 3 November between Croatia's President Franjo Tudjman and President Slobodan Milosevic of the Federal Republic of Yugoslavia (Serbia and Montenegro) to reinvigorate local negotiations. From those local negotiations emerged the Basic Agreement on the Region of Eastern Slavonia, Baranja and Western Sirmium, signed in Croatia on 12 November between the Government of Croatia and the local Croatian Serb authorities in Eastern Slavonia. The text was communicated by Croatia to the Secretary-General on 15 November.[59]

The negotiations were based on 11 principles embodied in a document titled "Guiding Basic Principles for Negotiations", signed also by the Government and the Croatian Serb authorities in Eastern Slavonia on 3 October in Erdut, Croatia, and transmitted to the Security Council on 6 October.[60] Agreement on those principles had been the result of discreet contacts made by the UN Co-Chairman of the ICFY Steering Committee with the parties throughout July and September.[61]

The objective of the Basic Agreement was the peaceful reintegration of the region in question into the country's constitutional and legal systems. To that end, the Basic Agreement provided for the following: a 12-month period of transition, which might be extended at most to another period of the same duration if so requested by one of the parties; a Transitional Administration to be authorized by the Security Council to govern the region during that period, to ensure the possible return of refugees and displaced persons to their homes of origin, to re-establish all public services, and to organize and train a temporary police force; an international force, also to be authorized by the Council, to demilitarize the region completely not later than 30 days after deployment; the presence of international monitors, to be authorized by the Government, along the region's international border to facilitate free movement of persons across existing border crossings; monitoring implementation of human rights and civil rights by interested countries and organizations; and, not later than 30 days before the end of the transition period, monitoring of local elections by international organizations and institutions, such as the Organization for Security and Cooperation in Europe (OSCE) (see "Cooperation with OSCE" below, under "Other issues"), and interested States.

#### SECURITY COUNCIL ACTION

The Security Council, having received the Basic Agreement, met on 22 November and adopted **resolution 1023(1995)**.

*The Security Council,*

*Recalling* all its earlier relevant resolutions,

*Reaffirming* its commitment to the search for an overall negotiated settlement of the conflicts in the former Yugoslavia, ensuring the sovereignty and territorial integrity of all the States there within their internationally recognized borders, and stressing the importance it attaches to the mutual recognition thereof,

*Reaffirming once again* its commitment to the independence, sovereignty and territorial integrity of the Republic of Croatia and emphasizing in this regard that the territories of Eastern Slavonia, Baranja and Western Sirmium, known as Sector East, are integral parts of the Republic of Croatia,

*Affirming* the importance it attaches to full respect for human rights and fundamental freedoms of all in those territories,

*Commending* the continuing efforts of the representatives of the United Nations, the European Union, the Russian Federation and the United States of America to facilitate a negotiated solution to the conflict in the Republic of Croatia,

1. *Welcomes* the Basic Agreement on the Region of Eastern Slavonia, Baranja and Western Sirmium, signed on 12 November 1995 between the Government of the Republic of Croatia and the local Serb representatives in the presence of the United Nations mediator and the United States Ambassador to the Republic of Croatia;

2. *Recognizes* the request to it contained in the Basic Agreement to establish a Transitional Administration and authorize an appropriate international force, stands ready to consider the above request expeditiously in order to facilitate the implementation of the Agreement, and invites the Secretary-General to maintain the closest possible contact with all those concerned in order to assist with its work on the matter;

3. *Stresses* the need for the Government of the Republic of Croatia and the local Serb party to cooperate fully on the basis of the Agreement and refrain from any military activity or any measure that might hinder the implementation of the transitional arrangements set out in it, and reminds them of their obligation to cooperate fully with UNCRO and to ensure its safety and freedom of movement;

4. *Decides* to remain actively seized of the matter.

Security Council resolution 1023(1995)

22 November 1995    Meeting 3596    Adopted unanimously

10-nation draft (S/1995/979).

*Sponsors:* Argentina, Czech Republic, France, Germany, Honduras, Italy, Russian Federation, Rwanda, United Kingdom, United States.

## Transition arrangements

**Report of the Secretary-General.** In his report[62] of 23 November, prepared to assist the Security Council in its deliberations on the future of the three UNPF missions before the expiration of their mandates on 30 November, the Secretary-General reported on UNCRO activities since his 29 September report,[56] and on arrangements to be made in the light of the Basic Agreement.

The Secretary-General noted that UNCRO continued its efforts to reduce the tension prevailing in Sector East and to monitor the situation of the Croatian Serb minorities in former Sectors North, South and West. At the same time, withdrawal and repatriation of all UN military personnel from those former Sectors were in progress, as was the closing of the three Sector headquarters, all of which should be completed no later than 21 December.

Against a background of Croatian troop build-up west of Sector East and repeated statements by Croatia of its intention to recapture the Sector should the ongoing negotiations for its peaceful reintegration be unsuccessful, UNCRO, in support of those negotiations, endeavoured to uphold the integrity of the zone of separation between the opposing forces and to initiate and foster confidence-building measures, such as family reunions and humanitarian visits. In cooperation with the UN High Commissioner for Human Rights, UNHCR, UNCRO and ECMM continued to document serious violations of the human rights of the Serb minorities.

The Secretary-General stated that Croatia had yet to respond positively to the Council's call, most recently made in **resolution 1019(1995)**, for lifting any time-limits placed on the return of refugees to Croatia to reclaim their property. The law on the temporary management of currently abandoned property in the formerly occupied territories, due to take effect on 3 December, allowed the Croatian Government to make abandoned houses and property available for housing displaced persons, unless their rightful owners returned to Croatia to reclaim them for personal use. Current administrative procedures and justified concerns for security, however, constituted virtually insurmountable obstacles to the return of Serbs to claim their property.

UNCRO had made a series of prison visits to follow up with regard to the approximately 800 Croatian Serbs who remained in detention, during which it received persistent complaints over the difficulty of access to lawyers and concerns over the lack of specificity of charges. UNCRO also provided civil affairs and civilian police assistance to the UNHCR operation at Kuplensko refugee camp in former Sector North, where there were more than 20,000 Bosnian refugees (loyal to Fikret Abdic) from Velika Kladusa.

In the context of the Basic Agreement's request for the establishment of a transitional administration and an international force, the Secretary-General identified two realistic options for the Council regarding UNCRO's future: terminate UNCRO on 30 November, when its mandate was due to expire, or authorize its continuation until the new arrangements had been emplaced.

President Tudjman had made clear to the Special Representative that he could not agree to a further extension of UNCRO, but would agree to retaining its two battalions in the region as a transitional arrangement, insisting that implementation of the Basic Agreement, particularly its demilitarization aspects, begin on 1 December. The Secretary-General thus suggested that the Council might confirm UNCRO's presence for two months as a transitional arrangement, pending the establishment of an international force; designate as quickly as possible a civilian transitional administrator for the region; and determine the date on which the Basic Agreement's implementation should begin. In this regard, the Secretary-General pointed to the absence of concurrence by the

Government to the continuation of UNCRO's current functions, except perhaps for the monitoring of the Prevlaka peninsula as a confidence-building measure.

The Security Council met on 30 November and adopted **resolution 1025(1995)**.

*The Security Council,*

*Recalling* all its previous relevant resolutions and in particular its resolution 981(1995) of 31 March 1995,

*Recalling also* the Secretary-General's report of 29 September 1995 and the letter of the President of the Security Council to the Secretary-General of 10 October 1995,

*Reaffirming* its resolution 1023(1995) of 22 November 1995,

*Reaffirming once again* its commitment to the independence, sovereignty and territorial integrity of the Republic of Croatia and emphasizing in this regard that the territories of Eastern Slavonia, Baranja and Western Sirmium, known as Sector East, are integral parts of the Republic of Croatia,

*Affirming* the importance it attaches to full respect for human rights and fundamental freedoms of all in those territories and elsewhere in the Republic of Croatia,

*Welcoming* again the Basic Agreement on the Region of Eastern Slavonia, Baranja and Western Sirmium, signed on 12 November 1995 between the Government of the Republic of Croatia and the local Serb representatives,

*Welcoming* the positive role played by UNCRO, and paying tribute to the personnel of UNCRO in the performance of their mandate,

*Having considered* the report of the Secretary-General of 23 November 1995,

*Reaffirming* its determination to ensure the security and freedom of movement of the personnel of United Nations peace-keeping operations in the territory of the former Yugoslavia, and, to these ends, acting under Chapter VII of the Charter of the United Nations,

1. *Welcomes* the report of the Secretary-General of 23 November 1995;

2. *Requests* the Secretary-General to submit for consideration by the Council at the earliest possible date and no later than 14 December 1995 a report on all aspects of the establishment by the Council of an operation consisting of a transitional administration and a transitional peace-keeping force to implement the relevant provisions of the Basic Agreement including on the possibilities for assistance from the host country in offsetting the costs of the operation;

3. *Decides* that, in order to allow for the orderly establishment of the operation referred to in paragraph 2 above, the mandate of UNCRO shall terminate after an interim period ending on 15 January 1996 or when the Council has decided on the deployment, including on the necessary period for the transfer of authority, of the transitional peace-keeping force referred to in that paragraph, whichever is sooner;

4. *Decides* to remain actively seized of the matter.

Security Council resolution 1025(1995)

30 November 1995    Meeting 3600    Adopted unanimously

9-nation draft (S/1995/994).

*Sponsors:* Argentina, Czech Republic, France, Germany, Honduras, Italy, Russian Federation, United Kingdom, United States.

**Further report of the Secretary-General.** In accordance with the foregoing resolution, the Secretary-General submitted for the Security Council's consideration a report dated 13 December on all aspects of the establishment of an operation comprising the transitional administration and peace-keeping force required to implement the Basic Agreement, as well as on the possibilities for host-country assistance to offset the operating costs involved.[63]

The Secretary-General considered the Basic Agreement a landmark accomplishment, meriting full international support for its effective and timely implementation. Only a substantial military force deployed at the outset, he felt, could generate the mutual confidence necessary for the parties to take the difficult steps required of them under the Agreement. A mechanized division of two brigades, with combat capability, air support and a strong mobile, armoured reserve, operating under Chapter VII of the UN Charter, would provide the minimum strength necessary to implement the Basic Agreement and to deter attacks from other forces in the region. It would have sufficient combat power and robust rules of engagement to endorse compliance if required, the Secretary-General said.

He emphasized that anything less than a well-armed division-sized force would only risk repeating the failures of the recent past. He said the concept of deterrence by mere presence, as attempted in the "safe areas" in Bosnia and Herzegovina, would not be more likely to succeed in this instance. Should there be a mismatch between the international force's mandate and its resources, there would be a risk of failure, of international casualties and of undermined credibility for those who had put the force in the field.

The force, which could include the current UNCRO troops in Sector East, could deploy in two self-sufficient task forces, north and south of the Drava River, reporting to a single headquarters. If it was to be a UN force, deployment would take up to 180 days; once declared deployed, demilitarization of the region would begin, to be completed within 30 days. Rather than collect weapons in storage points, the force would assist in the destruction or disposal of all weapons, ammunition and explosives and would oversee the disbanding of existing military, paramilitary and police forces in accordance with the Basic Agreement.

In this regard, one of two options presented by the Secretary-General was to authorize the deployment and command of a force comprising approximately 9,300 troops plus logistic support, under a Chapter VII mandate, entrusted to a coalition of Member States rather than to the United Nations and attached to the 60,000-strong multinational military Implementation Force to be deployed in Bosnia and Herzegovina (see "UN transition arrangements" above, under "Bosnia and Herzegovina"). The other option was to entrust such an operation to a UN force. The Secretary-General considered the first option to be the best, given his reservations about the current ability of the United Nations to undertake an enforcement operation of the kind described, as well as of the imprecise nature of the Basic Agreement and the consequent risk of differing interpretations of some of its provisions.

As for the transitional administration, whose specified tasks were of a magnitude and complexity not to be underestimated, the Secretary-General proposed that the administration head (the "transitional administrator") should be a UN official under the direction of and reporting to the Secretary-General. Should the international force be a multinational one, not subject to the transitional administrator's authority, the Council would have to request that troop-contributing States instruct the force commander to cooperate closely with the administrator and to respond appropriately, were the latter to ask the force to come to the aid of the civil power.

Also proposed was an advisory transitional council, to be chaired by the transitional administrator and to include one representative each of the Government, the local Serb population, the local Croat population and other local minorities. Executive power would be vested exclusively in the administrator, who would establish functional implementation committees, the composition of which would be determined in consultation with the parties. The implementation committees would address questions of police, civil administration, restoration of public services, education and culture, the return of refugees and displaced persons, human rights, elections and records. In view of the importance of implementing the civilian aspects of the Basic Agreement as soon as possible, the Secretary-General recommended that the Security Council authorize establishment of the transitional council and local implementation committees.

The Secretary-General warned that the operation envisaged by the Basic Agreement would not succeed unless two conditions were fulfilled: active and sustained political support from the Council, particularly from those Member States that had played a vital part in concluding the Agreement; and immediate provision by Member States of the necessary troops and guarantees that the financial resources needed would be made available. In that connection, the Secretary-General had received no indication from Croatia that it would be willing to contribute in any significant manner to defraying the costs of the operation.

(For the Secretary-General's recommendations on UNCRO's residual mandates, see below, under "Prevlaka peninsula".)

**Communication from the Security Council.** On 21 December, the President of the Security Council notified[64] the Secretary-General that the Council, having reviewed his report, stood ready to consider the option that both the transitional administration and the transitional international force be components of a UN operation, stressing that, if it so decided, the necessary financial resources should be made available in a timely fashion. The Council agreed that the force should operate under an appropriate mandate and be provided with the necessary protection. It encouraged the Secretary-General to accelerate discussions with possible troop contributors to allow deployment of the force at the earliest possible date.

Recognizing the complexity of the Basic Agreement and the danger that the two sides might have different interpretations of some of its provisions, the Council welcomed the Secretary-General's decision to send an envoy to the region as soon as convenient to discuss implementation of the Basic Agreement with the Croatian Government and the local Serbs, as well as the practical aspects of the proposed UN operation, including possible assistance from the host country in offsetting the cost.

### Prevlaka peninsula

In his 13 December report,[63] the Secretary-General pointed out that, in accordance with Council **resolution 1025(1995)**, the UNCRO mandate would be terminated on 15 January 1996. On the basis of consultations with the parties in the area, however, he recommended the continuation of UNMO monitoring of the demilitarization of the Prevlaka peninsula.[35] For the time being, the UNMOs would continue to report to UNPF-HQ in Zagreb. Given the dimensions of the "blue zone" in Prevlaka and of the "yellow zone", encompassing a demilitarized zone of 5 kilometres on either side of the tripartite border, and given also the need to establish a small local headquarters because of the isolation of the area, the Secretary-General recommended that the authorized strength of that UNMO operation be increased from 14 to 28. That would permit it to be self-sufficient, to patrol the areas concerned more reliably, and to maintain UNCRO's existing liaison teams in Dubrovnik and in Herceg Novi (Montenegro), some 45 kilometres south-east of Dubrovnik.

**Communications.** On 22 December, Yugoslavia (Serbia and Montenegro) drew attention[65] to what it claimed was an existing territorial dispute between it (specifically Montenegro) and Croatia, centred in the Prevlaka peninsula in Boka Kotorska Bay—a dispute the existence of which had been noted by both parties in Dubrovnik on 25 April. The legal status of the territory in question, encompassing Cape Ostri and part of the Prevlaka hinterland, was regulated by the 30 September and 20 October 1992 joint declarations by the Presidents of Yugoslavia (Serbia and Montenegro) and Croatia, as well as by Security Council resolutions 779(1992)[35] and **981(1995)**, pending a peaceful solution of the dispute.

Owing to the failure of its many attempts to resolve the dispute through negotiations with Croatia, including at the peace talks in Dayton, Ohio, Yugoslavia (Serbia and Montenegro) asked the Council to adopt a decision, prior to the expiry of the UNPF missions in the former Yugoslavia, to continue the UN monitoring mission in the disputed area.

Responding on 3 January 1996, Croatia stated[66] that the untrue claims by Yugoslavia (Serbia and Montenegro) were intended to justify its request for the prolongation of the UN presence in the Prevlaka peninsula in the Republic of Croatia beyond the expiration date of UNCRO. Croatia could not accept the notion of an existent "territorial dispute" as alleged, since the area in question had never been disputed or contested while Croatia was a constituent republic of the former Socialist Federal Republic of Yugoslavia. In accordance with international law, the borders of those constituent republics became recognized as international borders among the successor States of the former Yugoslavia, Croatia asserted, adding that that legal fact had also been confirmed by the European Community Arbitration Commission and the EU Badinter Commission.

Croatia went on to say that the issues discussed at the Dayton proximity talks were well known, and the Prevlaka peninsula was not among them. Rather, it had been raised unilaterally, and a unilateral claim to a part of another State's territory could in no way be construed as a "firm commitment to a peaceful solution of the dispute in accordance with the Charter of the United Nations", especially since Yugoslavia (Serbia and Montenegro) was still not prepared to recognize Croatia, despite the Council's numerous calls for such recognition. The Yugoslav claim was contrary to the spirit and letter of numerous Council and General Assembly resolutions protecting the territorial integrity of all successor States, including Croatia.

Croatia remained available to discuss all pertinent issues, including full normalization of relations with Yugoslavia (Serbia and Montenegro), but under one fair and objective condition: the discussion must be between two equal States that fully recognized each other within their internationally recognized borders. (See also other "Succession issues" under "General aspects", above.)

### Dubrovnik

On 13 April, Croatia drew attention[67] to an unprovoked artillery attack that day on Cilipi airport in Dubrovnik and nearby villages. The attack, Croatia alleged, had been launched by Bosnian Serb paramilitary units in Bosnia and Herzegovina, which had fired a total of twenty-two 130-millimetre shells, destroying a fuel depot at the airport. Croatia further alleged that, the day before, Serb paramilitary forces in the occupied territories of Croatia launched an SA-6 surface-to-air missile that had exploded in the village of Malik. Since such a missile was not in the arsenal of the occupied territories, Croatia could only conclude that its transportation from Yugoslavia (Serbia and Montenegro) had been allowed and was out of the control of UN peace-keepers. Croatia further reported[68] on 19 April that, on that day, the airport had again been shelled from Bosnian Serb-held territory.

On 14 August, Croatia wrote[69] of renewed shelling of the Dubrovnik region by Bosnian Serb paramilitary forces, with assistance from the Army of Yugoslavia (Serbia and Montenegro). The series of attacks, which began on 12 August and during which more than 3,000 impacts were recorded, had resulted in civilian casualties, numerous forest fires and severe damage to buildings and other property in the municipalities of Dubrovnik, Konavle and Ston. Cipili airport was closed due to heavy damage. Croatia urged the Security Council to bring such cross-border aggression to a halt.

A statement[70] by the EU Presidency on 19 August expressed the Union's deepest concern regarding the situation in and around Dubrovnik and urged the parties involved to stop all military activities forthwith and exercise restraint.

On 30 October, Croatia wrote[71] of yet another unprovoked attack on the Dubrovnik area by the Bosnian Serbs, regarding which it had lodged a protest with ECMM and UNCRO.

### Refugees and displaced persons

According to the Secretary-General's 18 October report,[22] about 116,000 people had been displaced from former Sectors North, South and West. Some 900 to 1,000 displaced Croats had returned to their homes in former Sector West. The number of those who returned to former Sectors North and South could not be confirmed, but was believed to be small. Accounting for that small number were the ongoing mopping-up operations by the Croatian Army and police, the looting and burning of Serb houses, the lack of economic prospects and the uncertain security environment, including the presence of mines.

Since early May, more than 480,000 persons had been forced from their homes. The movements directly involving Croatia included: in May, the more than 10,000 Croatian Serbs who fled Sector West for Sector East and the Banja Luka region (Bosnia and Herzegovina); in August, the exodus of about 200,000 Croatian Serbs from Sectors North and South, of whom 170,000 took refuge in Yugoslavia (Serbia and Montenegro) and the rest in Sector East and in Banja Luka; also in August, the 25,000 Bosnian-Muslim followers of Fikret Abdic who fled the Bihac pocket (Bosnia and Herzegovina) for Croatia, and the more than 20,000 Croat and Muslim minorities, expelled by the Bosnian Serbs from Banja Luka, who poured into Croatia.

Remaining in the previously Serb-held area of former Sector West were about 1,200 Serbs and between 4,000 and 5,000 in its northern part, which had always been under Croatian government control. An estimated 3,000 Krajina Serbs remained in former Sector North and about 2,000 in former Sector South. According to Croatian officials, the Serb population in Croatia fell from 12 per cent to less than 3 per cent of the national population as a result of the "liberation of the occupied territories" (of former Sectors North, South and West).

**SECURITY COUNCIL ACTION**

The Security Council met on 3 October to consider the question of the refugees and displaced persons who had fled Bosnia and Herzegovina for Croatia, as well as the ethnic Croatian Serbs who remained in former Sectors North, South and West or who had fled those areas and wished to return.

Following consultations among its members, the Council authorized the President to make the statement below[72] on the Council's behalf:

The Security Council expresses its concern at the humanitarian situation in and around the Republic of Croatia, including the situation of refugees from the Republic of Bosnia and Herzegovina.

The Security Council is particularly concerned at the withdrawal of refugee status from and the consequent ending of assistance to many refugees from the Republic of Bosnia and Herzegovina at present in the Republic of Croatia. The decisions of the Government of Croatia in this regard may lead to the involuntary return of tens of thousands of people to an area that is neither safe nor prepared to receive them. The Council stresses the importance of the principle of *non-refoulement* set out in the 1951 Geneva Convention on the Status of Refugees, to which Croatia is a party. The Council urges the Government of Croatia to continue to provide asylum to all refugees regardless of their origin.

The Security Council is also seriously concerned at the situation of the refugees from the Republic of Croatia wishing to return, as well as of those ethnic

Serbs who have chosen to remain in the Republic of Croatia. It reiterates its demands, contained *inter alia* in its resolution 1009(1995), that the Government of Croatia respect fully the rights of the local Serb population including their right to remain or return in safety, investigate all reports of human rights violations and take appropriate measures to put an end to such acts. The Council calls upon the Government of Croatia to lift any time-limits placed on the return of refugees to Croatia to reclaim their property. The Council also calls on the Government to cooperate with international humanitarian organizations in the creation of conditions conducive for the repatriation of refugees in safety and dignity.

The Security Council will remain actively seized of the matter.

*Meeting number.* SC 3584.

## Violations of human rights and international humanitarian law

In view of the humanitarian situation resulting from Croatia's offensives in May and August, as reported by the Secretary-General on 3 August[34] and 7 August,[48] the Security Council, by **resolution 1009(1995)**, demanded that Croatia respect fully the rights of the local Serb population, including their rights to remain, leave or return in safety; allow access to the population by international humanitarian organizations; and create conditions conducive to the return of persons who had left their homes. It reiterated that demand on 7 September[55] and, in its 3 October statement, urged Croatia to continue to provide asylum to all refugees regardless of their origin.

By **resolution 1019(1995)** of 9 November, the Council reaffirmed its demand that Croatia take urgent measures to put an end to violations of international humanitarian law and of human rights, and investigate all reports of such violations so that those responsible could be brought to justice. It reiterated its demand that Croatia respect fully the rights of the local Serb population, as well as its call for the lifting of any time-limits placed on the return of refugees to reclaim their property. It asked the Secretary-General to continue to inform the Council regularly on measures taken by Croatia to implement **resolutions 1009(1995)** and **1019(1995)**.

**Report of the Secretary-General (October).** As noted in the Secretary-General's report of 18 October,[22] the Special Rapporteur of the Commission on Human Rights conducted an on-site investigation of alleged human rights problems following the 1 May Croatian offensive on Sector West and, based on his findings, concluded that violations of human rights and humanitarian law had occurred during and after that offensive. Reports of such violations from Member States, EU, UNHCR, UNCRO and international human rights organizations persisted for more than eight weeks after the 4 August offensive on Sectors

North and South. During their investigations, UNPF action teams led by field officers of the Centre for Human Rights found evidence of extrajudicial executions, disappearances, ill-treatment and harassment of the remaining Serb population, and systematic and widespread destruction of Serb houses and entire villages in the Krajina by Croatia's Army and internal security forces. ECMM documented that, in the 243 villages it had investigated, 73 per cent of Serb houses had been burned and looted. In early October, incidents of armed robbery and personal threats were reported with increasing frequency, along with crimes against property.

While Croatian authorities maintained that the violations were perpetrated by uncontrolled elements, there were reports from international observers, including members of the press, who said they had witnessed the presence of the Croatian Army and special police units in several instances. Only after significant international criticism did President Tudjman announce investigations into 611 cases of looting, 27 bombings and seven murders. Under investigation by the authorities were another 36 murder cases, regarding which the President said it was not clear whether they were committed in war situations or in mopping-up operations or by "unbalanced individuals".

Confirmed reports of continuing human rights abuses had created a climate of deep apprehension hostile to the return of those wishing to do so. There were as yet no reliable government guarantees that returnees would enjoy safety and security, the Secretary-General said.

Furthermore, the Government had adopted a number of legislative measures since August that appeared incompatible with its stated intention to facilitate the return of refugees. Of grave concern was a decree of 31 August on the temporary expropriation and control by the Government of certain "abandoned" property in former Sectors North, South and West. The order was applicable to property anywhere in Croatia owned by individuals who had left the country since 17 August 1990 or who were residing in Sector East or Yugoslavia (Serbia and Montenegro) or in Serb-held areas of Bosnia and Herzegovina. It was also applicable to owners of such property who were citizens of Yugoslavia (Serbia and Montenegro).

The deadline for claims, as amended, required owners to claim their property "for possession and use" within 90 days from 4 September. Since return within that time-limit appeared neither feasible nor advisable under existing circumstances, that requirement constituted a potentially insurmountable obstacle to the return of Serbs currently outside Croatia, the Secretary-General observed. The UN High Commissioner for Human Rights had made representations to President Tudjman against this aspect of the decree, and, in its 3 October presidential statement, the Council had called for its lifting.

(The decree was the subject of an explanatory letter from Croatia on 7 September,[73] and of a protest lodged by Yugoslavia (Serbia and Montenegro) on 14 September.[74])

Other legislative measures adopted by Croatia's Parliament, before its dissolution in early September, modified the electoral law to reduce the number of Croatian Serb representatives from 12 to 3 (with effect from the elections scheduled for 29 October); suspended constitutional provisions with respect to the political autonomy of the Serb-majority districts of Glina (northern Krajina) and Knin (southern Krajina); and called for a new population census in 1996, the Secretary-General reported.

**Communication.** On 30 October, Yugoslavia (Serbia and Montenegro) transmitted a "Memorandum of October 1995 on the ethnic cleansing of and genocide against the Serb people of Croatia and Krajina".[75] The memorandum aimed to document mass killings, planned expulsions of the entire Serb population from Croatia and, in its words, the "systematic eradication of all traces of its centuries-long life" in the areas from which they were expelled. As a result of Croatia's policy of ethnic cleansing, it said, some 550,000 Serbs had been expelled from Krajina and other places between 1991 and 1995. Of those, 250,000 had been driven from former Sectors North, South and West. As a result, Yugoslavia (Serbia and Montenegro) said it was now faced with the problem of providing shelter for refugees from those parts.

**Further report of the Secretary-General.** In response to Council **resolution 1019(1995)**, the Secretary-General on 21 December reported[76] on Croatia's implementation of that resolution. Police-patrolling, a preventive measure which the Croatian authorities had assured would be increased throughout former Sectors North, South and West, was found inadequate. UN monitors in the countryside had observed only a few patrols, except in the area of Vrlika. On 9 October, UN officials were informed that joint Croatian-UN police patrols would be cancelled for lack of manpower and vehicles. In the week ending 19 November, substantial reductions in Croatian police checkpoints in former Sector South were reported, but were to be replaced by mobile patrols, which had so far not been in evidence.

The Secretary-General noted that the Government had been providing data showing the number of investigations undertaken with respect to killings, arson and looting, of the prosecutions under way, and the steps to trace suspected perpetrators. The Government had also established a special commission under the auspices of the Ministry of the Interior to follow up on serious crimes. A significant discrepancy existed between the number of suspicious deaths recorded by the United Nations and the number of murders registered by the Croatian authorities. Efforts to determine the number of civilians killed during and following the 4 August Croatian offensive had been impeded by the authorities' refusal of access to burial records concerning more than 750 freshly dug graves found by UN personnel in former Sectors North and South.

Likewise, a significant discrepancy existed between the UN estimate of at least 5,000 properties set on fire and the 2,787 cases of arson registered by the Government, which included 2,072 buildings said by Croatia to have been partly affected by combat operations and 715 partly or entirely destroyed in deliberate actions; only 11 persons had been charged with arson, it was reported. Government figures did not indicate the degree of military and police involvement. Croatia's claim that nearly 75 per cent of the buildings burned had been "affected by combat operations" was also inconsistent with UN reports documenting numerous fires in areas where hostilities had ceased days, weeks and sometimes even months before.

The Government established 1,054 cases of looting, of which 770 had been clarified. The number of persons charged—1,260—was high. A number of those cited were released, however, and Government figures did not indicate the number of Croatian soldiers and police involved. Efforts of Croatian authorities to confiscate and return property appeared insufficient to address the magnitude of the problem.

The right of the Krajina Serbs to remain in their homes had not been adequately safeguarded. Remaining Serbs had faced extensive harassment and intimidation; looters and armed thieves had robbed them of both their property and sense of security. Victims of those abuses who had complained to the Croatian police had been met with apathy or inaction or action that was neither timely nor sufficient.

The humanitarian situation of the more than 9,000 Serbs remaining in former Sectors North and South was reported to be grave, as was the situation of those remaining in former Sector West. Composed mainly of elderly and disabled people living in small villages deep in the countryside, those Serbs were in desperate need of food, medical assistance, hospitalization and proper shelter. The Croatian authorities reported having conducted a survey of 5,270 people and an assessment of their needs, described by one official as overwhelming.

The return of Croatian Serbs continued to be hampered by practical, legal, administrative and bureaucratic obstacles. Under a humanitarian policy of family reunification, only 59 of the 100 elderly Serb refugees stranded in Barc, Hungary, had been authorized to return to Croatia under UNHCR auspices, and only a handful of Croatian Serbs had returned on their own. The Government had stated that a mass return would not be possible in the absence of a specific agreement between it and Yugoslavia (Serbia and Montenegro).

Of concern was the failure to respect the right to a fair trial of the more than 700 Serbs who remained in detention on grounds of having committed "war crimes" or "armed rebellion". Inadequate access to legal counsel, vagueness of charges, trials in absentia and an excessive delay in preparing indictments appeared to be major problems. Court-appointed attorneys were reluctant to fulfil their duties and had little or no contact with defendants.

In September, the Croatian Parliament temporarily suspended several articles of the "Constitutional Law on Human Rights and Freedoms and the Rights of National and Ethnic Communities in the Republic of Croatia", namely, those guaranteeing the special status of districts predominantly populated by national minorities, providing for separate educational institutions, and providing for proportional representation in the parliament, government and the judiciary. The Secretary-General recalled that adoption of the foregoing articles was an essential condition for the international recognition of Croatia. Also suspended was the article providing for establishment of the Provisional Human Rights Court. The Ministry of Justice had created a working group, however, to consider relevant legal issues for the establishment of such a court.

**SECURITY COUNCIL ACTION**

In the light of the Secretary-General's report of 21 December, the Security Council met on 22 December and, following consultations among its members, authorized the President to make the statement below[(77)] on the Council's behalf:

> The Security Council takes note of the report of the Secretary-General of 21 December 1995, which it has just received.
>
> The Security Council, as a matter of urgency, expresses its grave concern that, according to information in that report, the Government of the Republic of Croatia has ignored the call of the Council in the statement of its President of 3 October 1995 that it lift any time-limits placed on the return of refugees to reclaim their property. The requirement that owners must reclaim their property by 27 December 1995 constitutes a virtually insurmountable obstacle for most Serb refugees.
>
> The Security Council strongly demands that the Government of the Republic of Croatia lift immediately any time-limits placed on the return of refugees to reclaim their property.

The Security Council shall continue its consideration of the report of the Secretary-General.

*Meeting number.* SC 3615.

**Communication.** On 27 December, Croatia stated[78] that it found the Secretary-General's 21 December report to be incorrect to the point of being biased, unnecessary and extremely unproductive. Rather than giving the relevant information requested in paragraph 12 of Security Council **resolution 1019(1995)**, it merely recycled material submitted in previous reports and already acted upon by the Council and General Assembly.

The Secretary-General's report and the hastily issued presidential statement, Croatia said, had created a wrong impression of the actual situation in Croatia, which could affect the ongoing peace process, including implementation of the Basic Agreement, and engender reluctance on the part of Member States to contribute troops for the transitional military force. Croatia claimed it had fulfilled most of the demands in Council **resolutions 1009(1995)** and **1019(1995)**. In particular, the Government had suspended the time-limit for reclaiming property and would propose to the Parliament that it amend the 21 August decree so as to extend the deadline *sine die*.

Croatia restated its commitment to the peaceful reintegration of its remaining occupied territories, to fostering confidence-building measures and to normalizing relations with Yugoslavia (Serbia and Montenegro).

### Croatia–Yugoslavia (Serbia and Montenegro)

During the year, Croatia addressed a number of letters to the Secretary-General alleging the active involvement of the Army of Yugoslavia (Serbia and Montenegro) (JA) in the Serb-occupied territories of Croatia and charging Yugoslavia (Serbia and Montenegro) with the violation of, among other things, the UN Charter, owing to its intervention across the international border of a sovereign State and its violation of the border closure referred to in Security Council resolution 943(1994).[79]

On 28 June, Croatia restated[80] the charges it had made on 27 and 28 March and on 18 May[81] regarding: the incremental transport of JA troops and *matériel* into the occupied territories; the assignment to the "Army of Serb Krajina" of a detachment of some 6,000 JA commissioned officers to direct the Krajina paramilitary units; the payment by Belgrade of the wages of those officers and members of the "proxy government and military", as evidenced by recently discovered payroll lists regularly forwarded to Belgrade; and the forcible mobilization, on a large scale, of Yugoslav citizens and Serb citizens of Croatia and Bos-

nia and Herzegovina for military service in the occupied territories. Croatia on 27 July further spoke of a sharp increase of JA assistance, particularly in Vukovar in Sector East.[82]

In the meantime, on 4 April, Yugoslavia (Serbia and Montenegro) lodged a strong protest[83] against what it labelled as Croatia's tendentious and untrue charges and conveyed a strong denial by the JA Joint Chiefs of Staff that any military units or equipment were in deployment outside Yugoslavia (Serbia and Montenegro).

In a series of charges and countercharges by the two countries, each accused the other of carrying out attacks on its territory.

On 13 August, Yugoslavia (Serbia and Montenegro) charged[84] that Croatian armed forces, in joint operations with the "Muslims", continued to fight the Serbs "along the entire line of the front" of what it called the "former Bosnia and Herzegovina" at the same time that Croatia was carrying out attacks against the "territory of the Federal Republic of Yugoslavia", the "territory" in question being the line of separation in Sector East near Osijek and the Trebinje, Debela Ljut and Kozen Do areas. Responding[85] on 28 August, Croatia expressed its indignation that Yugoslavia (Serbia and Montenegro) should be laying claim to parts of Croatian territory (Osijek in the Vukovar region in Sector East), as well as to parts of Bosnia and Herzegovina (Trebinje, Debela Ljut, Kozen Do), stressing that it regarded the claim to the Vukovar region as a hostile act against Croatia's sovereignty and territorial integrity.

Croatia on 20 August reported[86] that Croatian Serb paramilitaries, assisted by the JA Novi Sad Corps, had launched a terrorist attack on Osijek from their positions in occupied Vukovar, killing three civilians and wounding 10 others, and inflicting material damage. Yugoslavia (Serbia and Montenegro) on 24 August called that charge baseless and malicious, adding that Croatia was setting the stage for an offensive on Eastern Slavonia and on the Trebinje area.[87]

On 30 August, Yugoslavia (Serbia and Montenegro) alleged[88] that, two days before, the Croatian Army had launched three 82-millimetre mortar shells on Prasna Rupa, approximately 500 metres deep into Yugoslav territory, warning of grave consequences that might arise from Croatia's repeated criminal acts. Croatia, on 6 September, denied[89] the allegation, affirming it had no intention of raising tensions along the Croatia–Yugoslavia (Serbia and Montenegro) border, committed as it was to the ongoing peace process.

*REFERENCES*
[1]A/50/64-S/1995/28. [2]YUN 1994, p. 491. [3]YUN 1992, p. 327. [4]A/50/111-S/1995/206. [5]YUN 1994, p. 563. [6]Ibid., p. 569.

(7)S/PRST/1995/2. (8)S/1995/56. (9)A/50/77-S/1995/93. (10)S/PRST/1995/6. (11)YUN 1994, p. 495, SC res. 947(1994), 30 Sep. 1994. (12)S/1995/38. (13)YUN 1993, p. 433. (14)YUN 1994, pp. 491 & 494. (15)S/1995/222 & Corr.1,2. (16)YUN 1992, p. 343. (17)S/1995/320. (18)S/1995/339. (19)YUN 1992, p. 333, SC res. 743(1992), 21 Feb. 1992. (20)YUN 1994, p. 564. (21)Ibid., p. 565, GA res. 49/43, 9 Dec. 1994. (22)A/50/648. (23)A/50/613. (24)S/1995/626. (25)S/PRST/1995/23. (26)S/PRST/1995/26. (27)S/1995/358. (28)S/1995/360. (29)S/1995/363. (30)S/1995/467 & Corr.1. (31)A/50/219-S/1995/482. (32)A/50/221. (33)S/PRST/1995/30. (34)S/1995/650. (35)YUN 1992, p. 343, SC res. 779(1992), 6 Oct. 1992. (36)S/PRST/1995/37. (37)YUN 1994, p. 565, GA res. 49/43, 9 Dec. 1994. (38)S/1995/647. (39)S/1995/601. (40)A/50/306-S/1995/609. (41)S/PRST/1995/38. (42)S/1995/651. (43)S/1995/654. (44)A/50/331-S/1995/656. (45)S/1995/655. (46)S/1995/660. (47)A/50/336-S/1995/663. (48)S/1995/666. (49)S/1995/672. (50)S/1995/681. (51)A/50/344-S/1995/682. (52)S/1995/675. (53)S/1995/730. (54)S/1995/748. (55)S/PRST/1995/44. (56)S/1995/835. (57)S/1995/859. (58)S/1995/687. (59)A/50/757-S/1995/951. (60)S/1995/843. (61)S/1996/4. (62)S/1995/987. (63)S/1995/1028 & Add.1. (64)S/1995/1053. (65)S/1995/1059. (66)S/1996/3. (67)S/1995/301. (68)S/1995/314. (69)S/1995/695. (70)S/1995/721. (71)S/1995/896. (72)S/PRST/1995/49. (73)S/1995/775. (74)S/1995/792. (75)A/50/707-S/1995/907. (76)S/1995/1051. (77)S/PRST/1995/63. (78)S/1995/1060. (79)YUN 1994, p. 557, SC res. 943(1994), 4 Aug. 1994. (80)A/50/260-S/1995/518. (81)A/50/119-S/1995/223, A/50/124-S/1995/229, A/50/185-S/1995/401. (82)A/50/318-S/1995/628. (83)A/50/99-S/1995/258. (84)A/50/352-S/1995/693 & Corr.1,2. (85)A/50/389-S/1995/745. (86)S/1995/717. (87)S/1995/733. (88)S/1995/757. (89)S/1995/770.

## The former Yugoslav Republic of Macedonia

At the end of March 1995, the Security Council decided that the UNPROFOR operation in the former Yugoslav Republic of Macedonia should be known as the United Nations Preventive Deployment Force (UNPREDEP), reflecting by that name the essentially preventive mandate of the operation; that is, to monitor and report any developments along its borders that could undermine confidence and stability in the country.

The effective role of UNPREDEP was of major importance to the country, whose political situation remained divided across ideological and ethnic lines, whose economy remained precarious notwithstanding considerable government efforts with some outside assistance, and where a potential for confrontation still existed at its borders, as the Secretary-General had pointed out. Accordingly, the UNPREDEP mandate was extended beyond 30 November 1995 to 30 May 1996.

An event of major significance during the year was the signing of an Interim Accord on 13 September between Greece and the former Yugoslav Republic of Macedonia, which strengthened the latter's international standing and paved the way for the establishment of diplomatic relations with its neighbours and for its admission to a number of European organizations. Most importantly, implementation of the Accord would normalize relations between the two countries and, it was hoped, resolve the contentious dispute between

them over the name of the former Yugoslav Republic of Macedonia.

### UNPROFOR activities

Pursuant to Security Council resolution 947(1994),[1] the Secretary-General submitted a report[2] on 22 March 1995 describing developments affecting UNPROFOR's implementation of its mandate in the main theatres of its operation— Bosnia and Herzegovina, Croatia and the former Yugoslav Republic of Macedonia—to assist the Council in its consideration of that mandate before its expiration on 31 March.

In his observations relating to the former Yugoslav Republic of Macedonia, the Secretary-General stated that, in the recent past, ethnic Albanian leaders had stepped up demands for improvements in their political, economic, social, cultural and educational status, including recognition of Albanian as the Republic's second official language. A project to establish an Albanian-language university in Tetovo had led to a confrontation between the Government and the project's ethnic Albanian proponents, who argued that the State's two universities in Skopje and Bitola, as well as the restoration of some instruction in the Albanian language within the Pedagogical Academy in Skopje, were insufficient. The Government held that to establish such a university outside the State system was against the Constitution and laws of the Republic and charged its advocates with using purportedly educational issues to advance their political ambitions. Police had intervened on several occasions to halt the Tetovo project. Such intervention at a 17 February demonstration for the project resulted in the death of an ethnic Albanian and injuries to a number of policemen. In addition, ethnic Albanians holding 19 of the 120 seats in Parliament boycotted parliamentary sessions in support of their demand for Albanian as the second official language.

Internal political, social and inter-ethnic difficulties continued to be exacerbated by the fragile state of the country's economy. Approximately 30 per cent of the workforce was unemployed; the 1994 inflation rate was 50 per cent. The 1994 trade embargo imposed by Greece[3] and the UN sanctions against Yugoslavia (Serbia and Montenegro) continued to disrupt the country's principal export/import routes on its southern and northern borders. With some assistance from the International Monetary Fund, the World Bank, EU and individual Member States, the economy was showing signs of strength in some areas, but still needed further international support.

Following the 1994 border incidents arising from the non-recognition of the country's international borders by Yugoslavia (Serbia and Montenegro),[4]

UNPROFOR negotiated a military administrative boundary between the two countries which determined the northern limit of the area of operation for UNPROFOR troops, and both sides used that boundary for the reporting and management of border-crossing incidents. While UNPROFOR's monitoring of the boundary crossings by military patrols of both sides had revealed no tension between them, the potential for confrontation remained in the absence of a mutually recognized international border. The Secretary-General thus reiterated that a joint border commission should begin work forthwith to resolve that long-standing issue.

Summing up, he stated that the situation in the country was marked by a complex network of external and internal factors contributing to economic and political uncertainty and rising social tension. The country continued to labour under the combined constraints of the economic blockade imposed by Greece and the effects of sanctions against Yugoslavia (Serbia and Montenegro), the non-recognition of its borders by the latter, and inter- and intra-ethnic tensions, all of which continued to undermine its stability and pose a threat to its fragile democracy. Should threats to its peace and stability, either external or internal, increase to such an extent that a new mandate and reinforcements were judged necessary, the Secretary-General stood ready to submit appropriate recommendations to the Council.

**Communications.** On 27 March, the former Yugoslav Republic of Macedonia transmitted a number of suggested revisions to the Secretary-General's report that, it said, reflected a more objective representation of the situation in the country.[5] On the same date, Greece conveyed its objections to the report's reference not only to the "economic blockade" but also to the "trade embargo imposed by Greece". Continued use of those terms, Greece claimed, could mislead the Security Council and Member States, since they did not give the full picture, particularly with regard to the Skopje Government's long series of provocative acts that had preceded Greece's response.[6]

### UN Preventive Deployment Force

**Report of the Secretary-General (March).** As noted in his 22 March report,[2] the Secretary-General, responding to the wishes of the host Governments of Bosnia and Herzegovina, Croatia and the former Yugoslav Republic of Macedonia, proposed that the UNPROFOR operations in those countries be replaced by three distinct but interlinked peace-keeping operations (for details, see "UN peace forces: UNCRO, UNPROFOR, UNPREDEP" under "General aspects" above). The proposal in respect of the peace-keeping operation in the former Yugoslav Republic of Macedo-

nia was approved by the Security Council in the resolution below.

SECURITY COUNCIL ACTION (31 March)

On 31 March, the Security Council adopted **resolution 983(1995)**.

*The Security Council,*

*Recalling* its resolution 795(1992) and all subsequent relevant resolutions,

*Affirming* its commitment to the search for an overall negotiated settlement of the conflicts in the former Yugoslavia ensuring the sovereignty and territorial integrity of all the States there within their internationally recognized borders, and stressing the importance it attaches to the mutual recognition thereof,

*Reaffirming* its commitment to the independence, sovereignty and territorial integrity of the former Yugoslav Republic of Macedonia,

*Recalling* its concern about possible developments which could undermine confidence and stability in the former Yugoslav Republic of Macedonia or threaten its territory,

*Welcoming* the positive role played by the United Nations Protection Force (UNPROFOR) in the former Yugoslav Republic of Macedonia, and paying tribute to the personnel of UNPROFOR in the performance of its mandate in the former Yugoslav Republic of Macedonia,

*Noting* the report of the Secretary-General of 22 March 1995,

1. *Welcomes* the report of the Secretary-General of 22 March 1995, and in particular approves the arrangements contained in paragraph 84;

2. *Decides* that UNPROFOR within the former Yugoslav Republic of Macedonia shall be known as the United Nations Preventive Deployment Force (UNPREDEP) with the mandate set out in paragraph 85 of the report of the Secretary-General of 22 March 1995, and that the mandate of UNPREDEP shall continue for a period terminating on 30 November 1995;

3. *Urges* UNPREDEP to continue the current cooperation between UNPROFOR and the mission of the Organization for Security and Cooperation in Europe;

4. *Calls upon* Member States to consider favourably requests by the Secretary-General for necessary assistance to UNPREDEP in the performance of its mandate;

5. *Requests* the Secretary-General to keep the Council regularly informed of any developments on the ground and other circumstances affecting the mandate of UNPREDEP;

6. *Decides* to remain seized of the matter.

Security Council resolution 983(1995)

31 March 1995     Meeting 3512     Adopted unanimously

8-nation draft (S/1995/244).

*Sponsors:* Argentina, Czech Republic, France, Germany, Italy, Russian Federation, United Kingdom, United States.

**Report of the Secretary-General (November).** In a report[7] of 23 November, the Secretary-General brought the Security Council up to date on developments in the former Yugoslav Republic of Macedonia and reviewed progress in the implementation of UNPREDEP's mandate, which was to expire on 30 November.

The Secretary-General noted that, fortunately, the 3 October attempt on the life of President Kiro Gligorov had neither destabilized national life nor slowed down internal reforms and foreign policy initiatives. Although opposition parties continued to challenge the outcome of the 1994 parliamentary elections,[3] the ruling coalition in the legislature had made possible passage of several significant laws in the areas of democratization, privatization, formation of political parties, local self-government and education.

To meet the concerns of the ethnic Albanian minority, the Government had released all persons imprisoned in connection with the 17 February demonstration for the Tetovo project, instituted a special four-year teachers' course in Albanian at the Pedagogical Academy in Skopje, reserved a 10 per cent quota for ethnic minority students at institutions of higher learning, and appointed the first ethnic Albanian general in the army.

Externally, there was little evidence of any imminent military threat to the territorial integrity of the country. Three of its four neighbouring countries had officially recognized it; recognition by the fourth, Yugoslavia (Serbia and Montenegro), remained pending.

The Interim Accord (see below), which had strengthened the international standing of the country, was immediately followed by its establishment of full diplomatic relations with several other States, by its admission to OSCE and the Council of Europe, and by its participation in the "Partnership for Peace" initiative and other international and regional arrangements.

Government measures to stabilize the economy had met with partial success: whereas the inflation rate had been reduced and privatization and banking reforms were proceeding, industrial production had considerably declined and unemployment had increased to 50 per cent of the workforce.

The effective role of UNPREDEP had been of major importance to the country's highest authorities. UNPREDEP's regular contacts with a number of government ministries, as well as with all political parties including the opposition and ethnic minorities, had proved of special value to the functioning of UNPREDEP and to the implementation of its mandate. Mutually beneficial contacts had also been initiated by the UNPREDEP Commander with the military authorities of Albania and of Yugoslavia (Serbia and Montenegro). There was consent that greater tolerance should be displayed during encounters along their common border with the former Yugoslav Republic of Macedonia. Consequently, border incidents had significantly decreased.

It was the Secretary-General's assessment that the continued presence of UNPREDEP, with the same mandate, strength and troop composition, was vital to the maintenance of peace and stability in the country. It was his intention to revert to the Council as soon as practicable to propose putting UNPREDEP on a fully independent footing, reporting directly to New York. That would entail adjustments to its administrative, logistic and military support and thus to its authorized strength. In the meantime, he recommended that UNPREDEP be renewed for a further 12-month period, irrespective of developments elsewhere in the theatre.

**SECURITY COUNCIL ACTION (30 November)**

In the light of the Secretary-General's foregoing report, the Security Council met on 30 November and adopted **resolution 1027(1995)**.

*The Security Council,*

*Recalling* all its previous relevant resolutions and in particular its resolution 983(1995) of 31 March 1995,

*Reaffirming* its commitment to the independence, sovereignty and territorial integrity of the former Yugoslav Republic of Macedonia,

*Recalling* its concern about possible developments which could undermine confidence and stability in the former Yugoslav Republic of Macedonia or threaten its territory,

*Welcoming* the positive role played by the United Nations Preventive Deployment Force (UNPREDEP), and paying tribute to the personnel of UNPREDEP in the performance of their mandate,

*Having considered* the report of the Secretary-General of 23 November 1995,

1. *Welcomes* the report of the Secretary-General of 23 November 1995;

2. *Decides* to extend the mandate of UNPREDEP for a period terminating on 30 May 1996;

3. *Urges* UNPREDEP to continue its cooperation with the mission of the Organization for Security and Cooperation in Europe;

4. *Calls upon* Member States to consider favourably requests by the Secretary-General for necessary assistance to UNPREDEP in the performance of its mandate;

5. *Requests* the Secretary-General to keep the Council regularly informed of any developments on the ground and other circumstances affecting the mandate of UNPREDEP, and in particular to submit, if possible by 31 January 1996, a report on all aspects of UNPREDEP in the light of developments in the region, for review by the Council;

6. *Decides* to remain actively seized of the matter.

Security Council resolution 1027(1995)

30 November 1995     Meeting 3602     Adopted unanimously

9-nation draft (S/1995/996).

*Sponsors:* Argentina, Czech Republic, France, Germany, Honduras, Italy, Russian Federation, United Kingdom, United States.

## ICFY activities

According to the biannual reports of the Co-Chairmen of the ICFY Steering Committee, transmitted to the Security Council on 27 July 1995[8] and on 2 January 1996,[9] the ICFY Working Group on Ethnic and National Communities and Minorities intensified its efforts during 1995 to promote a series of legislative and practical improvements in favour of the ethnic Albanian and other minorities in the former Yugoslav Republic of Macedonia.

The Working Group had organized 10 rounds of two-day talks, in which representatives of all Albanian parties and the Ministers of the Interior, Justice and Education participated. To supplement those talks, numerous individual meetings were held with representatives of Parliament, other government agencies, other minority groups (Muslims, Romas, Serbs, Turks, Vlachs), opposition groups outside Parliament, and the media. The talks focused on new legislation under consideration for all three levels of education (elementary, secondary, university) and on local self-government. Also discussed were language and citizenship issues, and display of national symbols.

In the media sector, the Working Group sponsored an agreement between the Governments of Denmark and Switzerland, on the one hand, and ''Macedonian Radio and Television'', on the other, providing for the delivery of television equipment and for the tripling of broadcast time in the Albanian language, as well as for a considerable increase in air time for languages of other nationalities. A similar radio project had been prepared by specialists from the European Broadcasting Union.

### Relations with Greece

On 3 April, Greece registered its objection[10] to the fact that the former Yugoslav Republic of Macedonia, in its statement before the Security Council on the occasion of the adoption of **resolution 983(1995)** on 31 March, referred to itself as the ''Republic of Macedonia''. Greece recalled that the admission of that republic to the United Nations was provisionally as ''the former Yugoslav Republic of Macedonia'', pending settlement of the dispute with Greece over its name.

Responding[11] on 5 April, the former Yugoslav Republic of Macedonia asserted that the name of any Member State was that State's exclusive right, which was respected and established in international legal norms and in the basic principles of the United Nations.

### *Interim Accord*

The Secretary-General, by a letter of 13 September, informed the Security Council that the Ministers for Foreign Affairs of Greece and the former Yugoslav Republic of Macedonia had signed an Interim Accord that day at UN Headquarters in New York. The Accord, the result of more than two years' mediation by the Secretary-General's Special Envoy Cyrus Vance (United States), pursuant to Council resolution 845(1993),[12] was also signed by the Special Envoy as witness to the event. Annexed to the Secretary-General's letter[13] was the text of the Accord.

The Accord contained a series of articles governing: friendly relations between the parties and confidence-building measures (articles 1 to 8); human rights and cultural rights (9 and 10); international, multilateral and regional institutions (11); treaty relations (12 to 14); and economic, commercial, environmental and legal relations (15 to 20). The final clauses (articles 21 to 23) concerned settlement of disputes exclusively by peaceful means, non-infringement by the Accord of existing bilateral and multilateral agreements with other States, and the Accord's duration and effective date, namely, the thirtieth day following the date of its signature on 13 September.

Under the Accord, the two neighbouring States agreed to respect each other's sovereignty, territorial integrity and political independence and to establish diplomatic relations, ultimately at the ambassadorial level. They confirmed their common existing frontier as an inviolable international border. They agreed to refrain from the threat or use of force, to continue negotiations under the auspices of the Secretary-General on the contentious issue of the name of the former Yugoslav Republic of Macedonia, and that the latter should cease to use in any way the symbol currently displayed on its national flag. They further agreed to refrain from imposing any impediment to the movement of people or goods between their territories.

In a statement[14] on 14 September, the President of the former Yugoslav Republic of Macedonia informed the Secretary-General that the signing of the Interim Accord had been preceded by the establishment of full diplomatic relations with the United States.

SECURITY COUNCIL ACTION

The Security Council, having received the Interim Accord, met on 15 September and, after consultations among its members, authorized the President to make the following statement[15] on the Council's behalf:

> The Security Council welcomes the signing of the Interim Accord between Greece and the former Yugoslav Republic of Macedonia and looks forward to the establishment of a new relationship between the parties based on international law and peaceful, friendly relations. The Council believes the Accord will promote the strengthening of stability in the region.
>
> The Security Council commends both parties, the Secretary-General, the Secretary-General's Special

Envoy, Cyrus Vance, and the United States envoy, Matthew Nimetz, for their efforts in bringing about this important achievement, pursuant to Security Council resolutions 817(1993) and 845(1993). The Council encourages them to continue their efforts to resolve the remaining differences between the parties and urges the parties to implement fully the Interim Accord.

*Meeting number.* SC 3579.

**Further communication.** On 1 December, Greece, recalling the Interim Accord between it and the former Yugoslav Republic of Macedonia, stated[16] that the Accord constituted an unmistakable proof of its resolve to settle disputes peacefully and to ensure harmonious relations with its neighbours, for which the former Yugoslav Republic of Macedonia, along with other States, had expressed appreciation.

In this context, Greece was unpleasantly surprised that the former Yugoslav Republic of Macedonia, in its statement before the Council on 22 November on the occasion of the suspension of sanctions against Yugoslavia (Serbia and Montenegro), had once again referred to itself as the "Republic of Macedonia" and made other references that ran counter to the spirit and letter of the Interim Accord.

*REFERENCES*

[1]YUN 1994, p. 495, SC res. 947(1994), 30 Sep. 1994. [2]S/1995/222 & Corr.1,2. [3]YUN 1994, p. 571. [4]Ibid., p. 570. [5]A/49/875-S/1995/235. [6]S/1995/253. [7]S/1995/987. [8]S/1995/626. [9]S/1996/4. [10]S/1995/257. [11]S/1995/260. [12]YUN 1993, p. 209, SC res. 845(1993), 18 June 1993. [13]S/1995/794. [14]A/50/435-S/1995/793. [15]S/PRST/1995/46. [16]S/1995/1005.

## Federal Republic of Yugoslavia (Serbia and Montenegro)

In 1995, the Federal Republic of Yugoslavia (Serbia and Montenegro), together with both Croatia and Bosnia and Herzegovina, played a key role in contributing to the successful outcome of the peace process that led to their formal signing, on 14 December, of the General Framework Agreement for Peace in Bosnia and Herzegovina (the Peace Agreement). It had similarly contributed to the negotiations that had led to the earlier signing, on 12 November, of the Basic Agreement on the Region of Eastern Slavonia, Baranja and Western Sirmium, concluded between Croatia and the local Serb authorities in Eastern Slavonia.

As when the Security Council had acknowledged the significant step taken by Yugoslavia (Serbia and Montenegro) in 1994—closing its borders to the Bosnian Serbs to induce them to accept a negotiated settlement—by partially suspending the sanctions imposed against it, so too had the Council acknowledged, as early as the initialling on 22 November of the Peace Agreement,

that country's spirit of cooperation and compromise during the peace process by suspending indefinitely and with immediate effect all sanctions imposed against it.

### UNPF liaison office

Throughout 1995, the United Nations continued to maintain a liaison office in Belgrade, Yugoslavia (Serbia and Montenegro), under UNPROFOR until 31 March and under UNPF thereafter, in order to conduct political liaison and public information functions. In addition, the office performed tasks relevant to the monitoring of the Prevlaka peninsula, as mandated by Security Council resolution 779(1992),[1] and, until 20 December, of the country's airfields, as mandated by resolution 786(1992).[2]

The liaison office enjoyed a level of cooperation with the Federal Government that proved vital to the effective functioning of UNCRO in Croatia, UNPROFOR in Bosnia and Herzegovina and UNPREDEP in the former Yugoslav Republic of Macedonia. Given the necessity of a continued UN presence in Belgrade, the Secretary-General said in a 23 November report[3] to the Council that he felt it important for the Federal Government to extend to the United Nations, its personnel, property, funds and assets the necessary privileges and immunities deriving from Article 105 (1) of the UN Charter, the Convention on the Privileges and Immunities of the United Nations[4] and the customary principles and practices applicable to UN peace-keeping or similar operations.

### Kosovo, Sandjak (Raska) and Vojvodina

**Reports of ICFY Steering Committee Co-Chairmen.** The biannual reports of the Co-Chairmen of the ICFY Steering Committee, transmitted to the Security Council on 27 July 1995[5] and on 2 January 1996,[6] indicated that ICFY had renewed its efforts to re-establish a dialogue between leaders of non-Serb ethnic communities in Kosovo, Sandjak (Sandzak or Raska) and Vojvodina. To that end, consultations had been held with leaders of the Kosovo Albanians and Sandjak Muslims, as well as with the municipal authorities in Pristina and Novi Pazar. Those contacts were continuing and possible modalities for dialogue were under consideration, it was reported.

**Communications.** Yugoslavia (Serbia and Montenegro) transmitted to the Secretary-General on 24 March an *aide-mémoire* regarding Kosovo and Metohija, asserting that that province was an integral part of the Republic of Serbia and, hence, of Yugoslavia (Serbia and Montenegro).[7]

Yugoslavia (Serbia and Montenegro) drew attention to what it termed Albania's recognition of the non-existent "Republic of Kosovo" in October

1991 and the successor Government's subsequent endorsement of that recognition in April 1992, as well as to the opening of a "representative office of the Republic of Kosovo" in Tirana. Albania, the *aide-mémoire* stated, was according Kosovo's separatist leaders treatment befitting State representatives and had presented them as such to the national and international public. Albanian diplomatic missions in international organizations and forums (United Nations, OSCE, EU, European Parliament, Council of Europe, NATO) were representing the "Republic of Kosovo" and organizing the visits and meetings of its separatist leaders. A point in case was when the Permanent Mission of Albania to the United Nations had organized a press conference for Ibrahim Rugova on 8 December 1994, presenting him as "the President of the Republic of Kosovo".

The *aide-mémoire* went on to say that Albania continued to encourage Kosovo's Albanian minority to be disloyal to the State in which they lived and to boycott its general elections and educational system. By its official statements, Albania sought to internationalize the question of Kosovo and Metohija and to promote secession of the province from Serbia.

On 19 April, Yugoslavia (Serbia and Montenegro) reported[8] that Albania continued to seize lands owned by ethnic Serbian and Montenegrin minorities (the Vracani and Podgoricani) in the villages of Stari and Mladi Boric, where they had lived for centuries. The official explanation was that those lands were being taken in exchange for other parcels of land as part of an administrative reorganization. Yugoslavia (Serbia and Montenegro) expressed regret that international human rights organizations had tolerated that policy.

On 15 August, Albania charged[9] that Yugoslavia (Serbia and Montenegro) had begun to resettle Serb refugees from Croatia and from Bosnia and Herzegovina in Kosovo with the aim of changing the predominant ethnic Albanian composition of the population there. As that could aggravate an already tense situation in Kosovo, Albania asked the Security Council to take steps to stop what it called the ethnic cleansing of Kosovo's Albanians and include the Kosovo situation in the overall solution of the crisis in the former Yugoslavia. On the same date, Bosnia and Herzegovina drew attention[10] to the resettlement of Serb refugees in Sandjak (Raska) and Vojvodina, in addition to Kosovo, with the obvious intention of changing the ethnic character of those areas in favour of the Serb population.

Replying on 18 August, Yugoslavia (Serbia and Montenegro) declared[11] that instead of expressing compassion for the plight of the Serbs expelled from Krajina, Albania was using that humanitarian tragedy as an opportunity to generate fear among ethnic Albanians in Kosovo and provoke a spillover of the conflict to the entire region. It accused Bosnia and Herzegovina of interfering in the right of a sovereign Government to decide where in its territory—of which Raska (Sandjak) was an integral part—refugees would be accommodated. Similar points were made in a second letter[12] of the same date.

On 6 October, Yugoslavia (Serbia and Montenegro) raised its objection[13] over Hungary's statement before the General Assembly on 28 September, wherein Hungary voiced concern over the settlement of Serb refugees in areas traditionally inhabited by other national minorities so as to change the composition of the population in those areas, and suggested that forcible means and intimidation had been used against Croat and Hungarian minorities in Vojvodina, an autonomous province of Serbia. Yugoslavia (Serbia and Montenegro) labelled the suggestion baseless and reiterated its right as a sovereign State to decide where in its territory to resettle the refugees.

### Yugoslavia (Serbia and Montenegro)–Croatia

In a number of communications addressed to the Secretary-General and the President of the Security Council between July and October, Yugoslavia (Serbia and Montenegro) charged Croatia with many incidents of unprovoked attacks in flagrant violation of its sovereignty and territorial integrity.

The alleged incidents included Croatian Army attacks by anti-aircraft machine-gun fire and artillery at border positions of the Army of Yugoslavia (Serbia and Montenegro) near Greda in the region of Boka Kotorska (4 and 9 July),[14] as well as in the areas of Debela Ljut, Kozen Do (12 August)[15] and Dunave Krajnje (Konavli) (12 August).[16] Also reported were: two separate firings at JA border units from the Butkovina region (19 August),[17] shelling of Sitnica village and the Borovik forest (21 August),[18] renewed shelling of Sitnica (23 August),[19] and mortar-fire attacks in the areas of Gusarska Jama (26 August)[20] and Prasna Rupa, approximately 500 metres deep into Yugoslav territory (28 August).[21]

Responding to the alleged attack on Prasna Rupa, Croatia countercharged that the area in question was 1,100 metres inside the territory, not of Yugoslavia (Serbia and Montenegro), but of Bosnia and Herzegovina.[22]

Further allegations of Croatian Army attacks during September, almost all launched from Cesmina Glava, claimed repeated shelling of Gusarska Jama, as well as sniper fire, penetrating Yugoslav territory some 300 metres and 250 metres, respectively (13 and 14 September);[23] and anti-aircraft gunfire on JA positions in the area of Sitnica village, 12 kilometres north-west of Herceg Novi (19 September),[24] and of Prasna Rupa.[25]

On 22 September, Croatia denied[26] that its Army had launched any of the September attacks as charged, and pointed out, on the basis of an enclosed map, that Gusarska Jama, Sitnica and Borovik were all located within the territory of Bosnia and Herzegovina. In connection with the letters containing the allegations, Croatia on 2 October drew attention to the fact that their author had signed his name as an official of the "Permanent Mission of Yugoslavia to the United Nations"; Croatia objected to the publication of the letters as UN documents, stating that the author did not represent a Member State and as such had no authority to request their publication.[27]

On 9 October, Yugoslavia (Serbia and Montenegro) further alleged that Croatia's attacks were aimed at provoking a response from JA so as to portray Yugoslavia (Serbia and Montenegro) as an aggressor engaged in military activity on that part of the border; it also pointed out that the administrative borders of the republics of the former Yugoslavia had never been precisely delineated, making it possible for all "secessionist Yugoslav republics to interpret them in an arbitrary fashion".[28]

*REFERENCES*

[1]YUN 1992, p. 343, SC res. 779(1992), 6 Oct. 1992. [2]Ibid., p. 373, SC res. 786(1992), 10 Nov. 1992. [3]S/1995/987. [4]YUN 1946-47, p. 100, GA res. 22 A (I), annex, 13 Feb. 1946. [5]S/1995/626. [6]S/1996/4. [7]A/50/97. [8]A/50/162-S/1995/324. [9]S/1995/700. [10]S/1995/698. [11]S/1995/708. [12]S/1995/715. [13]A/50/530. [14]S/1995/591. [15]A/50/353-S/1995/694. [16]A/50/351-S/1995/692. [17]S/1995/727. [18]S/1995/732. [19]S/1995/734. [20]S/1995/749. [21]S/1995/757. [22]S/1995/770. [23]S/1995/802, S/1995/809. [24]S/1995/814. [25]S/1995/832. [26]S/1995/818. [27]S/1995/838. [28]S/1995/850.

## Other States

The Secretary-General in 1995 continued efforts towards an overall settlement of the Cyprus problem. The mandate of the UN peace-keeping force there was extended until 30 June 1996.

In accordance with an informal understanding between the United Nations and OSCE with respect to conflicts involving members of the Commonwealth of Independent States (CIS), the United Nations continued its lead in peacemaking efforts in Abkhazia, Georgia, while OSCE retained its lead in Nagorny Karabakh, an enclave in Azerbaijan, as well as in South Ossetia, Georgia.

In April, the Security Council reiterated its support for the efforts of the Co-Chairmen of the OSCE Conference to assist in the conclusion of a political agreement of the armed conflict in and around the Nagorny Karabakh region. In September, the Secretary-General decided to send his Special Adviser for special assignments on preventive and peacemaking efforts on a goodwill mission to the region, to demonstrate the Secretary-General's concern over the conflict and to underline his support for the peacemaking efforts of the OSCE Minsk Group.

Despite efforts of the Secretary-General's Special Envoy for Georgia and Deputy Special Envoy, appointed in October, no agreement was reached in 1995 on a political status for Abkhazia, Georgia, acceptable to both sides. However, the parties complied with their 1994 agreement on a cease-fire and separation of forces, as verified by the UN Observer Mission in Georgia (UNOMIG). In May, the Council extended the Mission's mandate until 12 January 1996.

### Cyprus

During 1995, the Secretary-General's mission of good offices in Cyprus continued, within the overall framework set out by the Security Council in 1994.[1] It sought to achieve progress on both the substance of the Cyprus problem and the implementation of the package of confidence-building measures between the two Cypriot communities, which had been recommended by the Council in 1992,[2] defined by the parties at the practical level in 1993[3] and accepted by them in principle in 1994.[4]

The Secretary-General's Special Representative, Joe Clark, and Deputy Special Representative, Gustave Feissel, continued contacts with the leaders of both sides as well as with the Governments of Greece and Turkey and with other interested Governments, with a view to finding a basis for the resumption of direct talks. To that end, the Special Representative travelled to the region in March and May, visiting Nicosia, Cyprus, Ankara, Turkey and Athens, Greece. In a 5 June briefing, he informed the Security Council that it had not been possible to define a basis for resumed talks. Further efforts did not succeed in breaking the impasse by year's end, despite the presence on the negotiating table of almost all elements required for a just and lasting settlement.

UN efforts were supported by activities of the European Union (EU) and individual Member States. Missions to Cyprus were undertaken by senior government officials and special representatives from Italy, the Russian Federation, the United Kingdom and the United States; fact-finding visits were made by senior officials of France, Germany, Ireland, Spain and the European Commission. From 21 to 23 May, the United States, in cooperation with the United Kingdom, convened a meeting in London with representatives of the Cypriot leaders; however, no progress towards the resumption of direct talks was achieved.

The United Nations Peace-keeping Force in Cyprus (UNFICYP), established in 1964,[5] continued to monitor the cease-fire, maintain the military status quo to prevent a recurrence of fighting, and carry out humanitarian and economic activities to promote a return to normal conditions on the island. The Security Council extended UNFICYP's mandate in June, and again in December, until 30 June 1996.

On 18 September, the General Assembly deferred consideration of the question of Cyprus and included it in the provisional agenda of its fiftieth session (**decision 49/502**).

**Communications.** During 1995, Cyprus, Greece and Turkey addressed a number of communications to the Secretary-General and the Security Council President on various aspects of the Cyprus question. Most of the letters from Turkey transmitted communications from representatives of the Turkish Cypriot community.

In a 20 January letter,[6] the Turkish Cypriot side expressed its readiness to implement the package of confidence-building measures, which included the reopening of the fenced area of Varosha and of Nicosia International Airport under UN administration, as well as 12 additional measures. In that regard, the letter set forth several proposals for action, including implementation of unmanning arrangements along the cease-fire lines; establishment of a transitional bicommunal body to develop and realize joint projects; and commencement, upon the conclusion of the confidence-building measures agreement, of substantive talks on a bicommunal and bizonal federal settlement and of negotiations on other measures, such as those of a military nature. In the meantime, the Turkish Cypriot side declared its unilateral implementation of measures to improve the living conditions of Greek Cypriots and Maronites in the northern part of the island, as well as procedures for family visits to the north by students studying in the south, and to promote bicommunal contacts. On 23 January, Turkey supported[7] those proposals.

In its reply,[8] communicated on 23 January, Cyprus pointed to the existing substantial differences between the two sides on all major aspects of the Cyprus question, including the political status and representation of both communities in a federal State, demilitarization, treaties of guarantees, settlers, territorial and constitutional issues, and accession of Cyprus to EU. The Greek Cypriot side was of the view that implementation of the confidence-building measures without finding a common basis on the main issues would not contribute to the solution, but rather would perpetuate the status quo.

In a 13 March letter,[9] Greece referred to Turkey's position that the opening of negotia-

tions on the membership of Cyprus in EU before an overall settlement of the Cyprus problem was undesirable and would lead to integration of the northern part of the island into Turkey. Greece stated that such a position undermined international efforts to promote the peace process on the island. In a similar vein, Cyprus on 15 March denounced[10] what it termed recent threats by Turkish government officials to integrate the occupied part of Cyprus into Turkey, bringing about the permanent division of the island. On 29 March, the Turkish Cypriot side responded[11] that the application to join EU had been made unilaterally by the Greek Cypriot side and was therefore devoid of legal basis and not binding on the other side or on Cyprus as a whole. In further communications on the issue, the Turkish Cypriot side accused[12] the other party of shifting the negotiating process to settle the Cyprus problem from the United Nations to the EU platform and of stepping up its militarization campaign. It also claimed[13] that the Greek Cypriot side, while rejecting the implementation of the confidence-building measures and continuing an excessive rearmament, was trying to achieve enosis (union with Greece), by way of membership in EU, before a resolution of the Cyprus question.

On 20 October, Cyprus stated[14] that the agreement on legal matters, concluded between what it termed the illegal entity in the occupied part of Cyprus—the "Turkish Republic of Northern Cyprus"—and Turkey, constituted a violation of the sovereignty and jurisdiction of the Republic of Cyprus and contravened UN resolutions on the question of Cyprus. In a letter transmitted on 1 November,[15] the Turkish Cypriot side responded that Turkey and the Turkish Republic of Northern Cyprus were two sovereign countries which formally recognized each other and that any interference with their reciprocal relationship was unwarranted. Acts of vandalism and desecration against places of worship in the northern part of the island was the subject of a 7 November communication[16] from Cyprus, which accused the other party of systematic destruction of the cultural heritage in the north; in its reply,[17] the Turkish Cypriot side countered that authorities in the north did their best to protect and preserve all cultural property regardless of origin, and that individual acts of vandalism or theft, which were a worldwide phenomenon, were partly due to the existence of a lucrative stolen-art market in the southern part of the island.

In several letters, Cyprus complained about violations of its airspace by Turkish military aircraft; the Turkish Cypriot side replied that all flights over the northern part of the island were made with full knowledge and consent of the authorities there, pointing out that Greek fighter planes had flown over the south during joint military exercises between the Greek Cypriot administration and Greece. A number of other communications from both parties dealt with excavations near the Old City of Nicosia, carried out by the Turkish Cypriot authorities (see below, under "Communications from the Secretary-General"). The Turkish Cypriot side also forwarded letters challenging the statements made by the other party in the General Assembly, and clarifying its position on the Cyprus question.

## UNFICYP

**Report of the Secretary-General (June).** In a 15 June report[18] on UNFICYP activities, covering the period from 13 December 1994 to 15 June 1995, the Secretary-General stated that the Force continued to monitor the cease-fire lines and to keep the area between the lines, known as the buffer zone, under constant surveillance from 22 permanent observation posts, two posts for daytime surveillance and 19 patrol bases for periodic daily surveillance. It also carried out periodic surveillance from 118 additional observation posts, conducted vehicle, foot and air patrols, and maintained surveillance of the seaward extension of the cease-fire lines.

During the period under review, both sides had generally respected the cease-fire and the military status quo; however, UNFICYP intervened in a number of minor incidents to correct violations and prevent any escalation, and reported the firing of weapons on numerous occasions. On 6 and 7 June, as part of a religious ceremony, the Greek Cypriot side temporarily deployed a sizeable armed guard of honour in the buffer zone near Athienou. It also continued with an extensive programme of strengthening its military positions and increasing their number along and behind its cease-fire line. Some excavations encroached upon the buffer zone but were filled in after representations by UNFICYP. The integrity of the buffer zone was also violated during a small number of Greek Cypriot demonstrations. For their part, the Turkish Forces in Cyprus carried out maintenance and some minor improvements of military positions along or behind their cease-fire line. Turkish Cypriot authorities also modified access to the fenced area of Varosha, despite UNFICYP protests, so as to allow public visits to a church located within the area, which was inaugurated on 2 May as an icon museum.

The number of air violations increased during the reporting period; in May, Turkish fighter aircraft entered Cypriot airspace in the north of the island as part of a military exercise, which was protested by the Greek Cypriot authorities. At the same time, Greek Cypriot tourist and fishing boats continued to cross the seaward extension of the Turkish Forces cease-fire line, and on two occasions crews of fishing vessels were apprehended by a Turkish Cypriot patrol.

Despite the Security Council's 1994 resolution[19] urging a significant reduction in the number of foreign troops in Cyprus, both sides continued to improve their military capabilities through the acquisition or upgrading of armaments and equipment and the recruitment of additional personnel. Nor was progress achieved in respect of the Council's calls for unmanning of other parts of the buffer zone, a ban on live ammunition or weapons other than hand-held weapons along the cease-fire lines, or the prohibition of the firing of weapons within sight or hearing of the buffer zone. The Turkish Forces refused to enter into discussions on those issues, referring UNFICYP instead to the Turkish Cypriot authorities, whereas the United Nations maintained that the Turkish Forces were a party to the cease-fire established in 1974[20] and could not abrogate their responsibility in that regard. Difficulties also remained regarding UNFICYP's freedom of movement in the northern part of the island.

The Force continued to facilitate a wide spectrum of humanitarian activities with agencies and authorities on both sides. It promoted bicommunal contacts and projects, delivered food and other supplies to the 520 Greek Cypriots and the 234 Maronites residing in the northern part of the island, assisted in organizing family visits across the buffer zone and in ensuring that permanent moves to the other side were voluntary, and engaged in discussions with authorities with regard to the living conditions of Greek Cypriots and Maronites located in the north and of Turkish Cypriots located in the south. UNFICYP also monitored the situation in the mixed village of Pyla in the buffer zone.

As at 1 June, the Force consisted of 1,138 military personnel from Argentina, Austria, Canada, Finland, Ireland and the United Kingdom, and 35 civilian police from Australia and Ireland. It was supported by 366 civilian staff, 42 of whom were recruited internationally. UNFICYP remained under the command of Brigadier-General Ahti T. P. Vartiainen (Finland), while the Secretary-General's Special Representative continued to act as Chief of Mission, with the resident Deputy Special Representative assuming that responsibility in his absence.

UN efforts to restore normal conditions in Cyprus included activities of various bodies and agencies of the UN system, coordinated by the United Nations Development Programme (UNDP). They involved programmes of technical assistance, UN fellowships and planning for future bicommunal projects. During the period under review, the Government of Cyprus received assistance in the areas of health care, radiation protection, financial management, statistics, industrial competitiveness, human development, capital investment, energy, family relations and the rights of women. UNDP administered 30 training fellowships for Cypriot nationals, totalling $80,500, and provided support to six UN workshops in Cyprus. Humanitarian assistance continued to be coordinated by UNHCR, and included bicommunal programmes in health care, forestry, pest control, the environment, water resources, architecture, civil engineering and education. Those programmes were funded through a $10-million annual grant provided to UNHCR by the United States Agency for International Development. UNHCR also cooperated with UNFICYP in addressing the needs of Turkish Cypriots in the south and Greek Cypriots in the north, and assisted in the operation of an exchange point to facilitate routine services between the two communities.

The Committee on Missing Persons did not meet during the reporting period, due to differences between the two sides over criteria for the conclusion of investigations; however, the Third Member of the Committee held regular bilateral meetings with both sides in an effort to find a compromise solution, and in March reported to the Secretary-General, who forwarded to the two leaders on 17 May his own proposals for the criteria in question. The Turkish Cypriot leader had replied positively to the proposed criteria; a response from the Greek Cypriot side was still pending.

The Secretary-General concluded that, in view of the prevailing circumstances, UNFICYP's presence on the island remained indispensable to achieving the objectives set by the Security Council. Accordingly, he recommended an extension of its mandate until the end of 1995, noting that the Governments of Cyprus, Greece and the United Kingdom had indicated their concurrence with that recommendation, while Turkey continued to support the position of the Turkish Cypriot side, as expressed in previous Council meetings on the extension of the mandate. At the same time, the Secretary-General pointed out that the continuing quiet in Cyprus should not obscure the fact that there was only a cease-fire, not peace, on the island. In the absence of progress towards an overall settlement, the situation remained subject to sudden tensions. He also stressed that the excessive levels of armaments and forces in Cyprus and the rate at which they were being strengthened were a cause for serious concern.

**SECURITY COUNCIL ACTION (June)**

On 23 June, the Security Council adopted **resolution 1000(1995)**.

*The Security Council,*

*Welcoming* the report of the Secretary-General on the United Nations operation in Cyprus of 15 June 1995,

*Taking note* of his recommendation that the Security Council extend the mandate of the United Nations Peace-keeping Force in Cyprus (UNFICYP) for a further period of six months,

*Noting* that the Government of Cyprus has agreed that in view of the prevailing conditions in the island it is necessary to keep the Force in Cyprus beyond 30 June 1995,

*Reaffirming* its earlier relevant resolutions on Cyprus, and in particular resolutions 186(1964) of 4 March 1964 and 969(1994) of 21 December 1994,

*Expressing its concern* that there has been no progress towards a final political solution,

*Noting* that no progress has been made on extending the 1989 unmanning agreement,

*Noting also* that a review of the situation on the Secretary-General's mission of good offices in Cyprus remains in progress and looking forward to receiving a definitive report at an appropriate time,

1. *Decides* to extend the mandate of UNFICYP for a further period ending on 31 December 1995;

2. *Calls upon* the military authorities on both sides to ensure that no incidents occur along the buffer zone and to extend their full cooperation to UNFICYP;

3. *Requests* the Secretary-General to keep under review the structure and strength of UNFICYP with a view to its possible restructuring, bearing in mind the possible implications of an agreement on the extension of the 1989 unmanning agreement;

4. *Expresses concern* about the modernization and upgrading of military forces in the Republic of Cyprus and the lack of progress towards a significant reduction in the number of foreign troops in the Republic of Cyprus, urges once again all concerned to commit themselves to such a reduction and to a reduction of defence spending in the Republic of Cyprus to help restore confidence between the parties and as a first step towards the withdrawal of non-Cypriot forces as described in the set of ideas, and calls upon the Secretary-General to promote efforts in this direction;

5. *Expresses concern also* about the failure by the military authorities on both sides to take reciprocal measures to prohibit along the cease-fire lines live ammunition or weapons other than those which are hand-held and to prohibit also the firing of weapons within sight or hearing of the buffer zone, and calls upon those authorities to enter into discussions with UNFICYP on this matter in line with paragraph 3 of resolution 839(1993) of 11 June 1993;

6. *Regrets* the failure to reach agreement on the extension of the 1989 unmanning agreement to cover all areas of the buffer zone where the two sides are in close proximity to each other, and calls upon the military authorities on both sides to cooperate urgently with UNFICYP to this end;

7. *Urges* the leaders of both communities to promote tolerance and reconciliation between the two communities as recommended in the relevant reports of the Secretary-General;

8. *Welcomes* the Secretary-General's decision to continue contacts with the two leaders, to make every effort to find common ground for the basis for a resumption of direct talks;

9.   *Reaffirms* the importance it attaches to early progress being made on the substance of the Cyprus question and on the implementation of the confidence-building measures as called for in resolution 939(1994) of 29 July 1994;

10.   *Requests* the Secretary-General to submit a report by 10 December 1995 on the implementation of the present resolution and on any obstacles he may have encountered;

11.   *Decides* to remain actively seized of the matter.

Security Council resolution 1000(1995)

23 June 1995     Meeting 3547     Adopted unanimously

Draft prepared in consultations among Council members (S/1995/503).

**Communications from the Secretary-General (July).** On 7 July, the Secretary-General informed[21] the Security Council that the Turkish Cypriot authorities had begun large-scale excavations immediately behind the Turkish Forces' cease-fire line in an area adjacent to the walls of the Old City of Nicosia known as the Roccas Bastion. He said that the area was specifically covered by the 1989 unmanning agreement. Although the declared purpose of the excavations was to build a playground, the extensive digging of trenches raised questions as to the real purpose. As provided for in the 1989 agreement, UNFICYP requested regular access to the excavations and a detailed briefing on construction plans; however, both requests were denied. For its part, the Government of Cyprus indicated that, if the existing situation was not rectified, it would deem the unmanning agreement to have been breached and would consider taking countermeasures. Despite UN representations to the Turkish Cypriot side, no progress was achieved towards a resolution of the problem.

On 11 July, the Security Council President replied[22] that Council members supported fully the efforts being made to secure UNFICYP inspection of the excavations, and requested the Secretary-General to inform the Council of the inspection's outcome.

In a 25 July letter,[23] the Secretary-General reported that his Deputy Special Representative had received a detailed briefing by Turkish Cypriot authorities on 13 July and that two UNFICYP inspections of the site were carried out on the following two days. The letter provided findings of the inspections as well as a construction sketch. It was concluded that, while the construction appeared unnecessarily elaborate and costly for its stated purpose, work carried out to date did not correspond to normal military specifications or to any evident military logic. The Turkish Cypriot authorities maintained that the trenches would serve to provide access to underground facilities for the planned public park and recreational area and to facilitate repair of the water and sewage pipes as well as electricity and telephone wires.

They agreed to provide UNFICYP with unhindered regular access to the site. The first follow-up inspection was carried out on 22 July.

**Report of the Secretary-General (December).** In his report covering developments from 16 June to 10 December,[24] the Secretary-General stated that both sides had generally respected the cease-fire and the military status quo, but continued to upgrade their military capabilities. The Greek Cypriot side proceeded with a programme to improve its military positions along and behind the cease-fire line, while the Turkish Cypriot side stated that it intended to convert an UNFICYP observation post within the fenced area of Varosha to a student dormitory, a violation of the status quo in that area. UNFICYP maintained close liaison and cooperation with the military and civilian authorities on both sides; however, in three instances involving detention of persons who had crossed the buffer zone into the northern part of the island, UNFICYP received neither timely nor accurate information from the Turkish Forces and the Turkish Cypriot authorities. By 1 December, the total strength of the Force had increased to 1,184, including 1,150 military personnel and 34 civilian police. Hungary resumed its contribution to the Force on 14 November.

A number of incidents occurred during the reporting period. On several occasions, Greek Cypriot hunters discharged firearms in the buffer zone at Force members, causing slight injuries to one soldier and damage to an UNFICYP patrol vehicle; furthermore, military and police personnel from both sides occasionally entered the zone without authorization from UNFICYP. The integrity of the zone was also violated during Greek Cypriot demonstrations in August and November, resulting in minor injuries to 15 UNFICYP members. On 15 November, during the opening of the newly constructed park and playground near the Old City of Nicosia (see also above), Turkish Cypriots showered stones and other objects into the buffer zone and at Greek Cypriot residences and offices; the authorities subsequently assured UNFICYP that such actions would not be allowed to recur. They also agreed to provide the Force with unhindered monthly access to the site, to ensure that it was used for exclusively civilian purposes.

The Secretary-General expressed concern at the growing incidence of overflights by military aircraft, noting that Turkish fighter planes had entered Cypriot airspace in October as part of an annual land and sea exercise, and repeatedly overflew the northern part of Nicosia and, on one occasion, the buffer zone. On 14 November, UNFICYP received reports that two Turkish military aircraft had entered the Nicosia flight information region, circumnavigated the island and overflew the Karpas peninsula before returning to

Turkey. The Government of Cyprus protested those actions; for their part, the Turkish Cypriot authorities and Turkey condemned the participation of Greek aircraft, using live ordnance, in an annual military exercise on the Greek Cypriot side.

In October, UNFICYP organized within the buffer zone in Nicosia an "open house" for children of both communities and their families, attended by more than 5,000 people—the largest bicommunal gathering since 1974—as well as a bicommunal friendship concert, with the participation of more than 1,000 persons. On both occasions, the Turkish Cypriot authorities waived restrictions on the movement of Turkish Cypriot civilians across the cease-fire line. The Force also continued to discharge humanitarian functions in respect of Greek Cypriots and Maronites located in the northern part of the island, whose numbers had decreased to 492 and remained at 234 respectively. UNFICYP discharged similar functions for Turkish Cypriots in the south, some 362 of whom had made themselves known to the Force. Following its review of the living conditions of those population groups, the Force made a number of recommendations for remedial action to authorities on both sides. The review found that Turkish Cypriots in the south, while enjoying the same legal rights as other citizens, were often victims of capricious discrimination or police harassment; there were also reports of maltreatment of detainees by the Cyprus police. At the same time, Greek Cypriots and Maronites living in the north were subject to severe restrictions, which curtailed the exercise of many basic freedoms and some economic and social rights.

In a series of replies concerning the review, the Government of Cyprus stated its commitment to equal treatment of all Cypriot citizens and its readiness to examine carefully complaints or reasonable demands by Turkish Cypriots residing in the south. It declared that it had initiated an inquiry into police misconduct, and announced a number of additional steps in response to UNFICYP recommendations. The Turkish Cypriot authorities, in their response to UNFICYP, cited the existing regulations concerning north-south family visits of Greek Cypriots and Maronites, as well as measures to be taken for improving their living conditions in the north, including the upkeep of their places of worship and education, possible restoration of holy places, installation of telephones, improvements to the water supply and road systems, and establishment of a medical centre.

The report further noted that bodies and agencies of the UN system continued their economic and social activities in Cyprus. UNDP carried out bicommunal projects in the field of health, including the campaign against AIDS, and arranged UN fellowships for Cypriots outside the country. UNHCR administered a bicommunal humanitarian programme in the areas of sanitation, agriculture, health, forestry, environmental monitoring and architecture; convened regular bicommunal meetings on its premises in Cyprus; and sponsored bicommunal seminars and training sessions both within and outside the island. As for the Committee on Missing Persons, the Secretary-General stated that both sides had responded positively to his 17 May proposal (see above), agreed that no further cases would be submitted after the end of 1995, and decided to resume the Committee's activities.

The Secretary-General concluded that UNFICYP's presence on the island remained indispensable, and recommended an extension of its mandate for a further six months, until 30 June 1996. The Council was informed that the Governments of Cyprus, Greece and the United Kingdom had indicated their concurrence with the proposed extension, while Turkey continued to support the position of the Turkish Cypriot side, as expressed in previous Council meetings on the extension of the mandate.

**SECURITY COUNCIL ACTION (December)**

On 19 December, the Security Council adopted **resolution 1032(1995)**.

*The Security Council,*

*Welcoming* the report of the Secretary-General on the United Nations operation in Cyprus of 10 December 1995,

*Taking note* of his recommendation that the Security Council extend the mandate of the United Nations Peace-keeping Force in Cyprus (UNFICYP),

*Noting* that the Government of Cyprus has agreed that in view of the prevailing conditions in the island it is necessary to keep the Force in Cyprus beyond 31 December 1995,

*Reaffirming* its earlier relevant resolutions on Cyprus, and in particular resolutions 186(1964) of 4 March 1964 and 1000(1995) of 23 June 1995,

*Expressing its concern* that there has been no progress towards a final political solution,

*Noting* that no progress has been made on extending the 1989 unmanning agreement,

1. *Decides* to extend the mandate of UNFICYP for a further period ending on 30 June 1996;

2. *Calls upon* the military authorities on both sides to ensure that no incidents occur along the buffer zone and to extend their full cooperation to UNFICYP;

3. *Requests* the Secretary-General to keep under review the structure and strength of UNFICYP with a view to its possible restructuring, and to present any new considerations he may have in this regard;

4. *Welcomes* the humanitarian review undertaken by UNFICYP with regard to the living conditions of the Greek Cypriots and the Maronites living in the northern part of the island and of Turkish Cypriots living in the southern part of the island, supports UNFICYP's

recommendations contained in the Secretary-General's report, and decides to keep the matter under review;

5.    *Expresses concern* about the continuing modernization and upgrading of military forces in the Republic of Cyprus and the lack of progress towards a significant reduction in the number of foreign troops in the Republic of Cyprus, urges once again all concerned to commit themselves to such a reduction and to a reduction of defence spending in the Republic of Cyprus to help restore confidence between the parties and as a first step towards the withdrawal of non-Cypriot forces as described in the set of ideas, and calls upon the Secretary-General to promote efforts in this direction;

6.    *Expresses concern also* about the failure by the military authorities on both sides to take reciprocal measures to prohibit along the cease-fire lines live ammunition or weapons other than those which are hand-held and to prohibit also the firing of weapons within sight or hearing of the buffer zone, and calls upon those authorities to enter into discussions with UNFICYP on this matter in line with paragraph 3 of resolution 839(1993) of 11 June 1993;

7.    *Regrets* the failure to reach agreement on the extension of the 1989 unmanning agreement to cover all areas of the buffer zone where the two sides are in close proximity to each other, and calls upon the military authorities on both sides to cooperate urgently with UNFICYP to this end;

8.    *Welcomes* the initiative of UNFICYP in organizing successful bicommunal events, urges the leaders of both communities to promote tolerance, confidence and reconciliation between the two communities as recommended in the relevant reports of the Secretary-General, and calls upon them to promote further bicommunal contacts and to remove obstacles to such contacts;

9.    *Welcomes* the Secretary-General's decision to continue contacts with the two leaders, to make every effort to find common ground for the basis for a resumption of direct talks;

10.    *Reaffirms* the importance it attaches to early progress being made on the substance of the Cyprus question and on the implementation of the confidence-building measures as called for in resolution 939(1994) of 29 July 1994;

11.    *Requests* the Secretary-General to submit a report during the coming mandate period on his mission of good offices, including a full assessment of his efforts towards reaching a settlement of the situation in Cyprus;

12.    *Also requests* the Secretary-General to submit a report by 10 June 1996 on the implementation of the present resolution;

13.    *Decides* to remain actively seized of the matter.

Security Council resolution 1032(1995)

19 December 1995     Meeting 3608     Adopted unanimously

Draft prepared in consultations among Council members (S/1995/1045).

## Financing

**Reports of the Secretary-General and ACABQ (April-June).** In a 25 April report on financing of UNFICYP,[25] the Secretary-General noted that the resources made available to the Force from 16 June to 15 December 1994 had totalled $22,800,000 gross ($22,357,700 net), including the one-third share of the cost met through voluntary

contributions from the Government of Cyprus ($7.6 million) and one half of the annual pledge of $6.5 million from the Government of Greece. Expenditures for the period from 16 June to 31 December 1994 amounted to $22,550,100 gross ($22,166,800 net), leaving an unencumbered balance of $249,900 gross ($190,900 net). Pursuant to a 1994 General Assembly resolution,[26] Member States' respective share in that balance was set off against their assessment for the period from 1 January to 30 June 1995. Accordingly, no further Assembly action was required. The report also noted that outstanding assessed contributions due from Member States for the period from 16 June 1993 to 31 December 1994 totalled $5.1 million as at 31 March 1995.

In a 30 May report,[27] the Advisory Committee on Administrative and Budgetary Questions pointed to the distortions between the Secretary-General's April report and his October 1994 report[28] containing preliminary estimates for the period ending 31 December 1994, and recommended that, in the future, financial performance reports for any given period should be submitted after the conclusion of that period. ACABQ did not recommend any change in the level of appropriations for UNFICYP.

In his June report on UNFICYP[18] (see above), the Secretary-General estimated the cost of maintaining the operation from 1 July to 31 December 1995 at $21.7 million, of which $11.2 million was to be assessed on Member States in accordance with a 1993 Assembly resolution.[29] As at 31 May 1995, unpaid contributions to the UNFICYP Special Account amounted to $9.6 million.

**GENERAL ASSEMBLY ACTION (July)**

On 12 July, the General Assembly, by **decision 49/484,** approved ACABQ's observations and recommendations.

**Reports of the Secretary-General and ACABQ (November/December).** On 6 November, the Secretary-General reported[30] that UNFICYP's financial performance from 1 January to 30 June 1995 had resulted in an overexpenditure of $333,000 gross ($344,800 net), owing primarily to the change in the supplier of rations from the British Forces Cyprus to a commercial supplier, as well as to pre-employment medical examinations of 300 locally employed civilian personnel who were converted to locally recruited UNFICYP staff on 1 July. There were also unforeseen additional requirements for utilities, contractual services, and medical treatment and services. Accordingly, the Secretary-General proposed appropriation and assessment of the overexpended amount.

ACABQ, in a 4 December report,[31] noted that the change in the rations supplier had been expected during the mandate period in question and that the anticipated additional expenditure should have been included in the budget for that period. In that regard, ACABQ believed that, in a long-established operation such as UNFICYP, unplanned activities should be at a minimum, and that greater managerial control should be exercised. In its opinion, no additional appropriation was needed at the current time, especially since the question of indemnity payment to locally employed civilians was still under legal review. Such additional appropriation as might be necessary should be reflected in the performance report for the period July to December 1995.

According to the Secretary-General's December report on UNFICYP[24] (see above), the Force's estimated costs from 1 January to 30 June 1996 amounted to $21.7 million, with $11.2 million to be borne by Member States, while outstanding assessed contributions totalled $9.2 million as at 30 November 1995.

**GENERAL ASSEMBLY ACTION (December)**

On 22 December, the General Assembly, by **decision 50/448**, endorsed ACABQ's observations and recommendations.

On 23 December, the Assembly decided that the Fifth (Administrative and Budgetary) Committee should continue its consideration of the item on financing of UNFICYP at its resumed fiftieth session (**decision 50/469**).

*REFERENCES*

[1]YUN 1994, p. 600, SC res. 939(1994), 29 July 1994. [2]YUN 1992, p. 269, SC res. 789(1992), 25 Nov. 1992. [3]YUN 1993, p. 385. [4]YUN 1994, p. 598. [5]YUN 1964, p. 165, SC res. 186(1964), 4 Mar. 1964. [6]S/1995/62. [7]S/1995/71. [8]A/49/836-S/1995/73. [9]A/49/862-S/1995/199. [10]A/49/865-S/1995/202. [11]A/49/873-S/1995/233. [12]A/50/544-S/1995/862. [13]A/50/801-S/1995/1008. [14]A/50/667-S/1995/878. [15]A/50/717-S/1995/919. [16]A/50/738-S/1995/938. [17]A/50/800-S/1995/1007. [18]S/1995/488 & Add.1. [19]YUN 1994, p. 604, SC res. 969(1994), 21 Dec. 1994. [20]YUN 1974, p. 267. [21]S/1995/561. [22]S/1995/562. [23]S/1995/618. [24]S/1995/1020 & Add.1. [25]A/49/590/Add.1. [26]YUN 1994, p. 607, GA res. 49/230, 23 Dec. 1994. [27]A/49/781/Add.1. [28]YUN 1994, p. 607. [29]YUN 1993, p. 394, GA res. 47/236, 14 Sep. 1993. [30]A/50/722 & Corr.1. [31]A/50/802.

## Armenia-Azerbaijan

The unresolved situation in and around the enclave of Nagorny Karabakh in Azerbaijan continued in 1995 to draw that country and Armenia into conflict. With support from the United Nations, the Co-Chairmen of the OSCE Minsk Conference continued their efforts, through the OSCE Minsk Group, to bring that conflict to a speedy resolution and to facilitate the delivery of humanitarian assistance to refugees and displaced persons.

**Communications (22 January–9 March).** On 22 January, Armenia drew attention[1] to what it described as Azerbaijan's increased military activities along their common border over the past

20 days, and asked the international community to defuse the resultant tension. In addition to new military deployments along the front line, rearrangement of artillery positions, redeployment of four regiments from Nakhichevan to the Horadiz front and increased sniping, Armenia accused Azerbaijan of engaging in a new wave of hostile propaganda and of once more blowing up a section of the gas pipeline running through Georgia to Armenia.

Azerbaijan in turn on 26 January charged[2] Armenia with regrouping and redeploying troops along the cease-fire line, moving equipment and troops towards Azerbaijani positions at the Geranboy and Terter sectors of the front, stepping up ground and air reconnaissance activities, resettling Armenians in the occupied territories of Azerbaijan and organizing provocative official visits to those territories. By such acts, Azerbaijan claimed, Armenia was derailing the ongoing peace process within the framework of OSCE, just when the latter had intensified efforts to organize a peace-keeping force aimed at creating conditions for a political settlement of the conflict.

In a statement on 24 February, Azerbaijan, in connection with the forthcoming seventh anniversary of Armenia's undeclared war on the country aimed at seizing its Nagorny Karabakh region, recalled what it said were crimes committed by Armenia in pursuit of that objective.[3]

On 6 March, Azerbaijan issued a press release stating that beginning on the night of 4/5 March, Armenian forces had subjected the border settlements in the Tauz, Kazakh and Akstafa districts to intense shelling through the morning of 6 March; Armenia was reportedly destabilizing the situation along the country's north-western border to divert attention from a projected attack on northern Karabakh.[4] None the less, on 9 March, Azerbaijan reaffirmed[5] its commitment to a political settlement; Armenia, however, in Azerbaijan's view, maintained its destructive position, refusing to discuss the question of liberating the occupied Azerbaijani territories, including the Lachin and Shusha districts, thus stalling the OSCE Minsk negotiating process. Referring to the possible deployment of a multinational peace-keeping force as an essential element of a political agreement on the cessation of armed conflict under the auspices of the OSCE Minsk Group, Azerbaijan proposed inclusion in that agreement of a provision guaranteeing safe passage along the Hankendi/Stepanakert-Shusha-Lachin-Goris road, the complete withdrawal of armed forces from Lachin, and a fixed date for the return of displaced persons to that district.

**Reports of the Co-Chairmen, OSCE Minsk Conference.** On 21 March, the Co-Chairmen (Sweden and the Russian Federation) of the OSCE Minsk Conference reported on progress made towards a peaceful settlement of the Nagorny

Karabakh conflict since the OSCE Budapest decision of 6 December 1994 to intensify action to resolve that conflict.[6] The Co-Chairmen reported that the 1994 cease-fire,[7] reconfirmed several times, remained largely respected; that, through an exchange of letters the parties had undertaken to strengthen the cease-fire through direct contacts and other confidence-building measures; but that the understanding within the Minsk Group to establish an OSCE presence in the region remained unimplemented. An agreed basis for further negotiations presented to the parties was discussed at a round of negotiations held in Moscow in February.

It remained the view of the parties that a peace-keeping operation was necessary to give maximum guarantee to a political agreement. The High-level Planning Group, established by the Budapest decision, was in the process of formulating recommendations for such a force.

On 20 April, the Co-Chairmen pointed out[8] that continuing support from the Security Council for the possible deployment of an OSCE peace-keeping force, as well as continued UN technical advice and expertise, would be required, should such an operation materialize. The Co-Chairmen continued to pursue implementation of agreed measures for confidence-building and strengthening the cease-fire. They continued to seek the release of civilian detainees, including the sick, the wounded and persons over 50 years old, as well as of POWs. They asked all States to respond generously to the recently launched UN inter-agency appeal for humanitarian assistance to the Caucasus, where the number of war refugees and displaced persons had reached more than a million.

### SECURITY COUNCIL ACTION

In the light of the foregoing reports, the Security Council met on 26 April and, following consultations among its members, authorized the President to make the statement below[9] on the Council's behalf:

The Security Council has considered the reports of the Co-Chairmen of the OSCE Minsk Conference on Nagorny Karabakh presented in accordance with paragraph 8 of its resolution 884(1993). It expresses its satisfaction that the cease-fire in the region agreed upon on 12 May 1994 through the mediation of the Russian Federation in cooperation with the OSCE Minsk Group has been holding for almost a year.

At the same time, the Council reiterates the concern it has previously expressed at the conflict in and around the Nagorny Karabakh region of the Azerbaijani Republic and at the tensions between the Republic of Armenia and the Azerbaijani Republic. In particular, it expresses its concern at recent violent incidents and emphasizes the importance of using the mechanism of direct contacts for the settlement of incidents as agreed upon on 6 February 1995. It strongly urges the parties to the conflict to take all necessary measures to prevent such incidents in future.

The Council reaffirms all its relevant resolutions, *inter alia*, on the principles of sovereignty and territorial integrity of all States in the region. It also reaffirms the inviolability of international borders and the inadmissibility of the use of force for the acquisition of territory.

The Council reiterates its full support for the efforts of the Co-Chairmen of the Minsk Conference to assist in conducting speedy negotiations for the conclusion of a political agreement on the cessation of the armed conflict, the implementation of which will eliminate major consequences of the conflict for all parties, *inter alia*, ensuring withdrawal of forces, and permit the convening of the Minsk Conference.

The Council stresses that the parties to the conflict themselves bear the main responsibility for reaching a peaceful settlement. It stresses the urgency of concluding a political agreement on the cessation of the armed conflict on the basis of the relevant principles of the Charter of the United Nations and of the OSCE. It strongly urges those parties to constructively conduct negotiations without preconditions or procedural obstacles and to refrain from any actions that may undermine the peace process. It emphasizes that the achievement of such an agreement is a prerequisite for the deployment of a multinational OSCE peace-keeping force.

The Council welcomes the decision of the Budapest summit of the CSCE of 6 December 1994 on the "Intensification of CSCE action in relation to the Nagorny Karabakh conflict". It confirms its readiness to provide continuing political support, *inter alia*, through an appropriate resolution regarding the possible deployment of a multinational OSCE peace-keeping force following agreement among the parties for cessation of the armed conflict. The United Nations also stands ready to provide technical advice and expertise.

The Council underlines the urgency of the implementation by the parties of confidence-building measures, as agreed upon within the Minsk Group on 15 April 1994, in particular in the humanitarian field, including the release of all prisoners of war and civilian detainees by the first anniversary of the cease-fire. It calls upon the parties to prevent suffering of the civilian populations affected by the armed conflict.

The Council reiterates its request that the Secretary-General, the Chairman-in-Office of the OSCE and the Co-Chairmen of the OSCE Minsk Conference continue to report to the Council on the progress of the Minsk process and on the situation on the ground, in particular, on the implementation of its relevant resolutions and on present and future cooperation between the OSCE and the United Nations in this regard.

The Council will keep the matter under consideration.

*Meeting number.* SC 3525.

**Further communications.** Azerbaijan on 17 May labelled as unverified and a product of Armenia's propaganda machinery a 15 May broadcast by "Svoboda" radio in the Armenian-occupied Azerbaijani town of Hankendi, alleging Azerbaijani troop movements in the Barda, Agjabedi and Beilagan areas along the confrontation line.[10]

Armenia reported[11] another explosion on 21 May that destroyed a section of the gas pipeline running through the Azeri-populated Marneuli district of Georgia into Armenia, stressing that since 1992 this was the sixteenth such explosion, in addition to 34 acts of sabotage on the railway and seven explosions on the rail bridge over the Khram River connecting Armenia to Georgia. As a result, not only had Armenia been deprived of natural gas supply for close to 200 days, but its economy had also suffered incalculable damage.

Azerbaijan on 23 May responded[12] to Armenia's decision to suspend its participation in the negotiations under the auspices of the OSCE Minsk Group due to the gas-pipeline explosions attributed by Armenia to "agents of the Azerbaijani Government". Azerbaijan stated that as a country which had experienced the consequences of such acts, it had condemned, as it was condemning on this occasion, such acts of "international terrorism". On 6 June, Azerbaijan welcomed[13] Armenia's decision to continue to participate in the negotiations, as well as Georgia's statement that, pending completion of an investigation into the explosion, attributions of responsibility for it were premature and groundless.

Armenia on 2 June welcomed[14] the condemnation of the pipeline explosion by the OSCE Chairman-in-Office, as well as the latter's request that the OSCE Mission in Georgia work closely with that country's authorities to investigate the incident. Armenia insisted, however, that such "terrorist acts" were "acts of war" and contrary to the spirit and letter of the cease-fire agreement.

Azerbaijan, by letters[15] of 21 and 30 November and 5 December, drew attention to a what it called a flagrant political mistake in a Joint Inspection Unit (JIU) report[16]—namely, that it had ignored the fact that Nagorny Karabakh was an integral part of the Republic of Azerbaijan, while correctly identifying Abkhazia and South Ossetia as parts of the Republic of Georgia. Azerbaijan found it perplexing that the JIU inspectors, while abundantly citing Security Council and General Assembly resolutions that unequivocally reaffirmed the status of Nagorny Karabakh as an integral part of Azerbaijan, had ignored that fact, thus undermining the sovereignty of a State Member of the United Nations. Azerbaijan rejected as invalid the inspectors' explanation that their report's treatment of the region was analogous to the use of the title "Nagorny Karabakh" for a separate subsection in the Secretary-General's draft report on the work of the Organization, which, in its final version,[17] Azerbaijan pointed out, did not contain that title.

**Further report of the Co-Chairmen, OSCE Minsk Conference.** The Co-Chairmen of the OSCE Minsk Conference reported on 5 July that two other rounds of talks had taken place (Moscow, 15-18 May; Helsinki, Finland, 15-19 June), followed by consultations among members of the Minsk Group and representatives of the parties.[18] Discussions focused on the various elements for a draft political agreement.

On 12 May, the first anniversary of the cease-fire agreement, Armenia released all POWs and detainees and repatriated them to Baku, Azerbaijan. Azerbaijan had reciprocated accordingly, as had the Nagorny Karabakh leadership. The Minsk Group had followed up those reciprocal gestures of good will with a call on the conflicting parties to declare an amnesty for those who had participated in the armed conflict.

The OSCE Chairman-in-Office continued endeavours to obtain the necessary international support for a multinational OSCE peace-keeping operation.

**Statement for the Secretary-General.** According to a statement issued by his Spokesman on 8 September, the Secretary-General had decided to send his Special Adviser for special assignments on preventive and peacemaking efforts, Under-Secretary-General Aldo Ajello, on a goodwill mission in connection with the conflict over Nagorny Karabakh. The mission's purpose was to demonstrate the Secretary-General's concern about the conflict and to underline his support for the continuing peacemaking efforts of the OSCE Minsk Group, which had the leading role in assisting the parties to reach a peaceful solution to the conflict.

Mr. Ajello's itinerary was to include Moscow, where he would attend a meeting of the OSCE Minsk Group on Nagorny Karabakh (11-12 September); Armenia and Azerbaijan, to consult with senior government officials of those two countries and meet with representatives in the Azerbaijani region of Nagorny Karabakh; and Vienna, to consult with the Chairman-in-Office of OSCE and other officials of its secretariat.

*REFERENCES*

[1]S/1995/63. [2]S/1995/84. [3]S/1995/162. [4]S/1995/182. [5]S/1995/196. [6]S/1995/249. [7]YUN 1994, p. 577. [8]S/1995/321. [9]S/PRST/1995/21. [10]S/1995/399. [11]S/1995/408. [12]S/1995/413. [13]S/1995/464. [14]S/1995/455. [15]A/50/780-S/1995/980, A/50/793-S/1995/1000, A/50/805-S/1995/1009. [16]A/50/571. [17]A/50/1. [18]S/1995/558.

## Georgia

During 1995, despite efforts by the United Nations and the Russian Federation as facilitator, the political process to achieve a comprehensive settlement of the conflict in Abkhazia—a region located on the Black Sea in the north-western part of Georgia—remained deadlocked. The Secretary-General's Special Envoy, Edouard Brunner (Switzerland), convened a new round of talks in February and held separate consultations with the Georgian Government and Abkhaz authorities on a number of occasions. However, no agreement was reached on a status for Abkhazia which would be acceptable to both sides. Formal repatriation of refugees and displaced persons to Abkhazia under UNHCR auspices, within the framework of the 1994 quadripartite agreement,[(1)] was also at a standstill, although spontaneous returns continued.

Both sides had complied with the 14 May 1994 agreement on a cease-fire and separation of forces.[(2)] The UN Observer Mission in Georgia (UNOMIG), established in 1993,[(3)] continued to monitor and verify implementation of the agreement and to fulfil other tasks mandated by the Security Council in 1994,[(4)] in close coordination with the CIS peace-keeping force. The Council extended the Mission's mandate in January and again in May, until 12 January 1996. During 1995, UNOMIG maintained its full authorized strength of 136 military observers. On 28 October, Major-General Per Källström (Sweden) replaced Brigadier-General John Hvidegaard (Denmark) as Chief Military Observer. Also in October, Liviu Bota (Romania) was appointed resident deputy to the Special Envoy and Head of UNOMIG.

**Report of the Secretary-General (January).** In a 6 January report concerning the situation in Abkhazia, Georgia,[(5)] the Secretary-General informed the Security Council of political and humanitarian developments that had occurred from October through December 1994.[(6)] He noted that the parties continued to comply with the 14 May agreement, with all armed forces and heavy military equipment having been withdrawn from the security zone and no heavy military equipment remaining in the restricted weapons zone. He described the situation in UNOMIG's area of operations as generally stable but tense, due to the high crime rate, the regular occurrence of sporadic shooting, robbery and looting, and the inability of local authorities to control banditry. Operating at its full authorized strength of 136 had allowed UNOMIG to intensify activities in the area west of Zugdidi, where most refugees were returning, and along the Gali Canal, to observe and possibly prevent the infiltration of armed personnel into the security zone. It continued to monitor the weapons storage sites on both sides, and conducted regular patrols in the Kodori valley until weather conditions prevented it from doing so. Those activities were undertaken in close coordination with the CIS peace-keeping force. UNOMIG maintained three sector headquarters, in Sukhumi, Gali and Zugdidi, and two semi-static observation posts in the Gali sector; in addition, its liaison office in Tbilisi, Georgia's capital, became operational. On 6 January, the Chairman of the CIS Council of Heads of State confirmed his agreement with the Secretary-General's proposals regarding the respective roles and responsibilities of UNOMIG and the CIS peace-keeping force.

At the same time, the political process to reach a comprehensive settlement of the conflict remained at a standstill over the question of a political status for Abkhazia acceptable to both sides. Nevertheless, the Secretary-General expressed his conviction that negotiations between the parties were the only way to resolve the issue, and recommended that UNOMIG's mandate be extended until 15 May 1995, to coincide with the duration of the mandate of the CIS peace-keeping force. He pointed out that in case of extension, the monthly cost of maintaining the Mission would be limited to the commitment authority approved by the General Assembly in December 1994.[(7)] The Secretary-General also noted that the voluntary fund in support of the implementation of the 14 May agreement, established in response to a 1994 Security Council request,[(4)] had to date received no contributions.

SECURITY COUNCIL ACTION (January)

On 12 January, the Security Council adopted **resolution 971(1995)**.

_The Security Council,_

_Reaffirming_ its resolutions 849(1993) of 9 July 1993, 854(1993) of 6 August 1993, 858(1993) of 24 August 1993, 876(1993) of 19 October 1993, 881(1993) of 4 November 1993, 892(1993) of 22 December 1993, 896(1994) of 31 January 1994, 906(1994) of 25 March 1994, 934(1994) of 30 June 1994 and 937(1994) of 21 July 1994,

_Having considered_ the report of the Secretary-General of 6 January 1995,

_Reaffirming_ its commitment to the sovereignty and territorial integrity of the Republic of Georgia, and in this context recalling the statement by the President of the Security Council of 2 December 1994,

_Reaffirming also_ the right of all refugees and displaced persons affected by the conflict to return to their homes in secure conditions in accordance with international law and as set out in the Quadripartite Agreement on voluntary return of refugees and displaced persons, signed in Moscow on 4 April 1994,

_Urging_ the parties to refrain from any unilateral actions which could complicate or hinder the political process aimed at an early and comprehensive settlement of the conflict,

_Deeply concerned_ about the lack of progress regarding a comprehensive political settlement as well as the slow pace of return of refugees and displaced persons,

_Calling upon_ the parties to intensify efforts, under the auspices of the United Nations and with the assistance of the Russian Federation as facilitator and with the participation of representatives of the Organization for Security and Cooperation in Europe (OSCE), to achieve an early and comprehensive political settlement of the conflict, including on the political status of Abkhazia, fully respecting the sovereignty and territorial integrity of the Republic of Georgia,

*Expressing* its satisfaction with the close cooperation and coordination between the United Nations Observer Mission in Georgia (UNOMIG) and the Commonwealth of Independent States (CIS) peace-keeping force in the performance of their respective mandates,

*Commending* the contribution of the CIS peace-keeping force and of UNOMIG to the maintenance of a cease-fire and to the stabilization of the situation in the zone of the Georgian-Abkhaz conflict,

1. *Welcomes* the report of the Secretary-General of 6 January 1995;

2. *Decides* to extend the mandate of UNOMIG, as set out in its resolution 937(1994), for an additional period terminating on 15 May 1995;

3. *Requests* the Secretary-General to report within two months of the adoption of this resolution on all aspects of the situation in Abkhazia, Republic of Georgia;

4. *Encourages* the Secretary-General to continue his efforts aimed at achieving a comprehensive political settlement of the conflict, including on the political status of Abkhazia, respecting fully the sovereignty and territorial integrity of the Republic of Georgia and calls upon the parties to reach substantive progress in the negotiations under the auspices of the United Nations and with the assistance of the Russian Federation as facilitator and with participation of representatives of the OSCE;

5. *Calls upon* the parties to comply with their commitments with regard to the return of refugees and displaced persons, as undertaken in the Quadripartite Agreement, and in particular calls upon the Abkhaz side to accelerate the process significantly;

6. *Decides* to undertake, on the basis of a report from the Secretary-General submitted by 4 May 1995 and in the light of any progress achieved towards a political settlement and the return of refugees and displaced persons, a thorough review of the situation in Abkhazia, Republic of Georgia;

7. *Requests also* the Secretary-General to examine, within UNOMIG's existing mandate, in cooperation with the relevant representatives of the CIS peace-keeping force the possibility of additional steps to contribute to conditions conducive to the safe and orderly return of refugees and displaced persons;

8. *Reiterates* its encouragement to Member States to contribute to the voluntary fund in support of the implementation of the Agreement on a Cease-fire and Separation of Forces signed in Moscow on 14 May 1994 and/or for humanitarian aspects including demining, as specified by the donors;

9. *Decides* to remain actively seized of the matter.

Security Council resolution 971(1995)

12 January 1995     Meeting 3488     Adopted unanimously

Draft prepared in consultations among Council members (S/1995/23).

**Further report of the Secretary-General (March).** On 6 March, the Secretary-General reported[8] that his Special Envoy for Georgia had convened a further round of negotiations in Geneva from 7 to 9 February. The two sides reached an understanding on certain provisions of a future agreement concerning a State within the boundaries of the former Georgian Soviet Socialist Republic as at 21 December 1991, including the establishment of a ''federal legislative organ'' and a ''supreme organ of executive power'' acting within the bounds of agreed competences. During subsequent expert group meetings in Moscow, from 15 to 17 February and from 1 to 3 March, further progress was achieved on formulations for basic provisions of an agreement on a political settlement; however, the parties continued to diverge on the issues of recognition of Georgia's territorial integrity, characterization of the union State as federal in nature, the question of a joint army, and popular legitimization of an agreement.

Following the talks, the Quadripartite Commission, overseeing the implementation of the agreement on the return of refugees, met in Moscow on 16 February for the first time in two months. The Government of Georgia and the Abkhaz authorities agreed to consider a pragmatic repatriation timetable and to adopt measures to restore acceptable security conditions in the areas of return. However, due to Abkhaz unwillingness to accept returnees in any significant numbers, as well as to the deteriorating security situation in the Gali region, organized repatriation remained at a standstill, with only 311 refugees returning under UNHCR procedures, while the number of people leaving Abkhazia for safer areas exceeded that of people returning to the region, according to a UNOMIG assessment. In addition, the lack of funding for humanitarian programmes in Georgia had compelled UNHCR to reduce its presence in the country.

The situation on the ground remained tense, except in the Kodori valley. Both sides attempted to reintroduce heavy military equipment and armaments into the security and restricted weapons zones, while uncontrolled armed elements continued to commit human rights violations and clashed with the local police. The number of ambushes in the Gali region had increased; those involved 23 casualties, including one fatality, among CIS soldiers. In addition, six people, including four CIS soldiers, were killed by mines, and 15 others were killed or wounded in other incidents. In an effort to improve the security situation, the CIS peace-keeping force imposed a curfew in the area. At the same time, UNOMIG continued to monitor the weapons storage sites and to conduct daily patrols, and expanded the area patrolled on a 24-hour basis. The Mission's permanent presence and frequent patrolling in areas of high criminality had a certain deterrent effect and instilled a sense of safety in the population, while its protests against violations of the 14 May agreement, coupled with action by the CIS peace-keeping force, helped to reduce their number and duration.

The Secretary-General concluded that the presence of both UNOMIG and the CIS peace-keeping force in the region had contributed greatly to preventing a renewal of hostilities and paved the way for continued political negotiations. He observed, however, that the lack of progress on the refugee question could result in explosive developments likely to derail the political process and lead to the resumption of conflict, a point which was brought to the attention of Abkhaz leader Vladislav Ardzinba by the Secretary-General's Special Envoy. At the same time, the Secretary-General remained confident that, with patience and perseverance, solutions to the situation could be found.

### SECURITY COUNCIL ACTION (March)

On 17 March, the Council President made the following statement[9] on behalf of the Council:

The Security Council welcomes the interim report of the Secretary-General concerning the situation in Abkhazia, Republic of Georgia. The Council also welcomes the recent efforts of the Secretary-General's Special Envoy which enjoy the Council's full support.

The Security Council reaffirms its commitment to the sovereignty and territorial integrity of the Republic of Georgia and calls upon the parties to achieve a comprehensive settlement of the conflict, including on the political status of Abkhazia.

The Security Council notes that there has been little overall progress in achieving a comprehensive political settlement and that a stalemate exists with respect to the return of refugees and displaced persons.

The Security Council takes note of the movement which has occurred in the political talks which resumed in Geneva from 7 to 9 February 1995 and calls upon the parties to exert determined efforts towards achieving substantive progress during the next round of talks.

The Security Council notes with concern that despite the efforts of the United Nations Observer Mission in Georgia (UNOMIG) and the CIS peace-keeping force, the security situation, in the Gali region in particular, has deteriorated, causing great difficulty in the delivery of humanitarian supplies. The Council also notes with concern that reports of human rights abuses, largely against the Georgian population, have become more frequent. The Council calls upon the parties to provide a secure environment, *inter alia*, to provide security for returning refugees and displaced persons and to ensure that international relief supplies can be delivered safely.

The Security Council is deeply concerned about the lack of progress regarding the return of refugees and displaced persons. The Council deplores the continued obstruction on this issue displayed by the Abkhaz authorities and, in particular, the position taken by those authorities in the recent meeting of the Quadripartite Commission in Moscow. The Council expects the parties to implement fully their obligations under the Quadripartite Agreement on voluntary return of refugees and displaced persons. The Council urges the Abkhaz authorities to agree to a timetable on the basis of that proposed by UNHCR. The Council notes that

cooperation between UNOMIG and UNHCR is critical to the safe and orderly return of refugees and displaced persons.

The Security Council, while welcoming the pledge that has been announced to the voluntary fund in support of the implementation of the Agreement on a Cease-fire and Separation of Forces, notes the lack of contributions to this fund and reiterates its encouragement to Member States to make contributions to the voluntary fund in support of the implementation of the Agreement on a Cease-fire and Separation of Forces and/or for humanitarian aspects including demining, as specified by the donors. The Council also welcomes all other relevant humanitarian contributions of Member States.

The Security Council welcomes the steps taken by UNOMIG and the CIS peace-keeping force aimed at improving conditions for the safe and orderly return of refugees and displaced persons. The Council notes UNOMIG's increased patrolling and looks forward to further information on intensification of its activities within its mandate. The Council also welcomes the strengthening of cooperation between UNOMIG and the OSCE representatives in Georgia.

The Security Council agrees with the observation of the Secretary-General that, with patience and perseverance, solutions can be found to the situation in Abkhazia, Republic of Georgia. The Council underlines that without progress in this direction it will not be possible to maintain the support of the international community.

The Security Council will remain seized of the matter.

*Meeting number.* SC 3509.

**Communications and report of the Secretary-General (March and May).** On 13 March, Georgia transmitted[10] a statement by its State Commission for Investigation of the Policy of Ethnic Cleansing/Genocide against the Georgian Population in Abkhazia, Republic of Georgia. In a foreword to the statement, Eduard Shevardnadze, Head of State of the Republic of Georgia, called for bringing to justice those responsible for crimes against humanity in the territory of Abkhazia and expressed his hope that the United Nations would create an international body to investigate and punish the perpetrators of such crimes. On 20 March, Georgia communicated[11] a 15 March statement by Mr. Shevardnadze regarding the escalation of the situation in Abkhazia. The statement said that between 11 and 14 March, more than 500 militiamen, led by some leaders of the Abkhaz separatists, had intruded into and burned Georgian villages in the Gali region, stealing cattle and other property, executing 24 people, capturing more than 150 and torturing many others. According to the statement, international observers in the area were indifferent towards the crimes committed and were not providing information to their Governments and relevant international organizations. The neutrality of commanders of the CIS peace-keeping force was inconsistent with its mandate of creating necessary conditions for the secure return of refugees, the statement said.

In a 1 May report,[12] the Secretary-General noted that the situation in the security and restricted weapons zones had been extremely unstable from March to mid-April, during which time 28 people had died, 17 had been wounded and some 20 others kidnapped as a result of criminal activities, and incidents of looting and burning of houses and tea plantations were reported. Most of those acts were committed by armed elements on both sides, beyond the control of either the Government of Georgia or the Abkhaz authorities. However, in March and early April, the Abkhaz authorities carried out two militia operations in the Gali region, reportedly to "clamp down on subversive elements" and to "check identification cards" of residents. In the wake of the first operation, which involved some 400 militia personnel, UNOMIG observed the bodies of 13 men, several of whom showed signs of having been tortured; in addition, some 200 civilians were detained but later released. Following the Mission's protest, the Abkhaz authorities admitted to having been unable to exercise full control over the militia and other elements present in the area. The second operation, involving some 170 militia personnel and provoked by an ambush on an Abkhaz funeral procession that had resulted in three fatalities and several injuries, had been more closely controlled by the authorities and monitored by both UNOMIG and the CIS peace-keeping force, but had led, nevertheless, to one death and seven arrests. On the other hand, the situation in the Kodori valley remained calm.

The Secretary-General further reported that his Special Envoy had visited Moscow on 19 and 20 April to hold separate consultations with representatives of the Russian Federation, the Georgian side and the Abkhaz side. The two parties received a draft text which developed elements discussed on earlier occasions, providing for a solution on the basis of a federal State within the borders of Georgia as at 21 December 1991, with certain competences for Abkhazia. The Abkhaz side rejected the draft, stating that fundamental principles of a possible solution had been set out in the 1994 declaration on measures for a political settlement,[1] and that the competences being offered to Abkhazia were less than those given to it in 1978 by the USSR. The Georgian side said that, in recognizing a federal solution to the conflict, the draft text went as far as Georgia was prepared to go. It also reaffirmed the utmost importance of a prompt and massive return of refugees and displaced persons to their homes. The Abkhaz side, while stating that the grave security situation in the area precluded it from accepting large numbers of refugees, had nevertheless communicated to UNHCR on 17 April an offer to register some

40,000 spontaneous returnees and to consider UNHCR-sponsored returnees at the rate of 200 per week.

As of April 1995, contributions to the UNHCR assistance programme for refugees and displaced persons in Georgia amounted to $943,424, only 10.3 per cent of the 1995 budget requirements, jeopardizing continuation of that programme. An inter-agency mission visited the country from 29 January to 4 February to assess the humanitarian situation and finalize a consolidated inter-agency appeal for the period from 1 April 1995 to 31 March 1996. Contributions under the appeal covering the preceding 12 months represented only 50.1 per cent of total funding requirements for Georgia (see PART FOUR, Chapter III). At the same time, no further pledges had been made or contributions received for the voluntary fund in support of the implementation of the 14 May agreement.

The report noted that UNOMIG's concept of operations had been adjusted to allow for closer monitoring of the situation and a more flexible response to developments on the ground, and was now based on mobile patrols operating from the three sector headquarters and four team-site bases, including three in the Gali region and one in the Zugdidi region. However, the Mission was being prevented by the Georgian side from monitoring its weapons storage site and by the Abkhaz side from patrolling parts of the Gali Canal; in addition, two warning shots had been fired at military observers, and a wire-commanded mine had been detonated in the vicinity of a UNOMIG vehicle. The Mission continued to cooperate with the OSCE office in Tbilisi, UNHCR and other humanitarian agencies; its cooperation with the CIS peace-keeping force involved regular exchanges of information, mutual assistance and joint patrolling.

The Secretary-General observed that security conditions in the region would remain unstable without an agreement on the number and type of personal weapons allowed in the security zone and in the absence of an earnest attempt by the parties to control armed elements in the area. In that regard, he intended to instruct the Chief Military Observer of UNOMIG to discuss with both sides the definition of personal weapons. The Secretary-General further pointed out that the untimely withdrawal of the CIS peace-keeping force and UNOMIG would lead to the resumption of conflict, and recommended that the Mission's mandate be extended until 15 November 1995, subject to revision in the light of the decision on the mandate of the CIS peace-keeping force. In case of extension, the monthly cost of maintaining UNOMIG until 13 July would be limited to the commitment authority approved by the Assembly in 1994.[7]

On 12 May, the Security Council adopted **resolution 993(1995)**.

*The Security Council,*

*Reaffirming* all its relevant resolutions, in particular resolution 971(1995) of 12 January 1995,

*Having considered* the report of the Secretary-General of 1 May 1995,

*Reaffirming* its commitment to the sovereignty and territorial integrity of the Republic of Georgia,

*Concerned* that insufficient progress has been achieved towards a comprehensive political settlement,

*Welcoming and encouraging* continuing consultations regarding a new constitution for the Republic of Georgia based on federal principles in the context of a comprehensive political settlement,

*Reaffirming* the right of all refugees and displaced persons affected by the conflict to return to their homes in secure conditions in accordance with international law and as set out in the Quadripartite Agreement on voluntary return of refugees and displaced persons, signed in Moscow on 4 April 1994, deploring the continued obstruction of such return by the Abkhaz authorities and underlining that return of refugees and displaced persons to the Gali region would be a welcome first step,

*Expressing concern* over the critical funding shortages which may result in suspension of important humanitarian programmes,

*Recalling* the conclusions of the Budapest summit of the Conference on Security and Cooperation in Europe regarding the situation in Abkhazia, Republic of Georgia,

*Reaffirming* the need for the parties to comply with international humanitarian law,

*Noting* that the Agreement on a Cease-fire and Separation of Forces signed in Moscow on 14 May 1994 has been generally respected by the parties over the past year with the assistance of the Commonwealth of Independent States (CIS) peace-keeping force and the United Nations Observer Mission in Georgia (UNOMIG), but expressing concern at the continued lack of a secure environment, in particular recent attacks on civilians in the Gali region,

*Further expressing concern* about the safety and the security of UNOMIG and CIS personnel and stressing the importance it attaches to their freedom of movement,

*Stressing also* the importance it attaches to restrictions on the number and type of weapons which may be borne by the parties in the security zone, and welcoming the intention of the Secretary-General to pursue this question with the parties,

*Expressing its satisfaction* with the close cooperation and coordination between UNOMIG and the CIS peace-keeping force in the performance of their respective mandates and commending the contribution both have made to stabilization of the situation in the zone of conflict,

*Paying tribute* to those members of the CIS peace-keeping force who have lost their lives in the exercise of their duties,

1. *Welcomes* the report of the Secretary-General of 1 May 1995;

2. *Decides* to extend the mandate of UNOMIG for an additional period terminating on 12 January 1996, subject to review by the Council in the event of any changes that may be made in the mandate of the CIS peace-keeping force;

3. *Expresses* its full support for the efforts of the Secretary-General aimed at achieving a comprehensive political settlement of the conflict, including on the political status of Abkhazia, respecting fully the sovereignty and territorial integrity of the Republic of Georgia, as well as for the efforts that are being undertaken by the Russian Federation in its capacity as facilitator to intensify the search for a peaceful settlement of the conflict, and encourages the Secretary-General to continue his efforts, with the assistance of the Russian Federation as facilitator, and with the support of the Organization for Security and Cooperation in Europe (OSCE), to that end;

4. *Calls upon* the parties to reach substantive progress in the negotiations under the auspices of the United Nations and with the assistance of the Russian Federation as facilitator and with participation of representatives of OSCE;

5. *Urges* the parties to refrain from any unilateral actions which could complicate or hinder the political process aimed at an early and comprehensive political settlement;

6. *Reiterates* its call to the Abkhaz side to accelerate significantly the process of the voluntary return of refugees and displaced persons by accepting a timetable on the basis of that proposed by the Office of the United Nations High Commissioner for Refugees, and to guarantee the safety of spontaneous returnees already in the area and regularize their status in accordance with the Quadripartite Agreement;

7. *Welcomes* the additional measures implemented by UNOMIG and the CIS peace-keeping force in the Gali region aimed at improving conditions for the safe and orderly return of refugees and displaced persons;

8. *Calls upon* the parties to improve their cooperation with UNOMIG and the CIS peace-keeping force in order to provide a secure environment for the return of refugees and displaced persons and also calls upon them to honour their commitments with regard to security and freedom of movement of all United Nations and CIS personnel;

9. *Requests* the Secretary-General, in the context of paragraph 7 of resolution 971(1995), to consider ways of improving observance of human rights in the region;

10. *Reiterates* its encouragement to States to contribute to the voluntary fund in support of the implementation of the Agreement on a Cease-fire and Separation of Forces signed in Moscow on 14 May 1994 and/or for humanitarian aspects including demining, as specified by the donors;

11. *Encourages* States to respond to the consolidated inter-agency appeal, in particular for the urgent needs of UNHCR, and welcomes all relevant humanitarian contributions of States;

12. *Requests* the Secretary-General to report every three months from the date of the adoption of this resolution on all aspects of the situation in Abkhazia, Republic of Georgia, including the operations of UNOMIG, and decides to undertake, on the basis of those reports, further reviews of the situation;

13. *Decides* to remain actively seized of the matter.

Security Council resolution 993(1995)

12 May 1995      Meeting 3535      Adopted unanimously

Draft prepared in consultations among Council members (S/1995/384).

**Further communication and report of the Secretary-General (June and August).** On 2 June, the Russian Federation communicated[13] decisions and a statement adopted on 26 May by the Council of the CIS Heads of State in Minsk, Belarus. The Council defined more precisely the mandate of the Collective Peace-keeping Forces in the conflict zone in Abkhazia, Republic of Georgia, and extended its validity and the length of stay of the Forces until 31 December 1995. In the statement, the Council affirmed its commitment to the territorial integrity of the Republic of Georgia, advocated the continuation and an early conclusion of talks, and called on the parties to strive for a comprehensive settlement of the conflict within the framework of a unified federative State. It also welcomed the readiness of Georgia to hold consultations on its new constitution, to serve as the basis for an appropriate resolution of all the contentious issues of State organization.

On 7 August, the Secretary-General reported[14] that his Special Envoy had visited the region from 15 to 18 July to meet with representatives of the Russian Federation and the parties to the conflict. The basis for discussions was a draft protocol aimed at identifying an acceptable status for Abkhazia within the borders of the former Georgian Soviet Socialist Republic, including competences of federal authorities, the establishment of a federal legislative body and the treatment by it of questions directly affecting Abkhaz interests, as well as issues concerning the early and safe return of refugees and displaced persons. The Abkhaz side found that without a number of changes the draft was unacceptable, and stated that a federative arrangement had to be between two equal entities. It also found unacceptable that the CIS peace-keeping force should take an active part in providing security for returnees, asserting that there could be no police functions for anyone other than the Abkhaz authorities. The Georgian side, on the other hand, felt that further concessions on its part would be unacceptable. The Special Envoy also met in Tbilisi with representatives of displaced persons, ambassadors of the "Friends of Georgia" group of States (France, Germany, Russian Federation, United States), as well as representatives of OSCE, ICRC and UN agencies operating in Georgia.

The Secretary-General informed the Security Council of his decision to appoint a resident deputy to the Special Envoy, who would be also the Head of UNOMIG, following the model of other operations, as in Cyprus and Tajikistan. He further described the humanitarian situation in the region, noting that the Quadripartite Commission had met in Moscow on 19 May to explore possibilities for resuming the voluntary repatriation programme under UNHCR auspices. During the meeting, the Abkhaz side maintained its position of allowing only 200 returnees per week, which continued to be unacceptable to the other parties. Subsequently, the Abkhaz authorities announced the beginning of their own repatriation programme as well as of registration of all inhabitants of the Gali district; UNHCR dissociated itself from that action. In July, the Abkhaz side claimed to have registered some 2,600 of the 30,000 to 40,000 refugees and displaced persons it asserted had returned spontaneously. In the meantime, UNHCR distributed clothes, high-protein biscuits and World Food Programme (WFP) provisions to more than 7,000 children, and continued to monitor, to the best of its ability, the situation of returnees and the local population. The Secretary-General noted that, while Georgia continued to suffer from the scarcity of basic foods and energy supply and to lack resources for basic social services, with its health care almost entirely dependent on international assistance, the second consolidated inter-agency appeal for that country, launched on 23 March, had collected no more than $5 million as at 30 June.

Efforts were undertaken by the Special Envoy and the UN High Commissioner for Human Rights to secure agreement for the establishment of a human rights monitoring mission in the Gali region, including a visit by a senior human rights officer to Georgia from 24 June to 2 July. While the Georgian side supported the proposal, the Abkhaz side strongly objected to the establishment of such a mission in Gali, and expressed the view that periodic visits by human rights monitors would be more acceptable for the time being. At the same time, the situation in the security zone remained unstable, with 7 killings and 12 kidnappings recorded from May through July. Looting and destruction of property also continued, albeit at a lower level; nevertheless, the number of spontaneous returns to the Gali region had increased. According to UNOMIG, significant quantities of weapons remained in the area despite a weapons-permit regime administered by the CIS peace-keeping force, and not all elements of interior forces present in the region were under the full control of the Georgian authorities. The Abkhaz side continued defensive preparations in the restricted weapons zone, and occasional violations of its northern boundary were reported. UNOMIG established two additional team-site bases, in the Zugdidi region and in the Kodori valley, and continued to cooperate closely with the CIS peace-keeping force.

**SECURITY COUNCIL ACTION (August)**

On 18 August, the Security Council President made the following statement[15] on behalf of the Council:

The Security Council welcomes the report of the Secretary-General on the situation in Abkhazia, Georgia, of 9 August 1995 pursuant to its resolution 993(1995).

The Security Council notes there has been little overall progress in achieving a comprehensive political settlement and that a stalemate exists with respect to the return of refugees and displaced persons.

The Security Council expresses its full support for the efforts of the Secretary-General and those of the Russian Federation in its capacity as facilitator aimed at achieving a comprehensive political settlement of the conflict, including on the political status of Abkhazia, respecting fully the sovereignty and territorial integrity of the Republic of Georgia. The Council renews its call to the parties, in particular the Abkhaz side, to reach substantive progress in the political negotiations as a matter of urgency.

The Security Council remains deeply concerned at the continued obstruction of the return of the refugees and displaced persons by the Abkhaz authorities, which is totally unacceptable. Reaffirming its resolution 993(1995), the Council reiterates its call to the Abkhaz authorities to accelerate the return process significantly, to guarantee the safety of all returnees and to regularize the status of spontaneous returnees, in accordance with internationally accepted practice and in cooperation with the Office of the United Nations High Commissioner for Refugees.

The Security Council welcomes the continuing close cooperation and coordination between UNOMIG and the CIS peace-keeping force in the performance of their respective mandates. It reminds the parties of their obligations to cooperate fully with UNOMIG and the CIS peace-keeping force and to ensure the safety and freedom of movement of all United Nations and CIS personnel.

The Security Council takes note with appreciation of the decision of the Secretary-General regarding the resident Deputy to his Special Envoy. The Council also supports the Secretary-General's efforts with regard to the establishment of a human rights monitoring mission in the area. It encourages the Secretary-General to continue his consultations with the parties to this end.

*Meeting number.* SC 3567.

## Communications and report of the Secretary-General (October/November).

On 2 October,[16] the Secretary-General informed the Security Council that he had appointed Liviu Bota (Romania) as resident deputy to the Special Envoy and Head of UNOMIG. The Council's agreement to the appointment was communicated to the Secretary-General on 5 October.[17] The Deputy Special Envoy arrived in the area at the beginning of October.

In an 8 November report,[18] the Secretary-General observed that the political process remained deadlocked. The Special Envoy had met with the parties in Moscow on 28 and 29 August; however, the Abkhaz side refused to accept the draft protocol (see above) as a basis for negotiation. At a further meeting, convened under the auspices of the Russian Federation on 24 October, the Abkhaz delegation made the resumption of negotiations conditional on the lifting of the Russian-imposed naval blockade of Sukhumi. Subsequently, both sides agreed to a new round of talks, under the same auspices, which began on 2 November. In the meantime, the Georgian Parliament adopted on 24 August the text of a new constitution, declaring the Republic of Georgia to be an independent, single and indivisible State, with internal territorial arrangements to be defined upon restoration of the Government's jurisdiction over the State's whole territory.

The humanitarian situation also remained largely unchanged. UNHCR reported that the number of displaced persons crossing the Inguri River in both directions continued to be high, but the official Abkhaz claim that 50,000 persons had returned to the Gali district appeared to be excessive. Since August, UNHCR had discontinued monitoring the situation in the area after an attack on one of its vehicles, maintaining only an intermittent presence. It provided construction material to a number of returnees whose houses had been destroyed, and distributed school kits in the district. As at 1 September, some $20 million, or 52.3 per cent of the total requested, had been received under the consolidated inter-agency appeal. The situation on the ground was tense, except in the Kodori valley, and involved 15 violent incidents against the civilian population, mainly robberies. Six people were killed and 12 injured; in addition, there were six mine casualties, including five civilians and one CIS force member. A new system of weapon permits was introduced in the security zone.

The Mission had recently changed its disposition on the ground, the Secretary-General reported, to increase the number of military observers positioned permanently in the security zone and to redeploy military staff from Pitsunda to Sukhumi, while maintaining administrative headquarters at Pitsunda. The main headquarters at Sukhumi retained responsibility for patrolling the Kodori valley, but passed its patrolling function in the restricted weapons zone to the sector headquarters in Gali; a small forward headquarters, co-located with the sector headquarters, was set up in Zugdidi. The Mission continued to experience difficulties with regard to access to the weapons storage sites on both sides; its ability to implement mandated tasks was adversely affected by the pervasive lawlessness in the security and restricted weapons zones. On the Abkhaz side, there were incidents of restriction on the freedom of movement of UNOMIG personnel and of armed robberies committed against them, mostly in the restricted weapons zone; however, all of the robberies were deemed to be criminally motivated.

**Further developments.** In the light of the continuing stalemate in the political process, the Georgian side stated that new initiatives were needed, while the Abkhaz side maintained its position that the 1994 declaration on measures for a political settlement of the conflict and Quadripartite Agreement on voluntary return of refugees and displaced persons[1] were the only basis for a successful continuation of the talks, and that a union agreement between Georgia and Abkhazia in which both sides enjoyed equal rights would represent a guarantee against the renewal of hostilities. On 5 November, Eduard Shevardnadze was elected President of Georgia; a new Parliament was formed, which held its first session on 25 November. Georgia and the Russian Federation reached a number of agreements relevant to the conflict, concerning consular affairs, trade facilities and restoration of railway lines, among other matters. The Special Envoy and his Deputy initiated consultations with the Abkhaz authorities and the UN High Commissioner for Human Rights on a programme for the protection and promotion of human rights in Abkhazia. As for the humanitarian situation, WFP assisted some 2,500 people in the Kodori valley, UNICEF launched an emergency diphtheria control campaign in Abkhazia, and on 20 December UNHCR resumed its monitoring activities in the Gali region. There were 23 violent incidents reported in UNOMIG's area of responsibility, mainly robberies and kidnappings, of which 21 occurred on the Abkhaz side; those resulted in seven fatalities and as many injuries, and two cases involved torture. In addition, there were two mine casualties, involving an Abkhaz soldier and a soldier of the CIS peace-keeping force.

## UNOMIG financing

**Reports of the Secretary-General and ACABQ (May/June).** On 19 May, the Secretary-General reported[19] that UNOMIG's financial performance for the period since its inception until 15 May 1995 resulted in an unencumbered balance of $3,714,186 gross ($3,612,298 net) from the total of $20,261,036 gross ($19,372,636 net) made available for its maintenance for that period. An unencumbered balance for the most recent period, from 1 July 1994 to 13 January 1995, amounted to $3,280,600 gross ($3,227,900 net). At the same time, outstanding contributions by Member States in respect of UNOMIG stood at $1,501,301 as at 30 April 1995. The Secretary-General noted that his current commitment authority was until 13 July 1995, and requested the General Assembly to make appropriate provision for the Mission's expenses beyond that date.

He estimated the cost of maintaining UNOMIG from 14 July 1995 to 30 June 1996, at a strength

of 135 military observers and 136 civilian staff, at $16,115,300 gross ($15,088,700 net), which represented a 19 per cent decrease on a monthly basis from the commitment authorized by the Assembly in 1994.[7] The Secretary-General set out specific proposals concerning the appropriation and assessment of resources for the periods from 14 January to 15 May 1995 and from 16 May 1995 to 12 January 1996, and requested commitment authorization at a monthly rate of $1,334,500 gross ($1,246,000 net) after 12 January 1996. He also requested that special arrangements regarding the Financial Regulations, approved by the Assembly in 1993[20] in respect of UNPROFOR, be applied to UNOMIG as well.

ACABQ, in a 2 June report,[21] recommended acceptance of the Secretary-General's proposals.

**GENERAL ASSEMBLY ACTION (July)**

On 12 July, the General Assembly adopted **resolution 49/231 B** on the financing of UNOMIG.

*The General Assembly,*

*Having considered* the report of the Secretary-General on the financing of the United Nations Observer Mission in Georgia and the related report of the Advisory Committee on Administrative and Budgetary Questions,

*Recalling* Security Council resolution 854(1993) of 6 August 1993, by which the Council approved the deployment of an advance team of up to ten United Nations military observers for a period of three months and the incorporation of the advance team into a United Nations observer mission if such a mission was formally established by the Council,

*Recalling also* Security Council resolution 858(1993) of 24 August 1993, by which the Council decided to establish the United Nations Observer Mission in Georgia, and the subsequent resolutions by which the Council extended the mandate of the Observer Mission, the most recent of which was resolution 993(1995) of 12 May 1995,

*Recalling further* its decisions 48/475 A of 23 December 1993 and 48/475 B of 5 April 1994 and its resolutions 48/256 of 26 May 1994 and 49/231 A of 23 December 1994 on the financing of the Observer Mission,

*Reaffirming* that the costs of the Observer Mission are expenses of the Organization to be borne by Member States in accordance with Article 17, paragraph 2, of the Charter of the United Nations,

*Recalling* its previous decision regarding the fact that, in order to meet the expenditures caused by the Observer Mission, a different procedure is required from that applied to meet expenditures of the regular budget of the United Nations,

*Taking into account* the fact that the economically more developed countries are in a position to make relatively larger contributions and that the economically less developed countries have a relatively limited capacity to contribute towards such an operation,

*Bearing in mind* the special responsibilities of the States permanent members of the Security Council, as indicated in General Assembly resolution 1874(S-IV) of 27 June 1963, in the financing of such operations,

*Mindful* of the fact that it is essential to provide the Observer Mission with the necessary financial resources to enable it to fulfil its responsibilities under the relevant resolutions of the Security Council,

1. *Takes note* of the status of contributions to the United Nations Observer Mission in Georgia as at 12 June 1995, including the contributions outstanding in the amount of 4,015,801 United States dollars, and urges all Member States concerned to make every possible effort to ensure the payment of their outstanding assessed contributions;

2. *Expresses concern* about the financial situation with regard to peace-keeping activities, due to overdue payments by Member States of their assessments, particularly Member States in arrears;

3. *Urges* all Member States to make every possible effort to ensure payment of their assessed contributions to the Observer Mission promptly and in full;

4. *Endorses* the observations and recommendations contained in the report of the Advisory Committee on Administrative and Budgetary Questions;

5. *Approves*, on an exceptional basis, the special arrangements for the Observer Mission with regard to the application of article IV of the Financial Regulations of the United Nations, whereby appropriations required in respect of obligations owed to Governments providing contingents and/or logistic support to the Mission shall be retained beyond the period stipulated under financial regulations 4.3 and 4.4, as set out in the annex to the present resolution;

6. *Requests* the Secretary-General to take all necessary action to ensure that the Observer Mission is administered with a maximum of efficiency and economy;

7. *Decides* to appropriate to the Special Account for the United Nations Observer Mission in Georgia the amount of 6,880,136 dollars gross (6,468,136 dollars net) for the period from 14 January to 15 May 1995, authorized and apportioned under the terms of its resolution 49/231 A;

8. *Decides also* to appropriate to the Special Account a total amount of 11,948,718 dollars gross (11,220,568 dollars net), inclusive of the amount of 3,440,068 dollars gross (3,234,068 dollars net) authorized and apportioned under the terms of resolution 49/231 A, for the maintenance of the Observer Mission for the period from 16 May 1995 to 12 January 1996;

9. *Decides further*, as an ad hoc arrangement, and taking into account the amount of 3,440,068 dollars gross (3,234,068 dollars net) already apportioned in accordance with resolution 49/231 A, to apportion an additional amount of 8,508,650 dollars gross (7,986,500 dollars net) for the period from 16 May 1995 to 12 January 1996 among Member States in accordance with the composition of groups set out in paragraphs 3 and 4 of General Assembly resolution 43/232 of 1 March 1989, as adjusted by the Assembly in its resolutions 44/192 B of 21 December 1989, 45/269 of 27 August 1991, 46/198 A of 20 December 1991 and 47/218 A of 23 December 1992, and its decision 48/472 A of 23 December 1993, and taking into account the scale of assessments for the years 1995, 1996 and 1997 as set out in Assembly resolution 49/19 B of 23 December 1994;

10. *Decides* that, in accordance with the provisions of its resolution 973(X) of 15 December 1955, there shall be set off against the apportionment among Member States, as provided for in paragraph 9 above, their respective share in the Tax Equalization Fund of the estimated additional staff assessment income of 522,150 dollars approved for the Observer Mission for the period from 16 May 1995 to 12 January 1996;

11. *Decides also* that there shall be set off against the apportionment among Member States, as provided for in paragraph 9 above, their respective share in the unencumbered balance of 3,714,186 dollars gross (3,612,298 dollars net) in respect of the period from 7 August 1993 to 13 January 1995;

12. *Decides further*, with regard to the period beyond 12 January 1996, to authorize the Secretary-General to enter into commitments for a period of 5.7 months, at a monthly rate not to exceed 1,334,500 dollars gross (1,246,000 dollars net), in connection with the maintenance of the Observer Mission, to be apportioned in accordance with the scheme set out in the present resolution, subject to the decision of the Security Council to extend the mandate of the Observer Mission beyond 12 January 1996;

13. *Invites* voluntary contributions to the Observer Mission in cash and in the form of services and supplies acceptable to the Secretary-General, to be administered, as appropriate, in accordance with the procedure established by the General Assembly in its resolutions 43/230 of 21 December 1988, 44/192 A of 21 December 1989 and 45/258 of 3 May 1991;

14. *Decides* to include in the provisional agenda of its fiftieth session the item entitled "Financing of the United Nations Observer Mission in Georgia".

## ANNEX
### Special arrangements with regard to the application of article IV of the Financial Regulations of the United Nations

1. At the end of the twelve-month period provided for in regulation 4.3, any unliquidated obligations of the financial period in question relating to goods supplied and services rendered by Governments for which claims have been received or which are covered by established reimbursement rates shall be transferred to accounts payable; such accounts payable shall remain recorded in the Special Account for the United Nations Observer Mission in Georgia until payment is effected.

2. *(a)* Any other unliquidated obligations of the financial period in question owed to Governments for goods supplied and services rendered, as well as other obligations owed to Governments, for which required claims have not yet been received shall remain valid for an additional period of four years following the end of the twelve-month period provided for in regulation 4.3;

*(b)* Claims received during this four-year period shall be treated as provided for in paragraph 1 of the present annex, if appropriate;

*(c)* At the end of the additional four-year period, any unliquidated obligations shall be cancelled and the then remaining balance of any appropriations retained therefor shall be surrendered.

General Assembly resolution 49/231 B

12 July 1995     Meeting 105     Adopted without vote

Approved by Fifth Committee (A/49/798/Add.1) without vote, 23 June (meeting 58); draft by Chairman (A/C.5/49/L.54), based on informal consultations; agenda item 126.

*Meeting numbers.* GA 49th session: 5th Committee 56, 58; plenary 105.

**Reports of the Secretary-General and ACABQ (November/December).** On 7 November,[22] the Secretary-General reported that the Mission's financial performance from 14 January to 15 May 1995 resulted in an unencumbered balance of $1,966,500 gross ($1,858,600 net); he requested the General Assembly to retain that amount in the light of outstanding assessed contributions from Member States.

In a 4 December report,[23] ACABQ pointed out that outstanding contributions to UNOMIG amounted to $2.4 million as at 15 November, and recalled that under the current practice, an unencumbered balance was to be returned to Member States, unless the Assembly decided otherwise.

**GENERAL ASSEMBLY ACTION (December)**

On 22 December, the General Assembly decided that Member States' respective shares in the unencumbered balance of $1,966,500 gross ($1,858,600 net) for the period from 14 January to 15 May 1995 should be set off against their future apportionment if they had fulfilled financial obligations to the Mission and against their outstanding obligations if they had not (**decision 50/449**).

*REFERENCES*

[1]YUN 1994, p. 581. [2]Ibid., p. 583. [3]YUN 1993, p. 509, SC res. 858(1993), 24 Aug. 1993. [4]YUN 1994, p. 584, SC res. 937(1994), 21 July 1994. [5]S/1995/10 & Add.1,2. [6]YUN 1994, p. 587. [7]YUN 1994, p. 589, GA res. 49/231 A, 23 Dec. 1994. [8]S/1995/181. [9]S/PRST/1995/12. [10]S/1995/200. [11]S/1995/212. [12]S/1995/342. [13]S/1995/459. [14]S/1995/657. [15]S/PRST/1995/39. [16]S/1995/839. [17]S/1995/840. [18]S/1995/937. [19]A/49/429/Add.3. [20]YUN 1993, p. 435, GA res. 47/210 B, 14 Sep. 1993. [21]A/49/766/Add.1. [22]A/50/731. [23]A/50/802.

# Other issues

## Relations among Balkan States

**Report of the Secretary-General.** In keeping with a 1993 General Assembly resolution,[1] the Secretary-General, by a note verbale, sought the views of Member States, particularly those from the Balkan region, on the development of good-neighbourly relations in the region and on measures and preventive activities aimed at the creation of a stable zone of peace and cooperation in the Balkans by the year 2000.

In a report of 7 September 1995, with a later addendum, the Secretary-General reproduced the replies received from nine States, among them five from the Balkan region: Albania, Bulgaria, Croatia, the former Yugoslav Republic of Macedonia, and Yugoslavia (Serbia and Montenegro).[2]

**Communications.** On 23 October, Yugoslavia (Serbia and Montenegro) referred to Albania's reply, noting the latter's statement to the effect that its foreign policy was aimed at respecting sovereignty, territorial integrity and political independence, and not at changing borders by force. Underscoring the political significance of that statement, Yugoslavia (Serbia and Montenegro) said it expected Albania to revoke, as a matter of urgency, its 1991 decision recognizing the province of Kosovo and Metohija—an integral part of the Republic of Serbia and thus of Yugoslavia (Serbia and Montenegro)—as a sovereign and independent State.[3]

In connection with the call for the development of good-neighbourly relations, Yugoslavia (Serbia and Montenegro) on 30 October transmitted a "declaration for a better future" and a joint communiqué adopted at an international conference, held in its capital, of municipal organizations of socialist and social-democratic parties from the Balkans (Belgrade, 22-24 September).[4]

**GENERAL ASSEMBLY ACTION**

On 12 December, the General Assembly adopted **resolution 50/80 B**.

**Development of good-neighbourly relations among Balkan States**

*The General Assembly,*

*Recalling* its resolution 2625(XXV) of 24 October 1970, the annex to which contains the Declaration on Principles of International Law concerning Friendly Relations and Cooperation among States in accordance with the Charter of the United Nations, and its resolutions 46/62 of 9 December 1991 and 48/84 B of 16 December 1993,

*Affirming its determination* that all nations should live together in peace with one another as good neighbours,

*Emphasizing* the urgency of the consolidation of the Balkans as a region of peace, security, stability and good-neighbourliness, thus contributing to the maintenance of international peace and security and so enhancing the prospects for sustained development and prosperity for all its peoples,

*Noting* the desire of the Balkan States to develop good-neighbourly relations among themselves and friendly relations with all nations in accordance with the Charter of the United Nations,

*Welcoming* the present international efforts aimed at achieving an overall political settlement of the conflict in the former Yugoslavia,

*Having considered* the report of the Secretary-General on the development of good-neighbourly relations among the Balkan States,

*Stressing* the importance of the ongoing cooperation between the United Nations and the Organization for Security and Cooperation in Europe,

*Taking note* of its deliberations on the subject at its present session,

1. *Notes with interest* the views of some States on the development of good-neighbourly relations among the Balkan States contained in the report of the Secretary-General;

2. *Urges* relevant international organizations and competent bodies and organizations of the United Nations system to submit to the Secretary-General their views on the subject;

3. *Calls upon* all Balkan States to endeavour to promote good-neighbourly relations and continually to undertake unilateral and joint activities, particularly confidence-building measures as appropriate, in particular within the framework of the Organization for Security and Cooperation in Europe;

4. *Emphasizes* the importance for all Balkan States to promote mutual cooperation in all fields;

5. *Stresses* that closer engagement of Balkan States in cooperation arrangements on the European continent will favourably influence the political and economic situation in the region, as well as the good-neighbourly relations among all Balkan States;

6. *Urges* normalization of the relations among all States of the Balkan region;

7. *Requests* the Secretary-General to continue to seek the views of the Member States, particularly those from the Balkan region, and of international organizations, as well as of competent organs of the United Nations, on the development of good-neighbourly relations in the region and on measures and preventive activities aimed at the creation of a stable zone of peace and cooperation in the Balkans by the year 2000, and to submit a report to the General Assembly at its fifty-second session taking into account, *inter alia*, the views expressed by Member States;

8. *Decides* to consider the report of the Secretary-General on the subject at its fifty-second session.

General Assembly resolution 50/80 B

12 December 1995     Meeting 90     Adopted without vote

Approved by First Committee (A/50/601) without vote, 16 November (meeting 23); 29-nation draft (A/C.1/50/L.43); agenda item 81.

*Meeting numbers.* GA 50th session: 1st Committee 3-11, 17, 23; plenary 90.

## Cooperation with OSCE

**Report of the Secretary-General.** Pursuant to General Assembly resolution 49/13,[5] the Secretary-General issued a report[6] on 16 October noting a further enhancement and consolidation of the cooperation and coordination between the United Nations and the Organization for Security and Cooperation in Europe (OSCE) (formerly the Conference on Security and Cooperation in Europe).

In continuation of the informal tripartite consultations initiated in 1994,[7] the Chairman-in-Office (Hungary) hosted a round of consultations in Budapest in February 1995, which gave an important impetus to the dialogue between OSCE and humanitarian organizations. In accordance with the agreement reached at the meeting to strengthen the tripartite process by target-oriented meetings on major humanitarian operations, two such meetings were subsequently held, one in April, on Chechnya, and another in May, on the Caucasus and Tajikistan.

The report noted that the tripartite consultation process was a useful forum for regular information sharing and coordination of action, as well

as for ensuring participation by OSCE institutions and the Chairman-in-Office in regular dialogue with humanitarian organizations, thereby assuring an essential link between prevention/conflict resolution processes and humanitarian operations. The process was further enhanced by a meeting in June of all OSCE field mission heads and humanitarian agencies. Given the emphasis of the process on humanitarian activities, participation in the consultations also included ICRC, the International Organization for Migration and the EU Commission, on the basis of their involvement in the areas under discussion.

**Communication.** On 11 December, Hungary transmitted the texts of the summary of the fifth meeting of the Ministerial Council of OSCE (Budapest, 7-8 December) and of the meeting's decisions on OSCE action for peace, democracy and stability in Bosnia and Herzegovina, as well as on the question of the Nagorny Karabakh conflict.[8]

According to the summary's account of activities in respect of the former Yugoslavia, OSCE welcomed the role envisaged for it by the General Framework Agreement for Peace in Bosnia and Herzegovina (see that topic above, under "Bosnia and Herzegovina") and agreed to supervise the preparation, conduct and monitoring of elections in Bosnia and Herzegovina, certifying when conditions would permit elections to take place. It would closely monitor human rights throughout the country and, to that end, had appointed an international human rights ombudsman. It would assist in arms control negotiations, in confidence- and security-building and in implementation and verification of resulting agreements, with the aim of promoting long-term stability through reduced and verified armament levels.

At the invitation of Croatia, two missions visited that country for the purpose of exploring the possible establishment of a long-term OSCE presence there, in order to assist central and local authorities in building democracy, protecting human and minority rights and promoting the safe return of refugees. The OSCE mission in the former Yugoslav Republic of Macedonia continued to be at the Government's disposal to assist with addressing issues relating to education, minority rights, confidence-building measures and economic development. Regarding human and minority rights in Kosovo, Sandjak (Raska) and Vojvodina in Yugoslavia (Serbia and Montenegro), OSCE underlined the urgent need for the return to those provinces of OSCE missions of long duration.

As to certain CIS members, while agreement on basic principles for the resolution of the Nagorny Karabakh conflict continued to elude the OSCE Minsk process, the sole forum for the settlement of that conflict, OSCE had succeeded in establishing a long-term presence in Chechnya in the form of its assistance group, whose role was to facilitate negotiations between the warring parties and to monitor human rights.

The summary also noted, among other matters, that the Pact on Stability in Europe, with its Baltic and Central European tables, had been passed on to OSCE, where discussions were continuing on sustaining and, when possible, expanding the efforts initiated by the Pact, and building on its regional approach.

**GENERAL ASSEMBLY ACTION**

At its meeting on 18 December, the General Assembly, having considered the Secretary-General's report of 16 October 1995 and the Document of the OSCE Budapest Summit of 1994,[(9)] adopted **resolution 50/87**.

**Cooperation between the United Nations and the Organization for Security and Cooperation in Europe**

*The General Assembly,*

*Recalling* its resolution 48/5 of 13 October 1993 on observer status for the Conference on Security and Cooperation in Europe, and the framework for cooperation and coordination between the United Nations and the Conference on Security and Cooperation in Europe signed on 26 May 1993, as well as its resolution 49/13 of 15 November 1994 on cooperation between the two organizations,

*Recalling also* the declaration at the 1992 Helsinki Summit by the heads of State or Government of the participating States of the Conference on Security and Cooperation in Europe of their understanding that the Conference is a regional arrangement in the sense of Chapter VIII of the Charter of the United Nations and as such provides an important link between European and global security,

*Taking note* of the Document of the Budapest Summit of 1994 of the Conference, in particular the decision that, in order to reflect the fundamental change in the Conference and the dramatic growth in its role in shaping a common security area, the Conference would henceforth be known as the Organization for Security and Cooperation in Europe,

*Having examined* the report of the Secretary-General of 16 October 1995 on cooperation between the United Nations and the Organization for Security and Cooperation in Europe,

*Acknowledging* the increasing contribution of the Organization for Security and Cooperation in Europe to the establishment and maintenance of international peace and security in its region through activities in early warning, preventive diplomacy, crisis management, arms control and disarmament, and post-crisis stabilization and rehabilitation measures, and its efforts in supporting the economic dimension, as well as its crucial role in the human dimension,

*Taking note* of the statement of the Budapest Summit of 1994 in which it was agreed that participating States might, in exceptional circumstances, jointly decide that a dispute would be referred to the Security Council on behalf of the Organization for Security and Cooperation in Europe,

*Welcoming* the fact that, since the Budapest Summit of 1994, cooperation between the United Nations and the Organization for Security and Cooperation in Europe has developed further on both the political and organizational levels and that joint efforts in several areas are being undertaken, such as humanitarian activities, monitoring of human rights, election monitoring and the implementation of sanctions regimes,

*Welcoming also* the progress made in the development and consolidation of contacts and cooperation between the United Nations and the Organization for Security and Cooperation in Europe with regard to the activities of the field missions of the latter,

*Recalling* that the Organization for Security and Cooperation in Europe has already established a long-term presence in several countries, including the conflict zones in its region,

*Stressing* the importance of the full implementation of Security Council resolution 855(1993) of 9 August 1993, as well as the decisions of the Organization for Security and Cooperation in Europe concerning the resumption of the activities of its mission to Kosovo, the Sandzak and Vojvodina in the Federal Republic of Yugoslavia (Serbia and Montenegro),

*Underlining* the possibilities for regional action by the Organization for Security and Cooperation in Europe for the maintenance of international peace and security as provided for under Chapter VIII of the Charter,

*Welcoming* the ongoing work within the framework of the Organization for Security and Cooperation in Europe on the elaboration of a common and comprehensive security model for the Europe of the twenty-first century,

*Welcoming also* the further development of closer contacts between the Organization for Security and Cooperation in Europe and the non-participating Mediterranean States with special regard to their seminar at Cairo on the experience of the Organization in confidence-building measures, as well as the increased cooperation between the Organization and States in Asia, and looking forward to the continuation of those contacts,

*Welcoming further* the decision of the Permanent Council of the Organization for Security and Cooperation in Europe, which met at Budapest on 7 December 1995, that the above-mentioned Mediterranean States would be known henceforth as "Mediterranean Partners for Cooperation" and the above-mentioned States in Asia as "Partners for Cooperation",

1. *Takes note with satisfaction* of the report of the Secretary-General;

2. *Welcomes* the intensified cooperation and coordination between the United Nations and the Organization for Security and Cooperation in Europe on the basis of the framework agreement, and requests the Secretary-General of the United Nations to explore with the Chairman-in-Office and the Secretary-General of the Organization for Security and Cooperation in Europe possibilities for further improvement, with special regard to the mutual provision in advance of information in those areas where both organizations have their own respective roles to play;

3. *Also welcomes* the support extended by the United Nations in sharing its experience with the Organization

for Security and Cooperation in Europe in conflict prevention and peace-building and peace-keeping activities;

4. *Supports* the activities of the Organization for Security and Cooperation in Europe aimed at contributing to stability and the maintenance of peace and security within its region, and stresses the importance of the work done by its field missions;

5. *Encourages* the States members of the Organization for Security and Cooperation in Europe to make every effort to achieve peaceful settlement of disputes in the region, through conflict prevention and crisis management by the Organization, including peace-keeping;

6. *Welcomes* the General Framework Agreement for Peace in Bosnia and Herzegovina and the annexes thereto, signed in Paris on 14 December 1995 by the Presidents of the Republic of Bosnia and Herzegovina, the Republic of Croatia and the Federal Republic of Yugoslavia, and the important role it assigns to the Organization for Security and Cooperation in Europe to supervise the preparation and conduct of free and fair elections in Bosnia and Herzegovina, to monitor, in cooperation with other international organizations, the human rights situation, to help guide the negotiating process to bring about regional stability and to build mechanisms to increase confidence and security;

7. *Also welcomes* the Basic Agreement on the Region of Eastern Slavonia, Baranja and Western Sirmium, signed on 12 November 1995, and acknowledges the important role of the Organization for Security and Cooperation in Europe in the implementation of that agreement and the future role of the Organization in other regions of Croatia;

8. *Decides* to include in the provisional agenda of its fifty-first session the item entitled "Cooperation between the United Nations and the Organization for Security and Cooperation in Europe", and requests the Secretary-General to submit to the General Assembly at its fifty-first session a report on cooperation between the United Nations and the Organization for Security and Cooperation in Europe in implementation of the present resolution.

General Assembly resolution 50/87

18 December 1995     Meeting 94     Adopted without vote

51-nation draft (A/50/L.62 & Add.1); agenda item 30.

*Meeting numbers.* GA 50th session: plenary 6, 7, 9, 11, 24, 94.

## OSCE chairmanship

On 18 October, Hungary informed the President of the General Assembly that Switzerland would hold the office of Chairman of OSCE for one year, beginning on 1 January 1996. Thus, in conformity with the framework for cooperation and coordination between the UN Secretariat and OSCE, the Permanent Observer of Switzerland to the United Nations would serve as the OSCE contact at UN Headquarters.[10]

To enable Switzerland to carry out the responsibilities of that office, Hungary requested that the Assembly grant it the necessary authorization to transmit OSCE communications for circulation as UN documents, to represent OSCE at UN meet-

ings and to participate in Assembly discussions of direct concern to OSCE.

By **decision 50/423** of 18 December, the General Assembly decided to authorize Switzerland, on an ad hoc basis, as the State holding the chairmanship of OSCE from 1 January to 31 December 1996, to submit communications on behalf of the States members of OSCE for circulation as UN documents and to participate in Assembly discussions during that period.

## Strengthening of security and cooperation in the Mediterranean region

In response to a 1994 General Assembly resolution,[11] the Secretary-General submitted a report[12] reproducing replies from five States to his request for their views and suggestions on means to strengthen security and cooperation in the Mediterranean region.

On 12 December, the General Assembly adopted **resolution 50/75**.

### Strengthening of security and cooperation in the Mediterranean region

*The General Assembly,*

*Recalling* its previous resolutions on the subject, including resolution 49/81 of 15 December 1994,

*Reaffirming* the primary role of the Mediterranean countries in strengthening and promoting peace, security and cooperation in the Mediterranean region,

*Bearing in mind* all the previous declarations and commitments, as well as all the initiatives taken by the riparian countries at the recent summits, ministerial meetings and various forums concerning the question of the Mediterranean region,

*Recognizing* the efforts made so far and the determination of the Mediterranean countries to intensify the process of dialogue and consultations with a view to resolving the problems existing in the Mediterranean region and to eliminate the causes of tension and the consequent threat to peace and security,

*Recognizing also* the indivisible character of security in the Mediterranean and that the enhancement of cooperation among Mediterranean countries with a view to promoting the economic and social development of all peoples of the region will contribute significantly to stability, peace and security in the region,

*Recognizing further* that prospects for closer Euro-Mediterranean cooperation in all spheres can be enhanced by positive developments worldwide, in particular in Europe, in the Maghreb and in the Middle East,

*Noting with satisfaction* the positive developments in the Middle East peace process that will lead to achieving a comprehensive, just and lasting peace in the region and therefore to promoting confidence-building measures and a good-neighbourly spirit among the countries of the area,

*Expressing satisfaction* at the growing awareness of the need for more joint efforts by all Mediterranean countries so as to strengthen economic, social, cultural and environmental cooperation in the region,

*Reaffirming* the responsibility of all States to contribute to the stability and prosperity of the Mediterranean region and their commitment to respect the purposes and principles of the Charter of the United Nations, as well as the provisions of the Declaration on Principles of International Law concerning Friendly Relations and Cooperation among States in accordance with the Charter of the United Nations,

*Expressing its concern* at the persistent tension and continuing military activities in parts of the Mediterranean that hinder efforts to strengthen security and cooperation in the region,

*Taking note* of the report of the Secretary-General on this item,

1. *Reaffirms* that security in the Mediterranean is closely linked to European security as well as to international peace and security;

2. *Expresses its satisfaction* at the continuing efforts by Mediterranean countries to contribute actively to the elimination of all causes of tension in the region and to the promotion of just and lasting solutions to the persistent problems of the region through peaceful means, thus ensuring the withdrawal of foreign forces of occupation and respecting the sovereignty, independence and territorial integrity of all countries of the Mediterranean and the right of peoples to self-determination, and therefore calls for full adherence to the principles of non-interference, non-intervention, non-use of force or threat of use of force and the inadmissibility of the acquisition of territory by force, in accordance with the Charter and the relevant resolutions of the United Nations;

3. *Commends* the efforts by the Mediterranean countries in meeting common challenges through coordinated overall responses, based on a spirit of multilateral partnership, towards the general objective of turning the Mediterranean basin into an area of dialogue, exchanges and cooperation, guaranteeing peace, stability and prosperity;

4. *Recognizes* that the elimination of the economic and social disparities in levels of development as well as other obstacles in the Mediterranean area will contribute to enhancing peace, security and cooperation among Mediterranean countries through the existing forums;

5. *Calls upon* all States of the Mediterranean region that have not yet done so to adhere to all the multilaterally negotiated legal instruments related to the field of disarmament, thus creating the necessary conditions for strengthening peace and cooperation in the region;

6. *Encourages* all States of the region to favour the necessary conditions for strengthening the confidence-building measures among them by promoting genuine openness and transparency on all military matters, by participating, *inter alia*, in the United Nations system for the standardized reporting of military expenditures as well as by providing accurate data and information to the United Nations Register of Conventional Arms;

7. *Encourages* the Mediterranean countries to strengthen further their cooperation in combating terrorism, which poses a serious threat to peace, security and stability in the region and therefore to the improvement of the current political, economic and social situation;

8. *Invites* all States of the region to address, through various forms of cooperation, problems and threats posed to the region, such as terrorism, international crime and illicit arms transfers, as well as illicit drug production, consumption and trafficking, which jeopardize the friendly relations among States, hinder the development of international cooperation and result in the destruction of human rights, fundamental freedoms and the democratic basis of pluralistic society;

9. *Also encourages* the continued widespread support among the Mediterranean countries for the convening of a conference on security and cooperation in the Mediterranean, as well as the ongoing regional consultations to create the appropriate conditions for its convening;

10. *Requests* the Secretary-General to submit a report on means to strengthen security and cooperation in the Mediterranean region;

11. *Decides* to include in the provisional agenda of its fifty-first session the item entitled ''Strengthening of security and cooperation in the Mediterranean region''.

General Assembly resolution 50/75

12 December 1995     Meeting 90     Adopted without vote

Approved by First Committee (A/50/595) without vote, 10 November (meeting 18); 31-nation draft (A/C.1/50/L.36/Rev.1); agenda item 75.

*Meeting numbers.* GA 50th session: 1st Committee 3-11, 16, 18; plenary 90.

*REFERENCES*

[1]YUN 1993, p. 497, GA res. 48/84 B, 16 Dec. 1993. [2]A/50/412 & Add.1. [3]A/C.1/50/4. [4]A/C.1/50/5. [5]YUN 1994, p. 611, GA res. 49/13, 15 Nov. 1994. [6]A/50/564. [7]YUN 1994, p. 610. [8]A/50/813-S/1995/1030. [9]YUN 1994, p. 612. [10]A/50/652. [11]YUN 1994, p. 609, GA res. 49/81, 15 Dec. 1994. [12]A/50/300.

Chapter VI

# Middle East

During 1995, the Arab-Israeli peace process, which was launched in October 1991 in Madrid, Spain, proceeded despite a number of difficulties. An important further step in that process was the signing of the Israeli-Palestinian Interim Agreement on the West Bank and the Gaza Strip in September. In accordance with this and previous accords, the Palestinian Authority pursued its efforts to establish and maintain central institutions of administration, not only in the self-rule areas of the Gaza Strip and the West Bank area of Jericho, but throughout the West Bank.

The United Nations continued to support the overall peace process and remained involved in the Middle East in a number of ways—through its peace-keeping operations, through the good offices of the Secretary-General and its active participation in the multilateral negotiations on regional issues, and through significantly broadened programmes of economic, social and other assistance. The Special Committee to Investigate Israeli Practices Affecting the Human Rights of the Palestinian People and Other Arabs of the Occupied Territories reported to the General Assembly on situations in the Golan Heights, the West Bank (including East Jerusalem) and the Gaza Strip. The Committee on the Exercise of the Inalienable Rights of the Palestinian People continued to mobilize support and assistance to the Palestinians, expanding its cooperation with non-governmental organizations.

The Special Coordinator in the Occupied Territories served as the focal point for United Nations assistance to the Palestinians. The United Nations Relief and Works Agency for Palestine Refugees in the Near East (UNRWA) continued to provide a wide-ranging programme of education, health, relief and social services to Palestinian refugees. On various occasions throughout the year, UN bodies expressed their support for the ongoing negotiations, which were sometimes hampered by repeated delays and acts of violence, reaching a critical juncture with the assassination on 4 November of Yitzhak Rabin, the Prime Minister of Israel.

The ongoing construction and expansion of settlements in the occupied territories, and Israel's orders in April to expropriate 53 hectares of land in East Jerusalem, caused an outcry in many quarters. The Security Council met in February and again in May to consider those matters, but did not adopt resolutions in either case. Both the Economic and Social Council and the General Assembly discussed the economic and social repercussions of the Israeli settlements on the Palestinian people.

The situation in southern Lebanon remained both tense and volatile. The United Nations Interim Force in Lebanon (UNIFIL) continued efforts to limit the conflict and protect inhabitants from its consequences. Upon Lebanon's request, the Security Council in 1995 twice extended the UNIFIL mandate. It also extended the mandate of the United Nations Disengagement Observer Force (UNDOF) in the Golan Heights. The United Nations Truce Supervision Organization, headquartered in Jerusalem, continued to assist both peace-keeping operations in their tasks.

On 18 September, the General Assembly deferred (**decision 49/500**) consideration of the agenda item entitled "Armed Israeli aggression against the Iraqi nuclear installations and its grave consequences for the established international system concerning the peaceful uses of nuclear energy, the non-proliferation of nuclear weapons and international peace and security", and placed it on the provisional agenda of its fiftieth session. On 21 December, the Assembly again deferred (**decision 50/444**) the item and included it in the provisional agenda of its fifty-first (1996) session. The item had been inscribed yearly on the Assembly's agenda since 1981, following the bombing by Israel of a nuclear research centre near Baghdad.[a]

## Peace process

### Overall situation

A further step in the peace process was taken on 28 September 1995, in Washington, D.C., with the signing of the historic Israeli-Palestinian Interim Agreement on the West Bank and the Gaza Strip,[1] which superseded all earlier agreements in implementation of the 1993 Declaration of Principles on Interim Self-Government Arrangements.[2] On 27 August 1995, the parties had signed in Cairo, Egypt, the Protocol on Further Transfer of Powers and Responsibilities.

[a]YUN 1981, p. 275.

The September accord, which set out self-government arrangements in its 31 articles and six annexes, provided for the dissolution of the Israeli civil administration and the withdrawal of the Israeli military government, with a scheduled transfer of powers and responsibilities to the Palestinian Interim Self-Governing Authority, which was to replace the Palestinian Authority established under the May 1994 Agreement on the Gaza Strip and the Jericho Area.[3] The new Interim Self-Governing Authority was to be composed of an 82-member Council and the Head of its Executive Authority, both elected in January 1996 for a transitional period until May 1999 at the latest. The new Agreement further contained modalities for participation in the elections by the Palestinians of the West Bank, Jerusalem and the Gaza Strip, and made provision for international observation of the election process.

Prior to the elections, Israeli military forces were scheduled to be redeployed, first from the cities of Jenin, Nablus, Tulkarm, Kalkiliya, Ramallah and Bethlehem, and then from 450 towns, villages, refugee camps and hamlets. Redeployment would also take place in Hebron, with special security arrangements, including a temporary international presence. The Agreement provided for the gradual assumption of civil powers and responsibilities by the Palestinian Council. Further Israeli military redeployments were to take place at six-month intervals (for a period of 18 months) following the Council's inauguration, with concomitant extensions of the territorial jurisdiction of the Council except for areas subject to final-status negotiations. Arrangements were set out for the transfer of agreed-upon powers and responsibilities from the Israeli civil administration to the Council; the establishment of a Palestinian police force; and other provisions regarding legal matters, religious sites, human rights, water, a phased release of Palestinian detainees and prisoners, and cooperation in the areas of environment, economics, technology and science, and in fostering dialogue and mutual understanding.

The Agreement reaffirmed the parties' understanding that the interim self-government arrangements provided therein were an integral part of the whole peace process and that the negotiations on the permanent status, scheduled to start no later than 4 May 1996, would lead to the implementation of Security Council resolutions 242(1967)[4] and 338(1973).[5]

Throughout 1995, the Palestinian Authority pursued its efforts to establish and maintain central institutions of administration, not only in the self-rule areas of the Gaza Strip and the West Bank area of Jericho, but throughout the West Bank, in five key delegated spheres: civil administration, including education and culture, health, social welfare, tourism and direct taxation.

The peace process was affected throughout the year by acts of violence and terrorist incidents.

### Terrorist acts

On 22 January 1995, the fundamentalist organization Islamic Jihad claimed responsibility for two explosions, several minutes apart, at a crowded bus stop at the Sharon Junction (Beit Lid) in central Israel. Rescuers assisting victims of the first explosion themselves became victims of the second. Some 19 people were killed and another 66 wounded. Israel, reporting the incident to the Secretary-General on 23 January,[6] said that 110 Israelis had been killed by Palestinian terrorists in 49 separate incidents since the signing of the Declaration of Principles in 1993.[2]

#### SECURITY COUNCIL ACTION

After consultations of the Security Council held on 24 January 1995, the President of the Council made the following statement to the media on behalf of the Council members:[7]

> The members of the Security Council strongly condemn the terrorist attack which took place in Nordiya, Israel, last Sunday, 22 January 1995, with the clear purpose of trying to undermine the Middle East peace efforts.
> The members of the Security Council extend their condolences to the families of those who died as a consequence of the explosions and wish a speedy recovery of the wounded.
> The members of the Security Council call upon all parties to continue their efforts to consolidate the peace process. The members of the Security Council believe that common ground can only be found through the practice of dialogue, respect and tolerance.

### Rabin assassination

On 4 November, Israeli Prime Minister Yitzhak Rabin was assassinated at a pro-Government rally in Tel Aviv. In a statement on the same day, the Secretary-General strongly condemned the assassination as an outrageous act of terror which had struck one of the greatest leaders in Israel's history.

The General Assembly and its Third (Social, Humanitarian and Cultural) Committee, on 6 November, paid tribute to Prime Minister Rabin and, on 5 December, the Assembly held a special meeting in his memory. The assassination was also condemned by the Bureau of the Committee on Exercise of the Inalienable Rights of the Palestinian People (Committee on Palestinian Rights).

#### ECONOMIC AND SOCIAL COUNCIL ACTION

On 28 July, the Economic and Social Council adopted **resolution 1995/52**.

### Middle East peace process

*The Economic and Social Council,*

*Recalling* General Assembly resolution 49/88 of 16 December 1994,

*Reaffirming* its resolution 1994/44 of 29 July 1994,

*Recalling* the convening of the Peace Conference on the Middle East at Madrid on 30 October 1991, on the basis of Security Council resolutions 242(1967) of 22 November 1967 and 338(1973) of 22 October 1973, and the subsequent bilateral negotiations, as well as the meetings of the multilateral working groups, and noting with satisfaction the broad international support for the peace process,

*Noting* the continuing positive participation of the United Nations as a full extraregional participant in the work of the multilateral working groups,

*Bearing in mind* the Declaration of Principles on Interim Self-Government Arrangements, signed by the Government of the State of Israel and the Palestine Liberation Organization in Washington, on 13 September 1993, and the subsequent Agreement on the Gaza Strip and the Jericho Area, signed by the Government of the State of Israel and the Palestine Liberation Organization, the representative of the Palestinian people, at Cairo on 4 May 1994,

*Also bearing in mind* the Agreement between Israel and Jordan on the Common Agenda, signed in Washington, on 14 September 1993, the Washington Declaration signed by the Governments of Jordan and Israel on 25 July 1994, and the Treaty of Peace signed by the Governments of Jordan and Israel on 26 October 1994,

*Welcoming* the Declaration of Casablanca, adopted at the Middle East/North Africa Economic Summit, held at Casablanca from 30 October to 1 November 1994,

1.  *Welcomes* the peace process started at Madrid, and supports the subsequent bilateral negotiations;

2.  *Stresses* the importance of, and need for, achieving a comprehensive, just and lasting peace in the Middle East;

3.  *Expresses its full support* for the achievements of the peace process thus far, in particular the Declaration of Principles on Interim Self-Government Arrangements, signed by the Government of the State of Israel and the Palestine Liberation Organization, the subsequent Agreement on the Gaza Strip and the Jericho Area, signed by the Government of the State of Israel and the Palestine Liberation Organization, the representative of the Palestinian people, their 29 August 1994 agreement on the preparatory transfer of powers and responsibilities, the Agreement between Israel and Jordan on the Common Agenda, the Washington Declaration, signed by Jordan and Israel on 25 July 1994, and the Treaty of Peace signed by the Governments of Jordan and Israel on 26 October 1994, which constitute important steps in achieving a comprehensive, just and lasting peace in the Middle East, and urges all parties to implement the agreements reached;

4.  *Also expresses its support* for the ongoing negotiations between Israel and the Palestine Liberation Organization on modalities for elections in the West Bank and Gaza Strip, the redeployment of Israeli forces and the further transfer of responsibilities in the West Bank to the Palestinian Authority, and urges the parties to conclude these negotiations as soon as possible;

5.  *Welcomes* the results of the Conference to Support Middle East Peace, convened in Washington, on 1 October 1993, including the establishment of the Ad Hoc Liaison Committee, and the subsequent work of the World Bank Consultative Group, welcomes also the appointment by the Secretary-General of the United Nations Special Coordinator in the Occupied Territories,

and urges Member States to expedite and to increase economic, financial and technical assistance to the Palestinian people during the interim period;

6.  *Stresses* the need to achieve rapid progress on the other tracks of the Arab-Israeli negotiations within the peace process;

7.  *Calls upon* all Member States to extend economic, financial and technical assistance to parties in the region and to render support for the peace process;

8.  *Welcomes* the Middle-East/North Africa Economic Summit to be held at Amman from 29 to 31 October 1995, and expresses the hope that this Summit will contribute to the promotion of regional and international cooperation in the Middle East and North Africa;

9.  *Considers* that an active United Nations role in the Middle East peace process and in assisting in the implementation of the Declaration of Principles can make a positive contribution;

10.  *Encourages* regional development and cooperation in the areas where work has already begun within the framework of the Madrid Conference.

Economic and Social Council resolution 1995/52

28 July 1995          Meeting 57          47-1-1 (roll-call vote)

34-nation draft (E/1995/L.39); agenda item 7.
*Meeting numbers.* ESC 45, 46, 49, 57.

Roll-call vote in Council as follows:

*In favour:* Australia, Bahamas, Belarus, Bhutan, Brazil, Bulgaria, Canada, Chile, China, Colombia, Côte d'Ivoire, Cuba, Denmark, Egypt, France, Gabon, Germany, Ghana, Greece, India, Indonesia, Ireland, Jamaica, Japan, Luxembourg, Mexico, Netherlands, Nigeria, Norway, Pakistan, Philippines, Poland, Portugal, Republic of Korea, Romania, Russian Federation, Senegal, South Africa, Sri Lanka, Thailand, Uganda, Ukraine, United Kingdom, United Republic of Tanzania, United States, Venezuela, Zimbabwe.
*Against:* Libyan Arab Jamahiriya.
*Abstaining:* Malaysia.

Speaking before the vote, the Libyan Arab Jamahiriya objected to the text on the grounds that it was a purely political matter unrelated to the Council's terms of reference. With regard to the declarations signed in Casablanca and Washington, it noted that not all the States in the region had been present. The Syrian Arab Republic remarked that paragraph 3 lacked any mention of two basic principles on which the Peace Conference on the Middle East had been based: the principles of land for peace, and Israel's immediate and unconditional withdrawal from Lebanon. The Sudan explained that it would not participate in the vote as it had reservations concerning what it called loopholes in the peace process that did not serve the purposes of peace in the region.

After the vote, Israel stated that the resolution did what the Council should be doing, namely, putting its weight and that of the international community behind the peace process. Israel hoped that States which had not yet done so would join the multilateral, regional track of that process which, as underlined in paragraphs 6 and 10, was designed to bring the parties closer by dealing with social and economic issues of concern to all.

**Report of the Secretary-General.** On 7 November, the Secretary-General reported[8] to the General Assembly on his efforts to promote peace in the Middle East. Pursuant to a request made in a 1994 Assembly resolution on the peaceful settlement of the Palestine question,[9] he had in September sought the views of the Security Council and the parties concerned—i.e., Egypt, Israel, Jordan, Lebanon, the Syrian Arab Republic and the Palestine Liberation Organization (PLO)—on continuing efforts to advance the search for peace. On 25 September, the Security Council stated that it continued to be determined to provide the necessary backing to the Middle East peace process, giving full support to its achievement, including the 1993 Declaration of Principles on Interim Self-Government Arrangements between Israel and PLO, as well as subsequent implementation agreements. The Council believed that the parties should be further encouraged to adhere to and fully implement those agreements.

On 11 September, Israel recalled that it had voted against the 1994 resolution (49/62 D) and that its position remained unchanged. It had long advocated direct negotiations without preconditions, freely agreed on by all parties, as the only framework to advance peace. The peace process begun in Madrid was based on that principle and, within its framework, Israel and PLO had signed the 1993 Declaration of Principles, the May 1994 Agreement on the Gaza Strip and the Jericho Area and the August 1994 Agreement on Preparatory Transfer of Powers and Responsibility.[3] In addition, Israel and Jordan had signed a peace treaty on 26 October 1994.[10] Bilateral and multilateral negotiations between Israel and its neighbours continued, and Israel looked forward to progress on all tracks of the peace process.

Israel believed that resolution 49/62 D stood in direct contradiction to the principle of direct negotiations without preconditions; moreover, its paragraph 5 (stressing the need for resolving the problem of the Palestinian refugees in conformity with Assembly resolution 149(III) of 11 December 1948[11]) was intended to predetermine the outcome of the final-status talks agreed upon in the Declaration of Principles, as well as the results of the negotiations on the other tracks, and was therefore contrary to any notion of genuine negotiations.

Conveying the position of the PLO leadership and the Palestinian National Authority, the Permanent Observer of Palestine on 16 October noted that the sponsors of the 1994 resolution, while retaining essential principles, had introduced important changes to accommodate the positions of some Member States and, as a result, received overwhelming support from the Assembly Members. The resolution provided support for the peace process, a more active and expanded UN role in that process, and the basis for a just settlement of the Palestine question. Since the adoption of that reso-

lution, further positive developments had taken place, in particular the signing on 28 September 1995 of the Interim Agreement on the West Bank and Gaza Strip (the second implementation agreement of the Declaration of Principles), which provided for the extension of the self-government arrangements to the rest of the West Bank and the holding of general and democratic Palestinian elections.

There had been various delays in the implementation of the Declaration of Principles and some lack of compliance with the provisions of the September agreement; both sides, however, had recently indicated their firm commitment to implementing the agreement in good faith, fully and according to the agreed timetable. They had also reaffirmed their intention to enter into the final-status negotiations in accordance with the Declaration of Principles.

The Palestine side strongly believed that the international community and the Assembly should always uphold the principles of the Charter of the United Nations, international law, international humanitarian law and the validity of Security Council resolutions. The Assembly had to uphold its positions with regard to the inalienable rights of the Palestinians and should maintain its positions related to the final-status issues, where Israel had already created illegal, de facto situations, until negotiations on those issues took place and a final settlement was achieved.

The Palestinian side hoped that the United Nations would become more involved in the peace process itself. In that context, it regarded United Nations participation in the steering committee of the multilateral working groups as a normal step forward; another step would be United Nations participation in the supervision of the upcoming Palestinian elections, and further involvement of the Security Council would be a very important element.

Finally, the Secretary-General, in the 7 November report, observed that the past year had seen important progress in the Middle East peace process. The September 1995 Interim Agreement had been a significant step forward and provided a solid basis for the realization of Palestinian rights, a long-sought goal of the United Nations. He hoped that the resolve and dedication to peace shown by Israeli and Palestinian leaders would continue to guide them through the transitional stage until a permanent settlement on the basis of Security Council resolutions 242(1967) and 338(1973) was reached.

The Secretary-General further hoped that those developments, together with the ongoing implementation of the October 1994 Israeli-Jordanian peace accord, would generate momentum for progress on the Israeli-Syrian and Israeli-Lebanese tracks of the peace talks, leading to a comprehensive, just and lasting solution of the Arab-Israeli conflict.

The United Nations, he added, would continue to support the peace process, politically and economically, in order to reinforce what was achieved in the negotiations and to help build the foundations for a new post-conflict Middle East. It already participated actively in the multilateral negotiations on regional economic, security, environment, water and refugee issues. Its agencies and programmes were doing their utmost to assist the Palestinians in Gaza and the West Bank. The United Nations Special Coordinator in the Occupied Territories and his Office (UNSCO) were instrumental in supporting and facilitating those peace-building activities and during the transitional period would continue to serve as a focal point for United Nations economic, social and other assistance to the Palestinians throughout the occupied territories.

**GENERAL ASSEMBLY ACTION**

On 4 December, the General Assembly adopted **resolution 50/21**.

### Middle East peace process

*The General Assembly,*

*Recalling* its resolution 49/88 of 16 December 1994 and Economic and Social Council resolution 1995/52 of 28 July 1995,

*Stressing* that the achievement of a comprehensive, just and lasting settlement of the Middle East conflict will constitute a significant contribution to strengthening international peace and security,

*Recalling* the convening of the Peace Conference on the Middle East at Madrid on 30 October 1991, on the basis of Security Council resolutions 242(1967) of 22 November 1967 and 338(1973) of 22 October 1973, and the subsequent bilateral negotiations, as well as the meetings of the multilateral working groups, and noting with satisfaction the broad international support for the peace process,

*Noting* the continuing positive participation of the United Nations as a full extraregional participant in the work of the multilateral working groups,

*Bearing in mind* the Declaration of Principles on Interim Self-Government Arrangements, signed by the Government of the State of Israel and the Palestine Liberation Organization, the representative of the Palestinian people, in Washington on 13 September 1993, and the subsequent Agreement on the Gaza Strip and the Jericho Area, signed by the Government of the State of Israel and the Palestine Liberation Organization at Cairo on 4 May 1994, their 29 August 1994 Agreement on the Preparatory Transfer of Powers and Responsibilities, the Protocol on Further Transfer of Powers and Responsibilities signed by the Government of Israel and the Palestine Liberation Organization at Cairo on 27 August 1995, and the Interim Agreement on the West Bank and Gaza Strip, signed by the Government of Israel and the

Palestine Liberation Organization in Washington on 28 September 1995,

*Also bearing in mind* the Agreement between Israel and Jordan on the Common Agenda, signed in Washington on 14 September 1993, the Washington Declaration, signed by Jordan and Israel on 25 July 1994, and the Treaty of Peace between the State of Israel and the Hashemite Kingdom of Jordan, of 26 October 1994,

*Welcoming* the Declaration of the Middle East/North Africa Economic Summit held at Casablanca from 30 October to 1 November 1994, as well as the Declaration of the Middle East/North Africa Economic Summit held at Amman from 29 to 31 October 1995,

1. *Welcomes* the peace process started at Madrid, and supports the subsequent bilateral negotiations;

2. *Stresses* the importance of, and need for, achieving a comprehensive, just and lasting peace in the Middle East;

3. *Expresses its full support* for the achievements of the peace process thus far, in particular the Declaration of Principles on Interim Self-Government Arrangements, signed by the Government of the State of Israel and the Palestine Liberation Organization, the representative of the Palestinian People, the subsequent Agreement on the Gaza Strip and the Jericho Area, signed by the Government of the State of Israel and the Palestine Liberation Organization, their 29 August 1994 Agreement on the Preparatory Transfer of Powers and Responsibilities, the Protocol on Further Transfer of Powers and Responsibilities signed by the Government of Israel and the Palestine Liberation Organization at Cairo on 27 August 1995, the Interim Agreement on the West Bank and Gaza Strip, signed by the Government of Israel and the Palestine Liberation Organization in Washington on 28 September 1995, the Agreement between Israel and Jordan on the Common Agenda, the Washington Declaration, signed by Jordan and Israel on 25 July 1994, and the Treaty of Peace between the State of Israel and the Hashemite Kingdom of Jordan, of 26 October 1994, which constitute important steps in achieving a comprehensive, just and lasting peace in the Middle East, and urges all parties to implement the agreements reached;

4. *Stresses* the need to achieve rapid progress on the other tracks of the Arab-Israeli negotiations within the peace process;

5. *Welcomes* the results of the Conference to Support Middle East Peace, convened in Washington on 1 October 1993, including the establishment of the Ad Hoc Liaison Committee, and the subsequent work of the World Bank Consultative Group, welcomes also the appointment by the Secretary-General of the "United Nations Special Coordinator in the Occupied Territories", and urges Member States to expedite economic, financial and technical assistance to the Palestinian people during the interim period;

6. *Calls upon* all Member States to extend economic, financial and technical assistance to parties in the region and to render support for the peace process;

7. *Considers* that an active United Nations role in the Middle East peace process and in assisting in the implementation of the Declaration of Principles can make a positive contribution;

8. *Encourages* regional development and cooperation in areas where work has begun within the framework of the Madrid Conference.

General Assembly resolution 50/21

4 December 1995    Meeting 79    148-4-1 (recorded vote)

76-nation draft (A/50/L.24 & Add.1); agenda item 44.
*Meeting numbers.* GA 50th session: plenary 76, 77, 79.

Recorded vote in Assembly as follows:

*In favour:* Albania, Algeria, Andorra, Antigua and Barbuda, Argentina, Armenia, Australia, Austria, Azerbaijan, Bahamas, Bahrain, Bangladesh, Barbados, Belarus, Belgium, Belize, Benin, Bhutan, Bolivia, Bosnia and Herzegovina, Botswana, Brazil, Brunei Darussalam, Bulgaria, Burkina Faso, Burundi, Cameroon, Canada, Cape Verde, Chad, Chile, China, Colombia, Congo, Costa Rica, Côte d'Ivoire, Croatia, Cuba, Cyprus, Czech Republic, Denmark, Djibouti, Dominica, Ecuador, Egypt, El Salvador, Eritrea, Estonia, Ethiopia, Finland, France, Gabon, Georgia, Germany, Ghana, Greece, Grenada, Guatemala, Guinea, Guyana, Haiti, Honduras, Hungary, Iceland, India, Indonesia, Ireland, Israel, Italy, Jamaica, Japan, Jordan, Kazakstan, Kenya, Kuwait, Lao People's Democratic Republic, Latvia, Lesotho, Liechtenstein, Lithuania, Luxembourg, Madagascar, Malawi, Malaysia, Maldives, Mali, Malta, Marshall Islands, Mauritania, Mauritius, Mexico, Micronesia, Monaco, Mongolia, Morocco, Mozambique, Myanmar, Namibia, Nepal, Netherlands, New Zealand, Nicaragua, Niger, Norway, Oman, Pakistan, Panama, Papua New Guinea, Paraguay, Peru, Philippines, Poland, Portugal, Qatar, Republic of Korea, Romania, Russian Federation, Samoa, Saudi Arabia, Senegal, Singapore, Slovakia, Slovenia, Solomon Islands, South Africa, Spain, Sri Lanka, Suriname, Swaziland, Sweden, Tajikistan, Thailand, the former Yugoslav Republic of Macedonia, Togo, Tunisia, Turkey, Uganda, Ukraine, United Arab Emirates, United Kingdom, United Republic of Tanzania, United States, Uruguay, Venezuela, Viet Nam, Yemen, Zambia, Zimbabwe.

*Against:* Iran, Lebanon, Libyan Arab Jamahiriya, Syrian Arab Republic.

*Abstaining:* Sudan.

Explaining its vote, the Libyan Arab Jamahiriya said the contents of the text did not include the full prerequisites of a just and comprehensive Middle East peace, failing to call on Israel to withdraw from southern Lebanon in accordance with Security Council resolution 425(1978).[12] Also, the text did not mention the return of the Palestinians to their country and homes. The Syrian Arab Republic noted that the text did not refer to Council resolutions 425(1978), 242(1967)[4] and 338(1973),[5] the foundations on which the peace process was built. France considered the omission of references to resolution 425(1978) regrettable, as it attached particular importance to the principles enshrined in it.

Introducing the draft on behalf of sponsors, Norway said the past year had seen great achievements in the Middle East peace process. The Interim Agreement was a major accomplishment and produced remarkable results. Important consequences had been the Palestinian elections to be held on the West Bank and in the Gaza Strip in January 1996, as well as the Israeli redeployment from the West Bank town of Jenin. It was hoped that the final-status negotiations would begin as scheduled in spring 1996. Another milestone along the road to comprehensive peace was the Economic Summit held in October in Amman, Jordan, in which 1,500 international businessmen and politicians, including those from the Middle East and North Africa, had participated. The new climate of coexistence and cooperation must be protected and expanded. The tragic death of Prime Minister Rabin was a reminder that the peace process demanded not only commitment and a clear vision of the future, but also considerable courage.

Israel declared that despite the pain of Mr. Rabin's assassination, the Government of Prime Minister Shimon Peres was determined to push forward and achieve a comprehensive peace; terrorists would not be allowed to stop that process. The peace which was being created would translate into full regional cooperation that had begun last year with the convening in Casablanca, Morocco, of the first Middle East/North Africa economic summit, followed by the second summit in Amman.

From such tragic times, said the United States, must come a renewed determination to go forward on the path of peace.

In the view of the Observer of Palestine, Mr. Rabin's assassination was proof that terrorism had grown in a climate nurtured by Israeli parties. The Committee on Palestinian Rights hoped that that tragic act would not lead to a setback in the peace process; the outpouring of support by the international community, as well as by Israeli public opinion, showed that the path which the parties were following was the correct one.

## Jerusalem

Since ancient times, Jerusalem has been a city at the heart of three major world religions—Christianity, Judaism and Islam. The November 1947 General Assembly plan for partition had specified that Jerusalem was to be placed under international status, with Palestine to be partitioned into an Arab State and an Israeli State. The plan was not accepted by the Palestinian Arabs and the Arab States, and hostilities ensued after Israel declared its independence on 14 May 1948. During the early fighting in Jerusalem, a neutral zone was established in the area of the building and grounds of Government House—the headquarters of the former British Mandatory Administration—which later became the headquarters of the UN Truce Supervision Organization (UNTSO). On 7 October 1948, following renewed fighting, during which the status of the neutral zone was violated by both Israeli and Jordanian forces, Government House and its surrounding grounds were transferred to United Nations protection by the International Committee of the Red Cross (ICRC), which had been holding the area in trust for a successor administration. Both States parties were informed of those arrangements and did not raise any objections. A cease-fire agreement of 30 November 1948 left that arrangement in place. The General Armistice Agreement concluded between Israel and Jordan on 3 April 1949 provided that in the Jerusalem sector the Armistice Demarcation Lines should correspond to the lines defined in the cease-fire agreement of 30 November 1948, and therefore the status of Government House and the neutral zone remained unaltered.

On 5 June 1967, after fighting erupted in Jerusalem during the six-day war, Israeli forces occupied Government House and escorted UNTSO staff out of its premises. When a cease-fire went into effect on 10 June, Israel was occupying parts of the Sinai Desert, the Golan Heights, the West Bank, the Gaza Strip and East Jerusalem. After negotiations, Israel agreed on 22 August 1967 that UNTSO personnel could return to their headquarters at Government House.

Jerusalem since the 1967 six-day war has been the subject of many UN resolutions, with the Security Council and the General Assembly calling on Israel to rescind measures to alter the status of the Holy City and not to take further actions which might alter its status, and declaring as invalid any changes in its status. Demonstrations, outbreaks of violence, excavations at holy sites and, most recently, expropriation of land for residential construction in East Jerusalem have been the subject of discussion and action at the UN. Questions centring on Jerusalem are considered a "final-status" negotiation issue in the ongoing Middle East peace process, and the status of the Holy City in 1995 continued to be a central focal point of United Nations concern.

**Report of the Secretary-General.** On 24 October 1995, the Secretary-General submitted a report[13] containing replies of four Member States to his request for information on steps taken or envisaged to implement a 1994 General Assembly resolution[14] dealing with the transfer by some States of their diplomatic missions to Jerusalem and calling on them to abide by the relevant UN resolutions. Of the responding States, Austria and Mexico said they maintained embassies in Tel Aviv. Cape Verde stated that it had not taken any action contrary to the 1994 resolution. Japan expressed support of that resolution, as it had adhered to previous resolutions on the subject.

**GENERAL ASSEMBLY ACTION**

On 4 December, the General Assembly adopted **resolution 50/22 A**.

### Jerusalem

*The General Assembly,*

*Recalling* its resolutions 36/120 E 10 December 1981, 37/123 C of 16 December 1982, 38/180 C of 19 December 1983, 39/146 C of 14 December 1984, 40/168 C of 16 December 1985, 41/162 C of 4 December 1986, 42/209 D of 11 December 1987, 43/54 C of 6 December 1988, 44/40 C of 4 December 1989, 45/83 C of 13 December 1990, 46/82 B of 16 December 1991, 47/63 B of 11 December 1992, 48/59 A of 14 December 1993 and 49/87 A of 16 December 1994, in which it determined that all legislative and administrative measures and actions taken by Israel, the occupying Power, which had altered or purported to alter the character and status of the Holy City of Jerusalem, in particular the so-called "Basic Law" on Jerusalem and the proclamation of

Jerusalem as the capital of Israel, were null and void and must be rescinded forthwith,

*Recalling also* Security Council resolution 478(1980) of 20 August 1980, in which the Council, *inter alia*, decided not to recognize the "Basic Law" and called upon those States that had established diplomatic missions at Jerusalem to withdraw such missions from the Holy City,

*Having considered* the report of the Secretary-General of 24 October 1995,

1. *Determines* that the decision of Israel to impose its laws, jurisdiction and administration on the Holy City of Jerusalem is illegal and therefore null and void and has no validity whatsoever;

2. *Deplores* the transfer by some States of their diplomatic missions to Jerusalem in violation of Security Council resolution 478(1980), and their refusal to comply with the provisions of that resolution;

3. *Calls once more upon* those States to abide by the provisions of the relevant United Nations resolutions, in conformity with the Charter of the United Nations;

4. *Requests* the Secretary-General to report to the General Assembly at its fifty-first session on the implementation of the present resolution.

General Assembly resolution 50/22 A

4 December 1995      Meeting 79      133-1-13 (recorded vote)

19-nation draft (A/50/L.37 & Add.1); agenda item 44.
*Meeting numbers.* GA 50th session: plenary 76, 77, 79.

Recorded vote in Assembly as follows:

*In favour:* Albania, Algeria, Andorra, Argentina, Armenia, Australia, Austria, Azerbaijan, Bahrain, Bangladesh, Barbados, Belarus, Belgium, Belize, Benin, Bhutan, Bolivia, Bosnia and Herzegovina, Botswana, Brazil, Brunei Darussalam, Bulgaria, Burkina Faso, Burundi, Cameroon, Canada, Cape Verde, Chad, Chile, China, Colombia, Croatia, Cuba, Cyprus, Czech Republic, Denmark, Djibouti, Ecuador, Egypt, Eritrea, Estonia, Ethiopia, Finland, France, Gabon, Georgia, Germany, Ghana, Greece, Guinea, Guyana, Haiti, Honduras, Hungary, Iceland, India, Indonesia, Iran, Ireland, Jamaica, Japan, Jordan, Kazakstan, Kenya, Kuwait, Lao People's Democratic Republic, Latvia, Lebanon, Lesotho, Libyan Arab Jamahiriya, Liechtenstein, Lithuania, Luxembourg, Malawi, Malaysia, Maldives, Mali, Malta, Mauritania, Mauritius, Mexico, Monaco, Mongolia, Morocco, Mozambique, Myanmar, Namibia, Nepal, Netherlands, New Zealand, Niger, Norway, Oman, Pakistan, Panama, Paraguay, Peru, Philippines, Poland, Portugal, Qatar, Republic of Korea, Romania, Russian Federation, Saudi Arabia, Senegal, Singapore, Slovakia, Slovenia, South Africa, Spain, Sri Lanka, Sudan, Suriname, Sweden, Syrian Arab Republic, Tajikistan, Thailand, the former Yugoslav Republic of Macedonia, Togo, Tunisia, Turkey, Uganda, Ukraine, United Arab Emirates, United Kingdom, United Republic of Tanzania, Uruguay, Venezuela, Viet Nam, Yemen, Zambia, Zimbabwe.

*Against:* Israel.

*Abstaining:* Antigua and Barbuda, Bahamas, Congo, Costa Rica, Côte d'Ivoire, Dominica, Marshall Islands, Micronesia, Papua New Guinea, Samoa, Solomon Islands, Swaziland, United States.

After the vote, the United States said it had abstained, as Jerusalem had to remain undivided; the Assembly should not interject itself into that most complex issue when the parties themselves had decided to defer its discussion to their already scheduled permanent-status negotiations. Swaziland held the view that resolutions which sounded harsh and reprimanding were no longer rewarding or productive.

In Palestine's view, the resolution sent a clear message to the international community to the effect that all parties must refrain from taking measures that would introduce changes on the ground which might influence the negotiation process on Jerusalem.

Iran expressed reservations on the parts of the resolution which might be construed as any recognition of Israel. Iraq noted that the text was incomplete, as it ignored the United States' decision to move its embassy to Jerusalem in 1999, which it called a provocation. The Libyan Arab Jamahiriya also regarded that decision as a flagrant violation of international legality, as embodied in Security Council and Assembly resolutions.

(For the question of Israeli settlements and land expropriation in East Jerusalem, see below, under "Occupied territories".)

## Occupied territories

### Special Committee on Israeli Practices

The situation in territories occupied by Israel as a result of armed conflicts in the Middle East continued to be of concern to the United Nations in 1995. The three-member Special Committee to Investigate Israeli Practices Affecting the Human Rights of the Palestinian People and Other Arabs of the Occupied Territories, established in 1968,[15] reported for the twenty-seventh time to the General Assembly on events in those territories it considered to be occupied, namely the Golan Heights of the Syrian Arab Republic, the West Bank (including East Jerusalem) and the Gaza Strip.

In addition to that annual report,[16] two periodic reports were also prepared in 1995 by the Special Committee at the request of the General Assembly,[17] one in May,[18] the other in July.[19] The three reports, which covered developments between 26 August 1994 and 18 August 1995, contained information obtained from: the Arab and Israeli press; testimony given at hearings held in Amman (Jordan), Cairo (Egypt) and Damascus (Syrian Arab Republic) between 13 and 23 May 1995; Israeli government policy statements; and other communications and reports. The Committee reported that the Governments of Egypt, Jordan and the Syrian Arab Republic had provided information. As in the past, it said, Israel had not responded to requests for cooperation with the Committee.

Chairman Herman Leonard de Silva of Sri Lanka said the Special Committee presented a composite picture of the realities in the occupied territories as they affected the human rights of the civilian population. Recent historic events—the signing of the Declaration of Principles on Interim Self-Government Arrangements, on 13 September 1993,[2] and the Israel-PLO Agreement on the Gaza Strip and the Jericho Area, on 4 May 1994,[20] and the subsequent establishment of the Palestinian National Authority, as well as the September 1995 agreement on the West Bank and Gaza—had given rise to very high expectations concerning the improvement of the human rights situation in the occupied territories among their population, he said. It was expected that those agreements would usher in a new era, with the establishment of peace, justice, understanding and respect for human rights in the region. The information in the twenty-seventh report showed, however, that the general situation of human rights in the territories still remained very serious and a matter for grave concern.

A major factor contributing to the lack of improvement in the human rights situation was the repeated closures of the territories by the Israeli authorities after serious security incidents in Israel, caused by groups on both sides opposed to the peace process, the Chairman stated.

The closures had entailed a significant deterioration in the economic and social situation in the occupied territories, in particular the Gaza Strip, he went on, and had resulted in a significant reduction in the number of Palestinians allowed to work in Israel. Restrictions on freedom of movement had also had adverse consequences in the fields of health and education, and on freedom of worship.

A continuing source of tension was the existence of Israeli settlements in the occupied territories, the Chairman declared. The situation regarding expropriation of Arab-owned land and the expansion of the settlements was particularly serious in Jerusalem. While the overall level of violence and number of deaths had declined, the nature of the violence perpetrated by the Israel Defence Forces was of an aggravated kind. Also, situations of prisoners and conditions at places of detention had not improved. Deficiencies continued to be noted in the administration of justice by Israeli authorities.

The Committee welcomed several positive developments: the transfer to the Palestinians of additional responsibilities in the fields of statistics, fuel, insurance, commerce and industry, labour and local government; the allocation of additional water resources to the territories' inhabitants; the decrease in demolition orders for Palestinian-owned houses; the increase in approvals of requests for family reunification; and the approval of a number of requests, made by Palestinians expelled by the security forces before the *intifadah*, to return to their homes in the West Bank.

Unless progress was made with regard to the enjoyment of human rights by all the inhabitants of the occupied territories, the Chairman declared, support for the peace process would erode further and give way to despair. All parties concerned must endeavour to build a truly meaningful culture of respect for human rights in the occupied territories so that the recent significant achievements might enable the people of the region to live together in dignity, peace, security and mutual respect. Progress in the peace process, he concluded, must go hand in hand with full compliance with all relevant UN resolutions and all universally accepted standards of human rights.

The Committee, in its report, stated that it hoped its findings would be taken into account when concrete measures were drawn up in order to give life to the spirit of the recent important developments. In the meantime, it recommended once more measures for safeguarding the basic human rights of the Palestinians and other Arabs in the territories, including full application by Israel of the fourth Geneva Convention and compliance with all UN resolutions pertinent to the territories; Israeli cooperation with UNSCO and the UN Relief and Works Agency for Palestine Refugees in the Near East (UNRWA), and full support by Member States of the activities of UNRWA and ICRC; access by ICRC representatives to detained persons; renewed efforts to convince Israel of the need for increased human rights protection through international monitoring; and Israeli cooperation with the UN Centre for Human Rights with regard to implementation of human rights advisory assistance in areas falling under the Interim Self-Government Arrangements.

The Committee appealed to Israel to act in conformity with the spirit animating the peace process, by giving serious consideration to the following concrete measures: *(a)* establishing clear rules of engagement for its security forces; exercising restraint in responding to outbreaks of violence and investigating all shooting incidents; and ending immediately the activities of undercover units, in particular, extrajudicial and summary executions; *(b)* controlling violence and abuses by settlers and bringing those responsible to justice; *(c)* reviewing its settlements policy, halting the expansion of settlements and ending land confiscation; and ending pressure on Arabs in East Jerusalem to sell their houses; *(d)* enforcing the law equitably and ensuring all legal safeguards for the Arab population and prompt and impartial administration of justice; *(e)* ending torture and ill-treatment and investigating those responsible; making guidelines concerning interrogation procedures transparent and conforming them to international human rights standards; *(f)* reviewing the situation of Palestinian and Arab prisoners, especially political detainees or those having committed non-violent crimes, and expediting their release; refraining from detaining residents of the territories within Israel; and improving conditions of detention, to conform with the Standard Minimum Rules for the Treatment of Prisoners adopted in 1955 by the first United Nations Congress on the Prevention of Crime and the Treatment of Of-

fenders;[21] *(g)* allowing all deported or expelled persons to return to the territories and have their properties restored; and *(h)* ending all measures of collective punishment, which affected adversely the economic and social situation of the population of the territories and hindered the enjoyment of fundamental rights and freedoms of movement, education, religion and expression; and refraining from imposing curfews and closures, destroying property, demolishing houses and uprooting trees, as well as from discriminatory measures concerning the use of water resources.

During consideration by the General Assembly's Fourth Committee, the representative of Israel and the Observer from Palestine made statements on 17 November regarding the Special Committee report.

Israel said the Fourth Committee should note that certain resolutions adopted when the Arab-Israeli conflict was at its height did not reflect the new reality in the Middle East. Israel considered that the Special Committee on Israeli Practices wasted the limited financial resources of the UN without bringing any benefit at all to the Palestinian people.

Palestine expressed regret regarding the refusal of the Israeli authorities to cooperate with the Special Committee, believing the current situation warranted the continued work of the Committee. It hoped the report for next year would reflect further progress and positive change on the ground.

During the year, Israel had reported a number of terrorist incidents to the Secretary-General, including three bomb attacks against Israeli public buses, on 9 April,[22] on 24 July[23] and on 21 August.[24] On 10 April, Israel stated[22] that since the signing of the 1993 Declaration of Principles on Interim Self-Government Arrangements, 125 Israelis had been killed by Palestinian terrorists in 52 separate attacks, most committed by Islamic fundamentalist organizations which received support and guidance from like-minded States in the region, especially Iran.

On 12 April, Iran, in a letter to the Secretary-General,[25] rejected that allegation, stressing that the course of events and developments in the occupied territories had nothing to do with Iran, but rather stemmed from the inherent expansionist agenda of the Zionist regime, which had serious repercussions for the peace and security of the region.

**Report of the Secretary-General.** On 20 October 1995, the Secretary-General reported[26] that all necessary facilities had been provided to the Special Committee on Israeli Practices, as requested by the General Assembly in 1994.[17] Arrangements had been made for meetings in March, May and August, and field missions to Egypt, Jordan and the Syrian Arab Republic were carried out in May. Committee reports were circulated to Member States, and press releases in English and French had been issued.

GENERAL ASSEMBLY ACTION

Following consideration of the reports of the Committee on Israeli Practices, the General Assembly on 6 December 1995 adopted four resolutions under the general title ''Report of the Special Committee to Investigate Israeli Practices Affecting the Human Rights of the Palestinian People and Other Arabs of the Occupied Territories'', among them **resolution 50/29 A**.

*The General Assembly,*

*Guided* by the purposes and principles of the Charter of the United Nations,

*Guided also* by the principles of international humanitarian law, in particular the Geneva Convention relative to the Protection of Civilian Persons in Time of War, of 12 August 1949, as well as international standards of human rights, in particular the Universal Declaration of Human Rights and the International Covenants on Human Rights,

*Recalling* its relevant resolutions, including resolution 2443(XXIII) of 19 December 1968, and relevant resolutions of the Commission on Human Rights,

*Recalling also* relevant resolutions of the Security Council,

*Aware* of the uprising (*intifadah*) of the Palestinian people,

*Convinced* that occupation itself represents a primary violation of human rights,

*Having considered* the reports of the Special Committee to Investigate Israeli Practices Affecting the Human Rights of the Palestinian People and Other Arabs of the Occupied Territories and the relevant reports of the Secretary-General,

*Noting* the signing of the Declaration of Principles on Interim Self-Government Arrangements, including its Annexes and its Agreed Minutes, by the Government of the State of Israel and the Palestine Liberation Organization in Washington, on 13 September 1993, as well as the subsequent implementation agreements, including the Agreement on the Gaza Strip and the Jericho Area signed at Cairo on 4 May 1994 and the Interim Agreement on the West Bank and the Gaza Strip signed in Washington on 28 September 1995,

*Expressing the hope* that, with the progress of the peace process, the Israeli occupation will be brought to an end and therefore violation of the human rights of the Palestinian people will cease,

1. *Commends* the Special Committee to Investigate Israeli Practices Affecting the Human Rights of the Palestinian People and Other Arabs of the Occupied Territories for its efforts in performing the tasks assigned to it by the General Assembly and for its impartiality;

2. *Demands* that Israel cooperate with the Special Committee in implementing its mandate;

3. *Deplores* those policies and practices of Israel which violate the human rights of the Palestinian people and other Arabs of the occupied territories, as reflected in the reports of the Special Committee covering the reporting period;

4. *Expresses the hope* that, in the light of the recent positive political developments, those policies and practices will be brought to an end immediately;

5. *Requests* the Special Committee, pending complete termination of the Israeli occupation, to continue to investigate Israeli policies and practices in the occupied Palestinian territory, including Jerusalem, and other Arab territories occupied by Israel since 1967, to consult, as appropriate, with the International Committee of the Red Cross according to its regulations in order to ensure that the welfare and human rights of the peoples of the occupied territories are safeguarded and to report to the Secretary-General as soon as possible and whenever the need arises thereafter;

6. *Also requests* the Special Committee to submit regularly to the Secretary-General periodic reports on the current situation in the occupied Palestinian territory;

7. *Further requests* the Special Committee to continue to investigate the treatment of prisoners in the occupied Palestinian territory, including Jerusalem, and other Arab territories occupied by Israel since 1967;

8. *Requests* the Secretary-General:

(a) To provide all necessary facilities to the Special Committee, including those required for its visits to the occupied territories, so that it may investigate the Israeli policies and practices referred to in the present resolution;

(b) To continue to make available such additional staff as may be necessary to assist the Special Committee in the performance of its tasks;

(c) To circulate regularly to Member States the periodic reports mentioned in paragraph 6 above;

(d) To ensure the widest circulation of the reports of the Special Committee and of information regarding its activities and findings, by all means available, through the Department of Public Information of the Secretariat and, where necessary, to reprint those reports of the Special Committee that are no longer available;

(e) To report to the General Assembly at its fifty-first session on the tasks entrusted to him in the present resolution;

9. *Decides* to include in the provisional agenda of its fifty-first session the item entitled ''Report of the Special Committee to Investigate Israeli Practices Affecting the Human Rights of the Palestinian People and Other Arabs of the Occupied Territories''.

General Assembly resolution 50/29 A

6 December 1995     Meeting 82     69-2-80 (recorded vote)

Approved by Fourth Committee (A/50/606) by recorded vote (63-2-65), 30 November (meeting 25); 12-nation draft (A/C.4/50/L.18); agenda item 85.
*Meeting numbers.* GA 50th session: 4th Committee 24, 25; plenary 82.

Recorded vote in Assembly as follows:

*In favour:* Afghanistan, Algeria, Azerbaijan, Bahrain, Bangladesh, Benin, Botswana, Brazil, Brunei Darussalam, Burkina Faso, Cameroon, Chad, Chile, China, Colombia, Côte d'Ivoire, Cuba, Djibouti, Democratic People's Republic of Korea, Egypt, Ghana, Guinea, Guyana, Haiti, India, Indonesia, Iran, Jordan, Kuwait, Lao People's Democratic Republic, Lebanon, Libyan Arab Jamahiriya, Malawi, Malaysia, Maldives, Mali, Mauritania, Mauritius, Mexico, Morocco, Myanmar, Nepal, Niger, Nigeria, Oman, Pakistan, Philippines, Qatar, Saint Lucia, Saudi Arabia, Senegal, Sierra Leone, Singapore, South Africa, Sri Lanka, Sudan, Syrian Arab Republic, Thailand, Togo, Trinidad and Tobago, Tunisia, Turkey, United Arab Emirates, Uganda, Venezuela, Viet Nam, Yemen, Zambia, Zimbabwe.
*Against:* Israel, United States.
*Abstaining:* Albania, Antigua and Barbuda, Argentina, Armenia, Australia, Austria, Bahamas, Barbados, Belarus, Belgium, Belize, Bolivia, Bosnia and Herzegovina, Bulgaria, Cambodia, Canada, Croatia, Cyprus, Czech Republic, Denmark, Dominica, Ecuador, El Salvador, Estonia, Ethiopia, Fiji, Finland, France, Gabon, Georgia, Germany, Greece, Grenada, Guatemala,

Guinea-Bissau, Honduras, Hungary, Iceland, Ireland, Italy, Jamaica, Japan, Kazakstan, Kenya, Latvia, Liechtenstein, Lithuania, Luxembourg, Malta, Marshall Islands, Micronesia, Monaco, Mongolia, Netherlands, New Zealand, Nicaragua, Norway, Panama, Papua New Guinea, Paraguay, Peru, Poland, Portugal, Republic of Korea, Republic of Moldova, Romania, Russian Federation, Samoa, Slovakia, Slovenia, Solomon Islands, Spain, Suriname, Swaziland, Sweden, the former Yugoslav Republic of Macedonia, Ukraine, United Kingdom, Uruguay, Vanuatu.

## Fourth Geneva Convention

**Committee report.** The Special Committee on Israeli Practices, in its annual report,[16] reiterated that the relevant provisions of the fourth Geneva Convention remained the main international instrument in humanitarian law that applied to the occupied territories, and its applicability to those territories had repeatedly been reaffirmed by the Security Council, the General Assembly and other UN organs.

**Report of the Secretary-General.** On 20 October, the Secretary-General informed[27] the General Assembly that Israel had not replied to his May request for information on steps taken or envisaged to implement a 1994 Assembly resolution[28] demanding that Israel accept *de jure* applicability of the fourth Geneva Convention and comply scrupulously with its provisions.

### GENERAL ASSEMBLY ACTION

On 6 December, the General Assembly adopted **resolution 50/29 B** under the general title ''Report of the Special Committee to Investigate Israeli Practices Affecting the Human Rights of the Palestinian People and Other Arabs of the Occupied Territories''.

*The General Assembly,*

*Recalling* its relevant resolutions,

*Bearing in mind* the relevant resolutions of the Security Council,

*Having considered* the reports of the Special Committee to Investigate Israeli Practices Affecting the Human Rights of the Palestinian People and Other Arabs of the Occupied Territories and the relevant reports of the Secretary-General,

*Considering* that the promotion of respect for the obligations arising from the Charter of the United Nations and other instruments and rules of international law is among the basic purposes and principles of the United Nations,

*Stressing* that Israel, the occupying Power, should comply strictly with its obligations under international law,

1. *Reaffirms* that the Geneva Convention relative to the Protection of Civilian Persons in Time of War, of 12 August 1949, is applicable to the occupied Palestinian territory, including Jerusalem, and other Arab territories occupied by Israel since 1967;

2. *Demands* that Israel accept the *de jure* applicability of the Convention in the occupied Palestinian territory, including Jerusalem, and other Arab territories occupied by Israel since 1967, and that it comply scrupulously with the provisions of the Convention;

3. *Calls upon* all States parties to the Convention, in accordance with article 1 common to the four Geneva Conventions, to exert all efforts in order to ensure re-spect for its provisions by Israel, the occupying Power, in the occupied Palestinian territory, including Jerusalem, and other Arab territories occupied by Israel since 1967;

4. *Requests* the Secretary-General to report to the General Assembly at its fifty-first session on the implementation of the present resolution.

General Assembly resolution 50/29 B

6 December 1995      Meeting 82      147-2-4 (recorded vote)

Approved by Fourth Committee (A/50/606) by recorded vote (127-2-4), 30 November (meeting 25); 12-nation draft (A/C.4/50/L.19); agenda item 85.
*Meeting numbers.* GA 50th session: 4th Committee 24, 25; plenary 82.

Recorded vote in Assembly as follows:

*In favour:* Afghanistan, Albania, Algeria, Antigua and Barbuda, Argentina, Armenia, Australia, Austria, Azerbaijan, Bahamas, Bahrain, Bangladesh, Barbados, Belarus, Belgium, Belize, Benin, Bolivia, Bosnia and Herzegovina, Botswana, Brazil, Brunei Darussalam, Bulgaria, Burkina Faso, Burundi, Cameroon, Canada, Cape Verde, Chad, Chile, China, Colombia, Côte d'Ivoire, Croatia, Cuba, Cyprus, Czech Republic, Democratic People's Republic of Korea, Denmark, Djibouti, Dominica, Ecuador, Egypt, El Salvador, Eritrea, Estonia, Ethiopia, Fiji, Finland, France, Gabon, Georgia, Germany, Ghana, Greece, Grenada, Guatemala, Guinea, Guinea-Bissau, Guyana, Haiti, Honduras, Hungary, Iceland, India, Indonesia, Iran, Ireland, Italy, Jamaica, Japan, Jordan, Kazakstan, Kenya, Kuwait, Lao People's Democratic Republic, Latvia, Lebanon, Libyan Arab Jamahiriya, Liechtenstein, Lithuania, Luxembourg, Malawi, Malaysia, Maldives, Mali, Malta, Mauritania, Mauritius, Mexico, Monaco, Mongolia, Morocco, Myanmar, Nepal, Netherlands, New Zealand, Niger, Nigeria, Norway, Oman, Pakistan, Panama, Papua New Guinea, Paraguay, Peru, Philippines, Poland, Portugal, Qatar, Republic of Korea, Republic of Moldova, Romania, Saint Lucia, Samoa, Saudi Arabia, Senegal, Sierra Leone, Singapore, Slovakia, Slovenia, Solomon Islands, South Africa, Spain, Sri Lanka, Sudan, Suriname, Swaziland, Sweden, Syrian Arab Republic, Thailand, the former Yugoslav Republic of Macedonia, Togo, Trinidad and Tobago, Tunisia, Turkey, Uganda, Ukraine, United Arab Emirates, United Kingdom, Uruguay, Vanuatu, Venezuela, Viet Nam, Yemen, Zambia, Zimbabwe.

*Against:* Israel, United States.

*Abstaining:* Marshall Islands, Micronesia, Nicaragua, Russian Federation.

## Palestinian prisoners

**Committee report.** According to the annual report of the Special Committee on Israeli Practices,[16] the release of Palestinian prisoners in accordance with the May 1994 agreement had fallen behind schedule, with some 5,400 Palestinians still in Israeli detention centres, a fact that remained a considerable source of tension. The so-called ''exceptional dispensations'' accorded to the Israeli General Security Service were a source of particular concern to the Committee, which also noted deficiencies in the administration of justice, notably in the severity of sentences handed down to Palestinians as compared with those given to Israelis.

Large-scale arrests of members of the Hamas movement had been undertaken in the wake of suicide bombings and other attacks on Israeli civilians and military personnel. More than 4,000 Hamas activists were reported to have been apprehended since a suicide bus bombing in Tel Aviv in October 1994. Members of the Islamic Jihad had also been arrested during similar operations, with several hundred of those arrested reportedly placed in administrative detention. On 5 February 1995, the maximum period of administrative detention was extended from six months to one year, on a renewable basis. At the end of 1994, there were 239 persons in administrative detention. The maximum period that a person could be held before being brought before a judge was officially reduced from 18 to 11 days. According to Amnesty International, detainees were held without access to lawyers for up to 30 days, and without access to families for up to 140 days.

Conditions of detention and treatment of detainees in Israeli prisons had deteriorated during the period under review, the Committee reported. Aggravated forms of torture were frequently used during interrogations of persons arrested for security reasons, sometimes resulting in their deaths. Torture had become more severe after the October 1994 suicide bombing in Tel Aviv, the Committee stated.

**Report of the Secretary-General.** In a 20 October report,[29] the Secretary-General stated that he had not received any response from Israel to his May request for information on steps taken or envisaged to implement relevant provisions of a 1994 General Assembly resolution[30] calling on Israel to accelerate the release of all remaining Palestinians arbitrarily detained or imprisoned, in line with agreements reached, and to facilitate the return of the remaining deportees to the occupied territories.

GENERAL ASSEMBLY ACTION

In **resolution 50/29 C**, under the general title "Report of the Special Committee to Investigate Israeli Practices Affecting the Human Rights of the Palestinian People and Other Arabs of the Occupied Territories", the General Assembly called on Israel to accelerate the release of all remaining Palestinians arbitrarily detained or imprisoned, in line with agreements reached.

*Palestinian women*

**Report of the Secretary-General.** In March 1995, the Secretary-General reported[31] to the Commission on the Status of Women on the situation of and assistance to Palestinian women, as requested by the Commission in 1994.[32] The report addressed the problem of violence related to occupation as it affected women, and monitored the participation of women in development and political decision-making, as well as women's situation in health, education and employment.

Women were victims of violence by Israeli soldiers and settlers, and experienced violence during interrogation and imprisonment. In addition, Palestinian women were confronted with various kinds of physical, sexual or psychological violence from the family or from society in general, the report stated. With the launching of Palestinian self-rule, however, women's contribution to institution-building and legislation had gained importance and public awareness of women's status had increased. Respect for and acceptance of the work

of women's organizations was high and women were prepared to play an active role in government. The number of women in leadership positions was growing. After implementation of the self-rule agreement, a woman had been appointed Minister for Social Affairs of the Palestinian Authority and another had become head of the 70-strong women's police force. At the request of women's organizations, the Palestinian Authority had established a women's affairs technical committee, with the objective of ensuring equal participation in future legislative, executive and judicial structures.

The report concluded that, as the peace process in the occupied territories and the self-rule area of Jericho and the Gaza Strip was being consolidated, the importance of integrating the gender perspective in all areas of legislation, infrastructure development and human resource and economic development was being recognized. Preparing for de facto and *de jure* equality between men and women was of primary importance at this juncture. Palestinian women needed practical support and assistance at all levels, from inside and outside the territories. There was potential for development, and resources and support had to be made available immediately in order to create the necessary infrastructure, especially in education, health and employment.

**Action by the Commission on the Status of Women.** The Commission on the Status of Women, in 1995, adopted a resolution on the integration of women in the Middle East peace process,[33] emphasizing that the achievement of a comprehensive, just and lasting peace was vital for the implementation of the human rights of women in the area. The Commission urged Governments, intergovernmental bodies and NGOs to include women in the peace process, to support the Declaration of Principles and to help ensure Palestinian women's political development and participation. It urged Member States to expedite economic, financial and technical assistance to Palestinian women.

The Commission also recommended a draft resolution on Palestinian women for adoption by the Economic and Social Council (see below).

ECONOMIC AND SOCIAL COUNCIL ACTION

On 25 July, the Economic and Social Council adopted **resolution 1995/30**.

**Palestinian women**

*The Economic and Social Council,*

*Having considered with appreciation* the report of the Secretary-General on the situation of and assistance to Palestinian women,

*Recalling* the Nairobi Forward-looking Strategies for the Advancement of Women, in particular paragraph 260 concerning Palestinian women and children,

*Recalling also* Commission on the Status of Women resolution 38/4 of 18 March 1994 and other relevant United Nations resolutions,

*Further recalling* the Declaration on the Elimination of Violence against Women as it concerns the protection of civilian populations,

*Welcoming* the signing by the Government of the State of Israel and the Palestine Liberation Organization of the Declaration of Principles on Interim Self-Government Arrangements, in Washington, on 13 September 1993, as well as the implementation of the agreements reached between the two sides,

*Deeply concerned* about the continuing deterioration of all aspects of the situation of the Palestinian women in the occupied Palestinian territory, including Jerusalem,

*Gravely concerned* about the severe consequences of the continuous Israeli illegal settlements activities, as well as the measures which isolate Jerusalem from the West Bank and Gaza Strip, on the situation of Palestinian women and their families,

1.  *Reaffirms* that the Israeli occupation constitutes a major obstacle for Palestinian women with regard to their advancement, self-reliance and integration in the development plan of their society;

2.  *Demands* that Israel, the occupying Power, comply fully with the provisions and principles of the Universal Declaration of Human Rights, the Regulations annexed to the Hague Convention IV of 18 October 1907 and the Geneva Convention relative to the Protection of Civilian Persons in Time of War of 12 August 1949, in order to protect the rights of Palestinian women and their families;

3.  *Calls upon* Israel to facilitate the return of all refugee and displaced Palestinian women and children and those who are political deportees to their homes and properties in the occupied Palestinian territory, in compliance with the relevant United Nations resolutions;

4.  *Urges* Member States, international financial organizations of the United Nations system, non-governmental organizations and other relevant institutions to intensify their efforts to provide financial and technical assistance to Palestinian women for the creation of projects responding to their needs, especially during the transitional period;

5.  *Requests* the Commission on the Status of Women to continue to monitor and take action with regard to the implementation of the Nairobi Forward-looking Strategies for the Advancement of Women, in particular paragraph 260 concerning Palestinian women and children;

6.  *Requests* the Secretary-General to continue to review the situation and to assist Palestinian women by all available means, and to submit to the Commission, at its fortieth session, a report on the progress made in the implementation of the present resolution.

Economic and Social Council resolution 1995/30

25 July 1995          Meeting 51          43-1-4 (roll-call vote)

Draft by Commission on women (E/1995/26); agenda item 5 *(e)*.
*Meeting numbers.* ESC 49-51.

Roll-call vote in Council as follows:

*In favour:* Australia, Bahamas, Bhutan, Brazil, Bulgaria, Chile, China, Colombia, Costa Rica, Cuba, Denmark, Egypt, France, Germany, Ghana, Greece, India, Indonesia, Ireland, Jamaica, Japan, Libyan Arab Jamahiriya, Luxembourg, Malaysia, Mexico, Netherlands, Nigeria, Pakistan, Philippines, Poland, Portugal, Republic of Korea, Romania, Russian Federation, Sene-

gal, South Africa, Sri Lanka, Sudan, Thailand, Uganda, United Kingdom, Venezuela, Zimbabwe.

*Against:* United States.

*Abstaining:* Canada, Côte d'Ivoire, Norway, Ukraine.

Explaining its vote, the United States said it believed that Council consideration of issues which the parties to the peace process should address only distracted from those efforts and complicated the ongoing search for peace. Spain, on behalf of the European Union (EU), noted that some language did not properly reflect recent developments; it would have been more appropriate to examine the text in conjunction with the consensus resolution adopted by the Commission on the Status of Women on the integration of women in the Middle East peace process (see above). Iran said it was concerned over both the continuing deterioration of the situation of Palestinian women and the major obstacle which Israeli occupation constituted for Palestinian women with regard to advancement, self-reliance and integration into the development plans of their society.

### Israeli settlements

**Committee report.** In its annual report,[16] the Special Committee on Israeli Practices stated that Israel's policy of establishing Jewish settlements in the occupied territories had been, since its inception in 1968, at the heart of the Arab-Israeli conflict. Although Prime Minister Yitzhak Rabin had declared, when his Government came to power in 1992, that no new settlements would be built, the expansion of existing ones had continued unabated, the Committee stated. Israel, it was stated, had circumvented its pledge not to build new settlements by withholding official financial support but not preventing private funding. The time-frame for the completion of most projects was three to five years, i.e., before the negotiations on the final status of the territories. It had been reported that an average 1,500 acres of Arab land had been confiscated each month since the signing of the September 1994 Oslo agreement on the economic and social development of the Palestinians.[3]

The situation regarding expropriation of Arab land and the expansion of settlements was considered particularly serious in East Jerusalem, where intensive priority construction was taking place. The Committee felt Israel's policy was aimed at reducing the number of Arabs there and creating a new demographic, geographic and political situation. If completed, it went on, "Greater Jerusalem" would stretch to Jericho, converting the Palestinian villages in its vicinity into isolated islands. It had been estimated that some 50,000 Palestinians had ceased to live within Jerusalem's municipal boundaries since 1967.

The largest settlement in the occupied territories was Maaleh Adumim, east of Jerusalem in the

West Bank, with an estimated population of 20,000. In December 1994, it was reported that the Ministry of Housing and Construction was building 2,000 housing units there and that others were in the planning stage. As a result, some 800 members of the Jahalin Bedouin tribe faced forcible eviction, having already been evicted in 1950 from the Arad area.

An additional problem linked to the settlements was the behaviour of their inhabitants, who had become, the Committee said, more violent and aggressive, in both harassing the Arab population and staking claims on land. The tension was particularly felt in Hebron where settlers lived in the centre of that West Bank town. Settlers from Hebron and Kiryat Arba had repeatedly attacked Palestinians and vandalized their property with complete impunity, the Committee stated.

**Committee report.** The Committee on Palestinian Rights, in its annual report,[1] had noted with concern that the presence of large numbers of armed Israeli settlers in the immediate vicinity of densely populated Palestinian areas generated tension often resulting in acts of violence. According to the Committee, the campaign launched by settlers in opposition to the new agreements added to the sense of insecurity and lack of protection felt by Palestinians living near the settlements. Further, the Committee noted plans for the construction of additional settler housing and for roads linking the settlements that would lead to the fragmentation of the West Bank and the isolation of East Jerusalem.

The Committee noted Israel's positive decision, in May, to suspend the planned confiscation of Palestinian land in East Jerusalem. It also reaffirmed that the settlement policy was in contradiction to Israel's obligations as the occupying Power under the fourth Geneva Convention and called on the Government to end that policy once and for all.

## SECURITY COUNCIL CONSIDERATION

The situation in the occupied Arab territories was discussed in the Security Council in February and again in May. A debate was held on 28 February centring on Israel's settlement policy; no action was taken. Following debate held between 12 and 17 May on expropriation of land in East Jerusalem, the Council voted on a draft resolution calling the expropriation action invalid. The text was not adopted due to the negative vote of a permanent member.

## 28 February debate

Djibouti, in its capacity as Chairman of the Arab Group, on 22 February requested[34] a Council meeting to consider the question of "the establishment of Israeli settlements in the territories occupied since 1967, including Jerusalem, and

the dangerous consequences of those activities on the Palestinian people and on the Middle East peace process."

Sixteen States—Algeria, Brunei Darussalam, Djibouti, Egypt, Iran, Israel, Japan, Jordan, Malaysia, Morocco, Pakistan, the Sudan, the Syrian Arab Republic, Tunisia, Turkey and the United Arab Emirates—were invited under Council provisional rule 37[b] to participate in the debate. Under provisional rule 39,[c] the Permanent Observers of Palestine and of the Organization of the Islamic Conference (OIC), as well as the Chairman of the Committee on Palestinian Rights, were also invited to participate.

Leading off the debate on 28 February, the Observer from Palestine stated that throughout recent history the Palestinian people had been subjected to grave injustices, including the uprooting of a large proportion of them from their land and homes and the subjugation of those who remained to occupation, repression and the denial of their right to self-determination.

One of the harshest things endured was the campaign of settler colonialism waged on Palestinian lands occupied by Israel since 1967, including Jerusalem, Palestine said. Since the early days of occupation, Israel had confiscated Palestinian and State-owned land for the purpose of constructing many settlements, and had transferred large numbers of Israeli settlers to those settlements in an obvious campaign to change the land's demographic structure, thus paving the way to total or partial annexation.

The failure of the Council to impose its will, Palestine continued, had allowed Israel to pursue its settlement policy—resulting in approximately 140 settlements inhabited by about 300,000 settlers, including those brought to East Jerusalem. The settlers were a major source of repression, injustice and outright harassment, stealing land and water from the Palestinians and interfering in and even destroying their daily lives, the Observer maintained.

The minimum requirement for negotiations in good faith was that the parties desist from creating facts on the ground that affect and pre-empt the negotiating process. Any settlement activity in the occupied Palestinian territory, including

[b]Rule 37 of the Council's provisional rules of procedure states: "Any Member of the United Nations which is not a member of the Security Council may be invited, as the result of a decision of the Security Council, to participate, without vote, in the discussion of any question brought before the Security Council when the Security Council considers that the interests of that Member are specially affected, or when a Member brings a matter to the attention of the Security Council in accordance with Article 35(1) of the Charter."

[c]Rule 39 of the Council's provisional rules of procedure states: "The Security Council may invite members of the Secretariat or other persons, whom it considers competent for the purpose, to supply it with information or to give other assistance in examining matters within its competence."

Jerusalem, constituted a flagrant violation of the letter and spirit of the 1993 Declaration of Principles, the fourth Geneva Convention and relevant Security Council resolutions, Palestine declared.

Djibouti, speaking for the Arab Group, said that a widespread and pervasive mood of mounting disenchantment had begun to permeate the Arab world—the direct consequence of the near-total lack of progress in negotiations between the Palestinians and the Israeli authorities since 1993. Few impediments to progress were more implacable and emotional than that of Israeli settlers. For the peace process to resume in a meaningful way, settlements in the West Bank must be immediately frozen and those in Gaza dismantled.

Israel considered the PLO initiative to discuss the issue of settlements in the Council as incompatible with its signed commitments to resolve all permanent-status issues, such as settlements and Jerusalem, in direct and bilateral negotiations with Israel. The present Government, formed in July 1992, had substantially changed Israel's settlement policy, based on its profound belief that the best alternative was peace based on security, understanding and cooperation. Therefore, no new settlements had been established in the territories since then, nor would they be. The Government had stopped allocating public resources to support the extension of existing settlements. No land had been or would be confiscated to establish new settlements. Yes, Israel said, it had continued to build in Jerusalem, as the Arabs had. "They have not stopped building, and this is their right. We have not stopped building, and this is our right."

Direct dialogue was the only way "to solve the issues that divide us", Israel declared. Military conflict and solutions imposed from the outside had not solved the Arab-Israeli conflict. New problems did not distinguish between Arab and Israeli: economic, environmental, humanitarian and so on. "We can solve them only by working together."

Terrorism was now the main obstacle to peace. Radical fundamentalists with ties to Iran had the goal of derailing the peace process. Their strategy was to provoke a cycle of violence and sow anger, hatred and resentment towards further progress, Israel stated. Their method was to kill Israeli men, women and children going about their daily lives. Israel could not view such attacks with indifference. Morally and humanly, it was obligated to protect its people's lives. Within Israel, the most important task before all supporters of peace was credibly to address the growing sense in Israeli public opinion that the Palestinians were unable to meet their commitments to fighting terrorism. Israel expected the Palestinian Authority to disarm all those who were forbidden to possess arms, and to do all in its power to combat terrorism and to

bring to justice all those involved in murderous activities.

Israel believed that great progress, irreversible progress, had been made with its Palestinian partners; their shared goals and hopes had to be pursued in a commitment to a comprehensive peace.

During the debate, many speakers called into question Israel's settlement policy. It was stated that the policy was hampering the ongoing peace process and seriously compromising recent agreements reached between major parties, including the 1993 Declaration of Principles, the May 1994 Gaza-Jericho Agreement, the August 1994 Agreement on the Preparatory Transfer of Powers and Responsibilities, and the October 1994 peace treaty between Israel and Jordan.

Some speakers stressed that the settlement activity was undermining not only the confidence of the Palestinians in the peace process, but the process as a whole. The continued construction of settlements not only would jeopardize ongoing negotiations between Israel and PLO, but would also threaten and jeopardize the overall peace process in the region. An end to the settlement policy, it was generally felt, could be a determining factor in a successful progression towards the achievement of a just and lasting peace. It was stated that if progress to remove the settlements was not made, support for the anti-peace camps on both sides would increase.

Some countries of the region charged that Israel was using the issue of security as a pretext for continuing its settlement policy; it was stated that Israel had no justification for continuing to build and expand its settlements. Many others stated that the issue was just one aspect of the complex relations between Israel and the Palestinians and should be left to bilateral negotiations, outside the spotlight of international attention.

Still other nations felt the debate might provide an appropriate forum for expressing support for the peace process; they called for redoubled efforts to attain peace.

**Views of permanent Council members.** China expressed concern over the suddenly sharpened discord between the parties regarding Israeli settlements. With the peace process at a very critical moment, both sides must exercise restraint, build mutual trust, continue removing obstructions and persist in settling disputes through negotiations.

France encouraged Israel to find a way to halt work on expanding the settlements, which was being carried out by private interests and with private financing. It understood that Israeli public opinion was traumatized by the resurgence of terrorism, and called on the Palestinian Authority to do all it could to prevent and punish such acts. Later, speaking for EU, France vigorously condemned blind violence, and stated that the question of security must not become an obstacle to progress in the negotiations.

The Russian Federation said it believed in timely and complete compliance, in good faith, with the letter and spirit of the 1993 Declaration of Principles. The parties should refrain from any acts to disturb the status quo and prejudice a Palestinian-Israeli settlement.

The United Kingdom understood the frustration felt by the Palestinians over Israel's settlement activity, which it considered illegal. The Declaration of Principles had defined settlements as a final-status issue, and the implication of that was that the status quo would remain in the meantime. Any expansion, therefore, went against the spirit of the Declaration. At the same time, the United Kingdom did not underestimate or seek to belittle Israel's legitimate security concerns.

The United States said that Israel and Palestinian negotiators were seeking a balance to address both Israeli security concerns and Palestinian political and economic concerns. Council debate at such a sensitive time could only sour the atmosphere and deflect the parties from the need to work on the path they had set for themselves. The United States opposed any activity that would only complicate efforts to spur the negotiation process.

**Views of non-permanent members.** Argentina wanted the Israeli and Palestinian authorities to speed up the joint quest for a solution to the sensitive question of settlements. Botswana said that whatever action might be taken should in no way accentuate the complications or difficulties currently encountered by the negotiations. The Czech Republic, which considered the settlements to be illegal and not conducive to the peace process, nevertheless conceded that Israel had effected important changes in its policy.

Germany said both sides had to understand the other's concerns and fears and should redouble their efforts through direct negotiations: increased acts of terrorism legitimately concerned Israelis; settlement activities were of major concern to Palestinians. Honduras declared that the achievement of peace in the region had to be based on the principle of "land for peace" and withdrawal from all occupied territories. Indonesia called for a speedy dismantlement of settlements, leading to a mutually supportive and positively reinforcing approach, such as that which had resulted in important breakthroughs in the past.

Italy said the debate ought not to interfere with ongoing negotiations between Israel and PLO, but rather provide an opportunity for a constructive exchange of thoughts. Nigeria warned that the continued settlement activities could lead to an entrenchment of extremist views within radical sections of Middle East society. In Oman's opinion, there could be no potential breakthrough in the course of bilateral or other negotiations unless Israel ended its settlement policy immediately and resolved the question of existing settlements through peaceful negotiations.

*Meeting number.* SC 3505.

### May meetings

Morocco, as Chairman of the Islamic Group,[35] and the United Arab Emirates[36] on 8 May requested an urgent Council meeting, to discuss in particular a recent Israeli confiscation order in respect of Palestinian land in East Jerusalem. Urgent measures by the Council had been called for earlier by Palestine, which had reported, in a 28 April letter to the Secretary-General,[37] that on the previous day Israel had ordered the confiscation of 53 hectares of Palestinian land within East Jerusalem.

At meetings held on 12, 15, 16 and 17 May, the Council considered the situation in the occupied Arab territories. Twenty-six nations were invited, under Council provisional rule 37,[b] to participate in the debate without vote: Algeria, Australia, Bangladesh, Canada, Cuba, Djibouti, Egypt, Iran, Iraq, Israel, Japan, Jordan, Kuwait, Lebanon, the Libyan Arab Jamahiriya, Malaysia, Mauritania, Morocco, Pakistan, Qatar, Saudi Arabia, the Sudan, the Syrian Arab Republic, Tunisia, Turkey and the United Arab Emirates. Under provisional rule 39,[c] the Observer from Palestine and the Acting Chairman of the Committee on Palestinian Rights also were invited to participate.

Opening the debate on 12 May, the Observer from Palestine said the Council was addressing a dangerous Israeli action: the recent order to confiscate 53 hectares of land in the area of occupied East Jerusalem. Under Security Council resolution 181(II),[38] a demilitarized Jerusalem had been designated as a *corpus separatum* under the UN Trusteeship Council. The land confiscated by Israel in an expanded East Jerusalem through the years added up to 2,400 hectares, on which 35,000 units for settlement had been built and allocated to Jewish settlers; by 1993, Jewish settlers in Jerusalem numbered 150,000. The Palestinians had been left with minimal land—14 per cent of East Jerusalem in its expanded municipal boundaries.

Negotiation in good faith required that the parties did not make changes on the ground that would prejudge the results of the negotiations or influence it, Palestine said. By ordering the confiscation and announcing plans for constructing more residential units for settlers, Israel had violated international law, as well as its obligations under recent agreements.

Israel could not go on with its occupation mentality; it could not achieve peace and demand normal relations with its neighbours and their friends while continuing to maintain its grip on Jerusalem. The Council must guarantee the rescinding of the confiscation orders through adopting a clear resolution and make Israel understand the importance of not repeating such acts in the future, Palestine concluded.

Israel responded that its recent decision to expropriate, not confiscate, barren land for construction, not for settlements, was based on its long-standing policy to ensure that development in Jerusalem kept pace with the changes that were a natural feature of any living city. Construction and development for all residents had always been regular features of Jerusalem life and would continue to be in the future. The people of the city—Jews and Arabs alike—could not be deprived of sufficient schools, roads, housing and workplaces. Some of the designated land was under Jewish ownership. All owners had the right to appeal the expropriation orders. If expropriation was upheld, owners would be compensated.

Jerusalem had been established by King David as the capital of Israel 3,000 years ago. Its centrality had sustained the Jews as a people in their darkest days. Israel was sensitive to the importance of Jerusalem to Christians and Moslems and in 1967 had opened the city, for the first time, to pilgrims and worshippers of all religions.

There was, in Israel's view, no contradiction between the peace process and continued development in Jerusalem for the benefit of all its residents, both Jewish and Arab. The 1993 Declaration of Principles did not prohibit development activity in the city. If the PLO leadership felt otherwise, the issue should be addressed in bilateral negotiations; any attempts to do so outside the agreed-upon framework contradicted the letter and spirit of agreements between both parties. Israel called on the Council not to take any action.

During the course of the debate, most speakers considered that the expropriation orders contravened the spirit of UN resolutions and recent agreements between Israel and PLO. Many, while expressing concern over their effect on the peace process, called on Israel to rescind its recent decision and make the necessary compromises with the Palestinians in order to accelerate implementation of the relevant agreements.

On 17 May, the Council did not adopt, due to the negative vote of a permanent member, a draft resolution[39] submitted by Botswana, Honduras, Indonesia, Nigeria, Oman and Rwanda. By that text, the Council, stating its awareness of the negative impact of the expropriation on the Middle East peace process, would have: confirmed that the expropriation of land in East Jerusalem by Israel was invalid and violated relevant Council resolutions and the fourth Geneva Convention; called on Israel to rescind the expropriation orders and refrain from such action in the future; expressed full support for the peace process and its achievements, including the 1993 Declaration of Principles and subsequent agreements; and urged the parties to adhere to them and follow up with their full implementation.

The vote was 14 in favour (Argentina, Botswana, China, Czech Republic, France, Germany, Honduras, Indonesia, Italy, Nigeria, Oman, Russian Federation, Rwanda, United Kingdom) to 1 against (United States).

In explanation of vote, the United States, noting that it was the first time in five years that it had cast a veto, said it was compelled to oppose the resolution because the Council had sought to declare itself on a permanent-status issue—Jerusalem—and had thus violated the principle that the only path to achieving a just and lasting peace was through direct talks between the parties. *Meeting numbers.* SC 3536, 3538.

Palestine, in identical letters of 24 May to the Secretary-General and to the Security Council President,[40] referred to the unanimous expression of disagreement, during Council debate, by all members, including the United States, with Israel's confiscation orders. It noted an Israeli Cabinet decision on 22 May to suspend the expropriation of 53 hectares of land in Jerusalem, and cited a 15 May statement by Israel that the Cabinet had no intention of carrying out additional expropriation of land in Jerusalem for housing purposes. While those could be considered as steps in the right direction, they were hardly enough to satisfy previous Council resolutions and international law. Palestine believed that the Council should remain seized of the matter and keep itself apprised of any further Israeli measures with regard to the land in question, to ensure that the confiscation orders were not being carried out and no building would take place on that or any other land in the occupied Palestinian territory, including Jerusalem.

**Report of the Secretary-General.** In a 20 October report,[29] the Secretary-General informed the General Assembly that no reply had been received from Israel to his May request for information on steps it had taken or envisaged to implement the 1994 Assembly resolution[30] reaffirming that Israeli settlements in the territories, including Jerusalem, were illegal and an obstacle to a comprehensive settlement.

**GENERAL ASSEMBLY ACTION**

On 6 December, the Assembly adopted **resolution 50/29 C** under the general title ''Report of the Special Committee to Investigate Israeli Practices Affecting the Human Rights of the Palestinian People and Other Arabs of the Occupied Territories''.

*The General Assembly,*

*Recalling* its relevant resolutions and the resolutions of the Commission on Human Rights,

*Bearing in mind* the relevant resolutions of the Security Council, the most recent of which is resolution 904(1994) of 18 March 1994,

*Having considered* the reports of the Special Committee to Investigate Israeli Practices Affecting the Human Rights of the Palestinian People and Other Arabs of the Occupied Territories and the reports of the Secretary-General,

*Aware* of the responsibility of the international community to promote human rights and ensure respect for international law,

*Reaffirming* the principle of the inadmissibility of the acquisition of territory by force,

*Reaffirming also* the applicability of the Geneva Convention relative to the Protection of Civilian Persons in Time of War, of 12 August 1949, to the occupied Palestinian territory, including Jerusalem, and other Arab territories occupied by Israel since 1967,

*Welcoming* the signing of the Declaration of Principles on Interim Self-Government Arrangements, including its Annexes and its Agreed Minutes, by the Government of the State of Israel and the Palestine Liberation Organization in Washington on 13 September 1993, as well as the subsequent implementation agreements, including the Agreement on the Gaza Strip and the Jericho Area signed at Cairo on 4 May 1994 and the Interim Agreement on the West Bank and the Gaza Strip signed in Washington on 28 September 1995,

*Noting* the withdrawal of the Israeli army, which took place in the Gaza Strip and the Jericho area in accordance with the agreements reached between the parties, and the initiation of the Palestinian Authority in those areas,

*Concerned* about the continuing violation of the human rights of the Palestinian people by Israel, the occupying Power, especially in the use of collective punishment, closure of areas, annexation and establishment of settlements, and the continuing actions by it designed to change the legal status, geographical nature and demographic composition of the occupied Palestinian territory,

*Concerned in particular* about the dangerous situation resulting from actions taken by the illegal, armed Israeli settlers in the occupied territory, as illustrated by the massacre of Palestinian worshippers by an illegal Israeli settler in Al-Khalil on 25 February 1994,

*Convinced* of the positive impact of a temporary international or foreign presence in the occupied Palestinian territory for the safety and protection of the Palestinian people,

*Expressing its appreciation* to the countries that participated in the Temporary International Presence in Hebron for their positive contribution,

*Also convinced* of the need for the full implementation of Security Council resolution 904(1994),

1. *Determines* that all measures and actions taken by Israel, the occupying Power, in the occupied Palestinian territory, including Jerusalem, in violation of the relevant provisions of the Geneva Convention relative to the Protection of Civilian Persons in Time of War, of 12 August 1949, and contrary to the relevant resolutions of the Security Council are illegal and have no validity, and demands that Israel desist forthwith from taking any such measures or actions;

2. *Reaffirms in particular* that the Israeli settlements in the occupied Palestinian territory, including Jerusalem, and the other Arab territories occupied by Israel since 1967 are illegal and an obstacle to achieving comprehensive peace;

3. *Notes with satisfaction* the return of a number of deportees to the occupied Palestinian territory and calls upon Israel to facilitate the return of the remainder;

4. *Calls upon* Israel, the occupying Power, to accelerate the release of all remaining Palestinians arbitrarily detained or imprisoned, in line with agreements reached;

5. *Calls* for complete respect by Israel, the occupying Power, of all fundamental freedoms of the Palestinian people, pending the extension of the self-government arrangements to the rest of the West Bank;

6. *Requests* the Secretary-General to report to the General Assembly at its fifty-first session on the implementation of the present resolution.

General Assembly resolution 50/29 C

6 December 1995     Meeting 82     144-2-7 (recorded vote)

Approved by Fourth Committee (A/50/606) by recorded vote (122-2-8), 30 November (meeting 25); 12-nation draft (A/C.4/50/L.20); agenda item 85.
*Meeting numbers.* GA 50th session: 4th Committee 24, 25; plenary 82.

Recorded vote in Assembly as follows:

*In favour:* Afghanistan, Albania, Algeria, Antigua and Barbuda, Armenia, Australia, Austria, Azerbaijan, Bahamas, Bahrain, Bangladesh, Barbados, Belarus, Belgium, Belize, Benin, Bolivia, Bosnia and Herzegovina, Botswana, Brazil, Brunei Darussalam, Bulgaria, Burkina Faso, Burundi, Cameroon, Canada, Cape Verde, Chad, Chile, China, Colombia, Côte d'Ivoire, Croatia, Cuba, Cyprus, Czech Republic, Denmark, Djibouti, Dominica, Democratic People's Republic of Korea, Ecuador, Egypt, El Salvador, Eritrea, Estonia, Ethiopia, Fiji, Finland, France, Gabon, Georgia, Germany, Ghana, Greece, Grenada, Guatemala, Guinea, Guinea-Bissau, Guyana, Haiti, Honduras, Hungary, Iceland, India, Indonesia, Iran, Ireland, Italy, Jamaica, Japan, Jordan, Kazakstan, Kenya, Kuwait, Lao People's Democratic Republic, Latvia, Lebanon, Libyan Arab Jamahiriya, Liechtenstein, Lithuania, Luxembourg, Malawi, Malaysia, Maldives, Mali, Malta, Mauritania, Mauritius, Mexico, Monaco, Mongolia, Morocco, Myanmar, Nepal, Netherlands, New Zealand, Niger, Nigeria, Norway, Oman, Pakistan, Papua New Guinea, Paraguay, Peru, Philippines, Poland, Portugal, Qatar, Republic of Korea, Republic of Moldova, Romania, Saint Lucia, Samoa, Saudi Arabia, Senegal, Sierra Leone, Singapore, Slovakia, Slovenia, Solomon Islands, South Africa, Spain, Sri Lanka, Sudan, Suriname, Swaziland, Sweden, Syrian Arab Republic, Thailand, the former Yugoslav Republic of Macedonia, Togo, Trinidad and Tobago, Tunisia, Turkey, United Arab Emirates, Uganda, Ukraine, United Kingdom, Vanuatu, Venezuela, Viet Nam, Yemen, Zambia, Zimbabwe.

*Against:* Israel, United States.

*Abstaining:* Argentina, Marshall Islands, Micronesia, Nicaragua, Panama, Russian Federation, Uruguay.

### Economic and social repercussions

A report[41] prepared by the Economic and Social Commission for Western Asia (ESCWA) and submitted in July by the Secretary-General, in accordance with 1994 requests of the Economic and Social Council[42] and the General Assembly,[43] dealt with the economic and social repercussions of Israeli settlements on the Palestinians in the Palestinian territory, including Jerusalem, occupied since 1967, and on the Arab population of the Syrian Golan.

The report stated that construction activities in West Bank settlements had proceeded at an unprecedented rate during the review period from April 1994 to March 1995, in contrast to the policy adopted by the Israeli Government. A study by Israeli experts had determined that building operations were being carried out by private companies, without government financing but with permits from the local councils and Israeli ministry officials. The study's findings showed that the Government was facilitating the sale of privately built housing units and continued to provide the necessary public utilities and infrastructure.

ESCWA reported that the stepped-up settlement policy and relocation of thousands of Jews to Jerusalem were at the expense of the Palestinian residents. Many of them had had to build homes without permits owing to the limited land allocated for construction by Arabs, and the Israeli authorities continued to destroy about 50 such homes each year.

In the Golan Heights, a new Israeli settlement in August 1994 brought the total built since 1967 to 33; total inhabitants numbered 13,160 in March 1994.

The use of water resources in the territories had negatively affected the lives of Palestinians, with per capita water consumption among Palestinians in the West Bank ranging between 22 and 28 cubic metres as compared with 165 cubic metres for the Israeli population. The disparity, it was stated, was due to military orders restricting the use of water by Palestinians and preventing them from drilling new wells or developing existing ones, while allowing Israeli settlers to do so and to pump large quantities of water without restriction.

According to Palestinians, the Israeli water policy in the Gaza Strip had led to a dangerous and distressing situation. Water experts believed that the depletion of water reserves in the Gaza Strip and sea-water intrusion had caused the salinity of the water to be six times higher than the internationally accepted level, with 60 per cent of the water no longer suitable for drinking or irrigation.

The uprooting of fruit trees was a daily Israeli practice in the West Bank, as it had been previously in the Gaza Strip. During the *intifadah*, an estimated 117,000 olive trees had been uprooted for construction and security reasons. Sewage leaking from Israeli settlements had spoilt more than 500 dunums of vineyards in the West Bank. The resulting annual loss was an estimated $1.5 million, with the overall loss exceeding $10 million.

**ECONOMIC AND SOCIAL COUNCIL ACTION**

On 28 July, the Economic and Social Council adopted **resolution 1995/49**.

**Economic and social repercussions of the Israeli settlements on the Palestinian people in the Palestinian territory, including Jerusalem, occupied since 1967, and on the Arab population of the occupied Syrian Golan**

*The Economic and Social Council,*

*Recalling* General Assembly resolution 49/132 of 19 December 1994,

*Recalling also* its resolution 1994/45 of 29 July 1994,

*Reaffirming* the principle of the permanent sovereignty of people under foreign occupation over their national resources,

*Guided* by the principles of the Charter of the United Nations, affirming the inadmissibility of the acquisition of territory by force and recalling Security Council resolutions 242(1967) of 22 November 1967 and 497(1981) of 17 December 1981,

*Recalling* Security Council resolution 465(1980) of 1 March 1980 and other resolutions affirming the applicability of the Geneva Convention relative to the Protection of Civilian Persons in Time of War, of 12 August 1949, to the occupied Palestinian territory, including Jerusalem, and other Arab territories occupied by Israel since 1967,

*Recalling also* Security Council resolution 904(1994) of 18 March 1994, in which, among other things, the Council called upon Israel, the occupying Power, to continue to take and implement measures, including, *inter alia*, confiscation of arms, with the aim of preventing illegal acts of violence by Israeli settlers, and called for measures to be taken to guarantee the safety and protection of the Palestinian civilians in the occupied territory,

*Aware* of the negative and grave economic and social repercussions of the Israeli settlements on the Palestinian people in the Palestinian territory, including Jerusalem, occupied since 1967, and on the Arab population of the occupied Syrian Golan,

*Welcoming* the ongoing Middle East peace process started at Madrid, in particular the signing at Cairo, on 4 May 1994, by the Government of Israel and the Palestine Liberation Organization, the representative of the Palestinian people, of the first agreement on the implementation of the Declaration of Principles on Interim Self-Government Arrangements, namely, the Agreement on the Gaza Strip and the Jericho Area,

1. *Takes note* of the report of the Secretary-General;

2. *Reaffirms* that Israeli settlements in the Palestinian territory, including Jerusalem, and other Arab territories occupied since 1967 are illegal and an obstacle to economic and social development;

3. *Recognizes* the economic and social repercussions of the Israeli settlements on the Palestinian people in the Palestinian territory, including Jerusalem, occupied by Israel since 1967, and on the Arab population of the occupied Syrian Golan;

4. *Reaffirms* the inalienable right of the Palestinian people and the population of the Syrian Golan to their natural and all other economic resources, and regards any infringement thereof as being illegal;

5. *Requests* the Secretary-General to submit to the General Assembly at its fifty-first session, through the Economic and Social Council, a report on the progress made in the implementation of the present resolution.

Economic and Social Council resolution 1995/49

28 July 1995          Meeting 57          45-1-5 (roll-call vote)

6-nation draft (E/1995/L.42), orally corrected; agenda item 8.
Sponsors: Bahrain, Egypt, Morocco, Oman, Qatar, United Arab Emirates.
Meeting numbers. ESC 53, 56, 57.

Roll-call vote in Council as follows:

In favour: Australia, Bahamas, Bhutan, Brazil, Bulgaria, Canada, Chile, China, Colombia, Cuba, Denmark, Egypt, France, Gabon, Germany, Ghana, Greece, India, Indonesia, Ireland, Jamaica, Japan, Libyan Arab Jamahiriya, Luxembourg, Malaysia, Mexico, Netherlands, Nigeria, Norway, Pakistan, Philippines, Poland, Portugal, Republic of Korea, Romania, Senegal, South Africa, Sri Lanka, Sudan, Thailand, Uganda, United Kingdom, United Republic of Tanzania, Venezuela, Zimbabwe.
Against: United States.
Abstaining: Belarus, Costa Rica, Côte d'Ivoire, Russian Federation, Ukraine.

After the vote, the United States said the intemperate and unbalanced criticism of Israel was unhelpful to the search for a solution to the Arab-Israeli conflict; it was the Council's duty to promote peace, not to adopt inflammatory resolutions. The Russian Federation considered that issues such as those contained in the text would be more appropriately discussed in other forums. In Israel's view, the resolution reflected the thinking of those opposed to the peace process.

GENERAL ASSEMBLY ACTION

On 20 December, the General Assembly adopted **resolution 50/129**.

**Economic and social repercussions of the Israeli settlements on the Palestinian people in the Palestinian territory, including Jerusalem, occupied since 1967, and on the Arab population of the occupied Syrian Golan**

The General Assembly,

Recalling Economic and Social Council resolution 1995/49 of 28 July 1995,

Reaffirming the principle of the permanent sovereignty of people under foreign occupation over their national resources,

Guided by the principles of the Charter of the United Nations, affirming the inadmissibility of the acquisition of territory by force, and recalling Security Council resolutions 242(1967) of 22 November 1967 and 497(1981) of 17 December 1981,

Recalling Security Council resolution 465(1980) of 1 March 1980 and other resolutions affirming the applicability of the Geneva Convention relative to the Protection of Civilian Persons in Time of War, of 12 August 1949, to the occupied Palestinian territory, including Jerusalem, and other Arab territories occupied by Israel since 1967,

Recalling also Security Council resolution 904(1994) of 18 March 1994, in which, among other things, the Council called upon Israel, the occupying Power, to continue to take and implement measures, including, inter alia, confiscation of arms, with the aim of preventing illegal acts of violence by Israeli settlers, and called for measures to be taken to guarantee the safety and protection of the Palestinian civilians in the occupied territory,

Aware of the negative and grave economic and social repercussions of the Israeli settlements on the Palestinian people in the Palestinian territory, occupied since

1967, including Jerusalem, and on the Arab population of the occupied Syrian Golan,

Welcoming the ongoing Middle East peace process started at Madrid, in particular the two implementation agreements embodied in the Agreement on the Gaza Strip and Jericho Area, of 4 May 1994, and the interim agreement on the West Bank and Gaza Strip of 28 September 1995,

1. Takes note of the report of the Secretary-General;

2. Reaffirms that Israeli settlements in the Palestinian territory, including Jerusalem, and other Arab territories occupied since 1967 are illegal and an obstacle to economic and social development;

3. Recognizes the economic and social repercussions of the Israeli settlements on the Palestinian people in the Palestinian territory occupied by Israel since 1967, including Jerusalem, and on the Arab population of the occupied Syrian Golan;

4. Reaffirms the inalienable right of the Palestinian people and the population of the occupied Syrian Golan to their natural and all other economic resources, and regards any infringement thereupon as illegal;

5. Requests the Secretary-General to submit to the General Assembly at its fifty-first session, through the Economic and Social Council, a report on the progress made in the implementation of the present resolution.

General Assembly resolution 50/129

20 December 1995          Meeting 96          126-2-28 (recorded vote)

Approved by Second Committee (A/50/615/Add.1) by recorded vote (91-2-22), 30 November (meeting 40); 5-nation draft (A/C.2/50/L.13); agenda item 12.
Sponsors: Bangladesh, Cuba, Egypt (as Chairman of Arab Group), Indonesia, Malaysia.
Meeting numbers. GA 50th session: 2nd Committee 15, 16, 29, 32, 40; plenary 96.

Recorded vote in Assembly as follows:

In favour: Afghanistan, Albania, Algeria, Andorra, Angola, Argentina, Armenia, Australia, Austria, Azerbaijan, Bahrain, Bangladesh, Belgium, Belize, Bhutan, Bolivia, Bosnia and Herzegovina, Botswana, Brazil, Brunei Darussalam, Bulgaria, Burkina Faso, Cameroon, Canada, Cape Verde, Chad, Chile, China, Colombia, Cuba, Cyprus, Denmark, Djibouti, Democratic People's Republic of Korea, Ecuador, Egypt, Ethiopia, Fiji, Finland, France, Germany, Ghana, Greece, Guinea, Guyana, Haiti, Honduras, India, Indonesia, Iran, Ireland, Italy, Jamaica, Japan, Jordan, Kazakstan, Kenya, Kuwait, Kyrgyzstan, Lao People's Democratic Republic, Lebanon, Lesotho, Libyan Arab Jamahiriya, Liechtenstein, Lithuania, Luxembourg, Malawi, Malaysia, Maldives, Mali, Malta, Mauritania, Mauritius, Mexico, Monaco, Mongolia, Morocco, Mozambique, Myanmar, Namibia, Netherlands, New Zealand, Nicaragua, Niger, Norway, Oman, Pakistan, Papua New Guinea, Paraguay, Peru, Philippines, Portugal, Qatar, Republic of Korea, Republic of Moldova, Saint Lucia, Samoa, Saudi Arabia, Senegal, Singapore, Slovakia, Slovenia, Solomon Islands,* South Africa, Spain, Sri Lanka, Sudan, Swaziland, Sweden, Syrian Arab Republic, Thailand, the former Yugoslav Republic of Macedonia, Togo, Trinidad and Tobago, Tunisia, Turkey, United Arab Emirates, Uganda, United Kingdom, United Republic of Tanzania, Venezuela, Viet Nam, Yemen, Zambia, Zimbabwe.
Against: Israel, United States.
Abstaining: Antigua and Barbuda, Bahamas, Barbados, Belarus, Benin, Cambodia, Costa Rica, Côte d'Ivoire, Croatia, Czech Republic, Dominica, El Salvador, Federated States of Micronesia, Gabon, Georgia, Grenada, Guatemala, Hungary, Latvia, Marshall Islands, Nepal, Panama, Poland, Romania, Russian Federation, Suriname, Ukraine, Uruguay.
*Later advised the Secretariat it had intended to abstain.

Speaking before the vote, Israel urged that the text be deferred, since the criteria for adopting resolutions on the Middle East should reflect the positive developments in the peace process and the hopes for a better future in the region.

The United States considered that rather than participating in a meaningless exercise, it would be more appropriate for Member States to express their strong support for the peace process and encourage the parties as they proceeded with their negotiations. The resolution was flawed because it purported to deal with an issue which, in accordance with the 1993 Declaration of Principles, was to be covered in negotiations no later than the third year of the interim period, or May 1996.

In Australia's view, any infringement of Palestinian water rights, as mentioned in paragraph 4, was illegal, but the matter should be resolved in negotiation.

Iran emphasized that its positive vote should not be construed as recognition of the State of Israel. Similarly, the Libyan Arab Jamahiriya expressed reservations on all points of the text that could be taken as recognition of Israel or the Middle East peace process; the only way to achieve peace, it added, was by repatriating the Palestinian people.

According to the Observer for Palestine, the illegal settlements were a major obstacle to peace and their mere presence would lead to extremism and violence. Adoption of the resolution was not a meaningless exercise since the text reaffirmed the international community's position with regard to a dangerous element that might jeopardize the peace process.

### REFERENCES

[1]A/50/35. [2]YUN 1993, p. 521. [3]YUN 1994, p. 616. [4]YUN 1967, p. 257, SC res. 242(1967), 22 Nov. 1967. [5]YUN 1973, p. 213, SC res. 338(1973), 22 Oct. 1973. [6]A/50/67-S/1995/64. [7]S/PRST/1995/3. [8]A/50/725-S/1995/930. [9]YUN 1994, p. 619, GA res. 49/62 D, 14 Dec. 1994. [10]A/50/73-S/1995/83. [11]YUN 1948-49, p. 174, GA res. 194(III), 11 Dec. 1948. [12]YUN 1978, p. 312, SC res. 425(1978), 19 Mar. 1978. [13]A/50/574. [14]YUN 1994, p. 624, GA res. 49/87 A, 16 Dec. 1994. [15]YUN 1968, p. 555, GA res. 2443(XXIII), 19 Dec. 1968. [16]A/50/463. [17]YUN 1994, p. 646, GA res. 49/36 A, 9 Dec. 1994. [18]A/50/170. [19]A/50/282. [20]YUN 1994, p. 614. [21]YUN 1955, p. 209. [22]A/50/133-S/1995/282. [23]A/50/305-S/1995/608. [24]A/50/359-S/1995/718. [25]A/50/135-S/1995/293. [26]A/50/657. [27]A/50/658. [28]YUN 1994, p. 655, GA res. 49/36 B, 9 Dec. 1994. [29]A/50/659. [30]YUN 1994, p. 649, GA res. 49/36 C, 9 Dec. 1994. [31]E/CN.6/1995/8. [32]YUN 1994, p. 1191. [33]E/1995/26-E/CN.6/1995/14 (res. 39/3). [34]S/1995/151. [35]S/1995/367. [36]S/1995/366. [37]A/50/168-S/1995/341. [38]YUN 1947-48, p. 247, GA res. 181(II) A, 29 Nov. 1947. [39]S/1995/394. [40]A/50/191-S/1995/418. [41]A/50/262-E/1995/59. [42]YUN 1994, p. 651, ESC res. 1994/45, 29 July 1994. [43]Ibid., p. 652, GA res. 49/132, 19 Dec. 1994.

# Issues related to Palestine

## General aspects

During 1995, the General Assembly continued to grapple with the question of Palestine. Following consideration of the annual report of the Committee on Palestinian Rights, the Assembly in December adopted four resolutions, reaffirming, among

other things, the necessity of achieving a peaceful settlement of the question of Palestine—the core of the Arab-Israeli conflict—in all its aspects and again stressing the need for the realization of the inalienable rights of the Palestinians, primarily the right to self-determination, as well as for Israeli withdrawal from the Palestinian territory occupied since 1967.

In commemoration of the International Day of Solidarity with the Palestinian People, celebrated annually in accordance with a 1977 Assembly resolution,[1] the Committee held a solemn meeting on 29 November to which all Member States, specialized agencies and observers were invited.

**GENERAL ASSEMBLY ACTION**

On 15 December, the General Assembly adopted **resolution 50/84 D**.

### Peaceful settlement of the question of Palestine
*The General Assembly,*

*Recalling* its relevant resolutions,

*Recalling also* the relevant Security Council resolutions, including resolutions 242(1967) of 22 November 1967 and 338(1973) of 22 October 1973,

*Having considered* the report of the Secretary-General of 7 November 1995, submitted pursuant to the request made in its resolution 49/62 D of 14 December 1994,

*Convinced* that achieving a final and peaceful settlement of the question of Palestine, the core of the Arab-Israeli conflict, is imperative for the attainment of a comprehensive and lasting peace in the Middle East,

*Aware* that the principle of equal rights and self-determination of peoples is among the purposes and principles of the Charter of the United Nations,

*Affirming* the principle of the inadmissibility of the acquisition of territory by war,

*Affirming also* the illegality of the Israeli settlements in the territory occupied since 1967 and of Israeli actions aimed at changing the status of Jerusalem,

*Affirming once again* the right of all States in the region to live in peace within secure and internationally recognized borders,

*Aware* of the mutual recognition between the Government of the State of Israel and the Palestine Liberation Organization, the representative of the Palestinian people, and the signing by the two parties of the Declaration of Principles on Interim Self-Government Arrangements in Washington on 13 September 1993, as well as the subsequent implementation agreements, including the Interim Agreement on the West Bank and the Gaza Strip signed in Washington on 28 September 1995,

*Noting with satisfaction* the withdrawal of the Israeli army, which took place in the Gaza Strip and the Jericho area in accordance with the agreements reached by the parties, and the initiation of the Palestinian Authority in those areas, as well as the beginning of the redeployment of the Israeli army in the rest of the West Bank,

*Aware also* that the United Nations has participated as a full, extraregional participant in the work of the multilateral working groups of the Middle East peace process,

*Noting* the appointment of the United Nations Special Coordinator in the Occupied Territories by the Secretary-General, and the positive contribution in this regard,

*Welcoming* the convening of the Conference to Support Middle East Peace at Washington on 1 October 1993 and all follow-up meetings,

1. *Reaffirms* the necessity of achieving a peaceful settlement of the question of Palestine, the core of the Arab-Israeli conflict, in all its aspects;

2. *Expresses its full support* of the ongoing peace process which began in Madrid and the Declaration of Principles on Interim Self-Government Arrangements, as well as the subsequent implementation agreements, and expresses the hope that the process will lead to the establishment of a comprehensive, just and lasting peace in the Middle East;

3. *Calls* for the timely and scrupulous implementation of the agreements reached between the parties towards the negotiation of the final settlement;

4. *Stresses* the need for:

*(a)* The realization of the inalienable rights of the Palestinian people, primarily the right to self-determination;

*(b)* The withdrawal of Israel from the Palestinian territory occupied since 1967;

5. *Stresses also* the need for resolving the problem of the Palestine refugees in conformity with its resolution 194(III) of 11 December 1948;

6. *Urges* Member States to expedite the provision of economic and technical assistance to the Palestinian people during this critical period;

7. *Emphasizes* the importance for the United Nations to play a more active and expanded role in the current peace process and in the implementation of the Declaration of Principles, including the monitoring of the forthcoming Palestinian elections;

8. *Requests* the Secretary-General to continue his efforts with the parties concerned, and in consultation with the Security Council, for the promotion of peace in the region and to submit progress reports on developments in this matter.

General Assembly resolution 50/84 D

15 December 1995     Meeting 93     143-3-3 (recorded vote)

17-nation draft (A/50/L.50 & Add.1); agenda item 42.
*Meeting numbers.* GA 50th session: plenary 74, 75, 93.

Recorded vote in Assembly as follows:

*In favour:* Afghanistan, Albania, Algeria, Andorra, Angola, Antigua and Barbuda, Argentina, Armenia, Australia, Austria, Azerbaijan, Bahamas, Bahrain, Bangladesh, Belarus, Belgium, Belize, Benin, Bhutan, Bolivia, Botswana, Brazil, Brunei Darussalam, Bulgaria, Burkina Faso, Cambodia, Cameroon, Canada, Cape Verde, Chile, China, Colombia, Côte d'Ivoire, Croatia, Cuba, Cyprus, Czech Republic, Denmark, Djibouti, Ecuador, Egypt, El Salvador, Eritrea, Estonia, Ethiopia, Fiji, Finland, France, Gabon, Georgia, Germany, Ghana, Greece, Grenada, Guatemala, Guinea, Guyana, Haiti, Honduras, Iceland, India, Indonesia, Ireland, Italy, Jamaica, Japan, Jordan, Kazakstan, Kenya, Kuwait, Kyrgyzstan, Lao People's Democratic Republic, Lebanon, Lesotho, Libyan Arab Jamahiriya, Liechtenstein, Lithuania, Luxembourg, Malawi, Malaysia, Maldives, Mali, Malta, Mauritania, Mauritius, Mexico, Monaco, Mongolia, Morocco, Mozambique, Myanmar, Namibia, Nepal, Netherlands, New Zealand, Niger, Nigeria, Norway, Oman, Pakistan, Panama, Papua New Guinea, Peru, Philippines, Poland, Portugal, Qatar, Republic of Moldova, Romania, Samoa, Saudi Arabia, Senegal, Singapore, Slovakia, Slovenia, Solomon Islands, South Africa, Spain, Sri Lanka, Sudan, Suriname, Swaziland, Sweden, Syrian Arab Republic, the former Yugoslav Republic of Macedonia, Thailand, Togo, Trinidad and Tobago, Tunisia, Turkey, United Arab Emirates, Uganda, Ukraine, United Kingdom, United Republic of Tanzania, Uruguay, Uzbekistan, Vanuatu, Venezuela, Viet Nam, Yemen, Zambia, Zimbabwe.

*Against:* Israel, Micronesia, United States.

*Abstaining:* Costa Rica, Marshall Islands, Russian Federation.

In the view of the United States, it was both inappropriate and unhelpful for the General Assembly to take a position and speak conclusively on issues under direct negotiation between the parties. The Assembly should support the negotiation process rather than focus on divisive and polarizing issues and statements. Three of the texts adopted under the agenda item were remnants of an earlier time and had been overtaken by events. They promoted institutions and activities whose approach to Middle East peace was both unbalanced and outdated and did little to support the negotiations under way; nor did those texts reflect, except in perfunctory ways, the remarkable progress that had been achieved. Those institutions and activities, which absorbed about $7 million worth of financial and human resources, could be better used in another way, for example through UNSCO for programmes directly benefiting Palestinians.

Speaking after the vote, Palestine expressed regret over the positions taken by Israel and the United States which, it said, appeared to aim principally at setting aside international law and at forcing the Palestinians to accept the results of illegal Israeli policies that had been condemned by the international community for many years, subjecting the final settlement to an imbalance of power in favour of Israel.

The Syrian Arab Republic said its favourable vote did not mean that it supported or opposed the Declaration of Principles referred to in the text. Iran expressed reservations on those parts of the resolutions adopted under the agenda item which might be construed as any recognition of Israel. The Libyan Arab Jamahiriya stated similar reservations; it also reserved its position on the provisions welcoming or supporting the current peace process. That process, it felt, did not provide a just, comprehensive and final solution.

The right of the Palestinians to self-determination was reaffirmed by the Commission on Human Rights (see PART THREE, Chapter II) and by the Assembly in **resolution 50/140**. The Assembly expressed the hope that they could soon be exercising that right within the peace process and urged for continued support in their quest for self-determination.

## Committee on Palestinian Rights

As mandated by the General Assembly in 1994,[2] the Committee on Palestinian Rights, established in 1975,[3] kept under review the situation relating to the Palestine question, reported on it and made suggestions to the Assembly or the Security Council. The Committee continued to promote the exercise of the rights of the Palestinians and heighten international awareness of the facts relating to the question, making adjustments in its approach and work programme as necessary in order to promote implementation of the agreements reached and to mobilize support and assistance to the Palestinians. In carrying out its mandate, the Committee also expanded its cooperation with non-governmental organizations (NGOs). During the year, it organized regional seminars and meetings and oversaw the preparation of studies and publications. As in the past, it invited Palestinian and Israeli personalities to participate in all events organized under its auspices, with a view to promoting constructive debate and analysis of the most important issues relating to the Palestine question, the transition period and the peace process.

In establishing its 1995 work programme, the Committee decided not to hold any North American seminar and to devote some of the resulting savings to the North American NGO symposium. It also decided to devote resources earmarked for a European seminar to one on Palestinian administrative, managerial and financial needs and challenges (see Committee report below, under "Assistance to Palestinians"). The Committee initiated consultations with regard to identifying a venue for an Asian seminar and NGO symposium; that event and an event in Africa, however, could not be held during 1995.

The Latin American and Caribbean Regional Seminar (Rio de Janeiro, Brazil, 20-23 March), held in support of the peace process, was attended by 17 panellists from that region, as well as Palestinians and Israelis, representatives of 17 Governments, 3 United Nations organs and intergovernmental organizations, 16 NGOs, media representatives, and faculty and students of universities and institutes. A regional NGO symposium on the same theme was held in conjunction with that seminar, as were workshops on mobilizing NGOs to promote assistance to the Palestinians and on NGO activities to mobilize public opinion for a just and lasting solution to the Palestine question.

The twelfth United Nations North American NGO Symposium on the Question of Palestine (New York, 19-21 June), held in cooperation with the North American Coordinating Committee for NGOs on the Question of Palestine, was attended by 73 NGOs, 18 panellists and workshop leaders, 11 Governments and 2 intergovernmental organizations. Panel topics included: Jerusalem and settlements; the situation of the refugees; securing respect for international humanitarian law; building civil society; advancing women's concerns; promoting social development; and the continuing commitment of NGOs to the Palestine question.

The twelfth United Nations International NGO Meeting and Ninth European NGO Symposium on the Question of Palestine were combined (Vienna, 29 August–1 September) and attended by 26 panellists and workshop leaders, 51 NGOs, 37 Governments, 10 UN agencies and bodies, 3 intergovernmental organizations, 5 NGO coordinating committees and a delegation from Palestine. Participating NGOs adopted a communiqué, welcoming the positive developments in the Middle East peace process as a result of the 1993 Declaration of Principles,[4] noting with concern the delays in implementing the agreement and exhorting Israel to honour its commitments in a timely manner.

In its 1995 report to the Assembly,[5] the Committee continued to stress that a comprehensive, just and lasting solution to the Palestine question—the core of the Arab-Israeli conflict—had to be based on the relevant United Nations resolutions and the following principles: Israeli withdrawal from the Palestinian territory occupied since 1967, including Jerusalem, and from the other occupied Arab territories; respect for the right of all States in the region to live in peace within secure and internationally recognized boundaries; and recognition and exercise of the inalienable rights of the Palestinians, primarily the right to self-determination.

The Committee noted with satisfaction that the peace process continued despite many difficulties and that the parties had affirmed its irreversibility. As an important further step in that process, the Committee welcomed the signing in September of the Interim Agreement.

The Committee expressed its commitment to continue and intensify its support for the Palestinian people and its leadership during the transition. It reaffirmed that the United Nations had a permanent responsibility with respect to the Palestine question until a comprehensive, just and lasting settlement was reached, and reiterated that the involvement of the United Nations in the peace process, both as guardian of international legitimacy and in mobilizing and providing international assistance, was essential for the successful outcome of the peace efforts. During the interim period, the Committee believed, Israel had to recognize and respect its obligations as the occupying Power under the 1949 Geneva Convention relative to the Protection of Civilian Persons in Time of War (fourth Geneva Convention).

Despite positive developments, the Committee noted that the situation in the areas still under Israeli occupation gave reason for concern and continued to create facts on the ground that had potential negative effects on the future exercise of Palestinian rights and the peace process itself. Of utmost importance was the issue of land confiscation and settlements, including in East Jerusalem (see above, under "Occupied territories").

The Committee expressed profound concern at the repeated closures, for security reasons, of the occupied territory and the self-rule areas and at the isolation of East Jerusalem, which had a devastating effect on the overall livelihood of the Palestinian population in an economy much intertwined with that of Israel, as well as on Palestinian education and health. The Committee was also concerned that thousands of Palestinian prisoners and detainees remained in Israeli prisons, under conditions that had been repeatedly decried by human rights organizations. It called on Israel to implement the planned releases speedily and work to ameliorate conditions of detention (see above).

The Committee voiced concern at the continued deterioration of the living conditions of the Palestinians in the West Bank, including East Jerusalem, and particularly in the Gaza Strip. It stressed that the destruction of the Palestinian economic infrastructure as a result of the prolonged occupation required the urgent attention of the international community.

An important first step towards integrating the Palestinian economy into a wider regional economic framework was, in the Committee's view, the first Middle East/North Africa Economic Summit (Casablanca, Morocco, 30 October–1 November 1994) and the adoption of the Declaration of Casablanca,[6] as a dynamic economy and prosperity were important underpinnings of peace and stability, ideas that were reaffirmed in a joint communiqué issued on 12 February 1995 by the United States, Egypt, Israel, Jordan and the Palestinian Authority. The Committee welcomed the convening of the Second Middle East/North Africa Economic Summit (Amman, 29-31 October) which, it believed, would facilitate the expansion of investment in the region and enhance regional cooperation and development, thereby promoting stability and an atmosphere conducive to peace.

The Committee expressed great appreciation to those States that had supported its work and facilitated the organization of events held under its auspices; it believed that the time had come for all States to recognize its contribution as a valuable forum for dialogue, analysis, exchange of expertise, mobilization of public opinion and action in support of the peace efforts and the rights of the Palestinians, as well as their socio-economic development. The Committee considered that a broadening of its membership to include countries that supported its objective but had not hitherto participated in its work would greatly enhance the contribution of the United Nations to promote peace.

The Committee further considered that its seminars on economic and social issues confronting the Palestinians in the occupied territory had been particularly useful in bringing together experts, donor countries, UN departments, agencies and organizations, NGOs and others. In view of the new situation created by the 1993 Declaration of Principles and subsequent implementation agreements and mindful of the measures taken by the Palestinian Authority to establish an effective administration, which required continued international support, the Committee felt that an event under its auspices should be held as soon as possible to address various aspects of the transition period.

The Committee stressed the value of its role as a catalyst in bringing together and developing a network of NGOs interested in the Palestine question, and in promoting solidarity activities as well as concrete assistance. Noting the increasing interest and participation of Governments, in particular of donor countries, and UN organizations and agencies in NGO events organized under its auspices, the Committee also intended to continue its meetings in the various regions, seeking to structure them for maximum usefulness and to cooperate with NGOs with a view to developing effective follow-up mechanisms and encouraging a wider and more active participation of NGOs.

The Committee also made recommendations regarding the activities of the UN Division for Palestinian Rights and the special information programme on the question of Palestine of the Department of Public Information (DPI) (see below).

Finally, the Committee said it would continue to strive to achieve maximum effectiveness in implementing its mandate and to adjust its work programme in the light of developments, in order to continue to contribute, to the extent possible, to the realization of the common UN objective of achieving a just and lasting solution to the question of Palestine.

**GENERAL ASSEMBLY ACTION**

On 15 December, the General Assembly adopted **resolution 50/84 A**.

### Committee on the Exercise of the Inalienable Rights of the Palestinian People

*The General Assembly,*

*Recalling* its resolutions 181(II) of 29 November 1947, 194(III) of 11 December 1948, 3236(XXIX) of 22 November 1974, 3375(XXX) and 3376(XXX) of 10 November 1975, 31/20 of 24 November 1976, 32/40 A of 2 December 1977, 33/28 A and B of 7 December 1978, 34/65 A of 29 November 1979 and 34/65 C of 12 December 1979, ES-7/2 of 29 July 1980, 35/169 A and C of 15 December 1980, 36/120 A and C of 10 December 1981, ES-7/4 of 28 April 1982, 37/86 A of 10 December 1982, 38/58 A of 13 December 1983, 39/49 A of 11 December 1984, 40/96 A of 12 December 1985, 41/43 A of 2 December 1986, 42/66 A of 2 December 1987, 43/175 A of 15 December 1988, 44/41 A of 6 December 1989, 45/67 A of 6 December 1990, 46/74 A of 11 December 1991, 47/64 A of 11 December 1992, 48/158 A of 20 December 1993 and 49/62 A of 14 December 1994,

*Having considered* the report of the Committee on the Exercise of the Inalienable Rights of the Palestinian People,

*Welcoming* the signing of the Declaration of Principles on Interim Self-Government Arrangements, including its Annexes and Agreed Minutes, by the Government of the State of Israel and the Palestine Liberation Organization in Washington on 13 September 1993, as well as the subsequent implementation agreements, in particular the Agreement on the Gaza Strip and the Jericho Area, signed at Cairo on 4 May 1994, and the Interim Agreement on the West Bank and the Gaza Strip, signed in Washington on 28 September 1995,

*Reaffirming* that the United Nations has a permanent responsibility with respect to the question of Palestine until the question is resolved in all its aspects in a satisfactory manner, in accordance with international legitimacy,

1. *Expresses its appreciation* to the Committee on the Exercise of the Inalienable Rights of the Palestinian People for its efforts in performing the tasks assigned to it by the General Assembly;

2. *Considers* that the Committee can continue to make a valuable and positive contribution to international efforts to promote the effective implementation of the Declaration of Principles on Interim Self-Government Arrangements and to mobilize international support for and assistance to the Palestinian people during the transitional period;

3. *Endorses* the recommendations of the Committee contained in chapter VII of its report;

4. *Requests* the Committee to continue to keep under review the situation relating to the question of Palestine and to report and make suggestions to the General Assembly or the Security Council, as appropriate;

5. *Authorizes* the Committee to continue to exert all efforts to promote the exercise of the inalienable rights of the Palestinian people, to make such adjustments in its approved programme of work as it may consider appropriate and necessary in the light of developments, to give special emphasis to the need to mobilize support and assistance for the Palestinian people, and to report thereon to the General Assembly at its fifty-first session and thereafter;

6. *Also requests* the Committee to continue to extend its cooperation to non-governmental organizations in their contribution towards heightening international awareness of the facts relating to the question of Palestine and promoting support and assistance to meet the needs of the Palestinian people, and to take the necessary steps to involve additional non-governmental organizations in its work;

7. *Requests* the United Nations Conciliation Commission for Palestine, established under resolution 194(III), and other United Nations bodies associated with the question of Palestine to continue to cooperate fully with the Committee and to make available to it, at its request, the relevant information and documentation which they have at their disposal;

8. *Requests* the Secretary-General to circulate the report of the Committee to all the competent bodies of the United Nations and urges them to take the necessary action, as appropriate;

9. *Also requests* the Secretary-General to continue to provide the Committee with all the necessary facilities for the performance of its tasks.

General Assembly resolution 50/84 A

15 December 1995      Meeting 93      95-2-52 (recorded vote)

17-nation draft (A/50/L.47 & Add.1); agenda item 42.
*Meeting numbers.* GA 50th session: plenary 74, 75, 93.

Recorded vote in Assembly as follows:

*In favour:* Afghanistan, Algeria, Angola, Antigua and Barbuda, Azerbaijan, Bahamas, Bahrain, Bangladesh, Belarus, Belize, Benin, Bhutan, Bolivia, Botswana, Brazil, Brunei Darussalam, Burkina Faso, Cameroon, Cape Verde, Chile, China, Colombia, Costa Rica, Cuba, Cyprus, Djibouti, Egypt, El Salvador, Eritrea, Ethiopia, Fiji, Gabon, Ghana, Guatemala, Guinea, Guyana, Haiti, Honduras, India, Indonesia, Iran, Jamaica, Jordan, Kenya, Kuwait, Lao People's Democratic Republic, Lebanon, Libyan Arab Jamahiriya, Malawi, Malaysia, Maldives, Mali, Malta, Mauritania, Mauritius, Mexico, Mongolia, Morocco, Mozambique, Myanmar, Namibia, Nepal, Nicaragua, Niger, Nigeria, Oman, Pakistan, Panama, Peru, Philippines, Qatar, Saudi Arabia, Senegal, Singapore, South Africa, Sri Lanka, Sudan, Suriname, Syrian Arab Republic, Thailand, Togo, Trinidad and Tobago, Tunisia, Turkey, United Arab Emirates, Uganda, Ukraine, United Republic of Tanzania, Uruguay, Vanuatu, Venezuela, Viet Nam, Yemen, Zambia, Zimbabwe.

*Against:* Israel, United States.

*Abstaining:* Andorra, Argentina, Armenia, Australia, Austria, Belgium, Bulgaria, Canada, Croatia, Czech Republic, Denmark, Dominica, Ecuador, Estonia, Finland, France, Georgia, Germany, Greece, Grenada, Iceland, Ireland, Italy, Japan, Kazakstan, Kyrgyzstan, Lesotho, Liechtenstein, Lithuania, Luxembourg, Marshall Islands, Micronesia, Monaco, Netherlands, New Zealand, Norway, Papua New Guinea, Poland, Portugal, Republic of Moldova, Romania, Russian Federation, Samoa, Slovakia, Slovenia, Solomon Islands, Spain, Swaziland, Sweden, the former Yugoslav Republic of Macedonia, United Kingdom, Uzbekistan.

## Division for Palestinian Rights.

Under the guidance of the Committee on Palestinian Rights, the Division for Palestinian Rights of the UN Secretariat continued to function as a centre for research, monitoring, preparation of studies, and collection and dissemination of information on all issues related to the Palestine question. In cooperation with relevant technical services of the Secretariat, the Division had made progress towards establishing a UN computer-based information system on the question of Palestine (UNISPAL), as requested by the Committee and endorsed by the General Assembly. The Committee stressed the usefulness of UNISPAL for its own work and for that of the United Nations, as well as for other members of the international community, and called for intensified efforts to advance towards the full operation of the system and its further expansion as required.

The Committee requested the Division to continue its programme of publications, with particular attention to preparing or updating studies on various issues subject to final status negotiations. It noted with satisfaction the progress made in incorporating into UNISPAL documentation on relevant activities of the UN system and NGOs, as well as other information material, including documents related to the peace process.

**GENERAL ASSEMBLY ACTION**

On 15 December, the General Assembly adopted **resolution 50/84 B**.

**Division for Palestinian Rights of the Secretariat**

*The General Assembly,*

*Having considered* the report of the Committee on the Exercise of the Inalienable Rights of the Palestinian People,

*Taking note in particular* of the relevant information contained in chapter V.B of that report,

*Recalling* its resolutions 32/40 B of 2 December 1977, 33/28 C of 7 December 1978, 34/65 D of 12 December 1979, 35/169 D of 15 December 1980, 36/120 B of 10 December 1981, 37/86 B of 10 December 1982, 38/58 B of 13 December 1983, 39/49 B of 11 December 1984, 40/96 B of 12 December 1985, 41/43 B of 2 December 1986, 42/66 B of 2 December 1987, 43/175 B of 15 December 1988, 44/41 B of 6 December 1989, 45/67 B of 6 December 1990, 46/74 B of 11 December 1991, 47/64 B of 11 December 1992, 48/158 B of 20 December 1993 and 49/62 B of 14 December 1994,

1. *Notes with appreciation* the action taken by the Secretary-General in compliance with its resolution 49/62 B;

2. *Considers* that the Division for Palestinian Rights of the Secretariat continues to make a useful and constructive contribution through the organization of seminars and meetings of non-governmental organizations, as well as through its research and monitoring activities, the preparation of studies and publications and the collection and dissemination of information in printed and electronic form on all issues pertaining to the question of Palestine;

3. *Requests* the Secretary-General to continue to provide the Division with the necessary resources, including for the further development of the United Nations information system on the question of Palestine, and to ensure that it continues to discharge the tasks detailed in paragraph 1 of resolution 32/40 B, paragraph 2 (*b*) of resolution 34/65 D, paragraph 3 of resolution 36/120 B, paragraph 3 of resolution 38/58 B, paragraph 3 of resolution 40/96 B, paragraph 2 of resolution 42/66 B, paragraph 2 of resolution 44/41 B, paragraph 2 of resolution 46/74 B and paragraph 2 of resolution 48/158 B, in consultation with the Committee on the Exercise of the Inalienable Rights of the Palestinian People and under its guidance;

4. *Also requests* the Secretary-General to ensure the continued cooperation of the Department of Public Information and other units of the Secretariat in enabling the Division to perform its tasks and in covering adequately the various aspects of the question of Palestine;

5. *Invites* all Governments and organizations to lend their cooperation to the Committee and the Division in the performance of their tasks;

6. *Notes with appreciation* the action taken by Member States to observe annually on 29 November the International Day of Solidarity with the Palestinian People and requests them to continue to give the widest possible publicity to the observance, and requests the Committee to continue to organize, as part of the observance of the Day of Solidarity, an annual exhibit on Palestinian rights in cooperation with the Permanent Observer Mission of Palestine to the United Nations.

General Assembly resolution 50/84 B

15 December 1995     Meeting 93     96-2-53 (recorded vote)

17-nation draft (A/50/L.48 & Add.1); agenda item 42.
*Meeting numbers.* GA 50th session: plenary 74, 75, 93.

Recorded vote in Assembly as follows:

*In favour:* Afghanistan, Algeria, Angola, Antigua and Barbuda, Azerbaijan, Bahamas, Bahrain, Bangladesh, Belarus, Belize, Benin, Bhutan, Bolivia, Botswana, Brazil, Brunei Darussalam, Burkina Faso, Cameroon, Cape Verde, Chile, China, Colombia, Congo, Costa Rica, Cuba, Cyprus, Djibouti, Egypt, El Salvador, Eritrea, Ethiopia, Fiji, Gabon, Ghana, Guatemala, Guinea, Guyana, Haiti, Honduras, India, Indonesia, Iran, Jamaica, Jordan, Kenya, Kuwait, Lao People's Democratic Republic, Lebanon, Libyan Arab Jamahiriya, Malawi, Malaysia, Maldives, Mali, Malta, Mauritania, Mauritius, Mexico, Mongolia, Morocco, Mozambique, Myanmar, Namibia, Nepal, Nicaragua, Niger, Nigeria, Oman, Pakistan, Panama, Peru, Philippines, Qatar, Saudi Arabia, Senegal, Singapore, South Africa, Sri Lanka, Sudan, Suriname, Syrian Arab Republic, Thailand, Togo, Trinidad and Tobago, Tunisia, Turkey, United Arab Emirates, Uganda, Ukraine, United Republic of Tanzania, Uruguay, Vanuatu, Venezuela, Viet Nam, Yemen, Zambia, Zimbabwe.

*Against:* Israel, United States.

*Abstaining:* Andorra, Argentina, Armenia, Australia, Austria, Belgium, Bulgaria, Canada, Côte d'Ivoire, Croatia, Czech Republic, Denmark, Dominica, Ecuador, Estonia, Finland, France, Georgia, Germany, Greece, Grenada, Iceland, Ireland, Italy, Japan, Kazakstan, Kyrgyzstan, Lesotho, Liechtenstein, Lithuania, Luxembourg, Marshall Islands, Micronesia, Monaco, Netherlands, New Zealand, Norway, Papua New Guinea, Poland, Portugal, Republic of Moldova, Romania, Russian Federation, Samoa, Slovakia, Slovenia, Solomon Islands, Spain, Swaziland, Sweden, the former Yugoslav Republic of Macedonia, United Kingdom, Uzbekistan.

### Public information activities

As requested by the General Assembly in 1994,[7] DPI continued its special information programme on the Palestine question, with particular emphasis on public opinion in Europe and North America. In doing so, it provided press coverage of all meetings of the Committee on Palestinian Rights, as well as of seminars and symposia. It cooperated with the Division for Palestinian Rights in media promotion and other arrangements for the International Day of Solidarity with the Palestinian People, held annually on 29 November. The Department distributed various publications covering Palestinian issues, including *Prerequisites for Peace in the Middle East: An Israeli-Palestinian Dialogue,* based on the proceedings of a 1994 international encounter for journalists.[8]

DPI's Public Inquiries Unit responded to requests for information on Palestine and the Middle East. The subject was included in presentations made to visitors taking guided tours of the United Nations, and the DPI Group Programme Unit organized seven briefings on the question.

A wide range of information material was disseminated through the Internet and other electronic networks.

A video with the working title "Palestine: Fifty Years On" was produced by the Media Division and distributed to all UN information centres (UNICs) and services and United Nations Development Programme (UNDP) libraries. DPI's Video Section produced four "UN in Action"/CNN World Report segments on: the Palestinian Broadcasting Corporation in Jericho; training of the Palestinian police force; Palestinian women setting up business in the West Bank; and a UNDP-assisted banana plantation in Jericho.

The Radio Section produced a number of feature programmes and covered various aspects of the Palestine question in news and current affairs radio programmes in official and non-official languages worldwide.

The global network of UNICs continued to disseminate information on the Palestine question to mass media, academics, NGOs and the general public, through newsletters, press releases and briefings.

In cooperation with the United Nations Educational, Scientific and Cultural Organization (UNESCO) and with the support of the Institute for Cooperation with the Arab World of the Spanish Ministry of Foreign Affairs, DPI organized a Seminar on Assistance to the Palestinian People in the Field of Media Development (Madrid, Spain, 29-31 March). Palestinian media practitioners participated, together with representatives of international media organizations, training institutions and foundations, with the aim of strengthening Palestinian media capability. DPI also organized a training programme for Palestinian media practitioners at Headquarters (7 October–22 November).

The Committee on Palestinian Rights, in its 1995 report,[5] stated that DPI's special information programme was very useful in raising the awareness of the international community concerning the complexities of the Palestine question and the Middle East situation. The Committee believed that the programme was contributing effectively to an atmosphere conducive to dialogue and supportive of the peace process, and should follow and reflect the new realities, assist Palestinian media development and continue to inform about the cause of the Palestinians, in addition to supporting dialogue in the effort to build peace.

**GENERAL ASSEMBLY ACTION**

On 15 December, the General Assembly adopted **resolution 50/84 C**.

**Department of Public Information of the Secretariat**

*The General Assembly,*

*Having considered* the report of the Committee on the Exercise of the Inalienable Rights of the Palestinian People,

*Taking note in particular* of the information contained in chapter VI of that report,

*Recalling* its resolution 49/62 C of 14 December 1994,

*Convinced* that the worldwide dissemination of accurate and comprehensive information and the role of non-governmental organizations and institutions remain of vital importance in heightening awareness of and support for the inalienable rights of the Palestinian people,

*Aware* of the Declaration of Principles on Interim Self-Government Arrangements signed by the Government of the State of Israel and the Palestine Liberation Organization in Washington on 13 September 1993, and of the subsequent implementation agreements, in particular the Interim Agreement on the West Bank and the Gaza Strip signed in Washington on 28 September 1995, and their positive implications,

1. *Notes with appreciation* the action taken by the Department of Public Information of the Secretariat in compliance with resolution 49/62 C;

2. *Considers* that the special information programme on the question of Palestine of the Department of Public Information is very useful in raising the awareness of the international community concerning the complexities of the question and the situation in the Middle East in general, including the achievements of the peace process, and that the programme is contributing effectively to an atmosphere conducive to dialogue and supportive of the peace process;

3. *Requests* the Department, in full cooperation and coordination with the Committee on the Exercise of the Inalienable Rights of the Palestinian People, to continue, with the necessary flexibility as may be required by developments affecting the question of Palestine, its special information programme on the question of Palestine for the biennium 1996-1997, with particular emphasis on public opinion in Europe and North America and, in particular:

*(a)* To disseminate information on all the activities of the United Nations system relating to the question of Palestine, including reports on the work carried out by the relevant United Nations organizations;

*(b)* To continue to issue and update publications on the various aspects of the question of Palestine in all fields, including materials concerning the recent developments in that regard and, in particular, the achievements of the peace process;

*(c)* To expand its audiovisual material on the question of Palestine, including the production of such material;

*(d)* To organize and promote fact-finding news missions for journalists to the area, including the territories under the jurisdiction of the Palestinian Authority and the occupied territories;

*(e)* To organize international, regional and national encounters for journalists;

*(f)* To provide, in cooperation with specialized agencies of the United Nations system, particularly the United Nations Educational, Scientific and Cultural Organization, assistance to the Palestinian people in the field of media development.

General Assembly resolution 50/84 C

15 December 1995     Meeting 93     142-2-7 (recorded vote)

17-nation draft (A/50/L.49 & Add.1); agenda item 42.
*Meeting numbers.* GA 50th session: plenary 74, 75, 93.

Recorded vote in Assembly as follows:

*In favour:* Afghanistan, Albania, Algeria, Andorra, Angola, Antigua and Barbuda, Argentina, Armenia, Australia, Austria, Azerbaijan, Bahamas, Bahrain, Bangladesh, Belarus, Belgium, Belize, Benin, Bhutan, Bolivia, Botswana, Brazil, Brunei Darussalam, Bulgaria, Burkina Faso, Cameroon, Canada, Cape Verde, Chile, China, Colombia, Congo, Costa Rica, Croatia, Cuba, Cyprus, Czech Republic, Denmark, Djibouti, Egypt, El Salvador, Eritrea, Estonia, Ethiopia, Fiji, Finland, France, Gabon, Georgia, Germany, Ghana, Greece, Guatemala, Guinea, Guyana, Haiti, Honduras, Iceland, India, Indonesia, Iran, Ireland, Italy, Jamaica, Japan, Jordan, Kazakstan, Kenya, Kuwait, Kyrgyzstan, Lao People's Democratic Republic, Lebanon, Libyan Arab Jamahiriya, Liechtenstein, Lithuania, Luxembourg, Malawi, Malaysia, Maldives, Mali, Malta, Mauritania, Mauritius, Mexico, Monaco, Mongolia, Morocco, Mozambique, Myanmar, Namibia, Nepal, Netherlands, New Zealand, Nicaragua, Niger, Nigeria, Norway, Oman, Pakistan, Panama, Papua New Guinea, Peru, Philippines, Poland, Portugal, Qatar, Republic of Moldova, Romania, Samoa, Saudi Arabia, Senegal, Singapore, Slovakia, Slovenia, Solomon Islands, South Africa, Spain, Sri Lanka, Sudan, Suriname, Swaziland, Sweden, Syrian Arab Republic, Thailand, the former Yugoslav Republic of Macedonia, Togo, Trinidad and Tobago, Tunisia, Turkey, Uganda, Ukraine, United Arab Emirates, United Kingdom, United Republic of Tanzania, Uruguay, Uzbekistan, Vanuatu, Venezuela, Viet Nam, Yemen, Zambia, Zimbabwe.

*Against:* Israel, United States.

*Abstaining:* Côte d'Ivoire, Ecuador, Grenada,* Lesotho, Marshall Islands, Micronesia, Russian Federation.

*Later advised the Secretariat it had intended to vote in favour.

## Assistance to Palestinians

### UN involvement

**Report of the Secretary-General.** On 13 July, the Secretary-General reported[9] on assistance to the Palestinians, specifying needs, ongoing programmes and proposals for additional assistance. According to the report, the Palestinian Authority faced growing financial difficulties, with a projected budget deficit of $136 million. On 27 April in Paris, the Palestinian Authority, Israel and, on behalf of the donors, the Chair of the Ad Hoc Liaison Committee (the main donor-led body overseeing the assistance effort) concluded a Tripartite Plan of Action elaborating commitments and responsibilities for each party to bridge the budget deficit.

At that meeting, a Joint Liaison Committee was re-established to provide a forum for discussing with the Palestinian Authority economic policy and practical matters related to donor assistance. That Committee was comprised of: the Palestinian Authority as gavel holder; Norway, in its capacity as Chair of the Ad Hoc Liaison Committee, as shepherd; the United Nations and the World Bank as joint secretariat; as well as the United States and EU. Japan was also asked to take part in the meetings. In addition to taking up bilateral issues relating to donor assistance, the Joint Liaison Committee was to discuss progress in implementing the Tripartite Programme of Action. The Joint Liaison Committee, which began meeting on 15 May, decided to create a Task Force on Project Implementation—comprised of the Palestinian Economic Council for Development and Reconstruction as gavel holder, the United States and the European Commission as co-shepherds, UNSCO as secretariat, and the World Bank, UNDP and UNRWA—to examine technical and other obstacles to timely project implementation and to seek solutions for addressing such obstacles. The Task Force reported to the Joint Liaison Committee, which then would discuss obstacles with the appropriate party, whether the Palestinian Authority, Israel, donors or the implementing agencies.

Terje Roed Larsen (Norway), the Special Coordinator in the Occupied Territories, appointed in June 1994,[10] convened a second inter-agency meeting in Gaza in June 1995 to examine the evolving role of the United Nations in the West Bank and the Gaza Strip and to review progress made in implementing the UN coordinating mechanisms agreed on at the first inter-agency meeting, held in December 1994. A central objective of the meeting was to discuss draft sectoral strategy papers under preparation by the priority sector focal points in consultation with interested UN organizations. Those sectoral papers and accompanying project documents were to form the core of a strategy coordinated, targeted and unified by the UN to expand its ongoing programmes and undertake new initiatives for the benefit of the Palestinian Authority and the Palestinians in the West Bank and Gaza. More than 20 UN agencies and programmes participated. The sectoral papers and project documents were also to provide a basis for fund-raising by the Special Coordinator, on behalf of and in coordination with implementing agencies.

Among the ongoing assistance programmes (see below), UNDP's was oriented towards water supply, sanitation, agriculture, industry and housing, while UNRWA had provided basic infrastructure facilities for more than 450,000 Palestinian refugees in camps throughout the West Bank and Gaza. Under its Peace Implementation Programme (PIP), launched in 1993, UNRWA carried out environmental and health projects, constructed and improved educational institutions, and rehabilitated shelters. Some 5,000 UNRWA teachers provided primary, preparatory and vocational schooling to 145,000 students. The Agency offered basic health and social services to more than 1 million registered refugees, operating 230 outpatient facilities and employing more than 500 health-care workers, including 100 doctors. In the Gaza Strip, UNRWA provided monthly in-kind support to almost 100,000 of the poorest refugees.

The United Nations also assisted the Palestinian Authority in institution-building. UNDP gave public-sector support at municipal and local levels. It supported rural infrastructure investments, and provided start-up funding and procurement support to the 14 ministries of the Palestinian Authority, as well as to the Palestinian Economic Council for Development and Reconstruction, the Palestinian Central Bureau of Statistics, the Palestinian Computer Centre, the Civil Defense Department, Palestinian TV and the Palestinian Environmental Protection Agency. A key starting point in public administration development was the May 1995 UNDP mission to work with the Palestinian Authority to identify needs for action in public administration development and to begin the process of formulating an overall national strategy.

Since early 1995, UNDP had managed TOKTEN (Transfer of Knowledge Through Expatriate Nationals Programme), which sponsored the return of Palestinian expatriates living abroad for short-term missions to provide advisory services, consultancy studies and training to the Palestinian Authority ministries and private-sector institutions.

In late 1994, the United Nations Industrial Development Organization (UNIDO) developed a programming strategy for services to the Palestinian people, to provide technical assistance in the areas of private-sector development, development of small- and medium-scale enterprises, human resources development for the industrial sector, acquisition and application of technology to enhance competitiveness and industrial regional cooperation and integration.

The International Labour Organisation's (ILO) ongoing activities included reintegration, through employment, of ex-detainees; assistance in the creation of a Ministry of Labour and the development of labour policy and legislation; capacity-building for the Federation of Palestinian Chambers of Commerce and for the Palestinian trade union federation; an income-generating programme for the disabled; assistance to the Palestinian Central Bureau of Statistics, including a regular labour force survey; and technical assistance for labour-intensive infrastructure.

UNRWA also increased its job creation activities, from $1 million to $2 million per year prior to September 1993 to about $35 million in 1994, while UNDP's activities doubled to $22 million. Under its income generation programme, UNRWA supplied credit to small businesses, 170 of them in the Gaza Strip alone. Working closely with the Agency, the Palestinian Economic Council for Development and Reconstruction was managing over $15 million worth of infrastructure projects.

Based on consultations with the Ministry of Education, a United Nations inter-agency meeting (Gaza, 15-16 June) agreed on principles for a UN education strategy, which included: UN compliance with the strategies and priorities established by the Ministry of Education; cooperation among UN agencies, in close coordination with the Special Coordinator, the donor community and NGOs; consultations among agencies to emphasize complementarity of programmes; sharing of expertise and experiences between UN agencies and the Palestinian Authority; and coordinated fund-raising efforts.

The activities of the United Nations Children's Fund (UNICEF) focused on four key areas: primary health care, primary education, early childhood development, and youth and community development. Since the establishment of the Palestinian Authority, those priorities had shifted towards a long-term institution-building approach. UNICEF supported the Palestinian Authority in developing a national programme of action for the Palestinian child, to provide a broad policy framework for addressing children's issues.

In partnership with the Palestinian Authority, UNESCO developed a programme of assistance consisting of more than 20 priority projects which included strengthening of the Ministries of Education and Culture.

As a result of several missions, the Food and Agriculture Organization of the United Nations (FAO) and ESCWA jointly recommended an action programme for the restructuring, development and strengthening of the Palestinian public agricultural institutions.

The World Health Organization (WHO) focused principally on institutional development and building infrastructure for primary and secondary health care and environmental health, particularly in the Gaza Strip. It provided resources for the establishment and operation of a number of departments of the Palestinian Health Authority and assisted in the transfer of health services from the Palestinian Council for Health to the Palestinian Authority.

The Department for Development Support and Management Services of the Secretariat undertook two needs assessment missions at the invitation of the Palestinian Authority, one on strengthening the capacities of the Ministry of Planning and International Cooperation and the Ministry of Local Government Affairs, and another on developing the institutional capacity of the Palestinian Authority in terms of civil service training and strengthening the administrative functioning of the various ministries. The Special Coordinator oversaw the training of and other assistance to the Palestinian Police Force (see below).

The United Nations Institute for Training and Research (UNITAR) designed a training programme on the use of information system techniques for map production. During an April mission to the occupied territories, the International Civil Aviation Organization (ICAO) emphasized the need to restructure the Palestinian Civil Aviation Authority and to establish a comprehensive training programme with the technical assistance of ICAO.

The Economic and Social Council, by **decision 1995/314** of 28 July, took note of the Secretary-General's report. In **resolution 1995/30** (see above), the Council called for intensified financial and technical assistance to Palestinian women. The situation of and assistance to Palestinian women was the subject of a March report of the Secretary-General to the Commission on the Status of Women (see above, under "Occupied territories").

**Committee report.** In its annual report,[5] the Committee on Palestinian Rights noted with satisfaction that a coordination mechanism for international assistance had been established and a plan of action elaborated. The Committee called on the international donor community to increase assistance as a matter of high priority and urgency. It noted with appreciation the contribution of funds by donor countries and EU to the Palestinian Police Force, as well as to various development projects.

The Committee noted the diversified assistance to the Palestinians by the UN system, which had significantly widened over the years. It expressed appreciation for the efforts by the Special Coordinator to mobilize and coordinate such assistance. It continued to give priority to promoting international assistance to the Palestinians in order to meet their socio-economic and development needs and to support the Palestinian Authority in its institution-building efforts. The Committee structured its programme of regional meetings to that end and convened at UNESCO headquarters a seminar on Palestinian administrative, managerial and financial needs and challenges (Paris, 28-30 June 1995). It was attended by donor countries, intergovernmental and non-governmental organizations, UN bodies and agencies, as well as by Palestinian, Israeli and other experts. The final report[11] of the seminar was submitted to the Economic and Social Council in July.

In closing remarks, the Chairman said the Committee would continue to act primarily in the international political arena and address such fundamental issues as the question of Jerusalem, Israeli settlements in the occupied territories, and Palestine refugees. At the same time, the Committee increasingly felt the need to contribute to promoting international assistance for reconstruction and development and for strengthening Palestinian institutions on the ground during the transition period. Meeting the needs of the Palestinians in establishing a viable and effective administration in the area under the Palestinian Authority was an essential stepping-stone in the struggle for self-determination, he said. Well-functioning government institutions, a developing economy, the creation of employment opportunities and the effective provision of social services were interrelated issues which, if addressed satisfactorily, would provide solid foundations for the new stages of the peace process.

**GENERAL ASSEMBLY ACTION**

On 20 December, the General Assembly adopted **resolution 50/58 H**.

### Assistance to the Palestinian people

*The General Assembly,*

*Recalling* its resolution 49/21 N of 20 December 1994,

*Recalling also* previous resolutions on the question,

*Welcoming* the signing at Cairo on 4 May 1994 by the Government of the State of Israel and the Palestine Liberation Organization, the representative of the Palestinian people, of the first implementation agreement of the Declaration of Principles on Interim Self-Government Arrangements, namely the Agreement on the Gaza Strip and the Jericho Area, and the Agreement on the Preparatory Transfer of Powers and Responsibilities of 29 August 1994, and the Interim Agreement on the West Bank and the Gaza Strip of 28 September 1995,

*Gravely concerned* about the difficult economic and employment conditions facing the Palestinian people throughout the Occupied Territory,

*Conscious* of the urgent need for improvement in the economic and social infrastructure of the Occupied Territory and the living conditions of the Palestinian people,

*Aware* that development is difficult under occupation and best promoted in circumstances of peace and stability,

*Noting,* in the light of the recent developments in the peace process, the great economic and social challenges and needs facing the Palestinian people and their leadership,

*Conscious* of the urgent necessity for international assistance to the Palestinian people, taking into account the Palestinian priorities,

*Noting* the convening of the United Nations Seminar on Palestinian Administrative, Managerial and Financial Needs and Challenges in the light of the new developments, held at the headquarters of the United Nations Educational, Scientific and Cultural Organization from 28 to 30 June 1995,

*Welcoming* the signing of the agreements between the Palestine Liberation Organization and the United Nations Development Programme, the United Nations Relief and Works Agency for Palestine Refugees in the Near East, the United Nations Educational, Scientific and Cultural Organization and the International Labour Organization,

*Stressing* the need for the full engagement of the United Nations in the process of building Palestinian institutions and in providing broad assistance to the Palestinian people, including assistance in the fields of elections, police training and public administration,

*Noting* the appointment by the Secretary-General in June 1994 of the United Nations Special Coordinator in the Occupied Territories,

*Welcoming* the results of the Conference to Support Middle East Peace, convened in Washington on 1 October 1993, and the establishment of the Ad Hoc Liaison Committee and the work being done by the World Bank as its secretariat, as well as the establishment of the consultative group and the convening of an international conference on economic assistance to the Palestinian people to be held in Paris,

*Welcoming also* the results of the meetings of the Ad Hoc Liaison Committee on 29 and 30 November 1994 at Brussels, and on 27 April 1995 in Paris,

*Having considered* the report of the Secretary-General of 13 July 1995,

1. *Takes note* of the report of the Secretary-General;

2. *Expresses its appreciation* to the Secretary-General for his rapid response and efforts regarding assistance to the Palestinian people;

3. *Also expresses its appreciation* to the Member States, United Nations bodies and intergovernmental and non-governmental organizations that have provided and continue to provide assistance to the Palestinian people;

4. *Stresses* the importance of the appointment of the United Nations Special Coordinator in the Occupied Territories and of the steps taken under the auspices of the Secretary-General to ensure the achievement of a coordinated mechanism for United Nations activities throughout the Occupied Territories;

5. *Urges* Member States, international financial institutions of the United Nations system, intergovernmental and non-governmental organizations and regional and interregional organizations to extend, as rapidly and as generously as possible, economic and social assistance

to the Palestinian people in order to assist in the development of the West Bank and Gaza, and to do so in close cooperation with the Palestine Liberation Organization and through official Palestinian institutions;

6. *Calls upon* relevant organizations and agencies of the United Nations system to intensify their assistance in response to the urgent needs of the Palestinian people in accordance with the Palestinian priorities set forth by the Palestinian Authority, with emphasis on national execution and capacity-building;

7. *Urges* Member States to open their markets to exports from the West Bank and Gaza and on the most favourable terms, consistent with appropriate trading rules;

8. *Calls upon* the international donor community to expedite the delivery of pledged assistance to the Palestinian people to meet their urgent needs;

9. *Suggests* the convening in 1996 of a United Nations-sponsored seminar on building the Palestinian economy;

10. *Requests* the Secretary-General to submit a report to the General Assembly at its fifty-first session, through the Economic and Social Council, on the implementation of the present resolution, containing:

*(a)* An assessment of the assistance actually received by the Palestinian people;

*(b)* An assessment of the needs still unmet and specific proposals for responding effectively to them;

11. *Decides* to include in the provisional agenda of its fifty-first session, under the item entitled "Strengthening of the coordination of humanitarian and disaster relief assistance of the United Nations, including special economic assistance", the sub-item entitled "Assistance to the Palestinian people".

General Assembly resolution 50/58 H

20 December 1995     Meeting 96     Adopted without vote

16-nation draft (A/50/L.54 & Add.1); agenda item 20 *(b)*.

### UNDP action

In March 1995, the UNDP Administrator reported[12] on activities during 1994 within the framework of the UNDP Programme of Assistance to the Palestinian People (PAPP). He noted that after the signing of the May 1994 Agreement on the Gaza Strip and the Jericho Area, which established Palestinian self-rule, the Programme had placed high priority on providing start-up support to the Palestinian Authority and its various sectoral departments and supporting institutions. The Programme strategy in 1994, formulated in full collaboration with the Authority, had focused on four broad objectives: protection and management of the environment; encouragement of sustainable human development; support of economic development; and strengthening of public administration. UNDP continued to play a major role in placing its experience at the disposal of the Special Coordinator.

Taking note of the report, the UNDP/United Nations Population Fund (UNFPA) Executive Board in April[13] encouraged the international donor community to increase contributions to the Programme and to take full advantage of its unique and effective delivery capacity.

In 1995, PAPP was enlarged considerably in response to the developments in the peace process between Israel and PLO.[14] The Programme strategy in 1995 was to mobilize and target bilateral donor contributions to meet rapidly emerging priorities, emanating from the changes in Palestinian society and institutions. It was aimed at translating those changes into immediate and tangible impacts. Within that context, PAPP activities in 1995 had three overriding objectives: to support the Palestinian Authority's institution- and capacity-building; to progress from direct PAPP programme execution, which had been necessary before the establishment of the Authority, to a new generation of projects where PAPP's role centred on technical support, supervision and facilitation; and to focus on poverty elimination by helping create employment opportunities, especially in Gaza, where widespread unemployment was the primary obstacle impeding economic growth.

In extensive consultations with the Authority, bilateral donors, UN agencies, EU and the World Bank, PAPP formulated a comprehensive and forward-looking framework to guide its activities over the coming three years (1996-1998), providing strategies and concrete initiatives in six key areas: public administration management; gender in development; agricultural development; private-sector development; employment-generating public works programme; and environmental and social infrastructure. The total programme was projected at $94 million for the three-year period.

Total PAPP expenditures in 1995 were estimated at $34 million, an increase of more than 50 per cent over 1994 expenditures of $22 million, made possible through large-scale bilateral contributions. During 1995, PAPP received contributions from various donors for programme activities in 1996: $11 million from Japan; $4 million from Norway; $2.1 million from Italy; $1.75 million from Sweden; $350,000 from Finland; $20,000 from the Netherlands; $400,000 from the United States Agency for International Development (USAID); $1.5 million from the United Nations Capital Development Fund (UNCDF); and $35,000 from UNFPA. In addition, eight donors (USAID, Canada, Finland, France, Japan, Norway, Sweden, Switzerland and the United States) pledged a total of an additional $25 million.

In order to deliver its greatly expanded programme, PAPP's operational capacity was considerably strengthened during 1995, primarily through the recruitment of highly skilled Palestinian technical, engineering and programming professionals. Two new technical sections, in public administration management and rural development, were added. The Gaza Office was given a large degree of delegated responsibility and was also significantly reinforced, as 60 per cent of ongoing PAPP programme activities were based in the Gaza Strip. Another important trend in the latter half of 1995 was the integration of UNDP-financed expertise into the emerging Palestinian public administration.

Despite increased expenditures, PAPP was still hindered in its programme delivery during the year for two primary reasons: frequent closures of the border between the Gaza Strip and Israel, which at times severely restricted a free flow of goods and persons; and the difficulty experienced by many newly established counterpart Palestinian institutions to define clearly their mandates, priorities and needs for technical cooperation and capital assistance, an aspect UNDP attempted to mitigate through advisory services in public administration management.

A multi-project employment-generation programme, begun as an emergency scheme in 1994 primarily to provide immediate employment opportunities in the Gaza Strip, had become a major infrastructure rehabilitation programme involving numerous Palestinian contractors. In 1995, donors committed a total of $19 million to that programme. PAPP's large-scale infrastructure development programme included construction, rehabilitation and extension of water-supply systems in rural villages and cities in the West Bank and Gaza; continued construction of two main West Bank hospitals; the launching of a small-scale infrastructure rehabilitation and maintenance programme in partnership with the Municipality of Gaza; and construction and renovation work at the Jericho school and sports complex.

PAPP's gender-in-development programme, aimed at promoting the role of Palestinian women in decision-making processes and empowering them through leadership and gender training, continued to expand in 1995. A number of advocacy initiatives were carried out, including a comparative review of existing legislation from a gender perspective with suggested refinements to make the legal system more gender sensitive, and support for a coalition of Palestinian women's health professionals working on women's health policy.

PAPP also initiated activities in 1995 related to formulating a human development profile in the West Bank and Gaza Strip as a crucial step towards defining long-term development goals and facilitating dialogue between the Palestinian Authority, civil society, the United Nations and donors. As part of its capacity-development efforts, PAPP responded to the most urgent needs of the Palestinian Authority by providing emergency start-up support of more than $10 million to more than 20 major institutions, primarily the ministries. PAPP subsequently launched a public administration development programme to support further the Palestinian Authority institutions in

operational, administrative and human resources management tasks. The PAPP water resources action programme provided key technical support to facilitate the establishment of a central Palestinian Water Authority in April 1995. Two new programmes in 1995 aimed primarily at developing the capacities of Palestinian institutions. In private-sector development, in close consultation with the Special Coordinator, PAPP sponsored a pioneering mission to help the Palestinian Authority define its strategy for establishing industrial parks. An integrated rural development programme, introduced in 1994, continued to expand in the poorest area of the West Bank, utilizing participatory development planning and implementation tools and focusing on strengthening village-level planning, financial and project management capacities.

In an effort to support the progressive integration of the West Bank and Gaza Strip into the region, PAPP promoted Palestinian participation in regional conferences and training seminars. UNDP facilitated implementation of a regional project against desertification, involving experts from the Palestinian Authority, Israel and Jordan. It also initiated an exchange of experts in agricultural research and extension.

PAPP supported UNFPA in preparatory work for a population and housing census, to provide essential data and information for developing economic and social policies. In addition, PAPP worked with FAO to provide policy advisory support in the field of agriculture, with collaborative relationships with UNICEF, UNRWA, UNIDO and ILO.

### UNCTAD activities

In July, the secretariat of the UN Conference on Trade and Development (UNCTAD) reported[15] on developments in the economy of the occupied Palestinian territory and proposed a programme of technical assistance. Once Israel had granted UNCTAD staff access to the Palestinian territory in March, its secretariat consulted with the Palestinian Authority, as well as with UNDP and the Special Coordinator. During a follow-up mission in May, consultations were held on substantive issues related to private investment.

The programme aimed to provide Palestinians with support in the areas of trade, finance and transport, and specifically to help them: strengthen the technical, managerial and information capacities of the public and private-sector institutions responsible for formulating and implementing policies; formulate policy and strategy options; enhance the capacity of the commodity-producing sectors; establish the necessary infrastructures for an efficient transport system for trade; reform the overall legal and regulatory framework, along with institutional capacities, for mobilizing financial resources, promoting investments and improving the performance of public utilities; and strengthen technical and institutional capacities in management of financial flows and maximization of insurance resources and their efficient allocation. Ultimately, the programme would be presented to the Palestinian Authority for approval and then to potential bilateral and multilateral sources for funding.

The Trade and Development Board, at its September session, took note[16] of the report and the proposed programme of technical assistance.

### Financing of the Palestinian Police Force

On 6 April, the Secretary-General reported[17] that UNRWA would continue to be responsible for disbursing donor contributions for salaries and other start-up costs of the Palestinian Police Force, with the cooperation of the Special Coordinator and UNDP. From September 1994, when a Memorandum of Understanding was signed in Gaza by representatives of the Palestinian Police Force and UNRWA,[18] through March 1995, seven donor countries (Denmark, Japan, Netherlands, Norway, Saudi Arabia, Sweden, United Kingdom) and EU contributed funds, channelled through UNRWA.

Under the May 1994 Agreement on the Gaza Strip and Jericho Area, the Force had an authorized strength of 9,000 policemen. The cost for their net salaries, from September through March, the Secretary-General reported, was $30.2 million, of which $29.8 million had been funded.

Although the Memorandum of Understanding included other recurrent costs of about $1.9 million per month, there were not always sufficient donor contributions for them. UNRWA reviewed monthly expenditures by the Force only when funds were available to offset them.

Total costs incurred by UNRWA, acting as the disbursement mechanism, amounted to $134,000 by March 1995. The Agency had received, either as reimbursement for costs or in programme support costs or earned interest, about $521,000.

GENERAL ASSEMBLY ACTION

On 13 April 1995, following consideration of the Secretary-General's report, the General Assembly adopted **resolution 49/21 O**, under the general title "Special economic assistance to individual countries or regions".

**Financing of the Palestinian Police Force**

*The General Assembly,*

*Recalling* its resolution 49/21 B of 2 December 1994 on the financing of the Palestinian Police Force,

*Taking note* of the report of the Secretary-General of 6 April 1995 and his designation of the United Nations Relief and Works Agency for Palestine Refugees in the Near East in pursuance of paragraph 1 of resolution 49/21 B,

1. *Requests* the Secretary-General to designate once again the United Nations Relief and Works Agency for Palestine Refugees in the Near East to disburse, with due attention to the need for thorough accounting, the voluntary contributions given by donors in light of the activities of the Ad Hoc Liaison Committee for salaries and other start-up costs of the Palestinian Police Force, for a period ending not later than 31 December 1995;

2. *Encourages* all Member States to contribute funds for this purpose through the Agency;

3. *Requests* the Secretary-General to report on the implementation of the present resolution.

General Assembly resolution 49/21 O

13 April 1995          Meeting 101          Adopted without vote

19-nation draft (A/49/L.65 & Add.1); agenda item 37 *(b)*.

Before the vote, the United States said the UN mechanism had been a crucial and effective instrument in facilitating much needed support to the Palestinian Police Force which was in the mutual interest of both Israel and the Palestinians and was critical to the successful implementation of the Declaration of Principles and its follow-on agreements.

**Report of the Secretary-General.** The Secretary-General on 17 November 1995 reported[19] that at his request, pursuant to Assembly **resolution 49/21 O** (see above), UNRWA, in coordination with the Special Coordinator, had effected payment of salaries to the Palestinian Police Force for the month of July. Contributions for the months April through June had not been received, nor had they for months after July. UNRWA had therefore not been involved in disbursing Palestinian police salaries during those months. The July disbursement was for contributions from the Netherlands ($3,434,066 net of UNRWA programme support costs), Norway ($1,995,335 net) and Greece ($89,286 net). Of those contributions, UNRWA disbursed $4,508,091 in net salaries for 9,000 policemen and $375,264 in salary deductions for the Police Force pension, health and social security funds. The unutilized surplus of $635,332 was paid to the Police Force to cover other running costs for July, as agreed to by the donors.

In August, an independent review was conducted, on behalf of the European Commission, of the 10 million European currency units disbursed by UNRWA for salaries and running costs of the Police Force for December 1994 and January 1995. The report concluded that those funds had been disbursed in accordance with relevant agreements and that controls and procedures continued to be implemented effectively by the Palestinian Authority and UNRWA in months when donor funds were involved.

## The UN and Palestine refugees

In 1995, the United Nations Relief and Works Agency for Palestine Refugees in the Near East

(UNRWA) marked 45 years of humanitarian service to persons displaced from their homes and property as a result of four major conflicts in the Middle East. In June, more than 3 million refugees were registered with UNRWA, living both in and outside camps in the West Bank and the new Self-Rule Area of Jericho (517,000) and Self-Rule Area of the Gaza Strip (683,000), as well as in Jordan (1.3 million), Lebanon (346,000) and the Syrian Arab Republic (337,000).

The future of UNRWA was under discussion as the Palestinian Authority, headquartered in the Gaza Strip, took over some of the services previously provided by UNRWA, which took steps to move its headquarters from Vienna to Gaza in 1995. Major areas of service by UNRWA continued to be in the areas of education, health, and relief and social services.

Introducing his annual report[20] on the work of the Agency (1 July 1994–30 June 1995) to the General Assembly's Fourth Committee on 30 October, the UNRWA Commissioner-General said that the Agency was in the contradictory position of planning for its own eventual dissolution while expanding its programmes and operations. UNRWA had been closely associated with the fate of the Palestine refugees for 45 years, trying to mitigate their sufferings, helping them preserve their cultural identity, educating their children, providing them with primary health care and hospitalization, creating employment opportunities and assisting their poorest.

Tens of thousands of Palestinians had served as UNRWA staff over the years with exceptional dedication to their own community and to the United Nations, he said. Now, the Palestine refugees, among them the 21,000-strong staff of UNRWA, eagerly awaited a solution to the refugee problem as foreseen in the agreements between Israel and the Palestinians. They were feeling the inevitable strain of a transition period and of the imponderables of a not-yet-defined future. The situation facing UNRWA in the West Bank and Gaza Strip was evolving rapidly. As the Palestinian Authority had taken greater responsibilities for education, health and social services, it had become UNRWA's exclusive interlocutor in the West Bank and Gaza Strip. At the same time, the effective running of Agency operations required the support of the Israeli authorities which remained in control of borders, customs, security and movement into and out of the Gaza Strip and the West Bank. Restrictions on movement and security measures by Israeli authorities had affected UNRWA operations, in particular causing delays in receiving equipment and supplies. However, in comparison to the previous year, there had been a marked reduction in the number of incursions into Agency installations by members of the Israeli security forces.

## The work of UNRWA

The UNRWA Commissioner-General, in his annual report, observed that during the ongoing Middle East peace process, UNRWA had broadened its efforts to substantively improve the socioeconomic conditions of Palestine refugees in the transitional period. UNRWA had entered into a close working relationship with the new Palestinian Authority, focusing on harmonizing mutual activities in education, health, and relief and social services in preparation for an eventual handover of the administration of those areas. As the seat of both the Chairman of PLO and the Palestinian Authority, the Gaza Strip was the focal point of UNRWA relations with the Palestinian leadership.

Palestine refugees in the self-rule areas, comprising 22 per cent of all refugees registered with UNRWA, benefited from the absence of daily tension that had characterized the period prior to the Israel-PLO agreements. UNRWA schools, clinics and community centres functioned with minimal disruption for the first time since the *intifadah* and Israeli countermeasures, which began in December 1987. UNRWA established coordination mechanisms with Palestinian Authority counterparts in the education, health, and relief and social services sectors. In education, the focus was on the admission of returnee children to UNRWA schools, the introduction of a tenth year in the basic education cycle, teacher training and vocational programmes. In health, priority issues included medical insurance, treatment of refugee patients in Palestinian Authority hospitals, school health services and immunization policies. Coordination in relief and social services was sought in the areas of direct relief assistance, housing and land use in Gaza camps, housing for returnees, and national plans for youth and children.

### Peace Implementation Programme

By mid-1995, most projects UNRWA had introduced through its Peace Implementation Programme (PIP) were under way.[21] A comprehensive investment programme begun in 1993 to improve infrastructure and stabilize socioeconomic conditions, PIP aimed at making the results of the peace process felt at the local level. Its main focus was infrastructure development—through construction and renovation of schools, clinics and community centres, rehabilitation of shelters, and provision of adequate sewage and drainage systems in camps. PIP also gave priority support to the Palestinian private sector through income-generation initiatives. It was estimated that during the first phase of PIP, which ended in September 1994, more than 5,500 jobs had been created in the Gaza Strip alone, each for an average period of four months. The Programme's second phase (PIP II) consisted of projects valued at $311 million in mid-1995, including $78 million in unfunded projects transferred from PIP I. PIP II was developed in conjunction with relevant ministries of the Palestinian Authority, as well as with the Palestinian Economic Council for Development and Reconstruction (PECDAR).

Special emphasis was placed on assisting the Palestinian Authority in addressing the needs of returnees, particularly additional schools and classrooms. In conjunction with local municipalities, UNRWA developed comprehensive project proposals for internal sewage and storm-water drainage systems, treatment plants and pumping stations for 11 camps in the West Bank and Gaza Strip, valued at more than $124 million. By 30 June 1995, the Agency had received $29.5 million in funds and pledges for PIP II, of which $24.5 million was for the Gaza Strip, $1 million for the West Bank and $4 million for the Agency's other three fields of operation.

A separately funded project, well under way by the end of 1995, was the construction of the 232-bed European Gaza Hospital, an UNRWA initiative financed by EU. Construction also began on the Gaza College of Nursing and Allied Health Sciences, to be affiliated with the Gaza Hospital. UNRWA also was improving and expanding infrastructure newly taken over by the Palestinian Authority from the Israeli civil administration, building one secondary school, renovating 14 Palestinian Authority schools, upgrading municipal garbage depository sites and undertaking maintenance on existing water and sewerage systems.

### Major service areas

#### Education

The UNRWA education programme, covering schools, vocational training and teacher education, in 1995 remained UNRWA's largest single activity, accounting for about half of the Agency's regular budget. More than 408,000 elementary, preparatory and secondary school pupils attended UNRWA's 644 schools, an increase of 10,000 pupils over the preceding school year. Vocational training, comprising two-year, post-preparatory trade courses and two-year, post-secondary technical courses, was available to some 4,500 persons, with some new courses introduced. UNRWA schools followed the host Governments' curricula and operated with assistance from UNESCO.

To improve academic achievement levels, UNRWA had developed remedial plans, including diagnostic tests, curriculum enrichment materials and self-learning kits. The Agency worked closely with the Palestinian Authority Ministry of Education in the Gaza Strip and the Jericho Area, with the Authority assuming control in 1995 of the school system formerly run by the Israeli civil administration. Following the establishment of the Authority, thousands of refugees had returned to the Gaza Strip from other countries in the region, markedly increasing the student population there. An UNRWA proposal to provide in-service training for 12,000 teaching staff in West Bank and Gaza Strip public schools was withdrawn after the Palestinian Authority undertook its own initiative in that regard. A joint study with the Palestinian Authority identified areas for improvement in vocational and technical training programmes in the West Bank and Gaza.

In Jordan, 202 UNRWA schools provided basic education to 149,932 pupils, 1,675 fewer than in the preceding year. The decrease was attributed to the transfer of refugee pupils to new government schools opened in or near refugee camps at the beginning of the academic year, which offered smaller class sizes, superior facilities and a five-day school week. By contrast, severely overcrowded UNRWA schools operated on a six-day week, with 93 per cent running on a double shift, effectively depriving pupils of extracurricular activities. A quarter of UNRWA schools were still using rented premises, usually with inadequate classroom space, laboratories, libraries and playgrounds. In 1995, UNRWA constructed a 20-classroom girls' school in Baqa'a camp and work progressed on six other schools, the last to be replaced by UNRWA in Jordan. All new schools were being provided with fully equipped computer laboratories. Special classes for children with learning difficulties were established in schools at the Marka and Souf camps. Some 600 disabled and slow learners were integrated into the regular education programme after attending remedial classes. In-service training was given to 365 UNRWA teachers, and pre-service teacher training was also provided. UNRWA's Amman and Wadi Seer training centres offered places to 1,224 students in trades and semi-professional courses. UNRWA awarded scholarships to 231 Palestine refugee students, including 89 women, to universities in Jordan.

The improved security situation in Lebanon allowed the 75 UNRWA schools there to operate without disruption, with no days lost owing to strikes and disturbances. A total of 35,207 pupils were enrolled in UNRWA elementary, preparatory and secondary schools, 1,560 pupils more than the preceding year. That unusually high increase was attributed to transfers from tuition-based private schools. The Siblin Training Centre provided vocational and technical instruction to 624 trainees. UNRWA in 1995 awarded 54 university scholarships to Palestine refugees in Lebanon.

Some 60,000 students were enrolled in 108 UNRWA elementary and preparatory schools in the Syrian Arab Republic in the 1994-1995 school year, a decrease of 520 pupils from the preceding year. Overcrowding remained a serious problem, with 98 per cent of elementary classes and 91 per cent of preparatory classes operating on a double-shift basis. UNRWA's Damascus Training Centre offered vocational courses and semi-professional courses to 767 trainees. The Agency provided university scholarships to 208 Palestine refugee students, including 74 women, to study at Syrian universities.

In the West Bank, 100 UNRWA schools served 44,573 pupils, about 2,000 more than during the preceding school year. The return of families to the West Bank after the establishment of the Palestinian Authority was considered the principal reason for the increase.

UNRWA reported that schools within the municipal boundary of Jerusalem were adversely affected by movement restrictions imposed in February 1994 on Palestinians holding West Bank identity cards. As a result, many West Bank residents employed as teachers or education staff at Jerusalem-area schools could not reach their place of work. To help compensate for lost teaching time and improve achievement levels, UNRWA offered remedial classes, particularly in core subjects such as reading, writing, mathematics and English. Three UNRWA training centres in the West Bank provided 1,248 vocational and technical training places. At the Ramallah Women's Training Centre, courses were offered in hairdressing, clothing production, business administration, ceramics production, social work and computer studies, as well as programmes to prepare for jobs as laboratory technicians, assistant pharmacists, physiotherapy assistants and executive secretaries. The Ramallah Men's Training Centre provided instruction in business administration, computer science, financial management and marketing. The Kalandia Training Centre offered training in the building, electrical and mechanical trades and post-secondary technical courses for construction technicians and land surveyors. A new workshop was constructed for a diesel engine and heavy equipment mechanics course. UNRWA awarded university scholarships to 150 West Bank students, including 88 women, to attend universities in the region.

In the Gaza Strip, UNRWA's 159 elementary and preparatory schools served 118,406 pupils, some 8,000 more than the preceding year. That sizeable increase was due to returning refugee families. To accommodate the increase, the Agency hired 276 extra teachers on one-year contracts.

UNRWA schools in the Gaza Strip continued to be overcrowded, with classes averaging 47.2 pupils, the highest classroom occupancy rate in UNRWA's five fields of operation. Many schools were still housed in cement-brick buildings dating from the 1950s and 1960s, originally built as temporary structures. Three schools operated on a triple-shift basis after some premises were declared unsafe.

Donor countries provided $27.7 million through PIP for expanding and upgrading educational infrastructure and other projects in Gaza. During the reporting period, construction was completed on 7 new school buildings and 2 specialized rooms; work was under way on an additional 21 schools and 86 more classrooms. At the Gaza training centre, 629 men and 25 women were enrolled in 16 two-year vocational and semi-professional courses. In response to growing demand for skilled labour in the local construction sector, the centre offered 12-week vocational courses in aluminium fabrication, concrete forming and plumbing. UNRWA awarded university scholarships to 220 Palestine refugee students from Gaza, including 102 women.

For the first time in more than 15 years, UNRWA teachers participated in administering secondary (*tawjihi*) examinations, in cooperation with colleagues from the Palestinian Authority.

Health

The Agency's network of 123 health centres or points provided a full range of preventive, curative, support and community health services, including paediatrics, obstetrics and gynecology, cardiology and ophthalmology. Special care was available for treatment of chest diseases and ear, nose and throat illnesses, as well as for the management of diabetes mellitus and hypertension. Maternal and child health programmes and family-planning services were available. Seventy-six centres offered comprehensive dental care; 84 had medical laboratories.

Some 6.5 million patient visits a year were handled by the Agency, with a relatively high average of 94 consultations per doctor per day and a continuing heavy workload for dental consultations and other support services. The UNRWA health programme employed 3,296 professional and support staff, the majority locally recruited Palestinians. UNRWA continued to cooperate with WHO, which provided staff, including the Director of Health.

In spring 1995, UNRWA participated in a national immunization campaign against poliomyelitis throughout its areas of operations, implemented according to a WHO regional strategy in coordination with UNICEF and local health authorities. In all, 200,000 refugee children received oral polio vaccines. UNRWA also developed a special curriculum on HIV/AIDS prevention for schools in coordination with WHO, and it developed a youth-centred programme against tobacco use.

More than 205,000 children under three years of age, 73,000 pregnant women and 31,000 family-planning acceptors received health care at UNRWA mother and child health and family-planning clinics. Supplementary nutritional assistance was provided to 74,000 pregnant and nursing women and 121,000 children under the age of two; immunization and growth monitoring were provided to children under the age of three. An expanded maternal health and family-planning programme in the West Bank and Gaza Strip, under joint implementation since 1992 by UNRWA and UNFPA, was deemed successful upon completion of its implementation.

The Agency participated in a tripartite mission in March 1995 to assess the needs of the Palestinian health authorities. As a result, a strategic plan and operational framework for a sustainable women's health programme, including reproductive health and family planning, was developed.

To ensure acceptable environmental health standards within refugee communities, UNRWA provided services related to sewage disposal, storm water run-off, safe drinking water, refuse disposal, insect control and rodent infestation. Feasibility studies and preliminary designs for improving sewerage, drainage and solid-waste management were completed for 11 camps in the West Bank and Gaza Strip. UNRWA undertook efforts to strengthen primary health-care facilities and sought more economical options for provision of essential hospital care.

In preparing for an eventual handover of UNRWA's health-care system to the Palestinian Authority, the Agency focused on maintaining and upgrading infrastructure at the primary level, coordinating and harmonizing health policies and services with those of the Palestinian Authority, and gradually re-deploying resources to Palestinian Authority hospitals. Significant progress was achieved during the reporting year in the construction of Gaza General Hospital and other health facilities which would become part of the Palestinian health infrastructure.

### Relief and social services

UNRWA's relief and social services programme continued to provide direct relief to those refugees unable to meet their own life-sustaining needs. Under the UNRWA special hardship programme, more than 181,000 refugees were receiving basic bimonthly food rations, shelter rehabilitation, subsidized medical care, preferential access to vocational training and assistance in establishing income-generating projects. Many other families were reported as facing extreme socio-economic difficulties but were ineligible for the programme, since their problem stemmed not from the absence of an employable male adult, but from the lack of employment opportunities, especially in the

Gaza Strip and Lebanon. Moreover, for the first time in several years there was marked growth in demand for welfare assistance from refugees in Jordan. Cash assistance was provided on an ad hoc basis to special hardship families facing extreme difficulty.

More than 4,000 shelters were upgraded—mostly in the West Bank and Gaza Strip—as part of UNRWA's multimillion dollar programme to rehabilitate substandard refugee housing. The funds were provided under PIP, which as at 30 June 1995 had received a total of $31.2 million for that purpose. The Agency continued to cooperate with the Palestinian Authority in studying how to harmonize direct relief assistance programmes, and they were coordinating other issues such as shelter rehabilitation, land use and housing for returnees.

In Lebanon, UNRWA's main concern was the rehousing of displaced refugees evicted from properties where they had been illegally squatting. Under the Palestinian Women's Initiative Fund, four new projects provided for functional literacy classes in Lebanon, training in maintenance and repair of sewing and knitting machines in Gaza, a community-run kindergarten at a women's programme centre in the West Bank, and a food production unit in a refugee camp in Jordan. A fund-raising campaign was launched in February for phase two of the Fund, which supported projects aimed at self-reliance for women and women's institutions.

Activities within UNRWA community centres included promotion of legal literacy, civic education and early childhood development through women's programme centres; linking community rehabilitation programmes with mainstream UNRWA services, especially the integration of disabled children into the regular school education system; and participation in such multidisciplinary campaigns as the Agency's HIV/AIDS awareness campaign. UNRWA refugee community centres provided training, technical assistance and partial financial support to 17,000 persons in 71 women's programme centres and 29 community rehabilitation centres in the five fields of operation, as well as 27 youth activity centres in the West Bank and Gaza Strip.

Increasing attention was given to income-generation initiatives. UNRWA reported that as a result of the Persian Gulf War, remittances from expatriate workers to their families had dwindled, eroding household purchasing power and causing local economies to stagnate. Simultaneously, growing domestic pressure on Governments of the region had significantly reduced employment opportunities for refugees, particularly in Lebanon, the West Bank and Gaza Strip. UNRWA's revolving loan fund for small businesses, initiated in 1991, created employment for Palestine refugees by making finance capital available at reasonable interest rates to be used to expand existing enterprises or establish new ones. The programme aimed to support small-scale entrepreneurs in the formal and informal sectors of the economy producing goods for sale locally and abroad. Often ineligible for formal banking credit, most entrepreneurs raised investment capital from individual and family savings. Since 1991, the revolving loan fund had made loans to more than 800 small-scale enterprises and had acquired a total capital base of $7.2 million. In many cases, enterprises were owned and managed by skilled labourers who had previously been unemployed. The leading field-based income-generation programme was in Gaza, which utilized more capital than the other three fields served by UNRWA combined. Its capital base was more than $4 million; the overall loan recovery rate was 98 per cent.

In Gaza, UNRWA also operated a solidarity-group lending programme, providing credit to women working in micro-enterprises and as street vendors. Some 400 loans averaging $400 were provided to individual women organized in 74 solidarity groups.

UNRWA's poverty alleviation programme was established in 1993 for special hardship cases of working age. While the revolving loan fund was intended to generate employment opportunities within the refugee community at large, the poverty elimination programme specifically sought to raise the income of the neediest families so they could be removed from the special hardship rolls. The programme included skill-training, apprenticeships and access to credit. Low-interest loans averaging $3,000 were provided on an individual, family or group-guaranteed basis for the establishment of self-support projects. To assist loan applicants, courses on starting a business were offered in the West Bank, Gaza Strip and Jordan. Special attention was devoted to the needs of women income-earners and to the development of sustainable income-generating enterprises to support affiliated community organizations.

In the wake of the restrictions on movement in the Gaza Strip in early 1995, UNRWA reported serious hardship to many families, and distributed flour rations to 26,000 families in the West Bank and 14,000 families in the Gaza Strip. In Lebanon, some basic commodities and cash assistance were given to refugee families with emergency needs.

## Future of UNRWA

At an informal meeting with major donor and host Governments, held in Amman, Jordan, in March 1995, UNRWA proposed a five-year financial and planning horizon, coinciding with the interim period set out in the Declaration of Principles, to establish for donors, host countries and the Palestinian Authority a financial framework for UNRWA services during the interim period. A clear consensus arose that UNRWA services would continue to be required until a political solution to the refugee problem was found. Participants considered it premature to place a time limit on UNRWA's existence, as the period for which its services would be required could not be predicted until there was such an agreed solution. Participants concurred that the eventual transfer of UNRWA operations to the Palestinian Authority should be made when political, economic and financial conditions so permitted, and at the Authority's request. Until then, UNRWA should focus on harmonization of services and coordination and cooperation with other agencies operating in the field. (See also "UNRWA financing" below.)

### Move to Gaza

UNRWA took steps to relocate its Vienna headquarters to Gaza, in accordance with a decision of the Secretary-General[22] endorsed by the General Assembly in December 1994.[23] UNRWA developed a budget and plan for the move, including the design of a new headquarters building in Gaza town. The Agency estimated the move would cost $13.5 million, to be funded through special voluntary contributions. By mid-1995, over $4 million in pledges or contributions having been received, construction of the new headquarters was begun.

## General Assembly resolutions related to Palestine refugees

On 6 December, the General Assembly adopted seven resolutions relating to Palestine refugees: assistance to Palestine refugees (50/28 A); financing of UNRWA (50/28 B); displaced persons (50/28 C); scholarships for higher education and vocational training (50/28 D); operations of UNRWA (50/28 E); revenues from Palestinian refugee properties (50/28 F); and the proposed University of Jerusalem "Al-Quds" for Palestine refugees (50/28 G).

By an 8 June note,[24] Israel stated that its position on the resolutions on Palestine refugees had been set forth in successive annual replies, the latest of which was included in a 1994 report by the Secretary-General.[25] Israel also said that while the number of resolutions regarding UNRWA had been reduced in the previous year from 10 to 7, their content remained occupied with political issues irrelevant to the Agency's work. While Israel believed that UNRWA could play an important role in promoting the social and economic advancement foreseen in agreements between Israel and PLO, and accordingly looked forward to continuing cooperation with UNRWA, it considered it essential that the Assembly consolidate the UNRWA resolutions into one directly related to the Agency's humanitarian tasks.

### General aspects

The General Assembly on 6 December adopted **resolution 50/28 E.**

**Operations of the United Nations Relief and Works Agency for Palestine Refugees in the Near East**

*The General Assembly,*

*Recalling* its resolutions 194(III) of 11 December 1948, 212(III) of 19 November 1948, 302(IV) of 8 December 1949 and all subsequent related resolutions,

*Recalling also* the relevant Security Council resolutions,

*Having considered* the report of the Commissioner-General of the United Nations Relief and Works Agency for Palestine Refugees in the Near East covering the period from 1 July 1994 to 30 June 1995,

*Taking note* of the letter dated 4 October 1995 from the Chairman of the Advisory Commission of the United Nations Relief and Works Agency for Palestine Refugees in the Near East addressed to the Commissioner-General, contained in the report of the Commissioner-General,

*Having considered* the reports of the Secretary-General submitted in pursuance of its resolutions 48/40 E, 48/40 H and 48/40 J of 10 December 1993 and 49/35 C of 9 December 1994,

*Recalling* Articles 100, 104 and 105 of the Charter of the United Nations and the Convention on the Privileges and Immunities of the United Nations,

*Affirming* the applicability of the Geneva Convention relative to the Protection of Civilian Persons in Time of War, of 12 August 1949, to the Palestinian territory occupied since 1967, including Jerusalem,

*Aware* of the fact that Palestine refugees have, for over four decades, lost their homes, lands and means of livelihood,

*Also aware* of the continuing needs of Palestine refugees throughout the occupied Palestinian territory and in the other fields of operation, namely in Lebanon, Jordan and the Syrian Arab Republic,

*Expressing its appreciation* for the role which has been played by the United Nations Relief and Works Agency for Palestine Refugees in the Near East over the years in the service of the Palestine refugees, and aware of the importance of its presence and the increase in its work in the new circumstances,

*Further aware* of the valuable work done by the refugee affairs officers of the Agency in providing protection to the Palestinian people, in particular Palestine refugees,

*Deeply concerned* about the critical financial situation of the Agency and its effect on the continuity of provision of necessary Agency services to the Palestine refugees, including the emergency-related programmes,

*Aware* of the initiation of the new peace implementation programme of the Agency,

*Convinced* of the necessity of the transfer of the headquarters of the Agency to the occupied Palestinian territory as part of the area of operation of the Agency,

*Welcoming* the signing in Washington on 13 September 1993 of the Declaration of Principles on Interim Self-Government Arrangements by the Government of the State of Israel and the Palestine Liberation Organization, and the subsequent implementation agreements, including the Agreement on the Gaza Strip and the Jericho Area signed at Cairo on 4 May 1994 and the Interim Agreement on the West Bank and the Gaza Strip signed in Washington on 28 September 1995,

*Taking note* of the agreement reached on 24 June 1994, embodied in an exchange of letters between the Agency and the Palestine Liberation Organization,

*Recalling* its decision 48/417 of 10 December 1993 on the establishment of a working relationship between the Advisory Commission of the Agency and the Palestine Liberation Organization,

1. *Expresses its appreciation* to the Commissioner-General of the United Nations Relief and Works Agency for Palestine Refugees in the Near East, as well as to all the staff of the Agency, for their tireless efforts and valuable work;

2. *Expresses its appreciation also* to the Advisory Commission of the United Nations Relief and Works Agency for Palestine Refugees in the Near East, and requests it to continue its efforts and to keep the General Assembly informed on its activities, including the full implementation of decision 48/417;

3. *Acknowledges* the support of the host Governments and the Palestine Liberation Organization for the Agency in the discharge of its duties;

4. *Calls upon* Israel, the occupying Power, to accept the *de jure* applicability of the Geneva Convention relative to the Protection of Civilian Persons in Time of War, of 12 August 1949, and to abide scrupulously by its provisions;

5. *Also calls upon* Israel to abide by Articles 100, 104 and 105 of the Charter of the United Nations and the Convention on the Privileges and Immunities of the United Nations with regard to the safety of the personnel of the Agency and the protection of its institutions and the safeguarding of the security of the facilities of the Agency in the occupied Palestinian territory, including Jerusalem;

6. *Calls once again upon* the Government of Israel to compensate the Agency for damages to its property and facilities resulting from actions by the Israeli side;

7. *Requests* the Commissioner-General to proceed with the issuance of identification cards for Palestine refugees and their descendants in the occupied Palestinian territory;

8. *Notes* that the new context created by the signing of the Declaration of Principles on Interim Self-Government Arrangements by the Government of the State of Israel and the Palestine Liberation Organization and subsequent implementation agreements has had major consequences for the activities of the Agency, which is henceforth called upon, in close cooperation with the United Nations Special Coordinator in the Occupied Territories, the specialized agencies and the World Bank, to continue to contribute towards the development of economic and social stability in the occupied territory;

9. *Notes also* that the functioning of the Agency remains essential in all fields of operation;

10. *Notes further* the significant success of the peace implementation programme of the Agency during the first year following the signing of the Declaration of Principles;

11. *Urges* all States, specialized agencies and non-governmental organizations to continue and to increase their contributions to the Agency so as to ease current financial constraints and to support the Agency in maintaining the provision of the most basic and effective assistance to the Palestine refugees.

General Assembly resolution 50/28 E

6 December 1995      Meeting 82      146-2-3 (recorded vote)

Approved by Fourth Committee (A/50/605) by recorded vote (138-2-3), 30 November (meeting 25); 10-nation draft (A/C.4/50/L.15); agenda item 84.
*Sponsors:* Djibouti, Egypt, Indonesia, Jordan, Malaysia, Senegal, Sudan, Tunisia, United Arab Emirates, Yemen.
*Meeting numbers.* GA 50th session: 4th Committee 12, 13, 25; plenary 82.

Recorded vote in Assembly as follows:

*In favour:* Afghanistan, Albania, Algeria, Antigua and Barbuda, Argentina, Armenia, Australia, Austria, Azerbaijan, Bahamas, Bahrain, Bangladesh, Barbados, Belarus, Belgium, Belize, Benin, Bolivia, Bosnia and Herzegovina, Botswana, Brazil, Brunei Darussalam, Bulgaria, Burkina Faso, Burundi, Cambodia, Cameroon, Canada, Cape Verde, Chad, Chile, China, Colombia, Congo, Côte d'Ivoire, Croatia, Cuba, Cyprus, Czech Republic, Democratic People's Republic of Korea, Denmark, Djibouti, Dominica, Ecuador, Egypt, El Salvador, Eritrea, Estonia, Ethiopia, Fiji, Finland, France, Gabon, Georgia, Germany, Ghana, Greece, Guatemala, Guinea, Guyana, Haiti, Honduras, Hungary, Iceland, India, Indonesia, Iran, Ireland, Italy, Jamaica, Japan, Jordan, Kazakstan, Kenya, Kuwait, Lao People's Democratic Republic, Latvia, Lebanon, Libyan Arab Jamahiriya, Liechtenstein, Lithuania, Luxembourg, Malawi, Malaysia, Maldives, Mali, Malta, Mauritius, Mexico, Monaco, Mongolia, Myanmar, Nepal, Netherlands, New Zealand, Nicaragua, Niger, Nigeria, Oman, Pakistan, Panama, Papua New Guinea, Paraguay, Peru, Philippines, Poland, Portugal, Qatar, Republic of Korea, Republic of Moldova, Romania, Saint Lucia, Samoa, Saudi Arabia, Senegal, Sierra Leone, Singapore, Slovakia, Slovenia, Solomon Islands, South Africa, Spain, Sri Lanka, Sudan, Suriname, Swaziland, Sweden, Syrian Arab Republic, Thailand, the former Yugoslav Republic of Macedonia, Togo, Trinidad and Tobago, Tunisia, Turkey, Uganda, Ukraine, United Arab Emirates, United Kingdom, Uruguay, Vanuatu, Venezuela, Viet Nam, Yemen, Zambia, Zimbabwe.

*Against:* Israel, United States.

*Abstaining:* Marshall Islands, Micronesia, Russian Federation.

Explaining its abstention, the Russian Federation said in the Committee that the text went beyond UNRWA's strictly humanitarian mandate.

On 6 December 1995, the General Assembly adopted **resolution 50/28 A**.

### Assistance to Palestine refugees

*The General Assembly,*

*Recalling* its resolution 49/35 A of 9 December 1994 and all its previous resolutions on the question, including resolution 194(III) of 11 December 1948,

*Taking note* of the report of the Commissioner-General of the United Nations Relief and Works Agency for Palestine Refugees in the Near East covering the period from 1 July 1994 to 30 June 1995,

*Welcoming* the signature by the Government of the State of Israel and the Palestine Liberation Organization of the Declaration of Principles on Interim Self-Government Arrangements in Washington on 13 September 1993,

*Welcoming also* the signature by the Government of the State of Israel and the Palestine Liberation Organization of the Interim Agreement on the West Bank and the Gaza Strip in Washington on 28 September 1995,

*Commending* the work of the Multilateral Working Group on Refugees of the Middle East peace process,

1. *Notes with regret* that repatriation or compensation of the refugees, as provided for in paragraph 11 of its resolution 194(III), has not yet been effected and that, therefore, the situation of the refugees continues to be a matter of concern;

2. *Expresses its thanks* to the Commissioner-General and to all the staff of the United Nations Relief and Works Agency for Palestine Refugees in the Near East, recognizing that the Agency is doing all it can within the limits of available resources, and also expresses its thanks to the specialized agencies and to private organizations for their valuable work in assisting refugees;

3. *Notes with regret* that the United Nations Conciliation Commission for Palestine has been unable to find a means of achieving progress in the implementation of paragraph 11 of resolution 194(III), and requests the Commission to exert continued efforts towards the implementation of that paragraph and to report to the General Assembly as appropriate, but not later than 1 September 1996;

4. *Notes* the significant success of the peace implementation programme of the Agency since the signing of the Declaration of Principles on Interim Self-Government Arrangements;

5. *Urges* all Member States to extend and expedite aid and assistance with a view to the economic and social development of the Palestinian people and the occupied territories;

6. *Also notes* the progress achieved to date in the transfer of the Agency's headquarters to its area of operations, and requests the Secretary-General, in consultation with the Commissioner-General, to present to the Working Group on the Financing of the United Nations Relief and Works Agency for Palestine Refugees in the Near East an updated plan for the transfer;

7. *Reiterates its concern* about the continuing seriousness of the financial position of the Agency, as outlined in the report of the Commissioner-General;

8. *Notes with profound concern* that the structural deficit problem confronting the Agency portends an almost certain decline in the living conditions of Palestine refugees and therefore has possible consequences for the peace process;

9. *Calls upon* all Governments, as a matter of urgency, to make the most generous efforts possible to meet the anticipated needs of the Agency, including the costs of moving the headquarters to Gaza, and urges non-contributing Governments to contribute regularly and contributing Governments to consider increasing their regular contributions;

10. *Decides* to extend the mandate of the Agency until 30 June 1999, without prejudice to the provisions of paragraph 11 of resolution 194(III).

General Assembly resolution 50/28 A

6 December 1995      Meeting 82      145-1-1 (recorded vote)

Approved by Fourth Committee (A/50/605) by recorded vote (140-1-1), 30 November (meeting 25); 11-nation draft (A/C.4/50/L.11); agenda item 84.
*Meeting numbers.* GA 50th session: 4th Committee 12, 13, 25; plenary 82.

Recorded vote in Assembly as follows:

*In favour:* Afghanistan, Albania, Algeria, Antigua and Barbuda, Argentina, Armenia, Australia, Austria, Azerbaijan, Bahamas, Bahrain, Bangladesh, Barbados, Belarus, Belgium, Belize, Benin, Bolivia, Bosnia and Herzegovina, Botswana, Brazil, Brunei Darussalam, Bulgaria, Burkina Faso, Cambodia, Cameroon, Canada, Chad, Chile, China, Colombia, Congo, Côte d'Ivoire, Croatia, Cuba, Cyprus, Czech Republic, Democratic People's Republic of Korea, Denmark, Djibouti, Dominica, Ecuador, Egypt, Eritrea, Estonia, Ethiopia, Fiji, Finland, France, Gabon, Georgia, Germany, Ghana, Greece, Guatemala, Guinea, Guyana, Haiti, Honduras, Hungary, Iceland, India, Indonesia, Iran, Ireland, Italy, Jamaica, Japan, Jordan, Kazakstan, Kenya, Kuwait, Lao People's Democratic Republic, Lebanon, Libyan Arab Jamahiriya, Liechtenstein, Lithuania, Luxembourg, Malawi, Malaysia, Maldives, Mali, Malta, Marshall Islands, Mauritius, Mexico, Micronesia, Monaco, Mongolia, Morocco, Myanmar, Nepal, Netherlands, New Zealand,

Nicaragua, Niger, Nigeria, Oman, Pakistan, Panama, Papua New Guinea, Paraguay, Peru, Philippines, Poland, Portugal, Qatar, Republic of Korea, Republic of Moldova, Romania, Russian Federation, Saint Lucia, Samoa, Saudi Arabia, Senegal, Sierra Leone, Singapore, Slovakia, Slovenia, Solomon Islands, South Africa, Spain, Sri Lanka, Sudan, Suriname, Swaziland, Sweden, Syrian Arab Republic, Thailand, the former Yugoslav Republic of Macedonia, Togo, Trinidad and Tobago, Tunisia, Turkey, Uganda, Ukraine, United Arab Emirates, United Kingdom, Uruguay, Vanuatu, Venezuela, Viet Nam, Yemen, Zambia, Zimbabwe.

*Against:* Israel.

*Abstaining:* United States.

In the Committee, Spain, on behalf of EU, said that members voted for the text as UNRWA was in a prominent position to complement and consolidate the peace process. Unfortunately, support for the renewal of UNRWA's mandate had not been unanimous and therefore EU had not been able to submit the draft resolution as in previous years.

The United States, saying that it would continue to support important educational, health, social and humanitarian programmes of UNRWA, was disappointed that efforts to reach a consensus on the renewal of the Agency mandate had not been successful. Sponsors had chosen to introduce the text in a manner that had forced the United States to abstain. UNRWA's mission should not be tied to a political agenda.

Israel said it had voted against the text, as it had addressed political issues which had nothing to do with UNRWA and were contrary to the spirit of the agreements between Israel and Palestinians. However, it was important for UNRWA to continue providing humanitarian assistance to Palestine refugees and Israel supported the proposed extension of the Agency's mandate.

## Displaced persons

The Secretary-General reported[24] on 20 September on compliance with a 1994 General Assembly resolution[26] calling for the accelerated return of all persons displaced as a result of the June 1967 and subsequent hostilities to their homes or former places of residence in the territories occupied by Israel since 1967.

He said that since the Agency was not involved in arrangements for either refugees or displaced persons not registered with it, UNRWA information was based on requests by returning registered refugees for transfer of their entitlements for services to their areas of return. The Agency was unable to estimate the total number of displaced inhabitants who had returned, as it kept records only of registered refugees, which might be incomplete, particularly with regard to the location of such refugees. Displaced refugees known by UNRWA to have returned to the West Bank and the Gaza Strip since June 1967 numbered about 14,170. Between 1 July 1994 and 30 June 1995, 244 registered refugees had returned to the West Bank, and 726 to the Gaza Strip. Some of the refugees might not have been displaced in 1967, but might be family members

of a displaced registered refugee whom they either had accompanied on return or joined later.

**GENERAL ASSEMBLY ACTION**

On 6 December, the General Assembly adopted **resolution 50/28 C**.

### Persons displaced as a result of the June 1967 and subsequent hostilities

*The General Assembly,*

*Recalling* its resolutions 2252(ES-V) of 4 July 1967, 2341 B(XXI) of 19 December 1967 and all subsequent related resolutions,

*Recalling also* Security Council resolutions 237(1967) of 14 June 1967 and 259(1968) of 27 September 1968,

*Taking note* of the report of the Secretary-General submitted in pursuance of its resolution 49/35 C of 9 December 1994,

*Taking note also* of the report of the Commissioner-General of the United Nations Relief and Works Agency for Palestine Refugees in the Near East covering the period from 1 July 1994 to 30 June 1995,

*Concerned* about the continuing human suffering resulting from the June 1967 and subsequent hostilities,

*Taking note* of the relevant provisions of the Declaration of Principles on Interim Self-Government Arrangements, signed in Washington on 13 September 1993 by the Government of the State of Israel and the Palestine Liberation Organization, with regard to the modalities for the admission of persons displaced in 1967,

1. *Reaffirms* the right of all persons displaced as a result of the June 1967 and subsequent hostilities to return to their homes or former places of residence in the territories occupied by Israel since 1967;

2. *Expresses the hope* for an accelerated return of displaced persons through the mechanism agreed upon by the parties in article XII of the Declaration of Principles on Interim Self-Government Arrangements;

3. *Endorses,* in the meanwhile, the efforts of the Commissioner-General of the United Nations Relief and Works Agency for Palestine Refugees in the Near East to continue to provide humanitarian assistance, as far as practicable, on an emergency basis, and as a temporary measure, to persons in the area who are currently displaced and in serious need of continued assistance as a result of the June 1967 and subsequent hostilities;

4. *Strongly appeals* to all Governments and to organizations and individuals to contribute generously to the Agency and to the other intergovernmental and non-governmental organizations concerned for the above purposes;

5. *Requests* the Secretary-General, after consulting with the Commissioner-General, to report to the General Assembly before its fifty-first session on the progress made with regard to the implementation of the present resolution.

General Assembly resolution 50/28 C

6 December 1995　　　　Meeting 82　　　　147-2 (recorded vote)

Approved by Fourth Committee (A/50/605) by recorded vote (140-2-0), 30 November (meeting 25); 10-nation draft (A/C.4/50/L.13); agenda item 84.

*Sponsors:* Brunei Darussalam, Djibouti, Egypt, Indonesia, Jordan, Malaysia, Sudan, Tunisia, United Arab Emirates, Yemen.

*Meeting numbers.* GA 50th session: 4th Committee 12, 13, 25; plenary 82.

Recorded vote in Assembly as follows:

*In favour:* Afghanistan, Albania, Algeria, Antigua and Barbuda, Argentina, Armenia, Australia, Austria, Azerbaijan, Bahamas, Bahrain, Bangladesh, Barbados, Belarus, Belgium, Belize, Benin, Bolivia, Bosnia and Herzegovina, Botswana, Brazil, Brunei Darussalam, Bulgaria, Burkina Faso, Burundi, Cambodia, Cameroon, Canada, Chad, Chile, China, Colombia, Congo, Côte d'Ivoire, Croatia, Cuba, Cyprus, Czech Republic, Democratic People's Republic of Korea, Denmark, Djibouti, Dominica, Ecuador, Egypt, El Salvador, Eritrea, Estonia, Ethiopia, Fiji, Finland, France, Gabon, Georgia, Germany, Ghana, Greece, Guatemala, Guinea, Guyana, Haiti, Honduras, Hungary, Iceland, India, Indonesia, Iran, Ireland, Italy, Jamaica, Japan, Jordan, Kazakstan, Kenya, Kuwait, Lao People's Democratic Republic, Lebanon, Libyan Arab Jamahiriya, Liechtenstein, Lithuania, Luxembourg, Malawi, Malaysia, Maldives, Mali, Malta, Marshall Islands, Mauritius, Mexico, Micronesia, Monaco, Mongolia, Morocco, Myanmar, Nepal, Netherlands, New Zealand, Nicaragua, Niger, Nigeria, Oman, Pakistan, Panama, Papua New Guinea, Paraguay, Peru, Philippines, Poland, Portugal, Qatar, Republic of Korea, Republic of Moldova, Romania, Russian Federation, Saint Lucia, Samoa, Saudi Arabia, Senegal, Sierra Leone, Singapore, Slovakia, Slovenia, Solomon Islands, South Africa, Spain, Sri Lanka, Sudan, Suriname, Swaziland, Sweden, Syrian Arab Republic, Thailand, the former Yugoslav Republic of Macedonia, Togo, Trinidad and Tobago, Tunisia, Turkey, Uganda, Ukraine, United Arab Emirates, United Kingdom, Uruguay, Vanuatu, Venezuela, Viet Nam, Yemen, Zambia, Zimbabwe.

*Against:* Israel, United States.

### Education, training and scholarships

In September, the Secretary-General reported[27] on responses to the General Assembly's 1994 appeal[28] to augment special allocations for scholarships and grants to Palestine refugees, for which UNRWA acted as recipient and trustee.

In the 1994/95 academic year, Japan offered 10 vocational fellowships for study in that country to Palestine refugees in UNRWA's employ. Under a five-year grant of $400,000 made by Japan in 1992, 205 Palestinian students were participating in the UNRWA university programme in 1994/95. Contributions from Switzerland in 1994 and 1995 totalling nearly $500,000 allowed some 250 Palestinians to pursue university studies. UNRWA and the United World Colleges provided four scholarships in 1995.

**GENERAL ASSEMBLY ACTION**

On 6 December, the General Assembly adopted **resolution 50/28 D**.

**Offers by Member States of grants and scholarships for higher education, including vocational training, for Palestine refugees**

*The General Assembly,*

*Recalling* its resolution 212(III) of 19 November 1948 on assistance to Palestine refugees,

*Recalling also* its resolutions 35/13 B of 3 November 1980, 36/146 H of 16 December 1981, 37/120 D of 16 December 1982, 38/83 D of 15 December 1983, 39/99 D of 14 December 1984, 40/165 D of 16 December 1985, 41/69 D of 3 December 1986, 42/69 D of 2 December 1987, 43/57 D of 6 December 1988, 44/47 D of 8 December 1989, 45/73 D of 11 December 1990, 46/46 D of 9 December 1991, 47/69 D of 14 December 1992, 48/40 D of 10 December 1993 and 49/35 D of 9 December 1994,

*Cognizant* of the fact that the Palestine refugees have, for the last four decades, lost their homes, lands and means of livelihood,

*Having considered* the report of the Secretary-General,

*Having also considered* the report of the Commissioner-General of the United Nations Relief and Works Agency for Palestine Refugees in the Near East covering the period from 1 July 1994 to 30 June 1995,

1. *Urges* all States to respond to the appeal in its resolution 32/90 F of 13 December 1977 and reiterated in subsequent relevant resolutions in a manner commensurate with the needs of Palestine refugees for higher education, including vocational training;

2. *Strongly appeals* to all States, specialized agencies and non-governmental organizations to augment the special allocations for grants and scholarships to Palestine refugees, in addition to their contributions to the regular budget of the United Nations Relief and Works Agency for Palestine Refugees in the Near East;

3. *Expresses its appreciation* to all Governments, specialized agencies and non-governmental organizations that responded favourably to its resolutions 41/69 D, 42/69 D, 43/57 D, 44/47 D, 45/73 D, 46/46 D, 47/69 D, 48/40 D and 49/35 D;

4. *Invites* the relevant specialized agencies and other organizations of the United Nations system to continue, within their respective spheres of competence, to extend assistance for higher education to Palestine refugee students;

5. *Appeals* to all States, specialized agencies and the United Nations University to contribute generously to the Palestinian universities in the Palestinian territory occupied by Israel since 1967, including, in due course, the proposed University of Jerusalem "Al-Quds" for Palestine refugees;

6. *Appeals also* to all States, specialized agencies and other international bodies to contribute towards the establishment of vocational training centres for Palestine refugees;

7. *Requests* the Agency to act as the recipient and trustee for the special allocations for grants and scholarships and to award them to qualified Palestine refugee candidates;

8. *Requests* the Secretary-General to report to the General Assembly at its fifty-first session on the implementation of the present resolution.

General Assembly resolution 50/28 D

6 December 1995     Meeting 82     150-0-1 (recorded vote)

Approved by Fourth Committee (A/50/605) by recorded vote (142-0-1), 30 November (meeting 25); 12-nation draft (A/C.4/50/L.14); agenda item 84.
*Meeting numbers.* GA 50th session: 4th Committee 12, 13, 25; plenary 82.

Recorded vote in Assembly as follows:

*In favour:* Afghanistan, Albania, Algeria, Antigua and Barbuda, Argentina, Armenia, Australia, Austria, Azerbaijan, Bahamas, Bahrain, Bangladesh, Barbados, Belarus, Belgium, Belize, Benin, Bolivia, Bosnia and Herzegovina, Botswana, Brazil, Brunei Darussalam, Bulgaria, Burkina Faso, Burundi, Cambodia, Cameroon, Canada, Cape Verde, Chad, Chile, China, Colombia, Congo, Côte d'Ivoire, Croatia, Cuba, Cyprus, Czech Republic, Democratic People's Republic of Korea, Denmark, Djibouti, Dominica, Ecuador, Egypt, El Salvador, Eritrea, Estonia, Ethiopia, Fiji, Finland, France, Gabon, Georgia, Germany, Ghana, Greece, Guatemala, Guinea, Guyana, Haiti, Honduras, Hungary, Iceland, India, Indonesia, Iran, Ireland, Italy, Jamaica, Japan, Jordan, Kazakstan, Kenya, Kuwait, Lao People's Democratic Republic, Lebanon, Libyan Arab Jamahiriya, Liechtenstein, Lithuania, Luxembourg, Madagascar, Malawi, Malaysia, Maldives, Mali, Malta, Marshall Islands, Mauritius, Mexico, Micronesia, Monaco, Mongolia, Morocco, Myanmar, Nepal, Netherlands, New Zealand, Nicaragua, Niger, Nigeria, Oman, Pakistan, Panama, Papua New Guinea, Paraguay, Peru, Philippines, Poland, Portugal, Qatar, Republic of Korea, Republic of Moldova, Romania, Russian Federation, Saint Lucia, Samoa, Saudi Arabia, Senegal, Sierra Leone, Singapore, Slovakia, Slovenia, Solomon Islands, South Africa, Spain, Sri Lanka, Sudan, Suriname, Swaziland, Sweden, Syrian Arab Republic, Thailand, the former Yugoslav Republic of Macedonia, Togo, Trinidad and Tobago, Tunisia, Turkey, Uganda, Ukraine, United Arab Emirates, United Kingdom, United States, Uruguay, Vanuatu, Venezuela, Viet Nam, Yemen, Zambia, Zimbabwe.

*Against:* None.

*Abstaining:* Israel.

### Proposed University of Jerusalem "Al-Quds"

In keeping with a General Assembly request of 1994,[29] the Secretary-General reported[30] in October 1995 on the proposal to establish a university for Palestine refugees at Jerusalem. First considered by the Assembly in 1980,[31] it had been the subject of annual reports by the Secretary-General.

To assist in the preparation of a feasibility study and at the Secretary-General's request, the Rector of the United Nations University asked Dr. Mihaly Simai to visit the area and meet with competent Israeli officials. By a note verbale of 11 September, the Secretary-General requested Israel to facilitate the expert's visit.

Israel replied on 18 September that its position remained unchanged. It had voted consistently against resolutions on the proposed university, whose sponsors, it said, sought to exploit higher education for political purposes extraneous to genuine academic pursuits. Accordingly, Israel was of the opinion that the proposed visit would serve no useful purpose.

The Secretary-General reported that it had not been possible to complete the feasibility study as planned.

**GENERAL ASSEMBLY ACTION**

On 6 December, the General Assembly adopted **resolution 50/28 G**.

#### University of Jerusalem "Al-Quds" for Palestine refugees

*The General Assembly,*

*Recalling* its resolutions 36/146 G of 16 December 1981, 37/120 C of 16 December 1982, 38/83 K of 15 December 1983, 39/99 K of 14 December 1984, 40/165 D and K of 16 December 1985, 41/69 K of 3 December 1986, 42/69 K of 2 December 1987, 43/57 J of 6 December 1988, 44/47 J of 8 December 1989, 45/73 J of 11 December 1990, 46/46 J of 9 December 1991, 47/69 J of 14 December 1992, 48/40 I of 10 December 1993 and 49/35 G of 9 December 1994,

*Having considered* the report of the Secretary-General,

*Having also considered* the report of the Commissioner-General of the United Nations Relief and Works Agency for Palestine Refugees in the Near East covering the period from 1 July 1994 to 30 June 1995,

1. *Emphasizes* the need for strengthening the educational system in the Palestinian territory occupied by Israel since 5 June 1967, including Jerusalem, and specifically the need for the establishment of the proposed university;

2. *Requests* the Secretary-General to continue to take all necessary measures for establishing the University of Jerusalem "Al-Quds", in accordance with General Assembly resolution 35/13 B of 3 November 1980, giving due consideration to the recommendations consistent with the provisions of that resolution;

3. *Calls once more upon* Israel, the occupying Power, to cooperate in the implementation of the present resolution and to remove the hindrances that it has put in the way of establishing the University of Jerusalem "Al-Quds";

4. *Also requests* the Secretary-General to report to the General Assembly at its fifty-first session on the progress made in the implementation of the present resolution.

**General Assembly resolution 50/28 G**

6 December 1995     Meeting 82     148-2-2 (recorded vote)

Approved by Fourth Committee (A/50/605) by recorded vote (138-2-1), 30 November (meeting 25); 12-nation draft (A/C.4/50/L.17); agenda item 84.
*Meeting numbers.* GA 50th session: 4th Committee 12, 13, 25; plenary 82.

Recorded vote in Assembly as follows:

*In favour:* Afghanistan, Albania, Algeria, Antigua and Barbuda, Argentina, Armenia, Australia, Austria, Azerbaijan, Bahamas, Bahrain, Bangladesh, Barbados, Belarus, Belgium, Belize, Benin, Bolivia, Bosnia and Herzegovina, Botswana, Brazil, Brunei Darussalam, Bulgaria, Burkina Faso, Burundi, Cambodia, Cameroon, Canada, Cape Verde, Chad, Chile, China, Colombia, Congo, Côte d'Ivoire, Croatia, Cuba, Cyprus, Czech Republic, Democratic People's Republic of Korea, Denmark, Djibouti, Dominica, Ecuador, Egypt, El Salvador, Eritrea, Estonia, Ethiopia, Fiji, Finland, France, Gabon, Georgia, Germany, Ghana, Greece, Guatemala, Guinea, Guinea-Bissau, Guyana, Haiti, Honduras, Hungary, Iceland, India, Indonesia, Iran, Ireland, Italy, Jamaica, Japan, Jordan, Kazakstan, Kenya, Kuwait, Lao People's Democratic Republic, Latvia, Lebanon, Libyan Arab Jamahiriya, Liechtenstein, Lithuania, Luxembourg, Malawi, Malaysia, Maldives, Mali, Malta, Marshall Islands, Mauritius, Mexico, Micronesia, Monaco, Mongolia, Morocco, Myanmar, Nepal, Netherlands, New Zealand, Nicaragua, Niger, Nigeria, Norway, Oman, Pakistan, Panama, Papua New Guinea, Paraguay, Peru, Philippines, Poland, Portugal, Qatar, Republic of Korea, Republic of Moldova, Romania, Saint Lucia, Samoa, Saudi Arabia, Senegal, Sierra Leone, Singapore, Slovakia, Slovenia, Solomon Islands, South Africa, Spain, Sri Lanka, Sudan, Suriname, Sweden, Syrian Arab Republic, Thailand, the former Yugoslav Republic of Macedonia, Togo, Trinidad and Tobago, Tunisia, Turkey, Uganda, Ukraine, United Arab Emirates, United Kingdom, Uruguay, Venezuela, Viet Nam, Yemen, Zambia, Zimbabwe.

*Against:* Israel, United States.

*Abstaining:* Russian Federation, Swaziland.

The Russian Federation said the text contained provisions that went beyond UNRWA's strictly humanitarian mandate.

### Property rights

**Report of the Secretary-General.** In response to a 1994 General Assembly resolution,[32] the Secretary-General in September 1995 reported[33] on steps taken to protect and administer Arab property, assets and property rights in Israel and to establish a fund for income derived therefrom, on behalf of the rightful owners. He indicated that he had transmitted the resolution to Israel and to all other Member States, requesting information on any steps taken or envisaged with regard to its implementation.

In an 8 June reply, reproduced in the report, Israel stated its view that while the number of resolutions regarding UNRWA had been reduced from 10 to 7, their content remained occupied with political issues irrelevant to the Agency's work. While it believed that UNRWA could play an important role in promoting the social and economic advancement foreseen in agreements between Israel and PLO, and accordingly looked forward to continuing cooperation with UNRWA, Israel considered it essential that the Assembly consolidate its resolutions into one directly related to UNRWA's humanitarian tasks.

In 1995, UNRWA reported that no progress had been made with regard to various claims against Governments.

**Report of the Conciliation Commission.** The United Nations Conciliation Commission for Palestine, in its forty-ninth report, covering the period from 1 September 1994 to 31 August 1995,[34] stated that it had nothing new to report since the submission of its October 1994 report.[35]

**GENERAL ASSEMBLY ACTION**

On 6 December, the General Assembly adopted **resolution 50/28 F**.

### Revenues derived from Palestine refugees' properties

*The General Assembly,*

*Recalling* its resolutions 194(III) of 11 December 1948, 36/146 C of 16 December 1981 and all its subsequent resolutions on the question,

*Taking note* of the report of the Secretary-General in pursuance of resolution 49/35 F of 9 December 1994,

*Taking note also* of the report of the United Nations Conciliation Commission for Palestine covering the period from 1 September 1994 to 31 August 1995,

*Recalling* that the Universal Declaration of Human Rights and the principles of international law uphold the principle that no one shall be arbitrarily deprived of his or her private property,

*Considering* that the Palestine Arab refugees are entitled to their property and to the income derived therefrom, in conformity with the principles of justice and equity,

*Recalling in particular* its resolution 394(V) of 14 December 1950, in which it directed the Conciliation Commission, in consultation with the parties concerned, to prescribe measures for the protection of the rights, property and interests of the Palestine Arab refugees,

*Taking note* of the completion of the programme of identification and evaluation of Arab property, as announced by the Conciliation Commission in its twenty-second progress report, and of the fact that the Land Office had a schedule of Arab owners and file of documents defining the location, area and other particulars of Arab property,

1. *Requests* the Secretary-General to take all appropriate steps, in consultation with the United Nations Conciliation Commission for Palestine, for the protection of Arab property, assets and property rights in Israel and to establish a fund for the receipt of income derived therefrom, on behalf of the rightful owners;

2. *Calls once more upon* Israel to render all facilities and assistance to the Secretary-General in the implementation of the present resolution;

3. *Calls upon* the Governments of all the other Member States concerned to provide the Secretary-General with any pertinent information in their possession concerning Arab property, assets and property rights in Israel which would assist the Secretary-General in the implementation of the present resolution;

4. *Also requests* the Secretary-General to report to the General Assembly at its fifty-first session on the implementation of the present resolution.

General Assembly resolution 50/28 F

6 December 1995     Meeting 82     98-2-48 (recorded vote)

Approved by Fourth Committee (A/50/605) by recorded vote (91-2-48), 30 November (meeting 25); 12-nation draft (A/C.4/50/L.16); agenda item 84.

*Meeting numbers.* GA 50th session: 4th Committee 12, 13, 25; plenary 82.

Recorded vote in Assembly as follows:

*In favour:* Afghanistan, Algeria, Antigua and Barbuda, Azerbaijan, Bahamas, Bahrain, Bangladesh, Barbados, Belize, Benin, Bolivia, Bosnia and Herzegovina, Botswana, Brazil, Brunei Darussalam, Burkina Faso, Cameroon, Cape Verde, Chad, Chile, China, Colombia, Congo, Côte d'Ivoire, Cuba, Cyprus, Democratic People's Republic of Korea, Djibouti, Ecuador, Egypt, El Salvador, France, Gabon, Ghana, Greece, Guatemala, Guinea, Guinea-Bissau, Guyana, Haiti, Honduras, India, Indonesia, Iran, Ireland, Jordan, Kenya, Kuwait, Lao People's Democratic Republic, Lebanon, Libyan Arab Jamahiriya, Malawi, Malaysia, Maldives, Mali, Malta, Mauritius, Mexico, Monaco, Morocco, Myanmar, Nepal, Nicaragua, Niger, Nigeria, Oman, Pakistan, Panama, Papua New Guinea, Paraguay, Peru, Philippines, Qatar, Republic of Korea, Saint Lucia, Saudi Arabia, Senegal, Sierra Leone, Singapore, South Africa, Spain, Sri Lanka, Sudan, Suriname, Syrian Arab Republic, Thailand, Togo, Trinidad and Tobago, Tunisia, Uganda, United Arab Emirates, Uruguay, Vanuatu, Venezuela, Viet Nam, Yemen, Zambia, Zimbabwe.

*Against:* Israel, United States.

*Abstaining:* Albania, Argentina, Armenia, Australia, Austria, Belarus, Belgium, Bulgaria, Canada, Croatia, Czech Republic, Denmark, Dominica, Estonia, Ethiopia, Fiji, Finland, Georgia, Germany, Hungary, Iceland, Italy, Jamaica, Japan, Kazakstan, Latvia, Liechtenstein, Lithuania, Luxembourg, Marshall Islands, Micronesia, Netherlands, New Zealand, Poland, Portugal, Republic of Moldova, Romania, Russian Federation, Samoa, Slovakia, Slovenia, Solomon Islands, Swaziland, Sweden, the former Yugoslav Republic of Macedonia, Turkey, Ukraine, United Kingdom.

Explaining its abstention, Canada said the text might prejudice the outcome of the multilateral negotiations under way. The Russian Federation felt that the resolution contained provisions that went beyond UNRWA's strictly humanitarian mandate.

## UNRWA financing

Voluntary contributions remained the principal means of financing UNRWA's operations, accounting for 97 per cent of Agency funding. The remaining 3 per cent represented the core of UNRWA's international staff costs—92 international posts during the period from 1 July 1994 to 30 June 1995, funded by the United Nations. Most contributions were received in cash, although 12.5 per cent of UNRWA's total funding was received in kind, usually in the form of food for distribution to needy refugees.

The Commissioner-General reported[20] that UNRWA's ability to provide expanded services was constrained by financial shortfalls for the third consecutive year. The inability of some donors to increase their contributions commensurate with the Agency's annual budget growth rate of 5 per cent—needed to offset natural population growth and inflation—was a matter of concern.

At the end of the 1994-1995 budget biennium, UNRWA recorded a deficit of $8.4 million in its General Fund budget, which covered its core programmes. In December 1994, the Agency had a deficit of $6 million, which had reduced working capital from $22.6 million at the beginning of 1994 to $16.6 million. By June 1995, working capital had again been reduced, standing at $8.2 million, and the 1995 deficit was projected at $16 million—which, if realized, would virtually eliminate its working capital. An accumulated deficit of $17.8 million in the fund for Extraordinary Measures in Lebanon and the Occupied Territory (EMLOT) could, however, be accommodated only by drawing on the working capital.

Furthermore, the estimated shortfall did not include the cost of lifting the remaining austerity measures, which would require an additional $11.2 million. The lack of working capital would mean reduced services, not merely a freeze on growth. The Agency's budget had to expand over time even to maintain current levels of services. Austerity measures included a general salary freeze and cuts in the budget for additional teacher posts. Funding requirements for 1996 would be $342.3 million, including $2.25 million for EMLOT, as well as the value of needed in-kind donations.

In response to changing political circumstances and the prospect of an eventual handover of Agency services, a five-year financial and policy planning framework was adopted to establish the Agency's minimum financial requirements for the period 1995-1999. The framework provided for an unavoidable 5 per cent annual increase. In addition, a certain sum was to be set aside each year towards payment of an estimated $127 million in termination indemnities accruing to area staff upon dissolution of the Agency. Project funding was not covered by the framework. The five-year planning horizon had been endorsed by the major donor and host Governments at an informal meeting in Amman in March (see ''Future of UNRWA'' above). The 1996-1997 biennial budget was prepared in accordance with those basic assumptions. The move of UNRWA's Vienna headquarters to the area of operations—primarily the Gaza Strip with some units in Amman—was budgeted at $13.5 million. In approving relocation of the headquarters, major donors stipulated that the move should not be financed from the regular budget. Consequently, UNRWA took steps to raise the required funds directly from donors.

**Working Group on financing.** The Working Group on the Financing of UNRWA held two meetings in 1995, on 14 September and 13 October. In its 19 October report to the General Assembly,[36] the Working Group noted that by the end of 1994, UNRWA's recorded financial balance for the year showed expenditures of $265.8 million on regular programmes, against income from contributions of $298.2 million, leaving a book surplus of $32.4 million. Included in that book surplus, however, were late contributions of $38.4 million, received and recorded in 1994 but intended for the 1993 regular programme. If applied to the 1994 accounts, that amount would account for the resulting deficit of $6 million and the reduction in working capital to $16.6 million (see above). In addition, some $13.4 million had been spent on EMLOT activities in 1994, against a total income of $7.9 million, leaving a deficit of $5.5 million which had to be funded from working capital. The Agency also operated three extrabudgetary project funds in 1994: the Expanded Programme of Assistance (EPA), the European Gaza Hospital fund and PIP. EPA, which had become redundant with the establishment of PIP, was being phased out as projects were completed.

Having begun 1995 with such a deficit, the Agency's financial prospects for the year were not favourable, the Working Group stated. The growth of contributions was not keeping pace with the rising number of UNRWA beneficiaries and cost increases due to inflation. Unexpected emergency needs required additional funds. Austerity measures were having a negative impact on the quality of UNRWA services. By the last quarter of 1995, UNRWA's estimated deficit was $4 million, but if one included the $12 million reserve for salary increases for 21,000 area staff which was frozen as a result of the deficit, that figure would be $16 million.

In meetings with major donors and other concerned government representatives, the Commissioner-General had once again appealed for help in finding ways to alleviate the structural deficit problem. While some additional and special contributions were received by the Agency for its regular budget during the year, they fell short of the amounts required to address the Agency's current requirements and projected future needs, and the situation remained serious.

The Working Group noted that the past year had continued to see dramatic political developments in UNRWA's area of operations. Donors had supported the ongoing peace process by devoting unprecedented resources to projects benefiting Palestinians, particularly in the West Bank and Gaza Strip. PIP had met with a particularly generous response from donors. The budgets for PIP projects included programme support costs, which alleviated some of the burden on UNRWA's own resources and infrastructure. Nevertheless, some of the additional tasks which the Agency was asked to carry out would inevitably have financial implications. The prospect of eventually phasing out UNRWA, which would become more apparent as the political process unfolded, also raised the issue of termination indemnities that would have to be paid to the area staff once the Agency began to cease operations and handed over its functions to other authorities; donors had agreed that UNRWA should begin to include a provision for those termination indemnities in its budget, beginning with $25.4 million in the 1996-1997 biennium. The planned relocation of UNRWA's headquarters also had potential financial implications, as it could not be financed out of the regular budget. However, contributions to the special fund established for that purpose had fallen considerably short of the budget for the move arrived at in consultation between UNRWA and the United Nations Secretariat. While proceeding with the first phases of the move as funds became available, the Commissioner-General had appealed to donors to help make up that shortfall.

The Working Group expressed concern that UNRWA had been able to carry out its regular activities once again only by drawing on its working capital reserves in 1994 and expected again to sustain a budget deficit in 1995. The Group voiced special concern about the negative cumulative effect of austerity measures, but commended the Commissioner-General for his fund-raising efforts, particularly those for PIP, which had succeeded in attracting financial support from some donors surpassing their previous contributions. The Working Group shared the Commissioner-General's concern that UNRWA's core activities—education, health care, and relief and social services—were increasingly threatened by chronic deficits, and stressed that it would be unfortunate if the substantial social and economic benefits promised by programmes such as PIP were undermined by the inability of the international community to provide the resources needed to preserve those regular services. The Group urged Governments to continue contributing generously and consider additional contributions in support of both emergency-related and special programmes, as well as current and future phases of PIP, the operating costs of the European Gaza Hospital and the special fund for the relocation of UNRWA's headquarters.

**GENERAL ASSEMBLY ACTION**

On 6 December, the General Assembly adopted **resolution 50/28 B**.

**Working Group on the Financing of the United Nations Relief and Works Agency for Palestine Refugees in the Near East**
*The General Assembly,*
*Recalling* its resolutions 2656(XXV) of 7 December 1970, 2728(XXV) of 15 December 1970, 2791(XXVI) of 6 December 1971, 49/35 B of 9 December 1994 and the previous resolutions on this question,
*Recalling also* its decision 36/462 of 16 March 1982, by which it took note of the special report of the Working Group on the Financing of the United Nations Relief and Works Agency for Palestine Refugees in the Near East,
*Having considered* the report of the Working Group,
*Taking into account* the report of the Commissioner-General of the United Nations Relief and Works Agency for Palestine Refugees in the Near East covering the period from 1 July 1994 to 30 June 1995,

*Deeply concerned* about the critical financial situation of the Agency, which has affected and affects the continuation of the provision of the necessary Agency services to the Palestine refugees, including the emergency-related programmes,
*Emphasizing* the continuing need for extraordinary efforts in order to maintain, at least at the current minimum level, the activities of the Agency, as well as to enable the Agency to carry out essential construction,
1. *Commends* the Working Group on the Financing of the United Nations Relief and Works Agency for Palestine Refugees in the Near East for its efforts to assist in ensuring the financial security of the Agency;
2. *Takes note with approval* of the report of the Working Group;
3. *Requests* the Working Group to continue its efforts, in cooperation with the Secretary-General and the Commissioner-General, for the financing of the Agency for a further period of one year;
4. *Requests* the Secretary-General to provide the necessary services and assistance to the Working Group for the conduct of its work.

General Assembly resolution 50/28 B
6 December 1995     Meeting 82     Adopted without vote

Approved by Fourth Committee (A/50/605) without vote, 30 November (meeting 25); 18-nation draft (A/C.4/50/L.12); agenda item 84.
*Meeting numbers.* GA 50th session: 4th Committee 12, 13, 25; plenary 82.

Iran expressed reservations concerning any provisions in this and other UNRWA resolutions that could be construed as indicating recognition of Israel.

*REFERENCES*
(1)YUN 1977, p. 304, GA res. 32/40 B, 2 Dec. 1977. (2)YUN 1994, p. 620, GA res. 49/62 A, 14 Dec. 1994. (3)YUN 1975, p. 248, GA res. 3376(XXX), 10 Nov. 1975. (4)YUN 1993, p. 521. (5)A/50/35. (6)A/49/645, annex. (7)YUN 1994, p. 622, GA res. 49/62 C, 14 Dec. 1994. (8)YUN 1994, p. 622. (9)A/50/286-E/1995/113. (10)YUN 1994, p. 624. (11)A/50/278-E/1995/114. (12)DP/1995/20/Rev.1. (13)E/1995/34 (dec. 95/8). (14)DP/1996/15. (15)TD/B/42(1)/8. (16)TD/B/42(1)/19 (Vol.I). (17)A/49/885. (18)YUN 1994, p. 628. (19)A/50/763. (20)A/50/13 & Add.1 & Add.1/Corr.1. (21)YUN 1993, p. 569. (22)YUN 1994, p. 656. (23)Ibid., p. 660, GA res. 49/35 A, 9 Dec. 1994. (24)A/50/451. (25)YUN 1994, p. 667. (26)YUN 1994, p. 667, GA res. 49/35 C, 9 Dec. 1994. (27)A/50/450. (28)YUN 1994, p. 668, GA res. 49/35 D, 9 Dec. 1994. (29)Ibid., p. 669, GA res. 49/35 G, 9 Dec. 1994. (30)A/50/531. (31)YUN 1980, p. 443, GA res. 35/13 B, 3 Nov. 1980. (32)YUN 1994, p. 670, GA res. 49/35 F, 9 Dec. 1993. (33)A/50/428. (34)A/50/500. (35)YUN 1994, p. 670. (36)A/50/491.

# Peace-keeping operations

UN peace-keeping operations were born in the Middle East, with the establishment in May 1948 of the Organization's first and oldest operation—the UN Truce Supervision Organization (UNTSO), originally established to monitor the cease-fire called for by the Security Council in May 1948 in newly partitioned Palestine. Over the course of nearly four decades, its unarmed military observers have fulfilled changing mandates—from supervising the original four armistice agreements between Israel and its Arab neighbors—Egypt, Jordan, Lebanon and Syria—to observing and monitoring other cease-fires, as well as other tasks. In the wake of regional wars in 1956, 1967 and 1973, its functions have been adapted to changing circumstances. UNTSO headquarters are located at Government House in Jerusalem.

In 1995, UNTSO personnel worked with the two remaining UN peace-keeping forces in the Middle East—its Observer Group Golan (OGG) with the UN Disengagement Force (UNDOF) in the Golan Heights, and Observer Group Lebanon (OGL) with the UN Interim Force in Lebanon (UNIFIL). UNTSO observers in 1995 also maintained a presence in the Sinai peninsula—Observer Group Egypt (OGE), with headquarters in Ismailia. In addition, UNTSO in 1995 had offices in Amman, Beirut and Gaza. The Amman office was closed in July following the Israeli-Jordanian peace agreement of October 1994.

### Lebanon

A report[1] by the Secretary-General described the situation at the end of 1995 as tense and volatile, with Israel continuing to maintain its occupation of parts of south Lebanon. The Israeli Defence Forces (IDF) and their local Lebanese auxiliary, the so-called de facto forces (DFF), continued to be targets of attacks in that area by groups proclaiming their resistance to the occupation. The United Nations Interim Force in Lebanon (UNIFIL), established in 1978[2] to confirm the withdrawal of Israeli forces, restore international peace and security, and assist the Government of Lebanon in ensuring the return of its effective authority in the area, maintained its efforts in 1995 to limit the conflict and to protect the inhabitants from the fighting. The Secretary-General stated that the Force, through a network of checkpoints and observation posts and active patrolling, was doing its best to prevent its area of operations from being used for hostile activities. It also was deployed as necessary to provide a measure of protection to the villages and to farmers working in the fields. Its mandate, although repeatedly reaffirmed over the years, nevertheless remained unfulfilled.

In notes issued on 17 January[3] and on 10 July,[4] both requesting the extension of the mandate of UNIFIL (see below), Lebanon declared that national reconstruction and rehabilitation were proceeding (see PART FOUR, Chapter III). Efforts to rebuild the new commercial centre in downtown Beirut and to modernize the nation's infrastructure were ongoing, with priority given to such basic services as electricity, telecommunications, transportation, waterworks, schools and hospitals. Despite those positive developments and coordinated efforts by UNIFIL and the Lebanese authorities to deploy the Lebanese army throughout the southern part of the country, Lebanon said that Israel's occupation and its continued aggression against Lebanon and its citizens remained the major obstacle to national recovery. Constant shelling of villages and towns in the south and aerial bombardments of different parts of the country continued to result in deaths and injuries of many civilians and the destruction of property. Furthermore, Lebanon said, Israel still refused to allow ICRC to visit hundreds of Lebanese detainees held for years in Israeli jails and detention camps in Al-Khiam and Marjayoun, in violation of the fourth Geneva Convention.

In view of Israel's continued aggressions, Lebanon went on, and the threat to the peace process, implementation of resolution 425(1978) remained the only way to stop the violence. By taking long-overdue measures towards that end, the Security Council could play a positive role in securing peace for the region and enabling the Lebanese Government to extend its authority up to its internationally recognized boundaries and to re-establish law and order throughout the entire south of the country.

On 1 March, Lebanon reported[5] that an Israeli naval blockade had spread to all southern Lebanese port cities. In addition, Israeli naval patrols were preventing Lebanese fishermen from fishing in Lebanese territorial waters. Daily artillery shelling and air raids had resulted in numerous civilian casualties and considerable material damage. Lebanon requested[6] that the Security Council take all necessary action to bring about the lifting of the illegal blockade, cessation of bombarding civilians, and respect by Israel of Lebanon's sovereignty, territorial integrity and territorial waters, in accordance with Council resolutions 425(1978),[2] 426(1978)[7] and 509(1982).[8] Throughout the year, Lebanon continued to report Israeli attacks and other operations against southern Lebanon and the Bekaa.

In a 5 July letter,[9] the Foreign Minister of Lebanon called for the release of 225 Lebanese detainees held in Israeli detention camps since 1984, in defiance of resolution 425(1978), against whom, he said, no legal charge had been brought while they continued to be subjected to inhumane treatment and torture. He specifically called for the closure of the Al-Khiam camp.

Israel, in an 18 January letter,[10] had confirmed its position on the situation in southern Lebanon, as previously outlined in August 1994,[11] when it had stated that its measures there had to be viewed in the light of its right to self-defence and were intended solely to prevent acts of terror against the Israeli population. Terrorist organizations such as Hezbollah and others were openly intent on undermining the peace process; they functioned with impunity in Lebanon where they were free to plan and carry out their attacks, Israel declared.

By a 7 March resolution,[12] the Commission on Human Rights deplored the continued Israeli violation of human rights in the occupied zone of southern Lebanon and the western Bekaa, demonstrated in particular by the kidnapping and arbitrary detention of civilians, the destruction of their dwellings, confiscation of their property, expulsion from their land, and the bombing of villages and civilian areas. It called on Israel immediately to end such practices, which were manifested recently by an escalation of air raids and the use of prohibited weapons such as fragmentation bombs, and to release immediately all kidnapped and detained Lebanese.

The Economic and Social Council, by **decision 1995/278**, approved the Commission's request that the Secretary-General bring its resolution to Israel's attention and invite Israel to provide information concerning the extent of its implementation.

## UNIFIL

The Security Council in 1995 twice extended the mandate of UNIFIL, in January and July, each time for a six-month period.

Established by the Council in March 1978[2] following Israel's invasion of Lebanon,[13] UNIFIL originally was entrusted with confirming the withdrawal of Israeli forces, restoring international peace and security, and assisting the Lebanese Government in ensuring the return of its effective authority in the area. A second Israeli invasion in June 1982[14] radically altered the situation in which UNIFIL had to function. Shortly thereafter, the Council authorized the Force to carry out, in addition to its original mandate, the interim tasks of providing protection and humanitarian assistance to the local population, while maintaining its positions in its area of deployment.[15] During 1995, UNIFIL continued to carry out its mandated tasks.

The Force maintained close contact and cooperated with the Lebanese authorities on matters of mutual concern. Those authorities provided valuable assistance in connection with the rotation of troops and the increasing volume of logistic activities in Beirut. The Lebanese army was particularly helpful in defusing confrontations with armed elements. UNIFIL also continued to cooperate with the Lebanese gendarmerie on matters pertaining to the maintenance of law and order.

In January 1995, UNIFIL's military personnel numbered 5,001. They were provided by nine countries: Fiji, Finland, France, Ghana, Ireland, Italy, Nepal, Norway and Poland. Civilian support was provided by a staff of 521, of whom 136 were recruited internationally and 385 locally. By July, at the beginning of the second 1995 mandate period, troop strength had decreased slightly, to 4,967, and civilian staff numbers had changed to 524, 159 and 365, respectively.

Major-General Trond Furuhovde of Norway ended his tour of duty as Force Commander on 22 February and was succeeded on 1 April by Major-General Stanislaw F. Wozniak of Poland.

UNIFIL was assisted by 59 military observers of the United Nations Truce Supervision Organization (UNTSO) organized as Observer Group Lebanon, under the operational control of the UNIFIL Commander. UNTSO observers manned five observation posts along the Lebanese side of the Israel-Lebanon armistice demarcation line and operated five mobile teams in the part of the area of operation controlled by Israel (ICA, Israeli-controlled area).

### Activities

**Report of the Secretary-General (January).** In a 23 January report[16] on developments from 21 July 1994 to 20 January 1995 in the UNIFIL area of operation, the Secretary-General stated that Israel continued to control an area, manned by IDF and DFF, whose boundaries were not clearly defined but determined by the forward positions of those forces. ICA included territory adjacent to the armistice demarcation line, parts of the Fijian, Finnish, Ghanaian, Irish and Nepalese battalion sectors, and the entire Norwegian battalion sector, as well as sizeable areas to the north of the UNIFIL area. Within those areas, IDF/DFF manned 69 military positions. Within ICA, Israel maintained a civil administration and a security service. Movement between ICA and the rest of Lebanon was strictly controlled; crossings were closed frequently. ICA remained economically dependent on Israel. An estimated 3,000 jobs in Israel were held by Lebanese from ICA; access to those jobs was controlled by DFF and the security services. There were continued reports of forced recruitment to DFF, including that of persons under the age of 18, the Secretary-General reported.

During the period under review, UNIFIL observers reported 87 operations against IDF/DFF by armed elements who had proclaimed their resistance against Israeli occupation. Numerous attacks took place against IDF/DFF positions north of the Litani River. The armed elements employed roadside bombs, rockets, mortars, rocket-propelled grenades and anti-tank missiles. IDF/DFF continued their attacks and retaliatory firing against armed elements. UNIFIL recorded more than 16,000 artillery, mortar and tank rounds fired by

IDF/DFF, compared to 10,500 during the previous six months.

In some cases, IDF/DFF fire was directed at villages, causing damage and casualties. In two incidents, armed elements reportedly responded by firing rockets into northern Israel. On 4 October, an Israeli aircraft bombed a village near the town of Nabatiyeh, killing and injuring several civilians; the bombing, which Israeli authorities said was a mistake, was followed by the firing of several rockets into northern Israel, injuring three civilians. On 20 October, IDF/DFF artillery and tank fire killed seven civilians and wounded six others in villages near Nabatiyeh, to the north of the UNIFIL area of deployment. The shelling was strongly protested to Israeli authorities. Several rockets were fired into northern Israel in response to that shelling.

During the period under review, there were 197 instances of firing by IDF/DFF at or close to UNIFIL positions and personnel; all such firings were routinely protested to the Israeli authorities.

UNIFIL continued to oppose attempts by armed elements to use its area for hostile purposes. At times, that led to friction at UNIFIL checkpoints, followed by harassment and threats directed at Force members. Such cases were generally resolved through negotiations. There were 17 instances of firing at or close to UNIFIL positions by Lebanese armed elements; they were protested through the Lebanese army. On 22 September, three Fijian soldiers were wounded and their vehicle seriously damaged by a roadside bomb explosion. In a similar incident on 7 November, south of the village of Al Hinniyah in the Nepalese sector, two Polish soldiers were lightly wounded and their vehicle seriously damaged.

As in the past, UNIFIL detonated mines, roadside bombs and unexploded remnants of war and dismantled ordnance of various types in the area of deployment; a total of 412 controlled explosions were carried out.

Within available resources, UNIFIL continued to extend humanitarian assistance to the civilian population in its area, in the form of medical supplies, water, clothes, blankets, food, fuel and electricity. Engineering work was executed and repairs were made to buildings damaged by firing. Force personnel escorted farmers to their fields within range of IDF/DFF positions. Troop-contributing Governments made available resources for water projects, equipment or services for schools, and supplies for social services and needy people. UNIFIL medical centres and mobile teams provided care for about 2,500 civilian patients per month. Some 500 patients per month were treated under a field dental programme. In those areas, UNIFIL cooperated closely with the Lebanese authorities, UN agencies and programmes operating in Lebanon, ICRC and NGOs.

Also during the period under review, two Ghanaian soldiers died of natural causes. Since UNIFIL's establishment, 202 military members of the Force had died, 76 as a result of firing or mine or bomb explosions, 82 in accidents and 44 from other causes. A total of 312 were wounded by firing or by mine or bomb explosions.

The Secretary-General concluded that, although there had been no progress towards implementation of the UNIFIL mandate, the Force's contribution to stability in the area and protection for the inhabitants remained important. He therefore recommended that the Security Council accept Lebanon's request and extend UNIFIL's mandate for another six months, until 31 July 1995.

**SECURITY COUNCIL ACTION (January)**

Following consideration of the Secretary-General's report, the Security Council on 30 January adopted **resolution 974(1995)**.

*The Security Council,*

*Recalling* its resolutions 425(1978) of 19 March 1978, 426(1978) of 19 March 1978, 501(1982) of 25 February 1982, 508(1982) of 5 June 1982, 509(1982) of 6 June 1982 and 520(1982) of 17 September 1982, as well as all its resolutions on the situation in Lebanon,

*Having studied* the report of the Secretary-General on the United Nations Interim Force in Lebanon of 23 January 1995, and taking note of the observations expressed therein,

*Taking note* of the letter dated 16 January 1995 from the Permanent Representative of Lebanon to the United Nations addressed to the Secretary-General,

*Responding* to the request of the Government of Lebanon,

1. *Decides* to extend the present mandate of the United Nations Interim Force in Lebanon for a further interim period of six months, that is, until 31 July 1995;

2. *Reiterates* its strong support for the territorial integrity, sovereignty and independence of Lebanon within its internationally recognized boundaries;

3. *Re-emphasizes* the terms of reference and general guidelines of the Force as stated in the report of the Secretary-General of 19 March 1978, approved by resolution 426(1978), and calls upon all parties concerned to cooperate fully with the Force for the full implementation of its mandate;

4. *Reiterates* that the Force should fully implement its mandate as defined in resolutions 425(1978), 426(1978) and all other relevant resolutions;

5. *Endorses* the Secretary-General's intention to pursue the possibilities for streamlining and achieving economies in the areas of maintenance and logistic support;

6. *Requests* the Secretary-General to continue consultations with the Government of Lebanon and other parties directly concerned with the implementation of the present resolution and to report to the Security Council thereon.

Security Council resolution 974(1995)
30 January 1995     Meeting 3495     Adopted unanimously

Draft prepared in consultations among Council members (S/1995/81).

In a 30 January statement[17] complementing the resolution on the mandate extension for UNIFIL, the Council reaffirmed its commitment to Lebanon's full sovereignty, independence, integrity and national unity within its internationally recognized boundaries. In that context, any State should refrain from the threat or use of force against the political independence of any State, or in any other manner inconsistent with the purposes of the United Nations, the statement said. In extending UNIFIL's mandate, the Council again stressed the urgent need for implementing resolution 425(1978) in all its aspects. It reiterated its full support for the 1989 Taif Agreement and for the continued efforts of the Lebanese Government to consolidate peace, national unity and security in the country while successfully carrying out the reconstruction process. The Council commended the Government for its successful effort to extend its authority in the south of the country in full coordination with UNIFIL.

The Council again expressed concern over the continuing violence in southern Lebanon, regretted the loss of civilian life and urged all parties to exercise restraint. Finally, it expressed appreciation for the continuing efforts of the Secretary-General and his staff in that regard, and commended UNIFIL's troops and troop-contributing countries for their sacrifices and commitment to the cause of international peace and security under difficult circumstances.

**Report of the Secretary-General (July).** In a 19 July report[18] to the Security Council on developments during the period from 21 January to 20 July 1995, the Secretary-General noted that the level of hostilities in the UNIFIL area had increased and that civilians on both sides had been killed or injured. Exchanges were sparked by indiscriminate fire or the targeting of populated areas by IDF/DFF, followed by the firing of rockets into Israel, for which a group known as the Islamic Resistance claimed responsibility. In some instances, armed elements launched attacks from the vicinity of villages in the UNIFIL area of deployment, drawing retaliatory fire. There had been 51 instances of firing at or close to UNIFIL positions and personnel by armed elements, compared to 17 during the July-to-January reporting period just past. Such firings had been reported to the Lebanese army and, where possible, were protested to the leadership of the groups involved. On 19 March, a Nepalese soldier was seriously injured when an anti-personnel mine exploded at a newly established observation post at Yatar. A similar mine was found at the same location a few days later. There were 208 instances of firing by IDF/DFF at or close to UNIFIL positions and personnel, which were protested to the Israeli authorities.

UNIFIL observers reported on 129 operations against IDF/DFF by armed elements who had proclaimed their resistance against Israel's occupation. There were also numerous reports of attacks against IDF/DFF positions north of the Litani River, mostly carried out by the Islamic Resistance. IDF/DFF continued their attacks and retaliatory firing against armed elements; UNIFIL recorded more than 16,500 artillery, mortar and tank rounds fired by them. IDF also stepped up night-time ambushes and long-range patrolling and increasingly made use of assault helicopters. While air attacks were less frequent than during the previous periods, flights by Israeli military aircraft over Lebanese territory continued. From February on, Israel imposed restrictions on the movement of Lebanese fishermen in southern Lebanese territorial waters, enforcing those restrictions by naval vessels—which, at times, involved firing at fishing boats and temporary detention of fishermen.

In its efforts to detonate mines, roadside bombs and unexploded remnants of war, UNIFIL carried out 105 controlled explosions during the period under review. It also continued to protect and assist the population, helping to execute a school project financed by UNICEF and UNESCO, and assisting UNDP in its South Lebanon Emergency Rehabilitation Programme (see PART FOUR, Chapter III), among many other activities.

On 16 April, Israel deported to Lebanon two Palestinians who had just been released from prison. However, they were denied entry into the country by the Lebanese authorities and were subsequently turned over to UNIFIL. Since 18 April, the two men had been accommodated at UNIFIL headquarters, the report stated, and efforts continued to arrange passage to a country or territory willing to accept them.

Expressing particular concern at the targeting of civilians and the number of those killed or injured, the Secretary-General said he had urged the parties to exercise restraint. He was also conscious of the risk of escalation inherent in the exchanges of hostilities, observing that UNIFIL continued to make every effort to limit the conflict. Although there had been no progress towards implementation of its mandate, the Force's contribution to stability in the area and the protection it afforded the inhabitants remained important. The Secretary-General recommended that the Council accept Lebanon's request and extend the UNIFIL mandate for another six months, until 31 January 1996.

**SECURITY COUNCIL ACTION (July)**

On 28 July, the Security Council adopted **resolution 1006(1995)**.

*The Security Council,*

*Recalling* its resolutions 425(1978) and 426(1978) of 19 March 1978, 501(1982) of 25 February 1982, 508(1982) of 5 June 1982, 509(1982) of 6 June 1982 and 520(1982) of 17 September 1982, as well as all its resolutions on the situation in Lebanon,

*Having studied* the report of the Secretary-General on the United Nations Interim Force in Lebanon of 19 July 1995 and taking note of the observations expressed therein,

*Taking note* of the letter dated 10 July 1995 from the Permanent Representative of Lebanon to the United Nations addressed to the Secretary-General,

*Responding* to the request of the Government of Lebanon,

1. *Decides* to extend the present mandate of the United Nations Interim Force in Lebanon for a further period of six months, that is, until 31 January 1996;

2. *Reiterates* its strong support for the territorial integrity, sovereignty and independence of Lebanon within its internationally recognized boundaries;

3. *Re-emphasizes* the terms of reference and general guidelines of the Force as stated in the report of the Secretary-General of 19 March 1978, approved by resolution 426(1978), and calls upon all parties concerned to cooperate fully with the Force for the full implementation of its mandate;

4. *Reiterates* that the Force should fully implement its mandate as defined in resolutions 425(1978), 426(1978) and all other relevant resolutions;

5. *Condemns* the increase in acts of violence committed in particular against the Force and urges the parties to put an end to them;

6. *Concurs* with the streamlining of the Force, described in paragraph 11 of the report of the Secretary-General, and stresses that its implementation will not affect the operational capacity of the Force;

7. *Requests* the Secretary-General to continue consultations with the Government of Lebanon and other parties directly concerned with the implementation of the present resolution and to report to the Security Council thereon.

Security Council resolution 1006(1995)

28 July 1995     Meeting 3558     Adopted unanimously

Draft prepared in consultations among Council members (S/1995/619).

Also on 28 July, complementing the Council's extension of UNIFIL, its President made a statement[19] similar to that made on 30 January (see above).

## Financing

**Report of the Secretary-General (May).** In May 1995, the Secretary-General provided financial information[20] on UNIFIL for the period from 1 February 1994 to 31 January 1995, which reflected an overall unencumbered balance of $1,755,000 gross ($16,000 net), due mainly to savings from lower military personnel costs. As at 31 March 1995, outstanding assessments for UNIFIL from its inception in 1978 to 31 January 1995 amounted to $206.6 million. The Secretary-General proposed that the General Assembly credit Member States with the unencumbered net balance of $16,000 against their assessments in respect of any future mandate periods. The Advisory Committee on Administrative and Budgetary Questions (ACABQ), in a June report,[21] concurred with the proposal.

Following consideration of reports by the Secretary-General and ACABQ, the General Assembly on 12 July (**decision 49/483**) decided that there should be set off against the apportionment among Member States, in respect of future mandate periods of UNIFIL as might be approved by the Security Council, their respective shares in the unencumbered balance of $1,755,000 gross ($16,000 net) for the period from 1 February 1994 to 31 January 1995. The Assembly's decision was adopted without vote, after the Fifth (Administrative and Budgetary) Committee, on 23 June, had approved, also without vote, a draft[22] submitted by its Chairman following informal consultations.

**Report of the Secretary-General (October).** In an 11 October report,[23] the Secretary-General presented cost estimates of $53,874,000 gross ($52,448,000 net) for the maintenance of UNIFIL from 1 February to 30 June 1996, conforming with the new budget cycle from 1 July to 30 June decided on by the General Assembly in 1994.[24] Those cost estimates provided for a phased reduction of contingent personnel from 5,015 to 4,513 by May 1996, as well as for a reduction of 37 civilian staff, down to 143 internationally recruited and 193 locally recruited staff.

Those reductions resulted in a decrease of 4.1 per cent on a monthly basis in gross terms; monthly requirements were estimated at $10,774,800 gross ($10,489,600 net), down from $11,234,500 gross ($10,870,830 net) authorized by the Assembly in December 1994.[25]

The Secretary-General noted that as at 30 September 1995, a total of $2,575.6 million had been appropriated for UNIFIL from its inception to 31 January 1996. Assessed contributions received for the same period amounted to $2,312.8 million, leaving an outstanding balance of $232 million. As a result of the withholding or delay in payment of assessed contributions, UNIFIL was unable to meet its obligations on a current basis or in full, in particular those due to the troop-contributing countries. However, full reimbursement had been made to them up to the period ending 31 January 1995.

ACABQ[26] concurred with the Secretary-General's proposal that the Assembly authorize entering into commitments not to exceed $10,774,800 gross ($10,489,600 net) per month. The Advisory Committee noted that, as at 31 August, $30.7 million was due to troop-contributing countries.

On 19 December, the General Assembly adopted **resolution 50/89 A**.

### Financing of the United Nations Interim Force in Lebanon

*The General Assembly,*

*Having considered* the report of the Secretary-General on the financing of the United Nations Interim Force in Lebanon, and the related report of the Advisory Committee on Administrative and Budgetary Questions,

*Bearing in mind* Security Council resolution 425(1978) of 19 March 1978, by which the Council established the United Nations Interim Force in Lebanon, and the subsequent resolutions by which the Council extended the mandate of the Force, the latest of which was resolution 1006(1995) of 28 July 1995,

*Recalling* its resolution S-8/2 of 21 April 1978 on the financing of the Force and its subsequent resolutions and decisions thereon, the latest of which were resolution 49/226 of 23 December 1994 and decision 49/483 of 12 July 1995,

*Reaffirming* that the costs of the Force are expenses of the Organization to be borne by Member States in accordance with Article 17, paragraph 2, of the Charter of the United Nations,

*Recalling also* its previous decisions regarding the fact that, in order to meet the expenditures caused by the Force, a different procedure is required from the one applied to meet expenditures of the regular budget of the United Nations,

*Taking into account* the fact that the economically more developed countries are in a position to make relatively larger contributions and that the economically less developed countries have a relatively limited capacity to contribute towards such an operation,

*Bearing in mind* the special responsibilities of the States permanent members of the Security Council, as indicated in General Assembly resolution 1874(S-IV) of 27 June 1963, in the financing of such operations,

*Mindful* of the fact that it is essential to provide the Force with the necessary financial resources to enable it to fulfil its responsibilities under the relevant resolutions of the Security Council,

*Recalling* its resolution 34/9 E of 17 December 1979 and the subsequent resolutions in which it decided that the provisions of regulations 5.2 *(b)*, 5.2 *(d)*, 4.3 and 4.4 of the Financial Regulations of the United Nations should be suspended, the latest of which was resolution 49/226,

*Concerned* that the Secretary-General continues to face difficulties in meeting the obligations of the Force on a current basis, including reimbursement to current and former troop-contributing States,

*Concerned also* that the surplus balances in the Special Account for the United Nations Interim Force in Lebanon have been used up for meeting expenses of the Force in order to compensate for the lack of income resulting from non-payment and late payment by Member States of their contributions and have consequently been exhausted,

1. *Takes note* of the status of contributions to the United Nations Interim Force in Lebanon as at 13 December 1995, including the contributions unpaid in the amount of 216,216,752 United States dollars, representing 9 per cent of the total assessed contributions from the inception of the Force to the period ending 31 January 1996, notes that some 22 per cent of the Member States have paid their assessed contributions in full, and urges all other Member States concerned, particularly those in arrears, to ensure the payment of their outstanding assessed contributions;

2. *Expresses concern* about the financial situation with regard to peace-keeping activities, particularly as regards the reimbursement of troop contributors, notably those troop-contributing Member States that have paid their assessed contributions in full, which bear an additional burden owing to overdue payments by Member States of their assessments;

3. *Urges* all Member States to make every possible effort to ensure the payment of their assessed contributions to the Force promptly and in full;

4. *Endorses* the observations and recommendations contained in the report of the Advisory Committee on Administrative and Budgetary Questions;

5. *Requests* the Secretary-General to take all necessary action to ensure that the Force is administered with a maximum of efficiency and economy;

6. *Decides* to appropriate to the Special Account for the United Nations Interim Force in Lebanon the amount of 67,407,000 United States dollars gross (65,224,980 dollars net) authorized and apportioned by the General Assembly in paragraph 10 of its resolution 49/226 for the operation of the Force from 1 August 1995 to 31 January 1996, inclusive;

7. *Authorizes* the Secretary-General to enter into commitments for the operation of the Force at a rate not to exceed 10,774,800 dollars gross (10,489,600 dollars net) per month for a period of up to five months beginning 1 February 1996, and to assess the amount of 32,324,400 dollars gross (31,468,800 dollars net) on Member States in accordance with the scheme set out in the present resolution, should the Security Council decide to continue the Force beyond the period of six months authorized under its resolution 1006(1995);

8. *Decides,* as an ad hoc arrangement, to apportion the amount referred to in paragraph 7 above among Member States in accordance with the composition of groups set out in paragraphs 3 and 4 of General Assembly resolution 43/232 of 1 March 1989, as adjusted by the Assembly in its resolutions 44/192 B of 21 December 1989, 45/269 of 27 August 1991, 46/198 A of 20 December 1991 and 47/218 A of 23 December 1992 and its decision 48/472 A of 23 December 1993, and taking into account the scale of assessments for the year 1996, subject to the decision of the Security Council to extend the mandate of the Force beyond 31 January 1996 and the mandate periods to be decided upon by the Council;

9. *Decides also* that there shall be set off against the apportionment among Member States, as provided for in paragraph 8 above, their respective share in the estimated income of 4,800 dollars other than staff assessment income for the period from 1 February to 30 April 1996, inclusive;

10. *Decides further* that, in accordance with the provisions of its resolution 973(X) of 15 December 1955, there shall be set off against the apportionment among Member States, as provided for in paragraph 8 above, their respective share in the Tax Equalization Fund of the estimated staff assessment income of 850,800 dollars for the period from 1 February to 30 April 1996, inclusive;

11. *Invites* voluntary contributions to the Force in cash and in the form of services and supplies acceptable to the Secretary-General, to be administered, as appropriate, in accordance with the procedure established by the General Assembly in its resolutions 43/230 of 21 December 1988, 44/192 A of 21 December 1989 and 45/258 of 3 May 1991;

12.    *Decides* to keep the sub-item entitled "United Nations Interim Force in Lebanon" under the agenda item entitled "Financing of the United Nations peace-keeping forces in the Middle East" under review during its fiftieth session.

General Assembly resolution 50/89 A

19 December 1995      Meeting 95      Adopted without vote

Approved by Fifth Committee (A/50/824) without vote, 17 December (meeting 41); draft by Chairman (A/C.5/50/L.11), orally amended by Latvia; agenda item 122 *(b)*.
*Meeting numbers.* GA 50th session: 5th Committee 26, 41; plenary 95.

By **decision 50/469** of 23 December, the General Assembly decided that the Fifth Committee should continue its consideration of agenda item 122, the financing of UN peace-keeping forces in the Middle East, at its resumed fiftieth session.

## The Syrian Arab Republic

The General Assembly in 1995 continued to call for Israel's withdrawal from the Golan Heights, an area in the southern part of the Syrian Arab Republic near its borders with Israel and Lebanon. Israel occupied the Golan Heights following the 1967 war, effectively annexing that area when it extended its laws, jurisdiction and administration to the territory towards the end of 1981.[27] The annexation was confirmed by the Israeli Knesset in November 1991.[28]

Israeli practices affecting the human rights of the population in the Golan Heights and other occupied territories have been monitored by the Special Committee on Israeli Practices since 1968 (see below) and have also been the subject of resolutions adopted by the Commission on Human Rights (see PART THREE, Chapter III) and the General Assembly.

### The Golan Heights

**Committee report.** In its annual report,[29] the Special Committee on Israeli Practices noted that the situation in the Syrian Arab Golan did not change significantly during the period under review (August 1994–August 1995), despite continuing negotiations. The problems linked to the affirmation by the citizens of the Golan of their Syrian national identity continued, and a number of persons were arrested in that connection. Practices amounting to administrative harassment also continued. Israel, it was stated, had relentlessly pursued its settlement policy and continued to impose restrictions on the use of water, the consumption of which was said to be subjected to full Israeli control and was reportedly managed through a quota system, with settlers receiving an annual per capita volume of 600 cubic metres, while Syrian citizens were allocated 120 cubic metres. Orders were issued to demolish rainwater reservoirs used for irrigation. Meanwhile, settlers from the Golan Heights had launched a campaign aimed at sensitizing Israeli opinion to the need for the Golan to remain under Israeli control, and investment in both housing and industry was increasing.

The Special Committee recalled the position taken by the General Assembly and the Security Council that the annexation by Israel of the occupied Golan was illegal, and therefore, null and void. It hoped for further progress in the near future in the negotiations concerning the Golan within the framework of the Middle East peace process.

**Report of the Secretary-General.** In October, the Secretary-General reported[30] that he had received no reply from Israel to his May request for information on steps it had taken or envisaged to implement a 1994 Assembly resolution[31] calling on Israel to desist from changing the physical character, demographic composition, institutional structure and legal status of the occupied Syrian Golan, and in particular to desist from establishing settlements.

### GENERAL ASSEMBLY ACTION

On 6 December, the General Assembly adopted **resolution 50/29 D** under the general title "Report of the Special Committee to Investigate Israeli Practices Affecting the Human Rights of the Palestinian People and Other Arabs of the Occupied Territories".

*The General Assembly,*

*Deeply concerned* that the Syrian Golan occupied since 1967 has been under continued Israeli military occupation,

*Recalling* Security Council resolution 497(1981) of 17 December 1981,

*Recalling also* its previous relevant resolutions, the last of which was 49/36 D of 9 December 1994,

*Having considered* the report of the Secretary-General of 20 October 1995,

*Recalling further* its previous relevant resolutions in which, *inter alia*, it called upon Israel to put an end to its occupation of the Arab territories,

*Reaffirming once more* the illegality of the decision of 14 December 1981 taken by Israel to impose its laws, jurisdiction and administration on the occupied Syrian Golan, which has resulted in the effective annexation of that territory,

*Reaffirming* that the acquisition of territory by force is inadmissible under the Charter of the United Nations,

*Reaffirming also* the applicability of the Geneva Convention relative to the Protection of Civilian Persons in Time of War, of 12 August 1949, to the occupied Syrian Golan,

*Bearing in mind* Security Council resolution 237(1967) of 14 June 1967,

*Welcoming* the convening at Madrid of the Peace Conference on the Middle East on the basis of Security Council resolutions 242(1967) of 22 November 1967 and 338(1973) of 22 October 1973 aimed at the realization of a just, comprehensive and lasting peace, and stressing the need for rapid progress in all bilateral negotiations,

1. *Calls upon* Israel, the occupying Power, to comply with the relevant resolutions on the occupied Syrian Golan, in particular Security Council resolution 497(1981), in which the Council, *inter alia*, decided that the Israeli decision to impose its laws, jurisdiction and administration on the occupied Syrian Golan was null and void and without international legal effect, and demanded that Israel, the occupying Power, should rescind forthwith its decisions;

2. *Also calls upon* Israel to desist from changing the physical character, demographic composition, institutional structure and legal status of the occupied Syrian Golan and in particular to desist from the establishment of settlements;

3. *Determines* that all legislative and administrative measures and actions taken or to be taken by Israel, the occupying Power, that purport to alter the character and legal status of the occupied Syrian Golan are null and void, constitute a flagrant violation of international law and of the Geneva Convention relative to the Protection of Civilian Persons in Time of War, of 12 August 1949, and have no legal effect;

4. *Further calls upon* Israel to desist from imposing Israeli citizenship and Israeli identity cards on the Syrian citizens in the occupied Syrian Golan, and to desist from its repressive measures against the population of the occupied Syrian Golan;

5. *Deplores* the violations by Israel of the Geneva Convention relative to the Protection of Civilian Persons in Time of War, of 12 August 1949;

6. *Calls once again upon* Member States not to recognize any of the legislative or administrative measures and actions referred to above;

7. *Requests* the Secretary-General to report to the General Assembly at its fifty-first session on the implementation of the present resolution.

General Assembly resolution 50/29 D

6 December 1995    Meeting 82    139-1-13 (recorded vote)

Approved by Fourth Committee (A/50/606) by recorded vote (121-1-11), 30 November (meeting 25); 12-nation draft (A/C.4/50/L.21); agenda item 85.
*Meeting numbers.* GA 50th session: 4th Committee 24, 25; plenary 82.

Recorded vote in Assembly as follows:

*In favour:* Afghanistan, Albania, Algeria, Armenia, Australia, Austria, Azerbaijan, Bahrain, Bangladesh, Belarus, Belgium, Belize, Benin, Bolivia, Bosnia and Herzegovina, Botswana, Brazil, Brunei Darussalam, Bulgaria, Burkina Faso, Burundi, Cameroon, Canada, Cape Verde, Chad, Chile, China, Colombia, Côte d'Ivoire, Croatia, Cuba, Cyprus, Czech Republic, Denmark, Djibouti, Democratic People's Republic of Korea, Ecuador, Egypt, Eritrea, Estonia, Ethiopia, Fiji, Finland, France, Gabon, Georgia, Germany, Ghana, Greece, Grenada, Guatemala, Guinea, Guinea-Bissau, Guyana, Haiti, Honduras, Hungary, Iceland, India, Indonesia, Iran, Ireland, Italy, Jamaica, Japan, Jordan, Kazakstan, Kuwait, Lao People's Democratic Republic, Latvia, Lebanon, Libyan Arab Jamahiriya, Liechtenstein, Lithuania, Luxembourg, Malawi, Malaysia, Maldives, Mali, Malta, Mauritania, Mauritius, Mexico, Monaco, Mongolia, Morocco, Myanmar, Nepal, Netherlands, New Zealand, Niger, Nigeria, Norway, Oman, Pakistan, Panama, Papua New Guinea, Paraguay, Peru, Philippines, Poland, Portugal, Qatar, Republic of Korea, Republic of Moldova, Romania, Saint Lucia, Samoa, Saudi Arabia, Senegal, Sierra Leone, Singapore, Slovakia, Slovenia, Solomon Islands, South Africa, Spain, Sri Lanka, Sudan, Suriname, Swaziland, Sweden, Syrian Arab Republic, Thailand, the former Yugoslav Republic of Macedonia, Togo, Trinidad and Tobago, Tunisia, Turkey, Uganda, Ukraine, United Arab Emirates, United Kingdom, Vanuatu, Venezuela, Viet Nam, Yemen, Zambia, Zimbabwe.

*Against:* Israel.

*Abstaining:* Antigua and Barbuda, Argentina, Bahamas, Barbados, Dominica, El Salvador, Kenya, Marshall Islands, Micronesia, Nicaragua, Russian Federation, United States, Uruguay.

**Report of the Secretary-General.** On 24 October, the Secretary-General issued a report[32]

reproducing replies from States responding to his 31 August notes verbales requesting information from Israel and other Member States on steps taken or envisaged to implement a 1994 General Assembly resolution[33] demanding Israel's withdrawal from all the occupied Syrian Golan. In the report, Austria expressed the hope that the question of Israeli occupation of the Golan Heights would be resolved in the near future through intensified negotiations. Japan stated that it did not recognize the occupation of the Syrian Golan by Israel as legitimate, and hoped to see a peaceful solution of the problem. In that connection, the Japanese Prime Minister had encouraged direct negotiations on the occasion of his visit to both countries in September 1995.

GENERAL ASSEMBLY ACTION

On 4 December 1995, under the agenda item on the situation in the Middle East, the General Assembly adopted **resolution 50/22 B**.

### The Syrian Golan

*The General Assembly,*

*Having considered* the item entitled "The situation in the Middle East",

*Taking note* of the report of the Secretary-General of 24 October 1995,

*Recalling* Security Council resolution 497(1981) of 17 December 1981,

*Reaffirming* the fundamental principle of the inadmissibility of the acquisition of territory by force,

*Reaffirming once more* the applicability of the Geneva Convention relative to the Protection of Civilian Persons in Time of War, of 12 August 1949, to the occupied Syrian Golan,

*Deeply concerned* that Israel has not withdrawn from the Syrian Golan, which has been under occupation since 1967, contrary to the relevant Security Council and General Assembly resolutions,

*Noting with satisfaction* the convening at Madrid of the Peace Conference on the Middle East on the basis of Security Council resolutions 242(1967) of 22 November 1967 and 338(1973) of 22 October 1973, with the hope that substantial and concrete progress will be achieved on the Syrian and Lebanese tracks for the realization of a just, comprehensive and lasting peace in the region,

1. *Declares* that Israel has failed so far to comply with Security Council resolution 497(1981);

2. *Declares also* that the Knesset decision of 11 November 1991 annexing the occupied Syrian Golan constitutes a grave violation of resolution 497(1981) and therefore is null and void and has no validity whatsoever, and calls upon Israel to rescind it;

3. *Reaffirms its determination* that all relevant provisions of the Regulations annexed to the Hague Convention of 1907, and the Geneva Convention relative to the Protection of Civilian Persons in Time of War, of 12 August 1949, continue to apply to the Syrian territory occupied by Israel since 1967, and calls upon the parties thereto to respect and ensure respect for their obligations under those instruments in all circumstances;

4. *Determines once more* that the continued occupation of the Syrian Golan and its de facto annexation constitute a stumbling-block in the way of achieving a just, comprehensive and lasting peace in the region;

5. *Demands once more* that Israel withdraw from all the occupied Syrian Golan to the line of 4 June 1967 in implementation of the relevant Security Council resolutions;

6. *Requests* the Secretary-General to report to the General Assembly at its fifty-first session on the implementation of the present resolution.

General Assembly resolution 50/22 B

4 December 1995     Meeting 79     66-2-79 (recorded vote)

20-nation draft (A/50/L.38 & Add.1); agenda item 44.
*Meeting numbers.* GA 50th session: plenary 76, 77, 79.

Recorded vote in Assembly as follows:

*In favour:* Algeria, Armenia, Azerbaijan, Bahrain, Bangladesh, Benin, Bhutan, Bolivia, Bosnia and Herzegovina, Brunei Darussalam, Burkina Faso, Burundi, Chad, Chile, China, Colombia, Cuba, Cyprus, Djibouti, Ecuador, Egypt, Ethiopia, Guinea, Guyana, Haiti, Honduras, India, Indonesia, Iran, Jordan, Kazakstan, Kuwait, Lao People's Democratic Republic, Lebanon, Libyan Arab Jamahiriya, Malawi, Malaysia, Maldives, Mauritania, Mauritius, Morocco, Mozambique, Myanmar, Namibia, Nepal, Niger, Oman, Pakistan, Panama, Philippines, Qatar, Saudi Arabia, Senegal, South Africa, Sri Lanka, Sudan, Syria, Thailand, Tunisia, Turkey, Uganda, United Arab Emirates, United Republic of Tanzania, Viet Nam, Yemen, Zambia, Zimbabwe.

*Against:* Israel, United States.

*Abstaining:* Albania, Andorra, Antigua and Barbuda, Argentina, Australia, Austria, Bahamas, Barbados, Belarus, Belgium, Belize, Botswana, Brazil, Bulgaria, Cameroon, Canada, Congo, Costa Rica, Côte d'Ivoire, Czech Republic, Denmark, Dominica, El Salvador, Estonia, Finland, France, Gabon, Georgia, Germany, Ghana, Greece, Haiti, Hungary, Iceland, Ireland, Italy, Jamaica, Japan, Kenya, Latvia, Lesotho, Liechtenstein, Lithuania, Luxembourg, Mali, Malta, Marshall Islands, Mexico, Micronesia, Monaco, Mongolia, Netherlands, New Zealand, Nicaragua, Norway, Papua New Guinea, Paraguay, Peru, Poland, Portugal, Republic of Korea, Romania, Russian Federation, Samoa, Singapore, Slovakia, Slovenia, Solomon Islands, Spain, Suriname, Swaziland, Sweden, Tajikistan, the former Yugoslav Republic of Macedonia, Togo, Ukraine, United Kingdom, Uruguay, Venezuela.

Explaining its vote, the United States said the text served only to complicate the achievement of a mutually acceptable outcome and made the goal of a comprehensive peace much more difficult to attain, as Israel and the Syrian Arab Republic were engaged in a negotiating process to resolve their differences and achieve a lasting agreement. Among those abstaining, Canada regretted not only that the text remained largely unchanged from previous years, but also that a reference to a specific boundary had been added to it (see paragraph 5). In Australia's view, the resolution's new language did not sufficiently reflect the importance of both parties redoubling their efforts to reach agreement on a lasting peace and could complicate their negotiations. Argentina could have voted in favour, had the text not included new elements, such as the reference to the line of 4 June 1967. On behalf of EU, Spain expressed regret over the new wording in paragraph 5, which it felt tried to prejudice the peace negotiations between the parties. Swaziland held the view that harsh-sounding and reprimanding resolutions were no longer rewarding or productive.

Iraq, while supporting the objectives of the resolution, voiced reservations with regard to the last preambular paragraph of the text. Iran had reser-

vations on parts of the text which might be construed as any recognition of Israel. Similarly, the Libyan Arab Jamahiriya stressed that its positive vote should not be construed as any recognition of what was called Israel.

## UNDOF

The United Nations Disengagement Observer Force (UNDOF), established by the Security Council in 1974,[34] as called for under the Agreement on Disengagement of Forces between Israel and the Syrian Arab Republic concluded that year,[35] was charged with supervising the observance of the cease-fire between Israel and Syria in the Golan Heights area and ensuring the separation of their forces. Assisting UNDOF as required were observers from UNTSO.

The Force's mandate was renewed twice in 1995, in May and November, each time for a six-month period.

### Composition and deployment

In November 1995, UNDOF personnel numbered 1,038 troops (down from 1,041 in May) from Austria, Canada and Poland, plus four military observers from UNTSO. In addition, it was assisted by more than 80 observers of the Observer Group Golan of UNTSO assigned to the Israel-Syria Mixed Armistice Commission. By a 6 December letter,[36] the Secretary-General proposed that Japan be added to the list of Member States providing troops to UNDOF. The Security Council President, in a reply on 8 December,[37] expressed the Council members' agreement with the proposal.

UNDOF headquarters were at Camp Faouar, with an office in Damascus. The Force was deployed within, and close to, the area of separation, with base camps and a logistics unit. The Austrian battalion, deployed in the northern part of the area, maintained 16 positions and nine outposts. The Polish battalion, in the southern part, maintained 14 positions and eight outposts. Both battalions conducted mine-clearing under the operational control of headquarters. The Canadian logistics unit—based, like the Polish battalion, in Camp Ziouani—had a detachment at Camp Faouar and performed second-line general transport tasks, rotation transport, control and management of goods received by UNDOF and maintenance of heavy equipment. First-line logistic support, which included the transport of supplies to the positions, was internal to the contingents. Third-line support was provided through normal supply channels by the United Nations. Damascus International Airport served as UNDOF's airhead, with Tel Aviv International Airport also being used. In-theatre air support was provided by UNTSO on request. The ports of La-takia and Haifa were used for shipments by sea.

On 17 January, Major-General Johannes C. Kosters of the Netherlands assumed command of UNDOF, taking over from Colonel Jan Kempara of Poland, who had been acting Force Commander since the departure of Major-General Roman Misztal, also of Poland, in November 1994.

### Activities

UNDOF in 1995 continued to supervise the area of separation between Israeli and Syrian troops in the Golan Heights, to ensure that no military forces of either party were deployed there, by means of permanently manned positions and ob-servation posts and by foot and mobile patrols operating at irregular intervals on predetermined routes by both day and night. In addition, tem-porary outposts were established and patrols con-ducted as necessary. UNDOF made fortnightly in-spections of armament and force levels in the areas of limitation. Liaison officers from the party con-cerned accompanied the inspection teams, whose movements were, however, restricted by both sides and which were denied access to some positions.

The Force Commander and his staff maintained close contact with the military liaison staff of Is-rael and the Syrian Arab Republic. Both parties cooperated with the Force in the execution of its tasks.

UNDOF also assisted ICRC with mail facilities and the passage of persons through the area of separation. Within the means available, medical treatment was provided on request to the local population.

**Reports of the Secretary-General (May and November).** Before the expiration on 31 May and again on 30 November of the UNDOF mandate, the Secretary-General reported to the Security Council on UNDOF activities which had taken place since 22 November 1994,[38] and again from 17 May to 17 November 1995.[39] Both reports noted that UNDOF continued to fulfil its functions effectively, with the cooperation of the parties.

In concluding observations, the Secretary-General noted that despite the quiet in the Israel-Syria sector, the situation in the Middle East con-tinued to be potentially dangerous and was likely to remain so, unless and until a comprehensive set-tlement covering all aspects of the Middle East problem could be reached. He hoped for deter-mined efforts by all concerned to tackle the prob-lem in all its aspects, with a view to arriving at a just and durable peace settlement, as called for by the Security Council in resolution 338(1973).[40] Stating that he considered UNDOF's continued presence in the area to be essential, the Secretary-General, with the agreement of both Syria and Is-rael, each time recommended that the UNDOF mandate be extended for a further six months,

until 30 November 1995 in the first instance and 31 May 1996 in the second.

**SECURITY COUNCIL ACTION (May and November)**

Meeting on 30 May, the Security Council, with-out debate, adopted **resolution 996(1995)**.

*The Security Council,*

*Having considered* the report of the Secretary-General on the United Nations Disengagement Observer Force of 17 May 1995,

*Decides:*

*(a)* To call upon the parties concerned to implement immediately its resolution 338(1973) of 22 October 1973;

*(b)* To renew the mandate of the United Nations Disengagement Observer Force for another period of six months, that is, until 30 November 1995;

*(c)* To request the Secretary-General to submit, at the end of this period, a report on the development in the situation and the measures taken to implement Secu-rity Council resolution 338(1973).

Security Council resolution 996(1995)

30 May 1995     Meeting 3541     Adopted unanimously

Draft prepared in consultations among Council members (S/1995/430).

On 28 November, the Council, also without de-bate, adopted **resolution 1024(1995)**.

*The Security Council,*

*Having considered* the report of the Secretary-General on the United Nations Disengagement Observer Force of 17 November 1995;

*Decides:*

*(a)* To call upon the parties concerned to implement immediately its resolution 338(1973) of 22 October 1973;

*(b)* To renew the mandate of the United Nations Disengagement Observer Force for another period of six months, that is, until 31 May 1996;

*(c)* To request the Secretary-General to submit, at the end of this period, a report on the development in the situation and the measures taken to implement Secu-rity Council resolution 338(1973).

Security Council resolution 1024(1995)

28 November 1995     Meeting 3599     Adopted unanimously

Draft prepared in consultations among Council members (S/1995/990).

After the adoption of each resolution, the Pres-ident made the following statement on behalf of the Council:[41]

As is known, the report of the Secretary-General on the United Nations Disengagement Observer Force states, in paragraph 18 [14 in the November report]: "Despite the present quiet in the Israel-Syria sector, the situation in the Middle East continues to be poten-tially dangerous and is likely to remain so, unless and until a comprehensive settlement covering all aspects of the Middle East problem can be reached". That statement of the Secretary-General reflects the view of the Security Council.

### Financing

**Report of the Secretary-General (April).** In April 1995, the Secretary-General provided information[42] on the financial performance of UNDOF for the period from 1 December 1993 to 30 November 1994, reflecting overall savings of $805,000 gross ($891,000 net), due mainly to savings from lower personnel costs. As at 31 March 1995, for the period from UNDOF's inception in 1974 to 30 November 1994, outstanding assessments amounted to $61.4 million.

The Secretary-General proposed that the General Assembly credit Member States with the unencumbered net balance of $891,000 against their assessments in respect of any future mandate period. ACABQ, in a June report,[21] concurred with the proposal.

Following consideration of those reports from the Secretary-General and the Advisory Committee, the General Assembly on 12 July decided that there should be set off against the apportionment among Member States, in respect of future mandate periods of UNDOF as might be approved by the Security Council, their respective share in the unencumbered balance of $891,000 net for the period from 1 December 1993 to 30 November 1994. The Assembly adopted **decision 49/413 B** without vote, after the Fifth Committee, on 23 June, had approved, also without vote, the draft[43] submitted by its Chairman following informal consultations.

**Report of the Secretary-General (September).** In a 7 September report,[44] the Secretary-General presented cost estimates of $18,753,000 gross ($18,221,000 net) for the maintenance of UNDOF from 1 December 1995 to 30 June 1996, conforming with the new budget cycle from 1 July to 30 June decided on by the General Assembly in 1994.[24] The cost estimates provided for the continuation of an average mission strength of 1,036 military personnel, 36 international civilian staff and 84 locally recruited staff.

Those estimates reflected an increase of 0.4 per cent over the monthly commitments of $2,677,583 gross authorized in December 1994 by the Assembly[45] for the period from 1 June 1995.

The Secretary-General noted that as at 31 July 1995, a total of $1,116.6 million had been appropriated for UNDOF and the United Nations Emergency Force (UNEF) from inception to 30 November 1995. Assessed contributions for the same period amounted to $1,083.5 million, while contributions received totalled $1,015.5 million, leaving an outstanding balance of $68 million. Troop contributors had been fully reimbursed through 31 May 1995.

ACABQ in October recommended[46] that the Assembly appropriate $16,065,498 gross ($15,564,000 net) for the period from 1 June to 30 November 1995. Additionally, should the Security

Council decide to continue the Force beyond that date, the Committee recommended that the Secretary-General be authorized to enter into monthly commitments of $2,679,000 gross ($2,603,000 net) for the period from 30 November 1995 to 30 June 1996, and that the Assembly assess such amounts.

On 1 December 1995, the General Assembly adopted **resolution 50/20 A**.

### Financing of the United Nations Disengagement Observer Force

*The General Assembly,*

*Having considered* the report of the Secretary-General on the financing of the United Nations Disengagement Observer Force and the related report of the Advisory Committee on Administrative and Budgetary Questions,

*Bearing in mind* Security Council resolution 350(1974) of 31 May 1974, by which the Council established the United Nations Disengagement Observer Force, and the subsequent resolutions by which the Council extended the mandate of the Force, the latest of which was resolution 996(1995) of 30 May 1995,

*Recalling* its resolution 3211 B(XXIX) of 29 November 1974 on the financing of the United Nations Emergency Force and the United Nations Disengagement Observer Force, and its subsequent resolutions thereon, the latest of which was resolution 49/225 of 23 December 1994, and decision 49/413 B of 12 July 1995,

*Reaffirming* that the costs of the United Nations Disengagement Observer Force are expenses of the Organization to be borne by Member States in accordance with Article 17, paragraph 2, of the Charter of the United Nations,

*Recalling also* its previous decisions regarding the fact that, in order to meet the expenditures caused by the United Nations Disengagement Observer Force, a different procedure is required from the one applied to meet expenditures of the regular budget of the United Nations,

*Taking into account* the fact that the economically more developed countries are in a position to make relatively larger contributions and that the economically less developed countries have a relatively limited capacity to contribute towards such an operation,

*Bearing in mind* the special responsibilities of the States permanent members of the Security Council, as indicated in General Assembly resolution 1874(S-IV) of 27 June 1963, in the financing of such operations,

*Mindful* of the fact that it is essential to provide the United Nations Disengagement Observer Force with the necessary financial resources to enable it to fulfil its responsibilities under the relevant resolutions of the Security Council,

*Concerned* that the Secretary-General continues to face difficulties in meeting the obligations of the United Nations Disengagement Observer Force on a current basis, including reimbursement to current and former troop-contributing States,

*Concerned also* that the surplus balances in the Suspense Account for the United Nations Disengagement Observer Force have been used to meet expenses of the

Force in order to compensate for the lack of income resulting from non-payment and late payment by Member States of their contributions,

1. *Takes note* of the status of contributions to the United Nations Disengagement Observer Force as at 20 November 1995, including the contributions unpaid in the amount of 64,565,741 United States dollars, representing 6 per cent of the total assessed contributions from the inception of the Force to the period ending 30 November 1995, notes that some 30 per cent of the Member States have paid their assessed contributions in full, and urges all other Member States concerned, particularly those in arrears, to ensure the payment of their outstanding assessed contributions;

2. *Expresses concern* about the financial situation with regard to peace-keeping activities, particularly as regards the reimbursement of troop contributors, owing to overdue payments by Member States of their assessments;

3. *Urges* all Member States to make every possible effort to ensure the payment of their assessed contributions to the United Nations Disengagement Observer Force promptly and in full;

4. *Endorses* the observations and recommendations contained in the report of the Advisory Committee on Administrative and Budgetary Questions;

5. *Requests* the Secretary-General to take all necessary action to ensure that the United Nations Disengagement Observer Force is administered with a maximum of efficiency and economy;

6. *Decides* to appropriate to the Special Account for the United Nations Disengagement Observer Force the amount of 16,065,498 dollars gross (15,564,000 dollars net), authorized and apportioned by the General Assembly in paragraph 11 of its resolution 49/225 for the operation of the Force for the period from 1 June to 30 November 1995, inclusive;

7. *Authorizes* the Secretary-General to enter into commitments for the United Nations Disengagement Observer Force at a rate not to exceed 2,679,000 dollars gross (2,603,000 dollars net) per month for a period up to seven months from 1 December 1995, should the Security Council decide to continue the Force beyond the period of six months authorized under its resolution 996(1995), the said amount to be apportioned among Member States in accordance with the scheme set out in the present resolution;

8. *Decides*, as an ad hoc arrangement, to apportion the amount referred to in paragraph 7 above among Member States in accordance with the composition of groups set out in paragraphs 3 and 4 of General Assembly resolution 43/232 of 1 March 1989, as adjusted by the Assembly in its resolutions 44/192 B of 21 December 1989, 45/269 of 27 August 1991, 46/198 A of 20 December 1991 and 47/218 A of 23 December 1992 and its decision 48/472 A of 23 December 1993, and taking into account the scale of assessments for the years 1995 and 1996, subject to the decision of the Security Council to extend the mandate of the United Nations Disengagement Observer Force beyond 30 November 1995 and the mandate periods to be decided upon by the Council;

9. *Decides also* that, in accordance with the provisions of its resolution 973(X) of 15 December 1955, there shall be set off against the apportionment among Member States, as provided for in paragraph 8 above, their respective share in the Tax Equalization Fund of the estimated staff assessment income of 532,000 dollars for the period from 1 December 1995 to 30 June 1996, inclusive;

10. *Decides further* that there shall be set off against the apportionment among Member States, as provided for in paragraph 8 above, their respective share in the estimated other income of 9,000 dollars for the period from 1 December 1995 to 30 June 1996, inclusive;

11. *Decides* that there shall be set off against the apportionment among Member States, as provided for in paragraph 8 above, their respective share in the unencumbered balance of 805,000 dollars gross (891,000 dollars net) for the period from 1 December 1993 to 30 November 1994, inclusive, pursuant to General Assembly decision 49/413 B;

12. *Invites* voluntary contributions to the United Nations Disengagement Observer Force in cash and in the form of services and supplies acceptable to the Secretary-General, to be administered, as appropriate, in accordance with the procedure established by the General Assembly in its resolutions 43/230 of 21 December 1988, 44/192 A of 21 December 1989 and 45/258 of 3 May 1991;

13. *Decides also* to keep the sub-item entitled "United Nations Disengagement Observer Force", under the agenda item entitled "Financing of the United Nations peace-keeping forces in the Middle East", under review during its fiftieth session.

General Assembly resolution 50/20 A

1 December 1995     Meeting 76     Adopted without vote

Approved by Fifth Committee (A/50/792) without vote, 29 November (meeting 33); draft by Chairman (A/C.5/50/L.5), based on informal consultations; agenda item 122 *(a)*.
*Meeting numbers.* GA 50th session: 5th Committee 26, 33; plenary 76.

By **decision 50/469** of 23 December, the General Assembly decided that the Fifth Committee should continue its consideration of agenda item 122, the financing of UN peace-keeping forces in the Middle East, at its resumed fiftieth session.

*REFERENCES*
[1]S/1996/45. [2]YUN 1978, p. 312, SC res. 425(1978), 19 Mar. 1978. [3]S/1995/45 & Corr.1. [4]S/1995/554. [5]A/50/88-S/1995/167. [6]S/1995/170. [7]YUN 1978, p. 312, SC res. 426(1978), 19 Mar. 1978. [8]YUN 1982, p. 450, SC res. 509(1982), 6 June 1982. [9]A/50/283-S/1995/570. [10]S/1995/58. [11]YUN 1994, p. 629. [12]E/1995/23-E/CN.4/1995/176 (res. 1995/67). [13]YUN 1978, p. 296. [14]YUN 1982, p. 428. [15]Ibid., p. 450, SC res. 511(1982), 18 June 1982. [16]S/1995/66. [17]S/PRST/1995/4. [18]S/1995/595. [19]S/PRST/1995/35. [20]A/49/644/Add.1. [21]A/49/785/Add.1 & Add.1/Corr.1. [22]A/C.5/49/L.52. [23]A/50/543. [24]YUN 1994, p. 1338, GA res. 49/233 A, 23 Dec. 1994. [25]Ibid., p. 636, GA res. 49/226, 23 Dec. 1994. [26]A/50/694. [27]YUN 1981, p. 309. [28]YUN 1992, p. 415. [29]A/50/463. [30]A/50/660. [31]YUN 1994, p. 654, GA res. 49/36 D, 9 Dec. 1994. [32]A/50/574. [33]YUN 1994, p. 638, GA res. 49/87 B, 16 Dec. 1994. [34]YUN 1974, p. 205, SC res. 350(1974), 31 May 1974. [35]Ibid., p. 198. [36]S/1995/1022. [37]S/1995/1023. [38]S/1995/398. [39]S/1995/952. [40]YUN 1973, p. 213, SC res. 338(1973), 22 Oct. 1973. [41]S/PRST/1995/29, S/PRST/1995/59. [42]A/49/553/Add.1. [43]A/C.5/49/L.51. [44]A/50/386 & Corr.1. [45]YUN 1994, p. 642, GA res. 49/225, 23 Dec. 1994. [46]A/50/694.

PART THREE


Human rights

Chapter I

# Promotion of human rights

Over the last half century, the United Nations has created a strong and effective infrastructure to support its Charter goals of reaffirming faith in fundamental human rights, in the dignity and worth of the human person, in the equal rights of men and women and of nations large and small, and to establish conditions under which justice and respect for the obligations arising from treaties and other sources of international law can be maintained.

Each year, the Commission on Human Rights, its subsidiary body—the Subcommission on Prevention of Discrimination and Protection of Minorities—and human rights treaty-monitoring bodies report to the Economic and Social Council and the General Assembly on their work to promote respect for human rights. In addition, the Office of the UN High Commissioner for Human Rights, with the assistance of the UN Centre for Human Rights, supports activities to alleviate human suffering and ensure human dignity and equality in all regions of the world.

A panoply of human rights instruments has also been assembled by the United Nations over the years to complement and to further efforts to protect and promote human rights. The adoption in 1948 of the 30-article Universal Declaration of Human Rights was a landmark action by the United Nations. Two International Covenants, covering a wide spectrum of civil, political, economic, social and cultural rights, were adopted by the General Assembly in 1966, and, together with the Universal Declaration, are known as the "International Bill of Human Rights". Other UN human rights instruments deal with specific problems, such as genocide and torture, and specific groups of people, such as women, children and migrant workers; the implementation of some human rights instruments is monitored by expert committees which meet under UN auspices. A host of advisory services are offered to assist countries in ensuring human rights protection.

World conferences on human rights were convened by the United Nations in 1968 in Tehran, during the International Year for Human Rights, and in Vienna in June 1993. A World Public Information Campaign for Human Rights was launched in 1994 and a UN Decade for Human Rights Education began on 1 January 1995. Human Rights Day is observed each year on 10 December.

## UN machinery

### Commission on Human Rights

The Commission on Human Rights held its fifty-first session in Geneva from 30 January to 10 March 1995,[1] during which it adopted 93 resolutions and 15 decisions. Another 56 texts—8 draft resolutions and 48 draft decisions—were recommended for adoption by the Economic and Social Council. On 28 July, the Council, by **decision 1995/314**, noted the Commission's report on its fifty-first session.

On 31 January, the Commission invited[2] experts, special rapporteurs, special representatives and chairmen/rapporteurs of various working groups to participate in the discussion of their reports at Commission meetings.

On 3 February, the Commission invited[3] the representative of the Working Group on Enforced or Involuntary Disappearances dealing with the issue of enforced disappearances in the territory of the former Yugoslavia to participate in meetings dealing with the agenda item on enforced or involuntary disappearances.

#### Organization of work in 1996

On 3 March, the Human Rights Commission, in accordance with a 1994 Economic and Social Council decision,[4] recommended[5] that its next regular session be rescheduled, to later in the year, on a one-year trial basis (from 18 March to 26 April 1996). The Council approved that recommendation on 25 July, by **decision 1995/296**.

The Commission on 10 March recommended[6] that the Council authorize 40 fully serviced additional meetings, to be used only if necessary, for the Commission's fifty-second (1996) session. By **decision 1995/301** of 25 July, the Council approved that recommendation.

#### Thematic procedures

As requested by the Commission in 1994,[7] the Secretariat issued in February a note[8] containing the conclusions and recommendations of the Commission's thematic special rapporteurs and working groups.

**Commission action.** On 8 March, the Human Rights Commission encouraged[9] Governments encountering human rights problems to cooperate more closely with it through thematic procedures, particularly by inviting a thematic special rapporteur or working group to visit their countries. Governments were invited to study carefully recommendations addressed to them under thematic procedures and to keep relevant mechanisms informed on progress made in their implementation. Special rapporteurs and working groups were asked to provide comments on problems of responsiveness and the results of analyses, and to make suggestions on areas that might use the advisory services of the Centre for Human Rights. They should also include in their reports gender-disaggregated data and information on human rights violations directed against women. The Secretary-General should consider convening a meeting of all thematic special rapporteurs and working group chairmen to enable an exchange of views and closer cooperation; to issue annually the conclusions and recommendations of special rapporteurs and working groups; to ensure the availability of resources for effective implementation of all thematic mandates; and to provide in 1996 a list of all persons currently constituting the thematic and country procedures, including their country of origin.

## Subcommission on Prevention of Discrimination and Protection of Minorities

### Forty-seventh session

The Subcommission on Prevention of Discrimination and Protection of Minorities, at its forty-seventh session (Geneva, 31 July–25 August),[10] adopted 40 resolutions and 19 decisions, and recommended for adoption by the Commission on Human Rights two draft resolutions and 10 draft decisions.

The Subcommission adopted decisions relating to its organization of work,[11] its methods of work,[12] the composition of its pre-sessional working groups[13] and its 1995 agenda.[14]

**Report of Subcommission Chairman.** In January, the Subcommission's 1994 Chairman, Judith Sefi Attah (Nigeria), reported[15] on progress made in implementing a 1994 Commission resolution[16] on improving the Subcommission's work.

**Commission action.** On 3 March, the Human Rights Commission called on[17] the Subcommission, in fulfilling its functions and duties, to be guided by relevant resolutions of the Economic and Social Council. The Subcommission was asked to implement the guidelines annexed to a 1992 Subcommission resolution,[18] including those related to the number of studies and require-

ments for submission. It asked the Subcommission to re-evaluate its 1994 decision[16] regarding item 6 entitled "Question of the violation of human rights and fundamental freedoms, including policies of racial discrimination and segregation and of apartheid, in all countries, with particular reference to colonial and other dependent countries and territories: report of the Subcommission under Commission on Human Rights resolution 8(XXIII)". Also, the Subcommission was to ensure that each completed study was accompanied by a short summary, to help secure the widest possible dissemination.

On 25 July, the Economic and Social Council, by **decision 1995/261**, approved a Commission invitation to the 1994 Subcommission Chairman to consult with Bureau members and to invite the 1995 Subcommission Chairman to report on progress made regarding the Subcommission's work.

**Subcommission action.** On 24 August, the Subcommission decided[19] to continue the practice of considering agenda item 6 as soon as its agenda was approved.

### Review of Subcommission work

In a June note,[20] the Secretary-General provided a review of developments between 15 June 1994 and 1 May 1995 in areas of concern to the Subcommission. These related to: the 1965 International Convention on the Elimination of All Forms of Racial Discrimination;[21] the 1966 International Covenants on Human Rights;[22] the 1973 International Convention on the Suppression and Punishment of the Crime of Apartheid;[23] the 1984 Convention against Torture and Other Cruel, Inhuman or Degrading Treatment or Punishment;[24] the 1989 Convention on the Rights of the Child;[25] and the 1990 International Convention on the Protection of the Rights of All Migrant Workers and Members of Their Families.[26] The Subcommission also dealt with effective implementation of international instruments on human rights, including reporting obligations of States parties.

## Office of the High Commissioner for Human Rights

**Reports of the High Commissioner.** In 1995, the Commission on Human Rights had before it a February report[27] submitted by the UN High Commissioner for Human Rights, José Ayala Lasso (Ecuador), appointed in 1994,[28] in which he discussed activities undertaken to fulfil his mandate.

In accordance with a 1993 General Assembly request,[29] the High Commissioner in July provided updated information on his activities and on policy matters.[30] On 28 July, the Economic and Social Council, by **decision 1995/314**, noted the High Commissioner's report.

In a November report,[31] the High Commissioner described activities related to the promotion and protection of human rights, thematic issues and various elements of UN human rights machinery. Since submitting his first report in 1994,[28] the High Commissioner had visited Burundi and Rwanda (March) to review the ongoing UN human rights activities there (see PART TWO, Chapter II and PART THREE, Chapter III). He also visited Australia, Canada, Colombia, Costa Rica, Cuba, the Holy See and Italy, India, Panama, Spain and the United States.

The success of the human rights programme and of the High Commissioner depended on support and understanding from the international community and on cooperation with Governments, international organizations, non-governmental organizations (NGOs) and people throughout the world. Adequate human and financial resources had to be provided to implement the Vienna Declaration and Programme of Action, adopted by the 1993 World Conference on Human Rights,[32] and the activities of both the High Commissioner and the Centre for Human Rights.

**Commission action.** On 7 March, the Commission asked[33] for additional resources to enhance the capability of the High Commissioner and the Centre to fulfil effectively their respective mandates. Noting a February announcement by the High Commissioner[27] of a review of Secretariat structures dealing with human rights, particularly the Centre, the Commission asked that he continue to keep Member States informed. The Secretary-General, in preparing the proposed 1996-1997 programme budget, was to take into account recommendations resulting from the review.

## Centre for Human Rights

**Commission action.** On 10 March, the Human Rights Commission stressed[34] that restructuring of the Centre for Human Rights should ensure full implementation of the 1993 Vienna Declaration and Programme of Action and of all mandates established by human rights bodies. It requested the Secretary-General to convene, at least twice yearly in Geneva, meetings with all interested States to provide information on Centre activities and restructuring process.

The Economic and Social Council, by **decision 1995/293** of 25 July, approved the Commission's request.

**Secretary-General reports.** In response to a 1994 General Assembly request,[35] the Secretary-General in January submitted to the Commission an interim report[36] on developments to strengthen the Centre for Human Rights. In

October, he reported[37] to the Assembly regarding the allocation of resources to the Centre.

## Composition of staff

**Commission action.** On 7 March, the Commission, by a roll-call vote of 35 to 16, with 1 abstention, asked[38] the Secretary-General to adopt measures regarding recruitment for the Centre of personnel from developing countries. In signing agreements with countries on the hiring of junior professional officers (JPOs), those countries should ensure financial resources to guarantee that personnel from developing countries were able to work as JPOs, with a view to conforming to the principle of equitable geographical distribution. The Secretary-General was to report to the Assembly in 1995 on the geographical composition and functions of Centre staff, and to make recommendations to improve the current situation.

ECONOMIC AND SOCIAL COUNCIL ACTION

In July, the Economic and Social Council adopted **decision 1995/275**.

### Composition of the staff of the Centre for Human Rights

At its 52nd plenary meeting, on 25 July 1995, the Economic and Social Council, taking note of Commission on Human Rights resolution 1995/61 of 7 March 1995, endorsed the Commission's request to the Secretary-General to submit a comprehensive report to the General Assembly at its fiftieth session on the geographical composition and functions of the staff of the Centre for Human Rights and other categories of officers involved in its activities, including measures adopted and their results, and recommendations for improving the current situation.

Economic and Social Council decision 1995/275

29-20 (roll-call vote)

Draft by Commission on Human Rights (E/1995/23/Corr.2); agenda item 5 *(d)*. *Meeting numbers.* ESC 51, 52.

Roll-call vote in Council as follows:

*In favour:* Bahamas, Bhutan, Brazil, Chile, China, Colombia, Costa Rica, Côte d'Ivoire, Cuba, Egypt, India, Indonesia, Jamaica, Libyan Arab Jamahiriya, Malaysia, Mexico, Nigeria, Pakistan, Philippines, Republic of Korea, Senegal, South Africa, Sri Lanka, Sudan, Thailand, Uganda, United Republic of Tanzania, Venezuela, Zimbabwe.

*Against:* Australia, Belarus, Bulgaria, Canada, Denmark, France, Germany, Greece, Ireland, Japan, Luxembourg, Netherlands, Norway, Poland, Portugal, Romania, Russian Federation, Ukraine, United Kingdom, United States.

**Note by the Secretary-General.** In accordance with the Commission's request, the Secretary-General in October provided information to the Assembly on the current geographical distribution of Professional-level posts of the Centre.[39]

GENERAL ASSEMBLY ACTION

On 22 December, the General Assembly, by **decision 50/462**, noted part six of the Third (Social, Humanitarian and Cultural) Committee's report.[40] In addition, by **decision 50/464**, also adopted on 22 December, the Assembly included in its provisional agenda for 1996 and subsequent sessions a sub-item entitled ''Report of the United Nations High Commissioner for Human Rights'' under the item entitled ''Human rights questions''.

On the same date, the Assembly adopted **resolution 50/187**.

### Strengthening of the Office of the United Nations High Commissioner for Human Rights/ Centre for Human Rights

*The General Assembly,*

*Recalling* its resolutions 44/135 of 15 December 1989, 45/180 of 21 December 1990, 46/111 and 46/118 of 17 December 1991, 47/127 of 18 December 1992, 48/129 and 48/141 of 20 December 1993 and 49/195 of 23 December 1994, and bearing in mind all relevant resolutions of the Economic and Social Council and the Commission on Human Rights,

*Considering* that the promotion of universal respect for and observance of human rights and fundamental freedoms is one of the basic purposes of the United Nations enshrined in the Charter of the United Nations and a priority activity of the Organization,

*Taking into account* the fact that in the Vienna Declaration and Programme of Action, the World Conference on Human Rights, held at Vienna from 14 to 25 June 1993, concerned by the growing disparity between the activities of the Centre for Human Rights of the Secretariat and the human, financial and other resources available to carry them out, and bearing in mind the resources needed for other important United Nations programmes, requested the Secretary-General and the General Assembly to take immediate steps to increase substantially the resources for the human rights programme, from within the existing and future regular budgets of the United Nations, and to take urgent steps to seek increased extrabudgetary resources,

*Noting* that in the Vienna Declaration and Programme of Action, the World Conference on Human Rights stressed the importance of strengthening the Centre,

*Taking into account* the establishment of the post of the United Nations High Commissioner for Human Rights, as well as the mandate for the post, including its coordinating role and its overall supervision of the Centre, as well as the request by the General Assembly in resolution 48/141 for appropriate staff and resources to enable the High Commissioner to fulfil his mandate,

*Noting with concern* that the response to these requests has not been commensurate with the needs, resulting in a serious imbalance between the mandates assigned to the High Commissioner and the Centre by the competent bodies of the United Nations system in the field of human rights and the resources available to fulfil all of these mandates,

*Taking into account* the fact that, in the Vienna Declaration and Programme of Action, the World Conference on Human Rights urged all United Nations organs, bodies and the specialized agencies whose activities deal with human rights to cooperate in order to strengthen, rationalize and streamline their activities, taking into account the need to avoid unnecessary duplication,

*Noting* that the High Commissioner and the Centre are a unity whereby the High Commissioner, in accordance with resolution 48/141, sets the policy directions and the priority of action and the Centre implements those policies under the direction of the head of the Centre, the Assistant Secretary-General for Human Rights,

*Taking into account* the fact that the responsibilities of the High Commissioner include, *inter alia*, engaging in a dialogue with all Governments in the implementation of his mandate with a view to the promotion and protection of all human rights, and rationalizing, adapting, strengthening and streamlining the United Nations machinery in the field of human rights with a view to improving its efficiency and effectiveness,

*Acknowledging* that, while further improvement in the functioning and efficiency of the Centre, together with a strong emphasis on good management practices, is needed in order to enable the Centre to cope with its constantly increasing workload, good management practices need to be complemented by additional resources commensurate with additional mandates,

*Taking note* of the information provided by the High Commissioner with regard to the ongoing process aimed at increasing the efficiency and effectiveness of the Centre, and bearing in mind, in this context, the request of the Commission on Human Rights in its resolution 1995/93 of 10 March 1995 to the Secretary-General to convene, at least twice a year at Geneva, meetings with all interested States to provide information on the activities conducted by the Centre and its process of restructuring,

*Recognizing* that this process should contribute to the strengthening of the functional framework for integrated and consolidated activities of the Secretariat in the field of human rights,

*Recalling* that in its report to the Special Commission of the Economic and Social Council, the Commission on Human Rights reaffirmed that the paramount consideration in the employment of staff at every level was the need for the highest standards of efficiency, competence and integrity, and that it was convinced that that was compatible with the principle of equitable geographical distribution, and bearing in mind Article 101, paragraph 3, of the Charter of the United Nations,

*Taking note* of the report of the Secretary-General on the strengthening of the Centre for Human Rights of the Secretariat and the note by the Secretary-General on the geographical composition and functions of the staff of the Centre, as well as the report of the United Nations High Commissioner for Human Rights,

1. *Supports and encourages* the efforts of the Secretary-General to enhance the role and further improve the functioning of the Centre for Human Rights of the Secretariat, under the overall supervision of the United Nations High Commissioner for Human Rights;

2. *Reiterates* the need to ensure that all the necessary human, financial, material and personnel resources are provided without delay to the High Commissioner and the Centre to enable them to carry out efficiently, effectively and expeditiously the mandates assigned to them;

3. *Requests* the Secretary-General to make available additional human and financial resources, within the overall regular budget of the United Nations, to enhance the capability of the High Commissioner and of the Centre to fulfil effectively their respective mandates and their ability to carry out mandated operational activities and to coordinate efficiently with other relevant departments of the Secretariat, as well as other organs,

bodies and specialized agencies of the United Nations system, including on logistical and administrative questions, having due regard to the need to finance and implement activities of the United Nations related to development;

4. *Supports* fully the High Commissioner in his efforts to strengthen the human rights activities of the United Nations, *inter alia*, through measures aimed at restructuring the Centre to improve its efficiency and effectiveness;

5. *Also requests* the Secretary-General to submit an interim report to the Commission on Human Rights at its fifty-second session and a final report to the General Assembly at its fifty-first session on the strengthening of the human rights programme and on the measures taken to implement the present resolution.

General Assembly resolution 50/187

22 December 1995     Meeting 99     Adopted without vote

Approved by Third Committee (A/50/635/Add.2) without vote, 14 December (meeting 58); 74-nation draft (A/C.3/50/L.62/Rev.1), orally revised; agenda item 112 *(b)*.

*Meeting numbers.* GA 50th session: 3rd Committee 35, 38-51, 55, 58; plenary 99.

## Strengthening UN action

On 22 December, the General Assembly adopted **resolution 50/174**.

**Strengthening of United Nations action in the human rights field through the promotion of international cooperation and the importance of non-selectivity, impartiality and objectivity**
*The General Assembly,*

*Reaffirming its faith* in fundamental human rights, in the dignity and worth of the human person and the equal rights of men and women and of nations large and small, and reaffirming also its determination to promote social progress and better standards of living in greater freedom,

*Bearing in mind* that among the purposes of the United Nations are those of developing friendly relations among nations based on respect for the principle of equal rights and self-determination of peoples and taking other appropriate measures to strengthen universal peace, as well as achieving international cooperation in solving international problems of an economic, social, cultural or humanitarian character and in promoting and encouraging respect for human rights and fundamental freedoms for all without distinction as to race, sex, language or religion,

*Recalling* that, in accordance with Article 55 of the Charter of the United Nations, the Organization shall promote universal respect for and observance of human rights and fundamental freedoms for all, with a view to the creation of conditions of stability and well-being that are necessary for peaceful and friendly relations among nations, based on respect for the principle of equal rights and self-determination of peoples and that, in accordance with Article 56, all Members pledge themselves to take joint and separate action in cooperation with the Organization for the achievement of the purposes set forth in Article 55,

*Reiterating* that Member States should continue to act in the human rights field in conformity with the provisions of the Charter,

*Desirous* of achieving further progress in international cooperation in promoting and encouraging respect for human rights and fundamental freedoms,

*Considering* that such international cooperation should be based on the principles embodied in international law, especially the Charter, as well as the Universal Declaration of Human Rights, the International Covenants on Human Rights and other relevant instruments,

*Deeply convinced* that United Nations action in this field should be based not only on a profound understanding of the broad range of problems existing in all societies but also on full respect for the political, economic and social realities of each of them, in strict compliance with the purposes and principles of the Charter and for the basic purpose of promoting and encouraging respect for human rights and fundamental freedoms through international cooperation,

*Reaffirming* all its resolutions in this regard,

*Bearing in mind* its resolutions 2131(XX) of 21 December 1965, 2625(XXV) of 24 October 1970 and 36/103 of 9 December 1981,

*Reaffirming* the importance of ensuring the universality, objectivity and non-selectivity of the consideration of human rights issues, as affirmed in the Vienna Declaration and Programme of Action, adopted by the World Conference on Human Rights on 25 June 1993,

*Aware* of the fact that the promotion, protection and full exercise of all human rights and fundamental freedoms as legitimate concerns of the world community should be guided by the principles of universality, non-selectivity, impartiality and objectivity and should not be used for political ends,

*Affirming* the importance of the objectivity, independence and discretion of the special rapporteurs and representatives on thematic issues and countries, as well as of the members of the working groups, in carrying out their mandates,

*Affirming also* the need to cooperate so as to strengthen, rationalize and streamline United Nations activities on human rights, taking into account the need to avoid unnecessary duplication,

*Underlining* the obligation that Governments have to promote and protect human rights and to carry out the responsibilities that they have undertaken under international law, especially the Charter, as well as various international instruments in the field of human rights,

1. *Reiterates* that, by virtue of the principle of equal rights and self-determination of peoples enshrined in the Charter of the United Nations, all peoples have the right freely to determine, without external interference, their political status and to pursue their economic, social and cultural development, and that every State has the duty to respect that right within the provisions of the Charter, including respect for territorial integrity;

2. *Reaffirms* that it is a purpose of the United Nations and the task of all Member States, in cooperation with the Organization, to promote and encourage respect for human rights and fundamental freedoms and to remain vigilant with regard to violations of human rights wherever they occur;

3. *Calls upon* all Member States to base their activities for the protection and promotion of human rights, including the development of further international cooperation in this field, on the Charter of the United Nations, the Universal Declaration of Human Rights,

the International Covenant on Economic, Social and Cultural Rights, the International Covenant on Civil and Political Rights, and other relevant international instruments, and to refrain from activities that are inconsistent with that international framework;

4. *Considers* that international cooperation in this field should make an effective and practical contribution to the urgent task of preventing mass and flagrant violations of human rights and fundamental freedoms for all and to the strengthening of international peace and security;

5. *Affirms* that the promotion, protection, and full realization of all human rights and fundamental freedoms, as legitimate concerns of the world community, should be guided by the principles of non-selectivity, impartiality and objectivity, and should not be used for political ends;

6. *Requests* all human rights bodies within the United Nations system, as well as the special rapporteurs and representatives, independent experts and working groups, to take duly into account the contents of the present resolution in carrying out their mandates;

7. *Expresses its conviction* that an unbiased and fair approach to human rights issues contributes to the promotion of international cooperation as well as to the effective promotion, protection and realization of human rights and fundamental freedoms;

8. *Stresses*, in this context, the continuing need for impartial and objective information on the political, economic and social situations and events of all countries;

9. *Invites* Member States to consider adopting, as appropriate, within the framework of their respective legal systems and in accordance with their obligations under international law, especially the Charter, and international human rights instruments, the measures that they may deem appropriate to achieve further progress in international cooperation in promoting and encouraging respect for human rights and fundamental freedoms;

10. *Requests* the Commission on Human Rights to take duly into account the present resolution and to consider further proposals for the strengthening of United Nations action in the human rights field through the promotion of international cooperation and the importance of non-selectivity, impartiality and objectivity;

11. *Decides* to consider this matter at its fifty-first session under the item entitled "Human rights questions".

General Assembly resolution 50/174

22 December 1995      Meeting 99      Adopted without vote

Approved by Third Committee (A/50/635/Add.2) without vote, 13 December (meeting 55); 31-nation draft (A/C.3/50/L.34), orally revised; agenda item 112 *(b)*.
*Meeting numbers.* GA 50th session: 3rd Committee 35, 38-51, 55; plenary 99.

## Right to promote and protect human rights

**Working Group activities.** The tenth session of the working group to draft a declaration on the right and responsibility of individuals, groups and organs of society to promote and protect universally recognized human rights and fundamental freedoms was held in Geneva from 16 to 27 January and on 27 February.[40]

The group considered the preambular part of the draft and adopted, at second reading, three operative articles, including the texts of articles 1 and 2 of chapter I, and a third text (referred to as "X"), whose position in the document had not been determined. Annexed to the group's report were a first reading text of the draft declaration as amended during the second reading as well as a compilation of second reading proposals.

**Commission action.** On 8 March, the Commission urged[41] the working group to submit the completed draft declaration in 1996, and decided that its elaboration should continue in 1996.

### ECONOMIC AND SOCIAL COUNCIL ACTION

On 25 July, the Economic and Social Council adopted **resolution 1995/38**.

**Question of a draft declaration on the right and responsibility of individuals, groups and organs of society to promote and protect universally recognized human rights and fundamental freedoms**

*The Economic and Social Council,*

*Recalling* Commission on Human Rights resolution 1995/84 of 8 March 1995,

1. *Authorizes* an open-ended working group of the Commission on Human Rights to meet for a period of one week prior to the fifty-second session of the Commission in order to continue work on the elaboration of a draft declaration on the right and responsibility of individuals, groups and organs of society to promote and protect universally recognized human rights and fundamental freedoms;

2. *Requests* the Secretary-General to extend all necessary facilities, within existing United Nations resources, to the working group for its meetings.

Economic and Social Council resolution 1995/38

25 July 1995      Meeting 52      Adopted without vote

Draft by Commission on Human Rights (E/1995/23); agenda item 5 *(d)*.
*Meeting numbers.* ESC 51-53.

**Subcommission action.** On 24 August,[42] the Subcommission urged the Commission to ask Governments to investigate alleged cases of persecution of individuals or members of groups legitimately, peacefully and non-violently exercising the rights referred to in the draft declaration.

## Advancement of human rights

The Third Committee considered various human rights questions during the fiftieth (1995) session of the General Assembly. By **decision 50/460** of 22 December, the Assembly took note of part one of the Committee's report.[43]

*REFERENCES*

[1]E/1995/23 & Corr.1,2 & Add.1. [2]E/1995/23 (dec. 1995/101). [3]Ibid. (dec. 1995/102). [4]YUN 1994, p. 1042, ESC dec. 1994/297, 29 July 1994. [5]E/1995/23 (dec. 1995/106). [6]Ibid. (dec. 1995/115). [7]YUN 1994, p. 1043. [8]E/CN.4/1995/ 47. [9]E/1995/23 (res. 1995/87). [10]E/CN.4/1996/2. [11]Ibid. (dec. 1995/104). [12]Ibid. (dec. 1995/112 & 1995/114). [13]Ibid. (dec. 1995/119). [14]Ibid. (dec. 1995/102). [15]E/CN.4/1995/83. [16]YUN 1994, p. 1044. [17]E/1995/23 (res. 1995/26). [18]YUN 1992, p. 759. [19]E/CN.4/1996/2 (dec. 1995/113). [20]E/CN.4/

Sub.2/1995/3. (21)YUN 1965, p. 440, GA res. 2106 A (XX), annex, 21 Dec. 1965. (22)YUN 1966, pp. 419 & 423, GA res. 2200 A (XXI), annex, 16 Dec. 1966. (23)YUN 1973, p. 103, GA res. 3068(XXVIII), annex, 30 Nov. 1973. (24)YUN 1984, p. 813, GA res. 39/46, annex, 10 Dec. 1984. (25)GA res. 44/25, annex, 20 Nov. 1989. (26)GA res. 45/158, annex, 18 Dec. 1990. (27)E/CN.4/1995/98. (28)YUN 1994, p. 1049. (29)YUN 1993, p. 906, GA res. 48/141, 20 Dec. 1993. (30)E/1995/112. (31)A/50/36. (32)YUN 1993, p. 908. (33)E/1995/23 (res. 1995/64). (34)Ibid. (res. 1995/93). (35)YUN 1994, p. 1045, GA res. 49/195, 23 Dec. 1994. (36)E/CN.4/1995/113. (37)A/50/678. (38)E/1995/23 (res. 1995/61). (39)A/50/682. (40)E/CN.4/1995/93. (41)E/1995/23 (res. 1995/84). (42)E/CN.4/1996/2 (res. 1995/25). (43)A/50/635.

# Human rights instruments

## General aspects

At the outset of 1995, there were seven human rights treaty instruments in force, which required monitoring of their implementation by expert bodies. Those instruments and their treaty bodies were: the 1965 International Convention on the Elimination of All Forms of Racial Discrimination[1] (Committee on the Elimination of Racial Discrimination (CERD)); the 1966 International Covenant on Economic, Social and Cultural Rights (Committee on Economic, Social and Cultural Rights) and the 1966 International Covenant on Civil and Political Rights[2] (Human Rights Committee); the 1973 International Convention on the Suppression and Punishment of the Crime of Apartheid[3] (Group of Three); the 1979 Convention on the Elimination of All Forms of Discrimination against Women[4] (Committee on the Elimination of Discrimination against Women); the 1984 Convention against Torture and Other Cruel, Inhuman or Degrading Treatment or Punishment[5] (Committee against Torture); and the 1989 Convention on the Rights of the Child[6] (Committee on the Rights of the Child).

On 17 February 1995, the Commission on Human Rights, in view of developments in South Africa, decided[7] to suspend meetings of the Group of Three as at 17 February (see PART THREE, Chapter III).

**Commission action.** On 8 March, the Commission urged[8] States parties to meet their reporting obligations and to contribute to identifying and implementing ways to streamline further and improve reporting procedures. It urged treaty bodies to examine ways to reduce both duplication of reporting and the reporting burden on Member States and presented measures for doing so. It recommended that reporting guidelines be amended to identify gender-specific information. The UN Department of Public Information was asked to publish at the end of each year a compilation of all concluding observations adopted during that year by the treaty bodies.

The High Commissioner for Human Rights was asked to prepare an inventory of all international human rights standard-setting activities to facilitate better-informed decision-making. The *Manual on Human Rights Reporting*[9] should be made available in all official languages at the earliest opportunity, and due regard paid to recommendations concerning that publication made at the 1994 meeting of persons chairing the human rights treaty bodies.[10] The Secretary-General was to report on measures taken to establish a computerized database to improve the efficiency and effectiveness of the functioning of the treaty bodies, and to expedite implementation of the 1990 recommendations of the Task Force on Computerization[11] by asking Member States to contribute voluntarily to cover the cost of the proposed system. He was also to report on financing and staff resource issues to the General Assembly in 1995 and the Commission in 1996.

**Reports of the Secretary-General.** In 1995, the Commission considered a report of the Secretary-General containing an inventory of all international human rights standard-setting activities,[12] covering work and activities that fell under the purview of the Commission.

As requested by the General Assembly in 1994,[13] the Secretary-General reported[14] in October on ensuring financing and adequate staffing resources for the operations of the human rights treaty bodies. Also in October,[15] he transmitted the report of the sixth meeting of persons chairing the human rights treaty bodies (Geneva, 18-22 September 1995), convened pursuant to a 1994 Assembly resolution.[13]

On 22 December, the General Assembly adopted **resolution 50/170**.

**Effective implementation of international instruments on human rights, including reporting obligations under international instruments on human rights**

*The General Assembly,*

*Recalling* its resolution 49/178 of 23 December 1994, as well as other relevant resolutions,

*Recalling also* the relevant paragraphs of the Vienna Declaration and Programme of Action, adopted by the World Conference on Human Rights on 25 June 1993,

*Welcoming* the call in the Platform for Action, adopted by the Fourth World Conference on Women on 15 September 1995, both for intensified efforts to integrate the equal status and the human rights of all women and girls into the mainstream of United Nations system-wide activities and to address these issues regularly and systematically throughout relevant bodies and mechanisms, and for the related actions to be taken by, *inter alia*, the human rights treaty-monitoring bodies,

*Taking note* of the recommendations proposed by the expert group on the integration of gender perspectives into United Nations human rights activities and programmes, which met at Geneva from 3 to 7 July 1995,

*Reaffirming* that the full and effective implementation of United Nations human rights instruments is of major importance to the efforts of the Organization, pursuant to the Charter of the United Nations and the Universal Declaration of Human Rights, to promote universal respect for and observance of human rights and fundamental freedoms,

*Considering* that the effective functioning of the treaty bodies established pursuant to United Nations human rights instruments is indispensable for the full and effective implementation of such instruments,

*Conscious* of the importance of coordination of the human rights promotion and protection activities of the United Nations bodies active in the field of human rights,

*Noting with appreciation* the initiatives taken by a number of treaty bodies to elaborate early-warning measures and urgent procedures, within their mandates, with a view to preventing the occurrence, or reoccurrence, of serious human rights violations,

*Recalling* the reports of the five meetings of persons chairing the human rights treaty bodies, held from 1988 to 1994,

*Expressing concern* about the non-fulfilment by many States parties of their financial obligations under the relevant United Nations instruments on human rights,

*Also expressing concern* that the underresourcing of the Centre for Human Rights of the Secretariat is one impediment to the human rights treaty bodies in their ability to carry out their mandates effectively,

*Reaffirming* its responsibility to ensure the effective functioning of human rights treaty bodies established pursuant to instruments adopted by the General Assembly, and in this connection further reaffirming the importance of:

(*a*) Ensuring the effective functioning of the periodic reporting by States parties to these instruments;

(*b*) Securing sufficient financial, human and information resources to overcome existing difficulties with their effective functioning;

(*c*) Promoting greater efficiency and effectiveness through better coordination of the activities of the United Nations bodies active in the field of human rights, taking into account the need to avoid unnecessary duplication and overlapping of their mandates and tasks;

(*d*) Addressing questions of both reporting obligations and financial implications whenever elaborating any further instruments on human rights,

1. *Welcomes* the report of the persons chairing the human rights treaty bodies on their sixth meeting, held at Geneva from 18 to 22 September 1995, and takes note of their conclusions and recommendations;

2. *Emphasizes* the need to ensure financing and adequate staff and information resources for the operations of the human rights treaty bodies and, with this in mind:

(*a*) Reiterates its request that the Secretary-General provide adequate resources in respect of each treaty body;

(*b*) Calls upon the Secretary-General to make the most efficient use of existing resources and to seek the resources necessary to give the treaty bodies adequate administrative support, access to technical expertise and access to appropriate databases and on-line information services;

(*c*) Requests that the Secretary-General report on this question to the Commission on Human Rights at its fifty-second session and to the General Assembly at its fifty-first session;

3. *Welcomes* efforts to identify measures for more effective implementation of the United Nations human rights instruments, and in this regard takes note with interest of the plan of action of the United Nations High Commissioner for Human Rights to strengthen the implementation of the Convention on the Rights of the Child;

4. *Urges* States parties to notify the Secretary-General, as depository of the International Convention on the Elimination of All Forms of Racial Discrimination and the Convention against Torture and Other Cruel, Inhuman or Degrading Treatment or Punishment, of their acceptance of the amendments approved by the States parties and the General Assembly in its resolution 47/111 of 16 December 1992;

5. *Calls upon* all States parties to fulfil without delay and in full their financial obligations, including their arrears, under the International Convention on the Elimination of All Forms of Racial Discrimination and the Convention against Torture and Other Cruel, Inhuman or Degrading Treatment or Punishment until the amendments enter into force;

6. *Requests* the Secretary-General to continue to take the necessary measures to ensure that the two committees established under the International Convention on the Elimination of All Forms of Racial Discrimination and the Convention against Torture and Other Cruel, Inhuman or Degrading Treatment or Punishment meet as scheduled until the amendments enter into force;

7. *Welcomes* the continuing efforts by the treaty bodies and the Secretary-General aimed at streamlining, rationalizing and otherwise improving reporting procedures, and urges the treaty bodies and the meetings of persons chairing the human rights treaty bodies to continue to examine ways of reducing the duplication of reporting required under the different instruments, without impairing the quality of reporting, and of generally reducing the reporting burden on Member States, including through:

(*a*) Identifying where cross-referencing can be used in report writing;

(*b*) Recommending, where appropriate, the designation of specific national administrative units to coordinate reports to all treaty bodies;

(*c*) Establishing coordination between the treaty bodies and the International Labour Organization to identify overlap between their respective instruments and conventions;

(*d*) Considering the utility of single comprehensive reports and of replacing periodic reports with specifically tailored reports and thematic reports;

8. *Urges* States parties to contribute, individually and through meetings of States parties, to identifying and implementing ways of further streamlining, rationalizing, avoiding duplication in and otherwise improving reporting procedures;

9. *Encourages* the United Nations High Commissioner for Human Rights, in accordance with his mandate, to request the independent expert to finalize his interim report on possible long-term approaches to enhancing the effective operation of the human rights treaty system in time for the final report to be considered by the Commission on Human Rights, as requested by the General Assembly in resolution 48/120 of 20 December 1993, at its fifty-second session;

10. *Requests* the United Nations High Commissioner for Human Rights to ensure, from within existing resources, that the revision of the United Nations *Man-*

*ual on Human Rights Reporting* is completed as soon as possible, that the revised manual is available in all official languages at the earliest opportunity and that due regard is paid to the recommendations concerning the manual made by the fifth meeting of persons chairing the human rights treaty bodies;

11. *Expresses concern* about the increasing backlog of reports on implementation by States parties to United Nations instruments on human rights and about delays in consideration of reports by the treaty bodies, and again urges States parties to make every effort to meet their reporting obligations;

12. *Invites* States parties that have been unable to comply with the requirements to submit their initial report to avail themselves of technical assistance;

13. *Encourages* the efforts of the human rights treaty bodies to examine the progress made in achieving the fulfilment of human rights treaty undertakings by all States parties, without exception;

14. *Urges* States parties to address, as a matter of priority, at their next scheduled meetings, the issue of States parties consistently not complying with their reporting obligations;

15. *Urges* all States parties whose reports have been examined by treaty bodies to provide adequate follow-up to the observations and final comments of the treaty bodies on their reports;

16. *Welcomes* the emphasis placed by the persons chairing the human rights treaty bodies and by the Commission on Human Rights on the importance of technical assistance and advisory services, and to this end:

*(a)* Welcomes the plans of the United Nations High Commissioner for Human Rights to report regularly to the Commission on possible technical assistance projects identified by the treaty bodies;

*(b)* Encourages the treaty bodies to continue to identify possibilities for technical assistance in the regular course of their work of reviewing the periodic reports of States parties;

17. *Welcomes also* the recommendation by the meeting of persons chairing the human rights treaty bodies that treaty bodies urge each State party to translate, publish and make widely available in its territory the full text of the concluding observations on its reports to the treaty-monitoring bodies, and requests the United Nations High Commissioner for Human Rights to make every effort to ensure that recent reports and the summary records of committee discussions pertaining to them, as well as concluding observations and final comments of the treaty bodies, are made available in the United Nations information centres in the countries submitting those reports;

18. *Welcomes further* the contribution to the work of the human rights treaty bodies made by the specialized agencies and other United Nations bodies, and invites the specialized agencies, other United Nations bodies and the treaty bodies to continue to pursue further cooperation between them, bearing in mind the responsibilities of the United Nations High Commissioner for Human Rights and the desirability of avoiding unnecessary duplication;

19. *Invites* the United Nations High Commissioner for Human Rights to consult the human rights treaty bodies in his efforts to promote cooperation with regional intergovernmental organizations where appropriate for the promotion and protection of human rights;

20. *Recognizes* the important role played by non-governmental organizations in the effective implementation of all human rights instruments, and encourages the exchange of information between the human rights treaty bodies and such organizations;

21. *Endorses* the recommendation of the persons chairing the human rights treaty bodies that each treaty body, in its examination of States' reports, place emphasis on the implementation by States parties of their obligations regarding human rights education and the provision of public information on human rights;

22. *Welcomes* the emphasis by the persons chairing the human rights treaty bodies that the enjoyment of the human rights of women should be closely monitored by each treaty body within the competence of its mandate;

23. *Welcomes also* all appropriate measures the human rights treaty bodies may take, within their mandates, in response to situations of massive human rights violations, including bringing those violations to the attention of the United Nations High Commissioner for Human Rights, the Secretary-General and the competent bodies of the United Nations in the field of human rights, and requests the High Commissioner, acting within his mandate, to coordinate and consult throughout the United Nations system in this regard;

24. *Requests* the Secretary-General to report to the General Assembly at its fifty-first session on measures taken to implement the present resolution and on obstacles to its implementation;

25. *Decides* to continue giving priority consideration, at its fifty-first session, to the conclusions and recommendations of the meetings of persons chairing human rights treaty bodies, in the light of the deliberations of the Commission on Human Rights, under the item entitled ''Human rights questions''.

General Assembly resolution 50/170

22 December 1995     Meeting 99     Adopted without vote

Approved by Third Committee (A/50/635/Add.1) without vote, 14 December (meeting 58); 33-nation draft (A/C.3/50/L.47/Rev.1), orally revised; agenda item 112 *(a)*.

*Meeting numbers.* GA 50th session: 3rd Committee 35, 38-49, 56, 58; plenary 99.

## Successor States and human rights treaties

As requested by the Commission in 1994,[16] the Secretary-General presented information on successor States that were UN Members regarding action taken with respect to their accession to or ratification of international human rights treaties to which the predecessor States had not been parties.[17]

On 24 February, the Commission requested[18] the human rights treaty bodies to consider further the applicability of the respective international human rights treaties to successor States, with the aim of assisting them in meeting their obligations. It asked the Secretary-General to encourage successor States to confirm their obligations under the treaties to which their predecessors had been parties, and to report in 1996 on action taken.

## Support for International Covenants

On 24 February, the Commission asked[19] the Secretary-General to consider assisting States parties to the International Covenants on Human Rights[2] in preparing their reports, including holding seminars or workshops to train government officials responsible for doing so, and to explore other possibilities under the programme of advisory services. It also asked him to report in 1996 on the status of the Covenants.

In October, the Secretary-General provided information[20] on the status of the Covenants as at 1 September. He also reported[21] to the Commission on their status as at 1 November.

**GENERAL ASSEMBLY ACTION**

On 22 December, the General Assembly adopted **resolution 50/171**.

### International Covenants on Human Rights

*The General Assembly,*

*Recalling* its resolution 48/119 of 20 December 1993, and taking note of Commission on Human Rights resolution 1995/22 of 24 February 1995,

*Mindful* that the International Covenants on Human Rights constitute the first all-embracing and legally binding international treaties in the field of human rights and, together with the Universal Declaration of Human Rights, form the core of the International Bill of Human Rights,

*Taking note* of the report of the Secretary-General on the status of the International Covenant on Economic, Social and Cultural Rights, the International Covenant on Civil and Political Rights and the Optional Protocols to the International Covenant on Civil and Political Rights,

*Noting* that many States Members of the United Nations have yet to become parties to the International Covenants on Human Rights,

*Recalling* the International Covenant on Economic, Social and Cultural Rights and the International Covenant on Civil and Political Rights, and reaffirming that all human rights and fundamental freedoms are indivisible and interrelated and that the promotion and protection of one category of rights should never exempt or excuse States from the promotion and protection of the other rights,

*Recognizing* the important role of the Human Rights Committee and the Committee on Economic, Social and Cultural Rights in the implementation of the International Covenants on Human Rights and the Optional Protocols to the International Covenant on Civil and Political Rights,

*Welcoming* the submission to the General Assembly of the annual report of the Human Rights Committee and the report of the Committee on Economic, Social and Cultural Rights,

*Considering* that the effective functioning of treaty bodies established in accordance with the relevant provisions of international instruments on human rights plays a fundamental role and hence represents an important continuing concern of the United Nations,

*Noting with concern* the critical situation with regard to overdue reports from States parties to the International Covenants on Human Rights,

1. *Reaffirms* the importance of the International Covenants on Human Rights as major parts of international efforts to promote universal respect for and observance of human rights and fundamental freedoms;

2. *Appeals strongly* to all States that have not yet done so to become parties to the International Covenants on Human Rights as well as to accede to the Optional Protocols to the International Covenant on Civil and Political Rights and to make the declaration provided for in article 41 of the Covenant;

3. *Invites* the Secretary-General to intensify systematic efforts to encourage States to become parties to the International Covenants on Human Rights and, through the programme of advisory services in the field of human rights, to assist such States, at their request, in ratifying or acceding to the Covenants and to the Optional Protocols to the International Covenant on Civil and Political Rights;

4. *Emphasizes* the importance of the strictest compliance by States parties with their obligations under the International Covenant on Economic, Social and Cultural Rights and the International Covenant on Civil and Political Rights and, where applicable, the Optional Protocols to the International Covenant on Civil and Political Rights;

5. *Stresses* the importance of avoiding the erosion of human rights by derogation, and underlines the necessity of strict observance of the agreed conditions and procedures for derogation under article 4 of the International Covenant on Civil and Political Rights, bearing in mind the need for States parties to provide the fullest possible information during states of emergency so that the justification for the appropriateness of measures taken in these circumstances can be assessed;

6. *Also stresses* the importance of fully taking into account the gender perspective in the implementation of the International Covenants on Human Rights at the national level, including the national reports, and in the work of the Human Rights Committee and the Committee on Economic, Social and Cultural Rights;

7. *Encourages* the States parties to consider limiting the extent of any reservations they lodge to the International Covenants on Human Rights, to formulate any reservations as precisely and narrowly as possible and to ensure that no reservation is incompatible with the object and purpose of the relevant treaty or otherwise contrary to international law;

8. *Also encourages* the States parties to review regularly any reservations made in respect of the provisions of the International Covenants on Human Rights with a view to withdrawing them;

9. *Takes note with appreciation* of the annual reports of the Human Rights Committee submitted to the General Assembly at its forty-ninth and fiftieth sessions;

10. *Also takes note with appreciation* of the report of the Committee on Economic, Social and Cultural Rights on its tenth and eleventh sessions;

11. *Expresses its satisfaction* with the serious and constructive manner in which both Committees are carrying out their functions;

12. *Invites* the Committees to identify specific needs of States parties that might be addressed through the advisory services and technical assistance programme of the Centre for Human Rights of the Secretariat, with the possible participation of members of the Committees where appropriate;

13. *Welcomes* the continuing efforts of the Human Rights Committee and the Committee on Economic, Social and Cultural Rights to strive for uniform standards in the implementation of the provisions of the International Covenants on Human Rights, and appeals to other bodies dealing with similar human rights questions to respect these uniform standards, as expressed in the general comments of the Human Rights Committee;

14. *Urges* States parties to fulfil in good time such reporting obligations under the International Covenants on Human Rights as may be requested and to make use of gender-disaggregated data in their reports;

15. *Also urges* States parties to take duly into account, in implementing the provisions of the International Covenants on Human Rights, the observations made at the conclusion of the consideration of their reports by the Human Rights Committee and by the Committee on Economic, Social and Cultural Rights;

16. *Invites* States parties to give particular attention to the dissemination at the national level of the reports they have submitted to the Human Rights Committee and the Committee on Economic, Social and Cultural Rights, the summary records relating to the examination of those reports by the Committees and the observations made by the Committees at the conclusion of the consideration of the reports;

17. *Encourages once again* all Governments to publish the texts of the International Covenant on Economic, Social and Cultural Rights, the International Covenant on Civil and Political Rights and the Optional Protocols to the International Covenant on Civil and Political Rights in as many local languages as possible and to distribute them and make them known as widely as possible in their territories;

18. *Requests* the Secretary-General to consider ways and means of assisting States parties to the International Covenants on Human Rights in the preparation of their reports, including seminars or workshops at the national level for the purpose of training government officials engaged in the preparation of such reports, and the exploration of other possibilities available under the regular programme of advisory services in the field of human rights;

19. *Also requests* the Secretary-General to ensure that the Centre for Human Rights effectively assists the Human Rights Committee and the Committee on Economic, Social and Cultural Rights in the implementation of their respective mandates;

20. *Once again urges* the Secretary-General, taking into account the suggestions of the Human Rights Committee, to take determined steps to give more publicity to the work of that Committee and, similarly, to the work of the Committee on Economic, Social and Cultural Rights;

21. *Further requests* the Secretary-General to submit to the General Assembly at its fifty-second session, under the item entitled "Human rights questions", a report on the status of the International Covenant on Economic, Social and Cultural Rights, the International Covenant on Civil and Political Rights and the Optional Protocols to the International Covenant on Civil and Political Rights, including all reservations and declarations.

General Assembly resolution 50/171

22 December 1995    Meeting 99    Adopted without vote

Approved by Third Committee (A/50/635/Add.1) without vote, 11 December (meeting 54); 29-nation draft (A/C.3/50/L.53), orally revised; agenda item 112 *(a)*.

*Meeting numbers.* GA 50th session: 3rd Committee 35, 38-49, 52, 54; plenary 99.

## Covenant on Civil and Political Rights and Optional Protocols

### Accessions and ratifications

As at 31 December 1995, parties to the International Covenant on Civil and Political Rights and the Optional Protocol thereto, adopted by the General Assembly in 1966[22] and in force since 1976,[23] totalled 132 and 87 States, respectively.[24] Chad, Uganda and Uzbekistan became parties to the Covenant in 1995; Bosnia and Herzegovina, Chad, Croatia, El Salvador, Paraguay, Uganda and Uzbekistan acceded to or ratified the Optional Protocol.

Parties to the Second Optional Protocol, aiming at the abolition of the death penalty—adopted by the Assembly in 1989[25] and in force since 1991[26]—totalled 29 States as at 31 December 1995.[24] Croatia, Italy and the former Yugoslav Republic of Macedonia ratified or acceded to it in 1995.

On 24 February, the Human Rights Commission appealed[27] to States that had not done so to become parties to the Covenant and Optional Protocols and to consider making the declaration provided for in article 41 of the Covenant. The Commission requested the Secretary-General to provide the Human Rights Committee—the expert body responsible for monitoring implementation of the Covenant—with additional means to deal with its increasing workload and to report in 1996 on the status of the Covenant and its Protocols.

**Fair trial protocol.** On 3 March, the Commission decided[28] to consider in 1996 the establishment of an open-ended working group to draft a third optional protocol to the Covenant, aiming at guaranteeing the right to a fair trial and a remedy.

**Monitoring body.** The Human Rights Committee, established under article 28 of the Covenant on Civil and Political Rights, held three sessions in 1995: its fifty-third from 20 March to 7 April in New York, and its fifty-fourth from 3 to 28 July and fifty-fifth from 16 October to 3 November, both in Geneva.

At those sessions, the Committee considered reports from 14 States—Afghanistan, Argentina, Estonia, Haiti, Latvia, New Zealand, Paraguay, Russian Federation, Sri Lanka, Sweden, Ukraine, United Kingdom, United Kingdom concerning Hong Kong, United States, Yemen—under article 40 of the Covenant. It adopted views on 18 communications from individuals claiming that their rights under the Covenant had been violated, and decided that 15 other such communications were inadmissible. Those views and decisions were annexed to the Committee's report.[29]

In April, the Secretary-General transmitted to the Economic and Social Council the text of a general comment[30] adopted by the Committee in 1994 concerning issues related to reservations made upon accession to or ratification of the Covenant.[31]

## Covenant on Economic, Social and Cultural Rights

On 24 February, the Commission on Human Rights encouraged[32] States parties to the 1966 International Covenant on Economic, Social and Cultural Rights[33] to support and cooperate with the Committee on Economic, Social and Cultural Rights. Noting steps taken by the Committee to draft an optional protocol to the Covenant granting the right of individuals or groups to submit communications concerning non-compliance, it asked the Committee to report in 1996 thereon.

The Commission recommended that, as a follow-up to the 1993 seminar on indicators to measure achievements in realizing economic, social and cultural rights,[34] the UN Centre for Human Rights convene expert seminars to clarify the content of specific economic, social and cultural rights for chairmen of the human rights treaty-monitoring bodies and representatives of States, specialized agencies and NGOs. Taking note of the reports of the Special Rapporteur on the realization of economic, social and cultural rights, submitted in 1990,[35] 1991[36] and 1992,[37] the Commission requested the Secretary-General to ensure the publication of the reports in a single document. It also asked him to invite international financial institutions to consider organizing an expert seminar on their role in realizing economic, social and cultural rights. It asked the UN High Commissioner for Human Rights to continue to promote coordination of UN human rights activities and those of development agencies, with a view to drawing on their expertise and support.

On 25 July, the Economic and Social Council, by **decision 1995/257**, approved the Commission's recommendation that the Centre for Human Rights convene expert seminars for the chairmen of the human rights treaty-monitoring bodies and representatives of specialized agencies, NGOs and States.

### Accessions and ratifications

As at 31 December 1995, the International Covenant on Economic, Social and Cultural Rights, adopted by the General Assembly in 1966[33] and in force since 1976,[23] had been ratified, acceded to or succeeded to by 133 States. Chad and Uzbekistan became parties in 1995.[24]

### Implementation

**Commission action.** On 24 February, the Human Rights Commission appealed[38] to all States that had not done so to become parties to the Covenant. It welcomed the efforts of the Committee on Economic, Social and Cultural Rights to strive for uniform standards in implementing Covenant provisions and encouraged Governments to publish the Covenant in as many languages as possible and to disseminate it widely. It asked the Secretary-General to report in 1996 on the status of the Covenant.

**Monitoring body.** The Committee on Economic, Social and Cultural Rights[39] held its twelfth and thirteenth sessions in Geneva, from 1 to 19 May and from 20 November to 8 December, respectively.[40] The holding of an additional session during the second half of 1995 was authorized on 10 February by the Economic and Social Council by **decision 1995/217**. The Committee's pre-sessional, five-member working group, established in 1988,[41] met in Geneva from 12 to 16 December 1994 and from 22 to 26 May 1995, to identify issues that might most usefully be discussed with representatives of reporting States.

Under Covenant articles 1 to 15, the Committee examined reports from Algeria,[42] Colombia,[43] Mauritius,[44] Norway,[45] Portugal,[46] the Republic of Korea,[47] Suriname,[48] Sweden[49] and Ukraine.[50] Rights covered by articles 10 to 12 were examined in a report from the Philippines.[51]

The Committee had two days of general discussion. In May, it focused on the interpretation and practical application of the obligations incumbent upon States parties to the Covenant. In December, the general discussion was devoted to the draft optional protocol on communications to the Covenant.

As a follow-up to its technical assistance mission to Panama (16-22 April 1995) to look into the right to adequate housing, the Committee considered information submitted by NGOs concerned with human rights. The report of the two-member mission was annexed to the Committee's report.

On 24 November, the Committee adopted a general comment on the economic, social and cultural rights of older persons,[52] which was intended to guide States parties to understand better their obligations in implementing respect for those rights.

Concerning a draft optional protocol to the Covenant providing for an optional communications procedure, the Committee requested its Chairman to revise his 1994 report on the subject,[53] with a view to forwarding a final report to the Commission on Human Rights in 1996.

Annexed to the Committee's report was a list of States parties to the Covenant and the status of their submission of reports as at 8 December 1995, as well as the Committee's general comment on older persons.

In accordance with a 1976 Economic and Social Council resolution,[54] the Secretary-General transmitted the eighteenth,[55] nineteenth[56] and twentieth[57] reports of the International Labour Organization concerning implementation of the Covenant.

### ECONOMIC AND SOCIAL COUNCIL ACTION

On 25 July, the Economic and Social Council adopted **resolution 1995/39**.

#### Annual sessions of the Committee on Economic, Social and Cultural Rights

*The Economic and Social Council,*

*Recalling* its resolution 1985/17 of 28 May 1985, by which it established the Committee on Economic, Social and Cultural Rights to assist it in relation to the various functions entrusted to it under the International Covenant on Economic, Social and Cultural Rights,

*Recalling also* that in its resolution 1985/17 it decided to review the composition, organization and administrative arrangements of the Committee every five years beginning in 1990,

*Noting* that since its first session in 1987 the Committee has held 12 sessions, examined 103 reports of States parties and adopted five very detailed general comments,

*Recognizing* that the Committee has succeeded in developing constructive and effective methods of work, including in relation to its dialogue with States parties,

*Recalling* the emphasis contained in the Programme of Action of the World Summit for Social Development on the important role of the Committee in monitoring those aspects of the Copenhagen Declaration on Social Development and the Programme of Action that relate to compliance by States parties with the Covenant,

*Noting* that the number of States parties to the Covenant has increased by more than 50 per cent since the Council resolved to establish the Committee and that there are now 131 States parties,

*Noting also* that the Committee has consistently needed to hold two annual sessions in recent years in order to cope with its workload and that it continues to be faced with a backlog of reports to be considered,

1. *Authorizes* the holding of two annual sessions by the Committee on Economic, Social and Cultural Rights, in May and November-December, each of three weeks' duration, in addition to a pre-sessional working group of five members to meet for five days immediately after each session to prepare the list of issues for consideration at the subsequent session;

2. *Requests* the Committee to give careful consideration to the possible means by which it might contribute to the implementation of the Copenhagen Declaration on Social Development and the Programme of Action of the World Summit for Social Development, having particular regard to the commitments contained in the latter concerning the adoption of national strategies for social development and the definition of time-bound goals and targets for reducing overall poverty.

Economic and Social Council resolution 1995/39

25 July 1995     Meeting 52     Adopted without vote

Draft by Committee on Economic, Social and Cultural Rights (E/1995/L.21); agenda item 5 *(d)*.

By **decision 1995/303**, the Council on 25 July endorsed the Committee's proposal to include annually $10,000 within the overall budget of the Centre for Human Rights to enable the Committee to bring in specialists to participate in its days of general discussion and to commission papers dealing with technical aspects of its work. The Council noted that the relevant funds would not be spent on Committee members and would be committed only with the approval of the Assistant Secretary-General for Human Rights.

Concerning the payment of honorariums to Committee members, the Council, by **decision 1995/302 A** of 25 July, recalled its 1993 decision[30] endorsing the Committee's request to the General Assembly to authorize payment to each Committee member of an honorarium equivalent to that payable to the members of other treaty bodies, noted that the Assembly had taken no action and urged it to do so. On the same date, by **decision 1995/302 B**, the Council, noting that members of all human rights treaty bodies, except for those of the Committee on Economic, Social and Cultural Rights, were receiving or would soon receive a modest honorarium, urged the Assembly to authorize payment to each Committee member of an honorarium equivalent to that payable to the members of other treaty bodies.

On 28 July, the Council, by **decision 1995/314**, took note of the reports of the Committee on Economic, Social and Cultural Rights on its 1994 sessions.[53]

*REFERENCES*

[1]YUN 1965, p. 440, GA res. 2106 A (XX), annex, 21 Dec. 1965. [2]YUN 1966, pp. 419 & 423, GA res. 2200 A (XXI), annex, 16 Dec. 1966. [3]YUN 1973, p. 103, GA res. 3068(XXVIII), annex, 30 Nov. 1973. [4]YUN 1979, p. 895, GA res. 34/180, annex, 18 Dec. 1979. [5]YUN 1984, p. 813, GA res. 39/46, annex, 10 Dec. 1984. [6]GA res. 44/25, annex, 20 Nov. 1989. [7]E/1995/23 (res. 1995/10). [8]Ibid. (res. 1995/92). [9]*Manual on Human Rights Reporting*, Sales No. E.91.XIV.1. [10]YUN 1994, p. 1060. [11]E/CN.4/1990/39. [12]E/CN.4/1995/81. [13]YUN 1994, p. 1060, GA res. 49/178, 23 Dec. 1994. [14]A/50/755. [15]A/50/505. [16]YUN 1994, p. 1062. [17]E/CN.4/1995/80. [18]E/1995/23 (res. 1995/18). [19]Ibid. (res. 1995/22). [20]A/50/472. [21]E/CN.4/1996/75. [22]YUN 1966, p. 423, GA res. 2200 A (XXI), annex, 16 Dec. 1966. [23]YUN 1976, p. 609. [24]*Multilateral Treaties Deposited with the Secretary-General: Status as at 31 December 1995* (ST/LEG/SER.E/14), Sales No. E.96.V.5. [25]GA res. 44/128, annex, 15 Dec. 1989. [26]YUN 1991, p. 544. [27]E/1995/23 (res. 1995/22). [28]Ibid. (dec. 1995/110). [29]A/50/40. [30]E/1995/49. [31]YUN 1994, p. 1010. [32]E/1995/23 (res. 1995/15). [33]YUN 1966, p. 419, GA res. 2200 A (XXI), annex, 16 Dec. 1966. [34]YUN 1993, p. 890. [35]E/CN.4/Sub.2/1990/19. [36]YUN 1991, p. 568. [37]YUN 1992, p. 752.

(38)E/1995/23 (res. 1995/22). (39)YUN 1985, p. 878, ESC res. 1985/17, 28 May 1985. (40)E/1996/22. (41)YUN 1988, p. 527, ESC res. 1988/4, 24 May 1988. (42)E/1990/5/Add.22. (43)E/1994/104/Add.2. (44)E/1990/5/Add.21. (45)E/1994/104/Add.3. (46)E/1990/6/Add.6. (47)E/1990/5/Add.19. (48)E/1990/5/Add.20. (49)E/1994/104/Add.1. (50)E/1994/104/Add.4. (51)E/1986/3/Add.17. (52)E/C.12/1995/16/Rev.1. (53)YUN 1994, p. 1031. (54)YUN 1976, p. 615, ESC res. 1988(LX), 11 May 1976. (55)E/1995/5. (56)E/1995/39. (57)E/1995/127.

## Other human rights instruments

In addition to the 1966 Covenants, which together with the 1948 Universal Declaration of Human Rights constitute what is known as the ''International Bill of Human Rights'', there exist scores of instruments which deal with protection of human rights in many areas, many of which were formulated before the birth of the United Nations in 1945 and predate even the League of Nations. Taken together, they form a strong frontline of defence against human rights abuses worldwide. The following are rights instruments which were the subject of direct United Nations action in 1995.

### Convention against racial discrimination

*Accessions and ratifications*

As at 31 December 1995,[1] there were 146 parties to the International Convention on the Elimination of All Forms of Racial Discrimination, adopted by the General Assembly in 1965[2] and in force since 1969.[3] Japan, Monaco, Tajikistan and Uzbekistan acceded during 1995.

*Implementation*

**Monitoring body.** The Committee on the Elimination of Racial Discrimination, set up under article 8 of the Convention, held two sessions in 1995, both in Geneva: the forty-sixth from 27 February to 17 March and the forty-seventh from 31 July to 18 August.[4]

CERD mainly devoted its work to examining reports submitted by States parties on measures taken to implement the Convention's provisions. It considered periodic reports submitted by 22 States parties; reviewed the implementation of the Convention by three States parties based on their previous reports; and examined further information submitted by two States parties in reply to a 1993 request of the Committee.[5] In its report, CERD summarized its members' views on each country report and the statements made by the States parties concerned.

Under an item dealing with the prevention of racial discrimination, including early-warning measures and urgent procedures, the Committee in March requested the urgent submission of periodic reports from: Algeria, in view of continuing violence; Burundi, due to reports of continuing ethnic tension; Papua New Guinea, in view of reports of serious human rights violations in Bougainville; the Russian Federation, in view of human rights violations in Chechnya; and the former Yugoslav Republic of Macedonia, due to reports of ethnic tension. In a statement adopted by the Committee, Israel was requested to submit its periodic reports, which were due in 1992 and 1994. In another decision, CERD requested Mexico to submit further information regarding reports of serious conflicts in the State of Chiapas which affected some indigenous populations. In a further decision, the Committee endorsed the conclusions of the Special Rapporteur on the situation of human rights in Rwanda[6] and underlined the conclusions of the representative of the Secretary-General on internally displaced persons,[7] asking that its decision be transmitted to the UN High Commissioner for Human Rights.

In August, CERD asked the General Assembly and the Security Council to take steps with a view to stopping all violence and preventing another conflict in Burundi and to begin implementing its recommendations, which called for: creating a new police force; reducing and reorganizing the army; reorganizing and retraining the judiciary and civil administration; halting incitement to or promotion of racial or ethnic hatred disseminated by the mass media; rehabilitating ethnically mixed residential neighbourhoods in Bujumbura; establishing a national institution to promote and protect human rights; and maintaining an international presence, including a team of human rights observers. It also asked the Assembly to appeal to all States and the Council to halt the supply of arms to all parties until law and order were secured. (See also PART TWO, Chapter II.)

In a decision on the situation in Bosnia and Herzegovina, CERD demanded that all parties to the conflict ensure the safety of detained persons and disclose information concerning those missing; demanded that persons be given the opportunity to return safely to the places they inhabited before the beginning of the conflict; called on the international community to assist refugees and detained persons through the UN High Commissioner for Refugees, the International Committee of the Red Cross and other refugee assistance organizations; called on States to cooperate with the International Tribunal for the Prosecution of Persons Responsible for Serious Violations of International Humanitarian Law Committed in the Territory of the Former Yugoslavia since 1991, established by the Security Council in 1993;[8] demanded that States implement legislation to ensure their cooperation with the Tribunal; called for the provision to Bosnia and Herzegovina of all means to protect itself in accordance with Article 51 of the UN Charter; and expressed its solidarity with the former Special Rapporteur on the situation. It decided to transmit its decision to the Secretary-General for his attention and, through him, to the Assembly and the Council, and recommended that the United Nations take measures to provide for the strict implementation of resolutions in the areas referred to and to undertake urgent efforts to assist refugees and detained persons. (See also PART TWO, Chapter V.)

Concerning the situation in Papua New Guinea, the Committee regretted the Government's failure to submit outstanding reports or to respond to its request to renew a dialogue, and noted that the information on the human rights situation received was not sufficient to assess the situation in Bougainville. The Committee brought its decision to the attention of the UN High Commissioner for Refugees and asked her to take any action possible under her mandate to implement it. The Committee deferred further consideration of the Russian Federation and the former Yugoslav Republic of Macedonia until 1996.

In conformity with article 14 of the Convention, CERD considered communications from individuals or groups of individuals claiming violation of their rights under the Convention by a State party recognizing CERD's competence to receive and consider such communications. Twenty-two States parties (Algeria, Australia, Bulgaria, Chile, Costa Rica, Cyprus, Denmark, Ecuador, Finland, France, Hungary, Iceland, Italy, Netherlands, Norway, Peru, Russian Federation, Senegal, Slovakia, Sweden, Ukraine, Uruguay) had declared such recognition. The Committee's opinion on one communication, declared inadmissible, was annexed to its report.

Under article 15, the Secretary-General transmitted to CERD documents related to Trust and Non-Self-Governing Territories. CERD observed that it found it impossible to fulfil its function under article 15 as the documents did not include copies of petitions and did not contain valid information concerning legislative, judicial, administrative or other measures directly related to the Convention's principles and objectives. The Committee asked that appropriate information be furnished.

On 17 August, the Committee adopted a general recommendation concerning article 3 (prevention, prohibition and eradication of all practices of racial segregation and apartheid).

The Committee issued a commentary to a 1994 report of the Secretary-General[9] concerning the UN Decade for Human Rights Education (1995-2004), in which it stated its position on various proposals contained therein.

In a September report,[10] the Secretary-General informed the Assembly that, as at 5 September 1995, 17 States parties had accepted an amendment to the Convention regarding the financing of CERD. The amendment, adopted in 1992,[11] was to enter into force when accepted by a two-thirds majority of States parties. The Secretary-General reported that as at 31 July outstanding assessments and arrears totalled $232,725.

On 8 March,[12] the Commission on Human Rights urged States parties to notify the Secretary-General, as depositary of the Convention, of their acceptance of the amendment and called on them to fulfil their outstanding financial obligations under the Convention.

GENERAL ASSEMBLY ACTION

On 21 December, the General Assembly adopted **resolution 50/137**.

### Report of the Committee on the Elimination of Racial Discrimination

*The General Assembly,*

*Recalling* its previous resolutions concerning the reports of the Committee on the Elimination of Racial Discrimination and its resolutions on the status of the International Convention on the Elimination of All Forms of Racial Discrimination,

*Reiterating* the importance of the Convention, which is one of the most widely accepted human rights instruments adopted under the auspices of the United Nations,

*Aware* of the importance of the contributions of the Committee to the efforts of the United Nations to combat racism and all other forms of discrimination based on race, colour, descent or national or ethnic origin,

*Reiterating once again* the need to intensify the struggle for the elimination of all forms of racism and racial discrimination throughout the world, especially its most brutal forms,

*Emphasizing* the obligation of all States parties to the Convention to take legislative, judicial and other measures in order to secure full implementation of the provisions of the Convention,

*Bearing in mind* the Vienna Declaration and Programme of Action, adopted by the World Conference on Human Rights on 25 June 1993, in particular section II.B, relating to equality, dignity and tolerance, and General Assembly resolution 49/208 of 23 December 1994, in particular paragraph 7 thereof,

*Concerned* that the amendment to the Convention regarding the financing of the Committee, as decided upon at the Fourteenth Meeting of States Parties to the International Convention on the Elimination of All Forms of Racial Discrimination on 15 January 1992 and endorsed by the General Assembly in its resolution 47/111 of 16 December 1992, has not yet entered into force,

*Welcoming* efforts of the Secretary-General to ensure interim financial arrangements for the financing of the expenses incurred by the Committee,

*Stressing* the importance of enabling the Committee to function smoothly and to have all necessary facilities for the effective performance of its functions under the Convention,

*Having considered* the report of the Secretary-General on the financial situation of the Committee,

1. *Commends* the Committee on the Elimination of Racial Discrimination for its work with regard to the implementation of the International Convention on the Elimination of All Forms of Racial Discrimination and the Programme of Action for the Second Decade to Combat Racism and Racial Discrimination and its contribution to the preparation for the Third Decade to Combat Racism and Racial Discrimination;

2. *Encourages* the Committee to contribute fully to the implementation of the Third Decade and its revised Programme of Action, including by the continued collaboration and flow of information between the Committee and the Subcommission on Prevention of Discrimination and Protection of Minorities and the Special Rapporteur of the Commission on Human Rights on contemporary forms of racism, racial discrimination, xenophobia and related intolerance;

3. *Welcomes* the cooperation and exchange of information between the Committee and the relevant structures and mechanisms of the United Nations, such as meetings held with the Special Rapporteur of the Commission on Human Rights on the situation of human rights in the territory of the former Yugoslavia and the Special Rapporteur of the Commission on Human Rights on contemporary forms of racism, racial discrimination, xenophobia and related intolerance and encourages their continuation in the future, including with the United Nations High Commissioner for Human Rights;

4. *Encourages* the use of innovatory procedures by the Committee for reviewing the implementation of the Convention in States whose reports are overdue and the formulating of concluding observations on reports of States parties to the Convention;

5. *Commends* the Committee for its continuous efforts to improve its contribution to the prevention of racial discrimination, including early warning and urgent procedures, and welcomes its relevant decisions and action thereon;

6. *Welcomes* decision 9(46) of 17 March 1995 adopted by the Committee, entitled "Contribution of the Committee on the Elimination of Racial Discrimination to the United Nations Decade for Human Rights Education" and general recommendation XIX(47) on article 3 of the Convention;

7. *Urges* all States which have not yet ratified or acceded to the Convention to do so as soon as possible;

8. *Encourages* States to limit the extent of any reservation they lodge to the Convention and to formulate any reservation as precisely and as narrowly as possible while ensuring that no reservation is incompatible with the object and purpose of the Convention or otherwise contrary to international law;

9. *Expresses its profound concern* at the fact that a number of States parties have still not fulfilled their financial obligations, as shown in the report of the Secretary-General;

10. *Urges* States parties to accelerate their domestic ratification procedures with regard to the amendment to the Convention concerning the financing of the Committee and expeditiously to notify the Secretary-General in writing of their agreement to the amendment, as decided upon at the Fourteenth Meeting of States Parties to the International Convention on the Elimination of All Forms of Racial Discrimination on 15 January 1992 and endorsed by the General Assembly in its resolution 47/111 of 16 December 1992;

11. *Takes note with appreciation* of the report of the Committee on the work of its forty-sixth and forty-seventh sessions;

12. *Requests* the Secretary-General to continue to ensure adequate financial arrangements and appropriate means to enable the functioning of the Committee;

13. *Calls upon* States parties to fulfil their obligations under article 9, paragraph 1, of the Convention, to submit in due time their periodic reports on measures taken to implement the Convention and to pay their outstanding contributions;

14. *Strongly appeals* to all States parties which are in arrears to fulfil their outstanding financial obligations under article 8, paragraph 6, of the Convention;

15. *Requests* the Secretary-General to invite those States parties which are in arrears to pay the amounts in arrears and to report thereon to the General Assembly at its fifty-first session;

16. *Decides* to consider at its fifty-first session, under the item entitled "Elimination of racism and racial discrimination", the report of the Secretary-General on the financial situation of the Committee and the report of the Committee;

17. *Requests* the Secretary-General to draw the present resolution to the attention of States parties to the International Convention on the Elimination of All Forms of Racial Discrimination.

General Assembly resolution 50/137

21 December 1995      Meeting 97      Adopted without vote

Approved by Third Committee (A/50/626) without vote, 2 November (meeting 18); 41-nation draft (A/C.3/50/L.9), orally revised; agenda item 103.
*Meeting numbers.* GA 50th session: 3rd Committee 3-8, 15, 18; plenary 97.

## Convention against torture

As at 31 December 1995,[1] 93 States had become parties to the 1984 Convention against Torture and Other Cruel, Inhuman or Degrading Treatment or Punishment,[13] seven of them (Chad, Côte d'Ivoire, Cuba, Republic of Korea, Republic of Moldova, Tajikistan, Uzbekistan) in 1995. The Convention entered into force in 1987.[14] Amendments to articles 17 and 18, adopted in 1992,[15] had been accepted by 17 States parties by the end of the year. The optional provisions of articles 21 and 22 (under which a party recognizes the competence of the Committee against Torture to receive and consider communications to the effect that a party claims that another is not fulfilling its obligations under the Convention, and to receive communications from or on behalf of individuals claiming to be victims of a violation of the Convention by a State party) also entered into force in 1987; 38 parties had made the required declarations.

The Secretary-General reported on the status of the Convention as at 15 November 1995.[16]

**Commission action.** On 3 March, the Commission urged[17] all States to become parties to the Convention and invited all ratifying or acceding States and those States parties that had not done so to make the declaration provided for in articles 21 and 22 and to consider withdrawing their reservations to article 20. States parties were encouraged to notify the Secretary-General of their acceptance of the amendments to articles 17 and 18.

### Draft optional protocol

On 3 March, the Commission welcomed[18] progress made by the working group at its 1994 session[19] to elaborate a draft optional protocol to the Convention. The protocol would establish a system of visits to be carried out by a committee of experts to places of detention within the jurisdiction of States parties to the protocol. The Commission asked the group to meet for a two-week period prior to its 1996 session and to submit a new report. It requested the Secretary-General to transmit the group's report to Governments, specialized agencies, chairmen of the human rights treaty bodies, intergovernmental organizations and NGOs, and to invite them to submit their observations to the group. It also requested him to invite Governments, specialized agencies, NGOs, the Chairman of the Committee against Torture and the Special Rapporteur to participate in the group's activities and to extend all the necessary facilities to the group for its meeting.

On 25 July, the Economic and Social Council, by **resolution 1995/33**, authorized the working group to meet for a two-week period prior to the Commission's 1996 session.

**Working group activities.** The working group on the draft optional protocol to the Convention (Geneva, 30 October–10 November 1995)[20] examined and revised the text of articles 10 and 11 and 14 to 21 of the draft as submitted by Costa Rica in 1991.[21] The group adopted new articles, 18 *bis*, 19 *bis*, 19 *tertio* and 20 *bis*. Annexed to the group's report was the text of the first reading of draft articles 1 to 21.

### Implementation

**Monitoring body.** The Committee against Torture, established as a monitoring body under the Convention, held its fourteenth session in Geneva from 24 April to 5 May.[22] It examined reports submitted by Italy, Jordan, Mauritius and the Netherlands under article 19 of the Convention. It postponed consideration of a report by Guatemala.

In four closed meetings devoted to its activities under article 20, the Committee studied confidential information that appeared to contain well-founded indications that torture was systematically practised in a State party to the Convention. Under article 22, the Committee adopted its views on a communication considered in 1990[23] and

declared three others inadmissible, one of which was considered in 1994.[19]

The Committee held its fifteenth session, also in Geneva, from 13 to 24 November,[24] at which it examined reports submitted by Colombia, Denmark, Guatemala and the United Kingdom. It postponed consideration of reports from Armenia and Guatemala. Concerning a procedure relating to article 20, the Committee decided to ask a working group to draft a new proposal, based on texts concerning the participation of a member in the examination of the report of his own country, confidential investigations and the confidential examination of communications regarding his country.

## Convention on Elimination of Discrimination against Women

After many years of negotiation, the General Assembly in 1979 adopted the Convention on the Elimination of All Forms of Discrimination against Women.[25] The Committee on the Elimination of Discrimination against Women was established in 1982 to monitor its implementation. In 1995, the General Assembly adopted **resolution 50/202** on 22 December, urging approval of an amendment to the Convention, as called for at the Fourth World Conference on Women. (For details, see PART FOUR, Chapter X; for other aspects concerning women's rights, see next chapter.)

## Convention on the rights of the child

### Accessions and ratifications

As at 31 December,[1] there were 185 parties to the 1989 Convention on the Rights of the Child,[26] which entered into force on 2 September 1990. During 1995, 17 States became parties to the Convention. The Secretary-General reported on the status of the Convention as at 1 November.[27]

### Implementation

**Monitoring body.** In 1995, the Committee on the Rights of the Child (CRC) held its eighth (9-27 January),[28] ninth (22 May–9 June)[29] and tenth (30 October–17 November)[30] sessions, all in Geneva.

Under article 44 of the Convention, the Committee considered initial reports from 17 States parties: Belgium, Canada, Colombia, Denmark, Germany, Holy See, Italy, Jamaica, Nicaragua, Philippines, Poland, Portugal, Senegal, Sri Lanka, Tunisia, Ukraine, United Kingdom. It planned to consider in 1996 the initial report of the Federal Republic of Yugoslavia (Serbia and Montenegro).

At its eighth and tenth sessions, respectively, the Committee held thematic discussions on the situation and human rights of girls and on the administration of justice.

In accordance with article 43, the Secretary-General convened the fifth meeting of the States parties to the Convention (New York, 21 February) to elect five Committee members to replace those whose terms were due to expire on 28 February.[31] The terms of the remaining five Committee members were to expire on 28 February 1997.

**Commission action.** On 8 March, the Commission urged[32] States that had not done so to sign and ratify or accede to the Convention as a matter of priority and urged States parties that had made reservations to review the compatibility of their reservations with article 51 of the Convention and other relevant rules of international law. It asked UN bodies and organs, intergovernmental organizations and NGOs to disseminate information on the Convention, promote its understanding and assist Governments in its implementation. The Secretary-General was asked to ensure the provision of staff and facilities for the effective performance of the Committee and to report on the status of the Convention in 1996.

GENERAL ASSEMBLY ACTION

The General Assembly on 21 December 1995 adopted **resolution 50/153**.

### The rights of the child

*The General Assembly,*

*Recalling* its resolutions 49/209, 49/210, 49/211 and 49/212 of 23 December 1994,

*Recalling also* the recommendation in the Vienna Declaration and Programme of Action, adopted by the World Conference on Human Rights on 25 June 1993, that measures be taken to achieve, by 1995, universal ratification of the Convention on the Rights of the Child, adopted by the General Assembly in its resolution 44/25 of 20 November 1989, and the universal signing of the World Declaration on the Survival, Protection and Development of Children and the Plan of Action for Implementing the World Declaration on the Survival, Protection and Development of Children in the 1990s adopted by the World Summit for Children, as well as their effective implementation,

*Recalling further* Commission on Human Rights resolutions 1995/78 and 1995/79 of 8 March 1995,

*Convinced* that the Convention on the Rights of the Child, as a standard-setting accomplishment of the United Nations in the field of human rights, makes a positive contribution to protecting the rights of children and ensuring their well-being,

*Seriously concerned* about those reservations to the Convention that are contrary to the object and purpose of the Convention or otherwise contrary to international treaty law, and recalling that the Vienna Declaration and Programme of Action urges States to withdraw such reservations,

*Reaffirming* the Vienna Declaration and Programme of Action, which states that national and international mechanisms and programmes should be strengthened for the defence and protection of children, in particu-

lar the girl child, abandoned children, street children, economically and sexually exploited children, including through child pornography, child prostitution or sale of organs, children victims of diseases including acquired immunodeficiency syndrome, refugee and displaced children, children in detention, children in armed conflict and children victims of famine, drought and other emergencies, and also requires measures against female infanticide and harmful child labour,

*Reaffirming also* that the best interests of the child shall be a primary consideration in all actions concerning children,

*Mindful* of the important role of the United Nations and of the United Nations Children's Fund in promoting the well-being of children and their development,

*Noting with appreciation* the important work carried out by the United Nations, in particular the Committee on the Rights of the Child, the Special Rapporteur of the Commission on Human Rights on the sale of children, child prostitution and child pornography and the expert designated by the Secretary-General to undertake the study on the effect of armed conflicts on children,

*Recognizing also* the valuable work done by relevant intergovernmental and non-governmental organizations for the promotion and protection of the rights of the child,

*Reaffirming* that the rights of children require special protection and call for continuous improvement of the situation of children all over the world, as well as for their development and education in conditions of peace and security,

*Profoundly concerned* about the continuing deterioration in the situation of children in many parts of the world as a result of armed conflicts, and convinced that immediate action is called for,

*Convinced* that children affected by armed conflicts require the special protection of the international community and that there is a need for all States to work towards the alleviation of their plight,

*Profoundly concerned also* that the situation of children in many parts of the world remains critical as a result of inadequate social and economic conditions, natural disasters, armed conflicts, exploitation, intolerance, unemployment, rural-to-urban migration, illiteracy, hunger and disability, and convinced that urgent and effective national and international action is called for,

*Deeply concerned* by the persistence of the practice of the use of children for prostitution, sexual abuse and other activities, which may also often constitute exploitation of child labour,

*Recognizing* the existence of a market which encourages the increase of such criminal practices against children,

*Concerned* by the exploitation of child labour and by the fact that it prevents a large number of children from an early age, especially in poverty-stricken areas, from receiving basic education and may unduly imperil their health and even their lives,

*Alarmed*, in particular, by the exploitation of child labour in its most extreme forms, including forced labour, bonded labour and other forms of slavery,

*Encouraged* by measures taken by Governments to eradicate the exploitation of child labour,

*Determined* to safeguard children's right to life, and recognizing the duty and responsibility of Governments to investigate all cases of offences against children, including killing and violence, and to punish offenders,

*Deeply concerned* about the growing number of street children worldwide and the squalid conditions in which these children are often forced to live,

*Welcoming* the efforts made by some Governments to take effective action to address the question of street children,

*Recognizing* that legislation *per se* is not enough to prevent violations of human rights and that Governments should implement their laws and complement legislative measures with effective action, *inter alia*, in the fields of law enforcement and in the administration of justice, and in social, educational and public health programmes,

## I
### Implementation of the Convention on the Rights of the Child

1.   *Welcomes* the unprecedented number of one hundred and eighty-three States which have ratified or acceded to the Convention on the Rights of the Child as a universal commitment to the rights of the child;

2.   *Urges* all States which have not yet done so to sign and ratify or accede to the Convention as a matter of priority, with a view to reaching universal adherence by the end of 1995;

3.   *Emphasizes* the importance of the full implementation by States parties of the provisions of the Convention;

4.   *Urges* States parties to the Convention which have made reservations to review the compatibility of their reservations with article 51 of the Convention and other relevant rules of international law, with the aim of withdrawing them;

5.   *Calls upon* States parties to the Convention to ensure that the education of the child shall be carried out in accordance with article 29 of the Convention and that the education be directed, *inter alia*, to the development of respect for human rights and fundamental freedoms, for the Charter of the United Nations and for different cultures, and to the preparation of the child for responsible life in a free society, in the spirit of understanding, peace, tolerance, equality of the sexes and friendship among peoples, ethnic, national and religious groups and persons of indigenous origin;

6.   *Also calls upon* States parties to the Convention, in accordance with their obligation under article 42, to make the principles and provisions of the Convention widely known to adults and children alike;

## II
### Protection of children affected by armed conflicts

7.   *Calls upon* States fully to respect the dispositions contained in the Geneva Conventions of 12 August 1949 and the Additional Protocols thereto of 1977, as well as those in the Convention on the Rights of the Child, which accord children affected by armed conflicts special protection and treatment;

8.   *Takes note* of the report of the Secretary-General on concrete measures taken to alleviate the situation of children in armed conflict;

9.   *Takes note with appreciation* of the report of the Committee on the Rights of the Child on its eighth session and the recommendations contained therein concerning the situation of children affected by armed conflict;

10.   *Expresses its support* for the work of the expert designated by the Secretary-General to undertake a comprehensive study of the situation of children affected by armed conflicts, with the mandate established by the General Assembly in its resolution 48/157 of 20 December 1993;

11.   *Urgently requests* that appropriate measures be taken by Member States and United Nations agencies, within the scope of their respective mandates, to facilitate the extension of humanitarian assistance and relief and humanitarian access to children in situations of armed conflict and in the immediate aftermath of such conflict;

12.   *Invites* the open-ended inter-sessional working group of the Commisssion on Human Rights on the elaboration of a draft optional protocol to the Convention on the Rights of the Child related to the involvement of children in armed conflicts to pursue its mandate;

## III
### International measures for the prevention and eradication of the sale of children, child prostitution and child pornography

13.   *Welcomes* the provisional report of the Special Rapporteur of the Commission on Human Rights on the sale of children, child prostitution and child pornography;

14.   *Expresses its support* for the work of the Special Rapporteur appointed by the Commission on Human Rights to examine, all over the world, the question of the sale of children, child prostitution and child pornography;

15.   *Takes note* of the establishment by the Economic and Social Council in its resolution 1994/9 of 22 July 1994 of an open-ended inter-sessional working group of the Commission on Human Rights responsible for elaborating, as a matter of priority and in close cooperation with the Special Rapporteur and the Committee on the Rights of the Child, guidelines for a possible draft optional protocol to the Convention on the Rights of the Child related to the sale of children, child prostitution and child pornography, as well as the basic measures needed for the prevention and eradication of those abnormal practices;

16.   *Requests* that all States support efforts in the context of the United Nations system aimed at adopting efficient international measures for the prevention and eradication of all those practices and consider contributing to the drafting of an optional protocol to the Convention on the Rights of the Child;

17.   *Welcomes* the convening of the first world congress against the commercial sexual exploitation of children, to be held at Stockholm from 26 to 31 August 1996;

## IV
### Elimination of exploitation of child labour

18.   *Encourages* Member States which have not yet done so to ratify the conventions of the International Labour Organization relating to the elimination of exploitation of child labour, in particular those concerning the minimum age for employment, the abolition of forced labour and the prohibition of particularly hazardous work for children, and to implement them;

19.   *Calls upon* Governments to take legislative, administrative, social and educational measures to ensure the protection of children from economic exploitation, in particular the protection from performing any work that is likely to be hazardous or to interfere with the child's education or to be harmful to the child's health or physical, mental, spiritual, moral or social development;

20. *Urges* Governments to take all necessary measures to eliminate all extreme forms of child labour, such as forced labour, bonded labour and other forms of slavery;

21. *Requests* that measures be taken by Governments, at the national and international levels, within the framework of multisectoral approaches, to end exploitation of child labour in line with the commitments undertaken at the World Summit for Social Development, held at Copenhagen in March 1995, and the Fourth World Conference on Women, held at Beijing in September 1995, and taking into account the results of other relevant United Nations conferences;

22. *Requests* the Secretary-General, in cooperation with the International Labour Organization, the United Nations Children's Fund and other relevant actors, to report on current initiatives and programmes of the United Nations and its affiliated agencies which address the exploitation of child labour and on how to improve cooperation at the national and international levels in this field;

### V
### The plight of street children

23. *Expresses grave concern* at the continued growth in the number of cases worldwide and at reports of street children being involved in and affected by serious crime, drug abuse, violence and prostitution;

24. *Urges* Governments to continue actively to seek comprehensive solutions to tackle the problems of street children and to take measures to restore their full participation in society and to provide, *inter alia*, adequate nutrition, shelter, health care and education;

25. *Strongly urges* all Governments to guarantee the respect for all human rights and fundamental freedoms, particularly the right to life, and to take urgent measures to prevent the killing of street children and to combat torture and violence against them;

26. *Emphasizes* that strict compliance with the provisions of the Convention on the Rights of the Child and other relevant human rights instruments constitutes a significant step towards solving the problems of street children, and recommends that the Committee on the Rights of the Child and other relevant treaty-monitoring bodies give attention to this growing problem when examining reports from States parties;

27. *Calls upon* the international community to support, through effective international cooperation, the efforts of States to improve the situation of street children, and encourages States parties to the Convention on the Rights of the Child, in preparing their reports to the Committee on the Rights of the Child, to bear this problem in mind and to consider requesting technical advice and assistance for initiatives aimed at improving the situation of street children, in accordance with article 45 of the Convention;

### VI

28. *Invites* Governments, United Nations bodies and organizations, including the United Nations Children's Fund and relevant mechanisms of the Commission on Human Rights, and intergovernmental and non-governmental organizations to cooperate to ensure greater awareness and more effective action to solve the problem of children living in exceptionally difficult conditions by, among other measures, initiating and supporting development projects which can have a positive impact on the situation of those children;

29. *Requests* the Special Rapporteur of the Commission on Human Rights on the sale of children, child prostitution and child pornography to submit an interim report to the General Assembly at its fifty-first session;

30. *Requests* the Secretary-General to submit a report on the rights of the child to the General Assembly at its fifty-first session, containing information on the status of the Convention on the Rights of the Child; the findings of the expert designated by the Secretary-General to undertake the study on the effect of armed conflicts on children; and the problems of exploitation of child labour, its causes and consequences, in accordance with paragraph 22 above;

31. *Decides* to continue its consideration of this question at its fifty-first session under the item entitled "The rights of the child".

General Assembly resolution 50/153

21 December 1995      Meeting 97      Adopted without vote

Approved by Third Committee (A/50/633) without vote, 5 December (meeting 50); draft by 79 nations and Latin American and Caribbean Group (A/C.3/50/L.28), orally revised; agenda item 110.
*Meeting numbers.* GA 50th session: 3rd Committee 32-37, 45, 48, 50; plenary 97.

(For further information on sale of children and child labour, see next chapter.)

### Conference of States Parties

The Conference of States Parties to the Convention on the Rights of the Child (New York, 12 December) considered an amendment to article 43 of the Convention put forth by Costa Rica proposing that the CRC membership be increased from 10 to 18 experts.[33] A Secretariat statement[34] indicated that the increase would cost $518,000 for the 1996-1997 biennium. Until the amendment was approved by the General Assembly and accepted by a two-thirds majority of States parties, the Committee would continue to consist of 10 members in accordance with the existing text of the Convention.

**GENERAL ASSEMBLY ACTION**

On 21 December, the General Assembly adopted **resolution 50/155**.

### Conference of States Parties to the Convention on the Rights of the Child

*The General Assembly,*

*Recognizing* the importance of the Committee on the Rights of the Child and the valuable contribution of its members to the evaluation and monitoring of the implementation of the Convention on the Rights of the Child by its States parties,

*Noting with satisfaction* that there are now one hundred and eighty-three States parties to the Convention on the Rights of the Child, a figure approaching universal ratification,

*Noting* that the amendment to article 43, paragraph 2, of the Convention was adopted by the Conference of States Parties to the Convention,

1. *Approves* the amendment to article 43, paragraph 2, of the Convention on the Rights of the Child, replacing the word "ten" with the word "eighteen";

2. *Urges* States parties to take appropriate measures so that acceptance by a two-thirds majority of the States parties can be reached as soon as possible in order for the amendment to enter into force.

General Assembly resolution 50/155

21 December 1995    Meeting 97    Adopted without vote

Draft by Costa Rica (A/50/L.61/Rev.1); agenda item 110.
*Financial implications.* 5th Committee, A/50/832; S-G, A/C.5/50/46.
*Meeting numbers.* GA 50th session: 5th Committee 42; plenary 97.

### Children in armed conflicts

**Reports of the Secretary-General.** In 1995, the Commission on Human Rights had before it a report of the Secretary-General[35] describing action taken pursuant to a 1993 General Assembly resolution.[36]

As requested by the Assembly in 1994,[37] the Secretary-General in October submitted a second progress report[38] on the study on the impact on children of armed conflict. A first progress report on the study was submitted in 1994.[39] The Secretary-General stated that the expert appointed to undertake the study, Graça Machel (Mozambique), working closely with the Centre for Human Rights and the UN Children's Fund, had visited Angola, Cambodia, Lebanon and Rwanda. Other field visits were planned. An inter-agency task force met periodically to ensure a coordinated response, and regional consultations were under way. A final report was to be made to the Assembly in 1996.

Also in October, the Secretary-General summarized[40] the replies of two UN bodies and one NGO on measures taken to alleviate the situation of children in armed conflicts.

**Commission action.** On 8 March, the Human Rights Commission asked[32] the Secretary-General to transmit the report, on its first (1994) session,[41] of the working group for the elaboration of a draft optional protocol on involvement of children in armed conflict to Governments, relevant specialized agencies, intergovernmental organizations, NGOs, CRC, the International Committee of the Red Cross and the expert appointed to undertake the study on the impact of armed conflicts on children, and to invite their comments thereon in time for circulation prior to the group's second session in 1996. The Commission invited CRC to offer comments on the draft optional protocol and to be represented at future sessions of the working group.

ECONOMIC AND SOCIAL COUNCIL ACTION

On 25 July, the Economic and Social Council adopted **resolution 1995/37**.

**Question of a draft optional protocol to the Convention on the Rights of the Child on the involvement of children in armed conflicts**
*The Economic and Social Council,*
*Recalling* Commission on Human Rights resolution 1995/79 of 8 March 1995,

1. *Authorizes* the working group on a draft optional protocol to the Convention on the Rights of the Child on the involvement of children in armed conflicts to meet for a period of two weeks prior to the fifty-second session of the Commission;
2. *Requests* the Secretary-General to extend to the working group all the necessary services it requires to permit it to meet prior to the fifty-second session of the Commission on Human Rights.

Economic and Social Council resolution 1995/37

25 July 1995    Meeting 52    Adopted without vote

Draft by Commission on Human Rights (E/1995/23); agenda item 5 *(d)*.
*Meeting numbers.* ESC 51-53.

### Sale of children

By a roll-call vote of 42 to none, with 11 abstentions, the Human Rights Commission, on 8 March, decided[42] that the open-ended intersessional working group to elaborate guidelines on a possible draft optional protocol to the Convention on the sale of children, child prostitution and child pornography should elaborate such a protocol as a matter of priority, in cooperation with CRC and the Special Rapporteur on the subject and on the basis of guidelines provided by the group in 1994.[43] It asked the Secretary-General to invite Governments, intergovernmental organizations, NGOs, the Special Rapporteur and CRC to submit comments on the guidelines for circulation to Governments. It invited the Special Rapporteur and a representative of CRC to attend the group's next meeting and asked the Secretary-General to provide assistance needed to enable them to participate in the development of the draft optional protocol.

ECONOMIC AND SOCIAL COUNCIL ACTION

On 25 July, the Economic and Social Council adopted **resolution 1995/35**.

**Question of a draft optional protocol to the Convention on the Rights of the Child on the sale of children, child prostitution and child pornography, and the basic measures needed for their prevention and eradication**
*The Economic and Social Council,*
*Recalling* Commission on Human Rights resolution 1995/78 of 8 March 1995,

1. *Authorizes* the open-ended inter-sessional working group of the Commission on Human Rights for the elaboration of guidelines on a possible optional protocol on the sale of children, child prostitution and child pornography to elaborate, as a matter of priority and in close cooperation with the Special Rapporteur of the Commission on Human Rights on the sale of children, child prostitution and child pornography and the Committee on the Rights of the Child, and on the basis of the guidelines contained in its report, a draft optional protocol to the Convention on the Rights of the Child on the sale of children, child prostitution and child pornography, and to meet for two weeks before the fifty-second session of the Commission on Human Rights;

2. _Requests_ the Secretary-General to provide the working group with all the necessary assistance to enable it to meet and to fulfil its task.

Economic and Social Council resolution 1995/35

25 July 1995    Meeting 52    34-0-15 (roll-call vote)

Draft by Commission on Human Rights (E/1995/23); agenda item 5 _(d)_.
_Meeting numbers._ ESC 51-53.

Roll-call vote in Council as follows:

_In favour:_ Australia, Bahamas, Bhutan, Brazil, Bulgaria, Chile, China, Colombia, Costa Rica, Côte d'Ivoire, Cuba, Egypt, France, Gabon, Ghana, India, Indonesia, Ireland, Jamaica, Libyan Arab Jamahiriya, Luxembourg, Mexico, Nigeria, Pakistan, Philippines, Russian Federation, Senegal, South Africa, Sudan, Thailand, Uganda, United Republic of Tanzania, Venezuela, Zimbabwe.

_Against:_ None.

_Abstaining:_ Canada, Denmark, Germany, Greece, Japan, Malaysia, Netherlands, Norway, Poland, Portugal, Republic of Korea, Romania, Ukraine, United Kingdom, United States.

### Programme of action

The Secretary-General submitted in March 1995 a report[44] to the Working Group on Contemporary Forms of Slavery containing replies received from eight Governments on measures adopted to implement the 1992 Programme of Action for the Prevention of the Sale of Children, Child Prostitution and Child Pornography.[45] Four additional replies were contained in a June report to the Subcommission.[46] In December, the Secretariat drew the attention[47] of the Commission to the June report.

## Convention on migrant workers

### Accession and ratifications

As at 31 December 1995,[1] the International Convention on the Protection of the Rights of All Migrant Workers and Members of Their Families, adopted by the General Assembly in 1990,[48] had been ratified by Morocco and the Philippines, acceded to by Colombia, Egypt, Seychelles and Uganda, and signed by Chile and Mexico.

The Secretary-General reported to the General Assembly on the status of the Convention as at 31 August 1995[49] and to the Commission on Human Rights as at 1 November.[50]

**Commission action.** On 24 February, the Commission called on[51] all Member States to sign and ratify or accede to the Convention as a matter of priority, and invited UN agencies and organizations, intergovernmental organizations and NGOs to disseminate information on it and promote its understanding. The Secretary-General was to provide all assistance necessary to promote the Convention through the World Public Information Campaign for Human Rights and the programme of advisory services in the field of human rights and to report in 1996 on the Convention's status and on efforts made by the Secretariat to promote it and the protection of the rights of migrant workers.

(For further information on migrant workers, see next chapter.)

On 22 December, the General Assembly adopted **resolution 50/169**.

### International Convention on the Protection of the Rights of All Migrant Workers and Members of Their Families

_The General Assembly,_

_Reaffirming once more_ the permanent validity of the principles and norms set forth in the basic instruments regarding the international protection of human rights, in particular the Universal Declaration of Human Rights, the International Covenants on Human Rights, the International Convention on the Elimination of All Forms of Racial Discrimination, the Convention on the Elimination of All Forms of Discrimination against Women and the Convention on the Rights of the Child,

_Bearing in mind_ the principles and norms established within the framework of the International Labour Organization and the importance of the work done in connection with migrant workers and members of their families in other specialized agencies and in various organs of the United Nations,

_Reiterating_ that, despite the existence of an already established body of principles and norms, there is a need to make further efforts to improve the situation and to guarantee respect for the human rights and dignity of all migrant workers and members of their families,

_Aware_ of the situation of migrant workers and members of their families and the marked increase in migratory movements that has occurred, especially in certain parts of the world,

_Considering_ that, in the Vienna Declaration and Programme of Action, adopted by the World Conference on Human Rights on 25 June 1993, all States are urged to guarantee the protection of the human rights of all migrant workers and members of their families,

_Underlining_ the importance of the creation and promotion of conditions to foster greater harmony and tolerance between migrant workers and the rest of the society of the State in which they reside, with the aim of eliminating the growing manifestations of racism and xenophobia taking place in segments of many societies and perpetrated by individuals or groups against migrant workers,

_Recalling_ its resolution 45/158 of 18 December 1990, by which it adopted and opened for signature, ratification and accession the International Convention on the Protection of the Rights of All Migrant Workers and Members of Their Families,

_Bearing in mind_ that, in the Vienna Declaration and Programme of Action, States are invited to consider the possibility of signing and ratifying the Convention at the earliest possible time,

_Recalling_ that, in its resolution 49/175 of 23 December 1994, it requested the Secretary-General to submit to it at its fiftieth session a report on the status of the Convention,

1. _Expresses its deep concern_ at the growing manifestations of racism, xenophobia and other forms of discrimination and inhuman or degrading treatment directed against migrant workers in different parts of the world;

2. _Welcomes_ the signature or ratification of, or accession to, the International Convention on the Protection

of the Rights of All Migrant Workers and Members of Their Families by some Member States;

3. *Calls upon* all Member States to consider signing and ratifying or acceding to the Convention as a matter of priority, and expresses the hope that it will enter into force at an early date;

4. *Requests* the Secretary-General, within existing resources, to provide all facilities and assistance necessary for the promotion of the Convention through the World Public Information Campaign on Human Rights and the programme of advisory services in the field of human rights;

5. *Invites* the organizations and agencies of the United Nations system and intergovernmental and non-governmental organizations to intensify their efforts with a view to disseminating information on and promoting understanding of the Convention;

6. *Takes note* of the report of the Secretary-General, and requests him to submit to it at its fifty-first session an updated report on the status of the Convention;

7. *Decides* to consider the report of the Secretary-General at its fifty-first session under the sub-item entitled "Implementation of human rights instruments".

General Assembly resolution 50/169

22 December 1995     Meeting 99     Adopted without vote

Approved by Third Committee (A/50/635/Add.1) without vote, 11 December (meeting 53); 23-nation draft (A/C.3/50/L.39), orally corrected; agenda item 112 *(a)*.
*Meeting numbers.* GA 50th session: 3rd Committee 35, 38-49, 51, 53; plenary 99.

### Convention on genocide

As at 31 December 1995,[1] 120 States were parties to the 1948 Convention on the Prevention and Punishment of the Crime of Genocide.[52] During the year, Côte d'Ivoire, Kuwait, Singapore and Uganda acceded to the Convention.

*REFERENCES*
[1]*Multilateral Treaties Deposited with the Secretary-General: Status as at 31 December 1995* (ST/LEG/SER.E/14), Sales No. E.96.V.5. [2]YUN 1965, p. 440, GA res. 2106 A (XX), annex, 21 Dec. 1965. [3]YUN 1969, p. 488. [4]A/50/18. [5]YUN 1993, p. 858. [6]E/CN.4/1995/71. [7]E/CN.4/1995/50/Add.4. [8]YUN 1993, p. 438, SC res. 808(1993), 22 Feb. 1993. [9]YUN 1994, p. 1038. [10]A/50/467. [11]YUN 1992, p. 714. [12]E/1995/23 (res. 1995/92). [13]YUN 1984, p. 813, GA res. 39/46, annex, 10 Dec. 1984. [14]YUN 1987, p. 755. [15]YUN 1992, p. 735. [16]E/CN.4/1996/34. [17]E/1995/23 (res. 1995/37 A). [18]Ibid. (res. 1995/33). [19]YUN 1994, p. 1017. [20]E/CN.4/1996/28. [21]YUN 1991, p. 555. [22]A/50/44. [23]A/45/44. [24]A/51/44. [25]YUN 1979, p. 895, GA res. 34/180, annex, 18 Dec. 1979. [26]GA res. 44/25, annex, 20 Nov. 1989. [27]E/CN.4/1996/99. [28]CRC/C/38. [29]CRC/C/43. [30]CRC/C/46. [31]CRC/SP/14 & Add.1,2. [32]E/1995/23 (res. 1995/79). [33]CRC/SP/18/Rev.1. [34]CRC/SP/19. [35]E/CN.4/1995/112. [36]YUN 1993, p. 966, GA res. 48/157, 20 Dec. 1993. [37]YUN 1994, p. 1119, GA res. 49/209, 23 Dec. 1994. [38]A/50/537. [39]YUN 1994, p. 1119. [40]A/50/672. [41]YUN 1994, p. 1116. [42]E/1995/23 (res. 1995/78). [43]YUN 1994, p. 1117. [44]E/CN.4/Sub.2/AC.2/1995/4. [45]YUN 1992, p. 814. [46]E/CN.4/Sub.2/1995/29 & Add.1. [47]E/CN.4/1996/98. [48]GA res. 45/158, annex, 18 Dec. 1990. [49]A/50/469. [50]E/CN.4/1996/70. [51]E/1995/23 (res. 1995/21). [52]YUN 1948-49, p. 959. GA res. 260 A (III), annex, 9 Dec. 1948.

## Other activities

### Follow-up to 1993 World Conference

**Commission action.** On 8 March, the Commission on Human Rights asked[1] the Secretary-General to distribute as widely as possible the 1993 Vienna Declaration and Programme of Action.[2] States were urged to continue to give those documents widespread publicity. Special representatives, special rapporteurs, independent experts and thematic working groups were called on to take into account the recommendations of the Declaration and Programme of Action within their respective mandates. The Commission also asked the UN High Commissioner for Human Rights, the General Assembly and other UN entities related to human rights to take further action with a view to implementing fully all recommendations of the 1993 World Conference on Human Rights. The High Commissioner was to continue to coordinate human rights promotion and protection activities and to report on measures taken and progress achieved in implementing the Declaration and Programme of Action. The Secretary-General was asked to propose adequate resources in the 1996-1997 programme budget to implement them.

**Reports of the High Commissioner.** As requested by the Commission on Human Rights in 1994,[3] the High Commissioner reported[4] on progress made towards full implementation of the recommendations of the Vienna Declaration and Programme of Action. Those documents, he said, provided a dynamic and creative framework for action at all levels to promote and protect human rights. The UN organs had placed their human rights activities within the perspective of the Declaration and had resolved to achieve its objectives. Governments had reaffirmed the relevance of the Declaration to national needs and the importance of cooperating internationally within its framework. NGOs had been inspired by the Declaration and many reported adopting new methods and initiating new activities to achieve its objectives. The High Commissioner stated that the creation of his post had been the most concrete result of the Declaration and that he had taken that Declaration and its objectives as the foundation of his activities.

In November, the High Commissioner noted[5] that under the impact of the Declaration and Programme of Action and the mandate entrusted to him, the UN human rights programme was undergoing a profound transformation. In coordinated efforts aimed at implementing the Declaration and Programme of Action, emphasis was placed on strengthening UN human rights machinery and adapting it to new challenges, including human rights field operations and follow-up of recommendations and decisions of human rights organs and bodies; assistance to vulnerable groups; enhancement of various forms of activities taken by Governments and civil society to promote and protect human rights; and strengthening cooperation in implementing the Declaration and Programme of Action.

In October, the High Commissioner transmitted the report[6] of a meeting of special rapporteurs, representatives, experts and chairmen of working groups of the special procedures and advisory services of the Commission (Geneva, 29-31 May), as called for in the Vienna Declaration and Programme of Action. The participants reviewed items addressed at their first meeting in 1994[3] and discussed: cooperation with the High Commissioner; working relations with the Commission; coordination of extra-conventional mechanisms, with particular emphasis on implementation of additional thematic resolutions adopted by the Commission; integrating the human rights of women; resources and administration; and restructuring the Centre for Human Rights.

Participants regretted the scarcity of resources allotted for the protection of human rights. The situation was even more disturbing in the light of the widening discrepancy between real growth, if any, in Secretariat resources and the exponential growth in mandates requiring Secretariat servicing. They recommended greater administrative and technical support for participants' activities.

In an addendum,[7] the High Commissioner transmitted the text of his address and that of the UN Assistant Secretary-General for Human Rights at the meeting.

The next meeting was scheduled for May 1996 in Geneva.

**GENERAL ASSEMBLY ACTION**

On 22 December, the General Assembly adopted **resolution 50/201**.

**Comprehensive implementation of and follow-up to the Vienna Declaration and Programme of Action**
*The General Assembly,*

*Recalling* its resolution 48/121 of 20 December 1993, in which it endorsed the Vienna Declaration and Programme of Action, adopted by the World Conference on Human Rights, held at Vienna from 14 to 25 June 1993, as well as its resolution 49/208 of 23 December 1994 on the comprehensive implementation of and follow-up to the Vienna Declaration and Programme of Action,

*Recalling also* Commission on Human Rights resolution 1994/95 of 9 March 1994, in which the Commission decided to review annually the progress towards the full implementation of the recommendations contained in the Vienna Declaration and Programme of Action,

*Reaffirming* the view of the World Conference on Human Rights that the promotion and protection of human rights is a matter of priority for the international community,

*Considering* that the promotion of universal respect for and observance of human rights and fundamental freedoms is one of the basic purposes of the Charter of the United Nations and one of the main priorities of the Organization,

*Recognizing* the urgency of eliminating denials and violations of human rights, as expressed in the Vienna Declaration and Programme of Action,

*Convinced* that the Vienna Declaration and Programme of Action has to be translated into effective action by States, the competent United Nations organs and organizations and other organizations concerned, including non-governmental organizations,

*Recognizing* the importance of dialogue and cooperation between Governments and non-governmental organizations in the field of human rights,

*Noting* that the activities envisaged in the Vienna Declaration and Programme of Action add further to the workload and the responsibilities of the United Nations human rights system and that so far only initial steps have been taken towards bridging the gap between resources and the mandated outputs,

*Recalling* the request of the Conference to the Secretary-General and the General Assembly to take immediate steps to increase substantially the resources for the human rights programme from within the existing and future regular budgets of the United Nations,

*Welcoming* the fact that the call of the Conference for a United Nations system-wide approach to human rights issues has been reflected in the recommendations of major international conferences organized by the United Nations in the economic, social and related fields, in particular in the Programme of Action of the International Conference on Population and Development, held at Cairo from 5 to 13 September 1994, the Copenhagen Declaration on Social Development and the Programme of Action of the World Summit for Social Development, held at Copenhagen from 6 to 12 March 1995 and the Beijing Declaration and the Platform for Action of the Fourth World Conference on Women, held at Beijing from 4 to 15 September 1995,

*Noting* the ongoing efforts to ensure a coordinated follow-up to major international conferences in the economic, social and related fields,

*Recognizing* that the interdependence of democracy, development and respect for human rights, as stated in the Vienna Declaration and Programme of Action, requires a comprehensive and integrated approach to the promotion and protection of human rights,

*Recalling* that in its resolution 48/141 the General Assembly decided to create the post of United Nations High Commissioner for Human Rights as the United Nations official with principal responsibility for United Nations human rights activities, including coordination of the human rights promotion and protection activities throughout the United Nations system,

*Noting* that at the first regular session of 1994 of the Administrative Committee on Coordination, in April 1994, the executive heads of all United Nations agencies discussed the implications of the results of the Conference for their respective programmes and committed themselves to supporting the United Nations High

Commissioner for Human Rights in the coordination of the United Nations organs, bodies and the specialized agencies whose activities deal with human rights, as set out in resolution 48/141,

*Noting also* that the High Commissioner has established a permanent dialogue with the United Nations programmes and agencies whose activities deal with human rights in order to maintain systematic exchanges of information, experience and expertise,

*Having considered* the report of the High Commissioner,

1. *Takes note with appreciation* of the report of the United Nations High Commissioner for Human Rights;

2. *Endorses* the reaffirmation in the Vienna Declaration and Programme of Action of the importance of the promotion of universal respect for, and observance and protection of, all human rights and fundamental freedoms in accordance with the Charter of the United Nations;

3. *Reaffirms* the views of the World Conference on Human Rights on the urgency of eliminating denials and violations of human rights;

4. *Recognizes* that the international community should devise ways and means to remove current obstacles and meet the challenges to the full realization of all human rights and to prevent the continuation of human rights violations resulting therefrom throughout the world;

5. *Calls upon* all States to take further action with a view to the full realization of all human rights in the light of the recommendations of the Conference;

6. *Urges* all States to continue to give widespread publicity to the Vienna Declaration and Programme of Action in order to promote increased awareness of human rights and fundamental freedoms;

7. *Reiterates* the request of the Conference that immediate steps be taken to increase substantially the resources for the human rights programme from within existing and future regular budgets of the United Nations;

8. *Welcomes with appreciation* the work of the High Commissioner accomplished thus far, and expresses its commitment to continue to cooperate with and support the High Commissioner in the discharge of his mandate, as set out in resolution 48/141;

9. *Requests* the High Commissioner, the General Assembly, the Commission on Human Rights and other organs and bodies of the United Nations system related to human rights to take further action with a view to the full implementation of all the recommendations of the Conference;

10. *Also requests* the High Commissioner to continue to coordinate the human rights promotion and protection activities throughout the United Nations system, as set out in resolution 48/141, including through a permanent dialogue with the United Nations agencies and programmes whose activities deal with human rights;

11. *Invites* the Administrative Committee on Coordination to continue to discuss the implications of the Vienna Declaration and Programme of Action for the United Nations system;

12. *Requests* the High Commissioner to continue to report on the measures taken and the progress achieved in the comprehensive implementation of the Vienna Declaration and Programme of Action;

13. *Decides* to consider this question at its fifty-first session under the sub-item "Comprehensive implementation of and follow-up to the Vienna Declaration and Programme of Action".

General Assembly resolution 50/201

22 December 1995    Meeting 99    Adopted without vote

Approved by Third Committee (A/50/635/Add.4) without vote, 11 December (meeting 53); 90-nation draft (A/C.3/50/L.50), orally revised; agenda item 112 (d).

*Meeting numbers.* GA 50th session: 3rd Committee 35, 38-53; plenary 99.

## Advisory services

In 1995,[8] under the UN programme of advisory services in human rights established in 1955,[9] some 215 activities were implemented, compared with 130 in 1994. In addition, 19 countries benefited from the 1995 fellowship programme. Supplementing that were 13 global programme development activities; two interregional project formulation activities; four regional projects; and four regional project formulation activities. Activities were funded by the UN regular budget and by the Voluntary Fund for Technical Cooperation in the Field of Human Rights, established in 1987.[10] They covered national plans of action for human rights; constitutions; elections; legislative reform; national human rights institutions; law enforcement; the judiciary; the armed forces; conflict resolution; parliament; curriculum development; teacher training; treaty reporting and international obligations; NGOs and civil society; the mass media; information and documentation; regional institutions and arrangements, human rights support in peace-keeping and human rights training for international civil service; national needs assessment; and the annual UN Human Rights Fellowship Programme.

**Commission action.** On 3 March, the Human Rights Commission, noting the Secretary-General's report on advisory services in human rights during 1994, including the Voluntary Fund,[11] called[12] for implementation of all advisory service activities on the basis of clearly defined objectives and themes; allocation of more human and financial resources to widen advisory services; an inventory and analysis of available advisory services and technical cooperation in the field of human rights from all sources; and an annual report to the Commission on progress in implementing the programme and on operation and administration of the Voluntary Fund. The Commission asked the High Commissioner for Human Rights to explore the possibilities offered by cooperation between the Centre and UN specialized bodies and other organizations, as well as NGOs.

More efficient management of the Voluntary Fund was requested, as was strict and transparent project management rules, periodical evaluations of the programme and projects, dissemination of evaluation results and the holding of annual information meetings. Those requests were approved by the Economic and Social Council by

**decision 1995/269** of 25 July. The Commission asked the Fund's Board of Trustees to exercise its full mandate as an advisory body to promote and solicit contributions and to assist the High Commissioner in monitoring, reviewing and improving the process of selecting and implementing technical assistance projects, the conduct of needs assessments and project evaluation. The Secretary-General was to provide the Board with administrative assistance and to arrange Board meetings so that the Board's report could be included in his annual report to the Commission on advisory services and technical cooperation. It also asked for the incorporation into his next report of Board activities.

### Board of Trustees of Voluntary Fund

The Board of Trustees of the Voluntary Fund for Technical Cooperation in the Field of Human Rights in 1995 held its third and fourth sessions (Geneva, 20-24 March, 30 October–3 November).[8]

At its fourth session, the Board agreed on priority for financing of the following categories of endorsed projects: projects complementing other initiatives or constituting an integral part of a large programme, financed by different bi- or multi-lateral donors; projects which were reviewed previously and given favourable response by the Board; projects responding to specific mandates of the High Commissioner for Human Rights or to a special programme developed by the Centre for Human Rights; and projects addressing issues relating to the mandates emanating from the Vienna Declaration and Plan of Action. The Board also recommended that the existing administrative and financial procedures of the UN Development Fund and other agencies providing technical cooperation be applied *mutatis mutandis* to the technical cooperation projects financed under the Voluntary Fund. Projects were endorsed for Argentina, Armenia, Azerbaijan, Bhutan, El Salvador, Georgia, Haiti, Latvia, Malawi, Nepal, Palestine, Paraguay, Rwanda and Togo. In addition, the Board endorsed a project for regional training in human rights for heads of military academies in Africa; interregional human rights training for heads of military academies from African Lusophone and Commonwealth of Independent States countries; and for a global human rights training programme for the armed forces.

Funds available within the Voluntary Fund to cover 1995 activities amounted to $5,732,383. Also, in 1995, a new full-time Fund Coordinator was appointed.

### Albania

In 1995, the Commission on Human Rights considered a report of the Secretary-General on the human rights situation in Albania,[13] as requested by the Commission in 1994.[14] He stated he had received no reply from the Government to his request for information on implementation of the Commission's 1994 resolution. The Secretary-General summarized advisory services and technical assistance provided to Albania since its 1992 agreement with the Centre for Human Rights.[15]

### Cambodia

In a January report,[16] the Special Representative of the Secretary-General for human rights in Cambodia, Michael Kirby (Australia), described his fourth visit to the country (16-18 November 1994) to take stock of the most recent human rights developments since July 1994. He presented an overview of activities implemented by the Centre for Human Rights in Cambodia from July to November 1994 and discussed the Centre's administrative and financial problems resulting from inadequate budgets approved by the General Assembly.

In a February addendum to that report,[17] the Special Representative presented recommendations following his fifth visit to Cambodia (19-27 January 1995). These related to cultural rights; the rights to health, education, work, a healthy environment and sustainable development; new laws and practices; judicial independence and the rule of law; prisons and other custodial institutions; freedom of expression and the press law; the right to be elected and take part in government; vulnerable groups; Cambodia's fulfilment of its reporting obligations under the conventions to which it was a party; security issues; and ongoing technical support and assistance.

**Commission action.** On 3 March, the Commission asked[18] the Secretary-General to assure the protection of the rights of all people in Cambodia and to ensure sufficient resources for the enhanced functioning of the presence in the country of the Centre for Human Rights. Expressing concern at the serious human rights violations detailed by the Special Representative, the Commission endorsed his conclusions and recommendations and asked him to evaluate the extent to which the recommendations were followed up and implemented. It noted with appreciation the Secretary-General's use of the UN Trust Fund for a Human Rights Education Programme in Cambodia to finance Centre activities. The Commission decided to review in 1996 the programmes and mandates set out in a 1993 resolution.[19] It asked the Centre, in cooperation with relevant UN specialized agencies and development programmes, to develop and implement programmes, with the consent and cooperation of the Government, in priority areas identified by the Special Representative, paying particular attention to vulnerable groups. The Special Representative was to report to the Commission in 1996 and to the General Assembly in 1995. The Secretary-General was asked to renew the Special Representative's mandate, to provide resources to enable him to fulfil his tasks, and to report in 1996 on the role of the Centre in assisting Cambodia and on the Special Representative's recommendations.

On 25 July, the Economic and Social Council, by **decision 1995/271**, approved the Commission's request to the Secretary-General to renew the Special Representative's mandate and to provide the necessary resources. It also approved the request for reports from the Special Representative.

**Report of the Secretary-General.** In an October report,[20] the Secretary-General reviewed human rights activities in Cambodia carried out by the UN system. He also discussed the Special Representative's recommendations and the role of the Centre for Human Rights in assisting the Government and people of Cambodia to promote and protect human rights. The Special Representative's recommendations submitted between August 1994 and August 1995 were annexed to the report together with a summary of any action known to have been taken by the Government. The Secretary-General also discussed the Special Representative's sixth visit to Cambodia (5-16 August 1995) and reviewed his earlier recommendations and action subsequently taken.

The Secretary-General updated data on human rights issues concerning health care, education, the right to work, housing, the right to a healthy environment and to sustainable development, new laws and practices, judicial independence and the rule of law, conditions in prisons and other custodial institutions, freedom of expression and the press law, the right to be elected and to participate in government, the situation of vulnerable groups, including women, children and minorities, Cambodia's reporting obligations under international covenants to which it was a party and security issues. He made recommendations regarding the rights to health, education, housing and a healthy environment; new laws and practices; judicial independence; prisons and other custodial institutions; press law and freedom of expression; the right to be elected and take part in government; vulnerable groups; Cambodia's reporting obligations under international instruments; security issues; and ongoing technical advice and assistance.

Activities and programmes implemented in Cambodia by the Centre for Human Rights between December 1994 and 31 July 1995 were described. Most were to be financed from voluntary contributions to the Trust Fund for a Human Rights Education Programme in Cambodia which, as at 30 June 1995, had received some $1.3 million. The Centre assisted in creating a legal framework consistent with international human

rights standards and securing the promotion and protection of human rights; developing and strengthening national institutions; establishing a system for the administration of justice consistent with international human rights standards; developing expertise in preparing reports to UN treaty bodies; developing human rights curricula and teacher training; organizing training on freedom of expression for journalists; disseminating human rights information and documentation; training health officials; organizing meetings concerning children in armed conflict; and strengthening human rights activities at the local and provincial levels.

GENERAL ASSEMBLY ACTION

On 22 December, the General Assembly adopted **resolution 50/178**.

**Situation of human rights in Cambodia**

*The General Assembly,*

*Guided* by the purposes and principles embodied in the Charter of the United Nations, the Universal Declaration of Human Rights and the International Covenants on Human Rights,

*Taking note* of the Agreement on a Comprehensive Political Settlement of the Cambodia Conflict, signed in Paris on 23 October 1991, including part III thereof, relating to human rights,

*Taking note also* of Commission on Human Rights resolution 1995/55 of 3 March 1995, and recalling General Assembly resolution 49/199 of 23 December 1994 and previous relevant resolutions, including Commission on Human Rights resolution 1993/6 of 19 February 1993, in which the Commission recommended the appointment of a special representative for Cambodia, and the subsequent appointment by the Secretary-General of a special representative,

*Bearing in mind* the role and responsibilities of the United Nations and the international community in the process of the rehabilitation and reconstruction of Cambodia,

*Recognizing* that the tragic recent history of Cambodia requires special measures to assure the promotion and protection of the human rights of all people in Cambodia and the non-return to the policies and practices of the past, as stipulated in the Agreement signed in Paris on 23 October 1991,

*Commending* the continued operation in Cambodia of the office of the Centre for Human Rights of the Secretariat,

*Welcoming* the understanding reached between the Special Envoy of the Secretary-General and the Government of Cambodia in May 1995 regarding increased consultations between the Centre for Human Rights and the Government of Cambodia,

1. *Requests* the Secretary-General to assure the protection of the human rights of all people in Cambodia and to ensure adequate resources, from within existing United Nations resources, for the enhanced functioning of the operational presence in Cambodia of the Centre for Human Rights of the Secretariat;

2. *Welcomes* the report of the Secretary-General on the role of the Centre for Human Rights in assisting

the Government and people of Cambodia in the promotion and protection of human rights;

3. *Welcomes also* the continuing role of the United Nations High Commissioner for Human Rights in the promotion and protection of human rights in Cambodia;

4. *Welcomes and encourages* the efforts of individuals, non-governmental organizations, Governments and international organizations involved in human rights activities in Cambodia;

5. *Takes note with appreciation* of the most recent report submitted by the Special Representative of the Secretary-General for human rights in Cambodia, and endorses his recommendations and conclusions, including those aimed at ensuring the independence of the judiciary and the establishment of the rule of law, good governance, freedom of expression and the promotion of an effectively functioning multi-party democracy;

6. *Notes* that communal elections are due to be held in 1996 or early 1997 and National Assembly elections in 1998, and urges the Government of Cambodia to promote and uphold the effective functioning of multi-party democracy, including the right to form political parties, stand for election, take part freely in a representative government and to freedom of expression, in accordance with the principles set out in paragraphs 2 and 4 of annex 5 to the Agreement signed in Paris on 23 October 1991;

7. *Requests* the Special Representative, in collaboration with the office in Cambodia of the Centre for Human Rights, to continue his evaluation of the extent to which the recommendations made by the Special Representative in his report, and those contained in his previous reports, are followed up and implemented, and strongly encourages the Government of Cambodia to continue to cooperate with the Special Representative;

8. *Requests* the Secretary-General to provide all necessary resources, from within the regular budget of the United Nations, to enable the Special Representative to continue to fulfil his tasks expeditiously;

9. *Welcomes* the efforts made by the Government of Cambodia to promote and protect human rights, in particular in the essential area of creating a functioning system of justice, urges that efforts continue in this area, and also encourages the Government to improve the conditions of prisons;

10. *Expresses grave concern* about the atrocities that continue to be committed by the Khmer Rouge, including the taking and killing of hostages, and other deplorable incidents detailed in the reports of the Special Representative;

11. *Also expresses grave concern* about the serious violations of human rights as detailed by the Special Representative in his report, and calls upon the Government of Cambodia to prosecute in accordance with the due process of the law and international standards relating to human rights all those who have perpetrated human rights violations;

12. *Expresses particularly grave concern* at the comments made by the Special Representative concerning the reluctance of the courts to charge members of the military and other security forces for serious criminal offences, and encourages the Government of Cambodia to address this problem, which in effect places persons in authority above the principle of equality before the law;

13. *Further expresses grave concern* at the devastating consequences and destabilizing effects of the indiscriminate use of anti-personnel land-mines on Cambodian society, encourages the Government of Cambodia to continue its support and efforts for the removal of these mines, and welcomes the intention of the Government of Cambodia to ban all anti-personnel land-mines;

14. *Calls upon* the Government of Cambodia to ensure the full observance of human rights for all persons within its jurisdiction in accordance with the International Covenants on Human Rights and other human rights instruments to which Cambodia is a party;

15. *Encourages* the Government of Cambodia to continue its efforts to meet its reporting obligations under international human rights instruments, drawing on the assistance of the office in Cambodia of the Centre for Human Rights;

16. *Also encourages* the Government of Cambodia to request the Centre for Human Rights to provide advice and technical assistance with respect to the creation of an independent national institution for the promotion and protection of human rights;

17. *Further encourages* the Government of Cambodia to maintain constructive dialogue and consultation with the Centre for Human Rights concerning its activities in Cambodia;

18. *Commends* the ongoing efforts of the office in Cambodia of the Centre for Human Rights in supporting and assisting the Government of Cambodia, as well as non-governmental organizations and others involved in the promotion and protection of human rights in cooperation with the Government of Cambodia;

19. *Condemns unreservedly* attacks on and threats against staff of the United Nations, non-governmental organizations and the Cambodian Government, as well as individuals, and calls upon the Government of Cambodia to investigate those attacks and threats and to prosecute those who are responsible, in accordance with the due process of the law and international standards relating to the administration of justice;

20. *Notes with appreciation* the use by the Secretary-General of the United Nations Trust Fund for a Human Rights Education Programme in Cambodia to finance the programme of activities of the office in Cambodia of the Centre for Human Rights as defined in resolutions of the General Assembly and the Commission on Human Rights, and invites Governments, intergovernmental and non-governmental organizations, foundations and individuals to consider contributing funds to the Trust Fund;

21. *Requests* the Centre for Human Rights, in cooperation with the relevant specialized agencies and development programmes, to develop and implement programmes, with the consent and cooperation of the Government of Cambodia, in the priority areas identified by the Special Representative, paying particular attention to vulnerable groups, including women, children and minorities;

22. *Requests* the Secretary-General to report to the General Assembly at its fifty-first session on the role of the Centre for Human Rights in assisting the Government and people of Cambodia in the promotion and protection of human rights and on the recommendations made by the Special Representative on matters within his mandate;

23. *Decides* to continue its consideration of the situation of human rights in Cambodia at its fifty-first session.

General Assembly resolution 50/178

22 December 1995      Meeting 99      Adopted without vote

Approved by Third Committee (A/50/635/Add.2) without vote, 11 December (meeting 53); 18-nation draft (A/C.3/50/L.40), orally revised; agenda item 112 *(b)*.
*Meeting numbers.* GA 50th session: 3rd Committee 35, 38-51, 53; plenary 99.

### El Salvador

On 7 March, the Commission on Human Rights, noting the January report of independent expert Pedro Nikken (Venezuela),[21] commended[22] him for his work and welcomed his proposal for the conclusion of a technical cooperation agreement between the Government of El Salvador and the Centre for Human Rights. The High Commissioner for Human Rights was asked to facilitate the implementation of the agreement. The Voluntary Fund for Technical Cooperation in the Field of Human Rights was urged to support the technical cooperation programme agreed upon. The Commission decided to conclude consideration of the matter.

**Other action.** A March note by the Secretariat[23] contained a 23 February letter from the Director of the Human Rights Division of the UN Observer Mission in El Salvador (ONUSAL) addressed to the Chairman of the Commission on Human Rights, referring to the independent expert's proposal that the Centre's technical assistance programme be carried out in close coordination with the mechanism to be elaborated by the Secretary-General and the Security Council after the withdrawal of ONUSAL. The Director pointed out that, following ONUSAL's withdrawal on 30 April, the Secretary-General had proposed that the UN establish, for an initial period of six months, an on-site team to provide good offices, verify implementation of outstanding points on the peace agreements and provide information to the Secretary-General. Council members welcomed the proposal (see PART TWO, Chapter III).

### Guatemala

**Commission action.** Noting the report by independent expert Mónica Pinto (Argentina) on the situation of human rights in Guatemala,[24] the Commission on 3 March asked[25] the Secretary-General to continue to provide that country and NGOs with advisory services. It also asked that the expert's mandate be extended so that she could continue to examine the situation, provide assistance to the Government and report in 1996 on measures taken by Guatemala.

By **decision 1995/268** of 25 July, the Economic and Social Council approved the Commission's requests.

**Subcommission action.** On 18 August, the Subcommission asked[26] the Government of Guatemala to enable elections to take place in an appropriate political climate and asked parties to the negotiations to consider measures to ensure unrestricted exercise of political rights. The Government was requested to support the Supreme Electoral Tribunal's programmes and to give priority to the expansion of economic and social development programmes. The Commission of the European Union, the Organization of American States and the UN were asked to provide the economic and practical support that the Supreme Electoral Tribunal might seek to ensure a clear and transparent electoral process. The Subcommission asked the General Assembly to look favourably on the extension of the mandate of the UN Mission for the Verification of Human Rights and of Compliance with the Commitments of the Comprehensive Agreement on Human Rights in Guatemala (see PART TWO, Chapter III), established in 1994.[27] It also asked the Government and Unidad Revolucionaria Nacional Guatemalteca to step up efforts to apply the 1994 Comprehensive Agreement on Human Rights[28] and called on them to pursue the negotiating process. The Secretary-General was called on to provide the necessary means for that process, and the Assembly of Civil Society was asked to continue to take part in it.

### Romania

In a March report,[29] the Secretary-General evaluated the first comprehensive country programme of advisory services and technical assistance in the field of human rights implemented in Romania. Two external experts appointed by the Centre for Human Rights and two experts appointed by the Government had conducted interviews with selected categories of beneficiaries of the programme, such as ministry staff, professionals, NGOs and the Romanian Institute for Human Rights (IRDO).

The team concluded that the seminars had provided a basis for or complement to wider reform efforts. Laws to protect human rights had been drafted and institutions were being strengthened. However, the extent to which knowledge of human rights had been spread within the society at large remained unclear. The team noted that the ultimate responsibility for enhancing the effects of the programme must be assumed by the Government, which was the guarantor of its sustainability.

The team also made recommendations concerning coordination and planning; NGOs; participation of civilians; international and national experts; decentralization of programme activities; topic selection for seminars; and programme evaluation and cost. An independent review of IRDO was urged to take stock of its experience and examine its priorities.

## Somalia

On 3 March, the Commission, recalling its 1994 request for the independent expert to report on conditions in Somalia,[30] and noting that the expert had not been able to carry out his mandate owing to the circumstances in Somalia, called on[31] all parties to the conflict to work towards a peaceful solution to the crisis (see PART TWO, Chapter II). The Commission urged them to respect the human rights and fundamental freedoms of all, to prevent violations of international humanitarian law and human rights, to apply criminal justice standards and to protect UN personnel. It asked the independent expert to study how best to implement a programme of advisory services for Somalia, upon request. The Secretary-General was asked to provide resources to fund the activities of the independent expert and the Centre, and Governments and organizations in a position to do so were invited to respond positively to requests by the Secretary-General for assistance. The Secretary-General was asked to report to the Commission in 1996. The requests to the Secretary-General and the expert were appproved by the Economic and Social Council by **decision 1995/272** of 25 July.

On 31 July, the Secretary-General approved the appointment of Mohamed Charfi (Tunisia) as independent expert on Somalia.

## Togo

On 3 March, the Human Rights Commission welcomed[32] the forthcoming dispatch to Togo of an evaluation mission of the Centre for Human Rights, with a view to developing a programme of technical assistance to strengthen human rights promotion and protection under the Centre's programme of advisory services and technical assistance. The Secretary-General was to report to the Commission in 1996, with a view to ending consideration of the question.

## Public information

Pursuant to a 1994 request of the Commission on Human Rights,[33] the Secretary-General reported[34] on public information activities in the area of human rights, including the World Public Information Campaign for Human Rights, launched by the General Assembly in 1988[35] and carried out by the Centre for Human Rights and the Department of Public Information (DPI). Campaign activities included: the publications programme; the translation programme; briefings, exhibitions and human rights observances; fellow-

ships and internships; and workshops, seminars and training courses.

The Secretary-General stated that the Campaign was firmly in place and that a strategy had been developed to ensure its continued, effective implementation. However, currently the Centre was unable to guarantee the strategy's full implementation. Adequate resources were needed to ensure that the opportunity offered by an upsurge in public interest in UN work in the area of human rights was not wasted.

**Commission action.** On 3 March, the Commission urged[36] the Centre for Human Rights to finalize its comprehensive review of the programme of information and publications, including the elaboration of a new information strategy, to assess the effectiveness of the programme and to report in 1997. The Centre should continue to develop training courses and materials, including targeted training manuals for professional audiences. DPI was urged to utilize more effectively UN information centres (UNICs) for the timely dissemination of basic information and reference materials on human rights and fundamental freedoms, and to ensure that UNICs were supplied with adequate materials in UN official languages and relevant national languages and that available resources were used to produce factual information materials on human rights in all regions. Member States were encouraged to provide and promote publicity for UN human rights activities and to accord priority to disseminating, in their national and local languages, the 1948 Universal Declaration of Human Rights,[37] the 1966 International Covenants on Human Rights[38] and other international instruments.

The Commission called on the High Commissioner for Human Rights to coordinate and harmonize human rights information strategies, to ensure close cooperation between the Centre and DPI in implementing the aims of the World Public Information Campaign, and to coordinate with the UN Educational, Scientific and Cultural Organization regarding education for human rights. It asked the Secretary-General to take advantage of the collaboration of NGOs in implementing the Campaign, to consider making available resources from the UN regular budget to allow the Centre to implement fully its publications programme and to submit in 1997 a report on public information activities.

## Human rights education

**Commission action.** On 3 March, the Commission called[39] on Governments to contribute, in cooperation with NGOs, educators and the media, to the implementation of the Plan of Action for the UN Decade for Human Rights Education (1995-2004), proclaimed by the General Assembly in 1994.[40] The High Commissioner was to submit proposals in 1996 to supplement the Plan, taking into account the views submitted by Governments, and to coordinate implementation of the Plan and carry out other tasks enumerated therein. He was also asked to conduct the survey of human rights education and prepare a preliminary report provided for in the Plan as soon as possible; and to convene the international planning conference for the Decade. The Centre for Human Rights was to support the High Commissioner's efforts in implementing the Plan. The Commission requested the Secretary-General to consider the possibility of establishing a voluntary fund within the High Commissioner's Office to be used in implementing the Plan. It asked human rights monitoring bodies to emphasize implementation by Member States of their obligation to promote human rights education. It invited the specialized agencies to contribute to the implementation of the Plan for the Decade and called on NGOs to increase their involvement in education in human rights and to cooperate with the Centre in implementing the Plan.

**Report of the High Commissioner.** In October, the Secretary-General transmitted a report[41] of the High Commissioner on implementation of the Plan of Action by States, the Secretariat, human rights treaty bodies, UN specialized agencies and programmes, NGOs and other institutions. Future activities included: an international consultation to consider the relevance of education theories and practices to human rights education, to be organized by Costa Rica; a preliminary survey on existing human rights education programmes and initiatives; a survey of existing versions (printed, pictorial, audiovisual, etc.) of the Universal Declaration of Human Rights; and the establishment of a media advisory board for public information and education on human rights.

GENERAL ASSEMBLY ACTION

On 22 December, the General Assembly adopted **resolution 50/173**.

**United Nations Decade for Human Rights Education: towards a culture of peace**

*The General Assembly,*

*Recognizing* that, in the context of respect for the permanent values on which the United Nations system is based, the United Nations Educational, Scientific and Cultural Organization has, since its founding, worked to ensure the free circulation of ideas, to bring individuals and cultures closer together and to ensure respect for human rights, the effective exercise of democracy, justice and freedom,

*Bearing in mind* its resolutions 48/126 of 20 December 1993 and 49/213 of 23 December 1994 on the proclamation of the United Nations Year for Tolerance, and

its resolution 49/184 of 23 December 1994 proclaiming the United Nations Decade for Human Rights Education,

*Welcoming with appreciation* resolution 5.3 adopted by the General Conference of the United Nations Educational, Scientific and Cultural Organization at its twenty-eighth session, which invites the Director-General to implement the activities of the transdisciplinary project entitled "Towards a culture of peace", in particular unit 1, entitled "Education for peace, human rights, democracy, international understanding and tolerance",

*Considering* that the Plan of Action for the United Nations Decade for Human Rights Education, 1995-2004 will make a fundamental contribution to understanding and peaceful coexistence among individuals and nations and is consistent with the transdisciplinary project entitled "Towards a culture of peace",

1. *Expresses its satisfaction* at resolution 5.3 adopted by the General Conference of the United Nations Educational, Scientific and Cultural Organization at its twenty-eighth session, which contains the transdisciplinary project entitled "Towards a culture of peace";

2. *Encourages* countries, regional organizations, non-governmental organizations and the Director-General of the United Nations Educational, Scientific and Cultural Organization to take all necessary action to ensure education for peace, human rights, democracy, international understanding and tolerance;

3. *Requests* the Secretary-General, in consultation with the Director-General of the United Nations Educational, Scientific and Cultural Organization, to report to the General Assembly at its fifty-first session on the progress of educational activities in the framework of the transdisciplinary project entitled "Towards a culture of peace".

General Assembly resolution 50/173

22 December 1995     Meeting 99     Adopted without vote

Approved by Third Committee (A/50/635/Add.2) without vote, 11 December (meeting 53); 66-nation draft (A/C.3/50/L.33); agenda item 112 *(b)*.
Meeting numbers. GA 50th session: 3rd Committee 35, 38-51, 53; plenary 99.

On the same date, the Assembly adopted **resolution 50/177**.

**United Nations Decade for Human Rights Education**

*The General Assembly,*

*Guided* by the Charter of the United Nations and the Universal Declaration of Human Rights,

*Reaffirming* article 26 of the Universal Declaration of Human Rights, according to which "education shall be directed to the full development of the human personality and to the strengthening of respect for human rights and fundamental freedoms",

*Recalling* the provisions of other international human rights instruments, such as those of article 13 of the International Covenant on Economic, Social and Cultural Rights and article 28 of the Convention on the Rights of the Child, that reflect the aims of the aforementioned article,

*Taking into account* Commission on Human rights resolution 1993/56 of 9 March 1993, in which the Commission recommended that knowledge of human rights, both in its theoretical dimension and its practical application, should be established as a priority in educational policies,

*Convinced* that human rights education should involve more than the provision of information and should constitute a comprehensive life-long process by which people at all levels in development and in all strata of society learn respect for the dignity of others and the means and methods of ensuring that respect in all societies,

*Convinced also* that human rights education contributes to a concept of development consistent with the dignity of women and men of all ages that takes into account the diverse segments of society such as children, indigenous people, minorities and disabled persons,

*Taking into account* the efforts to promote human rights education made by educators and non-governmental organizations in all parts of the world, as well as by intergovernmental organizations, including the United Nations Educational, Scientific and Cultural Organization, the International Labour Organization and the United Nations Children's Fund,

*Convinced further* that each woman, man and child, to realize their full human potential, must be made aware of all their human rights—civil, cultural, economic, political and social,

*Believing* that human rights education constitutes an important vehicle for the elimination of gender-based discrimination and ensuring equal opportunities through the promotion and protection of the human rights of women,

*Aware* of the experience in human rights education of United Nations peace-building operations, including the United Nations Observer Mission in El Salvador and the United Nations Transitional Authority in Cambodia,

*Considering* the World Plan of Action on Education for Human Rights and Democracy, adopted by the International Congress on Education for Human Rights and Democracy convened by the United Nations Educational, Scientific and Cultural Organization at Montreal from 8 to 11 March 1993, according to which education for human rights and democracy is itself a human right and a prerequisite for the realization of human rights, democracy and social justice,

*Bearing in mind* the Vienna Declaration and Programme of Action, adopted by the World Conference on Human Rights on 25 June 1993, in particular section II, paragraphs 78 to 82 thereof,

*Recalling* that it is the responsibility of the United Nations High Commissioner for Human Rights to coordinate relevant United Nations education and public information programmes in the field of human rights,

*Recalling* its resolution 49/184 of 23 December 1994, by which it proclaimed the ten-year period beginning on 1 January 1995 the United Nations Decade for Human Rights Education, welcomed the Plan of Action for the Decade, and requested the High Commissioner to coordinate the implementation of the Plan of Action,

*Taking note* of the report of the High Commissioner to the General Assembly, in which he stated that human rights education was essential for the encouragement of harmonious intercommunity relations, for mutual tolerance and understanding and, finally, for peace,

1. *Takes note with appreciation* of the report of the United Nations High Commissioner for Human Rights on the implementation of the Plan of Action for the United Nations Decade for Human Rights Education, submitted in accordance with General Assembly resolution 49/184;

2. *Appeals* to all Governments to contribute to the implementation of the Plan of Action, and in particular,

in accordance with national conditions, to establish a national focal point (national committee) for human rights education and a resource and training centre for human rights education or, where such a centre already exists, to work towards its strengthening, and to develop and implement an action-oriented national plan for human rights education, as foreseen in the Plan of Action;

3. *Requests* the High Commissioner to coordinate the implementation of the Plan of Action and to carry out the tasks enumerated therein;

4. *Requests* the Centre for Human Rights of the Secretariat and the Commission on Human Rights, in cooperation with the existing human rights monitoring bodies, United Nations specialized agencies and programmes and other competent intergovernmental and non-governmental organizations, to support efforts by the High Commissioner in the implementation of the Plan of Action;

5. *Requests* the existing human rights monitoring bodies to place emphasis on the implementation by Member States of their international obligation to promote human rights education;

6. *Invites* all relevant specialized agencies, in particular the United Nations Educational, Scientific and Cultural Organization and the International Labour Organization, United Nations bodies, especially the United Nations Children's Fund, and other intergovernmental organizations to contribute, within their respective spheres of competence, to the implementation of the Plan of Action and to cooperate with the High Commissioner for that purpose;

7. *Calls upon* international, regional and national non-governmental organizations, in particular those concerned with women, labour, development and the environment, as well as other social justice groups, human rights advocates, educators, religious organizations and the media, to increase their involvement in formal and non-formal education in human rights and to cooperate with the High Commissioner and the Centre for Human Rights in implementing the Plan of Action;

8. *Requests* the Secretary-General to consider the possibility of establishing a voluntary fund for human rights education, with special provision for the support of the human rights education activities of non-governmental organizations, to be administered by the Centre for Human Rights;

9. *Also requests* the Secretary-General to bring the present resolution to the attention of all members of the international community and to intergovernmental and non-governmental organizations concerned with human rights and education;

10. *Decides* to consider this matter at its fifty-first session under the item entitled "Human rights questions".

General Assembly resolution 50/177

22 December 1995     Meeting 99     Adopted without vote

Approved by Third Committee (A/50/635/Add.2) without vote, 11 December (meeting 53); 85-nation draft (A/C.3/50/L.38); agenda item 112 *(b)*.
*Meeting numbers.* GA 50th session: 3rd Committee 35, 38-51, 53; plenary 99.

## National institutions and regional arrangements

### National institutions for human rights protection

**Reports of the Secretary-General.** In a January report,[42] the Secretary-General presented the views of six Governments and five national institutions concerning possible forms of participation by national institutions in UN meetings dealing with human rights. Most States felt that national institutions should act with complete independence and that they might participate in UN meetings in their own right, which would imply that they were credible. The national institutions wished to participate in the annual sessions of the Commission on Human Rights and of the Sub-commission, periodic meetings of treaty bodies and meetings of the General Assembly's Third Committee.

The Secretary-General recommended that if the Commission decided that national institutions should participate in meetings of UN human rights bodies, it should state that their structure and operation must conform with the principles relating to the status of national institutions as adopted by the Assembly in 1993.[43] He also recommended that the Commission should be informed whenever a national institution was established in order to accord it the appropriate status.

In September, the Secretary-General submitted a report[44] on activities taken by the Centre for Human Rights to establish and strengthen national institutions for the promotion and protection of human rights. The Centre held an international workshop (see below) and assisted national institutions under its programme of advisory services and technical assistance. The Coordination Committee for national institutions, set up to promote the establishment and strengthening of national human rights mechanisms, held its second session (Geneva, 22-23 February 1995), at which it emphasized strengthening its links with the High Commissioner and the Centre. The Secretary-General described action taken at the national and regional levels by national institutions and measures taken by Governments to promote those institutions. As to the status of the institutions, the Secretary-General noted that, according to the Coordination Committee, national institutions should be granted the same status as the specialized agencies and space should be made available so that their representatives could express their views as representatives of independent bodies. The Committee also asked that it should be consulted by the Centre about which national institutions should be entitled to participate in meetings of UN human rights bodies. The Secretary-General replied that he believed that the question of the status of national institutions at such meetings was a matter for the Commission and the Economic and Social Council to decide and he expected them to reach an appropriate decision. He would report to the Commission in 1996 and the Commission would decide on the status of national institutions in relation to UN human rights bodies.

**Commission action.** On 3 March, the Human Rights Commission asked[45] the Secretary-General to give high priority to requests from Member States for assistance in establishing and strengthening national institutions for the promotion and protection of human rights as part of the programme of advisory services and technical assistance in the field of human rights. It also asked him to invite Member States that had not done so to inform him of their views concerning possible forms of participation by national institutions in UN meetings dealing with human rights, and to include that information in his 1996 report; and to ensure that national institutions were informed about the relevant activities of the Centre for Human Rights. The Centre was asked to provide technical assistance for States wishing to establish or strengthen their national institutions and to organize training programmes.

**International workshop.** The third International Workshop on National Institutions for the Promotion and Protection of Human Rights (Manila, 18-21 April),[46] organized by the Centre for Human Rights in cooperation with the Philippine Commission for Human Rights, was held to assess the implementation of the 1993 principles and to consider ways of strengthening existing national institutions and encouraging their creation in countries where they did not exist. It also addressed national institutions and the fight against racism and racial discrimination, national institutions and the protection of migrant workers, national institutions and indigenous peoples, and relations between national institutions and the Commission on Human Rights and other UN forums. On 21 April, the Workshop adopted the Manila Declaration and recommendations for the Commission. The first two workshops were held in 1991[47] and 1993.[48]

On 22 December, the General Assembly adopted **resolution 50/176**.

### National institutions for the promotion and protection of human rights

*The General Assembly,*

*Recalling* the relevant resolutions of the General Assembly and the Commission on Human Rights concerning national institutions for the promotion and protection of human rights,

*Stressing* the importance of the Universal Declaration of Human Rights, the International Covenants on Human Rights and other international instruments for promoting respect for and observance of human rights and fundamental freedoms,

*Convinced* of the important role national institutions play in promoting and protecting human rights and fundamental freedoms and in developing and enhancing public awareness of those rights and freedoms,

*Mindful* in this regard of the guidelines on the structure and functioning of national and local institutions for the promotion and protection of human rights endorsed by the General Assembly in its resolution 33/46 of 14 December 1978,

*Recalling* the Vienna Declaration and Programme of Action, in which the World Conference on Human Rights reaffirmed the important and constructive role played by national institutions for the promotion and protection of human rights, in particular in their advisory capacity to the competent authorities, in their role in remedying human rights violations, in the dissemination of human rights information and in education in human rights,

*Noting* the diverse approaches adopted throughout the world for the promotion and protection of human rights at the national level, emphasizing the universality, indivisibility and interdependence of all human rights, and emphasizing and recognizing the value of such approaches to promoting universal respect for and observance of human rights and fundamental freedoms,

*Recalling* the principles relating to the status of national institutions for the promotion and protection of human rights, as contained in the annex to General Assembly resolution 48/134 of 20 December 1993, and recognizing the need for their continued dissemination,

*Welcoming* the growing interest shown worldwide in the creation and strengthening of independent and pluralistic national institutions,

*Recognizing* that the United Nations plays an important role in assisting the development of national institutions,

*Noting with satisfaction* the constructive participation of representatives of a number of national institutions for the promotion and protection of human rights in international seminars and workshops,

1. *Takes note with satisfaction* of the updated report of the Secretary-General;

2. *Reaffirms* the importance of the development of effective, independent and pluralistic national institutions for the promotion and protection of human rights in keeping with the Vienna Declaration and Programme of Action and, *inter alia*, the principles relating to the status of national institutions for the promotion and protection of human rights contained in the annex to General Assembly resolution 48/134, and recognizes that it is the right of each State to choose the framework that is best suited to its particular needs at the national level;

3. *Encourages* Member States to establish or, where they already exist, to strengthen national institutions for the promotion and protection of human rights, as outlined in the Vienna Declaration and Programme of Action, and, where appropriate, to incorporate those elements in national development plans or in their preparation of national action plans;

4. *Encourages* national institutions for the promotion and protection of human rights established by Member States to prevent and combat all violations of human rights as enumerated in the Vienna Declaration and Programme of Action and relevant international instruments;

5. *Affirms* the role of national institutions, where they exist, as appropriate agencies for the dissemination of human rights materials and public information activities, including those of the United Nations;

6. *Requests* the Secretary-General to give high priority to requests from Member States for assistance in the establishment and strengthening of national institutions for the promotion and protection of human rights as part of the programme of advisory services and technical assistance in the field of human rights, and invites Governments to contribute to the United Nations Voluntary Fund for Advisory Services and Technical Assistance in the Field of Human Rights for these purposes;

7. *Notes* the role of the coordinating committee created by national institutions at the second International Workshop on National Institutions for the Promotion and Protection of Human Rights, held at Tunis from 13 to 17 December 1993, in close cooperation with the Centre for Human Rights of the Secretariat, to assist Governments and institutions, when requested, to follow up on relevant resolutions and recommendations concerning the strengthening of national institutions;

8. *Also notes* the importance of finding an appropriate form of participation by national institutions in relevant United Nations meetings dealing with human rights;

9. *Recognizes* the important and constructive role that non-governmental organizations may play, in cooperation with national institutions, for the better promotion and protection of human rights;

10. *Encourages* all Member States to take appropriate steps to promote the exchange of information and experience concerning the establishment and effective operation of such national institutions;

11. *Requests* the Secretary-General to report to the General Assembly at its fifty-second session on the implementation of the present resolution.

General Assembly resolution 50/176

22 December 1995    Meeting 99    Adopted without vote

Approved by Third Committee (A/50/635/Add.2) without vote, 11 December (meeting 53); 28-nation draft (A/C.3/50/L.37), orally revised; agenda item 112 *(b)*.

*Meeting numbers.* GA 50th session: 3rd Committee 35, 38-53; plenary 99.

## Regional arrangements

The Commission on Human Rights had before it in 1995 a report of the Secretary-General on regional arrangements for the promotion and protection of human rights,[49] in which he drew the Commission's attention to a report he had submitted to the General Assembly in 1994.[50]

**Commission action.** On 3 March, the Commission asked[51] the Secretary-General to continue to strengthen exchanges between the UN and regional intergovernmental organizations dealing with human rights. He was to submit in 1997 a report on the state of regional arrangements for the promotion and protection of human rights, to formulate concrete proposals and recommendations on ways to strengthen the cooperation between the UN and regional arrangements in the field of human rights and to include the results of action taken in pursuance of the Commission's resolution.

### Asia and the Pacific

**Report of the Secretary-General.** As requested by the Commission in 1994,[52] the Secretary-

General submitted a report[53] on regional arrangements for the promotion and protection of human rights in Asia and the Pacific. He discussed cooperation with the Economic and Social Commission for Asia and the Pacific (ESCAP) (Bangkok, Thailand), and contacts with Bhutan, Cambodia, Indonesia, Japan, Mongolia, Nepal and the Republic of Korea, which were pursued and strengthened by the High Commissioner and the Centre through the programme of advisory services and technical assistance. The Secretary-General described activities of NGOs and summarized the views of States in the region regarding the Commission's 1994 resolution.

**Commission action.** On 3 March, the Commission asked[54] the Secretary-General to facilitate the exchange of ideas and information regarding matters of common human rights interest in Asia and the Pacific and to give attention to countries in the region by allocating more resources from existing UN funds to enable them to benefit from all activities under the programme of advisory services and technical assistance. It called on the Centre for Human Rights to facilitate better access to and fuller utilization of the programmes by all countries in the region. The Secretary-General was asked to report in 1996 on progress achieved in implementing the Commission's resolution.

The Commission's requests to the Secretary-General were approved by the Economic and Social Council by **decision 1995/267** of 25 July. The Council also endorsed the conclusions of the third workshop for the Asia and Pacific region on human rights issues,[52] contained in the Chairman's concluding remarks, that such workshops should be organized regularly and if possible annually.

## Cooperation with UN human rights bodies

As requested by the Commission in 1994,[55] the Secretary-General in February 1995 summarized information on specific cases, received and processed by UN human rights bodies, in which persons alleged that they had been intimidated or prevented from availing themselves of UN procedures established for the protection of human rights or had suffered reprisals for having done so or for having provided information on human rights violations.[56] The reported reprisals ranged from veiled threats to extrajudicial executions and the alleged victims were private individuals or members of NGOs that were or had been sources of information about human rights violations for UN human rights bodies.

On 8 March, the Commission urged[57] Governments to refrain from acts of intimidation or reprisal against: persons who sought to cooperate or had cooperated with representatives of UN human rights bodies, or who had provided testimony or information to them; individuals who availed themselves of UN procedures and those who had provided legal assistance to them for that purpose; those who submitted communications under procedures established by human rights instruments; and relatives of victims of human rights violations. It requested representatives of UN human rights bodies and treaty bodies monitoring the observance of human rights to help prevent the hampering of access to UN human rights procedures and to continue to take urgent steps to prevent the occurrence of intimidation or reprisal. It also requested them to include in their reports a reference to allegations of intimidation or reprisal, as well as an account of action taken. The Commission asked the Secretary-General to draw its resolution to the attention of UN human rights and treaty bodies and to report in 1996.

*REFERENCES*

[1]E/1995/23 (res. 1995/80). [2]YUN 1993, p. 908. [3]YUN 1994, p. 1050. [4]E/CN.4/1995/98. [5]A/50/36. [6]E/CN.4/1996/50. [7]E/CN.4/1996/50/Add.1. [8]E/CN.4/1996/90. [9]YUN 1955, p. 164, GA res. 926(X), 14 Dec. 1955. [10]YUN 1987, p. 790, ESC dec. 1987/147, 29 May 1987. [11]YUN 1994, p. 1054. [12]E/1995/23 (res. 1995/53). [13]E/CN.4/1995/85. [14]YUN 1994, p. 1095. [15]YUN 1992, p. 767. [16]E/CN.4/1995/87. [17]E/CN.4/1995/87/Add.1. [18]E/1995/23 (res. 1995/55). [19]YUN 1993, p. 874. [20]A/50/681 & Add.1 & Add.1/Corr.1. [21]E/CN.4/1995/88. [22]E/1995/23 (res. 1995/63). [23]E/CN.4/1995/157. [24]E/CN.4/1995/15. [25]E/1995/23 (res. 1995/51). [26]E/CN.4/1996/2 (res. 1995/7). [27]YUN 1994, p. 408, GA res. 48/267, 19 Sep. 1994. [28]Ibid., p. 407. [29]E/CN.4/1995/90/Add.1. [30]YUN 1994, p. 1059. [31]E/1995/23 (res. 1995/56). [32]Ibid. (res. 1995/52). [33]YUN 1994, p. 1053. [34]E/CN.4/1995/46 & Add.1. [35]YUN 1988, p. 539, GA res. 43/128, 8 Dec. 1988. [36]E/1995/23 (res. 1995/49). [37]YUN 1948-49, p. 535, GA res. 217 A (III), 10 Dec. 1948. [38]YUN 1966, pp. 419 & 423, GA res. 2200 A (XXI), annex, 16 Dec. 1966. [39]E/1995/23 (res. 1995/47). [40]YUN 1994, p. 1039, GA res. 49/184, 23 Dec. 1994. [41]A/50/698. [42]E/CN.4/1995/48. [43]YUN 1993, p. 900, GA res. 48/134, annex, 20 Dec. 1993. [44]A/50/452. [45]E/1995/23 (res. 1995/50). [46]E/CN.4/1996/8. [47]YUN 1991, p. 573. [48]YUN 1993, p. 898. [49]E/CN.4/1995/51. [50]YUN 1994, p. 1065. [51]E/1995/23 (res. 1995/46). [52]YUN 1994, p. 1067. [53]E/CN.4/1995/44. [54]E/1995/23 (res. 1995/48). [55]YUN 1994, p. 1028. [56]E/CN.4/1995/53. [57]E/1995/23 (res. 1995/75).

Chapter II

# Protection of human rights

In 1995, the United Nations continued to devote significant efforts to protecting the citizens of the world from basic human rights abuses and to seek redress and protection for victims. Explosive regional conflicts, often ethnic-based, and continuing political and social upheavals in many countries spurred extensive UN involvement in human tragedies involving mass exoduses, terrorism, genocide and other human rights–related areas.

During the year, progress was made on a draft declaration on the right and responsibility of individuals, groups and organs of society to promote and protect universally recognized human rights and fundamental freedoms.

Racial and ethnic discrimination—a particularly odious and widespread human rights abuse—continued in many parts of the world, despite relentless efforts by the United Nations. One success in this area was the elimination of apartheid, the institutionalized system of racial separation in South Africa, due in large part to more than four decades of UN activity, including economic and other types of strictly enforced global sanctions.

Details of the ongoing work of the United Nations in 1995 to address human rights problems follow.

## Racial discrimination and racism

### Third Decade against racism

The General Assembly in 1993 proclaimed the Third Decade to Combat Racism and Racial Discrimination (1993-2003) and adopted the Decade's Programme of Action.[1] The Third Decade's goals and objectives were those adopted by the Assembly in 1973 for the first Decade.[2]

The Second Decade to Combat Racism and Racial Discrimination (1983-1993), proclaimed by the Assembly in 1983,[3] was carried out in accordance with the plan of activities for 1985-1989 put forward in 1984[4] and the plan, approved by the Assembly in 1987,[5] covering the remainder of the Decade, 1990-1993.

#### Implementation of Programme for the Decade

**Reports of the Secretary-General.** In January, the Secretary-General provided information on activities to combat racism and racial discrimination carried out by two Governments, one UN body and six non-governmental organizations (NGOs).[6]

In response to a 1993 General Assembly request,[1] the Secretary-General submitted in July to the Economic and Social Council a report[7] describing activities undertaken or planned by UN bodies and the specialized agencies to combat racism and racial discrimination within the framework of the Third Decade. In an addendum,[8] he provided similar information received from 10 Governments, three intergovernmental organizations and an NGO.

The Secretary-General stated that the Centre for Human Rights had not been in a position to initiate the implementation of the plan of activities for the first third of the Decade (1994-1997) due to a lack of resources. In that regard, he noted the need to establish a focal point to coordinate activities for the Decade. He concluded that contributions to the work of the Decade made by UN bodies and organizations, Governments, intergovernmental organizations and NGOs represented global and concerted efforts to address the issues and to provide long-lasting solutions. He recommended government implementation of the Plan of Action for the UN Decade for Human Rights Education (1995-2004) (see preceding chapter); measures to promote information and publications about human rights; strengthening national institutions for the promotion and protection of human rights; and establishing "community relations commissions" to identify the seeds of future tension and take preventive action. The Secretary-General proposed that the Special Rapporteur on contemporary forms of racism and racial discrimination, xenophobia and related intolerance take account of all types of information, including from the mass media, and that the Centre build up its database and access information from diverse sources to support his work.

As requested by the Assembly in 1994,[9] the Secretary-General supplemented[10] in October information submitted to the Economic and Social Council in July. He described efforts taken by the UN and NGOs to prevent and combat racism, racial discrimination, xenophobia and related intolerance.

On 21 December, the Assembly, by **decision 50/441**, took note of the Secretary-General's report.

**Commission action.** On 24 February, the Commission on Human Rights appealed[11] to all States that had not ratified or acceded to the relevant international instruments to combat racism and racial discrimination to do so. It urged Governments to combat new forms of racism and asked them, international organizations and NGOs to increase activities to combat racism and racial discrimination and to assist the victims of those phenomena. It asked the Secretary-General to coordinate the programmes of UN bodies with a view to achieving the objectives of the Third Decade; to accord special attention to the situation of migrant workers and their families and to include information on them in his reports; to continue to study the effects of racial discrimination on children of minorities and those of migrant workers in the areas of education, training and employment, and to submit recommendations on measures to combat those effects; and to publish and distribute as soon as possible the revised model legislation for the guidance of Governments in the enactment of further legislation against racial discrimination, submitted to the General Assembly in 1993.[12] The Commission asked the UN Educational, Scientific and Cultural Organization to expedite the preparation of teaching materials and aids to promote educational and training activities on human rights and against racism and racial discrimination.

Regretting that some activities scheduled for the Second Decade had not been implemented due to a lack of resources, the Commission called on the international community to provide financial resources for efficient action against racism and racial discrimination, appealed for generous contributions to the Trust Fund for the Programme for the Decade to Combat Racism and Racial Discrimination, and asked the Secretary-General to ensure that financial resources were provided to implement the activities of the Third Decade in the 1994-1995 and 1996-1997 bienniums. It asked Governments, UN bodies and specialized agencies, other intergovernmental organizations and NGOs to participate in activities of the Third Decade. The Commission recommended that activities to be carried out in the first third of the Decade (1994-1997), detailed in a 1994 report of the Secretary-General,[13] be implemented. The Secretary-General should establish a focal point within the Centre for Human Rights to review information concerning activities carried out under the Third Decade and to make recommendations on activities to be undertaken. He was to submit an annual report on all activities of Member States, UN bodies, specialized agencies and NGOs, analysing information received on activities to combat racism and racial discrimination, and on measures to improve the coordination of the activities of the Programme of Action or to supplement it.

**ECONOMIC AND SOCIAL COUNCIL ACTION**

On 28 July, the Economic and Social Council adopted **resolution 1995/59**.

**Implementation of the Programme of Action for the Third Decade to Combat Racism and Racial Discrimination**

*The Economic and Social Council,*

*Reaffirming* the obligation of States under the Charter of the United Nations to promote universal respect for, and observance of, human rights and fundamental freedoms for all without distinction as to race, sex, language or religion,

*Reaffirming* its conviction that racism and racial discrimination constitute a total negation of the purposes and principles of the Charter and the Universal Declaration of Human Rights,

*Reaffirming* its firm determination and its commitment to eradicate racism in all its forms and racial discrimination totally and unconditionally,

*Recalling* the Universal Declaration of Human Rights, the International Convention on the Elimination of All Forms of Racial Discrimination and the Convention against Discrimination in Education adopted by the United Nations Educational, Scientific and Cultural Organization on 14 December 1960,

*Bearing in mind* General Assembly resolutions 3057(XXVIII) of 2 November 1973 on the first Decade for Action to Combat Racism and Racial Discrimination, and 38/14 of 22 November 1983 on the Second Decade to Combat Racism and Racial Discrimination,

*Recalling* the recommendations of the two World Conferences to Combat Racism and Racial Discrimination, held at Geneva from 14 to 25 August 1978 and from 1 to 12 August 1983,

*Welcoming* the outcome of the World Conference on Human Rights, held at Vienna from 14 to 25 June 1993, and, in particular, the attention given in the Vienna Declaration and Programme of Action to the elimination of racism, racial discrimination, xenophobia and related intolerance,

*Noting with grave concern* that, despite the efforts of the international community, the principal objectives of the two Decades to Combat Racism and Racial Discrimination have not been attained and that millions of human beings continue to this day to be the victims of varied forms of racism and racial discrimination,

*Aware* of the importance and magnitude of the phenomenon of migrant workers, as well as the efforts made by the international community to improve the protection of the fundamental rights of migrant workers and members of their families,

*Recalling* the adoption by the General Assembly, at its forty-fifth session, of the International Convention on the Protection of the Rights of All Migrant Workers and Members of Their Families,

*Aware* that indigenous populations are at times victims of particular forms of racism and racial discrimination,

*Welcoming* General Assembly resolution 48/91 of 20 December 1993, whereby the Assembly decided to proclaim the Third Decade to Combat Racism and Racial Discrimination, beginning in 1993, and to adopt the Programme of Action for the Third Decade,

*Taking note* of Commission on Human Rights resolution 1995/11 of 24 February 1995,

*Stressing* the importance of the activities of the Special Rapporteur of the Commission on Human Rights on contemporary forms of racism, racial discrimination, xenophobia and related intolerance,

1.   *Declares* that all forms of racism or racial discrimination, whether institutionalized or resulting from official doctrines of racial superiority or exclusivity, such as ethnic cleansing, are among the most serious violations of human rights in the contemporary world and must be combated by all possible means;

2.   *Commends* all States that have ratified or acceded to the international instruments to combat racism and racial discrimination;

3.   *Appeals* to those States that have not yet done so to consider ratifying, acceding to and implementing the relevant international instruments, particularly the International Convention on the Elimination of All Forms of Racial Discrimination and the Convention against Discrimination in Education;

4.   *Urges* all Governments to take all requisite measures to combat new forms of racism, in particular by ongoing adjustment of the methods used to combat them;

5.   *Invites* all Governments and international and nongovernmental organizations to increase and intensify their activities to combat racism and racial discrimination and to provide relief and assistance to victims of these evils;

6.   *Invites* the Secretary-General to take action to coordinate all the programmes currently being implemented by United Nations bodies with a view to achieving the objectives of the Third Decade to Combat Racism and Racial Discrimination;

7.   *Requests* the Secretary-General to continue to accord special attention to the situation of migrant workers and members of their families and to include regularly in his reports full information on such workers;

8.   *Also requests* the Secretary-General to continue the study on the effects of racial discrimination on the children of minorities, particularly those of migrant workers, in the fields of education, training and employment and to submit, *inter alia*, specific recommendations for the implementation of measures to combat the effects of that discrimination;

9.   *Calls upon* all Member States to consider signing and ratifying or acceding to the International Convention on the Protection of the Rights of All Migrant Workers and Members of Their Families as a matter of priority, so that it can enter into force as soon as possible;

10.   *Urges* the Secretary-General, United Nations bodies and specialized agencies, all Governments, intergovernmental organizations and relevant nongovernmental organizations, in implementing the Programme of Action for the Third Decade, to pay particular attention to the situation of indigenous peoples;

11.   *Requests* the Secretary-General to publish and distribute, as soon as possible, the model legislation on racism and racial discrimination for the guidance of Governments in the enactment of further legislation against racial discrimination;

12.   *Invites* the United Nations Educational, Scientific and Cultural Organization to expedite the preparation of teaching materials and teaching aids to promote teaching, training and education activities on human rights and against racism and racial discrimination, with particular emphasis on activities at the primary and secondary levels of education;

13.   *Regrets* that some of the activities for the Second Decade to Combat Racism and Racial Discrimination have not been implemented for lack of adequate resources;

14.   *Calls upon* the international community to provide the Secretary-General with appropriate financial resources for efficient action against racism and racial discrimination;

15.   *Invites* all Governments, United Nations bodies, the specialized agencies and other intergovernmental organizations, as well as interested non-governmental organizations in consultative status with the Economic and Social Council, to participate fully in the Third Decade;

16.   *Considers* that voluntary contributions to the Trust Fund for the Programme for the Decade to Combat Racism and Racial Discrimination are indispensable for the implementation of the Programme;

17.   *Strongly appeals*, therefore, to all Governments, organizations and individuals in a position to do so to contribute generously to the Trust Fund, and to this end requests the Secretary-General to continue to undertake appropriate contacts and initiatives to encourage contributions;

18.   *Requests* the Secretary-General to ensure that the necessary financial resources are provided for the implementation of the activities of the Third Decade during the bienniums 1994-1995 and 1996-1997;

19.   *Takes note* of the report of the Secretary-General on the Programme of Action for the Third Decade to Combat Racism and Racial Discrimination;

20.   *Recommends* that the activities mentioned in the plan of activities to be carried out during the first third of the Third Decade (1994-1997), as set out in the previous report of the Secretary-General, should be implemented;

21.   *Invites* the Secretary-General to do his utmost to establish a focal point within the Centre for Human Rights of the Secretariat, which will be responsible for reviewing information concerning specific recommendations on activities to be undertaken;

22.   *Decides* to maintain the item entitled "Third Decade to Combat Racism and Racial Discrimination" in its agenda and to give it the highest priority at its substantive session of 1996.

Economic and Social Council resolution 1995/59

28 July 1995        Meeting 57        Adopted without vote

20-nation draft (E/1995/L.56); agenda item 5 *(b)*.
*Meeting numbers.* ESC 51, 57.

**GENERAL ASSEMBLY ACTION**

On 21 December, the General Assembly adopted **resolution 50/136.**

### Third Decade to Combat Racism and Racial Discrimination

*The General Assembly,*

*Reaffirming its objectives* set forth in the Charter of the United Nations to achieve international cooperation in solving problems of an economic, social, cultural or humanitarian character and in promoting and encouraging respect for human rights and fundamental freedoms for all without distinction as to race, sex, language or religion,

*Reaffirming also its firm determination and its commitment* to eradicate totally and unconditionally racism, in all its forms, and racial discrimination,

*Recalling* the Universal Declaration of Human Rights, the International Convention on the Elimination of All Forms of Racial Discrimination and the Convention against Discrimination in Education adopted by the United Nations Educational, Scientific and Cultural Organization on 14 December 1960,

*Recalling also* the outcome of the two World Conferences to Combat Racism and Racial Discrimination, held at Geneva in 1978 and 1983,

*Recalling with satisfaction* the outcome of the World Conference on Human Rights, held at Vienna from 14 to 25 June 1993, and, in particular, the attention given in the Vienna Declaration and Programme of Action to the elimination of racism, racial discrimination, xenophobia and other forms of intolerance,

*Stressing* the importance of the activities of the Special Rapporteur of the Commission on Human Rights on contemporary forms of racism, racial discrimination, xenophobia and related intolerance,

*Recalling* its resolution 49/146 of 23 December 1994, the annex to which contains the revised Programme of Action for the Third Decade to Combat Racism and Racial Discrimination (1993-2003),

*Noting with grave concern* that, despite the efforts of the international community, the principal objectives of the two Decades for Action to Combat Racism and Racial Discrimination have not been attained and that millions of human beings continue to this day to be the victims of varied forms of racism and racial discrimination,

*Deeply concerned* about the current trend of the evolution of racism into discriminatory practices based on culture, nationality, religion or language,

*Recalling in particular* its resolution 48/91 of 20 December 1993, by which it proclaimed the Third Decade to Combat Racism and Racial Discrimination,

*Having considered* the reports submitted by the Secretary-General within the framework of the implementation of the Programme of Action for the Third Decade,

*Firmly convinced* of the need to take more effective and sustained measures at the national and international levels for the elimination of all forms of racism and racial discrimination,

*Recognizing* the importance of strengthening national legislation and institutions for the promotion of racial harmony,

*Deeply concerned* about the fact that the phenomenon of racism and racial discrimination against migrant workers continues to increase despite efforts undertaken by the international community to improve the protection of the human rights of migrant workers and members of their families,

*Recalling* the adoption at its forty-fifth session of the International Convention on the Protection of the Rights of All Migrant Workers and Members of Their Families,

*Acknowledging* that indigenous people are at times victims of particular forms of racism and racial discrimination,

1. *Declares once again* that all forms of racism and racial discrimination, whether in their institutionalized form or resulting from official doctrines of racial superiority or exclusivity, such as ethnic cleansing, are among the most serious violations of human rights in the contemporary world and must be combated by all available means;

2. *Recalls with satisfaction* the proclamation of the Third Decade to Combat Racism and Racial Discrimination,

which began in 1993, and requests the Secretary-General to make a further review of the Programme of Action with a view to making it more effective and action-oriented;

3. *Calls upon* Governments to cooperate more closely with the Special Rapporteur of the Commission on Human Rights on contemporary forms of racism, racial discrimination, xenophobia and related intolerance to enable him to fulfil his mandate;

4. *Urges* all Governments to take all necessary measures to combat new forms of racism, in particular by adapting constantly the means provided to combat them, especially in the legislative, administrative, educational and information fields;

5. *Decides* that the international community in general and the United Nations in particular should give the highest priority to programmes for combating racism and racial discrimination and should intensify their efforts, during the Third Decade, to provide assistance and relief to the victims of racism and all forms of racial discrimination;

6. *Requests* the Secretary-General to continue to accord special attention to the situation of migrant workers and members of their families and to include regularly in his reports all information on such workers;

7. *Calls upon* all Member States to consider signing and ratifying or acceding to the International Convention on the Protection of the Rights of All Migrant Workers and Members of Their Families as a matter of priority;

8. *Commends* all States which have ratified or acceded to the international instruments to combat racism and racial discrimination;

9. *Also requests* the Secretary-General to continue the study on the effects of racial discrimination on the children of minorities, in particular those of migrant workers, in the fields of education, training and employment, and to submit, *inter alia*, specific recommendations for the implementation of measures to combat the effects of that discrimination;

10. *Urges* the Secretary-General, United Nations bodies, the specialized agencies, all Governments, intergovernmental organizations and relevant non-governmental organizations, in implementing the Programme of Action for the Third Decade, to pay particular attention to the situation of indigenous people;

11. *Requests* States to consider the relevant decisions of the Economic and Social Council on the integrated follow-up to previous world conferences and the need to make optimum use of all available mechanisms in the struggle against racism;

12. *Further requests* the Secretary-General to consult Member States and intergovernmental, as well as non-governmental, organizations on the possibility of holding a world conference to combat racism, racial discrimination, xenophobia and other related contemporary forms of intolerance;

13. *Renews its invitation* to the United Nations Educational, Scientific and Cultural Organization to expedite the preparation of teaching materials and teaching aids to promote teaching, training and educational activities on human rights and against racism and racial discrimination, with particular emphasis on activities at the primary and secondary levels of education;

14. *Considers* that all the parts of the Programme of Action for the Third Decade should be given equal attention in order to attain the objectives of the Decade;

15. *Regrets* that some of the activities scheduled for the Second Decade to Combat Racism and Racial Discrimination have not been implemented for lack of adequate resources;

16. *Considers* that voluntary contributions to the Trust Fund for the Programme for the Decade for Action to Combat Racism and Racial Discrimination are indispensable for the implementation of the Programme;

17. *Requests* the Secretary-General to ensure that the necessary financial resources are provided for the implementation of the activities of the Third Decade during the biennium 1996-1997;

18. *Also requests* the Secretary-General to accord the highest priority to the activities of the Programme of Action for the Third Decade;

19. *Further requests* the Secretary-General to submit each year to the Economic and Social Council a detailed report on all activities of United Nations bodies and the specialized agencies, containing an analysis of information received on such activities to combat racism and racial discrimination;

20. *Invites* the Secretary-General to submit proposals to the General Assembly with a view to supplementing, if necessary, the Programme of Action for the Third Decade;

21. *Invites* all Governments, United Nations bodies, the specialized agencies and other intergovernmental organizations, as well as interested non-governmental organizations in consultative status with the Economic and Social Council, to participate fully in the Third Decade;

22. *Notes* that unless a supplementary financial effort is made very few of the activities planned for the period 1994-1997 will be carried out;

23. *Strongly appeals* to all Governments, intergovernmental and non-governmental organizations and individuals in a position to do so to contribute generously to the Trust Fund for the Programme for the Decade for Action to Combat Racism and Racial Discrimination, and to this end requests the Secretary-General to continue to undertake appropriate contacts and initiatives to encourage contributions;

24. *Decides* to keep the item entitled "Elimination of racism and racial discrimination" on its agenda and to consider it as a matter of the highest priority at its fifty-first session.

General Assembly resolution 50/136

21 December 1995     Meeting 97     Adopted without vote

Approved by Third Committee (A/50/626) without vote, 2 November (meeting 18); draft by Philippines, for Group of 77 and China (A/C.3/50/L.6), orally revised; agenda item 103.
*Meeting numbers.* GA 50th session: 3rd Committee 3-8, 15, 18; plenary 97.

(For information on the International Convention on the Elimination of All Forms of Racial Discrimination, see preceding chapter.)

## Contemporary forms of racism

**Report of the Special Rapporteur (January).** As requested by the Commission on Human Rights in 1994,[14] Special Rapporteur Maurice Glélé-Ahanhanzo (Benin) submitted in January a progress report describing his activities in 1994 and those planned for 1995, with detailed information on incidents of contemporary manifestations of racism and racial discrimination brought to his attention.[15] The Special Rapporteur also presented information on measures taken by seven Governments and one intergovernmental body to prevent and punish racist and xenophobic acts and practices.

In an addendum,[16] the Special Rapporteur discussed his 1994 visit to the United States (9-22 October) to verify allegations of racism and racial discrimination against various ethnic groups and in the administration of criminal justice.

**Commission action.** On 24 February, the Human Rights Commission appealed[17] to Governments to promote measures to eradicate all forms of racism, racial discrimination, xenophobia and related intolerance by making efforts to harmonize their domestic legislation, and to Governments, UN organizations, intergovernmental organizations and NGOs to supply information to the Special Rapporteur. It asked him to continue to examine incidents of contemporary forms of racism, racial discrimination, any form of discrimination against blacks, Arabs and Muslims, xenophobia, negrophobia, anti-Semitism and related intolerance, as well as governmental measures to overcome them, and to report in 1996. The Commission also asked him to exchange views with relevant mechanisms and UN treaty bodies and to use sources of information, including country visits and an evaluation of mass media, and to elicit the responses of Governments regarding allegations of violations. It encouraged him to present further recommendations concerning human rights education and recommendations on measures to prevent and eradicate problems within the purview of his mandate. The Commission asked the Secretary-General to seek the views of Governments on the possibility of using existing voluntary funds and of establishing a voluntary fund for the rehabilitation and social reintegration of victims of racism, racial discrimination, xenophobia and related intolerance, and to report to the General Assembly in 1995. Regretting the difficulties encountered by the Special Rapporteur in preparing his 1995 report due to the lack of necessary resources, it asked the Secretary-General to assist him to provide an interim report to the Assembly in 1995 and a comprehensive report to the Commission in 1996; those requests were approved by the Economic and Social Council by **decision 1995/255** of 25 July.

The Commission took note of a 1994 recommendation[14] of its Subcommission on Prevention of Discrimination and Protection of Minorities relating to the possible convening in 1997 of a world conference against racism, racial and ethnic discrimination, xenophobia and other related contemporary forms of intolerance.

In March, Cuba introduced in the Commission a draft text entitled "Violation of human rights in the United States of America as a result of racism and racial discrimination persisting in United States society".[18] At the request of the United States, a roll-call vote was taken by which the draft was rejected (32 to 3, with 18 abstentions).

**Report of the Special Rapporteur (September).** In September, the Secretary-General transmitted to the General Assembly a progress report of the Special Rapporteur,[19] describing his activities in 1995; summarizing problems faced in efforts to combat racism, together with recent incidents of racism and racial discrimination brought to his attention; and providing information on measures taken by Governments to remedy situations. The Special Rapporteur concluded that racism and racial discrimination were on the rise, fed by economic, religious and social causes, and xenophobia was becoming commonplace. He recommended compulsory human rights teaching and mobilizing the mass media to ensure the dissemination of human rights information. He stated that the Assembly should establish a mechanism for monitoring the use of the media to incite hatred and that States should be more liberal in granting visas to nationals of the South and call on their populations to be more receptive to foreigners and cultural interchange.

On 21 December, the Assembly, by **decision 50/441**, took note of the Special Rapporteur's report.

**Other action.** In August, the Committee on the Elimination of Racial Discrimination (CERD) held a joint meeting with the Subcommission and the Special Rapporteur on contemporary forms of racism, racial discrimination and xenophobia,[20] as decided in 1994.[14] At the conclusion of the meeting, the CERD and Subcommission Chairmen issued an agreed declaration for joint and cooperative action whereby: the bureaux of the two bodies would meet annually and the two bodies might hold joint meetings in the future; a speedy and efficient flow of information would start immediately; a joint study would begin concerning article 7 (dealing with the adoption of measures to combat prejudices leading to racial discrimination and the promotion of understanding, tolerance and friendship among nations and racial or ethnic groups) of the 1965 International Convention on the Elimination of All Forms of Racial Discrimination;[21] and the two bodies would issue a joint statement concerning massive and gross occurrences of racial and related discrimination.

In their declaration,[10] the Chairmen, among other things, declared their determination to mobilize their efforts to eliminate all forms of racism, racial discrimination, xenophobia and related intolerance, and reiterated their condemnation of human rights violations, in particular genocide and ethnic cleansing. They called for firm and urgent measures by the United Nations and the international community to end the violations, to continue to fight policies and practices of racial discrimination, to help save human lives, to stop ethnic cleansing, to help the voluntary and safe return of refugees to their homes, and to find just political solutions to existing racial, ethnic and related conflicts.

On 21 December, the General Assembly adopted **resolution 50/135**.

**Measures to combat contemporary forms of racism, racial discrimination, xenophobia and related intolerance**

*The General Assembly,*

*Recalling* its resolution 49/147 of 23 December 1994 and taking note of Commission on Human Rights resolution 1995/12 of 24 February 1995,

*Bearing in mind* the outcome of the World Conference on Human Rights, held at Vienna from 14 to 25 June 1993, and, in particular, the attention given in the Vienna Declaration and Programme of Action to the elimination of racism, racial discrimination, xenophobia and other forms of intolerance,

*Aware* that racism, being one of the exclusionist phenomena plaguing many societies, requires resolute action and cooperation for its eradication,

*Having examined* the report of the Special Rapporteur of the Commission on Human Rights on contemporary forms of racism, racial discrimination, xenophobia and related intolerance, including its conclusions and recommendations,

*Deeply concerned* that, despite continued efforts, racism, racial discrimination, xenophobia and related intolerance, as well as acts of racial violence, persist and even grow in magnitude, incessantly adopting new forms, including tendencies to establish policies based on racial, religious, ethnic, cultural and national superiority or exclusivity,

*Conscious* of the fundamental difference between, on the one hand, racism and racial discrimination as governmental policy or resulting from official doctrines of racial superiority or exclusivity and, on the other hand, other manifestations of racism, racial discrimination, xenophobia and related intolerance taking place in segments of many societies and perpetrated by individuals or groups, some of which are directed against migrant workers and members of their families,

*Underlining* the importance of creating conditions which foster greater harmony and tolerance within societies,

1. *Welcomes* the report of the Special Rapporteur of the Commission on Human Rights on contemporary forms of racism, racial discrimination, xenophobia and related intolerance;

2. *Expresses its full support* for the work of the Special Rapporteur, and requests him to continue his exchange of views with relevant mechanisms, related United Nations organs and specialized agencies in order to further their effectiveness and mutual cooperation;

3. *Expresses its profound concern at and unequivocal condemnation of* all forms of racism and all racist violence, including related acts of random and indiscriminate violence;

4. *Expresses its deep concern at and condemnation of* manifestations of racism, racial discrimination, xenophobia and related intolerance against migrant workers and members of their families and other vulnerable groups in many societies;

5. *Encourages* all States, in accordance with the conclusions and recommendations of the Special Rapporteur in his most recent report, to include in their educational curricula and social programmes, at all levels, as appropriate, knowledge of and tolerance and respect for foreign cultures, peoples and countries;

6. *Supports* the efforts of Governments in taking measures aimed at the eradication of all forms of racism, racial discrimination, xenophobia and related intolerance;

7. *Recognizes* that Governments should implement and enforce legislation to prevent acts of racism and racial discrimination;

8. *Calls upon* all Governments and intergovernmental organizations, with the assistance of non-governmental organizations, as appropriate, to continue to cooperate with and to supply relevant information to the Special Rapporteur;

9. *Urges* all Governments to cooperate fully with the Special Rapporteur, with a view to enabling him to fulfil his mandate;

10. *Requests once again* the Secretary-General promptly to provide the Special Rapporteur with all the necessary human and financial assistance in carrying out his mandate and enabling him to submit, in a timely manner, a preliminary report to the General Assembly at its fifty-first session on this question.

General Assembly resolution 50/135

21 December 1995     Meeting 97     Adopted without vote

Approved by Third Committee (A/50/626) without vote, 2 November (meeting 18); draft by Mexico, Philippines (for Group of 77 and China) and Turkey (A/C.3/50/L.5/Rev.1), orally revised; agenda item 103.
*Meeting numbers.* GA 50th session: 3rd Committee 3-8, 15, 18; plenary 97.

### World conference

On 24 February,[22] the Commission, taking note of a 1994 Subcommission resolution,[14] decided to recommend, through the Economic and Social Council, that the General Assembly consider at its fiftieth (1995) session the possibility of convening a world conference against racism, racial and ethnic discrimination, xenophobia and other related contemporary forms of intolerance.

By **decision 1995/294** of 25 July, the Council approved the Commission's recommendation. No action was taken on the matter by the Assembly in 1995.

*REFERENCES*

[1]YUN 1993, p. 853, GA res. 48/91, 20 Dec. 1993. [2]YUN 1973, p. 524, GA res. 3057(XXVIII), annex, 2 Nov. 1973. [3]YUN 1983, p. 806, GA res. 38/14, 22 Nov. 1983. [4]YUN 1984, p. 785. [5]YUN 1987, p. 732, GA res. 42/47, annex, 30 Nov. 1987. [6]E/CN.4/1995/77. [7]E/1995/111. [8]E/1995/111/Add.1. [9]YUN 1994, p. 988, GA res. 49/146, 23 Dec. 1994. [10]A/50/493. [11]E/1995/23 (res. 1995/11). [12]YUN 1993, p. 851. [13]YUN 1994, p. 987. [14]Ibid., p. 992. [15]E/CN.4/1995/78. [16]E/CN.4/1995/78/Add.1. [17]E/1995/23 (res. 1995/12). [18]E/CN.4/1995/L.26/Rev.2. [19]A/50/476. [20]A/50/18. [21]YUN 1965, p. 440, GA res. 2106 A (XX), annex, 21 Dec. 1965. [22]E/1995/23 (dec. 1995/104).

# Other aspects of intolerance

## Discrimination against minorities

### Declaration

**Commission action.** On 3 March, the Human Rights Commission authorized[1] the Subcommission to establish, initially for three years, an intersessional working group, consisting of five of its members, to meet each year for five working days to promote the rights of persons belonging to national or ethnic, religious and linguistic minorities, as set out in the 1992 Declaration on the Rights of Persons Belonging to National or Ethnic, Religious and Linguistic Minorities,[2] particularly to: review the promotion and practical realization of the Declaration; examine possible solutions to problems involving minorities; and recommend further measures to promote and protect the rights of minorities. It asked the Subcommission to make available the working group's annual report and called on States, intergovernmental organizations, UN bodies, specialized agencies and NGOs to participate in the group's work. The Commission asked the Secretary-General to provide the group, within existing UN resources, with the services and facilities necessary to fulfil its mandate and to submit a report in 1996.

The Commission urged States and the international community to promote and protect the rights of persons belonging to national or ethnic, religious and linguistic minorities, as set out in the Declaration, and to give effect to the Declaration. It appealed to them to consider making bilateral and multilateral arrangements or agreements to protect the rights of such minorities. It called on the High Commissioner for Human Rights to promote the implementation of the Declaration and urged treaty bodies and special representatives, special rapporteurs and working groups of the Commission to give due regard to it. The Commission called on the Secretary-General to make available, as part of the programme of advisory services and technical assistance of the Centre for Human Rights, qualified expertise on minority issues, including prevention and resolution of disputes to assist situations involving minorities. The Commission called on the Subcommission to examine ways to promote and protect the rights of minorities, as set out in the 1992 Declaration.

On 25 July, the Economic and Social Council adopted **resolution 1995/31**.

### Rights of persons belonging to national or ethnic, religious and linguistic minorities

*The Economic and Social Council,*

*Recalling* Commission on Human Rights resolution 1995/24 of 3 March 1995,

1. *Decides* to authorize the Subcommission on Prevention of Discrimination and Protection of Minorities to establish an inter-sessional working group of the Subcommission, consisting of five of its members, which shall meet each year for five working days, initially for a three-year period, in order to promote the rights of persons belonging to national or ethnic, religious and linguistic minorities, as set out in the Declaration on the Rights of Persons Belonging to National or Ethnic, Religious and Linguistic Minorities, and in particular:

*(a)* To review the promotion and practical realization of the Declaration;

*(b)* To examine possible solutions to problems involving minorities, including the promotion of mutual understanding between and among minorities and Governments;

*(c)* To recommend further measures, as appropriate, for the promotion and protection of the rights of persons belonging to national or ethnic, religious and linguistic minorities;

2. *Requests* the Secretary-General to provide the Working Group, within existing resources, with all the necessary services and facilities to fulfil its mandate.

Economic and Social Council resolution 1995/31

25 July 1995      Meeting 52      Adopted without vote

Draft by Commission on Human Rights (E/1995/23), orally amended by Japan; agenda item 5 *(d)*.
*Meeting numbers.* ESC 51-53.

**Working Group activities.** The Working Group on Minorities at its first session (Geneva, 28 August–1 September 1995)[3] reviewed the promotion and practical realization of the Declaration and decided that at its next session it would give priority attention to the constitutional and main legal provisions protecting the existence and identity of minorities; the rights to use their own language, profess and practise their religion and enjoy their own culture; the effective participation of minorities; educational issues; national recourse and conciliation machineries; regional mechanisms for the protection of minorities; the contribution of advisory services and technical assistance; and cooperation and coordination with the international community.

As to possible solutions to problems involving minorities, the Group considered recommendations contained in a 1993 report of its Chairman/Rapporteur concerning measures to facilitate the peaceful and constructive solution of problems involving minorities.[4] It decided to discuss at its next session the causes and nature of the problems affecting minorities, the facilitation of dialogue

between minorities and Governments, technical cooperation, prevention and early-warning systems, and the role of the media. Recommendations for further measures to protect minorities included: the provision of advisory services and technical assistance following the identification of minority problems; the establishment of an early-warning and rapid-action system; and the coordination between UN bodies and organs, Governments, the specialized agencies, international and intergovernmental organizations and NGOs.

**Reports of the Secretary-General.** As requested by the General Assembly in 1994,[5] the Secretary-General in October described measures for the effective promotion of the Declaration undertaken by 15 Governments, four UN bodies, a UN specialized agency, two UN treaty bodies, four special rapporteurs of the Commission on Human Rights, two intergovernmental bodies and two NGOs.[6]

In December, the Secretary-General presented information on issues relating to the promotion and implementation of the Declaration received from one Government and one NGO,[7] as requested by the Commission in 1994.[8]

On 22 December, the General Assembly adopted **resolution 50/180**.

### Effective promotion of the Declaration on the Rights of Persons Belonging to National or Ethnic, Religious and Linguistic Minorities

*The General Assembly,*

*Recalling* its resolution 47/135 of 18 December 1992, by which it adopted the Declaration on the Rights of Persons Belonging to National or Ethnic, Religious and Linguistic Minorities, as well as its resolution 49/192 of 23 December 1994,

*Conscious* of the need effectively to promote and protect the rights of persons belonging to minorities, as set out in the Declaration,

*Taking note* of Commission on Human Rights resolution 1995/24 of 3 March 1995 on the rights of persons belonging to national or ethnic, religious and linguistic minorities, in which the Commission, *inter alia*, decided to authorize the Subcommission on Prevention of Discrimination and Protection of Minorities to establish, initially for a three-year period, an inter-sessional working group consisting of five of its members, to meet each year for five working days in order to promote the rights of persons belonging to national or ethnic, religious and linguistic minorities,

*Taking note also* of Economic and Social Council resolution 1995/31 of 25 July 1995, in which the Council authorized the establishment of the working group,

*Noting* that the working group held its first session from 28 August to 1 September 1995, and that its report will be made available to the Commission on Human Rights,

*Aware* of the provisions of article 27 of the International Covenant on Civil and Political Rights concerning the rights of persons belonging to ethnic, religious or linguistic minorities,

*Acknowledging* that the United Nations has an increasingly important role to play regarding the protection of minorities by, *inter alia,* taking due account of and giving effect to the Declaration,

*Concerned* by the growing frequency and severity of disputes and conflicts concerning minorities in many countries, and their often tragic consequences,

*Affirming* that effective measures and the creation of favourable conditions for the promotion and protection of the rights of persons belonging to national or ethnic, religious and linguistic minorities, ensuring effective non-discrimination and equality for all, contribute to the prevention and peaceful solution of human rights problems and situations involving minorities,

*Considering* that the promotion and protection of the rights of persons belonging to national or ethnic, religious and linguistic minorities contribute to political and social stability and peace and enrich the cultural heritage of society as a whole of the States in which such persons live,

*Reaffirming* the obligation of States to ensure that persons belonging to minorities may exercise fully and effectively all human rights and fundamental freedoms without any discrimination and in full equality before the law in accordance with the Declaration,

*Noting* the positive initiatives of many countries as well as regional organizations to protect minorities and promote mutual understanding,

*Having considered* the report of the Secretary-General,

1. *Takes note with appreciation* of the report of the Secretary-General;

2. *Urges* States and the international community to promote and protect the rights of persons belonging to national or ethnic, religious and linguistic minorities, as set out in the Declaration on the Rights of Persons Belonging to National or Ethnic, Religious and Linguistic Minorities, including through the facilitation of their full participation in all aspects of the political, economic, social, religious and cultural life of society and in the economic progress and development in their country;

3. *Urges* States to take, as appropriate, all the necessary constitutional, legislative, administrative and other measures to promote and give effect to the principles contained in the Declaration;

4. *Appeals* to States to make bilateral and multilateral efforts, as appropriate, in order to protect the rights of persons belonging to national or ethnic, religious and linguistic minorities in their countries, in accordance with the Declaration;

5. *Recognizes* that respect for human rights and the promotion of understanding and tolerance by Governments as well as between and among minorities is central to the protection and promotion of the rights of persons belonging to minorities;

6. *Calls upon* the Secretary-General to make available, at the request of Governments concerned, qualified expertise on minority issues, including the prevention and resolution of disputes, to assist in existing or potential situations involving minorities;

7. *Requests* the Secretary-General, in the implementation of the present resolution, to provide human and financial resources for such advisory services and technical assistance by the Centre for Human Rights of the Secretariat, within existing resources;

8. *Calls upon* the United Nations High Commissioner for Human Rights to promote, within his mandate, the implementation of the Declaration and to continue to engage in a dialogue with Governments concerned for that purpose;

9. *Urges* all treaty bodies and special representatives, special rapporteurs and working groups of the Commission on Human Rights and the Subcommission on Prevention of Discrimination and Protection of Minorities to give due regard, within their respective mandates, to the promotion and protection of the rights of persons belonging to minorities;

10. *Invites* States, interested intergovernmental and non-governmental organizations, special representatives, special rapporteurs and working groups of the Commission on Human Rights to continue to submit, as appropriate, contributions as to how they promote and give effect to the Declaration;

11. *Invites* the Secretary-General to continue the dissemination of information on the Declaration and the promotion of understanding thereof, including through activities within the framework of the United Nations Decade for Human Rights Education;

12. *Calls upon* States and the Secretary-General to give due regard to the Declaration in their respective training programmes for officials;

13. *Encourages* intergovernmental as well as non-governmental organizations to continue to contribute to the promotion and protection of the rights of persons belonging to national or ethnic, religious and linguistic minorities;

14. *Requests* the Secretary-General to report to the General Assembly at its fifty-first session on the implementation of the present resolution under the item entitled "Human rights questions".

General Assembly resolution 50/180

22 December 1995     Meeting 99     Adopted without vote

Approved by Third Committee (A/50/635/Add.2) without vote, 11 December (meeting 53); 60-nation draft (A/C.3/50/L.48), orally revised; agenda item 112 *(b).*

*Meeting numbers.* GA 50th session: 3rd Committee 35, 38-53; plenary 99.

## Preventing minority discrimination

In a June report with later addenda,[9] the Secretary-General provided comments on recommendations in the final report of Special Rapporteur Asbjorn Eide (Norway), submitted in 1993,[4] concerning possible ways of facilitating the peaceful and constructive solution of problems involving minorities. Seven Governments, one UN body, one intergovernmental body and two NGOs had reported.

On 18 August,[10] the Subcommission, taking into account a working paper prepared by Special Rapporteur Eide in 1994,[11] asked him to prepare, for submission in 1996, a second working paper containing further suggestions for a comprehensive programme for the prevention of discrimination and protection of minorities. It asked him to take into account the discussion and proposals of the joint meeting of the Subcommission and CERD (see above, under "Contemporary forms of racism").

## Enclaved groups

As requested by the Subcommission in 1994,[12] Special Rapporteur Eide, in a July working paper[13] on the concept and issues relating to enclaved groups, stated that the notion of enclaved groups had not been formally defined under international law. Following a comparison of enclaved groups to inhabitants of international enclaves and to autonomies, and a discussion of situations where enclaved groups existed, he defined an enclaved group as persons belonging to a national or ethnic, religious or linguistic group who had traditionally lived in the area; who differed from the general population surrounding them; who were subject to special hardships due to restrictions imposed on them which were more severe than restrictions affecting members of the majority group in the area concerned; or who experienced fear of attack and maltreatment from members of the majority group, without being able to rely on effective and impartial protection by the local police and other agents of law. He also discussed various indicators of the existence of an enclaved group.

## Religious intolerance

**Report of the Secretary-General.** As requested by the Commission on Human Rights in 1994,[14] the Secretary-General reported[15] on activities carried out by the Centre for Human Rights and NGOs to implement the 1981 Declaration on the Elimination of All Forms of Intolerance and of Discrimination Based on Religion or Belief.[16]

**Report of the Special Rapporteur.** The Commission on Human Rights considered a report[17] of Abdelfattah Amor (Tunisia), the Special Rapporteur on religious intolerance. Allegations of intolerance or discrimination based on belief that he had transmitted in 1994 to 49 Governments were reproduced in his report, as were responses received from Governments. The majority of allegations concerned violations of the right to have the religion or belief of one's choice, the right to change one's religion or belief, the right to manifest and practise one's religion in public and in private, and the right not to be subjected to discrimination on those grounds by any State, institution or group of persons. The Special Rapporteur also described his visit to China (21-30 November 1994) where he noted developments in the human rights situation.

The Special Rapporteur deplored the serious infringement of the rights of persons belonging to religious minorities in countries with an official or clearly predominant majority religion. In certain cases, he had difficulty in distinguishing between religious conflicts and ethnic conflicts and between religious intolerance and political persecution. He noted the continuing extremism and religious fanaticism in certain countries, and expressed concern over: the abuse of legislation against blasphemy and groundless accusations; many cases of harm caused to places of worship, special religious sites and religious property of all denominations; and the role played by the media in some countries in developing a climate of religious intolerance. He emphasized education as the essential means of opposing intolerance and discrimination based on religion or belief, and stressed the importance of establishing a continuing interfaith dialogue to combat all forms of religious extremism. He recommended the use of advisory services for specific purposes; seminars to publicize or ensure better understanding of existing principles, norms and remedies regarding freedom of religion and belief; training courses for teachers; workshops for representatives of specific religions and ideologies and of non-governmental human rights organizations; and workshops for members of the media.

The report contained a questionnaire addressed to States on issues relating to freedom of religion and belief in primary and secondary schools.

**Commission action.** In 1995, the Commission continued to consider measures to implement the Declaration, as requested by the General Assembly in 1994.[18] On 24 February, it urged[19] States to: provide adequate constitutional and legal guarantees of freedom of thought, conscience, religion and belief; ensure that no one, on account of their religion or belief, was deprived of the right to life or the right to liberty and security of person, or was subjected to torture or arbitrary arrest or detention; combat hatred, intolerance and acts of violence, including those motivated by religious extremism; and ensure that members of law enforcement bodies, civil servants, educators and other public officials respected different religions and beliefs. The Commission called on States to recognize, as provided in the Declaration, the right of all persons to worship or assemble for religious purposes, establish and maintain places to do so, and ensure that such places were fully respected and protected. The Commission extended the Special Rapporteur's mandate for three years and called on Governments to cooperate with him. It asked the Secretary-General to submit an interim report to the General Assembly in 1995 and to report in 1996. Those requests and the Commission's decision to extend the Special Rapporteur's mandate were approved on 25 July by the Economic and Social Council in **decision 1995/260**.

**Interim report of the Special Rapporteur.** As requested by the General Assembly in 1994,[18] the Secretary-General in September transmitted the Special Rapporteur's interim report[20] on the elimination of all forms of religious intolerance. The Special Rapporteur discussed legislation to restrict religious intolerance and discrimination, based on replies to a 1990 questionnaire received from Governments in 1991[21] and 1992,[22] and additional responses[23] received in view of the Commission's 1994 request[14] to Governments to communicate all new information falling within the Special Rapporteur's mandate, as well as any other observations they wished to make. He stressed the importance of country visits, noting his visit to Pakistan (12-22 June 1995) where he paid particular attention to studying legislation and its application. The Special Rapporteur carried out consultations and projects regarding the role of education in combating intolerance and discrimination, and stated that he had received replies from 64 Governments to his questionnaire on issues relating to freedom of religion and belief in primary and secondary schools.[17] The report contained tables giving the status of communications sent to Governments from 1988, the year in which the mandate was established, to 1995.

GENERAL ASSEMBLY ACTION

On 22 December, the General Assembly adopted **resolution 50/183**.

### Elimination of all forms of religious intolerance
*The General Assembly,*

*Recalling* that all States have pledged themselves, under the Charter of the United Nations, to promote and encourage universal respect for and observance of human rights and fundamental freedoms for all without distinction as to race, sex, language or religion,

*Recognizing* that these rights derive from the inherent dignity of the human person,

*Emphasizing* that the right to freedom of thought, conscience, religion and belief is far-reaching and profound and that it encompasses freedom of thought on all matters, personal conviction and the commitment to religion or belief, whether manifested individually or in community with others,

*Recalling* article 18 of the International Covenant on Civil and Political Rights,

*Reaffirming* that discrimination against human beings on the grounds of religion or belief constitutes an affront to human dignity and a disavowal of the principles of the Charter,

*Reaffirming also* its resolution 36/55 of 25 November 1981, by which it proclaimed the Declaration on the Elimination of All Forms of Intolerance and of Discrimination Based on Religion or Belief,

*Reaffirming further* the call of the World Conference on Human Rights for all Governments to take all appropriate measures in compliance with their international obligations and with due regard to their respective legal systems to counter intolerance and related violence based on religion or belief, including practices of discrimination against women and the desecration of religious sites, recognizing that every individual has the right to freedom of thought, conscience, expression and religion,

*Recalling* that the World Conference on Human Rights recognized that the process of promoting and protecting human rights should be conducted in conformity with the purposes and principles of the Charter and international law,

*Calling upon* all Governments to cooperate with the Special Rapporteur of the Commission on Human Rights on religious intolerance to enable him to carry out his mandate fully,

*Recognizing* that it is desirable to enhance the promotional and public information activities of the United Nations in matters relating to freedom of religion or belief and that both Governments and non-governmental organizations have an important role to play in this domain,

*Emphasizing* that non-governmental organizations and religious bodies and groups at every level have an important role to play in the promotion of tolerance and the protection of freedom of religion or belief,

*Conscious* of the importance of education in ensuring tolerance of religion and belief,

*Welcoming* the inclusion of events relating to tolerance and religious diversity among the activities undertaken during the United Nations Year for Tolerance,

*Alarmed* that serious instances of intolerance and discrimination on the grounds of religion or belief, including acts of violence, intimidation and coercion motivated by religious extremism, occur in many parts of the world and threaten the enjoyment of human rights and fundamental freedoms,

*Deeply concerned* that, as reported by the Special Rapporteur, the rights violated on religious grounds include the right to life, the right to physical integrity and to liberty and security of person, the right to freedom of expression, the right not to be subjected to torture or other cruel, inhuman or degrading treatment or punishment, and the right not to be arbitrarily arrested or detained,

*Believing* that further efforts are therefore required to promote and protect the right to freedom of thought, conscience, religion and belief and to eliminate all forms of hatred, intolerance and discrimination based on religion or belief,

1. *Reaffirms* that freedom of thought, conscience, religion and belief is a human right derived from the inherent dignity of the human person and guaranteed to all without discrimination;

2. *Urges* States to ensure that their constitutional and legal systems provide adequate and effective guarantees of freedom of thought, conscience, religion and belief to all without discrimination, including the provision of effective remedies in cases where the right to freedom of religion or belief is violated;

3. *Also urges* States to ensure, in particular, that no one within their jurisdiction is, because of their religion or belief, deprived of the right to life or the right to liberty and security of person, or is subjected to torture or arbitrary arrest or detention;

4. *Condemns* all instances of hatred, intolerance and acts of violence, intimidation and coercion motivated by religious extremism and intolerance of religion or belief;

5. *Further urges* States, in conformity with international standards of human rights, to take all necessary action to prevent such instances, to take all appropriate measures to combat hatred, intolerance and acts of violence, intimidation and coercion motivated by religious extremism and to encourage understanding, tolerance

and respect in matters relating to freedom of religion or belief;

6. *Recognizes* that legislation alone is not enough to prevent violations of human rights, including the right to freedom of religion or belief;

7. *Emphasizes* that, as underlined by the Human Rights Committee, restrictions on the freedom to manifest religion or belief are permitted only if limitations are prescribed by law; are necessary to protect public safety, order, health or morals or the fundamental rights and freedoms of others; and are applied in a manner that does not vitiate the right to freedom of thought, conscience and religion;

8. *Urges* States to ensure that, in the course of their official duties, members of law enforcement bodies, civil servants, educators and other public officials respect different religions and beliefs and do not discriminate against persons professing other religions or beliefs;

9. *Calls upon* all States to recognize, as provided in the Declaration on the Elimination of All Forms of Intolerance and of Discrimination Based on Religion or Belief, the right of all persons to worship or assemble in connection with a religion or belief, and to establish and maintain places for those purposes;

10. *Expresses its grave concern* at any attack upon religious places, sites and shrines, and calls upon all States, in accordance with their national legislation and in conformity with international human rights standards, to exert utmost efforts to ensure that such places, sites and shrines are fully respected and protected;

11. *Recognizes* that the exercise of tolerance and non-discrimination by persons and groups is necessary for the full realization of the aims of the Declaration;

12. *Considers it desirable* to enhance the promotional and public information activities of the United Nations in matters relating to freedom of religion or belief and to ensure that appropriate measures are taken to this end, including the dissemination, as a matter of high priority, of the text of the Declaration by United Nations information centres, as well as by other interested bodies;

13. *Encourages* the continued efforts on the part of the Special Rapporteur appointed to examine incidents and governmental actions in all parts of the world that are incompatible with the provisions of the Declaration and to recommend remedial measures as appropriate;

14. *Invites* the Special Rapporteur, within the terms of his mandate and in the context of recommending remedial measures, to take into account the experiences of various States as to which measures are most effective in promoting freedom of religion and belief and countering all forms of intolerance;

15. *Encourages* Governments to give serious consideration to inviting the Special Rapporteur to visit their countries so as to enable him to fulfil his mandate even more effectively;

16. *Recommends* that the promotion and protection of the right to freedom of thought, conscience, religion and belief be given appropriate priority in the work of the United Nations programme of advisory services in the field of human rights, including with regard to the drafting of legal texts in conformity with international instruments on human rights and taking into account the provisions of the Declaration;

17. *Welcomes and encourages* the efforts of non-governmental organizations to promote the implemen-

tation of the Declaration, and invites them to consider what further contribution they could make to its implementation and dissemination in all parts of the world;

18. *Requests* the Commission on Human Rights to continue its consideration of measures to implement the Declaration;

19. *Requests* the Special Rapporteur of the Commission on Human Rights to submit an interim report to the General Assembly at its fifty-first session;

20. *Requests* the Secretary-General to ensure that the Special Rapporteur receives the necessary staffing and financial and material resources to enable him to discharge his mandate;

21. *Decides* to consider the question of the elimination of all forms of religious intolerance at its fifty-first session under the item entitled "Human rights questions".

General Assembly resolution 50/183

22 December 1995      Meeting 99      Adopted without vote

Approved by Third Committee (A/50/635/Add.2) without vote, 13 December (meeting 55); 69-nation draft (A/C.3/50/L.55), orally revised; agenda item 112 *(b)*.

*Meeting numbers.* GA 50th session: 3rd Committee 35, 38-51, 53, 55; plenary 99.

## HIV- and AIDS-related discrimination

**Report of the Secretary-General.** The Commission on Human Rights had before it a report[24] of the Secretary-General describing international and domestic measures taken to protect human rights and prevent discrimination in the context of human immunodeficiency virus/acquired immunodeficiency syndrome (HIV/AIDS), based on information received from 19 Governments, six UN bodies, two regional commissions, four UN specialized agencies, four intergovernmental bodies and nine NGOs.

The Secretary-General concluded that the protection of human rights and prevention of discrimination had been accepted in principle in many national AIDS programmes, yet a dramatic gap seemed to exist between national policies and legislation and their implementation. Furthermore, many national policies actively interfered with the human rights of the individual and were generally carried out without legal justification. He recommended that national AIDS programmes include measures to combat social stigmatization, discrimination and violence directed against persons with HIV or AIDS and develop a supportive legal and social environment necessary for AIDS prevention and care. The Secretary-General advocated education, outreach and the dissemination of information as effective means to prevent and control HIV/AIDS. Governments were urged to take special measures to reach disadvantaged groups with prevention information and education and with care programmes and to increase support to action-oriented social and behavioural research.

The Secretary-General welcomed the establishment of the Joint and Co-sponsored UN Programme on HIV/AIDS (UNAIDS) (see PART FOUR, Chapter XIII). He recommended that the Commission on Human Rights consider the elaboration of a set of guidelines or principles to assist Governments in shaping their national policies regarding the human rights dimension of HIV/AIDS. The guidelines, he stated, could provide an international framework for discussion of human rights considerations at the national, regional and international levels.

**Commission action.** On 3 March, the Commission called[25] on States to ensure that their laws, policies and practices, including those concerning HIV/AIDS, respected human rights standards and did not inhibit programmes dealing with HIV/AIDS prevention and care. It also called on them to take steps to ensure the full enjoyment of civil, political, economic, social and cultural rights by people living with HIV or AIDS, their families, those associated with them, and people presumed to be at risk of infection, paying particular attention to women, children and other vulnerable groups, and to address such concerns within their activities in the context of the UN Year for Tolerance in 1995 (see PART FOUR, Chapter IX). The Commission further called on States to strengthen their efforts to advance the legal, economic and social status of women, children and vulnerable groups in order to render them less vulnerable to the risk of HIV infection and to the adverse socio-economic consequences of the AIDS pandemic, and to take steps to facilitate informed and responsible behaviour.

The Commission called on the Special Rapporteur on the sale of children, child prostitution and child pornography, the Committee on the Rights of the Child, the Commission on the Status of Women and the Working Group on Contemporary Forms of Slavery to pay attention to the risk that the exploitation of children posed for HIV transmission. It asked the Human Rights Committee, the Committee on Economic, Social and Cultural Rights and similar bodies to monitor States parties' compliance with their commitments under the relevant human rights instruments regarding the rights of people infected with HIV or AIDS, their families and associates, or people presumed to be at risk. It called on the Subcommission to keep the issue of AIDS-related discrimination under review under all relevant agenda items, as well as within the work of its relevant working groups and special rapporteurs. The Commission called on relevant professional bodies to re-examine their codes of professional practice to strengthen respect for human rights and dignity in the context of HIV/AIDS and to develop training in that regard. It asked the agencies co-sponsoring UNAIDS to integrate a strong human

rights component throughout the programme. The Commission asked the High Commissioner for Human Rights to consider methods to keep under review the protection of human rights in the context of the pandemic and to undertake with the Centre, in cooperation with UNAIDS, non-governmental agencies and others, the elaboration of guidelines on promoting and protecting respect for human rights in the context of HIV/AIDS, and to reflect on organizing a second international expert consultation on human rights and AIDS, the first such consultation having been held in 1989.[26] The Secretary-General was asked to consult with Governments, relevant UN bodies, specialized agencies and NGOs with a view to keeping under review the protection of human rights in the context of the pandemic, and to submit in 1996 a progress report on the development of a human rights component in UNAIDS and on the status of future guidelines.

**Subcommission action.** On 24 August, the Subcommission called[27] on States to review their laws, policies and practices to ensure that they respected human rights standards and the full enjoyment of human rights and freedoms by people with HIV/AIDS, their families and those associated with them. It also called for strengthened efforts to advance the legal, economic and social status of women, children, minorities, migrants and other groups in order to render them less vulnerable to HIV infection and to the adverse socio-economic consequences of the pandemic. The Subcommission asked the Commission to request the Centre for Human Rights to maximize its efforts in combating HIV/AIDS-related discrimination and to build close links with UNAIDS for on-going collaboration. It stressed the importance of organizing a second international expert consultation to consider developments on the matter, including the production of guidelines for preventing HIV/AIDS-related discrimination. The Subcommission urged the Commission to keep under review the issue of HIV/AIDS-related human rights violations and discrimination and asked UNAIDS to ensure the integration of a strong human rights component in all its activities.

*REFERENCES*

[1]E/1995/23 (res. 1995/24). [2]YUN 1992, p. 723, GA res. 47/135, annex, 18 Dec. 1992. [3]E/CN.4/Sub.2/1996/2. [4]YUN 1993, p. 869. [5]YUN 1994, p. 1007, GA res. 49/192, 23 Dec. 1994. [6]A/50/514. [7]E/CN.4/1995/84. [8]YUN 1994, p. 1006. [9]E/CN.4/Sub.2/1995/33 & Add.1,2. [10]E/CN.4/1996/2 (dec. 1995/110). [11]YUN 1994, p. 1008. [12]Ibid., p. 1098. [13]E/CN.4/Sub.2/1995/34. [14]YUN 1994, p. 996. [15]E/CN.4/1995/92. [16]YUN 1981, p. 881, GA res. 36/55, 25 Nov. 1981. [17]E/CN.4/1995/91. [18]YUN 1994, p. 997, GA res. 49/188, 23 Dec. 1994. [19]E/1995/23 (res. 1995/23). [20]A/50/440. [21]YUN 1991, p. 535. [22]YUN 1992, p. 715. [23]E/CN.4/1995/91/Add.1. [24]E/CN.4/1995/45. [25]E/1995/23 (res. 1995/44). [26]HR/PUB/90/2. [27]E/CN.4/1996/2 (res. 1995/21).

# Civil and political rights

## The right to self-determination

In 1995, the Commission on Human Rights reaffirmed the right to self-determination of the people of Palestine[1] and of Western Sahara.[2] Two other resolutions adopted under the item pertained to the Middle East peace process[3] and the use of mercenaries as a means of impeding the exercise of the right of peoples to self-determination.[4]

In September, the Secretary-General summarized action taken by the Commission on the right of peoples to self-determination.[5]

### GENERAL ASSEMBLY ACTION

On 21 December 1995, the General Assembly adopted **resolution 50/139**.

### Universal realization of the right of peoples to self-determination

*The General Assembly,*

*Reaffirming* the importance, for the effective guarantee and observance of human rights, of the universal realization of the right of peoples to self-determination enshrined in the Charter of the United Nations and embodied in the International Covenants on Human Rights, as well as in the Declaration on the Granting of Independence to Colonial Countries and Peoples contained in its resolution 1514(XV) of 14 December 1960,

*Welcoming* the progressive exercise of the right to self-determination by peoples under colonial, foreign or alien occupation and their emergence into sovereign statehood and independence,

*Deeply concerned* at the continuation of acts or threats of foreign military intervention and occupation that are threatening to suppress, or have already suppressed, the right to self-determination of an increasing number of sovereign peoples and nations,

*Expressing grave concern* that, as a consequence of the persistence of such actions, millions of people have been and are being uprooted from their homes as refugees and displaced persons, and emphasizing the urgent need for concerted international action to alleviate their condition,

*Recalling* the relevant resolutions regarding the violation of the right of peoples to self-determination and other human rights as a result of foreign military intervention, aggression and occupation, adopted by the Commission on Human Rights at its thirty-sixth, thirty-seventh, thirty-eighth, thirty-ninth, fortieth, forty-first, forty-second, forty-third, forty-fourth, forty-fifth, forty-sixth, forty-seventh, forty-eighth, forty-ninth, fiftieth and fifty-first sessions,

*Reaffirming* its resolutions 35/35 B of 14 November 1980, 36/10 of 28 October 1981, 37/42 of 3 December 1982, 38/16 of 22 November 1983, 39/18 of 23 November 1984, 40/24 of 29 November 1985, 41/100 of 4 December 1986, 42/94 of 7 December 1987, 43/105 of 8 December 1988, 44/80 of 8 December 1989, 45/131 of 14 December 1990, 46/88 of 16 December 1991, 47/83 of 16 December 1992, 48/93 of 20 December 1993 and 49/148 of 23 December 1994,

*Taking note* of the report of the Secretary-General on the right of peoples to self-determination,

1. *Reaffirms* that the universal realization of the right of all peoples, including those under colonial, foreign and alien domination, to self-determination is a fundamental condition for the effective guarantee and observance of human rights and for the preservation and promotion of such rights;

2. *Declares its firm opposition* to acts of foreign military intervention, aggression and occupation, since these have resulted in the suppression of the right of peoples to self-determination and other human rights in certain parts of the world;

3. *Calls upon* those States responsible to cease immediately their military intervention in and occupation of foreign countries and territories and all acts of repression, discrimination, exploitation and maltreatment, particularly the brutal and inhuman methods reportedly employed for the execution of those acts against the peoples concerned;

4. *Deplores* the plight of the millions of refugees and displaced persons who have been uprooted as a result of the aforementioned acts, and reaffirms their right to return to their homes voluntarily in safety and honour;

5. *Requests* the Commission on Human Rights to continue to give special attention to the violation of human rights, especially the right to self-determination, resulting from foreign military intervention, aggression or occupation;

6. *Requests* the Secretary-General to report on this question to the General Assembly at its fifty-first session under the item entitled "Right of peoples to self-determination".

General Assembly resolution 50/139

21 December 1995     Meeting 97     Adopted without vote

Approved by Third Committee (A/50/627) without vote, 2 November (meeting 18); 24-nation draft (A/C.3/50/L.7); agenda item 104.
*Meeting numbers.* GA 50th session: 3rd Committee 3-8, 15, 18; plenary 97.

## The rights of Palestinians

On 17 February, the Commission, by a roll-call vote of 27 to 1, with 22 abstentions, reaffirmed[1] the right of the Palestinians to self-determination and called on Israel to withdraw from the Palestinian and other Arab territories, including Jerusalem, in accordance with UN resolutions. It asked the Secretary-General to transmit its resolution to Israel and all other Governments, to distribute it as widely as possible and to make available to the Commission, prior to its 1996 session, all information pertaining to its implementation by Israel.

As requested by the Commission in 1994,[6] the Secretary-General reported[7] that he had received no reply to his request to Israel for information on implementation of the Commission's 1994 resolution on the situation in occupied Palestine.

### GENERAL ASSEMBLY ACTION

On 21 December, the General Assembly adopted **resolution 50/140**.

dom of opinion and expression and recommended to the Commission that it consider the provision of adequate financial and human resources for his work.

**Commission action.** On 3 March,[41] the Commission, expressing concern at the inadequate resources provided to the Special Rapporteur, reiterated its 1994 request[42] to the Secretary-General to provide all the assistance necessary to the Special Rapporteur to fulfil his mandate effectively. The Secretary-General was asked to consider ways to publicize the Special Rapporteur's work, and Governments were urged to cooperate with and assist him. The Special Rapporteur was to report in 1996, to develop further his commentary on the right to seek and receive information and to expand on his observations arising from communications.

### Conscientious objectors

The Commission on Human Rights in 1995 considered a report of the Secretary-General[43] summarizing replies from 23 Governments to a 1993 Commission request[44] for comments or information on conscientious objection to military service.

On 8 March, the Commission appealed[45] to States to enact legislation and to take measures aimed at exemption from military service on the basis of a genuinely held conscientious objection to armed service. It urged them not to differentiate between conscientious objectors on the basis of the nature of their beliefs nor to discriminate against recognized conscientious objectors for failing to perform military service. It asked the Secretary-General to transmit its resolution to all Member States and to include the right of conscientious objection to military service in UN public information activities, including the UN Decade for Human Rights Education (1995-2005) (see preceding chapter). The Commission also asked for an update in 1997 of information provided in the annexes to a 1983 report on the subject.

### Administration of justice

On 3 March, the Commission called on[46] Member States to provide effective legislation and other mechanisms to ensure implementation of UN standards on human rights in the administration of justice. It urged the High Commissioner for Human Rights to consider favourably requests by States for assistance in the administration of justice and to strengthen coordination of activities.

As requested by the Commission in 1994,[47] the Secretary-General, in a February note,[48] drew the attention of the Commission to a report containing information on the provision to Governments of technical assistance and advisory services in the field of the administration of justice.[49]

**Working group activities.** The five-member sessional working group on the administration of justice and the question of compensation met in Geneva on 2, 9 and 10 August.[50] The group considered draft articles 8 to 11, concerning forms of reparation, of the principles and guidelines proposed by the Special Rapporteur in 1993. It recommended that the Subcommission request the Special Rapporteur to prepare a revised version of the proposed basic principles and guidelines before the Subcommission met in 1996. On 24 August,[51] the Subcommission requested the working group to continue consideration of the subject and asked the Special Rapporteur to submit a revised set of proposed basic principles and guidelines on remedies in time for its 1996 session.

Regarding follow-up measures to the 1992 Declaration on the Protection of All Persons from Enforced Disappearance,[52] the Chairman/Rapporteur proposed that the group in 1996 keep him informed of the status report prepared by the Working Group on Enforced or Involuntary Disappearances concerning measures taken by Governments to give effect to the Declaration and of the action taken by NGOs to encourage the implementation of the Declaration, facilitate its dissemination and contribute to the work of the Subcommission in that area. He also proposed that the group submit in 1996 a preliminary draft international convention on the prevention and punishment of enforced disappearances and that a meeting of experts be organized to prepare a working paper on the subject.

The group decided to request the Special Rapporteur on human rights and states of emergency to prepare a working paper on rights not subject to derogation during states of emergency and exceptional circumstances so that the group could examine the subject in depth at its next session.

Following discussion of the death penalty, the group recommended that the subject remain on its agenda and that special attention be given to the imposition of the death penalty on minors and on persons with mental and physical disabilities.

In order to decide whether the Subcommission had amply fulfilled its mandate on the question of juvenile justice and if the item could consequently be removed from the agenda to make way for a new item, the Chairman/Rapporteur requested the Secretariat to prepare an information note for 1996, recapitulating the reports, studies and other documents submitted by UN bodies since the issuance of the final report prepared in 1992 by the Special Rapporteur responsible for the matter.[53]

**GENERAL ASSEMBLY ACTION**

On 22 December, the General Assembly adopted **resolution 50/181**.

## Human rights in the administration of justice

*The General Assembly,*

*Recalling* its resolution 48/137 of 20 December 1993, and taking note of Commission on Human Rights resolution 1995/41 of 3 March 1995 on human rights in the administration of justice, in particular of children and juveniles in detention,

*Bearing in mind* the principles embodied in articles 3, 5, 9, 10 and 11 of the Universal Declaration of Human Rights and the relevant provisions of the International Covenant on Civil and Political Rights and the Optional Protocols thereto, in particular article 6 of the Covenant, which explicitly states that no one shall be arbitrarily deprived of his life and prohibits the imposition of the death penalty for crimes committed by persons below eighteen years of age,

*Bearing in mind also* the relevant principles embodied in the Convention against Torture and Other Cruel, Inhuman or Degrading Treatment or Punishment, the International Convention on the Elimination of All Forms of Racial Discrimination and the Convention on the Rights of the Child,

*Mindful* of the Convention on the Elimination of All Forms of Discrimination against Women, in particular of the obligation of States to treat men and women equally in all stages of procedures in courts and tribunals,

*Calling attention* to the numerous international standards in the field of the administration of justice,

*Recognizing* that the rule of law and the proper administration of justice are important elements for sustainable economic and social development and play a central role in the promotion and protection of human rights,

*Welcoming* the important work of the Commission on Human Rights and of the Subcommission on Prevention of Discrimination and Protection of Minorities in the field of human rights in the administration of justice, in particular regarding the independence of the judiciary, the independence of judges and lawyers, the right to a fair trial, habeas corpus, human rights and states of emergency, the question of arbitrary detention, the human rights of juveniles in detention, the privatization of prisons and the question of the impunity of perpetrators of violations of human rights,

*Welcoming also* Commission on Human Rights resolution 1995/36 of 3 March 1995 on the independence and impartiality of the judiciary, jurors and assessors and the independence of lawyers,

*Welcoming further* the important work of the Commission on Crime Prevention and Criminal Justice in the field of human rights in the administration of justice, as reflected, *inter alia*, in Economic and Social Council resolution 1995/13 on United Nations standards and norms in crime prevention and criminal justice and resolution 1995/15 on technical cooperation and interregional advisory services in crime prevention and criminal justice, of 24 July 1995,

*Emphasizing* the importance of coordinating the activities in this field carried out under the responsibility of the Commission on Human Rights with those under the responsibility of the Commission on Crime Prevention and Criminal Justice,

*Noting* that many human rights violations in the administration of justice are specifically or primarily directed against women and that the identification and reporting of those violations demand special vigilance,

*Aware* of the specific situation of children and juveniles in detention and their special needs while deprived of their liberty, in particular their vulnerability to various forms of abuse, injustice and humiliation,

1. *Reaffirms* the importance of the full and effective implementation of all United Nations standards on human rights in the administration of justice;

2. *Acknowledges* that the administration of justice, including law enforcement and prosecutorial agencies, and, especially, an independent judiciary and legal profession in full conformity with applicable standards contained in international human rights instruments are essential to the full and non-discriminatory realization of human rights and indispensable to democratization processes and sustainable development;

3. *Once again reiterates its call* to all Member States to spare no effort in providing for effective legislative and other mechanisms and procedures, as well as adequate resources, to ensure full implementation of those standards;

4. *Appeals* to Governments to include in their national development plans the administration of justice as an integral part of the development process and to allocate adequate resources for the provision of legal-aid services with a view to the promotion and protection of human rights;

5. *Invites* Governments to provide training in human rights in the administration of justice, including juvenile justice, to all judges, lawyers, prosecutors, social workers and other professionals concerned, including police and immigration officers;

6. *Encourages* States to make use of technical assistance offered by the United Nations programmes of advisory services and technical assistance, in order to strengthen national capacities and infrastructures in the field of the administration of justice;

7. *Urges* the Secretary-General to consider favourably requests by States for assistance in the field of the administration of justice and to strengthen system-wide coordination in this field, in particular between the United Nations programme of advisory services and technical assistance in the field of human rights and the technical cooperation and advisory services of the United Nations crime prevention and criminal justice programme;

8. *Invites* the international community to respond favourably to requests for financial and technical assistance for the enhancement and strengthening of the administration of justice, with a view to ensuring the promotion and protection of human rights in the administration of justice;

9. *Calls upon* special rapporteurs, special representatives and working groups of the Commission on Human Rights to continue to give special attention to questions relating to the effective protection of human rights in the administration of justice and to provide, wherever appropriate, specific recommendations in this regard, including proposals for concrete measures of advisory services and technical assistance;

10. *Acknowledges* the important role of the regional commissions, specialized agencies and United Nations institutes in the area of human rights and crime prevention and criminal justice, and of other organizations of the United Nations system, as well as intergovernmental and non-governmental organizations, including national professional associations concerned with promoting United Nations standards in this field;

11. *Invites* the Commission on Human Rights and the Commission on Crime Prevention and Criminal Justice to coordinate closely their activities relating to the administration of justice;

12. *Decides* to consider the question of human rights in the administration of justice at its fifty-second session under the item entitled "Human rights questions".

General Assembly resolution 50/181

22 December 1995     Meeting 99     Adopted without vote

Approved by Third Committee (A/50/635/Add.2) without vote, 11 December (meeting 53); 53-nation draft (A/C.3/50/L.49), orally revised; agenda item 112 *(b)*.
*Meeting numbers.* GA 50th session: 3rd Committee 35, 38-53; plenary 99.

### Compensation for victims

**Commission action.** On 3 March, the Human Rights Commission encouraged[54] its Subcommission to continue to consider at its 1995 session the proposed basic principles and guidelines contained in the 1993 report of the Special Rapporteur on the right to restitution, compensation and rehabilitation for victims of gross violations of human rights and fundamental freedoms.[55] It requested States to provide the Secretary-General with information about legislation they had adopted, or were in the process of adopting, relating to restitution, compensation and rehabilitation for such victims. The Secretary-General was requested to submit in 1996 a report based on the information received.

**Report of the Secretary-General.** In a May report with later addenda,[56] the Secretary-General summarized comments on the Special Rapporteur's proposed principles and guidelines[55] received from nine Governments, two specialized agencies, two intergovernmental organizations and one NGO. Annexed to the report were the proposed basic principles and guidelines.

**Subcommission action.** On 1 August, the Subcommission, recalling its 1994 decision,[47] decided[57] to establish a sessional working group on the right to compensation.

### Rule of law

**Commission action.** On 3 March, the Human Rights Commission, noting that the programme of advisory services and technical assistance did not have funds to assist projects with a direct impact on the realization of human rights and the maintenance of the rule of law, asked[58] the Secretary-General to explore the possibilities of obtaining from all relevant institutions of the UN system technical and financial means to strengthen the capacity of the Centre for Human Rights to provide such assistance and to report to the General Assembly in 1995.

By **decision 1995/270** of 25 July, the Economic and Social Council approved the Commission's request to the Secretary-General.

**Report of the Secretary-General.** In an October report,[59] the Secretary-General described efforts to strengthen the rule of law.

He called attention to the continuing lack of funds to assist States committed to strengthening the rule of law but also facing economic hardship. Efforts were initiated to encourage the international community to support the advisory services programme. The UN High Commissioner for Human Rights had sought to explore possibilities for obtaining from all relevant UN agencies and financial institutions technical and financial assistance. In addition, the High Commissioner initiated consultations with other UN entities; met with executive heads of UN agencies and programmes; had meetings and working-level contacts with agencies and programmes on thematic issues; held field-level meetings in connection with human rights field missions and projects; and concluded memoranda of understanding with various agencies and programmes. Support for capital and technical assistance funds, the Secretary-General stated, might be facilitated by supplementing the Voluntary Fund for Technical Cooperation in the Field of Human Rights; establishing a separate, complementary fund for capital assistance in the area of human rights; or encouraging increased support from development agencies and funds and financial institutions. To strengthen the rule of law, he advocated additional and dedicated resources to support programme development activities within the Centre for Human Rights.

The success of UN efforts to strengthen the rule of law, he went on, relied on the response of the international community to the urgencies he had described.

#### GENERAL ASSEMBLY ACTION

On 22 December, the General Assembly adopted **resolution 50/179**.

**Strengthening of the rule of law**
*The General Assembly,*

*Recalling* that, by adopting the Universal Declaration of Human Rights, Member States have pledged themselves to achieve, in cooperation with the United Nations, the promotion of universal respect for and observance of human rights and fundamental freedoms,

*Firmly convinced* that, as stressed in the Universal Declaration of Human Rights, the rule of law is an essential factor in the protection of human rights,

*Convinced* that through their own national legal and judicial systems States must provide appropriate civil, criminal and administrative remedies for violations of human rights,

*Recognizing* the importance of the role that can be played by the Centre for Human Rights of the Secretariat in supporting national efforts to strengthen the institutions of the rule of law,

*Bearing in mind* that, in its resolution 48/141 of 20 December 1993, the General Assembly entrusted the

United Nations High Commissioner for Human Rights with, *inter alia*, providing through the Centre and other appropriate institutions advisory services and technical and financial assistance in the field of human rights, enhancing international cooperation for the promotion and protection of all human rights and coordinating human rights activities throughout the United Nations system,

*Recalling* the recommendation of the World Conference on Human Rights that a comprehensive programme be established within the United Nations and under the coordination of the Centre with a view to helping States in the task of building and strengthening adequate national structures that have a direct impact on the overall observance of human rights and the maintenance of the rule of law,

*Recalling also* its resolution 49/194 of 23 December 1994, and taking note of Commission on Human Rights resolution 1995/54 of 3 March 1995,

1. *Takes note with satisfaction* of the report of the Secretary-General;

2. *Takes note with interest* of the proposals contained in the report of the Secretary-General for strengthening the programme of advisory services and technical assistance of the Centre for Human Rights of the Secretariat in order to comply fully with the recommendations of the World Conference on Human Rights concerning assistance to States in strengthening their institutions in the rule of law;

3. *Praises* the efforts made by the United Nations High Commissioner for Human Rights and the Centre to accomplish their ever-increasing tasks with the limited financial and personnel resources at their disposal;

4. *Expresses its deep concern* at the scarcity of means at the disposal of the Centre for the fulfilment of its tasks;

5. *Notes* that the programme of advisory services and technical assistance does not have assistance funds sufficient to provide any substantial financial assistance to national projects that have a direct impact on the realization of human rights and the maintenance of the rule of law in countries that are committed to those ends, but which face economic hardship;

6. *Affirms* that the High Commissioner, with the assistance of the Centre, remains the focal point for coordinating system-wide attention for human rights, democracy and the rule of law;

7. *Welcomes* the consultations and contacts initiated by the High Commissioner with other relevant bodies and programmes of the United Nations system aiming at the enhancement of inter-agency coordination and cooperation in providing assistance for the strengthening of the rule of law;

8. *Encourages* the High Commissioner to pursue these consultations, taking into account the need to explore new synergies with other organs and agencies of the United Nations system with a view to obtaining increased financial assistance for human rights and the rule of law;

9. *Requests* the High Commissioner to continue to explore the possibilities of obtaining from all relevant institutions of the United Nations system, including financial institutions, acting within their mandates, technical and financial means to strengthen the capacity of the Centre to provide assistance to national projects aiming at the realization of human rights and the maintenance of the rule of law;

10. *Requests* the Secretary-General to submit a report to the General Assembly at its fifty-first session on the results of the contacts established in accordance with paragraph 9 above, as well as on any other developments pertaining to the implementation of the above-mentioned recommendation of the World Conference on Human Rights.

General Assembly resolution 50/179

22 December 1995    Meeting 99    Adopted without vote

Approved by Third Committee (A/50/635/Add.2) without vote, 11 December (meeting 53); 41-nation draft (A/C.3/50/L.42); agenda item 112 *(b)*. *Meeting numbers.* GA 50th session: 3rd Committee 35, 38-51, 53; plenary 99.

## Impunity

The Special Rapporteur on the question of the impunity of perpetrators of violations of human rights (civil and political rights), Louis Joinet (France), in June provided a progress report on the subject,[60] following submission of a preliminary report in 1994.[42] He outlined certain points under discussion concerning the scope of impunity and its definition and the role of society in combating impunity, including the capacity of victims to organize themselves and secure reparation and the need to improve the effectiveness of UN mechanisms for the protection of human rights. The Special Rapporteur also discussed States' responsibility in combating impunity.

On 24 August, the Subcommission asked[61] the Special Rapporteur to submit his final report in 1996.

In June, the Special Rapporteur on opposition to the impunity of perpetrators of human rights violations (economic, social and cultural rights), El Hadji Guissé (Senegal), submitted an interim report[62] in which he discussed practices that might give rise to the violation of those rights, such as slavery, colonization, apartheid and cultural looting. He also discussed certain practices which were sources of violations of economic, social and cultural rights, including debt, structural adjustment programmes, corruption, and fiscal and customs fraud and other economic offences. Violations of economic, social and cultural rights affected a variety of specific rights: to development, to a healthy environment, to work, to health, to adequate food, to adequate housing and to education. The Special Rapporteur presented preventive measures and repressive or remedial action aimed at penalizing violations that had already been committed. He recommended broadening the scope of the study and holding an international meeting to gather information from various sources to prepare his final report.

On 24 August, the Subcommission asked[63] the Special Rapporteur to submit his final report in 1996.

## Independence of the judicial system

In February, the Special Rapporteur on the independence of judges and lawyers, Dato' Param

Cumaraswamy (Malaysia), submitted his first report,[64] in which he discussed his activities and examined his mandate and the legal framework of the issue. Issues of special importance concerned the principle of the separation of powers; judicial review of the constitutionality or legality of executive decisions, administrative orders and legislative acts; the criterion of independence; states of emergency; anti-terrorism measures; and the relationship between the media and the judiciary. The Special Rapporteur wanted to be apprised of requests for advisory services and technical assistance from the Centre for Human Rights with regard to the independence and impartiality of the judiciary; he recommended that the Centre publish a fact sheet on the subject.

On 3 March, the Commission, welcoming the Special Rapporteur's report, endorsed[65] his wish to be kept informed of the programme of advisory services and technical assistance, and requested him to report in 1996.

### Right to a fair trial

On 3 March, the Commission on Human Rights endorsed[66] a Subcommission proposal that the 1994 study on the right to a fair trial[67]— prepared by Special Rapporteurs Stanislav Chernichenko (Russian Federation) and William Treat (United States)—be published in all official UN languages, taking into account comments received from Governments and Subcommission members, as well as recent developments. It decided to consider in 1996 the establishment of an open-ended working group to draft a third optional protocol to the 1966 International Covenant on Civil and Political Rights,[40] aiming at guaranteeing the right to a fair trial and a remedy.

On 25 July, the Economic and Social Council, by **decision 1995/299**, approved the Commission's endorsement of the Subcommission's proposal and asked that the Secretary-General provide all the assistance needed to compile and publish the report.

### Detention of juveniles

**Commission action.** On 3 March, the Human Rights Commission called on[46] States to give high priority to promoting and protecting all rights of the child and juveniles, and to take into account in their national legislation and practices and to disseminate widely the 1985 UN Standard Minimum Rules for the Administration of Juvenile Justice (The Beijing Rules),[68] the 1990 UN Guidelines for the Prevention of Juvenile Delinquency (The Riyadh Guidelines)[69] and the UN Rules for the Protection of Juveniles Deprived of their Liberty.[70] States were urged to ensure compliance with the principle that depriving children and juveniles of their liberty should be used only as

a measure of last resort. The Commission also noted the recommendations of an expert meeting on children and juveniles in detention, held in 1994 (see below).

The Commission recommended that States use technical assistance offered by UN programmes of advisory services and technical assistance to strengthen national capacities and infrastructures in juvenile justice. It asked the High Commissioner for Human Rights to pay special attention to the subject and, in cooperation with the UN Crime Prevention and Criminal Justice Branch, the Committee on the Rights of the Child and the UN Children's Fund, to develop strategies to ensure effective coordination of relevant technical cooperation programmes. The Secretary-General was to report in 1996.

(See also preceding chapter, under "Other human rights instruments".)

**Notes by the Secretary-General.** In June, the Secretary-General transmitted to the Subcommission his report[71] on the 1994 expert meeting on children and juveniles in detention.[72]

As requested by the Subcommission in 1994,[72] the Secretary-General, in a July note with a later addendum,[73] provided information received from seven Governments, one specialized agency, one UN body and one intergovernmental organization describing the situation of children deprived of their liberty and the implementation of provisions and standards designed to ensure their protection.

### Detained UN staff members

**Report of the Secretary-General.** In January, the Secretary-General submitted to the Commission a report updating developments pertaining to the detention of international civil servants and their families.[74] Annexed to the report was a consolidated list of staff members under arrest and detention or missing and the text of the 1994 Convention on the Safety of United Nations and Associated Personnel.[75]

**Commission action.** On 3 March, the Commission appealed[76] to Member States to respect and ensure respect for the rights of staff members and others acting under UN authority and their families, and urged them to provide adequate and prompt information concerning their arrest or detention; grant immediate access to the detained by representatives of international organizations; allow independent medical teams to investigate the health of detained staff members, experts and their families and afford them medical assistance; allow representatives of international organizations to attend hearings; and ensure the release of detained UN staff members, experts and members of their families. Member States were urged to consider promptly signing the 1994 Convention on the

Safety of United Nations and Associated Personnel. The Commission asked the Secretary-General to report in 1996 on the status of the Convention, on the situation of UN staff members, experts and their families detained, imprisoned, missing or held in a country against their will, and on cases which had been successfully settled since his last report. It also asked him to take steps to ensure the application of the recommendations contained in the 1992 final report of the Special Rapporteur on the protection of the human rights of UN staff members, experts and their families.[77]

## Capital punishment

As requested by the Economic and Social Council in 1990,[78] the Secretary-General submitted in June 1995 the fifth quinquennial report on capital punishment,[79] which also covered the implementation of safeguards guaranteeing the protection of the rights of those facing the death penalty. The report was drawn from all available data, including current criminological research, and included comments from specialized agencies, intergovernmental organizations and NGOs. The Secretary-General provided information received from 60 Governments and three NGOs about the implementation of the safeguards and death penalty from 1989 to 1993.

ECONOMIC AND SOCIAL COUNCIL ACTION

On 28 July, the Economic and Social Council adopted **resolution 1995/57**.

### Capital punishment

*The Economic and Social Council,*

*Recalling* General Assembly resolutions 2857(XXVI) of 20 December 1971, 32/61 of 8 December 1977, 39/118 of 14 December 1984 and 44/128 of 15 December 1989,

*Recalling also* its resolutions 1745(LIV) of 16 May 1973, 1930(LVIII) of 6 May 1975, 1984/50 of 25 May 1984 and 1990/51 of 24 July 1990,

*Having considered* the fifth quinquennial report of the Secretary-General on capital punishment and the implementation of the safeguards guaranteeing the protection of the rights of those facing the death penalty, submitted to it in pursuance of its resolution 1990/51 and its decision 1994/206 of 3 February 1994,

*Conscious* of the fact that only sixty-three Governments replied to the questionnaire which the Secretary-General sent to them asking them to provide the information required for the preparation of the fifth quinquennial report,

1. *Invites* Member States to reply to the questionnaire which the Secretary-General will send them with a view to the preparation of the sixth quinquennial report in the year 2000, providing him with the information requested;

2. *Notes* that, during the period covered by the report of the Secretary-General, an increasing number of countries abolished the death penalty and others followed a policy of reducing the number of capital offences and declared that they had not sentenced any offender to that penalty, while others retained it;

3. *Requests* the Commission on Crime Prevention and Criminal Justice to examine the report of the Secretary-General at its fifth session;

4. *Requests* the Secretary-General, in preparing the sixth quinquennial report, to draw on all available data, including current criminological research, and to invite the comments of specialized agencies, intergovernmental organizations and non-governmental organizations in consultative status with the Economic and Social Council on this question;

5. *Recommends* that the quinquennial reports of the Secretary-General, like the one submitted to the Economic and Social Council in 1995, should continue to cover also the implementation of the safeguards guaranteeing protection of the rights of those facing the death penalty.

Economic and Social Council resolution 1995/57

28 July 1995    Meeting 57    Adopted without vote

11-nation draft (E/1995/L.47), orally revised following informal consultations; agenda item 5 *(g)*.

*Meeting numbers.* ESC 47-49, 53, 57.

## Other issues

### Terrorism

**Commission action.** On 3 March, the Human Rights Commission condemned[80] all acts, methods and practices of terrorism in all its forms and manifestations. Expressing its solidarity with victims of terrorism, the Commission encouraged States to respond to the Secretary-General's request, made pursuant to a 1994 General Assembly resolution,[81] to submit views on the establishment of a UN voluntary fund for victims. It called on States to take effective measures, in accordance with international human rights standards, to prevent, combat and eliminate terrorism, and urged the international community to enhance cooperation in the fight against terrorism. The Commission asked the Secretary-General to continue to collect information on terrorism from relevant sources and make it available to the special rapporteurs and working groups concerned and to the Commission. It welcomed the Subcommission's 1994 decision[82] to entrust one of its members with preparing a working paper on terrorism and human rights, and invited States that so wished to forward relevant information to him.

**Report of the Secretary-General.** As requested by the General Assembly in 1994,[81] the Secretary-General in October reported[83] the views of eight Governments on the establishment of a voluntary fund for victims of terrorism.

GENERAL ASSEMBLY ACTION

On 22 December, the General Assembly adopted **resolution 50/186**.

### Human rights and terrorism

*The General Assembly,*

*Guided* by the Charter of the United Nations, the Universal Declaration of Human Rights, the Declaration on Principles of International Law concerning Friendly Relations and Cooperation among States in accordance with the Charter of the United Nations and the International Covenants on Human Rights,

*Bearing in mind* the Declaration on the Occasion of the Fiftieth Anniversary of the United Nations,

*Taking into account* the fact that acts of terrorism in all its forms and manifestations aimed at the destruction of human rights have continued despite national and international efforts,

*Bearing in mind* that the most essential and basic human right is the right to life,

*Bearing in mind also* that terrorism creates an environment that destroys the freedom from fear of the people,

*Recalling* the Vienna Declaration and Programme of Action, adopted by the World Conference on Human Rights on 25 June 1993,

*Recalling also* its resolutions 48/122 of 20 December 1993 and 49/185 of 23 December 1994,

*Taking note* of Commission on Human Rights resolution 1995/43 of 3 March 1995,

*Reiterating* that all States have an obligation to promote and protect human rights and fundamental freedoms, and also that every individual should strive to secure their universal and effective recognition and observance,

*Seriously concerned* at the gross violations of human rights perpetrated by terrorist groups,

*Profoundly deploring* the increasing number of innocent persons, including women, children and the elderly, killed, massacred and maimed by terrorists in indiscriminate and random acts of violence and terror, which cannot be justified under any circumstances,

*Noting with great concern* the growing connection between the terrorist groups and other criminal organizations engaged in the illegal traffic in arms and drugs at the national and international levels, as well as the consequent commission of serious crimes such as murder, extortion, kidnapping, assault, taking of hostages and robbery,

*Mindful* of the need to protect human rights of and guarantees for the individual in accordance with the relevant international human rights principles and instruments, particularly the right to life,

*Reaffirming* that all measures to counter terrorism must be in strict conformity with international human rights standards,

1. *Expresses its solidarity* with the victims of terrorism;

2. *Reiterates its unequivocal condemnation* of the acts, methods and practices of terrorism as activities aimed at the destruction of human rights, fundamental freedoms and democracy, threatening the territorial integrity and security of States, destabilizing legitimately constituted Governments, undermining pluralistic civil society and having adverse consequences on the economic and social development of States;

3. *Calls upon* States to take all necessary and effective measures in accordance with international standards of human rights to prevent, combat and eliminate all acts of terrorism wherever and by whomever committed;

4. *Urges* the international community to enhance cooperation at regional and international levels in the fight against terrorism in accordance with relevant international instruments, including those relating to human rights, with the aim of its eradication;

5. *Condemns* incitement of ethnic hatred, violence and terrorism;

6. *Requests* the Secretary-General to continue to seek the views of Member States on the possible establishment of a United Nations voluntary fund for victims of terrorism, as well as ways and means to rehabilitate the victims of terrorism and to reintegrate them into society, and to submit to the General Assembly at its fifty-second session, for its consideration, a report containing comments made by Member States on the subject;

7. *Also requests* the Secretary-General to transmit the text of the present resolution to all Member States and to competent specialized agencies and intergovernmental organizations for their consideration;

8. *Encourages* special rapporteurs, special representatives and working groups of the Commission on Human Rights, as well as treaty bodies, to pay appropriate attention, within their mandates, to the consequences of the acts, methods and practices of terrorist groups;

9. *Decides* to consider this question at its fifty-second session under the item entitled "Human rights questions".

General Assembly resolution 50/186

22 December 1995      Meeting 99      Adopted without vote

Approved by Third Committee (A/50/635/Add.2) without vote, 13 December (meeting 56); 32-nation draft (A/C.3/50/L.61/Rev.1), orally revised; agenda item 112 *(b)*.

Meeting numbers. GA 50th session: 3rd Committee 35, 38-51, 53, 56; plenary 99.

## State of siege or emergency

**Commission action.** On 3 March, the Human Rights Commission endorsed[84] a 1994 resolution[85] of its Subcommission on Prevention of Discrimination and Protection of Minorities and recommended to the Economic and Social Council a draft resolution (see below).

On 24 February,[86] the Commission underlined the necessity for strict observance of the agreed conditions and procedure for derogation under article 4 of the Covenant and the need for States parties to provide full and timely information during states of emergency, so that the justification and appropriateness of measures taken in those circumstances could be assessed.

**ECONOMIC AND SOCIAL COUNCIL ACTION**

On 25 July 1995, the Economic and Social Council adopted **resolution 1995/34**.

**Question of human rights and states of emergency**

*The Economic and Social Council,*

*Recalling* Commission on Human Rights resolution 1995/42 of 3 March 1995 and Subcommission on Prevention of Discrimination and Protection of Minorities resolution 1994/36 of 26 August 1994,

1. *Approves* the request of the Subcommission on Prevention of Discrimination and Protection of Minorities to the Special Rapporteur on human rights and states of emergency, Mr. Leandro Despouy, to fulfil his mandate, notably relating to the holding of an expert meeting to study non-derogable rights in states or situations of emergency and the international principles to be taken into account in drafting national legal rules,

and to establish a database on states of emergency and related human rights questions;

2. *Requests* the Secretary-General to provide the Special Rapporteur with all the necessary assistance for the fulfilment of his mandate.

Economic and Social Council resolution 1995/34

25 July 1995      Meeting 52      Adopted without vote

Draft by Commission on Human Rights (E/1995/23), orally amended by Japan; agenda item 5 *(d)*.
*Meeting numbers.* ESC 51-53.

**Report of the Special Rapporteur.** In June, the Special Rapporteur, Leandro Despouy (Argentina), submitted his eighth annual report,[87] containing information on 87 States or territories which, since 1 January 1985, had proclaimed, extended or terminated a state of emergency. He discussed progress made on establishing a database on states of emergency. Annexed to his report was a report of a meeting of experts (Geneva, 17-19 May) on rights not subject to derogation during states of emergency and exceptional circumstances. Previous reports were issued by the Special Rapporteur in 1987,[88] 1988,[89] 1989,[90] 1991,[91] 1992,[92] 1993[93] and 1994.[85]

In November,[94] the Secretary-General transmitted to the Commission additional information on two countries in which measures had been taken that constituted the proclamation, introduction, extension, maintenance or termination of emergency regimes in various forms.[95]

**Subcommission action.** On 24 August, the Subcommission encouraged[96] the Special Rapporteur to submit in his ninth report conclusions and recommendations on non-derogable rights in states or situations of emergency, and asked him to pursue and broaden consultations on the subject of receiving, storing and retrieving information, through a database, on states of emergency and related human rights issues and to report in 1996 on the results.

### Humanitarian standards

**Commission action.** On 3 March, the Human Rights Commission, recognizing the need to address principles applicable to situations of internal and related violence, disturbance, tension and public emergency in a manner consistent with international law and the UN Charter, invited[97] States to consider reviewing their national legislation relevant to situations of public emergency with a view to ensuring that it met the requirements of the rule of law and that it did not involve discrimination. The Commission asked the Secretary-General to transmit the text of the Declaration of Minimum Humanitarian Standards, adopted by a group of experts (Turku, Finland, December 1990),[98] to Governments, intergovernmental organizations and NGOs for their comments and to submit a report in 1996.

Also, noting a 1994 Subcommission resolution,[99] the Commission decided[100] not to forward to the Economic and Social Council the Subcommission's draft decision to authorize a study on the question of the implications for human rights of UN action, including humanitarian assistance, in addressing international humanitarian problems and in the promotion of human rights.

### Arbitrary detention

**Commission action.** On 7 March, the Commission, taking note of the report of the Working Group on Arbitrary Detention on its 1994 sessions,[72] expressed concern[101] that, according to the Group, most cases of arbitrary deprivation of liberty were motivated by denial of the exercise of the right to freedom of opinion and expression. It requested Governments concerned to give the necessary attention to urgent appeals addressed to them on a strictly humanitarian basis and without prejudging the character of the detention. The Commission asked the Group to continue to seek and gather information from Governments, intergovernmental organizations and NGOs, as well as from individuals concerned, their families or their legal representatives; to submit a report in 1996; and to make suggestions which would enable it to discharge its mandate in the best possible way.

**Working Group activities.** The Working Group on Arbitrary Detention held its twelfth, thirteenth and fourteenth sessions in Geneva in 1995 (29 May–2 June, 11-19 September, 29 November–8 December).[102] The activities of the five independent experts included transmitting letters to Governments of countries where cases of alleged arbitrary detention were reported to have occurred and asking them to make inquiries and inform the Group of the results within 90 days. During the year, the Group sent communications to 28 countries concerning 829 new cases of arbitrary detention, to which 14 countries replied. The Group received three replies to letters transmitted prior to 1995. It also addressed 62 urgent-action appeals to 38 countries concerning 215 individuals. In addition, the Group addressed urgent appeals jointly with other thematic and country special rapporteurs to three Governments. In cases where the alleged arbitrary detention had endangered the health or life of the detainees, or in view of other particular circumstances, the Group appealed to the Governments concerned to consider releasing those persons without delay.

The Group proposed that the Commission recommend that Governments maintaining declared states of emergency strictly apply the principle of proportionality and limitation in time, considering the frequency with which arbitrary detentions occurred in those conditions. It suggested that the Commission request Governments to eliminate from their legislation precepts which sanctioned modes of conduct without describing them with sufficient clarity; ask States to incorporate habeas corpus in their legislation as an individual right; and renew the mandate of the Special Rapporteur on the question of states of emergency. The Group asked the Commission to recommend that the Subcommission transmit the draft declaration on habeas corpus, as soon as it was approved. It proposed the provision of advisory services related to individual freedom.

Annexed to the Group's report were its revised methods of work and statistical data regarding cases of detention in which the Group adopted a decision as to whether they were arbitrary or not.

In 1995, the Group adopted 49 decisions concerning 847 persons in 22 countries, as well as in the territory controlled by the Palestinian Authority. Decisions adopted in December 1994 and in June and September 1995 were contained in a separate addendum.[103]

### Extra-legal executions

**Reports of the Special Rapporteur.** The Commission on Human Rights considered a report submitted by its Special Rapporteur on summary or arbitrary executions, Bacre Waly Ndiaye (Senegal),[104] updating activities undertaken by him since the submission of his 1994 report.[105] He discussed issues related to his mandate and described situations where urgent appeals and other communications had been transmitted to Governments, together with any replies or observations received from them. He stated that, as in the past, impunity was the key to the perpetuation of violations of the right to life.

The Special Rapporteur recommended action concerning capital punishment, death threats, deaths in custody, deaths due to use of force by law enforcement officials, violations of the right to life during armed conflicts, extradition of persons to a country where their life was in danger, and impunity.

He made further recommendations concerning violations of the right to life directed against certain groups, including minors, particularly street children; women; persons belonging to national or ethnic, religious and linguistic minorities; UN and specialized agency staff members; and persons exercising their right to freedom of opinion and expression and to the right to life and the administration of justice. Other recommendations concerned terrorism, civil defence forces, mass exoduses, forensic experts, the 1993 World Conference on Human Rights,[106] and prevention of violations of the right to life.

The Special Rapporteur in 1995 visited Burundi (19-29 April)[107] to gather additional information about violations of the right to life which had oc-

curred following the October 1993 *coup d'état*[108] and which had continued, although to a lesser extent. He concluded that the serious human rights situation in Burundi resulted from abuses against the right to life which had taken root among the Hutu and Tutsi populations, the violence into which Burundi had been plunged and impunity. The Special Rapporteur expressed concern over the massacres and extrajudicial, summary or arbitrary executions among civilians, especially women and children, and the situation of refugees and the displacement and dispersion of people throughout the country. He called for action at the national level to provide security and protection and, at the international level, to improve the human rights situation. (See also next chapter.)

The Special Rapporteur in 1995 also visited the island of Bougainville in Papua New Guinea (23-28 October),[109] where he noted that violence, against the background of an armed conflict between the Papua New Guinea Defence Force and the Bougainville Revolutionary Army, had decreased considerably since a 1994 cease-fire (see next chapter). Noting that human rights violations continued, he gathered information regarding alleged extrajudicial executions, torture, harassment and ill-treatment by those in charge of care centres, and violations of the right to freedom of movement, and noted deficiencies in the right to education and the right to health and in the administration of justice. He made recommendations concerning peace and reconciliation, education and training for youth and the administration of justice.

**Commission action.** On 8 March, the Human Rights Commission strongly condemned[110] extrajudicial, summary or arbitrary executions and demanded that Governments ensure that those practices were ended and that they took effective action to combat and eliminate them. It asked the Special Rapporteur to: continue examining extrajudicial, summary or arbitrary executions and report annually; respond to information he received; enhance further his dialogue with Governments, as well as follow up on recommendations made in his reports; continue to pay special attention to extrajudicial, summary or arbitrary executions of children and women and to allegations concerning violations of the right to life; and continue monitoring the implementation of international standards on safeguards and restrictions relating to the imposition of capital punishment. The Commission extended the Special Rapporteur's mandate for three years and asked the Secretary-General to assist him in his work. The Economic and Social Council approved those actions on 25 July by **decision 1995/284**. The Commission also asked the Secretary-General to continue to use his best endeavours in cases where the minimum standard of legal safeguards provided for in articles 6, 9, 14 and 15 of the 1966 International Covenant on Civil and Political Rights[40] appeared not to be respected, and to continue to ensure that personnel specializing in human rights and humanitarian law formed part of UN missions in order to deal with serious human rights violations.

## Population movements

### Mass exoduses

**Commission action.** On 8 March, the Commission, strongly deploring ethnic and other forms of intolerance as one of the major causes of forced migratory movements, urged[111] States to take steps to ensure respect for human rights, especially the rights of persons belonging to minorities. It again invited Governments and intergovernmental and humanitarian organizations to intensify their cooperation in addressing problems resulting from mass exoduses of refugees and displaced persons and the causes of such exoduses. The Commission invited special rapporteurs, special representatives and working groups studying human rights violations to seek information on problems resulting in mass exoduses and to include such information in their reports. It asked all UN bodies, the specialized agencies, governmental and intergovernmental organizations and NGOs to cooperate with it and to provide information on the human rights situations creating or affecting refugees and displaced persons. The High Commissioner for Human Rights was asked to pay attention to situations causing or threatening to cause mass exoduses. The Commission urged the Secretary-General to allocate resources to consolidate the system for early-warning activities in the humanitarian area in order to ensure that effective action was taken to identify human rights abuses contributing to mass exoduses, and to invite comments thereon. The Commission requested the Secretary-General to ask Governments, intergovernmental organizations, specialized agencies and NGOs for information and to submit in 1996 an update of his report (see below).

**Reports of the Secretary-General.** Pursuant to its 1994 decision,[112] the Commission considered in 1995 a report of the Secretary-General[113] containing information and views on solutions found to be effective in the area of mass exoduses provided by seven Governments, five UN bodies, two UN specialized agencies, four intergovernmental bodies and two NGOs. The report also contained a compilation of information and recommendations from human rights mechanisms on problems resulting in mass exoduses or impeding voluntary return home submitted by the special rapporteurs on the human rights situations in Afghanistan, Iraq, Myanmar, Rwanda, the Sudan, the territory of the former Yugoslavia and Zaire;

the representative of the Secretary-General on internally displaced persons; the Special Rapporteur on violence against women; the Special Rapporteur on extrajudicial, summary or arbitrary executions; and the Committee on the Rights of the Child, the Committee on the Elimination of Racial Discrimination, the Human Rights Committee and the Working Group on the Right to Development.

Expressing his views on the matters referred to in the report, the Secretary-General stated that the problems of mass exoduses and their possible solutions transcended the human rights mechanisms of the UN system. He noted that the work of the Commission and the Subcommission needed a sharper focus. There was no single information-gathering system on the question and there was no single mechanism on the issue reporting to the Commission or Subcommission. The mandates of the High Commissioner for Human Rights and the representative of the Secretary-General on internally displaced persons could be amplified, but that called for commensurate resources. Activities of the human rights mechanisms should be encouraged and further developed and coordinated, with priority accorded to the systematization of early-warning information collected in the Centre for Human Rights. Again, he noted that increased resources would be necessary.

In accordance with a 1993 General Assembly request,[114] the Secretary-General, in an October report,[115] described action taken by the UN Department of Humanitarian Affairs (DHA) as focal point and facilitator of the early-warning network of new mass flows of refugees and displaced persons, noting that the project was fully operational and able to generate data on more than 100 countries. Early-warning activities were also being taken by the High Commissioner and the Centre for Human Rights. Preventive action was taken by the High Commissioner, a number of special rapporteurs and working groups and human rights treaty bodies. The Secretary-General also discussed the recommendations contained in a 1986 report of the Group of Governmental Experts on International Cooperation to Avert New Flows of Refugees[116] and the recommendations made by the Joint Inspection Unit in 1990.[117]

(For other information on refugees, see PART FOUR, Chapter XII.)

**GENERAL ASSEMBLY ACTION**

On 22 December, the General Assembly adopted **resolution 50/182**.

### Human rights and mass exoduses
*The General Assembly,*

*Deeply disturbed* by the escalating scale and magnitude of exoduses of refugees and displacements of population in many regions of the world and by the human suffering of millions of refugees and displaced persons,

*Recalling* its previous relevant resolutions, as well as those of the Commission on Human Rights, in particular Commission resolution 1995/88 of 8 March 1995, and the conclusions of the World Conference on Human Rights, which recognized that gross violations of human rights, including in armed conflicts, are among the multiple and complex factors leading to displacement of people, and the need for a comprehensive approach by the international community to address root causes and effects of movements of refugees and other displaced persons and the strengthening of emergency preparedness and response mechanisms,

*Conscious* of the fact that mass exoduses of populations are caused by multiple and complex factors, such as human rights violations, political, ethnic and economic conflicts, famine, insecurity, violence, poverty and environmental degradation, which indicate that any approach to early warning requires an intersectoral and multidisciplinary approach,

*Noting* that the Secretary-General, in his report entitled "An Agenda for Peace", identifies the protection of human rights and the promotion of economic well-being as important elements of peace, security and development,

*Noting* the continuation of the inter-agency consultations on early warning regarding new mass flows of refugees and displaced persons,

*Recognizing* the important aspects of complementarity between the system for the protection of human rights and humanitarian action, and that humanitarian agencies make an important contribution to the achievement of human rights,

*Stressing* the need for strengthening international cooperation aimed at averting new massive flows of refugees while providing durable solutions to actual refugee situations,

*Recognizing* that the human rights machinery of the United Nations, including the mechanisms of the Commission on Human Rights and the human rights treaty bodies, has important capabilities to address human rights violations that cause movements of refugees and displaced persons or prevent durable solutions to their plight,

*Recognizing also* that women and children constitute approximately 80 per cent of most refugee populations and that, in addition to the problems and needs they share with all refugees, women and girls in such circumstances are vulnerable to gender-based discrimination and gender-specific violence and exploitation,

*Reiterating* that development and rehabilitation assistance is essential in addressing some of the causes of mass exoduses and also in the context of the development of prevention strategies,

*Welcoming* the continuing efforts of the United Nations High Commissioner for Refugees to meet the protection and assistance needs of refugees and other persons of concern to her Office worldwide,

1. *Takes note* of the report of the Secretary-General;

2. *Recalls with satisfaction* its endorsement, in its resolution 41/70 of 3 December 1986, of the call upon all States to promote human rights and fundamental freedoms and to refrain from denying these to individuals in their population because of nationality, ethnicity, race, religion or language;

3. *Strongly deplores* ethnic and other forms of intolerance as one of the major causes of forced migratory movements, and urges States to take all necessary steps to ensure respect for human rights, especially the rights of persons belonging to minorities;

4. *Invites again* all Governments and intergovernmental, humanitarian and non-governmental organizations concerned to intensify their cooperation and assistance in worldwide efforts to address the serious problems resulting from mass exoduses of refugees and displaced persons and the causes of such exoduses;

5. *Encourages* States that have not already done so to consider acceding to the 1951 Convention and the 1967 Protocol relating to the Status of Refugees and to other relevant regional refugee instruments, as applicable, and relevant international human rights instruments;

6. *Notes with appreciation* the contribution made by the United Nations High Commissioner for Human Rights and the Centre for Human Rights of the Secretariat to the development of the humanitarian early-warning system of the Department of Humanitarian Affairs of the Secretariat, and takes note of ongoing consultations in this regard;

7. *Invites* the special rapporteurs, special representatives and working groups of the Commission on Human Rights and the United Nations human rights treaty bodies, acting within their mandates, to continue seeking information, where appropriate, on problems resulting in mass exoduses of populations or impeding their voluntary return home and, where appropriate, to include such information, together with recommendations thereon, in their reports and to bring such information to the attention of the United Nations High Commissioner for Human Rights, for appropriate action within his mandate, in consultation with the United Nations High Commissioner for Refugees;

8. *Requests* all United Nations bodies, including the human rights treaty bodies, the specialized agencies and governmental, intergovernmental and non-governmental organizations, to cooperate fully with all mechanisms of the Commission and, in particular, to provide them with all relevant information in their possession on the human rights situations creating or affecting refugees and displaced persons;

9. *Requests* the United Nations High Commissioner for Human Rights, in accordance with his mandate, as set out in General Assembly resolution 48/141 of 20 December 1993, and in cooperation with the United Nations High Commissioner for Refugees, to pay attention to situations that cause or threaten to cause mass exoduses and to address effectively such situations through emergency preparedness and response mechanisms, including information-sharing with United Nations early-warning mechanisms, and the provision of technical advice, expertise and cooperation;

10. *Invites* the Secretary-General to attach high priority and to make available the necessary resources within the regular budget of the United Nations for the consolidation and strengthening of emergency preparedness and response mechanisms, including early-warning activities in the humanitarian area, for the purpose of ensuring, *inter alia*, that effective action is taken to identify all multiple and complex factors, including human rights violations, that contribute to mass outflows of persons;

11. *Requests* the Secretary-General to prepare and submit to the General Assembly at its fifty-second session a report containing detailed information on the programmatic, institutional, administrative, financial and managerial efforts instituted to enhance the capacity of the United Nations to avert new flows of refugees and to tackle the root causes of such outflows;

12. *Decides* to continue its consideration of this question at its fifty-second session.

General Assembly resolution 50/182

22 December 1995     Meeting 99     Adopted without vote

Approved by Third Committee (A/50/635/Add.2) without vote, 13 December (meeting 56); 30-nation draft (A/C.3/50/L.51/Rev.1), orally revised; agenda item 112 *(b)*.

*Meeting numbers*. GA 50th session: 3rd Committee 35, 38-51, 54, 56; plenary 99.

### Population displacement

On 18 August, the Subcommission urged[118] Governments and others involved to do everything possible to cease all practices of forced displacement, population transfer and ethnic cleansing. It urged States parties to the 1951 Convention relating to the Status of Refugees[119] to safeguard and give effect to the right to seek and to enjoy in other countries asylum from persecution. It asked its inter-sessional Working Group on Minorities to examine possible solutions to problems involving minorities, issues relating to forcible displacement of populations, including threats of removal, and the return of displaced persons (see above, under ''Other aspects of intolerance'').

### Internally displaced persons

**Commission action.** On 3 March, the Human Rights Commission extended[120] the mandate of the representative of the Secretary-General on internally displaced persons and asked the Secretary-General to provide assistance in order for him to fulfil his mandate. It asked the representative to continue to submit reports annually to the General Assembly and the Commission. On 25 July, the Economic and Social Council, by **decision 1995/273**, approved all the above actions.

Calling on the High Commissioner for Human Rights, DHA, the UN High Commissioner for Refugees, the UN Development Programme, the UN Children's Fund, the UN Development Fund for Women, the International Committee of the Red Cross, the International Organization for Migration and all other humanitarian agencies to continue to cooperate with the representative, to provide him with relevant information and to assist him, the Commission encouraged the representative to continue to cooperate and coordinate with them. It also called on relevant rapporteurs, working groups, experts and the High Commissioner for Human Rights to seek information on situations that could lead to internal displacement and to include that information and recommendations thereon in their reports.

**Reports of the representative of the Secretary-General.** In accordance with a 1994 Commission resolution[121] encouraging the Secretary-General's representative on internally displaced persons, Francis Deng (Sudan), to continue his compilation and analysis of existing rules and norms relating to internal displacement, the representative, in a January report,[122] drew the attention of the Commission to a document containing two papers undertaken at his request by three institutions—the Ludwig Boltzmann Institute for Human Rights (Austria), the American Society of International Law (United States) and the International Human Rights Law Group (United States)—which were reviewed at a meeting of legal experts (Vienna, October 1994). The representative planned to present a complete version of the work in 1996.

In a February report,[123] the representative summarized his main findings since his appointment in 1992,[124] as well as the activities undertaken, the progress made, the difficulties encountered and the conclusions reached on the issue of protection and assistance for the internally displaced. He reviewed his missions to nine countries and follow-up activities to those missions, discussed the issue of legal standards, analysed relevant institutional mechanisms and capacities, and examined strategies being developed to provide better assistance and protection. He also outlined the fundamentals for a plan of action to address the protection and assistance needs of the internally displaced. He concluded that in spite of new and increased approaches to meet the needs of internally displaced persons, the challenge far exceeded the international community's response, which still remained largely ad hoc and grossly inadequate. He made a series of recommendations to address the crises of internal displacement.

In October,[125] the Secretary-General transmitted to the General Assembly an update of the representative's February report, describing his activities since then to improve the situation of internally displaced persons.

In a later report,[126] the representative described his visit to Peru (12-25 August) where the forced displacement of almost 1 million people had been the result of a 15-year armed conflict between various armed groups and the armed forces of the Government. The vast majority of the displaced were from the indigenous and native communities. The report cited the lack of personal documentation which increased the risk of arbitrary detention, false charges and forced recruitment by the armed forces, and the need to register land, provide property titles and enhance the system of adjudication of land disputes. The representative's recommendations focused on economic and social reform and pacification, enhanced cooperation between the Government and

NGOs, human rights promotion and protection at the local level, preventive strategies, increased material support from the Government, voluntary return and alternative areas of settlement, and international assistance.

GENERAL ASSEMBLY ACTION

On 22 December, the General Assembly adopted **resolution 50/195**.

### Protection of and assistance to internally displaced persons

*The General Assembly,*

*Deeply disturbed* by the growing number of internally displaced persons throughout the world who receive inadequate protection and assistance, and conscious of the serious problems this is creating for the international community,

*Recalling* the relevant norms of international human rights instruments and of international humanitarian law,

*Bearing in mind* the Vienna Declaration and Programme of Action, adopted by the World Conference on Human Rights on 25 June 1993, which calls for a comprehensive approach by the international community with regard to refugees and displaced persons,

*Reiterating its call* for a more concerted response by the international community to the needs of internally displaced persons while emphasizing that activities on their behalf must not undermine the institution of asylum,

*Conscious* of the continuing need for the United Nations system to gather information comprehensively on the issue of the protection of human rights of and assistance to internally displaced persons,

*Welcoming* the decision of the Commission on Human Rights in its resolution 1995/57 of 3 March 1995, in which it extended the mandate of the representative of the Secretary-General on internally displaced persons for another three years to continue his review of the need for protection of and assistance to internally displaced persons, including his compilation and analysis of legal norms, the root causes of internal displacement, prevention and long-term solutions,

*Noting* the progress made thus far by the representative of the Secretary-General in developing a legal framework, studying the causes and manifestations of internal displacement and analysing institutional arrangements, undertaking dialogue with Governments, issuing a series of reports on particular country situations together with proposals for remedial measures, and raising the level of awareness, at both the national and international levels, concerning the problem of internal displacement,

*Welcoming* the cooperation already established between the representative of the Secretary-General and the United Nations humanitarian assistance and development organizations engaged in protecting and assisting internally displaced persons, as well as the International Committee of the Red Cross, the International Federation of Red Cross and Red Crescent Societies and other relevant organizations,

*Welcoming in particular* the decision by the Executive Committee of the Programme of the United Nations High Commissioner for Refugees to promote further consultations with the representative of the Secretary-

General, as well as the decision by the Inter-Agency Standing Committee and its working group to invite the representative to participate in relevant meetings and in its Task Force on Internally Displaced Persons,

*Recalling* the report of the representative of the Secretary-General submitted to the Commission on Human Rights at its fifty-first session, and the conclusions and recommendations contained therein with regard to improving protection of, assistance to and development for internally displaced persons,

1. *Takes note with appreciation* of the report of the representative of the Secretary-General on internally displaced persons;

2. *Commends* the representative for the catalytic role he is playing in raising the level of consciousness about the plight of internally displaced persons;

3. *Notes* the efforts of the representative to develop a framework and to promote strategies for better protection, assistance and development for internally displaced persons;

4. *Encourages* the representative to continue his analysis of the causes of internal displacement, the needs of those displaced, measures of prevention and ways to increase protection, assistance and solutions for internally displaced persons;

5. *Also encourages* the representative to continue to pay specific attention in his review to the protection and assistance needs of women and children, bearing in mind the relevant strategic objective in the Beijing Declaration and the Platform for Action, adopted by the Fourth World Conference on Women, held at Beijing from 4 to 15 September 1995;

6. *Calls upon* the representative to continue to study the problem of internally displaced persons and to invite, with the approval of Governments, specialists and consultants to contribute expert assistance during missions and to make use of research facilities;

7. *Invites* the representative to finalize his compilation and analysis of existing legal norms for inclusion in his report to the Commission on Human Rights at its fifty-second session;

8. *Calls upon* the Commission on Human Rights to consider the question of establishing a framework in this regard on the basis of the report of the representative and the recommendations contained therein;

9. *Calls upon* all Governments to continue to facilitate the activities of the representative, encourages them to give serious consideration to inviting the representative to visit their countries so as to enable him to study and analyse more fully the issues involved, and thanks those Governments which have already done so;

10. *Invites* Governments to give due consideration, in dialogue with the representative, to the recommendations and suggestions made to them by him, in accordance with his mandate, and to inform him of measures taken thereon;

11. *Urges* all relevant United Nations humanitarian assistance and development organizations concerned to establish frameworks of cooperation with the representative so as to provide all possible assistance and support to him in the implementation of his programme of activities, and invites the representative to report thereon;

12. *Calls upon* the representative and regional intergovernmental organizations, such as the Organization of African Unity, the Organization of American States

and the Organization for Security and Cooperation in Europe, to intensify their cooperation with a view to encouraging their undertaking initiatives to facilitate assistance to and protection of internally displaced persons;

13. *Requests* the Secretary-General to give all necessary assistance to the representative to carry out his mandate effectively;

14. *Decides* to continue its consideration of this question at its fifty-second session.

General Assembly resolution 50/195

22 December 1995     Meeting 99     Adopted without vote

Approved by Third Committee (A/50/635/Add.3) without vote, 13 December (meeting 56); 56-nation draft (A/C.3/50/L.54), orally revised; agenda item 112 *(c)*.

*Meeting numbers.* GA 50th session: 3rd Committee 35, 38-51, 54, 56; plenary 99.

### Population transfer

In a June note,[127] the Secretary-General stated that the Special Rapporteur on the human rights dimensions of population transfer, including the implantation of settlers and settlements, Awn Shawkat Al-Khasawneh (Jordan), was unable to submit in 1995 a final report as the Subcommission had requested in 1994.[42]

On 24 August,[128] the Subcommission, recalling its request for a final report in 1995 and bearing in mind that the Special Rapporteur had not been in a position to provide that report, asked him to report in 1996.

### Disappearance of persons

#### Working Group on Enforced or Involuntary Disappearances

On 3 March, the Commission extended[129] for a three-year period the mandate of the five-member Working Group on Enforced or Involuntary Disappearances, established in 1980,[130] to enable it to consider information concerning such disappearances. It asked the Group to pay particular attention to cases of children subjected to enforced disappearance and children of disappeared persons and to cooperate closely with the Governments concerned to search for and identify those children. It urged Governments to take action concerning communications of alleged enforced disappearances transmitted to them by the Group, and to assist the Group, in particular by replying to its requests for information. It also urged them to intensify cooperation with the Group on any action taken pursuant to recommendations addressed to them; to take steps to protect the families of disappeared persons against any instances of intimidation or ill-treatment to which they might be subjected; and to take steps to ensure that, when a state of emergency was introduced, the protection of human rights was guaranteed, particularly regarding the prevention of enforced disappearances. The Commission invited States to implement the principles of the 1992 Declaration on the Protection of All Persons from Enforced Disappearance.[131] It asked the Group to report in 1996. The Secretary-General was requested to ensure that the Group received all the assistance it needed and to keep the Group and the Commission informed of the steps he had taken to promote the Declaration.

The Economic and Social Council on 25 July, by **decision 1995/266**, approved the extension of the Working Group's mandate and the request to the Secretary-General for assistance.

**Working Group activities.** The Working Group on Enforced or Involuntary Disappearances held three sessions in 1995: its forty-fifth in New York (5-9 June) and its forty-sixth and forty-seventh in Geneva (21-25 August, 13-17 November).[132] The Group examined information on enforced or involuntary disappearances received from Governments and NGOs and decided on the transmission of the reports or observations received thereon to the Governments concerned. It also requested Governments to provide complementary information whenever necessary to clarify cases.

In 1995, the total number of cases worldwide under active consideration stood at 43,508. Of the 824 newly reported cases transmitted to the Governments concerned, some 359 were reported to have occurred in 1995. The Group also transmitted to Governments 163 cases under its urgent-action procedure, of which 39 were clarified during the year.

The Group concluded that acts of enforced disappearance had spread to all regions and must be considered a worldwide phenomenon, occurring mainly in situations of internal armed conflict and ethnic strife. It noted that more and more Governments were cooperating with it in its efforts to deal with the problem. However, progress in the domestic implementation of the Declaration on the Protection of All Persons from Enforced Disappearance seemed to be extremely slow, with only a few countries enacting special legislation to make acts of enforced disappearance a specific offence under criminal law and to implement other provisions. The Group urgently called on the Commission to allocate more resources for its work.

#### Missing persons in the former Yugoslavia

As proposed by a Working Group member in 1993[133] and requested by the Commission on Human Rights in 1994,[134] a special process was established on missing persons in the territory of the former Yugoslavia as a joint mandate of the Special Rapporteur on the situation of human rights in that territory and a member of the Working Group. The process dealt with all cases of missing persons, regardless of whether the victim was a civilian or a combatant or whether the perpetrators were connected to the Government or not.

**Commission action.** On 3 March, the Commission commended and thanked[135] the Group's expert member for his first report, submitted in 1994, on the special process on missing persons in the territory of the former Yugoslavia.[136] It asked the Governments of Bosnia and Herzegovina and of Croatia to continue and extend cooperation with the special process and invited them, as well as other parties in a position to help, to continue searching for those missing on their territory. It urged the Government of the Federal Republic of Yugoslavia (Serbia and Montenegro) to allow the expert member to visit Belgrade to discuss cooperation, and to cooperate by disclosing all relevant available information and documentation.

The Commission requested: the expert member to report in 1996; UN bodies, including the Office of the UN High Commissioner for Refugees and the UN Protection Force, the International Committee of the Red Cross and national Red Cross and Red Crescent societies to continue their cooperation with the special process; and the Secretary-General to continue to provide the resources needed to the special process. The Commission's requests were approved by Economic and Social Council **decision 1995/264** of 25 July. (For further details, see next chapter.)

### Torture and cruel treatment

**Report of the Special Rapporteur.** In January, Special Rapporteur Nigel S. Rodley (United Kingdom) reported to the Commission on questions relevant to torture.[137] He made urgent appeals on behalf of persons who were allegedly being tortured or about whom fears were expressed that they might be. He transmitted 144 urgent appeals to 45 Governments concerning some 716 individuals. Details on the contents of those appeals and of government replies were given in the report. The Special Rapporteur recommended that countries not party to the 1984 Convention against Torture and Other Cruel, Inhuman or Degrading Treatment or Punishment[138] sign and ratify or accede to it (for details, see preceding chapter).

He further recommended: abolishing secret places of detention; regular inspection of places of detention; making illegal incommunicado detention and releasing without delay persons held incommunicado; granting persons under administrative detention the same degree of protection as those under criminal detention; permitting all detainees the ability to challenge the lawfulness of detention through habeas corpus or *amparo*; compensation to victims of torture or to their relatives; providing training courses and manuals to police and security personnel and assistance, on request,

by the UN programme of advisory services and technical assistance; enforcing strict measures against medical personnel that played a role in torture; and prohibiting the return, expulsion or extradition of a person to another State where there were grounds for believing that the individual would be in danger of being subjected to torture.

The Special Rapporteur visited Chile (21-26 August) to collect first-hand information to enable him to evaluate better the situation regarding the practice of torture.[139]

**Commission action.** On 3 March, the Human Rights Commission, commending the Special Rapporteur for his report, stressed[140] the recommendations made by him. It asked him to examine questions concerning torture directed against women and children and conditions conducive to such torture and to make recommendations to prevent those acts. The Commission extended the Special Rapporteur's mandate for three years, while maintaining the annual reporting cycle; it requested him to report in 1996. By **decision 1995/265** of 25 July, the Economic and Social Council approved the Commission's decision to extend the mandate and requested the Secretary-General to assist the Special Rapporteur.

### Voluntary Fund for torture victims

On 3 March, the Commission on Human Rights appealed[141] to Governments, organizations and individuals to contribute to the UN Voluntary Fund for Victims of Torture, which had been established in 1981.[142] It asked the Secretary-General to: transmit to Governments its appeals for contributions; assist the Fund's Board of Trustees to make the Fund and its humanitarian work better known and in its appeal for contributions; continue to include the Fund among the programmes for which funds were pledged at the UN Pledging Conference for Development Activities; ensure the provision of adequate staff and technical equipment to operate the Fund; and inform the Commission annually of the Fund's operations. The Commission called on the Board of Trustees to report in 1996 on the increasing need for overall rehabilitation services for torture victims.

In his annual report to the General Assembly on the status of the Fund,[143] the Secretary-General noted that the total amount available to the Board of Trustees in May 1995 for grants to projects to assist victims of torture came to $2.7 million, some $1 million less than in 1994. Following the fourteenth session of the Board of Trustees (Geneva, 15-24 May), the Secretary-General approved its recommendations regarding grants totalling $2.7 million to 104 projects submitted by 93 humanitarian organizations. Projects focused on supporting programmes providing direct medical, psychological, social and other assistance to torture victims and their families. Requests for assistance totalling $5.7 million had been received.

By November, 16 States had contributed or pledged $1,289,565 to the Fund for the year.[144]

### Anti-personnel land-mines

On 24 August, by 16 votes to 2, with 2 abstentions, the Subcommission requested[145] Governments and the international community to pursue a policy of information, prevention, rehabilitation and reintegration for victims of anti-personnel mines and to take economic and social measures necessary for that purpose. It called on States to participate actively in the conference to review the 1980 Convention on Prohibitions or Restrictions on the Use of Certain Conventional Weapons Which May Be Deemed to Be Excessively Injurious or to Have Indiscriminate Effects and the Protocols thereto[146] with a view to strengthening the instrument and giving it universal scope. The Subcommission asked the Secretary-General to transmit to Governments its appeal for voluntary contributions to the mine-clearance programme and to the Voluntary Trust Fund for Assistance in Mine Clearance, established in 1994,[147] and to transmit its resolution to the 1995 Review Conference of the States Parties to the Convention (see PART ONE, Chapter II).

*REFERENCES*

[1]E/1995/23 (res. 1995/4). [2]Ibid. (res. 1995/7). [3]Ibid. (res. 1995/6). [4]Ibid. (res. 1995/5). [5]A/50/485. [6]YUN 1994, p. 1013. [7]E/CN.4/1995/28. [8]YUN 1994, p. 616. [9]YUN 1993, p. 521. [10]Ibid., p. 523. [11]YUN 1994, p. 614. [12]E/CN.4/1996/2 (res. 1995/2). [13]YUN 1994, p. 199. [14]Ibid., p. 198, SC res. 907(1994), 29 Mar. 1994. [15]Ibid., p. 200. [16]GA res. 44/34, annex, 4 Dec. 1989. [17]YUN 1994, p. 1014, GA res. 49/150, 23 Dec. 1994. [18]A/50/390. [19]YUN 1994, p. 1014. [20]A/50/390/Add.1. [21]E/CN.4/1996/27. [22]YUN 1994, p. 1062, GA res. 49/190, 23 Dec. 1994. [23]A/50/736. [24]YUN 1991, p. 588, GA res. 46/137, 17 Dec. 1991. [25]YUN 1994, p. 1064, GA res. 49/180, 23 Dec. 1994. [26]A/50/495. [27]E/1995/23 (res. 1995/74). [28]Ibid. (res. 1995/70). [29]Ibid. (res. 1995/72). [30]Ibid. (res. 1995/8 & 1995/9). [31]Ibid. (res. 1995/52). [32]Ibid. (res. 1995/7). [33]Ibid. (res. 1995/69). [34]Ibid. (res. 1995/60). [35]YUN 1994, p. 251, GA res. 49/30, 7 Dec. 1994. [36]E/CN.4/Sub.2/1995/49. [37]E/CN.4/1996/2 (dec. 1995/116). [38]E/CN.4/1995/32. [39]YUN 1948-49, p. 535, GA res. 217 A (III), 10 Dec. 1948. [40]YUN 1966, p. 423, GA res. 2200 A (XXI), annex, 16 Dec. 1966. [41]E/1995/23 (res. 1995/40). [42]YUN 1994, p. 1028. [43]E/CN.4/1995/99 & Add.1. [44]YUN 1993, p. 888. [45]E/1995/23 (res. 1995/83). [46]Ibid. (res. 1995/41). [47]YUN 1994, p. 1015. [48]E/CN.4/1995/30. [49]YUN 1994, p. 1054. [50]E/CN.4/Sub.2/1995/16 & Corr.1. [51]E/CN.4/1996/2 (dec. 1995/117). [52]YUN 1992, p. 744, GA res. 47/133, 18 Dec. 1992. [53]YUN 1992, p. 738. [54]E/1995/23 (res. 1995/34). [55]YUN 1993, p. 962. [56]E/CN.4/Sub.2/1995/17 & Add.1,2. [57]E/CN.4/1996/2 (dec. 1995/103). [58]E/1995/23 (res. 1995/54). [59]A/50/653. [60]E/CN.4/Sub.2/1995/18. [61]E/CN.4/1996/2 (res. 1995/35). [62]E/CN.4/Sub.2/1995/19. [63]E/CN.4/1996/2 (res. 1995/34). [64]E/CN.4/1995/39. [65]E/1995/23 (res. 1995/36). [66]Ibid. (dec. 1995/110). [67]YUN 1994, p. 1029. [68]YUN 1985, p. 747, GA res. 40/33, annex, 29 Nov. 1985. [69]GA res. 45/112, annex, 14 Dec. 1990. [70]GA res. 45/113, annex, 14 Dec. 1990. [71]E/CN.4/Sub.2/1995/21. [72]YUN 1994, p. 1020. [73]E/CN.4/Sub.2/1995/30

& Add.1. [74]E/CN.4/1995/40. [75]YUN 1994, p. 1289, GA res. 49/59, annex, 9 Dec. 1994. [76]E/1995/23 (res. 1995/39). [77]YUN 1992, p. 739. [78]ESC res. 1990/29 & 1990/51, 24 May & 24 July 1990. [79]E/1995/78 & Add.1 & Add.1/Corr.1. [80]E/1995/23 (res. 1995/43). [81]YUN 1994, p. 1112, GA res. 49/185, 23 Dec. 1994. [82]Ibid., p. 1112. [83]A/50/685. [84]E/1995/23 (res. 1995/42). [85]YUN 1994, p. 1011. [86]E/1995/23 (res. 1995/22). [87]E/CN.4/Sub.2/1995/20 & Corr.1. [88]YUN 1987, p. 741. [89]YUN 1988, p. 499. [90]E/CN.4/Sub.2/1989/30/Rev.2. [91]YUN 1991, p. 545. [92]YUN 1992, p. 727. [93]YUN 1993, p. 871. [94]E/CN.4/1996/30. [95]E/CN.4/Sub.2/1995/20/Add.1. [96]E/CN.4/1996/2 (res. 1995/33). [97]E/1995/23 (res. 1995/29). [98]E/CN.4/Sub.2/1991/55. [99]YUN 1994, p. 1068. [100]E/1995/23 (dec. 1995/107). [101]Ibid. (res. 1995/59). [102]E/CN.4/1996/40. [103]E/CN.4/1996/40/Add.1. [104]E/CN.4/1995/61. [105]YUN 1994, p. 1021. [106]YUN 1993, p. 908. [107]E/CN.4/1996/4/Add.1. [108]YUN 1993, p. 262. [109]E/CN.4/1996/4/Add.2. [110]E/1995/23 (res. 1995/73). [111]Ibid. (res. 1995/88). [112]YUN 1994, p. 1111. [113]E/CN.4/1995/49. [114]YUN 1993, p. 960, GA res. 48/139, 20 Dec. 1993. [115]A/50/566. [116]YUN 1986, p. 851. [117]A/45/649 & Corr.1. [118]E/CN.4/1996/2 (res. 1995/13). [119]YUN 1951, p. 520. [120]E/1995/23 (res. 1995/57). [121]YUN 1994, p. 1067. [122]E/CN.4/1995/50/Add.3. [123]E/CN.4/1995/50. [124]YUN 1992, p. 777. [125]A/50/558. [126]E/CN.4/1996/52/Add.1. [127]E/CN.4/Sub.2/1995/35. [128]E/CN.4/1996/2 (dec. 1995/111). [129]E/1995/23 (res. 1995/38). [130]YUN 1980, p. 843. [131]YUN 1992, p. 744, GA res. 47/133, 18 Dec. 1992. [132]E/CN.4/1996/38 & Corr.1. [133]YUN 1993, p. 884. [134]YUN 1994, p. 1096. [135]E/1995/23 (res. 1995/35). [136]YUN 1994, p. 1025. [137]E/CN.4/1995/34. [138]YUN 1984, p. 813, GA res. 39/46, annex, 10 Dec. 1984. [139]E/CN.4/1996/35/Add.2. [140]E/1995/23 (res. 1995/37 B). [141]E/1995/23 (res. 1995/37 A). [142]YUN 1981, p. 906, GA res. 36/151, 16 Dec. 1981. [143]A/50/512. [144]E/CN.4/1995/33 & Add.1, E/CN.4/1996/33. [145]E/CN.4/1996/2 (res. 1995/24). [146]YUN 1980, p. 76. [147]YUN 1994, p. 173, GA res. 49/215, 23 Dec. 1994.

# Economic, social and cultural rights

## Right to development

**Commission action.** On 24 February, by a roll-call vote of 36 to 15, with 1 abstention, the Human Rights Commission welcomed[1] the efforts made by the Working Group on the Right to Development at its 1994 sessions,[2] which were oriented towards establishing a permanent evaluation mechanism to follow up the implementation of the 1986 Declaration on the Right to Development.[3] It asked the Secretary-General to take steps to implement the Group's recommendations, particularly by providing the Centre for Human Rights with a focal unit to follow up on the Declaration and its implementation. The Commission urged him to take measures to disseminate the Declaration's provisions and the Group's work. It decided that the Group would hold two 2-week sessions, in April and September 1995, and urged the Group to continue to identify ways and to suggest further measures to promote an economic environment more responsive to the needs of developing countries, particularly the least developed.

The Commission decided that the Group's reports, along with other documentation relating to development, should be made available to the General Assembly in the context of the celebration of the fiftieth anniversary of the United Nations. The High Commissioner for Human Rights was asked to continue to promote the implementation of the right to development and the 1986 Declaration by working closely with the Group and making recommendations for enhancing the support of relevant bodies of the UN system.

The Commission recommended that the Economic and Social Council dedicate the high-level segment of one of its substantive sessions to evaluating the implementation of the Declaration within the United Nations. It asked that the Council continue to consider the implementation of the Declaration's provisions at its 1995 substantive session, and recommended that the realization of the right to development be reflected adequately in the work and the final outcome of the 1995 World Summit for Social Development (see PART FOUR, Chapter IX). Consideration should be given to including the topic on the agenda of other UN conferences. The Centre for Human Rights was called on to make the right to development a subprogramme of its 1992-1997 programme of activities and of its future activities. The Secretary-General was asked to report in 1996 on the implementation of the Commission's resolution.

### ECONOMIC AND SOCIAL COUNCIL ACTION

In July, the Economic and Social Council adopted **decision 1995/258**.

#### The right to development

At its 52nd plenary meeting, on 25 July 1995, the Economic and Social Council, taking note of Commission on Human Rights resolution 1995/17 of 24 February 1995:

*(a)* Approved the Commission's request to the Secretary-General to take steps to implement the recommendations made by the Working Group on the Right to Development at its second and third sessions, particularly by providing the Centre for Human Rights of the Secretariat with a focal unit with the specific task of following up on the Declaration on the Right to Development and its implementation;

*(b)* Approved the Commission's decision that the Working Group would hold two sessions, each for a two-week period, in April and September 1995 respectively, to formulate its recommendations for submission to the Commission at its fifty-second session;

*(c)* Approved the Commission's request to the Council to continue to consider the question of the implementation of the provisions of the Declaration on the Right to Development under the item entitled "Human rights questions";

*(d)* Reiterated the Commission's request to the Secretary-General to ensure that the Working Group would be granted all the necessary assistance, in particular human and financial resources, to carry out its mandate.

Economic and Social Council decision 1995/258

30-8-11 (roll-call vote)

Draft by Commission on Human Rights (E/1995/23); agenda item 5 *(d)*.
*Meeting numbers.* ESC 51, 52.

Roll-call vote in Council as follows:

*In favour:* Bahamas, Bhutan, Brazil, Chile, China, Colombia, Costa Rica, Côte d'Ivoire, Cuba, Egypt, Gabon, Ghana, India, Indonesia, Jamaica, Libyan Arab Jamahiriya, Malaysia, Mexico, Nigeria, Pakistan, Philippines, Senegal, South Africa, Sri Lanka, Sudan, Thailand, Uganda, United Republic of Tanzania, Venezuela, Zimbabwe.

*Against:* Canada, Germany, Japan, Poland, Russian Federation, Ukraine, United Kingdom, United States.

*Abstaining:* Australia, Bulgaria, Denmark, France, Greece, Ireland, Luxembourg, Netherlands, Norway, Portugal, Romania.

**Working Group activities.** In 1995, the Working Group on the Right to Development held its fourth (15-26 May)[4] and fifth (27 September-6 October)[5] sessions, both in Geneva.

In May, the 15-member Working Group discussed the implementation of the 1986 Declaration by Governments, and contributions to its implementation by treaty-monitoring bodies, regional commissions, and world conferences and summits. It exchanged views on: obstacles to the realization of the right to development and ways to eliminate them; the need to encourage Member States, UN bodies and organs and NGOs to incorporate the right to development in their programmes; the need to establish a follow-up mechanism for the realization of the right to development; and the need for recommendations for the realization of that right at the local level. The Group had before it two April reports of the Secretary-General, presenting the views of five Governments[6] and one NGO[7] on obstacles to the implementation and realization of the Declaration.

At its September/October session, the Group considered the scope and implications of the Declaration and obstacles to its implementation. Recommendations to eliminate those obstacles included, among others: disseminating the Declaration and establishing a programme for that purpose within the Centre for Human Rights; encouraging Governments to send voluntarily periodic reports on the Declaration's application and to appoint existing administrative units or to create such units to serve as focal points for collecting, receiving and disseminating information on the application of the Declaration; and activities by NGOs. It made recommendations for action by human rights treaty-monitoring bodies, the UN system, intergovernmental organizations, the Economic and Social Council, the Commission on Human Rights, the Centre for Human Rights and the High Commissioner for Human Rights. As to the realization of the right to development, the Group proposed that the Commission set up a group of experts to make recommendations on a long-term strategy. It recommended according priority to the adoption of national and international measures that would include the creation of domestic and international conditions conducive to the realization of the right to development.

**Subcommission action.** On 24 August, the Subcommission drew the attention[14] of Member States to the importance of organizing a world summit on humanitarian assistance, in order to strengthen their development and to coordinate better their action in that area. The Subcommission recommended that the Commission authorize it to appoint a special rapporteur on the question of the implications for human rights of UN action under the Charter, including humanitarian assistance, in addressing international humanitarian problems and in the promotion and protection of human rights.

**Reports of the Secretary-General.** In January, the Secretary-General reported[8] on the implementation of a 1994 Commission resolution[2] concerning the right to development. He also drew to the attention of Commission members[9] a 1994 document[10] on the implementation of the Declaration, as requested by the General Assembly.[11]

By a note of 7 November,[12] the Secretary-General drew to the attention of the General Assembly the reports of the Working Group on the Right to Development on its first (1993),[13] second and third (1994),[2] and fourth and fifth (1995) sessions (see above). He also drew to the Assembly's attention his report covering the right to an adequate standard of living (see below).

GENERAL ASSEMBLY ACTION

On 22 December, the General Assembly adopted **resolution 50/184**.

### Right to development

*The General Assembly,*

*Reaffirming* the Declaration on the Right to Development, which it proclaimed at its forty-first session,

*Recalling* its resolutions 45/97 of 14 December 1990, 46/123 of 17 December 1991, 47/123 of 18 December 1992, 48/130 of 20 December 1993 and 49/183 of 23 December 1994 and those of the Commission on Human Rights relating to the right to development, and taking note of Commission resolution 1995/17 of 24 February 1995,

*Recalling also* the report on the Global Consultation on the Realization of the Right to Development as a Human Right,

*Recalling further* the principles proclaimed in the Rio Declaration on Environment and Development of 14 June 1992,

*Mindful* that the Commission on Human Rights continues to consider this matter, which is directed towards the implementation and further enhancement of the right to development,

*Noting* the need for coordination and cooperation throughout the United Nations system for a more effective promotion of the right to development,

*Recognizing* that the United Nations High Commissioner for Human Rights and the Centre for Human Rights of the Secretariat have important roles to play in the promotion and protection of the right to development,

*Reaffirming* the need for action at the national and international levels by all States to realize all human rights, and the need for relevant evaluation mechanisms to ensure the promotion, encouragement and reinforcement of the principles contained in the Declaration on the Right to Development,

*Welcoming* the Vienna Declaration and Programme of Action, adopted by the World Conference on Human Rights on 25 June 1993, which reaffirms the right to development as a universal and inalienable right and an integral part of all fundamental human rights and reaffirms that the human person is the central subject of development,

*Recalling* that the Vienna Declaration and Programme of Action examined the relationship between democracy, development and human rights, and recognizing the importance of creating a favourable environment in which everyone may enjoy their human rights as set out in the Vienna Declaration and Programme of Action,

*Recalling also* that lasting progress towards the implementation of the right to development requires effective development policies at the national level, as well as equitable economic relations and a favourable economic environment at the international level,

*Recalling further* that, in order to promote development, equal attention and urgent consideration should be given to the implementation, promotion and protection of civil, political, economic, social and cultural rights, and recognizing that all human rights are universal, indivisible, interdependent and interrelated and that the universality, objectivity, impartiality and non-selectivity of the consideration of human rights issues must be ensured,

*Noting* that aspects of the Programme of Action of the International Conference on Population and Development, the Copenhagen Declaration on Social Development and the Programme of Action of the World Summit for Social Development, adopted by the World Summit on 12 March 1995, and the Beijing Declaration and the Platform for Action, adopted by the Fourth World Conference on Women on 15 September 1995, are relevant to the universal realization of the right to development,

*Welcoming* the convening of the United Nations Conference on Human Settlements (Habitat II) in 1996, and affirming that this Conference constitutes another important international step towards the realization of the right to development, within the context of promoting and protecting all human rights,

*Taking note* of the work of the Working Group on the Right to Development during its fourth and fifth sessions, held at Geneva from 15 to 26 May and from 27 September to 6 October 1995,

*Having considered* the note by the Secretary-General, prepared pursuant to General Assembly resolution 49/183,

1. *Reaffirms* the importance of the right to development for every human person and all peoples in all countries, in particular the developing countries, as an integral part of fundamental human rights;

2. *Takes note* of the note by the Secretary-General;

3. *Requests* the Secretary-General to submit to the Commission on Human Rights at its fifty-second session a report on the implementation of Commission resolution 1995/17;

4. *Calls upon* the Commission on Human Rights to consider carefully the reports of the Working Group on the Right to Development, to assess whether the Working Group has been able to complete its mandate and to consider thoroughly the necessity to reconvene the Working Group;

5. *Also requests* the Secretary-General to continue coordination of the various activities with regard to the implementation of the Declaration on the Right to Development;

6. *Further requests* the Secretary-General to ask the Centre for Human Rights of the Secretariat to provide a programmatic follow-up on the implementation of the Declaration on the Right to Development, as part of the efforts to implement the Vienna Declaration and Programme of Action;

7. *Requests* the United Nations High Commissioner for Human Rights, within his mandate, to continue to take steps for the promotion and protection of the right to development by, *inter alia*, working in conjunction with the Centre for Human Rights and drawing on the expertise of the funds, programmes and specialized agencies of the United Nations system related to the field of development;

8. *Supports* the current initiatives of the United Nations High Commissioner for Human Rights, within his mandate, to consult with all relevant bodies, funds, programmes and specialized agencies of the United Nations system on how they may promote the right to development;

9. *Invites* the regional commissions and regional intergovernmental organizations to consider how they may contribute to the realization of the right to development, including through convening meetings of governmental experts and representative non-governmental and grass-roots organizations for the purpose of seeking arrangements or agreements for the implementation of the Declaration on the Right to Development through international cooperation;

10. *Requests* the Secretary-General to inform the Commission on Human Rights at its fifty-second session and the General Assembly at its fifty-first session of the activities of the organizations, funds, programmes and specialized agencies of the United Nations system for the implementation of the Declaration on the Right to Development;

11. *Calls upon* the Commission on Human Rights to continue to make proposals to the General Assembly, through the Economic and Social Council, on the future course of action on the question, in particular on practical measures for the implementation and enhancement of the Declaration on the Right to Development, taking into account the conclusions and recommendations of the Global Consultation on the Realization of the Right to Development as a Human Right and the reports of the Working Group on the Right to Development;

12. *Reiterates its commitment* to implementing the results of the World Conference on Human Rights, which reaffirm that all human rights are universal, indivisible, interdependent and interrelated and that democracy, development and respect for human rights and fundamental freedoms are interdependent and mutually reinforcing;

13. *Calls upon* all States to address, within the declarations and programmes of action adopted by the relevant international conferences convened by the United Nations, the elements for the promotion and protection of the principles of the right to development, as set out in the Declaration on the Right to Development;

14. *Decides* to consider this question at its fifty-first session under the sub-item entitled "Human rights questions, including alternative approaches for improving the effective enjoyment of human rights and fundamental freedoms".

General Assembly resolution 50/184

22 December 1995     Meeting 99     Adopted without vote

Approved by Third Committee (A/50/635/Add.2) without vote, 13 December (meeting 55); draft by 26 nations and Non-Aligned Movement (A/C.3/50/L.57); agenda item 112 *(b)*.

*Meeting numbers.* GA 50th session: 3rd Committee 35, 38-51, 53, 55; plenary 99.

## Effects of debt on living standards

**Reports of the Secretary-General.** In a January report,[15] the Secretary-General summarized comments and proposals on measures to be implemented to find a durable solution to the debt crisis of developing countries so that they might fully enjoy all human rights. These had been provided by 16 Governments, five UN specialized agencies, one intergovernmental organization and 16 NGOs.

In July, the Secretary-General presented a preliminary set of basic policy guidelines to be applied to structural adjustment programmes.[16] Policy guidelines at the national level dealt with popular participation and equality of opportunity and access to productive resources and to social services. At the international level, they concerned external pressure or intervention in the internal or external affairs of a State, the availability of external resources, foreign debt, external trade, transnational corporations, development assistance, adjustment in developed countries, military expenditure and international institutions.

**Commission action.** On 24 February, the Commission, by a roll-call vote of 33 to 15, with 4 abstentions, asked[17] the Working Group on the Right to Development to continue to pay attention to the social repercussions of the policies adopted to face situations of external debt on the enjoyment of economic, social and cultural rights and to make recommendations thereon. Recognizing that there was a need for more transparency in the activities of international financial institutions, it asked those institutions to report periodically to the General Assembly and the Economic and Social Council on the social repercussions of their policies on the full enjoyment of economic, social and cultural rights in developing countries. The High Commissioner for Human Rights was asked to pay particular attention to the problem of the debt burden of developing countries.

The Commission requested the Secretary-General to recommend ways to carry out a political dialogue between creditor and debtor countries in the UN system, based on the principle of shared responsibility, and to report in 1996. It also asked him to establish a programme unit in the Centre for Human Rights for the promotion of economic, social and cultural rights, particularly those related to the debt burden of developing countries and the implementation of the right to development.

ECONOMIC AND SOCIAL COUNCIL ACTION

In July, the Economic and Social Council adopted **decision 1995/256**.

**Effects on the full enjoyment of human rights of the economic adjustment policies arising from foreign debt and, in particular, of the implementation of the Declaration on the Right to Development**

At its 52nd plenary meeting, on 25 July 1995, the Economic and Social Council, taking note of Commission on Human Rights resolution 1995/13 of 24 February 1995, approved the Commission's request to the Secretary-General to establish a programme unit in the Centre for Human Rights of the Secretariat for the promotion of economic, social and cultural rights, in particular those related to the debt burden of developing countries and the implementation of the right to development.

Economic and Social Council decision 1995/256

31-18-1 (roll-call vote)

Draft by Commission on Human Rights (E/1995/23); agenda item 5 *(d)*.
*Meeting numbers.* ESC 51, 52.

Roll-call vote in Council as follows:

*In favour:* Bahamas, Bhutan, Brazil, Chile, China, Colombia, Costa Rica, Côte d'Ivoire, Cuba, Egypt, Gabon, Ghana, India, Indonesia, Jamaica, Libyan Arab Jamahiriya, Malaysia, Mexico, Nigeria, Pakistan, Philippines, Republic of Korea, Senegal, South Africa, Sri Lanka, Sudan, Thailand, Uganda, United Republic of Tanzania, Venezuela, Zimbabwe.

*Against:* Australia, Canada, Denmark, France, Germany, Greece, Ireland, Japan, Luxembourg, Netherlands, Norway, Poland, Portugal, Romania, Russian Federation, Ukraine, United Kingdom, United States.

*Abstaining:* Bulgaria.

**Subcommission action.** On 24 August, the Subcommission asked[18] the Commission to authorize an open-ended working group to meet for one week prior to its 1997 session to elaborate policy guidelines, in close cooperation with the Committee on Economic, Social and Cultural Rights, based on the preliminary set of policy guidelines on structural adjustment programmes and economic, social and cultural rights contained in the Secretary-General's report. It requested the Commission to ask the Secretary-General to invite Governments, intergovernmental organizations and NGOs, as well as the Committee, to contribute to the draft policy guidelines by providing their comments thereon for consideration by the working group. The Subcommission recommended that the Commission consider the matter in 1996.

### Income distribution

**Commission action.** On 24 February, the Commission, endorsing a 1994 Subcommission resolution,[19] approved[20] the decision to appoint José Bengoa (Chile) as Special Rapporteur on the relationship between the enjoyment of human rights, in particular economic, social and cultural rights, and income distribution, at national and international levels, and approved the request that he submit a preliminary report in 1995, a progress report in 1996 and a final report in 1997.

On 25 July, by **decision 1995/295**, the Economic and Social Council endorsed those approvals.

**Report of the Special Rapporteur.** In a preliminary report,[21] submitted in July, the Special Rapporteur stated that the right to life, to the development of the human body and to individual dignity was the foundation of civil and political rights and of economic, social and cultural rights. He noted that economic, social and cultural rights constituted the necessary minimum to guarantee the effective exercise of civil and political rights. The Special Rapporteur pointed to the growing globalization of the economy and world society as giving rise to increasing integration which tended to give universal bearing to minimum requirements in respect of both economic, social and cultural rights and civil and political rights. Income distribution, he stated, was the principal indicator of social integration and of the fulfilment of minimum requirements in respect of economic, social and cultural rights, enabling human beings to live in society. The Special Rapporteur also discussed the relationship between the enjoyment of human rights and income distribution at the international level, and presented a work plan.

**Subcommission action.** On 24 August, the Subcommission endorsed[22] the conclusion established by Asbjorn Eide (Norway), in a preparatory document he had prepared in 1994 at the request of the Commission on Human Rights,[19] and repeated by Special Rapporteur Bengoa that the concentration of wealth constituted a serious obstacle to the realization of human rights and that equality of opportunity was essential for participating effectively in the development process and for obtaining a share of the benefits deriving from it. It expressed its agreement with the work plan presented in the preliminary report and asked the Special Rapporteur to pay particular attention to the impact of the enjoyment of human rights, and that of the right to education in particular, on income distribution. It also asked him to take special care to analyse the indicators needed for the gradual full satisfaction of economic, social and cultural rights and to submit a progress report in 1996 and a final one in 1997. The Secretary-General was asked to invite Governments, UN bodies and specialized agencies, intergovernmental organizations and NGOs to provide the Special Rapporteur with information for the preparation of his report.

## Transnational corporations

**Report of the Secretary-General.** As requested by the Subcommission in 1994,[23] the Secretary-General submitted in July a report[24] examining the relationship between the enjoyment of human rights, in particular international labour and trade union rights, and the working methods and activities of transnational corporations (TNCs). He described the working methods and activities of TNCs and the human rights that might be affected by those practices, which included the rights: of peoples to self-determination and to permanent sovereignty over their natural wealth and resources; to development; of everyone to a standard of living adequate for the health and well-being of himself and his family and to the continuous improvement of living conditions; of everyone to the enjoyment of the highest attainable standard of physical and mental health; to full and productive employment; of everyone to the enjoyment of just and favourable conditions of work; to form and join trade unions, to strike and to bargain collectively; of everyone to social security; of everyone to enjoy the benefits of scientific progress and its applications; and of everyone to a social and international order.

**Subcommission action.** On 24 August, the Subcommission asked[25] the Secretary-General to prepare for its 1996 session a report on the impact of the activities and working methods of TNCs on the full enjoyment of all human rights, in particular economic, social and cultural rights and the right to development, bearing in mind existing international guidelines, rules and standards relating to the subject. It also asked him to invite Governments, intergovernmental organizations and NGOs to submit information on the topic for consideration in the preparation of his report.

## Unilateral coercive measures

**Report of the Secretary-General.** As requested by the Commission on Human Rights in 1994,[26] the Secretary-General in January reported[27] on coercive measures unilaterally implemented against developing countries, on the basis of the views of eight Governments, one UN body and three NGOs.

**Commission action.** By a roll-call vote of 24 to 17, with 12 abstentions, the Human Rights Commission, on 3 March, expressing grave concern that the use of unilateral coercive measures adversely affected the socio-humanitarian activities of developing countries, called on[28] the international community to reject the use by certain

countries of such measures. It asked States to refrain from adopting unilateral coercive measures in contradiction with international law and the UN Charter that created obstacles to trade relations among States. The Secretary-General was asked, in consultation with Governments and specialized agencies, as well as with intergovernmental organizations and NGOs, to report in 1996 on the coercive measures unilaterally implemented against developing countries.

## Scientific and technological concerns

### Human rights and the environment

On 24 February, the Commission on Human Rights, taking note of the final report[29] of the Special Rapporteur on human rights and the environment, Fatma Zohra Ksentini (Algeria), asked[30] that it be published in all UN official languages. It asked the Secretary-General to submit in 1996 a report containing the opinions of Governments, specialized agencies, intergovernmental organizations and NGOs on the issues raised in the Special Rapporteur's report.

**Subcommission action.** On 24 August, the Subcommission urged[31] the Commission to request again that the Special Rapporteur's final report be published in all the UN official languages and that it be widely disseminated. It also asked the Commission to extend the time in which it asked the Secretary-General to report on opinions based on the Special Rapporteur's report until at least one session following its publication.

### Rapporteur on toxic wastes

On 8 March, by a roll-call vote of 31 to 15, with 6 abstentions, the Commission on Human Rights decided[32] to appoint a special rapporteur for a three-year period to investigate and examine the effects of the illicit dumping of toxic and dangerous products and wastes in African and other developing countries on the enjoyment of human rights; to investigate, monitor, examine and receive communications and gather information on illicit dumping; to make recommendations and proposals on measures to control, reduce and eradicate illicit traffic in, transfer to and dumping of toxic and dangerous products and wastes in African and other developing countries; and to produce annually a list of the countries and TNCs engaged in the illicit dumping and a census of persons killed, maimed or otherwise injured in developing countries through that act.

The Special Rapporteur was to report in 1996. The Secretary-General was requested to establish a focal unit in the Centre for Human Rights to follow up on the Rapporteur's findings and other issues related to the effects of the illicit movement and dumping of toxic and dangerous products and wastes on the enjoyment of human rights.

Subsequently, the Commission appointed Fatma Zohra Ksentini (Algeria) as Special Rapporteur.

### ECONOMIC AND SOCIAL COUNCIL ACTION

In July, the Economic and Social Council adopted **decision 1995/288.**

**Adverse effects on the enjoyment of human rights of the illicit movement and dumping of toxic and dangerous products and wastes**

At its 52nd plenary meeting, on 25 July 1995, the Economic and Social Council, taking note of Commission on Human Rights resolution 1995/81 of 8 March 1995, approved the Commission's decision to appoint, for a three-year period, a special rapporteur on the adverse effects on the enjoyment of human rights of the illicit movement and dumping of toxic and dangerous products and wastes, and requested the Secretary-General to provide the Special Rapporteur with all the necessary assistance for the fulfilment of his or her mandate.

Economic and Social Council decision 1995/288

29-17-5 (roll-call vote)

Draft by Commission on Human Rights (E/1995/23); agenda item 5 *(d)*. *Meeting numbers.* ESC 51, 52.

Roll-call vote in Council as follows:

*In favour:* Bahamas, Belarus, Bhutan, Brazil, Chile, China, Colombia, Costa Rica, Côte d'Ivoire, Cuba, Egypt, Gabon, Ghana, India, Indonesia, Jamaica, Libyan Arab Jamahiriya, Nigeria, Pakistan, Philippines, Senegal, South Africa, Sri Lanka, Sudan, Thailand, Uganda, United Republic of Tanzania, Venezuela, Zimbabwe.

*Against:* Australia, Bulgaria, Canada, Denmark, France, Germany, Greece, Japan, Luxembourg, Netherlands, Norway, Poland, Portugal, Romania, Russian Federation, United Kingdom, United States.

*Abstaining:* Ireland, Malaysia, Mexico, Republic of Korea, Ukraine.

## Bioethics

**Report of the Secretary-General.** In 1995, the Commission on Human Rights considered a report of the Secretary-General on human rights and bioethics,[33] based on information received from Governments, UN specialized agencies and intergovernmental organizations. The Secretary-General provided background information on measures taken by the United Nations since 1968 and reviewed national and regional legislation and other measures taken to ensure that the life sciences developed in a manner respectful of human rights. He stated that legislation reinforcing certain ethical principles had been introduced in a number of States, but that the rapid development of science and its technological applications had not been accompanied by a consideration of their implications for human rights.

The Secretary-General concluded that there was a pressing need for the elucidation and universal adoption of basic bioethical principles in a manner that acknowledged the world's diverse moral and cultural perspectives, priorities and values.

**Commission action.** On 8 March, the Human Rights Commission invited[34] Governments, the specialized agencies and other UN organizations, intergovernmental organizations and NGOs to inform the Secretary-General of activities being carried out to ensure that the life sciences developed in a manner respectful of human rights and beneficial to humanity. States were invited to inform the Secretary-General of legislative and other measures taken. The Commission asked the Subcommission to consider, under the agenda item on human rights and scientific and technological developments, ways of ensuring that the life sciences developed in a manner respectful of human rights and beneficial to humanity and to make recommendations thereon. The Secretary-General was asked to report in 1997.

**Subcommission action.** On 31 July, the Subcommission postponed[35] consideration of the item on human rights and scientific and technological developments until its 1996 session.

## Computerized personal files

**Report of the Secretary-General.** In 1995, the Commission considered a report of the Secretary-General,[36] in which he discussed the application within the UN system of the guidelines for the regulation of computerized personal data files,[37] adopted by the General Assembly in 1990.[38] He presented information received from 13 States and three intergovernmental organizations concerning the follow-up to the guidelines at the regional and national levels. The guidelines were annexed to the Secretary-General's report.

**Commission action.** On 8 March, the Commission, referring to the guidelines and noting the Secretary-General's report, asked[39] States and intergovernmental, regional and non-governmental organizations to cooperate with him in the application of the guidelines; and asked the Secretary-General to continue to ensure implementation of the guidelines in the UN system and to report in 1997.

## Extreme poverty

**Commission action.** On 24 February, the Commission endorsed[40] a 1994 Subcommission resolution,[41] noted a Subcommission draft decision adopted by the Commission in 1995[20] and recommended that it be considered in the light of the conclusions of the current study on human rights and extreme poverty. It welcomed the holding in 1994 of a seminar on extreme poverty and denial of human rights[41] and noted the seminar's conclusions and recommendations. The Special Rapporteur was asked to continue to give attention to: the effects of extreme poverty on the enjoyment and exercise of human rights and fundamental freedoms of those affected by it; efforts by the poorest to exercise their rights and participate in the development of the society in which they lived; conditions in which the poorest could convey their experiences and ideas and become partners in the enjoyment of human rights; and means to promote a better understanding of the experiences and ideas of the poorest and those committed to working alongside them. It also asked him to give attention to the declaration and programme of action to be adopted by the World Summit for Social Development (see PART FOUR, Chapter IX).

**Report of the Special Rapporteur.** In July, Special Rapporteur Leandro Despouy (Argentina), in his second interim report on human rights and extreme poverty,[42] discussed the elements of extreme poverty, the human rights dimension of extreme poverty and the seriousness and scale of the phenomenon. He also described the work plan for his final report. Reports on the subject had been submitted in 1993[43] and 1994.[19]

**Subcommission action.** On 24 August, the Subcommission asked[44] the Special Rapporteur to submit a final report in 1996, focusing on his consultations with persons living in extreme poverty and persons working alongside them.

### Right to adequate housing

**Commission action.** On 24 February, the Commission, welcoming the 1994 progress report[45] of the Special Rapporteur on promoting the realization of the right to adequate housing, asked[46] him to submit a final report in 1995. It requested the Secretary-General to provide the Special Rapporteur with all the assistance he needed.

The Economic and Social Council approved that request on 25 July by **decision 1995/259**.

**Report of the Special Rapporteur.** In July, Special Rapporteur Rajindar Sachar (India) submitted his final report on the right to adequate housing,[47] in which he stated that, despite some meaningful steps forward, he regretted that housing rights had unjustifiably remained an empty promise for far too many people. Forced evictions continued to displace millions of persons yearly and national budgets devoted to housing those most in need continued to decline. In addition, armed conflicts had led to the massive destruction of homes and properties and to millions of internally displaced persons or refugees. Blatant discrimination denied certain groups the right to dwell in peace and security.

The Special Rapporteur presented indicators to assess State compliance with provisions in human rights instruments concerning the right to adequate housing. The indicators included: the state of the right to information; the state of living conditions and of natural resources; the state of local government; security of land tenure, the state of

evictions and the state of landlessness; economic parity and the state of economic well-being and resource accessibility; the state of cultural identity and skills; and the state of housing as a human right, the state of policy formulation and the question of illegality. He noted that it was crucial that all core indicators take into account the adverse impact that violations of the right to housing had on women and the contribution that women made in gaining and retaining that right.

The Special Rapporteur made recommendations for action by States, States parties to the Covenant on Economic, Social and Cultural Rights, the UN human rights programme, human rights treaty bodies, regional human rights organs, UN specialized agencies, other UN bodies, regional organizations, world conferences, and NGOs and community-based organizations.

**Subcommission action.** On 24 August, the Subcommission asked[48] the Secretary-General to compile in one document all reports of the Special Rapporteur[49] and to publish them as part of the Human Rights Study Series. It also asked him to solicit from States, UN bodies, specialized agencies and relevant NGOs and community-based organizations their comments on the draft international convention on housing rights presented by the Special Rapporteur in 1994[45] and the indicators contained in his final report. The Subcommission further asked the Secretary-General to submit in 1996 a compilation of and an analytical commentary on the views received on all aspects of the right to adequate housing and to develop further the analysis contained in the Special Rapporteur's final report regarding the use of indicators in monitoring compliance. The Secretary-General was asked to distribute the final report to all entities concerned, with a view to informing them of the recommendations contained therein and to receiving their views on any plans or programmes they might have or would develop to implement the recommendations.

### Forced evictions

**Report of the Secretary-General.** In a July report,[50] the Secretary-General submitted preliminary observations about the drafting of guidelines on international events and forced evictions. Examples of such acts included mass evictions prior to the visit of a foreign dignitary, the Olympic Games and the convening of international conferences. He stated that UN guidelines should be based on human rights considerations, such as the principle of non-discrimination, the need for participation, the need for taking decisions with the informed and free consent of the people concerned, the unlawfulness of force and coercion, access to courts, the right to appeal, and the right to compensation and to seek remedial action. He presented elements to be considered in drafting guidelines, which included: discouraging external donors if evictions were likely to result from the planned event; conducting public hearings prior to the adoption of plans for international events; permitting persons threatened with forced evictions to have the right to bring the matter before a court of law and the right to appeal before a higher court; and, in situations where no alternative to eviction existed, guaranteeing minimum periods of warning, possibilities for relocation and adequate financial compensation and participation.

**Subcommission action.** On 24 August, the Subcommission recommended[51] that Governments provide immediate restitution, compensation and/or sufficient alternative accommodation or land to persons and communities that had been forcibly evicted. It asked the High Commissioner for Human Rights to give attention to the practice of forced evictions, and the 1996 UN Conference on Human Settlements (see PART FOUR, Chapter VIII) to include in its final declaration and plan of action references to the nonacceptability of the practice and concrete measures to prevent it. The Subcommission asked the UN Centre for Human Settlements to do everything possible to prevent forced evictions by using the good offices of the Secretary-General to persuade Governments to refrain from carrying out forced evictions and by compiling annual lists of all eviction cases brought to its attention. Taking note of the Secretary-General's report, the Subcommission asked him to submit an updated report in 1996. It also asked him to convene an expert seminar on the practice of forced evictions and its relationship to internationally recognized human rights, with a view to developing comprehensive human rights guidelines on development-based displacement.

### Slavery and related issues

**Commission action.** On 3 March, the Human Rights Commission asked[52] its Subcommission on Prevention of Discrimination and Protection of Minorities to continue to strengthen its involvement in the activities of the Working Group on Contemporary Forms of Slavery. It endorsed the Subcommission's 1989 recommendations[53] regarding the review of the implementation of the three slavery conventions—the 1926 Slavery Convention, the 1956 Supplementary Convention on the Abolition of Slavery, the Slave Trade and Institutions and Practices Similar to Slavery,[54] and the 1949 Convention for the Suppression of the Traffic in Persons and of the Exploitation of the Prostitution of Others[55]—with the proviso that the proposed three-year term of office of Group

members should not be extended beyond their four-year Subcommission term. The Commission requested the Secretary-General to ask those States that had not ratified or acceded to the conventions to do so, or to explain in writing why they felt unable to do so, and to consider providing information concerning national legislation and practices in that regard. It asked the Secretary-General to reassign to the Working Group a Professional staff member of the Centre for Human Rights to ensure continuity and close coordination on issues relating to contemporary forms of slavery. The Commission recalled its request to designate the Centre as the focal point for coordinating UN activities to suppress contemporary forms of slavery. It asked the newly appointed Special Rapporteur on the sale of children to examine ways of cooperating with the Working Group, and asked Governments to pursue a policy of information, prevention and rehabilitation of women victims of prostitution and to take appropriate economic and social measures to that effect. The Subcommission was asked to review the draft programme of action for the prevention of traffic in persons and the exploitation of the prostitution of others in the light of comments received and to submit in 1996 a final text for Commission approval (see below).

**Working Group activities.** The Subcommission's five-member Working Group on Contemporary Forms of Slavery, at its twentieth session (Geneva, 19-28 April),[56] reviewed the status and implementation of the three conventions on slavery and the UN Voluntary Trust Fund on Contemporary Forms of Slavery (see below). It reviewed developments in this area, including the suppression of traffic in persons and the exploitation of the prostitution of others, organ transplants, bonded and child labour, forced labour, migrant workers, incest, early marriages and slavery during wartime. In addition, it considered the activities of the Special Rapporteur on the sale of children, child prostitution and child pornography (see PART THREE, Chapter I).

A July note[57] by the Secretariat contained information provided by the Netherlands to the Chairman of the Subcommission clarifying that country's policies on prostitution, which, it said, were not presented accurately and completely in the Working Group's report.

**Reports of the Secretary-General.** In March, the Secretary-General provided information from 10 Governments on implementation of the slavery conventions in their respective countries.[58]

In another March report,[59] he presented information received from three Governments, a specialized agency, a UN body and an intergovernmental organization on developments in contemporary forms of slavery and measures to prevent and eradicate all such forms.

Also in March, the Secretary-General provided replies received from one Government, a UN office, a specialized agency and an intergovernmental organization regarding allegations of child victimization or killing for the removal of organs for commercial transplants.[60]

**Subcommission action.** On 18 August, the Subcommission adopted[61] a resolution on issues under consideration by the Working Group.

### Fund on slavery

On 3 March, the Commission on Human Rights expressed regret[52] that, owing to a lack of contributions, the Board of Trustees of the UN Voluntary Trust Fund on Contemporary Forms of Slavery had been able to meet only once since it was appointed by the Secretary-General in 1993.[62] It appealed to Governments, organizations and individuals to respond favourably to requests for contributions to the Fund, established by the General Assembly in 1991,[63] and asked the Secretary-General to transmit its appeal to all Governments.

On 18 August, the Subcommission appealed[64] to Governments, governmental organizations and NGOs to respond favourably to requests for contributions to the Fund. It urged them and the Secretary-General to publicize the Fund and the latter to facilitate the holding of the meeting of the Board of Trustees so that a fund-raising campaign could be effectively carried out. He was also asked to study ways to draw the attention of potential donors to the Fund's role, and to cite both public and private donors on any list of such donors. The Subcommission recommended that the Board of Trustees consider renaming the Fund to reflect its aims better.

**Fund activities.** Following the first session in 1993 of the Fund's Board of Trustees,[65] the Fund received a number of contributions, but not enough to enable the Board to meet for a second session, which was therefore postponed.

At its second session (Geneva, 28 August–1 September 1995), the Board examined applications for assistance to NGO representatives to enable them to participate in the Working Group, and considered requests for financial assistance for NGO projects to benefit victims of contemporary forms of slavery. Guidelines and criteria for application and selection were annexed to the Board's report.[66] Two NGOs from each of four regions—Africa, Asia, Eastern Europe and Latin America—were selected for assistance to participate in the Working Group. Assistance to benefit victims was provisionally earmarked for a two-week fact-finding mission of the International League for Human Rights to document and report on trafficking in women and girls for the purpose of forced labour and prostitution in South-East Asia.

Since the Board's establishment, Governments, NGOs and individuals had contributed $60,750 to the Fund. The Board expressed grave concern at the Fund's situation and its management, and asked for an accurate and updated official statement on its financial status.

The Board recalled that the current members' term of office would end on 31 December 1995 and expressed the hope that the Secretary-General would take timely action to appoint members for the next term.

### Draft programme of action

On 18 August, the Subcommission decided[67] to transmit to the Commission the draft programme of action on the traffic in persons and the exploitation of the prostitution of others, as reformulated by the Working Group.[68]

The Secretariat transmitted in December the final draft programme of action for approval by the Commission in 1996.[69]

### Sexual exploitation of women during wartime

In July, Linda Chavez (United States) submitted to the Subcommission a working paper on systematic rape, sexual slavery and slavery-like practices during wartime,[70] in which she outlined issues that might be the subject of a further in-depth study.

On 18 August, the Subcommission decided[71] to appoint Ms. Chavez as Special Rapporteur with the task of undertaking an in-depth study of the situation of systematic rape, sexual slavery and slavery-like practices during periods of armed conflict. She was requested to submit a preliminary report in 1996 and a final one in 1997.

## Vulnerable groups

### Women

The advancement of the status of women and the protection of their rights have been central concerns of the United Nations since the Organization's inception. On 11 December 1946, the General Assembly adopted a resolution urging that women be granted the same political rights as men. The Commission on the Status of Women began work in February 1947. Over two decades, four world conferences on women's rights were convened by the UN, in 1975 in Mexico City, in 1980 in Copenhagen, in 1985 in Nairobi and in 1995 in Beijing (see PART FOUR, Chapter X). Strategies and programmes of action to expand women's rights, as well as international human rights instruments, including the 1979 Convention on the Elimination of Discrimination against Women (see preceding chapter), have contributed to securing equality for women in all areas of life and society. (For a comprehensive report on UN action for women, see PART FOUR, Chapter X.)

**Commission action.** On 8 March, the Human Rights Commission called[72] for intensified effort to integrate the equal status of women and the human rights of women into UN system-wide activity and to address those issues throughout relevant UN bodies and mechanisms. It encouraged the strengthening of cooperation and coordination among human rights treaty bodies, special rapporteurs, representatives, experts, working groups and other mechanisms of the Commission and its Subcommission concerned with the human rights of women, and requested that they report on violations of those rights. It also encouraged close monitoring by human rights treaty bodies of the enjoyment of the human rights of women; welcomed an initiative of the Committee on the Elimination of Discrimination against Women (CEDAW) to enhance cooperation with other human rights treaty bodies; endorsed a recommendation that each treaty body consider obtaining gender-specific information from States parties; requested that special rapporteurs, representatives, experts and chairmen of the working groups of the Commission address violations of the human rights of women; and called on those mechanisms to cooperate with the Special Rapporteur on violence against women.

The Commission also called on the High Commissioner for Human Rights, in convening a meeting of persons chairing the human rights treaty bodies and working groups, as well as special rapporteurs, representatives and experts, to consider ways in which the human rights of women could be integrated into the work of the UN system and to report on progress made at the Fourth World Conference on Women and to the Commission in 1996. That request was approved by the Economic and Social Council on 25 July by **decision 1995/289**. Governments and the UN were asked to include in their human rights education activities information on the human rights of women.

**Report of the Secretary-General.** In a June report,[73] the Secretary-General described action taken by special rapporteurs, experts, working groups, treaty bodies and other mechanisms of the Commission on Human Rights to integrate women's human rights into the UN system. He also reviewed the status of implementation of recommendations of the 1993 World Conference on Human Rights[74] and presented violations of women's rights as documented in the reports of special rapporteurs and working groups, including the right to life, participation in politics and decision-making, the right to full legal status and legal protection, freedom of opinion and expression, the right to liberty and security, freedom of movement, prohibition of sexual exploitation,

gender-based torture and degrading treatment, the right to education, the right to work, freedom of religion and the right to health care.

The Secretary-General concluded that some progress had been made in promoting and protecting the human rights of women, as well as in integrating women's rights into existing mechanisms and procedures. However, information available from the special rapporteurs indicated that gender equality in the full enjoyment of human rights had not been achieved, and an analysis of the current situation showed that public awareness of the importance of respecting the human rights of women remained low. He noted that the Centre for Human Rights would strengthen gender-sensitive training within the programme of technical assistance in human rights issues. The Centre was in the process of establishing a data-collection system, and a cooperative network was to be developed by the Focal Point for the Human Rights of Women with UN agencies, Member States and NGOs.

**Expert group meeting.** In November, the High Commissioner for Human Rights transmitted the report of an expert group meeting on the development of guidelines for the integration of gender perspectives into UN human rights activities and programmes (Geneva, 3-7 July 1995),[75] organized by the Centre for Human Rights and the UN Development Fund for Women. The group recommended using gender-inclusive language in formulating new human rights instruments and in existing standards and proposed that the Centre for Human Rights establish a guideline on gender inclusivity in all UN official languages. It also advocated the identification, collection and use of gender-disaggregated data; the revision of working methods by all UN bodies to incorporate a creative and comprehensive gender analysis of information, as well as a gender-sensitive interpretation of all human rights mechanisms; an evaluation of information and training materials published by the Centre; ensuring that activities related to the UN Decade for Human Rights Education (see preceding chapter) were gender sensitive; provision by the Centre of more accessible information on current activities and more aggressive steps to disseminate it; training for Centre management and staff and other personnel involved in UN human rights activities; more Centre-wide coordination of work on women's human rights; promotion by the High Commissioner of system-wide coordination and collaboration on the human rights of women within the UN; cooperation and collaboration by the Centre in efforts to mainstream women's human rights with women-specific bodies of the UN system; equal representation of women and men, as well as gender-trained individuals, on expert committees that monitored implementation of treaties, as well as among the independent experts and working groups of the Commission and Subcommission; consideration by the Centre of long-term, ongoing ways to produce and review information on women and action to protect women's human rights; and convening a meeting within 18 months to evaluate how work was progressing.

### Violence against women

**Report of the Special Rapporteur.** In response to a 1994 action,[76] the Commission considered a preliminary report submitted by Radhika Coomaraswamy (Sri Lanka), the Special Rapporteur on violence against women, its causes and consequences.[77] She discussed the nature of the problem of violence against women, existing international legal standards and general issues arising from violence in the family, in the community and perpetrated or condoned by the State. Her recommendations included that States be called upon to: condemn violence against women; ratify the 1979 Convention on the Elimination of All Forms of Discrimination against Women;[78] formulate national plans of action to combat violence against women; initiate strategies to develop legal and administrative mechanisms to ensure effective justice for victims; train and sensitize judicial and police officials; reform educational curricula; promote research in the field; and ensure proper reporting of the problem of violence against women to international human rights mechanisms.

**Commission action.** On 8 March, the Human Rights Commission commended[79] the Special Rapporteur for her analysis of the problem and specific causes and consequences of violence against women and encouraged her to make recommendations concerning situations in which advisory services and technical assistance might assist Governments concerned. Condemning all acts of gender-based violence against women, the Commission called for its elimination in the family, within the general community and where perpetrated or condoned by the State. It also condemned all human rights violations against women in situations of armed conflict and called for an effective response to those actions. The Commission stressed the recommendations made by the Special Rapporteur and asked that her report[77] be made available to the Fourth World Conference on Women and brought to the attention of the Commission on the Status of Women and CEDAW (see PART FOUR, Chapter X).

### Violence against women migrant workers

**Commission action.** On 24 February, the Human Rights Commission, expressing grave concern at the plight of women migrant workers who were victims of physical, mental and sexual harassment and abuse, called on[80] the sending and receiving countries to ensure that law enforcement officials assisted in guaranteeing the full protection of the rights of women migrant workers, consistent with international obligations of Member States. It urged sending and host countries to ensure that women migrant workers were protected from unscrupulous recruitment practices and encouraged Member States to consider signing and ratifying or acceding to the 1990 International Convention on the Protection of the Rights of All Migrant Workers and Members of Their Families.[81] The Commission called on UN bodies and specialized agencies, intergovernmental organizations and NGOs to inform the Secretary-General of the extent of the problem and to recommend further measures in that area. It also called for seminars and training programmes on human rights instruments, particularly those pertaining to migrant workers. Treaty-monitoring bodies and NGOs concerned with violence against women were to include the situation of women migrant workers in their deliberations and to supply relevant information to UN bodies and Governments. The Commission asked the Special Rapporteur on violence against women to continue to include among the issues pertaining to her mandate the violence perpetrated against women migrant workers and to consider including her findings in her 1996 report.

(See PART FOUR, Chapter X, for General Assembly action.)

### Traditional practices affecting the health of women and children

**Commission action.** On 3 March, the Commission, noting a 1994 Subcommission resolution,[29] endorsed[82] the Subcommission's recommendations regarding a two-year extension of the mandate of the Special Rapporteur on traditional practices affecting the health of women and children, Halima Embarek Warzazi (Morocco); the submission of her preliminary report in 1995 and her final report in 1996; and the request to the Secretary-General to assist the Special Rapporteur.

By **decision 1995/300** of 25 July, the Economic and Social Council approved the Commission's action.

**Report of the Special Rapporteur.** In a July report,[83] the Special Rapporteur discussed the similarities and differences between traditional practices affecting the health of women and children in various parts of the world, based on regional seminars held in Africa in 1991[84] and in Asia in 1994.[29] She called on States, UN bodies and organs, relevant specialized agencies, NGOs and grass-roots movements to implement the Plan of Action for the Elimination of Harmful Traditional Practices Affecting the Health of Women and Children[29] and to report on progress achieved and the obstacles encountered in doing so.

**Subcommission action.** On 24 August, the Subcommission called on[85] States, UN bodies and organs, relevant specialized agencies, NGOs and grass-roots movements to implement the Plan of Action and to inform the Special Rapporteur of progress achieved and obstacles encountered. It welcomed the Special Rapporteur's report and looked forward to her final report in 1996.

### Traffic in women and girls

On 3 March, the Commission, expressing grave concern at the worsening problem of trafficking, particularly the increasing syndication of the sex trade and the internationalization of the traffic in women and girl children, encouraged[86] Governments, relevant UN bodies and specialized agencies, intergovernmental organizations and NGOs to share information in order to develop anti-trafficking measures. It urged Governments to address the problem and to ensure that victims were provided with the necessary assistance, support, legal advice, protection, treatment and rehabilitation. The Commission called on them to prevent the misuse and exploitation by traffickers of economic activities, such as the development of tourism and the export of labour. The Commission asked the Secretary-General to provide it with his preliminary report[87] in 1996. (See PART FOUR, Chapter X, for details of the Secretary-General's report and General Assembly action.)

### Children

In 1959, the General Assembly adopted a Declaration of the Rights of the Child, setting out 10 principles aimed at ensuring special protection against abuse and guarantees of fundamental freedoms and human rights. Twenty years later, the Assembly declared 1979 as the International Year of the Child. In 1989, the world body adopted the Convention on the Rights of the Child. In 1995, consideration continued of two draft optional protocols to that Convention—one concerning the involvement of children in armed conflict, and a second related to the sale of children, child prostitution and child pornography. The Assembly also acted with regard to the girl child (see below), child labour and the plight of street children, and traffic in women and children (see preceding chapter and PART FOUR, Chapter X).

### Sale of children

As requested by the General Assembly in 1993,[88] Special Rapporteur Vitit Muntarbhorn (Thailand) submitted a preliminary report in 1994 on the sale of children and related issues.[89] The Human Rights Commission in 1994[90] had asked him to report in 1995. A note by the secretariat[91] stated that, owing to the resignation of the Special Rapporteur in October 1994, only the preliminary report would be available to the Commission in 1995.

Ofelia Calcetas-Santos (Philippines) was appointed as Special Rapporteur in January 1995.

**Commission action.** On 8 March, the Human Rights Commission renewed[92] the Special Rapporteur's mandate for a three-year period and asked the Secretary-General to enable her to submit an interim report to the General Assembly in 1995 and a report to the Commission in 1996. It appealed to Governments to assist the Special Rapporteur, including by inviting her to make country visits. The Commission invited the Special Rapporteur to cooperate with the Committee on the Rights of the Child, the Subcommission and its Working Group on Contemporary Forms of Slavery, as well as with other UN bodies dealing with questions covered by her mandate, and invited her to participate in the next sessions of those bodies.

**ECONOMIC AND SOCIAL COUNCIL ACTION**

On 25 July, the Economic and Social Council adopted **resolution 1995/36**.

**Special Rapporteur of the Commission on Human Rights on the sale of children, child prostitution and child pornography**

*The Economic and Social Council,*

*Taking note* of Commission on Human Rights resolution 1995/79 of 8 March 1995,

1. *Approves* the Commission's decision to extend the mandate of the Special Rapporteur of the Commission on Human Rights on the sale of children, child prostitution and child pornography for three years, while maintaining the annual reporting cycle;

2. *Also approves* the Commission's request to the Secretary-General to provide the Special Rapporteur with all necessary human and financial assistance, from within existing resources, so as to make possible the full discharge of the mandate.

Economic and Social Council resolution 1995/36

25 July 1995      Meeting 52      Adopted without vote

Draft by Commission on Human Rights (E/1995/23), orally amended by Japan; agenda item 5 *(d)*.
*Meeting numbers.* ESC 51-53.

**Provisional report.** In accordance with a 1994 General Assembly request,[93] the Special Rapporteur in September submitted a report on the sale of children, child prostitution and child pornography.[94] She discussed her mandate, setting out more precise definitions to avoid confusion and overlapping among the issues of sale, prostitution and pornography, and reviewed the causes giving rise to those concerns. The Special Rapporteur identified three catalysts in instituting reforms to benefit children: the education system, the justice system and the media. She presented preventive, interventive and rehabilitative strategies for the three catalysts. Recommendations were made for international action, including conducting an inventory and making a systematic analysis of recommendations, initiatives and programmes of the UN, its agencies and NGOs, and of bilateral, regional or international agreements addressing the concerns of her mandate. She also recommended organizing regional or international conferences for the persons and organizations representing the three catalysts.

### Programme on child labour

By a January note,[95] the Secretary-General drew attention to his 1994 report[96] describing action taken by States to implement the Programme of Action for the Elimination of the Exploitation of Child Labour, adopted by the Commission on Human Rights in 1993.[97]

**Commission action.** On 3 March, the Commission asked[98] the Subcommission to consider further its proposed appointment of Halima Embarek Warzazi (Morocco) as Special Rapporteur on the exploitation of child labour and debt bondage and to make the appointment subject to the submission of a preparatory document. It also asked the Subcommission to determine the need for a Special Rapporteur and, if it considered the appointment appropriate, to identify specific activities in order to avoid duplication with others within the UN system. The Commission encouraged Governments, within the context of the Programme of Action for the Elimination of the Exploitation of Child Labour, to consider adopting measures to protect child labourers and to ensure that their labour was not exploited.

### The girl child

The General Assembly in 1995 urged all States to eliminate all forms of discrimination against the girl child, noting that the advancement and development of women throughout their life cycle must begin with the girl child.

On 24 August, the Subcommission on Prevention of Discrimination and Protection of Minorities decided[99] to consider the human rights of women and the girl child under every item of its agenda, as well as in relevant studies, and asked that all reports submitted in 1996 contain a gender perspective in their analyses and recommendations. It asked the Secretary-General to obtain the views of CEDAW and the Commission on the Status of Women on the desirability of having an advisory opinion on the value and legal effect of reservations concerning the 1979 Convention on the Elimination of All Forms of Discrimination

against Women,[78] and to invite those bodies to formulate any other observations on the question. It also asked him to ensure that UN human rights and humanitarian relief personnel recognized and dealt with the human rights violations particular to women and to establish and reinforce mechanisms in the Centre for Human Rights in order to implement the recommendations and decisions adopted at the Fourth World Conference on Women (see PART FOUR, Chapter X).

GENERAL ASSEMBLY ACTION

On 21 December, the General Assembly adopted **resolution 50/154**.

#### The girl child

*The General Assembly,*

*Recalling* the Beijing Declaration and the Platform for Action of the Fourth World Conference on Women, the Copenhagen Declaration on Social Development and the Programme of Action of the World Summit for Social Development, the Programme of Action of the International Conference on Population and Development, the Vienna Declaration and Programme of Action of the World Conference on Human Rights, Agenda 21 adopted by the United Nations Conference on Environment and Development, the Plan of Action for Implementing the World Declaration on the Survival, Protection and Development of Children in the 1990s of the World Summit for Children, the World Declaration on Education for All and the Framework for Action to Meet Basic Learning Needs adopted at the World Conference on Education for All: Meeting Basic Learning Needs,

*Recalling also* that discrimination against the girl child and the violation of the rights of the girl child was identified as a critical area of concern in the Platform for Action of the Fourth World Conference on Women in the achievement of equality, development and peace for women, and that the advancement and empowerment of women throughout their life-cycle must begin with the girl child,

*Noting with appreciation* that the World Summit for Children sensitized the entire world to the plight of children,

*Reaffirming* the equal rights of women and men as enshrined in the Preamble to the Charter of the United Nations, and recalling the Convention on the Elimination of All Forms of Discrimination against Women and the Convention on the Rights of the Child,

1. *Urges* all States to eliminate all forms of discrimination against the girl child and to eliminate the violation of the human rights of all children, paying particular attention to the obstacles faced by the girl child;

2. *Also urges* all States, international organizations as well as non-governmental organizations individually and collectively to set goals and to develop and implement gender-sensitive strategies to address the needs of children, in particular those of girls, in accordance with the Convention on the Rights of the Child and the goals, strategic objectives and actions contained in the Platform for Action of the Fourth World Conference on Women;

3. *Requests* all States, international organizations as well as non-governmental organizations to increase awareness of the potential of the girl child and to pro-

mote the participation of girls and young women, on an equal basis and as partners with boys and young men, in social, economic and political life and in the development of strategies and in the implementation of actions aimed at achieving gender equality, development and peace;

4. *Calls upon* Member States and organizations and bodies of the United Nations system, in particular, the United Nations Children's Fund, the United Nations Educational, Scientific and Cultural Organization, the Food and Agriculture Organization of the United Nations and the World Health Organization, to take into account the rights and the particular needs of the girl child, especially in education, health and nutrition, and to eliminate negative cultural attitudes and practices against the girl child;

5. *Further urges* all States to eliminate all forms of violence against children, in particular the girl child;

6. *Calls upon* States, international organizations as well as non-governmental organizations to help mobilize the necessary financial resources and political support to achieve goals, strategies and actions relating to the survival, development and protection of the girl child in all programmes for children;

7. *Requests* the Secretary-General to ensure that the goals and actions relating to the girl child receive full attention in the implementation of the Platform for Action of the Fourth World Conference on Women through the work of all organizations and bodies of the United Nations system;

8. *Also requests* the Secretary-General, as Chairman of the Administrative Committee on Coordination, to urge all the organizations and bodies of the United Nations system focusing on the advancement of women to make commitments to goals and actions relating to the girl child in the revision and implementation of the system-wide medium-term plan for the advancement of women for the period 1996-2001, as well as in the medium-term plan for the period 1998-2002.

General Assembly resolution 50/154

21 December 1995     Meeting 97     Adopted without vote

Approved by Third Committee (A/50/633) without vote, 5 December (meeting 50); 81-nation draft (A/C.3/50/L.31/Rev.1); agenda item 110.
*Meeting numbers.* GA 50th session: 3rd Committee 32-37, 45, 48, 50; plenary 97.

## Indigenous populations

**Commission action.** On 3 March, the Human Rights Commission expressed appreciation and satisfaction[100] to the Working Group on Indigenous Populations for its work, particularly for the completed draft of the UN declaration on the rights of indigenous peoples,[101] and asked the Group to consider ways to enhance the contribution to its work of expertise from indigenous people. The Commission urged the Group to continue its review of developments and of the situation of indigenous people, asking it to take into account the work of all thematic special rapporteurs, special representatives, independent experts and working groups as it pertained to indigenous people. It recommended to the Economic and Social Council that the Group be authorized to meet for five days prior to the 1995 session of the Subcom-

mission. It asked the Secretary-General to assist the Group, to transmit its reports to Governments, indigenous and intergovernmental organizations and NGOs for comments and suggestions, and to ensure that the Group's meetings were provided with interpretation and documentation. The Commission appealed to Governments, organizations and individuals to consider favourably requests for contributions to the UN Voluntary Fund for Indigenous Populations (see below).

On 25 July, by **decision 1995/263**, the Economic and Social Council authorized the Working Group to meet for five days prior to the Subcommission's 1995 session. It approved the Commission's request that the Secretary-General assist the Group, transmit its reports and ensure servicing for the Group's meetings.

**Working Group activities.** At its thirteenth session (Geneva, 24-28 July),[102] the Working Group on Indigenous Populations recommended to the Subcommission that: the Group's Chairman/ Rapporteur prepare a note on criteria for a definition of indigenous peoples; the Special Rapporteur on treaties, agreements and other constructive arrangements between States and indigenous populations be given adequate resources so that he could submit his final report to the Group and to the Subcommission in 1996; a workshop be held prior to the Group's 1996 session to discuss the establishment of a permanent forum, in the United Nations, for indigenous people; and the Secretary-General review existing arrangements and programmes within the UN system which might be used by indigenous people. The Group also decided to highlight in 1996 the issue of indigenous peoples and health.

(See below for the Group's action on the International Decade of the World's Indigenous People.)

**Subcommission action.** On 24 August, the Subcommission asked[103] the Secretary-General to transmit the Working Group's report on its 1995 session to indigenous people's organizations, Governments, intergovernmental organizations and NGOs, as well as to all thematic rapporteurs, special representatives, independent experts and working groups, and to prepare an annotated agenda for the Group's 1996 session. Endorsing the Group's recommendation to focus on specific topics at future sessions and on indigenous health in 1996, the Subcommission asked the Secretary-General to invite Governments, intergovernmental and indigenous people's organizations and NGOs to provide information, particularly on matters relating to indigenous health. It asked the Group's Chairman/Rapporteur to inform the Board of Trustees of the UN Voluntary Fund for Indigenous Populations that the Group would highlight health issues in 1996, so that the Board could bear that in mind when it met in April 1996. The Subcommission recommended that the Chairman/Rapporteur prepare a working paper on the concept of indigenous people, to be transmitted to Governments and intergovernmental and indigenous people's organizations for their comments. It also recommended that the Commission ask the Economic and Social Council to authorize the Group to meet for eight days prior to the Subcommission's 1996 session.

### International Decade of the World's Indigenous People

**Commission action.** On 3 March, the Human Rights Commission welcomed[104] the General Assembly's 1994 decision[105] to adopt the 1995 short-term programme of activities for the International Decade of the World's Indigenous People (1994-2004), as contained in a report of the Secretary-General.[106] The Decade was proclaimed by the Assembly in 1993.[107] The Commission asked Governments to consider the final comprehensive programme of action to be considered by the Assembly in 1995. It took note of the Assembly's request for the establishment of a unit within the Centre for Human Rights to support Centre activities related to indigenous people, and the Assembly recommendation that a second technical meeting on the planning of the Decade be convened prior to the 1995 session of the Working Group on Indigenous Populations. It also noted the decision to consider at a later session the convening of meetings for planning and review purposes at intervals during the Decade. Annexed to the Commission's resolution was the Decade's 1995 programme of activities.

**Technical meeting.** As requested by the General Assembly in 1994,[105] a second technical meeting on the planning of the International Decade was held (Geneva, 20-21 July).[108] Activities were proposed for implementation by the Coordinator of the Decade and the Centre for Human Rights, the United Nations, regional organizations, Governments, NGOs and indigenous peoples. The first technical meeting was held in 1994.[106]

**Working Group activities.** In July, the Working Group on Indigenous Populations endorsed[102] the programme of activities proposed at the technical meeting, and recommended including in the final programme of activities the holding of a world conference on indigenous peoples and an expert meeting on problems arising from nuclear testing and dumping on indigenous lands. It recommended that the members of the Board of Trustees of the Voluntary Fund for the Decade be appointed as soon as possible to consider projects submitted during the Decade.

**Subcommission action.** On 24 August, the Subcommission welcomed[109] the General As-

sembly's 1994 decision to observe annually on 9 August the International Day of Indigenous People.[105] It recommended that a Board of Trustees for the Voluntary Trust Fund for the International Decade be established as soon as possible to consider projects submitted by indigenous and other organizations during the Decade and that the Board's members include representatives of indigenous people. The Subcommission asked the Secretary-General to include in his report to the Assembly suggestions made in the debate on the Decade at the Working Group's 1995 session.

**Reports of the Secretary-General.** In response to a 1994 General Assembly request,[105] the Secretary-General in October submitted a final report on a comprehensive programme of action for the Decade,[110] summarizing the views of two Governments on his preliminary report.[106] The report contained the proposals adopted by the technical meeting and recommendations made by the Working Group on Indigenous Populations regarding the Decade (see above), as well as a proposed calendar of activities for the Coordinator of the Decade and the Centre for Human Rights during the period 1996-1999.

Also in October, the Secretary-General reported[111] on progress made at the national, regional and international levels in accomplishing the objectives set out in a 1994 Assembly resolution.[105] The Secretary-General summarized information about Decade activities by three Governments, four UN bodies, five UN specialized agencies, one regional organization and 17 indigenous organizations and other NGOs.

**GENERAL ASSEMBLY ACTION**

On 21 December, the Assembly adopted **resolution 50/157**.

#### Programme of activities for the International Decade of the World's Indigenous People

*The General Assembly,*

*Bearing in mind* that one of the purposes of the United Nations, as set forth in the Charter, is the achievement of international cooperation in solving international problems of an economic, social, cultural or humanitarian character and in promoting and encouraging respect for human rights and fundamental freedoms for all without distinction as to race, sex, language or religion,

*Recalling* its resolutions 48/163 of 21 December 1993 and 49/214 of 23 December 1994 on the International Decade of the World's Indigenous People, and Commission on Human Rights resolution 1995/28 of 3 March 1995,

*Recalling also* that the goal of the Decade is to strengthen international cooperation for the solution of problems faced by indigenous people in such areas as human rights, the environment, development, education and health, and that the theme of the Decade is "Indigenous people: partnership in action",

*Recognizing further* the importance of consultation and cooperation with indigenous people in planning and implementing the programme of activities for the Decade, the need for adequate financial support from the international community, including support from within the United Nations and the specialized agencies, and the need for adequate coordination and communication channels,

*Recalling further* its invitation to organizations of indigenous people and other non-governmental organizations concerned to consider the contributions they can make to the success of the Decade, with a view to presenting them to the Working Group on Indigenous Populations of the Subcommission on Prevention of Discrimination and Protection of Minorities,

*Taking note* of Economic and Social Council decision 1992/255 of 20 July 1992, in which the Council requested United Nations bodies and specialized agencies to ensure that all technical assistance financed or provided by them was compatible with international instruments and standards applicable to indigenous people, and encouraged efforts to promote coordination in this field and greater participation of indigenous people in the planning and implementation of projects affecting them,

*Mindful* of the relevant recommendations of the World Conference on Human Rights, the United Nations Conference on Environment and Development, the International Conference on Population and Development, the Fourth World Conference on Women and the World Summit for Social Development, and of the Declaration on the Occasion of the Fiftieth Anniversary of the United Nations,

*Recognizing* the value and diversity of the cultures and forms of social organization of indigenous people, and convinced that the development of indigenous people within their countries will contribute to the socioeconomic, cultural and environmental advancement of all the countries of the world,

1. *Takes note* of the final report of the Secretary-General on a comprehensive programme of action for the International Decade of the World's Indigenous People and the annexes to that report;

2. *Decides* to adopt the programme of activities for the Decade contained in the annex to the present resolution;

3. *Also decides* that the programme of activities for the Decade may be reviewed and updated throughout the Decade and that at the mid-point of the Decade the Economic and Social Council and the General Assembly should review the results of the activities to identify obstacles to the achievement of the goals of the Decade and to recommend solutions for overcoming those obstacles;

4. *Affirms* as a major objective of the Decade the adoption by the General Assembly of a declaration on the rights of indigenous people;

5. *Welcomes* the establishment of an open-ended intersessional Working Group of the Commission on Human Rights with the sole purpose of elaborating a draft declaration, considering the draft contained in the annex to resolution 1994/45 of 26 August 1994 of the Subcommission on Prevention of Discrimination and Protection of Minorities, entitled "Draft United Nations declaration on the rights of indigenous peoples", for consideration and adoption by the General Assembly within the Decade;

6. *Also welcomes* the decisions of the Economic and Social Council to approve the participation of some organizations of indigenous people in the Working Group, and encourages the continuing cooperation of the Council, the Committee on Non-Governmental Organizations and the Centre for Human Rights of the Secretariat in processing further applications as a matter of priority in accordance with the relevant resolutions of the Commission on Human Rights and the Council;

7. *Recognizes* among the important objectives of the Decade the consideration of the possible establishment of a permanent forum for indigenous people within the United Nations, as recommended in the Vienna Declaration and Programme of Action, adopted by the World Conference on Human Rights, held from 14 to 25 June 1993, and welcomes the report of the workshop on the possible establishment of a permanent forum for indigenous people held at Copenhagen from 26 to 28 June 1995 and the ongoing dialogue on this subject;

8. *Recommends* that the Secretary-General, drawing on the expertise of the Commission on Human Rights as well as the Commission for Sustainable Development and other relevant bodies, undertake a review, in close consultation with Governments and taking into account the views of indigenous people and of the existing mechanisms, procedures and programmes within the United Nations concerning indigenous people, and report to the General Assembly at its fifty-first session;

9. *Also recommends* that the Commission on Human Rights, drawing on the results of the review and the Copenhagen workshop, consider the convening of a second workshop on the possible establishment of a permanent forum for indigenous people with the participation of independent experts as well as representatives of Governments, organizations of indigenous people and other non-governmental organizations concerned and United Nations bodies and specialized agencies;

10. *Recognizes* the importance of strengthening the human and institutional capacity of indigenous people to develop their own solutions to their problems, and, for these purposes, recommends that the United Nations University consider the possibility of sponsoring, in each region, one or more institutions of higher education as centres of excellence and the diffusion of expertise, and invites the Commission on Human Rights to recommend appropriate means of implementation;

11. *Further recommends* that special attention be given to improving the extent and effectiveness of the participation of indigenous people in planning and implementing the activities for the Decade, including through the recruitment, where appropriate, by relevant United Nations bodies and specialized agencies, of staff from among indigenous nationals of Member States, consistent with Article 101 of the Charter of the United Nations and within existing resources and staff levels;

12. *Recommends* that the Secretary-General:

*(a)* Request United Nations representatives in countries where there are indigenous people to promote, through the appropriate channels, greater participation of indigenous people in the planning and implementation of projects affecting them;

*(b)* Ensure coordinated follow-up to the recommendations concerning indigenous people of relevant world conferences, namely the World Conference on Human Rights, the United Nations Conference on Environment and Development, the International Conference on

Population and Development, the Fourth World Conference on Women and the World Summit for Social Development;

(c) Urge relevant United Nations conferences to promote and facilitate, to the extent possible and as appropriate, the effective input of the views of indigenous people;

(d) Ensure that information about the programme of activities for the Decade and opportunities for indigenous people to participate in those activities is disseminated in all countries and to the greatest possible extent in indigenous languages, to be financed from within existing budgetary resources;

(e) Report on progress made at the national, regional and international levels in accomplishing these objectives to the General Assembly at its fifty-first session;

13. *Requests* the United Nations High Commissioner for Human Rights to promote the objectives of the Decade, taking into account the special concerns of indigenous people, in the fulfilment of his functions;

14. *Requests* the Assistant Secretary-General for Human Rights, in his capacity as Coordinator of the Decade, bearing in mind the contribution that indigenous people have the capacity to make, to establish, within existing resources, a unit within the Centre for Human Rights of the Secretariat, including indigenous persons, to support its activities related to indigenous people, in particular to plan, coordinate and implement activities for the Decade;

15. *Invites* the Assistant Secretary-General for Human Rights to consider the appointment of a fundraiser who could develop new sources of funding for the Decade;

16. *Requests* the Administrative Committee on Coordination, through its inter-agency process, to consult and coordinate on the Decade, with a view to assisting the Coordinator of the Decade to fulfil his function, and to report on activities of the United Nations system in relation to the Decade to the General Assembly in each year of the Decade;

17. *Invites* the United Nations financial and development institutions, operational programmes and specialized agencies, in accordance with the existing procedures of their governing bodies:

(a) To give increased priority and resources to improving the conditions of indigenous people, with particular emphasis on the needs of those people in developing countries, including by the preparation of specific programmes of action for the implementation of the goals of the Decade, within their areas of competence;

(b) To launch special projects, through appropriate channels and in collaboration with indigenous people, for strengthening their community-level initiatives and to facilitate the exchange of information and expertise among indigenous people and other relevant experts;

(c) To designate focal points for coordination with the Centre for Human Rights of activities related to the Decade;

18. *Emphasizes* the important role of international cooperation in promoting the goals and activities of the Decade and the rights, well-being and sustainable development of indigenous people;

19. *Also emphasizes* the importance of action at the national level to the implementation of the goals and activities of the Decade;

20. *Encourages* Governments to support the Decade by:

(a) Contributing to the United Nations Trust Fund for the Decade;

(b) Preparing relevant programmes, plans and reports in relation to the Decade, in consultation with indigenous people;

(c) Seeking means, in consultation with indigenous people, of giving indigenous people greater responsibility for their own affairs and an effective voice in decisions on matters which affect them;

(d) Establishing national committees or other mechanisms involving indigenous people to ensure that the objectives and activities of the Decade are planned and implemented on the basis of full partnership with indigenous people;

21. *Also encourages* Governments to consider contributing, as appropriate, to the Fund for the Development of Indigenous Peoples of Latin America and the Caribbean, in support of the achievement of the goals of the Decade;

22. *Appeals* to Governments and intergovernmental and non-governmental organizations to support the Decade by identifying resources for activities designed to implement the goals of the Decade, in cooperation with indigenous people;

23. *Decides* to include in the provisional agenda of its fifty-first session the item entitled "Programme of activities of the International Decade of the World's Indigenous People".

### ANNEX
#### Programme of activities for the International Decade of the World's Indigenous People

#### A. Objectives

1. Taking into account General Assembly resolution 48/163 of 21 December 1993, the main objective of the International Decade of the World's Indigenous People is the strengthening of international cooperation for the solution of problems faced by indigenous people in such areas as human rights, the environment, development, health, culture and education.

2. The specialized agencies of the United Nations system and other international and national agencies, as well as communities and private enterprises, should devote special attention to development activities of benefit to indigenous communities.

3. A major objective of the Decade is the education of indigenous and non-indigenous societies concerning the situation, cultures, languages, rights and aspirations of indigenous people. In particular, efforts should be made to cooperate with the United Nations Decade for Human Rights Education.

4. An objective of the Decade is the promotion and protection of the rights of indigenous people and their empowerment to make choices which enable them to retain their cultural identity while participating in political, economic and social life, with full respect for their cultural values, languages, traditions and forms of social organization.

5. An objective of the Decade is to further the implementation of the recommendations pertaining to indigenous people of all high-level international conferences, including the United Nations Conference on Environment and Development, the World Conference on Human Rights, in particular its recommendation

that consideration be given to the establishment of a permanent forum for indigenous people in the United Nations system, the United Nations Conference on Population and Development and the World Summit for Social Development as well as all future high-level meetings.

6. An objective of the Decade is the adoption of the draft United Nations declaration on the rights of indigenous peoples and the further development of international standards as well as national legislation for the protection and promotion of the human rights of indigenous people, including effective means of monitoring and guaranteeing those rights.

7. The objectives of the Decade should be assessed by quantifiable outcomes that will improve the lives of indigenous people and that can be evaluated halfway through the Decade and at its end.

B. Activities to be undertaken by the major actors

1. *United Nations observances*

8. A formal observance each year on the International Day of the World's Indigenous People, in New York, Geneva and at other offices of the United Nations.

9. Official observance of the Decade as part of the Fourth World Conference on Women, the United Nations Conference on Human Settlements (Habitat II) and other international conferences related to the aims and themes of the Decade.

10. Issuance of a special series of stamps by the United Nations Postal Administration highlighting the goals and themes of the Decade.

2. *Activities of the Coordinator and the Centre for Human Rights*

11. Establish, as a matter of urgency, an adequately staffed and resourced indigenous people's unit.

12. Request Governments to second qualified indigenous people, in consultation with interested national indigenous organizations, to assist in the administration of the Decade.

13. Create a fellowship programme, in collaboration with the Advisory Services of the Centre for Human Rights of the Secretariat and Governments, to assist indigenous people wishing to gain experience in the different branches of the Centre and in other parts of the United Nations system. Such fellowships might be available for indigenous research and other similar activities.

14. Open a roster of indigenous experts in various fields who might be available to assist United Nations agencies, in collaboration with Governments, as appropriate, as partners or consultants.

15. Create an advisory group of persons with relevant knowledge of indigenous issues, acting in their personal capacity, to advise the Coordinator for the Decade and United Nations organizations, at their request. The members of this advisory group could include eminent indigenous persons, governmental representatives, independent experts and officials of the specialized agencies.

16. Consider the need to hold coordination meetings of Governments, organizations of the United Nations system and indigenous and non-governmental organizations, as necessary, to consider, examine and evaluate Decade activities and to develop an integrated, action-oriented strategy to advance the interests of indigenous people. The Economic and Social Council should hold mid-term and end-term reviews of the Decade in accordance with its resolution 1988/63 of 27 July 1988. The Working Group on Indigenous Populations of the Subcommission on Prevention of Discrimination and Protection of Minorities should review international activities undertaken during the Decade and receive information from Governments on the implementation of the goals of the Decade in their respective countries.

17. Compile, on the basis of communications of the focal points in the United Nations system, a regular news-sheet containing information about meetings of interest, major or innovatory projects, new sources of funding, policy developments and other news to be widely distributed.

18. Encourage the development of partnership projects in association with Governments to address specific regional or thematic issues bringing together Governments, indigenous people and appropriate United Nations agencies.

19. Establish an information programme linking the Coordinator of the Decade to focal points of the United Nations system, national committees for the Decade and, through appropriate channels, indigenous networks; also develop a database of indigenous organizations and other relevant information, in cooperation with indigenous people, Governments, academic institutions and other relevant bodies.

20. Organize meetings on relevant themes of concern to indigenous people with indigenous participation.

21. Launch a series of publications on indigenous issues to inform policy makers, opinion-formers, students and other interested people.

22. Develop, in collaboration with Governments, training programmes on human rights for indigenous people, including the preparation of relevant training materials, when possible in indigenous languages.

23. Establish a board of trustees or advisory group, including indigenous people, to assist the Coordinator of the Voluntary Fund for the International Decade.

24. Encourage the development of projects and programmes, in collaboration with Governments and taking into account the views of indigenous people and the appropriate United Nations agencies, for support by the Voluntary Fund for the Decade.

25. Ensure, in coordination with Governments and indigenous organizations, the necessary measures to guarantee financing of the objectives of the Decade.

3. *United Nations public information activities*

26. Produce and disseminate a series of posters on the Decade using designs by indigenous artists.

27. Organize a lecture series at United Nations information centres and campuses linked to the United Nations University, using indigenous speakers.

28. Publish in indigenous languages the Universal Declaration of Human Rights, international human rights conventions and, upon its adoption, the United Nations declaration on the rights of indigenous people, considering the use of audiovisual material for this purpose. Consider also the involvement of indigenous experts and their own information networks in disseminating information about the Decade.

29. Prepare, in collaboration with the Centre for Human Rights, information about indigenous people for distribution to the general public.

*4. Operational activities of the United Nations system*

30. Establish focal points for indigenous issues in all appropriate organizations of the United Nations system.

31. Encourage the governing bodies of specialized agencies of the United Nations system to adopt programmes of action for the Decade in their own fields of competence, in close cooperation with indigenous people.

32. Urge Governments to ensure that the programmes and budgets of relevant intergovernmental organizations give priority and devote sufficient resources to furthering the aims of the Decade, and request that regular reports on the action taken be submitted to the governing body or executive council of each organization.

33. Prepare, publish and disseminate a manual containing practical information for indigenous people on the operations and procedures of United Nations agencies.

34. Develop research on the socio-economic conditions of indigenous people, in collaboration with indigenous organizations and other appropriate partners, with a view to publishing regular reports in order to contribute to the solution of problems faced by indigenous people, taking into account paragraph 6.26 of the Programme of Action of the International Conference on Population and Development, held at Cairo from 5 to 13 September 1994.

35. Encourage Governments to establish appropriate mechanisms and practices to ensure the participation of indigenous people in the design and implementation of national and regional programmes of concern to them.

36. Hold regular inter-agency consultations, in collaboration with Governments and indigenous people, to exchange views and develop strategies on the programme of action for the Decade.

37. Hold consultations with Governments to examine, with national committees and development agencies, possibilities of cooperation in the activities of the Decade.

38. Develop training materials for indigenous people on human rights, including the translation of the main international instruments into different indigenous languages, and give them wide distribution. Consider the possibility of using radio programmes to gain access to indigenous communities not having written languages.

39. Prepare a database on national legislation on matters of particular relevance to indigenous people.

40. Hold consultations of all interested parties on the themes of human rights, the environment, development, health, culture and education, with a view to elaborating programmes in these areas.

*5. Activities of regional organizations*

41. Implement existing and develop new regional programmes of action to promote and support the objectives of the Decade.

42. Hold regional meetings on indigenous issues with existing regional organizations with a view to strengthening coordination, taking advantage of the machinery of the United Nations system and promoting the direct and active participation of indigenous people of different regions in collaboration with Governments.

The Working Group on Indigenous Populations could consider the possibility of holding its sessions in conjunction with these meetings.

43. Develop training courses and technical assistance programmes for indigenous people in areas such as project design and management, environment, health and education, and promote the exchange of skills and experiences of indigenous people from different regions.

44. Make funds available at the regional level to activities benefiting indigenous people.

45. Encourage regional organizations to draw up regional instruments for the promotion and protection of indigenous people in the framework of their own structures and promote existing regional instruments.

*6. Activities of Member States*

46. Establish national committees for the Decade or similar mechanisms, including indigenous people, all relevant departments and other interested parties duly convened by Governments, to mobilize public support for the various activities connected with the Decade.

47. Intensify coordination and communication at the national level between relevant ministries, agencies and regional and local authorities by establishing focal points or other mechanisms for coordination and dissemination of information.

48. Use part of the resources of existing programmes and of international assistance for activities of direct benefit to indigenous people and, where possible, provide additional funds for specific activities.

49. Develop, in collaboration with indigenous communities, national plans for the Decade, including main objectives and targets, fixing quantitative outcomes and taking into account the need for resources and possible sources of financing.

50. Provide appropriate resources for indigenous institutions, organizations and communities to develop their own plans and actions according to their own priorities.

51. Adopt measures, in cooperation with indigenous people, to increase knowledge, starting at the elementary-school level and in accordance with the age and development of schoolchildren, concerning the history, traditions, culture and rights of indigenous people, with special emphasis on the education of teachers at all levels, and adopt measures to restore indigenous place names.

52. Consider ratification and implementation of the Indigenous and Tribal Peoples Convention of the International Labour Organization (No. 169) and other international and regional instruments, in close consultation with the indigenous organizations of each country.

53. Recognize the existence, identity and rights of indigenous people through constitutional reforms or the adoption of new laws, when appropriate, to improve their legal status and guarantee their economic, social, cultural, political and civil rights.

54. Implement chapter 26 of Agenda 21, adopted by the United Nations Conference on Environment and Development, and the relevant provisions of the Convention on Biological Diversity, the Vienna Declaration and Programme of Action, adopted by the World Conference on Human Rights, the Programme of Action of the International Conference on Population and Development and the Programme of Action of the World

Summit for Social Development, as well as the relevant provisions of future high-level conferences.

### 7. *Activities of organizations of indigenous people*

55.   Establish an information network which can be linked to the Coordinator of the Decade and facilitate communications between the United Nations system, relevant governmental departments and indigenous communities.

56.   Indigenous organizations and international indigenous networks should develop information for local communities concerning the goals of the Decade and the activities of the United Nations.

57.   Establish and support indigenous schools and university-level institutions and collaborate with the relevant United Nations agencies; participate in the revision of school texts and the contents of programmes of study in order to eliminate discriminatory content and promote the development of indigenous cultures and, where appropriate, in indigenous languages and scripts; develop indigenous curricula for schools and research institutions.

58.   Create documentation centres, archives and *in situ* museums concerning indigenous people, their cultures, laws, beliefs and values, with material that could be used to inform and educate non-indigenous people on these matters. Indigenous people should participate on a preferential basis in the administration of these centres.

59.   Establish and promote networks of indigenous journalists and launch indigenous periodicals at the regional and international levels.

60.   Indigenous people may transmit their views on the programmes concerning their priority rights to Governments, the United Nations and the specialized agencies and regional organizations.

### 8. *Activities of non-governmental organizations and other interested parties, including education establishments, the media and business*

61.   Cooperate with indigenous organizations, communities and people in the planning of activities for the Decade.

62.   Non-governmental organizations working with indigenous people should involve indigenous people in their activities.

63.   Create radio and television centres in indigenous regions, when appropriate and in accordance with national legislation, to provide information on the problems and proposals of indigenous people and to improve communications between indigenous communities.

64.   Promote indigenous cultures, with due respect for intellectual property rights, through the publication of books, the production of compact discs and the organization of various artistic and cultural events which enhance knowledge of and serve to develop indigenous cultures and establish indigenous cultural and documentation centres.

65.   Involve different social and cultural groups in the activities planned for the Decade.

General Assembly resolution 50/157

21 December 1995      Meeting 97      Adopted without vote

Approved by Third Committee (A/50/634) without vote, 5 December (meeting 50); 26-nation draft (A/C.3/50/L.30), orally revised; agenda item 111.
*Meeting numbers.* GA 50th session: 3rd Committee 32-37, 45, 50; plenary 97.

### *Draft declaration*

**Human Rights Commission action.** By a 3 March resolution,[112] the Commission established an open-ended inter-sessional working group to elaborate a draft declaration on the rights of indigenous peoples, considering the draft annexed to a 1994 Subcommission resolution.[101] It asked the Group to meet for 10 days in 1995, to recommend to the Commission the time and duration of its meetings in subsequent years, and to submit a progress report in 1996. The Commission asked relevant UN bodies, programmes and specialized agencies and NGOs in consultative status with the Economic and Social Council which were interested in contributing to the activities of the Group to participate in its work. The Commission decided that participation of other relevant indigenous people's organizations, in addition to NGOs in consultative status with the Council, should be in accordance with the relevant provisions of a 1968 Council resolution[113] and procedures it annexed to its resolution; the Commission invited those organizations to submit applications as soon as possible. It requested the Secretary-General to ask Governments, intergovernmental organizations and NGOs in consultative status with the Council and indigenous people's organizations authorized to participate to submit, for the Group's consideration, comments on the draft declaration submitted by the Subcommission. The Commission recommended that the Council take steps to expedite its resolution.

#### ECONOMIC AND SOCIAL COUNCIL ACTION

On 25 July, the Economic and Social Council adopted **resolution 1995/32**.

**Establishment of a working group of the Commission on Human Rights to elaborate a draft declaration in accordance with paragraph 5 of General Assembly resolution 49/214**

*The Economic and Social Council,*

*Recalling* Commission on Human Rights resolution 1995/32 of 3 March 1995,

*Reaffirming* its resolution 1296(XLIV) of 23 May 1968, on arrangements for consultation with non-governmental organizations, in particular its paragraphs 9, 19 and 33,

*Recalling* the mandate of the Committee on Non-Governmental Organizations, especially as contained in paragraph 40 *(e)* of resolution 1296(XLIV),

1.   *Endorses* Commission on Human Rights resolution 1995/32;

2.   *Authorizes* the establishment, as a matter of priority and from within existing overall resources, of an open-ended inter-sessional working group of the Commission on Human Rights, operating in accordance with the procedures established by the Commission in the annex to its resolution 1995/32, with the sole purpose of elaborating a draft declaration, considering the draft United Nations declaration on the rights of indigenous peoples annexed to resolution

1994/45 of 26 August 1994 of the Subcommission on Prevention of Discrimination and Protection of Minorities, for consideration and adoption by the General Assembly within the International Decade of the World's Indigenous People;

3. *Also authorizes* the open-ended working group to meet for ten working days at the earliest possible date in 1995;

4. *Invites* applications from organizations of indigenous people not in consultative status with the Economic and Social Council that are interested in participating in the working group;

5. *Requests* the Coordinator of the Decade, in accordance with the procedures established by the Commission in its resolution 1995/32 and following consultations with the States concerned, and in accordance with Article 71 of the Charter of the United Nations, to forward all applications and information received to the Committee on Non-Governmental Organizations;

6. *Requests* the Committee on Non-Governmental Organizations to meet as necessary to examine the applications and, having considered all relevant information, including any views received from the States concerned, to recommend to the Economic and Social Council those organizations of indigenous people which should be authorized to participate in the working group, including at its first session in 1995;

7. *Decides*, on the basis of the recommendations of the Committee on Non-Governmental Organizations, to authorize the participation in the work of the working group of interested organizations of indigenous people, in accordance with rules 75 and 76 of the rules of procedure of the functional commissions of the Council;

8. *Requests* the Commission on Human Rights, at its fifty-second session, to review the progress of the working group and to transmit its comments to the Economic and Social Council at its substantive session of 1996;

9. *Requests* the Secretary-General to provide the necessary services and facilities for the implementation of the present resolution.

Economic and Social Council resolution 1995/32

25 July 1995     Meeting 52     Adopted without vote

Draft by Commission on Human Rights (E/1995/23); agenda item 5 *(d)*.
*Meeting numbers.* ESC 51-53.

On 25 October, by **decision 1995/317 A**, the Council approved the participation in the Working Group of 44 indigenous people's organizations, not in consultative status with the Council, and requested the Committee on NGOs to meet urgently to continue its consideration of the remaining applications. Governments were invited to submit their views on the applications.

In **decision 1995/317 B** of 2 November, the Council approved the participation of an additional 34 organizations not in consultative status.

**Subcommission action.** On 24 August, the Subcommission recommended[114] that the Commission recommend, through the Economic and Social Council, that the General Assembly update a 1985 resolution[115] by adding in its subpara-

graph *(b)* the words "and the working group established by the Commission on Human Rights in its resolution 1995/32 of 3 March 1995" after the words "Working Group on Indigenous Populations".

**Working Group activities.** The Working Group established to consider a UN draft declaration on the rights of indigenous peoples met in Geneva from 20 November to 1 December.[116] As requested by the Commission (see above), the Group had before it comments on the draft declaration submitted by 11 Governments,[117] two UN bodies and three specialized agencies,[118] and four non-governmental and indigenous organizations.[119]

The Group discussed the scope of application of the draft, its title and preambular paragraphs, and reviewed the draft declaration part by part.

### Voluntary Fund

On 21 December, the General Assembly adopted **resolution 50/156**.

#### United Nations Voluntary Fund for Indigenous Populations

*The General Assembly,*

*Recalling* its resolution 40/131 of 13 December 1985 establishing the United Nations Voluntary Fund for Indigenous Populations,

*Taking note* of Commission on Human Rights resolution 1995/32 of 3 March 1995, as endorsed by the Economic and Social Council in its resolution 1995/32 of 25 July 1995, which authorized the establishment of an open-ended inter-sessional working group of the Commission on Human Rights with the sole purpose of elaborating a draft declaration, considering the draft United Nations declaration on the rights of indigenous peoples annexed to resolution 1994/45 of 26 August 1994 of the Subcommission on Prevention of Discrimination and Protection of Minorities, for consideration and adoption by the General Assembly within the International Decade of the World's Indigenous People,

*Taking note also* of the provisions in Commission on Human Rights resolution 1995/32 regarding the participation of organizations of indigenous people in the Working Group,

*Emphasizing* the importance and special nature of the draft declaration as a standard-setting exercise specifically for indigenous people,

*Recognizing* the desirability of assisting organizations of indigenous people to participate in the Working Group,

1. *Decides* that the United Nations Voluntary Fund for Indigenous Populations should also be used to assist representatives of indigenous communities and organizations to participate in the deliberations of the open-ended inter-sessional Working Group of the Commission on Human Rights established by the Commission in its resolution 1995/32, as endorsed by the Economic and Social Council on 25 July 1995, as well as in the deliberations of the Working Group on Indigenous Populations of the Subcommission on Prevention of Discrimination and Protection of Minorities;

2. *Requests* the Secretary-General to bring the present resolution to the attention of Member States and to invite them to consider contributing to the Fund.

General Assembly resolution 50/156

21 December 1995    Meeting 97    Adopted without vote

Approved by Third Committee (A/50/634) without vote, 5 December (meeting 50); 19-nation draft (A/C.3/50/L.29); agenda item 111.
*Meeting numbers.* GA 50th session: 3rd Committee 32-37, 45, 50; plenary 97.

### Permanent forum for indigenous people

**Commission action.** On 3 March, the Commission endorsed[120] a 1994 Subcommission recommendation[121] that the Centre for Human Rights organize a workshop on establishing within the UN system a permanent forum for indigenous people. It recommended that the workshop be held for a three-day period prior to the 1995 session of the Working Group on Indigenous Populations and that its outcome be transmitted to the Group at that session. It asked the Secretary-General to transmit to the Group comments and suggestions on the possible establishment of a permanent forum received from Governments and indigenous people's organizations. The Group was to submit its views and suggestions, through the Subcommission, to the Commission in 1996.

On 25 July, the Economic and Social Council, by **decision 1995/262**, endorsed the recommendation for a workshop, that it be for a three-day period and that its outcome be transmitted to the Group in 1995.

**Workshop.** The workshop on the possible establishment of a permanent forum for indigenous people within the UN (Copenhagen, Denmark, 26-28 June) considered the scope of a permanent forum; the UN body to which it would report and its relationship with the UN; its mandate and terms of reference and activities that might be undertaken; membership and participation of indigenous people; the forum's relationship with the Working Group on Indigenous Populations; financial and secretariat implications; and the forum's location.[122]

The report of the workshop was transmitted to the Working Group, as were separate addenda containing the views of five Governments on the establishment of a permanent forum (as at 1 June 1995),[123] the views of three indigenous people's organizations,[124] and background papers on the subject prepared by independent experts.[125]

**Working Group activities.** In July,[102] the Working Group on Indigenous Populations expressed appreciation to the Government of Denmark and the Homerule Government of Greenland for organizing the workshop. It supported the idea that such a permanent forum should be established during the Decade; report to the Economic and Social Council; include in its mandate issues relating to human rights, development, environment, health, education and culture; and consist of a membership of representatives of Governments and indigenous peoples, as well as independent experts. The Group stated that if the permanent forum was open to non-members, it should be attended by representatives of all indigenous people's organizations regardless of their consultative status.

The Group recommended that another workshop be held, prior to its 1996 session, for continued discussions on the forum, with invitations sent to relevant UN departments and organizations, requesting that they consider how a new forum might cooperate with them. The Secretary-General was to review existing arrangements and programmes within the UN system which might be used by indigenous people.

**Subcommission action.** On 24 August, the Subcommission asked[126] the Secretary-General to invite Governments and indigenous organizations to express their views on establishing a permanent forum and to report to the Working Group in 1996 on comments and suggestions received. It also wanted a review of existing mechanisms, procedures and programmes within the UN for promotion and coordination of the rights of indigenous people. The Subcommission recommended that the forum be established early in the Decade and that its mandate include issues relating to human rights, development, environment, health, education and culture. Regarding membership, the Subcommission recommended that it consist of independent experts and representatives of Governments and indigenous peoples' organizations and, subject to its being open to non-members, that it also be open to representatives of all indigenous people's organizations without regard to consultative status. It also recommended that the Centre for Human Rights organize a second workshop on the subject.

### Study on treaties, agreements and other constructive arrangements

**Commission action.** On 3 March, the Human Rights Commission endorsed[127] a 1994 Subcommission recommendation[121] to Special Rapporteur Miguel Alfonso Martínez (Cuba) to submit in 1995 a second progress report on treaties, agreements and other constructive arrangements between States and indigenous populations to the Working Group on Indigenous Populations and the Subcommission and a final report to them in 1996. The Commission also endorsed the recommendation to the Secretary-General to assist the Special Rapporteur and provide the resources needed for a research mission to the Vatican archives in Rome. On 25 July, the Economic and Social Council endorsed those recommendations by **decision 1995/298**.

**Report of the Special Rapporteur.** In July, the Special Rapporteur submitted his second progress report,[128] describing research and other activities carried out between the last quarter of 1992 and the first quarter of 1995. He discussed the distinction between minorities and indigenous populations and analysed ways in which there had been a gradual erosion of the sovereign status of indigenous nations in Africa and Asia/Oceania. He recommended that advisory assistance from the Centre for Human Rights be guaranteed to him and that he be authorized to submit a third progress report in 1996 and a final report in 1997.

**Subcommission action.** On 24 August, the Subcommission requested[129] the Special Rapporteur to submit a third progress report to it and the Group in 1996 and a final report in 1997. It asked the Secretary-General to assist the Special Rapporteur and provide the resources needed for specialized research assistance, for visits to Geneva for consultation with the Centre for Human Rights and for a field mission to examine the contemporary significance of a historic treaty in one country, to be determined in consultation with the Government concerned, as a practical example for inclusion in the final report. It recommended that the Commission ask the Economic and Social Council to endorse its decision.

### Protection of indigenous heritage

**Commission action.** On 3 March, the Human Rights Commission endorsed[130] a 1994 Subcommission request[131] to the Secretary-General to submit the principles and guidelines for the protection of the heritage of indigenous people to indigenous people's organizations, nations and communities, Governments, specialized agencies, intergovernmental organizations and NGOs for their comments. It requested the Special Rapporteur, Erica-Irene A. Daes (Greece), to submit in 1995 her final report based on comments and information received, and the Secretary-General to assist her.

On 25 July, the Economic and Social Council, by **decision 1995/297**, welcomed the Special Rapporteur's preliminary report submitted in 1994,[131] authorizing her to prepare a final report for submission in 1995 and approving the Commission requests to the Secretary-General.

**Report of the Special Rapporteur.** In June, the Special Rapporteur submitted her final report[132] containing comments on the principles and guidelines for the protection of the heritage of indigenous people received from two Governments, two UN bodies, three UN specialized agencies and five indigenous people's organizations. She recommended that the Subcommission consider the revised principles and guidelines, as annexed to her report, in order to transmit them to the Commis-

sion in 1996. She further recommended the convening of a UN technical meeting to propose practical ways for the cooperation of relevant UN bodies and specialized agencies in protecting the heritage of indigenous people.

**Subcommission action.** On 25 August, the Subcommission expressed its appreciation[133] to the Special Rapporteur for her report, noting the limited number of replies received from Governments, indigenous communities and organizations and other parties concerned. It asked the Secretary-General to submit her report to Governments, specialized agencies, indigenous people's communities and organizations, intergovernmental organizations and NGOs concerned for their comments, and the Special Rapporteur to prepare in 1996 a supplementary report, based on those comments. The Subcommission also asked the Special Rapporteur to include in the supplementary report a chapter on activities taken in other forums, such as UNDP, UNESCO, FAO, WIPO and WTO, and to take into consideration the 1992 Convention on Biological Diversity,[134] the 1994 UN Convention to Combat Desertification in Those Countries Experiencing Serious Drought and/or Desertification, particularly in Africa,[135] and other relevant international instruments. The Subcommission recommended that the basic and comprehensive study on the protection of the cultural and intellectual property of indigenous peoples, prepared in 1993,[136] be published in all official UN languages and disseminated widely.

### Relocation of Navajo and Hopi families

In July, the Secretary-General reported[137] that, pursuant to a 1994 Subcommission request,[101] he had sought information regarding the human rights aspects of the case of the relocation of Navajo and Hopi families from northern Arizona (United States) from the Permanent Mission of the United States to the United Nations Office at Geneva, the Hopi Tribal Council, the Navajo Nation and the Indian Law Resource Center. No replies were received.

## Migrant workers

The situation of migrant workers has been a UN concern for many years, initially through the work of the International Labour Organization. This concern culminated in the adoption by the General Assembly in 1990 of the International Convention on the Protection of the Rights of All Migrant Workers and Members of Their Families (see preceding chapter).

In 1995, the Commission on Human Rights, the Economic and Social Council and the General Assembly adopted resolutions of particular concern to migrant workers, including those on family reunification and universal freedom of travel (see below) and violence against women migrant workers (see above and PART FOUR, Chapter X).

### Family reunification

**Commission action.** By a roll-call vote of 27 to 9, with 17 abstentions, the Human Rights Commission on 7 March called on[138] States to allow, in conformity with international legislation, the free flow of financial remittances by foreign nationals residing in their territory to relatives in the country of origin, and to discourage or repeal legislation that adversely affected the family reunification of documented migrants and the transfer of such remittances. It also called on them to ensure the universally recognized freedom of travel to all foreign nationals legally residing in their territory. It recommended that the General Assembly, through the Economic and Social Council, consider the matter in 1995.

#### ECONOMIC AND SOCIAL COUNCIL ACTION

In July, the Economic and Social Council adopted **decision 1995/276**.

#### Respect for the universal freedom of travel and the vital importance of family reunification

At its 52nd plenary meeting, on 25 July 1995, the Economic and Social Council, taking note of Commission on Human Rights resolution 1995/62 of 7 March 1995, approved the Commission's recommendation to the General Assembly, through the Council, that the Assembly consider at its fiftieth session the question of respect for the universal freedom of travel and the vital importance of family reunification.

Economic and Social Council decision 1995/276

20-7-23 (roll-call vote)

Draft by Commission on Human Rights (E/1995/23/Corr.2); agenda item 5 *(d)*.
*Meeting numbers.* ESC 51, 52.

Roll-call vote in Council as follows:

*In favour:* Brazil, Chile, China, Colombia, Costa Rica, Côte d'Ivoire, Cuba, Egypt, India, Indonesia, Jamaica, Libyan Arab Jamahiriya, Mexico, Nigeria, Pakistan, Sri Lanka, Sudan, Uganda, United Republic of Tanzania, Venezuela.

*Against:* Australia, Canada, Germany, Japan, Netherlands, United Kingdom, United States.

*Abstaining:* Bahamas, Belarus, Bhutan, Bulgaria, Denmark, France, Gabon, Greece, Ireland, Luxembourg, Malaysia, Norway, Philippines, Poland, Portugal, Republic of Korea, Romania, Russian Federation, Senegal, South Africa, Thailand, Ukraine, Zimbabwe.

#### GENERAL ASSEMBLY ACTION

On 22 December, the General Assembly adopted **resolution 50/175**.

#### Respect for the right to universal freedom of travel and the vital importance of family reunification

*The General Assembly,*

*Reaffirming* that all human rights and fundamental freedoms are universal, indivisible, interdependent and interrelated,

*Recalling* the provisions of the Universal Declaration of Human Rights,

*Stressing* that, as stated in the Programme of Action of the International Conference on Population and Development, family reunification of documented migrants

is an important factor in international migration, and that remittances by documented migrants to their countries of origin often constitute a very important source of foreign exchange and are instrumental in improving the well-being of relatives left behind,

*Recalling also* its resolution 49/182 of 23 December 1994,

1. *Once again calls upon* all States to guarantee the universally recognized freedom of travel to all foreign nationals legally residing in their territory;

2. *Reaffirms* that all Governments, particularly those of receiving countries, must recognize the vital importance of family reunification and promote its incorporation into national legislation in order to ensure protection of the unity of families of documented migrants;

3. *Calls upon* all States to allow, in conformity with international legislation, the free flow of financial remittances by foreign nationals residing in their territory to their relatives in the country of origin;

4. *Also calls upon* all States to refrain from enacting, and to repeal if it already exists, legislation intended as a coercive measure that discriminates against individuals or groups of legal migrants by adversely affecting family reunification and the right to send financial remittances to relatives in the country of origin;

5. *Decides* to continue its consideration of this question at its fifty-first session under the item entitled "Human rights questions".

General Assembly resolution 50/175

22 December 1995    Meeting 99    86-4-80 (recorded vote)

Approved by Third Committee (A/50/635/Add.2) by recorded vote (75-4-74), 13 December (meeting 55); draft by Cuba (A/C.3/50/L.36), orally revised; agenda item 112 *(b)*.
*Meeting numbers.* GA 50th session: 3rd Committee 35, 38-51, 55; plenary 99.

Recorded vote in Assembly as follows:

*In favour:* Afghanistan, Algeria, Angola, Armenia, Bangladesh, Benin, Bolivia, Bosnia and Herzegovina, Botswana, Brazil, Brunei Darussalam, Burkina Faso, Burundi, Cape Verde, Chad, Chile, China, Colombia, Costa Rica, Côte d'Ivoire, Cuba, Cyprus, Djibouti, Democratic People's Republic of Korea, Ecuador, Egypt, El Salvador, Gabon, Gambia, Ghana, Guinea, Guinea-Bissau, Guyana, Haiti, Honduras, India, Indonesia, Iran, Jamaica, Jordan, Kenya, Kuwait, Lao People's Democratic Republic, Lebanon, Lesotho, Libyan Arab Jamahiriya, Mali, Mauritania, Mauritius, Mexico, Morocco, Myanmar, Namibia, Nepal, Nicaragua, Niger, Nigeria, Oman, Pakistan, Papua New Guinea, Paraguay, Peru, Philippines, Qatar, Rwanda, Saint Lucia, Saudi Arabia, Senegal, Sri Lanka, Sudan, Swaziland, Syrian Arab Republic, Togo, Tunisia, Turkey, United Arab Emirates, Uganda, United Republic of Tanzania, Uruguay, Vanuatu, Venezuela, Viet Nam, Yemen, Zaire, Zambia, Zimbabwe.

*Against:* Canada, Israel, Japan, United States.

*Abstaining:* Albania, Andorra, Antigua and Barbuda, Argentina, Australia, Austria, Azerbaijan, Bahamas, Barbados, Belarus, Belgium, Belize, Bhutan, Bulgaria, Cambodia, Cameroon, Croatia, Czech Republic, Denmark, Dominica, Equatorial Guinea, Eritrea, Estonia, Ethiopia, Fiji, Finland, France, Georgia, Germany, Greece, Grenada, Hungary, Iceland, Ireland, Italy, Kazakstan, Kyrgyzstan, Latvia, Liechtenstein, Lithuania, Luxembourg, Malawi, Malaysia, Maldives, Malta, Marshall Islands, Micronesia, Monaco, Mongolia, Mozambique, Netherlands, New Zealand, Norway, Panama, Poland, Portugal, Republic of Korea, Republic of Moldova, Romania, Russian Federation, Saint Kitts and Nevis, Saint Vincent and the Grenadines, Samoa, San Marino, Sierra Leone, Singapore, Slovakia, Slovenia, Solomon Islands, South Africa, Spain, Suriname, Sweden, Tajikistan, Thailand, the former Yugoslav Republic of Macedonia, Trinidad and Tobago, Ukraine, United Kingdom, Uzbekistan.

### Disabled

**Commission action.** On 3 March, the Human Rights Commission called on[139] the Secretary-General to maintain the integrity of programmes within the UN relating to disabled persons and asked him to report biennially to the General Assembly on progress made to ensure the full recognition and enjoyment of their human rights. The Commission's request was approved by the Economic and Social Council by **decision 1995/274** of 25 July.

**Subcommission action.** On 18 August, the Subcommission asked[140] the Secretary-General to report in 1996 and to help ensure a wider distribution of the 1991 report[141] on disabled persons made by its Special Rapporteur Leandro Despouy (Argentina).

*REFERENCES*

[1]E/1995/23 (res. 1995/17). [2]YUN 1994, p. 1032. [3]YUN 1986, p. 717, GA res. 41/128, annex, 4 Dec. 1986. [4]E/CN.4/1996/10. [5]E/CN.4/1996/24. [6]E/CN.4/AC.45/1995/2 & Add.1. [7]E/CN.4/AC.45/1995/3. [8]E/CN.4/1995/26. [9]E/CN.4/1995/114. [10]YUN 1994, p. 1033. [11]Ibid., GA res. 49/183, 23 Dec. 1994. [12]A/50/729. [13]YUN 1993, p. 892. [14]E/CN.4/1996/2 (res. 1995/19). [15]E/CN.4/1995/25 & Add.1,2. [16]E/CN.4/Sub.2/1995/10. [17]E/1995/23 (res. 1995/13). [18]E/CN.4/1996/2 (res. 1995/32). [19]YUN 1994, p. 1035. [20]E/1995/23 (dec. 1995/105). [21]E/CN.4/Sub.2/1995/14. [22]E/CN.4/1996/2 (res. 1995/30). [23]YUN 1994, p. 1031. [24]E/CN.4/Sub.2/1995/11. [25]E/CN.4/1996/2 (res. 1995/31). [26]YUN 1994, p. 1068. [27]E/CN.4/1995/43. [28]E/1995/23 (res. 1995/45). [29]YUN 1994, p. 1123. [30]E/1995/23 (res. 1995/14). [31]E/CN.4/1996/2 (res. 1995/23). [32]E/1995/23 (res. 1995/81). [33]E/CN.4/1995/74. [34]E/1995/23 (res. 1995/82). [35]E/CN.4/1996/2 (dec. 1995/101). [36]E/CN.4/1995/75. [37]E/CN.4/1990/72. [38]GA res. 45/95, 14 Dec. 1990. [39]E/1995/23 (dec. 1995/114). [40]E/1995/23 (res. 1995/16). [41]YUN 1994, p. 1036. [42]E/CN.4/Sub.2/1995/15. [43]YUN 1993, p. 894. [44]E/CN.4/1996/2 (res. 1995/28). [45]YUN 1994, p. 1037. [46]E/1995/23 (res. 1995/19). [47]E/CN.4/Sub.2/1995/12. [48]E/CN.4/1996/2 (res. 1995/27). [49]YUN 1992, p. 756; YUN 1993, p. 895; YUN 1994, p. 1037; E/CN.4/Sub.2/1995/12. [50]E/CN.4/Sub.2/1995/13. [51]E/CN.4/1996/2 (res. 1995/29). [52]E/1995/23 (res. 1995/27). [53]E/CN.4/Sub.2/1989/37. [54]YUN 1956, p. 228. [55]YUN 1948-49, p. 613, GA res. 317(IV), annex, 2 Dec. 1949. [56]E/CN.4/Sub.2/1995/28. [57]E/CN.4/Sub.2/1995/ 39. [58]E/CN.4/Sub.2/AC.2/1995/5. [59]E/CN.4/Sub.2/AC.2/ 1995/7. [60]E/CN.4/Sub.2/AC.2/1995/6. [61]E/CN.4/1996/2 (res. 1995/16). [62]YUN 1993, p. 887. [63]YUN 1991, p. 563, GA res. 46/122, 17 Dec. 1991. [64]E/CN.4/1996/2 (res. 1995/15). [65]E/CN.4/1996/85. [66]E/CN.4/1996/86. [67]E/CN.4/1996/2 (dec. 1995/109). [68]E/CN.4/Sub.2/1995/28/Add.1. [69]E/CN.4/1996/82. [70]E/CN.4/Sub.2/1995/38. [71]E/CN.4/1996/2 (res. 1995/14). [72]E/1995/23 (res. 1995/86). [73]E/CN.4/Sub.2/1995/22. [74]YUN 1993, p. 908. [75]E/CN.4/1996/105. [76]YUN 1994, p. 1122. [77]E/CN.4/1995/42. [78]YUN 1979, p. 895, GA res. 34/180, annex, 18 Dec. 1979. [79]E/1995/23 (res. 1995/85). [80]Ibid. (res. 1995/20). [81]GA res. 45/158, annex, 18 Dec. 1990. [82]E/1995/23 (dec. 1995/112). [83]E/CN.4/Sub.2/1995/6. [84]YUN 1991, p. 619. [85]E/CN.4/1996/2 (res. 1995/20). [86]E/1995/23 (res. 1995/25). [87]A/50/369. [88]YUN 1993, p. 964, GA res. 48/156, 20 Dec. 1993. [89]YUN 1994, p. 1117. [90]Ibid., p. 1118. [91]E/CN.4/1995/94. [92]E/1995/23 (res. 1995/79). [93]YUN 1994, p. 1118, GA res. 49/210, 23 Dec. 1994. [94]A/50/456. [95]E/CN.4/ 1995/106. [96]YUN 1994, p. 1119. [97]YUN 1993, p. 965. [98]E/1995/23 (res. 1995/27). [99]E/CN.4/1996/2 (res. 1995/26). [100]E/1995/23 (res. 1995/31). [101]YUN 1994, p. 999. [102]E/CN.4/Sub.2/1995/24. [103]E/CN.4/1996/2 (res. 1995/38). [104]E/1995/23 (res. 1995/28). [105]YUN 1994, p. 1001, GA res. 49/214, 23 Dec. 1994. [106]Ibid., p. 1000. [107]YUN 1993, p. 865, GA res. 48/163, 21 Dec. 1993. [108]E/CN.4/Sub.2/AC.4/1995/5. [109]E/CN.4/1996/2 (res. 1995/37). [110]A/50/511. [111]A/50/565. [112]E/1995/23 (res. 1995/32). [113]YUN 1968, p. 647, ESC res. 1296(XLIV), 23 May 1968. [114]E/CN.4/1996/2 (res. 1995/36). [115]YUN 1985, p. 848, GA res. 40/131, 13 Dec. 1985. [116]E/CN.4/1996/84. [117]E/CN.4/1995/WG.15/2 & Add.1,2. [118]E/CN.4/1995/WG.15/3. [119]E/CN.4/1995/WG.15/4. [120]E/1995/23 (res. 1995/30). [121]YUN 1994, p. 1004. [122]E/CN.4/Sub.2/AC.4/1995/7. [123]E/CN.4/Sub.2/AC.4/1995/ 7/Add.1. [124]E/CN.4/Sub.2/AC.4/1995/7/Add.3. [125]E/CN.4/ Sub.2/AC.4/1995/7/Add.2. [126]E/CN.4/1996/2 (res. 1995/39). [127]E/1995/23 (dec. 1995/109). [128]E/CN.4/Sub.2/1995/27. [129]E/CN.4/1996/2 (dec. 1995/118). [130]E/1995/23 (dec. 1995/108). [131]YUN 1994, p. 1003. [132]E/CN.4/Sub.2/1995/26. [133]E/CN.4/1996/2 (res. 1995/40). [134]YUN 1992, p. 683. [135]YUN 1994, p. 944. [136]YUN 1993, p. 862. [137]E/CN.4/ Sub.2/1995/25. [138]E/1995/23 (res. 1995/62). [139]Ibid. (res. 1995/58). [140]E/CN.4/1996/2. (res. 1995/17). [141]YUN 1991, p. 627.

Chapter III

# Human rights violations

Alleged violations of human rights in specific countries in 1995 were again the subject of United Nations scrutiny in a number of forums, including the General Assembly, the Economic and Social Council, the Commission on Human Rights and its Subcommission on Prevention of Discrimination and Protection of Minorities, as well as by special bodies and officials appointed to examine the charges.

## General aspects

In addition to review in UN bodies of reported human rights violations in countries and other areas in Africa, Asia and the Pacific, Europe and the Mediterranean, Latin America and the Caribbean and the Middle East (see below), the United Nations also considered allegations in closed meetings and by secret ballot. Under a procedure established by the Economic and Social Council in 1970 to deal with communications alleging denial or violation of human rights,[1] the Commission on Human Rights held closed meetings to study confidential documents and a confidential report by a working group set up in 1990.[2] The documents dealt with human rights situations in Albania, Armenia, Azerbaijan, Chad, the Lao People's Democratic Republic, Latvia, the Republic of Moldova, Rwanda, Saudi Arabia, Slovenia, Thailand and Uganda. The Commission decided to discontinue consideration of the human rights situations in Albania, the Lao People's Democratic Republic, Latvia, the Republic of Moldova, Rwanda, Slovenia, Thailand and Uganda.

On 18 August,[3] the Subcommission decided, pursuant to a 1991 Council resolution,[4] to vote by secret ballot on proposals pertaining to allegations of human rights violations in countries, whenever such a vote was requested, including proposals of a procedural nature relating to proposals of a substantive nature.

On 24 August,[5] the Subcommission decided to consider in 1996 how best to carry out its mandate in examining item 6 of its agenda concerning violations of human rights and fundamental freedoms, while taking into account all reliable sources. The Subcommission asked the Secretariat to make the reports of Special Rapporteurs and Chairmen/Rapporteurs of working groups of the Commission available to the experts who requested them in 1996

and to undertake consultations with the Special Rapporteurs and Chairmen/Rapporteurs during their annual joint meeting. The Subcommission asked the Secretary-General to report in 1996.

With regard to recognition of gross and large-scale human rights violations, the Commission on 3 March,[6] noting a 1994 Subcommission resolution,[7] asked the Subcommission, bearing in mind the work of the other UN bodies on the issue, to reconsider its recommendation to appoint a special rapporteur to prepare a report on the recognition as an international crime of gross and large-scale violations of human rights, perpetrated on the orders of Governments or sanctioned by them.

On 24 August,[8] the Subcommission, reaffirming its recommendation that the Commission appoint Stanislav Chernichenko (Russian Federation) as the Special Rapporteur to prepare the report, decided to consider that report in 1996. It recommended that the Special Rapporteur take into account the comments made on his working papers submitted in 1992[9] and 1993,[10] as well as the work of the International Law Commission (see PART FIVE, Chapter III) and include in his report a draft declaration on the question.

*REFERENCES*

[1]YUN 1970, p. 530, ESC res. 1503(XLVIII), 27 May 1970. [2]ESC res. 1990/41, 25 May 1990. [3]E/CN.4/1996/2 (dec. 1995/106). [4]YUN 1991, p. 575, ESC res. 1991/32, 31 May 1991. [5]E/CN.4/1996/2 (dec. 1995/115). [6]E/1995/23 (dec. 1995/111). [7]YUN 1994, p. 1113. [8]E/CN.4/1996/2 (res. 1995/22). [9]YUN 1992, p. 810. [10]YUN 1993, p. 962.

## Africa

### Burundi

**Report of the Secretary-General.** In February, the Secretary-General discussed his good offices mission during the period from November 1993 to January 1995 to search for a peaceful solution in Burundi.[1] He described the activities of the UN High Commissioner for Human Rights who had conducted two missions to the country in 1994 and who had signed an agreement with the Government to execute a programme of advisory services. The programme emphasized human rights training, assistance to institutions and activities for young people.

The Secretary-General also described the activities of his Special Representative on internally displaced persons (see preceding chapter), special rapporteurs and working groups of the Commission and treaty bodies. He presented information received from the UN High Commissioner for Refugees and non-governmental organizations (NGOs).

**Commission action.** On 8 March,[2] the Commission strongly condemned the break in the democratic process initiated in Burundi, demanded an immediate end to violent acts and called on civilians and the military to respect the country's Constitution and Convention. It appealed to political groups, the army, the media and civilians to show moderation and a spirit of conciliation, and to restore full respect for and the promotion of human rights. It applauded the decision of the Special Rapporteur on extrajudicial, summary or arbitrary executions to undertake a mission to Burundi, which he did from 19 to 29 April (see PART THREE, Chapter I). The Commission called on its Chairman to appoint a special rapporteur to report in 1996 on the human rights situation in Burundi.

On 25 July, the Economic and Social Council approved the Commission's request to its Chairman by **decision 1995/291**.

Subsequently, Paulo Sérgio Pinheiro (Brazil) was appointed Special Rapporteur.[3]

**Subcommission action.** On 18 August,[4] the Subcommission appealed to the Commission to reinforce the activities of the Special Rapporteur.

On the same date,[5] the Subcommission condemned the existence of a radio station calling itself "Radio Démocratie–La Voix du Peuple", transmitting from the Uvira region of Zaire and broadcasting with complete impunity, under cover of anonymity, information inciting racial hatred among Burundi citizens and stirring up genocidal hatred. It urged the authorities of Zaire to take steps to close down the radio station, prosecute its sponsors and reporters, order an investigation and place under seal all materials and recordings which might serve as evidence, and to bring the reporters and their sponsors before the competent courts. The Subcommission suggested that the Special Rapporteur on Zaire, in conjunction with the Special Rapporteur on Burundi, accord priority in his observations on the role of such media in the propagation of genocidal behaviour. The Secretary-General was asked to transmit its resolution to the authorities of Zaire; the High Commissioner for Human Rights was to use his good offices to facilitate its implementation by them.

**Report of the Special Rapporteur.** In November, the Special Rapporteur submitted his report,[6] covering the period from 1 March to 31 October, reviewing his mandate, summarizing his activities and discussing the human rights situation in Burundi based on his visit from 21 June to 2 July.

The Special Rapporteur stated that the situation in Burundi was deteriorating, with the ethnic tension between the Hutus and Tutsis giving rise to systematic racist practices on both sides. A steady increase in serious human rights violations and criminal attacks on the security and lives of the population was due to widespread impunity. He discussed violations of the right to life and physical integrity, including: attacks on military positions, acts of violence against individuals, violence in primary and secondary schools and attacks against expatriates, NGOs and UN agencies; disturbances and killings at the Collège du Saint-Esprit in Kamenge and the University of Bujumbura in June and July; abuses by the army and forces of order; violations of the right to liberty of movement and freedom to choose one's residence within a State; arbitrary detentions; and violations of freedom of expression and freedom of the press.

The Special Rapporteur remained convinced that the best approach was to establish an international commission of inquiry, which had been called for by the Security Council (**resolution 1012(1995)**) and was subsequently established by the Secretary-General (see PART TWO, Chapter II). He recommended the consolidation of democratic institutions to eradicate impunity; measures to put an end to insecurity; the strengthening of civil society; and the promotion of the enjoyment of human rights.

## Equatorial Guinea

**Report of the Special Rapporteur.** In January,[7] Special Rapporteur Alejandro Artucio (Uruguay) described his visit to Equatorial Guinea in May and the human rights situation there, notably the situation of prisoners and detainees; the administration of justice; the unlimited encroachment of military jurisdiction into criminal matters; the legal structure of the State; failure to publicize laws and governmental acts; arrests, detentions and torture of political activists and others; freedom of expression; religious freedom; freedom of movement and freedom to travel; the situation of women; ethnic discrimination; and political rights. He concluded that progress had been made in the situation and enjoyment of human rights but that there were still serious human rights violations as well as disparities between the different parts of the country. He proposed technical assistance consisting of training courses and seminars.

**Commission action.** On 8 March,[8] the Commission called on the Government of Equatorial Guinea to promote the harmonious coexistence of all ethnic groups, to continue improving the conditions of prisoners and detainees, to continue taking measures to stop the practice of arbitrary arrest and detention, torture and cruel, inhuman or degrading treatment and to ensure that those responsible were investigated and punished. It appealed to the Government to improve the legal and social situation of women. The Commission decided to renew the Special Rapporteur's mandate for one year and asked him to report in 1996. The Secretary-General was asked to provide the Government with the technical assistance suggested by the Special Rapporteur and to assist him.

On 25 July, the Economic and Social Council, by **decision 1995/282**, approved the renewal of the Special Rapporteur's mandate, the Commission's request to him to report in 1996 and its request to the Secretary-General to assist him.

## Nigeria

On 8 March, the Commission on Human Rights, by a roll-call vote of 21 against to 17 in favour, with 15 abstentions, rejected a draft concerning the human rights situation in Nigeria.[9]

**GENERAL ASSEMBLY ACTION**

On 22 December, the General Assembly adopted **resolution 50/199**.

### Situation of human rights in Nigeria

*The General Assembly,*

*Guided* by the Charter of the United Nations, the Universal Declaration of Human Rights, the International Covenants on Human Rights, the Vienna Declaration and Programme of Action and other human rights instruments,

*Reaffirming* that all Member States have the duty to fulfil the obligations they have freely undertaken under the various international instruments in this field,

*Mindful* that Nigeria is a party to the International Covenant on Civil and Political Rights,

*Expressing concern* that the absence of representative government in Nigeria has led to violations of human rights and fundamental freedoms, and recalling in this regard the popular support for democratic rule as evidenced in the 1993 elections,

*Noting with interest* that the Government of Nigeria, on 1 October 1995, affirmed the principle of multi-party democracy, announcing its intent to accept the principle of power-sharing, lift the ban on political activity and the press, devolve power to local levels of government and subordinate the military to civilian authority, but disappointed that only limited action in this regard has followed,

*Noting with alarm* the recent arbitrary executions of nine persons, namely Ken Saro-Wiwa, Barinem Kiobel, Saturday Dobee, Paul Levura, Nordu Eawo, Felix Nwate, Daniel Gbokoo, John Kpuimen and Baribor Bera,

*Noting* the decision of the heads of Government of the Commonwealth countries to suspend Nigeria from membership in the Commonwealth,

*Noting also* the decisions of the European Union, as well as those of other States or groups of States with regard to Nigeria,

*Deeply concerned* about the human rights situation in Nigeria and the suffering caused thereby to the people of Nigeria,

1. *Condemns* the arbitrary execution, after a flawed judicial process, of Ken Saro-Wiwa and his eight co-defendants, and emphasizes that everyone charged with a penal offence has the right to be presumed innocent until proved guilty according to law in a public trial with all the guarantees necessary for defence;

2. *Expresses its deep concern* about other violations of human rights and fundamental freedoms in Nigeria, and calls upon the Government of Nigeria urgently to ensure their observance, in particular by restoring habeas corpus, releasing all political prisoners, guaranteeing freedom of the press and ensuring full respect for the rights of all individuals, including trade unionists and persons belonging to minorities;

3. *Calls upon* the Government of Nigeria to abide by its freely undertaken obligations under the International Covenant on Civil and Political Rights and other international instruments on human rights;

4. *Urges* the Government of Nigeria to take immediate and concrete steps to restore democratic rule;

5. *Welcomes* the decisions by the Commonwealth and other States individually or collectively to take various actions designed to underline to the Government of Nigeria the importance of return to democratic rule and observance of human rights and fundamental freedoms, and expresses the hope that these actions and other possible actions by other States, consistent with international law, will encourage the Government of Nigeria to achieve that specific purpose;

6. *Invites* the Commission on Human Rights at its fifty-second session to give urgent attention to the situation of human rights in Nigeria, and recommends, in this regard, that its relevant mechanisms, in particular the Special Rapporteur on extrajudicial, summary or arbitrary executions, report to the Commission prior to its fifty-third session;

7. *Requests* the Secretary-General, in the discharge of his good offices mandate and in cooperation with the Commonwealth, to undertake discussions with the Government of Nigeria and to report on progress in the implementation of the present resolution and on the possibilities for the international community to offer practical assistance to Nigeria in achieving the restoration of democratic rule.

General Assembly resolution 50/199

22 December 1995     Meeting 99     101-14-47 (recorded vote)

Approved by Third Committee (A/50/635/Add.3) by recorded vote (98-12-42), 14 December (meeting 57); 57-nation draft (A/C.3/50/L.66), orally revised; agenda item 112 *(c)*.

*Meeting numbers.* GA 50th session: 3rd Committee 35, 38-51, 54, 56-58; plenary 99.

Recorded vote in Assembly as follows:

*In favour:* Albania, Andorra, Antigua and Barbuda, Argentina, Armenia, Australia, Austria, Bahamas, Barbados, Belarus, Belgium, Belize, Bolivia, Bosnia and Herzegovina, Botswana, Brazil, Bulgaria, Cambodia, Canada, Chile, Colombia, Costa Rica, Croatia, Czech Republic, Denmark, Dominica, Ecuador, El Salvador, Estonia, Finland, France, Georgia, Germany, Greece, Grenada, Guatemala, Guyana, Haiti, Honduras, Hungary, Iceland, Ireland, Israel, Italy, Jamaica, Japan, Kazakstan, Latvia, Lesotho, Liechtenstein, Lithuania, Luxembourg, Malawi, Mali, Malta, Mauritius, Mexico, Micronesia, Monaco, Mongolia, Nepal, Netherlands, New Zealand, Norway, Panama, Paraguay, Peru, Philippines, Poland, Portugal, Qatar, Republic of Korea, Republic of Moldova, Romania, Russian Federation, Saint Kitts and Nevis, Saint Lucia, Saint Vincent and the Grenadines, Samoa, San Marino, Slovakia, Slovenia, Solomon Islands, South Africa, Spain, Suriname, Sweden, Tajikistan, the former Yugoslav Republic of Macedonia,

Trinidad and Tobago, Turkey, Uganda, Ukraine, United Kingdom, United States, Uruguay, Uzbekistan, Vanuatu, Venezuela, Zambia, Zimbabwe.

*Against:* Burundi, Chad, China, Cyprus,* Gambia, Iran, Libyan Arab Jamahiriya, Marshall Islands,* Myanmar, Niger, Nigeria, Sierra Leone, Sudan, Togo.

*Abstaining:* Afghanistan, Algeria, Angola, Bahrain, Bangladesh, Benin, Bhutan, Brunei Darussalam, Burkina Faso, Cameroon, Cape Verde, Congo, Côte d'Ivoire, Cuba, Democratic People's Republic of Korea, Djibouti, Egypt, Equatorial Guinea, Fiji, Gabon, Ghana, Guinea, Guinea-Bissau, India, Indonesia, Jordan, Kenya, Kyrgyzstan, Lebanon, Madagascar, Malaysia, Morocco, Mozambique, Namibia, Nicaragua, Pakistan, Papua New Guinea, Rwanda, Saudi Arabia, Senegal, Singapore, Sri Lanka, Swaziland, Thailand, Tunisia, United Arab Emirates, United Republic of Tanzania.

*Later advised the Secretariat it had intended to vote in favour.

A motion by Nigeria for a vote on paragraphs 1, 5 and 6 and on the draft as a whole was rejected by a recorded vote of 32 in favour to 80 against, with 30 abstentions.

### Rwanda

**Commission action.** On 8 March,[10] the Commission condemned genocide, violations of international humanitarian law and all human rights violations and abuses in Rwanda, as well as the kidnapping and killing of military peacekeeping personnel attached to the United Nations Assistance Mission for Rwanda (UNAMIR), the killing of personnel attached to humanitarian organizations, the killing of innocent civilians and the destruction of property. It urged all States concerned to cooperate fully with the International Tribunal for Rwanda, taking into account the obligations contained in a 1994 Security Council resolution[11] and another adopted in 1995 (**resolution 978(1995)**), and to take all measures for the early and effective functioning of the Tribunal. Welcoming the efforts of the Government of Rwanda to reconstruct the civil administration and the social, legal, economic and human rights infrastructure of the country, the Commission noted that efforts were hampered by a lack of resources. It commended the efforts of the High Commissioner for Human Rights to ensure that UN efforts aimed at conflict resolution and peacebuilding were accompanied by a strong human rights component and effectively supported by a comprehensive human rights programme.

Condemning attacks against persons in refugee camps near the Rwanda borders and demanding that such attacks cease immediately, the Commission called on States to prevent them and welcomed the efforts of UNAMIR, the Office of the UN High Commissioner for Refugees (UNHCR) and the human rights field operation in Rwanda. It also condemned those who obstructed the access of humanitarian relief. It welcomed the commitments of Governments to help resolve the problems of refugees and called on them to ensure the safety of refugees and the personnel providing humanitarian assistance. The Commission urged Governments in the region to prevent their territory from being used to pursue a strategy of destabilization of Rwanda.

The Commission extended the Special Rapporteur's mandate for another year and asked him to make recommendations concerning situations in which technical assistance might be appropriate. It asked the High Commissioner for Human Rights and the Centre for Human Rights to provide continuing and further technical assistance, upon request, particularly in the area of the administration of justice. It asked the Secretary-General to ensure adequate resources for the delivery of programmes of technical assistance and advisory services, especially in the area of the administration of justice as requested by the Government of Rwanda.

On 25 July, the Economic and Social Council, by **decision 1995/292**, approved the Commission's decision to extend the Special Rapporteur's mandate and its request to him to make recommendations regarding technical assistance. It also approved the Commission's request to the Secretary-General to assist the Special Rapporteur and to ensure resources for programmes of technical assistance and advisory services.

**Reports of the Special Rapporteur.** In June, Special Rapporteur René Degni-Ségui (Côte d'Ivoire) presented his findings resulting from his visits to Rwanda (27 March–3 April and 25-28 May).[12] He also travelled to Belgium, Canada, France and the United States.

The Special Rapporteur stated that the human rights situation in Rwanda had barely changed and was still characterized by serious violations of property rights, personal security and the right to life. In addition, there had been no obvious progress towards a solution to the problem of displaced persons or refugees.

Concerning the inquiry into genocide, the Special Rapporteur stated that substantial progress had been made in the deployment of observers, but that the human rights operation suffered from a shortage of financial resources and political difficulties which focused on relations between the operation and the Rwandan authorities and between the operation and the Special Rapporteur. The Special Rapporteur presented eyewitness accounts of incidents of genocide. The special investigation unit succeeded in identifying several hundred mass graves throughout the country and obtained and examined documents related to the planning of massacres.

The Special Rapporteur made recommendations for UN action regarding the repression of genocide, the cessation of human rights violations, the fate of the victims of human rights violations, the fate of refugees and displaced persons, and reconstruction and social harmony.

In a later report,[13] the Special Rapporteur described two further visits to Rwanda (24-28 August and 4-9 December). In August, he investigated the situation created by the expulsion of Rwandan refugees from the camps in Zaire and in December he familiarized himself with recent developments in the human rights situation. He stated that the human rights situation, notably violations of property rights, personal security and the right to life, seemed to be deteriorating owing to the addition of violations of the right to freedom of expression. The human rights observers were continuing to collect information on genocide and other human rights violations, and the inquiry had been extended to special situations concerning vulnerable groups, including women, children and the Twas, an ethnic group which accounted for some 1 per cent of the population. The problem of returnees arose only in relation to refugees since the closure of camps and the forced repatriation of displaced persons to their communes of origin. No substantial progress had been made in that respect, and the problem had been further complicated by the forced repatriations of refugees from Zaire and by the threat of new expulsions.

The Special Rapporteur presented recommendations for UN action concerning assistance for victims of genocide and other crimes belonging to vulnerable groups; the rehabilitation of the Rwandan judicial and prison system; the opening of trials at the International Tribunal for Rwanda and the cooperation of States; the punishment of human rights violations; and the strengthening of reception, resettlement and security facilities for returnees.

**Subcommission action.** On 18 August,[14] the Subcommission condemned the genocide committed in Rwanda and demanded an end to all action aimed at arming and training the militias and extremist elements in the refugee camps for the resumption of the war. It called for measures to reorganize the Rwandan judicial system; punishment of individuals implicated in the war crimes, and the adoption of measures by States which had granted asylum or other refuge to the individuals implicated in the genocide and massacres so that they did not escape justice. The Subcommission called on the international community to provide the necessary assistance so that the International Tribunal for Rwanda could function and begin the trials of those accused of genocide and appealed to it to make a financial contribution to the human rights development and education programmes. It demanded that the Government and the international community use all means possible to contain the epidemics of dysentery, pneumonia and gangrene, which were decimating detainees in Rwandan prisons. The Subcommission paid tribute to the work of the UN High Commissioner for Human Rights in Rwanda, especially the programmes he had established to reorganize the ju-

dicial system, promote education, human rights and technical cooperation and investigate genocide, and to the work accomplished by the Special Rapporteur.

Also on 18 August,[5] the Subcommission condemned the role played by some printed or audiovisual media in inciting genocidal hatred, as revealed by the Special Rapporteur.

**Notes of the Secretary-General.** On 2 November, the Secretary-General transmitted to the General Assembly and the Security Council the reports of the Special Rapporteur prepared since the forty-ninth (1994) session of the Assembly.[15] On 30 November, he transmitted[16] to the Assembly the report of the UN High Commissioner for Human Rights on the Human Rights Field Operation in Rwanda (see PART TWO, Chapter II).

GENERAL ASSEMBLY ACTION

On 22 December, the General Assembly adopted **resolution 50/200**.

### Situation of human rights in Rwanda

*The General Assembly,*

*Guided* by the Charter of the United Nations, the Universal Declaration of Human Rights, the International Covenants on Human Rights, the Convention on the Prevention and the Punishment of the Crime of Genocide and other applicable human rights and humanitarian law standards,

*Recalling* its resolution 49/206 of 23 December 1994, and taking note of Commission on Human Rights resolution 1995/91 of 8 March 1995, in which the Commission renewed the mandate of the Special Rapporteur to investigate the human rights situation in Rwanda,

*Welcoming* the commitments of the Government of Rwanda to protect and promote respect for human rights and fundamental freedoms and to eliminate impunity, recalling the efforts to restore the rule of law and reconstruct the civil administration and the social, legal and human rights infrastructure, and noting that these efforts are hampered by a lack of resources,

*Noting* the concerns of the Special Rapporteur, as set out in his report of 28 June 1995, that the human rights situation is exacerbated by the inadequate system for the administration of justice, characterized by a shortage of both human and material resources, and that there are threats and violence against the physical integrity of individuals, arrest, detention and treatment and conditions of detention, which do not conform to international standards,

*Expressing its grave concern* at the tragedy of Kibeho in April 1995, and bearing in mind the conclusions of the Independent International Commission of Inquiry in its report of 18 May 1995,

*Recalling* the obligations of all States to punish all persons who commit or authorize genocide or other grave violations of international humanitarian law or those who are responsible for grave violations of human rights and, pursuant to Security Council resolution 978(1995) of 27 February 1995, to exert every effort, without delay, to bring those responsible to justice in accordance with international principles of due process, and to honour their obligations under international law in this regard, particularly under the Convention on the Prevention and Punishment of the Crime of Genocide,

*Welcoming* the measures taken by the United Nations High Commissioner for Human Rights to put in place the Human Rights Field Operation in Rwanda and to coordinate its activities with those of the Special Representative of the Secretary-General, the United Nations High Commissioner for Refugees, the United Nations Development Programme, the United Nations Assistance Mission for Rwanda, the International Criminal Tribunal for the Prosecution of Persons Responsible for Genocide and Other Serious Violations of International Humanitarian Law Committed in the Territory of Rwanda and Rwandan Citizens Responsible for Genocide and Other Such Violations Committed in the Territory of Neighbouring States, between 1 January and 31 December 1994, the Department of Humanitarian Affairs of the Secretariat, and other United Nations agencies and intergovernmental and non-governmental organizations, and the International Committee of the Red Cross,

*Recognizing* the valuable contribution that the human rights officers deployed by the United Nations High Commissioner for Human Rights to Rwanda have made towards the improvement of the overall situation,

*Deeply concerned* by the reports of the Special Rapporteur and the United Nations High Commissioner for Human Rights, according to which genocide and systematic, widespread and flagrant violations of international humanitarian law, including crimes against humanity and grave violations and abuses of human rights, were committed in Rwanda,

*Welcoming* the policy of the Government of Rwanda to facilitate the process of voluntary and safe return, resettlement and reintegration of refugees, as reaffirmed in the Cairo Declaration on the Great Lakes Region of 29 November 1995,

*Noting* the United Nations support for all efforts to reduce tension and restore stability in the Great Lakes region, and supporting initiatives of the Secretary-General in this regard, particularly in implementing the Cairo Declaration on the Great Lakes Region and continuing consultations with the aim of convening a conference on security, stability and development in the Great Lakes region, as appropriate,

*Recalling* Security Council resolution 1029(1995) of 12 December 1995, in which the Council renewed the mandate of the United Nations Assistance Mission for Rwanda to exercise its good offices to assist in achieving the voluntary and safe repatriation of Rwandan refugees within the frame of reference of the recommendations of the Bujumbura Conference and the Cairo Summit of the heads of State of the Great Lakes region, and in promoting genuine national reconciliation, to assist the Office of the United Nations High Commissioner for Refugees and other international agencies in the provision of logistical support for the repatriation of refugees, to contribute, with the agreement of the Government of Rwanda, to the protection of the International Tribunal for Rwanda as an interim measure until alternative arrangements agreed with the Government of Rwanda can be put in place,

*Acknowledging* the responsibility of the Government of Rwanda for the safety and security of all personnel attached to the United Nations Assistance Mission for Rwanda, United Nations agencies and humanitarian organizations and other international staff operating in the country,

*Recognizing* the important role played by non-governmental organizations in providing humanitarian assistance and contributing to the reconstruction and rehabilitation of Rwanda,

*Recognizing also* that effective action must be taken to ensure that the perpetrators of genocide and crimes against humanity are promptly brought to justice,

*Recognizing further* that effective action to prevent further violations of human rights and fundamental freedoms must be a central and integral element of the overall Rwandan and United Nations responses to the situation in Rwanda and that a strong human rights component is indispensable to the political peace process and the post-conflict reconstruction of Rwanda,

1. *Welcomes* the report of the United Nations High Commissioner for Human Rights on the Human Rights Field Operation in Rwanda, and takes note of the reports of the Special Rapporteur of the Commission on Human Rights on violations committed during the tragedy in Rwanda and on the current situation of human rights in Rwanda;

2. *Condemns in the strongest terms* the acts of genocide, violations of international humanitarian law and all violations and abuses of human rights that occurred during the tragedy in Rwanda, especially following the events of 6 April 1994, which resulted in a massive loss of human life, up to one million people;

3. *Expresses its deep concern* at the intense suffering of the victims of genocide and crimes against humanity, recognizes the ongoing suffering of their survivors, particularly the extremely high number of traumatized children and women victims of rape and sexual violence, and urges the international community to provide adequate assistance to them;

4. *Condemns* the killing of personnel attached to the United Nations Assistance Mission for Rwanda, United Nations agencies and humanitarian organizations operating in the country, including Rwandan personnel working with them;

5. *Calls upon* the Government of Rwanda to take all necessary measures to ensure the safety and security of all personnel attached to the United Nations Assistance Mission for Rwanda, United Nations agencies and humanitarian organizations and other international staff operating in the country;

6. *Reaffirms* that all persons who commit or authorize genocide or other grave violations of international humanitarian law or those who are responsible for grave violations of human rights are individually responsible and accountable for those violations;

7. *Urges* all States, pursuant to Security Council resolution 978(1995), to exert, without delay, every effort, including arrest and detention, in order to bring those responsible to justice in accordance with international principles of due process, and also urges States to honour their obligations under international law in this regard, particularly under the Convention on the Prevention and Punishment of the Crime of Genocide;

8. *Recognizes* that effective action must be taken by all States concerned to ensure that the perpetrators of genocide and crimes against humanity are promptly brought to justice, and urges all States concerned to

cooperate fully with the International Criminal Tribunal for the Prosecution of Persons Responsible for Genocide and Other Serious Violations of International Humanitarian Law Committed in the Territory of Rwanda and Rwandan Citizens Responsible for Genocide and Other Such Violations Committed in the Territory of Neighbouring States, between 1 January 1994 and 31 December 1994, taking into account the obligations contained in Security Council resolutions 955(1994) of 8 November 1994 and 978(1995), and to intensify efforts for the effective functioning of the Tribunal without delay;

9.  *Commends* the efforts of the United Nations High Commissioner for Human Rights, working in cooperation with and assisting the Government of Rwanda, to ensure that human rights monitoring, a comprehensive programme of human rights assistance and confidence-building measures form integral parts of Rwandan and United Nations efforts aimed at conflict prevention and peace-building in Rwanda, drawing as appropriate on the expertise and capacities of all parts of the United Nations system, thus contributing to the promotion and protection of human rights in Rwanda;

10.  *Encourages* the Government of Rwanda, in a spirit of national reconciliation, to intensify efforts to protect and promote respect for human rights and fundamental freedoms and to create an environment conducive to the realization of civil, political, economic, social and cultural rights and the voluntary and safe return of refugees to their homes;

11.  *Takes note with concern* of the findings of the Special Rapporteur as set out in his report of 28 June 1995, and of the Human Rights Field Operation in Rwanda, that the human rights situation is exacerbated by the inadequate system for the administration of justice, characterized by a shortage of both human and material resources;

12.  *Notes with concern* the arrest, detention and treatment and conditions of detention that do not conform to international standards, as set out in the report of the Special Rapporteur;

13.  *Also notes with concern* that a situation still exists, evidenced by reports of threats and violence against the physical integrity of individuals, which is sometimes exacerbated by incursions;

14.  *Urges* Governments in the region to take measures to prevent their territory from being used to pursue a strategy of destabilization of Rwanda, and, in this regard, urges all States concerned to cooperate fully with the International Commission of Inquiry on arms flows in the Great Lakes region, established in pursuance of Security Council resolution 1013(1995) of 7 September 1995;

15.  *Condemns* the mass killings of civilians at Kibeho in April 1995, takes note of the conclusions of the Independent International Commission of Inquiry in its report, and expresses its grave concern at the events in Kanama in September 1995;

16.  *Welcomes* the efforts of the Government of Rwanda to reconstruct the civil administration and the social, legal, economic and human rights infrastructure of Rwanda, encourages the Government to intensify its efforts, with the assistance of the international community, the Human Rights Field Operation in Rwanda and other United Nations bodies, to expedite the processing of cases, to ensure conditions and treatment in detention in conformity with international standards, and to train civilian police in the legal procedures governing arrest and detention, and notes that efforts in this regard are hampered by a lack of human and financial resources;

17.  *Invites* Member States, the organizations and bodies of the United Nations system and intergovernmental and non-governmental organizations to continue and intensify their efforts to contribute financial and technical support to the efforts of the Government of Rwanda to reconstruct the civil administration and the social, legal, economic and human rights infrastructure of Rwanda, particularly in the areas of the administration of justice, and welcomes the contributions made, including those at the Round Table Conference at Geneva and its mid-term review, and urges States and donor agencies to fulfil their earlier commitments;

18.  *Condemns* all violence and intimidation against persons in the refugee camps in neighbouring countries, calls upon the appropriate authorities to ensure security in such camps, and welcomes the commitments undertaken by the Governments in the region in the Cairo Declaration on the Great Lakes Region;

19.  *Welcomes* the joint efforts of the Government of Rwanda, neighbouring countries and the United Nations High Commissioner for Refugees to assist the voluntary and safe return of refugees through, *inter alia*, the work of the Tripartite Commission and the agreements reached at Nairobi in January 1995, Bujumbura in February 1995 and Cairo in November 1995, and welcomes also the efforts of the United Nations High Commissioner for Refugees, the United Nations High Commissioner for Human Rights, the United Nations Assistance Mission for Rwanda and the United Nations Development Programme to coordinate their efforts to ensure protection of the human rights of refugees during their return, resettlement and reintegration;

20.  *Also welcomes* the measures taken by the United Nations High Commissioner for Human Rights, working in cooperation with and assisting the Government of Rwanda, to put in place the Human Rights Field Operation in Rwanda, which has as its objective:

(a)  The investigation of violations of human rights and humanitarian law, including acts of genocide and crimes against humanity;

(b)  The monitoring of the human rights situation and the prevention of future violations;

(c)  Cooperation with other international agencies in re-establishing confidence and thus facilitating the voluntary return and resettlement of refugees and displaced persons;

(d)  The rebuilding of civil society, through programmes of human rights education and technical cooperation, particularly in the areas of the administration of justice and conditions of arrest, detention and treatment in detention, and through programmes of cooperation with Rwandan human rights organizations; and requests the High Commissioner to report regularly on all of these activities of the Field Operation and to cooperate and share information with the Special Rapporteur in order to assist him in fulfilling his mandate;

21.  *Further welcomes* the cooperation the Government of Rwanda has extended to the United Nations High Commissioner for Human Rights, the Human Rights Field Operation in Rwanda and the Special Rappor-

teur and the acceptance by the Government of Rwanda of the deployment of human rights field officers throughout the country;

22. *Requests* the Secretary-General to take appropriate steps to ensure adequate financial and human resources and logistical support for the Human Rights Field Operation in Rwanda, taking into account the need to deploy a sufficient number of human rights field officers and the need for programmes of technical assistance and advisory services for the Government of Rwanda and Rwandan human rights organizations, especially in the field of the administration of justice;

23. *Requests* the United Nations High Commissioner for Human Rights to report on the activities of the Human Rights Field Operation in Rwanda to the Commission on Human Rights at its fifty-second session and to the General Assembly at its fifty-first session.

General Assembly resolution 50/200

22 December 1995      Meeting 99      Adopted without vote

Approved by Third Committee (A/50/635/Add.3) without vote, 14 December (meeting 58); 42-nation draft (A/C.3/50/L.67), orally revised; agenda item 112 (c).

*Meeting numbers.* GA 50th session: 3rd Committee 35, 38-51, 55, 58; plenary 99.

## South Africa

On 3 February,[17] the Commission decided not to hold a general debate on the final report[18] of the Ad Hoc Working Group of Experts on southern Africa.

On 17 February,[19] the Commission took note with appreciation of the final report of the Ad Hoc Working Group, which was established by the Commission in 1967,[20] and expressed its appreciation to the Group for the important role it had played in support of the efforts to eliminate apartheid in South Africa and to establish a non-racial and democratic society. The Commission considered that the Group's mandate had been successfully concluded and decided to terminate it as of 17 February. It decided to remove from its agenda, as from its 1996 session, the item "Violations of human rights in southern Africa: report of the Ad Hoc Working Group of Experts".

### Transition to democracy

**Commission action.** On 3 February,[17] the Commission decided not to hold a general debate on the final report[21] of the Special Rapporteur to monitor the transition to democracy in South Africa, Judith Sefi Attah (Nigeria).

On 17 February,[22] the Commission, taking note of the Special Rapporteur's final report, expressed its appreciation to her for monitoring the transition to democracy in South Africa and for the important role she had played in support of the efforts to eliminate apartheid and to establish a non-racial society. It considered that the Special Rapporteur's mandate had been successfully concluded and terminated it as at 17 February. The Commission removed from its agenda, as from its 1996 session, the item "Monitoring and assisting the transition to democracy in South Africa".

**Subcommission action.** On 4 August,[23] the Subcommission took note of the Special Rapporteur's final report and decided not to hold a general debate on the item.

On 18 August,[24] the Subcommission expressed its appreciation to the Special Rapporteur for the important role she had played in support of the efforts to eliminate apartheid and to establish a non-racial society. It considered that her mandate had been successfully concluded and decided to remove the item from its agenda as from its 1996 session.

### 1973 Convention against apartheid

As at 31 December 1995,[25] there were 99 parties to the International Convention on the Suppression and Punishment of the Crime of Apartheid, which was adopted by the General Assembly in 1973[26] and entered into force in 1976.[27] In 1995, there were no new parties to the Convention. In his annual report to the General Assembly on its status,[28] the Secretary-General provided a list of States that had signed, ratified, acceded or succeeded to it as at 31 August.

The Assembly, by **decision 50/441** of 21 December, took note of the Secretary-General's report.

**Activities of the Group of Three.** The Group of Three—established under article IX of the Convention to consider reports by States parties on measures taken to implement the Convention's provisions and in 1995 composed of Ecuador, the Philippines and Romania—held its sixteenth session in Geneva from 23 to 27 January.[29]

The Group noted with satisfaction that, with the entry into force in 1994[30] of South Africa's first non-racial and democratic Constitution and the holding of free elections, the system of apartheid had ended. As at 30 June 1994, it noted, 213 reports were overdue. Since its last session held in 1993,[31] no reports had been submitted under article VII of the Convention. In view of these and other developments, the Group recommended that the Commission suspend for the time being further meetings of the Group.

**Commission action.** On 3 February,[17] the Commission decided not to hold a general debate on the report of the Group of Three.

On 17 February,[32] the Commission, taking note of the Group's report, decided to suspend its meetings as at 17 February and to remove from its own 1997 agenda the item "Implementation of the International Convention on the Suppression and Punishment of the Crime of Apartheid".

## Sudan

**Report of the Special Rapporteur.** In January, Special Rapporteur Gáspár Bíró (Hungary) reported[33] on human rights violations in northern Sudan, including violations of freedom of conscience, freedom of expression, association and peaceful assembly, the rights of the child, the rights of women, and freedom of movement and residence. He discussed cases of slavery, servitude, slave trade, forced labour and similar practices and incidents relating to the distribution of relief in which all parties to the conflict bore responsibility and which constituted grave violations of international humanitarian law. He drew attention to specific cases of human rights violations occurring in central and eastern Sudan.

The Special Rapporteur stated that the human rights situation in the Sudan had deteriorated owing to intensified and regular bombardment of civilians by the Government. Human rights violations by government agents, as well as by members of factions of the Sudan People's Liberation Army, continued to take place, including extrajudicial killings, systematic torture and widespread arbitrary arrest of suspected opponents. The Special Rapporteur considered the situation of women and children to be alarming.

He suggested to the Commission on Human Rights that he be authorized to consult with the Secretary-General on the placement of monitors in locations which would facilitate information flow and assessment and help the independent verification of reports on the human rights situation. He recommended that the Commission urge all parties to the conflict to begin negotiations on enlarging the tranquillity corridors so as to decrease the flow of Sudanese refugees to neighbouring countries. The Special Rapporteur also recommended that the Government abide by its human rights obligations under international law; cease immediately the aerial bombardment of civilians; ratify the 1984 Convention against Torture and Other Cruel, Inhuman or Degrading Treatment or Punishment;[34] accede to the 1979 Convention on the Elimination of All Forms of Discrimination against Women;[35] sign the first Optional Protocol to the 1966 International Covenant on Civil and Political Rights,[36] and Protocol II to the Geneva Conventions of 12 August 1949 for the protection of war victims, adopted in 1977;[37] ensure proper training for its security and police forces, army, paramilitary and civil defence groups; revise its policy concerning children living or working in the street; grant free access to regional and international humanitarian and human rights organizations; carry out investigations into human rights violations in the Nuba Mountains and towns of southern Sudan; and address the problem of displaced persons. The Special Rapporteur proposed that the parties to the conflict be urged to agree on a cease-fire and called on them to prevent violence by their agents against

civilians and to apply strictly the agreements reached with Operation Lifeline Sudan (see PART FOUR, Chapter III) regarding unimpeded delivery of relief.

**Commission action.** By a roll-call vote of 33 to 7, with 10 abstentions, the Commission on 8 March,[38] expressing its deep concern at the serious human rights violations in the Sudan, urged the Government to respect human rights and called on all parties to the hostilities to cooperate to ensure such respect. It expressed outrage at the use of military force to disrupt or attack relief efforts and called for an end to such practices and for those responsible to be brought to justice. The Commission also called on the Government to allow the judiciary and other legal institutions to exercise their functions free from government restrictions and interference; to comply with applicable international human rights instruments and to bring its national legislation into accordance with the instruments to which the Sudan was a party; to work actively for the eradication of practices that were directed against and violated the human rights of women and girls; to cease immediately the aerial bombardment of civilian targets; and to ensure a thorough investigation by the independent judicial inquiry commission of the killings of Sudanese employees of foreign relief organizations, to bring to justice those responsible and to provide just compensation to the victims' families. The Commission called on the Government and all parties to permit international agencies, humanitarian organizations and donor Governments to deliver humanitarian assistance and to cooperate with the UN Department of Humanitarian Affairs and Operation Lifeline Sudan. It also called on the parties to respect the provisions of international humanitarian law, including the 1949 Geneva Conventions for the protection of war victims and the Additional Protocols thereto,[37] to halt the use of weapons against the civilian population and to protect civilians from violations.

The Commission extended the Special Rapporteur's mandate for one year and asked him to report to the General Assembly in 1995 and to the Commission in 1996. It called on the Sudan to cooperate fully with the Special Rapporteur and to ensure that he had free and unlimited access to any person with whom he wished to meet, with no threats or reprisals. The Commission recommended that the Special Rapporteur begin consultations with the Secretary-General on modalities leading to the placement of monitors.

**ECONOMIC AND SOCIAL COUNCIL ACTION**

In July, the Economic and Social Council adopted **decision 1995/287**.

### Situation of human rights in the Sudan

At its 52nd plenary meeting, on 25 July 1995, the Economic and Social Council, taking note of Commission on Human Rights resolution 1995/77 of 8 March 1995, approved the Commission's decision to extend for an additional year the mandate of the Special Rapporteur on the situation of human rights in the Sudan, also approved its request to him to report his findings and recommendations to the General Assembly at its fiftieth session and to the Commission at its fifty-second session, and further approved the Commission's request to the Secretary-General to give the Special Rapporteur all necessary assistance in the discharge of his mandate.

Economic and Social Council decision 1995/287

33-8-10 (roll-call vote)

Draft by Commission on Human Rights (E/1995/23); agenda item 5 *(d)*. *Meeting numbers.* ESC 51, 52.

Roll-call vote in Council as follows:

*In favour:* Australia, Bahamas, Belarus, Brazil, Bulgaria, Canada, Chile, Colombia, Costa Rica, Côte d'Ivoire, Denmark, France, Gabon, Germany, Greece, Ireland, Jamaica, Japan, Luxembourg, Mexico, Netherlands, Norway, Poland, Portugal, Romania, Russian Federation, South Africa, Uganda, Ukraine, United Kingdom, United States, Venezuela, Zimbabwe.

*Against:* China, Cuba, India, Indonesia, Libyan Arab Jamahiriya, Pakistan, Sri Lanka, Sudan.

*Abstaining:* Bhutan, Egypt, Ghana, Malaysia, Nigeria, Philippines, Republic of Korea, Senegal, Thailand, United Republic of Tanzania.

**Interim report of the Special Rapporteur.** In October, the Secretary-General transmitted to the General Assembly an interim report[39] of the Special Rapporteur. The Special Rapporteur carried out a fact-finding mission to Kenya, Uganda and Eritrea between 30 July and 15 August. He reported no response from the Government of the Sudan to his request of 28 July to visit the country.

The Special Rapporteur received information regarding extrajudicial killings and summary executions, enforced or involuntary disappearances, torture and other cruel, inhuman or degrading treatment, arbitrary arrest and detention, slavery, servitude, slave trade, forced labour and similar practices. Also reported were violations of the right to freedom of thought, conscience and religion, freedom of expression, association and peaceful assembly and freedom of movement and residence. Concerning violations and abuses against children and women, the Special Rapporteur stated that no improvement had taken place. He described abuses by parties to the conflict in southern Sudan, other than the Government.

The Special Rapporteur noted with regret that he could not report any improvement of the human rights situation in the Sudan between January and October. To the contrary, he stated, information from the Nuba Mountains indicated that atrocities on the indigenous population there had intensified. He recommended that the Government abide by its human rights obligations under international law; cease aerial bombardments of civilians; release detainees and prisoners, cease acts of torture and cruel, inhuman and degrading punishment and close secret detention

centres; ensure training for its security and police forces, army, paramilitary or civil defence groups; stop rounding up children from the streets in major towns under its control, release all children being held against their will, make efforts to reunite them with their families and ensure decent living conditions for orphans; grant free access to regional and international humanitarian and human rights organizations; carry out investigations into human rights violations in the Nuba Mountains and towns in the south; agree on a cease-fire with other parties to the conflict; and address the problem of displaced persons. The Special Rapporteur recommended providing human rights monitors at the earliest possible date.

**GENERAL ASSEMBLY ACTION**

On 22 December, the General Assembly adopted **resolution 50/197**.

### Situation of human rights in the Sudan

*The General Assembly,*

*Guided* by the Charter of the United Nations, the Universal Declaration of Human Rights, the International Covenants on Human Rights, the International Convention on the Elimination of All Forms of Racial Discrimination and the Convention on the Rights of the Child,

*Reaffirming* that all Member States have an obligation to promote and protect human rights and fundamental freedoms and to comply with the obligations laid down in the various instruments in this field,

*Recalling* the obligation by all parties to respect international humanitarian law,

*Recalling also* its resolution 49/198 of 23 December 1994, and taking note of Commission on Human Rights resolution 1995/77 of 8 March 1995,

*Noting with deep concern* reports of grave human rights violations in the Sudan, particularly summary executions, detentions without trial, forced displacement of persons and torture, as described in reports submitted to the Commission on Human Rights by the Special Rapporteur on the question of torture, the Special Rapporteur on extrajudicial, summary or arbitrary executions and the Special Rapporteur on the question of religious intolerance,

*Welcoming* the third and latest interim report of the Special Rapporteur on the situation of human rights in the Sudan, and noting with concern the continuing violations of human rights in the Sudan,

*Concerned* about continuing indiscriminate and deliberate aerial bombardments by the Government of the Sudan of civilian targets in southern Sudan, in clear violation of international humanitarian law, which have added to the suffering of the civilian population and resulted in casualties to civilians, including relief workers,

*Deeply concerned* that access by the civilian population to humanitarian assistance continues to be impeded, which represents a threat to human life and constitutes an offence to human dignity,

*Expressing the hope* that the continuing dialogue between the Government of the Sudan and other parties and donor Governments, Operation Lifeline Sudan and international private voluntary agencies will result in improved cooperation for the delivery of humanitarian assistance to all persons in need,

*Alarmed* by the large number of internally displaced persons and victims of discrimination in the Sudan, including members of ethnic minorities who have been forcibly displaced in violation of their human rights and who are in need of relief assistance and protection,

*Alarmed also* by the mass exodus of refugees into neighbouring countries and conscious of the burden that this places on those countries, but expressing its appreciation for the efforts of host countries and of the international community to assist the refugees,

*Deeply concerned* by the conclusion of the Special Rapporteur, also stated in his previous reports, that grave and widespread violations of human rights by government agents, as well as abuses by members of parties to the conflict in southern Sudan other than the Government of the Sudan, continue to take place, including extrajudicial killings, enforced or involuntary disappearances, abductions, slavery, systematic torture and widespread arbitrary arrests of suspected political opponents,

*Alarmed further* by the continuing failure of the Sudanese authorities to investigate human rights violations and abuses brought to their attention over the past years,

*Gravely alarmed* that since February 1994 there have been increasing reports from a wide variety of sources indicating that atrocities by the Government of the Sudan against the local population in the area of the Nuba Mountains have intensified,

*Concerned* by reports of religious persecution in areas of the conflict zone controlled by the Government of the Sudan and of discrimination based upon religion in the provision of shelter and relief,

*Deeply concerned* by the Special Rapporteur's conclusion that the abduction of persons, mainly women and children, belonging to ethnic and religious minorities from southern Sudan, the Nuba Mountains and the Ingessana Hills area, and their subjection to the slave trade, servitude and forced labour are taking place with the knowledge of the Government of the Sudan,

*Also deeply concerned* about the problem of unaccompanied minors and the use of children as soldiers by all parties despite repeated calls from the international community to put an end to this practice, as described in the report of the Special Rapporteur,

*Recognizing* the fact that the Sudan has been hosting large numbers of refugees from several neighbouring countries over the past three decades,

*Welcoming* the release of some of the political prisoners by the Government of the Sudan in August 1995, and noting its recent announcement of open, free and fair elections in 1996,

*Also welcoming* the efforts of the United Nations and other humanitarian organizations to provide humanitarian relief to those Sudanese in need,

*Further welcoming* the dialogues and contacts between non-governmental organizations and the religious minorities in the Sudan, aimed at developing a more balanced relationship between the Government of the Sudan and the religious minority groups,

1. *Expresses deep concern* at the serious, widespread and continuing human rights violations in the Sudan, including extrajudicial killings and summary executions; detentions without due process; forced displacement of persons; enforced or involuntary disappearances; torture and other forms of cruel and unusual punishment; slavery, practices similar to slavery and forced labour; and denial of the freedoms of expression, association and peaceful assembly;

2. *Urges* the Government of the Sudan to investigate without delay the cases of slavery, servitude, slave trade, forced labour and similar practices brought to its attention and to take all appropriate measures to put an immediate end to these practices;

3. *Takes note with appreciation* of the interim report of the Special Rapporteur;

4. *Welcomes* the recommendation of the Special Rapporteur that human rights monitors be placed at the earliest possible date in such locations as will facilitate improved information flow and assessment and independent verification of reports on the situation of human rights in the Sudan;

5. *Calls upon* the Government of the Sudan to comply with applicable international human rights instruments to which the Sudan is a party, in particular the International Covenants on Human Rights, the International Convention on the Elimination of All Forms of Racial Discrimination, the Convention on the Rights of the Child, the Slavery Convention, as amended, and the Supplementary Convention on the Abolition of Slavery, the Slave Trade and Institutions and Practices Similar to Slavery, to implement those instruments to which it is a party and to ensure that all individuals in its territory and subject to its jurisdiction, including members of all religious and ethnic groups, enjoy fully the rights recognized in those instruments;

6. *Urges* the Government of the Sudan to cease immediately all aerial attacks on civilian targets and other attacks that are in violation of international humanitarian law;

7. *Calls upon* parties to the hostilities to respect fully the applicable provisions of international humanitarian law, including article 3 common to the Geneva Conventions of 12 August 1949, and the Additional Protocols thereto, of 1977, to halt the use of weapons against the civilian population and to protect all civilians, including women, children and members of ethnic and religious minorities, from violations, including forcible displacement, arbitrary detention, ill-treatment, torture and summary executions, and deplores the consequences for innocent civilians of the use of land-mines by government and rebel forces alike;

8. *Again calls upon* the Government of the Sudan and all parties to permit international agencies, humanitarian organizations and donor Governments to deliver humanitarian assistance to the civilian population and to cooperate with the initiatives of the Department of Humanitarian Affairs of the Secretariat and United Nations agencies working in the field, in particular Operation Lifeline Sudan, to deliver humanitarian assistance to all persons in need;

9. *Reiterates its call upon* the Government of the Sudan to ensure a full, thorough and prompt investigation by an independent judicial inquiry commission of the killings of Sudanese nationals employed by foreign relief organizations and foreign Governments;

10. *Welcomes* the decision of the Commission on Human Rights to extend the mandate of the Special Rapporteur for an additional year;

11. *Requests* the Secretary-General to continue to provide the Special Rapporteur with all necessary assistance in the discharge of his mandate;

12. *Deplores* the continuing refusal of the Government of the Sudan to cooperate in any manner with the Special Rapporteur and the unacceptable threats against his person;

13. *Calls upon* the Government of the Sudan to extend its full and unreserved cooperation to the Special Rapporteur and to assist him in the ongoing discharge of his mandate and, to this end, to take all necessary steps to ensure that the Special Rapporteur has free and unlimited access to any person in the Sudan with whom he wishes to meet, with no threats or reprisals;

14. *Invites* the Special Rapporteurs of the Commission on Human Rights on the questions of religious intolerance and freedom of expression to consult with the Special Rapporteur on the situation of human rights in the Sudan and to consider and report on the situation in the Sudan, and calls upon the Government of the Sudan to extend to them its full cooperation, including inviting them to visit the Sudan;

15. *Recommends* the continued monitoring of the serious human rights situation in the Sudan and of the regional efforts to end the hostilities and human suffering in the south, and invites the Commission on Human Rights, at its fifty-second session, to give urgent attention to the situation of human rights in the Sudan;

16. *Decides* to continue its consideration of this question at its fifty-first session.

General Assembly resolution 50/197

22 December 1995     Meeting 99     94-15-54 (recorded vote)

Approved by Third Committee (A/50/635/Add.3) by recorded vote (93-15-47), 13 December (meeting 56); 29-nation draft (A/C.3/50/L.58); agenda item 112 *(c)*.

*Meeting numbers.* GA 50th session: 3rd Committee 35, 38-51, 53, 56; plenary 99.

Recorded vote in Assembly as follows:

*In favour:* Albania, Andorra, Antigua and Barbuda, Argentina, Armenia, Australia, Austria, Bahamas, Barbados, Belarus, Belgium, Belize, Bolivia, Botswana, Brazil, Bulgaria, Canada, Chile, Croatia, Cyprus, Czech Republic, Denmark, Dominica, Ecuador, Egypt, El Salvador, Eritrea, Estonia, Ethiopia, Finland, France, Georgia, Germany, Greece, Guyana, Haiti, Honduras, Hungary, Iceland, Ireland, Israel, Italy, Jamaica, Japan, Kazakstan, Latvia, Liechtenstein, Lithuania, Luxembourg, Malta, Marshall Islands, Mauritius, Mexico, Micronesia, Monaco, Mongolia, Namibia, Netherlands, New Zealand, Nicaragua, Norway, Panama, Paraguay, Peru, Poland, Portugal, Republic of Moldova, Romania, Russian Federation, Saint Lucia, Saint Vincent and the Grenadines, Samoa, Singapore, Slovakia, Slovenia, Solomon Islands, South Africa, Spain, Suriname, Sweden, Tajikistan, the former Yugoslav Republic of Macedonia, Trinidad and Tobago, Turkey, Uganda, Ukraine, United Kingdom, United Republic of Tanzania, United States, Uruguay, Uzbekistan, Venezuela, Zambia, Zimbabwe.

*Against:* Afghanistan, China, Cuba, India, Indonesia, Iran, Libyan Arab Jamahiriya, Myanmar, Nigeria, Pakistan, Qatar, Saudi Arabia, Sudan, Syrian Arab Republic, Viet Nam.

*Abstaining:* Algeria, Angola, Bahrain, Bangladesh, Benin, Bhutan, Brunei Darussalam, Burkina Faso, Burundi, Cambodia, Cameroon, Cape Verde, Chad, Colombia, Congo, Côte d'Ivoire, Democratic People's Republic of Korea, Equatorial Guinea, Fiji, Gabon, Gambia, Ghana, Grenada, Guatemala, Guinea, Guinea-Bissau, Jordan, Kenya, Kuwait, Kyrgyzstan, Lao People's Democratic Republic, Lebanon, Lesotho, Malaysia, Maldives, Mali, Mauritania, Morocco, Nepal, Niger, Oman, Papua New Guinea, Philippines, Republic of Korea, Rwanda, Saint Kitts and Nevis, Sierra Leone, Sri Lanka, Swaziland, Thailand, Togo, Tunisia, United Arab Emirates, Vanuatu.

In the Committee, paragraphs 2, 4 and 12 were adopted by separate recorded votes of 83 to 14, with 44 abstentions, 86 to 16, with 40 abstentions, and 87 to 15, with 40 abstentions, respectively. In the Assembly, the same paragraphs were adopted by recorded votes of 87 to 15, with 50 abstentions, 85 to 17, with 49 abstentions, and 85 to 14, with 50 abstentions, respectively.

## Togo

**Report of the Secretary-General.** In February, the Secretary-General described action taken by the UN High Commissioner for Human Rights and reviewed action taken by special rapporteurs and working groups of the Commission and treaty mechanisms in respect of Togo.[40] Information received from the Government of Togo was reproduced concerning national reconciliation, its obligation to submit periodic reports under the international human rights instruments to which Togo was a party and the use of technical assistance through the programme of advisory services of the Centre for Human Rights. NGOs brought information to the Secretary-General's attention regarding the overall situation in Togo in 1994, human rights violations by the armed forces, violations of the right to life and to physical integrity, and violations of freedom of expression and press freedom.

**Commission action.** On 3 March,[41] the Commission, urging the authorities in Togo to continue to improve the human rights situation, called on them to comply with their obligations under the international human rights instruments to which Togo was a party.

(See PART THREE, Chapter I, for Commission action on advisory services in Togo.)

## Zaire

**Report of the Special Rapporteur.** In his first report,[42] Special Rapporteur Roberto Garretón (Chile), appointed in 1994,[43] discussed his mandate, described his activities, which included a visit to Zaire in 1994, and presented general background information on Zaire. He reviewed the political regime in the country, the Government's legislative, judiciary and executive branches, the armed forces, security forces and police, and the impunity enjoyed by the security services. The Special Rapporteur described ethnic conflicts in Northern Kivu, the situation of Rwandese refugees in Kivu and regional conflicts in the Shaba (Katanga) region. Allegations of human rights violations involved the rights to life, to security, to physical and mental integrity and not to be subjected to torture, to liberty of person, to freedom of movement, to a fair trial, to freedom of assembly, to freedom of association, and to freedom of opinion and expression. Violations of economic, social and cultural rights dealt with the rights to work, to housing, to public health and sanitation and to education.

The Special Rapporteur declared that children were among those most affected by the country's social and economic disintegration and that the role of women was circumscribed by a number of ancient traditions that relegated them to a domestic role. He recommended that the High Commissioner for Human Rights send two human rights specialists to monitor the human rights situation in Zaire and to gather information on allegations of violations, follow up on complaints and visit places of detention. The specialists would also advise governmental authorities and NGOs on measures to strengthen institutions for the protection and advancement of human rights. He recommended that the authorities of Zaire: establish control over the State security apparatus; adopt a language of pacification; prevent the armed forces from conducting repressive or public order function; enact laws to regulate the electoral process; ratify the 1984 Convention against Torture and Other Cruel, Inhuman or Degrading Treatment or Punishment;[34] strengthen the judiciary through training; cooperate with UN mechanisms for human rights protection; and offer to host a subregional meeting of the Committee on the Rights of the Child which could consider the situation of children. He made further recommendations for action by NGOs and the international community.

**Commission action.** On 8 March,[44] the Commission deplored the continuing serious violations of human rights and fundamental freedoms in Zaire, noted with concern that the army and security forces continued to use force against civilians and enjoyed impunity, and condemned discriminatory measures affecting persons belonging to minority groups. It called on the Government to reinforce the judiciary and its independence and also called for continued and broadened efforts to assure full respect for the right to freedom of opinion and expression, in particular for all mass media, as well as freedom of association, assembly and peaceful demonstration. It asked the High Commissioner for Human Rights to consider the Special Rapporteur's recommendation to send, in consultation with the Government, two human rights experts to monitor the human rights situation and to give advice to governmental authorities and NGOs.

The Commission extended the Special Rapporteur's mandate for another year and asked him to report in 1996. The Secretary-General was asked to assist him. The Economic and Social Council approved these actions by **decision 1995/280** of 25 July.

*REFERENCES*

[1]E/CN.4/1995/66. [2]E/1995/23 (res. 1995/90). [3]E/1995/54. [4]E/CN.4/1996/2 (res. 1995/11). [5]Ibid. (res. 1995/4). [6]E/CN.4/1996/16. [7]E/CN.4/1995/68. [8]E/1995/23 (res. 1995/71). [9]E/CN.4/1995/L.100. [10]E/1995/23 (res. 1995/91). [11]YUN 1994, p. 299, SC rcs. 955(1994), 8 Nov. 1994. [12]E/CN.4/1996/7. [13]E/CN.4/1996/68. [14]E/CN.4/1996/2 (res. 1995/5). [15]A/50/709-S/1995/915. [16]A/50/743. [17]E/1995/23 (dec. 1995/103). [18]YUN 1994, p. 1076. [19]E/1995/23 (res. 1995/8). [20]YUN 1967, p. 509. [21]YUN 1994, p. 1077. [22]E/1995/23 (res. 1995/9). [23]E/CN.4/1996/2 (dec. 1995/105). [24]Ibid. (res. 1995/12). [25]*Multilateral Treaties Deposited with the Secretary-General: Status as at 31 December 1995* (ST/LEG/SER.E/14), Sales No. E.96.V.5. [26]YUN 1973, p. 103, GA res. 3068(XXVIII), annex, 30 Nov. 1973. [27]YUN 1976, p. 575. [28]A/50/468. [29]E/CN.4/1995/76. [30]YUN 1994, p. 262. [31]YUN 1993, p. 925. [32]E/1995/23 (res. 1995/10). [33]E/CN.4/1995/58. [34]YUN 1984, p. 813, GA res. 39/46, annex, 10 Dec. 1984. [35]YUN 1979, p. 895, GA res. 34/180, annex, 18 Dec. 1979. [36]YUN 1966, p. 423, GA res. 2200 A (XXI), annex, 16 Dec. 1966. [37]YUN 1977, p. 706. [38]E/1995/23 (res. 1995/77). [39]A/50/569. [40]E/CN.4/1995/16. [41]E/1995/23 (res. 1995/52). [42]E/CN.4/1995/67. [43]YUN 1994, p. 1082. [44]E/1995/23 (res. 1995/69).

# Asia and the Pacific

## Afghanistan

**Report of the Special Rapporteur.** In a January report,[1] Special Rapporteur Felix Ermacora (Austria) outlined events that had taken place in Afghanistan since his report to the General Assembly in 1994[2] and examined the human rights situation there, based on his 1994 visit to Pakistan (16-17 December) and Afghanistan (18-22 December).

The Special Rapporteur noted that the human rights situation continued to be conditioned by the absence of an effective central government and depended on the intensity of the power struggle between the rival groups which was conducted without due respect for international law and humanitarian law. Hundreds of secret places of detention continued to operate and the judicial system was not unified. The enjoyment of economic, social and cultural rights was maintained at a minimum level. The conflict between the armed groups had deprived Afghans of the full exercise of their right to self-determination; no progress had been made on the creation of a national army or the drafting of an Islamic constitution.

The Special Rapporteur recommended visits to prisons by the International Committee of the Red Cross (ICRC); efforts by the international community to collect illegally held weapons; drafting an Islamic constitution; establishing a constitutional council to guarantee the respect of human rights; after a cease-fire in Kabul, requesting the international community to plan the reconstruction of the parts of Kabul which had been destroyed; requesting the UN Educational, Scientific and Cultural Organization (UNESCO) to contribute to reconstructing the Kabul Museum and to establishing the education system in the provinces; requesting the World Health Organization (WHO) to provide assistance to Bamyan and Badakhshan provinces; requesting international agencies to assist with the problem of malnourished children; treating Afghan refugees living in other countries in conformity with the 1988 Geneva Agreements on the Settlement of the Situation relating to Afghanistan;[3] respecting the amnesty decree proclaimed in 1992;[4] and translating his report into the Dari and Pashtu languages.

**Commission action.** On 8 March,[5] the Commission urged the Afghan parties to intensify efforts to achieve a comprehensive political solution, establish a democratic government and respect the humanitarian rules set out in the 1949 Geneva Conventions and their Additional Protocols of 1977.[6] It called on them to work with the UN Special Mission to Afghanistan, established in 1993,[7] and invited the mission and the Special Rapporteur to exchange information and to consult and cooperate with each other. The Commission further called on the Afghan parties to ensure respect for the human rights and fundamental freedoms of women. It called for the unconditional and simultaneous release of all prisoners of war, including former Soviet prisoners, for tracing the many Afghans still missing and for the abolition of prisons run by political parties and armed groups. The Commission called on the authorities in Afghanistan to investigate the fate of disappeared persons, apply amnesty decrees equally to all detainees, reduce the period during which prisoners awaited trial, treat all prisoners in accordance with the 1955 Standard Minimum Rules for the Treatment of Prisoners[8] and apply to all suspected or convicted persons the relevant articles of the 1966 International Covenant on Civil and Political Rights.[9] It urged them to provide effective remedies to victims of grave human rights violations and to continue to extend to the Special Rapporteur and the Commission their full cooperation.

The Commission asked Member States and the international community to respond positively to the Secretary-General's appeal for financial support for the rehabilitation of Afghanistan, including support for activities such as mine detection and clearance and repatriation projects undertaken by UNHCR (see PART FOUR, Chapter XII), the UN Coordinator for Humanitarian and Economic Assistance Programmes (see PART FOUR, Chapter III) and other UN agencies or humanitarian NGOs. It urged all parties to ensure the safety of personnel of humanitarian organizations and media representatives.

The Commission extended the Special Rapporteur's mandate for one year and asked him to report to the Assembly in 1995 and to the Commission in 1996. The Secretary-General was asked to give him all necessary assistance. By **decision 1995/285** of 25 July, the Economic and Social Council approved those actions.

**Interim report of the Special Rapporteur.** In October, the Secretary-General transmitted to the General Assembly an interim report[10] on the human rights situation in Afghanistan, submitted by Special Rapporteur Choong-Hyun Paik (Republic of Korea), who was appointed following the death of Mr. Ermacora in February.

The Special Rapporteur visited Afghanistan and Pakistan in August. He stated that despite sporadic disturbances, peace was gradually gaining ground in Kabul and other areas controlled by local authorities. However, murders, disappearances and violations of the right to life and the right to be free from torture, cruel, inhuman or degrading treatment persisted, as did a lack of resources needed to provide safe water, food and sanitation, and the disruption of general health services country-wide. The lack of a central government posed extreme difficulty in redressing human rights violations and the collapse of an impartial judicial system prevented the administration of justice. The cultural heritage of Afghan society was exposed to wanton destruction. The Special Rapporteur made recommendations for peace-building, the provision of humanitarian assistance, rebuilding the Afghan society and the protection of vulnerable populations and of cultural property.

(For details on the political situation in Afghanistan, see PART TWO, Chapter IV.)

**GENERAL ASSEMBLY ACTION**

On 22 December, the General Assembly adopted **resolution 50/189**.

**Situation of human rights in Afghanistan**

*The General Assembly,*

*Guided* by the Charter of the United Nations, the Universal Declaration of Human Rights, the International Covenants on Human Rights and accepted humanitarian rules, as set out in the Geneva Conventions of 12 August 1949 and the Additional Protocols thereto, of 1977,

*Reaffirming* that all Member States have an obligation to promote and protect human rights and fundamental freedoms and to fulfil the obligations they have freely undertaken under the various international instruments,

*Recalling* all its relevant resolutions, as well as the resolutions of the Commission on Human Rights and the decisions of the Economic and Social Council,

*Taking note in particular* of Commission on Human Rights resolution 1995/74 of 8 March 1995, in which the Commission decided to extend the mandate of its Special Rapporteur on the situation of human rights in Afghanistan for one year and requested him to consider submitting a report to the General Assembly at its fiftieth session, and of Economic and Social Council decision 1995/285 of 25 July 1995, in which the Council approved the Commission's decision,

*Noting* that armed confrontation persists in certain parts of the territory of Afghanistan,

*Aware* that peace and security in Afghanistan are conducive to the full restoration of all human rights and fundamental freedoms, the voluntary return of refugees to their homeland in safety and dignity, the clearance of minefields in many parts of the country and the reconstruction and rehabilitation of Afghanistan,

*Deeply concerned* at reports of human rights abuses and violations of humanitarian law and human rights, including the rights to life, liberty and security of person and to freedom of opinion, expression and association,

*Concerned in particular* at reports of abuses and violations of the human rights of women, including acts of violence and denial of access to primary and basic education, training and employment, affecting their effective participation in political and cultural life throughout the country,

*Concerned* that a unified judicial system cannot be established throughout the country under the prevailing circumstances,

*Commending* the activities carried out for the welfare of the Afghan people by various agencies and programmes of the United Nations and by the International Committee of the Red Cross and other humanitarian organizations,

*Noting with satisfaction* that the voluntary repatriation of the Afghan refugees has resumed,

*Taking note with appreciation* of the interim report of the Special Rapporteur of the Commission on Human Rights on the situation of human rights in Afghanistan, of the conclusions and recommendations contained therein and of the translation of previous reports into the Dari and Pashtu languages,

1. *Welcomes* the cooperation that the Government and local authorities in Afghanistan have extended to the Special Rapporteur of the Commission on Human Rights on the situation of human rights in Afghanistan and to humanitarian agencies;

2. *Urges* all the Afghan parties to work with the United Nations Special Mission to Afghanistan with a view to achieving a comprehensive political solution leading to the cessation of armed confrontation and the eventual establishment of a democratic Government elected through free and fair elections based on the right to self-determination of the people of Afghanistan;

3. *Recognizes* that the promotion and protection of human rights should be an essential element in the achievement of a comprehensive solution to the crisis in Afghanistan, and therefore invites the Special Mission and the Special Rapporteur to exchange relevant information and to consult and cooperate with each other;

4. *Also urges* all the Afghan parties to respect accepted humanitarian rules and all human rights and fundamental freedoms, including the rights of women and children, and calls upon the Afghan authorities to take measures to ensure the effective participation of women in social, political and cultural life throughout the country;

5. *Calls* for the unconditional and simultaneous release of all prisoners of war, wherever they may be held, including former Soviet prisoners of war, and for the tracing of the many Afghans still missing as a result of the war;

6. *Calls upon* the Afghan authorities to investigate thoroughly the fate of those persons who have disappeared during the conflict, to apply the amnesty decree issued in 1992 by the Transitional Islamic State of Afghanistan in a strictly non-discriminatory manner, to

reduce the period during which prisoners await trial and to treat all suspected, convicted or detained persons according to relevant international instruments;

7. *Urges* the Afghan authorities to provide sufficient and effective remedies to the victims of grave violations of human rights and accepted humanitarian rules and to bring their perpetrators to trial in accordance with internationally accepted standards;

8. *Appeals* to Member States and to the international community to continue to provide adequate humanitarian assistance to the people of Afghanistan and to the Afghan refugees in the neighbouring countries, pending their voluntary repatriation according to relevant international instruments, in particular through the support of activities such as mine detection and clearance and repatriation projects undertaken by the United Nations High Commissioner for Refugees, the Coordinator for Humanitarian and Economic Assistance Programmes Relating to Afghanistan as well as by United Nations agencies or non-governmental humanitarian organizations;

9. *Strongly urges* all parties to the conflict to take all necessary measures to ensure the safety of all personnel of humanitarian organizations and representatives of the media in Afghanistan;

10. *Invites* the United Nations to offer, upon the request of the Afghan authorities and with due regard for Afghan tradition, advisory services and technical assistance concerning the drafting of a constitution, which should embody internationally accepted human rights principles, and the holding of direct elections;

11. *Encourages* the United Nations Educational, Scientific and Cultural Organization to study, with the contribution of its competent committees, appropriate ways and means to restore the Afghan system of education and the Afghan cultural heritage, in particular the restoration of the Kabul Museum;

12. *Urges* the Afghan authorities to continue to extend their full cooperation to the Commission on Human Rights and its Special Rapporteur;

13. *Requests* the Secretary-General to give all necessary assistance to the Special Rapporteur;

14. *Decides* to keep the situation of human rights in Afghanistan under consideration at its fifty-first session, in the light of additional elements provided by the Commission on Human Rights and the Economic and Social Council.

General Assembly resolution 50/189

22 December 1995     Meeting 99     Adopted without vote

Approved by Third Committee (A/50/635/Add.3) without vote, 11 December (meeting 54); draft by Chairman (A/C.3/50/L.41), orally revised; agenda item 112 *(c)*.

*Meeting numbers.* GA 50th session: 3rd Committee 35, 38-52, 54; plenary 99.

## Cambodia

The Commission on Human Rights expressed concern about the protection of human rights in Cambodia (see PART THREE, Chapter I).

## China

On 7 March, the Commission on Human Rights, by a roll-call vote of 21 against to 20 in favour, with 12 abstentions, rejected a draft concerning the human rights situation in China.[11]

## East Timor

**Report of the Secretary-General.** In a January report,[12] the Secretary-General updated his good-offices activities aimed at achieving a just, comprehensive and internationally acceptable settlement of the question of East Timor. He also described action taken by the Special Rapporteurs on the question of torture,[13] and on extrajudicial, summary or arbitrary executions,[14] and the Working Groups on Arbitrary Detention and on Enforced or Involuntary Disappearances in 1994.[15] Annexed to the report was information received from the Government of Indonesia regarding the trials surrounding the November 1991 incidents of violence at Dili, which resulted in loss of life, injuries and disappearances among civilians,[16] and a further incident that occurred in 1994 in East Dili involving demonstrations and arrests (see also PART ONE, Chapter III).

**Commission action.** On 1 March, the Commission adopted by consensus a statement concerning the human rights situation in East Timor, by which, among other things, it asked the Secretary-General to keep it informed of the situation.[17]

## Iran

**Report of the Special Representative.** In January, Special Representative Reynaldo Galindo Pohl (El Salvador) submitted to the Commission on Human Rights a report[18] on the human rights situation in Iran. He had received information on alleged incidents and cases concerning the right to life; enforced or involuntary disappearances; the right to freedom from torture or cruel, inhuman or degrading treatment or punishment; the administration of justice; the excessive use of force by security forces; freedom of expression and opinion and the press; freedom of religion and the Baha'i community; the situation of women; freedom of association; political rights; the situation of refugees; and two incidents of alleged military aggression by Iran against Iraq in November 1994.[19] He discussed the murders of three Protestant ministers and an attack in Mashhad where 5 kilograms of explosives were set off in the prayer halls of the tomb of Imam Reza, one of the holiest sanctuaries and pilgrimage sites, leaving 26 people dead and 170 wounded.

The Special Representative concluded that the situation of human rights and fundamental freedoms in Iran should remain under international scrutiny. He recommended, among other things, that Iran abide by the terms of a 1991 agreement concluded with ICRC concerning visits to prisons

and prisoners;[20] ensure due process of law; end discrimination against the Baha'is and Protestants; ensure freedom of opinion and expression and the rights of assembly and association; and solicit the cooperation of UN organs and humanitarian organizations in sending observers to politically sensitive trials involving police investigation and criminal prosecution.

**Commission action.** On 8 March,[21] by a roll-call vote of 28 to 8, with 17 abstentions, the Commission, expressing concern at continuing reports of human rights violations in Iran, urged Iran to refrain from activities such as those cited in the report of the Special Representative and to intensify its efforts to investigate and rectify the human rights issues raised by him. It also urged Iran to abide by international human rights instruments to which it was a party and to investigate the assassination of the three Christian ministers mentioned in the Special Representative's report. The Commission called on Iran to implement existing agreements with international humanitarian organizations and to cooperate with the Special Representative and allow him to revisit the country. The Commission extended the Special Representative's mandate for another year and asked him to report to the General Assembly in 1995 and to the Commission in 1996.

**ECONOMIC AND SOCIAL COUNCIL ACTION**

The Economic and Social Council adopted **decision 1995/279** in July.

### Situation of human rights in the Islamic Republic of Iran

At its 52nd plenary meeting, on 25 July 1995, the Economic and Social Council, taking note of Commission on Human Rights resolution 1995/68 of 8 March 1995, approved the Commission's decision to extend for a further year the mandate of the Special Representative on the situation of human rights in the Islamic Republic of Iran, as contained in Commission resolution 1984/54 of 14 March 1984, also approved the Commission's request to the Special Representative to submit an interim report to the General Assembly at its fiftieth session on the situation of human rights in the Islamic Republic of Iran, including the situation of minority groups such as the Baha'ís, and to report to the Commission at its fifty-second session, and further approved the Commission's request to the Secretary-General to give all necessary assistance to the Special Representative.

Economic and Social Council decision 1995/279

28-8-15 (roll-call vote)

Draft by Commission on Human Rights (E/1995/23); agenda item 5 *(d)*.
*Meeting numbers.* ESC 51, 52.

Roll-call vote in Council as follows:

*In favour:* Australia, Bahamas, Brazil, Bulgaria, Canada, Chile, Colombia, Costa Rica, Côte d'Ivoire, Denmark, France, Germany, Greece, Ireland, Jamaica, Japan, Luxembourg, Mexico, Netherlands, Norway, Poland, Portugal, Romania, Russian Federation, South Africa, United Kingdom, United States, Venezuela.

*Against:* China, Cuba, India, Indonesia, Libyan Arab Jamahiriya, Malaysia, Pakistan, Sudan.

**Subcommission action.** On 24 August,[22] the Subcommission, by a secret ballot of 13 votes to 7, with 2 abstentions, condemned the human rights violations in Iran and asked the Government to cease any involvement in or toleration of murder and State-sponsored terrorism against Iranians living abroad and nationals of other States. It also asked the Government to withdraw its support for and cease condoning repeated threats to the lives of persons of whose opinions, writings or publications it disapproved. The Subcommission called on Iran to cooperate with the judicial authorities in countries which were investigating incidents of international terrorism. It asked the Secretary-General to inform it of relevant reports and UN measures to prevent human rights violations in Iran, particularly those concerning the Kurds, the Arab minority and the Baha'i and Christian communities.

**Interim report of the Special Representative.** In October, the Secretary-General transmitted to the General Assembly the interim report[23] on the human rights situation in Iran, prepared by Special Representative Maurice Danby Copithorne (Canada), who replaced Mr. Galindo Pohl following his resignation in March. Mr. Copithorne stated that in September he had requested a visit to Iran, but had not received a reply. He noted that he was not in a position to discuss questions of substance but expected to report to the Commission in 1996 and hoped that report would include information obtained from a visit to the country.

The report contained letters of 8 and 23 May and 10 June from Iran to the Special Representative presenting Iran's replies to his allegations of human rights violations.

**GENERAL ASSEMBLY ACTION**

On 22 December, the General Assembly adopted **resolution 50/188**.

### Situation of human rights in the Islamic Republic of Iran

*The General Assembly,*

*Guided* by the Charter of the United Nations, the Universal Declaration of Human Rights and the International Covenants on Human Rights,

*Recalling* the Vienna Declaration and Programme of Action, as endorsed by the General Assembly in its resolution 48/121 of 20 December 1993, in particular section I, paragraph 1, in which the World Conference on Human Rights reaffirmed, *inter alia*, that human rights and fundamental freedoms were the birthright of all human beings and that their protection and promotion was the first responsibility of Governments,

*Reaffirming* that all Member States have a duty to fulfil the obligations they have undertaken under the various international instruments in this field,

*Mindful* that the Islamic Republic of Iran is a party to the International Covenants on Human Rights,

*Recalling* Commission on Human Rights resolution 1984/54 of 14 March 1984, in which the Commission requested its Chairman to appoint a special representative to make a thorough study of the human rights situation in the Islamic Republic of Iran, based on such information as the special representative might deem relevant, including comments and material provided by the Government of the Islamic Republic of Iran,

*Noting* the appointment by the Chairman of the Commission on Human Rights of Mr. Maurice Danby Copithorne as Special Representative of the Commission on Human Rights on the situation of human rights in the Islamic Republic of Iran, and paying tribute to his predecessor Mr. Reynaldo Galindo Pohl,

*Recalling* its previous resolutions expressing concern at the violations of human rights by the Government of the Islamic Republic of Iran, including the most recent, resolution 49/202 of 23 December 1994, and the resolutions of the Commission on Human Rights, including the most recent, resolution 1995/68 of 8 March 1995, and those of the Subcommission on Prevention of Discrimination and Protection of Minorities, including the most recent, resolution 1995/18 of 24 August 1995,

*Reaffirming* that Governments are accountable for assassinations and attacks by their agents against persons in the territory of another State, as well as for the incitement, approval or wilful condoning of such acts,

*Noting* that in the view of the Special Representative the significant number of communications received by the Centre for Human Rights of the Secretariat for the attention of the Special Representative and the important concerns reflected therein will need careful scrutiny,

*Welcoming* the announcement by the Special Representative that he has been invited to visit the Islamic Republic of Iran and the high priority given by the Special Representative to visiting the country,

*Noting* the stated readiness of the Government of the Islamic Republic of Iran to invite the Special Rapporteur of the Commission on Human Rights on religious intolerance and the Special Rapporteur of the Commission on Human Rights on freedom of expression to visit the Islamic Republic of Iran,

*Noting also* the concluding observations of the Committee on the Elimination of Racial Discrimination, the Human Rights Committee and the Committee on Economic, Social and Cultural Rights on the human rights situation in the Islamic Republic of Iran,

*Noting further* that the Subcommission on Prevention of Discrimination and Protection of Minorities, in its resolution 1995/18, condemned the flagrant violations of human rights in the Islamic Republic of Iran,

*Taking note* of the interim report of the Special Representative of 20 October 1995, and his intention to present a substantive report to the Commission on Human Rights,

*Taking into account* the reports of the former Special Representative, including his report of 16 January 1995,

*Considering* that continued international scrutiny of human rights and fundamental freedoms in the Islamic

Republic of Iran is warranted and that the subject should remain on the agenda of the General Assembly,

1. *Expresses its concern* at violations of human rights in the Islamic Republic of Iran, in particular the high number of executions, cases of torture and cruel, inhuman or degrading treatment or punishment, the failure to meet international standards with regard to the administration of justice, the absence of guarantees of due process of law, the discriminatory treatment of minorities by reason of their religious beliefs, notably the Baha'is, whose existence as a viable religious community in the Islamic Republic of Iran is threatened, lack of adequate protection for the Christian minorities, some members of which have been the target of intimidation and assassinations, excessive force in suppressing demonstrations, restrictions on the freedom of expression, thought, opinion and the press and widespread discrimination against women;

2. *Urges* the Government of the Islamic Republic of Iran, as a State party to the International Covenants on Human Rights, to abide by its obligations freely undertaken under the Covenants and under other international instruments on human rights and to ensure that all individuals within its territory and subject to its jurisdiction, including religious groups, enjoy the rights recognized in those instruments;

3. *Calls upon* the Government of the Islamic Republic of Iran to implement existing agreements with international humanitarian organizations;

4. *Also calls upon* the Government of the Islamic Republic of Iran to take the necessary steps so that the visit of the Special Representative of the Commission on Human Rights on the situation of human rights in the Islamic Republic of Iran can take place as soon as possible and without conditions;

5. *Expresses its grave concern* that there are continuing threats to the life of Mr. Salman Rushdie, as well as to individuals associated with his work, which appear to have the support of the Government of the Islamic Republic of Iran;

6. *Urges* the Government of the Islamic Republic of Iran to refrain from activities against members of the Iranian opposition living abroad and to cooperate wholeheartedly with the authorities of other countries in investigating and punishing offences reported by them;

7. *Requests* the Secretary-General to give all necessary assistance to the Special Representative to enable him to discharge his mandate fully;

8. *Decides* to continue the examination of the situation of human rights in the Islamic Republic of Iran, including the situation of minority groups such as the Baha'is, during its fifty-first session under the item entitled "Human rights questions", on the basis of the report of the Special Representative and in the light of additional elements provided by the Commission on Human Rights and the Economic and Social Council.

General Assembly resolution 50/188

22 December 1995     Meeting 99     78-27-58 (recorded vote)

Approved by Third Committee (A/50/635/Add.3) by recorded vote (74-26-49), 13 December (meeting 55); 28-nation draft (A/C.3/50/L.35); agenda item 112 (c).

*Meeting numbers.* GA 50th session: 3rd Committee 35, 38-51, 53, 55; plenary 99.

Recorded vote in Assembly as follows:

*In favour:* Algeria, Andorra, Antigua and Barbuda, Argentina, Australia, Austria, Bahamas, Barbados, Belgium, Belize, Bolivia, Botswana, Brazil, Bulgaria, Canada, Costa Rica, Czech Republic, Denmark, Dominica, Ecuador, El Salvador, Estonia, Finland, France, Germany, Greece, Grenada, Guyana, Haiti, Honduras, Hungary, Iceland, Ireland, Israel, Italy, Jamaica, Japan, Latvia, Liechtenstein, Lithuania, Luxembourg, Malawi, Malta, Marshall Islands, Mauritius, Mexico, Micronesia, Monaco, Mongolia, Netherlands, New Zealand, Norway, Panama, Paraguay, Peru, Poland, Portugal, Romania, Russian Federation, Saint Lucia, Saint Vincent and the Grenadines, Samoa, San Marino, Slovakia, Slovenia, Solomon Islands, South Africa, Spain, Suriname, Swaziland, Sweden, Trinidad and Tobago, Tunisia,* United Kingdom, United States, Vanuatu, Venezuela, Zambia.

*Against:* Afghanistan, Armenia, Azerbaijan, Bangladesh, Brunei Darussalam, China, Cuba, Democratic People's Republic of Korea, Gambia, Ghana, India, Indonesia, Iran, Libyan Arab Jamahiriya, Malaysia, Maldives, Myanmar, Nigeria, Oman, Pakistan, Qatar, Sri Lanka, Sudan, Syrian Arab Republic, Turkmenistan, United Republic of Tanzania, Viet Nam.

*Abstaining:* Albania, Angola, Bahrain, Belarus, Benin, Bhutan, Burkina Faso, Burundi, Cambodia, Cameroon, Cape Verde, Chad, Colombia, Congo, Côte d'Ivoire, Cyprus, Egypt, Equatorial Guinea, Eritrea, Ethiopia, Fiji, Gabon, Guatemala, Guinea, Guinea-Bissau, Jordan, Kazakstan, Kenya, Kuwait, Kyrgyzstan, Lao People's Democratic Republic, Lebanon, Lesotho, Mali, Mauritania, Mozambique, Namibia, Nepal, Niger, Papua New Guinea, Philippines, Republic of Korea, Republic of Moldova, Rwanda, Saint Kitts and Nevis, Saudi Arabia, Sierra Leone, Singapore, Tajikistan, Thailand, the former Yugoslav Republic of Macedonia, Togo, Uganda, Ukraine, United Arab Emirates, Uruguay, Zaire, Zimbabwe.

*Later advised the Secretariat it had intended to abstain.

## Iraq

**Report of the Special Rapporteur (February).** In a February report,[24] Special Rapporteur Max van der Stoel (Netherlands) described his activities and reported on the human rights situation in Iraq. He stated that the politico-legal structures of Iraq, in which power was concentrated in extremely few hands, was the essential cause of human rights violations. He concluded that human rights violations were inevitable, since guarantees for protection were absent and the scope for abuse of power was enormous. He referred to allegations of violations he had received regarding summary or arbitrary execution; arbitrary arrest and detention; enforced or involuntary disappearances; freedom of opinion, expression and association; freedom of movement; and the right to food and health care. He pointed out that minority protection in the form of cultural and educational rights was generally not accorded. He presented examples of repressive decrees issued by the Revolution Command Council, which had the power to override the Provisional Constitution at any time and without judicial review. He also described the situation of refugees.

The Special Rapporteur recommended that Iraq: bring the activities of its security services into conformity with the standards of international law; abrogate laws granting impunity to specified forces or persons killing or injuring individuals for any purpose beyond the administration of justice; set up a commission on disappearances and cooperate with the Working Group on Enforced or Involuntary Disappearances; stop the practices of torture and other cruel, inhuman and degrading treatment or punishment; release detainees; abrogate laws and abolish policies implementing punishments imposed on persons for the alleged crimes of family members; restore the independence of the judiciary; facilitate the enjoyment of the freedoms of opinion, expression and association; remove restrictions relating to the entry and exit of citizens to and from the country; review its citizenship law; abrogate discriminatory laws regarding the enjoyment of property; end its internal economic embargoes; take advantage of the food-for-oil formula to purchase food and medical supplies; abrogate discriminatory laws against women; eliminate the death penalty for minors; ensure the recognition and enjoyment of minority rights; cease periodic shelling of Kurdish agricultural lands; cease its military activities against the Marsh Arab population; end its interference in the religious activities of the Shiah community and compensate it for damages; and agree to the stationing of human rights monitors throughout the country.

The report also contained selected decrees issued by Saddam Hussein, Chairman of the Revolution Command Council.

**Commission action.** By a roll-call vote of 31 to 1, with 21 abstentions, the Commission on 8 March[25] expressed strong condemnation of massive human rights violations by Iraq, in particular: summary and arbitrary executions; systematic torture; decrees prescribing cruel and unusual punishment; enforced or involuntary disappearances; suppression of freedom of thought, expression and association; and lack of responsibility concerning economic and social rights. It called on Iraq to resolve cases of disappearances of Kuwaitis and nationals of other States by providing detailed information on persons deported from or arrested in Kuwait between 2 August 1990 and 26 February 1991 and on those who were executed or died in detention during or after that period, as well as on the location of their graves. It also called on Iraq to release detained Kuwaitis and nationals of other States, improve cooperation with humanitarian organizations and compensate families of persons who died while in the custody of Iraqi authorities. It again called on Iraq, as a State party to the International Covenants on Human Rights,[26] to abide by its obligations under them. Demanding that the Government restore the independence of the judiciary and abrogate all laws granting impunity to specified forces or persons killing or injuring individuals for any purpose beyond the administration of justice, the Commission urged Iraq bring the action of its security apparatus into line with the standards of international law. It further urged the Government to release all persons arbitrarily arrested and detained and to set up an independent commission of inquiry to look into the fate of tens of thousands of disappeared persons.

The Commission demanded that Iraq ensure the recognition and enjoyment of human rights of persons belonging to minorities; abrogate decrees prescribing cruel and unusual punishments, and cease repressive practices aimed at the Iraqi Kurds. Regretting Iraq's failure to provide satisfactory replies concerning human rights violations brought to the attention of the Special Rapporteur, the Commission called on Iraq to reply without delay to enable him to formulate recommendations to improve the human rights situation. It urged Iraq to cooperate with him, notably during his next visit.

The Commission extended for one year the Special Rapporteur's mandate. It asked him to report to the Commission periodically, to submit an interim report to the General Assembly in 1995 and to report to the Commission in 1996. The Commission asked the Secretary-General to take measures to send monitors to verify reports on the human rights situation, to provide funding to do so and to give the Special Rapporteur all the assistance he needed. On 25 July, the Economic and Social Council, by **decision 1995/286**, approved those actions.

**Subcommission action.** By a secret ballot of 15 votes to 5, with 4 abstentions, the Subcommission on 18 August[27] strongly condemned the human rights violations by the Government of Iraq and requested it to abide by various Security Council resolutions, particularly **resolution 986(1995)**, which would permit it to sell some of its oil to meet the health and food needs of its people (see PART TWO, Chapter IV). It asked the Special Rapporteur to visit the border and the marshlands and to report on the situation in those areas to the General Assembly. It asked the Secretary-General to call on the Government to cooperate with the Special Rapporteur.

Also on 18 August,[28] the Subcommission, expressing deep concern at the serious consequences that the embargo imposed on Iraq for the past five years was having on civilians, appealed to the international community to facilitate the supply of food and medicines.

**Reports of the Special Rapporteur (September and November).** In his first periodic report,[29] submitted in September, the Special Rapporteur stated that he had received comments on the significance of decrees of the Revolution Command Council and felt obliged to study them and submit the texts to the Commission together with an analysis of their importance. The decrees in question, Nos. 61 and 64, granted amnesty to specified categories of persons and were promulgated during the latter part of July 1995. Decree No. 61 remitted the remainder of the sentences of Iraqi prisoners and detainees, commuted death sentences to life imprisonment and pardoned persons liable to the penalty of amputation of the hand or the ear. Decree No. 64 granted a general amnesty to Iraqis living in or outside the country in respect of the penalties imposed on them following their conviction for political reasons. The texts of the decrees were annexed to the report. The Special Rapporteur concluded that the conditions set out in the decrees greatly reduced their value. Moreover, he stated, in the absence of great change in the legal and political order of Iraq, the decrees warranted no confidence.

In November, the Secretary-General transmitted to the General Assembly an interim report[(30)] by the Special Rapporteur, in which he described two missions: to Kuwait (22-30 June), by two staff members of the UN Centre for Human Rights, to follow up on the situation of Kuwaitis and third-country nationals who had disappeared during the 1990/91 Iraqi occupation of Kuwait;[(31)] and to Lebanon (24-30 July), also taken by two Centre staff members, to interview Iraqis who had recently arrived there.

The Special Rapporteur recommended that Iraq: abrogate decrees prescribing cruel and unusual punishment or treatment and abolish that practice; cooperate to discover the whereabouts or resolve the fate of the several hundred Kuwaitis and third-country nationals who disappeared under the 1990/91 Kuwaiti occupation; cooperate with the United Nations to organize a sale of oil to purchase humanitarian goods; and abrogate laws penalizing the free expression of competing views and ideas.

**GENERAL ASSEMBLY ACTION**

On 22 December, the General Assembly adopted **resolution 50/191**.

### Situation of human rights in Iraq

_The General Assembly_,

_Guided_ by the Charter of the United Nations, the Universal Declaration of Human Rights and the International Covenants on Human Rights,

_Reaffirming_ that all Member States have an obligation to promote and protect human rights and fundamental freedoms and the duty to fulfil the obligations they have undertaken under the various international instruments in this field,

_Mindful_ that Iraq is a party to the International Covenants on Human Rights and to other international human rights instruments,

_Recalling_ its resolution 49/203 of 23 December 1994, in which it expressed its strong condemnation of the massive violations of human rights of the gravest nature in Iraq,

_Recalling also_ Commission on Human Rights resolution 1991/74 of 6 March 1991, by which the Commission requested its Chairman to appoint a special rapporteur to make a thorough study of the violations of human rights by the Government of Iraq, based on all information the special rapporteur might deem relevant, including information provided by intergovernmental and non-governmental organizations and any comments and material provided by the Government of Iraq,

_Recalling further_ the pertinent resolutions of the Commission on Human Rights condemning the flagrant violations of human rights by the Government of Iraq, including its most recent, resolution 1995/76 of 8 March 1995, by which the Commission extended the mandate of the Special Rapporteur on the situation of human rights in Iraq for a further year and requested him to submit an interim report to the General Assembly at its fiftieth session and a final report to the Commission at its fifty-second session,

_Bearing in mind_ Security Council resolution 688(1991) of 5 April 1991, in which the Council demanded an end to the repression of the Iraqi civilian population and insisted that Iraq cooperate with humanitarian organizations and ensure that the human and political rights of all Iraqi citizens were respected,

_Recalling_ Security Council resolutions 687(1991) of 3 April 1991, 706(1991) of 15 August 1991, 712(1991) of 19 September 1991 and 778(1992) of 2 October 1992,

_Recalling also_ Security Council resolution 986(1995) of 14 April 1995, by which the Council authorized States to permit imports of Iraqi oil up to the amount of one billion United States dollars every ninety days, on a renewable basis, to be used to purchase essential food and medical supplies for humanitarian purposes,

_Deeply concerned_ by the persisting massive and grave violations of human rights by the Government of Iraq, regarding which there are no signs of improvement, such as summary and arbitrary executions, the enactment and implementation of decrees prescribing cruel and inhuman punishments, torture and other cruel, inhuman or degrading treatment, arbitrary arrests and detentions, lack of due process, non-respect for the rule of law and the suppression of freedom of thought, expression and association, as well as the persistence of specific discrimination within the country as regards access to food and health care, which amounts to a violation of the economic and social rights of Iraqis,

_Deeply disturbed_ by the observation by the Special Rapporteur that Iraqi armed forces have continued their attacks on the farming communities throughout the region adjoining northern Iraq and in the south of the country, resulting in the destruction of their crops and livestock,

_Deeply disturbed also_ by reports about the climate of oppression and the dire economic and social situation in the south of Iraq,

_Noting_ the responsibility of the Iraqi authorities with regard to persons missing and detained as a result of the Iraqi occupation of Kuwait, and also noting that Iraq has recently renewed its participation in the Tripartite Commission established pursuant to the cease-fire agreement of 1991,

_Deploring_ the refusal of the Government of Iraq to cooperate with the United Nations human rights mechanisms, in particular by receiving a return visit of the Special Rapporteur to Iraq and allowing the stationing of human rights monitors throughout Iraq pursuant to the relevant resolutions of the General Assembly and the Commission on Human Rights,

1. _Takes note with appreciation_ of the interim report on the situation of human rights in Iraq submitted by the Special Rapporteur of the Commission on Human Rights on the situation of human rights in Iraq and the observations, conclusions and recommendations contained therein;

2. *Expresses its strong condemnation* of the massive and extremely grave violations of human rights for which the Government of Iraq is responsible, resulting in an all-pervasive order of repression and oppression which is sustained by broad-based discrimination and widespread terror;

3. *Expresses its condemnation* with regard to the violations of human rights and international humanitarian law, in particular of:

(*a*) Summary and arbitrary executions, including political killings;

(*b*) The widespread routine practice of systematic torture in its most cruel forms;

(*c*) The enactment and implementation of decrees prescribing cruel and unusual punishment, namely mutilation, as a penalty for certain offences and the abuse and diversion of medical-care services for the purpose of such mutilations;

(*d*) Enforced or involuntary disappearances, routinely practised arbitrary arrests and detention and consistent and routine failure to respect due process and the rule of law;

(*e*) Suppression of freedom of thought, information, expression, association and assembly, through fear of arrest, imprisonment and other sanctions, including the death penalty, as well as harsh limitations to freedom of movement;

4. *Urges* the Government of Iraq to cooperate with the United Nations with a view to arranging for the export of oil in order to purchase essential food and medical supplies for humanitarian purposes, as authorized by the Security Council in its resolution 986(1995);

5. *Strongly condemns* the continued refusal of the Government of Iraq to take advantage of resources available to alleviate the suffering of the people, which includes long-term disabilities of millions of people and the death of many thousands more;

6. *Again expresses its special alarm* at the policies of the Government of Iraq, which discriminate between regions and prevent the equitable enjoyment of basic foodstuffs and medical supplies, and calls upon Iraq, which has sole responsibility in this regard, to take steps to cooperate with international humanitarian agencies in the provision of relief to those in need throughout Iraq;

7. *Calls once again upon* Iraq, as a State party to the International Covenant on Economic, Social and Cultural Rights and to the International Covenant on Civil and Political Rights, to abide by its obligations freely undertaken under the Covenants and under other international instruments on human rights, and particularly to respect and ensure the rights of all individuals, irrespective of their origin, within its territory and subject to its jurisdiction;

8. *Demands* that the Government of Iraq restore the independence of the judiciary and abrogate all laws granting impunity to specified forces or persons killing or injuring individuals for any purpose beyond the administration of justice under the rule of law as prescribed by international standards;

9. *Also demands* that the Government of Iraq abrogate any and all decrees that prescribe cruel and inhuman punishment or treatment and take every step necessary to ensure that the practice of torture and cruel and unusual punishments and treatment no longer occur;

10. *Urges* the Government of Iraq to abrogate all laws and procedures, including Revolution Command Council decree No. 840 of 4 November 1986, that penalize the free expression of competing views and ideas and to ensure that the genuine will of the people shall be the basis of authority in the State;

11. *Also urges* the Government of Iraq to improve its cooperation with the Tripartite Commission with a view to establishing the whereabouts or resolving the fate of the remaining several hundred missing persons and prisoners of war, Kuwaitis and third-country nationals victims of the illegal Iraqi occupation of Kuwait;

12. *Requests* the Secretary-General to provide the Special Rapporteur with all necessary assistance in carrying out his mandate and to approve the allocation of sufficient human and material resources for the sending of human rights monitors to such locations as would facilitate improved information flow and assessment and help in the independent verification of reports on the situation of human rights in Iraq;

13. *Decides* to continue its consideration of the situation of human rights in Iraq during its fifty-first session under the item entitled "Human rights questions", in the light of additional elements provided by the Commission on Human Rights and the Economic and Social Council.

General Assembly resolution 50/191

22 December 1995     Meeting 99     111-3-53 (recorded vote)

Approved by Third Committee (A/50/635/Add.3) by recorded vote (104-4-49), 13 December (meeting 56); 30-nation draft (A/C.3/50/L.44), orally revised; agenda item 112 (c).

*Meeting numbers.* GA 50th session: 3rd Committee 35, 38-51, 53, 56; plenary 99.

Recorded vote in Assembly as follows:

*In favour:* Albania, Andorra, Antigua and Barbuda, Argentina, Armenia, Australia, Austria, Azerbaijan, Bahamas, Barbados, Belarus, Belgium, Belize, Bhutan, Bolivia, Bosnia and Herzegovina, Botswana, Brazil, Bulgaria, Cambodia, Canada, Chile, Colombia, Costa Rica, Croatia, Cyprus, Czech Republic, Denmark, Dominica, Ecuador, El Salvador, Estonia, Fiji, Finland, France, Georgia, Germany, Ghana, Greece, Grenada, Guinea, Guyana, Haiti, Honduras, Hungary, Iceland, Iran, Ireland, Israel, Italy, Jamaica, Japan, Kazakstan, Kuwait, Kyrgyzstan, Latvia, Lebanon, Liechtenstein, Lithuania, Luxembourg, Malawi, Maldives, Malta, Marshall Islands, Mauritius, Mexico, Micronesia, Monaco, Mongolia, Netherlands, New Zealand, Nicaragua, Norway, Panama, Papua New Guinea, Paraguay, Peru, Poland, Portugal, Republic of Korea, Republic of Moldova, Romania, Russian Federation, Saint Kitts and Nevis, Saint Lucia, Saint Vincent and the Grenadines, Samoa, San Marino, Saudi Arabia, Senegal, Singapore, Slovakia, Slovenia, Solomon Islands, South Africa, Spain, Suriname, Swaziland, Sweden, Syrian Arab Republic, Tajikistan, the former Yugoslav Republic of Macedonia, Trinidad and Tobago, Turkey, Ukraine, United Kingdom, United States, Uruguay, Uzbekistan, Venezuela, Zambia.

*Against:* Libyan Arab Jamahiriya, Nigeria, Sudan.

*Abstaining:* Afghanistan, Algeria, Angola, Bahrain, Bangladesh, Benin, Brunei Darussalam, Burkina Faso, Burundi, Cameroon, Cape Verde, Chad, China, Côte d'Ivoire, Cuba, Democratic People's Republic of Korea, Egypt, Equatorial Guinea, Eritrea, Ethiopia, Gabon, Guatemala, Guinea-Bissau, India, Indonesia, Jordan, Kenya, Lao People's Democratic Republic, Lesotho, Malaysia, Mali, Mauritania, Morocco, Mozambique, Myanmar, Namibia, Nepal, Niger, Pakistan, Philippines, Rwanda, Sierra Leone, Sri Lanka, Thailand, Togo, Tunisia, Uganda, United Arab Emirates, United Republic of Tanzania, Vanuatu, Viet Nam, Zaire, Zimbabwe.

## Myanmar

**Report of the Special Rapporteur.** In a January report,[32] Special Rapporteur Yozo Yokota (Japan) reported on the human rights situation in Myanmar and described his 1994 visit (7-16 November) to the country. He met with high-level government officials and leaders of political parties and visited governmental institutions and facilities. He also met with representatives of national organizations and institutions. He was disappointed that he was not allowed to meet with Daw Aung San Suu Kyi, the 1991 Nobel Peace Prize Laureate detained without trial for the last six years.

The Special Rapporteur received information of alleged human rights violations relating to extrajudicial, summary or arbitrary executions; arbitrary arrest and detention; torture and other cruel, inhuman or degrading treatment; freedom of movement; freedom of expression; labour rights; and the rights of the child. He discussed the repatriation from Bangladesh of Muslims of Rakhine State and the 1993 National Convention, which was held to lay down the basic principles for elaborating a new constitution.

The Special Rapporteur stated that the people did not generally enjoy freedom of thought, opinion, expression, publication and peaceful assembly and association. He was pleased to note the continued release of political detainees, but regretted the long prison terms of five persons arrested in 1994 for engaging in political activities. He welcomed progress in the repatriation of refugees and training programmes for military officers and soldiers.

He recommended that the Government of Myanmar fulfil its obligations under Articles 55 and 56 of the UN Charter; consider acceding to the 1966 International Covenants on Human Rights,[26] the 1984 Convention against Torture and Other Cruel, Inhuman or Degrading Treatment or Punishment[33] and the 1977 Protocols to the Geneva Conventions of 1949;[6] bring Myanmar law concerning the protection of physical-integrity rights into line with accepted international standards; guarantee the freedoms of opinion, expression and association; try, by an independent civilian court in an accessible judicial process, those arrested or detained following demonstrations in 1988 and 1990 or as a result of the National Convention; bring the conduct of the military into line with accepted international standards; refrain from recruiting into the armed forces persons under the age of 15 years; train military and law enforcement personnel as to their responsibilities; condemn human rights violations committed by government authorities; revise its Citizenship Law; cooperate with UNHCR in ensuring the voluntary and safe return of Rakhine Muslims; and continue its cooperation with NGOs.

**Commission action.** On 8 March,[34] the Commission, deploring the continued seriousness of the human rights situation in Myanmar and the fact that political leaders, including Daw Aung San Suu Kyi and other leaders of the National League for Democracy, remained deprived of their liberty, urged the Government to release her, other detained political leaders and all political prisoners. The Commission further urged the Government to: take measures to guarantee democracy; take measures to allow all citizens to participate freely in the political process and accelerate the process of transition to democracy by transferring power to democratically elected representatives, lifting restraining orders on political leaders, releasing detainees, and ensuring the normal function of political parties; guarantee the freedom of expression and opinion and the rights of association and assembly; and cooperate with the Special Rapporteur. It asked the Government to ensure that all persons were afforded the minimum guarantees for a fair trial, that laws were given due publicity and that the principle of non-retroactivity was respected.

The Commission extended the Special Rapporteur's mandate for one year and asked him to report to the General Assembly in 1995 and to the Commission in 1996. The Secretary-General was asked to assist him. The Economic and Social Council approved those actions by **decision 1995/283** of 25 July.

**Interim report of the Special Rapporteur.** In October, the Secretary-General transmitted to the General Assembly the Special Rapporteur's interim report[35] on the human rights situation in Myanmar. He stated that in early September he had transmitted to the Government a summary of allegations of human rights violations concerning summary or arbitrary execution; arbitrary arrest and detention; torture and other cruel, inhuman or degrading treatment; forced labour; and the situation of women. He also transmitted allegations of human rights abuses along the Thai/Myanmar border areas, notably in Manerplaw and Kawmoora, both strongholds of the Karen National Union. The report contained Myanmar's response to those allegations.

Following the lifting of restrictions against Daw Aung San Suu Kyi, the Special Rapporteur asked the Government in July for permission to visit Myanmar, which he did from 8 to 17 October.[36]

**Report of the Secretary-General.** In response to a 1994 General Assembly request,[37] the Secretary-General submitted a report[38] in November, describing the good-offices activities he had undertaken to assist Myanmar to respond to concerns with respect to the human rights situation and to achieve national reconciliation.

**GENERAL ASSEMBLY ACTION**

On 22 December, the General Assembly adopted **resolution 50/194**.

**Situation of human rights in Myanmar**
*The General Assembly,*

*Reaffirming* that all Member States have an obligation to promote and protect human rights and fundamental freedoms as stated in the Charter of the United Nations and elaborated in the Universal Declaration of Human Rights, the International Covenants on Human Rights and other applicable human rights instruments,

*Aware* that, in accordance with the Charter, the Organization promotes and encourages respect for human rights and fundamental freedoms for all and that the Universal Declaration of Human Rights states that the will of the people shall be the basis of the authority of government,

*Recalling* its resolution 49/197 of 23 December 1994,

*Recalling also* Commission on Human Rights resolution 1992/58 of 3 March 1992, in which the Commission, *inter alia*, decided to nominate a special rapporteur to establish direct contacts with the Government and with the people of Myanmar, including political leaders deprived of their liberty, their families and their lawyers, with a view to examining the situation of human rights in Myanmar and following any progress made towards the transfer of power to a civilian Government and the drafting of a new constitution, the lifting of restrictions on personal freedoms and the restoration of human rights in Myanmar,

*Taking note* of Commission on Human Rights resolution 1995/72 of 8 March 1995, in which the Commission decided to extend for one year the mandate of the Special Rapporteur on the situation of human rights in Myanmar,

*Gravely concerned* that the Government of Myanmar still has not implemented its commitment to take all necessary steps towards democracy in the light of the results of the elections held in 1990,

*Noting* the recent developments regarding the composition of the National Convention,

*Welcoming* the release without conditions, on 10 July 1995, of Nobel Peace Prize Laureate Aung San Suu Kyi and a number of other political prisoners, as called for by the General Assembly,

*Also gravely concerned*, however, at the continued violations of human rights in Myanmar, as reported by the Special Rapporteur, including killings of civilians, arbitrary arrest and detention, restrictions on freedom of expression and association, torture, forced labour, forced portering, human rights abuses in border areas in the course of military operations, forced relocations and development projects, abuse of women and the imposition of oppressive measures directed in particular at ethnic and religious minorities,

*Welcoming* the continuing cooperation between the Government of Myanmar and the Office of the United Nations High Commissioner for Refugees on the voluntary repatriation of refugees from Bangladesh to Myanmar,

*Noting*, however, that the human rights situation in Myanmar has resulted in flows of refugees to neighbouring countries, thus creating problems for the countries concerned,

1. *Expresses its appreciation* to the Special Rapporteur of the Commission on Human Rights on the situation of human rights in Myanmar for his interim report;

2. *Also expresses its appreciation* to the Secretary-General for his report;

3. *Deplores* the continued violations of human rights in Myanmar;

4. *Welcomes* the release without conditions of Nobel Peace Prize Laureate Aung San Suu Kyi and other prominent political leaders;

5. *Strongly urges* the Government of Myanmar to release immediately and unconditionally detained political leaders and all political prisoners, to ensure their physical integrity and to permit them to participate in the process of national reconciliation;

6. *Urges* the Government of Myanmar to engage, at the earliest possible date, in a substantive political dialogue with Aung San Suu Kyi and other political leaders, including representatives of ethnic groups, as the best means of promoting national reconciliation and the full and early restoration of democracy;

7. *Welcomes* the discussions between the Government of Myanmar and the Secretary-General, and further encourages the Government of Myanmar to cooperate fully with the Secretary-General;

8. *Again urges* the Government of Myanmar, in conformity with its assurances given at various times, to take all necessary steps towards the restoration of democracy in accordance with the will of the people as expressed in the democratic elections held in 1990 and to ensure that political parties can function freely;

9. *Expresses its concern* that most of the representatives duly elected in 1990 are still excluded from participating in the meetings of the National Convention, created to prepare basic elements for the drafting of a new constitution, and that one of its objectives is to maintain the participation of the armed forces in a leading role in the future political life of the State, and notes with concern that the working procedures of the National Convention do not permit the elected representatives of the people freely to express their views;

10. *Strongly urges* the Government of Myanmar to take all appropriate measures to allow all citizens to participate freely in the political process, in accordance with the principles of the Universal Declaration of Human Rights, and to accelerate the process of transition to democracy, in particular through the transfer of power to democratically elected representatives;

11. *Also strongly urges* the Government of Myanmar to ensure full respect for human rights and fundamental freedoms, including freedom of expression and assembly, and the protection of the rights of persons belonging to ethnic and religious minorities, and to put an end to violations of the right to life and integrity of the human being, to the practices of torture, abuse of women, forced labour and forced relocations, and to enforced disappearances and summary executions;

12. *Appeals* to the Government of Myanmar to consider becoming a party to the International Covenant on Civil and Political Rights, the International Covenant on Economic, Social and Cultural Rights and the Convention against Torture and Other Cruel, Inhuman and Degrading Treatment or Punishment;

13. *Urges* the Government of Myanmar to fulfil its obligations as a State party to the Forced Labour Convention, 1930 (No. 29), and to the Freedom of Association and Protection of the Right to Organize Convention, 1948 (No. 87), of the International Labour Organization;

14. *Stresses* the importance for the Government of Myanmar to give particular attention to conditions in the country's jails and to allow the International Committee of the Red Cross to communicate freely and confidentially with prisoners;

15. *Calls upon* the Government of Myanmar to respect fully the obligations of the Geneva Conventions

of 12 August 1949, and to make use of such services as may be offered by impartial humanitarian bodies;

16.  *Expresses its grave concern* at the attacks by Myanmar army soldiers on the Karens and the Karennis during the past year, resulting in further refugee flows to a neighbouring country;

17.  *Welcomes* the cessation of hostilities following the conclusion of cease-fire agreements between the Government of Myanmar and several ethnic groups;

18.  *Encourages* the Government of Myanmar to create the necessary conditions to ensure an end to the movements of refugees to neighbouring countries and to create conditions conducive to their voluntary return and their full reintegration, in conditions of safety and dignity;

19.  *Requests* the Secretary-General to continue his discussions with the Government of Myanmar in order to assist in its efforts for national reconciliation and in the implementation of the present resolution and to report to the General Assembly at its fifty-first session and to the Commission on Human Rights at its fifty-second session;

20.  *Decides* to continue its consideration of this question at its fifty-first session.

General Assembly resolution 50/194

22 December 1995      Meeting 99      Adopted without vote

Approved by Third Committee (A/50/635/Add.3) without vote, 11 December (meeting 54); 31-nation draft (A/C.3/50/L.52), orally revised; agenda item 112 (c).

Meeting numbers. GA 50th session: 3rd Committee 35, 38-52, 54; plenary 99.

### Papua New Guinea

**Report of the Secretary-General.** In February, the Secretary-General transmitted to the Commission on Human Rights information on activities undertaken by UN human rights treaty-monitoring bodies regarding the human rights situation on the island of Bougainville, Papua New Guinea,[39] where violence had erupted against the background of an armed conflict between the Papua New Guinea Defence Forces and the Bougainville Revolutionary Army (for action by the Committee on the Elimination of Racial Discrimination in 1995, see PART THREE, Chapter I). He described the evolution of the situation since March 1994. The report contained a copy of a cease-fire agreement signed on 8 September 1994 by the Bougainville Revolutionary Army and a representative of an organization known as the Bougainville Interim Government (BIG). It also contained the Government's response to the Human Rights Commission on alleged human rights violations, which indicated that all the peace processes embarked upon by all parties in Bougainville and the member States of the South Pacific Forum had culminated in the Mirigini Charter, signed on 25 November 1994. The Charter was to lead to the establishment of the Bougainville Transitional Government (BTG).

In an addendum to his report,[40] the Secretary-General described a visit in 1995 by his Representative, Francesc Vendrell, to Papua New Guinea (23-28 January) and Solomon Islands (29-31 January). The Secretary-General concluded that important steps had been taken by the Government of Papua New Guinea towards a peaceful settlement of the conflict. Although specific allegations of human rights violations were brought to the Representative's attention, the Secretary-General was of the impression that the number of violations had substantially decreased since September 1994.

(For details of a visit to Bougainville by the Special Rapporteur on extrajudicial, summary and arbitrary executions, see PART THREE, Chapter I.)

**Commission action.** On 7 March,[41] the Commission asked all parties in Bougainville to implement the instrument of cease-fire and called on all parties to the conflict to adhere strictly to the paragraph calling for the immediate lifting of the restrictions on the provision of medical and other humanitarian services. It asked the Secretary-General to bring its resolution to the attention of the Government of Papua New Guinea and all parties to the peace process and to continue to lend his good offices. The Commission asked the Government of Papua New Guinea to invite the relevant thematic rapporteurs and working groups to visit Bougainville to monitor the peace process and to report on the human rights situation. It urged the Government to cooperate with the Secretary-General's Representative and the relevant thematic rapporteurs and working groups so that they could report in 1996.

**Further report of the Secretary-General.** The Secretary-General reported[42] that a 27-member Transitional Government was installed in April in Bougainville. In June, the Parliament passed the Organic Law on Provincial Governments and Local-Level Governments, which was to come into effect in 1997. The Law, which recognized provincial and local governments by doing away with elected provincial assemblies and strengthening local-level governments, exempted BTG from its provisions until 1997, in recognition of the special circumstances of the province. Representatives of BTG and BIG held preliminary talks (Cairns, Australia, 9-12 September) to identify problems and lay the groundwork for a meeting of the leaders of Bougainville, with the participation, subject to the concurrence of the Government of Papua New Guinea, of UN and Commonwealth representatives. Annexed to the report was a joint communiqué issued by the All-Bougainville Leaders' Talks (Cairns, 14-18 December).

*REFERENCES*

[1]E/CN.4/1995/64.  [2]YUN 1994, p. 1083.  [3]YUN 1988, p. 185.  [4]YUN 1992, p. 263.  [5]E/1995/23 (res. 1995/74).  [6]YUN 1977, p. 706.  [7]YUN 1993, p. 732, GA res. 48/208, 21 Dec. 1993.  [8]YUN 1955, p. 209.  [9]YUN 1966, p. 423, GA

res. 2200 A (XXI), annex, 16 Dec. 1966. [10]A/50/567. [11]E/CN.4/1995/L.86. [12]E/CN.4/1995/72. [13]E/CN.4/1995/34. [14]E/CN.4/1995/61 & Add.1. [15]YUN 1994, pp. 1020 & 1024. [16]YUN 1991, p. 798. [17]E/1995/23. [18]E/CN.4/1995/55. [19]YUN 1994, p. 456. [20]YUN 1991, p. 601. [21]E/1995/23 (res. 1995/68). [22]E/CN.4/1996/2 (res. 1995/18). [23]A/50/661. [24]E/CN.4/1995/56. [25]E/1995/23 (res. 1995/76). [26]YUN 1966, pp. 419 & 423, GA res. 2200 A (XXI), annex, 16 Dec. 1966. [27]E/CN.4/1996/2 (res. 1995/3). [28]Ibid. (dec. 1995/107). [29]E/CN.4/1996/12. [30]A/50/734. [31]YUN 1991, p. 167. [32]E/CN.4/1995/65 & Corr.1. [33]YUN 1984, p. 813, GA res. 39/46, annex, 10 Dec. 1984. [34]E/1995/23 (res. 1995/72). [35]A/50/568. [36]E/CN.4/1996/65. [37]YUN 1994, p. 1093, GA res. 49/197, 23 Dec. 1994. [38]A/50/782. [39]E/CN.4/1995/60. [40]E/CN.4/1995/60/Add.1. [41]E/1995/23 (res. 1995/65). [42]E/CN.4/1996/58.

# Europe and the Mediterranean

## Cyprus

In February, the Secretary-General, pursuant to a 1994 Commission decision,[1] reported on human rights in Cyprus.[2] He described action taken by him in response to Security Council requests and by the Committee on Missing Persons in Cyprus (see PART TWO, Chapter V).

On 8 March,[3] the Commission postponed debate on the question of human rights in Cyprus until 1996, on the understanding that action required by previous resolutions would continue to remain operative, including its request to the Secretary-General to provide a report on their implementation.

## The former Yugoslavia

### Human rights situation

**Tenth periodic report of the Special Rapporteur.** As requested by the Commission, Special Rapporteur Tadeusz Mazowiecki (Poland) submitted a series of periodic reports on the human rights situation in the former Yugoslavia. Previous reports were submitted in 1993[4] and 1994.[5]

In his tenth periodic report,[6] submitted on 16 January, the Special Rapporteur updated his ninth (November 1994) report[5] based on information received from the field staff assigned to him in Sarajevo and Zagreb. He discussed the situations in Bosnia and Herzegovina, Croatia, the Federal Republic of Yugoslavia (Serbia and Montenegro) and the former Yugoslav Republic of Macedonia, as well as disappearances and field operations.

Concerning Bosnia and Herzegovina, the Special Rapporteur reiterated the conclusions and recommendations made in his ninth periodic report and added that the Bosnian Serb forces had escalated the military targeting of civilians, resulting in daily loss of life and injury. He condemned those practices and called for their immediate cessation.

He called on the Bosnian Croat local authorities in the Mostar region who were hampering the re-establishment of civil society to abide by the spirit of the Federation of Bosnia and Herzegovina—established in 1994[7]—its Constitution and associated agreements. In view of severe difficulties in the delivery of humanitarian aid, the Special Rapporteur reminded those who interfered that they were violating the human rights of those who relied on such aid for survival.

In his update of the situation in Croatia, the Special Rapporteur repeated the conclusions and recommendations made in his ninth periodic report. He emphasized that the obstruction of the delivery of humanitarian aid in the enclave of Bihac and the refugee camps in Batnoga and Turanj constituted a flagrant violation of fundamental humanitarian principles and called for the cessation of all interference.

The Special Rapporteur reported increased ethnic discrimination in the Federal Republic of Yugoslavia (Serbia and Montenegro). Human rights violations in Kosovo continued, as did tensions between the local Muslim community and authorities in the region of Sandjak (also known as Raska). In addition, the Bulgarian minority in Serbia was subject to harassment. Trade union freedoms and rights were restricted by labour and social legislation and the freedom of the media was threatened. The Special Rapporteur repeated the recommendations made in his ninth periodic report and additionally called on the Government to: remove obstacles preventing the development of a free trade union movement; take measures to respect the rights of ethnic, religious or linguistic minorities; and cooperate with the expert on missing persons designated by the Working Group on Enforced or Involuntary Disappearances (see PART THREE, Chapter I). He also recommended full respect for freedom of the media.

As for the former Yugoslav Republic of Macedonia, the Special Rapporteur discussed, among other things, the situation of ethnic Albanians, difficulties faced by the Serbian population in registering its religious community, and the peaceful atmosphere of the first round of presidential and parliamentary elections.

As to the problem of disappearances, the Special Rapporteur stated that in Croatia the situation of many missing persons had been clarified. However, in Bosnia and Herzegovina, disappearances continued with varied degrees of intensity and it was impossible to ascertain the total number.

The current human rights field operation, set up by the Centre for Human Rights, had functioned since March 1993. With offices in Zagreb, Sarajevo and Skopje, much of its work centred on on-site investigations and field missions to gather first-hand information.

On 26 January, the Secretary-General transmitted[8] the Special Rapporteur's report to the General Assembly, the Security Council and the International Conference on the Former Yugoslavia (ICFY), which began work in 1992[9] to achieve a final settlement of the problems in the former Yugoslavia.

**Report of the Secretary-General.** In February, the Secretary-General reported on the situation of human rights in Bosnia and Herzegovina,[10] as requested by the Commission in 1994. He described the activities of the UN High Commissioner for Human Rights and the Special Rapporteur and action taken by the Commission of Experts, which was established in 1992[11] and concluded its work in April 1994;[12] the International Tribunal for the Prosecution of Persons Responsible for Serious Violations of International Humanitarian Law Committed in the Territory of the Former Yugoslavia since 1991, established by the Security Council in 1993[13] (see PART FIVE, Chapter II); ICFY; and the United Nations Protection Force (UNPROFOR). He also discussed the situation concerning the voluntary return of displaced persons and the problem of disappearances (see PART THREE, Chapter I).

On 9 November, the Security Council, in **resolution 1019(1995)**, condemned all violations of international humanitarian law and of human rights in the territory of the former Yugoslavia.

**Commission action.** By a roll-call vote of 44 to none, with 7 abstentions, the Commission on 8 March[14] condemned all violations of human rights and international humanitarian law and specific violations identified by the Special Rapporteur—including mass killing, torture, disappearances, rape and other sexual abuses against women and children, the use of civilians as human shields, arbitrary executions, the destruction of houses, religious objects and cultural and historical heritage, forced and illegal evictions, detentions, arbitrary searches and other acts of violence. It demanded immediate, firm and resolute action by all concerned parties and the international community to stop those violations and breaches of international law, to secure a just and lasting peace in Bosnia and Herzegovina and to bring war criminals to trial. It also demanded the immediate internationally supervised release of all persons arbitrarily or illegally detained and the immediate closure of all detention facilities not authorized by or in compliance with the 1949 Geneva Conventions and the 1977 Additional Protocols thereto.[15] The Commission further demanded that all parties ensure that all persons under their control cease the deliberate impeding of the delivery of food and medical and other supplies essential for civilians.

Denouncing once again the deliberate and unlawful attacks and use of military force against civilians and other protected persons by all sides, the Commission condemned the besieging of cities and other civilian areas; the terrorization and murder of non-combatants; the destruction of vital services; the use of military force against relief operations; the obstruction of relief convoys; violations of the Agreement on Complete Cessation of Hostilities concluded on 31 December 1994;[16] and ethnic cleansing, particularly in the areas of Banja Luka, Prijedor and Bijeljina.

Strongly condemning discriminatory practices against and human rights violations of ethnic Albanians in Kosovo, the Commission demanded that the Federal Republic of Yugoslavia (Serbia and Montenegro) respect their human rights and fundamental freedoms; cease all human rights violations, discriminatory measures and practices; release political prisoners and cease the persecution of political leaders and members of local human rights organizations; respect the will of the inhabitants of Kosovo; guarantee freedom of the media and cease the obstruction of the Albanian-language media in Kosovo; abrogate the Government's official settlement policy; allow the Special Rapporteur to visit Kosovo; and cooperate with the Organization for Security and Cooperation in Europe (OSCE) to enable the mission to resume its activities immediately by permitting its return to Kosovo. The Secretary-General was urged to explore ways to establish an international monitoring presence in Kosovo.

The Commission deplored and condemned the continual refusal of the Bosnian Serb authorities to permit the Special Rapporteur to conduct investigations in territory under their control. It demanded that the Federal Republic of Yugoslavia (Serbia and Montenegro) permit entry into Kosovo, Sandjak and Vojvodina of UN observer missions and field officers of the Special Rapporteur and resumption of the missions of long duration of OSCE. The Commission also demanded that the Government of the Federal Republic of Yugoslavia (Serbia and Montenegro), as well as the Governments of Serbia and of Montenegro, end the violence and harassment directed against the Muslim community in Sandjak. It expressed grave concern at renewed reports of human rights violations in Vojvodina concerning the Bulgarian and Croatian minorities. It noted with concern that many of the Special Rapporteur's past recommendations had not been fully implemented. It recommended the inclusion of a human rights component in any internationally negotiated arrangements for Bosnia and Herzegovina and that implementation of such a component be conducted in close cooperation with the Special Rapporteur and the Centre for Human Rights.

Welcoming the expanding activities of the International Tribunal for the former Yugoslavia, the

Commission asked States to make available to the Tribunal resources, services and expert personnel. It commended the expert member of the Working Group on Enforced or Involuntary Disappearances for his first report,[17] in 1994, on the special process on missing persons in the territory of the former Yugoslavia (see also PART THREE, Chapter I).

The Commission, extending the Special Rapporteur's mandate for one year, asked him to continue to submit periodic reports. The Secretary-General was requested to make those reports available to the Security Council and to ICFY. It asked the Secretary-General to assist in obtaining the cooperation of all UN bodies in implementing its resolution and, pursuant to a 1994 General Assembly request,[18] to provide the Special Rapporteur with the necessary assistance to enable him to fulfil his mandate and, in particular, to appoint field staff in the former Yugoslavia to provide first-hand, timely reports on the human rights situation there. The Commission's requests were approved by the Economic and Social Council on 25 July by **decision 1995/290**.

**Further periodic reports of the Special Rapporteur.** In response to the Commission's request (see above), the Special Rapporteur on the human rights situation in the former Yugoslavia prepared a series of periodic reports in 1995.

In April, he described the situation of the non-Serb population in the Banja Luka region of northern Bosnia and Herzegovina, which had reached a critical point in February when certain towns suffered sustained campaigns of violence directed against Muslims and Bosnian Croats.[19] He stated that non-Serbs had been subjected to unrelenting discrimination and terrorization, and it appeared that virtually none wished to remain in the area. Local authorities in Banja Luka reaped revenue from fees imposed on persons applying to leave, but authorities in Pale—the capital of the so-called "Serbian Republic"—seemed to have moved to slow down the exodus, possibly to retain some non-Serbs for forced labour and to have people available for inclusion in negotiated population exchanges. The de facto authorities continued to compel non-Serbs to serve in forced-labour brigades. So-called criminal gangs increased their operations, with one purpose appearing to be to carry out ethnic cleansing without directly implicating the authorities. The Special Rapporteur stated that the de facto authorities had violated their obligations under the cease-fire agreements of December 1994[16] to allow access of human rights monitors into territories they controlled. He called on the de facto authorities to stop the ethnic cleansing, to provide adequate protection to groups subjected to discrimination and to facilitate the restitution of property. He urged that those

responsible for crimes be brought to justice and that conditions be created for the return in safety and dignity of displaced persons and refugees. He called on the international community to exercise pressure to obtain access of UN civilian police officers and human rights monitors to territories controlled by the Bosnian Serb authorities.

In July, the Secretary-General transmitted the Special Rapporteur's April report to the General Assembly, the Security Council and ICFY.[20]

Also in July, the Special Rapporteur described his visit to Croatia and central and south Bosnia and Herzegovina (22 May–3 June).[21] In addition, he provided information on human rights developments in areas he was unable to visit—such as Sarajevo, other UN-designated safe areas and Banja Luka—owing to the security situation or denial of access.

In May, the Republic of Croatia, in violation of the cease-fire agreement of 29 March 1994,[22] launched a major military operation in Western Slavonia (Sector West)—an area defined as a UN Protected Area and subject to UN protection and monitoring, which constituted the so-called "Republic of Serb Krajina" ("RSK"). Croatian Army troops, supported by some 30 tanks, moved into Sector West on 1 May and took most Serb-controlled territory within 36 hours and the entire Sector by 4 May. On 4 May, the Croatian Minister of Defence stated that between 350 and 450 "RSK" soldiers had been killed and 1,200 wounded; the Croatian forces were reported to have suffered 37 fatalities, with some 150 wounded. On 22 May, the Croatian Government set the number of Serb dead at 188; of those, it was claimed that some 54 might be civilians. The Special Rapporteur's field staff on 16 May observed burial sites in Vrbovljani and Okucani which bore the appearance of possible mass graves. By the end of May, these sites had been altered, with individual mounds created and marked with crosses. The Croatian Government refused to release data on the identities of most of the war dead. It claimed that only 10 wounded from "RSK" had been treated in Croatian hospitals, but the UN estimated that about 500 wounded from "RSK" had fled into the Serb-held territory of Bosnia and Herzegovina. More than 100 houses were destroyed and, according to a reliable report, some houses in Vrbovljani, Covac and Okucani were intentionally blown up because, in the past, those villages had been well known for terrorist activities. There were also numerous incidents of looting by the advancing Croatian forces and, to a lesser extent, by retreating "RSK" forces. Also, "RSK" authorities had ordered a series of artillery and rocket attacks against several Croatian cities, carried out on 2 and 3 May. After recovering control over Western Slavonia, Croatian authorities detained virtually all males, particularly from the area around Pakrac (Gavrinica). A total of 1,494 men were taken into custody in three community centres in the towns of Bjelovar, Pozega and Varazdin.

The Special Rapporteur concluded that the Croatian authorities were responsible for violations of human rights and humanitarian law, many of which were of a serious nature but had not occurred on a massive scale. ''RSK'' authorities were responsible for shelling civilians, the Rapporteur said. Serious doubts existed as to the credibility of data provided by Croatian authorities concerning the number of persons killed; credible data, the Rapporteur stated, indicated that the number of civilian dead exceeded that reported by the Government. While it appeared that the majority of detainees had been treated correctly, there had been some alleged cases of physical and verbal abuse and other forms of degrading treatment.

Croatian authorities and international organizations had failed to prevent an exodus of the Serbian population from Western Slavonia, the Rapporteur continued. The exodus was due to fear of possible repercussions. The authorities had taken steps to restore confidence and to facilitate coexistence among the population, but those measures did not appear to have met existing needs. An important confidence-building role had been played by the Coordination of Organizations for Human Rights, composed of NGOs from all over Croatia. The Special Rapporteur recommended that Croatian authorities identify those killed and provide information to the families about cause of death and place of burial, pursue criminal proceedings against persons suspected of having committed war crimes, and accelerate the process of integrating representatives of the Serbian population into local administrative structures. He also recommended: clarifying doubts about the events during the military operation; taking into account the cultural identity of the Serb population in the Western Slavonia school system; monitoring by international and local organizations of the human rights situation in the region; and organizing the process of the return of displaced persons so as to guarantee the human rights of all of the population, including the right to property.

The Special Rapporteur reported that in Sarajevo targeting of civilian areas by Bosnian Serb forces continued, resulting in deaths and injuries. Since the beginning of 1995, there had been an ongoing pattern of humiliation of and attacks against UN personnel and representatives of other organizations, including targeting resulting in death and injury, detention, hostage-taking and restrictions on freedom of movement. The humanitarian aid situation in Sarajevo had reached a desperate stage, owing to the blockade by Bosnian Serb forces.

UN-designated safe areas—including Bihac, Gorazde, Srebrenica, Tuzla and Sarajevo—were shelled on 25 May by Bosnian Serb forces in retaliation for airstrikes by the North Atlantic Treaty Organization (see PART TWO, Chapter V).

Following the Croatian offensive in Western Slavonia, there were further reports in Banja Luka of human rights abuses against the non-Serbian population, particularly Croats; there was also a proliferation of attacks on Catholic clergy and buildings. In Mostar, human rights violations, particularly against the Muslim population in Croat-controlled West Mostar, continued to be a cause for concern. In addition, the human rights of the Serb community in East and West Mostar were not adequately safeguarded. Freedom of movement between the two parts of the city was restricted, and limited progress was made in terms of joint institutional developments.

In his conclusions and recommendations, the Special Rapporteur stated that snipers should be among those tried and sentenced for grave breaches of humanitarian law. He called on those responsible for civilian attacks to cease them immediately. Calling on the Bosnian Serb de facto authorities to ensure that human rights violations against minorities in Banja Luka were stopped, the Special Rapporteur asked that he and his field staff be granted access to the area to assess first-hand the human rights situation there. As for Mostar, he urged a speedy reunification of the city as that would greatly assist the human rights situation. He recommended that immediate steps be taken to facilitate decisions at the federal level concerning the return of refugees and displaced persons in the Federation of Bosnia and Herzegovina.

In July, the Secretary-General transmitted the Special Rapporteur's July report to the General Assembly, the Security Council and ICFY.[23]

In an August report,[24] the Special Rapporteur discussed violations of human rights and humanitarian law following the fall of Srebrenica on 11 July 1995, which saw the expulsion of the entire Muslim population, estimated at between 38,000 and 42,000. The Special Rapporteur's report was based on his mission to Tuzla from 22 to 24 July, as well as on an investigation by staff of the Centre for Human Rights in conjunction with the civil affairs component of the UN Peace Forces. About 25,000 people fled from Srebrenica and began to arrive in Potocari on 11 July. There were accounts of physical violence by Bosnian Serb soldiers, executions and abductions of young women. The Special Rapporteur described the journey by bus and truck from Potocari to the edge of Bosnian Serb–held territory near Tisca; the evacuation of 65 wounded persons from Potocari by medical convoy; and the journey on foot of some 15,000 draft-age men from Srebrenica to Bosnian Government territory., He discussed the situation in Tuzla, where, from about 13 July, displaced persons had begun to arrive.

The Special Rapporteur concluded that there was evidence of summary executions and possibly of mass executions. There were credible accounts that women had been raped, as well as evidence of physical assaults and inhuman and degrading treatment against the entire population. Civilians had been targeted by shelling and other forms of military activity, and prisoners of war were badly mistreated. The Special Rapporteur said that there had been complete disregard for the mental suffering caused by the expulsion of the population from Srebrenica and credible reports of looting and destruction of Muslim property following the fall of that enclave. Thousands of people were still missing. Finally, there was an indication that reprisal attacks had taken place against Serbians living in Tuzla by Muslim displaced persons from Srebrenica.

The Special Rapporteur recommended continuing investigations and making available to competent UN bodies information derived from military intelligence sources relevant to uncovering violations of international humanitarian law. He also recommended that: the Bosnian Serb de facto authorities account for the thousands of persons reportedly still missing; ICRC be granted access to detention facilities; the international community make efforts to ensure that displaced persons returned in safety and dignity and provide assistance and financial support to them; and local authorities in Tuzla continue to safeguard the rights of the Serbian minority. He called for an investigation under international supervision of accusations against UNPROFOR in Srebrenica.

The Special Rapporteur discussed the concept of safe areas and a meeting he organized in Szeged, Hungary, on 8 and 9 July to collect information on the human rights situation in the Federal Republic of Yugoslavia (Serbia and Montenegro). With 32 representatives of NGOs participating, the meeting elaborated and substantiated allegations concerning irregularities in the judicial system; irregularities in citizenship law; discrimination based on ethnicity and nationality; impediments surrounding the activities of independent trade unions; restrictions on the freedom of the media and the dominance of the State-sponsored media; systematic suppression of cultural heritage; and deportation of citizens and individuals seeking refuge in the Federal Republic of Yugoslavia (Serbia and Montenegro).

The Special Rapporteur stated that the human rights situation in Montenegro had improved; there was no indication of significant or systematic discrimination. During the Szeged meeting, his attention was drawn to the existence of a Bosnian

Government-operated detention facility in Tarcin, where a few hundred individuals had been detained for three years. He urged the Government of Bosnia and Herzegovina to release all detainees at the facility.

The Special Rapporteur's report contained a 27 July letter, by which he informed the Chairman of the Commission on Human Rights of his resignation. On 3 August, the Subcommission expressed its solidarity and support for the Special Rapporteur for his moral and courageous stand, and for his resignation in protest at the perpetuation of gross violations in Bosnia and Herzegovina.[25]

In September, the Secretary-General transmitted the Special Rapporteur's August report to the General Assembly, the Security Council and ICFY.[26]

On 27 September, the Commission Chairman appointed Elisabeth Rehn (Finland) as Special Rapporteur, whose periodic report the Secretary-General transmitted to the Assembly, the Security Council and ICFY on 7 November.[27] She visited Bosnia and Herzegovina, Croatia and the Federal Republic of Yugoslavia (Serbia and Montenegro) from 9 to 15 October. Her report dealt mainly with the human rights problems arising from operation "Storm", launched by the Croatian army on 4 August in former sectors North and South (see PART TWO, Chapter V). Evidence gathered indicated that violations of human rights and humanitarian law committed during and after operation "Storm" included the killing of fleeing civilians; targeting of heavy weapons against militarily insignificant sites in towns, including the residential areas of Glina and Knin; lack of protection of the remaining members of the minority population; threats against and ill-treatment of the Serb minority by Croatian soldiers, policemen and civilians; and looting, burning and occupation of Serb houses. The Special Rapporteur recommended that the Government of Croatia fulfil its responsibilities to secure the human rights of the remaining Serb population in the retaken territories and remove all legal and administrative obstacles preventing the return of refugees and displaced persons.

In Bosnia and Herzegovina, military activities in recent months and accompanying territorial changes had yielded new evidence of human rights violations, past and present. Allegations of human rights violations committed by all sides to the conflict required further investigation. Of immediate concern was the fate of some 8,000 Bosnian Muslims, mainly males, from Srebrenica who were still unaccounted for. Noting that there was ongoing persecution and harassment of the remaining Bosnian Muslim and Bosnian Croat minorities in Banja Luka and other areas controlled by Bosnian

Serb forces, the Special Rapporteur recommended that the de facto Bosnian Serb authorities provide prompt access for human rights monitors to territories controlled by them, in particular to Banja Luka and Srebrenica. She stated that proper conditions for the return of some 25,000 Bosnian Muslim refugees from the Velika Kladusa region had not been created by the authorities of Bosnia and Herzegovina and recommended that the Government take steps to do so.

The Federal Republic of Yugoslavia (Serbia and Montenegro), the Special Rapporteur stated, was facing serious humanitarian problems owing to the influx of over 100,000 refugees from Croatia. She had received allegations regarding the ethnic Albanian community in Kosovo, which she intended to investigate on a subsequent mission. A monitoring presence must be established, such as an office of the Centre for Human Rights, to obtain first-hand information concerning the human rights situation there.

In a later report,[28] the Special Rapporteur described another mission (26 November–2 December), during which she visited: the Federal Republic of Yugoslavia, with stops in Belgrade and Pristina, the capital of Kosovo; Bosnia and Herzegovina, with visits to Bjeljina and Banja Luka in the Republika Srpska; and the towns of Jajce and Bogojno and the region of Eastern Slavonia in Croatia.

By a 12 December letter,[29] the Special Rapporteur informed the Commission Chairman of observations she made during her visit. In Bosnia and Herzegovina, the humanitarian situation of several thousands of Serbs displaced from other areas in Bosnia and Herzegovina and from the Republic of Croatia was very serious. The human rights situation of the remaining Muslim and Croat population, despite improvements, was still difficult. Insignificant progress had been achieved regarding the return of displaced persons within the Federation of Bosnia and Herzegovina, but substantial progress had been made concerning freedom of movement in Mostar. In central Bosnia and Herzegovina, the Special Rapporteur witnessed the burning and looting of houses by Bosnian Croat soldiers. She noted that the Centre for Human Rights had taken preliminary steps to open a human rights monitoring office in Banja Luka.

During her visit to the Federal Republic of Yugoslavia (Serbia and Montenegro), the Special Rapporteur focused on the problem of the human rights situation of Albanians in Kosovo, where children were deprived of a regular school system and adequate health protection and there were still cases of police brutality, harassment of the local population and restrictions on freedom of movement. During meetings in Belgrade, she raised the question of opening an office of the Centre for Human Rights in the country.

The main concern in the Republic of Croatia was the situation of the Serbian population, the majority of whom belonged to vulnerable groups and required immediate assistance.

The Special Rapporteur stated that one of the most serious problems was the question of missing persons. Without progress in that area, she noted that it would be impossible to create conditions for peaceful coexistence.

**GENERAL ASSEMBLY ACTION**

On 22 December, the General Assembly adopted **resolution 50/193**.

**Situation of human rights in the Republic of Bosnia and Herzegovina, the Republic of Croatia and the Federal Republic of Yugoslavia (Serbia and Montenegro)**

*The General Assembly,*

*Guided* by the purposes and principles of the Charter of the United Nations, the Universal Declaration of Human Rights, the International Covenants on Human Rights, the International Convention on the Elimination of All Forms of Racial Discrimination, the Convention on the Rights of the Child, the Convention on the Prevention and Punishment of the Crime of Genocide, the Convention against Torture and Other Cruel, Inhuman or Degrading Treatment or Punishment, the Convention on the Elimination of All Forms of Discrimination against Women and other instruments of international humanitarian law, including the Geneva Conventions of 12 August 1949 for the protection of victims of war and the Additional Protocols thereto, of 1977, as well as the principles and commitments undertaken by States members of the Organization for Security and Cooperation in Europe,

*Reaffirming* that all Member States have an obligation to promote and protect human rights and fundamental freedoms and to fulfil the obligations they have under the human rights instruments to which they are party, and reaffirming also the obligation of all to respect international humanitarian law,

*Welcoming* the General Framework Agreement for Peace in Bosnia and Herzegovina initialled by the Republic of Bosnia and Herzegovina, the Republic of Croatia and the Federal Republic of Yugoslavia (Serbia and Montenegro), representing also the Bosnian Serb party, at Dayton, Ohio, on 21 November 1995 which commits the parties to the conflict to ending the war and starting to build peace with justice; enables Bosnia and Herzegovina to continue its legal existence as a single State within its internationally recognized borders with full respect for its sovereignty, territorial integrity and political independence by its neighbours; and commits the parties in Bosnia and Herzegovina to respect fully human rights,

*Welcoming also* the basic agreement on the region of Eastern Slavonia, Baranja and Western Sirmium, signed on 12 November 1995 by the Government of the Republic of Croatia and the local Serb representatives,

*None the less gravely concerned* at the human tragedy that has occurred in the territories of the Republic of Bosnia and Herzegovina, the Republic of Croatia and the Federal Republic of Yugoslavia (Serbia and Montenegro) and at the massive and systematic violations of human rights and international humanitarian law,

*Recalling* its resolution 49/196 of 23 December 1994, Commission on Human Rights resolution 1995/89 of 8 March 1995 and all relevant resolutions of the Security Council,

*Recalling specifically* the Security Council resolutions in which the Council demanded, *inter alia*, that all parties and others concerned in the former Yugoslavia immediately cease and desist from all breaches of international humanitarian law, requested the Secretary-General to establish a commission of experts to examine and analyse information relating to serious violations of such law being committed in the territory of the former Yugoslavia, established an international tribunal for the prosecution of persons responsible for such violations and condemned in particular the unacceptable practice of ethnic cleansing perpetrated in areas of the Republic of Bosnia and Herzegovina under the control of Bosnian Serb forces,

*Recalling also* additional Security Council resolutions, in particular resolutions 824(1993) of 6 May 1993 and 836(1993) of 4 June 1993, in which the Council declared that Sarajevo, Tuzla, Zepa, Gorazde, Bihac, Srebrenica and their surroundings should be treated as safe areas, that international humanitarian agencies should be given free and unimpeded access to those areas and that there should be freedom of movement for the civilian population and humanitarian goods to, from and within the areas,

*Recalling further* Security Council resolution 1019(1995) of 9 November 1995, in which the Council demanded that the Bosnian Serb party give immediate and unimpeded access to representatives of the United Nations High Commissioner for Refugees, the International Committee of the Red Cross and other international agencies to persons displaced and to persons detained or reported missing from Srebrenica, Zepa and the regions of Banja Luka and Sanski Most,

*Gravely concerned* at attacks and capture by the Bosnian Serbs and Croatian Serb forces of safe areas, in violation of the relevant Security Council resolutions,

*Recalling* Security Council resolution 1009(1995) of 10 August 1995, in which the Council demanded that the Government of the Republic of Croatia respect fully the rights of the local Serb population, including their rights to remain, leave or return in safety, allow access to this population by international humanitarian organizations and create conditions conducive to the return of those persons who have left their homes,

*Noting with appreciation* the efforts of the United Nations Peace Forces to help to create the conditions for the peaceful settlement of the conflicts in the Republic of Bosnia and Herzegovina and the Republic of Croatia and to provide protection for the delivery of humanitarian aid and the protection of human rights, and also noting the obstacles faced by those forces in the performance of their mandates,

*Acknowledging* the progress made by the Bosnian Federation as a model for ethnic reconciliation in the region,

*Encouraging* the international community, acting through the United Nations and other international organizations as well as bilaterally, to enhance significantly humanitarian support for the people of the region and to promote human rights, economic reconstruction, the repatriation of refugees and the holding of free elections in the Republic of Bosnia and Herzegovina,

*Welcoming* the efforts of the European Union to promote respect for human rights and fundamental freedoms, and endorsing the recommendation of the Special Rapporteur of the Commission on Human Rights on the situation of human rights in the territory of the former Yugoslavia that economic and other aid must be made conditional upon meaningful progress in human rights,

*Gravely concerned* at the human rights violations in the Republic of Bosnia and Herzegovina, the Republic of Croatia and the Federal Republic of Yugoslavia (Serbia and Montenegro), in particular at those committed in the context of the odious practice of ethnic cleansing, which has been the direct cause of the vast majority of human rights violations there and whose principal victims have been the Muslim population, as well as the Croats and others,

*Also gravely concerned* at reports, including by the Special Representative of the Secretary-General, of grave violations of international humanitarian law and of human rights in and around Srebrenica, and in the areas of Banja Luka and Sanski Most, including reports of mass murder, unlawful detention and forced labour, rape and deportation of civilians,

*Dismayed* by the huge number of missing persons still unaccounted for, particularly in Bosnia and Herzegovina and in Croatia,

*Deeply concerned* by the situations reflected in the report of the Secretary-General on rape and abuse of women in the areas of armed conflict in the former Yugoslavia, and stressing the need for detailed reporting on this subject,

*Alarmed* that the conflict in the Republic of Bosnia and Herzegovina and in the Republic of Croatia has also been characterized by the systematic destruction and profanation of mosques, churches and other places of worship, religious buildings and sites of cultural heritage,

*Expressing its particular concern* for the situation of the children and the elderly as well as other vulnerable groups in the area,

*Calling attention* to the reports and recommendations of the Special Rapporteur on the situation of human rights in the territories of the Republic of Bosnia and Herzegovina, the Republic of Croatia and the Federal Republic of Yugoslavia (Serbia and Montenegro), including the most recent report by the newly appointed Special Rapporteur, Mrs. Elisabeth Rehn,

*Expressing its deep appreciation* for the activity and efforts of the previous Special Rapporteur, Mr. Tadeusz Mazowiecki, in the discharge of his mandate,

*Noting* the recommendations of the Special Rapporteur that respect for human rights should be given priority during and after the peace negotiations and that, without genuine improvements in the human rights situation in the area, any peace agreement will not have a solid foundation,

1. *Commends* both the former and the current Special Rapporteurs of the Commission on Human Rights on the situation of human rights in the territory of the former Yugoslavia for their efforts, and notes that the presence of the Special Rapporteur can be a positive factor towards reducing the instances of all human rights violations in the region;

2.  *Expresses its outrage* at the instances of massive and systematic violations of human rights and humanitarian law as described in the reports of the Special Rapporteur, including ethnic cleansing, killings, disappearances, torture, rape, detentions, beatings, arbitrary searches, destruction of houses, illegal evictions and other acts of violence aimed at forcing individuals from their homes;

3.  *Condemns in the strongest terms* all violations of human rights and international humanitarian law by the parties to the conflict, recognizing that the leadership in territories under the control of Serbs in the Republic of Bosnia and Herzegovina and formerly Serb-held areas of the Republic of Croatia, the commanders of Serb paramilitary forces and political and military leaders in the Federal Republic of Yugoslavia (Serbia and Montenegro) bear primary responsibility for most of those violations and that persons who commit such acts will be held personally responsible and accountable;

4.  *Condemns* the attacks on the safe areas of Srebrenica and Zepa by Bosnian Serb forces, which led to gross abuses of human rights and grave breaches of international humanitarian law and the disappearance of thousands of persons, as detailed in the reports of the former and the current Special Rapporteurs;

5.  *Also condemns* the indiscriminate shelling of civilians in the safe areas of Sarajevo, Tuzla, Bihac and Gorazde and the use of cluster bombs on civilian targets by Bosnian Serb and Croatian Serb forces;

6.  *Further condemns* violations of human rights and international humanitarian law, including killings, the burning and looting of houses, the shelling of residential areas, harassment of and attacks on refugees, the elderly and the infirm perpetrated by members of the Croatian armed forces and civilians in the formerly Serb-controlled regions of Croatia during and subsequent to the military operations there in August 1995;

7.  *Welcomes* the withdrawal of the heavy weapons surrounding Sarajevo following the decision to implement Security Council resolution 836(1993), reinforced by the London conference of 21 July 1995, to respond to attacks on safe areas, and notes that this opened Sarajevo to badly needed humanitarian relief;

8.  *Notes with appreciation* the efforts of the International Tribunal for the Prosecution of Persons Responsible for Serious Violations of International Humanitarian Law Committed in the Territory of the Former Yugoslavia since 1991, established pursuant to Security Council resolutions 806(1993) of 5 February 1993 and 827(1993) of 25 May 1993, notes the issuance of indictments against individuals, and urges that the Tribunal be given the resources it needs;

9.  *Requests* States, as a matter of urgency, to continue to make available to the International Tribunal expert personnel, adequate resources and services to aid in the investigation and prosecution of persons accused of having committed serious violations of international humanitarian law;

10.  *Reminds* all States of their obligation under Security Council resolution 827(1993) to cooperate with the International Tribunal, including through compliance with requests for assistance and orders issued by a trial chamber of the Tribunal, and, in this regard, urges the parties to allow the establishment of offices of the Tribunal in their territories and draws the attention of the Federal Republic of Yugoslavia (Serbia and Monte-

negro), the Republic of Croatia and the Republic of Bosnia and Herzegovina to their obligation to cooperate with the Tribunal, in particular to arrest, detain and facilitate the transfer to the custody of the Tribunal any and all indicted war criminals who reside in or transit through or are otherwise present in their respective territories;

11.  *Demands* that all parties refrain from any action intended to destroy, alter, conceal or damage any evidence of violations of human rights and international humanitarian law and that they preserve such evidence;

12.  *Expresses its complete support* for the victims of violations of human rights and international humanitarian law, recognizes the right of refugees and displaced persons freely to return to their homes of origin in safety and dignity, to have restored to them property of which they were deprived in the course of hostilities since 1991 and to be compensated for any such property that cannot be restored to them, considers null any commitments made under duress, and urges all parties to fulfil their agreements to this end;

13.  *Condemns* all deliberate obstruction of the delivery of food and medical and other supplies essential for the civilian population, which constitutes a serious violation of international humanitarian law and international human rights law, and of medical evacuations, and demands that all parties ensure that all persons under their control cease such acts;

14.  *Also condemns* all attacks on the United Nations Peace Forces and on personnel working with the Office of the United Nations High Commissioner for Refugees and other humanitarian organizations by parties to the conflict;

15.  *Expresses its outrage* that the systematic practice of rape has been used as a weapon of war against women and children and as an instrument of ethnic cleansing, and recognizes that rape in this context constitutes a war crime;

16.  *Condemns* police violence against the non-Serb populations in Kosovo, the Sandjak, Vojvodina and other areas of the Federal Republic of Yugoslavia (Serbia and Montenegro), particularly the systematic acts of harassment, beatings, torture, warrantless searches, arbitrary detention and unfair trials, including those directed mainly against members of the Muslim population;

17.  *Strongly urges* the authorities of the Federal Republic of Yugoslavia (Serbia and Montenegro) to take appropriate measures to respect fully all human rights and fundamental freedoms and to take urgent action to ensure the rule of law in order to prevent arbitrary evictions and dismissals and discrimination against any ethnic or national, religious and linguistic group, including in the fields of education and information;

18.  *Cautions* against any attempts to use Serb refugees to alter the population balance in Kosovo, the Sandjak, Vojvodina and any other part of the country, thus further suppressing the enjoyment of human rights in those areas;

19.  *Strongly encourages* all parties to fulfil the commitments made at Dayton, Ohio, to release without delay all civilians and combatants held in prison or detention in relation to the conflict, in conformity with international humanitarian law and the provisions of the General Framework Agreement for Peace in Bosnia and Herzegovina, and demands that the parties cooperate fully with the International Committee of the Red Cross,

the Special Rapporteur and her staff, the United Nations High Commissioner for Refugees, the United Nations High Commissioner for Human Rights and the monitoring and other missions of the European Union and the Organization for Security and Cooperation in Europe;

20. *Urges* Member States to consider positively the Special Rapporteur's recommendation that economic and other aid must be made conditional upon meaningful progress in human rights;

21. *Recognizes* that the Bosnian Federation should be further developed to serve as a model for ethnic reconciliation in the region;

22. *Urges* all parties, in particular the Government of the Federal Republic of Yugoslavia (Serbia and Montenegro), to cooperate with the ''special process'' dealing with the problem of missing persons in the territory of the former Yugoslavia established pursuant to paragraph 24 of Commission on Human Rights resolution 1994/72 of 9 March 1994, and reiterated in its resolution 1995/35 of 3 March 1995, by disclosing information and documentation on inmates in prisons, camps and other places of detention;

23. *Also urges* all parties to provide full access for monitoring the human rights situation, including by allowing access to the missions of the Organization for Security and Cooperation in Europe, including in Kosovo, as called for by the General Assembly in resolution 49/196 and by the Security Council in resolution 855(1993) of 9 August 1993, and in the Sandjak, Vojvodina and other affected areas, and requests that the Federal Republic of Yugoslavia (Serbia and Montenegro) permit the opening of a field office of the Centre for Human Rights of the Secretariat as called for by the General Assembly in resolution 49/196;

24. *Urges* the Secretary-General to take all necessary steps to ensure the full and effective coordination of the activities of all United Nations bodies in implementing the present resolution, and urges those bodies concerned with the situation in the territories of Bosnia and Herzegovina, Croatia and the Federal Republic of Yugoslavia (Serbia and Montenegro) to coordinate closely with the United Nations High Commissioner for Human Rights, the Special Rapporteur and the International Tribunal, and to provide to the Special Rapporteur on a continuing basis all relevant and accurate information in their possession on the situation of human rights in Bosnia and Herzegovina, Croatia and the Federal Republic of Yugoslavia (Serbia and Montenegro);

25. *Draws attention* to the need for an immediate and urgent investigation by qualified investigators of several mass grave sites near Srebrenica and Vukovar and other mass grave sites and places where mass killings are reported to have taken place, and requests the Secretary-General, within existing resources, to make available the necessary means for this undertaking;

26. *Also urges* the Secretary-General, within existing resources, to make all necessary resources available for the Special Rapporteur to carry out her mandate and in particular to provide her with adequate staff based in the territories of Bosnia and Herzegovina, Croatia and the Federal Republic of Yugoslavia (Serbia and Montenegro) to ensure effective continuous monitoring of the human rights situation there and coordination with other United Nations bodies involved, including the United Nations Peace Forces;

27. *Welcomes* the effort by the Government of Bosnia and Herzegovina to uphold human rights in its territory, and urges it to fulfil the human rights commitments it has made;

28. *Notes with concern* that many of the past recommendations of the Special Rapporteur have not been fully implemented, in some cases because of resistance by the parties on the ground, and urges the parties, all States and relevant organizations to give immediate consideration to them, in particular the calls of the former and the current Special Rapporteurs:

*(a)* For the de facto Bosnian Serb authorities to provide prompt access for humanitarian monitors to territories controlled by them, in particular to the Banja Luka region and to Srebrenica, emphasizing that the fate of thousands of missing persons from Srebrenica requires immediate clarification;

*(b)* For the Government of Croatia to fulfil its responsibilities to secure the human rights of the remaining ethnic Serb population in all recently retaken territories and to remove all legal and administrative hurdles which are preventing the return of refugees and displaced persons;

*(c)* For greater cooperation between Governments and non-governmental organizations, recognizing that the work and role of non-governmental organizations is vital to the promotion and protection of the rights of the individual and respect and protection of human rights in the region;

*(d)* For the Federal Republic of Yugoslavia (Serbia and Montenegro) to undertake measures to respect fully the rights of persons belonging to national or ethnic, religious and linguistic minorities;

29. *Invites* the Commission on Human Rights, at its fifty-second session, to request the Special Rapporteur to report to the General Assembly at its fifty-first session;

30. *Decides* to continue its examination of this question at its fifty-first session under the item entitled ''Human rights questions''.

General Assembly resolution 50/193

22 December 1995     Meeting 99     144-1-20 (recorded vote)

Approved by Third Committee (A/50/635/Add.3) by recorded vote (124-1-18), 14 December (meeting 58); 38-nation draft (A/C.3/50/L.46), orally revised; agenda item 112 (c).

*Meeting numbers.* GA 50th session: 3rd Committee 35, 38-52, 58; plenary 99.

Recorded vote in Assembly as follows:

*In favour:* Afghanistan, Albania, Algeria, Andorra, Antigua and Barbuda, Argentina, Australia, Austria, Azerbaijan, Bahamas, Bahrain, Bangladesh, Barbados, Belgium, Belize, Benin, Bhutan, Bolivia, Bosnia and Herzegovina, Botswana, Brazil, Brunei Darussalam, Bulgaria, Burundi, Cambodia, Cameroon, Canada, Cape Verde, Chad, Chile, Colombia, Costa Rica, Croatia, Cyprus, Czech Republic, Denmark, Djibouti, Dominica, Ecuador, Egypt, El Salvador, Equatorial Guinea, Estonia, Fiji, Finland, France, Gabon, Gambia, Georgia, Germany, Ghana, Guatemala, Guinea, Guinea-Bissau, Guyana, Haiti, Honduras, Hungary, Iceland, Indonesia, Iran, Ireland, Israel, Italy, Jamaica, Japan, Jordan, Kazakstan, Kuwait, Kyrgyzstan, Latvia, Lebanon, Lesotho, Libyan Arab Jamahiriya, Liechtenstein, Lithuania, Luxembourg, Malawi, Malaysia, Maldives, Mali, Malta, Marshall Islands, Mauritania, Mauritius, Mexico, Micronesia, Monaco, Mongolia, Morocco, Myanmar, Nepal, Netherlands, New Zealand, Nicaragua, Niger, Nigeria, Norway, Oman, Pakistan, Panama, Papua New Guinea, Paraguay, Peru, Philippines, Poland, Portugal, Qatar, Republic of Korea, Republic of Moldova, Romania, Rwanda, Saint Kitts and Nevis, Saint Lucia, Saint Vincent and the Grenadines, Samoa, San Marino, Saudi Arabia, Senegal, Singapore, Slovakia, Slovenia, Solomon Islands, South Africa, Spain, Sri Lanka, Sudan, Suriname, Swaziland, Sweden, Syrian Arab Republic, Thailand, the former Yugoslav Republic of Macedonia, Trinidad and Tobago, Tunisia, Turkey, Uganda, United Arab Emirates, United Kingdom, United States, Uruguay, Uzbekistan, Vanuatu, Venezuela.

*Against:* Russian Federation.

## Ethnic Albanians in Kosovo

**Subcommission action.** On 18 August,[30] by a secret ballot of 17 votes to 3, with 4 abstentions, the Subcommission, strongly condemning the discriminatory practices and human rights violations committed by the authorities of the Federal Republic of Yugoslavia (Serbia and Montenegro) against ethnic Albanians in Kosovo, requested that these authorities cease all such violations and practices; revoke all discriminatory legislation; release all political prisoners; establish democratic institutions in Kosovo; reopen all cultural and scientific institutions of ethnic Albanians; and pursue a dialogue with the representatives of ethnic Albanians in Kosovo, under ICFY auspices. It demanded that the authorities of the Federal Republic of Yugoslavia (Serbia and Montenegro) cooperate with the Special Rapporteur and urged them to allow the return of the OSCE mission to Kosovo. The Subcommission asked the Secretary-General to seek ways to establish an international monitoring presence in Kosovo and called on the Special Rapporteur to continue to monitor the human rights situation there.

**Report of the Secretary-General.** In a November report,[31] the Secretary-General described action taken by the General Assembly, the Commission on Human Rights and the Subcommission, regarding the situation of human rights in Kosovo. He reviewed efforts to establish a monitoring presence in the Federal Republic of Yugoslavia (Serbia and Montenegro) and the reinstatement of the OSCE mission, which had ceased in July 1993.[32]

The Secretary-General concluded that with the renewed willingness of the Federal Republic of Yugoslavia (Serbia and Montenegro) to cooperate with the UN High Commissioner for Human Rights and the Special Rapporteur, the establishment of an international monitoring presence appeared to be more attainable.

**GENERAL ASSEMBLY ACTION**

On 22 December, the General Assembly adopted **resolution 50/190**.

### Situation of human rights in Kosovo

*The General Assembly,*

*Guided* by the Charter of the United Nations, the Universal Declaration of Human Rights, the International Covenants on Human Rights, the International Convention on the Elimination of All Forms of Racial Discrimination, the Convention on the Prevention and Punishment of the Crime of Genocide and the Convention against Torture and Other Cruel, Inhuman or Degrading Treatment or Punishment,

*Welcoming* the General Framework Agreement for Peace in Bosnia and Herzegovina reached on 21 November 1995 at Dayton, Ohio, and hoping that it will have a positive impact also on the human rights situation in Kosovo,

*Recalling* its resolution 49/204 of 23 December 1994 and other relevant resolutions,

*Taking note* of Commission on Human Rights resolution 1995/89 of 8 March 1995 and recalling previous Commission resolutions 1992/S-1/1 of 14 August 1992, 1992/S-2/1 of 1 December 1992, 1993/7 of 23 February 1993 and 1994/76 of 9 March 1994,

*Taking note also* of the reports of the Special Rapporteurs of the Commission on Human Rights on the situation of human rights in the territory of the former Yugoslavia, in which they describe the situation in Kosovo, the various discriminatory measures taken in the legislative, administrative and judicial areas, acts of violence and arbitrary arrests perpetrated against ethnic Albanians in Kosovo and the continuing deterioration of the human rights situation in Kosovo, including:

(a) Police brutality against ethnic Albanians, the killing of ethnic Albanians resulting from such violence, arbitrary searches, seizures and arrests, forced evictions, torture and ill-treatment of detainees and discrimination in the administration of justice, including the recent trials of ethnic Albanian former policemen;

(b) Discriminatory and arbitrary dismissals of ethnic Albanian civil servants, notably from the ranks of the police and the judiciary, mass dismissals of ethnic Albanians, confiscation and expropriation of their properties, discrimination against ethnic Albanian pupils and teachers, the closing of Albanian-language secondary schools and the university, as well as the closing of all Albanian cultural and scientific institutions;

(c) The harassment and persecution of political parties and associations of ethnic Albanians and their leaders and activities, their maltreatment and imprisonment;

(d) The intimidation and imprisonment of ethnic Albanian journalists and the systematic harassment and disruption of the news media in the Albanian language;

(e) The dismissals from clinics and hospitals of doctors and members of other categories of the medical profession of Albanian origin;

(f) The elimination in practice of the Albanian language, particularly in public administration and services;

(g) The serious and massive occurrence of discriminatory and repressive practices aimed at ethnic Albanians in Kosovo, as a whole, resulting in widespread involuntary migration;

and noting that the Subcommission on Prevention of Discrimination and Protection of Minorities, in its resolutions 1993/9 of 20 August 1993 and 1995/10 of 18 August 1995, considered that those measures and practices constituted a form of ethnic cleansing,

*Concerned* at any attempt to use Serb refugees and other means to alter the ethnic balance in Kosovo, thus further suppressing the enjoyment of human rights there, and, in this context, noting with concern the new citizenship law awaiting approval by the Parliament of the Federal Republic of Yugoslavia (Serbia and Montenegro),

*Reaffirming* that the long-term mission of the Organization for Security and Cooperation in Europe to Kosovo played a positive role in monitoring the human rights situation and in preventing an escalation of conflict there, and recalling in this context Security Council resolution 855(1993) of 9 August 1993,

*Considering* that the re-establishment of the international presence in Kosovo to monitor and investigate the situation of human rights is of great importance in preventing the situation in Kosovo from deteriorating into violent conflict, and, in this context, taking note of the report of the Secretary-General submitted pursuant to General Assembly resolution 49/204,

1. *Strongly condemns* the measures and practices of discrimination and the violations of the human rights of ethnic Albanians in Kosovo committed by the authorities of the Federal Republic of Yugoslavia (Serbia and Montenegro);

2. *Condemns* the large-scale repression by the police and military of the Federal Republic of Yugoslavia (Serbia and Montenegro) against the defenceless ethnic Albanian population and the discrimination against the ethnic Albanians in the administrative and judiciary branches of government, education, health care and employment, aimed at forcing ethnic Albanians to leave;

3. *Urgently demands* that the authorities of the Federal Republic of Yugoslavia (Serbia and Montenegro):

*(a)* Take all necessary measures to bring to an immediate end all human rights violations against ethnic Albanians in Kosovo, including, in particular, the discriminatory measures and practices, arbitrary searches and detention, the violation of the right to a fair trial and the practice of torture and other cruel, inhuman or degrading treatment, and to revoke all discriminatory legislation, in particular that which has entered into force since 1989;

*(b)* Release all political prisoners and cease the persecution of political leaders and members of local human rights organizations;

*(c)* Allow the establishment of genuine democratic institutions in Kosovo, including the parliament and the judiciary, and respect the will of its inhabitants as the best means of preventing the escalation of the conflict there;

*(d)* Abrogate the official settlement policy as far as it is conducive to the heightening of ethnic tensions in Kosovo;

*(e)* Reopen the cultural and scientific institutions of the ethnic Albanians;

*(f)* Pursue dialogue with the representatives of ethnic Albanians in Kosovo, including under the auspices of the International Conference on the Former Yugoslavia;

4. *Demands once again* that the authorities of the Federal Republic of Yugoslavia (Serbia and Montenegro) cooperate fully and immediately with the Special Rapporteur of the Commission on Human Rights on the situation of human rights in the territory of the former Yugoslavia in the discharge of her functions, as requested by the Commission in its resolution 1994/76 and in other relevant resolutions;

5. *Encourages* the Secretary-General to pursue his humanitarian efforts in the former Yugoslavia, in liaison with the Office of the United Nations High Commissioner for Refugees, the United Nations Children's Fund and other appropriate humanitarian organizations, with a view to taking urgent practical steps to tackle the critical needs of the people in Kosovo, especially of the most vulnerable groups affected by the conflict, and to assist in the voluntary return of displaced persons to their homes;

6. *Urges* the authorities of the Federal Republic of Yugoslavia (Serbia and Montenegro) to allow the immediate unconditional return of the long-term mission of the Organization for Security and Cooperation in Europe to Kosovo, called for in Security Council resolution 855(1993);

7. *Welcomes* the report of the Secretary-General submitted pursuant to General Assembly resolution 49/204;

8. *Requests* the Secretary-General to continue to seek ways and means, including through consultations with the United Nations High Commissioner for Human Rights and relevant regional organizations, to establish an adequate international monitoring presence in Kosovo and to report thereon to the General Assembly at its fifty-first session;

9. *Emphasizes* the importance of laws and regulations concerning citizenship applied by the authorities of the Federal Republic of Yugoslavia (Serbia and Montenegro) being in accordance with the standards and principles of non-discrimination, equal protection before the law and the reduction and avoidance of statelessness, as set out in the relevant international human rights instruments;

10. *Calls upon* the Special Rapporteur to continue to monitor closely the situation of human rights in Kosovo and to continue to pay due attention to this matter in her reporting;

11. *Decides* to continue examination of the human rights situation in Kosovo at its fifty-first session under the item entitled "Human rights questions".

General Assembly resolution 50/190

22 December 1995    Meeting 99    115-2-43 (recorded vote)

Approved by Third Committee (A/50/635/Add.3) by recorded vote (107-2-35), 11 December (meeting 54); 38-nation draft (A/C.3/50/L.43); agenda item 112 *(c)*.

*Meeting numbers.* GA 50th session: 3rd Committee 35, 38-51, 54; plenary 99.

Recorded vote in Assembly as follows:

*In favour:* Afghanistan, Albania, Algeria, Andorra, Antigua and Barbuda, Argentina, Australia, Austria, Azerbaijan, Bahrain, Bangladesh, Barbados, Belgium, Belize, Benin, Bolivia, Bosnia and Herzegovina, Brazil, Brunei Darussalam, Bulgaria, Cambodia, Canada, Cape Verde, Chile, Colombia, Costa Rica, Croatia, Cyprus, Czech Republic, Denmark, Djibouti, Dominica, Ecuador, Egypt, El Salvador, Estonia, Fiji, Finland, France, Germany, Grenada, Guatemala, Guyana, Haiti, Honduras, Hungary, Iceland, Indonesia, Iran, Ireland, Israel, Italy, Japan, Jordan, Kazakstan, Kuwait, Kyrgyzstan, Latvia, Lebanon, Lesotho, Libyan Arab Jamahiriya, Liechtenstein, Lithuania, Luxembourg, Malaysia, Maldives, Mali, Malta, Marshall Islands, Mauritania, Mauritius, Mexico, Micronesia, Monaco, Mongolia, Morocco, Mozambique, Netherlands, New Zealand, Nicaragua, Niger, Norway, Oman, Pakistan, Panama, Papua New Guinea, Paraguay, Poland, Portugal, Qatar, Republic of Korea, Saint Lucia, Saint Vincent and the Grenadines, Samoa, San Marino, Saudi Arabia, Senegal, Sierra Leone, Slovenia, Solomon Islands, South Africa, Spain, Sudan, Suriname, Swaziland, Sweden, Thailand, Tunisia, Turkey, United Arab Emirates, United Kingdom, United States, Uruguay, Uzbekistan, Vanuatu.

*Against:* India, Russian Federation.

*Abstaining:* Angola, Bahamas, Belarus, Bhutan, Botswana, Burundi, Cameroon, China, Congo, Côte d'Ivoire, Equatorial Guinea, Gabon, Gambia, Ghana, Greece, Guinea, Guinea-Bissau, Jamaica, Kenya, Malawi, Myanmar, Namibia, Nepal, Nigeria, Peru, Philippines, Republic of Moldova, Romania, Rwanda, Saint Kitts and Nevis, Singapore, Slovakia, Sri Lanka, Syrian Arab Republic, Tajikistan, Togo, Trinidad and Tobago, Uganda, Ukraine, United Republic of Tanzania, Venezuela, Zaire, Zimbabwe.

## Rape and abuse of women

As requested by the General Assembly in 1994,[33] the Secretary-General in August 1995 submitted a report on rape and abuse of women in the areas of armed conflict in the former Yugoslavia.[34] He gave an overview of efforts to end those practices taken by Governments and a wide range of UN bodies and other organizations, including the Commission of Experts, the Commission on Human Rights, the Committee on the Elimination of Discrimination against Women, the International Tribunal for the Prosecution of Persons Responsible for Serious Violations of International Humanitarian Law Committed in the Territory of the Former Yugoslavia since 1991, the United Nations Children's Fund, UNHCR, UNESCO, WHO, the European Community Task Force (an implementing arm of the European Community Humanitarian Office), ICRC, and the International Federation of Red Cross and Red Crescent Societies and other NGOs.

The Secretary-General stated that reports of rape and sexual violence continued to be received, although to a lesser extent than earlier in the conflict. He noted that activities being undertaken by the international community were welcomed, but that caution should be exercised in assuming that the needs of the victims were being adequately met. (See also PART FOUR, Chapter X.)

On 22 December, the General Assembly, by **decision 50/461**, took note of the Secretary-General's report.

**GENERAL ASSEMBLY ACTION**

On 22 December, the General Assembly adopted **resolution 50/192**.

### Rape and abuse of women in the areas of armed conflict in the former Yugoslavia

*The General Assembly,*

*Guided* by the purposes and principles of the Charter of the United Nations, the Universal Declaration of Human Rights, the International Covenants on Human Rights, the Convention on the Prevention and Punishment of the Crime of Genocide, the Convention against Torture and Other Cruel, Inhuman or Degrading Treatment or Punishment, the Convention on the Elimination of All Forms of Discrimination against Women, the Convention on the Rights of the Child and other instruments of human rights and international humanitarian law, including the Geneva Conventions of 12 August 1949 and the Additional Protocols thereto, of 1977,

*Recalling* its resolution 3074(XXVIII) of 3 December 1973, entitled ''Principles of international cooperation in the detection, arrest, extradition and punishment of persons guilty of war crimes and crimes against humanity'', as well as Commission on Human Rights resolution 1994/77 of 9 March 1994, entitled ''Rape and abuse of women in the territory of the former Yugoslavia'', General Assembly resolutions 48/143 of 20 December 1993 and 49/205 of 23 December 1994, both entitled ''Rape and abuse of women in the areas of armed conflict in the former Yugoslavia'', and relevant resolutions of the Commission on the Status of Women,

*Reaffirming* the relevant Security Council resolutions, in particular resolution 798(1992) of 18 December 1992, in which, *inter alia*, the Council strongly condemned those acts of unspeakable brutality,

*Welcoming* the initialling of the General Framework Agreement for Peace in Bosnia and Herzegovina and the annexes thereto by the Republic of Bosnia and Herzegovina, the Republic of Croatia and the Federal Republic of Yugoslavia (Serbia and Montenegro) and other parties thereto at Dayton, Ohio, on 21 November 1995,

*Noting with deep concern* all reports of the Special Rapporteur of the Commission on Human Rights on the situation of human rights in the territory of the former Yugoslavia, regarding rape and abuse of women in the territory of the former Yugoslavia, particularly in the Republic of Bosnia and Herzegovina,

*Convinced* that this heinous practice constitutes a deliberate weapon of war in fulfilling the policy of ethnic cleansing carried out by Serbian forces in the Republic of Bosnia and Herzegovina, and recalling General Assembly resolution 47/121 of 18 December 1992, in which the Assembly stated, *inter alia*, that the abhorrent policy of ethnic cleansing was a form of genocide,

*Desirous* of ensuring that persons accused of authorizing, aiding and perpetrating rape and sexual violence as a weapon of war in the areas of armed conflict in the former Yugoslavia will be brought to justice without further delay by the International Tribunal for the Prosecution of Persons Responsible for Serious Violations of International Humanitarian Law Committed in the Territory of the Former Yugoslavia since 1991, where appropriate,

*Underlining*, in this context, the need for the protection of the rape victims and the provision of effective guarantees of privacy and confidentiality of the rape victims, and desirous of facilitating their participation in the proceedings of the International Tribunal and ensuring that further traumatization will be prevented,

*Deeply alarmed* at the situation facing victims of rape in armed conflicts in different parts of the world and any use of rape as a weapon of war, in particular in the Republic of Bosnia and Herzegovina,

*Noting with appreciation* the efforts of Governments and the work of the United Nations High Commissioner for Refugees, the United Nations Educational, Scientific and Cultural Organization, humanitarian organizations, and non-governmental organizations aimed at supporting the victims of rape and abuse and alleviating their suffering,

*Welcoming* the report of the Secretary-General of 4 August 1995, submitted pursuant to resolution 49/205,

1. *Strongly condemns* the abhorrent practice of rape and abuse of women and children in the areas of armed conflict in the former Yugoslavia, which constitutes a war crime;

2. *Expresses its outrage* that the systematic practice of rape has been used as a weapon of war and an instrument of ethnic cleansing against women and children in the Republic of Bosnia and Herzegovina;

3. *Reaffirms* that rape in the conduct of armed conflict constitutes a war crime and that under certain circumstances it constitutes a crime against humanity and an act of genocide as defined in the Convention on the Prevention and Punishment of the Crime of Genocide, and calls upon States to take all measures required for the protection of women and children from such acts and to strengthen mechanisms to investigate and punish all those responsible and bring the perpetrators to justice;

4. *Also reaffirms* that all persons who perpetrate or authorize crimes against humanity or other violations of international humanitarian law are individually responsible for those violations and that those in positions of authority who have failed to ensure that persons under their control comply with the relevant international instruments are accountable, together with the perpetrators;

5. *Reminds* all States of their obligation to cooperate with the International Tribunal for the Prosecution of Persons Responsible for Serious Violations of International Humanitarian Law Committed in the Territory of the Former Yugoslavia since 1991 and also with the Office of the Prosecutor in the investigation and prosecution of persons accused of using rape as a weapon of war;

6. *Calls upon* States to put experts, including experts in the prosecution of crimes of sexual violence, as well as adequate resources and services, at the disposal of the Chief Prosecutor and the International Tribunal;

7. *Urges* all States and relevant organizations to continue to give serious consideration to the recommendations in the reports of the Special Rapporteur of the Commission on Human Rights on the situation of human rights in the former Yugoslavia, in particular the recommendation concerning provision for the continuation of necessary medical and psychological care to victims of rape within the framework of programmes to rehabilitate women and children traumatized by war, as well as the provision of protection, counselling and support to victims and witnesses;

8. *Recognizes* the extraordinary suffering of the victims of rape and sexual violence and the necessity for an appropriate response to provide assistance to those victims, and expresses its concern, in particular, for the welfare of those victims who are currently among the internally displaced or otherwise affected by the war and who have experienced severe trauma and require psychosocial and other assistance;

9. *Also urges* all States and all relevant intergovernmental and non-governmental organizations, as well as the United Nations Children's Fund, the Office of the United Nations High Commissioner for Refugees, the United Nations High Commissioner for Human Rights, the United Nations Educational, Scientific and Cultural Organization and the World Health Organization, to continue to provide to the victims of such rape and abuse appropriate assistance for their physical and mental rehabilitation and to extend their support to the community-based assistance programmes;

10. *Demands* that the parties cooperate fully with the International Committee of the Red Cross, the United Nations High Commissioner for Human Rights, the Special Rapporteur of the Commission on Human Rights and her staff, as well as other mechanisms of the Commission on Human Rights, the United Nations High Commissioner for Refugees, the monitoring and other missions of the European Union and the Organization for Security and Cooperation in Europe, including by providing full access;

11. *Encourages* the new Special Rapporteur to continue to pay particular attention to the use of rape as a weapon of war, particularly in the Republic of Bosnia and Herzegovina;

12. *Requests* the Secretary-General to submit a report, as appropriate, to the General Assembly at its fifty-first session on the implementation of the present resolution;

13. *Decides* to continue its consideration of this question at its fifty-first session.

General Assembly resolution 50/192

22 December 1995    Meeting 99    Adopted without vote

Approved by Third Committee (A/50/635/Add.3) without vote, 13 December (meeting 56); 72-nation draft (A/C.3/50/L.45), orally revised; agenda item 112 (c).
*Meeting numbers.* GA 50th session: 3rd Committee 35, 38-51, 53, 56; plenary 99.

The Committee adopted the sixth preambular paragraph by a recorded vote of 133 to 1, with 11 abstentions. The General Assembly adopted it by a recorded vote of 146 to 1, with 10 abstentions.

### The media

In a special report on the media,[35] Special Rapporteur Tadeusz Mazowiecki stated that most of the media in the former Yugoslavia were controlled, directly or indirectly, by Governments and ruling parties. Nationalistic rhetoric and attacks against other peoples had been the dominant feature of the news since the start of the conflicts. Some journalists had willingly accepted the restrictions placed on their profession, either because of their support for the nationalist cause or merely for reasons of self-advancement. The Special Rapporteur noted that the situation of the media was not entirely bad, and each republic offered examples of courageous journalists, media enterprises and NGOs.

The Special Rapporteur recommended eliminating expressions of hatred from the media and improving legislation concerning the media. He also advocated government responsibility for human rights violations perpetrated in accordance with editorial policy and contributions published or broadcast in the State-owned media. He encouraged projects which provided assistance from democratic countries to the media in the former Yugoslavia.

In January,[36] the Secretary-General transmitted the report to the General Assembly, the Security Council and ICFY.

## Russian Federation

### Republic of Chechnya

On 27 February,[37] the Chairman of the Commission on Human Rights read out a statement indicating the Commission's consensus agreement in connection with the situation of human rights in Chechnya. By it, the Commission, among other things, expressed deep concern over the disproportionate use of force by the Russian armed forces and deplored grave violations of human rights and humanitarian law. It called for an immediate cessation of the fighting and of human rights violations and for the holding of a dialogue with the aim of achieving a peaceful solution to the crisis, with respect for the territorial integrity and the constitution of the Russian Federation, as well as a guarantee of human rights. The Commission supported OSCE efforts to seek a durable solution and urged the Russian Federation to cooperate to further efforts within the framework of OSCE. Noting that it would continue to follow the situation in Chechnya, the Commission asked the Secretary-General to report in 1996 on the human rights situation there.

### Turkey

On 18 August,[38] by a secret ballot of 11 votes to 9, with 2 abstentions, the Subcommission, taking note of the positive initiatives taken by Turkey regarding freedom of expression, decided to postpone consideration of the question until 1996 in expectation of the implementation of those measures.

*REFERENCES*

[1]YUN 1994, p. 1095. [2]E/CN.4/1995/69. [3]E/1995/23 (dec. 1995/113). [4]YUN 1993, p. 944. [5]YUN 1994, p. 1097. [6]E/CN.4/1995/57. [7]YUN 1994, p. 550. [8]A/50/69-S/1995/79. [9]YUN 1992, p. 327. [10]E/CN.4/1995/62. [11]YUN 1992, p. 370, SC res. 780(1992), 6 Oct. 1992. [12]YUN 1994, p. 505. [13]YUN 1993, p. 440, SC res. 827(1993). 25 May 1993. [14]E/1995/23 (res. 1995/89). [15]YUN 1977, p. 706. [16]YUN 1994, p. 551. [17]Ibid., p. 1025. [18]Ibid., p. 1098, GA res. 49/196, 23 Dec. 1994. [19]E/CN.4/1996/3. [20]A/50/296-S/1995/597. [21]E/CN.4/1996/6. [22]YUN 1994, p. 563. [23]A/50/287-S/1995/575. [24]E/CN.4/1996/9. [25]E/CN.4/1996/2 (res. 1995/1). [26]A/50/441-S/1995/801. [27]A/50/727-S/1995/933. [28]E/CN.4/1996/63. [29]E/CN.4/1996/107. [30]E/CN.4/1996/2 (res. 1995/10). [31]A/50/767. [32]YUN 1993, p. 495. [33]YUN 1994, p. 1104, GA res. 49/205, 23 Dec. 1994. [34]A/50/329. [35]E/CN.4/1995/54 & Corr.1. [36]A/50/71-S/1995/80. [37]E/1995/23. [38]E/CN.4/1996/2 (dec. 1995/108).

# Latin America and the Caribbean

### Colombia

On 6 March, the Chairman of the Commission on Human Rights made a statement acknowledging receipt of a written communication from Colombia, pledging the cooperation of the Government with the thematic special procedures of the Commission, and with the Office of the UN High Commissioner for Human Rights.[1]

On 18 August,[2] the Subcommission called on the Government to implement the recommendations made by the thematic rapporteurs and the Working Group on Enforced or Involuntary Disappearances, and to report to the Commission in 1996 on measures taken. It recommended that the Commission consider in 1996 the developments in Colombia by examining the measures taken by the Government.

### Cuba

**Report of the Special Rapporteur.** In January, Special Rapporteur Carl-Johan Groth (Sweden) reported[3] on the human rights situation in Cuba. As he had received no reply from the Government of Cuba to his request to visit the country, he based his report on information received from Cubans living outside the country, mainly in the United States, and from representatives of groups and organizations concerned with human rights in Cuba. He discussed allegations of human rights abuses dealing with prison conditions and with the rights to freedom of expression and association, trade union freedom, press freedom and the right to enter and leave the country. Concerning economic, social and cultural rights, the Special Rapporteur stated that the Cuban economy had suffered a breakdown over the past four years, but that the Government had taken tentative steps to remedy the situation. He discussed the issue of "dangerousness", defined in Cuba's Penal Code as a state of habitual inebriation and dipsomania, drug addiction or antisocial behaviour, which might warrant security measures involving therapy, re-education or surveillance by the National Revolutionary Police.

The Special Rapporteur recommended that Cuba end persecution for reasons related to the freedom of peaceful expression and association; release those serving sentences for offences against State security and for trying to leave the country unlawfully; permit legalization of independent groups; ratify the principal human rights instruments to which it was not a party; review legal provisions relating to the concept of a "dangerous state"; repeal legal provisions which entailed discrimination between citizens on political grounds and those concerning the right freely to enter or leave the country; respect the guarantees of due process; ensure greater transparency and guarantees in prisons; and allow NGOs concerned with human rights to enter the country.

**Commission action.** By a roll-call vote of 22 to 8, with 23 abstentions, the Commission on 7 March[4] called on Cuba to permit the Special Rapporteur to carry out his mandate in full, particularly by allowing him to visit the country. It expressed concern that Cuba had failed to cooperate with it, and regretted the numerous unanswered reports of human rights violations described by the Special Rapporteur, particularly intolerance for freedom of speech and assembly. It called on Cuba to bring the observance of human rights and fundamental freedoms up to universally recognized standards and to end all human rights violations as recommended by the Special Rapporteur. The Commission extended the Special Rapporteur's mandate for one year, and asked him to maintain direct contact with the Government and citizens of Cuba, to submit an interim report to the Assembly in 1995 and to report to the Commission in 1996.

In July, the Economic and Social Council adopted **decision 1995/277**.

### Situation of human rights in Cuba

At its 52nd plenary meeting, on 25 July 1995, the Economic and Social Council, taking note of Commission on Human Rights resolution 1995/66 of 7 March 1995, approved:

(a) The Commission's decision to extend for one year the mandate of the Special Rapporteur on the situation of human rights in Cuba;

(b) The Commission's request to the Special Rapporteur to maintain direct contacts with the Government and citizens of Cuba as specified in previous resolutions of the Commission;

(c) The Commission's request to the Special Rapporteur to carry out his mandate, bearing in mind, *inter alia*, the Universal Declaration of Human Rights, to submit an interim report to the General Assembly at its fiftieth session and to report to the Commission at its fifty-second session on the results of his endeavours pursuant to Commission resolution 1995/66;

(d) The Commission's request to the Secretary-General to provide all necessary assistance to the Special Rapporteur.

Economic and Social Council decision 1995/277

23-10-18 (roll-call vote)

Draft by Commission on Human Rights (E/1995/23); agenda item 5 *(d)*. *Meeting numbers.* ESC 51, 52.

Roll-call vote in Council as follows:

*In favour:* Australia, Bulgaria, Canada, Chile, Costa Rica, Côte d'Ivoire, Denmark, France, Germany, Greece, Ireland, Japan, Luxembourg, Netherlands, Norway, Poland, Portugal, Republic of Korea, Romania, Russian Federation, United Kingdom, United States, Venezuela.

*Against:* China, Cuba, India, Indonesia, Libyan Arab Jamahiriya, Nigeria, South Africa, Sudan, Uganda, United Republic of Tanzania.

*Abstaining:* Bahamas, Belarus, Bhutan, Brazil, Colombia, Egypt, Gabon, Ghana, Jamaica, Malaysia, Mexico, Pakistan, Philippines, Senegal, Sri Lanka, Thailand, Ukraine, Zimbabwe.

**Interim report of the Special Rapporteur.** In October, the Secretary-General transmitted to the Assembly the Special Rapporteur's interim report[5] on the situation of human rights in Cuba. The Special Rapporteur's request to visit Cuba remained unanswered, thus once again his report was based on meetings with individuals and representatives of organizations and groups concerned with human rights in Cuba. He had travelled to New York and Washington, D.C. (28 August–1 September), where he met with Cuban citizens in exile and representatives of human rights organizations.

The Special Rapporteur received information on alleged violations of freedom of expression and association, press freedom, the administration of justice, the right to leave and return to the coun-

try and prison conditions. He discussed the serious economic crisis in Cuba and its impact on the enjoyment of economic, social and cultural rights.

The Special Rapporteur proposed that Cuba end persecution for reasons related to the freedom of peaceful expression and association; release those serving sentences imposed for offences against State security and for trying to leave the country unlawfully; permit legalization of independent groups; ratify the human rights instruments to which it was not a party; review the legal provisions relating to "dangerousness" and the relevant security measures with a view to eliminating those aspects liable to infringe individual rights and freedoms; repeal legal provisions which implied discrimination between citizens on political grounds; repeal legal provisions which barred Cuban citizens from entering and leaving the country freely without requiring prior administrative authorization; respect the guarantees of due process; investigate events surrounding the sinking of the tugboat *13 de Marzo* in the Straits of Florida on 13 July 1994, resulting in fatalities, with a view to punishing those responsible and providing compensation to victims' relatives; ensure greater transparency and guarantees in prisons; and allow NGOs concerned with human rights to enter the country.

On 22 December, the General Assembly adopted **resolution 50/198**.

### Situation of human rights in Cuba

*The General Assembly,*

*Reaffirming* that all Member States have an obligation to promote and protect human rights and fundamental freedoms as stated in the Charter of the United Nations and elaborated in the Universal Declaration of Human Rights, the International Covenants on Human Rights and other applicable human rights instruments,

*Reaffirming also* that all States have an obligation to fulfil the commitments they have freely undertaken under the various international instruments,

*Taking particular note* of Commission on Human Rights resolution 1995/66 of 7 March 1995, in which the Commission recognized with deep appreciation the efforts of the Special Rapporteur to carry out his mandate concerning the situation of human rights in Cuba,

*Expressing concern* about continuing serious violations of human rights in Cuba, of which the majority are violations of civil and political rights, as outlined in the interim report on the situation of human rights in Cuba submitted to the General Assembly by the Special Rapporteur,

*Welcoming* the authorization granted to a delegation comprising representatives of four international human rights organizations to visit Cuba, and encouraging the Government of Cuba to grant further access to such organizations,

*Also welcoming* the release of a number of political prisoners,

*Recalling* the continued failure of the Government of Cuba to cooperate with the Commission on Human Rights with regard to its resolution 1995/66, including its refusal to permit the Special Rapporteur to visit Cuba,

1. *Commends* the Special Rapporteur of the Commission on Human Rights for his interim report on the situation of human rights in Cuba;

2. *Expresses its full support* for the work of the Special Rapporteur;

3. *Calls once more upon* the Government of Cuba to cooperate fully with the Special Rapporteur by permitting him full and free access to establish contact with the Government and the citizens of Cuba so that he may fulfil the mandate entrusted to him;

4. *Regrets profoundly* the numerous violations of human rights and fundamental freedoms in Cuba, as described in the report of the Special Rapporteur to the Commission on Human Rights and in his interim report;

5. *Urges* the Government of Cuba to ensure freedom of expression and assembly and the freedom to demonstrate peacefully, including by allowing political parties and non-governmental organizations to function freely in the country and by reforming legislation in this area;

6. *Welcomes* the ratification by the Government of Cuba of the Convention against Torture and other Cruel, Inhuman or Degrading Treatment or Punishment;

7. *Calls especially upon* the Government of Cuba to release the numerous persons detained for activities of a political nature, including those specifically mentioned in the report of the Special Rapporteur who suffer from inadequate medical care while imprisoned or whose rights as journalists or jurists are impeded or denied;

8. *Calls upon* the Government of Cuba to adopt the other measures proposed in the interim report of the Special Rapporteur to bring the observance of human rights and fundamental freedoms in Cuba into conformity with international law and international human rights instruments and to end all violations of human rights by, *inter alia*, ratifying and effectively implementing those international human rights instruments to which it is not yet party, ceasing the persecution and punishment of citizens for reasons related to freedom of expression and peaceful association, respecting due process, and granting permission for access to the prisons by non-governmental humanitarian organizations and international humanitarian agencies;

9. *Decides* to continue its consideration of this question at its fifty-first session.

General Assembly resolution 50/198

22 December 1995    Meeting 99    66-22-78 (recorded vote)

Approved by Third Committee (A/50/635/Add.3) by recorded vote (62-23-73), 13 December (meeting 56); 26-nation draft (A/C.3/50/L.60); agenda item 112 (c).

Meeting numbers. GA 50th session: 3rd Committee 35, 38-51, 53, 56; plenary 99.

Recorded vote in Assembly as follows:

*In favour:* Albania, Andorra, Argentina, Armenia, Australia, Austria, Belgium, Bosnia and Herzegovina, Bulgaria, Canada, Chile, Costa Rica, Croatia, Cyprus, Czech Republic, Denmark, Ecuador, El Salvador, Estonia, Finland, France, Georgia, Germany, Greece, Honduras, Hungary, Iceland, Ireland, Israel, Italy, Japan, Kuwait, Latvia, Liechtenstein, Lithuania, Luxembourg, Malta, Marshall Islands, Monaco, Netherlands, New Zealand, Nicaragua, Norway, Panama, Paraguay, Poland, Portugal, Republic of Korea, Republic of Moldova, Romania, Russian Federation, Rwanda,* Samoa, Saudi Arabia, Slovakia, Slovenia, Solomon Islands, Spain, Sweden, Tajikistan, the former Yugoslav Republic of Macedonia, Turkey, United Kingdom, United States, Uzbekistan, Vanuatu.

*Against:* China, Cuba, Democratic People's Republic of Korea, Gambia, Ghana, India, Indonesia, Iran, Lao People's Democratic Republic, Lesotho, Libyan Arab Jamahiriya, Myanmar, Namibia, Nigeria, South Africa, Sudan, Syrian Arab Republic, Uganda, United Republic of Tanzania, Viet Nam, Zambia, Zimbabwe.

*Abstaining:* Afghanistan, Algeria, Antigua and Barbuda, Azerbaijan, Bahamas, Bahrain, Bangladesh, Barbados, Belarus, Belize, Benin, Bhutan, Bolivia, Botswana, Brazil, Brunei Darussalam, Burkina Faso, Burundi, Cambodia, Cameroon, Cape Verde, Chad, Colombia, Congo, Côte d'Ivoire, Dominica, Egypt, Equatorial Guinea, Eritrea, Ethiopia, Fiji, Gabon, Grenada, Guinea, Guinea-Bissau, Guyana, Haiti, Jamaica, Jordan, Kazakstan, Kenya, Kyrgyzstan, Lebanon, Malawi, Malaysia, Maldives, Mali, Mauritania, Mauritius, Mexico, Micronesia, Mongolia, Morocco, Mozambique, Nepal, Niger, Oman, Pakistan, Papua New Guinea, Peru, Philippines, Qatar, Saint Kitts and Nevis, Saint Lucia, Saint Vincent and the Grenadines, Sierra Leone, Singapore, Sri Lanka, Suriname, Swaziland, Thailand, Togo, Trinidad and Tobago, Tunisia, Ukraine, Uruguay, Venezuela, Zaire.

*Later advised the Secretariat it had intended to vote against.

## Haiti

**Report of the Special Rapporteur.** In a February report,[6] Special Rapporteur Mario Tulio Bruni Celli (Venezuela) updated the human rights situation in Haiti based on his visit to the country (9-14 January). He discussed events leading to the return of President Jean-Bertrand Aristide on 15 October 1994 and the subsequent enactment of various legal instruments and military appointments by him upon his return. A main concern expressed to the Special Rapporteur during his visit related to disarming the paramilitary groups and civilians; another related to the slowness of international development cooperation programmes.

Since the return of President Aristide and the appointment and approval of a new Prime Minister, the situation in Haiti had begun to return to normal, with a real decrease in the number of abuses and violations of human rights, the Special Rapporteur stated. The normalization was due to a combination of factors, including the presence of the multinational force, authorized by the Security Council in 1994,[7] police monitors, reduction of the Haitian Armed Forces, the dismantling and partial disarming of the paramilitary groups, the return of the members of the International Civilian Mission to Haiti (MICIVIH), and, presumably, the restoration of the legitimate Government and the appeals by the President to his party members to respect human rights and contribute to reconciliation.

The Special Rapporteur recommended that the Commission on Human Rights: once again condemn human rights violations in Haiti; express satisfaction at the effort of the international community to resolve the question concerning Haiti; express its satisfaction at the cooperation established between various bodies of the UN and of the inter-American system and between the latter and democratic Governments in Latin America; express gratitude to the Special Envoy of the Secretaries-General of the UN and the Organization of American States (OAS), to MICIVIH, to international development organizations, to other

UN and OAS bodies and to others whose efforts had led to the restoration of the legitimate authorities; reaffirm previous Commission statements to the effect that the political changes and the return of the legitimate authorities constituted only the beginning of changes necessary to promote human rights; and request the High Commissioner for Human Rights to ensure that the situation was evaluated and studied, priorities were established, programmes were formulated, guidance was provided, responsibilities were defined and coordinated activities were initiated.

**Commission action.** On 8 March,[8] the Commission expressed satisfaction at the return of President Aristide, at the re-establishment of constitutional order and at the support given by the President to national reconciliation and efforts to end violence. Condemning the human rights violations that took place during the de facto regime, the Commission called on the Government of Haiti to take measures to improve the administration of justice and the prison system. It urged the Haitian authorities to implement the Special Rapporteur's recommendations, particularly updating civil and criminal legislation, complete separation of the police from the armed forces, establishment of a civilian police force, and separation of and mutual respect for the various powers of the State. It also urged the Government to create favourable conditions for reconstruction and development programmes and called on the international community to cooperate fully towards that end.

The Commission asked the Secretary-General to appoint an independent expert to assist the Government in the area of human rights, to examine the development of human rights in Haiti and to monitor the fulfilment by Haiti of its obligations in that area. The independent expert was to submit a report on the implementation of the Commission's resolution to the General Assembly in 1995 and to the Commission in 1996. The Secretary-General was requested to provide, at the Government's request, advisory services in the area of human rights. The requests to the Secretary-General and the independent expert were approved by the Economic and Social Council by **decision 1995/281** of 25 July. The Commission decided to consider the question of Haiti in 1996 under the item "Advisory services in the field of human rights".

On 31 July, the Secretary-General appointed Adama Dieng (Senegal) as the independent expert.

**Report of the independent expert.** Independent expert Dieng presented to the General Assembly a preliminary overview and recommendations[9] on the human rights situation in Haiti following his first visit to the country (23 September–6 October) and discussions held in neighbouring countries.

He noted that the human rights situation in Haiti had improved considerably since the return of the President. However, common crime had skyrocketed, although the situation had improved somewhat due to the presence of the UN Mission in Haiti (UNMIH). Pre-trial detention was the rule rather than the exception, contributing to overcrowding in prisons. The judicial system was outdated and needed reform. The preamble of the presidential decree of 28 March 1995 setting up the National Commission of Truth and Justice constituted a key to understanding the commitment to end the culture of impunity and to respect the Haitian people's desire to make Haiti a State subject to the rule of law. However, the expert noted that the National Commission could be undermined by a lack of funds. Efforts were under way to rehabilitate Haitian women who still suffered from domestic violence. Children who worked as servants were a major concern.

He recommended investigating political killings; reducing overcrowded conditions in prisons; providing funds to the National Commission; prioritizing support for judicial reform; evaluating the aptitude and independence of the government commissioners appointed by the illegal Governments; organizing retraining sessions for judges and government commissioners; adding instruction in international human rights law to the curricula of the Ecole de la Magistrature and the Police Academy; developing, in cooperation with Haitian human rights organizations, a programme of rural legal services to train paralegals; revising the Code of Criminal Investigation; establishing an institution and a national committee on the rights of the child; keeping the UNMIH civil police in Haiti with a maximum of 300 police officers for a minimum period of five years; extending the MICIVIH mandate; coordinating the technical assistance activities of MICIVIH and the Centre for Human Rights; and providing greater support for programmes to reintegrate former soldiers into civilian life.

**GENERAL ASSEMBLY ACTION**

On 22 December, the General Assembly adopted **resolution 50/196**.

**Human rights in Haiti**

*The General Assembly,*

*Recalling* its resolution 49/201 of 23 December 1994,

*Guided* by the principles embodied in the Charter of the United Nations, the Universal Declaration of Human Rights and the International Covenants on Human Rights,

*Taking note* of Commission on Human Rights resolution 1995/70 of 8 March 1995, in which the Commission requested the Secretary-General to appoint an independent expert with the mandate to furnish assistance to the Government of Haiti in the area of human rights, to examine the development of the situation of human rights in that country, to monitor the fulfilment by Haiti of its obligations in this field and to submit a report to the General Assembly at its fiftieth session and to the Commission on Human Rights at its fifty-second session,

*Recognizing* the work carried out by the International Civilian Mission to Haiti for the defence of human rights, and recalling General Assembly resolution 49/27 B of 12 July 1995, in which it decided to authorize the extension of the mandate of the Mission,

1. *Expresses its thanks* for the efforts of the Secretary-General and his Special Representative for Haiti in favour of the consolidation of democratic institutions in Haiti and the respect for human rights in that country;

2. *Welcomes* the satisfactory evolution of the political process in Haiti and the holding of legislative and municipal elections and the forthcoming presidential elections, in accordance with the Constitution, as indispensable elements in the strengthening of democratic institutions;

3. *Takes note with appreciation* of the report of the independent expert of the Commission on Human Rights, Mr. Adama Dieng, on the situation of human rights in Haiti and the recommendations contained therein;

4. *Expresses its concern* about the recent incidents of violence, in particular the assassination of a member of the Haitian Parliament, and hopes that such acts and other incidents of violence will not impede continued progress in the field of human rights and the consolidation of constitutional democracy;

5. *Welcomes* the establishment of the programme of technical cooperation prepared by the Centre for Human Rights of the Secretariat aimed at strengthening the institutional capacity in the field of human rights, particularly in the areas of legislative reform, training for justice administration personnel and human rights education;

6. *Requests* the Secretary-General, through the United Nations High Commissioner for Human Rights and the Centre for Human Rights, to take appropriate steps to ensure financial and technical resources for the implementation of such a programme;

7. *Expresses its support* for the work currently undertaken by the National Commission of Truth and Justice, with the cooperation of the International Civilian Mission to Haiti, in its investigation of past human rights abuses, and looks forward to its report at the end of 1995;

8. *Decides* to continue its consideration of the situation of human rights and fundamental freedoms in Haiti at its fifty-first session, on the basis of information provided by the Commission on Human Rights and the Economic and Social Council.

General Assembly resolution 50/196

22 December 1995      Meeting 99      Adopted without vote

Approved by Third Committee (A/50/635/Add.3) without vote, 11 December (meeting 53); 51-nation draft (A/C.3/50/L.56), orally corrected; agenda item 112 *(c)*.

*Meeting numbers.* GA 50th session: 3rd Committee 35, 38-53; plenary 99.

*REFERENCES*

[1]E/1995/23. [2]E/CN.4/1996/2 (res. 1995/6). [3]E/CN.4/1995/52. [4]E/1995/23 (res. 1995/66). [5]A/50/663. [6]E/CN.4/1995/59. [7]YUN 1994, p. 426, SC res. 940(1994), 31 July 1994. [8]E/1995/23 (res. 1995/70). [9]A/50/714.

# Middle East

## Lebanon

**Commission action.** On 7 March,[1] the Commission, by a roll-call vote of 48 to 1, with 4 abstentions, deplored the ongoing Israeli violations of human rights in southern Lebanon and the western Bekaa, demonstrated by the kidnapping and arbitrary detention of civilians, destruction of their homes, confiscation of their property, expulsion from their land and the bombardment of their villages. It called on Israel to end such practices immediately and to implement relevant Security Council resolutions requiring its immediate, total and unconditional withdrawal from all Lebanese territory and respect for Lebanon's sovereignty, independence and territorial integrity. It also called on Israel to comply with the 1949 Geneva Convention relative to the Protection of Civilian Persons in Time of War (fourth Geneva Convention), to release Lebanese and other prisoners detained in Israeli prisons and detention centres contrary to the Geneva Convention and other provisions of international law, and to facilitate the humanitarian mission of ICRC and similar organizations, allowing them to visit the detention centres of Khiyam and Marjayoun. It asked the Secretary-General to bring the resolution to Israel's attention and to invite Israel to provide information on its implementation. He was to report to the General Assembly in 1995 and to the Commission in 1996 on the results of his efforts.

**ECONOMIC AND SOCIAL COUNCIL ACTION**

In July, the Economic and Social Council adopted **decision 1995/278**.

### Human rights situation in southern Lebanon and the western Bekaa

At its 52nd plenary meeting, on 25 July 1995, the Economic and Social Council, taking note of Commission on Human Rights resolution 1995/67 of 7 March 1995, approved the Commission's request to the Secretary-General to bring the resolution to the attention of the Government of Israel and to invite it to provide information concerning the extent of its implementation thereof, and to report to the General Assembly at its fiftieth session and to the Commission on Human Rights at its fifty-second session on the results of his efforts in this regard.

Economic and Social Council decision 1995/278

47-1-1 (roll-call vote)

Draft by Commission on Human Rights (E/1995/23/Corr.2); agenda item 5 *(d)*. *Meeting numbers.* ESC 51, 52.

Roll-call vote in Council as follows:

*In favour:* Australia, Bahamas, Belarus, Bhutan, Brazil, Bulgaria, Canada, Chile, China, Colombia, Costa Rica, Côte d'Ivoire, Cuba, Denmark, Egypt, France, Gabon, Germany, Greece, India, Indonesia, Ireland, Jamaica, Japan, Libyan Arab Jamahiriya, Luxembourg, Malaysia, Mexico, Netherlands, Nigeria, Norway, Poland, Portugal, Republic of Korea, Romania, Russian Fed-

eration, Senegal, South Africa, Sri Lanka, Sudan, Thailand, Uganda, Ukraine, United Kingdom, United Republic of Tanzania, Venezuela, Zimbabwe.
*Against:* United States.
*Abstaining:* Philippines.

**Reports of the Secretary-General.** In response to a 1994 Commission request,[2] the Secretary-General reported[3] that he had asked Israel for information on the implementation of the Commission's 1994 resolution on the human rights situation in southern Lebanon and had received no reply.

Similarly, the Secretary-General in October reported[4] that he had asked Israel for information on the implementation of the Commission's 1995 resolution and had received no reply. On 22 December, the General Assembly, by **decision 50/461**, noted the Secretary-General's report.

### Territories occupied by Israel

In 1995, the question of human rights violations in the territories occupied by Israel as a result of the 1967 hostilities in the Middle East was again considered by the Commission. Political and other aspects were considered by the General Assembly, its Special Committee to Investigate Israeli Practices Affecting the Human Rights of the Palestinian People and Other Arabs of the Occupied Territories (Committee on Israeli practices) and other bodies (see PART TWO, Chapter VI).

**Report of the Special Rapporteur.** In 1995, the Commission on Human Rights had before it a report of René Felber (Switzerland), the Special Rapporteur on the question of the violation of human rights in the occupied Arab territories.[5] He described his activities in 1994, including his visit to the Middle East in October (Jerusalem, Tel Aviv, Ramallah, Gaza, Hebron and the Negev desert).

He received information from NGOs and the Committee on Israeli practices concerning torture and ill-treatment of Palestinian detainees, prison conditions, violations of freedom of movement, the issue of land and the sealing of houses.

The Special Rapporteur stated that neither the General Assembly nor the Commission on Human Rights had had any particular success in enforcing human rights in the occupied territories. No specific measures had been taken and political condemnation was not proving effective. The solution lay in the establishment of normal peaceful relations between States to guarantee the existence and security of each of them. That did not mean that human rights violations should not be denounced or that interventions should not be made in countries where human rights were under threat. He suggested changing the method by possibly doing away with the services of a Special Rapporteur altogether. A report might soothe con-

sciences, he said, but its effectiveness should be measured by the impact of the points it made and by how seriously they were taken by those to whom they were addressed.

**Reports of the Secretary-General.** The Secretary-General reported[6] that he had brought the Commission's 1994 resolutions on human rights violations in the Israeli-occupied territories to the attention of Israel and other Governments, the Committee on Israeli practices and the Committee on the Exercise of the Inalienable Rights of the Palestinian People. They had also been transmitted to the specialized agencies, the UN Relief and Works Agency for Palestine Refugees in the Near East, international humanitarian organizations and NGOs. Information had also been disseminated through UN press releases, documents and UN information centres and services.

The Secretary-General submitted to the Commission a list of all General Assembly and other reports issued since 11 March 1994 on the situation of the population of the occupied Arab territories.[7]

**Commission action.** On 17 February,[8] by a roll-call vote of 26 to 2, with 21 abstentions, the Commission, deeply regretting the continued human rights violations in the occupied Palestinian territory since the 1993 signing of the Declaration of Principles on Interim Self-Government Arrangements by the Government of Israel and the Palestine Liberation Organization,[9] called on Israel to desist from all human rights violations in the Palestinian and other occupied Arab territories, to respect the principles of international law and its commitments to the UN Charter, and to withdraw from the Palestinian territory, including Jerusalem, and other occupied Arab territories in accordance with UN and Commission resolutions. The Commission asked the Secretary-General to bring its resolution to the attention of the Government of Israel and to all other Governments, concerned UN organs, the specialized agencies, regional intergovernmental organizations and international humanitarian organizations, to disseminate it as widely as possible and to report in 1996 on its implementation by Israel. The Commission also asked him to provide it with all UN reports issued between its sessions that dealt with conditions in which the Palestinians were living under Israeli occupation.

In another 17 February resolution,[10] adopted by a roll-call vote of 25 to 1, with 23 abstentions, the Commission called on Israel to comply with UN resolutions on the Syrian Golan and demanded that Israel rescind its decision to impose its laws, jurisdiction and administration on that occupied territory. Calling on Israel to desist from changing the physical character, demographic composition, institutional structure and legal status of the Syrian Golan, the Commission emphasized that displaced persons must be allowed to return to their homes and to recover their properties. The Commission further called on Israel to desist from imposing Israeli citizenship and identity cards on Syrians in the Golan and to desist from its repressive measures against them. It determined that all Israeli measures that altered the character and legal status of the Syrian Golan were null and void, violated international law and the fourth Geneva Convention and had no legal effect. It again called on Member States not to recognize any of the legislative or administrative measures or actions mentioned in its resolution. The Secretary-General was asked to bring the Commission's resolution to the attention of all Governments, UN organs, specialized agencies, regional intergovernmental organizations and international humanitarian organizations, to give the resolution wide publicity and to report in 1996.

In a third text,[11] adopted on 17 February by a roll-call vote of 46 to 1, with 3 abstentions, the Commission reaffirmed that the installation of Israeli civilians in the occupied territories was illegal and constituted a violation of the relevant provisions of the fourth Geneva Convention. It regretted that Israel had not complied with its resolutions adopted in 1990,[12] 1991,[13] 1992,[14] 1993[15] and 1994.[16] It urged Israel to abstain from and prevent any installation of settlers in the occupied territories.

**Subcommission action.** On 18 August,[17] the Subcommission, by a secret ballot of 17 votes to 2, with 4 abstentions, called on Israel: to comply with its international obligations, respect the rules of international law and apply the fourth Geneva Convention to the Palestinian and other occupied Arab territories; to desist from establishing Israeli settlements; to comply with relevant General Assembly and Security Council resolutions; and to desist from changing the physical character, demographic composition, institutional structure and legal status of the occupied Syrian Golan and from imposing Israeli citizenship and identity cards on the Syrian citizens in the occupied Syrian Golan, and to desist from its repressive measures against them. It called on Member States not to recognize any of the legislative or administrative measures referred to in its resolution. The Subcommission called on the Palestinian Authority to comply with all international human rights norms, to provide greater access to its prisons and interrogators through international organizations, to avail itself of the advisory services offered by the Centre for Human Rights, and to hold free elections.

*REFERENCES*

[1]E/1995/23 (res. 1995/67). [2]YUN 1994, p. 1110. [3]E/CN.4/1995/63. [4]A/50/662. [5]E/CN.4/1995/19. [6]E/CN.4/1995/20 & E/CN.4/1995/21. [7]E/CN.4/1995/22. [8]E/1995/23 (res. 1995/1). [9]YUN 1993, p. 521. [10]E/1995/23 (res. 1995/2). [11]Ibid. (res. 1995/3). [12]E/1990/22 (res. 1990/1). [13]YUN 1991, p. 612. [14]YUN 1992, p. 809. [15]YUN 1993, p. 959. [16]YUN 1994, p. 1111. [17]E/CN.4/1996/2 (res. 1995/9).

PART FOUR

# Economic and social questions

Chapter I

# Development policy and international economic cooperation

The beginning of 1995 saw the global economy in strong condition. Although the growth of output rate—around 3 per cent—was not very rapid, it was unusually widespread and appeared to be sustainable. The developed market economies had emerged from the recession of the early 1990s, the situation in the transition economies was encouraging, and the developing countries were in their fourth year of relatively strong economic growth. Latin America, however, was experiencing a contractionary phase following the exchange-rate crisis in Mexico in late 1994, which spread financial shock over the region. Although growth was expected to strengthen in Africa in 1995, economic activity was affected by civil strife in a number of countries, and inadequate or irregular rainfall curtailed agricultural production in others.

Work continued on an agenda for development, initially proposed by the Secretary-General in 1992 as an integrated approach towards the wide range of economic and social issues confronting the United Nations. An Ad Hoc Open-ended Working Group was established and held three sessions in 1995 to advance efforts towards an international consensus on cooperation for development.

The need for strategies to eradicate poverty was discussed by the Commission on Sustainable Development and by the Standing Committee on Poverty Alleviation of the United Nations Conference on Trade and Development. The Assembly, in December, adopted a resolution on the observance of the International Year for the Eradication of Poverty (1996). It also proclaimed the first United Nations Decade for the Eradication of Poverty (1997-2006).

The implementation of Agenda 21, adopted at the 1992 United Nations Conference on Environment and Development, continued to be monitored by the Commission on Sustainable Development. During the Commission's April session, a high-level meeting with ministerial participation discussed, among other things, the concept of sustainable development. In December, the General Assembly decided to hold a special session in 1997 to carry out a review and appraisal of Agenda 21.

In July, the Economic and Social Council, having considered the report of the Commission on Science and Technology for Development, which held its second session in May, recommended that Governments adopt the Declaration of Intent on Gender, Science and Technology for Sustainable Development. In other action, the Council invited the Commission on Science and Technology for Development to continue to contribute to the work of the Commission on Sustainable Development on the science and technology components of Agenda 21. The Assembly, in December, called on those two bodies to interact more effectively, through the Council, in carrying out their mandates.

The problems of the 48 officially designated least developed countries (LDCs) were discussed at the High-level Intergovernmental Meeting on the Mid-term Global Review of the Implementation of the Programme of Action for LDCs for the 1990s, held in September/October. The Assembly endorsed the Meeting's recommendations, which it annexed to its December resolution on the subject, and stressed the critical importance of providing multilateral assistance for LDCs.

The special challenges facing small island developing States were also considered by the Assembly as it reviewed action being taken to implement the 1994 Programme of Action for the Sustainable Development of Small Island States. The Secretary-General was asked to ensure that the Secretariat's Small Island Developing States Unit include in its work programme provision for the development and compilation of a vulnerability index for that group of countries.

In the public administration area, the Twelfth Meeting of Experts on the United Nations Programme in Public Administration and Finance, which took place in July/August, acted as the preparatory meeting for the resumed fiftieth session of the Assembly (1996) to be devoted to the question of public administration and development.

## International economic relations

### Development and international economic cooperation

During 1995, several United Nations bodies, including the General Assembly and the Economic and Social Council, considered development and international economic cooperation issues.

The Assembly's Second (Economic and Financial) Committee discussed matters relating to macroeconomic policy questions and sustainable development and international economic cooperation and made recommendations on a number of topics. By **decision 50/425** of 20 December, the Assembly took note of part one of the Committee's report on sustainable development and international economic cooperation.[1]

By **decision 50/468** of 22 December, the Assembly deferred consideration of the launching of global negotiations on international economic cooperation for development and decided to include it in the provisional agenda of its fifty-first (1996) session.

### Agenda for development

An agenda for development—an integrated approach to the many and varied economic and social issues dealt with by the United Nations—was first proposed by the Secretary-General in his report on the work of the Organization in 1992.[2] Later that year, the General Assembly asked[3] that a report on that proposal be prepared by the Secretary-General. In May 1994, he presented a wide-ranging document, "An agenda for development",[4] presenting initial approaches and broad themes to be pursued. It was subsequently discussed at World Hearings on Development held in June 1994 in New York.[5]

In accordance with a 1994 General Assembly resolution,[6] the Ad Hoc Open-ended Working Group of the General Assembly on an Agenda for Development was established in early 1995 under the chairmanship of the Assembly President. The Working Group held three sessions during the year (21-24 February; 8-19 May; and 28 August–8 September)[7] to elaborate further an agenda for development.

At its first session, the Working Group exchanged views on a tentative outline for an agenda for development and asked the Secretariat to provide a compendium containing the goals, targets and commitments of major UN conferences, agreements and meetings that had been held during the preceding five years and an assessment of their status of implementation. At its second session, the Working Group had before it an outline proposed by its two Vice-Chairmen, the compendium and contributions from a number of groups and States. Based on the outline, the Working Group agreed that the proposed agenda for development should comprise three chapters: setting and objectives; policy framework, including means of implementation; and institutional issues and follow-up. Subsequently, the Working Group discussed the first two chapters and asked for preparation of a synthesis text to take into account both debate and written contributions. Interested groups and/or States were invited to make contributions on all three chapters. At its third session, the Working Group reviewed the synthesis text and

exchanged views on the third chapter. A revised synthesis text, including the third chapter, was requested.

At a meeting on 8 September, the Working Group recommended that work on the agenda for development continue during the Assembly's fiftieth session.

By **decision 49/497** of 14 September, the Assembly noted the progress report of the Ad Hoc Working Group[7] and decided that the Group should continue its work during the Assembly's fiftieth session, with a view to finalizing an agenda for development.

The Assembly's Second Committee discussed an agenda for development on 19 October[8] but took no action. By **decision 50/437** of 20 December, the Assembly noted the report of the Second Committee on that same subject.

**Economic and Social Council consideration.** In accordance with a 10 February decision **(1995/216)**, the Economic and Social Council extended an invitation to the General Assembly President to make a statement at the Council's substantive session on the work of the Ad Hoc Open-ended Working Group of the General Assembly on an Agenda for Development. In a 3 July address,[9] he informed the Council of progress achieved by the Working Group at its first and second sessions and described the proposed outline for the agenda for development (see above).

### Development through partnership

In response to a 1994 General Assembly request,[10] the Secretary-General submitted an October 1995 report on renewal of the dialogue on strengthening international economic cooperation for development through partnership.[11] He observed that progress on several fronts had confirmed the validity of the approach to development through partnership suggested in his 1994 note on the subject.[12] On 28 July,[13] the Economic and Social Council had agreed on elements of a coordinated approach to the follow-up to major UN conferences (see PART SIX, Chapter IV). Also, the Ad Hoc Open-ended Working Group on an Agenda for Development (see above) had embraced the emergence of globalization and interdependence as the key elements of the agenda's setting and objectives, and the fiftieth anniversary of the United Nations was providing impetus to the effort to renew the Organization's role in harmonizing the interests of nations. In particular, the policy framework being developed in the agenda and the issues identified for priority attention should set the stage for the renewal and pursuit of a constructive dialogue based on partnership.

The report listed the elements of the policy framework identified in the proposed agenda for development. It also suggested some themes that could be drawn on by the partners in the dialogue on the management of global change: globalization and the rules of the game; competition; regional integration and the global economy; new information technologies and the global economy; international migration; prevention and management of emergencies and post-conflict peace-building; and crime, drugs, violence and global stability. Modalities were proposed for conducting a dialogue on broad intersectoral themes in the context of a high-level plenary session of the General Assembly, as suggested by the Secretary-General in 1994.[12]

The October 1995 report concluded that a high-level dialogue conducted in a constructive spirit in the Assembly would help to reinvigorate the Assembly's policy-making role in the economic, social and related fields and enable the United Nations to contribute to improving the management and governance of the world economy.

**GENERAL ASSEMBLY ACTION**

On 20 December, the General Assembly adopted **resolution 50/122**.

### Renewal of the dialogue on strengthening international economic cooperation for development through partnership

*The General Assembly,*

*Recalling* its resolutions 48/165 of 21 December 1993 and 49/95 of 19 December 1994 on renewal of the dialogue on strengthening international economic cooperation for development through partnership,

*Noting with appreciation* the efforts of the Secretary-General to encourage a constructive dialogue for enhancing development and to facilitate actions in that regard,

*Noting also* the ongoing work of the Ad Hoc Open-ended Working Group of the General Assembly on an Agenda for Development,

*Recognizing* that the continued trend towards deepening interdependence among countries and the increasing globalization of economic issues and problems present risks and uncertainties as well as opportunities and challenges for dialogue on international economic cooperation,

1. *Takes note* of the report of the Secretary-General on renewal of the dialogue on strengthening international economic cooperation for development through partnership;

2. *Reaffirms* that such a dialogue should be conducted in response to the imperatives of mutual interests and benefits, genuine interdependence, shared responsibility and the partnership for achieving sustained economic growth and sustainable development as well as improving the international economic environment that is conducive to such development, and that the United Nations should reinforce its activities in order to facilitate such a dialogue;

3. *Stresses* the need to put development at the centre of United Nations activities and that the United Nations has a central role to play in promoting international economic cooperation for development and in bringing development issues to the attention of the international community;

4. *Recognizes* that the ongoing discussions in the Ad Hoc Open-ended Working Group on an Agenda for Development and its outcome aim at strengthening constructive dialogue with a view to enhancing and revitalizing international economic cooperation through increased partnership among and between countries;

5. *Agrees* to hold a high-level dialogue for a period of two days at the fifty-first session of the General Assembly—the date, modalities and focus of the discussion to be decided on in the context of the outcome of the work of the Ad Hoc Open-ended Working Group on an Agenda for Development and the decision taken on the adoption of the agenda—on the theme of the social and economic impact of globalization and interdependence and their policy implications, and requests the Secretary-General, in close cooperation with Governments, relevant organizations and other development actors, to make initial preparations for such a dialogue;

6. *Requests* the Secretary-General to submit further recommendations for enhancing the dialogue, taking into consideration the agreed conclusions of the Economic and Social Council on coordinated follow-up by the United Nations system and implementation of the results of the major international conferences organized by the United Nations in the economic, social and related fields, the outcome of the ongoing discussions in the Ad Hoc Open-ended Working Group on an Agenda for Development, and on restructuring and revitalization of the United Nations in the economic, social and related fields;

7. *Also requests* the Secretary-General to submit to the General Assembly at its fifty-first session, for its consideration, recommendations on possible future themes for dialogue, including the issues of regional integration and of new information technology and the global economy;

8. *Further requests* the Secretary-General to elaborate his proposals to convene special sessions of the General Assembly, on major issues relevant to the dialogue on international economic cooperation for development, including those identified in an Agenda for Development;

9. *Decides* to include in the provisional agenda of its fifty-first session a sub-item entitled ''Renewal of the dialogue on strengthening international economic cooperation for development through partnership'' under the item entitled ''Agenda for development''.

General Assembly resolution 50/122

20 December 1995     Meeting 96     Adopted without vote

Approved by Second Committee (A/50/622) without vote, 8 December (meeting 42); draft by Vice-Chairman (A/C.2/50/L.67), orally revised, based on informal consultations on draft introduced by Philippines for Group of 77 and China, Colombia for Non-Aligned Movement, and Kyrgyzstan (A/C.2/50/L.11); agenda item 100.

*Meeting numbers.* GA 50th session: 2nd Committee 17, 29, 42; plenary 96.

## UN initiative on opportunity and participation

In accordance with a 1993 General Assembly resolution,[14] the Secretary-General appointed the members of the UN Panel on Opportunity and Participation, which met in New York from 15 to 19 May 1995. By an October note,[15] the Secretary-General transmitted the Panel's report to the Assembly. The Panel stated that although concepts of opportunity and participation encompassed a wide range of economic, social and political issues, it had concentrated on aspects related to economic opportunity within the framework of sustainable development. The Panel discussed the concepts of opportunity and participation and factors shaping the policy environment at both the international and national levels. It also highlighted the complementary roles of the overall economic environment and the importance of appropriate economy-wide policies at the national level. As a way to increase opportunity and participation in developing countries, with special reference to poverty eradication and the situation of disadvantaged groups, the Panel also considered the relevance of, and scope for, the promotion of micro-enterprises and small and medium-sized enterprises (SMEs), including the need for targeted approaches. It further discussed the positive impact of environmentally sustainable agriculture on rural development and the relevance of the participatory approach in its promotion.

The Panel concluded that the continuous creation and exploitation of opportunity and the widening of participation were required for sustainable development. The participatory approach was found to be particularly effective in programmes aimed at poverty alleviation and in promoting sustainable agriculture and fisheries. The promotion of micro-enterprises and SMEs was found to be an important way to enhance opportunity and broaden participation, primarily through creating employment. That required sound macroeconomic policies and other economy-wide policies at the national level supported by a favourable international environment. The Panel further concluded that targeted policies for promoting SMEs were also necessary owing to the vulnerability of the sector. Finally, it considered that the United Nations could play an important role in disseminating the concepts of opportunity and participation and the development strategies embodying them.

**GENERAL ASSEMBLY ACTION**

On 20 December, the General Assembly adopted **resolution 50/108**.

### United Nations initiative on opportunity and participation

*The General Assembly,*

*Recalling* its resolution 48/60 of 14 December 1993 and its decision 49/434 of 19 December 1994 on a United Nations initiative on opportunity and participation,

*Reaffirming* that one of the fundamental prerequisites of the achievement of sustainable development is broad-based public participation in decision-making,

*Acknowledging* the relevance of opportunity and participation in the economic and social development agenda

of the United Nations, as reflected in the various international conferences and agreements related to the follow-up of the Rio process,

*Commending* the South Pacific Forum Vision Statement, adopted by the Twenty-sixth South Pacific Forum, held at Madang, Papua New Guinea, from 13 to 15 September 1995, which promotes opportunities for international and regional cooperation leading to growth with equity, broad-based participation and capacity-building for self-reliance,

*Noting* that the United Nations Panel on Opportunity and Participation met at United Nations Headquarters from 15 to 19 May 1995,

1. *Welcomes* the report of the United Nations Panel on Opportunity and Participation;

2. *Takes note* of the Panel's contribution to the completion of an agenda for development and the follow-up arrangements to the World Summit for Social Development, held at Copenhagen from 6 to 12 March 1995;

3. *Invites* Member States and relevant organizations and agencies of the United Nations system to consider the insights and the recommendations of the Panel, particularly the sections of its report related to the efforts to be made for the development of small and medium-sized enterprises in developing countries as an effective measure for promoting opportunity and participation in the context of national development and the economic and social development of all peoples;

4. *Invites* the Commission for Sustainable Development, in the overall framework of trade, environment and sustainable development, alleviating poverty and promoting sustainable agriculture and rural development and small-scale fisheries development, to draw upon the work of the Panel;

5. *Invites* the Committee for Development Planning, in accordance with its mandate, to take into account the recommendations of the Panel in its work in 1996 in the context of the International Development Strategy for the Fourth United Nations Development Decade;

6. *Encourages* the relevant agencies and organizations of the United Nations system, in particular the United Nations Development Programme and the regional commissions, to increase their efforts to promote opportunity and participation, and to develop those concepts and incorporate them into their strategies and programmes, including regional and national workshops and seminars;

7. *Invites* Member States and international organizations to make voluntary contributions to these efforts;

8. *Encourages* support for the widest possible dissemination of the report of the Panel to the international community.

General Assembly resolution 50/108

20 December 1995     Meeting 96     Adopted without vote

Approved by Second Committee (A/50/617/Add.10) without vote, 8 December (meeting 42); draft by Vice-Chairman (A/C.2/50/L.60), based on informal consultations on 17-nation draft (A/C.2/50/L.36); agenda item 95 (j).

Meeting numbers. GA 50th session: 2nd Committee 35, 36, 39, 42; plenary 96.

## Rural development and management of land resources

**Commission on Sustainable Development.** The Secretary-General transmitted to the Commission on Sustainable Development (New York, 11-28 April) a report on promoting sustainable agriculture and rural development (SARD),[16] prepared by the Food and Agriculture Organization of the United Nations (FAO). The report discussed progress made in implementing chapter 14 ("Promoting sustainable agriculture and rural development") of Agenda 21, adopted in 1992[17] by the UN Conference on Environment and Development (UNCED), and was the result of consultations among designated focal points in various UN organizations and international and national non-governmental organizations (NGOs). It described the current situation with regard to agricultural production, nutrition and food security and assessed progress in different SARD programme areas. The report noted that major SARD issues varied in each group of countries and identified gaps in implementing SARD, such as lack of an overall SARD policy, the failure to address both poverty-environment links and environmental problems associated with uncontrolled agricultural commercialization, and slow progress in promoting off-farm employment and attracting financial resources.

The report reviewed the experience and progress achieved at the country level and by major groups, such as NGOs and farmers' and women's organizations, and discussed recent developments in international cooperation between Governments, within the UN system and between organizations outside the United Nations. Addressing matters related to finance and technology, the report noted that financing efforts to promote SARD was a key issue, especially in developing countries. In Agenda 21, it was estimated that the average annual cost (1993-2000) of implementing SARD would be about $31.8 billion, of which some $5.075 billion was to come from the international community as grants or concessional loans. As for technology, case-studies had demonstrated that sustainable production techniques existed and that farmers in both developed and developing countries were showing an interest in adopting them.

The report concluded that productive agriculture was an essential prerequisite of SARD, with its multiple objectives of reducing poverty and improving livelihoods, while conserving and protecting the natural resource base. However, achieving SARD was a complex and slow-moving process. Within the majority of developing countries and economies in transition, an incentive environment was needed to promote private-sector investment in agriculture and to reward environmental protection. In all countries, policies oriented towards promoting food and agricultural production and rural development and raising or maintaining farm incomes, while protecting the natural resource base, needed to be coherent, consistent and

mutually supportive. In addition, there was a need for a deeper understanding of socio-gender-cultural-economic relationships between the farmer and his or her environment, for better sharing of information on both sustainable indigenous and modern technologies and for reorientation of data-collecting and information management systems at the national level in parallel with the development of sustainability indicators.

The report set forth general strategy and specific proposals for action for implementing SARD.

In April, the Commission on Sustainable Development noted[18] that disappointment had been widely expressed at the slow progress in moving towards SARD in many countries. It recommended that FAO, the United Nations Development Fund for Women and the United Nations Development Programme (UNDP), together with government agencies, NGOs and people's representative organizations, promote an exchange of experiences with participatory mechanisms, with a view to enhancing their effectiveness. FAO, in collaboration with the United Nations Conference on Trade and Development (UNCTAD), the World Trade Organization (WTO), UNDP, the United Nations Environment Programme (UNEP) and other organizations, was asked to analyse the implications for SARD of the 1994 Final Act Embodying the Results of the Uruguay Round of Multilateral Trade Negotiations[19] at national, regional and international levels. In that context, the Commission noted the importance of a comprehensive examination of the environmental consequences of agricultural practices and policies, including agricultural subsidies, and their impact on SARD. The Commission stressed the importance of developing internationally agreed agri-environmental criteria and indicators; urged Governments to work out their own comprehensive agricultural policies and programmes to take full account of environmental concerns and capacity-building, encouraged them to integrate action on energy into their SARD efforts and urged them to support the efforts of developing countries in their transition towards the sustainable use of a mix of fossil and renewable sources of energy for rural communities; urged support for research and technology development, for strengthened national and international action to bring international cooperation for the conservation and sustainable use of animal genetic resources to a level similar to that for plant genetic resources and for strengthened coordination and cooperation efforts related to SARD; and recommended steps by all countries to reduce the environmental impact of pesticide use and that there should be a synthesis and exchange of information and practical experience among Governments, intergovernmental agencies and agricultural research institutions, and non-governmental and farmers' organizations, with a view to identifying models that could be applied in other situations.

In another report[20] to the Commission, the Secretary-General detailed progress in implementing chapter 10 ("Integrated approach to the planning and management of land resources") of Agenda 21.[17] He presented a number of proposals for action at the international and national levels for Commission consideration.

In April, the Commission noted[18] with concern the convergence of poverty, hunger and the degradation of terrestrial resources in environmentally more fragile marginal lands, and called on Governments, bilateral donors, multilateral financial institutions, technical specialized agencies and NGOs to give high priority to rural development in such lower-potential areas. Governments were urged to develop national and/or local land-use planning systems containing a statement of objectives and a detailed timetable for implementation spread over a period of years. They were also urged to pay particular attention to: establishing stable land-use systems in areas where important ecosystems or ecoregions were endangered by human activities; applying integrated planning and development approaches in regions subject to intensified settlement and agricultural production; and bringing about integrated approaches to capacity-building. The Secretary-General was asked to strengthen coordination and cooperation within the UN system through joint approaches and collaborative programmes. FAO, in partnership with UNEP, UNDP, other international bodies and Governments, and with contributions from NGOs, should develop tools and recommend actions for integrated land management. Such action should involve the Commission in its capacity as a forum for exchanging knowledge and experience, with the full participation of developing countries.

The Commission noted with appreciation the outcome of an international workshop dealing with integrated planning and management of land resources (Wageningen, the Netherlands, 20-22 February 1995)[21] and invited the Government of the Netherlands and FAO to disseminate the workshop's report and recommendations.

**ACC Subcommittee.** The Subcommittee on Rural Development of the Administrative Committee on Coordination (ACC) met in Paris from 31 May to 2 June.[22] It adopted revised terms of reference, which it submitted to the ACC Consultative Committee on Programme and Operational Questions (CCPOQ), and examined reports of agencies on experiences in rural areas in promoting income-generating activities and on the rehabilitation of returnees. It also considered the reports of the Panel on Monitoring and Evaluation (Paris, 23 and 24 March) and the Working Group on Industrial Contribution to Rural Development (Paris, 30 May).

Papers were presented on environment and rural development, rural/urban linkages and their importance for rural development, and development, public action and rural poverty alleviation.

CCPOQ (New York, 19-22 September)[23] recommended to ACC the adoption of the Subcommittee's revised terms of reference.

## Business and development

In response to a 1993 General Assembly request,[24] the Secretary-General submitted a September 1995 report on entrepreneurship and privatization for economic growth and sustainable development.[25] The report described the private sector's contributions towards economic growth and sustainable development and summarized responses from 37 UN entities that had been asked to provide information on: activities in promoting entrepreneurship and privatization programmes and implementing demonopolization and administrative deregulation; technical assistance programmes on development of national capacities to promote entrepreneurship, design and implementation of privatization policies and creation of enabling environments; and partnerships between private and public entities.

The report concluded that, with regard to privatization, Governments were encouraged to use the sectoral and cross-sectoral agencies of the UN to evaluate and assess their privatization policies and programmes. Concerning the commercialization of State-owned enterprises, Governments should pay greater attention to possible performance improvement in parastatals not scheduled for sale or liquidation and seek technical assistance from the international community. Regulatory policies should be stable as frequent changes added to investment risks and deterred new investment. With regard to private-sector development, the UN system should assist Governments to create an enabling environment for small and medium-size enterprise start-ups and expansion by special programmes targeted at that sector. As to military conversion to civilian goods and services, the UN should continue and expand assistance to Member States by collecting and analysing data, managing an information clearing house, developing enterprise conversion models from case-studies of successes and failures, and providing technical assistance support.

On 20 December, the General Assembly adopted **resolution 50/106**.

### Business and development

*The General Assembly,*

*Reaffirming* its resolution 48/180 of 21 December 1993,

*Taking note* of the report of the Secretary-General concerning policies and activities related to entrepreneurship, privatization, demonopolization and administrative deregulation,

*Also taking note* of chapter VI of the *World Economic and Social Survey, 1995*,

*Further taking note* of the report of the Committee on an International Agreement on Illicit Payments on its first and second sessions, the report of the Commission on Transnational Corporations on efforts by the United Nations to address the issue of corrupt practices and work undertaken in other international forums on the issue of corrupt practices,

*Looking forward* to the review by the Economic and Social Council of the report of the Twelfth Meeting of Experts on the United Nations Programme in Public Administration and Development,

*Aware* of the need to increase private-sector involvement in the provision of infrastructure services, *inter alia*, through joint ventures between public and private entities, particularly in countries with economies in transition, while protecting essential services and safeguarding the environment,

*Recognizing* the important role of Governments in creating, through transparent and participatory processes, an enabling environment supportive of entrepreneurship and facilitative of privatization, in particular in establishing the judicial, executive and legislative frameworks necessary for a market-based exchange of goods and services and for good management,

*Taking note* of the World Ministerial Conference on Organized Transnational Crime (Naples, 21-23 November 1994 and Buenos Aires, November 1995), and of the Ninth United Nations Congress on the Prevention of Crime and the Treatment of Offenders (Cairo, 29 April-8 May 1995), in particular the consideration by those conferences of the issue of illicit payments in international business transactions,

*Acknowledging* the need for international cooperation to deal with the problem of illicit payments in international business transactions, such as in the ongoing work on its draft international agreement on illicit payments, so as to promote accountability and a stable and predictable international business environment, and acknowledging further that international efforts in that field require the cooperation of all countries concerned,

1. *Values* the promotion of entrepreneurship in the development of small and medium-sized enterprises and industries by various actors throughout civil society, and of privatization, demonopolization and the simplification of administrative procedures;

2. *Invites* Member States, requests the Secretary-General and calls upon and encourages the relevant organs, organizations and programmes of the United Nations system to continue to foster active participation in support of entrepreneurship, privatization, demonopolization and the simplification of administrative procedures, as described in General Assembly resolution 48/180;

3. *Also invites* Member States, requests the Secretary-General and calls upon and encourages the relevant organs, organizations and programmes of the United Nations system, in their respective activities for the provision of infrastructure services, to encourage private-sector cost-effective involvement in the efficient construction, use and maintenance of infrastructure;

4. *Looks forward* to its resumed session in March and April 1996, during which it will examine public adminis-

tration and development, and address the issues contained in its agenda, including the role of public administration in promoting partnership for development;

5. *Welcomes* the continuation of work on illicit payments in relevant international forums, including the United Nations, taking account of progress already achieved on that issue;

6. *Recommends* that the Economic and Social Council, at its organizational session of 1996, consider the appropriate time-frame and procedure for the continuation of the work with a view to completing the draft international agreement on illicit payments, including consideration of the draft at the substantive session of 1996 of the Council, and recommends that the Council report to the Assembly at its fifty-first session;

7. *Decides* to include in the provisional agenda of its fifty-second session the item "Sustainable development and international economic cooperation: business and development".

**General Assembly resolution 50/106**

20 December 1995     Meeting 96     Adopted without vote

Approved by Second Committee (A/50/617/Add.8) without vote, 12 December (meeting 43); 4-nation draft (A/C.2/50/L.41/Rev.1), orally revised; agenda item 95 *(h)*.

*Sponsors:* Poland, Russian Federation, Ukraine, United States.

*Meeting numbers.* GA 50th session: 2nd Committee 35-37, 40, 43; plenary 96.

## Role of enterprises in development

The Ad Hoc Working Group on the Role of Enterprises in Development, established by the UNCTAD Trade and Development Board in 1994,[26] held two sessions in 1995, both in Geneva. At its first session (3-7 April),[27] the Working Group analysed the State's role in creating an enabling environment for promoting entrepreneurship and enterprises, especially small and medium-size enterprises, with reference to the regulatory framework and incentive structure, human resources development, institution building and institutional support, and the integration of the informal sector into the formal economy. It also examined the role of SMEs in export development, giving due consideration to possible advantages arising from the globalization process. The Working Group had before it UNCTAD reports on creating an enabling environment for the development of enterprises, particularly SMEs,[28] and on the role of SMEs in export development.[29]

At its second session (3-7 July), the Working Group focused on interactions between the development of SMEs and of capital markets and banking systems, with particular reference to the generation of domestic savings and access to capital markets and other sources of financing. It also sought to identify areas where technical cooperation in support of policy development to enhance the role of SMEs could be strengthened. The Working Group had before it UNCTAD secretariat reports on issues concerning SMEs' access to finance[30] and on strengthening technical cooperation for policy development to enhance the role of SMEs.[31] In 1995, the Working Group reviewed studies or presentations on the role of enterprise in development submitted by 22 countries.

In conclusions and recommendations in its final report,[32] which also covered the work of its second session, the Working Group welcomed the consensus reached on the important role of SMEs in the development process and the need to provide a supportive infrastructure for SME development, including: establishment of favourable macroeconomic conditions and a sound policy and commercial framework for business development, resource mobilization, financial institutional development and the promotion of long-term lending for enterprise development; policy and support measures to enhance the availability and efficient utilization of essential inputs of SMEs, including finance, market information and training, as well as to strengthen enterprise capabilities and linkages in order to facilitate the development of enterprises and their expansion into export markets; the promotion of various types of financial institutions, including community-based banks, taking into account the importance of personal contact in mobilizing domestic savings, as well as of a dialogue among policy makers, development banks and other financial institutions and SMEs; and technical cooperation in support of policy development, institution building and inter-firm cooperation for enhancing the role of SMEs in the development process.

The Working Group recommended that technical cooperation be continued and strengthened by both multilateral and bilateral support for SME development and for their role in trade development, including in the following areas: policy and commercial framework for enterprise development; institutional support for SME development; promotion of inter-firm linkages and modernization of SMEs, including the improvement of marketing capabilities; and regional cooperation on SME development, including networking of SME development support agencies. The Working Group noted that the provisional agenda for the ninth session (1996) of UNCTAD (UNCTAD IX) contained an item on promoting enterprise development and competitiveness in developing countries and countries in transition and considered that the following topics were worthy of further study: nature and causes of market imperfections that inhibit the viable development of SMEs; cost and benefit analysis of incentive structure and programmes, such as policy-based lending and credit guarantees, for SME development; effectiveness of different types of technical cooperation activities for SME development; improvement and diversification of the financial sector in order to promote enterprise development; and facilitation of inter-firm linkages, including through networking and promotion of standards for information exchange. The Working Group considered that the results of its work would provide useful inputs for the UNCTAD IX preparatory process.

At its eighteenth special session (Geneva, 11-15 December), the Trade and Development Board decided[33] to transmit the Ad Hoc Working Group's final report to the Board's executive session in February/March 1996 so it could be taken into account in relation to the substantive content of the document to be prepared for UNCTAD IX.

## Coercive economic measures

In response to a 1993 General Assembly request,[34] the Secretary-General submitted a September report on economic measures as means of political and economic coercion against developing countries.[35] The report contained a summary of responses received from seven States (Colombia, Cuba, Ecuador, Estonia, Iraq, Japan, Madagascar) on the issue of coercive economic measures and a review of actions taken by UN bodies and other international instruments. The report also summarized the main findings of an expert group meeting on coercive economic measures, convened by the Department for Economic and Social Information and Policy Analysis (New York, 22 and 23 June).

GENERAL ASSEMBLY ACTION

On 20 December, the General Assembly adopted **resolution 50/96**.

**Economic measures as a means of political and economic coercion against developing countries**

*The General Assembly,*

*Recalling* the relevant principles set forth in the Charter of the United Nations,

*Reaffirming* that no State may use or encourage the use of economic, political or any other type of measures to coerce another State in order to obtain from it the subordination of the exercise of its sovereign rights,

*Bearing in mind* the general principles governing the international trading system and trade policies for development contained in relevant resolutions, rules and provisions of the United Nations Conference on Trade and Development, the General Agreement on Tariffs and Trade and the World Trade Organization,

*Reaffirming* its resolutions 44/215 of 22 December 1989, 46/210 of 20 December 1991 and 48/168 of 21 December 1993,

*Gravely concerned* that the use of coercive economic measures adversely affects the economy and development efforts of developing countries and has a general negative impact on international economic cooperation and on worldwide efforts to move towards a nondiscriminatory and open trading system,

1. *Takes note* of the report of the Secretary-General, which contains a summary of the deliberations of the group of experts on coercive economic measures;

2. *Urges* the international community to adopt urgent and effective measures to eliminate the use by some developed countries of unilateral coercive economic measures against developing countries which are not authorized by relevant organs of the United Nations or are inconsistent with the principles contained in the Charter of the United Nations, as a means of forcibly imposing the will of one State on another;

3. *Requests* the Secretary-General to assign to the Department for Economic and Social Information and Policy Analysis of the Secretariat, in cooperation with the United Nations Conference on Trade and Development, the task of continuing to monitor the imposition of measures of this nature and to prepare possible methodologies or criteria for evaluating the impact of such measures on the affected countries, including the impact on trade and development, for the consideration of Member States;

4. *Also requests* the Secretary-General to submit a report to the General Assembly at its fifty-second session on the implementation of the present resolution.

General Assembly resolution 50/96

20 December 1995    Meeting 96    100-30-22 (recorded vote)

Approved by Second Committee (A/50/617/Add.1) by recorded vote (79-27-19), 5 December (meeting 41); draft by Philippines, for Group of 77 and China (A/C.2/50/L.18), agenda item 95 *(a)*.
*Meeting numbers.* GA 50th session: 2nd Committee 30-32, 36, 41; plenary 96.

Recorded vote in Assembly as follows:

*In favour:* Algeria, Angola, Antigua and Barbuda, Argentina, Bahrain, Bangladesh, Barbados, Belize, Benin, Bhutan, Bolivia, Botswana, Brazil, Brunei Darussalam, Burkina Faso, Cambodia, Cameroon, Chad, Chile, China, Colombia, Costa Rica, Côte d'Ivoire, Cuba, Democratic People's Republic of Korea, Djibouti, Dominica, Ecuador, Egypt, El Salvador, Ethiopia, Fiji, Ghana, Guinea, Guyana, Haiti, Honduras, India, Indonesia, Iran, Jamaica, Jordan, Kenya, Kuwait, Kyrgyzstan, Lao People's Democratic Republic, Lebanon, Lesotho, Libyan Arab Jamahiriya, Madagascar, Malawi, Malaysia, Maldives, Mali, Marshall Islands, Mauritania, Mauritius, Mexico, Micronesia, Mongolia, Morocco, Mozambique, Myanmar, Namibia, Nepal, Nicaragua, Niger, Nigeria, Oman, Pakistan, Panama, Papua New Guinea, Paraguay, Peru, Philippines, Qatar, Samoa, Saudi Arabia, Senegal, Singapore, Solomon Islands, South Africa, Sri Lanka, Sudan, Suriname, Swaziland, Syrian Arab Republic, Thailand, Togo, Trinidad and Tobago, Tunisia, Uganda, Ukraine, United Arab Emirates, Uruguay, Venezuela, Viet Nam, Yemen, Zambia, Zimbabwe.

*Against:* Australia, Austria, Belgium, Canada, Croatia, Czech Republic, Denmark, Finland, France, Germany, Hungary, Iceland, Ireland, Israel, Italy, Japan, Latvia, Liechtenstein, Lithuania, Luxembourg, Monaco, Netherlands, New Zealand, Norway, Poland, Republic of Moldova, Slovakia, Sweden, United Kingdom, United States.

*Abstaining:* Albania, Andorra, Armenia, Azerbaijan, Bahamas, Belarus, Bulgaria, Cyprus, Gabon, Georgia, Greece, Kazakstan, Malta, Portugal, Republic of Korea, Romania, Russian Federation, Slovenia, Spain, Tajikistan, the former Yugoslav Republic of Macedonia, Turkey.

## Sustainable development

### Commission on Sustainable Development

The Commission on Sustainable Development held its third session in New York from 11 to 28 April.[18] In accordance with a 1992 General Assembly recommendation,[36] a high-level meeting with ministerial participation was held on 26, 27 and 28 April to review the implementation of Agenda 21,[17] adopted by UNCED in 1992,[37] to consider emergency policy issues and to provide political impetus to the implementation of UNCED decisions and commitments.

In a March report,[38] the Secretary-General presented a number of issues that he felt the high-level meeting might wish to address: the concept of sustainable development; national-level experience in achieving sustainable development; the cluster of finance, changing production and consumption patterns and trade; technology; integrated land management; and forests. The high-level meeting also considered the report of the third (1994) session of the High-level Advisory Board on Sustainable Development.[39]

Reports before the Commission dealt with a variety of subjects: an integrated approach to the planning and management of land resources and promoting sustainable agriculture and rural development (see above); combating deforestation, managing fragile ecosystems, conservation of biological diversity and information for decision-making and Earthwatch (see PART FOUR, Chapter VII); financial resources and mechanisms for sustainable development and trade, environment and sustainable development (see PART FOUR, Chapter IV); poverty eradication and sustainable development (see below); demographic dynamics and sustainability (see PART FOUR, Chapter VIII); and science for sustainable development, transfer of environmentally sound technologies and environmentally sound management of biotechnology (see below).

By **decision 1995/235** of 17 July, the Economic and Social Council noted the Commission's report on its 1995 session and endorsed the recommendations pertaining to cross-sectoral issues, the programme of work for the ad hoc open-ended intersessional working groups and the provisional agenda for the Commission's 1996 session.

**Full EC participation.** As agreed in 1994,[40] the Economic and Social Council, at its organizational session, considered the question of the full participation by the European Community (EC) in the Commission on Sustainable Development. The Council had before it a note by the Secretariat[41] that addressed various legal and procedural questions pertaining to EC participation.

By **decision 1995/201** of 8 February, the Council adopted modalities for EC's full participation in the Commission. While not a member of the Commission, EC's participation would include the rights to speak and reply and to introduce proposals and amendments. It would also include the right to raise as a point of order the fact that consultations were under way among Community member States on a matter on which a decision was to be made and for which EC was the representative on the Commission; that right would not include the right to challenge the Chairman's decision in response to the point of order. EC would not have the right to vote but could submit proposals to be put to the vote if requested by a Commission member. Subject to Council approval, similar arrangements would apply to other regional or subregional economic integration organizations to which their member States had transferred competence over a range of matters within the Commission's purview.

*Cross-sectoral issues*

In a March report,[42] the Secretary-General summarized an analysis of submissions from 41 major group organizations, 20 Governments and 17 UN and non-UN intergovernmental organizations, on the role and contribution of major groups in the follow-up to Agenda 21,[17] particularly during 1994-1995. Country information indicated some positive steps regarding major group participation in such areas as the national Agenda 21 coordination mechanisms. The intergovernmental sphere showed significant support for participation of major groups in various regular and conference-related meetings; continued support for training, information dissemination and research collaboration activities; and some support for participation in policy-making and project design.

The report concluded that overall interest and participation of major groups in Agenda 21 follow-up had increased in the period 1994-1995 compared with previous years. There was also a trend among Governments and international organizations to include multiple sectors of major groups in efforts to identify problems. It could be argued, the report stated, that the political and practical significance of the major groups concept had influenced the way individuals, organizations and institutions at all levels were looking at economic and social challenges. However, the existence of numerous activities, programmes and projects did not necessarily mean that problems were solved. Positive examples reflected the experiences of relatively few major groups compared with the full spectrum of organizations around the world. Also, national information was limited, with only 20 of 183 UN Member States providing information.

Based on proposals for action contained in the Secretary-General's report, the Commission[18] brought a number of matters to the attention of the Economic and Social Council. It reiterated the importance of enabling and empowering partnerships between the governmental, intergovernmental and non-governmental sectors in achieving Agenda 21 goals, emphasized national-level participation of major groups in implementing and monitoring Agenda 21 through national coordination mechanisms, including national councils on sustainable development or national networks of major groups, and recommended that such participation be encouraged, strengthened and ex-

panded. The Commission recommended that existing and future national coordination mechanisms should strive to achieve representation of all major group sectors and that, in establishing those mechanisms, national and local major group organizations should choose their own representatives. It also recommended that major groups should continue to be involved in inter-sessional events and encouraged partnerships among Governments, intergovernmental organizations and major groups in organizing inter-sessional activities and other meetings. The Commission recognized the desirability of additional funding to increase major-group participation in its sessions, inter-sessional activities and other meetings concerning Agenda 21 follow-up and urged interested institutions to explore the possibility of creating suitable arrangements. It requested Governments and international organizations, together with major groups such as business and industry and academic communities, to explore ways to increase the availability of and access to electronic information systems and urged all countries to seek and enable public-private partnerships. Noting the need to ensure that information submitted by major-group organizations was fully utilized, the Commission asked the Inter-Agency Committee on Sustainable Development to consider that issue and to report to the Commission in 1996. The Secretary-General was asked to include information on recognizing and strengthening the role of major groups at the national and local levels in his 1996 report.

Other reports dealing with cross-sectoral issues included notes on activities of FAO and the World Food Programme in sustainable development[43] and on integrating environment and development in decision-making,[44] reports on changing consumption and production patterns (see below),[45] on national information,[46] and on progress in implementing the decisions and recommendations of the Commission's second (1994) session,[47] a March ACC statement to the Commission[48] and the report of the Workshop on Indicators of Sustainable Development for Decision-making (Ghent, Belgium, 9-11 January 1995).[49]

Changing consumption and production patterns

In a March report,[45] the Secretary-General described progress made in implementing chapter 4 of Agenda 21 ("Changing consumption patterns"), with special reference to recommendations made by the Commission in 1994.[50] In a general overview, the report identified the environmental, social and economic impact of existing production and consumption patterns with a view to assisting Governments to establish national priorities. It also summarized the results of recent projections and perspective studies, addressed the relevance of data and information collection for monitoring, evaluating and reviewing performance, and analysed policy measures aimed at promoting sustainable production and consumption patterns, with a focus on the use of economic instruments. Progress by Governments, major groups and international organizations in implementing the Commission's 1994 decisions was reviewed.

The report concluded that considerable progress had been made, especially in developed countries, in reducing the intensity of energy use and of metals and minerals per unit of gross domestic product (GDP). However, problems relating to excessive fertilizer and pesticide and to soil quality had only just begun to be addressed, and deforestation continued to be unsustainably high. Environmental monitoring data and other information, including consumer information—currently lacking in many developing countries—needed to be developed to provide a sound base for policy formulation and decision-making on changing unsustainable production and consumption patterns. The analysis underscored the need to continue the traditional emphasis on the supply side, while strengthening efforts on the demand side. The emphasis on consumers also reflected the conviction that changing consumption habits and lifestyle would eventually persuade manufacturers to develop new products and production processes. A number of problems called for further discussion, including agreement on a conceptual and methodological framework for a more systematic and standardized study of consumption and production issues; the need to build or improve infrastructure to facilitate a shift to more sustainable consumption and production patterns by household and other end-users; and how Governments and major groups could most effectively contribute to progress in changing consumption patterns, in addition to participating in ''green'' consumer movements. Those and other questions were included in a proposed work programme on sustainable consumption and production patterns.

The Commission[18] noted with concern the significant gaps in per capita income between developing and developed countries and the continuing current imbalances in the global patterns of consumption and production. It further noted that the growing recognition that patterns of production and consumption should be addressed had not been matched by a full understanding of the implications of such patterns on economic, social and environmental conditions at the local, national and global levels. Governments, business and industry and consumers were urged to intensify efforts to reduce the energy and material intensities of production and consumption through improving energy efficiency, energy-saving measures, technological innovations and transfer, increased waste recovery and reuse and recycling of materials. Developed countries were urged to intensify efforts to encourage the transfer of appropriate technologies to developing countries. The Commission adopted a work programme, for its future consideration of changing production and consumption patterns, that covered the following: identification of the policy implications of projected trends in consumption and production patterns; assessment of the impact on developing countries, especially the least developed countries (LDCs) and small island developing States, of changes in consumption and production in developed countries; evaluation of the effectiveness of policy measures intended to change consumption and production patterns, such as command-and-control, economic and social instruments, and government procurement policies and guidelines; eliciting a time-bound, voluntary commitment from countries to make measurable progress on sustainable development goals having an especially high priority at the national level; and revision of the guidelines for consumer protection.

### Sectoral issues

The Ad Hoc Inter-sessional Working Group on Sectoral Issues of the Commission on Sustainable Development met in New York from 27 February to 3 March.[51] It noted proposals for action included in the Secretary-General's reports on the following chapters of Agenda 21: chapters 10 (integrated approach to the planning and management of land resources) and 14 (promoting sustainable agriculture and rural development) (see above); and chapters 11 (forests), 12 (combating desertification and drought), 13 (sustainable mountain development) and 15 (conservation of biological diversity) (see PART FOUR, Chapter VII). The Working Group also addressed issues common to all topics under consideration (approaches, tools, finance, technology transfer, cooperation and capacity-building, and the relationship between existing conventions and other related processes) and put forward a number of proposals for the Commission's consideration.

### Inter-Agency Committee

The ACC Inter-Agency Committee on Sustainable Development (IACSD) held its fifth (New York 1-3 February) and sixth (Geneva, 12-14 July) sessions in 1995. In February,[52] IACSD considered preparations for the April session of the Commission on Sustainable Development, progress in coordination within the UN system and preparation of joint initiatives to implement Agenda 21, and support for Agenda 21 coordination and planning activities at the national level. It also reviewed its own functioning.

In July,[53] IACSD considered the outcome of the Commission's April session and follow-up action, preparations for the Commission's 1996 session, system-wide coordination in implementing the 1994 Programme of Action for the Sustainable Development of Small Island Developing States,[54] support for Agenda 21 coordination and planning activities at the national level, and a review of its own functioning, a note on which it submitted to ACC.

At its October session,[55] ACC adopted the note on IACSD functioning and annexed it to its report.

## High-level Advisory Board

The High-level Advisory Board on Sustainable Development held its fourth session in New York from 30 May to 1 June,[56] at which it examined three topics: mobilizing finance for sustainable development; enhancing cooperation and coordination in the UN system; and building alliances between the UN and non-governmental partners.

With regard to mobilizing finance, the Board noted that a three-pronged attack was needed: to review official development assistance (ODA) strategy in donor countries; to examine national policies in developing countries; and to explore new and innovative funding. Debt remission and the use of the World Bank/UNDP/UNEP Global Environment Facility were both considered important, but secondary by comparison. Although the World Bank and other Bretton Woods institutions (the International Monetary Fund, the International Development Association and the International Finance Corporation) were changing their approach and entering into partnerships with the UN system and NGOs, changes were needed in the governance of those institutions to provide UN Member States with greater influence on their policy agenda and greater equality among States. The impact on those institutions of the growing strength of the private sector as a source of investment in developing countries also needed appraisal.

The cooperative relationship among UN bodies and between the United Nations and major groups of NGOs should also be strengthened. UN agencies and the secretariats of major international environmental conventions should review their machinery for cooperation with the non-governmental world, while major non-governmental groups should develop their arrangements for dialogue and partnership with the UN system.

## Implementation of Agenda 21

In a September report,[57] prepared in response to a 1992 request,[58] the Secretary-General submitted to the General Assembly proposals on the format, scope and organizational aspects of the 1997 special Assembly session on the overall review and appraisal of Agenda 21, adopted by UNCED in 1992.[17] In addition to outlining priority issues for and the institutional framework of the special session, the report covered questions of documentation, the possible outcome of the review exercise, organizational aspects, the level of representation, participation of major groups, and the preparatory process.

**GENERAL ASSEMBLY ACTION**

On 20 December, the General Assembly adopted **resolution 50/113**.

### Special session for the purpose of an overall review and appraisal of the implementation of Agenda 21

*The General Assembly,*

*Recalling* its resolution 47/190 of 22 December 1992, in which it decided to convene, not later than 1997, a special session for the purpose of an overall review and appraisal of the implementation of Agenda 21,

*Having considered* the report of the Secretary-General containing proposals on the format, scope and organizational aspects of such a special session,

1. *Decides* to convene the special session envisaged in resolution 47/190 for a duration of one week during the month of June 1997 at the highest possible level of participation;

2. *Encourages* participants at the high-level meeting of the Commission on Sustainable Development to be held during its fourth session, in 1996, to address, *inter alia*, matters related to the special session of the General Assembly decided on above;

3. *Invites* the Commission to devote its Ad Hoc Open-ended Inter-Sessional Working Group meeting, to be held in February 1997, to assisting the Commission in undertaking the review for the special session;

4. *Welcomes* the decision of the Commission to devote its fifth session, in 1997, to preparations for the special session, and decides that that session of the Commission will be open-ended in its deliberations, allowing for the full participation of all States;

5. *Invites* the Commission to make available to the General Assembly at the special session all relevant reports prepared under the aegis of the Commission, along with the recommendations of the Commission thereon;

6. *Welcomes* the decisions of the Governing Council of the United Nations Environment Programme, in which the Council emphasized the need for the Programme, in accordance with its mandate in the implementation of Agenda 21, to continue to provide effective support to the work of the Commission on Sustainable Development, and in which the Council decided to hold its nineteenth session early in 1997 with a view to making a contribution to the special session;

7. *Invites* Governments as well as relevant regional and subregional organizations to consider undertaking reviews of progress achieved since the United Nations Conference on Environment and Development at the national, subregional, regional and interregional levels with a view to contributing to the preparations for the special session;

8. *Welcomes* the preparation of hemispheric, regional and subregional conferences on sustainable development, and in that context invites the Governments concerned to contribute to the special session the outcomes of such conferences;

9. *Also invites* all other relevant organizations and bodies of the United Nations system, including the United Nations Conference on Trade and Development, the specialized agencies and other multilateral organizations, including the multilateral financial institutions and the World Trade Organization, to contribute to the special session, and requests the Inter-Agency Committee on Sustainable Development, in close coordination with the Commission on Sustainable Development, to ensure an effective and coordinated system-wide response to the preparation of the special session;

10. *Further invites* the conferences of parties or other regulatory bodies of the United Nations Framework Convention on Climate Change, the Convention on Biological Diversity and the United Nations Convention to Combat Desertification in Those Countries Experiencing Serious Drought and/or Desertification, Particularly in Africa, as well as the regulatory bodies of other relevant instruments, as appropriate, and the Global Environment Facility, to provide their inputs to the special session;

11. *Recognizes* the important role played by major groups, including non-governmental organizations, at the United Nations Conference on Environment and Development and in the implementation of its recommendations, and recognizes the need for their active involvement in preparations for the special session, as well as the need to ensure appropriate arrangements for their contribution during the special session;

12. *Invites* Governments to assist the developing countries, in particular the least developed among them, in participating fully and effectively in the special session and its preparatory process, and in that regard invites them to make appropriate contributions to the Trust Fund to Support the Work of the Commission on Sustainable Development;

13. *Requests* the Secretary-General to prepare, for the consideration of the Commission on Sustainable Development at its fifth session, a comprehensive report containing an overall assessment of the progress achieved since the United Nations Conference on Environment and Development in the implementation of Agenda 21 at all levels, and in the implementation of related outcomes, as well as recommendations for future actions and priorities, and requests that the report include:

*(a)* Concise reports containing an assessment of the progress achieved in specific sectoral and cross-sectoral areas;

*(b)* Country profiles providing a concise presentation of progress made and constraints encountered in implementing Agenda 21 at the national level, compiled on the basis of national information received and in close cooperation with the Governments concerned;

*(c)* Major and emerging trends and issues within the framework of Agenda 21 and related outcomes of the Conference in the area of sustainable development, including the environmental impact of activities that are gravely hazardous to the environment, taking into account the views of States;

*(d)* Recommendations on the future role of the Commission in the follow-up to the outcome of the Conference and related outcomes, building on experience gained since 1992;

14. *Requests* the Secretary-General to mount a public information programme to raise global awareness of both the special session to review the implementation of Agenda 21 and the work undertaken by the United Nations in the follow-up to the Conference;

15. *Decides* that the preparations for the special session and the special session itself shall be kept within the agreed appropriation level for the 1996-1997 biennium;

16. *Decides* to include a sub-item entitled "Special session for the purpose of an overall review and appraisal of the implementation of Agenda 21" in the provisional agenda of its fifty-first session, and requests the Secretary-General to submit to it at that session a progress report on the state of preparations for the 1997 special session.

General Assembly resolution 50/113

20 December 1995      Meeting 96      Adopted without vote

Approved by Second Committee (A/50/618/Add.1) without vote, 12 December (meeting 43); draft by Vice-Chairman (A/C.2/50/L.78), based on informal consultations on draft by Philippines, for Group of 77 and China (A/C.2/50/L.23); agenda item 96 *(a)*.

*Financial implications.* 5th Committee, A/50/831; S-G, A/C.2/50/L.82, A/C.5/50/43.

*Meeting numbers.* GA 50th session: 2nd Committee 18-23, 37, 43; 5th Committee 41; plenary 96.

## Eradication of poverty
### Commission on Sustainable Development.

In a report on poverty eradication and sustainable development[59] considered in April by the Commission on Sustainable Development (see above), the Secretary-General described progress in implementing the provisions of chapter 3 of Agenda 21, adopted by UNCED in 1992,[17] and presented proposals for future action for poverty eradication.

The report concluded that systematic action was needed to implement the recommendations of UN organizations and agencies within a reasonable timeframe, taking into account the targets set at the 1995 World Summit for Social Development (see PART FOUR, Chapter IX). While economic growth would continue to be important, there was an urgent need to implement an explicit, poverty-reducing growth strategy incorporating measures to ensure environmental sustainability. Just as measures to combat poverty needed to be environmentally sound, the eradication of poverty was a necessary condition for sustainable development and for long-term socio-political stability—itself a precondition for sustained socio-economic development. Efforts to eliminate poverty should not be viewed as acts of charity but as an economic necessity to mobilize the productive potential of the poor for their own benefit and for that of society generally. To eradicate poverty and achieve environmental sustainability, it would be necessary to shift from traditional top-down approaches to development to bottom-up approaches that included the participation of all citizens in socio-political processes and in planning and implementing development programmes. In developing countries, the success of strategies to eradicate poverty and safeguard environmental integrity would depend on the extent of international cooperation, especially in terms of international trade, transfer of environmentally sound technologies and financial and technical support. The report suggested a number of themes to which the Commission on Sustainable Development could restrict itself when considering linkages between poverty and the natural environment.

In April,[18] the Commission on Sustainable Development adopted a decision on combating poverty, which it brought to the attention of the Economic and Social Council. It stressed that the promotion of full employment and the sustainable use of resources was an essential requirement for combating poverty and promoting social integration, noting that this was the primary responsibility of States themselves. Governments should create an enabling economic environment to promote more equitable access for all to income, resources and social services. The Commission recognized that women, who constituted the majority of those living in abject poverty, should be a central focus of poverty eradication efforts and urged the introduction of programmes focusing on the specific needs of children and youth. It recognized the need to promote access to food, water, employment, shelter, education, health, information, transportation and other essential public services. People living in poverty should have access to productive resources and sustainable livelihoods, including credit, land, education and training, and technology, and should be empowered to participate in formulating and implementing policies and decisions affecting them.

The Commission reaffirmed that a favourable international economic environment and the provision of financial and technical assistance were essential catalysts towards poverty eradication. Better terms of trade and better access to markets including on concessional and preferential terms—particularly for labour-intensive products, agricultural and agri-based products, and for those of medium- and small-scale enterprises, access to and transfer of environmentally sound technology on favourable terms—were also important conditions for sustainability. A durable solution to the external debt problems of heavily indebted LDCs and other low-income countries, particularly sub-Saharan countries, would help to free resources for poverty eradication programmes. Transfer of environmentally sound technologies was also indispensable for adopting sustainable production patterns, both in industry and agriculture. The Commission stressed that activities geared towards poverty eradication should be accompanied by programmes to reduce environmentally and socially unsustainable patterns of production and consumption.

The Commission reiterated the need for the full implementation of commitments, agreements and targets agreed upon by the international community to eradicate poverty and called on Governments, the international community, international financial institutions and NGOs to implement the poverty eradication commitments adopted at the World Summit for Social Development (see PART FOUR, Chapter IX) and at UNCED in Agenda 21. It recommended that the Economic and Social Council, when considering a common framework for implementing the outcome of UN conferences in the economic and social fields, examine how to ensure synergy and cooperation between the Commission and other functional commissions with responsibilities in the area of poverty eradication, including the proper division of labour among them.

**UNCTAD action.** The UNCTAD Standing Committee on Poverty Alleviation held its third session in Geneva from 12 to 16 June.[60] The Committee considered reports by the UNCTAD secretariat on international trade and poverty alleviation[61] and on aid effectiveness in international development cooperation for poverty alleviation.[62] Also before the Committee was an UNCTAD secretariat review of the implementation of the Standing Committee's work programme and proposed future orientation of its work[63] and a report on the workshop on poverty alleviation through international trade (Santiago, Chile, 10-13 January).[64]

In a series of agreed conclusions, the Standing Committee addressed the issues of the effects on the livelihood of the poor of elimination of trade barriers, increased competitiveness, trade flows, external shocks, diversification of exports, particularly of labour-intensive goods, and market access for such goods. It expressed concern over losses that could be incurred by LDCs and net food-importing developing countries due to possible price increases of imported food resulting from the Uruguay Round of multilateral trade negotiations, the Final Act of which was signed in 1994.[65] There would be a need for adequate food aid and for technical and financial assistance. The Standing Committee expressed concern over the decline in the quantity of ODA directed to developing countries and emphasized the need to meet internationally agreed aid targets. Consideration should be given to institutional methods such as targeting, decentralization, appraisal, monitoring and evaluation and an enabling environment and sustainability, so that ODA could reach and benefit the poor. Focusing on women was especially important if aid was to benefit the poor more effectively since women comprised the poorest of the poor and also used their incomes to feed, clothe and educate their children. It was agreed that food aid could play a major short-term role in relieving poverty, particularly for women and children; it could help eliminate present hunger among the poor and catalyze their self-reliant growth. However, access to income and other forms of purchasing power would be a more appropriate long-term strategy. Debt relief could be a principal element in helping poverty reduction if the freed resources were properly mobilized and channelled for developmental and poverty-alleviation purposes.

With regard to its work programme, the Standing Committee agreed that it had done valuable work on various issues since its establishment following UNCTAD VIII in 1992[66] and decided to transmit its recommendations and conclusions to UNCTAD IX, to be held in 1996. There was consensus that UNCTAD should continue its work on poverty issues, and agreement that the question of whether the existing form of intergovernmental machinery for addressing poverty alleviation was the appropriate one should be deferred to UNCTAD IX for consideration.

**Report of the Secretary-General.** In response to a 1993 General Assembly request,[67] the Secretary-General submitted a September 1995 report[68] on international cooperation for the eradication of poverty in developing countries. Based on information provided by UN organizations and bodies, the report discussed poverty eradication as a common theme of major international conferences: UNCED, the 1994 International Conference on Population and Development[69] and the 1995 Fourth World Conference on Women (see PART FOUR, Chapter X). It also took up the World Summit for Social Development (see PART FOUR, Chapter IX) as the framework for inter-agency cooperation for the eradication of poverty and gave an overview of policies, multisectoral strategies and programmes relating to poverty, providing examples of poverty eradication programmes and coordination mechanisms at the country level— Indonesia, Jamaica, Malawi, Pakistan, Philippines, Sri Lanka and Zimbabwe.

In concluding observations and recommendations, the report stated that although the primary responsibility for coordination belonged to Governments, the UN system could assist in strengthening the capacity of Governments for such coordination. Governments had to demonstrate a firm commitment to the goal of poverty eradication and be willing to mobilize and allocate the required domestic financial and human resources for that purpose. UN agencies could play an advocacy role, provide financial and technical assistance and help develop coherent and complementary poverty-eradication programmes. UN agencies must work together to help build the capacity of Governments to carry out their leadership and coordinating responsibilities, it was stated. A key question was the relationship between the United Nations, its funds and programmes and the specialized agencies on the one hand, and the Bretton Woods institutions on the other. An integrated poverty agenda could move forward if the Bretton Woods institutions and the rest of the system could develop common approaches, definitions, poverty-assessment indicators and data collection and also work towards greater complementarity and integration between economic and social policies.

However, even the best formulated strategies and well-coordinated programmes required resources in order to be implemented effectively. Determined efforts had to be made at the national and international levels to mobilize and reallocate resources towards the goal of poverty eradication. In that regard, the commitments and goals of major international conferences, particularly the World Summit for Social Development, should be fully adhered to and implemented by all countries.

**Joint Meetings of CPC and ACC.** Participants in the twenty-ninth Joint Meetings of the Committee for Programme and Coordination (CPC) and ACC (New York, 16 October)[70] discussed coordination of activities of the UN system for the eradication of poverty. They reviewed a background paper on the subject,[71] prepared by the Secretariat.

It was concluded that the eradication of poverty was a top priority for UN system work and should be pursued in the coordinated follow-up to global conferences, particularly the World Summit for Social Development. Since efforts to eradicate poverty should be based on individual country goals and plans, the success of UN coordination efforts had to be measured at the country level. There was a need to identify and assess practical measures to enhance coordination within the UN system and to mobilize adequate resources and use them effectively and efficiently. The Meetings noted that ACC (New York, 12 and 13 October)[72] had established three inter-agency task forces on three topics, closely related to the eradiction of poverty, to follow up on recent global conferences: basic social services for all; employment and sustainable livelihoods; and an enabling environment for social and economic development. They noted that consideration was being given to establishing an inter-agency task force to follow up on the outcome of the Fourth World Conference on Women. The efforts of the UN system had to be integrated with those of Governments and NGOs at community and national levels and the resident coordinator had a key role to play at the field level, the Meetings stated.

By **decision 1995/321** of 12 December, the Economic and Social Council decided that the coordination segment of its 1996 substantive session should be devoted to coordination of the activities of the UN system for the eradication of poverty.

## International Year and
## UN Decade for the Eradication of Poverty

In response to a 1994 General Assembly request,[73] the Secretariat submitted to the Economic and Social Council a June note[74] containing elements of a draft programme for the International Year for the Eradication of Poverty, to be observed in 1996. In outlining the principles, objectives and themes for the Year, the report took into account the commitments contained in the Copenhagen Declaration and Programme of Action of the World Summit for Social Development (see PART FOUR, Chapter IX). The report described activities envisaged for observing the Year at the international level and provided some examples of possible activities at the national level.

In **decision 1995/234** of 17 and 19 July, the Council took note of the Secretariat's note.

In an October report[75] to the General Assembly, the Secretary-General elaborated on the proposals contained in the Secretariat note to the Council, taking into account observations and suggestions received from Member States, as well as additional information provided from within the UN system and by non-governmental and other intergovernmental organizations.

**GENERAL ASSEMBLY ACTION**

On 20 December, the General Assembly adopted **resolution 50/107**.

### Observance of the International Year for the Eradication of Poverty and proclamation of the First United Nations Decade for the Eradication of Poverty

*The General Assembly,*

*Reaffirming* its resolutions 43/195 of 20 December 1988, 44/212 of 22 December 1989, 45/213 of 21 December 1990, 46/141 of 17 December 1991, 47/197 of 22 December 1992, 48/184 of 21 December 1993 and 49/110 of 19 December 1994, all related to international cooperation for the eradication of poverty in developing countries,

*Recalling* its resolution 48/183 of 21 December 1993, in which it proclaimed 1996 International Year for the Eradication of Poverty,

*Recalling also* its resolution 49/110, in which it requested that a draft programme on the preparations for and observance of the Year be elaborated at an early date,

*Emphasizing* the necessity for Governments to focus their efforts and policies on addressing the root causes of poverty and providing for the basic needs of all,

*Recognizing* that the eradication of poverty requires ensuring universal access to economic opportunities that will promote sustainable livelihood and making basic

efforts to facilitate access to opportunities and services for the disadvantaged, and that people living in poverty and vulnerable groups must be empowered through organization and social life, in particular in the planning and implementation of policies that affect them, thus enabling them to become genuine partners in development,

*Also recognizing* that economic development, social development and environmental protection are interdependent and mutually reinforcing components of sustainable development, which is the framework for efforts to achieve a higher quality of life for all people, and that equitable social development, which empowers people living in poverty to utilize environmental resources sustainably, is a necessary foundation for sustainable development,

*Stressing* the necessity to promote and implement policies to create a supportive external economic environment, through, *inter alia*, cooperation in the formulation and implementation of macroeconomic policies, trade liberalization, mobilization and/or the provision of new and additional financial resources that are both adequate and predictable and mobilized in a way that maximizes the availability of such resources for sustainable development, using all available funding sources and mechanisms, enhanced financial stability and ensuring increased access of developing countries to global markets, productive investments and technologies, and appropriate knowledge,

*Also stressing* that the United Nations system should play a central role in enhancing support and assistance for developing countries, in particular African countries and least developed countries, in their efforts to achieve the objectives set forth in the Copenhagen Declaration and Programme of Action of the World Summit for Social Development, as well as in the major United Nations conferences organized since 1990 towards the eradication of poverty,

*Emphasizing* that empowering women will be a critical factor in the eradication of poverty, since women constitute a majority of people living in poverty and since they contribute to the economy and to combating poverty through both their remunerated and their unremunerated work at home, in the community and in the workplace,

*Considering* that the international community at the highest political level has already reached a consensus and committed itself to the eradication of poverty in recent major United Nations conferences, including the United Nations Conference on Environment and Development, the International Conference on Population and Development, the Fourth World Conference on Women and in particular the World Summit for Social Development, which addressed the eradication of poverty as one of its three major themes, as well as the expected contributions from the forthcoming United Nations Conference on Human Settlements (Habitat II) and the ninth session of the United Nations Conference on Trade and Development and the World Food Summit,

*Noting* the importance attached at the summit meeting of seven major industrialized countries, held at Halifax, Canada, from 15 to 17 June 1995, in considering measures towards the eradication of poverty,

*Bearing in mind* that Governments decided to adopt the appropriate measures and mechanisms for implementing and monitoring the outcome of the World Summit for Social Development, with the assistance, upon request, of the specialized agencies, programmes, funds and regional commissions of the United Nations system, with broad participation of all sectors of civil society,

*Recalling* the Copenhagen Declaration and Programme of Action of the World Summit for Social Development, in particular paragraph 95(c) of the Programme of Action, in which it is recommended that the General Assembly, at its fiftieth session, declare the first United Nations Decade for the Eradication of Poverty, following the International Year for the Eradication of Poverty (1996), with a view to considering further initiatives on the eradication of poverty,

*Having considered* the reports of the Secretary-General on the draft programme for the observance of the International Year for the Eradication of Poverty and on international cooperation for the eradication of poverty in developing countries,

*Taking note* of the Secretary-General's proposal in response to resolution 49/110 of 19 December 1994, that the theme of the international year for the eradication of poverty be "Poverty can be and must be eradicated throughout the World",

I. Observance of the International Year for the Eradication of Poverty (1996)

1. *Urges* all Governments, the international community, including the United Nations system, and all other actors in society to pursue seriously the objective of the eradication of poverty within the context of the International Year for the Eradication of Poverty (1996);

2. *Reaffirms* that the activities for the observance of the Year shall be undertaken at all levels, and that assistance should be provided by the United Nations system with a view to creating among States, policy makers and international public opinion a greater awareness of the fact that the eradication of poverty is both a complex and multidimensional problem, and is fundamental to reinforcing peace and achieving sustainable development;

3. *Decides* that the aim of the activities during the Year shall be to support a longer-term, sustained effort to implement fully and effectively the commitments, recommendations and measures undertaken, and the basic provisions already agreed upon at major United Nations conferences since 1990, in particular the World Summit for Social Development and the Fourth World Conference on Women;

4. *Also decides* that, in order to achieve the goal of eradicating poverty, activities during the Year, at all levels, shall be guided, *inter alia*, by the following principles:

(a) A sustained, collective commitment and effort shall be mounted by Governments, local administrations, all relevant actors of civil society, including non-governmental organizations, business and corporations, supported by the international community, including the United Nations system and relevant subregional, regional and other international organizations, and anti-poverty strategies and programmes shall be designed, implemented and monitored with the full and effective participation of people living in poverty;

(b) Measures shall be adopted to ensure that people living in poverty have access to the resources and opportunities necessary to escape from poverty, and policies shall be adopted to ensure that all people have adequate economic and social protection during unemployment, ill health, maternity, child-rearing, widowhood, disability and old age;

(c) Access of all people living in poverty to basic social services shall be ensured, as well as their participation in the economic, social, cultural and political life of society;

(d) Women shall be given the economic and social opportunities to contribute to development, and anti-poverty strategies and programmes shall be designed with a gender dimension;

(e) Targeted programmes shall be developed to meet the special needs of particular social and demographic groups, including young people, disadvantaged older persons, persons with disabilities and other vulnerable and disadvantaged groups of persons;

(f) The international community shall provide continued and effective support to broad-based development in developing countries, in particular in Africa and the least developed countries;

(g) The efforts of the United Nations system to achieve the overall goal of eradicating poverty should be well coordinated in order to ensure that activities of relevant organizations are complementary and cost-effective;

5. *Recommends* that all States, as set out in the Copenhagen Declaration on Social Development and Programme of Action of the World Summit for Social Development, undertake the following, preferably by 1996:

(a) Develop a precise definition and assessment of absolute poverty;

(b) Elaborate the measurements, criteria and indicators for determining the extent and distribution of absolute poverty;

(c) Formulate or strengthen, as a matter of urgency, national policies and strategies geared to substantially reducing overall poverty in the shortest possible time, reducing inequalities and eradicating absolute poverty by a target date to be specified by each country in its national context;

(d) Increase public efforts to eradicate absolute poverty and to reduce overall poverty substantially by, *inter alia*, formulating or strengthening and implementing national poverty eradication plans to address the structural causes of poverty, encompassing action on the local, national, subregional, regional and international levels;

(e) Attach particular attention, in the context of national plans, to employment creation as a means of eradicating poverty, while also giving appropriate consideration to health and education, assigning a higher priority to basic social services, generating household income and promoting access to productive assets and economic opportunities;

6. *Urges* Governments to review, adopt and maintain macroeconomic policies and development strategies that address the needs and efforts of women living in poverty, in particular in rural areas, as set out in paragraph 58 of the Platform for Action adopted by the Fourth World Conference on Women;

7. *Reaffirms* the agreement to a mutual commitment between interested developed and developing country partners to allocate, on average, 20 per cent of official

development assistance and 20 per cent of the national budget, respectively, to basic social programmes;

8. *Stresses* that, during the Year and beyond, people living in poverty and their organizations should be empowered by being fully involved in the setting of targets and in the design, implementation, monitoring and assessment of national strategies and programmes for the eradication of poverty and the development of community bases, ensuring that such programmes reflect their priorities;

9. *Notes* the activities for the observance of the Year planned by the organizations and bodies of the United Nations system, as contained in the report of the Secretary-General, and invites them to take further initiatives;

10. *Urges* multilateral financial and development institutions to intensify and accelerate their investments in social sectors and poverty eradication programmes;

11. *Takes note* of decision 95/22 of the Executive Board of the United Nations Development Programme, in which the Board decided to give poverty elimination the overriding priority in Programme activities and to concentrate its programmes on the most needy regions and countries, in particular the least developed countries, especially in Africa;

12. *Invites* all relevant specialized agencies, funds, programmes and related organizations of the United Nations system to strengthen and adjust their activities, programmes and strategies, as appropriate, in order to achieve the overall goal of eradicating poverty and meeting the basic human needs of all;

13. *Welcomes* the recent decision taken by the Administrative Committee on Coordination to establish task forces on different aspects of the follow-up to United Nations major conferences with a view to considering issues related to the eradication of poverty;

14. *Takes note* of the decision taken by the Administrator of the United Nations Development Programme to establish an eradication of poverty fund for the duration of the International Year for the Eradication of Poverty in order to help developing countries, in particular African countries and the least developed countries, in the elaboration of national plans during 1996 to combat poverty;

15. *Requests* the Secretary-General to take all relevant measures to arrange for the wide and effective dissemination of the present resolution and the programme for the observance of the Year, and in this regard invites all States, organizations of the United Nations system, relevant international organizations, concerned national organizations, non-governmental organizations and other interested groups of civil society to give the necessary attention to the observance of the Year;

II.  First United Nations Decade for the
Eradication of Poverty (1997-2006)

16. *Proclaims* the first United Nations Decade for the Eradication of Poverty (1997-2006);

17. *Urges* all Governments and the international community, including the United Nations system, and all other actors in society to pursue effectively the implementation of the outcomes of major United Nations conferences related to the eradication of poverty, in particular the World Summit for Social Development;

18. *Welcomes* the arrangements, within the agreed appropriation level for the biennium 1996-1997 made by

the Secretary-General regarding the entity within the Secretariat required to undertake the functions needed in support of the system-wide implementation of the International Year for the Eradication of Poverty, including activities of the Decade;

19. *Requests* the Secretary-General to invite those organs, organizations, programmes, funds and bodies of the United Nations system that have not already done so to consider the establishment of focal points and other similar mechanisms so that they may effectively implement the provisions, agreements and outcomes of major United Nations conferences relevant to the eradication of poverty;

20. *Recalls* the coordinating role of the Economic and Social Council in the activities of the United Nations system towards eradication of poverty in the context of the coordinated follow-up of the outcome of the major United Nations conferences and summits organized since 1990 in the economic, social and related fields;

21. *Stresses* the importance of ensuring, at the intergovernmental and inter-agency levels, coherent, comprehensive and integrated activities for the Year and Decade, according to the outcome of the major United Nations conferences and summits organized since 1990 in the economic, social and related fields;

22. *Invites* the Administrative Committee on Coordination to ensure, in particular through the inter-agency task forces, the involvement and coordination of all relevant organs, organizations and bodies of the United Nations system for a full and effective implementation of the present resolution and to submit to the General Assembly, at its fifty-first session, through the Economic and Social Council, reports on activities envisaged in support of the Decade, taking into account the outcome of the major United Nations conferences and summits organized since 1990 in the economic, social and related fields;

23. *Calls upon* States, the United Nations system, relevant international organizations and all other actors concerned with the Decade to participate actively in the financial and technical support of the Decade, in particular with a view to translating all measures and recommendations into operational and concrete poverty eradication programmes and activities;

24. *Decides* that the trust fund of the World Summit for Social Development established in accordance with General Assembly resolution 47/92 of 16 December 1992 to finance preparatory activities be continued and renamed the Trust Fund for the Follow-up to the World Summit for Social Development, under the authority of the Secretary-General, with the aim of supporting programmes, seminars and activities for the promotion of social development in the implementation of the Copenhagen Declaration and Programme of Action of the World Summit for Social Development, which include activities of the first United Nations Decade for the Eradication of Poverty, and invites all States to contribute to the Fund;

25. *Requests*, therefore, that the Secretary-General ensure that the outcomes of major United Nations conferences are disseminated as widely as possible and also to ensure that the documents related to the Year and the United Nations Decade for the Eradication of Poverty, once adopted, are transmitted to all States, relevant international and regional organizations, multilateral financial institutions and regional development

banks in order to secure their active and substantial contributions;

26. *Recommends* that donor countries give greater priority to the eradication of poverty in their assistance programmes and budgets, on either a bilateral or multilateral basis;

27. *Encourages* developing countries to mobilize domestic and external resources for poverty eradication programmes and activities, and to facilitate their full and effective implementation;

28. *Requests* the Secretary-General to submit to the General Assembly at its fifty-first session, in one document, a progress report on action taken by the United Nations system to implement the programme for the observance of the Year and action envisaged to be taken in preparation for the Decade;

29. *Decides* to include in the provisional agenda of its fifty-first session an item entitled "First United Nations Decade for the Eradication of Poverty (1997-2006)".

General Assembly resolution 50/107

20 December 1995     Meeting 96     Adopted without vote

Approved by Second Committee (A/50/617/Add.9) without vote, 12 December (meeting 43); draft by Vice-Chairman (A/C.2/50/L.80), based on informal consultations on draft by Philippines, for Group of 77 and China (A/C.2/50/L.39) and orally revised; agenda item 95 *(i)*.

*Meeting numbers.* GA 50th session: 2nd Committee 35-37, 40, 43; plenary 96.

## Economic cooperation among developing countries

**UNCTAD action.** The UNCTAD Standing Committee on Economic Cooperation among Developing Countries (ECDC) held its third session in Geneva from 19 to 23 June.[76] It had before it UNCTAD secretariat reports on enlarging and deepening monetary, financial and investment cooperation among developing countries and promoting cooperation of the enterprise sectors of developing countries;[77] evaluation of major developments in the area of ECDC, including implications of the Uruguay Round results on ECDC arrangements and regular consultations, technical support, assistance and skill development;[78] and review of the work programme of the Standing Committee with special emphasis on the preparations for UNCTAD IX.[79]

In a series of agreed conclusions, the Committee stated that: trade financing was an essential facet of ECDC, which, in addition to trade, underpinned business, investment and technological cooperation; capital market cooperation was of major importance for mobilizing financial resources; among regional partners, predictable monetary policies were prerequisites for stable and realistic foreign exchange rates; the attainment of currency convertibility by some developing countries did not diminish the importance of their clearing and payments arrangements, which continued to play an important role in credit extension and monetary-policy coordination; direct investment among developing countries should be en-

couraged, as should cross-border business activities and export-processing, industrial and special economic zones in developing countries; it was important to expand contacts and linkages among business enterprises of developing countries, and participation of the enterprise sector in meetings of ECDC arrangements and other international forums, such as UNCTAD and the International Trade Centre (ITC), should be encouraged, as should joint multi-enterprise and multi-country technological cooperation efforts encompassing research institutes, universities and venture capital financing associations; emphasis should be placed on exchanges of experiences among the various regions; special attention needed to be given to Africa, particularly to LDCs; and UNCTAD coordination with other UN agencies, including UNDP, the regional commissions and ITC was important.

The Standing Committee felt that it had carried out a valuable work programme during its three sessions. As for future work on ECDC, UNCTAD had a role to play and should continue its work on issues where it had expertise and competence. It was agreed that the question of institutional reform should be deferred to UNCTAD IX for consideration.

### South-South cooperation

**Intergovernmental Meeting of Experts.** Pursuant to a 1994 General Assembly resolution,[80] the Intergovernmental Meeting of Experts on South-South Cooperation was convened in New York from 31 July to 4 August 1995.[81] The Meeting considered reports on the status of South-South cooperation and the emerging issues[82] and on expanding South-South cooperation: some suggested issues and modalities.[83] It also considered reports of the UNCTAD Standing Committee on ECDC (see above) and the report of the High-level Committee on the Review of Technical Cooperation among Developing Countries on the work of its ninth (1995) session (see next chapter).

In a summary of the Meeting's discussions, the Chairman stated that South-South cooperation was a viable mode of international economic and technical cooperation. The resurgence of interest shown by developing countries in South-South cooperation through ECDC and technical cooperation among developing countries (TCDC) had been characterized by an increase in an open and flexible framework for such cooperation. It was emphasized that South-South cooperation was a dynamic process which needed to be examined in the light of a new and emerging international environment; such cooperation could facilitate the integration of developing countries into the world economy. Areas addressed during the Meeting's deliberations included: regional economic cooperation and integration; globalization and liberalization; trade among developing countries; the impact of the Uruguay Round; information, communication and technology; the special needs of Africa, LDCs and land-locked developing countries; the special needs of small island States; follow-up to UN conferences; and donor and UN system support to South-South cooperation. The Meeting also listed a number of elements of successful South-South cooperation strategies.

**Report of the Secretary-General.** In response to General Assembly requests of 1993[84] and 1994,[80] the Secretary-General submitted a September 1995 report on the state of South-South cooperation.[85] The report assessed the state of institutional arrangements for South-South cooperation at the subregional, regional and global levels, the state of cooperation in trade and monetary and financial cooperation, and the state of other priority functional areas (industry and enterprises; agriculture and food security; transport and communications; natural resources, including commodities, energy and the environment; education, science and technology; and social development).

The addendum contained information received from UN organizations and agencies on action taken to promote and strengthen South-South cooperation.

**GENERAL ASSEMBLY ACTION**

On 20 December, the General Assembly adopted **resolution 50/119**.

**Economic and technical cooperation among developing countries and a United Nations conference on South-South cooperation**

*The General Assembly,*

*Reaffirming* its resolutions 33/134 of 19 December 1978, in which it endorsed the Buenos Aires Plan of Action for Promoting and Implementing Technical Cooperation among Developing Countries, and 46/159 of 19 December 1991 on technical cooperation among developing countries, as well as other relevant resolutions of the General Assembly on economic and technical cooperation among developing countries,

*Reaffirming also* its resolution 49/96 of 19 December 1994 on a United Nations conference on South-South cooperation,

*Recalling* Economic and Social Council resolution 1992/41 of 30 July 1992, in which the Council called upon all parties in the development effort to make concerted, planned and vigorous endeavours to benefit from utilization of the capacities of developing countries by giving their full support and first consideration to the use of the modality of technical cooperation among developing countries,

*Taking note* of the decisions and recommendations contained in the Final Document of the Eleventh Conference of Heads of State or Government of the Non-Aligned Countries, held at Cartagena de Indias, Colombia, from 18 to 20 October 1995,

*Bearing in mind* the Ministerial Declaration of the Group of 77, adopted at the nineteenth annual meeting of the Ministers for Foreign Affairs of the Group of 77, held in New York on 29 September 1995, which emphasized the importance of South-South cooperation, particularly the convening of a United Nations conference on South-South cooperation no later than 1997,

*Reaffirming* that South-South cooperation constitutes an important element of international cooperation for development as well as an essential basis for national and collective self-reliance and a means of promoting the integration of developing countries into the world economy,

*Reaffirming also* that South-South cooperation is not a substitute for, but is complementary to, North-South cooperation,

*Noting with satisfaction* the increase in economic and technical cooperation among developing countries reported by both developing countries and the United Nations development system,

*Recognizing* the need for the international community to support the developing countries in optimizing opportunities for expanding South-South cooperation,

*Welcoming* the report on new directions for technical cooperation among developing countries, prepared in response to General Assembly resolution 49/96 of 19 December 1994, whose recommendations were endorsed by the High-level Committee on the Review of Technical Cooperation among Developing Countries at its ninth session, and subsequently endorsed by the Economic and Social Council,

*Noting with satisfaction* the launching of the South Centre as an intergovernmental organization, and its important contribution to the promotion and strengthening of South-South cooperation,

*Recognizing* that recent advances in communications technology have created new opportunities for South-South cooperation,

*Taking note* of the report of the Intergovernmental Meeting of Experts on South-South Cooperation, convened by the Secretary-General in New York from 31 July to 4 August 1995, and of the reports of the Standing Committee on Economic Cooperation among Developing Countries of the United Nations Conference on Trade and Development and of the High-level Committee on the Review of Technical Cooperation among Developing Countries on the work of its ninth session, at which substantive issues were presented and practical modalities for strengthening South-South economic and technical cooperation at the global level were recommended,

1. *Takes note* of the report of the Secretary-General on the state of South-South cooperation and its supplement entitled *State of South-South Cooperation: Statistical Pocket Book and Index of Cooperation Organizations,*[a] which provide a comprehensive and systematic overview and analysis of South-South cooperation worldwide and of United Nations system support for such cooperation;

2. *Endorses* the recommendations contained in the report on new directions for technical cooperation among developing countries, which among other things call for the adoption of a more strategic orientation for technical cooperation among developing countries focusing on

---

[a]Sales No. E.95.II.D.18.

priority issues, such as trade and investment, debt, the environment, poverty alleviation, production and employment, and macroeconomic policy coordination, as well as education, health, the transfer of technology and rural development, which are likely to have a major development impact on a large number of developing countries;

3. *Welcomes* the decision of the Executive Board of the United Nations Development Programme to increase the allocation of resources for technical cooperation among developing countries during the next programming cycle;

4. *Calls upon* all Governments and relevant United Nations organizations, including the multilateral financial institutions, to consider increasing allocations for economic and technical cooperation among developing countries and to identify new funding modalities to promote South-South cooperation such as triangular cooperation and private-sector funding;

5. *Invites* the United Nations Development Programme to establish a voluntary trust fund for the promotion of South-South cooperation and invites all countries to contribute to the fund;

6. *Calls upon* the developing countries and their institutions to increase joint efforts in technology cooperation, broader technological development such as encompasses scientific and technological management capabilities and information networks that are demand-oriented and involve participation by users of technology or by those involved in the process of technological development, infrastructure and human resources development;

7. *Welcomes* the decision of the United Nations Conference on Trade and Development to address at its ninth session the issue of new approaches to South-South economic cooperation, as well as the role and potential impact on development of regional economic groupings in the globalizing and liberalizing world economy;

8. *Invites*, in this context, the United Nations Conference on Trade and Development, at its ninth session, to be held in South Africa, to consider strengthening economic and technical cooperation among developing countries as a strategy for promoting growth and development and for ensuring the effective integration of the developing countries into the world economy, and to formulate concrete policy recommendations in this regard;

9. *Requests* the Secretary-General to present to the General Assembly, on a biennial basis, a report entitled "State of South-South cooperation" containing a comprehensive overview and analysis of South-South economic and technical cooperation worldwide and international support in this regard, including quantitative data and indicators on all aspects of South-South cooperation as well as recommendations for strengthening such cooperation, keeping in view the importance of the proposal to convene a United Nations conference on South-South cooperation;

10. *Invites* all other organs, organizations and agencies of the United Nations system, in particular the United Nations Conference on Trade and Development and the regional commissions, to provide analytical and empirical material for the preparation of the above-mentioned report;

11. *Decides* to include in the provisional agenda of its fifty-second session the sub-item entitled "Economic and technical cooperation among developing countries".

General Assembly resolution 50/119

20 December 1995     Meeting 96     Adopted without vote

Approved by Second Committee (A/50/619) without vote, 5 December (meeting 41); draft by Vice-Chairman (A/C.2/50/L.48), based on informal consultations on draft by Colombia (for Non-Aligned Movement) and Philippines (for Group of 77 and China) (A/C.2/50/L.24); agenda item 97.
*Meeting numbers.* GA 50th session: 2nd Committee 24-29, 37, 41; plenary 96.

## Science and technology for development

**Commission on Science and Technology for Development.** The Commission on Science and Technology for Development, at its second session (Geneva, 15-24 May),[86] had before it an overview[87] of the reports of panels of experts that had met in 1994 and 1995 to discuss the following subjects: technology for small-scale economic activities to address the basic needs of low-income populations, which met twice in 1994[88] and again from 18 to 20 January 1995;[89] gender implications of science and technology for developing countries;[88] the science and technology aspects of the sectoral issue to be discussed by the Commission on Sustainable Development in 1995 (science and technology for integrated land management);[90] and the contribution of technologies, including new and emerging technologies, to industrialization in developing countries.[90] Other substantive reports considered by the Commission dealt with: coordination mechanisms in science and technology within the UN system;[91] activities of the UN system in the field of science and technology for development, including cooperation in technology assessment;[92] information technologies for development;[93] progress achieved and problems encountered in the application of science and technology for sustainable development;[94] and scientific and technological aspects of the conversion of military capacities for civilian use and sustainable development.[95] By a March note,[96] the UNCTAD secretariat transmitted the final report (1994) of the Ad Hoc Working Group on the Interrelationship between Investment and Technology Transfer[90] and, by a February note,[97] it transmitted the report of the 1994 Consultative Meeting on a Coalition of Resources for Science and Technology for Development.[98] Following consideration of those reports, the Commission recommended to the Economic and Social Council for adoption an omnibus draft resolution on science and technology for development (**resolution 1995/4**). The Commission also recommended to the Council for adoption a draft decision on the report of its second session and a provisional agenda and documentation for the third (1997) session.

In other action, the Commission adopted two resolutions and two decisions, which it brought to the Council's attention. By the first resolution,[99] it decided to set up, for a duration of four years and on the basis of extrabudgetary resources, an Advisory Board on Gender Issues as an expert group to facilitate the Commission's future deliberations on the gender implications of science and technology for developing countries. By the second resolution,[(100)] the Commission decided to promote and authorize the broadest dissemination of the reports and documentation of its panels and working groups. Such dissemination should follow the principles and guidelines of UN publications, acknowledging that the contents represented the views of experts and that their work had been conducted under the auspices of the Commission. In its first decision,[(101)] the Commission set out working methods to be used in implementing its work programme and requested the secretariat to report to it on the use of all resources made available for the work programme. The secretariat was also asked to provide a spending plan on an annual basis, indicating proposed expenditure and allocation of resources for the work programme and a six-month progress report on the work programme and its financial aspects. By its second decision,[(102)] the Commission called the Council's attention to the problem of lack of synchronization of the terms of Commission members with the timing of the Commission's third (1997) session. It recommended that the Council take steps to resolve this problem to ensure the Commission's efficient functioning.

### ECONOMIC AND SOCIAL COUNCIL ACTION

On 19 July, the Economic and Social Council adopted **resolution 1995/4**.

### Science and technology for development

*The Economic and Social Council,*

*Recognizing* the unique role of the Commission on Science and Technology for Development as a global forum for the examination of science and technology questions, for improving understanding of science and technology policies for development and for the formulation of recommendations and guidelines on science and technology matters within the United Nations system, all in relation to development,

*Recognizing further* that the Commission, in carrying out its work, should pay special attention to the needs and requirements of developing countries, in particular the least developed countries, and that it should also take into consideration the relevant problems of countries with economies in transition,

*Noting* the efforts of the Commission to adopt a new working style consisting of panels and working groups that take advantage of the available expertise of representatives of States Members of the Commission and have responsibility for preparing draft reports for consideration by the Commission,

*Taking note with appreciation* of the reports prepared by the panels and working groups of the Commission, pursuant to decisions taken at its first session, entitled "Science and technology for basic needs: a bridge", "Science and technology for sustainable human devel-

opment: the gender dimension", "Science and technology for integrated land management" and "Strengthening of linkages between the national research and development systems and industrial sectors", and the recommendations contained therein,

*Noting also* the other relevant documents submitted to the Commission for consideration at its second session,

*Recognizing* the need to focus the future inter-sessional activities of the Commission on a limited number of substantive themes,

*Recognizing further* that information and communication are important requisites for planning, development and decision-making in science and technology, and also recognizing the far-reaching implications of information technologies for society,

*Basic needs, gender, land management, research and development, industrialization, coordination, financing and other matters arising from the first session of the Commission and work programme for the inter-sessional period 1995-1997*

1. *Invites* Governments to undertake systematic reviews of each major component of their macroeconomic policy frameworks and to take measures to address any unwarranted disincentives for healthy and progressive informal and small and medium-sized productive sectors, and to create an enabling environment for the scientific and technological community to take initiatives to link technologies, in a participatory manner, with entrepreneurs from those sectors;

2. *Decides* to draw the attention of Member States to the importance of targeted research and development and the application of science and technology in helping to satisfy basic needs, requests the relevant United Nations bodies and donor organizations to assist interested countries in formulating policies and action plans to implement, evaluate and improve efforts for that purpose, and requests Member States and relevant organizations to report on the outcome of those endeavours to the Commission on Science and Technology for Development at its third session;

3. *Decides* that the Commission should assist the United Nations system in identifying and promoting replicable demonstration activities and programmes, involving different countries from diverse regions, that apply science and technology to the satisfaction of basic needs, and recommends that the operational mechanisms of the United Nations system, including the Department for Development Support and Management Services of the United Nations Secretariat, the regional commissions and other relevant organizations, such as the United Nations Development Programme, disseminate information and facilitate the application of science and technology in meeting basic needs;

4. *Recognizes* that the role of the United Nations in promoting better awareness of relationships between gender and science and technology is crucial, and requests the Secretary-General and United Nations organs and bodies to consider and take the necessary action to implement the recommendations addressed to the United Nations system contained in the report of the Panel on the Gender Implications of Science and Technology for Developing Countries, and to report thereon to the Commission at its subsequent sessions;

5. *Recommends* that all Governments adopt the Declaration of Intent on Gender, Science and Technology for Sustainable Human Development set out in the annex

to the present resolution, conduct reviews of the national situation regarding gender and science and technology through special committees within or outside existing suitable mechanisms, formulate action plans, and report publicly and to the Commission on progress in achieving the goals of the declaration of intent by the end of 1996 and 1998, and calls upon donor countries and agencies to assist the follow-up activities of the committees;

6. *Recommends* that the principles set out in the report of the Panel on the Science and Technology Aspects of the Sectoral Issue on science and technology for integrated land management be further elaborated to provide guidelines for the application of technologies that support integrated land management under site- and region-specific conditions, and, for that purpose, invites the Food and Agriculture Organization of the United Nations, the United Nations Environment Programme, the United Nations Centre for Human Settlements (Habitat) and the International Fund for Agricultural Development, in cooperation with the regional commissions, where appropriate, to elaborate such guidelines and work together with a view to designing programmes to address specific land-management problems and assisting developing countries and economies in transition in implementing such programmes and sharing the information thus obtained;

7. *Notes* that the research and development systems in most developing countries, in particular the least developed countries, and in some countries with economies in transition, do not provide sufficient support to the improvement of sustainable industrial development in those countries, and recommends that the international community, through multilateral and bilateral aid and, generally, through the enhancement of linkages with enterprises, universities, foundations, research institutes, scientific laboratories, trade and professional associations, and other channels and mechanisms for international scientific and technological cooperation, should strengthen its support for countries undertaking reforms in their research and development systems and their efforts in building innovative capacities;

8. *Requests* Governments and intergovernmental and non-governmental organizations to give priority to effective access to networks, such as the Internet, by scientific and technical institutions in developing countries, in particular the least developed countries, and countries with economies in transition, through the provision of technical and other support for related investments, and to facilitate appropriate electronic communication among institutions engaged in science and technology for development;

9. *Requests* the Commission on Science and Technology for Development and the United Nations Conference on Trade and Development to liaise in establishing a programme of country reviews on science, technology and innovation policy for interested countries, also requests the Commission to consider providing advisory inputs, analytical support and evaluation, as need be, in the carrying out of such country reviews, and requests the United Nations Development Programme to explore the possibilities of contributing to the funding of such activities from its centrally controlled resources;

10. *Recognizes* that technological capacity-building is a major factor in the process of effective technology transfer and long-term growth, and invites the United Nations system and the international community to support the implementation of projects specially designed to foster technological capacity-building in interested countries, including least developed countries;

11. *Recalls* the agreed conclusions on coordination of the policies and activities of the specialized agencies and other bodies of the United Nations system related to science and technology for development adopted at its substantive session of 1994, and, in that context, decides that the Commission, in its substantive work, should maximize coordination in undertaking its inter-sessional studies on specific issues by relating actively to competent United Nations organs and agencies, as well as other multilateral organizations;

12. *Decides* that the Commission, in reviewing the activities of the United Nations system in science and technology, should highlight innovative programme concepts and designs of common interest and bring them to the attention of the science and technology community, with an indication of their resource implications, and should use them as a basis for building ad hoc resource coalitions;

13. *Decides also* that the main substantive theme that will constitute the focus of the work of the Commission during the inter-sessional period 1995-1997 will be information technologies and their implications for development;

14. *Decides further* to set up panels and/or working groups to analyse, elaborate and make recommendations on issues related to information technologies, possibly including:

(*a*) Analysis of the application of information technologies in different groups of countries with a view to making recommendations to enhance the diffusion of information technologies in key sectors of their economies;

(*b*) The implications of the revolutionary improvements in the cost effectiveness of information technologies for the development of a global information infrastructure;

(*c*) Implications for the promotion of sustainable development, including the sustainable use of natural resources and the reduction of environmental degradation;

(*d*) The implications of such improvements for more effectively meeting basic human needs, such as education, health, water and food;

(*e*) The effects of information technology on social cohesion, economic growth and cultural values, including such issues as gender, employment, small-scale economic activities, production capability, improved governance and increased participation in the decision-making process;

(*f*) Public policy, legal, regulatory, institutional, financial, market, human resource and infrastructural requirements for the diffusion and application of information technology;

(*g*) Examination of the programmes of the organs, organizations and bodies of the United Nations system that relate to the global information infrastructure and their impacts, and the ways in which improved coordination and new avenues to be opened up for the coalition of resources could better assist developing countries and countries with economies in transition in gaining more effective access to information technology and participating to a greater extent in the development and application of information technology;

*(h)* Assessment of experiences and progress made with regard to access to networks, as referred to in paragraph 8 of the present resolution;

15. *Notes* the recommendations adopted at the Consultative Meeting on a Coalition of Resources for Science and Technology for Development; recommends that, at the international level, a coalition of resources should focus on specific themes and common goals among recipients, donors and international financing institutions, including the World Bank and the regional development banks; that such themes and common goals should be based on voluntary and informal mechanisms that promote the full interaction of both donors and recipients; and that the feasibility of building science and technology into existing and broader coordination schemes should be considered; and also recommends that the Commission should provide a forum for exchanging views and interaction among partners of different networks and coordination schemes in the area of science and technology for development, drawing lessons from past experience in that area, a forum that could be held either as a segment of its biennial sessions or as an inter-sessional activity, as required and defined by the Commission in consultation with relevant United Nations bodies and international organizations;

16. *Welcomes* the important contribution to the work of the Commission on Sustainable Development made by the Commission on Science and Technology for Development in the area of integrated land management, and invites the Commission on Science and Technology for Development to continue contributing substantively and constructively to the work of the Commission on Sustainable Development on the science and technology components of Agenda 21;

17. *Invites* the Commission on Science and Technology for Development to give consideration to ways and means of taking advantage of the twentieth anniversary of the United Nations Conference on Science and Technology for Development, held at Vienna from 20 to 31 August 1979, for the formulation of a common vision for the future contribution of science and technology for development;

18. *Recognizes* the importance of clean and safe energy technologies in the pursuit of sustainable development, and recommends that the Commission secretariat, in consultation with the Committee on New and Renewable Sources of Energy and on Energy for Development and other relevant international bodies, submit to the Commission at its third session an issues note that should identify scientific and technological aspects of sustainable energy systems that might be considered by the Commission in defining its future work programme;

19. *Takes note* of the report by the secretariat of the United Nations Conference on Trade and Development entitled "Scientific and technological aspects of the conversion of military capacities for civilian use and sustainable development: an overview of the main issues", and recommends the continuation of the work of the Commission on scientific and technological aspects of the conversion of military capacities in close cooperation with other relevant bodies of the United Nations system and with other organizations;

20. *Expresses* its appreciation to the Commission secretariat for its work in preparing timely and substantive documentation for the second session, reiterates its earlier decision that responsibility for implementation of the Commission's programme rests with members of the Commission, and that the secretariat is responsible for servicing the Commission, and emphasizes, furthermore, that the Commission should implement its future work programme and its priorities in a transparent manner;

21. *Requests* the Secretary-General to provide the necessary resources for convening at least four intersessional ad hoc panels/workshops on specific issues in the field of science and technology, which will provide crucial input into the work of the Commission in terms of independent, specialized and expert advice;

22. *Recognizes with appreciation* the financial contributions made by Governments, foundations, institutions and individual donors to the work of the panels, as well as the important support received to that end from individuals, experts and non-governmental groups and United Nations bodies, and encourages them and all appropriate institutions to continue and enhance their support of the activities of the Commission in the intersessional period 1995-1997.

### ANNEX
#### Declaration of intent on gender, science and technology for sustainable human development

All Governments agree to work actively towards the following goals:

1. To ensure basic education for all, with particular emphasis on scientific and technological literacy, so that all women and men can effectively use science and technology to meet basic needs.

2. To ensure that women and men have equal opportunities to acquire advanced training in science and technology and to pursue careers as technologists, scientists and engineers.

3. To achieve gender equity within science and technology institutions, including policy and decision-making bodies.

4. To ensure that the needs and aspirations of women and men are equally taken into account in the setting of research priorities and in the design, transfer and application of new technologies.

5. To ensure that all women and men have equal access to the information and knowledge, particularly scientific and technological knowledge, that they need to improve their standard of living and quality of life.

6. To recognize local knowledge systems, where they exist, and their gender-specific nature as a source of knowledge that is complementary to modern science and technology and is also valuable for sustainable human development.

Economic and Social Council resolution 1995/4

19 July 1995      Meeting 44      Adopted without vote

Draft by Commission on Science and Technology for Development (E/1995/31); agenda item 6 *(d)*.
*Meeting numbers.* ESC 42-44.

On 28 July, the Council adopted **resolution 1995/54**.

### Science and technology for development

*The Economic and Social Council,*

*Considering* the critical and catalytic role of science and technology for development,

*Recognizing* the specific needs and requirements of developing countries, in particular the least developed countries, especially those in Africa, and countries with economies in transition,

*Recognizing* the unique role of the Commission on Science and Technology for Development as a global forum for the examination of science and technology questions, for improving understanding of science and technology policies for development and for the formulation of recommendations and guidelines on science and technology matters within the United Nations system, all in relation to development,

*Recognizing further* that the Commission, in carrying out its work, should pay special attention to the needs and requirements of developing countries, in particular the least developed countries, and that it should also take into consideration the relevant problems of countries with economies in transition,

*Taking note* of the report of the Commission on Science and Technology for Development on its second session,

*Recognizing* the need to support activities of the United Nations system in the field of science and technology for development and considering that the level of funding for science and technology as a generic field is limited, being only a small percentage of total United Nations system resources for development,

1. *Urges* all countries to increase their support for science and technology for development and for the activities of relevant organizations, funds and programmes of the United Nations in this sphere;

2. *Urges* the Commission on Science and Technology for Development to ensure greater transparency in its working methods and decision-making processes, including the allocation and utilization of resources, in accordance with Commission decision 2/101 of 24 May 1995;

3. *Requests* the relevant organizations, funds and programmes of the United Nations, in the spirit of coordination which should prevail in the actions of the United Nations system in the field of science and technology for development:

*(a)* To sensitize the international community regarding the critical and catalytic role of science and technology for development;

*(b)* To consider strengthening their capability to contribute to strengthening capacities in developing countries to generate applied research and development activities and results, and the application of those results to the industry and the actual user, including through pilot-scale projects;

*(c)* To consider facilitating and financing, including by catalysing other forms of financial support, South-South technology transfer and cooperation as an effective ingredient of self-sustaining development; in this context, possibilities of cooperation between developing countries and countries with economies in transition should also be explored;

*(d)* To work in a coordinated manner to develop a catalogue of proved technologies to enable effective choice by developing countries of state-of-the-art technologies;

*(e)* To continue to promote more effective technology cooperation between developed countries, developing countries and countries with economies in transition, in particular by providing better access to technology and transfer of technology through, *inter alia*, fostering foreign direct investment from developed to developing countries, as well as to countries with economies in transition, including in the areas of new and emerging technologies;

*(f)* To consider enhancing research and development institutions of developing countries, in particular the least developed countries, in order to encourage and implement activities that reduce technological dependence on developed countries and promote South-South cooperation;

4. *Invites* the Commission on Science and Technology for Development to continue contributing substantively and constructively to the work of the Commission on Sustainable Development on the science and technology components of Agenda 21.

Economic and Social Council resolution 1995/54

28 July 1995          Meeting 57          Adopted without vote

Draft by Vice-President (E/1995/L.59), based on informal consultations on draft by Philippines, for Group of 77 and China (E/1995/L.32); agenda item 6 *(d)*.

*Meeting numbers.* ESC 39-44, 47, 57.

In other action, the Council, by **decision 1995/237** of 19 July, noted the report on the second session of the Commission on Science and Technology for Development, endorsing its resolutions and decisions. It also approved the provisional agenda and documentation for the Commission's third (1997) session. By **decision 1995/312** of 27 July, the Council extended the terms of office of the members of the Commission to 31 December 1997.

**Commission on Sustainable Development.** At its April session,[18] the Commission on Sustainable Development had before it the Secretary-General's report on science for sustainable development,[103] which focused on the experiences of national Governments, the UN system, other international organizations and the scientific community in implementing science-related policies and programmes at the national, regional and international levels. The report, prepared for the Commission's review of chapter 35 of Agenda 21,[17] covered four of the chapter's programme areas: strengthening the scientific basis for sustainable management; enhancing scientific understanding; improving long-term scientific assessment; and building scientific capacity and capability. It identified priority issues within those areas for specific action by national Governments, with the support of international organizations and major groups, in particular the scientific community. Several policy recommendations to encourage and promote those actions were presented for Commission consideration.

The Commission urged countries and international organizations to accord high priority to measures aimed at capacity-building and sharing of know-how in science, with particular emphasis on the needs of developing countries. Governments, UN organizations and other intergovernmental organizations should share information on scientific capacities and know-how and its impact on achieving sustainable development objectives in developing countries, particularly LDCs, and make that information available to the Commission. They should implement activities that would enhance the scientific capacities and capabilities of developing countries in the following priority areas: promoting scientific education and training, particularly for women; enhancing the status of science; enhancing the capabilities of decision makers to use existing scientific information in developing sustainable development policies; improving the integration of science into national development policies and plans; promoting interdisciplinary approaches and use of new technologies; and increasing training in specialized scientific areas.

The Commission encouraged Governments to enhance international scientific cooperation, including North-South and South-South cooperation, for example through networking of national and international centres of excellence that would build on existing national and regional research, education and development institutions, organizations and programmes; and enhancing participation of developing countries in international research programmes on global environmental issues.

The donor community was invited to consider targeted financial support for activities related to scientific capacity-building in identified priority areas.

In a report on the environmentally sound management of biotechnology,[104] the Secretary-General reviewed the implementation of chapter 16 of Agenda 21,[17] which focused on the need to increase the availability of food, feed and renewable raw materials; improve human health; enhance environmental protection; enhance safety and develop international mechanisms for cooperation; and establish enabling mechanisms for the development and environmentally sound application of biotechnology. Based on analyses received from Governments, the UN system and other intergovernmental organizations, NGOs, the scientific and academic communities, the business community, donors and others, the report presented several proposals for action by the Commission to support and initiate activities at the national level and promote international cooperation.

Following consideration of the report, the Commission urged Governments to: increase the involvement of business and industry, and financial, academic and research institutions, NGOs and other major groups in national, regional and international consultations on biotechnology development trends and on impact assessments; encourage case-studies on "best practice" in the environmentally sound and safe development, application and management of biotechnology, and

make their results available, especially to developing countries; support the establishment of biotechnology associations, particularly in developing countries, with a view to facilitating the safe commercialization and application of biotechnology products and processes; and mobilize financial resources for biotechnology research, development and work on safety and for its sustainable use and management, especially in developing countries.

Countries and international organizations were urged to accord high priority to measures aimed at integrating biotechnology, including biosafety concerns, into national and regional sustainable development policies and programmes and to make the experiences gained in the environmentally sound application and management of biotechnology available in order to facilitate the Commission's work.

**Report of the Secretary-General.** In response to a 1993 General Assembly request,[105] the Secretary-General submitted an October 1995 report on science and technology for development.[106] He described measures taken to ensure implementation of the programme on science and technology for development in the UN medium-term plan for the period 1992-1997, and coordination efforts among the UN organizations and entities in science and technology.

With regard to financing, the report noted that the focus of the UN Fund for Science and Technology for Development (UNFSTD) in 1994 and 1995 had continued to be endogenous capacity-building, including technology assessment, technology innovation and entrepreneurship, quality control, and technology information and information technologies. The Endogenous Capacity-building Programme, carried out in Cape Verde, Jamaica, Pakistan, Uganda and Viet Nam, concluded in 1995 with the third round of policy dialogues among stakeholders, based on which technology portfolios for each country were being prepared; funding would be provided through a coalition of domestic and international resources. Based on experience gained by UNFSTD from the Technology Incubator Programme, which had concluded in 1994, a manual on technology business incubator centres was being prepared. Within the interregional programme on the maintenance and repair of scientific instruments, 60 Bangladesh nationals were trained as technicians and users and formed a national network. Similar training was carried out in Cameroon. Core contributions to UNFSTD for the period 1993-1995 came exclusively from developing countries, while project-related funding was provided by several European countries and Japan.

The follow-up to the 1994 Consultative Meeting on a Coalition of Resources for Science and

Technology for Development[98] was described, including the recommendation of the Economic and Social Council (**resolution 1995/4**) that a coalition of resources should focus on specific themes and common goals among recipients, donors and international financing institutions, including the World Bank and the regional development banks.

The report stated that activities for 1996-1997 under the science and technology programme of the medium-term plan would focus on areas that could provide fresh insights into the consideration of science, technology and innovation policies. They would also include work on monitoring developments in science and technology, particularly those with implications for society at large, on production, employment and competitiveness, including assessment and diffusion of scientific and technological knowledge.

**GENERAL ASSEMBLY ACTION**

On 20 December, the General Assembly adopted **resolution 50/101**.

### Science and technology for development
*The General Assembly,*

*Reaffirming* the continuing validity of the Vienna Programme of Action on Science and Technology for Development, and recalling the relevant paragraphs of the Declaration on International Economic Cooperation, in particular the Revitalization of Economic Growth and Development of the Developing Countries, the International Development Strategy for the Fourth United Nations Development Decade, the Cartagena Commitment, adopted by the United Nations Conference on Trade and Development at its eighth session, the relevant recommendations and decisions adopted by the United Nations Conference on Environment and Development, particularly those contained in Agenda 21, and the relevant resolutions and decisions adopted by organizations and bodies of the United Nations system concerning science and technology for development,

*Bearing in mind* the vital contribution of science and technology, including new and emerging technologies, to the promotion of economic growth and development, particularly in developing countries, and stressing the importance of monitoring new developments in science and technology and their implications for society, on production, employment and international competitiveness, especially for developing countries,

*Recognizing* the importance for developing countries of having access to science and technology so as to enhance their productivity and competitiveness in the world market, and stressing the need to promote, facilitate and finance, as appropriate, access to and transfer of environmentally sound technologies and the corresponding know-how, in particular to the developing countries, on favourable terms, including on concessional and preferential terms as mutually agreed, taking into account the need to protect intellectual property rights as well as the special needs of developing countries,

*Stressing* the primary responsibility of all countries for their own science and technology policies, and the need to further promote endogenous capacity-building in science and technology in developing countries so as to enable them to participate in, benefit from and contribute to the rapid advances in science and technology,

*Recognizing* that information technologies are important requisites for planning, development and decision-making in science and technology, and recognizing also their far-reaching implications for society,

*Recognizing* the importance of developing countries' own efforts in the field of science and technology for development,

*Reaffirming* that the United Nations should play an important role in the promotion of cooperation in science and technology, and in the enhancement of support and assistance to developing countries in their efforts to achieve the objectives set forth by the United Nations Conference on Environment and Development in this regard,

*Recognizing* the work of the Commission on Science and Technology for Development in promoting the developing countries' endogenous capacity in science and technology, and recognizing its unique function as a global forum for the examination of science and technology questions, for the improvement of the understanding of science and technology policies for development and for the formulation of recommendations and guidelines on science and technology matters within the United Nations system, all in relation to development,

*Recognizing* the role of the United Nations Conference on Trade and Development in science and technology for development, as reaffirmed in General Assembly resolution 48/179 of 21 December 1993,

*Recognizing* the need for adequate resources to be devoted to fostering science and technology for development,

*Recognizing* the special needs and requirements of developing countries, in particular the least developed countries, especially those in Africa,

*Also recognizing* the relevant problems of countries with economies in transition in the sphere of the transformation and development of their scientific and technological potentials,

*Taking note* of the report of the Secretary-General on the implementation of programme 17, Science and technology for development, of the medium-term plan for the period 1992-1997,

1. *Reaffirms* the relevant resolutions and decisions adopted by the Economic and Social Council at its substantive session of 1995 on the basis of the report of the Commission on Science and Technology for Development on its second session;

2. *Reaffirms* that capacity-building in science and technology in developing countries should remain a priority issue in the United Nations agenda, and urges that international cooperation efforts be intensified and strengthened towards developing countries' endogenous capacity-building in science and technology, including their capacity to utilize scientific and technological developments from abroad and to adapt them to suit local conditions;

3. *Calls upon* the international community to meet all the objectives as reaffirmed in chapter 34 of Agenda 21, in particular those dealing with effective access to and transfer of environmentally sound technologies, including new and emerging technologies and publicly owned technologies, to developing countries on favour-

able terms, including on concessional and preferential terms, as mutually agreed, taking into account the need to protect intellectual property rights as well as the special needs of developing countries, so as to contribute to enabling those developing countries to meet their development-related challenges;

4. *Stresses* that it is important for developing countries to adopt and implement their own science and technology policies that support the national effort to achieve sustained economic growth and sustainable development in the light of their respective national conditions, needs, priorities and objectives;

5. *Stresses* the need to strengthen the important role of the United Nations in the field of science and technology, particularly through effective policy guidance and better coordination, including in international cooperation in technology assessment, monitoring and forecasting;

6. *Recognizes* the role of the private sector in science and technology for development, in particular in the transfer and development of science and technology capabilities;

7. *Also recognizes* the role of Governments in science and technology for development, in particular in providing appropriate regulatory frameworks and incentives for the development of science and technology capabilities;

8. *Requests* the relevant organizations, funds and programmes of the United Nations, in the spirit of coordination that should prevail in the activities of the United Nations system in the field of science and technology for development, to work in a coordinated manner to develop a catalogue of proved technologies that will enable developing countries to make effective choices from among state-of-the-art technologies;

9. *Calls upon* the Commission on Science and Technology for Development and the Commission on Sustainable Development to interact more effectively, through the Economic and Social Council, in carrying out their respective mandates;

10. *Calls upon* the supporting secretariats of the Commission on Science and Technology for Development and the Commission on Sustainable Development to improve their interaction;

11. *Takes note* of the developments at the Consultative Meeting on a Coalition of Resources for Science and Technology for Development and the recommendation of the Economic and Social Council that the Commission on Science and Technology for Development provide a forum for exchanging views and interaction among partners of different networks and coordination schemes;

12. *Reaffirms* the need for adequate financial resources on a continuous and assured basis to foster science and technology for development, in particular to promote endogenous capacity-building in developing countries in accordance with their priorities;

13. *Notes with appreciation* the measures taken by the Secretary-General in response to paragraph 6 of General Assembly resolution 48/179 and invites him to continue to take all necessary measures, including to explore the possibility of organizing a more effective coalition of resources within the United Nations development system, multilateral financial institutions, regional development banks and bilateral funding agencies to ensure the full implementation of programme 17, Science and technology for development, of the medium-term plan for the period 1992-1997 and the activities planned for 1996-1997 in the field of science and technology for de-

velopment, in accordance with specific mandates provided for in the relevant Assembly resolutions;

14. *Takes note* that enhanced cooperation could help focus the activities of the United Nations system in the field of science and technology for development for greater impact;

15. *Recognizes* the importance of cooperation among developing countries in the field of science and technology, building on their complementarities, and the need for further advancing such cooperation through the establishment and/or the strengthening of national technology and information centres in developing countries and their networking on regional, subregional, interregional and global levels to promote technology research, training and dissemination as well as joint projects in developing countries, and urges the organizations and bodies of the United Nations system and other relevant international, regional and subregional organizations and programmes to provide continued and enhanced support, through technical assistance and financing for such efforts;

16. *Requests* the relevant organizations, funds and programmes of the United Nations system to continue to promote the development of effective and mutually beneficial technological cooperation between countries with economies in transition and all other countries, including in the area of new and emerging technologies;

17. *Notes* the endorsement by the Economic and Social Council of the decision of the Commission on Science and Technology for Development to select information technologies as the main substantive theme of its work during the inter-sessional period 1995-1997 and to set up panels and/or working groups to analyse, and elaborate and make recommendations on issues pertaining to information technologies and their implications for development;

18. *Takes note* of the decision of the Economic and Social Council to invite the Commission on Science and Technology for Development to consider ways and means for the formulation of a common vision regarding the future contribution of science and technology for development, taking advantage of the twentieth anniversary of the United Nations Conference on Science and Technology for Development, held at Vienna in 1979;

19. *Stresses* the potentially important role that the United Nations Fund for Science and Technology for Development should play in enhancing endogenous capacity-building in science and technology in developing countries, and calls on all countries in a position to do so to contribute generously to the Fund;

20. *Reaffirms* the need for Governments and regional and international bodies to take measures to ensure that women have equal access to and equal opportunity to participate in scientific and technological areas, especially in areas where they are not represented or are underrepresented;

21. *Requests* the Secretary-General to submit a report to the General Assembly at its fifty-second session on progress in the implementation of the present resolution.

General Assembly resolution 50/101

20 December 1995     Meeting 96     Adopted without vote

Approved by Second Committee (A/50/617/Add.4) without vote, 8 December (meeting 42); draft by Vice-Chairman (A/C.2/50/L.68), based on informal consultations on draft by Philippines, for Group of 77 and China (A/C.2/50/L.25) and orally revised; agenda item 95 *(d)*.

*Meeting numbers.* GA 50th session: 2nd Committee 30-32, 37, 42; plenary 96.

## Technology transfer

**Commission on Sustainable Development.** In a report on the transfer of environmentally sound technologies (ESTs), cooperation and capacity-building,[107] the Secretary-General covered three priority areas which the Commission on Sustainable Development had identified as requiring specific action: access to and dissemination of information on environmentally sound technologies; institutional development and capacity-building for managing technological changes; and financial and partnership arrangements. The report presented elements of a work programme for the promotion of EST transfer, cooperation and capacity-building.

In April,[18] the Commission welcomed the elements of a work programme in that report and highlighted the need to develop a programme of work on the transfer of ESTs, cooperation and capacity-building, with the objective of reporting on its implementation by 1997. Organizations of the UN system, other intergovernmental organizations, the secretariats of various international conventions, and major groups, particularly business and industry, were urged to make clear commitments to undertake specific elements of the work programme, which the Commission included in its report.[18]

### Draft code of conduct

In response to a 1993 General Assembly request,[108] the Secretary-General, in a 6 October note,[109] transmitted the report of the UNCTAD Secretary-General on negotiations on an international code of conduct on the transfer of technology. The UNCTAD Secretary-General reviewed recent developments in the discussion on the draft code, including the work of the Ad Hoc Working Group on the Interrelationship between Investment and Technology Transfer, the mandate of which ended in 1994,[98] and the Agreement on Trade-Related Aspects of Intellectual Property Rights, which was included in the Final Act of the Uruguay Round of multilateral trade negotiations.[19]

The report noted that the international milieu had changed drastically since the negotiations on an international code of conduct began in the 1970s. It was important to assess the implications of conceptual and policy shifts for the international transfer of technology, particularly for developing countries, and assess their possible effects on enterprise and intergovernmental cooperation in technology transfer, including the identification of possible rules and principles that could enhance the stability and predictability required for such cooperation.

The UNCTAD Secretary-General suggested, therefore, that negotiations on the existing draft code should be formally suspended. Alternatively, the Assembly could close discussions on the code by disseminating to interested groups the outcome of the work so far achieved. He further suggested that Governments consider convening a round-table meeting of eminent persons to examine recent developments, so as to reconcile past differences and achieve a better understanding of the principles that should govern international cooperation in the area of technology.

By **decision 50/427** of 20 December, the Assembly took note of the Secretary-General's note.

### Coordination in science and technology

In response to a 1994 Economic and Social Council request,[110] the Secretary-General submitted in May a report on inter-agency coordination in science and technology for development.[111] He noted that focal points for science and technology had been designated in 26 major UN organizations and agencies and that inter-agency coordination bodies had discussed how best to deal with science and technology issues. At regional and national levels, the role of the UNDP Resident Coordinator was being given increased attention. It was recommended that the Council review progress in science and technology coordination within five years.

*REFERENCES*

[1]A/50/617. [2]YUN 1992, p. 15. [3]Ibid., p. 528, GA res. 47/181, 22 Dec. 1992. [4]A/48/935. [5]YUN 1994, p. 758. [6]YUN 1994, p. 759, GA res. 49/126, 19 Dec. 1994. [7]A/49/45. [8]A/C.2/50/SR.14. [9]E/1995/SR.22. [10]YUN 1994, p. 761, GA res. 49/95, 19 Dec. 1994. [11]A/50/480. [12]YUN 1994, p. 760. [13]A/50/3/Rev.1 (Agreed conclusions 1995/1). [14]YUN 1993, p. 659, GA res. 48/60, 14 Dec. 1993. [15]A/50/501. [16]E/CN.17/1995/6. [17]YUN 1992, p. 672. [18]E/1995/32. [19]YUN 1994, p. 868. [20]E/CN.17/1995/2. [21]E/CN.17/1995/33. [22]ACC/1995/12. [23]ACC/1995/18. [24]YUN 1993, p. 663, GA res. 48/180, 21 Dec. 1993. [25]A/50/417. [26]YUN 1994, p. 900. [27]TD/B/42(1)/2. [28]TD/B/WG.7/2. [29]TD/B/WG.7/3. [30]TD/B/WG.7/6. [31]TD/B/WG.7/7. [32]TD/B/42(1)/17. [33]TD/B(S-XVIII)/3 (dec. 433(S-XVIII)). [34]YUN 1993, p. 665, GA res. 48/168, 21 Dec. 1993. [35]A/50/439. [36]YUN 1992, p. 676, GA res. 47/191, 22 Dec. 1992. [37]Ibid., p. 670. [38]E/CN.17/1995/21. [39]YUN 1994, p. 770. [40]YUN 1994, p. 1269. [41]E/1995/7. [42]E/CN.17/1995/9. [43]E/CN.17/1995/28. [44]E/CN.17/1995/19. [45]E/CN.17/1995/13. [46]E/CN.17/1995/24. [47]E/CN.17/1995/22. [48]E/CN.17/1995/31. [49]E/CN.17/1995/32. [50]YUN 1994, p. 767. [51]E/CN.17/1995/10. [52]ACC/1995/3. [53]ACC/1995/17. [54]YUN 1994, p. 783. [55]ACC/1995/23. [56]E/CN.17/1996/2. [57]A/50/453. [58]YUN 1992, p. 675, GA res. 47/190, 22 Dec. 1992. [59]E/CN.17/1995/14. [60]TD/B/42/(1)/10. [61]TD/B/CN.2/13. [62]TD/B/CN.2/14. [63]TD/B/CN.2/15. [64]UNCTAD/ECDC/PA/1. [65]YUN 1994, p. 1474. [66]YUN 1992, p. 536. [67]YUN 1993, p. 670, GA res. 48/184, 21 Dec. 1993. [68]A/50/396. [69]YUN 1994, p. 955. [70]E/1996/4 & Corr.1. [71]E/1995/120. [72]ACC/1995/23. [73]YUN 1994, p. 771, GA res. 49/110, 19 Dec. 1994. [74]E/1995/92. [75]A/50/551. [76]TD/B/42(1)/7. [77]TD/B/CN.3/13. [78]TD/B/CN.3/14. [79]TD/B/CN.3/15. [80]YUN 1994, p. 773, GA res. 49/96, 19 Dec. 1994. [81]A/AC.246/3. [82]A/AC.246/1. [83]A/AC.246/2. [84]YUN 1993, p. 666, GA res. 48/164, 21 Dec. 1993. [85]A/50/340 & Add.1. [86]E/1995/31. [87]E/CN.16/1995/5. [88]YUN 1994, p. 929. [89]E/CN.16/1995/2. [90]YUN 1994,

p. 930. [91]E/CN.16/1995/6. [92]E/CN.16/1995/7. [93]E/CN.16/1995/9 & Corr.1,2. [94]E/CN.16/1995/12. [95]E/CN.16/1995/13. [96]E/CN.16/1995/10. [97]E/CN.16/1995/11. [98]YUN 1994, p. 931. [99]E/1995/31 (res. 2/1). [100]Ibid. (res. 2/2). [101]Ibid. (dec. 2/101). [102]Ibid. (dec. 2/102). [103]E/CN.17/1995/16. [104]E/CN.17/1995/20. [105]YUN 1993, p. 793, GA res. 48/179, 21 Dec. 1993. [106]A/50/649. [107]E/CN.17/1995/17. [108]YUN 1993, p. 802, GA res. 48/167, 21 Dec. 1993. [109]A/50/486. [110]YUN 1994, p. 933. [111]E/1995/62 & Corr.1.

# Economic and social trends and policy

## Economic surveys and trends

The *World Economic and Social Survey 1995*,[1] prepared by the Department for Economic and Social Information and Policy Analysis (DESIPA) and issued in mid-1995, stated that the world economy appeared to have attained a "cruising speed" in growth of output of about 3 per cent a year—a rate that seemed to be sustainable. Although the rate of growth was not very rapid—about at the average of the 1980s—it was unusually widespread. The industrialized economies had emerged from recent recessions and were in expansionary phases, while inflation remained relatively under control. However, there was concern about the strength of the recovery in some countries and the limited impact it was having in reducing unemployment. An increasing number of economies that were in transition to the market system showed clear signs of having turned the corner from economic contraction to recovery. Nevertheless, economic and social conditions continued to be difficult and unemployment was inordinately high, as was inflation. In the developing countries, average economic growth had been maintained at a relatively high rate since 1992 and efforts to tame inflation had borne fruit. Even in Africa, where economic growth had been painfully slow, the pace of output growth had increased and per capita output was expected not to fall in 1995 for the first time in the decade. Latin America was experiencing the contractionary side to the inflows of volatile international portfolio investment that it had been enjoying in recent years.

The economic recovery in the developed market economies was well established and their pace of expansion was likely to show little change in 1995 from the 3 per cent recorded in 1994. In addition, the difference in growth rates among countries was becoming smaller. The growth of the economies of Australia, New Zealand, the United Kingdom and the United States was forecast to slow down in 1995, to a more sustainable rate, while in continental Europe economic growth was expected to proceed at or marginally above the 1994 rate. Japan was projected to continue its recovery, although it could

be unusually weak by the standards of previous upswings. In most of the industrialized economies, the unemployment problem remained intractable; it was expected to average 7.5 per cent of the labour force of the industrialized economies as a whole in 1995.

In 1994, for the first time since 1989, the overall economic situation in the transition economies of central and eastern Europe brightened. In all countries of the region and in the Baltic States, GDP grew and a similar result was forecast for 1995. Unemployment, however, was in double digits in all countries of the region except the Czech Republic. The strong performance of industry and the dynamism of newly established private firms were common sources of growth in most transition economies. However, among the higher-income economies, the two countries with the fastest rates of growth showed different experiences. Supply-side adjustment, most notably in industry, appeared to be the leading domestic source of economic growth in Poland, where industrial output grew by 12 per cent in 1994 and by 23 per cent in the industrial private sector, while in Slovakia, domestic factors played a negligible role in the strong GDP growth in 1994, which was mostly attributable to the growth of exports and the improving balance of trade.

For the Russian Federation and the other countries of the Commonwealth of Independent States (CIS), the situation was one of continued and unremitting economic decline, according to reports from their statistical authorities. The cumulative fall in production between 1990 and 1994 totalled 47 per cent of the level of output in 1989 and the reported rate of decline actually accelerated in 1994 in two thirds of the countries. However, the *Survey* noted, the level of reliability of the statistical data received from the CIS countries was very low and analysis of the economic situation was thus difficult. It was clear, though, that macroeconomic stabilization had largely eluded CIS since the breakup of the Soviet Union, although significant progress in certain countries was within reach in 1995. The Russian Federation had reduced the annual increase in consumer prices to below 300 per cent in 1994 from the almost 1,000 per cent rate of 1993. In Ukraine, prices rose more than 10,000 per cent in 1993 but the rate of increase fell to 500 per cent in 1994.

The developing countries entered their fourth year of 5 per cent growth of GDP in 1995—an important trend when set against the average annual growth of 3 per cent in the 1980s. However, behind that steady average increase were strong contrasts. In Africa, economic growth picked up in 1994, stimulated by agricultural production and an increase in demand for Africa's exports from the recovering developed market economies. Improved export prices of non-oil commodities contributed to growth, but depressed oil prices dampened it in the oil-exporting countries. The GDP of the sub-Saharan Africa grouping grew in 1994 for the first time in two years, but the population grew faster. There were cases in Africa, however, where adjustment programmes had begun to pay off in economic expansion. Ghana, Mauritius, Tunisia and Uganda had had a string of years of substantial growth of GDP and the economy of Côte d'Ivoire began to grow following the CFA franc devaluation in 1994. Nevertheless, sustained high rates of growth were exceptions.

As in years past, the rapidly growing developing economies were concentrated in Asia. The 15 countries with the highest expected growth rates in 1995 were all in Asia, with forecast growth ranging from 5.8 per cent (the Philippines) to 10 per cent (China).

Latin America's growth rate, which had finally been gathering steam after the "lost decade" of the 1980s, was expected to drop precipitously in 1995 to less than half the 1994 rate. Creditor Governments and the financial community, including investors who lost considerable sums in the wake of the exchange-rate crisis in Mexico in late 1994, were asking whether better international surveillance of domestic policy might avert future crises.

By **decision 1995/234** of 17 and 19 July, the Economic and Social Council took note of the *Survey.*

In a note giving an update of the world economy based on information available as at 15 December,[2] the Secretary-General stated that the world economy had grown by some 2.6 per cent during 1995, a slightly slower rate than the 3 per cent forecast in the *Survey.* In part because of the effort to hold inflation at bay, the growth rate in the developed economies dropped by about half a percentage point in 1995, with the slow-down most pronounced in Australia, Canada, New Zealand, the United Kingdom and the United States, which had been the first countries to emerge from the previous recession. In continental Europe, the recovery of 1994 and early 1995 slowed or paused later in the year, but growth was expected to be in the 2.5 to 3 per cent range during 1996. After four years of almost no growth of output, the Japanese economy was expected to begin modest growth in 1996.

The 5 per cent growth of GDP of the developing countries in 1995 and the 5.5 per cent forecast for 1996 reflected the capacity of many of those countries to capture and effectively utilize growth impulses, many of which arose in the international economy in 1995. In many developing countries, the translation into economic growth was enhanced by progress in domestic economic adjustment and, in some cases, by the quieting of political instability and civil disorder. Of 94 developing

countries monitored regularly, only 7 were estimated to have had outright reduction of output in 1995 compared with 17 in 1994.

By the close of 1995, the deep economic decline of the early stages of the economic transition process in central and eastern Europe and the countries that had constituted the former USSR finally seemed to be ending. The countries of central and eastern Europe and the Baltic States, joined by Armenia, continued the growth that began in 1994. Although output was reported to have dropped again in almost all CIS nations, the rate of decline fell in 1995; the Russian Federation's economy was forecast to grow in 1996.

The *Trade and Development Report, 1995*[3] noted that world output growth had accelerated sharply in 1994, to reach 3.1 per cent, compared to 1.7 per cent in 1993. The increase was due to the recovery in the developed market-economy countries and continued high rates of expansion in developing countries and in China. In keeping with recent trends, production continued to be outpaced by trade, which rose in volume by close to 9 per cent in 1994, thanks to expansion of trade in manufactures (see also PART FOUR, Chapter IV).

### Human Development Report 1995

The real wealth of a nation is its people and the purpose of development is to create an enabling environment for people to enjoy long, healthy and creative lives. So stated the *Human Development Report 1995,* prepared by UNDP. It noted that the human development concept had gone beyond its basic premises to emphasize the sustainability of the development process. Having considered the process of human development over the preceding three decades, the *Report* drew four major conclusions: the developing world had witnessed unprecedented improvements in human development in those 30 years; despite progress, considerable human deprivation remained in both the developing and the industrial world; rapid human progress was possible, development cooperation worked, and much more could be done by focusing national and international energy on essential targets; and the key human development challenges for the next century would require global compacts. The *Report* ranked 174 countries in its human development index.

In light of the Fourth (1995) World Conference on Women (see PART FOUR, Chapter X), the theme selected for the 1995 report was gender and human development.

**UNDP action.** In accordance with a 1994 UNDP/UNFPA Executive Board decision,[4] the UNDP Administrator submitted a report[5] on steps taken to improve the process of consultation with Member States and international bodies to refine methodologies used in the *Human Develop-*

*ment Report* with a view to improving its quality and accuracy without compromising its editorial independence. He noted that consultations on the 1995 *Report* began with meetings in November 1994, followed by consultations and informal meetings in 1995. In addition, two expert advisory groups were established, consisting of experts from all parts of the world on gender and development, the theme of the 1995 report. Regarding international bodies, a policy of strengthening professional collaboration was pursued, particularly on statistics. As to assuring accuracy, attention was paid to improving data by reviewing data series and providing more detailed recording of sources and definitions.

By a 16 June decision,[6] the Executive Board noted the report on the *Human Development Report.*

### Long-term trends in social and economic development

In accordance with a 1988 General Assembly request,[7] the Secretary-General submitted in September 1995 a report on long-term trends in social and economic development.[8] The document, which had been requested in time for the midpoint of the Fourth United Nations Development Decade (1991-2000) on the basis of the updated *Overall Socio-economic Perspective of the World Economy to the Year 2000,*[9] addressed selected aspects of long-term changes in the world economy to assist the Assembly in its deliberations on long-term sustainable development.

The report discussed demographic changes and some social implications of those changes, noting that the world's population, which had been 2.52 billion in 1950, was estimated to be 5.72 billion by mid-1995. The total population was expected to exceed 6 billion by the year 2000, with almost all of the increase occurring in less developed regions. It went on to consider the determinants of and prospects for long-term economic growth and sectoral changes in the world economy.

The report concluded that although the rate of world population growth was slowing, prolonged large increments in its size would require policy efforts to facilitate the supply of adequate education, employment, health care and financial support appropriate to various age groups and in countries at different stages of development. To deal effectively with economic, social, political and environmental pressures for rapid international migration, especially from developing to developed countries, the international community should increase its efforts to promote rapid, equitable, sustained and sustainable development of the developing countries.

Technical innovations would continue to set in motion new cycles of product development that would spread across countries and change their competitiveness. The commitment of countries to free trade and international cooperation was critical to that process and the conclusion of the Uruguay Round of multilateral trade negotiations was a hopeful portent that the international community could keep abreast of the rapid evolution of global production and trade systems with appropriate international accords. With regard to food production, policies were required to ease environmental constraints in certain regions and to generate a green revolution in Africa, which would soon be the region with the largest number of undernourished people. Since the atmospheric concentration of carbon dioxide due to growing energy consumption was expected to rise considerably by 2010, adherence to international agreements on the environment was of crucial importance.

By **decision 50/424** of 20 December, the Assembly took note of the Secretary-General's report.

*REFERENCES*

[1]*World Economic and Social Survey 1995: Current Trends and Policies in the World Economy* (E/1995/50), Sales No. E.95.II.C.1. [2]E/1995/INF/1. [3]*Trade and Development Report, 1995* (UNCTAD/TDR/15), Sales No. E.95.II.D.16. [4]YUN 1994, p. 1138. [5]DP/1995/34. [6]E/1995/34 (dec. 95/24). [7]YUN 1988, p. 323, GA res. 43/194, 20 Dec. 1988. [8]A/50/429. [9]*Overall Socio-economic Perspective of the World Economy to the Year 2000* (ST/ESA/215), Sales No. E.90.II.C.2.

# Development planning and public administration

## Development planning

The Committee for Development Planning (CDP)—a 24-member expert group appointed by the Economic and Social Council to advise it on development issues—did not meet in 1995. However, the Council considered the body's methods of work.

### ECONOMIC AND SOCIAL COUNCIL ACTION

In February, the Economic and Social Council adopted **decision 1995/215**.

#### Committee for Development Planning

At its 5th plenary meeting, on 10 February 1995, the Council, recalling General Assembly resolutions 2084(XX) and 2096(XX) of 20 December 1965, 2564(XXIV) of 13 December 1969, 44/212 of 22 December 1989 and 46/206 of 20 December 1991 and Economic and Social Council resolutions 1035(XXXVII) of 15 August 1964, 1079(XXXIX) of 28 July 1965, 1089(XXXIX) of 31 July 1965 and 1625(LI) of 30 July 1971, by which the Committee for Development Planning was established and entrusted with, *inter alia*, a broad mandate to assess world development trends and prospects, decided:

*(a)* To request the Secretary-General to submit nominations to the Council at its resumed organizational session in May 1995 or, at the latest, at its substantive session of 1995, for reconstitution of the membership of the Committee for Development Planning and to reconvene the reconstituted Committee before the end of 1995. In making the nominations, after consultations with interested Governments, the Secretary-General is requested to take into account the need for balanced representation and the diversity of issues dealt with by the Council and the General Assembly in the economic, social, environment and related fields;

*(b)* To request the Secretary-General to submit a comprehensive report to the Council at its substantive session of 1995 to enable it to review the working methods of the Committee, in line with the provisions of General Assembly resolution 48/162 of 20 December 1993;

*(c)* That the Committee should examine its working procedures with a view to improving them, in particular to reflect the ongoing work of the Council and the General Assembly and their subsidiary bodies;

*(d)* That the Committee should continue its work, in particular with regard to issues relating to the least developed countries;

*(e)* That the Chairperson of the Committee should address the Council on the major findings and conclusions of the Committee, starting in 1996.

Economic and Social Council decision 1995/215

Adopted without vote

Draft by Vice-President (E/1995/L.3), based on informal consultations; agenda item 4.
*Meeting numbers.* ESC 2, 5.

In response to the Council's request, the Secretary-General submitted a June report[1] on the methods of work of CDP. The report discussed the Committee's terms of reference and the evolution of its mandate and described the thematic content of CDP reports and its role within the UN system. The report's quality and dissemination were also addressed, as was the Committee's organization of work as regards selection of themes and pattern of meetings.

By **decision 1995/234** of 17 and 19 July, the Council took note of the Secretary-General's report.

## Public administration

In accordance with Economic and Social Council **decision 1995/212** of 10 February, the Twelfth Meeting of Experts on the United Nations Programme in Public Administration and Finance was held in New York from 31 July to 11 August.[2] The session was a preparatory meeting for the General Assembly's resumed fiftieth session (April 1996), which, in accordance with a 1994 Assembly resolution,[3] was to be devoted to the question of public administration and development. The Meeting was preceded, on 28 July, by an informal inter-agency working group that reviewed the activities of UN departments, regional commissions, funds and agencies under their public administration and finance programmes.

The Meeting concluded that there were three central ideas that guided public administration in developed, developing and transition economies: (1) rapidly changing domestic and international conditions and demands for services would require innovative policies at the strategic level and improved service delivery systems at the operational level; (2) public administration would continue to fulfil critical functions in development, moving from supporting measures for economic growth to protecting the environment, to determining the relationship between the public and private sector, to reducing poverty and illiteracy and other social development activities, thereby achieving the goals of sustainable development; and (3) to fulfil critical future-shaping functions, public administration should bring about dynamic people-oriented systems through strategic restructuring and outstanding professionalism by attracting top-quality people into administration.

The Meeting's report contained 103 recommendations for action for national Governments and 96 for the United Nations under the following topics: strengthening government capacity for policy development, administrative restructuring, civil service reform, human resources development and public administration training; improving performance in the public sector; financial management; public-private interaction; social development; developing infrastructure and protecting the environment; government legal capacity; post-conflict rehabilitation and reconstruction of government machinery; and management of development programmes.

By **decision 1995/325** of 12 December, the Council postponed consideration of the question of public administration and development until 1996.

*REFERENCES*

[1]E/1995/82. [2]A/50/525-E/1995/122. [3]YUN 1994, p. 777, GA res. 49/136, 19 Dec. 1994.

# Developing countries

## Least developed countries

During 1995, the General Assembly, the UNCTAD Trade and Development Board and the UNDP/UNFPA Executive Board reviewed the problems of the officially designated LDCs. The Mid-term Global Review of the Implementation of the Programme of Action for the Least Developed Countries was held in September/October.

The number of countries on the UN list of offically designated LDCs remained at 48, namely: Afghanistan, Angola, Bangladesh, Benin, Bhutan, Burkina Faso, Burundi, Cambodia, Cape Verde, Central African Republic, Chad, Comoros, Djibouti, Equatorial Guinea, Eritrea, Ethiopia, Gambia, Guinea, Guinea-Bissau, Haiti, Kiribati, Lao People's Democratic Republic, Lesotho, Liberia, Madagascar, Malawi, Maldives, Mali, Mauritania, Mozambique, Myanmar, Nepal, Niger, Rwanda, Samoa, Sao Tome and Principe, Sierra Leone, Solomon Islands, Somalia, Sudan, Togo, Tuvalu, Uganda, United Republic of Tanzania, Vanuatu, Yemen, Zaire, Zambia.

**UNDP action.** In response to a 1993 request,[1] the UNDP Administrator submitted to the April session of the UNDP/UNFPA Executive Board a report on matters relating to LDCs.[2] With regard to aid coordination and economic management, the Administrator noted that assistance had been provided to LDCs through the use of Special Programme Resources (SPR) that were used to finance technical support and logistics for national aid coordination processes, such as the round-table process, consultative groups or thematic or sectoral meetings, and to help build national capacities for improved coordination and management of aid. Two major umbrella projects supported aid coordination in the Africa and Asia/Pacific regions. Nearly all country programmes in Africa stressed capacity-building and public sector reform; in 1994, UNDP had supported such programmes in Angola, Burkina Faso, Malawi, Mozambique, Namibia and Zambia, among others. Activities had also been carried out under the African Capacity-Building Initiative, the National Long-term Perspective Studies Programme and the NATCAP (national technical cooperation assessment and programmes) exercises.

UNDP efforts sought to deal with the priority areas of environment, poverty alleviation and human development in LDCs in an integrated and mutually reinforcing manner in country and regional programmes, as well as in other special initiatives, so as to promote sustainable human development. Many country programmes in LDCs included environmental management, and focal points for the environment had been designated in each of the country offices in LDCs. Poverty reduction was the key objective in most country programmes in LDCs. In several of them, UNDP collaborated with key partners in formulating participatory and innovative approaches to reducing poverty.

The Administrator stated that UNDP, over time, had allocated the majority share of its core resources to LDCs. For the fifth programming cycle (1992-1996), the percentage of total country indicative planning figures (IPFs) allocated to LDCs

reached 58.2 per cent. The Special Measures Trust Fund for LDCs, however, had not received any contributions since 1993.

Other initiatives included the establishment of an operational link between UNDP and UNCTAD—the UN focal point for LDC matters—for coordination and exchange of information. Also, UNDP would participate in the Mid-term Global Review of the Implementation of the Programme of Action to be held in September/October and would assist Governments to mobilize resources to permit their participation in the review. UNDP was decentralizing programme responsibilities to the country level, which would increase its responsiveness to changing national priorities and make support to aid coordination the central concern of country offices in LDCs.

On 7 April,[3] the Executive Board asked UNDP to assist in the preparations for the mid-term review of the Programme of Action for LDCs and in mobilizing funding for the participation of LDCs. It urged the Administrator to ensure that poverty eradication was further strengthened in UNDP activities and that priority was given to LDCs, bearing in mind the commitments made at the 1995 World Summit for Social Development (see PART FOUR, Chapter IX). The Administrator was asked to keep under review the outcomes of relevant UN conferences and of the mid-term review of the Programme of Action and the implications for interventions by UNDP in LDCs, and to report to the Board as necessary.

### Programme of Action for the 1990s

**UNCTAD action.** At its March session, the UNCTAD Trade and Development Board (TDB) conducted its fifth annual review of progress in implementing the Programme of Action for the Least Developed Countries for the 1990s, adopted in 1990 at the Second UN Conference on the Least Developed Countries (Paris Conference)[4] and endorsed by the General Assembly later that year.[5]

TDB had before it *The Least Developed Countries—1995 Report*,[6] prepared in the context of the forthcoming High-level Intergovernmental Meeting on the Mid-term Global Review of the Programme of Action for LDCs (see below). It noted that the overall economic conditions of LDCs in the early 1990s continued to be bleak. Instead of reversing the economic deterioration in LDCs, those years had actually marked a period of decline following two decades of stagnation. The combined annual average growth rate of LDCs during 1990-1993 was 1.6 per cent and was estimated to be even lower for 1994—at around 1.4 per cent. Although LDC economies faced almost identical structural problems and similar difficulties of access to product markets and external finance, their development experience had become more heterogeneous. As many as 12 LDCs (Bangladesh, Benin, Cambodia, Equatorial Guinea, Guinea-Bissau, Lao People's Democratic Republic, Lesotho, Mozambique, Myanmar, Sao Tome and Principe, Solomon Islands, Sudan) had improved their performance, with strong expansion of agricultural production, internal stability, strong government commitments, and a sound political and regulatory framework for development, complemented by significant external support, contributing to raising economic growth rates. At the other end of the spectrum were several countries whose development experiences were dominated by a range of non-economic factors such as civil conflicts, political instability, increased flows of refugees and internally displaced persons, recurrent droughts, floods and devastating cyclones.

In agreed conclusions of 31 March,[7] TDB asked the UNCTAD secretariat to prepare an update of the *Least Developed Countries Report 1995* in time for the High-level Meeting in September. In an exchange of views on LDC issues, attention was drawn to the progressive deterioration of economic and social conditions in LDCs despite vigorous efforts by them to implement the economic reforms envisaged in the Programme of Action. Inadequacy of external finance, impediments to market access and persistence of debt-servicing difficulties were cited by many participants as major contributory factors to the deterioration in economic performance. Attention was drawn to possible lessons that could be learned from the experience of LDCs that had performed relatively well and TDB urged the secretariat to identify gaps in implementing reforms and additional measures and to analyse more fully the question of whether such experience could be replicated in other LDCs.

The Board noted that the proceedings of the High-level Intergovernmental Meeting could be enhanced if an assessment of progress in implementing the Programme of Action by Governments was available to it. It outlined various issues that such an assessment should include. TDB recommended that UNCTAD IX, to be held in 1996, take the outcome of the Mid-term Global Review fully into account and recommended for adoption by the High-level Intergovernmental Meeting a draft provisional agenda and proposals for organization of its work, which it annexed to the agreed conclusions.

The Meeting of Governmental Experts of Donor Countries and Multilateral and Bilateral Financial and Technical Assistance Institutions with Representatives of the Least Developed Countries—the main preparatory exercise for the Mid-term Global Review—took place in Geneva from 29 May to 2 June.[8] As requested by TDB, the Meeting prepared a draft assessment of pro-

gress in implementing the Programme of Action at the national level and progress in international support measures, which it annexed to its report as a contribution to the High-level Intergovernmental Meeting (see below). The draft assessment covered: the main economic developments during the early 1990s as they affected the performance of LDCs; the policy reform process; civil strife and political instability; developments in the productive sectors; human resources development; external trade and the implications of the Final Act of the Uruguay Round of multilateral trade negotiations; external finance; external debt and relief measures; and arrangements for implementation, follow-up and monitoring of the Programme of Action. The Meeting also presented possible recommendations covering a number of key areas of concern for LDCs: reforms; external trade and investment; external finance; and external debt.

Also in preparation for the Mid-term Global Review, the UNCTAD secretariat organized a series of expert group meetings: on women in development in LDCs (Niamey, Niger, 24-26 January);[9] on fiscal policy reforms in LDCs (Geneva, 16 and 17 March);[10] and on trade diversification in LDCs (Geneva, 10 and 11 April).[11] The issues of external finance, debt and trade were the subject of a special high-level panel organized during the Donor-Recipient Meeting in May.

### Mid-term Global Review

In accordance with a 1994 General Assembly resolution,[12] the High-level Intergovernmental Meeting on the Mid-term Global Review of the Implementation of the Programme of Action for the Least Developed Countries for the 1990s was held in New York from 26 September to 6 October 1995.[13] It was preceded, on 25 September, by a one-day Meeting of Senior Officials, which addressed outstanding issues related to the Meeting's organization of work. Among documents before the Meeting was, as requested by TDB (see above), an addendum[14] to *The Least Developed Countries 1995 Report*, which examined why some LDCs had performed better than others and provided more recent data and analysis concerning trends in providing development finance to LDCs and in the evolution of their external debt and debt service.

The Meeting adopted: an assessment of progress in the implementation of the Programme of Action at the national level, and progress in international support measures; and recommendations covering a number of key areas of concern for LDCs. It also adopted a Declaration on the Mid-term Global Review of the Programme of Action.

**Report of the Secretary-General.** In response to requests contained in General Assembly resolutions of 1993[15] and 1994,[12] the Secretary-

General submitted a November 1995 report[16] on the outcome of the High-level Intergovernmental Meeting on the Mid-term Global Review. The report summarized the Meeting's recommendations (see annex to resolution 50/103 below) and described the preparatory process for the review.

By **decision 50/429** of 20 December, the Assembly took note of the Secretary-General's report on the Mid-term Global Review.

GENERAL ASSEMBLY ACTION

The General Assembly, on 20 December, adopted **resolution 50/103**.

### Implementation of the Programme of Action for the Least Developed Countries for the 1990s

*The General Assembly,*

*Recalling* its resolutions 45/206 of 21 December 1990, in which it endorsed the Paris Declaration and the Programme of Action for the Least Developed Countries for the 1990s, and 49/98 of 19 December 1994, in which it decided to convene the High-level Intergovernmental Meeting on the Mid-term Global Review of the Implementation of the Programme of Action for the Least Developed Countries for the 1990s,

*Reaffirming* the Paris Declaration and the Programme of Action, the prime objective of which is to arrest the further deterioration in the socio-economic situation of the least developed countries, to reactivate and accelerate growth and development in those countries and, in the process, to set them on the path of sustained economic growth and sustainable development,

*Expressing serious concern* that the least developed countries as a group have not been able to achieve many of the objectives of the Programme of Action and that their overall socio-economic situation has continued to deteriorate,

*Noting with concern* the reduced flow of development resources to the least developed countries, the resulting need to accord them priority in the allocation of concessional resources and their continued marginalization in world trade, as well as the fact that many least developed countries face serious debt problems and more than half are considered debt-distressed,

*Taking note* of agreed conclusions 423(XLI) of 31 March 1995 of the Trade and Development Board on the annual review of progress in the implementation of the Programme of Action for the Least Developed Countries for the 1990s, which was underpinned by *The Least Developed Countries 1995 Report,*

*Taking note* of the note by the Secretary-General transmitting the report of the High-level Intergovernmental Meeting on the Mid-term Global Review of the Implementation of the Programme of Action for the Least Developed Countries for the 1990s,

1. *Reaffirms* the Programme of Action for the Least Developed Countries for the 1990s as the basis for continuing cooperation between the least developed countries, which have the responsibility for their own development, and their development partners, based on shared responsibility and strengthened partnership, as well as its commitment to the full and effective implementation of the Programme of Action;

2. *Endorses* the measures and recommendations contained in the note by the Secretary-General transmitting the report of the High-level Intergovernmental Meeting on the Mid-term Global Review of the Implementation of the Programme of Action for the Least Developed Countries for the 1990s, as annexed hereto, which are designed to ensure the full implementation of the Programme of Action over the second half of the decade;

3. *Calls upon* all Governments, international and multilateral organizations, financial institutions and development funds, the organs, organizations and programmes of the United Nations system, and all other organizations concerned to take immediate, concrete and adequate steps to implement the Programme of Action, taking full account of the measures and recommendations of the mid-term global review so as to ensure sustained economic growth and sustainable development in the least developed countries and to enable them to participate in and benefit from the process of globalization and liberalization;

4. *Notes* that many least developed countries, for their part, have been implementing courageous and far-reaching policy reforms and adjustment measures in line with the Programme of Action, and in that regard emphasizes the need for national policies and measures aimed at establishing macroeconomic stability by rationalizing public expenditure and adopting sound monetary and fiscal policies so as to ensure a dynamic private sector by such means as providing a sound legal framework and improving human resources development, living standards, health and the status of women, and calls upon the international community to provide adequate support thereto;

5. *Strongly urges* all donor countries to implement fully and expeditiously their commitments in all relevant areas, including the agreed menu of aid targets and commitments as set out in the Programme of Action and support to reinforce structural adjustment reform, as well as the measures agreed upon at the mid-term global review so as to provide a significant and substantial increase in the aggregate level of external support for the least developed countries, keeping in mind the increased needs of those countries as well as the requirements of the countries added to the list of the least developed countries following the Second United Nations Conference on the Least Developed Countries;

6. *Stresses* the critical importance of providing multilateral assistance for the least developed countries, in the form of grant-based multilateral programmes, and in that regard calls attention to the need to ensure adequate replenishment of the International Development Association and the soft-term windows of the regional development banks;

7. *Emphasizes* the serious debt problems of the least developed countries, which necessitate strengthened efforts to formulate an international debt strategy that should include concrete measures to alleviate the debt burden and increased concessional financing in support of appropriate economic policy measures, which will be critical to the revitalization of the growth and development of the least developed countries, and encourages the Bretton Woods institutions to expedite the ongoing consideration of ways to address the issue of multilateral debt, including those concerning the least developed countries;

8. *Reiterates* that increased opportunities for trade can help reactivate economic growth in the least developed countries, calls for significantly improved market access for their products and emphasizes the importance of applying effectively the provisions of the Final Act Embodying the Results of the Uruguay Round of Multilateral Trade Negotiations, and further emphasizes in that context the importance of taking concrete action, as appropriate, to fully and expeditiously implement the Marrakesh Declaration as it relates to the least developed countries and the ministerial decision on measures in favour of the least developed countries, as well as the measures agreed to at the mid-term global review, with a view to enabling the least developed countries to maximize their benefit from the Final Act and to cope with any adverse effects arising therefrom;

9. *Also reiterates* the importance attached to the implementation of the ministerial decision on measures concerning possible negative effects of reform programmes on the least developed countries and net food-importing developing countries;

10. *Reaffirms* the importance of the follow-up and monitoring mechanisms for implementation of the Programme of Action at the national, regional and global levels as crucial to the implementation of the Programme of Action;

11. *Recalls* that in its resolution 49/98, it invited the Secretary-General to make recommendations to the General Assembly at its fiftieth session, with a view to ensuring that the secretariat of the United Nations Conference on Trade and Development had sufficient capacity to undertake an effective follow-up of the outcome of the mid-term global review and to follow up the conclusions and recommendations relating to the least developed countries adopted by major United Nations conferences, and in this regard takes note of the relevant proposals of the Secretary-General related to the programme budget for the biennium 1996-1997;

12. *Emphasizes* the importance of the annual reviews by the Trade and Development Board of progress in the implementation of the Programme of Action and the pressing need for enabling representatives of the least developed countries to participate in such annual reviews, and to that end requests the Secretary-General to defray the cost of participation of representatives of least developed countries by mobilizing extrabudgetary resources for that purpose and by reallocating existing resources of the regular budget, if required;

13. *Recalls* that at the end of the decade, a global review and appraisal of the implementation of the Programme of Action will be carried out, in accordance with paragraph 140 of the Programme of Action and operative paragraph 7 (*c*) of General Assembly resolution 45/206 regarding the consideration by the Assembly at its fifty-second session of the holding of a third United Nations conference on the least developed countries;

14. *Calls upon* the United Nations Conference on Trade and Development at its ninth session to take into account the outcome of the High-level Intergovernmental Meeting on the Mid-term Global Review of the Programme of Action for the Least Developed Countries for the 1990s;

15. *Requests* the Secretary-General to submit to the General Assembly at its fifty-second session a report on the implementation of the present resolution.

## ANNEX
### Mid-term global review of progress towards the implementation of the Programme of Action for the Least Developed Countries for the 1990s

*Part One*

Declaration of the High-level Intergovernmental Meeting on the Mid-term Global Review of the Implementation of the Programme of Action for the Least Developed Countries for the 1990s

*The Meeting*

*Declares*, in particular, the following:

(*a*) The participants in the Meeting have undertaken an assessment of progress in the implementation of the Programme of Action and agreed on concrete recommendations to ensure that the Programme is more effectively implemented throughout the remaining part of the decade.

(*b*) They reaffirmed their commitment to work cooperatively towards achieving the prime objective of the Programme of Action which is to arrest the further deterioration in the socio-economic situation of the least developed countries, to reactivate and accelerate growth and development in these countries and, in the process, to set them on the path of economic growth and sustainable development based on shared responsibility and strengthened partnership.

(*c*) The least developed countries as a group have not been able to meet many of the objectives of the Programme of Action and their overall socio-economic situation has continued to deteriorate. This deeply concerned the participants at the Meeting. At the domestic level, civil strife and recurrent natural disasters in some of the least developed countries and the resulting social economic burdens, macroeconomic imbalances and poor performance of the productive sectors, *inter alia* the lack of adequate physical and institutional infrastructures, have contributed to this deterioration. Persistent and serious debt and debt-servicing problems, very low levels of exports, and a declining share in world trade and the insufficiency of external finance have had unfavourable consequences on their growth and development.

(*d*) However, the least developed countries have continued to implement, under many difficulties, wide-ranging and far-reaching reforms. In some countries these efforts, complemented by a favourable external climate, have shown encouraging results. Many development partners have provided increased support to least developed countries, although the commitment to provide them with a significant and substantial increase in the aggregate level of external support has not happened.

(*e*) The participants are determined to pursue their efforts to implement the measures and recommendations agreed at the present Meeting. They are confident that the success of these efforts would lead to a reactivation and acceleration of growth and development in the least developed countries, and enable them to participate in and benefit from the processes of globalization and liberalization.

(*f*) They call upon all Governments, the United Nations system, regional and subregional organizations and the competent non-governmental organizations to combine their efforts in implementing the measures and recommendations agreed upon by the present Meeting so as to ensure the success of the Programme of Action.

(*g*) They firmly believe that, given political will on the part of the least developed countries, which have the primary responsibility for their development, and the support of the international community, the least developed countries will be able to enter the next century with better prospects for their peoples.

*Part Two*
Assessment of progress in the implementation of the Programme of Action for the Least Developed Countries for the 1990s at the national level, and progress in international support measures

Introduction

1. The Second United Nations Conference on the Least Developed Countries, held in Paris in 1990, adopted the Paris Declaration and the Programme of Action for the Least Developed Countries for the 1990s. The basic principles and aims of the Programme of Action are as valid today as when they were drawn up. The prime objective of the Programme of Action is to arrest the further deterioration in the socio-economic situation of least developed countries (LDCs), to reactivate and accelerate growth and development in these countries and, in the process, to set them on the path of sustained growth and development. The policies and measures in support of these objectives set out in the Programme of Action revolve around the following major areas: establishment of a macroeconomic policy framework conducive to sustained economic growth and long-term development; development and mobilization of human resources; development, expansion and modernization of the productive base; reversing the trend towards environmental degradation; promotion of an integrated policy of rural development aimed at increasing food production, enhancing rural income and enhancing non-agricultural sector activities; and the provision of adequate external support.

2. It was noted with great concern that only one country, i.e., Botswana, has graduated from the group of LDCs since the early 1970s. At the same time the number of LDCs has increased from 41 at the time of the Paris Conference in September 1990 to 48 countries at present, without a proportionate increase in support measures despite national and international efforts.

I. Main developments during the early 1990s

3. Despite vigorous efforts by LDCs to implement economic reforms as envisaged by the Programme of Action, the LDCs as a group have not been able to meet many of the objectives of the Programme of Action and their overall socio-economic situation has continued to deteriorate. Several factors, both domestic and external, have contributed to the overall socio-economic deterioration in the LDCs. The domestic factors include: civil strife and recurrent natural disasters in some LDCs and the resulting social and economic burdens, political instability, macroeconomic imbalances, manifested in large fiscal and balance-of-payments deficits, in many cases the unfavourable short-term impact of macroeconomic policy adjustments on specific areas, in particular the most disadvantaged and vulnerable sections of the population, and poor performance of the productive sectors including lack of adequate physical infrastructure. The external factors include: persistent debt and debt-servicing problems; the decline in the share of LDCs in world trade and their continued marginalization; the inadequacy of external finance; and the emergence of new claimants for aid.

4. According to United Nations Conference on Trade and Development (UNCTAD) statistics, the real GDP growth rate of the LDCs averaged only 1.7 per cent per annum during the first four years of the 1990s, having declined from the growth rate of 2.3 per cent achieved during the 1980s. Despite the recovery in the world economy, the situation in the LDCs continues to be precarious, although a few of them made limited progress. With population growing at an average annual rate of 2.9 per cent, GDP per capita suffered an annual 1.1 per cent decline, thus threatening to worsen the already precarious income and consumption levels, as well as to widen the savings-investment gap in these countries.

5. While the slow-down in economic growth rates was common to both Asian and African LDCs, the former, which benefited, *inter alia*, from a relatively favourable regional environment, attained an average per capita output growth of 1.4 per cent in the 1990s, as compared with a 2.1 per cent per annum fall suffered by the latter. There have also been significant inter-country variations in growth performance. Thus, it is encouraging to note that, despite the poor performance for the group as a whole, nearly one quarter of LDCs were able to attain positive per capita income gains in the early 1990s. A strong expansion of agricultural production, internal stability, strong government commitments, a sound political and regulatory framework for development, complemented by significant external support, among other factors, have contributed to raising economic growth rates.

6. The worsening of socio-economic conditions in many LDCs in the 1990s has increasingly been translated into a marked deterioration in human welfare as reflected in reduced caloric intakes, increased mortality and morbidity, the re-emergence and spread of diseases, lower school enrolment, further marginalization of the weakest members of society, and other signals of acute social distress, as further reviewed below in section V.

7. Overall, the external environment facing LDCs has remained difficult. As these countries moved into the 1990s, despite an increase in exports of manufactured goods, their share in world exports and imports fell by more than three eighths and one third from the already low levels of 0.7 per cent and 1.0 per cent respectively in 1980. Despite vigorous efforts to diversify the largely commodity-based composition of their exports, the LDCs' economies continued to be vulnerable to vicissitudes and instability in commodity markets. Official development assistance (ODA), on which LDCs depend principally for their external financing, registered a decline over the early 1990s, and the aid outlook remains uncertain. Although a large number of LDCs have adopted national regulatory frameworks conducive to foreign investment, they have not yet attracted significant foreign direct investment (FDI). Despite measures adopted to alleviate their external debt burden, this burden continued to be unsustainably high for many LDCs and seriously compromises their adjustment and development efforts.

8. Some developing countries are also important development partners of LDCs. They have technical assistance and training programmes from which the latter have benefited. The potential for expanded economic and technical cooperation between LDCs and other de-

veloping countries merits further exploration and support by the international community, especially in view of the new opportunities emerging with the dynamic growth experience of a number of those other developing countries. As a means of maximizing the potential for such South-South cooperation, triangular funding arrangements which include the active contribution of developed countries and relevant international organizations can be initiated.

9. Several LDCs have been taking a number of measures to promote trade with neighbouring countries. For example, a number of African LDCs, especially land-locked ones, have sought to establish some form of free trade area or customs union at the subregional level. However, the establishment of such subregional arrangements has encountered a number of obstacles which have limited their effectiveness.

10. In sum, therefore, the requisite progress has not been made in most LDCs during the first half of the 1990s in realizing the overall objective of the Programme of Action, although some progress has been recorded in a number of LDCs as a result of the implementation of appropriate policies. Furthermore, the ongoing processes of economic globalization and liberalization are likely to have profound consequences for the future development of the LDCs. These processes, which offer great opportunities for growth and development, also entail risks of instability and marginalization. LDCs as a whole have made limited progress in overcoming structural constraints, infrastructural insufficiencies, debt overhang, promoting and diversifying the enterprise and export sectors, attracting foreign investment and creating a sufficient technological base. In this context, most of the LDCs will face globalization and liberalization from the situation of a constrained environment.

## II. The policy reform process

11. In recent years, most LDCs have embarked on a process of structural adjustment and wide-ranging reforms, often under internationally agreed frameworks for structural and sectoral adjustment. Important areas of policy focus have been towards coping with fiscal and balance-of-payments deficits, improved mobilization and use of domestic resources, through tax reforms, improving the effectiveness of the public sector and providing greater opportunities for the private sector. LDCs have also initiated reforms in critical areas such as population, education, health, food security and trade policy.

12. There are, however, some cases where the pace and scope of these reforms contrast with the limited progress achieved. In particular, despite success in securing short-term macroeconomic stability, certain situations sometimes existed where the reforms appear neither to have helped in lifting structural constraints facing the economies of LDCs nor to have improved supply capacity and export diversification. Thus, while it was recognized that the reform process sometimes could not guarantee immediate results, it was emphasized that the efforts of LDCs provided a context in which, over the longer term, growth and structural transformation could reinforce each other under more favourable circumstances.

13. The experience of LDCs points towards a number of factors which determined the success or otherwise of reform measures. Prime among them has been government commitment to reforms, the appropriateness of national policy contents, sequencing of reforms and the level of external financial support to underpin reform efforts. Problems inherent in policy design, particularly the neglect of structural conditions and endowment-related considerations, retarded and even reversed the momentum of reforms. Inadequate domestic and external resource mobilization has been a particularly critical constraint for development in the LDCs.

14. The socio-economic difficulties of most LDCs have been further exacerbated by a specific set of environmental problems, such as land degradation and erosion, drought and desertification, which impair prospects for their development. These environmental problems have been aggravated in LDCs by a number of complex and interrelated factors, which include poverty and poverty-linked population pressures and cross-border refugee movements resulting from man-made and natural disasters. A noteworthy development has been that LDCs have demonstrated growing awareness of environmental issues and problems and many have implemented policies, strategies and institutional mechanisms to deal with them. The special situation and needs of the LDCs should be given special priority. International cooperation for sustainable development should be strengthened in order to support and complement the efforts of the LDCs. In particular, new and additional financial resources from all sources, both public and private, that are both adequate and predictable are necessary for environmentally sound development programmes and projects. However, adequate international support is needed to facilitate the transition from emergency relief to rehabilitation and development, and in particular in the context of activities under the International Decade for Natural Disaster Reduction and the promotion of national capacity-building to help prevent and mitigate future emergencies.

15. In many LDCs, it is encouraging to note that far-reaching changes in the system of governance, ranging from free elections to democratic constitutional reforms, have ushered in new possibilities for establishing more participatory and transparent systems of government. Generally, LDCs which achieved a revival of economic growth were those where greater progress has been made in securing popular participation and respect of human rights. In a number of LDCs, the consequences of man-made and other disasters have continued to drain resources, hampering overall long-term development. In some of these LDCs, armed conflict has often resulted in large-scale displacement of population, food emergencies and the unleashing of other destabilizing forces. The developmental task of Governments in meeting the socio-economic challenges posed became highly constrained under these circumstances. Besides destabilization caused by the presence of a large number of refugees, some LDCs have been obliged to provide asylum, with far-reaching implications for the budget, the environment impacts, other resource needs and related security problems which require urgent concrete international support for those countries hosting the refugees. The LDCs undergoing fundamental political, economic and social transformation, in the process of consolidating peace and democracy, require the support of the international community.

## III. Developments in the productive sectors

16. During the early 1990s, agriculture in most LDCs has been characterized by lags in production

growth relative to that of the population, continued declines in terms of trade and loss of market shares for traditional agricultural commodities. Agricultural production in LDCs fell by 1.1 per cent per annum in per capita terms during the period 1990-1993. Several LDCs responded to the continued poor performance of the sector by introducing reform measures, particularly reforming producer price incentives and marketing systems and the provision of essential agricultural inputs. While the overall thrust of these measures has been the removal of barriers to the private sector in agriculture, they have been unable to provide support services. A particularly disquieting trend in many LDCs is the growing incidence of man-made and recurrent natural disasters such as drought, flood, and devastating cyclones, which are the most important causes of food insecurity in many African LDCs. The situation has been further exacerbated by declines in food output and limited capacity to offset shortfalls through imports.

17.   Notwithstanding the wide variations in manufacturing growth rates among LDCs, the performance of the manufacturing sector on the whole has weakened in recent years, manufacturing activities have remained relatively undiversified, and the utilization of capacity and resources has been low. The sector growth rate decelerated to 1.4 per cent per annum during the early 1990s, from 2.1 per cent per annum in the 1980s. While some one third of LDCs maintained a positive growth of manufacturing value added (MVA) in the 1980s and early 1990s, most LDCs experienced stagnation and even declines in manufacturing output. The response of the LDCs to deteriorating manufacturing performance has been through adjustments of macroeconomic policies and instruments, and sectoral measures to augment manufacturing output and efficiency. At the sectoral level, the LDCs have reoriented their incentive structure and introduced changes in institutional policies and regulatory arrangements in order to improve the macroeconomic environment for manufacturing production.

18.   The LDCs have made major efforts to improve their transport and transit infrastructure systems during the last decade. The budgetary constraints faced by LDCs have, however, gradually undermined the financial capabilities of Governments to maintain the momentum of these efforts. These constraints are particularly felt in land-locked and island LDCs, where inadequate physical infrastructure poses major obstacles to structural transformation and economic development.

IV.   Land-locked and island least developed countries

19.   Sixteen of the 48 least developed countries are also land-locked. The high transport costs which result from their particular geographical handicaps continue to have a significant adverse impact on their international trade performance and overall economic development. In order to alleviate the particular problems which these countries face, the land-locked and transit developing countries, as well as the donor community, adopted a Global Framework for Transport Cooperation, which contains a comprehensive set of recommendations for concrete action at the national and subregional levels designed to improve the efficiency of transit transport systems. The Framework underscores the need for extensive financial and technical support by the donor community. The donor community recognizes this. Furthermore, the Framework calls upon

UNCTAD and the regional economic commissions to play a leading role in promoting the implementation of the agreed actions.

20.   Island least developed countries continue to face particular problems resulting from their smallness, insularity and remoteness from the major economic centres. They are vulnerable to a number of adverse factors, including environmental degradation. Poor internal and external transport links to world markets negatively compound their ability to participate effectively in world trade. The Programme of Action for the Sustainable Development of Small Island Developing States, adopted in Barbados in May 1994, outlines a range of measures that need to be undertaken in order to alleviate the particular problems which these countries face. The Programme calls for increased support by the international community to ensure effective implementation of these measures in conjunction with national measures in support of sustainable development.

V.   Human resources development

21.   LDCs have adopted and are implementing policies, measures and programmes to tackle key problems in human resources development. However, the expansion of national population programmes within the overall framework of human resources development has been difficult for a number of reasons, such as funding constraints, among others. These programmes have been complemented by strong efforts to change attitudes, including persuasion and campaigns relying on traditional and modern information techniques.

22.   Despite major difficulties, there have been some encouraging results achieved by some LDCs, particularly in the areas of health and education. However, in many LDCs, mortality rates continue to be high. The situation is exacerbated by poor sanitation and hygienic conditions and the lack of safe drinking-water supplies. Acquired immunodeficiency syndrome (AIDS) and tropical epidemic and endemic diseases have become a major cause of death in recent years in some LDCs, as these countries have limited resources to deal effectively with such endemics and epidemics. The economic crisis faced by LDCs has further undermined health conditions in many countries as living standards have fallen, health services have been cut owing to budgetary pressures, and the availability of imported medicines and other medical supplies has dwindled. Education services continue to be affected by deteriorating economic conditions, in particular by budgetary constraints. There is need for investment in the development of human capacities, particularly in programmes of health, nutrition, education and training and population activities.

23.   Although women constitute half of human resources in the LDCs, they have continued to be hampered by their marginal position from playing their full role in socio-economic development. Despite measures being taken to enhance their role in development, women in the LDCs still lag behind their male counterparts as well as women from other developing countries in all areas of social and economic development. They face particular problems related to gender discrimination, such as limited access to productive resources, restricted education and training opportunities, poor health status, low representation in strategic decision-making positions, as well as having to bear a high dependency burden: the more so, as deepening pov-

erty is felt more acutely by women-headed households. In addition, prevalent attitudes regarding women's abilities and their proper socio-economic role, and women's own lack of knowledge about their rights, have kept them away from mainstream development. The lack of follow-up of decisions and internationally agreed recommendations aiming at the advancement of the status of women has also been a major cause of the poor prevailing situation.

## VI. External trade and the implications of the Final Act of the Uruguay Round

24. The Programme of Action underlined that it is essential that all countries contribute to developing a more open, credible and durable multilateral trading system, recognizing that the results of this process could be a reflection, *inter alia*, of their respective weight in world trade. It is encouraging to note that the LDCs have contributed to this process by implementing important trade liberalization measures. The Programme of Action also called for important support measures in favour of LDCs in such areas as duty-free treatment of their exports, exemptions from quotas and ceilings and the use of simplified and flexible rules of origin. Progress made in the provision of such support has been important in the case of a number of countries. While a number of LDCs have been able to increase their exports, the overall trade situation of the LDCs has deteriorated, in that their share in global trade has continued to decline. Although globalization and liberalization offer opportunities to LDCs, these processes also pose major challenges, particularly in the form of increased global competition. Despite recent improvements, world commodity markets have remained volatile and depressed. As a result the LDCs have become further marginalized and this trend needs to be reversed.

25. The extremely low export capacity of most LDCs has continued to be one of the major obstacles to growth and a source of the high dependence on ODA for financing the necessary investment, imports and technical support for development. Difficulties have persisted in expanding the external trading opportunities of LDCs, as commodity and market diversification measures have been rendered difficult principally by lack of investment, technology and skills to augment levels of production and efficiency.

26. LDCs have been granted special tariff preferences under various Generalized System of Preferences (GSP) schemes and other preferential arrangements. Following the conclusion of the Uruguay Round, a number of countries have taken steps to improve their GSP schemes in favour of LDCs. However, some schemes still exclude a number of products of export interest to LDCs (e.g., textiles, clothing, carpets, footwear, leather goods, etc.) and have rigid rules of origin. As the ability of many LDCs to utilize such facilities remains constrained, only a part of GSP-covered imports from LDCs has received preferential treatment. Thus the use of GSP schemes, in particular by African LDCs, has remained limited.

27. The adoption of the Final Act of the Uruguay Round will have significant consequences for the trading prospects of LDCs, in particular as regards preferences and the competitiveness of LDC exports. Increased transparency of trade regimes and the reduction of trade barriers, particularly tariff-binding on agricultural products and reduction in tariff escalation, as foreseen in the

Marrakesh arrangements, provide LDCs with increased opportunities in the long run. On the other hand, concerns have been expressed that LDCs may suffer erosion of preferential margins in relation to many of their exports to major markets and a possible consequential loss in export market shares and export earnings. In addition, the net food-importing LDCs may face higher import bills, at least in the short run, resulting from the agreement on agriculture. In the long run, the Final Act poses to LDCs the twin challenges of, first, developing and strengthening institutional and human capacities to formulate and manage legislation implementing the complex set of agreements of the Round, and secondly, building capacities for maximizing opportunities arising from these agreements. In this regard, the provisions of the Marrakesh Declaration and the ministerial decisions in favour of LDCs should be fully implemented.

28. A number of developed countries have set up in their own countries import promotion agencies in order to promote more trade with LDCs. Such agencies have played a helpful role in providing support services and in acting as contact points for business/trade missions from LDCs, undertaking market research and giving publicity to LDC products.

29. Trade among the LDCs, on the one hand, and that between LDCs and other developing countries within the same subregional or regional economic groupings, on the other hand, remains insignificant as a share of international trade. Only a few LDCs at present receive preferential treatment for their exports under the Global System of Trade Preferences among Developing Countries (GSTP) on a non-reciprocal basis. Additionally, subregional and regional trade is constrained by a number of obstacles, such as the fact that most countries produce similar export products, that subregional transport infrastructure is geared to trade with developed countries, that progress in tariff reduction is limited due to fiscal revenue implications for preference-giving countries, and that international support remains limited.

## VII. External finance

30. It was noted with concern that ODA remains the single most important source of external financing for LDCs. While welcoming improved aid performance by some donors, at the same time it was noted that overall aid performance by donors fell short of the commitments undertaken in the Programme of Action. ODA flows (actual disbursements) from Development Assistance Committee (DAC) countries, and multilateral agencies mainly financed by them, to the LDCs declined sharply in 1993. In absolute terms, ODA flows fell by $1.5 billion. Almost $1 billion of this was due to a drop in multilateral aid flows to LDCs. In view of the important role of multilateral funding in meeting the financial needs of LDCs and the uncertain resource outlook for some of the major multilateral financial institutions and grant-based programmes, this is a particularly worrying development. The ODA/GNP ratio for DAC donors as a whole declined to 0.08 per cent in 1993 as compared with 0.09 per cent in 1990. Moreover, this shortfall has to be seen against the agreed menu of aid targets and/or commitments as set out in paragraph 23 of the Programme of Action for the Least Developed Countries for the 1990s which call for a significant and substantial increase in resources

to LDCs and include, *inter alia*, the targets of 0.15 per cent and 0.20 per cent of donor GNP as ODA.

31. Donors have modified and improved their policies in the area of aid modalities. Most DAC donors have now shifted to a grant basis in their aid programmes for LDCs, resulting in a further increase in the grant element of bilateral ODA (which averaged 97 per cent in 1993). Most multilateral funding to LDCs is also on highly concessional terms. Multilateral funding constitutes an important complement to bilateral ODA for the LDCs and it is crucial that the base of this multilateral funding be sufficiently broadened. International efforts should continue to mobilize resources to LDCs implementing structural adjustment programmes, such as the World Bank–led Special Programme of Assistance (SPA) process, which in some cases have resulted in limited progress.

VIII. External debt and relief measures

32. The external debt and its servicing burden remains a crucial issue for the majority of LDCs. According to Organization for Economic Cooperation and Development/Development Assistance Committee (OECD/DAC) information, LDC total debt stock amounted to $127 billion in 1993, corresponding to 76 per cent of their combined GDP. It appears that for half of these countries, their external debt is equal to or exceeds their respective GDP. The difficulties many LDCs have in meeting their external obligations, in the context of the critical current economic situation and their poor export performance, are reflected in the relatively low levels of debt service paid in relation to scheduled payments. The share of multilateral debt in total long-term debt, as well as debt service, has increased considerably in recent years. Thus, in 1993 the multilateral debt constituted around 36 per cent of total debt of LDCs as compared with 27 per cent in 1984. The corresponding share in total debt service during this period increased even more, from less than 30 per cent to almost 50 per cent. This increase partly reflects the "lender of last resort function" of the international financial institutions and the fact that an increasing number of bilateral creditors are relinquishing many of their ODA claims to LDCs and have shifted from credit lending to grants. Debt-relief measures taken so far have not yet fully provided an effective and durable solution to the outstanding debt and debt-servicing burden of LDCs, although important relief measures have been taken to reduce their debt stock and debt-service obligations. In particular, following the adoption of the Toronto terms in 1988 (and enhanced Toronto terms in 1991), from which 19 LDCs benefited, the Paris Club in 1994 improved the debt treatment of the poorest countries by adopting the "Naples terms". These may constitute a step forward for the LDCs but might not be sufficient by themselves to resolve their external debt problem. Eight LDCs have already benefited from these provisions, which notably offer the possibilities to reduce the eligible debt of the poorest and most indebted countries by 50 to 67 per cent.

IX. Arrangements for implementation, follow-up and monitoring of the Programme of Action

A. The national level

33. At the national level, review arrangements, including United Nations Development Programme (UNDP)–sponsored round tables and the World Bank consultative and aid groups, have been further consolidated during the early 1990s, with additional countries joining or rejoining the process and meetings taking place more frequently and on a more regular basis. A strengthened country review process was considered the principal means of policy dialogue, and for coordinating the aid efforts of development partners with the development programmes of LDCs as well as mobilizing the required resources for their implementation. In all, over 60 full-scale consultative aid groups and round table or similar meetings were organized from the adoption of the Programme of Action until early 1995. While results in terms of resource mobilization have varied between countries, these meetings no doubt have an important role to play in improving aid flows to LDCs and in aid coordination. An important aspect of the country review process in recent years has been the attempt to link these arrangements more closely to national policy-making and programming.

B. The regional level

34. At the regional level, the Programme of Action called for monitoring progress in economic cooperation between LDCs and other developing countries, particularly those in the same region. It also called for organizing cluster meetings to improve and strengthen existing cooperation arrangements at the regional and subregional levels. The United Nations regional commissions have, as part of their ongoing work, continued to follow up and monitor the implementation of the Programme of Action in LDCs in their respective regions. The Economic and Social Commission for Asia and the Pacific (ESCAP) has established a Special Body on Least Developed and Land-locked Developing Countries. The Economic Commission for Africa (ECA) has continued to consider progress in the implementation of the Programme of Action in African LDCs during the annual meetings of the Commission. However, owing to resource constraints in the United Nations the cluster meeting process has not been initiated.

C. The global level

35. At the global level, UNCTAD has responsibility as the focal point for the monitoring, follow-up and review of the implementation of the Programme of Action. In addition to the regular follow-up, monitoring and review of progress in the implementation of the Programme of Action at the global level by the UNCTAD Trade and Development Board, efforts have also been made to promote the full mobilization and coordination of all organs, organizations and bodies of the United Nations system for the purpose of the implementation and follow-up of the Programme of Action, but more remains to be done. Individual agencies have continued to develop and implement assistance programmes for the LDCs and pursued their advocacy and policy advisory missions with regard to these countries. There is need for regular reporting of progress made by various agencies.

*Part Three*

Recommendations

36. The present recommendations are based on the assessment of progress in the implementation of the Programme of Action for the Least Developed Countries for the 1990s presented above, as well as on informa-

tion contained in *The Least Developed Countries 1995 Report*, and recommendations made by the expert groups convened by the UNCTAD secretariat as part of the preparations for the High-level Intergovernmental Meeting on the Mid-term Global Review of the Implementation of the Programme of Action for the Least Developed Countries for the 1990s. These recommendations cover a number of key areas of concern for the LDCs.

### I. Major challenges

37. The challenges facing LDCs in the second half of the 1990s are to reverse the decline in economic and social conditions, to promote sustainable economic growth, development and structural transformation and to avoid becoming further marginalized in the international economy. An intensified policy commitment by both LDC Governments and the international community will be required to meet these challenges. In implementing domestic policies, LDCs should endeavour to focus on measures to restore and maintain macroeconomic stability; to promote the growth and diversification of exports; to strengthen an enabling environment for private-sector investment and entrepreneurship; to enhance human resources development; to continue to implement population and development programmes with full respect for the various religious and ethical values and cultural background of each country's people; to adhere to basic human rights recognized by the international community which strike an optimal balance in the interrelationship between their population, their natural resource base and the environment, taking into account economic imperatives; to strengthen the infrastructure; to promote good governance as mentioned in the Programme of Action; to broaden popular participation in the development process; and to ensure the full utilization of human resources along with democratization, promotion of good governance, observance of the rule of law and peaceful resolution of any civil conflicts where such conditions exist. The broad outlines of a domestic economic policy framework conducive to meeting the challenges facing the LDCs are delineated below.

### II. The economic policy framework

38. *(a)* Macroeconomic stability would require rationalization and sound management of public expenditure, properly planned monetary growth and maintenance of appropriate exchange rates commensurate with ensuring a sustainable external balance;

*(b)* Policies to increase export earnings, including appropriate exchange rate and trade policy reforms to reverse the decline in the share of world trade of the LDCs, diversify the composition of their export structure and to facilitate their ability to exploit opportunities arising from the Final Act of the Uruguay Round, are essential;

*(c)* This will entail strengthening of existing policies and measures for the promotion and support of the private sector complemented with public investment, including policy-based incentives or the adoption of new policies and measures where necessary;

*(d)* The potential for economic and technical cooperation between LDCs and other developing countries merits further exploration. The international community should help LDCs promote trade links and should take appropriate measures to support such trade links, particularly subregional and regional trade. Such trade could be promoted by identifying complementarities in production structures among countries, strengthening the institutional and human capacities for the operation of subregional trading arrangements, establishing subregional trade information networks, and associating the private sector more closely with the integration process. There are potential gains for the LDCs in participating in the Global System of Trade Preferences among Developing Countries (GSTP). LDCs should be encouraged to accede to GSTP and be provided with appropriate technical assistance to enable them to benefit fully from the system. Least developed countries should strengthen subregional, regional and interregional cooperation in order to benefit from economies of scale and to attract foreign direct investment more easily from developed and other developing countries. More attention should be given to promoting triangular cooperation and technical cooperation among developing countries (TCDC) as well as South-South joint ventures and economic cooperation among developing countries (ECDC) investment in these countries;

*(e)* The growth of a dynamic private enterprise sector requires an appropriate economic, fiscal and legal framework. Essential features of this framework are stable and predictable policies, tax, monetary and trade policies which ensure adequate incentives for investment, and a legal system which protects property rights and commercial contracts. These features are also needed to tap into international capital flows in the form of direct and portfolio investments;

*(f)* Enhancing human resources development is imperative if LDCs are to raise productivity, output and living standards. With the support of the international community, LDC Governments should intensify their efforts to raise education and training standards, promote life-long learning, improve the health status of their populations, and strengthen the status of women, by implementing appropriate policies in accordance with the provisions of the International Conference on Population and Development and the Fourth World Conference on Women;

*(g)* To enable women in LDCs to play their full role in development, efforts should focus on legislative and administrative reforms to give women full and equal access to economic resources, including the right to inheritance and to ownership of land and other property, credit, natural resources and appropriate technologies, and to involve women directly in planning, decision-making, implementation and development of macroeconomic and social policies, programmes and projects. Special initiatives and innovative schemes which can give women increased access to credit, training, information on marketing channels, as well as other support services, to alleviate the burden of their role as mothers and housewives, should be adopted;

*(h)* The economic policy strategies adopted by the LDCs should be consistent with the need to eradicate the chronic levels of poverty afflicting these countries, in particular by promoting the development of the private sector and entrepreneurship, by ensuring that all people have access to productive resources, and benefit from a policy and regulatory environment that enhances their overall capacities and empowers them to benefit from expanding employment and economic opportunities;

*(i)* LDC Governments are attempting to implement comprehensive structural adjustment reforms in very

difficult circumstances, often in the face of severe administrative and financial constraints. Many of the constraints that they face are structural, deep-seated and not amenable to short-term solutions. Consequently, successful structural adjustment reforms require a government commitment to reform, and a medium-term to long-term perspective for implementation;

*(j)* In order to ensure that structural adjustment programmes include social development goals, in particular the eradication of poverty, the generation of productive employment and the enhancement of social integration, LDC Governments, in cooperation with the international financial institutions and other international organizations, should:

(i) Protect basic social programmes and expenditure, in particular those affecting the poor and vulnerable segments of society, from budget reductions;

(ii) Review the impact of structural adjustment programmes on social development by means of gender-sensitive social-impact assessments and other relevant methods, and develop policies to reduce their negative effects and improve their positive impact;

(iii) Further promote policies enabling small enterprises, cooperatives and other forms of microenterprises to develop their capacities for income generation and employment creation;

*(k)* Agreeing on a mutual commitment between interested developed and developing country partners to allocate, on average, 20 per cent of ODA and 20 per cent of the national budget, respectively, to basic social programmes, and in this context, the proposal of the Government of Norway to host a meeting in 1996 among interested countries and representatives of relevant international institutions, with a view to considering how the 20/20 initiative can be applied operationally, is welcomed;

*(l)* Commitment of the LDCs and the assistance of the international community are essential components for the success of structural adjustment programmes. Without such support, the long-term objectives and the sustainability of the programmes will be jeopardized. In this regard, therefore, renewed commitments by the international community as defined by the Programme of Action adopted in Paris and other relevant instruments to support the efforts of the LDCs with adequate resources are vital.

III. External trade and investment

39. The extremely low export capacity of LDCs, their very low level of export receipts, and the fluctuation and the resulting sharp limitation on their capacity to import, are the major structural constraints to developing LDC trade. This situation is more acute in the case of land-locked and island least developed countries, as their external trade is further impeded by high transportation costs.

40. Action by the international community, including increased technical assistance as foreseen in the Marrakesh Ministerial Decision on Measures in Favour of LDCs, complemented by adequate financial support, can help LDC efforts to increase export earnings through increased production in both the traditional and the modern sectors of the economy, through diversification of the commodity structure and export markets, and thereby help to obtain better prices for their export commodities. It can also help LDCs to mitigate any adverse

effects of the implementation of the Uruguay Round agreements and to integrate themselves better into the international trading system. The interest of LDCs regarding the idea of considering the setting up of a "safety net" to help them cope with any such effects in the immediate and short term was noted. The Final Act of the Uruguay Round of multilateral trade negotiations, including the special clauses providing differential and more favourable treatment, and the decision on measures in favour of least developed countries provide the institutional framework for these matters.

A

41. All provisions of the Final Act of the Uruguay Round should be effectively applied. In this regard, concrete action, as appropriate, should be taken, consistent with the Final Act, to fully and expeditiously implement the Marrakesh Declaration as it relates to LDCs, and the Ministerial Decision on Measures in Favour of LDCs, and to give effect to the Ministerial Decision on Measures Concerning the Possible Negative Effects of the Reform Programme on Least Developed and Net Food-importing Countries, with a view to enhancing LDC participation in the multilateral trading system, taking into account the impact of trade liberalization, and the relatively weak capacities of LDCs to participate in an increasingly competitive global market in goods and services.

42. Consideration shall be given to further improving GSP schemes and other schemes for products of particular export interest to LDCs, e.g., agricultural products, fish and fish products, leather and footwear, and textiles and clothing, through, where possible, the widening of product coverage; the reduction of procedural complexities, and the avoidance of frequent changes in the schemes. Consideration should also be given to a significant reduction in tariff escalation.

43. The rules set out in the various agreements and instruments and the transitional provisions of the Uruguay Round, including those relating to anti-dumping, countervailing duties, safeguards, and rules of origin, should be applied in a flexible and supportive manner for the least developed countries.

44. As for textiles and clothing, consideration should be given, to the extent possible, to permitting meaningful increases in the possibilities of access for exports from LDCs.

45. In the area of services, efforts should be directed at building and strengthening the efficiency and competitiveness of the weak domestic service sectors of the LDCs. Their participation in trade in services could be enhanced by effective application of article IV of the General Agreement on Trade in Services (GATS) with special priority given to LDCs. Furthermore, ways should be explored to facilitate LDC access to information technology and networks and distribution channels, and to give easy access to information to LDC service suppliers through contact points to be established, in accordance with GATS. It was noted that the movement of labour for the provision of services to other countries is an area of interest to LDCs.

46. Care should be taken so that domestic laws and regulations of importing countries in areas such as labour and the environment do not constrain the export opportunities of LDCs in a manner inconsistent with the Final Act of the Uruguay Round.

47. The home countries of foreign investment are urged to encourage investment in LDCs by taking appropriate supportive action.

48. South-South cooperation at the subregional and regional levels should be promoted to enhance regional and subregional trade by providing market access for LDCs by neighbouring countries. Appropriate measures should be taken to promote, support and strengthen trade initiatives of LDCs in subregional and regional groupings. Efforts of the LDCs to diversify their exports need to be supported so that their trading prospects become more viable. Such cooperation can be critical in complementing actions by LDCs and their development partners to attract foreign investment to LDCs. Measures should be taken to grant preferential access to the exports of LDCs on a non-reciprocal basis by developing countries under the GSTP, and also to augment resources, where appropriate, for promoting economic cooperation among developing countries (ECDC) and technical cooperation among developing countries (TCDC) through multilateral and bilateral institutions. Developing countries should, *inter alia*, introduce preferential schemes for LDCs under the GSTP.

### B

49. Technical assistance should be refocused and wherever necessary intensified to help LDCs adapt to and take advantage of the new trading environment created by the conclusion of the Uruguay Round. Common efforts of donors, international organizations as well as the LDCs themselves are needed in the implementation of the commitments undertaken and for maximizing the opportunities arising from the Uruguay Round agreements. Main areas of technical assistance in this regard should include:

*(a)* Enhancing institutional and human capacities to comply with the new obligations arising from membership of the World Trade Organization (WTO) or to assist LDCs to accede to WTO, as well as to formulate and implement future trade policy;

*(b)* Developing and strengthening supply capabilities in relation to tradeable goods and services, and the competitiveness of enterprises;

*(c)* Improving the microeconomic trading environment and expanding the use of new communications technologies in the service of trade through the UNCTAD Trade Efficiency Programme;

*(d)* Enhancing the capability to make full use of GSP schemes;

*(e)* Supporting commodity diversification and marketing efforts;

*(f)* Expanding the trading and investment opportunities of LDCs, in particular, by identifying new trading opportunities which could be carried out, *inter alia*, through import promotion agencies by developed and other countries, developing an environment conducive to attracting foreign investment, and through advice and technical support.

50. With a view to achieving these aims, it is essential to eliminate duplication and strengthen cooperation between relevant international organizations, in particular UNCTAD, WTO and the International Trade Centre UNCTAD/GATT, in order to conserve scarce resources and make full use of the existing and potential synergies among these organizations. Among the measures that should be considered is the establishment of a technical assistance fund administered by WTO in order to help LDCs participate actively in WTO.

### IV. External finance

51. The overwhelming dependence of LDCs on official development assistance (ODA) is likely to continue during the rest of the present decade and beyond. The basic policy issues that the international community faces in this respect in the current climate of budgetary stringency and ODA scarcity, are: *(a)* how to improve aid allocations to the LDCs; and *(b)* how to enhance the quality and effectiveness of assistance to these countries. Donors need to expeditiously implement the agreed menu of aid targets and/or commitments as set out in paragraph 23 of the Programme of Action and fulfil their commitments to provide a significant and substantial increase in the aggregate level of external support to LDCs, keeping in mind the increased needs of these countries, as well as the requirements of the new countries included in the list of LDCs following the Paris Conference. The various provisions of the relevant resolutions adopted in the General Assembly in recent years, as well as the various relevant provisions adopted by recent major United Nations conferences, in particular the World Summit for Social Development, should also be taken into account, as adopted.

52. In view of the enhanced assistance capacities of a number of developing countries over the last few years, they should be invited to join the traditional donor countries in providing assistance to the LDCs.

53. The following measures and actions by donors can be highlighted:

*(a)* Specific measures to incorporate the agreed menu of aid targets and/or commitments as set out in paragraph 23 of the Programme of Action more explicitly into the national aid strategies and budgetary planning mechanisms of donors;

*(b)* Ensure adequate funding of the multilateral institutions and programmes which are major sources of financing for LDCs. Particular attention will have to be paid to replenishment of the International Development Association (IDA) and the soft-term windows of the regional development banks, and other grant-based multilateral programmes. The relevant multilateral financial institutions are also invited to explore the possibility of tapping new sources of funds to help support LDC development efforts;

*(c)* Support United Nations development efforts by substantially increasing the resources for operational activities on a predictable, continuous and assured basis commensurate with the increasing needs of developing countries as stated in General Assembly resolutions 47/199 of 22 December 1992 and 48/162 of 20 December 1993, while giving particular consideration to the special needs of LDCs as underlined in the programmes of action of major United Nations conferences organized since 1990;

*(d)* Continue to give high priority to LDCs in the operational activities of all parts of the United Nations system for development, bearing in mind decision 95/23 of 16 June 1995 of the Executive Board of the United Nations Development Programme and of the United Nations Population Fund, in which it is stated that 60 per cent of UNDP programme resources in its future programming arrangement should be allocated to LDCs;

*(e)* Continue to provide financial support to adjustment programmes in LDCs on a timely basis and on terms adapted to the special needs and circumstances of LDCs, adequate external financing for the development and diversification of the productive sector, as well as additional support for poverty eradication, environmental conservation and social programmes;

*(f)* An increased level of technical assistance should be provided to LDCs and priority should be given to skill transfer, with a view to developing national capacity;

*(g)* Ensure the maintenance of mutual transparency and accountability in the management of aid resources by the aid officials of donor countries/organizations and managers in recipient countries, as well as ensure the active support of the donor countries/organizations towards the promotion of ownership of development programmes by the recipient countries;

*(h)* The international community should support the measures being taken in the LDCs towards the eradication of poverty. Increased resources should be made available from all possible sources, public and private, in this regard.

### V.  External debt

54.  Many LDCs face serious debt problems and more than half are considered debt-distressed. The serious debt problem of the LDCs necessitates strengthened efforts on the international debt strategy. This strategy should include concrete measures to alleviate the debt burden and increased concessional financing, in support of appropriate economic policy measures, which will be critical to the revitalization of growth and development. Debt-distressed LDCs should benefit from substantial debt-relief schemes.

#### A.  Official bilateral debt

55.  *(a)*  All donors that have not already done so are urged to implement Trade and Development Board resolution 165(S-IX) of 11 March 1978 by cancelling or providing equivalent relief for ODA debt as a matter of priority in such a way that the net flows of ODA are improved for the recipient. Those creditors still holding such claims, including non-OECD creditors, are urged to take similar measures;

*(b)*  Adopt measures to substantially reduce the bilateral debt of the LDCs, in particular the countries of Africa, as soon as possible;

*(c)*  Paris Club creditors are invited to continue to implement expeditiously and in a flexible manner the very concessional treatment under the Naples terms;

*(d)*  Other non-Paris Club creditors are also invited to take similar measures in order to alleviate the debt burden of debt-distressed LDCs, including by setting up special debt-reduction programmes and debt-relief mechanisms.

#### B.  Multilateral debt

56.  In order to address the multilateral debt problems of LDCs, the Bretton Woods institutions are encouraged to develop a comprehensive approach to assist countries with multilateral debt problems, through the flexible implementation of existing instruments and new mechanisms where necessary. In this respect the Bretton Woods institutions are encouraged to expedite the ongoing consideration of ways to address the issue of multilateral debt. Other international financial institutions are invited to consider, within the scope of their mandates, appropriate efforts with a view to assisting LDCs with multilateral debt problems.

#### C.  Commercial debt

57.  *(a)*  Invites creditor countries, private banks and multilateral financial institutions, within their prerogatives, to consider continuing the initiatives and efforts to address the commercial debt problems of the LDCs;

*(b)*  Mobilize the resources of the Debt Reduction Facility of the International Development Association in order to help eligible least developed countries to reduce their commercial debt, considering alternative mechanisms to complement that Facility.

58.  In accordance with the Copenhagen Declaration on Social Development, techniques of debt conversion applied to social development programmes and projects should be developed and implemented.

### VI.  Arrangements for implementation, follow-up and monitoring of the Programme of Action

59.  It is important that UNCTAD, which is the focal point at the global level for the monitoring, follow-up and review of the implementation of the Programme of Action, has sufficient capacity and resources to follow up the outcome of the mid-term global review. In this regard, it is recalled that the General Assembly, in resolution 49/98, invited the Secretary-General to make recommendations to the General Assembly at its fiftieth session with a view to ensuring that the UNCTAD secretariat has sufficient capacity to undertake an effective follow-up of the outcome of the mid-term review as well as the follow-up of the conclusions and recommendations relating to LDCs adopted by major global conferences, as appropriate.

General Assembly resolution 50/103

20 December 1995     Meeting 96     Adopted without vote

Approved by Second Committee (A/50/617/Add.5) without vote, 12 December (meeting 43); draft by Vice-Chairman (A/C.2/50/L.72), orally corrected, based on informal consultations on draft by Philippines, for Group of 77 and China (A/C.2/50/L.31); agenda item 95 *(e).*
*Financial implications.* S-G, A/C.2/50/L.77.
*Meeting numbers.* GA 50th session: 2nd Committee 30-32, 38, 43; plenary 96.

## Island developing countries

In response to a 1994 General Assembly request,[17] the Secretary-General submitted a September 1995 report[18] on action taken by UN organs, organizations and bodies to implement the 1994 Programme of Action for the Sustainable Development of Small Island Developing States (SIDS).[19] In addition to providing details of the plans and programmes adopted within the UN system to implement the Programme of Action, the report reviewed the institutional arrangements either already in place or envisaged to support such implementation.

In concluding observations, the report stated that organizations and bodies of the UN system had incorporated elements of the Programme of Action that fell within their mandates into their work programmes and had begun to implement projects to meet the Programme of Action's priorities.

In an addendum to the report,[20] the Secretary-General provided, in tabular form, project-related information supplied by UN organizations.

GENERAL ASSEMBLY ACTION

The General Assembly, on 20 December, adopted **resolution 50/116**.

### Implementation of the outcome of the Global Conference on the Sustainable Development of Small Island Developing States

*The General Assembly,*

*Recalling* its resolution 49/122 of 19 December 1994 on the Global Conference on the Sustainable Development of Small Island Developing States,

*Recalling also* its resolution 49/100 of 19 December 1994 on specific measures in favour of island developing countries,

*Reaffirming* that, because the development options of small island developing States are limited, there are special challenges to devising and implementing sustainable development plans, and that small island developing States will be constrained in meeting such challenges without the cooperation of the international community,

1. *Notes with appreciation* the report of the Secretary-General on action taken by the organs, organizations and bodies of the United Nations system to implement the Programme of Action for the Sustainable Development of Small Island Developing States, and welcomes in particular the action that has been taken by the Department for Policy Coordination and Sustainable Development of the United Nations Secretariat to support the system-wide implementation of the Programme of Action;

2. *Takes note* of the establishment of the Small Island Developing States Unit within the Department, and requests the Secretary-General to maintain the level of staffing and the structure and organization of the Unit in accordance with General Assembly resolution 49/122;

3. *Welcomes* the action that has been taken to enable the regional commissions to support activities to coordinate the outcome of the Global Conference on the Sustainable Development of Small Island Developing States;

4. *Takes note* of the interim measures that have been instituted to strengthen the capacity of the United Nations Conference on Trade and Development to enable it to complement the functions of the Department with respect to the implementation of the Programme of Action, and requests the Secretary-General to implement fully the relevant provisions of General Assembly resolution 49/122;

5. *Calls upon* Governments, as well as the organs, organizations and bodies of the United Nations system, other intergovernmental organizations and non-governmental organizations, to continue to implement fully all the commitments and recommendations that were made at the Conference, and to continue to take the action necessary for effective follow-up to the Programme of Action, including action to ensure the provision of the means of implementation under chapter XV thereof;

6. *Welcomes,* in particular, the progress made by the United Nations Development Programme in implementing General Assembly resolution 49/122, and invites the Programme to continue to implement all the provisions of both the technical assistance programme and the information network for small island developing States, as appropriate;

7. *Takes note* of the support that has been provided by the Commission on Sustainable Development to following up the implementation of the Programme of Action in accordance with General Assembly resolution 49/122 and the Programme of Action itself, and invites the Commission at its fourth session to consider giving due attention to small island developing States in the national presentations on coastal zone management;

8. *Notes* the initial action that has been taken by the United Nations Conference on Trade and Development and by the Department for Policy Coordination and Sustainable Development in preparation for the high-level panel that is being convened to discuss the challenges faced by island developing countries, particularly in the area of external trade, and invites the Conference and the Department to complete their arrangements in time for the fourth session of the Commission on Sustainable Development, and to make the report of the panel available to the Conference at its ninth session;

9. *Requests* the Secretary-General to ensure that the Small Island Developing States Unit of the Department include in its work programme, along with an indication of the resources of its activities and programmes, provision for the development and compilation of a vulnerability index for small island developing States, to be prepared in collaboration with the United Nations Conference on Trade and Development and other relevant organizations;

10. *Requests* the Secretary-General to submit to the General Assembly at its fifty-third session a report on the plans, programmes and projects for the sustainable development of small island developing States that have been implemented in response to the Programme of Action, as well as those that are under implementation and those that are envisaged for implementation within five years of the date of the report;

11. *Decides* to include in the provisional agenda of its fifty-first session, under the item entitled "Environment and sustainable development", the sub-item entitled "Implementation of the outcome of the Global Conference on the Sustainable Development of Small Island Developing States";

12. *Requests* the Secretary-General to submit to the General Assembly at its fifty-first session a report on action taken to implement the present resolution.

General Assembly resolution 50/116

20 December 1995     Meeting 96     Adopted without vote

Approved by Second Committee (A/50/618/Add.4) without vote, 30 November (meeting 40); draft by Vice-Chairman (A/C.2/50/L.47), based on informal consultations on draft by Australia, Austria, Belgium, Canada, Denmark, Finland, France, Germany, Greece, Ireland, Italy, Japan, Luxembourg, Netherlands, New Zealand, Philippines (for Group of 77 and China), Portugal, Spain, Sweden, United Kingdom and United States (A/C.2/50/L.32); agenda item 96 (e).

*Meeting numbers.* GA 50th session: 2nd Committee 34, 35, 38, 40; plenary 96.

## Land-locked developing countries

**UNCTAD action.** In accordance with a 1993 General Assembly request,[21] the Second Meeting of Governmental Experts from Land-locked and Transit Developing Countries and Representatives of Donor Countries and Financial and Development Institutions was held in New York from 19 to 22 June 1995,[22] the first having been held in 1993.[23] The Meeting was preceded by a Symposium for Land-locked and Transit Developing Countries which addressed specific regional problems faced by those countries in their efforts to improve their transit transport systems (New York, 14-16 June).[24] The Symposium, which was also convened in response to a 1993 Assembly request,[21] made proposals for the development of a global framework for transit transport cooperation between land-locked and transit developing countries and the donor community and submitted them to the Second Meeting for consideration.

On 22 June, the Meeting adopted the Global Framework for Transit Transport Cooperation between Land-locked and Transit Developing Countries and the Donor Community and annexed it to its report.[22]

**Report of the Secretary-General.** In response to a 1993 General Assembly request,[21] the Secretary-General, by a September note,[25] submitted the UNCTAD Secretary-General's report on progress in implementing specific actions related to the particular needs and problems of land-locked developing countries. The report described UNCTAD's activities, including the Second Meeting of Governmental Experts, the Symposium for Land-locked and Transit Developing Countries and its technical cooperation projects on behalf of those countries. It also summarized replies received from individual countries and from international and intergovernmental organizations in response to a request for information on action taken related to the particular needs and problems of land-locked developing countries.

The report concluded that the replies received underlined the fact that rail and road services were particularly relevant for transit transport operations. Although physical infrastructure development remained a priority concern, the removal of non-physical barriers to the smooth movement of transit cargoes was assuming significant importance. That related largely to the simplification and harmonization of customs and administrative procedures in ports and along the transit transport corridors, as well as to the simplification of other controls for the movement of cargo. Inter-State cooperation was considered essential for efficient transit transport operations, and bilateral agreements were the most common instruments for such cooperation. In Africa,

regional agreements within the context of regional integration schemes were a major vehicle for promoting cooperative arrangements. Technical assistance from UNCTAD and other international agencies was generally viewed as a critical support measure to improve the efficiency of transit transport operations.

GENERAL ASSEMBLY ACTION

The General Assembly, on 20 December, adopted **resolution 50/97**.

### Specific actions related to the particular needs and problems of land-locked developing countries

_The General Assembly,_

_Recalling_ the provisions of its resolutions 44/214 of 22 December 1989, 46/212 of 20 December 1991 and 48/169 of 21 December 1993,

_Recognizing_ that the lack of territorial access to the sea, aggravated by remoteness and isolation from world markets, and prohibitive transit costs and risks impose serious constraints on the overall socio-economic development efforts of the land-locked developing countries,

_Recognizing also_ that 16 of the land-locked developing countries are also classified by the United Nations as least developed countries and that their geographical situation is an added constraint on their overall ability to cope with the challenges of development,

_Recognizing further_ that most transit countries are themselves developing countries facing serious economic problems, including the lack of adequate infrastructure in the transport sector,

_Recalling_ that measures to deal with the transit problems of land-locked developing countries require closer and even more effective cooperation and collaboration between those countries and their transit neighbours,

_Welcoming_ the entry into force on 16 November 1994 of the United Nations Convention on the Law of the Sea,

_Recognizing_ the important role played by bilateral cooperative arrangements and regional and subregional cooperation and integration in alleviating the transit problems of the land-locked developing countries and improving the transit transport systems in land-locked and transit developing countries,

_Recognizing also_ the importance of continuing the activities of the regional commissions to improve the transit transport infrastructure in the land-locked and transit developing countries,

_Noting_ the importance of strengthening the existing international support measures with a view to addressing further the problems of land-locked developing countries,

1. _Reaffirms_ the right of access of land-locked developing countries to and from the sea and freedom of transit through the territory of transit States by all means of transport, in accordance with international law;

2. _Also reaffirms_ that transit developing countries, in the exercise of their full sovereignty over their territory, have the right to take all measures necessary to

ensure that the rights and facilities provided for land-locked developing countries should in no way infringe upon their legitimate interests;

3. *Calls upon* both the land-locked developing countries and their transit neighbours, in the spirit of South-South cooperation, including bilateral cooperation, to implement measures to strengthen further their cooperative and collaborative efforts in dealing with their transit problems;

4. *Appeals once again* to all States, international organizations and financial institutions to implement, as a matter of urgency and priority, the specific actions related to the particular needs and problems of land-locked developing countries envisaged in the previous resolutions adopted by the General Assembly and the United Nations Conference on Trade and Development and in the International Development Strategy for the Fourth United Nations Development Decade and the Declaration on International Economic Cooperation, in particular the Revitalization of Economic Growth and Development of the Developing Countries, adopted at the eighteenth special session of the General Assembly and contained in the annex to its resolution S-18/3 of 1 May 1990, as well as the relevant provisions of the Programme of Action for the Least Developed Countries for the 1990s and the outcomes of recent major United Nations conferences relevant to land-locked developing countries;

5. *Invites* the land-locked developing countries and their transit neighbours to intensify further their cooperative arrangements for the development of transit infrastructures, institutions and services to facilitate the faster movement of goods in transit, with financial and technical assistance from donors and financial institutions;

6. *Emphasizes* that assistance for the improvement of transit transport facilities and services should be integrated into the overall economic development strategies of the land-locked and transit developing countries and that donor assistance should consequently take into account the requirements for the long-term restructuring of the economies of the land-locked developing countries;

7. *Invites* donor countries and multilateral financial and development institutions to provide land-locked and transit developing countries with appropriate financial and technical assistance in the form of grants or concessional loans for the construction, maintenance and improvement of their transport, storage and other transit-related facilities, including alternative routes and improved communications;

8. *Invites* the United Nations Development Programme further to promote, as appropriate, subregional, regional and interregional projects and programmes and to expand its support in the transport and communications sectors to the land-locked and transit developing countries and its technical cooperation for development geared towards promoting national and collective self-reliance among them;

9. *Takes note* of the report of the Second Meeting of Governmental Experts from Land-locked and Transit Developing Countries and Representatives of Donor Countries and Financial and Development Institutions, held in New York from 19 to 22 June 1995, and endorses the Global Framework for Transit Transport

Cooperation between Land-locked and Transit Developing Countries and the Donor Community contained therein;

10. *Requests* the Secretary-General of the United Nations Conference on Trade and Development, in collaboration with the donor countries and institutions, in particular the United Nations Development Programme, the regional commissions and relevant subregional institutions, to organize, within existing resources, specific consultative groups, when requested by the land-locked and transit developing countries concerned, to identify priority areas for action at the national and subregional level and draw up action programmes for the period 1996-1997;

11. *Requests* the Secretary-General to convene in 1997, within the overall level of resources for the biennium 1996-1997, another meeting of governmental experts from land-locked and transit developing countries and representatives of donor countries and financial and development institutions, including relevant regional and subregional economic organizations and commissions, to review progress in the development of transit systems in the land-locked and transit developing countries, taking into account, *inter alia*, the results of the consultative group meetings referred to in paragraph 10 of the present resolution, with a view to exploring the possibility of formulating specific action-oriented measures and the ongoing study undertaken by the United Nations Conference on Trade and Development on the implications of the globalization and liberalization of the world economy for the development prospects of land-locked developing countries;

12. *Requests* the Secretary-General of the United Nations Conference on Trade and Development to seek voluntary contributions to ensure participation of representatives from land-locked and transit developing countries in the meeting of governmental experts from land-locked and transit developing countries and representatives of donor countries and financial and development institutions referred to in paragraph 11 of the present resolution;

13. *Notes with appreciation* the contribution of the United Nations Conference on Trade and Development in formulating international measures to deal with the special problems of the land-locked developing countries, and urges the Conference, *inter alia*, to keep under constant review the evolution of transit transport infrastructure facilities, institutions and services, monitor the implementation of agreed measures, collaborate in all relevant initiatives, including those of the private sector and non-governmental organizations, and serve as a focal point on cross-regional issues of interest to land-locked developing countries;

14. *Invites* the Secretary-General of the United Nations, in consultation with the Secretary-General of the United Nations Conference on Trade and Development, to take appropriate measures for the effective implementation of the activities called for in the present resolution and of existing measures in support of land-locked developing countries, within the context of the ninth session of the Conference;

15. *Welcomes* the note by the Secretary-General and the progress report of the secretariat of the United Na-

tions Conference on Trade and Development on specific actions related to the particular needs and problems of land-locked developing countries, and requests the Secretary-General of the United Nations, together with the Secretary-General of the United Nations Conference on Trade and Development, to prepare a report on the implementation of the present resolution and submit it to the Trade and Development Board and to the General Assembly at its fifty-second session.

General Assembly resolution 50/97

20 December 1995     Meeting 96      Adopted without vote

Approved by Second Committee (A/50/617/Add.1) without vote, 8 December (meeting 42); draft by Vice-Chairman (A/C.2/50/L.59), based on informal consultations on draft by Kyrgyzstan, Philippines, for Group of

77 and China, and the former Yugoslav Republic of Macedonia (A/C.2/50/L.19), agenda item 95 *(a)*.

*Meeting numbers.* GA 50th session: 2nd Committee 30-32, 36, 42; plenary 96.

## REFERENCES

[1]YUN 1993, p. 677. [2]DP/1995/19. [3]E/1995/34 (dec. 95/12).[4]A/CONF.147/18. [5]GA res. 45/206, 21 Dec. 1990. [6]*The Least Developed Countries—1995 Report* (TD/B/41/(2)/4), Sales No. E.95.II.D.2. [7]A/50/15, vol. I (agreed conclusions 423(XLI)). [8]TD/B/42(1)/9. [9]TD/B/LDC/GR/2. [10]TD/B/LDC/GR/1. [11]TD/B/LDC/GR/3. [12]YUN 1994, p. 780, GA res. 49/98, 19 Dec. 1994. [13]A/50/745. [14]TD/B/41(2)/4/Add.1. [15]YUN 1993, p. 677, GA res. 48/171, 21 Dec. 1993. [16]A/50/746. [17]YUN 1994, p. 784, GA res. 49/122, 19 Dec. 1994. [18]A/50/422. [19]YUN 1994, p. 783. [20]A/50/422/Add.1. [21]YUN 1993, p. 681, GA res. 48/169, 21 Dec. 1993. [22]TD/B/42(1)/11. [23]YUN 1993, p. 680. [24]TD/B/LDC/AC.1/8 & Add.1. [25]A/50/341.

Chapter II

# Operational activities for development

In 1995, the estimated income of the United Nations Development Programme (UNDP)—the central funding body of the UN system for providing technical assistance to developing countries—fell to $1,624 million from $1,818 million in 1994. Voluntary contributions to the Programme declined to $903 million, from $932 million in 1994.

The UNDP/United Nations Population Fund (UNFPA) Executive Board instituted a major change in UNDP's programming arrangements in 1995 when it replaced the five-year programming cycle with a three-year rolling planning scheme for activities, to begin in 1997. The year also saw the introduction of UNDP's first corporate plan—the 1995 UNDP Plan—which was a means to enhance UNDP's management and make operational the initiatives for change adopted by the Board in 1994.

A comprehensive policy review of UN operational activities for development took place in 1995. The Economic and Social Council considered a preliminary report in July, while the triennial policy review itself was carried out by the General Assembly later in the year. In December, the Assembly stressed the need for a substantial increase in resources for operational activities for development on a predictable, continuous and assured basis, commensurate with the increasing needs of developing countries.

The United Nations, mainly through its Department for Development Support and Management Services, delivered a technical cooperation programme amounting to some $80.1 million in 1995, compared to $100.6 million in 1994. Expenditures by the UN Capital Development Fund (UNCDF), a multilateral agency providing small-scale capital assistance to least developed countries, totalled $40.6 million.

The UN Office for Project Services (UNOPS), formerly part of UNDP, became a separate, identifiable entity within the United Nations in January 1995. During the year, UNOPS concluded cooperation agreements with a number of UN partners other than UNDP and, by year's end, had incurred project expenditures totalling some $383 million.

A total of 3,263 United Nations Volunteers (UNV)—specialists and field workers from 134 nations—served in 139 countries during the year. In January, the UNDP/UNFPA Executive Board endorsed the Secretary-General's proposal to relocate UNV headquarters from Geneva to Bonn, Germany, from mid-1996.

At its ninth session, the High-level Committee on the Review of Technical Cooperation among Developing Countries (TCDC) endorsed recommendations for new directions for TCDC. The new directions were also endorsed by the Executive Board, which reaffirmed the important role that they could play in increasing the use of both TCDC and economic cooperation among developing countries as dynamic instruments for South-South cooperation.

In 1995, UNCDF continued to support small-scale credit and rural infrastructure, stressing direct partnership with local government and community groups, especially those of the rural poor.

## General aspects

### Operational activities segment of the Economic and Social Council

At its 1995 substantive session (Geneva, 26 June–28 July),[1] the Economic and Social Council considered the question of operational activities of the United Nations for international development cooperation. Among the documents before it was a Secretariat note[2] transmitting an interim report on the triennial comprehensive policy review of operational activities for development of the UN system. The final report was submitted to the General Assembly later in the year (see below). The interim report covered changing trends in operational activities for development, programme development and implementation, UN system coordination mechanisms at the global level in support of country action, the resident coordinator system and programme support.

Other documents considered during the operational activities segment included: the annual report of UNDP to the Council,[3] which detailed information on measures taken to implement the provisions of the triennial policy review of operational activities (General Assembly resolutions 44/211 of 1989[4] and 47/199 of 1992[5]), and the report of the UNDP/UNFPA Executive Board on the work of its first and second regular sessions of 1995 and its annual session.[6] UNDP's annual report was transmitted to the Council by an Executive Board decision of 8 June.[7] Also in that decision, the Board requested UNDP and UNFPA to ensure that future reports on implementation of the triennial policy review addressed more thoroughly problems and opportunities that had been identified, particularly at the field level, and contained recommendations and requests for guidance from the Board. It also requested the UNDP Administrator and the UNFPA Executive Director, together with the Executive Director of the United Nations Children's Fund (UNICEF), to consider producing a common report on the implementation of the triennial policy review for both the UNDP/UNFPA and UNICEF Executive Boards.

**ECONOMIC AND SOCIAL COUNCIL ACTION**

On 28 July, the Economic and Social Council adopted **resolution 1995/50**.

**Operational activities of the United Nations for international development cooperation segment**
*The Economic and Social Council,*

*Recalling* General Assembly resolutions 44/211 of 22 December 1989, 46/219 of 20 December 1991 and, in particular, resolution 47/199 of 22 December 1992, in which the Assembly requested the Secretary-General to submit to it, through the Economic and Social Council, a comprehensive analysis of the implementation of the resolution,

*Recalling also* General Assembly resolution 48/162 of 20 December 1993 and Economic and Social Council resolution 1994/33 of 28 July 1994,

*Recalling* that, in accordance with resolution 48/162, the role of the Council in the operational activities of the United Nations for international development cooperation segment includes the provision to the United Nations system of cross-sectoral coordination and overall guidance on a system-wide basis,

*Recognizing* that appropriate recommendations regarding the need to increase substantially resources for operational activities for development on a predictable, continuous and assured basis, commensurate with the increasing needs of developing countries, should be further considered in the open-ended working group of the General Assembly on a new funding system for operational activities for development, established pursuant to Assembly resolution 48/162, annex I, section III.B,

*Having considered* the note by the Secretariat on the triennial policy review of operational activities for development within the United Nations system and the report on the annual sessions of the United Nations funds and programmes,

*Deeply concerned* about the decrease in resources allocated to the operational activities for development of the United Nations system,

1. *Takes note* of the note by the Secretariat;
2. *Reaffirms* that the strengthening of the efficiency and effectiveness of the operational activities of the United Nations system in the delivery of its assistance for development requires a real commitment to implementing General Assembly resolutions 47/199 and 48/162, including the need to increase substantially the availability of resources on a predictable, continuous and assured basis, commensurate with the needs of developing countries;

3. *Considers* that there is a need for additional measures to improve the efficiency and effectiveness of the operational activities for development of the United Nations system, including, *inter alia*, programmes focused on meeting the specific needs of developing countries; giving priority in resource allocation to developing countries, in particular the least developed countries and Africa; appropriate cooperation among United Nations programmes and between them and those of other donors; and keeping administrative costs to a level that allows effective programme delivery;

4. *Requests* the Secretary-General to finalize the report requested in paragraph 55 of General Assembly resolution 47/199 and to submit to the Assembly at its fiftieth session, in consultation with Member States, a comprehensive analysis of the implementation of resolution 47/199, with appropriate recommendations, also taking into account the work and outcome of the open-ended working group of the General Assembly on a new funding system for operational activities for development and the need to implement paragraph 3 of resolution 47/199;

5. *Reiterates* that the United Nations funds and programmes should submit their reports to the Council in all the official languages of the United Nations in good time, to enable the Council to carry out its policy guidance functions, and should schedule their Executive Board meetings so as to ensure this;

6. *Decides* that in 1996 the high-level meeting of the operational activities segment should focus on strengthening collaboration between the United Nations development system and the Bretton Woods institutions in the areas of social and economic development, at all levels, including the field level;

7. *Also decides* that the themes for the working-level meetings of the operational activities segment should include:

(*a*) Field-level coordination issues relating to the follow-up of the theme of the high-level segment of the previous substantive session of the Council;

(*b*) Issues relating to the budgets of the United Nations funds and programmes, with the aim of:
(i) Promoting greater budgetary transparency with respect to resources, including administrative costs of different funds and programmes;
(ii) Addressing the linkages between administrative expenditure and programme expenditure;
(iii) Ensuring the most efficient use of resources;
(iv) Promoting budgetary transparency with respect to resources mobilized by developing countries for operational activities for development of the United Nations, including resources from the private sector;

(*c*) Issues relating to:
(i) Strengthening national capacity for management and coordination of international assistance;
(ii) Improving national participation in the process of evaluation of the efficiency and effectiveness of assistance provided by United Nations funds and programmes;
(iii) Promoting greater collaboration among United Nations funds and programmes in the evaluation of their activities;

(*d*) Issues relating to procurement, in particular from developing countries;

*(e)* Issues relating to the use of national experts and local technologies;

*(f)* Issues relating to the priorities to be given in particular to the least developed countries and Africa;

8. *Further decides* to review these themes at its organizational session for 1996, in the light of the discussion on the triennial policy review at the fiftieth session of the General Assembly.

Economic and Social Council resolution 1995/50

28 July 1995    Meeting 57    Adopted without vote

Draft by Vice-President (E/1995/L.65), based on informal consultations on draft by Philippines, for Group of 77 and China (E/1995/L.30); agenda item 4.
*Meeting numbers.* ESC 30-38, 45, 57.

Also on 28 July, the Council adopted **resolution 1995/51.**

### Overall guidance on operational activities for development to the United Nations funds and programmes

*The Economic and Social Council*

1. *Decides,* in accordance with General Assembly resolution 48/162 of 20 December 1993, to provide to the United Nations funds and programmes the following policy guidance on operational activities for development, so as to ensure that the policies formulated by the General Assembly, particularly during the triennial policy review of operational activities, are appropriately implemented on a system-wide basis;

2. *Requests* the United Nations funds and programmes, in their response to the increasing needs of developing countries, to take into account General Assembly resolutions 45/206 of 21 December 1990 on the implementation of the Programme of Action for the Least Developed Countries for the 1990s and 46/151 of 18 December 1991, to which is annexed the United Nations New Agenda for the Development of Africa in the 1990s, and to continue to give high priority in their budget allocations to the least developed countries, low income countries and Africa;

3. *Also requests* the United Nations funds and programmes to take into account the specific needs and requirements of the countries with economies in transition;

4. *Further requests* the United Nations funds and programmes to take into account the specific needs and requirements of different regions;

5. *Requests* the Executive Boards of the United Nations funds and programmes, in establishing their priorities, to take fully into account the relevant conclusions and recommendations of United Nations conferences in the economic, social and related fields, in accordance with their respective mandates, also bearing in mind national plans and priorities and relevant General Assembly resolutions;

6. *Requests* the United Nations funds and programmes to improve coherence in their country programmes, *inter alia,* by considering the possibility of joint or consecutive meetings of the Executive Boards, where practicable, on country programmes, and by improving the link between their country programmes and the country strategy notes, where in place, bearing in mind the need for cooperation between external donors and the United Nations funds and programmes in this field;

7. *Requests* the heads of the United Nations funds and programmes to report to the Economic and Social Council at its substantive session of 1996, through their Executive Boards, on the steps taken to further refine and effectively apply procedures for:

*(a)* The overall impact and performance of United Nations funds and programmes and measures to ensure that higher priority is given to monitoring and evaluation activities and to the implementation of findings, in accordance with General Assembly resolution 47/199 of 22 December 1992;

*(b)* Strengthening national capacity for the management and coordination of international assistance;

*(c)* Improving national participation in the process of evaluation of the efficiency and effectiveness of assistance provided by the United Nations funds and programmes;

*(d)* Promoting greater collaboration among United Nations funds and programmes in the evaluation of their activities;

8. *Requests* the Executive Boards of the United Nations Funds and Programmes, in their reports to the Council, to identify specific problems, opportunities and areas in which the Council could provide cross-sectoral coordination and overall guidance on a system-wide basis, and to make appropriate proposals, which should be further analysed as a basis for recommendations to the Council, to ensure that the policies formulated by the General Assembly, particularly during the triennial policy review of operational activities, are appropriately implemented on a system-wide basis;

9. *Invites* the specialized agencies, where appropriate, to identify specific problem areas for consideration by the Council in line with paragraph 8 above;

10. *Requests* the United Nations funds and programmes, in the context of the Joint Consultative Group on Policy, to report jointly to the Council through the Secretary-General on questions relating to coordination, cooperation and the division of labour, and on other issues they consider appropriate;

11. *Also requests* the United Nations funds and programmes, and invites specialized agencies, to explore the scope for improving the cost-effectiveness of administrative services, including the possible use of common administrative services at the field level, with the aim of strengthening programme delivery, and to report thereon to the Council at its substantive session of 1996;

12. *Urges* the United Nations funds and programmes to improve the personnel management system for resident coordinators and other senior managers.

Economic and Social Council resolution 1995/51

28 July 1995    Meeting 57    Adopted without vote

Draft by Vice-President (E/1995/L.66), based on informal consultations on draft by Spain, for EU (E/1995/L.31); agenda item 4.
*Meeting numbers.* ESC 30-38, 45, 57.

In other action, the Council, by **decision 1995/233** of 13 July, noted the report of the UNDP/UNFPA Executive Board on the work of its first and second regular sessions of 1995 and its annual session[6] and the annual report of UNDP to the Council.[3]

### Triennial policy review

In accordance with a 1992 General Assembly resolution,[5] the Secretary-General in 1995 reported on the triennial comprehensive policy review of operational activities for development of the UN system.[8] The report was based on completed questionnaires received from Governments, UN organizations and resident coordinators, and on case-studies drawn up on the basis of country missions. Policy recommendations in the report benefited from the 1995 deliberations and resolutions of the Economic and Social Council (see above).

The report described changing trends in operational activities and discussed the broad themes of programme development and implementation, UN system coordination mechanisms at the global level in support of country actions, the resident coordinator system and programme support. The report noted the shift from individual projects to support of and inputs to national goals and strategies, the broadened reach and range of UN operational activities, the growing importance of humanitarian aid, and the imperative of enhanced cooperation with the Bretton Woods institutions (the World Bank Group and the International Monetary Fund). Also addressed were the growing upstream role of the UN system in some countries; the increasing specificity of country contexts; the differing perceptions as to how and where UN system assistance could make a development difference; evaluation, monitoring and review; and the cross-cutting nature of capacity-building. There was broad consensus that developing countries' capacities required selective strengthening in order to achieve greater self-reliance. That needed to be done in new and more effective ways to promote a coordinated response that was effectively integrated into national priority programmes.

A number of coordination mechanisms and operational modalities were reviewed, such as the country strategy note (CSN), harmonization of programming cycles, programme approach and national execution. CSN had been generally welcomed as a promising basis for better and more coordinated UN system operational activities in support of national plans, strategies and priorities. Six States had completed CSNs and 85 States were in the process of preparing them. Six other States had formally decided that they did not wish to implement this measure.

Increasingly, developing countries were shifting from project technical cooperation towards modalities that emphasized support for national programmes, around which UN system inputs were mobilized in a flexible manner and often linked to other sources of external financing. There were more requests for upstream policy advice and technical support, resulting in policy-making, normative analysis and technical assistance being brought together. National execution had been widely welcomed by recipient countries as a major means to promote the national management of

UN development assistance and was increasingly the preferred modality of the UN system. While traditional agency-executed activities had diminished with regard to their involvement in nationally executed activities, their technical services were being obtained more selectively, particularly through short-term expertise. The resident coordinator system had undergone considerable strengthening and enhancement over the preceding three years, including widening the pool for recruiting resident coordinators; developing a new statement on the role and functioning of the resident coordinator system; providing substantial financial support; and intensifying the number and frequency of training workshops.

Many UN system organizations had introduced changes in their organizational and management structures and practices as an ongoing process of streamlining, simplifying and enhancing the impact and effectiveness of their activities. Decentralization and empowerment of field offices were key elements in those efforts.

The report also contained recommendations regarding the role of the Economic and Social Council; improved substantive dialogue at the country level; resources; the resident coordinator system; CSN; the programme approach; national execution; harmonization and simplification of rules and procedures; staffing at the country level; regional coordination; capacity-building; evaluation, monitoring and review; cooperation with the Bretton Woods institutions; strengthened national coordination; and common premises and shared services.

The report's addenda provided comprehensive statistical data on operational activities for development for 1993 and 1994 and summarized action taken by the executive boards of UN development funds and programmes and UN bodies in implementing a 1994 Economic and Social Council resolution[9] requesting them to contribute to the triennial policy review and to standardize their annual reports to the Council.

**ACC consideration.** The Consultative Committee on Programme and Operational Questions (CCPOQ) of the Administrative Committee on Coordination (ACC) discussed the implementation of General Assembly resolution 47/199 at its fifth session (Geneva, 31 January–2 February).[10] It approved "Guiding principles for a monitoring and evaluation methodology in the context of the programme approach", which it annexed to its report. It also approved revised terms of reference for its Advisory Panel on Operational Activities Training in order to enhance its advisory role for the International Training Centre in Turin, Italy, and to facilitate harmonized approaches between and within agencies on training and operational activities. CCPOQ further adopted a statement on the role and functioning of the resident coordinator system, agreeing that all system organizations would circulate it to field representatives.

The triennial policy review was discussed by CCPOQ at its fifth,[(10)] inter-sessional sixth (New York, 30 May–1 June)[(11)] and resumed sixth (Geneva, 25-26 July)[(12)] and seventh (New York, 19-22 September)[(13)] sessions.

**GENERAL ASSEMBLY ACTION**

On 20 December, the General Assembly adopted **resolution 50/120**.

**Triennial policy review of operational activities for development of the United Nations system**

*The General Assembly,*

*Recalling* its resolutions 44/211 of 22 December 1989 and 47/199 of 22 December 1992, as well as other relevant resolutions,

*Reaffirming* that operational activities for development within the United Nations system have a critical and unique role to play in enabling developing countries to continue to take a lead role in the management of their own development process,

*Bearing in mind* that the effectiveness of operational activities should be measured by their impact on the sustained economic growth and sustainable development of developing countries,

*Stressing* that national plans and priorities constitute the only viable frame of reference for the national programming of operational activities for development within the United Nations system, and that programmes should be based on such development plans and priorities, and should therefore be country-driven,

*Also stressing* in that context the need to take into account the outcomes and commitments of relevant United Nations conferences, as well as the individual mandates and complementarities of the organizations and bodies of the United Nations development system, bearing in mind the need to avoid duplication,

*Further stressing* that the fundamental characteristics of the operational activities of the United Nations system should be, *inter alia*, their universal, voluntary and grant nature, their neutrality and their multilateralism, as well as their ability to respond to the needs of developing countries in a flexible manner, and that the operational activities of the United Nations system are carried out for the benefit of the developing countries, at the request of those countries and in accordance with their own policies and priorities for development,

*Recognizing* the urgent and specific needs of the low-income countries, in particular the least developed countries,

*Noting* the progress that has been achieved in a number of areas in the implementation of its resolution 47/199, while stressing the need for individual organs, organizations and bodies of the United Nations system, as well as coordination mechanisms of the United Nations system, to continue to work towards the full and coordinated implementation of that resolution,

*Also recognizing* that the United Nations development system should take into account the specific needs and requirements of the countries with economies in transition and other recipient countries,

*Recalling* that the General Assembly is the highest intergovernmental mechanism for the formulation and appraisal of policy matters relating to the economic, social and related fields, in accordance with Chapter IX of the Charter of the United Nations, and that the functions and powers of the Economic and Social Council are provided for in Chapters IX and X of the Charter and are elaborated in relevant Assembly resolutions, including resolutions 45/264 of 13 May 1991 and 48/162 of 20 December 1993, in which the Assembly defined the relationship between the Assembly, the Council and the executive boards of the funds and programmes, in particular the Council function of overall guidance and coordination of the operational activities for development of the United Nations system,

1. *Takes note* of the report of the Secretary-General on the triennial comprehensive policy review of operational activities for development of the United Nations system and welcomes its user-friendly format;

2. *Reaffirms* its resolution 47/199 and stresses the need to implement fully all the elements of that resolution in a coherent manner, keeping in mind their interlinkages;

3. *Endorses* Economic and Social Council resolution 1995/51 of 28 July 1995 on overall guidance on operational activities for development to the United Nations funds and programmes;

4. *Notes with regret* that, although significant progress has already been made on the restructuring and rationalization of the governance and functioning of the United Nations development funds and programmes, there has not been, as part of the overall reform process, any substantial increase in resources for operational activities for development on a predictable, continuous and assured basis, nor have the consultations on prospective new modalities for financing reached a conclusion;

5. *Strongly reaffirms* that the efficiency, effectiveness and impact of the operational activities of the United Nations system must be enhanced by, *inter alia*, a substantial increase in their funding on a predictable, continuous and assured basis, commensurate with the increasing needs of developing countries, as well as through the full implementation of resolutions 47/199 and 48/162;

6. *Urges* developed countries, in particular those countries whose overall performance is not commensurate with their capacity, taking into account established official development assistance targets, including targets established at the Second United Nations Conference on the Least Developed Countries and their current levels of contribution, to increase substantially their official development assistance, including contributions to the operational activities of the United Nations system;

7. *Notes with appreciation* the sustained contributions of many donors and recipient countries to the operational activities for development in a spirit of partnership;

8. *Expresses serious concern* at the persistent insufficiency of resources for the operational development activities of the United Nations, in particular the decline in contributions to core resources;

9. *Stresses* the need for a substantial increase in resources for operational activities for development on a predictable, continuous and assured basis, commensurate with the increasing needs of developing countries;

10.   *Decides* that intensified consultations and negotiations on prospective new specific modalities for financing operational activities for development on a predictable, continuous and assured basis, in accordance with paragraphs 31 to 34 of annex I to resolution 48/162 on the restructuring and revitalization of the United Nations in the economic and social fields, should lead to an agreed outcome in the framework of the review process of that resolution;

11.   *Reaffirms* the need for priority allocation of scarce grant resources to programmes and projects in low-income countries, particularly the least developed countries;

12.   *Emphasizes* that recipient Governments have the primary responsibility for coordinating, on the basis of national strategies and priorities, all types of external assistance, including that provided by multilateral organizations, in order to integrate effectively such assistance into their development process;

13.   *Urges* the members of the United Nations development system to continue to develop an agreed division of responsibility, in accordance with their respective mandates, under the coordination of Governments as well as greater complementarity in their respective roles at the field level in response to the needs and priorities of recipient countries;

14.   *Stresses* the need for the United Nations system to take full account of the interests and concerns of all recipient countries, and, in that context, stresses the need for it to give serious consideration to ways of ensuring a more coherent response by the system to the national plans and priorities of recipient Governments;

15.   *Also stresses* the need for all organizations of the United Nations development system to focus their efforts at the field level on priority areas, in accordance with the priorities identified by recipient countries and the mandates, mission statements and relevant decisions of their governing bodies, in order to avoid duplication and enhance the complementarity and impact of their work;

16.   *Further stresses* that, in the context of the reform of the United Nations Secretariat and the restructuring and revitalization of the intergovernmental process, the mandates of the separate sectoral and specialized entities, funds, programmes and specialized agencies should be respected and enhanced, taking into account their complementarities;

17.   *Reaffirms* that the country strategy note remains a voluntary initiative of recipient countries that should be formulated by interested recipient countries in accordance with their development plans and priorities, with the assistance of and in cooperation with the United Nations system under the leadership of the resident coordinator, in all recipient countries where the Government so decides;

18.   *Decides* that, where in place, the country strategy note should be the common framework for country programmes of United Nations system organizations and for programming, monitoring and evaluating United Nations system activities in such countries, and that the country strategy note should outline the United Nations system contribution, including, where appropriate, an indication of the level of resources needed to meet the requirements therein;

19.   *Requests* the Secretary-General, in consultation with interested Member States and in order to be able to respond more effectively to the needs of recipient countries, to undertake further work on:

*(a)*   Broad common guidelines, with the aim of promoting greater consistency and clarity in the United Nations system contribution to country strategy notes;

*(b)*   Enhancing its operational relevance by ensuring that the development of individual country programmes takes fully into account the framework provided by the country strategy note, where it exists, so as to promote an agreed division of responsibility within the United Nations system in accordance with paragraph 13 of the present resolution;

*(c)*   Promoting the exchange of experiences gained in producing country strategy notes among recipient countries;

20.   *Requests* the Secretary-General, in consultation with Member States and United Nations organizations, to consider ways of enhancing the coordination of United Nations development activities at the regional and subregional levels, including ways of enhancing the role of the regional commissions and of promoting the national ownership of regional programmes;

21.   *Stresses* that the United Nations system, where requested by interested Governments, should support the establishment of the forums and mechanisms that facilitate and guide policy dialogue among the partners in the development process, primarily in order to ensure that their programmes are integrated with national plans and strategies;

22.   *Decides* that the objective of capacity-building and its sustainability should continue to be an essential part of the operational activities of the United Nations system at the country level, with the aim of integrating their activities and providing support to efforts to strengthen national capacities in the fields of, *inter alia*, policy and programme formulation, development management, planning, implementation, coordination, monitoring and review;

23.   *Recalls* the importance of accountability as well as of simplifying reporting requirements, which should be in line with national systems;

24.   *Decides* that, where Governments so desire, the United Nations system should be ready to engage in providing an enabling environment to strengthen the capacity of civil societies and national non-governmental organizations that are involved in development activities, in accordance with national priorities;

25.   *Also decides* that the United Nations system should use, to the fullest extent possible, available national expertise and indigenous technologies;

26.   *Calls for* further work on the development of common guidelines at the field level for the recruitment, training and remuneration of national project personnel, including national consultants in the formulation and implementation of development projects and programmes supported by the United Nations development system in order to enhance the coherence of the system;

27.   *Decides* that the United Nations development system should continue to work on promoting a common understanding and the operationalization of capacity-building concepts, as well as on ways of enhancing the sustainability of capacity-building;

28.   *Also decides* that the United Nations development system should continue to work on improving the definition and guidelines for national execution and the programme approach;

29. *Requests* the organizations and bodies of the United Nations system to undertake efforts in the context of national execution and capacity-building to enhance the absorptive capacity in developing countries, in particular in the least developed countries and Africa, and to assist similar efforts undertaken by those countries;

30. *Stresses* the important role of the specialized agencies of the United Nations system in transferring and facilitating the necessary technical and substantive expertise to support the national execution of United Nations–funded programmes and projects, and invites the Secretary-General, in collaboration with the heads of specialized agencies, to inform the Economic and Social Council of the measures taken by those specialized agencies in response to General Assembly resolution 47/199, in particular as regards national execution;

31. *Also stresses* that the governing bodies of all funds, programmes and specialized agencies should make further progress in order to ensure that the prescribed limits on field-level authority for cancelling, modifying and adding activities within approved programmes and shifting resources within approved budget lines of individual components of a programme and among components of a programme, with the approval of national authorities, should be expanded to become equal and uniform, to the maximum extent possible, in the context of enhanced accountability;

32. *Recognizes* that monitoring and evaluation processes, including joint evaluations, should continue to be nationally led, and that the United Nations system should therefore support, where requested by Governments, the strengthening of national evaluation capacities;

33. *Also recognizes* in that context the need to strengthen capacities to perform both effective programme, project and financial monitoring and impact evaluations of operational activities funded by the United Nations;

34. *Requests* the United Nations system to strengthen its efforts, in consultation with recipient countries, to ensure that:

(a) Monitoring is carried out in a way that ensures the timely identification of problems and effective remedial action;

(b) Organizations of the United Nations system, operating at the country level, coordinate their periodic programme reviews and evaluations;

(c) The lessons learned from both monitoring and evaluation exercises are systematically applied into programming processes at the operational level, and that responsibility for such application is clearly assigned;

(d) Evaluation criteria are built into all projects and programmes at their design stage, bearing in mind the need for adequate training;

35. *Underlines* the importance of promoting, under the leadership of Governments, greater collaboration on issues relating to evaluation among recipient Governments, the United Nations development system and relevant development partners at the country level;

36. *Requests* the Secretary-General to make the resident coordinator system more participatory in its functioning at the field level by, *inter alia*, making greater use of thematic groups and adopting a more consultative approach;

37. *Also requests* the Secretary-General to:

(a) Identify ways of encouraging wider participation in the pool of candidates for resident coordinator positions;

(b) Promote greater governmental involvement in the selection process for resident coordinators, in particular by ensuring that national Governments are consulted before the post profile for resident coordinators is passed to the Joint Consultative Group on Policies, and keeping up to date the selection criteria for resident coordinators and, through the respective executive heads, for senior representatives of United Nations agencies in the field, bearing in mind the specific circumstances of individual countries;

(c) Develop common guidelines for staff performance appraisal for the funds and programmes, including ways of assessing the contribution of staff members to United Nations system coordination;

(d) Urge all members of the United Nations development system to give clear guidance and direction to their country representatives to promote the effective functioning of the resident coordinator system;

(e) Promote training in the areas of team-building and interpersonal skills;

38. *Invites* the United Nations system, including the funds and programmes, specialized agencies and the Secretariat, to provide, as appropriate, support to the resident coordinator system;

39. *Reaffirms* that resident coordinators, in full consultation with national Governments, should facilitate a coherent and coordinated United Nations follow-up to major international conferences at the field level;

40. *Decides* that in order to promote coordination and a better division of labour resident coordinators should, at an early stage of formulation, be informed of planned programme activities of the United Nations agencies, funds, programmes and bodies;

41. *Also decides* that the field-level committees organized by the United Nations system country team, which were established in accordance with paragraph 40 of General Assembly resolution 47/199, should review substantive activities—including draft country programmes, sectoral programmes and projects—prior to their approval by individual organizations, and should exchange experience acquired, on the understanding that the result of the work of the review committee should be submitted to national Governments for final approval through the national focal points;

42. *Reaffirms* the need to enhance the responsibility and authority of resident coordinators for the planning and coordination of programmes, as well as to allow them to propose, in full consultation with Governments, to the heads of the funds, programmes and specialized agencies, the amendment of country programmes and major projects and programmes, where required, in order to bring them into line with country strategy notes;

43. *Requests* the Secretary-General and the United Nations development system to take the need for gender balance fully into account when making appointments, including at the senior level and in the field, in accordance with relevant General Assembly resolutions;

44. *Requests* the Joint Consultative Group on Policies and, to the maximum extent possible, the specialized agencies, to raise substantially the target for achieving common premises on the basis of cost-benefit analysis and avoiding an increased burden on host countries;

45. *Calls for* further simplification and harmonization of rules of procedure used by the United Nations development system in its operational activities, in particular by the promotion of greater consistency in the presentation of budgets at the headquarters level, as well as in sharing administrative systems and services in the field, where possible, and in developing common databases, in consultation with national Governments;

46. *Urges* the members of the United Nations development system to adopt a more collaborative approach in preparing reports at all levels;

47. *Requests* the Secretary-General to promote the creation or further development of common guidelines on procedures relating to, *inter alia*, programme components and project formulation, appraisal, implementation, monitoring, evaluation and administration, in fulfilment of paragraph 33 of General Assembly resolution 47/199;

48. *Takes note* of Economic and Social Council resolution 1995/50 of 28 July 1995, in which the Council decided that the high-level meeting of the operational activities segment of its substantive session of 1996 should focus on strengthening collaboration between the United Nations development system and the Bretton Woods institutions in the area of social and economic development at all levels, including the field level;

49. *Also takes note* of the mission statement of the World Food Programme and the decision of the executive boards of the United Nations Development Programme/United Nations Population Fund and of the United Nations Children's Fund to establish mission statements for their respective organizations;

50. *Emphasizes* the importance of disseminating the experience of effective and efficient cooperation with the United Nations development system, *inter alia*, through interregional projects of technical cooperation, and urges the United Nations system to give support to such activities;

51. *Calls upon* the United Nations system, in implementing the present resolution, to bear in mind the specific requirements of the continuum from humanitarian assistance through rehabilitation to development;

52. *Requests* the Secretary-General, after consultations with the funds, programmes and specialized agencies of the United Nations system, to present to the Economic and Social Council at its substantive session of 1996 an appropriate management process containing clear guidelines, targets, benchmarks and time-frames for the full implementation of the present resolution;

53. *Invites* the Economic and Social Council, during the operational activities segment of its substantive sessions of 1996 and 1997, to examine the operational activities of the United Nations system with a view to ensuring the full implementation of the present resolution;

54. *Also invites* the Economic and Social Council, at its substantive session of 1996, to consider, *inter alia*, the issues of harmonization and administrative services, common premises and monitoring and evaluation, and, at its substantive session of 1997, to consider, *inter alia*, capacity-building, field and regional-level coordination, and resources, on the basis of progress reports by the Secretary-General, including appropriate recommendations;

55. *Reaffirms* that the governing bodies of the funds, programmes and specialized agencies of the United Nations system should take appropriate action for the full

implementation of the present resolution, and requests the executive heads of those funds, programmes and specialized agencies, bearing in mind paragraph 46 of the present resolution, to submit a yearly progress report to their governing bodies on measures taken and envisaged for the implementation of the present resolution, as well as appropriate recommendations;

56. *Decides* that, as an integral part of the next comprehensive triennial policy review, there should be, in consultation with Member States, an evaluation of the impact of operational activities for development, and requests the Secretary-General to submit to the Economic and Social Council at its substantive sessions of 1996 and 1997 information on progress in that regard;

57. *Requests* the Secretary-General to submit to the General Assembly at its fifty-third session, through the Economic and Social Council, a comprehensive analysis of the implementation of the present resolution in the context of the triennial policy review, and to make appropriate recommendations.

General Assembly resolution 50/120

20 December 1995     Meeting 96     Adopted without vote

Approved by Second Committee (A/50/619) without vote, 12 December (meeting 43); draft by Vice-Chairman (A/C.2/50/L.79), orally corrected and based on informal consultations; agenda item 97 (a).
*Meeting numbers.* GA 50th session: 2nd Committee 24-29, 43; plenary 96.

## Financing of operational activities

### Expenditures

During 1994,[14] the most recent year for which complete figures were available, expenditures by the UN system on operational activities totalled $18.7 billion. Of that, $4.6 billion was distributed in development grants through UNDP, UNFPA, UNICEF, the World Food Programme (WFP) and specialized agencies and other organizations. Another $4.9 billion was disbursed in concessional loans by the International Development Association (IDA) ($4.7 billion) and the International Fund for Agricultural Development (IFAD) ($188.5 million), and $9.2 billion was disbursed in nonconcessional loans through the International Bank for Reconstruction and Development (IBRD) ($7 billion) and the International Finance Corporation (IFC) ($2.2 billion). In addition, $1.2 billion was spent on refugee, humanitarian, special economic and disaster relief activities, and $143.8 million was channelled through UNOPS management service agreements.

Of total expenditures on grant-financed development activities, $1.4 billion was channelled through WFP (extrabudgetary expenditures and project expenditures for development activities and emergency operations), $1.2 billion through UNDP (central resources and administered funds), $800.6 million through UNICEF and $201.4 million through UNFPA. A total of $688.4 million was financed by specialized agencies and other organizations from extrabudgetary sources and $280.3

million was financed by regular budgets (mostly the World Health Organization).

## Contributions

Contributions from Governments and other sources for operational activities of the UN system, including IFAD and the World Bank Group (IBRD, IDA, IFC), totalled $11.1 billion in 1994.[14]

In addition, contributions for refugees, humanitarian, special economic and disaster relief activities totalled $896.7 million.

### UN Pledging Conference for Development Activities

The 1995 UN Pledging Conference for Development Activities (New York, 1-2 November)[15] received government pledges for 1996 to UN funds and programmes concerned with development and related assistance. More than $2.1 billion was pledged in real or anticipated contributions, some $950 million of which was for UNDP.

The Secretary-General listed[16] contributions pledged or paid, as at 30 June 1995, to 27 UN funds and programmes at the 1994 Pledging Conference, totalling approximately $1.2 billion, with an estimated $638 million designated for UNDP.

*REFERENCES*

[1]A/50/3/Rev.1. [2]E/1995/98. [3]E/1995/89. [4]GA res. 44/211, 22 Dec. 1989. [5]YUN 1992, p. 552, GA res. 47/199, 22 Dec. 1992. [6]E/1995/34. [7]Ibid. (dec. 95/17). [8]A/50/202-E/1995/76 & Add.1-3. [9]YUN 1994, p. 789, ESC res. 1994/33, 28 July 1994. [10]ACC/1995/1 & Corr.1. [11]ACC/1995/11. [12]ACC/1995/11/Add.1. [13]ACC/1995/18. [14]A/50/202/Add.1-E/1995/76/Add.1. [15]A/CONF.178/3. [16]A/CONF.173/2.

## Technical cooperation through UNDP

In his annual report covering 1995,[1] the UNDP Administrator assessed achievements and areas for improvement in implementing the five operational objectives of the UNDP Plan, launched in June 1995: strengthening country offices for the operationalization of sustainable human development; resource mobilization and constituency-building; the 1996-1997 biennial budget strategy and the successor programming arrangements; improving support to the UN system; and improving management accountability and information systems.

The Administrator stated that 1995 had seen bold and imaginative steps by UNDP to maintain its position as a leader in institutional reform within the UN system. Changes were introduced to: focus UNDP on high-priority development objectives; build a leaner, more accountable organization; strengthen the quality, responsiveness and impact of the UNDP programme; support the UN

system and resident coordinators; enhance UNDP services to people in crisis; and create new partnerships for development cooperation.

With its first organization-wide plan (the 1995 UNDP Plan), the Administrator stated, UNDP had developed a useful framework for aligning its human, financial and technical resources with its overall vision, objectives and strategies. In the process, UNDP had developed a human resources strategy for investing in core competencies to manage change and accomplish its new mission successfully. Results achieved and those yet to be achieved would influence the choice of goals to be set in the next plan period and the pace to be set for their attainment.

Total UNDP resources for the fifth programming cycle (1992-1996) were estimated at $8.2 billion, significantly above both the original and revised earmarking of $7.5 billion, reflecting a significant increase in cost-sharing and trust funds to a level of about $3.2 billion. Contributions to UNDP core resources were estimated at $4.7 billion, considerably lower than the $6.3 billion projected by the Governing Council in 1990[2] when it had called for an 8 per cent annual increase during the fifth cycle.

In 1995, estimated UNDP income was almost $1.7 billion, a decrease from $1.8 billion in 1994. Of the 1995 total, some $900 million came from voluntary pledges, compared to $928 million in 1994. Other major sources included cost-sharing contributions by recipient Governments ($601 million), trust funds established by the Administrator, excluding the Global Environment Facility ($158 million), contributions to local office costs ($19 million), government cash counterpart contributions ($8 million), extrabudgetary activities ($9 million) and contributions to the Special Measures Fund for the Least Developed Countries ($8,631). An additional $128 million was received through management service agreements.

UNDP also administered eight funds that provided an additional $72.6 million. Those funds were the UN Capital Development Fund, the UN Revolving Fund for Natural Resources Exploration, the Office to Combat Desertification and Drought, UN Volunteers (UNV), the UN Fund for Science and Technology for Development, the UN Development Fund for Women (UNIFEM), the UNDP Energy Account and the UNDP Study Programme.

Of donor countries that were members of the Development Assistance Committee of the Organisation for Economic Cooperation and Development, Japan and the Netherlands announced increases in their contributions for 1996; Australia, Belgium, Denmark, Germany, Norway, Spain, Sweden, Switzerland and the United Kingdom maintained their 1996 contributions at the previous year's levels. Among smaller countries, New Zealand and Portugal provided substantial increases, while contributions from France and the United States were estimated to be lower than those for 1995. Increasing their contributions substantially were Andorra, Benin, Costa Rica, the Czech Republic, Honduras, India, Mauritania, Namibia, the Philippines, the Republic of Korea, Romania, Turkey and Viet Nam. Countries resuming support for UNDP included Djibouti, Kenya, Nicaragua, the Niger, the Sudan, Ukraine, Yemen and Zambia. Slovenia made a pledge to UNDP for the first time.

Field programme expenditures from central resources (voluntary · contributions and cost-sharing) totalled $1,014 million in 1995. Of total field programme expenditures, 46.5 per cent went for project personnel, 19.5 per cent for subcontracts, 15.9 per cent for equipment, 9.7 per cent for training, and the remainder for technical support services and miscellaneous expenses, including maintenance and operational costs.

By region, Latin America and the Caribbean used 45.4 per cent of field programme expenditures; Asia and the Pacific, 21.2 per cent; Africa, 19.4 per cent; the Arab States, 6.4 per cent; and Europe, 2.6 per cent. Global and interregional projects used 5 per cent.

## UNDP/UNFPA Executive Board

In 1995, the UNDP/UNFPA Executive Board held four sessions, all in New York: three regular sessions (10-13 January, 3-7 April and 11-15 September) and its annual session (5-16 June).[3]

In January, the Board adopted seven decisions (the text on the UN Sudano-Sahelian Office is dealt with in the next chapter). On 13 January, the Board decided[4] that its segment on UNFPA should take place at the beginning or end of regular and annual sessions, bearing in mind the need for a more coordinated approach to the discussion of country programmes. The UNDP Administrator and UNFPA Executive Director were asked to enhance collaboration between their organizations in the Board's secretariat and to consider appointing a UNFPA staff member to it. They were also asked to consider ways to strengthen their cooperation in matters relating to the Board's functioning. By another 13 January decision,[5] which included an overview of decisions adopted at the session, the Board elected its Bureau for 1995 and agreed to a schedule for its 1995 sessions and to subjects to be discussed. It also noted a number of reports.

In April, the Board adopted six decisions, one including an overview of session decisions.[6] It also noted a number of reports. Other April decisions dealt with: assistance to the Palestinian peo-

ple (see PART TWO, Chapter VI); UNCDF (see below); UNIFEM (see PART FOUR, Chapter X); the Joint and Co-sponsored UN Programme on HIV/AIDS (see PART FOUR, Chapter XIII); and matters relating to the least developed countries (LDCs) (see preceding chapter).

At its annual session in June, the Board adopted 11 decisions, one dealing with the follow-up to General Assembly resolution 47/199 (see above). Those covered in other chapters dealt with UNFPA matters (see PART FOUR, Chapter VIII) and UNIFEM (see PART FOUR, Chapter X). By a 16 June decision,[7] which included an overview of decisions adopted at the session, the Board noted a number of reports, including the Administrator's report for 1994.[8]

By **decision 1995/233** of 13 July, the Economic and Social Council noted the report of the UNDP/UNFPA Executive Board on the work of its first and second regular sessions and its annual session of 1995.

In September, the Board adopted 13 decisions, including an overview of decisions adopted at that session,[9] in which it took note of a number of reports and established a schedule for its 1996 sessions. Decisions covered in other chapters dealt with UNFPA matters (see PART FOUR, Chapter VIII), UNIFEM (see PART FOUR, Chapter X) and UN efforts following a series of hurricanes in the Caribbean (see next chapter).

## UNDP operational activities

### Country and intercountry programmes

On 13 January, the Executive Board approved[5] the first country programme for the Czech Republic. On 7 April, it approved[6] the cooperation framework with Indonesia; the first country programmes for Belarus, Estonia, Kyrgyzstan, Latvia, Lithuania, the Republic of Moldova, Ukraine and Uzbekistan; the third country programme for the British Virgin Islands; and the fifth country programmes for Barbados and Turkey. On 15 September, the Board approved[9] the first country programmes for Azerbaijan and the Russian Federation and the fifth country programme for Haiti. It also endorsed the reorientation of fifth country programmes for Burundi and Rwanda.

**Mid-term reviews.** On 7 April, the Board noted[6] the mid-term reviews of the fifth country programmes for Bangladesh,[10] Chad,[11] Malawi[12] and Tunisia,[13] and the sixth country programme for Guatemala.[14] All reviews were carried out in 1994.

In 1995, mid-term reviews were executed for some 75 country programmes, including those of Brazil, the Lao People's Democratic Republic, Mozambique, Romania and Yemen.[15]

The Board, in September, had before it the Administrator's report on mid-term reviews.[16] The report—the fourth submitted in response to a 1992 request[17]—covered mid-term reviews of regional programmes undertaken between January and June 1995. Addenda contained reviews of: the global and interregional programme; the regional programme for Africa; the regional programme for Asia and the Pacific; the regional programme for the Arab States; the regional programme for Latin America and the Caribbean; and the regional programme for Europe and the Commonwealth of Independent States (CIS). Collectively, those programmes accounted for approximately $380 million (or 12 per cent) of fifth cycle indicative planning figure (IPF) entitlements.

The Administrator concluded that regional programmes remained the most viable mechanism through which UNDP could effectively address development challenges that transcended national boundaries, such as economic integration, health concerns, especially HIV/AIDS, environmental and resource management issues, transfer of technology and development-related research.

On 13 September, the Board encouraged[18] the Administrator to continue the trend towards the programme approach by promoting fewer and larger interventions in support of clearly defined regional, interregional and global objectives. It stressed the need to enhance UNDP capability to ensure improved design and implementation of intercountry programmes and strengthen linkages between national programmes and global, interregional and regional ones. The Administrator was also encouraged to identify and enhance the subregional, regional and national ownership of the elements of regional programmes in a more systematic manner through the decentralized management of activities and increased use of regional and national entities in implementing and establishing linkages. He was asked to: ensure that future UNDP-supported regional, interregional and global programmes were based on a results-oriented approach in order to improve their impact and incorporate clear performance criteria for effective evaluation; and enhance resource mobilization efforts in all areas, including intercountry programmes.

On 15 September,[9] the Board took note of the Administrator's report on mid-term reviews.[16]

**Field visits.** In accordance with a 1994 Board decision,[19] the Executive Board secretariat submitted to the January 1995 session a note containing draft revised terms of reference for UNDP/UNFPA Executive Board field visits.[20] On 13 January,[5] the Board noted them and the comments made thereon.

Based on further discussion in January and February, the terms of reference were again revised and renamed as guidelines for the field visits of the UNDP/UNFPA Executive Board. On 7 April,[6] the Board adopted those guidelines.[21]

In 1995, field visits took place to Colombia, Ghana, Nicaragua, the Niger and Turkey.

### Country programmes by region

#### Africa

Through its Regional Bureau for Africa, UNDP support for African development focused on indigenous capacity-building and utilization to enable countries to manage their own development. In Lesotho, the Grass-roots Initiative Support project, launched in 1991, helped to train 948 village district council members in project planning, management and implementation. In Ethiopia and the Gambia, UNDP helped to train several staff of line ministries in policy formulation and implementation.

UNDP also supported specific initiatives on capacity-building. The aim of the African Capacity-Building Initiative (ACBI), launched jointly in 1990 by UNDP, the World Bank and the African Development Bank, was to assist Governments to build and use national capacities, mainly for economic management. Donors had pledged $86.9 million to ACBI (based in Harare, Zimbabwe, and managed by the African Capacity-Building Foundation), of which $35.5 million had been received by late 1994. By late 1995, 26 projects had been initiated in 18 countries for a total commitment of some $60 million.

The aim of National Long-Term Perspective Studies was to help African countries to define national priorities and enhance strategic thinking and planning in order to guide their development over a 25-year period. The exercise, under way in several countries, had been completed in Côte d'Ivoire and Mauritius; significant advances had been made in Cape Verde, Gabon, Guinea-Bissau, Madagascar and Zambia. More than 30 countries participated in the national technical cooperation assessment and programmes (NATCAP) exercise. Many had completed the first phase and had formulated a comprehensive database and a policy framework paper. Some had finished the second phase, which required the preparation of a technical cooperation programme, making possible the incorporation of technical cooperation resources into overall budget planning. To strengthen capacity-building further, UNDP had reduced the availability of long-term international experts and had enhanced the application of national expertise. A policy to reduce long-term overseas training was also being implemented, while in-country and in-region training was being promoted.

UNDP supported African efforts to establish systems of government that were transparent and accountable and that met all the other criteria of good governance. In Mozambique, a special elections team was assembled to train registration and civic education agents, as well as polling station and electoral officers. UNDP also assisted Benin in the reform of its judiciary system and in conducting parliamentary elections.

Poverty eradication was the key element in most African country programmes, going beyond income poverty to access to basic services and power structures. In 1995, numerous sub-Saharan African countries, with UNDP assistance and the collaboration of other development partners, launched comprehensive cross-sectoral poverty eradication programmes. UNDP provided assistance to Burkina Faso, Côte d'Ivoire, Ghana, Malawi, Togo and Zimbabwe in preparing or implementing poverty alleviation programmes.

With regard to women's participation in development, there was a shift from the concept of women in development to that of gender in development, the latter taking into account the interdependence of women and men as defined by their relationships, roles and responsibilities. Workshops were organized in 18 countries to sensitize planners, policy makers and other groups to the gender-in-development concept, as well as to concentrate greater national focus on gender issues. In collaboration with UNIFEM, UNDP launched a programme, ''Strengthening Gender and Development Capacity in Africa'', to develop an integrated strategy for mainstreaming gender issues into African development planning and programming.

There was renewed emphasis on generating private-sector initiatives in Africa, focusing on small and medium enterprise development. Several sensitization meetings were organized with African entrepreneurs and, in collaboration with other agencies, UNDP held two regional forums, in Botswana and Cameroon, which led to two subregional initiatives in East and West Africa.

During 1995, UNDP organized round-table meetings—the key mechanism for policy dialogue and resource mobilization—for Angola, Burkina Faso, the Gambia, Lesotho, Namibia, Rwanda and Seychelles. Sectoral round-table meetings were convened in Benin, Burkina Faso, Cape Verde, Mali and the Niger. In the case of Angola, total pledges made at the round-table meeting and follow-up consultations amounted to more than $1 billion, while $630 million was pledged for Rwanda at the round-table meeting, an amount that rose to $1.2 billion during follow-up activities.

Of 184 new projects approved in 1995, valued at $120.7 million, a total of 135, valued at $69.9 million, were nationally executed, increasing the proportion of nationally executed projects to 70 per cent from 50 per cent in 1994.

## Arab States

The UNDP Regional Bureau for Arab States conducted a strategic planning workshop in March 1995, which identified the five top developmental targets in the region: governance; high population growth rate; scarcity of water; sustainable livelihood (with special emphasis on poverty eradication, employment creation and environmental protection); and diversified economic growth. Special situations, including security, sanctions and emergencies facing a number of Arab countries, created especially challenging circumstances for programme development and delivery, UNDP reported. Nevertheless, 80 per cent of all country and regional funds were committed as of the end of November 1995.

Although sustainable human development (SHD) as the focus of UNDP programming had been introduced to the region when the majority of resources had already been allocated, many countries introduced the concept through highlighting SHD elements in approved projects and refocusing others, as well as by using remaining IPF resources and Special Programme Resources (SPR). In collaboration with the Government of Egypt, UNDP continued to consolidate and elaborate its SHD programme through a second national human development report and a platform for monitoring and evaluating all the Governorates of Egypt. UNDP also assisted SHD activities in Tunisia and Lebanon. SHD programming was boosted by an SPR allocation to the Regional Bureau of $1 million. Ten country initiatives were launched, the majority aimed at preparing national human development reports, situation analyses and/or country profiles. In addition, the Bureau decided to use the full 1995-1996 TSS-1 (technical support services-1) allocation to enhance SHD operationalization, with the focus on poverty elimination.

With regard to community-based activities, UNDP continued support for programmes in Somalia despite uncertain political conditions. Assistance ranged from small-credit agricultural-extension activities, education and health to labour-intensive rehabilitation of basic community infrastructure where security conditions permitted. Area development schemes remained a key effort in the Sudan. In the Syrian Arab Republic, UNDP continued to support an agricultural investment programme aimed at raising standards of living of rural populations through increasing agricultural production and creating other income-generating activities, with a strong component for improving the status of women.

Although support to macroeconomic reform was a major area of concentration of the country programme for the Sudan, it was only in 1995 that the first significant UNDP project in that field was approved. Technical support was provided to economic reform programmes in Yemen, which included assistance to the five-year economic plan, privatization, support to Yemen Free Trade Zones and assistance for economic and financial management. Efforts to support the programme of economic revitalization of Lebanon continued to gain momentum in 1995 and UNDP's ongoing programme of support to administrative rehabilitation there continued to show positive results.

With regard to resource mobilization, UNDP, based on the recommendations of a 1994 inter-agency mission to Djibouti, committed $200,000 to foster consensus on key policy reforms and long-term development strategies for that country. That led to the formulation of a comprehensive national economic reform programme. In Morocco, a sectoral round-table meeting on drinking-water was successfully organized under the auspices of UNDP and the Government.

Of newly approved projects and programmes in 1995, almost 50 per cent were nationally executed.

## Asia and the Pacific

Although the Asia and Pacific region continued to experience dynamic rates of economic growth, poverty was the dominant issue in many countries and the region as a whole was home to the majority of the world's poor. Greater programme focus was achieved through the closing of old projects and a systematic clustering of ongoing initiatives within the framework of SHD. Inter-agency working groups identified focus themes in several countries. In India, discussions identified four gender-related areas as follow-up to the 1995 Fourth World Conference on Women, held in Beijing, China (see PART FOUR, Chapter X): advocacy for the ninth development plan; influencing the 2001 census exercise; supporting government and non-governmental organization (NGO) efforts to implement the Beijing Platform for Action; and showcasing UN system best practices. Inter-agency task forces were also set up in Indonesia, Iran, Pakistan and the Philippines to follow up on a UN system response to poverty eradication and gender concerns. In Thailand, inter-agency groups were established on gender, decentralization for poverty eradication, children, environment, HIV/AIDS and disaster management.

In the field of poverty eradication, UNDP conducted three studies as a contribution to Thailand's eighth national plan (1997-2001). They provided guidelines for a holistic approach to human development, suggested ways to strengthen development capacity and described steps to be taken to emphasize participation. National poverty alleviation programme coordination mechanisms were improved in Mongolia, where local staff were trained in social development methodol-

ogies and in computer and electronic communications. UNDP was to finance projects to assist poor women to overcome structural and other barriers to full participation in the development process. The reformulation of UNDP support to the Cambodian resettlement and reintegration programme culminated in the approval in November of a $40 million four-year experimental project in decentralized planning and financing of participatory rural development. It aimed at eradicating poverty, strengthening civil society and promoting dialogue between the constituents of Cambodian society.

Environmental projects in the region included UNDP assistance to a Bhutan biodiversity conservation plan and a grant to India to phase out chlorofluorocarbons in the foams sector.

In the area of advancement of women and gender equality, UNDP supported a review of the institutional capability of Bangladesh to mainstream gender issues in development. A UNDP-sponsored study on women leaders recommended measures for advancement of the role and socio-economic position of women in Maldives. A programme exercise for the further integration of gender concerns into UNDP activities in India was undertaken in 1995; proposals included support to a projected Indian Centre for Women in Politics, responding to the Constitutional amendment according local governance institutions statutory status, and reserving a third of seats in elected bodies for women. Grass-roots initiatives in Myanmar were supported under the Human Development Initiative, which focused on deprived rural communities participating in income-generation activities and training, and the expansion of opportunities for women and girls to participate actively in the economy.

In the area of public institutions, UNDP supported several large donor-funded projects under the national Public Administration Reform Programme in Viet Nam. Three new projects were formulated to strengthen key governance institutions in the country: the National Assembly, the court system and the procuracy system. UNDP–World Bank policy studies included a major research endeavour on corporate governance issues and structures necessary for China's rapidly changing State-owned enterprise sector.

A total of 104 nationally executed programmes/projects were approved during 1995 for approximately $51 million, representing 73 per cent of the total value of new UNDP projects approved during the year.

## Europe and the Commonwealth of Independent States

During 1995, UNDP strengthened its role in the Eastern Europe and CIS region, approving 12 country programmes and, under the theme of

SHD, focusing on six priority themes: environment; democracy, governance and participation; small and medium enterprises; aid coordination; and gender in development. UNDP supported preparation of national human development reports in 21 countries of the region. Published in May 1995, these documents introduced the concept of SHD to countries in transition, providing much useful data and statistics disaggregated by region, gender, age and ethnic groups.

UNDP organized an eight-day train trip—the "Beijing Express"—bringing more than 200 women (from Governments and NGOs of the region) from Warsaw, Poland, to Beijing for the Fourth World Conference on Women. Its goal was to increase the participation of gender-related NGOs in the region in follow-up activities to the Conference.

With UNDP support, the Interstate Council for the Aral Sea organized in September 1995 the Nukus (Uzbekistan) Conference on the sustainable development of the Aral Sea Basin States. There, Central Asian heads of State signed the Nukus Declaration to renew efforts to combat the Aral Sea environmental crisis. UNDP led the capacity-development efforts within the framework of the jointly managed UNDP/World Bank/UNEP $200 million multi-year rehabilitation programme.

The first Central Asian conference on regional cooperation took place in June 1995 at Lake Issyk-Kul, Kyrgyzstan. Assisted by UNDP, the five Central Asian republics (Kazakstan, Kyrgyzstan, Tajikistan, Turkmenistan, Uzbekistan) addressed three principal issues of mutual concern: economic and social development and regional cooperation; demographic issues, including migration and displaced persons; and environmental problems and natural disasters.

With regard to aid coordination, a major three-year UNDP regional training programme on building national capacities for aid management was launched in 1995 in 15 countries of Eastern Europe and CIS. Austria and Japan provided financial support.

Another regional programme to strengthen democracy, governance and participation covered both regional and country-specific activities and included issues such as: democratization; sound governance; strengthening government agencies; human rights; support to the electoral process; and the promotion of civil society, grass-roots organizations and NGOs.

During 1995, cost-sharing budgets for national projects in the region totalled $19 million, including new cost-sharing contributions of $10 million, a 300 per cent increase over 1994. Major donors included Austria, Japan, the Netherlands, Switzerland and the Nordic countries. In addition, management services agreements were approved

to support the health reform process in Turkey (with funding from the World Bank) and for gender in development in Albania (with funding from Italy).

### Latin America and the Caribbean

UNDP-supported programmes in Latin America and the Caribbean in 1995 fell largely within the areas of: governance; support for peace processes; social reform and development/follow-up to the 1995 World Summit for Social Development (see PART FOUR, Chapter IX); and environment and management of natural resources.

The Regional Bureau for Latin America and the Caribbean continued to cooperate with the UNDP Management Development and Governance Division to promote national and regional governance initiatives. These included a conference on governance and development (Santiago, Chile, September) and the preparation of two books: *Democracy, Markets and Equity* and *Governance in Latin America and the Caribbean on the Threshold of the Year 2000.*

UNDP consolidated its presence in Guatemala as facilitator and source of technical support for peace efforts. The UN Human Rights Verification Mission in Guatemala/UNDP Joint Unit was created to oversee the institutional strengthening requirements of the Peace Accords on Human Rights and Indigenous Rights. UNDP was also responsible for administering all technical cooperation programmes in support of the Peace Accord Concerning Displaced Persons. (See PART TWO, Chapter III.)

The SHD programme at the local level was created to combat poverty in areas most affected by war. In El Salvador, UNDP supported commitments emanating from the Peace Accords by mobilizing technical and financial resources. Efforts were directed to projects to strengthen nascent democratic institutions, such as the Human Rights Ombudsman Office, the National Civilian Police and its training facility, and the Academy for Public Security. In Nicaragua, UNDP was commended by leading donor Governments for coordinating a support group of major donor countries to assist Nicaragua in consolidating peace with development. UNDP coordinated all activities in the area of governance in Haiti. A programme for reforming and strengthening the executive, legislative and judicial branches of government was considered particularly notable.

In the area of poverty eradication, UNDP assisted Jamaica in preparing a poverty reduction strategy, convening a poverty workshop and formulating a programme support document for poverty reduction. In Trinidad and Tobago, it supported a highly participatory and bottom-up approach for restructuring the delivery system of social services. An agreement was signed between UNDP and Guyana in December, aimed at preparing and implementing a national SHD initiative. Direct UNDP technical cooperation in Guyana concentrated on improving the delivery and quality of social services.

In the environment sector, a project was approved in Mexico to increase the participation of civil society organizations in formulating environmental policies and their follow-up. In line with the SHD concept, which encompassed both social and ecological aspects, ongoing projects in Brazil included: assistance for a national environmental plan; institutional and policy support to the new Ministry of the Environment and Inter-Ministerial Commission for Sustainable Development; projects emphasizing participatory approaches with large environmental components in vulnerable areas such as the Amazon Basin; control of industrial pollution through a large cost-sharing project with the National Environmental Management Institute and support for implementing environmental accords; and innovative technological developments, such as a gas turbine using biomass resources. During 1995, the first year of the Global Environment Facility Operational Phase, 11 UNDP projects were approved for funding in the region for a total of $15.35 million.

The Regional Bureau's resource mobilization strategy continued its upward trend in 1995. Total fifth cycle non-core and approved resources were $2.8 billion, comprising $2.6 billion non-core resources and $198 million in approved IPF resources. Approved cost-sharing resources, closely linked to the national execution modality, accounted for approximately 64.2 per cent of entire programme resources in the region; IPFs for 9.6 per cent; management services agreements for 11.4 per cent; and miscellaneous trust funds for 14.8 per cent.

### Global and interregional programmes

Following reorganization in mid-1994, the Division for Global and Interregional Programmes was dissolved and most of its activities transferred to the Science, Technology and the Private Sector Division. The mandate of the HIV and development programme included increasing awareness of the HIV epidemic and strengthening the capacity of countries to respond to the multiple consequences of the increasing infection worldwide. The UN Joint and Co-sponsored Programme on HIV/AIDS, of which UNDP was a co-sponsor, was established in 1995 to coordinate assistance to countries in developing multisectoral HIV strategies.

Following a UNDP-sponsored feasibility study, the International Vaccine Institute was being created within the framework of the Children's Vaccine Initiative. The Institute, which would focus on Asia, would assist countries to produce quality vaccines, ensure effective regulation of their production and use, conduct clinical trials and epidemiological surveillance, and engage in and coordinate research and development for new and improved vaccines against diseases of particular concern to the region.

The UNDP–World Bank Water and Sanitation Programme, a collaborative initiative emerging from the International Drinking Water Supply and Sanitation Decade (1981-1990), served to strengthen national and local efforts to improve poor people's access to safe water and sanitation. Investment projects in 17 countries totalled close to $1 billion, primarily funded by the World Bank.

Demand for UNDP's capacity-building for sustainable water development programme, established in 1993, had surged, with 18 countries participating or expressing interest in its concept and approach. By November 1995, water-sector assessments had been completed in Bolivia, China and Peru, and fact-finding missions had taken place in another 15 countries.

Research was under way to improve the productivity of staple food crops in developing countries and to reduce the need for commercial synthetic pesticides. UNDP supported projects to improve sustainable tropical maize production by resource-poor farmers; progress was achieved in the breeding and testing of locally consumed bananas and plantains.

Under the aegis of the Global Technology Group, some 40 projects were concluded with the support of international teams and active NGO interest. UNDP continued to seek appropriate new technologies for poor countries and their poorest sectors, with the Group uncovering 1,150 such technologies, mainly in construction, medical equipment, waste management and food products. Technology transfer to at least nine LDCs had demonstrated the pivotal role it could play in generating employment, enabling market-competitive, unique product development and eradicating poverty.

The International Network on Genetics in Aquaculture showed some results, with over 10 intercountry fish exchanges during 1994/95. Using the Network, Ghana was able to characterize genetically DNA from fish and had offered its expertise to other Network members. The Philippine national tilapia-breeding programme had also offered to share its experiences through the Network.

Under the Private Sector Development Programme, a framework was designed to create industrial parks in the occupied Palestinian territories through an initiative by the private sector, thus alleviating severe unemployment in the Gaza border area. In Mongolia, a programme was designed to restructure and support enterprises undertaken by newly privatized companies, while in Poland and Slovakia, a project was launched to develop new enterprises, using the assets of large State-owned organizations that had been difficult to privatize.

## Programme planning and management

In response to a 1994 Executive Board request,[22] the Administrator reported[23] on initiatives for change he had proposed that year. He described efforts to focus UNDP resources on key dimensions of SHD, noting that UNDP had addressed the need to: develop focused programme strategies; establish a framework for resource programming that reflected that focus; and develop pilot and demonstration programmes in the four main areas of poverty elimination, employment, environmental regeneration and advancement of women. Linkages between those areas had been built into all activities, he noted.

The Administrator also outlined efforts to strengthen both UN and international cooperation for SHD and to strengthen UNDP capacity to perform its new mission. Constraints to reform included: declining official development assistance; the fact that the call for reform had come towards the end of the fifth programming cycle (1992-1996) when uncommitted resources were scarce; and staff cuts caused by reductions in core contributions.

The Administrator said that five key goals had been drawn up for UNDP in 1995/96: strengthening country offices for implementation of SHD; resource mobilization and constituency-building; preparation of the 1996-1997 biennial budget strategy and fifth cycle successor arrangements; improving management accountability and information systems; and improving support to the UN system and fulfilling the role of the UNDP continuum.

He told the Board on 13 June that he would launch consultations in New York and at the regional level so he could present to the Board in 1996 a more definitive outline of the longer-term programme focus for UNDP.

On 16 June, the Board welcomed[24] the consultations mentioned by the Administrator and asked for a report on their outcome. It urged UNDP through the initiatives for change process—in the framework of the goals and priority areas supported by the Board in its 1994 decision[22] and given poverty elimination as the overriding priority in UNDP programmes—to concentrate on areas where it had demonstrable comparative advantage, particularly capacity-building in the most needed regions and countries, in particular LDCs, especially in Africa. It noted the elaboration of a strategic plan as a means to enhance UNDP management and make operational the initiatives for change, and looked forward

to receiving in 1996 a further elaborated concise version, including the following elements: a concise mission statement, a clear hierarchy of operational objectives and a comprehensive action plan.

### Fifth programming cycle

#### Independence bonus

In the context of discussions on the fifth programming cycle (1992-1996), the Executive Board in September had before it a note by the Administrator on eligibility for an independence bonus for new programme countries.[25] In it, he stated that the UN Office of Legal Affairs had been asked to furnish a legal interpretation of the eligibility for an independence bonus of 23 countries that had been granted recipient status during the fifth programming cycle (Armenia, Azerbaijan, Belarus, Bosnia and Herzegovina, Croatia, Czech Republic, Estonia, Eritrea, Georgia, Kazakstan, Kyrgyzstan, Latvia, Lithuania, Republic of Moldova, Russian Federation, Slovakia, Slovenia, South Africa, Tajikistan, the former Yugoslav Republic of Macedonia, Turkmenistan, Ukraine, Uzbekistan).

The Legal Office noted that the UNDP Governing Council had established the independence bonus in 1976 and had decided that each recipient country that had gained independence since the start of 1973 should have its IPF increased by $500,000, plus 15 per cent of its approved IPF. However, the history of the application of the provision revealed that it was the Council's intention to grant the bonus only to newly independent States that could be classified as LDCs. The Legal Office was therefore of the opinion that, of the countries listed, only Eritrea would qualify for the bonus, as it was the only one that was both an LDC and had gained independence since 1973. Estonia, Latvia and Lithuania had already been granted the bonus.

On 14 September, the Executive Board decided[26] that 15 countries (Armenia, Azerbaijan, Bosnia and Herzegovina, Croatia, Eritrea, Georgia, Kazakstan, Kyrgyzstan, Palau, Republic of Moldova, Slovenia, Tajikistan, the former Yugoslav Republic of Macedonia, Turkmenistan, Uzbekistan) were eligible for an independence bonus, which should be financed immediately from fifth cycle resources, provided that existing allocations for country and intercountry programmes were fully honoured. The Administrator was asked to report on the implementation of the decision in 1996.

#### Haiti

In response to a 1994 Executive Board request,[19] the UNDP Administrator reported on Haiti's development needs and activities[27] so the Board could consider a revision of the fifth programming cycle (1992-1996) IPF. The political crisis that originated in Haiti in 1991 had limited the use of the

IPF of $26.375 million, plus the carry-over of $6.31 million from the fourth cycle, to some $11.2 million over the three-year period 1992-1994. The Administrator described Haiti's technical cooperation needs for 1995-1996, noting that UNDP could play a strategic role as a major contributor and catalytic agent for mobilizing other donors. For UNDP to perform its functions, the undisbursed amount of the fifth cycle IPF was insufficient. The Executive Board was asked to consider an exceptional and one-time restoration of Haiti's fifth cycle IPF, either to the original level established in 1990,[2] resulting in an increase of $11.3 million, or on a pro-rated level for the remaining two years of the fifth cycle, resulting in an increase of $4.5 million.

On 13 January, the Board decided[28] to restore Haiti's IPF to the level established in 1990, an increase of $11.3 million, and to release 50 per cent of that funding immediately and the remainder following further discussion in September on the basis of a report by the Administrator on the use of all available UNDP resources. The Administrator was asked to make proposals on how to enhance UNDP capacity to respond financially to exceptional and emergency situations.

In response to the Board's January request, the Administrator submitted a note[29] to the September session describing UNDP activities in Haiti during the transition period following the reestablishment of the constitutional Government in 1994. He also submitted the fifth country programme for Haiti for the remainder of the fifth cycle,[30] which proposed that UNDP assistance target promotion of national consensus and preparation of reform policies and laws; formulation of national programmes and mobilization of resources for their implementation; and coordination of the various actors involved in implementing integrated packages for SHD at the local level.

On 15 September, the Executive Board approved[9] the fifth country programme for Haiti, took note of the Administrator's note on Haiti's development needs and activities, and authorized the release of the remaining 50 per cent of the restored IPF for programming.

**Successor programming arrangements**

At its January session, the Executive Board had before it the Administrator's report on a framework for UNDP's next programming period,[31] which followed from the Board's 1994 discussions on the subject.[32] The report focused on the broad assignment of resources and on the elaboration of the three-year planning cycle and its relationship to the programming process. The Administrator described the advantages of a rolling three-year resource planning scheme compared with the five-year IPF programming cycle cur-

rently in place. He also discussed the assignment of resources at the aggregate level, showing the relative shares of resources earmarked for three major components (programmes/projects; programme development and technical services; and support to the UN system and aid coordination) and applying them to two possible resource scenarios for the next programming period.

On 13 January,[5] the Board noted the Administrator's report.

The Administrator reported to the Board's April session on a further elaboration of the framework for the next programming period.[33] The document, which discussed resource earmarkings for the next programming period and resource distribution alternatives, was considered in informal consultations.

In June, the Board considered the Administrator's report on successor programming arrangements,[34] in which he stated that pivotal among his recommendations for change was the structure for financial allocations in the next programming period, including the allocation of country-level resources under a three-tier target for resource assignment from the core (TRAC). The report examined the three-tier TRAC scheme, successor programming arrangements, resource allocation structure and resource distribution.

On 16 June, the Board adopted a wide-ranging decision[35] on successor programming arrangements that covered principles for the programming cycle, mobilization of resources, programming arrangements, the financing mechanism, distribution of resources and Executive Board review.

With regard to mobilization of resources, the Board adopted for planning purposes the initial figure of $3.3 billion for core resources for the three-year period starting in 1997 and asked the Administrator to take measures to secure those resources. It stressed that increasing voluntary contributions to core resources should remain the central effort of all donors and of the Administrator's mobilization efforts. It also recognized the importance of non-core resources, including cost-sharing and non-traditional sources of financing as a means to enhance the capacity and supplement the means of UNDP to achieve the Board's 1994 goals and priorities.[32] The Administrator was urged to explore further non-traditional sources of financing, such as multilateral and regional banks and NGOs, in order to mobilize additional resources.

As to programming arrangements, the Board accepted in principle the three-year rolling planning scheme proposed by the Administrator.[34] New country cooperation frameworks (country programmes) should be developed by recipient Governments, in consultation with UNDP, and submitted to the Board for endorsement. It also decided to consider further, in 1996, its involvement in programming processes and procedures.

In connection with the financing mechanism, the Board decided to introduce a new, more flexible three-tier target for resource assignment from the core scheme for allocating resources to the country level and endorsed earmarkings for UNDP core resources, which it included in its decision. The Board allocated an additional 0.5 per cent of total resources for the Europe and CIS region, given the special needs of the countries with economies in transition. It authorized the Administrator to allocate $3 million for 1997, on a one-time basis, to facilitate the smooth phase-out of UNDP funding for the UN Industrial Development Organization Country Director Programme.

The Board approved the methodology for distribution of resources for country programmes as described by the Administrator,[34] including gross national product per capita and total population, using existing weights and 1994 data (or latest estimates thereof); elimination of supplementary points; increased graduation thresholds; adjusted floors; and an appropriate bonus rate for LDCs. Countries exceeding graduation thresholds during any year of the next cycle would continue to be recipients for three years and their target for resource assignment from the core would be phased out progressively during those years. The Board decided that the Administrator should ensure that 88 per cent of all targets for resource assignments from the core would be allocated to the low-income countries and 60 per cent to LDCs, and urged him to take account of those goals in all UNDP programme activities. He was to report annually on the management of the programming arrangements and on the actual resource assignments made to each country.

The Board decided to apply its decision during the period July 1995 to June 1997 for the programming of activities for the years 1997 onwards to enable the Administrator to implement the initiatives for change and support national endeavours towards poverty elimination and achievement of SHD. It asked the Administrator to submit an interim report in 1996 on the implementation of the programming arrangements, and decided to carry out a full-scale review of the July 1995 to June 1997 introductory period for the purpose of assessing experience and determining necessary changes.

### Programme evaluation

In a report to the Executive Board's April session,[36] the Administrator summarized the findings and recommendations of major evaluations carried out in 1994, including those on NATCAPs, the resident coordinator function and national execution. He also discussed evaluation methodology, building national capacity for monitoring and evaluation and outreach and support activities, and provided information on evaluations undertaken by UNDP-administered funds and programmes (UNCDF, UNIFEM and UNSO). Annexed to the report were the conclusions of an examination of the UNDP evaluation system, "Rethinking evaluation for feedback, learning and strategy formulation", which included proposals for priority actions to be carried out during 1995.

On 7 April, the Board noted[6] the Administrator's report.

### National execution

In 1995, the Secretary-General transmitted to the General Assembly a report by the Joint Inspection Unit (JIU) on national execution of projects,[37] discussing the theory underlying national execution by Governments and the role of partners in such project execution. It also gave some examples of dysfunction in national execution.

JIU concluded that national execution of programmes and projects had become the norm for multilateral projects financed by UN organizations and that the number of projects so executed was growing in all regions. Although all partners—Governments, UNDP and specialized agencies—had adopted the principle of national execution, noteworthy cases of dysfunction in its application called for adjustments, particularly regarding the roles and relationships of the various partners. At the country level, the new procedures and rules of UNDP and the specialized agencies had to be explained and decision makers and senior staff trained, so as to enable Governments to discharge their responsibilities as executing agents and steadily develop their national capacities. Within UNDP, coordination between all partners and their involvement at all levels of the process should be promoted, and the degree of transparency should be raised in the choice of implementing agencies. New financial arrangements for technical support services should be simplified and explained, so they would not reduce the use of technical support from the specialized agencies. The agencies themselves should make an effort to transfer constantly developing know-how and advanced technologies to developing countries at affordable prices.

The Secretary-General also transmitted to the Assembly the comments of ACC on the JIU report.[38]

By **decision 50/436** of 20 December, the Assembly noted the JIU report and the ACC comments.

### Financing

In his annual review of the financial situation,[39] the UNDP Administrator reported that total income in 1995 was $1.62 billion, a decrease of $18 million compared to 1994, with income exceeding expenditures by $223 million. The balance of general resources increased from $311 million at the end of 1994 to $462 million at the end of 1995. Income from voluntary contributions amounted to $903 million, a decrease from $932 million in 1994. Miscellaneous income increased to $76 million ($58 million in 1994), mostly due to improved interest earnings. After several years of rapid growth, cost-sharing income remained stable, growing by less than 1 per cent to $601 million ($596 million in 1994). Extrabudgetary income fell to $40 million ($49 million in 1994), solely because of the separation of UNOPS income from that of UNDP.

Total expenditure (inclusive of cost-sharing) decreased by $11 million, to $1,379 million in 1995. Programme expenditure declined to $994 million from $1,020 million. Within that amount, IPF expenditure declined to $438 million from $489 million, a 10 per cent reduction. SPR expenditure also declined, from $43 million to $41 million. Cost-sharing expenditure increased by 6 per cent, from $475 million in 1994 to $504 million, representing slightly less than 51 per cent of total programme delivery.

On 15 September, the Executive Board, following its review of the financial situation in 1994,[40] noted[41] with concern the projected decline in the balance of UNDP general resources in 1996 and called on Governments to increase their voluntary contributions on a predictable, continuous and assured basis. It also noted with concern the continued overcommitment and overexpenditure in the Reserve for Field Accommodation and asked for an update in 1996 on the progress of the three-year plan on use of the Reserve. The Administrator was also asked to submit in 1996 an up-to-date analysis of the risk situation of the operational reserve.

The Board noted the summary of observations and audit reports[42] of external auditors of the executing agencies on their 1993 accounts relating to UNDP-funded expenditures, and decided that in future only significant observations of those auditors on UNDP-funded expenditures should be included as part of the annual review of the financial situation.

## Budgets

### Revised 1994-1995 budget

In September, the Executive Board had before it revised budget estimates for 1994-1995,[43] along with observations of the Advisory Committee on Administrative and Budgetary Questions (ACABQ).[44] Estimates for UNDP core activities totalled $472 million gross ($435.3 million net),

$14.1 million (3 per cent) less than original estimates approved in 1993.[45] Revised estimates for programme support and development activities included a volume increase of $0.2 million pertaining to UNV due to the application of its staffing formula. The net effect of the volume, various cost, inflation, and currency adjustments on the programme support and development activities budget, excluding support to UN operational activities, was an upward adjustment of $2.8 million, to $77.5 million. Total revised estimates against UNDP resources thus amounted to $549.6 million—$12 million (2.1 per cent) less than the original approved estimates.

Combined revised estimates for the UNDP-administered funds (UNCDF, UNSO, UNIFEM, UN Fund for Science and Technology for Development/UN Revolving Fund for Natural Resources Exploration (UNFSTD/UNRFNRE) were also adjusted downwards to $24.8 million, representing a reduction of $5.9 million (19.3 per cent) compared to original estimates.

On 15 September, the Executive Board took note[46] of the realignments and adjustments incorporated into the revised 1994-1995 budget estimates, including the fact that UNOPS estimates were no longer included in the UNDP budget presentation. It endorsed the proposal, in respect of CIS and the Baltic States, to cover from savings the anticipated shortfall in extrabudgetary income generated from co-financing and cash contributions towards local office costs.

The Board approved revised appropriations in the amount of $574.4 million gross to finance the 1994-1995 budget, and resolved that income estimates in the amount of $36.7 million should be used to offset the gross appropriations, resulting in net appropriations of $537.7 million.

### 1996-1997 budget

In budget estimates for 1996-1997,[43] presented in September, the Administrator stated that, in addition to new successor programming arrangements (see above), his proposals represented a second important component of UNDP's strategic response to a changing environment. The 1996-1997 estimates for core activities, including support to UN operational activities, amounted to $470.5 million gross ($432.5 million net). Major volume features were: the overall volume reduction of $52 million comprised a headquarters reduction of $14.8 million and a country offices reduction of $37.2 million; the reduction in headquarters included the elimination of 20 Professional and 30 General Service posts—a 10.4 per cent reduction. The post reduction in country offices was 8.4 per cent and included the phasing out of 85 international Professional and 229 General Service posts. The reduction in international Professional posts was partly offset by an increase of 20 national Professional posts.

The proposed programme support and development activities budget totalled $83.6 million. One increase related to the Office of UN System Support and Services, established by the Administrator in response to the Secretary-General's request to ensure policy coherence and enhanced coordination of operational activities for development. In the case of UNV, savings resulting from the move to Bonn, Germany (see below), were fully incorporated into the 1996-1997 proposals.

With regard to UNDP-administered funds, the Administrator proposed volume reductions for UNCDF, UNFSTD/UNRFNRE and UNIFEM.

On 15 September, the Board noted[46] with concern the decline in UNDP core resources and called on Governments to increase their voluntary contributions on a predictable, continuous and assured basis. It approved appropriations in the amount of $576.8 million gross to finance the 1996-1997 biennial budget and resolved that income estimates of $38 million should be used to offset the gross appropriations, resulting in net appropriations of $538.8 million.

With regard to core activities, the Board appreciated the Administrator's proposal to continue a restrictive budget policy and to implement volume reductions with the aim of maximizing resources available for programme and programme support activities and, in that connection, emphasized the importance of: safeguarding accountability and ensuring that programme delivery was not negatively affected; the policy to reduce a larger percentage of headquarters than field posts and using functional analyses and consistent and transparent criteria to contribute to an effective process of rationalization; placing capacities and functions in optimal locations through decentralization and outsourcing; and maximizing benefits through improved management of communications and information. The Administrator was asked to assess the impact of the Board's budget decision on UNDP's organizational capacity, particularly the adequacy of human resources both at headquarters and country level. The Board was to be kept informed on progress made in clustering and networking, as well as on steps to promote common services with other UN agencies at the country level.

As to programme support and development activities, the Administrator was to report in 1996 on the specific functions of envisaged new posts in the Office of UN System Support and Services, and to report on assistance to the Secretary-General to ensure system-wide coordination and policy coherence. He was also to review, in the context of future biennial budget presentations, the

estimated workload related to support to UN operational activities.

The Board approved the Administrator's budget and staffing proposals relating to UNCDF, UNIFEM, UNFSTD/UNRFNRE and UNSO and asked him to report on steps taken to integrate UNSO's work into the UNDP core programme and on steps taken to reflect that integration in 1998-1999 budget proposals.

### Harmonization of budget presentations

In response to a 1994 Executive Board request,[47] the UNDP Administrator and the UNFPA Executive Director reported[48] on harmonization of presentation of budgets and accounts. A working party on financial statements had been established, with full participation of senior financial officials of UNDP, UNFPA and UNICEF; it would report to the General Assembly in 1996.

As for biennial budgets, a consultant engaged by the three agencies was identifying differences between existing budget presentations, and a first report was being reviewed. Also, a recent study of UNICEF budgetary matters would affect the manner in which the joint UNDP/UNFPA/UNICEF study could progress.

On 15 September, the Board requested[49] the UNDP Administrator and the UNFPA Executive Director to provide it with draft appropriation decisions on the budgets prior to its discussions. They were also asked to accelerate efforts to contribute to the harmonization of budget presentations and to provide the Board in 1996 with: an oral progress report, including identification of common features in the budgets of UNDP, UNFPA and UNICEF, and an explanation of areas not common in the budgets; an oral progress report on steps for further harmonization, which, together with Board views on the issue, would be presented to the Economic and Social Council's 1996 substantive session; and initial action proposals by the Executive Board, through ACABQ. The Administrator and Executive Director were also to ensure that the proposals for harmonization and budget presentation further promoted the provision of user-friendly and transparent budget documents and preparation procedures.

### Audit reports

In January, the Executive Board reviewed the Administrator's report[50] on follow-up to recommendations of the Board of Auditors for the biennium 1992-1993.[51] An addendum to the Administrator's report[52] provided a framework and estimated targets to help develop an implementation plan for the Reserve for Field Accommodation covering 1994-1996.

On 11 January, the Board noted[53] the Administrator's actions to address all recommendations made by the Board of Auditors. It noted the three-year plan on the use of the Reserve for Field Accommodation and asked the Administrator to report annually on the status of the Reserve as part of the annual review of the financial situation.

## Procurement

In response to a 1993 UNDP Governing Council decision,[54] the Administrator reported to the Executive Board in September on procurement from developing countries.[55] UN system-wide procurement from developing countries had reached $1.3 billion in 1994, or 35 per cent of total procurement volume, compared to 30 per cent in 1991, he stated. The report described measures already taken by the UN system to increase geographical distribution of procurement. Although important progress had been made in increasing procurement from developing countries, many external constraints remained, varying from export, currency and other regulatory barriers to commercial constraints limiting competitiveness, such as lack of quality control, limited production and servicing capacity and packing.

Progress had been made in upgrading and maintaining supplier rosters in the common vendor database (CVD), used extensively in the UN system. Distribution of CVD to country offices for decentralized use would be pursued, and country offices would be aided in establishing local vendor rosters. The Inter-Agency Procurement Services Office (IAPSO) would promote further use of advertising by UN agencies through its publication ''Procurement update'', which contained information on business opportunities and contract awards, and would seek means to facilitate global distribution of that information.

In April, meeting in Harare, Zimbabwe, the Inter-Agency Procurement Working Group (IAPWG) had stressed that measures to increase procurement from developing and underutilized major donor countries should be subordinate to considerations of competitiveness.

On 14 September, the Executive Board encouraged[56] IAPSO to continue to coordinate, through the IAPWG mechanism, efforts within the UN system to increase procurement from developing and underutilized major donor countries. The Economic and Social Council should encourage UN organizations and agencies to cooperate with IAPSO in improving the accuracy and timeliness of data for annual reporting on procurement to the Board and the Council. The Administrator was asked to streamline reporting on procurement to ensure a clear distinction between activities aimed at promoting procurement from developing countries and those from underutilized major donors, and to organize statistical data accordingly.

*REFERENCES*

[1]DP/1996/18 & Add.1-4. [2]E/1990/29 (dec. 90/34). [3]E/1995/34. [4]Ibid. (dec. 95/5). [5]Ibid. (dec. 95/7). [6]Ibid. (dec. 95/13). [7]Ibid. (dec. 95/24). [8]DP/1995/30 & Add.1-5. [9]E/1995/34 (dec. 95/37). [10]DP/1995/17/Add.1. [11]DP/1995/17/Add.2. [12]DP/1995/17/Add.4. [13]DP/1995/17/Add.5. [14]DP/1995/17/Add.3. [15]DP/1996/12 & Add.1-5. [16]DP/1995/47 & Add.1-6 & Add.1/Corr.1. [17]YUN 1992, p. 559. [18]E/1995/34 (dec. 95/25). [19]YUN 1994, p. 794. [20]DP/1995/5. [21]DP/1995/14. [22]YUN 1994, p. 799. [23]DP/1995/31. [24]E/1995/34 (dec. 95/22). [25]DP/1995/46. [26]E/1995/34 (dec. 95/26). [27]DP/1995/4. [28]E/1995/34 (dec. 95/4). [29]DP/1995/48. [30]DP/CP/HAI/5. [31]DP/1995/3. [32]YUN 1994, p. 799. [33]DP/1995/15 & Add.1. [34]DP/1995/32. [35]E/1995/34 (dec. 95/23). [36]DP/1995/18. [37]A/50/113. [38]A/50/113/Add.1. [39]DP/1996/28. [40]YUN 1994, p. 802. [41]E/1995/34 (dec. 95/29). [42]DP/1995/53 & Add.1. [43]DP/1995/51 & Add.1. [44]DP/1995/52. [45]YUN 1993, p. 698. [46]E/1995/34 (dec. 95/28). [47]YUN 1994, p. 805. [48]DP/1995/29. [49]E/1995/34 (dec. 95/30). [50]DP/1995/10. [51]A/49/5/Add.1. [52]DP/1995/10/Add.1. [53]E/1995/34 (dec. 95/3). [54]YUN 1993, p. 700. [55]DP/1995/55. [56]E/1995/34 (dec. 95/27).

# Other technical cooperation

## UN programmes

### DDSMS activities

During 1995, the UN Department for Development Support and Management Services (DDSMS) was executing more than 1,400 technical cooperation projects, with a total project expenditure of some $80.1 million. Projects financed by UNDP represented $34.6 million; those by trust funds, $36.2 million; by UNFPA, $4.8 million; and by the UN regular programme of technical cooperation, $4.5 million. These included expenditures of $19.1 million for interregional and global programmes, $31.3 million in Africa, $12.2 million in Asia and the Pacific, $4.1 million in the Americas, $11.1 million in the Arab States and $2.3 million in Europe. Africa had the largest share—39.1 per cent of total delivery.

Distribution of expenditures by substantive sectors was as follows: natural resources and environment planning, $17.4 million; national execution and capacity-building, $12.7 million; development policies and planning, $12.2 million; governance and public administration, $7.4 million; statistics, $5.2 million; energy, $4.4 million; public finance and enterprise management, $3.9 million; social development management, $3.3 million; the UN Educational and Training Programme for Southern Africa, $2.7 million; and population, $1.9 million.

On a component basis, DDSMS delivery in 1995 included $53.8 million for project personnel, $3.9 million for subcontracted services, $9.9 million for training, $9.5 million for equipment and $3 million for miscellaneous expenses.

## UN Office for Project Services

On 1 January 1995, in accordance with a 1994 General Assembly decision,[1] the UN Office for Project Services, formerly part of UNDP, became a separate and identifiable entity within the United Nations.

In response to a 1994 Executive Board request,[2] the UNDP Administrator and the UNOPS Executive Director reported on the proposed scope and objectives of UNOPS.[3] The proposed objective was to provide high-quality, timely and cost-effective development services to help UN Member States successfully implement projects. Services would include: comprehensive project management, including contracting for technical expertise and backstopping; implementation of project components being executed by other UN organizations or by national institutions; project supervision and loan administration on behalf of international financial institutions; and management services for multilateral, bilateral and beneficiary-financed projects.

The report described the role and functions of the Management Coordination Committee (MCC)—providing operational guidance and management direction to UNOPS—*vis-à-vis* the Executive Board—the governing body for UNOPS—and the role and functions of the Users Advisory Group, which would provide feedback on the quality, effectiveness and responsiveness of UNOPS services and promote the dissemination of lessons learned and new approaches developed.

The Administrator and the Executive Director also presented proposed financial regulations governing the operations of UNOPS.[4] An ACABQ report on the financial regulations was also before the Board.[5]

On 10 January, the Board approved[6] financial regulations for UNOPS as an annex to the UNDP Financial Rules and Regulations and endorsed the definition of the roles of MCC and the Users Advisory Group. It decided that the UNOPS operational reserve should be initially established at a level equal to 20 per cent of the annual administrative budget of UNOPS, rounded to the nearest $100,000.

The UNOPS Executive Director and MCC were asked to keep the Financial Regulations and Rules under review, taking into account the experience of their operation and ACABQ observations. The Board asked the Executive Director to report in June on the review's outcome.

The UNOPS Executive Director provided an update[7] on the ongoing review of the status and application of the Financial Regulations and the development of new financial rules. Pending finalization of the new rules, UNDP Rules would apply to UNOPS operations. In January, a UNOPS contracts committee was established, consisting of staff from UNDP and UNOPS, to review proposed contracts exceeding $100,000. UNOPS had launched a study of the risks and liabilities inherent in the business process of a self-financing entity providing development services.

### Budget estimates

In September, the Executive Director presented revised budget estimates for the biennium 1994-1995 and budget estimates for the biennium 1996-1997 for UNOPS.[8] Revised income projections for 1994-1995 amounted to some $59 million, about $9 million less than originally anticipated.

With regard to the 1996-1997 biennium, UNOPS anticipated a total delivery of some $810 million, $20 million more than for 1994-1995. It was estimated that delivery would generate income totalling some $61.5 million. Administrative expenditures were anticipated at $61.4 million.

The Executive Board also reviewed an ACABQ report[9] on revised budget estimates for 1994-1995 and estimates for 1996-1997.

On 15 September, the Board approved[10] three additional General Service posts, bringing the total to 244 established posts. The Executive Director was to review existing posts to determine which ones were to be maintained or reallocated, and to report in 1996.

The Board approved revised budget estimates for 1994-1995 in the amount of $58.4 million and budget estimates for 1996-1997 of $61.4 million. It noted that UNDP and UNOPS were reviewing the nature of and conditions under which central administrative services were made available to UNOPS by UNDP, and instructed the Executive Director to report in 1996 on arrangements for such services during the 1996-1997 biennium. The Board noted the financial management model developed by UNOPS to establish and monitor its administrative budget. The Executive Director was to report, through MCC, any significant changes in income projections. The future direction of UNOPS was to be considered in 1996.

### 1995 activities

During 1995, UNOPS concluded cooperation agreements with UN partners other than UNDP, including the UN High Commissioner for Refugees, the UN Department for Policy Coordination and Sustainable Development, the UN International Drug Control Programme (UNDCP), the International Fund for Agricultural Development and the International Labour Organization.

At year's end, UNOPS had incurred project expenditures totalling $382,924,263. Income from all sources totalled $30,425,868; administrative expenditures were $27,688,064. Some 48 per cent of income was from UNDP-funded projects; 5 per cent from services provided by UNOPS as either cooperating or associated agency; 5 per cent from UNDCP-funded projects; 20 per cent from projects financed by UNDP-administered trust funds; and 22 per cent from management fees for projects funded under the Management Service Agreement modality.

## UN Volunteers

In his annual report on the work of UNDP,[11] the UNDP Administrator stated that during 1995 a total of 3,263 UNV specialists and field workers from 134 nations served in 139 countries. New major programme areas included poverty eradication, support to the peace-building and democratization processes, assistance to countries in transition and strengthening civil society.

In the fight against poverty, one of the largest UNV programmes was in the United Republic of Tanzania, where 60 UNV specialists and field workers focused on health, agriculture and strengthening local community groups. In Burkina Faso, 51 volunteers worked in the areas of rural development, education and skills training, health and food security, while in the Niger, 31 volunteers were assigned to programmes linked to employment and income-generating activities, preservation of natural resources, women in development and economic management. A multisectoral project in Togo, based on promoting people's participation at the village level, served as a model for UNDP and the Government for a larger participatory approach to poverty eradication.

In the areas of peace-building and democratization, 74 UNV specialists supported the UN Assistance Mission in Rwanda, and an additional 65 volunteers participated as human rights monitors in the field. Logistical support was provided to the UN Mission in Haiti by 29 UNV specialists; another 30 specialists served as human rights observers there. In addition, 12 electoral assistance and logistical support officers worked in Haiti in 1995. In Guatemala, UNV provided the UN Human Rights Verification Mission with 105 human rights monitors, indigenous rights monitors, and human rights promotion and education officers.

UNV assistance to countries in transition included supporting innovative poverty eradication efforts, working with communities in environmentally degraded areas, strengthening human resources and mobilizing external financial resources. A continuing UNV presence in Cambodia played a significant role in the transition from emergency and rehabilitation to development. In the Aral Sea region, 10 UNV specialists assisted communities to develop self-help initia-

tives through programmes addressing issues of environment and biodiversity, nutrition, soil and water management, and small business and agro-business development. In Kyrgyzstan, indigenous UNV specialists were building self-management capacities of indigenous NGOs to support local initiatives.

With regard to strengthening civil society, UNV worked with NGOs and community-based organizations (CBOs) in Latin America to facilitate sharing experiences and knowledge of indigenous crafts, technologies and medicine. In Africa, UNV collaborated extensively with NGOs and CBOs, using mixed teams of international and national UNV specialists to advocate community support in HIV/AIDS care. In Lebanon, UNV promoted the return of some 450,000 displaced persons.

### Relocation of UNV headquarters

In January, the Administrator outlined[12] to the Executive Board the Secretary-General's proposal to relocate UNV headquarters from Geneva to Bonn, a proposal already discussed in 1994.[13] A working group established to consider the relocation's technical, financial and legal aspects had identified human resource, administrative, legal and financial implications. Its report was annexed to the Administrator's report to the Board. ACABQ also reported on the proposal.[14]

On 10 January, the Board endorsed[15] the Secretary-General's proposal to accept Germany's offer to relocate UNV headquarters to Bonn from mid-1996 onwards. The Administrator was authorized to continue discussions on the terms and provisions of the offer to resolve outstanding issues and complete arrangements to enable the transfer by July 1996.

### Technical cooperation among developing countries

In his annual report covering 1995,[11] the Administrator stated that activities funded from the SPR allocation for technical cooperation among developing countries (TCDC) fell into four subprogrammes: sensitization and information on the TCDC modality; capacities and needs-matching exercises and subject-specific workshops; studies and evaluation; and enhancement of capacities for the application of TCDC. Activities within those subprogrammes focused on priority areas to promote SHD: TCDC and poverty eradication; jobs and sustainable livelihood; environment; gender in development; and the TCDC Information Referral Service.

## TCDC Committee action

At the ninth session of the High-level Committee on the Review of Technical Cooperation among Developing Countries (New York, 30 May–2 June),[16] experts reviewed progress made in implementing the 1978 Buenos Aires Plan of Action for Promoting and Implementing TCDC[17] and decisions of the High-level Committee and implementation of the recommendations of the South Commission.[18] Also considered were a report on new directions for TCDC, with an addendum containing the Bandung (Indonesia) Framework for Asia-Africa Cooperation, adopted at the Asia-Africa Forum in December 1994;[19] and a document dealing with organizational matters.[20]

On 2 June, the Committee adopted six decisions. Regarding progress made in implementing the Buenos Aires Plan of Action,[21] the Committee called on all parties in the development effort to give the highest priority to implementing the 1992 Economic and Social Council resolution on TCDC,[22] giving first consideration to the use of the TCDC modality in their technical cooperation programmes. It urged those parties to continue to accord high priority to key elements in the South Commission report,[23] including strengthening national commitment to South-South cooperation, the use of developing country training and education facilities, promotion of South-South trade, cooperation between enterprises in the South and strengthening food security. The Committee called on Governments, the UN development system and relevant intergovernmental organizations to continue to improve the quality and timeliness of reporting on the promotion and application of TCDC activities at subregional, regional, interregional and international levels. The UNDP Administrator was asked to report in 1997 on the implementation of its decision.

In a decision on new directions for TCDC,[24] the Committee welcomed the report on the subject,[19] prepared in response to a 1994 General Assembly request.[25] It also expressed its belief that the report was an important contribution to the Secretary-General's report on the state of South-South cooperation (see preceding chapter). It endorsed the report's recommendations on new directions, particularly those on adopting a more strategic focus for TCDC and on selecting priority issues, such as trade and investment, debt, the environment, poverty alleviation, production and employment and macroeconomic policy coordination, as well as education, health, transfer of technology and rural development. The Committee urged Governments and UN organizations, as well as other institutions and entities in both public and private sectors, particularly in developed countries, to incorporate new directions for TCDC into their programmes for technical cooperation. Governments and UN organizations were called on to consider increasing budget allocations for TCDC and to identify new funding arrangements such as triangular funding and private-sector funding, as well as mobilizing contributions to ensure that adequate resources were available to implement the recommendations on new directions. The UNDP Administrator was asked to ensure that the Special Unit for TCDC played a proactive role within the UN system to expand the application of TCDC and effectively implement the strategy for new directions, while endeavouring to reduce the delivery cost of future TCDC programmes. The Committee called on the Intergovernmental Meeting of Experts on South-South Cooperation (see preceding chapter) to take fully into account the report of the High-level Committee, with special emphasis on the decision on new directions, and to propose practical application recommendations for TCDC. The UNDP Administrator was to report in 1997 on progress in implementing the Committee's decision.

With regard to an overall framework for promoting and applying TCDC, the Committee endorsed[26] the recommendation of its Bureau[20] that existing arrangements for the Committee be maintained. UN agencies should consider how to refine and improve the guidelines for the review of TCDC policies and procedures, and report on the subject for ACC consideration. The Committee supported the Administrator's decision to maintain the separate identity of the Special Unit for TCDC, for which the UNDP/UNFPA Executive Board was to provide adequate staff and support.

In a decision on strengthening TCDC,[27] the Committee welcomed the Administrator's efforts to increase TCDC resources and the commitment to the South Centre—an intergovernmental organization in Geneva—and his commitment to help expand the core capital of the Perez-Guerrero Trust Fund (formerly the Trust Fund for Economic Cooperation among Developing Countries (ECDC)/TCDC).

By another decision,[28] the Committee welcomed the establishment of the Group of 77/UNDP Award for ECDC/TCDC, on the occasion of the commemoration in June 1994 of the thirtieth anniversary of the founding of the Group of 77 developing countries, to promote greater awareness of the importance of South-South cooperation and to support ECDC/TCDC activities. The Committee also approved the agenda for its tenth (1997) session.[29]

By **decision 1995/233** of 13 July, the Economic and Social Council took note of the Committee's report.

**Executive Board action.** On 14 June, the Executive Board endorsed[30] the new directions for TCDC as recommended by the High-level Committee. It reaffirmed the important role they could play in increasing the use of both TCDC and ECDC as dynamic instruments for expanded South-South cooperation. UNDP efforts to promote a more strategic orientation for TCDC by focusing on high-impact activities were welcomed. The Administrator was to take action regarding the promotion and implementation of TCDC, pursuant to a 1992 Economic and Social Council resolution,[22] which called on parties in the development effort to give the TCDC option first consideration in technical cooperation activities. He was also asked to ensure that the Special Unit for TCDC played a proactive role within the UN system to expand the application of TCDC and effectively implement the strategy for new directions for TCDC, while endeavouring to reduce the delivery cost of future programmes.

GENERAL ASSEMBLY ACTION

By **decision 50/436** of 20 December, the General Assembly noted the Secretary-General's report on ECDC/TCDC,[31] which drew attention to the report of the High-level Committee on the Review of TCDC on its ninth session and to the report on the state of South-South cooperation (see preceding chapter).

In **resolution 50/119** of 20 December, the Assembly endorsed the recommendations in the report[19] on new directions for TCDC and welcomed the Executive Board decision to increase the allocation of resources for TCDC during the next programming cycle. UNDP was invited to establish a voluntary trust fund for the promotion of South-South cooperation, to which all countries were invited to contribute (see preceding chapter).

*REFERENCES*
[1]YUN 1994, p. 806, GA dec. 48/501, 19 Sep. 1994. [2]Ibid., p. 807. [3]DP/1995/6. [4]DP/1995/7 & Add.1. [5]DP/1995/13. [6]E/1995/34 (dec. 95/1). [7]DP/1995/37. [8]DP/1995/60. [9]DP/1995/45. [10]E/1995/34 (dec. 95/31). [11]DP/1996/18/Add.1. [12]DP/1995/11. [13]YUN 1994, p. 809. [14]DP/1995/12. [15]E/1995/34 (dec. 95/2). [16]A/50/39. [17]YUN 1978, p. 467. [18]TCDC/9/2 & Corr.1. [19]TCDC/9/3 & Add.1. [20]TCDC/9/4. [21]A/50/39 (dec. 9/1). [22]YUN 1992, p. 573, ESC res. 1992/41, 30 July 1992. [23]A/45/810 & Corr.1. [24]A/50/39 (dec. 9/2). [25]YUN 1994, p. 773, GA res. 49/96, 19 Dec. 1994. [26]A/50/39 (dec. 9/3). [27]Ibid. (dec. 9/4). [28]Ibid. (dec. 9/5). [29]Ibid. (dec. 95/6). [30]E/1995/34 (dec. 95/19). [31]A/50/421.

# UN Capital Development Fund

The UN Capital Development Fund, in a policy paper published in 1995 entitled ''Poverty Reduction, Participation and Local Government: The Role for UNCDF'',[1] outlined the Fund's future direction and tied its core mandate—poverty reduction in LDCs—to experience accumulated over the years. While continuing to emphasize its traditional role in providing small-scale credit and rural infrastructure in LDCs, UNCDF was placing increased importance on developing direct partnerships with newly empowered local governments and the community groups they served, particularly the rural poor.

The policy paper stated that many new and planned UNCDF programmes aimed at building capacity and responded to needs at the local level. These included projects in Cambodia, Malawi, Togo, the United Republic of Tanzania and the West Bank.

UNCDF continued to collaborate with UNDP, members of the International Union of Local Authorities, the French NGO Cités Unies Développement, the Association of Dutch Municipalities and the Local Government International Bureau (United Kingdom) to help strengthen the development work of local authorities.

The implementation of UNCDF credit activities improved significantly in 1995 and a guarantee facility was launched in Madagascar. A regional unit was established in West Africa.

During 1995, UNCDF received $30.6 million in voluntary pledges, $3.8 million for sub-trust funds and $20,279 in cost-sharing. Expenditures during the year totalled $40.6 million.

On 6 April, the UNDP/UNFPA Executive Board appealed[2] to all interested donor countries, organizations and other parties to make voluntary contributions to UNCDF. It encouraged the Administrator to continue to refine the Fund's community development focus, which would include a strong emphasis on projects involving local authorities, the private sector and civil society in the context of its assigned mandate.

*REFERENCES*
[1]DP/1996/18/Add.1. [2]E/1995/34 (dec. 95/9).

Chapter III

# Humanitarian and special economic assistance

During 1995, with a growing number of major emergencies of all varieties requiring international assistance, the United Nations, through the Department of Humanitarian Affairs, continued to strengthen its coordination support capacity and to act as a focal point for the development of new initiatives to be undertaken by the international emergency response community for the improved effectiveness of international relief operations. Consolidated inter-agency appeals were launched for Afghanistan, Angola, the Caucasus, Chechnya in the Russian Federation, Iraq, Liberia, Rwanda and countries receiving refugees from Rwanda, the Sudan and the former Yugoslavia, but the international response often fell short of the set targets.

Regarding special economic assistance, the Economic and Social Council devoted the high-level segment of its substantive session of 1995 to the consideration of the development of Africa, including the implementation of the UN New Agenda for the Development of Africa in the 1990s. The General Assembly established an ad hoc committee during its fiftieth session to prepare a mid-term review in 1996 of the implementation of the New Agenda and the Administrative Committee on Coordination decided to launch the System-wide Special Initiative on Africa in 1996.

Having entered the second half of the International Decade for Natural Disaster Reduction (1990-2000), the international community accelerated efforts towards integrating disaster reduction into national development planning. The Assembly called for international assistance for the Caribbean region, which was hard hit by Hurricane Luis, and for Madagascar, which was struggling to recover from the cyclones and floods of 1994.

## Humanitarian assistance

Increasingly, humanitarian organizations were compelled to operate in war-torn societies where conflicting parties were often openly contemptuous of fundamental humanitarian norms. In such circumstances, a major challenge was the need to safeguard the well-being of civilians while providing assistance in a manner consistent with humanitarian principles.

At the World Summit on Humanitarian Assistance (Madrid, Spain, 14 December), convened by the European Commissioner for Humanitarian Aid, heads of the world's 10 major humanitarian agencies called for decisive international action to resolve and prevent the crises. The Summit's Madrid Declaration appealed to the international community at large for, among other things, the development of a global system of proactive crisis prevention; urgent steps to address the deliberate targeting of civilians in conflicts; and urgent attention to the needs and protection of all victims, with priority to women, children and the elderly. The agencies also appealed to all concerned to respect the humanitarian and non-political nature of their work, to ensure the safety of humanitarian personnel and to provide them with a more secure basis for funding.

### Humanitarian activities

#### Africa

*Angola*

In January, a UN Consolidated Inter-Agency Appeal for Angola for the period January to December 1995 was launched. It sought $213 million, of which $145 million was for resettlement and repatriation of the internally displaced and refugees; $56 million for the demobilization of former combatants and their reintegration into civilian society; and $12 million for a mine action programme. Approximately 3.2 million Angolans were in need of humanitarian assistance, including 1.1 million internally displaced persons, 100,000 potential returnees, and 1.9 million conflict-affected persons. In July, the Appeal's programme for demobilization and reintegration was revised, reflecting the demobilization exercise agreed upon between the Government of Angola and the National Union for the Total Independence of Angola (UNITA) (see below). The revised requirements for the programme covering the period January 1995 to December 1996 amounted to $102.3 million.

The round-table conference for Angola (Brussels, Belgium, 25-26 September) reviewed the community rehabilitation programme, which involved measures to facilitate national reconciliation, rehabilitation, reconstruction and economic revitalization. The donor community responded with pledges of over $993 million. The International Monetary Fund (IMF) collaborated with Angola in the implementation of a new economic and social programme, while the World Bank helped to prepare an emergency reconstruction programme.

**Report of the Secretary-General.** In response to a 1993 General Assembly request,[1] the Secretary-General reported[2] in September 1995 on international assistance for the economic rehabilitation of Angola. The report described emergency assistance during the civil conflict and developments following the signing of the Lusaka Protocol in 1994,[3] and outlined future humanitarian assistance.

Opening of the roads, which had been closed for more than two years, facilitated humanitarian assistance to previously inaccessible areas. Easier access to land, markets and food supply contributed to a dramatic decline in the number of people served by the World Food Programme (WFP) to 1.1 million in July. While the main coordination responsibility for humanitarian assistance remained with the Unit for Coordination of Humanitarian Assistance (UCHA) of the Department of Humanitarian Affairs (DHA), a Humanitarian Coordination Group was established as a step to transfer the responsibility to the Government of Angola.

Under the Lusaka Protocol, as many as 100,000 combatants, including 30,000 disabled and under-age soldiers, were to be demobilized and reintegrated into civilian life. UCHA created a Demobilization and Reintegration Office to conduct feasibility studies on reintegration projects for under-age and disabled soldiers, quick-impact projects for the resettlement of demobilized soldiers in rural areas, and a survey of 600 soldiers concerning their social profile and social and economic expectations of reintegration into civilian life. The Government of Angola and UNITA agreed to demobilize troops in stages over a period of approximately 27 months. The section of the Consolidated Inter-Agency Appeal covering demobilization and reintegration was accordingly readjusted in July to take account of the agreement, seeking $102.3 million for the revised programme, of which $52.3 million was for the crucial first quartering phase. As at 22 August, $4.2 million had been pledged for the revised programme. The selection of 15 quartering areas for UNITA troops was completed and the quartering launched in November.

A draft mine action plan was prepared by UCHA's Central Mine Action Office to conduct extensive surveys of mined areas; public education and awareness about mines; training of Angolans in mine action; and mine clearance in priority areas. Demining activities were carried out in the quartering areas along access roads and around bridges designated for reconstruction. A Demining School, established by the Central Mine Action Office and the Angolan National Institute for the Removal of Explosive Devices, had begun a course to train Angolans. The Secretary-General observed that massive destruction of physical infrastructure, severe disruption of socio-economic activities and pollution of land-mines and unexploded ordnance would affect the activities and lives of thousands of Angolans for decades.

In December, the security situation deteriorated, especially in UNITA-controlled areas; none the less, humanitarian assistance continued wherever possible, including deliveries of food, seeds and medical supplies, as well as nutritional assessments and the repair of medical equipment.

GENERAL ASSEMBLY ACTION

On 12 December, the General Assembly adopted **resolution 50/58 D**.

**International assistance for the economic rehabilitation of Angola**

*The General Assembly,*

*Recalling* its previous resolutions appealing to the international community to continue to render material, technical and financial assistance for the economic rehabilitation of Angola,

*Recalling also* that the Security Council, in its resolutions 922(1994) of 31 May 1994, 932(1994) of 30 June 1994, 945(1994) of 29 September 1994, 952(1994) of 27 October 1994, 966(1994) of 8 December 1994, 976(1995) of 8 February 1995 and 1008(1995) of 7 August 1995, in the presidential statements on Angola of 11 May 1995 and 12 October 1995, and in other resolutions on international assistance for the economic rehabilitation of Angola, had, *inter alia*, requested the international community to render assistance to Angola,

*Deeply concerned* about the critical economic and social situation prevailing in Angola, aggravated by the tremendous consequences of war which have destroyed the economic and social infrastructure,

*Stressing* the fact that the ongoing implementation of the peace agreements, including the Lusaka Protocol, will foster peace and stability, thus creating favourable conditions for the economic and social rehabilitation of the country,

*Welcoming* the results of the first Round-Table Conference of Donors, held at Brussels from 25 to 27 September 1995, conducted in a spirit of reconciliation and intended to mobilize funds for the Community Rehabilitation and National Reconciliation Programme, and aware of the important role to be played by the international community in assisting Angola in rehabilitating its economy and its basic and social infrastructures, as well as the development of human resources,

*Recognizing* that the social and economic reintegration of demobilized combatants is essential for the establishment of lasting peace and sustainable development in Angola,

*Stressing* the need the strengthen the process of demining of all roads, as well as areas of productive activities, by means of appropriate international assistance and the continued commitment of all parties in Angola,

1. *Takes note* of the report of the Secretary-General of 12 September 1995;

2. *Calls upon* all parties to do their utmost to achieve the full and effective implementation of the Peace Accords for Angola in order to bring peace and stability to Angola, thus creating conditions conducive to its economic rehabilitation;

3. *Expresses its appreciation* to all States, United Nations organizations and other donors for the substantial humanitarian assistance rendered to Angola during the last two years, and appeals for continued and generous contributions in support of humanitarian activities facilitating the current transition to peace;

4. *Appeals* to all Governments and international and private institutions that announced their contributions at the Round-Table Conference of Donors to honour their commitments, and encourages the Government of Angola to proceed with its programme of economic rehabilitation, including through the implementation of the Community Rehabilitation and National Reconciliation Programme, and to overcome its social, economic and financial crisis;

5. *Requests* the Secretary-General, in cooperation with the international community, to continue to mobilize organizations and organs of the United Nations system in order to ensure an appropriate level of economic assistance for Angola;

6. *Commends* all Governments, non-governmental organizations and United Nations specialized agencies involved in the mine-action programme in Angola, and requests the international community to consider increasing its support in this domain;

7. *Urges* Member States and other donors to provide support for the programme of demobilization and reintegration of excess combatants, as outlined in the appeal issued by the Department of Humanitarian Affairs of the Secretariat in July 1995;

8. *Requests* the Secretary-General to report to the General Assembly at its fifty-second session on the implementation of the present resolution;

9. *Decides* to review at its fifty-second session the question of international assistance for the economic rehabilitation of Angola.

General Assembly resolution 50/58 D

12 December 1995	Meeting 89	Adopted without vote

34-nation draft (A/50/L.31 & Add.1); agenda item 20 *(b)*.
*Meeting numbers.* GA 50th session: plenary 70, 89.

### Burundi

In January, DHA launched the UN Consolidated Inter-Agency Appeal for Persons Affected by the Crisis in Rwanda, seeking a total of $805 million to assist Burundi, Rwanda, Uganda, the United Republic of Tanzania and Zaire. Assistance to Burundi targeted 110,000 returnees and 100,000 internally displaced persons, as well as 294,000 Burundese refugees in Rwanda, the United Republic of Tanzania and Zaire. The Office of the Humanitarian Coordinator, established in November, had primary responsibility for the coordination of emergency relief activities of the UN system in Burundi. During 1995, the Office

of the UN High Commissioner for Refugees (UNHCR) provided assistance to returnees, displaced persons and 5,000 urban poor in the country. The United Nations Children's Fund (UNICEF) provided basic drugs for health centres and integrated supplementary feeding into health centre activities. Its activities also included basic and hygiene education, as well as identification of and assistance to unaccompanied children. The United Nations Development Programme (UNDP) helped the Government to plan reconstruction and development projects and initiated technical assistance with the World Health Organization (WHO) in the rehabilitation of the health system, and with the Food and Agriculture Organization of the United Nations (FAO) in agricultural production.

The issue of assistance to countries receiving refugees from Rwanda, such as Burundi, was discussed at the Regional Conference on Assistance to Refugees, Returnees and Displaced Persons in the Great Lakes Region (see below, under ''Rwanda'').

**Report of the Secretary-General.** In response to requests made by the General Assembly in October[4] and December[5] 1994, the Secretary-General submitted an October 1995 report[6] on special emergency assistance for the economic recovery and reconstruction of Burundi. He found it encouraging that none of the 12 political parties that had signed the 1994 Convention on Governance[7] had withdrawn from the agreement aimed at promoting peace, security and power-sharing between the Hutu and Tutsi communities. Despite increasing attempts by extremists to disrupt life throughout the country, Burundi's governmental institutions, agricultural sector, schools, banks, telephone communications and public transport continued to function. The general consensus of the relief community in Burundi was that the humanitarian crisis was over. However, health and educational services remained impaired by continuous ethnic turmoil, forcing the international community to set up parallel administrative structures. Dwindling international emergency resources and the absence of follow-up development assistance raised concerns about the Government's capacity to provide basic services. The Secretary-General concluded that the international community should continue to coordinate its efforts so that the message to the political leaders of Burundi was consistent and unanimous.

By December, the humanitarian situation had deteriorated as political violence resumed in the country. A series of attacks targeted representatives of UN agencies, the International Committee of the Red Cross (ICRC) and non-governmental organizations (NGOs).

**GENERAL ASSEMBLY ACTION**

On 22 December, the General Assembly adopted **resolution 50/58 K**.

## Special emergency assistance for the economic recovery and reconstruction of Burundi

*The General Assembly,*

*Recalling* its resolutions 48/17 of 3 November 1993, 49/7 of 25 October 1994 and 49/21 C of 2 December 1994,

*Having considered* the report of the Secretary-General of 11 October 1995,

*Considering* that Burundi continues to face a social, human rights and political crisis that has existed since October 1993, the adverse effects of which are endangering the national economy, as evidenced by the destruction of economic and social infrastructures, declining production and trade and, as a result, shrinking public revenue,

*Concerned* about the instability of the situation in a number of areas, and acknowledging the need to ensure the safety and security of humanitarian and other international personnel,

*Concerned also* about the acts of violence that have the negative effect of stifling the national economy, in particular by disturbing the movement of persons, goods and services,

*Recognizing* that the coalition Government that emerged from the Convention on Governance is making efforts to redress the economic and social situation through its plan of action of March 1995,

*Convinced* that the country has the capacity to achieve appreciable economic results, particularly through its structural adjustment programme, and that an improved economic situation would contribute to the consolidation of peace,

*Bearing in mind,* however, that, in view of Burundi's inadequate economic and financial resources, the continued and increased assistance of the international community is still essential for the implementation of the plans and programmes of the Government,

1. *Expresses its gratitude* to all States, United Nations institutions and intergovernmental and non-governmental organizations that responded favourably to the appeal made at the forty-ninth session;

2. *Invites* once again all States, United Nations institutions and intergovernmental and non-governmental organizations to continue to provide Burundi with economic, financial, material and technical assistance for economic recovery and for the reconstruction of the various infrastructures destroyed or damaged during the crisis and to facilitate the voluntary repatriation of refugees;

3. *Calls upon* all parties not to hinder in any way efforts by international, intergovernmental and non-governmental aid organizations to transport and distribute humanitarian assistance to the people of Burundi and to take all necessary measures to ensure the safety and security of all humanitarian personnel operating in the country;

4. *Requests* the Secretary-General of the United Nations, in close cooperation with the Secretary-General of the Organization of African Unity, to coordinate the activities being implemented by the United Nations system to meet the needs of the people of Burundi adequately and to mobilize the assistance of the international community;

5. *Requests* the Government of Burundi to continue its efforts geared towards the achievement of national reconciliation and the maintenance of lasting peace, *inter alia,* through adherence to the principles of the Convention on Governance, provisions that are essential for the successful and sustainable implementation of humanitarian aid and economic, financial, material and technical assistance to the people of Burundi;

6. *Calls upon* the Secretary-General to report to the General Assembly at its fifty-first session on the implementation of the present resolution;

7. *Decides* to consider at its fifty-first session the question of special emergency assistance for the economic recovery and reconstruction of Burundi.

General Assembly resolution 50/58 K

22 December 1995     Meeting 98     Adopted without vote

22-nation draft (A/50/L.58/Rev.1 & Rev.1/Add.1); agenda item 20 *(b)*.

### Liberia

In January, a UN Consolidated Inter-Agency Appeal for Liberia was issued, seeking $65.3 million for the period until June 1995. It was later extended to the end of August. The largest sum of $45 million was requested for assistance in food aid and nutrition, followed by $7 million in health. As at 30 August, $53 million had been contributed. Another Inter-Agency Appeal for $110 million was issued in October, covering the period from September 1995 to August 1996. Priority areas for assistance included food security ($44.6 million); displacement, repatriation and resettlement/reintegration ($43 million); and health ($12 million). It was estimated that 1.8 million Liberians required humanitarian assistance, of whom 1.5 million had access to relief organizations.

**Report of the Secretary-General.** In response to a 1994 General Assembly request,[8] the Secretary-General submitted in October 1995 a report[9] on assistance for the rehabilitation and reconstruction of Liberia. He described support provided for the Liberian peace process (see PART TWO, Chapter II), reviewed sectoral assistance in areas of food and nutrition, agriculture, health and medical care, water and sanitation, education and training, and aid to specific target groups, and outlined contributions from Member States. He stated that contributions to the Trust Fund established to enable the Economic Community of West African States (ECOWAS) Monitoring Group (ECO-MOG) to fulfil its mandate had been minimal.

Continued fighting during 1995, notably between the Liberia Peace Council and the National Patriotic Front of Liberia and between rival branches of the United Liberation Movement for Democracy, resulted in further large-scale population displacements and prevented humanitarian assistance agencies from helping those civilians unable to flee the affected areas. However, as ECO-MOG secured the roads north-east as well as north and west of Monrovia in June, UN agencies and NGOs started to expand operations into those areas where credible security was guaranteed. In addition to 1.5 million Liberians in the country, more than 700,000 Liberian refugees (367,300 in Côte d'Ivoire, 395,000 in Guinea, 14,000 in Ghana, 4,600 in Sierra Leone and 4,000 in Nigeria) required humanitarian assistance.

Following the signing of the Abuja Agreement in August, a Humanitarian Assistance Coordinator was appointed to support the efforts of UN operational agencies and non-governmental, international and multilateral organizations. Towards the end of the year, steps were taken to link emergency relief activities to rehabilitation; a joint UNDP/World Bank mission to Liberia examined short-term grant assistance and possible long-term stabilization measures, WFP began preparations for feeding 60,000 ex-combatants during the demobilization period, and FAO distributed seeds and tools to increase household food security.

The Secretary-General concluded that any plan for sustainable progress in rehabilitating Liberia would have to include the demobilization and integration of combatants into civil society, including under-aged fighters.

On 27 October, the Secretary-General, in collaboration with the President of Ghana as Chairman of ECOWAS and the Chairman of the Liberian Council of State, convened in New York a conference on assistance to Liberia. Attended by more than 100 participants, the objectives of the conference were to consolidate the peace process through renewed support for humanitarian assistance and the demobilization process, recovery and rehabilitation needs and assistance to ECOMOG. A total of $145.7 million was pledged.

**GENERAL ASSEMBLY ACTION**

On 12 December, the General Assembly adopted **resolution 50/58 A**.

### Assistance for the rehabilitation and reconstruction of Liberia

*The General Assembly,*

*Taking note* of Security Council resolution 1020 (1995) of 10 November 1995, in which, *inter alia*, the Council called upon all of the Liberian parties to respect and implement fully and expeditiously all the agreements and commitments they had entered into, in particular with regard to the maintenance of the cease-fire, disarmament and demobilization of combatants, and national reconciliation, as the restoration of peace and democracy in Liberia was primarily the responsibility of those parties which signed the Abuja Agreement on 19 August 1995,

*Having considered* the report of the Secretary-General of 9 October 1995,

*Deeply concerned* about the adverse effects of the protracted conflict on the socio-economic development of Liberia, and noting the urgent need to restore peace and stability so as to make possible the rehabilitation and reconstruction of basic sectors of the country,

*Recognizing* the recent progress made by the Liberian parties towards the peaceful resolution of the conflict, including the re-establishment of a cease-fire, the instal-

lation of a new Council of State on 1 September 1995 and the agreement reached on a timetable for the implementation of the peace process from the cease-fire to the holding of executive and legislative elections in August 1996,

*Noting with concern* that the lack of logistics and security guarantees continues to impair the delivery of relief assistance, particularly in the areas not yet under the control of the Economic Community of West African States Monitoring Group, thereby hampering the transition from emergency to development activities,

*Commending* the concerted and determined efforts of the Economic Community of West African States to restore peace, security and stability in Liberia,

1. *Expresses its gratitude* to the States and intergovernmental and non-governmental organizations that have rendered assistance to the Liberian National Transitional Government in its relief and rehabilitation efforts, and urges that such assistance be continued;

2. *Expresses its appreciation* to the Secretary-General for his continuing efforts to mobilize relief and rehabilitation assistance for Liberia, expresses its gratitude to him for convening a pledging conference on assistance to Liberia in New York on 27 October 1995, and in this regard encourages States that pledged assistance to fulfil their commitments;

3. *Calls upon* all States and intergovernmental and non-governmental organizations to continue to provide Liberia with technical, financial and other assistance for the repatriation and resettlement of Liberian refugees, returnees and displaced persons and the rehabilitation of combatants so as to facilitate the restoration of peace and normalcy in Liberia;

4. *Reiterates its appeal* to all States to contribute generously to the Trust Fund for Liberia established by the Secretary-General, *inter alia*, to assist the Economic Community of West African States Monitoring Group to fulfil its mandate and to provide assistance for the reconstruction of Liberia;

5. *Emphasizes* the urgent need for all parties and factions in Liberia to respect fully the security and safety of all personnel of the United Nations, its specialized agencies, non-governmental organizations and the Economic Community of West African States Monitoring Group by ensuring their complete freedom of movement throughout Liberia and to take all measures necessary to create an atmosphere conducive to the successful resolution of the conflict;

6. *Requests* the Secretary-General:

(a) To continue his efforts to mobilize all possible assistance within the United Nations system to help the Government of Liberia in its reconstruction and development efforts;

(b) To undertake, when conditions permit, in close collaboration with the authorities of Liberia, an overall assessment of needs, with the objective of holding a round-table conference of donors for the reconstruction and development of Liberia;

7. *Also requests* the Secretary-General to report to the General Assembly at its fifty-first session on the progress made in the implementation of the present resolution;

8. *Decides* to consider at its fifty-first session the question of international assistance for the rehabilitation and reconstruction of Liberia.

General Assembly resolution 50/58 A
12 December 1995    Meeting 89    Adopted without vote

Draft by South Africa (A/50/L.27/Rev.1); agenda item 20 *(b)*.
*Meeting numbers.* GA 50th session: plenary 70, 71, 89.

### Rwanda

During 1995, a climate of relative security and stability prevailed within Rwanda, despite the absence of any discernible effort towards national reconciliation. The humanitarian situation improved, with steady progress in the transition from emergency relief to rehabilitation, reconstruction and development.

At a round-table conference (Geneva, 18-19 January) organized by UNDP in cooperation with the Government of Rwanda, a Programme for National Reconciliation and Socio-Economic Rehabilitation and Recovery was presented to the donor community. In response to the Government's request for $764.1 million for the implementation of the Programme, donor countries pledged $587 million. At the round-table mid-term review (Kigali, 6-7 July), the donors announced that they would make available an additional $128 million. The implementation of the Programme was supported by UNDP.

In January, the UN Consolidated Inter-Agency Appeal for Persons Affected by the Crisis in Rwanda was issued, seeking $805 million, of which $229 million was for Rwanda ($576 million was for the subregion—Burundi, Rwanda, Uganda, United Republic of Tanzania and Zaire), for the period ending December 1995. Projects in the Consolidated Appeal reflected the Government's framework for the Programme set forth at the round-table conference. Of the $229 million for Rwanda, the largest request was for food aid and nutrition ($73.4 million), followed by assistance to repatriates and internally displaced persons ($55.5 million).

**Reports of the Secretary-General.** In response to a 1994 General Assembly request,[10] the Secretary-General reported[11] in October 1995 on emergency assistance for a solution to the problem of refugees, the restoration of total peace, reconstruction and socio-economic development in Rwanda. The Joint Commission for the Repatriation of Rwandan Refugees was officially launched in May to propose repatriation plans, assist the Government in mobilizing resources and facilitate cooperation among the various partners in the area—measures that should result in stability and harmony in Rwanda and the region as a whole.

The United Nations Rwanda Emergency Office (UNREO) issued frequent reports and analysis for the humanitarian and donor communities so as to ensure a more effective humanitarian response. As emergency relief gave way to rehabilitation, UNREO was closed in October and its functions

were integrated into the Resident Coordinator's Office. During the first half of 1995, WFP distributed 28,726 million tons of food aid to a monthly average of 520,000 beneficiaries, including returnees, hospital patients and orphans. Since January, WFP had also been feeding 3,300 refugees from Burundi and 1,700 internally displaced persons. Several World Bank missions visited Rwanda in 1995 with a view to restructuring the project portfolio in place before the 1994 crisis. Eleven development projects were restarted in the areas of education, communications, transport, energy and agricultural services. The total value of the World Bank's project portfolio was $233 million as at 31 July 1995. Of the 95,000 unaccompanied children in Rwanda, more than 7,000 had been reunited with their families since February 1995. More than 1 million children were attending school as a result of efforts by the Government, UNICEF and the United Nations Educational, Scientific and Cultural Organization (UNESCO) in re-establishing primary education. The problem of mines continued to be a concern as people returned and began to till their land. Following a bilateral agreement between Rwanda and the United States, a national demining programme was established in July. The Secretary-General concluded that repatriation, reconciliation and reconstruction were under way at the grass-roots level, and sustained donor support was required to accelerate the process and build needed government capacity. He expressed concern about the tensions between some government ministries and their international partners, including NGOs.

In a December report[12] to the Security Council, the Secretary-General stated that the humanitarian situation in Rwanda continued to improve, with steady progress in the transition from emergency to rehabilitation, reconstruction and development. During September and October, a total of 32,190 refugees returned to Rwanda. The main deterrents to the return of greater numbers of refugees were the continuing campaign of intimidation and misinformation in the camps, fear of reprisal or imprisonment upon return and the shortage of adequate housing.

**GENERAL ASSEMBLY ACTION**

On 22 December, the General Assembly adopted **resolution 50/58 L**.

**Situation in Rwanda: international assistance for a solution to the problem of refugees,
the restoration of total peace, reconstruction and socio-economic development in Rwanda**

*The General Assembly,*

*Recalling* its resolutions 48/211 of 21 December 1993, entitled "Emergency assistance for the socio-economic rehabilitation of Rwanda", and 49/23 of 2 December 1994, entitled "Emergency international assistance for a solution to the problem of refugees, the restoration of total peace, reconstruction and socio-economic development in war-stricken Rwanda'',

*Recalling also* Security Council resolution 1029(1995) of 12 December 1995 concerning the final extension of the mandate of the United Nations Assistance Mission for Rwanda and calling upon States and donor agencies to fulfil their earlier commitments to give assistance for Rwanda's rehabilitation efforts, to increase such assistance and in particular to support the early and effective functioning of the International Tribunal for Rwanda and the rehabilitation of the Rwandan judicial system,

*Taking note* of the report of the Secretary-General of 1 December 1995 and of the statement by the President of the Security Council of 17 October 1995 in connection with the consideration by the Council of the item entitled ''The situation concerning Rwanda'',

*Having considered* the report of the Secretary-General of 19 October 1995 on emergency international assistance for a solution to the problem of refugees, the restoration of total peace, reconstruction and socio-economic development in war-stricken Rwanda,

*Taking into consideration* the serious consequences of genocide and other mass killings and of the destruction of the economic, social, educational and administrative infrastructure,

*Expressing its grave concern* over the disastrous humanitarian situation of the Rwandan population, including 1.6 million refugees who need to be reintegrated into society and employment, and noting that several categories of refugees are also involved,

*Welcoming* the summit of Heads of State of the Great Lakes region, held at Cairo on 28 and 29 November 1995, and their declaration of 29 November 1995,[a] and noting the United Nations support for all efforts to reduce tension and restore stability in the Great Lakes region, in particular implementation of the Cairo Declaration on the Great Lakes Region and other previously adopted commitments, and for continuing consultations with the aim of convening a conference on security, stability and development in the Great Lakes region, as appropriate,

*Emphasizing* the need to consider the crisis in Rwanda in a regional context, in view of its implications for the countries of the region, through the implementation of the plan of action recommended by the Government of Rwanda, the Office of the United Nations High Commissioner for Refugees and the Organization of African Unity within the framework of the Peace Agreement between the Government of the Rwandese Republic and the Rwandese Patriotic Front, signed at Arusha, United Republic of Tanzania, on 4 August 1993,

*Conscious* that technical assistance and advisory services will assist the Government of Rwanda in reconstructing the social, legal and economic infrastructure, and that extensive assistance is required for this,

*Recognizing* that the Arusha Peace Agreement provides an appropriate framework for national reconciliation,

*Expressing its gratitude* to those States and intergovernmental and non-governmental organizations which have responded positively and continue to respond positively to the humanitarian and development needs of Rwanda, and to the Secretary-General, who has mobilized and coordinated the distribution of humanitarian assistance,

1. *Encourages* the Government of Rwanda to pursue its efforts with a view to creating conditions that would be conducive to the return of the refugees to their country and their resettlement and to the recovery by displaced persons of their property in peace, security and dignity;

2. *Congratulates* the Secretary-General on the efforts he has made to draw the attention of the international community to the humanitarian situation in Rwanda, requests him to provide all possible assistance and encourages him and his Special Representative to continue to coordinate the activities of the United Nations in Rwanda, including those of the organizations and agencies active in the humanitarian and developmental field and of the human rights officers;

3. *Welcomes* the increased commitments and funds pledged for the Government's Programme of National Reconciliation and Socio-Economic Rehabilitation and Recovery, and calls on the international community to continue to support Rwanda's rehabilitation process and to translate these pledges into urgent concrete assistance;

4. *Also welcomes* the commitment of the Government of Rwanda to cooperate with and to take all necessary measures to ensure the safety and security of all humanitarian personnel, including personnel of non-governmental organizations, operating in the country;

5. *Urges* all States, United Nations organizations, specialized agencies and other intergovernmental and non-governmental organizations and the international financial and development institutions to continue to provide all possible financial, technical and material assistance, bearing in mind that sound economic foundations are vital for achieving lasting stability in Rwanda and for the return and resettlement of Rwandan refugees;

6. *Calls upon* the international community to continue its assistance with a view to alleviating the intolerable conditions in Rwandan prisons and to expediting the processing of cases, and encourages the Government of Rwanda to continue its efforts to improve the situation in the prisons and to expedite the processing of cases;

7. *Welcomes* the indictments recently issued by the International Tribunal for Rwanda, calls upon all States to cooperate with the Tribunal, in accordance with Security Council resolutions 955(1994) of 8 November 1994 and 978(1995) of 27 February 1995, by arresting and detaining persons suspected of genocide and other serious violations of international humanitarian law, and encourages the Government of Rwanda to work cooperatively with the Secretary-General and the Tribunal to establish an effective protective force for the Tribunal;

8. *Urges* all States, in particular donor countries, to contribute generously to the trust fund established by the Secretary-General on 14 July 1994 to finance humanitarian relief and rehabilitation programmes to be implemented in Rwanda;

9. *Calls upon* all States to act in accordance with the recommendations adopted by the Nairobi Summit of January 1995 and the Regional Conference on Assistance to Refugees, Returnees and Displaced Persons in the Great Lakes Region, held at Bujumbura in February 1995, and with those contained in the Cairo Decla-

---

[a]S/1995/1001.

ration, and to continue efforts with regard to the search for peace in the Great Lakes region;

10. *Requests* the Secretary-General to consult with the Government of Rwanda and with the relevant United Nations agencies on the nature of a continued United Nations presence in Rwanda after 8 March 1996 and on the role such a United Nations presence might play in furthering the search for peace and stability through justice, reconciliation and refugee return and in assisting the Government of Rwanda in its pressing task of rehabilitation and reconstruction, and to report to the General Assembly by 1 February 1996 on the results of those consultations in addition to submitting to the Assembly at its fifty-first session a report on the implementation of the present resolution;

11. *Decides* to consider at its fifty-first session the question of the situation in Rwanda: international assistance for a solution to the problem of refugees, the restoration of total peace, reconstruction and socio-economic development in Rwanda.

General Assembly resolution 50/58 L

22 December 1995     Meeting 98     Adopted without vote

11-nation draft (A/50/L.64/Rev.2 & Rev.2/Add.1); agenda item 20 *(b)*.
*Meeting numbers.* GA 50th session: plenary 71, 98.

### Countries receiving refugees from Rwanda

In 1995, there were some 1.8 million Rwandese refugees still outside the country. By late 1995, their prolonged presence, together with 354,000 Burundese refugees, continued to affect stability and security in the neighbouring countries of the Great Lakes region. The UN Consolidated Inter-Agency Appeal for Persons Affected by the Crisis in Rwanda (see above) requested $576 million to assist Burundi, Rwanda, Uganda, the United Republic of Tanzania and Zaire through December 1995. The largest sum, $324 million, was requested by WFP, followed by $235 million by UNHCR. The issue of assistance to countries receiving refugees from Rwanda was also discussed at the Regional Conference on Assistance to Refugees, Returnees and Displaced Persons in the Great Lakes Region (Bujumbura, Burundi, 15-17 February) (see also PART THREE, Chapter XII). In response to a request made by the Conference for UNDP to hold a round-table donor's meeting for the countries of the region, UNDP and UNHCR jointly undertook the preparations for consultations with donors. UNDP dispatched a preliminary mission to the region, which identified priority needs and gauged the response of the donor community to a call for financial assistance. The mission confirmed the likelihood of an environmental catastrophe in the region, should the current trends continue unabated.

Substantial amounts of food, including targeted food assistance and food-for-work programmes, were provided by WFP to the internally displaced, returnees, orphans, hospital patients and other vulnerable groups. WHO and UNICEF continued to focus on re-establishing the health-care system.

Water programmes were continued, benefiting more than 2.5 million people. In addition to supplying seeds and tools, FAO undertook a seeds multiplication programme and launched actions to enhance disease control and livestock management. As part of efforts to help build a regional capacity to manage the crisis, DHA established in November its Integrated Regional Information Network in Nairobi, Kenya. The Network was to enhance effective coordination of humanitarian assistance, as well as early warning.

### Sierra Leone

In 1995, the humanitarian situation in Sierra Leone remained critical. Estimates indicated that the conflict, which began in 1991, had forced nearly 50 per cent of Sierra Leone's population of 4.4 million to flee their homes, 1.6 million being internally displaced and nearly 370,000 seeking refuge in neighbouring countries. Local communities, which had been absorbing some 1.4 million of the internally displaced, were supported by UN agencies and NGOs. However, the relief effort was hindered by the lack of access to affected communities and the lack of security assistance to humanitarian road convoys.

Following a 24 January attack on the town of Kambia and the ensuing abduction of approximately 100 residents, 45,000 refugees from the area sought asylum in Guinea. With this new influx, the total number of Sierra Leonean refugees in Guinea rose to more than 200,000. The security situation led to a withdrawal of UN organizations and their partners to Freetown, although humanitarian activities continued on a limited scale. In March, the United Nations issued an Inter-Agency Appeal to deal with new refugee outflows and populations affected by the humanitarian situation in the country, requesting $14.7 million for the period ending December 1995. Among new and unmet needs identified within Sierra Leone were food aid and nutrition ($5.7 million), health ($2.2 million), and water and sanitation ($562,000). A total of $4.6 million was requested to provide the newly arrived refugees in Guinea with food, shelter, domestic items, water and sanitation as well as emergency health care. In late 1995, DHA established a Humanitarian Assistance Coordination Unit in Freetown. The Unit became active in five areas: establishment of coordination mechanisms and agreements; assessment of humanitarian needs; engaging in humanitarian advocacy; carrying out emergency information dissemination; and supporting the Government's National Relief and Rehabilitation Committee.

### Somalia

The Under-Secretary-General for Humanitarian Affairs, in an oral report[13] to the Economic and Social Council in July, stated that there was a great need to assist in the reconstruction and rehabilitation efforts in Somalia since the humanitarian situation was still fragile and unpredictable. The Council, by **decision 1995/314** of 28 July, took note of the report.

During 1995, the target amount requested in the 1994 Appeal[14] for emergency relief and short-term rehabilitation activities for Somalia was increased by $22.8 million, to reflect the full UNHCR and UNICEF requirements for the period January to December 1995.

**Security Council consideration.** In a 28 March report[15] to the Security Council, the Secretary-General assessed, among other things, what had been achieved by UN humanitarian activities in Somalia since 1991. He stated that the experience of the United Nations Operation in Somalia (UNOSOM II) had demonstrated the vital link between humanitarian assistance and efforts to achieve national reconciliation, and that UN agencies and NGOs would continue humanitarian operations in Somalia after the withdrawal of UNOSOM II at the end of March. In a 6 April statement made on behalf of the Council,[16] the President said that it was important to sustain UN humanitarian activities in Somalia, but their success would depend on the degree of cooperation and security offered by the Somali parties.

**Report of the Secretary-General.** In response to a 1994 General Assembly request,[17] the Secretary-General submitted a September 1995 report[18] on assistance for humanitarian relief and the economic and social rehabilitation of Somalia. The report described relief and rehabilitation programmes provided by the UN system, and the impact of security problems on the ability of the UN and NGOs to deliver humanitarian relief; it also summarized information received from Member States on assistance to Somalia.

Food aid requirements for 1995/96 were estimated at 129,500 tons, of which 77,500 tons had previously been pledged. In 1994/95, WFP helped Somalia generate over $5 million through the sale of high-value food commodities not produced in the country. These funds were used to provide non-food inputs to 240 rehabilitation projects, creating about 4,000 jobs. In January, a Food Security Assessment Unit was established to monitor weather conditions, food production, market prices, consumption and food availability trends, as well as the nutritional and health status of populations throughout Somalia. Cholera, which resurfaced in February, was rapidly contained by WHO, UNICEF, WFP and UNESCO. WHO provided more than 54 tons of treatment drugs and other supplies. Between September 1994 and July 1995, more than 95,000 children were immunized against measles, 125,000 against tuberculosis and

another 143,000 against four other preventable diseases. More than 106,000 women of child-bearing age were vaccinated against tetanus.

There were still some 457,000 Somalis living as refugees in neighbouring countries and 300,000 to 400,000 internally displaced persons country-wide. UNESCO and UNHCR continued to implement a mine-awareness programme in 36 towns and villages.

As a result of a review of the criteria for continuing their rehabilitation and development assistance, the Somalia Aid Coordination Body—composed of donors, UN agencies and international organizations—adopted a Code of Conduct for International Rehabilitation and Development Assistance to Somalia. Coordination of relief and rehabilitation activities by UN agencies and their partners was carried out by the UN Coordination Team, which had been established in October 1994 in anticipation of UNOSOM II's withdrawal in March 1995. While the political and security situation in Mogadishu had not stabilized sufficiently to allow the return of UN staff on a permanent basis, most parts of the country remained stable enough for relief and rehabilitation activities to continue.

Finally, the Secretary-General said that, following the departure of UNOSOM II, eight organizations of the UN system had maintained, and in some cases expanded, their activities and, in addition, some 40 international NGOs maintained a presence in the country. He asked donors to support generously efforts to assist the Somali people.

**GENERAL ASSEMBLY ACTION**

On 20 December, the General Assembly adopted **resolution 50/58 G**.

**Assistance for humanitarian relief and the economic and social rehabilitation of Somalia**

*The General Assembly,*

*Recalling* its resolutions 43/206 of 20 December 1988, 44/178 of 19 December 1989, 45/229 of 21 December 1990, 46/176 of 19 December 1991, 47/160 of 18 December 1992, 48/201 of 21 December 1993 and 49/21 L of 20 December 1994 and the resolutions and decisions of the Economic and Social Council on emergency assistance to Somalia,

*Recalling also* Security Council resolution 733(1992) of 23 January 1992 and all subsequent relevant resolutions, in which the Council, *inter alia*, urged all parties, movements and factions in Somalia to facilitate the efforts of the United Nations, its specialized agencies and humanitarian organizations to provide urgent humanitarian assistance to the affected population in Somalia and reiterated the call for the full respect of the security and safety of the personnel of those organizations and the guarantee of their complete freedom of movement in and around Mogadishu and other parts of Somalia,

*Recalling in particular* Security Council resolution 954(1994) of 4 November 1994, in which the Council, *inter alia*, decided to withdraw all the forces of the United

Nations Operation in Somalia II before 31 March 1995 and expressed its confidence in the willingness of the United Nations to remain ready to provide, through its various agencies, rehabilitation and reconstruction assistance,

*Taking note* of the presidential statement of 6 April 1995, in which the Security Council, *inter alia*, noted the successful conclusion of the withdrawal from Somalia of the forces of the United Nations Operation in Somalia II and welcomed the willingness expressed by the international humanitarian agencies and the non-governmental organizations to continue to provide rehabilitation and reconstruction assistance in areas where security is guaranteed by the Somalis,

*Noting* the cooperation between the United Nations, the Organization of African Unity, the League of Arab States, the Organization of the Islamic Conference, the countries of the Horn of Africa and the States members of the Movement of Non-Aligned Countries in their efforts to resolve the humanitarian, security and political crisis in Somalia,

*Noting with appreciation* the continued efforts made by the Secretary-General to assist the Somali people in their efforts to promote peace, stability and national reconciliation,

*Noting with concern* that the political instability and the absence of central authority that continue to characterize Somalia provide a breeding ground for new emergencies,

*Reaffirming* the importance it attaches to the need for effective coordination and cooperation among the United Nations agencies and their partners since the withdrawal of the United Nations Operation in Somalia in March 1995,

*Taking note* of the report of the Secretary-General of 19 September 1995 on assistance for humanitarian relief and the economic and social rehabilitation of Somalia,

*Deeply appreciative* of the humanitarian assistance and rehabilitation support rendered by a number of States to alleviate the hardship and suffering of the affected Somali population,

*Noting with appreciation* that, following the departure of the United Nations Operation in Somalia and despite the ongoing difficulties, the country is slowly moving towards recovery and reconstruction,

*Recognizing* that, while the humanitarian situation remains fragile, there is a need to undertake efforts to begin the process of rehabilitation and reconstruction alongside the process of national reconciliation, without prejudice to the provision of emergency relief assistance wherever and whenever required, as the security situation allows,

*Re-emphasizing* the importance of the further implementation of its resolution 47/160 to rehabilitate basic social and economic services at local and regional levels throughout the country,

1. *Expresses its gratitude* to all States and the intergovernmental and non-governmental organizations that have responded to the appeals of the Secretary-General and others by extending assistance to Somalia;

2. *Expresses its appreciation* to the Secretary-General for his continued and tireless efforts to mobilize assistance to the Somali people;

3. *Welcomes* the ongoing efforts of the United Nations, the Organization of African Unity, the League of Arab States, the Organization of the Islamic Conference, the countries of the Horn of Africa and the States members of the Movement of Non-Aligned Countries to resolve the situation in Somalia;

4. *Also welcomes* the current strategy of the United Nations focusing on the implementation of community-based interventions aimed at rebuilding local infrastructures and increasing the self-reliance of the local population, as well as the ongoing efforts by the United Nations agencies and their partner organizations to establish and maintain close coordination and cooperation mechanisms for relief, rehabilitation and reconstruction in the period following the departure of the United Nations Operation in Somalia;

5. *Urges* all States and relevant intergovernmental and non-governmental organizations to continue the further implementation of resolution 47/160 in order to assist the Somali people in embarking on the rehabilitation of basic social and economic services as well as institution-building aimed at the restoration of civil administration at the local level in all those parts of the country where peace, security and stability prevail;

6. *Appeals* to all the Somali parties concerned to terminate hostilities and to engage in a national reconciliation process that will allow for the transition from relief to reconstruction and development;

7. *Calls upon* all parties, movements and factions in Somalia to respect fully the security and safety of personnel of the United Nations and its specialized agencies and of non-governmental organizations and to guarantee their complete freedom of movement throughout Somalia;

8. *Calls upon* the Secretary-General to continue to mobilize international humanitarian, rehabilitation and reconstruction assistance for Somalia;

9. *Requests* the Secretary-General, in view of the critical situation in Somalia, to take all measures necessary for the implementation of the present resolution, to apprise the Economic and Social Council at its substantive session of 1996 of the progress made and to report thereon to the General Assembly at its fifty-first session.

General Assembly resolution 50/58 G

20 December 1995     Meeting 96     Adopted without vote

36-nation draft (A/50/L.41/Rev.1); agenda item 20 *(b)*.

### Sudan

In 1995, armed conflict between the Government of the Sudan and the rebel factions continued. The delivery of humanitarian assistance was hindered by hostage-taking of relief workers, misappropriation of relief supplies, frequent evacuation of relief workers due to security reasons, and restrictions imposed on flight operations.

In January, the United Nations launched the Consolidated Inter-Agency Appeal for the Sudan, seeking $101.1 million for the remainder of the year. The Appeal was for activities in the areas of emergency food aid ($26.4 million); nutrition, health and water ($35.4 million); refugees and returnees ($15.6 million); agriculture, livestock and fishing ($11 million); other relief activities ($9.1 million); and inter-agency coordination and support ($3.5 million). The emergency food aid targeted an estimated 1.2 million war-affected and displaced persons in the south, the transitional zone and Khartoum, while the non-food programmes targeted 4.25 million accessible war-affected persons.

**Report of the Secretary-General.** In a September report[19] on emergency assistance to the Sudan, submitted in response to a 1994 General Assembly request,[20] the Secretary-General provided an update on the humanitarian situation in the Sudan and on the emergency response provided through the UN system, notably Operation Lifeline Sudan (OLS). Despite interruptions caused by widespread insecurity, loss of flight access to some key locations and a complex working relationship with parties to the conflict, OLS continued to maintain basic access to the majority of the populations in need, and the number of locations served by OLS increased from eight in 1989 to more than 100.

As a result of the record harvest year of 1994, only 109,409 tonnes of emergency food aid was required for 1995, compared with 487,000 tonnes for 1994. Carry-over relief food stocks of 149,134 tonnes were sufficient to cover 1995 emergency food aid needs except supplies of supplementary foods. From January to mid-June, WFP distributed about 8,500 tonnes of food.

UNICEF, the main provider of non-food assistance for the Sudan, targeted 4.25 million people, 2.5 million from its operations in Khartoum and 1.7 million from Nairobi. Together with ICRC and NGOs, UNICEF distributed more than 3,600 tonnes of seeds and more than 1 million hand tools to an estimated 300,000 households in time for the 1995 growing season; however, low rainfall levels led to crop failure in the eastern and western parts of the country. Under the livestock programme, 242,000 cattle had been vaccinated against rinderpest as at mid-1995 and training of vaccinators was being expanded. In the health sector, Guinea-worm disease eradication, an expanded programme of immunization and barge-based health activities received priority attention.

In conclusion, the Secretary-General stated that OLS, which had begun in 1989 as a short-term programme to deliver life-saving provisions, had evolved to undertake a much broader range of activities, such as household food security, water and sanitation, basic shelter, food-for-work in support of agricultural production, and capacity-building. While cooperation among national, UN and non-governmental organizations remained excellent, the rash of kidnapping and the misappropriation of relief supplies had negatively affected humanitarian operations in the Sudan. The Secretary-General said that concerned parties should desist from actions that would prevent humanitarian aid from reaching people in need.

On 22 December, the General Assembly adopted **resolution 50/58 J.**

### Emergency assistance to the Sudan
*The General Assembly,*

*Recalling* its resolutions 43/8 of 18 October 1988, 43/52 of 6 December 1988, 44/12 of 24 October 1989, 45/226 of 21 December 1990, 46/178 of 19 December 1991, 47/162 of 18 December 1992, 48/200 of 21 December 1993 and 49/21 K of 20 December 1994 on assistance to the Sudan,

*Noting* that, despite the progress made in Operation Lifeline Sudan, considerable relief needs still remain to be addressed, particularly in the areas of non-food assistance, including assistance to combat malaria and for logistics, emergency recovery, rehabilitation and development,

*Taking note* of the ongoing review of Operation Lifeline Sudan, intended to assess the effectiveness and efficiency of the operation since its launching in 1989,

*Recognizing* the need in emergency situations to address the continuum of relief, rehabilitation and development so as to reduce dependence on external food aid and other relief services,

*Taking note* of the report of the Secretary-General of 22 September 1995 on emergency assistance to the Sudan and of the statement made by the representative of the Sudan before the General Assembly on 27 November 1995,

1. *Acknowledges* the cooperation by the Government of the Sudan with the United Nations, including the agreements and arrangements achieved to facilitate relief operations through improvement of United Nations assistance to affected areas, and encourages the Government of the Sudan to continue its cooperation in this regard;

2. *Stresses* the need for the ongoing review of Operation Lifeline Sudan to assess the effectiveness and the efficiency of the operation, as well as its transparency, and for the involvement of the Government of the Sudan in its operation;

3. *Calls upon* the international community to continue to contribute generously to the emergency needs, recovery and development of the country;

4. *Calls upon* the donor community and the United Nations system to provide financial, technical and medical assistance, guided by the actions called for by the General Assembly, in its relevant resolutions, to combat malaria in the Sudan;

5. *Appeals* to all parties concerned to continue to pursue dialogue and negotiations and to terminate hostilities so as to allow for the re-establishment of peace, order and stability, and also to facilitate relief efforts;

6. *Stresses* the importance of assuring safe access for personnel providing relief assistance to all in need;

7. *Urges* all parties involved to continue to offer all feasible assistance, including facilitating the movement of relief supplies and personnel, so as to guarantee maximum success of Operation Lifeline Sudan in all parts of the country;

8. *Stresses also* that Operation Lifeline Sudan should operate within the principle of national sovereignty and the framework of international cooperation in accordance with relevant international law;

9. *Requests* the Secretary-General to continue to mobilize and coordinate resources and support for Operation Lifeline Sudan, to assess the emergency situation in the country and to report thereon, as well as on the recovery and rehabilitation of the country, to the General Assembly at its fifty-first session.

General Assembly resolution 50/58 J

22 December 1995     Meeting 98     Adopted without vote

10-nation draft (A/50/L.43/Rev.1 & Rev.1/Add.1); agenda item 20 *(b)*.
*Sponsors:* China, Honduras, India, Indonesia, Jordan, Oman, Qatar, Sudan, Syrian Arab Republic, Yemen.
*Meeting numbers.* GA 50th session: plenary 70, 98.

## Asia

### Afghanistan

In response to the October 1994 UN Consolidated Inter-Agency Appeal for Humanitarian Assistance to Afghanistan for the period up to September 1995,[21] which had sought $106.4 million, the international community contributed or pledged $79.3 million as at 1 October 1995. A new Appeal was launched in October, seeking $124 million for the period October 1995 to September 1996. The largest sum was requested by UNHCR ($35 million), followed by the UN Office for the Coordination of Humanitarian Assistance to Afghanistan (UNOCHA) ($23.5 million). The components of the Appeal included assistance to internally displaced persons, mine clearance, voluntary repatriation, food aid, agriculture, health, water and sanitation, emergency rehabilitation of physical infrastructure, social programmes and coordination.

**Report of the Secretary-General.** Pursuant to a 1994 General Assembly request,[22] the Secretary-General reported[23] in November 1995 on emergency assistance to Afghanistan. He provided an update on the political situation, including the work undertaken by the UN special mission to Afghanistan (see PART TWO, Chapter IV), and described rehabilitation and development activities carried out and emergency humanitarian assistance provided.

During 1995, UNOCHA continued to coordinate humanitarian programmes under the direction of the UN Coordinator for the Emergency Humanitarian Programme for Afghanistan. Since April, 150,000 internally displaced persons and refugees had returned to Kabul. With the complete lifting of the economic blockade in March, humanitarian activities were substantially expanded. From January to June 1995, WFP distributed 53,200 tons of food aid: 35 per cent was for rehabilitation activities, 35 per cent for the internally displaced and refugees, and 29 per cent for food-for-work-based rehabilitation programming. During an immunization campaign, nearly 2.4 million children under five years old were immunized against polio, and more than 800,000 under two against measles. More than 700,000 women of child-bearing age

were immunized against tetanus. UNICEF established 46 mini-health centres and supported the repair of wells.

The UNOCHA mine-clearance programme had identified 490 square kilometres of mined areas in Afghanistan. Of the 128 square kilometres categorized as high-priority areas, it had cleared 89 square kilometres. Of $18 million requested for the programme in the October 1994 Consolidated Appeal, $17.4 million had been made available as at 30 September 1995.

In 1995, UN operational activities for rehabilitation and development focused on rural infrastructure, food production, health improvement, animal health services, rehabilitation of disabled people and human settlements. Rural economic production was being rehabilitated through projects in irrigation systems and flood protection. In the urban areas, with funding from UNDP, the UN Centre for Human Settlements assisted 10,000 families in rebuilding their houses and supplied 280 shallow-well pumps to bring safer water to 13,800 urban families. The UN Office for Project Services, also with UNDP funding, trained 65,000 disabled Afghans, leading to their reintegration into community life. WFP supported the rehabilitation of schools, vocational training and income-generating projects, reaching more than 3,000 youth, women and orphans.

A briefing of donors (Stockholm, Sweden, 1-2 June), attended by 20 organizations of the UN system and 24 NGOs, updated the donor community on the work of the UN system in Afghanistan and its potential to serve as a vehicle for intensified donor assistance.

GENERAL ASSEMBLY ACTION

On 19 December, the General Assembly adopted **resolution 50/88 A**.

**Emergency international assistance for peace, normalcy and reconstruction of war-stricken Afghanistan**

*The General Assembly,*

*Recalling* its resolutions 47/119 of 18 December 1992, 48/208 of 21 December 1993 and 49/140 of 20 December 1994 concerning emergency international assistance for the reconstruction of war-stricken Afghanistan,

*Taking note* of the report of the Secretary-General of 8 November 1995,

*Concerned* about the renewal of armed conflict and the attendant displacement of families and interruptions in the process of repatriating refugees,

*Deeply concerned* about the massive loss of human life, the aggravated suffering of the most vulnerable groups, the destruction of property and the serious damage to the economic and social infrastructure of Afghanistan caused by sixteen years of war, and stressing the importance of a return to peace and stability for the rehabilitation and reconstruction of Afghanistan, bearing in mind that the country continues to suffer from an extremely critical economic situation as a land-locked, least developed and war-stricken country,

*Welcoming* the efforts of the United Nations Special Mission to Afghanistan headed by Mahmoud Mestiri to bring about the restoration of peace, normalcy and national reconciliation and the reconstruction and rehabilitation of war-stricken Afghanistan,

*Deeply concerned also* about the problem of millions of anti-personnel land-mines and unexploded ordnance in Afghanistan which continue to prevent many Afghan refugees from returning to their villages and working in their fields, and disturbed by reports of new mines being laid,

*Concerned* for the well-being of the unarmed civilian population of Afghanistan, in particular of Kabul, who face a long winter possibly deprived of basic foods, fuel and medicine owing to a renewal of hostilities around the capital,

*Bearing in mind* the close interrelationship between ensuring peace and normalcy in Afghanistan and the ability of the country to take effective steps towards revitalizing the economy, and stressing that a cessation of armed hostilities between the warring parties in Afghanistan is indispensable if reconstruction measures are to have a lasting effect,

*Affirming* the urgent need to continue international action to assist Afghanistan in restoring basic services and the infrastructure of the country, and welcoming the efforts of the United Nations Development Programme and other United Nations agencies in this respect,

*Expressing its appreciation* for the assistance of the Office of the United Nations High Commissioner for Refugees in its continuing support for the repatriation of Afghan refugees from neighbouring countries,

*Reaffirming* the principle of *non-refoulement* as contained in article 33 of the Convention relating to the Status of Refugees,

*Expressing its gratitude* to all Governments that have rendered assistance to Afghan refugees, in particular the Governments of Pakistan and the Islamic Republic of Iran, and recognizing the need for continuing international assistance for the maintenance abroad and the voluntary repatriation and resettlement of refugees and internally displaced persons,

*Expressing its appreciation* to the States and intergovernmental and non-governmental organizations that have responded positively and continue to respond to the humanitarian needs of Afghanistan, as well as to the Secretary-General for his efforts to draw the attention of the international community to the acute problems of reconstruction in Afghanistan and for mobilizing and coordinating the delivery of appropriate humanitarian assistance,

1.  *Takes note* of the report of the Secretary-General and endorses the observations and recommendations set out therein;

2.  *Requests* the Secretary-General to authorize the United Nations Special Mission to Afghanistan, established under resolution 48/208, to continue its efforts to facilitate national reconciliation and reconstruction in Afghanistan;

3.  *Also requests* the Secretary-General to continue efforts to develop plans for national reconstruction and rehabilitation beginning in areas of peace and security, on the basis of the recommendations set out in his report;

4.  *Calls upon* all Afghan parties not to hinder in any way efforts by the United Nations and associated organizations to transport and distribute emergency humanitarian assistance to the Afghan population, particularly to the city of Kabul, and urges them to ensure full freedom of movement for the United Nations Special Mission;

5.  *Urgently appeals* to all States, organizations and programmes of the United Nations system, specialized agencies and other intergovernmental and non-governmental organizations to continue to provide, on a priority basis and as far as conditions on the ground permit, all possible financial, technical and material assistance for the restoration of the basic services and the reconstruction of Afghanistan and the voluntary, safe and secure return of refugees and internally displaced persons, and appeals to the international financial and development institutions to assist in the planning of the reconstruction of Afghanistan;

6.  *Calls upon* the international community to respond to the inter-agency consolidated appeal for emergency humanitarian and rehabilitation assistance for Afghanistan launched by the Secretary-General for the period from 1 October 1995 to 30 September 1996, bearing in mind the availability also of the Afghanistan Emergency Trust Fund;

7.  *Requests* the Secretary-General to submit to the General Assembly at its fifty-first session a report on the actions taken pursuant to the present resolution;

8.  *Decides* to include in the provisional agenda of its fifty-first session, under the cluster of items on coordination of humanitarian assistance, the item entitled "Emergency international assistance for peace, normalcy and reconstruction of war-stricken Afghanistan".

General Assembly resolution 50/88 A

19 December 1995     Meeting 95     Adopted without vote

54-nation draft (A/50/L.60 (part A) & Add.1); agenda item 20 *(d)*.

## Iraq

Since the Gulf crisis in 1990, the humanitarian situation in Iraq had been steadily deteriorating, more so in 1995. In addition to 2 million people in dire need of humanitarian aid, there were over half a million internally displaced persons and some 116,000 refugees in Iraq. Despite the increased need for humanitarian assistance, response to the April 1994 Appeal for the Inter-Agency Humanitarian Programme in Iraq[24] had been inadequate, with approximately 50 per cent of overall programme requirements met.

In March 1995, a new Consolidated Appeal for Iraq, covering the period April 1995 to March 1996, was launched. Seeking $183.3 million, the Appeal addressed only the most essential needs to sustain relief and rehabilitation activities as well as to prevent a further deterioration of the conditions affecting the most vulnerable population groups throughout the country. The largest sum of $60.1 million was requested for food assistance and nutrition, followed by $25 million each for agricultural assistance and rehabilitation, and basic health and water and sanitation. The total budget requirement was later revised to $169 million.

With regard to food aid, in addition to a case-load of 1 million beneficiaries identified in the 1995/96 Appeal, WFP added some 30,000 destitute persons and 1.1 million people in families with malnourished children under five years old, as well as pregnant women and nursing mothers. Approximately 23 per cent of children under five suffered from malnutrition and constituted 39 per cent of the monthly deaths of about 11,000.

**Security Council action.** On 14 April, by **resolution 986(1995)**, the Security Council, concerned by the serious nutritional and health situation of the Iraqi population and by the risk of a further deterioration in that situation, authorized States, under certain conditions, to import petroleum and petroleum products originating in Iraq, up to a total of $1 billion, to meet humanitarian needs and to cover various Iraq-related programmes mandated by the Council.

*Lebanon*

In response to a 1994 Economic and Social Council request,[25] the Secretary-General, in May 1995, reported[26] on assistance for the reconstruction and development of Lebanon. The report summarized developments with regard to the Government, the economy and reconstruction efforts. It also described the role and activities of UN organizations active in Lebanon.

Economic performance continued to be strong, and financial indicators, such as the exchange rate of the Lebanese pound to the United States dollar and interest rates, were generally positive in 1995. Annual inflation was between 11 and 13 per cent, and gross domestic product (GDP) increased by 7 per cent. At the end of the year, more than 20,000 families had regained their villages of origin and, with $27 million disbursed, 13,800 housing units had been repaired and 3,160 units reconstructed. Under the framework of the 10-year National Emergency Recovery Programme (1993-2002),[27] the rehabilitation work accelerated in many sectors during 1995. By the end of August, construction and supply contracts, amounting to $2.6 billion, had been approved; of that amount, $440 million had been disbursed. The sectoral distribution of contracts authorized by the Council for Development and Reconstruction, a national coordination agency, went to basic infrastructure (64.3 per cent); airport and ports (16 per cent); social infrastructure (8.1 per cent); public services (6.6 per cent); and public buildings and institutions (5 per cent). Total secured foreign financing for the recovery amounted to $2.5 billion at the end of August.

On 31 March, the Office of the Coordinator of UN Assistance for Reconstruction and Development of Lebanon was closed and its role and functions were transferred to the UNDP Resident Coordinator. In May, the Resident Coordinator organized a workshop for the UN system, the Government and other development partners to discuss their respective roles and to identify priority support by the UN system. Under the programme of operational activities for development of UN system organizations, a total of $17 million was disbursed in 1995. Technical assistance grants and loan disbursements by the World Bank were not included in that figure. UNDP disbursed $4.7 million, which was distributed among social reconstruction ($1.9 million), balanced economic development ($1.2 million), and public administration ($0.9 million). In addition, WFP provided $3.3 million worth of food assistance; UNICEF, $2.3 million for primary health care, basic education and water quality; and the UN International Drug Control Programme (UNDCP), $1.8 million for demand reduction and integrated development of areas that had been involved with illicit crop production. The World Bank committed $55 million for solid waste/environmental management and $20 million for administrative rehabilitation. The first phase of the Baalbeck-Hermel Integrated Rural Development Programme established an operational mechanism to provide urgent support to farmers and began work on crop replacement. UNDP, in close collaboration with UNDCP, formulated the second phase, and a donor meeting on the Programme (Paris, 20 June) was convened by the Government of France.

The Secretary-General noted in his conclusions that the UN system was called upon increasingly to focus its activities on core areas; to adopt a programme approach for operational activities for development; to collaborate planning and implementation of activities; and to undertake high-profile support of priority themes. He stated that more resources were required for capacity-building, urgent rehabilitation of south Lebanon, the Baalbeck-Hermel Programme and social reconstruction programmes.

**ECONOMIC AND SOCIAL COUNCIL ACTION**

On 27 July, the Economic and Social Council adopted **resolution 1995/42**.

**Assistance for the reconstruction and development of Lebanon**

*The Economic and Social Council,*

*Recalling* General Assembly decision 48/450 of 21 December 1993,

*Also recalling* its resolutions in which it called upon the specialized agencies and other organizations and bodies of the United Nations system to expand and intensify their programmes of assistance in response to the urgent needs of Lebanon,

*Reaffirming* its resolution 1994/35 of 29 July 1994,

*Aware* of the magnitude of the requirements of Lebanon resulting from the extensive destruction of its infrastructure, which is impeding national rehabilitation and reconstruction efforts and adversely affecting economic and social conditions,

*Reaffirming* the pressing need to continue to assist the Government of Lebanon in the reconstruction of the country and the recovery of its human and economic potential,

*Expressing its appreciation* of the efforts of the Secretary-General in mobilizing assistance for Lebanon,

1. *Appeals* to all Member States and all organizations of the United Nations system to intensify their efforts to mobilize all possible assistance for the Government of Lebanon in its reconstruction and development efforts;

2. *Calls upon* all organizations and programmes of the United Nations system to intensify their assistance in response to the urgent needs of Lebanon, especially in the technical and training fields;

3. *Requests* the Secretary-General to inform the Council at its substantive session of 1996 of the progress achieved in the implementation of the present resolution.

Economic and Social Council resolution 1995/42

27 July 1995      Meeting 56      Adopted without vote

29-nation draft (E/1995/L.41); agenda item 5 *(a).*
*Meeting numbers.* ESC 47-49, 50, 56.

On 28 July, the Council, in **decision 1995/314**, took note of the report of the Secretary-General.

## Americas

### Central America

In response to a 1994 General Assembly resolution,[28] the Secretary-General submitted an October 1995 report[29] on international assistance to and cooperation with the 1994 Alliance for the Sustainable Development of Central America,[30] a comprehensive regional initiative in the political, moral, economic, social and ecological fields. The report described economic developments in the countries of the region, including Belize, Costa Rica, El Salvador, Guatemala, Honduras, Nicaragua and Panama, and discussed the cooperation activities undertaken by UNDP.

Based on priorities and undertakings established by the Presidents of Central America at their recent summit meetings and commitments made at the 1989 International Conference on Central American Refugees, UNDP prepared a new programme in support of the Alliance, focusing on peace and governability; economic and social development; and sustainable development of the environment. Under the peace and governability programme, UNDP's support included a consensus-building forum, strengthening NGOs, restructuring of democratic institutions, and economic and social reintegration of former combatants. In the area of sustainable human development, national coordination and support groups were established in Belize, Costa Rica, El Salvador and Nicaragua to focus on populations affected by uprootedness, conflicts and extreme poverty. The Programme for Displaced Persons, Refugees and Returnees in Central America wound up its operations on 31 July; it consisted of six national and two regional projects, with total funding of $148 million. At the request of the Governments of Central America, UNDP was taking steps to launch a new initiative on social development. The agricultural development project, under the leadership of the World Bank, assisted countries in their policies and programmes of agricultural modernization and institutional and rural-sectoral reform, while the poverty alleviation project dealt with the social sector, especially basic education, health, nutrition and increased funding for social investment. With regard to the environment and sustainable development of natural resources, UNDP support was provided in the areas of forestry development, conservation of biodiversity and the protection of wilderness areas.

**GENERAL ASSEMBLY ACTION**

On 12 December, the General Assembly adopted **resolution 50/58 B**.

**International assistance to and cooperation with the Alliance for the Sustainable Development of Central America**

*The General Assembly,*

*Bearing in mind* the relevant resolutions on the importance of international economic, financial and technical cooperation and assistance during the transition period, a process of peace-keeping and post-conflict peace-building, in particular its resolutions 49/137 and 49/21 I of 19 and 20 December 1994, respectively, which emphasize the compelling need to design a new programme for international economic, financial and technical cooperation and assistance for Central America geared to the new circumstances in the region and based on the priorities established by the Governments of the region,

*Recalling* its resolutions 48/7 of 19 October 1993 and 49/215 A of 23 December 1994 on assistance in mine clearance, and recognizing with concern that the presence of mines and other unexploded devices on Central American territory has social, economic and humanitarian consequences that constitute an obstacle to the restoration of normal conditions for development throughout the region,

*Recalling also* the efforts and aspirations of the peoples and Governments of the isthmus to make Central America a region of peace, freedom, democracy and development,

*Recognizing* the valuable and effective contribution made by the United Nations, and by the various governmental and non-governmental mechanisms, towards enabling the Central American peoples fully to achieve their objectives of peace, freedom, democracy and development, and the importance of the political dialogue and economic cooperation taking place within the ministerial conference between the European Union and the Central American countries and the joint initiative of the industrialized countries of the Group of Twenty-four and the countries of the Group of Three as cooperating countries, through the Association for Democracy and Development in Central America and other institutions,

*Taking note with satisfaction* of the very important results achieved by the Programme for Displaced Persons, Refugees and Returnees in Central America (PRODERE) for sustainable social and economic development in Central America, and stressing the relevance of the contribution made by the Programme to the peace process in the region,

*Also taking note with satisfaction* of the report of the Secretary-General on international assistance to and cooperation with the Alliance for the Sustainable Development of Central America, which describes the international cooperation activities implemented since January 1995 in support of the new regional development programme, following the conclusion of the Special Plan of Economic Cooperation for Central America,

*Recognizing* the validity of the Declaration of Commitments in favour of populations affected both by uprootedness and by conflicts and extreme poverty, adopted at Mexico City on 29 June 1994, as well as the functions of lead agency assumed by the United Nations Development Programme, in replacement of the mandate previously carried out by the Office of the United Nations High Commissioner for Refugees, which are concentrated in priority social spheres,

*Recognizing also* that, notwithstanding the progress made, it is necessary to continue monitoring the situation in Central America until the underlying structural causes that gave rise to the deep crisis into which the region was plunged have been overcome, and to avoid set-backs in the process and consolidate a firm and lasting peace in Central America,

*Recognizing further* the importance and validity of the commitments assumed by the Central American Presidents from the Esquipulas II summit meeting of 7 August 1987 to the present, in particular at the fifteenth summit meeting held at Guácimo, Costa Rica, from 18 to 20 August 1994, the Central American Environment Summit for Sustainable Development held at Managua on 12 and 13 October 1994, the International Conference on Peace and Development in Central America held at Tegucigalpa on 24 and 25 October 1994 and the sixteenth summit meeting of Central American Presidents held in El Salvador in March 1995, at which the priorities of the subregion were set which constitute the framework for the new programme of international assistance and cooperation for Central America,

*Underlining* the establishment of the Alliance for the Sustainable Development of Central America, which constitutes the new comprehensive strategy for national and regional development and defines political, economic, social and environmental priorities, and the signing, at the El Salvador summit meeting on 30 March 1995, of the Treaty on Central American Social Integration,[a] one of the main objectives of which is to increase investment in human capital, and taking into account that the Central American Integration System is the institutional framework that makes it possible to promote integral development in an effective, orderly and coherent manner,

*Taking into consideration* the will of the Central American Presidents to adopt a national and regional strategy entitled "Alliance for the Sustainable Development of Central America" as a comprehensive initiative in the political, moral, economic, social and ecological fields, which includes a redefining of the relations of Central America with the international community and is aimed at improving the well-being of the peoples of the subregion,

1. *Emphasizes* the importance of supporting and strengthening the new programme for international economic, financial and technical cooperation and assistance for Central America geared to the new circumstances in the region and based on the priorities laid down in the Declaration of Commitments adopted by the Follow-up Committee of the International Conference on Central American Refugees and in the new subregional development strategy, the Alliance for the Sustainable Development of Central America;

2. *Notes with satisfaction* the efforts and achievements relating to mine clearance in Central America, and appeals to the organs of the United Nations system and to the international community, and in particular to the Secretary-General, to provide the material, technical and financial support needed by the Central American Governments to complete mine-clearance activities in the region, including those activities among the priorities of the new programme of international assistance to and cooperation with Central America, so as to create improved conditions for promoting the process of reconstruction and sustainable development and, hence, lasting and permanent peace in the region;

3. *Supports* the efforts of the Central American countries in their commitments to the alleviation of extreme poverty and the fostering of sustainable human development, and urges their Governments to continue their efforts to formulate and implement policies and programmes, especially those of a social and environmental character and those relating to investment in human capital;

4. *Stresses* the importance of international economic, financial and technical cooperation and assistance, both bilateral and multilateral, in supporting the efforts of the Central American Governments to implement the new programme for the sustainable development of Central America;

5. *Requests* the Secretary-General, the United Nations system and, in particular, the United Nations Development Programme, to continue their efforts to mobilize resources in order to put into effect the new strategy for integral development in Central America contained in the Alliance for Sustainable Development and in the Declaration of Commitments, through arrangements that the Central American countries are to determine jointly with the cooperating community;

6. *Urges* all States, intergovernmental organizations, international financial institutions, the organs and specialized agencies of the United Nations system and regional and subregional organizations to continue the necessary support for the implementation of the goals and objectives of the new strategy for integral development in Central America;

---

[a]A/49/901-S/1995/396.

7. *Again stresses* the urgent need for the international community to maintain its cooperation with the Central American countries and to provide them with the necessary financial resources, in a sustained manner and on soft terms, where appropriate, with a view to promoting effectively the economic growth and development of the region;

8. *Supports* the decision of the Central American Governments to concentrate their efforts on the implementation of updated programmes with strategies for sustainable human development in previously determined priority areas, which help to consolidate peace and remedy social inequalities, extreme poverty and the social explosion;

9. *Reiterates* that only by solving the political, economic, social and environmental problems that are the cause of tensions and conflicts in society will it be possible to avoid a reversal of the achievements and guarantee a firm and lasting peace in Central America;

10. *Requests* the Secretary-General to report to the General Assembly at its fifty-second session on the implementation of the present resolution;

11. *Decides* to consider at its fifty-second session the question of international assistance to and cooperation with the Alliance for the Sustainable Development of Central America.

General Assembly resolution 50/58 B

12 December 1995     Meeting 89     Adopted without vote

36-nation draft (A/50/L.29/Rev.1 & Rev.1/Add.1); agenda item 20 *(b)*.
*Meeting numbers.* GA 50th session: plenary 70, 89.

### El Salvador

Pursuant to a 1994 General Assembly request,[31] the Secretary-General reported[32] in October 1995 on assistance for the reconstruction and development of El Salvador. The report outlined the economic situation in 1994, the economic outlook for 1995-1996, and the Government's economic and social development plan for 1995-1999. It examined the obstacles to, prospects for, and advances made in reconstruction and the strengthening of democratic institutions. Annexed to the report was a progress report on the implementation, in 1994-1995, of the principal programmes and projects related to national reconstruction.

The economic and social reintegration of former combatants in rural areas continued to be among the more complex items on the agenda of the peace agreements because of difficulties in resolving some of the underlying issues, such as poverty alleviation, expansion of employment and social integration. The land transfer programme, considered the cornerstone of rural integration efforts, was plagued with delays, with only 71.7 per cent of the total transfer process completed by mid-September. Agricultural training, housing and latrine facilities were provided by UNDP to support former combatants who were beneficiaries of the land transfer process. The support provided to those former combatants who opted for urban reintegration had been channelled largely through training programmes in the industrial and serv-

ices sector, in the form of administrative/entrepreneurial and technical/vocational training, and through a scholarship programme. The wounded and disabled had been receiving pensions and the relevant compensation from the Fund for the Protection of the Wounded and War-Disabled as a consequence of the Armed Conflict, established by the Government of El Salvador in 1992.

Under the Government's National Reconstruction Plan, over 2,500 infrastructure projects were implemented from January 1992 to July 1995 at a cost of $68 million, generating over 16,000 jobs. The projects were in the areas of access roads, schools, health, water-supply and sewerage systems, municipal buildings, electrification, and community housing. In 1995, $40.3 million had been budgeted to finance projects for former combatants, the basic infrastructure programme, and support for NGOs, micro-enterprises and agriculture. Through an agricultural development project, financed by the International Fund for Agricultural Development, UNDP and the Central American Bank for Economic Integration, technical assistance and credit were provided to small farmers. Thirty "model farms" had been set up and were being run by lead families, who, in 1995, trained farmers in environmental protection, women's equal participation, agricultural diversification and management capacity-building for the marketing of agricultural products. WFP supported the project through the modality of food-for-work in the areas of soil conservation and upgrading housing and roads.

GENERAL ASSEMBLY ACTION

On 12 December, the General Assembly adopted **resolution 50/58 C**.

### Assistance for the reconstruction and development of El Salvador

*The General Assembly,*

*Recalling* the Security Council resolutions relating to the peace process in El Salvador, and reaffirming its resolutions 47/158 of 18 December 1992, 48/203 of 21 December 1993, 49/21 J of 20 December 1994 and 50/7 of 31 October 1995,

*Having considered* the report of the Secretary-General of 23 October 1995 on assistance for the reconstruction and development of El Salvador and of 6 October 1995 on the Mission of the United Nations in El Salvador,[a]

*Noting with satisfaction* the renewed expression by the Government of El Salvador and all the political forces involved in the peace process of their political will to implement the remaining commitments under the Chapultepec Agreement, and the efforts to develop programmes and projects of social benefit aimed at the maintenance and consolidation of peace, democratization and sustainable development,

---

[a]A/50/517.

*Noting* that, in spite of national efforts and the support given by the international community to the implementation of the priority programmes in fulfilment of the Peace Agreement, including the strengthening of democratic institutions, the national reconstruction plan and the economic and social development plan, the implementation of certain programmes and projects basic to the process has continued to be affected by, *inter alia*, the limited availability and the reduction of financial resources in support of the consolidation of peace,

*Recognizing* that El Salvador is at a complex stage in the process of consolidating peace, which calls not only for the implementation of the remaining commitments under the Peace Agreement but also for a new approach involving the implementation and consolidation of medium-term and long-term national development programmes and strategies aimed at resolving the structural problems that are the cause of tension and social instability, and emphasizing the importance and necessity of international technical and financial assistance, both bilateral and multilateral, for the development of those programmes in support of national efforts to achieve the objective of a firm and lasting peace,

*Taking into account* the need to ensure the continuity of the process of democratization and national reconciliation, to complete national reconstruction and to promote sustainable development, as well as the need to strengthen the national machinery which will monitor the consolidation of the peace process before the completion of the mandate of the Mission of the United Nations in El Salvador,

1. *Again expresses its appreciation* to the Secretary-General and his representatives for their effective and timely participation, to the Group of Friends of the Secretary-General, Colombia, Mexico, Spain and Venezuela, and to the United States of America and other interested States for their contribution to the consolidation of the peace process, democratization and the promotion of economic and social development in El Salvador;

2. *Again expresses its gratitude* to the international community, especially the cooperating community, to the specialized agencies of the United Nations system and to international development and financing institutions, both governmental and non-governmental, for the technical and financial assistance they have provided to El Salvador to complement the effort to consolidate peace and to bring about democracy, reconstruction and national development;

3. *Reaffirms* that the implementation of the remaining commitments of the Peace Agreement, the continuation of programmes of national reconstruction, the strengthening of democratic institutions and the promotion of sustainable development constitute the collective goals, aspirations and needs of the country in overcoming the root causes of the crisis and consolidating peace, democracy and human development;

4. *Urges* the Government of El Salvador and all the political forces involved in the peace process to make every effort to finish complying with the remaining commitments of the Peace Agreement and to continue to develop medium-term and long-term national programmes and strategies, particularly social welfare projects, designed to improve the lives of the most vulnerable segments of the population;

5. *Encourages* the international community, in particular the donor community and international institutions of the United Nations system active in the field of development, cooperation and financing, to continue to contribute to the consolidation of peace in El Salvador by responding flexibly and generously with sufficient resources in support of the efforts of the Government of El Salvador effectively to promote and achieve the aspirations and objectives of the people of El Salvador, in accordance with the spirit of the Peace Agreement;

6. *Again invites* the international financial organizations to work with the Government of El Salvador in considering measures to harmonize the economic adjustment and stabilization programmes with the priority programmes of the national reconstruction plan and the economic and social development plan targeting the population affected by the conflict and the most vulnerable segments of Salvadoran society;

7. *Again requests* the Secretary-General to take the necessary measures and make every possible effort to mobilize the material and financial resources needed to meet the requirements of the priority programmes in El Salvador that are critical to the successful outcome and consolidation of the peace process;

8. *Requests* the Secretary-General to report to the General Assembly at its fifty-second session on the implementation of the present resolution, and decides to consider at that session the question of assistance for the reconstruction and development of El Salvador.

**General Assembly resolution 50/58 C**

12 December 1995     Meeting 89     Adopted without vote

24-nation draft (A/50/L.30/Rev.1 & Rev.1/Add.1); agenda item 20 *(b)*.
*Meeting numbers.* GA 50th session: plenary 70, 89.

### Nicaragua

Since the internationally monitored presidential election in 1990, Nicaragua had made substantial achievements in reconciliation, macroeconomic stabilization, the consolidation of democracy and the organization of civil society, but deterioration of the social situation was becoming the main obstacle to the Nicaraguan transition, the Secretary-General stated in an October report[33] on international assistance for the rehabilitation and reconstruction of Nicaragua in the aftermath of war and natural disasters. The report, submitted in response to a 1994 General Assembly request,[34] described the activities of the UN system in Nicaragua during 1994-1995.

In 1995, Nicaragua, for the first time, had no politically motivated armed groups and constitutional reform was promulgated in July. The complex issue of property was dealt with at the Conference on Property in Nicaragua (4-5 July) and agreements were reached on, among others, security for occupants of small rural and urban properties; speedy and fair compensation for victims of confiscation; and the need for occupants of large urban properties to pay to receive titles. Subsequently, a joint committee, bringing together members of the Government, the legislative Assembly, victims of confiscation, beneficiaries and agricultural associations, was established to follow up on the agreements. UNDP served as the secretariat of the joint committee.

Various UN agencies, in particular UNDP, continued to provide support to Nicaragua. UNDP assisted in the organization and transformation of the Government, the rule of law and State reform, education and culture, economic reactivation, community participation and improvement of living conditions, and sustainable development and environmental conservation. The Development Programme for Disabled Persons, Refugees and Returnees in Central America, implemented by UNDP in the former conflict zone, completed its operations in June.

**GENERAL ASSEMBLY ACTION**

On 15 December, the General Assembly adopted **resolution 50/85**.

### International assistance for the rehabilitation and reconstruction of Nicaragua: aftermath of the war and natural disasters

*The General Assembly,*

*Recalling* its resolutions 45/15 of 20 November 1990, 46/109 A and B of 17 December 1991, 47/118 of 18 December 1992, 48/161 of 20 December 1993 and 49/137 of 19 December 1994 concerning the situation in Central America,

*Recalling also* its resolutions 47/169 of 22 December 1992, 48/8 of 22 October 1993 and 49/16 of 17 November 1994 concerning the item entitled "International assistance for the rehabilitation and reconstruction of Nicaragua: aftermath of the war and natural disasters", in which it requested the international community to continue providing support to Nicaragua, taking into account the exceptional circumstances faced by that country, and requested the Secretary-General, in coordination with the Nicaraguan authorities, to provide the assistance necessary in the process of consolidation of peace,

*Deeply concerned* at the fact that the recent natural disasters that have occurred in Nicaragua, the burden of the foreign debt, despite its reduction and renegotiation achieved with the collaboration of the international community, and the harmful effects on its economy of the prolonged periods of drought followed by excessive rain and floods that have afflicted the Central American region impede the efforts being made by Nicaragua to overcome the consequences of war within the framework of a democracy and under the macroeconomic conditions already achieved,

*Deeply concerned also* at the serious effects of the volcanic eruption of Cerro Negro in Nicaragua, which has created a social and ecological emergency in the affected areas, as well as the urgent requirement for humanitarian assistance and the need to restore the normal conditions of the population,

*Taking into account* the central role of all parties in Nicaragua, in particular the Government and the Nicaraguan people, in seeking lasting solutions to consolidate the achievements of their transition,

*Expressing its appreciation* for the work of the Support Group for Nicaragua, which, under the coordination of the Secretary-General, is playing an active role in supporting that country's efforts towards economic recovery and social development,

*Recognizing* the efforts of the international community and the Government of Nicaragua to provide relief to the persons affected by the aftermath of the war and natural disasters,

*Recognizing also* the intensive efforts by the Government of Nicaragua to promote a sustained economic recovery and the considerable progress made in securing a broad social consensus by means of a process of national dialogue for the adoption of measures to lay the foundations for reconstruction and economic and social development through a comprehensive transition process that will be further consolidated with the holding of free and democratic elections at the end of 1996,

*Taking into account* the commitments adopted by the Central American Presidents at the Central American Environment Summit for Sustainable Development, through the Alliance for the Sustainable Development of Central America, and, in this context, the special attention required by Nicaragua because of its exceptional situation in order that those important commitments may begin to be implemented,

*Taking note with satisfaction* of the report of the Secretary-General of 10 October 1995 on the measures adopted pursuant to resolution 49/16,

1. *Commends* the efforts made by the international community, including the organs and organizations of the United Nations system, to supplement the action undertaken by the Government of Nicaragua and by other parties concerned in the task of rehabilitation and national reconstruction as well as in providing emergency assistance;

2. *Requests* the Secretary-General, within existing resources, to support the efforts of the Government of Nicaragua in the affected areas, and invites Member States, organizations, specialized agencies and programmes of the United Nations to continue to provide assistance and to respond generously while the emergency situation persists;

3. *Expresses its gratitude* to the Secretary-General for his report on the measures adopted pursuant to resolution 49/16;

4. *Encourages* the Government of Nicaragua to continue its efforts for reconstruction and national reconciliation, in particular those related to poverty alleviation, economic and social development and the solution of property problems, with a view to the consolidation of a stable democracy;

5. *Requests* all Member States, the international funding agencies and regional, intraregional and non-governmental organizations to continue to provide, in a broad and flexible form, support to Nicaragua at the required levels, giving particular attention to the exceptional circumstances of Nicaragua, and to stimulate a greater effort in the process of reconstruction, social investment, stabilization and development;

6. *Calls upon* all Member States, the international funding agencies, regional and intraregional organizations and, in particular, the Secretary-General, taking into account the explicit request of the Government of Nicaragua, to provide the technical cooperation and assistance needed in support of the electoral process which will take place in Nicaragua in 1996;

7. *Requests* the Secretary-General, in cooperation with the relevant organs and organizations of the United Nations system and in close cooperation with the Nicaraguan authorities, to continue to provide all necessary assistance to activities for the reconstruction, stabilization and development of Nicaragua and to continue to ensure the timely, comprehensive, flexible and effective formulation and coordination of programmes of the United Nations system in Nicaragua, given the importance of those activities for the consolidation of peace, democracy and sustainable development;

8. *Also requests* the Secretary-General to provide Nicaragua, at the request of its Government, with all possible assistance to support the consolidation of peace, democracy and sustainable development in such areas as caring for displaced persons, land ownership and land tenure in rural areas, appropriate care for war-disabled persons, mine clearance and the overcoming of difficulties in the restoration of the productive areas of the country, and, in general, a process of sustained economic and social recovery and development so that the peace and democracy already achieved become irreversible;

9. *Further requests* the Secretary-General to submit to the General Assembly at its fifty-first session a report on the action taken to implement the present resolution;

10. *Decides* to include in the provisional agenda of its fifty-first session the item entitled "International assistance for the rehabilitation and reconstruction of Nicaragua: aftermath of the war and natural disasters", and thereafter to consider this issue on a biennial basis, under the item entitled "Special economic assistance to individual countries or regions".

General Assembly resolution 50/85

15 December 1995     Meeting 93     Adopted without vote

29-nation draft (A/50/L.18/Rev.1 & Rev.1/Add.1); agenda item 33.
*Meeting numbers.* GA 50th session: plenary 55, 93.

## Europe

### Croatia

In June, the United Nations launched a Consolidated Inter-Agency Appeal for $261.5 million to meet a funding shortfall for humanitarian assistance for the former Yugoslavia in 1995. The Appeal updated a November 1994 Appeal,[35] which had covered requirements for the first half of 1995. The updated total funding requirements for humanitarian assistance to be provided were $470 million. The Appeal was further revised in September to reflect the dramatic escalation of the humanitarian needs in the region. Of the revised total target of $514.8 million, the funding requirement for Croatia was $97.9 million. The largest sum was requested by WFP ($47.1 million), followed by UNHCR ($36.3 million). In November, the United Nations announced requirements of $208 million to fund humanitarian assistance in the former Yugoslavia from January to April 1996.

In a December report[36] to the Security Council, the Secretary-General described the humanitarian situation of approximately 9,000 Serbs who remained in former Sectors North and South following the May and August 1995 Croatian mili-

tary offensive (see PART TWO, Chapter V). He said that many of them were elderly and disabled people and received inadequate attention, at times with fatal consequences. He warned that many more might die during the winter if adequate assistance was not provided in a timely manner.

**Technical Fact-finding Mission.** Pursuant to a 1994 General Assembly request,[37] the Secretary-General dispatched a Technical Fact-finding Mission to Croatia from 22 October to 5 November 1995, and submitted a report[38] on the Mission to the Assembly in December. The outbreak of war in 1991 had necessitated the restructuring of the Croatian economy into a war economy. An immediate effect was a decline in GDP from $14 billion to $10 billion in 1993. Due to a lack of investments, main economic indicators had declined during the period 1990 to 1995: GDP by 31 per cent; industrial production by 44 per cent; construction by 56 per cent; agriculture by 31 per cent; tourism by 62 per cent; employment by 33 per cent. Unemployment had increased by 51 per cent. According to the Government, the estimated damage amounted to $22 billion since 1991. Military events in May and August 1995 added further damage costs of $5 billion to $8 billion. The Government's investments in support of rehabilitation and reconstruction amounted to approximately $1 billion, of which the largest expenditures were for housing (24 per cent), roads (21 per cent) and industry (13 per cent). During the first quarter of 1995, the Croatian economy showed signs of improvement, with an increase of GDP to $14 billion per annum and a stabilized inflation rate of 2 per cent per annum.

The Mission assessed war damages by region and by sector, including social infrastructure and health, housing, agriculture, land-mines, environment, cultural heritage and tourism.The war had caused severe structural damage to 1,500 civil buildings and 16,000 deaths, and for 24,000 individuals had resulted in long-term disabilities. There were more than 400,000 displaced persons and refugees. The assessment of war damage to housing, carried out by the State Commission for War Damage Inventory and Assessment, was limited due to the inaccessibility of some areas for security reasons and recurring and sustained damage. Of a $205.1 million loan from the World Bank for an emergency reconstruction project, $54.7 million had been allocated for housing. The war and hostilities had taken place mostly in agricultural areas, driving an estimated 105,000 farmers from their land. There were 2 million to 4 million land-mines laid in Croatia, causing deaths, casualties and a loss of production from contaminated agricultural land and industrial plants, and preventing displaced persons from returning to mined areas. The environment had been affected by

chemicals released during shelling of industrial facilities, and there was serious oil spillage, uncontrolled disposal of industrial and household waste,
destroyed ionic detectors and other radioactive
sources. Damage to Croatia's cultural heritage encompassing Roman, medieval, Renaissance and
baroque architecture was assessed at $300 million.
Tourism, which had represented 25 per cent of
Croatia's GDP prior to 1991, suffered a serious loss
of 300 million tourist/nights between 1991 and
1995.

The Mission concluded that the future reconstruction of Croatia would require action to deal
with needs of individuals and society as a whole,
investment in human resource development, restoration of major infrastructure systems, re-
establishment of productive farms, problems of
land-mines and improvement of production technology.

*Other territories of former Yugoslavia*

Since the first UN Inter-Agency Appeal in
1991[39] for humanitarian assistance for the countries of the former Yugoslavia, up to 4 million people had been assisted. During 1995, the United
Nations launched Consolidated Inter-Agency
Appeals for the former Yugoslavia in June, September and November (see above). Of $514.8 mil-
lion requested in the revised Appeal of September, $261.9 million was for Bosnia and
Herzegovina, $85 million for the Federal Repub-
lic of Yugoslavia (Serbia and Montenegro), $8 mil-
lion for the former Yugoslav Republic of Macedonia and $3.1 million for Slovenia.

In February, the consideration of applications
concerning legitimate humanitarian assistance to
the former Yugoslavia was expedited by the measures implemented by the Security Council Committee established pursuant to resolution 724(1991)
concerning Yugoslavia.[40]

In the Federal Republic of Yugoslavia (Serbia
and Montenegro), the arrival of 170,000 Croatian
refugees in August had a far-reaching impact on
the assistance programme in the country where
the case-load more than doubled. A UNHCR emergency relief team in Serbia assessed the needs of
the refugees and coordinated the distribution of
food and non-food items and fuel, together with
emergency assistance. In the supplement to the revised Consolidated Inter-Agency Appeal of September, UNHCR requested an additional $24 mil-
lion to meet the new requirements in the sectors
of transport and logistics, domestic needs and
household support, health and nutrition, shelter
and community services.

In the former Yugoslav Republic of Macedonia,
the refugee situation remained relatively stable.
While government statistics recorded nearly 15,000

refugees, the planning figure for beneficiaries of
international assistance was 6,500 in September.

During 1995, the assisted population in Slovenia decreased from 27,500 to 24,000, including
20,800 registered and 3,200 unregistered refugees
who also received support. The decrease was due
to departure to third countries and a limited number of returnees to Bosnia and Herzegovina.

In Bosnia and Herzegovina, since the 1994 cessation of hostility agreement[41] between the
Government and the Bosnian Serb authorities,
overall deliveries of aid supplies were successful at
the beginning of 1995. UNHCR was consistently
able to exceed its monthly target in Sarajevo and
elsewhere in central Bosnia. However, a series of
offensives since May by Croat forces against Serbs
in Croatia had resulted in an influx of refugees to
Bosnia and Herzegovina and onwards to the Federal Republic of Yugoslavia (Serbia and Montenegro). The airstrike by the North Atlantic
Treaty Organization in late May, the ensuing escalation of the conflict and the hostage crisis deeply
affected UNHCR's ability to continue to provide
assistance in Bosnia and Herzegovina. The fall of
the eastern enclaves of Srebrenica and Zepa in July
to the Bosnian Serb force resulted in the exodus
of 36,000 displaced persons to the Tuzla and Zenica regions. Access to Sarajevo was very irregular
during the summer months, with only 15 per cent
of the target for assistance delivery met in June,
30 per cent in July and 45 per cent in August. The
humanitarian airlift operation which had been resumed in September was temporarily suspended
in November to allow for a build-up of stock in
Ancona (Italy) by 10 December, before discontinuation of the operation in early 1996.

At the Peace Implementation Conference for
Bosnia and Herzegovina (London, 8-9 December)
(see PART TWO, Chapter V), the main tasks of humanitarian assistance were identified as the continued provision of food, shelter and medicines,
and a repatriation operation to allow for the early,
phased, safe and orderly return of refugees and
displaced persons. Other tasks included the release
of prisoners and detainees, and the provision of
information on the fate of persons unaccounted
for. Reconstruction of the country was also discussed at the Conference.

*The Caucasus*

Continuing conflicts in the countries in the
Caucasus—Armenia, Azerbaijan and Georgia—
resulted in more than a million refugees and internally displaced persons in the region, including approximately 380,000 in Armenia, 890,000
in Azerbaijan and more than 280,000 in Georgia.
Contributions to the UN Consolidated Inter-
Agency Appeal for the Caucasus, launched in
April 1994[42] for the period through March 1995,

amounted to $77.3 million by the end of February 1995. The funding received covered 71 per cent of requirements for activities in Armenia, 76 per cent in Azerbaijan, 50 per cent in Georgia and 50 per cent for regional projects. In March, the second Consolidated Inter-Agency Appeal for $118 million was launched to fund humanitarian programmes in the region from April 1995 to March 1996. Of that total, $13.6 million was required for regional logistics activities, $5.3 million for control of vaccine-preventive diseases in the region, as well as $28 million for Armenia, $34.5 million for Azerbaijan and $36.5 million for Georgia. The Appeal was based on an assessment by a UN interagency mission to the three countries in January/February 1995.

In Georgia, organized repatriation of refugees remained at a standstill, owing to the unwillingness of the authorities of the region of Abkhazia to accept returnees and the deteriorating security situation. However, minor improvements in security conditions later resulted in increased daily movements back and forth across the Inguri River by displaced persons to work in the fields, trade or repair houses. After a government offer to repatriate 200 persons a week was rejected by other parties including UNHCR as inflexible, Abkhazia started its own repatriation programme with strict conditions for returning inhabitants of the Gali district. Between March and July, UNHCR distributed children's clothes, high-protein biscuits and WFP provisions to more than 7,000 highly vulnerable cases. Many primary-health-care units and hospitals were unable to function owing to shortages of medicine and equipment. Large numbers of orphans, abandoned children and people in need of special education lived in extremely poor circumstances, lacking adequate food, bedding, warm clothes and learning materials. In order to meet the food needs during the winter months, WFP assisted some 2,500 persons in the Kodori valley. UNICEF initiated an emergency diphtheria control campaign in Abkhazia. As at 1 September, approximately $20 million had been received from the international community, in response to the second Appeal.

With regard to the conflict between Armenia and Azerbaijan over the status of Nagorny Karabakh, the cease-fire agreement of May 1994[43] had been observed during 1995. In Armenia, in addition to refugees from Azerbaijan and internally displaced persons from the areas bordering Azerbaijan, there were over half a million victims of the 1988 earthquake and some 1.5 million economically vulnerable persons. They were critically dependent on humanitarian assistance for food, as they were unable to afford to buy necessary quantities even at subsidized prices and with the compensation programme initiated

by the Government. In Azerbaijan, many of the refugees and internally displaced persons continued to live under extremely difficult conditions and had little or no access to cash resources, leaving them entirely dependent on external sources of help. The identification of target beneficiaries, the monitoring of aid, mobilization of basic foodstuffs, and provision of medical assistance were some of the problems faced in meeting the humanitarian needs of Azerbaijan.

### Chechnya, Russian Federation

The outbreak of fighting at the end of 1994 between Russian federal forces and Chechen separatists displaced approximately 220,000 persons from Chechnya into the neighbouring republics of Daghestan, Ingushetia and North Ossetia. Food and other resource reserves of local families, which hosted more than 90 per cent of the displaced, were reported to be nearing exhaustion. UN agencies began assistance efforts in January 1995 in response to a request from the Government of the Russian Federation for aid to those displaced. A emergency appeal was issued in February, followed by a Consolidated Inter-Agency Appeal in March. The latter Appeal sought a total of $25.1 million for the period January to June; the largest sum was requested by UNHCR ($10.4 million), followed by WFP ($6.8 million).

UNHCR provided assistance to the displaced from Chechnya and the Prigorodny District of North Ossetia, as well as to refugees from Georgia. Its food assistance met immediate needs pending the larger programmes of WFP and ICRC. In April, DHA issued an urgent alert regarding the situation of internally displaced persons fleeing Chechnya. It was reported that an estimated 30,000 to 50,000 Chechens were moving towards the Daghestani border. In July, some operations initiated under the Consolidated Appeal were extended until the end of 1995 and the targeted populations were reduced to 152,000. As at 30 June, 77 per cent of the required funds was covered by $17.4 million in pledges and contributions.

### Tajikistan

In Tajikistan, UN agencies, including UNDP, UNHCR, UNICEF, WFP and WHO, had worked to meet the needs of conflict-affected populations and to repatriate refugees and internally displaced persons since 1992. Assistance activities were supported by contributions received through the Inter-Agency Consolidated Appeals for 1993, 1994 and 1995, which amounted to $64 million. By the end of 1995, the refugees remaining in northern Afghanistan numbered 20,000, compared to 60,000 in 1993, and fewer than 10,000 displaced remained within Tajikistan. With the country's emergency needs largely met, UNHCR's field office and DHA's

Field Coordination Unit were closed in December 1995. Although WFP would continue emergency food aid programmes mainly in the south, targeting a total of 500,000 persons, UNDP would coordinate future assistance, placing emphasis on rehabilitation and development projects.

## Humanitarian coordination

The growth in the frequency and brutality of conflicts in recent years had led to increasing numbers of civilian casualties and a commensurate rise in humanitarian assistance needs. However, disregard for humanitarian norms, the scourge of land-mines and the diminishing amount of resources available had undermined effective implementation of humanitarian action, the Secretary-General said in a June report[44] on strengthening the coordination of emergency humanitarian assistance of the United Nations. The report examined issues arising from coordination efforts, focusing on DHA, the Inter-Agency Standing Committee, the Central Emergency Revolving Fund (see below), support for in-country coordination, the consolidated appeals process and information-sharing. Also discussed were operational and financial capacities of the UN humanitarian system, issues of recovery and transition, and disaster prevention and preparedness (see below under "Disaster relief").

The Secretary-General stated that the limited regular budget funding available to DHA had posed limitations on its capacity in the face of accelerated incidence of humanitarian emergencies. UN organizations had adapted their operational capacity to the growing demands either through reorganization to give more focus to emergency response or through the development of new structures within, but in an ad hoc manner. The Secretary-General recommended that Member States ensure greater coherence in the direction given to the governing bodies of UN agencies and programmes. Among other recommendations were the use of influence by Member States with parties to an armed conflict to strengthen compliance with international humanitarian law; adequate security arrangements for humanitarian workers; additional unearmarked contributions for a particular crisis; greater use of local NGOs; and earmarking a percentage of donors' contributions to consolidated appeals for DHA's coordination activities.

**Central Emergency Revolving Fund.** As at 31 May 1995, operational organizations of the United Nations had utilized the Central Emergency Revolving Fund (CERF)—a cash-flow mechanism to ensure rapid and coordinated response by UN organizations to humanitarian emergencies—on 38 occasions since its establishment in 1992,[45]

drawing some $115.8 million, of which $100 million had been reimbursed. During the first five months of 1995, three advances totalling $6.41 million were made. The Fund's balance stood at $35.8 million as at 31 May 1995. Maintaining the level of resources of the Fund at the minimum level of $50 million had been difficult, owing to delayed reimbursements caused by weak responses to certain consolidated appeals.

In his June report,[44] the Secretary-General said that CERF had proved its value in facilitating a rapid and joint response by UN organizations to fast-breaking emergencies. In order to maintain the Fund at the minimum level, he recommended that Member States respond favourably to the proposal to replenish the Fund to cover advances that had been outstanding for more than a year in the amount of $6.12 million. Emphasizing the need for quick access to funds for rehabilitation activities, he also recommended that a separate window with an additional $30 million be opened within the Fund to act as a catalyst for such activities. Other recommendations included expansion of the Fund's scope to facilitate the provision of emergency assistance in the case of protracted emergencies, and the use of interest accrued in the Fund to support security arrangements for humanitarian workers.

**Post-conflict situations.** The International Colloquium on Post-Conflict Reconstruction Strategies (Schlaining, Austria, 23-24 June),[46] organized by the Department for Development Support and Management Services (DDSMS) of the UN Secretariat, explored the capacity of the UN system to help countries recover and reconstruct in the aftermath of armed conflict. The Colloquium's recommendations covered strategic issues, needs and capabilities, an integrated post-conflict reconstruction framework and mobilization of resources.

The recommendations of the Colloquium were considered at the seventh session[47] of the Consultative Committee on Programme and Operational Questions of the Administrative Committee on Coordination in September. UNDP, DDSMS and DHA agreed to initiate the articulation of a comprehensive integrated post-conflict framework and strategy; the development of criteria and operational guidelines for involvement of the UN system in post-conflict recovery; and a review of the UN system's capabilities and modalities for ensuring a rapid and effective response to post-conflict recovery needs, including new sources and methods of funding and new forms of partnerships.

## Consolidated appeals

Consolidated inter-agency humanitarian assistance appeals launched or ongoing during 1995 related to Afghanistan, Angola, the Caucasus (including Armenia, Azerbaijan and Georgia),

Chechnya, Iraq, Liberia, Rwanda and its subregion, Sierra Leone and Guinea, Somalia, the Sudan, Tajikistan and the former Yugoslavia, requiring total funding of $2,342,024,676 to assist some 28.3 million people. Approximately 74 per cent of the requirements were covered.

ECONOMIC AND SOCIAL COUNCIL ACTION

On 28 July, the Economic and Social Council adopted **resolution 1995/56**.

**Strengthening of the coordination of emergency humanitarian assistance of the United Nations**
*The Economic and Social Council,*

*Reaffirming* the guiding principles for providing humanitarian assistance as outlined in the annex to General Assembly resolution 46/182 of 19 December 1991,

*Recalling* other relevant General Assembly resolutions, in particular resolutions 47/168 of 22 December 1992, 48/57 of 14 December 1993 and 49/139 A of 20 December 1994, and the relevant agreed conclusions of the coordination segment of the substantive session of 1993 of the Economic and Social Council,

*Taking note* of the report of the Secretary-General,

*Noting* the differences and the limitations in the capacity of agencies, organizations, programmes and funds of the United Nations system to address effectively and in a comprehensive and coordinated manner the need for preparedness and humanitarian response, as well as prevention, rehabilitation, recovery and development, in accordance with their mandates,

*Recognizing* the need to review and strengthen the capacity of the United Nations system for humanitarian assistance,

1. *Requests* the Secretary-General, in close cooperation with relevant organizations of the United Nations system, to submit, at a date to be determined by the Council at its substantive session of 1996, a comprehensive and analytical report, including options, proposals and recommendations for a review and strengthening of all aspects of the capacity of the United Nations system for humanitarian assistance;

2. *Decides*, in order to facilitate that process:

*(a)* To encourage Governments to ensure coherence in the direction given to the governing bodies of relevant agencies, organizations, programmes and funds of the United Nations system, with the aim of improving the coordination and effectiveness of humanitarian assistance in the United Nations system;

*(b)* To urge the governing bodies of relevant organizations of the United Nations system to review, during the period from 1995 to 1997, issues concerning the role and operational responsibilities, as well as the operative and financial capacities, of their respective organizations to respond, within their mandates, in the context of broad and comprehensive humanitarian programmes, bearing in mind section VII of the annex to General Assembly resolution 46/182 and the indicative list of issues contained in the annex to the present resolution;

*(c)* To request the Secretary-General and relevant agencies, organizations, programmes and funds of the United Nations system to include in their reports to the Economic and Social Council at its substantive session of 1996 a section on the progress achieved in the review

of those issues and on the full implementation of General Assembly resolution 46/182;

3. *Calls upon* the Department of Humanitarian Affairs of the Secretariat, in this context, to convene regular, informal and open information meetings with Member States, observer States and relevant intergovernmental and other organizations on the review of the above-mentioned issues so as to ensure that they are coherently addressed and appropriately reflected in the report of the Secretary-General.

ANNEX
**Indicative list of issues for consideration by the governing bodies of the appropriate agencies, organizations, programmes and funds of the United Nations system**

Specific measures to strengthen local capacity and coping mechanisms.

Role and operational responsibilities of each specific organization in humanitarian situations, in regard to prevention, preparedness, humanitarian response, rehabilitation, recovery and development, as applicable.

Impact of the allocation of resources on the relationship between life-saving needs, prevention, preparedness and recovery.

Development of operative memoranda of understanding between different organizations to ensure interlinkages between, and coherence of, the operational activities of relevant actors.

Operational and financial capacity of each organization to act in a timely and effective manner in relation to its role and mandate.

Practical implications for each agency of participating fully in the coordinated programming of the Department of Humanitarian Affairs and in related consolidated appeals.

Development of strategies for comprehensive staff development, including inter-agency training modules.

Reporting, both operational and financial, and evaluation of programmes undertaken.

Administrative and other procedures which provide flexibility and facilitate rapid response.

Levels of delegation of authority to the field level.

Economic and Social Council resolution 1995/56

28 July 1995      Meeting 57      Adopted without vote

Draft by Vice-President (E/1995/L.62), orally corrected and based on informal consultations on 30-nation draft (E/1995/L.45); agenda item 5 *(a)*.
*Meeting numbers.* ESC 47-49, 52, 57.

GENERAL ASSEMBLY ACTION

On 12 December, the General Assembly adopted **resolution 50/57**.

**Strengthening of the coordination of emergency humanitarian assistance of the United Nations**
*The General Assembly,*

*Recalling* its resolutions 46/182 of 19 December 1991, 47/168 of 22 December 1992, 48/57 of 14 December 1993 and 49/139 of 20 December 1994,

*Taking note* of the report of the Secretary-General of 14 June 1995

*Taking note also* of Economic and Social Council resolution 1995/56 of 28 July 1995,

*Decides* to refer further deliberations on these matters, including those related to the Central Emergency Revolving Fund, to the Economic and Social Council at its substantive session of 1996.

General Assembly resolution 50/57

12 December 1995     Meeting 89     Adopted without vote

Draft by Sweden (A/50/L.39); agenda item 20 *(a)*.
*Meeting numbers.* GA 50th session: plenary 35-37, 70-72, 89.

## Participation of volunteers in humanitarian efforts

In response to a 1994 General Assembly request,[48] the Secretary-General submitted in June 1995 a report[49] on participation of volunteers, ''White Helmets'', in activities of the UN in the field of humanitarian relief, rehabilitation and technical cooperation for development.

Based on past experience—more than 2,000 United Nations volunteers had assisted in a diverse range of activities—the Secretary-General suggested that ''White Helmets'' deployment could include: the delivery of urgent relief supplies and services; support to local emergency relief coordinating units; assistance in arrangements for return, resettlement and repatriation of refugees and internally displaced persons; and monitoring of respect for human rights. The United Nations Volunteers (UNV) would handle managerial and administrative aspects of the deployment of volunteers, while DHA would provide overall coordination in the field. Issues of concern arising from the implementation of the ''White Helmets'' initiative included the need for additional arrangements to recruit and field teams of volunteers in the earliest stages of emergency, training for volunteers, and financing for their training and deployment. The Secretary-General concluded that the ''White Helmets'' initiative presented a new opportunity for creative and resourceful programme design, formulation and implementation. Once several volunteer teams had served successfully under UN auspices, experiences gained would help identify the gaps in the evolving volunteer service scheme, and ways and means to enhance the effectiveness of the deployment. He invited Governments to provide the necessary financial support and to set up national volunteer teams in order to achieve the objectives of the initiative.

### ECONOMIC AND SOCIAL COUNCIL ACTION

On 27 July, the Economic and Social Council adopted **resolution 1995/44**.

#### Participation of volunteers, 'White Helmets', in activities of the United Nations in the field of humanitarian relief, rehabilitation and technical cooperation for development

*The Economic and Social Council,*

*Recalling* General Assembly resolution 49/139 B of 20 December 1994 on the participation of volunteers, ''White Helmets'', in activities of the United Nations in the field of humanitarian relief, rehabilitation and technical cooperation for development,

*Reaffirming* the guiding principles on humanitarian assistance contained in the annex to General Assembly resolution 46/182 of 19 December 1991,

*Recognizing* the importance of voluntary national and regional actions aimed at providing the United Nations system on a stand-by basis with specialized human and technical resources for the purposes mentioned above, on a stand-by basis,

*Noting* that, pursuant to General Assembly resolution 49/139 B, a distinct window has been opened within the Special Voluntary Fund of the United Nations Volunteers programme to channel funds for operationalizing the activities of the ''White Helmets'',

*Taking note* of the information submitted to the Council on recent developments related to the implementation of the ''White Helmets'' initiative by Governments, specialized agencies and relevant bodies,

1. *Expresses its satisfaction* with the growing number of Governments involved in the ''White Helmets'' initiative;

2. *Takes note with interest* of the report of the Secretary-General, in particular the statement that the ''White Helmets'' initiative represents an innovative opportunity for the effective, efficient and economical provision of assistance to the intended beneficiaries of the operations of the United Nations system in the field of humanitarian relief, rehabilitation and technical cooperation for development, and that it presents a new opportunity for creative and resourceful programme design, formulation and implementation in such areas, in accordance with General Assembly resolution 46/182;

3. *Invites* Governments able to do so to set up and make available their existing national volunteer teams and individuals, taking into account the ''White Helmets'' initiative;

4. *Encourages* the Department of Humanitarian Affairs of the Secretariat, as part of its functions of coordination of humanitarian assistance, and the relevant bodies of the United Nations, in accordance with their respective mandates, to continue to make use of the ''White Helmets'' and other volunteers in appropriate United Nations relief, humanitarian and development operations;

5. *Requests* the Secretary-General, in view of the information related to the ''White Helmets'' initiative that has recently become available, to prepare an updated report on recent developments regarding the implementation of the initiative for submission to the General Assembly at its fiftieth session;

6. *Recommends* that the General Assembly include the ''White Helmets'' initiative and the consideration of the report mentioned in paragraph 5 above as a separate item in the agenda of its fiftieth session.

Economic and Social Council resolution 1995/44

27 July 1995     Meeting 56     Adopted without vote

70-nation draft (E/1995/L.46), orally revised; agenda item 5 *(a)*.
*Meeting numbers.* ESC 47-49, 52, 56.

Pursuant to the Council's request, the Secretary-General submitted an October note[50] to the General Assembly, updating the developments regarding the initiative. He reported that since June specific project activities had been identified by UNV to involve ''White Helmets'' volunteers in Angola, Armenia, Gaza, Haiti and Jamaica, and that the first ''White Helmets'' team, composed of Argentine, Bolivian and Dominican volunteers was to be deployed in Haiti shortly.

On 28 November, the General Assembly adopted **resolution 50/19**.

### Participation of volunteers, 'White Helmets', in activities of the United Nations in the field of humanitarian relief, rehabilitation and technical cooperation for development

*The General Assembly,*

*Reaffirming* its resolution 49/139 B of 20 December 1994,

*Reaffirming also* its resolutions 46/182 of 19 December 1991, in particular the guiding principles on humanitarian assistance embodied in the annex thereto, 47/168 of 22 December 1992 and 48/57 of 14 December 1993,

*Recalling* Economic and Social Council decision 1993/205 of 12 February 1993 and the agreed conclusions of the coordination segment of the Council of 1993, and Council resolution 1995/44 of 27 July 1995,

*Recognizing*, in the light of the increasing number and growing magnitude and complexity of natural disasters and other emergencies, the need to utilize fully the national potential of countries in providing the United Nations system, on a stand-by basis, with support for its activities in the area of humanitarian emergency assistance, as well as in the promotion of a smooth transition from relief to rehabilitation, reconstruction and development, which should contribute to more coordinated responses in these fields,

1. *Takes note with interest* of the report of the Secretary-General and the note by the Secretariat, prepared in pursuance of Economic and Social Council resolution 1995/44, on the participation of volunteers, "White Helmets", in activities of the United Nations in the field of humanitarian relief, rehabilitation and technical cooperation for development, as well as of the initial projects undertaken in the implementation of resolution 49/139 B;

2. *Commends* the activities and experiences of the United Nations Volunteers, including the White Helmets, deployed in the context of the implementation of resolution 49/139 B, as well as other experiences developed to improve, in accordance with resolutions 46/182 and 49/139 B, the capability for a quick and coordinated response to natural disasters and other emergencies, while preserving the non-political, neutral and impartial character of humanitarian action;

3. *Encourages* voluntary national and regional actions aimed at making available to the United Nations system, through the United Nations Volunteers, national volunteer corps such as the White Helmets on a stand-by basis, in accordance with accepted United Nations procedures and practices, in order to provide specialized human and technical resources for emergency relief and rehabilitation, and in this regard notes with satisfaction the establishment, in particular in developing countries, of national volunteer corps such as the White Helmets;

4. *Encourages also* the Department of Humanitarian Affairs of the Secretariat, as part of its function of coordination of humanitarian assistance, and the relevant bodies of the United Nations, in accordance with their respective mandates, to make use of the White Helmets and other United Nations volunteers in the area of humanitarian emergency assistance, as well as to support

a smooth transition from relief to rehabilitation, reconstruction and development;

5. *Recognizes*, in this context, the operational role of the United Nations Volunteers in the selection, training, deployment and effective utilization of the White Helmets at the field level;

6. *Calls upon* countries in a position to do so to contribute to the distinct window created to this end, in accordance with paragraph 6 *(b)* of resolution 49/139 B, within the Special Voluntary Fund of the United Nations Volunteers;

7. *Requests* the Secretary-General to report to the General Assembly at its fifty-second session, in the context of the cluster of issues related to the item "Strengthening of the coordination of humanitarian and disaster relief assistance of the United Nations, including special economic assistance", on the technical, institutional and financial viability of the initiative.

General Assembly resolution 50/19

28 November 1995     Meeting 72     Adopted without vote

69-nation draft (A/50/L.23 & Add.1); agenda item 154.
*Meeting numbers.* GA 50th session: plenary 70-72.

### Mine clearance

Responding to a 1994 General Assembly request,[51] the Secretary-General submitted a September 1995 report[52] on assistance in mine clearance. The report discussed UN activities in providing assistance in mine clearance, and described an integrated approach of and resources for UN mine-action programmes.

Estimates indicated that there were between 95 million and 110 million land-mines scattered throughout 68 countries. An estimated 30 people were killed daily by uncleared land-mines and perhaps as many as 60 people were maimed. Land-mines that sold for as little as $3 cost the international community between $300 and $1,000 to clear. With DHA as the focal point, UN entities engaged in land-mine-related activities during 1995 in Afghanistan, Angola, Cambodia, Chad, El Salvador, Georgia, Guatemala, Mozambique, Rwanda, Somalia, the former Yugoslavia and Yemen. In Afghanistan, Angola, Cambodia and Mozambique, the United Nations took an integrated approach, involving mine clearance, national capacity-building, mine surveys, education and training in mine awareness, and treatment and rehabilitation of land-mine victims. Those activities were funded by consolidated appeals, assessed peace-keeping contributions and the Voluntary Trust Fund for Assistance in Mine Clearance, established in 1994.[53] DHA was working to establish a demining stand-by capacity for tapping into personnel, equipment and facilities maintained by Member States.

The Secretary-General stated that he had convened an International Meeting on Mine Clearance (Geneva, 5-7 July), which had discussed the technical aspects of mine clearance and mine-related issues, and strengthening the stand-by capacity of the

United Nations in mine clearance. Participants pledged more than $20 million to the Voluntary Trust Fund and $7 million for the stand-by capacity.

The Secretary-General concluded that clearing all the mines already laid could not be accomplished within the existing funding and technology. He called for increased efforts to develop demining and mine-clearance technologies, and emphasized that only a total ban would effectively stop their spread once and for all.

GENERAL ASSEMBLY ACTION

On 14 December, the General Assembly adopted **resolution 50/82.**

### Assistance in mine clearance
*The General Assembly,*

*Recalling* its resolutions 48/7 of 19 October 1993 and 49/215 of 23 December 1994 on assistance in mine clearance, both adopted without a vote,

*Reaffirming its deep concern* at the tremendous humanitarian problem caused by the presence of mines and other unexploded devices that have serious and lasting social and economic consequences for the populations of mine-infested countries and constitute an obstacle to the return of refugees and other displaced persons, to humanitarian aid operations and to reconstruction and economic development, as well as to the restoration of normal social conditions,

*Reiterating its dismay* at the high number of victims of mines, especially among civilian populations, particularly children, and recalling in this context Commission on Human Rights resolution 1995/79 of 8 March 1995 on the rights of the child,

*Deeply alarmed* that the number of mines being laid each year, as well as the presence of a large number of mines and other unexploded devices as a result of armed conflicts, exponentially outweighs the number of such mines that can be cleared during that time, and thus convinced of the necessity and urgency of a significant increase in mine-clearance efforts by the international community,

*Recognizing* the importance of recording the location of mines and of retaining all such records and making them available to concerned parties upon cessation of hostilities, in accordance with international law,

*Bearing in mind* the serious threat that mines and other unexploded devices pose to the safety, health and lives of personnel participating in humanitarian, peace-keeping and rehabilitation programmes and operations,

*Conscious* of the limited availability of safe and cost-effective mine-clearance techniques, and the need for improvements thereof, and of the lack of global coordination in the field of research to improve mine-clearance technology and the urgent need to foster international technical cooperation in this field,

*Aware* that the rate of mine clearance needs to improve substantially if the global land-mine problem is to be tackled effectively,

*Recalling* its resolution 50/74 of 12 December 1995 on the Convention on Prohibitions or Restrictions on the Use of Certain Conventional Weapons Which May Be Deemed to Be Excessively Injurious or to Have Indiscriminate Effects and the convening by the Secretary-

General of the Review Conference of the States Parties to that Convention at Vienna from 25 September to 13 October 1995, taking note, in this regard, of the decision of the Review Conference to continue its work in order to conclude negotiations on the strengthening of the Protocol on Prohibitions or Restrictions on the Use of Mines, Booby Traps and Other Devices (Protocol II), and welcoming in this regard the additional ratifications of or accessions to the Convention,

*Recalling also* its resolutions 48/75 K of 16 December 1993, 49/75 D of 15 December 1994 and 50/70 O of 12 December 1995 calling for a moratorium on the export of anti-personnel land-mines, and welcoming in this regard the export moratorium adopted by several States,

*Bearing in mind* that significant progress needs to be achieved in these fields,

*Recognizing* that, in addition to the primary role of States, the United Nations has an important role in the field of assistance in mine clearance,

*Noting with satisfaction* the inclusion in the mandates of several peace-keeping operations of provisions relating to mine-clearance work carried out under the direction of the Department of Peace-keeping Operations of the Secretariat in the context of such operations,

*Commending* the activities already undertaken by the United Nations system, donor and recipient Governments, the International Committee of the Red Cross and non-governmental organizations to coordinate their efforts and seek solutions to the problems related to the presence of mines and other unexploded devices,

*Also commending* the role of the Secretary-General, through the work of the Department of Humanitarian Affairs of the Secretariat, in increasing public awareness of the problem of land-mines and for the establishment of the Central Land-Mine Database and its inventories of mine-awareness materials and mine-clearance techniques,

*Commending in particular* the outcome of the International Meeting on Mine Clearance held at Geneva from 5 to 7 July 1995, in which notable financial pledges were gathered for the Voluntary Trust Fund for Assistance in Mine Clearance and for the development of a demining stand-by capacity by the United Nations,

1. *Expresses its appreciation* to the Secretary-General for his comprehensive report of 6 September 1995 on the activities of the United Nations in providing assistance in mine clearance and on the operation of the Voluntary Trust Fund for Assistance in Mine Clearance, and takes note with interest of the proposals contained therein;

2. *Welcomes,* in particular, the efforts made by the United Nations to foster the establishment of national mine-clearance capacities in countries where mines constitute a serious threat to the safety, health and lives of the local population, and urges all Member States, particularly those that have a capacity to do so, to assist afflicted countries in the establishment and development of their national mine-clearance capacities;

3. Expresses its appreciation to Member States, United Nations organizations and intergovernmental and non-governmental organizations that participated in the International Meeting on Mine Clearance for their strong expression of cooperation in the field of assistance in mine clearance, and particularly to States and regional organizations for their financial contribu-

tions to the Voluntary Trust Fund as well as for providing the necessary means to establish a de-mining standby capacity within the United Nations;

4. *Appeals* to Member States as well as to intergovernmental organizations and foundations to continue to contribute to the Voluntary Trust Fund and to continue to supply the necessary means to the United Nations to foster its de-mining stand-by capacity;

5. *Invites* all relevant multilateral and national programmes and bodies to include, in coordination with the United Nations, activities related to mine clearance in their humanitarian, social and economic assistance activities;

6. *Emphasizes again*, in this connection, the importance of coordination by the United Nations of activities related to mine clearance, including those by regional organizations, in particular activities related to information and training;

7. *Welcomes* the efforts of the Department of Humanitarian Affairs of the Secretariat to coordinate mine-related activities and, in particular, the establishment, in cooperation with other relevant United Nations organizations, of comprehensive mine-action programmes, and encourages the Department to continue and enhance those efforts within existing resources with a view to improving the effectiveness of assistance in mine clearance by the United Nations;

8. *Calls upon* the Secretary-General to designate the Department of Humanitarian Affairs, the focal point in the United Nations for coordinating de-mining and related issues, as the repository of information and for encouraging and facilitating international research to improve mine-clearance methods;

9. *Urges* Member States, regional organizations, governmental and non-governmental organizations and foundations to continue to extend full assistance and cooperation to the Secretary-General and, in particular, to provide him with information and data as well as other appropriate resources which could be useful in strengthening the coordination role of the United Nations in the field of mine awareness, training, surveying, mine detection and clearance, scientific research on mine detection and clearance technology, and information on and distribution of medical equipment and supplies;

10. *Calls upon* Member States, especially those that have a capacity to do so, to provide the necessary information and technical and material assistance, as appropriate, and to locate, remove, destroy or otherwise render ineffective minefields, mines, booby traps and other devices, in accordance with international law;

11. *Urges* Member States, intergovernmental organizations and non-governmental organizations and foundations that have the ability to do so to provide, as appropriate, technological assistance to mine-afflicted countries as well as to promote scientific research and development on humanitarian mine-clearance techniques and technology so that mine-clearance activities may be more effectively carried out at lower cost and through safer means, and to promote international collaboration in this regard;

12. *Requests* the Secretary-General to submit to the General Assembly at its fifty-first session a report on the progress achieved on all relevant issues outlined in his reports to the Assembly at its forty-ninth and fiftieth sessions on assistance in mine clearance and on the operation of the Voluntary Trust Fund;

13. *Decides* to include in the provisional agenda of its fifty-first session the item entitled "Assistance in mine clearance".

General Assembly resolution 50/82

14 December 1995     Meeting 92     Adopted without vote

63-nation draft (A/50/L.57 & Add.1); agenda item 46.
*Meeting numbers.* GA 50th session: plenary 91, 92.

*REFERENCES*

[1]YUN 1993, p. 724, GA res. 48/202, 21 Dec. 1993. [2]A/50/424. [3]YUN 1994, p. 346. [4]Ibid., p. 280, GA res. 49/7, 25 Oct. 1994. [5]Ibid., p. 829, GA res. 49/21 C, 2 Dec. 1994. [6]A/50/541 & Add.1. [7]YUN 1994, p. 278. [8]Ibid., p. 830, GA res. 49/21 E, 20 Dec. 1994. [9]A/50/522. [10]YUN 1994, p. 834, GA res. 49/23, 2 Dec. 1994. [11]A/50/654. [12]S/1995/1002. [13]E/1995/SR.47. [14]YUN 1994, p. 837. [15]S/1995/231. [16]S/PRST/1995/15. [17]YUN 1994, p. 836, GA res. 49/21 L, 20 Dec. 1994. [18]A/50/447. [19]A/50/464. [20]YUN 1994, p. 838, GA res. 49/21 K, 20 Dec. 1994. [21]Ibid., p. 839. [22]Ibid., GA res. 49/140, 20 Dec. 1994. [23]A/50/737. [24]YUN 1994, p. 840. [25]Ibid., p. 841, ESC res. 1994/35, 29 July 1994. [26]E/1995/53. [27]YUN 1993, p. 733. [28]YUN 1994, p. 845, GA res. 49/21 H, 20 Dec. 1994. [29]A/50/534. [30]YUN 1994, p. 845. [31]Ibid., p. 847, GA res. 49/21 J, 20 Dec. 1994. [32]A/50/455. [33]A/50/535. [34]YUN 1994, p. 849, GA res. 49/16, 17 Nov. 1994. [35]Ibid., p. 843. [36]S/1995/1051. [37]YUN 1994, p. 842, GA res. 49/21 G, 20 Dec. 1994. [38]A/50/812. [39]YUN 1991, p. 218. [40]Ibid., p. 219, SC res. 724(1991), 15 Dec. 1991. [41]YUN 1994, p. 551. [42]Ibid., p. 844. [43]Ibid., p. 577. [44]A/50/203-E/1995/79. [45]YUN 1992, p. 584. [46]A/50/345. [47]ACC/1995/18. [48]YUN 1994, p. 827, GA res. 49/139 B, 20 Dec. 1994. [49]A/50/203/Add.1-E/1995/79/Add.1. [50]A/50/542. [51]YUN 1994, p. 173, GA res. 49/215, 23 Dec. 1994. [52]A/50/408. [53]YUN 1994, p. 172.

# Special economic assistance

## African economic recovery and development

### New Agenda for the Development of Africa

In 1995, a number of UN bodies continued to implement or monitor the implementation of the United Nations New Agenda for the Development of Africa in the 1990s, adopted by the General Assembly in 1991.[1] They included the United Nations Conference on Trade and Development (UNCTAD), UNDP, the Economic and Social Council and the General Assembly.

**UNCTAD action.** At its March session, the Trade and Development Board had before it a January progress report[2] on UNCTAD's contribution to the implementation of the New Agenda. The report addressed the issues of policy research and analysis, and technical cooperation in the areas of trade; commodities; debt management and negotiations; economic cooperation among developing countries; privatization; foreign direct investment; shipping, ports and multimodal transport; insurance; technology; and human resources development. UNCTAD's ongoing work had focused increasingly on the problems facing Africa and had emphasized that they were largely structural. The dramatic changes in the world economy and trading system had also placed the African countries in a relatively weaker position in international competition. UNCTAD also studied the impact of the 1994 Uruguay Round agreements on multilateral trade[3] on low-income developing countries, particularly the African ones, with a view to strengthening its technical cooperation activities in that field. It reported that additional resources in support of Africa's development endeavours were urgently required, with a view to achieving lasting effect and long-term sustainability of policy reforms.

In agreed conclusions of 31 March,[4] the Board stated that the economic situation in most of Africa continued to deteriorate and official resource flows for development purposes to Africa, including official development assistance (ODA), had fallen significantly since 1990. The Board invited African countries to strengthen industrial strategies so as to encourage economic growth and employment opportunities, to create domestic stability and to improve the business environment for both domestic and foreign direct investment. The international community was called on to support the commodity diversification efforts of Africa; to fulfil the agreed target of 0.7 per cent of gross national product for overall ODA; and to implement urgently existing debt-relief agreements and negotiate further initiatives. The UNCTAD secretariat was requested to propose recommendations to facilitate access to, and acquisition of, appropriate existing and new technologies, emphasizing the utility of scientific and technological knowledge to meet basic needs and requirements for sustainable development.

**UNDP activities.** In response to a 1994 request,[5] the UNDP Administrator submitted to the Executive Board of UNDP and of the United Nations Population Fund (UNFPA) an April report[6] on UNDP's role in the implementation of the New Agenda. The report outlined activities and achievements during 1994.

In a later report on the subject,[7] the Administrator stated that, during 1995, UNDP provided support to a number of African countries, with particular emphasis on priorities established in the New Agenda. It coordinated its interventions with other partners, including the Office to Combat Desertification and Drought (see below, under "Disaster relief") in the environmental field; the Africa 2000 Network on grass-roots activities in the management of natural resources; and the Global Environment Facility in biodiversity conservation and the protection of coastal areas from pollution. UNDP continued to provide assistance to the joint Organization of African Unity/Economic Commission for Africa (ECA)/African Development Bank (AfDB)

secretariat charged with establishing the African Economic Community. Under the multi-donor-funded African Capacity-Building Initiative, support was extended to key training institutions in Benin, Ghana, Guinea, Nigeria, Uganda, the United Republic of Tanzania and Zimbabwe. In 1995, national long-term perspective studies were completed in Mauritius and were under way in Cape Verde, Cote d'Ivoire, Gabon, Guinea-Bissau, Mauritania, Senegal, Swaziland, the United Republic of Tanzania, Zambia and Zimbabwe. In the area of private sector development, the African Project Development Facility, co-sponsored by UNDP, AfDB, the World Bank and bilateral donors, had completed 130 projects in 25 countries.

**Economic and Social Council consideration.** As decided by **decision 1995/203** of 10 February, the Economic and Social Council devoted the high-level segment (Geneva, 3-6 July) of its substantive session of 1995 to the development of Africa, including the implementation of the New Agenda.

The Council had before it a 20 June report[8] of the Secretary-General on the subject. The report analysed some critical issues facing Africa in the implementation of the New Agenda, such as trade and finance, external assistance and debt, Africa's competitiveness, foreign direct investment flows to Africa, poverty eradication and human development, crisis prevention and management, capacity-building and South-South cooperation. The Secretary-General concluded that Africa needed significant and sustained support from the international community for the development of its immense natural and human resources, and Africa's needs for external assistance went well beyond the region's emergency needs. He also provided an assessment of the implementation of the New Agenda and suggested some measures for consideration that could contribute to enabling African countries and the international community to confront those issues and put the continent on the path of sustainable development.

The President of the Council, in his summary of the high-level segment,[9] stated that despite Africa's economic, social and political achievements, progress had been slow and insufficient. While Africa's development was first and foremost the responsibility of the African countries themselves, it could be sustained only with the support of the international community. The President stated that African economic development had to be considered in the context of an increasingly globalized world economy, and that all the critical issues, including increasing the role of women in development, should be addressed simultaneously.

The Council, in **decision 1995/309** of 27 July, took note of the report[10] of the twenty-eighth series (New York, 27 October 1994) of Joint Meetings of the Committee for Programme and Coordination and the Administrative Committee on Coordination. The report included the Chairman's summary of the consideration of the critical situation of Africa.

**Reports of the Secretary-General.** The Secretary-General submitted two reports to the General Assembly relating to the implementation of the New Agenda. The first report,[11] prepared in response to a 1993 Assembly request,[12] discussed financial intermediation in Africa. It reviewed the state of financial systems and practices, categorizing countries under three broad stages of intermediation—primary, intermediate and advanced—and proposed a course of future action, including support measures that the international community could provide. Although the regions's performance in both the financial and real sectors had improved substantially, financial systems were still among the weakest sectors in African countries; of the 41 countries, nearly 20 were still at the primary stage, 19 at the intermediate stage and only 2 might be at the advanced stage. Neglect of the informal sector, limited operational independence and inadequate capacity of central banks, incomplete restructuring and rehabilitation of banks and non-banks, and the lack of real sector restructuring were the constraints facing African financial systems. The report said that sustainable progress in advancing financial intermediation and its continued effectiveness required certain preconditions to be met. The foremost among them was the restoration and maintenance of a reasonable degree of macroeconomic stability; among others were the development of human capital and management systems, the building of expertise in maintaining an appropriate portfolio of financial assets, and the establishment of information channels.

Noting that the informal finance system mediated a significant amount of financial transactions in most African countries, the Secretary-General proposed that the informal and semi-informal systems, including the postal system, credit unions, other cooperatives and a variety of financial institutions run by NGOs, be preserved and encouraged, while addressing their limitations through appropriate policy initiatives and developing and strengthening the formal financial system. With respect to the formal financial sector, the Secretary-General suggested a three-pronged development strategy of strengthening financial institutions; devising a variety of financial paper; and implementing indirect instruments of monetary policy.

The second report,[13] submitted pursuant to a 1994 Assembly request,[14] outlined steps taken by AfDB, the UN system and Member States towards the establishment of a diversification facility and national diversification councils at the country level. Organized by ECA, the lead agency for the

UN system's support programmes on diversification of African economies, an inter-agency workshop (Yaounde, Cameroon, 13-17 February) made recommendations on the development of private small and medium-sized enterprises, establishment of a special facility for commodity diversification, and functions of the national diversification councils. The workshop also recommended that UN organizations and agencies continue to assess the impact of the Uruguay Round on African economies and initiate measures to enhance their diversification.

During 1995, the UN Office of the Special Coordinator for Africa and the Least Developed Countries organized or co-sponsored a number of meetings on the development of Africa. They included an international workshop on development of Africa's informal sector (New York, 13-15 June); a regional workshop for eastern and southern Africa on the operationalization of the principles of the Tokyo Declaration on African Development (Harare, Zimbabwe, 26-27 July); a high-level symposium on peace and development in Africa (Tokyo, 11-12 October); and an Asia-Africa Forum core group meeting of African experts on the operationalization of the principles of the Tokyo Declaration (Seychelles, 19-21 December).

**GENERAL ASSEMBLY ACTION**

On 22 December, the General Assembly adopted **resolution 50/160 A**.

**Implementation of the United Nations New Agenda for the Development of Africa in the 1990s**

*The General Assembly,*

*Reaffirming* its resolution 46/151 of 18 December 1991, the annex to which contains the United Nations New Agenda for the Development of Africa in the 1990s, in paragraphs 43 *(c)* and *(e)* and 44 of which it decided, *inter alia,* to conduct a mid-term review and a final review and assessment of the implementation of the New Agenda,

*Reaffirming also* its resolutions 48/214 of 23 December 1993 and 49/142 of 23 December 1994 concerning the implementation of the New Agenda,

*Recalling* its resolution 45/253 of 21 December 1990 on programme planning, in which the economic recovery and development of Africa was stated to be one of the five overall priorities in the medium-term plan for the period 1992-1997,

*Taking note* of the document entitled "Relaunching Africa's economic and social development: the Cairo Agenda for Action" adopted by the Council of Ministers of the Organization of African Unity at its seventeenth extraordinary session, held at Cairo from 25 to 28 March 1995, and endorsed by the Assembly of Heads of State and Government of the Organization of African Unity in its resolution AHG/Res.236(XXXI) of 28 June 1995,[a]

---

[a]A/50/647.

*Taking note also* of resolution CM/Res.1596(LXII) of 23 June 1995 of the Council of Ministers of the Organization of African Unity on the implementation of the New Agenda, endorsed by the Assembly of Heads of State and Government,

*Bearing in mind* the report of the Secretary-General of 20 June 1995 to the high-level segment of the Economic and Social Council at its substantive session of 1995, devoted to the consideration of the development of Africa, including the implementation of the New Agenda, and the summary made by the President of the Council of the debate during the high-level segment,

*Having considered* the report of the Secretary-General of 6 October 1995 on advancing financial intermediation in Africa and of 11 October 1995 on diversification of Africa's commodities,[a]

*Recalling* that the prime objective of the New Agenda is to stop and reverse the continuing deterioration in the socio-economic situation of African countries and to renew the commitment of the international community to support Africa's own efforts to achieve sustained economic growth and sustainable development,

*Expressing serious concern* about the limited progress made so far in the implementation of the New Agenda and the continuing deterioration of the economic and social situation in Africa,

*Mindful* of the urgent need for African countries to increase and mobilize internal resources for the implementation of the New Agenda through, *inter alia*, policies for the promotion of domestic savings, improved and accessible banking facilities and further improvements in traditional practices of capital formation at local levels, as well as to continue creating an enabling environment for domestic and foreign investment,

*Acknowledging* that effective, equitable, development-oriented and durable solutions have to be found to the problems of external debt and the burden of debt which continue to impede the socio-economic development of African countries despite measures taken on both a bilateral and a multilateral basis to reduce or reschedule their debt,

*Recognizing* the possible adverse effects and looking forward to the challenges and opportunities for African countries of the implementation of the agreements of the Uruguay Round of multilateral trade negotiations and the urgent need for further technical and financial assistance to African countries, with a view, *inter alia*, to identifying the adverse effects and alleviating them through appropriate measures, including possible supportive measures, as appropriate, in order to maximize their participation in the world trading system,

*Recognizing also* the urgent need to continue to assist African countries in their efforts to diversify their economies,

*Recognizing further* that the mid-term review of the implementation of the New Agenda should provide an opportunity for the international community to conduct an in-depth assessment of the actions so far taken in the implementation of the New Agenda and the measures needed for sustained economic growth and sustainable development in Africa beyond the 1990s, and to continue to develop policies and measures, including new and/or corrective policies and measures, as appropriate, and continued external support to the efforts of African countries in all areas, so as to ensure the timely, effective and full implementation of the New Agenda during the remaining part of the decade,

*Bearing in mind* its resolution 42/163 of 8 December 1987 on the critical economic situation in Africa, in which it established an Ad Hoc Committee of the Whole of the General Assembly as the most appropriate mechanism to prepare the review and appraisal of the United Nations Programme of Action for African Economic Recovery and Development 1986-1990, and its resolutions 43/27 of 18 November 1988 and 45/178 A of 19 December 1990 on that review and appraisal,

1. *Takes note with appreciation* of the reports of the Secretary-General on advancing financial intermediation in Africa and on diversification of Africa's commodities;

2. *Takes note also* of the summary made by the President of the Economic and Social Council of the debate during the high-level segment of the Council at its substantive session of 1995, devoted to the consideration of the development of Africa, including the implementation of the United Nations New Agenda for the Development of Africa in the 1990s;

3. *Reaffirms* the need for the effective implementation of the New Agenda and, to that effect, calls upon the donor countries and all other parties concerned to fulfil their respective commitments as stated in the New Agenda, and calls upon African countries to implement the measures necessary to achieve the goals of the New Agenda;

4. *Decides* to establish an ad hoc committee of the whole of the fiftieth session of the General Assembly as the most appropriate mechanism to prepare the mid-term review in 1996 of the implementation of the New Agenda, as provided for in the annex to resolution 46/151;

5. *Also decides* to convene an organizational session of the Ad Hoc Committee of the Whole as soon as possible but not later than 30 June 1996, for two working days, to consider and adopt the necessary arrangements for its work regarding, *inter alia*, the mid-term review of the implementation of the New Agenda, and that the Ad Hoc Committee should have its Bureau constituted at the highest appropriate level and composed of a Chairman, three Vice-Chairmen and a Rapporteur;

6. *Further decides* that the Ad Hoc Committee should meet for a period of up to seven working days in September 1996, prior to the fifty-first session of the General Assembly, to prepare the mid-term review on the basis of a report to be prepared by the Secretary-General, including relevant inputs from Governments and/or organizations and programmes of the United Nations system and other intergovernmental organizations, in particular the Organization of African Unity and non-governmental organizations, regarding their efforts and experiences in implementing the New Agenda;

7. *Invites* the Economic Commission for Africa to submit a report to the Secretary-General by June 1996 on actions taken and progress achieved by African countries in the implementation of the New Agenda;

8. *Decides* that the Ad Hoc Committee, in carrying out its mandate, should submit its findings to the General Assembly at its fifty-first session and propose concrete measures and recommendations for sustained economic growth and sustainable development in Africa beyond the 1990s;

---

[a]A/50/520.

9. *Urges* Member States and organs and bodies of the United Nations system to be represented at the highest appropriate level and to participate actively in the work of the Ad Hoc Committee;

10. *Requests* the Secretary-General to submit to the Ad Hoc Committee a report on the implementation of the New Agenda, including a summary and assessment of national efforts based on relevant inputs from African countries, and to continue ensuring close cooperation and coordination with the Secretary-General of the Organization of African Unity concerning the contributions of the relevant organs, organizations and bodies of the United Nations system, including the Economic Commission for Africa, the United Nations Development Programme, the Food and Agriculture Organization of the United Nations, the United Nations Industrial Development Organization, the United Nations Conference on Trade and Development, the Office of the United Nations High Commissioner for Refugees and the United Nations Children's Fund, in the context of his report on the preparation of the mid-term review of the implementation of the New Agenda;

11. *Also requests* the Secretary-General to include in his report to the Ad Hoc Committee estimates of the projected resource requirements from all sources, public and private, domestic and international, needed for the full implementation of the New Agenda, the amount expected to be mobilized and proposals for filling any resource gaps, taking into account the specific economic and development situation of African countries;

12. *Further requests* the Secretary-General, in close cooperation with the organs and organizations of the United Nation system concerned, to ensure the necessary preparation of the meetings of the Ad Hoc Committee;

13. *Requests* the Secretary-General to submit to the General Assembly at its fifty-first session a report on the work of the Ad Hoc Committee and on the implementation of the present resolution.

General Assembly resolution 50/160 A

22 December 1995     Meeting 98     Adopted without vote

Draft by Sudan (A/50/L.40/Rev.1); agenda item 24.
*Meeting numbers.* GA 50th session: plenary 78, 79, 98.

### System-wide Special Initiative on Africa

The issue of African economic recovery and development remained a priority concern of the Administrative Committee on Coordination (ACC) in 1995. In February, the Secretary-General, as a follow up to the consideration of the subject by ACC during 1994,[15] proposed establishing a steering committee to develop further practical initiatives to maximize the support provided by the UN system to African development, and raise the priority given to African development in the international agenda. A number of UN bodies participated in the work of the Steering Committee and five working groups were formed dealing with water, food security, governance, social and human development, and resource mobilization. The result was a System-wide Special Initiative on Africa containing a set of specific development actions to be undertaken jointly by UN organizations, and a year-long campaign for political and resource mobilization.

ACC, at its second regular session of 1995 (New York, 12-13 October),[16] decided to launch the Initiative in early 1996 and extended the Steering Committee's mandate for a further year to monitor it. The Steering Committee was requested to submit a progress report to ACC at its first regular session of 1996.

### Special assistance to Djibouti

The situation of Djibouti had been adversely affected by the evolving critical situation in the Horn of Africa, the presence of tens of thousands of refugees, the extremes of local climate and cyclical droughts, torrential rains and floods, as well as the extremely limited financial capacity to implement reconstruction and development programmes, the Secretary-General said in his July report[17] on assistance for the reconstruction and development of Djibouti, submitted in response to a 1994 General Assembly request.[18]

The organizations of the UN system, including UNDP, UNHCR, UNESCO, UNICEF and WFP, dealt with the growing social and economic problem of the refugees by developing activities related to repatriation, food distribution and education, by initiating regrouping efforts to resettle refugees in camps, and by clean-up operations in the capital. The Secretary-General stated that the most feasible long-term solution to the presence of the refugees in Djibouti would require the formal political commitment of the concerned countries. In addition, there were urgent needs to support the Government's demobilization programme through budgetary support and to reconstruct damaged or destroyed social infrastructures.

**GENERAL ASSEMBLY ACTION**

On 12 December, the General Assembly adopted **resolution 50/58 F**.

#### Assistance for the reconstruction and development of Djibouti

*The General Assembly,*

*Recalling* its resolution 49/21 F of 20 December 1994 and its previous resolutions on economic assistance to Djibouti,

*Recalling also* the Paris Declaration and the Programme of Action for the Least Developed Countries for the 1990s, adopted by the Second United Nations Conference on the Least Developed Countries on 14 September 1990, as well as the mutual commitments undertaken on that occasion and the importance attached to the follow-up to that Conference,

*Distressed* by the large number of persons afflicted by the torrential rains and unprecedented flooding in Djibouti in November 1994 and by the significant damage and devastation to property and infrastructure,

*Noting* that the economic and social development efforts of Djibouti, which is included in the list of least developed countries, are constrained by the extremes of the local climate, in particular cyclical droughts and torrential rains and floods such as those which occurred in 1989 and 1994, and that the implementation of reconstruction and development programmes, as well as of the demobilization programme, requires the deployment of substantial resources which exceed the real capacity of the country,

*Noting with concern* that the situation in Djibouti has been made worse by the deteriorating situation in the Horn of Africa and in particular in Somalia, and noting the presence of over 100,000 refugees and persons displaced from their countries, which has, on the one hand, placed serious strains on the fragile economic, social and administrative infrastructure of Djibouti and, on the other, caused serious security problems in the country,

*Noting also* the difficult economic and financial situation of Djibouti resulting in part from the number of priority development projects that have had to be suspended in view of serious developments in the international situation and in part from the prolonged effects of the previous regional conflicts, notably in Somalia, which have disrupted services, transport and trade and which are draining the State of most of its revenues,

*Noting with satisfaction* the progress made by the Government of Djibouti and the International Monetary Fund on the negotiations concerning the structural adjustment programme, and convinced of the necessity to support that financial recovery programme and to take effective measures to alleviate the consequences, in particular the social consequences, of that adjustment policy, which is in the course of implementation, in order that the country may achieve appreciable economic results in the context of the programme,

*Noting with appreciation* the efforts of the United Nations Inter-Agency Assessment Mission to Djibouti organized in April 1994 and led by the United Nations Development Programme, and having considered its recommendations in the light of the new realities of the country,

*Noting with gratitude* the support provided to relief and rehabilitation operations by various countries and by intergovernmental and non-governmental organizations,

*Taking note* of the report of the Secretary-General of 26 July 1995,

1. *Declares its solidarity* with the Government and people of Djibouti in the face of the devastating consequences of the torrential rains and floods and the new economic realities of Djibouti, resulting in particular from the continuing critical situation in the Horn of Africa, especially in Somalia;

2. *Welcomes* the progress made by the Government of Djibouti and the International Monetary Fund on the negotiations concerning the structural adjustment programme, and in that context appeals to all Governments, international financial institutions, the specialized agencies of the United Nations system and non-governmental organizations to respond in an appropriate manner, as a matter of urgency, to the financial and material needs of the country;

3. *Considers* that implementation of the demobilization programme and of the national rehabilitation

plan and reinforcement of democratic institutions require appropriate assistance in the form of financial and material support;

4. *Requests* a review of the recommendations of the United Nations Inter-Agency Assessment Mission to Djibouti with a view to their implementation;

5. *Expresses its appreciation* to the Secretary-General for his efforts to make the international community aware of the difficulties faced by Djibouti;

6. *Requests* the Secretary-General to continue his efforts to mobilize the resources necessary for an effective programme of financial, technical and material assistance to Djibouti;

7. *Also requests* the Secretary-General to prepare a study of the progress made with economic assistance to Djibouti, in time for the question to be considered by the General Assembly at its fifty-first session.

General Assembly resolution 50/58 F

12 December 1995     Meeting 89     Adopted without vote

27-nation draft (A/50/L.33/Rev.1 & Rev.1/Add.1); agenda item 20 *(b)*.
*Meeting numbers.* GA 50th session: plenary 71, 89.

## Other economic assistance

### States affected by sanctions against Yugoslavia (Serbia and Montenegro)

During 1995, a number of countries continued to experience special economic problems as a result of the severance of their economic relations with the Federal Republic of Yugoslavia (Serbia and Montenegro) and especially the disruption of traditional transport and communications links in that part of Europe. In response to a 1994 General Assembly request,[19] the Secretary-General submitted in September 1995 a report[20] on economic assistance to States affected by the implementation of the Security Council resolutions imposing sanctions against the Federal Republic of Yugoslavia. The report reviewed the relevant action taken by the Council and its Sanctions Committee concerning Yugoslavia, with a view to alleviating the special economic problems of neighbouring and other States (see PART TWO, Chapter V). The report also summarized the information received from States, organizations of the UN system and regional organizations, namely the Organization for Security and Cooperation in Europe and the European Union, regarding economic assistance to the affected States.

UNDP, with a contribution of more than $5.7 million from the United States, continued to carry out a programme to ease the critical obstacles to commercial traffic around the territory of the Federal Republic. In the area of trade facilitation and foreign-investment promotion, UNCTAD was implementing an Automated System for Customs Data in Hungary, Romania and Slovakia, and assisted the Albanian Centre for Foreign Investment Promotion in financing study tours and developing a promotional brochure for foreign investment in Albania. The World Bank continued to provide assistance to the affected countries through balance-of-payments support, project financing and technical cooperation, while IMF provided policy advice, including assessment of the impact of the sanctions and the design of an appropriate policy response in the context of the countries' overall economic situations. From May 1992 to June 1995, the Fund's disbursements to the eight affected countries—Albania, Bulgaria, Hungary, Romania, Slovakia, the former Yugoslav Republic of Macedonia, Uganda and Ukraine—amounted to $2.3 billion.

The report concluded that the World Bank and IMF, as well as relevant UN bodies and organs, continued to implement substantial programmes of financial and technical assistance in the affected countries, and that those programmes had been reviewed in order to make them as responsive as possible to the particular problems of the countries concerned. Most important, however, remained the need to mobilize new and additional funds from all potential funding sources, in particular bilateral donors and the regional development banks.

**GENERAL ASSEMBLY ACTION**

On 12 December, the General Assembly adopted **resolution 50/58 E**.

**Economic assistance to States affected by the implementation of the Security Council resolutions imposing sanctions against the Federal Republic of Yugoslavia (Serbia and Montenegro)**

*The General Assembly,*

*Recalling* the provisions of Articles 25, 48, 49 and 50 of the Charter of the United Nations,

*Recalling also* Security Council resolution 843(1993) of 18 June 1993, in which the Council entrusted the Committee established pursuant to its resolution 724(1991) of 15 December 1991 with the task of examining requests by Member States for assistance under the provisions of Article 50 of the Charter, and the recommendations of the Committee in response to requests for assistance addressed to the Council by certain States confronting special economic problems arising from the implementation of Council trade and economic sanctions against the Federal Republic of Yugoslavia (Serbia and Montenegro),

*Recalling further* Security Council resolution 943(1994) of 23 September 1994, in which the Council invited the Committee established pursuant to resolution 724(1991) to adopt appropriate streamlined procedures for expediting its consideration of applications concerning legitimate humanitarian assistance,

*Expressing its appreciation* that in the last few months the Committee established pursuant to resolution 724(1991) has undertaken measures aimed at improving and accelerating the processing of applications put forward to the Committee,

*Reaffirming* its resolutions 48/210 of 21 December 1993 and 49/21 A of 2 December 1994 on economic assistance to States affected by the implementation of the Security Council resolutions imposing sanctions against the

Federal Republic of Yugoslavia (Serbia and Montenegro),

*Taking note* of the letter on behalf of the Ministers for Foreign Affairs of five States directly affected addressed to the Secretary-General[a] and in particular the proposals for taking concrete steps contained therein,

*Commending* the efforts of the international financial institutions, other international organizations and those States that responded to the appeal of the Secretary-General by taking into consideration the special economic problems arising from the implementation of the sanctions in their support programmes to the affected States,

*Commending also* the continuing attention by the intergovernmental and regional organizations, in particular the Organization for Security and Cooperation in Europe and the European Union, as well as through the Central European Initiative, to the needs of the affected States for assistance in developing regional transport and communication infrastructures,

*Taking note* of the report of the Secretary-General of 25 January 1995 entitled "Supplement to An Agenda for Peace: position paper of the Secretary-General on the occasion of the fiftieth anniversary of the United Nations",[b] in particular its chapter III.E, on the issue of United Nations sanctions,

*Taking note also* of the report of the Secretary-General of 12 September 1995 on the implementation of resolution 49/21 A and, in particular, of the conclusions and recommendations contained therein,

1. *Commends* the States bordering on the Federal Republic of Yugoslavia (Serbia and Montenegro), the other Danube riparian States and all other States for the measures they have taken to comply with Security Council resolutions 713(1991) of 25 September 1991, 757(1992) of 30 May 1992, 760(1992) of 18 June 1992, 787(1992) of 16 November 1992, 820(1993) of 17 April 1993 and 1021(1995) and 1022(1995) of 22 November 1995, and urges all States to continue to observe those resolutions strictly;

2. *Expresses concern* at the persisting special economic problems confronting States, in particular the States that border the Federal Republic of Yugoslavia (Serbia and Montenegro), the other Danube riparian States and all other States adversely affected by the severance of their economic relations with the Federal Republic of Yugoslavia (Serbia and Montenegro) and the disruption of traditional transport and communications links in that part of Europe and their long-term adverse impact on the economies of those States;

3. *Reaffirms* the urgent need of a concerted response from the international community to deal in a more effective manner with the special economic problems of the affected States in view of their magnitude and the adverse impact of the sanctions on those States;

4. *Renews its invitation* to the international financial institutions, in particular the International Monetary Fund, the International Bank for Reconstruction and Development and the European Bank for Reconstruction and Development, to continue to pay special attention to the economic problems of the affected States and their adverse social impact and to consider ways and means for mobilizing and providing resources on ap-

---

[a]A/50/189-S/1995/412.

[b]A/50/60-S/1995/1.

propriate terms for mitigating the continuing negative impact of the sanctions on the efforts of the affected States for financial stabilization as well as for development of regional transport and communications infrastructure;

5. *Renews its request* to the competent organs, programmes and specialized agencies of the United Nations system to take into consideration, in programming their development activities, the special needs of the affected States and to consider providing assistance to them from their special programme resources;

6. *Renews its appeal* to all States, on an urgent basis, to provide technical, financial and material assistance to the affected States to mitigate the adverse impact of the sanctions on their economies, *inter alia*, through the consideration of measures for the promotion of exports of the affected countries and for the promotion of investments in their economies;

7. *Encourages* the States of the region affected by the implementation of the Security Council resolutions imposing sanctions against the Federal Republic of Yugoslavia (Serbia and Montenegro) to continue, *inter alia*, to cooperate actively on a regional basis in such fields as cross-border infrastructure projects or promotion of trade, thus alleviating the adverse impact of the sanctions;

8. *Urges* the organizations and specialized agencies of the United Nations system rendering humanitarian assistance to Bosnia and Herzegovina and the Federal Republic of Yugoslavia (Serbia and Montenegro), including material and food supply for the United Nations Protection Force and other United Nations peace-keeping contingents, to take appropriate steps to broaden access for suppliers, particularly from the States affected by the implementation of the Security Council mandatory sanctions against the Federal Republic of Yugoslavia (Serbia and Montenegro);

9. *Requests* the Secretary-General to take all appropriate measures to increase the opportunity for countries affected by the sanctions to participate actively in the post-conflict reconstruction and rehabilitation of the crisis-stricken areas of former Yugoslavia after the achievement of a peaceful, lasting and just political solution of the conflict in the Balkans;

10. *Also requests* the Secretary-General to continue to seek on a regular basis information from States and regional organizations and the concerned organs and agencies of the United Nations system on action taken to alleviate the special economic problems of those States and to report thereon to the Security Council, as well as to submit to the General Assembly at its fifty-first session a report on the implementation of the present resolution.

General Assembly resolution 50/58 E

12 December 1995      Meeting 89      Adopted without vote

35-nation draft (A/50/L.32 & Add.1); agenda item 20 *(b)*.
*Meeting numbers.* GA 50th session: plenary 70-72, 89.

## Yemen

On 27 July, the Economic and Social Council adopted **resolution 1995/41**.

**Provision of assistance for the repair of war damage in the Republic of Yemen**

*The Economic and Social Council,*

*Noting* the unification of the two parts of Yemen and the formation of the Republic of Yemen in May 1990

as a unified State exercising national sovereignty over all Yemeni territory,

*Also recalling* General Assembly resolution 45/222 of 21 December 1990, Economic and Social Council resolution 1991/62 of 26 July 1991 and other resolutions concerning the provision of assistance to the Republic of Yemen,

*Appreciating* the difficulties that the Republic of Yemen is facing in its endeavours to preserve its national unity, strengthen democracy and respect for human rights and boost its economic development,

*Mindful* of the essential needs of the process of repairing the damage caused by the recent war and meeting development requirements in the Republic of Yemen,

1. *Appeals* to all Member States, all organizations and programmes of the United Nations system and all other international organizations and institutions to provide the requisite support and assistance to the Government of the Republic of Yemen to repair the war damage suffered by the economic infrastructure;

2. *Calls upon* those bodies to intensify their efforts to assist the Republic of Yemen to implement national reconstruction and development programmes;

3. *Requests* the Secretary-General to inform the Council at its substantive session of 1996 of the progress achieved in the implementation of the present resolution.

Economic and Social Council resolution 1995/41

27 July 1995      Meeting 56      Adopted without vote

9-nation draft (E/1995/L.35), orally revised following informal consultations; agenda item 5 *(a)*.
*Sponsors:* Algeria, Egypt, Lebanon, Libyan Arab Jamahiriya, Morocco, Qatar, Sudan, Syrian Arab Republic, Yemen.
*Meeting numbers.* ESC 47-49, 52, 56.

**Report of the Secretary-General.** Responding to a 1993 General Assembly request,[21] the Secretary-General reported[22] in July 1995 on assistance to Yemen. Unification, the return of Yemeni expatriates, the flow of refugees and natural disasters in recent years had led the Government of Yemen to request large-scale foreign assistance in 1993.[23] The World Bank and the Government, together with UNDP and other UN agencies, had developed a multisectoral emergency recovery programme in the amount of $245 million for road construction, education, agriculture and housing. To date, the World Bank had mobilized $60 million in credits and grants while UNDP had provided $400,000. Activities targeted to programme objectives by the UN Capital Development Fund, UNICEF, the Netherlands and others brought total funds available for the programme to $86 million.

UNDP's country programme for Yemen concentrated on strategic planning, management and human development and natural resources management. Seed money had been provided to support strategic planning for the private sector, health development and women in development. Although studies had been carried out on vocational training, environment, water and privatization, approvals and budget build-up had been slow owing to internal political conflict. WFP continued to provide food aid to 13,000 Ethiopian and

Somali refugees in Yemen. In addition, it supported development of rural community infrastructure, soil and water conservation, primary education, maternal and child health-care centres, and health-care units and hospitals. Control of diarrhoeal diseases, health education and vaccinations were provided by WHO.

*REFERENCES*

[1]YUN 1991, p. 402, GA res. 46/151, annex, part II, 18 Dec. 1991. [2]TD/B/41(2)/9. [3]YUN 1994, p. 1474. [4]A/50/15, vol. I (agreed conclusions 424(XLI)). [5]YUN 1994, p. 813. [6]DP/1995/35. [7]DP/1996/20. [8]E/1995/81. [9]E/1995/117. [10]E/1995/4. [11]A/50/490. [12]YUN 1993, p. 712, GA res. 48/214, 23 Dec. 1993. [13]A/50/520. [14]YUN 1994, p. 814, GA res. 49/142, 23 Dec. 1994. [15]Ibid., p. 817. [16]ACC/1995/23. [17]A/50/311. [18]YUN 1994, p. 818, GA res. 49/21 F, 20 Dec. 1994. [19]Ibid., p. 821, GA res. 49/21 A, 2 Dec. 1994. [20]A/50/423. [21]YUN 1993, p. 716, GA res. 48/195, 21 Dec. 1993. [22]A/50/301. [23]YUN 1993, p. 715.

# Disaster relief

In 1995, DHA coordinated the international response in support of 55 countries faced with the sudden impact of 82 natural disasters and environmental emergencies. In 28 cases, disaster-affected countries requested DHA to launch appeals for international assistance on their behalf. Contributions of $7,399,378 were channelled through DHA, while emergency grants came to $1.21 million. UN Disaster Assessment and Coordination Teams were dispatched to nine countries. Under the Disaster Management Training Programme, jointly managed since 1990 by DHA and UNDP, country workshops were held in Azerbaijan, Cuba, Eritrea, Mozambique and Papua New Guinea, and a subregional workshop was organized in Morocco for countries of the Arab Maghreb Union.

Major natural disasters during the year included earthquakes in Indonesia, Japan, the Russian Federation and Turkey; floods in the Lao People's Democratic Republic and the Democratic People's Republic of Korea; a hurricane in the Caribbean; a volcano eruption in Cape Verde; chemical accidents and environmental emergencies in Guyana, Rwanda and Seychelles; and a chemical waste dumping-site fire in Slovenia.

## International Decade for Natural Disaster Reduction

**Report of the Secretary-General (June).** In response to a 1994 General Assembly resolution,[1] the Secretary-General reported[2] in June 1995 on progress made in programme activities of the International Decade for Natural Disaster Reduction (IDNDR) (1990-2000), proclaimed by the Assembly in 1989.[3] He also discussed the International Framework of Action for IDNDR and the programme for the period 1995-2000.

The 1994 World Conference on Natural Disaster Reduction[4] had provided the impetus and exerted a strong influence on programme activity for the second half of the Decade. With renewed emphasis on practical applications at the national and local levels, the importance of regional and subregional organizations was growing. In addition, there was recognition of the interdependency between natural disaster reduction, environmental and natural resources management and sustainable development. The IDNDR secretariat placed emphasis on integrating disaster reduction into national development planning. Despite contributions in cash and kind, the Trust Fund for the Decade remained under-funded, barely able to support essential functions of the International Framework of Action for the Decade,[3] including the Special High-level Council, the Scientific and Technical Committee and the secretariat, and equally limited its capacity to support disaster-reduction projects.

The Secretary-General stated that, while the objective of the Decade and targets of the programme of the Decade remained valid, policy orientation should be shifted from promotional aspects of disaster reduction, which had been the main focus of activities before the Conference, to a much greater commitment to the practical implementation of disaster-reduction measures. He recommended an action plan composed of core activities in the areas of development of national capacities; application of knowledge and technology; information management, public information and promotion; and international collaboration. With regard to a proposed second world conference to be held not later than the year 2000, the Secretary-General suggested that it should be used to arrange continuous interdisciplinary and cross-sectoral interaction of all partners in the Decade. The IDNDR secretariat would serve as the conference secretariat.

**ECONOMIC AND SOCIAL COUNCIL ACTION**

By **decision 1995/238** of 19 July, the Economic and Social Council took note of the report of the Secretary-General and endorsed its conclusions and recommendations.

On 27 July, it adopted **resolution 1995/47 B** on the International Decade.

*The Economic and Social Council*

1. *Recognizes* that disaster reduction forms an integral part of sustainable development strategies and national development plans of vulnerable countries and communities;

2. *Also recognizes* that concerted international action is required to promote and apply disaster reduction ef-

fectively and that it must be supported by effective coordination of the day-to-day activities for which the secretariat of the International Decade for Natural Disaster Reduction is responsible;

3. *Commends* the work of the bodies comprising the International Framework of Action for the International Decade for Natural Disaster Reduction, in particular their contribution to the implementation of the Yokohama Strategy for a Safer World: Guidelines for Natural Disaster Prevention, Preparedness and Mitigation and the Plan of Action contained therein;

4. *Takes note with appreciation* of the report of the Secretary-General on the implementation of General Assembly resolution 49/22 A of 2 December 1994;

5. *Takes note in particular* of the recommendations contained in the report of the Secretary-General concerning the development of a coordinated international programme for disaster reduction, including the strengthening of the International Framework of Action for the Decade and the closing event of the Decade;

6. *Again urges* all United Nations bodies that are involved in disaster reduction activities to give priority to integrating, coordinating and strengthening their work to build the capacities of disaster-prone countries and regions in the field of disaster prevention, mitigation and preparedness, with particular consideration for the needs of the least developed countries and small island and land-locked developing States;

7. *Expresses its concern* about the continuing financial limitations with regard to effective support for the International Framework of Action for the Decade and in relation to the national, subregional, regional and international activities for the implementation of the Yokohama Strategy and the Plan of Action contained therein, as endorsed by the General Assembly in its resolution 49/22 A;

8. *Calls upon* Member States, relevant intergovernmental bodies and all others involved in the Decade to provide adequate financial resources and technical support for the activities of the Decade;

9. *Requests* the Secretary-General, therefore, to include in his report to the General Assembly at its fiftieth session an examination of options from all existing sources for an adequate funding of the core functions of the secretariat of the Decade, and to specify those functions in his report;

10. *Recommends* that the General Assembly, at its fiftieth session, consider the question of the International Decade for Natural Disaster Reduction as a separate sub-item under the item entitled ''Environment and sustainable development'';

11. *Also recommends* to the General Assembly the adoption of the draft resolution annexed to the present resolution.

### ANNEX
**International Decade for Natural Disaster Reduction**
[For text, see General Assembly resolution 50/117 A below.]

Economic and Social Council resolution 1995/47 B

27 July 1995      Meeting 56      Adopted without vote

Draft by Vice-President (E/1995/L.50), based on informal consultations on draft by Philippines, for Group of 77 and China (E/1995/L.33); agenda item 6 *(n)*.

*Meeting numbers.* ESC 42-44, 47, 56.

## Report of the Secretary-General (November).
Pursuant to the Council's request (above), the Secretary-General submitted a November report,[5] describing the core functions, staff and cost of the IDNDR secretariat. Established for the period of the Decade, the secretariat supported and coordinated the International Framework of Action for the Decade; implemented the goals of the Decade; followed up on the 1994 World Conference; and supported all aspects of promotion of the Decade's goals and objectives, and advocacy of natural disaster reduction. With additional responsibilities entrusted to the secretariat for the implementation of the Yokohama Strategy for a Safer World and the Plan of Action, both adopted at the World Conference, as well as for preparatory work for the second conference to be held at the end of the Decade, it had a larger staff than originally foreseen. All activities and secretariat costs had been financed exclusively from extra-budgetary resources made available to the Trust Fund for the Decade. Out of $8 million contributed to the Trust Fund to date, an overall expenditure of $7.1 million had been incurred, about 87 per cent of which was staff and operational costs, limiting the secretariat's efforts to undertake necessary and additional activities that had financial implications beyond the available resources.

The Secretary-General suggested several funding options to attain financial security for the secretariat: the private sector, broadening the donor base, pledging for the remaining period of the Decade until 1999, the use of the Trust Fund as a channelling mechanism for voluntary contributions, and strengthening the secondment of specialist expertise.

**GENERAL ASSEMBLY ACTION**

On 20 December, the General Assembly adopted **resolution 50/117 A**.

**International Decade for Natural Disaster Reduction**
*The General Assembly,*

*Recalling* its resolutions 44/236 of 22 December 1989, 48/188 of 21 December 1993, 49/22 A of 2 December 1994 and 49/22 B of 20 December 1994,

*Expressing its solidarity* with the people and countries that suffer as a result of natural disasters,

*Emphasizing once again* the urgent need for concrete measures to reduce the vulnerability of societies to natural hazards, the loss of human lives and the heavy physical and economic damage that occur as a result of natural disasters, in particular in developing countries, small island States and land-locked countries,

*Reiterating* the validity of the conclusions of the first World Conference on Natural Disaster Reduction, held at Yokohama, Japan, from 23 to 27 May 1994, in particular with regard to its call for increased bilateral, subregional, regional and multilateral cooperation in the field of disaster prevention, preparedness and mitigation,

*Commending* those countries, national and local institutions, organizations and associations that have adopted policies, allocated resources and initiated action programmes, including international assistance, for disaster reduction and, in this context, welcoming the participation of private companies and individuals,

*Also commending* all countries and intergovernmental and regional organizations that have actively engaged in regional and subregional assessments of vulnerability to natural hazards and have consequently initiated regional and subregional cooperation in the field of disaster reduction, including the exchange of data and technology, as well as the development of joint administrative, technological and scientific approaches for applied disaster reduction,

*Further commending* those organizations of the United Nations system and other international organizations, scientific associations and non-governmental organizations which, in accordance with decisions of their governing bodies, have incorporated the recommendations of the General Assembly relating to disaster reduction and those of the World Conference on Natural Disaster Reduction in their programmes of work, thus contributing towards effective progress in disaster reduction in their mandated responsibilities and respective fields of activity, including the allocation of budgetary resources for disaster reduction,

1. *Takes note with appreciation* of the report of the Secretary-General concerning the specific measures for the implementation of the Yokohama Strategy for a Safer World: Guidelines for Natural Disaster Prevention, Preparedness and Mitigation and its Plan of Action, and requests the secretariat of the International Decade for Natural Disaster Reduction to continue to promote and monitor their translation into concrete activities, in close cooperation with all bodies comprising the International Framework of Action for the Decade, so as to ensure timely and effective implementation;

2. *Commends* those developing and least developed countries that have mobilized domestic resources for disaster reduction activities and have facilitated the effective implementation of such activities, and encourages all developing countries concerned to continue in this direction;

3. *Recommends* that all countries, with appropriate support, continue to study conventional and non-conventional ways and means of financing disaster reduction measures, both at the national level and with respect to subregional, regional and international technical cooperation;

4. *Calls upon* Member States, relevant intergovernmental bodies and all others involved in the Decade to participate actively in the financial and technical support of Decade activities, in order to ensure the implementation of the International Framework of Action for the Decade, in particular with a view to translating the Yokohama Strategy and the Plan of Action contained therein into concrete disaster reduction programmes and activities;

5. *Requests* the Commission on Sustainable Development to pay appropriate attention at its fourth session to the issue of disaster reduction when considering the relevant chapters of Agenda 21 and of the Programme of Action for the Sustainable Development of Small Island Developing States;

6. *Welcomes* the measures proposed by the Secretary-General to bring the International Framework of Action for the Decade into line with the Yokohama Strategy and its Plan of Action, in order to provide disaster reduc-

tion activities worldwide and regionally with authoritative and effective programme guidance so as to ensure stronger cohesion of disaster reduction programmes and the joint participation of concerned sectors in their implementation;

7. *Notes* the initiative for an informal mechanism between the secretariat of the Decade and Member States, intended to facilitate and support the promotion of Decade activities and the regular exchange of information between Governments, organizations of the United Nations system and other organizations;

8. *Welcomes*, in pursuance of its resolution 49/22 A, the restructuring of the Special High-Level Council and the Scientific and Technical Committee for the Decade so that for the second half of the Decade they will provide the necessary support to global, regional and national policy and strategy development, public awareness-building and resource mobilization, and at the same time provide links with the scientific community and support the national committees for the Decade and national authorities in their cooperative efforts to integrate disaster reduction programmes into national activities for sustainable development;

9. *Endorses* the decision of the Secretary-General to extend until the end of the Decade the mandate of the United Nations Steering Committee for the Decade, established in pursuance of General Assembly resolutions 42/169 of 11 December 1987 and 44/236;

10. *Emphasizes* that effective and efficient coordination and servicing of the above-mentioned components of the International Framework of Action for the Decade require a financially and structurally stable secretariat of the Decade, reporting to the Secretary-General through the Emergency Relief Coordinator;

11. *Decides*, in pursuance of its resolution 49/22 A, to convene a closing event of the Decade, through coordinated sectoral and cross-sectoral meetings at all levels, in order to facilitate the full integration of disaster reduction into the substantive efforts for sustainable development and environmental protection by the year 2000;

12. *Decides also* that the secretariat of the Decade will serve as the substantive secretariat for the preparation of the closing event of the Decade, working with the full support of relevant bodies of the United Nations Secretariat and drawing on the contributions of the organizations of the United Nations system concerned, other international organizations and Governments;

13. *Requests* the Secretary-General to ensure the availability of resources for the preparatory process, including the necessary enhancement of the capacity of the secretariat, and to appeal for additional voluntary contributions to the Trust Fund for the Decade;

14. *Also requests* the Secretary-General to submit to the General Assembly at its fifty-first session, through the Economic and Social Council, a report on the implementation of the International Framework of Action for the Decade;

15. *Further requests* the Secretary-General to submit to the General Assembly at its fifty-first session a report containing proposals on how the distinct programme and coordination capability of the secretariat of the Decade might be enhanced so as to enable it to coordinate effectively the activities of the Decade and the integration of natural disaster reduction into the sustainable development process;

16. *Decides* to consider the question of the International Decade for Natural Disaster Reduction at its fifty-first session, as a separate sub-item under environmental questions related to the environment and sustainable development.

General Assembly resolution 50/117 A

20 December 1995     Meeting 96     Adopted without vote

Approved by Second Committee (A/50/618/Add.5) without vote, 5 December (meeting 41); draft recommended by ESC in res. 1995/47 B (A/C.2/50/L.5); agenda item 96 *(f)*.
*Meeting numbers.* GA 50th session: 2nd Committee 39, 41; plenary 96.

By **decision 50/435**, also of 20 December, the Assembly took note of the Secretary-General's November report.

### Early-warning capacities of the UN system

On 27 July, the Economic and Social Council adopted **resolution 1995/47 A** on the International Decade.

*The Economic and Social Council*
1. *Recognizes* the importance of reliable and hazard-resistant telecommunications for natural disaster reduction, in particular in support of early warning at the community, national, regional and international levels;
2. *Invites* the Secretary-General, in pursuance of General Assembly resolution 49/22 B of 20 December 1994, to include, in his report to the Assembly at its fiftieth session on the early-warning capacities of the United Nations system with regard to natural disasters, proposals for further improvements in the field of disaster-related telecommunications;
3. *Invites* the Secretary-General to ensure, in pursuance of resolution 36 of the Plenipotentiary Conference of the International Telecommunication Union, held at Kyoto, Japan, in 1994, close cooperation between the International Framework of Action for the International Decade for Natural Disaster Reduction, the Department of Humanitarian Affairs of the Secretariat and the International Telecommunication Union.

Economic and Social Council resolution 1995/47 A

27 July 1995     Meeting 56     Adopted without vote

34-nation draft (E/1995/L.38); agenda item 6 *(n)*.
*Meeting numbers.* ESC 42-44, 49, 56.

**Report of the Secretary-General.** Pursuant to a 1994 General Assembly request[6] and the Economic and Social Council's 1995 request (above), the Secretary-General reported[7] in October on early-warning capacities of the UN system with regard to natural disasters. He reviewed the current early-warning activities of UN organizations and proposed improvements and ways in which they might be coordinated more effectively. Consideration was given to the roles of technology and telecommunications in the warning process.

Numerous activities had been under way within the UN system, contributing to different aspects of the early-warning process, such as for meteorological and hydrological hazards (hurricane, cyclone), geophysical hazards (earthquake, volcanic activity, tsunami), environmental hazards

(drought) and technological hazards (industrial accidents). However, a review of early-warning activities of UN organizations revealed gaps and requirements for future improvements in effectiveness and coordination of early warning. The Secretary-General proposed that an informal mechanism be established to develop international doctrine and operational standards for better coordinated global early-warning analysis, forecasting and dissemination. He encouraged Governments to assess how adequately existing international, regional and national warning systems addressed their own needs to provide ready access to warnings for all citizens, and to designate a national body as the focus for the coordination of early warnings based on an all-hazards approach.

**GENERAL ASSEMBLY ACTION**

On 20 December, the General Assembly adopted **resolution 50/117 B** on the International Decade.

*The General Assembly,*
*Reaffirming* its resolutions 44/236 of 22 December 1989, 46/182 of 19 December 1991, 49/22 A of 2 December 1994 and 49/22 B of 20 December 1994,
*Taking note* of Economic and Social Council resolutions 1995/47 A and B of 27 July 1995,
*Concerned* about the continued threat posed by natural disasters and similar disasters with an adverse impact on vulnerable communities, including their environments, particularly in developing countries,
*Concerned also* about the continuing threat posed by natural disasters and similar disasters with an adverse impact on the environment,
*Recalling* the Yokohama Strategy for a Safer World: Guidelines for Natural Disaster Prevention, Preparedness, and Mitigation and its Plan of Action, adopted by the World Conference on Natural Disaster Reduction on 27 May 1994,
*Taking into account* already existing early-warning capacities within the United Nations system, in particular within the Department of Humanitarian Affairs of the Secretariat, the United Nations Environment Programme, the World Meteorological Organization, the World Health Organization and the Food and Agriculture Organization of the United Nations,
*Conscious* of the need to avoid duplication of work among United Nations bodies dealing with early-warning capacities,
*Emphasizing* that early warnings of impending natural disasters and similar disasters with an adverse impact on the environment, linked to effective disaster preparedness measures and their effective dissemination, using, in particular, telecommunications, including broadcast services, are key factors to successful disaster prevention and preparedness,
*Reaffirming* that sustained economic growth and sustainable development are essential for the prevention of and preparedness for natural disasters and similar disasters with an adverse impact on the environment and that special attention should be given to disaster preven-

tion and preparedness by the Governments concerned as well as by the international community,

1. *Takes note* of the report of the Secretary-General on early-warning capacities of the United Nations system with regard to natural disasters and similar disasters with an adverse impact on the environment;

2. *Commends* the secretariat of the International Decade for Natural Disaster Reduction, as part of the Department of Humanitarian Affairs of the United Nations Secretariat, and all concerned agencies and organizations of the United Nations system for the constructive inter-agency approach they have applied, which has led to this initial overview and analysis of early-warning concepts, capacities and gaps and to proposals for improvements in coordination and capacity-building with regard to such disasters;

3. *Requests* the Scientific and Technical Committee of the Decade to continue, within the scope of its work on early-warning capabilities, to examine and study new scientific and experimental concepts and methodologies for accurate and timely short-term forecasting of earthquakes, other natural disasters and similar disasters with an adverse impact on the environment, with a view to making recommendations on their applicability and development in the context of international cooperation to improve preparedness for and minimize the risks of such disasters;

4. *Takes note* of the conclusions and proposals made by the Secretary-General in his report with respect to the improvement of early-warning capabilities, better international coordination in their use, and more effective and beneficial exchange of knowledge and technology;

5. *Invites* the Secretary-General, in particular, to facilitate, within the existing International Framework of Action for the International Decade for Natural Disaster Reduction, an internationally concerted framework for improvements in early-warning capacities by developing a concrete proposal for an effective international mechanism on early warning, to include the transfer of technologies related to early warning to developing countries, under the auspices of the United Nations and as part of the implementation of the International Framework, the Yokohama Strategy for a Safer World and its Plan of Action;

6. *Also invites* the Secretary-General to take the steps necessary to make the early-warning data gathered under the United Nations auspices readily available to the decision makers concerned at the international, national, regional and subregional levels;

7. *Encourages* all Governments to undertake, with the full support of the United Nations system, regular reviews of early-warning requirements and capabilities at national and community levels, within the framework of the development of national disaster reduction policies in order to enhance protection of their national populations and assets;

8. *Calls on* the secretariat of the Decade to continue to facilitate a concerted international approach to improvements in early-warning capacities for natural disasters and similar disasters with an adverse impact on the environment, within the process leading towards the closing event of the Decade;

9. *Recommends* that donor countries give greater priority to disaster prevention, preparedness and mitigation in their assistance programmes and budgets, on either a bilateral or multilateral basis, including through increasing contributions to the Trust Fund for the Decade, and promote and facilitate the transfer of technologies related to early warning to developing countries within the framework of the implementation of the Yokohama Strategy and its Plan of Action;

10. *Encourages* improved efforts, in the context of international technical assistance and cooperation within the framework of the implementation of the Yokohama Strategy and its Plan of Action, towards facilitating the availability of appropriate technology and reliable data, along with the corresponding training, and access to network systems related to early warning, particularly to developing countries;

11. *Requests* the Secretary-General to report to the General Assembly at its fifty-second session on progress made in the implementation of the present resolution.

General Assembly resolution 50/117 B

20 December 1995      Meeting 96      Adopted without vote

Approved by Second Committee (A/50/618/Add.5) without vote, 8 December (meeting 42); draft by Vice-Chairman (A/C.2/50/L.71), orally revised and based on informal consultations on 25-nation draft (A/C.2/50/L.35); agenda item 96 *(f)*.

*Meeting numbers.* GA 50th session: 2nd Committee 39, 42; plenary 96.

## Drought-stricken areas

### Sudano-Sahelian region

Pursuant to a 1995 decision of the Executive Board of UNDP/UNFPA,[8] the United Nations Sudano-Sahelian Office (UNSO), the central entity within UNDP in the area of desertification control and drought preparedness, was renamed the Office to Combat Desertification and Drought, while keeping its acronym. The Economic and Social Council, by **decision 1995/232** of 13 July, took note of the change of name.

In his annual report covering 1995,[9] the UNDP Administrator stated that UNSO supported 43 affected countries (24 in Africa and 19 in Asia and Latin America) in preparing for implementation of the 1994 International Convention to Combat Desertification in Countries Experiencing Serious Drought and/or Desertification, particularly in Africa.[10] UNSO provided catalytic funding and training and capacity-building. It also provided technical advice for: the national and subregional action programme processes, development of guidelines and tools for operationalizing the Convention, awareness-raising, building partnerships and resource mobilization. African Governments were assisted in strengthening the capacity of country offices and national focal points to build genuine partnership arrangements and national compacts as required by the Convention. UNSO provided technical and catalytic support to Cape Verde, where the first national forum since the adoption of the Convention was held in November 1995. In Argentina, UNSO supported the preparation and realization of the first national conference on desertification.

UNSO made $625,000 available to the Permanent Inter-State Committee on Drought Control in the Sahel, the Intergovernmental Authority for Drought and Development, the Arab Maghreb Union and the Southern African Development Community for joint conceptualization and initiation of the subregional action programme. UNSO played a leading role in promoting and defining the concept of national desertification funds, which were viewed as a key tool for mobilizing and channelling resources to the local level. Its awareness-raising activities included catalytic support to 47 countries for the first World Day to Combat Desertification (17 June).

In April, UNDP and the United Nations Environment Programme signed an agreement forming a partnership to combat desertification, under which the two organizations were to develop joint programme packages in areas of complementary expertise, broaden their geographic scope to cover all affected countries and mobilize the necessary resources.

## Hurricanes and cyclones

### The Caribbean region

On 4, 5 and 6 September, Hurricane Luis hit a group of small island States and a territory of the eastern Caribbean, namely Antigua and Barbuda, Dominica, Montserrat and Saint Kitts and Nevis and Sint Maarten. It caused damage of more than $1 billion to businesses, homes, schools, churches and government buildings, and destroyed electricity and telephone systems. At the request of Antigua and Barbuda, DHA issued an international appeal, to which the international community responded by contributing $17.8 million as at 24 October.

**UNDP action.** On 15 September,[11] the Executive Board of UNDP/UNFPA, acknowledging the fragile ecosystems of small island countries and their particular vulnerability to natural disasters, requested the Administrator to continue to support the effective coordination of response measures and contribute to the mobilization of resources for the response effort.

GENERAL ASSEMBLY ACTION

On 18 September, the General Assembly adopted **resolution 49/21 P**.

**Emergency Assistance to Antigua and Barbuda, Dominica, Montserrat, Saint Kitts and Nevis and Sint Maarten (Netherlands Antilles)**

*The General Assembly*,

*Recalling* its resolutions 42/169 of 11 December 1987, 43/202 of 20 December 1988, 44/236 of 22 December 1989, 45/185 of 21 December 1990, 46/149 of 18 December 1991, 46/182 of 19 December 1991, 48/188 of 21 December 1993 and 49/22 A of 2 December 1994,

*Deeply distressed* by the large number of afflicted persons and the destruction wrought by Hurricane Luis, which on 4 and 5 September 1995 devastated Antigua and Barbuda, Dominica, Montserrat, Saint Kitts and Nevis, and Sint Maarten (Netherlands Antilles),

*Conscious* of the efforts of the Governments and peoples of Antigua and Barbuda, Dominica, Montserrat and Saint Kitts and Nevis and the people of Sint Maarten (Netherlands Antilles) to save lives and alleviate the sufferings of the victims of Hurricane Luis,

*Noting* the enormous effort that will be required to alleviate the grave situation caused by this natural disaster,

*Conscious* of the prompt response being made by Governments, the bodies and agencies of the United Nations system, international and regional agencies, non-governmental organizations and private individuals to provide relief,

*Recognizing* that the magnitude of the disaster and its medium-term and long-term effects will require, as a complement to the efforts being made by the Governments and peoples of Antigua and Barbuda, Dominica, Montserrat and Saint Kitts and Nevis and the people of Sint Maarten (Netherlands Antilles), a demonstration of international solidarity and humanitarian concern to ensure broad multilateral cooperation in order to meet the immediate emergency situation in the affected areas and to initiate the process of reconstruction,

1. *Expresses its solidarity and support* to the Governments and peoples of Antigua and Barbuda, Dominica, Montserrat and Saint Kitts and Nevis and the people of Sint Maarten (Netherlands Antilles);

2. *Expresses its appreciation* to all States of the international community, international agencies and non-governmental organizations that are providing emergency relief to the affected countries;

3. *Urges* all States of the international community, as a matter of urgency, to contribute generously to the relief, rehabilitation and reconstruction efforts in the affected countries;

4. *Requests* the Secretary-General, in collaboration with the international financial institutions and bodies and agencies of the United Nations system, to assist the Governments of Antigua and Barbuda, Dominica, Montserrat and Saint Kitts and Nevis and the people of Sint Maarten (Netherlands Antilles) in identifying their medium-term and long-term needs and in mobilizing resources, as well as to help with the task of reconstruction of the affected countries undertaken by their respective Governments;

5. *Also requests* the Secretary-General to submit to the General Assembly at its fiftieth session a report on the collaborative effort referred to in paragraph 4 above and on progress made with the relief, rehabilitation and reconstruction efforts in the affected countries.

General Assembly resolution 49/21 P

18 September 1995     Meeting 108     Adopted without vote

46-nation draft (A/49/L.70 & Add.1 & Add.1/Corr.1), orally revised; agenda item 37 *(b)*.

### Madagascar

Pursuant to a 1994 Economic and Social Council request,[12] the Secretary-General submitted in July 1995 a report[13] summarizing measures taken following the cyclones and floods in Madagascar in 1994.

A network of regional disaster relief centres created under a joint DHA/UNDP project from 1987 to 1993, and staff training and stockpiling of relief materials for emergency operations undertaken by DHA turned out to be very viable, the Secretary-General reported. In addition, the centres were given responsibility for monitoring food situations and carrying out food relief operations. A national fund, established to meet the costs relating to rehabilitation and reconstruction activities remained modest, while a national highways fund, solely for the reconstruction of highway infrastructure damaged by natural disasters, had 1.3 million Malagasy francs set aside for 1995. A programme for the regular maintenance of the highway infrastructure had been implemented. The World Bank supported a government project that addressed the conservation, development and restoration of cultivated areas. Other areas of support included disaster-monitoring, early warning and a statistical information system to monitor the availability of rice, the staple food of Madagascar.

The Secretary-General concluded that, in spite of all those efforts, Madagascar remained vulnerable to the impact of natural disasters. The main factor was lack of resources, which had also constrained adequate reconstruction and rehabilitation of the cyclone- and flood-affected areas. Resource limitations had also affected the development of effective coordination and management of relief and reconstruction activities.

**ECONOMIC AND SOCIAL COUNCIL ACTION**

On 27 July, the Economic and Social Council adopted **resolution 1995/43**.

**Assistance for the reconstruction of Madagascar following the natural disasters of 1994**
*The Economic and Social Council,*
*Recalling* General Assembly resolution 48/234 of 14 February 1994 on emergency assistance to Madagascar and Economic and Social Council resolution 1994/36 of 29 July 1994 concerning the measures to be taken following the cyclones and floods that had affected Madagascar,
*Having considered* the report of the Secretary-General on the implementation of resolution 1994/36,
*Noting with concern* that, despite the efforts made by the Government of Madagascar and by the international community, in particular the organizations of the United Nations system, the resources mobilized are inadequate and that Madagascar remains vulnerable to the impact of natural disasters,
*Bearing in mind* the fact that, apart from the immediate damage, such repeated climatic phenomena have residual effects which weaken the country's economic base, hold up its economic and social progress, and frustrate its development policy,
*Considering* that the country's sustainable development requires a capacity to overcome the after-effects of nat-

ural disasters and that disaster aid and relief should accordingly include a long-term dimension,
1. *Urges* all States to continue and intensify their participation in the implementation of the programmes for the recovery and reconstruction of the areas and sectors affected by the cyclones and floods;
2. *Requests* international and regional organizations, the specialized agencies, financial institutions and voluntary institutions to support, within the framework of their respective programmes, the requests for assistance formulated by the Government of Madagascar during the recovery and reconstruction phase;
3. *Invites* international cooperation to take into account, in the objectives of its assistance operations, the need to reduce the country's vulnerability to natural disasters and to safeguard its development process;
4. *Requests* the Secretary-General to take the necessary measures to help the Government of Madagascar to mobilize the resources needed to overcome the effects of the natural disasters and neutralize their repercussions on the development process;
5. *Also requests* the Secretary-General to inform the Council at its substantive session of 1996 of the progress made in the implementation of the present resolution.

Economic and Social Council resolution 1995/43

27 July 1995    Meeting 56    Adopted without vote

9-nation draft (E/1995/L.48), orally revised following informal consultations; agenda item 5 (a).
*Sponsors:* Cameroon, Côte d'Ivoire, Gabon, India, Lebanon, Madagascar, Mauritius, Senegal, Uganda.
*Meeting numbers.* ESC 47-49, 53, 56.

**GENERAL ASSEMBLY ACTION**

On 20 December, the General Assembly adopted **resolution 50/58 I**.

**Assistance for the reconstruction of Madagascar following the natural disasters of 1994**
*The General Assembly,*
*Recalling* its resolution 48/234 of 14 February 1994,
*Recalling also* Economic and Social Council resolutions 1994/36 of 29 July 1994 and 1995/43 of 27 July 1995,
*Having considered* the report of the Secretary-General of 14 July 1995 relating to the implementation of resolution 48/234 and in particular the conclusions reached therein,
*Noting with concern* that, despite the efforts made by the Government of Madagascar and by the international community, in particular the organizations of the United Nations system, the resources mobilized are still inadequate, and that Madagascar remains vulnerable to the impact of natural disasters,
*Noting* that the implementation of the programmes for disaster prevention and for the reconstruction and rehabilitation of the areas affected by natural disasters requires the mobilization of substantial resources that are beyond the country's real means,
*Noting also* that each country has responsibility for natural disaster prevention and that reconstruction and rehabilitation efforts will be enhanced by continuing national development efforts,
*Considering* that Madagascar's sustainable development requires a long-term capacity to prepare for and prevent disasters and to overcome the residual effects of these repeated climatic phenomena, and recognizing that the assistance provided should take this into account,

1. *Expresses its appreciation* to the Secretary-General and the international community, the Department of Humanitarian Affairs of the Secretariat and the United Nations Development Programme for the efforts they have made to supplement the action of the Government of Madagascar in the implementation of programmes for disaster prevention and for the reconstruction and rehabilitation of the areas and sectors affected by natural disasters;

2. *Urges* all States and governmental and non-governmental organizations, together with United Nations organizations, programmes and specialized agencies, in particular the international financial institutions, to increase their support to the Government of Madagascar with a view to preventing disasters and mitigating their effects on Madagascar's development process;

3. *Requests* the Secretary-General to continue his efforts to mobilize the necessary resources to assist the Government of Madagascar in the reconstruction of Madagascar;

4. *Also requests* the Secretary-General to report to the General Assembly at its fifty-second session on the progress made in the implementation of the present resolution.

General Assembly resolution 50/58 I

20 December 1995     Meeting 96     Adopted without vote

10-nation draft (A/50/L.56/Rev.1 & Rev.1/Add.1); agenda item 20 *(b)*.
*Sponsors:* Burkina Faso, Congo, Cuba, France, Gabon, India, Madagascar, Mauritius, Mongolia, South Africa.

## Chernobyl aftermath

**Communications.** In a letter of 8 June,[14] the President of Ukraine informed the Secretary-General that Ukraine had decided to close down the Chernobyl nuclear plant before the year 2000 but would require relevant technical, technological and financial assistance from the seven major industrialized Powers, the European Union, international organizations and the financial institutions. On 9 October,[15] Ukraine further communicated that it deemed it extremely important that a thorough and in-depth study be undertaken on the consequences of the Chernobyl accident. To that end, Ukraine proposed the establishment of an International Scientific and Technological Centre for Nuclear and Radiological Accidents and solicited suggestions regarding the orientation of scientific research, the organization of work and the participation of representatives of foreign States in its activities.

**Report of the Secretary-General.** Pursuant to a 1993 General Assembly request,[16] the Secretary-General submitted a September 1995 report,[17] in which he described the extent of the humanitarian disaster facing the three most affected countries—Belarus, the Russian Federation and Ukraine—and the broader social and economic context in which the protracted humanitarian crisis had, and was continuing to be, played out. He also summarized the international response to date in eliminating the consequences of the Chernobyl accident.

While at least 400,000 people had chosen or been forced to leave their homes because of radioactive contamination, health risks continued to affect a great number of people. Thyroid cancers, immunological deficiencies, anaemia, neurocirculatory problems and respiratory ailments had shown an increase and, according to WHO, morbidity and mortality rates among Chernobyl recovery workers were growing. While the shrinkage of the absolute size of GDP continued in all three affected countries, they had been forced to dedicate enormous portions of their budgets to addressing Chernobyl's consequences. Huge tracts of formerly productive agricultural and forest land had been rendered uninhabitable and unusable for generations.

The response of the international community had been particularly inconsistent with a large imbalance between research activities and financial and material assistance offered to the three countries. The UN Trust Fund for Chernobyl became virtually empty, exhausting funds raised at the 1991 pledging conference,[18] and WHO lacked funds to extend its International Programme on the Health Effects of the Chernobyl Accident beyond the pilot phase. At a meeting of the Expanded Quadripartite Committee for Coordination on Chernobyl (New York, 29 November), convened by the UN Coordinator of International Cooperation on Chernobyl, it was agreed that the tenth (1996) anniversary of the accident was to be used both to bring worldwide attention back to Chernobyl and to mark a change in the international approach to Chernobyl's problems; the focus had to be shifted from humanitarian to redevelopment assistance.

Expressing concern about the lack of resources, the Secretary-General said that Chernobyl was still a major humanitarian tragedy and the magnitude of its effects would continue to grow over the next 10 years. He stressed that a limited but effective range of practical, health-related projects should receive first priority, while economic projects should focus on creating a full legal framework for foreign investment.

GENERAL ASSEMBLY ACTION

On 20 December, the General Assembly adopted **resolution 50/134**.

**Strengthening of international cooperation and coordination of efforts to study, mitigate and minimize the consequences of the Chernobyl disaster**

*The General Assembly,*

*Reaffirming* its resolutions 45/190 of 21 December 1990, 46/150 of 18 December 1991, 47/165 of 18 December 1992 and 48/206 of 21 December 1993,

*Recalling* Economic and Social Council resolutions 1990/50 of 13 July 1990, 1991/51 of 26 July 1991 and

1992/38 of 30 July 1992 and Council decision 1993/232 of 22 July 1993,

*Taking note* of the decisions adopted by the organs, organizations and programmes of the United Nations system in the implementation of General Assembly resolutions 45/190, 46/150, 47/165 and 48/206,

*Noting with appreciation* the contribution made by Member States and by organizations of the United Nations system to the development of cooperation to mitigate and minimize the consequences of the Chernobyl disaster, and the activities of regional and other organizations, in particular the Commission of the European Communities, as well as bilateral activities and those of non-governmental organizations,

*Welcoming* the commitments made by Member States in the Declaration on the Occasion of the Fiftieth Anniversary of the United Nations, adopted on 24 October 1995, to intensify cooperation on natural disaster reduction and major technological and man-made disasters, disaster relief, post-disaster rehabilitation and humanitarian assistance in order to enhance the capabilities of affected countries to cope with such situations,

*Conscious* of the forthcoming tenth anniversary of the disaster at the Chernobyl nuclear power plant, which became the largest technological catastrophe in terms of its scope and created humanitarian, environmental, social, economic and health consequences and problems of common concern, requiring for their solution wide and active international cooperation and coordination of efforts in this field at the international and national levels,

*Expressing profound concern* about the ongoing effects on the lives and health of people, particularly children, in the affected areas of Belarus, the Russian Federation and Ukraine, as well as in other countries most affected by the Chernobyl disaster,

*Noting* the readiness of Ukraine in principle to close the Chernobyl nuclear power plant by the year 2000, bearing in mind the need for adequate support from relevant countries and international organizations for that purpose,

*Taking note* of the report of the Secretary-General of 8 September 1995 on the implementation of resolution 48/206,

1. *Requests* the Secretary-General to continue his efforts in the implementation of General Assembly resolutions 45/190, 46/150, 47/165 and 48/206 and, through existing coordination mechanisms, in particular the United Nations Coordinator of International Cooperation on Chernobyl, to continue to maintain close cooperation with the agencies of the United Nations system, as well as with regional and other relevant organi-

zations, with a view to encouraging the regular exchange of information, cooperation and coordination of multilateral and bilateral efforts in those areas, while implementing programmes and specific projects, *inter alia*, in the framework of relevant agreements and arrangements;

2. *Invites* Member States, in particular donor States, relevant multilateral financial institutions and other concerned parties of the international community, including non-governmental organizations, to provide support to the ongoing efforts made by Belarus, the Russian Federation and Ukraine to cope with the consequences of the Chernobyl disaster, and requests the Secretary-General to appeal to Member States to continue and intensify that assistance;

3. *Notes* the establishment in Ukraine of an International Scientific and Technological Centre for Nuclear and Radiological Accidents as an important step towards enhancing the capabilities of the international community to study, mitigate and minimize the consequences of such accidents, and invites all interested parties to take part in its activities;

4. *Declares* 26 April 1996 International Day Commemorating the Tenth Anniversary of the Chernobyl Nuclear Power Plant Accident, and invites Member States to conduct appropriate activities to commemorate this tragic event and to enhance public awareness of the consequences of such disasters for human health and the environment throughout the world;

5. *Requests* the Secretary-General to submit to the General Assembly at its fifty-second session, under a separate sub-item, a report on the implementation of the present resolution.

General Assembly resolution 50/134

20 December 1995     Meeting 96     Adopted without vote

6-nation draft (A/50/L.26/Rev.1 & Rev.1/Add.1); agenda item 20 *(c)*.
*Sponsors:* Belarus, Japan, Kazakstan, Kyrgyzstan, Russian Federation, Ukraine.
*Meeting numbers.* GA 50th session: plenary 70-72, 96.

*REFERENCES*

[1]YUN 1994, p. 852, GA res. 49/22 A, 2 Dec. 1994. [2]A/50/201-E/1995/74. [3]GA res. 44/236, 22 Dec. 1989. [4]YUN 1994, p. 851. [5]A/50/521. [6]YUN 1994, p. 853, GA res. 49/22 B, 20 Dec. 1994. [7]A/50/526. [8]E/1995/34/Rev.1 (dec. 95/6). [9]DP/1996/18/Add.1. [10]YUN 1994, p. 944. [11]E/1995/34/Rev.1 (dec. 95/33). [12]YUN 1994, p. 855, ESC res. 1994/36, 29 July 1994. [13]A/50/292-E/1995/115. [14]A/50/265. [15]A/50/546. [16]YUN 1993, p. 747, GA res. 48/206, 21 Dec. 1993. [17]A/50/418. [18]YUN 1991, p. 419.

Chapter IV

# International trade, finance and transport

In keeping with the recent trend, international trade again exceeded world output in 1994, rising in volume by close to 9 per cent, mainly due to expansion of trade in manufactures. The prices of many non-oil commodities rose sharply during the year, partly because of an upsurge in demand but also because of speculative trading and a declining dollar. The United States and Western Europe received a strong impetus from exports, especially to the developing countries in East and South-East Asia and Latin America. Although Africa showed a slight improvement in terms of trade, long-term development performance remained depressed by commodity dependence, poor infrastructure, over-indebtedness, low levels of domestic investment and caution by foreign investors, as well as by political instability and conflicts.

Preparations for the ninth session of the United Nations Conference on Trade and Development (UNCTAD IX), to be held in 1996, began with the approval in March 1995 by the UNCTAD Trade and Development Board (TDB) of a development-oriented provisional agenda. Following an offer from South Africa, received during TDB's September session, the General Assembly in December decided to convene UNCTAD IX in Midrand, Gauteng Province. The Conference was to have the unifying theme: "Promoting growth and sustainable development in a globalizing and liberalizing world economy".

Following consideration of international trade and development issues in December, the Assembly invited UNCTAD to follow developments in the international trading system, particularly their implications for developing countries, and to identify new trading opportunities arising from the implementation of the 1994 Uruguay Round agreements.

Questions of trade, environment and sustainable development were discussed by the Commission on Sustainable Development and by UNCTAD's Ad Hoc Working Group on Trade, Environment and Development, which completed its work in 1995. The Assembly invited UNCTAD and the UN Environment Programme to continue their joint programme on trade and environment issues.

The Third UN Conference to Review All Aspects of the Set of Multilaterally Agreed Equitable Principles and Rules for the Control of Restrictive Business Practices took place in November.

The Conference requested the UNCTAD secretariat to revise periodically the commentary to the model law on restrictive business practices and to disseminate widely the model law and its commentary. In the area of commodities, the International Natural Rubber Agreement, 1995, was adopted in February and opened for signature in April.

The debt of low-income and some middle-income countries continued to cause concern during 1995. The Assembly in December called on the international community to implement the commitments of the major UN conferences and summits on development, organized since the beginning of the 1990s, addressing the question of external debt.

The newly named Commission on International Investment and Transnational Corporations met in April to discuss trends in foreign direct investment (FDI) and related issues. It recognized the role of investment for development, especially for Africa, and supported international activities to increase FDI flows.

With regard to transport, the Economic and Social Council, having reviewed the work of the Committee of Experts on the Transport of Dangerous Goods, requested the Committee to elaborate proposals for globally harmonized criteria for the classification of flammable, explosive and reactive materials.

## Preparations for UNCTAD IX

As requested by TDB in 1994,[1] the Officer-in-Charge of UNCTAD carried out informal, open-ended consultations on the provisional agenda for the ninth session of UNCTAD, to be held in 1996. At the second part of its forty-first session (Geneva, 20-31 March 1995),[2] TDB approved the provisional agenda and agreed annotations for UNCTAD IX, requested the Officer-in-Charge to complete the provisional agenda with the customary procedural and administrative items and annexed to its report a background note on the agenda, prepared by the secretariat. On 31 March, TDB noted the Final Communiqué of the Eighteenth Meeting of the Chairmen and Coordinators of the Group of 77 (developing countries) Chapters (Geneva, 14-15 March)[3] and annexed it to its report.

At its tenth executive session on 4 May, TDB agreed[4] that exploratory work should be undertaken on new and emerging issues on the international trade agenda within the preparatory process of UNCTAD IX, in accordance with the provisional agenda and agreed annotations for the Conference. The UNCTAD secretariat was encouraged to take into account relevant work being done in other forums.

On 18 September, during the first part of TDB's forty-second session (Geneva, 11-20 September), a teleconference was held between Addis Ababa (Ethiopia), Geneva, Johannesburg (South Africa) and New York, in the course of which the Premier of Gauteng Province announced South Africa's offer to host UNCTAD IX in Midrand from 27 April to 11 May 1996.

Also on 18 September, TDB agreed[5] that UNCTAD IX should take place in Midrand from 27 April to 11 May 1996, preceded by a one-day senior officials' meeting, and recommended the location and dates to the General Assembly. The UNCTAD Secretary-General was asked to make the necessary arrangements for the Conference.

**GENERAL ASSEMBLY ACTION**

On 20 December, the General Assembly adopted **resolution 50/98**.

### Ninth session of the United Nations Conference on Trade and Development

*The General Assembly,*

*Recalling* its resolution 1995(XIX) of 30 December 1964, as amended, on the establishment of the United Nations Conference on Trade and Development as an organ of the General Assembly,

*Reaffirming* its resolution 47/183 of 22 December 1992 in which it, *inter alia,* emphasized the importance of the Cartagena Commitment, adopted by the United Nations Conference on Trade and Development at its eighth session, held at Cartagena de Indias, Colombia, from 8 to 25 February 1992,

*Expressing its satisfaction* with the early and unanimous agreement reached by the Trade and Development Board, at the second part of its forty-first session, on the development-oriented provisional agenda for the ninth session of the United Nations Conference on Trade and Development, pursuant to which, under the unifying theme "Promoting growth and sustainable development in a globalizing and liberalizing world economy", the Conference will be addressing the following topics:

(a) Development policies and strategies in an increasingly interdependent world economy in the 1990s and beyond:
  (i) Assessment of the development *problématique* in the current context;
  (ii) Policies and strategies for the future;
(b) Promoting international trade as an instrument for development in the post-Uruguay-Round world;
(c) Promoting enterprise development and competitiveness in developing countries and countries in transition;

(d) Future work of the United Nations Conference on Trade and Development in accordance with its mandate: institutional implications,

*Considering* that the ninth session of the United Nations Conference on Trade and Development is a major intergovernmental economic and development event of 1996 within the United Nations,

*Taking note* of the recommendation of the Trade and Development Board that the ninth session of the United Nations Conference on Trade and Development should be held at Midrand, Gauteng Province, South Africa, from 27 April to 11 May 1996, preceded by a one-day meeting of senior officials on 26 April 1996,

1. *Welcomes with appreciation* the generous offer made by the Government of South Africa to host the ninth session of the United Nations Conference on Trade and Development;

2. *Decides* to convene the ninth session of the United Nations Conference on Trade and Development at Midrand, Gauteng Province, South Africa, from 27 April to 11 May 1996, to be preceded by a one-day meeting of senior officials at the same place on 26 April 1996;

3. *Stresses* the crucial importance of the ninth session of the United Nations Conference on Trade and Development in considering the topics of its provisional agenda, and affirms the need to achieve through the session a constructive and action-oriented outcome;

4. *Calls upon* all Governments to ensure their full participation, at the highest possible political level, in the ninth session of the United Nations Conference on Trade and Development;

5. *Invites* the Secretary-General to establish a fund to which voluntary contributions can be made with a view to contributing to the participation of representatives of the least developed countries in the ninth session of the United Nations Conference on Trade and Development;

6. *Urges* all Governments to take appropriate steps to ensure adequate preparations at the national, regional and interregional levels and within the framework of the permanent machinery of the United Nations Conference on Trade and Development for the purpose of facilitating a positive and action-oriented outcome.

General Assembly resolution 50/98

20 December 1995      Meeting 96      Adopted without vote

Approved by Second Committee (A/50/617/Add.1) without vote, 5 December (meeting 41); draft by Vice-Chairman (A/C.2/50/L.50), based on informal consultations on draft by Philippines, for Group of 77 and China (A/C.2/50/L.20) and orally revised; agenda item 95 (a).
*Meeting numbers.* GA 50th session: 2nd Committee 30-32, 36, 41; plenary 96.

*REFERENCES*

[1]YUN 1994, p. 903. [2]A/50/15, vol. I. [3]TD/B/41(2)/13. [4]TD/B/EX(10)/2 (dec. 426(EX-10)). [5]TD/B/42(1)/19(Vol.I) (dec. 430(XLII)).

# International trade

World trade rose in volume by close to 9 per cent in 1994, outpacing global output, which reached 3.1 per cent, according to the *Trade and Development Report, 1995*[1]—a review of international economic issues, published annually by the UNCTAD secretariat. The trade increase was the highest for two decades and was largely due to the continued expansion of trade in manufactures. Trade in services appeared to have risen much less than merchandise trade during 1994, reversing a decade-long trend. There was continued strong expansion in Asia and the Americas and a rapid recovery in Western Europe, where trade rose nearly three times faster than output. The share of intra-regional trade also rose most markedly in those regions where total trade grew most (Asia and the western hemisphere).

World trade grew even more rapidly in current dollar terms, largely because of the sharp increase in prices of many non-oil primary commodities, but also because of the fall in the value of the dollar *vis-à-vis* other major currencies.

In the United States, output growth accelerated from 3 per cent in 1993 to 4.1 per cent in 1994—the highest increase in 10 years. The volume of exports rose sharply, by 9 per cent, which was double the growth of the previous year, but the increase of imports was even larger (13 per cent). Depreciation of the dollar and increased productivity were major factors behind the fast expansion of United States exports, which also benefited from continued strong demand from the developing countries and the recovery in Western Europe, as well as appreciation of the Japanese yen. The spillover of domestic demand into imports was particularly marked for office machinery and telecommunication equipment, sectors in which domestic investment was strong.

Strong export demand was the main factor behind recovery in the European Union (EU) and that recovery contributed much to the rapid expansion of world trade in 1994. While trade among EU countries helped to sustain the fast pace of exports from Western Europe (a 10.1 per cent increase over 1993), most of the increase was accounted for by strong demand in third countries, especially from developing countries in Asia, but also from North America and countries of Central and Eastern Europe. Export performance was also affected by changes in competitiveness brought about by currency realignments.

Growth in Japan was weak and erratic in 1994 in spite of supportive fiscal and monetary policies. While exports were well sustained in value, due to the high yen, their volume growth was small. By contrast, the strong yen favoured imports, particularly of labour-intensive consumer goods from overseas subsidiaries of domestic firms. The volume increase in imports was as high as 12 per cent.

For developing countries as a whole, output continued to expand in 1994, but there was much variation among countries and regions. For African developing countries, output growth was higher in 1994 than in 1993, but at around 2 per cent it remained lower than population growth, resulting in a further decline in per capita gross domestic product (GDP). There was a sharp increase in prices of a wide variety of non-fuel primary commodities in 1994, which, combined with the recovery in Western Europe, benefited African countries to a varying extent. The major exporters of petroleum continued to suffer from depressed prices and the trade deficit of the African region widened further.

Trade grew rapidly in Latin America in 1994 and was most buoyant for imports. Exports benefited not only from the strength of demand in major trading partners, especially the United States, but also from large increases in the prices of many commodities, especially tropical beverages and metals, which led to an improvement in the terms of trade. However, the growth of exports continued to lag behind that of imports, particularly in Argentina, Brazil, Colombia and Mexico.

In developing Asia, trade, including intra-regional trade, continued to be buoyant in 1994. In a few countries of East Asia, imports rose in volume by over 30 per cent and exports by over 20 per cent. Strong import demand in East Asia also contributed to sustaining export expansion in other developing countries, especially those in South Asia. Despite substantially increased export earnings, many Asian developing countries continued to incur trade deficits due to their large imports of capital goods and industrial raw materials. China ran up a trade deficit in 1993 for the first time since 1990, but devaluation brought about a reduction of imports in 1994.

In countries of Central and Eastern Europe, trade, especially exports, rose markedly in value in 1994, leading to a general improvement in trade balances. The surplus of the Russian Federation rose to a record level of almost $20 billion. The recovery of demand, particularly in Western Europe, was the principal factor behind the improved export performance, but supply factors also contributed in many instances, such as improved competitiveness resulting from lower production costs or devaluation. Intraregional trade also showed renewed growth, especially that involving the Czech Republic and Poland.

**GENERAL ASSEMBLY ACTION**

On 20 December, the General Assembly adopted **resolution 50/95**.

### International trade and development

*The General Assembly,*

*Reaffirming* the Declaration on International Economic Cooperation, in particular the Revitalization of Economic Growth and Development of the Developing Countries, the International Development Strategy for the Fourth United Nations Development Decade, the

United Nations New Agenda for the Development of Africa in the 1990s, the Programme of Action for the Least Developed Countries for the 1990s, the Cartagena Commitment, Agenda 21, and the various agreements and conferences that provide an overall policy framework for sustained economic growth and sustainable development to address the challenges of the 1990s,

*Recalling* its resolutions 1995(XIX) of 30 December 1964, as amended, on the establishment of the United Nations Conference on Trade and Development as an organ of the General Assembly, 47/183 of 22 December 1992 on the eighth session of the Conference, and 48/55 of 10 December 1993 and 49/99 of 19 December 1994 on international trade and development,

*Welcoming* the appointment of the Secretary-General of the United Nations Conference on Trade and Development,

*Noting* the progress made by the Conference in the implementation of the outcome of its eighth session, in particular its contribution, within its mandate, to trade and development,

*Emphasizing* the importance of an open, rule-based, equitable, secure, non-discriminatory, transparent and predictable multilateral trading system,

*Emphasizing also* that a favourable and conducive international economic and financial environment and a positive investment climate are necessary for the economic growth of the world economy, including the creation of employment, in particular for the sustained economic growth and sustainable development of the developing countries, and emphasizing further that each country is responsible for its own economic policies for development,

*Welcoming* the successful conclusion of the Uruguay Round of multilateral trade negotiations at the Ministerial Meeting of the Trade Negotiations Committee, held at Marrakesh, Morocco, from 12 to 15 April 1994, and noting that the Uruguay Round agreements represent a historic achievement, which is expected to contribute to strengthening the world economy and to lead to more trade, investment, employment and income growth throughout the world and in particular to the promotion of sustained economic growth and sustainable development, especially in the developing countries,

*Emphasizing* the importance of strengthening and attaining a greater universality of the international trading system and welcoming the process directed towards the accession to the World Trade Organization of economies in transition and developing countries that are not members of the General Agreement on Tariffs and Trade, thereby contributing to their rapid and full integration into the multilateral trading system,

*Noting* the assessment and recommendations adopted at the Mid-term Global Review of the Implementation of the Programme of Action for the Least Developed Countries for the 1990s, held in New York from 25 September to 6 October 1995,

*Noting also* that the Uruguay Round agreements should lead, *inter alia*, to a substantial liberalization of international trade, the strengthening of multilateral rules and disciplines to ensure more stability and predictability in trade relations, and the establishing of rules and disciplines in new areas, and noting further the founding of a new institutional framework in the form of the World Trade Organization, with an integrated dispute settlement mechanism which should prevent the application of unilateral actions against international trade rules,

*Recognizing* that the developing countries have made a major contribution to the success of the Uruguay Round, in particular by accepting the challenges of trade liberalization reforms and measures, and stressing that there is a need for positive efforts designed to ensure that developing countries, especially the least developed among them, secure a share in the growth in international trade commensurate with their economic development needs,

*Recognizing also* that the subregional and regional economic integration processes, including those among developing countries, which have intensified in recent years, impart substantial dynamism to global trade and enhance trade and development possibilities for all countries, and stressing that, in order to maintain the positive aspects of such integration arrangements and to assure the prevalence of their dynamic growth effects, Member States and groupings should be outward oriented and supportive of the multilateral trading system,

*Expressing concern* about possible adverse effects for the least developed countries, particularly those in Africa and net food-importing developing countries, arising from the implementation of the Uruguay Round agreements, as agreed in the Final Act Embodying the Results of the Uruguay Round of Multilateral Trade Negotiations, signed at Marrakesh, and recognizing the need to assist those disadvantaged developing countries so that they benefit fully from the implementation of the Uruguay Round,

*Welcoming* the generous offer of the Government of South Africa to act as host for the United Nations Conference on Trade and Development at its ninth session,

*Recognizing* the role of the United Nations Conference on Trade and Development in identifying and analysing new and emerging issues in the international trade agenda in accordance with agreed conclusions 410(XL) of 29 April 1994 of the Trade and Development Board on the Uruguay Round, agreed conclusions 419(XLI) of 30 September 1994 of the Board on the Uruguay Round, and decision 426(XLII) of 4 May 1995 of the Board, and with the provisional agenda for the ninth session of the United Nations Conference on Trade and Development,

*Noting* the importance of the inaugural Ministerial Conference of the World Trade Organization, to be held in Singapore in December 1996,

*Stressing* the need to promote, facilitate and finance, as appropriate, access to and the transfer of environmentally sound technologies and the corresponding know-how in particular to the developing countries, on favourable terms, including concessional and preferential terms, as mutually agreed, taking into account the need to protect intellectual property rights, as well as the special needs of the developing countries in the implementation of Agenda 21,

*Taking note with satisfaction* of the recommendation on trade, environment and sustainable development made by the Commission on Sustainable Development at its third session, and recognizing, in the spirit of a new global partnership for sustainable development, the need for a balanced and integrated approach to environment, trade and development issues,

1. *Takes note* of the reports of the Trade and Development Board on the second part of its forty-first session and the first part of its forty-second session, and calls upon all States to take appropriate action to implement the outcome of those sessions;

2. *Also takes note* of the *Trade and Development Report, 1995,* and recognizes the contribution such reports have made to the international trade and development dialogue;

3. *Emphasizes* the importance of follow-up and monitoring of the implementation of the policies and measures contained in the Cartagena Commitment, adopted by the United Nations Conference on Trade and Development at its eighth session, held at Cartagena de Indias, Colombia, from 8 to 25 February 1992;

4. *Stresses* the urgent need to continue trade liberalization, including liberalization through a substantial reduction of tariff and other barriers to trade, in particular non-tariff barriers, and the elimination of discriminatory and protectionist practices in international trade relations, and to improve access to the markets of all countries, in particular those of the developed countries, so as to generate sustained economic growth and sustainable development;

5. *Also stresses* the need for the full integration of the economies in transition, as well as other countries, into the world economy, in particular through improved market access for their exports and elimination of discriminatory tariff and non-tariff measures and further liberalization of their trade regimes, including *vis-à-vis* developing countries, and recognizes in this respect the importance of open regional economic integration of interested economies in transition among themselves as well as with developed and/or developing countries in creating new possibilities for expanding trade and investment;

6. *Further stresses* the importance of the timely and full implementation of the agreements contained in the Final Act Embodying the Results of the Uruguay Round of Multilateral Trade Negotiations and the significance of the entering into force on 1 January 1995 of the Agreement Establishing the World Trade Organization;

7. *Emphasizes* the importance of the full and continuing implementation of the provisions contained in the Final Act that confer special and differential treatment for developing countries, including decisions giving special attention to the situation of the least developed countries and the net food-importing developing countries;

8. *Notes* the work that has been undertaken jointly and separately by the United Nations Conference on Trade and Development and the World Trade Organization on the impact of the Uruguay Round on developing countries, and looks forward to the integration of this analysis into discussions, including those at ministerial conferences;

9. *Invites* the United Nations Conference on Trade and Development at its ninth session to transmit its assessment of challenges and opportunities arising from the Uruguay Round agreements from a development perspective to the Ministerial Conference of the World Trade Organization;

10. *Emphasizes* the need for continued review and evaluation of the implementation of the Uruguay Round agreements to ensure that the benefits of the evolving multilateral trade system promote sustained economic growth and sustainable development;

11. *Also emphasizes* the significance of the Ministerial Conference of the World Trade Organization, to be held in Singapore in December 1996, in helping to set the future direction of a rule-based multilateral trading system;

12. *Deplores* any attempt to bypass or undermine multilaterally agreed measures of trade liberalization, through resort to unilateral actions over and above those agreed to in the Uruguay Round, and reaffirms that environmental and social concerns should not be used for protectionist purposes;

13. *Notes* the work of the United Nations Conference on Trade and Development on trade and environment, in particular the outcome of its Ad Hoc Working Group on Trade, Environment and Development, and also notes the work of the Committee on Trade and Environment of the World Trade Organization;

14. *Also notes* the progress achieved by the joint United Nations Environment Programme/United Nations Conference on Trade and Development programme in the consideration of trade and environment issues, and invites the two organizations to continue their work in accordance with paragraph 59 of chapter I of the report of the Commission on Sustainable Development on its third session;

15. *Reaffirms* the need as a matter of priority to implement the Programme of Action for the Least Developed Countries for the 1990s, taking into account the assessment and recommendations adopted at the Midterm Global Review of the Implementation of the Programme of Action for the Least Developed Countries for the 1990s, held in New York from 25 September to 6 October 1995;

16. *Emphasizes* the urgent need for assistance to African countries, *inter alia*, for evaluation of the impact of the Final Act Embodying the Results of the Uruguay Round of Multilateral Trade Negotiations and to enable them to identify and implement adaptive measures to enhance their competitiveness;

17. *Requests* preference-giving countries to improve their preferential schemes, and invites the 1996 policy review of the generalized system of preferences to examine possible adaptations to the system, taking into account paragraphs 134 to 140 of the Cartagena Commitment, as well as the results of the Uruguay Round;

18. *Reaffirms* the role that the United Nations Conference on Trade and Development has been playing as the focal point within the United Nations for the integrated treatment of development and interrelated issues in the areas of trade, finance, technology, investment, services and sustainable development and, within this context, stresses that there should be constructive and effective cooperation between the Conference and the World Trade Organization, based on the complementarity of their functions;

19. *Decides* to enable the United Nations Conference on Trade and Development to discharge its mandate, thereby making it a more effective and efficient instrument for promoting development;

20. *Recognizes* that the Conference at its ninth session will, *inter alia*, consider its future role, including its relationship with other international institutions, to generate synergies among them and, on the basis of its mandate and with a view to strengthening the United Nations system, the ninth session should enable the United Nations Conference on Trade and Development

to become a more effective instrument for promoting development;

21. *Invites* the United Nations Conference on Trade and Development to consider, in close cooperation with other competent organizations, new and emerging issues in the international trade agenda, taking into account the new multilateral trade framework, with a view to fostering international consensus-building among Member States in such areas as trade and environment and competition policy, and, in this regard, recognizes the role of the Conference in preparing the background work and consensus-building on such issues in accordance with agreed conclusions 410(XL) and 419(XLI) and decision 426(XLII) of the Trade and Development Board;

22. *Also invites* the United Nations Conference on Trade and Development, in close cooperation with other competent organizations, to follow developments in the international trading system, in particular their implications for developing countries, and to identify new trading opportunities arising from the implementation of the Uruguay Round agreements so as to provide information and technical support with a view to facilitating the integration of those countries into the system and to assist them in taking full advantage of new trading opportunities, in accordance with agreed conclusions 410(XL) of the Trade and Development Board;

23. *Requests* the United Nations Conference on Trade and Development to monitor, analyse and review the development of trade between economies in transition and developing countries and to recommend appropriate measures for its revival, thus contributing to the strengthening of the multilateral trading system;

24. *Welcomes* the measures taken by the secretariats of the United Nations Conference on Trade and Development and the World Trade Organization and invites them to continue to develop their working relationship, mutual cooperation and complementarity;

25. *Emphasizes* the importance to the international trading system of the inclusion in multilateral trade agreements of all countries that are not members of the World Trade Organization, and urges the international community to assist appropriately and adequately those countries that are not members of the World Trade Organization in the steps towards acceding to that Organization;

26. *Requests* the United Nations Conference on Trade and Development, and invites the World Trade Organization, in accordance with their respective mandates and competence and in close cooperation with other competent United Nations bodies and the regional commissions, to address trade and environment matters comprehensively and to report, through the Commission on Sustainable Development, to the Economic and Social Council and to the General Assembly at its special session in 1997 on the concrete progress achieved on the issue of trade and environment;

27. *Also requests* the United Nations Conference on Trade and Development to continue its special role in the field of trade and environment, including analytical and empirical work, conceptual and empirical studies, policy analysis, and consensus-building, with a view to ensuring transparency and coherence in making environmental and trade policies mutually supportive, taking into account the need for continuing close cooperation and complementarity in the work of the Conference,

the United Nations Environment Programme and the World Trade Organization;

28. *Further requests* the United Nations Conference on Trade and Development to focus and intensify, where necessary, its technical assistance in the light of the Uruguay Round agreements, in cooperation with relevant international organizations, in particular the International Trade Centre and the World Trade Organization, with the aim of increasing the capacities of developing countries, especially the least developed countries, African countries, and small island developing States, so that they may participate effectively in the international trading system;

29. *Requests* the United Nations Conference on Trade and Development to continue to provide technical assistance to economies in transition, bearing in mind the needs of developing countries, in particular with regard to their full integration into the multilateral trading system, so as to contribute to the expansion of their external trade, *inter alia*, with developing countries.

General Assembly resolution 50/95

20 December 1995     Meeting 96     Adopted without vote

Approved by Second Committee (A/50/617/Add.1) without vote, 12 December (meeting 43); draft by Vice-Chairman (A/C.2/50/L.73), based on informal consultations on draft by Philippines (for Group of 77 and China) and Colombia (for Non-Aligned Movement) (A/C.2/50/L.17) and orally revised; agenda item 95 *(a)*.

*Meeting numbers.* GA 50th session: 2nd Committee 30-32, 36, 43; plenary 96.

## Trade policy

Using the *Trade and Development Report, 1995* [1] as a major resource, TDB in September discussed a number of general policy issues concerning global interdependence, including the special topic of linkages between global financial and trade flows, development and levels of economic activity and employment, and the future implications following the Uruguay Round. In a section dealing with unemployment and interdependence, the *Report* stated that despite growing support for globalization, liberalization and outward-oriented development in industrialized countries, joblessness there was increasingly blamed on imports of manufactured products from the South (the developing countries). Proposed solutions ranged from raising import barriers to imposing higher labour standards on southern producers to lowering labour standards in the North. Although trade and technology, both identified as causes of unemployment, had indeed tended to reduce the demand for unskilled labour, dislocations of labour as a result of new competition or new technology were not new in economic history; in addition, demand for skilled labour had been weak. The *Report* took the view that the root of the problem was the slow pace at which demand, output and investment had expanded over the preceding two decades. It saw the remedy in international cooperation to accelerate world economic growth, noting that such a strategy would create jobs in the North while benefiting the South. It would also remove the main threat to the liberalization of trade. By contrast, a strategy of adjusting unemployment by pitting worker against worker in competitive labour markets would exacerbate conflicts among social classes and among nations. Turning labour back into another commodity was not seen as a viable recipe for advancing towards an open world economy; on the contrary, it would invigorate the forces that would prefer to go in the opposite direction, the *Report* stated.

The TDB President prepared a summing-up of the debate on interdependence, which the Board incorporated into the report on the first part of its forty-second session (Geneva, 11-20 September).[2] While interdependence among unemployment, trade and development was generally recognized, some delegations expressed concern that the *Report* devoted too much attention to economic problems in the industrialized countries as compared to trade and development issues and problems of economic policy in developing countries. There was general optimism about the longer-term prospects for the world economy. The strong growth of exports in 1994, along with the perspectives of further trade liberalization opened by the successful conclusion of the Uruguay Round of multilateral trade negotiations, provided excellent prospects for a more open world economy. Although it was agreed that the problem of unemployment in developed countries was very real, it was suggested that the *Report*'s figure of 34 million unemployed in the advanced industrial economies, although high by historical standards, was small compared with the number of unemployed and underemployed in developing countries. Delegations from economies in transition also pointed to historically high rates of unemployment in their own countries. There was broad agreement with the *Report*'s conclusion that the rise of manufactured exports from developing countries was not the cause of labour-market problems in developed countries. However, it was also stated that the problem of labour-market rigidities merited greater attention. The importance of exports to developing countries was noted by many delegations as a major source of job creation in developed economies; better commodity price trends, increased development assistance and further debt relief, by enhancing the import capacity of developing countries, would help reduce unemployment in developed countries.

### Structural adjustment policies

In March, TDB had before it an UNCTAD secretariat report on developments relating to structural adjustment policies in developed countries and their implications.[3] The report assessed major features of structural adjustment policies of developed countries against the backdrop of a world economic setting characterized by the gradual opening of frontiers to free trade, growing economic integration across national borders, rapid technological changes, and equally fast changes in the skill requirements of the workforce.

In its conclusions, the report stated that developed countries would need to adjust in response to growing competition resulting from the implementation of Uruguay Round commitments, from the increasing liberalization of highly protected production sectors and, in the case of some countries, from growing regional integration. Continuous investment, disinvestment and relocation in line with changes in comparative advantage, as well as technological innovation and human skill development, were at the heart of the structural adjustment process. Enterprises were increasingly pursuing global corporate strategies to take best advantage of each country's ability to produce.

Governments of developed countries were emphasizing the importance of support for investment in technological innovation, basic research and human skill development to promote shifts in production patterns into new technology- and skill-intensive industries. They were also providing support for traditional industries to move into competitive higher-value products. Such adjustment assistance could encourage developed countries to move out of production in many low- and middle-market segments of traditional industries where many developing countries and economies in transition had competitive supply capabilities. However, import protection and subsidies in support of unviable lines of production were still being provided in response to political and social constraints. Such aid denied new market opportunities to competitive suppliers in lower-cost countries and Governments needed to resist pressure to grant wasteful subsidization. For their part, a growing number of developing countries were moving their export supply capabilities into more skill- and technology-intensive industries; they would gain new market opportunities through intra-industry specialization. Liberal market access would be a crucial prerequisite. Policy makers in developed countries had to pay greater attention to structural adjustment policies for industries in which liberalization was likely to lead to increased imports from developing countries and economies in transition. Important cases in point were agriculture, textiles and clothing.

In agreed conclusions of 31 March,[4] TDB stated that structural adjustment was a global issue with a crucial part to play in ensuring the enhanced participation in the world economy of developing countries and countries in transition. All countries would have to face growing competition and pressures on economic agents to adjust as the world economy became more global and trade liberalization continued. The full implementation of the Uruguay Round agreements would further increase adjustment pressures. The main responsibility of Governments in the process was to create stable framework conditions to allow for structural adjustment. Efforts had been made by countries in all regions to: introduce deregulation and privatization; open markets to competition; and provide a more liberal framework for enterprises to produce, trade and invest. TDB noted that Governments should take a positive approach to structural adjustment and adopt a global perspective favouring a dynamic process in production and trade beyond national boundaries in order to improve transparency and coherence at the multilateral level. Shifts from sectors with declining international competitiveness towards more capital- and skill-intensive activities should be encouraged. Such an approach not only would benefit the developed countries, but would have an impact on the world economy as a whole and especially on trade and development opportunities of developing countries.

Structural adjustment policies, said TDB, should not aim to maintain inefficient production structures, but should allow a positive approach to promote shifts in patterns of production and trade in line with changes in comparative advantage. That approach could support measures such as vocational training, retraining in new skills, research, technical development and technological innovation. Measures to restore the international competitiveness of enterprises could also contribute to tackling unemployment and create room for expansion of production and trade in developing countries and countries in transition in sectors where they had gained a comparative advantage. A policy framework favourable to structural adjustment could facilitate the implementation of the Uruguay Round agreements, lower resistance to further liberalization and make economies better prepared for future negotiations on improving market access. Sectors of particular concern to developing countries and countries in transition included textiles, clothing, hides and skins, footwear, steel, marine products, agriculture, agro-based industries and certain rapidly expanding services industries. Improving market access for products and services of those countries would, in turn, increase their import capacity and benefit exports and structural adjustment in developed countries.

### Structural adjustment
### for transition to disarmament

The Ad Hoc Working Group to Explore the Issue of Structural Adjustment for the Transition to Disarmament (SATD), established by TDB in 1992[5] and whose terms of reference were agreed upon in 1994,[6] met in Geneva from 17 November to 2 December 1995.[7] The Group had before it a report by the UNCTAD secretariat on SATD,[8] which noted that world military expenditure had fallen from a peak of $995 billion in 1987 to $767 billion in 1994. As a share of gross national product (GNP), the decline was substantial in both developed and developing countries. Between 1987 and 1993, the ratio of military expenditure to GNP declined from 5.4 per cent to 3.4 per cent in the developed countries and from 4.7 per cent to 3.1 per cent in the developing countries. It was noted that the UN Development Programme (UNDP) referred to military expenditure not incurred during 1988-1994 relative to the 1987 baseline as a peace dividend.

The report discussed: the questions of the conversion from military to civilian use of three types of resources—facilities producing goods and services for the military, military installations and bases, and manpower; the effects of decreasing military expenditures on the production and export of some commodities; and the impact of disarmament and conversion on world economic growth and development, international technology flows and the exchange of experience with respect to national technology policy.

Experience since the end of the cold war, the Group concluded, showed that the cost of transition to disarmament had been greater than expected, while benefits had been slower to emerge and were smaller than had been hoped. International cooperation could help individual countries to minimize costs and maximize the benefits of SATD, including conversion. Such cooperation could take a number of forms, such as targeted increases in official development assistance (ODA). Reduced military expenditure in developed countries could release resources to support SATD and conversion in developing countries and countries in transition or to promote world economic growth and development generally.

SATD had different implications in different types of countries. In the developed countries or economies in transition, military production was the sector most at issue, while in developing countries, the demobilization of armed forces was the major question.

In summarizing the debate, the Ad Hoc Working Group Chairman stated that delegations had agreed that all countries should consider the possibilities that existed in their specific situations for reducing military expenditures and channelling the savings towards socially productive uses. Notwithstanding the uncertainties associated with the conversion process, it would be possible to realize some savings that could be rechannelled to increase the availability of development finance and ODA. Different views were expressed concerning the relationship between SATD and ODA; several delegations argued that the relationship between the two was multifaceted and that to posit a mechanical relationship between falling military expenditure in developed countries and ODA was misleading. Other matters discussed included: the use of armed forces for civilian purposes; demobilization and reintegration of ex-combatants; the accumulation of small arms in politically unstable regions; conversion of former foreign military bases; the importance of market access for the output of converted activities; access to technology; and the role of the State in SATD.

The Ad Hoc Working Group also discussed institutional issues and recommended that, in the preparation process for UNCTAD IX, TDB should examine whether a work programme on SATD should be envisaged.

**Trade and environment**

In March, TDB considered a report[9] prepared by the UNCTAD secretariat to assist the Board in its policy review of UNCTAD activities on sustainable development. The report concluded that although UNCTAD's institutional machinery was sufficiently flexible to allow sustainable development issues to be integrated into the work programmes of the Standing Committees and Ad Hoc Working Groups, gaps remained in overall coverage. Although the Board had decided to consider the theme of trade and development at the first part of its annual sessions and another theme or themes on sustainable development at the second part, it had also established an Ad Hoc Working Group on Trade, Environment and Development. Assuming that Governments would wish TDB discussions to be reserved for matters of high policy, it would seem reasonable that technical work on sustainable development should be conducted primarily in its subsidiary bodies, the report stated.

On 31 March,[10] TDB took note of the UNCTAD secretariat report.

**Commission on Sustainable Development consideration.** For its general discussion on progress in implementing Agenda 21, adopted by the UN Conference on Environment and Development in June 1992,[11] the Commission on Sustainable Development (New York, 11-28 April 1995) had before it a report of the Secretary-General on trade, environment and sustainable development.[12] Prepared by the UNCTAD secretariat as task manager for sustainable development and trade issues, the report described progress in implementing Agenda 21 objectives related to trade, particularly programme areas dealing with promoting sustainable development through trade and making trade and environment mutually supportive.

The report concluded that positive measures, such as improved market access, improved access to technology and finance, capacity-building and special provisions for small firms, were the most effective instruments for supporting developing countries and countries in transition in their efforts to internalize environmental externalities. An analysis of potential effects of recent product-specific policies, such as eco-labelling and certain packaging and recycling requirements, was needed. Measures such as financial and technical assistance were preferable to trade measures in encouraging the widest participation in multilateral environmental agreements. Several suggestions were made to strengthen the positive linkages between trade and environmental policies. In many cases, however, there was no clear relationship between trade and environment and, in general, trade policy should not be used for the attainment of environmental objectives, it was stated. In pursuing environmental sustainability, countries should use direct measures that addressed the specific distortions or market failures.

Also before the Commission was the report of a High-level Meeting on Trade, Environment and Sustainable Development, held in 1994,[13] submitted by the secretariats of UNCTAD and the UN Environment Programme (UNEP).

Following consideration of the Secretary-General's report, the Commission brought a number of trade, environment and sustainable development–related matters to the attention of the Economic and Social Council.[14] The potential effects of product-specific policies should be analysed, particularly those based on life-cycle approaches, such as eco-labelling and certain packaging and recycling requirements, especially their potential impacts on the exports of developing countries and countries with economies in transition. The Commission considered that trade liberalization, along with sustained economic growth, could be expected to pave the way for the gradual raising of environmental standards at the national and global levels, but that needed to be complemented by the adoption of sound environmental policies.

The Commission invited UNCTAD, as task manager for trade and environment, in cooperation with UNEP, the World Trade Organization (WTO), the Food and Agriculture Organization of the United Nations, the World Health Organization, the Department for Policy Coordination and Sustainable Development of the UN Secretariat and other institutions, to prepare a background paper for the Commission that would review the growing volume of research on trade, environment and sustainable development linkages carried out by international organizations, academic institutions and non-governmental organizations (NGOs) in developed and developing countries.

As called for in Agenda 21, the Commission recommended that Governments of developed countries and multilateral aid agencies strengthen efforts to improve access to markets and finance and access to and transfer of technology and to build capacity to support developing countries and countries with economies in transition in their efforts to internalize environmental costs. UNCTAD, in cooperation with other international bodies, was asked to undertake further work in that area with a view to identifying innovative approaches. UNCTAD was also asked to carry out an analytical study on the relationship of environmental protection to international competitiveness, job creation and development. UNCTAD and UNEP were asked to analyse how transparency and international cooperation could be strengthened with respect to product-specific policies, particularly eco-labelling and certain packaging and recycling requirements, so as to avoid adverse trade effects.

In **resolution 50/95**, the General Assembly noted progress achieved by the joint UNEP/UNCTAD programme on trade and environment issues and invited the two organizations to continue their work.

### Ad Hoc Working Group on
### Trade, Environment and Development

The Ad Hoc Working Group on Trade, Environment and Development held its second and third sessions in 1995, the first having been held in 1994.[15] The second session (Geneva, 6-9 June)[16] had before it reports by the UNCTAD secretariat on trade, environment and development aspects of establishing and operating eco-labelling programmes[17] and on conceptual and empirical issues of environmental policies, trade and competitiveness.[18]

In a summary of the Working Group's discussions, the Chairman stated that, with regard to market access and competitiveness, the Group focused on the competitiveness of firms, particularly those of developing countries, in the international markets. At the firm level, while short-term competitiveness effects could be negative, in many sectors the long-term effects were more likely to be positive. At the national level, it was felt that the loss in competitiveness of some sectors might be compensated by gains in others, but those possibilities were higher in dynamic economies. It was also recognized that those options were more limited in countries whose export basket comprised a few products. More analysis was called for to support alternative measures for dealing with the negative impact of environmental policies, standards and regulations on competitiveness. The importance of transparency in respect of environmental standards and regulations was emphasized. In addition, the identification of appropriate technical and/or financial assistance required by developing countries was stressed, with special attention being given to the least developed countries (LDCs).

With regard to the trade and competitiveness effects of multilateral environmental agreements, it was agreed that further work on both positive and negative impacts was necessary. Such work should run parallel with the analysis of compensatory/cooperative measures under different agreements. UNCTAD's further work on the subject could encompass: costs of late implementation of multilateral environmental agreements; the competitiveness effects of environmental policies, standards and regulations on small and medium-sized firms; and studies on sectors that produced low-value-added products and those that produced homogeneous products of export interest to developing countries. As to economic instruments, three topics were identified for further research: the trade and competitiveness effects of eco-taxes; the environmental effectiveness of border tax adjustment in the case of process taxes; and the trade effects of the use of regulatory versus incentive-based mechanisms in addressing environmental problems.

The Group's discussions on eco-labelling focused on three sets of issues: trade, environment and development effects of eco-labelling; the use of criteria related to process and production methods; and measures to take account of developing countries' interests in determining eco-labelling criteria.

The final report of the Ad Hoc Working Group also incorporated the report on its third session (Geneva, 6-10 November),[19] at which the discussion of the trade and competitiveness effects of environmental policies, standards and regulations was continued and a preliminary discussion on newly emerging environmental policy instruments with a trade impact was held. The Group had before it UNCTAD secretariat reports on the latter topic,[20] and on the policy debate on trade, environment and development.[21]

The Working Group recommended that UNCTAD's work on trade, environment and development be pursued, at an adequately high level in the organization's future structure, after UNCTAD IX. It recommended policies and measures to promote sustainable development for consideration by Governments; identified areas for future UNCTAD activities in trade, environment and development; and encouraged donors and UNCTAD to provide technical assistance to developing countries to help them to promote sustainable development.

In **resolution 50/95**, the General Assembly noted the outcome of the sessions of the Ad Hoc Working Group.

### Trade preferences

#### Generalized system of preferences

TDB's Special Committee on Preferences held its twenty-second session in Geneva from 23 to 27 October.[22] It carried out a comprehensive policy review of the generalized system of preferences (GSP), with the objective of revitalizing that multilateral trade policy instrument.

In preparation for the policy review, the second Ad Hoc Expert Group on GSP met (Geneva, 15-16 May)[23] to follow up on the first (1994) meeting[24] and to have a more detailed discussion of the subjects addressed. It agreed on conclusions and recommendations covering: the objectives of GSP; product coverage; graduation; erosion of the preferential margin resulting from most-favoured-nation tariff reductions under the Uruguay Round; special measures in favour of LDCs; a possible extension of the GSP concept to new areas, particularly services and investment; the GSP rules of origin; and technical assistance.

The Special Committee had before it an UNCTAD secretariat report on policy options and proposals for the revitalization of GSP,[25] which drew on those conclusions and recommendations.

Also before the Special Committee was the eighteenth general report[26] by the UNCTAD secretariat on the implementation of GSP, which described changes and improvements in the system, updated information on its trade effects, and provided information on technical cooperation activities during 1994 and the first half of 1995. It also described EU's new GSP scheme for industrial products, brought into effect on 1 January 1995 for the period 1995 to 1998. Changes from the previous scheme included the replacement of quotas on GSP imports by "tariff modulation" and the introduction of an open policy of graduation. Estonia, Latvia and Lithuania on 1 January were deleted from the EU beneficiary list, following the entry into force of the free-trade area with EU. South Africa was added to the list, with an extended list of exceptions, and Eritrea was added to the list of LDCs.

Changes with regard to the beneficiary lists of other countries included the addition by Japan of Albania, Armenia, Belarus, Estonia, Georgia, Kazakstan, Latvia, Lithuania, the Republic of Moldova, South Africa, the former Yugoslav Republic of Macedonia, Turkmenistan and Ukraine; the addition by the Czech Republic and Slovakia of those countries plus Antigua and Barbuda, Azerbaijan, Belize, Bosnia and Herzegovina, Brunei Darussalam, Chile, China, Croatia, Eritrea, Kyrgyzstan, the Marshall Islands, Micronesia, Namibia, the Republic of Korea, the Russian Federation, Saint Kitts and Nevis, Tajikistan and Uzbekistan; the addition by Hungary and Norway of South Africa; the addition by the United States of Armenia, the West Bank and the Gaza Strip; the addition by Poland of Algeria, the Congo, the Dominican Republic, Guyana, Peru and Zimbabwe; the removal by New Zealand of Cyprus; the suspension by the United States of the Bahamas and Israel; and the removal by Poland of Argentina, Belize, Botswana, Dominica, Fiji, Grenada, Saint Lucia and the Syrian Arab Republic.

The report also provided information on tariff rate changes made by certain countries on specific products as a consequence of the Uruguay Round commitments and changes made with regard to the duration of some schemes.

Summarizing the Special Committee's discussions,[22] the Chairman stated that there was agreement that GSP was fulfilling an important role as a multilateral tool for development. Preference-receiving countries called on preference-giving countries to expand product coverage for those sectors that were being fully integrated into the multilateral trading system. Extension of GSP to agricultural products, processed food, textiles, clothing, leather and footwear products would substantially improve the match between GSP benefits and the export capacities of developing countries, particularly LDCs. Preference-giving countries considered that it would be difficult to arrive at multilaterally agreed criteria for all of them in view of the basic differences in their GSP schemes. There was broad consensus that priorities for UNCTAD's further work in the area of GSP should include: effective utilization of existing preferences; further special measures in favour of LDCs; strengthening of technical cooperation in coordination with other institutions, particularly in favour of LDCs; and improvement of the information base on GSP and of channels for dissemination to the enterprises concerned, including the use of information technologies and stronger involvement of GSP focal points and of the Trade Point system.

#### Rules of origin

The Intergovernmental Group of Experts on Rules of Origin met in Geneva from 19 to 21 July.[27] It had before it an UNCTAD secretariat study containing options and proposals for harmonization, simplification and improvement of the rules of origin[28] and a summary of replies received from preference-giving and preference-receiving countries to a questionnaire prepared by the UNCTAD secretariat.[29] The Group adopted agreed conclusions, which it brought to the attention of the Special Committee on Preferences for its policy review of GSP.

In October,[22] the Special Committee endorsed the Group's recommendations and recommended that TDB adopt them and arrange for their follow-up.

## Trade promotion and facilitation

During 1995, UN bodies continued to assist developing countries to promote their exports and to facilitate the movement of their goods in international commerce. The International Trade Centre (ITC) was the main originator of technical cooperation projects in that area.

### International Trade Centre

In 1995, ITC, which was formerly under the joint sponsorship of UNCTAD and the General Agreement on Tariffs and Trade (GATT) and known as the International Trade Centre UNCTAD/GATT, became the International Trade Centre UNCTAD/WTO, following an exchange of letters between the UN Secretary-General and the WTO Director-General setting out a framework for cooperation between the two organizations (see PART SIX, Chapter IV). By **decision 1995/322** of 12 December, the Economic and Social Council noted the recommendation in the exchange of letters that current arrangements governing the status of ITC as a joint body should be confirmed and renewed with WTO and that the name of the Centre would become International Trade Centre UNCTAD/WTO.

ITC's expenditures in 1995,[30] the funds for which came from the regular budget (contributed equally by the United Nations and WTO), trust funds, UNDP and support costs, totalled $41.8 million, an increase from $38.2 million in 1994. Trust fund delivery reached $9.8 million, compared with $9.7 million in 1994. Delivery of UNDP funding totalled $5.7 million, a drop from $6.2 million in 1994.

During the year, ITC work focused on six main programme areas or core services: product and market development; development of trade support services; trade information; human resource development; international purchasing and supply management; and needs assessment and programme design for trade promotion. Those activities were carried out with a wide variety of target groups, with particular emphasis on LDCs. Within its programme areas, ITC gave special attention to working directly with individual business enterprises, in the light of the increasing role of the private sector in economic development, and to specific follow-up actions to the Uruguay Round agreements of benefit to the business community. In addition, several issues of common concern to the international community were of particular relevance to ITC during 1995, as they had a direct link with trade promotion and export development and permeated all ITC core services. They were environmental considerations, entrepreneurship development, advancement of women, poverty alleviation, and economic and technical cooperation among developing countries.

In the core service of product and market development, ITC carried out a study on the selection of priority products for its future work. The purpose was to determine the mix of product-related expertise to be maintained; develop a methodology for selecting and updating that range of priority products; and propose a concrete selection of priority product clusters. Under that new structure, ITC's product work in 1995 covered agricultural commodities and agro-based products (coffee, tea, cocoa, spices, sugar, jute, hard fibres, fresh fruits and vegetables, floricultural products, edible nuts and processed fruits and vegetables) and manufactured products and services (textiles and clothing, wood and wood products, hides and skins, leather and leather products, rubber and plastic products, engineering products and environmental technologies, artisanal products and services).

In trade support services, ITC's main task in 1995 was to assess programme strengths and their relevance to the economic and trade environment in the post–Uruguay Round period and to draw up strategies to enable the Centre to satisfy current and future requirements with greater efficacy. Work in trade support services covered export quality and export packaging; the legal aspects of foreign trade; trade financing services; enhancing public-private partnership in institution-building; and international competitiveness for small and medium-sized enterprises.

Trade information activities were directed towards creating or strengthening trade information services and networks in developing countries and economies in transition, as well as the direct supply of information in areas in which ITC had comparative advantages over other information providers. The programme focused on building capacity in the management of trade information, bridging information gaps, and providing prices and market information on a wide range of products through ITC's Market News Service.

Human resource development activities concentrated on programmes at the national level, stressing capacity-building for in-career training. A major Uruguay Round follow-up programme involving information dissemination, needs identification and capacity-building was designed and approved for implementation in 1996. The human resource dimension was incorporated into ITC's new international competitiveness programme for small and medium-sized enterprises, one focus of which was enterprise and trade entrepreneurship training.

Under ITC's international purchasing and supply management core service, an important area of work was public procurement reform. ITC supported central tender boards through the implementation of computer-based management information systems. Procurement training was a central concern, as were the establishment and strengthening of purchasing and supply management associations, since such institutions often served as anchor points for national trading programmes and as sources of local expertise.

ITC prepared a three-year comprehensive strategy and action plan for international purchasing and supply management to focus on the key areas of: modular learning systems; management tools; information systems; national purchasing associations; regulatory and institutional aspects of importing; and quality ·and environmental concerns in international purchasing and supply.

As to programme development, UNDP-funded interregional projects and trust fund donors enabled ITC to execute missions to refine wider-scope programmes of technical cooperation in high-priority areas.

**JAG action.** The Joint Advisory Group (JAG) on ITC held its twenty-eighth session in Geneva from 29 May to 2 June.[31] Documentation before it included: a review of the ITC priority-setting exercise[32] and reports on a 1992 ITC technical meeting on setting up a global trust fund,[33] on the ITC role in trade and the environment[34] and on ITC activities in 1994.[35]

JAG strongly supported ITC's ongoing work in the area of revitalization; it gave ITC a mandate to operationalize priorities as presented in the priority-setting review[32] through restructuring, redeployment of resources, and design and implementation of work programmes.

Informal consultations on a global trust fund were concluded, as JAG adopted a revised proposal for its establishment, which it annexed to its report.

The new Global Trust Fund was launched later in 1995, with the objectives of increasing resources for technical cooperation with developing countries and economies in transition, enhancing the transparency of their use, and facilitating a more efficient and effective technical cooperation programme within JAG priorities. The Fund augmented other ITC extrabudgetary financial mechanisms: bilateral trust funds and separate trust-fund-financed projects.

A Consultative Committee was established to advise the ITC secretariat and ensure transparency in the use of Fund resources. It held its first meeting on 5 November, discussing working procedures, reviewing a proposal on use of funds and considering general conditions for implementing the Trust Fund. Two further meetings were held in 1995 to review specific programme proposals.

JAG endorsed the main purpose of strategy proposals for ITC activities on trade and the environment, as set out in an ITC report.[34] The need for a specific action programme was stressed.

ITC should coordinate and cooperate fully with its parent bodies and other organizations on trade and environment matters, JAG stated.

Trust-fund contributions were pledged by Canada, China, Finland, France, Germany, India, Italy, Japan, the Netherlands, Norway, Sweden, Switzerland and the United States.

**Trade efficiency**

At its resumed eighth executive session on 29 June, TDB continued its discussion of the follow-up to the 1994 UN International Symposium on Trade Efficiency.[36] The Board adopted[37] texts on an international federation of Trade Points, conclusions on technical cooperation, and criteria for establishing and operating Trade Points.

With regard to the feasibility of establishing an international federation of Trade Points, TDB asked the UNCTAD secretariat to prepare proposals for articles of association of such a federation and to circulate them, as well as to convene the Intergovernmental Meeting of Trade Point Officials and Experts to examine secretariat proposals and comments.

In another text, the Board stated that support for establishing/strengthening Trade Points and their interconnections should continue to be an important part of technical cooperation work in trade efficiency. Since a large number of countries wanted such technical cooperation, fund-raising should be an area for rapid action by the secretariat. In countries where phase one of the Trade Point programme was complete, a second phase, with a focus on reducing transaction costs, should begin. Urgent action was particularly required in telecommunications, as effective interconnection of Trade Points was critical for their long-term success. Technical cooperation should also incorporate training, and coordination with ITC, the Economic Commission for Europe and other international and national bodies should continue in order to avoid duplication of effort.

The criteria for establishing and operating Trade Points covered basic services, operative principles and organization; an appendix to the TDB decision dealt with the creation of local Trade Point associations.

**Trading opportunities**

The Ad Hoc Working Group on Trading Opportunities in the New International Trading Context, established by TDB in 1994,[38] held its first session in 1995 (Geneva, 9-13 October).[39] Documents before the Group included UNCTAD secretariat reports on an analysis of trading opportunities resulting from the Uruguay Round in agriculture, textiles, clothing and other industrial products,[40] and on issues and policy requirements for translating Uruguay Round special provisions for LDCs into concrete action.[41]

Summarizing the discussions, the Chairman said that the Ad Hoc Working Group recognized that Uruguay Round results presented significant increases in global trading opportunities of interest to developing countries in many sectors, both agricultural and industrial. However, an assessment of the potential for developing countries and countries in transition to benefit from those opportunities must take account of such elements as: less-than-average tariff reductions, tariff peaks and tariff escalation in a number of sectors of interest to developing countries, prohibitively high tariff rates in those agricultural products subject to tariffication, and postponement of the integration programme for textile and clothing products of interest to developing countries.

To identify trading opportunities in a more concrete manner, greater effort should be made to relate the concessions of developed countries to the supply capacity and export interests of developing countries and LDCs, with a view to enabling them to benefit from those opportunities. In addition, technical assistance was needed to assist individual countries to use fully opportunities presented by the Uruguay Round agreements, including strengthening their institutional and administrative capacities.

The Working Group also discussed possible actions, as components of a safety-net package of measures, to assist LDCs to confront the problems of adjustment to the post–Uruguay Round trading system and to avoid further marginalization. It was noted that elements of the outcome of the High-level Meeting on the Mid-term Global Review of the Programme of Action for LDCs (see PART FOUR, Chapter I) could be incorporated into the Group's final report. Those included the need for: financial resources to strengthen export capacities, develop skills and overcome infrastructural deficiencies; flexible application of anti-dumping and countervailing duty provisions, safeguard measures and rules of origin; more favourable treatment in market access in the area of textiles and in improving GSP; facilitating the export of manpower; and financial aid, measures to improve access to technology, and assistance for developing incentive schemes to promote FDI in LDCs. It was suggested that UNCTAD's work to assist LDCs in that respect could focus on identifying opportunities for, and concretizing the special provisions in favour of, those countries and on devising appropriate government policies to create an exporting community that could take advantage of those opportunities. Institutional and negotiating capacities and human resources should be strengthened.

## Restrictive business practices

The Intergovernmental Group of Experts on Restrictive Business Practices held its fourteenth session in 1995 (Geneva, 6-10 March).[42] As agreed in 1994,[43] the session was devoted to preparations for the Third UN Conference to Review All Aspects of the Set of Multilaterally Agreed Equitable Principles and Rules for the Control of Restrictive Business Practices (see below). The Group of Experts had before it an UNCTAD secretariat note[44] containing an annotated outline of a study on the scope, coverage and enforcement of competition laws and policies in member States and an analysis of the provisions of the Uruguay Round agreements relevant to competition policy, including their implications for developing and other countries. It also included a preliminary list of selected cases of restrictive business practices that had an effect in more than one country, particularly developing countries and countries in transition, and preliminary findings relative to the feasibility of developing a bibliography of relevant materials dealing with restrictive business practice issues, and the implementation of a database facility relating to decisions by competition authorities and courts.

On 10 March, the Group of Experts adopted agreed conclusions in which it requested the UNCTAD secretariat to prepare reports for the Third Review Conference. It also put forward proposals for consideration by the Conference and listed other proposals on which it could not reach agreement.

### Third Review Conference

In accordance with a 1993 General Assembly decision,[45] the Third UN Conference to Review All Aspects of the Set of Multilaterally Agreed Equitable Principles and Rules for the Control of Restrictive Business Practices was held under UNCTAD auspices in Geneva from 13 to 21 November 1995.[46] The first conference to review the 1980 Set of Multilaterally Agreed Equitable Principles and Rules for the Control of Restrictive Business Practices (known as the Set)[47] was held in 1985,[48] and a second took place in 1990.[49]

The Conference considered UNCTAD secretariat studies on: the role of competition policy in economic reforms in developing and other countries;[50] the scope, coverage and enforcement of competition laws and policies and analysis of the provisions of the Uruguay Round agreements relevant to competition policy, including their implications for developing and other countries;[51] and the feasibility of developing a bibliography and database facility on restrictive business practices.[52] It also had before it UNCTAD secretariat notes on preparations for a handbook on restrictive business practices legislation,[53] a review of 15 years of application and implementation of the Set,[54] and restrictive business practices that had an effect in more than one country, in particular developing and other countries, with overall conclusions regarding the issues raised by those cases.[55] The Conference also considered draft commentaries to possible elements for articles of a model law or laws on restrictive business practices.[56]

In addition, the secretariat transmitted the Declaration of Tunis, adopted at the African workshop on competition policy (Tunis, Tunisia, 17-18 October),[57] the conclusions of a meeting on competition policies in Latin America and the Caribbean (Caracas, Venezuela, 23-24 October)[58] and the Declaration and Protocol Decision of the Interstate Council for Anti-monopoly Policies of the Commonwealth of Independent States and the Commission for the Protection of Competition of the Republic of Bulgaria (Kishinev, Republic of Moldova, 6-7 November).[59] At the request of Turkey, the secretariat transmitted the texts of the Act on the Protection of Competition No. 4054 of 7 December 1994 and of the Law on the Protection of Consumers No. 4077 of 8 March 1995.[60]

On 21 November, the Conference adopted a wide-ranging resolution, by which it requested the secretariat to review technical cooperation activities undertaken by UNCTAD and other international organizations, as well as by States bilaterally, with a view to strengthening its ability to provide technical assistance for capacity-building in the area of competition law and policy, and to prepare a report thereon for consideration by the Intergovernmental Group of Experts. The Conference urged intergovernmental organizations and financing programmes and agencies to provide resources for technical assistance activities, and appealed to States, particularly developed countries, to increase voluntary financial contributions and provide expertise for the implementation of such activities.

The UNCTAD secretariat was asked to prepare, for submission in 1996 to the Group of Experts, a draft outline of a study on empirical evidence of the benefits (including for consumers) to be gained by developing countries, LDCs and countries in transition from applying competition law and policy principles to economic development in order to attain greater efficiency in international trade and development. The Conference decided that future sessions of the Group of Experts should include at least three days for informal multilateral consultations among participants on competition law and policy issues and that several small workshops should be organized as part of such consultations. In addition, the Group should embark on an exercise, at the request of member States and in collaboration with national and regional competition law and policy authorities, to map and strengthen common ground among States in the area of competition law and policy in identifying restrictive business practices affecting economic development.

The Conference invited Governments to clarify the scope or application of their competition laws and policies, with a view to improving mutual understanding about substantive principles and procedures of competition law and policy, taking into account relevant provisions of the Uruguay Round agreements. It called on States to strive to implement all provisions of the Set to ensure its effective application.

The UNCTAD secretariat was asked to revise periodically the commentary to the model law on restrictive business practices in the light of legislative developments and comments made by member States for consideration by future sessions of the Intergovernmental Group of Experts and to disseminate widely the model law and its commentary as revised.

The Conference recommended the continuation of the work programme within UNCTAD's intergovernmental machinery addressing competition law and policy issues and a change of title of the Intergovernmental Group of Experts on Restrictive Business Practices to Intergovernmental Group of Experts on Competition Law and Policy. The Conference further recommended that the Assembly convene a fourth review conference in the year 2000.

## Commodities

The *Trade and Development Report, 1995* [1] stated that because of an upsurge in demand, speculative trading and a declining dollar, the nominal prices in dollar terms of many non-oil commodities had risen sharply during most of 1994. After falling to record lows at the beginning of the 1990s, the terms of trade of non-oil primary commodities with respect to manufactures also went up substantially during the year. Petroleum prices, however, continued to drop and their terms of trade with manufactures were at a new low. Many price changes also reflected vagaries in supply. For example, frost in Brazil and lower production in Colombia, Côte d'Ivoire and Indonesia resulted in a tight supply situation in coffee. Prices of cotton and copra also rose due to reduced supplies. Price increases were both sizeable and widespread: among foodstuffs and tropical beverages, they rose in coffee, cocoa, rice and sugar; among agricultural raw materials, they rose in cotton, rubber, hides and skins; and among minerals, they rose in aluminium, tungsten ores, copper and nickel.

However, other commodity prices continued to fare badly, notably tea, beef and bananas, as well as iron ore.

Despite many substantial increases in nominal terms, for most commodities the declining trend in real terms since 1970 was only slightly affected. Moreover, the expected slow-down of industrial expansion in many major markets and sluggish recovery in Western Europe, in combination with the expected expansion of supply, would tend to dampen the price movements of many commodities, the *Report* stated.

### Standing Committee on Commodities

The Standing Committee on Commodities in 1995 held its fourth session (Geneva, 30 October–3 November).[61] It reviewed reports by the UNCTAD secretariat on: sustainable development and the possibilities for the reflection of environmental costs in prices;[62] the Uruguay Round and international commodity trade and prices;[63] and a review of the Standing Committee's work programme, with special emphasis on preparations for UNCTAD IX.[64] It also considered reports on the third (1994) sessions[65] of intergovernmental groups of experts on both tungsten and iron ore, as well as the report of the iron ore group's fourth (1995) session (see below).

In agreed conclusions adopted on 3 November, the Standing Committee stated that the expected growth of world commodity demand in the foreseeable future was likely to be accompanied by persisting traditional and newly emerging problems of the international commodity economy. Those problems, including depressed prices, faced commodity exporters and, especially, developing countries and LDCs, which were heavily dependent on commodities for their export earnings, domestic employment and food production.

Export diversification was well recognized as a key prerequisite if commodity-dependent developing economies were to succeed in moving towards sustainable development with higher growth and standards of living. There was general consensus that expanded market access for developing countries' exports was an important condition for durable expansion in their export earnings and gains in market shares. Domestic policy reform and economic and technical cooperation from the international community were crucial if developing countries were to take full advantage of available opportunities and niches in commodity production and trade. The need to assist developing countries, particularly LDCs, in that regard was emphasized.

To achieve sustainable development, it was important to take into account all relevant costs and benefits of economic activity, including those related to the environment. Existing distortions in the price system, particularly those caused by subsidies in commodity production, should be eliminated as a prerequisite for internalizing externalities. Moreover, clarifying the concept of internalization and its significance for sustainable development would contribute to both implementation at the national level and advancement of an international dialogue.

Producer-consumer cooperation was an important element of commodity policy that needed to be pursued where feasible, taking into account the particular needs of developing countries and the characteristics of individual commodities. Such cooperation could be enhanced by taking market forces more fully into account; involving both the private sector and industry experts; improving research and development; and promoting consideration of environmental issues and sustainable development.

The Standing Committee agreed that UNCTAD had an important role to play in the commodity area. It should concentrate its future work on issues where it had expertise and competence in promoting sound, compatible and consistent policies with a view to achieving the improved functioning of the international commodity economy and an enhanced role for the developing countries in that economy. Special attention was needed for highly commodity-dependent, low-income countries and other weaker economies, such as those in Africa, particularly for LDCs.

The Standing Committee agreed that, after UNCTAD IX, UNCTAD should continue to address commodity issues, which could be conceptualized in terms of the macroeconomic, sectoral, microeconomic and international dimensions. Meeting those challenges required a three-pronged approach: research and analysis; policy dialogue; and technical and economic cooperation. It was recommended that UNCTAD develop a work programme within the intergovernmental machinery that addressed commodity issues and proceeded only with the active support and participation of relevant government ministries and enterprises of member countries and other concerned organizations.

**State participation and privatization in the minerals sector.** The Ad Hoc Group of Experts on State Participation and Privatization in the Minerals Sector of the Standing Committee on Commodities met in 1995 (Geneva, 26-27 October).[66] It had before it an UNCTAD secretariat report on such State participation and privatization,[67] which discussed changes in State control of non-fuel mineral production over the preceding decades and performance of State-controlled companies and presented arguments for privatization. It also suggested the following structure for the Group's discussions: the rationale for State participation and for privatization; the conditions, policies and instruments required; and the roles of the public and private sectors.

Summarizing the Group's discussions, the Chairman said that there was no one path to privatization. In one case, minority equity participation was most appropriate; in another, full State ownership was preferred in order not to divert from the private sector the immense amounts of capital required to purchase existing State assets; in yet another, existing State assets were being capitalized in such a way as to capture more sucessfully for the State and society the full market value of State assets as opposed to the book value of the assets.

Whatever the path to privatization or continued State participation, the successful exploitation of mineral assets would depend on the existence of a good legislative, administrative and regulatory framework and clear and enforced labour, legal and environmental regimes. Privatization in the minerals sector was complex and lengthy and had to be seen in the context of the whole economy and include both macro- and micro-level considerations. Local communities that were largely dependent on minerals activities were stakeholders in the privatization process and should be involved. Decisions regarding the role of the State and the choices made concerning the degree and form of ownership were ultimately political in nature. Therefore, there was criticism and public debate surrounding every privatization or State participation decision. That was particularly true when the mineral asset was central to the national economy or when it was the leading economic activity of a particular area. The political objective was clear, however: to achieve the most economically efficient and socially responsible exploitation and use of the natural resource base of the nation.

The Standing Committee on Commodities took note of an oral report on the meeting presented by the Group's Chairman.

### Common Fund for Commodities

The 1980 Agreement Establishing the Common Fund for Commodities,[68] a mechanism intended to stabilize the commodities market by helping to finance buffer stocks of specific commodities as well as commodity development activities such as research and marketing, entered into force in 1989, and the Fund became operational later that year.

As at 31 December 1995,[69] the Agreement had been signed by 115 States and the European Community (European Union), and 103 States and the European Community had become parties to it. Turkey's withdrawal from the Fund became effective on 1 August.

### Individual commodities

#### Agricultural commodities

**Natural rubber.** The UN Conference on Natural Rubber, 1994, met in its third part in Geneva from 6 to 17 February 1995,[70] the first two parts having taken place in 1994.[71] On 17 February, 31 countries representing nearly 90 per cent of world trade in natural rubber adopted the International Natural Rubber Agreement, 1995, which aimed at stabilizing prices. The 1995 Agreement, the third on rubber to be negotiated under the aegis of UNCTAD, succeeded the International Natural Rubber Agreement, 1987,[72] which expired on 28 December 1995.

By its final resolution,[73] the Conference, having established the text of the Agreement in Arabic, Chinese, English, French, Russian and Spanish, decided that those texts were equally authentic and requested that they be forwarded to the UN Secretary-General. He was asked to forward copies of the Agreement to all Governments invited to the Conference and to arrange for it to be open for signature in New York during the period laid down in article 57 (3 April–28 December 1995). The attention of Governments was drawn to the procedures laid down in articles 59 (ratification, acceptance and approval) and 61 (entry into force). They were urged to sign the Agreement and deposit instruments of ratification, acceptance, approval or accession before 1 January 1997, or to notify that they would apply the Agreement provisionally.

As at 31 December 1995,[69] 19 States and the European Community had signed the Agreement, one State had formally accepted it and two States had given notification of its provisional application.

#### Minerals and metals

**Iron ore.** The Intergovernmental Group of Experts on Iron Ore of the Standing Committee on Commodities held its fourth session in 1995 (Geneva, 23-25 October).[74] It had before it iron ore statistics for 1987-1994,[75] an annotated bibliography on iron ore,[76] and a review of the current situation and outlook for iron ore,[77] all prepared by the UNCTAD secretariat.

On 25 October, the Group adopted a text stating that governmental representatives, industry experts and iron ore companies reaffirmed that the work of the Group was unique and extremely useful to producers and consumers. It recalled that the statistical work and the exchange of views within the Group was an important contribution to increasing market transparency.

The Group agreed that a possible application by it to the Common Fund for Commodities for designation as an eligible International Commodity Body should be considered following UNCTAD IX. It proposed that its fifth session be held in October 1996.

**Tungsten.** The Standing Committee on Commodities considered the report of the third (1994) session of the Intergovernmental Group of Experts on Tungsten,[65] by which it had remitted to the Standing Committee the determination of the date for its fourth session. The Committee also had before it an UNCTAD secretariat review of the current market situation and outlook in tungsten.[78]

The Standing Committee recommended to TDB that it suspend the activities of the Group until the Board could determine that there was adequate support to re-initiate it in the future.

### Services

The third session of the Standing Committee on Developing Services Sectors: Fostering Competitive Services Sectors in Developing Countries took place in Geneva from 25 to 29 September.[79] It had before it reports by the UNCTAD secretariat on: ways of enhancing access to and use of information networks and distribution channels;[80] the impact of progressive liberalization and of service imports on the development of competitive services sectors, and the difficulties faced by developing countries which prevented them from increasing their participation in world trade in services;[81] and the work programme of the Standing Committee, with special emphasis on the preparations for UNCTAD IX.[82]

On 29 September, the Standing Committee adopted agreed recommendations, which it annexed to its report. It stated that UNCTAD's future work should be oriented towards assisting developing countries to strengthen their capacities in the services sector and to identify clearly the opportunities for their services exports, as well as the barriers and impediments to their ability to compete in world markets. Work should focus on measures to overcome those difficulties, including by enhancing the negotiating capacity of developing countries in obtaining greater market access in sectors and modes of supply of export interest to them. LDCs should receive particular attention.

It was agreed that future work could focus on the following issues: the impact of subsidies, government procurement, safeguards and anti-competitive practices on development of competitive services sectors in developing countries and trade in specific services sectors and the improvement of information on current practice in those areas; analysis of trading opportunities made available as a result of market access commitments on temporary movement of natural persons in the General Agreement on Trade in Services (GATS); a sustained result-oriented approach in dealing

with problems faced by developing countries in enhancing their access to and use of information networks and distribution channels; strengthening and making operational the Database on Measures Affecting Service Trade (MAST), giving priority to areas of ongoing negotiations at the multilateral and regional levels, responding to requests for cooperation from countries and regional and subregional arrangements, and disseminating MAST, particularly to the private sector; analysis of how to achieve the development objectives of GATS; the implications of environmental measures for the services trade of developing countries; evaluation of modalities and policies aimed at promoting regional, subregional and interregional cooperation on services, including among countries at different levels of economic development; the impact of economic integration arrangements on the services sectors of other countries, particularly those of developing countries; improvement of statistics on trade in services; strengthening UNCTAD's technical assistance capacity; and studying problems and opportunities faced by countries undergoing transition to a market economy in improving the role of services in their economies.

### Insurance

The Standing Committee on Developing Services Sectors: Fostering Competitive Services Sectors in Developing Countries held its third session on insurance (Geneva, 13-17 November).[83] It considered the following documents prepared by the UNCTAD secretariat: a study on the establishment of effective insurance regulatory and supervisory systems;[84] a review of activities of the secretariat pertaining to the work programme;[85] and a summary of the major components and structures for catastrophe insurance schemes.[86] The Standing Committee also had before it, in addition to a number of background documents, the report of an expert group meeting on prudential regulation and supervision of insurance markets in developing countries and countries in transition to market economies (Geneva, 19-20 June).[87]

In agreed conclusions adopted on 17 November, the Standing Committee stated that future UNCTAD work on insurance should focus on the following issues: the establishment of an appropriate framework for the functioning of a competitive market; catastrophe insurance; the specific needs of developing countries; and information and technical assistance.

### Consumer protection

In accordance with a 1990 Economic and Social Council request,[88] the Secretary-General submitted in May a report on consumer protection.[89] The report covered activities relating to the implementation of the guidelines for consumer protection, adopted by the General Assembly in 1985.[90] It described action taken within the UN system, implementation of the guidelines by Governments, regional and international cooperation and activities of NGOs. In a section on the future scope of the guidelines, the report noted that at its April 1995 session, the Commission on Sustainable Development (see PART FOUR, Chapter I) had adopted a work programme on changing production and consumption patterns, which included a call for the expansion of the guidelines for consumer protection to include those for sustainable consumption patterns. Such guidelines might cover schemes for the dissemination of properly researched information and advice on the environmental impact of consumer products, including eco-labelling and eco-profile schemes; the promotion of joint environmental testing; educational programmes on sustainable consumption; and standards on environmental claims.

**ECONOMIC AND SOCIAL COUNCIL ACTION**

On 28 July, the Economic and Social Council adopted **resolution 1995/53**.

### Consumer protection

_The Economic and Social Council,_

_Recalling_ General Assembly resolution 39/248 of 9 April 1985, in which the Assembly adopted guidelines for consumer protection,

_Recalling also_ its resolutions 1988/61 of 27 July 1988 and 1990/85 of 27 July 1990, as well as resolution 48/7 of 23 April 1992 of the Economic and Social Commission for Asia and the Pacific, in which Governments were urged to implement the guidelines for consumer protection and the Secretary-General was requested to provide assistance to Governments in that regard,

_Noting_ that the Commission on Sustainable Development, at its third session, recommended that the guidelines for consumer protection be expanded to include guidelines for sustainable consumption patterns,

_Aware_ that the need for assistance in the area of consumer protection, particularly in developing countries and countries with economies in transition, remains great,

1. _Commends_ the Secretary-General for his report on consumer protection, prepared pursuant to Council resolution 1990/85, containing information on the efforts currently being made within the United Nations system to promote the implementation of the guidelines for consumer protection;

2. _Notes with appreciation_ the impact the guidelines have had in the decade since their adoption in promoting just, equitable and sustainable economic and social development through their implementation by Governments;

3. _Recognizes_ the role of civil societies and non-governmental organizations in promoting the implementation of the guidelines;

4. _Urges_ all Governments to continue their efforts to implement the guidelines, create the appropriate legal framework and establish the means to develop, implement and monitor policies and programmes for consumer protection;

5. _Requests_ the Secretary-General, in cooperation with the development funds and programmes of the United Nations, the regional commissions and other relevant organizations and bodies of the United Nations system, to continue to provide assistance to Governments, at their request, in implementing the guidelines for consumer protection, to elaborate guidelines in the area of sustainable consumption patterns, taking into account the work undertaken in other intergovernmental forums, and to examine the possible extension of those guidelines into other areas;

6. _Also requests_ the Secretary-General to report to the Council at its substantive session of 1997 on the implementation of the present resolution.

Economic and Social Council resolution 1995/53

28 July 1995     Meeting 57     Adopted without vote

16-nation draft (E/1995/L.27), orally revised following informal consultations; agenda item 6.

_Meeting numbers._ ESC 39-41, 45, 57.

*REFERENCES*

[1]_Trade and Development Report, 1995_ (UNCTAD/TDR/15), Sales No. E.95.II.D.16. [2]TD/B/42(1)/19(Vol.I). [3]TD/B/41(2)/8. [4]A/50/15, vol. I (agreed conclusions 422(XLI)). [5]YUN 1992, p. 613. [6]YUN 1994, p. 875. [7]TD/B/42(2)/7. [8]TD/B/WG.9/2. [9]TD/B/41(2)/10. [10]A/50/15, vol. I. [11]YUN 1992, p. 672. [12]E/CN.17/1995/12. [13]YUN 1994, p. 871. [14]E/1995/32. [15]YUN 1994, p. 873. [16]TD/B/42(1)/6. [17]TD/B/WG.6/5. [18]TD/B/WG.6/6. [19]TD/B/42(2)/9. [20]TD/B/WG.6/9 & Add.1. [21]TD/B/WG.6/10 & Add.1. [22]TD/B/42(2)/4. [23]TD/B/SCP/15. [24]YUN 1984, p. 877. [25]TD/B/SCP/13 & Corr.1,2 & Add.1. [26]TD/B/SCP/12. [27]TD/B/SCP/14. [28]TD/B/SCP/AC.1/2. [29]TD/B/SCP/AC.1/2/Add.1. [30]ITC/AG(XXIX)/152 & Add.1. [31]ITC/AG(XXVIII)/150. [32]ITC/AG(XXVIII)/148. [33]YUN 1992, p. 620. [34]ITC/AG(XXVIII)/147. [35]YUN 1994, p. 878. [36]YUN 1994, p. 880. [37]TD/B/EX(8)/2 (dec. 427(EX-8)). [38]YUN 1994, p. 861. [39]TD/B/42(2)/3. [40]TD/B/WG.8/2 & Add.1. [41]TD/B/WG.8/3 & Add.1. [42]TD/B/42(1)/3. [43]YUN 1994, p. 883. [44]TD/B/RBP/105 & Add.1. [45]YUN 1993, p. 759, GA dec. 48/442, 21 Dec. 1993. [46]TD/B/RBP/CONF.4/15. [47]YUN 1980, p. 626. [48]YUN 1985, p. 563. [49]TD/RBP/CONF.3/9. [50]TD/RBP/CONF.4/2. [51]TD/RBP/CONF.4/8. [52]TD/RBP/CONF.4/7. [53]TD/RBP/CONF.4/3. [54]TD/RBP/CONF.4/5. [55]TD/RBP/CONF.4/6. [56]TD/B/RBP/81/Rev.4. [57]TD/RBP/CONF.4/10. [58]TD/RBP/CONF.4/11. [59]TD/RBP/CONF.4/12. [60]TD/RBP/CONF.4/9. [61]TD/B/42(2)/5. [62]TD/B/CN.1/29. [63]TD/B/CN.1/30 & Add.1,2. [64]TD/B/CN.1/31. [65]YUN 1994, p. 888. [66]TD/B/CN.1/35. [67]TD/B/CN.1/GE.2/2. [68]YUN 1980, p. 621. [69]_Multilateral Treaties Deposited with the Secretary-General: Status as at 31 December 1995_ (ST/LEG/SER.E/14), Sales No. E.96.V.5. [70]TD/RUBBER.3/11/Rev.1. [71]YUN 1994, p. 887. [72]YUN 1987, p. 482. [73]TD/RUBBER.3/10. [74]TD/B/CN.1/33. [75]TD/B/CN.1/IRON ORE/17. [76]TD/B/CN.1/IRON ORE/19. [77]TD/B/CN.1/IRON ORE/18. [78]TD/B/CN.1/TUNGSTEN/12. [79]TD/B/42(2)/2. [80]TD/B/CN.4/42. [81]TD/B/CN.4/43. [82]TD/B/CN.4/44. [83]TD/B/42(2)/6. [84]TD/B/CN.4/52. [85]TD/B/CN.4/53. [86]TD/B/CN.4/54. [87]UNCTAD/SDD/INS/12. [88]ESC res. 1990/85, 27 July 1990. [89]E/1995/70. [90]YUN 1985, p. 571, GA res. 39/248, annex, 9 Apr. 1985.

# Finance

## Financial policy

In 1994 and early 1995, according to the _Trade and Development Report, 1995,_[1] there were marked differences in the growth of the major categories of external financing from the international financial markets. Those differences largely reflected the impact of unsettled conditions on issues of debt securities. Consequently, 1994 had been characterized by a slow-down in new external bond issues after the first quarter, accompanied by indications of greater reluctance among investors to purchase instruments with long maturities. The more difficult conditions in financial markets had led to a very large decrease in new bond issues by Latin American entities in the first four months of 1995 and to the postponement of international equity issues by companies from developing countries. The ripple effects from the Mexican currency crisis in late 1994 were also generally viewed as having contributed, together with such factors as rising interest rates, to ubiquitous declines in prices that took place in major emerging financial markets between mid-December 1994 and mid-January 1995.

Flows to developing countries of some major categories of financing broadly followed the movements experienced by other borrowers. However, the international equity issues of developing countries increased to more than $15.5 billion in 1994, almost double the level of the previous year; that was largely due to an increase in issues originating in South and South-East Asia. Total external purchases of developing-country equities also included those of shares in local markets, and figures for net inflows in that form (i.e., purchases less sales) showed a fall from over $60 billion in 1993 to about $40 billion in 1994.

Total claims on developing countries of banks in the Bank for International Settlements (BIS) reporting area increased more rapidly in 1994 than those on all borrowers. Their faster expansion reflected a substantial rise for countries of South and South-East Asia, a much smaller one for those of Latin America, and falls for those of Africa and West Asia. Claims also decreased for countries of Eastern Europe.

During the first half of 1994, the vigorous growth of the previous two years in the net flow of export credits to developing countries was not sustained. Indeed, total net flows to Africa and Latin America were actually negative. The costs and other terms of official insurance were especially important in depressing the levels of such credits to African countries, of which more than 50 per cent in 1993 and 60 per cent in the first half of 1994 experienced net outflows. There were also increases in the frequency of net outflows from countries in Latin America and West Asia during early 1994.

Access to major categories of financing from international financial markets in 1994 continued to be concentrated on a relatively small group of de-

veloping countries and economies in transition. For example, three Latin American countries (Argentina, Brazil, Mexico) received approximately 40 per cent of sums raised in the form of external bond issues by countries and territories other than certain major offshore financial centres. A similar proportion was centred in South and South-East Asia (China, Indonesia, Republic of Korea, Taiwan, Thailand). Of the economies in transition, only Hungary was a major borrower in this form.

Monies raised through new syndicated bank credits were still more concentrated. Five countries of South and South-East Asia (China, Indonesia, Republic of Korea, Malaysia, Thailand) accounted for 70 per cent and four of those (excluding Malaysia) accounted for almost the entire growth in 1994 of the value of claims of banks in the BIS reporting area on developing countries and territories. Borrowing in the form of various other instruments was heavily concentrated among a few Latin American countries. Argentina, Brazil and Mexico were responsible for more than 90 per cent of funds raised by developing countries through announced medium-term Euronote facilities, and they also accounted for most of developing countries' issues of Eurocommercial paper.

Between mid-1994 and April 1995, a number of countries, including Barbados, Bolivia, Ghana, Guatemala, Lebanon, Pakistan and Tunisia, issued external bonds either for the first time or after lengthy absences from the markets for such instruments. Similarly, in the spring of 1995, Romania returned to the market for syndicated international bank credits after an absence of about 15 years. However, the accession of such countries had not yet had a major effect on the distribution of financing from the international financial markets for developing countries and economies in transition.

A number of countries of South and South-East Asia, which had been left largely unscathed by the 1980s debt crisis, had increasingly been integrated into the global system of financial markets and could raise money there relatively easily. However, the spillover effects of the Mexican crisis served as a reminder of the continuing vulnerability of their financial markets to speculative international investors still inclined to lump them with emerging markets elsewhere in the developing world. Those effects were evident in downward pressures on share prices and exchange rates and contributed to substantial declines in external bond and equity issues.

### Net transfer of resources

In response to a 1994 General Assembly request,[2] the *World Economic and Social Survey 1995*[3] reported on the question of the net transfer of resources between developing and developed countries. It stated that the developing countries taken together had, in 1994, enjoyed a fourth straight year of large net financial transfers, although the transfer was almost $15 billion less than in 1993. Coupled with strong growth of export earnings, it facilitated a double-digit growth of import volumes.

The level of official reserves rose by almost $80 billion. Some of that increase represented the larger dollar value of the stock of non-dollar reserves, owing to the depreciation of the dollar exchange rate against the yen and other reserve currencies. But the increase of reserves at constant exchange rates was over $50 billion. Not all countries shared in that experience. Mexico, in particular, saw its reserves fall from their peak of $29 billion at the end of February 1994 to $6 billion by the end of the year. Indeed, the fall in Latin America's reserves was fully accounted for by Mexico's decline. Excluding Mexico, Latin America's reserves rose by $8 billion at constant exchange rates. The reserves of sub-Saharan Africa (excluding Nigeria and South Africa) also rose, both nominally and as a share of imports.

On the whole, the quality of the financial components of the flows to the developing countries improved in 1994. For the sample of 93 capital-importing countries whose data were sufficient to construct reasonable estimates, there had been a smaller net inflow of short-term and speculative funds. Instead, net inflows of direct investment and medium- and long-term credit from private sources (particularly bonds and syndicated loans), as well as official and private grants, were larger. The bulk of the improvement was enjoyed by Asia, although direct investment in Latin America rose as well. While there was little change in the overall net transfers of sub-Saharan Africa, Africa as a whole experienced a negative transfer, as more funds were used on interest and capital outflows than were received from abroad. The net transfer to Africa through official credit was positive in 1994, and significantly positive to the sub-Saharan region, while Latin America experienced its eighth consecutive year of negative transfers on account of official credits. However, in January 1995, the International Monetary Fund (IMF) agreed to an 18-month stand-by arrangement for Mexico of almost $18 billion, far more than the Fund's total lending commitments in 1994.

More generally, developing countries were still repaying IMF loans on a net basis in 1994, although there were net disbursements of about $1 billion of concessional loans through the Enhanced Structural Adjustment Facility. Net disbursements by the World Bank to developing countries and transition economy borrowers remained positive, but when interest payments in the order of $8 billion were subtracted from the net capital flow, the resulting net transfer of the Bank was negative, as it had been throughout the decade. Nevertheless, lending commitments at IMF and the World Bank Group rose in 1994. Loan arrangements by all the regional development banks fell in 1994, however, except at the European Bank for Reconstruction and Development, which was only in its fourth year of making loan commitments. The sharpest cut-backs were by the African Development Bank and the International Fund for Agricultural Development.

**GENERAL ASSEMBLY ACTION**

On 20 December, the General Assembly adopted **resolution 50/91**.

### Global financial integration: challenges and opportunities

*The General Assembly,*

*Reaffirming* its resolutions S-18/3 of 1 May 1990, the annex to which contains the Declaration on International Economic Cooperation, in particular the Revitalization of Economic Growth and Development of the Developing Countries, and 45/199 of 21 December 1990, the annex to which contains the International Development Strategy for the Fourth United Nations Development Decade, and the Cartagena Commitment, adopted by the United Nations Conference on Trade and Development at its eighth session,

*Recalling* its resolution 49/93 of 19 December 1994 on net flows and transfer of resources between developing and developed countries,

*Stressing* the importance at the national level in the countries concerned of a favourable climate for private financial flows, sound macroeconomic policies and appropriate functioning of markets,

*Recognizing* that the international community should continue to give strong support to the efforts of the developing countries to solve their grave economic and social problems as well as to promote a favourable climate for private financial flows through the creation of a favourable international economic environment,

*Noting with satisfaction* that the process of economic growth, in a number of developing countries, has been positively affected by the recent increase in international private capital flows,

*Commending* continuing efforts made by developing countries to create a more favourable national framework and stressing that a considerable number of developing countries, in particular the least developed countries, especially in Africa, have not benefited from the aforementioned capital flows,

*Expressing concern*, within such a context, at the decline in real terms in the past three years in the overall level of official development assistance to developing countries,

*Expressing concern also* that a significant number of developing countries have become more vulnerable, in the course of liberalizing their external economic and financial regimes, to the volatile fluctuations of private capital flows in international financial markets,

*Noting* the necessity of promoting the creation of favourable conditions for achieving international stability in private capital flows and of preventing the destabilization arising from swift movements of private capital flows, in order, *inter alia*, to enhance development, in particular of developing countries,

*Aware* of the role of the International Monetary Fund in the promotion of a stable international financial environment conducive to economic growth, and taking into account the strengthening of the cooperative relationship between the United Nations and the Fund,

1. *Stresses* that global financial integration presents new challenges and opportunities for the international community and that it should constitute a very important element of the dialogue between the United Nations system and the Bretton Woods institutions;

2. *Underscores* the need for encouragement of private flows to all countries, in particular to developing countries, especially long-term flows, while reducing the risks of volatility;

3. *Recognizes* that, in a globalized world, sound fiscal and monetary policy in each country is among the elements essential in preventing crises relating to capital flows;

4. *Emphasizes* the need to explore ways to broaden appropriate enhanced cooperation and, where appropriate, coordination of macroeconomic policy among interested countries, monetary and financial authorities and institutions, so as to enhance preventive consultation arrangements between such institutions as a means of promoting a stable international financial environment conducive to economic growth, particularly in developing countries, taking into account the needs of developing countries as well as situations that may have a significant impact upon the international financial system;

5. *Reiterates* the need for broadening and strengthening the participation of developing countries in the international economic decision-making process;

6. *Welcomes* the steps taken by the International Monetary Fund and recognizes the need for a stronger and central role for the Fund in surveillance of all countries, in a symmetrical manner, in accordance with paragraph 4 of the communiqué of the Interim Committee of the Board of Governors of the Fund, dated 26 April 1995, with regard to potential sources of destabilization of capital markets with a view to promoting transparency and stability in international financial markets and promoting economic growth, such surveillance including, among other elements, the regular and timely provision of economic and financial data;

7. *Reaffirms* the objective of promoting greater transparency and openness, including increasing participation of developing countries in the work of the International Monetary Fund, an objective that involves, among other elements, the regular and timely provision of economic and financial data by all Fund members;

8. *Requests* the Secretary-General to report to the General Assembly, at its fifty-first session, in cooperation with the Bretton Woods institutions and the United Nations Conference on Trade and Development, on the implementation of the present resolution.

General Assembly resolution 50/91

20 December 1995     Meeting 96     Adopted without vote

Approved by Second Committee (A/50/616) without vote, 5 December (meeting 41); draft by Vice-Chairman (A/C.2/50/L.56), based on informal consultations on draft by Philippines, for Group of 77 and China (A/C.2/50/L.6) and orally revised; agenda item 94.

*Meeting numbers.* GA 50th session: 2nd Committee 11-13, 23, 24, 32, 41; plenary 96.

## Debt problems of developing countries

The *Trade and Development Report, 1995* [1] noted that the official debt of low-income debtor countries and some middle-income countries continued to cause concern. In December 1994, the Paris Club (a group of creditor Governments) had adopted the new Naples terms in favour of the poorest and most indebted countries. The terms included the option of reducing the stock of debt, provision for the level of debt reduction to be raised to 67 per cent, and more generous coverage of debt. During the first six months of 1995, nine low-income countries (Bolivia, Cambodia, Guinea, Guinea-Bissau, Haiti, Nicaragua, Senegal, Togo, Uganda) and two middle-income countries (Croatia, Russian Federation) rescheduled their debt at the Paris Club.

The multilateral debt of 41 highly indebted low-income countries more than tripled from 1982 to 1993, reaching a level of $55.5 billion, which was more than 24 per cent of their total debt outstanding. The share of multilateral debt service exceeded 46 per cent for those countries and for 28 of them the share was more than half. The higher share of debt service compared to the share of debt outstanding was indicative of the preferred creditor status of multilateral institutions which protected their claims from rescheduling or reduction. Multilateral debt had often been serviced by accumulating arrears on other types of debt.

The World Bank Group accounted for over half the multilateral debt outstanding at the end of 1993. While lending by the World Bank declined, that was more than offset by high International Development Association loans. By contrast, there was a dramatic drop in the share of IMF lending, from over 29 per cent in the period 1980-1983 to less than 12 per cent in 1993. Net transfers from IMF were negative from 1984 to 1993, but it reported positive net transfers of over $365 million in 1994. Other multilateral institutions, particularly the regional development banks, were also an important source of financing, accounting for a third of the multilateral debt of the low-income countries.

The *Report* concluded that, following the initiatives taken by bilateral official creditors, the debt problem had shifted to that of outstanding debt owed to multilateral financial institutions. With few exceptions, a decade of adjustment policies supported by financing from multilateral financial institutions had not halted or reversed the economic stagnation of the heavily indebted low-income countries or increased their capacity to service external debt. There was little doubt that those countries would have to rely for some time on highly concessional finance. How to use those funds to increase their export earnings and enhance their development prospects was the real challenge for both recipient countries and the rest of the international community.

**Report of the Secretary-General.** In response to a 1994 General Assembly request,[4] the Secretary-General submitted a report on the developing-country debt situation as of mid-1995.[5] The report updated the current strategy in terms of new measures launched by private, bilateral official and multilateral creditors to deal with persistent difficulties faced by developing countries in servicing their external debt obligations, analysed recent debt indicators and discussed the situation of countries that were still classified as severely indebted despite the initiatives adopted.

The report concluded that although significant relief had been accorded to some countries and for certain classes of debt, the international strategy had not comprehensively addressed the full stock of debt, leaving vulnerable those countries whose debt-servicing obligations still exceeded their capacity to pay. Removing the debt overhang would not by itself solve the development problems of the debt-crisis countries, but while it remained even the most rigorous and effective domestic economic stabilization and structural adjustment programmes would leave the countries in question with serious obstacles to moving to a sustained and sustainable development path.

**Group of Seven Summit.** The seven major industrialized nations (Canada, France, Germany, Italy, Japan, United Kingdom, United States), in the communiqué adopted at their 1995 Summit meeting (Halifax, Canada, 15-17 June),[6] urged full and constructive implementation of the Naples terms. They stated that they would encourage the Bretton Woods institutions (IMF and the World Bank Group) to develop a comprehensive approach to assist countries with multilateral debt problems through flexible implementation of existing instruments and new mechanisms where necessary. They would further encourage better use of all existing World Bank and IMF resources and adoption of appropriate measures in the multilateral development banks to advance that objective and to continue concessional Enhanced Structural Adjustment Facility lending operations.

**Group of 77 annual meeting.** In the declaration adopted at the nineteenth annual meeting of Ministers for Foreign Affairs of the Group of 77 developing countries (New York, 29 September),[7] the Ministers regretted that, despite the implementation of several approaches undertaken by the international community, the debt crisis continued to persist as one of the main constraints for the development of developing countries. They reiterated the urgent need for the international community, particularly the donor countries and international financial institutions, to adopt an effective, comprehensive and equitable, once-and-for-all development-oriented and durable solution to the debt problems of the developing countries, including debt reduction and increased concessional financial flows for LDCs and Africa. They stressed that structural adjustment policies should not divert resources from social priorities in debtor countries.

**GENERAL ASSEMBLY ACTION**

On 20 December, the General Assembly adopted **resolution 50/92**.

**Enhancing international cooperation towards a durable solution to the external debt problem of developing countries**

*The General Assembly,*

*Recalling* its resolutions 41/202 of 8 December 1986, 42/198 of 11 December 1987, 43/198 of 20 December 1988, 44/205 of 22 December 1989, 45/214 of 21 December 1990, 46/148 and 46/151 of 18 December 1991 and 47/198 of 22 December 1992, and reaffirming its resolutions 48/182 of 21 December 1993 and 49/94 of 19 December 1994,

*Reaffirming* its resolutions 48/165 of 21 December 1993 on renewal of the dialogue on strengthening international economic cooperation for development through partnership and 48/166 of 21 December 1993 on an agenda for development,

*Noting* the improvement in the debt situation of a number of developing countries since the second half of the 1980s and the contribution that the evolving debt strategy has made to this improvement,

*Noting with appreciation* the debt-relief measures undertaken by creditor countries both within the framework of the Paris Club and through their cancellation and equivalent relief of bilateral official debt, and welcoming the even more favourable terms of the debt-relief measures recently envisaged by the Paris Club, namely the Naples terms of December 1994, for the poorest and heavily indebted countries, to help them exit from the rescheduling process, thus contributing to the prospects of those countries for resuming growth and development,

*Reaffirming* the urgent need for effective, equitable, development-oriented and durable solutions to the external debt and debt-servicing problems of developing countries, and to help them exit from the rescheduling process,

*Emphasizing* the importance for debtor countries of continuing to pursue and intensify their efforts with respect to economic reforms, stabilization and structural adjustment programmes, in order to raise savings and investments, reduce inflation and improve economic efficiency, taking into account the need to address the social aspects of development, including the eradication of poverty, and their individual characteristics, as well as the vulnerability of the poorer strata of their populations,

*Stressing* the urgent need for further assisting developing countries, in particular the poorest and heavily indebted countries, especially in Africa, in their efforts to improve their debt situation in view of their continued very high level of total debt stock and servicing burdens,

*Noting* the urgent need for full, constructive and expeditious implementation of various debt-relief measures undertaken by creditor countries both within the framework of the Paris Club and through their cancellations and equivalent relief of bilateral official debt,

*Noting also* that, owing to uneven developments within the context of the evolving international debt strategy, further progress, including new and concrete measures and innovative approaches, is essential as regards contributing to effective, equitable, development-oriented and durable solutions to the external debt and debt-servicing problems of developing countries, particularly the poorest and heavily indebted countries,

*Noting with concern* the continuing debt and debt-servicing problems of indebted developing countries as constituting an element adversely affecting their development efforts and economic growth, and stressing the importance of alleviating the onerous debt and debt-service burdens connected with various types of debt of many developing countries, on the basis of an effective, equitable, development-oriented and durable approach and, where appropriate, addressing the full stock of debt of the poorest and most indebted developing countries as a matter of priority,

*Noting* that multilateral lending operations are excluded from debt restructuring and, in this regard, emphasizing the need for the consideration of comprehensive approaches to assist low-income countries with substantial multilateral debt problems through the flexible implementation of existing instruments and new mechanisms where necessary,

*Expressing its concern* that, in a number of developing countries that are making continuous and strenuous economic reform efforts, the burden of debt and debt service continues to constitute a major obstacle to the revitalization of the economic growth and development of those countries, in particular the least developed among them,

*Noting* that those developing countries that have continued, at great cost to themselves, to meet their international debt and debt-service obligations in a timely fashion have done so despite serious external and domestic financial constraints,

*Also expressing its concern* that debt-relief measures taken so far have not yet fully provided effective, equitable, development-oriented and durable solutions to the outstanding debt and debt-servicing problems of a large number of developing countries, in particular the poorest and heavily indebted countries,

*Reaffirming* the results, as agreed, of all major United Nations conferences and summits held since the beginning of the 1990s on development, relating to effective, equitable, development-oriented and durable solutions to the external debt and debt-servicing problems of developing countries, as well as the consideration of appropriate measures relating to the mobilization of substantial, new and additional resources to enable developing countries to achieve sustained economic growth and sustainable development,

*Noting*, while addressing the external debt and debt-servicing problems of developing countries, the situation in some creditor countries with economies in transition,

*Stressing* the need for continuing global economic growth and the necessity for a continuing supportive international economic environment with regard to, *inter alia*, terms of trade, commodity prices, improved market access, trade practices, access to technology, exchange rates and international interest rates, and noting the continued need for resources for sustained economic growth and sustainable development of the developing countries,

*Taking note* of the results of the Eleventh Conference of Heads of State or Government of the Non-Aligned Countries, held at Cartagena de Indias, Colombia, from 18 to 20 October 1995, in particular, chapter III, entitled "Economic issues", of the Final Document of the Conference,

*Taking note also* of the communiqué of the Summit of the seven major industrialized countries, held at Halifax, Canada, from 15 to 17 June 1995,

*Taking note further* of the communiqué of the Interim Committee of the Board of Governors of the International Monetary Fund, held at Washington on 8 October 1995,

*Taking note* of the Ministerial Declaration of the Group of 77 adopted at the nineteenth annual meeting of Ministers for Foreign Affairs of the Group of 77 and China, held in New York on 29 September 1995,

1. *Takes note* of the report of the Secretary-General on the developing country debt situation as of mid-1995;

2. *Recognizes* that effective, equitable, development-oriented and durable solutions to the external debt and debt-servicing problems of developing countries can contribute substantially to the strengthening of the global economy and to the efforts of developing countries to achieve sustained economic growth and sustainable development;

3. *Also recognizes* that the evolving international debt strategy has to be supplemented by appropriate external financial flows to indebted developing countries;

4. *Emphasizes* the importance for developing countries of continuing their efforts to promote a favourable environment for attracting foreign investment, thereby promoting economic growth and sustainable development, and stresses the need for the international community to promote a conducive external economic environment through, *inter alia*, improved market access, stabilization of exchange rates, effective stewardship of international interest rates and increased resource flows, as well as improved access to technology for the developing countries;

5. *Stresses* the need for finding effective, equitable, development-oriented and durable solutions to the continuing debt and debt-servicing problems of the poorest and most indebted developing countries and the importance of a full, constructive and expeditious implementation of the Naples terms, agreed upon in the Paris Club in December 1994, for such countries, with a view to helping them exit from the rescheduling process on the basis of sound economic policies in those countries, thus contributing to the promotion of their prospects for resuming growth and development;

6. *Recognizes* the efforts of indebted developing countries in fulfilling their commitments on debt servicing despite the incurring of a high social cost and, in this regard, encourages private creditors and, in particular, commercial banks to continue their initiatives and efforts to address the commercial debt problems of middle-income developing countries;

7. *Invites* creditor countries, private banks and multilateral financial institutions, within their prerogatives, to consider continuing the initiatives and efforts to address the commercial debt problems of the least developed countries and the requests for continued mobilization of resources through the Debt-reduction Facility

of the International Development Association in order to help eligible least developed countries reduce their commercial debt;

8.  *Notes* the high proportion of multilateral debt of a number of developing countries and invites international financial institutions to examine proposals to tackle the problems of those countries with regard to multilateral debt, taking into account the specific situation of each country, while preserving the preferred creditor status of the multilateral financial institutions, in order to ensure that they can continue to provide concessional financing to those developing countries to assist their development;

9.  *Reaffirms* the mid-term global review of the implementation of the Programme of Action for the Least Developed Countries for the 1990s, in particular the appropriate actions in favour of least developed countries concerning their official bilateral, commercial and multilateral debt;

10.  *Notes with concern* the continuing burden of debt and debt-service obligations of middle-income countries, including in particular those in Africa, and encourages creditors, including multilateral financial institutions and commercial banks, to continue to address their obligations effectively;

11.  *Stresses* the importance of continued concessional Enhanced Structural Adjustment Facility lending operations for low-income countries;

12.  *Also stresses* the need for existing facilities to provide debt-relief measures through various debt conversion programmes, where possible, such as debt-equity swaps, debt-for-nature swaps, debt-for-child-development swaps, and other debt-for-development swaps, to be widely implemented so that the countries concerned may be ably assisted in their development efforts, as well as to support measures in favour of the most vulnerable segments of the societies of those countries and to develop techniques of debt conversion applied to social development programmes and projects, in conformity with the priorities of the World Summit for Social Development, held at Copenhagen in March 1995;

13.  *Further stresses* the need for, in addition to debt-relief measures that include debt and debt-service reduction, new financial flows to debtor developing countries, and urges creditor countries and multilateral financial institutions to continue to extend concessional financial assistance, particularly to the least developed countries, in order to support the implementation of economic reforms, stabilization and structural adjustment programmes and the eradication of poverty by the developing countries so as to enable them to extricate themselves from the debt overhang and to assist them in achieving sustained economic growth and sustainable development;

14.  *Stresses* the need for the expeditious conclusion of the ongoing work of the International Monetary Fund, in close collaboration with the World Bank, on the steps to address the problems of those low-income countries that are undertaking strong adjustment and reform programmes but whose debt situation, including debt to multilateral institutions, may prove unsustainable, even after debt reduction on the Naples terms, within this context urging donor countries to fulfil promptly their commitments to the tenth replenishment of the International Development Association and to support a significant replenishment through the elev-

enth replenishment of the Association, and requests the Secretary-General to report to the General Assembly at its fifty-first session on the outcome of the meeting of the Development Committee scheduled for April 1996;

15.  *Notes* the initiative to develop new, parallel financing arrangements, complementary to the General Arrangements to Borrow, with the aim of doubling the resources currently available under the General Arrangements to Borrow;

16.  *Recognizes* that the evolving debt strategy must be accompanied by a favourable and supportive international environment, including the full implementation of the results of the Uruguay Round of multilateral trade negotiations, and the Marrakesh ministerial decisions in favour of the least developed countries and net food-importing developing countries;

17.  *Invites* the International Monetary Fund to continue devising concrete policy measures and actions to address the problems faced by indebted developing countries;

18.  *Underscores* the need for encouragement of private flows to all countries, in particular developing countries, while reducing the risks of volatility;

19.  *Stresses* the urgent need to continue to provide social safety nets to vulnerable groups most adversely affected by the implementation of economic reform programmes in the debtor countries, in particular low-income groups;

20.  *Urges* the international community, particularly the creditor countries and multilateral institutions, as well as commercial banks and other lending institutions, when continuing the implementation of various measures aimed at contributing to effective, equitable, development-oriented and durable solutions to the external debt and debt-servicing problems of developing countries, as well as when exploring the need for additional and innovative measures to alleviate substantially the external debt and debt-service burden of developing countries, to ensure that the debt strategy evolved through the years is fully implemented and taken into account;

21.  *Recognizes* the urgent need for the international community to assist developing countries, in particular the poorest and heavily indebted countries, in mobilizing the resources needed for their development efforts, and also recognizes that effective, equitable, development-oriented and durable solutions to the external debt and debt-servicing problems of developing countries could contribute towards releasing domestic resources and sustaining their development efforts, in particular those for social development;

22.  *Calls upon* the international community, including the relevant institutions, to build upon the momentum gained from the various meetings that have addressed debt issues and to address the external debt and debt-servicing problems of developing countries, particularly those of the least developed countries, in the elaboration of an agenda for development;

23.  *Also calls upon* the international community, including the United Nations system, and invites the Bretton Woods institutions, as well as the private sector, to take urgent measures and action for the implementation of the commitments, agreements and decisions of the major United Nations conferences and summits organized since the beginning of the 1990s on develop-

ment, addressing, *inter alia*, and where appropriate, the question of external debt;

24. *Requests* the Secretary-General to report to the General Assembly at its fifty-first session on the implementation of the present resolution.

General Assembly resolution 50/92

20 December 1995     Meeting 96     Adopted without vote

Approved by Second Committee (A/50/616) without vote, 12 December (meeting 43); draft by Vice-Chairman (A/C.2/50/L.75), based on informal consultations on draft by Colombia (for Non-Aligned Movement), Kyrgyzstan and Philippines (for Group of 77 and China) (A/C.2/50/L.7); agenda item 94.
*Meeting numbers.* GA 50th session: 2nd Committee 11-13, 23, 24, 32, 41, 43; plenary 96.

## Taxation

As decided by the Economic and Social Council in 1994,[8] the Ad Hoc Group of Experts on International Cooperation in Tax Matters held its seventh meeting in 1995 (Geneva, 11-15 December).[9] The Group's Steering Committee had met in New York from 5 to 7 June,[10] proposing four areas for special attention: the tax treatment of teachers and students, with reference to the possible deletion of two articles of the 1980 United Nations Model Double Taxation Convention between Developed and Developing Countries; the tax treatment of transfer pricing; the tax treatment of financial instruments and derivatives; and the updating of the Model Convention and the *Manual for the Negotiation of Bilateral Tax Treaties between Developed and Developing Countries*. The Steering Committee also considered expanding the Group's role to include the provision of technical assistance and support in the areas of tax administration, international taxation, transfer pricing and the negotiation of tax treaties. The Group of Experts included those topics on its agenda.

The Group of Experts did not reach a consensus on the deletion of articles from the Model Convention, but agreed that an addition could be made to the commentary providing advice for bilateral negotiations on visiting teachers. It was also agreed that a drafting committee should make recommendations on activities to be undertaken by the Group in the area of transfer pricing. The Group noted that consideration of the important issue of new financial instruments was in its introductory stages and further analysis was needed. In view of the lengthy process involved in revising the Model Convention, the Group indicated that it would be useful to have it reprinted and the Secretariat was asked to facilitate that task. As to expanding its role relating to technical assistance in international taxation, the Group considered a proposal for the organization of five annual interregional workshops, which had been developed by the Secretariat in response to a Steering Committee request. The Group noted the need to coordinate the proposed technical assistance programme with the efforts of other organizations.

## Financing of development

In response to a 1993 General Assembly request,[11] the Secretary-General submitted a report on the sources of finance for development at mid-decade,[12] which focused on the levels of saving that could be used to finance investment and the channels for allocating savings to particular investments. The report noted that recent developments in private and official flows had put the long-standing questions of development financing in a new context, in which the volatility of private flows was more highly appreciated and the significant future growth of official flows, particularly ODA, could not be taken for granted. Policy makers in some developing countries had, therefore, begun to focus on the disparate characteristics of different types of private financial inflows, and many questioned the wisdom of early and complete liberalization of the capital account in international transactions. Meanwhile, in some developed countries, the prospective role of development assistance itself was being re-examined. A related concern was that the foreign debt difficulties of developing countries—debt owed to both private and official creditors—had not been resolved more than a decade after the debt crisis burst onto the international political stage (see above).

The report's main conclusion was that in the short to medium term the world economy seemed able to generate the savings needed to finance global investment, including that of the developing countries. It was not so clear, however, whether those savings would find their way in adequate amounts to the more desirable places and would be used for the more desirable projects in terms of equitable, sustainable and efficient development. That would depend on: the development of the financial sector in developing countries; economic reform and socio-economic policy more generally; the ability of private and public investors in developing countries to tap international financial resources; and the flow of official resources for development.

**GENERAL ASSEMBLY ACTION**

On 20 December, the General Assembly adopted **resolution 50/93**.

### Sources for the financing of development

*The General Assembly*,

*Reaffirming* the Declaration on International Economic Cooperation, in particular the Revitalization of Economic Growth and Development of the Developing Countries, contained in the annex to its resolution S-18/3 of 1 May 1990, and the International Development Strategy for the Fourth United Nations Development Decade, contained in the annex to its resolution 45/199 of 21 December 1990,

*Recalling* its resolution 45/234 of 21 December 1990 on the implementation of the commitments and policies agreed upon in the Declaration,

*Recalling also* its resolution 48/187 of 21 December 1993, particularly as it relates to the decision to continue to explore the issue of the financing of development and its potential funding sources,

*Decides* to consider at the fifty-second session of the General Assembly the convening of an international conference on the financing of development, and requests the Secretary-General to submit to it at its fifty-second session a report on substantive areas, including the consideration of aspects of interrelatedness and coordination necessary as a basis for the full consideration of the issue of financing of development and its potential funding sources.

General Assembly resolution 50/93

20 December 1995      Meeting 96      Adopted without vote

Approved by Second Committee (A/50/616) without vote, 12 December (meeting 43); draft by Vice-Chairman (A/C.2/50/L.74), based on informal consultations on draft by Kyrgyzstan and Philippines, for Group of 77 and China (A/C.2/50/L.15); agenda item 94.
*Meeting numbers.* GA 50th session: 2nd Committee 11-13, 23, 24, 32, 41, 43; plenary 96.

Also on 20 December, the Assembly, by **decision 50/424**, took note of the Secretary-General's report on the sources of finance for development at mid-decade.

## International investment and transnational corporations

International production by transnational corporations (TNCs)—some 40,000 parent firms and some 250,000 foreign affiliates—was increasingly influencing the size and nature of cross-border transactions, stated the *World Investment Report 1995: Transnational Corporations and Competitiveness.*[13] In the 1990s, the rate of growth of FDI stock substantially exceeded that of world output (GDP) and world exports. The size and scope of international production were amplified further by the activities of TNCs in forms other than FDI, such as subcontracting, licensing and franchising, through which markets for goods, services and factors of production could be reached and international production organized. Global sales in international markets associated with that more broadly defined international production amounted to an estimated $7 trillion in 1992, compared to some $3 trillion in arm's-length trade.

Investment stocks and flows remained concentrated primarily in the developed world and particularly in the Triad (EU, Japan and the United States), as far as both their origin and their destination were concerned. That distribution of inward FDI stock mirrored market size, with the developing countries accounting for between one fifth and one quarter of both world GDP and global inward FDI stock. However, the FDI stock in developing countries was highly concentrated: the 10 largest developing host countries accounted for about two thirds of the total stock in developing countries, more than would be expected from their share in developing-country output or trade. As far as outward stock was concerned, firms from developing countries generated only 6 per cent of the world FDI stock in 1994. As with inward investment, the outward developing-country FDI stock was largely accounted for by firms from only a handful of developing countries.

As far as FDI flows were concerned, the share of developing countries in world inflows was higher than their share in world imports (about 30 per cent in the early 1990s). In terms of FDI outflows, the developing-country share was about half of their share in world exports. By the end of 1993, FDI outflows had largely recovered from the FDI recession (reaching $222 billion) and, in 1994, maintained that level. Preliminary estimates for 1995 ($230 billion) suggested that the recovery had been further consolidated.

## Commission on International Investment and TNCs

In accordance with a 1994 General Assembly resolution,[14] by which the Commission on Transnational Corporations became a commission of TDB and was renamed the Commission on International Investment and Transnational Corporations, the Board, by a 31 March decision,[15] adopted the terms of reference of the Commission and annexed them to its decision. The Board also decided that the rules of procedure of its main committees should apply to the Commission.

The Commission held its twenty-first session in Geneva from 24 to 28 April.[16] It had before it a report by the UNCTAD secretariat on trends in FDI,[17] which noted that the increase of FDI outflows by 5 per cent in 1993 to $193 billion (and by an additional 6 per cent in 1994 to an estimated $204 billion) marked the end of the FDI recession. The global FDI stock stood at an estimated $2.1 trillion at the end of 1993; sales associated with some 207,000 foreign affiliates were around $5.8 trillion in 1992. The recovery of the developed economies and the continuing strong growth of several major recipient developing countries were the principal factors in the turn-around in investment flows. Underlying those cyclical factors were the ongoing liberalization of investment regimes (including the adoption of privatization programmes) and the decline of majority foreign-owned cross-border mergers and acquisitions, particularly among the developed countries. Flows into developing countries, at a record $71 billion in 1993 (and an estimated $80 billion in 1994), continued to grow, even as the economies of developed countries began to recover, thus boosting their share of total inflows to some 39 per cent. However, 80 per cent of the inflows were to 10 developing countries, in particular China. Outward FDI from several developing countries, including inter-developing-country FDI (and increasingly investments from developing to developed countries), was growing, especially from countries whose firms recognized the importance of investing abroad to remain competitive. The levels of FDI flows and stocks were not indicative of the importance of other modalities of servicing markets and accessing assets internationally. The proliferation of alliances, licensing agreements and subcontracting added more dimensions to international transactions undertaken by TNCs, diminished the risks embedded in those transactions because of diversification, and strengthened the relationship and multiplied the links between producers and consumers in different countries.

Other documentation before the Commission included UNCTAD secretariat reports on FDI in developing countries[18] and on experience gained in technical cooperation activities relating to the commercialization of science and technology.[19] The Commission also considered the report of the Working Group of Experts on International Standards of Accounting and Reporting on its 1995 session (see below) and a number of background documents.

In the course of the Commission session, four informal panel discussions were organized on: the international framework for FDI; recent developments in international investments and TNCs; incentives and FDI; and the FDI impact on the Mexican crisis.

On 28 April, the Commission adopted agreed conclusions, in which it stated that it would continue to review recent developments in the areas of investment, resource mobilization, particularly savings, and the interlinkages among FDI, trade, competition, technology and other international transactions. It would seek the active participation of the private sector in the context of specific topics in those areas. The Commission noted the relatively low levels of both foreign and domestic investment in Africa. It recognized the role of investment for development, with special attention to Africa, with a view to improving the climate for investment; supported international activities aimed at increasing FDI flows; and encouraged the organization of such activities in conjunction with UNCTAD IX. The Commission was prepared to undertake policy reviews of member States that so desired. Such reviews would be an occasion to familiarize other Governments and the private sector with an individual country's investment environment and policies and should be undertaken on the basis of a common format and include inputs from the private sector and non-governmental experts.

The Commission stated that it would deepen its analysis of incentives and their costs and benefits as part of the overall investment climate, as well as patterns of investment. It requested the UNCTAD secretariat to undertake the necessary analytical work and to explore the possibility of preparing pilot presentations of information on incentives for a small number of countries that wished to participate. TDB was asked to explore the possibility of making the *World Investment Report* available in all UN official languages in time for the Commission's session.

### Standards of accounting and reporting

At its thirteenth session (Geneva, 13-17 March),[20] the Intergovernmental Working Group of Experts on International Standards of Accounting and Reporting had before it reports of the UNCTAD secretariat covering a review of national environmental accounting laws and regulations;[21] incentives and disincentives for the adoption of sustainable development by TNCs;[22] disclosure by TNCs of environmental matters at the national level in annual reports;[23] and the integration of environmental performance indicators with financial information by TNCs.[24] It also considered a case-study on accounting for sustainable forestry management.[25]

The Group concluded that the UNCTAD Secretary-General should be asked to convene a group of experts and to prepare a report on environmental accounting. It requested the secretariat to report on environmental accounting in 1996 and welcomed voluntary contributions by Governments and/or organizations for research and studies on the subject. The Group further concluded that the 1996 work programme, to be reported on in 1997, should include research on a conceptual framework for environmental accounting and a study of the implications of the accounting standards work performed by the International Organization of Securities Commissions and the International Accounting Standards Committee. With regard to the establishment of a subgroup to investigate the development of global qualification standards for accountants and auditors to be endorsed by the United Nations, which the Group had recommended for adoption by the Commission on TNCs in 1994,[26] that recommendation was still before the Commission for consideration. The Group agreed that if the subgroup was established, work on accreditation should initially focus not on the professional accountancy level but rather on a level referred to as management and financial accountants; depending on available resources, consideration might be given to a combined approach involving parallel focus on management accountants and/or (statutory) auditors.

With regard to assistance for accountancy development, the Group, having considered the outcome of the Ad Hoc Working Group of Experts on Accountancy Training and Development, which met in 1994,[26] concurred with that Group's recommendation that the proposal for an accounting education project in Senegal should be selected for further work, together with an effort to strengthen the accounting profession in one African country.

*REFERENCES*

[1]*Trade and Development Report, 1995* (UNCTAD/TDR/15), Sales No. E.95.II.D.16. [2]YUN 1994, p. 892, GA res. 49/93, 19 Dec. 1994. [3]*World Economic and Social Survey 1995* (E/1995/50), Sales No. E.95.II.C.1. [4]YUN 1994, p. 895, GA res. 49/94, 19 Dec. 1994. [5]A/50/379 & Corr.1. [6]A/50/254-S/1995/501. [7]A/50/518. [8]YUN 1994, p. 897, ESC dec. 1994/211, 3 Feb. 1994. [9]E/1996/62. [10]ST/SG/AC.8/1995/L.7. [11]YUN 1993, p. 762, GA res. 48/187, 21 Dec. 1993. [12]A/50/397. [13]*World Investment Report 1995: Transnational Corporations and Competitiveness* (UNCTAD/DTCI/26), Sales No. E.95.II.A.9. [14]YUN 1994, p. 904, GA res. 49/130, 19 Dec. 1994. [15]A/50/15, vol. I (dec. 425(XLI)). [16]TD/B/42(1)/4. [17]TD/B/ITNC/2. [18]TD/B/ITNC/3. [19]TD/B/ITNC/4. [20]TD/B/ITNC/5. [21]TD/B/ITNC/AC.1/2. [22]TD/B/ITNC/AC.1/3. [23]TD/B/ITNC/AC.1/4. [24]TD/B/ITNC/AC.1/5. [25]UNCTAD/DTCI/4. [26]YUN 1994, p. 906.

# Transport

## Maritime transport

### Shipping services

The third session of the Standing Committee on Developing Services Sectors: Fostering Competitive Services in Developing Countries—Shipping was held in Geneva from 6 to 9 June.[1] It considered UNCTAD secretariat reports on competitive services in multimodal transport;[2] technical cooperation and human resource development in shipping, ports and multimodal transport;[3] and the work programme of the Standing Committee, with special emphasis on preparations for UNCTAD IX.[4]

The Committee also reviewed work accomplished since UNCTAD VIII in 1992,[5] and outlined work that remained to be done before UNCTAD IX in 1996. It suggested possible future activities that TDB might take into account for consideration by UNCTAD IX: technical cooperation and human resource development; shipping aimed at fostering progressive liberalization and facilitating the provision of free and fair competitive shipping services; ports; multimodal transport involving a sealeg; and maritime and transport legislation aimed at fostering international trade and transport of developing countries.

### Maritime legislation

#### Maritime liens and mortgages

The Joint UNCTAD/International Maritime Organization (IMO) Intergovernmental Group of Experts on Maritime Liens and Mortgages and Related Subjects held its eighth session in 1995 (London,

9-12 October).[6] It considered a possible review of the International Convention for the Unification of Certain Rules relating to the Arrest of Sea-going Ships, 1952. The Group had before it a note[7] by the UNCTAD and IMO secretariats on such a review, which comprised a set of draft articles for a convention on arrest of ships, taking into account discussions by the Group in 1994.[8] The Group established an informal Sessional Group of the Whole, which adopted the UNCTAD/IMO draft articles as its basic text. The Sessional Group introduced several amendments to the draft and decided to consider it again in 1996.

## Transport of dangerous goods

The Secretary-General submitted to the Economic and Social Council a report[9] on the work during 1993-1994 of the Committee of Experts on the Transport of Dangerous Goods. The Committee adopted new and amended recommendations on the transport of dangerous goods and finalized the rationalization of its *Manual of Tests and Criteria* for the classification of dangerous goods. It requested that the new and amended recommendations be compiled in a new revised edition (the ninth revised edition) of the *Recommendations on the Transport of Dangerous Goods*, and that that revised edition be published, in all official languages, not later than the end of 1995. The Committee also requested that the *Manual of Tests and Criteria* be published in English and French not later than the end of 1995, and in all the other official languages as soon as possible.

The Committee took steps to give effective follow-up to Agenda 21, adopted by the UN Conference on Environment and Development in 1992,[10] particularly chapter 19 dealing with environmentally sound management of toxic chemicals, including prevention of illegal international traffic in toxic and dangerous products.

In 1995, the Committee's Subcommittee of Experts on the Transport of Dangerous Goods held its tenth (Geneva, 10-20 July)[11] and eleventh (Geneva, 4-15 December)[12] sessions, while the Committee itself was scheduled to meet again in 1996.

ECONOMIC AND SOCIAL COUNCIL ACTION

On 19 July, the Economic and Social Council adopted **resolution 1995/5.**

#### Work of the Committee of Experts on the Transport of Dangerous Goods

*The Economic and Social Council,*

*Recalling* its resolution 1993/50 of 29 July 1993,

*Noting* the increasing volume of dangerous goods in worldwide commerce and the rapid expansion of technology and innovation,

*Bearing in mind* the continuing need to meet the growing concern for the protection of life, property and the environment through the safe transport of dangerous goods, while facilitating trade,

*Aware* that, in order to achieve internationally harmonized laws, the Economic Commission for Europe, the specialized agencies, other international organizations involved in activities related to the transport of dangerous goods and interested Member States have responded positively to the Council's various resolutions adopted since 15 April 1953, and that, being committed to taking the recommendations of the Committee of Experts on the Transport of Dangerous Goods as a basis for the formulation of their requirements and regulations, including those concerning labelling and classification, those organizations therefore rely on the work of the Committee,

*Noting* the activities of the Economic Commission for Europe and the Central Office for International Railway Transport, as well as projects of other international organizations for restructuring their regulations applicable to the transport of dangerous goods,

*Noting also* the advice of the Committee to the effect that reformatting the provisions applicable to all modes of transport contained in the *Recommendations on the Transport of Dangerous Goods* into a model regulation, annexed to a basic recommendation, that could be directly integrated into all modal national and international regulations would enhance harmonization, facilitate regular updating of all instruments concerned by the relevant organizations or regulatory authorities, and result in overall considerable resource savings for the Governments of the Member States, the United Nations, the specialized agencies and other international organizations,

1. *Takes note* of the report of the Secretary-General on the work of the Committee of Experts on the Transport of Dangerous Goods during the biennium 1993-1994 and of the new and amended recommendations approved by the Committee for inclusion in its existing recommendations, including a rationalized *Manual of Tests and Criteria;*

2. *Commends* the Secretary-General for the timely publication of the eighth revised edition of the *Recommendations on the Transport of Dangerous Goods* in all the official languages of the United Nations;

3. *Requests* the Secretary-General:

*(a)* To incorporate within the existing recommendations of the Committee of Experts on the Transport of Dangerous Goods all the new and amended recommendations approved by the Committee at its eighteenth session;

*(b)* To publish the new and amended recommendations in all the official languages of the United Nations, in the most cost-effective manner, not later than the end of 1995;

*(c)* To publish, in the most cost-effective manner, the rationalized *Manual of Tests and Criteria* in English and French not later than the end of 1995, and in all the other official languages of the United Nations as soon as possible;

*(d)* To circulate the new and amended recommendations, including the *Manual of Tests and Criteria*, immediately after their publication to the Governments of Member States, the specialized agencies, the International Atomic Energy Agency and other international organizations concerned;

4. *Invites* all Governments, the specialized agencies, the International Atomic Energy Agency and the other international organizations concerned to transmit to the Secretary-General their views on the Committee's work, together with any comments that they may wish to make on the amended recommendations;

5. *Invites* all interested Governments, regional commissions and specialized agencies and the international organizations concerned, when developing appropriate codes and regulations, to take full account of the recommendations of the Committee;

6. *Requests* the Secretary-General to take all necessary steps for ensuring representation of the secretariat of the Committee at appropriate meetings of international organizations committed to implementing the recommendations of the Committee or involved in the process of global harmonization of classification and labelling systems for chemicals;

7. *Approves* the programme of work of the Committee and its Subcommittee of Experts on the Transport of Dangerous Goods for the biennium 1995-1996, and the working arrangements and the priorities of work for that biennium, as follows:

*(a)* Global harmonization of classification criteria (implementation of chapter 19 of Agenda 21), in accordance with Council resolution 1995/6 of 19 July 1995 on the role of the Committee in the development of a harmonized system of classification and labelling of chemicals for implementing chapter 19 of Agenda 21;

*(b)* Reformatting of the *Recommendations on the Transport of Dangerous Goods* into a model regulation;

*(c)* Review of the recommendations on the transport of dangerous goods in multimodal portable tanks;

*(d)* New or revised recommendations on the transport of dangerous goods;

8. *Requests* the Secretary-General to maintain the appropriate staff resources for the service of meetings related to the work of the Committee and its Subcommittee, in view of the new programme of work which includes as a high priority the global harmonization of classification criteria;

9. *Also requests* the Secretary-General to submit a report to the Council in 1997 on the implementation of the present resolution.

Economic and Social Council resolution 1995/5

19 July 1995          Meeting 44          Adopted without vote

Draft by Committee of Experts on the Transport of Dangerous Goods (E/1995/56); agenda item 6 *(j)*.
Meeting numbers. ESC 42-44.

Also on 19 July, the Council adopted **resolution 1995/6**.

**Role of the Committee of Experts on the Transport of Dangerous Goods in the development of a harmonized system of classification and labelling of chemicals for implementing chapter 19 of Agenda 21**

*The Economic and Social Council,*

*Recalling* its resolution 468 G (XV) of 15 April 1953, in which it established the terms of reference of the Committee of Experts on the Transport of Dangerous Goods, in particular with regard to its role in recommending and defining groupings or classifications of dangerous goods on the basis of the character of risk involved, and recommending marks or labels for each grouping or classification which should identify the risk graphically and without regard to printed text,

*Recalling also* its resolution 645 G (XXIII) of 26 April 1957, in which it invited the Secretary-General to continue his consultations with the Director-General of the International Labour Office on the best means of avoiding any overlapping of the work of the Committee with any work being undertaken in this field by the International Labour Organization,

*Recalling further* its resolution 1993/50 of 29 July 1993, in which it invited all Governments and the international organizations concerned with the implementation of chapter 19 of Agenda 21, and participating in the development of a globally harmonized system of classification and labelling of chemicals, to avoid duplication of work and to ensure that, to the greatest extent possible, the new system drew on, or was compatible with, the internationally well-recognized and implemented system developed by the Committee,

*Bearing in mind* that the Commission on Sustainable Development, at its second session, when reviewing progress in the implementation of Agenda 21 and, in particular, the sectoral cluster "Toxic chemicals and hazardous wastes", endorsed the priorities for action for the implementation of chapter 19 of Agenda 21, adopted by the International Conference on Chemical Safety, held at Stockholm from 25 to 29 April 1994, and welcomed in particular the targets and timetables agreed upon, including the date of 1997 for finalization of the technical work on classification criteria, and that the Commission called upon United Nations bodies and other international organizations to improve international coordination to avoid unnecessary duplication of efforts and to strengthen the International Programme on Chemical Safety,

*Recalling* its decision 1994/300 of 29 July 1994, in which it endorsed the decisions and recommendations contained in the report of the Commission on Sustainable Development, with the exception of that contained in chapter I, paragraph 24, and invited, *inter alia*, organs of the United Nations system to implement those decisions and recommendations and to take the necessary action to give them effective and transparent follow-up,

*Noting* that the Committee, to accelerate the work on global harmonization, is already cooperating with the International Labour Office, the World Health Organization, the United Nations Environment Programme and the Organisation for Economic Cooperation and Development with regard to criteria for health hazards and hazards to the environment,

*Noting also* that the Committee, after four years of fruitful work, has just finalized an extensive revision of its *Manual of Tests and Criteria*, related to the classification of flammable, explosive and reactive materials,

*Noting further* that the Director of the International Programme on Chemical Safety and the Director of the Working Conditions and Environment Department of the International Labour Office have requested the Committee to elaborate proposals for globally harmonized criteria for the classification of flammable, explosive and reactive materials, on the basis of the newly revised *Manual of Tests and Criteria*, which should take account of aspects not necessarily covered under transport safety regulations, that is, of other aspects such as the protection of workers, consumers and the general environment, in collaboration with experts in those aspects,

*Confirming* the need for the Committee to participate actively in relevant activities associated with the implementation of Agenda 21, and to cooperate not only with international bodies involved in activities related to the transport of dangerous goods but also with those involved in other aspects of chemical safety,

1. *Notes with satisfaction* that the Committee of Experts on the Transport of Dangerous Goods has taken the necessary steps to collaborate with the international bodies and international organizations concerned with the implementation of chapter 19 of Agenda 21, in particular for the purpose of establishing and elaborating a harmonized classification and labelling system for chemicals, and to strengthen its links with the International Programme on Chemical Safety;

2. *Requests* the Committee, as a high priority in its work programme in accordance with Council resolution 1995/5 of 19 July 1995 on the work of the Committee:

(a) To elaborate, by the end of 1996, as requested by the International Programme on Chemical Safety and the International Labour Organization, proposals for globally harmonized criteria for the classification of flammable, explosive and reactive materials, on the basis of the newly revised *Manual of Tests and Criteria*, taking account of aspects not necessarily covered under transport safety regulations, such as the protection of workers, consumers and the general environment, in collaboration with experts from the International Labour Organization and the Programme;

(b) To continue collaboration with the International Programme on Chemical Safety for the implementation of chapter 19 of Agenda 21;

3. *Requests* the Secretary-General to convene, in consultation with the Director-General of the International Labour Office, meetings of experts in the classification of physical hazards during sessions of the Subcommittee of Experts on the Transport of Dangerous Goods, or in conjunction with those sessions, taking into account, on the one hand, the programme of work of the Committee and its Subcommittee and, on the other, the calendar of conferences and the availability of resources to service such meetings.

Economic and Social Council resolution 1995/6

19 July 1995          Meeting 44          Adopted without vote

Draft by Committee of Experts on the Transport of Dangerous Goods (E/1995/56); agenda item 6 *(j)*.
*Meeting numbers.* ESC 42-44.

*REFERENCES*
[1]TD/B/42(1)/5. [2]TD/B/CN.4/46. [3]TD/B/CN.4/47. [4]TD/B/CN.4/48. [5]YUN 1992, p. 611. [6]TD/B/CN.4/GE.2/10. [7]TD/B/CN.4/GE.2/5. [8]YUN 1994, p. 899. [9]E/1995/56. [10]YUN 1992, p. 672. [11]ST/SG/AC.10/C.3/20 & Add.1,2. [12]ST/SG/AC.10/C.3/22 & Add.1,2.

# UNCTAD institutional and organizational questions

## UNCTAD programme

In 1995, the Trade and Development Board—the executive body of UNCTAD—held two regular sessions, one special session and three executive sessions, all in Geneva. It also resumed its eighth executive session, which had commenced in 1994.[1] The second part of TDB's forty-first session took place from 20 to 31 March;[2] the first part of its forty-second session from 11 to 20 September;[3] and its eighteenth special session from 11 to 15 December.[4] In March, TDB established the provisional agenda and agreed annotations for UNCTAD IX and adopted agreed conclusions on structural adjustment policies (see above). It also adopted agreed conclusions on the implementation of the Programme of Action for LDCs for the 1990s (see PART FOUR, Chapter I) and on the UN New Agenda for the Development of Africa in the 1990s (see preceding chapter). By a March decision, TDB adopted the terms of reference of the Commission on International Investment and TNCs (see above).

In September, the Board decided that UNCTAD IX should be held in Midrand, South Africa, from 27 April to 11 May 1996. It also discussed linkages between global financial and trade flows, development and levels of economic activity and employment, and the future implications of the outcome of the Uruguay Round (see above).

At the eighteenth special session in December, TDB reviewed the functioning of UNCTAD's intergovernmental machinery (see below). By a 15 December decision,[5] it transmitted the reports of its subsidiary bodies to its February/March 1996 executive session on substantive preparations for UNCTAD IX, so that they could be taken into account in relation to the substantive content of the document to be prepared for the Conference.

At the ninth executive session (17 March),[6] TDB discussed the terms of reference of the Commission on International Investment and TNCs. It considered the 1994 reports of its subsidiary bodies, and endorsed their agreed conclusions. At the tenth executive session (4 May),[7] TDB agreed that exploratory work should be undertaken on new and emerging issues on the international trade agenda within the preparatory process for UNCTAD IX. At the resumed eighth executive session (29 June),[8] the Board adopted a decision on the follow-up to the 1994 UN International Symposium on Trade Efficiency (see above) and endorsed the recommendations of the Working Party on the Medium-term Plan and the Programme Budget (see below). It also adopted a decision[9] on the status of the European Community (EC) in the Special Committee on Preferences, noting that the Standing Committee rules of procedure stated that intergovernmental organizations having competence in the area of GSP should be accorded the same participation rights as States, except for the right to vote. That principle would be applied *mutatis mutandis* in accordance with Economic and Social Council **decision 1995/201** on the full participation of EC in the Commission on Sustainable Development. At the eleventh executive session (5 September),[10] TDB noted the reports of its subsidiary bodies and dealt with a number of institutional matters.

By **decision 1995/207 A** of 10 February, the Economic and Social Council decided to consider at its 1995 substantive session TDB's report on the second part of its forty-first session and to authorize the Secretary-General to transmit directly to the General Assembly's fiftieth session the Board's report on the first part of its forty-second session. In **decision 1995/234** of 17 and 19 July, the Council noted TDB's report on the second part of its forty-first session.

## Medium-term plan and programme budget

The UNCTAD Working Party on the Medium-term Plan and the Programme Budget held two sessions in 1995, both in Geneva. At its twenty-fifth session (26-28 June),[11] the Working Party reviewed the UNCTAD section of the proposed UN programme budget for the biennium 1996-1997[12] and recommended agreed conclusions and recommendations to TDB for approval.

At its resumed eighth executive session on 29 June, TDB endorsed the agreed conclusions and recommendations, annexing them to its decision.[13] In part A of the conclusions and recommendations, which TDB requested the Advisory Committee on Administrative and Budgetary Questions to take into account in considering the proposed programme budget, it was felt that since UNCTAD IX was likely to affect the content and orientation of the UNCTAD work programme, it would be necessary to review the programme budget soon after the Conference in order to assess the budgetary implications of decisions taken there. Although the UNCTAD secretariat had made efforts to redeploy resources to programmes designated as high priority, it was noted that the correlation between the allocation of resources and designated priority areas was not totally satisfactory in some cases and needed further examination. Concern was voiced that there appeared to be duplications among various subprogrammes, and it was noted that presentation of the budget by subprogrammes should reflect the cross-sectoral approach needed in dealing with those issues. The Working Party experienced difficulty in reviewing the science and technology for development programme, as the Commission on Science and Technology for Development remained a subsidiary body of the Economic and Social Council and was outside the jurisdiction of UNCTAD intergovernmental machinery.

In part B, which TDB was asked to consider in its preparations for UNCTAD IX, the Working Party welcomed the Board's decision, at its ninth executive session,[6] to review the matter of the large number of subprogrammes designated as high priority after the Conference. It was noted that more comprehensive information on the demand for and usage of various UNCTAD products and services would facilitate consideration of the work programmes. Further efforts were recommended to implement a 1994 Board recommendation on transparent and equitable allocation of UNCTAD's technical cooperation support costs. It was also recommended that TDB review the Working Party's role and functioning.

At its twenty-sixth session (5-8 December),[14] the Working Party had before it a report by the UNCTAD secretariat on the technical cooperation programme of UNCTAD in 1994,[15] and an in-depth study by the secretariat on UNCTAD's ASYCUDA (Automated System for Customs Data) programme.[16]

In agreed conclusions, the Working Party noted with concern the adverse impact on several of UNCTAD's technical cooperation activities of continued reduced levels of UNDP funding. It welcomed the increasing financial support for technical cooperation programmes by member States and other donors. The secretariat was encouraged to improve the exchange of information on such activities by and with other organizations providing technical cooperation in trade and development, and to seek to conclude memoranda of understanding with them, with a view to improving cooperation and ensuring synergy and complementarity. The Working Party commended the secretariat for the rapidly growing ASYCUDA progamme, which had proved to be an effective instrument for customs reform and modernization worldwide in the context of the Trade Point programme and the Trade Efficiency initiative. It stressed the need for the ASYCUDA programme to be maintained on a regular and sustainable basis within the context of UNCTAD's overall resource constraints and programmatic priorities.

### OIOS review

In December, the Secretary-General transmitted to the General Assembly a review by the UN Office of Internal Oversight Services on the programme and administrative practices of the UNCTAD secretariat.[17] The report covered programmatic issues; quality and complementarities; technical cooperation; organization and staffing; programme support and management; and programme oversight.

In conclusions and recommendations on issues of substance, the report stated that UNCTAD's programme of work should be given a fresh look by shifting emphasis from activities that had ceased to attract significant interest from member countries to those that had attracted a high level of interest. New activities should not result in duplication of the work of other UN organizations. Rather, the secretariat should focus on areas in which its competence and comparative advantage were undisputed, namely, research and policy analysis of emerging issues. The programming and budgeting process should be used more effectively. Financial constraints required strict selectivity of issues to be covered and a greater integration of the work programme into fewer mutually supporting activities. They also required issues of overlap and complementarity with other organizations to be addressed at the programme formulation stage. A related issue concerned technical cooperation activities. The report suggested that UNCTAD should endeavour to integrate its regular programme activities with those financed from extrabudgetary sources. It also suggested that the bulk of extrabudgetary resources was used for funding few successful operational projects; it was therefore recommended that greater emphasis be given to mobilizing resources towards advisory services in the areas of policy adjustments and institutional development. Also, the secretariat should address problems relating to the use of overhead resources and to administrative support to technical cooperation activities.

In conclusions and recommendations relating to administration and organization, the report stated that the UNCTAD secretariat was functioning in an environment that did not facilitate efficiency and effectiveness. It was overstaffed and top-heavy and the organizational structure was artificial and not adequately aligned to programme content. Divisional functional responsibilities were not clear and organizational linkages had clouded accountability. That situation was compounded by the limited effectiveness of programme oversight and inefficiencies at the level of administration. The report contained recommendations for action by UNCTAD's management, including streamlining the organizational structure; reducing Professional staff by 10 per cent, giving special attention to posts at the D-2, D-1 and P-5 levels; analysing the workload of the General Service staff with a view to reducing that category; and introducing a benchmark system for administrative services.

### Intergovernmental machinery

At its eighteenth special session in December, TDB reviewed the functioning of the intergovernmental machinery of UNCTAD in accordance with the Cartagena Commitment, adopted by UNCTAD VIII in 1992.[18] On 15 December,[19] the Board recommended to UNCTAD IX that UNCTAD's intergovernmental machinery be based on the following: greater coherence and simplicity in intergovernmental structures, functions and reporting lines; decision-making commensurate with the level of each body in the hierarchy; improved transparency and supervision of the budget and programme of work and of technical cooperation activities; effective follow-up and evaluation of actions agreed upon; greater attention to handling cross-sectoral issues; better use of short expert meetings to deal with technical issues; technical matters discussed at the expert level to be reported to the relevant parent body; a better-regulated calendar of meetings and a reduced number of meetings; enhanced cooperation with and participation by non-governmental interests and the business/private sector; improved participation by developing-country experts in technical meetings; and strengthened cooperation and coordination with other international organizations, such as WTO and ITC. The Board also made recommendations regarding the length and number of its regular and executive sessions.

By a 15 December decision,[20] TDB requested its President to initiate informal consultations, in the context of the UNCTAD IX preparatory process, on the participation of experts in UNCTAD intergovernmental meetings. The UNCTAD secretariat was asked to update a 1994 note on the financial implications of providing travel assistance to experts from developing countries, notably LDCs, and to provide statistical information on the participation, including financing, of experts in post-Cartagena UNCTAD meetings.

## UNCTAD Secretary-General

By **decision 49/325** of 14 September, the General Assembly, on the proposal of the Secretary-General,[21] confirmed the appointment of Rubens Ricupero as UNCTAD Secretary-General for a term of office of four years, beginning on 15 September 1995 and ending on 14 September 1999.

*REFERENCES*

[1]YUN 1994, p. 901. [2]A/50/15, vol. I. [3]TD/B/42(1)/19(Vol.I). [4]TD/B(S-XVIII)/3. [5]Ibid. (dec. 433(S-XVIII)). [6]TD/B/EX(9)/2. [7]TD/B/EX(10)/2. [8]TD/B/EX(8)/2. [9]Ibid. (dec. 428(EX-8)). [10]TD/B/EX(11)/2. [11]TD/B/42(1)/12. [12]A/50/6 (Sect. 10A). [13]TD/B/EX(8)/2 (dec. 429(EX-8)). [14]TD/B/42(2)/8. [15]TD/B/WP/92 & Add.1. [16]TD/B/WP/93. [17]A/50/719. [18]YUN 1992, p. 641. [19]TD/B(S-XVIII)/3 (recs. 431(S-XVIII)). [20]Ibid. (dec. 432(S-XVIII)). [21]A/49/242.

Chapter V

# Regional economic and social activities

In 1995, the five UN regional commissions continued efforts to promote economic and social development in their respective regions. Four commissions met for regular sessions during the year: the Economic Commission for Africa (ECA) in Addis Ababa, Ethiopia; the Economic and Social Commission for Asia and the Pacific (ESCAP) in Bangkok, Thailand; the Economic Commission for Europe (ECE) in Geneva; and the Economic and Social Commission for Western Asia (ESCWA) in Beirut, Lebanon. The Economic Commission for Latin America and the Caribbean (ECLAC) did not meet in 1995, having held its most recent biennial session in 1994.

In July, the Economic and Social Council amended the terms of reference of ESCAP, so as to include the Russian Federation within the geographical scope of the Commission. The General Assembly dealt with a number of regional issues, calling for support for cooperative efforts in such areas as economic cooperation, transport and communications and industrial development, among others.

## Regional cooperation

In 1995, efforts continued to strengthen the role of the regional commissions as part of the restructuring and revitalization of the United Nations in the economic, social and related fields. The Executive Secretaries of the regional commissions, meeting in New York on 20 February, discussed coordination and decentralization of activities between the regions and Headquarters, and relations with the United Nations Conference on Trade and Development (UNCTAD) as well as with UN funds and specialized agencies. The meeting emphasized that the commissions possessed an array of comparative advantages which, in the context of proper coordination and cooperation, could enhance their contribution to the Organization. The advantages included: the commissions' geographical proximity to the field; their mid-way position between UN entities operating at the global level and at the country level; work programmes tailored to the specific needs of each region; the commissions' expertise and experience in a range of economic and social sectors, which enabled them to take up regional issues of a cross-sectoral nature and act as a catalyst for the integration of economic cooperation and development in their regions; their role as a forum in which all countries of the region could participate on an equal footing and without conditions; and their cost effectiveness.

The Executive Secretaries reaffirmed that the relationship within the UN system should be founded on the principle of "subsidiarity", whereby the centre concentrated on issues and programmes which could not be pursued effectively at the local level. They noted that the establishment of regional coordination arrangements, in the context of administrative committees on coordination chaired by the Executive Secretaries, allowed the commissions to facilitate interagency cooperation among regional representatives. However, a number of obstacles to such cooperation were identified, including: the absence of an institutional structure for the exchange of information on work programmes; discrepancies in the geographical areas of responsibility among agencies; differences in budget and programme cycles of the agencies; the need for a common approach to decentralization of authority in programming matters; and the need to foster cooperation with non-UN bodies, using the technical and political comparative advantages of the United Nations.

The meeting examined the progress made in cooperative arrangements between the regional commissions and specific global entities. It welcomed a cooperation agreement worked out with the UN Development Programme (UNDP) concerning the preparation of the UNDP programming cycle, mobilization of resources, cooperation with non-UN partners, and collaboration on specific issues on a non-project basis. Considering the affinity between the activities of the commissions and UNCTAD, it was suggested that ways of joint programming should be investigated and that cooperation should be enhanced in the areas of trade, environment, macroeconomic policies, privatization, foreign direct investment, technology transfer, transport, and assistance to the least developed countries (LDCs). The executive secretaries noted the decline in resources from the UN Population Fund (UNFPA) for the implementation of joint population activities, and discussed ways of collaborating with UNFPA in the follow-up to the

1994 International Conference on Population and Development (see PART FOUR, Chapter VIII). They also considered the impact of the decision by the Food and Agriculture Organization of the United Nations (FAO) to strengthen its regional offices by withdrawing resources available to the commissions, and expressed the hope that alternative collaborative arrangements could be found to alleviate the situation.

The Executive Secretaries reviewed the implementation of decentralization measures aimed at strengthening the functions of the regional commissions and increasing their responsibilities. Noting that initial measures had already been implemented, they were of the opinion that the decentralization debate should be pursued to identify additional areas where duplication of work existed between global programmes and the commissions, and to ensure an appropriate distribution of labour and resources. The meeting noted a delayed implementation of measures in the area of natural resources and energy, and agreed to seek new sources of additional funding for joint programming exercises. It also supported planned initiatives for the decentralization of authority for some administrative matters.

It was pointed out that the Secretary-General's proposals for an integrated approach towards the wide range of economic and social issues confronting the United Nations—known as "An agenda for development"—firmly established the commissions as the regional arm of the Organization, which implied their much closer interaction with global programmes. In that regard, the executive secretaries considered possible contributions by the commissions to efforts towards an international consensus on cooperation for development (see PART FOUR, Chapter I). They further discussed regional preparations for the commemoration of the UN fiftieth anniversary as well as for the 1995 World Summit for Social Development and the 1995 Fourth World Conference on Women (see PART ONE, Chapter III and PART FOUR, Chapters IX and X, respectively). Preparations were reviewed for launching the regional commissions' project on interregional cooperation in social development, concerning the impact of international migration in countries of destination and countries of origin. Consideration of that subject by the Economic and Social Council, initially proposed by the executive secretaries in 1994 as a subject of common interest to all regions, had been postponed due to time constraints. By **decision 1995/206** of 10 February, the Council included it for consideration at its 1995 substantive session.

**Report of the Secretary-General.** In a June report[1] to the Economic and Social Council on regional cooperation, the Secretary-General outlined the work of the regional commissions, including matters requiring action by or brought to the attention of the Council, and provided a detailed account of the February meeting of the executive secretaries. The report also dealt with the impact of international migration in countries of destination and countries of origin, and examined current and proposed activities of the regional commissions as part of interregional cooperation in that field.

**Reports of the Office of Internal Oversight Services.** Pursuant to a 1994 General Assembly resolution,[2] the Secretary-General, by a 19 April note,[3] transmitted reports of the Office of Internal Oversight Services (OIOS) on programme and administrative practices in ECA, ESCWA and ECE.

The report on ECA concluded that there was a need for greater coherence at the levels of substance, programme and administration. It was recommended that: in elaborating a new development strategy for Africa, emphasis be placed on an analysis of trade patterns within the region and with outside trading blocks; the quality of staff be improved through increased training and greater horizontal communication; a single oversight mechanism be created to programme and coordinate all ECA activities, irrespective of the source of funding; financial authorization for all funds be centralized; the capacity of administrative staff be enhanced and administrative performance upgraded; and the audit function be strengthened. In addition, the report pointed out that Headquarters should provide urgent assistance to the ECA Division of Administration by sending a short-term mission of knowledgeable staff.

As for ESCWA, the Office stated that its programme of work appeared to lack direction and focus, activities did not seem to be coordinated, a system for feedback and self-evaluation of performance was absent, as was a system of priority setting, and the quality of outputs was irregular. Noting the seriousness of the situation, which provided no assurance that resources allocated to the Commission were being used efficiently, the report recommended that a fundamental reappraisal and restructuring of the work programme take place, to be followed by a consequential reorganization of the secretariat and that, in the meantime, a freeze be imposed on personnel appointments and movements.

The report concerning ECE recommended that: the research capability of the secretariat be strengthened and more emphasis given to research and analysis of the transition problems in Eastern Europe; a single oversight mechanism be created to programme and coordinate all ECE activities; the monitoring of programme implementation be perceived as a performance evaluation tool, not as a mere reporting mechanism; new initiatives be reconciled with the priorities and objectives of the medium-term plan and the programme budget; the Administrative Unit be transformed into a full-fledged Executive Office; and a greater transparency and a more informative approach be introduced in all matters relating to the availability of resources and their redeployment between programmes.

By a 26 October note,[4] the Secretary-General transmitted comments of the Joint Inspection Unit (JIU) on the OIOS reports. The Unit emphasized the need to eliminate duplication and reinforce collaboration between ECA and specialized agencies, regional organizations and global secretariat entities in the economic and social sectors, and proposed a number of measures in that regard. It also noted that the OIOS main recommendations concerning ESCWA had been endorsed by the Commission at its 1994 session and that ESCWA's revised work programme had been endorsed by the Committee for Programme and Coordination (CPC), also in 1994.[5] The Inspectors concurred in general with the recommendations pertaining to ECE, but considered that the Commission should develop stronger relationships with other relevant European organizations, especially the European Commission, the European Bank for Reconstruction and Development and the Organisation for Economic Cooperation and Development. They also considered that the ECE secretariat could do more to play a team leadership role in coordinating UN programmes and activities in support of the economies in transition.

ECONOMIC AND SOCIAL COUNCIL ACTION

On 24 July, by **decision 1995/250**, the Economic and Social Council took note of the Secretary-General's report on regional cooperation[1] and other documents considered in connection with the question of regional cooperation in the economic, social and related fields, including, *inter alia*, summaries of: the economic survey of Europe in 1994-1995;[6] survey of economic and social conditions in Africa, 1994;[7] survey of economic and social conditions in Asia and the Pacific, 1995;[8] survey of economic conditions in the region of Latin America and the Caribbean, 1994;[9] and survey of economic and social developments in the ESCWA region, 1994.[10]

In its 1995 agreed conclusions,[11] the Council acknowledged that the regional commissions should play an important role in assisting countries in each region in the implementation of the recommendations of global conferences and that the Council and the General Assembly should take measures to ensure that the commissions could carry out that task effectively. It was also acknowledged that the Council should enhance coordination with and among the regional commissions, including through their more effective

participation in its substantive work relating to conference follow-up. In that regard, the Council felt that, in its consideration of the chosen theme related to conference follow-up, it could benefit from the active participation of the regional commissions, among others, and that it should develop a more focused dialogue with them.

### Regional institutes

On 4 December, the Secretary-General submitted to the General Assembly a report[12] on funding of regional institutes from the regular UN budget. He noted that there were eight regional institutes and centres currently in receipt of resources from the regular budget, including the Latin American and Caribbean Institute for Economic and Social Planning (ILPES), the Latin American Demographic Centre (CELADE), the Latin American Centre for Economic and Social Documentation (CLADES), the African Institute for Economic Development and Planning (IDEP), the UN African Institute for the Prevention of Crime and the Treatment of Offenders (UNAFRI), as well as the UN regional centres for peace and disarmament in Africa and in Asia and the Pacific and for peace, disarmament and development in Latin America and the Caribbean.

The Secretary-General pointed out that a policy whereby regional institutes and centres should be funded had not been elaborated by the Assembly, as most of them were initially to operate and be financed without recourse to the regular budget. However, due to their financial difficulties, for lack of voluntary contributions, and on the urging of intergovernmental organizations, the Assembly eventually agreed to provide resources, primarily for posts. The Secretary-General was of the opinion that activities funded under the regular budget should be undertaken only by the Secretariat and that the creation of centres and institutes such as those in question should be subject to the availability of financial sources outside the budget. However, he recommended that the institutes and centres currently receiving resources from the regular budget should continue to be funded in 1996-1997.

*REFERENCES*

(1)E/1995/40. (2)YUN 1994, p. 1362, GA res. 48/218 B, 29 July 1994. (3)A/49/891. (4)A/50/459/Add.1. (5)YUN 1994, p. 753. (6)Ibid., p. 722. (7)Ibid., p. 676. (8)Ibid., p. 699. (9)Ibid., p. 735. (10)Ibid., p. 746. (11)A/50/3/Rev.1. (12)A/C.5/50/33.

## Africa

The Economic Commission for Africa held its thirtieth session/twenty-first meeting of the Conference of Ministers in Addis Ababa, Ethiopia, from 1 to 3 May 1995.[1] The Conference theme was "Promoting accelerated growth and sustainable development in Africa through the building of critical capacities". The Ministers reviewed perspectives of Africa's socio-economic development; the continent's economic and social situation; progress on a framework of building and utilizing African critical capacities; issues relating to regional economic integration and regional cooperation for development; and programme, administrative and organizational issues.

In his message to the Conference, the UN Secretary-General stressed that African countries must seize and retain the initiative for their own development, which required furthering economic and social reforms as well as a more supportive political environment for development, including greater democracy, better governance and increased political stability. The international community had committed itself to supporting Africa's development efforts in the UN New Agenda for the Development of Africa in the 1990s (UNNADAF), adopted by the General Assembly in 1991,[2] and the UN system remained committed to implementation of the New Agenda and of the System-wide Plan of Action for African Economic Recovery and Development, formulated in 1992[3] and revised in 1994.[4] The Secretary-General noted that the Economic and Social Council would devote its high-level segment in 1995 to the continent's economic recovery and development (see PART FOUR, Chapter III), and emphasized the importance of the regional commissions as key actors in the development of their regions, stressing that ECA should continue to be a source of creative solutions for Africa's development challenges.

The Acting Executive Secretary of ECA observed that the Conference was taking place at a time when the Commission secretariat was acquiring a new structure, to become operational in June, when a new ECA Executive Secretary, Kingsley Amoako, would assume his duties. The economic and social situation in the region, he went on, remained disturbing and modest improvements in the rate of economic growth had to be seen against other factors: the continuing fall in per capita income, weak productive sectors, low savings and investment rates, little and declining contribution to world trade, minimal attraction of foreign private investments, accumulation of external debt, and worsening social conditions as a result of civil disturbances and inequalities; all had contributed to Africa's widespread poverty, he concluded.

At the same time, he pointed out that the region had made significant progress in terms of democracy, human rights, transparency in the management of public affairs, pursuit of economic reforms, and regional and subregional economic integration. Sustainable growth and development in the region required enhanced commitment of African Governments and peoples, their intergovernmental and non-governmental organizations and their development partners, as well as the active participation of the private sector. The issues of external debt, trade, and development financing remained of major importance, and high-level negotiations should be conducted to find a long-term solution to the region's external debt.

The Conference of Ministers was preceded by the sixteenth meeting of the Technical Preparatory Committee of the Whole (Addis Ababa, 24-28 April), which reviewed the continent's economic performance in 1994 and the outlook for 1995;[5] prospects for the implementation of the Abuja Treaty establishing the African Economic Community, adopted in 1991 by the Organization of African Unity (OAU); progress towards elaborating a framework agenda for building and utilizing critical capacities in Africa, as requested by the ECA Conference of Ministers in 1994;[6] preparations for and follow-up to regional and international conferences and programmes; as well as regional cooperation in trade and development finance, human development, empowerment of women, and poverty alleviation through sustainable development. The Committee also considered the Commission's programme of work and priorities.

The Conference of Ministers reviewed, amended and adopted the Committee report,[7] including a special memorandum concerning the programme of action for LDCs. It also adopted a declaration on Africa's external debt and a motion of appreciation to Layashi Yaker, former Executive Secretary of ECA, whose term of office ended on 28 February 1995. On 3 May, the Conference decided[8] to include in its next agenda the issue of technical cooperation among African countries; the Executive Secretary was asked to conduct a study on the subject, for submission in 1996.

## Economic and social trends

### Economic trends

According to a summary of the survey of economic and social conditions in Africa in 1995,[9] the region's gross domestic product (GDP) increased by 2.3 per cent, compared with 2.1 per cent in 1994; however, per capita income declined by 0.6 per cent, due to population growth. The increase in output was mainly attributable to the good performance of manufacturing and a modest rebound in the mining sector. Beverage-exporting countries registered the highest growth of 5.5 per cent, up from 1.8 per cent in the previous year, while output of mineral exporters rose by 2.8 per cent, compared with 1.5 per cent in 1994. The economies of both oil-exporting States and non-oil exporters expanded by 2.3 per cent, representing an increase from 1.6 per cent in 1994 for the former group, but a slight decline of 0.2 per cent for the latter. GDP in the franc-zone countries grew by 3.6 per cent, an improvement over the 1.5 per cent rate of 1994, whereas the economies of African LDCs rebounded with a 2.4 per cent growth, having contracted by 1.6 per cent in the previous year. Output fell in only 3 countries in 1995, compared to 14 in 1994, but rose by more than 6 per cent in 8 States, up from only 2 in the previous year.

Manufacturing value-added (MVA) continued to grow at a 4.2 per cent rate, as a result of better input supplies and improvements in imports of raw materials for agro-allied industries. It rose by 6.9 per cent in southern Africa, compared with 2.6 per cent in 1994, and by 6.4 per cent in sub-Saharan Africa as a whole, up from 2.4 per cent; LDCs registered a 3.4 per cent growth, as against a 2.1 per cent increase in the previous year. On the other hand, MVA growth slowed, from 6.1 per cent in 1994 to 3.9 per cent in 1995 in East Africa and from 6.6 per cent to 0.9 per cent in North Africa, with negative rates recorded in Algeria and the Sudan. MVA contracted by 0.4 per cent in central Africa, after a 1.4 per cent decline in the previous year. Manufacturing sector performance in West Africa was adversely affected by the situation in Nigeria, characterized by a battered infrastructure, collapsing consumer demand, inflation and internal political difficulties. At the country level, South Africa registered its highest MVA growth since 1990, the manufacturing production index rising by an annualized 12.8 per cent during the first half of 1995, and capacity utilization increasing to some 83 per cent in the first quarter. MVA grew by 13.5 per cent in Namibia, against 4.1 per cent in 1994, but declined in Zimbabwe due to high input costs, weak domestic demand, loss of competitiveness in textile export markets and cash-flow problems of manufacturing companies.

Value-added in the mining sector, having declined by 3.7 per cent in 1994, rose by 2.7 per cent in 1995, due mostly to a 4.4 per cent increase in crude oil output after virtual stagnation the previous year. Higher oil production volumes were recorded in Angola, Egypt and the Libyan Arab Jamahiriya. At the same time, exploration and mining investments, particularly in precious metals and minerals such as gold, diamonds and other gemstones, increased in several countries as a result of extensive reforms in the mining sector.

The consumer price index in Africa, with 1990 as baseline, was up 43.4 per cent in 1995, compared to 60.6 per cent in 1994. Zaire succeeded

in bringing its annual inflation rate down from 9,797 per cent in 1994 to 370.3 per cent in 1995 by reducing money supply and rationalizing public finances. In Ghana, on the other hand, average inflation more than doubled, from 34.2 per cent to 70.8 per cent, owing to inadequate food supply and adverse price effects as a result of the introduction of the value-added tax.

While policy reforms had some impact on economic stabilization in the region, in most African countries external resources needed to stimulate and accelerate economic growth were insufficient. Net flows of official development assistance (ODA) to the continent declined from $25 billion in 1992 to $23.5 billion in 1994, due to the growing demand for aid from economies in transition, fiscal constraints in donor countries and reorientation of their aid policies. Foreign direct investment to sub-Saharan Africa alone fell by almost 27 per cent, from $2.9 billion in 1994 to $2.2 billion in 1995. Only a few middle-income countries recorded encouraging volumes of inflows. Tunisia and South Africa appeared to offer the most attractive environment for foreign investment and attracted more private capital resources than other countries.

Civil conflicts and political stalemates in governance continued to disrupt and paralyse production, especially in Burundi, Liberia, Rwanda, Sierra Leone, Somalia, the Sudan and Zaire. Instability caused by significant population migration and displacement in some countries adversely affected economic activities in neighbouring States as well, placing a further burden on their physical infrastructure, despite considerable humanitarian efforts for economic rehabilitation and for repatriation and resettlement of refugees. On the other hand, economic policies in most countries remained focused on creating an enabling environment for the private sector and an efficient operation of the market economy. Overall growth prospects for the region indicated that it had begun to gather momentum towards economic recovery. The region's total output and its agricultural production were both expected to increase in 1996, boosted by efforts to reduce macroeconomic imbalances and to return investors' confidence.

### External debt

Africa's external debt, which had been $312.2 billion in 1994, continued to pose a major threat to economic recovery in 1995, due to the negative impact of debt-servicing obligations on availability of resources. A number of African middle-income countries rescheduled their commercial debt, while Nigeria succeeded in debt conversion and Chad, Comoros, Côte d'Ivoire, Ethiopia and Morocco were granted various cancellations from bilateral creditors.

In a Declaration on Africa's external debt, adopted on 3 May, the ECA Conference of Ministers noted the poor results of the various international initiatives to reduce the African debt burden, and observed that the debt crisis was partly due to an international financial crisis and therefore could not be resolved through debt rescheduling agreements only. The Ministers requested that African efforts for economic reforms be met with substantial debt forgiveness and an increase in concessional flows, and appealed for an 80 per cent reduction in total non-concessional debt and accumulated interest, the cancellation of rescheduled concessional debt, and innovative measures to reduce both multilateral and commercial debt. They also proposed that negotiations be held between indebted countries and their bilateral creditors and multilateral financial institutions to find a positive solution to the African debt problem.

### Agriculture

Growth of output in agriculture—the mainstay of the regional economy—decelerated from 4.2 per cent in 1994 to 1.5 per cent in 1995. Value-added declined by an estimated 0.7 per cent in the North, East and southern Africa subregions, against the 1994 growth of 6.1 per cent, 1.1 per cent and 3 per cent, respectively. On the other hand, West Africa registered a 4.2 per cent increase, although lower than the 5.8 per cent rate in the previous year, and Central Africa rebounded with a 0.9 per cent rise, after a 1.9 per cent contraction in 1994. Rice production grew from 14.2 million tons to 14.9 million tons, and that of roots and tubers, constituting some 20 per cent of Africa's total food supply, reached 157.3 million tons, up from 154.7 million tons in 1994. Livestock production, however, was on the decline in 43 countries, due to the policy of rebuilding cow herds in drought-affected areas. The production of pulses stagnated between 6.5 million tons and 7 million tons, while that of fruits and vegetables increased by less than 2 per cent.

The food situation remained a serious cause of concern, with the food deficit for the region as a whole estimated at 19.6 million metric tons of cereals. Drought brought about famine conditions in 10 countries in the northern, eastern and southern subregions, while in a number of other States the decline in food production was the consequence of civil strife, displacements and insecurity.

### Trade

Africa's terms of trade index, with 1990 as baseline, was up 1.5 per cent in 1995, as against 1.2 per cent in 1994. Export earnings rose by about 11 per cent, compared to 4.9 per cent in the previous year. Improved trade performance was attributable to an 8 per cent increase in oil prices, averaging $17 per barrel, and to the sustained recovery in mineral and metal prices. The aggregate price index for metals rose by 19 per cent over 1994, with copper prices growing by more than 27 per cent, whereas food prices increased by an average of 8 per cent. At the same time, growth in beverage prices was less than 1 per cent, as price increases of 6 per cent for coffee and 3 per cent for cocoa were offset by a 10 per cent decline in the price of tea.

While the 11 per cent growth in regional export value brought earnings to $98 billion, imports increased by 15 per cent to $109 billion, leading to an $11 billion deficit in trade balance and an $8.4 billion deficit in the service balance. Although the region received $16.3 billion in unrequited transfers, income net outflows, which reflected dependence on external capital, amounted to $13.6 billion and pushed the current account deficit to $16.8 billion, an increase of 46 per cent over 1994.

Despite improving terms of trade, Africa continued to lose its global market share, due to reliance on primary commodities as a source of export earnings and the failure to diversify its exports composition into secondary and tertiary commodities. As a result, the region's share fell by 30 per cent between 1990 and 1995 in relation to world trade, from 3.1 per cent to 2.2 per cent, and by 45 per cent in relation to trade of the developing countries, from 11 per cent to 6 per cent.

### Subregional economic performance

The West, East and southern Africa subregions registered GDP growth rates in excess of the regional average in 1995, owing to improved performance in their agricultural and mining sectors. Economic output in East Africa grew by 4.8 per cent, compared to 4.2 per cent in 1994, while economies of West and southern Africa expanded by 4.1 per cent and 2.9 per cent, respectively, as against 1 per cent and 2.6 per cent in the previous year. In sub-Saharan Africa as a group, the growth rate of GDP increased to 3 per cent from 1.5 per cent, or from a 0.3 per cent decline, if measured without including Nigeria and South Africa.

At the same time, the rate of growth decelerated from 2.9 per cent to 1 per cent in North Africa and stagnated at 1.9 per cent in Sahelian countries as a group, while economies of central Africa contracted by 1.1 per cent, compared with a 2.5 per cent decline in 1994, due to continuing poor performances in Burundi, Cameroon, the Congo, Rwanda and Zaire.

### Policy developments

During 1995, many African countries carried out domestic reforms concerning fiscal, monetary and trade policies, aimed at both reducing government intervention in the economy and improving the productivity of public expenditure and investment. Kenya, Nigeria, Uganda and Zambia implemented measures to strengthen their regulatory framework and prudential guidelines for banking and non-banking financial institutions. Value-added tax and presumptive taxation were introduced in Ghana, Nigeria and Zambia to broaden the tax base, while tax reform in other countries involved rationalization of the tariff structure, lowering of import duties and excise taxes and devolution of tax collection to lower levels of government. New land and mineral legislation were adopted in an effort to deregulate and liberalize the mining sector, along with measures to enhance the role of the private sector in the development of mineral resources. Several Governments discontinued price support policies in 1995 in favour of price and exchange rate liberalization. By mid-year, 24 States had adopted various types of floating foreign exchange rate systems and 5 countries had a "composite currency basket" system, while 29 Governments retained a "single currency reserve" system. In addition, measures were introduced to improve fiscal discipline by prioritizing, streamlining and rationalizing government budgets.

## Social trends

The crisis in the social sector remained severe in most African countries in 1995, highlighting the critical need to reorient policies towards enhanced social development and poverty reduction. The health sector continued to bear a disproportionate burden of socio-economic difficulties, with the exodus of doctors, nurses and technicians, compounded by declining or stagnating public expenditure on health, culminating in a virtual collapse of health infrastructures in many States. A large proportion of public health expenditure, sometimes up to 60 per cent, was devoted to curative services. Preventive and primary health care still did not receive proper attention in African health policies, while district and community focus in health-care provision, promoted by the World Health Organization (WHO), also lacked universal endorsement in the region.

Severe budgetary cutbacks and rapid population growth also exacerbated the crisis in the education sector. Public expenditure on education in sub-Saharan Africa was the lowest in the world. Capital and recurrent expenditures for new construction, supplies, furniture, science laboratory equipment and repair and maintenance were hit hardest, while available resources were disproportionately skewed in favour of higher education. The situation was further aggravated by low salaries and poor working conditions, leading to the flight of teachers and closure of premises due to labour disputes. In many African countries, primary education received practically no funding from central Governments, except for teachers' salaries and allowances; as a result, the growth in non-formal education and literacy programmes could not compensate for the shortfalls in the formal educational system.

Problems of unemployment remained critical, particularly among educated people, including university graduates; the unemployment rate of women also continued to be relatively high for the formal sector. While the situation of women as main income earners was generally improving, their marginalization in the development process was still apparent in low rates of participation in education and the labour force and their lack of access to credit for investment in self-employment activities. The extremely high number of refugees and displaced persons in Africa placed an additional burden on its social sector, with about 7 million people formally categorized as refugees and many others displaced. Ethnic conflicts, civil wars, drought and famine were among primary causes for large-scale displacements of population in the region. On the positive side, democratic forms of governance and popular participation were gaining ground and were seen as powerful portents of a more peaceful political atmosphere on the continent.

## Activities in 1995

The biennial report of the Executive Secretary for 1994-1995[10] noted that ECA activities to promote African economic and social development focused on advocating economic and social policies, formulating plans and strategies, strengthening institutions for development, and providing technical assistance to member States and intergovernmental organizations. The Commission's substantive work was carried out under nine subprogrammes: development issues and policies; trade, regional economic cooperation and integration; poverty alleviation through sustainable development; development administration and management; human resources and social transformation; statistical and information systems development; natural resources and energy development; infrastructural and structural transformation; and women in development. Issues related to capacity-building, economic cooperation and integration, and gender were cross-sectoral themes incorporated into each subprogramme.

## Development policy and regional economic cooperation

ECA activities concerning development issues and policies included research for macroeconomic policy analysis and development, aimed at improving national mechanisms for the appraisal of socioeconomic conditions and of development policies and programmes; review of the debt and development finance situation in the region, including promotion of capital markets and strategies for mitigating the impact of external shocks on African monetary zones; development planning and economic modelling; and policies in support of African LDCs. The first volume of the *Economic Bulletin for Africa* was produced, and a number of technical publications were issued, dealing with the effectiveness of debt management and techniques for debt reduction and conversion, financial sector liberalization, exchange rate management policies, and foreign direct investment in the least developed, island and land-locked African countries.

Activities to promote regional economic cooperation and integration focused on strengthening regional economic communities at the institutional and sectoral level, as well as institutional capacity to accelerate monetary and financial integration. The secretariat published a framework for the rationalization, harmonization and coordination of activities of African economic groupings and studies on, *inter alia*, harmonization of monetary and financial policies at the subregional level, the effectiveness of subregional financial insititutions for development, coordination of intergovernmental and subregional programmes in different sectors, and the role of monetary and financial institutions in enhancing national and subregional self-reliance.

ECA continued to provide technical support and assistance to member States and regional intergovernmental organizations; its Multidisciplinary Regional Advisory Group extended advisory and training services on the institutional and substantive issues of economic cooperation and integration, including the development of cooperative arrangements, economic management, macroeconomics and policy reform, and policy and programme formulation.

### Programmes for African recovery and development

At its 1995 meeting, the ECA Technical Preparatory Committee of the Whole underscored the importance of the UN system as Africa's full partner in the implementation of the UN New Agenda for Africa, and noted the steps taken to strengthen coordination and harmonization of activities both within the UN Inter-Agency Task Force and the Administrative Committee on Coordination (ACC). The Technical Committee further noted that the OAU Council of Ministers, at its seventeenth extraordinary session (Cairo, Egypt, 27-28 March), had approved the Cairo Agenda for Action for relaunching Africa's economic and social development. Subsequently, the Agenda for Action was adopted by the OAU Assembly of Heads of State and Government at its thirty-first ordinary session (Addis Ababa, 26-28 June).[11] The ECA Acting Executive Secretary, in his statement[1] to the Conference of Ministers in May, noted that the Cairo Agenda placed special emphasis on peace, stability, human resource development and critical capacity-building, food self-sufficiency and security, development financing, the structural transformation of African economies, and regional cooperation and integration (see also PART FOUR, Chapter III).

In his biennial report,[10] the Executive Secretary pointed out that ECA had organized a regional seminar on the role of non-governmental organizations (NGOs) in the implementation of the UN New Agenda, and prepared studies on key factors of the region's economic recovery, including resource flows, commodity diversification, and capacity-building for the diversification of African economies. He also noted the Commission's contribution to the Asia-Africa Forum (Bandung, Indonesia, 12-16 December 1994),[12] which adopted the Bandung Framework for Asia-Africa Cooperation, and follow-up activities for implementation of the Framework in eastern and southern African countries (see also PART FOUR, Chapter II).

### Implementation of the Programme of Action for LDCs in the 1990s

The Technical Preparatory Committee had before it a progress report on the implementation by African least developed countries of the Programme of Action for LDCs in the 1990s, adopted in 1990 by the second UN Conference on LDCs[13] and endorsed by the General Assembly later that year.[14] The report,[15] submitted further to a 1994 Assembly resolution[16] on the global mid-term review of the Programme's implementation, provided a situation analysis and evaluation of external support measures, outlined a development vision for African LDCs, and examined international cooperation and support measures as well as follow-up and monitoring mechanisms.

On 3 May, the ECA Conference of Ministers, on the recommendation of the Committee, adopted a Special Memorandum on the mid-term global review, which gave an overview of the socioeconomic performance of African LDCs; assessed the status of the Programme's implementation in the region; and proposed national and international support measures for its accelerated implementation in 1995-2000, as well as measures to improve follow-up and monitoring mechanisms. The Ministers recognized that reversing the socioeconomic decline of African LDCs was an ethical imperative and that stronger efforts were needed by both the LDCs and their development partners to implement the Programme of Action. By a resolution[17] of the same date, the Conference requested the Executive Secretary to intensify regional coordination of programmes and special measures in favour of the least developed and landlocked countries, and to transmit the progress report[15] and the Special Memorandum as Africa's contribution to the high-level intergovernmental meeting on the mid-term global review, to be held in New York in September/October 1995 (see PART FOUR, Chapter I).

During 1994-1995, the ECA secretariat provided technical assistance and advisory services to 23 of the 33 African LDCs in the areas of statistical and infrastructural development, agriculture, natural resources, and industrial development.

### Framework agenda for capacity-building

In April, the Technical Preparatory Committee considered a progress report[18] on a framework agenda for building and utilizing critical capacities in Africa, submitted in response to a 1994 Commission resolution.[6] The report provided further findings and conclusions in the eight priority areas critical for the region's development, identified in 1994: good governance, human rights, political stability, peace and security; socioeconomic policy analysis and management; human capacities; entrepreneurial capacities for public and private sector management; physical infrastructure; exploitation of natural resources and diversification of African economies into processing and manufacturing; sustainable food and agricultural production; and mobilization and efficient allocation of financial resources.

The Committee reaffirmed that systematic action for building, strengthening and utilizing critical capacities in Africa was the missing link to sustained economic growth and development, and renewed its endorsement of a broad framework agenda which would propose a regional programme of action incorporating policy measures and activities in each priority area. It noted that such a programme needed to be supported by a programme of technical cooperation involving Africa's external bilateral and multilateral development partners.

The Committee also underscored the importance of capacity-building in science and technology, including information and telematics, and in environmental management, and endorsed the proposal to establish "think-tanks" at the national, subregional and regional levels to address development problems and provide policy advice. It recommended that increased utilization of African indigenous expertise and the issue of personnel motivation be given full attention in the framework agenda, and urged that the agenda be linked to the existing development initiatives for Africa.

The Framework Agenda was subsequently finalized at a high-level expert group meeting, which identified two additional priority areas for capacity-building: managing African environmental and ecological resources, and harnessing science and technology for accelerated growth.

### ECA support for the African Economic Community

At its 1995 session, the ECA Technical Preparatory Committee of the Whole had before it a progress report[19] on implementation of the Abuja Treaty establishing the African Economic Community. The report noted that the Treaty, adopted by OAU in 1991, had entered into force in 1994 and that it had been ratified to date by 36 States. The ECA secretariat had conducted sectoral studies in various subregions on infrastructural development, production and trade liberalization, and had prepared draft protocols for consideration by the OAU Permanent Steering Committee, relating to: the free movement of persons, rights of residence and establishment; transport and communications; the rules of origin; customs cooperation within the Community; industry; and relations between the Community and subregional economic groupings. The report further described the steps taken or envisaged to harmonize and rationalize activities of subregional economic integration institutions, and examined the question of financing the integration process in Africa.

The Committee expressed concern over the slow pace of integration and urged member States to commit themselves to accelerating that process. It underlined the need to strengthen subregional integration groupings and to harmonize national legislation with the Treaty's provisions, as well as the urgent need to establish mechanisms for the mobilization of domestic funds.

On 3 May, the ECA Conference of Ministers urged[20] member States and regional and subregional communities to rationalize and harmonize trade liberalization policies through the progressive unification of trade liberalization rules; establish common external tariffs and an efficient domestic taxation system and pricing policy; and institute indigenous resource mobilization mechanisms. The Ministers called for external financial assistance to implement the Treaty, for conclusion of the drafting of Treaty protocols, and for support to subregional economic communities in the rationalization of their activities and in resource mobilization.

### UN Trust Fund for African Development

The Technical Preparatory Committee had before it a report[21] on strengthening the operational capacity of ECA's programme of technical cooperation under the UN Trust Fund for African Development (UNTFAD). The Trust Fund, established by the Secretary-General in 1977, served to mobilize additional resources necessary for African development through biennial pledging conferences. The report described utilization of UNTFAD resources in 1993-1994 and provided resource requirements for 1996-1997, estimated at $600,000. It also set forth recommendations for revitalizing the Fund.

The Committee urged member States to honour their pledges to the Fund and requested their active participation in the 1995 pledging conference. The conference, held on 3 May in conjunction with the ECA session, received $515,000 and 9.5 million Zambian Kwachas in pledged contributions. In a resolution[22] of the same date, the ECA Conference of Ministers invited African countries and institutions, as well as multilateral and bilateral donors, to continue support for the Fund, and requested the Executive Secretary to review UNTFAD operations and to study the possibility of negotiating a schedule for the phased payment of pledged contributions or their outright cancellation, and of merging biennial pledging conferences with the annual General Pledging Conference of the United Nations, organized in New York.

### Statistical and information systems development

ECA work in statistics was defined by the Addis Ababa Plan of Action for Statistical Development in Africa in the 1990s, adopted by ECA in 1992.[23] The secretariat carried out research and analysis of measures to rehabilitate, revitalize and develop statistical capacities and systems in the region, including evaluation of the Statistical Training Programme for Africa (STPA), research in national statistical services and STPA centres, current practices in statistical needs assessment and planning, and statistical data processing practices. Major publications during the year included an African compendium of environment statistics, directories of statistical databases in the region and of STPA training centres, guidelines for the improvement of statistics on elderly persons, and studies dealing with tourism statistics, selected demographic and social indicators, development of national statistical systems, and statistics on manufacturing in Africa. The secretariat also continued to update its directory of African statisticians and to publish African socio-economic indicators, the series on foreign trade statistics, the *African Statistical Yearbook* and the *Statistical Newsletter*.

On 3 May, the ECA Conference of Ministers urged[24] member States to take steps to build national information networks for decision-making and planning, as part of the infrastructure for Africa's "information highway", and requested the Executive Secretary to set up a high-level work-

ing group on information technologies and communications in Africa. The working group subsequently met under the auspices of the Pan-African Development Information System (PADIS) to elaborate an action plan for exploiting information technology to accelerate the region's socio-economic development.

Among other activities to promote information for development was an African regional symposium on telematics for development (Addis Ababa, April), co-sponsored by ECA. PADIS continued to advocate replacement of inadequate telecommunications systems and reform of laws and regulations impeding the flow of information and information technology, and to publish its *PADIS Newsletter* on development information systems. It also provided training in data management, networking, information policy formulation and information systems development, and assisted member States in strengthening national databases and developing norms and standards to facilitate information exchange.

### Public administration and finance

ECA activities in development administration and management in 1995 were aimed at promoting good governance and fostering policies for the development of the private sector, as well as enhancing the efficiency of the public service and of the use of resources, improving accountability, and increasing awareness of the need for decentralization of political and administrative authority. A study was prepared on the informal economy in Africa and its implications for appropriate fiscal policies, and national training workshops were held on integrated public financial management and related issues. Activities under a project for reinforcing the participation of civil society in socio-economic development included workshops and other meetings to facilitate the dialogue between Governments and NGOs.

### International trade and development finance

In April, the ECA Technical Preparatory Committee of the Whole considered a report[25] on policies, strategies and programmes for reviving private investments in Africa. The report examined the existing constraints on investment flows, pointing out that current structural adjustment programmes—the basis of the macroeconomic policy framework in most African countries—had not succeeded in reversing the decline in investments. Noting that political stability and appropriate economic reforms were important prerequisites to an increased investment flow, the report underscored the need to develop infrastructural and human capacities, to further regional economic integration, to promote dynamic financial sectors and to adopt monetary and credit policies conducive to investments in productive sectors, as well as efficient communication strategies focusing on the region's economic potential and opportunities for capital redeployment. Efforts of African Governments should be supported by relevant international assistance programmes, increased concessional flows, and alleviation of the continent's debt burden.

The Committee observed that improving the investment climate required the right macroeconomic policy frameworks to provide the public sector with a proper role in defining and implementing incentive packages, tackling the problems of domestic and external debt, optimizing rates of investment, increasing public investment in human development and infrastructure, enhancing financial intermediation, enlarging markets and promoting regionalism, improving the world's perception of Africa and building reliability through political stability, appropriate rules and regulations and continuity in the supply of foreign exchange for imports and transfers. The Committee also noted information concerning an international conference on reviving private investment in Africa, to be organized in Accra, Ghana, from 7 to 10 November, including the planned launching during the conference of an African capital markets forum. It further requested the ECA secretariat to take into account additional factors affecting investment in the region, such as the need for land reform in many African countries; the role of privatization programmes, domestic investment and South-South cooperation in the private sector development; and the impact of internal debt on the development process.

On 3 May, the ECA Conference of Ministers called[26] for intensified efforts to create and maintain an enabling environment for private sector development and the growth of private investment inflows, by improving infrastructural and human development capacities through the necessary macroeconomic policy framework. The Conference also called for support from Africa's development partners in improving investment conditions and for international technical and financial assistance.

During the year, ECA activities in trade and development finance were geared towards revitalizing African domestic and external trade and strengthening intra-African trade, particularly in minerals and agricultural products. A workshop was held to consider a study on gemstone development and marketing strategies in eastern and southern Africa, leading to the establishment of an African Gemstone Development Association in October 1995. A further study was prepared on the possible impact on African economies of the 1994 Uruguay Round of multilateral trade agreements.[27] Technical publications were issued

dealing with ECA's strategic objectives in trade promotion, Africa's participation in future multilateral trade negotiations, prospects for expanding South-South trade and cooperation, liberalization of trade in domestically produced goods, external trade financing techniques, promotion of trade in the agricultural and industrial sectors, the establishment of a trade information data bank, and Africa's expectations under the 1989 Lomé IV Convention on trade between the African, Caribbean and Pacific Group and the European Union. The secretariat also continued to publish the *African Trade Bulletin* and its newsletter on trade opportunities.

## Industrial development

Efforts continued in 1995 to diversify Africa's economic base by building industrial capacities for processed and semi-processed products, in order to reduce reliance on primary commodities. Studies were carried out on the region's potential industrial comparative advantage in an emerging new world order, modalities for South-South industrial cooperation, and the development of specific industries. The secretariat published the annual bulletin entitled *Focus on African Industry*, a directory of project profiles for small-scale industries, and surveys of the continent's basic industries and selected agro-based industries.

The Conference of African Ministers of Industry, at its twelfth meeting (Gaborone, Botswana, 6-8 June),[28] adopted the Gaborone Declaration, by which the Ministers committed themselves to: creating an enabling environment and policy framework for industrial development; building key human and institutional capacities to support industrialization; mobilizing necessary financial resources; promoting entrepreneurship and the development of the private sector and facilitating private sector participation in the industrialization process; improving competitiveness; strengthening regional and subregional cooperation; removing obstacles for women's full involvement in development; and integrating environmental issues in development programmes. The Conference also adopted the African Common Position for the sixth session of the General Conference of the United Nations Industrial Development Organization (UNIDO) (see PART SEVEN, Chapter XVII), and resolutions on, among others, mobilization of resources and the development of the private sector for industrialization in Africa, in line with the Gaborone Declaration.

### Second Industrial Development Decade for Africa

ECA continued its cooperation with UNIDO in implementing the programme for the Second Industrial Development Decade for Africa (IDDA II),

1993-2002, which was endorsed by the Economic and Social Council in 1992[29] and adopted by the General Assembly later that year.[30] In June, the Conference of African Ministers of Industry appealed for full implementation of national and subregional programmes for the Decade as well as for allocation of increased resources to support their implementation, and called on African countries to incorporate the IDDA II programme in their national development plans and to identify industrial projects for inclusion in the programme, taking into account their environmental impact. ECA, UNIDO and OAU were requested to undertake in 1997 a mid-term evaluation of the programme's implementation, to revise their respective programmes and to elaborate pertinent action plans. The Conference also urged African Governments to formulate policies geared towards increasing the participation of women in industrial development and called on them to take measures to enhance women's contribution to IDDA II.

**Report of the Secretary-General.** On 2 November, the Secretary-General submitted to the General Assembly a progress report[31] on implementation of the IDDA II programme, prepared by ECA and UNIDO in response to a 1994 Assembly request.[32] The report provided an overview of the industrial situation in Africa, described the progress made, and examined cooperation, coordination and harmonization of activities among ECA, OAU, UNIDO, UNDP and other UN agencies and international organizations. It also reviewed key issues relevant to the programme's implementation, including private sector development, impact of the CFA franc devaluation on the industrial sector and implications of the Uruguay Round multilateral trade agreements for that sector, competitiveness, national programmes for the Second Decade, the role of the Ministry of Industry, and regional and subregional cooperation.

UNIDO undertook a series of missions to review industrial sector programmes in 14 African countries and approved $750,000 for follow-up action. Five ad hoc expert group meetings were held during the period under review, dealing with the production of basic chemicals from natural gas in Africa, promotion of investment and industrial projects in the context of the Decade, technology transfer and acquisition, development of African metal industries based on South-South cooperation, and integrated development of natural resources and the production of phosphate. Technical cooperation projects and programmes carried out by UNIDO in Africa totalled $20.2 million in 1994, while those approved during the first eight months of 1995 amounted to $23.2 million. A new pre-screening process for project concepts was adopted, based on the five main development objectives of UNIDO: industrial and technological growth and competitiveness; development of human resources for industry; equitable development through industrial development; environmentally sustainable industrial development; and international cooperation in industrial investment and technology. The report further described activities geared towards meeting those objectives.

ECA provided technical advisory services to 15 countries to improve their IDDA II strategy formulation capabilities, while UNIDO assisted 21 countries in revising and updating national and subregional programmes for the Decade, preparing implementation plans and projects for presentation to investors and donors, and promoting investments and technology development and acquisition. It was also preparing short-term support strategies for the industrial sector of individual countries, focusing on agro-related as well as small- and medium-scale industries.

The report reaffirmed that African countries had the primary responsibility for implementing the IDDA II programme, and recommended that national and subregional committees be set up to follow up the programme's implementation.

GENERAL ASSEMBLY ACTION

On 20 December, the General Assembly, by **decision 50/426**, took note of the Secretary-General's report. On the same date, the Assembly adopted **resolution 50/94**.

**Second Industrial Development Decade for Africa**

*The General Assembly,*

*Reaffirming* its resolution 49/107 of 19 December 1994 on the programme for the Second Industrial Development Decade for Africa, in which it requested the Secretary-General to report to it at its fiftieth session on the implementation of the resolution,

*Reaffirming also,* in particular, paragraph 2 of its resolution 49/107,

*Stressing* the renewed urgency for promoting industrialization as a key element in the development of developing countries and the important role of the United Nations system, including the United Nations Industrial Development Organization, which is undergoing a process of reform, and recalling the declarations of the Group of 77, of the Organization of African Unity and of the Non-Aligned Movement, on 29 September 1995, 20 October 1995 and 28 June 1995, respectively, on the essential role of the United Nations Industrial Development Organization in this regard,

*Recognizing* the need for enhanced cooperation between African countries, the United Nations system and bilateral and multilateral financial institutions, as well as African regional and subregional organizations, in the implementation of the programme for the Second Decade,

*Recognizing also* the important role of industrialization in promoting sustained economic growth and sustainable development in Africa in the context of the United Nations New Agenda for the Development of Africa in the 1990s,

*Recognizing further* the importance of intercontinental, interregional, regional and subregional cooperation in the implementation of the programme for the Second Decade,

*Noting* the far-reaching implications of the fundamental developments in the international environment for development cooperation, including the conclusion of the Uruguay Round of multilateral trade negotiations, and for the implementation of the programme for the Second Decade, as well as the need for concerted national and international action to enable African countries to cope with the challenges posed by, and benefit fully from, the opportunities provided by recent developments in international trade, among other things, and the role of the United Nations Conference on Trade and Development in this regard,

*Emphasizing* the continuing need for the mobilization of adequate resources through domestic and international initiatives for the implementation of the programme for the Second Decade, including a favourable climate for foreign direct investment, private sector development, small and medium-sized enterprises and enhanced market access,

*Recognizing* the need for African countries to use both human and financial resources more effectively in the process of industrialization,

*Noting with appreciation* the various regional and subregional initiatives and meetings that have taken place, including the Conference of African Ministers of Industry, held at Gaborone from 6 to 8 June 1995, and the contribution made by the United Nations Industrial Development Organization in convening and organizing industrial investment forums aimed at the implementation of the programme for the Second Decade,

1. *Takes note* of the report of the Secretary-General on the implementation of the programme for the Second Industrial Development Decade for Africa (1993-2002);

2. *Emphasizes* the importance of industrial development cooperation and a positive investment and business climate, at the international, regional, subregional and national levels, in promoting the expansion, diversification and modernization of productive capacities in developing countries;

3. *Requests* the United Nations system, in particular the United Nations Industrial Development Organization and the Economic Commission for Africa, as well as the Organization of African Unity and all other partners in the development process, to continue to play an active and more effective role in the implementation of the programme for the Second Decade, bearing in mind the undertakings made in this regard in the United Nations New Agenda for the Development of Africa in the 1990s;

4. *Encourages* African Governments to strengthen national committees for the Second Decade in order to monitor its implementation effectively and to fashion effective policy responses to the challenges and the demands posed and the opportunities offered by changes in the domestic and international environment for industrialization;

5. *Emphasizes* the continuing need for technical and financial assistance from the United Nations system and from bilateral and multilateral sources to complement the efforts of African countries in achieving the objectives of the Second Decade, as well as the need for African countries to enhance cooperation among themselves in the areas of industrial policy, institutional development, human resources development, technology and investments;

6. *Requests* the United Nations Industrial Development Organization to facilitate the exchange of information among African Governments on activities carried out nationally in collaboration with the United Nations system and with the support of bilateral and multilateral partners in connection with the implementation of the programme for the Second Decade as a contribution to subsequent reports of the Secretary-General on the implementation of the programme;

7. *Calls upon* the United Nations Industrial Development Organization, the Economic Commission for Africa and the Organization of African Unity to enhance their assistance and coordinate their activities in human resources development for industry, with a view to improving the competitiveness of the industrial sector in Africa in the light of the globalization of production and the growth of related trade, investment and technology flows;

8. *Requests* the Secretary-General, in collaboration with all the relevant organizations, funds and programmes of the United Nations system, to take into account the implementation of the programme for the Second Decade when preparing for the mid-term review, in 1996, of the United Nations New Agenda for the Development of Africa in the 1990s;

9. *Also requests* the Secretary-General to submit to the General Assembly at its fifty-second session a report on the implementation of the present resolution.

**General Assembly resolution 50/94**

20 December 1995     Meeting 96     Adopted without vote

Approved by Second Committee (A/50/617/Add.12) without vote, 12 December (meeting 43); draft by Vice-Chairman (A/C.2/50/L.76), based on informal consultations on draft by Philippines, for Group of 77 and China (A/C.2/50/L.40); agenda item 95.
*Meeting numbers.* GA 50th session: 2nd Committee 30-37, 39, 43; plenary 96.

## Transport and communications

Activities in the area of transport and communications focused on assisting member States and intergovernmental organizations with their infrastructural and structural transformation programmes, stressing the development of their scientific and technological bases. The secretariat undertook studies of major developments in the postal services and the telecommunications sector in Africa, which made recommendations for extending postal services to rural areas and improving their competitiveness, as well as for promoting cross-border mobility with the introduction of cellular telecommunications services, establishing regulatory structures to enhance private sector participation in the development of telecommunications, and applying cellular technology to extend telecommunications services to remote areas. Other publications dealt with institutional reforms and organizational restructuring in the transport and communications sector and with cooperation in rail transport. Advisory services were provided in drafting a regional telecommunications strategy and legislation on national telecommunications policies. A training programme was carried out for postal workers from English-speaking African countries.

The Conference of African Ministers of Transport and Communications, at its tenth meeting (Addis Ababa, 20-21 March),[33] considered the question of reactivating the Trans-African Highway Bureau and decided that the Bureau's Statutes, adopted in 1993,[34] be amended to reduce from 26 to 18 the number of ratifications required for their entry into force. The Conference also appealed to member States to pursue the implementation of the Yamoussoukro Declaration on a New African Air Transport Policy, adopted in 1988 at the Special Conference of African Ministers responsible for Civil Aviation.[35]

In April, the ECA Technical Preparatory Committee of the Whole urged member States to ratify the Statutes of the Trans-African Highway Bureau.

### Transport and Communications Decade

ECA in 1995 continued activities aimed at implementing the programme for the Second United Nations Transport and Communications Decade in Africa, 1991-2000 (UNTACDA II), adopted by the Economic and Social Council in 1991[36] and endorsed by the General Assembly later that year.[37] Efforts focused on facilitating inter-State transport and communications, accelerating institutional reforms and improving human resources and other critical capacities through, *inter alia*, a regional programme on human resources and institutional development and a transport database project. The secretariat published two issues of the *UNTACDA II Newsletter* and produced a list of projects approved in the context of the Decade.

In March, the Conference of African Ministers of Transport and Communications reviewed the programme's implementation and adopted a programme of action for 1995-1997. The Conference urged member States to establish or strengthen national transport and communications databases and to adopt harmonized and standardized methodologies for data collection and calculation of performance indicators. It also recommended a resolution on implementation of phase II of the UNTACDA II programme, for adoption by the ECA Conference of Ministers.

In April, the Technical Preparatory Committee observed that the first mid-term evaluation of the programme, carried out in 1994, revealed unsatisfactory results due to the low priority accorded by African countries to projects approved under the programme, and to inadequate functioning of national coordination committees. The Committee noted the recommendations that the UNTACDA II programme should be focused on regional and subregional activities, scaled down to realistic levels and linked to available resources; that efforts should be concentrated only on activities of common benefit to most countries; that there should be greater reliance on mobilization of internal resources; and that the ECA regular budget be supplemented to implement the Decade's activities.

On 3 May, the ECA Conference of Ministers recommended a resolution[38] for adoption by the Economic and Social Council (below). Annexed to the resolution were its programme budget implications, estimated at $224,520.

**ECONOMIC AND SOCIAL COUNCIL ACTION**

On 24 July, the Council adopted **resolution 1995/23**.

**Implementation of phase II of the programme for the Second Transport and Communications Decade in Africa**

*The Economic and Social Council,*

*Recalling* resolution 710(XXVI) of 12 May 1991 of the Conference of Ministers of the Economic Commission for Africa, by which the Conference of Ministers adopted the programme for the Second Transport and Communications Decade in Africa,

*Referring* to General Assembly decision 46/456 of 20 December 1991, by which the Assembly approved the programme for the Second Decade, and Assembly decision 48/455 of 21 December 1993 concerning the provision of resources for its implementation,

*Recalling* resolution 93/89 of 13 March 1993 of the Conference of African Ministers of Transport, Communications and Planning on the implementation of the programme for the Second Decade,

*Having considered* the mid-term evaluation of the programme for the Second Decade and the action programme derived therefrom,

*Reaffirming* the continuing relevance and critical importance of the Second Decade, especially for achieving the goals of the Treaty Establishing the African Economic Community,

*Noting with concern* the low level of programme implementation due to a lack of resources,

*Recalling* that new projects to be proposed for inclusion in the programme for the Second Decade should conform to the principles and criteria already adopted and be submitted to the executing agencies concerned, specifying, among other things, the:

*(a)* Time-frame for implementation,

*(b)* Resource requirements, resource availability and prospective sources,

*(c)* Description of tasks to be performed and their assignment among the various partners,

1. *Urges* Member States to make every effort to implement the programme for the Second Transport and Communications Decade in Africa by undertaking, *inter alia*, the following specific activities:

*(a)* Facilitating and encouraging national coordinating committees to carry out activities by providing those committees with the necessary human and financial

resources to enable them to accomplish their assigned tasks;

(b) According priority to national projects that contribute to the achievement of the objectives of the Second Decade;

(c) Coordinating and strengthening national efforts in fund-raising, so as to be able to gain access to regional indicative planning figures through such sources as the Lomé IV Convention, for the implementation of the programme for the Second Decade;

(d) Taking into account the environmental impact of all transport and communications development projects;

2. *Invites* Member States and intergovernmental organizations to involve the subregional and subsectoral working groups in the design of regional action programmes concerning transport and communications and to provide them with all the assistance necessary to participate effectively in the implementation of the programme for the Second Decade;

3. *Requests* intergovernmental organizations to take an active part in the programme for the Second Decade by carrying out, within their regular work programmes, the activities set out in that programme, giving priority to those activities that promote regional integration;

4. *Invites* the United Nations Development Programme to consider favourably increasing the level of its support for the Second Decade by funding part of the regional action programme for the implementation of the second phase of the programme for the Second Decade;

5. *Invites* all donors to contribute further to the implementation of the programme approved by the Conference of African Ministers of Transport, Communications and Planning at its tenth meeting, held at Addis Ababa on 20 and 21 March 1995;

6. *Invites* the General Assembly to consider providing the Economic Commission for Africa with additional resources, allocated within the regular budget, to enable it to pursue the major activities of the programme for the Second Decade;

7. *Requests* the African, Caribbean and Pacific Coordinating Ministers of the European Development Fund to give appropriate priority to the projects and programmes for the Second Decade in the preparation of their national and regional indicative programmes under the second financial protocol of the Lomé IV Convention;

8. *Calls upon* the development banks and participating financial institutions to continue to work with the programme machinery of the Second Decade to provide coordinated and efficient support to the development of transport and communications in Africa;

9. *Appeals* to the World Bank to maintain a high level of involvement in and contribution to the implementation of the programme for the Second Decade;

10. *Requests* African financial institutions to provide further support to the programme for the Second Decade, in particular by systematically taking into account the guidelines and priorities of the Second Decade in the preparation of the action plans for African countries;

11. *Requests* the subsectoral working groups to initiate such regional action as would provide a framework for intervention by those countries that plan to commer-

cialize or privatize their transport and communications sector;

12. *Decides* that the Resource Mobilization Committee for the Second Transport and Communications Decade in Africa shall henceforth be known as the Advisory Committee on Programme Promotion for the Second Transport and Communications Decade in Africa, and adopts the terms of reference of that Committee, as set out in the report of the Conference of African Ministers of Transport, Communications and Planning on its tenth meeting;

13. *Requests* the Advisory Committee to emphasize assistance for Member States in seeking, arranging and mobilizing funds for projects approved under the programme for the Second Decade;

14. *Appeals* to all financial institutions that are members of the Advisory Committee to play a more active role in the efforts geared to supporting the Committee's mission by providing it with the required technical expertise;

15. *Requests* the subsectoral working groups to assist in the evaluation of projects falling within their areas of competence, and in the coordination and integration of the Africa regional work programmes of the specialized agencies with those of the Second Decade;

16. *Requests* the Executive Secretary of the Economic Commission for Africa to:

(a) Disseminate systematically among all partners in the Second Decade information on the implementation of the Decade through workshops, seminars, symposia, other forums and information bulletins;

(b) Play a far more active bullein in coordinating the programme for the Second Decade and to strengthen the capacity of the Commission to provide the necessary technical support of programme implementation;

(c) Ensure that future evaluations of the implementation of the programme for the Second Decade are based on a critical analysis of the degree to which the objectives of the Decade have been achieved;

(d) Prepare a consolidated report on the status of implementation of all the projects for the Second Decade, based on reports prepared by Member States and intergovernmental organizations on the status of their projects.

Economic and Social Council resolution 1995/23

24 July 1995          Meeting 50          Adopted without vote

Draft by ECA (E/1995/40), orally amended by Spain for EU; agenda item 7.
*Meeting numbers.* ESC 45, 46, 50.

### Europe-Africa permanent link through the Strait of Gibraltar

In response to a 1993 Economic and Social Council request,[39] the Secretary-General in May submitted a report,[40] prepared by the Executive Secretaries of ECA and ECE, on the project for a Europe-Africa permanent link through the Strait of Gibraltar. The report analysed studies carried out during 1993-1994 under 1980 and 1989 cooperation agreements between Morocco and Spain and dealing with the project's geophysical, technical and socio-economic aspects, including the options of constructing a bridge or a tunnel as well as traffic forecasting. It also reviewed project baseline and evaluation studies and other related activities, such as the fourth international colloquium on the permanent link, scheduled to take place in Seville, Spain, from 16 to 18 May. The report concluded that the tunnel option appeared to be preferable; however, its technical feasibility had to be confirmed by a current off-shore drilling survey.

ECONOMIC AND SOCIAL COUNCIL ACTION

The Economic and Social Council took note of the Secretary-General's report by **decision 1995/250** of 24 July. On 27 July, the Council adopted **resolution 1995/48**.

### Europe-Africa permanent link through the Strait of Gibraltar

*The Economic and Social Council,*

*Recalling* its resolutions 1982/57 of 30 July 1982, 1983/62 of 29 July 1983, 1984/75 of 27 July 1984, 1985/70 of 26 July 1985, 1987/69 of 8 July 1987, 1989/119 of 28 July 1989, 1991/74 of 26 July 1991 and 1993/60 of 30 July 1993,

*Recalling also* General Assembly resolution 43/179 of 20 December 1988, by which the Assembly declared the period 1991-2000 the Second Transport and Communications Decade in Africa,

*Referring* to resolution 912(1989) adopted on 1 February 1989 by the Parliamentary Assembly of the Council of Europe regarding measures to encourage the construction of a major traffic artery in south-western Europe and to study thoroughly the possibility of a permanent link through the Strait of Gibraltar,

*Also referring* to the conclusions of the special meeting on the permanent link organized at Cairo on 5 April 1994 by the International Tunnelling Association on the occasion of its General Assembly, pursuant to Council resolution 1993/60,

*Taking note* of the recommendations and conclusions of the evaluation report on the studies relating to the project prepared in accordance with resolution 1991/74 and the follow-up report prepared in accordance with resolution 1993/60, in which substantial support for the project from the European Union is recommended,

*Also taking note* of the conclusions of the Fourth International Colloquium on the Permanent Link, held at Seville, Spain, from 16 to 18 May 1995 and attended by international experts and representatives of specialized international organizations,

*Recalling* the strategy adopted by the European Union at the Essen Summit in December 1994, consisting in the setting-up of a European-Mediterranean partnership through the establishment of a free-trade zone,

*Recalling also* the conclusions of the first meeting of the Ministers of Transport of the six western Mediterranean countries, namely, Algeria, France, Italy, Morocco, Spain and Tunisia, held in Paris on 20 January 1995, at which the Ministers undertook to identify priority projects, among them the permanent link through the Strait of Gibraltar, to be proposed to the European Union for consideration of the possibilities of financing and execution,

1. *Welcomes* the cooperation on the project for the link through the Strait of Gibraltar established between the Economic Commission for Africa, the Economic Com-

mission for Europe, the Governments of Morocco and Spain and specialized international organizations;

2. *Commends* the Economic Commission for Africa and the Economic Commission for Europe on the work done in preparing the project follow-up report requested by the Council in its resolution 1993/60, even though necessary resources were not forthcoming from the General Assembly;

3. *Thanks* the International Tunnelling Association for organizing a special meeting on the project at Cairo on 5 April 1994, pursuant to Council resolution 1993/60;

4. *Repeats its invitation* to the competent organizations of the United Nations system to participate in the studies and work on the permanent link through the Strait of Gibraltar;

5. *Invites* the European Commission to consider the possibility of participating in the development of the project both institutionally and financially;

6. *Requests* the Executive Secretaries of the Economic Commission for Africa and the Economic Commission for Europe to take an active part in the follow-up to the project and to report to the Council at its substantive session of 1997;

7. *Requests* the Secretary-General to provide formal support and, to the extent that priorities permit, necessary resources, within the regular budget, to the Economic Commission for Africa and the Economic Commission for Europe in order to enable them to carry out the above-mentioned activities.

Economic and Social Council resolution 1995/48

27 July 1995    Meeting 56    Adopted without vote

2-nation draft (E/1995/L.37), orally revised following informal consultations; agenda item 7.

*Sponsors:* Morocco, Spain.

*Meeting numbers.* ESC 45, 46, 49, 56.

## Tourism

Activities aimed at mobilization of tourism resources for Africa's overall development included a publication on modernization of handicraft production and its adaptation to the requirements of African tourism and a study on the role of tourism in the regional integration process, which recommended the establishment of a cooperation mechanism for promoting tourism development and proposed measures for improving the airline industry and accommodation facilities, increasing participation of local entrepreneurs in the tourist sector and using Africa's cultural heritage for tourist purposes.

## Science and technology

ECA continued to promote science and technology development and application in Africa through meetings, studies and advisory services geared towards strengthening infrastructural capacities, formulating appropriate policies and enhancing science and technology impact and effectiveness for Africa's overall development. Technical assistance in establishing national policy frameworks and coordination mechanisms was provided to the Central African Republic, the Congo, Mozambique, Senegal and the Sudan, while research activities remained focused on identifying appropriate science and technology indicators for Africa, analysing the role of foreign direct investment in technological capacity-building and examining incentives for science and technology promotion.

The first African Regional Conference on Science and Technology (Addis Ababa, 6-10 November)[41] made a number of recommendations dealing with, *inter alia*, adoption of appropriate legislation; the use of incentives to foster scientific progress and technological innovation; accelerated technology acquisition, absorption and assimilation; institutional capacity-building for technology transfer and technology assessment and forecasting; containment of brain drain; implementation of the protocol on science and technology of the African Economic Community; strengthened acquisition and application of nuclear science and technology; participation of women; and incorporation of science and technology issues in school curricula. The Conference also decided to create five subregional conferences on science and technology, and recommended an amendment to its terms of reference to include a call for special attention to the needs of women and children.

**JIU report.** By a 29 March note,[42] the Secretary-General transmitted to the General Assembly and the Economic and Social Council a JIU report on UN system support for science and technology in Africa, and comments of the Administrative Committee on Coordination thereon. The report described the concept and methodology of the JIU evaluation, examined the regional setting for science and technology development and the role of the UN system, and presented main findings and recommendations arising from the evaluation.

In comments on the report, ACC supported in principle the recommendation that a normative framework be established by the UN system for the design, execution and evaluation of institution-building projects in low-income countries, particularly LDCs, and agreed with the idea that long-term financial sustainability should be a main prerequisite for UN system support for such projects. The Committee also agreed that the programme approach to technical cooperation should be applied more systematically and comprehensively to those projects, and that the end-users targeted by the projects should be involved in their design and planning. It recognized the importance of the proposal to initiate discussions at the highest level of ACC for increasing UN system policy and programmatic collaboration in support of science and technology capacity-building in Africa, and considered that it could be appropriate to devote

one OAU summit meeting to the problems of science and technology for development in Africa. However, reservations were expressed concerning the other recommendations.

The Economic and Social Council, by **decision 1995/234** of 17 and 19 July, took note of the Secretary-General's note transmitting the JIU report and the ACC comments.

**GENERAL ASSEMBLY ACTION**

On 20 December, the General Assembly adopted **resolution 50/102**.

### United Nations system support for science and technology in Africa

*The General Assembly,*

*Reaffirming* the Vienna Programme of Action on Science and Technology for Development, adopted by the United Nations Conference on Science and Technology for Development and subsequently endorsed and reaffirmed by the General Assembly,

*Reaffirming also* its resolution 46/151 of 18 December 1991, the annex to which contains the United Nations New Agenda for the Development of Africa in the 1990s, having as its priority objectives the accelerated transformation, integration, diversification and growth of the African economies, in order to strengthen them within the world economy,

*Having considered* the report of the Joint Inspection Unit entitled "United Nations system support for science and technology in Africa", and the conclusions and recommendations contained therein,

*Recognizing* the crucial significance of science and technology, including the related information technologies, for planning, development and decision-making in science and technology and the promotion of endogenous capacity-building in science and technology in the process of growth and development,

*Recognizing also* that the fundamental objective of science and technology to meet basic needs should be to create conditions that increase the ability of people living in poverty to gain access to, fully understand, integrate, use and generate knowledge and technology creatively in order to satisfy their basic needs,

*Stressing* the importance of South-South cooperation in the promotion of science and technology in Africa in the context of, *inter alia*, modalities for economic and technical cooperation among developing countries,

*Noting* the efforts being undertaken by African leaders within the Presidential Forum on the Management of Science and Technology for Development in Africa, 1995-2005,

*Taking note* of the Cairo Agenda for Action, adopted on 28 June 1995 by the Assembly of Heads of State and Government of the Organization of African Unity at its thirty-first ordinary session,

1. *Takes note* of the report of the Joint Inspection Unit entitled "United Nations system support for science and technology in Africa", and the comments of the Administrative Committee on Coordination thereon;

2. *Requests* the Secretary-General to continue to promote and implement activities in support of science and technology in Africa in the context of the United Na-

tions New Agenda for the Development of Africa in the 1990s;

3.  *Also requests* the Secretary-General, in consultation with the organizations, funds and programmes of the United Nations system, to make concrete proposals on activities, in the context of the mid-term review of the United Nations New Agenda for the Development of Africa in the 1990s, to be carried out in 1996, aimed at strengthening United Nations system support for science and technology in Africa, taking into account the views and recommendations contained in the reports mentioned above and other relevant resolutions of the General Assembly, and to report thereon to the Assembly at its fifty-first session.

General Assembly resolution 50/102

20 December 1995     Meeting 96     Adopted without vote

Approved by Second Committee (A/50/617/Add.4) without vote, 8 December (meeting 42); draft by Vice-Chairman (A/C.2/50/L.62), based on informal consultations on draft by Philippines, for Group of 77 and China (A/C.2/50/L.38); agenda item 95 (d).

*Meeting numbers.* GA 50th session: 2nd Committee 35-37, 39, 42; plenary 96.

## Natural resources, energy and marine affairs

ECA continued to promote the development and management of energy, water, mineral and marine resources, as well as cartography and remote sensing services. Studies were carried out on rural electrification in the region, manufacturing of turbines and generators for mini-hydropower in African countries, the situation in the mining sector, geographic and land information systems, and marine pollution and strategies for intercountry cooperation. The secretariat continued to publish *MAJI* (an information bulletin on water resources) and the *Cartographic and Remote Sensing Bulletin for Africa*, and produced a digital geographic atlas, catalogues of maps, a directory of African experts in natural resources, and a list of charts and remote sensing imageries.

Other activities addressed such issues as privatization and deregulation of the energy sector, its role in poverty alleviation, and regional economic integration through energy trade and power pooling; a framework for water resources development in a global perspective; mining legislation and improvement of small-scale mining; development and management of ocean resources; and assistance to member States and subregional institutions in building their capacity to generate and access adequate information, and to diagnose problems and propose remedial action.

On 3 May, the ECA Conference of Ministers urged[43] African countries to adopt the strategy and plan of action for water resources assessment in Africa, formulated in March by an ECA/World Meteorological Organization (WMO) international conference on water resources. The Ministers also called for an integrated approach in sustainable water resources development and management, closer cooperation for the development of trans-boundary river/lake groundwater basins, and action to promote the strategy and plan of action.

The first Regional Conference of African Ministers responsible for the Development and Utilization of Mineral Resources and Energy (Accra, 20-23 November)[44] recommended measures for building relevant capacities through studies, policies and strategies as well as cooperation and integration.

## Food and agriculture

ECA activities in food and agriculture focused on enhancing national capacities for food security policy analysis and planning as well as on improving the food security situation. Measures were recommended to ensure sustainable production and rational use of food, fishery, forestry and livestock resources and to improve delivery systems. Subregional meetings were held to consider harmonization of food production and pricing policies, establishment of subregional information systems on food markets, development of credit schemes for the private sector and improvement of marketing infrastructures. The secretariat continued to publish the *Rural Progress* newsletter and a series on food security and its outlook in Africa, and conducted studies dealing with poverty alleviation, rural development, and cooperation in fisheries.

In April, the ECA Technical Preparatory Committee of the Whole considered a report[45] on food and agricultural production, food security and food self-sufficiency in Africa. The report examined the food security situation and related constraints, and identified priorities for sustainable agricultural food production and security. The Committee recognized that improvement in food security would entail effective policies for promoting local food production and greater popular participation and improving agricultural delivery systems, credit programmes and market efficiency, and emphasized the urgent need for land reform, water development and irrigation management systems, crop diversification, and farm storage facilities. Other important areas were research and training, improved climatic and early warning systems, subregional and regional cooperation, and promotion of strong linkages between the agricultural and industrial sectors.

On 3 May, the ECA Conference of Ministers called[46] on member States to create a macroeconomic environment conducive to the enhancement of all required capacities for food and agricultural production; urged subregional economic communities to build an appropriate cooperation framework; appealed for international measures to mitigate the impact of agricultural price liberalization on Africa's food and agriculture sector; and called on ECA and FAO to develop a strategy for sustainable agricultural and rural development. In another resolution,[47] the Conference requested the Executive Secretary to undertake studies on food security and self-sufficiency in North Africa, and called for international assistance in analysing the impact of trade liberalization in agricultural commodities on the subregion's exports and imports.

### Cooperation in fisheries

By a 13 June note,[48] the Secretary-General transmitted to the Economic and Social Council a report on cooperation in fisheries in Africa, prepared by the Director-General of FAO in response to a 1994 Council request.[49] The report reviewed the status of the FAO Regional Convention on Fisheries Cooperation among African States Bordering the Atlantic Ocean, adopted in 1991, and described FAO activities in support of the Ministerial Conference on the same subject, including its advisory project on improving the legal framework of West African coastal States for fisheries cooperation, management and development.

The third session of the Ministerial Conference was held in Praia, Cape Verde, on 17 and 18 July. The Regional Convention entered into force on 11 August, having received seven instruments of ratification, acceptance, approval or accession.

The Economic and Social Council, by **decision 1995/234** of 17 and 19 July, took note of the Secretary-General's note transmitting the report.

### Environment

Agenda 21,[50] the wide-ranging action plan adopted in 1992 by the UN Conference on Environment and Development,[51] continued to be at the centre of ECA work in that area. The ECA secretariat carried out a number of activities under the African Strategies to implement Agenda 21, which had been approved by the ECA Conference of Ministers in 1993.[52] Technical assistance was provided to the African Centre of Meteorological Applications for Development in strengthening its operations and work programme, and measures were recommended in support of efforts to combat desertification. The secretariat also continued to publish the *ECA Environment Newsletter*.

### Social development and humanitarian affairs

In April, the ECA Technical Preparatory Committee of the Whole considered a report[53] on human development in Africa—the first in a biennial series launched in 1995. The report examined the concept and measurement of human development and its current state in the region, reviewed regional goals concerning children, health and basic education for all, and outlined future per-

spectives. The Committee underscored the importance of the well-being of both children and women, noted the need to restore or improve the quality of services, such as basic health care and education, as well as to address gender gaps in terms of service access and socio-economic and political status, and emphasized the need to monitor the human situation in Africa on a continuous basis. It also discussed the Declaration adopted at the 1995 World Summit for Social Development, held in Denmark in March (see PART FOUR, Chapter IX), and stressed the importance of establishing follow-up mechanisms.

On 3 May, the ECA Conference of Ministers urged[54] member States to monitor human development indicators, called for international financial and technical cooperation in preparing human development reports, and requested the Executive Secretary to promote the cause of human development in Africa and to monitor progress in attaining regional targets for education, children and social development. In other action, the Conference, on the recommendation of the Governing Board of the UN African Institute for the Prevention of Crime and the Treatment of Offenders (fourth meeting, Addis Ababa, 4-5 January), approved[55] the Board's composition for 1995-1999, endorsed a biennial rotational basis for its membership, urged Governments to accede to the Statute of the Institute, and appealed for financial and programme support for UNAFRI.

ECA continued to assist Governments in developing human resources, building and strengthening institutional capacities, and fostering popular participation in social development. The secretariat provided policy guidance and extended technical assistance to member States through seminars, workshops and advisory services. Studies were undertaken on South African labour policy and on the socio-economic impact of AIDS on households and families, and manuals were produced on management and administration of education, planning for human development, and planning and implementation of curricula for peace and nation-building. The secretariat issued guidelines for improving the informal sector's productivity and its linkages with other sectors of the economy, and continued to analyse trends and issues in human resources planning, development and utilization in Africa and to publish its *People First* series and training information notices.

### Population

At its 1995 meeting, the ECA Technical Preparatory Committee of the Whole stressed the importance of implementing the Cairo Programme of Action adopted by the International Conference on Population and Development (ICPD) in

1994[56] and the Dakar/Ngor Declaration on Population, Family and Sustainable Development, adopted by the third African Population Conference in 1992[57] and endorsed by ECA in 1993.[58]

A workshop of experts and NGOs on the implementation of the Dakar/Ngor Declaration and the ICPD Programme of Action (Abidjan, Côte d'Ivoire, 6-9 June) approved[59] recommendations to African Governments and NGOs, as well as to subregional, regional and international organizations, on the formulation and implementation of national population policies and programmes, monitoring and evaluation of their implementation, and relevant capacity-building; promotion of education about family life and its inclusion in educational curricula, and outreach to vulnerable population groups; and facilitation of pertinent information exchange as well as support to activities of national population commissions at the subregional, regional and international levels.

ECA secretariat activities continued to address the issues of family planning, migration, ageing, the interrelationship between population and sustainable development, and management of population programmes. Two issues of the *African Population Newsletter* were published, and technical publications were produced on the integration of population variables into development planning, consequences of teenage pregnancy and measures to reduce the magnitude of the problem, contraceptive prevalence and practice in ECA member States, and linkages among the environment, urbanization and migration in Africa.

**Human settlements**

As part of regional preparations for the second United Nations Conference on Human Settlements (Habitat II), to be held in Turkey in 1996 (see PART FOUR, Chapter VIII), a second Special Meeting of African Ministers responsible for Human Settlements (Johannesburg, South Africa, 16-18 October) adopted a declaration embodying a common African position on key issues of interest to the region. The declaration identified critical problems common to human settlements in Africa, such as inadequate shelter, lack of proper maintenance of urban infrastructure and services, poor sanitation, unemployment and poverty, as well as factors exacerbating those problems, including social and political conflicts and instability, wars, external debt burdens, natural disasters, desertification, population pressures, and an unfavourable macroeconomic climate.

By the declaration, the Ministers also underscored the need to create an enabling environment and promote strategies for the land and housing sector development; pledged support for efforts to increase production, supply and accessibility of shelter for all segments of the population, especially the poor; emphasized the importance of rural-urban development balance and the necessity of human settlements planning; decided to revise legal and regulatory systems of land administration and management and give priority to land-tenure reform; and urged Governments to ensure decentralization of responsibilities to local authorities, strengthen administrative and revenue-generation capacity at all levels of government, and develop innovative financial mechanisms.

The secretariat's work focused on the formulation and implementation of human settlements policies aimed at mitigating rural/urban imbalances in African countries and promoting the implementation of the Global Strategy for Shelter to the Year 2000, adopted by the General Assembly in 1988.[60] Guidelines were issued for improving human settlements management, elaborating and implementing policies on shelter provision for the urban and rural poor, and developing sustainable energy and transport systems in human settlements. A technical publication was produced on a strategy for building materials and construction industries development.

Preparations for Habitat II were also reviewed in 1995 by subregional ministerial meetings for eastern, central and southern Africa.

**Integration of women in development**

In April, the Technical Preparatory Committee reviewed regional activities in preparation for the Fourth World Conference on Women, which was subsequently held in Beijing in September (see PART FOUR, Chapter X). It also considered a progress report[61] on a proposed African bank for women and promotion of women entrepreneurship. The Committee noted that a meeting of experts on practical modalities for establishing an African bank for women, held in 1994,[62] had recommended the establishment of a regional institution—an "Africa Women's Bank"—with affiliates at the national level, and that the idea had gained prominence in nearly all African countries. However, it was deemed necessary to conduct an additional study on the bank's structure and capital, its legal aspects and its impact on the advancement of African women, particularly rural women.

On 3 May, the ECA Conference of Ministers, on the recommendation of the Africa Regional Coordinating Committee for the Integration of Women in Development (sixteenth meeting, Addis Ababa, 20-22 April),[63] adopted[64] the African Platform for Action: African Common Position for the Advancement of Women, approved by the fifth African Regional Conference on Women in 1994,[62] and urged member States to give full support to its implementation. In another resolution,[65] the Ministers urged African countries to make adequate financial appropriations in their national budgets for implementing the Platform for Action, and called for strengthening national institutions for the advancement of women and for assistance from regional financial institutions and business associations, Africa's development partners and the international community.

The ECA secretariat produced technical publications on gender issues in Africa, African women and leadership, participation of women in the economic sector, and international legal instruments relevant to women in the region. It issued guidelines for implementing the African Platform for Action, continued to publish the *ATRCW Update* newsletter of the African Training and Research Centre for Women, and established an African Women Leadership Fund as a follow-up to the Fourth World Conference on Women.

## Programme, administrative and organizational questions

The ECA Technical Preparatory Committee of the Whole reviewed a new organizational chart of the Commission's secretariat and a proposed programme of work and priorities for 1996-1997[66] clustered, as in 1994-1995, around nine subprogrammes (see above, under "Activities in 1995"). The programme also incorporated activities of policy-making organs and those related to executive direction and management and to programme support. The Committee observed that the proposed programme did not pay adequate attention to conflict resolution, and urged closer cooperation with OAU in that regard. It also urged the secretariat to expand and update its programme evaluation methods, and proposed that there should be enhanced communication between the ECA Conference of Ministers and the African Group in the General Assembly and in other principal UN organs so as to ensure continuity in Africa's position on major issues.

On 3 May, the ECA Conference of Ministers recommended a resolution[67] for adoption by the Economic and Social Council (below).

ECONOMIC AND SOCIAL COUNCIL ACTION

On 24 July, the Economic and Social Council adopted **resolution 1995/24**.

**Programme of work and priorities of the Economic Commission for Africa for the biennium 1996-1997**

*The Economic and Social Council,*

*Recalling* General Assembly resolution 41/213 of 19 December 1986 and subsequent relevant resolutions on programme planning,

*Recalling* its resolution 1992/52 of 31 July 1992, entitled "Restructuring and revitalization of the United Nations in the economic and social fields: strengthening the role and functions of the Economic Commission for Africa", and resolution 769(XXVIII) of 6 May 1993 of

the Conference of Ministers of the Economic Commission for Africa on strengthening the role of the Commission to provide team leadership and coordination of United Nations system activities with a regional perspective in Africa,

*Reaffirming* that measures to improve the efficiency of the administrative and financial functioning of the Secretariat and to improve the planning, programming and budgeting process, as called for by the General Assembly in its resolution 47/212 of 23 December 1992, would significantly contribute to enhancing the effectiveness of the Commission in dealing with the development challenges facing the Africa region,

*Conscious* of the importance of the ongoing measures to improve the effectiveness of the United Nations resulting from General Assembly resolution 46/235 of 13 April 1992, on the basis of which resources and activities have been decentralized from Headquarters to the Commission during the biennium 1994-1995,

*Having examined* the proposed programme of work and priorities of the Commission for the biennium 1996-1997,

*Taking note* of the new organizational structure which, among other things, is aimed at enhancing the effectiveness of the Commission,

*Appreciative* of the redeployment of resources to the Commission's regular programme of technical cooperation to enhance the multidisciplinary regional advisory services it renders to member States,

*Noting with appreciation* the grant made available to the African Institute for Economic Development and Planning, which has contributed significantly to the operational capacity of the Commission,

1. *Endorses* the proposed programme of work and priorities of the Economic Commission for Africa for the biennium 1996-1997;

2. *Requests* the Secretary-General to ensure, through the Administrative Committee on Coordination, that United Nations programmes and activities for the Africa region are coordinated and harmonized for cost-effectiveness, synergy and greater impact;

3. *Urges* the Secretary-General, in making his proposals for the programme budget for the biennium 1996-1997, to take into consideration the special development needs of the Africa region, by stressing the need to make available to the Commission adequate resources to enable it to carry out fully those activities under programme 30 (Regional cooperation for development in Africa) and programme 45 (Africa: critical economic situation, recovery and development), in particular subprogramme 2 thereof (Monitoring, assessment and follow-up of the implementation of action programmes, including their financial aspects), of the medium-term plan for the period 1992-1997;

4. *Urgently appeals* to the General Assembly to consider the possibility of converting, within existing resources, the grant provided to the African Institute for Economic Development and Planning to establish core posts in the regular budget, as called for by the Economic and Social Council in its resolutions 1992/51 of 31 July 1992 and 1993/68 of 30 July 1993;

5. *Endorses* the appeal of the Economic Commission for Africa to the Committee for Programme and Coordination to consider these proposals favourably and to recommend, through the Economic and Social Council, their adoption by the General Assembly at its fiftieth session;

6. *Calls upon* the General Assembly, through its Second and Fifth Committees, to take the necessary action to ensure that adequate resources are made available to the Commission for the implementation of its work programme;

7. *Requests* the Executive Secretary of the Economic Commission for Africa to endeavour to maintain and strengthen the cohesion of the programme of technical cooperation, especially at the implementation level.

Economic and Social Council resolution 1995/24

24 July 1995    Meeting 50    Adopted without vote

Draft by ECA (E/1995/40), orally amended by Spain for EU; agenda item 7. *Meeting numbers.* ESC 45, 46, 50.

## Programme evaluation

The Technical Preparatory Committee considered a progress report[68] on programme evaluation in ECA, which described steps taken to implement the Commission's recommendations emanating from its 1994 review[69] of the ECA Multinational Programming and Operational Centres (MULPOCs) and PADIS, an in-depth evaluation of the programme for African recovery and development under the 1992-1997 UN medium-term plan, and self-evaluation of ECA sub-programmes in marine affairs (non-living resources); least developed, land-locked and island developing countries; environment and development; trade development and cooperation; natural resources; and energy, including new and renewable sources of energy.

The Committee noted the progress made and urged the secretariat to ensure full implementation of Commission recommendations. It also acted on recommendations of intergovernmental committees of experts of the five MULPOCs, adopted at their meetings in March and April 1995.

At its 1995 session,[70] the Committee for Programme and Coordination recommended that the General Assembly review the level of resources devoted to implementing the programme for African recovery and development, taking into account the enormous needs of that region.

## Cooperation between SADC and the United Nations

In response to a 1993 General Assembly request,[71] the Secretary-General submitted in October a report[72] on cooperation between the United Nations and the Southern African Development Community (SADC), established in 1992 as successor to the 10-member Southern African Development Coordination Conference. The report described assistance provided to southern African countries by the UN system and various Member States.

The UN Secretariat had 118 ongoing development cooperation projects in SADC countries,

focusing on human resources development and institution-building in the areas of public administration and governance, electoral assistance, support to aid coordination, development programming, and water and other natural resources for development. The UN Children's Fund (UNICEF) extended assistance in formulating national programmes of action and goals for children and facilitating a review of the progress made; developing analytical materials on major issues affecting southern African children; promoting human resources development in basic education; and assessing health, nutrition and water needs arising from the 1994/1995 drought, in preparation for the launching by SADC of a regional drought programme and consolidated appeal. UNCTAD assisted in drafting an SADC protocol on trade cooperation, provided advisory services on matters related to rules of origin and enterprise cooperation, and carried out a programme on multimodal transport and trade facilitation in Mozambique.

UNDP funded projects totalling $16.4 million in support of various sectors such as transport, petroleum, mining, food security and education, while the World Food Programme (WFP) delivered food aid valued at $226 million, committed $49 million for commodities and transport in the countries most affected by the 1994/95 drought, and purchased $108 million worth of commodities from the region. Projects financed by the World Bank focused on structural adjustment, private sector development, poverty alleviation, private investment and foreign direct investment, development of human resources and physical infrastructure, and economic integration. The Bank's commitments to SADC members for 1991-1995 totalled $4.5 billion. Activities of the International Monetary Fund (IMF) were aimed at opening SADC economies to the advantages of larger markets and fostering market integration.

The UN Environment Programme (UNEP) provided assistance in environmental monitoring and assessment, expansion of environmental networks and information systems, development of environmental legislation, and personnel training. The UN Centre for Human Settlements (Habitat) cooperated with Governments in formulating effective housing finance systems and programmes for human settlements development, rehabilitation of the housing and urban development sector, and environmentally sound management. The UN Educational, Scientific and Cultural Organization (UNESCO) and SADC finalized a memorandum of understanding on cooperation and collaborated in the area of water use management training and research, among others. SADC members received assistance from other UN programmes and agencies, such as the International Trade Centre, the

International Labour Organization (ILO), FAO, WHO, the Universal Postal Union, WMO, the World Intellectual Property Organization (WIPO) and UNIDO.

On 20 December, the General Assembly adopted **resolution 50/118.**

**Cooperation between the United Nations and the Southern African Development Community**

*The General Assembly,*

*Reaffirming* its resolutions 37/248 of 21 December 1982, 38/160 of 19 December 1983, 39/215 of 18 December 1984, 40/195 of 17 December 1985, 42/181 of 11 December 1987, 44/221 of 22 December 1989, 46/160 of 19 December 1991 and 48/173 of 21 December 1993, in which, *inter alia,* it requested the Secretary-General to promote cooperation between the organs, organizations and bodies of the United Nations system and the Southern African Development Coordination Conference, and urged intensification of contacts in order to accelerate the achievement of the objectives of the Lusaka Declaration of 1 April 1980, by which the Conference was established,

*Having considered* the report of the Secretary-General,

*Welcoming* the strengthening of the Southern African Development Community through the admission of South Africa and Mauritius as member States,

*Commending* member States of the Community for demonstrating their support and commitment to deeper and more formal arrangements for cooperation within the new Community,

*Commending also* the efforts made by the Community to implement its programme of action,

*Reaffirming* that the successful implementation of the development programmes of the Community can be achieved only if the Community has adequate resources at its disposal,

*Noting* that the effects of war, loss of life and destruction of economic and social infrastructure in southern Africa demand the continuation and strengthening of rehabilitation programmes to regenerate the economies of the countries of the region,

*Noting with grave concern* the recurrence of drought in the region and the increase of poverty as a result, especially in rural communities,

*Recognizing* the strengthening of democratic governance and other positive developments in the region, including the holding of elections and installation of a democratic Government in South Africa, and the restoration of democratic rule in Lesotho in September 1994, as well as the holding of multi-party elections in Malawi and recently in the United Republic of Tanzania,

*Welcoming with satisfaction* the reintegration of Walvis Bay and the offshore islands into Namibia, and noting the impact of Walvis Bay as a major harbour on regional economic cooperation,

*Also noting* that despite the positive developments in the political and military situation in Angola, the economic, social and humanitarian situation remains dire, and reaffirming both the importance of and the need for a continued and effective United Nations presence in promoting a negotiated settlement in Angola with a view to fostering the peace process,

*Noting with satisfaction* the successful implementation of the General Peace Agreement for Mozambique, which has created favourable conditions for the establishment of lasting peace, the enhancement of democracy, the promotion of national reconciliation, and the implementation of a programme of national reconstruction and development in Mozambique,

*Recognizing* the valuable and effective economic and financial contribution that some organs, organizations and bodies of the United Nations system have made to complement national and subregional efforts for the advancement of the process of democratization, rehabilitation and development in southern Africa,

*Welcoming* the outcome of recent United Nations conferences, in particular the Fourth World Conference on Women, and recognizing the important role that women play in development in the region,

1. *Takes note* of the report of the Secretary-General, in which he describes progress made in the implementation of General Assembly resolutions dealing with cooperation between the United Nations and the Southern African Development Community;

2. *Commends* the States Members of the United Nations and organs, organizations and bodies of the United Nations system that have maintained, enhanced and initiated development cooperation with the Community;

3. *Calls upon* the States Members of the United Nations and organs, organizations and bodies of the United Nations system that have not yet established contact and relationships with the Community to explore the possibility of doing so;

4. *Commends also* the members of the Community for the progress that has been achieved to date in implementing its programme of action, and encourages perseverance with those efforts;

5. *Expresses appreciation* to the international community for the financial, technical and material support given to the Community;

6. *Renews its appeal* to the international community to maintain current levels of, and increase, where appropriate, its financial, technical and material support to the Community in order to enable it to implement fully its programme of action and to meet the reconstruction and rehabilitation needs of the region;

7. *Appeals* to the international community and to relevant organizations and bodies of the United Nations system to extend appropriate assistance to the Community in order to enable it to advance further the process of regional economic integration;

8. *Appeals* to the United Nations, its related organs and the international community to assist the Community with appropriate resources to implement the programmes and decisions adopted by various United Nations world conferences, with specific emphasis on the enhancement of the role of women in the development process;

9. *Welcomes* the economic and political achievements and reforms undertaken within the Community, which are intended to address better the challenges of regional cooperation and integration in the 1990s and beyond;

10. *Appeals* to the international community to extend the needed assistance to the newly democratized South African nation to enable it to implement its reconstruction and development programme as speedily as possible;

11. *Calls upon* the United Nations to intensify its efforts to assist the Government of Angola and the National Union for the Total Independence of Angola in the rapid implementation of the Lusaka Protocol in all its aspects;

12. *Expresses its appreciation* for the substantial contributions of Member States, United Nations agencies and non-governmental organizations to meet the needs of the Angolan people, and encourages additional substantial contributions;

13. *Calls upon* the international community to continue to extend its support to the people of Mozambique in their efforts to consolidate their newfound peace and democracy based on national reconstruction and development in that country;

14. *Reaffirms its appeal* to the international community to continue rendering assistance to Namibia to enable it to implement its national development programmes;

15. *Commends* the Secretary-General and members of the international community for their timely response to the drought situation in southern Africa, which has averted famine in the region;

16. *Appeals* to the United Nations and the international community for continued assistance in addressing the drought situation in the southern African region, especially through strengthening the capacity of the Community in drought mitigation, drought monitoring, early warning and preparedness;

17. *Invites* the donor community and other cooperating partners to participate at a high level in the Annual Consultative Conference of the Southern African Development Community, to be held at Johannesburg on 1 and 2 February 1996;

18. *Requests* the Secretary-General, in consultation with the Executive Secretary of the Southern African Development Community, to continue to intensify contacts aimed at promoting and harmonizing cooperation between the United Nations and the Community;

19. *Also requests* the Secretary-General to report to the General Assembly at its fifty-second session on the implementation of the present resolution.

General Assembly resolution 50/118

20 December 1995     Meeting 96     Adopted without vote

Approved by Second Committee (A/50/619) without vote, 30 November (meeting 40); 12-nation draft (A/C.2/50/L.16), orally amended following informal consultations; agenda item 97.

*Meeting numbers.* GA 50th session: 2nd Committee 24-29, 37, 40; plenary 96.

*REFERENCES*

(1)E/1995/38. (2)YUN 1991, p. 402, GA res. 46/151, annex II, 18 Dec. 1991. (3)YUN 1992, p. 577. (4)YUN 1994, p. 817. (5)E/ECA/CM.21/3. (6)YUN 1994, p. 681. (7)E/ECA/CM.21/16/Rev.1. (8)E/1995/38 (res. 796(XXX)). (9)E/1996/47. (10)E/ECA/CM.22/9. (11)A/50/647. (12)TCDC/9/3/Add.1. (13)A/CONF.147/18. (14)GA res. 45/206, 21 Dec. 1990. (15)E/ECA/CM.21/15. (16)YUN 1994, p. 780, GA res. 49/98, 19 Dec. 1994. (17)E/1995/38 (res. 797(XXX)). (18)E/ECA/CM.21/5. (19)E/ECA/CM.21/4. (20)E/1995/38 (res. 794(XXX)). (21)E/ECA/CM.21/14 & Corr.1. (22)E/1995/38 (res. 808(XXX)). (23)YUN 1992, p. 465. (24)E/1995/38 (res. 795(XXX)). (25)E/ECA/CM.21/7. (26)E/1995/38 (res. 798(XXX)). (27)YUN 1994, p. 868. (28)CAMI.12/13. (29)YUN 1992, p. 468, ESC res. 1992/44, 31 July 1992. (30)Ibid., p. 469, GA res. 47/177, 22 Dec. 1992. (31)A/50/487. (32)YUN 1994, p. 689, GA res. 49/107, 19 Dec. 1994. (33)E/ECA/TCD/MIN/95-100. (34)YUN 1993, p. 599. (35)YUN 1988, p. 273. (36)YUN 1991, p. 301, ESC res. 1991/83, 26 July 1991. (37)Ibid., p. 302, GA dec. 46/456, 20 Dec. 1991. (38)E/1995/38 (res. 804(XXX)). (39)YUN 1993, p. 600, ESC res. 1993/60, 30 July 1993. (40)E/1995/46. (41)E/ECA/NRD/S&T/ARCS/1. (42)A/50/125-E/1995/19 & Add.1. (43)E/1995/38 (res. 800(XXX)). (44)ECA/NRD/RC/DUMRE/MIN/6. (45)E/ECA/CM.21/10. (46)E/1995/38 (res. 801(XXX)). (47)Ibid. (res. 805(XXX)). (48)E/1995/94. (49)YUN 1994, p. 694, ESC dec. 1994/264, 25 July 1994. (50)YUN 1992, p. 672. (51)Ibid., p. 670. (52)YUN 1993, p. 603. (53)E/ECA/CM.21/8. (54)E/1995/38 (res. 799(XXX)). (55)Ibid. (res. 806(XXX)). (56)YUN 1994, p. 956. (57)YUN 1992, p. 476. (58)YUN 1993, p. 605. (59)E/ECA/CM.22/7/Add.1. (60)YUN 1988, p. 478, GA res. 43/181, 20 Dec. 1988. (61)E/ECA/CM.21/9. (62)YUN 1994, p. 696. (63)E/ECA/ACW/ARCC.XVI/95/L. (64)E/1995/38 (res. 802(XXX)). (65)E/1995/38 (res. 803(XXX)). (66)E/ECA/CM.21/12 & Add.1. (67)E/1995/38 (res. 807(XXX)). (68)E/ECA/CM.21/13. (69)YUN 1994, p. 697. (70)A/50/16. (71)YUN 1993, p. 607, GA res. 48/173, 21 Dec. 1993. (72)A/50/664.

## Asia and the Pacific

The Economic and Social Commission for Asia and the Pacific, at its fifty-first session (Bangkok, Thailand, 24 April–1 May),[1] had as its theme topic ''Strengthening of regional cooperation in human resources development, with special reference to the social implications of sustainable economic growth in Asia and the Pacific''. The Commission also reviewed recent economic and social developments and their likely impact on the region, and considered issues pertaining to regional economic cooperation; the environment and sustainable development; poverty alleviation through economic growth and social development; transport and communications; statistics; the situation in the least developed, land-locked and island developing countries; inter-organizational cooperation to promote regional development; as well as programme and organizational questions (see below, under specific subject headings).

In his message to the session, the UN Secretary-General noted that there had been increasing awareness in recent years of the fundamental importance of economic and social development to international welfare and referred to efforts to find solutions to economic and social problems and to formulate and implement a global strategy in support of social progress. Asia and the Pacific, despite its economic dynamism, faced many challenges posed by those problems, he said, adding that the Commission represented a valuable forum to address those issues. The Secretary-General was confident that Commission decisions would help to bring the region closer to a future of social strength and shared prosperity.

In his policy statement, the ESCAP Executive Secretary drew attention to the region's success in sustaining its economic growth, underpinned by the continued momentum of economic reform in most countries. He also emphasized the need to assist

States with slower economic growth through increased regional cooperation in a wide range of areas, exchanges of experience on policies, and more intraregional transfers of technology and investment. He noted that the most serious challenges confronting Asian and Pacific countries pertained to providing macroeconomic stability with generally low rates of inflation, resolving growing infrastructural bottlenecks, and mitigating emerging social concerns. The Executive Secretary called for efforts to establish cooperative relationships among countries at different stages of development; to sustain development of intraregional trade and investment; to implement measures aimed at poverty alleviation and provision of social security services; to protect the environment and promote sustainable development; and to ensure the development of human resources and of transport, communications and power infrastructures. He concluded that ESCAP should focus its work on three basic functions: in-depth research on the region's pressing problems, mobilization of the intergovernmental machinery to foster the exchange of experience, and provision of technical and advisory assistance.

## Economic and social trends

### Economic trends

The *Economic and Social Survey of Asia and the Pacific 1996*[2] reviewed world economic developments in 1995 and their implications for the ESCAP region. It discussed the region's macroeconomic performance and policies, regional trade performance and balance of payments, as well as the role of the private sector in development and of public expenditure in the provision of social services.

A summary[3] of the survey noted that the region's developing countries recorded a 7.8 per cent growth rate in 1995, compared with 8 per cent in 1994. A small deceleration in growth was expected to continue through 1996 and 1997, as some economies were overcoming constraints, such as shortages of labour, skills and infrastructure that had emerged as a result of years of rapid expansion. At the same time, annual inflation decreased from 10.4 per cent in 1994 to 8.4 per cent in 1995, due to anti-inflationary policies put in place in most countries. Economic performance remained uneven among individual States, subregions and economic groups, with LDCs and island economies registering growth rates well below the regional average and negative growth rates persisting in the Central Asian republics.

Among the region's three developed economies, Australia and New Zealand had emerged from their earlier 1990-1992 slowdown and had experienced strong economic growth in 1993 and 1994, leading to some rise in inflationary pressures (up from 1.9 per cent in 1994 to 4.6 per cent in 1995 in Australia and from 1.7 per cent to 2.3 per cent in New Zealand) and a consequent tightening of monetary policy in the second half of 1994 that brought about the beginnings of a new slowdown. Growth of GDP fell in 1995 compared to 1994, from 4.9 per cent to 2.1 per cent, and from 4.3 per cent to 2.2 per cent, respectively, with a subdued performance of the manufacturing sector in both countries and, in New Zealand, drought in some regions that negatively impacted agriculture.

Japan's economy, on the other hand, remained weak after experiencing a fall in output in 1993, and had eased both monetary and fiscal policy in efforts to stimulate the economy. Growth of Japanese GDP was only 0.7 per cent, following a 0.6 per cent growth in the previous year. Inflation, which had increased by 0.7 per cent in 1994, was expected to register zero growth in 1995, due to a continued decline in asset prices, the increase in low-cost imports with the rise of the yen, and the prolonged recession. Other major concerns during the year related to the reconstruction after the Kobe earthquake, a massive trade surplus, implementation of further deregulation measures, and the debt overhang in the financial sector.

Private consumption and investment in Australia and New Zealand, which had been strong in 1994, slowed somewhat early in 1995 after the tighter monetary policies dampened consumer confidence, but were expected to increase following continued wage and employment gains in the year. Unemployment dropped about 1 per cent in both countries, to 8.7 per cent and 7.2 per cent, respectively. Unemployment in Japan, while lower than those rates, was rising and had reached 3.1 per cent compared to 2.9 per cent the previous year, and personal consumption showed a downward trend.

In the Asian and Pacific least developed countries, half a decade of economic reforms aimed at enhancing the role of the private sector in development and promoting greater efficiency in resource mobilization and allocation had had a favourable impact on overall economic performance, which showed improvement during 1990-1995 over a comparable period in the previous decade. In 1994, GDP had grown by 6.8 per cent in Myanmar, 6.5 per cent in Bhutan, 5.5 per cent in Maldives and 4.9 per cent in Cambodia, an increase over the previous year for all those countries except Maldives. Growth rates were expected to accelerate from 4.6 per cent in 1994 to 5 per cent in 1995 in Bangladesh, but to decline from 8 per cent to 7 per cent in the Lao People's Democratic Republic and from 7 per cent to 2.6 per cent in Nepal.

The agricultural sector, which provided the largest share of GDP and remained the main source of employment in LDCs, thus playing an important role in poverty alleviation and overall development, expanded by 2.6 per cent in Bangladesh, up from 1.8 per cent in 1994, but contracted by 1 per cent in Nepal, after a 7.7 per cent growth in the previous year. Agricultural output had rebounded in 1994 with 6.1 per cent growth in Myanmar, and was up 2.4 per cent in Maldives, 2 per cent in Bhutan, and 1.4 per cent in Cambodia.

The continuing civil strife in Afghanistan had had severe effects on major economic sectors and on the economic and social infrastructure in that country, it was reported. Dislocations and disruptions in agricultural production required food imports of up to 650 thousand tons a year, while production in major industries, such as textiles, cement and food processing, was drastically reduced or had ceased altogether; the transport sector was seriously disrupted by the lack of spare parts and extensive war damage. The economic situation was also characterized by high inflation and a volatile exchange rate, fueled by large fiscal and current account deficits and a rapid rise in the money supply. In the remainder of LDCs, inflation rates remained mostly in double digits. They did fall from 8.9 per cent to 8 per cent in Nepal but accelerated from 1.8 per cent to 4 per cent in Bangladesh and from 6.9 per cent to more than 15 per cent in the Lao People's Democratic Republic. Most LDCs also continued to face constraints imposed by inadequate infrastructure, a low level of human resource development, widening budget deficits, a narrow tax base, low savings rates and growing environmental concerns.

The Pacific island economies generally failed to improve their economic performance—although the rapid exploitation of natural resources boosted growth in some countries—and remained vulnerable to exogenous shocks. Poor performance of public enterprises, coupled with continuing large budget deficits, highlighted the need to enhance the role of the private sector in development. While most island economies managed to sustain high rates of investment relative to GDP, much of it was undertaken by the public sector and financed by external aid. In addition, little success was achieved in expanding their export bases. With high population growth rates not matched by economic expansion, per capita GDP continued to decline.

In 1994, total output had fallen by 7.1 per cent in Samoa and 0.4 per cent in Kiribati, and had increased at rates lower than in 1993 in the Cook Islands (1.5 per cent), the Solomon Islands (4.2 per cent), Tuvalu (2.6 per cent) and Vanuatu (2 per cent), improving only in Tonga (5.7 per cent). GDP was expected to grow in 1995 by 2.7 per cent in Fiji, down from 5.2 per cent in 1994, and to fall

by 4.6 per cent in Papua New Guinea, after growth of 3 per cent the previous year and 16.6 per cent in 1993, owing to a contraction of its mining and industrial sectors. Some positive achievements in economic performance were recorded by Guam, New Caledonia, the Northern Mariana Islands and Palau, due mainly to increased tourism. Guam's economy had recovered from a 1992 typhoon and a 1993 earthquake with 3.2 per cent growth in 1994, while, at last report, Palau's GDP had increased by an estimated 5.3 per cent in 1993.

Most Pacific island economies experienced low and falling inflation rates, owing to declining inflation in their major suppliers (Australia, New Zealand, United States); the rates were expected to remain below 3 per cent in 1995 in the Cook Islands, Fiji, Tonga, Tuvalu and Vanuatu and at around 5 per cent in Kiribati, but to reach 16 per cent in Papua New Guinea, compared with 2.9 per cent in 1994, due to a sharp depreciation of the local currency and an increase in import and excise duty rates. Samoa's inflation was expected to decrease. Following the introduction of value-added tax and shortfalls in the taro crop there, the rate had reached 18.4 per cent in 1994, a tenfold rise over 1993.

*Subregional economic performance*

The economies of East Asia grew by 9.3 per cent in 1995, compared with 9.9 per cent in 1994, while annual inflation for the subregion as a whole fell from 14.6 per cent to 10.6 per cent. The rate of growth in China decreased from 11.8 per cent to 10 per cent, due to austerity measures to counter inflationary pressures, but nevertheless remained the highest in the ESCAP region; at the same time, China's inflation was brought down from 21.7 per cent in 1994 to the targeted 15 per cent in 1995. Agricultural production, affected by heavy floods in 1994, increased by 4 per cent in 1995, up from 3.5 per cent in the previous year, while the services sector maintained the 1994 expansion rate of 10 per cent. Industrial output was expected to rise at a slower rate of 12 per cent, against 16.3 per cent in 1994.

The high growth rate of the Chinese economy had a stimulating effect on neighbouring countries, as well as on the rest of the region. GDP rose by 9.3 per cent in the Republic of Korea, compared with 8.4 per cent in the previous year; its agriculture rebounded with an estimated 7.4 per cent growth rate, having gained only 1.2 per cent in 1994, while rates of increase in the industrial and services sectors were expected to accelerate. Following the introduction of a tight monetary policy to curb excessive domestic demand, inflation was estimated at 5 per cent, a 1 per cent drop from the previous year. The economy of Hong Kong maintained a 5.5 per cent growth rate, despite a sharp slowdown in consumer spending. The services sector was the main source of growth, along with a strong stimulus from expanding construction activities. Inflation increased slightly, from 8.1 per cent in 1994 to 8.5 per cent in 1995, owing to such factors as high inflation rates in China, rising import costs of commodities, and rising labour and housing costs.

Mongolia, an economy in transition to a market system, reversed the output contraction experienced in the early 1990s, registering growth rates of 2.1 per cent in 1994 and 3.5 per cent in 1995. The recovery was attributed to strong improvements in agricultural and industrial production, a modest expansion of the mining sector, growing private participation in trading and retail activities, and an encouraging upturn in the volume of trade, investment and foreign aid. Efforts to restrict monetary and credit expansion against a background of gradual price liberalization had led to a fall in inflation from 268 per cent in 1993 to 88 per cent in 1994 and below 30 per cent in 1995. The Democratic People's Republic of Korea, on the other hand, seemed to be facing economic difficulties, aggravated by flood damage to agricultural production, which necessitated substantial rice shipments to the country.

In South-East Asia, the average rate of growth accelerated slightly to 8 per cent in 1995, compared with 7.9 per cent in 1994, while inflation rose by 0.1 per cent to reach 6.4 per cent. The subregion's growth was underpinned by strong domestic demand and high savings and investment rates. The economy of the Philippines maintained its recovery, growing by 5.3 per cent, a 1 per cent increase over the previous year. A downturn in that country's agricultural sector, which expanded by 1.9 per cent against 2.3 per cent in 1994, was offset by stronger performance of industry and services. The pace of economic growth also accelerated in Viet Nam, with GDP growth estimated at 9.5 per cent in 1995 against 8.8 per cent in 1994, as its industrial and services sectors maintained high expansion rates of some 14 per cent and 10 per cent, respectively, while agriculture grew by 5.2 per cent, up from 3.9 per cent.

Growth rates in Malaysia accelerated from 9.2 per cent in 1994 to 9.6 per cent in 1995 but decreased in Indonesia from 7.3 per cent to 7.1 per cent and in Singapore from 10.1 per cent to 9 per cent. Thailand's economy grew by 8.6 per cent, only an estimated 0.1 per cent improvement over the previous year. Most countries registered higher growth rates than in 1994 in their agricultural, industrial and services sectors; however, agricultural output expanded more slowly in Singapore, while industrial performance was below 1994 levels in Indonesia, Malaysia and Singapore. Inflation rates in Malaysia were expected to decline from 3.7 per

cent in 1994 to 3.5 per cent in 1995, from 9.1 per cent to 8 per cent in the Philippines, and from 3.1 per cent to 2.2 per cent in Singapore, but increased from 9.2 per cent to 10 per cent in Indonesia, 5 per cent to 5.5 per cent in Thailand and 14.4 per cent to 14.9 per cent in Viet Nam. Brunei Darussalam stood in marked contrast to the rest of the subregion, having achieved growth rates of only 0.5 per cent in 1993 and 1.8 per cent in 1994, after a contraction in 1992. However, its inflation rate had dropped to 2.4 per cent in 1994, from 4.3 per cent in 1993.

The South Asian economies registered a slight improvement in their performance, with the GDP growth rate increasing from 5.1 per cent in 1994 to 5.5 per cent in 1995 and inflation declining from 9.9 per cent to 8.4 per cent. Despite recent economic reforms in the subregion, savings and investment activities remained relatively weak and budget deficits large.

The economy of India expanded by 5.7 per cent, up from 5.3 per cent in 1994, as the growth rate in its services sector rose from 5.5 per cent to 7.5 per cent; however, rates of increase decelerated from 8.3 per cent in 1994 to 6.9 per cent in 1995 for industry and from 2.4 per cent to 2.1 per cent for agriculture. GDP was expected to grow by 5.1 per cent in Iran, compared with 3 per cent in the previous year, with a 3.9 per cent recovery in its industrial sector after a decline of 0.3 per cent in 1994, and a 7.4 per cent expansion in services. Pakistan's output rose by 4.7 per cent, against 3.8 per cent in the previous year, due to a revival in agricultural production, which grew by 4.9 per cent—2 per cent faster than in 1994—as well as improved performance of both the industrial and services sectors. In Sri Lanka, GDP expanded by 5.4 per cent, down from 5.6 per cent in 1994, with its agriculture and industry performing below the 1994 level and services maintaining a growth rate of some 5.3 per cent.

Inflation decreased from 10.3 per cent in 1994 to 8 per cent in 1995 in India, but rose from 11.2 per cent to 12.9 per cent in Pakistan and from 8.4 per cent to 9.1 per cent in Sri Lanka. It was expected to exceed the 1994 level of 35.2 per cent in Iran.

The situation in several Central Asian economies in transition showed the first signs of improvement since 1991, although Armenia was the only country in the group to have recorded a positive growth rate—5.2 per cent—after a 2 per cent contraction in 1994. The fall in GDP and in industrial production slowed in most countries. Output dropped 8.9 per cent in Kazakstan, 7.5 per cent in Turkmenistan, 6.2 per cent in Kyrgyzstan and 0.5 per cent in Uzbekistan, compared with respective 1994 decreases of 25 per cent, 12 per cent, 26 per cent and 4 per cent. However, rates of decline continued at the 1994 level of some 17 per cent in Azerbaijan and 12 per cent in Tajikistan. Agricultural production continued to suffer from shortages of fuel, fertilizers and spare parts for machinery; in 1994, it had contracted by 25 per cent in Tajikistan, 17 per cent in Kazakstan, 13 per cent in Azerbaijan and 1 per cent in Uzbekistan, but had expanded by 3 per cent in Armenia and 2 per cent in Turkmenistan, in the latter after a 9 per cent growth rate in 1993. At the same time, the fall in agricultural output slowed in Kyrgyzstan, from 15 per cent in 1994 to an estimated 4.5 per cent in 1995.

Armenia was also the only country to have maintained growth in its industrial sector, although at a lower rate of 2.4 per cent, compared with 6.9 per cent in the previous year. In other economies, the rates of decline in industrial production decelerated from 24 per cent in 1994 to 21.4 per cent in 1995 in Azerbaijan, 28.5 per cent to 7.9 per cent in Kazakstan, 24.5 per cent to 12.5 per cent in Kyrgyzstan, 30.8 per cent to 5.1 per cent in Tajikistan and 25 per cent to 6.9 per cent in Turkmenistan; in Uzbekistan, industrial output contracted 0.2 per cent after a 1 per cent increase in 1994. The services sector proved more resilient to the adverse economic climate, with retailing and financial services showing positive growth rates. Measures to contain inflation yielded results in most countries as annual rates fell from 5,060 per cent to 280 per cent in Armenia, from 1,760 per cent to 510 per cent in Azerbaijan, from 1,980 per cent to 280 per cent in Kazakstan, from 380 per cent to 150 per cent in Kyrgyzstan, and from 1,650 per cent to 420 per cent in Uzbekistan. In Tajikistan, however, inflation was expected to rise from 340 per cent to about 500 per cent. At the same time, budget deficits remained a principal concern, ranging from 1.5 per cent of GDP in Turkmenistan to between 3 per cent and 5 per cent in Kazakstan and Azerbaijan and more than 12 per cent in Armenia and Kyrgyzstan.

### External sector

Both the export and import trade of the region's developing countries continued to grow strongly in 1995, although the overall rate of growth was estimated to be somewhat lower than in 1994, when exports from those countries totalled $677.5 billion, a 19.6 per cent increase over the previous year, while imports grew by 18.2 per cent to reach $714.5 billion. Exports in 1994 rose by 19.1 per cent in East Asia and 22.2 per cent in South-East Asia, to respective totals of $368.6 billion and $261.6 billion. China and Hong Kong accounted for the bulk of export receipts, followed by Singapore and the Republic of Korea. South Asian countries increased their exports by 14.3 per cent to $40.5 billion, with India's share amounting to $25 billion.

Trade of the ESCAP LDCs, Pacific island countries and economies in transition, on the other hand, continued to suffer from structural weaknesses such as a narrow export base limited to a few primary commodities or simple manufactured goods—textiles or garments. Consequently, their trade sector, although recording high growth rates, constituted a very small part of GDP. In 1994, exports grew by 19.9 per cent in LDCs and by 7 per cent in Pacific island countries, but their value totalled only $4.7 billion and $3.7 billion, respectively. At the same time, export value declined in Central Asian republics from $3.8 billion in 1993 to $3.3 billion in 1994. Bangladesh, Papua New Guinea and Kazakstan were the leading exporters in their respective groups. Importers were led by Bangladesh, Papua New Guinea and Uzbekistan. In most countries imports far outstripped exports.

Imports to Asian and Pacific LDCs reached $8.5 billion, 18.3 per cent more than the previous year and $3.8 billion more than exports. Pacific island countries registered a 14.3 per cent increase in their imports to about $3.7 billion, only slightly less than exports. Central Asian imports rose from $2.6 billion in 1993 to $2.8 billion in 1994 and continued to climb in 1995, approaching the level of exports.

In other developing economies of the region, both export and import expansion were significant. Import values increased in 1994 by 16.3 per cent to $379.9 billion for East Asia, by 22.1 per cent to $279.8 billion for South-East Asia and by 12.4 per cent to $48.4 billion for South Asia. The leading importers in those subregions were, respectively, China and Hong Kong; Singapore; and India.

The balance-of-payments situation raised concerns in several countries, as continuing liberalization and openness of trade regimes, as well as easier access to credit and capital, including offshore facilities, contributed to a rapid growth of imports, while exports faced more intense competition due to differences in costs and efficiency. Higher labour production costs, stemming from shortages of labour and skills, highlighted the need to improve labour productivity in a number of Asian and Pacific countries and to make their production more technology-intensive. The management of the balance of payments in open and deregulated trade and financial environments also posed new challenges, necessitating greater reliance on market forces. The balance of trade and payments deteriorated in a number of more advanced developing economies, including India, Indonesia, Malaysia, Pakistan, the Philippines, the Republic of Korea, Sri Lanka and Thailand, with their merchandise trade deficits aggravated by the deficits incurred in trade in invisibles. The balance of payments suffered from structural disequilibrium in most LDCs, Pacific island countries and economies in transition, with merchandise imports generally exceeding exports by a margin of two to one. China and Singapore, on the other hand, recorded surpluses in both their merchandise and invisible trade accounts; trade surpluses were also expected in Kazakstan, Kyrgyzstan, Tajikistan and Uzbekistan.

Private capital inflows to the region remained relatively small. In 1994, Asia received $26.6 billion, or 10.5 per cent, of the global total announced by syndicated credit facilities. China, Indonesia and Thailand alone accounted for $21 billion of that. The region also received $15.4 billion, or 4 per cent, of global bond issues, with more than half channelled to China and the Republic of Korea. In 1993, China alone had received 45 per cent of total flows to Asian developing countries, while Singapore had accounted for an additional 20 per cent, followed by Indonesia, Malaysia and Thailand. India and Viet Nam also emerged recently as recipients of substantial flows of foreign direct investment (FDI).

### Policy developments

Most countries in the ESCAP region showed strong commitment to reform aimed at restructuring, stabilizing and liberalizing their economies. Privatization of public enterprises and accelerated measures of trade and investment liberalization constituted the cornerstone of reform programmes, which differed, however, in their immediate objectives. The Asian and Pacific LDCs gave high priority to promoting savings and investment and accelerating growth with macroeconomic stability. Pacific island countries faced the need to reduce government involvement in their economies, control substantially public expenditure, improve economic management, and strengthen decision-making and planning machineries. Reform measures in Central Asia focused on establishing a legal framework to facilitate the functioning of market-oriented economies, carrying out privatization, and increasing the role of financial intermediation, as well as containing expenditure and increasing budget revenues. Similar reforms also continued in Mongolia and Viet Nam.

In South Asia, India and Iran implemented a range of stabilization and adjustment policies, while Pakistan and Sri Lanka continued efforts towards deregulation and liberalization of their economies. South-East Asian policies were geared towards enhancing efficiency, competitiveness and the growth process. In May, Indonesia introduced a reform package for its import tariff structure, while Malaysia in June announced measures to develop its capital market. Policy efforts in East Asian countries centred on curtailing a further rise in inflation and enhancing external competitiveness.

Most policy reforms were aimed at encouraging the development of the private sector and enhancing its role in economic activities. Measures already implemented highlighted the need for an appropriate legal framework, dealing with property rights and contract enforcement, among others; price liberalization and incentives promotion; improvement of tax systems and deregulation of financial sectors; liberalization of trade and investment regimes; promotion of competition; and the development of entrepreneurship and of small and medium-sized enterprises.

Inflation concerns prevailed in Australia and New Zealand, while Japan pursued measures to stimulate economic growth and to bring its economy out of recession, although at the expense of a balanced budget.

### Social trends

The social situation in the ESCAP region was characterized by growing awareness of the importance of human and social development in the overall development process and increasing demand for social services, which in turn enhanced the traditional role of the public sector in the delivery of such services. As a result, public spending on health, education, housing, water supply and sanitation, and social protection had risen since the early 1990s to more than 20 per cent of total budgetary expenditures, representing between 5 per cent and 10 per cent of GDP in most countries. Although inequities in social allocations persisted in many countries, with higher education and curative health care receiving a greater share than primary education and preventive services, the situation in the social sector improved considerably, as reflected in the growing number of schools, teachers, hospitals, doctors and other relevant institutions and personnel. Public health and sanitation programmes were expanded to cover the majority of the population, while increased accessibility of various services led to a rise in school enrolment ratios and literacy rates and reductions in morbidity and mortality.

Life expectancy at birth in the period 1990-1995 was 67.3 to 75.6 years for men and 74.9 to 81.8 years for women in newly industrializing economies (NIEs) (Hong Kong, Republic of Korea, Singapore); 61.5 to 69.5 years and 68.5 to 75.5 years, respectively, in Central Asian republics; 43 to 67.3 years and 44 to 65.2 years in the region's LDCs; and 55.2 to 69.7 years and 60.4 to 74.2 years in other developing countries of Asia and the Pacific. Crude death rates ranged between 5.6 and 6.2 deaths per 1,000 in NIEs and between 6.1 and 7.5 in Central Asia to between 7.2 and 21.8 in LDCs and between 4.5 and 10.7 in other developing countries. Newly industrializing economies also had the lowest infant mortality rates, 6 to 11 deaths per 1,000 live births, compared with 21 to 57 in Central Asian States, 84 to 163 in LDCs and 13 to 91 in other countries. In addition to the Central Asian republics, universal or near-universal access of the population to health services was achieved in NIEs, China, Mongolia, Papua New Guinea, Sri Lanka, Thailand and Viet Nam. Countries where only about half the population or less had health services were Afghanistan (29 per cent), Bangladesh (45 per cent), Cambodia (53 per cent) and Pakistan (55 per cent).

Quantitative and qualitative deficiencies persisted in many other social areas. School enrolment rates were still relatively low and drop-out rates high in several countries, particularly for female and underprivileged children in rural areas and depressed urban locations, and the quality of education often remained poor due to a lack of teachers and an inadequate supply of educational equipment. For countries lacking public health coverage, infectious and communicable diseases continued to be a major health hazard, and they also experienced high infant and maternal mortality rates. In addition, HIV/AIDS emerged as a new major threat to public health. Those challenges highlighted the need for increased allocation of public resources to expand and improve the social services infrastructure, as well as for involvement of the private sector, NGOs and local communities in developing and maintaining facilities and delivering many social services, which in turn required considerable decentralization and devolution to the local level of activities, resources and decision-making powers.

## Activities in 1995

ESCAP activities in 1995 were implemented under six thematic subprogrammes approved by the Commission in 1994:[4] regional economic cooperation; environment and sustainable development; poverty alleviation through economic growth and social development; transport and communications; statistics; and least developed, land-locked and island developing countries.

### Development policy and regional economic cooperation

At its 1995 session, the Commission had before it a study on strengthening regional cooperation in human resources development, with special reference to the social implications of sustainable economic growth in Asia and the Pacific,[5] as well as its summary.[6] Those documents analysed key aspects of the human resources development situation in the region, examined emerging challenges, reviewed institutional arrangements and provided proposals for regional cooperation in that area. The Commission noted that the study had

been considered by a panel of eminent persons in 1994,[7] which subsequently adopted the Bangkok Statement on Regional Cooperation in Human Resources Development. The Commission affirmed that continued and increased investment in the region's human resources through education, skills formation and improved health was crucial to enhancing the quality of life in Asia and the Pacific and to maintaining its competitive edge.

In a May resolution[8] on the subject, the Commission invited its members to strengthen the scope and effectiveness of their human resources development policies, plans and programmes and to identify their potential for regional cooperation in that area. The Executive Secretary was requested to examine the feasibility of organizing a regional network of centres to promote regional cooperation in human resources development and to seek advice of the Panel of Eminent Persons on further action in that regard; to highlight human resources development as a strategy to alleviate poverty in the medium-term plan for 1998-2001; to devote particular attention to promoting women's human resources development as a means of ensuring gender equity; and to report in 1999 on progress made.

In another resolution,[9] the Commission welcomed the major recommendations made at an expert group meeting (New Delhi, India, April) on follow-up to implementation of the Delhi Declaration on Strengthening Regional Economic Cooperation in Asia and the Pacific towards the Twenty-first Century, adopted by ESCAP in 1994.[10] It requested the Committee for Regional Economic Cooperation and its Steering Group to propose further measures to strengthen regional cooperation, with a view to preparing a comprehensive strategy in that respect, and recommended that the feasibility of establishing a number of regional mechanisms and networks be examined for enhancing trade, investment, technology transfer and economic cooperation. Other recommendations dealt with linking trade and environment-related as well as social issues, human resources development and the ESCAP secretariat's leading role in assisting States to take advantage of emerging information and communication technologies. The Executive Secretary was to report in 1996 on the progress made.

The Committee for Regional Economic Cooperation, at its fourth session (Bangkok, 8-9 February),[11] endorsed the text of the revised draft New Delhi Action Plan on Infrastructure Development in Asia and the Pacific, recommended by its Steering Group at the sixth meeting (Jakarta, Indonesia, 23-26 January) pursuant to a 1994 Commission request.[12] The Action Plan was subsequently adopted by the Commission (see below). The Committee also adopted ESCAP's draft work programme for 1996-1997, pertaining to regional economic cooperation. Later in the year, the Committee's Steering Group held its seventh meeting (Ulaanbaatar, Mongolia, 19-22 September) to consider issues relating to regional economic cooperation in trade and investment, technology transfer, promotion of industrial restructuring in Asia and the Pacific, and economic cooperation in North-East Asia.

In 1995, the ESCAP secretariat organized a second consultative meeting of executive heads of subregional organizations (Jakarta, January), which reiterated the need to pursue inter-subregional cooperation in trade and investment, transport and communications, human resources development, and energy. The Regional Inter-agency Committee for Asia and the Pacific (RICAP), established by the Inter-agency Meeting on Strengthening Coordination at the Regional Level in May 1994, held its second meeting on 22 June 1995 to consider emerging priority issues of the region. Several subcommittees were constituted under RICAP, including those on disability-related concerns, the advancement of women, population and development, urbanization, water, environment and sustainable development, regional space applications programme, HIV/AIDS, poverty alleviation, and industry and technology, as well as the Inter-Agency Steering Group on Phase II (1992-1996) of the Transport and Communications Decade for Asia and the Pacific. Most of those subcommittees met during the year (see below, under specific subject headings).

The secretariat provided advisory services to Bangladesh on major trends in macroeconomic policy developments in the region and to Myanmar on macroeconomic modelling and policy analysis, and issued publications dealing with management of economic reforms, privatization issues and prospects, social accounting models for policy analysis, tax system reforms, strategies for technological transformation through regional cooperation, and technological transaction patterns for enhancing regional cooperation in biotechnology. It also continued to publish the *Asia-Pacific Development Journal*.

### Action plan on infrastructure development

At its 1995 session, the Commission considered issues relating to infrastructure development in Asia and the Pacific, stressing the importance of regional and subregional cooperation in that respect, as well as the need to mobilize domestic private capital and FDI for infrastructure development. It proposed the establishment of a regional information system on infrastructure. The Commission also supported the decision of the World Infrastructure Forum–Asia 1994[12] to establish an Asia Infrastructure Development Alliance (AIDA), and endorsed the sugges-

tion that the ESCAP secretariat participate actively in the work of the Alliance.

On 1 May, the Commission adopted[13] the New Delhi Action Plan on Infrastructure Development in Asia and the Pacific, 1997-2006, and decided to convene in 1996 a ministerial conference on infrastructure to launch the Action Plan and to review phase II of the Transport and Communications Decade for Asia and the Pacific, as well as to hold, in conjunction with the conference, the World Infrastructure Forum–Asia 1996. It invited member States to adopt policies making the provision of infrastructure more sensitive to user demand and to establish national focal points for infrastructure development; requested them to identify areas for action in promoting their infrastructural development; and urged them to promote the active involvement of the public sector in the process and to strengthen the public-private sector partnership. The Committee on Transport and Communications was requested to review its terms of reference, including its name, to cover aspects relating to the development of physical infrastructure and tourism. The Commission called for international assistance in implementing the Action Plan and asked the Executive Secretary, *inter alia*, to support preparations for the ministerial conference on infrastructure and to report annually on the implementation of the Action Plan.

The Action Plan, annexed to the Commission resolution, provided an overview of infrastructure requirements and issues to be addressed, and included proposals for action relating to infrastructure planning and policy; administration and management; private sector participation; logistics and facilitation; environment and safety; human resources development; poverty alleviation, rural areas and disadvantaged population groups; and infrastructure needs of the least developed, land-locked and island developing countries, as well as economies in transition. The Action Plan also outlined implementation modalities, time-frame, priorities, monitoring mechanisms, and strategies for resource mobilization.

As requested by the Commission, the secretariat participated in a meeting to establish AIDA (Bangkok, May) and in the first meeting of the Steering Committee for Establishment of AIDA (New Delhi, September). In November, the Committee on Transport and Communications endorsed a regional programme for the implementation of the New Delhi Action Plan and recommended that its title and terms of reference be changed (see below, under "Transport and communications").

### Least developed and land-locked developing countries

The Special Body on Least Developed and Land-locked Developing Countries, at its second session (Bangkok, 17-19 April),[14] made a number of recommendations to strengthen regional input to the global mid-term review of the implementation of the UN Programme of Action for LDCs for the 1990s, adopted in 1990 by a United Nations conference held in Paris[15] and endorsed by the General Assembly later that year.[16] The Special Body noted that the overall growth rate of the region's LDCs had been insufficient to have an impact on the main social and economic problems facing those countries, and expressed concern over their low domestic savings and investment rates. It also reviewed sectoral developments and welcomed initiatives towards deregulation and liberalization, particularly measures to boost the growth of the agricultural and industrial sectors. The Special Body further pointed out that relatively high population growth rates in LDCs, the status of women, and education and health remained areas of continuing concern, and called for the commitment of adequate resources to those areas, their better use, and delivery of improved services.

In 1995, the Commission expressed concern over the slow progress in implementing the 1990 Programme of Action and identified priorities in its implementation for the remaining years of the decade, including poverty alleviation, human resources development and capacity-building for effective environmental planning and management. In a resolution,[17] the Commission endorsed recommendations of the Special Body, urged active participation of member States in the High-level Intergovernmental Meeting on the Mid-term Global Review of the Implementation of the Programme of Action for LDCs for the 1990s (see PART FOUR, Chapter I), and called on the ESCAP secretariat to prepare regional input for that meeting. It reaffirmed that progress in the Programme's implementation required effective national policies of LDCs for their socio-economic development and urged adequate international assistance in support of LDC development efforts.

During the year, the secretariat organized a meeting of senior officials and experts on the mid-term review (Bangkok, April). It provided advisory services and technical assistance to LDCs and land-locked countries through workshops, seminars, expert group meetings and training courses, in such areas as macroeconomic management; trade, technology and industrial development; social development and poverty alleviation; environment, energy and natural resources; transport and communications; and statistical development. The first in a series of national workshops in LDCs to assist in policy design for enhanced access of women to formal credit was held in Bhutan in December. Publications were issued on lessons for LDCs to be derived from early development experience of NIEs and on public expenditure and the provision of social services in Bangladesh and Nepal, among others.

### Special problems of Pacific island countries

The Special Body on Pacific Island Developing Countries, at its third session (Bangkok, 20-21 April),[18] recognized the urgent need for those countries to attract increased flows of foreign investment and made recommendations in that regard. It also recommended action to expand trade and investment relations between Pacific island countries and the Asian region, by increasing the flows of information on export products and investment opportunities, enhancing business contacts, promoting exchange of experience in policy areas and identifying potential export products for Asia. Measures were proposed for the development of the local private sector. The need was underlined for more training for both public and private sectors. The Special Body further reviewed implications for the region of the first Global Conference on the Sustainable Development of Small Island Developing States (the Barbados Conference), held in 1994,[19] pointing out that Pacific island countries needed assistance in implementing Conference recommendations. In that regard, it called for improved cooperation and coordination between ESCAP and Pacific subregional organizations.

At its 1995 session, the Commission endorsed the conclusions and recommendations of the Special Body and emphasized that ESCAP should act as a bridge between the Pacific and Asia to assist Pacific island countries in expanding trade and investment links. It also reaffirmed the usefulness of the Pacific Trust Fund in facilitating those countries' participation in Commission sessions.

During the year, the ESCAP Pacific Operations Centre provided advisory services focusing on programming, corporate planning, central banking, macroeconomic policy formulation, development planning and financial systems, trade promotion, planning and improvement of port infrastructure, and computerization. The ESCAP secretariat undertook studies of Fiji's export potential and of energy and urban development issues in the Solomon Islands and Vanuatu, and launched a project on enhancing cooperation in trade and investment between Pacific island countries and economies of East and South-East Asia. ESCAP also cooperated with the South Pacific Forum and the South Pacific Regional Environment Programme in the follow-up to the 1994 Barbados Conference.[19]

### ESCAP transition economies

During the year, the ESCAP secretariat continued to provide assistance to the Asian and Pacific disadvantaged economies in transition to a market system. National workshops on economic reform were held in Armenia, Azerbaijan, Kyrgyzstan, Tajikistan and Turkmenistan. A publication was issued on lessons of East and South-East Asian growth experience for macroeconomic reforms in economies in transition. In addition, agencies in Kyrgyzstan and Turkmenistan were advised on the role of ESCAP in promoting regional economic cooperation and on existing opportunities for such cooperation, as well as benefits to be derived from it.

In 1995, the Commission noted the continuing need of economies in transition for analytical and technical assistance in the areas of macroeconomic management and policy, trade and investment, privatization, industrial restructuring and technological upgrading, transport and human resources development. It further observed the need for coordination between ESCAP and ECE in the use of resources, in view of the shared membership in those two regional commissions of several economies in transition.

### Economic and technical cooperation

During 1995, ESCAP received $22.4 million in contributions for technical cooperation activities, a marginal decrease of some $23,000 from 1994, including $9.12 million from sources within the UN system and $13.25 million from donor States, developing member countries and organizations.[20] Australia, Finland, France, Germany, Japan, the Netherlands, New Zealand and Sweden contributed 86.13 per cent of total bilateral assistance received. China, India, Indonesia and the Republic of Korea were the largest contributors among developing member countries that provided assistance in 1995. In addition to cash contributions, donor States and developing member countries provided 372 work-months of expert services, compared with 221 in 1994. Financial requirements for the 140 new project proposals recommended for bilateral funding in 1996 amounted to $11.65 million. Bilateral donors approved 99 projects, totalling $8.18 million, for execution under ESCAP's work programme, excluding special projects and regional institutions. A corps of 14 regional advisers undertook 144 missions to 48 developing countries of the region.

#### Technical cooperation among developing countries

The Commission in 1995 commended the ESCAP secretariat on its catalytic role in promoting technical cooperation among developing countries (TCDC) and recommended that efforts be intensified to mobilize additional resources for TCDC activities, to strengthen TCDC national focal points, and to streamline and prioritize TCDC programmes, which should be related to development

schemes, address the most common critical needs and capitalize on local resources. The importance of follow-up activities was also emphasized.

During the year, the secretariat carried out some 130 promotional TCDC activities, financed from extrabudgetary resources and complemented by resources under the UN regular programme of technical cooperation. With the support of China, the Netherlands and the Republic of Korea, 51 operational TCDC activities were implemented through the TCDC supplementary fund. Those activities, aimed at promoting self-reliance and strengthening South-South cooperation through an exchange of information and the sharing of experience and expertise, covered a broad range of subjects including, *inter alia*, water resources management, computer applications systems in customs documentation, telecommunications, port management and operations, population information, flood and storm forecasting, energy conservation, manufacturing of agricultural machinery, information technology management, banking operations in a market economy, housing construction, reinsurance management and social issues relating to the disabled.

Ten training courses were offered by China and six by Singapore under their TCDC programmes. Kazakstan entered into a long-term TCDC agreement on water resources management with Thailand, and two exchange visits were undertaken to discuss water resources development and planning. The secretariat continued efforts to promote exchanges of population programme managers, to establish a women's information network and networks of trade-related research institutions and of human settlements management authorities, and to strengthen TCDC national focal points. In 1995, its TCDC programme was thematically reoriented to focus on trade and investment, the environment, poverty alleviation, macroeconomic policy coordination, human resources development, transfer of technology, small and medium-sized enterprises, rural development, and tourism.

### International trade and finance

At its 1995 session, the Commission noted the progress made in implementing the Action Programme for Regional Economic Cooperation in Trade and Investment, which it had endorsed in 1993,[21] including activities to promote export-oriented small and medium-sized enterprises and to strengthen the regional investment information and promotion service. It approved proposed revisions to the Action Programme, directed the secretariat to carry out studies on commodity trade problems of concern to the region, and recommended that issues relating to trade in primary products and raw materials be examined within the framework of the Action Programme. The

Commission also recommended the revitalization of the 1975 Bangkok Agreement on trade negotiations among ESCAP developing member States, and stressed that the Agreement's membership needed to be expanded and the national list of concessions under the Agreement extended. In that regard, it noted that China was in the process of acceding to the Agreement and that Papua New Guinea was at the final stage of ratifying its accession.

On 1 May, the Commission adopted a resolution[22] on Asia-Pacific International Trade Fairs (ASPAT), in which it requested member States to participate actively in ASPAT'96, to be held in the Philippines, called on them and other UN Members, as well as UNDP, to extend full support to that and subsequent fairs, and asked the Executive Secretary to support the participation in those fairs of least developed, Pacific island and landlocked countries and economies in transition.

During the year, consultative meetings, seminars and workshops were held on: the Bangkok Agreement, agricultural trade, the networking of trade-related research institutions, the use of information technologies for trade and investment, intraregional trade in rice, trade facilitation and promotion in the ESCAP region, exploitation of trade and investment complementarities in North-East Asia, integration of Asian and Pacific countries not members of the World Trade Organization into the international trading system, promotion of foreign investment, export credit and finance, country-specific models for trade policy analysis, electronic applications in international trade, export marketing, and expansion of trade in pulses. Advisory services were provided to ESCAP member States on the regional investment information and promotion service, promotion of trade and investment flows between subregions, preparations for ASPAT'96, investment promotion, and assistance to industry for export promotion.

The secretariat updated the directory of trade and investment-related organizations of developing countries and areas; issued publications on electronic commerce initiatives of ESCAP, foreign investment incentive schemes and regional implications of the Uruguay Round multilateral trade agreements, signed in 1994;[23] prepared a number of studies on trade and investment issues; and continued to publish the *TISNET Trade Information Bulletin.*

## Transport and communications

In 1995, the Commission reviewed activities relating to land, railway, urban, multimodal, maritime and inland water transport; freight forwarding; commercialization and private sector involvement in ports, dredging and inland waterways; and

phase II (1992-1996) of the Transport and Communications Decade for Asia and the Pacific (see below). The Commission reiterated its strong support for the integrated Asian Land Transport Infrastructure Development (ALTID) project, comprising the Asian Highway, the Trans-Asian Railway Network and transport facilitation measures, and stressed the need for countries to consider acceding to international conventions on road and rail transport modes in relation to facilitation measures, as it had recommended in 1992.[24] It noted the inauguration of the railway route Bafq-Bandar Abbas, which served the needs of Central Asian republics; progress in constructing a railway link between Iran and Turkmenistan; and a feasibility study on various railway linkages between China, Kazakstan, the Korean peninsula, Mongolia and the Russian Federation.

The Committee on Transport and Communications, at its second session (Bangkok, 6-10 November),[25] considered developments in the transport, communications and tourism sectors, as well as issues relating to infrastructure development in the region. The Committee endorsed a plan of action for phase II (1996-1997) of the ALTID project and a regional programme for the implementation of the New Delhi Action Plan on Infrastructure Development in Asia and the Pacific, adopted by the Commission in May (see above, under "Development policy and regional economic cooperation). It recommended that the ALTID project should constitute a priority item under the Action Plan. It also stressed the need for further action in implementing the 1992 Commission resolution[24] on road and rail transport modes in relation to facilitation measures, and endorsed a proposal to develop guidelines for port commercialization and privatization. As requested by the Commission in May, the Committee recommended that its title be changed to the "Committee on Transport, Communications, Tourism and Infrastructure Development" and that its terms of reference be adjusted accordingly.

During the year, the secretariat organized a series of national, subregional and regional workshops, seminars and expert group meetings on freight forwarding, multimodal transport, international maritime traffic, inland water transport and locomotive and rolling stock maintenance, and another on commercialization and private sector participation in ports, related activities, dredging and inland waterways. Under the ALTID project, a policy-level meeting was held (Bangkok, October) to consider the feasibility of connecting the rail networks of China, Mongolia, Kazakstan, the Russian Federation and the Korean peninsula, and expert group meetings were convened on the development of a highway network in Asian republics and on trans-Asian railway route requirements in the southern corridor (Bangladesh, India, Iran, Myanmar, Nepal, Pakistan).

The secretariat provided advisory services to Kyrgyzstan, Sri Lanka and Thailand on road taxation systems and on commercial aspects of railway modernization. It continued to publish the *Transport and Communications Bulletin for Asia and the Pacific*. A map of the Asian highway route was produced, and studies were undertaken on commercial aspects of inland water transport, land transport linkages from Central Asia to seaports in South and East Asia, maritime manpower for the shipping industry, the railway break-of-gauge problem, road safety in Asia and the Pacific, and the development of freight forwarding and multimodal and urban transport in the region.

### Transport and Communications Decade for Asia and the Pacific

At its 1995 session, the Commission expressed concern about the lack of funding for 13 activities under the regional action programme for phase II (1992-1996) of the Transport and Communications Decade for Asia and the Pacific, and urged donor countries and agencies to support priority projects. The Decade, proclaimed by the General Assembly in 1984[26] and extended in 1991[27] until 1996, promoted infrastructure improvements in both the ESCAP and ESCWA regions.

The Decade programme's implementation was reviewed in 1995 by the Inter-Agency Steering Committee on Phase II of the Decade at its fourth session (Bangkok, 2-3 November). Also in November, the Committee on Transport and Communications endorsed the Steering Committee's recommendations and called for continuing coordinated efforts to implement the remaining part of the programme, noting that it was of considerable benefit to the countries in the region.

Decade-related information continued to be disseminated during the year in *Decade News*, published by the ESCAP secretariat.

### Tourism

In 1995, the Commission reaffirmed the important role of tourism in the region's socio-economic development and urged the ESCAP secretariat to intensify its activities in that sector. It supported recommendations for convening an intergovernmental meeting on tourism development and establishing a regional network of tourism training institutes. In November, those recommendations were endorsed by the Committee on Transport and Communications.

Activities to promote tourism included the first two meetings of a working group on the Greater Mekong subregion tourism sector, workshops on ecotourism development in Asia and the Pacific and on integrated tourism planning in Pacific is-

land countries, and national seminars on integrated tourism planning and tourism marketing in the Marshall Islands and Nauru. The secretariat carried out studies on foreign investment in the tourism sectors of Samoa and Vanuatu, and continued to publish the *ESCAP Tourism Review* and the *ESCAP Tourism Newsletter*.

### Industrial and technological development

The Commission reviewed activities for implementing the mandates of the Seoul Plan of Action for Promoting Industrial Restructuring in Asia and the Pacific, adopted in 1992,[28] and the Tehran Declaration on Strengthening Regional Cooperation for Technology-led Industrialization in Asia and the Pacific, as well as the Regional Strategy and Action Plan for Industrial and Technological Development, both endorsed in 1993.[29] The Commission emphasized the need to pursue open multilateral policies to accelerate the pace of industrial and technological development in the region, expressed concern at persisting and growing disparities in that sector, and identified target areas for further action, including FDI, technology transfer, private-sector development and privatization, the development of small and medium-sized enterprises, industrial relocation and complementarities, industrial and technological skills development, information sharing, and quality control and standardization.

The ESCAP secretariat organized a subregional workshop on assistance in matching investment and industrial relocation, an expert group meeting on promoting regional cooperation for industrial and technological skills development, and a symposium on strengthening private sector involvement in enhancing manufacturing competitiveness. It also published a small industry bulletin for Asia and the Pacific and provided advisory services to Indonesia on coconut industry development and to Nepal on policy measures to promote small- and medium-scale enterprises. Issues relating to industrial and technological development were discussed at a regional meeting of Asian and Pacific ministers of industry (New Delhi, October), convened in cooperation with UNIDO.

### Asian and Pacific Development Centre

The year 1995 marked the beginning of programme phase VI (1995-1998) in the work of the Asian and Pacific Development Centre (APDC), located in Kuala Lumpur, Malaysia. The Centre issued seven publications and carried out 27 research and training activities in the programme areas of economic management and information technology, energy and the environment, gender and human development, poverty alleviation and employment, and public management. The Centre's institutional fund for 1995 totalled $2,914,480. Centre activities were reviewed in 1995 by the APDC Management Board (fourteenth meeting, Kuala Lumpur, 13-14 July).

## Natural resources and marine affairs

### Mineral resources

Mineral resources activities included publications on the development of industrial minerals in the region and on the mineral resources potential and development policy in Asian LDCs, as well as preparation of mineral resources atlases of Afghanistan and Myanmar. The ESCAP secretariat provided advisory services to Cambodia in drafting its mining law and strengthening its institutional capacity for mineral resources development and offered training in mining and environmental management in Viet Nam. Meetings were convened on trends and policies in sustainable development of land and mineral resources, environmental and urban geology of fast-growing cities, and urban geology in the ESCAP region.

The Coordinating Committee for Coastal and Offshore Geoscience Programmes in East and South-East Asia (CCOP) continued to focus on the sectors of energy, minerals and coastal zones. In 1995, projects dealt with resource data management and dynamic basin analyses, application of computer technology to regional map compilation and the interpretation of geoscientific data, a geoscience programme for integrated management and development of South-East and East Asian coastal zones, and a symposium on geological aspects of sustainable development in coastal and offshore areas.

### Water resources

ESCAP secretariat activities related to water resources development and management included an assessment of water resources and water demand by user sectors in Myanmar and a study on the protection of water resources, water quality and aquatic ecosystems in Asia and the Pacific. The secretariat also continued to publish the *Water Resources Journal*. It organized an expert meeting on the implications of Agenda 21[30] for integrated water management in the region and an international workshop on water-related problems in low-lying coastal areas. Other projects dealt with water pricing policies and structure for sustainable management of water demand, guidelines on water and sustainable development, urban water management, and promotion of women's role in the protection and management of water resources. Advisory services were provided to Brunei Darussalam, Iran and the Philippines in water resources development and management and to Kyrgyzstan and Uzbekistan on management and funding arrangements in addressing the Aral Sea

crisis. The inter-agency Subcommittee (formerly Task Force) on Water for Asia and the Pacific met in Bangkok in June and December.

### Marine affairs

ESCAP activities in the area of marine affairs included a workshop on coastal and marine environmental management, a consultative meeting on coastal and marine environmental management in the South China Sea, a training seminar on the removal and disposal of obsolete offshore installations and structures in the exclusive economic zone and on the continental shelf, and a publication on integrated coastal zone management, under the series on development and management of non-living resources in the region's coastal zones.

### Mekong River basin development

Negotiations within the framework of the Interim Committee for Coordination of Investigations of the Lower Mekong Basin culminated in 1995 in the signing, at a conference of plenipotentiaries (Chiang Rai, Thailand, 5 April), of the Agreement on Cooperation for Sustainable Development of the Mekong River Basin among the four riparian States (Cambodia, the Lao People's Democratic Republic, Thailand and Viet Nam). The Agreement established the Mekong River Commission to replace the Interim Committee, with the mandate of promoting and coordinating the development, use, conservation and management of Mekong River water and related resources, as well as the socio-economic development of the riparian States, ensuring environmental protection in the region and strengthening cooperative relations with other international organizations to that end. At its 1995 session, the Economic and Social Commission for Asia and the Pacific welcomed the establishment of the Mekong River Commission; noted its intention to emphasize a basin-wide programme approach and activities while maintaining core functions of basic data collection and analysis and water quality and environmental monitoring; and urged UNDP and other donors to provide financial and technical support.

The Mekong River Commission consisted of three permanent bodies—the Council, the Joint Committee and the Secretariat. In addition, three permanent subcommittees were set up: to formulate the Mekong Basin development plan, to elaborate rules for water utilization and inter-basin diversion, and to establish a donor consultative group. Some 46 projects received funding in 1995, including those dealing with sustainable protection of resources in the basin, watershed classification, improvement of the hydrometeorological network, the role of women in water resources development, development of the Upper Srepok basin, the access channel to the Bassac River, and legal aspects of international cooperation for water resources development. The Commission also adopted a strategy for the development of human resources.

New donor commitments totalled $27 million in 1995, compared with $9.6 million in 1994. The Mekong work programme for 1996 included 97 projects, with a funding requirement of $217 million. Funding requirements were 68.6 per cent basin-wide and 31.4 per cent national, reflecting a continuing shift from national to basin-wide and regional priorities.

### Energy

Activities in energy development and management included workshops, seminars and symposia on energy conservation and efficiency, wind energy development and utilization, renewable energy, demand-side management in integrated resource planning of the power sector, integration of environmental considerations into energy planning, investment promotion in the domestic manufacturing of energy-efficient products, energy-efficient design and operation of commercial buildings, and gas pricing and investment. Other meetings and training courses focused on marketing of energy efficiency services in China, energy conservation in Mongolia, energy resiliency and the integration of the environment into energy policy and planning. An advisory group meeting under the UNDP-funded Programme for Asian Cooperation on Energy and the Environment was held in December in Bangkok.

Advisory services on natural gas activities were provided to Iran, and training for energy/power utility personnel was completed in Cambodia. Guidebooks and manuals were prepared on energy efficiency, energy and environment planning, energy survey, analysis of energy and environment data, as well as sectoral energy demand analysis and long-term forecasting for developing countries. Studies were undertaken on electric power in Asia and the Pacific, promotion of energy end-use efficiency in Asian developing countries, and environmental consequences of private sector participation in power generation. The secretariat issued a directory of energy consultants, service companies, manufacturers and distributors of energy-efficient equipment and appliances in Asia, and continued to disseminate information through the publication of the energy, environment and sustainable development series and *ESCAP Energy News*.

### Agriculture and rural development

In 1995, ESCAP reviewed a secretariat note[31] containing proposals for action in, *inter alia*, rural industrialization and the introduction of science and technology in rural areas, as well as popular participation in the alleviation of rural poverty. In endorsing those proposals, the Commission called for enhancing regional cooperation in technology transfer and industrialization of rural areas and emphasized the need for developing the agricultural and non-agricultural sectors in those areas as a means of expanding employment opportunities and accelerating rural poverty alleviation. In that regard, it recommended that the secretariat continue assisting small and medium-scale industries in promoting their competitiveness. The Commission also cited the critical importance of people's participation in the design and implementation of rural poverty alleviation programmes and endorsed a project on poverty alleviation in South Asian countries through sister-district arrangements to enhance the participation of the poor.

The Committee on Poverty Alleviation through Economic Growth and Social Development, at its second session (Bangkok, 25-29 September),[32] considered policy issues related to agriculture and rural development and other issues. The Committee emphasized the need for adopting an integrated approach to rural development, including the introduction of science and appropriate technology in rural areas. Such technology should address basic needs, be environmentally friendly and take into account the natural, human and financial resource endowments, market environment and competitive advantage of each locality. In calling for measures to facilitate rural industrialization, it emphasized that special steps should be taken to assist small and medium-scale industries through technological upgrading and capacity-building, skills development, marketing and access to credit (see also below, under "Social development").

Studies were made of programmes for popularizing food-processing and storage technology and of modalities for the use of targeting in poverty alleviation programmes. A safety guide on handling and application of agro-pesticides and a compendium of UN programmes on rural poverty alleviation were issued and the *Agro-chemicals News in Brief* and *Poverty Alleviation Initiatives* were published. National workshops were held in China, India, Indonesia, Malaysia, Thailand and Viet Nam on the effects of price liberalization and market reform on rural poverty, and in Mongolia and Nepal on poverty alleviation through market-generated rural employment. An expert group meeting was organized on the role of the informal service sector in poverty alleviation.

Workshops and seminars were held on fertilizer legislation, balanced fertilizer use to increase crop yields and improve the environment, fertilizer development and marketing management, environment aspects, and fertilizer sector development in Kazakstan, Kyrgyzstan and Uzbekistan. A regional fertilizer conference for Asia and the Pacific was held in Perth, Australia, in November. A monthly information bulletin was published on fertilizer trade.

The Regional Network for Agricultural Machinery (RNAM) continued to assist members in the development of agricultural machinery and its local manufacture, testing and popularization, as well as in mechanization policy formulation, enhancement of employment opportunities for rural women, and promotion and development of agro-related metalworking industries in LDCs and Pacific island countries. Other projects in 1995 included a regional workshop on the manufacture and extension of agricultural machinery (Tehran, Iran, September) and an agricultural machinery exhibition and symposium, AGRIMACH'95 (Nakorn Ratchasima, Thailand, November).

The Regional Coordination Centre for Research and Development of Coarse Grains, Pulses, Roots and Tuber (CGPRT) Crops in the Humid Tropics of Asia and the Pacific continued to expand in 1995.[33] It conducted training seminars on socio-economic methodologies for agricultural research and on forecasting and modelling methods in agricultural planning. A regional conference on women's role in upland farming development was held in Chiang Mai, Thailand. Projects continued on farmers' agricultural diversification strategies, synthesis of soybean studies, sustainable upland agriculture in South-East Asia, market prospects of upland crop products and policy analysis in selected Asian countries, and implications of agricultural diversification and food-crop trade for agricultural policies in South-East Asia. The Centre published monographs, working papers and project reports as well as its quarterly *Palawija News*.

In 1995, the Commission suggested that the Centre should undertake new activities on rural poverty alleviation, market development, crop diversification and the effects of trade liberalization on CGPRT producers. Centre activities were reviewed in 1995 by its Governing Board (fourteenth session, Bogor, Indonesia, 4-6 December).

### Science and technology

In 1995, the Commission noted progress in implementing the Action Programme for Regional Economic Cooperation in Investment-related Technology Transfer, which it had endorsed in 1994,[34] and stressed the importance of technology transfer in the development and industrialization process. Such transfer should be undertaken at minimum cost, taking into account local absorption capabilities, with particular attention to rural areas and to small and medium-scale enterprises,

it stated. Regional cooperation in science and technology should give priority to building endogenous capacities for the development, assessment, transfer, adaptation and use of technology, including new and clean technology, as well as to increasing the role of the private sector and upgrading the overall technological capabilities, particularly in less dynamic economies.

In a resolution concerning regional cooperation on space applications,[35] the Commission endorsed recommendations of the Ministerial Conference on Space Applications for Development in Asia and the Pacific, held in 1994,[34] as well as the Beijing Declaration on Space Technology Applications for Environmentally Sound and Sustainable Development in Asia and the Pacific, the Strategy for Regional Cooperation in Space Applications, and the Action Plan on Space Applications for Sustainable Development in Asia and the Pacific, adopted by the Conference, and called for their early implementation. It urged active participation of member States in the Regional Space Applications Programme, launched by the Conference, and recommended that the Intergovernmental Consultative Committee on the Regional Remote Sensing Programme reconstitute itself as the Ad Hoc Intergovernmental Consultative Committee on the Regional Space Applications Programme for Sustainable Development, under the purview of the UN Committee on Environment and Sustainable Development. The Commission further called for inclusion of the Programme in the next intercountry programme of UNDP.

During the year, activities in science and technology comprised efforts for strengthening national capabilities to receive, transfer, adopt and develop technologies as well as for promoting the integrated application of remote sensing and geographic information systems (GIS). Expert group meetings, workshops and seminars were held on space technology applications for sustainable development; regional economic cooperation for industrial and technological skills development, including requirements for adapting new and emerging technologies; enhancement of technology flows from advanced developing countries to Asian and Pacific LDCs; elaboration of guidelines for GIS standards and standardization procedures; remote sensing and GIS for land and marine resources and environment management in the Pacific subregion; and remote sensing in tropical ecosystem management.

The secretariat also organized a working group meeting on the regional information services and education networks of the Regional Space Applications Programme as well as an expert consultation on a prefeasibility study for the establishment of an Earth space information network in Asia and the Pacific, and provided advisory services to

Samoa on institutional issues in connection with GIS development and applications. GIS and remote-sensing guidelines were prepared for planners and decision-makers, and a study was made on patent laws, regulations and organizational structure for acquisition and use of selected technologies in the region. The *Asia-Pacific Remote Sensing Journal* and *Remote Sensing Newsletter* continued to be published.

Activities in space applications were reviewed at meetings of directors of national remote-sensing centres and programmes in the region and of the Intergovernmental Consultative Committee on Space Applications for Sustainable Development (formerly on the Regional Remote Sensing Programme). The inter-agency Subcommittee on the Regional Space Applications Programme for Sustainable Development, meeting in October, identified areas for inter-agency cooperation, including databases and information networks; satellite information for natural resources and environment management; and standardization of project outputs for improved information sharing.

### Centre for technology transfer

During the year, the Asian and Pacific Centre for Transfer of Technology organized or co-sponsored 10 regional workshops, five national training programmes, two expert group meetings, three exhibitions, two business needs programmes, and two women's entrepreneurship development programmes.[36] It continued to promote environmentally sound technologies under the Mechanism for Exchange of Technology Information, to strengthen technology management, to promote technological information and technology utilization, and to encourage more effective participation of women in the field of technology. Findings were published in the bi-monthly *Asia-Pacific Tech-Monitor* and *Value Added Technology Information Service*.

The Centre's work was reviewed by its Governing Board at its tenth session (New Delhi, 7-8 December), which endorsed proposals to set up a regional association for commercialization of research and development results and a panel of experts to assist the Centre in technology selection and evaluation.

**JIU report.** By a 6 November note,[37] the Secretary-General transmitted to the General Assembly a JIU report on UN system support for science and technology in Asia and the Pacific, recommending: that UNDP and other UN agencies publicize, on a regular basis, technical cooperation achievements; additional measures to strengthen regional cooperation in science and technology, including training programmes, especially to benefit Pacific island countries, LDCs and economies in transition; periodic evaluation of UN agencies' science and technology information, eas-

ier accessibility by potential users in developing regions, linkage with the UNDP global information referral system and with data banks of the regional commissions; and more systematic use of UN agencies' experience, projects and institutional capacities in science and technology to expand cooperation with developing regions, which should be reflected in their technical cooperation budgets. Also recommended were specific administrative and organizational measures by regional commissions to strengthen interregional cooperation in science and technology.

### Social development

On 1 May, the Commission welcomed[38] the Manila Declaration and endorsed the Agenda for Action on Social Development in the ESCAP Region, both adopted in 1994 by the Asian and Pacific Ministerial Conference in Preparation for the World Summit for Social Development.[39] It also welcomed the Copenhagen Declaration and Programme of Action adopted by the World Summit in March 1995 (see PART FOUR, Chapter IX), and urged its members to implement those documents. The Commission called for financial support to implement the Agenda for Action, and requested the Executive Secretary to assist States and ensure UN inter-agency coordination in the Agenda's implementation and to convene a regional ministerial conference on social development in 1997 to assess the progress achieved. In that regard, it welcomed the interest of Sri Lanka in hosting a meeting of senior officials in 1996 on implementation of the Agenda for Action, with special reference to poverty alleviation.

The Commission also considered an ESCAP overview[31] of policy issues related to social security, drug abuse and HIV/AIDS, disabled and elderly persons, youth, urban poverty and the informal sector, and information, education and communication for poverty alleviation. The Commission noted the need to promote the participation of the destitute in anti-poverty programmes and recommended that social protection be an important aspect of development policies aimed at achieving growth with equity. Governments should consider alternative approaches to the provision of social protection for the poor, based on self-help and community participation, the Commission stated, and it called for concerted action to combat youth unemployment.

In a resolution on regional cooperation to eradicate the demand for drugs subject to abuse,[40] the Commission urged its members to accord priority to the development and implementation of policies and programmes to reduce such demand, as well as to promote activities and methods for the treatment and rehabilitation of drug abusers. It invited them to establish or strengthen national focal points on demand aspects of drug abuse control and called for intensified collaboration with UN agencies, NGOs and community-based organizations. The Executive Secretary was asked to assist Pacific countries in exploring the possibility of establishing a subregional training centre for drug demand reduction and to consider convening a regional expert meeting on drug abuse control.

The Committee on Poverty Alleviation through Economic Growth and Social Development, meeting in September at its second session,[32] reviewed the regional poverty situation and recommended that ESCAP members adopt a holistic and integrated approach to the reduction of poverty and that policies and programmes targeted to the poor follow a decentralized approach, be responsive to local needs, enable the poor to participate in the decision-making process and recognize the necessity of special measures to assist disadvantaged groups of the population. The Committee also recommended that policies and programmes for the poor give due attention to income generation and distribution, asset creation and basic needs provision, including social safety nets. It reviewed the recommendations contained in recent global and regional mandates, including, *inter alia*, the Programme of Action adopted by the World Summit for Social Development and the Agenda for Action on Social Development in the ESCAP Region, and provided guidance to the secretariat on further follow-up activities. The Committee endorsed the proposed medium-term plan, 1998-2001, for the subprogramme on poverty alleviation.

During the year, the secretariat issued a review of the incidence of poverty in the region and target-oriented poverty alleviation programmes, an Asia-Pacific fact sheet on drug demand reduction and HIV/AIDS prevention, and an overview of five demonstration projects on community-based drug demand reduction and a manual on the subject; it also continued to publish the *Social Development Newsletter*. Studies were undertaken on the informal sector and urban poverty alleviation in the region and on the role of NGOs in implementation of the Agenda for Action on Social Development in the ESCAP Region, and advisory services were provided to member States on the formulation of national policies for poverty alleviation and for youth, the treatment of prisoners and their education and classification, as well as other issues relating to correctional management, the role of the community in the prevention of crime and the treatment of offenders, and juvenile vocational training. National training workshops on youth participation in development were organized in Cambodia, the Lao People's Democratic Republic and Sri Lanka. Expert group meetings were convened on training local officials in concepts and issues of public participation and on enhancing social security for the poor in the ESCAP region. The inter-agency Subcommittee on HIV/AIDS held its first meeting in June to consider ways to assist countries in planning and implementing national HIV/AIDS programmes.

### Disabled persons

In 1995, the Commission underscored the value of the Agenda for Action for the Asian and Pacific Decade of Disabled Persons, 1993-2002, adopted in 1993,[41] and urged the secretariat to strengthen its efforts to promote regional cooperation on disability issues and the participation of rural people with disabilities in poverty alleviation programmes. It endorsed guidelines on the promotion of non-handicapping physical environments for disabled persons, adopted by a regional meeting on the subject in 1994,[7] and called for their national application.

The progress of the Asian and Pacific Decade of Disabled Persons was reviewed at a meeting on the subject (Bangkok, 26-30 June), which adopted targets and recommendations for implementing the Decade's Agenda for Action, endorsed in September by the Committee on Poverty Alleviation through Economic Growth and Social Development. Inter-agency cooperation in implementing the Agenda for Action was considered by the Subcommittee on Disability-related Concerns in October. Workshops were organized on the indigenous production and distribution of assistive devices, on pilot projects to promote non-handicapping environments, and on women with disabilities. The ESCAP secretariat provided advisory services to India and Singapore concerning the Decade and to Viet Nam on development of self-help organizations of people with diverse disabilities. It undertook case studies on the promotion of non-handicapping environments and on women and girls with disabilities in the ESCAP region, and issued a regional review of legislation on equal opportunities and full participation in development of disabled persons.

### Human resources development

At its 1995 session, the Commission adopted a resolution on regional cooperation in human resources development (see above, under "Development policy and regional economic cooperation") and reiterated its endorsement of the Jakarta Plan of Action on Human Resources Development in the ESCAP Region, as Revised in 1994.[7]

Activities during the year included a regional training seminar on promoting human resources development services for the poor (Manila, Philippines, September) and a regional workshop on distance education as an aspect of human resources development (Shanghai, China, October). The secretariat also issued a publication on promoting the role of the private sector in human resources development.

### Women in development

On 1 May, the Commission endorsed[42] the Plan of Action for the Advancement of Women in Asia and the Pacific, contained in the Jakarta Declaration, adopted in 1994 by the Second Asian and Pacific Ministerial Conference on Women in Development.[43] It urged its members to implement the Declaration and Plan of Action, and called for financial support in their implementation. It asked that an inter-agency task force be established to promote intersectoral participation and coordination of activities within the UN system.

The Committee on Poverty Alleviation through Economic Growth and Social Development, in 1995, reviewed national activities towards implementation of the Jakarta Declaration and Plan of Action, as well as the Beijing Declaration and Platform for Action, adopted at the Fourth World Conference on Women in September 1995 (see PART FOUR, Chapter X). The Committee agreed that the feminization of poverty in the region had to be addressed by empowering women and promoting women's access to productive resources, such as education, training, credit and asset endowment, wage employment and skill generation programmes.

During the year, the ESCAP secretariat organized a training course on entrepreneurship for women; expert group meetings on the implementation of the Jakarta Declaration in LDCs, the status of women in poverty, and promotion of women's participation in decision-making; and workshops on the enhancement of employment opportunities for women, women with disabilities, promotion and implementation of the Jakarta Declaration, and a women's information network. It issued a directory of national focal points for the advancement of women in Asia and the Pacific, and prepared a study on functional literacy for women's empowerment in South Asia. As recommended by the Commission, an inter-agency Subcommittee on the Advancement of Women in Asia and the Pacific was established and held its first meeting in October.

### Population

ESCAP population activities in 1995 were geared towards implementing the Bali Declaration on Population and Sustainable Development, endorsed by the Commission in 1993,[44] in accordance with targets and goals adopted in 1994,[43] as well as the Programme of Action adopted by the 1994 International Conference on Population and Development.[45] An expert group meeting was organized on the linkages between population and poverty, and a number of workshops on population information were held within the framework of the Asia-Pacific Population Information Network (POPIN). The ESCAP secretariat conducted seminars on population ageing and development, migration and development, and population change, development and women's role and status, as well as a training workshop on selected population topics and information technology. Publications included an ESCAP population data sheet, an annotated bibliography on policy and programme issues in the field of ageing, a POPIN directory, a manual for preparing computerized population information directories, and a study of trends, patterns and implications of rural-urban migration in India, Nepal and Thailand. Population information was disseminated through the *Asia-Pacific Population Journal* and the *Population Headliners* newsletter. An Inter-organizational Subcommittee on Population and Development in Asia and the Pacific was established and held its first meeting in November.

### Human settlements

ESCAP's work in the area of human settlements focused on the implementation of the Regional Action Plan on Urbanization, adopted by the Commission in 1994,[46] as well as preparations for the second United Nations Conference on Human Settlements (Habitat II), to be held in Turkey in 1996 (see PART FOUR, Chapter VIII). Seminars, workshops and expert group meetings were organized on community-based housing, land management in Asia, preparation of regional documentation for Habitat II, the use of urban forums for urban planning and policy-making, and coordination in the Rawalpindi-Islamabad metropolitan area in Pakistan. The ESCAP secretariat conducted an international training course on dwelling construction technology and prepared a diagnostic manual on "healthy" cities in Asia and a review of current research in urban issues in the form of a computer database. The Inter-organizational Committee on Urbanization held its second meeting in February.

### Environment

Activities under the ESCAP environment subprogramme continued to focus on implementation of Agenda 21[30] and the Regional Strategy on Environmentally Sound and Sustainable Development, endorsed by the Commission in 1991.[47] In 1995, the Commission endorsed the 1994 recommendations of the Committee on Environment and Sustainable Development[48] and adopted a resolution[49] urging the strengthening of the

Regional Network of Research and Training Centres on Desertification Control in Asia and the Pacific. It also urged ESCAP members to become signatories to the UN Convention to Combat Desertification in those Countries Experiencing Serious Drought and/or Desertification, particularly in Africa, concluded in 1994,[50] and requested the Executive Secretary to convene a high-level meeting of the Regional Network to develop its work programme.

The third Ministerial Conference on Environment and Development in Asia and the Pacific (Bangkok, 22-28 November)[51] adopted the Ministerial Declaration and the Regional Action Programme for Environmentally Sound and Sustainable Development 1996-2000, calling for concerted action to arrest the rapid deterioration of the environment in the region, including a massive loss of resources and increased pollution of air, water and soil. The Conference stressed the need to strengthen regional cooperation in order to address such issues as transboundary and marine pollution and acid rain. It recommended that cooperative agreements be concluded on the exchange of information in technology transfer and capacity-building and welcomed the proposal to establish a new trust fund as a regional funding mechanism for the implementation of the Regional Action Programme. It also recommended that the private sector be actively involved in implementation activities and that modalities and mechanisms be developed for both Governments and the private sector with regard to the promotion and transfer of environmentally sound technologies.

The Regional Action Programme identified 24 programme areas, grouped under four objectives: pollution reduction and prevention, as well as control and enhancement of environmental quality; conservation and management of natural resources and ecosystems; improvement of sustainable development policy; and sustainable development indicators and assessment.

The NGO/Media Symposium on Environment and Development and the Sustainable Development Asia-Pacific Forum 1995, both organized by the private sector, were held in conjunction with the Conference. The Conference was preceded by a preparatory meeting of senior officials on environment and development and other preparatory meetings. Other activities in 1995 included the fourth Asia-Pacific seminar on climate change; an Asia-Pacific meeting on follow-up to the International Convention to Combat Desertification; expert group meetings on the feasibility of establishing a regional waste exchange data bank and on the environmental impact of coastal development; a training course on wind erosion control; seminars on tropical ecosystem management and on environmentalist business management; and a panel of experts and a workshop on desertification control in Asia and the Pacific.

The secretariat carried out studies on incorporating sustainable development considerations into economic decision-making and on the state of the environment in the region, launched a new *Asia-Pacific Environment* quarterly, and continued to publish *Environmental News Briefing*. The Interagency Subcommittee on Environment and Sustainable Development in Asia and the Pacific met in July and in August, both times in Bangkok.

### Natural disaster reduction

The Typhoon Committee (twenty-eighth session, Kuala Lumpur, 5-11 December)[52] reviewed activities undertaken in 1995 under the meteorological, hydrological, disaster prevention and preparedness, training and research components of its work programme. It considered, *inter alia*, issues relating to typhoon forecasting and analysis, as well as flood forecasting and flood-loss prevention and management. Member States were urged to enhance the coverage of upper-air observation data. The Committee reviewed the Regional Cooperation Programme Implementation Plan on natural disaster reduction and stressed the need for better international cooperation and agreement on protocols for the exchange of warnings.

During the year, ESCAP issued a publication on natural hazards and natural disaster reduction in Asia and the Pacific, organized a training workshop on flood risk analysis and mapping (Nepal, September), and concluded an assessment of current preparedness programmes, forecasting systems and operational methods for water-related natural disaster reduction in the region. A new project proposal, dealing with land-use planning and practices in watershed management and disaster reduction, was submitted to potential donors for funding. The WMO/ESCAP Panel on Tropical Cyclones held its twenty second session (Colombo, Sri Lanka, March).

### Statistics

At its 1995 session, the Commission endorsed the 1994 recommendations of the Committee on Statistics[53] and the work programme in statistics for 1996-1997, and decided to proclaim the period 1995-1999 the quinquennium for improving civil registration and vital statistics in the ESCAP region. It emphasized the importance of implementing the 1993 System of National Accounts (SNA 1993) (see PART FOUR, Chapter XV), noted progress made in developing the ESCAP Statistical Information System (ESIS), and made recommendations concerning social and economic, demographic, poverty and gender, and environment statistics.

Activities during the year included seminars, workshops and meetings on environment statistics, statistics on trade in services, gender statistics, review of data under the 1993 International Comparison Programme for national accounts (see PART FOUR, Chapter XV), and computerization development in the public sector. Advisory services were provided to member States on organizational and institutional issues affecting national statistical services, statistical database development, the 1996 population census, collection and compilation of industrial statistics, processing of multiround surveys, and demographic data analysis. Publications were issued under the series on statistical indicators for Asia and the Pacific, as well as on foreign trade statistics in the region; an overview entitled "Asia-Pacific in Figures 1995", the *Statistical Newsletter* and the *Government Computerization Newsletter* were also published.

### Statistical Institute for Asia and the Pacific

Pursuant to a 1994 Commission recommendation,[53] the Statistical Institute for Asia and the Pacific in Tokyo acquired the legal status of an ESCAP subsidiary body as of 1 April 1995, with the host country agreement between the UN and Japan taking effect on that date. On 1 May, the Commission adopted[54] the Statute of the Institute, as recommended by the Committee on Statistics, which provided, *inter alia*, for the establishment of the Institute's Governing Board.

During the year, the Institute conducted training courses on practical statistics, automatic data processing, analysis and interpretation of statistics, sample design for household and establishment surveys, statistical methodology, and human development indicators.

## Programme and organizational questions

In 1995, the Commission reviewed the implementation of the 1994-1995 programme of work,[55] noting that it was the first biennium in which the programme had been restructured in line with a thematic programme approach. It stated that it appreciated initiatives for reorganizing the secretariat's structure and setting up six working groups on each of the subprogrammes, but observed that implementation rates were relatively low in respect of subprogrammes on transport and communications and on least developed, land-locked and island developing countries. The Commission endorsed a tentative calendar of meetings for 1995/96[56] and approved proposed programme changes for 1995[57] affecting the six thematic subprogrammes. It also considered and endorsed a proposed programme of work and priorities for 1996-1997.[58]

The Commission further reviewed activities of the Advisory Committee of Permanent Represen-

tatives and Other Representatives Designated by Members of the Commission,[59] and proposed that its role should be enhanced, particularly regarding the preparation of draft resolutions. The Advisory Committee was requested to make recommendations for improving the functioning of the Committee for Regional Economic Cooperation in relation to its Steering Group.

### Annual sessions

The Commission endorsed[60] Advisory Committee recommendations on the organization of ESCAP's future sessions[61] and decided to: meet annually for up to seven working days, with the last three days meeting at the ministerial level, to discuss and decide upon important issues concerning economic and social development in the region, to endorse recommendations of its subsidiary bodies and of the Executive Secretary, to examine and approve the programme of work and to take any other decisions required; upgrade the Informal Working Group on Draft Resolutions to enable it to function along with the three Committees of the Whole; and review new arrangements for holding its sessions in 1996.

### Terms of reference

The Commission, having considered a proposed amendment to its terms of reference,[62] recommended that the Russian Federation, already a member State under paragraph 3, be included within the geographical scope of ESCAP as defined in paragraph 2, so as to allow Commission programme activities to be extended to that country, particularly its Siberian and far-eastern regions.

On 24 July, the Economic and Social Council, by **resolution 1995/22**, decided to amend paragraph 2 of the ESCAP terms of reference accordingly.

### Fifty-second session of ESCAP

At its fifty-first session, the Commission decided to hold its fifty-second session in Bangkok in March or April 1996, and chose as its theme for that session "Sustainable development and poverty alleviation in Asia and the Pacific".

## Cooperation between the United Nations and the Economic Cooperation Organization

By an 8 June letter,[63] States members of the Economic Cooperation Organization (ECO)—Afghanistan, Azerbaijan, Iran, Kazakstan, Kyrgyzstan, Pakistan, Tajikistan, Turkey, Turkmenistan, Uzbekistan—requested the inclusion in the provisional agenda of the General Assembly's fiftieth (1995) session of an item on cooperation between the United Nations and ECO. The explanatory memorandum accompanying that letter noted that ECO, which was granted observer status with the Assembly in 1993,[64] had made significant progress in promoting cooperation with ESCAP and several UN bodies and specialized agencies, and described those activities.

**GENERAL ASSEMBLY ACTION**

On 12 October, the General Assembly adopted **resolution 50/1**.

## Cooperation between the United Nations and the Economic Cooperation Organization

*The General Assembly,*

*Recalling* its resolution 48/2 of 13 October 1993, by which it granted observer status to the Economic Cooperation Organization,

*Recalling also* that one of the purposes of the United Nations is to achieve international cooperation in solving international problems of an economic, social, cultural or humanitarian nature,

*Recalling further* that the Charter of the United Nations provides for the existence of regional arrangements or agencies for dealing with such matters as maintenance of international peace and security as are appropriate for regional action, provided that their activities are consistent with the purposes and principles of the United Nations,

*Bearing in mind* that the Treaty of Izmir, signed at Izmir, Turkey, on 12 March 1977, created a permanent body for intraregional cooperation, consultation and coordination in order to enhance economic, social and cultural development,

*Taking note* of the communiqué of the Third Meeting of the Heads of Government of the member States of the Economic Cooperation Organization, held at Islamabad on 14 and 15 March 1995,

*Affirming* the need to strengthen the cooperation that already exists between entities of the United Nations system and the Economic Cooperation Organization in the areas of economic and social development,

*Convinced* of the need for the coordinated utilization of available resources to promote common objectives of the two organizations,

1. *Takes note* of the decision of the heads of Government of the member States of the Economic Cooperation Organization on the desirability of strengthening cooperation and coordination between the Secretariat of the United Nations and the Economic Cooperation Organization;

2. *Invites* the Secretary-General of the United Nations to take the necessary measures, in consultation with the Secretary-General of the Economic Cooperation Organization, to promote and expand cooperation and coordination between both secretariats in order to increase the capacity of the two organizations to attain their common objectives;

3. *Requests* the Secretary-General of the United Nations, in consultation with the Secretary-General of the Economic Cooperation Organization, to promote meetings between their representatives for consultation on policies, projects, measures and procedures that will facilitate and broaden cooperation and coordination between them;

4. *Urges* the specialized agencies and other organizations and programmes of the United Nations system to cooperate with the Secretary-General of the United Nations and the Secretary-General of the Economic Cooperation Organization in order to initiate, maintain and increase consultation and programmes with the Economic Cooperation Organization and its associated institutions in the attainment of their objectives;

5. *Requests* the Secretary-General to submit to the General Assembly at its fifty-first session a report on the implementation of the present resolution;

6. *Decides* to include in the provisional agenda of its fifty-first session the item entitled "Cooperation between the United Nations and the Economic Cooperation Organization".

General Assembly resolution 50/1

12 October 1995     Meeting 30     Adopted without vote

9-nation draft (A/50/L.1); agenda item 153.

*Sponsors:* Afghanistan, Azerbaijan, Iran, Kazakstan, Kyrgyzstan, Pakistan, Tajikistan, Turkey, Turkmenistan.

### REFERENCES

[1]E/1995/37. [2]*Economic and Social Survey of Asia and the Pacific 1996* (ST/ESCAP/1616), Sales No. E.96.II.F.18. [3]E/1996/48. [4]YUN 1994, p. 720. [5]ST/ESCAP/1467. [6]E/ESCAP/978. [7]YUN 1994, p. 715. [8]E/1995/37 (res. 51/2). [9]Ibid. (res. 51/6). [10]YUN 1994, p. 699. [11]E/ESCAP/979. [12]YUN 1994, p. 703. [13]E/1995/37 (res. 51/8). [14]E/ESCAP/998. [15]A/CONF.147/18. [16]GA res. 45/206, 21 Dec. 1990. [17]E/1995/37 (res. 51/9). [18]E/ESCAP/997. [19]YUN 1994, p. 783. [20]E/ESCAP/1035. [21]YUN 1993, p. 609. [22]E/1995/37 (res. 51/5). [23]YUN 1994, p. 868. [24]YUN 1992, p. 485. [25]E/ESCAP/1026. [26]YUN 1984, p. 624, GA res. 39/227, 18 Dec. 1984. [27]YUN 1991, p. 313, GA dec. 46/453, 20 Dec. 1991. [28]YUN 1992, p. 486. [29]YUN 1993, p. 617. [30]YUN 1992, p. 672. [31]E/ESCAP/991. [32]E/ESCAP/1023. [33]E/ESCAP/1025. [34]YUN 1994, p. 713. [35]E/1995/37 (res. 51/11). [36]E/ESCAP/1019. [37]A/50/721. [38]E/1995/37 (res. 51/4). [39]YUN 1994, p. 714. [40]E/1995/37 (res. 51/10). [41]YUN 1993, p. 621. [42]E/1995/37 (res. 51/7). [43]YUN 1994, p. 716. [44]YUN 1993, p. 622. [45]YUN 1994, p. 956. [46]Ibid., p. 717. [47]YUN 1991, p. 318. [48]YUN 1994, p. 718. [49]E/1995/37 (res. 51/12). [50]YUN 1994, p. 944. [51]E/ESCAP/1020. [52]E/ESCAP/1040. [53]YUN 1994, p. 719. [54]E/1995/37 (res. 51/1). [55]E/ESCAP/1004 & Corr.1. [56]E/ESCAP/1006. [57]E/ESCAP/1005 & Corr.1. [58]E/ESCAP/1007. [59]E/ESCAP/1011 & Add.1. [60]E/1995/37 (res. 51/3). [61]E/ESCAP/1010. [62]E/ESCAP/1013 & Add.1. [63]A/50/143. [64]YUN 1993, p. 219, GA res. 48/2, 13 Oct. 1993.

# Europe

The fiftieth session of the Economic Commission for Europe (ECE) was held in Geneva from 3 to 11 April 1995,[1] at a time when the rapid pace of political, economic and social change in the ECE region continued to pose challenges to Governments and international institutions. The Commission noted important developments in the scope and structure of regional cooperation that had occurred since its 1994 session, including the enlargement of the European Union to 15 member States and the succession of the Conference on Security and Cooperation in Europe (CSCE) by the Organization for Security and Cooperation in

Europe (OSCE) and of the General Agreement on Tariffs and Trade (GATT) by the World Trade Organization (WTO). It was also noted that economic performance in most of Eastern Europe showed a marked improvement as the European economies in transition to a market system continued to implement legislative, economic and restructuring measures to pursue further the reform process. At the same time, policy problems pertaining to transition persisted, as had the difficulties of overcoming macroeconomic imbalances and of making progress in structural reforms, highlighting the need for investment, project financing and improved market access, as well as for Western financial and technical assistance in supporting reforms. The transition process was also threatened by conflicts in the region, which continued despite international efforts to restore peace and stability.

The Commission reviewed its implementation of the relevant provisions of the Final Act of the 1975 Conference on Security and Cooperation in Europe (Helsinki Conference)[2] and of the Concluding Document adopted by the CSCE Review Conference in 1994,[3] as well as economic cooperation in the Mediterranean region in the light of the Final Act. The Executive Secretary was asked[4] to take steps to strengthen cooperation between ECE and OSCE in implementing provisions of OSCE documents, to participate in the OSCE Economic Forum, and to establish close cooperation with OSCE in the economic dimension. The Commission called on its subsidiary bodies to contribute to follow-up activities in that area. In another decision,[5] the Commission reiterated its requests to the Executive Secretary to identify means of enhancing economic cooperation in the Mediterranean in all areas of the ECE programme of work and to pursue efforts for increasing cooperation on matters within the competence of ECE and of common interest to Mediterranean countries. The Executive Secretary was also asked to continue cooperation with other regional commissions and relevant UN bodies to secure interaction with Mediterranean countries not members of ECE, and to cooperate with the informal open-ended contact group on the Mediterranean, to be established within the framework of the OSCE Permanent Council in Vienna. The Commission further took note of follow-up activities to the project on the Europe-Africa permanent link through the Strait of Gibraltar (see above, under "Africa").

During the year, ECE participated in the third OSCE Economic Forum (Prague, Czech Republic, 7-9 June), which focused on regional economic cooperation in the fields of trade, investment and infrastructure. It also contributed to a seminar on the trans-European role of infrastructure in maintaining stability and security in the Black Sea re-gion, held in Sofia, Bulgaria. The ECE secretariat prepared a study on the implementation of commitments contained in the final document of the 1990 Bonn Conference on Economic Cooperation in Europe. It also supported or followed closely activities and initiatives for the Mediterranean region, including a seminar on the OSCE experience in confidence-building, conflict prevention and crisis management (Cairo, Egypt, 26-28 September), the Euro-Mediterranean Ministerial Conference (Barcelona, Spain, 27-28 November) and an international expert group meeting on integrated coastal area management in the Mediterranean and Adriatic (Ljubljana, Slovenia, November).

In April, the Commission approved[6] its work programme for 1995-1996 and endorsed the programme for 1995-1999, subject to review at its 1996 session. The work programme included sub-programmes on policy and coordination of work, environment, transport, statistics, trade facilitation, economic analysis, energy, development of international trade, industry and technology, agriculture and timber, and human settlements.

The Commission asked the Executive Secretary to: bring to the attention of the Secretary-General the need for resources necessary to fulfil the Commission's mandate; explore ways of increasing the visibility and outside perception of ECE activities; and take steps towards establishing close cooperation with the Council of Europe and its Parliamentary Assembly. The Secretary-General was urged to consider the possibility of strengthening the Commission, while the ECE principal subsidiary bodies were requested to rationalize their proceedings so as to make optimal use of available resources. The Commission also decided to convene in 1997 a high-level fifty-second jubilee session with a view to adopting a Declaration on strengthening of economic cooperation in Europe, which would define strategic directions of future ECE activities.

At a special session (Geneva, 20 September),[7] the Commission reviewed its cooperation with FAO and with the Council of Europe, and considered measures to enhance its programme of work and achieve greater efficiency and savings. In a decision on the Declaration on strengthening of economic cooperation in Europe,[8] it established an ad hoc Working Group to define strategic directions of future ECE activities, and specified the Group's mandate. It also adopted a decision on the future work of its Committee on Agriculture (see below, under "Activities in 1995").

In response to a 1991 Commission request,[9] its Chairman continued to convene ad hoc informal meetings of ECE to consult on policy matters, assist with preparations for the annual sessions, monitor progress in work programmes and offer guidance to the Executive Secretary. The Chairman also arranged consultations between the Executive Secretary and ECE subsidiary bodies, in accordance with a 1992 Commission decision on the provision of adequate resources.[10]

### Economic trends

In 1995, economic developments in various parts of the ECE region became increasingly divergent, according to a summary of the economic survey of Europe in 1995.[11] Economic growth slowed in both Western Europe and North America. Although annual averages showed GDP rising by 2.7 per cent in Western Europe, compared with 2.5 per cent in the previous year, preliminary statistics for the last quarter of 1995 actually fell slightly. Sluggish private consumption, reflecting weak consumer confidence and held down also by higher taxes and social security charges and reductions in governmental transfers, was a contributing factor. Consumption grew on average by 2 per cent in 1995, compared with annual rates well over 3 per cent between 1986 and 1990. GDP growth rates decelerated from 4.6 per cent in 1994 to 2.2 per cent in 1995 in Canada, from 3.8 per cent to 2.4 per cent in the United Kingdom, from 3.5 per cent to 2.1 per cent in the United States, and from 2.9 per cent in both France and Germany to 2.4 per cent and 1.9 per cent, respectively. Economic performance improved slightly in Italy, where GDP grew by 3 per cent, up from 2.2 per cent in the previous year; at the same time, some smaller economies, such as Belgium and Switzerland, registered negative growth for two consecutive quarters during the year.

The weakening of demand led to a steady reduction in investment plans, although fixed investment still rose on average by 4 per cent, against 1.6 per cent in 1994. However, rather than focusing on expansion of productive capacity, investment concentrated on cost reduction and the modernization of the capital stock. Limited progress was achieved in reducing unemployment, which averaged 10.5 per cent in Western Europe in 1995—below its 1994 peak of 10.9 per cent, but still above the recession year of 1993. Its weaker rate of job creation contrasted sharply with the more buoyant expansion in North America, where the number of new jobs had increased by 3 per cent in 1994 and 2 per cent in 1995. Unemployment declined from 6 per cent in 1994 to 5.6 per cent in 1995 in the United States, from 8.4 per cent to 8.2 per cent in Germany, from 9.5 per cent to 8.7 per cent in the United Kingdom, from 10.3 per cent to 9.5 per cent in Canada, and from 12.3 per cent to 11.6 per cent in France, but rose from 11.4 per cent to 11.8 per cent in Italy. Several countries implemented

early retirement schemes and other measures to encourage withdrawals from the labour force. At the same time, unemployment among young people, although slightly reduced due to special labour market programmes in some countries, remained at 20 per cent or more and constituted a major social problem.

Annual inflation dropped from 2.7 per cent in 1994 to 1.8 per cent in 1995 in Germany, remained at 1.7 per cent in France and increased from 2.6 per cent to 2.8 per cent in the United States and from 2.5 per cent to 3.4 per cent in the United Kingdom. Canada and Italy, on the other hand, recorded larger increases, from 0.2 per cent to 2.1 per cent and from 3.9 per cent to 5.4 per cent, respectively. Domestic activity in Western Europe continued to be supported by export growth, although its net effect was smaller than in the previous year because of a slowdown in intraregional trade and, in early 1995, exchange rate turbulence. Nevertheless, the region continued to benefit from the strong global demand for investment goods and from the rapid growth of imports into transition economies and developing countries.

Economic performance of the European countries in transition was uneven. Aggregate real GDP in Eastern Europe grew by 5.4 per cent in 1995, compared with 4 per cent in the previous year. Rates of growth accelerated from 4.8 per cent to 7.4 per cent in Slovakia, from 5.2 per cent to 7 per cent in Poland, from 3.9 per cent to 6.9 per cent in Romania, and from 2.6 per cent to 5.2 per cent in the Czech Republic, but declined from 5.3 per cent to 4.8 per cent in Slovenia. Albania also showed strong economic expansion, and some recovery was registered in Yugoslavia (Serbia and Montenegro) following the success of its 1994 programme to end hyperinflation. On the other hand, GDP increased only by 2 per cent in Hungary, down from 2.9 per cent in the previous year, and by 2.5 per cent in Bulgaria, and continued to fall in Croatia, the former Yugoslav Republic of Macedonia, and almost certainly in Bosnia and Herzegovina, for which no data were available.

The recovery in Eastern Europe was largely based on the revival of industrial production, which rose by more than 7 per cent. The recovery of industry was accompanied by large annual gains in productivity—between 10 and 16 per cent in many countries. Agricultural output also expanded by between 2 and 5 per cent in most countries except Poland, where agricultural production increased by 13 per cent after a 9.3 per cent decline in 1994.

The performance of the Baltic States continued to lag behind most of Eastern Europe; in 1995, their economies grew by some 1 per cent. Nevertheless, a modest recovery was registered in Lithuania, where output grew by 2 per cent, up from 1 per cent in the previous year, while Estonia's GDP increased by 2.5 per cent, compared with a 2.7 per cent contraction in 1994. At the same time, Latvia experienced a further setback as its economy contracted by 1.6 per cent, partly due to a major crisis in the banking sector, after a 0.6 per cent growth in the previous year. GDP continued to fall in most countries of the Commonwealth of Independent States (CIS), but the rate of decline decelerated considerably in 1995, while Armenia and Georgia experienced positive growth. Output decreased by 3 per cent in the Republic of Moldova, 4 per cent in the Russian Federation, 10 per cent in Belarus and 12 per cent in Ukraine, compared with respective declines of 31.2 per cent, 12.6 per cent, 15.8 per cent and 23 per cent in 1994 (for economies of Central Asia and the Caucasus, see above, under "Asia and the Pacific").

According to preliminary data, domestic demand, strong in Eastern Europe and weak in CIS member States, had a major impact on the economic situation in those countries. Private consumption, supported by rising real incomes, increased in the Czech Republic, Poland, Romania and Slovakia. They also experienced substantial growth in fixed investment, at rates ranging from 13 per cent in Romania to 22 per cent in Slovakia. On the other hand, austerity programmes and income policies held consumption down in Bulgaria, Croatia and Hungary, while in the Russian Federation it fell by 7 per cent, due to declining real wages. Another important development was a sharp drop in inflation, except in Tajikistan and Yugoslavia (Serbia and Montenegro), but the actual annual rates remained high, at between 25 and 40 per cent in Hungary, Poland, Romania and the Baltic States and even higher in Bulgaria. Among CIS countries, inflation rates varied from 30 per cent in the Republic of Moldova to 197 per cent in the Russian Federation, 377 per cent in Ukraine and 709 per cent in Belarus.

Unemployment was a major problem in almost all transition economies, although the strong economic growth in Eastern Europe led to a marked slowdown in the fall of employment levels and an increase in Albania, Bulgaria, the Czech Republic, Poland and Slovakia. However, average unemployment remained high at 13 per cent, with rates ranging from 3 per cent in the Czech Republic and 9 per cent in Romania to 18 per cent in Croatia. There were exceptionally high levels in Yugoslavia (Serbia and Montenegro) and the former Yugoslav Republic of Macedonia. In the Baltic States, unemployment remained largely unchanged in Estonia and Latvia, but rose sharply in Lithuania. It averaged 5.4 per cent in CIS countries, although actual unemployment in that group was believed to be much higher than "registered unemployment". Young people accounted for between 26 and 40 per cent of the unemployed, and the number of long-term unemployed people continued to grow rapidly. The problem was also aggravated by the weakening of traditional safety nets in those countries.

Foreign trade of transition economies continued to expand rapidly in the first three quarters of 1995. The volume of Eastern European exports was estimated to have risen by between 10 and 12 per cent and imports by between 13 and 15 per cent, while their value increased by some 28 per cent for exports and by about one third for imports. The prevalence of imports over exports, due to the recovery of domestic demand, led to a sharp deterioration in trade deficits, which grew from $7 billion to $13 billion in Eastern Europe and from $0.6 billion to $0.9 billion in the Baltic States. As a result, the aggregate current account deficit in Eastern Europe almost doubled, reaching $8.8 billion. On the other hand, both the value and volume of exports from the Russian Federation and other CIS countries grew much faster than imports, and their trade surpluses increased from nearly $15 billion to $22 billion and from $1.5 billion to $3.5 billion, respectively. Western Europe became the major trading partner of most transition economies, taking some 50 to 70 per cent of their exports and accounting for a similar share of imports. At the same time, trade among transition economies also strengthened, except for intra-CIS trade, the volume of which was reported to have continued to fall.

In 1995, net capital flows to Eastern Europe tripled to reach more than $31 billion, from $10.6 billion in 1994, which was more than what was required to finance current account deficits and, consequently, constituted large additions to foreign-currency reserves in most countries. The inflows consisted of a wide range of types of capital, from FDI and portfolio investment to medium- and long-term bank credits, while short-term obligations accounted for just a small portion of the total. However, the Czech Republic, Hungary and Poland alone received nearly 90 per cent of total inflows.

### Activities in 1995

The transition process in Central and Eastern European countries and their integration into the European and global economies remained a focus of ECE activities in 1995.[12] Since the inception of its programme to assist economies in transition in 1990, ECE had organized a total of 183 workshops on issues relating to human settlements, environment, industrial development, energy, transport, statistics, forestry, economic analysis and population, including women and elderly persons. Their conclusions often influenced work programmes of ECE subsidiary bodies and were incorporated into follow-up activities pertaining to ECE programmes, national policies or specific technical assistance projects. The Trust Fund on Assistance to Countries in Transition continued to help those States to defray the costs of their participation in ECE workshops and experts' meetings. The ECE secretariat also contributed to technical cooperation programmes and projects funded by other organizations and agencies, completed a list of experts and specialists in the problems of privatization, and took part in activities focusing on reconstruction of war-torn areas in Europe. Initial contacts were established with the European Training Foundation, an autonomous agency of EU created in 1995 in Turin, Italy, to coordinate training activities in economies in transition. The secretariat also continued cooperation with the ILO Centre in Turin in developing training manuals.

Under the ECE regional advisory services programme,[13] 144 missions were carried out between July 1994 and September 1995, including 50 to CIS members, 48 to Central and Eastern European economies in transition, 8 to the Baltic States and 38 to donor countries. The missions covered a broad range of issues relating to strategic policy formulation and implementation in the areas of privatization, industrial restructuring and energy, development of entrepreneurship, institution-building for a market economy, and attraction of foreign direct investment. The regional advisers assisted Georgia in elaborating a medium-term strategy of economic reconstruction, recovery and reform, and organized workshops on the expansion of trade in transition economies and on harmonization of transport infrastructure networks and transport regulations. The programme also contributed to a regional workshop of CIS and Baltic States on regional trade and enterprise cooperation and major challenges of increased participation in international trade (Chisinau, Republic of Moldova, January). Regional advisory services on population and development were initiated in February.

In an April[14] decision the Commission asked the Executive Secretary to report on the objectives and activities of the regional advisory services programme, including ways to improve its effectiveness; to request allocation of adequate resources; and to intensify cooperation of the ECE regional advisory services with other relevant organizations. In another decision,[15] the Commission recommended that the Executive Secretary, in consultation with UNDP and other international and regional organizations, explore the possibility of establishing, in one of the interested countries in transition, training courses in matters of market economy for the administration and business community of transition economies. It requested him to study the feasibility of cooperation between ECE and international and regional organizations in the collection and sharing of data on FDI projects in those economies, confirmed the importance of continuing the programme of workshops and seminars, and invited member States and international organizations to finance it through the Trust Fund.

Other areas of activity included ECE's participation in OSCE meetings,[16] cooperation with other organizations and subregional groupings active in the region,[17] and its contribution to UN global programmes, as well as to programmes of assistance to developing countries of other regions.[18] On 11 April, the Commission recommended[15] that the Secretary-General consider the possibility of using ECE as a focal point to promote and enhance mutual cooperation with UN global programmes, organs and specialized agencies. It also noted the ECE contribution to preparations for UN global conferences, including the 1994 high-level regional preparatory meeting[19] for the 1995 Fourth World Conference on Women (see PART FOUR, Chapter X), and invited[6] the Executive Secretary to focus work in the field of population on follow-up activities to implement the Programme of Action adopted by the International Conference on Population and Development in 1994.[20]

As part of preparations for the World Summit for Social Development, held in Denmark in March (see PART FOUR, Chapter IX), the secretariat organized a workshop on population ageing in Europe and North America (Geneva, 13-14 February), which adopted a message to the World Summit entitled "Towards a mature society for all ages", containing recommendations for action on the issues of poverty, employment, integration in society, and data and research. ECE also took part in an NGO meeting on links between social and economic development and the role and experience of NGOs in promoting civil society, focusing on Central and Eastern European economies in transition and held in conjunction with the World Summit.

## International trade

At its 1995 session, the Commission held a round table to consider a study on ways of promoting the expansion of trade in transition economies,[21] prepared by the Executive Secretary in response to a 1994 Commission request.[22] The study analysed the importance and structure of trade in those countries, examined the main factors affecting their trading competitiveness, and proposed specific measures to facilitate trade. It also provided recommendations for a coordinated

Regional Action Programme to Boost Trade in Transition Economies. The round table endorsed the recommendations in general and suggested that the study be disseminated to a wider audience after revision. On 11 April, the Commission took note[6] of the study and invited the Committee on the Development of Trade and other subsidiary bodies concerned to continue their work geared towards promoting the expansion of trade in transition economies, including improvements in market access and market competitiveness. The Commission also stressed the importance of continuing policies aimed at further trade liberalization and expansion among Western countries and economies in transition, reducing the remaining constraints to trade among ECE countries, improving the export competitiveness of economies in transition and facilitating their integration into the international trading system.

The ECE Committee on the Development of Trade, at its forty-fourth session (Geneva, 5-7 December),[23] reviewed its work and the activities of its Working Parties relating to trade analysis, facilitation and promotion, and held a panel discussion on ways of financing trade and investment in transition economies. It supported the general direction of work towards establishing a centre for facilitation of procedures and practices for administration, commerce and transport, as well as proposals concerning the production of legal guides on international contract practices in industry. The Committee agreed on its programme of work for 1996-1999 and on future directions for its activities, and asked the secretariat to prepare a study on the institutional, legal and business framework for developing more efficient systems to finance trade and promote more dynamic intraregional trade between ECE countries.

The Working Party on International Contract Practices in Industry (forty-fourth session, Geneva, 13-15 November) organized a forum on attracting private investment for large-scale infrastructure projects in the transition economies of Central and Eastern Europe, which adopted recommendations concerning the development of guidelines on new project financing and construction budget techniques, information and training seminars on those techniques, confidence-building measures to lower investment risks, private-sector experience sharing, and comparability of financing terms for infrastructure projects in developed countries and economies in transition. Acting on those recommendations, the Working Party decided to establish an expert group of private- and public-sector representatives charged with developing project financing guidelines, and requested the secretariat to explore other proposals with the Organisation for Economic Cooperation and Development (OECD). It also decided to convene such forum

meetings annually and to build its future work around them, and agreed on the procedure for holding those meetings.

The Working Party further reviewed the text and amended the title of a guide for the transition economies of Central and Eastern Europe and the CIS on adapting property laws, and agreed on a timetable for finalizing and publishing the guide. It also noted that the secretariat had finalized a guide for the transition economies on financing trade and private companies, to be published in 1996.

The Working Party on Facilitation of International Trade Procedures held two sessions in Geneva in 1995 (forty-first, 21-24 March; forty-second, 18-22 September). It reviewed matters arising from its restructuring process and agreed to set up three groups to develop policy and overall objectives as well as a framework for procedures to "empower" technical bodies, and to undertake an evaluation of possible organizational structures. It was also agreed that the general direction of the process should be towards the establishment of a centre for facilitation of procedures and practices for administration, commerce and transport. The Working Party approved recommendations of its meetings of experts on: data elements, automatic data interchange, procedures and documentation relating to the development of messages for the UN Electronic Data Interchange for Administration, Commerce and Transport (UN/EDIFACT) as a standard for world trade; activities of the steering group to develop models for international trade transactions; trade facilitation of the transport of dangerous goods; facilitation measures related to international trade procedures; and various trade-related codes.

The Working Party also dealt with trade facilitation and UN/EDIFACT in economies in transition, including activities of the regional adviser on trade facilitation. It approved two draft UN/EDIFACT directories and confirmed the appointment of rapporteurs for the Africa, Asia, Australia/New Zealand, Central and Eastern European, Pan American and West European EDIFACT Boards.

During the year, the secretariat prepared a study on trade and investment finance in transition economies, published four issues of *East-West Investment News*, compiled its trade facilitation recommendations into a single volume, and launched a trade facilitation "home page" on the Internet. The regional advisor on trade facilitation assisted economies in transition in promoting intra-CIS and Baltic trade, organizing in the Russian Federation the first Eastern European conference on electronic data interchange and UN/EDIFACT, and strengthening or establishing national trade facilitation bodies.

## Industry

On 11 April, the Commission, further to its 1994 decision to consider convening a European Forum on Sustainable Industrial Development,[22] decided[24] to hold in 1996 a Round Table Conference on cooperation and sustainable industrial development, and invited the Executive Secretary to make the necessary preparations.

The Working Party on the Chemical Industry, at its fifth session (Geneva, 27-29 September),[25] reviewed the implementation of the regional programme on sustainable economic and ecological development of the chemical industry and held a round-table discussion on the chlorine industry and sustainable development. It endorsed the reports of its meetings of experts on the pilot project demonstrating the environmental clean-up of selected sites polluted by chemicals and on the periodic survey of the chemical industry, as well as the report on activities of the Regional Environmental Management Centre for the Chemical Industry. The Working Party approved the first version of the comparative study of chemical legislation in ECE member countries and changed the project's title to "comparative data bank"; noted the progress in the study on trends in structural and ownership changes in the chemical industries of the economies in transition; agreed that the secretariat should publish *The Chemical Industry in 1995—Annual Review* and continue publishing statistics on aromatic hydrocarbons and olefins; and requested that efforts be pursued to publish the *Directory of Chemical Producers and Products.* It also considered preparations for or follow-up to workshops, seminars and study tours organized under its work programme, and adopted the programme of work for 1996-2000.

Activities during the year included a seminar on the complex utilization of raw materials using advanced low- and non-waste process technologies (Moscow, 12-15 September), an international workshop on technologies for soil decontamination and remediation of soils polluted by chemical products (Paris, 5-7 December), and a study tour in the Czech Republic, Hungary and Slovakia (19-24 June). The secretariat produced a publication on the current economic situation and outlook in the plastics sector and issued the annual review of the chemical industry for 1994 and the second edition, Part I, of the directory of chemical producers and products, dealing with chemical enterprises in Central and Eastern Europe.

The Working Party on Engineering Industries and Automation, which did not meet in 1995, focused its activities on economic analysis and industrial statistics, environmental protection and sustainable industrial development, and assistance to economies in transition. It organized a seminar on national experiences of conversion to international classification standards in industrial statistics (Geneva, 19-20 October), whose recommendations were approved at the seventeenth Meeting on Questions of Statistics concerning Engineering Industries and Automation (Geneva, 20 October).

The first open-ended meeting of experts on robotics (Geneva, 4 September) endorsed a draft publication on world industrial robots, dealing with statistics for 1983-1994 and forecasts to 1998. The ECE secretariat published an overview of performance and prospects in world engineering industries and automation for 1993-1995 and prepared a review of industrial restructuring in selected countries in transition, considered by an advisory workshop (Geneva, 8-9 June), which focused on strategic planning for industrial restructuring in different countries. The ECE regional adviser on industry and technology provided assistance to economies in transition in elaborating industrial policies, including a round table on national industrial policy in Hungary, and launched a project for the development of small and medium-sized enterprises (SMEs) in those countries. A workshop on SMEs was held in Moscow in September.

The Working Party on Steel, at its fifth session (Geneva, 25-27 October),[26] considered a report of its meeting of experts on the steel market in 1994 and prospects for 1995, the status of annual bulletins of steel statistics and studies on iron and steel scrap and on restructuring and changing ownership in the steel industry, as well as issues relating to the steel industry and the environment, including the preparation of a directory of environmental organizations in the steel sector. It heard a report on a global review of the steel industry in Europe undertaken by several regional and international organizations and endorsed the secretariat's participation in a study on opportunities for regional cooperation in the steel industry in Europe. The Working Party also reviewed preparations for or follow-up to seminars, workshops and study tours organized under its programme of work and adopted its programme of work for 1996-2000.

During the year, the secretariat issued a publication on iron and steel scrap and the annual bulletin of statistics of world trade in steel. Among other activities were a seminar on the steel industry and recycling (Düsseldorf, Germany, 24-27 April) and a study tour of the steel industry in the Russian Federation (September).

## Transport

The Inland Transport Committee, at its fifty-seventh session (Geneva, 16-20 January),[27] analysed the transport situation in member countries, reviewed the results of the second Pan-European

Transport Conference (Crete, Greece, 14-16 March 1994) and preparations for the 1996 Regional Conference on Transport and the Environment, as well as the status of application of international UN/ECE transport agreements and conventions. It also considered activities to assist economies in transition, and discussed issues relating to transport trends and policy and economics; road, rail, inland water and combined transport; customs questions; international trade procedures related to transport; transport of dangerous goods and perishable foodstuffs; transport statistics, including the preparation of the 1995 census of road traffic; measures to facilitate the movement of persons with reduced mobility; and the development of electronic procedures and documentation.

The Committee noted proposals for the follow-up to the second Pan-European Conference and requested its subsidiary bodies to study the possibilities of their implementation. It endorsed the decisions of its Working Party on Transport Trends and Economics to convene an ad hoc session in 1995 to consider ways and forms of rendering assistance to Central and Eastern European countries and to examine transport flow indices and the interface between land and sea transport. The Committee approved the report on the methodological basis for the definition of common criteria regarding bottlenecks, missing links and the quality of service of infrastructure networks, and decided that regulatory and infrastructural measures to improve the transport situation should be designed as a follow-up to the report. The Working Party should attach greater importance to transport problems in the Mediterranean region, it was stated. The importance of updating further the European Agreement on Main International Traffic Arteries was stressed. The Committee called for simplification of procedures to obtain a visa for professional drivers in international road traffic and noted the draft amendments to the 1958 Agreement concerning the Adoption of Uniform Conditions of Approval and Reciprocal Recognition of Approval for Motor Vehicle Equipment and Parts. The Working Party on the Construction of Vehicles was asked to consider proposals for a global agreement on the subject, as well as for environmental standards for vehicles in international road traffic. Governments were invited to follow the recommendations for the installation of child restraint systems. The amendments subsequently entered into force on 16 October 1995, thereby modifying the title of the 1958 Agreement to read the "Agreement Concerning the Adoption of Uniform Technical Prescriptions for Wheeled Vehicles, Equipment and Parts which can be Fitted and/or be Used on Wheeled Vehicles and the Conditions for Reciprocal Recognition of Approvals Granted on the Basis of these Prescriptions".

The Committee endorsed the decisions of its Working Party on Rail Transport to postpone modification of the infrastructure parameters under the European Agreement on Main International Railway lines and to set up a Steering Group and an ad hoc group on railway facilitation. The Working Party was asked to propose measures for harmonizing existing legal regimes in different rail transport systems. It also endorsed the decision of its Working Party on Inland Water Transport to convene a special session in 1995 to consider a draft European Agreement on Main Inland Waterways of International Importance; took note of a map of European inland waterways based on a new classification, and decided to revise it on a regular basis; and approved the conclusions of a study on the role of coastal shipping and its potential as an alternative for land transport in Europe, noting that provisions on coastal shipping could be incorporated into a legal instrument along with provisions on inland water transport using combined transport techniques. The Committee initiated an urgent revision of the Customs Convention on the International Transport of Goods under Cover of TIR Carnets (TIR Convention), welcomed progress in preparing a convention on international customs transit procedures for the carriage of goods by rail, and decided to set up an international working group to draft a European agreement concerning the international carriage of dangerous goods by inland waterways. In April, the Commission endorsed that decision. Noting the continuing revision of provisions concerning the carriage of gases under the European Agreement concerning the International Carriage of Dangerous Goods by Road, the Committee stressed the importance of concluding the restructuring of that Agreement as early as possible.

The Preparatory Committee for the 1996 Regional Conference on Transport and the Environment, established in 1994,[28] held five sessions during 1995 to elaborate the draft final documents of the Conference, including guidelines for a common strategy on transport and the environment, a programme of action and a political declaration. The Preparatory Committee also identified issues on which binding agreement could be achieved, such as environmental standards for vehicles in international transport, periodic technical inspections of vehicles and development of combined transport on inland waterways and coastal shipping.

In April, the Commission supported[29] the Preparatory Committee's findings and requested it to continue its work. It noted the conclusions of the Inland Transport Committee at its fifty-seventh session, urging it to complete at its next sessions regulations for combined transport on inland waterways and possibly for coastal shipping. The

Commission also welcomed the holding of the second Road Safety Week in the ECE region (27 March–2 April), and emphasized the necessity of an urgent revision of the TIR Convention.

In 1995, the European Agreement on Main Inland Waterways of International Importance was finalized, bringing the total number of ECE agreements and conventions in the field of transport to 51. During the year, 29 States, of which 13 were economies in transition and 2 were non-ECE members, became contracting parties to one or more legal instruments. Forty ECE members agreed to carry out the 1995 census of motor traffic on main international traffic arteries in Europe. The consolidated text of the revised European Provisions concerning the International Carriage of Dangerous Goods by Inland Waterway was finalized. Work began on the revision of the TIR Convention. Activities continued under the Trans-European North-South Motorway (TEM) and Trans-European Railways (TER) projects, aimed at the coordinated development of international road and rail as well as combined transport infrastructure in Central and Eastern Europe, including the updating of existing networks, development of databases, preparation of studies and organization of workshops and training seminars. A seminar on ECE work in the field of transport, including legal instruments, was held for the benefit of CIS members (Geneva, September). The regional adviser on transport issues assisted economies in transition in formulating programmes of transport development planning and of economic regulatory activities and advised them on transport pricing, transport funds and railway restructuring. The secretariat continued to publish the annual bulletin of transport statistics for Europe and North America.

### Energy

At its 1995 session, the Commission emphasized[30] the growing importance of energy in the development of economic cooperation in the region, noted the report and conclusions of the fourth session of the Committee on Energy, held in 1994,[28] and confirmed the importance of continuing the programme of workshops and seminars in the field of energy for countries in transition. The Commission welcomed activities under the technical cooperation programme for the promotion and development of a market-based gas industry in transition economies within the framework of a Gas Centre, as well as under the Energy Efficiency 2000 project, aimed at reducing the gap between energy-intensive industries in Eastern Europe and energy-saving technologies of the West through trade and cooperation. Member States and international organizations were invited to

participate in the project and the Centre and to contribute to their trust funds.

The Committee on Energy, at its fifth session (Geneva, 7-9 November),[31] reviewed the energy situation and policies in the region, particularly in the economies in transition, and activities assisting the transition of the coal, gas and electric power industries in Central and Eastern Europe, including efforts to enhance energy efficiency and to promote and develop a market-based gas industry, as well as workshops on energy aspects of economic reforms. The Committee also considered cooperation in the field of renewable sources of energy and held a round table on restructuring, privatization and deregulation. It endorsed the recommendations of its Working Parties concerning the preparation of explicit studies in the gas and energy fields, the restructuring policies of the coal industry and sustainable development of coal-mining regions, as well as further development of the implementation programme on accelerating clean coal technology. It requested the secretariat to examine ways of mobilizing resources for the programme, including the creation of a trust fund. The Committee also endorsed a programme of work in the area of renewable sources of energy, and decided to promote international technical cooperation in the establishment of energy efficiency demonstration zones and projects using such sources.

The Working Parties on Coal, Gas and Electric Power held their fifth sessions in Geneva. The Working Party on Coal (18-20 October) considered general energy problems in the ECE region of relevance to coal; economic reforms and restructuring of the coal industry in Europe; sustainable coal development and policies; environmental protection related to coal-mining and coal utilization; and mine safety. It approved the reports of an ad hoc meeting on the elaboration of market-oriented UN classification for assessment of coal and mineral deposits (Geneva, 13-15 March) and of its expert meetings on research, management and transition in the coal industry; on coal trade, statistics and transport; and on clean coal technologies. The Working Party adopted recommendations concerning the restructuring of the coal industry, development and modernization of profitable mining operations, further privatization of coal-mining companies and development of the stock market, creation of vertical structures between coal producers and coal users, regulations and financial support for the closure of uneconomic coal mines, promotion of new economic activities in the slowdown mining regions, and larger community participation in decision-making and in the programme of retraining and investment. It also endorsed the recommendations of a symposium on sustainable development of opencast coal-mining regions (Krasnojarsk, Russian Federation, 12-16 June). The Working Party held a round table on coal in the European energy market, considered the results of workshops on coal-related issues, and approved its programme of work for 1995-1999.

Activities during the year included workshops on geodynamic zoning, development of clean small-sized boilers for industrial household and farming sectors, market adaptation of the coal industry in Central and Eastern Europe, and reassessment of coal and mineral deposits under market conditions, the latter focusing on the development of a UN classification for reserves and resources of solid fuels and mineral commodities.

The Working Party on Gas (23-25 January) reviewed developments in the gas industry and implications of reforms and restructuring in Central and Eastern Europe for gas markets and the gas industry in the region, and considered issues relating to the gas industry and the environment and the rational use of gas, including conservation and efficiency measures. It adopted the reports of its meetings of experts on natural gas resources, the use and distribution of gas and the transport and storage of gas, and decided to reinforce the role of the Gas Centre in its programme of assistance to economies in transition, as well as to update the study of gas grids, dealing with interconnections and extensions. The Working Party requested the secretariat to examine the feasibility of organizing a joint interregional symposium with ESCWA and ECA on developments and prospects of the gas industry and gas markets, as well as a symposium on the use of gaseous fuels for motor vehicles, and to explore the prospects of cooperation in implementing the European Energy Charter in the field of gas.

During 1995, seminars were organized on the gas industry and the European market economies and on gas contracting principles and practices, and a workshop was held on rehabilitation and enhancement techniques of natural gas transmission and distribution systems. Publications were issued on gas industry operations, gas pricing, rate-making and tariff design. The secretariat completed a glossary on national gas reserves, prepared a study on measures of gas conservation dealing with household gas consumption and appliances, and began developing a database and training manuals for the Gas Centre.

The Working Party on Electric Power (3-5 May) reviewed the electric power situation in the region and considered the interconnection of electric power transmission systems and problems of improving efficiency, environmental issues, and energy-related activities of the Black Sea Economic Cooperation Council. It took note of the progress made on the study of prospects of natural gas demand for electric power generation and their impact on the development of natural gas and electric power industries. It asked that statistical information on national equipment plans and policies be published and a note be prepared on programmes of other organizations to support demand-side management. The Working Party approved its programme of work for 1995-1999, including a project on the regulation of electric power industry.

A symposium on coal-fired power generation, the environment and public acceptance was held in Turkey (Ankara, 30 May–1 June), and a workshop on achievement and future development of cogeneration and district heating, in Romania (Poiana Brasov, 10-12 October). A meeting of experts on electric power generation and the environment held its fifth session (Geneva, 25-26 September).

The Steering Committee of the Energy Efficiency 2000 project, at its sixth session (Geneva, 22-24 May), reviewed activities under the second phase (1994-1997) of the project and preparations for the UNDP/ECE energy efficiency demonstration zones project, and approved the proposed budget of the energy efficiency project trust fund for 1995-1996 as well as proposed project activities for 1995/96. It recommended that training courses using the manuals on financial engineering and business planning be set up for energy efficiency demonstration zone managers and that the item on harmonization of energy efficiency standards and labels throughout the ECE region be integrated in the work under the project and activities in that area be coordinated with other bodies, particularly the Working Party on Standardization Policies (see below, under "Standardization"). The Steering Committee also agreed on the transfer of activities and experience-sharing between the two projects.

Other activities during 1995 included an ad hoc meeting on business opportunities in energy efficiency demonstration zones and the conversion of military industries to the manufacture of energy-efficient technologies (Minsk, Belarus, 24-27 October), a workshop on the use of solar energy (Bet Berl, Israel, July/August), as well as symposia and trade fairs of energy-efficient technologies. An ECE/EU project was implemented on energy efficiency standards in Belarus, Bulgaria, Hungary and Ukraine, as was a UNDP/ILO/ECE project on the conversion of military bases into zones of employment, entrepreneurship and energy conservation in Belarus. The regional adviser on energy assisted economies in transition in assessing the current status and prospects of their fuel and energy complex, upgrading energy production, elaborating energy conservation policies, and selecting energy efficiency zone sites and promoting their commercialization. The secretariat continued to publish annual statistical bulletins for coal, electric energy and gas.

## Agriculture

At its special session,[7] the Commission considered matters relating to the future work of the Committee on Agriculture in the light of a 1994 decision by FAO to strengthen its regional and subregional offices by withdrawing staff from the regional commissions, including ECE. During the discussion, FAO reaffirmed its readiness to consider the ECE proposal to establish a new joint body to deal with agriculture issues of particular interest to the European region. The Commission decided to postpone action on the future of the Committee on Agriculture until 1996. In a related decision,[32] the Commission invited the Committee to adapt its 1996 programme of work to the limited ECE resources currently available for work on agriculture, pending a Commission decision on its future work in that field. The Executive Secretary was invited to continue consultations with FAO on modalities of further cooperation.

The Committee on Agriculture, at its forty-sixth session (Geneva, 20-23 November),[33] examined two options regarding its future status: one calling for its discontinuance, the other suggesting its merger with the FAO European Commission on Agriculture. It recommended that ECE consider the proposal for merging its activities with FAO, and adjusted its programme of work for 1995-1996 in accordance with the Commission's decision (above). The Committee also reviewed recent developments in agriculture and agricultural policies, particularly in transition countries; discussed the impact of institutions and policies relating to agricultural markets on regional trade; and considered issues relating to standardization of perishable produce and quality development, economics of the agri-food sector and farm management, relations between agriculture and the environment, and food and agricultural statistics in Europe. It accepted that the Working Party on Standardization of Perishable Produce and Quality Development be integrated into activities of the Committee on Development of Trade, and noted a training workshop on private farming in Eastern Europe (Rambouillet, France, 6-10 November).

The Timber Committee, at its fifty-third session (Geneva, 13-16 November),[34] reviewed activities to assist economies in transition, discussed market developments for forest products in 1995 and prospects for 1996, and considered the follow-up to UNCED and to the 1993 Helsinki Ministerial Conference on the Protection of Forests in Europe.[35] It welcomed the review by the Joint FAO/ECE/ILO Committee on Forest Technology, Management and Training of its structure, objectives, methods and programme of work, and noted

a long-term strategy for Joint Committee activities, prepared by its Steering Committee (twelfth session, Geneva, 26-27 June). The Committee endorsed the report of the Joint FAO/ECE Working Party on Forest Economics and Statistics (twentieth session, Geneva, 20-22 June), and approved the redesign of the annual *Timber Bulletin*, published by the secretariat. It stressed the importance of developing standard global terms and definitions for key parameters under the project on global resource assessment 2000 (temperate zone); endorsed the mandate for a team of specialists on the supply and demand of non-wood goods and services; extended for one year the mandate of the team of specialists on certification of forest products; and asked the secretariat to prepare a policy workshop on timber markets, recycling and energy generation from wood. The Committee noted the finalization of the fifth study of European timber trends and prospects (ETTS V) and requested the ECE secretariat to develop a proposal for evaluating the ETTS V process. It approved its work programme for 1996-2000, requested its office holders to propose a modified programme adapted to the new priorities and challenges and to the availability of resources, and endorsed the incorporation of its secretariat into the ECE Trade Division.

During the year, the regional adviser on forestry and forest products undertook missions to six economies in transition to identify areas for possible international cooperation, and provided assistance to facilitate follow-up to the Ministerial Conference on the Protection of Forests in Europe. Draft project outlines were developed on forest ecosystem monitoring and on establishing extension services for small-scale private forestry. An international forestry seminar (Prince George, British Columbia, Canada, 9-15 September) proposed that international guidelines be prepared for drawing up codes of practice on multiple use forestry. The secretariat issued publications on the milk and dairy products markets, the role of farmers and professional agricultural organizations as partners of Governments in policy development and implementation, prices of agricultural products and selected inputs in Europe and North America, and the human factor in agriculture, among others. It prepared a survey of the structure of the sawmilling industry in the ECE/FAO region and a country profile of forest and forest products in Armenia.

## Economic analysis

The Senior Economic Advisers to ECE Governments, at their thirty-first session (Geneva, 19-23 June),[36] exchanged information on the development of national economies and on policies and programmes, reviewed long-term projections and perspectives for the world economy, and considered selected structural economic issues relating to trends and policies in interregional and intraregional trade, sustainable economic development, and the impact of structural changes in the region on employment, labour productivity, working patterns and income distribution. The Advisers also discussed maintaining the momentum of the recovery and mobilizing resources for sustained growth in transition economies, and adopted their programme of work for 1995-1999. They recommended that work be undertaken on macroeconomic development scenarios for the global and ECE economies and their implications for countries in transition, the relation between industrial restructuring and international trade, and access of exports from transition economies to world markets. The Advisers noted the results of a workshop on the contact zone of Bratislava-Brno-Györ-Vienna (Bratislava, Slovakia, 17 May), dealing with transboundary cooperation in that geo-economic subregion and held in preparation for an international conference on the subject.

During 1995, ECE secretariat activities in economic analysis and projections focused on trends in transition countries, as well as on population research dealing with international and regional migration issues, fertility and family surveys, and ageing. It continued to publish the annual *Economic Bulletin for Europe* and prepared a study on the role of agriculture in the transition process towards a market economy.

### Environment

The Commission in 1995 endorsed[37] the recommendations prepared in 1994[38] by the Committee on Environmental Policy on problems and bottlenecks in ECE activities in the field of environment and sustainable development. It noted the clarification provided to the Committee by the secretariat concerning resource implications of the draft ECE Action Plan to implement Agenda 21.[39] It also stressed the need to strengthen ECE activities in the field of environment and sustainable development, requested the Committee on Environmental Policy to make a decision concerning both the development and provision of resources for an ECE programme of country environmental performance reviews, and called on it to cooperate with the Inland Transport Committee in promoting sustainable development and preparing the Regional Conference on Transport and the Environment (see above, under "Transport"). The Commission reiterated its call for the ratification of or accession to ECE environmental conventions and their protocols, and invited its members and international organizations to consider the needs of economies in transition in implementing the provisions of the conventions.

The Committee on Environmental Policy, at its second session (Geneva, 29-31 May),[40] reviewed preparations for the Ministerial Conference "Environment for Europe" and for the Regional Conference on Transport and the Environment, follow-up to UNCED in the ECE region, implementation of the environmental conventions pending their entry into force, and progress in specific areas of cooperation. The Committee also discussed its future role in international environmental legislation and retained the subject for further consideration. It noted reports of the Joint Working Group on Environment and Economics (fifth session, Geneva, 25-26 January) and of the workshop on interaction between privatization processes and the environment (Geneva, 23-24 January), organized by Estonia, Lithuania and Norway, as well as the results of the first session (Bilthoven, Netherlands, 13-14 March) of the European Environment and Health Committee, established in 1994[38] to implement the Environmental Health Action Plan for Europe. The Committee adopted guidelines on the prevention and control of water pollution from fertilizers and pesticides in agriculture, recommendations concerning management of hazardous chemicals, and recommendations for action by ECE Governments and EU in the implementation of the 1992 Convention on the Transboundary Effects of Industrial Accidents, pending its entry into force. It noted progress made in developing the initial ECE programme of country environmental performance reviews, including a review mission to Estonia in May, and invited its Bureau to consider a peer-review mechanism for ECE reviews, criteria for country selection and other relevant issues.

The Working Group of Senior Governmental Officials "Environment for Europe" held four sessions in Geneva in 1995 (13-15 February, 31 May–2 June, 31 July–3 August and 11-12 September). It considered substantive preparations and practical arrangements for the Ministerial Conference and prepared draft documents for the Conference.

The Third Ministerial Conference "Environment for Europe" (Sofia, 23-25 October) considered measures to improve environmental conditions in transition economies as well as issues relating to harmonization and convergence of environmental policies in the region, including policies for the involvement of business and industry in securing environmentally sustainable development, conservation of biological and landscape diversity, and public participation in environmental decision-making. The Conference adopted a Ministerial Declaration reaffirming their commitment to cooperation in the field of environmental protection in Europe, welcoming the progress in implementing the Environmental Action Programme for Central and Eastern Europe, and endorsing the Environmental Programme for Europe, highlighting a number of long-term environmental priorities at a pan-European level, as well as the ECE Guidelines on Access to Environmental Information and Public Participation in Environmental Decision-Making. The Conference supported initiatives to follow up recommendations of the ECE Integrated Report on Environmental Financing, and called for better implementation of and compliance with ECE environmental conventions.

The Executive Body for the 1979 Convention on Long-range Transboundary Air Pollution, at its thirteenth session (Geneva, 28 November–1 December), adopted and approved for publication the 1995 annual review of strategies and policies for air pollution abatement and reviewed activities of the Working Groups on Strategies (Geneva, fourteenth session, 6-8 March; fifteenth session, 28-31 August), on Effects (fourteenth session, Geneva, 10-12 July) and on Technology, which did not meet in 1995. It noted progress made in developing a strategy to reduce nitrogen compounds and related substances, elaborating options for reducing emissions of ammonia and implementing activities concerning the effects of major air pollutants on human health and the environment. It agreed to begin negotiations on three protocols: a second step to the protocol on the control of nitrogen oxide emissions, and protocols on heavy metals and on persistent organic pollutants.

The Executive Body adopted the amended mandate of the Working Group on Abatement Techniques and revised mandates of the ad hoc preparatory working groups on heavy metals and on persistent organic pollutants. It established expert groups on implementation of the protocol for the control of nitrogen oxide emissions and on amendments to the technical annexes to the protocols concerning emissions of nitrogen oxides and of volatile organic compounds from mobile sources other than road vehicles. It called for harmonizing approaches and emission reduction levels concerning the air pollution from ship and air traffic, and approved for publication reports on the effects of nitrogen and ozone, on the calculation of critical loads of nitrogen as a nutrient, and on forest condition in Europe. The Executive Body considered the work of the Steering Body to the Cooperative Programme for Monitoring and Evaluation of the Long-range Transmission of Air Pollutants in Europe (EMEP) (nineteenth session, Geneva, 4-6 September), and requested the Steering Body to evaluate the performance of EMEP centres. It also made decisions on long-term financing of EMEP, of the International Cooperative Programmes for the Assessment and Monitoring of Air Pollution Effects and of the Mapping Programme.

By the end of 1995, there were 40 parties to the Convention. There were 25 parties to its protocol on the control of nitrogen oxide emissions, 13 parties to its protocol on the control of emissions of volatile organic compounds, and 3 parties to its protocol on further reduction of sulphur emissions. The 1992 Convention on the Protection and Use of Transboundary Watercourses and International Lakes and the 1991 Convention on Environmental Impact Assessment in a Transboundary Context, whose status and implementation were reviewed in 1995 at the fourth meeting of its signatories (Geneva, 14-17 March), were expected to enter into force in 1996. The status and implementation of the 1992 Convention on the Transboundary Effects of Industrial Accidents were also reviewed in 1995 by its signatories (fourth meeting, Geneva, 8-10 February). Recommendations were made concerning: the use of the ECE accident notification system, the work of the ECE regional coordinating centres for industrial accident training and exercise (Warsaw, Poland) and the prevention of industrial accidents (Budapest, Hungary), and efforts to set up a network of relevant centres in ECE countries.

The Working Party on Water Problems held its eighth session in 1995 (Geneva, 28 February–3 March), and workshops were organized on chemical accidents (Divonne-les-Bains, France, 6-7 February) and on trends in effects of air pollution on the environment (Oslo, Norway, 15-16 March), as was a seminar on the prevention and control of groundwater pollution from the storage of chemicals and from waste disposal (Madrid, Spain, 11-15 September). The secretariat participated in the pilot OECD environmental performance review of Bulgaria, conducted the first pilot ECE review of Estonia, and selected Slovenia as the next country to be reviewed. It prepared guidelines on public participation in environmental decision-making and issued publications on effects and control of long-range transboundary air pollution and on the protection and sustainable use of waters. The regional adviser on environmental protection provided assistance in formulating projects and programmes dealing with transboundary water management and protection, industrial safety, sustainable investment in water management, and mitigation of environmental effects of the military complex and its conversion to peaceful uses.

## Human settlements

At its 1995 session, the Commission reviewed preparations for the second UN Conference on Human Settlements (Habitat II), to be held in Turkey in 1996 (see PART FOUR, Chapter VIII), including the outcome of the ECE Regional Preparatory Meeting for Habitat II, organized in 1994.[41] The Commission called[42] on the Committee on Human Settlements to provide policy guidance and practical expertise in reforming the housing and construction sector in transition countries, developing schemes for financing housing and infrastructure investments, accelerating the modernization and improving the maintenance of the housing stock, creating and improving land registration/cadastre, and developing guidelines for urban planning and the provision of local infrastructure and services.

The Committee on Human Settlements, at its fifty-sixth session (Geneva, 18-20 September),[43] noted activities of the task force established in 1994[41] to implement ECE preparations for Habitat II and the outcome of the fourth Meeting of Ministers Responsible for Human Settlements in Countries in Transition (Budapest, 13-14 June), and adopted a document entitled "Towards sustainable human settlements development in the ECE region" as the regional contribution to Habitat II. It requested the task force to pursue the preparatory process and welcomed in principle the proposal to hold, in conjunction with the Conference, one or more special events on key issues of Committee activity.

The Committee reviewed the human settlements situation and trends and activities relating to sustainable human settlements planning and management, policies on urban renewal and housing modernization, cadastre and land registration systems, and human settlements statistics. It endorsed guidelines on sustainable human settlements planning and management, strategies to implement human settlements policies on renewal and modernization, and land administration guidelines, prepared by its task forces, and agreed to set up a task force on a framework of activities to promote sustainable human settlements development. The Committee also noted progress made in the project on country profiles of the housing sector and decided to prepare a glossary on housing finance and related policy issues and a study on major trends influencing human settlements development, and to publish the revised ECE compendium of model provisions for building regulations. Acting on the recommendations of the expert meeting on human settlements problems in southern Europe (Bucharest, Romania, 4-6 September), the Committee confirmed the necessity to continue convening such meetings, approved its synthesis report and agreed to include it with the regional contribution to Habitat II.

In 1995, the Working Parties on Housing Development, Modernization and Management and on Sustainable Human Settlements Planning held their third sessions in Geneva (10-12 May and 22-24 May, respectively). They considered housing financing; country profiles of the housing sector; housing statistics and urban indicators; cadastre and land registration systems; promotion of sustainable human settlements policies; implementation of policies for the renewal and modernization of human settlements; major trends influencing human settlements development; and management of real property and land information systems. In September, the Committee on Human Settlements endorsed their reports.

During the year, the secretariat published the annual bulletin of housing and building statistics for Europe and North America, and a number of workshops were held on cadastre and land registration and on urban renewal and housing modernization.

### Standardization

The Working Party on Standardization Policies, at its fifth session (Geneva, 22-24 May),[44] reviewed developments in the field of standardization, including coordination, harmonization, conformity assessment and metrology in testing, and agreed on its revised terms of reference and the change of its title to the Working Party on Technical Harmonization and Standardization Policies. It noted the establishment of a list of contact points within ECE member States for information on national standards documentation, conformity assessment procedures and metrology, as well as progress made in the fourth revision of the ECE standardization list and in the elaboration of harmonized international standards for calibration and testing, inspection, codification, and accreditation of laboratories. The Working Party also considered possible cooperation with the group of experts on energy efficiency standards under the "Energy Efficiency 2000" project (see above, under "Energy"), and adopted its programme of work for 1995-1999, including a new element on quality policy and competitiveness.

A first training seminar on metrology was organized in Paris in March, and a workshop on quality assurance was held in Iasi, Romania, in May. At an October meeting of office-bearers, coordinators and rapporteurs, agreement was reached on a study of the possibility of transforming some ECE recommendations on standardization policies into more binding legal forms, such as intergovernmental agreements.

### Statistics

The Conference of European Statisticians, at its forty-third session (Geneva, 12-15 June),[45] considered an integrated presentation of international statistical work in the ECE region, dealing with the organization and operation of statistical services, technical infrastructure and other cross-cutting issues, economic statistics, social and demographic statistics, natural resources and environment statistics, dissemination and support for secretariat activities, and its future work. The

Conference also reviewed issues relating to ECE statistical publications, the analytical use of national statistics at the international level, the statistical treatment of persons on leave, data protection, and possible statistical description of the effects of ongoing integration processes in Europe. It approved planned activities of the ECE secretariat under a UNDP-funded project on the development of social and demographic statistics in economies in transition, launched in 1995; requested its Bureau to consider including in its programme of work a project on statistical services in the Mediterranean region and to examine the possibility of international coordination in tourism statistics; urged accelerated harmonization of concepts on migration statistics, including statistics on refugees; suggested that higher priority be given to work on classifications in environment statistics and physical environmental accounting; and urged statistical institutes to make better use of available statistics to describe the situation of youth. The Conference approved its programme of work for 1995/96 and 1996/97 and agreed to consider new statistical and analytical approaches to labour market dynamics as a substantive topic in 1996.

The Joint ECE/OECD Meeting on National Accounts (Paris, 9-12 May) reviewed the implementation of the 1993 System of National Accounts (see PART FOUR, Chapter XV) and other related issues, including accounting for the hidden economy. Among other activities during the year were meetings on energy statistics, consumer price indices, food and agricultural statistics and gender statistics. The Working Parties on Transport Statistics and on Electronic Data Processing also held sessions in 1995. The secretariat published the first volume of the *Statistical Yearbook of the ECE—Trends in Europe and North America, 1995*, as well as a volume of gender-specific statistics in Europe and North America for 1995, and continued to issue the *Statistical Journal*. The regional adviser on economic statistics assisted 13 countries in transition in implementing the system of national accounts, improving the quality of basic data used for the estimation of major macroeconomic aggregates, and accounting for the hidden economy.

*REFERENCES*

[1]E/1995/36. [2]YUN 1975, p. 100. [3]YUN 1994, p. 721. [4]E/1995/36 (dec. F(50)). [5]Ibid. (dec. D(50)). [6]Ibid. (dec. A(50)). [7]E/1995/36 (dec. 1(1995-S)). [8]Ibid. (dec. 1(1995-S)). [9]YUN 1991, p. 320. [10]YUN 1992, p. 493. [11]E/1996/46. [12]E/ECE/1310, E/ECE/1328 & Add.1. [13]E/ECE/1329 & Add.1. [14]E/1995/36 (dec. C(50)). [15]Ibid. (dec. B(50)). [16]E/ECE/1333 & Add.1. [17]E/ECE/1334. [18]E/ECE/1343. [19]YUN 1994, p. 724. [20]Ibid., p. 956. [21]E/ECE/1311 & Add.1,2. [22]YUN 1994, p. 725. [23]ECE/TRADE/199. [24]E/1995/36 (dec. E(50)). [25]ECE/CHEM/101. [26]ECE/STEEL/91. [27]ECE/TRANS/111 & Add.1. [28]YUN 1994, p. 727. [29]E/1995/36 (dec. H(50)). [30]Ibid. (dec. I(50)). [31]ECE/ENERGY/28. [32]E/1995/36/Add.1 (dec. 2(1995-S)). [33]ECE/AGRI/134. [34]ECE/TIM/85. [35]YUN 1993, p. 632. [36]ECE/EC.AD/48 & Add.1. [37]E/1995/36 (dec. G(50)). [38]YUN 1994, p. 731. [39]YUN 1992, p. 672. [40]ECE/CEP/14 & Add.1. [41]YUN 1994, p. 732. [42]E/1995/36 (dec. J(50)). [43]ECE/HBP/93. [44]ECE/STAND/42. [45]ECE/CES/48.

# Latin America and the Caribbean

The Economic Commission for Latin America and the Caribbean did not meet in 1995. In accordance with a 1994 Economic and Social Council decision,[1] the Commission's twenty-sixth session was to be held in San José, Costa Rica, in 1996.

## Economic trends

According to a summary of the 1995 economic survey of Latin America and the Caribbean,[2] the region's economic panorama during the year was dominated by three features: the financial crisis in Mexico, which had begun at the end of 1994 and produced major after-effects in Argentina; consolidation of the stabilization programme in Brazil; and the similarity of economic performance in other countries to that of 1994, characterized by moderate growth rates, moderate and diminishing inflation, large current account deficits covered by external capital, and low domestic savings rates. Due to the Mexican financial crisis, which caused an economic contraction of 7 per cent in Mexico and of 2.5 per cent in Argentina, the region's GDP grew by a mere 0.6 per cent, compared with 4.6 per cent in 1994, marking a pause in the recovery begun in 1991. Per capita GDP fell by 1.1 per cent, in contrast to the increases of the four preceding years. However, excluding those two countries, regional output recorded a gain of slightly more than 4 per cent—nearly equal to the 1994 level, the highest in 15 years.

The economies of four countries expanded by more than 5 per cent—8 per cent in Chile, 7.5 per cent in Peru, 6.5 per cent in El Salvador and somewhat more than 5 per cent in Colombia. Four other countries recovered after the poor results of previous years, their growth rates ranging from 2 per cent in Venezuela to 3.5 per cent in Haiti and Honduras and 4 per cent in Nicaragua. GDP rose by some 5 per cent in the Dominican Republic, 4.5 per cent in Guatemala, 4 per cent in Brazil, 3.5 per cent in Bolivia, 3 per cent in Panama and in Trinidad and Tobago, 2.5 per cent in Costa Rica and in Ecuador, 2 per cent in Barbados, and 0.5 per cent in Jamaica. Economic activity in Cuba increased by 2.5 per cent, owing to the growth in manufacturing, tourist and electricity services, mining, nonsugar agriculture and construction; however, the deep economic crisis, which had persisted there for several years, continued.

Apart from Argentina and Mexico, which were affected by a sharp devaluation of the local currency, a reversal of capital inflows and the resultant decline in domestic demand and in aggregate output, Uruguay was the only other country to have registered a drop in GDP, of around 1.5 per cent, attributable to the steep decline in demand from Argentina and the abrupt downturn in domestic demand as a result of fiscal adjustment. Per capita GDP also fell in those three countries and in Jamaica, and remained unchanged in Venezuela; however, despite relatively high population growth rates, it increased by 3 per cent or more in Chile, Colombia, El Salvador and Peru, and by between 1 per cent and 3 per cent in the rest of the region. At the subregional level, the growth rate dropped to 2.9 per cent in South America, down from 5.1 per cent in 1994, but rose to 3.4 per cent in Central America and the Caribbean, compared to 2.5 per cent in the previous year.

With Brazil recording a marked decline in its annual inflation rate—to 22 per cent, down from 129 per cent in 1994 and 489 per cent in 1993—inflation in the region as a whole plummeted to 25 per cent in 1995, from 340 per cent in 1994 and 890 per cent in 1993. The consumer price index fell or remained stable in 17 of the 22 countries observed; apart from Mexico, where inflation accelerated from 7.1 per cent in 1994 to 48.5 per cent in 1995, it grew only in three countries, compared with the previous year: from 8.5 per cent to 10.7 per cent in Bolivia, from 8.9 per cent to 11.4 per cent in El Salvador, and from 19.9 per cent to 24.9 per cent in Costa Rica. In other countries, inflation rates varied from less than 2 per cent in Argentina, Barbados and Panama and less than 10 per cent in Chile, Guatemala and Trinidad and Tobago to between 11 per cent and 16 per cent in the Dominican Republic, Jamaica, Nicaragua, Paraguay and Peru, and between 20 per cent and 30 per cent in Colombia, Ecuador, Haiti and Honduras. Although below the 1994 level, inflation remained high in Venezuela, at 52.9 per cent, and in Uruguay, at 36.8 per cent.

The decline in economic growth had a considerable impact on labour markets. The regional open unemployment rate increased from 6.4 per cent in 1994 to 7.4 per cent in 1995, rising significantly in Argentina, Mexico and Venezuela. Real wages stagnated or fell in most countries; in Mexico, they had fallen by 13 per cent up to July. At the same time, average and minimum wages went up in real terms by some 4 per cent in Chile, and unemployment rates decreased, albeit modestly, in Brazil, Chile, Colombia, Guatemala, Honduras, Nicaragua and Peru.

As in the previous year, terms of trade improved in most of Latin America and the Caribbean—

rising by 1.8 per cent, against the 2.7 per cent increase in 1994—owing largely to higher commodity prices. Chile, Colombia, Honduras and Peru registered increases of 10 to 12 per cent, while the Dominican Republic and El Salvador improved their terms of trade by 14.4 per cent and 15.7 per cent, respectively. On the other hand, terms of trade stagnated in Brazil and declined in Bolivia, Ecuador, Mexico, Panama and Uruguay. Regional merchandise exports expanded by 10.5 per cent in volume and by 23 per cent in value—the highest value growth since 1980, with Argentina and Mexico accounting for 60 per cent of the increase. In addition to those countries, the value of exports grew by more than 30 per cent in Chile, El Salvador, Guatemala, Haiti and Nicaragua; on the other hand, growth rates were less than 10 per cent in Bolivia, Brazil, Panama, Paraguay and Uruguay. The unit value of exports rose in all countries, increasing by 11.1 per cent for the region as a whole, compared with 6.6 per cent in 1994.

Due to the positive evolution of prices and export quantities, the value of regional imports reached $220 billion—a record high and up from $174 billion in the previous year; however, the rate of increase was 12 per cent, lower than the 1994 level of 18.5 per cent. Excluding Argentina and Mexico, where imports declined by, respectively, 10 per cent and 7.7 per cent in value and 17.4 per cent and 14.9 per cent in volume, the growth rate stood at 33 per cent. Much of the increase was attributable to the success of the stabilization plan and a growing demand in Brazil, which expanded its imports by 51 per cent in value and by 36.7 per cent in volume, compared with a respective 28.8 per cent and 24.9 per cent in 1994. The value of imports also expanded by more than 30 per cent in Chile, the Dominican Republic, Haiti, Peru and Venezuela, owing variously to such factors as a fast-growing domestic demand, exchange-rate appreciation, or a surge in industrial activity.

The unit value of imports rose by 9.1 per cent in 1995, up from 3.6 per cent in 1994, while import volume for the region as a whole grew by only 2.8 per cent, compared to 14.3 per cent in the previous year. In addition to Argentina and Mexico, the volume of imports declined or remained unchanged in Bolivia, Costa Rica, Nicaragua, Panama, Paraguay and Uruguay. As export growth outstripped slower growing imports, the region's balance of merchandise trade showed a surplus of $2.3 billion for the first time since 1991. Significant surpluses accumulated by Argentina and Mexico more than offset the shift in the opposite direction in Brazil, which swung from a $10 billion surplus in 1994 to a $3 billion deficit in 1995. In addition, the regional deficit of net service payments was reduced from nearly $27 billion in 1994 to some $6 billion in 1995.

Latin America's current account deficit declined to $34.5 billion, from some $50 billion in the previous year, due entirely to the improved balance of goods and services. All countries except the Dominican Republic and Venezuela registered a deficit; Venezuela's considerable surplus of 1994 dropped by more than half, from $4.1 billion to $1.7 billion. The deficit was reduced from $10.2 billion in 1994 to $3.3 billion in 1995 in Argentina and from $28.9 billion to $0.2 billion in Mexico, but ballooned in Brazil from $1.7 billion to $17.9 billion.

Net capital inflows to the region, not including exceptional financial assistance provided to Argentina and Mexico to mitigate the consequences of the financial crisis, declined to $22.4 billion in 1995, compared to some $45 billion in 1994. However, excluding outflows from Mexico and Venezuela, the region's capital account balance was $43 billion. Capital inflows increased substantially to Brazil, which received $28 billion, up from $9 billion in 1994. According to the 1995 preliminary overview of the Latin American and Caribbean economy,[3] Colombia's net inflows increased from $3 billion to $4.2 billion—a record figure for that country, with more than half in direct investment, while those in Peru remained at the previous year's exceptional level of $4.6 billion. At the same time, Argentina and Mexico recorded net outflows of $0.4 billion and $16.9 billion, respectively, after inflows of some $11 billion each in 1994. The capital flight also continued from Venezuela, with outflows totalling $3.7 billion—lower than the 1994 outflow of $4.9 billion.

During the year, all countries had to adjust their macroeconomic policy in response to the Mexican financial crisis. In addition to Mexico, the solvency of the financial system was jeopardized in Argentina, Brazil, Ecuador, Nicaragua, Paraguay and Venezuela. Despite the diversity of prevailing economic climates, the achievement of domestic price stability and fiscal equilibrium remained a priority in all countries. Mexico changed its exchange-rate policy, allowing the local currency to float; Brazil and Ecuador adopted flotation band systems; and Honduras implemented an auction mechanism with intervention by its central bank.

### External debt

In 1995, the external debt of Latin America and the Caribbean approached $574 billion, an increase of 7.5 per cent over 1994, attributable mainly to a 14 per cent growth in Brazil and a 12.7 per cent growth in Mexico, after respective increases of only 1.8 per cent and 6.2 per cent in the previous year. Rates of increase declined significantly in a number of countries, including from 15.6 per cent in 1994 to 6.4 per cent in 1995 in Colombia, from 14.4 per cent to 0.3 per cent in Uruguay, from 11.6 per cent to 5 per cent in Bolivia, and from 10.1 per cent to 2.4 per cent in Argentina. Several other countries reduced their debt: Guatemala by 0.3 per cent, after the 1994 growth of 3.4 per cent; Chile and Ecuador by almost 5 per cent, having increased it by 11.3 per cent and 7 per cent, respectively, in the previous year; Nicaragua by some 11 per cent, compared to a 6.4 per cent rise in 1994. The Dominican Republic's debt continued to decline, dropping by 10.8 per cent in 1995, but grew in the rest of the region at rates ranging from 1.1 per cent in Jamaica and 1.8 per cent in Haiti to between 3 per cent and 5 per cent in Guyana, Honduras, Panama, Paraguay and Peru, and between 6 per cent and 7 per cent in Costa Rica, El Salvador and Trinidad and Tobago.

The regional debt burden continued the downward trend of several years. The ratio of total interest due to exports of goods and services, although unchanged at 16 per cent for the region as a whole, went down in most countries, except Bolivia, Brazil, Colombia, Haiti and Uruguay, which experienced a moderate rise. That indicator was below 10 per cent in Chile, Costa Rica, the Dominican Republic, El Salvador, Guatemala and Paraguay, and between 14 per cent and 17 per cent in Bolivia, Colombia, Ecuador, Haiti, Honduras, Mexico, Uruguay and Venezuela. The highest ratios were in Nicaragua (80 per cent), Peru (32 per cent), Argentina (23 per cent) and Brazil (22 per cent). At the same time, the debt/export ratio fell from 250 per cent in 1994 to 220 per cent in 1995, the lowest level since 1980, including drops from 448 per cent to 392 per cent in Peru, from 439 per cent to 346 per cent in Argentina, from 348 per cent to 300 per cent in Honduras, and from 327 per cent to 272 per cent in Ecuador. In seven countries (Chile, Costa Rica, Dominican Republic, El Salvador, Guatemala, Paraguay, Uruguay), external debt was practically equal to or less than the annual level of exports of goods and services. The ratio continued to improve in Colombia, Mexico and Venezuela, but remained high at 1,664 per cent in Nicaragua, despite a substantial reduction from 1994.

During the year, most of the region's heavily indebted countries renegotiated their external debt. Panama signed an agreement to restructure its commercial external debt, while Peru reached a preliminary restructuring agreement. Nicaragua repurchased 80 per cent of its debt at 7 per cent of its nominal value, using funds from the Inter-American Development Bank, the World Bank and a number of European Governments. Bolivia, Haiti and Nicaragua signed agreements to restructure their bilateral debt, and Honduras was also negotiating a restructuring. However, while those measures brought some relief to the most indebted countries, the level of their debt burden still remained high.

## Activities in 1995

### Development policy and regional economic cooperation

According to the report on Commission activities between its 1994 and 1996 sessions,[4] the ECLAC Economic Development Division in 1995 continued to monitor economic trends in the region, as reflected in its annual publications— *Economic Survey of Latin America and the Caribbean*, *Economic Panorama of Latin America* and *Preliminary Overview of the Economy of Latin America and the Caribbean*. The Division continued to study the distributive aspects of economic development, including the effects of adjustment processes on income distribution and the effectiveness of government policies for changing production patterns and promoting sustainable development and social equity. Seminars, workshops and meetings were held on fiscal policy, stabilization and adjustment, privatization in Bolivia and Nicaragua, fiscal decentralization and decentralized management in the region, and decentralizing and financing social spending on education and health services. Training courses were offered on fiscal decentralization in Latin America, statistics on regional trade and external finances, and financial relations between the central Government and territorial entities.

The Latin American Centre for Economic and Social Development (CLADES), which focused on strengthening the management of information and documentation for development, continued to provide technical assistance to Governments and to publish the periodicals *PLANINDEX* and *Informativo Terminológico*. The Latin American and Caribbean Institute for Economic and Social Planning (ILPES) conducted international and related national courses on development issues, advisory assistance missions to Governments and to academic institutions, a seminar on economic reforms and strategic public management and a workshop on the public decision-making process and resource allocation. The Institute's activities were reviewed at the seventeenth meeting of the Presiding Officers of the Regional Council for Planning (Caracas, Venezuela, 28-29 August), which considered the proposed work programme of ILPES for 1996 and its financial situation in 1994-1996, as well as matters relating to the public decision-making process in the region. Following the meeting's recommendation, the publication of the *Boletín del Instituto* was resumed at the end of September.

Activities in the area of regional integration and cooperation included publications dealing with the Latin American economic integration process,

technical cooperation assistance to Governments and integration agencies, and seminars on complementarity of production between members of the Southern Common Market (MERCOSUR), the social dimension of regional integration, and development of trade between Latin America and EU.

### Industrial, scientific and technological development

The Joint ECLAC/UNIDO Industrial and Technological Development Unit focused on the industrial restructuring process and policy formulation to enhance competitiveness of Latin American and Caribbean countries. It continued to provide technical assistance on policies for export promotion, human resources development and technological innovation and dissemination, as well as on the design of industrial policies and modernization of business associations. Studies were produced on interactions between micro- and macroeconomics and on the automobile, pharmaceutical, petrochemical and pulp and paper industries in selected countries. Computer programs were developed to evaluate the export competitiveness of individual countries and industrial performance in the region; 13 training course-workshops were conducted on the use of the programs. International seminars were held on industrial policy, successful experiences in government-private sector cooperation, and the new role of business associations in the development of production. Training courses were offered on structural adjustment in the region, innovation theory and technological change, industrial analysis of paper and pulp, and the Cuban pharmaceuticals industry. To promote the exchange of information on restructuring and industrial policy, a regional network of researchers in that field was established.

As part of a joint ECLAC/International Development Research Centre (IDRC) project, a conference was held on productivity, technological change and mechanisms for innovation in Latin America in the 1990s. Other activities included a national forum on competitive industrial development in Venezuela, a meeting on restructuring public institutions, and publication of the *Desarrollo Productivo* series on restructuring and competitiveness.

### International trade and development finance

During 1995, ECLAC activities to foster the continued expansion and improvement of the region's commercial links with the world economy included a seminar on new developments in and promotional strategies for foreign direct investment in Latin America, and publications on the agricultural agreement reached in 1994 in the Uruguay Round of multilateral trade negotiations,[5] the world market for bananas, Latin American exports of fish products, trade liberalization and growth in Chile and Uruguay, measures to attract foreign capital, trade in services, the region's economic relations with China and EU, and trade relations between Latin American and Eastern European countries. In addition, training courses were offered on the theory of international trade and monetary and financial policy, the region's linkages with the global economy, capital movements, and international trade statistics.

In the area of development finance, work began on a project dealing with reforms of health systems financing, and an expert workshop was held on a methodology for evaluating the distributive consequences of macroeconomic policies. Case studies of Argentina, Brazil and Colombia were completed under a new project on income distribution and recent stabilization and adjustment policies. Studies commenced on regulation and supervision of financial conglomerates, the access of low- and medium-income strata to housing finance, and financial institutions and capital formation in the region. National seminars were held on policies to support financing of small firms in Bolivia, Brazil, Colombia, Costa Rica and Ecuador, and training courses on public policies, economic reforms and strategic public management.

New developments and initiatives in international trade and development finance continued to be reflected in ECLAC periodic publications, such as *CEPAL News* and *Financiamiento del desarrollo*.

## Natural resources and energy

Activities of the ECLAC Natural Resources and Energy Unit in the areas of water, marine and mineral resources, hazardous wastes and energy focused on institutional management issues; defining the role of the State, particularly with regard to privatization and regulation; the design and application of public policies for integrated natural resources management; and the regional implementation of international environmental agreements, such as Agenda 21.[6] National seminars were held on energy and development in Chile, Colombia and El Salvador; regional seminars on private-sector participation in water utilities and on the role of new and renewable sources of energy, such as geothermal energy, in sustainable development of the region; and an expert group meeting on the implementation of Agenda 21 concerning integrated water resources management. Training courses were offered on management of watersheds and coastal areas, sustainable development models and their applications, natural resources management, and methods and models for determining energy requirements. Advisory services were provided on coastal manage-ment, mining operations, and the application of international regulations concerning biodiversity, transportation of hazardous products and wastes, high-seas fisheries, seabed regime, and protection of marine resources. Studies were made on those issues and information in a mining databank was compiled and updated.

## Transport

The work of ECLAC in the field of transport concentrated on research, technical cooperation and institutional support in the areas of railways operation, road maintenance, port management, and urban transport. Technical assistance was provided to Governments within the framework of the Operational Network of Regional Cooperation among Maritime Authorities in South America, Mexico and Panama. Cooperation projects were carried out with the Central American Bank for Economic Integration in preparing guidelines for its investments in port infrastructure and services in Central American countries. Assistance was extended to regional organizations in, *inter alia*, drafting international agreements on land and multimodal transport. ECLAC organized a seminar on public works in Chile and an expert meeting concerning the impact of ports on the exporting process, and continued to publish its *Boletín FAL* on the facilitation of trade and transport in the region.

## Social development

In 1995, the ECLAC Social Development Division, acting as the regional coordinating centre for youth and social policy activities in the UN system, completed regional preparations for the World Summit for Social Development, held in Copenhagen, Denmark, in March (see PART FOUR, Chapter IX). The 1995 edition of the *Social Panorama of Latin America* was prepared, describing recent social trends in the region, and the *Políticas sociales* series on social policies continued to be published. A project was launched to assess the impact of social policies and the progress made by Latin American countries in the socio-economic sphere. A high-level expert meeting was convened on coordination of social and economic policies in the region. Goverments were assisted in the formulation and evaluation of social programmes and projects, and training courses offered on the social impact of recent economic changes in Latin America, social effects of economic globalization in the region, and poverty and social policies.

Activities in the area of youth focused on strengthening inter-agency action on youth issues and conducting research on policies regarding youth, particularly from rural areas. The Division analysed educational policies designed to reduce inequalities in the opportunities available to youth from different social backgrounds, and studied alternatives for improving both the quality and equity of the educational system, which was the subject of several meetings and a new research project. Seminars were held on the social dimension of regional integration on adolescent health and on economic and social development policies in Latin America, the Russian Federation and several European countries.

### Integration of women

The Presiding Officers of the Regional Conference on the Integration of Women into the Economic and Social Development of Latin America and the Caribbean (twenty-first meeting, Santiago, Chile, 3-4 July)[7] reviewed regional and national preparations for the Fourth World Conference on Women (Beijing, September) (see PART FOUR, Chapter X). They analysed the Regional Programme of Action for the Women of Latin America and the Caribbean, 1995-2001, adopted in 1994[8] as a regional contribution to the World Conference.

During the year, the ECLAC Women and Development Unit continued to study the situation of women in the region with regard to work, education, health, political participation, violence and human resource training, among other matters. Its activities were geared in particular towards strengthening regional cooperation and improving coordination among ECLAC members and with NGOs and the UN system, and aimed at promoting integration of women in development.

### Environment

The Joint ECLAC/UNEP Development and Environment Unit focused on the application of economic policy instruments for environmental management and sustainable development in Latin American and Caribbean countries, international trade and the environment, and environmentally sound waste management. Activities were carried out in Argentina, Bolivia, Chile, Colombia, Costa Rica, the Dominican Republic, El Salvador, Guatemala and Mexico to identify socio-economic factors affecting soil erosion, deforestation, declining biodiversity and deterioration of inland waters, and to recommend economic policy instruments to deal with those processes. A regional symposium was held on environmental information and indicators, and a seminar on economic instruments for environmental management in the region. A publication was issued on free trade agreements and environmental issues, and assistance provided to Argentina, Colombia and Chile in formulating waste management policies, with an emphasis on the institutional and legal framework, technological policy and urban planning.

### Human settlements

The ECLAC/UNCHS Unit on Human Settlements began the second phase of a project on urban management in selected medium-sized cities of Latin America, and launched a new project dealing with changing production patterns in the region's housing sector. Under the new project, two subregional seminars were held during the year—at La Paz, Bolivia in August, and Havana, Cuba, in December. Technical studies were prepared on the design of indicators and models as an aid to decision-making in human settlements and on the development of corresponding statistical bases for the region.

In preparation for the UN Conference on Human Settlements (Habitat II), to be held in Turkey in 1996 (see PART FOUR, Chapter VIII), a regional meeting was held in November to review regional trends in human settlements and to adopt a common position before the Conference. The meeting adopted[9] a Regional Plan of Action on Human Settlements, containing recommendations for action in achieving social equity and alleviating urban poverty, raising the productivity of human settlements for improving the quality of life, improving the human settlements environment, as well as governability and participation, and increasing the efficiency of urban and housing policy and management.

In conjunction with that meeting, the fourth Regional Meeting of Ministers and High-level Authorities of the Housing and Urban Development Sector of Latin America and the Caribbean was held on 16 and 17 November to review progress made in such areas as sectoral statistics, institutional structure, financing of housing and urban services, land management, and housing technology and production. The Meeting agreed to initiate new activities relating to, *inter alia*, housing subsidies, decentralization, urban poverty and monitoring of housing policies.

### Population

ECLAC population activities were organized around the areas of population and development, demographic analysis and projections, processing of population data and documentation, and training and special programmes. They were designed to reflect the integrated perspective of changing production patterns with social equity, as well as the Latin American and Caribbean Regional Plan of Action on Population and Development, approved in 1994[10] as a regional contribution to the International Conference on Population and Development held that year.[11]

Seminars and workshops were organized on information concerning population and poverty for social programmes, future trends in mortality and the application of a population database programme. Training activities included a fifth postgraduate course on population and development under the UNFPA Global Programme of Training in Population and Development and the eighteenth intensive regional course on demographic analysis for development. The Latin American Demographic Centre continued to: provide technical assistance and advisory services to national public-sector organizations; collaborate with universities, public institutions, NGOs and international organizations in the training of national officials and in the exchange of teachers and research fellows; and conduct research and issue publications on population issues, including periodicals such as *DOCPAL: Latin American Population Abstracts*, and *Notas de Población*.

### Food and agriculture

The ECLAC Agricultural Development Unit focused on policy formulation for transforming agricultural production in the region, as well as promoting the socio-economic integration of small- and medium-scale farmers into agro-industry. National seminars on the latter subject were held during the year in Colombia, Ecuador, El Salvador, Peru, and Trinidad and Tobago. Case studies and thematic studies were prepared on agro-industrial relations and the transformation of agriculture, national systems of technological innovation in agriculture, and technological applications in the forestry sector and in agricultural markets. In addition, information continued to be compiled and analysed on biotechnology research, land and labour markets, and agricultural situations and policies outside the region.

### Statistics and economic projections

The ECLAC Statistics and Economic Projections Division continued to analyse the region's position in the global economy, carry out activities to expand the regional network of statistical information and regional cooperation in statistics, and undertake studies on Latin American and Caribbean development. Thematic databases were used, and a system of retrieval and analysis of information from the External Trade Data Bank for Latin America and the Caribbean was set up.

Special emphasis was placed on implementation of the revised System of National Accounts (SNA 1993) (see PART FOUR, Chapter XV). A seminar was organized on dissemination of statistical information (3-7 July) and an expert group meeting was held on international price comparison in the framework of SNA 1993 (4-7 December). Technical cooperation projects focused on household surveys, social policies and programmes, and production of basic statistics, including environmental and poverty statistics and indicators. Stud-

ies were undertaken on outside factors affecting the evolution of Latin American and Caribbean economies and on potential economic growth trends for individual countries and the region as a whole. National macroeconomic projections were updated and the regional economy monitored in the context of Project Link, which coordinated world economic projections.

### Transnational corporations

The Joint ECLAC/UNCTAD Unit on TNCs carried out activities concerning transnational corporations relating to information, economic research and technical cooperation. Work continued on development of an electronic system for a statistical database on foreign investment, and research was conducted on economic and institutional reforms and the investment process in major national and transnational companies. The contribution of TNCs to industrial restructuring and international competitiveness was analysed, and a study prepared on industrial restructuring and the role of TNCs in Argentina, Brazil, Chile and Mexico. Comparative studies were also conducted on the legal and contractual framework of the petroleum sectors in Argentina, Bolivia, Brazil, Colombia, Ecuador, Peru, Venezuela and Mexico, as well as on foreign investment and technology transfer in several countries of Asia and Latin America.

### Technical cooperation and assistance

During the year, the ECLAC Programme Planning and Operations Division completed 21 regional, 2 subregional and 24 country projects financed from extrabudgetary funds. It launched 22 new projects, 8 of which were completed in 1995; an additional 17 were in progress. New regional and subregional projects focused on decentralization of fiscal policy and management, environmentally sound waste management, health systems financing reform, improvement of the petroleum supply to Central America, trade and investment promotion, public financing and provision of social services, human resources training in development planning, urban management in selected medium-sized cities, study of small and medium-sized enterprises (SMEs), and social policies evaluation, support and promotion. Agreements were concluded between ECLAC and the Latin American Confederation of Pulp and Paper Industry, the municipality of La Plata in Argentina, and universities in Chile and Colombia. Country projects dealt with support for regional planning in Bolivia, business development strategies and the 1994 economic census in Argentina, regional development in Brazil, and local development and a project and operations bank in Colombia.

*Technical cooperation among developing countries*

The Programme Planning and Operations Division continued to carry out activities within the framework of the 1978 Buenos Aires Plan of Action for Promoting and Implementing Technical Cooperation among Developing Countries.[12] Its efforts focused on the incorporation of TCDC elements in projects to strengthen national institutions, establish and support cooperation networks, improve information systems to expedite the match-up of technical cooperation supply and demand between countries, and consolidate national TCDC focal points. The Division also supported seminars and technical meetings to exchange experiences, prepared studies to identify opportunities for cooperation, and facilitated provision of services by local experts and consultants.

ECLAC collaborated with the Latin American Economic System (SELA) and UNDP within the framework of a regional coordination mechanism for TCDC. In that context, a cooperation project was carried out on instruments and mechanisms to create linkages between the private and public sectors; the project results pertaining to instruments of support to SMEs led to a joint SELA/UNDP initiative on intraregional cooperation in that area. The Commission also continued to publish the newsletter *Cooperation and Development*.

In 1995, TCDC issues were considered at the tenth meeting of national directors for international technical cooperation in March, which adopted the Montevideo (Uruguay) Declaration in support of TCDC subject areas and projects proposed for the next UNDP regional programming cycle (see PART FOUR, Chapter II), as well as at the eleventh meeting of the Coordination Mechanism for Regional Bodies and Forums Engaged in TCDC Activities (Montevideo, 15-17 May).

## Subregional activities

### Caribbean

The ECLAC subregional headquarters for the Caribbean, located in Port of Spain, Trinidad and Tobago, continued to analyse socio-economic development in the subregion and to support activities of subregional bodies, including the Caribbean Development and Cooperation Committee (CDCC) and the Caribbean Council for Science and Technology (CCST). High priority was accorded to promoting cooperation in functional and sectoral areas both among CDCC member States and between them and other Latin American countries. In that context, assistance was provided for the establishment of the Association of Caribbean States. The subregional headquarters carried out preparatory and follow-up activities with regard to global conferences organized under UN auspices, and assisted Governments in conduct-

ing research on issues relating to environmentally sustainable development programmes, as well as in formulating their science and technology and population policies, and in analysing census data and population projections.

Studies were prepared on socio-economic and sustainable development issues, public sector reform, structural adjustment and privatization policies in the subregion. New databases were established on intra-CDCC trade, social statistics and environmental data. Expert group meetings took place on population and development (Bahamas, 3-5 May) and on the implementation of the Programme of Action for Small Island Developing Countries (Port of Spain, 17-19 May) (see PART FOUR, Chapter I), as did a workshop for ECLAC/CDCC focal points and seminars on agro-industry and small-scale agriculture and on the promotion of competitiveness. The bulletin *External Sector Briefing Notes* and the *Focus* newsletter were issued.

ECLAC activities in the Caribbean were reviewed at the seventh meeting of the CDCC Monitoring Committee and at the thirteenth session of CCST (Cuba, 22-27 September).

### Mexico and Central America

The activities of the ECLAC subregional headquarters in Mexico City continued to focus on the analysis of economic change experienced during the year by Central American countries, Cuba, the Dominican Republic, Haiti and Mexico. Efforts were made to elaborate on various aspects of the integrated approach and the concept of open regionalism as development options for the subregion. The subregional headquarters also supported integration efforts of Central American organizations, such as the Central American Bank for Economic Integration and the Central American Economic Cooperation Committee (CCE). ECLAC convened a special consultation meeting of CCE (Mexico City, 10 March) and its eleventh regular meeting (Guatemala City, 28-29 September) to exchange ideas and review the progress made in the areas of open regionalism and effective protection in Central America, hemispheric integration, and investment and its links with trade.

Technical cooperation activities dealt with macroeconomic policy, institutional change, national accounts, non-traditional agricultural exports, assessment of industrial competitiveness and electrical integration. A seminar was held on the role of investment and financing in changing production patterns in Central America (Tegucigalpa, Honduras, 3 and 4 July), and an expert meeting took place (Mexico City, May) on the issue of social security. Studies were prepared on the status of women in relation to human resources, poverty, the urban informal sector and the "maquiladora" industry; the effects of the North American Free Trade Agreement on the economies of the subregion; and public investment. Privatization programmes, industrial development and the food situation were other areas of concern.

## Cooperation between the United Nations and the Latin American Economic System

In response to a 1994 General Assembly request,[13] the Secretary-General reported[14] on 18 September on cooperation between the UN and the Latin American Economic System, reiterating that collaboration between the two organizations had intensified over the years since the establishment of SELA in 1975 and had become more diversified in terms of both the activities and the participation of UN bodies.

Some essential activities were carried out jointly with ECLAC, which participated in SELA meetings and supported various SELA projects, particularly those on integrated social policies, demographics, training in information management, international trade, and industrial policy. A meeting of experts was held under a joint project for coordination of economic and social policies in the region (Cartagena de Indias, Colombia, 21-23 June), and a working mechanism was established for convening an annual meeting of trade policy officials. The two organizations launched a cooperative project to identify and describe the current status of industrial policy in countries in the region.

FAO continued to collaborate with SELA through action committees dealing with marine and freshwater products, fertilizers, the economic and social development of Central America, and plant genetic resources. The two organizations discussed establishing a cooperation framework for the regional programme on vegetal germplasm and the project on biotechnology and food security. Cooperation also continued with ILO, which participated in the dialogue of high-level government officials on new orientations for international macroeconomic coordination and gave lectures on labour-market issues and changing production patterns and on competitiveness concepts and labour costs. SELA received technical assistance from the International Maritime Organization (IMO) in the area of shipping, and was finalizing a cooperation agreement with the International Fund for Agricultural Development (IFAD).

UNESCO participated in a regional meeting on challenges of urban youth, co-sponsored by SELA (Caracas, 12-13 June). A network of Latin American economic dailies was initiated under the UNESCO-SELA agreement on communication for integration, and UNESCO links were established with projects for the development of the regional handicraft industry. UNESCO continued to cooperate with SELA in the area of intellectual property, as did the World Intellectual Property Organization.

UNIDO was involved in follow-up to the Regional Forum on Industrial Policy in Latin America and the Caribbean, held in October 1994, through the work of the Coordination Committee established on the Forum's recommendation. It attended an inter-agency meeting on investment promotion and technological innovation and a regional meeting on human resources training in support of processes to modernize production and competitiveness. Agreement was reached on activities to promote the development of the handicraft sector in the region. A joint meeting was being organized on privatization processes in Latin America. SELA was preparing a new initiative on privatization, supported by the World Bank.

UNDP collaborated with SELA in identifying and improving mechanisms to facilitate economic links and industrial modernization among SELA members; a series of studies and meetings were conducted on trade and the environment, industrialization and technological development, and integration and regional cooperation. Cooperation with UNCTAD was aimed at implementing the LATINTRADE project, disseminating the Uruguay Round results and identifying new business opportunities, modernizing and updating legislative and regulatory frameworks for trade relations, as well as improving information management, human resources development and training, and institution-building, national administration and coordination mechanisms.

**GENERAL ASSEMBLY ACTION**

On 15 November, the General Assembly adopted **resolution 50/14**.

**Cooperation between the United Nations and the Latin American Economic System**

*The General Assembly,*

*Recalling* its resolution 49/6 of 21 October 1994 on cooperation between the United Nations and the Latin American Economic System,

*Having considered* the report of the Secretary-General of 18 September 1995 on cooperation between the United Nations and the Latin American Economic System,

*Bearing in mind* the Agreement between the United Nations and the Latin American Economic System, in which the parties agree to strengthen and expand their cooperation in matters which are of common concern in the field of their respective competence pursuant to their constitutional instruments,

*Considering* that the Economic Commission for Latin America and the Caribbean has developed ties of cooperation with the Latin American Economic System which have grown stronger in recent years,

*Bearing in mind also* that the Permanent Secretariat of the Latin American Economic System has carried out several programmes with the support of the United Nations Development Programme in areas that are considered of priority for the economic development of the region,

*Considering also* that the Latin American Economic System is developing joint activities with the specialized agencies and other organizations and programmes of the United Nations system, such as the United Nations Conference on Trade and Development, the United Nations Educational, Scientific and Cultural Organization, the United Nations Industrial Development Organization, the World Meteorological Organization, the World Health Organization, the World Intellectual Property Organization, the United Nations Environment Programme, the Department for Economic and Social Information and Policy Analysis of the Secretariat, the Office of the United Nations Disaster Relief Coordinator, the United Nations Institute for Training and Research and the International Telecommunication Union,

*Welcoming* the continued monitoring of changes in the treatment of topics relating to the United Nations system, in close contact with the delegations of the Member States participating in such deliberations,

1. *Takes note with satisfaction* of the report of the Secretary-General;

2. *Urges* the Economic Commission for Latin America and the Caribbean to continue broadening and deepening its coordination and mutual support activities with the Latin American Economic System;

3. *Urges* the United Nations Development Programme to strengthen and expand its support to the programmes that the Permanent Secretariat of the Latin American Economic System is carrying out, aimed at complementing the technical assistance activities conducted by the Latin American Economic System;

4. *Urges* the specialized agencies and other organizations and programmes of the United Nations system to continue and intensify their support for, and cooperation in the activities of, the Latin American Economic System;

5. *Requests* both the Secretary-General of the United Nations and the Permanent Secretary of the Latin American Economic System to assess, at the appropriate time, the implementation of the Agreement between the United Nations and the Latin American Economic System and to report thereon to the General Assembly at its fifty-second session;

6. *Requests* the Secretary-General to submit to the General Assembly at its fifty-second session a report on the implementation of the present resolution.

General Assembly resolution 50/14

15 November 1995      Meeting 60      Adopted without vote

28-nation draft (A/50/L.16); agenda item 25.

*REFERENCES*
[1]YUN 1994, p. 744, ESC dec. 1994/287, 26 July 1994. [2]E/1996/49. [3]*Preliminary Overview of the Economy of Latin America and the Caribbean, 1995* (LC/G.1892-P), Sales No. E.95.II.G.18. [4]LC/G.1900(SES.26/5). [5]YUN 1994, p. 868. [6]YUN 1992, p. 672. [7]LC/L.904(MDM.21/3). [8]YUN 1994, p. 739. [9]LC/G.1889(CONF.85/4). [10]YUN 1994, p. 740. [11]Ibid., p. 955. [12]YUN 1978, p. 467. [13]YUN 1994, p. 745, GA res. 49/6, 21 Oct. 1994. [14]A/50/438.

# Western Asia

In accordance with a 1994 Economic and Social Council resolution,[1] the Economic and Social Commission for Western Asia held its eighteenth session in Beirut, Lebanon, on 24 and 25 May 1995.[2] The Commission's session was preceded by the ninth session of its Technical Committee (Beirut, 22-23 May). ESCWA and the Technical Committee assessed progress in implementing the work programme for 1994-1995, reviewed follow-up action on Commission resolutions adopted in 1994, and examined regional preparations for and follow-up to UN world conferences and ESCWA regional meetings, cooperation among developing countries and regional organizations and the impact of the single European market on ESCWA member States, as well as programme and organizational matters. The Commission reviewed, amended and adopted the Technical Committee's report,[3] including its draft resolutions.

In July, the Economic and Social Council, acting on Commission recommendations, decided to establish within ESCWA committees on energy and on water resources (see below).

## Economic and social trends

### Economic trends

Overall economic performance in Western Asia improved in 1995, according to a summary of economic and social developments in the ESCWA region for that year.[4] The region's GDP, excluding Iraq, grew 2.8 per cent, compared with an adjusted rate of 0.8 per cent in 1994. The growth was attributable to increases in oil prices, as well as the past several years' economic and structural reforms carried out in many countries. Owing to a relatively high population growth rate, however, per capita GDP stagnated, after a 1.8 per cent decline in the previous year. At the same time, the continuation of UN sanctions against Iraq and the low level of regional economic cooperation restrained further growth and development in Western Asia.

Economies of the Gulf Cooperation Council (GCC)—Bahrain, Kuwait, Oman, Qatar, Saudi Arabia and the United Arab Emirates—after contracting by 0.5 per cent in 1994, expanded by 2 per cent due to the development of the oil sector which offset reductions in government expenditures on some other economic sectors. On the other hand, the group's per capita GDP was estimated to have decreased another 1 per cent, after falling 3.2 per cent the previous year. Growth rates increased from 0.1 per cent in 1994 to 1.3 per cent in 1995 in the United Arab Emirates, from 2 per cent to 2.7 per cent in Bahrain and from 3.5 per cent to 4.5 per cent in Oman, while the economies of Kuwait, Qatar and Saudi Arabia, which recorded respective declines of 0.4 per cent, 1.5 per cent and 1.1 per cent in 1994, rebounded with growth rates of 2.9 per cent, 1 per cent and 1.7 per cent, respectively. Saudi Arabia's economic performance was boosted mainly by the growth of the oil sector, but was adversely affected by the reduction in subsidies of public goods and services, higher costs of imports, significant cutbacks in government expenditures, and the outflow of expatriate workers' remittances, which increased from $15.2 billion in 1994 to $17.2 billion in 1995.

Total output of the region's more diversified economies (Egypt, Iraq, Jordan, Lebanon, the Syrian Arab Republic, Yemen, the West Bank and Gaza Strip), with the exception of Iraq, rose 5.2 per cent, up from 4.3 per cent in the previous year, while their per capita GDP grew 2.3 per cent, compared with 1.7 per cent in 1994. Among contributing factors were: the rejuvenation of the private sector following economic reform and liberalization measures, improved conditions for private investment, increased revenues from tourism, large inflows of workers' remittances, and a declining debt-servicing burden. Egypt's growth rate accelerated from 3.9 per cent in 1994 to 4.9 per cent in 1995, due to an expansion in both oil and non-oil exports, a 21 per cent increase in the number of tourists and growing revenues from the Suez Canal, among other factors. Jordan registered a 6.3 per cent growth, up from 5.7 per cent in the previous year, with its exports rising by 20 per cent and tourism revenues by 24 per cent. Economic growth in Lebanon slowed, from 8 per cent to 7 per cent but remained the highest in the region for the second consecutive year as that country continued to benefit from large-scale reconstruction activities, capital inflows and a boom in the services sector, particularly tourism and banking. The Beirut Stock Exchange reopened in 1995, having been closed for 13 years because of civil strife. The Syrian Arab Republic recorded a 6 per cent growth rate, a 1 per cent increase over 1994, while Yemen's GDP grew by 0.5 per cent, as against a 0.5 per cent decline in the previous year. Economic conditions in Iraq, already among the world's lowest in per capita GDP, deteriorated further as a result of UN sanctions and were characterized by hyper-inflation and vast underutilization of productive capacities due to the oil embargo and a lack of raw materials, spare parts, seeds, fertilizers, pesticides and herbicides. Economic performance of the West Bank and Gaza Strip was adversely affected by a poor olive crop and restrictions on the employment of Palestinian workers in Israel; the GDP growth rate decelerated from 7.3 per cent in 1994 to 3 per cent in 1995.

Inflation rates jumped in the GCC countries, where, except for Kuwait, all currencies were pegged to the United States dollar. Coupled with the reduction in subsidies of public goods and services, the weakening of the US dollar led to higher inflation in that economic group in 1995, ranging from 1 per cent in Oman to 4.8 per cent in Saudi Arabia and 5 per cent in the United Arab Emirates. Among the more diversified economies implementing IMF-supported structural adjustment programmes, Jordan experienced a steady inflation rate of 3.5 per cent. The rate declined in Egypt from 8.2 per cent in 1994 to some 4.9 per cent in November 1995, and fell from 100 per cent to 45 per cent in Yemen. Inflation decreased from 16 per cent to 12.5 per cent in Lebanon and from 30 per cent to 25 per cent in the West Bank and Gaza Strip, but was estimated to have risen in the Syrian Arab Republic from 15 per cent in the previous year. Hyper-inflation persisted in Iraq as its currency continued to depreciate and its money supply increased. Unemployment remained a major regional problem, with Yemen and the West Bank and Gaza Strip registering the highest rates, estimated at 30 per cent.

Most ESCWA countries continued to carry out economic reform and structural adjustment programmes in 1995, aimed at correcting internal and external imbalances and enhancing efficiency and productivity. New investment and tax laws were formulated to encourage private investment, particularly FDI, which remained modest compared to other developing regions; several States also began privatization of public enterprises, albeit at a slow pace for fear of higher unemployment and inflation. Most GCC countries restrained spending and adopted policies to increase non-oil revenues by raising fees on public services or privatizing parts of public-sector enterprises. As a result, their aggregate budget expenditures declined from $72 billion in 1994 to some $68 billion in 1995, and their budget deficit from $17.3 billion to $9.6 billion. In the more diversified economies, Egypt's targeted 2 per cent ratio of budget deficit to GDP was expected to rise by some 6 per cent and Lebanon's budget expenditures were almost double its revenues. On the other hand, the deficit was kept close to budgeted figures in Jordan, and dropped to 7 per cent of GDP in Yemen, down from 17 per cent the previous year. In the West Bank and Gaza Strip, the Palestinian Authority, which took over taxation from Israel in 1995, covered its $200 million deficit by collecting $70 million in tax revenues and using $130 million received from foreign funding sources.

Banking-sector activities, characterized by tight conditions in the first half of 1995, eased significantly and led to record profits for the banks by the end of the year. The share of consumer banking in the region's banking market rose from 45 per cent in 1994 to 55 per cent in 1995. Advances were also recorded in the region's stock markets, which proved to be an adequate vehicle for raising private capital for banks, other financial institutions and corporations; however, their insufficiently developed legal, administrative and institutional infrastructures inhibited their ability to finance the development process effectively.

The external debt of ESCWA countries, excluding Iraq, remained in 1995 at about $182 billion. Jordan's debt dropped from $7 billion to $6 billion due to its partial cancellation by a number of creditors, and the debts of Kuwait and of Saudi Arabia were reduced significantly. On the other hand, Egypt's debt reached $33 billion, a 7 per cent increase over 1994, while that of Lebanon rose by some 68 per cent, to $1.3 billion.

## Oil

Crude oil production in oil-exporting ESCWA countries grew in 1995 by almost 1 per cent, to 15.89 million barrels per day. Output rose 6.3 per cent in Oman, 5 per cent in Iraq, 4.5 per cent in Qatar, 4.3 per cent in the Syrian Arab Republic, and 1.5 per cent in Yemen, but remained unchanged in the rest of the region, owing either to quota limitations established by the Organization of Petroleum Exporting Countries (OPEC) or to limited production capacity.

Due mostly to the upward adjustment in oil prices, to an average $16.88 per barrel, compared with $15.53 per barrel in 1994, oil revenues rebounded with a 9.3 per cent increase to reach $78.4 billion, after a 5 per cent decline the previous year. Revenues grew in all oil-exporting countries, with Oman, Qatar and Yemen registering the greatest increases of 14 per cent, 13.7 per cent and 10.3 per cent, respectively. While the refining capacity of oil exporters remained largely unchanged from its 1990 level, several States embarked on a number of projects to expand it during 1997-2000.

Proven oil reserves in the region were estimated at 570 billion barrels, or 57 per cent of the world total and some 74 per cent of OPEC's total.

## Agriculture

The ESCWA region's production of cereals was estimated at 30.8 million tons in 1995, a 7.6 per cent increase over 1994, owing to favourable weather conditions in most of the region. The GCC countries recorded a 4.8 per cent growth, mostly in Saudi Arabia, and accounted for 14 per cent of the region's total. In more diversified economies, cereal output rose by 8 per cent, to 26.5 million tons, including 17 million tons—an 11.1 per cent increase—in Egypt alone, which represented some 55.2 per cent of the region's total. Egypt in-

creased its wheat production by 28 per cent, to a record 5.7 million tons, mainly by using high-yield varieties, while its output of paddy (rice before threshing) was expected to have grown by 113,000 tons to reach 4.7 million tons.

The Syrian Arab Republic registered growth rates in the year of 8 per cent for cereals and 10 per cent for barley, and its output of wheat expanded by 330,000 tons to a total of 4 million tons. In Jordan, the aggregate production of wheat and barley rose 8 per cent, owing to a marked expansion of the area planted, while output of lentils more than doubled to reach 5,000 tons. Combined production of wheat and barley was estimated at 73,000 tons in Lebanon, an increase of 10,000 tons over the previous year; however, its cereal output covered only about 10 per cent of total requirements, and the country remained dependent on imports to meet the demand for rice, sugar and milk powder. In Saudi Arabia, wheat production declined, from 3.4 million tons in 1993 to 2.5 million tons in 1995, as the country continued its water-conservation policy of reducing wheat production to the level of local demand; the production of barley increased only slightly. Cereal output continued to decline in Yemen, with imports of cereals estimated at 2 million tons in 1995, a 19 per cent increase over 1994. In Iraq, cereal production dropped 10 per cent due to the lack of foreign exchange, which led to a significant reduction in the use of agricultural inputs such as spare parts, fertilizers and pesticides and extreme shortages of basic food items; the country needed an estimated $2.7 billion to meet its import requirements for 1995/96.

The value of regional food imports was estimated to have risen by 7.8 per cent in 1995 and was projected to grow annually by an average 8.9 per cent during 1996-2000. In addition, the European Union's new trade policy of applying the entry price system, particularly for fresh vegetables and fruits, was expected to affect adversely exports from Egypt, Jordan, Lebanon and the Syrian Arab Republic.

While food imports in the region rose 2.5 per cent to $11.8 billion in 1994, the region's food gap (net imports) also increased, by 2.9 per cent, to reach $10 billion, and that gap was expected to widen further as a result of world agricultural trade liberalization following the Uruguay Round of multilateral trade negotiations, concluded in 1994.[5]

In the light of those developments, the reform of agricultural sectors continued in several ESCWA countries. Egypt liberalized production and marketing activities for agricultural inputs; Jordan was removing producer subsidies on crops and planned to liberalize trade in barley; and the Palestinian Authority began to build up institutional capabilities to rehabilitate the agricultural sector in the West Bank and Gaza Strip, and focused on establishing a Ministry of Agriculture.

### Industrial development

The region's overall manufacturing value-added, excluding Iraq and the West Bank and Gaza Strip, grew 3.6 per cent in 1995, compared with more than 4 per cent in 1994. In GCC countries that rate was unchanged from the previous year, whereas the more diversified economies experienced a decline in growth from the 1994 rate of 5 per cent. Developments in the manufacturing sector were influenced by structural adjustment programmes and public-sector reform, continued economic recovery of major export markets, and a rise in the production and export value of major products, such as petrochemicals, fertilizers, aluminium and textiles. The expansion was restrained, however, by trade barriers in EU and other major markets, increased international competition especially from East Asia, reduced public investment in manufacturing projects and still insufficient involvement of the private sector, which was hindered by the slow pace of economic reforms. In many countries, a lack of electricity-generation capacity was another obstacle to manufacturing development.

Long-standing challenges confronting the transport sector persisted in 1995, including the need to rehabilitate networks damaged by war and civil strife, standardization of technical specifications, harmonization of border-crossing procedures, removal of trade barriers and improved maintenance of existing infrastructure and equipment. A number of transport projects were considered by ESCWA member States, dealing with a subregional rail network linked to Europe and to North Africa, a bridge over the Suez Canal, and development of seaports and airports in the Gulf of Aqaba, as well as several other international airports.

### Trade

Regional exports and imports, excluding Iraq, were positively affected by rising oil prices and higher GDP growth rates. Exports expanded by 8.4 per cent to $109.8 billion. Imports rose 9.2 per cent to $93.4 billion, representing a reversal of the previous year's downward trend. Agricultural exports grew from $2.9 billion in 1994 to an estimated $3.5 billion in 1995, while agricultural imports increased from $14.4 billion to some $16.2 billion over the same period. The region's export/import ratio, a measure of its ability to finance imports from export proceeds, remained at 1.18 in 1995; it grew from 1.53 to 1.57 in the GCC countries, but declined from 0.43 to 0.40 in the more diversified economies.

Exports from the GCC countries, amounting to $97 billion—an 8 per cent increase over 1994—accounted for 88 per cent of the region's total. Within that group, Kuwait, Qatar and Saudi Arabia registered increases of more than 9 per cent. The growth in exports from the more diversified economies exceeded 11.6 per cent, reaching more than $12.4 billion, largely due to the performances of Egypt, Jordan and Lebanon.

Imports of the GCC countries grew by almost 6 per cent, to some $62 billion, with rates of increase ranging from 8 to 5 per cent in Kuwait, Qatar, Saudi Arabia and the United Arab Emirates. Bahrain was the only country to record a slight decrease. The more diversified economies witnessed a 16.6 per cent rise in imports, totalling $31 billion; however, rates varied from more than 12 per cent in Egypt, Jordan and Lebanon to between 5 per cent and less than 1 per cent in other countries of the group.

The current account deficit (excluding Iraq, Lebanon, Qatar, the United Arab Emirates and Yemen, where data were not available) declined further in 1994 to $7.1 billion from $15.1 billion a year earlier; it dropped by one third of the 1993 level in Jordan, while in Saudi Arabia the deficit fell from $17.3 billion in 1993 to $9.1 billion in 1994 and was estimated to have declined to $5 billion in 1995. The combined current account of the more diversified economies showed a deficit of $1 billion in 1994 after a surplus in 1993, as Egypt's surplus decreased from $2.3 billion to $31 million. The deficit in the balance of goods and services in the more diversified economies declined only slightly in 1994, as inflows of expatriate workers' remittances, counted on to finance the overall trade deficit, fell from $9 billion to $6.7 billion, including from $7 billion to $4.62 billion for Egypt alone. GCC countries, however, regained a surplus as Kuwait made a full return to the oil market, while outflows of remittances from that group dropped from $18.4 billion to $17.7 billion.

The region's international reserves, excluding Iraq, the Syrian Arab Republic and Yemen, rose from $45.7 billion in 1994 to $50 billion in 1995, or 9.4 per cent. GCC countries accounted for $24.2 billion in reserves, with Saudi Arabia ($9.8 billion) and the United Arab Emirates ($7.6 billion) being the largest holders. Reserves of the more diversified economies totalled $25.9 billion, of which Egypt held $18 billion.

### Social trends

The population of the ESCWA region was expected to reach 150.2 million by mid-1996, growing at a yearly rate of about 2.7 per cent. Annual growth rates ranged from 7.07 per cent in Kuwait and 3.91 per cent in the West Bank and Gaza Strip to 1.79 per cent in Egypt and 1.31 per cent in

Qatar. Also by mid-1996, 40.36 per cent of the total population was projected to be under age 15, and 3.45 per cent over age 65. The crude birth rate was expected to decrease slightly, from 31.3 to 30.1 births per 1,000 over 1994-1995, exceeding that of the less developed regions of the world (25 per 1,000) and more than twice the rate in the more developed regions (13 per 1,000). The crude death rate declined to 6.98 deaths per 1,000 in mid-1994, less than the world's average of 9.3 deaths per 1,000, and was expected to decrease to 6.82 deaths per 1,000 by mid-1996. Life expectancy at birth in the region remained at 65.58 years.

The total fertility rate was expected to drop to 4.5 births per woman by mid-1996, owing mostly to a fertility decline in Egypt, the region's most populous country, as well as in Jordan and the Syrian Arab Republic. In mid-1994, averages varied from between 6 and 7.5 births per woman in Kuwait, Oman, Saudi Arabia, the West Bank and Gaza Strip and Yemen to less than 4 in Egypt and less than 3 in Lebanon. By mid-1996, Yemen was expected to have the highest rate, at 7.5 births per woman, and Lebanon the lowest, at 2.76 births per woman. The infant mortality rate stood regionally at 58.38 deaths per 1,000 live births, and ranging up to 90 per 1,000 in Iraq and more than 80 in Yemen, but as low as 16 deaths per 1,000 in Kuwait.

The urban population accounted for 53 per cent of the region's total in 1993 and was projected to reach 58 per cent by the year 2000. In addition to such factors as a natural increase in population and rural-urban migration, rapid urbanization in the ESCWA region was boosted by a massive flow of population between labour-sending and labour-absorbing countries. Its impact on urban areas manifested itself in a boom in housing construction, coupled with soaring land and housing prices. As a result, high vacancy rates in luxurious dwellings in large cities of the more diversified economies were paralleled by the spread of squatter settlements, increasing overcrowding, and substandard housing for the growing category of low-income people. In GCC countries, however, high vacancy rates reflected their dependence on expatriate labour, which made them vulnerable to fluctuations in the job market and affected their ability for efficient planning of urban expansion and public service delivery. Between 75 and 90 per cent of households in that group of countries had access to water, a sewerage network and electricity, and more than 95 per cent were connected to kitchen and bathroom facilities.

Environmental conditions deteriorated further in many areas of the ESCWA region in 1995, owing to rapid population growth, inappropriate economic and social policies, weak regulatory and administrative systems, and insufficient public awareness. Increasing water demand strained the region's limited water resources and exacerbated the problem of water scarcity, as substantial volumes drawn from rivers and aquifers were shared among countries both within and outside the ESCWA region. To overcome the problem, several States were desalinating sea water and brackish water, reusing renovated waste water and utilizing non-conventional water sources. Significant efforts were made to update and implement national water plans, and laws were enacted to protect existing water sources and to regulate excessive water utilization. Most countries were also formulating strategies or plans to combat environmental degradation; however, their implementation was hindered by financial constraints and reduced public spending.

## Activities in 1995

During 1995, ESCWA activities under its programme of work and priorities for 1994-1995 focused on five thematic subprogrammes, established pursuant to the 1994 programme revision:[6] management of natural resources and environment; improvement of the quality of life; economic development and cooperation; regional development and global changes; and special programmes and issues.

### Development planning, development finance and international trade

At its 1995 session, the Technical Committee considered the Executive Secretary's note[7] regarding the impact of the single European market on ESCWA member countries. The note summarized the single market's implications for the region's foreign trade, agriculture, manufacturing, banking and finance, and science and technology, and provided recommendations for action in each of those areas. The Technical Committee requested the secretariat to undertake studies of obstacles to the creation of an Arab common market, reasons for the decline in trade relations between the ESCWA region and EU, possibilities and relative advantages of early agricultural production for export to EU, and the potential for developing scientific and technological institutions in member States in conformity with their counterparts in the industrialized countries. The secretariat was also requested to monitor and assess developments in the world trade system, assist in building awareness of the importance of concerted Arab action in dealing with economic coalitions, and establish coordination mechanisms with international and regional organizations to enhance Arab cooperation until the creation of an Arab common market.

Implications of the single European market for the economic sectors covered in the Executive Secretary's note were the subject of a series of studies published during the year. The secretariat also issued the annual survey of economic and social developments in the region and an overview of the region's stock markets, and undertook studies on the establishment of business incubators and on privatization in the Gulf countries as well as in the more diversified economies. Publications on international trade and development finance included annual reviews of developments and issues in the external trade and payments situation of ESCWA countries, and of developments and trends in the monetary and financial sectors in the region.

## Food and agriculture

Activities in the area of agriculture included training workshops on food and agricultural policy analysis, agricultural sector management, project planning and environmental considerations in agriculture, and monitoring and evaluation of rural development projects. ESCWA continued to issue its annual publication *Agriculture and Development in Western Asia*, and carried out studies on resource conservation policies for agriculture in the Syrian Arab Republic, the impact of structural adjustment measures on food production and consumption in Egypt, the impact of population growth and urbanization on food consumption patterns in Jordan, and agricultural integration among Iraq, Jordan, Lebanon and the Syrian Arab Republic. Other publications dealt with the development of fisheries statistics in the United Arab Emirates and agricultural extension and its future prospects in Yemen.

The secretariat also contributed to the formulation of an action programme for restructuring agriculture institutions in the occupied territories by preparing a national farm data handbook for the West Bank and Gaza Strip as well as studies on prospective developments of agricultural institutions in the occupied Palestinian territories and on the cropping pattern in the Gaza Strip and prospects for development.

## Industrial development and technology

In 1995, the secretariat published a review of recent developments in manufacturing activities and prospects in the ESCWA region for 1994, and produced studies on industrial strategies and policies in the region, investment environment in the industrial sector in Yemen, and the use of cleaner industrial production technologies in selected ESCWA countries. Expert group meetings on industrial strategies and policies and on entrepreneurial and managerial skills were organized in Bahrain, and a workshop was held on micro- and small-enterprise development in the occupied Pal-

estinian territories. A regional seminar was held on total quality management based on International Organization for Standardization (ISO) requirements. The Second Arab Conference and Expo for Electronics, Software and Communications Industries in the Arab Countries was organized in cooperation with the Arab Industrial Development and Mining Organization, UNIDO and other agencies.

In the area of science and technology, expert group meetings were held on revitalization of research and development activities in ESCWA countries and on techno-economic aspects of the commercial application of new materials technologies, and related studies on those subjects were issued.

## Natural resources, energy and environment

### Water resources

In the area of water resources, the secretariat published an assessment of water quality in the ESCWA region, organized a training course on using remote-sensing techniques in hydrology, and undertook studies of shared basalt aquifers in Jordan and the Syrian Arab Republic and on the introduction of appropriate mechanisms to promote regional cooperation in the water sector. Expert group meetings reviewed regional activities for integrated water management in implementation of relevant provisions of Agenda 21,[8] and provided recommendations for the establishment of a regional training network in the water sector.

In 1995, the Commission decided to establish a committee on water resources and recommended a resolution[9] for adoption by the Economic and Social Council.

**ECONOMIC AND SOCIAL COUNCIL ACTION**

On 24 July, the Council adopted **resolution 1995/26**.

**Establishment of a committee on water resources within the Economic and Social Commission for Western Asia**

*The Economic and Social Council,*

*Conscious* of the importance of water security in view of the scarcity of water resources in the States members of the Economic and Social Commission for Western Asia,

*Conscious also* of the importance of developing the water resources of those States and rationalizing their use,

*Taking into account* the need to monitor scientific and technological developments in the use of both traditional and non-traditional water sources,

*Also taking into account* the importance of the participation of the competent authorities of the States members of the Commission in the planning, development and monitoring of the programmes of the secretariat of the Commission in the field of water resources,

1. *Decides* to establish, within existing resources, a Committee on Water Resources within the Economic and Social Commission for Western Asia, made up of

representatives of States members of the Commission who are specialists in the field of water resources, which will undertake the following tasks:

(*a*) Participation in the establishment and formulation of priorities for the programme of work and medium-term plan in the field of water resources;

(*b*) Monitoring of developments in the field of water resources in the States members of the Commission;

(*c*) Monitoring of the progress achieved in the activities of the secretariat of the Commission in the field of water resources;

(*d*) Follow-up of international and regional conferences, participation of member States in them and coordination of regional efforts relating to the implementation of resolutions and recommendations;

2. *Also decides* that the Committee on Water Resources will hold its meetings every two years, starting in 1996;

3. *Requests* the Executive Secretary of the Economic and Social Commission for Western Asia to follow up the implementation of the present resolution and report thereon to the Commission at its nineteenth session.

Economic and Social Council resolution 1995/26

24 July 1995      Meeting 50      Adopted without vote

Draft by ESCWA (E/1995/40), orally amended by United States; agenda item 7.
*Meeting numbers.* ESC 45, 46, 50.

## Energy

The secretariat continued to issue its annual *ESCWA Energy Bulletin* and prepared a compilation of energy information and a study of recent projects on the development of oil and natural gas in Jordan and Yemen.

In May, the Commission decided to establish a committee on energy and recommended a resolution[10] for adoption by the Economic and Social Council.

**ECONOMIC AND SOCIAL COUNCIL ACTION**

On 24 July, the Council adopted **resolution 1995/25**.

**Establishment of a committee on energy within the Economic and Social Commission for Western Asia**

*The Economic and Social Council,*

*Aware* that petroleum and gas are not the only energy resources available in States members of the Economic and Social Commission for Western Asia, but that renewable sources of energy are also available, and aware also that close regional cooperation is needed to strengthen the capabilities of those States for developing the use of renewable sources of energy,

*Aware* of the importance of coordinating activities in the field of energy with efforts to protect the environment in States members of the Commission, as well as the importance of related issues pertaining to the development, transport and use of energy sources, the rationalization of their use and the impact of their use on the environment and on the sustainable development of those States,

*Conscious* of the importance of the participation of the competent authorities of the States members of the Com-

mission in the planning and development of the programmes of the secretariat of the Commission in the field of energy and in monitoring their implementation,

*Inspired* by the steps taken by other regional commissions for the establishment of specialized committees on various energy areas to ensure the coordination of action at the regional level,

1. *Decides* to establish, within existing resources, a Committee on Energy within the Economic and Social Commission for Western Asia, made up of representatives of the States members of the Commission who are specialists in the field of energy, which will undertake the following tasks:

(*a*) Participation in the establishment and formulation of priorities for the programme of work and medium-term plan in the field of energy;

(*b*) Monitoring of developments in the field of energy in the States members of the Commission;

(*c*) Monitoring of the progress achieved in the activities of the secretariat of the Commission in the field of energy;

(*d*) Follow-up of international and regional conferences, participation of member States in them and coordination of regional efforts relating to the implementation of resolutions and recommendations;

2. *Also decides* that the Committee on Energy will hold its meetings every two years, starting in 1996;

3. *Requests* the Executive Secretary of the Economic and Social Commission for Western Asia to follow up the implementation of the present resolution and report thereon to the Commission at its nineteenth session.

Economic and Social Council resolution 1995/25

24 July 1995      Meeting 50      Adopted without vote

Draft by ESCWA (E/1995/40), orally amended by United States; agenda item 7.
*Meeting numbers.* ESC 45, 46, 50.

## Environment

Activities in the area of environment were geared towards regional implementation of Agenda 21[8] within the framework of the Joint Committee on Environment and Development in the Arab World, established in 1993,[11] and the Arab Programme of Action for Sustainable Development, adopted in 1992 by the Council of Arab Ministers Responsible for Environment. Work focused on implementing 1994 Joint Committee recommendations[12] aimed at building an environmental information system for policy makers in the region, convening an expert meeting on biological diversity, and creating a regional mechanism to monitor and deal with illegal traffic in hazardous wastes. Other activities included those on: combating desertification and increasing the green area in the region; improving environmental education, awareness and information; and reducing industrial pollution. A workshop on popular participation in environmental protection programmes was held (Tunis, Tunisia, 10-13 January) to review the role of the family, women and children in that respect and to consider practical ways of protecting the environment in the Arab world.

## Transport and communications

The ESCWA work programme for transport was linked to activities under the second phase (1992-1996) of the Transport and Communications Decade for Asia and the Pacific (see above, under "Asia and the Pacific"). An expert group meeting was held on development of a multimodal transport chain in the ESCWA region, which formulated a regional strategy for multimodal transport development. A study was conducted on upgrading the performance level and the quality of services in transport and port management in Egypt, a port pricing model for the region was prepared and the *Transport Bulletin* was published.

## Social development, population and human settlements

The secretariat continued to monitor progress in social programmes of member States and took steps to implement a 1994 Economic and Social Council resolution[13] establishing a committee on social development within ESCWA, and to define national focal points for coordination of various social activities. ESCWA countries were assisted in preparations for the World Summit for Social Development (Denmark, March) (see PART FOUR, Chapter IX); publications were issued on human development and its socio-cultural specificity in the Arab world and on social dimensions of human development; and studies prepared on a social perspective of poverty in Western Asia and the impact of macroeconomic and social policies on poverty in Egypt, Jordan and Yemen. ESCWA was also formulating a follow-up to the recommendations of the expert group meeting on the Arab family, held in 1994.[12]

Population activities were linked to implementation of the Programme of Action adopted by the International Conference on Population and Development in 1994.[14] A regional expert group meeting on population estimates and projections was organized (Cairo, 10-14 June), and biennial demographic and related socio-economic indicators were published. The annual *Population Bulletin* was issued.

In preparation for the second UN Conference on Human Settlements (Habitat II), to be held in Turkey in 1996 (see PART FOUR, Chapter VIII), a regional expert group meeting was convened (Amman, 23-26 January) to review urbanization trends and the housing situation in the Arab world; assess policies relating to sustainable development of human settlements; draft a general outline for national reports to be presented at the Conference; and discuss a regional contribution to Habitat II. Recommendations were formulated concerning the form and content of a draft Arab Declaration on Sustainable Development for Human Settlements. The Declaration, subsequently approved by the third Arab Preparatory Meeting for Habitat II (Rabat, Morocco, 25-30 September) and adopted by the Council of Arab Ministers of Housing and Reconstruction at its thirteenth session (Cairo, 13-14 November), confirmed that adequate housing was a fundamental right and requirement. It included commitments aimed at ensuring, *inter alia*, balanced urban-rural development and infrastructure development, popular participation in housing policy formulation, optimum land utilization, the strengthening of the role of the media and local authorities as well as of women and youth, shelter provision to all population categories, appropriate housing finance mechanisms, establishment of real estate systems, development of adequate construction technologies, capacity-building for human settlements management, promotion of community-based efforts for poverty alleviation, rational energy consumption, incorporation of environmental considerations into urbanization projects, reconstruction and development of settlements damaged by conflicts, and preservation of the architectural heritage and historical sites.

A case study was made of technological and social aspects of upgrading and revitalizing settlements, and a report prepared on technical assistance activities to improve the quality of life in human settlements.

## Role of women

Activities in the area of women and development included a study on the situation of disabled women, including their marginalization and measures for social integration in the ESCWA region, and a compilation of statistical data on Arab women. As part of final preparations for the Fourth World Conference on Women (Beijing, September) (see PART FOUR, Chapter X), a regional workshop was organized for Arab official delegations to the Conference. ESCWA participated in national workshops held in Kuwait and in Lebanon as a follow-up to the Conference.

## Statistics

The ESCWA Statistical Committee, established in accordance with a 1993 Economic and Social Council resolution,[15] held its first session in 1995 (Amman, 6-9 November).[16] The Committee discussed and recommended for adoption 10 fundamental principles of official statistics; assessed regional activities and global developments in the area of statistics; considered progress made in 1994-1995, a work programme for 1996-1997 and the ESCWA subprogramme on statistics within the medium-term plan for 1998-2001; examined technical cooperation in statistics, a national household survey capability programme and gender statistics in the Arab countries; and reviewed matters relating to international statistical programmes, including the 1993 System of National Accounts, the International Comparison Programme and a programme for vital statistics and civil registration systems (see PART FOUR, Chapter XV). The Committee adopted recommendations concerning each of those areas.

During the year, ESCWA continued to publish its annual *Statistical Abstract of the ESCWA Region* and *National Account Studies of the ESCWA Region* and its biennial *Prices and Financial Statistics in the ESCWA Region*. It also produced a second issue of the bulletin of industrial statistics for the Arab countries, and organized workshops on computer processing of statistical data, the International Comparison Programme, and uses of geographic information systems in statistics.

## Programme and organizational questions

At its 1995 session, the Commission approved[17] its programme of work and priorities for 1996-1997.[18] It noted that the programme had incorporated changes proposed by member States and reflected an integrated approach to Commission activities, based on its five thematic subprogrammes (see above, under "Activities in 1995"). The programme also included proposals concerning technical cooperation activities.

The Commission, having considered a report[19] on the meeting (Amman, 3 May) of the Advisory Committee established pursuant to a 1989 ESCWA resolution,[20] amended[21] paragraph 1 *(a)* of that resolution to read: "To invite member States to set up an advisory body comprising the heads of their diplomatic missions in the host country, or such persons as may be delegated by their Governments and a representative of the host country, to assist the Executive Secretary in the study of problems connected with the work of the Commission."

The Technical Committee, at its ninth session, noted the text of the Executive Secretary's note[22] on the financial status of ESCWA programmes, which provided information on activities financed under the regular UN budget, from extra-budgetary resources, and from the Trust Fund for ESCWA Regional Activities.

## Permanent headquarters

The Commission had before it a report[23] of the Executive Secretary on follow-up action concerning relocation of ESCWA to its permanent headquarters in Beirut, in accordance with a 1994 Economic and Social Council resolution.[24] The report described arrangements with regard to the permanent headquarters building and to the previous headquarters building in Baghdad, Iraq. The Commission called[25] on member States to take measures in support of the Secretary-General's efforts to secure the necessary resources for ESCWA's relocation.

*REFERENCES*

[1]YUN 1994, p. 753, ESC res. 1994/26, 26 July 1994. [2]E/1995/84. [3]E/ESCWA/18/4. [4]E/1996/50. [5]YUN 1994, p. 868. [6]Ibid., p. 753. [7]E/ESCWA/C.1/18/8. [8]YUN 1992, p. 672. [9]E/1995/84 (res. 205(XVIII)). [10]Ibid. (res. 204(XVIII)). [11]YUN 1993, p. 650. [12]YUN 1994, p. 751. [13]Ibid., p. 752, ESC res. 1994/27, 26 July 1994. [14]Ibid., p. 956. [15]YUN 1993, p. 652, ESC res. 1993/2, 2 Feb. 1993. [16]E/ESCWA/STAT/1995/IG.1/16. [17]E/1995/84 (res. 206(XVIII)). [18]E/ESCWA/C.1/18/9 & Corr.1. [19]E/ESCWA/18/6. [20]E/1989/36 (res. 175(XV)). [21]E/1995/84 (res. 208 (XVIII)). [22]E/ESCWA/C.1/18/10 & Corr.1. [23]E/ESCWA/C.1/18/5/Add.1. [24]YUN 1994, p. 753, ESC res. 1994/43, 29 July 1994. [25]E/1995/84 (res. 207(XVIII)).

Chapter VI

# Natural resources and energy

The use and conservation of natural resources and energy were considered by a number of United Nations bodies in 1995, with the environmental aspects of increased exploitation receiving particular attention. The Committee on New and Renewable Sources of Energy and on Energy for Development held a special session in February and adopted a series of recommendations for sustainable energy in the rural areas of developing countries.

Having considered a report by the Secretary-General on progress made in providing safe water supply and sanitation for all during the first half of the 1990s, the General Assembly and the Economic and Social Council called on Governments to develop and implement, in the context of a national sustainable development strategy, measures for drinking water supply and sanitation. Organizations of the UN system were called on to intensify their financing and technical support efforts for developing countries and countries in transition in that regard.

In his annual address to the Assembly, the Director General of the International Atomic Energy Agency observed that nuclear power could provide part of the solution to the problem of providing sufficient energy for developing countries without increased emissions of carbon dioxide, sulphur dioxide or nitrogen oxides. The main obstacle to increased use was public concern with safety, radioactive waste and non-proliferation.

## Natural resources

### Exploration

The United Nations Revolving Fund for Natural Resources Exploration (UNRFNRE) was undergoing revitalization in 1995 with support from the Government of Japan, said the Administrator of the United Nations Development Programme in his annual report covering 1995.[1] Proposals for the Fund's revitalization included that it should: maintain its unique characteristic—the replenishment feature—which embodied the concept of self-reliance and enabled the Fund to take a cost/benefit approach; have a catalytic role in teaming developing country Governments with mining companies from around the world for mining activities in harmony with environmental protection; focus on deposits appropriate for small-scale mining among the less stable developing countries; establish close collaboration within the UN system, as well as with external organizations that could provide support; and diversify the Fund's activities to include information services, through mining forums, round-table conferences and other mechanisms.

In 1995, two projects were operational and the project pipeline was structured to reach a level of five operational projects by 1998. At the same time, UNRFNRE was streamlining its activities so that strategic interventions in areas of poverty eradication, job generation and environmental protection would be made.

Following the discovery in 1993[2] of a gold deposit in the United Republic of Tanzania worth some $400 million, UNRFNRE assisted the Government in an international bidding exercise for discoveries made by the Fund. Of 40 mining companies that expressed interest in the project, 3 were selected to bring the discoveries to the feasibility and production stage. A successful placer-gold project in Peru was sold to a Brazilian company for $5 million, with start-up estimated to begin in 1998.

### Technical cooperation

In his report covering UN technical cooperation activities in 1995,[3] the Secretary-General observed that artisanal mining was an economic mainstay of many rural communities in developing countries, providing income for local economic and social development. Many developing countries and economies in transition were interested in formalizing artisanal mining into legal, small-scale mining so as to maximize revenue and minimize environmental degradation. The Department for Development Support and Management Services (DDSMS) was acting as a catalyst in several such national efforts, through activities emphasizing legislative approaches and community mobilization.

### Water resources

#### Water supply and sanitation

In response to a 1990 General Assembly request,[4] the Secretary-General submitted a report,[5] through the Economic and Social Council, on progress made in providing safe water supply and sanitation for all during the first half of the 1990s. The report provided information on the water supply and sanitation service coverage situation from 1990 to 1994 in Africa, Asia and the Pacific, Latin America and the Caribbean, and Western Asia, and on the level of services that would be achieved by the year 2000, should the 1990-1994 trend in service delivery continue. It was noted that, in 1994, some 1.11 billion people lacked access to safe water and 2.87 billion lacked access to sanitation. An additional 783 million people were provided with access to safe water during the four-year period and the total number of people without clean water decreased by 472 million. It appeared that the annual rates of increase in water supply over the four years constituted an acceleration of the pace witnessed during the previous decade.

The challenge of providing full water supply and sanitation coverage to the urban areas of developing countries remained daunting, especially because of high rates of population growth and urbanization. The neglect of urban sanitation was particularly critical in Africa, where only an additional 1 million people were reported to have gained access to safe sanitation. The ranks of those without such services swelled by as many as 36 million. In all four developing regions, the proportion of people with access to safe sanitation remained considerably lower than in the case of water supply.

Progress with regard to the provision of clean water to rural areas was significant. About 611 million people were added to the ranks of those having access to safe water; the number without services decreased by 504 million. By contrast, rural sanitation was totally neglected. With the exception of Western Asia, the levels of sanitation services to rural areas remained dismally low. Africa reported some progress, having increased by 23 million the number of people with access. Nevertheless, those without services increased by 23 million. No gains were made in Latin America; an apparent decrease in coverage for Asia and the Pacific was due to a reported drastic change in criteria in the larger countries of the region.

Despite calls to action dating back to the Mar del Plata Action Plan, adopted by the UN Water Conference in 1977,[6] the situation concerning urban water supply and sanitation had steadily deteriorated. It was particularly alarming with regard to neglect of sanitation and inadequate attention to pollution from urban waste. The problem of providing services to rural areas was closely linked to the fact that these accounted for a large proportion of people living at or below the level of absolute poverty.

The report concluded that no real solution to the problem of water supply and sanitation would be at hand without significant infusions of funding. In the case of urban water supply, the problem was compounded by the need for considerable additional capital investments in infrastructure and increasing costs in the light of a growing demand for water from rapidly expanding cities. The 1994 Ministerial Conference on Drinking Water Supply and Environmental Sanitation[7] had stressed the need for a partnership approach to water resources development in general, and drinking water supply and environmental sanitation in particular. It had recommended that Governments develop detailed guidelines for investments in order to rationalize resource generation and use. With regard to issues requiring the attention of the international community, it was clear that priority needed to be given to the African region. Urgent attention was equally required to achieve significant progress with regard to sanitation in urban and rural areas, with special attention given to problems confronting large and rapidly growing urban concentrations.

ECONOMIC AND SOCIAL COUNCIL ACTION

On 27 July, the Economic and Social Council adopted **resolution 1995/46**.

### Water supply and sanitation

*The Economic and Social Council*

*Recommends* to the General Assembly the adoption of the following draft resolution:

*The General Assembly,*

*Recalling* its resolution 35/18 of 10 November 1980, by which it proclaimed the period 1981-1990 as the International Drinking Water Supply and Sanitation Decade,

*Recalling also* its resolution 45/181 of 21 December 1990, in which it expressed its deep concern about the slow rate of progress in the provision of services in water and sanitation,

*Bearing in mind* that the Second United Nations Conference on the Least Developed Countries, held in Paris from 3 to 14 September 1990, the World Summit for Children, held in New York on 29 and 30 September 1990, the Global Strategy for Shelter to the Year 2000 and the United Nations Conference on Environment and Development, held at Rio de Janeiro from 3 to 14 June 1992, reiterated the need to provide, on a sustainable basis, access to safe water in sufficient quantities and proper sanitation for all,

*Deeply concerned* that at the current rate of progress the provision of drinking water will be insufficient to satisfy the needs of a very large number of people by the year 2000 and that the lack of progress in the provision of basic sanitation services is likely to have dramatic environmental and health consequences in the near future,

1. *Takes note with appreciation* of the report of the Secretary-General on progress made in providing safe water supply and sanitation for all during the first half of the 1990s;

2. *Takes note* of the programme strategies in water and environmental sanitation adopted by the Executive

Board of the United Nations Children's Fund at its annual session for 1995[a] and of resolution AFR/RC 43/R2 of the Regional Committee for Africa of the World Health Organization, in which the Committee endorsed the Africa 2000 initiative for water supply and sanitation in Africa;

3. *Calls upon* Governments to implement fully the provisions concerning water resources in general and water supply and sanitation in particular contained in chapter 18 of Agenda 21, and the recommendations made by the Commission on Sustainable Development at its second and third sessions, including the recommendations for action contained in the Action Programme of the Ministerial Conference on Drinking Water and Environmental Sanitation convened by the Government of the Netherlands on 22 and 23 March 1994, in particular:

*(a)* To develop, review or revise by 1997 and implement, in the context of a national sustainable development strategy consistent with Agenda 21, measures for drinking water supply and environmental sanitation, taking into account the goals set by the World Summit for Children;

*(b)* To undertake, as appropriate, legal, regulatory and institutional reforms designed to bring about the management of water resources at the lowest appropriate level, including stake-holder participation and the involvement of the private sector, and to adopt strategies for capacity-building;

*(c)* To assign high priority to programmes designed to provide basic sanitation and excreta disposal systems to urban and rural areas and to the treatment of waste waters, with provisions for community involvement;

*(d)* To formulate and implement investment strategies and cost recovery policies aimed at generating a flow of financial resources commensurate with needs, taking into account the needs and conditions of the peri-urban and rural poor;

*(e)* To establish or strengthen a nationwide water and sanitation monitoring system, making full use, as appropriate, of the information support system developed by the Joint Monitoring Programme of the World Health Organization and the United Nations Children's Fund;

4. *Calls upon* the organizations of the United Nations system and other relevant organizations to intensify their efforts concerning financial and technical support for developing countries and countries with economies in transition;

5. *Urges* donor Governments, multilateral financial and development institutions and non-governmental organizations to give favourable and appropriate consideration to requests for grants and concessional financing, particularly with regard to environmental sanitation and sewerage and to waste-water treatment projects, which are intended to implement programmes consistent with the provisions and recommendations referred to in paragraph 3 of the present resolution;

6. *Decides* to review at its fifty-fifth session the situation at the end of the 1990s and requests the Secretary-General to submit a report to it, through the Commission on Sustainable Development and the Economic and Social Council, containing an assessment of the water supply and sanitation situation in developing countries, including proposals for action for the ensuing decade at the national and international levels.

Economic and Social Council resolution 1995/46

27 July 1995      Meeting 56      Adopted without vote

Draft by Philippines, for Group of 77 and China (E/1995/L.36), orally revised following informal consultations; agenda item 6 *(m)*.
Meeting numbers. ESC 42-44, 50, 56.

On 19 July, the Council, by **decision 1995/234**, took note of the Secretary-General's report.

### Inter-agency coordination

The Subcommittee on Water Resources of the Administrative Committee on Coordination held its sixteenth session in New York from 4 to 6 October.[8] It was preceded by the Inter-Agency Steering Committee for Water Supply and Sanitation (2-3 October). Issues discussed included measures to strengthen coordination, a comprehensive assessment of the freshwater resources of the world, water resources management in Africa, public information with particular reference to the World Day for Water (22 March), and facilitation of information flows concerning programmes and activities of the UN system and non-governmental organizations.

**GENERAL ASSEMBLY ACTION**

On 20 December, the General Assembly adopted **resolution 50/126**.

### Water supply and sanitation

*The General Assembly,*

*Recalling* its resolution 35/18 of 10 November 1980, by which it proclaimed the period 1981-1990 as the International Drinking Water Supply and Sanitation Decade,

*Recalling also* its resolution 45/181 of 21 December 1990, in which it expressed its deep concern about the slow rate of progress in the provision of services in water and sanitation,

*Recalling further* its resolution 47/193 of 22 December 1992, in which it declared 22 March of each year World Day for Water,

*Bearing in mind* that the Second United Nations Conference on the Least Developed Countries, held in Paris from 3 to 14 September 1990, the World Summit for Children, held in New York on 29 and 30 September 1990, the Global Strategy for Shelter to the Year 2000 and the United Nations Conference on Environment and Development, held at Rio de Janeiro from 3 to 14 June 1992, reiterated the need to provide, on a sustainable basis, access to safe water in sufficient quantities and proper sanitation for all,

*Deeply concerned* that at the current rate of progress the provision of drinking water will be insufficient to satisfy the needs of a very large number of people by the year 2000 and that the lack of progress in the provision of basic sanitation services is likely to have dramatic environmental and health consequences in the near future,

---

[a]E/1995/33/Rev.1 (dec. 1995/22).

1. *Takes note with appreciation* of the report of the Secretary-General on progress made in providing safe water supply and sanitation for all during the first half of the 1990s;

2. *Takes note* of the programme strategies in water and environmental sanitation adopted by the Executive Board of the United Nations Children's Fund at its annual session for 1995[a] and of resolution AFR/RC 43/R2 of the Regional Committee for Africa of the World Health Organization, in which the Committee endorsed the Africa 2000 initiative for water supply and sanitation in Africa;

3. *Calls upon* Governments to implement fully the provisions concerning water resources in general and water supply and sanitation in particular contained in chapter 18 of Agenda 21, and the recommendations made by the Commission on Sustainable Development at its second and third sessions, including the recommendations for action contained in the Action Programme of the Ministerial Conference on Drinking Water and Environmental Sanitation convened by the Government of the Netherlands on 22 and 23 March 1994, in particular:

(*a*) To develop, review or revise by 1997 and implement, in the context of a national sustainable development strategy consistent with Agenda 21, measures for drinking water supply and environmental sanitation, taking into account the goals set by the World Summit for Children;

(*b*) To undertake, as appropriate, legal, regulatory and institutional reforms designed to bring about the management of water resources at the lowest appropriate level, including stakeholder participation and the involvement of the private sector, and to adopt strategies for capacity-building;

(*c*) To assign high priority to programmes designed to provide basic sanitation and excreta disposal systems to urban and rural areas and to the treatment of waste waters, with provisions for community involvement;

(*d*) To formulate and implement investment strategies and cost-recovery policies aimed at generating a flow of financial resources commensurate with needs, taking into account the needs and conditions of the peri-urban and rural poor;

(*e*) To establish or strengthen a nationwide water and sanitation monitoring system, making full use, as appropriate, of the information support system developed by the Joint Monitoring Programme For the Water and Sanitation Sector of the World Health Organization and the United Nations Children's Fund;

4. *Calls upon* the organizations of the United Nations system and other relevant organizations to intensify their efforts concerning financial and technical support for developing countries and countries with economies in transition;

5. *Urges* donor Governments, multilateral financial and development institutions and non-governmental organizations to give favourable and appropriate consideration to requests for grants and concessional financing, particularly with regard to environmental sanitation and sewerage and to waste-water treatment projects, which are intended to implement programmes consistent with the provisions and recommendations referred to in paragraph 3 of the present resolution;

6. *Decides* to review at its fifty-fifth session the situation at the end of the 1990s and requests the Secretary-

General to submit a report to it, through the Commission on Sustainable Development and the Economic and Social Council, containing an assessment of the water supply and sanitation situation in developing countries, including proposals for action for the ensuing decade at the national and international levels.

---

[a]E/1995/33/Rev.1 (dec. 1995/22).

General Assembly resolution 50/126

20 December 1995     Meeting 96     Adopted without vote

Approved by Second Committee (A/50/615/Add.1) without vote, 30 November (meeting 40); draft recommended by ESC in res. 1995/46 (A/C.2/50/L.3), orally amended following informal consultations; agenda item 12.
*Meeting numbers.* GA 50th session: 2nd Committee 15, 16, 40; plenary 96.

### Technical cooperation activities

Through DDSMS, the United Nations carried out water resource planning and management projects—from simple provision of rural water supply and training of technicians to complex interventions involving models, computer software packages, capacity-building and community empowerment.[3] In several West African countries, work was focusing on the participation of all basin stakeholders in decision-making and the introduction of new regulatory principles. For capacity-building in water resource organizations, DDSMS assisted in training national multidisciplinary teams and using advanced tools for integrated water resources management. It helped to establish networks for assessing water supply and demand, which provided essential inputs to planners formulating strategies for water and land use, protection and conservation, and for making decisions on water allocations. Examples were the establishment of computer-based economic planning models in China and the Sudan, incorporating geographical information systems databases with water resource allocation techniques that reflected social, environmental and economic criteria.

*REFERENCES*

[1]DP/1996/18/Add.1. [2]YUN 1993, p. 782. [3]DP/1996/8. [4]GA res. 45/181, 21 Dec. 1990. [5]A/50/213-E/1995/87. [6]YUN 1977, p. 555. [7]YUN 1994, p. 920. [8]ACC/1995/22.

# Energy

## Committee on New and Renewable Sources of Energy and on Energy for Development

In accordance with a 1994 Economic and Social Council decision,[1] the Committee on New and Renewable Sources of Energy and on Energy for Development held a special session in New York from 6 to 17 February.[2] As decided by the Council in 1994,[3] the Committee discussed the issues of energy for rural development, biomass for energy and energy coordination.

In recommendations to the Commission on Sustainable Development, to be taken into account during its consideration of the implementation of Agenda 21, adopted by the 1992 Conference on Environment and Development[(4)] (see PART FOUR, Chapter I), the Committee noted that adequate energy inputs were required to raise standards of living and the productivity of human labour and for income-generation in rural areas in developing countries. To that end, rural energy policies and technologies should promote a mix of cost-effective options to improve the efficiency of energy consumption and the utilization of fossil and renewable energy sources. With regard to energy for rural development, the Committee described the major problems of rural development, the importance of energy in solving those problems, the existing status and recent trends in rural energy conversion, and the present and future patterns of energy services in rural areas. In its consideration of energy options, the Committee discussed energy and material efficiency, renewable energy technologies (photovoltaic systems, solar thermal energy conversion, wind energy, biomass energy, hydropower), fossil fuels and system aspects.

The strategy recommended by the Committee for sustainable rural energy development included the establishment of national sustainable energy action programmes for agriculture and rural development, priority-setting, capacity-building, new directions in management and institutional arrangements, new financial and investment arrangements, accelerated development and implementation of new technologies, new international actions for rural energy development and strengthening sustainable energy activities within the UN system.

By **decision 1995/240** of 19 July, the Council took note of the Committee's report and approved the revised provisional agenda for its second (1996) session.

By **decision 1995/234** of 19 July, the Council took note of an oral report by the Director of the Division for Sustainable Development on the format in which the Committee on Natural Resources and the Committee on New and Renewable Sources of Energy and on Energy for Development should present their work.

## Nuclear energy

On 21 August,[(5)] the Secretary-General transmitted the 1994 report of the International Atomic Energy Agency (IAEA) to the General Assembly. Presenting and updating the report in the Assembly on 1 November, the IAEA Director General addressed the issues of nuclear non-proliferation, the possibility of a comprehensive nuclear test-ban treaty, the IAEA nuclear safeguards system and verification of States' compliance with nuclear-arms-control pledges, including inspection missions in Iraq and verification activities in the Democratic People's Republic of Korea (see PART TWO, Chapter IV), nuclear-weapon-free zones, nuclear safety and waste disposal, and illicit trafficking in nuclear materials.

The Director General stated that a great challenge facing the international community was to find the proper means of providing sufficient energy for sustainable development—energy without unacceptable damage to the environment. The Agency was cooperating with several international organizations in drawing up methodologies and databases for a comparative assessment of different options for producing electric power. Solar power, wind power, biomass and other renewable forms of energy would bring a valuable but minor contribution to the global energy supply, but it was evident that developing countries would need energy in much greater amounts. Expansion of nuclear power, which was providing about 8 per cent of the world's energy and 17 per cent of its electricity, could provide a part of the solution on the supply side without increasing emissions of carbon dioxide, sulphur dioxide or nitrogen oxides. The main obstacle to increased use was public concern with safety, radioactive waste and non-proliferation. Few developing countries had the technological level and infrastructure to allow them to make use of the existing types of nuclear power reactors. It was to be hoped that smaller and less costly nuclear reactors would become available in the future for generating electricity and also for the desalination of water to compensate for scarce freshwater resources. It was obvious that the increasing number of cities with more than a million, even more than 10 million, inhabitants in developing countries could not be provided with electricity generated by solar cells, windmills or biomass, for example. Their real choice for decades to come would be between fossil fuels and nuclear power.

**GENERAL ASSEMBLY ACTION**

On 1 November, the General Assembly adopted **resolution 50/9**.

**Report of the International Atomic Energy Agency**

*The General Assembly,*

*Having received* the report of the International Atomic Energy Agency to the General Assembly for the year 1994,

*Noting* the statement of the Director General of the International Atomic Energy Agency of 1 November 1995, in which he provided additional information on the main developments in the activities of the Agency during 1995,

_Reaffirming_ that the Agency is the competent authority responsible for verifying and assuring, in accordance with the statute of the Agency and the Agency's safeguards system, compliance with its safeguards agreements with States parties undertaken in fulfilment of their obligations under article III, paragraph 1, of the Treaty on the Non-Proliferation of Nuclear Weapons, with a view to preventing diversion of nuclear energy from peaceful uses to nuclear weapons or other nuclear explosive devices, and also reaffirming that nothing should be done to undermine the authority of the Agency in this regard and that States parties that have concerns regarding non-compliance with the safeguards agreement of the Treaty by the States parties should direct such concerns, along with supporting evidence and information, to the Agency to consider, investigate, draw conclusions and decide on necessary actions in accordance with its mandate,

_Recognizing_ the importance of the work of the Agency in promoting the further application of nuclear energy for peaceful purposes, as envisaged in its statute and in accordance with the inalienable right of States parties to the Treaty on the Non-Proliferation of Nuclear Weapons and other relevant internationally legally binding agreements that have concluded relevant safeguards agreements with the Agency to develop research, production and use of nuclear energy for peaceful purposes without discrimination and in conformity with articles I and II of the Treaty, with other relevant articles and with the objectives and purposes of the Treaty,

_Also recognizing_ the special needs of the developing countries for technical assistance from the Agency and the importance of funding in order to benefit effectively from the transfer and application of nuclear technology for peaceful purposes as well as from the contribution of nuclear energy to their economic development,

_Conscious_ of the importance of the work of the Agency in the implementation of the safeguards provisions of the Treaty on the Non-Proliferation of Nuclear Weapons and other international treaties, conventions and agreements designed to achieve similar objectives, as well as in ensuring, as far as it is able, that the assistance provided by the Agency or at its request or under its supervision or control is not used in such a way as to further any military purpose, as stated in article II of its statute,

_Further recognizing_ the importance of the work of the Agency on nuclear power, applications of nuclear methods and techniques, nuclear safety, radiological protection and radioactive waste management, including its work directed towards assisting developing countries in all these fields,

_Again stressing_ the need for the highest standards of safety in the design and operation of nuclear installations so as to minimize risks to life, health and the environment,

_Taking note_ of the report of the Director General to the General Conference on the developments which took place in August 1995 related to Iraq's nuclear-weapons programme and of resolution GC(39)/RES/5 of 22 September 1995 of the General Conference,

_Taking note also_ of resolutions GOV/2711 of 21 March 1994 and GOV/2742 of 10 June 1994 of the Board of Governors and GC(39)/RES/3 of 22 September 1995 of the General Conference in connection with the implementation of the Agreement between the Government

of the Democratic People's Republic of Korea and the International Atomic Energy Agency for the application of safeguards in connection with the Treaty on the Non-Proliferation of Nuclear Weapons, the statements by the President of the Security Council of 31 March, 30 May and 4 November 1994, and the authorization by the Board of Governors, on 11 November 1994, to the Director General to carry out all the tasks requested of the Agency in the statement by the President of the Security Council of 4 November 1994,

_Bearing in mind_ resolutions GC(39)/RES/14 on the strengthening of the Agency's technical cooperation activities, GC(39)/RES/15 on a plan for producing potable water economically, GC(39)/RES/16 on extensive use of isotope hydrology for water resources management, GC(39)/RES/17 on strengthening the effectiveness and improving the efficiency of the safeguards system, GC(39)/RES/18 on measures against the illicit trafficking in nuclear materials, GC(39)/RES/4 on a nuclear-weapon-free zone in Africa, GC(39)/RES/5 on the implementation of Security Council resolutions 687(1991), 707(1991) and 715(1991) relating to Iraq, GC(39)/RES/24 on application of Agency safeguards in the Middle East, GC(39)/RES/21 and GC(39)/RES/22 on the amendment of article VI of the statute relating to the membership of the Board of Governors, GC(39)/RES/13 on the Convention on Nuclear Safety, GC(39)/RES/19 on the staffing of the Agency's secretariat and GC(39)/RES/23 on nuclear testing, adopted on 22 September 1995 by the General Conference of the Agency at its thirty-ninth regular session,

_Also bearing in mind_ resolution GC(39)/RES/20 on women in the secretariat adopted on 22 September 1995 by the General Conference, calling upon the Director General to examine the Platform for Action developed at the Fourth World Conference on Women and to integrate, where applicable, the elements of this Platform into the Agency's relevant policies and programmes,

1. _Takes note_ of the report of the International Atomic Energy Agency;

2. _Affirms its confidence_ in the role of the Agency in the application of nuclear energy for peaceful purposes;

3. _Welcomes_ the measures and decisions taken by the Agency to maintain and strengthen the effectiveness and cost efficiency of the safeguards system in conformity with the Agency's statute, and calls upon States to cooperate in implementing the decisions taken by the Agency to that end;

4. _Urges_ all States to strive for effective and harmonious international cooperation in carrying out the work of the Agency, pursuant to its statute; in promoting the use of nuclear energy and the application of the necessary measures to strengthen further the safety of nuclear installations and to minimize risks to life, health and the environment; in strengthening technical assistance and cooperation for developing countries; and in ensuring the effectiveness and efficiency of the safeguards system of the Agency;

5. _Welcomes also_ the measures and decisions taken by the Agency to strengthen and fund its technical cooperation activities, and calls upon States to cooperate in implementing the measures and decisions pursuant thereto;

6. _Commends_ the Director General and the secretariat of the Agency for their continuing impartial efforts to implement the safeguards agreement in force between

the Agency and the Democratic People's Republic of Korea, including their efforts to monitor the freeze of specified facilities in the Democratic People's Republic of Korea as requested by the Security Council, expresses concern over the continuing non-compliance of the Democratic People's Republic of Korea with the safeguards agreement, and urges the Democratic People's Republic of Korea to cooperate fully with the Agency in the implementation of the safeguards agreement and to take all steps the Agency may deem necessary to preserve, intact, all information relevant to verifying the accuracy and completeness of the initial report of the Democratic People's Republic of Korea on the inventory of nuclear material subject to safeguards until the Democratic People's Republic of Korea comes into full compliance with its safeguards agreement;

7. *Also commends* the Director General of the Agency and his staff for their strenuous efforts in the implementation of Security Council resolutions 687(1991) of 3 April, 707(1991) of 15 August and 715(1991) of 11 October 1991, expresses deep concern that Iraq has, since 1991, withheld from the Agency information about its nuclear-weapons programme in violation of its obligations under resolutions 687(1991), 707(1991) and 715 (1991), and stresses the need for Iraq to cooperate fully with the Agency in achieving the complete implementation of the relevant Security Council resolutions;

8. *Appeals* to all States to ratify or accede to the Convention on Nuclear Safety;

9. *Welcomes* the measures taken by the Agency in support of efforts to prevent illicit trafficking in nuclear materials and other radioactive sources;

10. *Requests* the Secretary-General to transmit to the Director General of the Agency the records of the fiftieth session of the General Assembly relating to the activities of the Agency.

General Assembly resolution 50/9

1 November 1995     Meeting 47     144-1-8 (recorded vote)

41-nation draft (A/50/L.11 & Add.1); agenda item 14.
*Meeting numbers.* GA 50th session: plenary 46, 47.

Recorded vote in Assembly as follows:

*In favour:* Albania, Algeria, Argentina, Armenia, Australia, Austria, Bahamas, Bahrain, Bangladesh, Barbados, Belarus, Belgium, Belize, Benin, Bhutan, Bolivia, Bosnia and Herzegovina, Botswana, Brazil, Brunei Darussalam, Bulgaria, Burkina Faso, Burundi, Cambodia, Cameroon, Canada, Chad, Chile, Colombia, Congo, Costa Rica, Côte d'Ivoire, Croatia, Cyprus, Czech Republic, Denmark, Djibouti, Ecuador, Egypt, El Salvador, Eritrea,

Estonia, Ethiopia, Fiji, Finland, France, Gabon, Georgia, Germany, Greece, Grenada, Guatemala, Guinea, Guinea-Bissau, Guyana, Haiti, Honduras, Hungary, Iceland, India, Indonesia, Iran, Ireland, Israel, Italy, Jamaica, Japan, Jordan, Kazakstan, Kenya, Kuwait, Latvia, Lesotho, Libyan Arab Jamahiriya, Liechtenstein, Lithuania, Luxembourg, Madagascar, Malaysia, Maldives, Mali, Malta, Marshall Islands, Mauritania, Mauritius, Mexico, Micronesia, Monaco, Mongolia, Morocco, Mozambique, Myanmar, Namibia, Nepal, Netherlands, New Zealand, Nicaragua, Niger, Nigeria, Norway, Oman, Pakistan, Panama, Papua New Guinea, Peru, Philippines, Poland, Portugal, Qatar, Republic of Korea, Republic of Moldova, Romania, Russian Federation, Rwanda, Saint Lucia, Samoa, San Marino, Saudi Arabia, Senegal, Singapore, Slovakia, Slovenia, Solomon Islands, South Africa, Spain, Sri Lanka, Suriname, Swaziland, Sweden, Thailand, the former Yugoslav Republic of Macedonia, Togo, Trinidad and Tobago, Tunisia, Turkey, Uganda, Ukraine, United Arab Emirates, United Kingdom, United States, Uruguay, Venezuela, Zambia, Zimbabwe.

*Against:* Democratic People's Republic of Korea.

*Abstaining:* China, Cuba, Ghana, Lao People's Democratic Republic, Sudan, Syrian Arab Republic, United Republic of Tanzania,* Viet Nam.

*Subsequently advised the Secretariat it had intended to vote in favour.

Before the adoption of the resolution, a recorded vote was taken on an amendment to operative paragraph 7, proposed by Iraq, which was rejected by 95 votes against to 8 in favour, with 22 abstentions. By that amendment, the following words would have been added after 715(1991) "notes in paragraph 13 of the Agency's report of 6 October 1995 to the Security Council (S/1995/844) that 'of the information which has been reviewed and analysed to date, nothing suggests that a change is warranted in IAEA's conclusion that Iraq's nuclear-weapon programme has been, for all practical purposes, destroyed, removed or rendered harmless'''. The words "Iraq to cooperate fully" would have been replaced with "Iraq to continue its cooperation".

Separate recorded votes were taken on the fourth and eleventh preambular paragraphs, which were adopted by 128 to 3, with 7 abstentions, and by 121 to none, with 10 abstentions, respectively. Operative paragraph 7 was adopted by a recorded vote of 128 to none, with 10 abstentions.

*REFERENCES*

[1]YUN 1994, p. 922, ESC dec. 1994/305, 29 July 1994. [2]E/1995/25/Rev.1. [3]YUN 1994, p. 922, ESC dec. 1994/309, 3 Nov. 1994. [4]YUN 1992, p. 672. [5]A/50/360.

Chapter VII

# Environment

In 1995, the United Nations continued to work towards overcoming the challenges of environmental degradation, particularly through the work of the United Nations Environment Programme (UNEP).

The first session of the Conference of the Parties to the 1992 United Nations Framework Convention on Climate Change adopted the Berlin Mandate, under which talks were launched on a protocol or another legal instrument that would contain stronger commitments for Parties included in Annex I of the Convention (developed and transition countries) after the year 2000. The UNEP Governing Council, having noted the Climate Agenda—a proposal for an integrating framework for international climate-related programmes, which encompassed all the climate-related activities of international organizations—endorsed the proposal that UNEP should be responsible for coordinating international activities with regard to studies of climate impact assessments and response strategies to reduce vulnerabilities.

Stressing the need to further assess actions taken to combat deforestation and forest degradation and to promote management, conservation and sustainable development of all types of forests, the Commission on Sustainable Development recommended the establishment of an open-ended ad hoc Intergovernmental Panel on Forests, under its aegis. In June, the Economic and Social Council approved the establishment of the panel.

The Intergovernmental Conference to Adopt a Global Programme of Action for the Protection of the Marine Environment from Land-based Activities, convened in October/November by the UNEP Executive Director, adopted the Programme of Action, which was designed to guide national and/or regional authorities in devising and implementing sustained action to prevent, reduce, control and/or eliminate marine degradation from land-based activities.

The second meeting of the Conference of the Parties to the 1992 Convention on Biological Diversity decided that a protocol on biosafety should be developed, and established an open-ended ad hoc working group to do so.

The UNEP Governing Council held its eighteenth session at UNEP headquarters in Nairobi, Kenya, from 15 to 26 May.

# United Nations Environment Programme

At its eighteenth session, held at the headquarters of the United Nations Environment Programme (UNEP), (Nairobi, Kenya, 15-26 May), the UNEP Governing Council adopted decisions on environmental and administrative matters, which were contained in its report on the session.[1] That report was taken note of by the Economic and Social Council in July in **decision 1995/234**.

By **decision 1995/207/B** of 10 February, the Council had decided that, when reviewing the UNEP Governing Council's report on its eighteenth session, it would not consider new draft proposals, except for specific recommendations that required action by the Council and proposals on matters relating to the coordination aspects of UNEP's work.

In **resolution 50/110** of 20 December, the General Assembly endorsed the Governing Council's report and the decisions contained therein.

### Role and priorities

By a 26 May decision,[2] the UNEP Governing Council stated the Programme should concentrate on assessing and addressing emerging critical environmental issues; promoting international cooperation and recommending, as appropriate, policies to that end; acting as a catalyst to address major threats to the environment; monitoring the status of the global environment; facilitating the coordination of activities of all UN bodies on environmental matters; supporting, upon request, the work of environment ministries and other national environmental authorities in formulating their policies and related capacity-building activities; furthering the development of international environmental law; providing expert advice on the development and use of environmental economic concepts and instruments; and developing environmental regional programmes. It decided that the major results of UNEP activities should be international arrangements to enhance environmental protection; periodic and scientifically sound forecasts designed to support decision-making and the creation of an international consensus on the main environmental threats and responses; more effective coordination within the UN system; policy options and advice to Governments, multilateral organizations and others, incorporating the environmental dimension into the sustainable process and strengthening environmental protection; and higher public awareness and greater capacity for environmental management and effective responses to threats of environmental degradation. The Executive Director was asked to take the Council's decision into account in shaping and executing future UNEP programmes and to bring the Governing Council's report on its eighteenth session[1] to the attention of the Secretary-General, as a contribution to his preparations for the special session of the General Assembly in 1997 to review the follow-up of Agenda 21 (for General Assembly action on the special session, see PART FOUR, Chapter I).

In a decision[3] of the same date, the Council, taking note of the Executive Director's report on international environment technology centres,[4] including the progress report on the UNEP International Environmental Technology Centre, asked her to make proposals on UNEP's own role and its partnership role in the context of international environmental technology centres, and on ways to financing endogenous capacity-building of scientific and technological centres, in particular of developing countries and countries with economies in transition. The Council asked her to report in 1997.

**Governing structures**

By a 26 May decision,[5] the Governing Council decided to review in 1997 UNEP's governing structures, with a view to taking action or, where necessary, recommending that the General Assembly take action to modify and streamline the structures to produce greater efficiency, effectiveness and transparency. It asked the Executive Director to propose options in this regard to the Council in 1997, following consultations with Governments.

**In-depth evaluation of programme on environment**

At its May session, the Governing Council considered a note by the Executive Director[6] transmitting a report on the in-depth evaluation of the programme on the environment prepared by the UN Office of Internal Oversight Services (OIOS) and transmitted by the Secretary-General to the Committee for Programme and Coordination (CPC), and another document comprising the draft report of CPC on its discussion of the report

at its May/June session[7] and its conclusions on it. By a 26 May decision,[8] the Council asked the Executive Director to consider and take action on the OIOS recommendations and to take due consideration of the CPC conclusions and recommendations.

The OIOS recommendations aimed at refocusing UNEP activities by strengthening its partnership with other organizations within and outside the UN system, with due regard to its role as a global environment programme.

*Role of NGOs*

The Governing Council, having noted the OIOS recommendations,[6] asked the Executive Director, by a 26 May decision,[9] to give high priority to developing a policy framework and mechanisms within the secretariat for working with non-governmental organizations (NGOs) involved in the environment, including the assigning of the function of coordinator to an existing senior position.

**Globalization and the environment**

The Governing Council, in a 26 May decision,[10] urged the Executive Director to pay special attention to regional and national particularities and the implications and impact of sustainable development for developing countries and countries with economies in transition, when (1) evaluating the link between trade and environment policies, international agreements and trade, trade rules, and the development of themes to assess the effectiveness of policy instruments; (2) providing technical assistance to Governments, where requested, for the analysis and formulation of environmental regulations and legislation to facilitate the implementation of international agreements at the national level; and (3) ensuring that the work under the sub-programme, globalization and the environment, included activities that UNEP was invited to undertake by the Commission on Sustainable Development in its decisions on trade, environment and sustainable development and consumption and production patterns, adopted at its 1994[11] and 1995 (see PART FOUR, Chapter I) sessions. In so doing, UNEP was to cooperate with all relevant international organizations, the Council stated.

**Regional support**

UNEP maintained regional offices in Africa (Nairobi), Asia and the Pacific (Bangkok, Thailand), Europe (Geneva), Latin America and the Caribbean (Mexico City), North America (New York) and West Asia (Manama, Bahrain). (For

UNEP regional activities, see below under "Regional concerns".)

## Coordination and cooperation

### UNEP and Commission
### on Sustainable Development

The Governing Council, having considered a March report of the Executive Director on environment and sustainable development,[12] adopted a decision[13] in which it stressed the need for UNEP to focus on the system-wide activities for which it had been assigned a special responsibility by Agenda 21, adopted by the UN Conference on Environment and Development in 1992,[14] and the major policy issues and challenges in the environment, as determined by the Council. UNEP should continue to support the work of the Commission on Sustainable Development by providing scientific, technical and policy information and advice on the environment, the Council stated.

### UNEP and small island
### developing States

The Governing Council, in a 26 May decision,[15] welcomed the action taken by the Executive Director in response to the 1994 Global Conference on the Sustainable Development of Small Island Developing States,[16] including the establishment of a focal point and a task force within UNEP to coordinate activities relevant to the Programme of Action adopted by the Conference. It urged the Executive Director to ensure that attention was given to the needs and vulnerabilities of small island developing States and to encourage an integrated approach within UNEP to addressing issues of relevance to those States.

### UNEP and Habitat

The Commission on Human Settlements (see next chapter) adopted a 1 May decision[17] in which it commended the UN Centre for Human Settlements (UNCHS) (Habitat) and UNEP on their decision to join forces in the Sustainable Cities Programme (SCP) and supported an agreement between them to mobilize their scientific and technical resources. It asked the Executive Director of UNCHS (Habitat) to extend SCP support to additional cities and to accelerate SCP operations.

## International events

In a March report,[18] the Executive Director summarized the conclusions of major international events since the Council's 1993 session, and submitted proposals for follow-up strategies by UNEP for the Council's consideration. The report cited the Secretary-General's 1992 report "An Agenda for Peace",[19] the agenda for development initiative (see PART FOUR, Chapter I), the 1994 Global

Conference on the Sustainable Development of Small Island Developing States,[16] the 1994 International Conference on Population and Development,[20] the 1982 United Nations Convention on the Law of the Sea,[21] which entered into force in 1994,[22] and the 1995 World Summit for Social Development (see PART FOUR, Chapter IX).

On 25 May, the Governing Council took note of the Executive Director's report and endorsed her proposals regarding follow-up action by UNEP.[23]

## General Assembly issues

The Executive Secretary, in March, provided information on issues emanating from resolutions adopted by the General Assembly in 1993 and 1994 that were relevant to UNEP.[24] Those issues concerned Antarctica,[25] the effects of atomic radiation,[26] strengthening UNEP,[27] drought and desertification,[28] the elaboration of an international convention to combat desertification,[29] monitoring global environmental problems,[30] the 1994 report of the Commission on Sustainable Development,[31] the Convention on Biological Diversity,[32] early warning capacities of the United Nations system with regard to natural disasters,[33] the International Day for the Preservation of the Ozone Layer,[34] observance of the World Day to Combat Desertification and Drought,[35] the International Year of the Ocean (1998),[36] the Global Learning and Observations to Benefit the Environment Programme,[37] the dissemination of the principles of the Rio Declaration on Environment and Development,[38] protection of global climate,[39] the Global Conference on Sustainable Development of Small Island Developing States,[40] fisheries by-catch and discards and their impact on the sustainable use of the world's living marine resources,[41] the United Nations Conference on Straddling Fish Stocks and Highly Migratory Fish Stocks,[42] an agenda for development,[43] and the report of the 1994 International Conference on Population and Development.[44]

On 25 May, the Governing Council took note of the Executive Director's report and authorized her to submit to future sessions her report on issues arising from General Assembly resolutions as an information document.[45]

The General Assembly's Second (Economic and Financial) Committee discussed matters relating to environment and sustainable development and made recommendations on a number of issues. By **decision 50/430** of 20 December, the Assembly took note of part one of the Committee's report.

## Telecommunications services

The Governing Council had before it the report of the Executive Director on the Mercure satellite telecommunications system.[46] The system, which was being provided by several European countries to generate and deliver environmental data to UNEP's global participants, was under implementation. By a 25 May decision,[47] the Council asked the Executive Director to ensure that a full review and cost-benefit analysis of the system and experience gained in its initial operation be carried out as soon as technically feasible. She was asked to report on the matter in 1997. The Council decided that the Mercure agreement should be submitted to the General Assembly for endorsement, in accordance with UN procedures.

## UNEP Fund

In a report to the Governing Council,[48] the Executive Director discussed the use of the resources of the Environment Fund in the bienniums 1992-1993 and 1994-1995 and the proposed use of projected resources in the 1996-1997 biennium. By a 26 May decision,[49] the Council approved a $90 million appropriation for Fund programme activities for the 1996-1997 biennium and apportioned the appropriation between subprogrammes, with $35.1 million earmarked for sustainable management and use of natural resources; $27 million for global and regional servicing and support; $10.8 million for a better environment for human health and well-being; $9.9 million for sustainable production and consumption; and $7.2 million for globalization and the environment. It approved an additional $15 million for Fund programme activities if sufficient resources became available and $5 million to the Fund programme reserve for the 1996-1997 biennium. The Council asked the Executive Director to prepare, for the 1998-1999 biennium, two alternative programmes for Fund activities, of $105 million and $130 million, and to report to the Committee of Permanent Representatives at its regular meetings on matters of programme implementation and planning.

By another decision of the same date,[50] the Council, noting with deep concern that 1995 pledges and contributions had not only fallen short of the target established by the Council, but might be insufficient to finance the Fund programme of activities approved by it in 1993,[51] asked the Executive Director to undertake a process of negotiating the amount and timing of pledges and contributions with Member States.

She was also asked to analyse the causes of falling contributions, recommend solutions and study ways to raise additional financial resources, periodically to inform the Committee of Permanent Representatives of the progress made and to report in 1997.

Following consideration of a March report of the Executive Director on the financial report and audited accounts of the Fund for the 1992-1993 biennium ended 31 December 1993,[52] and having noted comments of the Executive Director on the 1994 report of the Board of Auditors and on the observations of the Advisory Committee on Administrative and Budgetary Questions (ACABQ),[53] the Governing Council, by a 25 May decision,[54] asked the Executive Director to report in 1997 on measures taken to respond to queries raised by the auditors and views expressed at the Council's 1995 session.

Also on 25 May,[55] the Governing Council, having considered the Executive Director's March report containing the performance report on the programme and programme support costs budget for the 1994-1995 biennium and the proposed management and administrative support costs budget for the 1996-1997 biennium,[56] together with the relevant comments of ACABQ, noted that ACABQ had subsequently acknowledged the receipt of a response from the Executive Director.[57] The Council asked the Executive Director to transmit to ACABQ her report on the UN Office at Nairobi[58] and her note on ACABQ's report. It also asked her to ensure that ACABQ received sufficient and timely information for its purposes in future. The Council approved a revised appropriation of $41.05 million for the programme and programme support costs for the 1994-1995 biennium, and provisionally approved the staff redeployment and upgrading and the creation of the Ombudsman Unit, as proposed by the Executive Director in her reports,[56],[58] on the condition that there was no overall increase in posts and budgetary allocations. The Council asked the Executive Director to report annually on the activities of the Ombudsman, including any comments of UN/OIOS on those activities. It decided to review in 1997 provisional transfers, upgrades and personnel changes, with a view to final approval. As to the management and administrative support costs for the 1996-1997 biennium, the Council approved an appropriation of some $42 million.

Following consideration of a March report of the Executive Director on Fund programme activities for the 1996-1997 biennium,[59] the Governing Council, by a 26 May decision,[60] provisionally approved the work programme and a core appropriation of $90 million for Fund programme activities, with an additional supplementary appropriation of $15 million, if and when funds became available. It decided to apportion the appropriation for Fund programme activities as outlined in an annex to its decision. The Executive Director was asked to continue mobilizing resources for the 1996-1997 work programme.

**ACABQ action.** ACABQ met from 15 to 19 May[61] to discuss, among other things, the availability and use of Fund resources, the revised estimates for the 1994-1995 biennium for the Fund's programme and programme support costs budget, the Fund's proposed budget for the 1996-1997 biennium for management and administrative support costs, and its financial report and audited accounts for the 1992-1993 biennium, ended 31 December 1993. The Committee also considered the management of trust funds, new developments in conference-servicing, and the establishment of a UN office in Nairobi (see below for Governing Council action on these issues).

## Trust funds

Taking note of a report of the Executive Director providing details on newly established trust funds and those on which the Governing Council was being requested to take action,[62] the Council, by a 25 May decision,[63] approved the establishment of 11 trust funds and the extension of another 10. It provisionally approved the extension of 14 trust funds and closed three others.

Also on 25 May, the Council, in a decision[64] in which it expressed concern that contributions to the trust funds were not being paid ahead of the year in which they were required, resulting in temporary advances from the Fund, asked donors to abide strictly by the terms of the trust funds and asked the Executive Director to conduct a cost-management study of expenditure on administering trust funds, of resource shortfalls and of possible ways to overcome such shortfalls, if any, and to report thereon in 1997. It also asked her to keep the Committee of Permanent Representatives informed of the measures taken on the matter.

## Implementation of Agenda 21

In a March report,[65] the Executive Director estimated that the costs for UNEP to implement fully the parts of Agenda 21, adopted by UNCED in 1992,[14] specifically recommended for UNEP's attention was $105 million for the 1996-1997 biennium. On 26 May,[66] the Governing Council took note of the Executive Director's report and asked her to present broad-based estimates to the Council in 1997.

## Administrative matters

### UNEP Governing Council

*Sessions*

In a March report,[67] the Executive Director proposed that the Governing Council revert to annual sessions and limit the sessions to three working days. She discussed the possibility of setting up a preparatory committee of the Council to serve as its primary subsidiary organ to meet on a permanent basis every two years in odd years in sessions immediately preceding the Council session itself. She proposed maintaining the month of May for the sessions and that the Council recommend that the Commission on Sustainable Development be invited to schedule its meetings in order to allow the Council's deliberations to offer timely policy contributions to Commission meetings. In an April addendum,[68] the Executive Director clarified her proposals.

On 25 May, the Governing Council decided to hold its nineteenth session in Nairobi from 27 January to 7 February 1997 and approved its provisional agenda for that session.[1]

GENERAL ASSEMBLY ACTION

On 20 December, the General Assembly adopted **resolution 50/110.**

### Report of the Governing Council of the United Nations Environment Programme

*The General Assembly,*

*Recalling* its resolution 2997(XXVII) of 15 December 1972, in which it decided to establish the Governing Council of the United Nations Environment Programme,

*Recalling also* its resolution 47/191 of 22 December 1992, in which it endorsed the recommendations on international institutional arrangements to follow up the United Nations Conference on Environment and Development, as contained in chapter 38 of Agenda 21, in which, *inter alia*, the need for a strengthened role for the United Nations Environment Programme and its Governing Council was stressed and priority areas on which the Programme should concentrate were elaborated,

*Having considered* the report of the Governing Council of the United Nations Environment Programme on its eighteenth session, the report of the Secretary-General on the strengthening of the Programme, the note by the Secretary-General on the activities of the Programme in environmental monitoring, and the note by the Secretary-General on international conventions and protocols in the field of the environment,

1. *Endorses* the report of the Governing Council of the United Nations Environment Programme on its eighteenth session and the decisions contained therein;

2. *Recognizes*, in particular, Governing Council decisions 18/1 on the role and priorities of the United Nations Environment Programme, 18/5 on the in-depth evaluation of the programme on environment and 18/7 on environment and sustainable development, all of 26 May 1995, and decision 18/10 of 25 May 1995 on good environmental housekeeping within the United Nations system;

3. *Requests* the Governing Council to prepare a report on the role and activities of the United Nations Environment Programme in the implementation of Agenda 21, in accordance with its mandate, and to submit that report to the General Assembly at its special session on the overall review and appraisal of the implementation of Agenda 21;

4. *Notes* the importance of sufficient and timely contributions to the Environment Fund, and calls upon Governments to make contributions in a timely fashion in order to allow for the full and effective implementation of the work programmes;

5. *Welcomes* the efforts of the United Nations Environment Programme to promote maximum and cost-effective utilization of the conference facilities at its headquarters at Nairobi, and calls upon Governments and relevant intergovernmental bodies to support such efforts to ensure optimum utilization of the capacity of all United Nations conference facilities;

6. *Requests* the Secretary-General to inform the General Assembly at its fifty-second session on the implementation of the present resolution.

General Assembly resolution 50/110

20 December 1995      Meeting 96      Adopted without vote

Approved by Second Committee (A/50/618/Add.6) without vote, 8 December (meeting 42); draft by Vice-Chairman (A/C.2/50/L.69), based on informal consultations on draft by Philippines, for Group of 77 and China (A/C.2/50/L.28); agenda item 96.
*Meeting numbers.* GA 50th session: 2nd Committee 18-23, 34, 35, 38, 39, 42; plenary 96.

## UN Office at Nairobi

In a May report,[58] the Executive Director described how a UN Office in Nairobi (UNON) would be established as from 1 January 1996 by combining the administrative and conferences services of UNEP with those of UNCHS (Habitat) and the UN Common Services in Nairobi.

By a 25 May decision,[69] the Governing Council approved the attachment of administrative and conference services staff of UNEP to UNON, as set out in the Executive Director's report, and the payment of the costs of their emoluments from the management and administrative support costs budget of the Environment Fund. It asked that the Committee of Permanent Representatives be kept informed of the Council's decision and requested the Executive Director to report in 1997 on progress made.

## Conference-servicing

By a 25 May decision,[70] the Governing Council, taking note of the Executive Director's March report on new developments in conference-servicing,[71] asked her to provide adequate communications facilities for the use of government representatives at UNON and to keep under review the financial viability of establishing a team of interpreters in Nairobi, and, if found financially advantageous, to establish a team on a pilot basis. She was also asked to offer, at cost, interpretation services wherever possible to UNCHS (Habitat) and the Economic Commission for Africa. Endorsing the Executive Director's efforts to limit documents for the Governing Council to a maximum of four pages, it asked her to encourage convention secretariats administered by UNEP to do the same.

## Human resources

The Governing Council, by a 25 May decision,[72] asked the Executive Director to present to the Committee of Permanent Representatives a quarterly report on consultancies and to submit to the Committee a statement listing the procedures to be followed in identifying the need for consultancies, selecting consultancies and assessing that their duties had been properly performed. It asked the Executive Director to take into account a series of principles when selecting consultancies and to ensure that the results of consultancies were evaluated by UNEP.

On 26 May, the Council asked the Executive Director to examine how the level of expertise in UNEP might be further improved, and to keep the Committee of Permanent Representatives informed of her efforts and report in 1997.[73]

## Waste, fraud and mismanagement

On 25 May, the Governing Council asked the Executive Director, in consultation with OIOS, to draw up and enact a specific plan of action to heighten the awareness of UNEP staff members concerning the need to combat waste, fraud and mismanagement and establish measures that would enable them to do so.[74] The Council presented measures to be included in the plan of action and recommended the production and dissemination of an administrative handbook containing the plan of action and a guide to the administrative manuals regulating UNEP and highlighting the practices that could be most subject to waste, fraud and mismanagement. In the interests of transparency, the Council stated that Governments should have access to information on the status of all audit investigations, their results and recommendations, and the response of UNEP management. The Executive Director was asked to implement the Council's decision in consultation with the Committee of Permanent Representatives and to report thereon in 1997. The biennial report of the UNEP Board of Auditors was to be submitted to the Governing Council at its regular sessions.

## Strengthening UNEP

In response to a 1993 General Assembly request,[75] the Secretary-General submitted a report on strengthening of UNEP,[76] in which he described steps taken to strengthen the liaison function for the Commission on Sustainable Development and efforts to increase UNEP's financial resources. He also discussed progress made in ensuring maximum use of conference facilities in Nairobi and in improving their cost-effectiveness.

In **resolution 50/110** of 20 December, the Assembly noted the importance of sufficient and timely contributions to the Environment Fund and called on Governments to make contributions in a timely fashion. It also called on Governments to support UNEP's efforts to ensure optimum use of the capacity of UN conference facilities.

*REFERENCES*

[1]A/50/25. [2]Ibid. (dec. 18/1). [3]Ibid. (dec. 18/22). [4]UNEP/GC.18/15. [5]A/50/25 (dec. 18/2). [6]UNEP/GC.18/Inf.7. [7]A/50/16. [8]A/50/25 (dec. 18/5). [9]A/50/25 (dec. 18/4). [10]Ibid. (dec. 18/3). [11]YUN 1994, p. 765. [12]UNEP/GC.18/27 & Corr.1. [13]A/50/25 (dec. 18/7). [14]YUN 1992, p. 672. [15]A/50/25 (dec. 18/34). [16]YUN 1994, p. 783. [17]A/50/8 (dec. 15/8). [18]UNEP/GC.18/26. [19]YUN 1992, p. 35. [20]YUN 1994, p. 955. [21]YUN 1982, p. 178. [22]YUN 1994, p. 1301. [23]A/50/25 (dec. 18/16). [24]UNEP/GC.18/28. [25]YUN 1993, p. 204, GA res. 48/80, 16 Dec. 1993. [26]Ibid., p. 202, GA res. 48/38, 10 Dec. 1993 & YUN 1994, p. 238, GA res. 49/32, 9 Dec. 1994. [27]YUN 1993, p. 819, GA res. 48/174, 21 Dec. 1993. [28]Ibid., p. 816, GA res. 48/175, 21 Dec. 1993. [29]Ibid., p. 814, GA res. 48/191, 21 Dec. 1993 & YUN 1994, p. 945, GA res. 49/234, 23 Dec. 1994. [30]YUN 1993, p. 812, GA res. 48/192, 21 Dec. 1993. [31]YUN 1994, p. 767, GA res. 49/111, 19 Dec. 1994. [32]Ibid., p. 939, GA res. 49/117, 19 Dec. 1994. [33]Ibid., p. 853, GA res. 49/22 B, 20 Dec. 1994. [34]Ibid., p. 940, GA res. 49/114, 19 Dec. 1994. [35]Ibid., p. 947, GA res. 49/115, 19 Dec. 1994. [36]Ibid., p. 951, GA res. 49/131, 19 Dec. 1994. [37]Ibid., p. 936, GA res. 49/112, 19 Dec. 1994. [38]Ibid., p. 935, GA res. 49/113, 19 Dec. 1994. [39]Ibid., p. 938, GA res. 49/120, 19 Dec. 1994. [40]Ibid., p. 784, GA res. 49/122, 19 Dec. 1994. [41]Ibid., p. 949, GA res. 49/118, 19 Dec. 1994. [42]Ibid., p. 948, GA res. 49/121, 19 Dec. 1994. [43]Ibid., p. 759, GA res. 49/126, 19 Dec. 1994. [44]Ibid., p. 963, GA res. 49/128, 19 Dec. 1994. [45]A/50/25 (dec. 18/17). [46]UNEP/GC.18/21 & Corr.1. [47]A/50/25 (dec. 18/47). [48]UNEP/GC.18/14 & Corr.1 & Add.1 & Corr.1. [49]A/50/25 (dec. 18/41 B). [50]A/50/25 (dec. 18/41 A). [51]YUN 1993, p. 818. [52]UNEP/GC.18/16. [53]YUN 1994, p. 952. [54]A/50/25 (dec. 18/41 C). [55]Ibid. (dec. 18/42). [56]UNEP/GC.18/32 & Corr.1. [57]UNEP/GC.18/32/Add.2. [58]UNEP/GC/32/Add.1. [59]UNEP/GC.18/9 & Add.1. [60]A/50/25 (dec. 18/40). [61]UNEP/GC.18/38. [62]UNEP/GC.18/13 & Corr.1. [63]A/50/25 (dec. 18/44 A). [64]Ibid. (dec. 18/44 B). [65]UNEP/GC.18/30. [66]A/50/25 (dec. 18/18). [67]UNEP/GC.18/22 & Corr.1. [68]UNEP/GC.18/22/Add.1. [69]A/50/25 (dec. 18/43). [70]A/50/25 (dec. 18/45). [71]UNEP/GC.18/10. [72]A/50/25 (dec. 18/49). [73]Ibid. (dec. 18/48). [74]Ibid. (dec. 18/46). [75]YUN 1993, p. 819, GA res. 48/174, 21 Dec. 1993. [76]A/50/171.

# International conventions and mechanisms

In a report to the UNEP Governing Council,[1] the Executive Director gave the status, as at 30 November 1994, of new and existing conventions dealing with the environment.

By a 25 May decision,[2] the Council authorized the Executive Director to transmit her report, on its behalf, to the General Assembly at its 1995 session, which the Secretary-General did by a note of 28 September.[3] The Council asked the Executive Director to continue the regular publication of the Register of International Treaties and Other Agreements in the Field of Environment and called on States that had not yet done so to sign,

ratify or accede to those conventions and protocols dealing with the environment to which they were eligible to become parties.

## Climate change convention

As at 31 December 1995,[4] there were 151 States parties to the United Nations Framework Convention on Climate Change, which was opened for signature in 1992,[5] and entered into force in 1994.[6] The Convention aimed at stabilizing atmospheric concentrations of greenhouse gases at levels that would prevent human activities from interfering dangerously with the global climate system.

The Intergovernmental Negotiating Committee for a Framework Convention on Climate Change held its eleventh session (New York, 6-17 February), during which it continued to prepare for the first session of the Conference of the Parties to the Convention.[7] The Committee remitted the draft rules of procedure to the Conference for consideration. Recommendations approved dealt with temporary arrangements between the Committee and the Global Environment Facility (GEF) and guidelines for parties in creating inventories on national greenhouse gases and assessing climate change impacts. A draft protocol on greenhouse gas emissions reduction was introduced. In addition, the Committee considered options for the site of the permanent secretariat of the Convention. In accordance with a 1992 General Assembly resolution,[8] the Secretary-General, by an October note,[9] transmitted the final report of the Chairman of the Committee.

The Conference of the Parties, at its first session (Berlin, Germany, 28 March-7 April),[10] adopted the Berlin Mandate, by which talks were launched on a protocol or another legal instrument containing stronger commitments for Parties included in Annex I of the Convention (developed and transition countries) after the year 2000. The Conference established the Ad Hoc Group on the Berlin Mandate (see below). It adopted the Convention budget for the 1996-1997 biennium and decided to accept the offer of Germany to host the Convention secretariat in Bonn. The Conference outlined the functions of the Convention's subsidiary bodies—the Subsidiary Body for Scientific and Technological Advice (SBSTA), which held its first session (Geneva, 28 August-1 September),[11] primarily of an organizational nature, and the Subsidiary Body for Implementation (SBI), which at its first session (Geneva, 31 August-1 September) considered communications from Annex I Parties[12] and discussed its proposed programme of work.[13]

In other action, the Conference considered the GEF report containing information on the development of an operational strategy in the climate change area and on initial activities in that area,[14] and decided to adopt a mixed strategy, whereby projects would be selected with a double set of programme priorities, if they met either one of the long-term programme priorities or one of the short-term programme priorities. The Conference also took action on communications from Parties, activities implemented jointly under the Convention, the maintenance of interim arrangements, the transfer of technology, funding, and financial procedures and mechanisms.

**Ad Hoc Group meetings.** The Ad Hoc Group on the Berlin Mandate (AGBM) met twice in 1995 in Geneva (21-25 August[15] and 30 October-3 November[16]), to identify possible policies and measures for Annex I Parties that could contribute to limiting and reducing emissions by sources and protecting and enhancing sinks and reservoirs of greenhouse gases. Under the Berlin Mandate process, quantified emission limitation and reduction objectives were to be set within specified time-frames. AGBM invited Parties to make preliminary submissions to the secretariat by 15 January 1996, offering ideas and comments on policies and measures. In addition, it held an initial exchange of views on the establishment of quantified limitation and reduction objectives within specified time-frames, such as 2005, 2010 and 2020, for anthropogenic emissions by sources and removals by sinks of greenhouse gases for Annex I Parties.

**Report of the Secretary-General.** As requested by the General Assembly in 1994,[17] the Secretary-General submitted a November report on protection of global climate for present and future generations of mankind,[18] in which he described action taken, including activities by States to ratify, accept, approve or accede to the Convention. He also described initial communications submitted by Annex I Parties, the work of the Intergovernmental Negotiating Committee, and activities of the interim secretariat. The Secretary-General discussed decisions taken at the first session of the Conference of Parties and their institutional, administrative and financial implications for the United Nations.

**GENERAL ASSEMBLY ACTION**

On 20 December, the General Assembly adopted **resolution 50/115**.

**Protection of global climate for present and future generations of mankind**

*The General Assembly,*

*Recalling* its resolutions 45/212 of 21 December 1990, 46/169 of 19 December 1991, 47/195 of 22 December 1992, 48/189 of 21 December 1993 and 49/120 of 19 December 1994,

*Noting with satisfaction* that a large number of States and one regional economic integration organization have ratified the United Nations Framework Convention on Climate Change and calling upon other States to take appropriate action to that end,

*Noting* that, in accordance with paragraphs 1 and 2 of General Assembly resolution 48/189, the first session of the Conference of the Parties to the United Nations Framework Convention on Climate Change was convened from 28 March to 7 April 1995 in Berlin, and that it was attended by one hundred and sixteen of the then one hundred and eighteen Parties to the Convention, as well as by a large number of governmental, intergovernmental and non-governmental observers,

*Expressing its deep appreciation* to the Government of Germany for the generous manner in which it hosted the first session of the Conference of the Parties,

*Looking forward* to the ongoing work of the Conference of the Parties and its subsidiary bodies in addressing climate change within the framework of the Convention and to the successful conclusion of the Berlin Mandate process at the third session of the Conference of the Parties,

*Noting* the important scientific contribution of the World Meteorological Organization/United Nations Environment Programme Intergovernmental Panel on Climate Change to the Convention process and looking forward to the completion of its second assessment report,

*Recognizing* the contribution to the Convention process of the interim secretariat of the Convention, within the framework of the Department for Policy Coordination and Sustainable Development of the Secretariat, as well as the support provided to that secretariat by the World Meteorological Organization, the United Nations Environment Programme, the United Nations Conference on Trade and Development, the United Nations Development Programme and bilateral contributors,

*Taking note* of the advice of the Secretary-General on an institutional linkage for the secretariat of the Convention with the United Nations, including the procedures indicated therein for the application of the Financial Regulations and the Staff Regulations and Staff Rules of the United Nations and for the appointment and accountability of the head of that secretariat,

*Taking note also* of the decision of the Conference of the Parties, on the basis of the advice of the Secretary-General, that the Convention secretariat shall be institutionally linked to the United Nations, while not being fully integrated into the work programme and management structure of any particular department or programme,

*Taking note further* of the financial procedures for the Conference of the Parties to the United Nations Framework Convention on Climate Change, its subsidiary bodies and its permanent secretariat adopted at its first session, whereby, *inter alia*, the Secretary-General is asked to establish trust funds for the purposes of the Convention, to be managed by the head of the Convention secretariat in accordance with duly delegated authority,

*Taking note further* of the decision of the Conference of the Parties whereby the General Assembly is requested, bearing in mind the institutional linkage of the Convention secretariat to the United Nations and the large number of States that are Parties to the Convention, to decide to finance from the regular programme budget of the United Nations the conference-servicing costs arising from sessions of the Conference of the Parties and its subsidiary bodies for the duration of the institutional linkage mentioned above,

*Having considered* the report of the Secretary-General on the implementation of General Assembly resolution 49/120, with particular reference to the implications arising from the report of the Conference of the Parties on its first session,

1. *Takes note with appreciation* of:

(a) The report of the Intergovernmental Negotiating Committee on a Framework Convention on Climate Change on its eleventh session;

(b) The final report prepared on behalf of the Committee, by its Chairman, on the completion of the Committee's work;

(c) The report of the Conference of the Parties to the Convention on its first session and its presentation on behalf of the President of the Conference;

2. *Endorses* the institutional linkage between the Convention secretariat and the United Nations, as advised by the Secretary-General and adopted by the Conference of the Parties;

3. *Requests* the Secretary-General to review the functioning of this institutional linkage not later than 31 December 1999, in consultation with the Conference of the Parties, with a view to making such modifications as may be considered desirable by both parties and to report thereon to the General Assembly;

4. *Notes* that the Conference of the Parties has decided to accept the offer of the Government of Germany to host the Convention secretariat and expresses its appreciation for the support offered by the future host Government for the relocation and effective functioning of the Convention secretariat;

5. *Notes with appreciation* contributions made to the extrabudgetary funds established under paragraphs 10 and 20 of General Assembly resolution 45/212, and maintained in accordance with its resolution 47/195;

6. *Urges* Member States that are Parties to the Convention to pay promptly and in full for each of the years 1996 and 1997, in accordance with the indicative scale adopted by consensus by the Conference of the Parties, the contributions required for the trust fund for the core budget of the Convention envisaged in paragraph 13 of its financial procedures, so as to ensure continuity in the cash flow required to finance the ongoing work of the Conference of the Parties, the subsidiary bodies and the Convention secretariat;

7. *Calls upon* Member States that are Parties to the Convention to also contribute generously to the trust fund for participation in the Convention process envisaged in paragraph 15 of its financial procedures, as well as to the trust funds envisaged for supplementary activities under the Convention;

8. *Decides* to include in the calendar of conferences and meetings for 1996-1997 the sessions of the Conference of the Parties and its subsidiary bodies envisaged for that biennium entailing twelve weeks of conference-servicing facilities;

9. *Requests* the Secretary-General to make the necessary arrangements to include in the calendar of conferences and meetings for the biennium 1998-1999 those sessions of the Conference of the Parties and its subsidiary bodies that the Conference may need to convene in that period;

10. *Takes note* of the transitional arrangement for administrative support to the Convention secretariat, outlined in the report of the Secretary-General on the implementation of General Assembly resolution 49/120,

with particular reference to the implications arising from the report of the Conference of the Parties, on its first session, which should facilitate the establishment and relocation of the Convention secretariat and assist it in addressing any initial financial and personnel problems that may be encountered within this context, and also takes note of the financing arrangements contained in paragraphs 8 and 9 above, and requests the Secretary-General to review these arrangements towards the end of the biennium 1996-1997 and to report upon the results of this review to the Assembly at its fifty-second session;

11. *Notes* that the Secretary-General intends:

(a) To transfer the end-1995 balance in the trust fund for the negotiating process established under paragraph 20 of General Assembly resolution 45/212 into the trust fund for the core budget of the Convention envisaged in paragraph 13 of its financial procedures;

(b) To transfer the end-1995 balance in the special voluntary fund for participation in the negotiating process established under paragraph 10 of the same resolution into the trust fund for participation in the Convention process envisaged in paragraph 15 of the aforementioned financial procedures;

12. *Requests* the Secretary-General to report to the General Assembly at its fifty-first session on the implementation of the present resolution;

13. *Decides* to include in the provisional agenda of its fifty-first session the item entitled "Protection of global climate for present and future generations of mankind".

**General Assembly resolution 50/115**

20 December 1995　　　　Meeting 96　　　　Adopted without vote

Approved by Second Committee (A/50/618/Add.3) without vote, 5 December (meeting 41); draft by Vice-Chairman (A/C.2/50/L.33), based on informal consultations; agenda item 96 *(d)*.

*Financial implications.* 5th Committee, A/50/823; S-G, A/C.2/50/L.49, A/C.5/50/39.

*Meeting numbers.* GA 50th session: 2nd Committee 34, 35, 41; 5th Committee 41; plenary 96.

## Convention on Biological Diversity

The Convention on Biological Diversity, which was opened for signature in 1992,[19] and entered into force in 1993,[20] had been ratified or acceded to by 137 States as at 31 December 1995.[4]

In accordance with a 1994 General Assembly request,[21] the Executive Secretary of the Convention submitted a June report on progress achieved in implementing the Convention.[22] He discussed decisions adopted at the first (1994) meeting of the Conference of the Parties[23] relating to financial resources and financial mechanism; technical and scientific matters; the statement to the Commission on Sustainable Development for submission to its third (1995) session; the 1995-1997 medium-term programme of work; and organizational matters.

The Open-ended Ad Hoc Group of Experts on Biosafety (Madrid, Spain, 24-28 July)[24] met to consider the need for a protocol setting out procedures, including advance informed agreement, in the area of safe transfer, handling and use of any living modified organism (LMO) resulting from biotechnology that might have an adverse effect on the conservation and sustainable use of biological diversity. It also considered existing knowledge, experience and legislation in the area of biosafety. A panel of 15 Government-nominated experts (Cairo, Egypt, 1-5 May) prepared a background document describing current approaches to risk assessment and management, a survey of existing national, regional and international guidelines/regulations, and recommendations on further action to be taken to improve safety in biotechnology. The report was annexed to the Group's report. The Group stressed the immediate need for international action to achieve adequate safety of LMOs and suggested items to be considered in an international framework on biosafety. It presented options for an international framework that were relevant for the Conference of the Parties in considering the need for a protocol.

The second meeting of the Conference of the Parties to the Convention (Jakarta, Indonesia, 6-17 November)[25] decided to develop a protocol on biosafety and established an open-ended ad hoc working group to do so. It adopted decisions concerning, among other things, the transfer and development of technology, forests and biological diversity, marine and coastal biological diversity, access to genetic resources, intellectual property rights, cooperation with other biodiversity-related conventions, the convening of an intergovernmental workshop on cooperation between the Convention and other international conventions on related issues, the Food and Agriculture Organization of the United Nations (FAO) Global System for the Conservation and Utilization of Plant Genetic Resources, national reports by Parties, the 1996-1997 medium-term programme of work of the Conference, and the financing and budget for the Convention. It decided to locate the Convention secretariat in Montreal, Canada. The Conference considered the report of the first meeting of the Subsidiary Body on Scientific, Technical and Technological Advice (SBSTTA) (Paris, 4-8 September).[26] SBSTTA had designed the Convention's programme of work for 1995-1997, which the Conference approved. At its two-day ministerial segment (14 and 15 November), the Conference of Parties adopted the Jakarta Ministerial Statement on the implementation of the Convention. The third meeting of the Conference was scheduled to take place from 4 to 15 November 1996 in Buenos Aires, Argentina.

**Commission on Sustainable Development.** At its third session (New York, 11-28 April),[27] the Commission on Sustainable Development urged Governments that had not yet done so to ratify, accede to and begin implementing the Convention. It encouraged the Conference of the Parties to explore means for coordinating relevant global and regional agreements related to the Convention and establishing effective cooperation mecha-

nisms. The Commission called on multilateral organizations and other intergovernmental and non-governmental organizations to cooperate with the Convention and Governments in developing coordinating mechanisms. It welcomed the decision of the Conference to include in its medium-term programme consideration of the knowledge, innovations and practices of indigenous and local communities. Welcoming the decision of the Conference to establish the clearing-house mechanism of the Convention, the Commission urged Governments and non-governmental and intergovernmental organizations to collect, analyse and disseminate more reliable and adequate data for measuring achievements at the national, regional and global levels.

**UNEP Governing Council action.** On 26 May, the Governing Council welcomed the designation of UNEP to carry out the functions of the secretariat of the Convention.[28]

**GENERAL ASSEMBLY ACTION**

On 20 December, the General Assembly adopted **resolution 50/111**.

### Convention on Biological Diversity

*The General Assembly,*

*Reaffirming* its resolutions 49/117 on the Convention on Biological Diversity and 49/119 on the International Day for Biological Diversity, of 19 December 1994,

*Recalling* the Convention on Biological Diversity,

*Recalling also* Agenda 21, particularly its chapter 15 on the conservation of biological diversity, and related chapters,

*Recalling further* the recommendations made at the third session of the Commission on Sustainable Development on the review of chapter 15 of Agenda 21 on the conservation of biological diversity,

*Deeply concerned* by the continuing loss of the world's biological diversity and, on the basis of the provisions of the Convention, reiterating the commitment to the conservation of biological diversity, and the sustainable use of its components, as well as the fair and equitable sharing of benefits arising from the use of genetic resources,

1. *Welcomes* the results of the first meeting of the Conference of the Parties to the Convention on Biological Diversity, held at Nassau from 28 November to 9 December 1994, as reflected in the report of the Executive Secretary of the Convention,[a] submitted in accordance with paragraph 4 of General Assembly resolution 49/117;

2. *Takes note* that the Conference of the Parties to the Convention on Biological Diversity has decided to accept the offer of the Government of Canada to host the secretariat of the Convention, and expresses its appreciation for the support offered by the Canadian authorities to ensure the effective functioning of the secretariat;

3. *Also takes note* of the results of the first meeting of the Subsidiary Body on Scientific, Technical and Technological Advice, held at the headquarters of the United

---

[a] A/50/218.

Nations Educational, Scientific and Cultural Organization in Paris from 4 to 8 September 1995, including
its medium-term programme of work for 1996-1997 and
its contribution to the Open-ended Ad Hoc Intergovernmental Panel on Forests of the Commission on Sustainable Development;

4. *Calls upon* those States that have not yet ratified
the Convention to expedite their internal procedures of
ratification, acceptance or approval;

5. *Invites* the Executive Secretary of the Convention
on Biological Diversity to report, through the Economic
and Social Council, to the General Assembly at its fifty-
first session on the results of the second meeting of the
Conference of the Parties to the Convention, held at
Jakarta from 6 to 17 November 1995, and also invites
the Secretary to make the reports of the Conference of
the Parties to the Convention available to the Commission on Sustainable Development.

General Assembly resolution 50/111

20 December 1995      Meeting 96      Adopted without vote

Approved by Second Committee (A/50/618/Add.1) without vote, 30 November
(meeting 40); draft by Vice-Chairman (A/C.2/50/L.45), based on informal consultations on draft by Philippines, for Group of 77 and China
(A/C.2/50/L.8); agenda item 96 *(a)*.
*Meeting numbers.* GA 50th session: 2nd Committee 18-23, 40; plenary 96.

## Montreal Protocol and Ozone Convention

At their seventh meeting (Vienna, 5-7 December),[29] the Parties to the 1987 Montreal Protocol
on Substances that Deplete the Ozone Layer[30]
considered the reports of the Scientific Assessment
Panel, the Environmental Effects Panel, and the
Technology and Economic Assessment Panel; the
report of the Co-Chairs of the Open-ended Working Group of the Parties to the Protocol on the outcome of the preparatory meeting on the issues before its 1995 meeting; the report of the President
of the Implementation Committee; and the report
of the Chairman of the Executive Committee of
the Multilateral Fund for the Implementation of
the Protocol. Decisions adopted by the Parties
dealt with, among other things, adjustments and
reductions of production and consumption of the
controlled substances listed in Annexes to the Protocol; provision of financial support and technology transfer; the definition of "quarantine applications" with respect to methyl bromide and of
"pre-shipment applications"; the reduction of
methyl bromide emissions; trade in methyl bromide; review of methyl bromide controls; uses of
controlled substances as chemical process agents
after 1996; alternatives to controlled substances
used for laboratory and analytical purposes; limitations on the use of halon; the Multilateral Fund
of the Montreal Protocol; and other financial and
administrative matters.

The Administrator of the United Nations Development Programme (UNDP) stated that, as at
the end of December 1995, UNDP was assisting
41 countries to eliminate ozone-depleting substances (ODS) under the Protocol.[31] During the

year, $32.4 million in UNDP work programmes
had been approved and funded by the Executive
Committee of the Multilateral Fund of the Montreal Protocol, thus raising the UNDP 1991-1995 cumulative project portfolio to $110 million. The
portfolio comprised 398 projects, including 207
technology transfer investment projects, which
would eliminate 14,128 tons of ODS per year. The
regional shares of the cumulative programme
were: Africa and the Middle East, 13 per cent; Asia
and the Pacific, 51 per cent; Latin America and the
Caribbean, 33 per cent; and regional and global
programmes, 3 per cent. The foam and refrigeration sectors accounted for four-fifths of the total
programme.

As at 31 December,[4] 152 States and the European Community (EC) were parties to the 1985
Vienna Convention for the Protection of the
Ozone Layer,[32] which had entered into force in
1988.[33] At the same date,[4] 150 States and EC
were parties to the 1987 Montreal Protocol,[30]
103 States and EC were parties to the 1990
Amendment to the Protocol,[34] and 50 States and
EC were parties to the 1992 Amendment.[35]

## Convention to Combat Desertification

As at 31 December 1995,[4] the UN Convention
to Combat Desertification in those Countries Experiencing Serious Drought and/or Desertification,
particularly in Africa, which was adopted in
1994[36] and was opened for signature in October
of that year, had been signed by 114 countries and
the European Community and been ratified, accepted or acceded to by 19 States.

In accordance with a 1994 General Assembly
decision,[37] the Intergovernmental Committee
continued to function, pending the entry into force
of the Convention, which would occur 90 days
after the deposit of the fiftieth instrument of ratification. It held its sixth (New York, 9-18 January)
and seventh (Nairobi, 7-17 August) sessions in
1995. By notes of January[38] and February[39] the
Secretary-General transmitted the reports of those
sessions to the Assembly, which, by **decision
50/432** of 20 December, took note of them.

In January, the Intergovernmental Committee
adopted resolutions relating to the work programme for the period leading to the first session
of the Conference of Parties and observance of the
World Day to Combat Desertification and
Drought (17 June), proclaimed by the General Assembly in 1994.[40] It also adopted a decision on
accreditation of NGOs. Annexed to the Committee's January report were the conclusions of the
Committee Chairman regarding urgent action for
Africa and action taken in other regions, and the
review of the situation regarding extrabudgetary
funds.

At its August session, the Committee recommended to the Assembly that the Committee hold its eighth and ninth sessions in 1996 from 5 to 16 February in Geneva and from 3 to 13 September in New York, respectively. It also recommended to the Assembly the convening in 1997 of its tenth session in New York from 6 to 17 January and its eleventh session in April, the exact dates and venue to be determined. It requested the Assembly to review the financial situation of the Trust Fund to support the work of the Committee and the interim secretariat and the Special Voluntary Fund. The Committee recommended that, upon the Convention's entry into force, the Conference of Parties be convened in either June or August 1997. It adopted decisions regarding accreditation of NGOs, the identification of an organization to house the Global Mechanism, financial rules, programme and budget, the location and designation of a permanent secretariat, the draft rules of procedures of the Conference of the Parties, procedures for communication of information and review of implementation and organization of scientific and technological cooperation.

**Reports of the Secretary-General.** Pursuant to a 1993 General Assembly request,[41] the Secretary-General submitted an August report,[42] stating that support for the implementation of the Convention was urgently required, since more than 900 million people lived under the shadow of desertification and drought. He noted that it was especially important to support immediate actions in Africa. The Secretary-General hoped that greater efforts could be made to increase contributions for multilateral funding for the Convention and appealed for donors to support subregional programmes and active subregional organizations.

In response to a 1994 Assembly request,[37] the Secretary-General reported in October on the work of the Intergovernmental Negotiating Committee in 1995 (see above), activities on urgent measures for Africa and interim action in other regions, and future work concerning the Convention.[43].

**Executive Board action.** The Executive Board of UNDP/United Nations Population Fund, in a 13 January decision,[44] expressed support for the UNDP Administrator's initiatives to promote UNDP measures in support of the implementation of the Convention and its regional annexes. The Executive Board encouraged the Administrator, in light of the Convention, to take the necessary steps to change the name of the United Nations Sudano-Sahelian Office (UNSO), while keeping its acronym. UNSO was subsequently renamed the Office to Combat Desertification and Drought (see also PART FOUR, Chapter III).

**GENERAL ASSEMBLY ACTION**

On 20 December, the General Assembly adopted **resolution 50/112**.

### Elaboration of an international convention to combat desertification in those countries experiencing serious drought and/or desertification, particularly in Africa

*The General Assembly,*

*Recalling* its resolutions 44/172 of 19 December 1989 and 44/228 of 22 December 1989 and its other relevant resolutions and decisions, and the recommendations made in Agenda 21, adopted by the United Nations Conference on Environment and Development,

*Recalling also* its resolution 47/188 of 22 December 1992, by which it decided to establish the Intergovernmental Negotiating Committee for the Elaboration of an International Convention to Combat Desertification in Those Countries Experiencing Serious Drought and/or Desertification, particularly in Africa,

*Recalling further* its resolution 49/234 of 23 December 1994, in which it decided that the Intergovernmental Negotiating Committee should continue to function in order, *inter alia*, to prepare for the first session of the Conference of the Parties to the Convention, as specified in the United Nations Convention to Combat Desertification in Those Countries Experiencing Serious Drought and/or Desertification, particularly in Africa,

*Having considered* the reports of the Secretary-General on the implementation of resolution 49/234 and on possible requirements for intergovernmental and secretariat work on the implementation of the Convention and its regional implementation annexes, and having also considered Intergovernmental Negotiating Committee resolution 7/1 of 17 August 1995 on dates and venue of the sessions of the Committee during the period up to and including the first session of the Conference of the Parties to the Convention,

*Expressing its concern* about the present level of the Special Voluntary Fund for participation in the negotiation process of developing countries affected by desertification and drought, in particular the least developed countries,

*Noting* that the Intergovernmental Negotiating Committee has established two working groups in order to be able to discharge its responsibilities in the preparation for the first session of the Conference of Parties to the Convention,

*Also expressing its concern* about the present level of the Trust Fund, established pursuant to its resolution 47/188, to support the work of the Intergovernmental Negotiating Committee and the interim secretariat,

*Considering* that the Convention is one of the main steps in the implementation and follow-up to the United Nations Conference on Environment and Development,

1. *Welcomes* the signing of the United Nations Convention to Combat Desertification in Those Countries Experiencing Serious Drought and/or Desertification, particularly in Africa, by a large number of States and one regional economic integration organization and the ratification of the Convention by a growing number of States, and urges States that have not yet signed or ratified the Convention to do so, so that it may enter into force as soon as possible;

2. *Decides* that the Intergovernmental Negotiating Committee for the Elaboration of an International Convention to Combat Desertification in Those Countries Experiencing Serious Drought and/or Desertification, particularly in Africa, shall continue to prepare for the first session of the Conference of the Parties to the Convention as specified in the Convention;

3. *Also decides*, for this purpose, to convene two sessions of the Intergovernmental Negotiating Committee in 1996, each of up to two weeks' duration, the eighth session to be held at Geneva from 5 to 16 February and the ninth session in New York from 3 to 13 September;

4. *Further decides* to convene the tenth session of the Intergovernmental Negotiating Committee, which is to be held in New York from 6 to 17 January 1997 and, pending the entry into force of the Convention, to convene, as necessary, a further session of the Committee in 1997, of up to two weeks' duration, the exact dates and venue of which shall be determined at a later stage;

5. *Recommends* that, upon the entry into force of the Convention, a session of the Conference of the Parties to the Convention be convened in the second and third weeks of June 1997 or, alternatively, in the second and third weeks of August 1997, the exact dates and venue of the session to be determined at a later stage;

6. *Requests* all countries, the United Nations system, including the regional commissions, relevant subregional and regional organizations, appropriate scientific and business communities, trade unions, relevant non-governmental organizations and other interested groups, to take action for the prompt implementation of the Convention and its relevant regional implementation annexes upon its entry into force and in this regard to respond effectively to the needs in the African, Asian and Latin American and Caribbean regions;

7. *Urges* all countries, the United Nations system, including the regional commissions, relevant subregional and regional organizations and all other relevant actors to undertake actions and measures for the full and effective implementation of the provisions of Intergovernmental Negotiating Committee resolution 5/1 of 17 June 1994 on urgent action for Africa, as well as to promote actions for other affected developing countries and regions, and invites all States to continue to communicate to the interim secretariat of the Convention, in addition to the information they have already provided, information on actions undertaken and/or envisaged for the implementation of the provisions of resolution 5/1;

8. *Decides* that the work of the Intergovernmental Negotiating Committee and the interim secretariat shall continue to be funded through existing United Nations budgetary resources, without negatively affecting its programmed activities, and through voluntary contributions to the Trust Fund established pursuant to General Assembly resolution 47/188 specifically for that purpose and administered by the head of the interim secretariat under the authority of the Secretary-General, with the possibility of using the Fund, as appropriate, to support the participation of representatives of non-governmental organizations in the work of the Committee and of carrying over resources contributed from one fiscal year to the other;

9. *Urges* States, regional economic integration organizations and other interested organizations to reinforce the capacity of the interim secretariat of the Convention through substantial contributions to the Trust Fund;

10. *Renews its appeals* to Governments, regional economic integration organizations and other interested organizations, including non-governmental organizations, to make early contributions to the Special Voluntary Fund in order to ensure an enhanced effective participation in the negotiation process of developing countries affected by desertification and/or drought, in particular the least developed countries;

11. *Notes* the arrangements and contributions made by the Secretary-General and relevant organizations active in the fields of desertification, drought and development, including the United Nations Development Programme/Office to Combat Desertification and Drought, the United Nations Environment Programme, the Food and Agriculture Organization of the United Nations, the United Nations Conference on Trade and Development, the United Nations Educational, Scientific and Cultural Organization and the World Bank, as regards the Intergovernmental Negotiating Committee and the interim secretariat in the conduct of their mandate, and invites them to intensify and expand such support and collaboration in the future, as appropriate;

12. *Also notes* the arrangements concluded between the interim secretariat of the Convention and the International Fund for Agricultural Development and the World Meteorological Organization, whereby appropriate actions are taken for an active collaboration and support of activities at the national and regional levels in affected developing countries, in particular those in Africa, and the least developed countries;

13. *Requests* the Chairman of the Intergovernmental Negotiating Committee to submit progress reports on the work of the Committee to the General Assembly, the Commission on Sustainable Development and other appropriate bodies of the United Nations;

14. *Requests* the Secretary-General to bring the present resolution to the attention of all Governments, the relevant specialized agencies and programmes of the United Nations, international financial institutions, other intergovernmental and non-governmental organizations and other relevant institutions;

15. *Also requests* the Secretary-General to submit to the General Assembly at its fifty-first session a report on the implementation of the present resolution relative to the United Nations Convention to Combat Desertification in Those Countries Experiencing Serious Drought and/or Desertification, particularly in Africa, under the item entitled "Implementation of decisions and recommendations of the United Nations Conference on Environment and Development".

General Assembly resolution 50/112

20 December 1995      Meeting 96      Adopted without vote

Approved by Second Committee (A/50/618/Add.1) without vote, 5 December (meeting 41); draft by Vice-Chairman (A/C.2/50/L.54), based on informal consultations on draft by Philippines, for Group of 77 and China (A/C.2/50/L.22); agenda item 96 (a).

*Meeting numbers.* GA 50th session: 2nd Committee 18-23, 36, 41; plenary 96.

*REFERENCES*

[1]UNEP/GC.18/23 & Corr.1 & Add.1,2. [2]A/50/25 (dec. 18/25). [3]A/C.2/50/2. [4]*Multilateral Treaties Deposited with the Secretary-General: Status as at 31 December 1995* (ST/LEG/SER.E/14), Sales No. E.96.V.5. [5]YUN 1992, p. 681. [6]YUN 1994, p. 938. [7]A/AC.237/91 & Add.1. [8]YUN 1992, p. 682, GA res. 47/195, 22 Dec. 1992. [9]A/50/536. [10]FCCC/CP/1995/7 & Add.1. [11]FCCC/SBSTA/1995/3. [12]FCCC/SBI/1995/1. [13]FCCC/SBI/1995/2. [14]FCCC/CP/1995/4.

(15)FCCC/AGBM/1995/2. (16)FCCC/AGBM/1995/7. (17)YUN 1994, p. 939, GA res. 49/120, 19 Dec. 1994. (18)A/50/716 & Add.1. (19)YUN 1992, p. 683. (20)YUN 1993, p. 810. (21)YUN 1994, p. 939, GA res. 49/117, 19 Dec. 1994. (22)A/50/218. (23)YUN 1994, p. 939. (24)UNEP/CBD/COP/2/7. (25)UNEP/ CBD/COP/2/19. (26)UNEP/CDB/COP/2/5. (27)E/1995/32. (28)A/50/25 (dec. 18/36 A). (29)UNEP/OzL.Pro.7/12. (30)YUN 1987, p. 686. (31)DP/1996/18/Add.1. (32)YUN 1985, p. 804. (33)YUN 1988, p. 810. (34)UNEP/OzL.Pro.2/3. (35)YUN 1992, p. 684. (36)YUN 1994, p. 944. (37)YUN 1994, p. 945, GA res. 49/234, 23 Dec. 1994. (38)A/50/74. (39)A/50/74/Add.1. (40)YUN 1994, p. 947, GA res. 49/115, 19 Dec. 1994. (41)YUN 1993, p. 816, GA res. 48/175, 21 Dec. 1993. (42)A/50/347. (43)A/50/515. (44)E/1995/34 (dec. 95/6).

# Environmental activities

## The atmosphere

### The Climate Agenda

In March, the UNEP Executive Director submitted to the Governing Council a summary of a proposal for an integrating framework for the 1979 World Climate Programme (WCP).[1] Entitled "Climate Agenda",[2] the proposal for international climate-related programmes was presented jointly by the six international organizations involved in implementing WCP—UNEP, FAO, the International Union of Scientific Unions, the United Nations Educational, Scientific and Cultural Organization and its Intergovernmental Oceanographic Commission (IOC), and the World Meteorological Organization (WMO). It suggested action to be taken by international organizations and Governments and summarized achievements to date. It stated that the Agenda would be developed along four main thrusts: new frontiers in climate science and production; climate services for sustainable development; studies of climate impact assessments and response strategies to reduce vulnerability; and dedicated observations of the climate system.

By a 26 May decision,[3] the UNEP Governing Council endorsed the proposal that UNEP should be responsible for coordinating international activities under thrust 3 of the Agenda (studies of climate impact assessments and response strategies to reduce vulnerabilities) of the four thrusts identified. It urged relevant international organizations to align their climate-related activities according to the Agenda's priorities and to implement those activities, and to establish reporting and coordinating mechanisms for WCP. It asked Governments to undertake those parts of the programme for which they had the required expertise; to strengthen or establish national climate programmes required by the 1992 United Nations Framework Convention on Climate Change[4] and the Intergovernmental Meeting on WCP;[5] to

cooperate in building the scientific and technical capacity of developing countries and countries with economies in transition; and to provide a modest amount of additional resources to international organizations to coordinate the implementation of the Climate Agenda and to manage the programmes, through the inter-agency Coordinating Committee of WCP.

### Intergovernmental Panel on Climate Change

By a 25 May decision,[6] the Governing Council, taking note of a report of the Executive Director on the work of the Intergovernmental Panel on Climate Change (IPCC) during 1994,[7] asked her, jointly with the Secretary-General of WMO, to continue arrangements to support IPCC and to ensure the participation of specialists in its activities. It asked IPCC to continue to update the assessments on the science, impacts, response options and technical aspects of the socio-economics of climate change. Governments were urged to continue to support the Panel's activities and to contribute to its trust fund. The Council also asked the Panel to report to the Governing Council in 1997.

IPCC (Rome, December 1995) approved the 1995 Second Assessment Report, which was expected to improve the world's understanding of the causes of global climate change.

## Terrestrial ecosystems

### Biological diversity

**Report of the Secretary-General.** The Commission on Sustainable Development (New York, 11-28 April), considered a February report of the Secretary-General[8] reviewing the progress made in implementing the aims set out in Chapter 15 (conservation of biological diversity) of Agenda 21, since its adoption by UNCED in 1992.[4] The Secretary-General concluded that there appeared to have been no major initiatives on the issues of technology transfer and financial mechanisms that would ensure the additional financial resources needed by developing countries. Some issues that still needed to be addressed included the harmonization of principles and obligations; implementation of methods and procedures for better understanding and identification of various components of biodiversity and the conservation and management of indigenous species; the mobilization and exchange of information relevant to conservation and the sustainable use of biodiversity; coordinated promotion of public awareness; and the determination of the potential impact of intended projects and programmes on the delicate balance and well-being of fragile and complex ecosystems worldwide. The Secretary-General noted, however, that significant progress had been made on most issues pertaining to the Convention on Biological Diversity.

Proposals for action dealt with cooperation programmes and collaborative arrangements; information exchange and networking; education, science, human resources development, technology transfer and capacity-building; policy reforms; UN assessment of the impacts of macroeconomic and other issues affecting biodiversity; government assessment of existing information systems; and improving and increasing understanding of the role of biodiversity in sustainable development.

**Commission action.** In April,[9] the Commission on Sustainable Development urged the international community to support efforts towards capacity-building, human resource development and the transfer of technology to developing countries for the conservation of biodiversity. Countries were urged to take measures with the aim of having the private sector facilitate access to joint development of technology. The international community should make efforts to develop economic mechanisms to determine the costs and benefits of the conservation of biological diversity and sustainable use of its components. Governments were asked to undertake policies aimed at the implementation of the objectives of chapter 15 of Agenda 21, and to integrate actions to conserve biodiversity and to promote sustainable development. The Commission further urged Governments to promote the fair and equitable sharing of benefits accruing from the utilization of biological resources.

### Biosafety

In a 25 May decision,[10] the UNEP Governing Council expressed support for the holding of a global expert consultation on International Technical Guidelines for Safety in Biotechnology and Related Capacity-Building Requirements and endorsed and supported UNEP sponsorship of regional consultations on the subject. It asked the Executive Director to consult with the secretariat of the 1992 Convention on Biological Diversity[11] in implementing its decision and to report in 1997.

The UNEP International Guidelines for Safety in Biotechnology were adopted at the Global Consultation of Government-designated Experts (Cairo, Egypt, December 1995) following a consensus building process involving seven regional and subregional consultations and encompassing a wide spectrum of stakeholders including the biotechnology industry. A capacity-building programme related to the implementation of the Guidelines was formulated by UNEP for submission to potential donors for financial and technical support to assist developing countries and countries with economies in transition developing national biosafety mechanisms.

### Desertification and drought control

**Report of the Secretary-General.** In accordance with a 1993 General Assembly request,[12] the Secretary-General submitted an August report[13] on desertification and drought. He noted that cooperation between UNEP and UNDP had been strengthened, with the two organizations having signed, on 26 April 1995, a new partnership agreement to refocus the joint venture into the Partnership to Combat Desertification and Drought. Under the agreement the two organizations would develop programme packages and jointly mobilize resources in areas where they had complementary expertise. He described support activities undertaken by the international community to combat desertification and drought.

### Plan of Action to Combat Desertification

On 26 May, the Governing Council, having considered the Executive Director's report on progress achieved in 1993 and 1994[14] in implementing the 1977 Plan of Action to Combat Desertification (PACD),[15] including implementation in the Sudano-Sahelian region, adopted a decision[16] in which it expressed support for UNEP efforts concerning the development of an updated assessment method for drylands and desertification, as well as its efforts to increase awareness of desertification and disseminate information materials to a range of media. It asked the Executive Director to continue promoting cooperation and coordination of efforts to combat desertification and intensifying research and development in collaboration with relevant institutions and centres. The Council asked the Executive Director to submit her report on PACD, through the Economic and Social Council, to the General Assembly at its fiftieth (1995) session. It also requested her to participate in assisting Governments and intergovernmental and non-governmental organizations to implement the 1994 United Nations Convention to Combat Desertification in those Countries Experiencing Serious Drought and/or Desertification, particularly in Africa,[17] and to support the Convention's interim secretariat. The Executive Director was further asked to: report to the Council in 1997 on the implementation of the April 1995 UNEP/UNDP Partnership to Combat Desertification; contribute to implementing the 1994 Convention and to urgent action for Africa; invite other UN organizations and agencies, financial institutions, funds and other interested parties to join the Partnership and contribute to efforts of developing countries to combat desertification and mitigate the effects of drought; and to report to the Council in 1997 on the activities undertaken.

By a June note,[18] the Secretary-General transmitted the Executive Director's report to the Economic and Social Council and the Assembly. In June, the Council, by **decision 1995/234**, took note of the Secretary-General's note and, by **decision 50/434** of 20 December, the Assembly took note of it.

(For the activities of the United Nations Sudano-Sahelian Office, renamed in 1995 the Office to Combat Drought and Desertification, see PART FOUR, Chapter III.)

**Commission on Sustainable Development action.** At its April session,[9] the Commission on Sustainable Development expressed concern that, according to a February report of the Secretary-General on combating desertification and drought,[19] the economic loss caused by desertification worldwide, in terms of average income foregone, was estimated in 1991 to be more than $42 billion annually, most of it in Africa ($9.3 billion) and Asia ($20.9 billion). The Commission urged Governments to take an integrated approach to combating desertification and drew their attention to the potential of the 1994 Convention[17] to provide an in-country coordinating mechanism for integrated land management in arid, semi-arid and sub-humid lands. It also urged them to enhance public awareness of the issue. The Commission recommended that organizations of the UN system take steps to facilitate the financing of programmes and projects in dry and sub-humid areas and urged developed countries to agree on policies and resource allocations for fulfilling their commitments towards implementing the 1994 Convention. Affected countries and regional and subregional organizations were urged to: set up institutional arrangements and policy frameworks for developing, managing and implementing national strategies and action programmes; encourage Governments to improve national coordination among agencies to combat desertification and manage drought more effectively and for the sustainable use of natural resources; and establish, as a matter of highest priority, coordinating arrangements and to create partnerships with donors and national stakeholders, within the context of the 1994 Convention.

**GENERAL ASSEMBLY ACTION**

On 20 December, the General Assembly adopted **resolution 50/114**.

### Desertification and drought

*The General Assembly,*

*Recalling* its resolution 48/175 of 21 December 1993 in which it recalled the decisions of the United Nations Conference on Environment and Development set forth in chapter 12 of Agenda 21, entitled "Managing fragile ecosystems: combating desertification and drought", and took note of the recommendation contained in paragraph 38.27 of Agenda 21 and of decision 93/33 of 18 June 1993 of the Governing Council of the United Nations Development Programme,

*Noting* the work being undertaken by the Intergovernmental Negotiating Committee for the Elaboration of an International Convention to Combat Desertification in Those Countries Experiencing Serious Drought and/or Desertification, particularly in Africa,

*Referring* to its resolution 48/175, in which it recalled the appeals to the United Nations Development Programme and the United Nations Environment Programme to continue and strengthen their cooperation in combating desertification, notably through support for the Office to Combat Desertification and Drought by the joint venture programme,

*Having considered* the report of the Secretary-General on the implementation of its resolution 48/175,

*Expressing its concern* at the present level of resources available to relevant United Nations bodies, including the Office to Combat Desertification and Drought of the United Nations Development Programme, to support activities to combat desertification and mitigate the effects of drought in all affected developing countries and regions,

1. *Welcomes* the efforts made by the United Nations Environment Programme and the United Nations Development Programme to strengthen their cooperation in combating desertification through the United Nations Environment Programme/United Nations Development Programme partnership to combat desertification;

2. *Renews its appeal* to Governments, regional economic integration organizations and other interested organizations, as well as non-governmental organizations, to make contributions to relevant United Nations bodies, including the Office to Combat Desertification and Drought of the United Nations Development Programme, to strengthen their capacity to support activities to combat desertification and mitigate the effects of drought in all affected developing countries and regions;

3. *Requests* the Secretary-General to submit to the General Assembly at its fifty-second session a report on the implementation of the present resolution, which would be considered under one unified sub-item on the agenda entitled "Implementation of decisions and recommendations of the United Nations Conference on Environment and Development", under the item entitled "Environment and sustainable development".

General Assembly resolution 50/114

20 December 1995          Meeting 96          Adopted without vote

Approved by Second Committee (A/50/618/Add.2) without vote, 5 December (meeting 41); draft by Vice-Chairman (A/C.2/50/L.52), based on informal consultations on draft by Philippines, for Group of 77 and China (A/C.2/50/L.29); agenda item 96 (b).

*Meeting numbers.* GA 50th session: 2nd Committee 18-23, 38, 41; plenary 96.

### World Day to Combat Desertification and Drought

In a June report to the General Assembly,[20] the Secretary-General described activities undertaken by the interim secretariat of the 1994 Convention and UN programmes and specialized agencies to observe the first World Day to Combat Desertification and Drought (17 June 1995), which was proclaimed by the General Assembly in 1994.[21] The purpose of the activities was to raise public awareness with a view to ensuring the successful implementation of the Convention. The Secretary-General outlined ways and means by which the interim secretariat could assist Member States in organizing their national activities.

On 20 December, the General Assembly by **decision 50/433** took note of the Secretary-General's report.

### Deforestation and forest degradation

The Secretary-General submitted to the Commission on Sustainable Development a February report,[22] prepared by FAO as task manager for chapter 11 (combating deforestation) of Agenda 21, adopted by UNCED in 1992.[23] Chapter 11 and the Non-legally Binding Authoritative Statement of Principles for a Global Consensus on the Management, Conservation and Sustainable Development of All Types of Forests (Forest Principles), also an outcome of UNCED, both aimed to achieve the sustainable management of all types of forests, with an equal emphasis on conservation and management. The report summarized information on progress made and experiences reported by 34 Governments, 20 NGOs, 5 private-sector associations, 14 UN agencies and 6 non-UN intergovernmental organizations and presented proposals for action by the Commission.

At its April session,[9] the Commission urged Governments and interested organizations and groups to mobilize financial resources and the transfer of environmentally sound technology for the effective implementation of the Forest Principles and chapter 11 of Agenda 21. It considered further concrete actions, on the management, conservation and sustainable development of forests, particularly by Governments, to be an urgent priority. Stressing the need to further assess actions taken to combat deforestation and forest degradation and to promote management, conservation and sustainable development of all types of forests, the Commission decided to establish an open-ended ad hoc intergovernmental panel on forests, under its aegis. The Panel's mandate, modalities for its establishment and terms of reference for the Panel were annexed to the Commission's report.

In a May note to the Economic and Social Council,[24] the Secretariat outlined the priority areas for the proposed panel, which were to include elements based on chapter 11 of Agenda 21 and the Forest Principles. The panel would consider the following main issues: implementation of UNCED decisions related to forests; international cooperation in financial assistance and technology transfer; scientific research, forest assessment and development of criteria and indicators for sustainable forest management; trade and environment relating to forest products and services; and international organizations and multilateral institutions and instruments, including legal mechanisms. The note discussed the Panel's work programme, composition and programme budget implications.

The Council, by **decision 1995/226** of 1 June, approved the estabishment of an open-ended ad hoc intergovernmental panel on forests. By **decision 1995/316** of 28 July, the Council decided that the Panel should meet in New York from 11 to 15 September 1995.

The open-ended Ad Hoc Intergovernmental Panel on Forests (IPF), at its first session (New York, 11-15 September),[25] elected its officers, adopted its agenda and decided on the dates and venues of future meetings. The Panel considered suggestions regarding its future work programme as contained in an August report of the Secretary-General.[26] It decided to extend the duration of its second session, to be held in Geneva, by one week so that the dates would be from 11 to 22 March 1996, and that its third session would be from 2 to 13 September 1996, at a venue to be determined. That decision was approved by the Economic and Social Council by **decision 1995/318** of 25 October 1995.

**UNEP Governing Council action.** On 25 May, the Governing Council requested the Executive Director to place UNEP's experience and expertise in environmental issues related to forests at the disposal of the Panel, and to further develop and strengthen that expertise through the relevant elements of the UNEP work programme so as to contribute effectively to the Panel's work.[27]

### Sustainable mountain development

The Secretary-General submitted to the Commission on Sustainable Development a February report on progress made in implementing the aims set out in chapter 13 of Agenda 21 (managing fragile ecosystems: sustainable mountain development).[28] The report was prepared by FAO, as task manager of the issue, in consultation with the Secretariat. It focused on new approaches concerning the integrated management of the natural resource base, the interaction between rural mountain populations and resources in terms of sustainable livelihoods, and efforts to ensure environmentally sound and sustainable development of mountain areas. Proposals for action dealt with poverty eradication; strengthening a global information network and database; strengthening country capacity; raising awareness through the preparation and organization of a world conference on sustainable mountain development; and formulating and negotiating regional or subregional mountain conventions and developing a global mountain charter.

At its April session,[9] the Commission called on Governments and the international community to take action to combat poverty in mountain areas, diversify mountain economies, protect the environment and food security of local communities, strengthen global information networks and databases, addressing environmental problems, and create new livelihood opportunities. It urged expanding the network of protected mountain areas to cover all types of mountain ecosystems, strengthening existing management capabilities for conserving mountain ecosystems, species and genetic diversity and promoting local and non-governmental organizations' participation in the management of those areas. It urged interested Governments to prepare and implement comprehensive national and/or local mountain development programmes.

**Land resources**

The Commission on Sustainable Development considered a February report,[29] submitted by the Secretary-General describing progress made in implementing the aims set out in chapter 10 of Agenda 21 (Integrated approach to the planning and management of land resources). The report, prepared by FAO in consultation with the Secretariat, concluded that advances had been made in developing tools and technology to support more productive sustainable land use, but much less progress had been made in creating the capacity to apply the tools routinely in all countries. It noted that attention needed to be paid to developing linkages between traditional knowledge and land management systems on the one hand, and the application of science and technology on the other. A series of proposals for action by the Commission were presented.

The Commission, at its April session,[9] noting with concern the convergence of poverty, hunger and the degradation of terrestrial resources in environmentally more fragile marginal lands, where the large majority of poor smallholder farmers were increasingly located, called on Governments, bilateral donors, multilateral financial institutions, technical specialized agencies, and NGOs to give high priority to rural development in such lower-potential areas. It asked the Secretary-General to strengthen coordination and cooperation within the UN system by developing and implementing joint approaches and collaborative programmes. The Commission urged Governments, with the cooperation and support of UN bodies and organizations, to pay particular attention to establishing stable land-use systems in areas where important ecosystems or ecoregions were being endangered by human activities; applying integrated planning and development approaches in regions that were becoming open to intensified settlement and agricultural production; and bringing about integrated approaches to capacity-building. Noting with appreciation the outcome of the International Workshop on Integrated Land Management (Wageningen, the Netherlands, 20-22 February 1995),[30] organized by FAO and hosted by the Government of the Netherlands, the Commission invited the Government and FAO to disseminate the workshop's report and recommendations as widely as possible.

## Marine ecosystems

### Protection of the marine environment from land-based activities

**UNEP action.** By a 25 May decision,[31] the Governing Council called on all States and relevant international and non-governmental organizations to consider the draft Global Programme of Action for the Protection of the Marine Environment from Land-based Activities,[32] and to communicate any proposals for amendment to the Executive Director for submission to the Intergovernmental Conference to Adopt a Global Programme of Action for the Protection of the Marine Environment from Land-based Activities (see below). It called on States participating in the Conference to consider how attention could be given to support national and regional activities on urban waste-water management and treatment and persistent organic pollutants (POPs).

**Intergovernmental Conference.** The Intergovernmental Conference to Adopt a Global Programme of Action for the Protection of the Marine Environment from Land-based Activities (Washington, D.C., 23 October–3 November 1995)[33] was convened by the UNEP Executive Director pursuant to a 1993 Governing Council decision.[34] The Conference was preceded by a preparatory meeting (Reykjavik, Iceland, 6-10 March)[35] and a Consultation on Financial and Capacity-building Issues related to the Global Programme of Action (Washington, D.C., 16-18 August 1995).[36]

Following consideration of the draft Global Programme of Action[32] and the comments submitted thereon,[37] the Conference adopted the Programme of Action, which was designed to guide national and/or regional authorities in devising and implementing sustained action to prevent, reduce, control and/or eliminate marine degradation

from land-based activities. Actions for consideration by States dealt with sewage, POPs (polychlori-
nated biphenyls (PCBs), dioxans and furans,
aldrin, dieldrin, DDT, endrin, chlordane, hexa-
chlorobenzene, mirex, toxaphene, heptachlor),
radioactive substances, heavy metals, oils
(hydrocarbons), nutrients, sediment mobilization,
litter, and physical alterations and destruction of
habitats.

The High-Level Segment of the Conference was
held on 31 October and 1 November. It discussed
institutional follow-up and preparations for consideration of oceans issues by the Commission on
Sustainable Development, the mobilization of
resources finance and the importance of the oceans
and the marine environment to life on Earth and
the serious degradation afflicting them. At the
close of the High-Level Segment, the Washington
Declaration on Protection of the Marine Environment from Land-based Activities was adopted. By
the Declaration, the 109 countries participating in
the Conference declared their commitment to protect and preserve the marine environment from
the impacts of land-based activities through
numerous measures.

As to future activities, it was stated that during
the first two months of 1996, the UNEP secretariat
would review the status of activities dealing with
the protection of the marine environment from
land-based activities in the 13 regions of the UNEP
Regional Seas Programme and other regional seas
and activities. Based on that review, a series of
regional workshops would be organized to identify the activities and projects that individual nations and regions would have to carry out to develop and begin implementation of regional
strategic programmes.

**Living marine resources**

*Drift-net fishing*

In response to a 1994 General Assembly request,[38] the Secretary-General submitted, in
October, information received from States, intergovernmental and non-governmental organizations and scientific institutions on activities undertaken with regard to large-scale pelagic drift-net
fishing and its impact on the living marine
resources of the world's oceans and seas.[39]

*Unauthorized fishing in
zones of national jurisdiction*

In accordance with a 1994 General Assembly
request,[40] the Secretary-General, in an October
report,[41] presented information provided by
States, UN bodies and organizations, intergovernmental organizations, regional and subregional
fisheries organizations and arrangements, and
NGOs on the issue of unauthorized fishing in zones

of national jurisdiction and its impact on living
marine resources.

*Fisheries by-catch and discards*

Pursuant to a 1994 General Assembly request,[42] the Secretary-General, by an October
note,[43] transmitted a report by FAO on fisheries
by-catch and discards and their impact on the sustainable use of the world's living marine resources.
The report presented an assessment of fisheries by-
catch and discards and noted that the Rome
Consensus on World Fisheries, adopted by the
Ministerial Meeting on Fisheries (Rome, 14 and
15 March), stated that improved fisheries conservation and management, along with better protection from harmful sea- and land-based activities, were crucial to maintaining world fish
resources and aquatic ecosystems. The Meeting
urged Governments and international organizations to take prompt action to adopt policies, apply
measures and develop techniques to reduce by-
catches, fish discards and post-harvest losses. Concerning high seas fisheries, the report pointed out
that information was poor and incomplete, and as
a result conservation and management of high seas
resources was weak. The United Nations Conference on Straddling Fish Stocks and Highly Migratory Fish Stocks, which met in 1993[44] and
1994,[14] sought to improve and strengthen the
conservation and management of those two types
of stocks and to ensure that data and the timeliness of the provision of data were greatly enhanced. (For action concerning the 1995 meetings
of the Conference and the Agreement for the Implementation of the Provisions of the 1982 United
Nations Convention on the Law of the Sea relating to the Conservation and Management of
Straddling Fish Stocks and Highly Migratory Fish
Stocks, see PART FIVE, Chapter IV.) The draft international code of conduct for responsible fisheries, which was currently open for revision, addressed matters pertaining to by-catch and
discards. FAO estimated that a significant reduction in discards by the year 2000 of around 60 per
cent could be achieved by improving the selectivity
of fishing gear; developing international standards
for research, and additional research designed specifically to address problems resulting from by-
catch; greater interaction between research staff,
industry and fisheries managers; and by applying
appropriate technology through fisheries regulations. As a consequence of a June decision of the
FAO Council, an open-ended Technical Committee was set up to review and agree on the form
and content of the code of conduct for responsible fisheries and any follow-up action that might
be required to finalize the code prior to its submission to the 1995 FAO Conference (see also PART
SEVEN, Chapter III).

On 5 December, the General Assembly adopted **resolution 50/25**.

**Large-scale pelagic drift-net fishing and its impact on the living marine resources of the world's oceans and seas; unauthorized fishing in zones of national jurisdiction and its impact on the living marine resources of the world's oceans and seas; and fisheries by-catch and discards and their impact on the sustainable use of the world's living marine resources**

*The General Assembly*,

*Reaffirming* its resolutions 44/225 of 22 December 1989, 45/197 of 21 December 1990 and 46/215 of 20 December 1991, as well as its decisions 47/443 of 22 December 1992, 48/445 of 21 December 1993 and 49/436 of 19 December 1994, on large-scale pelagic drift-net fishing and its impact on the living marine resources of the world's oceans and seas,

*Recalling* its resolution 49/116 of 19 December 1994 on unauthorized fishing in zones of national jurisdiction and its impact on the living marine resources of the world's oceans and seas,

*Recalling also* its resolution 49/118 of 19 December 1994 on fisheries by-catch and discards and their impact on the sustainable use of the world's living marine resources,

*Recognizing* the efforts that international organizations and members of the international community have made to reduce by-catch and discards in fishing operations,

*Conscious* of the need to promote and facilitate international cooperation, especially at the regional and subregional levels, in order to ensure the sustainable development and use of the living marine resources of the world's oceans and seas, consistent with the present resolution,

*Noting* that the Agreement for the Implementation of the Provisions of the United Nations Convention on the Law of the Sea of 10 December 1982 relating to the Conservation and Management of Straddling Fish Stocks and Highly Migratory Fish Stocks, adopted by the United Nations Conference on Straddling Fish Stocks and Highly Migratory Fish Stocks, provides in its general principles that States shall minimize pollution, waste, discards, catch by lost or abandoned gear, catch of non-target species, both fish and non-fish species, and impacts on associated or dependent species, in particular endangered species, through measures including, to the extent practicable, the development and use of selective, environmentally safe and cost-effective fishing gear and techniques, and further provides that States shall take measures, including the establishment of regulations, to ensure that vessels flying their flags do not conduct unauthorized fishing within areas under the national jurisdiction of other States,

*Noting also* that the Food and Agriculture Organization of the United Nations has adopted a Code of Conduct for Responsible Fisheries, which sets out principles and global standards of behaviour for responsible practices to conserve, manage and develop fisheries, including guidelines for fishing on the high seas and in areas under the national jurisdiction of other States, and on fishing gear selectivity and practices, with the aim of reducing by-catch and discards,

*Expressing deep concern* at the detrimental impact of unauthorized fishing in areas under national jurisdiction, where the overwhelming proportion of the global fish catch is harvested, on the sustainable development of the world's fishery resources and on the food security and economies of many States, particularly developing States,

*Reaffirming* the rights and duties of coastal States to ensure proper conservation and management measures with respect to the living resources in areas under their national jurisdiction, in accordance with international law as reflected in the United Nations Convention on the Law of the Sea,

*Taking note* of the reports of the Secretary-General on large-scale pelagic drift-net fishing and its impact on the living marine resources of the world's oceans and seas, and unauthorized fishing in zones of national jurisdiction and its impact on the living marine resources of the world's oceans and seas,

*Taking note also* of the report of the Food and Agriculture Organization of the United Nations on fisheries by-catch and discards and their impact on the sustainable use of the world's living marine resources,

*Acknowledging with appreciation* the measures taken and the progress made by members of the international community, international organizations and regional economic integration organizations to implement and support the objectives of resolution 46/215,

*Expressing deep concern* that there are continuing reports of activities inconsistent with the terms of resolution 46/215 and unauthorized fishing inconsistent with the terms of resolution 49/116,

1. *Reaffirms* the importance it attaches to compliance with its resolution 46/215, in particular to those provisions of the resolution calling for full implementation of a global moratorium on all large-scale pelagic drift-net fishing on the high seas of the world's oceans and seas, including enclosed seas and semi-enclosed seas;

2. *Urges* all authorities of members of the international community to take greater enforcement responsibility to ensure full compliance with resolution 46/215 and to impose appropriate sanctions, consistent with their obligations under international law, against acts contrary to the terms of that resolution;

3. *Calls upon* States to take the responsibility, consistent with their obligations under international law as reflected in the United Nations Convention on the Law of the Sea and resolution 49/116, to take measures to ensure that no fishing vessels entitled to fly their national flags fish in areas under the national jurisdiction of other States unless duly authorized by the competent authorities of the coastal State or States concerned; such authorized fishing operations should be carried out in accordance with the conditions set out in the authorization;

4. *Urges* States, relevant international organizations and regional and subregional fisheries management organizations and arrangements to take action to adopt policies, apply measures, collect and exchange data and develop techniques to reduce by-catches, fish discards and post-harvest losses consistent with international law and relevant international instruments, including the Code of Conduct for Responsible Fisheries;

5. *Calls upon* development assistance organizations to make it a high priority to support, including through financial and/or technical assistance, efforts of developing coastal States, in particular the least developed coun-

tries and the small island developing States, to improve the monitoring and control of fishing activities and the enforcement of fishing regulations;

6. *Requests* the Secretary-General to bring the present resolution to the attention of all members of the international community, relevant intergovernmental organizations, the organizations and bodies of the United Nations system, regional and subregional fisheries management organizations, and relevant non-governmental organizations, and invites them to provide the Secretary-General with information relevant to the implementation of the present resolution;

7. *Also requests* the Secretary-General to ensure that reporting on all major fisheries-related activities and instruments is effectively coordinated and duplication of activities and reporting minimized and that relevant scientific and technical studies are disseminated to the international community, and invites the relevant specialized agencies, including the Food and Agriculture Organization of the United Nations, as well as regional and subregional fisheries organizations and arrangements, to cooperate with the Secretary-General to that end;

8. *Further requests* the Secretary-General to submit to the General Assembly at its fifty-first session a report on further developments relating to the implementation of resolutions 46/215, 49/116 and 49/118, taking into account the information provided by States, relevant specialized agencies, in particular the Food and Agriculture Organization of the United Nations, and other appropriate organs, organizations and programmes of the United Nations system, regional and subregional organizations and arrangements and other relevant intergovernmental and non-governmental organizations;

9. *Decides* to include in the provisional agenda of its fifty-first session, under the item entitled "Law of the sea", a sub-item entitled "Large-scale pelagic drift-net fishing and its impact on the living marine resources of the world's oceans and seas; unauthorized fishing in zones of national jurisdiction and its impact on the living marine resources of the world's oceans and seas; and fisheries by-catch and discards and their impact on the sustainable use of the world's living marine resources".

General Assembly resolution 50/25

5 December 1995     Meeting 81     Adopted without vote

19-nation draft (A/50/L.36 & Add.1); agenda item 96 *(c)*.
*Meeting numbers.* GA 50th session: plenary 80, 81.

### Coral reef initiative

In 1995, Australia, France, Jamaica, Japan, the Philippines, Sweden, the United Kingdom and the United States announced a major initiative to protect coral reefs in partnership with other coral reef nations around the world, NGOs, international organizations, multilateral developments banks, and private sector businesses. The eight nations hosted an international workshop (Dumaguete City, the Philippines, 29 May–2 June), during which they adopted a Call to Action which defined the purpose and urgency of the workshop and developed a Framework for Action to serve as a basis for national and local coral reef management efforts.

**UNEP action.** In a 26 May decision,[45] the UNEP Governing Council welcomed the inter-

national coral reef initiative, which was a partnership of Governments, international organizations and NGOs, to address capacity-building, research and monitoring and sustainable management and use of coral reefs and associated ecosystems. It supported the establishment of a global reef coral monitoring network, as proposed as part of the coastal zone and shelf module of the Global Ozone Observing System by UNEP, the World Conservation Union, IOC, WMO and the International Geosphere-Biosphere Programme, to monitor the status of reefs and enhance their management.

For Governing Council action regarding the Action Plan for the Protection and Management of the Marine and Coastal Environment of the South Asian Seas Region, see below.

### Conservation of wildlife

The Agreement on the Conservation of African-Eurasian Migratory Waterbirds was adopted at a meeting (The Hague, Netherlands, 12-16 June), held under the auspices of the Convention on Migratory Species. The Agreement covered species of birds that were ecologically dependent on wetlands for at least part of their annual cycle and included 172 species, among them, pelicans, storks, flamingoes, ducks and geese, and concerned 116 countries in Europe, parts of Asia and North America, the Middle East and Africa, in addition to the European Union. The Netherlands agreed to provide an interim secretariat for the Agreement and to host the first session of the meeting of the Parties. The secretariat functions were to be assumed by the secretariat of the Convention in Bonn, Germany, which was administered by UNEP.

The first meeting of the Parties to the Agreement on the Conservation of Bats in Europe (Bristol, United Kingdom, July) established a permanent secretariat and a work programme. The regional agreement was concluded in 1994 under the auspices of the Convention on Migratory Species.

Memoranda of Understanding on the conservation of two extremely endangered species, the Siberian crane and the slender-billed curlew, were signed in 1995.

### Protection against harmful products and wastes

The Secretary-General submitted to the Economic and Social Council and the General Assembly a May report[45] for the fourth triennial review of the Consolidated List of Products Whose Consumption and/or Sale Have Been Banned, Withdrawn, Severely Restricted or Not Approved by Governments. Previous reviews were submitted in 1992,[47] 1989,[48] and 1986.[49]

The Secretary-General presented an overview of recent developments regarding harmful products and their effects on human health and the environment. In order to enhance the efficiency of production and distribution of the List, the Secretary-General proposed publishing it in two parts, one for pharmaceuticals and the other for chemicals, and that the List be issued every two years with a supplement for the intervening year.

In July, the Council took note of the Secretary-General's report by **decision 1995/234**, as did the Assembly by **decision 50/431** of 20 December.

## Persistent organic pollutants

In a 25 May decision,[50] the UNEP Governing Council invited the Inter-Organization Programme for the Sound Management of Chemicals, working with the International Programme on Chemical Safety and the Intergovernmental Forum on Chemical Safety, to initiate an assessment process of POPs and asked the Executive Director to support the work of the process. It invited the Intergovernmental Forum to develop recommendations and information on international action, including an international legal mechanism on POPs to be considered in 1997 by the Council and the WHO World Health Assembly. The Council called on States, the United Nations and its specialized agencies, regional, organizations and other relevant organizations to participate and provide contributions for the assessment process and for the participation of developing countries and countries with economies in transition.

## Chemical safety

In a May addendum[51] to a report concerning activities related to measures beyond the prior informed consent (PIC) procedure for certain hazardous chemicals in international trade,[52] which might be considered in conjunction with the development of a PIC convention, the Executive Director stated that the issue was considered at the first meeting of the Intersessional Group of the Intergovernmental Forum on Chemical Safety (Bruges, Belgium, 20-23 March).[53] The meeting had expressed broad support for the development of a PIC convention. Trade-related issues that might be considered under the proposed convention were discussed at the first session of the UNEP Meeting of the Expert Group on International Environmental Agreements and Trade (New York, 30 and 31 March).

By a 26 May decision,[54] the UNEP Governing Council authorized the Executive Director to prepare for and convene, with FAO and in consultation with Governments and other relevant international organizations, an intergovernmental negotiating committee to prepare an international legally binding instrument for the application of the PIC Procedure. She was invited to convene also, in cooperation with FAO, a government-designated group of experts to consider the negotiations on the convention on PIC and the activities to be undertaken in accordance with the Council's decision on POPs (see above). The Council asked her to recommend further measures needed to reduce the risks from a limited number of hazardous chemicals, either within or beyond the scope of the existing PIC procedure, and to report thereon in 1997. The Council decided that it should consider in 1997 the need to develop further measures, including the possibility that the mandate of the intergovernmental negotiating committee for the legally binding PIC procedure be extended to provide a basis for developing such measures. It also decided that the committee should begin its work as soon as possible and not later than January 1996. The Executive Director was asked to invite relevant international organizations to participate in the negotiating process for the development of the instrument and to convene, together with the FAO Director-General, a diplomatic conference to adopt and sign an international legally binding instrument for the application of the PIC procedure, preferably not later than early 1997.

## Leaded gasoline

At its April session,[9] the Commission on Sustainable Development, taking note of an International Workshop on Phasing Lead Out of Gasoline (Washington, D.C., 14-15 March) hosted by Mexico and the United States, called on all countries to consider developing action plans with a view to phasing out or reducing the use of lead in gasoline and invited them to inform the Commission in 1996 of their decisions and progress.[7] Donor countries and international financial institutions should assist developing countries in the financing and transfer of relevant technologies and developing countries were encouraged to disseminate their knowledge in the reduction of or phasing out of leaded gasoline, including the use of biomass ethanol as an environmentally sound substitute. The Commission called on countries to guard against the replacement of lead in gasoline with the excessive use of aromatics that were also harmful to human health.

**UNEP action.** In a 26 May decision,[55] the Governing Council called on Governments to fully consider the costs and benefits of phasing out lead in gasoline, including the risks associated with increased aromatic components in the absence of catalytic converters. It urged countries that had already begun to phase out the use of lead in gasoline, as well as international organizations and international financial institutions to assist other countries in their efforts to achieve such a phase-out and to promote the transfer of technology towards the overall reduction of vehicular emissions. The Executive Director was invited to participate in those efforts as part of her broader efforts to promote more effective approaches to emissions control.

### Irradiated nuclear fuel

As requested by the UNEP Governing Council in 1993,[56] the Executive Director submitted a report[57] describing developments resulting from the work of the Joint International Atomic Energy Agency/International Maritime Organization (IMO)/UNEP Working Group on the carriage of irradiated nuclear fuel by sea. She stated that consultations were ongoing in the relevant IMO committees and subcommittees. In 1995, the IMO Assembly reviewed the Code for the Safe Carriage of Irradiated Nuclear Fuel, Plutonium and High-level Radioactive Wastes in Flasks on Board Ships, which was adopted in 1993.[58]

On 25 May, the Governing Council took note of the Executive Director's report and asked UNEP to continue its collaboration with the relevant organizations and to report on progress in 1997.[59]

### Environmental technologies

In a decision of 26 May,[60] the UNEP Governing Council took note of a report of the Executive Director on cleaner production, environmental technology assessment, awareness and preparedness for emergencies at the local level, and development of international guidelines on information on potential environmental impacts that exporters of a technology could feasibly provide to importers.[61] The Council called on the Executive Director to continue to support Governments and industry in developing cleaner production demonstration countries and to support and monitor the activities of the National Cleaner Production Centres. In collaboration with the United Nations Industrial Development Organization, the UNEP Industry and Environment/Programme Activity Centre was engaged in establishing National Cleaner Production Centres in a number of developing countries and countries with economies in transition to raise the awareness and strengthen the skills of government and industry managers, promote cooperation with other countries, and launch local demonstration projects and research. While noting progress made in those areas, the Council expressed concern that environmentally unfriendly technologies continued to remain in use. It asked the Executive Director to develop draft international guidelines on information on potential environmental impacts that technology exporters or suppliers should provide to technology importers or users and to develop initial

mechanisms of verification. It also requested her to report on progress in 1997.

### Hazardous wastes used by the military

Taking note of a February report of the Executive Director on the application of environmental norms by military establishments,[62] the UNEP Governing Council, on 25 May,[63] authorized the Executive Director to arrange, within available resources, regional meetings, in cooperation with the regional commissions and regional organizations, for implementing a 1993 Council decision[64] concerning the design and implementation of environmental plans for military establishments relating to hazardous waste management.

## Environmental monitoring and assessment

### Earthwatch

As requested by the General Assembly in 1993,[65] the Executive Director reported in February on the UN system-wide Earthwatch (environment assessment activities), environment monitoring and environment assessment within UNEP.[66] Earthwatch was first proposed at the 1972 United Nations Conference on the Human Environment[67] as a UN system-wide mechanism, coordinated by UNEP, to monitor major global disturbance in the environment and to give early warning of problems requiring international action. The first meeting of the inter-agency Earthwatch Working Party in 1994[52] redefined the mission of Earthwatch as being to coordinate, harmonize and integrate observing, assessment and reporting activities across the UN system to provide environmental and appropriate socioeconomic information, and for early warning of emerging problems requiring international action.

The Executive Director stated that Earthwatch was being revitalized as a collaborative set of international efforts to coordinate, harmonize and integrate observing, assessment and reporting activities. Regarding environment monitoring, she stated that building on the experience of the Global Environment Monitoring System (GEMS) and other efforts, international scientific planning and inter-agency cooperative efforts were underway to advance a set of complementary global observing systems—the Global Climate Observing System, the Global Ocean Observing System, and the Global Terrestrial Observing System. UNEP was a co-sponsor of those systems which intended to go beyond time-limited research programmes towards the operational data collection and assessment necessary to identify and respond to changes which might affect the human condition. Environmental assessment within UNEP included the assessment and reporting functions of GEMS, the data management functions of the Global Resource Information Database, the capacity-building and regional networking of the environment and natural resources information networks and UN system-wide Earthwatch coordination. The programme had been reshaped to attend more explicitly to the needs of policy makers and to the data- and information-handling capacities of countries. The Executive Director outlined a funding strategy for the programme.

By a 25 May decision,[68] the Governing Council endorsed the refocused strategy of the Programme to undertake, at the request of Governments or their representative bodies, policy-relevant asssessment and reporting of environment and development issues through cooperating networks of national and regional agencies, organizations or institutions, and to promote the development of data and information management capacity in the bodies situated in developing countries to ensure their full participation. It asked the Executive Director to continue to provide assistance, within available resources, to developing countries to build capacity to enable them to use and benefit from the data and information acquired through the Earthwatch programme. The Council authorized her to transmit her report and its decision through the Economic and Social Council, to the General Assembly at its fiftieth session. The report was transmitted by a note of the Secretary-General on 24 August[69] and was considered by the Assembly before its adoption of **resolution 50/110** of 20 December.

By a March note,[70] the Executive Director transmitted to the Governing Council a report of the Administrative Committee on Coordination (ACC), which recommended to the Council and interested UN organizations that sufficient resources be allocated to Earthwatch and to capacity-building for information gathering. ACC considered that the Council might wish to address ways to promote ready access to the environmental information essential to ensure a coordinated and efficient approach to informed decision-making for sustainable development, including the implementation of a UN system-wide Earthwatch. In that regard, the report stated that UNEP might be asked to convene an ad hoc governmental expert group to further clarify the matter. ACC recommended that UNEP and other organizations involved in Earthwatch should continue to develop approaches to linking socio-economic and environmental assessment and reporting, and that the Earthwatch Working Party give further attention to the conceptual issues involved. It also recommended that UNEP and concerned organizations of the UN system participate in the process underway to initiate a Development Watch, suggested by the 1994 Earth-

watch Working Party,[52] and to ensure its close interlinkage with Earthwatch.

On 25 May, the ACC recommendations were endorsed by the Governing Council.[68] On the same date, the Governing Council asked ACC to continue to report to the Council at its regular sessions.[71]

**Commission on Sustainable Development.** The Commission on Sustainable Development considered the Secretary-General's March report on information for decision-making,[72] in which he proposed that through the coordination of UNEP, the UN system, with NGOs, should support, strengthen and operationalize Earthwatch. He stated that UNDP, UNEP and the UN Department for Policy Coordination and Sustainable Development, in cooperation with other interested organizations, should further define Development Watch. The Secretary-General noted that Earthwatch and Development Watch should evolve as two closely linked support systems for monitoring and assessing sustainable development. A programme of work for Development Watch and its linkage to Earthwatch should be provided to the Commission in 1997.

At its April session,[9] the Commission requested UNEP, with the UN Department for Policy Coordination and Sustainable Development, UNEP, the World Bank, WHO and FAO, in cooperation with the regional commissions and other interested organizations, to further define Development Watch and to submit a progress report on the implementation of the programme of work for Development Watch in 1997, taking into account the need for a close linkage between Development Watch and Earthwatch. It urged Governments and major groups, as well as relevant international organizations and the scientific community, to participate in strengthening Earthwatch.

### State of the environment

*Statement on the environment*

In a March report,[73] the Executive Director presented to the UNEP Governing Council a statement on the environment, which covered the important new environmental challenges addressed in a proposed sub-programme on globalization trends and the environment, with particular emphasis on trade and environment. She proposed that future statements on the environment focus on one or two critical issues, such as major emerging environmental threats or driving forces of environmental change.

On 26 May, the Governing Council, having considered the Executive Director's statement, welcomed the proposed format of her statement and asked her to continue to improve it.[74]

### State of the environment report

In a 26 May decision,[75] the Governing Council requested the Executive Director to prepare a new, comprehensive report on the state of the world environment, consisting of three parts: the present state of the global environment; the state of the global environment in the year 2015; and findings, conclusions and recommendations. It recommended for inclusion in the first two parts issues dealing with essential problems of and threats to the environment and the global effects of expected development growth, population increase and main trends of consumption, production and urbanization patterns. For inclusion in the second part, it recommended the expected impact of population increase, consumption and production patterns and economic development on the environment. The third part should include recommended measures and actions that could effectively reverse unwelcome trends and challenge principal threats to the environment, and specific institutional and legal measures for the implementation of proposed actions. The Council asked that the preparation of the report be based on the existing data collected and prepared by UNEP, in cooperation with UNDP, WHO, FAO, the World Bank and other UN agencies and bodies, and on the results of research and studies by public and private scientific and statistical institutions engaged in the formulation of environmental and development assessments and forecasts. It asked the Executive Director to consult periodically with the Committee of Permanent Representatives regarding the preparation of the report and to submit a first report in 1997.

### Environmental indicators

On 25 May, the Governing Council, taking note of the Executive Director's progress report, including a plan of action, on the development and use of environmental indicators,[52] endorsed the plan of action on environmental and sustainable development indicators to be carried out in collaboration with other agencies and parties.[76]

## Other matters

### Global Environment Facility

In a March report,[77] the Executive Director reviewed UNEP's role in the Global Environmental Facility (GEF) on the basis of the Instrument for the Establishment of the Restructured GEF, which was adopted in 1994 by the three implementing agencies of GEF—UNDP, UNEP and the World Bank.[78] UNEP maintained a portfolio of five pilot-phase projects totalling $19.3 million and one pre-investment study of $0.1 million. Three projects were on biodiversity and two were on

climate change. Two additional projects were approved by the GEF Council in February, both dealing with climate change.

**UNDP action.** In his report covering 1995 activities,[79] the UNDP Administrator stated that all 55 UNDP-GEF pilot-phase projects, authorized between 1991 and 1994 and totalling $242.5 million, had been approved as at September 1995; 53 were being implemented. Twenty-one pre-investment projects, totalling $20.8 million, and $13 million for its Small Grants Programme were also approved, bringing the total of the UNDP pilot phase portfolio to $276.5 million. For the UNDP-GEF I portfolio, approvals were granted in 1995 for 31 technical cooperation projects; 20 GEF Project Development Facility (PDF) Block A projects; and 18 GEF PDF Block B projects, including a replenishment of the Small Grants Programme for $25.9 million, bringing the UNDP-GEF I portfolio to $76.5 million.

**World Bank.** As at the end of fiscal year 1995 (30 June 1995), 63 projects, valued at $558 million, were allocated for World Bank GEF investment projects. The allocation of the Bank's GEF investment project resources, by focal areas, was: 50 per cent for biodiversity; 30 per cent climate change; 12 per cent international waters; 7 per cent the reduction of ozone-depleting substances; and 1 per cent multiple thematic areas.

### Environmental law and sustainable development

In a 26 May decision,[80] the Governing Council, expressing concern that three years after UNCED's adoption of Agenda 21 in 1992,[23] only limited progress had been made in realizing its goals and objectives and that existing and proposed legal and institutional instruments and arrangements had so far been ineffective in halting the deterioration of the global environment, asked the Executive Director to monitor the implementation of international legal instruments concerning the environment, to elaborate and recommend, where necessary, means to enhance their effectiveness and to provide support to the convention secretariats. It also asked her to update, within available resources, a compilation of international environmental instruments and, in implementing the mandate for a database on national and international environmental law, to use the existing World Conservation Union database as the core archival system. It further asked her to develop a position paper for international environmental law aiming at sustainable development, to prepare a study on the need for and feasibility of new international environmental instruments aiming at sustainable development and to keep the Committee of Permanent Representatives informed of UNEP's progress and to submit a report thereon in 1997.

## Environmental standards within the UN

The Governing Council, by a 25 May decision,[81] called on the Executive Director to recommend strategies to promote environmental housekeeping by UNEP, and to advise and encourage the rest of the UN system to develop and apply similar strategies for improving their own environmental performance and promoting sustainable development. It asked the General Assembly to adopt a resolution calling for the application of good environmental housekeeping practices by the UN system as soon as possible and invited the Executive Director to report to the Council, at each of its regular sessions, on the steps taken and progress achieved by UNEP and other entities of the UN system.

## Environmental emergencies

In a February report,[82] the Executive Director described activities and services provided by the Joint UNEP/UN Department of Humanitarian Affairs Environment Unit, which was set up in 1994[83] to deal with environmental aspects of emergencies to Governments upon request. Annexed to the report were the draft terms of reference of the Advisory Group on Environmental Emergencies, which held its first meeting in January 1995.

By a 26 May decision,[84] the Governing Council welcomed the establishment of the Joint Unit and invited Governments and relevant UN agencies, bodies and programmes to cooperate with it in its efforts to assist countries, particularly developing countries, facing environmental emergencies. It asked the Executive Director to allocate the necessary resources for the 1996-1997 biennium for the administration and operation of the Joint Unit with strict regard to economy. It also asked her to submit in 1997 a progress report on the activities of the Joint Unit.

## Women and environment

The UNEP Governing Council, by a 26 May decision,[85] took note of a report of the Executive Director on the role of women in environment and development,[86] and of her intention to integrate fully a gender perspective and balance into UNEP's work and activities. It urged Governments to assist her in achieving those goals by proposing qualified candidates of both sexes for vacancies announced to Governments. The Council decided to send a message, which was annexed to its decision, to the Fourth World Conference on Women (see PART FOUR, Chapter X). The Executive Director was urged to ensure an input and contribution from UNEP on gender and environment in the preparation of other subsequent conferences, particularly the United Nations Conference on Human Settlements (see next chapter) and asked her to report in 1997 on the implementation of its decision.

## Occupied Palestinian and other Arab territories

Taking note of a report of the Executive Director on the environmental situation in the occupied Palestinian and other Arab territories,[87] the Governing Council, on 25 May,[88] asked her to update the report and to implement a 1993 Council decision,[89] which requested her to provide technical assistance in Palestinian institutional and self-capacity-building in the environment.

## Regional concerns

### Africa

On 26 May,[90] the UNEP Governing Council asked the Executive Director to ensure that in implementing the proposed programme of work and budget for the 1996-1997 biennium,[91] emphasis was placed on areas of concern to Africa, including land resources, with support for implementing the 1994 United Nations Convention to Combat Desertification in those Countries Experiencing Serious Drought and/or Desertification, particularly in Africa,[92] and conservation and rehabilitation strategies in conflict areas; water resources, including strengthening African inland water management groups and regional technical cooperation networks, and reclamation and rehabilitation of African lakes and wetlands areas; biological resources, with the promotion of the implementation of the 1992 Convention on Biological Diversity,[93] and related programmes in Africa; coastal and marine resources, including an updated inventory of coastal and marine resources of four African regional seas programmes, and ratification and implementation of African regional seas conventions and protocols; support to the African preparations for the follow-up to the Fourth World Conference on Women (1995) (see PART FOUR, Chapter X); and global and regional servicing and support, including support to the programmes of the 1993 African Ministerial Conference on the Environment[94] and capacity-building of its secretariat, strengthening of the Regional Office for Africa, a focus on capacity-building, and public awareness, information and participation programmes. It also asked her to implement the activities within available resources and to report in 1997.

In another decision of the same date,[95] the Council urged the Executive Director to work closely in partnership with UNDP to increase support for technical cooperation among African countries in the area of environmental management and sustainable development and to urge

UNDP to explore the possibility of opening a special window for technical cooperation among African countries; to facilitate measures to promote technical cooperation among African countries and capacity-building and utilization in environmental management and sustainable development for the African region; to collaborate with UNDP in seeking support for the mobilization of resources from within the UN system, bilateral and multilateral agencies, NGOs and the private sector to facilitate the development and implementation of further measures for technical cooperation among African countries. It asked her to urge the Economic Commission for Africa to incorporate environmental management and sustainable development into its capacity-building and utilization initiative for Africa and to urge the Organization of African Unity and subregional organizations to incorporate measures and mechanisms for technical cooperation among African countries and capacity-building and utilization for Africa into the programming of their resource mobilization and policy design strategies. The Executive Director was authorized to ask UNDP to carry out a study of the feasibility, modalities, approaches, measures and resource requirements for the successful implementation of technical cooperation among African countries and to collaborate with UNEP on those aspects of the study relating to environmental management and sustainable development; to request UNDP to submit the report of the study to the Economic and Social Council in 1996; and to report to the Governing Council in 1997 on the results of those efforts.

### Asia and the South Asian Seas region

By a 25 May decision,[96] the Governing Council asked the Executive Director to support, within available resources, the objectives of the North-East Asia Regional Environment Programme through technical and financial support to the third meeting on environmental cooperation in north-east Asia, scheduled for early 1996 in Mongolia, and through technical support to the priority project proposals adopted at the second meeting on environmental cooperation in north-east Asia.[97] On 26 May, the Council asked the Executive Director to support, within available resources, the Regional Office for West Asia.[98]

By another decision of the same date,[99] the Council called on the Executive Director to give due attention, within the context of UNEP's regional seas programme, to the further development and implementation of the Action Plan for the Protection and Management of the Marine and Coastal Environment of the South Asian Seas region, adopted at a Meeting of Plenipotentiaries (New Delhi, India, 24 March 1995), and to provide, within available resources, adequate finances and staff time for implementing the Action Plan.

### Council of Arab Ministers

The Governing Council, on 26 May, asked the Executive Director to support, within available resources, the aims of the Council of Arab Ministers Responsible for the Environment, particularly the Arab priority project proposals under Arab programmes for sustainable development approved for implementation by the Council of Arab Ministers.[98]

### Europe

In a March report,[100] the Executive Director described activities carried out within the "Environment for Europe" process for countries with economies in transition during the 1994-1995 biennium and presented activities planned for 1996-1997.

On 25 May, the Governing Council took note of the progress achieved in assisting countries in transition with their environmental problems and asked the Executive Director to continue those efforts.[101]

### Regional representation

On 26 May, the UNEP Governing Council adopted three decisions concerning UNEP's regional representation.

By the first,[102] the Council took note of the Executive Director's report on the role and function of the regional representation of UNEP;[103] endorsed the measures that she was taking to strengthen the regional office system and asked her to keep under review the configuration of regional offices, the relationship between regional and outposted offices of UNEP and the future development of subregional offices. It urged the Executive Director to consider locating, wherever possible and necessary, the regional offices of UNEP at the same venues as the regional commissions.

In another decision related to decentralizing and strengthening of the UNEP regional offices,[104] the Council asked the Executive Director to continue the process of decentralizing UNEP by strengthening the role and function of its regional offices and granting them greater functional and administrative capacities. The Council outlined a series of elements for that process and recommended that the Executive Director, at least once a year, include in the agenda of the Committee of Permanent Representatives the subject of strengthening the regional offices.

In the third decision, which dealt with strengthening regional coordination,[105] the Council called on the Executive Director, within available resources, to encourage the holding of annual meetings at the ministerial level to evaluate and design policies and strategies to guide the activities of the regional offices, and to hold consultations annually in Nairobi with the permanent representatives and delegations of countries to assess the progress of the programme.

## Training networks

On 26 May, the Governing Council urged the Executive Director to strengthen the environmental training networks in each region, with a view to achieving the implementation of environmental education and training.[106]

By another decision of the same date,[107] the Council asked the Executive Director to ensure that training courses in integrated environmental management aimed at strengthening the capacity of developing countries and countries with economies in transition, as well as courses in collaboration with other bilateral and multilateral organizations, continued to be organized.

### REFERENCES

[1]YUN 1979, p. 1312. [2]UNEP/GC.18/17 & Corr.1. [3]A/50/25 (dec. 18/20 A). [4]YUN 1992, p. 681. [5]YUN 1993, p. 1304. [6]A/50/25 (dec. 18/20 B). [7]YUN 1994, p. 938. [8]E/CN.17/1995/7. [9]E/1995/32. [10]A/50/25 (dec. 18/36 B). [11]YUN 1992, p. 683. [12]YUN 1993, p. 816, GA res. 48/175, 21 Dec. 1993. [13]A/50/347. [14]YUN 1994, p. 947. [15]YUN 1977, p. 509. [16]A/50/25 (dec. 18/26). [17]YUN 1994, p. 944. [18]A/50/227-E/1995/99. [19]E/CN.17/1995/4. [20]A/50/516. [21]YUN 1994, p. 945, GA res. 49/115, 19 Dec. 1994. [22]E/CN.17/1995/3. [23]YUN 1992, p. 672. [24]E/1995/72 & Add.1. [25]E/CN.17/IPF/1995/3. [26]E/CN.17/IPF/1995/2. [27]A/50/25 (dec. 18/30). [28]E/CN.17/1995/5. [29]E/CN.17/1995/2. [30]E/CN.17/1995/33. [31]A/50/25 (dec. 18/31). [32]UNEP(OCA)/LBA/IG.2/3. [33]A/51/116. [34]YUN 1993, p. 818. [35]UNEP(OCA)/LBA/IG.2/L.INF.4. [36]UNEP(OCA)/LBA/IG.2/4. [37]UNEP(OCA)/LBA/IG.2/3/Add.1-7. [38]YUN 1994, p. 950, GA dec. 49/436, 19 Dec. 1994. [39]A/50/553. [40]YUN 1994, p. 950, GA res. 49/116, 19 Dec. 1994. [41]A/50/549. [42]YUN 1994, p. 949, GA res. 49/118, 19 Dec. 1994. [43]A/50/552. [44]YUN 1993, p. 817. [45]A/50/25 (dec. 18/33). [46]A/50/182 & Corr.1-E/1995/66 & Corr.1. [47]YUN 1992, p. 685. [48]A/44/276-E/1989/78. [49]YUN 1986, p. 654. [50]A/50/25 (dec. 18/32). [51]UNEP/GC.18/7/Add.1. [52]YUN 1994, p. 942. [53]IGS/95.11. [54]A/50/25 (dec. 18/12). [55]Ibid. (dec. 18/35). [56]YUN 1993, p. 812. [57]UNEP/GC.18/35. [58]YUN 1993, p. 1310. [59]A/50/25 (dec. 18/21). [60]Ibid. (dec. 18/23). [61]UNEP/GC.18/5. [62]UNEP/GC.18/6 & Add.1. [63]A/50/25 (dec. 18/29). [64]YUN 1993, p. 820. [65]Ibid., p. 812, GA res. 48/192, 21 Dec. 1993. [66]UNEP/GC.18/4 & Corr.1. [67]YUN 1972, p. 322. [68]A/50/25 (dec. 18/27 A). [69]A/50/371. [70]UNEP/GC.18/33. [71]Ibid. (dec. 18/27 B). [72]E/CN.17/1995/18. [73]UNEP/GC.18/24. [74]A/50/25 (dec. 18/8). [75]Ibid. (dec. 18/27 C). [76]Ibid. (dec. 18/28). [77]UNEP/GC.18/20. [78]YUN 1994, p. 941. [79]DP/1996/18/Add.1. [80]A/50/25 (dec. 18/9). [81]Ibid. (dec. 18/10). [82]UNEP/GC.18/2. [83]YUN 1994, p. 944. [84]A/50/25 (dec. 18/19). [85]Ibid. (dec. 18/6). [86]UNEP/GC.18/11. [87]UNEP/GC.18/18 & Corr.1. [88]A/50/25 (dec. 18/11). [89]YUN 1993, p. 820. [90]A/50/25 (dec. 18/39 A). [91]UNEP/GC.18/9. [92]YUN 1994, p. 944. [93]YUN 1992, p. 683. [94]YUN 1993, p. 603. [95]A/50/25 (dec. 18/39 B). [96]Ibid. (dec. 18/39 D). [97]YUN 1994, p. 718. [98]A/50/25 (dec. 18/39 C). [99]Ibid. (dec. 18/39 E). [100]UNEP/GC.18/19 & Corr.1. [101]A/50/25 (dec. 18/24). [102]Ibid. (dec. 18/38 A). [103]UNEP/GC.18/31. [104]A/50/25 (dec. 18/38 B). [105]Ibid. (dec. 18/38 C). [106]Ibid. (dec. 18/37 A). [107]Ibid. (dec. 18/37 B).

Chapter VIII

# Population and human settlements

At mid-1995, world population stood at 5.75 billion and, while the rate of growth was declining, world population was increasing by more than 86 million persons annually. During the year, UN bodies, particularly the United Nations Population Fund (UNFPA), continued to implement the Programme of Action adopted at the 1994 International Conference on Population and Development. UNFPA strengthened its collaborative and coordination efforts with its partner agencies and organizations within the UN system and with bilateral agencies and non-governmental organizations. The Fund's population assistance expenditures in 1995 totalled some $311 million. By year's end, 2,479 projects were being assisted. In December, the General Assembly urged all countries to consider their current spending priorities with a view to making additional contributions for the Programme of Action's implementation.

The Commission on Population and Development, formerly the Population Commission, met in February/March to review population needs, policies and programmes, discuss follow-up action to the Conference and consider the programme of work in population. The Commission discussed the work carried out by the Population Division of the UN Department for Economic and Social Information and Policy Analysis, which included population projections and the analysis of demographic variables at the world level covering fertility and family planning, mortality, and international and internal migration. The Division provided technical assistance services to more than 80 projects in 45 developing countries and countries with economies in transition during the year.

In the area of human settlements, preparations continued for the 1996 UN Conference on Human Settlements (Habitat II), also known as "The City Summit". The Conference's Preparatory Committee held its second substantive session in April/May, when it considered progress made by the Conference secretariat in preparing for the Conference and progress in national preparations. It also worked on a draft statement of principles and global plan of action to be considered by the Conference.

In December, the Assembly renewed its appeal to all Governments, as well as to international and regional financial institutions, to make substantial contributions to the voluntary fund established for the purpose of financing the Conference's preparatory activities.

The Commission on Human Settlements, which held its fifteenth session in April/May, had as its major themes a review of national action on housing since the 1976 UN Conference on Human Settlements and sustainable human settlements in an urbanizing world. It also carried out a mid-term review of the 1988 Global Strategy for Shelter to the Year 2000 and transmitted a report on the subject to the Assembly, which endorsed it in December. The UN Centre for Human Settlements (Habitat) supported 193 technical cooperation programmes and projects in 79 countries and 42 global, regional and interregional programmes in 1995, with an overall budget of more than $19.6 million.

## Follow-up to the 1994 Conference on Population and Development

**Commission on Population and Development consideration.** In response to a 1994 General Assembly resolution,[1] the Secretary-General submitted to the Commission on Population and Development a report[2] on the implications of the recommendations of the 1994 International Conference on Population and Development (ICPD)[3] for the work programme of the UN Department for Economic and Social Information and Policy Analysis (DESIPA) on population. The report summarized the substantive results of the Conference, examined the programmatic implications of the results for DESIPA's medium-term plan of work and considered the institutional implications for the United Nations of the Conference recommendations.

The Commission adopted a decision,[4] which it brought to the Economic and Social Council's attention, in which it transmitted its views on the implications for the Commission of the follow-up to the Conference. Those views addressed the functioning of the Commission, including its proposed terms of reference and membership, secretariat support, management, inter-agency coordination and resource base, and its work programme.

**UNFPA programme priorities.** In response to a 1993 UNDP Governing Council request,[5] the

Executive Director of UNFPA submitted to the annual session (June) of the Executive Board of the United Nations Development Programme (UNDP)/UNFPA a report[6] on programme priorities and future directions of UNFPA in the light of ICPD. On 13 January,[7] the Board had taken note of an interim report on the same subject.[8]

The Executive Director noted that all activities in UNFPA-assisted programmes would be undertaken in accordance with the principles and objectives of the ICPD Programme of Action.[3] UNFPA proposed to concentrate its funding in three core areas: reproductive health and family planning; population policy; and advocacy. Within each area, support would be given for research, training, awareness creation and information dissemination. ICPD had recognized that there could be no sustainable development without the full and equal participation of women, gender equality and equity and the empowerment of women; gender concerns would therefore be integral components of all aspects of UNFPA programming.

With regard to its operational strategy, UNFPA, in all its programming, would work closely with Governments to assure that activities were tailored to their specific needs; build partnerships with implementing agencies, including non-governmental organizations (NGOs) and the private sector; and expand coordination with UN funds, programmes and organizations. It would also continue to provide technical assistance through UNFPA country support teams under inter-agency technical support service arrangements.

As to resource allocation, UNFPA would base its system on the principles and goals recommended in the ICPD Programme of Action: all countries seeking UNFPA assistance should adhere to the principles contained in the Programme of Action; technical assistance would be provided to all developing countries requesting it; financial assistance would be focused on countries with the lowest level of achievement with regard to ICPD goals related to access to reproductive health and family planning services, access to education by girls and women, and levels of infant and maternal mortality; financial assistance to countries that were close to or had surpassed ICPD goals would be phased out or limited; temporary financial assistance would be provided to countries with economies in transition, particularly for family planning and reproductive health; and South-South cooperation would be promoted.

On 25 July, the Inter-Agency Task Force for the Implementation of ICPD held its second meeting in New York. Its aim was to enhance inter-agency collaboration and coordination in implementing the ICPD Programme of Action at the country level, under the leadership of the resident coordinator. The Task Force had prepared a set of Guidelines for the UN Resident Coordinator System and developed a Common Advocacy Statement on Population and Development. At its second regular session of 1995 (12-13 October),[9] the Administrative Committee on Coordination (ACC) agreed that the Task Force should be expanded to focus more broadly on social services for all.

On 14 June, the UNDP/UNFPA Executive Board supported[10] the broad outline of the future programme of assistance of UNFPA. It endorsed the core programme areas and requested the Executive Director to concentrate assistance within those areas, while stressing that population policies were an integral part of a strategy for sustainable development and the need for UNFPA to cooperate with other partners in formulating its strategies. It took note of the approach proposed for allocating resources and invited the Executive Director to refine that approach, based on the relevant provisions of the ICPD Programme of Action, as well as on other qualitative and quantitative indicators, and taking into account the views of delegations and the need to give special attention to the least developed countries and Africa, and to report to the Board in 1996. The Executive Director was asked to submit to the Board in 1996: a background note on the issue of whether the Board should consider becoming a member of the United Nations Children's Fund (UNICEF)/World Health Organization (WHO) Joint Committee on Health Policy; and a draft mission statement for UNFPA based on her report,[6] taking into account the Board's discussion.

**Report of the Secretary-General.** In response to a 1994 General Assembly resolution,[1] the Secretary-General submitted, through the Economic and Social Council, a report[11] on the implementation of that resolution, which dealt with the report of ICPD. The report addressed the question of requirements for international assistance and flow of financial resources for assisting the implementation of the Programme of Action; institutional follow-up issues and reporting procedures; implementation by the specialized agencies and all related organizations of the UN system; implementation by the UNDP/UNFPA Executive Board; and implementation by the Commission on Population and Development.

ECONOMIC AND SOCIAL COUNCIL ACTION

On 28 July, the Economic and Social Council adopted **resolution 1995/55**.

**Implementation of the Programme of Action of the International Conference on Population and Development**
*The Economic and Social Council,*
*Recalling* General Assembly resolution 49/128 of 19 December 1994 on the report of the International Conference on Population and Development, in which the

Assembly endorsed the Programme of Action of the Conference, and taking note of Commission on Population and Development decisions 1995/1 and 1995/2 of 2 March 1995,

1. *Takes note* of the report of the Secretary-General on the implementation of General Assembly resolution 49/128;

2. *Notes* the action taken so far by Governments and the international community to implement the Programme of Action of the International Conference on Population and Development and encourages them to strengthen their efforts in this regard in a concerted and coordinated manner;

3. *Endorses* the terms of reference proposed by the Commission on Population and Development in its report on its twenty-eighth session, which reflect the comprehensive and integrated nature of population and development, and decides that, in addition to those terms of reference, the Commission should review the findings of research and analysis pertaining to the interrelationship between population and development at the national, regional and global levels and advise the Council thereon;

4. *Decides* that Government representatives nominated to serve on the Commission should have the relevant background in population and development;

5. *Also decides* that the Commission should monitor the progress made in achieving the targets for financial resources set out in chapters XIII and XIV of the Programme of Action, taking fully into account paragraph 7 of resolution 49/128;

6. *Further decides*, bearing in mind the new terms of reference, new mandate and work programme of the Commission, to enlarge the Commission's membership at a resumed session of the Council no later than 31 December 1995, recognizing the importance of adequate representation;

7. *Endorses* the multi-year work programme proposed by the Commission in its report on its twenty-eighth session;

8. *Recalls* that the General Assembly, in paragraph 28 (*c*) of its resolution 49/128, requested the Council to consider the submission of recommendations to the Secretary-General regarding the establishment of an appropriate inter-agency coordination, collaboration and harmonization mechanism for the implementation of the Programme of Action;

9. *Taking note* of the fact that the Secretary-General has established an Inter-Agency Task Force on the Implementation of the Programme of Action, with the United Nations Population Fund as the lead agency, and welcomes the intention of the Secretary-General to report through the Commission to the Council on the work of the task force, so as to ensure system-wide cooperation in the implementation of the Programme of Action;

10. *Notes* that the work programme of the Commission set out in its report contains a request that the work of the Inter-Agency Task Force be expanded to include migration issues;

11. *Invites* the Department for Economic and Social Information and Policy Analysis of the Secretariat and other relevant organizations and bodies, in particular the United Nations Population Fund, to work closely in the preparation of reports for the Commission;

12. *Also invites* the Department, in its report to the Commission, to analyse and evaluate relevant compara-

tive international information on population and development issues, to focus on issues that need further clarification and to submit suggestions for recommendations by the Commission;

13. *Recommends* that the General Assembly at its fiftieth session consider further, in the context of the comprehensive review of the implementation of its resolution 48/162 of 20 December 1993, the establishment of a separate executive board for the United Nations Population Fund, taking into account the role of the Fund in the follow-up of the implementation of the Programme of Action and bearing in mind the administrative, budgetary and programme implications of such a proposal.

Economic and Social Council resolution 1995/55

| 28 July 1995 | Meeting 57 | Adopted without vote |

Draft by Vice-President (E/1995/L.61), based on informal consultations on draft by Philippines, for Group of 77 and China (E/1995/L.28); agenda item 6 (*e*).

Meeting numbers. ESC 39-41, 45, 57.

**GENERAL ASSEMBLY ACTION**

On 20 December, the General Assembly adopted **resolution 50/124**.

### Implementation of the Programme of Action of the International Conference on Population and Development

*The General Assembly*,

*Recalling* its resolutions 49/128 of 19 December 1994 on the report of the International Conference on Population and Development, and 48/162 of 20 December 1993 on the restructuring and revitalization of the United Nations in the economic, social and related fields,

*Recalling also* Economic and Social Council decision 1994/227 of 14 July 1994, by which the Council approved the provisional agenda and documentation for the twenty-eighth session of the then Population Commission, including discussion of the implications of the recommendations of the International Conference on Population and Development,

*Recalling further* Economic and Social Council resolution 1995/55 of 28 July 1995 on the implementation of the Programme of Action of the International Conference on Population and Development, by which the Council endorsed the terms of reference proposed by the renamed Commission on Population and Development in its report on its twenty-eighth session, which reflect the comprehensive and integrated nature of population and development,

*Acknowledging* fully the integrated approach taken during the International Conference on Population and Development, which recognizes the interrelationship between population, sustained economic growth and sustainable development,

*Having considered* the report of the Secretary-General on the implementation of General Assembly resolution 49/128 on the report of the International Conference on Population and Development,

*Recognizing* that the implementation of the recommendations contained in the Programme of Action is the sovereign right of every country, in accordance with its national laws and development priorities, with full respect for the various religious and ethical values and cultural backgrounds of its peoples and in conformity with universally recognized international human rights,

*Reaffirming* the importance of the principles and concepts set out in the Rio Declaration on Environment and Development and Agenda 21 for the purpose of implementing the Programme of Action of the International Conference on Population and Development, and in that regard recognizing that chapter 5 of Agenda 21 and chapter III of the Programme of Action reinforce one another and together form a comprehensive and compelling up-to-date account of what needs to be done about the interface between population, environment and sustainable development,

*Noting with satisfaction* the contribution that the outcome of the International Conference on Population and Development has made to the World Summit for Social Development and the Fourth World Conference on Women, and expressing its belief in the contribution that the outcome of the International Conference on Population and Development will make to the forthcoming United Nations Conference on Human Settlements (Habitat II) and in the elaboration of an agenda for development, in particular with regard to the call for a greater investment in people,

1. *Notes* the action taken so far by Governments and the international community to implement the Programme of Action of the International Conference on Population and Development, and encourages them to strengthen their efforts in that regard;

2. *Reiterates* its commitment to the full implementation of the Programme of Action, and reaffirms that Governments should continue to commit themselves at the highest political level to achieving its goals and objectives, which reflect a new integrated approach to population and development, and to take a lead role in coordinating the implementation, monitoring and evaluation of the follow-up actions;

3. *Takes note with appreciation* of the report of the Secretary-General on the implementation of General Assembly resolution 49/128 and of the proposals contained therein;

4. *Takes note* of the following proposals made by the United Nations Population Fund in the above-mentioned report:

(a) To replace the biennial report of the Fund to the Commission on Population and Development on multilateral population assistance by an annual report on the amount of financial resources allocated for the implementation of the Programme of Action at the national and international levels;

(b) To refine and improve further, where necessary, the current system devoted to monitoring the amount of international assistance for programmes dealing with population and development so as to render it more accurate;

5. *Endorses* Economic and Social Council decision 1995/320 of 12 December 1995, by which it enlarged the membership of the Commission on Population and Development from 27 to 47 members, elected by the Council from among the members of the United Nations and members of its specialized agencies, in time to take part in the twenty-ninth session of the Commission, and that the regional representation would be 12 for African States, 11 for Asian States, 5 for Eastern European States, 9 for Latin American and Caribbean States and 10 for Western European and Other States, bearing in mind that the representatives of Governments that are to serve on the Commission should have a relevant back-ground in population and development, in order to ensure that it fulfils its functions as reflected in its updated and enhanced mandate, taking into account the integrated multidisciplinary and comprehensive approach of the Programme of Action and the membership of the other functional commissions of the Council;

6. *Takes note* of the report of the Secretary-General on monitoring world population trends and policies,[a] and of the Executive Director of the United Nations Population Fund on monitoring multilateral population assistance;[b]

7. *Renews its call* to all Governments, organizations of the United Nations system and other major groups concerned with population and development issues, including intergovernmental and non-governmental organizations, parliamentarians and other community leaders, to continue to give the widest possible dissemination to the Programme of Action, including the use of electronic data networks, to seek public support for its goals, objectives and actions, and to maintain and enhance partnership between Governments and non-governmental organizations so as to ensure their continued contributions and cooperation concerning all aspects of population and development;

8. *Urges* Governments that have not yet done so to establish appropriate national follow-up mechanisms, in partnership with non-governmental organizations, community groups and representatives of the media and the academic community, and to seek the support of parliamentarians so as to ensure the full implementation of the Programme of Action;

9. *Reaffirms* that the follow-up to the Conference, at all levels, should take fully into account that population, health, education, poverty, patterns of production and consumption, empowerment of women and the environment are closely interconnected and should be considered through an integrated approach;

10. *Urges* all countries to consider their current spending priorities with a view to making additional contributions for the implementation of the Programme of Action, taking into account the provisions of chapters XIII and XIV thereof and the economic constraints faced by developing countries, in particular the least developed among them, and emphasizes that international cooperation in the field of population and development is essential for the implementation of the recommendations adopted at the Conference; and in this context, calls upon the international community to continue to provide, both bilaterally and multilaterally, adequate and substantial support and assistance for population and development activities, including through the United Nations Population Fund and other organs and organizations of the United Nations system and the specialized agencies that will be involved in the implementation, at all levels, of the Programme of Action;

11. *Reiterates* the importance of South-South cooperation for the successful implementation of the Programme of Action;

12. *Reaffirms* that the effective implementation of the Programme of Action will require an increased commitment of financial resources, both domestically and externally, and, in this context, calls upon the developed

---

[a]E/CN.9/1995/2.
[b]E/CN.9/1995/4.

countries to complement the national financial efforts of developing countries on population and development and to intensify their efforts to transfer new and additional resources to the developing countries, in accordance with the relevant provisions of the Programme of Action, in order to ensure that population and development objectives and goals are met;

13. *Acknowledges* that countries with economies in transition should receive temporary assistance for population and development activities, in view of the difficult economic and social problems faced by those countries at present;

14. *Urges* the international community to promote a supportive international economic environment by adopting favourable macroeconomic policies aimed at promoting sustained economic growth and sustainable development;

15. *Emphasizes* the importance of the early identification and allocation of financial resources by all members of the international community, including regional financial institutions, to enable them to fulfil their commitments with regard to the implementation of the Programme of Action;

16. *Invites* the Secretary-General to ensure that adequate resources are provided for the Conference follow-up activities to be carried out by the Secretariat during 1996;

17. *Invites* the regional commissions, other regional and subregional organizations and the development banks to continue to examine and analyse the results of implementation of the Programme of Action at the regional level under their respective mandates;

18. *Welcomes* the work undertaken by the Inter-Agency Task Force on the Implementation of the Programme of Action, chaired by the Executive Director of the United Nations Population Fund, and stresses the importance of continued and enhanced cooperation and coordination by all relevant organs, organizations and programmes of the United Nations system and the specialized agencies in the implementation of the Programme of Action, and, in this context, notes the establishment of new inter-agency task forces for the follow-up to conferences, which could be relevant for the implementation and follow-up to the International Conference on Population and Development;

19. *Emphasizes the need* to maintain the momentum of the follow-up activities relating to the Conference and the Programme of Action so as to utilize, to the fullest extent possible, existing capacity within the United Nations system in the area of population and development, including the Commission on Population and Development, the Population Division of the Department for Economic and Social Information and Policy Analysis of the Secretariat and the United Nations Population Fund, other organizations, funds and programmes of the United Nations and the specialized agencies whose continued support and commitment are required for the successful implementation of the full range of activities outlined in the Programme of Action, and invites them to work closely in the preparation of reports for the Commission on Population and Development;

20. *Requests* the specialized agencies and all related organizations of the United Nations system to continue to take appropriate measures to ensure the full and effective implementation of the Programme of Action, taking into account the specific needs of developing countries, and welcomes the intention of the Secretary-General to report through the Commission on Population and Development to the Economic and Social Council at its substantive session of 1996 on the work of the Inter-Agency Task Force, for coordination purposes, and to the General Assembly at its fifty-first session, for policy implications;

21. *Requests* the Economic and Social Council:

(a) To consider relevant reports and give guidance on matters concerning harmonization, cooperation and coordination within the United Nations system regarding the implementation of the Programme of Action;

(b) To consider, as appropriate, the reports submitted by the different bodies and organs on various matters related to the Programme of Action;

(c) To consider the proposed report on the work of the Inter-Agency Task Force;

22. *Requests* the funds and programmes of the United Nations system and the regional commissions and funds to continue to provide their full and active support to the implementation of the Programme of Action, in particular at the field level, through the United Nations resident coordinator system, and invites the relevant specialized agencies to do the same;

23. *Requests* the Secretary-General to report, through the Economic and Social Council, to the General Assembly at its fifty-first session on the implementation of the present resolution;

24. *Decides* to include in the agenda of its fifty-first session, within existing clusters, the item entitled "Implementation of the Programme of Action of the International Conference on Population and Development".

**General Assembly resolution 50/124**

20 December 1995      Meeting 96      Adopted without vote

Approved by Second Committee (A/50/624) without vote, 12 December (meeting 43); draft by Vice-Chairman (A/C.2/50/L.58), orally revised and based on informal consultations on draft by Colombia (for Non-Aligned Movement), Kyrgyzstan and Philippines (for Group of 77 and China) (A/C.2/50/L.9); agenda item 102.

*Financial implications.* S-G, A/C.2/50/L.81.

*Meeting numbers.* GA 50th session: 2nd Committee 9, 10, 29, 43; plenary 96.

## International migration and development

In response to a 1994 General Assembly request,[12] the Secretary-General submitted to the Economic and Social Council a report on international migration and development.[13] The report gave an overview of migration trends and policies, described the economic and social aspects of international migration and gave the views of Governments regarding the convening of an international conference on international migration and development. In that context, the report discussed the organizational modalities of other UN conferences and described the relevant activities of UN bodies and other organizations.

On 27 July, by **decision 1995/313**, the Council took note of the Secretary-General's report and recommended that the Assembly continue consideration of the question, including the convening of a conference.

By a September note,[14] the Secretariat summarized the Council's decision and noted that the Secretary-General's report would be made available to the Assembly.

GENERAL ASSEMBLY ACTION

On 20 December, the General Assembly adopted **resolution 50/123**.

### International migration and development
*The General Assembly,*

*Recalling* the Programme of Action of the International Conference on Population and Development adopted at Cairo, in particular, chapter X on international migration,

*Recalling also* the relevant provisions contained in the Copenhagen Declaration on Social Development and the Programme of Action of the World Summit for Social Development and in the Platform for Action adopted by the Fourth World Conference on Women,

*Recalling further* its resolution 49/127 of 19 December 1994 and Economic and Social Council decision 1995/313 of 27 July 1995,

*Recognizing* the importance from an analytical and operational point of view of identifying the existing linkages among the social, economic, political and cultural factors related to international migration and development, and of taking appropriate steps to intensify the analysis of issues involved,

*Recognizing also* the important role of the United Nations Population Fund as the lead agency of the Inter-Agency Task Force on the Implementation of the Programme of Action adopted at Cairo,

*Recalling* that the General Assembly and the Economic and Social Council should carry out their respective responsibilities, as entrusted to them in the Charter of the United Nations, in the formulation of policies and the provision of guidance to and coordination of United Nations activities in the field of population and development,

*Recalling also* that the Economic and Social Council, in the context of its role under the Charter *vis-à-vis* the General Assembly and in accordance with Assembly resolutions 45/264 of 13 May 1991, 46/235 of 13 April 1992 and 48/162 of 20 December 1994, should assist the Assembly in promoting an integrated approach to the implementation of the Programme of Action in providing system-wide coordination and guidance in monitoring the implementation,

1. *Takes note* of the report of the Secretary-General on international migration and development, including the comments of Governments regarding the objectives and modalities for the convening of a United Nations conference on international migration and development;

2. *Urges* Member States and the United Nations system to strengthen international cooperation in the area of international migration and development in order to address the root causes of migration, especially those related to poverty, and to maximize the benefits of international migration to those concerned and increase the likelihood that international migration has positive consequences for the sustainable development of both sending and receiving countries;

3. *Calls upon* the international community to seek to make the option of remaining in one's country viable for all people; to that end, efforts to achieve sustainable economic and social development, ensuring a better economic balance between developed and developing countries, should be strengthened;

4. *Invites* the Commission on Population and Development to consider, in 1997, in the context of the follow-up to the Programme of Action of the International Conference on Population and Development, in particular chapter X, the interrelationship between international migration and development;

5. *Calls upon* all relevant organs, organizations and programmes of the United Nations system and other intergovernmental, regional and subregional organizations to address the issue of international migration and development, and invites them to submit their views to the Secretary-General;

6. *Invites* the Economic and Social Council to consider at its organizational session for 1997 including "International migration and development" as a theme in the context of its agenda for 1997;

7. *Requests* the Secretary-General to designate, within existing resources, a clearly identifiable, qualified and competent focal point and to prepare, following consultations with the International Organization for Migration and the International Labour Organization and other relevant organizations of the United Nations system and after soliciting the additional views of Governments, a report to be presented to the General Assembly at its fifty-second session containing concrete proposals on ways and means to address, from cross-sectoral, interregional, regional and subregional points of view, the issue of international migration and development, including aspects related to objectives and modalities for the convening of a United Nations conference on international migration and development;

8. *Decides* to include in the provisional agenda of its fifty-second session the item entitled "International migration and development, including the convening of a United Nations conference on international migration and development".

General Assembly resolution 50/123

20 December 1995    Meeting 96    Adopted without vote

Approved by Second Committee (A/50/623 & Corr.1) without vote, 30 November (meeting 40); draft by Philippines, for Group of 77 and China (A/C.2/50/L.12), orally amended following informal consultations; agenda item 101.

*Financial implications.* S-G, A/C.2/50/L.26.

*Meeting numbers.* GA 50th session: 2nd Committee 8, 9, 32, 40; plenary 96.

## UN Population Fund

### UNFPA activities

In her report for 1995[15] to the UNDP/UNFPA Executive Board, the Executive Director stated that, on 18 June, 240 UNFPA staff members had met in Rye, New York, for a four-day meeting on the future direction and programme priorities of the Fund, in the light of the 1994 ICPD (see above). UNFPA staff members from all over the world understood that, in order to meet the goals of the ICPD Programme of Action, the Fund would need to be more focused in its programmes and resource allocations, and welcomed the Executive Board's decision (see above) to focus on three priority areas: reproductive health, including family planning and sexual health (referred to as reproductive health); population and development strategies; and advocacy. In addition to the new programme directions, the Rye participants focused on the need for improved programme coordination and complementarity between and among UN agencies, bilateral donors and NGOs. They also agreed that full transparency and accountability in programme management was critical to the effectiveness and impact of UNFPA activities.

UNFPA support for reproductive health was based on a public health, pragmatic and participatory approach. Reproductive health initiatives covered reproductive tract infections, maternal mortality, female genital mutilation, reproductive health in emergency situations and the activities of the Global Initiative on Contraceptive Requirements and Logistics Management Needs. In addition, UNFPA began to elaborate ways in which men's responsibilities in the area of reproductive health could be fostered and in which adolescents could be encouraged to exercise responsible sexual behaviour. UNFPA also supported HIV/AIDS prevention and control activities within the global strategy of the Joint and Co-sponsored UN Programme on HIV/AIDS, developed programme initiatives with strong information, education and communication components, and promoted community participation in reproductive health programmes.

A primary focus of the UNFPA programme in population and development strategies during 1995 was to provide a framework to translate ICPD's global commitments and goals to the national level, outlining approaches as to how to integrate such commitments and goals into national population and development planning.

In the area of advocacy, the Fund worked with Governments, UN agencies, NGOs and other members of civil society in an effort to build broad-based support for population issues and the ICPD goals. Population, particularly reproductive health, continued to be the Fund's primary focus for advocacy activities, but it was also an advocate for human rights, including women's rights, and development issues such as education, poverty, basic health services, empowerment of women and people's participation. In addition, the Fund worked to mobilize political support and financial resources for population and development activities.

At year's end, UNFPA was assisting 2,479 projects—775 country and regional projects in Africa, 594 in Asia and the Pacific, 456 in Latin America and the Caribbean, 352 in the Arab States and Europe, and 302 interregional projects. During the year, 307 new country projects were approved, amounting to $56.4 million, compared to 448, amounting to $46 million, in 1994. UNFPA undertook programme review and strategy development missions to five countries—Cape Verde, Ghana, Honduras, Sri Lanka and the Syrian Arab Republic.

Family planning programmes received an allocation of $165.8 million, or 48.7 per cent of all programme allocations ($340.4 million). Communication and education received $64.9 million (19.1 per cent); formulation and evaluation of population policies, $29.2 million (8.6 per cent); special programmes, $26.8 million (7.9 per cent); basic data collection, $18.9 million (5.5 per cent); population dynamics, $17.4 million (5.1 per cent); multisector activities, $16 million (4.7 per cent); and implementation of policies, $1.5 million (0.4 per cent).

UNFPA's *The State of World Population 1995*, entitled "Decisions for Development: Women, Empowerment and Reproductive Health", contained chapters on progress in population and development; the empowerment of women; reproductive health and family planning; and conclusion: after Cairo, which discussed country responses to ICPD.

**UNDP/UNFPA Executive Board action.** On 16 June,[16] the Executive Board took note of the Executive Director's annual report for 1994.[17] By a 14 June decision, the Board recommended[18] that the Economic and Social Council and the General Assembly endorse the agreement between UNDP and UNFPA to designate UNFPA resident country directors as UNFPA representatives on the understanding that UNFPA would take measures to enhance cooperation with and active support for resident coordinators for operational activities of the United Nations and on the understanding that the agreement would not result in increased administrative expenditure for UNFPA.

In accordance with **decision 1995/224** of 5 May, the Council considered as a principal theme of its high-level meeting of the operational activities of the United Nations for international development cooperation segment (June) the implementation by the UN system of the ICPD Programme of Action. By **decision 1995/231** of 13 July, the Council endorsed and recommended to the Assembly for endorsement the agreement between UNDP and UNFPA to designate Fund resident country directors as Fund representatives under the same conditions as those outlined in the Board's decision. The Assembly, by **decision 50/438** of 20 December, also endorsed the agreement.

**Annual report to the Economic and Social Council.** In response to a 1994 Economic and Social Council request,[19] UNFPA prepared a report[20] outlining measures taken to implement the provisions of the 1992 triennial policy review of operational activities.[21] The report also covered follow-up to ICPD and to the World Summit for Social Development (see PART FOUR, Chapter IX).

On 8 June, the Executive Board transmitted[22] the report to the Council together with its comments. It requested UNFPA to ensure that future reports on the implementation of the triennial policy review addressed more thoroughly problems and opportunities that had been identified, particularly at the field level, and that they contained any appropriate recommendations and requests for guidance from the Board. It asked the Executive Director, together with the UNDP Administrator and the UNICEF Executive Director, to consider producing a common report on the triennial policy review implementation, which should contain both a common section and sections by each of the three bodies.

By **decision 1995/233** of 13 July, the Council took note of the annual report of UNFPA.

### Global Initiative on Contraceptive Requirements

In response to a 1994 Executive Board request,[23] the UNFPA Executive Director submitted a status report[24] on the Global Initiative on Contraceptive Requirements and Logistics Management Needs in Developing Countries in the 1990s, covering the Initiative's 1994 activities.

On 14 June, the Board requested[25] the Executive Director to submit to it in September a proposal, in the context of the UNFPA intercountry programme, for the continuation of the Initiative beyond 1995, including an outline of the objectives, modalities and procedures for a possible future global contraceptive arrangement. She was also asked to submit in 1996 a report containing a reappraisal of UNFPA's future role in assessing and meeting the unmet needs for contraceptives and the requirements for logistics management.

In response to that request, the Executive Director submitted a later report on the Global Initiative,[26] in which she proposed that the Initiative, funding for which would end in 1995, be continued. The Consultative Group on Contraceptive Requirements had recommended that the Initiative's secretariat should be made an integral part of UNFPA. The Fund therefore proposed that the secretariat (two Professional and one General Service staff) be continued. Activities proposed for the next four years included: medium-term followup to the in-depth studies already undertaken; technical assistance and training in logistics management and forecasting; development and regular updating of the contraceptive commodity database; publication of additional technical reports; development of mechanisms for coordinated procurement; and monitoring of country follow-up plans. The implementation of those activities was contingent upon continuation of the three-person secretariat and the provision of $2 million.

With regard to a possible global contraceptive arrangement, the Executive Director stated that the establishment of such a facility was deemed necessary to ensure that all developing countries were able to secure contraceptives at the lowest possible cost; to ensure that the contraceptives provided were of appropriate quality; and to facilitate a prompt response to urgent demands in order to avert potentially critical disruptions to contraceptive supply and the resultant problems.

Noting that three prerequisites were necessary for the establishment of the facility—funding, staffing and operational criteria—the Executive Director stated that UNFPA intended to set up a revolving fund and provide an initial $2 million to commence the arrangement. An additional $3 million would be sought from interested donor organizations.

On 15 September, the Executive Board emphasized[27] that contraceptive commodity procurement and logistics activities in UNFPA should be undertaken as an integral component of the Fund's overall work in strengthening reproductive health programmes, including family planning and sexual health, and that those activities should be monitored to ensure their adherence to technical standards of safety and quality. It noted that a strengthened role for UNFPA in contraceptive commodity procurement and logistics should support the objective of building national self-reliance, including financial and technical capacity for local production where feasible, and urged the Executive Director to take steps towards that objective. The Board agreed in principle to the establishment of a global contraceptive commodity programme whose objectives would be to anticipate demand and facilitate a prompt response in order to avert critical disruptions to contraceptive supplies; to achieve economies of scale and lower costs to recipient countries; to ensure the quality of contraceptives provided by UNFPA; and to build national capacity to manage and finance contraceptive procurement and logistics on a self-reliant basis, so that the programme would no longer be needed. The Executive Director was asked to submit in 1996 a comprehensive report on the envisaged global contraceptive commodity programme, including the objectives and scope, administrative and financial aspects, and the efforts made by UNFPA to promote national capacity-building, drawing on the experience of other UN agencies, particularly UNICEF, WHO, and the Inter-Agency Procurement Service Office, in order to take a final decision on the matter.

## Country and intercountry programmes

UNPFA's provisional project expenditures for country and intercountry (regional and inter-regional) programmes in 1995 totalled $230.6 million, compared to $202.1 million in 1994.[15] A total of 307 new country projects were approved in 1995, compared to 448 new projects in 1994. In accordance with the criteria approved by the UNDP Governing Council in 1988,[28] 58 countries had priority status (32 in Africa, 17 in Asia and the Pacific, 5 in Latin America and the Caribbean, and 4 in Arab States) and were allocated $192.7 million, compared to $154.2 million in 1994.

Allocations to programmes for sub-Saharan Africa totalled $109 million, with projected expenditures of between $67 million and $74 million, up considerably from the $57 million recorded in 1994. Most resources were allocated to the family planning (44.5 per cent) and communication and education (22.6 per cent) sectors. In the countries of the region, increased political and general awareness of population issues continued to translate into growing demand for population programmes and services. At the same time, institutional and operational capacity to deliver such services was constrained by events ranging from political instability in several countries to a more widespread economic malaise, often coupled with constraints associated with structural adjustment programmes. HIV/AIDS threatened to drain overall health budgets in many countries by drawing greater proportions of available resources into treatment and away from prevention. UNFPA convened a series of regional meetings during the year to develop strategies to implement the ICPD Programme of Action and the follow-up to the 1992 Dakar/Ngor Declaration on Population, Family and Sustainable Development.[29] Effecting the switch from a maternal and child health and family planning emphasis to a broader reproductive health approach was the common thread underlying regional consultations. The Fund also examined post-ICPD priorities in terms of information, education and communication, and demographic, population and development training needs and assessed the relative roles to be played by national and regional training institutions, in some instances with a view as to whether certain projects should be included or modified in the next regional programming cycle (1996-1999). Recommendations included training a cadre of qualified personnel at the national level and incorporating population and development concerns into undergraduate courses. At the country level, Mauritania and Uganda adopted national population policies, bringing to 17 the number of countries in the region to have done so. Mid-term reviews of 20 ongoing country programmes allowed for some reshaping to make programmes more responsive

to ICPD. Emergency situations continued to complicate UNFPA efforts to provide population assistance in Burundi, Liberia, Rwanda, Sierra Leone and Zaire. A first priority was given to providing reproductive health care, including family planning services, to afflicted but reachable populations. A second priority, for countries where major population movements had occurred, entailed support for quick surveys to ascertain their size and relocation sites as a help to critical humanitarian relief planning.

The Arab States and Europe were allocated $41.1 million in 1995, compared to expenditures of $19.4 million in 1994. Of the total, 50 per cent went to family planning and 15.2 per cent to communication and education. Almost all the national population policies adopted in the Arab States had a strong focus on increasing access to and improving the quality of reproductive health services as well as on promoting gender equity and equality and the empowerment of women. Jordan and Yemen updated their national population policies to integrate the ICPD goals, and the Syrian Arab Republic adopted the ICPD goals as its own and was in the process of adopting a national population policy. With regard to government structures, Egypt merged ministerial health and population portfolios and Morocco established a Ministry of Population. With UNFPA support, comprehensive reproductive health was being promoted through review and enhancement of current programmes and the formulation of new ones. Covering the entire region, the Amman-based country support team undertook more than 100 missions to 20 countries in 1995, advising on reproductive health; information, education and communication; gender; and data collection and analysis. It was also involved in the programme review and strategy development exercise in the Syrian Arab Republic and mid-term reviews in Egypt, Jordan, Morocco and Yemen. The second phase of the Gulf Family Health Survey Programme was launched at the beginning of 1995 to provide detailed information on the demographic and health status of the population in the Arab Gulf States. In 1995, UNFPA supplied humanitarian assistance for emergency situations in Iraq, Somalia and the Sudan.

Reflecting the ICPD Programme of Action's recognition that countries with economies in transition should receive temporary assistance for population and development activities given their difficult economic and social problems, 1995 saw a surge of requests for UNFPA assistance from Central and Eastern Europe. The Fund approved 26 projects totalling $5 million, covering country and regional activities in the reproductive health field. It also organized a regional workshop on how countries with economies in transition could follow through on the Programme of Action. To upgrade the skills and knowledge of modern family planning methods and management among 170 health care professionals from the region, UNFPA was working with the University Medical School of Debrecen, Hungary, to set up a three-year training course. In response to the humanitarian emergency situation, UNFPA and WHO were collaborating in sending reproductive health equipment and supply kits to government-run clinics in Bosnia and Herzegovina, where they were also training staff. In Croatia, UNFPA and Marie Stopes International were providing reproductive health and psycho-social care to refugees.

Some $98.4 million was allocated to Asia and the Pacific in 1995, representing almost 29 per cent of all UNFPA project assistance. Countries of the region quickly set about translating commitment to the Programme of Action into concrete population and development policy initiatives, in addition to promoting reproductive health care measures at the operational level and involving NGOs more closely in programme design and implementation.

Fiji, the Marshall Islands, Palau, Solomon Islands and Tonga led the way in the South Pacific in revising national population policies to reflect ICPD priorities. Cambodia and Myanmar upgraded government capacity to advise on population issues. UNFPA helped Pakistan to organize a national symposium on the population situation there that was addressed by the Prime Minister. In India, a new set of indicators designed to track social-sector spending and gauge progress towards the ICPD goals could strengthen the UN system's advocacy for increased government and donor support for population and development programmes. The Indian Government released one district in each state from method-specific family planning targets; the effect of that decision on family welfare services would be surveyed with UNFPA assistance. Male methods of contraception continued to be promoted in the region. Cambodia, Indonesia, Thailand and Viet Nam were among countries encouraging condom use both for family planning and for HIV/AIDS prevention. In India, UNFPA was assisting a project for the nationwide expansion of no-scalpel vasectomy. Two new country programmes were approved in 1995 for Azerbaijan and Kazakstan, totalling $23 million, $18 million from regular and $5 million from multi-bilateral resources. A project formulation mission was fielded in November to Kazakstan, Kyrgyzstan and Uzbekistan and programme review and strategy development missions were undertaken to Sri Lanka and Viet Nam. South-South cooperation—a regional strong point—was best evidenced by the continuing efforts of Indonesia, the Republic of Korea

and Thailand to facilitate regional colleagues seeking to study and learn lessons from their programmes.

UNFPA allocations to Latin America and the Caribbean in 1995 totalled $43.6 million, or 12.8 per cent of total project allocations. Despite an unfavourable economic climate, concerted efforts continued to sustain the momentum required to realize the targets set by the Programme of Action and increase resources available to address priority population issues, such as teenage pregnancy, maternal mortality and persistently high fertility rates among underserved segments of the population. Support from Governments was significant. In August, ministers and high-level government officials of the educational, cultural and youth ministries of the Central American region passed a strong declaration in favour of population education within the framework of the ICPD recommendations. Ecuador adopted a new National Action Plan on Population which would extend maternal health, including reproductive health, care to members of the armed forces and would bring services to adolescents and women. A parliamentary commission on population and development was established in Nicaragua, and in El Salvador UNFPA funded two reproductive health projects for adolescents. The region's new country programmes and those up for review and/or extension were reshaped during 1995 to accentuate reproductive health, increased involvement of NGOs and special emphasis on reaching young people. More countries in the region were involved in HIV/AIDS prevention, with Cuba and Haiti, in particular, having channelled their support into social mobilization campaigns.

Allocations for interregional programmes amounted to $36.6 million in 1995. UNFPA-supported projects offered opportunities for countries and organizations to confer, combine their knowledge and experience, and put useful and practical programmes into effect. UNFPA's Global Programme of Training in Population and Development started 10-month population and development training courses in Botswana and Morocco for mid-level civil servants, NGO staff and university students.

The UNFPA Executive Director presented proposals to the Executive Board's second regular session (April) for country programmes for Benin, the Comoros, Indonesia, Mauritius, Mozambique, the Sudan and Turkey and for Azerbaijan, Kazakstan, Kyrgyzstan, Tajikistan, Turkmenistan and Uzbekistan, all of which were approved[30] by the Board on 7 April, when it also approved assistance to Cambodia for the National Population Census and for institutional strengthening and family health improvement through birth spacing. At its annual session (June), the

Board approved[16] increased funding authority for the Namibia country programme by $3.7 million, as requested by the Executive Director. At its third regular session (September), the Board approved[31] the UNFPA intercountry programme for 1996-1999[32] and the country programme for Costa Rica.

### Assistance to Rwanda

On 8 June, the Executive Board approved[33] the continued implementation of its 1994 decision[34] allowing for flexibility in sectoral expenditure from Rwanda's third country programme resources and for overall expenditures of up to $7.8 million, to enable UNFPA to continue to respond to the evolving needs of the Government of Rwanda for reconstruction and development.

### Financial and administrative questions

UNFPA's estimated income in 1995 increased to $312.6 million from $265.3 million in 1994, said the Executive Director in her annual financial review, 1995.[35] Expenditures totalled $312.1 million, compared with $274.4 million the previous year. Total contributions pledged by 85 Governments in 1995 reached $302.8 million, an increase of $47.6 million in dollar terms over 1994. Of UNFPA's major donors, significantly increased contributions were received from Belgium, Denmark, Finland, Germany, Japan, the Netherlands, Norway and the United Kingdom. The cumulative outstanding balance of unpaid pledges for 1995 and prior years was $629,637.

By a 15 September decision,[36] the Executive Board took note of the UNFPA financial review for 1994.[37]

### 1996-1997 budget

The Executive Director submitted to the Executive Board budget estimates for UNFPA administrative and programme support services for the 1996-1997 biennium.[38] She requested net appropriations of $127.4 million for the biennium ($137.4 million gross). The proposed budget assumed an income level of $702 million for the biennium, as reflected in the Fund's work plan for 1996-1999.[39] That amount, which included $30 million in multi-bilateral resources, was calculated by assuming an average 8 per cent a year increase in most contributions.

By a 15 September decision,[36] the Board, having also considered the report of the Advisory Committee on Administrative and Budgetary Questions (ACABQ) on the budget estimates,[40] took note of ACABQ's concerns with respect to the accuracy of income projection and asked the Executive Director to keep them under continuous review. She was also asked to continue to make efforts to minimize administrative expenditure,

particularly at headquarters, and to report to the Board in 1996 on possible measures to increase the total volume reduction at headquarters and Geneva from 1.2 per cent to 2 per cent and on steps taken to reduce administrative expenditures should projected levels of income not be realized. The Board further asked the Executive Director to report in 1996 on the effectiveness of its publications programme, taking into account the need for publications to be available in a range of languages, and to conduct an evaluation of training activities, reporting to the Board through ACABQ no later than 1997. The Board approved appropriations in the amount of $137,346,000 gross to finance the 1996-1997 biennial budget for administrative and programme support services and agreed that overhead credits available to the Fund, estimated at $9 million, and the miscellaneous income from trust funds for support services, in the amount of $1 million, should be used to offset the gross appropriations, resulting in net appropriations of $127,346,000. The Board approved the reclassification or establishment of a number of posts and decided that the number of Country Directors at the D-1 level should not exceed 25 per cent of the total number of Country Directors. It endorsed the opening of a country office in South Africa.

### Technical Support Services

In a report to the Executive Board,[41] the Executive Director analysed the effectiveness of the successor support-cost arrangements, known as the Technical Support Services (TSS) arrangements, which were established in 1992 to replace the previous arrangements of providing technical assistance through regional advisers based in UN agency regional offices. The objectives were to provide effective and timely support for population programmes and policies in developing countries, to enhance and maximize the use of national and regional capacities in population activities, to use the most appropriate and competitive sources of technical assistance, to bring technical advice closer to field-level activities, to help Governments assume the management of UNFPA-funded programmes and projects, and to continue the practice of cost-sharing between UNFPA and the agencies of the UN system participating in the new successor arrangements. The report described the implementation of the TSS arrangements and their overall effectiveness. It presented proposals for strengthening the arrangements and gave the financial implications of those proposals.

On 15 September,[42] the Executive Board took note of the Executive Director's proposals and welcomed her plan to strengthen the TSS arrangements, particularly the country support teams. It requested her to enhance the contribution of the arrangements towards national capacity-building. Noting the heavy workloads of some staff of the country support teams, the Board asked the Executive Director to monitor carefully the adequacy of the arrangements proposed, especially in relation to Africa, and to consider further the probable need to reassign TSS specialist posts to country support teams. It stressed the need to ensure that those teams had staff with the skills and experience to contribute to national efforts to attain those goals of the ICPD Programme of Action for which UNFPA had responsibility, especially in relation to reproductive health. The Executive Director was asked to report annually to the Board, starting in 1997, on the implementation and monitoring of the TSS arrangements. She was also asked to include in her report in 1997: details of progress made in implementing the TSS arrangements with regard to the proposed change of coordinator posts to specialist posts at the United Nations and its regional commissions and at WHO regional offices; and an assessment of the appropriateness and effectiveness of the specialist posts, and details of measures taken to strengthen the teamwork between TSS specialists and country support teams and to strengthen the advocacy function of TSS specialists. The Executive Director was authorized to commit $107 million for the four-year period 1996-1999 to implement the TSS arrangements.

### Work plan for 1996-1999

In a report[39] to the Executive Board's annual session (June), the Executive Director examined the utilization of resources by UNFPA in 1994, described the work plan for 1996-1999, including information about projected resources and the proposed use of programmable resources among country and intercountry activities as well as among geographical regions, and presented the proposed programme expenditure authority for 1996 from regular resources, the estimates of new programmable regular resources for the 1997-1999 period and the estimates of new programmable resources from multi-bilateral funding. The proposed expenditure authority for 1996 amounted to $263 million, and the new programmable resources for 1997, 1998 and 1999 were estimated at $280 million, $298 million and $319 million, respectively.

On 8 June, the Board endorsed[43] the Executive Director's programme resource planning proposals, while taking into account its request[10] that UNFPA assistance be concentrated within the core programme areas (see above). It approved the request for 1996 programme expenditure authority at a level equal to new programmable resources for 1996, estimated at $263 million. The Board endorsed the use of the following estimates of new programmable resources from regular resources for the 1997-1999 period: $280 million for 1997; $298 million for 1998; and $319 million for 1999. It further endorsed the use of the following estimates of new programmable resources from multi-bilateral funding: $15 million per year for the years 1996-1999.

### UN Population Award

The 1995 United Nations Population Award was presented to Dr. Halfdan Mahler of Denmark, the Secretary-General of the International Planned Parenthood Federation, and to the Inter-African Committee on Traditional Practices Affecting the Health of Women and Children (IAC). Dr. Mahler, who was Director-General of WHO from 1973 to 1988, was chosen for his distinguished career in public health, which included strong leadership in reproductive health, family planning and worldwide population issues. IAC, an Ethiopia-based NGO, was chosen for its efforts to create the social, cultural and public health conditions that allowed women to exercise their reproductive rights, including the practice of family planning.

At a ceremony on 5 June, the laureates each received an award of $12,500. The Award was established by the General Assembly in 1981,[44] to be presented annually to individuals or institutions for outstanding contributions to increased awareness of population problems and to their solutions. The Award's Trust Fund totalled $630,078 as at 31 December 1994.

In an April report,[45] the Secretary-General transmitted to the Assembly the UNFPA Executive Director's report on the status of the Award. The Assembly took note of it by **decision 50/439** of 20 December.

## Other population activities

### Commission on Population and Development

The Commission on Population and Development (formerly the Population Commission and renamed by the General Assembly in 1994[1]), at its twenty-eighth session (New York, 21 February–2 March),[46] reviewed population trends, policies and programmes, discussed follow-up action to ICPD (see above), and considered the Organization's programme of work in population. By **decision 1995/209** of 10 February, the Economic and Social Council endorsed the Assembly's decision that the Population Commission should be renamed and that it should meet annually.

The Council, by **decision 1995/236** of 17 July, took note of the Commission's report on its twenty-eighth session and approved the provisional agenda for the twenty-ninth (1996) session. On 12 December, the Council decided (**decision 1995/320**) that the Commission's membership should be increased from 27 to 47 (see AP-PENDIX III).

### 1995 UN activities

In a report on the work of DESIPA during 1995,[47] the Secretary-General described the research and technical cooperation work and information activities carried out by the Population Division. The Division's analysis of demographic variables at the world level covered fertility and family planning, mortality and international and internal migration. Work on world population projections included the completion of *World Population Prospects: The 1994 Revision*[48] and continuation of the preparation of *The 1996 Revision*. *World Urbanization Prospects: The 1994 Revision*[49] was also completed and planning for *The 1996 Revision* commenced.

With regard to population policy and socio-economic development, a world survey of international migration policies and programmes continued, as did research on policy issues resulting from rapid population growth in the world's largest cities. *The Challenge of Urbanization: The World's Large Cities*,[50] which presented profiles of 100 of the world's largest agglomerations, was published and was expected to be an important input for the 1996 UN Conference on Human Settlements. The publication *Abortion Policies: A Global Review*, volume III, *Oman to Zimbabwe*[51] was issued in 1995. The population data bank maintained by the Division was being continuously updated. In 1995, the fifth edition of *Global Population Policy Database* and the companion volume *Population Policy Diskette Documentation, 1995* were completed and submitted for publication. A study of government views on the relationships between population and the environment was issued as a working paper pending its publication. The study was based on a review of official governmental statements, national reports and the draft and final documents adopted at major intergovernmental conferences dealing with population, environment and development issues from the early 1970s through ICPD in 1994, as well as of the international development strategies for the UN development decades since 1960. An updated version of the database on population, resources, the environment and development was issued, incorporating information from *The 1994 Revision* of population estimates and projections. It included updates of other data series and incorporated a number of additional indicators. Also ongoing during 1995 was a study of demographic aspects of poverty. The focus was methodological, with the long-term aim of increasing the amount of attention given to demographic factors in poverty research, and vice versa. The study included an overview of approaches to measuring poverty and a discussion of data requirements for linking poverty measurement to the study of demographic factors. It also considered ways in which measurement choices might affect the demographic profile of households classified as poor.

As to coordination and dissemination of population information, the global Population Information Network (POPIN) Coordinating Unit, in collaboration with the regional commissions, continued in 1995 to focus on strengthening the Network and its ability to collect and disseminate information among UN entities and NGOs. POPIN continued to promote the use of electronic mail and the Internet to facilitate and enhance communication among the regional networks, specialized agencies, NGOs and the broader population community. Meetings of the POPIN Advisory Committee and Information Technology Working Group were held in Bangkok, Thailand, from 12 to 21 June to review the status of POPIN activities and electronic computer networking in each of the regions, to present the POPIN work programme and future plans, and to draft a strategy for activities for the next biennium (1996-1997). The Population Division continued to publish the results of its research studies in a variety of formats to meet the needs of different audiences. It also continued to receive and respond to numerous requests for population information from UN organizations, research institutions and individual scholars.

During 1995, the Population Division provided technical assistance services to more than 80 projects in 45 developing countries and countries with economies in transition in the areas of population and development training, institutionalizing analysis and research on socio-economic and demographic data obtained from population censuses, surveys and vital registration systems, population policy, and population and development. TSS specialists in demographic analysis, population and development, population policy, fertility and family planning, and teaching and training in demography augmented substantive support provided to the eight country support teams. In addition, a number of missions were undertaken by TSS specialists to country support teams in Addis Ababa (Ethiopia), Dakar (Senegal), Harare (Zimbabwe), Santiago (Chile) and Suva (Fiji).

### Programme questions

The Commission on Population and Development had before it the proposed programme of work on population for the biennium 1996-1997. In a note to the Commission,[52] the Secretary-General stated that the programme of work had been designed to undertake follow-up activities relating to ICPD, to carry out research findings in the most effective manner possible, and to provide substantive support for technical cooperation projects in the field of population.

The Commission adopted a decision[53] by which it transmitted its views on programme questions to the Economic and Social Council for consideration. Those views, which were attached to the Commission's report, gave suggestions for the work programme. The Commission stressed that the Population Division should continue to work closely with States, organizations of the UN system, other intergovernmental organizations and NGOs in implementing programmes. It noted that the follow-up to ICPD would require the Division to be involved in new work, such as the elaboration of reproductive health indicators and the interrelationship between migration and development. The Commission recommended the strengthening of the Secretariat in the field of population, from within existing resources, in order to ensure adequate preparation and support for the Commission.

*REFERENCES*

[1]YUN 1994, p. 963, GA res. 49/128, 29 Dec. 1994. [2]E/CN.9/1995/5. [3]YUN 1994, p. 956. [4]E/1995/27 (dec. 1995/1). [5]YUN 1993, p. 836. [6]DP/1995/25 & Corr.1. [7]E/1995/34 (dec. 95/7). [8]DP/1995/8. [9]ACC/1995/23. [10]E/1995/34 (dec. 95/15). [11]A/50/190-E/1995/73. [12]YUN 1994, p. 966, GA res. 49/127, 19 Dec. 1994. [13]E/1995/69. [14]A/50/479. [15]DP/FPA/1996/17 (Part I & Part I/Corr.1 & Part II). [16]E/1995/34 (dec. 95/24). [17]YUN 1994, p. 967. [18]E/1995/34 (dec. 95/20). [19]YUN 1994, p. 789, ESC res. 1994/33, 28 July 1994. [20]E/1995/55. [21]YUN 1992, p. 552, GA res. 47/199, 22 Dec. 1992. [22]E/1995/34 (dec. 95/17). [23]YUN 1994, p. 970. [24]DP/1995/24 (Part II). [25]E/1995/34 (dec. 95/21). [26]DP/1995/62. [27]E/1995/34 (dec. 95/36). [28]YUN 1988, p. 474. [29]YUN 1992, p. 476. [30]E/1995/34 (dec. 95/13). [31]Ibid. (dec. 95/37). [32]DP/1995/44. [33]E/1995/34 (dec. 95/14). [34]YUN 1994, p. 972. [35]DP/FPA/1996/22. [36]E/1995/34 (dec. 95/35). [37]DP/1995/41. [38]DP/1995/42. [39]DP/1995/26. [40]DP/1995/43. [41]DP/1995/40. [42]E/1995/34 (dec. 95/34). [43]Ibid. (dec. 95/16). [44]YUN 1981, p. 792, GA res. 36/201, 17 Dec. 1981. [45]A/50/132. [46]E/1995/27. [47]E/CN.9/1996/7. [48]*World Population Prospects: The 1994 Revision* (ST/ESA/SER.A/145), Sales No. E.95.XIII.16. [49]*World Urbanization Prospects: The 1994 Revision* (ST/ESA/SER.A/150), Sales No. E.95.XIII.12. [50]*The Challenge of Urbanization: The World's Large Cities* (ST/ESA/SER.A/151), Sales No. E.96.XIII.4. [51]*Abortion Policies: A Global Review*, vol. III, *Oman to Zimbabwe*, Sales No. E.95.XIII.24. [52]E/CN.9/1995/7. [53]E/1995/27 (dec. 1995/2).

# Human settlements

## Preparations for Habitat II (1996)

### Preparatory Committee

The Preparatory Committee for the United Nations Conference on Human Settlements (Habitat II) held its second substantive session in Nairobi, Kenya, from 24 April to 5 May 1995.[1] The Conference, also known as "The City Summit'', was to take place in Istanbul, Turkey, in 1996, 20 years after the first UN Conference on Human Settlements.[2]

Among the documents before the Preparatory Committee were progress reports by the Conference Secretary-General on the activities of the Conference secretariat[3] and on national preparations,[4] a note by the secretariat on updated guidelines for national preparations,[5] and a draft statement of principles and global plan of action,[6] formulated in response to recommendations made by the Preparatory Committee at its first (1994) session.[7] Also before the Committee was a report by the Conference Secretary-General,[8] in which he reviewed contributions to the implementation of Agenda 21, adopted by the UN Conference on Environment and Development in 1992,[9] of national and international action in the area of human settlements.

On 5 May, the Preparatory Committee adopted nine decisions, the first four of which were referred to the General Assembly for further action. In a decision on financing of the Conference and its preparatory activities,[10] the Committee urgently called on Governments and international regional financial institutions to increase their in-cash and in-kind contributions to the two Trust Funds established to finance the preparatory process, and called on Governments to disburse undistributed resources pledged to the ad hoc secretariat of Habitat II. The Conference Secretary-General was called on to explore all avenues for funding, including the private sector and public foundations, and the Assembly was asked to allocate sufficient funds to cover the costs of general temporary assistance, advisory services, secretariat operations, communications, consultants, information dissemination and miscellaneous expenses for the period October 1995 to July 1996. The other decisions requiring action by the Assembly dealt with the Preparatory Committee's third session (February 1996),[11] recommendations on the Conference's organization of work, including the establishment of committees and procedural matters,[12] and adoption of the rules of procedure for the Conference.[13] Other decisions concerned preparatory activities at the national, regional and international levels;[14] substantive documentation for the Conference;[15] criteria for nominating and selecting best practices;[16] inter-sessional arrangements for drafting the statement of principles and commitments and the global plan of action;[17] and accreditation of NGOs.[18]

### Other preparatory activities

Regional preparations for Habitat II were carried out during the year in the UN regional commissions for Africa, Asia and the Pacific, Europe,

Latin America and the Caribbean and Western Asia (see also PART FOUR, Chapter V). In a note to the General Assembly,[19] submitted in response to a 1994 request,[20] the Secretary-General reviewed key activities carried out during the year.

The Economic Commission for Africa (ECA) participated in the subregional Ministerial Meeting for Eastern and Southern Africa on Preparations for the UN Conference on Human Settlements (Kampala, 26-28 February), which was jointly organized by the UN Centre for Human Settlements (UNCHS) and the Government of Uganda, with support from UNDP and Shelter Afrique. The Meeting resulted in the Kampala Declaration,[21] in which the Ministers committed themselves to design, adopt and implement enabling, participatory and innovative human settlements development strategies towards realizing the objectives of Habitat II: adequate shelter for all and sustainable human settlements development in an urbanizing world. ECA also participated in the subregional Ministerial Meeting for Central Africa on Preparations for the UN Conference on Human Settlements (Brazzaville, 10-12 April), which was jointly organized by UNCHS and the Government of the Congo, with support from UNDP and the Organization for the Promotion and Management of Real Estate in the Congo. The Ministers adopted the Brazzaville Declaration,[22] in which they pledged to adopt and implement enabling, participatory and innovative policies in the field of urban development, land and urban management and housing in order to achieve the goals of Habitat II. The Regional Ministerial Meeting for Africa Preparatory to Habitat II (Johannesburg, South Africa, 16-18 October) adopted the Johannesburg Declaration, which stated the consolidated African position for country, subregional and regional strategies for effective African participation in the Habitat II process.

The Economic Commission for Europe (ECE), in cooperation with the Government of Hungary and UNCHS, organized the fourth meeting of ministers from countries in transition responsible for human settlements (Budapest, 13-14 June), which formulated common goals and commitments to be achieved and implemented in connection with the Conference's two main themes. ECE's Committee on Human Settlements established a task force to assist it in carrying out the preparatory work for the Conference, and a regional workshop on housing and urban indicators for countries in transition was held in Budapest in June.

The Economic Commission for Latin America and the Caribbean organized the Regional Latin America and Caribbean Meeting Preparatory to Habitat II (Santiago, Chile, 13-17 November), which approved a Regional Plan of Action for Human Settlements.

The Economic and Social Commission for Western Asia helped to organize the Regional Preparatory Expert Group Meeting for the Conference (Amman, Jordan, 23-26 January). The meeting reviewed the housing situation in the Arab region, assessed policies and programmes on the sustainable development of human settlements and made relevant proposals and practical suggestions.

In a November progress report on the activities of the secretariat,[23] the Conference Secretary-General stated that the in-country preparatory process was in full swing. By 15 November, the secretariat had received progress reports from 89 countries, of which 47 had submitted reports of a substantial nature, including draft national plans of action, reviews of the current situation and identification of priority issues. The Best Practice Initiative had generated much interest and enthusiasm. By mid-November, 314 submissions for best practices had been received from 72 countries. With regard to information and awareness building, the secretariat continued to issue its series of regular publications that focused on the human settlements issues to be addressed at the Conference. Five issues of the newsletter _Countdown to Istanbul_ were issued during the year, as were four issues of _Habitat Debate_, the UNCHS journal on the Centre's substantive programmes. In collaboration with the UN Department of Public Information, a number of promotional activities were carried out.

The Dubai (United Arab Emirates) International Conference for Habitat II on Best Practices in Improving the Living Environment took place from 19 to 22 November.[24] Some 29 Best Practices were presented. The Conference adopted the Dubai Declaration, and the Dubai Municipality announced the establishment of the Dubai Award for Best Practices, which would be administered in collaboration with UNCHS, for an annual amount of $150,000.

**Report of the Secretary-General.** In response to a 1994 General Assembly request,[20] the UN Secretary-General, in consultation with the Conference Secretary-General, reported on progress made in the preparations for the Conference. He described the action taken at the second session of the Preparatory Committee (see above) and progress made since that session, noting that the first inter-sessional meeting of the informal drafting group for the draft statement of principles and commitments and the global plan of action met in Nairobi from 17 to 21 July.

On 20 December, the General Assembly adopted **resolution 50/100**.

### United Nations Conference on Human Settlements (Habitat II)

*The General Assembly,*

*Recalling* its resolution 47/180 of 22 December 1992, in which it decided to convene the United Nations Conference on Human Settlements (Habitat II) from 3 to 14 June 1996, and to establish both a preparatory committee and an ad hoc secretariat for the Conference,

*Reiterating its gratitude* to the Government of Turkey for offering to act as host to the Conference, which is to be held at Istanbul,

*Noting with satisfaction* the progress that has been made so far in the preparations for the Conference, as outlined in the report of the Preparatory Committee for the Conference on its second substantive session and the report of the Secretary-General on preparations for the Conference,

*Reaffirming* the importance of the principles and concepts set out in the Rio Declaration on Environment and Development and Agenda 21 for the purpose of guiding the implementation of the decisions and recommendations of the Conference,

*Recalling also* its resolution 49/109 of 19 December 1994, in which, *inter alia*, it decided that a third substantive session of the Preparatory Committee would be held at United Nations Headquarters early in 1996 to complete the preparatory work for the Conference,

1. *Endorses* the report of the Preparatory Committee for the United Nations Conference on Human Settlements (Habitat II) on its second substantive session (Nairobi, 24 April–5 May 1995), which contains, *inter alia*, decision II/1 on the financing of the Conference and its preparatory activities, decision II/3 on the recommendations of the Preparatory Committee on the organization of work of the Conference, including the holding of pre-conference consultations on 1 and 2 June 1996, the establishment of committees and other procedural matters and decision II/4 on the rules of procedure for the Conference;

2. *Decides* that the third session of the Preparatory Committee will be held at United Nations Headquarters from 5 to 16 February 1996;

3. *Requests* the Secretary-General to make the necessary provisions, within existing resources, so that the Preparatory Committee may, if it so decides, establish two working groups to meet in addition to plenary meetings for the duration of the third session;

4. *Notes with interest* the call by the Secretary-General of the United Nations to give the Conference the dimensions of a "city summit", and reaffirms that the Conference should be held at the highest possible level of participation;

5. *Expresses its sincere appreciation* to those States and organizations that have made or pledged financial or other contributions in support of the preparatory activities for the Conference, and requests the Secretary-General of the Conference to continue to make every effort to raise the extrabudgetary resources required for Conference activities and preparations;

6. *Renews its appeal* to all Governments, especially the Governments of developed countries and other Govern-

ments in a position to do so, as well as to international and regional financial institutions, to make substantial contributions to the voluntary fund established by the General Assembly in its resolution 47/180 for the purpose of financing preparatory activities for the Conference and supporting developing countries, in particular the least developed among them, in participating fully and effectively in the Conference and its preparatory process;

7. *Encourages* all relevant non-governmental organizations that are interested, especially organizations from developing countries, to participate in and contribute to the Conference and its preparatory process on the basis of the procedures adopted at recent United Nations conferences;

8. *Invites* the Secretary-General to report to the General Assembly at its fifty-first session on the implementation of and follow-up to the outcome of the Conference undertaken by the organizations and bodies of the United Nations system, including the role played by the United Nations Centre for Human Settlements in that process;

9. *Decides* to include in the provisional agenda of its fifty-first session under the item "Sustainable development and international economic cooperation" a subitem entitled "United Nations Conference on Human Settlements (Habitat II)".

General Assembly resolution 50/100

20 December 1995      Meeting 96      Adopted without vote

Approved by Second Committee (A/50/617/Add.3) without vote, 5 December (meeting 41); draft by Vice-Chairman (A/C.2/50/L.57), orally revised and based on informal consultations on draft by Philippines (for Group of 77 and China) and Turkey (A/C.2/50/L.27); agenda item 95 *(c)*.

*Financial implications.* S-G, A/C.2/50/L.44.

*Meeting numbers.* GA 50th session: 2nd Committee 33, 34, 38, 41; plenary 96.

Also on 20 December, the Assembly, by **decision 50/428**, took note of the Secretary-General's note[19] reviewing regional preparations for Habitat II.

## Commission on Human Settlements

The Commission on Human Settlements held its fifteenth session in Nairobi from 25 April to 1 May,[25] when it adopted 14 resolutions and six decisions. The Commission adopted a resolution on the Global Strategy for Shelter to the Year 2000[26] (see below) and recommended a draft text on the subject to the General Assembly for adoption. Other resolutions dealt with a housing rights strategy (see below);[27] promoting the participation of women in human settlements development (see below);[28] the role of UNCHS in assisting refugees, returnees and displaced persons and their families in Africa;[29] assistance to countries with economies in transition;[30] urban and housing performance indicators;[31] strengthening the presence of UNCHS in the Latin American and Caribbean region;[32] cooperation between UNCHS and the United Nations Environment Programme (UNEP) on the urban environment (see PART FOUR, Chapter VII);[33] the progress report of the UNCHS Executive Director on the activities of the Centre;[34] priorities for national action to provide housing for all (see below);[35] sustainable human settlements in an urbanizing world, including issues related to land policies and mitigation of natural disasters (see below);[36] coordination matters;[37] cooperation between Governments and NGOs in the field of human settlements development;[38] and concrete measures towards the full realization of children's housing rights.[39]

The Commission's decisions dealt with its fourth report to the Assembly on the implementation of the Global Strategy for Shelter to the Year 2000 (see below);[40] preparations for Habitat II;[41] the work programme of UNCHS for the biennium 1996-1997;[42] the budget of the UN Habitat and Human Settlements Foundation for the biennium 1996-1997;[43] the new objectives, role and place of UNCHS within the UN system;[44] and themes for consideration by the Commission at its sixteenth (1997) session (the contribution of the private and non-governmental sectors to shelter delivery to low-income groups and the management of natural resources in the context of human settlements).[45]

ECONOMIC AND SOCIAL COUNCIL ACTION

By **decision 1995/207 B** of 10 February, the Economic and Social Council decided that, when reviewing the report of the Commission on Human Settlements on its fifteenth session, it would not consider new draft proposals, except for specific recommendations contained in those reports that required action by the Council and proposals on matters relating to the coordination aspects of the work of those bodies.

On 17 July, by **decision 1995/234**, the Council took note of the report of the Commission on its fifteenth session.

GENERAL ASSEMBLY ACTION

On 20 December, the General Assembly adopted **resolution 50/99**.

### Commission on Human Settlements

*The General Assembly,*

*Recalling* its resolution 32/162 of 19 December 1977, by which it established the Commission on Human Settlements and its secretariat, the United Nations Centre for Human Settlements (Habitat), to serve as the institutional focus for human settlements activities within the United Nations system,

*Recalling also* its resolution 43/181 of 20 December 1988, in which it designated the Commission on Human Settlements as the United Nations intergovernmental body responsible for coordinating, evaluating and monitoring the implementation of the Global Strategy for Shelter to the Year 2000,

*Recalling further* its resolution 47/180 of 22 December 1992, by which it decided to convene the United Na-

tions Conference on Human Settlements (Habitat II) from 3 to 14 June 1996 and requested the Secretary-General to establish an ad hoc secretariat for the Conference, which should be organizationally part of the Centre,

*Noting with satisfaction* the positive role played by the Centre in the implementation of the Global Strategy and the human settlement aspects of Agenda 21,

*Aware* of the fact that two thirds of the entire increase in world population currently occurs in urban areas, so that by the year 2000 almost half of the world population will be living in towns and cities, and noting with concern that high-level urbanization is straining the capacity of Governments, at both the national and the local levels, to mobilize the financial, technical and managerial resources necessary to sustain such human settlements,

1. *Endorses* the report of the Commission on Human Settlements on the work of its fifteenth session (Nairobi, 25 April-1 May 1995), including its resolution 15/1 on the implementation of the Global Strategy for Shelter to the Year 2000, and the report of the Commission on the implementation of the Global Strategy;

2. *Takes note with appreciation* of the contribution of the Commission and of the United Nations Centre for Human Settlements (Habitat) to the preparations at the national, regional and global levels for the United Nations Conference on Human Settlements (Habitat II), to be held at Istanbul, Turkey, from 3 to 14 June 1996;

3. *Encourages* the Centre to submit its contributions to the preparations for the Conference to the Preparatory Committee for the Conference at its third session, to be held in New York between 5 and 16 February 1996.

General Assembly resolution 50/99

20 December 1995     Meeting 96     Adopted without vote

Approved by Second Committee (A/50/617/Add.2) without vote, 5 December (meeting 41); draft by Vice-Chairman (A/C.2/50/L.53), orally revised and based on informal consultations on draft by Philippines, for Group of 77 and China (A/C.2/50/L.30); agenda item 95 *(b)*.

*Meeting numbers.* GA 50th session: 2nd Committee 33, 34, 38, 41; plenary 96.

### Global Strategy for Shelter to the Year 2000

The Commission on Human Settlements had before it a report[46] by the Executive Director of UNCHS on the mid-term review of the Global Strategy for Shelter to the Year 2000, adopted by the General Assembly in 1988.[47] In undertaking the review, UNCHS analysed information obtained from a variety of sources. It had invited member countries to provide information on their experiences and issued a brief questionnaire to all Governments. Some 74 Governments responded and some provided additional information. Information was also received from international and non-governmental organizations. Another report by the Executive Director[48] described briefly the findings of the questionnaire and gave examples of "best practice" in each of the major components of enabling strategies in the shelter sector: political commitment to enabling strategies; policy and institutional framework; regulating land and housing development; property rights; developing long-term housing finance; rationalizing subsidies; providing infrastructure; and organizing the building industry. The report also summarized actions taken by external support agencies and by organizations within the UN system.

The review indicated that while a large number of countries had adopted an enabling approach to shelter in their policies, very few had put into action the full range of implementing mechanisms.

By a 1 May resolution,[26] the Commission adopted its report on the implementation of the Global Strategy,[49] including the proposed plan of action and timetable for 1996-1997, and requested the Executive Director to transmit it to the Assembly, through the Economic and Social Council. The Commission requested the Executive Director to report to it at its sixteenth (1997) session on the implementation of the next phase of the Global Strategy and urged the Preparatory Committee for Habitat II to take into account the conclusions of the mid-term review in preparing the Global Strategy Plan of Action. A draft resolution on the Strategy was recommended to the Assembly for adoption. Also on 1 May, the Commission adopted a decision,[40] by which it incorporated into its report on the implementation of the Global Strategy additions and amendments submitted by delegations relating to their respective countries.

On 17 July, by **decision 1995/234**, the Economic and Social Council took note of the Commission's report on the implementation of the Global Strategy.[49]

The Assembly took no action on the Commission's proposed text but, in **resolution 50/99**, endorsed both the resolution on the implementation of the Global Strategy[26] and the report on the subject.[49]

## UN Centre for Human Settlements

### Activities

In 1995, UNCHS, through its Technical Cooperation Division, supported 193 technical cooperation programmes and projects in 79 countries and 42 global, regional and interregional programmes, with an overall budget in excess of $29.6 million. Eleven new projects were approved and became operational during the year, while 10 others were completed.

The 1994-1995 UNCHS work programme comprised the following subprogrammes: global policies and strategies; national policies and instruments; managing human settlements development, including financial and land resources; improving infrastructure and the living environment; managing disaster mitigation,

reconstruction and development; housing for all; strengthening local communities; and reducing poverty and promoting equity.

During the year, preparations for Habitat II (see above) received the highest priority in the Centre's work on global policies and strategies. Those activities focused on expanding partnerships with national Governments, local authorities, UN agencies, NGOs and the scientific/professional community in defining the relevance of local human settlements issues to the global development agenda.

The global monitoring capacity of the Centre was strengthened. The *Compendium of Human Settlements Statistics 1995* and two wall charts on human settlements conditions in some 300 cities and 120 countries were published, as was the Human Settlements Statistical Database Version 4, which contained a pre-selected set of human settlements indicators to enable users to make a quick preview of a country's human settlements conditions.

Under the subprogramme on national human settlements policies and instruments, various capacity-building and training-of-trainers efforts were carried out. The "Localizing Agenda 21: Action Planning for Sustainable Urban Development" programme started operations in 1995. Its purpose was to support local authorities in undertaking consultative processes to develop and implement a local Agenda 21 for their communities. In a report to the Commission on developments in urban and housing indicators,[50] the Executive Director stated that, following further retesting and comments by member countries, the number of key urban indicators had been substantially reduced from 51 to 27, plus nine background information indicators, and the elements in the system had been renumbered. The final material for the Indicators Programme was issued. It included three volumes of the complete Programme, and an abridged Key Indicators Worksheet, which was translated into French and Spanish. Major country programmes had begun in Brazil, India, Nigeria and South Africa and smaller programmes were under way in other countries. Overall, some 130 countries were involved in the Programme by attending seminars, receiving worksheets or collecting information.

The subprogramme on managing human settlements development continued its technical cooperation efforts and its work on the Urban Management Programme. Integrated settlements management was the focus of 79 projects in 1995, ranging over 42 countries plus a number of global projects and programmes. Reports published under the first three subprogrammes included *Metropolitan Planning and Management in the Developing World*,[51] *A Reappraisal of the Planning Process*,[52] *The Place, Role and Prospects of Urban Planning*[53] and

*Guidelines for Settlements Planning in Disaster-prone Areas.*[54]

The improving infrastructure and the living environment subprogramme continued to implement three major global programmes: the Settlements Infrastructure and Environment Programme (SIEP), the Sustainable Cities Programme (SCP) and the Urban Management Programme (UMP). In 1995, SIEP implemented a demonstration project on a community-based environmental management information system in Ghana and Indonesia and publications were produced on major aspects of environmental infrastructure. UNCHS was identified by ACC in 1995 as the UN focal point for urban water issues and the lead agency for the World Day for Water (22 March). It began implementation of a global capacity-building project on the integrated management of water and environmental infrastructure. Throughout the year, SCP continued its activities in nine fully fledged city demonstration projects and initiated activities and pipeline projects in five more, building capacities at the local level in environmental planning and management, and developing networks of expertise and information-sharing at the national level. The agreement making SCP a joint UNCHS-UNEP facility enabled the Programme to draw on the resources and expertise of both agencies, while providing them with an efficient vehicle for on-the-ground project implementation. UMP activities included regional interchange of successful experiences of Brazil and Colombia on solid waste; ongoing demonstrations of urban environmental planning and management in Chile, Ecuador, Egypt, Ghana, India, Nigeria, Poland, Senegal and the United Republic of Tanzania; and city consultations in Concepción (Chile), Dar es Salaam (United Republic of Tanzania), Ibadan (Nigeria), Madras (India) and Tunis (Tunisia).

Under its subprogramme on managing disaster mitigation, reconstruction and development, UNCHS continued to assist countries in post-war and post-conflict situations. It embarked on a medium-term urban rehabilitation programme in Afghanistan, providing institutional strengthening, rehabilitation and development to its three principal urban centres. In Sierra Leone, UNCHS assisted the Government to develop and implement a programme for the reconstruction of war-torn areas. Assistance was also provided to Angola, Guatemala, Haiti, Palestine, the Philippines, Rwanda, Somalia, the United Republic of Tanzania and Yemen. The Centre organized the first UNDP-UNCHS consultation on African countries in crisis, covering Burundi, Rwanda, Uganda, the United Republic of Tanzania and Zaire.

As part of the Centre's strategy for reducing poverty and promoting equity, the Urban Poverty partnership with the International Labour Organization (ILO) and UNDP continued with support from the UN Volunteers. The Centre and ILO sent a joint call to the World Summit for Social Development (see PART FOUR, Chapter IX) for a poverty-eradication strategy joining the goals of shelter for all and full employment.

A new journal, *Habitat Debate*, was launched, with four issues appearing in 1995. A number of technical publications, audiovisual aids and information kits were also prepared.

The 1995 Habitat Scroll of Honour Awards for outstanding contributions by individuals, organizations and projects to the shelter delivery process were presented to the Comunidades Programme of the State Government of Ceará (Brazil), the Foundation in Support of Local Democracy (Poland), the Urban Community Development Office (Thailand), Gangadhar Rao Dattatri (India), the Projet de Taza, Agence Nationale de Lutte contre l'Habitat Insalubre (Morocco), La coopérative des veuves de Save "Duhozanye" (Rwanda), the Shanghai Municipal Housing Project (China) and Joe Slovo (deceased) (South Africa).

## Human settlements and political, economic and social issues

### The right to adequate housing

In response to a 1993 Commission request,[55] the Executive Director of UNCHS submitted a report on practical contributions that the Centre could make towards promoting, ensuring and protecting the full realization of the human right to adequate housing.[56] A detailed proposal for a consolidated approach was contained in a background paper.[57] The proposed strategy was premised on a six-point agenda: promotional activities; advisory services and technical cooperation; monitoring activities; promoting the housing rights of specific social groups; networking; and Habitat II and housing rights.

On 1 May,[27] the Commission asked the Executive Director to undertake a further examination and update of his report, taking into consideration the legal, social, economic, political and practical aspects of the subject and the views and concerns of Member States, including those regarding the existence and/or legal status of the right to adequate housing. He was asked to report on the matter in 1997.

### Women and human settlements

In response to a 1993 Commission request,[55] the Executive Director submitted a report on the activities of UNCHS on promoting the advancement of women in human settlements development.[58] The report described the focus of the

Centre's main achievements regarding women's participation and the inclusion of a gender perspective within its work at the national, regional and global levels in cooperation with member States, community-based organizations and NGOs. The Centre's contribution to the Fourth World Conference on Women (see PART FOUR, Chapter X) was outlined in an annex to the report.

On 1 May,[28] the Commission requested the Executive Director to continue to strengthen the role and competence of the Centre in gender-sensitive human settlements development and to include in the guidelines on legal rights to housing and land tenure and access to credit for women the issue of gender-impact analysis on human settlements programmes and policies. He was asked to incorporate those measures in all relevant parts of the Centre's work programme for 1996-1997 and to report to the Commission in 1997 on the implementation of those recommendations.

### Housing for all

In response to a 1993 Commission request,[59] the Executive Director submitted a report[60] in which he reviewed national action to provide housing for all since the 1976 UN Conference on Human Settlements.[2] The report described national and international action on developing and implementing shelter strategies, including a summary of their results. It analysed the main bottlenecks and successful approaches in the shelter process, paying particular attention to scale, sustainability and poverty-reach, and to the needs of particularly vulnerable groups. It also identified a series of common themes, issues and challenges that had emerged from the experience of the previous two decades and assessed the extent of progress made.

On 1 May,[35] the Commission urged the international community to pay greater attention to assisting developing countries to alleviate land market constraints, encourage shelter development and improve urban management, especially by concentrating on capacity-building to ensure sustainable progress. The Executive Director was asked to intensify the monitoring and evaluation of progress in national action to improve shelter conditions, to incorporate the findings of that research in the Centre's work programme and to report on the results in 1997.

### Sustainable human settlements

In response to a 1993 Commission request,[59] the Executive Director submitted a report on sustainable human settlements in an urbanizing world, including issues related to land policies and mitigation of natural disasters.[61] The report discussed the main environmental, technological, economic and socio-political dimensions of sustainable development and addressed land issues in the context of sustainable urban development, focusing on the rising demand for land, the physical degradation of land, and the need to utilize land for raising urban municipal finance. It also considered the issues of mitigation of natural disasters within urban settlements with regard to the location and land-use policies required to minimize encroachment into hazardous areas, and the building technologies suited to disaster mitigation. The report further discussed action necessary for implementing sustainable human settlements policies at local, national and international levels, including the specific needs of land use and the mitigation of disasters.

On 1 May,[36] the Commission recommended that Governments adopt and ensure implementation of the following measures for the sustainable development of human settlements: decentralization of decision-making and creation of an enabling environment to support the initiatives of local authorities and community organizations; formulation and implementation of local Agenda 21 plans and improvement of intersectoral coordination at the local, regional and national levels; establishment of regulatory and incentive structures to encourage sustainable use of resources; promotion of the use of non-polluting appropriate technologies in human settlements activities; and increased financial resources at the local level for promoting national sustainable urban development objectives.

As to sustainable urban land development and management, the Commission called on Governments to adopt the following measures: promotion of access to land and security of tenure for all urban residents, particularly the poor; decentralization and simplification of land registration and privatization of land survey departments; promotion of land-use planning; strengthening of conservation measures; strengthening the role of land as the cornerstone of urban municipal finance; and compiling national inventories of land and other ecological resources and formulating long-term spatial strategies to guide land resources development.

With regard to the mitigation of natural disasters, Governments were urged, taking into account the outcome of the 1994 World Conference on Natural Disaster Reduction,[62] to promote and implement the following measures: setting up of institutional structures and decision-making processes to ensure that mitigation of natural disasters became an integral part of sustainable human settlements development; building up of national collective memories of disasters; improving and regulating access to land for housing the poor in order to limit encroachment onto hazardous sites; encouragement of and assistance to local authorities to direct human settlements development onto vacant public land in relatively safe locations through the provision of infrastructure; identification of hazardous sites and their conversion into alternative uses; reduction and elimination of the threats of already identified hazardous sites; development and use of housing designs, building materials and construction methods that could mitigate the effects of natural disasters; and enhancement of technical assistance to regional and local institutions and provision of training in managing natural disasters to technicians, professionals and administrators.

The Executive Director was asked to review recent trends in the development of urban informal settlements in developing countries and in countries in transition, and to prepare further practical guidelines for sustainable human settlements planning and management in areas prone to natural disasters.

## Financing

During 1995, the UNCHS work programme continued to be financed from the UN regular budget and from extrabudgetary resources. Programme support income from projects financed by UNDP and trust funds amounted to $2.1 million, while income from the UN Habitat and Human Settlements Foundation was $7.7 million.

UNCHS project delivery amounted to $33.3 million, including projects financed by UNDP ($22.2 million), the Foundation ($5.5 million) and other sources ($5.6 million).

### UN Habitat and Human Settlements Foundation

During 1995, the combined income of the UN Habitat and Human Settlements Foundation, including contributions from Governments on the basis of firm pledges and from the Danish International Development Agency, totalled $12.5 million. Expenditures totalled $14.9 million.

*REFERENCES*

[1]A/50/37. [2]YUN 1976, p. 441. [3]A/CONF.165/PC.2/2. [4]A/CONF.165/PC.2/2/Add.2. [5]A/CONF.165/PC.2/2/Add.1/Rev.1. [6]A/CONF.165/PC.2/3 & Add.1. [7]YUN 1994, p. 978. [8]A/CONF.165/PC.2/8. [9]YUN 1992, p. 672. [10]A/50/37 (dec. II/1). [11]Ibid. (dec. II/2). [12]Ibid. (dec. II/3). [13]Ibid. (dec. II/4). [14]Ibid. (dec. II/5). [15]Ibid. (dec. II/6). [16]Ibid. (dec. II/7). [17]Ibid. (dec. II/8). [18]Ibid. (dec. II/9). [19]A/50/411. [20]YUN 1994, p. 979, GA res. 49/109, 19 Dec. 1994. [21]A/CONF.165/PC.2/INF.6. [22]A/CONF.165/PC.2/INF.10. [23]A/CONF.165/PC.3/3. [24]A/CONF.165/PC.3/INF.4. [25]A/50/8. [26]Ibid. (res. 15/1). [27]Ibid. (res. 15/2). [28]Ibid. (res. 15/3). [29]Ibid. (res. 15/4). [30]Ibid. (res. 15/5). [31]Ibid. (res. 15/6). [32]Ibid. (res. 15/7). [33]Ibid. (res. 15/8). [34]Ibid. (res. 15/9). [35]Ibid. (res. 15/10). [36]Ibid. (res. 15/11). [37]Ibid. (res. 15/12). [38]Ibid. (res. 15/13). [39]Ibid. (res. 15/14). [40]Ibid. (dec. 15/15). [41]Ibid. (dec. 15/16). [42]Ibid. (dec. 15/17). [43]Ibid. (dec. 15/18). [44]Ibid. (dec. 15/19). [45]Ibid. (dec. 15/20). [46]HS/C/15/3/Add.3. [47]YUN 1988, p. 478, GA res. 43/181, 20 Dec. 1988. [48]HS/C/15/3/Add.4. [49]A/50/8/Add.1. [50]HS/C/15/3/Add.6. [51]HS/380/95E. [52]HS/365/95E. [53]HS/360/95E. [54]HS/384/95E. [55]YUN 1993, p. 844. [56]HS/C/15/2/Add.2. [57]HS/C/15/INF.7. [58]HS/C/15/2/Add.1. [59]YUN 1993, p. 839. [60]HS/C/15/5. [61]HS/C/15/6. [62]YUN 1994, p. 851.

Chapter IX

# Social policy, crime prevention and human resource development

Major international conferences were organized by the United Nations in 1995 in the areas of social development and crime prevention. The World Summit for Social Development, which was held in March in Copenhagen, Denmark, adopted the Copenhagen Declaration on Social Development and the Programme of Action of the World Summit for Social Development, which were both endorsed by the General Assembly in December. The core issues addressed in those documents were the enhancement of social integration, poverty alleviation and expansion of productive employment.

The Ninth United Nations Congress on the Prevention of Crime and the Treatment of Offenders took place in Cairo, Egypt, in April/May. It adopted nine substantive resolutions, one of which dealt with the four major topics considered—international cooperation for strengthening the rule of law; action against national and transnational economic and organized crime; criminal justice and police systems; and crime prevention strategies. In December, the Assembly endorsed the Congress resolutions and invited Governments to be guided by them when formulating legislation and policy directives. Having considered the report of the Commission on Crime Prevention and Criminal Justice, which met in May/June, the Assembly requested the Secretary-General to continue strengthening the UN crime prevention and criminal justice programme by providing it with needed resources. As recommended by the Commission, the Economic and Social Council, in July, took note of the draft international code of conduct for public office holders and urged States to comment on it so as to facilitate further revision of the draft.

The United Nations Year for Tolerance was officially launched on 21 February 1995. On 20 November, the Assembly held a special commemorative meeting to mark the Year. The Secretary-General made a number of proposals to the Assembly with regard to the follow-up to the International Year of the Family (1994). The proposals were welcomed by the Assembly, which invited Governments to continue action to build family-friendly societies. The Assembly also considered a mid-decade review of the follow-up to International Literacy Year (1990) and appealed to Governments and economic and financial organizations to lend greater financial and material support to efforts to increase literacy and achieve education for all.

In its twentieth anniversary year, the United Nations University established the International Leadership Academy in Amman, Jordan, and the Institute of Advanced Studies in Tokyo, Japan.

## Social policy and cultural issues

### Social aspects of development

#### World Summit for Social Development

The World Summit for Social Development was held in Copenhagen, Denmark, from 6 to 12 March 1995,[1] as decided by the General Assembly in 1992.[2] The core issues addressed by the Summit were the enhancement of social integration, particularly of the more disadvantaged and marginal groups; alleviation and reduction of poverty; and expansion of productive employment.

The Summit was attended by representatives from 186 States, including 117 heads of State or Government, and the European Community, the observers for Macau, the Netherlands Antilles and Palestine, the five regional commissions, UN organizations and specialized agencies and intergovernmental organizations and non-governmental organizations (NGOs). During the Summit, a variety of special events (meetings, symposia, round tables, workshops and panel discussions) were held with a view to enriching the debate on social issues and the follow-up to the Summit. Parallel to the Summit, an NGO Forum was held in Copenhagen from 3 to 12 March.

The Summit elected as its President Poul Nyrup Rasmussen, Prime Minister of Denmark; it also elected a Rapporteur-General and 28 Vice-Presidents, one of them *ex officio* from Denmark. (See APPENDIX III.)

In his statement to the opening session, the Secretary-General said that the aim of the Summit was to make social development a major priority for the international community. It was part of the process of reflection and debate on which the international community had embarked— about itself and its future, and about the role of the individual human being. He identified as "priority objectives": providing social protection for the individual; assisting social integration; and maintaining social peace. He hoped that the United Nations might acquire the means to follow up the Conference and trusted that the Bretton Woods institutions (the World Bank and the International Monetary Fund) would play a full role in the social action that was being redefined and reinvented. Giving social issues the status of universal priorities showed the determination to accept responsibility for the collective destiny of international society and to establish a new planet-wide pact of solidarity.

On 12 March, the Summit adopted the Copenhagen Declaration on Social Development and the Programme of Action of the World Summit for Social Development,[a] which it recommended to the General Assembly for endorsement.

**Copenhagen Declaration on Social Development.** The Copenhagen Declaration comprised an overview of the current social situation, a section on principles and goals, and ten commitments for action at the national and international levels.

With regard to the current situation, the Summit acknowledged that while there had been progress in some areas of social and economic development, far too many people, particularly women and children, were vulnerable to stress and deprivation. The gap between rich and poor had increased in many societies and more than one billion people in the world lived in abject poverty, most of them going hungry every day. There were serious social problems in countries with economies in transition and those experiencing fundamental political, economic and social transformations. The major cause of continued deterioration of the global environment was the unsustainable pattern of consumption and production, which aggravated poverty and imbalances. At the same time, continued growth of the world population challenged the adaptive capacities of Governments, social institutions and the natural environment. Over 120 million people worldwide were officially unemployed and many more were underemployed, while millions of others were refugees or internally displaced persons. Women carried a disproportionate share of the problems of coping with poverty, social disintegration, unemployment, environmental degradation and the effects of war.

People with disabilities were too often forced into poverty, unemployment and social isolation and older persons could be particularly vulnerable to social exclusion, poverty and marginalization. The situation in developing countries, particularly in Africa and the least developed countries (LDCs), was critical and required special attention and action. Countries with economies in transition and those undergoing fundamental political, economic and social transformation also required the support of the international community. The challenge was to establish a people-centred framework for social development, to build a culture of cooperation and partnership, and to respond to the immediate needs of those most affected by human distress.

In the principles and goals contained in the Declaration, the heads of State and Government stated that they would create a framework for action that would, among other things: place people at the centre of development; ensure equity among generations and protect the integrity and sustainable use of the environment; recognize that social development could not be successfully achieved without the commitment and efforts of the international community; integrate economic, cultural and social policies and acknowledge the interdependence of public and private spheres of activity; recognize that achieving sustained social development required sound economic policies; promote democracy, human dignity, social justice and solidarity and ensure tolerance, non-violence, pluralism and non-discrimination; promote the equitable distribution of income and greater access to resources; recognize the family as the basic unit of society; ensure that disadvantaged and vulnerable persons and groups were included in social development; promote universal respect for human rights and fundamental freedoms for all, including the right to development; reaffirm the right of self-determination of all peoples; recognize and support indigenous people in their pursuit of economic and social development; underline the importance of transparent and accountable governance and administration; and recognize that empowering people, particularly women, to strengthen their own capacities was a main objective of development and its principal resource.

The ten commitments adopted, each containing actions to be taken at the national and international levels, dealt with: creating an environment to enable people to achieve social development; the eradication of poverty; promoting the goal of full employment; promoting social integration; promoting full respect for human dignity and equality and equity between men and women; promoting and attaining the goals of universal and equitable access to quality

---

[a]The following countries expressed reservations or made comments on parts of the Declaration and Programme of Action: Argentina, Azerbaijan, Costa Rica, Guatemala, Holy See, Iraq, Libyan Arab Jamahiriya, Malta, Oman, Qatar, Saudi Arabia, United Arab Emirates, United States.

education and the highest standards of physical and mental health; accelerating the economic, social and human resource development of Africa and LDCs; ensuring that structural adjustment programmes included social development goals; allocating adequate resources to social development; and improving and strengthening the framework for international, regional and subregional cooperation for social development.

**Programme of Action.** The five-chapter Programme of Action of the World Summit for Social Development, the draft text of which had been established by the Summit's Preparatory Committee (see below), outlined policies, actions and measures to implement the principles and fulfil the commitments enunciated in the Copenhagen Declaration.

Chapter I, which addressed the need for an enabling environment for sustainable development, listed actions required to promote a favourable national and international economic, political and legal environment. Those actions included: establishment of an open, equitable, cooperative and mutually beneficial economic environment; implementing sound and stable macroeconomic and sectoral policies; promoting enterprise, productive investment and expanded access to markets and to technologies; full implementation of the Final Act (1994) of the Uruguay Round of multilateral trade negotiations;[3] refraining from creating obstacles to trade relations among States; increasing food production and improving access to food by low-income people in developing countries; strengthening capacity-building in developing countries, particularly in Africa and LDCs; ensuring, in accordance with Agenda 21,[4] adopted by the United Nations Conference on Environment and Development in 1992, the need to protect the environment and the interests of future generations; and ensuring that the special needs of small island developing States were adequately addressed by implementing the 1994 Programme of Action for the Sustainable Development of Small Island Developing States.[5] Actions identified to ensure that the benefits of global economic growth were equitably distributed among countries included debt alleviation, strengthening technical and financial assistance to developing countries and changing unsustainable consumption and production patterns. Within the framework of support to developing countries, giving priority to the needs of Africa and LDCs, actions required included improving the functioning of commodity markets and supporting commodity diversification efforts; immediate implementation of the terms of debt forgiveness agreed on in the Paris Club of creditor Governments in 1994 (see PART FOUR, Chapter IV); increasing official development assistance (ODA) and improving its impact; and

striving to attain the agreed target of 0.7 per cent of gross national product for ODA and 0.15 per cent to LDCs. Recommendations were also made regarding actions to make economic growth and the interaction of market forces more conducive to social development and to ensure that fiscal systems and other public policies were geared towards poverty eradication and did not generate socially divisive disparities.

In order to ensure that the political framework supported social development, it was necessary, among other things, to ensure that government agencies responsible for social policies had the resources necessary to give high priority to social development. The full involvement of women at all levels in the economic and political decision-making and implementation process was needed, as was the removal of all legal impediments to the ownership of means of production and property by men and women. Human rights and fundamental freedoms should be promoted and protected, including the right to development, and an open political and economic system required access by all to knowledge, education and information. International support for national efforts to promote a favourable political and legal environment called for the following actions: making use of the capacity of the United Nations and other organizations to prevent and resolve armed conflicts and promote social progress and better standards of life; coordinating measures to combat terrorism, all forms of extremist violence, illicit arms trafficking, organized crime and illicit drug problems, money laundering and related crimes, and trafficking in women, adolescents, children, migrants, and human organs; international cooperation to support the efforts of developing countries for the full realization of the right to development and the elimination of obstacles to development; ensuring that human persons were at the centre of social development; reinforcing the capacity of national, regional and international organizations to promote the implementation of all human rights and fundamental freedoms; elaborating policies to support the objectives of social development and contribute to institutional development through capacity-building and other forms of cooperation; strengthening the capacities of Governments, the private sector and civil society (especially in Africa and LDCs) to enable them to meet their specific and global responsibilities; and reinforcing the capacities of those groups in countries with economies in transition, with a view to helping them to transform their economies from centrally planned to market-oriented ones.

Chapter II, on eradication of poverty, acknowledged that over 1 billion people lived under unacceptable conditions of poverty, mostly in developing countries. Poverty could not be eradicated through anti-poverty programmes alone but needed democratic participation and changes in economic structures and universal access to economic opportunities, as well as special efforts to facilitate access for the disadvantaged. The Programme of Action described actions required in that regard, grouping them under the headings: formulation of integrated strategies; improved access to productive resources and infrastructure; meeting basic human needs of all people; and enhanced social protection and reduced vulnerability. Governments should give greater focus to eradicating absolute poverty and reducing overall poverty substantially by formulating—preferably by 1996—and implementing national poverty eradication plans to address the structural causes of poverty, giving particular attention to employment creation, health and education, basic social services, generating household income and promoting access to productive assets and economic opportunities. Each country should develop a precise definition and assessment of absolute poverty (preferably by 1996, the International Year for the Eradication of Poverty) and elaborate the measurements, criteria and indicators for determining the extent and distribution of absolute poverty. Governments should implement the commitments made to meet the basic needs of all, including the following objectives to be accomplished by the year 2000: universal access to basic education and completion of primary education by at least 80 per cent of primary school–age children; life expectancy of not less than 60 years in any country; reduction of mortality rates of infants and children under five by one third of the 1990 level, or 50 to 70 per 1,000 live births, whichever was less; a reduction in maternal mortality by one half of the 1990 level; a reduction of severe and moderate malnutrition among children under five by one half the 1990 level; ensuring primary health care for all; reducing malaria mortality and morbidity by at least 20 per cent compared to 1995 levels in at least 75 per cent of affected countries; and eradicating or controlling major diseases in accordance with Agenda 21.[4] Particular efforts should be made to improve the situations of children, youth and ageing persons. People and communities should be protected from impoverishment and long-term displacement resulting from disasters by designing mechanisms to reduce the impact of natural disasters, developing contingency plans to mitigate natural disasters and famine and establishing logistical mechanisms to enable quick and effective response to provide food and care to victims. Governments should also reduce vulnerability to natural disasters through the development of early warning systems.

Chapter III of the Programme of Action addressed the expansion of productive employment

and reduction of unemployment. Full and adequately remunerated employment was an effective method of combating poverty and promoting social integration. It required that the State and the other parts of civil society at all levels cooperate to create conditions for everyone to participate in and benefit from productive work. Suggested actions to expand productive employment included placing the issue at the centre of sustainable development strategies and economic and social policies; minimizing the negative impact on jobs of measures for macroeconomic stability; promoting patterns of economic growth that maximized employment creation; and enhancing opportunities for the creation and growth of private-sector enterprises that would generate additional employment. It was also necessary to facilitate people's access to productive employment in the rapidly changing global environment and develop better quality jobs; and help workers to adapt and to enhance their employment opportunities under changing economic conditions. Governments should enhance the quality of work and employment and remove exploitation, abolish child labour, raise productivity and enhance the quality of life in order to achieve a healthy and safe working environment. Measures were also recommended for the full participation of women in the labour market and their equal access to employment opportunities. In terms of enhancing employment opportunities for groups with specific needs, action was suggested for improving the design of policies and programmes, better addressing the problem of short- and long-term unemployment through employment policies, establishing programmes for entry or re-entry into the labour market, and policies to guarantee all youth constructive options for their future. Action to promote the full participation of indigenous people in the labour market and their equal access to employment opportunities was advised, as were broadening the range of employment opportunities for persons with disabilities and intensifying international cooperation and national attention to migrant workers and their families. Recommendations were made for a broader recognition and understanding of work and employment and for developing additional socially useful new types of employment and work.

Chapter IV stated that the aim of social integration was to create a "society for all", based on respect for all human rights and fundamental freedoms, cultural and religious diversity, social justice and the special needs of vulnerable and disadvantaged groups, democratic participation and the rule of law. While progress, such as decolonization, the elimination of apartheid, the spread of democracy and the wider recognition of the need to respect human rights, was noted, violence was a growing threat to the security of individuals, families and communities everywhere. Actions recommended included the promotion and protection by Governments of all human rights and fundamental freedoms, including the right to development, bearing in mind the interdependent and mutually reinforcing relationship between democracy, development and respect for human rights; making public institutions more responsive to people's needs; and encouraging the fullest participation in society. At the national and international levels, it was necessary to eliminate discrimination and promote tolerance and mutual respect for the value of diversity. Governments should also promote equality and social justice and respond to the special needs of social groups, especially the vulnerable and the disadvantaged. In addition, they should address the special needs of refugees, displaced persons, and asylum-seekers; promote the equitable treatment and integration of documented migrants, particularly workers and their families; and address the concerns and basic needs of undocumented migrants. They should deal with the problems created by violence, crime, substance abuse and the production and use of and trafficking in illicit drugs and promote the rehabilitation of addicts. The family, as the basic unit of society, should be strengthened, with husband and wife as equal partners, and helped in its supporting, educating and nurturing roles.

Chapter V, which dealt with the implementation and follow-up to the Declaration and Programme of Action, stated that social development and the implementation of the Programme of Action of the Summit were primarily the responsibility of Governments, although international cooperation and assistance were essential. It required an integrated approach at the national level, in accordance with national specificities. Among the recommendations made were for the formulation or strengthening by 1996 of comprehensive cross-sectoral strategies and national strategies for social development for implementing the Summit outcome, and the development of quantitative and qualitative indicators of social development. Other action identified included international support for the formulation of national strategies for social development requiring action by bilateral and multilateral agencies. Effective implementation also required strengthening community organizations and non-profit NGOs in the spheres of education, health, poverty, social integration, human rights, improvement of the quality of life, and relief and rehabilitation, enabling them to participate constructively in policy-making and implementation. At the national level, substantial new and additional resources were needed in both the public and private sectors. Likewise, implementation in developing countries, particu-

larly in Africa and LDCs, would need additional financial resources and more effective development cooperation and assistance. That would require translating the commitments of the Summit into financial implications for social development programmes in those countries; striving for the fulfilment of the agreed target of 0.7 per cent of GNP for overall ODA and increasing the share of funding for social development programmes; agreeing on a mutual commitment between interested developed and developing country partners to allocate 20 per cent of ODA and 20 per cent of the national budget, respectively, to basic social programmes; giving high priority in ODA to the eradication of poverty in developing countries; and providing assistance, including in the form of grants and loans, for social-sector activities such as rehabilitation and development of social infrastructure. Economies in transition would need continued international cooperation and assistance, including assessing the financial implications of the commitments of the Summit for social development programmes. Substantial debt reduction was needed to enable developing countries to implement the Declaration and the Programme of Action. Building on the momentum of the 1994 meetings of the seven major industrialized nations and of the governors of the World Bank and IMF, further progress could be achieved by inviting the international community to continue to explore ways to implement additional measures to alleviate the debt burdens of developing countries; adopting measures to reduce substantially the bilateral debt of LDCs, particularly the countries of Africa; giving special consideration to developing countries where multilateral debt was an important part of total debt; and encouraging debt swaps for social development, with resources released by debt cancellation or reduction being invested in social development programmes. Governments should cooperate with international financial institutions and other international organizations to ensure that structural development programmes included social development goals, in particular the eradication of poverty, the generation of productive employment and the enhancement of social integration, including the protection of basic social programmes and expenditures, particularly those affecting the poor and vulnerable segments of society, from budget reductions. International financial institutions should contribute to the mobilization of resources for implementing the Declaration and Programme of Action by further integrating social development goals in their policies, programmes and operations, including giving higher priority to social-sector lending. The Bretton Woods institutions and the UN system should work with concerned countries to improve policy dialogues and develop new initiatives to ensure that structural adjustment programmes promoted sustained economic and social development, with particular attention to their impact on the poor and vulnerable groups. In addition, relevant UN bodies, particularly the Economic and Social Council, should consider new and innovative ideas for generating funds.

The Programme of Action also addressed the role of the UN system in its implementation. A framework for international cooperation should be developed in the context of an agenda for development[6] to ensure the integrated and comprehensive implementation, follow-up and assessment of the outcome of the Summit, together with the results of other recent and planned UN conferences related to social development. The financial and organizational implications of the commitments, goals and targets should be assessed, priorities established, and budgets and work programmes planned. As to considering social development at the intergovernmental level, the General Assembly should include the follow-up to the Summit in its agenda and, in 1996, review the effectiveness of the steps taken to implement the outcome of the Summit with regard to poverty eradication, as part of the activities of the International Year for the Eradication of Poverty. It should hold a special session in the year 2000 for an overall review and appraisal of the implementation of the outcome of the Summit and consider further action and initiatives and, at its fiftieth (1995) session, declare the first United Nations Decade for the Eradication of Poverty (see PART FOUR, Chapter I) and convene meetings of high-level representatives on critical social issues and on policies for addressing them. The Assembly should draw on the initial work of the Ad Hoc open-ended Working Group of the General Assembly on an Agenda for Development (see PART FOUR, Chapter I) on a common framework for implementing the outcome of conferences. The Economic and Social Council would oversee and make recommendations for system-wide coordination in implementing the Summit outcome and should look for ways to strengthen its role, authority, structures, resources and processes, bringing specialized agencies into a closer working relationship with it so that it could review progress in implementing the Summit's outcome. At its 1995 substantive session, the Council should review the mandate, agenda and composition of the Commission for Social Development, including strengthening the Commission. It should also review the reporting system in social development with a view to establishing a coherent system that would result in clear policy recommendations for Governments and international actors. The Council should consider holding joint meetings with the Development Committee of the World Bank and

IMF. The Secretary-General and the heads of IMF, the World Bank, the International Labour Organization (ILO), UN funds and programmes and other relevant agencies should hold joint meetings to consider implementation of the Declaration and Programme of Action prior to the Development Committee sessions. To promote implementation at the regional and subregional levels, the regional commissions, in cooperation with the regional intergovernmental organizations and banks, could convene biennial meetings to review progress. The UN system should provide technical cooperation and other forms of assistance to the developing countries, in particular in Africa and LDCs, in implementing the Declaration and Programme of Action. To that end, specialized agencies and related organizations of the system were invited to strengthen and adjust their activities, programmes and medium-term strategies to take into account the follow-up to the Summit, while relevant governing bodies should review their policies, programmes, budgets and activities. The Administrative Committee on Coordination (ACC) should consider how its participating agencies might best coordinate their activities to implement the objectives of the Summit. The UN system should also provide technical cooperation and other forms of assistance to the countries with economies in transition. To ensure coherence in implementing the Declaration and the Programme of Action, the General Assembly should strengthen coordination of UN system activities, the Bretton Woods institutions and the World Trade Organization (WTO), invite WTO to consider how it might contribute and request ILO to contribute to the implementation. UN operational activities for development should be strengthened and the UN Development Programme (UNDP) should organize UN efforts towards capacity-building, support the coordinated implementation of social development programmes through its network of field offices, and improve coordination at the country level through the resident coordinator system. UN developmental efforts should be supported by a substantial increase in resources for operational activities for development on a continuous and assured basis. The support of major groups, as defined in Agenda 21,[7] was essential for planning, elaboration, implementation and evaluation at the national and international levels. To that end, mechanisms were needed to support, promote and allow their effective participation in all relevant UN bodies, including mechanisms for reviewing the implementation of the Programme of Action.

**Other action.** In addition to adopting the Declaration and the Programme of Action, the Summit adopted a resolution expressing its gratitude to the Government and the people of Denmark for their hospitality. By another resolution, the Summit approved the report of its Credentials Committee.

**Documentation.** The Summit had before it a note by the Secretary-General transmitting the draft declaration and draft programme of action, as approved by the Preparatory Committee (see below)[8] and a note by the Secretariat transmitting the texts of additional proposals for those drafts.[9] By a 2 February note verbale,[10] Bangladesh, on behalf of the secretariat of the South Asian Association for Regional Cooperation (SAARC), submitted the report of the SAARC Workshop to Formulate a Collective Position for the World Summit for Social Development (New Delhi, India, 12-13 December 1994). Greece, in an 11 March note verbale[11] addressed to the Summit secretariat, requested that, at the World Summit, the former Yugoslav Republic of Macedonia should use that name and not that of "the Republic of Macedonia", in accordance with a 1993 Security Council resolution.[12] Also before the Summit was the report of the Credential Committee[13] and several notes by the Secretariat dealing with organizational and procedural matters,[14] accreditation of NGOs,[15] and participation of intergovernmental organizations.[16]

### Preparations for the Summit

The Preparatory Committee for the World Summit held its third and final session in New York from 16 to 28 January,[17] during which it approved the draft declaration and draft programme of action of the Summit[18] and a list of NGOs[19] for accreditation and recommended a provisional agenda and organization of work for adoption by the Summit. The Committee considered a number of contributions of organs, organizations and programmes of the UN system[20] to the Summit and also considered the status of the preparations for the Summit. It had before it a 1994 secretariat note[21] on the status of preparations for the Summit, the report of the 1994 Seminar on the Ethical and Spiritual Dimensions of Social Progress[21] and the report of the Symposium on Social Development (Beijing, China, 7-9 October 1994).[22]

### Follow-up to the Summit

**Commission for Social Development.** The Commission for Social Development, at its April (1995) session[23] (see below), considered the agenda item, "Priority subject: World Summit for Social Development". It had before it a note[24] by the Secretariat on follow-up to the Summit, which contained information on the Commission's establishment and functions and outlined those provisions of the Copenhagen Declaration and the Programme of Action that were of relevance to international cooperation and the follow-up to the

Summit, including Commitment 10 of the Declaration and Chapter V of the Programme of Action.

The Commission adopted a 20 April resolution,[25] by which it transmitted to the Economic and Social Council its views on the follow-up to the Summit. It considered that implementation of the commitments and policy recommendations involved Governments, the international community and all actors of civil society, as well as regional and international organizations, which had a responsibility to provide support to Governments. The Commission should have a central role to play in the follow-up, which should be compatible with that of other relevant bodies, organs and organizations of the UN system. The Council should review the Commission's mandate, agenda and composition, including an expansion of its membership and the annualization of its meetings, as well as its reporting system and methods of work, with a view to enhancing its contribution to the Summit follow-up. Its mandate should be adapted to ensure an integrated approach to social development, taking into account the relationship between social and economic development as defined by the Summit. The Commission should open its debates to experts and the main actors of civil society; update its methods of work; contribute to the review of the Declaration and Programme of Action by the Assembly and the Council; and develop a work programme for considering the Declaration and Programme of Action.

By an 11 May note,[26] the Secretariat submitted the views of the Commission to the Council.

**Economic and Social Council.** In accordance with **decision 1995/214** of 10 February, the Economic and Social Council, at its resumed organizational session, discussed the manner in which the discussion on the outcome of the World Summit for Social Development could be organized during the high-level meeting of the operational activities segment of its 1995 substantive session. In **decision 1995/224** of 5 May, the Council decided that the high-level meeting would have as one of its themes a preliminary exchange on the follow-up by the UN system to the Copenhagen Declaration on Social Development and the Programme of Action of the World Summit for Social Development. It would consider the direction to be taken by the UN system for adopting an approach to social development issues in accordance with the framework developed by the Summit.

In a 27 June note,[27] the Secretariat examined the general approach to the follow-up to the Summit, follow-up at the national level, involvement of civil society and follow-up at the regional and international levels. It identified the roles of the General Assembly, the Council and the Commission for Social Development and other subsidiary bodies of the Council. The report stated that follow-up to the Summit should be innovative, allowing existing mechanisms to be transformed and new approaches and arrangements to be put in place; open in its orientation; universal; and holistic. The Secretariat recommended that the Council provide for the Commission on Social Development a central role in the implementation and follow-up of the Summit, as well as roles for most of its subsidiary bodies and other organs of the UN system; approve the provisional agenda for the Commission's next session; consider aligning the periodicity of the Commission's session with that of other bodies engaged in the follow-up to major conferences, starting in 1996 with a special session on the follow-up to the Summit; and consider ways to involve experts and the main actors of civil society at the next session of the Commission and request the Secretary-General to report in 1996 on the experience gained. Also in 1996, it should review the membership of the Commission and the reporting system in the area of social development in the light of proposals made by the Secretary-General and taking into consideration the outcome of the General Assembly discussion and relevant developments in other forums. The Council should request other functional commissions and committees to place on their agendas relevant aspects of the follow-up to the Summit.

**UNDP action.** The United Nations Development Programme Administrator, in a 26 April report[28] to the UNDP/UN Population Fund (UNFPA) Executive Board and in UNDP's annual report[29] to the Council, discussed the follow-up to the Summit. In February, in anticipation of its role in supporting countries implementing the outcome of the Summit, UNDP had established a Summit follow-up strategy group to work with country officers and country-level partners in developing specific strategies and programmes for implementing the Programme of Action. The Summit's commitments closely paralleled UNDP's core mission and strategy as outlined in the Administrator's 1994 proposed initiatives for change.[30] UNDP was in a strong position to respond quickly and concretely to the challenges of the Summit follow-up. Its follow-up strategy included immediate support to countries in integrating the Summit commitments and related conference agreements into their long-term development plans and frameworks, particularly strategies for the eradication of poverty; dialogue among UN specialized agencies and other development partners on the integration of follow-up strategies and for improved aid coordination and cooperation; and a possible capacity development window for the Summit follow-up, comparable to Capacity 21, launched in 1992[31] as follow-up to the United Nations Conference on Environment and Devel-

opment. National partnership facilities would be a key element of that strategy, facilitating the mobilization of funds for national capacity-building and the coordination of activities in that area.

**UNFPA action.** The UNFPA Administrator, in a 20 April report[32] to the Executive Board and in UNFPA's annual report to the Council,[33] stated that, immediately following the Summit's conclusion, UNFPA had shared with its field and headquarters staff those elements of the Programme of Action related to the consensus reached at the 1994 International Conference on Population and Development.[34] It would implement all relevant recommendations that were within its mandate and would serve as a strong advocate for recommendations on other population-related social goals, objectives and commitments adopted at Copenhagen.

### ECONOMIC AND SOCIAL COUNCIL ACTION

On 28 July, the Economic and Social Council adopted **resolution 1995/60**.

#### Social development

*The Economic and Social Council,*

*Recalling* the Copenhagen Declaration on Social Development, in particular commitment 10, and the Programme of Action of the World Summit for Social Development, in particular chapter V on implementation and follow-up, in which, *inter alia*, the Economic and Social Council was invited to review, at its substantive session of 1995, the mandate, agenda and composition of the Commission for Social Development, including consideration of the strengthening of the Commission, taking into account the need for synergy with other related commissions and conference follow-up,

*Taking note* of the report of the Commission for Social Development on its thirty-fourth session, at which the World Summit for Social Development was the priority subject,

*Taking into account* Commission resolutions 34/4 and 34/5 of 20 April 1995, including the annexes thereto, concerning the follow-up to the World Summit for Social Development, in particular the recommendation that the Commission should have a central role in the follow-up to the Copenhagen Declaration and Programme of Action,

*Reaffirming* that the Economic and Social Council should oversee system-wide coordination in the implementation of the outcome of the World Summit for Social Development and make recommendations to the General Assembly in this regard,

*Reiterating* that the Commission for Social Development will assist the Council in the intergovernmental review of the implementation of the Copenhagen Declaration and Programme of Action so as to ensure an integrated approach to social development,

*Bearing in mind* the coordinated follow-up to major United Nations conferences and the overall responsibilities of the General Assembly and the Economic and Social Council,

*Considering* that all relevant organs, organizations and bodies of the United Nations system should be involved in the follow-up to the Summit, in accordance with their mandates,

1. *Takes note* of the note by the Secretariat;

2. *Decides* that the Commission for Social Development, as a functional commission of the Economic and Social Council, in promoting the integrated treatment of social development issues in the United Nations system, should review, on a periodic basis, issues related to the follow-up and implementation of the Copenhagen Declaration and Programme of Action, in a manner consistent with the functions and contributions of other relevant organs, organizations and bodies of the United Nations system, and that, to this end, the Commission should:

(a) Improve international understanding of social development, including through exchanges of information and experiences, and through discussions on emerging issues;

(b) Make recommendations regarding social development to the Economic and Social Council;

(c) Elaborate practical measures aimed at furthering the recommendations of the World Summit for Social Development;

3. *Decides also* that the Commission for Social Development should:

(a) Adapt its mandate so as to ensure an integrated approach to social development, taking into account the relationship between social and economic development as defined in the recommendations of the World Summit for Social Development; it should, *inter alia*, contribute to the identification of practical measures;

(b) Develop a multi-year programme of work to the year 2000, selecting specific themes and addressing them from an interrelated and integrated perspective;

(c) Establish the practice of opening its debates to experts and the main actors of civil society so as to enhance the exchange of information and experience, knowledge and understanding of social development;

(d) Review and update its methods of work;

(e) Review the reporting practices to and by the Commission in order to enhance the multi-year programme of work;

4. *Decides* that the Commission for Social Development should hold a special session in 1996 in order, *inter alia*:

(a) To review its mandate, terms of reference and scope of work;

(b) To elaborate its multi-year programme of work;

(c) To review the frequency of its meetings in the light of the above and make recommendations thereon to the Council;

5. *Also decides*, in the light of those recommendations and on the basis of the scope of work of the Commission, to consider in 1996 the composition of the membership of the Commission and the frequency of its sessions;

6. *Further decides* that the substantive theme to be considered during the special session of the Commission in 1996 should be determined at the resumed substantive session of 1995 of the Council;

7. *Requests* the Secretary-General to make the appropriate arrangements for the special session of the Commission in 1996;

8. *Reiterates* that the implementation of the Copenhagen Declaration and Programme of Action will require the mobilization of financial resources at the national and international levels, as set out in paragraphs 87 to 92 of the Programme of Action of the World Summit for Social Development;

9. *Requests* the General Assembly, at its fiftieth session, to give special consideration to the implications, including financial aspects, of the follow-up and the implementation by the United Nations system of the Copenhagen Declaration and Programme of Action and to adopt decisions thereon.

Economic and Social Council resolution 1995/60

28 July 1995      Meeting 57      Adopted without vote

Draft by Vice-President (E/1995/L.64), orally corrected and based on informal consultations on draft by Philippines, for Group of 77 and China (E/1995/L.44); agenda item 5 *(f)*.
*Financial implications.* S-G, E/1995/L.60.
*Meeting numbers.* ESC 47-49, 52, 57.

In **decision 1995/324** of 12 December, the Council decided that the special session of the Commission for Social Development would be held in New York from 21 to 30 May 1996 and that its theme would be strategies and actions for the eradication of poverty.

**Report of the Secretary-General.** In a 26 October report to the General Assembly on implementation of the outcome of the Summit,[35] the Secretary-General discussed an improved and strengthened framework for cooperation for social development and reviewed the roles of the UN system and the Assembly in implementing the Declaration and the Programme of Action. He had informed heads of State or Government who had participated at the Summit of his intention to ensure a coordinated UN response to the commitments agreed to there, based on a clear division of labour. He had suggested the designation of a national focal point on the implementation of the Summit and requested the views of leaders on ways to maintain the momentum towards the agreed objectives. He had also emphasized that the situation of LDCs should be taken into account in the Summit follow-up. In response, Governments had emphasized their determination to foster social development and to implement the objectives and commitments of the Summit. Focal points were being designated in central ministries, and some national committees established for the preparation of the Summit were being maintained, while in other cases new ones were being set up.

As Chairman of ACC, the Secretary-General wrote to the heads of UN programmes and specialized agencies and the Bretton Woods institutions, stressing the need for an integrated approach to the follow-up to UN conferences. At its second regular session of 1995 (New York, 12-13 October),[36] ACC considered proposals for mobilizing the UN system in support of programmes to implement the commitments and plans of action emanating from recent UN conferences, in particular at the country level, and in support of national follow-up. In that regard, the Secretary-General drew attention to the agreed conclusions of the Economic and Social Council at its coordination segment,[37] which provided a framework for follow-up arrangements (see PART SIX, Chapter IV).

The Secretary-General described follow-up action by UNDP, UNFPA, UNICEF, the United Nations High Commissioner for Refugees, the United Nations Centre for Human Settlements (Habitat) and the United Nations Environment Programme. He also indicated that the five United Nations regional commissions were planning activities in relation to poverty eradication and the observance of the International Year for the Eradication of Poverty (see PART FOUR, Chapter I), including the development of regional programmes of action. Following the adoption by the Rio Group (Argentina, Bolivia, Brazil, Chile, Colombia, Ecuador, Mexico, Paraguay, Peru, Uruguay and Venezuela) Buenos Aires, Argentina (4-5 May) of a declaration on the follow-up to the Summit and actions to be taken at the regional level, a regional meeting of the Rio Group, the UN system and lending institutions took place in Quito, Ecuador, in November. A regional project on social indicators was to be launched for the Latin American region with the Economic Commission for Latin America and the Caribbean and UNDP with the support of the World Bank and the Inter-American Development Bank.

The Development Committee of the World Bank and IMF considered, at its October meeting, the implications of the Summit for developing countries and countries with economies in transition. The two institutions identified activities in the area of poverty reduction, with emphasis on the role of public expenditure, aspects of their work to be strengthened and ways of enhancing cooperation between the Bretton Woods institutions and other multilateral and bilateral donors in support of poverty-reduction strategies of developing and transition economies. In November, the ILO Governing Body discussed action to be taken to follow up the Summit. It agreed that it would strengthen its dialogue and cooperation with the Bretton Woods institutions in the field of employment and undertake several national employment policy reviews. The UN Secretariat's contribution to implementing the Declaration and Programme of Action would be provided mainly through the technical and substantive servicing of the relevant intergovernmental bodies.

The Secretary-General suggested that the Assembly might wish to hold a special session in 2000 for an overall review and appraisal of the outcome of the Summit; include in its agenda, between 1996 and 2000, an item on the implementation of the outcome of the Summit; and consider convening in 1997 a meeting of high-level representatives to consider issues of social development, with particular emphasis on the commitments adopted at the Summit. In that context, the Assembly could invite the Economic and Social Council to consider arrangements to maximize its contribution to the review and appraisal of the Summit in 2000, including an assessment of technical assistance provided by the UN system. The Commission for Social Development should play a central role, and the Secretariat would report to the Council on the activities and findings of other relevant functional commissions. The Council would report to the Assembly on the results of the review and invite regional commissions to hold, between 1996 and 1998, a meeting at a high political level to review implementation of the outcome of the Summit so that the results could be used by the Council in 1999 and by the Assembly in 2000.

The Assembly might encourage Governments to prepare periodic national reports outlining successes, problems and obstacles, particularly with regard to defining time-bound goals and targets for reducing poverty and eradicating absolute poverty, expanding employment, reducing unemployment and enhancing social integration. It could request the Secretary-General to prepare a report on the implementation of the outcome of the Summit for the Assembly in 2000, and in 1997, in the context of its meeting of high-level representatives. The Assembly could ask him to report to the Council in 1999 on the activities of the United Nations system to promote international cooperation for the implementation.

**GENERAL ASSEMBLY ACTION**

On 22 December, the General Assembly adopted **resolution 50/161**.

### Implementation of the outcome of the World Summit for Social Development

*The General Assembly,*

*Recalling* its resolutions 46/139 of 17 December 1991, 47/92 of 16 December 1992 and 48/100 of 20 December 1993,

*Recalling also* Economic and Social Council decision 1991/230 of 30 May 1991, resolutions 1992/27 of 30 July 1992 and 1995/60 of 28 July 1995, and agreed conclusions 1995/1 of 28 July 1995,

*Having considered* the report of the World Summit for Social Development, held at Copenhagen from 6 to 12 March 1995,

*Expressing its profound gratitude* to the Government and people of Denmark for the hospitality extended to all participants at the Summit and for the facilities, staff and services placed at their disposal,

*Expressing its satisfaction* that for the first time in history, at the invitation of the United Nations, heads of State and Government gathered at Copenhagen to recognize the significance of social development and human well-being for all and to give to those goals the highest priority both now and into the twenty-first century by reaching a successful conclusion and adopting the Copenhagen Declaration on Social Development and Programme of Action of the World Summit for Social Development,

*Critical importance of national action and international cooperation for social development*

1. *Takes note with appreciation* of the report of the World Summit for Social Development;

2. *Takes note also* of the report of the Secretary-General of 26 October 1995 on implementation of the outcome of the World Summit for Social Development;

3. *Endorses* the Copenhagen Declaration on Social Development and the Programme of Action of the World Summit for Social Development, adopted on 12 March 1995;

4. *Reaffirms* the pledge by the heads of State and Government at the Summit to give highest priority to national, regional and international policies and actions for the promotion of social progress, justice and the betterment of the human condition, based on full participation by all;

5. *Recognizes* the necessity to create a framework for action to place people at the centre of development and direct economies to meet human needs more effectively;

6. *Stresses* the need for a renewed and massive political will at the national and international levels to invest in people and their well-being to achieve the objectives of social development;

7. *Emphasizes* that economic development, social development and environmental protection are interdependent and mutually reinforcing components of sustainable development;

8. *Recognizes* that social development and the implementation of the Programme of Action are primarily the responsibility of Governments, although international cooperation and assistance are essential for their full implementation;

9. *Reiterates* the call to Governments to define time-bound goals and targets for reducing overall poverty and eradicating absolute poverty, expanding employment and reducing unemployment, and enhancing social integration, within each national context;

10. *Emphasizes* that there is a need for promotion of an integrated and multidimensional approach for the implementation of the Declaration and Programme of Action at all levels;

11. *Also reiterates* the call for formulating or strengthening by 1996 comprehensive cross-sectoral strategies for implementing the outcome of the Summit and national strategies for social development, including government action, actions by States in cooperation with other Governments and international, regional and subregional organizations, and actions taken in partnership and cooperation with actors of civil society, the private sector and cooperatives, with specific responsibilities to be undertaken by each actor and with agreed priorities and time-frames;

12. *Further reiterates* the call for regularly assessing national progress towards implementing the outcome of the Summit, possibly in the form of periodic national reports, outlining successes, problems and obstacles;

such reports could be considered within the framework of an appropriate consolidated reporting system, taking into account the different reporting procedures in the economic, social and environmental fields;

13. *Reaffirms* the need for effective partnership and cooperation between Governments and the relevant actors of civil society, the social partners, the major groups as defined in Agenda 21, including non-governmental organizations and the private sector, in the implementation of and follow-up to the Declaration and Programme of Action, and for ensuring their involvement in the planning, elaboration, implementation and evaluation of social policies at the national level;

14. *Recognizes* that the implementation of the Declaration and Programme of Action will require the mobilization of financial resources at the national and international levels, as set out in commitments 8 and 9 of the Declaration and paragraphs 87 to 93 of the Programme of Action;

15. *Also recognizes* that the implementation of the Declaration and Programme of Action in developing countries, in particular in Africa and the least developed countries, will need additional financial resources and more effective development cooperation and assistance;

16. *Concurs* that substantial debt reduction is needed to enable developing countries to implement the Declaration and Programme of Action, as set out in commitment 9 *(o)* of the Declaration and paragraph 90 of the Programme of Action;

17. *Reaffirms* the importance of agreeing on a mutual commitment between interested developed and developing country partners to allocate, on average, 20 per cent of official development assistance and 20 per cent of the national budget, respectively, to basic social programmes;

18. *Recognizes* the necessity of providing appropriate technical cooperation and other forms of assistance to the countries with economies in transition, as set out in the provisions of the Declaration and Programme of Action;

19. *Urges* the Secretary-General, in cooperation with the World Bank, the International Monetary Fund and other multilateral development institutions, to study the impact of structural adjustment programmes on economic and social development and to assist adjusting countries in creating conditions for economic growth, job creation, poverty eradication and social development;

20. *Encourages* Governments as well as public and private institutions and organizations to take initiatives relevant to the high priority attached by the Summit to social development and to the implementation of the objectives and commitments adopted at the Summit;

*The role of the United Nations system*

21. *Calls upon* all relevant organs, organizations and bodies of the United Nations system to be involved in the follow-up to the Summit, and invites specialized agencies and related organizations of the United Nations system to strengthen and adjust their activities, programmes and medium-term strategies, as appropriate, to take into account the follow-up to the Summit;

22. *Reaffirms* that the follow-up to the Summit will be undertaken on the basis of an integrated approach to social development and within the framework of a

coordinated follow-up to and implementation of the results of the major international conferences in the economic, social and related fields;

23. *Decides* that the General Assembly, through its role in policy formulation, the Economic and Social Council, through its role in overall guidance and coordination, in accordance with their respective roles under the Charter of the United Nations and with Assembly resolution 48/162 of 20 December 1993, and a revitalized Commission for Social Development shall constitute a three-tiered intergovernmental process in the follow-up to the implementation of the Declaration and Programme of Action;

24. *Also decides* to hold a special session of the General Assembly in the year 2000 for an overall review and appraisal of the implementation of the outcome of the Summit and to consider further actions and initiatives;

25. *Also reaffirms* that the Economic and Social Council will provide overall guidance and oversee system-wide coordination in the implementation of the outcome of the Summit and make recommendations in this regard;

26. *Requests* the Economic and Social Council, so that it can review progress made towards implementing the outcome of the Summit as well as improving its own effectiveness, to continue examining ways, consistent with the mandates of the Charter and in accordance with General Assembly resolutions 45/264 of 13 May 1991, 46/235 of 13 April 1992 and 48/162, to strengthen its role, authority, structures, resources and processes, bringing specialized agencies into a closer working relationship with it;

27. *Invites* the Economic and Social Council to review the reporting system in the area of social development with a view to establishing a coherent system that could result in clear policy recommendations for Governments and international actors;

28. *Calls upon* the Commission for Social Development, as a functional commission of the Economic and Social Council with the primary responsibility for the follow-up to and review of the implementation of the Summit, to develop a multi-year programme of work to the year 2000, selecting specific themes and addressing them from an interrelated and integrated perspective, in a manner consistent with the functions and contributions of other relevant organs, organizations and bodies of the United Nations system, and to present its recommendations to the Council, which should ensure harmonization between such a multi-year programme of work and those of other relevant functional commissions of the Council;

29. *Endorses* Economic and Social Council resolution 1995/60, and calls upon the Commission for Social Development, when developing at its next session its multi-year programme of work for the follow-up to the Summit:

(a) To adapt its mandate in order to ensure an integrated approach to social development;

(b) To integrate the current sectoral issues on its agenda in the multi-year programme;

(c) To review and update its methods of work and to make recommendations to ensure an effective follow-up to the Summit;

(d) To establish the practice of inviting experts to contribute to its work;

(e) To consider integrating into its work high-level representatives on social development issues and policies;

30. *Requests* the Commission for Social Development, in view of the scope of its work, to consider at its next session the composition of the membership of the Commission and the frequency of its sessions and to make recommendations thereon to the Economic and Social Council;

31. *Also requests* the Commission for Social Development to establish the practice of involving the relevant actors of civil society in the field of social development to contribute to its work, and requests the Secretary-General to present proposals to the Commission for Social Development and the Economic and Social Council for consideration at their next sessions, taking into account the experience gained in other functional commissions, the Council and the International Labour Organization and at the Summit;

32. *Requests* the Economic and Social Council, without prejudice to the outcome of the review of consultative arrangements by the Open-ended Working Group on the Review of Arrangements for Consultations with Non-Governmental Organizations, to consider authorizing the participation at the next session of the Commission for Social Development of interested civil society organizations that participated, by accreditation, in the Summit;

33. *Invites*, within their mandates, the regional commissions, in cooperation with the regional intergovernmental organizations and banks, to consider convening, on a biennial basis, a meeting at a high political level to review progress made towards implementing the outcome of the Summit, to exchange views on their respective experiences and to adopt the appropriate measures;

34. *Emphasizes* the important role of the Committee on Economic, Social and Cultural Rights in monitoring those aspects of the Declaration and Programme of Action that relate to compliance by States parties with the International Covenant on Economic, Social and Cultural Rights;

35. *Notes* the establishment of task forces for the follow-up to the Summit and other related United Nations conferences, and invites the Administrative Committee on Coordination to bring system-wide coordination issues to the attention of the Economic and Social Council, in particular its coordination segment, and to make recommendations thereon;

36. *Reiterates* that United Nations operational activities should be strengthened in order to contribute to the implementation of the outcome of the Summit in accordance with relevant resolutions;

37. *Requests* the United Nations Development Programme to facilitate the efforts of the United Nations system towards capacity-building at the local, national and regional levels and to support the coordinated implementation of social development programmes through the resident coordinator system;

38. *Invites* the International Labour Organization, which, because of its mandate, tripartite structure and expertise, has a special role to play in social development in the field of employment, to continue to contribute to the implementation of the Programme of Action;

39. *Invites* the Bretton Woods institutions to be actively involved in the implementation of and follow-up

to the Summit and to enhance their cooperation with other parts of the United Nations system for this purpose;

40. *Invites* the World Trade Organization to consider how it might contribute to the implementation of the Programme of Action, including activities in cooperation with the United Nations system;

41. *Invites* the Secretary-General, including within the framework of the Administrative Committee on Coordination, to make appropriate arrangements, which may include joint meetings, for consultations with the heads of the International Monetary Fund, the World Bank, the International Labour Organization, the United Nations funds and programmes, and other relevant agencies, for the purpose of cooperating in the implementation of the Declaration and the Programme of Action in their respective organizations;

42. *Requests* the Secretary-General to ensure an effectively functioning secretariat, within which clear responsibility is assigned to assist with the implementation of and follow-up to the Summit and the servicing of the intergovernmental bodies involved;

43. *Also requests* the Secretary-General and the United Nations bodies to take appropriate measures, in a coordinated manner, to strengthen the United Nations capacity for gathering and analysing information and developing indicators of social development, taking into account the work carried out by different countries, in particular by developing countries, as well as for providing policy and technical support and advice, upon request, to improve national capacities in this regard;

44. *Decides* that the trust fund of the World Summit for Social Development, established in accordance with General Assembly resolution 47/92 of 16 December 1992 to finance preparatory activities, be continued and renamed the Trust Fund for the Follow-up to the World Summit for Social Development, under the authority of the Secretary-General, with the aim of supporting programmes, seminars and activities for the promotion of social development in implementation of the Declaration and Programme of Action, including activities of the United Nations Decade for the Eradication of Poverty, and invites all States to contribute to the Fund;

45. *Requests* the Economic and Social Council to consider new and innovative ideas for generating funds and to offer for this purpose any useful suggestions;

46. *Calls upon* the Secretary-General to disseminate as widely as possible the Copenhagen Declaration on Social Development and Programme of Action of the World Summit for Social Development, including to all competent organs of the United Nations and the specialized agencies;

47. *Decides* to include in the provisional agenda of its fifty-first session the item entitled "Implementation of the outcome of the World Summit for Social Development", and to consider the implications for a more coherent treatment of related items on its agenda in the appropriate forums.

General Assembly resolution 50/161

22 December 1995     Meeting 98     Adopted without vote

38-nation draft (A/50/L.66 & Add.1); agenda item 161.
*Meeting numbers.* GA 50th session: plenary 83-86, 98.

The draft programme for the observance of the International Year for the Eradication of Poverty

(1996)[38] (see PART FOUR, Chapter I) took into account, and followed closely, the Copenhagen Declaration and Programme of Action of the World Summit for Social Development.

The Assembly, in **resolution 50/107** of 20 December, as recommended in the Programme of Action, proclaimed the first United Nations Decade for the Eradication of Poverty (1997-2006).

## World social situation

In an interim report on the world social situation[39] submitted to the General Assembly and to the Economic and Social Council, in response to a 1989 Assembly request,[40] the Secretary-General updated the main social issues and trends of international concern that had emerged since the publication of the *Report on the World Social Situation 1993*[41] and set out the draft framework for the 1997 report.

It was noted that intense discussions of the world social situation since the 1993 *Report* had mostly related to the six major UN conferences dealing directly with social development questions, four of which had concluded—the 1992 International Conference on Nutrition,[42] the 1993 World Conference on Human Rights,[43] the 1994 International Conference on Population and Development[34] and the World Summit for Social Development (see above)—and two still to be held—the 1995 Fourth World Conference on Women (see PART FOUR, Chapter X) and the 1996 UN Conference on Human Settlements. That upsurge of interest was consequent upon a perceived deterioration of social conditions, the incapacity of current paradigms, institutions, policies and programmes to address effectively problems of social development and the earnest desire of Governments to harness national and international strengths to meet those challenges.

Claims for equality between men and women gained momentum during the course of preparations for the Fourth World Conference on Women, and much knowledge was gained on levels of well-being, access to income-earning assets and social services and sharing of power, whether in families, enterprises or institutions of Government. The scarcity of adequate employment opportunities continued to be a common feature. Even where the increase in the pace of economic growth was most pronounced, as in developed market economies, rates of unemployment, especially among the long-term unemployed, remained high. There was evidence that income distribution was more uneven than a decade before, with the exception of countries in Asia that were growing consistently at very high rates. In economies in transition, the worsening income distribution situation resulted from their abandonment of a set of economic and social institutions that set out to secure a high degree of equality in incomes and living conditions. Structural adjustment programmes in many developing countries had been slow to show salutary effects, and there was less enthusiasm for sudden sharp changes in policies than for slow and gradual changes. The increased incidence of crime and its adverse effect on individuals and communities was a growing concern in many societies. It posed challenges to policy makers in several areas and tested the capacity of the criminal justice system to dispose of cases and mete out deserved punishment.

The 1997 report would be written in the context of the conclusions of the six major UN conferences and the unusually rapid change in several fundamental social and political institutions and economies. The unifying theme would be the manner in which individuals responded to the challenge posed by those rapid and fundamental changes. It would deal with demographic changes and their social consequences; "traditional" social concerns: health, nutrition, housing, sanitation and education; economic transformation and adjustment policies and their consequences for the social situation and policies; social security; crime and policies for its prevention; the situation and policies relating to children, youth, the aged and the handicapped; aggravating situations caused by ethnic and religious conflicts; the nature of people's rights; and the relations between Government and the market, from the points of view of growth, efficiency and equity.

The Economic and Social Council, by **decision 1995/314** of 28 July, took note of the report of the Secretary-General, as did the General Assembly by **decision 50/442** of 21 December.

### Social welfare issues and activities

The Commission on Social Development, at its April session,[23] considered the monitoring of international plans and programmes of action. It had before it a report[44] of the Secretary-General on major issues and programme activities of the UN Secretariat and the regional commissions relating to social development and welfare, youth, ageing, disabled persons and the family. In an addendum,[45] the Secretary-General outlined the social welfare and social development activities of the regional commissions for 1993-1994. The Commission also had before it reports of the Secretary-General on the conceptual framework of a programme for the preparation and observance of the International Year of Older Persons (1999)[46] (see PART FOUR, Chapter XI); on measures taken to observe the International Day of Disabled Persons[47] (see PART FOUR, Chapter XIII); on the draft world programme of action for youth to the year 2000 and beyond;[48] (see PART FOUR, Chap-

ter XI) and on the International Year of the Family (1994)[49] (see below).

In accordance with a 1993 Economic and Social Council decision,[50] the Commission reconsidered the text of a draft decision[51] entitled "Contribution of comprehensive national social policies to societal management and to the solving of economic, environmental, demographic, cultural and political problems", which the Commission, at its 1993 session, had recommended for adoption by the Council.

On 20 April, the Commission decided to take no action on the draft decision.

### UN Year for Tolerance (1995)

The General Assembly in 1993 had proclaimed 1995 the UN Year for Tolerance,[52] and the Year was officially launched on 21 February 1995. In accordance with a 1994 resolution,[53] the General Conference of the United Nations Educational, Scientific and Cultural Organization (UNESCO), the lead organization for the Year, adopted a Declaration of Principles on Tolerance and a Follow-Up Plan of Action for the UN Year for Tolerance on 16 November 1995.[54] The Declaration recalled relevant human rights instruments and addressed intolerance in its many forms, including violence, terrorism, injustice and exclusion. It proclaimed 16 November the International Day for Tolerance and decided to submit the Declaration and the Follow-Up Plan of Action to the Assembly in 1996.

On 20 November, the Assembly, in accordance with a 1994 resolution,[53] held a special commemorative meeting to mark the UN Year for Tolerance. In a message to mark the occasion, the Assembly President said that intolerance was a complex human phenomenon where prejudice, feelings, impulses, social hierarchies and irrational fear of the "other" brought forces together to make it difficult to design clear strategies of action. The international community had a duty to create a climate favourable to tolerance through the construction of democratic institutions and the curbing of acts of intolerance, violence, discrimination and exclusion. He called on States to transcend differences in order to renew their determined commitment to promoting the concept of tolerance as a prerequisite for a peaceful and non-violent world. In his message, the Secretary-General called for a redoubling of efforts to close the apparent divides between peoples and overcome momentary differences and ideological and cultural barriers.

### Follow-up to the International Year of the Family

**Meeting of national coordinators.** As part of the follow-up to the 1994 observance of the International Year of the Family,[55] the UN Interregional Meeting of National Coordinators/Focal points for the Year, was held in Bratislava, Slovakia, from 4 to 7 February.[56] Organized by the secretariat for the Year, in collaboration with the Department for Policy Coordination and Sustainable Development, the meeting reviewed the global observances of the Year and their implications for national social policies in the process of sustainable development; considered concepts and forms of international cooperation on family issues, with emphasis on assistance to developing countries; and described national, regional and international follow-up to the Year. It adopted a number of specific conclusions and recommendations.

**Commission for Social Development.** In a 22 March note,[57] the Secretary-General reported to the Commission for Social Development on the status of the implementation of a 1993 General Assembly resolution on the International Year of the Family.[58] The report described the 1994 International Conference on Families,[55] outlined suggestions regarding a declaration on the role, responsibilities and rights of families and made specific proposals on the follow-up to the Year. Only eight responses had been received from Commission members to requests for their views on the proposed declaration. The Secretary-General would submit to the Assembly's fiftieth session proposals regarding the follow-up to the Year (see below).

On 20 April,[59] the Commission noted that the Secretary-General would submit to the Assembly specific proposals on the follow-up to the Year, intended to serve as an indicative guide for action, primarily at the local and material levels. It requested him to prepare a concise draft reflecting the outcome of the relevant UN conferences and national experiences of the International Year of the Family.

**Inter-agency meeting.** The Fifth Ad Hoc Inter-Agency Meeting on the International Year of the Family (Vienna, 22-23 May)[60] reviewed the implementation of inter-agency projects for the Year; carried out an assessment of the Year from the perspective of the UN system and NGOs and of the work of the ad hoc inter-agency mechanism; and discussed strategies and priorities for the follow-up to the Year.

The Meeting recommended that concerned organizations and agencies should continue to serve as important partners in the global effort to achieve long-term development objectives regarding families by providing substantive leadership on family-specific dimensions of their mandates and adequately reflecting a focus on family issues in their programmes and budgets. They should appoint permanent focal points on family issues to facilitate a coordinated system-wide follow-up to the Year. Based on the experience of the inter-agency

mechanism for the Year, ad hoc inter-agency meetings on family issues should be instituted on a biennial basis to coordinate the follow-up to the Year, facilitate the exchange of information and collaboration, harmonize approaches and understanding of relevant concepts and implement projects. The first meeting should be held in 1996. The ad hoc inter-agency meetings on family issues would also implement the long-term project on support for capacity-building and empowering families, led by the World Health Organization. The themes for the annual observances of the International Day of Families (15 May) in the years 1996 to 2000 would be, respectively: Families—victims of poverty and homelessness; Building families on equality and equity; Family—source of education for human rights; Families for all ages; Families—agents of development and social progress. UN organizations and agencies should give adequate attention to family issues in their substantive contributions to the Fourth World Conference on Women (see PART FOUR, Chapter X) and the UN Conference on Human Settlements (Habitat II), to be held in 1996. NGOs and institutions devoted to family issues should be allowed to participate as partners in family-related work of the UN system and NGOs should be represented as observers at meetings of the ad hoc inter-agency meetings on family issues.

**Report of the Secretary-General.** In response to a 1993 General Assembly request,[58] the Secretary-General submitted a September report[61] on the observance of the International Year of the Family. The report discussed the background and operational modalities to the Year, major instruments, campaigns and special initiatives, relevant intergovernmental conferences, action taken at the national and regional levels, and action by intergovernmental bodies, the Secretariat, the UN system and inter-agency cooperation, intergovernmental organizations, NGOs, and research and academic institutions. It also listed in-kind contributions made to the secretariat for the Year and to the Voluntary Fund for the Year. Among proposals made on the follow-up of the Year were translation of the increased awareness regarding families into concrete measures; implementation of family dimensions of the outcomes of major international conferences in the 1990s; elaboration of long-term national plans of action on families; exchange of information and experience, mobilization of resources and expertise and the provision of technical assistance, with a focus on the least developed and developing countries; the promotion of networks and partnerships in support of families; and the continuation of a voluntary fund for families as a means of resource mobilization and financial assistance, including from the private sector through innovative fund-raising approaches.

The Secretary-General stated that the Year's observance had resulted in a significant record of accomplishment. It increased the understanding of the interrelationship of families to society, and underscored the need for appropriate and timely policies. A major outcome was the greater awareness of the extent to which policy decisions affected families and the value of a family-sensitive perspective in policy development and implementation. He suggested that its achievements should be built upon through long-term action, including effective follow-up at all levels.

**GENERAL ASSEMBLY ACTION**

On 21 December, the General Assembly adopted **resolution 50/142**.

**Follow-up to the International Year of the Family**

*The General Assembly,*

*Recalling* its resolutions 44/82 of 8 December 1989, 45/133 of 14 December 1990, 46/92 of 16 December 1991 and 47/237 of 20 September 1993, concerning the proclamation, preparations for and observance of the International Year of the Family,

*Taking note with appreciation* of the report of the Secretary-General on the observance of the International Year of the Family,

*Bearing in mind* the results of the International Conference on Population and Development, the World Summit for Social Development and the Fourth World Conference on Women, within which it was noted that the family is the basic unit of society and as such should be strengthened, that it is entitled to receive comprehensive protection and support, that in different cultural, political and social systems various forms of family exist and that the rights, capabilities and responsibilities of family members must be respected,

*Noting* the accomplishments resulting from the observance of the International Year of the Family, *inter alia*, the new initiatives and long-term activities in support of the family all over the world, in particular at the local and national levels, and the value of international cooperation on family issues,

1. *Invites* Governments to continue their action to build family-friendly societies, *inter alia*, by promoting the rights of individual family members, in particular gender equality and the protection and development of the child;

2. *Urges* Governments to ratify or accede to and to ensure implementation of the Convention on the Elimination of All Forms of Discrimination against Women so that universal ratification can be achieved by the year 2000 and to take urgent measures to achieve universal ratification of or accession to the Convention on the Rights of the Child before the end of 1995, and urges those who have not yet done so to become party to the Convention in order to achieve universal implementation by the year 2000;

3. *Welcomes* the proposals, contained in the report of the Secretary-General, on the follow-up to the International Year of the Family;

4. *Invites* the Commission for Social Development to consider how best to integrate the follow-up to the International Year of the Family into its work programme

as laid out in Economic and Social Council resolution 1995/60 of 28 July 1995, taking into account the integrated follow-up of major United Nations conferences, to form part of a holistic approach to development and social progress;

5. *Requests* the Secretary-General:

*(a)* To submit proposals to the Commission for Social Development in order to assist the Commission in its work;

*(b)* To prepare a comprehensive document containing the family-related provisions from the outcome of the World Summit for Children, the United Nations Conference on Environment and Development, the World Conference on Human Rights, the International Conference on Population and Development, the World Summit for Social Development, the Fourth World Conference on Women, and the United Nations Conference on Human Settlements (Habitat II), to be submitted to the Commission for Social Development at its thirty-fifth session;

*(c)* To report to the General Assembly at its fifty-second session, through the Commission for Social Development and the Economic and Social Council, on the progress made on the follow-up to the International Year of the Family, taking into account the promotion of integrated reporting;

*(d)* To continue the operation of the Voluntary Fund for the International Year of the Family, to be renamed the United Nations Trust Fund on Family Activities, to provide financial assistance for activities specific to the family and projects of direct benefit to it, with special focus on least developed and developing countries, giving particular attention to non-traditional resources;

6. *Calls upon* Governments, as well as organizations, individuals and the private sector, to contribute generously to the United Nations Trust Fund on Family Activities.

General Assembly resolution 50/142

21 December 1995     Meeting 97     Adopted without vote

Approved by Third Committee (A/50/628) without vote, 8 November (meeting 21); 30-nation draft (A/C.3/50/L.10), orally revised; agenda item 105.
*Meeting numbers.* GA 50th session: 3rd Committee 8-12, 18, 21; plenary 97.

## Promotion of literacy

The Secretary-General, in response to a 1991 General Assembly request,[62] transmitted to the Assembly and the Economic and Social Council, the report of the Director-General of the United Nations Educational, Scientific and Cultural Organization (UNESCO) on progress made and problems encountered in the quest to achieve a literate world.[63] The report also summed up the existing situation and discussed action taken for improving future prospects. The UNESCO Director-General reported that progress could be seen in the rising literacy rates, approximately 0.5 per cent per year or 5.0 per cent per decade since 1960, despite rapid population growth; a dramatic increase in the number of literate adults, especially in the developing countries; and a steady expansion in educational enrolments, with average annual growth projected at 1.7 per cent in the 1990s.

The increase in enrolments was brought about in part by the renewed emphasis placed on primary education by Governments, international organizations and agencies following the 1990 World Conference on Education for All.[64] However, the problems were equally apparent: more than one adult in five was still illiterate, amounting to an estimated 885 million in 1995; more than three illiterates in five were women; an estimated 129 million primary school-age children were not enrolled in school; and many children who were enrolled attended schools inadequate in terms of staffing, equipment and facilities.

In terms of future prospects, the Director-General reported that ·UNESCO had pursued the follow-up to International Literacy Year, observed in 1990, and the World Conference on Education for All through a unified programme of initiatives and activities, including the establishment of an International Consultative Forum on Education for All to monitor progress towards education for all and to promote consultation and cooperation at the global level. It developed a core programme and an extended programme to support the education for all movement. In collaboration with UNICEF, UNESCO established a joint project for monitoring learning achievement, and was carrying out another project "Education for all: Making it work", with UNICEF, UNDP, Germany and other partners, to identify and make known effective and innovative educational strategies. UNESCO was also conducting a mid-term review of its 1989 Plan of Action, covering the decade 1990-1999.

The Director-General stated that the World Conference had encouraged additional aid to basic education and literacy and improved the effectiveness of such assistance. The World Bank increased aid to basic education fourfold; UNDP reported that basic education received 32 per cent or $43 million of total expenditures during 1993; and UNICEF increased the portion of its programme budget spent on education from 8 to 11 per cent and planned to achieve a 20 per cent rate of expenditure by the end of the decade. However, bilateral aid appeared to be receding.

By **decision 1995/314** of 28 July, the Economic and Social Council took note of the report.

**GENERAL ASSEMBLY ACTION**

On 21 December, the General Assembly adopted **resolution 50/143**.

**Progress made and problems encountered in the struggle against illiteracy: a mid-decade review—cooperation to achieve education for all**

*The General Assembly,*

*Recalling* that in the Universal Declaration of Human Rights and the International Covenant on Economic,

Social and Cultural Rights the inalienable right of every individual to education is recognized,

*Recalling also* its resolutions 42/104 of 7 December 1987, by which it proclaimed 1990 as International Literacy Year, and 44/127 of 15 December 1989 and 46/93 of 16 December 1991, in which it called for continuing international efforts to promote literacy,

*Recalling further* its resolution 45/126 of 14 December 1990, in which it called for strengthening efforts towards the elimination of illiteracy of women of all ages,

*Mindful* of the fact that the eradication of illiteracy is one of the paramount objectives of the International Development Strategy for the Fourth United Nations Development Decade,

*Convinced* that literacy, especially functional literacy and adequate education, represents an indispensable element for the development and harnessing of science, technology and human resources for economic and social progress,

*Confident* that the International Literacy Year and the World Conference on Education for All, held at Jomtien, Thailand, in 1990, resulted in increased awareness and support for literacy efforts and became a turning-point in the struggle for a literate world,

*Underlining* the importance of maintaining the momentum generated by the Year and the spirit of partnership forged at the Jomtien Conference,

*Welcoming* the setting up of the International Consultative Forum on Education for All entrusted with the task of monitoring the progress towards education for all and promoting consultation and cooperation at the global level,

*Recognizing* that, despite the significant advances registered in the growth of literacy rates in many parts of the world, major problems still persist which require greater mobilization of efforts at both national and international levels to achieve the goal of education for all,

*Stressing* the importance of the effective implementation of the World Declaration on Education for All, and the United Nations Educational, Scientific and Cultural Organization Plan of Action for the Eradication of Illiteracy by the Year 2000, as well as the relevant commitments and recommendations to promote literacy contained, *inter alia*, in the Plan of Action for Implementing the World Declaration on the Survival, Protection and Development of Children in the 1990s of the World Summit for Children, the Programme of Action of the International Conference on Population and Development, the Copenhagen Declaration on Social Development and the Programme of Action of the World Summit for Social Development, the Beijing Declaration and the Platform for Action of the Fourth World Conference on Women and the Delhi Declaration of the Education for All Summit of Nine High-Population Developing Countries,

1. *Takes note* of the report of the Secretary-General entitled "Progress made and problems encountered in the struggle against illiteracy: a mid-decade review";

2. *Notes with appreciation* the close collaboration and commendable work being pursued as a follow-up to the International Literacy Year and the World Conference on Education for All by the specialized agencies and other organizations of the United Nations system, including the United Nations Educational, Scientific and Cultural Organization, the United Nations Children's Fund and the United Nations Development Programme;

3. *Commends* those Governments which have launched national literacy programmes and attained notable progress in meeting the objectives of the International Literacy Year and those set forth in the World Declaration on Education for All;

4. *Invites* Member States, specialized agencies and other organizations of the United Nations system and relevant intergovernmental and non-governmental organizations to further intensify their efforts to effectively implement the World Declaration on Education for All, the United Nations Educational, Scientific and Cultural Organization Plan of Action for the Eradication of Illiteracy by the Year 2000, as well as the relevant commitments and recommendations to promote literacy contained, *inter alia*, in the Plan of Action for Implementing the World Declaration on the Survival, Protection and Development of Children in the 1990s of the World Summit for Children, the Programme of Action of the International Conference on Population and Development, the Copenhagen Declaration on Social Development and the Programme of Action of the World Summit for Social Development, the Beijing Declaration and the Platform for Action of the Fourth World Conference on Women, and the Delhi Declaration of the Education for All Summit of Nine High-Population Developing Countries, with a view to better coordinating their activities and increasing their contribution to development;

5. *Appeals anew* to Governments and economic and financial organizations and institutions, both national and international, to lend greater financial and material support to the efforts to increase literacy and achieve education for all;

6. *Calls upon* the United Nations Educational, Scientific and Cultural Organization to continue assuming the role of lead organization in ensuring an effective follow-up to the International Literacy Year and to pursue, in cooperation with other sponsors of the World Conference on Education for All, the implementation of the World Declaration on Education for All;

7. *Notes with satisfaction* the firm commitment and active involvement of many non-governmental organizations, the mass media and the private sector in support of and in the follow-up to the International Literacy Year;

8. *Requests* the Secretary-General, in cooperation with the Director-General of the United Nations Educational, Scientific and Cultural Organization, to submit to the General Assembly, at its fifty-second session, in 1997, through the Economic and Social Council, a progress report on the implementation process of the education for all objectives, including the recommendations of the International Consultative Forum on Education for All, taking into account the possible measures, if any, to improve the reporting procedure;

9. *Decides* to include in the provisional agenda of its fifty-second session the question of cooperation to achieve education for all under the item on social development.

General Assembly resolution 50/143

21 December 1995     Meeting 97     Adopted without vote

Approved by Third Committee (A/50/628) without vote, 10 November (meeting 25); 57-nation draft (A/C.3/50/L.11), orally revised; agenda item 105.
*Meeting numbers.* GA 50th session: 3rd Committee 8-12, 18, 25; plenary 97.

## Institutional machinery

### Commission for Social Development

The Commission for Social Development, at its thirty-fourth session (New York, 10-20 April),[23] recommended one draft resolution and one draft decision to the Economic and Social Council for adoption. It also adopted one resolution and one decision that called for action by the Council and four resolutions and one decision that it brought to the Council's attention.

The draft resolution dealt with the International Year of Older Persons (1999): towards a society for all ages (see PART FOUR, Chapter XI). The draft decision addressed the Commission's report on its thirty-fourth session and the agenda and documentation for the thirty-fifth (1997) session. The resolutions adopted concerned the tenth anniversary of International Youth Year and the world programme of action for youth to the year 2000 and beyond (see PART FOUR, Chapter XI); monitoring the implementation of the Standard Rules on the Equalization of Opportunities for Persons with Disabilities (see PART FOUR, Chapter XIII); the follow-up to the International Year of the Family (see above); the follow-up to the World Summit for Social Development (see above); and the proposed programme of work of the Division for Social Policy and Development for the biennium 1996-1997.[65]

On 24 July, the Council, by **decision 1995/248**, took note of the Commission's report, endorsed its resolutions and decisions and approved the provisional agenda and documentation for its 1997 session.

In **resolution 1995/60** of 28 July, the Council decided that the Commission should hold a special session in 1996 to review its mandate, terms of reference and scope of work; elaborate a multi-year programme of work; review the frequency of its meetings; and consider the composition of its membership and the frequency of its sessions.

On 12 December, by **decision 1995/324**, the Council decided that the theme to be considered by the Commission at its special session would be: Strategies and actions for the eradication of poverty. It also decided that the special session should be held in New York from 21 to 30 May 1996.

## Cultural issues

### Restitution of cultural property

As requested by the General Assembly in 1993,[66] the Secretary-General, by a 3 October note,[67] submitted the report of the UNESCO Director-General on action taken to promote the return and restitution of cultural property to the countries of origin, in particular through the application of the recommendations of the eighth session (Paris, 24-27 May 1994) of the Intergovernmental Committee for Promoting the Return of Cultural Property to its Countries of Origin or its Restitution in Case of Illicit Appropriation. The report discussed the promotion of bilateral negotiations for the return or restitution of cultural property; international technical cooperation; steps to curb traffic in cultural property; and public information activities.

**GENERAL ASSEMBLY ACTION**

On 11 December, the General Assembly adopted **resolution 50/56**.

### Return or restitution of cultural property to the countries of origin

*The General Assembly,*

*Recalling* its resolutions 3026 A(XXVII) of 18 December 1972, 3148(XXVIII) of 14 December 1973, 3187(XXVIII) of 18 December 1973, 3391(XXX) of 19 November 1975, 31/40 of 30 November 1976, 32/18 of 11 November 1977, 33/50 of 14 December 1978, 34/64 of 29 November 1979, 35/127 and 35/128 of 11 December 1980, 36/64 of 27 November 1981, 38/34 of 25 November 1983, 40/19 of 21 November 1985, 42/7 of 22 October 1987, 44/18 of 6 November 1989, 46/10 of 22 October 1991 and 48/15 of 2 November 1993,

*Recalling also* the Convention on the Means of Prohibiting and Preventing the Illicit Import, Export and Transfer of Ownership of Cultural Property adopted on 14 November 1970 by the General Conference of the United Nations Educational, Scientific and Cultural Organization,

*Taking note with satisfaction* of the report of the Secretary-General of 3 October 1995 submitted in cooperation with the Director-General of the United Nations Educational, Scientific and Cultural Organization,

*Noting with satisfaction* that, following its appeal, other Member States have become parties to the Convention,

*Aware* of the importance attached by the countries of origin to the return of cultural property which is of fundamental spiritual and cultural value to them, so that they may constitute collections representative of their cultural heritage,

1. *Commends* the United Nations Educational, Scientific and Cultural Organization and the Intergovernmental Committee for Promoting the Return of Cultural Property to Its Countries of Origin or Its Restitution in Case of Illicit Appropriation on the work they have accomplished, in particular through the promotion of bilateral negotiations, for the return or restitution of cultural property, the preparation of inventories of movable cultural property, the reduction of illicit traffic in cultural property and the dissemination of information to the public;

2. *Reaffirms* that the restitution to a country of its objets d'art, monuments, museum pieces, archives, manuscripts, documents and any other cultural or artistic treasures contributes to the strengthening of international cooperation and to the preservation and flowering of universal cultural values through fruitful cooperation between developed and developing countries;

3. *Requests* the Secretary-General, in collaboration with the United Nations Educational, Scientific and Cultural Organization, to continue to develop all possibilities for bringing about the attainment of the objectives of resolution 48/15;

4. *Also requests* the Secretary-General, in cooperation with the Director-General of the United Nations Educational, Scientific and Cultural Organization, to submit to the General Assembly at its fifty-second session a report on the implementation of the present resolution;

5. *Decides* to include in the provisional agenda of its fifty-second session the item entitled ''Return or restitution of cultural property to the countries of origin''.

General Assembly resolution 50/56

11 December 1995     Meeting 87     124-0-24 (recorded vote)

18-nation draft (A/50/L.28 & Add.1); agenda item 22.
*Meeting numbers.* GA 50th session: plenary 69, 87.

Recorded vote in Assembly as follows:

*In favour:* Afghanistan, Albania, Algeria, Angola, Antigua and Barbuda, Armenia, Australia, Azerbaijan, Bahrain, Bangladesh, Barbados, Belarus, Belize, Benin, Bhutan, Bolivia, Bosnia and Herzegovina, Botswana, Brazil, Brunei Darussalam, Bulgaria, Burkina Faso, Cambodia, Cameroon, Canada, Cape Verde, Chad, China, Colombia, Congo, Côte d'Ivoire, Croatia, Cuba, Cyprus, Czech Republic, Djibouti, Dominica, Ecuador, El Salvador, Estonia, Ethiopia, Fiji, Finland, Gabon, Ghana, Greece, Guatemala, Guinea, Guyana, Haiti, Honduras, Iceland, India, Indonesia, Iran, Kazakstan, Kenya, Kuwait, Kyrgyzstan, Lao People's Democratic Republic, Lebanon, Lesotho, Libyan Arab Jamahiriya, Liechtenstein, Lithuania, Madagascar, Malawi, Malaysia, Maldives, Mali, Malta, Marshall Islands, Mauritania, Mauritius, Mexico, Micronesia, Mongolia, Morocco, Mozambique, Myanmar, Namibia, Nepal, New Zealand, Nicaragua, Niger, Nigeria, Norway, Oman, Pakistan, Panama, Papua New Guinea, Peru, Philippines, Qatar, Republic of Korea, Samoa, Saudi Arabia, Senegal, Singapore, Solomon Islands, South Africa, Sri Lanka, Sudan, Suriname, Swaziland, Syrian Arab Republic, Thailand, the former Yugoslav Republic of Macedonia, Togo, Trinidad and Tobago, Tunisia, Turkey, Uganda, Ukraine, United Arab Emirates, United Republic of Tanzania, Uruguay, Vanuatu, Venezuela, Viet Nam, Yemen, Zaire, Zambia, Zimbabwe.

*Against:* None.

*Abstaining:* Andorra, Austria, Belgium, Denmark, France, Georgia, Germany, Ireland, Israel, Italy, Luxembourg, Monaco, Netherlands, Poland, Portugal, Republic of Moldova, Romania, Russian Federation, Slovakia, Slovenia, Spain, Sweden, United Kingdom, United States.

## The Olympic Ideal

By an 18 October letter,[68] Sierra Leone transmitted to the Secretary-General the resolutions of the sixty-second ordinary session of the Council of Ministers of the Organization of African Unity (Addis Ababa, Ethiopia, 21-23 June). One resolution adopted by the Council of Ministers dealt with the role of the Olympic ideal in the building of a peaceful world.

**GENERAL ASSEMBLY ACTION**

On 7 November, the General Assembly adopted **resolution 50/13**.

### The Olympic Ideal

*The General Assembly,*

*Recalling* its resolution 49/29 of 7 December 1994, in which it requested the Secretary-General to encourage ministers of youth and sport or concerned officials of Member States to participate in the consideration by the General Assembly at its fiftieth session of an item entitled ''Building a peaceful and better world through sport and the Olympic Ideal'' on the eve of the centenary of the revival of the Olympic Games in 1896 at Athens, on the initiative of a French educator, Baron

Pierre de Coubertin, and called upon Member States to reaffirm during the fiftieth session of the Assembly the observance of the Olympic Truce, during the next Summer Olympic Games,

*Recalling also* its resolution 48/11 of 25 October 1993, which, *inter alia*, revived the ancient Greek tradition of *ekecheria* or "Olympic Truce", calling for all hostilities to cease during the Games, thereby mobilizing the youth of the world in the cause of peace,

*Taking into account* resolution CM/Res.28(LXII), adopted by the Council of Ministers of the Organization of African Unity at its sixty-second ordinary session, held at Addis Ababa from 21 to 23 June 1995, and endorsed by the Assembly of Heads of State and Government of that organization, which supports the appeal for an Olympic Truce,

*Reaffirming* that the Olympic Ideal promotes international understanding, particularly among the youth of the world, through sport and culture in order to advance the harmonious development of humankind,

*Noting with satisfaction* the increasing number of joint endeavours of the International Olympic Committee and the United Nations system, such as recent meetings on "Sport against drugs" with the United Nations International Drug Control Programme, "Sport and the environment" with the United Nations Environment Programme, "Sport for all and health for all" with the World Health Organization and "Forum on physical activity and sport" with the United Nations Educational, Scientific and Cultural Organization,

1. *Calls upon* Member States to reaffirm the observance of an Olympic Truce during the Games of the XXVI Olympiad, the Centennial Games, to be held at Atlanta, United States of America, from 19 July to 4 August 1996, and also calls upon them to reaffirm the observance of the Olympic Truce in advance of each Summer and Winter Olympic Games;

2. *Commends* the International Olympic Committee, now in its one-hundred-and-first year, for promoting international understanding and equality among nations and thereby serving the cause of peace and the well-being of humankind by providing assistance for the development of sport and the Olympic Ideal;

3. *Welcomes* the participation of ministers of youth and sport and concerned officials and the presence of the President of the International Olympic Committee in its consideration of the item entitled "Building a peaceful and better world through sport and the Olympic Ideal" at its fiftieth session;

4. *Suggests* that national ministries of youth and sport consider collaborating with the Olympic Movement, in the spirit of Olympic ethics and fair play, on preventive education programmes such as anti-doping programmes, drug abuse prevention, environmental protection and enhancing the participation of women in all aspects of the sport movement;

5. *Requests* the Secretary-General to continue to cooperate with the International Olympic Committee in joint endeavours for the promotion of peace, equality among nations and the harmonious development of humankind;

6. *Decides* to include in the provisional agenda of its fifty-second session the item entitled "Building a peaceful and better world through sport and the Olympic Ideal" and to biennialize this item so that it will be considered in advance of each Summer and Winter Olympic Games.

General Assembly resolution 50/13

7 November 1995      Meeting 52      Adopted without vote

161-nation draft (A/50/L.15 & Add.1); agenda item 40.
*Meeting numbers.* GA 50th session: plenary 50-52.

*REFERENCES*

(1)A/CONF.166/9. (2)YUN 1992, p. 836, GA res. 47/92, 16 Dec. 1992. (3)YUN 1994, p. 868. (4)YUN 1992, p. 672. (5)YUN 1994, p. 783. (6)Ibid., p. 758. (7)YUN 1992, p. 674. (8)A/CONF.166/L.1. (9)A/CONF.166/L.2. (10)A/CONF.166/5. (11)A/CONF.166/8. (12)YUN 1993, p. 208, SC res.817 (1993), 7 April, 1993.(13)A/CONF.166/7. (14)A/CONF.166/3. (15)A/CONF.166/4. (16)A/CONF.166/6. (17)A/CONF.166/PC/28. (18)A/CONF.166/PC/L.22. (19)A/CONF.166/PC/11/Adds.2-3. (20)A/CONF.166/PC/20/Adds.12-19. (21)YUN 1994, p. 1142. (22)A/CONF.166/PC/26. (23)E/1995/24-E/CN.5/1995/9. (24)E/CN.5/1995/8. (25)E/1995/24 (res. 34/4). (26)E/AC.51/1995/4. (27)E/1995/102. (28)DP/1995/30/Add.3. (29)E/1995/89. (30)YUN 1994, p. 798. (31)YUN 1992, p. 680. (32)DP/1995/24 (Part III). (33)E/1995/55. (34)YUN 1994, p. 955. (35)A/50/670. (36)ACC/1995/23. (37)A/50/3 (agreed conclusion 1995/1). (38)A/50/551. (39)A/50/84-E/1995/12. (40)GA res. 44/56, 8 Dec. 1989. (41)YUN 1993, p. 999. (42)YUN 1992, p. 830. (43)YUN 1993, p. 908. (44)E/CN.5/1995/2. (45)E/CN.5/1995/2/Add.1. (46)A/50/114. (47)E/CN.5/1995/4. (48)E/CN.5/1995/3. (49)E/CN.5/1995/5. (50)YUN 1993, p. 1005, ESC dec. 1993/239, 27 July 1993. (51)E/CN.5/1995/L.3. (52)YUN 1993, p. 1002, GA res. 48/126, 20 Dec. 1993. (53)YUN 1994, p. 1144, GA res. 49/213, 23 Dec. 1994. (54)A/51/201. (55)YUN 1994, p. 1144. (56)IYF/NCFP/9. (57)E/CN.5/1995/5. (58)YUN 1993, p. 1003, GA res. 47/237, 20 Sept. 1993. (59) E/1995/24 (res. 34/3). (60)ACC/1995/10. (61)A/50/370. (62)YUN 1991, p. 646, GA res. 46/93, 16 Dec. 1991. (63)A/50/181-E/1995/65. (64)YUN 1991, p. 646. (65)E/CN.5/1995/L.4. (66)YUN 1993, p. 1027, GA res. 48/15, 2 Nov. 1993. (67)A/50/498. (68)A/50/647.

# Crime prevention

## Ninth UN Crime Congress

The Ninth United Nations Congress on the Prevention of Crime and the Treatment of Offenders was held in Cairo, Egypt, from 29 April to 8 May.(1) By **decision 1995/211** of 10 February, the Economic and Social Council had changed the Congress dates; instead of 29 April to 10 May with two days for pre-Congress consultations, it would be held from 28 April to 8 May with one day for consultations. The Congress, the theme of which was "Less crime, more justice: security for all", was attended by 138 States and by observers from Palestine, UN offices and organs and specialized agencies, intergovernmental organizations, NGOs, and 190 individual experts (see APPENDIX III).

Four major topics were considered: international cooperation and practical technical assistance for strengthening the rule of law: promoting the UN crime prevention and criminal justice programme; action against national and transnational economic and organized crime, and the role of criminal law in the protection of the environment: national experiences and international cooperation; criminal justice and police systems: management and improvement of police and other law enforcement agencies, prosecution, courts and corrections, and the role of lawyers; and crime prevention strategies, in particular as related to crime in urban areas and juvenile and violent criminality, including the question of victims: assessment and new perspectives. The Congress also held two special plenary sessions on experiences in practical measures aimed at combating corruption involving public officials and on technical cooperation.

During the Congress six workshops were held on the following subjects: extradition and international cooperation; mass media and crime prevention; urban policy and crime prevention; prevention of violent crime; environmental protection at the national and international levels: potentials and limits of criminal justice; and international cooperation and assistance in the management of the criminal justice system.

Farouk Seif El-Nasr, Minister of Justice of Egypt, was elected President of the Congress.

The Secretary-General, in his message to the Congress, noted that new and rapacious forms of criminality had been taking advantage of the very trends that had brought so many benefits: improvements in information and transportation technologies, relaxation of border controls, and internationalization of world markets. Every country had a duty to do whatever was possible to protect its children and future generations from the scourge of crime, which in some countries had reached the point of challenging legitimate Governments, jeopardizing their economic and social fabric. Rising crime was impairing the process of development and the general well-being of humanity. Crime in its various dimensions required coordinated, international action with close cooperation among States.

## Resolutions of the Congress

The Congress adopted nine substantive resolutions on a broad range of crime-related issues. It also adopted a resolution thanking the Government of Egypt for its hospitality and welcoming its proposal to establish a regional centre for training and research on crime prevention and criminal justice for the Mediterranean States in Cairo. Another resolution concerned the credentials of representatives attending the Congress.

In a resolution containing recommendations on its four substantive topics, the Congress, in the section relating to international cooperation and technical assistance, urged Member States to intensify efforts to improve the rule of law through international cooperation and practical technical assistance. It invited them to improve policy development, increase the use of bilateral or multilateral cooperation agreements and conduct more

extensive research on traditional organized crime, terrorist crimes and their links, violent activities in urban areas, illicit trafficking in drugs and arms, international trafficking in minors, alien smuggling, economic crime, forgery of currency, environmental crime, corruption, crime against cultural property, motor vehicle theft, computer and telecommunications-related crime, money laundering and the infiltration of legitimate economies by organized criminal groups and the effects of those activities on society. It called on Member States to establish integrated regional policies, programmes, plans and mechanisms and to intensify subregional and regional cooperation and invited them to support the UN crime prevention and criminal justice programme by extrabudgetary contributions. They were also called on to contribute to the UN Crime Prevention and Criminal Justice Fund. The Congress invited the Commission on Crime Prevention and Criminal Justice to call on UNDP, the World Bank and other international, regional and national funding agencies to support technical cooperation activities to strengthen the rule of law and cooperation with the UN crime prevention and criminal justice programme. It invited the Commission to encourage the Secretary-General to recommend the inclusion of the re-establishment and reform of criminal justice systems in peace-keeping operations, and to request him to strengthen operational activities in developing countries and countries in transition. The Commission should call on relevant international and intergovernmental organizations and NGOs to develop manuals and training curricula and organize courses in crime prevention and criminal justice.

In a section of the resolution that dealt with organized crime and the role of criminal law in the protection of the environment, the Congress urged Member States to cooperate for the prevention and control of transnational and organized crime, with emphasis on extradition and mutual assistance, to avoid the commission of offences fully or partially in different countries with impunity; to establish cooperation with regard to the institution of extradition; and to update domestic legislation in crime prevention and criminal justice. Member States should promote cooperation between their national crime prevention and criminal justice sectors and improve the exchange of information, particularly at the regional level; facilitate transnational criminal investigations by extending legal assistance to each other; study ways to promote prompt mutual assistance in criminal procedures and adopt penalties related to the possession of the proceeds of economic crime. They should establish multidisciplinary units specializing in the investigation of economic or financial crime; help to identify major commercial networks influenced by transnational criminal organizations; cooperate in identifying specific measures against corruption, bribery and the abuse of power and in identifying and combating new forms of transnational organized crime, terrorist crimes and their links; and provide further assistance to prevent and combat such crime effectively, including the conclusion of mutual-assistance agreements.

Member States should strengthen the exchange of information on transnational organized and terrorist crimes and their links, and supply information on experiences and practices to the Secretariat; enact legal provisions, including the establishment of enforcement and monitoring mechanisms, concerning economic crime; and consider developing legislation concerning the registration of unregistered imported motor vehicles and other measures to promote international cooperation in combating theft and illegal traffic of motor vehicles. The Commission should consider measures for the prevention and suppression of illegal traffic in motor vehicles. In the area of the environment, Member States were called on to enact environmental protection legislation and penal provisions on the protection of the environment, endangered species and cultural property; create special prosecutors and investigative bodies; and include the role of criminal law in the protection of the environment in curricula on criminal law and in the training of law enforcement and criminal justice personnel.

The Commission was asked to emphasize the development of strategies for the prevention and control of transnational and organized crime and the role of criminal law in the protection of the environment, and to request the Secretary-General to establish an integrated information system on national legislation in crime prevention and criminal justice. Member States were urged to provide the relevant data. The Secretary-General should be asked by the Commission to continue to study transnational and organized crime and effective measures for its control, and to assist Member States in adjusting their national legislation with a view to making the investigation, prosecution and adjudication of transnational crime more effective. He should be asked to ensure close coordination between the Crime Prevention and Criminal Justice Branch and other UN entities, in particular the UN International Drug Control Programme and the Centre for Human Rights, and to encourage further cooperation with the International Criminal Police Organization (ICPO/Interpol) and other international and intergovernmental bodies. Member States that had not yet done so were urged to ratify or accede to the 1988 UN Convention against Illicit Traffic in Narcotic Drugs and Psychotropic Substances.[2]

Concerning criminal justice and police systems, the Congress called on Member States to ensure the independence and impartiality of the judiciary and the proper functioning of prosecutorial and legal services; promote operational research on designing plans to curb crime and upgrade the skills of law enforcement and criminal justice personnel; increase the use of non-custodial measures to reduce the use of detention and the prison population; and ensure the most basic rights of detainees. It encouraged donor countries and international funding agencies to support developing countries' efforts to improve prison conditions. Member States were also asked to take measures against the spread of HIV/AIDS and other diseases among the prison population. Affirming that it was essential for law enforcement and criminal justice personnel to respect human rights, it called on Member States to adopt the community policing approach and forge partnerships with local communities and the private sector when undertaking crime prevention activities. It recommended that Member States strengthen the role of the office of the public prosecutor, in particular its autonomy, and adopt measures to enhance the professional calibre of staff in all sectors concerned with crime prevention and criminal justice.

The Congress urged Member States to review the penitentiary system and recommended enhancement of coordination between the prison system and the broader criminal justice system and closer involvement in research in policy development and drafting of legislation. It called for improving schools for training prison officers and personnel; the organization of regular training programmes and the exchange of information and personnel between the prison administration and the academic community; enhancement of the exchange of information and technical cooperation to further the training of correctional personnel; the use of alternatives to imprisonment of offenders; and reviewing and changing, as necessary, regulations governing prison systems. The Commission should request the Secretary-General to promote technical cooperation projects on penal law reform and on the modernization of criminal justice administration; urge developed countries to provide technical aid for law enforcement agencies in developing countries; and expedite the dissemination of the 1990 *Commentary on the United Nations Standard Minimum Rules for Non-custodial Measures (Tokyo Rules)*.[3]

The Congress invited Member States to develop strategies and programmes for the prevention and control of urban crime, juvenile delinquency and violent crime (including domestic violence) and for the reduction of levels of victimization, and to develop projects related to juvenile delinquency and on the prevention and control of crimes committed by children and young persons, with emphasis on the problem of street children and their exploitation for criminal purposes. They were invited to pay attention to crime prevention activities aimed at young children and to study the factors associated with criminality and establish prevention mechanisms, including counselling services. The Congress recommended that the Commission consider the impact of migratory flows on urban criminality, while Member States should consider the problems arising from such flows and take them into account when drawing up strategies for crime prevention in urban areas.

Member States were urged to adopt short- and medium-term preventive measures in urban planning, housing, education and vocational training, as well as recreational and sports facilities, in high-risk areas, and to adopt measures to combat racism, racial discrimination, xenophobia and related intolerance; promote the regulation of firearms and other high-risk weapons; and support the organization of workshops and training programmes on urban criminality, paying attention to its relationship to social development. They were further urged to develop educational, social and other programmes based on mutual tolerance, to give attention to public awareness and promote the role of information in crime prevention. The Commission was invited to request the Secretary-General to prepare a manual for public awareness campaigns to guide States in formulating national public awareness programmes.

The Congress recommended that Member States adopt policies on the prevention of juvenile delinquency and enact legislation on juvenile justice and invited the Commission to call on the regional commissions, the institutes of the UN crime prevention and criminal justice programme network and other relevant entities to plan and implement joint activities in the area of juvenile justice. Member States should establish local, regional and national bodies for crime prevention and criminal justice and allocate or reallocate resources to facilitate the development of such bodies for the implementation of crime prevention measures. The Commission was invited to continue studying the effects of criminality in urban areas, its contributing factors and prevention measures; organize seminars and training programmes to search for ways to prevent crime in urban and other areas; and promote technical cooperation projects on the improvement of juvenile justice systems.

In its resolution on international cooperation and practical assistance for strengthening the rule of law (resolution 2), the Congress urged the Commission to convene an intergovernmental expert group to examine recommendations for the further development and promotion of international cooperation, including UN model treaties on international cooperation in criminal matters. The group should develop model legislation on extradition and related forms of international cooperation in criminal matters; explore ways of increasing the efficiency of extradition and related mechanisms, including technical assistance in the development of bilateral and multilateral agreements based on UN model treaties and other sources; and draft model legislation or agreements, alternative or complementary articles for existing treaties and articles for possible model multilateral instruments. A report on the implementation of the resolution should be presented to the Commission at its fifth (1996) session.

In the resolution dealing with international instruments against organized transnational crime (resolution 3), the Congress invited the Commission to give priority to initiating the process called for by the 1994 World Ministerial Conference on Organized Transnational Crime, Naples Political Declaration and Global Action Plan against Organized Transnational Crime,[4] by requesting the views of Governments on elaborating new international instruments such as a convention or conventions. It was also asked to consider whether it would be useful to propose to Governments a list of issues and elements that could be dealt with in such instruments. Possible examples of such issues were listed in the resolution's annex.

The resolution on the link between terrorist crimes and transnational organized crimes (resolution 4) called on States to take measures to ensure the prevention and suppression of terrorist crimes and transnational organized crime, to enhance international cooperation to combat such crimes, to exchange technical information and share experiences in combating the use of the proceeds of crime, particularly organized crime, for financing terrorist crimes and to cooperate in the legal and judicial fields, particularly with regard to the extradition of offenders, by means of bilateral, regional or international conventions or other arrangements. The Commission was invited to request UN bodies to collect information on the links between transnational organized crime and terrorist crimes and facilitate the access of States to such information, and to establish an open-ended intergovernmental working group to consider measures to combat transnational organized crime, with due regard to the growing danger of links with terrorist crimes, with the aim of drafting a code of conduct or other legal instrument. The working group would report to the Commission, which would include in the agenda of its Tenth Congress an item entitled ''The links between transnational organized crime and terrorist crimes''.

In a resolution on the practical implementation of the 1955 Standard Minimum Rules for the

Treatment of Prisoners[5] (resolution 5), the Congress invited Member States to respond as a matter of urgency to the questionnaire on the Rules; exchange views on improving prison conditions and strengthen their cooperation; share information on conditions in penal institutions with the public, professional organizations, scientific institutions and NGOs; stimulate and support studies of prison systems undertaken by academia and NGOs; and enhance transparency in prison systems and their functioning by providing ways of monitoring them by independent national bodies. The Commission was invited to keep the matter under review. Its open-ended in-sessional working group on UN standards and norms in crime prevention and criminal justice should discuss, during the Commission's 1996 session (see below), the establishment of efficient information-gathering mechanisms to that end, taking into account the forthcoming results of the UN survey on the use and application of the Rules.

Concerning criminal justice management (resolution 6), the Congress called on Member States to intensify efforts to exchange experiences and innovations in criminal justice operations and encouraged States, intergovernmental organizations and professional NGOs to include in their programmes of work developmental projects dealing with criminal justice management issues in a more comprehensive manner. It requested the Commission to review the membership and databases of the UN Crime and Justice Information Network, with a view to increasing participation of Member States, intergovernmental organizations and NGOs and academic and other research institutions. It also asked developed countries to promote the broader participation of developing countries in the Network by assisting them in reviewing data and other information needs in their criminal justice operations, with a view to making them a more accountable part of public administration; financing the training of criminal justice and technical staff involved in collecting, providing and disseminating data and other information to be included in national criminal justice statistical databases and in the Network; and organizing study tours, donating computer equipment and programs and covering telecommunications expenses. The Commission was asked to consider establishing an ad hoc expert group on statistical and computerized criminal justice applications to advise it on related technical cooperation projects, including their funding; to improve the management and information functions of the Crime Prevention and Criminal Justice Branch and other elements of the UN crime prevention and criminal justice programme; and to request the Secretary-General to prepare a model plan on criminal justice management and to report to the

Tenth Congress on the implementation of that action plan.

In the resolution dealing with children as victims and perpetrators of crime and the UN criminal justice programme (resolution 7), the Congress recommended that the Commission invite the Secretary-General to elaborate a programme of action for promoting the use and application of relevant UN human rights instruments, standards and norms and integrate them into the information-gathering process. It called upon States to support the UN crime prevention and criminal justice programme in developing initiatives to promote universal recognition and application of these norms, in particular with regard to children; provide for legislative and other mechanisms and procedures, as well as adequate resources; and give due regard to the special situation of children. Those States that were not parties to the 1989 Convention on the Rights of the Child[6] were urged to become parties and those that were parties were urged to consider withdrawing those reservations that were incompatible with the object and purpose of the Convention, particularly those relevant to the issue of violence against children. States should enable children to participate in criminal justice proceedings, to be heard and to be given information about their status and any subsequent proceedings. States were invited to develop multidisciplinary training for law enforcement personnel and other professionals concerned with children; ensure that all structures, procedures and programmes in the administration of justice with regard to child offenders allowed children to take responsibility for their actions and encouraged, *inter alia*, reparation, mediation and restitution; and to foster the independent monitoring of juvenile detention and other custodial facilities.

The Congress urged States and relevant international bodies to promote research, collect data and compile statistics relating to the extent and incidence of violence against children including their exploitation and use in criminal activities; encourage research on the causes, nature, seriousness and consequences of such misuse and on the effectiveness of measures to prevent and redress such violence; and study and exchange information on the extent to which experiences of violence suffered by children contributed to their subsequent criminal or deviant behaviour or mental health problems. States were urged to implement prevention and early intervention and treatment programmes for perpetrators and victims. The Congress recommended a series of measures for States to adopt to eliminate all forms of violence against children, in the absence of existing laws. It urged States to ensure that children subjected to violence had access to assistance to promote their safety and physical and psychological recovery and social reintegration; develop programmes in schools that promoted non-violence, mutual respect and tolerance and that enhanced self-confidence and self-esteem and taught students how to resolve their conflicts in a peaceful manner; and support public education and information activities to heighten public awareness of violence against children and its criminal nature. It invited the Commission to request the views of States regarding the elaboration of an international convention on the illicit traffic in children and to protect children from violence in situations of armed conflict.

The Commission was asked to invite the Secretary-General to continue to include in the various advisory services and technical assistance programmes specific arrangements for technical assistance in the field of criminal justice and the administration of justice with regard to children. It recommended that such technical cooperation programmes should entail appropriate evaluation and follow-up procedures and should involve UN regional institutes, the United Nations Children's Fund and other relevant UN bodies, national institutions and NGOs. The Secretary-General should publish and distribute the draft UN manual on juvenile justice; ensure that *Strategies for Confronting Domestic Violence: a Resource Manual* was published in the other official languages of the UN; and enhance inter-agency cooperation in the area of administration of justice with regard to children. The in-sessional working group of the Commission, at its 1995 session, should develop and undertake activities, including training, research and advisory services, for preventing and eradicating violence against children. The Commission should make the elimination of such violence one of the priorities of the UN crime prevention and criminal justice programme in 1996-1997 and request the Secretary-General to submit a report on the subject to its sixth (1997) session.

In a resolution on elimination of violence against women (resolution 8), the Congress recommended a number of initiatives which it urged Member States to adopt in the absence of existing laws. It urged them to enforce their laws relating to violence against women; take action to eliminate violence against women in detention; promote access by women subjected to violence to assistance for their safety and physical and psychological healing; promote the involvement and participation of women in decision-making processes concerning crime prevention and criminal justice; develop intervention programmes and treatment services; promote multidisciplinary training and educational and information-sharing activities to sensitize law enforcement officials, justice personnel and other relevant professions to problems related to violence against women; promote and support public education and informa-

tion activities to ensure gender equality; and heighten public awareness of violence against women and of its criminal nature. Member States should also promote research, collect data and compile statistics on the various forms of violence against women and encourage research on its causes, nature, seriousness and consequences; invite the media, schools and other relevant partners to contribute to the eradication of violence against women and enhance respect for their dignity; and take special account of women's vulnerability to violence in situations of armed conflict. They were further asked to study, disseminate, and encourage utilization of the publication *Strategies for Confronting Domestic Violence: a Resource Manual*. The Congress requested the in-sessional working group of the Commission, at its 1995 session, to develop activities to achieve the goal of preventing and eradicating violence against women. It urged the Commission to consider the issue of violence against women as a priority in its programme's training and technical assistance efforts.

The Congress, in its resolution on firearms regulations for the purposes of crime prevention and public safety (resolution 9), requested the Commission urgently to consider the measures to regulate firearms commonly applicable in Member States, with a view to suppressing the use of firearms in criminal activities. It recommended that the Commission request the Secretary-General to establish close cooperation with Member States and intergovernmental and other organizations, especially ICPO/Interpol, which are active in the field of firearms regulation; initiate a study on, *inter alia*, criminal cases, accidents and suicides in which firearms were involved, transnational illicit trafficking in firearms, relevant national legislation and regulation, and initiatives for firearms regulation at the regional and inter-regional levels. The Congress reiterated the need for allocating sufficient resources to the Crime Prevention and Criminal Justice Branch to facilitate UN activities in the field of firearms regulation. It called on States to promote adequate regulation of firearms and take action against illicit trafficking in firearms and urged UN organs, bodies and specialized agencies to take up more seriously the issue of firearms regulation. The Congress recommended that the Commission request the Secretary-General to report to it, at its 1996 session, on the implementation of the resolution and submit recommendations for further action at the national and transnational levels, including the possibility of seeking the views of Member States on the preparation of a declaration.

**Secretariat working papers.** Among the documents considered by the Congress were four working papers submitted by the Secretariat on: international cooperation and practical technical assistance for strengthening the rule of law: promoting the UN crime prevention and criminal justice programme;[7] action against national and transnational economic and organized crime, and the role of criminal law in the protection of the environment: national experiences and international cooperation;[8] criminal justice and police systems: management and improvement of police and other law enforcement agencies, prosecution, courts and corrections, and the role of lawyers;[9] and crime prevention strategies, in particular as related to crimes in urban areas and juvenile and violent criminality, including the question of victims: assessment and ·new perspectives.[10]

## Follow-up to the Congress

The Commission on Crime Prevention and Criminal Justice, at its fourth session (30 May–9 June 1995)[11] considered the report of the Ninth United Nations Congress on the Prevention of Crime and the Treatment of Offenders[1] and recommended a draft resolution on the subject for the Economic and Social Council to recommend to the General Assembly for adoption, and a draft resolution on the implementation of Congress resolutions and recommendations, which it recommended to the Council for adoption.

**ECONOMIC AND SOCIAL COUNCIL ACTION**

On 24 July, the Economic and Social Council adopted **resolution 1995/8**.

### Ninth United Nations Congress on the Prevention of Crime and the Treatment of Offenders

*The Economic and Social Council*

*Recommends* to the General Assembly the adoption of the following draft resolution:

[See text of General Assembly resolution 50/145 below.]

Economic and Social Council resolution 1995/8

24 July 1995      Meeting 49      Adopted without vote

Draft by Commission on Crime Prevention and Criminal Justice (E/1995/30); agenda item 5 *(g)*.
*Meeting numbers.* ESC 47-49.

On the same date, the Council adopted **resolution 1995/27**.

### Implementation of the resolutions and recommendations of the Ninth United Nations Congress on the Prevention of Crime and the Treatment of Offenders

*The Economic and Social Council,*

*Recalling* its resolutions 1992/24 of 30 July 1992, 1993/32 of 27 July 1993 and 1994/19 of 25 July 1994 on preparations for the Ninth United Nations Congress on the Prevention of Crime and the Treatment of Offenders,

*Recalling also* General Assembly resolution 49/157 of 23 December 1994, in which the Assembly requested the Commission on Crime Prevention and Criminal Justice to give priority attention at its fourth session to the conclusions and recommendations of the Ninth Congress, with a view to recommending appropriate follow-up, through the Economic and Social Council, by the General Assembly at its fiftieth session,

*Determined* to give effect to the resolutions and recommendations of the Ninth Congress, taking into account the guidance provided by the Commission on Crime Prevention and Criminal Justice at its fourth session,

*Taking note* of the report of the Ninth Congress, considered by the Commission on Crime Prevention and Criminal Justice at its fourth session,

1. *Invites* Governments, in their efforts to combat crime and ensure justice, to draw on the resolutions and recommendations of the Ninth United Nations Congress on the Prevention of Crime and the Treatment of Offenders, held at Cairo from 29 April to 8 May 1995;

2. *Approves* the follow-up of the resolutions and recommendations concerning the topics of the Ninth Congress, as contained in the present resolution, and requests the Secretary-General to implement them in accordance with work plans of implementation and with the rules and regulations of the United Nations, including financial and programme planning rules and regulations, in the context of the priority themes determined by the Council in section VI of its resolution 1992/22 of 30 July 1992.

I. International cooperation and practical technical assistance for strengthening the rule of law: promoting the United Nations crime prevention and criminal justice programme

1. *Calls upon* the United Nations Development Programme, the World Bank and other international, regional and national funding agencies to support technical cooperation activities devoted to strengthening the rule of law, in cooperation with the United Nations crime prevention and criminal justice programme, in order to ensure proper coordination; and requests the Secretary-General to undertake vigorous fund-raising activities, also in accordance with Economic and Social Council resolution 1992/22;

2. *Encourages* the Secretary-General, as a way of strengthening the rule of law, to include upon request the re-establishment and reform of criminal justice systems in peace-keeping operations;

3. *Requests* the Secretary-General to further strengthen operational activities in developing countries and countries in transition, by providing advisory services and training programmes and by carrying out field studies at the national level, also drawing on extrabudgetary resources;

4. *Calls upon* all relevant international, intergovernmental and non-governmental organizations to continue cooperating with the United Nations in developing manuals and training curricula and in organizing courses in the various areas of crime prevention and criminal justice;

A. *International cooperation in criminal matters, including extradition*

5. *Requests* the Secretary-General to convene, utilizing extrabudgetary funds already offered for this purpose, and in accordance with the principle of equitable geographical distribution, a meeting of an intergovernmental expert group to examine practical recommendations for the further development and promotion of mechanisms of international cooperation, including the

United Nations model treaties on international cooperation in criminal matters, as well as for the development of model legislation on extradition and related forms of international cooperation in criminal matters;

6. *Recommends* that the expert group should, in the light of the discussion at the workshop held during the Ninth Congress, explore ways and means of increasing the efficiency of extradition and related mechanisms of international cooperation in criminal matters, having due regard to the rule of law and the protection of human rights, including, where appropriate, such measures as:

(a) The provision of technical assistance in the development of bilateral and multilateral agreements based on the United Nations model treaties and other sources;

(b) The drafting of model legislation or agreements on international cooperation in criminal matters, alternative or complementary articles for existing model treaties, and articles for possible model multilateral instruments;

7. *Recommends* that a report on the implementation of paragraph 5 above should be submitted to the Commission on Crime Prevention and Criminal Justice at its fifth session;

B. *Establishment of a regional centre for training and research in crime prevention and criminal justice for the Mediterranean States*

8. *Decides* to establish an open-ended intergovernmental working group within the framework of the Commission on Crime Prevention and Criminal Justice which would meet during the first and second days of the fifth session of the Commission with the aim of studying, with the assistance of the Secretary-General, the proposal for the establishment of a regional centre, to be based at Cairo, for training and research in crime prevention and criminal justice for the Mediterranean States, taking into consideration, *inter alia*, Economic and Social Council resolution 1994/23 of 25 July 1994 on criteria and procedures for the affiliation with the United Nations of institutes or centres and the establishment of United Nations subregional institutes in the field of crime prevention and criminal justice; that the working group should report to the Commission at its fifth session; and that the working group may invite other relevant entities or seek views from them, as appropriate.

II. Action against national and transnational economic and organized crime, and the role of criminal law in the protection of the environment: national experiences and international cooperation

1. *Requests* the Commission on Crime Prevention and Criminal Justice to consider measures on the prevention and suppression of illicit trafficking in motor vehicles and requests the Secretary-General to seek the views of Governments and relevant organizations on this matter and to report to the Commission at its sixth session;

2. *Also requests* the Commission on Crime Prevention and Criminal Justice, in its review of priority themes, to continue placing special emphasis on the development of strategies for the effective prevention and control of organized transnational crime;

3. *Calls upon* the Secretary-General, as well as the United Nations Interregional Crime and Justice Research Institute and the regional institutes for the prevention of crime and the treatment of offenders, to continue research, exchange of information, training and technical cooperation facilitating the development of preventive, regulatory and other strategies on the role of criminal law in the protection of the environment, with an emphasis on:

(a) Needs assessment and advisory services;

(b) Assistance in the review or redrafting of legislation and the development of effective infrastructure;

(c) Training of criminal justice and regulatory agency personnel;

4. *Requests* the Secretary-General to consider the feasibility of establishing an integrated system for the periodic gathering and dissemination of information on national legislation in crime prevention and criminal justice and its implementation, taking into account the current and planned capabilities of the United Nations Crime and Justice Information Network and the activities of other United Nations entities and relevant intergovernmental organizations, invites Member States to cooperate in this regard, with a view to encouraging progressive alignment regarding, *inter alia*, international cooperation, extradition and other bilateral and multilateral modalities of mutual assistance in criminal matters, and requests the Secretary-General to report thereon to the Commission on Crime Prevention and Criminal Justice at its fifth session;

5. *Also requests* the Secretary-General to continue studying the actual situation of organized transnational crime and effective measures for its control;

6. *Further requests* the Secretary-General to assist Member States, upon request, in adjusting their national legislation with a view to making the investigation, prosecution and adjudication of organized transnational crime more effective;

7. *Requests* the Secretary-General to ensure close coordination between the Crime Prevention and Criminal Justice Branch of the Secretariat and other United Nations entities, in particular, *inter alia*, the United Nations International Drug Control Programme, the Centre for Human Rights of the Secretariat, the United Nations Environment Programme and the United Nations Development Programme, including the sponsorship of joint activities, and to encourage further cooperation with the International Criminal Police Organization and other international and intergovernmental bodies concerned, through joint programmes and projects;

*Links between transnational organized crime and terrorist crimes*

8. *Calls upon* institutes and centres for crime prevention and criminal justice to devote the required attention to studying the links between transnational organized crime and terrorist crimes, their effects and appropriate means for countering them;

9. *Requests* the competent United Nations bodies to collect information on the links between transnational organized crime and terrorist crimes, to coordinate their activities and to facilitate the access of States to such information;

10. *Decides* to establish an open-ended intergovernmental working group, within the framework of the Commission, to consider, at the fifth session of the Commission, the views of Member States to be sought by the Secretary-General in the implementation of Ninth Congress resolution 3, paragraph 1, and to consider measures for combating transnational organized crime, including the drafting of a code of conduct or other legal

istrument, with due regard to the growing danger of links between organized crime and terrorist crimes, and that the working group should report to the Commission at its fifth session;

11. *Recommends* that the Commission should consider including in the agenda for the Tenth United Nations Congress on the Prevention of Crime and the Treatment of Offenders an item entitled ''The links between transnational organized crime and terrorist crimes''.

### III. Criminal justice and police systems: management and improvement of police and other law enforcement agencies, prosecution, courts and corrections; and the role of lawyers

1. *Requests* the Secretary-General to promote technical cooperation projects on penal law reform and on the modernization of criminal justice administration, particularly in the fields of data collection and computerization, the training of law enforcement officials, the promotion of non-custodial measures and prisoners' welfare, taking into account United Nations standards and norms such as the United Nations Standard Minimum Rules for Non-custodial Measures (the Tokyo Rules), the Basic Principles for the Treatment of Prisoners and the WHO Guidelines on HIV Infection and AIDS in Prisons;

2. *Also requests* the Secretary-General to play an active role in urging developed countries to provide support by supplying and maintaining technical aid for law enforcement agencies in developing countries;

3. *Further requests* the Secretary-General to expedite the dissemination of the Commentary on the United Nations Standard Minimum Rules for Non-custodial Measures (the Tokyo Rules), which was published pursuant to General Assembly resolution 45/110 of 14 December 1990, and welcomes the support of the United Nations Asia and Far East Institute for the Prevention of Crime and the Treatment of Offenders, the International Penal and Penitentiary Foundation and the Asia Crime Prevention Foundation in its preparation;

#### A. *Prison conditions*

4. *Invites* the Commission on Crime Prevention and Criminal Justice to keep the matter of prison conditions under regular review and, in particular, recommends that the open-ended in-sessional working group on United Nations standards and norms in crime prevention and criminal justice should discuss, at the fifth session of the Commission, the establishment of efficient information-gathering mechanisms to that end, taking into account the forthcoming results of the United Nations survey on the use and application of the Standard Minimum Rules for the Treatment of Prisoners, which were approved by the Economic and Social Council in its resolution 663 C(XXIV) of 31 July 1957;

5. *Invites* the Secretary-General, drawing upon extrabudgetary resources, to distribute the manual entitled Making Standards Work, prepared by Penal Reform International, among Member States for their use and consideration, and to seek their advice with a view to preparing a subsequent version of the manual for further consideration by the Commission;

#### B. *Information network and databases*

6. *Requests* the Commission on Crime Prevention and Criminal Justice to review the membership and databases of the United Nations Crime and Justice Infor-

mation Network, with a view to increasing the participation in the Network of Member States, relevant intergovernmental and non-governmental organizations and academic and other research institutions;

7. *Requests* the Secretary-General to seek the contributions of Member States in order to prepare, in cooperation with the institutes comprising the United Nations crime prevention and criminal justice programme network, for the consideration of the Commission at its fifth session, a draft action plan on international cooperation and assistance with regard to statistical and computerized applications in the management of the criminal justice system, commensurate with the priorities of the United Nations crime prevention and criminal justice programme;

8. *Also requests* the Secretary-General to include in the above-mentioned initiative recommendations for improving the management and information functions of the Crime Prevention and Criminal Justice Branch and other elements of institutes comprising the United Nations crime prevention and criminal justice programme network to reflect the resolve of the international community to pursue the programme priorities determined in accordance with the statement of principles and programme of action of the programme, annexed to General Assembly resolution 46/152 of 18 December 1991, and taking into account the proposals for improving the clearing-house capacity of the United Nations crime prevention and criminal justice programme, contained in the report of the Secretary-General;

9. *Requests* the Commission on Crime Prevention and Criminal Justice to consider the utilization of experts of interested Member States to advise the Secretary-General on technical cooperation projects related to paragraph 7 above, including their funding by the public and private sectors;

10. *Requests* the Commission on Crime Prevention and Criminal Justice and the Secretary-General, when implementing the above-mentioned recommendations, to take account of work already being carried out in the United Nations and other international organizations, such as the Council of Europe, in comparing national crime and criminal justice databases.

### IV. Crime prevention strategies, in particular as related to crimes in urban areas and juvenile and violent criminality, including the question of victims: assessment and new perspectives

1. *Recommends* that the Commission on Crime Prevention and Criminal Justice should consider the possible impact of migratory flows on urban criminality;

2. *Urges* Member States to give attention to public awareness and to promote the role of information in crime prevention, and requests the Secretary-General, in collaboration with specialized research centres and experts, to prepare a manual for public awareness campaigns, to be used to guide States in formulating national public awareness programmes;

3. *Approves* the guidelines for cooperation and technical assistance in the field of urban crime prevention, which were finalized by the Commission on Crime Prevention and Criminal Justice at its fourth session;

4. *Requests* the Secretary-General, within existing resources:

*(a)* To continue studying the effects of criminality in urban areas, the factors contributing to it and measures

for its effective prevention, taking into consideration recent developments in, *inter alia*, sociology, child and adolescent psychology, health, criminology and technology, including environmentally sound planning, city planning and housing design;

(*b*) To organize seminars and training programmes to search for ways and means to prevent crime in urban and other areas;

(*c*) To promote technical cooperation projects on the improvement of juvenile justice systems, taking into account the United Nations Standard Minimum Rules for the Administration of Juvenile Justice (the Beijing Rules), the United Nations Guidelines for the Prevention of Juvenile Delinquency (the Riyadh Guidelines) and the United Nations Rules for the Protection of Juveniles Deprived of Their Liberty;

5. *Calls upon* Member States, in cooperation with the institutes comprising the United Nations crime prevention and criminal justice programme network and other relevant bodies, to develop tried and tested crime prevention strategies that are capable of being adapted to local conditions, with particular reference to those presented at the workshops on urban policy and crime prevention, prevention of violent crime, and mass media and crime prevention held during the Ninth Congress;

A. *Firearms regulation for purposes of crime prevention and public safety*

6. *Requests* the Commission on Crime Prevention and Criminal Justice, at its fifth session, to consider, under a separate agenda item, the measures to regulate firearms commonly applicable in Member States, such as the prevention of transnational illicit trafficking in firearms, with a view to suppressing the use of firearms in criminal activities, taking into account the urgent need for effective strategies to ensure the proper regulation of firearms at both national and transnational levels;

7. *Requests* the Secretary-General to establish and maintain close cooperation with Member States and intergovernmental and other organizations, especially the International Criminal Police Organization, active in the field of firearms regulation, *inter alia*, by regularly exchanging data and other information, in accordance with specific circumstances of Member States, on, among other things, the following topics:

(*a*) Criminal cases, accidents and suicides in which firearms are involved, including the number of such cases and the number of victims involved, and the status of firearms regulation by the law enforcement authorities;

(*b*) The situation with regard to transnational illicit trafficking in firearms;

(*c*) National legislation and regulations relevant to firearms regulation;

(*d*) Relevant initiatives for firearms regulation at the regional and interregional levels;

8. *Also requests* the Secretary-General to initiate a study on, *inter alia*, the topics listed in paragraph 7 above, so as to provide the Commission on Crime Prevention and Criminal Justice at its fifth session with a basis for its consideration of measures to regulate firearms;

9. *Endorses* the work plan presented by the representative of the Secretary-General, as contained in paragraph 19 of the report of the Commission on its fourth session, to implement Ninth Congress resolution 9;

10. *Requests* the Secretary-General to collect information and consult with Member States on the implementation of the national measures outlined in Ninth Congress resolution 9, paragraphs 7 to 10;

11. *Invites* all United Nations organs, bodies and specialized agencies and intergovernmental and other organizations active in the field of firearms regulation to provide the Secretary-General with views and proposals on their possible contributions towards the full implementation of Ninth Congress resolution 9;

12. *Requests* the Secretary-General to report to the Commission on Crime Prevention and Criminal Justice, at its fifth session, on the implementation of Ninth Congress resolution 9, as well as the paragraphs above, and to submit to it recommendations for further concerted action at the national and transnational levels, including the possibility of seeking views of Member States on the preparation of a declaration;

B. *Children as victims and perpetrators of crime: effective application of United Nations standards and norms in juvenile justice*

13. *Decides* that the elimination of violence against children should be considered within the priority theme ''Crime prevention in urban areas, juvenile and violent criminality'' of the United Nations crime prevention and criminal justice programme in the biennium 1996-1997;

14. *Calls upon* the regional commissions, the institutes comprising the United Nations crime prevention and criminal justice programme network and other relevant entities to cooperate closely in planning and implementing joint activities in the area of juvenile justice;

15. *Recommends* that Strategies for Confronting Domestic Violence: a Resource Manual, which is based on a draft prepared by the Government of Canada, in cooperation with the Crime Prevention and Criminal Justice Branch of the Secretariat and the European Institute for Crime Prevention and Control, affiliated with the United Nations, and currently available in English only, should be published in the other official languages of the United Nations, subject to the availability of regular budgetary or extrabudgetary funds;

16. *Decides* to integrate United Nations standards and norms in juvenile justice into the current process of information-gathering;

17. *Requests* the Secretary-General to initiate the process of requesting the views of Member States on the elaboration of an international convention on the illicit traffic in children, which may embody elements necessary to efficiently combat this form of transnational organized crime;

18. *Also requests* the Secretary-General, subject to the availability of extrabudgetary funding, to organize a meeting of an expert group on the prevention of the sexual exploitation of children for commercial purposes within the context of international travel (sex tourism);

19. *Further requests* the Secretary-General to enhance inter-agency cooperation within the United Nations system in connection with the elimination of violence against children and the administration of justice with regard to children by, *inter alia*, using existing meeting possibilities, both at headquarters and at the regional and national levels, including the Crime Prevention and Criminal Justice Branch, the Centre for Human Rights,

the Office of the United Nations High Commissioner for Refugees, the United Nations Children's Fund, the United Nations Development Programme, the United Nations Educational, Scientific and Cultural Organization and the World Health Organization, as well as the Committee on the Rights of the Child and the Special Rapporteurs of the Commission on Human Rights concerned about this issue, with a view, in particular, to avoiding duplication and overlapping of activities;

20. *Requests* the Secretary-General to continue including in the various advisory services and technical assistance programmes specific arrangements for technical assistance in the field of criminal justice and the administration of justice, with regard to children; such assistance may include technical advice in law and criminal justice reform, including the promotion of alternative measures, such as alternatives to custody, diversionary programmes, alternative dispute resolution, restitution, family conferences and community services;

21. *Recommends* that technical cooperation programmes in the field of administration of justice with regard to children should entail appropriate evaluation and follow-up procedures and that the United Nations Children's Fund, other relevant United Nations bodies, institutes comprising the United Nations crime prevention and criminal justice programme network, national institutions and non-governmental organizations should be involved as appropriate;

22. *Invites* the Committee on the Rights of the Child, as well as the Special Rapporteur on the sale of children, child prostitution and child pornography and the Working Group on Arbitrary Detention of the Commission on Human Rights, to identify, in their reports, issues of particular concern with regard to the protection of children and juveniles in detention for their consideration under programmes of technical cooperation;

23. *Requests* the Secretary-General to include in his reports on technical assistance programmes and advisory services in the field of criminal justice and the administration of justice the following aspects:

(a) Existing possibilities for including specific needs of children and juveniles into concrete projects undertaken under those programmes;

(b) Existing arrangements for the coordination of those programmes;

(c) Current evaluation and follow-up procedures in that regard;

(d) The scope for including projects for the promotion of alternative measures, such as alternatives to custody, diversionary programmes, alternative dispute resolution, restitution, family conferences and community services, under those programmes;

(e) Possibilities for further strengthening United Nations action in this field through enhanced technical cooperation programmes;

24. *Invites* the Secretary-General, taking into account the conclusions of the reports referred to in paragraph 23 of the present resolution, to consider ways of elaborating a programme of action aimed at promoting the effective use and application of relevant United Nations human rights instruments in the administration of justice with regard to children and of United Nations standards and norms in juvenile justice, giving due regard to the work accomplished by the Commission on Human Rights and in cooperation with the Office of the United Nations High Commissioner for Human Rights, the United Nations Children's Fund and other agencies and organizations concerned, within existing resources;

25. *Requests* the Secretary-General to submit a report on the implementation of these recommendations to the Commission on Crime Prevention and Criminal Justice at its fifth session, including in particular that contained in paragraph 24 above, and decides that the open-ended in-sessional working group of the Commission, at its fifth session, should seek ways to develop and undertake practical activities, including training, research and advisory services, to achieve the goal of preventing and eradicating violence against children;

### C. *Elimination of violence against women*

26. *Requests* the Secretary-General to forward Ninth Congress resolution 8, on the elimination of violence against women, to the Fourth World Conference on Women: Action for Equality, Development and Peace, to be held at Beijing from 4 to 15 September 1995;

27. *Urges* the Commission on Crime Prevention and Criminal Justice to continue to consider the elimination of violence against women within its priority themes and within the training and technical assistance efforts of the United Nations crime prevention and criminal justice programme;

28. *Requests* the Secretary-General to seek the contributions of interested Member States, institutes comprising the United Nations crime prevention and criminal justice programme network, and intergovernmental and non-governmental organizations, in order to prepare a draft plan of action, in the context of crime prevention and criminal justice, on the elimination of violence against women that will provide practical and action-oriented suggestions on how to address this issue by means of, *inter alia*, legislative action, research and evaluation, technical cooperation, training and exchange of information;

29. *Also requests* the Secretary-General to seek the views of Member States, institutes comprising the United Nations crime prevention and criminal justice programme network, and intergovernmental and non-governmental organizations on the draft plan of action and, taking into account the views received and the outcome of the Fourth World Conference on Women, to submit the draft plan of action, as well as a report on the views received, to the Commission at its fifth session so that it may be considered by the open-ended in-sessional working group of the Commission;

30. *Urges* the Commission on Crime Prevention and Criminal Justice to cooperate closely on the issue of the elimination of violence against women with other United Nations bodies, such as the Commission on the Status of Women, the Committee on the Elimination of Discrimination against Women, the Commission on Human Rights, including the Subcommission on Prevention of Discrimination and Protection of Minorities and the Special Rapporteur on violence against women, its causes and its consequences, as well as with relevant experts and non-governmental organizations, as appropriate;

31. *Invites* the institutes in the United Nations crime prevention and criminal justice programme network to promote and undertake practical activities to eliminate violence against women, including the provision of training and advisory services, to develop proposals on other measures that could be taken in the field of crime preven-

tion and criminal justice to eliminate violence against women and to submit a report on those issues to the Commission on Crime Prevention and Criminal Justice at its fifth session;

### D. *Victims of crime*

32. *Requests* the Secretary-General to seek the views of Member States and relevant organizations on the advisability of preparing a manual on the use and application of the Declaration of Basic Principles of Justice for Victims of Crime and Abuse of Power.

Economic and Social Council resolution 1995/27

24 July 1995     Meeting 50     Adopted without vote

Draft by Commission on Crime Prevention and Criminal Justice (E/1995/30); agenda item 5 *(g)*.
*Financial implications.* S-G, E/1995/30/Add.1.
*Meeting numbers.* ESC 47-50.

**Report of the Secretary-General.** By a 24 August note,[12] the Secretary-General, in accordance with a 1994 General Assembly request,[13] transmitted the report of the Ninth United Nations Congress on the Prevention of Crime and the Treatment of Offenders.

**GENERAL ASSEMBLY ACTION**

On 21 December, the General Assembly, by **decision 50/443**, took note of the report of the Ninth United Nations Congress on the Prevention of Crime and the Treatment of Offenders.

On the same date, the Assembly adopted **resolution 50/145**.

#### Ninth United Nations Congress on the Prevention of Crime and the Treatment of Offenders

*The General Assembly,*

*Emphasizing* the responsibility assumed by the United Nations in the field of crime prevention and criminal justice in pursuance of Economic and Social Council resolution 155 C(VII) of 13 August 1948 and General Assembly resolution 415(V) of 1 December 1950,

*Acknowledging* that the United Nations congresses on the prevention of crime and the treatment of offenders, as major intergovernmental forums, have influenced national policies and practices and promoted international cooperation in this field by facilitating the exchange of views and experiences, mobilizing public opinion and recommending policy options at the national, regional and international levels,

*Recalling* its resolution 46/152 of 18 December 1991, in the annex to which Member States affirmed that the United Nations congresses on the prevention of crime and the treatment of offenders should be held every five years and should provide a forum for, *inter alia*, the exchange of views between States, intergovernmental and non-governmental organizations and individual experts representing various professions and disciplines, the exchange of experiences in research, law and policy development and the identification of emerging trends and issues in crime prevention and criminal justice,

*Bearing in mind* the theme for the Ninth United Nations Congress on the Prevention of Crime and the Treatment of Offenders, which was "Less crime, more justice: security for all", and the importance of achieving this goal at the national and international levels,

*Deeply concerned* about the rising levels of crime in many parts of the world, particularly transnational organized crime and its negative effects on socio-economic development, political stability and the internal and external security of States, as well as on the well-being of people,

*Convinced* that the United Nations crime prevention and criminal justice programme has a significant role to play in enhancing regional and interregional cooperation in crime prevention and criminal justice in order to achieve further progress in this area, including the mobilization and coordination of efforts by Member States to combat crime in all its forms and to ensure greater justice,

*Recalling* its resolution 49/157 of 23 December 1994, in which it requested the Commission on Crime Prevention and Criminal Justice to give priority attention at its fourth session to the conclusions and recommendations of the Ninth Congress, with a view to recommending, through the Economic and Social Council, appropriate follow-up by the General Assembly at its fiftieth session,

*Having considered* the report of the Ninth Congress and the related recommendations made by the Commission on Crime Prevention and Criminal Justice at its fourth session,

1. *Expresses its satisfaction* with the results achieved by the Ninth United Nations Congress on the Prevention of Crime and the Treatment of Offenders, held at Cairo from 29 April to 8 May 1995;

2. *Expresses its profound gratitude* to the Government and people of Egypt for the generous hospitality extended to the participants at the Ninth Congress and for the efficient facilities, staff and services placed at their disposal;

3. *Takes note with appreciation* of the report of the Ninth Congress, which contains the results of the Congress, including the recommendations and suggestions made at the workshops, at the special plenary meeting on combating corruption involving public officials and at the special plenary meeting on technical cooperation;

4. *Endorses* the resolutions adopted by the Ninth Congress, as approved by the Commission on Crime Prevention and Criminal Justice, and also endorses the recommendations made by the Commission, at its fourth session, and by the Economic and Social Council, at its substantive session of 1995, on the implementation of the resolutions and recommendations of the Ninth Congress, as contained in Council resolution 1995/27 of 24 July 1995;

5. *Invites* Governments to be guided by the resolutions and recommendations of the Ninth Congress in formulating legislation and policy directives and to make all efforts to implement the principles contained therein, in accordance with the economic, social, legal, cultural and political circumstances of each country;

6. *Requests* the Secretary-General to pay particular attention to the operational aspects of the follow-up to the Ninth Congress in order to assist interested States in strengthening the rule of law by reinforcing their national machinery, promoting human resource development, undertaking joint training activities and executing pilot and demonstration projects, and urges the Department for Development Support and Management

Services of the Secretariat, the United Nations Development Programme, the World Bank and other funding agencies to continue to provide financial support and assistance within the framework of their technical cooperation programmes;

7. *Urges* all entities of the United Nations system, including the regional commissions, the regional institutes for the prevention of crime and the treatment of offenders and the relevant intergovernmental and nongovernmental organizations to become actively involved in the implementation of the resolutions and recommendations of the Ninth Congress, paying particular attention to the needs and priorities identified by Member States;

8. *Expresses its appreciation* to those Member States, institutes and intergovernmental and non-governmental organizations which have provided human and financial resources, particularly on the occasion of the Ninth Congress, and invites Governments to lend their support to the United Nations crime prevention and criminal justice programme and to increase their financial contributions to the United Nations Crime Prevention and Criminal Justice Trust Fund;

9. *Requests* the Secretary-General to circulate the report of the Ninth Congress to Member States and intergovernmental and non-governmental organizations, so as to ensure that it is disseminated as widely as possible, and to conduct appropriate public information activities in this field;

10. *Also requests* the Secretary-General to submit to the General Assembly, at its fifty-first session, a report on the measures taken to implement the present resolution;

11. *Decides* to include in the provisional agenda of its fifty-first session the item entitled ''Crime prevention and criminal justice''.

General Assembly resolution 50/145

21 December 1995      Meeting 97      Adopted without vote

Approved by Third Committee (A/50/629) without vote, 10 November (meeting 25); draft recommended by ESC in res. 1995/8 (A/C.3/50/L.3); agenda item 106.
*Meeting numbers.* GA 50th session: 3rd Committee 12-17, 19, 25; plenary 97.

## Commission on Crime Prevention and Criminal Justice

The Commission on Crime Prevention and Criminal Justice, established by the Economic and Social Council in 1992,[14] held its fourth session in Vienna from 30 May to 9 June,[11] in accordance with Council **decision 1995/210** of 10 February. The Commission recommended one draft resolution for adoption by the General Assembly and eight draft resolutions and three draft decisions for adoption by the Council.

The Commission adopted three resolutions to be brought to the attention of the Council. By a resolution on the succession of States in respect of international treaties on combating crime,[15] the Commission urged successor States that had not yet done so to become parties to those treaties to which their predecessor States were not parties. It requested the Secretary-General to render ad-

visory services in that regard and to include in his report to the Commission's 1996 session information received from Member States on progress achieved. By a resolution on a proposal for the development of minimum rules for the administration of criminal justice,[16] the Commission requested the Secretary-General to seek more comments from States on the draft minimum rules and to submit an analytical report, including options on how to proceed, to the Commission in 1996. In a resolution on the provision of information in accordance with the plan for strategic management by the Commission of the UN crime prevention and criminal justice programme,[17] the Commission decided on, and set out in an annex, the type of information that would be useful in considering draft resolutions. It also decided that the Secretariat should report annually on progress in implementing any proposed activity and that a standing item should be included in its agenda so that it could review the extent to which activities had been successfully implemented.

**ECONOMIC AND SOCIAL COUNCIL ACTION**

On 24 July, the Economic and Social Council, by **decision 1995/243**, took note of the Commission's report on its fourth session[11] and approved the provisional agenda and documentation for its fifth (1996) session. On the same date, by **decision 1995/242**, the Council decided that the Commission's fifth session, in addition to plenary meetings, should be provided with full interpretation services for a total of 14 meetings for informal consultations on draft proposals and for meetings of open-ended working groups, on the understanding that no more than two meetings would be held concurrently, in order to ensure maximum participation of delegations.

## UN crime prevention and criminal justice programme

In a report on strengthening the United Nations crime prevention and criminal justice programme[18] submitted to the Commission on Crime Prevention and Criminal Justice, the Secretary-General recalled the various mandates of the Economic and Social Council and the General Assembly for strengthening the programme and referred to the proposed programme of work in crime prevention and criminal justice for 1996-1997 (see below),[19] including the Secretary-General's proposal to upgrade the Crime Prevention and Criminal Justice Branch of the Secretariat to a division and strengthen its staff with two additional posts at the Professional level.

In a 14 September report,[20] the Secretary-General described progress made in implementing a 1994 General Assembly resolution[21] on strengthening the United Nations crime prevention and criminal justice programme. He examined the critical need for crime prevention and criminal justice and reviewed programme activities during the year, especially research and information dissemination, implementation of UN standards and norms, operational activities, support to the Commission on Crime Prevention and Criminal Justice and collaborative initiatives. He discussed recent mandates and their programme implications and proposals and action to strengthen programme capacity.

The proliferation of requests for crime and justice-related assistance led to the provision of a second interregional adviser post under the regular programme of technical cooperation in the 1994-1995 programme budget so that short-term missions could be resumed in late 1994 after a hiatus of almost a year. Needs assessment missions were carried out by both advisers and the Ninth Congress provided opportunities for consultations with government officials regarding their requirements. Other needs assessments were carried out in the context of peace-keeping operations, as for Haiti and Rwanda. Some requests for interregional advisory services sought expert guidance in defining needs in a specific area or sub-sector. Needs assessments were carried out in Albania, Pakistan, Peru, and Caribbean countries. Advisory services were also provided by the Crime Prevention and Criminal Justice Branch to Belarus, the Russian Federation and Ukraine. A substantial number of training courses, seminars and workshops were organized and serviced during the year, a major initiative being a series of workshops for prison personnel in Argentina, Barbados, Brazil and Uganda.

The Secretary-General stated that the amount of resources for the Crime Prevention and Criminal Justice Branch (0.1 per cent of overall UN resources) was considered a bare minimum that did not redress the acute imbalance in the amount of work to be done *vis-à-vis* the means for doing it. Taking into account the additional mandates deriving from the Ninth Congress, the General Assembly and the Economic and Social Council, as well as the extensive crime and justice-related needs facing countries, a careful assessment of the steps to be taken was necessary in order to optimize and supplement programme capabilities. The programme required a recognized place in the mainstream of UN development assistance. The UNDP Administrator had noted new areas for UNDP aid, such as assistance in the reform of criminal codes and access to due process. Other international funding agencies, such as the World Bank and the International Development Association, had been called on to support efforts related to crime prevention and criminal justice, but so far to little avail. In addition, the United Nations Crime Prevention and Criminal Justice Fund was in a precarious situation.

The Secretary-General concluded that 1994/1995 had been significant in the history of the UN crime prevention and criminal justice programme, which was called upon to meet the unprecedented challenges that crime in its new forms and dimensions posed to the world. Although much had been done, much more remained to be done for improved crime prevention, greater justice and effective international cooperation against the mounting threat of transnational crime. The rising toll of violence linked to civil strife, terrorism and ordinary street crime, and the price exacted by organized, economic and environmental criminality, had jeopardized some of the gains of development and undermined future prospects. It was clear that security and justice were indispensable conditions for sustained development and human well-being, and for both national and world progress.

The Secretary-General also submitted an 18 September report[22] on the Naples Political Declaration and Global Action Plan against Organized Transnational Crime (see below).

**GENERAL ASSEMBLY ACTION**

On 21 December, the General Assembly adopted **resolution 50/146**.

**Strengthening the United Nations Crime Prevention and Criminal Justice Programme, particularly its technical cooperation capacity**

*The General Assembly,*

*Recognizing* the direct relevance of crime prevention and criminal justice to sustained development, stability, security and improved quality of life,

*Convinced* of the desirability of closer coordination and cooperation among States in combating crime, including drug-related crimes such as terrorist crimes, illicit arms trade and money laundering, and bearing in mind the role that could be played by both the United Nations and regional organizations in this respect,

*Bearing in mind* the goals of the United Nations in the field of crime prevention and criminal justice, specifically the reduction of criminality, more efficient and effective law enforcement and administration of justice, respect for human rights and promotion of the highest standards of fairness, humanity and professional conduct,

*Recognizing* the urgent need to increase technical cooperation activities to assist countries, particularly developing countries and countries in transition, with their efforts in translating United Nations policy guidelines into practice, including training and upgrading of national capacities,

*Noting* the continued increase in the workload of the Crime Prevention and Criminal Justice Branch of the Secretariat, as well as the considerable obstacles to the full and effective implementation of its programme activities, resulting from the lack of appropriate institutional capacity,

*Convinced* that the Crime Prevention and Criminal Justice Branch can be effective only if it is provided with resources commensurate to its requirements and adequate to allow it to implement its mandates and to respond in a timely and efficient manner to the increasing requests of Member States for its services,

*Recalling* its resolution 49/158 of 23 December 1994, in which it requested the Secretary-General, as a matter of urgency, to give effect to General Assembly resolutions 47/91 of 16 December 1992 and 48/103 of 20 December 1993, and to Economic and Social Council resolutions 1992/22 of 30 July 1992, 1993/31 and 1993/34 of 27 July 1993 and 1994/16 of 25 July 1994 by providing the United Nations crime prevention and criminal justice programme with sufficient resources for the full implementation of its mandates, in conformity with the high priority attached to the programme,

*Recalling also* its resolution 49/159 of 23 December 1994, in which it resolved to take decisions at its fiftieth session on the allocation of adequate resources to the United Nations crime prevention and criminal justice programme on the basis of proposals for the modification of the programme to be submitted by the Secretary-General, taking into account the responsibilities entrusted to the United Nations pursuant to the Naples Political Declaration and Global Action Plan against Organized Transnational Crime,

*Recalling further* its resolution 46/152 of 18 December 1991 on the creation of an effective United Nations crime prevention and criminal justice programme, in which it approved the statement of principles and programme of action annexed to the resolution, in which it was recommended to the Secretary-General that an upgrading of the Crime Prevention and Criminal Justice Branch into a division should be effected as soon as possible,

*Concerned* about the fact that despite the repeated calls by the General Assembly and the Economic and Social Council to upgrade the Crime Prevention and Criminal Justice Branch to a division, action has not been taken to give effect to the relevant Assembly and Council resolutions,

*Noting* that the Secretary-General, in section 13 (Crime control) of the proposed programme budget for the biennium 1996-1997, proposes the strengthening of the United Nations crime prevention and criminal justice programme in response to the repeated calls by the General Assembly and the Economic and Social Council to that effect,

*Noting also* the additional information provided in the introductory statement by the Director-General of the United Nations Office at Vienna on the proposed programme budget,

1. *Takes note with appreciation* of the reports of the Secretary-General on the progress made in the implementation of General Assembly resolution 49/158 on strengthening the United Nations crime prevention and criminal justice programme, particularly its technical cooperation capacity, and on the implementation of General Assembly resolution 49/159 on the Naples Political Declaration and Global Action Plan against Organized Transnational Crime;

2. *Reaffirms* the importance of the United Nations crime prevention and criminal justice programme and the crucial role it has to play in promoting international cooperation in crime prevention and criminal justice,

in responding to the needs of the international community in the face of both national and transnational criminality and in assisting Member States in achieving the goals of preventing crime within and among States and improving the response to crime;

3. *Also reaffirms* the priority of the United Nations crime prevention and criminal justice programme, in accordance with its resolutions 46/152, 47/91, 48/103 and 49/158, and the need for an appropriate share of the existing resources of the United Nations for the programme;

4. *Welcomes* the proposed strengthening of the United Nations crime prevention and criminal justice programme, in response to the repeated calls by the General Assembly and the Economic and Social Council to that effect and, in particular, welcomes the proposal of the Secretary-General to upgrade the Crime Prevention and Criminal Justice Branch of the Secretariat into a division, in accordance with Assembly resolutions 46/152, 47/91, 48/103 and 49/158;

5. *Requests* the Secretary-General to continue strengthening the United Nations crime prevention and criminal justice programme by providing it with the resources necessary for the full implementation of its mandates, including follow-up action to the Naples Political Declaration and Global Action Plan against Organized Transnational Crime and to the Ninth United Nations Congress on the Prevention of Crime and the Treatment of Offenders;

6. *Reaffirms* the high priority attached to technical cooperation and advisory services as a means for the United Nations crime prevention and criminal justice programme to respond to the needs of the international community in the face of both national and transnational criminality and to assist Member States in achieving the goals of preventing crime within and among States and improving the response to crime, in accordance with General Assembly resolution 46/152 and in line with the recommendations of the Ninth Congress on the Prevention of Crime and the Treatment of Offenders;

7. *Stresses* the importance of continuing to improve the operational activities of the United Nations crime prevention and criminal justice programme, particularly in developing countries and countries in transition, in order to meet the needs of Member States, at their request, for support in crime prevention and criminal justice;

8. *Calls upon* States and funding agencies to make significant financial contributions for operational activities for crime prevention and criminal justice, and encourages all States to make voluntary contributions for that purpose to the United Nations Crime Prevention and Criminal Justice Trust Fund, also taking into account the activities required for the implementation of the Naples Political Declaration and Global Action Plan against Organized Transnational Crime;

9. *Requests* the Secretary-General to facilitate, as appropriate, the creation of joint initiatives, including bilateral activities, and the joint formulation and implementation of technical assistance projects benefiting developing countries and countries in transition, involving interested donor countries and funding agencies, particularly the United Nations Development Programme and the World Bank, with a view to establishing and maintaining efficient criminal justice systems

on a country-by-country basis as an essential component of developmental efforts;

10. *Also requests* the Secretary-General to take all necessary measures to assist the Commission on Crime Prevention and Criminal Justice, as the principal policy-making body in the field of crime prevention and criminal justice, in performing its functions and to ensure the proper coordination of all relevant activities in the field, in particular with the Commission on Human Rights, the Commission on the Status of Women and the Commission on Narcotic Drugs;

11. *Calls upon* the United Nations Development Programme, the World Bank and other international, regional and national funding agencies to support technical cooperation activities devoted to crime prevention and criminal justice at country level and, in pursuance of their mandates, to include such activities in their programmes, emphasizing social development aspects and utilizing the expertise of the United Nations crime prevention and criminal justice programme in such activities and cooperating closely on relevant technical assistance projects and advisory missions;

12. *Expresses its appreciation* for the provision of services of two interregional advisers for crime prevention and criminal justice;

13. *Takes note with appreciation* of the contributions of the United Nations crime prevention and criminal justice programme to United Nations peace-keeping and special missions, as well as its contributions to the follow-up to those missions, *inter alia*, through advisory services, and encourages the Secretary-General, as a way of strengthening the rule of law, to recommend the inclusion of the re-establishment and reform of criminal justice systems in peace-keeping operations;

14. *Requests* the Secretary-General to continue to strengthen cooperation between the Crime Prevention and Criminal Justice Branch and the United Nations International Drug Control Programme;

15. *Also requests* the Secretary-General to take all necessary measures to provide improved services, at its future sessions, to the Commission on Crime Prevention and Criminal Justice, as the principal policy-making body in the field of crime prevention and criminal justice, with a view to ensuring full implementation of the relevant Commission resolutions on the strategic management by the Commission of the United Nations crime prevention and criminal justice programme in the context of United Nations rules and regulations;

16. *Reaffirms* the importance of rule 28 of the rules of procedure of the functional commissions of the Economic and Social Council, and urges the Secretary-General to provide the appropriate information to the Commission on Crime Prevention and Criminal Justice;

17. *Requests* the Secretary-General to submit a report on the implementation of the present resolution to the General Assembly at its fifty-first session.

General Assembly resolution 50/146

21 December 1995     Meeting 97     Adopted without vote

Approved by Third Committee (A/50/629) without vote, 10 November (meeting 25); 35-nation draft (A/C.3/50/L.15), orally revised; agenda item 106.
*Meeting numbers.* GA 50th session: 3rd Committee 12-17, 19, 25; plenary 97.

## Programme questions

The Secretary-General, in a 22 May note,[19] submitted to the Commission on Crime Prevention and Criminal Justice the proposed programme of work in crime prevention and criminal justice for 1996-1997. The proposed programme was also submitted to the General Assembly as part of the proposed UN programme budget for 1996-1997.[23] The programme would focus on providing Member States with assistance and advisory services and on enabling the Commission to perform as the principal UN policy-making body in the field of crime prevention and criminal justice. Member States would also be assisted in the implementation of the 1994 Naples Political Declaration and Global Action Plan against Transnational Organized Crime[4] and follow-up to the recommendations of the Ninth United Nations Congress on the Prevention of Crime and the Treatment of Offenders (see above). The Crime Prevention and Criminal Justice Branch would be upgraded to a division in order to reflect the programme's expanded mandate.

The Commission annexed to the report on its May/June session[11] the text of a draft resolution proposed by its Chairman concerning programme questions. It recommended that the Economic and Social Council take the proposed text into account in its consideration of programme questions relating to crime control.

On 28 July, the Council, by **decision 1995/315**, deferred consideration of a draft resolution[24] entitled "Programme of work in crime prevention and criminal justice" to its 1995 resumed substantive session. On 25 October, the draft resolution was withdrawn.

The General Assembly, in **resolution 50/214** of 23 December, approved the upgrading of the Crime Prevention and Criminal Justice Branch to a division. It requested the Secretary-General, in strengthening the Crime Prevention and Criminal Justice Division, to review the adequacy of resources for crime prevention activities at the regional level and to report to the Assembly in 1996. He was also asked to report on the implementation of the strategic management plan of the Division, including those activities that had achieved demonstrable results in combating international crime, assisting international law enforcement or otherwise meeting current mandates of the United Nations Congress on the Prevention of Crime and the Treatment of Offenders and of the Commission.

## Technical cooperation

In a 28 April report to the Commission on Crime Prevention and Criminal Justice,[25] the Secretary-General examined technical cooperation and advisory services of the United Nations crime prevention and criminal justice programme carried out or initiated between November 1993 and April 1995 by the Crime Prevention and Criminal Justice Branch, the two interregional advisers for Crime Prevention and Criminal Justice based in Vienna and the regional adviser based in Bangkok. He discussed increased technical cooperation in crime prevention and criminal justice; an overview of technical assistance activities; interregional advisory services; development of a database on technical assistance needs; and future technical assistance activities and their funding.

In his conclusions and recommendations, the Secretary-General stated that future operational activities of the programme would involve mobilizing resources for project implementation; collaborating with traditional partners and NGOs; preparing a needs assessment instrument to guide future technical assistance activities and development of an evaluation instrument; and expansion of the fellowship programme. He suggested that the Commission recommend that the high priority given to technical cooperation be reaffirmed; the interregional advisory service programme be strengthened, including resources for short-term advisory services, field projects, training and fellowships; Member States, funding agencies and other relevant institutions be called on to contribute human and material resources and the means for technical assistance projects; and that donors' meetings be held to encourage close cooperation among them, including joint implementation of technical assistance activities. In addition, the Secretary-General should make further use of the capacity of the programme in connection with peace-keeping operations, including training courses for peace-keeping police, needs assessment missions and advisory services for rebuilding national structures, including training criminal justice practitioners and helping local judges to render justice. The branch should be advised on the development of the database on technical cooperation.

ECONOMIC AND SOCIAL COUNCIL ACTION

On 24 July, the Economic and Social Council adopted **resolution 1995/15**.

### Technical cooperation and interregional advisory services in crime prevention and criminal justice

*The Economic and Social Council,*

*Recalling* its resolution 1994/22 of 25 July 1994, on technical cooperation in the field of crime prevention and criminal justice,

*Recalling also* its resolution 1994/16 of 25 July 1994, in which it requested the Secretary-General to provide adequate funds to build and maintain the institutional capacity of the United Nations crime prevention and criminal justice programme to respond to requests of Member States for assistance in the field of crime prevention and criminal justice, if necessary through the reallocation of resources,

*Recalling further* General Assembly resolution 49/158 of 23 December 1994, on strengthening the United Nations crime prevention and criminal justice programme, particularly its technical cooperation capacity,

*Convinced* that establishing the rule of law and maintaining efficient criminal justice systems is one of the essential elements of developmental efforts, and recognizing the direct relevance of crime prevention and criminal justice to sustained development, stability, security and improved quality of life,

*Underlining* the fact that one of the most effective ways to meet the needs of States in this area is through operational activities, such as advisory services, training programmes and the dissemination and exchange of information,

*Recognizing* the need, in making specific proposals on the resolutions of the Ninth United Nations Congress on the Prevention of Crime and the Treatment of Offenders related to technical cooperation and advisory services, to take into account the capacity of the United Nations crime prevention and criminal justice programme and its future role in providing services in that field,

1. *Takes note with appreciation* of the report of the Secretary-General on the technical cooperation and advisory services of the United Nations crime prevention and criminal justice programme;

2. *Welcomes* the call of the Ninth United Nations Congress on the Prevention of Crime and the Treatment of Offenders for intensified efforts to strengthen the rule of law by means of international cooperation and practical technical assistance;

3. *Reaffirms* the high priority attached to technical cooperation and advisory services as a means for the United Nations crime prevention and criminal justice programme to respond to the needs of the international community in the face of both national and transnational criminality and to assist Member States in achieving the goals of preventing crime within and among States and improving the response to crime, in accordance with General Assembly resolution 46/152 of 18 December 1991, on the creation of an effective United Nations crime prevention and criminal justice programme, and in line with the recommendations of the Ninth United Nations Congress on the Prevention of Crime and the Treatment of Offenders;

4. *Stresses* the importance of continuing to improve the operational activities of the United Nations crime prevention and criminal justice programme, particularly in developing countries and countries in transition, so as to meet the needs of Member States, at their request, for support in crime prevention and criminal justice, by undertaking advisory services and training programmes and by carrying out field studies and action-oriented research at the regional, subregional, national and local levels, also drawing upon extrabudgetary contributions;

5. *Expresses its appreciation* to Member States and other entities supporting the United Nations crime prevention and criminal justice programme, through contributions to the United Nations Crime Prevention and Criminal Justice Fund or by other means, and invites them to continue their support;

6. *Invites* Member States to contribute to the activities of the United Nations crime prevention and criminal justice programme by other means, for example by providing the services of associate experts, by providing the services of consultants and experts for training purposes and advisory missions, by developing training manuals and other material, by offering fellowship opportunities and by hosting problem-oriented workshops and expert group meetings;

7. *Calls upon* the United Nations Development Programme, the World Bank and other international, regional and national funding agencies to support technical cooperation activities devoted to crime prevention and criminal justice and, in pursuance of their mandates, to include such activities in their programmes, utilizing the expertise of the United Nations crime prevention and criminal justice programme in such activities and cooperating closely on relevant technical assistance projects and advisory missions;

8. *Calls upon* all relevant international, intergovernmental and non-governmental organizations to continue cooperating with the United Nations crime prevention and criminal justice programme in support of its operational and technical activities;

9. *Requests* the Secretary-General to facilitate, as appropriate, joint initiatives and the joint formulation and implementation of technical assistance projects, involving interested donor countries, funding agencies and other relevant entities, and to organize meetings of interested donor and recipient countries;

10. *Notes with appreciation* the contribution of the United Nations crime prevention and criminal justice programme to United Nations peace-keeping and special missions, as well as its contribution to the follow-up to those missions, *inter alia*, through advisory services, and encourages the Secretary-General, as a way of strengthening the rule of law, to recommend the inclusion of the re-establishment and reform of criminal justice systems in peace-keeping operations;

11. *Notes* the work of the crime prevention and criminal justice programme on collecting and disseminating data and other information on technical cooperation projects, and requests the Secretary-General further to strengthen the capacity of the Secretariat to establish and develop relevant databases, by cooperating in this endeavour with the United Nations Development Programme and the network of institutes cooperating with the United Nations crime prevention and criminal justice programme;

12. *Reiterates its appreciation* for the provision of the services of two interregional advisers for crime prevention and criminal justice and strongly recommends to the Secretary-General that those posts should be retained and that the interregional advisory services of the United Nations crime prevention and criminal justice programme should be further strengthened to support technical assistance activities, including short-term advisory services, needs assessment, feasibility studies, field projects, training and fellowships;

13. *Requests* the Secretary-General to provide, within the regular budget, appropriate resources for the United Nations crime prevention and criminal justice programme to provide better planning support and backstopping for the interregional advisory services, in accordance with General Assembly resolution 49/158 and Economic and Social Council resolutions 1994/16 and 1994/22.

Economic and Social Council resolution 1995/15
24 July 1995     Meeting 49     Adopted without vote
Draft by Commission on Crime Prevention and Criminal Justice (E/1995/30); agenda item 5 *(g)*.
*Meeting numbers.* ESC 47-49.

## Clearing-house capacity

The Secretary-General submitted to the Commission on Crime Prevention and Criminal Justice proposals[26] for improving the clearing-house capacity of the United Nations crime prevention and criminal justice programme. The improvement was based on a three-pronged strategy involving: a system for electronic exchange of information; computerization of criminal justice administration; and collection and dissemination of criminal justice data and information. Responding to a 1993 Economic and Social Council request,[27] the Secretariat initiated studies on the further development of the United Nations Crime and Justice Information Network, with a view to designing and implementing a properly functioning on-line crime and justice clearing-house. While its ultimate objective would be to strengthen the capacities of Governments to produce, acquire, store, analyse and disseminate electronic information on crime prevention and criminal justice, the intermediate goals of the strategy were several. It was designed to serve as an effective broker between intergovernmental, non-governmental and other relevant organizations, sectors of public administration and the private sector, including individual experts and other professionals. It was also to provide regularly electronic information on crime and justice; facilitate the computerization process by promoting the more widespread use of automated data processing in, and exchange of such data between, criminal justice systems, as well as assist developing countries in the transfer of know-how on such computerization; and collect and disseminate criminal justice data and information, analyse the results of periodic crime surveys and prepare the data for electronic dissemination. A further objective was to improve the survey of transnational crime and produce the report on crime and justice in the world, and in a format to permit electronic dissemination.

To achieve those goals, a number of major tasks were identified to be accomplished within the 1994-1995 and the 1996-1997 bienniums, including the transfer of the United Nations Crime and Justice Information Network from the State University of New York at Albany to the Vienna University and the UN Office in Vienna. In addition, a needs assessment study should be carried out to review existing and projected programme facilities and resources devoted to the clearing-house functions with a primary focus on electronic data exchange.

On 24 July, the Economic and Social Council adopted **resolution 1995/12**.

### Establishment of a clearing-house for international projects in the field of crime prevention and criminal justice

*The Economic and Social Council,*

*Recalling* General Assembly resolution 46/152 of 18 December 1991, in which the Assembly decided that the United Nations crime prevention and criminal justice programme should be devoted to providing States with practical assistance to achieve the goals of preventing crime and improving the response to crime,

*Recalling also* its resolution 1994/22 of 25 July 1994, in which it requested the Secretary-General to establish a database on technical assistance, integrating needs of Member States, particularly developing countries, as well as on existing collaborative arrangements and funding, taking into account regional concerns,

*Recognizing* the need for maximum efficiency and effective utilization of increasingly scarce developmental assistance at a time of growing difficulties in the prevention and control of crime,

*Recognizing also* that improving the clearing-house capacity of the United Nations crime prevention and criminal justice programme requires a steady and concerted effort on the part of Member States and other entities including institutes cooperating within the programme to work more closely and effectively in advancing the electronic exchange of information, the computerization of the administration of criminal justice, and the collection and dissemination of crime and justice information,

*Recognizing further* that the improvement of the clearing-house capacity of the United Nations crime prevention and criminal justice programme requires continuous efforts to create and maintain databases on current crime and justice developments globally, regionally and subregionally, the information from which should be made available through the computerized United Nations Crime and Justice Information Network, as part of a broader clearing-house function carried out by that programme,

*Conscious* that the present capacity of the Crime Prevention and Criminal Justice Branch of the Secretariat lags behind the growing need to provide timely information at the request of Member States and other interested parties, and that the management of the databases listed in the programme budget for the Branch requires a coordinated effort on the part of those parties,

*Having considered* the report of the Secretary-General on proposals for improving the clearing-house capacity of the United Nations crime prevention and criminal justice programme, prepared in response to resolution 3/3 of 5 May 1994 of the Commission on Crime Prevention and Criminal Justice,

*Noting* that, in recent years, many international projects on crime prevention and criminal justice have targeted States in Central and Eastern Europe,

*Fully aware* that international cooperation is essential to successful efforts against international criminal activity,

*Recognizing* that there is no existing central repository with information on planned, ongoing or projected training and other projects in the field of crime prevention and criminal justice,

*Taking note* of the report of the Secretary-General on proposals for improving the clearing-house capacity of the United Nations crime prevention and criminal justice programme, which consolidate the approach to relevant crime and justice information activities that should be further intensified and made operational,

*Taking note also* of the initiatives taken by the European Institute for Crime Prevention and Control, affiliated with the United Nations, in the areas to which the present resolution refers,

1.   *Requests* the Secretary-General, subject to the availability of extrabudgetary funds, to initiate a project to establish a regional database on international training and technical assistance projects in the field of crime prevention and criminal justice which, upon completion, would provide interested Governments, international organizations and other entities with information on concluded, ongoing or planned international projects in consultation and cooperation with the European Institute for Crime Prevention and Control, affiliated with the United Nations, which has offered to manage the database;

2.   *Invites* all Member States, international organizations and other entities engaged in collaborative training and technical assistance projects in Central and Eastern Europe in the field of crime prevention and criminal justice to provide, to the extent of their ability, information to the Secretary-General for a regional clearing-house to facilitate the exchange of information to assist policy makers in all Member States in better allocating resources, identifying potential partners in cooperative projects and opportunities for collaborative action and improving support for an incremental approach to better prevent crime and ensure criminal justice, on the understanding that all information provided to the database may be restricted at the request of the provider;

3.   *Takes note* of the form for providing information on technical assistance in the field of crime prevention and criminal justice, contained in annex II to the report of the Secretary-General on the technical cooperation and advisory services of the United Nations crime prevention and criminal justice programme;

4.   *Recommends* that the Secretary-General should view the project as a pilot project aimed at demonstrating the utility of a regional database on crime prevention and criminal justice, with a view to considering additional regional databases, or a global database;

5.   *Requests* the Secretary-General to submit the results of the pilot project to the Commission on Crime Prevention and Criminal Justice at its fifth session.

Economic and Social Council resolution 1995/12

24 July 1995          Meeting 49          Adopted without vote

Draft by Commission on Crime Prevention and Criminal Justice (E/1995/30); agenda item 5 *(g)*.
*Meeting numbers.* ESC 47-49.

## UN standards and norms

In response to a 1994 Economic and Social Council request,[28] the Secretary-General submitted to the Commission on Crime Prevention and Criminal Justice a report[29] which provided an overview of development activities in promoting the use and application of UN standards and norms. He stated that he had received replies from 31 countries to a questionnaire on the 1955 Standard Minimum Rules for the Treatment of Prisoners;[5] replies from 32 countries to the questionnaire on the 1979 Code of Conduct for Law Enforcement Officials, including the Basic Principles on the Use of Force and Firearms by Law Enforcement Officials;[30] replies from 17 countries to the questionnaire on the 1990 Declaration of Basic Principles of Justice for Victims of Crime and Abuse of Power;[31] and replies from 28 countries to the questionnaire on the 1985 Basic Principles on the Independence of the Judiciary.[32] Information collected would be used to establish databases on the respective subjects. The Secretary-General also reported that China, France, the Russian Federation and Spain had committed themselves to funding publication of the *Compendium of United Nations Standards and Norms in Crime Prevention and Criminal Justice*[33] in their languages, while the United Kingdom had provided resources for its reprinting in English and Portugal had agreed to publish it in Portuguese.

In response to a 1994 Economic and Social Council request,[34] the Secretary-General submitted an addendum to the report,[35] stating that, by 25 April, he had received replies from 27 Member States and comments from 6 interregional and regional institutes on the desirability of preparing and adopting United Nations minimum rules in the field covered by the draft minimum rules for the administration of justice, prepared by an expert commission.[36]

**ECONOMIC AND SOCIAL COUNCIL ACTION**

On 24 July, the Economic and Social Council adopted **resolution 1995/13**.

### United Nations standards and norms in crime prevention and criminal justice

*The Economic and Social Council,*

*Reaffirming* the importance of United Nations standards, norms and guidelines in crime prevention and criminal justice,

*Underlining* the need for further coordination and concerted action in translating those standards and norms into practice,

*Recalling* its resolution 1993/34 of 27 July 1993, in section III of which it requested the Secretary-General to commence without delay a process of information-gathering to be undertaken by means of surveys, such as reporting systems, and contributions from other sources,

*Recalling also* its resolution 1994/18 of 25 July 1994, in which it endorsed the questionnaires on the Standard Minimum Rules for the Treatment of Prisoners, the Code of Conduct for Law Enforcement Officials, including the Basic Principles on the Use of Force and Firearms by Law Enforcement Officials, the Declaration of Basic Principles of Justice for Victims of Crime and Abuse of Power and the Basic Principles on the Independence of the Judiciary and requested the Secretary-

General to submit to the Commission at its fifth session a report on the replies to those questionnaires,

1. *Notes* that the Secretary-General has received a number of replies from Governments and other sources to the questionnaires on the use and application of United Nations standards and norms on crime prevention and criminal justice, pursuant to Economic and Social Council resolutions 1993/34, section III, and 1994/18;

2. *Urges* Governments that have not yet replied to the questionnaires to submit their replies in time to be included in the report of the Secretary-General on the use and application of the United Nations standards and norms, pursuant to Economic and Social Council resolution 1994/18;

3. *Requests* the Secretary-General to develop questionnaires on the United Nations Standard Minimum Rules for the Administration of Juvenile Justice (the Beijing Rules), the United Nations Guidelines for the Prevention of Juvenile Delinquency (the Riyadh Guidelines) and the United Nations Rules for the Protection of Juveniles Deprived of their Liberty, to be considered by the Commission on Crime Prevention and Criminal Justice at its fifth session, taking into account the results of the above-mentioned surveys, with a view to requesting the Secretary-General to submit a report on the replies to the Commission at a subsequent session, in accordance with Economic and Social Council resolution 1993/34, section III, paragraph 7 *(c)*;

4. *Decides* that the Commission at its sixth session will consider the following United Nations standards, norms and guidelines in crime prevention and criminal justice with a view to requesting the Secretary-General to develop appropriate measures:

*(a)* The United Nations Standard Minimum Rules for Non-custodial Measures (the Tokyo Rules);

*(b)* The Guidelines on the Role of Prosecutors;

*(c)* The Basic Principles on the Role of Lawyers;

5. *Requests* the Secretary-General to ensure adequate time for consideration of the reports by the open-ended in-sessional working group of the Commission;

6. *Invites* the open-ended in-sessional working group of the Commission at its fifth session to undertake an overall review of the information-gathering system, pursuant to Economic and Social Council resolution 1993/34, section III, and to discuss ways of further improving that system;

7. *Recognizes* the importance of the publication of the English version of the *Compendium of United Nations Standards and Norms in Crime Prevention and Criminal Justice* and expresses its gratitude to the Government of the United Kingdom of Great Britain and Northern Ireland for its valuable contribution to the reprinting of that publication;

8. *Expresses its appreciation* of the valuable contribution of the Governments of China, France and the Russian Federation to the translation of the *Compendium* into other official languages of the United Nations;

9. *Welcomes* the publication of the *Compendium* in Portuguese by the Government of Portugal and encourages other Governments to publish it in the languages of their countries;

10. *Requests* the Secretary-General to continue to promote the use and application of United Nations standards and norms in crime prevention and criminal justice, *inter alia*, by providing advisory services and technical

cooperation, when requested by Member States, providing assistance to Member States in criminal justice and law reform and organizing seminars for training law enforcement and criminal justice personnel;

11. *Also requests* the Secretary-General to seek the views of Member States and relevant organizations on the advisability of preparing a manual on the use and application of the Declaration of Basic Principles of Justice for Victims of Crime and Abuse of Power;

12. *Further requests* the Secretary-General to encourage the coordination of activities related to the use and application of standards and norms between the Crime Prevention and Criminal Justice Branch of the Secretariat and other relevant United Nations entities, such as the United Nations International Drug Control Programme and the Office of the United Nations High Commissioner for Human Rights, so as to heighten their efficacy and avoid overlapping in the implementation of their programmes;

13. *Expresses its appreciation* to the United Nations network of institutes and intergovernmental and non-governmental organizations for their valuable contribution to the effective use and application of United Nations standards and norms in crime prevention and criminal justice.

Economic and Social Council resolution 1995/13

24 July 1995      Meeting 49      Adopted without vote

Draft by Commission on Crime Prevention and Criminal Justice (E/1995/30); agenda item 5 *(g)*.
*Meeting numbers.* ESC 47-49.

## Organized transnational crime

In a report[37] to the Commission on Crime Prevention and Criminal Justice, the Secretary-General made proposals related to the programmable aspects of the Naples Political Declaration and Global Action Plan against Organized Transnational Crime, adopted by the World Ministerial Conference on Organized Transnational Crime in 1994[4] and approved by the General Assembly later that year.[38] To improve the international community's knowledge of criminal organizations and their dynamics, it was proposed that the United Nations initiate a comprehensive comparative study of the situation in the various regions of the world by an expert team with experience in the field of prevention and control of organized crime. In addition, the United Nations could establish a central repository of existing legislative and regulatory measures and information on organizational structures designed to combat organized crime and, based on the information accumulated through the comprehensive comparative study, develop practical models of and guidelines for substantive and procedural legislation, in cooperation with relevant international organizations and individual States. It could assist States in assessing their immediate needs through the provision of advisory services to identify and put in place modalities for strength-

ening their capacity to respond to problems created by new manifestations of organized transnational crime; provide expert advice and options on establishing special investigative units and developing reliable evidence-gathering techniques; and assist in creating special mechanisms and implementing measures to strengthen the capacity of States to cooperate and exchange information, intelligence and experience. The UN crime prevention and criminal justice programme should be geared towards developing expertise and promoting the highest standards of professionalism and specialization.

On 25 May, Italy submitted to the Commission a preliminary report[39] of the first meeting (Rome, Italy, 17-18 May) of the international task-force to study the feasibility of establishing an international training centre for law enforcement and criminal justice personnel. A general agreement was reached that, in the short term, the most logical location for the centre would be the existing centre of advanced studies for personnel of law enforcement agencies in Rome. The setting up of a UN centre would not be advisable. Italy intended to provide the site for the centre, as well as administrative staff and infrastructure needed for its functioning. It was also considering offering accommodation and board to participants. Other Governments would be invited to contribute to the centre's activities on a voluntary basis.

**ECONOMIC AND SOCIAL COUNCIL ACTION**

On 24 July, the Economic and Social Council adopted **resolution 1995/11**.

**Implementation of the Naples Political Declaration and Global Action Plan against Organized Transnational Crime**

*The Economic and Social Council,*

*Recalling* General Assembly resolution 49/159 of 23 December 1994, in which the Assembly approved the Naples Political Declaration and Global Action Plan against Organized Transnational Crime, adopted by the World Ministerial Conference on Organized Transnational Crime, held at Naples, Italy from 21 to 23 November 1994, and urged States to implement them as a matter of urgency,

*Recalling also* General Assembly resolutions 44/71 of 8 December 1989, 45/121 and 45/123 of 14 December 1990, 47/87 of 16 December 1992 and 48/103 of 20 December 1993 and its own resolutions 1992/22 and 1992/23 of 30 July 1992, 1993/29 and 1993/30 of 27 July 1993 and 1994/12 and 1994/13 of 25 July 1994,

*Recalling further* General Assembly resolution 46/152 of 18 December 1991, in which the Assembly approved the statement of principles and programme of action of the United Nations crime prevention and criminal justice programme, contained in the annex to that resolution,

*Emphasizing* the need for strengthened and improved international cooperation at all levels and for more effective technical cooperation to assist States in their fight against organized transnational crime,

1. *Takes note* of the report of the Secretary-General on proposals related to the programmatic aspects of the Naples Political Declaration and Global Action Plan against Organized Transnational Crime;

2. *Requests* the Commission on Crime Prevention and Criminal Justice to ensure and monitor full implementation of the Naples Political Declaration and Global Action Plan;

3. *Requests* the Secretary-General to initiate the process of requesting the views of Governments on the opportunity and impact of international instruments such as a convention or conventions against organized transnational crime and on the issues and elements that could be covered therein, pursuant to the Naples Political Declaration and Global Action Plan;

4. *Also requests* the Secretary-General, for the purpose of assisting the international community in increasing its knowledge of criminal organizations and their dynamics, to collect and analyse information on the structure and dynamics of organized transnational crime and on the responses of States to this problem, building on the experience and expertise of States and drawing on contributions from Governments, which could include teamwork by highly qualified experts, relevant organizations and individuals, taking into account work already done in this area;

5. *Decides* that an open-ended intergovernmental working group should be established, within the framework of the Commission, at its fifth session, to consider the results of the work described in paragraph 4 above, and the views of Governments requested in paragraph 3 above, and to propose further action on the implementation of the Naples Political Declaration and Global Action Plan;

6. *Requests* the Secretary-General to submit to Member States for their consideration at the fifth session of the Commission a proposal on the creation of a central repository for existing legislative and regulatory measures and information on organizational structures designed to combat organized transnational crime, taking into account the capabilities of the United Nations Crime and Justice Information Network and the activities of other United Nations and relevant intergovernmental bodies, with a view to making this information available to requesting Member States;

7. *Urges* Member States, entities of the United Nations system and relevant intergovernmental and nongovernmental organizations to assist the Secretary-General in implementing the request contained in paragraph 6 above, also by providing relevant information and legislative and regulatory texts;

8. *Requests* the Secretary-General as necessary to submit concrete proposals to the Commission for approval, with a view to developing practical models and guidelines for substantive and procedural legislation, building on the experience and expertise of States and drawing on contributions from relevant organizations, in order to assist, in particular, developing countries and countries in transition, upon request, in reviewing and evaluating their legislation and in planning and undertaking reforms, taking into account existing practices and cultural, legal and social traditions;

9. *Also requests* the Secretary-General to provide advisory services and technical assistance to requesting Member States in needs assessment, capacity-building and training, as well as in the implementation of the Naples Political Declaration and Global Action Plan;

10. *Further requests* the Secretary-General to seek cooperation and to join efforts with other international, global and regional organizations and mechanisms that have played an active role in combating money-laundering so as to reinforce common regulatory and enforcement strategies in that area and to assist States, upon request, in assessing their needs in treaty development and the development of criminal justice infrastructure and human resources and to provide technical assistance and as necessary to compile, drawing upon the expertise of Member States, and of other relevant organizations, appropriate manuals, taking into account differences in legal systems, using the expertise and cooperation of all the institutes and other relevant entities of the United Nations crime prevention and criminal justice programme, including the International Scientific and Professional Advisory Council;

11. *Requests* the Secretary-General to avail himself of the assistance of experts with extensive experience in the field of prevention and control of organized crime indicated by Member States, who might be called upon in connection with technical cooperation activities;

12. *Welcomes with appreciation* the preliminary report of the international task force on the study of the feasibility of establishing an international training centre for law enforcement and criminal justice personnel, and encourages the Government of Italy and the Governments of the other States members of the task force to continue and finalize its work, in accordance with the resolution adopted by the World Ministerial Conference on Organized Transnational Crime, with a view to informing the General Assembly at its fiftieth session;

13. *Also requests* the Secretary-General to report to the Commission on Crime Prevention and Criminal Justice on the implementation of the present resolution, including proposals for further action aimed at the full implementation of the Naples Political Declaration and Global Action Plan.

Economic and Social Council resolution 1995/11

24 July 1995          Meeting 49          Adopted without vote

Draft by Commission on Crime Prevention and Criminal Justice (E/1995/30); agenda item 5 *(g)*.
*Meeting numbers.* ESC 47-49.

In response to a 1994 General Assembly resolution,[38] which dealt with the Naples Political Declaration and Global Action Plan, the Secretary-General submitted a report[22] on the implementation of that resolution. He discussed action taken by the Commission (see above); steps taken within the international community towards making action against organized transnational crime a global priority; the programmatic aspects and modalities of implementing the Naples Political Declaration, including strengthening international cooperation, increasing reliable knowledge, providing assistance in the legislative and regulatory fields; and technical cooperation.

In his conclusions, the Secretary-General said that States should specify the activities that needed to be undertaken for implementation of the Naples Political Declaration and Global Action Plan, agree on the pace of such implementation and devote their energies and attention to achieving the common goals identified therein. Such action would enable the Commission and the United Nations to undertake rational and effective planning. He had begun implementing the priority attached to the fight against organized transnational crime in the proposed programme budget for 1996-1997. However, there was need for the regular budget to be supplemented by extrabudgetary resources, due to the vast needs of developing countries and countries in transition.

In **resolution 50/146**, the Assembly called on States and funding agencies to make financial contributions for operational activities for crime prevention and criminal justice and encouraged States to contribute to the UN Crime Prevention and Criminal Justice Trust Fund, also taking into account activities required to implement the Naples Political Declaration and Global Action Plan.

## Action against corruption

Pursuant to a 1994 Economic and Social Council resolution,[40] the Ninth United Nations Congress on the Prevention of Crime and the Treatment of Offenders,[1] at a special session held on 4 and 5 May, considered experiences in practical measures aimed at combating corruption involving public officials, based on a background paper prepared by the Secretariat.[41]

Among practical measures to be adopted at the national level, which were proposed at the Congress, were that independent bodies be established to monitor the activities of various government agencies, free from interference and undue influence. The judiciary should exercise effective control over the executive branch of government. At the administrative level, measures were required to eliminate unnecessary and cumbersome procedures, and checks and balances should be instituted at various levels of management and administration. Budgetary allocations and expenditures should be closely monitored and subjected to professional and independent auditing.

International cooperation was essential to combat corruption. Several countries had already engaged in and supported multilateral activities. The potential of the United Nations in that regard was highlighted. The draft manual on practical measures against corruption[42] was considered a commendable initiative, particularly in the context of technical cooperation. The draft international code of conduct for public office holders, prepared by the Secretariat, would constitute a useful complement of relevant efforts when revised and further considered. Several delegations indicated their intention to provide their comments on the draft to the Secretariat. It was suggested that technical assistance in the training of public officials, law enforcement and judicial personnel, and the staff of regulatory agencies should be strengthened and that the United Nations designate an international year to the fight against corruption.

ECONOMIC AND SOCIAL COUNCIL ACTION

On 24 July, the Economic and Social Council adopted **resolution 1995/14**.

### Action against corruption
*The Economic and Social Council,*

*Concerned* at the seriousness of problems posed by corruption, which may endanger the stability and security of societies, undermine the values of democracy and morality and jeopardize social, economic and political development,

*Also concerned* about the links of corruption with other forms of crime, particularly organized crime, economic crime and money-laundering,

*Convinced* that since corruption is a phenomenon that can cross national borders and affect all societies and economies, international cooperation to prevent and control it is essential,

*Deeply concerned* about the problems faced by States in this regard,

*Also convinced* of the need to provide technical assistance to developing countries and countries in transition designed to improve public management systems and enhance accountability and transparency,

*Recalling* the resolution on corruption in government, adopted by the Eighth United Nations Congress on the Prevention of Crime and the Treatment of Offenders,

*Recalling also* General Assembly resolutions 45/121 of 14 December 1990 and 46/152 of 18 December 1991 and Economic and Social Council resolutions 1992/22 of 30 July 1992, 1993/32 of 27 July 1993 and 1994/19 of 25 July 1994,

*Welcoming* the results of the special plenary meeting on corruption involving public officials, held during the Ninth United Nations Congress on the Prevention of Crime and the Treatment of Offenders,

1. *Urges* States, as necessary, to develop and implement specific and comprehensive anti-corruption strategies to enhance accountability, by adopting and enforcing civil, administrative, fiscal and criminal law measures, emphasizing, *inter alia*, transparency and fairness, including legislation to regulate and sanction corrupt forms of corporate behaviour and provide for the forfeiture and/or confiscation of proceeds derived from corrupt practices;

2. *Also urges* States to increase their capacity for the prevention, detection, investigation and prosecution of corrupt practices, by promoting public awareness, by appropriately strengthening their criminal justice systems and by establishing, as appropriate, independent bodies for the prevention and control of corruption;

3. *Further urges* States to increase and improve international cooperation for the prevention and control of corruption, including the use of arrangements for extradition, mutual legal assistance, the sharing of information and the collection of evidence;

4. *Takes note* of the draft international code of conduct for public office holders, in its revised form, annexed to the present resolution, and of the work done

to date in revising the text on the basis of comments received from Governments, and requests the Secretary-General to continue his consultations with Governments to revise the text further and to submit it to the Commission on Crime Prevention and Criminal Justice at its fifth session for consideration and action;

5. *Urges* States to provide their comments to the Secretary-General so as to facilitate the further revision of the draft international code of conduct for public office holders;

6. *Requests* the Secretary-General to review and expand the manual on practical measures against corruption, seeking contributions from relevant international organizations, with a view to increasing its use, in advisory services, training and other technical assistance activities;

7. *Also requests* the Secretary-General to cooperate and coordinate with other entities of the United Nations system and relevant international organizations, within their respective mandates, in undertaking joint activities in the field of the prevention and control of corruption and in maximizing the effect of such activities;

8. *Calls upon* States, relevant international organizations and financing institutions to extend to the Secretary-General their full support and assistance in the implementation of the present resolution;

9. *Further requests* the Secretary-General, in cooperation with the interregional and regional institutes of the United Nations crime prevention and criminal justice programme network, to study the effects of anti-corruption strategies in order to provide a comparative review of the most effective practices and to develop training and awareness curricula;

10. *Requests* the Commission on Crime Prevention and Criminal Justice to keep the issue of action against corruption under regular review;

11. *Requests* the Secretary-General to report to the Commission on Crime Prevention and Criminal Justice at its sixth session on the implementation of the present resolution.

### Annex
#### Draft international code of conduct for public office holders

#### I. General principles

1. A public office, as defined by national law, is a position of trust, implying a duty to act in the public interest. Therefore, the primary loyalty of public office holders shall be to the public interests of their country as expressed through the democratic institutions of government, and not to persons, political parties or specific government departments or agencies.

2. Public office holders shall ensure that they perform their functions in an efficient and effective manner. They shall at all times seek to ensure that public resources for which they are responsible are administered in the most effective and efficient manner.

[2bis. Public office holders shall be responsible for the proper conduct of the functions assigned to them by their hierarchical superior. Public office holders shall be under the obligation not to obey orders which do not conform to law and to inform their hierarchical superior accordingly. If their hierarchical superior reiterates the order in writing, such order shall be executed. In this case, responsibility shall rest with the hierarchical superior. The order whose objective constitutes a crime shall not be executed under any circumstances.]

3. Public office holders shall be attentive, fair and impartial in the performance of their functions and, in particular, in their relations with the public. They shall at no time afford any undue preferential treatment to any group or individual, discriminate against any group or individual, or otherwise abuse the power and authority vested in them. [This provision should not be interpreted as excluding any officially approved affirmative action policies to assist disadvantaged groups.]

#### II. Conflicts of interest and disqualification

4. Public office holders shall never in any way use their official authority for the advancement of their own or their family's personal or financial interest. They shall not engage in any transaction, acquire any position or function, or have any financial, commercial or other comparable interest that is incompatible with their office, functions and duties, or the discharge thereof.

5. All public office holders designated under national law shall, unless exempted, declare relevant business, commercial and financial interests, or activities undertaken for financial gain upon entering the service. This information shall be updated regularly. In situations of possible or perceived conflict of interest between public office holders' public duties and private interests, they shall disqualify themselves from any decision-making process relating to such conflict of interest.

6. Public office holders shall at no time use public property, services, or information acquired in the performance of, or as a result of, their official duties for activities not related to their official work.

7. Within a stated period after separation from public service, public office holders holding managerial positions shall, within the framework of national law, obtain governmental permission prior to accepting employment or consultancy assignments from business or private concerns that are in financial relationship with the governmental department or agency in which such officials were employed. During the same period after separation, such permission shall also be required prior to engaging in any private or business activity related to, or dependent on, their previous position in public service.

#### III. Disclosure of assets

8. Public office holders holding managerial or policy-making positions as designated by and pursuant to procedures established by national law, shall disclose all personal property, assets and liabilities, as well as those of their spouses and/or other dependants. Such office holders shall also provide detailed information on the source of any property or asset acquired after their appointment to a senior post. All information provided shall be treated as confidential and may be disclosed only within the framework of special procedures.

#### IV. Acceptance of gifts or other favours

9. Public office holders shall not place themselves in a position of being under the moral obligation to accord preferential treatment of special consideration to any person or entity [, for instance by accepting directly or indirectly any gift, gratuity, favour, entertainment, loan or anything of monetary value, above a certain limit to be defined by their employer].

[*Alternative formulation:* Public office holders must, as a matter of principle, refuse any gift which may have an influence on the exercise of their functions, performance of their duties or their judgement.]

### V. Confidential information

10. Matters of a confidential nature in the possession of public office holders shall be kept confidential, unless the performance of duty or the needs of justice strictly require otherwise. Such restrictions shall apply also after separation from service.

### VI. Political activity

11. The political activity of public office holders shall not be such as to impair public confidence in the impartial performance of their functions and duties.

### VII. Reporting, disciplinary action and implementation

[12. Public officials should report violations of this code to the appropriate authorities.]

[13. Public officials who knowingly and deliberately, or recklessly disregard the provisions of this code shall be subject to the appropriate disciplinary and administrative measures.]

[14. Serious violations of the provisions of this code may also be punishable by criminal sanctions, including forfeiture and confiscation of illicit proceeds with compensation to any injured party.]

[*Alternative formulations for a single paragraph to replace paragraphs 13 and 14:*

*Alternative 1:*

Public office holders who violate the provisions of this code shall be subject to the appropriate disciplinary, administrative or penal measures, as determined by national legal principles and procedures.

*Alternative 2:*

Public office holders who deliberately or negligently violate the provisions of this code shall be subject to disciplinary measures. Serious violations may also be punishable by criminal sanctions, including forfeiture and confiscation of illicit proceeds with compensation to any injured party.]

Economic and Social Council resolution 1995/14

24 July 1995　　　　Meeting 49　　　　Adopted without vote

Draft by Commission on Crime Prevention and Criminal Justice (E/1995/30); agenda item 5 *(g)*.
*Meeting numbers.* ESC 47-49.

## Alien smuggling

In a report[43] to the Commission on Crime Prevention and Criminal Justice, the Secretary-General presented information received from Barbados, Brunei Darussalam, Cuba, France, Germany, Malawi, Nepal, Oman, Spain and the Syrian Arab Republic and from the International Organization for Migration on measures to combat alien smuggling. The report updated information on the subject that he supplied to the General Assembly in 1994.[44]

**ECONOMIC AND SOCIAL COUNCIL ACTION**

On 24 July, the Economic and Social Council adopted **resolution 1995/10**.

### Criminal justice action to combat the organized smuggling of illegal migrants across national boundaries

*The Economic and Social Council,*

*Recalling* that the General Assembly, in its resolution 48/102 of 20 December 1993, requested the Commis-

sion on Crime Prevention and Criminal Justice at its third session to consider giving special attention to the question of the smuggling of aliens, in order to encourage international cooperation to address that problem within the framework of its mandate,

*Recalling also* its resolution 1994/14 of 25 July 1994, adopted on the recommendation of the Commission on Crime Prevention and Criminal Justice at its third session, in which it, *inter alia*, condemned the practice of smuggling illegal migrants, recognized that such smuggling was a widespread criminal activity frequently involving highly organized international syndicates, acknowledged the substantial role played by organized transnational crime in such smuggling and called upon all States to take effective and expeditious measures, such as the enactment or amendment of domestic criminal law, providing appropriate penalties to combat all aspects of organized crime activities constituting such smuggling,

*Alarmed* by the significant increase in the activities of transnational criminal organizations that profit illicitly by smuggling illegal migrants and threatening the lives and human rights of migrants,

*Concentrating its attention* on crime prevention and criminal justice, in particular the activities of those who organize and facilitate the smuggling of illegal migrants,

*Recognizing* that organized international criminal groups are becoming increasingly active and successful in smuggling individuals across national boundaries,

*Recognizing also* that by trafficking in illegal migrants such criminal groups often make enormous profits that are frequently used to finance numerous other criminal activities, thus bringing great harm to the States concerned,

*Concerned* that such activities endanger the lives of the individual migrants involved and entail severe costs for the international community, including the costs of rescue, medical care, food, housing and transportation,

*Acknowledging* that socio-economic factors influence the problem of illegal migrant smuggling and also contribute to the complexity of current international migration,

*Aware* that smugglers, particularly in the State of destination of the illegal migrants being smuggled, often force migrants into forms of debt bondage or servitude, commonly involving criminal activities, in order to pay for their passage,

*Convinced* of the need for all States to provide humane treatment and to protect fully the human rights of migrants,

*Recognizing* that such illegal migrant smuggling has high social and economic costs, often contributing to official corruption, and burdens law enforcement agencies in all States where illegal migrants transit or are found,

*Recalling* the undertaking of States parties to the Supplementary Convention on the Abolition of Slavery, the Slave Trade, and Institutions and Practices Similar to Slavery, done at Geneva on 7 September 1956, to take all practicable and necessary legislative and other measures to bring about progressively and as soon as possible the complete abolition or abandonment of the practice of debt bondage,

*Reaffirming* respect for the sovereignty and territorial integrity of all States, including their right to control immigration flows,

*Concerned* that the smuggling of illegal migrants undermines public confidence in policies and procedures for lawful immigration and for ensuring the protection of genuine refugees,

*Noting* that the smuggling of illegal migrants can involve criminal activities in many States, including the State where the smuggling scheme was planned, the State of nationality of the migrants, the State where the means of transport was prepared, the flag State of any vessels or aircraft that transport the migrants, States through which the migrants transit to their destination or in order to be repatriated, and the State of destination,

*Commending* those States that have enacted effective domestic legislation permitting seizure and forfeiture of all property, both real and personal, that is knowingly used in organized criminal activities aimed at smuggling illegal migrants, as well as all property, both real and personal, that constitutes, or is derived from, the proceeds of the smuggling, illegal transport, or labour of illegal migrants,

*Gravely concerned* that a significant number of States have not yet enacted domestic criminal legislation to combat all aspects of the smuggling of illegal migrants,

1. *Condemns once again* the practice of smuggling illegal migrants in violation of international standards and national law, and without regard to the safety, well-being and human rights of the migrants;

2. *Recognizes* that the smuggling of illegal migrants continues to be a widespread international criminal activity frequently involving highly organized international syndicates that traffic in human cargo, without regard for the dangerous and inhumane conditions to which illegal migrants are subjected, and in flagrant violation of domestic laws and international standards;

3. *Acknowledges* the substantial and harmful role played by organized transnational crime in activities related to the smuggling of illegal migrants in many parts of the world;

4. *Urges* States to share information, to coordinate law enforcement activities between national authorities in cooperation with the competent international bodies and carriers engaged in international transport, and otherwise to cooperate, if their law permits, in order to trace and arrest those who organize the smuggling of illegal migrants and to prevent the illegal transport by smugglers of third-country nationals through their territory;

5. *Calls upon* Member States and relevant specialized agencies and international organizations to take into account socio-economic factors and to cooperate at the bilateral and multilateral levels in addressing all aspects of the problem of organized smuggling of illegal migrants, including by promoting technical assistance so as to assist countries, at their request, in developing and implementing policies to prevent and criminalize clandestine traffic in illegal migrants and to punish those who engage in organizing such activity;

6. *Reaffirms* the need fully to observe international and national law in dealing with the smuggling of illegal migrants, including the provision of humane treatment and strict observance of all human rights of migrants;

7. *Reiterates* that international efforts to prevent the smuggling of illegal migrants should not inhibit legal migration or freedom of travel, or undercut the protection provided by international law to refugees;

8. *Encourages* States to take prompt and effective preventive measures, such as increasing vigilance at coastal ports, airports and land borders, as well as enhancing the professional skills of relevant personnel, to frustrate the objectives and activities of those who organize the smuggling of illegal migrants, thus protecting would-be migrants from exploitation and loss of life;

9. *Calls upon* all States that have not yet done so to take effective and expeditious measures such as the enactment or amendment if necessary of domestic criminal law, with a range of enforcement measures, providing appropriate penalties to combat all aspects of organized criminal activities constituting the smuggling and transport of illegal migrants, such as the production or distribution of false travel documents, money-laundering, extortion and misuse of international commercial aviation and maritime transport in violation of international standards;

10. *Welcomes* the report of the Secretary-General and the note by the Secretariat on measures taken by Member States and relevant specialized agencies and intergovernmental organizations to combat the smuggling of illegal migrants, which were prepared pursuant to General Assembly resolution 48/102;

11. *Requests* the Secretary-General to remind Member States which have not yet done so of the importance of responding to the notes verbales sent to all Member States on 10 February and 9 June 1994 concerning the criminal legislation that they have enacted and other measures that they have taken to combat the smuggling of illegal migrants, and to submit to the Commission on Crime Prevention and Criminal Justice at its fifth session an updated report on measures to combat such smuggling, containing a compilation and an analysis of the responses of Member States;

12. *Decides* that the ever-growing problem of organized smuggling of illegal migrants across national borders requires the continuing scrutiny of the international community in general and should be considered by the Commission on Crime Prevention and Criminal Justice at its fifth session in the context of the broader problem of organized transnational crime.

Economic and Social Council resolution 1995/10

24 July 1995     Meeting 49     Adopted without vote

Draft by Commission on Crime Prevention and Criminal Justice (E/1995/30); agenda item 5 *(g)*.
*Meeting numbers.* ESC 47-49.

## International traffic in minors

In accordance with a 1994 Commission on Crime Prevention and Criminal Justice decision,[45] a report[46] on the world situation with regard to international traffic in minors, prepared by the Latin American Institute for the Prevention of Crime and the Treatment of Offenders, was submitted to the Commission's May/June 1995 session. The report described UN action to deal with criminal offences involving minors and various illicit practices in the international traffic in minors, and analysed current legislation at the international, regional and national levels in respect of each aspect of the traffic in minors.

The report concluded that international traffic in minors was conducted by criminal organizations with international connections. Although some progress had been made, the machinery for the trafficking in and sale of children was to a large extent still unknown and insufficiently controlled. Furthermore, there was no international convention specifically covering the traffic in and sale of children and adolescents, and national legislation in many cases was not applied.

The report suggested that the Commission might strengthen its role in combating international traffic in minors by bringing up to date research on the features of such offences and the measures that could be adopted to counter them; evaluate the scope and applicability of criminal law and initiate a pro-child and anti-crime network in association with ICPO/Interpol, national police, immigration authorities and local community groups to increase awareness of child abuse and exploitation; collaborate with bodies concerned with military matters to prevent children from being the object of abuse in situations of armed conflict; study ways to prevent the international traffic in minors and punish traffickers; show how criminal law should be used to eliminate discriminatory practices and promote changes in behaviour; mount publicity campaigns; and analyse the aspects that could form the basis of specific legislation to be adopted at the national level against the sale of and trafficking in children, exploitation of children at work, sexual exploitation of children and trafficking in organs.

### Urban crime

In 1995, the Commission on Crime Prevention and Criminal Justice finalized the proposed guidelines for the prevention of urban crime, as requested by the Economic and Social Council in 1994[(47)] and by the 1995 Ninth United Nations Congress on the Prevention of Crime and the Treatment of Offenders.[(1)]

**ECONOMIC AND SOCIAL COUNCIL ACTION**

On 24 July, the Economic and Social Council adopted **resolution 1995/9**.

**Guidelines for the prevention of urban crime**
*The Economic and Social Council,*

*Recalling* its resolutions 1979/20 of 9 May 1979, 1984/48 of 25 May 1984, 1990/24 of 24 May 1990 and 1993/27 of 27 July 1993 and General Assembly resolutions 45/121 of 14 December 1990 and 46/152 of 18 December 1991,

*Recalling also* its resolutions 1992/22 of 30 July 1992 and 1993/34 of 27 July 1993,

*Recalling further* its resolution 1994/20 of 25 July 1994, and resolution 1, section IV, of the Ninth United Nations Congress on the Prevention of Crime and the Treatment of Offenders, in which the Ninth Congress invited the Commission on Crime Prevention and

Criminal Justice, at its fourth session, to finalize and adopt the proposed guidelines for cooperation and technical assistance in the field of urban crime prevention, annexed to resolution 1994/20,

*Recalling* the Milan Plan of Action, the United Nations Standard Minimum Rules for the Administration of Juvenile Justice (the Beijing Rules), the United Nations Guidelines for the Prevention of Juvenile Delinquency (the Riyadh Guidelines), the United Nations Standard Minimum Rules for Non-custodial Measures (the Tokyo Rules), the Declaration of Basic Principles of Justice for Victims of Crime and Abuse of Power, and the resolution on the prevention of urban crime adopted by the Eighth United Nations Congress on the Prevention of Crime and the Treatment of Offenders,

*Aware* of the universal character of urban crime,

*Recognizing* the usefulness of establishing guidelines to facilitate the prevention of urban crime,

*Seeking* to respond to the call by many States for technical cooperation programmes adapted to local conditions and needs,

1. *Adopts* the guidelines for cooperation and technical assistance in the field of urban crime prevention, annexed to the present resolution, which were considered by the Commission on Crime Prevention and Criminal Justice at its second, third and fourth sessions and by the Ninth United Nations Congress on the Prevention of Crime and the Treatment of Offenders, held at Cairo from 29 April to 8 May 1995, and which are designed to make urban crime prevention more effective;

2. *Requests* the Commission on Crime Prevention and Criminal Justice to ensure the publication of the guidelines in the most appropriate form;

3. *Exhorts* Member States to report to the Secretary-General on their experiences in elaborating and evaluating projects dealing with urban crime prevention, taking into account the guidelines;

4. *Invites* the interregional, regional and affiliated institutes cooperating with the United Nations in the field of crime prevention and criminal justice and non-governmental organizations to share their experiences in urban crime prevention;

5. *Requests* the Secretary-General to transmit the guidelines to the United Nations Conference on Human Settlements (Habitat II), to be held at Istanbul from 3 to 14 June 1996;

6. *Requests* the Commission on Crime Prevention and Criminal Justice to consider practical ways of ensuring follow-up on the use and application of the guidelines;

7. *Calls upon* the United Nations Development Programme, other relevant United Nations organizations and bodies and international financial institutions to give appropriate consideration to the inclusion in their assistance programmes of projects dealing with urban crime prevention.

#### Annex
#### Guidelines for cooperation and technical assistance in the field of urban crime prevention

A. *Design and implementation of cooperation and assistance activities*

1. Cooperation projects for urban crime prevention should take account of the principles set out below.

    1. *Local approach to problems*

2. Urban crime is characterized by a multiplicity of factors and forms. A multi-agency approach and a

coordinated response at the local level, in accordance with an integrated crime prevention action plan, will often be helpful. This should involve:

(*a*)  A local diagnostic survey of crime phenomena, their characteristics, factors leading to them, the form they take and their extent;

(*b*)  The identification of all the relevant actors that could take part in compiling the above-mentioned diagnostic survey in crime prevention as well as in the fight against crime, for example public institutions (national or local), local elected officials, the private sector (associations, enterprises), the voluntary sector, community representatives etc.;

(*c*)  The establishment, wherever appropriate, of consultation mechanisms promoting closer liaison, the exchange of information, joint work and the design of a coherent strategy;

(*d*)  The elaboration of possible solutions to these problems in the local context.

### 2. *Integrated crime prevention action plan*

3.  The authors of an integrated crime prevention action plan, in order for it to be comprehensive and efficient, should:

(*a*)  Define:

(i)   The nature and types of crime problems to be tackled, such as theft, robbery, burglary, racial attacks, drug related crimes, juvenile delinquency and illegal possession of firearms, taking into account all the factors that may directly or indirectly cause such problems or contribute to them;

(ii)  The objectives being pursued and the time by which they should be attained;

(iii) The action envisaged and the respective responsibilities of those involved *vis-à-vis* the implementation of the plan (for example, whether local or national resources are to be mobilized);

(*b*)  Consider involving a range of actors representing in particular:

(i)   Social workers and education, housing and health workers, in addition to the police, the courts, public prosecutors and probation services etc.;

(ii)  The community: elected officials, associations, volunteers, parents, victims' organizations etc.;

(iii) The economic sector: enterprises, banks, business, public transport etc.;

(iv)  The media;

(*c*)  Consider the relevance to the crime prevention action plan of such factors as:

(i)   Relationships in the family, between generations or between social groups etc.;

(ii)  Education, religious, moral and civic values, culture etc.;

(iii) Employment, training, measures for combating unemployment and poverty;

(iv)  Housing and urbanism;

(v)   Health, drug and alcohol abuse;

(vi)  Government and community welfare aid for the least fortunate members of society;

(vii) Combating the culture of violence and intolerance;

(*d*)  Consider providing for action at various levels:

(i)   Primary prevention by:

a.   Promoting situational criminal prevention measures, such as target hardening and opportunity reduction;

b.   Promoting welfare and health development and progress and combating all forms of social deprivation;

c.   Promoting communal values and respect for fundamental human rights;

d.   Promoting civic responsibility and social mediation procedures;

e.   Facilitating the adaptation of the working methods of the police and the courts;

(ii)  Prevention of recidivism by:

a.   Facilitating the adaptation of methods of police intervention (rapid response, intervention within the local community etc.);

b.   Facilitating the adaptation of methods of judicial intervention and implementation of alternative remedies:

i.   Diversification of methods of treatment and of measures taken according to the nature and seriousness of the cases (diversionary schemes, mediation, a special system for minors etc.);

ii.  Systematic research on the reintegration of offenders involved in urban crime through the implementation of non-custodial measures;

iii. Socio-educational support within the framework of the sentence, in prison and as preparation for release from prison;

c.   Giving an active role to the community in the rehabilitation of offenders;

(iii) After the sentence has been served: aid and socio-educational support, family support etc.;

(iv)  Protection of victims by practical improvements in their treatment by means of the following:

a.   Raising awareness of rights and how to exercise them effectively;

b.   Reinforcing rights (in particular the right to compensation);

c.   Introducing systems of victim assistance.

### B.   *Implementation of the action plan*
#### 1.   *Central authorities*

4.  The central authorities, to the extent consistent with their competence, should:

(*a*)  Provide active support, assistance and encouragement to local actors;

(*b*)  Coordinate national policy and strategies with local strategies and needs;

(*c*)  Organize consultation and cooperation mechanisms between the various administrations concerned at the central level.

#### 2.   *Authorities at all levels*

5.  Competent authorities at all levels should:

(*a*)  Be constantly mindful of respect for the fundamental principles of human rights in promoting these activities;

(*b*)  Encourage and/or implement appropriate training and information to support all professionals involved in crime prevention;

(*c*)  Compare experiences and organize exchanges of know-how;

(*d*)  Provide a means of evaluating regularly the effectiveness of the strategy implemented and provide for the possibility of revising it.

Economic and Social Council resolution 1995/9

24 July 1995      Meeting 49      Adopted without vote

Draft by Commission on Crime Prevention and Criminal Justice (E/1995/30);
    agenda item 5 *(g)*.

*Meeting numbers.* ESC 47-49.

## Crime prevention institutes

In a report[48] to the Commission on Crime Prevention and Criminal Justice, the Secretary-General reviewed the 1994 activities of UN bodies and institutions concerned with crime prevention, including the UN Interregional Crime and Justice Research Institute (UNICRI), regional institutes affiliated with the United Nations—the African Institute for the Prevention of Crime and Treatment of Offenders (UNAFRI), the Asia and Far East Institute for the Prevention of Crime and the Treatment of Offenders, the European Institute for Crime Prevention and Control, affiliated with the UN, and the Latin American Institute for the Prevention of Crime and the Treatment of Offenders—and associate institutes, such as the Arab Security Studies and Training Centre, the Australian Institute of Criminology, the International Centre for Criminal Law Reform and Criminal Justice Policy and the International Institute of Higher Studies in Criminal Sciences. He also reported on the activities of the International Scientific and Professional Advisory Council. The Secretary-General drew a number of matters to the attention of the Commission and said that, despite the increasing demands made on it and without the human and financial resources to match them, the UN crime prevention and criminal justice programme network continued to support and reinforce the UN crime prevention and criminal justice programme.

In an addendum to his report,[49] the Secretary-General drew the attention of the Commission to the list of nominees to fill the three vacancies on the Board of Trustees of UNICRI.

On 24 July, by **decision 1995/241**, the Economic and Social Council endorsed the appointment by the Commission of Jan J. van Dijk (Netherlands), Karoly Bard (Hungary) and Adedokun A. Adeyemi (Nigeria) to fill the vacancies on the Board of UNICRI.

## UNAFRI

In response to a 1994 General Assembly request,[50] the Secretary-General submitted a report[51] on the status of UNAFRI's recent operations, its staffing, programme activities and funding.

UNAFRI continued to conduct training activities to upgrade the skills, knowledge and expertise of crime prevention and criminal justice personnel in the region. It conducted studies on the resettlement of street children in Kampala, Uganda, and on the rehabilitation of prisoners. The Governing Board approved two research activities for implementation in 1995: the continuation of the African crime, victimization and criminal justice administration survey, and a study on the resettlement of street children in other African countries. The Institute improved cooperation with other relevant organizations and agencies operating in the area and published its biannual newsletter. It expanded compilation of African country profiles and the roster of African experts in crime prevention and criminal justice and continued to develop a specialized reference library on crime prevention and the treatment of offenders.

In January, the Governing Board appointed Isam Abugideri as Director of the Institute.

### Financial situation

The financial situation of the Institute remained precarious in 1995. On 6 April, the General Assembly, by **decision 49/480**, redeployed the amount of $119,700 from section 3 of the 1994-1995 programme budget to section 15 (Economic Commission for Africa). That additional funding would enable UNAFRI to meet its 1995 administrative expenses.

The Conference of Ministers of the Economic Commission for Africa (Addis Ababa, Ethiopia, 26-27 April)[52] appealed to those States that had not done so to make timely contributions, including payment of arrears, within a reasonable time to guarantee the survival and the implementation of the work programme of the Institute. It also appealed to the Administrator of UNDP to renew its programme support to the Institute, taking into account the difficult economic and financial situation faced by most countries in the African region, and to continue its financial support to enable the Institute to meet its administrative obligations on a sustained basis. ECA also endorsed the recommendation of the Governing Board that the Chairmanship of the Board should be held by member States on a two-year rotational base from among members of the Board and approved the composition of the Board for 1995-1999.

In his report to the Assembly on the Institute,[51] the Secretary-General stated that major efforts had been made to mobilize financial, technical and political support for the Institute. However, while some limited contributions might be forthcoming, the financial situation of the Institute remained a matter of serious concern. He proposed that the Assembly authorize the appropriation of additional funds for the Institute in the 1996-1997 programme budget. In the meantime, the Institute would urge its members to speed up payment of their assessed contributions through a special appeal and mount a vigorous fundraising campaign for additional donations. It was also important that UNDP continue supporting the Institute beyond 1995.

**GENERAL ASSEMBLY ACTION**

On 21 December, the General Assembly adopted **resolution 50/147**.

**United Nations African Institute for the Prevention of Crime and the Treatment of Offenders**

*The General Assembly,*

*Recalling* its resolution 49/156 of 23 December 1994,

*Recalling also* Economic and Social Council resolution 1994/21 of 25 July 1994, .

*Aware* of the financial difficulties that the United Nations African Institute for the Prevention of Crime and the Treatment of Offenders continues to face as a result of the fact that many States of the African region are in the category of least developed countries and therefore lack the necessary resources with which to support the Institute,

*Conscious* of the efforts made thus far by the Institute in fulfilling its mandate through, *inter alia*, the organization of training programmes and regional seminars, as well as the provision of advisory services,

*Having considered* the report of the Secretary-General,

1. *Commends* the United Nations African Institute for the Prevention of Crime and the Treatment of Offenders for the activities it has undertaken, despite its difficulties in fulfilling its mandate, as reflected in the progress report of the Secretary-General on the activities of the United Nations Interregional Crime and Justice Research Institute and other institutes;

2. *Expresses its appreciation* to those Governments and intergovernmental bodies which have supported the Institute in the discharge of its responsibilities;

3. *Appeals* to Governments and intergovernmental and non-governmental organizations to provide financial and technical support to the Institute to enable it to fulfil its objectives, in particular those concerning training, technical assistance, policy guidance, research and data collection;

4. *Requests* the Secretary-General to ensure that the Institute is provided with adequate funds, within the overall appropriation of the programme budget and from extrabudgetary resources, and to submit proposals for any necessary additional funding of the Institute, in accordance with General Assembly resolution 49/156 and its decision 49/480 of 6 April 1995;

5. *Requests* the Administrator of the United Nations Development Programme to reconsider its decision with regard to its financial support to the Institute and to continue providing appropriate funds for the institutional strengthening and the implementation of the programme of work of the Institute, taking into account the difficult economic and financial situation faced by many countries in the African region;

6. *Also requests* the Secretary-General to ensure proper follow-up with all concerned on the implementation of the present resolution and to report thereon to the General Assembly at its fifty-first session and to the Commission on Crime Prevention and Criminal Justice at its fifth session.

General Assembly resolution 50/147

21 December 1995     Meeting 97     Adopted without vote

Approved by Third Committee (A/50/629) without vote, 29 November (meeting 42); draft by South Africa, for African Group (A/C.3/50/L.16), orally revised; agenda item 106.

*Meeting numbers.* GA 50th session: 3rd Committee 12-17, 25, 42; plenary 97.

*REFERENCES*

[1]A/CONF.169/16. [2]YUN 1988, p. 690. [3]ST/CSDHA/22. [4]YUN 1994, p. 1160. [5]*Human Rights: A Compilation of International Instruments*, Sales No. E.94.XIV.1. [6]GA res. 44/25, annex, 20 Nov. 1989. [7]A/CONF.169/4. [8]A/CONF.169/5. [9]A/CONF.169/6. [10]A/CONF.169/7. [11]E/1995/30 & Add.1. [12]A/50/373. [13]YUN 1994, p. 1172, GA res. 49/157, 23 Dec. 1994. [14]YUN 1992, p. 842, ESC res. 1992/1, 6 Feb. 1992. [15]E/1995/30 (res. 4/1). [16]Ibid. (res. 4/2). [17]Ibid. (res. 4/3). [18]E/CN.15/1995/12. [19]E/CN.15/1995/10. [20]A/50/432. [21]YUN 1994, p. 1151, GA res. 49/158, 23 Dec. 1994. [22]A/50/433. [23]A/50/6. [24]E/1995/L.55. [25]E/CN.15/1995/6. [26]E/CN.15/1995/6/Add.1. [27]YUN 1993, p. 1007, ESC res. 1994/34, 27 July 1993. [28]YUN 1994, p. 1155, ESC res. 1994/18, 25 July 1994. [28]E/CN.15/1995/7. [30]YUN 1979, p. 779, GA res. 34/169, annex, 17 Dec. 1979. [31]*Eighth United Nations Congress on the Prevention of Crime and the Treatment of Offenders, Havana, 27 August–7 September 1990: report prepared by the Secretariat*, Sales No. E.91.IV.2. [32]YUN 1985, p. 743, GA res. 40/34, annex, 29 Nov. 1985. [33]*Compendium of United Nations Standards and Norms in Crime Prevention and Criminal Justice*, Sales No. E.92.IV.1 & corrigendum. [34]YUN 1994, p. 1156, ESC res. 1994/17, 25 July 1994. [35]E/CN.15/1995/7/Add.1. [36]E/CN.15/1995/11. [37]E/CN.15/1995/2. [38]YUN 1994, p. 1161, GA 49/159, 23 Dec. 1994. [39]E/CN.15/1995/11. [40]YUN 1994, p. 1169, ESC res. 1994/19, 25 July 1994. [41]A/CONF.169/14. [42]*International Review of Criminal Policy*, Nos. 41 and 42, Sales No. E.93.IV.4. [43]E/CN.15/1995/3. [44]YUN 1994, p. 1167. [45]YUN 1994, p. 1149. [46]E/CN.15/1995/4. [47]YUN 1994, p. 1165, GA res. 1994/20, 25 July 1994. [48]E/CN.15/1995/9. [49]E/CN.15/1995/9/Add.1. [50]YUN 1994, p. 1175, GA res. 49/156, 23 Dec. 1994. [51]A/50/375. [52]E/1995/38 (res. 806(XXX)).

# Human resources

## Human resource development

In response to a 1993 General Assembly request,[1] the Secretary-General submitted a report[2] on developing human resources for development. He examined the status of human resource development: the concept, constraints and definitions; reviewed progress made by developing countries at the national level, described the operational activities of the UN system, the coordination of its activities and development of an integrated approach; and discussed the Copenhagen Declaration and Programme of Action of the World Summit for Social Development as they related to human resource development.[3]

The Secretary-General recommended that the UN system should continue to move towards greater specificity in its definitions and conceptualization of human resource development, and that the participating agencies in the Administrative Committee on Coordination Subcommittee on

Rural Development should explore ways to deepen their understanding and pool their knowledge and experiences on human resource development and design mechanisms for coordination at the regional and national level. The fundamental global changes in the areas of employment and work should be a major research and policy/priority for the UN system. Overall government frameworks were needed to provide useful structure, coordination and monitoring for national human resource development strategies, with a focus on involving organizations of civil society more directly to deliver services at all levels in social development efforts.

Regional initiatives to assist countries in making integrated human resource development strategies operational should be continued, with the UN system supporting those efforts by improving linkages and providing global communication of commonalities and differences across regions. The needs of women and girls, the vulnerable, the disabled and the ageing in the developing world should be given special attention by the UN system during the follow-up to the World Summit for Social Development. The United Nations should also ensure that training was focused on sustainable learning of lasting benefit to those trained, and that its support reached substantial portions of those in need of training. It should improve the monitoring of its own efforts and strengthen countries' abilities to monitor theirs. The UN Statistical Commission and the Department for Economic and Social Information and Policy Analysis should develop a common system of social development indicators, social impact assessment and performance appraisal methods. Countries and UN agencies should cooperate to identify resource and expenditure flows to permit identification of people-centred development costs as a proportion of total costs.

GENERAL ASSEMBLY ACTION

On 20 December, the General Assembly adopted **resolution 50/105**.

### Developing human resources for development
*The General Assembly,*

*Reaffirming* its resolutions 48/205 of 21 December 1993, 46/143 of 17 December 1991 and 45/191 of 21 December 1990, as well as its resolutions S-18/3 of 1 May 1990 and 45/199 of 21 December 1990,

*Reaffirming* that people are central to all activities related to development and that human resources development is an essential means of achieving sustainable development goals,

*Recognizing* that human resources development should contribute to total human development, which enlarges the choices available to people in developing their lives and fulfilling their aspirations, and that there is a need to integrate human resources development into comprehensive strategies for human development that main-

streams a gender perspective, taking into account the needs of all people, in particular the needs of women,

*Stressing* that there is need for a supportive and favourable international economic environment that will enhance human development in developing countries and promote economic growth and development,

*Recognizing* that, while economic reforms and structural adjustment programmes are intended to promote economic growth and development, elements of such programmes may have an adverse impact on human resources development, and also that there is a need to take action, in the formulation and implementation of these programmes, to mitigate any negative effects,

*Stressing* the need for adequate resources to enhance the capacity of Governments of developing countries to promote human resources development in pursuit of their national programmes, plans and strategies for development,

*Stressing also* that Governments of developing countries have the primary responsibility for defining and implementing appropriate policies for human resources development,

*Recognizing* the vital role that South-South and North-South cooperation play in supporting national efforts in human resources development, bilaterally as well as multilaterally,

*Emphasizing* the need for coordination and integration among the organs and organizations of the United Nations system in assisting developing countries to foster the development of their human resources, especially that of the most vulnerable, and for the United Nations to continue to give priority to human resources development in developing countries,

*Recognizing* the importance accorded in the Copenhagen Declaration on Social Development and in the Programme of Action of the World Summit for Social Development to the human component of development,

*Recognizing also* the importance of the Platform for Action adopted at the recently concluded Fourth World Conference on Women, held at Beijing from 4 to 15 September 1995,

1. *Takes note with appreciation* of the report of the Secretary-General on developing human resources for development;

2. *Emphasizes* that, in the development of human resources, an overall, well-conceived and integrated approach that mainstreams a gender perspective and takes into account the needs of all people should be adopted, incorporating such vital areas as population, health, nutrition, water, sanitation, housing, communications, education and training, and science and technology, as well as taking into account the need to create more opportunities for employment in an environment that guarantees opportunities for political freedom, popular participation, respect for human rights, justice and equity, all of which are essential for enhancing human capacity to meet the challenge of development;

3. *Encourages* all countries to accord priority, in particular in national budgets, to human resources development in the context of the adoption of economic and social policies;

4. *Emphasizes* the need to ensure the full participation of women in the formulation and implementation of national policies to promote human resources development;

5. *Calls upon* the international community to support national efforts to develop human resources for development by increasing the priority of resources for those activities;

6. *Calls upon* the relevant organs, organizations and bodies of the United Nations system to ensure the coordination of activities in support of national and regional action in the area of human resources development;

7. *Emphasizes* that structural adjustment programmes should include social development goals, in particular the eradication of poverty, the promotion of full and productive employment, and the enhancement of social integration;

8. *Also emphasizes* that Governments and relevant institutions should ensure, where appropriate, an adequate social safety net under structural adjustment programmes and should develop policies to reduce the negative effects of these programmes and to improve their positive impact, bearing in mind that social safety nets associated with economic restructuring are short-term by nature and should be considered as complementary strategies;

9. *Acknowledges* the action taken thus far by the United Nations system in operational activities in the area of human resources development, and urges further action in accordance with resolutions of the General Assembly on human resources for development;

10. *Notes with serious concern* the worrisome trend of a decrease in overall development assistance, which affects the level of resources for human resources development, and emphasizes that financial commitment to human resources development is of critical importance in contributing to the enhancement of the concept of people-centred sustainable development;

11. *Calls for* follow-up action to be taken as recommended in the Programme of Action of the World Summit for Social Development and in the Platform for Action adopted at Beijing, in order to ensure the strengthening of human resources development;

12. *Requests* the Secretary-General to take into account the outcome of the upcoming United Nations Conference on Human Settlements (Habitat II) in the context of human resources development;

13. *Also requests* the Secretary-General to continue to monitor the activities of the United Nations system in human resources development and to submit to the General Assembly at its fifty-second session a report on the implementation of the present resolution, including further action taken by the United Nations system with regard to human resources development and the enhancement of inter-agency coordination;

14. *Decides* to include in the provisional agenda of its fifty-second session, under the item entitled "Sustainable development and international economic cooperation", a sub-item entitled "Human resources development".

General Assembly resolution 50/105

20 December 1995     Meeting 96     Adopted without vote

Approved by Second Committee (A/50/617/Add.7) without vote, 8 December (meeting 42); draft by Vice-Chairman (A/C.2/50/L.70), based on informal consultations on draft by Philippines, for Group of 77 and China (A/C.2/50/L.34); agenda item 95 *(g)*.

*Meeting numbers.* GA 50th session: 2nd Committee 30-32, 38, 42; plenary 96.

## UN research and training institutes

### UN Institute for Training and Research

In a note to the General Assembly,[4] the Secretary-General submitted a summary of ongoing activities and a brief identification of potential developments of the United Nations Institute for Training and Research (UNITAR), prepared at the request of the Board of Trustees of the Institute. UNITAR had completed its restructuring phase and was entering a phase of consolidation. Programmes were developing and gaining credibility and the financial situation, though still fragile, was more stable. Training programmes in the areas of multilateral diplomacy and related disciplines and economic and social development had been continuously expanding and evolving through the restructuring process. As the number and range of activities increased, so did the need to better register and document methodology and end-results. There was a pressing need to have the capacity to design and develop appropriate training materials and to excel in the conduct of problem-clarification exercises with key players.

The Secretary-General stated that UNITAR now had the possibility to enhance its intellectual relevance, further strengthen the credibility of its training activities, and ensure that those, as well as the financial means of accomplishing them, reached a certain critical mass. However, a coherent and efficient funding strategy had to be designed to ensure a minimum of predictability and sustainability. Such a secure financial basis would also consolidate existing programmes and accelerate their development, thus enabling the Institute to respond more promptly to requests for training. To enhance and extend the quality and number of training services provided to Member States, the Board of Trustees had decided that the Institute would open, without delay, a liaison office in New York.

On 27 November, during consideration by the Assembly's Second (Economic and Financial) Committee, the Director of Financial Management, Department of Administration and Management, said that, following the Committee's decision to consider issues relating to UNITAR on a biennial basis, the Secretary-General would submit an oral report during the current year. In accordance with a 1994 General Assembly request,[5] the Secretary-General had provided office space for the Institute in Geneva as well as administrative and logistic support. As the financial situation had improved, the Board of Trustees had initiated discussions on the setting up of a liaison office in New York. Related expenditure would be covered by the Institute's resources, and the Board would ensure that the funds were available before proceeding. The Secretary-General had instructed the Head of the Training Service to coordinate the training programmes offered in New York, and the Board had set up a subcommittee to study the strengthening of cooperation between the Institute and other national and international institutions, including the International Training Centre of the International Labour Organization in Turin, Italy. UNITAR envisaged offering a training programme on international trade in collaboration with the World Trade Organization and was considering other subjects. It was also studying using the facilities in Turin.

**GENERAL ASSEMBLY ACTION**

On 20 December, the General Assembly adopted **resolution 50/121**.

**United Nations Institute for Training and Research**

*The General Assembly,*

*Recalling* its resolutions 47/227 of 8 April 1993, 48/207 of 21 December 1993 and 49/125 of 19 December 1994,

*Having considered* the report prepared upon the request of the Board of Trustees of the United Nations Institute for Training and Research, entitled "Summary of ongoing activities and brief identification of potential developments of the United Nations Institute for Training and Research", and taking into account the statements made before the Second Committee of the General Assembly,

*Recognizing* the successful implementation of the transfer of the headquarters of the United Nations Institute for Training and Research from New York to Geneva and the Institute's consolidating itself at its new location,

*Taking note with interest* of the measures taken to complete the restructuring process of the Institute,

*Welcoming* the measures already taken pursuant to resolution 49/125 in order to resolve the problem the Institute had been experiencing with respect to the rent of its Geneva headquarters,

*Recognizing* that training activities should be accorded a more visible and larger role in support of the management of international affairs and in the execution of the economic and social development programmes of the United Nations system,

1. *Reaffirms* the relevance of the United Nations Institute for Training and Research, particularly in view of the many training requirements of all Member States;

2. *Invites* the Institute to further develop its cooperation with United Nations institutes and other relevant national, regional and international institutes;

3. *Welcomes* the decision of the Board of Trustees of the Institute, at its thirty-third session and at its special session, inviting the Institute to open a liaison office in New York, in so far as this is possible within its existing resources and pursuant to General Assembly resolutions 47/227 and 49/125, in order to respond to the training needs of the Missions and delegations of Member States in New York and in order to strengthen its cooperative relationship with the United Nations Secretariat;

4. *Urges* all Member States to consider resuming or increasing their voluntary contributions to the restructured United Nations Institute for Training and Research, in particular to its General Fund;

5. *Encourages* the Secretary-General to take relevant measures with respect to the regularization of the Executive Director of the Institute, taking into account the recommendations of the Board of Trustees;

6. *Requests* the Secretary-General, duly taking into account the deliberations of the Board of Trustees, to submit a report to the General Assembly at its fifty-first session on possible ways to strengthen the training activities of the United Nations Institute for Training and Research and to better define its role.

General Assembly resolution 50/121

20 December 1995     Meeting 96     Adopted without vote

Approved by Second Committee (A/50/620) without vote, 8 December (meeting 42); draft by Vice-Chairman (A/C.2/50/L.63), based on informal consultations on draft by Argentina, Cameroon, Chile, China, Nigeria and Pakistan (A/C.2/50/L.43); agenda item 98.

*Meeting numbers.* GA 50th session: 2nd Committee 39, 40, 42; plenary 96.

## Financial report and audited financial statements

In the financial report and audited financial statements covering UNITAR for the year ended 31 December 1994,[6] the Board of Auditors welcomed the improved financial control of UNITAR operations. The UNITAR General Fund administrative expenditure was reduced to $595,977 in 1994 compared with $700,129 in 1993 and expenditure was substantially within the budget set by the Board of Trustees ($776,100). Total income generated by the General Fund was $800,430, resulting in an operating surplus for 1994 of $204,453.

The Board recommended that expenditure statements in respect of UNDP-financed projects should be submitted by UNITAR each year, to allow programme support income to be accounted for promptly. Also, UNITAR should follow UN procurement procedures and adhere more closely to UN Financial Regulations and Rules on procurement of goods and services.

**GENERAL ASSEMBLY ACTION**

On 23 December, the General Assembly adopted **resolution 50/204 D**.

*The General Assembly,*

*Recalling* its resolutions 47/211 of 23 December 1992 and 48/216 B of 23 December 1993, as well as previous relevant resolutions,

1. *Regrets* the delay in the submission of a report on measures taken or proposed to be taken by the United Nations Institute for Training and Research in response to the recommendations of the Board of Auditors for the year ended 31 December 1994;

2. *Requests* the Institute to submit such reports in a timely manner in order to allow Member States to consider them properly before the beginning of formal discussions during future sessions of the General Assembly.

General Assembly resolution 50/204 D

23 December 1995     Meeting 100     Adopted without vote

Approved by Fifth Committee (A/50/839) without vote, 21 December (meeting 44); draft by Vice-Chairman (A/C.5/50/L.20, part D) following informal consultations; agenda item 113.

*Meeting numbers.* GA 50th session: 5th Committee 21, 25, 27, 44; plenary 100.

## UN University

### UNU activities

The year 1995 marked the twentieth anniversary of the United Nations University (UNU), an autonomous academic institution within the UN system. During the year,[7] UNU continued to carry out its research on universal human values and global responsibilities; new directions in the world economy; sustaining global life-support systems; advances in science and technology; and population dynamics and human welfare. Four UNU research and training centres were fully operational: the World Institute for Development Economics Research (WIDER) (Helsinki, Finland); the Institute for New Technologies (INTECH) (Maastricht, the Netherlands); the International Institute for Software Technology (IIST) (Macau); and the Institute for Natural Resources in Africa (INRA) (Accra, Ghana). In addition, the University established a new International Leadership Academy in Amman, Jordan, in 1995. It also continued its Programme for Biotechnology in Latin America and the Caribbean (BIOLAC) in Caracas, Venezuela, and established a new research and training centre, the Institute of Advanced Studies (IAS) in Tokyo, Japan.

During 1995, 82 fellowships were awarded for training in UNU research and training centres and associated and other cooperating institutions. They included 23 in natural resources and the environment; 16 in geothermal energy; 15 in biotechnology at UNU/IIST and 12 at UNU/BIOLAC; 11 in food and nutrition; 1 in micro-informatics; and 4 in other fields. In addition, some 500 individuals attended UNU training workshops.

Among the 29 titles published during the year were *The United Nations System: The Policies of Member States*; *State, Society, and the United Nations System: Changing Perspectives on Multilateralism*; *Hydropolitics along the Jordan River: Scarce Water and Its Impact on the Arab-Israeli Conflict*; *Managing Water for Peace in the Middle East: Alternative Strategies*; *Steering Business Toward Sustainability*; *Amazonia: Resiliency and Dynamism of the Land and its People*; *Regions at Risk: Comparisons of Threatened Environments*; *In Place of the Forest: Environmental and Socio-economic Transformation in Borneo and the Eastern Malay Peninsula*; *Emerging World Cities in Pacific Asia*; *Global Employment: An International Investigation into the Future of Work*; and *Ethnicity and Power in the Contemporary World*.

### UNU Council

At its forty-second session (Tokyo, 4-8 December),[7] the UNU Council examined the University's work in the final year of its second Medium-Term Perspective (1990-1995) and reviewed the draft third Medium-Term Perspective (1996-2001). The Council noted the need for more systematic reporting of the work of the University to permit a more critical assessment by the Council of its activities. It expressed concern about the state of UNU/INRA and the lack of staff and financial resources which had hampered implementation of programme activities. The Council urged the Rector to continue to harmonize standards and procedures for electronic communication throughout the UNU system. It asked him to assess UNU fellowship and training activities and to develop a strategy to ensure a more coherent implementation of those activities, including an appropriate geographic balance in their distribution; and to study UNU's publishing activities with the aim of improving efficiency and cost-effectiveness. The Council designated members of a Nominating Committee to prepare a list of candidates for the post of Rector, who would begin his/her term in September 1997.

On 27 July, by **decision 1995/310**, the Economic and Social Council took note of the report of the UNU Council for 1994.[8]

## University for Peace

In accordance with a 1993 resolution,[9] the General Assembly considered at its 1995 session the item entitled "University for Peace".

GENERAL ASSEMBLY ACTION

On 8 December, the General Assembly adopted **resolution 50/41**.

#### University for Peace

*The General Assembly,*

*Recalling* that in its resolution 34/111 of 14 December 1979 it approved the idea of establishing the University for Peace as a specialized international centre for postgraduate studies, research and the dissemination of knowledge specifically aimed at training and education for peace and its universal promotion within the system of the United Nations University,

*Recalling also* that in its resolution 35/55 of 5 December 1980 it approved the establishment of the University for Peace in conformity with the International Agreement for the Establishment of the University for Peace,

*Recalling further* its resolutions 45/8 of 24 October 1990 and 46/11 of 24 October 1991, on the tenth anniversary of the University for Peace and the report of the Secretary-General on that anniversary, and its resolution 48/9 of 25 October 1993, in which it decided to include in the agenda of its fiftieth session the item entitled "University for Peace",

*Recognizing* that the University has suffered from financial limitations which have impeded the full development of the activities and programmes necessary for carrying out its important mandate,

*Recognizing also* the important and varied activities carried out by the University during the period 1993-1995, largely thanks to the financial contributions made by Canada, Costa Rica, the Netherlands and Spain and contributions by foundations and non-governmental organizations,

*Noting* that in 1991 the Secretary-General, with the assistance of the United Nations Development Programme, established a Trust Fund for Peace consisting of voluntary contributions in order to provide the University with the means necessary to extend its sphere of activity to the rest of the world, to take full advantage of its potential capacity for education, research and support of the United Nations and to carry out its mandate of promoting peace in the world,

*Noting also* that the University has placed special emphasis, in the context of the report of the Secretary-General entitled "An Agenda for Peace", on the area of conflict prevention, peace-keeping and peace-building, as well as on the peaceful settlement of disputes,

*Considering* the importance of promoting an education for peace which will help to foster respect for the values inherent in peace and universal coexistence among human beings, such as respect for life, friendship and solidarity between peoples and the dignity and integrity of persons irrespective of their nationality, race, sex, religion or culture,

*Taking into account* the efforts being made by the United Nations Educational, Scientific and Cultural Organization for the development and promotion of a new culture of peace,

*Noting further* the research activities for international peace and security being carried out by the United Nations University,

*Recalling* that Turkey acceded to the International Agreement for the Establishment of the University for Peace on 27 November 1995,

*Recalling also* that in its resolution 46/11 it decided to include in the agenda of its forty-eighth session and biennially thereafter an item entitled "University for Peace",

1. *Reiterates its appreciation* to the Secretary-General for the establishment of the new Council of the University for Peace, which held its ninth regular meeting on 3 October 1994;

2. *Requests* the Secretary-General to consider ways of strengthening cooperation between the United Nations and the University for Peace and to submit a report thereon to the General Assembly at its fifty-second session;

3. *Invites* Member States, non-governmental organizations and intergovernmental bodies, as well as interested individuals and organizations, to contribute directly to the Trust Fund for Peace and to the budget of the University;

4. *Invites* Member States to accede to the International Agreement for the Establishment of the University for Peace, thereby demonstrating their support for a global peace studies institution whose mandate is the promotion of a global culture of peace;

5. *Decides* to include in the agenda of its fifty-second session the item entitled "University for Peace".

General Assembly resolution 50/41

8 December 1995   Meeting 85   Adopted without vote

54-nation draft (A/50/L.42/Rev.1 & Rev.1/Add.1); agenda item 21.
*Meeting numbers.* GA 50th session: plenary 82, 85.

*REFERENCES*

[1]YUN 1993, p. 994, GA res. 48/205, 21 Dec. 1993. [2]A/50/330 & Corr.1. [3]A/CONF.166/9. [4]A/50/539. [5]YUN 1994, GA res. 49/125, 19 Dec. 1994. [6]A/50/5/Add.4. [7]A/51/31. [8]YUN 1994, p. 1140. [9]YUN 1993, p. 998, GA res. 48/9, 25 Oct. 1993.

Chapter X

# Women

Aiming to accelerate a process begun two decades earlier to advance the status of women worldwide, the United Nations in September 1995 convened the Fourth World Conference on Women in Beijing (4-15 September). The two-week global convocation culminated with the adoption of the Beijing Declaration and Platform for Action, a comprehensive, ground-breaking plan designed to speed implementation of the 1985 Nairobi Forward-looking Strategies for the Advancement of Women and to promote the goals of equality, development and peace.

Some 17,000 representatives of Governments, non-governmental organizations, international organizations and the media attended the gathering in Beijing's International Conference Centre, making it one of the largest UN conferences ever held. In addition, more than 30,000 participants attended a parallel forum organized by non-governmental organizations in suburban Huairou.

The Conference aimed to build upon and expand a process that formally began in 1975, during the UN-proclaimed International Women's Year, when the first UN conference on women, held in Mexico City, squarely placed women's issues on the international agenda. In 1979, the General Assembly adopted the Convention on the Elimination of All Forms of Discrimination against Women, which entered into force in 1981 and set an international standard to ensure equality between women and men. The second UN women's conference was held in Copenhagen, Denmark, in 1980. In 1985, the third women's conference convened in Nairobi to review the achievements of the UN Decade for Women (1976-1985), a worldwide effort to examine the status and rights of women and to bring women into decision-making at all levels. The conference adopted the Nairobi Forward-looking Strategies for the Advancement of Women to the year 2000, which provided a framework for action at the national, regional and international levels to promote empowerment of women and their enjoyment of human rights. A 1990 evaluation of the Strategies revealed that, while the international community had become more conscious of issues affecting women, there seemed to be some loss of momentum for implementation.

The Fourth World Conference on Women built also on agreements reached at a continuum of international meetings convened by the United Nations in the 1990s to address interrelated problems of economic and social development, human rights and other matters. In December 1995, the General Assembly endorsed the Beijing Declaration and Platform for Action. The Declaration recognized that the status of women had advanced in some important respects in the past decade, but that progress had been uneven, inequalities between women and men had persisted and major obstacles remained, with serious consequences for the well-being of all people. The Platform for Action described an agenda for women's empowerment which established a basic group of priority actions to be carried out by the year 2000, focusing in particular on 12 critical areas of concern. It reflected a review and appraisal of the 1985 Nairobi Forward-looking Strategies and expanded on the General Assembly's 1993 Declaration on the Elimination of Violence against Women, confronting issues such as domestic and sexual abuse, forced pregnancy and sexual slavery.

The Beijing Platform set forth new measures related to such matters as the right to inherit, parental responsibility, the role of the family, freedom of culture and religion, the rights of the girl child and women's rights to control and decide freely about matters such as sexuality and reproductive health, among others.

The Economic and Social Council addressed issues related to the Fourth World Conference on Women; commended the efforts of the International Research and Training Institute for the Advancement of Women to address all levels of poverty that hampered the advancement of women; and created a working group to consider elaboration of a draft optional protocol to the Convention on the Elimination of All Forms of Discrimination against Women. The Council also welcomed the intention of the Secretary-General to ensure implementation of the strategic plan of action to improve the status of women in the UN Secretariat.

The Commission on the Status of Women, as preparatory body for the Beijing Conference, formulated the draft Declaration and Platform for Action. In 1995, the Commission also urged the release of women and children taken hostage in armed conflicts, condemned the rape and abuse of women and children in the former Yugoslavia and addressed such issues as violence against women migrant workers, traffic in women and girls and integrating women into the development process.

In 1995, the Committee on the Elimination of Discrimination against Women at its fourteenth session examined reports from 13 States parties to the 1979 Convention.

# Fourth World Conference on Women

## Conference preparations

In 1990, the General Assembly had endorsed[1] a recommendation of the Economic and Social Council that the United Nations convene a world conference on women in 1995, and requested the Commission on the Status of Women to serve as the preparatory committee for the Fourth World Conference on Women. In December 1992, Gertrude Mongella, a former cabinet minister of the United Republic of Tanzania, was appointed Secretary-General of the Conference.

Preparatory activities were characterized by intense collaboration among Governments, the UN Secretariat and UN organizations, and by an unprecedented involvement of and strong support from other intergovernmental organizations and a broad spectrum of non-governmental actors at the international, regional, subregional and national levels.

Preparatory meetings for the Conference were convened by the five UN regional commissions, which resulted in regional plans or programmes providing perspectives for the draft Platform for Action.[2] Consultations with representatives of youth organizations at each regional meeting resulted in youth statements on the Platform for Action.

Support for the Conference at the international level was further provided by an Advisory Group composed of 19 eminent persons. Meeting three times prior to the Conference, the Group provided advice to the Secretary-General and assisted in mobilizing political interest and public attention for the Conference.

### Preparatory meeting

In 1995, the Commission on the Status of Women, at its third and final preparatory meeting, held during its thirty-ninth session (15 March–7 April),[3] set up a working group to finalize the draft Platform for Action as well as other matters related to Conference preparations, including draft rules of procedure, applications from non-governmental organizations for accreditation and issues related to Conference follow-up. The Commission had before it a report of the Secretary-General containing information on the status of preparations.[4]

After extending the session by three days, to 7 April, the Commission approved the draft Platform and decided[5] to transmit it to the World Conference for adoption. The Commission also approved the provisional agenda and organization of work for the Conference[6] and decided to transmit the provisional rules of procedure for the Conference[7] to the General Assembly, which approved them on 21 April by **decision 49/482**.

The Commission further decided[8] to establish an informal contact group to seek agreement on the commonly understood meaning of the term "gender" in the context of the draft Platform for Action. The group met twice in May and decided that the Conference President should read a statement at the Conference indicating the commonly understood meaning of the term.

**GENERAL ASSEMBLY ACTION**

On 21 April, the General Assembly adopted **resolution 49/243**.

**Accreditation of non-governmental organizations to the Fourth World Conference on Women: Action for Equality, Development and Peace**
*The General Assembly,*

*Recalling* Economic and Social Council resolution 1296(XLIV) of 23 May 1968 on arrangements for consultation with non-governmental organizations,

*Recalling also* Economic and Social Council resolution 1987/20 of 26 May 1987, in which the Council decided that the Commission on the Status of Women should be designated as the preparatory body for world conferences on women,

*Recalling further* resolution 37/7 of 25 March 1993 of the Commission on the Status of Women, concerning preparations for the Fourth World Conference on Women: Action for Equality, Development and Peace,

*Recalling* General Assembly resolution 48/108 of 20 December 1993, by which the Assembly adopted modalities for participation in and contribution to the Conference and its preparatory process by non-governmental organizations,

*Emphasizing* that the rules for accreditation of non-governmental organizations to the Conference, contained in the annex to resolution 48/108, should be applied transparently and fairly,

*Reaffirming* the importance of participation by non-governmental organizations in the Conference and its preparatory process,

*Noting* that there is need for more time and opportunity for many non-governmental organizations to clarify their qualifications for accreditation to the Conference,

1. *Requests* the secretariat of the Fourth World Conference on Women: Action for Equality, Development and Peace to communicate immediately in writing with each non-governmental organization which, by 15 March 1995, had applied for accreditation to the Conference but had not yet been accredited, listing the reasons why the secretariat had not forwarded the name of the organization to the Commission on the Status of Women for accreditation;

2. *Also requests* the secretariat of the Conference to invite those non-governmental organizations referred to in paragraphs 1 above and 4 below to submit, within four weeks of the date of transmittal of the secretariat's written communication, further relevant information concerning their qualifications for accreditation;

3. *Requests* that the secretariat of the Conference be responsible for the receipt and evaluation, in accordance with the provisions of the annex to General Assembly resolution 48/108, of all previously supplied information, as well as that submitted by non-governmental organizations under the terms of paragraph 2 above;

4. *Requests* the secretariat of the Conference to extend the deadline for application for accreditation by non-governmental organizations until 28 April 1995, to continue to consider applications received by that date and to ensure that those applications are considered in a transparent manner, in accordance with the criteria set forth in the annex to resolution 48/108;

5. *Also requests* the secretariat of the Conference, prior to the convening of the substantive session of 1995 of the Economic and Social Council, to prepare a list of those non-governmental organizations referred to in paragraphs 1 and 4 which, considering all available information, appear to have met the criteria set forth in the annex to resolution 48/108 for accreditation to the Conference;

6. *Further requests* the secretariat of the Conference to provide a list of those non-governmental organizations referred to in paragraphs 1 and 4 which the secretariat does not recommend for accreditation, together with the reasons for non-recommendation, to all members of the Economic and Social Council no later than one week prior to the substantive session of 1995 of the Council;

7. *Authorizes* the Economic and Social Council, at its substantive session of 1995, to decide on all pending proposals for accreditation of non-governmental organizations;

8. *Requests* the secretariat of the Conference, after the final consideration by the Economic and Social Council of the list of the non-governmental organizations referred to in paragraphs 1 and 4, promptly to notify those organizations of the final determination made by the Council.

General Assembly resolution 49/243

21 April 1995    Meeting 102    86-0-1 (recorded vote)

Draft by Commission on the Status of Women (A/49/887 & Corr.1); agenda item 97.

Recorded vote in Assembly as follows:

*In favour:* Algeria, Andorra, Argentina, Armenia, Australia, Austria, Azerbaijan, Bangladesh, Barbados, Belarus, Belgium, Benin, Bhutan, Bolivia, Brazil, Bulgaria, Cambodia, Canada, Chile, Colombia, Côte d'Ivoire, Cyprus, Denmark, Ecuador, Estonia, Finland, France, Gabon, Germany, Greece, Guyana, Honduras, Hungary, Iceland, India, Iran, Ireland, Italy, Jamaica, Japan, Kenya, Kuwait, Latvia, Lesotho, Liechtenstein, Lithuania, Luxembourg, Madagascar, Maldives, Malta, Mexico, Monaco, Morocco, Nepal, Netherlands, New Zealand, Nigeria, Norway, Pakistan, Panama, Peru, Philippines, Poland, Portugal, Romania, Russian Federation, San Marino, Singapore, Slovakia, Slovenia, South Africa, Spain, Suriname, Sweden, Thailand, the former Yugoslav Republic of Macedonia, Togo, Tunisia, Turkey, Ukraine, United Kingdom, United States, Uruguay, Venezuela, Viet Nam, Zimbabwe.

*Against:* None

*Abstaining:* China.

On 20 July, the General Assembly, on the recommendation of the secretariat of the Fourth

World Conference on Women,[9] by **decision 49/494** granted observer status to six intergovernmental organizations for attendance at the Conference.

On 29 June and 21 July, the Economic and Social Council, by **decision 1995/229**, approved the addition of 749 non-governmental organizations (NGOs) to the list of more than 2,000 NGOs already approved for accreditation to the Conference. By **decision 1995/225** of 1 June, the Council authorized the Chairman of the Commission on the Status of Women to conduct open-ended informal consultations prior to the Conference to further consider the draft Platform for Action, specifically those portions of the text that remained within brackets.

## Beijing Conference

The Fourth World Conference on Women (Beijing, 4-15 September 1995) addressed the interrelated issues of development, equality and peace, and defined an agenda for action to empower women socially, politically and economically, in both private and public life, and to eliminate all forms of discrimination against women. It emphasized the connection between the advancement of women and progress for society as a whole, and reaffirmed that societal issues must be addressed from a gender perspective in order to ensure sustainable development.

The Beijing Conference carried forward the themes of "Equality, Development and Peace", adopted at the first UN-sponsored global conference on women, held in Mexico City (1975), which were subsequently developed during the United Nations Decade for Women (1976-1985).[10] The second women's conference, held in Copenhagen (1980), added three sub-themes: education, employment and health,[11] and the third UN conference on women (1985) incorporated those themes into the "Nairobi Forward-looking Strategies for the Advancement of Women".[12] A major challenge before the Fourth World Conference was to find ways and means to accelerate the application of the Nairobi Forward-looking Strategies. Its mission was not further analysis, but a deeper level of action.

Consultations were held in Beijing on 2 and 3 September to consider procedural and organizational matters, and the Conference opened on 4 September with representatives of 189 Governments in attendance. At the first session, Chen Muhua, Vice Chairman of the Standing Committee of the Eighth National People's Conference of China and President of the Executive Committee of the All-China Women's Federation, was elected Conference President.

Addressing the opening of the Conference on 4 September, UN Secretary-General Boutros

Boutros-Ghali said that securing equality for women and men, in fact as well as in law, was the great political project of the twentieth century. Over the past decade, a continuum of global conferences had worked to define the new global agenda; it had become clear that progress would require the full and equal participation of women and men in promoting peace, safeguarding the environment, securing sustainable development, and making advances in human rights, population, health, education, government, the home and civil society. Conference Secretary-General Gertrude Mongella also spoke, describing the Platform for Action as a document for everyone. She said there could be no spectators or abstainers from the crucial social agenda affecting all humanity.

While the Conference's Main Committee addressed the chapter-by-chapter process of negotiating agreement on contentious issues, plenary sessions featured a general exchange of views on key issues affecting the realization of the rights of women. Statements were made by representatives of 186 Member States—including 5 heads of State or Government—as well as 3 associate members, 16 intergovernmental organizations, 32 UN agencies and programmes and 50 NGOs. Representatives of the European Union and other international and regional organization speakers also addressed the Conference.

Governments were invited to make use of the general exchange of views to express their commitments to the advancement of women. Most commitments dealt with improving the status of women through reform of national policies, numerical targets for the year 2000 and frameworks for international development cooperation. Commitments made during the general exchange of views, along with the Beijing Declaration and Platform for Action, constituted the major results of the Conference.

On 15 September, the Conference concluded with the unanimous adoption of the Beijing Declaration and Platform for Action,[13] which was recommended to the General Assembly for endorsement. After adoption of the final documents, general or interpretive statements were made or reservations expressed on the Beijing Declaration and Platform for Action by representatives of the following countries: Algeria, Argentina, Bahrain, Bangladesh, Benin, Bolivia, Brazil, Brunei Darussalam, Cambodia, Cameroon, Canada, Central African Republic, Chad, Colombia, Comoros, Costa Rica, Djibouti, Dominican Republic, Ecuador, Egypt, El Salvador, Ethiopia, France, Gabon, Ghana, Guatemala, Holy See, Honduras, India, Indonesia, Iran, Iraq, Jordan, Kuwait, Lebanon, Liberia, Libyan Arab Jamahiriya, Madagascar, Malaysia, Maldives, Mali, Malta, Mauritania, Morocco, Nicaragua, Niger, Nigeria, Oman,

Pakistan, Panama, Peru, Philippines, Qatar, South Africa, Sudan, Syrian Arab Republic, Togo, Tunisia, United Arab Emirates, United Republic of Tanzania, United States, Vanuatu, Venezuela and Yemen. The observer for Palestine also made a statement. Conference participants also expressed thanks to the people and Government of the People's Republic of China and approved the report of the Conference Credentials Committee.[14]

### Beijing Declaration

The Beijing Declaration[13] embodied the commitment of the international community to advance the goals of equality, development and peace and to implement the Platform for Action, ensuring that a gender perspective was reflected in all policies and programmes.

Among the 38 provisions of the Declaration, Governments declared that women's rights were human rights and expressed their determination to intensify efforts and actions to achieve the goals of the Nairobi Forward-looking Strategies for the Advancement of Women by the end of the century.

In the Declaration, Governments expressed determination to promote women's economic independence and employment; "people-centred" sustainable development, including sustained economic development through the provision of basic education, lifelong education, literacy and training; and primary health care for girls and women. Recognizing the leading role that women played in the peace movement, Governments committed themselves to working towards general and complete disarmament under strict and effective international control and supported negotiations on the conclusion, without delay, of a universal, multilaterally and effectively verifiable nuclear-test-ban treaty.

The Declaration called for elimination of all forms of violence against women and girls. Governments pledged to intensify efforts to ensure equal enjoyment of human rights and fundamental freedoms for women and girls. They committed themselves to implementing the Platform for Action and ensuring that a gender perspective was reflected in all their policies and programmes. They urged the UN system, regional and international financial institutions and all women and men to commit themselves to action as well.

### Platform for Action

The six chapters of the Platform for Action[13] set out measures for national and international action for the advancement of women, and aimed to hasten the removal of the remaining obstacles to women's full and equal participation in all spheres of life. It also strove to protect women's human rights and to integrate women's concerns into all aspects of sustainable development. It outlined strategic objectives and actions related to the critical areas of concern, and addressed institutional and financial arrangements.

The Platform's "Mission Statement" emphasized that women and men shared common concerns which could only be addressed by working together and in partnership towards the common goal of gender equality throughout the world. It asserted that the success of the Platform for Action would require a strong commitment on the part of Governments, international organizations and institutions at all levels.

The "Global Framework" stated that the Platform's implementation was the responsibility of each State and that their communities should contribute to the full enjoyment by women of their human rights in order to achieve equality, development and peace. It stated that structural adjustment programmes had led to a reduction in social expenditure, thereby adversely affecting women. While one fourth of all households worldwide were headed by women, and growing numbers of women had achieved economic independence through employment, women were not adequately represented in decision-making structures, including in the United Nations.

### Critical areas of concern

The third chapter of the Beijing Platform for Action outlined 12 critical areas of concern: poverty, education, health, violence against women, armed conflict, economic structures, power sharing and decision-making, mechanisms to promote the advancement of women, human rights, the media, the environment and the girl child. There was a need, according to the text, for mechanisms of accountability for all the areas of concern, which were interrelated, interdependent and of high priority.

The fourth chapter of the Platform contained the strategic objectives and actions for each critical area of concern. On women and poverty, the Platform set out actions to achieve four strategic objectives, such as: bringing about macroeconomic and development policies to address women in poverty; revising laws to ensure access to economic resources; providing women with access to savings and credit; and developing gender-based methodologies and conducting research to address the feminization of poverty.

Among the objectives outlined to promote education and training of women were equal access to education, eradication of illiteracy, development of non-discriminatory education and training and promotion of lifelong education. In the area of health, the Platform called for increasing women's access to appropriate, affordable and quality health care, strengthening preventive programmes, promoting research on women's health and undertaking gender-sensitive initiatives that addressed sexually transmitted diseases, human immunodeficiency virus/acquired immunodeficiency syndrome (HIV/AIDS) and reproductive health issues.

The Platform also described measures Governments, citizens' groups, employers, international organizations and others could and should take to prevent violence against women and to eliminate trafficking in women. Regarding armed conflict, the text called for increasing the participation of women in conflict resolution at decision-making levels and aimed to reduce excessive military expenditures, control the availability of armaments and reduce the incidence of human rights abuse in conflict situations. Other goals were to promote women's contribution to fostering a culture of peace and to provide protection, assistance and training to refugee women and other women in need of international protection.

With regard to economic matters, the Platform outlined actions to promote women's economic rights and independence; facilitate women's equal access to resources, employment, markets and trade; and provide business services, training and access to information and technology, particularly to low-income women. Other aims included strengthening women's economic capacity and commercial networks, eliminating occupational segregation and all forms of employment discrimination and promoting harmonization of work and family responsibilities for women and men.

The Platform sought to ensure women's equal access to and full participation in power structures, leadership and decision-making, and described actions to be taken by Governments, national bodies, the private sector, political parties, trade unions and others to increase women's capacity to participate in those areas.

Objectives related to institutional mechanisms for the advancement of women included creation of national machineries; integration of gender perspectives in legislation; and dissemination by Governments, the United Nations and other national, regional and international bodies of gender-disaggregated information for planning and evaluation.

To promote and protect the human rights of women, the Platform called for the full implementation of all human rights instruments, especially the Convention on the Elimination of All Forms of Discrimination against Women.[15] The Platform also aimed to ensure equality and non-discrimination under the law and in practice and to achieve legal literacy.

Goals related to the media included increasing access to expression and decision-making in and through the media and new communication technologies and promoting a balanced and nonstereotyped portrayal of women in the media. In terms of the environment, the Platform called for actions to involve women actively in environmental decision-making at all levels. It also aimed to integrate gender concerns and perspective in sustainable development programmes, as well as to establish mechanisms to assess the impact of development and environmental policies on women.

Among nine strategic objectives related to the girl child, the Platform called for eliminating negative cultural attitudes and practices against girls and eliminating discrimination against girls in education and health. It also outlined action to eradicate violence against the girl child; to promote the girl child's participation in social, economic and political life; and to eliminate the economic exploitation of child labour and protect young girls at work.

### Institutional and financial arrangements

In the Platform's chapters on institutional and financial arrangements for follow-up to the Fourth World Conference on Women, Governments were called on to develop strategies to implement the Platform by the end of 1996, with time-bound targets. Benchmarks for monitoring as well as proposals for allocating resources for implementation were included. The Secretary-General was invited to establish a high-level post to act as his adviser on gender issues and help ensure system-wide implementation of the Platform. Emphasis was placed on the role of the Commission on the Status of Women, which should have a clear mandate and necessary financial support to play a central role in monitoring the Platform's implementation. Ultimately, the Platform said, the Commission should serve as the gender-analysis arm of the Economic and Social Council.

## Reports of the Conference

### Second review and appraisal

The Fourth Women's Conference considered a report of the Secretary-General on the second review and appraisal of the implementation of the 1985 Nairobi Forward-looking Strategies for the Advancement of Women.[16] The first review and appraisal took place in 1990.

The report was based on information contained in national reports, the results of the regional conferences and information provided by UN specialized agencies, as well as other governmental and non-governmental organizations. The report reviewed progress achieved and persistent gaps in implementation of the Forward-looking Strategies from the perspective of each of the critical areas of concern contained in the Platform for Action. It also provided an overview of the social, political and economic framework against which progress should be assessed. According to the report, changes in the global economic, social and political framework had affected the work and lives of women all over the world. Democratization provided opportunities for women to participate in their societies on an equal footing with men. At the same time, the absence of democratic institutions in societies in transition led, at least initially, to the marginalization of vulnerable groups. Studies had shown that the short-term costs of adjustment and stabilization were often distributed disproportionately, so that women came to bear the greater share of the burden. On the other hand, there was evidence of a strong relationship between economic growth and the economic advancement of women.

### Other documents

Other documents before the Conference included the 1994 *World Survey on the Role of Women in Development*,[17] and *The World's Women: Trends and Statistics*.[18] The *World Survey*, the third to be published, examined the role of women in efforts to achieve sustainable development and international economic cooperation, and found that economic growth and development appeared to be intricately related to the advancement of women. Where women had advanced, economic growth had usually been steady; where women had not been allowed to be full participants, there had been stagnation. According to *The World's Women*, women had made significant progress in some areas since the first World Conference on Women was held in Mexico City in 1975; however, statistical data provided by the report also made it clear that greater efforts were required to achieve social, political and economic equality between genders.

Also before the Conference were: a preliminary report submitted by the Special Rapporteur on violence against women, its causes and consequences;[19] the Plan of Action for the Elimination of Harmful Traditional Practices Affecting the Health of Women and Children,[20] the report of the Committee on the Elimination of Discrimination against Women[21] and reports of the regional conferences and other international conferences.[22]

On 8 December, the General Assembly adopted **resolution 50/42**.

#### Fourth World Conference on Women

*The General Assembly,*

*Noting with satisfaction* the successful conclusion of the Fourth World Conference on Women, held at Beijing from 4 to 15 September 1995, which culminated in the adoption of the Beijing Declaration and the Platform for Action, aimed at accelerating the implementation of the Nairobi Forward-looking Strategies for the Advancement of Women to the year 2000,

1. *Expresses its profound gratitude* to the Government of the People's Republic of China for having made it possible for the Fourth World Conference on Women to be held at Beijing and for the excellent facilities, staff and services so graciously placed at the disposal of the Conference;

2. *Takes note* of the report of the Fourth World Conference on Women;

3. *Endorses* the Beijing Declaration and the Platform for Action as adopted at the Conference on 15 September 1995;

4. *Calls upon* all States and all bodies of the United Nations system and other international organizations, as well as non-governmental organizations, to take action for the effective implementation of the Beijing Declaration and the Platform for Action.

General Assembly resolution 50/42

8 December 1995     Meeting 86     Adopted without vote

105-nation draft (A/50/L.46 & Add.1); agenda item 165.

## Conference follow-up

**Report of Secretary-General.** In accordance with a 1994 request of the General Assembly,[23] the Secretary-General reported[24] in November on implementation of the outcome of the Fourth World Conference on Women. The Secretary-General said he would ensure that Conference recommendations addressed to him were implemented swiftly and effectively, and that he was committed to integrating the gender perspective into all aspects of the work of the Organization. He added that he would work with his colleagues, the executive heads of UN specialized agencies and UN programmes and funds to ensure a coordinated system-wide response, integrating the follow-up of the Fourth Conference with that of other global conferences.

The report said that deeply entrenched attitudes and practices perpetuated inequality and discrimination against women, in both public and private life, in all parts of the world. Accordingly, implementation of the Beijing Platform for Action would require changes in values, attitudes, practices and priorities at the national, regional and international levels. A clear commitment to international norms and standards of equality between men and women, as well as measures to protect and promote the human rights of women and girl children as an integral part of universal human rights, must underlie all action. Institutions at all levels must be reoriented to expedite implementation, and an active and visible policy of mainstreaming a gender perspective should be promoted by Governments, the UN system and all other relevant organizations.

### New senior adviser

Responding to a Conference recommendation that a new high-level post be established in the office of the Secretary-General to help ensure system-wide implementation of the Platform for Action, the Secretary-General on 28 December designated Assistant Secretary-General Rosario Green as his senior adviser on gender issues.

### Inter-agency meeting

The twentieth Ad Hoc Inter-Agency Meeting on Women (New York, 16-17 November) centred on revision of the system-wide medium-term plan for the advancement of women, 1996-2001, and included discussion of the role of the UN system in follow-up to the Conference.[25] Concern was expressed that roles and functions remained unclear, as did the mechanisms for interaction, coordination and reporting in the intergovernmental and inter-agency areas. In particular, the apparatus for women's and gender issues and for Conference follow-up under the Administrative Committee on Coordination (ACC) needed to be clarified. The Meeting decided to continue its discussion of the matter and to make recommendations for submission to ACC at its twenty-first meeting in March 1996.

GENERAL ASSEMBLY ACTION

On 22 December, the General Assembly adopted **resolution 50/203**.

**Follow-up to the Fourth World Conference on Women and full implementation of the Beijing Declaration and the Platform for Action**

*The General Assembly,*

*Recalling* its resolutions 45/129 of 14 December 1990, 46/98 of 16 December 1991 and 47/95 of 16 December 1992, as well as Economic and Social Council resolution 1990/12 of 24 May 1990 and Council decision 1992/272 of 30 July 1992, recommending that a world conference on women be held in 1995,

*Reaffirming* the importance of the outcome of the previous World Conferences on Women, held at Mexico City in 1975, at Copenhagen in 1980 and at Nairobi in 1985,

*Building* on the consensus reached and the progress made at previous United Nations conferences and summits, for children in New York in 1990, on environment and development at Rio de Janeiro in 1992, on human rights at Vienna in 1993, on population and development at Cairo in 1994 and on social development at Copenhagen in 1995, towards achieving equality, development and peace,

*Expressing its satisfaction* that the Fourth World Conference on Women: Action for Equality, Development and Peace reached a successful conclusion and adopted the Beijing Declaration and the Platform for Action,

*Expressing its profound gratitude* to the Government of the People's Republic of China for having made it possible for the Conference to be held at Beijing and for the excellent facilities, staff and services so graciously placed at the disposal of the Conference,

*Recognizing* the significance of the outcome of the Conference to make a real change for the empowerment of women and thus to the fulfilment of the goals adopted in the Nairobi Forward-looking Strategies for the Advancement of Women,

*Deeply convinced* that the Beijing Declaration and the Platform for Action are important contributions to the advancement of women worldwide and must be translated into effective action by all States, the United Nations system and other organizations concerned, as well as non-governmental organizations,

*Recognizing* that the implementation of the Platform for Action rests primarily at the national level, that Governments, non-governmental organizations and public and private institutions should be involved in the implementation process and that national mechanisms also have an important role to play,

*Bearing in mind* that promotion of international cooperation is essential for the effective implementation of the Beijing Declaration and the Platform for Action,

*Recognizing* that the implementation of the Platform for Action requires commitment from Governments and the international community,

*Recognizing also* the important role played by States, the United Nations, the regional commissions and other international organizations, as well as non-governmental organizations and women's organizations, in the preparatory process of the Conference and the importance of their involvement in the implementation of the Platform for Action,

*Taking into account* the fact that the follow-up to the Conference should be undertaken on the basis of an integrated approach to the advancement of women within the framework of a coordinated follow-up to and implementation of the results of the major international conferences in the economic, social and related fields, as well as the overall responsibilities of the General Assembly and the Economic and Social Council,

*Bearing in mind* its resolution 50/42 of 8 December 1995,

*Expressing its appreciation* to the Secretary-General, the Secretary-General of the Conference and the staff of the Secretariat for the effective preparations and services provided for the Conference,

1. *Takes note* of the report of the Fourth World Conference on Women, as adopted on 15 September 1995;

2. *Endorses* the Beijing Declaration and the Platform for Action as adopted by the Conference;

3. *Calls upon* States, the United Nations system and all other actors to implement the Platform for Action, in particular by promoting an active and visible policy of mainstreaming a gender perspective at all levels, including in the design, monitoring and evaluation of all policies, as appropriate, in order to ensure effective implementation of the Platform;

4. *Stresses* that Governments have the primary responsibility for implementing the Platform for Action, that commitment at the highest level is essential for its implementation and that Governments should take a leading role in coordinating, monitoring and assessing progress in the advancement of women;

5. *Calls upon* States, with the assistance of non-governmental organizations, to disseminate the Beijing Declaration and the Platform for Action widely;

6. *Emphasizes* that Governments should, as soon as possible and no later than 1996, develop comprehensive implementation strategies or plans of action, includ-

ing time-bound targets and benchmarks for monitoring, in order to implement the Platform for Action fully;

7. *Calls upon* Governments to create a national machinery where it does not exist and to strengthen, as appropriate, existing national machineries for the advancement of women;

8. *Encourages* non-governmental organizations to contribute to the design and implementation of these strategies or national plans of action in addition to their own programmes that complement government efforts;

9. *Recognizes* the importance attached to the regional monitoring of the global and regional platforms for action by regional commissions and other subregional or regional structures, within their mandates, in consultation with Governments, and the necessity of promoting cooperation among national Governments of the same region in this respect;

10. *Invites* the Economic and Social Council, in order to facilitate the regional implementation, monitoring and evaluation process, to consider reviewing the institutional capacity of the United Nations regional commissions, within their mandates, including their women's units or focal points, to deal with gender-related issues in the light of the Platform for Action, as well as the regional platforms and plans of action, and to give consideration, *inter alia*, and where appropriate, to strengthening the capacity in this respect;

11. *Calls upon* States to take action to fulfil the commitments made at the Conference for the advancement of women and for the strengthening of international cooperation, and reaffirms that adequate financial resources should be committed at the international level for the implementation of the Platform for Action in the developing countries, in particular in Africa, and in the least developed countries;

12. *Recognizes* that implementation of the Platform for Action in the countries with economies in transition requires continued international cooperation and assistance, as indicated in the Platform for Action;

13. *Stresses* that full and effective implementation of the Platform for Action will require a political commitment to make available human and financial resources for the empowerment of women, the integration of a gender perspective in budgetary decisions on policies and programmes, as well as adequate financing of specific programmes for securing equality between women and men;

14. *Reaffirms* that, in order to implement the Platform for Action, a reformulation of policies and reallocation of resources may be needed, but that some policy changes may not necessarily have financial implications;

15. *Reaffirms also* that, in order to implement the Platform for Action, adequate mobilization of resources at the national and international levels, as well as new and additional resources to the developing countries, in particular in Africa, and the least developed countries, from all available funding mechanisms, including multilateral, bilateral and private sources for the advancement of women, will also be required;

16. *Calls upon* those States committed to the 20:20 initiative to integrate a gender perspective fully into its implementation, as referred to in paragraph 358 of the Platform for Action;

17. *Recognizes* that the creation of an enabling environment is necessary to ensure the full participation of women in economic activities;

18. *Reaffirms further* that the implementation of the Platform for Action will require immediate and concerted action by all to create a peaceful, just and humane world based on all human rights and fundamental freedoms, including the principle of equality for all people of all ages and from all walks of life, and to this end, recognizes that broad-based and sustained economic growth in the context of sustainable development is necessary to sustain social development and social justice;

19. *Considers*, in relation to the United Nations, that the Platform for Action should be implemented through the work of all the bodies and organizations of the system during the period 1995-2000, specifically and as an integral part of wider programming;

20. *Considers also* that an enhanced framework for international cooperation for gender-related issues must be developed during the period 1995-2000 in order to ensure the integrated and comprehensive implementation, follow-up and assessment of the Platform for Action, taking into account the results of global United Nations summits and conferences;

21. *Decides* that the General Assembly, the Economic and Social Council and the Commission on the Status of Women, in accordance with their respective mandates and in accordance with Assembly resolution 48/162 of 20 December 1993 and other relevant resolutions, shall constitute a three-tiered intergovernmental mechanism that will play the primary role in the overall policy-making and follow-up, and in coordinating the implementation and monitoring of the Platform for Action, reaffirming the need for a coordinated follow-up to and implementation of the results of major international conferences in the economic, social and related fields;

22. *Also decides* to appraise the progress on a regular basis and to include in the agenda of its forthcoming sessions, starting from 1996, an item entitled ''Implementation of the outcome of the Fourth World Conference on Women'', with a view to assessing, in the year 2000, the progress achieved in the implementation of the Nairobi Forward-looking Strategies for the Advancement of Women and the Platform for Action in an appropriate forum;

23. *Invites* the Economic and Social Council to consider devoting to this matter one high-level segment, one coordination segment and one operational segment, before the year 2000, taking into account the multi-year programme of work of the Commission on the Status of Women and all other functional commissions of the Council;

24. *Also invites* the Economic and Social Council to review and strengthen the mandate of the Commission on the Status of Women, taking into account the Platform for Action as well as the need for synergy with all other related commissions and conference follow-up, and for a system-wide approach to its implementation;

25. *Decides* that the Commission on the Status of Women, as a functional commission assisting the Economic and Social Council, shall have a central role in the monitoring of the implementation of the Platform for Action within the United Nations system and in advising the Council thereon;

26. *Also decides* that the Economic and Social Council should oversee system-wide coordination in the implementation of the Platform for Action, ensure overall coordination of the follow-up to and implementation of the results of all United Nations international conferences in the economic, social and related fields and report thereon to the General Assembly;

27. *Requests* the Commission on the Status of Women to develop its multi-year programme of work for the period 1996-2000 at its fortieth session so that it can review the critical areas of concern in the Platform for Action and to consider how it could integrate into its programme of work the follow-up to the Conference and how it could develop its catalytic role in mainstreaming a gender perspective in United Nations activities, taking into account the need for a focused and thematic approach to the review of the Platform for Action and the contribution that can be made by all other functional commissions of the Council;

28. *Also requests* the Commission on the Status of Women to forward its recommendations on the multi-year programme of work to the Economic and Social Council so that the Council can take a decision on the programme of work at its meeting in 1996, reviewing, coordinating and harmonizing the different programmes of work, including the reporting systems of all the commissions in the area of the advancement of women;

29. *Invites* all other functional commissions of the Economic and Social Council, within their mandates, to take due account of the Platform for Action and to ensure the integration of gender aspects in their respective work;

30. *Requests* the Secretary-General to assume responsibility for the coordination of policy within the United Nations for the implementation of the Platform for Action and the mainstreaming of a system-wide gender perspective in all activities of the United Nations system, including training, in accordance with paragraph 326 of the Platform for Action;

31. *Also requests* the Secretary-General to disseminate the Beijing Declaration and the Platform for Action as widely as possible, including to the competent organs of the United Nations and the specialized agencies;

32. *Further requests* the Secretary-General to report, through the Commission on the Status of Women and the Economic and Social Council, to the General Assembly at its fifty-first session on ways to enhance the capacity of the Organization and of the United Nations system to support the ongoing follow-up to the Conference in the most integrated and effective way, including human and financial requirements;

33. *Requests* the Secretary-General to ensure the more effective functioning of the Division for the Advancement of Women of the Secretariat in order to carry out all the tasks foreseen for it in the Platform for Action by, *inter alia*, providing sufficient human and financial resources within the regular budget of the United Nations;

34. *Also requests* the Secretary-General, in cooperation with the Administrator of the United Nations Development Programme, to ask the resident coordinators fully to apply a gender perspective in integrating the follow-up to the Conference into the coordinated follow-up to recent global United Nations conferences;

35. *Further requests* the Secretary-General to report annually to the Commission on the Status of Women and to the General Assembly, through the Economic and Social Council, on the measures taken and the progress

achieved in the implementation of the Beijing Declaration and the Platform for Action;

36. *Requests* the Committee on the Elimination of Discrimination against Women, within its mandate, to take into account the Platform for Action when considering reports submitted by States parties, and invites States parties to include information on measures taken to implement the Platform for Action in their reports;

37. *Notes* the importance of the activities undertaken by the United Nations Development Fund for Women and the International Research and Training Institute for the Advancement of Women in the implementation of the Platform for Action;

38. *Encourages* international financial institutions to review and revise policies, procedures and staffing to ensure that investments and programmes benefit women and thus contribute to sustainable development;

39. *Invites* the World Trade Organization to consider how it might contribute to the implementation of the Platform for Action, including through activities in cooperation with the United Nations system.

General Assembly resolution 50/203

22 December 1995     Meeting 99     Adopted without vote

Approved by Third Committee (A/50/816) without vote, 13 December (meeting 56); draft by Chairman (A/C.3/50/L.64); agenda item 165.
*Financial implications.* 5th Committee, A/50/838; S-G, A/C.3/50/L.68, A/C.5/50/44.
*Meeting numbers.* GA 50th session: 3rd Committee 24, 26-31, 54, 56; 5th Committee 42, 43; plenary 99.

Also on 22 December, the General Assembly, in **decision 50/463**, took note of the Secretary-General's report on the implementation of the outcome of the Fourth World Conference on Women.

*REFERENCES*
[1]GA res. 45/129, 14 Dec. 1990. [2]YUN 1994, p. 1178. [3]E/1995/26. [4]E/CN.6/1995/4. [5]E/1995/26 (dec. 39/4). [6]Ibid. (res. 39/1). [7]A/49/887 & Corr.1. [8]E/1995/26 (dec. 39/3). [9]A/49/942. [10]YUN 1975, p. 666, GA res. 3520(XXX), 15 Dec. 1975. [11]YUN 1980, p. 890. [12]YUN 1985, p. 937. [13]A/CONF.177/20. [14]A/CONF.177/14. [15]YUN 1979, p. 895, GA res. 34/180, annex, 18 Dec. 1979. [16]E/CN.6/1995/3 & Add.1-10. [17]*World Survey on the Role of Women in Development*, Sales No. E.95.IV.1. [18]*The World's Women: Trends and Statistics*, Sales No. E.95.XVII.2. [19]E/CN.8/1995/42. [20]E/CN.4/Sub.2/1994/10 & Corr.1 & Add.1/Corr.1. [21]A/CONF.177/7. [22]E/CN.6/1995/5 & Add.1-7. [23]YUN 1994, p. 1179, GA res. 49/161, 23 Dec. 1994. [24]A/50/744. [25]ACC/1995/25.

# Advancement of the status of women

## UN mechanisms

### Convention on discrimination against women

The 30-article Convention on the Elimination of All Forms of Discrimination against Women, adopted in 1979 by the General Assembly,[1] spells out constitutional, legislative and other measures which aim to promote equality for women through affirmative action, maternity protection, équal education and employment opportunities, and equality before the law. It sets standards by which countries aim to improve the status of women in many areas and the conditions under which they work and live. (See also PART THREE, Chapter I.)

### CEDAW session

The Committee on the Elimination of Discrimination against Women (CEDAW), established in 1982[2] to monitor compliance with the 1979 Convention on the Elimination of All Forms of Discrimination against Women, held its fourteenth session in New York from 16 January to 3 February 1995.[3]

The 23-member Committee had before it initial and periodic reports of 13 States parties (Argentina, Bolivia, Chile, Finland, Hungary, Mauritius, Norway, Peru, Russian Federation, Saint Vincent and the Grenadines, Tunisia, Uganda, Ukraine). States parties to the Convention are required to submit an initial report within one year of accession to the Convention and periodic reports at least every four years, giving account of measures adopted and progress achieved by States towards implementing the Convention. The Committee also considered a report submitted by Croatia on an exceptional basis, pursuant to a 1993 CEDAW request[4] for reports from countries of the former Yugoslavia, regarding violence against women.

In 1995, CEDAW adopted a general recommendation[5] that would have States parties consider amending article 20 of the Convention in respect of the meeting time of the Committee, so as to allow it to meet annually for such duration as necessary for the effective performance of its functions under the Convention. It also recommended that the General Assembly authorize the Committee to meet exceptionally in 1996 for two sessions, each of three weeks' duration.

The Committee also adopted a suggestion[6] on elements of an optional protocol, which would introduce petition procedures to the Convention. The Committee suggested that States parties should have the option to ratify the optional protocol, which should include both a communications procedure and an inquiry procedure. The Committee recommended that communications be submitted by an individual, group or organization suffering detriment from a violation of rights in the Convention or claiming to be directly affected by the failure of a State party to comply with its obligations under the Convention or by a person or group having a sufficient interest in the matter. The State party should have the right to cooperate in examining the information and in submitting observations on it, after which the

Committee should have the power to designate one or more members to conduct an inquiry and report urgently to the Committee.

Another suggestion[7] related to follow-up to the 1994 International Conference on Population and Development. The Committee decided that CEDAW should develop a jurisprudence of standards of international law in the field of women's reproductive health, and that the Committee should employ its reporting procedures to follow implementation of the Programme of Action adopted at that Conference.

The Committee adopted decisions on ways to improve its work, including a request to locate the Committee in Geneva with servicing provided by the Centre for Human Rights. It also decided to transmit, as its contribution to the Fourth World Conference on Women, its report[8] on the progress achieved in implementing the Convention.

Annexed to the Committee's report were a list of States parties to the Convention and a chart showing the status of submission and consideration of reports by States parties under article 18 of the Convention, both as at 3 February.

**ECONOMIC AND SOCIAL COUNCIL ACTION**

On 24 July, the Economic and Social Council adopted resolution **1995/29**.

### Convention on the Elimination of All Forms of Discrimination against Women

*The Economic and Social Council,*

*Bearing in mind* that the Convention on the Elimination of All Forms of Discrimination against Women is a key international human rights instrument for the promotion of equality between women and men,

*Welcoming* the increasing number of States parties to the Convention, which has reached one hundred and thirty-nine,

*Noting with deep concern* that the Convention is still one of the human rights instruments with a large number of reservations, many of which run contrary to the object and purpose of the Convention, despite the fact that some States parties have withdrawn their reservations to it,

*Recalling* the Vienna Declaration and Programme of Action adopted by the World Conference on Human Rights, held from 14 to 25 June 1993, in which the Conference stipulated that the human rights of women and of the girl child were an inalienable, integral and indivisible part of universal human rights,

*Recalling also* that, in the Vienna Declaration and Programme of Action, the Conference recommended the adoption of new procedures to strengthen the implementation of the commitment to women's equality and human rights and called upon the Commission on the Status of Women and the Committee on the Elimination of Discrimination against Women to examine quickly the possibility of introducing the right of petition through the preparation of an optional protocol to the Convention on the Elimination of All Forms of Discrimination against Women,

*Taking note* of suggestion 7, on elements for an optional protocol to the Convention, adopted by the Committee on the Elimination of Discrimination against Women at its fourteenth session,

*Recalling* General Assembly resolution 47/94 of 16 December 1992, relating to the scheduling of the meetings of the Committee,

*Recalling also* its resolution 1994/7 of 21 July 1994 and relevant resolutions adopted by the General Assembly to support the work of the Committee,

*Welcoming* General Assembly resolution 49/164 of 23 December 1994 and decision 49/448 of 23 December 1994, providing for a meeting of States parties to the Convention in 1995 to consider the revision of article 20, paragraph 1, of the Convention,

*Aware* that the workload of the Committee has increased because of the growing number of States parties to the Convention, and that the annual session of the Committee is still the shortest of all the annual sessions of the human rights treaty bodies,

*Welcoming* the Committee's efforts further to improve its working methods, *inter alia*, by adopting concluding observations containing specific suggestions and recommendations,

1.  *Welcomes* the fact that the States parties to the Convention on the Elimination of All Forms of Discrimination against Women, at their eighth meeting, held on 22 May 1995, have already considered the revision of article 20, paragraph 1, of the Convention in order to allow the Committee on the Elimination of Discrimination against Women to meet annually with sufficient time for the effective performance of its functions under the Convention;

2.  *Supports* the request made by the Committee at its twelfth session for additional meeting time, with adequate support from the Secretariat, so as to allow the Committee to meet for three weeks for its fifteenth session, and recommends that the request made by the Committee at its fourteenth session to hold two sessions in 1996, each of three weeks' duration, be considered favourably, within the existing level of budgetary resources;

3.  *Welcomes* the efforts made by the Committee to improve its procedures and working methods, and encourages it to continue such efforts, within its mandate;

4.  *Notes* that suggestion 7, on elements for an optional protocol to the Convention, adopted by the Committee at its fourteenth session, was transmitted to the Commission on the Status of Women for consideration;

5.  *Requests* the Secretary-General to invite Governments and intergovernmental and non-governmental organizations to submit their views on an optional protocol to the Convention, including those related to feasibility, taking into account the elements suggested by the Committee in its suggestion 7;

6.  *Also requests* the Secretary-General to submit to the Commission on the Status of Women at its fortieth session a comprehensive report, including a synthesis, on the views expressed in accordance with paragraph 5 above, if possible six weeks prior to the commencement of the session;

7.  *Decides* that the Commission should establish an in-session open-ended working group for a two-week period at its fortieth session to consider the report requested in paragraph 6 above with a view to elaborating a draft optional protocol to the Convention;

8. *Once again urges* all States that have not yet done so to become parties to the Convention;

9. *Encourages* States to consider limiting the extent of any reservation they lodge to the Convention, to formulate any reservation as precisely and as narrowly as possible, and to ensure that no reservation is incompatible with the object and purpose of the Convention or otherwise contrary to international law;

10. *Requests* States parties to the Convention to review their reservations regularly with a view to withdrawing them expeditiously so that the Convention may be fully implemented;

11. *Also encourages* States parties that are behind schedule in submitting their periodic reports to the Committee to do so promptly, and requests the Committee to follow up this problem;

12. *Urges* the Secretary-General to continue to publicize widely the decisions and recommendations of the Committee.

Economic and Social Council resolution 1995/29

24 July 1995      Meeting 50      Adopted without vote

Draft by Commission on the Status of Women (E/1995/26), orally amended; agenda item 5 *(e)*.
*Meeting numbers.* ESC 49, 50.

On 28 July, in **decision 1995/314**, the Economic and Social Council took note of the report of CEDAW on its fourteenth session.

### CEDAW working methods

Pursuant to a 1994 request of the General Assembly,[9] States parties to the Convention convened their eighth meeting in May and decided by consensus to amend article 20 of the Convention so that the duration of the Committee's annual meetings would be determined by the States parties, subject to the General Assembly's approval, rather than restricted to two weeks in duration as originally specified. The amendment, which was proposed in December 1994[10] by Denmark, Finland, Iceland, Norway and Sweden, would enter into force following consideration by the Assembly and acceptance by a two-thirds majority of States parties.

**GENERAL ASSEMBLY ACTION**

On 22 December, the General Assembly adopted **resolution 50/202**.

**Amendment to article 20, paragraph 1, of the Convention on the Elimination of All Forms of Discrimination against Women**

*The General Assembly,*

*Recalling* its resolution 49/164 of 23 December 1994 on the Convention on the Elimination of All Forms of Discrimination against Women and its decision 49/448 of 23 December 1994 on the consideration of the request for the revision of article 20, paragraph 1, of the Convention,

*Noting* the decision of the States parties to the Convention on the Elimination of All Forms of Discrimination against Women of 22 May 1995 to amend article 20, paragraph 1, of the Convention,

*Welcoming* the call for broad ratification of this amendment in the Platform for Action of the Fourth World Conference on Women, held at Beijing from 4 to 15 September 1995,

*Reiterating* the importance of the Convention as well as the contribution of the Committee on the Elimination of Discrimination against Women to the efforts of the United Nations to eliminate discrimination against women,

1. *Takes note with approval* of the resolution regarding the amendment to article 20, paragraph 1, of the Convention on the Elimination of All Forms of Discrimination against Women, adopted by the States parties to the Convention on 22 May 1995;

2. *Urges* States parties to the Convention to take appropriate measures so that acceptance by a two-thirds majority of States parties can be reached as soon as possible in order for the amendment to enter into force.

General Assembly resolution 50/202

22 December 1995      Meeting 99      Adopted without vote

Approved by Third Committee (A/50/816) without vote, 11 December (meeting 54); 5-nation draft (A/C.3/50/L.63), orally revised; agenda item 165.
*Sponsors:* Denmark, Finland, Iceland, Norway, Sweden.
*Meeting numbers.* GA 50th session: 3rd Committee 24, 26-31, 54; plenary 99.

### Ratifications, accessions and signatures

As at 31 December 1995,[11] there were 151 States parties to the 1979 Convention on the Elimination of All Forms of Discrimination against Women. During the year, Azerbaijan, Chad, Côte d'Ivoire, Eritrea, Fiji, Lesotho, Liechtenstein, Malaysia, Papua New Guinea, Singapore, South Africa, Uzbekistan and Vanuatu became parties.

As at 31 December 1995, no States parties to the Convention had accepted the amendment to article 20, paragraph 1, which had been adopted by the States parties at their eighth meeting on 22 May and noted with approval by the General Assembly on 22 December. The amendment would enter into force when accepted by a two-thirds majority of States parties.

In August, the Secretary-General submitted his annual report[12] to the General Assembly on the status of the Convention, which contained information on signatures, ratifications, successions and accessions as at 1 August 1995 and on reservations, objections to reservations and withdrawals of reservations and declarations between 1 August 1994 and 1 August 1995. On 22 December, the General Assembly, by **decision 50/459**, took note of his report.

### Implementation of Nairobi Strategies

A major review of the Nairobi Forward-looking Strategies for the Advancement of Women[13] was conducted by participants in the Fourth World Conference on Women. Objectives and actions designed to accelerate implementation of the Strategies were contained in the final documents of the Conference, known as the Beijing Declaration and Platform for Action.[14]

In September, pursuant to requests in 1985[15] and 1994,[16] the Secretary-General reported[17] on measures taken by the UN system and inter-governmental and non-governmental organizations to implement the Strategies. The report included an assessment of recent developments relevant to the priority themes of equality, development and peace, as well as a review of progress made in finalizing the system-wide medium-term plan for the advancement of women for the period 1996-2000.

The Secretary-General also provided information on the integration of older women in development, pursuant to a request of the General Assembly in 1994.[18] He noted that a life-cycle approach to dealing with the advancement of women had become normal in the activities of the organizations of the UN system; the UN Development Fund for Women (UNIFEM), in particular, had projects targeting older women and addressing their needs and interests. The report also outlined the references to older women's concerns in the Copenhagen Declaration, adopted at the 1995 World Summit for Social Development, and in the Beijing Declaration and Platform for Action, adopted at the Fourth World Conference on Women.

**Commission on Status of Women**

Completing preparations for the Fourth World Conference on Women, especially the draft Platform for Action, was the focus of the thirty-ninth session of the Commission on the Status of Women, held at UN Headquarters from 15 March to 7 April.[19] The Commission considered the draft rules of procedure, applications from NGOs for accreditation and issues related to Conference follow-up. In its regular work of monitoring activities to advance the status of women worldwide, the Commission adopted eight resolutions and four decisions, and also recommended to the Economic and Social Council the adoption of three additional draft resolutions: on improvement of the status of women in the Secretariat (see PART SIX, Chapter III); on Palestinian women; and on the Convention on the Elimination of All Forms of Discrimination against Women.

During the three-week session, the Commission considered three priority themes related to equality, development and peace; expert meetings were held on each topic before the session was convened, and the results incorporated into reports submitted to the Commission by the Secretary-General. The reports dealt with equality in economic decision-making,[20] promotion of literacy, education and training,[21] and the involvement of women in international decision-making.[22]

The Commission also considered a note by the Secretary-General[23] transmitting an expert report on existing technical and financial programmes in favour of women. As part of the Commission's preparations for the Fourth World Conference, the report offered guidelines for overcoming constraints and increasing cooperation in critical areas of concern as well as recommendations for strengthening the impact of UN assistance and financing for the advancement of women. The recommended measures included strategies for integrating gender analysis in policy, planning and implementation, and for increased accountability for improving the status of women through technical cooperation and financial assistance programmes.

On 24 July, the Economic and Social Council, by **decision 1995/252**, took note of the report of the Commission on its thirty-ninth session, and approved the provisional agenda and documentation for the Commission's fortieth session. On 25 July, by **decision 1995/253**, the Council observed that, in paragraph 5 of the Commission's resolution on women in agriculture and rural development, the word ''equity'' should be replaced by the word ''equality''.

*Communications*

The Commission on the Status of Women at its thirty-ninth session had before it a confidential list of communications concerning the status of women, which was distributed in a sealed envelope to the representatives of each of its States members, as well as a non-confidential list of communications, which were considered by the Working Group on Communications on the Status of Women. The Group was appointed in 1994,[24] on the basis of a 1983 recommendation of the Economic and Social Council.[25] In March, the Rapporteur of the Working Group expressed support for the communication procedure, but said that the communications had not reflected all aspects of violations of the human rights of women worldwide. The Secretariat should give more publicity to the communication procedure, and the report of the group should be published, according to the Rapporteur.[19]

**UN Development Fund for Women**

The Consultative Committee on the United Nations Development Fund for Women at its thirty-fifth session (New York, 3-7 April) reviewed progress in UNIFEM's work in various areas during the 1993-1994 biennium, as well as initiatives related to the Fourth World Conference on Women and the financial situation of the Fund. UNIFEM, formerly the Voluntary Fund for the United Nations Decade for Women,[26] was created to address the economic and social advancement of women and provide direct technical and financial support to women in developing countries.

The Consultative Committee noted that the Fund had a critical role to play in the Fourth World Conference on Women and in implementation of the Platform for Action. It recommended that when post-Beijing institutional arrangements and mandates were discussed, the question of UNIFEM's role in Eastern Europe should be seriously considered. Since 1994, UNIFEM, within the confines of its mandate limiting the commitment of its financial resources to what had been traditionally understood as the developing world, had provided technical assistance to the countries of Eastern Europe.

Regarding a resolution of UNIFEM's financial problem, the Committee expressed approval for establishment of a line of credit from the UN Development Program (UNDP) and co-financing of UNIFEM projects by UNDP and other agencies and donors. The Committee recognized the importance of maintaining UNIFEM's presence in the developing world through its regional programme advisers.

In the biennium 1993-1994, UNIFEM initiatives included launching programmes in every developing region to help women gain the skills needed to make advances in the area of decision-making. An important emphasis of the Fund's work was in linking women's development initiatives at the grass-roots level with the macroeconomic policy formulation that shaped their future. In Africa, UNIFEM focused on promoting agriculture and food security, trade and industry and the protection of the environment. In Asia and the Pacific, the Fund aimed to develop mechanisms to link women to formal decision-making structures that closely affected their lives and livelihoods. In Latin America and the Caribbean, the programme addressed environmental management and education, citizenship development and democratization, the institutional capacity-building of women's organizations, advocacy and support for initiatives addressing violence and poverty alleviation.

In May, the UNDP Administrator reported[27] that the main reason for the current financial situation was inadequate performance and oversight by key UNIFEM staff as to financial reviews, monitoring and controls in connection with the partial funding system (which permitted the Fund to allocate funds to projects in excess of available resources) and the decision to reduce the unexpended resources. The resulting financial deficit had remained undetected until August 1994.

In September, the Secretary-General transmitted to the General Assembly the report of the UNDP Administrator on the 1994 activities of UNIFEM.[28] UNIFEM's work was organized around a frame-work, the women's development agenda, which aimed for the economic and political empowerment of women. Economically, UNIFEM programmes had focused on economic restructuring, sustainable livelihoods and building stable lives and healthy communities, while political empowerment was ensured through programmes in peace building, conflict resolution and ethical governance and respect for civil society. The report also reviewed UNIFEM's strategy for the Fourth World Conference on Women, which had focused on ensuring that the concerns of diverse groups of women were heard during all preparatory activities. (See also under "Human rights of women" below.)

### International Research and Training Institute

The Board of Trustees of the International Research and Training Institute for the Advancement of Women (INSTRAW) held its fifteenth session in Santo Domingo, Dominican Republic, from 24 to 28 April 1995.[29] INSTRAW is an autonomous institution undertaking research and training programmes in close cooperation with other agencies, both within the UN system and on national, regional and international levels. Its aims are to contribute to the advancement and mobilization of women in development, to raise awareness of women's issues worldwide and to better assist women to meet new challenges and directions.

In 1995, the Board gave special attention to its preparation for the Fourth World Conference on Women and recommended that close attention be paid to the critical areas of concern in the Platform for Action submitted to the Conference. It stressed that INSTRAW should retain its original mandate, as stipulated by the General Assembly in 1975,[30] as well as a distinct capacity to carry out research and training for the advancement of women. The Board decided that INSTRAW should continue its work and establish priorities in areas where it had already acquired valuable research and training expertise. It proposed that an international conference on research and training on gender issues be convened in early 1996, to be hosted by the International Labour Organization (ILO) in Turin, Italy.

The Board also adopted the work programme for the biennium 1996-1997, focusing on the economic and political empowerment of women; women, environment and sustainable development; women, communication and the media; statistics and indicators on gender issues; and issues related to different population groups, including older and displaced women, refugee and migrant women and women in rural areas.

### INSTRAW activities

INSTRAW organized two panels at the Fourth World Conference and four workshops at the parallel NGO forum. In 1995, the Institute addressed such topics as the performance of a gender impact analysis of credit; methods for valuing the contribution of women; and development of communications materials for women and development. Among activities related to women, environment and sustainable development, INSTRAW conducted national training seminars on women, water supply and sanitation in Ecuador, Guyana and Namibia. It also prepared, in cooperation with ILO, the modular training package *Women, Environmental Management and Sustainable Development*. Other IN-STRAW publications in 1995 included research studies and training manuals, two issues of *IN-STRAW News* and a handbook entitled *Content Discontent: Towards a Fair Portrayal of Women in the Media*.

## ECONOMIC AND SOCIAL COUNCIL ACTION

On 27 July, the Economic and Social Council adopted **resolution 1995/45**.

### International Research and Training Institute for the Advancement of Women

*The Economic and Social Council*,

*Recalling* its resolution 1994/30 of 27 July 1994, in which it took note of the report of the Board of Trustees of the International Research and Training Institute for the Advancement of Women on its fourteenth session,

*Recalling also* General Assembly resolution 49/163 of 23 December 1994,

*Recognizing* the important role that the Institute plays in the substantive preparations for the Fourth World Conference on Women: Action for Equality, Development and Peace, to be held in Beijing from 4 to 15 September 1995, and the role of the Institute with respect to the Conference,

*Also recognizing* the equally important contribution of the Institute in its area of expertise to activities related to the International Conference on Population and Development, the World Summit for Social Development, the fiftieth anniversary of the United Nations, the United Nations Conference on Human Settlements (Habitat II) and the International Year of Older Persons,

*Reaffirming* the original mandate and distinct capacity of the Institute to carry out research and training for the advancement of women, as stipulated in General Assembly resolution 3520(XXX) of 15 December 1975,

*Taking note* of the recommendation of the Board of Trustees that the Institute should implement the recommendations emanating from the Fourth World Conference on Women, especially those related to research and training needs for the advancement of women, and coordinate effectively with United Nations bodies and organizations to avoid duplication,

*Taking into account* the fact that the Fourth World Conference on Women will consider the issue of institutional arrangements in the Platform for Action,

1. *Takes note with satisfaction* of the report of the Board of Trustees of the International Research and Training Institute for the Advancement of Women on its fifteenth session and the decisions contained therein;

2. *Takes note* of the analysis done by the Board of Trustees and its recommendation that the Institute

should also report to the Second Committee of the General Assembly under relevant agenda items, in order to improve the coordination and synergy of its programmes with other economic and social issues;

3. *Commends* the efforts of the Institute to address all levels of poverty that hamper so dramatically the advancement of women, through research and training activities in the areas of empowerment of women; statistics and indicators in gender issues; communications; women, natural resources and sustainable development; water and sanitation; waste management; renewable sources of energy; and issues related to different population groups, such as older persons and displaced, refugee and migrant women;

4. *Also commends* the Institute for its efforts further to develop active and close cooperation with the specialized agencies and related organizations of the United Nations system, the International Training Centre of the International Labour Organization, the United Nations Children's Fund, the United Nations Educational, Scientific and Cultural Organization, the United Nations University, the regional commissions and other organs, programmes and institutions, in order to promote programmes that contribute to the advancement of women;

5. *Reiterates* the importance of maintaining the level of resources devoted to independent research and related training activities, which are crucial for the situation of women;

6. *Calls upon* States and intergovernmental and non-governmental organizations to contribute through voluntary contributions and pledges to the United Nations Trust Fund for the International Research and Training Institute for the Advancement of Women, thus enabling the Institute to continue to respond effectively to its mandate.

Economic and Social Council resolution 1995/45

27 July 1995      Meeting 56      Adopted without vote

Draft by Philippines, for Group of 77 and China (E/1995/L.51), orally revised following informal consultations; agenda item 5 *(e)*.
*Meeting numbers.* ESC 51, 56.

Pursuant to a 1993 General Assembly request,[31] the Secretary-General in October reviewed[32] the activities of INSTRAW for the biennium 1994-1995, focusing on the Institute's specific objectives for the Fourth World Conference on Women, as well as its efforts to establish stronger linkages between the improvement of the status of women and the achievement of equitable sustainable development goals.

## GENERAL ASSEMBLY ACTION

On 22 December, the General Assembly adopted **resolution 50/163**.

### International Research and Training Institute for the Advancement of Women

*The General Assembly*,

*Recalling* its resolution 48/105 of 20 December 1993,

*Taking note* of Economic and Social Council resolution 1995/45 of 27 July 1995,

*Taking note also* of the report of the Board of Trustees of the International Research and Training Institute for the Advancement of Women on its fifteenth session,

*Taking note further* of the analysis done by the Board of Trustees and its recommendation that the Institute should also report to the Second Committee of the General Assembly under relevant agenda items, in order to improve the coordination and synergy of its programmes with other economic and social issues,

*Reaffirming* the original mandate and distinct capacity of the Institute to carry out research and training for the advancement of women, as stipulated in General Assembly resolution 3520(XXX) of 15 December 1975,

*Stressing* the need for independent research to ensure that policy-making and project implementation address issues and emerging areas of concern to women, and the role of the activities of the Institute therein,

*Noting* the recommendation of the Board of Trustees that the Institute should implement the recommendations emanating from the United Nations Conference on Environment and Development, the International Conference on Population and Development, the World Summit for Social Development and the Fourth World Conference on Women, especially those related to research and training needs for the advancement of women, and coordinate effectively with United Nations bodies and organizations to avoid duplication,

*Convinced* that sustainable development cannot be achieved without the full participation of women,

*Taking into account* paragraph 334 of the Platform for Action adopted by the Fourth World Conference on Women at Beijing on 15 September 1995,

1. *Expresses its satisfaction* with the report of the Board of Trustees of the International Research and Training Institute for the Advancement of Women, and commends the Institute for its efforts to focus on problems that constitute barriers to improving the status of women and their full participation in the sustainable development process;

2. *Emphasizes* the unique function of the Institute as the only entity within the United Nations system devoted exclusively to research and training for the integration of women in development, and stresses the importance of making its research findings available for policy purposes and for operational activities;

3. *Commends* the efforts of the Institute to address all levels of poverty that hamper so dramatically the advancement of women, through the coordination of research and training activities in the areas of empowerment of women; statistics and indicators in gender issues; communications; women, natural resources and sustainable development; water, sanitation and waste management; renewable sources of energy; and issues related to different population groups, such as older and displaced women, refugee and migrant women and women in rural areas;

4. *Encourages* the Institute to further develop active and close cooperation with the specialized agencies and related organizations of the United Nations system and with other institutions, such as universities and research institutions, so as to promote programmes that contribute to the advancement of women;

5. *Reiterates* the importance of maintaining the level of resources devoted to independent research and related training activities which are crucial for the situation of women;

6. *Expresses its appreciation* to those Governments and organizations which have contributed to and supported the activities of the Institute;

7. *Invites* Member States and intergovernmental and non-governmental organizations to contribute, through voluntary contributions and pledges, to the United Nations Trust Fund for the International Research and Training Institute for the Advancement of Women, thus enabling the Institute to continue to respond effectively to its mandate;

8. *Requests* the Secretary-General to submit to the General Assembly at its fifty-second session a report on the activities of the Institute, especially on those activities related to research and training needs for the advancement of women as contained in the follow-up process of the plans and platforms emanating from the major United Nations conferences, under the item entitled "Advancement of women".

General Assembly resolution 50/163

22 December 1995     Meeting 99     Adopted without vote

Approved by Third Committee (A/50/630) without vote, 1 December (meeting 46); draft by 14 nations and Latin American and Caribbean Group (A/C.3/50/L.22), orally revised; agenda item 107.
*Meeting numbers.* GA 50th session: 3rd Committee 24, 26-31, 40-42, 44, 46; plenary 99.

Also on 22 December, the General Assembly, in **decision 50/459**, took note of the Secretary-General's report on the activities of INSTRAW.

## Proposed merger of INSTRAW and UNIFEM

In 1993, the Secretary-General transmitted to the Economic and Social Council a proposal for the merger of INSTRAW and UNIFEM (see below under "Women and development"), based on a recommendation made by the high-level panel of advisers on the restructuring of the economic and social sectors of the Organization.[33]

The Beijing Platform for Action[14] called for both INSTRAW and UNIFEM to review their work programmes but reaffirmed their individual mandates and set out separate roles. It called on INSTRAW to identify those types of education and training programmes that could be effectively supported by the Institute. It also stated that adequate resources should be made available to UNIFEM for it to carry out its functions, focusing on women's economic and political empowerment.

In November, pursuant to a 1994 request,[34] the Secretary-General submitted to the General Assembly and Economic and Social Council additional information on the administrative and financial implications of the proposed merger of INSTRAW and UNIFEM.[35] On 27 November, the Advisory Committee on Administrative and Budgetary Questions pointed out[36] that the Secretary-General's report had not specified the results of the Commission on the Status of Women at its thirty-ninth session and of the Fourth World Conference on Women concerning institutional arrangements in the UN system for the advancement of women, and that these deliberations were among the prerequisites set by the General Assembly for consideration of the issue by the Council and for the Assembly's final decision.

On 12 December the Council, by **decision 1995/323**, decided to refer the matter to the General Assembly for consideration.

GENERAL ASSEMBLY ACTION

On 22 December, the General Assembly adopted **resolution 50/162**.

**Proposed merger of the International Research and Training Institute for the Advancement of Women and the United Nations Development Fund for Women**

*The General Assembly,*

*Recalling* its resolution 48/111 of 20 December 1993 regarding the proposal to merge the International Research and Training Institute for the Advancement of Women and the United Nations Development Fund for Women,

*Recalling also* its resolution 49/160 of 23 December 1994 regarding the proposed merger,

*Bearing in mind* the report of the Secretary-General of 7 July 1994, submitted pursuant to resolution 48/111,

*Bearing in mind also* the report of the Advisory Committee on Administrative and Budgetary Questions of 7 September 1994, prepared in compliance with resolution 48/111,

*Taking into consideration* its request to the Secretary-General, in resolution 49/160, that he submit, through the Advisory Committee on Administrative and Budgetary Questions, an updated report which would contain, *inter alia*, the information requested by the Economic and Social Council in its decision 1993/235 of 27 July 1993 and by the General Assembly in paragraphs 2 and 3 of resolution 48/111, as well as the additional information requested by the Advisory Committee,

*Also taking into consideration* paragraph 5 of resolution 49/160, in which it requested the Economic and Social Council to re-examine the issue at a resumed session to take place after the Fourth World Conference on Women and before the Third Committee of the General Assembly considered the question of the advancement of women, taking into account the deliberations of the Commission on the Status of Women at its thirty-ninth session, the Fourth World Conference on Women and the Advisory Committee on Administrative and Budgetary Questions concerning institutional arrangements in the United Nations system for the advancement of women,

*Keeping in mind* that the Commission on the Status of Women did not give an opinion on this matter, as requested by the General Assembly in resolution 49/160, owing to the lack of the documents requested therein,

*Keeping in mind also* that the Fourth World Conference on Women did not discuss the proposed merger of the Institute and the Fund, but outlined their mandates separately and distinctly,

*Taking note* of the opinion expressed in the report of the Joint Inspection Unit, entitled "The advancement of women through and in the programmes of the United Nations system: what happens after the Fourth World Conference on Women?", that the vast majority of women, and the most pressing problems for women, are in the developing world and that therefore at least one of the specific United Nations women's units should also be based there,

1. *Takes note* of the note by the Secretariat prepared pursuant to General Assembly resolution 49/160;

2. *Takes note also* of the report of the Advisory Committee on Administrative and Budgetary Questions;

3. *Reaffirms* the view expressed in paragraph 360 of the Platform for Action adopted by the Fourth World Conference on Women at Beijing on 15 September 1995 that, recognizing the roles of United Nations funds, programmes and specialized agencies, in particular the special roles of the United Nations Development Fund for Women and the International Research and Training Institute for the Advancement of Women, in the promotion of the empowerment of women and, therefore, in the implementation of the Platform for Action within their respective mandates, *inter alia*, in research, training and information activities for the advancement of women, as well as technical and financial assistance to incorporate a gender perspective in development efforts, the resources provided by the international community need to be sufficient and should be maintained at an adequate level;

4. *Concurs* with the views expressed in paragraphs 334 and 335 of the Platform for Action concerning the mandates of the Institute and the Fund;

5. *Regrets* that, owing to the absence of sufficient information on the legal, technical and administrative implications of the proposed merger, it is currently unable to decide on the proposed merger;

6. *Urges* the Secretary-General to implement the mandates set out in its resolution 49/163 of 23 December 1994;

7. *Recommends* that the interaction between the Commission on the Status of Women, the International Research and Training Institute for the Advancement of Women, the Committee on the Elimination of Discrimination against Women, the Division for the Advancement of Women of the Secretariat and the United Nations Development Fund for Women should be reviewed and rationalized within the context of ongoing efforts to revitalize the Economic and Social Council in pursuance of a stronger, more unified programme for the advancement of women as requested in paragraph 2 of resolution 48/111;

8. *Also recommends* that any proposal dealing with the institutional structure and the mandates of the different United Nations bodies dealing with the advancement of women must be considered part of the general restructuring exercise of the United Nations.

General Assembly resolution 50/162

22 December 1995     Meeting 99     Adopted without vote

Approved by Third Committee (A/50/630) without vote, 13 December (meeting 55); draft by Philippines, for Group of 77 (A/C.3/50/L.21/Rev.1); agenda item 107.

*Meeting numbers.* GA 50th session: 3rd Committee 24, 26-31, 40-42, 44, 46, 50, 51, 55; plenary 99.

## Women and development

### Integration of women in economic development

Pursuant to a 1987 General Assembly request,[37] the Secretary-General submitted in September his fourth biennial report[38] on the effective mobilization and integration of women in development. The report focused on gender issues in entrepreneurship, macroeconomic policymaking and development planning. Selection of this theme reflected the growing recognition in academic circles and among development practitioners of the need to consider gender as a variable in the design of economic policies if their implementation was to produce an efficient and socially desirable outcome. In his conclusions, the Secretary-General suggested that taking gender into account would require a modification of the underlying assumptions of development, and that all economic policy questions should be subject to examination in terms of their gender dimensions.

In **decision 1995/234** of 19 July, the Economic and Social Council noted the report.

GENERAL ASSEMBLY ACTION

On 20 December, the General Assembly adopted **resolution 50/104**.

### Women in development

*The General Assembly,*

*Recalling* its resolutions 40/204 of 17 December 1985, 42/178 of 11 December 1987 and 44/171 of 19 December 1989, as well as all other relevant Assembly resolutions on the integration of women in development, and the resolutions adopted by the Commission on the Status of Women on the integration of women in development,

*Bearing in mind* the outcome of the Fourth World Conference on Women and other recent major United Nations conferences and summits,

*Recognizing* the significant contribution that women make to economic activities and the major force that they represent for change and development in all sectors of the economy, especially in key areas, such as agriculture, industry and services,

*Reaffirming* that women are key contributors to the economy and to combating poverty through both remunerated and unremunerated work at home, in the community and in the workplace, and that the empowerment of women is a critical factor in the eradication of poverty,

*Recognizing* that the difficult socio-economic conditions that exist in many developing countries have resulted in the rapid feminization of poverty, especially in rural areas and in female-headed households,

*Aware* that the continued discrimination against women, their continued lack of equal access to education and training, and their lack of control over land, capital, technology and other areas of production impede their full contribution to, and opportunity to benefit from, development,

*Recognizing* that the informal sector is a major source of entrepreneurship and employment for women in many developing countries,

*Noting* the importance of the organizations and bodies of the United Nations system in facilitating the advancement of women in development,

1. *Welcomes* the adoption of the Beijing Declaration and Platform for Action by the Fourth World Conference on Women;

2. *Takes note* of the report of the Secretary-General on the effective mobilization and integration of women in development;

3. *Calls* for the urgent implementation of the Platform for Action adopted at Beijing as well as the relevant provisions contained in the outcome of all other major United Nations conferences and summits;

4. *Stresses* that a favourable and conducive international and national economic and financial environment and a positive investment climate are necessary for the effective integration of women in development;

5. *Also stresses* the importance of developing national strategies for promoting sustainable and productive entrepreneurial activities to generate income among disadvantaged women and women living in poverty;

6. *Calls upon* all Governments and all actors of society to implement the commitment made in Beijing to create an enabling environment through, *inter alia*, removing discriminatory barriers and ensuring the full and equal participation of women in economic activities through, *inter alia*, the adoption of gender-sensitive policies and legal measures and the provision of other necessary structures;

7. *Urges* all Governments to ensure women's equal rights and access to economic resources, and to increase women's access to credit by instituting innovative lending practices, including practices that integrate credit with services and training for women, and that provide flexible credit facilities to women, in particular rural women, women in the informal sector, young women and women who lack access to traditional sources of collateral;

8. *Urges* Governments to develop and promote methodologies for incorporating a gender perspective into all aspects of policy-making, including economic policy-making;

9. *Calls upon* the United Nations system, in particular its funds and programmes and specialized agencies, and all other relevant organizations to promote an active and visible policy of mainstreaming gender perspective in the implementation, monitoring and evaluation of all policies and programmes;

10. *Urges* the international community, the United Nations system and other relevant organizations to give priority to assisting developing countries' efforts to ensure the full and effective participation of women in deciding and implementing development strategies, including through increased access to health care, capital, education, training and technology, as well as by women's wider participation in decision-making;

11. *Urges* multilateral donors, international financial institutions and regional development banks to review and implement policies in support of national efforts to ensure that a higher proportion of resources reach women, in particular in rural and remote areas;

12. *Requests* the United Nations development system to work towards establishing a more coherent approach to its support for women's income-generating activities, in particular credit schemes;

13. *Decides* to include in the provisional agenda of its fifty-second session a sub-item entitled ''Effective mobilization and integration of women in development'';

14. *Requests* the Secretary-General to submit to the General Assembly at its fifty-second session a report on action taken to implement the present resolution.

General Assembly resolution 50/104

20 December 1995    Meeting 96    Adopted without vote

Approved by Second Committee (A/50/617/Add.6) without vote, 8 December (meeting 42); draft by Vice-Chairman (A/C.2/50/L.66), orally revised and based on informal consultations on draft by Philippines, for Group of 77 and China (A/C.2/50/L.46); agenda item 95 (f).
*Meeting numbers*. GA 50th session: 2nd Committee 35-37, 40, 42; plenary 96.

## Women in rural areas

In March, the Commission on the Status of Women adopted a resolution appealing to Governments to pay special attention to the situation of rural women, with emphasis on those displaced from their place of origin owing to terrorist violence, drug trafficking or other causes related to situations of violence.[39] It also urged Governments, in their development programmes, to consider projects that had positive effects upon displaced rural women and were geared primarily to productive employment, in order to facilitate the integration of those women into their new social setting or their return to their place of origin or another place of their preference. The Commission decided to consider the question of the integration of displaced rural women into development processes at its fortieth session.

The Commission also urged Governments[40] to develop specific plans to support rural women's full participation in the economy and in the political system, and to set up monitoring and evaluation measures to appraise progress made. It urged them to integrate gender issues in mainstream research and policy initiatives; promote legislative initiatives that guarantee equity in the wage system and increase the status of women in agriculture, family enterprises, the professions and the informal sector; and to empower rural women to develop their potential and to actively engage, individually or in groups, in the fight for the enforcement of their rights.

In response to a 1993 General Assembly request,[41] the Secretary-General reported[42] on improvement in the situation of women in rural areas, and also examined the trends that would affect the status of women in the twenty-first century. Noting that by the beginning of the next century, half of the world's population would be living in urban areas and the proportion of women living in rural areas would continue to decline globally, the Secretary-General suggested that the importance of rural women in the next century would rest more on their impact on the economy and society than on their numbers. It would relate to their contribution to food security and to economic growth as well as to the maintenance of social cohesion.

In July, by **decision 1995/314**, the Economic and Social Council took note of the Secretary-General's report.

GENERAL ASSEMBLY ACTION

On 22 December, the General Assembly adopted **resolution 50/165**.

### Improvement of the situation of women in rural areas

*The General Assembly*,

*Recalling* its resolution 34/14 of 9 November 1979, in which it endorsed the Declaration of Principles and the Programme of Action as adopted by the World Conference on Agrarian Reform and Rural Development, and its resolutions 44/78 of 8 December 1989 and 48/109 of 20 December 1993,

*Recalling also* the importance attached to the problems of rural women by the Nairobi Forward-looking Strategies for the Advancement of Women and by the Beijing Declaration and the Platform for Action adopted by the Fourth World Conference on Women on 15 September 1995,

*Recalling further* its resolution 47/174 of 22 December 1992, in which it welcomed the adoption of the Geneva Declaration for Rural Women by the Summit on the Economic Advancement of Rural Women, held at Geneva in February 1992, and urged all States to work for the achievement of the goals endorsed in the Declaration,

*Welcoming* the growing awareness of Governments of the need for strategies and programmes to improve the situation of women in rural areas,

*Noting with deep concern* that the economic and financial crises in many developing countries have severely affected the socio-economic status of women, especially in rural areas, and the continuing rise in the number of rural women living in poverty,

*Recognizing* the urgent need to take appropriate measures aimed at further improving the situation of women in rural areas,

1. *Takes note* of the report of the Secretary-General;

2. *Invites* Member States, in their efforts to implement the outcome of the United Nations Conference on Environment and Development, the World Conference on Human Rights, the International Conference on Population and Development, the World Summit for Social Development and the Fourth World Conference on Women, bearing in mind also the Geneva Declaration for Rural Women, to attach greater importance to the improvement of the situation of rural women in their national development strategies, paying special attention to both their practical and their strategic needs, by, *inter alia*:

(*a*) Integrating the concerns of rural women into national development policies and programmes, in particular by placing a higher priority on budgetary allocation related to the interests of rural women;

(*b*) Strengthening national machineries and establishing institutional linkages among governmental bodies in various sectors and non-governmental organizations that are concerned with rural development;

(*c*) Increasing the participation of rural women in the decision-making process;

(*d*) Undertaking necessary measures to give rural women full and equal access to productive resources, including the right to inheritance and to ownership of land and other property, credit/capital, natural resources, appropriate technologies, markets and information, and meeting their basic requirements in water and sanitation;

*(e)* Investing in the human resources of rural women, particularly through health and literacy programmes and social support measures;

3. *Requests* the international community and relevant United Nations organizations and bodies to promote the realization of the programmes and projects aimed at the improvement of the situation of rural women within the overall framework of integrated follow-up to recent global conferences;

4. *Invites* the World Food Summit to be convened by the Food and Agriculture Organization of the United Nations in 1996 to give due consideration to the issue of improving the situation of rural women, taking into account their role in food production and food security, and the United Nations Conference on Human Settlements (Habitat II) to give due consideration to the gender aspects of rural-urban migration and its impact on the situation of rural women, in formulating relevant strategies and actions;

5. *Requests* the Secretary-General to prepare, in consultation with Member States and relevant United Nations organizations, a report on the implementation of the present resolution and to submit it, through the Economic and Social Council, to the General Assembly at its fifty-second session, taking into account possible measures to improve the reporting procedure.

General Assembly resolution 50/165

22 December 1995     Meeting 99     Adopted without vote

Approved by Third Committee (A/50/630) without vote, 6 December (meeting 51); 59-nation draft (A/C.3/50/L.24), orally revised; agenda item 107.
*Meeting numbers.* GA 50th session: 3rd Committee 24, 26-31, 40-42, 44, 46, 50, 51; plenary 99.

## Human rights of women

### Violence against women

At its thirty-ninth session,[19] the Commission on the Status of Women had before it a February report of the Secretary-General[43] on activities undertaken by UN bodies concerned with crime prevention with regard to the question of violence against women.

The preliminary report of the Special Rapporteur of the Commission on Human Rights on violence against women[44] included information on the dimensions of the problem of violence against women; the Commission on Human Rights, at its annual session, also considered the issue. (See PART THREE, Chapters I and II.)

### Violence against women migrant workers

In March, the Commission on the Status of Women adopted a resolution concerning continuing reports of grave abuses committed against women migrant workers by some of their employers in host countries.[45] The Commission called upon Member States to adopt measures for the effective implementation of the Declaration on the Elimination of Violence against Women,[46] including applying them to women migrant workers. It urged Member States to adopt and implement measures to eradicate all forms of racism and xenophobia and to promote education on human rights understanding and acceptance of cultural diversity. It called upon States to explore the possibility of adopting measures to prevent the victimization of women migrant workers by sexual traffickers and to penalize those traffickers, including ratifying the Convention for the Suppression of the Traffic in Persons and of the Exploitation of the Prostitution of Others.[47]

The Commission invited relevant UN bodies to monitor the situation of women migrant workers and repeated its request that the Secretary-General ensure development of concrete indicators as a basis for future action to determine the situation of women migrant workers in sending and receiving countries. The Secretary-General was also asked to consider establishing an expert group on the matter, which would submit recommendations for improving coordination of the various efforts of the United Nations on behalf of migrant workers.

In August, the Secretary-General reported[48] on steps taken to prevent violence against women migrant workers pursuant to a 1994 request of the General Assembly.[49] He noted that the short time between the Commission's 1995 session and the fiftieth session of the Assembly made it impossible to organize the requested expert group meeting on the topic of violence against women migrant workers, and that no information had been received from Governments on national measures taken to identify problem areas in protecting women migrant workers. He noted, however, that the Special Rapporteur of the Commission on Human Rights on violence against women intended to carry out a fact-finding mission to a receiving country in 1996 to permit an in-depth analysis of the problem.

**GENERAL ASSEMBLY ACTION**

On 22 December, the General Assembly adopted **resolution 50/168**.

#### Violence against women migrant workers

*The General Assembly,*

*Recalling* its resolutions 47/96 of 16 December 1992, 48/110 of 20 December 1993 and 49/165 of 23 December 1994, as well as Commission on the Status of Women resolution 38/7 of 18 March 1994, and taking note of Commission on the Status of Women resolution 39/7 of 31 March 1995 and Commission on Human Rights resolution 1995/20 of 24 February 1995,

*Taking note* of the report of the Secretary-General,

*Taking note with concern* of the report of the Working Group on Contemporary Forms of Slavery of the Subcommission on Prevention of Discrimination and Protection of Minorities on its twentieth session, in particular its observations with respect to the treatment of migrant workers,

*Acknowledging* the preliminary report of the Special Rapporteur of the Commission on Human Rights on violence against women, its causes and its consequences,

*Stressing* that the promotion of the human rights of women constitutes an integral part of human rights activities of the United Nations, as reaffirmed in the Vienna Declaration and Programme of Action, adopted by the World Conference on Human Rights on 25 June 1993,

*Affirming* the Programme of Action of the International Conference on Population and Development, which called upon all countries to take full measures to eliminate all forms of exploitation, abuse, harassment and violence against women,

*Welcoming* the Copenhagen Declaration on Social Development and the Programme of Action of the World Summit for Social Development, adopted by the World Summit on 12 March 1995, which declared that countries should take concrete measures against the exploitation of migrants,

*Welcoming also* the Beijing Declaration and the Platform for Action, adopted by the Fourth World Conference on Women on 15 September 1995, which recognized the vulnerability to violence and other forms of abuse of women migrants, including women migrant workers, whose legal status in the host country depends on employers who may exploit their situations,

*Noting* the large numbers of women from developing countries and from some countries with economies in transition who continue to venture forth to more affluent countries in search of a living for themselves and their families, as a consequence of poverty, unemployment and other socio-economic conditions, while acknowledging the primary duty of States to work for conditions that provide employment and security to their citizens,

*Concerned* by the continuing reports of grave abuses and acts of violence committed against the persons of women migrant workers by some employers in some host countries,

*Encouraged* by some measures adopted by some receiving countries to alleviate the plight of women migrant workers residing within their areas of jurisdiction,

*Reiterating* that acts of violence directed against women impair or nullify their enjoyment of their human rights and fundamental freedoms,

1. *Determines* to prevent and eliminate all forms of violence against women and girls;

2. *Calls upon* States Members of the United Nations to adopt measures for the effective implementation of the Declaration on the Elimination of Violence against Women, including applying them to women migrant workers, as well as all relevant measures emanating from recent world conferences;

3. *Encourages* Member States to enact and/or reinforce penal, civil, labour and administrative sanctions in domestic legislation to punish and redress the wrongs done to women and girls who are subjected to any form of violence, whether in the home, the workplace, the community or society;

4. *Also encourages* Member States to adopt and/or implement and periodically to review and analyse legislation to ensure its effectiveness in eliminating violence against women, emphasizing the prevention of violence and the prosecution of offenders, and to take measures to ensure the protection of women subjected to violence and that they have access to just and effective remedies, including compensation and indemnification and healing of victims, and for the rehabilitation of perpetrators;

5. *Reiterates* the need for States concerned, specifically the sending and receiving States of women migrant workers, to conduct regular consultations for the purpose of identifying problem areas in promoting and protecting the rights of women migrant workers and ensuring health, legal and social services for them, adopting specific measures to address these problems, setting up, as necessary, linguistically and culturally accessible services and mechanisms to implement these measures and, in general, creating conditions that foster greater harmony and tolerance between women migrant workers and the rest of the society in which they reside;

6. *Encourages* Member States to consider signing and ratifying or acceding to the International Convention on the Protection of the Rights of All Migrant Workers and Members of Their Families, as well as the Slavery Convention of 1926;

7. *Recommends* that the issue of violence against women migrant workers be included in the agenda of the inter-agency meeting that precedes the regular session of the Commission on the Status of Women;

8. *Requests* the Secretary-General to convene a meeting of an expert group, with the participation of the Special Rapporteur of the Commission on Human Rights on violence against women and under the regular programme of the Division for the Advancement of Women of the Secretariat, to submit recommendations for improving coordination of the various efforts of United Nations agencies on the issue of violence against women migrant workers and to develop concrete indicators as a basis for determining the situation of women migrant workers for submission, through normal channels, to the General Assembly at its fifty-first session;

9. *Requests* the United Nations High Commissioner for Human Rights, the Centre for Human Rights of the Secretariat and the Special Rapporteur, as well as all relevant bodies and programmes in the United Nations system, when addressing the issue of violence against women, to give particular attention to the issue of violence perpetrated against women migrant workers and to submit reports thereon to the General Assembly;

10. *Invites* trade unions to support the realization of the rights of women migrant workers by assisting them in organizing themselves so as to enable them better to assert their rights;

11. *Requests* the Secretary-General to report to the General Assembly at its fifty-first session on the implementation of the present resolution, including on reports received from all authorities and bodies in the United Nations system, Member States, intergovernmental organizations and other concerned bodies, with due regard for possible measures to improve the reporting procedure.

General Assembly resolution 50/168

22 December 1995    Meeting 99    Adopted without vote

Approved by Third Committee (A/50/630) without vote, 13 December (meeting 55); 13-nation draft (A/C.3/50/L.27), orally revised; agenda item 107.
*Meeting numbers.* GA 50th session: 3rd Committee 24, 26-31, 40-42, 44, 46, 50, 51, 55; plenary 99.

## Women and children in armed conflicts

On 31 March, the Commission on the Status of Women adopted a resolution calling for the release of women and children taken hostage in armed conflicts before the opening of the Beijing Conference on 4 September.[50] The Commission asked the Secretary-General and international agencies to help facilitate their release. The Secretary-General was also asked to report to the Fourth World Conference on Women as to the situation concerning their release and also to report to the Commission at its fortieth session on implementation of the resolution. (For other information, see PART THREE, Chapter II.)

### Rape and abuse in the former Yugoslavia

In March, the Commission on the Status of Women condemned the continuing abhorrent practice of rape and abuse of women and children in the areas of armed conflict in the former Yugoslavia, which constituted a war crime, and demanded that those involved immediately cease those outrageous acts.[51] The Commission voted 35 in favour to 1 against (Russian Federation), with 5 abstentions (Angola, Belarus, India, Madagascar and Namibia), to retain a preambular paragraph in that text by which the Commission expressed its conviction that the heinous practice of rape and abuse of women constituted a deliberate weapon of war fulfilling the policy of "ethnic cleansing" carried out by Serb forces in the Republic of Bosnia and Herzegovina.

The Commission also condemned the persistent denial of access by the Bosnian Serb forces to the Special Rapporteur, the Special Representative of the Secretary-General, the Office of the UN High Commissioner for Refugees and the UN Protection Force (UNPROFOR), as well as other agencies, and demanded that immediate and unimpeded access be granted. The Commission urged all States and relevant organizations to consider the recommendations of the Special Rapporteur, in particular for the continuation of necessary medical and psychological care to victims of rape, within the framework of programmes to rehabilitate women and children traumatized by war. It asked the Secretary-General to help enable any future missions to have free and secure access to places of detention.

**GENERAL ASSEMBLY ACTION**

On 22 December, the General Assembly adopted **resolution 50/166.**

**The role of the United Nations Development Fund for Women in eliminating violence against women**

*The General Assembly,*

*Welcoming* the Beijing Declaration and the Platform for Action, which called for the prevention and elimination of all forms of violence against women and girls and the promotion and protection of all human rights of women and girls, stressing that acts or threats of violence, whether occurring within the home or in the community or perpetrated or condoned by the State, instilled fear and insecurity in women's lives and were obstacles to the achievement of equality, development and peace,

*Recalling* that the Platform for Action called for action to eradicate violence against the girl child, recognizing that girls were more vulnerable to all kinds of violence,

*Recalling also* that the Vienna Declaration and Programme of Action affirmed that gender-based violence and all forms of sexual harassment and exploitation, including those resulting from cultural prejudice and international trafficking, were incompatible with the dignity and worth of the human person and must be eliminated,

*Recalling further* its resolution 48/104 of 20 December 1993, proclaiming the Declaration on the Elimination of Violence against Women, in which it recognized that violence against women violated and impaired or nullified the enjoyment by women of human rights and fundamental freedoms,

*Recognizing* the importance of the effective implementation of the Convention on the Elimination of All Forms of Discrimination against Women,

*Emphasizing* the need for full implementation by Governments and community organizations, non-governmental organizations, educational institutions, and the public and private sectors, as appropriate, of the measures set out in the Beijing Declaration and the Platform for Action,

*Urging* that Governments allocate adequate resources within their budgets and mobilize community resources for activities related to the elimination of violence against women, including resources for the implementation of plans of action at all appropriate levels, as called for in paragraph 124 (*p*) of the Platform for Action,

*Taking note* of Economic and Social Council resolution 1995/27 of 24 July 1995, in which the Council approved resolution 8 of the Ninth United Nations Congress on the Prevention of Crime and the Treatment of Offenders concerning the elimination of violence against women and urged the Commission on Crime Prevention and Criminal Justice to continue to consider the elimination of violence against women within its priority themes and within the training and technical assistance efforts of the United Nations Crime Prevention and Criminal Justice Programme,

*Recognizing* the importance of cooperation with the Special Rapporteur of the Commission on Human Rights on violence against women,

*Reaffirming* the importance of developing a holistic and multidisciplinary approach to the task of promoting families, communities and States that are free from violence against women, and affirming the need for coordinated and strengthened international support for this approach,

*Recalling* its resolution 48/107 of 20 December 1993, in which it reaffirmed the catalytic role that the United Nations Development Fund for Women has played in facilitating the efforts of Governments and non-governmental organizations at the national and community levels to support innovative activities that directly benefit and empower women and in increasing opportunities and options for women in developing countries to participate more effectively in the development of their countries, in line with national priorities,

1. *Reiterates its appreciation* for the advocacy initiatives of the United Nations Development Fund for Women, including its contribution to and participation in the follow-up to the Vienna Declaration and Programme of Action, in particular with respect to efforts to combat violence against women, commends the Fund for its support of catalytic and innovative projects that strengthen the national capacity to improve the situation of women, and takes note with appreciation of the Platform for Action which affirmed that the Fund had the mandate to increase options and opportunities for women's economic and social development in developing countries by providing technical and financial assistance to incorporate the women's dimension into development at all levels and that it should review and strengthen, as appropriate, its work programme in the light of the Platform for Action, focusing on women's political and economic empowerment;

2. *Requests* the Fund, as one of the operational bodies of the United Nations, to take into account the need to strengthen its activities to eliminate violence against women as part of system-wide efforts of the United Nations towards this goal, in accordance with the measures set out in the Beijing Declaration and the Platform for Action and the Declaration on the Elimination of Violence against Women and focusing on activities, particularly at the national and community levels, and calls upon Member States to promote cooperation with the Fund to these ends;

3. *Also requests* the Fund, in undertaking any relevant activities, to cooperate closely with the relevant United Nations organs and bodies, in particular the Division for the Advancement of Women of the Secretariat, the Special Rapporteur of the Commission on Human Rights on violence against women, the Centre for Human Rights of the Secretariat, the Crime Prevention and Criminal Justice Branch of the Secretariat and the United Nations Children's Fund, in order to ensure that its activities form part of the system-wide efforts of the United Nations to eliminate violence against women;

4. *Further requests* the Fund to include in its regular reports information regarding its activities to eliminate violence against women and girls and to provide such information to the Commission on the Status of Women and the Commission on Human Rights;

5. *Requests* the Administrator of the United Nations Development Programme, in consultation with the Secretary-General, as well as with the relevant United Nations organs and bodies, in particular the Division for the Advancement of Women, the Special Rapporteur of the Commission on Human Rights on violence against women, the Centre for Human Rights and the Crime Prevention and Criminal Justice Branch, to consider the possibility of establishing a trust fund, within the existing mandate, structure and management of the United Nations Development Fund for Women, in support of national, regional and international actions, including those taken by Governments and nongovernmental organizations, to eliminate violence against women;

6. *Requests* the Fund to include in its regular reports information on the implementation of the present resolution and also to provide such information to the Commission on the Status of Women and the Commission on Human Rights.

General Assembly resolution 50/166

22 December 1995     Meeting 99     Adopted without vote

Approved by Third Committee (A/50/630 & Corr.1) without vote, 5 December (meeting 50); 47-nation draft (A/C.3/50/L.25/Rev.1); agenda item 107.
*Meeting numbers.* GA 50th session: 3rd Committee 24, 26-31, 40-42, 44, 46, 50; plenary 99.

## Traffic in women and girls

In March, the Commission on the Status of Women invited Governments to combat trafficking in women and children through national and internationally coordinated measures, and at the same time to establish or strengthen institutions for the protection of the victims of such trafficking.[52] The Commission recommended that the problem be given consideration within the implementation of all relevant international legal instruments and that consideration be given to measures to strengthen them if necessary. The Commission requested that the International Day for the Abolition of Slavery (2 December 1996) focus on the problem of trafficking in human persons, especially women and children, and that one meeting of the fifty-first session of the General Assembly be devoted to the discussion of the problem.

As requested by the General Assembly in 1994,[53] the Secretary-General reported[54] in August on steps taken to address the problem of traffic in women and girls. He concluded that concern for trafficking in women as an international problem was growing and had been considered in a variety of forums, which in most cases addressed separately aspects such as human rights dimensions, migration and its regulation, crime prevention and social services. The steps requested by the General Assembly in 1994, including the gathering and sharing of information about all aspects of traffic in women and girls, the adoption of prevention and sanctioning measures and the provision of support, legal advice and other services for victims, all implied the desirability of a comprehensive approach to the issue. The Secretary-General suggested undertaking a full appraisal of the most appropriate means to ensure such an approach, which could include the preparation by the Secretary-General of a comprehensive report on measures to address international trafficking, both at the intergovernmental and inter-secretariat levels.

**GENERAL ASSEMBLY ACTION**

On 22 December, the General Assembly adopted **resolution 50/167**.

### Traffic in women and girls
*The General Assembly,*

*Reaffirming* the principles set forth in the Universal Declaration of Human Rights, the Convention on the Elimination of All Forms of Discrimination against

Women, the International Covenants on Human Rights, the Convention against Torture and Other Cruel, Inhuman or Degrading Treatment or Punishment, the Convention on the Rights of the Child and the Declaration on the Elimination of Violence against Women,

*Recalling* that the Vienna Declaration and Programme of Action, adopted by the World Conference on Human Rights on 25 June 1993, affirmed the human rights of women and the girl child as an inalienable, integral and indivisible part of universal human rights,

*Welcoming* the Programme of Action of the International Conference on Population and Development which, *inter alia*, called upon all Governments to prevent all international trafficking in migrants, especially for the purpose of prostitution, and for the adoption by Governments of both receiving countries and countries of origin of effective sanctions against those who organize undocumented migration, exploit undocumented migrants or engage in trafficking in undocumented migrants, especially those who engage in any form of international traffic of women and children,

*Recalling* the recognition by the World Summit for Social Development, held at Copenhagen from 6 to 12 March 1995, of the danger to society of the trafficking in women and children,

*Welcoming* the initiatives taken by the Commission on Crime Prevention and Criminal Justice and the Ninth United Nations Congress on the Prevention of Crime and the Treatment of Offenders, held at Cairo from 29 April to 8 May 1995, towards criminalizing clandestine traffic in illegal migrants,

*Concurring* with the conclusion in the Platform for Action adopted by the Fourth World Conference on Women at Beijing on 15 September 1995, that the effective suppression of trafficking in women and girls for the sex trade is a matter of pressing international concern,

*Recalling* its resolution 49/166 of 23 December 1994, and taking note of Commission on the Status of Women resolution 39/6 of 29 March 1995,

*Acknowledging* the work done by intergovernmental and non-governmental organizations in compiling information on the scale and complexity of the problem of trafficking, in providing shelters for trafficked women and children and in effecting their voluntary repatriation to their countries of origin,

*Noting with concern* the increasing number of women and girl children from developing countries and from some countries with economies in transition who are being victimized by traffickers, and acknowledging that the problem of trafficking also victimizes young boys,

*Convinced* of the need to eliminate all forms of sexual violence and sexual trafficking, including for prostitution and other forms of commercial sex, which are violations of the human rights of women and girl children and are incompatible with the dignity and worth of the human person,

*Realizing* the urgent need for the adoption of effective measures nationally, regionally and internationally to protect women and girl children from this nefarious traffic,

1. *Takes note with appreciation* of the report of the Secretary-General on the traffic in women and girls;

2. *Appeals* to Governments to take appropriate measures to address the root factors, including external factors, that encourage trafficking in women and girls for prostitution and other forms of commercialized sex, forced marriages and forced labour, so as to eliminate trafficking in women, including by strengthening existing legislation with a view to providing better protection of the rights of women and girls and to punishing perpetrators, through both criminal and civil measures;

3. *Invites* Governments to combat trafficking in women and children through nationally and internationally coordinated measures, at the same time establishing or strengthening institutions for the protection of the victims of trafficking of women and children, and to ensure for victims the necessary assistance, including legal support services that are linguistically and culturally accessible, for their full protection, treatment and rehabilitation;

4. *Also invites* Governments to consider the development of standard minimum rules for the humanitarian treatment of trafficked persons, consistent with human rights standards;

5. *Urges* concerned Governments to support comprehensive, practical approaches by the international community to assist women and children victims of transnational trafficking to return home and be reintegrated into their home societies;

6. *Encourages* Member States to consider signing and ratifying or acceding to the Convention for the Suppression of the Traffic in Persons and the Exploitation of the Prostitution of Others, international agreements on the suppression of slavery and other relevant international instruments;

7. *Invites* the United Nations High Commissioner for Human Rights, in addressing the obstacles to the realization of the human rights of women, in particular, through his contacts with the Special Rapporteur of the Commission on Human Rights on violence against women and the Special Rapporteur of the Commission on Human Rights on the sale of children, child prostitution and child pornography, to include the traffic in women and girls among his priority concerns;

8. *Also encourages* the Centre for Human Rights of the Secretariat to include the traffic in women and girls in its programme of work under its advisory, training and information services, with a view to providing assistance to member Governments, upon their request, in instituting preventive measures against trafficking through education and appropriate information campaigns;

9. *Requests* the Commission on Human Rights to encourage the Working Group on Contemporary Forms of Slavery of the Subcommission on Prevention of Discrimination and Protection of Minorities to continue to address the issue of the traffic in women and girls under its draft programme of action on the traffic in persons and the exploitation of the prostitution of others;

10. *Requests* the Commission on Crime Prevention and Criminal Justice to consider appropriate follow-up to the Ninth United Nations Congress on the Prevention of Crime and the Treatment of Offenders on measures to address the problem of trafficking in women and children and to submit a report thereon to the Secretary-General, through the usual channels, for inclusion in his report to the General Assembly;

11. *Invites* relevant intergovernmental and non-governmental organizations to provide advisory services to Governments, upon their request, in planning and setting up rehabilitation programmes for victims

of trafficking and in training personnel who will be directly involved in the implementation of these programmes;

12. *Decides* to focus the International Day for the Abolition of Slavery, 2 December 1996, on the problem of trafficking in human persons, especially women and children, and to devote one meeting of the fifty-first session of the General Assembly to the discussion of this problem;

13. *Requests* the Secretary-General to submit to the General Assembly at its fifty-first session, under the item entitled "Advancement of women", a comprehensive report on the implementation of the present resolution, with due regard for possible measures to improve the reporting procedure.

General Assembly resolution 50/167

22 December 1995     Meeting 99     Adopted without vote

Approved by Third Committee (A/50/630) without vote, 13 December (meeting 55); 33-nation draft (A/C.3/50/L.26/Rev.1); agenda item 107.
*Meeting numbers.* GA 50th session: 3rd Committee 24, 26-31, 40-42, 44, 46, 50, 51, 55; plenary 99.

## Women in the Middle East

In March, the Commission on the Status of Women adopted a resolution emphasizing that the achievement of a just and lasting peace in the Middle East was vital for the implementation of the human rights of women in the area.[55] It urged Governments and other bodies to ensure the political development and participation of Palestinian women and to expedite economic, financial and technical assistance to them.

### Palestinian women

In March, the Secretary-General reported[56] on progress made in implementing the Nairobi Forward-looking Strategies with regard to Palestinian women, highlighting in particular the issues of concern within the present political context. The report discussed such aspects as violence, governance, health, education and employment, placing emphasis on development aspects and the participation of women in political decision-making.

On 25 July, the Economic and Social Council adopted **resolution 1995/30** on Palestinian women (see PART TWO, Chapter VI).

## Human rights mechanisms

Pursuant to a 1994 General Assembly request, the Secretary-General in March outlined[57] steps to be taken by the UN Division for the Advancement of Women and the UN Centre for Human Rights to ensure that relevant UN human rights mechanisms regularly addressed violations of the rights of women. The report included the proposed joint work plan for the UN Centre for Human Rights and the Division for the Advancement of Women. The plan, which covered 1995, focused on three activities: training, advisory services and educational materials.

In March, the Commission on the Status of Women recommended[58] that the Division for the Advancement of Women provide input for the next meeting of chairmen of the human rights treaty bodies, in order to assist those bodies in addressing violations of women's rights, for example by amending their reporting guidelines. The Commission urged States to consider the gender composition of the treaty bodies when electing candidates and asked the Secretary-General, on an annual basis, to oversee preparation of a joint work plan on the human rights of women for the Centre for Human Rights and the Division for the Advancement of Women.

*REFERENCES*

[1]YUN 1979, p. 895, GA res. 34/180, annex, 18 Dec. 1979. [2]YUN 1982, p. 1149. [3]A/50/38. [4]YUN 1993, p. 1049. [5]A/50/30, gen. rec. 22. [6]A/50/38, sugg. 7. [7]Ibid., sugg. 8. [8]A/CONF.177/7. [9]YUN 1994, p. 1196, GA dec. 49/448, 23 Dec. 1994. [10]YUN 1994, p. 1195. [11]*Multinational Treaties Deposited with the Secretary-General: Status as at 31 December 1995* (ST/LEG/SER.E/14), Sales No. E.96.V.5. [12]A/50/346. [13]YUN 1985, p. 937. [14]A/CONF.177/20. [15]YUN 1985, p. 940, GA res. 40/108, 13 Dec. 1985. [16]YUN 1994, p. 1179, GA res. 49/161, 23 Dec. 1994. [17]A/50/398. [18]YUN 1994, p. 1186, GA res. 49/162, 23 Dec. 1994. [19]E/1993/26. [20]E/CN.6/1995/10. [21]E/CN.6/1995/11. [22]E/CN.6/1995/12. [23]E/CN.6/1995/6. [24]YUN 1994, p. 1193. [25]YUN 1983, p. 923, ESC res. 1983/27, 26 May 1983. [26]YUN 1976, p. 627, GA res. 31/137, 16 Dec. 1976. [27]DP/1995/33. [28]A/50/410. [29]E/1995/80. [30]YUN 1975, p. 666, GA res. 3520(XXX), 15 Dec. 1975. [31]YUN 1993, p. 1037, GA res. 48/105, 20 Dec. 1993. [32]A/50/538. [33]YUN 1993, p. 1038. [34]YUN 1994, p. 1184, GA res. 49/160, 23 Dec. 1994. [35]A/50/747-E/1995/126. [36]A/50/785-E/1995/128. [37]YUN 1987, p. 837, GA res. 42/178, 11 Dec. 1987. [38]A/50/399. [39]E/1995/26 (res. 39/8). [40]Ibid. (res. 39/9). [41]YUN 1993, p. 1042, GA res. 48/109, 20 Dec. 1993. [42]A/50/257-E/1995/61 Rev.1. [43]E/CN.6/1995/9. [44]E/CN.4/1995/42. [45]E/1995/26 (res. 39/7). [46]YUN 1993, p. 1046, GA res. 48/104, 20 Dec. 1993. [47]YUN 1948-49, p. 613, GA res. 317(IV), annex, 2 Dec. 1949. [48]A/50/378. [49]YUN 1994, p. 1189, GA res. 49/165, 23 Dec. 1994. [50]E/1995/26 (res 39/2). [51]Ibid. (res. 39/4). [52]Ibid. (res. 39/6). [53]YUN 1994, p. 1190, GA res. 49/166, 23 Dec. 1994. [54]A/50/369. [55]E/1995/26 (res. 39/3). [56]E/CN.6/1995/8. [57]E/CN.6/1995/13. [58]E/1995/26 (res. 39/5).

Chapter XI

# Children, youth and ageing persons

In 1995, the United Nations Children's Fund (UNICEF) pursued two major priorities: continuing support for its country programmes to help women and children, with particular focus on achieving in as many countries as possible the mid-decade goals for children and development set by the World Summit for Children in 1990; and strengthening UNICEF's management, accountability, cost-effectiveness and transparency. The Fund provided assistance totalling $804 million to developing countries and countries in transition to market economies in the areas of child health, planning, advocacy and programme support, education, water supply and sanitation, and nutrition. One quarter of the Fund's allocations went to emergency operations. New strategies were developed and adopted during the year for UNICEF programmes in health, basic education, and water and environmental sanitation.

On 10 April, the Secretary-General appointed Carol Bellamy, former Director of the United States Peace Corps, as the new Executive Director of UNICEF.

In December, the General Assembly adopted the World Programme of Action for Youth to the Year 2000 and Beyond. The Assembly also invited Member States to adopt the conceptual framework of a programme for the preparation of the International Year of Older Persons in 1999 and to formulate programmes for the Year.

## Children

### UN Children's Fund

In 1995, the United Nations Children's Fund (UNICEF) supported programmes in 161 countries, the greatest number of which were in Africa (46); followed by the Americas and the Caribbean (37); Asia (32); Central and Eastern Europe, the Commonwealth of Independent States (CIS) and the Baltic States (28); and the Middle East and North Africa (18).

Major components of UNICEF programmes in 1995 included primary health care, nutrition, basic education, water supply and sanitation, child protection and priority for Africa. Emergency operations also figured prominently, and the Conven-

tion on the Rights of the Child continued to provide the framework for programme development and advocacy. Among other issues having a bearing on UNICEF's work were capacity-building and sustainable development; participation and social mobilization; poverty alleviation; evaluation and monitoring; and follow-up to major international conferences.

Total programme expenditure amounted to $804 million—slightly higher than the $801 million in 1994—of which $212 million (26 per cent) was spent on child health; $203 million (25 per cent) on emergencies, down from $216 million in 1994; $137 million (17 per cent) on planning, advocacy and programme support; $85 million (11 per cent) on education; $71 million (9 per cent) on water supply and sanitation; and $31 million (4 per cent) on nutrition. The remainder of $65 million (8 per cent) was spent on other programme areas. Some 38 per cent of emergency assistance expenditure was for health; 16 per cent each for water and for planning, advocacy and programme support; 13 per cent for nutrition; 7 per cent for education; 1 per cent for general programme areas; and the rest (9 per cent) for other programme areas. UNICEF operations in 1995 were described in the *1996 UNICEF Annual Report* and the report of the Executive Director.[1].

The UNICEF Executive Board held three regular sessions and an annual session in 1995, all in New York. The first regular session met from 1 to 3 and on 6 February, the second from 20 to 23 March and the third from 18 to 21 September, in accordance with General Assembly **decision 50/403 A** of 19 September; the annual session was from 22 to 26 May. During those sessions, the Board adopted 38 decisions which, with its deliberations, were reflected in its report to the Economic and Social Council.[2]

In February, the Board paid tribute to former UNICEF Executive Director James P. Grant, who had died on 28 January at the age of 72, for his 15 years of service to the organization.

### Programme policies

During 1995, the Executive Board took a number of decisions pertaining to UNICEF programme policies.

In March, the Board requested[3] the secretariat to develop a strategy for including human immunodeficiency virus/acquired immunodeficiency syndrome (HIV/AIDS) components in its programmes and activities within the framework of the Joint and Co-sponsored United Nations Programme on HIV/AIDS (UNAIDS) (see PART FOUR, Chapter XIII). In May, it called for an active role of UNICEF in achieving the goals and objectives set by the 1990 World Summit for Children. Also in May, the Board endorsed frameworks for UNICEF education programmes and for the water supply and environmental sanitation programme (see below). In September, it endorsed[4] a UNICEF health strategy (see PART FOUR, Chapter XIII), as well as a framework for UNICEF follow-up to the 1994 International Conference on Population and Development (see below).

*Follow-up to 1990 World Summit for Children*

In May 1995, the Executive Board had before it an April report[5] on follow-up to the 1990 World Summit for Children, which summarized progress towards the decade and mid-decade goals enunciated in the World Declaration on the Survival, Protection and Development of Children and the Plan of Action for implementing the Declaration,[6] both adopted by the 1990 World Summit for Children. The report reviewed the status of national programmes of action and of the Convention on the Rights of the Child, major Summit follow-up activities globally and in each region, inter-agency collaboration, the role of non-governmental organizations (NGOs) and the private sector, and the resource situation.

The Board requested[7] the Executive Director to play an active and supportive role in helping implement the 1990 General Assembly resolution[8] on the achievement of the goals and objectives endorsed in the World Declaration and the Plan of Action, and to consult within the United Nations system and with members of the Board as to how UNICEF could best support that process. It proposed that the results of such a review be announced on 30 September 1996, the date of the sixth anniversary of the Summit, and urged Governments to assess, together with provincial and local authorities, NGOs, the private sector and civic groups, progress at mid-decade towards the Summit goals. International and national NGOs should provide input to the assessments and to steps needed for attaining the year 2000 goals. The Board requested the secretariat to support countries in gathering and analysing data, in a standardized and coordinated manner, on progress towards the mid-decade and decade goals and the overall assessment of their response to the World Summit Declaration and Plan of Action; such work should result in improved and sustainable national capacity in obtaining and analysing data on the situation of children. The results of national assessments should be systematized, in cooperation with other UN entities, with a view to presenting, by mid-1996, a comprehensive statement on the status of achievement of the mid-decade goals and of progress towards the goals for children and development by the year 2000.

*Basic education strategies*

In May, the Executive Board had before it an April report[9] on UNICEF strategies in basic education, focusing on universal primary education, with special attention to girls and women, and early childhood development and adult basic education as supporting components. The strategic objectives were: to increase enrolment, retention and completion rates of primary school-age children, reduce gender and geographic disparities, improve parents' knowledge of and skills in early child care, and enhance linkages between basic education and other programmes for children and women. Those global goals were adapted to the circumstances of each country through the country programme.

The Board endorsed[10] the framework for UNICEF education programmes and encouraged the secretariat, with other UN agencies, national partners and external providers of assistance, to continue to focus on universal access to basic education and support the improvement of the quality of basic education; to promote parents' knowledge and skills and community- and family-based approaches to early childhood development; and to increase allocations in country programmes for basic education, in line with the key role of basic education in promoting sustainable progress in the well-being and development of children.

The Board urged the secretariat to put greater emphasis on targeting the major systemic problems in basic education; building the capacity of countries to plan and implement education programmes by adopting a systemic and systematic approach to long-term education development, promoting cost-effective reforms, resource mobilization and sustainable strategies for universal opportunities; providing education services for children in emergencies; and expanding education opportunites for children in other difficult situations, including working children and children with disabilities. The Board requested the Executive Director to reorient and strengthen UNICEF's capacity to play its role effectively in assisting developing countries to reach the goals of Education for All.

*Water and environmental sanitation strategies*

The Executive Board considered at its May session an April report[11] detailing strategies to be followed by UNICEF in assisting Governments and

communities to achieve their goals in water supply and environmental sanitation. The report
provided an overall framework for country programming which could be adapted to each country's particular situation. Describing water as a
basic right and central to sustainable development, the report set the strategy within the
global context, reporting on the lessons learned
and the challenges remaining. It detailed the
UNICEF contribution in the sector and the implications for UNICEF in terms of staffing, organizational structure, the choice of partners and
funding.

Recognizing universal access to clean drinking
water as a fundamental human need and essential to the right of the child to enjoy the highest
attainable standard of health, the Board endorsed[12] the framework for the water supply and
environmental sanitation programme and encouraged the secretariat to continue supporting
countries in achieving universal access to water
supply and environmental sanitation by implementing national programmes; promoting and advocating public commitment, national policy and
accelerated actions for meeting the needs and
rights of children and the poor; setting, defining,
reviewing and monitoring national and local goals;
strengthening partnerships with Governments,
NGOs, the private sector, external support agencies and others; supporting the expansion of services through appropriate technologies; supporting
emergency programmes in the sector; allocating
appropriate resources for water supply, sanitation
and hygiene education, and improving the capacity of national counterparts; and promoting the
standardization of technologies for water supply
and sanitation to minimize installation costs, operations and maintenance.

The Board urged UNICEF to put greater emphasis on and allocate resources to environmental sanitation, hygiene and behavioural change;
community management of the "water environment" within the context of Agenda 21 of the 1992
Conference on Environment and Development[13]
and primary environmental care; capacity-
building; community cost-sharing; gender-
balanced and participatory approaches in planning, implementing, managing and monitoring
services; research, development and transfer of
technology; assistance to countries in standardizing the definition of coverage and improving
monitoring systems; enhanced linkages with
health, education, nutrition, environment and
other development programmes; and support for
the promotion of water supply and sanitation services in deprived, low-income urban areas.

The General Assembly, in **resolution 50/126**,
took note of the programme strategies in water and
environmental sanitation adopted by the Board.

*Follow-up to major conferences*

In March, the Executive Board had before it a
report[14] on UNICEF follow-up to the 1994 International Conference on Population and Development (ICPD),[15] which focused on strengthening
UNICEF's own strategies, advocacy and programme interventions to promote the reproductive health of women and youth. Beyond the health
sector, UNICEF would give added importance to
a wide range of activities for the advancement of
women and girls and would give increased priority
to support for basic education, with particular emphasis on equitable access by girls, and a major
effort to reduce illiteracy, especially among women.

The Board requested[16] the secretariat to submit to its third regular session in 1995 a revised
paper taking into account the comments of Board
members.

A revised report,[17] issued in July, identified
priority areas for UNICEF in the follow-up to ICPD
and implementation of its Programme of Action,
reflecting the report of the Conference and consultation with UNICEF partners and responding,
as requested, to guidance provided by the Board.

According to the report, UNICEF, in its follow-
up to ICPD, would pursue close collaboration with
partners in a variety of sectors, with particular
focus on girls' education; women's empowerment;
primary health care, including reproductive
health; and tracking progress in reducing child and
maternal mortality. In its commitment to contribute to the implementation of the ICPD Programme
of Action, it would continue its strong advocacy
in support of child protection, survival and development, and particularly reducing gender disparities. It would increase its support to country-level
action in girls' education, adolescent health, and
women's health and empowerment.

In addition to country-level collaboration,
UNICEF participated actively in the five working
groups of the Inter-Agency Task Force on the Implementation of the ICPD Programme of Action
(see PART FOUR, Chapter VIII) and was the lead
agency for the working group on "A Common Approach to Building National Capacity in Tracking Child and Maternal Mortality".

In September, the Board endorsed[18] the framework for UNICEF follow-up to ICPD and stressed the
need for its speedy implementation. It requested
the Executive Director to report in 1996 on the process to integrate ICPD follow-up in UNICEF country programmes and in 1998 on UNICEF follow-up
activities, including those in cooperation with other
donor agencies, and on their results.

In May, the Board also considered a report[19]
on UNICEF follow-up to the World Summit for Social Development (WSSD) (see PART FOUR, Chapter IX), which it decided[20] to transmit to the Economic and Social Council's 1995 substantive session.

The report stated that the Executive Director was committed to ensuring that UNICEF played an active and supportive role in the overall UN system follow-up and that field-level action needed to be a special area of focus. As proposed by the Secretary-General, the WSSD implementation processes should be seen as part of a continuum related closely to those for the 1990 World Summit for Children, the 1992 United Nations Conference on Environment and Development,[21] ICPD, etc., which offered UNICEF opportunities to help strengthen and accelerate the implementation of the goals of the World Summit for Children; its work in that regard formed a direct part of the implementation of the commitments of WSSD. In addition, the broad agenda of WSSD follow-up could help mobilize a wide range of action on poverty reduction, within which progress for children could be placed. Through its inter-agency participation and advocacy, UNICEF could help link the previously approved goals for basic services to the new goals related to the income side of poverty. WSSD also offered a unique opportunity to create an overall "anti-poverty initiative".

In a November report,[22] UNICEF outlined its follow-up action in the implementation of the Platform for Action adopted by the Fourth World Conference on Women in September (see PART FOUR, Chapter X), focusing on three priority areas: girls' education; adolescent girls' and women's health; and children's and women's rights.

## Follow-up to Economic and Social Council decisions

In August, the secretariat reported[23] on follow-up to decisions taken by the Economic and Social Council at its substantive 1995 session, focusing on operational activities for development and humanitarian affairs, two areas which the Council had dealt with at its operational and general segment, respectively (see PART FOUR, Chapters II and III).

The outcome of the Council's discussions were **resolutions 1995/50** on operational activities for development segment, **1995/51** on overall guidance on operational activities for development to the UN funds and programmes and **1995/56** on strengthening coordination of UN emergency humanitarian assistance.

The report noted that the first two resolutions would have implications for UNICEF in several areas, including priorities, country programmes, reporting to the Council and scheduling of Board sessions. With regard to implementation of resolution **1995/56**, which urged the governing bodies of the relevant UN organizations to review issues concerning their role and responsibilities, as well as their operational and financial capacities

to respond to emergency situations and support preventive action, the report said that the Executive Board had already decided to discuss emergency operations, including strategic issues and inter-agency coordination, during the first half of 1996.

The Board took note[24] of the report in September.

The secretariat in November submitted a more complete report,[25] stating that since the Council's substantive session and the Board's September session, UNICEF had held consultations with its partners. With regard to **resolution 1995/50**, in which the Council had reiterated the importance of receiving timely reports from the Executive Boards in all official languages, the UNICEF Board had decided that the Executive Director's annual report would be considered at the Board's second regular session in April 1996, to allow for the relevant parts of the Board's report to be made available to the Council's substantive session. On the subject of holding joint or consecutive meetings, the Executive Director brought to the Board's attention that the 1996 schedules placed the United Nations Development Programme (UNDP)/United Nations Population Fund (UNFPA) and the UNICEF Board sessions almost back to back. Also, he noted, 1996 would provide useful guidance concerning the new country programme approval process both for UNICEF and UNDP/UNFPA and how the Boards would like to organize their work in that respect. With regard to the Council's request to the Executive Boards to identify specific problems, opportunities and areas where the Council could provide useful coordination and guidance on a system-wide basis, the Executive Director suggested that the matter be placed before the Bureau of the UNICEF Board in January 1996.

In follow-up to **resolution 1995/56** and in the light of the Board's decision to discuss emergency operations, the report noted that UNICEF had reviewed its role and responsibilities, as well as operational and financial capacities to respond to emergency situations and support preventive actions. It had concluded that strengthening country-specific and particularly local coping mechanisms of communities affected by disasters, conflicts or wars would continue to be the main thrust of its emergency and humanitarian efforts. It was consulting with the United Nations, bilateral agencies and NGOs on collaboration in emergencies and was in the final stages of signing a Memorandum of Understanding (MOU) with the Office of the United Nations High Commissioner for Refugees. An MOU with the World Food Programme was close to completion and consultations with the World Health Organization on signing an MOU were progressing well. (For UNICEF assistance in emergency situations, see below.)

## Maurice Pate Memorial Award

In February, the Executive Board decided,[26] on a recommendation of the Executive Director,[27] to present the annual Maurice Pate Award, established in 1966[28] in memory of UNICEF's first Executive Director, to Professor Ihsan Dogramaci of Turkey. The $25,000 award was given in recognition of Professor Dogramaci's more than 50 years of service to children in Turkey and around the world, through his outstanding contributions in the fields of public health and child survival and development.

## Emergency operations

According to an overview report on UNICEF emergency operations in 1995,[29] UNICEF provided assistance to 21 major complex emergencies in Afghanistan, Angola, Armenia, Azerbaijan, Bosnia and Herzegovina, Burundi, Croatia, the Federal Republic of Yugosalvia (Serbia and Montenegro), Georgia, Haiti, Iraq, Liberia, Mozambique, the Russian Federation (Chechnya), Rwanda, Sierra Leone, Somalia, the Sudan, Tajikistan, the former Yugoslav Republic of Macedonia and Zaire. UNICEF aid targeted special needs of vulnerable groups, especially children and women. The Fund collaborated with its partners in assisting the reunification of over 26,000 unaccompanied children in Mozambique, Rwanda, the southern Sudan and eastern Zaire, and assisted 16 countries in counselling systems and the creation of family and community environment for recovery. It provided assistance in the health sector in Afghanistan, Angola, Burundi, Liberia, Rwanda and the former Yugoslavia. UNICEF with NGOs provided supplementary feeding in Burundi, distributed seeds and farm implements in Rwanda, provided therapy and rehabilitation to malnourished children in Sierra Leone and supported supplementary feeding centres in Afghanistan. In water and sanitation, UNICEF assisted Afghanistan, Angola, Burundi, Sierra Leone and Rwanda. It supplied basic classroom materials in Afghanistan, Angola, and Bosnia and Herzegovina, as well as materials and trained teachers for children in prison and for demobilized soldiers in Rwanda.

Programme expenditure for emergencies amounted to some $203 million, or 25 per cent of UNICEF's total programme expenditure. In addition, as of September 1995, $9 million had been disbursed to 17 countries for global activities under the Emergency Programme Fund.

During the year, UNICEF enhanced its programme and operational response capacity for emergency situations. It created a rapid response team (RRT) of 18 specially trained staff members on stand-by at regular duty stations for quick deployment to any emergency. That core group was to be augmented as necessary by national and international officers with special skills in administration, finance, personnel and setting up operations systems. An Operations Centre was set up in the Office of Emergency Programmes to provide contact between headquarters and field locations to support RRT and ongoing field operations. UNICEF reviewed and updated its emergency stockpiles of supplies and equipment for emergency situations and created a special RRT stockpile of essential supplies and equipment in Copenhagen, Denmark, valued at $3 million.

In November, UNICEF presented a strategy paper[30] on its emergency assistance, summarizing purpose, mandate, guiding principles and emergency response strategies and describing measures initiated in 1995 to reinforce its capacity as an effective humanitarian partner in emergency cooperation.

## UNICEF programmes by region

### Africa

In 1995, programme expenditure in Africa totalled $292 million, or 36 per cent of UNICEF's total programme expenditure.

For many of the countries in Eastern and Southern Africa, 1995 was a year of recovery and momentum-building. South Africa's Reconstruction and Development Programme spearheaded efforts to extend access to basic services. National goals for children were incorporated in the 1995 policy statement on the Programme. The Convention on the Rights of the Child was a symbol of recovery and growth for the whole region. With Botswana, South Africa and Swaziland ratifying the Convention, all countries of the region, except Somalia, had become parties. As a result, closer ties were facilitated between UNICEF and organizations concerned with children, including AIDS orphans and children affected by armed conflict. The devastating impact of the HIV/AIDS epidemic was increasingly felt in the region. Child mortality rates rose in Uganda, Zambia and Zimbabwe. Programmes aimed at changing sexual behaviour, controlling sexually transmitted diseases and providing clinical and psychological care were being implemented in many countries. Emphasis was given to improved monitoring of the condition of children as a basis for informed planning and advocacy. UNICEF supported surveys of progress towards mid-decade goals in 11 countries, in collaboration with the Economic Commission for Africa (ECA) and UNFPA. ECA and UNICEF worked with national statistical agencies to incorporate social indicators in routine data-gathering and jointly published the *Atlas of the African Child*, a cartographical depiction of social development. The adolescent girl communication initiative, a multimedia project to help adolescents develop life skills and become more involved in community affairs, was started.

Although large disparities remained between countries, broad improvements were evident in the prospects for many of the region's children. Almost all countries had national programmes of action (NPAs) for children or had incorporated such programmes into their national development plans. However, many countries faced challenges in terms of their capacity to raise primary school enrolment rates, provide access to safe water and sanitation, and improve child protection and nutrition. Major constraints on countries' efforts included chronic underfinancing of public services, the impact of the HIV/AIDS pandemic, weak administrative and financial capacity of national and local governments, and the rising level of crime in urban areas. UNICEF was increasingly involved in those issues in individual countries as an advocate for the rights of children and women and as a supporter of data collection and analysis linked to policy development. It introduced a gender development index as a means of consolidating statistical data on social developments affecting women.

In West and Central Africa, political instability and armed conflicts had disastrous effects on women and children in a number of countries. UNICEF stepped up its emergency assistance in Sierra Leone and supported rehabilitation efforts in Liberia. Although the region was the first in which all countries had ratified the Convention on the Rights of the Child, at the end of 1995, only four—Burkina Faso, the Niger, Nigeria and Senegal— had filed reports on their implementation of the Convention. With the increasing urbanization in the region, UNICEF intensified its advocacy for special protection of neglected and abused children, focusing on child workers, child prostitutes, street children, young girls working as domestic servants and boys forced into begging. Performance in terms of the mid-decade goals for children were mixed. The regional average of immunization coverage reached only 45 per cent, although a number of countries had achieved or were close to achieving the goal of immunizing 80 per cent of their children. Use of oral rehydration therapy (ORT) against diarrhoeal diseases was a low 35 per cent, but most countries had plans of action to increase its use. The incidence of dracunculiasis (guinea worm disease) had been dramatically reduced and was expected to be eradicated by the year 2000. Regional access to water and sanitation services remained low, with about 45 per cent of the people having access to safe drinking water and 25 per cent to sanitation. A large number of countries had laws or legislation requiring iodization of table salt and all countries increased

access to vitamin A. By the end of 1995, some 4,000 health centres (about 80 per cent of the target) had embraced the Bamako Initiative concept, originally adopted by the African Ministers of Health in 1987[31] to improve the concept of primary health care in sub-Saharan Africa through community participation in financing and managing local health services. The Initiative improved the quality of care and access to essential drugs and was a safety net for communities in situations of political instability. In 1995, policy makers turned a spotlight on education, with subregional meetings in Guinea and Mali, and an announcement by the Organization of African Unity (OAU) that 1996 would be the year of education for Africa. There were serious problems throughout the region in terms of education quality and the willingness of parents to put and keep their children in school. Policy reforms were also needed to support education for girls and involve communities in non-formal and adult education. UNICEF assisted innovative education projects aimed at achieving those goals in Benin, Burkina Faso, Ghana, Guinea, Mali and Senegal.

In May, the UNICEF Executive Board considered an April progress report[32] on ensuring child survival, protection and development in Africa, which discussed economic and political trends in sub-Saharan Africa as well as the main areas of UNICEF focus, including the Convention on the Rights of the Child, achievement of mid-decade and year 2000 goals, collaboration with different partners, response to emergencies and the HIV/AIDS pandemic.

The Board reaffirmed[33] its commitment to Africa as the region of greatest need and highest priority and requested the Executive Director to develop specific strategies for translating that priority into concrete actions, including increasing resource allocation for country programmes. It reaffirmed its commitment and support to the Special Initiative on Africa (see PART FOUR, Chapter III), and requested the Executive Director to ensure that UNICEF continued to play an active role in the inter-agency work on the implementation of the Initiative. Acknowledging the role of basic education in development, the Board urged African Governments to develop feasible and dynamic plans of action and allocate resources for reversing the falling rates of enrolment and moving towards the Education for All goals agreed to in 1990 at the World Conference on Education for All, co-sponsored by UNESCO, UNDP, UNICEF, the World Bank and others, and the World Summit for Children. It requested the Executive Director to support countries in formulating such plans and mobilizing external resources for their implementation. The Board called on African Governments to increase and strengthen the participation of communities in the planning, implementation and management of programmes for the delivery of social services, including the commitments of the World Summit for Children. It asked the Executive Director to coordinate UNICEF activities with those of other UN agencies, particularly the World Health Organization (WHO), and to participate in strengthening strategies and programmes in the implementation of the 1992 WHO Global Plan of Action on Malaria.[34] He should also develop partnerships with bilateral and multilateral donor agencies to support African countries' efforts to meet specific goals within their national programmes of action. The Board urged donor countries and international financial institutions to consider measures to reduce the official debt burden of African countries, including debt cancellation and conversions for social investment in health, education, water supply and sanitation, and encouraged the Executive Director to advocate at the highest possible levels the reduction of African bilateral and multilateral debt. The Board requested him to strengthen collaboration with regional and subregional organizations to improve the well-being of children and women in Africa; seek additional resources through, *inter alia*, strengthening cooperation with multilateral and bilateral funding institutions, including the World Bank and the African Development Bank; strengthen collaboration with African institutions and NGOs in developing and implementing UNICEF-supported country programmes; ensure that UNICEF operational capacity in Africa was further enhanced within the context of UNICEF's management reform (see below); and report on progress made in ensuring child survival, protection and development in Africa in 1997.

### Asia and the Pacific

Programme expenditure in Asia totalled $220 million, or 27 per cent of UNICEF's total programme expenditure in 1995.

In East Asia and the Pacific, UNICEF supported a wide range of innovative media programmes capitalizing on the capacity of the communications revolution to educate and encourage behavioural change. In Thailand, it promoted AIDS awareness, focusing on high-risk groups including hill tribes, children in urban slums, street children, the rural poor and workers in the informal sector. Its activities facilitated the willingness of Governments to confront the AIDS epidemic. In Malaysia, UNICEF supported the development of AIDS messages that were sensitive to the cultural and religious environment. Most of the mid-decade goals for children were within reach of the region as a whole and some had already been achieved in a number of countries. Some of the region's most encouraging results during 1995 were recorded in

its least developed countries. In Cambodia, UNICEF worked with the Government and NGOs on that country's first five-year programme of cooperation (1996-2000), with the focus shifting from emergency relief and rehabilitation to community action for the social development of children and women. The region achieved universal ratification of the Convention on the Rights of the Child.

In South Asia, UNICEF maintained its gender perspective in all regional and country programmes. Child labour, a major area of focus for UNICEF and almost every country in the region, remained a subject of close collaboration between UNICEF, the International Labour Organization (ILO), Governments and industry. UNICEF launched an initiative with the Bangladesh Garment Manufacturers and Exporters Association to eliminate gradually child labour in the garment industry and enrol released child workers in school. It supported a number of large-scale, cost-effective and culturally sensitive innovations in support of Education for All. One of UNICEF's concerns was the impact of war and conflict on children in Afghanistan and Sri Lanka. Its "education for peace" initiative reached more than 40,000 children in Sri Lanka. All countries gave greater attention to vaccination, although immunizations rates fell below 1990 levels. The nutrition initiative for South Asia, established in 1994, began to improve the understanding of malnutrition by Governments and development agencies. Activities included assessing nutrition projects, refocusing strategies and working with policy makers and donors, including the Asian Development Bank. Significant advances were also made against micronutrient deficiencies.

### Americas and the Caribbean

In 1995, programme expenditure in the Americas and the Caribbean totalled $93 million, or 12 per cent of UNICEF's total programme expenditure.

All countries in the region had ratified the Convention on the Rights of the Child and six (Bolivia, Brazil, the Dominican Republic, Ecuador, El Salvador and Peru) had integrated the Convention into legislation. UNICEF provided technical and financial support to Argentina, Mexico, Uruguay and Venezuela to bring national legislation into conformance with the Convention. It assisted Brazil, Colombia, Ecuador, Guatemala and Peru in studies of child labour, giving special attention to the link with basic education, and developed a framework for reform of juvenile justice systems to address the tendency to criminalize poverty, especially among street children. Recognizing the need for public embracement of reformed child policies, UNICEF encouraged the participation of civil society, not just Governments, in designing new policies for children. It cooperated with the World Bank in holding regional training workshops for teachers on the quality of schooling. With UNESCO, UNICEF supported regional authors and publishers in designing and producing materials for students and for training teachers in Chile, Costa Rica, the Dominican Republic, Ecuador, Guatemala, Honduras, Paraguay and Peru. At a global NGO symposium in Costa Rica on early childhood education in the context of poverty, UNICEF promoted strategies to improve knowledge of child development among parents and caregivers. UNICEF also collaborated on child labour with ILO, Save the Children, and the Inter-American Institute of the Child.

### Middle East and North Africa

Programme expenditure in the Middle East and North Africa totalled $91 million in 1995, or 12 per cent of UNICEF's total programme expenditure.

Although economic belt-tightening continued in much of the region, most countries reported progress towards their goals for children. The Palestinian Authority held a symposium on Palestinian children and women to review progress in the development of an NPA whose goals, strategies, project outlines and funding requirements were elaborated in a five-year programme to be implemented from January 1996 on. In a March 1995 review paper,[35] UNICEF outlined its programme cooperation in support of Palestinian children and women. To encourage investment in the region, Jordan hosted a regional economic summit in October. Subsequently, UNICEF and the Arab Thought Forum, a Pan-Arab NGO, followed up with a regional consultation on social change in the Middle East, which recommended steps to ensure that vulnerable groups were protected and that social development was a priority for policy makers, donors and the media. Agreements with groups in southern Sudan enabled UNICEF to maintain child protection services, especially immunization and dracunculiasis programmes, in most of the country. In collaboration with OAU, the League of Arab States and individual Governments, UNICEF helped generate a greater commitment to children's needs in planning and policy-making. Many countries, including Egypt, Jordan, Lebanon, the Libyan Arab Jamahiriya, Morocco, Oman and the Sudan established national commissions for children and Tunisia's Council of Ministers adopted a code for the protection of the child. All but two countries (Oman and the United Arab Emirates) had ratified the Convention on the Rights of the Child, and Lebanon, Tunisia and Yemen reported on their implementation activities. UNICEF financed a study in Lebanon analysing legislation in relation to the Convention, and in Jordan, it worked closely with the office of Queen Noor to establish a task force for children to monitor implementation of the Convention. More than half the countries had met the mid-decade goals on immunization and almost half had met ORT and sanitation goals.

### Central and Eastern Europe, CIS and the Baltic States

In 1995, programme expenditure in Central and Eastern Europe, CIS and the Baltic States totalled $72 million, or 9 per cent of UNICEF's total programme expenditure.

The region fell short of the mid-decade goals in safe water supply and sanitation, salt iodization and the baby-friendly initiative. Shortage of vaccines and other supplies resulted in a diphtheria epidemic in CIS. Large-scale emergency interventions were needed by mid-1995, funded through a $21 million appeal launched in July by WHO, UNICEF and the International Federation of Red Cross and Red Crescent Societies. Measles remained a major threat throughout the region. An encouraging factor was the breakthrough in the campaign to eradicate polio through a concerted immunization effort in 1995. Complex emergencies continued in the Caucasus, while the fall of safe havens in Bosnia and Herzegovina and Croatia led to the flight of thousands of civilians, mostly women and children. UNICEF's main role was to aid the rapid reinforcement of immunization and education services. It worked with Kazakstan, Turkmenistan and Uzbekistan, the World Bank and major NGOs to provide urgent support for the basic needs of children and women affected by health problems resulting from the pollution due to the over-exploitation of the Aral Sea for irrigation and the overuse of pesticides. UNICEF, the World Bank and other partners launched the Aral Sea Project for Environmental and Regional Assistance. Although all countries had ratified the Convention on the Rights of the Child, an increasing number of States were having difficulty submitting timely reports on implementation. A UNICEF-financed analysis of the situation of children in the Russian Federation found that the abuse of alcohol, tobacco and drugs by mothers contributed to a doubling of diseases among newborns and that 15 to 30 per cent of preschool children suffered from chronic diseases.

## UNICEF programmes by sector

### Primary health care

The 1987 Bamako Initiative[31] remained a benchmark for sustainable primary health care in 1995. Eight more countries (Azerbaijan, Ecuador, El Salvador, Georgia, Guatemala, Guyana, Honduras and Mongolia) adopted its basic principles, bringing the total number of countries that had signed on to it to to 41. With $8.5 million in supplementary funding for 1994-1995 from the Nippon (formerly Sasakawa) Foundation, UNICEF helped a number of countries revitalize community health systems by introducing the principles of the Bamako Initiative.

UNICEF assisted Zambia in the design and implementation of its comprehensive health policy reform and provided technical assistance to make health services more community-oriented, integrated and equitable in South Africa. In collaboration with the Harvard School of Public Health, it undertook a two-year study of China's rural health strategy. It developed a comprehensive training package for front-line health workers and community-elected health committee members and tested it in the Gambia and Uganda. Supplementary funding from the Australian and French National Committees enabled UNICEF to assist Benin, Burkina Faso, Guinea, Mali, the Senegal, Togo and Uganda in laying the groundwork to revitalize selected district hospitals. Results from that preliminary undertaking were expected to help in formulating a policy framework for strengthening district hospital services. UNICEF supported operations research into community participation, equitable access to basic health care, staff motivation, sustainable health structures and systems, drug management and quality assurance and improved health care. Partners like the European Union, WHO and the World Bank, provided undesignated assistance to respond to district health priorities rather than earmarking aid for specific programmes. Such strategies were helping Mali, Senegal and Zambia to use resources more efficiently.

### Immunization

Global infant immunization levels advanced beyond the 80 per cent level during 1995. However, relatively low rates persisted in half the countries of West and Central Africa, and in countries undergoing or recovering from conflict in Eastern and Southern Africa. Cambodia and the Lao People's Democratic Republic had lower immunization rates than their neighbours in South-East Asia, but both countries improved substantially over the previous year. Average rates for diphtheria/pertussis/tetanus (DPT3) ranged from 89 per cent for Asia, to 87 per cent in the Middle East and North Africa, 82 per cent in the Americas, 71 per cent in Central and Eastern Europe and the newly independent States, and 58 per cent for Africa. Haiti was the high-water mark for measles control in the Americas and the Caribbean region. Chile, Cuba and the English-speaking Caribbean also reported successful campaigns

against measles. Elsewhere, significant inroads were made on neonatal tetanus, particularly in Benin, Egypt and the United Republic of Tanzania. In Central Asia, Eastern Europe and the newly independent States, UNICEF, WHO and the International Committee of the Red Cross (ICRC) launched a global campaign for vaccines to contain an ongoing diphtheria epidemic. UNICEF continued collaborating with Rotary International and the United States Centres for Disease Control and Prevention in raising funds and procuring vaccines for the global eradication effort. Vaccination and monitoring continued in the polio-free zones to maintain their status. UNICEF and WHO produced promotional material to help stop the transmission of hepatitis B and HIV/AIDS through the use of sterilized syringes.

There was closer partnership with vaccine manufacturers under the Children's Vaccine Initiative to improve access to new and better vaccines and obtain price reductions. UNICEF continued to support field trials for a *Haemophilus influenzae* type B vaccine for bacterial meningitis in the Gambia. Under the Vaccine Independent Initiative, a revolving fund to bridge the time between payments, 12 countries were able to purchase vaccines at favourable bulk rates during 1995. Donors, including Australia, Japan, the Netherlands, New Zealand, Norway, the United Kingdom and the United States, contributed $47.5 million to the fund.

### Control of diarrhoeal diseases

In 1995, ORT was used in 60 per cent of diarrhoeal episodes worldwide, up from 44 per cent in 1994. The UNICEF mid-decade goal for ORT use in 80 per cent of diarrhoeal cases was achieved by about 25 developing countries, the most successful being Bangladesh, China and Nigeria. Thirty countries held national health/ORT weeks and 33 took part in international ORT symposia in Brazil, Burkina Faso and Cameroon. The production of oral rehydration salts (ORS) reached about 800 million packets a year, with UNICEF having become one of the largest distributors and promoters, particularly in Africa. A number of pharmaceutical manufacturers collaborated with UNICEF in marketing ORS through their distributors. A lack of timely and reliable national ORT data continued to hamper monitoring of diarrhoeal disease control, although many countries took action to redress the situation. Thirty countries initiated surveys and more than 50 others planned to follow.

### Acute respiratory infections

Acute respiratory infections (ARI) continued to be the major cause of death among children under five in developing countries, where in 1995 more than 3 million died of pneumonia and a further

1.1 million from ARI compounded by other ailments. Relatively few countries where children were at the greatest risk of infection gave sufficient priority to ARI, although 65 had active national programmes to combat ARI, but fewer than a quarter of them provided protection on a nationwide basis. UNICEF supported mass media campaigns in Egypt, Iran, Mexico, Pakistan, the Philippines and a number of other countries to ensure that parents knew precisely where to take their children for treatment. It also supported training of health care workers in ARI case management and efforts to make drugs more accessible in a number of countries, including Bangladesh, India and Pakistan.

## HIV/AIDS control

In 1995, HIV/AIDS continued its debilitating sweep. According to estimates of UNAIDS (see PART FOUR, Chapter XIII), 6 million people globally had developed AIDS and over 5 million had died. Half of all infections affected people aged 15 to 24 and about 1.5 million children were infected. Worldwide, UNAIDS estimated by the end of the century, AIDS would have robbed almost 5 million children of one or both parents. HIV/AIDS raised a number of complex challenges for UNICEF and other organizations fighting the pandemic. While UNICEF and its partners continued to strengthen preventive programmes against HIV infection and the care of victims, attention also turned to means of strengthening the capacity of families and communities to protect the rights of children against AIDS. UNICEF continued to support public AIDS education, emphasizing the need for tolerance as well as changes in human behaviour. Programmes helped identify and monitor the situation of the most vulnerable children, strengthen family coping capacity and community support, enable children affected by AIDS to remain in school, and make reproductive health services, together with care and counselling, more accessible and welcoming. Regional consultations with UNAIDS were held in Santiago, Chile; Dakar, Senegal; Nairobi, Kenya; Venice, Italy; and New Delhi, India. UNICEF and UNAIDS jointly published a booklet entitled *Children and Families Affected by AIDS: Guidelines for Action.*

In March, UNICEF provided the Executive Board with an update[36] on its participation in UNAIDS. The Board urged[37] the secretariat to participate actively in UNAIDS and to support the director of the programme; and that steps be taken to implement the Declaration of the 1994 Paris Summit on HIV/AIDS[38] in the context of UNAIDS. It requested the UNICEF secretariat to develop a strategy for including HIV/AIDS components in its programmes and regular activities within the framework of UNAIDS.

## Maternal health and family planning

In 1995, UNICEF policies and strategies in women's health were revised, taking into account current international knowledge regarding maternal health care and programme experiences of several UNICEF country offices. A new approach to estimating maternal mortality developed by WHO and UNICEF indicated that 585,000 women died each year from pregnancy-related causes, a significant increase over the past estimate of 500,000. UNICEF support focused on reducing maternal mortality, primarily through expanding access to quality prenatal, delivery and post-natal care. It refocused its efforts on strengthening the role of professional midwives in the light of the declining role of traditional birth attendants and worked with community-based women's groups to develop health promotion messages on issues such as family planning, breastfeeding, HIV/AIDS, violence against women and female genital mutilation. Examples of those approaches could be seen in Bangladesh, Benin, Ghana, India, Indonesia, Mali and Zambia. In Mexico, UNICEF supported the National Commission for Safe Motherhood and safe motherhood workshops were held in Amman, Jordan; Abidjan, Côte d'Ivoire; and New Delhi, India.

Global networking and advocacy continued through participation in the Joint Programme on National Capacity-building to Reduce Maternal Deaths and Disabilities (WHO, UNDP, UNFPA and UNICEF), the Inter-agency Working Group on Safe Motherhood, the Symposium on Reproductive Health in Refugee Situations, the International Maternal and Child Health Committee of the American Public Health Association, meetings with professional associations of midwives and obstetricians/gynaecologists, and the preparation with WHO of guidelines for monitoring progress in maternal mortality.

## Nutrition

The reduction of child malnutrition remained a key effort in many UNICEF country programmes. The nutrition focal points from all UNICEF regions and the Nutrition Section at headquarters reviewed the application of the UNICEF nutrition strategy and reaffirmed its value as an intersectoral programme framework. The review called for a greater focus on women's and girls' nutrition. The Nutrition Section developed guidelines on the conceptualization and evaluation of household food security activities and an inventory of household food security components in UNICEF programmes. UNICEF also contributed to the preparation of a background paper for the World Food Summit to be organized by FAO in 1996 (see PART FOUR, Chapter XIII). Several country programmes supported innovative approaches to household food security, such as Cambodia's effort to transform the family food production programme into a more integrated approach that helped rural women meet basic household needs. Global progress was made towards salt iodization in 1995 and technical guidelines for monitoring salt iodization programmes were developed. UNICEF supported surveys of Vitamin A status that resulted in widespread deficiency being recognized for the first time in Botswana, Egypt, Kenya and South Africa. With support from the Micronutrient Initiative in Canada, UNICEF launched projects in 14 countries to bring about innovations in distribution systems for Vitamin A supplements and improvements in monitoring the impact of supplementation on mortality and morbidity. UNICEF and WHO developed a statement on strategies for reducing iron deficiency anaemia, which called for iron supplementation in any population of pregnant women or young children where the prevalance of anaemia exceeded 30 per cent. It joined with other agencies in exploring ways of increasing the micronutrient content of foods in the breeding of high-yielding varieties of cereals such as rice.

In 1995, the Baby-Friendly Hospital Initiative reached the milestone of 4,000 baby-friendly hospitals in 170 countries. After a slow start, countries of Central and Eastern Europe joined the Initiative and were making considerable progress. The number of countries that adopted a law or some provisions of the International Code of Marketing of Breast Milk Substitutes increased by 10 in 1995. Four more countries adopted actions to end the practice of distributing free and low-cost supplies at health facilities, bringing to 101 the total number of countries taking legal steps or a practical measures in that direction. UNICEF also participated in the development of a new multi-agency statement on HIV and breast-feeding, a process that was to continue with UNAIDS in 1996.

UNICEF and WHO commissioned a review on issues related to complementary feeding as a key component of "care for nutrition". The review made recommendations on complementing breast milk from the age of six months; guidelines were to be distributed widely and promoted through regional workshops.

### Basic education

In May, the UNICEF Executive Board approved a new basic education strategy (see above) and urged UNICEF to promote universal participation in basic education, giving priority to ending the disadvantage of girls and with a focus on Africa, South Asia and countries in emergency situations. The new approach endorsed early childhood development and adult education as two major sup-

portive strategies. To implement them, UNICEF was working with multilateral and bilateral organizations, NGOs, private voluntary organizations and foundations concerned with young child development. In 1995, over 90 countries addressed issues of young child development in their educational programmes in some form. Adult education activities included paraprofessional training in Malawi, school training in Benin and gender training of rural school committees in Zimbabwe. In Uganda and Zimbabwe, work was carried out on HIV/AIDS education, in line with UNICEF emphasis on intersectoral linkages between education and health.

The mid-decade goals for universal primary education and reducing the gender gap were met in most of Latin America, the Middle East and East Asia, with some positive signs in South Asia. On the other hand, progress was uneven in Africa and even in regression in some cases. No progess was made in countries with recurrent crises and poverty. UNICEF responded by developing its Focus on Education for All in Africa (EFA) through the Accelerated Programme of Collaboration; the main strategies of that initiative were adopted in the United Nations System-Wide Initiative on Africa (see PART FOUR, Chapter III).

The year 1995 was the year of girls' education, which came to be recognized as the centre-piece for sustainable development, demographic balance and women's empowerment. A multi-country initiative for girls' education in Africa began with the support of the Canadian International Development Agency. Activities in 15 African countries helped to intensify national efforts to expand educational opportunities for girls. Discussions were under way for a broader partnership in girls' education with other partners, including Japan, Norway and the World Bank. UNICEF supported programmes in Bangladesh, Burkina Faso, Egypt, Morocco and Pakistan making girls the priority target group in programme design and delivery. In collaboration with UNESCO, UNICEF tackled obstacles to universal primary and basic education, addressing the monitoring of learning achievement in more than 15 countries and disseminating and promoting examples of educational change. It also assisted sub-Saharan countries in building capacity for education statistics and establishing educational management information systems.

UNICEF responded to complex emergencies around the world with the development of an intersectoral programme that included education. Education kits were used in Bosnia and Herzegovina, Rwanda, Somalia and a number of refugee camps.

In Namibia and Nicaragua, UNICEF supported studies on repetition to improve basic education planning. In Brazil, it collaborated on a project to improve student flow and reduce repetition. In Ecuador, it assisted programmes aimed at reducing repetitions in first and second grade where the problem was most severe. UNICEF also supported teacher training in a number of countries. "Joyful learning and teaching" activities, an important feature of a project in India, included monitoring of progress towards minimum levels of learning and other key indicators of effective learning. In Pakistan, UNICEF led an inter-agency mission to develop a programme for improving access to and the quality of primary schools and reaching millions of out-of-school children through non-formal programmes.

### Water supply and sanitation

The water and environmental sanitation strategy endorsed by the Executive Board in May (see above) provided a conceptual framework and guide for UNICEF country programmes, emphasizing behavioural change regarding sanitation and hygiene, integrated community management of the water environment, enhancing community ownership, and improving cost-effectiveness and sustainability. Regional consultations led to the design of effective implementation strategies; the first one was held at Cotonou, Benin, for West and Central Africa, to be followed by similar events in other regions.

In 1995, UNICEF supported regular water and environmental sanitation programmes in more than 90 countries through grants and technical assistance totalling $71 million. Its programmes provided direct support to Governments in their pursuit of mid-decade goals for water and sanitation. UNICEF completed a comprehensive review of global sanitation programmes with the United States Agency for International Development/Environmental Health Project and hygiene case studies in six countries, published a sanitation newsletter in South Asia and conducted a sanitation workshop for Eastern and Southern Africa. UNICEF continued to build its partnership with other multilateral and bilateral agencies and NGOs, undertaking joint missions to support programmes in India, Malawi, Papua New Guinea and Turkmenistan. With WHO, it continued to play a leading role in sector monitoring at the global level through the Joint Monitoring Programme. It provided support to 15 countries in emergency situations, where water and sanitation interventions remained crucial and developed water, sanitation and hygiene emergency service kits.

### Child protection

In 1995, UNICEF continued to review its policies and strategies for addressing child protection issues, with the aim of integrating concerns of children in especially difficult circumstances into mainstream programmes, leading to a holistic response. Among the priority concerns were child labour, children affected by armed conflict, sexual exploitation, childhood disability, and children and families affected by AIDS. Progress was made in giving the issue of child labour a higher priority. A Memorandum of Understanding was signed between the Bangladesh Garment Manufacturers and Exporters Association, ILO and UNICEF, to work towards the progressive elimination of child labour. In India, UNICEF joined with more than 100 carpet manufacturers and national and international NGOs to establish a trademark, RUGMARK, for carpets made without child labour; RUGMARK aimed at expanding child labour-free markets and assisting in the rehablitation and education of those released from the carpet industry.

With sexual exploitation of children emerging as a major global concern, a growing number of NGOs became involved in programmes for prevention, protection and rehabilitation, training of personnel and advocacy. UNICEF supported the efforts of several such local organizations in Brazil, Costa Rica, Sri Lanka, Thailand and other countries. Preparations continued for the convening of the World Congress on Commercial Sexual Exploitation, to be held in Stockholm, Sweden, in August 1996.

UNICEF response to children affected by armed conflict included technical assistance, such as in Rwanda, where it supported a national programme for trauma recovery. It played a leading role in providing support to the study on the impact of armed conflict on children, (see PART THREE, Chapter I) as requested by the General Assembly in 1993.[39]

Childhood disablity and children and families affected by AIDS received increased attention. A seminar on the rights of children with disabilities was organized in collaboration with Rehabilitation International in connection with the World Summit on Social Development (see PART FOUR, Chapter IX). The rights and needs of children affected by the AIDS epidemic were addressed through multisectoral approaches involving alternative care, education opportunities and life skills training for children orphaned by AIDS. Such efforts were supported in Uganda by a consortium of donors, NGOs and community groups. Within the framework of UNAIDS, a set of guidelines and programming approaches was developed and several regional consultations took place.

The Assembly, in **section IV of resolution 50/153**, requested the cooperation of ILO and UNICEF with the Secretary-General for a report on current initiatives and programmes addressing the exploitation of child labour and how to improve cooperation at the national and international levels.

## UNICEF finances

In 1995, UNICEF income totalled $1,011 million, $5 million more than in 1994. Contributions from Governments, intergovernmental organizations and the United Nations accounted for 65 per cent of total income, with the remainder coming from non-governmental sources. Of the total, $537 million went to general resources and $474 million to supplementary funds, including $163 million to emergency supplementary funds.

Expenditures totalled $1,022 million, $23 million more than in 1994. Of the total, $912 million was for programme expenditures, $99 million for administrative expenditures and $11 million for write-offs and other charges.

### Budget appropriations

In March,[40] the Executive Board approved the following respective amounts for general resources and supplementary funding for programme cooperation: Africa, $108,709,249 and $248,383,450; Americas and the Caribbean, $9,108,352 and $44,100,000; Asia, $344,074,941 and $430,500,000; Central and Eastern Europe, CIS and the Baltic States, $39,500,000 and $48,500,000; and the Middle East and North Africa, $5,000,000 and $5,000,000. It also approved $1,019,433 to cover overexpenditure.

In May,[41] the Board approved additional amounts of $49,870,615 and $48,281,000 for Africa; $36,697,002 and $84,800,000 for Central and Eastern Europe, CIS and the Baltic States; and $13,096,933 and $45,260,000 for the Middle East and North Africa.

Total amounts approved were $607,101,525 for general resources, including $25,000 for the Maurice Pate Award, and $954,824,450 for supplementary funding.

In February, the Board postponed[42] preparation of the administrative and programme support budget and the global funds budgets for 1996-1997 pending its decision on implementation of the management review of UNICEF (see below). It agreed that the budgets for 1994-1995 would serve as baseline budgets for 1996-1997 and that there would be no addition or upgrading of net additional core posts, except in connection with the new regional office for Central and Eastern Europe, CIS and the Baltic States, whose proposed budget would be considered later in 1995. The Board also agreed that the baseline budgets would be submitted to the Advisory Committee on Administrative and Budgetary Questions (ACABQ) and considered with the report of ACABQ at the Board's annual session. It decided to consider as necessary budget revisions submitted by the secretariat during the remainder of 1995 and in 1996 and 1997.

In September, the Board[43] approved an interim budget allocation of $126,852,592 for administrative and programme support in 1996 for headquarters and regional offices. It authorized the Executive Director to execute a thorough analysis of the administrative costs at headquarters and in the field, in line with the request of ACABQ in the context of the management review (see below). It noted the secretariat's intention to submit in 1996 an integrated budget for headquarters and regional offices for 1996-1997, incorporating the budgets of administrative and programme support and global funds into a unified budget, with the exception of the Emergency Programme Fund. The Board agreed that the interim budget allocation for headquarters and regional offices would cease when the integrated budget was approved.

Also in September, the Board approved[44] administrative and programme support for field offices totalling $174,820,301 for 1996-1997. It also approved[45] interim budgets for 1996 of $45 million for global funds and totalling $15 million for the Emergency Programme. It requested the Executive Director to inform it about plans for appropriations for global activities and the criteria for the allocation of funds, including to the programmes UNICEF was co-sponsoring. It noted the secretariat's intention to submit in 1996 an integrated budget for headquarters and regional offices for 1996-1997, and agreed that the global funds interim budget would cease upon approval of the integrated budget. It also approved[46] an interim supplementary-funded global funds programme budget of $76.7 million for 1996 and agreed that the interim budget would be replaced by final budgets in 1996.

The Board took note[47] of the interim financial report and statements for the biennium ended 31 December 1994[48] and the review of expenditures in excess of commitments and unspent commitments for completed projects financed by supplementary funds.[49] Also in September, it approved[50] the medium-term plan as a framework of projections for 1995-1998, including up to $582 million in programme expenditure from general resources, to be submitted to the Board in 1996.

### Harmonization of budgets and financial statements

In September, the Executive Board had before it a June progress report[51] on the harmonization of the presentation of financial statements and budgets of UNICEF, UNDP and UNFPA, prepared in response to a 1994 General Assembly request.[52]

According to the report, the Working Party on Financial Statements, established by the Administrative Committee on Coordination (ACC), through its Consultative Committee on Administrative Questions (Financial and Budgetary Questions) (CCAQ (FB)), was in the process of finalizing its work which was to be considered by CCAQ (FB) at its late August session. This would allow for finalization of statement formats and instructions, and any revisions to the Accounting Standards, in time for reporting to the General Assembly in 1996.

The report also stated that as a follow-up to a 1994 Executive Board decision,[53] the three organizations had initiated consultations on harmonizing their budgets with regard to presentation, common definitions, higher degree of financial transparency and comparability. A consultant, engaged to study existing presentations and identify differences, had provided a draft report as a basis for future discussions. The next step after a joint review of the report would be to identify common areas where harmonization was feasible. The recently completed management study of UNICEF (see below), which dealt extensively with budget matters, in particular recommendations to integrate programme and administrative budgets and develop a more analytical budgeting process, would also have a number of implications.

It was not expected that the final findings and conclusions on harmonization would have an impact on the 1996-1997 budgets, said the report. Nevertheless, the secretariat would continue to discuss the subject, particularly with regard to common terms and definitions, and would report to the Board through ACABQ.

The Board requested[54] the Executive Director to accelerate efforts towards harmonization and to provide in 1996 an oral progress report, including identification of common features in the budgets of UNICEF and UNFPA and an explanation of the areas that were not common; an oral progress report on steps needed for further harmonization which, together with an account of the debate on the issue, to the Economic and Social Council at its 1996 substantive session; and submission at the third regular 1996 session, through ACABQ, of initial proposals for action by the Board.

### Organizational and administrative questions

*Management review*

In February, the Executive Board had before it the executive summary of the final report of the UNICEF management review.[55] The study contained more than 80 recommendations, which proposed some 150 specific actions covering the following areas: UNICEF's mission and emergency policy, relations with NGOs and other agencies, human resources, programming, global goals, supply operations, fund raising, information and communication, information systems, UNICEF structure, accountability, financial systems, cost effectiveness, governance and implementation.

The Board called[56] on the secretariat to establish an internal process of management reform, including the designation of a task force to deal with the report and develop a plan of action; and to involve UNICEF staff in the work of the task force. It looked forward to maintaining close contact with the secretariat in formulating the plan of action and called for regular briefings of all interested parties by the secretariat between Board meetings on progress with implementing change. The Board established an informal inter-sessional consultation of interested parties to facilitate its own discussion and decision-making and requested the secretariat to provide information for its second regular session on an initial response to the recommendations of the review, including reference to any disagreements over matters of fact; advice on recommended priorities for action; outline of broad priority areas for implementation and an estimated monthly timetable for their consideration and action; and advice on the implications of the review for UNICEF's mandate and mission. It encouraged the secretariat, in its follow-up to the review, to take into consideration the recommendations of the multi-donor evaluation[57] as well as reform measures, both planned and under implementation, elsewhere in the UN system. The secretariat should submit to the Board a draft overall mission statement for UNICEF and a draft mission statement for emergency operations, as well as draft terms of reference for any further study relating to the review and submissions on any additional funding requirements arising from the study.

In response to the Board's February request, the secretariat submitted a March report[58] on strengthening management in UNICEF, which constituted its initial response to the recommendations of the review and included advice on recommended priorities for action, the initial implementation process, broad priority areas for implementation and funding requirements, as well as an annex covering some issues of perception and fact contained in the study. The report also contained a draft recommendation on the establishment of a management task force, including operating budget, as well as a budget for consultancies proposed in the study.

In March, the Board agreed[59] with the secretariat's intention to reallocate funds already approved for implementation of the review and requested it to elaborate further, taking into account the views of the Board members and the work plan for implementation of the review follow-up, and to submit it for the information and guidance of the Board. It called on the secretariat to redraft the terms of reference for further consultancies and decided to consider the question of the UNICEF mission, including emergencies, at its annual session.

In May, the Board had before it a report[60] outlining issues concerning the UNICEF mission and a further elaboration of the work plan for management reform activities,[61] as requested in March. In September, it was provided with an update[62] on the process and projects for promoting management excellence in UNICEF, including a strategic work plan outlining the time-frame for key activities and interrelationships among projects.

The Board welcomed[63] the Executive Director's plan to ensure its continued full involvement in the follow-up to the management review, in particular by sharing relevant documentation on progress; providing regular updates on resources spent and/or allocated implementation; sharing the mission statement document with Board members when available; scheduling inter-sessional meetings and establishing a time-table; keeping the management review on the agenda for upcoming Board meetings; and submitting, through ACABQ, recommendations for implementation that affected policy, structure, financial and/or staffing and required Board approval. The Board requested a summary at its first regular 1996 session explaining the link between management review recommendations and the strategic approach being taken and follow-up action proposed, including a time-frame for decision-making by the Board and that all future progress reports make that link; that each recommendation emerging from the management reform process presented to the Board for approval include an analysis of implications for other follow-up to the management review and explain how it contributed to UNICEF carrying out its mandate; that management review's recommendations on Greeting Card and related Operations be considered in the follow-up exercise; and that, following the deliberations of management excellence project 3 (concerning relations with National Committees), any implications for the agreement between UNICEF and its National Committees be brought to the Board's attention.

In a September report,[64] ACABQ made a number of recommendations in respect of the UNICEF management study and stated that further elaboration was needed of the terms of reference of the implementation structure, particularly with regard to the roles of the Executive Board, the Executive Director and the Steering Committee. Also needed was further clarification as to the role of the task force established to deal with the management study, *vis-à-vis* the Steering Committee, as well as the indication as to how the interests of the field would be represented in the task force; high priority should be given to the recommendations in the management study on human resources management, and UNICEF should report to the Board on a strategy for implementing those recommendations; a full cost estimate and analysis of all expenditures related to the management review should be prepared for submission through ACABQ to the Board at its next session; and an item on implementation of the management study should be part of the Board's agenda on a regular basis. There should be a work plan on a phased completion of the study; proposals to be discussed by the Board should be grouped in a comprehensive report and should focus on one area or aspect of UNICEF management and operations; and proposals of the Executive Director should indicate how they related to the management study, or should be explained if they differed or were in addition to what was contained in the study.

## Approval process for country programme recommendations

The UNICEF management review also considered ways to make the relationship between programming, countries and regions more effective, recommending more intense dedication to conceptual ''product design'', more integrated focus on field service delivery and more negotiation on programme and goals.

In February, the Executive Board decided[65] that the secretariat, in consultation with recipient Governments, should inform the Board at an early stage, through a brief country note, of its preliminary ideas regarding the mix and weight given in UNICEF country programmes to programme strategies and priorities, including a description of other activities within each sector explaining how UNICEF's proposals fit in with those, to be used as a basis for further discussion in the recipient country. The Board called on the UNICEF country-representative, in consultation with the recipient country and the UN resident coordinator, to organize periodic meetings to exchange views with the relevant partners on the status of country programmes in order to avoid duplication and strengthen mutual support. It requested the secretariat to submit a summary of the final country programme document for approval, not exceeding 15 pages and with a systematic presentation of strategy, inputs and outputs. Board approval would be given on a no-objection basis. Board members had to inform the secretariat before the meeting of any country programme they wished to have discussed by the Board. The Board requested the secretariat to submit a summary of the outcome of mid-term reviews and major evaluation reports, specifying, *inter alia*, results achieved, lessons learned and the need for adjustment in the country note. Those arrangements would take effect in 1996 and be reviewed in 1998.

## Strengthening accountability and oversight

In May, the Executive Director reported to the Executive Board on the major findings of an internal audit investigation of the Kenya country office, which revealed a number of irregularities, mismanagement and fraud amounting to some $9 million. The investigation confirmed gross violations of UNICEF rules and regulations, lack of financial and administrative controls, and excessively high overheads, including the opening of seven sub-offices without budget approval. Eight staff members had been dismissed, 15 charged with serious misconduct and placed on suspension without pay and another charged with mismanagement.

The Board noted[66] the findings and welcomed the measures taken by the Executive Director and her statement to the Board on 25 May on immediate steps to strengthen accountability and financial procedures within the organization. It requested her to ensure that those measures would prevent any recurrence of fraud or mismanagement throughout UNICEF and to provide a further progress report in September on the situation in Kenya and the steps being taken to strengthen financial management, accountability and oversight.

In August, UNICEF presented an update[67] on the results of the audit of the Kenya country office and measures taken to prevent the recurrence of fraud and/or mismanagement. A new representative to Kenya, with a strong background in financial management and personnel administration, had been appointed to provide strong leadership needed to strengthen financial management and accountability and restore order to programme delivery. Recruitment for existing staff vacancies would be carried out, but in the interim, the staff of the Eastern and Southern Africa Regional Office and other offices would provide short-term support.

The third phase of the audit was completed in June/July. The audit team issued a management letter to the Kenya country office leadership formalizing recommendations for specific improvements. Of the 67 issues raised, one half had been successfully addressed and progress on the remaining areas of concern was being monitored by the Office of Internal Audit and supervised by the Executive Director. With the consolidation of the regular and the emergency programmes, staff had been reduced to 137 and that number was to reach 100 by December. Six sub-offices were closed, and the remaining one at Garissa would support the emergency programme in the north-east. Action was taken regarding the delegation of authority, financial monitoring and reconciliations, streamlining programme delivery, and cash and supply assistance.

In terms of strengthening financial control and accountability throughout UNICEF, several reform projects were underway, including the redefinition of a UNICEF mission statement as well as initiatives to define the accountability structure, build capacity for effective field management, develop an integrated strategy for relations with National Committees and a set of professional standards for staff. Division directors and heads of offices were required to give specific attention to the follow-up of audit recommendations and were to be held accountable for their implementation. Training packages were developed to give managers the capacity to undertake regular participatory self-audits within their offices. Training was being oriented towards building staff capacity at all levels to implement regulations and procedures for protecting assets and managing people, programmes and money on an ongoing basis. The management of emergency operations was also strengthened. Special attention was given to agreements with NGOs to ensure their conformity with the principles of the standard project agreement. The Executive Director continued to discuss with regional directors and other senior staff steps to strengthen the oversight role of regional offices and clarify lines of reporting and accountability.

In September, the Board requested[68] the secretariat to report at each of its sessions on all future audit activity in the Kenya office until the matter was resolved, and UNICEF to organize an in-country briefing with interested partners on the implications of the Kenya office incident for its Kenya programme. It took note[69] of the measures to strengthen financial control and accountability and called on the Executive Director to report on how internal controls were being addressed through the follow-up to the management review; how UNICEF could use reports on overcommitment and overspending to examine the causes and take appropriate action; and to consider the eligibility criteria for classification as NGOs and review their role in implementing UNICEF programmes.

In response to the Board's request, UNICEF submitted a November progress report[70] on the audit of the Kenya country office. According to the report, eight additional cases of fraud identified during the third phase of the audit investigation were under review by the Division of Personnel and the UN Office of Legal Affairs. A total of 23 staff had been charged with fraud, one with mismanagement and one with misconduct, bringing the total number involved to 25. As of 15 November, 21 staff had separated from UNICEF—17, including one representative, had been summarily dismissed, 3 had resigned and one had opted for early retirement. The ongoing management reforms in the Kenya country office were on course. At the end of the exercise, the various instructions and guidelines would be constituted into two internal control manuals (operations and programmes), which would form the basis for the day-to-day operations in the office. The Office of Internal Audit was asked to review the various instructions and guidelines and to suggest improvements. With the closure of the six sub-offices, the total staffing level had been reduced to 90. An Internal Control Panel had been approved and certifying, authorizing, approving and paying officials had received relevant guidelines. In other related action, the recovery of longstanding cash assistance advances to government counterparts and NGOs was being pursued and overpayment to suppliers followed up.

### Reports and sessions

At a meeting in November 1994, UNICEF, UNDP, UNFPA and the World Food Programme (WFP) agreed to proceed on a common understanding with regard to the format and content of their annual reports. Earlier in the year, the Economic and Social Council had requested[71] UN development funds and programmes to develop a common structure for their reports, as had the General Assembly in 1993.[72]

In February 1995, the Executive Board decided[73] that one part of the annual report of the executive head of UNICEF to the Board would also be the report to the Council; that part would carry both Board and Council document symbols and contain the sections requested by the Council, namely, a section outlining measures taken to implement the provisions of the triennial policy review of operational activities and another on the activities and measures undertaken within the designated theme(s) for the high-level meeting of the Council's operational activities segment. The format of those two sections would be discussed with the Bureau of the Board, which at its annual session would consider them as distinct agenda items. The Board's comments and recommendations would be presented to the Council as part of the report on its annual session. The reports on the Board's sessions since July 1994 would be submitted to the Council at its 1995 substantive session, following the same procedure in 1994. A section summarizing the relevant recommendations of the Board would be included in the Secretary-General's annual report to the operational activities segment of the Council, as well as a short analytical overview of reports on the work of the funds and programmes, highlighting common themes, trends and problems.

In May, the Board took note[74] of the Executive Director's annual report to the Council[75] and decided to transmit it to the 1995 substantive session of the Council. The Council, by **decision 1995/233** of 13 July, took note of UNICEF's annual report[76], which dealt with measures taken to implement the triennial policy review of oper-

ational activities and UNICEF follow-up to the World Summit for Social Development (see PART FOUR, Chapter IX), as well as of the Board's report on its first and second regular sessions and its annual session of 1995.[77]

Also in May, the Board requested[78] the secretariat to consider the format of future Board decisions in order to facilitate an effective and businesslike conduct of work and to make recommendations to the September 1995 session of the Board. In September, it agreed[79] on the allocation of items for its 1996 sessions.

### Greeting Card Operation

In a financial report for the year ended 30 April 1995,[80] the Executive Director stated that in 1994 the contribution of the Greeting Card Operation to UNICEF general resources was $144 million and 158 million cards were sold, 4 million more than in 1993. Gross proceeds increased from $138.1 million to $153.6 million over the same period.

In May 1995, the Executive Board took note[81] of the Greeting Card and related Operations (GCO) provisional report for the period 1 May 1994-30 April 1995[82] and the GCO financial report and accounts for the year ended 30 April 1994.[83]

Also in May, the Board approved[84] budgeted GCO expenditures totalling $87.1 million for the fiscal year 1 May 1995 to 30 April 1996 and noted that for 1995-1996, GCO net proceeds were budgeted at $234 million. The Board also approved the changes in posts as presented in the proposed budget for 1995,[85] with the exception of the proposed transfer of the Personnel Unit and no reduction in the number of posts. It renewed the Fundraising Development Programme and the Market Development Programme, with $7 million and $4 million, respectively, for 1995. It authorized the expansion of the Central and Eastern European National Committees Development Programme to include the National Committees of Estonia, Latvia, Lithuania and Slovenia, and approved for that purpose a budget of $1.5 million, of which $0.2 million was for one-time investments. It noted the three different income statement formats presented by GCO and requested the Executive Director, in the interest of greater transparency and consistency, to use the income statement format as presented in the GCO work plan and budget[85] for all future GCO documents. The Board further decided that GCO should present a regional analysis of profitability, with recommendations, in its next work plan and budget and that it should no longer submit a provisional report. It further decided that the questions of moving the GCO Personnel Unit to the UNICEF Division of Personnel and of changing GCO's fiscal year from 1 May-

30 April to 1 January-31 December should be considered further by the Executive Director in the context of the UNICEF management review; and that a study, with recommendations, should be presented in the next GCO work plan, of the optimum structure and location of GCO, so as to reflect its main markets, business partners and areas of potential growth, not excluding the possibility of consolidating its staff in a single headquarters location.

### Headquarters conference facilities

As requested by the Executive Board in 1994,[86] UNICEF submitted an initial feasibility study[87] on developing a conference facility at UNICEF headquarters. The cost of constructing, furnishing and equipping such a facility were estimated at around $1.2 million, in addition to recurrent operating costs of $279,000 per year. At the current time, there was no source of funding for those costs, the report said. The United Nations could provide conference service staff for Executive Board meetings held at UNICEF headquarters, but the size of Labouisse Hall would limit participation of observer delegations. If the conference facility was not constructed, UNICEF would be able to use the United Nations conference facilities; with UNICEF, UNDP and Buildings Management Services reaching agreement on a minimal readjustment of the Economic and Social Council chamber, it would suit better the requirements of UNDP, UNFPA and UNICEF.

In February, the Executive Director informed the Board that Sweden, on behalf of the Nordic countries, had notified UNICEF that they would provide $1.2 million to cover the installation costs of conference facilities at UNICEF headquarters premises. The Board decided[88] to take a decision on the subject at a later date.

ACABQ, in a September report,[65] invited the Executive Board to request UNICEF to continue its negotiations with the UN Secretariat to obtain those conference-facilities within the UN premises identified by the Board to meet its specific requirements.

### Joint committees

At its thirtieth session (Geneva, 30-31 January 1995), the UNICEF/WHO Joint Committee on Health Policy (JCHP) reviewed[89] WHO policies and UNICEF decisions on the health of women and children, as well as the health goals established by the 1990 World Summit for Children. The Joint Committee made recommendations on immunization coverage, neonatal tetanus, measles, and poliomyelitis; oral rehydration therapy, and diarrhoeal case management; breast-feeding, iodine deficiency disorders, vitamin A

deficiency and the reduction of malnutrition; dracunculiasis (guinea-worm transmission); water and sanitation; HIV/AIDS-related preventive practices; reduction of maternal and infant mortality rates and of iron deficiency anaemia; and acute respiratory infections. It also discussed health systems development in a decentralizing situation: options for improving district health systems, and complementarity of UNICEF and WHO in emergency situations, with particular reference to women and children.

In March, the Executive Board took note[90] of the report and its recommendations. It requested the UNICEF secretariat to consult on the draft UNICEF health strategy document (see above and PART FOUR, Chapter XIII) with concerned parties such as JCHP, WHO, the World Bank, UNFPA and others, for submission to the Board and in order to promote its implementation at the country level.

In February, the Board considered the mechanisms for the review and implementation of future recommendations of JCHP and the UNESCO/UNICEF Joint Committee on Education (JEC). The Board decided[91] that in order to be more involved in the work of the joint committees, the draft agendas of the two bodies should be submitted to its representatives on the committees for their comments and approval; consultations should be institutionalized between the UNICEF secretariat and the Board representatives on the joint committees regarding agenda, issues and desired outcome; the President of the Board should present the report of the relevant joint committee to the Board, outlining the issues raised, the recommendations made and their context, and the future implications of those recommendations.

Also in February, the Board elected[92] the members and alternates to JEC from the African, Asian, Central and Eastern European, and the Western European and Others groups of States, and agreed that the Latin American and Caribbean group of States would advise the Board of its nominees at a later date. In May, it elected[93] the members and alternates from the latter group.

### Fiftieth anniversary of UNICEF

In a November 1995 report,[94] UNICEF outlined activities planned to commemorate its fiftieth anniversary in 1996. Under the overall theme ''Children First'', its offices around the world worked in consultation with other UN agencies and offices, Governments and UNICEF partners to develop regional and country-level anniversary activities. No global-level anniversary activities were planned, but UNICEF regional offices planned for ministerial-level conferences to review progress on regional priorities, as well as for interregional meetings of experts and professionals on education, children in especially difficult circumstances and child rights. UNICEF country offices made the acceleration of mobilization and advocacy efforts to achieve country-specific goals a central priority for the anniversary year. In 14 countries around the world, where children were affected by civil strife and war, they developed plans to accelerate programmes, thus generating global media exposure in concert with the 1996 Olympic Games and bringing public attention and support to the plight of those children. Activities were being organized by the National Committees and at headquarters, including a global advertising campaign to give additional fund-raising support to country-level efforts. Four special greeting card sets and anniversary-related products had been produced and support was given to private sector fund-raising initiatives both globally and at the country-level.

*REFERENCES*

[1]E/ICEF/1996/10 (Part I). [2]E/1995/33/Rev.1. [3]E/1995/33/Rev.1 (dec. 1995/13). [4]Ibid. (dec. 1995/28). [5]E/ICEF/1995/15. [6]A/45/625, Annex. [7]E/1995/33/Rev.1 (dec. 1995/14). [8]GA res. 45/217, 21 Dec. 1990. [9]E/ICEF/1995/16. [10]E/1995/33/Rev.1 (dec. 1995/21). [11]E/ICEF/1995/17 & Corr.1. [12]E/1995/33/Rev.1 (dec. 1995/22). [13]YUN 1992, p. 670. [14]E/ICEF/1995/12. [15]YUN 1994, p. 955. [16]E/ICEF/1995/33/Rev.1 (dec. 1995/11). [17]E/ICEF/1995/12/Rev.1. [18]E/ICEF/1995/33/Rev.1 (dec. 1995/29). [19]E/ICEF/1995/19. [20]E/ICEF/1995/33/Rev.1 (dec. 1995/17). [21]YUN 1992, p. 670. [22]E/ICEF/1996/3. [23]E/ICEF/1995/CRP.47. [24]E/ICEF/1995/33/Rev.1 (dec. 1995/36). [25]E/ICEF/1996/6. [26]E/ICEF/1995/33/Rev.1 (dec. 1995/2). [27]E/ICEF/1995/3. [28]YUN 1966, p. 385. [29]E/ICEF/1996/7. [30]E/ICEF/1996/4. [31]YUN 1987, p. 859. [32]E/ICEF/1995/18. [33]E/ICEF/1995/33/Rev.1 (dec. 1995/18). [34]YUN 1992, p. 1120. [35]E/ICEF/1995/P/L.40. [36]E/ICEF/1995/CRP.15. [37]E/ICEF/1995/33/Rev.1 (dec. 1995/13). [38]YUN 1994, p. 1129. [39]YUN 1993, p. 966, GA res. 48/157, 20 Dec. 1993. [40]E/ICEF/1995/33/Rev.1 (dec. 1995/9). [41]E/ICEF/1995/33/Rev.1 (dec. 1995/16). [42]E/ICEF/1995/33/Rev.1 (dec. 1995/6). [43]E/ICEF/1995/33/Rev.1 (dec. 1995/30). [44]Ibid. (dec. 1995/31). [45]Ibid. (dec. 1995/32). [46]Ibid. (dec. 1995/33). [47]Ibid. (dec. 1995/35). [48]E/ICEF/1995/AB/L.14. [49]E/ICEF/1995/AB/L.18. [50]E/ICEF/1995/33/Rev.1 (dec. 1995/34). [51]E/ICEF/1995/AB/L.15. [52]YUN 1994, p. 1370, 49/216 E, 23 Dec.1994. [53]YUN 1994, p. 1370. [54]E/ICEF/1995/33/Rev.1 (dec. (1995/37). [55]E/ICEF/1995/AB/L.1. [56]E/ICEF/1995/33/Rev.1 (dec. 1995/7). [57]E/ICEF/1995/6. [58]E/ICEF/1995/AB/L.4. [59]E/ICEF/1995/33/Rev.1 (dec. 1995/12). [60]E/ICEF/1995/AB/L.11. [61]E/ICEF/1995/CRP.24. [62]E/ICEF/1995/CRP.48. [63]E/ICEF/1956/33/Rev.1 (dec. 1995/25). [64]A/50/489. [65]E/1995/33/Rev.1 (dec. 1995/8). [66]Ibid. (dec. 1995/19). [67]E/ICEF/1995/AB/L.17. [68]E/ICEF/1995/33/Rev.1 (dec. 1995/27). [69]Ibid. (dec. 1995/26). [70]E/ICEF/1996/AB/L.1. [71]YUN 1994, p. 789, ESC res, 1994/33, 28 July 1994. [72]YUN 1993, p. 1118, GA res. 48/162, Annex I, 20 Dec. 1993. [73]E/1995/33/Rev.1 (dec. 1995/5). [74]Ibid. (dec. 1995/17). [75]E/ICEF/1995/14 (Part III). [76]E/1995/90 & Add.1. [77]E/1995/33. [78]E/ICEF/1995/33/Rev.1 (dec. 1995/24). [79]Ibid. (dec. 1995/38). [80]E/ICEF/1996/AB/L.12. [81]E/ICEF/1995/33/Rev.1 (dec. 1995/15). [82]E/ICEF/1996/AB/L.7 & Corr.1. [83]E/ICEF/1995/AB/L.6. [84]E/ICEF/1995/33/Rev.1 (dec. 1995/20). [85]E/ICEF/1995/AB/L.8. [86]YUN 1994, p. 1212. [87]E/ICEF/1995/AB/L.2. [88]E/ICEF/1995/33/Rev.1 (dec. 1995/3). [89]E/ICEF/1995/P/L.9. [90]E/ICEF/1995/33/Rev.1 (dec. 1995/10). [91]Ibid. (dec. 1995/4). [92]Ibid. (dec. 1995/1). [93]Ibid. (dec. 1995/23). [94]E/ICEF/1996/5.

# Youth

In an April 1995 report,[1] the Secretary-General presented to the Commission on Social Development a draft world programme of action for youth to the year 2000 and beyond, pursuant to a 1994 General Assembly resolution.[2] The draft was prepared on the basis of replies received from Governments, United Nations bodies and organizations, other intergovernmental organizations and non-governmental youth and youth-related organizations. The draft programme contained a statement of purpose, described the development setting, outlined strategies and policy specifics and identified priority areas and means of implementation at the national, regional and international levels.

The Commission at its April session adopted a resolution[3] on the tenth anniversary of the International Youth Year, recommending that the Economic and Social Council establish an open-ended working group to complete formulation of the draft programme of action.

In May, the Chairman of the Commission, on behalf of the Bureau, submitted to the Council a revised version[4] of the resolution and informed the Council that the Commission's Working Group on Youth had presented a revised text of the draft programme. The Commission recommended that the Council authorize the Working Group to formulate a final draft programme, for submission to the Council's 1995 resumed substantive session.

Following the Commission's recommendation, the Council, by **decision 1995/251** of 24 July, established an open-ended working group during its resumed substantive session, building on the process achieved by the Commission's Working Group, to complete formulation of the draft programme.

By an October note,[6] the Secretariat submitted to the Council the final draft of the world programme of action. The Council adopted it by **resolution 1995/64**. In November, the Secretary-General transmitted[7] to the General Assembly a draft resolution on the programme, recommended by the Council for adoption by the Assembly. The Assembly acted on it by adopting **resolution 50/81** (see below).

**ECONOMIC AND SOCIAL COUNCIL ACTION**

On 2 November, the Economic and Social Council adopted **resolution 1995/64**.

### World Programme of Action for Youth to the Year 2000 and Beyond

*The Economic and Social Council*

*Recommends* to the General Assembly the adoption of the following draft resolution:

[For text, see General Assembly resolution 50/81 below.]

Economic and Social Council resolution 1995/64

2 November 1995   Meeting 59   Adopted without vote

7-nation draft (E/1995/L.69), orally revised; agenda item 5 *(f)*.
*Sponsors:* Austria, Czech Republic, Netherlands, Nicaragua, Nigeria, Portugal, Romania.
*Meeting numbers.* ESC 58, 59.

### GENERAL ASSEMBLY ACTION

On 14 December, the General Assembly adopted **resolution 50/81**.

### World Programme of Action for Youth to the Year 2000 and Beyond

*The General Assembly,*

*Recognizing* that young people in all countries are both a major human resource for development and key agents for social change, economic development and technological innovation,

*Bearing in mind* that the ways in which the challenges and potentials of young people are addressed by policy will influence current social and economic conditions and the well-being and livelihood of future generations,

*Acknowledging* that young women and men in all parts of the world aspire to full participation in the life of society,

*Recognizing* that the decade since the observance of International Youth Year: Participation, Development and Peace has been a period of fundamental political, economic and sociocultural change in the world,

*Acknowledging* the contribution that non-governmental youth organizations could make in improving dialogue and consultations with the United Nations system on the situation of youth,

*Recalling* its resolution 45/103 of 14 December 1990, in which it requested the Secretary-General to prepare a draft world youth programme of action towards the year 2000 and beyond,

*Recalling also* its resolution 49/152 of 23 December 1994 on the International Youth Year, in which it requested the Commission for Social Development at its thirty-fourth session to consider further the draft world programme of action for youth towards the year 2000 and beyond,

*Having considered* the report of the Economic and Social Council,

1. *Adopts* the World Programme of Action for Youth to the Year 2000 and Beyond, annexed hereto, as an integral part of the present resolution, including the ten priority areas identified therein, namely, education, employment, hunger and poverty, health, environment, drug abuse, juvenile delinquency, leisure-time activities, girls and young women and the full and effective participation of youth in the life of society and in decision-making;

2. *Invites* Governments, with the support of the international community, non-governmental organizations and the public and private sectors, as well as youth organizations in particular, to implement the Programme of Action by undertaking the relevant activities outlined therein;

3. *Requests* the Secretary-General to report to it at its fifty-second session, through the Commission for Social Development and the Economic and Social Council, on the progress made in the implementation of the Programme of Action, taking into account the promotion of integrated reporting;

4. *Invites* Member States, once again, to include, whenever possible, youth representatives in their delegations to the General Assembly and other meetings of relevant United Nations bodies, with a view to stimulating the participation of young women and men in the implementation of the Programme of Action.

### ANNEX
**World Programme of Action for Youth
to the Year 2000 and Beyond**

Contents

### Preamble

1. The decade since the observance of International Youth Year: Participation, Development, Peace has been a period during which the world experienced fundamental political, economic and sociocultural changes. These changes will inevitably affect at least the first decade of the twenty-first century as well.

2. Young people represent agents, beneficiaries and victims of major societal changes and are generally confronted by a paradox: to seek to be integrated into an existing order or to serve as a force to transform that order. Young people in all parts of the world, living in countries at different stages of development and in different socio-economic settings, aspire to full participation in the life of society.

### Statement of purpose

3. The World Programme of Action for Youth provides a policy framework and practical guidelines for national action and international support to improve the situation of young people. It contains proposals for action to the year 2000 and beyond, aiming at achieving the objectives of the International Youth Year and at fostering conditions and mechanisms to promote improved well-being and livelihood among young people.

4. The Programme of Action focuses in particular on measures to strengthen national capacities in the field of youth and to increase the quality and quantity of opportunities available to young people for full, effective and constructive participation in society.

## I. United Nations Declaration of Intent on Youth: problems and potentials

5. The States Members of the United Nations have agreed to work towards achievement of the purposes and principles of the Charter of the United Nations, *inter alia*, the promotion of higher standards of living, full employment and conditions of economic and social progress and development. Young people in all parts of the world, living in countries at different stages of development and in different socio-economic situations, aspire to full participation in the life of society, as provided in the Charter, including:

(*a*) Attainment of an educational level commensurate with their aspirations;

(*b*) Access to employment opportunities equal to their abilities;

(*c*) Food and nutrition adequate for full participation in the life of society;

(*d*) A physical and social environment that promotes good health, offers protection from disease and addiction and is free from all types of violence;

(*e*) Human rights and fundamental freedoms without distinction as to race, sex, language, religion or any other forms of discrimination;

(*f*) Participation in decision-making processes;

(*g*) Places and facilities for cultural, recreational and sports activities to improve the living standards of young people in both rural and urban areas.

6. While the peoples of the United Nations, through their Governments, international organizations and voluntary associations, have done much to ensure that these aspirations may be achieved, including efforts to implement the guidelines for further planning and suitable follow-up in the field of youth endorsed by the General Assembly in 1985, it is apparent that the changing world social, economic and political situation has created the following conditions that have made this goal more difficult to achieve in many countries:

(*a*) Claims on the physical and financial resources of States, which have reduced the resources available for youth programmes and activities, particularly in heavily indebted countries;

(*b*) Inequities in social, economic and political conditions, including racism and xenophobia, which lead to increasing hunger, deterioration in living conditions and poverty among youth and to their marginalization as refugees, displaced persons and migrants;

(*c*) Increasing difficulty for young people returning from armed conflict and confrontation in integrating into the community and gaining access to education and employment;

(*d*) Continuing discrimination against young women and insufficient access for young women to equal opportunities in employment and education;

(*e*) High levels of youth unemployment, including long-term unemployment;

(*f*) Continuing deterioration of the global environment resulting from unsustainable patterns of consumption and production, particularly in industrialized countries, which is a matter of grave concern, aggravating poverty and imbalances;

(*g*) Increasing incidence of diseases, such as malaria, the human immunodeficiency virus and the acquired immunodeficiency syndrome (HIV/AIDS), and other threats to health, such as substance abuse and psychotropic substance addiction, smoking and alcoholism;

(*h*) Inadequate opportunities for vocational education and training, especially for persons with disabilities;

(*i*) Changes in the role of the family as a vehicle for shared responsibility and socialization of youth;

(*j*) Lack of opportunity for young people to participate in the life of society and contribute to its development and well-being;

(*k*) Prevalence of debilitating disease, hunger and malnutrition that engulfs the life of many young people;

(*l*) Increasing difficulty for young people to receive family life education as a basis for forming healthy families that foster sharing of responsibilities.

7. These phenomena, among others, contribute to the increased marginalization of young people from the larger society, which is dependent on youth for its continual renewal.

8. We, the peoples of the United Nations, believe that the following principles, aimed at ensuring the well-being of young women and men and their full and active participation in the society in which they live, are fundamental to the implementation of the World Programme of Action for Youth to the Year 2000 and Beyond:

(*a*) Every State should provide its young people with opportunities for obtaining education, for acquiring skills and for participating fully in all aspects of society, with a view to, *inter alia*, acquiring productive employment and leading self-sufficient lives;

(*b*) Every State should guarantee to all young people the full enjoyment of human rights and fundamental freedoms in accordance with the Charter of the United Nations and other international instruments related to human rights;

(*c*) Every State should take all necessary measures to eliminate all forms of discrimination against young women and girls and remove all obstacles to gender equality and the advancement and empowerment of women and should ensure full and equal access to education and employment for girls and young women;

(*d*) Every State should foster mutual respect, tolerance and understanding among young people with different racial, cultural and religious backgrounds;

(*e*) Every State should endeavour to ensure that its policies relating to young people are informed by accurate data on their situation and needs, and that the public has access to such data to enable it to participate in a meaningful fashion in the decision-making process;

(*f*) Every State is encouraged to promote education and action aimed at fostering among youth a spirit of peace, cooperation and mutual respect and understanding between nations;

(*g*) Every State should meet the special needs of young people in the areas of responsible family-planning practice, family life, sexual and reproductive health, sexually transmitted diseases, HIV infection and AIDS prevention, consistent with the Programme of Action adopted by the International Conference on Population and Development in September 1994, the Copenhagen Declaration on Social Development and the Programme of Action adopted by the World Summit for Social Development in March 1995, and the Beijing Declaration and the Platform for Action adopted by the Fourth World Conference on Women in September 1995;

*(h)* Environmental protection, promotion and enhancement are among the issues considered by young people to be of prime importance to the future welfare of society. States should therefore actively encourage young people and youth organizations to participate actively in programmes, including educational programmes, and actions designed to protect, promote and enhance the environment;

*(i)* Every State should take measures to develop the possibilities of education and employment of young people with disabilities;

*(j)* Every State should take measures to improve the situation of young people living in particularly difficult conditions, including by protecting their rights;

*(k)* Every State should promote the goal of full employment as a basic priority of its economic and social policies, giving special attention to youth employment. They should also take measures to eliminate the economic exploitation of children;

*(l)* Every State should provide young people with the health services necessary to ensure their physical and mental well-being, including measures to combat diseases such as malaria and HIV/AIDS, and to protect them from harmful drugs and the effects of addiction to drugs, tobacco and alcohol;

*(m)* Every State should place people at the centre of development and should direct their economies to meet human needs more effectively and to ensure that young people are active participants and beneficiaries in the process of development.

## II. Development setting

9. In 1995, the world youth population—defined by the United Nations as the age cohort 15-24—is estimated to be 1.03 billion, or 18 per cent of the total world population. The majority of the world youth population (84 per cent in 1995) lives in developing countries. This figure is projected to increase to 89 per cent by 2025. The difficult circumstances that people experience in many developing countries are often even more difficult for young people because of limited opportunities for education and training, viable employment and health and social services, and because of a growing incidence of substance abuse and juvenile delinquency. Many developing countries are also experiencing unprecedented rates of rural-urban migration by young people.

10. Apart from the statistical definition of the term "youth" mentioned above, the meaning of the term "youth" varies in different societies around the world. Definitions of youth have changed continuously in response to fluctuating political, economic and sociocultural circumstances.

11. Young people in industrialized countries comprise a relatively smaller proportion of the total population because of generally lower birth rates and longer life expectancy. They comprise a social group that faces particular problems and uncertainties regarding its future, problems that relate in part to limited opportunities for appropriate employment.

12. Young people in all countries are both a major human resource for development and key agents for social change, economic development and technological innovation. Their imagination, ideals, considerable energies and vision are essential for the continuing development of the societies in which they live. Thus, there is special need for new impetus to be given to the design and implementation of youth policies and programmes at all levels. The ways in which the challenges and potentials of young people are addressed by policy will influence current social and economic conditions and the well-being and livelihood of future generations.

## III. Strategies and policy specifics

13. In 1965, in resolution 2037(XX), the General Assembly endorsed the Declaration on the Promotion among Youth of the Ideals of Peace, Mutual Respect and Understanding between Peoples. From 1965 to 1975, both the General Assembly and the Economic and Social Council emphasized three basic themes in the field of youth: participation, development and peace. The need for an international policy on youth was emphasized as well. In 1979, the General Assembly, by resolution 34/151, designated 1985 as International Youth Year: Participation, Development, Peace. In 1985, by resolution 40/14, the Assembly endorsed the guidelines for further planning and suitable follow-up in the field of youth. The guidelines are significant for their focus on young people as a broad category comprising various subgroups, rather than a single demographic entity. They provide proposals for specific measures to address the needs of subgroups such as young people with disabilities, rural and urban youth and young women.

14. The themes identified by the General Assembly for International Youth Year: Participation, Development, Peace reflect a predominant concern of the international community with distributive justice, popular participation and quality of life. These were reflected in the guidelines, and they represent overall themes of the World Programme of Action for Youth to the Year 2000 and Beyond as well.

15. The Programme of Action also builds upon other, recent international instruments, including the Rio Declaration on Environment and Development, adopted by the United Nations Conference on Environment and Development, the Vienna Declaration and Programme of Action adopted by the World Conference on Human Rights, the Programme of Action of the International Conference on Population and Development, the Copenhagen Declaration on Social Development and the Programme of Action of the World Summit for Social Development, and the Platform for Action adopted by the Fourth World Conference on Women.

16. The Programme of Action is drawn from these international instruments generally and specifically related to youth policies and programmes. The Programme of Action is significant because it provides a cross-sectoral standard relating to both policy-making and programme design and delivery. It will serve as a model for integrated actions, at all levels, to address more effectively problems experienced by young people in various conditions and to enhance their participation in society.

17. The Programme of Action is divided into three phases: the first phase focused on analysis and on drafting the Programme of Action and on its adoption by the General Assembly at its fiftieth session, in 1995; the second phase is concerned with worldwide implementation of the Programme of Action to the year 2000; the

third phase, covering the period 2001 to 2010, will focus on further implementation and evaluation of progress made and obstacles encountered; it will suggest appropriate adjustments to long-term objectives and specific measures to improve the situation of young people in the societies in which they live.

### IV. Priority areas

18. Each of the ten priority areas identified by the international community is presented in terms of principal issues, specific objectives and the actions proposed to be taken by various actors to achieve those objectives. Objectives and actions reflect the three themes of International Youth Year: Participation, Development, Peace; they are interlinked and mutually reinforcing.

19. The ten fields of action identified by the international community are education, employment, hunger and poverty, health, environment, drug abuse, juvenile delinquency, leisure-time activities, girls and young women and the full and effective participation of youth in the life of society and in decision-making. The Programme of Action does not exclude the possibility of new priorities which may be identified in the future.

20. Implementation of the Programme of Action requires the full enjoyment by young people of all human rights and fundamental freedoms, and also requires that Governments take effective action against violations of these rights and freedoms and promote non-discrimination, tolerance, respect for diversity, with full respect for various religious and ethical values, cultural backgrounds and philosophical convictions of their young people, equality of opportunity, solidarity, security and participation of all young women and men.

### A. *Education*

21. Although progress towards universal basic education, beginning with literacy, has been impressive in recent times, the number of illiterate people will continue to grow and many developing countries are likely to fall short of universal primary education by the year 2000. Three main concerns regarding current systems of education may be expressed. The first is the inability of many parents in developing countries to send their children to schools because of local economic and social conditions. The second concerns the paucity of educational opportunities for girls and young women, migrants, refugees, displaced persons, street children, indigenous youth minorities, young people in rural areas and young people with disabilities. The third concerns the quality of education, its relevance to employment and its usefulness in assisting young people in the transition to full adulthood, active citizenship and productive and gainful employment.

22. To encourage the development of educational and training systems more in line with the current and future needs of young people and their societies, it would be helpful to share experience and to investigate alternative arrangements, such as informal arrangements for the provision of basic literacy, job skills training and lifelong education.

23. Opportunities for young people to pursue advanced or university education, engage in research or be trained for self-employment should be expanded in developing countries. Given the economic problems faced by such countries and the inadequacy of international assistance in this area, it is difficult to provide appropriate training for all young people, even though they are a country's chief economic asset.

24. Governments, intergovernmental and non-governmental organizations are called upon to assist young people from developing countries to obtain education and training at all levels in developed as well as in developing countries, as well as to participate in mutual academic exchanges among developing countries.

*Proposals for action*

1. *Improving the level of basic education, skill training and literacy among youth*

25. Priority should be given to achieving the goal of ensuring basic education for all (beginning with literacy), mobilizing for that purpose all channels, agents and forms of education and training, in line with the concept of lifelong education. Special emphasis should also be given to the reform of education content and curricula, especially curricula that reinforce traditional female roles which deny women opportunities for full and equal partnership in society, at all levels, focusing on scientific literacy, moral values and learning of skills, adapted to the changing environment and to life in multi-ethnic and multicultural societies. The importance of the development of information skills, that is, skills for researching, accessing and using information, and informatics should be emphasized, along with the importance of distance education. Non-governmental youth organizations and educational organizations should develop youth-to-youth programmes for basic education, skills training and literacy. Consideration should be given to developing programmes enabling retired and elderly people to teach literacy to young people. Particular attention should be given to specific groups of youth in distressed circumstances, including indigenous, migrant and refugee youth, displaced persons, street children and poor youth in urban and rural areas, as well as to special problems, including literacy problems, for blind youth and youth with other disabilities.

2. *Cultural heritage and contemporary patterns of society*

26. Governments should establish or strengthen programmes to educate young people in the cultural heritage of their own and other societies and the world. Governments should institute, in cooperation with non-governmental youth organizations, travel and exchange programmes and youth camps to help youth understand cultural diversity at both the national and international levels, develop intercultural learning skills and participate in the preservation of the cultural heritage of their own and other societies and the world around them. The United Nations Educational, Scientific and Cultural Organization, in cooperation with interested Governments and non-governmental organizations, is requested to expand international programmes, such as youth camps, by which young people, particularly those from developing countries, with different cultures, may help restore major international cultural sites and engage in other cultural activities.

3. *Promoting mutual respect and understanding and the ideals of peace, solidarity and tolerance among youth*

27. Programmes aimed at learning peacemaking and conflict resolution should be encouraged and designed by Governments and educational institutions for introduction to schools at all levels. Children and

youth should be informed of cultural differences in their own societies and given opportunities to learn about different cultures as well as tolerance and mutual respect for cultural and religious diversity. Governments and educational institutions should formulate and implement educational programmes which promote and strengthen respect for all human rights and fundamental freedoms and enhance the values of peace, solidarity, tolerance, responsibility and respect for the diversity and rights of others.

#### 4. *Vocational and professional training*

28. Governments and educational institutions, in cooperation with regional and international organizations, could establish or enhance vocational and technical training relevant to current and prospective employment conditions. Youth must be given the opportunity to access vocational and professional training and apprenticeship programmes that help them acquire entry-level jobs with growth opportunities and the ability to adjust to changes in labour demand.

#### 5. *Promoting human rights education*

29. Governments should ensure that the United Nations Decade for Human Rights Education, which began in 1995, is adequately observed in schools and educational institutions. In order to make youth aware of their civil, cultural, economic, political and social rights, as well as their societal responsibilities, and in order to develop harmonious intercommunity relations, mutual tolerance and respect, equality between women and men, and tolerance for diversity, Governments should develop human rights education strategies targeted at youth, taking particular account of the human rights of women.

#### 6. *Training for enterprise programmes*

30. Governments, in cooperation with regional and international organizations, should formulate model training programmes for youth in individual and cooperative enterprises. They are encouraged to establish self-contained enterprise centres where young people may plan and test their enterprise venture concepts.

#### 7. *Infrastructure for training youth workers and youth leaders*

31. Governments should assess the adequacy of facilities and programmes to train youth workers and youth leaders, including the adequacy of curricula and staff resources. On the basis of such assessments, Governments should plan and implement relevant training programmes. Non-governmental youth organizations should be encouraged and assisted in formulating and disseminating model training courses for use by member organizations.

32. Interested organizations should investigate possibilities of strengthening international youth worker and youth leadership training, with priority given to accepting participants from developing countries. In cooperation with concerned organizations that provide training opportunities for youth, including internships and volunteer programmes, establishment of an inventory of such programmes could also be explored.

#### B. *Employment*

33. Unemployment and underemployment among youth is a problem everywhere. It is, indeed, part of the larger struggle to create employment opportunities for all citizens. The problem has worsened in recent years because of the global recession which has affected developing countries the most seriously. The disturbing fact is that economic growth is not always accompanied by growth in employment. The difficulty of finding suitable employment is compounded by a host of other problems confronting young people, including illiteracy and insufficient training, and is worsened by periods of world economic slow-down and by overall changing economic trends. In some countries, the influx of young people into the employment market has brought with it acute problems. According to estimates of the International Labour Organization, more than one hundred million new jobs would have to be created within the next twenty years in order to provide suitable employment for the growing number of young people in the economically active populations of developing countries. The situation of girls and young women, as well as of young people with disabilities, refugee youth, displaced persons, street children, indigenous youth, migrant youth and minorities, warrants urgent attention, bearing in mind the prohibition of forced labour and child labour.

34. The crisis of youth unemployment deprives young people of the opportunity to secure independent housing or the accommodations necessary for the establishment of families and participation in the life of society. Advances in technology and communications, coupled with improved productivity, have imposed new challenges as well as new opportunities for employment. Young people are among the most severely affected by these developments. If effective solutions are not found, the cost to society will be much higher in the long run. Unemployment creates a wide range of social ills and young people are particularly susceptible to its damaging effects: the lack of skills, low self-esteem, marginalization, impoverishment and the wasting of an enormous human resource.

*Proposals for action*

#### 1. *Opportunities for self-employment*

35. Governments and organizations should create or promote grant schemes to provide seed money to encourage and support enterprise and employment programmes for young people. Businesses and enterprises could be encouraged to provide counterpart financial and technical support for such schemes. Cooperative schemes involving young people in production and marketing of goods and services could be considered. The formation of youth development banks could be considered. The Committee for the Promotion and Advancement of Cooperatives is encouraged to develop models for cooperatives run by youth in developed and developing countries. Such models could include guidelines for management training and training in entrepreneurial techniques and marketing.

#### 2. *Employment opportunities for specific groups of young people*

36. Within funds designated to promote youth employment, Governments should, as appropriate, designate resources for programmes supporting the efforts of young women, young people with disabilities, youth returning from military service, migrant youth, refugee youth, displaced persons, street children and indigenous youth. Youth organizations and young people themselves should be directly involved in the planning and implementation of these programmes.

### 3. *Voluntary community services involving youth*

37. Where they do not already exist, Governments should consider the establishment of voluntary service programmes for youth. Such programmes could provide alternatives to military service, or might constitute a required element in educational curricula, depending on national policies and priorities. Youth camps, community service projects, environmental protection and inter-generational cooperation programmes should be included among the opportunities offered. Youth organizations should be directly involved in designing, planning, implementing and evaluating such voluntary service programmes. In addition, international cooperation programmes organized between youth organizations in developed and developing countries should be included to promote intercultural understanding and development training.

### 4. *Needs created by technological changes*

38. Governments, in particular those of developed countries, should encourage the creation of employment opportunities for young people in fields that are rapidly evolving as a result of technological innovation. A subset of the employment data compiled by Governments should track the employment of youth into those fields marked by newly emerging technologies. Measures should be taken to provide ongoing training for youth in this area.

39. Special attention should be paid to developing and disseminating approaches that promote flexibility in training systems and collaboration between training institutions and employers, especially for young people in high-technology industries.

### C. *Hunger and poverty*

40. Over one billion people in the world today live in unacceptable conditions of poverty, mostly in developing countries, particularly in rural areas of low-income countries in Asia and the Pacific, Africa, Latin America and the Caribbean and the least developed countries. Poverty has various manifestations; hunger and malnutrition; ill health; limited or lack of access to education and other basic services; increased morbidity and mortality from illness; homelessness and inadequate housing; unsafe environments; and social discrimination and exclusion; it is also characterized by a lack of participation in decision-making and in civil and sociocultural life. Poverty is inseparably linked to lack of access to or loss of control over resources, including land, skills, knowledge, capital and social connections. Without those resources, people have limited access to institutions, markets, employment and public services. Young people are particularly affected by this situation. Therefore, specific measures are needed to address the juvenilization and feminization of poverty.

41. Hunger and malnutrition remain among the most serious and intractable threats to humanity, often preventing youth and children from taking part in society. Hunger is the result of many factors: mismanagement of food production and distribution; poor accessibility; maldistribution of financial resources; unwise exploitation of natural resources; unsustainable patterns of consumption; environmental pollution; natural and human-made disasters; conflicts between traditional and contemporary production systems; irrational population growth; and armed conflicts.

### *Proposals for action*

#### 1. *Making farming more rewarding and life in agricultural areas more attractive*

42. Governments should enhance educational and cultural services and other incentives in rural areas to make them more attractive to young people. Experimental farming programmes directed towards young people should be initiated and extension services expanded to maintain improvements in agricultural production and marketing.

43. Local and national Governments, in cooperation with youth organizations, should organize cultural events that enhance exchanges between urban and rural youth. Youth organizations should be encouraged and assisted in organizing conventions and meetings in rural areas, with special efforts to enlist the cooperation of rural populations, including rural youth.

#### 2. *Skill-training for income-generation by young people*

44. Governments, in cooperation with youth organizations, should develop training programmes for youth which improve methods of agricultural production and marketing. Training should be based on rural economic needs and the need to train young people in rural areas in techniques of food production and the achievement of food security. Attention should be given in such programmes to young women, youth retention in rural areas, youth returning to rural areas from the cities, young people with disabilities, refugee and migrant youth, displaced persons and street children, indigenous youth, youth returning from military service and youth living in areas of resolved conflicts.

#### 3. *Land grants for young people*

45. Governments should provide grants of land to youth and youth organizations, supported by financial and technical assistance and training. The Food and Agriculture Organization of the United Nations and the International Labour Organization are invited to document and disseminate information about national experience with land-grant and settlement schemes for use by Governments.

46. Governments, consistent with their rural development schemes and with the assistance of international organizations, as appropriate, are encouraged to work with volunteer youth organizations on projects which enhance and maintain the rural and urban environments.

#### 4. *Cooperation between urban and rural youth in food production and distribution*

47. Non-governmental organizations should organize direct-marketing groups, including production and distribution cooperatives, to improve current marketing systems and to ensure that young farmers have access to them. The aim of such groups should be to reduce food shortages and losses from defective systems of food storage and transport to markets.

### D. *Health*

48. Young people in some parts of the world suffer from poor health as a result of societal conditions, including such factors as customary attitudes and harmful traditional practices, and, in some cases, as a result of their own actions. Poor health is often caused by an unhealthy environment, by missing support systems in

everyday life for health-promoting patterns of behaviour, by lack of information and by inadequate or inappropriate health services. Problems include the lack of a safe and sanitary living environment, malnutrition, the risk of infectious, parasitic and water-borne diseases, the growing consumption of tobacco, alcohol and drugs, and unwarranted risk-taking and destructive activity, resulting in unintentional injuries.

49. The reproductive health needs of adolescents have been largely ignored. In many countries, there is a lack of information and services available to adolescents to help them understand their sexuality, including sexual and reproductive health, and to protect them from unwanted pregnancies and sexually transmitted diseases, including HIV/AIDS.

*Proposals for action*

### 1. *Provision of basic health services*

50. All young people should have access to basic health services in the interest of all and of society as a whole. It is the indispensable responsibility of each Government to mobilize the necessary awareness, resources and channels. These measures should be supported by a favourable international economic environment and by cooperation.

51. Efforts should be expedited to achieve the goals of national health-for-all strategies, based on equality and social justice, in line with the Declaration of Alma Ata on primary health care adopted on 12 September 1978 by the International Conference on Primary Health Care, by developing or updating country action plans or programmes to ensure universal, non-discriminatory access to basic health services, including sanitation and drinking water, to protect health, and to promote nutrition education and preventive health programmes.

52. Support should be provided for stronger, better-coordinated global actions against major diseases which take a heavy toll of human lives, such as malaria, tuberculosis, cholera, typhoid fever and HIV/AIDS; in this context, support should be continued for the Joint and Co-sponsored United Nations Programme on the human immunodeficiency virus/acquired immunodeficiency syndrome (HIV/AIDS).

53. Poor health is often caused by lack of information and lack of health services for youth, mostly in developing countries. The resulting problems are, among others, sexually transmitted diseases, including infection with HIV; early pregnancies; lack of hygiene and sanitation, leading to infection, infestation and diarrhoea; genetic and congenital diseases; psychological and mental diseases; narcotic and psychotropic drug abuse; misuse of alcohol and tobacco; unwarranted risk-taking and destructive activity, resulting in unintentional injuries; malnutrition; and poor spacing of births.

### 2. *Development of health education*

54. Governments should include, in the curricula of educational institutions at the primary and secondary levels, programmes focusing on primary health knowledge and practices. Particular emphasis should be placed on the understanding of basic hygiene requirements and the need to develop and sustain a healthy environment. These programmes need to be developed in full awareness of the needs and priorities of young people and with their involvement.

55. Cooperation among Governments and educational and health institutions should be encouraged in order to promote personal responsibility for a healthy lifestyle and provide the knowledge and skills necessary to adopt a healthy lifestyle, including teaching the legal, social and health consequences of behaviour that poses health risks.

### 3. *Promotion of health services, including sexual and reproductive health and development of relevant education programmes in those fields*

56. Governments, with the involvement of youth and other relevant organizations, should ensure the implementation of the commitments made in the Programme of Action of the International Conference on Population and Development, as established in the report of that Conference, in the Copenhagen Declaration on Social Development and the Programme of Action of the World Summit for Social Development, and in the Beijing Declaration and the Platform for Action of the Fourth World Conference on Women, as well as in the relevant human rights instruments, to meet the health needs of youth. The United Nations Population Fund and other interested United Nations organizations should continue to take effective steps on these issues. The reproductive health needs of adolescents as a group have been largely ignored to date by existing reproductive health services. The response of societies to the reproductive health needs of adolescents should be based on information that helps them attain a level of maturity required to make responsible decisions. In particular, information and services should be made available to adolescents to help them understand their sexuality and protect them from unwanted pregnancies, sexually transmitted diseases and the subsequent risk of infertility. This should be combined with the education of young men to respect women's self-determination and to share responsibility with women in matters of sexuality and reproduction. This effort is uniquely important for the health of young women and their children, for women's self-determination and, in many countries, for efforts to slow the momentum of population growth. Motherhood at a very young age entails a risk of maternal death that is much greater than average, and the children of young mothers have higher levels of morbidity and mortality. Early child-bearing continues to be an impediment to improvements in the educational, economic and social status of women in all parts of the world. Overall for young women, early marriage and early motherhood can severely curtail educational and employment opportunities and are likely to have a long-term adverse impact on the quality of life of young women and their children.

57. Governments should develop comprehensive sexual and reproductive health-care services and provide young people with access to those services including, *inter alia*, education and services in family planning consistent with the results of the International Conference on Population and Development, the World Summit for Social Development and the Fourth World Conference on Women. The United Nations Population Fund and other interested United Nations organizations are to be encouraged to continue assigning high priority to promoting adolescent reproductive health.

### 4. *HIV infection and AIDS among young people*

58. Governments should develop accessible, available and affordable primary health care services of high quality, including sexual and reproductive health care, as well as education programmes, including those related to sexually transmitted disease, including HIV/AIDS, for youth. Continued international cooperation and collective global efforts are necessary for the containment of HIV/AIDS.

### 5. *Promotion of good sanitation and hygiene practices*

59. Governments, in cooperation with youth and volunteer organizations, should promote the establishment of youth health associations to promote good sanitation and hygiene programmes.

### 6. *Prevention of disease and illness among youth resulting from poor health practices*

60. Governments, in cooperation with youth organizations, should promote healthier lifestyles and, in this context, should investigate the possibility of adopting policies for discouraging drug, tobacco and alcohol abuse, including possibly banning the advertisement of tobacco and alcohol. They should also undertake programmes to inform young people about the adverse effects of drug and alcohol abuse and tobacco addiction.

61. Programmes should be instituted, with the appropriate assistance of the United Nations bodies and organizations concerned, to train medical, paramedical, educational and youth work personnel in health issues of particular concern to young people, including healthy lifestyles. Research into such issues should be promoted, particularly research into the effects and treatment of drug abuse and addiction. Youth organizations should be enlisted in these efforts.

### 7. *Elimination of sexual abuse of young people*

62. As recommended by the Vienna Declaration and Programme of Action, the International Conference on Population and Development, the World Summit for Social Development and the Fourth World Conference on Women, and bearing in mind that young women are specially vulnerable, Governments should cooperate at the international level and take effective steps, including specific preventive measures to protect children, adolescents and youth from neglect, abandonment and all types of exploitation and abuse, such as abduction, rape and incest, pornography, trafficking and acts of paedophilia, as well as from commercial sexual exploitation resulting from pornography and prostitution. Governments should enact and enforce legislation prohibiting female genital mutilation wherever it exists and give vigorous support to efforts among non-governmental and community organizations and religious institutions to eliminate such practices.

### 8. *Combating malnutrition among young people*

63. Governments should promote post-primary-school and out-of-school health projects by individuals and youth organizations, emphasizing information on healthy eating practices. School lunch programmes, provision of food supplements and similar services should be available whenever possible to help ensure a proper diet for young people.

### E. *Environment*

64. The deterioration of the natural environment is one of the principal concerns of young people worldwide as it has direct implications for their well-being both now and in the future. The natural environment must be maintained and preserved for both present and future generations. The causes of environmental degradation must be addressed. The environmentally friendly use of natural resources and environmentally sustainable economic growth will improve human life. Sustainable development has become a key element in the programmes of youth organizations throughout the world. While every segment of society is responsible for maintaining the environmental integrity of the community, young people have a special interest in maintaining a healthy environment because they will be the ones to inherit it.

*Proposals for action*

### 1. *Integration of environmental education and training into education and training programmes*

65. Emphasis should be given in school curricula to environmental education. Training programmes should be provided to inform teachers of the environmental aspects of their subject-matter and to enable them to educate youth concerning environmentally friendly habits.

66. The participation of youth groups in gathering environmental data and in understanding ecological systems and actual environmental action should be encouraged as a means of improving both their knowledge of the environment and their personal engagement in caring for the environment.

### 2. *Facilitating the international dissemination of information on environmental issues to, and the use of environmentally sound technologies by, youth*

67. The United Nations Environment Programme, in cooperation with Governments and non-governmental youth organizations, is invited to intensify production of information materials illustrating the global dimension, its origins and the interrelated effects of environmental degradation, describing the outcome of initiatives undertaken in developing and developed countries as well as countries with economies in transition. The United Nations Environment Programme is requested to continue its efforts to disseminate information to and exchange information with youth organizations. Governments should encourage and assist youth organizations to initiate and develop youth-to-youth contacts through town-twinning and similar programmes in order to share the experience gained in different countries.

68. Relevant United Nations organizations and institutions and Governments of technologically advanced countries are encouraged to help spread the use of environmentally sound technologies in developing countries and in countries with economies in transition and to train youth in making use of such technologies in protecting and conserving the environment.

### 3. *Strengthening participation of youth in the protection, preservation and improvement of the environment*

69. Governments and youth organizations should initiate programmes to promote participation in tree planting, forestry, combating desert creep, waste reduction, recycling and other sound environmental practices. The participation of young people and their organizations in such programmes can provide good training and encourage awareness and action. Waste management

programmes may represent potential income-generating activities which provide opportunities for employment.

70. As recognized by the United Nations Conference on Environment and Development, the involvement of youth in environment and development decision-making is critical to the implementation of policies of sustainable development. Young people should be involved in designing and implementing appropriate environmental policies.

### 4. *Enhancing the role of the media as a tool for widespread dissemination of environmental issues to youth*

71. Governments should, to the extent consistent with freedom of expression, encourage the media and advertising agencies to develop programmes to ensure widespread dissemination of information on environmental issues in order to continue to raise awareness thereof among youth.

72. Governments should establish procedures allowing for consultation and possible participation of youth of both genders in decision-making processes with regard to the environment, at the local, national and regional levels.

### F. *Drug abuse*

73. The vulnerability of young people to drug abuse has in recent years become a major concern. The consequences of widespread drug abuse and trafficking, particularly for young men and women, are all too apparent. Violence, particularly street violence, often results from drug abuse and illicit drug networks.

74. As the number of psychotropic drugs increases steadily and their effects and appropriate prescriptive uses are often not fully known, some patients may not be adequately treated and others may become over-medicated. Abuse of prescription drugs and self-medication with tranquillizers, sleeping-pills and stimulants can also create serious problems, particularly in countries and regions where distribution controls are weak and habit-forming drugs are purchased abroad or diverted from licit channels of distribution. In this context, the vulnerability of young people raises a particular problem and specific measures are therefore needed.

75. The international community places particular emphasis on reducing the demand for and supply of illegal drugs and preventing abuse. Supply reduction includes combating international illicit drug trafficking. Drug abuse prevention initiatives range from discouraging people from taking drugs, thus preventing involuntary addiction, to helping those who are abusing drugs to stop doing so. Treatment programmes need to recognize that drug abuse is a chronic relapsing condition. It is essential for programmes to be adapted to the social and cultural context and for there to be effective cooperation between various approaches to treatment. To this end, national initiatives and measures to combat illicit drug trafficking should be fully supported and reinforced at the regional and international levels.

76. Drug control strategies at the national and international levels consistently emphasize initiatives aimed at reducing drug abuse among young people. This is reflected in the resolutions of the Commission on Narcotic Drugs and in the demand reduction programmes of the United Nations International Drug Control Programme.

*Proposals for action*

### 1. *Participation of youth organizations and youth in demand reduction programmes for young people*

77. To be effective, demand reduction programmes should be targeted at all young people, particularly those at risk, and the content of the programmes should respond directly to the interests and concerns of those young people. Preventive education programmes showing the dangers of drug abuse are particularly important. Increasing opportunities for gainful employment and activities which provide recreation and opportunities to develop a variety of skills are important in helping young people to resist drugs. Youth organizations can play a key role in designing and implementing education programmes and individual counselling to encourage the integration of youth into the community, to develop healthy lifestyles and to raise awareness of the damaging impact of drugs. The programmes could include training of youth leaders in communication and counselling skills.

78. Government entities, in cooperation with relevant agencies of the United Nations system and non-governmental organizations, particularly youth organizations, should cooperate in carrying out demand reduction programmes for illicit drugs, tobacco and alcohol.

### 2. *Training medical and paramedical students in the rational use of pharmaceuticals containing narcotic drugs or psychotropic substances*

79. The World Health Organization, associations of the medical, paramedical and pharmaceutical professions and pharmaceutical corporations and medical faculties and institutions could be asked to develop model training courses and disseminate information material for young medical and paramedical students on the proper handling of drugs and the early identification and diagnosis of substance abuse.

### 3. *Treatment and rehabilitation of young people who are drug abusers or drug-dependent and young alcoholics and tobacco users*

80. Research has been undertaken into the possibility of identifying medication to block cravings for specific drugs without creating secondary dependency, but much remains to be done in this area. The need for medical and social research in the prevention and treatment of substance abuse, as well as rehabilitation, has become more urgent, particularly with the worldwide increase in abuse and addiction among young people. In such research, emphasis should be given to the fact that intravenous substance abuse raises the risk of contracting communicable diseases, including HIV/AIDS and hepatitis, arising from the sharing of needles and other injection equipment. The fruits of all such research should be shared globally.

81. Research on issues such as the medical treatment and the rehabilitation of young drug abusers, including the combination of different types of treatment, the problem of recidivism and the administrative aspects of drug treatment, and the inclusion of students in the relevant faculties in such research, should be encouraged.

82. In cooperation with the institutions of civil society and the private sector, drug abuse prevention should be promoted, as should preventive education for children and youth and rehabilitation and education

programmes for former drug and alcohol addicts, especially children and youth, in order to enable them to obtain productive employment and achieve the independence, dignity and responsibility for a drug-free, crime-free productive life. Of particular interest is the development of treatment techniques involving the family setting and peer groups. Young people can make significant contributions by participating in peer group therapy to facilitate the acceptance of young drug-dependent persons and abusers upon their re-entry into society. Direct participation in rehabilitation therapy entails close cooperation between youth groups and other community and health services. The World Health Organization and other worldwide medical and mental health organizations could be requested to set guidelines for continuing research and for carrying out comparable programmes in different settings, whose effectiveness could be evaluated over a given period of time.

#### 4. *Care for young drug abusers and drug-dependent suspects and offenders in the criminal justice and prison system*

83. Authorities should consider strategies to prevent exposure to drug abuse and dependence among young people suspected or convicted of criminal offences. Such strategies could include alternative measures, such as daily reporting to police stations, regular visits to parole officers or the fulfilment of a specified number of hours of community service.

84. Prison authorities should cooperate closely with law enforcement agencies to keep drugs out of the prison system. Prison personnel should be discouraged from tolerating the presence of drugs in penal institutions.

85. Young prisoners who are already drug-dependent should be targeted as priority candidates for treatment and rehabilitation services and should be segregated as appropriate. Guidelines and standard minimum rules should be prepared to assist national authorities in law enforcement and prison systems in maintaining the necessary controls and initiating treatment and rehabilitation services. Action along these lines constitutes a long-term advantage to society, as the cycle of dependence, release, repeated offences and repeated incarcerations constitutes a heavy burden on the criminal justice system, quite apart from the wasted lives and personal tragedies which result from drug dependence and criminal behaviour.

### G. *Juvenile delinquency*

86. Juvenile crime and delinquency are serious problems all over the world. Their intensity and gravity depend mostly on the social, economic and cultural conditions in each country. There is evidence, however, of an apparent worldwide increase in juvenile criminality combined with economic recession, especially in marginal sectors of urban centres. In many cases, youth offenders are "street children" who have been exposed to violence in their immediate social environment, either as observers or as victims. Their basic education, when they have it, is poor; their primary socialization from the family is too often inadequate; and their socio-economic environment is shaped by poverty and destitution. Rather than relying solely on the criminal justice system, approaches to the prevention of violence and crime should thus include measures to support equality and justice, to combat poverty and to reduce hopelessness among young people.

*Proposals for action*

#### 1. *Priority to preventive measures*

87. Governments should give priority to issues and problems of juvenile delinquency and youth criminality, with particular attention to preventive policies and programmes. Rural areas should be provided with adequate socio-economic opportunities and administrative services which could discourage young people from migrating to urban areas. Youth from poor urban settings should have access to specific educational, employment and leisure programmes, particularly during long school holidays. Young people who drop out of school or come from broken families should benefit from specific social programmes that help them build self-esteem and confidence conducive to responsible adulthood.

#### 2. *Prevention of violence*

88. Governments and other relevant organizations, particularly youth organizations, should consider organizing information campaigns and educational and training programmes in order to sensitize youth to the personally and socially detrimental effects of violence in the family, community and society, to teach them how to communicate without violence and to promote training so that they can protect themselves and others against violence. Governments should also develop programmes to promote tolerance and better understanding among youth, with a view to eradicating contemporary forms of racism, racial discrimination, xenophobia and related intolerance and thereby preventing violence.

89. To prevent violence and crime, the development of social organization, particularly through youth organizations and community involvement, should be fostered by a supportive social policy and within a legal framework. Government assistance should focus on facilitating the ability of community and youth organizations to express and evaluate their needs concerning the prevention of violence and crime, to formulate and implement actions for themselves and to cooperate with each other.

#### 3. *Rehabilitation services and programmes*

90. Destitution, poor living conditions, inadequate education, malnutrition, illiteracy, unemployment and lack of leisure-time activities are factors that marginalize young people, which makes some of them vulnerable to exploitation as well as to involvement in criminal and other deviant behaviour. If preventive measures address the very causes of criminality, rehabilitation programmes and services should be made available to those who already have a criminal history. In general, youth delinquency begins with petty offences such as robbery or violent behaviour, which can be easily traced by and corrected through institutions and community and family environments. Indeed, law enforcement should be a part of rehabilitation measures. Finally, the human rights of young people who are imprisoned should be protected and principles of penal majority according to penal laws should be given great attention.

### H. *Leisure-time activities*

91. The importance of leisure-time activities in the psychological, cognitive and physical development of young people is recognized in all societies. Leisure-time activities include games, sports, cultural events, enter-

tainment and community service. Appropriate leisure programmes for youth are elements of any measure aimed at fighting social ills such as drug abuse, juvenile delinquency and other deviant behaviour. While leisure programmes can contribute greatly to the development of the physical, intellectual and emotional potential of young people, they should be designed with due care and concern so that they are not used as a means for excluding youth from participating in other aspects of social life or for indoctrinating them. Leisure-time activity programmes should be made freely available to young people.

*Proposals for action*

### 1. *Leisure-time activities as an integral part of youth policies and programmes*

92. Governments, in planning, designing and implementing youth policies and programmes, with the active involvement of youth organizations, should recognize the importance of leisure-time activities. The importance given to such activities should be reflected in appropriate funding.

93. Governments are invited to establish public libraries, cultural centres and other cultural facilities in rural and urban areas, with the aid of international organizations, and to provide assistance to young people active in the fields of drama, the fine arts, music and other forms of cultural expression.

94. Governments are invited to encourage the participation of young people in tourism, international cultural events, sports and all other activities of special interest to youth.

### 2. *Leisure-time activities as elements of educational programmes*

95. Governments, by providing adequate funding to educational institutions for the establishment of leisure-time activities, may accord priority to such activities. In addition, leisure-time activities could be integrated into the regular school curriculum.

### 3. *Leisure-time activities in urban planning and rural development*

96. National Governments as well as local authorities and community development agencies should incorporate leisure-time activity programmes and facilities in urban planning, giving particular attention to areas with a high population density. Equally, rural development programmes should pay due attention to the leisure needs of rural youth.

### 4. *Leisure-time activities and the media*

97. The media should be encouraged to promote youth understanding and awareness of all aspects of social integration, including tolerance and non-violent behaviour.

## I. *Girls and young women*

98. One of the most important tasks of youth policy is to improve the situation of girls and young women. Governments therefore should implement their obligations under international human rights instruments as well as implementing the Platform for Action of the Fourth World Conference on Women, the Programme of Action of the International Conference on Population and Development, the Vienna Declaration and Programme of Action of the World Conference on Human Rights and other programmes of relevant United Na-

tions conferences. Girls are often treated as inferior and are socialized to put themselves last, thus undermining their self-esteem. Discrimination and neglect in childhood can initiate a lifelong downward spiral of deprivation and exclusion from the social mainstream. Negative cultural attitudes and practices as well as gender-biased educational processes, including curricula, educational materials and practices, teachers' attitudes and classroom interaction, reinforce existing gender inequalities.

*Proposals for action*

### 1. *Discrimination*

99. Discrimination and neglect in childhood can initiate a lifelong exclusion from society. Action should be taken to eliminate discrimination against girls and young women and to ensure their full enjoyment of human rights and fundamental freedoms through comprehensive policies, plans of action and programmes on the basis of equality. Initiatives should be taken to prepare girls to participate actively, effectively and equally with boys at all levels of social, economic, political and cultural leadership.

### 2. *Education*

100. Universal and equal access to and completion of primary education for girls and young women as well as equal access to secondary and higher education should be ensured. A framework should be provided for the development of educational materials and practices that are gender-balanced and promote an educational setting that eliminates all barriers impeding the schooling of girls and young women, including married and/or pregnant girls and young women.

### 3. *Health*

101. Discrimination against girls and young women should be eliminated in health and nutrition. The removal of discriminatory laws and practices against girls and young women in food allocation and nutrition should be promoted, and their access to health services should be ensured in accordance with the Programme of Action of the International Conference on Population and Development and the Platform for Action of the Fourth World Conference on Women.

### 4. *Employment*

102. Girls and young women should be protected from economic and related forms of exploitation and from performing any work that is likely to be hazardous, to interfere with their education or to be harmful to their health or their physical, mental, spiritual, moral or social development, in conformity with the Convention on the Rights of the Child and the Convention on the Elimination of All Forms of Discrimination against Women. Equal access for young women to all employment opportunities should be promoted and their participation in the traditionally male-dominated sectors should be encouraged.

### 5. *Violence*

103. Governments should cooperate at the international level and enact and enforce legislation protecting girls and young women from all forms of violence, including female infanticide and prenatal sex selection, genital mutilation, incest, sexual abuse, sexual exploitation, child prostitution and child pornography. Age appropriate, safe and confidential programmes and sup-

port services to assist girls and young women who are subjected to violence should be developed in cooperation with relevant non-governmental organizations, particularly youth organizations, as appropriate.

### J. *Full and effective participation of youth in the life of society and in decision-making*

104. The capacity for progress of our societies is based, among other elements, on their capacity to incorporate the contribution and responsibility of youth in the building and designing of the future. In addition to their intellectual contribution and their ability to mobilize support, they bring unique perspectives that need to be taken into account.

105. Any efforts and proposed actions in the other priority areas considered in this programme are, in a certain way, conditioned by enabling the economic, social and political participation of youth, as a matter of critical importance.

106. Youth organizations are important forums for developing skills necessary for effective participation in society, promoting tolerance and increased cooperation and exchanges between youth organizations.

*Proposals for action*

107. The following actions are proposed:

*(a)* Improving access to information in order to enable young people to make better use of their opportunities to participate in decision-making;

*(b)* Developing and/or strengthening opportunities for young people to learn their rights and responsibilities, promoting their social, political, developmental and environmental participation, removing obstacles that affect their full contribution to society and respecting, *inter alia*, freedom of association;

*(c)* Encouraging and promoting youth associations through financial, educational and technical support and promotion of their activities;

*(d)* Taking into account the contribution of youth in designing, implementing and evaluating national policies and plans affecting their concerns;

*(e)* Encouraging increased national, regional and international cooperation and exchange between youth organizations;

*(f)* Inviting Governments to strengthen the involvement of young people in international forums, *inter alia*, by considering the inclusion of youth representatives in their national delegations to the General Assembly.

### V. Means of implementation

108. Effective implementation of the World Programme of Action for Youth to the Year 2000 and Beyond will require a significant expression of commitment by organizations and institutions responsible for its adoption and implementation and the involvement of such organizations and especially of youth from all sectors of society. Without such commitment by governmental, intergovernmental and non-governmental entities at the national, regional and international levels, the Programme of Action will remain little more than a global statement of intent and general standard for action.

109. Therefore the development of an overall system of enabling mechanisms is necessary in order for the Programme of Action to be implemented. Such mechanisms should engage, on a continuing basis, the human, political, economic, financial and sociocultural resources necessary to ensure that the Programme is implemented efficiently and effectively.

110. Implementation of the Programme of Action is ultimately the responsibility of Governments with the support of the international community and in cooperation, as appropriate, with the non-governmental and private sectors. Translation of the Programme's proposals for action into specific plans, targets and law will be influenced by national priorities, resources and historical experience. In this process, Governments can be assisted, at their request, by regional and international organizations.

111. In implementing the Programme of Action, Governments, youth organizations and other actors should promote an active and visible policy of mainstreaming a gender perspective in all policies and programmes in accordance with the results of the International Conference on Population and Development, the World Summit for Social Development and the Fourth World Conference on Women.

### A. *National level*

112. Governments which have not already done so are urged to formulate and adopt an integrated national youth policy as a means of addressing youth-related concerns. This should be done as part of a continuing process of review and assessment of the situation of youth, formulation of a cross-sectoral national youth programme of action in terms of specific, time-bound objectives and a systematic evaluation of progress achieved and obstacles encountered.

113. Reinforcing youth-related concerns in development activities can be facilitated through the existence of multilevel mechanisms for consultation, dissemination of information, coordination, monitoring and evaluation. These should be cross-sectoral in nature and multidisciplinary in approach and should include the participation of youth-related departments and ministries, national non-governmental youth organizations and the private sector.

114. Special and additional efforts may be required to develop and disseminate model frameworks for integrated policies and to identify and organize an appropriate division of responsibilities among both governmental and non-governmental entities concerned with youth-related issues. Special and additional efforts could also be directed towards strengthening national capacities for data collection and dissemination of information, research and policy studies, planning, implementation and coordination, and training and advisory services.

115. National coordinating mechanisms should be appropriately strengthened for integrated youth policies and programmes. Where such mechanisms do not exist, Governments are urged to promote their establishment on a multilevel and cross-sectoral basis.

### B. *Regional cooperation*

116. The activities of the United Nations regional commissions, in cooperation with concerned regional intergovernmental and non-governmental youth and youth-related organizations, are essential complements to national and global action aimed at building national capacities.

117. Regional commissions, within their existing mandates, are urged to promote the implementation of the Programme of Action through incorporation of its

goals in their plans, to undertake comprehensive reviews of the progress achieved and obstacles encountered and to identify options to further regional-level action.

118. Regional intergovernmental meetings of ministers responsible for youth, in cooperation with the concerned United Nations regional commissions, regional intergovernmental organizations and regional non-governmental youth organizations, can make particular contributions to the formulation, implementation, coordination and evaluation of action at the regional level, including periodic monitoring of regional youth programmes.

119. Data collection, dissemination of information, research and policy studies, inter-organizational coordination and technical cooperation, training seminars and advisory services are among the measures which can be provided on request at the regional level to promote, implement and evaluate youth programmes.

120. Regional non-governmental youth organizations, regional offices of bodies and organizations of the United Nations system and regional intergovernmental organizations concerned with youth are invited to consider meeting on a biennial basis to review and discuss issues and trends and to identify proposals for regional and subregional cooperation. United Nations regional commissions are also invited to play an essential role through the provision of a suitable venue and appropriate input regarding regional action.

### C. *International cooperation*

121. An essential role for international cooperation is to promote conditions conducive to the implementation of the Programme of Action at all levels. Means available include debates at the policy level and decisions at the intergovernmental level, global monitoring of issues and trends, data collection and dissemination of information, research and studies, planning and coordination, technical cooperation and outreach and partnership among interested constituencies from both the non-governmental and private sectors.

122. In its capacity as the subsidiary body of the Economic and Social Council responsible for global social development issues, the Commission for Social Development has an important role to play as the focal point for the implementation of the Programme of Action. The Commission is called upon to continue the policy-level dialogue on youth for policy coordination and for periodic monitoring of issues and trends.

123. Current regional and interregional conferences of ministers responsible for youth affairs in Africa, Asia, Europe, Latin America and the Caribbean and Western Asia are invited to intensify cooperation among each other and to consider meeting regularly at the international level under the aegis of the United Nations. Such meetings could provide an effective forum for a focused global dialogue on youth-related issues.

124. Youth-related bodies and organizations of the United Nations system are invited to cooperate with the above-mentioned conferences. In this connection, the existing ad hoc inter-agency working group on youth should meet annually and invite all concerned bodies and agencies of the United Nations system and related intergovernmental organizations to discuss ways and means by which they can promote the implementation of the Programme of Action on a coordinated basis.

125. Effective channels of communication between non-governmental youth organizations and the United Nations system are essential for dialogue and consultation on the situation of youth and implications for the implementation of the Programme of Action. The General Assembly has repeatedly stressed the importance of channels of communication in the field of youth. The Youth Forum of the United Nations system could contribute to the implementation of the Programme of Action through the identification and promotion of joint initiatives to further its objectives so that they better reflect the interests of youth.

### 1. *Data collection and dissemination of information*

126. Capacities to collect, analyse and present data in a timely and accurate fashion are essential for effective planning and target-setting, for monitoring issues and trends and for evaluating progress achieved in implementing the Programme of Action. Special attention should be directed towards building national capacities and institutions regularly to collect and compile socioeconomic data series that are both cross-sectional and disaggregated by cohort. To this end, interested centres and institutions may wish to consider the possibility of jointly strengthening or establishing, in cooperation with the United Nations, networks concerned with collection of data and publication of statistics and to realize thereby greater economies of scale in the development and dissemination of statistics in the field of youth.

127. Major contributions related to data and statistics in the field of youth are currently being made by the United Nations. Such contributions include the socio-economic data collection and statistical development activities of the Statistics Division of the Department for Economic and Social Information and Policy Analysis of the Secretariat; the youth policies and programmes information activities of the Division for Social Policy and Development of the Department for Policy Coordination and Sustainable Development of the Secretariat; the educational and literacy data collection activities of the United Nations Educational, Scientific and Cultural Organization; and the youth advisory networks of the United Nations Environment Programme. Concerned bodies and agencies of the United Nations system are urged to explore ways and means of achieving greater coherence in data collection and the publication of statistics. This could include programme planning and coordination on an inter-agency basis. For example, the data bank programme on adolescent health of the World Health Organization is coordinated with the work of the Statistics Division of the Secretariat. Other bodies and agencies of the United Nations system are invited to contribute data in their respective areas of expertise to an integrated socioeconomic data bank on youth. For instance, the international drug abuse assessment system of the United Nations International Drug Control Programme is urged to consider including a component on youth and drugs. An inventory of innovative youth policies, programmes and projects could be coordinated and made available to interested users by the Department for Policy Coordination and Sustainable Development. Other topics that could be considered for joint action include juvenile delinquency, runaways and homeless youth.

128. Public information and communications are equally important in building awareness of youth issues,

as well as a consensus on appropriate planning and action. The bodies and organizations of the United Nations system concerned are urged, as a matter of priority, to review publications currently produced and to identify ways in which these publications can better promote the Programme of Action and areas in which they may need to be complemented through the production of leaflets and posters in connection with special events.

129. To encourage widespread awareness of and support for the Programme of Action, Governments, non-governmental organizations and, as appropriate, the private sector are urged to consider the possibility of preparing both printed and audiovisual materials related to areas of concern in the Programme of Action. This could be carried out with the assistance of and in cooperation with the United Nations and materials could be disseminated through United Nations public information channels. In addition, young people and youth organizations are urged to identify and plan information activities that focus on priority issues, which they would undertake within the context of the Programme of Action.

### 2. *Research and policy studies*

130. Comparative studies on issues and trends concerning youth are essential to the continuous expansion and development of the global body of knowledge on relevant theories, concepts and methods. International, regional and national research centres and institutions concerned with youth-related issues are urged to consider the possibility of establishing cooperative relationships with the United Nations to ensure effective links between the implementation of the Programme of Action and relevant research and studies.

131. Cooperation in strengthening and improving national capacities for the research, design, conduct and dissemination of relevant studies on the situation of young people is a closely related concern.

132. A third concern is the improved planning and coordination of the scarce human and financial resources available so that appropriate attention is accorded to initiatives undertaken by young people at all levels, related to priority areas identified in the Programme of Action, to the identification and assessment of issues and trends and to the review and evaluation of policy initiatives.

### 3. *Planning and coordination*

133. Using the mechanisms currently available within the United Nations system for planning, programming and coordinating activities concerning youth, interested bodies and organizations of the United Nations system are urged to review their medium-term planning process to give appropriate consideration to reinforcing a youth perspective in their activities. They are also urged to identify current and projected programme activities that correspond to the priorities of the Programme of Action so that these activities can be reinforced throughout the system. Appropriate attention should be directed towards identifying opportunities for joint planning among interested members of the system so that joint action may be undertaken that reflects their respective areas of competence, that is of direct interest to young people or that responds to priority needs of young people in special circumstances.

134. A complementary mechanism for coordination is provided by the channels that have been developed between the United Nations and intergovernmental and non-governmental youth organizations. Such mechanisms require appropriate strengthening to enable them to respond better to priorities for action, as identified in the Programme of Action.

### 4. *Technical cooperation, training and advisory services*

135. Technical cooperation is an essential means for building national capacities and institutional capabilities. Bodies and organizations of the United Nations system that have not already done so are urged to review and assess their range of programmatic and operational activities in the light of the priorities for action identified in the Programme of Action and to reinforce a youth dimension in technical cooperation activities. In this regard, special attention should be directed towards measures that will serve to promote expanded opportunities for international technical assistance and advisory services in the field of youth as a means of building expanded and strengthened networks of institutions and organizations.

136. There is a need to continue to improve the impact of technical cooperation activities carried out by the United Nations system, including those that relate to youth activities. The United Nations system must continue to assist Governments, at their request, to ensure implementation of national plans and strategies within the national priorities and programmes to support youth activities. As administrative overheads can reduce the resources available for technical cooperation, these should be reduced. National execution should be the preferred modality for the implementation of projects and programmes and, where required, developing countries should be assisted in improving their national capacities for project and programme formulation and execution.

137. Countries with economies in transition, when required, should also be assisted in improving their national capacities for project and programme formulation and execution.

138. The organization, on an inter-agency basis, of missions to review, assess and plan technical cooperation concerning youth, available on request to Governments, represents a specific contribution by the United Nations system to the implementation of the Programme of Action.

139. The United Nations Youth Fund represents a unique resource to support catalytic and innovative action concerning youth. Programme implementation can be furthered through the Fund's support, in both a technical and a financial sense, of pilot action, studies and technical exchanges on issues concerning youth that encourage the participation of youth in devising and carrying out projects and whose short time-frames often make it difficult to obtain needed support from conventional budgeting processes. The capacities of the Fund for innovative action are, however, limited in the light of Programme priorities, and interested Governments, non-governmental organizations and the private sector are invited to consider the possibility of supporting the activities of the Fund on a predictable and sustained basis. To this end, the parties concerned may wish to consider the possibility of constituting an advisory body at an appropriate level to review the application of the terms of reference of the Fund and priorities and means of strengthening its capacities.

*5. Outreach and partnership among specialized constituencies*

140. A crucial element in implementing the Programme of Action is the recognition that governmental action alone is not sufficient to ensure its success, that rather it should be further complemented by the support of the international community. This process will also require both systematic outreach and partnership among the Programme's many constituencies in both the non-governmental and private sectors.

141. A critical first step is phased expansion and regularization of channels of communication between the United Nations and non-governmental youth organizations to include representatives of interested private sector organizations. This would build upon the provisions set forth in General Assembly resolution 45/103 of 14 December 1990 concerning the involvement of youth and non-governmental youth organizations in the formulation of the Programme of Action. Youth, youth-related organizations and interested private sector organizations are urged to identify, in partnership with Governments, ways in which they could contribute to action at the local level to implement the Programme, and to the periodic review, appraisal and formulation of options to achieve its goals and objectives.

142. Implementation of the Programme of Action offers important opportunities to expand technical and cultural exchanges among young people through new partnerships in both the public and private sectors; to identify and test improved ways to leverage public resources, in partnership with the non-governmental and private sectors, to further Programme priorities; and to encourage and jointly plan innovative approaches to critical issues concerning youth.

143. Relevant voluntary organizations, particularly those concerned with education, employment, juvenile justice, youth development, health, hunger, ecology and the environment, and drug abuse, can further the implementation of the Programme of Action by encouraging the involvement of young people in programme planning and field activities. The Programme of Action can contribute to the work of such organizations because it provides a global policy framework for consultation and coordination.

General Assembly resolution 50/81

14 December 1995     Meeting 91     Adopted without vote

Draft recommended by ESC in res. 1995/64 (A/50/728); agenda item 105.
*Meeting numbers.* GA 50th session: 3rd Committee 8-11; plenary 41-45, 91.

*REFERENCES*
[1]E/CN.5/1995/3. [2]YUN 1994, p. 1213, GA res 49/152, 23 Dec. 1994. [3]E/1995/24 (dec.34/1). [4]E/1995/58. [5]YUN 1993, p. 1065, ESC. res. 1993/24, 27 July 1993. [6]E/1995/123 & Corr.1,2. [7]A/50/728.

# Ageing persons

Responding to a 1993 General Assembly request,[1] the Secretary-General, in March 1995, presented[2] the conceptual framework of a programme for the preparation and observance of the International Year of Older Persons in 1999, declared by the Assembly in 1992.[3] As the over-all objective of the Year, the promotion of the 1991 UN Principles for Older Persons was proposed,[4] as well as their translation into policy and practical programmes of action. The four dimensions of the framework, within which those Principles could be promoted, were: situation of older persons; life-long individual development; multigenerational relationships; and development and the ageing of populations. The proposed theme for the Year was "a society for all ages".

The Department for Policy Coordination and Sustainable Development of the UN Secretariat was serving as focal point for the Year, to facilitate consultations on its objective, framework and theme and to devote its mandated activities on ageing to preparations for the Year. The report outlined also the global targets on ageing for the year 2000, adopted by the Assembly in 1992[3] and a timetable (1995-2000) of activities of the United Nations programme on ageing, adjusted to the needs of the Year.

In April, the Commission for Social Development recommended to the Economic and Social Council that it recommend to the Assembly for adoption a draft resolution entitled "International Year of Older Persons: towards a society for all ages". The Council did so by **resolution 1995/21**.

**ECONOMIC AND SOCIAL COUNCIL ACTION**

On 24 July, the Economic and Social Council adopted **resolution 1995/21**.

**International Year of Older Persons:
towards a society for all ages**
*The Economic and Social Council*
*Recommends* to the General Assembly the adoption of the following draft resolution:
[For text, see General Assembly resolution 50/141 below.]

Economic and Social Council resolution 1995/21

24 July 1995     Meeting 49     Adopted without vote

Draft by Commission for Social Development (E/1995/24); agenda item 5 *(f)*.
*Meeting numbers.* ESC 47-49.

**GENERAL ASSEMBLY ACTION**

On 21 December, the General Assembly adopted **resolution 50/141**.

**International Year of Older Persons:
towards a society for all ages**
*The General Assembly,*
*Recalling* its resolution 47/5 of 16 October 1992, the annex to which contains the Proclamation on Ageing, by which the Assembly decided to observe the year 1999 as the International Year of Older Persons,
*Recalling also* Economic and Social Council resolution 1993/22 of 27 July 1993, in which the Council invited Member States to strengthen their national mechanisms on ageing, *inter alia*, to enable them to serve as national focal points for the preparations for and observance of the Year,
*Recalling further* its resolution 45/106 of 14 December 1990, in which it recognized the complexity and rapid-

ity of the ageing of the world's population and the need to have a common basis and frame of reference for the protection and promotion of the rights of older persons, including the contribution that older persons could and should make to society,

*Bearing in mind* its resolution 49/162 of 23 December 1994 on the integration of older women in development,

1. *Takes note* of the conceptual framework of a programme for the preparation and observance of the International Year of Older Persons in 1999, as contained in the report of the Secretary-General;

2. *Invites* Member States to adapt the conceptual framework to national conditions and to consider formulating national programmes for the Year;

3. *Invites* the United Nations organizations and bodies concerned to examine the conceptual framework and identify areas for expanding upon it in keeping with their mandates;

4. *Requests* the Secretary-General to monitor activities for the Year and to make appropriate coordinating arrangements, bearing in mind that the Department for Policy Coordination and Sustainable Development of the Secretariat has been designated the United Nations focal point on ageing;

5. *Encourages* the Secretary-General to allocate sufficient resources for promoting and coordinating activities for the Year, bearing in mind resolution 47/5, in which it was decided that observance of the Year would be supported by the regular programme budget for the biennium 1998-1999;

6. *Invites* Member States, United Nations organizations and bodies and non-governmental organizations to assist the global coordinating entity for the Year;

7. *Invites* the regional commissions, within the existing mandates, to bear in mind the goals of the Year when convening regional meetings in 1998 and 1999 at which to mark the Year and formulate action plans on ageing for the twenty-first century;

8. *Encourages* relevant United Nations funds and programmes and the specialized agencies to support local, national and international programmes and projects for the Year;

9. *Encourages* the United Nations Development Programme to continue to ensure that the concerns of older persons are integrated into its development programmes;

10. *Invites* the International Research and Training Institute for the Advancement of Women, the United Nations Research Institute for Social Development and other relevant research institutes to consider preparing studies on the four facets of the conceptual framework, namely, the situation of older persons, lifelong individual development, multigenerational relationships and the relationship between the ageing of populations and development, and requests the International Research and Training Institute for the Advancement of Women to continue its research on the situation of older women, including those in the informal sector;

11. *Encourages* the Department of Public Information of the Secretariat to launch, within existing resources, an information campaign for the Year;

12. *Invites* the Committee on Economic, Social and Cultural Rights to continue its work on ageing and the situation of older persons, as described in its reports;

13. *Invites* non-governmental organizations to develop programmes and projects for the Year, particularly at the local level, in cooperation, *inter alia*, with local authorities, community leaders, enterprises, the media and schools;

14. *Decides* that henceforth the term "older persons" should be substituted for the term "the elderly", in conformity with the United Nations Principles for Older Persons, with the result that the Year and the Day concerned shall be called the International Year of Older Persons and the International Day of Older Persons;

15. *Requests* the Secretary-General to report to the General Assembly at its fifty-second session on the preparations being made by Member States, United Nations organizations and bodies and non-governmental organizations for the observance of the Year.

General Assembly resolution 50/141

21 December 1995      Meeting 97      Adopted without vote

Approved by Third Committee (A/50/628) without vote, 8 November (meeting 21); draft recommended by ESC in res. 1995/21 (A/C.3/50/L.2); agenda item 105.
*Meeting numbers.* GA 50th session: 3rd Committee 8-12, 21; plenary 97.

*REFERENCES*
[1]YUN 1993, p. 1069, GA res. 48/98, 20 Sept. 1993. [2]A/50/114. [3]YUN 1992, p. 889, GA res. 47/5, 16 Oct 1992. [4]YUN 1991, p. 698, GA res. 46/91, 16 Dec. 1991.

Chapter XII

# Refugees and displaced persons

In 1995, the Office of the United Nations High Commissioner for Refugees (UNHCR) was concerned with the fate of some 24 million persons, of whom 14 million were refugees, 3.2 million internally displaced persons, 2.8 million returnees, and 3.5 million were others with humanitarian needs. Prospects for a large-scale repatriation to the former Yugoslavia emerged towards the end of the year, while in Central Africa plans for a comprehensive voluntary repatriation faltered. In general, UNHCR focused on programmes and mechanisms launched in response to previous large-scale emergencies, the implementation of solutions where possible, and the elaboration of preventive strategies. It also continued to implement its international protection mandate and reinforced operational links with agencies and other partners, including various non-governmental organizations (NGOs) and UN human rights mechanisms.

During the year, UNHCR was involved in the repatriation of some 800,000 persons, notably to Afghanistan, Myanmar and Rwanda.

Africa in 1995 hosted 5.5 million refugees, some 2 million of whom were in the Great Lakes region and challenged the resources of both countries of asylum and UNHCR. Refugee flows also continued in Liberia, Sierra Leone and Somalia; in East Africa, repatriation efforts picked up, and were successfully concluded in Mozambique.

As durable solutions had been found to the majority of refugee situations in Central America, UNHCR concentrated on strengthening the capacity of Governments in the Americas region to deal with refugee-related matters. Some 1,121 Haitian refugees were repatriated from the Dominican Republic. The arrival of extra-continental asylum-seekers in South America and the Caribbean increased significantly.

In Europe, following the signing of the General Framework Agreeement for Peace in Bosnia and Herzegovina, UNHCR was entrusted with developing and implementing a repatriation plan to allow the orderly return of refugees and displaced persons. In Asia and Oceania, the voluntary repatriation of some 62,000 Myanmar refugees from Bangladesh took place and the implementation of the Comprehensive Plan of Action for Indo-Chinese Refugees was expected to be completed by the year's end. However, the impasse in finding a solution for Bhutanese asylum-seekers in Nepal and new displacements in Sri Lanka were causes for concern. In South-West Asia, North Africa and the Middle East, the UN continued efforts to assist some 3.6 million refugees.

In October, the UNHCR Executive Committee considered such topics as prevention and reduction of statelessness, refugee women, refugees and the environment, the situation of refugees, returnees and displaced persons in Africa, the Comprehensive Plan of Action for Indo-Chinese Refugees, voluntary repatriation to Afghanistan, humanitarian issues in the former Yugoslavia, and the budget structure and governance of UNHCR, as well as its working methods.

In December, the General Assembly called on States to promote conditions conducive to the return of refugees and to support their sustainable integration by providing countries of origin with rehabilitation and development assistance in conjunction with UNHCR and other development agencies.

## Office of the United Nations High Commissioner for Refugees

### Programme policy

**Executive Committee action.** At its forty-sixth session (Geneva, 16-20 October 1995),[1] the Executive Committee of the UNHCR Programme expressed its distress over the continued suffering of refugees for whom a solution had yet to be found, and urged the continued commitment of States to receive and host refugees and ensure their protection. It called on UNHCR to organize informal consultations on the development of guiding principles concerning measures to ensure international protection. The Committee called on the High Commissioner to support the development and implementation of criteria and guidelines on responses to persecution specifically aimed at women by sharing information on initiatives by States to develop such criteria and guidelines, and to ensure their fair and consistent application. It called on States to promote conditions conducive to the return of refugees and to support their reintegration by providing countries of origin with rehabilitation and development assistance in conjunction with UNHCR and relevant development agencies. The Committee encouraged UNHCR to cooperate with other international organizations on ways to facilitate the return of persons not in need of international protection and to inform the Standing Committee. It called on the High Commissioner to continue to expand and strengthen the Office's activities with regard to the promotion and dissemination of refugee law and protection principles and to explore ways to integrate its activities in the areas of documentation, research, publications and electronic dissemination. UNHCR was encouraged to strengthen its efforts in assisting host Governments to ensure the access of refugees to education. States were called on to manifest their international solidarity and burden-sharing with countries of asylum politically and in other tangible ways that reinforced their capacity to maintain generous asylum policies. The Committee welcomed the commissioning of an evaluation study and the UNHCR-sponsored consultations on resettlement, and encouraged UNHCR to strengthen its activities in that connection and provide regular reports to the Committee. It also called on States of refuge to ensure that the civilian and humanitarian character of refugee camps and settlements was maintained, and called on all other States to assist them; States of refuge should take measures to prevent the infiltration of armed elements, to provide effective physical protection to refugees and asylum-seekers, and to afford UNHCR and other organizations prompt and unhindered access to them.

Concerning the prevention and reduction of statelessness and the protection of stateless persons, the Committee called on States to adopt nationality legislation to reduce statelessness, to prevent the arbitrary deprivation of nationality, and to eliminate provisions permitting the renunciation of a nationality without prior possession or acquisition of another. It requested UNHCR to promote accession to the 1954 Convention relating to the Status of Stateless Persons[2] and the 1961 Convention on the Reduction of Statelessness,[3] and to provide to interested States technical and advisory services pertaining to the preparation and implementation of nationality legislation; to promote the prevention and reduction of statelessness through the dissemination of information and the training of staff and government officials; to enhance cooperation with other interested organizations; to provide the Committee biennially, beginning at its forty-seventh (1996) session, with information on activities undertaken on behalf of stateless persons, particularly with regard to the implementation of international instruments and principles relating to stateless persons, and including the magnitude of the problems of statelessness.

In her opening statement to the Committee, the High Commissioner stated that UNHCR had to prepare for a reappraisal of how it worked. Four priorities would be set for the coming years: revitalization of protection policies and strategies to reflect the dimension of solutions and respond to the needs of a growing range of beneficiaries; a rethinking of the way UNHCR planned its activities; reinforcement of the implementation and monitoring of UNHCR policies, guidelines and programmes, including the ability to monitor and control implementing partners; and restructuring of UNHCR work methods, so as to improve delivery, accountability and performance and to build a capacity to contract and expand in response to operational demands. In the light of the environmental damage caused by large concentrations of refugee populations, UNHCR proposed reformulating its environmental policy to make the environmental dimension an integral part of its operations.

By **decision 1995/314** of 28 July, the Economic and Social Council took note of the High Commissioner's report for 1994/1995.[4]

## UNHCR-NGO Partnership in Action

In 1995, UNHCR continued to follow up on the UNHCR/NGO Partnership in Action (PARINAC) process, launched in 1993[5] to establish a common agenda for field activities, and to implement the recommendations of the Oslo Declaration and Plan of Action, adopted at the 1994 PARINAC Global Conference.[6] To respond more effectively to the needs of NGOs, UNHCR made the NGO coordinator the focal point for all policy issues concerning NGOs at Headquarters and appointed NGO focal points in the Regional Bureaux. It undertook studies on safety of third countries, safety zones or safe areas and on minimum standards that Governments could apply concerning temporary protection. UNHCR concentrated on country/region-specific planning in emergency preparedness and was incorporating a systematic approach to inter-agency coordination, developed during recent emergencies, into emergency management training programme workshops. Guidelines governing cooperation with implementing partners, their choice and administrative support costs were issued and a programme and project management handbook for UNHCR implementing partners was being prepared. At the regional level, PARINAC follow-up meetings took place for southern Africa (South Africa, January), West Africa (Côte d'Ivoire, March), Asia and Oceania (Sri Lanka, May), and Central America (Costa Rica, December).

In October, the UNHCR Executive Committee adopted a conclusion[1] in which it reaffirmed the importance of the Oslo Declaration and Plan of Action as a joint agenda for humanitarian action. It encouraged UNHCR and NGOs to pursue activities in the field and at headquarters to enhance their partnership in protection and assistance and, together with Governments, to identify areas in the Plan of Action in which they could cooperate further to implement particular recommendations. The High Commissioner was asked to report in 1996 on the follow-up to the PARINAC process.

GENERAL ASSEMBLY ACTION

On 21 December, the General Assembly adopted **resolution 50/152**.

### Office of the United Nations High Commissioner for Refugees

*The General Assembly,*

*Having considered* the report of the United Nations High Commissioner for Refugees on the activities of her Office and the report of the Executive Committee of the Programme of the High Commissioner on the work of its forty-sixth session,

*Recalling* its resolution 49/169 of 23 December 1994,

*Reaffirming* the importance of the 1951 Convention and the 1967 Protocol relating to the Status of Refugees as the cornerstone of the international system for the protection of refugees, and noting with satisfaction that one hundred and thirty States are now parties to one or both instruments,

*Reaffirming also* the purely humanitarian and non-political character of the activities of the Office of the High Commissioner, as well as the crucial importance of the High Commissioner's functions of providing international protection to refugees and seeking solutions to refugee problems,

*Commending* the High Commissioner and her staff for the competent, courageous and dedicated manner in which they discharge their responsibilities, paying tribute to those staff members who have endangered or lost their lives in the course of their duties, and emphasizing the urgent need for effective measures to ensure the security of staff engaged in humanitarian operations,

*Distressed* at the continued suffering of refugees, for whom a solution has yet to be found, and noting with deep concern that refugee protection continues to be jeopardized in many situations as a result of denial of admission, unlawful expulsion, refoulement, unjustified detention, other threats to their physical security, dignity and well-being and failure to respect and ensure their fundamental freedoms and human rights,

*Welcoming* the continuing strong commitment of States to providing protection and assistance to refugees and the valuable support extended by Governments to the High Commissioner in carrying out her humanitarian tasks, and commending those States, particularly the least developed and those hosting millions of refugees over long periods of time, which, despite severe economic, development and environmental challenges of their own, continue to admit large numbers of refugees into their territories,

*Recognizing* that, in certain regions, misuse by individuals of asylum procedures jeopardizes the institution of asylum and adversely affects the prompt and effective protection of refugees,

*Concerned* that statelessness, including the inability to establish one's nationality, may result in displacement, and stressing, in this regard, that the prevention and reduction of statelessness and the protection of stateless persons are important also in the prevention of potential refugee situations,

1. *Strongly reaffirms* the fundamental importance and the purely humanitarian and non-political character of the function of the Office of the United Nations High Commissioner for Refugees of providing international protection to refugees and seeking solutions to refugee problems, and the need for States to cooperate fully with the Office in order to facilitate the effective exercise of that function;

2. *Calls upon* all States which have not yet done so to accede to and implement fully the 1951 Convention and the 1967 Protocol relating to the Status of Refugees and relevant regional refugee instruments, as applicable, for the protection of refugees;

3. *Also calls upon* all States to uphold asylum as an indispensable instrument for the protection of refugees, to ensure respect for the principles of refugee protection, including the fundamental principle of non-refoulement, as well as the humane treatment of asylum-seekers and refugees in accordance with internationally recognized human rights and humanitarian norms;

4. *Reaffirms* that everyone, without distinction of any kind, is entitled to the right to seek and enjoy in other countries asylum from persecution;

5. *Reiterates* the importance of ensuring access, for all persons seeking international protection, to fair and efficient procedures for the determination of refugee status or, as appropriate, to other mechanisms to ensure that persons in need of international protection are identified and granted such protection, while not diminishing the protection afforded to refugees under the terms of the 1951 Convention, the 1967 Protocol and relevant regional instruments;

6. *Reaffirms* the continued importance of resettlement as an instrument of protection;

7. *Reiterates* its support for the role of the Office of the High Commissioner in exploring further measures to ensure international protection to all who need it, consistent with fundamental protection principles reflected in international instruments, and looks forward to the informal consultations of the Office of the High Commissioner on the subject;

8. *Calls* for a more concerted response by the international community to the needs of internally displaced persons and, in accordance with its resolution 49/169, reaffirms its support for the High Commissioner's efforts, on the basis of specific requests from the Secretary-General or the competent principal organs of the United Nations and with the consent of the State concerned, and taking into account the complementarities of the mandates and expertise of other relevant organizations, to provide humanitarian assistance and protection to such persons, emphasizing that activities on behalf of internally displaced persons must not undermine the institution of asylum, including the right to seek and enjoy in other countries asylum from persecution;

9. *Reiterates* the relationship between safeguarding human rights and preventing refugee situations, recognizes that the effective promotion and protection of human rights and fundamental freedoms, including through institutions that sustain the rule of law, justice and accountability, are essential for States to address some of the causes of refugee movements and for States

to fulfil their humanitarian responsibilities in reintegrating returning refugees and, in this connection, calls upon the Office of the United Nations High Commissioner for Refugees, within its mandate and at the request of the Government concerned, to strengthen its support of national efforts at legal and judicial capacity-building, where necessary, in cooperation with the United Nations High Commissioner for Human Rights;

10. *Also reiterates* that development and rehabilitation assistance is essential in addressing some of the causes of refugee situations, as well as in the context of the development of prevention strategies;

11. *Condemns* all forms of ethnic violence and intolerance, which are among the major causes of forced displacements, as well as an impediment to durable solutions to refugee problems, and appeals to States to combat intolerance, racism and xenophobia and to foster empathy and understanding through public statements, appropriate legislation and social policies, especially with regard to the special situation of refugees and asylum-seekers;

12. *Welcomes* the Platform for Action adopted at the Fourth World Conference on Women, held at Beijing from 4 to 15 September 1995, particularly the strong commitment made by States in the Platform to refugee women and other displaced women in need of international protection, and calls upon the United Nations High Commissioner for Refugees to support and promote efforts by States towards the development and implementation of criteria and guidelines on responses to persecution, including persecution through sexual violence or other gender-related persecution, specifically aimed at women for reasons enumerated in the 1951 Convention and 1967 Protocol, by sharing information on States' initiatives to develop such criteria and guidelines and by monitoring to ensure their fair and consistent application by the States concerned;

13. *Reiterates* that, the grant of asylum or refuge being a peaceful and humanitarian act, refugee camps and settlements must maintain their exclusively civilian and humanitarian character and all parties are obliged to abstain from any activity likely to undermine this, condemns all acts which pose a threat to the personal security of refugees and asylum-seekers, and also those that may endanger the safety and stability of States, calls upon States of refuge to take all necessary measures to ensure that the civilian and humanitarian character of refugee camps and settlements is maintained, and further calls upon States of refuge to take effective measures to prevent the infiltration of armed elements, to provide effective physical protection to refugees and asylum-seekers and to afford the Office of the High Commissioner and other appropriate humanitarian organizations prompt and unhindered access to them;

14. *Encourages* the High Commissioner to continue her activities on behalf of stateless persons, as part of her statutory function of providing international protection and of seeking preventive action, as well as her responsibilities under General Assembly resolutions 3274(XXIV) of 10 December 1974 and 31/36 of 30 November 1976;

15. *Requests* the Office of the High Commissioner, in view of the limited number of States party to these instruments, actively to promote accession to the 1954 Convention relating to the Status of Stateless Persons and the 1961 Convention on the reduction of stateless-ness, as well as to provide relevant technical and advisory services pertaining to the preparation and implementation of nationality legislation to interested States;

16. *Calls upon* States to adopt nationality legislation with a view to reducing statelessness, consistent with the fundamental principles of international law, in particular by preventing arbitrary deprivation of nationality and by eliminating provisions that permit the renunciation of a nationality without the prior possession or acquisition of another nationality, while at the same time recognizing the right of States to establish laws governing the acquisition, renunciation or loss of nationality;

17. *Reaffirms* that voluntary repatriation, when it is feasible, is the ideal solution to refugee problems, and calls upon countries of origin, countries of asylum, the Office of the High Commissioner and the international community as a whole to do everything possible to enable refugees to exercise their right to return home in safety and dignity;

18. *Reiterates* the right of all persons to return to their country, and emphasizes in this regard the prime responsibility of countries of origin for establishing conditions that allow voluntary repatriation of refugees in safety and with dignity and, in recognition of the obligation of all States to accept the return of their nationals, calls upon all States to facilitate the return of their nationals who are not recognized as refugees;

19. *Calls upon* all States to promote conditions conducive to the return of refugees and to support their sustainable reintegration by providing countries of origin with necessary rehabilitation and development assistance in conjunction, as appropriate, with the Office of the High Commissioner and relevant development agencies;

20. *Recalls* Economic and Social Council resolution 1995/56 of 29 July 1995 on the strengthening of the coordination of emergency humanitarian assistance of the United Nations, and welcomes the decision of the Executive Committee of the Programme of the United Nations High Commissioner for Refugees to review, in the course of 1996, aspects of that resolution relevant to the work of the Office of the High Commissioner;

21. *Notes with appreciation* the programme policies established by the Executive Committee of the Programme of the High Commissioner, and underscores the importance of their implementation by the Office of the High Commissioner, implementing partners and other relevant organizations in order to ensure the provision of effective protection and humanitarian assistance to refugees;

22. *Reaffirms* the importance of incorporating environmental considerations into the programmes of the Office of the High Commissioner, especially in the least developed and developing countries which have hosted refugees over long periods of time, welcomes efforts by the Office of the High Commissioner to make a more focused contribution to resolving refugee-related environmental problems, and calls upon the High Commissioner to promote and enhance coordination and collaboration with host Governments, donors, relevant United Nations organizations, intergovernmental organizations, non-governmental organizations and other actors concerned to address refugee-related environmental problems in a more integrated and effective manner;

23. *Recognizes* the importance of the introduction of Russian as an official language of the Executive Com-

mittee of the Programme of the High Commissioner in facilitating the work of the High Commissioner and the implementation of the provisions of the 1951 Convention relating to the Status of Refugees, notably in the countries of the Commonwealth of Independent States;

24. *Calls upon* all Governments and other donors to demonstrate their international solidarity and burden-sharing with countries of asylum through efforts aimed at continuing to alleviate the burden borne by States which have received large numbers of refugees, in particular those with limited resources, and to contribute to the programmes of the Office of the High Commissioner and, taking into account the effect on countries of asylum of the increasing requirements of large refugee populations and the need to widen the donor base and to achieve greater burden-sharing among donors, to assist the High Commissioner in securing additional and timely income from traditional governmental sources, other Governments and the private sector in order to ensure that the needs of refugees, returnees and other displaced persons of concern to the Office of the High Commissioner are met.

General Assembly resolution 50/152

21 December 1995      Meeting 97      Adopted without vote

Approved by Third Committee (A/50/632) without vote, 22 November (meeting 36); 97-nation draft (A/C.3/50/L.20/Rev.1), orally corrected and revised; agenda item 109.

*Meeting numbers.* GA 50th session: 3rd Committee 19-23, 25, 32-34, 36; plenary 97.

## Financial and administrative questions

In 1995,[7] UNHCR's final budget was $1.17 billion, a decrease from the 1994 figure of $1.2 billion. Donors contributed some $1 billion in voluntary contributions in cash and kind towards General and Special Programmes, compared to $1.06 billion the previous year. Some $27.9 million from the UN regular budget went towards administrative support. The upward trend in the funding of General Programmes continued. Those programmes represented core activities for refugees and provided the High Commissioner with considerable flexibility to deal with emergencies and voluntary repatriations.

UNHCR expenditures in 1995 amounted to $1.14 billion: disbursements under General Programmes totalled $405.1 million and those under Special Programmes totalled $737.9 million. Some 31.7 per cent of Special Programme expenditures pertained to UNHCR's Programme of Humanitarian Assistance in the former Yugoslavia, and 31.8 per cent to the Burundi/Rwanda emergency operation. Other important expenditures related to the Mozambique repatriation programme and the Comprehensive Plan of Action for Indo-Chinese Refugees.

Regional apportionments were as follows: Africa, $482.6 million; Europe, $201.6 million; South-West Asia, North Africa and the Middle East, $105 million; Asia and Oceania, $95.8 million; and the Americas, $34.8 million.

Special operations accounted for some two thirds of UNHCR operational activities in 1995. Appeals were launched with the UN Department of Humanitarian Affairs (DHA) for operations in the former Yugoslavia, the Afghan repatriation programme, the Burundi/Rwanda emergency, Liberia, and programmes in the Horn of Africa and in the Republics of the former Soviet Union (see PART FOUR, Chapter III). UNHCR issued its own appeals for Central America, the Angolan and Mozambican repatriations, the repatriation to Myanmar, the Comprehensive Plan of Action for Indo-Chinese Refugees, and some other operations. The lack of funding for operations in the Great Lakes region of Africa was seen as the Office's greatest challenge during 1995, said the High Commissioner.[7] The Office raised some $662 million for special operations, repatriations and emergencies, in addition to the amounts under General Programmes.

A General Programmes budget target of $445.3 million was set for 1996, with Special Programme requirements estimated at $930.6 million, of which $288.4 million pertained to the Burundi/Rwanda operation and $348.3 million to the former Yugoslavia. Special Programme requirements for repatriation efforts in Africa and Asia, as well as for programmes in the former Yugoslavia, the Commonwealth of Independent States (CIS) and the Baltic States, remained urgent priorities.

At an extraordinary meeting held on 17 January,[8] the Executive Committee approved an increase in the 1995 General Programmes target from $415.4 million to $428.7 million, and noted that the revised proposed estimate for 1995 under General and Special Programmes amounted to $1,272,487,300

In an October decision,[1] the Committee approved the revised 1995 General Programmes budget amounting to $428,732,500 and noted that the estimate for 1995 General and Special Programmes was $1.3 billion. It also approved the country/area programmes, other programmes and the headquarters budgets amounting to $357,434,900, as well as $25 million for the Emergency Fund, $20 million for the Voluntary Repatriation Fund and a Programme Reserve of $42,892,100, constituting a 1996 total General Programmes budget of $445,327,000. The Committee requested the Commissioner to initiate informal consultations on the question of overhead costs for non-governmental implementing partners, particularly headquarters costs, for review at the first session of the Standing Committee in 1996, and authorized the Standing Committee to decide on the issue in the course of its deliberations during 1996. It also approved the creation of the post of Assistant High Commissioner (Policy, Planning and Operations) at the Assistant Secretary-General level and related staffing.

## UNHCR budget structure

Informal consultations on UNHCR's budget structure, funding and governance were launched at the 16 January inter-sessional meeting of the Subcommittee on Administrative and Financial Matters. At the heart of the consultations was the distinction between General and Special Programmes and governance by the Executive Committee, particularly over Special Programmes. In the light of those discussions, a series of conclusions covering the budget structure, General and Special Programmes, funds and reserves, governance, oversight reports, documentation, and future work were submitted to the Executive Committee for consideration.

In October,[1] the Executive Committee decided that the objectives of the UNHCR budget should be transparency, accountability and managerial control; flexibility to address emergency situations and unexpected changes to programmes; and assured funding for statutory activities. Further streamlining of the budget structure should be undertaken so that in a single, coherent structure, there would be a clear indication of overall, country-level and headquarters needs, as well as those of other programmes. To be included under General Programmes, activities should qualify as statutory, relate to situations that had stabilized, and be a funding priority. If, for a given year, all stabilized, statutory activities could not be included under General Programmes, the first priority for inclusion should be refugee situations that had stabilized. The High Commissioner should bear in mind the relative chances of funding for different activities and report to the Executive Committee the consideration which had determined the action. The Executive Committee should keep under review the levels of and criteria governing the Emergency Fund, the Programme Reserve, and the Voluntary Repatriation Fund. The Programme Reserve could be used to complement Special Programme funding for refugee situations, provided that the total of all such allocations did not exceed one third of the Programme Reserve in a given year. To support voluntary repatriation activities not included under General Programmes, the Voluntary Repatriation Fund should be enhanced by its extension to voluntary repatriation operations for refugees included under Special Programmes; in a given year, an allocation of up to $10 million could be made for any such operation. It was proposed that, as of 1997, the Programme Reserve should be constituted between 10 and 15 per cent of programmed activities under the Annual Programme for a given year; the level of the Voluntary Repatriation Fund for a given year should be set between $20 million and 10 per cent of the budgetary estimates for voluntary repatriation for the

previous year; the High Commissioner would propose the actual levels of the Programme Reserve and the Voluntary Repatriation Fund for approval by the Executive Committee. Any allocation from the Programme Reserve and the Voluntary Repatriation Fund could be cancelled if sufficient contributions were later received for relevant activities. The use of the Working Capital and Guarantee Fund could be extended to guarantee budget increases in the headquarters component of General Programmes, not exceeding 2 per cent of the approved General Programmes total target. The Executive Committee would thus allow the General Programmes approved budgetary target to rise by up to 2 per cent, with the adjustment of the General Programmes budget taking place at the end of a calendar year. If such use was made of the Working Capital and Guarantee Fund, it would be replenished in the subsequent year.

The inter-sessional meetings of the Executive Committee would review General and Special Programmes, consider updates on programme needs and funding, and review all country programmes in a particular region or regions and any Special Programmes covering a number of countries in a region. The Executive Committee would review the use made of the Emergency Fund, the Programme Reserve Fund and the Voluntary Repatriation Fund to ensure that their use was in accord with the governing criteria. Areas for further study and informal consultations to enhance UNHCR's budgetary structure and related matters were also proposed, including ways to ensure a better funding base for UNHCR activities.

## Accounts (1994)

The audited financial statements on funds administered by UNHCR for the year ending 31 December 1994 and the report of the Board of Auditors showed total expenditures of $1,167 million and total income of $1,192 million with a reserve balance of $363.9 million.[9]

The Board of Auditors noted that UNHCR's overall liquidity position was not fully satisfactory. It stated that UNHCR's control over its implementing partners was inadequate. Various aspects of programme management, including planning, programme formulation and appraisal, were deficient and the system adopted by field offices and implementing partners for budgeting, accounting and auditing of expenditures needed to be streamlined. The system of project reporting and monitoring was defective; the overhead costs of its implementing partners needed to be controlled. The Board suggested that the procurement system could be improved by streamlining the system of purchase planning and framework agreements and by giving adequate publicity to tenders and vendor performance analysis. In addition, weaknesses in property management procedures could be addressed through new asset management software. The Board also noted irregularities in the hiring of consultants, including the retrospective regularization of appointments, the engagement of consultants to perform the functions of regular staff, and the automatic extension of consultant contracts without the mandatory break in service and without a performance evaluation. The Board noted that while UNHCR had initiated action on many of its recommendations, implementation at the field level had not been satisfactory.

In its general decision on programme, administrative and financial matters,[1] the Executive Committee expressed serious concern about the observations of the Board of Auditors, especially those on management issues and, in particular, those relating to continuing problems regarding the lack of adequate managerial control by UNHCR of programmes implemented by its partners. It asked that the matters raised in the report be reviewed by the Standing Committee.

The Advisory Committee on Administrative and Budgetary Questions (ACABQ), in its 13 October report,[10] expressed concern that the Board's findings were not new and that it had had to reiterate previous recommendations because of non-compliance and lack of follow-up action by UNHCR in its field offices. ACABQ stated that significantly more budgetary and financial control over implementing partners needed to be exercised by field offices. It endorsed the view that UNHCR should establish norms to regulate and monitor the overhead costs of implementing partners and recommended that agreements with those partners should specify clearly UNHCR's responsibilities *vis a vis* those of the partners with respect to funding staff costs, including salary and allowances and separation payments. It did not believe that such payments should be chargeable to UNHCR and requested the High Commissioner to investigate the matter and include in her next report information on the findings and appropriate action taken on UNHCR activities. ACABQ believed that irregularities in consultancy services warranted immediate investigation and rectification and that existing rules and regulations should be enforced to prevent recurrences. If the current rules and regulations were, for the most part, not enforceable, proposals to amend them should be submitted rather than have programme managers circumvent or ignore the existing guidelines.

**GENERAL ASSEMBLY ACTION**

The General Assembly, in **resolution 50/204 A** of 23 December, accepted the audited financial statements for the year ending 31 December 1994

and the report of the Board of Auditors on UNHCR and the Board's conclusions and recommendations.

Also, on the same date, the Assembly adopted **resolution 50/204 B**.

*The General Assembly,*

*Recalling* its resolution 48/216 A of 23 December 1993, especially paragraph 6 thereof, as well as paragraph 2 of its resolution 48/216 C of 23 December 1993,

*Reaffirming* that the rectification of deficiencies and irregularities identified by the Board of Auditors will enhance the effective exercise of the functions of the Office of the United Nations High Commissioner for Refugees in providing international protection for refugees and will strengthen as well its crucial role in seeking solutions to refugee problems,

1. *Expresses serious concern* about the findings in the report of the Board of Auditors on the voluntary funds administered by the United Nations High Commissioner for Refugees, especially those concerning management issues, such as the continuing problems of the lack of adequate managerial control over the programmes carried out by implementing partners;

2. *Expresses particular concern* about the persistent nature of various problems and the non-implementation of the previous recommendations of the Board of Auditors;

3. *Requests* the High Commissioner to implement as a matter of urgency the recommendations of the Board of Auditors, taking into account the views expressed by the Member States and keeping the Board fully informed of the ongoing measures taken, and requests the Board to report thereon to the General Assembly at its fifty-first session;

4. *Also requests* the High Commissioner to work out and put in place, as a matter of urgency, procedures enhancing the efficiency of implementation of the recommendations of the Board of Auditors;

5. *Further requests* the High Commissioner to review with due diligence the content of the audit report, submitted to her before its issuance, in order to ensure the quality of the information issued for the use of the Member States;

6. *Notes with appreciation* that in the programme of work for 1996 recently adopted by the Executive Committee of the Programme of the United Nations High Commissioner for Refugees for its Standing Committee, the follow-up by the High Commissioner to the observations and recommendations of the Board of Auditors will be addressed in a systematic manner, in particular regarding issues related to implementing partners;

7. *Reiterates its request* that the Secretary-General and the executive heads of the United Nations organizations, funds and programmes comply with the common accounting standards approved by the General Assembly and that they address the specific recommendations made by the Board of Auditors in this regard;

8. *Requests* the High Commissioner to amend the term "funds available" in statement II of the audited financial statements of the voluntary funds administered by the High Commissioner, and in its annex, in order to correct the financial information disclosed and to reflect more accurately the financial resources available.

General Assembly resolution 50/204 B

23 December 1995     Meeting 100     Adopted without vote

Approved by Fifth Committee (A/50/839) without vote, 21 December (meeting 44); draft by Vice-Chairman (A/C.5/50/L.20, part B) following informal consultations; agenda item 113.

*Meeting numbers.* GA 50th session: 5th Committee 21, 25, 27, 44; plenary 100.

### Committee working methods

In 1995, the Executive Committee reviewed its working methods. In January, the Subcommittee on Administrative and Financial Matters established a working group to consider the issue, including the streamlining of documentation. At an extraordinary meeting on 20 June,[11] the Executive Committee adopted recommendations on documentation and the need for summary records.

By an October decision,[1] the Committee reconstituted its annual cycle of meetings to comprise one annual plenary session and a number of inter-sessional meetings of a Standing Committee of the Whole, which would replace the Subcommittee of the Whole on International Protection, the Subcommittee on Administrative and Financial Matters, and the informal meetings of the Executive Committee. The Standing Committee would discuss protection, programme and financial issues and would meet about four times a year; the penultimate annual meeting would focus on international protection and its programme implications. The annual plenary session of the Executive Committee would be held in mid-October and the general debate would be replaced by a debate on a focused annual theme. The Committee also made recommendations relating to decisions and conclusions, the structure of the agenda and timeliness and limitation of documentation. These arrangements would be implemented on an experimental basis for one annual cycle of meetings and reviewed in 1996.

It was also decided to introduce Russian as an official language of the Committee and to forward the matter to the General Assembly for approval.

### Subcommittee on Administrative and Financial Matters

The Executive Committee's Subcommittee on Administrative and Financial Matters met in Geneva on 16 January, 4 April, 20 June and 12 October.[12] It discussed a broad range of issues including an update of programmes and funding, UNHCR budget structure, the proposal to create a post of Assistant High Commissioner, policies and strategies for durable solutions, Executive Committee working methods, Rwanda "lessons learnt", UNHCR headquarters accommodation, human resources management, an update on voluntary repatriation movements, UNHCR telecommunications, an evaluation of the "women victims of violence" project in Kenya, the PARINAC progress re-

port, refugee children, refugee health, refugees and the environment, and implementing partners.

*REFERENCES*

[1]A/50/12/Add.1. [2]YUN 1954, p. 416. [3]YUN 1961, p. 533. [4]A/50/12. [5]YUN 1993, p. 1072. [6]YUN 1994, p. 1217. [7]E/1996/52. [8]A/AC.96/841. [9]A/50/5/Add.5. [10]A/50/560. [11]A/AC.96/843. [12]A/AC.96/859.

# Refugee protection and assistance

## Proposed conference on refugees

The Secretary-General, in response to a 1994 General Assembly request,[1] submitted a September 1995 report[2] on the comprehensive consideration and review of the problems of refugees, returnees, displaced persons and related migratory movements. In particular, the report discussed the preparatory process leading to the convening of a United Nations conference for the comprehensive consideration and review of the problems of refugees, returnees, displaced persons and migrants in the Commonwealth of Independent States (CIS) countries and relevant neighbouring States.

In January, UNHCR, the International Organization for Migration (IOM) and the Organization for Security and Cooperation in Europe (OSCE) Office for Democratic Institutions and Human Rights established a joint secretariat at UNHCR to prepare for such a conference. A joint UNHCR/IOM appeal for financial assistance for the secretariat was launched on 20 January. National consultations were held in February, March and April in Ukraine, Belarus and the Republic of Moldova, and the first regional consultation took place in March in Kyrgyzstan for the five Central Asian Republics. Consultations also took place in Armenia, Azerbaijan, Georgia, and the Baltic States. A first meeting of experts was held on 18 and 19 May in Geneva to identify issues of concern and to prepare a work plan for the conference. The experts identified the following types of movements to be addressed: refugees, displaced persons, resettlers, formerly deported peoples, irregular migration, trafficking in migrants, stranded migrants and ecological migration. The experts also raised the issues of the inadequacies of current terminology relating to refugees and displaced persons; national implementation of international instruments; emergency preparedness; a harmonized regional approach; root causes underlying displacement; strengthening the administrative systems of countries to deal with migration challenges; and cooperation among countries. A draft work plan envisaged a series of subregional meetings to be held between July and September 1995 to analyse issues of concern identified by the experts; a second meeting of experts was to be held in November to discuss possible solutions, in conjunction with the convening of a drafting committee to start work on a declaration of principles and a programme of action. A preparatory conference and the conference itself were planned for the first quarter of 1996.

The first two subregional meetings were held for the Transcaucasus region (Tbilisi, Georgia, 10-11 July) and for the Central Asian Republics (Ashkhabad, Turkmenistan, 27 July). The main objective of the conference process was to devise an integrated strategy for the region, through a declaration and plan of action and an accountability framework reflecting a shared commitment on roles and responsibilities. Consultations were held in July in Tbilisi and Moscow with local and international NGOs active in the region, and similar meetings were planned later in the year at Alma Ata (Almaty) (Kazakstan), Kiev (Ukraine) and Novosibirsk (Russian Federation).

In October,[3] the Executive Committee called on States concerned and relevant intergovernmental organizations to participate in the preparatory process leading to a CIS conference and urged Governments which had not yet done so to contribute to the common secretariat for the preparation of the conference. It requested the High Commissioner to report in 1996 on the outcome and follow-up of the conference.

**GENERAL ASSEMBLY ACTION**

On 21 December the General Assembly adopted **resolution 50/151.**

### Comprehensive consideration and review of the problems of refugees, returnees, displaced persons and related migratory movements

*The General Assembly,*

*Noting* the 1951 Convention and the 1967 Protocol relating to the Status of Refugees,

*Recalling* its resolutions 48/113 of 20 December 1993 and 49/173 of 23 December 1994,

*Having considered* the report of the Secretary-General and the report of the United Nations High Commissioner for Refugees,

*Reaffirming* the need for the international community to consider comprehensive approaches for the coordination of action with regard to refugees, returnees, displaced persons and related migratory movements,

*Considering* the magnitude of existing and potential refugee and related migratory movements in the countries of the Commonwealth of Independent States and relevant neighbouring States,

1. *Takes note* of the report of the Secretary-General, as well as the report of the United Nations High Commissioner for Refugees, in particular paragraph 30 of the addendum to the latter report;

2. *Calls upon* the United Nations High Commissioner for Refugees, in consultation with States concerned and in coordination with relevant intergovernmental, regional and non-governmental organizations, to continue to consider and develop comprehensive regional approaches to the problems of refugees and displaced persons;

3. *Expresses its appreciation* to the High Commissioner for her efforts to promote and develop a transparent preparatory process for a regional conference to address the problems of refugees, displaced persons and other forms of involuntary displacement and returnees in the countries of the Commonwealth of Independent States and relevant neighbouring States;

4. *Welcomes* the establishment of a common secretariat for the preparation of the conference, comprising the Office of the United Nations High Commissioner for Refugees, the International Organization for Migration and the Organization for Security and Cooperation in Europe and its Office for Democratic Institutions and Human Rights;

5. *Requests* the High Commissioner, in close cooperation with States and intergovernmental organizations concerned, to convene the conference in 1996;

6. *Expresses its appreciation* to United Nations bodies and agencies and other international organizations and institutions for their valuable contribution to the preparatory process leading to the conference;

7. *Urges* all States concerned and appropriate intergovernmental, regional and non-governmental organizations to support that process;

8. *Appeals* to all States and regional and intergovernmental organizations to provide the necessary support and resources needed by the secretariat for the preparation and holding of the conference;

9. *Requests* the Secretary-General to report to the General Assembly at its fifty-first session on the implementation of the present resolution.

General Assembly resolution 50/151

21 December 1995     Meeting 97     Adopted without vote

Approved by Third Committee (A/50/632) without vote, 21 November (meeting 34); 27-nation draft (A/C.3/50/L.19), orally corrected and revised; agenda item 109.

*Meeting numbers.* GA 50th session: 3rd Committee 19-23, 25, 32-34; plenary 97.

## Protection issues

While the numbers of refugees worldwide continued to decline slightly, concerns remained over the real, potential and perceived burden of protecting and assisting them. Those concerns caused some Governments to deny entry to asylum-seekers, or to forcibly return thousands of refugees to their countries of origin. Other States constricted entitlement to basic rights for various groups of victims of internal conflict, and still others attempted to streamline procedures in ways that precluded fair appeals before deportation. These and other developments in 1995 presented UNHCR with serious difficulties in undertaking its protection and assistance activities. Nevertheless, many Governments continued to uphold asylum as an indispensable instrument for the international protection of refugees and demonstrated their commitment to receive and host refugees in cooperation with UNHCR.

In a 1 September note[4] on international protection in mass influx, the High Commissioner examined current developments and explored protection strategies. She stated that, in 1995, a number of political and human rights factors highlighted the increased complexity and dimensions of refugee protection. The events of the year, whether in the former Yugoslavia, the Great Lakes region of Africa or the former Soviet Union, illustrated the value of the current international protection regime, while also revealing some of its shortcomings. The High Commissioner said that new and complementary strategies to ensure effective international protection should: first, reinforce the implementation of the the 1951 Convention relating to the Status of Refugees[5] and its 1967 Protocol[6] and existing regional instruments; strengthen the protection of persons falling outside the application of international legal instruments; and support protection measures taken by States not yet party to such instruments. While various possibilities for achieving that end could be kept under review, States did not appear prepared to undertake additional binding obligations towards refugees, the High Commissioner stated. She suggested that since the 1951 Convention and the 1967 Protocol, as well as international and regional refugee and human rights instruments, provided a broadly accepted overall framework for effective international protection, the inadequacies identified within that framework could be addressed through the further development and consolidation of non-binding standards.

In an October conclusion,[3] the UNHCR Executive Committee reiterated its support for UNHCR's role in exploring the development of guiding principles on measures to ensure international protection, consistent with fundamental protection principles reflected in international instruments. It called on UNHCR to organize informal consultations on the subject.

With regard to the protection of stateless persons, the Executive Committee encouraged UNHCR to continue its activities on their behalf as part of its statutory function of providing international protection and of seeking preventive action, as well as its responsibility to undertake the functions under article 11 of the 1961 Convention on the Reduction of Statelessness.[7]

The General Assembly, in **resolution 50/195** of 22 December, noted the efforts of the representative of the Secretary-General on internally displaced persons to develop a framework and to promote strategies for better protection, assistance and development for internally displaced persons (see PART THREE, Chapter II).

### International instruments

As at 31 December 1995,[8] the 1951 Convention relating to the Status of Refugees[5] had 126 States parties. Antigua and Barbuda, Namibia and the Solomon Islands became parties in 1995. The 1967 Protocol[6] to the Convention also had 126 States parties, with the accession in 1995 of Antigua and Barbuda and the Solomon Islands.

Other intergovernmental legal instruments of benefit to refugees included the 1969 OAU Convention governing the Specific Aspects of Refugee Problems in Africa, the 1957 Agreement relating to Refugee Seamen and its 1973 Protocol, the 1959 European Agreement on the Abolition of Visas to Refugees, the 1980 European Agreement on Transfer of Responsibility for Refugees, and the 1969 American Convention on Human Rights, Pact of San José, Costa Rica.

As at 31 December 1995,[8] there were 41 States parties to the 1954 Convention relating to the Status of Stateless Persons[9] and 17 States parties to the 1961 Convention on the Reduction of Statelessness.[7].

### Promotional activities

The UNHCR Centre for Documentation and Research provided users with a broad collection of refugee literature and legal and country-of-origin information. Its 14 databases, known collectively as REFWORLD, included country reports, UN documentation, case law, instruments, legislation, media reports and an on-line thesaurus. REFWORLD was available on the Internet and on CD-ROM.

UNHCR promotional activities included the organization of refugee law and protection courses for government officials, implementing partners and NGOs. It was also involved in the work of human rights treaty bodies and other human rights mechanisms. A memorandum was signed in 1995 between the UNHCR Branch Office in Rwanda and the Human Rights Field Operation in Rwanda to enhance complementarity of action regarding monitoring and institution building.

### Assistance measures

During 1995,[10] UNHCR considered programmes and mechanisms launched in response to previous large-scale emergencies, implemented solutions, and elaborated preventive strategies. The prospect of large-scale repatriation to the former Yugoslavia emerged near the end of the year as a distinct possibility, while in the Great Lakes region of Africa, plans for comprehensive, voluntary repatriation faltered. In the States of the former Soviet Union, the High Commissioner consolidated a wide-ranging strategy to address existing and potential population displacements. UNHCR continued to implement its international protection mandate to promote, safeguard and develop principles of refugee protection, strengthen international commitments, and promote durable solutions.

Worldwide, UNHCR was working to assist 24 million persons, of whom 14.2 million (60 per cent) were refugees; 3.2 million, internally displaced; 3.5 million, others of humanitarian concern; and 2.8 million, returnees. Overall, the number fell by 3.5 million during 1995, mainly in the internally displaced and returnee categories.

UNHCR continued to consolidate its emergency preparedness and response arrangements. The major deployment in 1995 of those resources was to the Russian Federation, in response to the crisis in Chechnya. Special attention was paid to contingency planning, particularly in Albania, Egypt, Ethiopia, Jordan, the Republic of Korea, Rwanda, Sri Lanka, the former Yugoslav Republic of Macedonia and Zaire. Following a meeting with NGOs in October, UNHCR began work to establish a database to better gauge and use NGO response capacity in refugee emergencies.

Following the emergency phase of a refugee operation, the basic needs of refugees were covered by care and maintenance activities. Total expenditures on such assistance in 1995 amounted to $696.2 million, including $454.4 million under Special Programmes.

UNHCR continued to regard voluntary repatriation as the preferable durable solution to refugee situations. In 1995, of more than 800,000 persons repatriated, 450,000 were directly assisted by UNHCR, notably to return to Afghanistan (170,000), Rwanda (110,000) and Myanmar (61,000). Expenditures of $191.9 million went to such efforts and another $126.4 million went to agricultural and non-agricultural activities to promote economic self-reliance and local integration of refugees.

Global expenditures on resettlement in 1995 amounted to $7,201.6 million. During the year, UNHCR resettled 10,000 refugees from the former Yugoslavia; 21,000 resettlers elsewhere departed to third countries. The majority of persons still needing resettlement originated in the Middle East and Africa. UNHCR met with major resettlement Governments and agencies in October.

### Refugee/returnee aid and development

UNHCR reinforced its operational linkages with agencies and partners to address the impact of refugee influxes on the development resources of asylum countries, as well as the multifaceted needs of countries into which refugees were least integrated. Jointly with the United Nations Development Programme (UNDP), UNHCR agreed on a Framework for Inter-agency Initiatives to promote a smooth transition from humanitarian assistance to sustainable human development. In a

new Memorandum of Understanding with the United Nations Children's Fund (UNICEF) and a revised Memorandum with the World Food Programme, the need was stressed to link operations involving the reintegration of refugees in situations of post-conflict recovery. The High Commissioner called for more flexible and predictable aid for post-conflict recovery to help bridge the gap between relief and development.

### Refugees and the environment

In 1995, UNHCR reformulated its policy concerning environmental matters associated with refugee situations, based on past experience and an assessment of its 1994 Interim Guidelines for Environment-Sensitive Management of Refugee Programmes. New overall environmental guidelines were developed and the related sectoral guidelines were being revised. The basic principles involved were: to assure an integrated approach; to prevent rather than cure; to be cost-effective and ensure overall benefit maximization; and to involve the refugee and local populations. The reformulated policy and operational outcomes, to be introduced in a step-by-step manner over the next three to four years, would help UNHCR to resolve refugee-related environmental problems, such as deforestation, soil erosion, depletion and degradation of water resources and their socio-economic impacts on refugees and local communities.

In an October conclusion,[3] the Executive Committee approved the UNHCR reformulated environmental policy, noting that proposed operational outcomes would enable UNHCR to make a more focused contribution to refugee-related environmental problems. The Committee requested the High Commissioner to revise the interim guidelines to give effect to the reformulated policy and to promote and enhance coordination and collaboration with host Governments, donors, relevant UN organizations, intergovernmental organizations and NGOs and other actors concerned to address refugee-related environmental problems in a more integrated and effective manner. The Committee called on the High Commissioner to keep it informed, through its Standing Committee, of the implementation of the policy, in particular financial implications and environmental actions in the field, and to report on results achieved in 1997.

Initiatives to promote the new policy included model projects on environmental education and training and participatory approaches to environmental problems, the development of an environmental database, and environmentally sound technologies. Efforts were also made to promote cooperation with other international organizations. One example was the UNDP/UNHCR Great

Lakes Initiative to address degradation of infrastructure and the environment in refugee-affected areas within Burundi, the United Republic of Tanzania and Zaire.

The General Assembly, in **resolution 50/152**, reaffirmed the importance of incorporating environmental considerations into UNHCR programmes, especially in least developed and developing countries hosting refugees over long periods of time. It called on the High Commissioner to promote and enhance coordination and collaboration with host Governments, donors, relevant UN organizations, intergovernmental organizations, NGOs and other actors concerned so that refugee-related environmental problems would be considered in a more integrated and effective manner.

### Refugee women

During 1995, UNHCR strengthened field implementation of existing policies and guidelines regarding refugee women, creating three regional refugee women coordinator posts. It also reinforced field focal points established in connection with preparations for the Fourth World Conference on Women (Beijing, China, 4-15 September) (see PART FOUR, Chapter X), and established a reference group to support field implementation by UNHCR of the Beijing Platform for Action, adopted by the Conference. The immediate focus of the group's work was women's access to and partnership in food distribution. UNHCR's gender training—People-Oriented Planning (POP)—continued to expand its stand-alone courses, while integrating aspects of that training into other courses. Independent replication of the training by NGOs increased and a network of POP trainers was formalized to support implementation of gender policies. UNHCR also developed a human rights awareness training module targeted at refugee women.

In terms of the implementation of the recommendations of the Working Group on Refugee Women and Children, which in 1994 had examined obstacles to carrying out UNHCR's Policies and Guidelines on Refugee Women and Refugee Children,[11] the High Commissioner had instituted a policy of recruiting only women for the next year and POP training was used to address attitudinal change among staff members. Concerning the integration of women's concerns into UNHCR emergency activities, it was now standard practice to include in emergency teams community services officers who would be responsible for identifying constraints to protection and assistance to women. An action-oriented research project was developed to establish the conditions necessary to place food distribution into the hands of refugee women and to assess the impact of such distribu-

tion on family level food security. Regarding physical protection and human rights, the UNHCR Guidelines on Preventing and Responding to Sexual Violence against Refugees, issued in March, were cited as a model in the Beijing Platform for Action. The annual protection reporting exercise was modified to ensure that specific concerns of women were addressed. Compliance with the UNHCR policy on refugee women was encouraged through the UNHCR-NGO PARINAC process and POP training of local and international NGOs and through the efforts of government ministries.

In an October conclusion,[3] the Executive Committee requested the High Commissioner to prepare a framework for implementation of the Beijing Platform for Action that would form the basis of future UNHCR planning on refugee women's issues, as well as reports to the Executive Committee and to the Commission on the Status of Women. It called on the High Commissioner to report in 1996 on the delivery of the implementation framework, with emphasis on field implementation of the policy and guidelines and on UNHCR implementation of the recommendations of the Working Group on Refugee Women and Refugee Children.

### Refugee children

UNHCR in 1995 provided the Committee on the Rights of the Child with information concerning the situation of refugee children and actively participated in the UN study on the Impact of Armed Conflict on Children to ensure an emphasis on refugee and displaced children (see also PART THREE, Chapter I).

UNHCR included much of its field work on the psychosocial well-being of children in its community services and education programmes. Professional mental health programmes were provided in collaboration with specialized NGOs. Assistance was provided to traumatized unaccompanied children in Central Africa. UNHCR brought to the attention of concerned authorities incidents of sexual exploitation involving children, including unaccompanied girls, and camp officials, security or military personnel. The development of guidelines and procedures, training activities and close monitoring of the well-being of the child were among measures to be taken to prevent such abuse.

UNHCR also intervened where refugee children were threatened with being recruited into armed groups, advocating that those not yet 15 years old should not be allowed to volunteer. A module on rights awareness training was being developed to inform refugee women and others about the right of children not to be recruited. As to educating refugee children, the use of distance education and other innovative approaches were being explored to meet the needs of older children. The policy of rapid educational response in emergencies bore fruit in the Kagera region of the United Republic of Tanzania, where 60,000 Rwandan refugee children were receiving non-formal education. A regional education workshop was held in Nairobi, Kenya, to train UNHCR and implementing partner staff from 15 countries.

Together with NGOs, UNHCR established or promoted projects in countries of origin to prepare the return of the child and to facilitate and monitor reintegration. In January, it established the Regional Support Unit for Refugee Children in Kigali, Rwanda, to provide technical assistance and programme support to its field offices and implementing partners in Burundi, Rwanda, the United Republic of Tanzania and Zaire. The importance of assessing children's needs from the earliest stages of emergencies to their integration into UNHCR protection and assistance activities was highlighted in the new UNHCR Handbook on Programme Management for UNHCR Implementing Partners.

**Report of the Secretary-General.** In response to a 1994 General Assembly request,[12] the Secretary-General submitted an October report on assistance to refugee children.[13] The report reviewed inter-agency cooperation; identification, registration and tracing of unaccompanied children; psychosocial rehabilitation; persistent protection problems; repatriation and reintegration; and lessons learnt.

The Secretary-General stated that unaccompanied children could constitute 3 to 5 per cent of the refugee or forcibly displaced population. In Rwanda, they represented 3.5 per cent in July. Some 300 Vietnamese unaccompanied children still lived in camps in exile in South-East Asia, while 6,000 unaccompanied children from the Sudan were living in Kenya. Few unaccompanied children were identified among Myanmar refugees in Bangladesh, Bhutanese refugees in Nepal or refugees in Chechnya, Russian Federation. However, the Burundi/Rwanda emergency created by far the highest number of unaccompanied minors in recent years; some 117,000 in July 1995. UNHCR established a Regional Support Unit for Refugee Children, based in Kigali, and UNICEF deployed specialists to advise agency staff, government counterparts and implementing partners. In Rwanda and Zaire, national NGOs were involved in the care of unaccompanied children.

In September, a meeting on family tracing and reunification was organized by the Save the Children Fund—UK, with the participation of UNHCR, UNICEF, the International Committee of the Red Cross, the International Federation of Red Cross and Red Crescent Societies and Governments responsible for large groups of unaccompanied children. Its purpose was to develop a framework for the management of unaccompanied children in future emergencies and to consolidate technical and professional practice in that area. In conjunction with NGOs, UNICEF developed a system for the registration, tracing and reunification of unaccompanied children, which was successfully implemented in Rwanda. Organizations working with unaccompanied children were exploring ways to support existing registration initiatives and share information so that implementing partners could begin active tracing as early as possible.

Among persistent problems confronting unaccompanied children, the Secretary-General said, were: allegations of recruitment of refugee children as combatants or assistants to the military or cases of children living with the military for alleged protection purposes; deprivation; neglect or abuse; sexual exploitation of unaccompanied girls; and evacuation and adoption of refugee children. UNHCR translated lessons learnt in providing protection and assistance to unaccompanied refugee children into handbooks and guidelines.

The Secretary-General concluded that progress had been made in the quality and timeliness of the international community's response to problems facing unaccompanied minors. Closer collaboration between UNHCR and UNICEF would further improve emergency response, ensuring compatibility with long-term solutions for the child, preferably in the country of origin.

**GENERAL ASSEMBLY ACTION**

On 21 December, the General Assembly adopted **resolution 50/150**.

**Assistance to unaccompanied refugee minors**
*The General Assembly,*

*Reaffirming* its resolution 49/172 of 23 December 1994,

*Aware* that the majority of refugees are children and women,

*Bearing in mind* that unaccompanied refugee minors are among the most vulnerable refugees and require special assistance and care,

*Mindful* of the fact that the ultimate solution to the plight of those unaccompanied minors is their return to and reunification with their families,

*Noting* that the Office of the United Nations High Commissioner for Refugees has developed revised Guidelines on Refugee Children, issued in May 1994,

*Noting also* the efforts of the High Commissioner to ensure the protection of and assistance to refugees, including children and unaccompanied minors, and that further efforts need to be exerted to this effect,

*Recalling* the provisions of the Convention on the Rights of the Child and the 1951 Convention and the 1967 Protocol relating to the Status of Refugees,

1. *Takes note* of the report of the Secretary-General;

2. *Expresses its deep concern* at the plight of unaccompanied refugee minors, and emphasizes the urgent need

for their early identification and for timely, detailed and accurate information on their number and whereabouts;

3. *Calls upon* all Governments, the Secretary-General, the United Nations High Commissioner for Refugees, all United Nations organizations, other international organizations and non-governmental organizations concerned to exert the maximum effort to assist and protect refugee minors and to expedite the return to and reunification with their families of unaccompanied refugee minors;

4. *Urges* the Office of the United Nations High Commissioner for Refugees, all United Nations organizations, other international organizations and non-governmental organizations concerned to take appropriate steps to mobilize resources commensurate to the needs and interests of the unaccompanied refugee minors and for their reunification with their families;

5. *Condemns* all acts of exploitation of unaccompanied refugee minors, including their use as soldiers or human shields in armed conflict and their recruitment in military forces, and any other acts that endanger their safety and personal security;

6. *Calls upon* the Secretary-General, the High Commissioner, the Department of Humanitarian Affairs of the Secretariat, the United Nations Children's Fund and other United Nations organizations and international organizations to mobilize adequate assistance to unaccompanied minors in the areas of relief, education, health and psychological rehabilitation;

7. *Requests* the Secretary-General to report to the General Assembly at its fifty-first session on the implementation of the present resolution.

General Assembly resolution 50/150

21 December 1995     Meeting 97     Adopted without vote

Approved by Third Committee (A/50/632) without vote, 21 November (meeting 34); 11-nation draft (A/C.3/50/L.18); agenda item 109.

*Meeting numbers.* GA 50th session: 3rd Committee 19-23, 25, 32-34; plenary 97.


## Regional activities

### Africa

In 1995, Africa hosted some 8.8 million persons of concern to UNHCR, of whom 5.5 million were refugees. The population displacements had been provoked mainly by political, ethnic and economic conflicts; in addition, widespread famine, insecurity, violence exacerbated by poverty and environmental degradation incited new population movements. Following the 1994 exodus of some 2 million people from Rwanda, the situation in the Great Lakes region remained fragile, and displacement continued. Refugee flows also continued in other parts of Africa, notably in Liberia, Sierra Leone, Somalia and the Sudan, with little hope of an early solution. In 1995, UNHCR expenditure in Africa totalled $482.6 million.

In February, UNHCR organized a regional conference on assistance to refugees, returnees and displaced persons in the Great Lakes region of Africa (Bujumbura, Burundi) (see below).

In a report[10] covering UNHCR activities during the year, the High Commissioner stated that in the Great Lakes region, some 1.7 million Rwandan refugees were living in Burundi, the United Republic of Tanzania and Zaire, and 208,000 Burundian refugees were in the United Republic of Tanzania and Zaire. In Rwanda, UNHCR efforts to facilitate voluntary repatriation and reintegration included the construction of shelters and implementation of quick-impact projects in the water, health, education and community services sectors in areas of return. However, major obstacles to large-scale repatriation remained, including continuing intimidation in camps in Burundi, the United Republic of Tanzania and Zaire, and the lack of a comprehensive political solution. On 10 February,[14] the Security Council expressed concern at reports of continuing intimidation and security problems in the Rwandan refugee camps, particularly those in Zaire, and asked the Secretary-General to make recommendations for ensuring their security (see PART TWO, Chapter II).

On 22 December, the General Assembly, in **resolution 50/58 L**, urged States, UN organizations, specialized agencies and other intergovernmental and non-governmental organizations, as well as the international financial and development institutions, to continue to provide financial, technical and material assistance, bearing in mind that sound economic foundations were vital for achieving lasting stability in Rwanda and for the return and resettlement of Rwandan refugees.

In Burundi, continuing armed conflicts provoked new flows of refugees into the United Republic of Tanzania and Zaire and within Burundi. Some 30,000 Rwandan refugees and Burundian asylum-seekers fled to the United Republic of Tanzania at the end of 1995, while 1,000 Burundians were arriving every month in Zaire.

Meanwhile, major asylum countries in the Great Lakes region expressed concern at the prolonged stay of the refugees. On 31 March, the Tanzanian Government closed its borders, and, in August, Zaire refouled some 16,000 refugees in one week, an action viewed with concern by the Security Council.[15] The Council called on Zaire to stand by its humanitarian obligations regarding refugees and supported the Secretary-General's decision to send the High Commissioner to the region to engage in discussions with Zaire and neighbouring States to resolve the situation.

The Tripartite Commissions on repatriation—involving Rwanda and UNHCR and the United Republic of Tanzania or Burundi—met regularly. Meetings involving Zaire, Rwanda and UNHCR were held in Geneva in September and December. Discussions focused on ways to enhance repatriation through mass information campaigns, separation of intimidators from refugees and cross-border visits.

In Central Africa, there were 27,000 Sudanese refugees in the Central African Republic and 111,870 in north-eastern Zaire, 91,545 of whom received assistance from UNHCR. The Office was also assisting 41,950 of the estimated 160,950 Angolan refugees in Zaire.

In West Africa, some spontaneous returns to Liberia were noted following the signing in August of the Abuja Peace Agreement (see PART TWO, Chapter II), but about 750,000 Liberian refugees remained, mostly in Côte d'Ivoire and Guinea. The number of refugees from Sierra Leone in Guinea and Liberia increased significantly, reaching 360,000, due to the ongoing civil war. With an improved situation in Togo, the number of refugees from that country in Benin and Ghana declined significantly in 1995; a total of 20,983 persons repatriated from Benin during the year. Likewise, a sizeable number of Tuaregs spontaneously returned to Mali in 1995, due to the improved security situation; however, some 100,000 Malians still remained in Algeria, Burkina Faso, Mauritania and Niger. The number of Mauritanian refugees in Senegal remained at 66,000.

In East Africa and the Horn of Africa, UNHCR activities focused mainly on care and maintenance for refugees in Eritrea, Ethiopia, Somalia and the Sudan; in Uganda and northern Zaire, the Office gradually phased out those activities. In June, some 24,235 Eritreans were successfully repatriated, completing the pilot phase of the Programme for Refugee Reintegration and Rehabilitation of Resettlement Areas in Eritrea. Starting in December, more than 19,000 Ethiopian refugees were repatriated from the Sudan, with an estimated 52,000 still remaining. Another 32,000 Ethiopians were repatriated from Djibouti. The number of Somali refugees in Kenya in 1995 stood at 126,060, with another 275,190 in Ethiopia.

In southern Africa, more than 1.7 million Mozambican refugees returned home from countries of asylum, successfully concluding the UNHCR-assisted repatriation effort there. Assistance in Mozambique had focused on the reintegration of returnees and other targeted populations by improving food security, road access, water and sanitation, and primary health care through some 750 quick-impact programmes. Meanwhile, UNDP and UNHCR established a framework for inter-agency initiatives to promote the transition from humanitarian assistance to sustainable human development.

In Angola, UNHCR launched a repatriation and reintegration operation for some 311,000 Angolan refugees over a 30-month period, beginning in June 1995.

The Council of Ministers of the Organization of African Unity (OAU) (Addis Ababa, 21-23 June),[16] in a resolution on refugees, returnees and displaced persons in Africa, appealed to the international community, and particularly UNHCR, to increase support to the countries involved in the programme of voluntary repatriation of refugees and to establish a link between emergency operations and those connected with rehabilitation and development.

On 28 July, by **decision 1995/314**, the Economic and Social Council took note of the oral report by UNHCR on assistance to refugees, returnees and displaced persons in Africa.[17]

In an October conclusion,[3] the Executive Committee called on UNHCR to intensify its protection activities by supporting African Governments in the training of officers and other capacity-building activities, disseminating information on refugee instruments and principles, and providing financial, technical and advisory services to accelerate the enactment/amendment and implementation of legislation relating to refugees. Also, in conjunction with OAU and concerned Governments, subregional groupings and other interested parties, UNHCR should continue to seek sustainable solutions to the refugee problems in Africa, in particular through facilitating voluntary return.

The Executive Committee appealed to Governments, UN agencies, NGOs and the international community to create conditions to facilitate the return and early rehabilitation and reintegration of refugees. UNHCR should assess the negative impacts of large refugee concentrations on hosting communities, with a view to initiating measures to prevent damage and to assist in repair, especially damage to the environment and ecosystems in host countries. It expressed concern over the long stay of refugees in certain African countries and called on the High Commissioner to keep under review programmes in those countries, taking into account the increasing requirements in the region.

**Report of the Secretary-General.** In response to a 1994 General Assembly request,[18] the Secretary-General submitted a September report[19] on assistance to refugees, returnees and displaced persons in Africa. Despite the sombre refugee picture, he said that the peaceful democratic changes that had occurred in several parts of Africa had created opportunities for large numbers of refugees to return to their homes, and prospects for voluntary repatriation of refugees and the reintegration of returnees had improved. However, more comprehensive, timely and sustained efforts were needed to rehabilitate war-torn societies. The international community had to press for new means to respond faster and to meet rehabilitation needs earlier. The persistence of population movements and refugee flows called for a comprehensive approach focusing on prevention, the adverse impact of refugees on asylum countries and the search for durable solutions.

### Great Lakes regional conference

A regional conference on assistance to refugees, returnees and displaced persons in the Great Lakes region of Africa was held in Bujumbura, Burundi, from 15 to 17 February[20] (see also PART FOUR, Chapter III). In accordance with a 1994 General Assembly resolution,[21] OAU and UNHCR jointly coordinated preparations for the Conference, including the establishment of a preparatory committee under their co-chairmanship. The aim of the Conference was to highlight the problems of refugees, returnees and displaced persons in the region; consider measures for their repatriation and safety; sensitize the international community to adverse socio-economic and environmental consequences; address root causes of the refugee problem; examine the impact on the civilian population of the presence of military personnel and militia in refugee camps and settlements; mobilize resources in support of the affected countries; and appeal for international assistance.

The Conference adopted a Plan of Action outlining a strategy for the peaceful resolution of the problem of displacement in the Great Lakes region, including voluntary return and reintegration of refugees and internally displaced persons. The Plan of Action included measures to be taken in and/or by the countries of origin and the countries of asylum and by the international community. The Conference requested UNDP to hold a donor's round table on countries of the region, which would provide a framework for coordinated and integrated approaches. It also established a Follow-up Committee, which, at its first meeting (Addis Ababa, Ethiopia, 26 May), noted that very little progress had been made in implementing the Plan of Action and that, in some areas, the situation had deteriorated. It agreed that consultations and discussion should continue, that political consultations should be encouraged to promote political accommodation, and that the proposed international conference on peace, security and development in the region (see PART TWO, Chapter II) would provide an impetus to humanitarian action in the region. In preparation for the round table, UNHCR and UNDP, in April, agreed that the consultations with donors should be a joint UNHCR/UNDP undertaking, in consultation with OAU. UNDP dispatched a preliminary mission to the subregion, which identified priority needs and, in collaboration with UNHCR, agreed to dispatch a comprehensive needs assessment and pro-

gramme project identification and formulation mission in September.

GENERAL ASSEMBLY ACTION

On 21 December, the General Assembly adopted **resolution 50/149.**

### Assistance to refugees, returnees and displaced persons in Africa

*The General Assembly,*

*Recalling* its resolution 49/174 of 23 December 1994,

*Having considered* the report of the Secretary-General and the report of the United Nations High Commissioner for Refugees,

*Bearing in mind* the fact that most of the affected countries are least developed countries,

*Convinced* of the necessity of strengthening the capacity within the United Nations system for the implementation and overall coordination of relief programmes for refugees, returnees and displaced persons,

*Welcoming* the prospects for voluntary repatriation and durable solutions to the refugee problems throughout Africa,

*Recalling* its resolution 49/7 of 25 October 1994, in which it endorsed the convening of a regional conference for assistance to refugees, returnees and displaced persons in the Great Lakes region,

*Taking into account* resolution CM/Res.1588(LXII) on refugees, returnees and displaced persons in Africa, adopted by the Council of Ministers of the Organization of African Unity at its sixty-second ordinary session, held at Addis Ababa from 21 to 23 June 1995,

*Recognizing* the need for States to create conditions conducive to the prevention of flows of refugees and displaced persons and to voluntary repatriation,

*Bearing in mind* that the majority of refugees and displaced persons are women and children,

1. *Takes note* of the report of the Secretary-General and the report of the United Nations High Commissioner for Refugees;

2. *Notes with concern* the effects of political instability, internal strife, human rights violations, foreign intervention, poverty and natural disasters, such as drought, in increasing the number of refugees and displaced persons in some countries of Africa;

3. *Expresses deep concern* at the serious and far-reaching consequences of the presence of large numbers of refugees and displaced persons in the receiving countries and the implications for their security, their long-term socio-economic development and the environment;

4. *Expresses its appreciation and strong support* for those African Governments and local populations which, in spite of the general deterioration of socio-economic and environmental conditions, as well as over-stretched national resources, continue to accept the additional burdens imposed by increasing numbers of refugees and displaced persons, in compliance with the relevant principles of asylum;

5. *Commends* the Governments concerned for their sacrifices, for providing assistance to refugees, returnees and displaced persons and for their efforts to promote voluntary repatriation and other measures taken to find appropriate and lasting solutions;

6. *Expresses its gratitude* to the international community for the humanitarian assistance it has continued

to render to refugees and displaced persons and to the countries of asylum, and calls upon it to continue to provide assistance to the millions of refugees and displaced persons in Africa;

7. *Expresses its concern* regarding instances, in some parts of Africa, where the fundamental principle of asylum is jeopardized as a result of unlawful expulsion, refoulement, or other threats to life, physical security, dignity and well-being;

8. *Welcomes* the strengthening of cooperation, at all levels, between the Office of the United Nations High Commissioner for Refugees and the Organization of African Unity, and urges both organizations, with relevant subregional bodies, United Nations and non-governmental organizations, the international community and the Governments concerned, to increase their efforts to address the root causes, work out strategies and find durable solutions to the problems of displacement in Africa;

9. *Also welcomes* the initiatives of the United Nations High Commissioner for Refugees to implement General Assembly resolution 49/7, and endorses the Plan of Action adopted by the Regional Conference on Assistance to Refugees, Returnees and Displaced Persons in the Great Lakes Region, held at Bujumbura from 15 to 17 February 1995, as a framework for solution-oriented approaches to the humanitarian problems in the Great Lakes region;

10. *Calls upon* the Office of the United Nations High Commissioner for Refugees to intensify its protection activities by, *inter alia*, supporting the efforts of African Governments through appropriate training of relevant officers and other capacity-building activities, disseminating information about refugee instruments and principles and providing financial, technical and advisory services to accelerate the enactment or amendment and implementation of legislation relating to refugees;

11. *Expresses its appreciation* for the efforts of Governments and for the important work being done by the Office of the United Nations High Commissioner for Refugees, United Nations organizations, the International Organization for Migration, non-governmental organizations and other cooperating bodies on the implementation of voluntary repatriation of refugees in Africa, and calls upon the Office of the High Commissioner, in conjunction with the Organization of African Unity and Governments concerned, subregional groupings and other interested parties, actively to continue to seek sustainable solutions to the refugee problem in Africa, in particular through facilitating voluntary return in a dignified and orderly manner;

12. *Appeals* to Governments, United Nations and non-governmental organizations and the international community to create conditions that can facilitate the voluntary return and the early rehabilitation and reintegration of refugees;

13. *Commends* the Governments of the Great Lakes region and the United Nations High Commissioner for Refugees on their initiatives to promote repatriation within the framework of tripartite agreements on voluntary repatriation of refugees in the region;

14. *Encourages* the Office of the United Nations High Commissioner for Refugees to continue to cooperate with the office of the United Nations High Commissioner for Human Rights in the promotion

and protection of human rights and fundamental freedoms in emergency humanitarian situations in Africa;

15. *Calls upon* the Office of the United Nations High Commissioner for Refugees, in conjunction with host Governments, United Nations and non-governmental organizations and the international community, to undertake an early assessment of the negative impacts of large refugee concentrations on the host communities, with a view to initiating timely and concrete measures to prevent damage and to assist in its repair, especially damage caused by mass refugee influxes to the environment and ecosystems in host countries;

16. *Notes with satisfaction* the voluntary return of millions of refugees to their homelands following the successful repatriation and reintegration operations carried out by the Office of the United Nations High Commissioner for Refugees, with the cooperation and collaboration of many countries hosting refugees, and looks forward to other programmes to assist the voluntary repatriation of all refugees in Africa;

17. *Expresses its concern* about the long stay of refugees in certain African countries, and calls upon the United Nations High Commissioner for Refugees to keep under review her programmes in those countries, taking into account the increasing requirements there;

18. *Expresses its appreciation* to the Secretary-General, the United Nations High Commissioner for Refugees, the specialized agencies, the International Committee of the Red Cross, the International Federation of Red Cross and Red Crescent Societies, donor countries and intergovernmental and non-governmental organizations for their assistance in mitigating the plight of the large number of refugees, returnees and displaced persons;

19. *Expresses the hope* that additional resources will be made available for general refugee programmes to keep pace with refugee needs;

20. *Calls upon* Governments, United Nations organizations, non-governmental organizations and the international community as a whole to strengthen the emergency response capacity of the Office of the United Nations High Commissioner for Refugees on the basis of the experience of the emergency in Rwanda, and to continue providing needed resources and operational support to Rwandese refugees and the host countries until a permanent solution can be implemented;

21. *Calls upon* the international donor community to provide material and financial assistance for the implementation of programmes intended for the rehabilitation of the environment and infrastructure in areas affected by refugees in countries of asylum;

22. *Calls upon* Member States and intergovernmental and non-governmental organizations to continue to provide the necessary support and financial assistance to the United Nations High Commissioner for Refugees to enhance her capacities and abilities to implement emergency operations, care and maintenance activities and repatriation and reintegration programmes for the benefit of refugees, returnees and, as appropriate, internally displaced persons;

23. *Appeals* to Member States and international and non-governmental organizations to provide adequate financial, material and technical assistance for relief and rehabilitation programmes for the large number of refugees, voluntary returnees and displaced persons and victims of natural disasters and to the affected countries;

24. *Requests* all Governments and intergovernmental and non-governmental organizations to pay particular attention to meeting the special needs of refugee women and children;

25. *Calls upon* the Secretary-General, the United Nations High Commissioner for Refugees, the Department of Humanitarian Affairs of the Secretariat, United Nations humanitarian organizations, the International Committee of the Red Cross, the International Federation of Red Cross and Red Crescent Societies, regional and international financial institutions, the International Organization for Migration and non-governmental organizations to increase the capacity for coordination and delivery of humanitarian emergency assistance and disaster relief in general, with States and others concerned in respect of asylum, relief, repatriation, rehabilitation and resettlement of refugees, returnees and displaced persons, including those refugees in urban areas;

26. *Requests* the United Nations High Commissioner for Refugees to review her general programmes in Africa to take account of the increasing requirements in that region and with a view to continuing her efforts and expanding her activities in close collaboration with the Organization of African Unity, regional organizations and governmental and non-governmental organizations in Africa, in order to consolidate aid and increase essential services to refugees, returnees and displaced persons;

27. *Requests* the Secretary-General to submit a comprehensive and consolidated report on the situation of refugees, returnees and displaced persons in Africa to the General Assembly at its fifty-first session, under the item entitled "Report of the United Nations High Commissioner for Refugees, questions relating to refugees, returnees and displaced persons and humanitarian questions", and an oral report to the Economic and Social Council at its substantive session of 1996.

General Assembly resolution 50/149

21 December 1995     Meeting 97     Adopted without vote

Approved by Third Committee (A/50/632) without vote, 21 November (meeting 34); draft by South Africa, for African Group (A/C.3/50/L.17), orally revised; agenda item 109.

*Meeting numbers.* GA 50th session: 3rd Committee 19-23, 25, 32-34; plenary 97.

In **resolution 50/58 K** of 22 December, the Assembly invited all States, UN institutions and intergovernmental and non-governmental organizations to continue to provide Burundi with assistance for economic recovery and to facilitate the voluntary repatriation of refugees.

In **resolution 50/58 L** of the same date, the Assembly encouraged Rwanda to pursue efforts to create conditions conducive to the return of refugees to their country.

### The Americas and the Caribbean

In a report on UNHCR's 1995 activities,[10] the High Commissioner stated that three developments had a major impact on UNHCR's work in the Americas and the Caribbean during the year. Political developments in Guatemala enhanced the repatriation process for the 12,000 Guatemalan refugees in Mexico; Mexico decided that Guatemalan refugees might stay in Mexico on a permanent basis; and the arrival of extra-continental asylum-seekers to countries in Latin America continued.

As durable solutions had been found for the majority of Central American refugees, UNHCR's task was to strengthen the capacity of Governments to deal with refugee-related matters and, as a means of prevention, to strengthen regional human rights institutions and ensure that development-oriented projects also targeted areas with major concentrations of persons of concern to UNHCR. In Belize, the quick-impact project (QIP) programme to facilitate the socio-economic integration of 8,100 refugees and undocumented persons continued. The QIP programme in El Salvador, which facilitated the integration of some 31,500 Salvadoran returnees, was completed in April. UNHCR continued with voluntary repatriation of individual cases and with the legal integration of those refugees opting to remain in their country of asylum. Some 9,500 Guatemalan refugees were repatriated from Mexico despite continuing security problems, the scarcity of available land, and the absence of a peace agreement, bringing the total number of returnees assisted by UNHCR since January 1993 to more than 20,000. The assistance programme in the Mexican states of Campeche and Quintana Roo increased the productivity of refugee settlements through joint programmes of credit and on-the-job training, helping refugees to become self-supporting. The transfer of responsibilities for infrastructure and services in those settlements to the Mexican authorities was initiated. Mexico, at the end of 1995, announced its intention to allow the local integration of those refugees not wishing to repatriate; the majority of them were expected to relocate to Campeche and Quintana Roo.

More than 1,100 Haitian refugees were repatriated during the year, leaving 937 still in the Dominican Republic, which continued discussions with UNHCR on finding durable solutions for them. The arrival of extra-continental asylum-seekers in South America and the Caribbean increased, reaching 80 per cent of all asylum-seekers compared to 13 per cent in 1994. The United States Congress was considering two proposed immigration bills. A Memorandum of Agreement between Canada and the United States on "Cooperation in Examination of Refugee Claims from Nationals of Third Countries" was also under consideration. In February, Canada announced that every adult immigrant and refugee must pay both "right-to-landing" and per-cost recovery fees.

Total UNHCR expenditures in the Americas and the Caribbean amounted to $34.9 million and the refugee population stood at just under 1 million.

## East and South Asia and Oceania

In a report covering 1995 UNHCR activities,[10] the High Commissioner stated that 62,000 Myanmar Muslim refugees had voluntarily repatriated from Bangladesh to their country's Rakhine State. Some 50,000 persons remaining in five camps in Bangladesh were expected to repatriate in 1996. More than 1,000 small-scale projects in returnee communities were funded by UNHCR. UNHCR staff monitored the welfare of the 93,250 refugees from Myanmar residing in Thailand. The Afghan urban refugee population in Delhi, India, decreased from 23,000 to 21,000 during the year. About 50 per cent of those refugees were receiving UNHCR assistance. Following the cessation of hostilities between Sri Lanka and the Liberation Tigers of Tamil Eelam in January, some 10,000 Sri Lankan refugees voluntarily repatriated from the Indian State of Tamil Nadu under UNHCR auspices. Some 52,000 refugees remained in camps in India and another 40,000 reportedly resided outside camps. Further repatriation of Sri Lankan refugees from India was hampered by the resumption of hostilities later in the year, precipitating the internal displacement of over 350,000 persons from the Jaffa peninsula. In December, Sri Lanka requested UNHCR assistance for up to 150,000 displaced persons in the Vanni region.

In Cambodia, UNHCR, in addition to assisting 20,300 vulnerable returnees, joined other UN agencies in providing relief to some 113,000 internally displaced persons. A total of 145 Cambodian refugees voluntarily returned home with UNHCR assistance, while some 370 remained in Association of South-East Asian Nations (ASEAN) countries pending return approval. UNHCR also monitored the safe return of 1,859 Cambodians of ethnic Vietnamese origin. The refugee population in China, as reported by the Government, increased slightly from 287,086 to 288,411 during the year. UNHCR assistance in China focused mainly on local settlement through support for revolving fund rural credit schemes.

In 1995, UNHCR expenditure in Asia and Oceania amounted to $95.8 million. The total number of refugees in the region stood at some 0.8 million.

### Comprehensive Plan of Action for Indo-Chinese Refugees

The Implementation of the Comprehensive Plan of Action for Indo-Chinese Refugees (CPA) continued in 1995. Agreements between Viet Nam, the host country, and UNHCR on modalities for the return of remaining Vietnamese non-refugees in camps were concluded in early 1995 with both Malaysia and the Philippines. Arrangements were discussed to simplify procedures for the return of all Vietnamese who did not qualify for refugee status. As of 31 March, there were 8,610

Lao in UNHCR-assisted camps in Thailand for whom durable solutions within the framework of CPA were being pursued. Voluntary repatriation was promoted for some 7,400 of them, while resettlement for 1,200 was being finalized. The Steering Committee of the International Conference on Indo-Chinese refugees (Geneva, 16 March) agreed that by the end of 1995 all CPA activities in first-asylum countries should be completed. The target would be met soon thereafter in Hong Kong. The Committee noted that a large number of Vietnamese who did not qualify for refugee status had refused voluntary repatriation. It recognized the significance of simplified procedures and the monthly target of the return to Viet Nam of at least 3,600 of remaining non-refugees in camps. UNHCR supported implementation of 109 community-based micro-projects, valued at $2.5 million, for returned Vietnamese refugees.

In an October conclusion,[3] the Executive Committee called on UNHCR to convene a meeting of the Steering Committee by the end of 1995 to assess the situation and to consider measures and durable solutions to ensure the successful conclusion of CPA. It appealed to the international community to support the repatriation of Indo-Chinese camp populations under voluntary repatriation and orderly return programmes, as well as developmental assistance to countries of origin for the reintegration of returnees. It called on countries of origin to continue to ensure reasonable access to returnees by intergovernmental and non-governmental organizations and requested all parties concerned to cooperate in implementing relevant memoranda of understanding and agreements relating to the repatriation of Indo-Chinese camp populations.

## Europe

In a report covering 1995 UNHCR activities,[10] the High Commissioner stated that the downward trend in requests from persons seeking asylum in Western Europe continued in 1995, due to restrictions by States on immigration. The number of applicants granted refugee status and those allowed to remain on special humanitarian grounds or under temporary protection also declined. The signing in December of the Peace Agreement for Bosnia and Herzegovina (see PART TWO, Chapter V) raised the question of the discontinuation of temporary protection for asylum-seekers from the former Yugoslavia in Europe and gave rise to the prospect of a large-scale return. UNHCR continued to engage in an informal dialogue with member States of the European Union (EU) on asylum and refugee matters.

In the former Yugoslavia, the worsening security situation in Bosnia and Herzegovina, following the failure of the warring parties to extend the

Cessation of Hostilities Agreement beyond March, adversely affected UNHCR's ability to provide assistance. The recapture of the Bihac pocket by the Bosnian Government from the Bosnian Serbs in August prompted the exodus of some 20,000 former inhabitants of Velaka Kladusa and Cazin who were loyal to the Bosnian rebel leader. When the situation improved, UNHCR launched a programme of voluntary repatriation to Bihac. In Banja Luka, continued pressure was placed on minority communities to leave the area, and the situation was further exacerbated by an influx of refugees from Western Slavonia. In May, 4,500 ethnic Serbs from Western Slavonia arrived in Sector East, while 2,500 fled to the Federal Republic of Yugoslavia (Serbia and Montenegro). The fall of the eastern Muslim enclaves of Srebrenica and Zepa in July to Bosnian Serb forces resulted in the forced exodus of 36,000 persons to the Tuzla and Zenica regions. The capture by Croat forces of Glamoc and Grahovo in late July also led to the flight of 14,000 Serbs to northern Bosnia, many of whom made their way to Banja Luka. In August, UNHCR aid supplies in Banja Luka were quickly exhausted, with a mass influx of some 200,000 refugees from Krajina. A major concern was the situation of the remaining Serb population in the Krajina. Human rights violations, including burning and looting of abandoned property, harassment and violence, were brought to the attention of Croatia, together with serious criticism from the international community. UNHCR supported the Federal Republic of Yugoslavia (Serbia and Montenegro) in efforts to cope with the influx of refugees from Krajina. It also requested the authorities to consider the estimated 800 Muslims from Zepa and Srebrenica detained in Mitrovo Polje and Slivovica in the Federal Republic as refugees.

In a 3 October statement,[22] the Security Council expressed concern at the withdrawal of refugee status from and the consequent ending of assistance to many refugees from Bosnia and Herzegovina in Croatia, as well as at the situations of refugees from Croatia wishing to return and of ethnic Serbs who had chosen to remain in Croatia. It urged Croatia to continue to provide asylum to all refugees regardless of their origin, and to lift any time-limits placed on the return of refugees to Croatia to claim their property.

In a 22 December statement,[23] the Council said that the requirement that owners should reclaim their property by 27 December 1995 was an insurmountable obstacle for most Serb refugees, and it demanded that Croatia lift the time-limit immediately (for details, see PART TWO, Chapter V).

The coming into effect of a cease-fire agreement towards the end of 1995 resulted in an agreement between the Croat and Muslim sides on return of displaced persons to contested areas in Central Bosnia and Sector East of Croatia. In accordance with the General Framework Agreement for Peace in Bosnia and Herzegovina, signed in Dayton, United States, in November, UNHCR was entrusted with the development and implementation of a repatriation plan for the orderly return of refugees and displaced persons.

In Central Europe, UNHCR efforts continued to be centred on influencing legislation with a view to establishing fair and accessible refugee status determination procedures. Its activities were also focused on institution- and capacity-building, training, and a limited assistance programme. The region was affected by large migratory movements where the distinction between migrants and genuine asylum-seekers was often blurred. UNHCR assisted refugee authorities in Central Europe by creating conditions conducive to integration; lack of affordable housing for asylum-seekers and refugees continued to be an obstacle.

In Eastern Europe, UNHCR continued to advocate strategies to pre-empt refugee-producing situations in the CIS countries. It assisted in developing an institutional capacity to provide solutions for displaced persons and was engaged in the search for a comprehensive approach to the problems of refugees, returnees, displaced persons and other forms of involuntary displacements in the CIS countries and neighbouring States in preparation for a regional conference (see above). In Armenia, UNHCR limited its intervention to the most vulnerable of the 150,000 refugees there. In October, Armenia adopted a law giving refugees of Armenian ethnic origin access to citizenship. UNHCR planned to facilitate the integration of the most needy among some 900,000 internally displaced persons and refugees in Azerbaijan, to strengthen Georgia's capacity to service its 200,000 internally displaced persons, and to initiate confidence-building measures to benefit the 35,000 persons who had returned to the Gali district in the Abkhaz region. UNHCR envisaged phasing out, by the end of 1995, its emergency operation in the North Caucasus for displaced populations from Chechnya in the Russian Federation, but new developments generated an additional influx of displaced persons into neighbouring republics. During the year, total UNHCR expenditure in Europe amounted to $291.9 million.

In an October conclusion,[3] the Executive Committee expressed concern for the fate of refugees and displaced and missing persons within and from the former Yugoslavia and called on countries of origin to create conditions for and to ensure the organized and phased return of refugees and displaced persons in safety and dignity, in cooperation with UNHCR, the host countries and the international community. The international community was asked to continue to contribute to ongoing humanitarian efforts, as well as to humanitarian and rehabilitation programmes to be undertaken within the framework of a possible peace settlement.

## South-West Asia, North Africa and the Middle East

In South-West Asia, North Africa and the Middle East, UNHCR programmes focused on capacity- and institution-building, particularly in the Central Asian Republics, the High Commissioner reported.[10] UNHCR bolstered its presence in Afghanistan in the hope of encouraging the repatriation of the 2.1 million Afghan refugees in Pakistan and Iran. In North Africa and the Middle East, incremental progress was made in planning and implementing durable solutions for relatively stable caseloads.

During 1995, 348,000 refugees returned to Afghanistan: 153,000 from Pakistan, of whom 77,000 were directly assisted by UNHCR, and 195,000 from Iran, with UNHCR assisting 92,000. Assistance activities to support repatriation shifted to communities inside Afghanistan. UNHCR implemented a total of 386 QIPs, mainly in the areas of education, irrigation and transport. The delivery of repatriation grants for returnees shifted from Quetta, Pakistan, to the southern Afghan city of Kandahar. A group-guaranteed lending programme for women in northern Afghanistan was initiated and additional credit programmes were under consideration. In Iran, host to the world's largest caseload of refugees—1,420,000 Afghans and 585,000 Iraqis (Kurds and Arabs)—the Government withdrew health and education subsidies, affecting both local and refugee populations. UNHCR initiated interim measures in those sectors to minimize any adverse impact on the welfare of the refugees.

The repatriation of refugees to Tajikistan from northern Afghanistan was lower in 1995 than projected, with 1,053 persons choosing to repatriate. The total number of returnees since 1993 was 43,000. Some 7,300 refugees remained in Sakhi Camp (Mazar), and an estimated 11,500 were scattered throughout the Kunduz province.

In North Africa, assistance continued for an estimated 50,000 refugees in southern Algeria, 28,000 from Mali and 22,000 from Niger. A pilot repatriation programme for Malians was initiated under a 1994 agreement signed by Algeria, Mali, IFAD and UNHCR,[24] but the situation in northern Mali delayed the implementation of mass organized repatriation. Still, some 8,000 Malians and 245 refugees from Niger were reported to have repatriated. The situation in northern Mali also impeded large-scale repatriation of refugees from Mauritania. In November, an UNHCR pilot proj-

ect for organized repatriation was implemented, benefiting 2,247 refugees. In the context of the plan to identify and register potential voters for the referendum in Western Sahara (see PART ONE, Chapter III), a UNHCR technical team visited various sites and potential repatriation locations in the territory, as well as the Tindouf (Algeria) camps, to collect information to update the 1991 UNHCR repatriation plan.[25]

In the Middle East, UNHCR helped 7,349 Iraqi Kurds to return home, notably from Iran. In Iraq, it assisted some 16,000 Turkish nationals of Kurdish origin; 38,500 Iranian refugees; and 556 refugees of other origins. No progress was reported in the exchange of refugees between Iran and Iraq. However, UNHCR continued to liaise with both parties to ensure an organized movement of those persons wanting to return. Saudi Arabia continued to assist Iraqi refugees in Rafha Camp. Some 4,430 persons were resettled in more than 10 countries, while 520 persons were repatriated. UNHCR also assisted Palestinians expelled from the Libyan Arab Jamahiriya and stranded at Salloum on the Egyptian border. A new camp location was identified at Shukrah in Yemen to host some 9,000 Somali refugees.

In the Central Asian Republics, the UNHCR objective was to assist Governments and operational partners to create conditions for the efficient management of population movements. In August/September, liaison offices were opened in Kazakstan, Kyrgyzstan and Turkmenistan. Of over 500,000 Tajik internally displaced persons who had left their homes in 1992, 95 per cent had returned to their places of origin by the end of 1995. Some 14,000 internally displaced persons remained in the Gorno-Badakhshan region and 43,000 refugees from Tajikistan who had fled to northern Afghanistan were repatriated with UNHCR assistance, leaving 17,600 Tajiks in Afghanistan. With the return of the majority of Tajik refugees and internally displaced persons to their places of origin, UNHCR in late 1995 neared the end of a three-year operation providing materials to reconstruct 18,000 houses for Tajik returnees. UNHCR launched resettlement projects in Kazakstan for refugees of Kazak ethnic origin and in Kyrgyzstan for those of Kyrgyz ethnic origin.

Total UNHCR expenditure for South-West Asia, North Africa and the Middle East amounted to some $106 million.

In an October conclusion,[3] the Executive Committee called for continued international support for the Afghan refugees in Iran and Pakistan and their early repatriation. The international community should support a comprehensive approach to the return of Afghan refugees and rehabilitation of affected areas. The High Commissioner was asked to: maintain UNHCR activities in

Afghanistan and its neighbouring countries still hosting large numbers of refugees and to collaborate with the Governments concerned, other international humanitarian agencies and NGOs to provide assistance to refugee areas; extend UNHCR activities to other areas of return, through collaborative ventures with UN agencies that would maximize benefits to communities receiving returnees; and continue to mobilize the involvement of international and multilateral organizations as part of the rehabilitation strategy to sustain repatriation.

*REFERENCES*

[1]YUN 1994, p. 1221, GA res. 49/173, 23 Dec. 1994. [2]A/50/414. [3]A/50/12/Add.1. [4]A/AC.96/850. [5]YUN 1951, p. 520. [6]YUN 1967, p. 477. [7]YUN 1961, p. 533. [8]*Multilateral Treaties Deposited with the Secretary General: Status as at 31 December 1995* (ST/LEG/SER.E/14), Sales No. E.96.V.5. [9]YUN 1954, p. 416. [10]E/1996/52. [11]YUN 1994, p. 1223. [12]Ibid., p. 1224, GA res. 49/172, 23 Dec. 1994. [13]A/50/555. [14]S/PRST/1995/7. [15]S/PRST/1995/41. [16]A/50/647. [17]E/1995/SR.47. [18]YUN 1994, p. 1226, GA res. 49/174, 23 Dec. 1994. [19]A/50/413. [20]A/50/541 & Add.1. [21]YUN 1994, p. 280, GA res. 49/7, 25 Oct. 1994. [22]S/PRST/1995/49. [23]S/PRST/1995/63. [24]YUN 1994, p. 1234. [25]YUN 1991, p. 793.

Chapter XIII

# Health, food and nutrition

In 1995, the United Nations continued to promote human health, deliver food aid and monitor trends in nutrition.

The Executive Board of the United Nations Children's Fund endorsed a strategy as a framework for UNICEF activities in the health sector. Further progress was made towards making the Joint and Co-sponsored UN Programme on Human Immunodeficiency Virus/Acquired Immunodeficiency Syndrome operational. In July, the Economic and Social Council endorsed arrangements for governing and managing the Joint Programme and for the participation of non-governmental organizations. The Council and the General Assembly also endorsed the strategies and workplans developed by the UN system to support countries in the prevention and control of malaria and diarrhoeal diseases, in particular cholera. In other action, the Assembly urged Governments and organizations to continue strengthening efforts to implement the Standard Rules on the Equalization of Opportunities for Persons with Disabilities and the Long-term Strategy to Implement the World Programme of Action concerning Disabled Persons to the Year 2000 and Beyond.

The World Food Programme (WFP)—a joint undertaking of the United Nations and the Food and Agriculture Organization of the United Nations—provided in 1995 over 2.8 million tons of food aid to some 50 million of the poorest people in the world, half of them victims of emergencies. The Assembly reconstituted the Committee on Food Aid Policies and Programmes of WFP into an Executive Board and approved revised General Regulations for the Programme. WFP also adopted on a trial basis, beginning in 1996, new policies designed to place its resources and long-term financing on a more sound and predictable basis. The Assembly invited Governments to participate at the level of heads of State or Government in the World Food Summit to be held in November 1996, and invited the international community to contribute to the fund established to facilitate the preparations for and holding of the Summit.

The United Nations University, an autonomous academic institution within the UN system, continued activities under its programme of food and nutrition for human and social development.

## Health

### Health policy

#### Health strategy for UNICEF

The United Nations Children's Fund (UNICEF) presented to its Executive Board in September a report on a health strategy for UNICEF,[1] proposing a framework for UNICEF activities in the context of community-focused health sector development. The report discussed how UNICEF strategies—which focused on reducing infant, child and maternal mortality and on improving children's health and nutrition through helping strengthen countries' capacities in health monitoring, promotion and essential health services within the primary health care approach—could be adapted and applied in diverse situations, including states of emergency. The report emphasized the complementarity between broader UNICEF advocacy, which addressed a range of child, adolescent and women's health issues, and programme support priorities within specific countries.

The implications for UNICEF of the proposed health strategy included the strengthening and rationalization of its core technical capacity, increased emphasis on strengthening technical partnerships and coordination with the World Health Organization (WHO) and other international and bilateral agencies, refinements in situation analyses, strengthened information and operations research capacities required to guide programming and partnership processes, and increased flexibility in supply and financial operations to better serve programme objectives.

The UNICEF Executive Board, in September, endorsed[2] the strategy as a framework for UNICEF activities in the health sector and stressed the need for speedy operationalization through the country programmes. It requested the Executive Director to report in 1996 on implementation of the strategy and emphasized that resources allocated for health programmes at the country level should be based on the priorities contained in the strategy. The Board urged UNICEF to participate with WHO and other partners in reviewing and updating the Global Strategy for Health for All by the Year 2000, adopted by the World Health Assembly in 1981[3] and endorsed by the General Assembly in the same year,[4] and to review implementation of the UNICEF health strategy and programme towards the goals of the 1990 World Summit for Children in the light of the revised Health for All Strategy.

### Human health and sustainable development

The UNICEF/WHO Joint Committee on Health Policy held its thirtieth session in Geneva, on 30 and 31 January,[5] to review WHO policies and UNICEF action; consider preparations for the 1995 mid-decade review of progress in implementing the goals of the 1990 World Summit for Children in the area of health; and discuss options for improving district health systems development in a decentralizing situation, and the complementarity of UNICEF and WHO in emergency situations, with particular reference to women and children.

The Joint Committee recommended that a message be conveyed to the World Summit for Social Development (see PART FOUR, Chapter IX), calling on heads of State to give high priority to monitoring progress towards health for all and the World Summit for Children goals, with national mid-decade reviews that gave special attention to the mid-decade health goals as stepping stones towards those for the year 2000. WHO, UNICEF and other international agencies should collaborate in assisting countries to monitor progress, using multiple indicator surveys in health and health-related sectors. The two organizations should also assess progress on the health goals at mid-decade as a basis for the Secretary-General's review in 1996. The Joint Committee further made recommendations for action aimed at achieving the mid-decade goals relating to immunization coverage, neonatal tetanus, measles deaths and cases, and poliomyelitis, as well as on oral rehydration therapy/diarrhoea case management; empowerment of women to breast-feed their children; iodine deficiency disorders; vitamin A deficiency and reduction of malnutrition; guinea-worm transmission; water and sanitation; knowledge of HIV/AIDS-related preventive practices; reduction of maternal and infant mortality rates and of iron deficiency anaemia; and acute respiratory infections.

The UNICEF Executive Board, in March, took note[6] of the Joint Committee's report and recommendations and requested the UNICEF secretariat to consult with concerned parties on the draft UNICEF health strategy in preparation for submission to the Board (see above), in order to promote its implementation at the country level.

In May, the WHO Executive Board endorsed[7] the Joint Committee's recommendations, in particular those pertaining to the end-of-decade goals set by the 1990 World Summit for Children.

**Action by the Commission on Sustainable Development.** At its third session in April,[8] the Commission on Sustainable Development (see PART FOUR, Chapter I) considered an April report of the Secretary-General[9] on progress in implementing the decisions and recommendations taken by the Commission at its May 1994 session, including those[10] relating to chapter 6 (protecting and promoting human health) of Agenda 21, adopted by the 1992 UN Conference on Environment and Development.[11]

The Commission noted that a joint WHO/United Nations Development Programme (UNDP) interregional initiative had so far succeeded in incorporating health- and environment-related concerns in the preparation of national plans for sustainable development in 12 countries. Regional initiatives relating health more closely to environment within the context of sustainable development had led to the creation of an Environment Health Action Plan for Europe and preparatory work for a Pan-American Conference on Health and the Environment in Sustainable Development.

The Commission also considered a March report of the Secretary-General,[12] which dealt with, among others, programme area B (improving human health) of chapter 16 (on the environmentally sound management of biotechnology) of Agenda 21.[11] The Commission urged Governments to take specific action, within the framework of the 1993 Convention on Biological Diversity,[13] aimed at enhancing the potential contribution of the private sector, financial, academic and research institutions, non-governmental organizations (NGOs) and other major groups to the implementation of the objectives of chapter 16.

### AIDS prevention and control

At its resumed organizational session in May 1995, the Economic and Social Council considered the Joint and Co-sponsored UN Programme on Human Immunodeficiency Virus/ Acquired Immunodeficiency Syndrome (UN-AIDS), which it had endorsed in 1994.[14] The Council had before it a May report[15] of the 1994 Council President, the Permanent Representative of Australia, on informal consultations on the question of the composition of the Programme Coordination Board (PCB) for UN-AIDS. He stated that agreement had been reached that the Board would comprise 22 members (5 each from African and Asian States, including Japan; 3 from Latin American and Caribbean States; 2 from Eastern European States and 7 from Western European and other States) elected for a three-year term. It was proposed that the first election be held by the

Council on 1 June, at which time it was expected that the Council would meet to consider further the programme of work of UNAIDS, on the basis, *inter alia*, of the report of the Committee of Co-sponsoring Organizations (CCO).

The Council, by **decision 1995/223** of 5 May, approved the composition of PCB as recommended and decided to continue informal consultations on the representation on the Board of the six co-sponsoring organizations (UNDP, the United Nations Educational, Scientific and Cultural Organization (UNESCO), the United Nations Population Fund (UNFPA), UNICEF, WHO and the World Bank) and NGOs; and on which body or bodies would conduct elections subsequent to the first, which would be conducted by the Council.

At its substantive session (June/July), the Council considered the report of CCO on UNAIDS, transmitted by the Secretary-General in May,[16] as requested by the Council in 1994.[14] The report examined the HIV/AIDS epidemic; the background to the establishment of the Joint Programme, its mission, priorities and strategies, and its functions; the terms and conditions of co-sponsorship, governance and management of the Programme; resource mobilization; and an outline of a proposed budget for 1996-1997. UNAIDS was to address the major strategic and policy issues of HIV/AIDS, advocate and catalyse a strong global response to the epidemic, ensure coordinated support by the co-sponsoring organizations to national AIDS programmes, and promote and support research of relevance to the developing countries. It was to act in partnership with other UN agencies, bilateral organizations, community-based groups, NGOs, the private sector and academic institutions, and would involve people with HIV infection and AIDS in all areas of its work. At the global level, UNAIDS would consist of staff representing a "critical mass" of expertise, and of activities in the areas of advocacy, strategic and policy guidance, research, support to country-level coordination, technical support to national AIDS programmes, and monitoring of the epidemic and of national and international responses to it. At the country level, where the mandate was to strengthen national capacity to respond to HIV/AIDS, the Joint Programme would work primarily through the theme groups on HIV/AIDS established by the resident coordinator. The policies developed by UN-AIDS would become part of each co-sponsor's mainstream activities at the country level, with HIV/AIDS-related activities being integrated into all relevant programme activities and the experience gained fed back into the Joint Programme.

The Programme's financial requirements in 1996-1997 were estimated at $180 million, excluding funds provided directly by the co-sponsoring agencies to the theme groups and national AIDS

programmes. PCB would serve as the governance structure, taking responsibility for all policy and budgetary matters and representing the interests and responsibilities of Governments, co-sponsoring organizations and other interested parties. CCO—composed of one representative from each of the co-sponsors—would serve as a standing committee of PCB to consider matters of major importance to the Programme. The Programme director would report to PCB, after consultation with CCO, on all major programmes and budget and operational issues, while the Council would review the annual report on the work of the Programme. A legal instrument setting out the conditions of co-ownership and co-sponsorship of the Joint Programme, its collaborating parties and resources, the functions and composition of its governing bodies and its financial arrangements was to be drafted by the co-sponsoring organizations. A memorandum of understanding between UN-AIDS and WHO, which would be responsible for the administration in support of the Programme, would also be drawn up.

The Council also had before it a report of the Director-General of WHO, transmitted in May by the Secretary-General,[17] on progress in implementing the global strategy for the prevention and control of AIDS, which described activities carried out by the WHO Global Programme on AIDS and by UN organizations and specialized agencies in 1993-1994. The Council, by **decision 1995/234** of 19 July, and the General Assembly, by **decision 50/439** of 20 December, took note of the report.

**UNDP/UNFPA action.** In a February report,[18] the UNDP Administrator stated that the recruitment process for HIV and Development National Professional Officers (NPOs), who worked in collaboration with their colleagues in the other co-sponsoring agencies of UNAIDS, was nearing completion, with more than half of the posts filled. The activities carried out by the HIV and Development NPOs reflected UNDP's focus on national capacity-strengthening and broad-based programming that was both effective and sustainable. Developing partnerships with civil society groups and institutions was also a feature of their work. NPOs played a crucial part in supporting efforts to improve the coordination of UN agencies in their HIV-related work, particularly in Honduras and Swaziland, through the provision of secretariat services for inter-agency HIV task forces and theme groups.

On 7 April, the UNDP/UNFPA Executive Board urged[19] that the UNDP Administrator and the Executive Director of UNFPA, in the framework of UNAIDS, implement the declaration of the 1994 Paris AIDS summit[20] and develop a strategy for including HIV/AIDS components in their regular activities. The Board urged the

Administrator to ensure that the HIV and Development NPOs carried out their duties in close collaboration and in accordance with the objectives of UNAIDS.

The Administrator, in a November report,[21] stated that UNDP had continued to support the development of UNAIDS. It had seconded a senior staff member to UNAIDS and was reviewing contributions in cash and in kind to global UNAIDS activities for 1996-1997. It continued to work closely with the Programme to develop an approach at the country level. The Administrator had requested all resident coordinators to begin in-country consultations on how best to support and/or strengthen UN theme groups on HIV/AIDS. In collaboration with UNAIDS, UNDP continued to undertake its HIV and development programme activities, including programme development, support and backstopping to integrate HIV activities more effectively into key UNDP programming areas. UNDP had given high priority to strengthening its country offices and to developing the capacity of resident representatives to mainstream HIV activities in a development context. The 22 NPOs were playing an important role in that regard. UNDP was also working with UNAIDS and its co-sponsoring partners to strengthen the implementation of UN HIV and AIDS personnel policy. Total UNDP HIV and development–related activities and staff support for 1994-1995 amounted to $71.8 million. Discussions were being held with UNAIDS and the other co-sponsors to fine-tune planned HIV activities for 1996-1997 and to ensure enhanced cooperation. Consultations were also going on regarding regional activities and to secure additional financing.

UNFPA, also in a November report,[22] outlined its support for and collaboration in UNAIDS, which included the secondment of a staff member to the Programme since December 1994 and a grant to the HIV/AIDS task force for the production of the biennial report on global activities. UNFPA, in agreement with WHO, considered that family planning, maternal care, prevention of abortion and prevention of reproductive-tract infections, including sexually transmitted diseases and HIV/AIDS, were the four most important components of reproductive health. By promoting and supporting effective intervention in those four areas, UNFPA said it would continue to work towards securing and safeguarding reproductive health for everyone.

**UNICEF action.** The UNICEF Executive Board, in March, urged[23] that the UNICEF secretariat participate actively in UNAIDS and support the Director of the Programme, and that steps be taken to implement the 1994 declaration of the Paris summit[20] in the context of UNAIDS. It requested the secretariat to develop a strategy for the inclusion of HIV/AIDS components in its programmes and regular activities within the framework of UNAIDS.

**Action by the Commission on Human Rights.** In March, the Commission on Human Rights adopted a resolution[24] on the protection of human rights in the context of HIV/AIDS (see PART THREE, Chapter II), by which it requested the co-sponsors of UNAIDS to integrate a strong human rights component throughout its strategies and work. It also requested the High Commissioner for Human Rights, in cooperation with UNAIDS, non-governmental agencies and other actors in the field, to elaborate guidelines on promoting and protecting respect for human rights in the context of HIV/AIDS and to consider convening a second international expert consultation on human rights and AIDS.

ECONOMIC AND SOCIAL COUNCIL ACTION

On 3 July, the Economic and Social Council adopted **resolution 1995/2**.

**Joint and Co-sponsored United Nations Programme on Human Immunodeficiency Virus/ Acquired Immunodeficiency Syndrome (HIV/AIDS)**

*The Economic and Social Council,*

*Recalling* its resolution 1994/24 of 26 July 1994 concerning the Joint and Co-sponsored United Nations Programme on Human Immunodeficiency Virus/Acquired Immunodeficiency Syndrome (HIV/AIDS) which was established to provide an internationally coordinated response to the HIV/AIDS pandemic, to provide global leadership in response to the epidemic and to achieve and promote global consensus on policy and programmatic approaches to the fight against HIV/AIDS.

*Recalling also* that the Programme is charged with promoting broad-based political and social mobilization to prevent and respond to HIV/AIDS within countries, ensuring that national responses involve a wide range of sectors and institutions and advocating greater political commitment in responding to the epidemic at the global and country levels, including the mobilization and allocation of adequate resources for HIV/AIDS-related activities.

*Emphasizing* the urgent need to make the Programme operational as soon as possible, but no later than January 1996,

1. *Welcomes* the report of the Committee of Co-sponsoring Organizations of the Joint and Co-sponsored United Nations Programme on HIV/AIDS, which will be of assistance in the further consideration of the operations of the new Programme, while recognizing the modifications that have been made to the arrangements set out in the report, as outlined by the Chairperson of the Committee, and the need for the Programme to operate in accordance with the provisions of Council resolution 1994/24;

2. *Endorses* the arrangements outlined in section VI of the report of the Committee (Governance and management) and decides to add the following to the functions of the Programme Coordination Board listed in paragraph 101 of the report:

*(a)* To establish broad policies and priorities for the Programme, taking into account the provisions of General Assembly resolution 47/199 of 22 December 1992;

*(b)* To make recommendations to the co-sponsoring organizations regarding their activities in support of the Programme, including those of mainstreaming;

3. *Requests* the Programme Coordination Board to give detailed consideration to the report of the Committee and to agree on the modalities for implementation of the arrangements set out in that report, taking into account the changes referred to in paragraphs 1 and 2 above;

4. *Calls upon* the co-sponsoring organizations, as soon as possible, to finalize and sign a legal document in the form of a memorandum of understanding outlining the responsibilities and functions of the co-sponsors, consistent with the provisions of Council resolution 1994/24, and to submit that document to the Council, through the Programme Coordination Board at its first substantive session, for consideration at a resumed session;

5. *Requests* the Executive Director of the Joint and Co-sponsored United Nations Programme on HIV/AIDS to report on the status of implementation of the new Programme, through the Board, to the Council early in 1996;

6. *Decides* that each of the six co-sponsors will participate in the work of the Programme Coordination Board and have full rights, except the right to vote;

7. *Decides also* that five non-governmental organizations will be invited to take part in the work of the Programme Coordination Board, in accordance with the report on the informal consultations on arrangements with regard to the participation of non-governmental organizations in the work of the Board, submitted to the Economic and Social Council by the Permanent Representative of Australia to the United Nations and annexed to the present resolution;

8. *Calls upon* each of the six co-sponsoring organizations to give their full support to the establishment of, transition to and smooth functioning of the Programme;

9. *Appeals* to all Governments, international institutions, non-governmental organizations and the private sector to support the Programme with adequate contributions to its resources;

10. *Decides* that the participation, as observers, of Member States and non-member States that are not members of the Board, in the work of the Board, should be consistent with the rules of procedure of the Council.

## ANNEX
**Arrangements for the participation of non-governmental organizations in the work of the Programme Coordination Board of the Joint and Co-sponsored United Nations Programme on Human Immunodeficiency Virus/ Acquired Immunodeficiency Syndrome (HIV/AIDS):**
### report on the informal consultation of the Economic and Social Council

1. The meeting on 9 June 1995 considered the question of the final arrangements for the Programme Coordination Board of the Joint and Co-sponsored United Nations Programme on Human Immunodeficiency Virus/Acquired Immunodeficiency Syndrome (HIV/AIDS), particularly the participation of nongovernmental organizations, and the report of the Committee of Co-sponsoring Organizations of the Joint and Co-sponsored United Nations Programme on

HIV/AIDS. The Board is a governance structure composed of Member States, with the participation of the six co-sponsors and eligible non-governmental organizations.

2. The deliberations of the meeting are summarized in the following terms:

*(a)* Non-governmental organizations would be invited to take part in the work of the Programme Coordination Board. Such invitations would need to be reviewed periodically. Non-governmental organizations invited should be those either in consultative status with the Economic and Social Council or in relationship with one of the six co-sponsoring organizations or on the roster of non-governmental organizations dealing with matters pertaining to HIV/AIDS, in accordance with the rules, procedures and well-established practice of the United Nations system;

*(b)* The process of identification of the nongovernmental organizations that sought to participate in the work of the Programme Coordination Board would be determined by the non-governmental organizations themselves. The Board would formally approve the nomination of those organizations;

*(c)* There would be five such non-governmental participants, three from developing countries and two from developed countries and countries with economies in transition;

*(d)* In making the selection, non-governmental organizations would be encouraged to seek competent and relevant representatives, for example participation by groups concerned with economic and social development and groups representing people affected by HIV/AIDS;

*(e)* The need for rotation among non-governmental organizations was recognized; the appointment of an individual organization should not exceed three years;

*(f)* Non-governmental organizations would be advised of the terms and conditions of their participation. It would be made clear to them that such participation would include:

A seat at the table with six representatives of the Committee of Co-sponsoring Organizations and the twenty-two Member States;

Non-governmental organizations would be able to speak;

Non-governmental organizations would have no negotiating role;

Non-governmental organizations would not participate in any part of the formal decision-making process, including the right to vote, which is reserved for representatives of Governments;

*(g)* These arrangements for the participation of nongovernmental organizations are not to be regarded as setting a precedent;

*(h)* Funding would be made available for the representatives of developing countries and for each of the three non-governmental organizations from developing countries to cover the costs of one representative each to attend meetings of the Programme Coordination Board. Such funds would cover the cost of daily subsistence allowance and travel only and would be based on existing eligibility criteria.

3. It was also recommended that the Economic and Social Council should review the Programme at its organizational session for 1996.

Economic and Social Council resolution 1995/2

3 July 1995          Meeting 21          Adopted without vote

Draft by Australia (E/1995/L.24/Rev.1); agenda item 6 (I).

**Follow-up action.** At its first meeting (Geneva, 13-14 July), PCB reviewed indicative budgetary proposals for 1996-1997 and requested that an overall budget be developed for the first biennium. It authorized the Executive Director of the Programme to proceed with the recruitment of staff and adopted the *modus operandi* for its operations. At its second meeting (Geneva, 13-15 November), PCB adopted the strategic plan for the Programme for 1996-2000 and approved the proposed programme budget for 1996-1997 in the amount of $120 million. The mode of operations for the Programme at the country level was endorsed, on the understanding that some of the operational issues would be further defined. The Board established informal working groups to discuss resource mobilization and indicators and evaluation.

The Memorandum of Understanding on the Programme was agreed on and signed by the six co-sponsoring organizations. A letter of agreement was signed between WHO and the Programme for the provision of administrative and financial services.

## Malaria and diarrhoeal diseases

The Secretary-General presented in May a report[25] on preventive action and intensification of the struggle against malaria in developing countries, particularly in Africa, as requested by the Economic and Social Council[26] and the General Assembly[27] in 1994. The report outlined the action plans for preventing and controlling malaria and diarrhoeal diseases, including cholera, developed in collaboration with relevant UN organizations, with WHO acting as task manager. The action plans covered goals and objectives, work plans, time-frames and resources needed.

The Secretary-General stressed that urgent action was needed to prevent and control those diseases that especially affected developing countries, impeding social and economic development and contributing to a vicious disease-malnutrition-poverty-disease cycle. Increased resources were needed from individual countries, the UN system and other bodies to apply and improve existing knowledge and tools. Progress in preventing and controlling malaria and diarrhoeal diseases provided an index of the success of current development policies. With concerted efforts, the world could enter the next century having made significant advances in conquering those diseases and reaffirming the efficacy of coordinated UN action in support of Member States.

On 28 July, the Economic and Social Council adopted **resolution 1995/63**.

**Malaria and diarrhoeal diseases,
in particular cholera**

*The Economic and Social Council,*

*Recalling* the agreed conclusions of the coordination segment of its substantive session of 1993, its resolution 1994/34 of 29 July 1994 and General Assembly resolution 49/135 of 19 December 1994,

1. *Welcomes* the report of the Secretary-General on preventive action and intensification of the struggle against malaria in developing countries, particularly in Africa;

2. *Endorses* the strategies and workplans which have been developed as a collaborative process involving relevant organizations, agencies, organs and programmes of the United Nations system, with the World Health Organization as task manager, to provide optimal support to countries in order to achieve the national and internationally accepted goals and objectives for the prevention and control of malaria and diarrhoeal diseases, in particular cholera;

3. *Stresses* the urgent need to prevent and control these diseases and, to that end, calls on the international community, especially industrialized countries, to expand, where possible, fund-raising channels and to provide adequate financial resources to countries where the diseases are endemic, especially the least developed countries, for the successful implementation of the workplans and the achievement of a significant impact in both the short and medium term, while recognizing that basic and applied research, including research on vaccines, is a priority component of such workplans;

4. *Welcomes with satisfaction* the agreement signed between Dr. Manual Elkin Patarroyo of Colombia and the World Health Organization during the forty-eighth World Health Assembly, in May 1995, by which Dr. Patarroyo donated to the World Health Organization the licence of the patent rights and know-how related to the SPf66 anti-malarial vaccine developed by him, and stresses the importance of the World Health Organization urgently taking full advantage of this donation;

5. *Notes* that the actions relating to the development and donation of this vaccine constitute an example of effective South-South cooperation for development through the United Nations system;

6. *Urges* the Director-General of the World Health Organization, the lead agency in international health, to continue to provide, in collaboration with the concerned United Nations agencies and programmes and within the United Nations resident coordinator system, technical expertise and support for the agreed strategies and workplans in support of national health development plans and actions in countries where malaria and diarrhoeal diseases, particularly cholera, are rife;

7. *Requests* the Secretary-General to submit to the Economic and Social Council, at its substantive session of 1998, the report of the Director-General of the World Health Organization on the implementation of the strategies and workplans presented to the Council at its substantive session of 1995, to be prepared in collabo-

ration with the other relevant organizations, organs, bodies and programmes of the United Nations system.

Economic and Social Council resolution 1995/63

28 July 1995          Meeting 57          Adopted without vote

Draft by Philippines, for Group of 77 and China (E/1995/L.54), orally revised following informal consultations; agenda item 9 *(d)*.
*Meeting numbers.* ESC 56, 57.

**GENERAL ASSEMBLY ACTION**

The General Assembly, on 20 December, adopted **resolution 50/128**.

**Preventive action and intensification of the struggle against malaria in developing countries, particularly in Africa**

*The General Assembly,*

*Reaffirming* its resolution 49/135 of 19 December 1994,

*Recalling* Economic and Social Council resolutions 1994/34 of 29 July 1994 and 1995/63 of 28 July 1995,

*Gravely concerned* by the fact that malaria causes the death of four million people annually, that hundreds of millions of cases of malaria are reported annually and that infants and children under age five are the major victims,

*Alarmed* by the loss of human life, the severe degradation in the quality of life and the fact that the social and economic development of developing countries is impeded as a result of malaria, and despite the development of new vaccines,

*Recalling* agreed conclusions 1993/2 of the coordination segment of the substantive session of 1993 of the Economic and Social Council on the coordination of the policies and activities of the specialized agencies and other bodies of the United Nations system in the fields of preventive action and intensification of the struggle against malaria and diarrhoeal diseases, in particular cholera,

*Acknowledging* the importance for countries where malaria is endemic of adopting national plans of action in conformity with the Global Malaria Control Strategy of the World Health Organization, endorsed by the Ministerial Conference on Malaria held at Amsterdam in 1992 and by the World Health Assembly in 1993,

1. *Welcomes* the report of the Secretary-General on preventive action and intensification of the struggle against malaria in developing countries, particularly in Africa;

2. *Reaffirms its endorsement* of the Global Malaria Control Strategy of the World Health Organization, as adopted;

3. *Expresses its appreciation* of the efforts of the World Health Organization and the specialized agencies concerned in assisting the developing countries in their efforts to combat endemic diseases;

4. *Notes with appreciation* the continuing efforts of the affected countries to control the disease, in spite of their meagre resources, through national plans and projects, and urges the affected countries that have not yet done so to adopt national plans to control malaria in conformity with the Global Strategy of the World Health Organization;

5. *Stresses* the need for strengthening national capacity-building within the context of primary health care so as to enable developing countries to meet the

objectives of the Global Strategy, with a view to contributing to the development of overall health;

6. *Endorses* the strategies and work plans that have been developed through a collaborative process involving relevant organs, organizations and programmes of the United Nations system, with the World Health Organization as task coordinator, to provide optimal support to affected developing countries in order to achieve the goals and objectives pertaining to the prevention and control of malaria and diarrhoeal diseases;

7. *Calls upon* the international community, in particular the donor countries, to expand, where possible, fund-raising channels and to provide adequate financial resources and medical and technical assistance to the affected developing countries, in particular African countries and least developed countries, for the successful implementation of work plans and projects and the achievement of significant progress in both the short and the medium term in controlling malaria, and to intensify basic and applied research on anti-malarial vaccines as a priority;

8. *Encourages* the Director-General of the World Health Organization, through the World Health Organization's Division of Control of Tropical Diseases, to continue his efforts to mobilize international organizations, multilateral financial institutions, the specialized agencies, organs and programmes of the United Nations system and non-governmental organizations as well as other groups to provide the affected developing countries, in particular African countries, with technical, medical and financial resources and assistance commensurate with the needs set forth in those countries' national plans to control malaria;

9. *Welcomes* the proposal of the Secretary-General related to the struggle against malaria in Africa contained in his initiatives for Africa;

10. *Welcomes with satisfaction* the agreement signed between Dr. Manual Elkin Patarroyo of Colombia and the World Health Organization, in May 1995, by which Dr. Patarroyo donated to the World Health Organization the licence of the patent rights and know-how related to the SPf66 anti-malarial vaccine developed by him, which constitutes an example of solidarity and effective South-South cooperation for development, and supports the request of the World Health Organization for the provision of additional resources for malaria research under the United Nations Development Programme/World Bank/World Health Organization Special Programme for Research and Training in Tropical Diseases in order to accomplish its goal of developing an effective vaccine for the control of malaria;

11. *Requests* the Secretary-General to transmit to the General Assembly at its fifty-first session the progress report of the Director-General of the World Health Organization on the implementation of the strategies and work plans to be prepared in collaboration with the other relevant organs, organizations, bodies and programmes of the United Nations system.

General Assembly resolution 50/128

20 December 1995          Meeting 96          Adopted without vote

Approved by Second Committee (A/50/615/Add.1) without vote, 30 November (meeting 40); draft by Vice-Chairman (A/C.2/50/L.42), based on informal consultations on draft by Philippines, for Group of 77 and China (A/C.2/50/L.10); agenda item 12.
*Meeting numbers.* GA 50th session: 2nd Committee 15, 16, 29, 40; plenary 96.

## Disabled persons

### _Implementation of the Programme of Action_

Responding to a 1993 General Assembly request,[28] the Secretary-General in September 1995 reported[29] on the implementation of the 1982 World Programme of Action concerning Disabled Persons,[30] and on the progress of efforts to ensure the equalization of opportunities and full inclusion of persons with disabilities in the various UN bodies. According to the report, a task force was established at UN Headquarters in January, at the initiative of the Department for Policy Coordination and Sustainable Development, to review steps that might increase the Organization's responsiveness to the needs of delegates, staff and visitors with disabilities. The task force would develop a phased approach and implementation plan covering the years 1996-2000 to ensure full accessibility to UN facilities. The Secretariat was informing the specialized agencies and other organizations of the experience gained and requesting information on measures taken and problems encountered in making buildings, conferences, information and documents fully accessible.

The General Assembly, by **decision 50/442** of 21 December, took note of the Secretary-General's report.

### _Standard Rules on the Equalization of Opportunities for Persons with Disabilities_

The World Summit for Social Development, in its Programme of Action (see PART FOUR, Chapter IX), recommended that governmental responses to special social needs should include, among others, promoting the United Nations Standard Rules on the Equalization of Opportunities for Persons with Disabilities, adopted in 1993,[31] and developing strategies for implementing those Rules. Governments, in collaboration with organizations of people with disabilities and the private sector, should work towards the equalization of opportunities so that people with disabilities could contribute to and benefit from full participation in society. An International NGO Conference for Disability (Copenhagen, 3 March), organized by the Danish Council of Organizations of Disabled People, was held in conjunction with the World Summit to create a human development index for disabled people, based on parameters corresponding to the 22 articles of the Rules.

In an April report[32] to the Commission for Social Development on major issues and UN programmes relating to social development and welfare and specific social groups, the Secretary-General summarized the substantive issues relating to disabled persons and outlined programme activities of the Department for Policy Coordina-

tion and Sustainable Development. He noted that the core issues of the World Summit were relevant to disability and offered the opportunity to interpret disability in the light of recent developments, placing it in the context of a broader political and social agenda. The issue of disability was linked to achieving a just and equitable society for all, and disability strategies must be considered in the framework of policies and practices to achieve social justice, equity and human rights.

The 1982 World Programme of Action concerning Disabled Persons[30] established a policy framework and guiding philosophy based on recognition of the human rights of disabled persons; the Standard Rules were an instrument for policy-making and action and provided a basis for technical cooperation among States, the United Nations and other international organizations; and the Long-term Strategy to Implement the World Programme of Action concerning Disabled Persons to the Year 2000 and Beyond, put forward by the Secretary-General in 1994,[33] was based on the understanding that effective change in attitudes and policies could not be achieved overnight, but was a creative process that needed to be generated and nurtured. Those three major initiatives, said the Secretary-General, were closely interrelated; progress in reaching the goals set by them could be achieved more quickly and effectively through close cooperation and coordination at every level.

To help advance those goals, the Secretary-General in 1994[34] had appointed Bengt Lindqvist (Sweden) as Special Rapporteur to monitor implementation of the Standard Rules. In April, the Commission for Social Development,[35] having heard an oral report of the Special Rapporteur, encouraged him to focus his monitoring efforts in the forthcoming two years on an appropriate number of priority areas, bearing in mind that the overall goal was to implement the Rules in their entirety. It urged States to continue to implement the Rules and establish or strengthen national coordinating committees or similar bodies to serve as national focal points on disability matters. It invited them to communicate to the Secretariat and to the Special Rapporteur information on their national focal point, in order to facilitate the exchange of information on the implementation of the Rules. The Commission also urged States, intergovernmental organizations and NGOs to respond to the Special Rapporteur's questionnaire on the Rules' implementation, and called on the Department for Policy Coordination and Sustainable Development, UNDP and other UN entities to cooperate with him in their implementation and monitoring. The Commission called on States to participate actively in international cooperation concerning policies for the equalization of opportunities for persons with disabilities and for the improvement of living conditions of persons with disabilities in developing countries.

**Report of the Special Rapporteur.** In August, the Secretary-General transmitted to the General Assembly the first report[(36)] of the Special Rapporteur, setting out activities undertaken to promote dissemination and understanding of the Rules worldwide and recommendations for future action, together with summaries of the submissions received in response to his questionnaire on their implementation. By the end of July, 42 replies had been received.

The Special Rapporteur noted that the Rules were being introduced in a large number of countries and already played an important role in influencing policy and thinking both internationally and at the national level. However, much remained to be done to implement them, especially in developing countries.

One interesting innovation in the mechanism for monitoring the Rules was the invitation by the United Nations to international organizations of persons with disabilities to establish among themselves a panel of experts to serve as an active part of the monitoring system. The 10-member panel was formed during the second half of 1994; it consisted of five men and five women, with various disabilities or experiences of disabilities, from all parts of the world. The first meeting of the panel (New York, 15-17 February) focused on the future activities of the monitoring exercise and adopted a number of recommendations.

In his report, the Special Rapporteur recommended, *inter alia*, that the major emphasis in the monitoring activity should be on assisting developing countries in their implementation efforts. Monitoring in the coming two years should focus on legislation, coordination of work, organization of persons with disabilities, accessibility, education and employment. The Rapporteur should consult with UNESCO and the International Labour Organization with regard to the survey in the areas of education and employment, and the offer by the panel of experts to evaluate the survey should be accepted. International disability organizations should be invited to participate in the survey. Other recommendations related to the involvement of the specialized agencies and the regional commissions in the implementation of the Rules; measures to stimulate the exchange of experience and information between countries; and promotion of awareness-raising. The Commission should suggest measures to secure resources and reopen the discussion on funding the monitoring mechanism through the UN regular budget.

The General Assembly, on 21 December, adopted **resolution 50/144**.

**Towards full integration of persons with disabilities in society: implementation of the Standard Rules on the Equalization of Opportunities for Persons with Disabilities and of the Long-term Strategy to Implement the World Programme of Action concerning Disabled Persons to the Year 2000 and Beyond**

*The General Assembly,*

*Recalling* its resolution 48/96 of 20 December 1993, by which it adopted the Standard Rules on the Equalization of Opportunities for Persons with Disabilities,

*Recalling also* its resolution 37/52 of 3 December 1982, by which it adopted the World Programme of Action concerning Disabled Persons,

*Recalling further* all its relevant resolutions, including resolutions 37/53 of 3 December 1982, 46/96 of 16 December 1991, 47/88 of 16 December 1992, 48/95 and 48/99 of 20 December 1993 and 49/153 of 23 December 1994,

*Taking note of* resolution 34/2 of 20 April 1995 of the Commission for Social Development, wherein it is stated, *inter alia*, that the Standard Rules are to be monitored within the framework of the sessions of the Commission, and that the purpose of such monitoring is to further their effective implementation,

*Noting with interest* the initiative taken by non-governmental organizations to develop a disability index based on the Standard Rules, as well as other activities related to the Standard Rules and activities in support of the World Programme of Action,

*Welcoming* the report of the Special Rapporteur of the Commission for Social Development on monitoring the implementation of the Standard Rules and his recommendation that, in the coming two years, the focus should be mainly on legislation, coordination of work, organizations of persons with disabilities, accessibility, education and employment,

*Welcoming also* the unreserved reaffirmation in the Vienna Declaration and Programme of Action, adopted by the World Conference on Human Rights on 25 June 1993, of all the human rights and fundamental freedoms of persons with disabilities, and the recognition in both the Programme of Action of the International Conference on Population and Development and the Programme of Action of the World Summit for Social Development of a pressing need, among others, for the realization of the goals of full participation in society and the equalization of opportunities for persons with disabilities, as well as the recognition by the Fourth World Conference on Women, held at Beijing from 4 to 15 September 1995, of the special needs of women with disabilities,

1. *Recalls* the recognition by the World Summit for Social Development of the need to promote the Standard Rules on the Equalization of Opportunities for Persons with Disabilities;

2. *Urges* all Governments and organizations to continue to strengthen their efforts to implement the Standard Rules by appropriate legal, administrative and other measures, taking into account the integrated social

development strategy set out in the Programme of Action of the World Summit for Social Development;

3. *Encourages* Governments of Member States to respond to the questionnaire sent by the Special Rapporteur of the Commission for Social Development;

4. *Encourages* Member States to make contributions to the United Nations Voluntary Fund on Disability to support initiatives on disability, including the important work of the Special Rapporteur;

5. *Calls upon* Governments, when implementing the World Programme of Action concerning Disabled Persons, to take into account the elements suggested in the Long-term Strategy to Implement the World Programme of Action concerning Disabled Persons to the Year 2000 and Beyond;

6. *Requests* the Secretary-General to ensure appropriate support for the effective functioning of the Long-term Strategy;

7. *Encourages* the use of communications networks for the dissemination to the general public of the Standard Rules, the World Programme of Action and the Long-term Strategy;

8. *Encourages* the Secretary-General, the Department for Policy Coordination and Sustainable Development of the Secretariat and the United Nations organizations concerned, particularly the United Nations Development Programme, to continue their efforts to facilitate the collection and transmission of relevant data to be used to finalize, in consultation with Member States, the development of global disability indicators, and requests the Secretary-General to submit a report on this question to the General Assembly at its fifty-second session.

General Assembly resolution 50/144

21 December 1995     Meeting 97     Adopted without vote

Approved by Third Committee (A/50/628) without vote, 16 November (meeting 30); 30-nation draft (A/C.3/50/L.12/Rev.1), orally revised; agenda item 105.
*Meeting numbers.* GA 50th session: 3rd Committee 8-12, 18, 30; plenary 97.

### International Day of Disabled Persons

The Secretary-General described in a March report[37] measures taken by Member States to observe the International Day of Disabled Persons (3 December) in 1994. He reported that many important initiatives were undertaken during the first two years of its observation. From the information received, he concluded that both Governments and organizations of disabled persons benefited from the opportunity to mark the Day and promote the World Programme of Action and the Standard Rules.

The Secretary-General made a number of recommendations for observance of the Day, i.e., to use it to initiate dialogue on the needs, interests and aspirations of the disabled community; take stock of the progress made and obstacles encountered in implementing disability policies and programmes; promote increased solidarity between people with disabilities and society as a whole; and explore options to encourage international organizations and potential donors to contribute to improvements in the situation of disabled persons.

### UN Voluntary Fund

The United Nations Voluntary Fund on Disability directed special attention to supporting activities relating to the Standard Rules (see above) and the development objectives of the World Programme of Action, according to an April 1995 report of the Secretary-General.[32] The Fund co-financed 24 assistance projects totalling $343,620, of which 20 per cent, or $72,500, was provided by the Arab Gulf Programme for UN Development Organizations. The Fund received numerous requests for assistance, with an increasing number from the non-governmental community, reflecting NGOs' growing partnership with Governments in action of benefit to persons with disabilities. More than half of the activities supported involved training and technical exchanges, including disability legislation, building national-level institutions and pilot action in income generation. Equally important was the seed-money role of the Fund, whose grants on average served to mobilize about five times as many resources.

### Tobacco or health

At its substantive session in June/July, the Economic and Social Council had before it a May report[38] of the Secretary-General on progress made in the implementation of multisectoral collaboration on tobacco or health, submitted in response to a 1994 Council request.[39] The report summarized replies from UN and other intergovernmental organizations, NGOs, Member States and government bodies to an invitation for comments and suggestions.

A United Nations focal point on the subject had been established in 1994[40] within the UN Conference on Trade and Development (UNCTAD), to coordinate multisectoral collaboration on the economic and social aspects of tobacco production and consumption, taking into particular account the serious health consequences of tobacco use, in accordance with a 1993 Council resolution.[41] The report stated that the focal point had accomplished its task of making every organization and Government aware of the objectives and purposes of the Council's initiative on tobacco or health. A consultation was held in New York in March, with the participation of several donor Governments, to consider a project proposal submitted by the focal point. The project was also distributed to other potential donors and technical cooperation organizations, including UNDP, and to the Bellagio (Italy) consultation of donors in June, sponsored by Health Canada, the International Development Research Centre of Canada and the Rockefeller Foundation.

Several developed countries, notably Canada, Norway and the United Kingdom, had formulated five-year action plans for tobacco control and others were in the process of doing so. Similarly, WHO was developing its five-year plan of action on tobacco or health for 1996-2000, as a follow-up to its 1988-1995 plan. The focal point hoped to draw from the experience of selected developed countries, as well as WHO, UNESCO, the United Nations Industrial Development Organization, the Food and Agriculture Organization of the United Nations (FAO), UNCTAD and other organizations, to coordinate assistance by the UN system to developing countries and countries in economic transition for the development and implementation of national plans of action on tobacco control. Some of those countries had requested technical support for diversification possibilities and the development of economic alternatives to tobacco agriculture.

Suggestions for future action included the provision of assistance for implementation of national plans of action; information collection, exchange and dissemination; and support in preparation for the Tenth World Conference on Tobacco and Health (Beijing, China, 1997). It was also suggested that UNCTAD prepare a study on the role of transnational tobacco corporations in the world tobacco economy and their impact on current trends in demand for tobacco products in different parts of the world.

In a July addendum,[42] the Secretary-General, at the request of the World Health Assembly, transmitted to the Council a resolution adopted by that body requesting the Director-General of WHO to study the feasibility of developing guidelines, a declaration or international convention on tobacco control to be adopted by the United Nations, taking into account existing trade and other conventions and treaties.

**ECONOMIC AND SOCIAL COUNCIL ACTION**

The Economic and Social Council, on 28 July, adopted **resolution 1995/62**.

### Tobacco or health

*The Economic and Social Council,*

*Recalling* its resolutions 1993/79 of 30 July 1993 and 1994/47 of 29 July 1994 and World Health Assembly resolutions WHA45.20 of 13 May 1992 and WHA46.8 of 10 May 1993,

*Taking note with appreciation* of the report of the Secretary-General on progress made in the implementation of multisectoral collaboration on tobacco or health,

*Taking note* of the adoption by the World Health Assembly of resolution WHA48.11 of 12 May 1995, in which the Assembly requested the Director-General of the World Health Organization to study the feasibility of developing an international instrument, such as guidelines, a declaration or an international convention on tobacco control to be adopted by the United Nations, taking into account existing trade and other conventions and treaties,

1. *Recognizes* that several United Nations organizations, agencies and offices have implemented World Health Assembly resolution WHA46.8 and banned the use of tobacco within the buildings of the United Nations system;

2. *Encourages* any organization of the United Nations system which has not yet done so to consider implementing resolution WHA46.8 before the end of 1995;

3. *Requests* the United Nations system focal point on tobacco or health to intensify the dialogue with organizations of the United Nations system and Member States in order to strengthen tobacco control policies;

4. *Encourages* organizations of the United Nations system to respond to the requests of the system focal point for further action to eliminate the negative impact of tobacco;

5. *Invites* Member States, bilateral and non-governmental organizations and organizations of the United Nations system to provide the necessary support to enable the United Nations system focal point to carry out his mandate in an effective manner;

6. *Requests* the Secretary-General to report to the Economic and Social Council at its substantive session of 1997 on progress made by the system focal point in the implementation of multisectoral collaboration on tobacco or health.

Economic and Social Council resolution 1995/62

| 28 July 1995 | Meeting 57 | Adopted without vote |

Draft by Vice-President (E/1995/L.63), orally amended by President and based on informal consultations on draft by United States (E/1995/L.52); agenda item 9 (c).

*Meeting numbers.* ESC 54, 57.

*REFERENCES*

[1]E/ICEF/1995/11/Rev.1. [2]E/1995/33/Rev.1 (dec. 1995/28). [3]YUN 1981, p. 802. [4]Ibid., p. 803, GA res. 36/43, 19 Nov. 1981. [5]E/ICEF/1995/P/L.9. [6]E/1995/33/Rev.1 (dec. 1995/10). [7]EB96/1995/REC/1 (dec. EB96(2)). [8]E/1995/32. [9]E/CN.17/1995/22. [10]YUN 1994, p. 1126. [11]YUN 1992, p. 672. [12]E/CN.17/1995/20. [13]YUN 1993, p. 819. [14]YUN 1994, p. 1126, ESC res. 1994/24, 26 July 1994. [15]E/1995/60. [16]E/1995/71. [17]A/50/175-E/1995/57. [18]DP/1995/21. [19]E/1995/34 (dec. 95/11). [20]YUN 1994, p. 1129. [21]DP/1996/10. [22]DP/FPA/1996/4. [23]E/1995/33/Rev.1 (dec. 1995/13). [24]E/1995/23 (res. 1995/44). [25]A/50/180-E/1995/63. [26]YUN 1994, p. 1129, ESC res. 1994/34, 29 July 1994. [27]Ibid., GA res. 49/135, 19 Dec. 1994. [28]YUN 1993, p. 974, GA res. 48/95, 20 Dec. 1993. [29]A/50/473. [30]YUN 1982, p. 981, GA res. 37/52, 3 Dec. 1982. [31]YUN 1993, p. 978, GA res. 48/96, annex, 20 Dec. 1993. [32]E/CN.5/1995/2. [33]A/49/435. [34]YUN 1994, p. 1130. [35]E/1995/24 (res. 34/2). [36]A/50/374. [37]E/CN.5/1995/4. [38]E/1995/67. [39]YUN 1994, p. 1132, ESC res. 1994/47, 29 July 1994. [40]Ibid., p. 1132. [41]YUN 1993, p. 989, ESC res. 1993/79, 30 July 1993. [42]E/1995/67/Add.1.

# Food and agriculture

## Food aid

### World Food Programme

The Secretary-General reported[1] to the Economic and Social Council in January 1995 that consultations had been held between the secretariats of the United Nations and FAO, in accordance

with a 1993 General Assembly resolution,[2] regarding transformation of the Committee on Food
Aid Policies and Programmes (CFA) of the World
Food Programme into an Executive Board and on
how to fulfil the requirements set out in the Assembly resolution.

By an April note,[3] the Secretary-General
transmitted to the Council the draft General Regulations of WFP, drawn up by an open-ended working group of the Committee, and a revised draft
resolution for adoption by the Assembly, both approved by CFA in December 1994.

The Council, by **decision 1995/227** of 6 June,
recommended to the Assembly for adoption a draft
resolution on revision of the General Regulations
and reconstitution of CFA as the Executive Board
of WFP, based on the draft approved by CFA.

In October, the Secretary-General informed[4]
the Assembly of the Council's decision and of a
parallel resolution adopted by the FAO Conference
at its twenty-eighth session on 31 October, according to which CFA would be constituted as the Executive Board of WFP with 36 members. The Conference also approved the revised regulations of
WFP as contained in the appendix to that resolution.

The Assembly, by **decision 50/439** of 20 December, took note of the Secretary-General's October note.

**GENERAL ASSEMBLY ACTION**

The General Assembly, on 1 November,
adopted **resolution 50/8**.

**Revision of the General Regulations of the
World Food Programme and reconstitution of the
Committee on Food Aid Policies and Programmes as
the Executive Board of the World Food Programme**

*The General Assembly,*

*Recalling* its resolutions 1714(XVI) of 19 December
1961, 2095(XX) of 20 December 1965 and 3404(XXX)
of 28 November 1975, concerning the establishment and
continuation of the United Nations/Food and Agriculture Organization of the United Nations World Food
Programme, and its resolution 46/22 of 5 December 1991
on the revision of the General Regulations of the World
Food Programme and enlargement of the Committee
on Food Aid Policies and Programmes of the World Food
Programme,

*Recalling also* its resolution 48/162 of 20 December 1993,
on further measures for the restructuring and revitalization of the United Nations in the economic, social and
related fields,

*Having considered* Economic and Social Council decision 1995/227 of 6 June 1995 adopted on the recommendation of the Committee on Food Aid Policies and Programmes of the World Food Programme concerning the
governance of the Programme, the revision of the
General Regulations of the World Food Programme, and
the reconstitution of the Committee on Food Aid Policies and Programmes as the Executive Board of the
World Food Programme,

1. *Decides,* subject to the concurrence of the Conference of the Food and Agriculture Organization of the
United Nations, that the Committee on Food Aid Policies and Programmes shall be reconstituted as the Executive Board of the World Food Programme, with
thirty-six members elected from among the States Members of the United Nations or the States members of the
Food and Agriculture Organization of the United Nations, and that the Economic and Social Council and
the Council of the Food and Agriculture Organization
of the United Nations shall elect eighteen members each,
as set forth in paragraph 2 below;

2. *Decides also* that the members of the Executive
Board of the World Food Programme shall be elected
on an interim basis for four years from among the States
included in the lists[a] set out in the Basic Texts of the
World Food Programme, in accordance with the following distribution of seats, it being understood that this
allocation of seats creates no precedent for the composition of other United Nations bodies of a limited membership:

(*a*)  Nine members from the States included in list
A, five members to be elected by the Economic and So-
cial Council and four by the Council of the Food and
Agriculture Organization of the United Nations;

(*b*)  Seven members from the States included in list
B, four members to be elected by the Economic and So-
cial Council and three by the Council of the Food and
Agriculture Organization of the United Nations;

(*c*)  Five members from the States included in list C,
two members to be elected by the Economic and Social
Council and three by the Council of the Food and
Agriculture Organization of the United Nations;

(*d*)  Twelve members from the States included in list
D, six members to be elected by the Economic and So-
cial Council and six by the Council of the Food and
Agriculture Organization of the United Nations;

(*e*)  Two members from the States included in list E,
one member to be elected by the Economic and Social
Council and one by the Council of the Food and Agriculture Organization of the United Nations;

(*f*)  One additional member alternating between the
States included in lists B and C, starting with list C,
to be elected by the Council of the Food and Agriculture Organization of the United Nations;

3. *Decides further* that the above-mentioned distribution of seats shall be reviewed within two years after the
establishment of the Executive Board with a view to
achieving its final outcome in accordance with paragraphs 25 and 30 and other relevant provisions of
General Assembly resolution 48/162; that the review
shall be conducted in parallel by the Assembly and the
Conference of the Food and Agriculture Organization
of the United Nations, taking into account the relevant
inputs of the Economic and Social Council and the
Council of the Food and Agriculture Organization of
the United Nations; and that its results shall enter into
force on 1 January 2000;

4. *Requests* the Economic and Social Council, at its
resumed substantive session of 1995, to elect eighteen
members of the Executive Board for a term beginning
on 1 January 1996 in accordance with the following distribution and terms of office:

---

[a]E/1995/L.11.

*(a)* Five members from the States included in list A, two for a term of three years, one for a term of two years and two for a term of one year;

*(b)* Four members from the States included in list B, one for a term of three years, two for a term of two years and one for a term of one year;

*(c)* Two members from the States included in list C, one for a term of three years and one for a term of one year;

*(d)* Six members from the States included in list D, two for a period of three years, two for a period of two years and two for a period of one year;

*(e)* One member from the States included in list E, for a period of two years;

5. *Decides* that thereafter all members of the Executive Board shall be elected for a term of three years and requests the Economic and Social Council to make such provisions as ensure that the terms of office of six members elected by the Economic and Social Council and the Council of the Food and Agriculture Organization of the United Nations shall expire in each calendar year;

6. *Decides* to approve the revised General Regulations of the World Food Programme contained in annex I of the note by the Secretary-General on the transformation of the Committee on Food Aid Policies and Programmes of the World Food Programme into an executive board, as endorsed by the Economic and Social Council in its decision 1995/227 and by the Council of the Food and Agriculture Organization of the United Nations at its one hundred and eighth session, on 12 June 1995;

7. *Decides*, subject to the concurrence of the Conference of the Food and Agriculture Organization of the United Nations, that the revised General Regulations shall enter into force on 1 January 1996.

General Assembly resolution 50/8

1 November 1995      Meeting 46      Adopted without vote

Approved by Second Committee (A/50/615) without vote, 12 October (meeting 9); draft recommended by ESC in dec. 1995/227 (A/C.2/50/L.2); agenda item 12.

### CFA activities

In 1995, the Committee on Food Aid Policies and Programmes (CFA), the governing body of WFP, held two sessions in Rome, Italy.

At its thirty-ninth session (22-26 May),[5] CFA approved 12 new projects recommended by its Subcommittee on Projects (fourteenth session, Rome, 15-19 May), as well as budget increases for previously approved projects. These related to food assistance for refugees and returnees, integrated agricultural development, improvement of food security, rural community infrastructure upgrading and rehabilitation, fruit-tree planting and feeding of vulnerable groups. CFA endorsed the Executive Director's proposal to prepare a four-year Strategic and Financial Plan every two years on a rolling basis and provided advice and guidance to the Executive Director on policy and operational principles for the 1996-1997 budget, the future Strategic and Financial Plans and other related matters. It approved the interim recommendations of the Working Group on Op-

tions for WFP Resource Policies and Long-term Financing regarding bilateral services support costs.

At its fortieth session (13-16 November),[6] CFA approved a further 10 new projects recommended by the Subcommittee (fifteenth session, 6-9 November), as well as budget increases.

The total cost to WFP of development projects approved in 1995 (including projects approved by the Executive Director under her delegated authority and budget increases) amounted to $279.8 million, with a total commitment of 999,500 tons of food for 8.7 million beneficiaries. Protracted relief operations (PROs) for refugees and internally displaced persons totalled $462.5 million (including those approved by the Executive Director and budget increases), with a total commitment of 1,054,000 tons of food for 9.5 million people. The total cost of emergency operations was $682.7 million (including budget increases), to provide 1,323,100 tons of food for 13.1 million beneficiaries.

The Committee endorsed the recommendations of the Working Group on Options for WFP Resource Policies and Long-term Financing, including a new model consisting of three elements: funding windows (multilateral, directed multilateral and bilateral), programme categories and costs. The principle of full-cost recovery would apply to all programme categories and the secretariat would be requested to prepare necessary changes in WFP General and Financial Regulations. The secretariat would implement the new model on a trial basis, commencing 1 January 1996, and develop by 31 March 1996 a concise paper on contributions made under the new model for the guidance of donors. The secretariat should also review the working of the new model and its associated policies at the end of the first biennium of operation and report on its effectiveness and efficiency.

The Committee also provided guidance to the newly constituted Executive Board of WFP on its rules of procedure, abolition of CFA's Subcommittee on Projects, official languages, venue of meetings and, on a provisional basis, the number and sequence of sessions (there should be three: a regular organizational session; an annual meeting, together with a regular session; and a third regular session), composition of the Bureau (which should consist of five members), reports and documentation, and the participation of non-members. Concerning implementation of the country programme approach, CFA agreed that the country programme cycle would involve Executive Board decision-making at four stages: strategy formulation, country programme approval, mid-term progress report and end-of-term evaluation.

On 13 July, the Economic and Social Council, by **decision 1995/233**, took note of the twentieth annual report of CFA.[7]

### WFP activities

In 1995, WFP helped some 50 million people in the world, half of them victims of emergencies, providing over 2.8 million tons of food at a cost of $1.2 billion, including 250,000 tons on behalf of bilateral donors. Some 25 million poor and hungry people were reached through development projects. Over 1.6 million tons of food went to victims of disasters.[8]

Total new commitments in 1995 amounted to 3.2 million tons; commitments totalled $248 million for development assistance and $1.1 billion for emergency operations.

At the end of the year, WFP's global portfolio of ongoing activities consisted of 204 development projects valued at $2.28 billion, and 89 relief operations valued at $1.77 billion. The biggest share was allocated to Africa (56 per cent), followed by Asia (28 per cent), the Americas (12 per cent), and Eastern Europe and the former USSR (4 per cent). The composition of the portfolio for the geographic regions differed greatly. The highest proportion of development assistance was reached in the Americas (99 per cent); in Asia it accounted for 80 per cent, while the portfolio for Africa consisted of 60 per cent of relief operations. In Eastern Europe and the former USSR, relief operations accounted for 100 per cent.

A number of steps were taken towards a more people-centred approach to food aid, involving the design of implementation strategies to better target development resources, and increasing people's participation in project design and implementation. WFP also strengthened its readiness to respond to emergencies, and several initiatives were introduced to improve WFP's food-procurement capability. New operational procedures were developed and specialist purchasing officers were stationed in countries that were strategically located for WFP operations.

The first WFP-NGO consultation was held in November. A Memorandum of Understanding with NGOs, clarifying respective responsibilities, was signed, and negotiations were initiated for others. WFP was working with more than 1,000 national and international NGOs.

### Relief activities

In 1995, WFP provided over 1.6 million tons of food to victims of emergencies, including 7 million refugees, 14 million internally displaced and nearly 4 million victims of drought and other natural disasters. That assistance was almost one quarter less than in 1994, as for the first time in several years, there was no dramatic new emergency situation. New commitments for emergency operations and PROs amounted to $1.1 billion, involving 2.3 million tons of food commodities, almost the same as in 1994.

In Africa, some 21 million persons received help from WFP, with relief food reaching over 15 million victims of disasters in 28 countries. Support for victims of civil conflict continued in Rwanda/Burundi and Liberia/Sierra Leone, as well as in Ethiopia, Kenya, Somalia, southern Sudan and Uganda. In Angola, Ghana, Mozambique and Rwanda/Burundi, the political situation allowed a shift from relief to reconstruction and rehabilitation activities. Drought-related food aid needs emerged in southern Africa and continued in Ethiopia. Relief operations were phased out in the Central African Republic, Guinea-Bissau, Senegal and Togo.

In Asia, WFP helped over 19 million people. Total WFP food aid deliveries amounted to over 900,000 tons. Some 14 million people participated in 58 WFP-supported development projects in 16 countries. WFP relief food reached another 5 million people. Emergency food assistance was provided for the first time to the Democratic People's Republic of Korea. Food assistance was also provided for rehabilitation in Cambodia, reintegration in Myanmar, relief and repatriation of refugees/returnees in Bangladesh, Nepal and Viet Nam, assistance for the displaced in Sri Lanka and flood victims in the Lao People's Democratic Republic. Support continued for vulnerable groups in Iraq, refugees in Yemen and relief, rehabilitation and reintegration in Afghanistan, Iraq and Pakistan.

WFP assisted almost 5 million people in Latin America and the Caribbean. Of the more than 200,000 tons of food delivered, some 95 per cent was for 55 development projects in 24 countries. The emphasis of WFP's work in the region was on community development through food-for-work programmes, primary education, and mother and child health and nutrition programmes. Food assistance continued for returnees and vulnerable groups in Haiti, while assistance was being phased out in Mexico, as refugees and returnees were repatriated or resettled.

In Eastern Europe and the Republics of the former USSR, relief at a total value of $168 million was provided to victims of ethnic strife and economic collapse, particularly in Armenia, Azerbaijan, Georgia, the Russian Federation (Chechnya), Tajikistan and the former Yugoslavia. In the Caucasus and Central Asia, WFP and NGOs used relief food aid to support the poorest groups after the collapse of the economies and the social security systems. Within the framework of emergency operations, WFP food aid also supported rehabilitation and infrastructure neglected or damaged by war. Almost 4 million people in the region received a total of 240,000 tons of food commodities in 1995.

### Resources and financing

In 1995, the total level of resources available to WFP fell to $1.2 billion, from $1.5 billion in 1994. Due to a shortfall in cash contributions, the Programme was forced to operate at a funding level below the one approved. To manage the scarcity of resources, WFP de-earmarked resources for some operational projects, limited budget increases for approved projects and did not extend projects beyond their duration.

In May, CFA endorsed[5] the Executive Director's proposal of a pledging target for 1997-1998 amounting to $1.3 billion and recommended it for endorsement by the FAO Council and the Economic and Social Council and subsequent approval by the General Assembly and the FAO Conference. The Committee noted that there were signs that additional resources might not become available and that some major donors were not expecting any significant improvement in their funding capacity in the next biennium. It noted with concern that prevailing resource constraints and possible future shortfalls would have serious implications for food-assisted development projects, affecting the pace of implementation of ongoing projects and the approval of new commitments.

WFP's new resource policies and financing were approved[6] by CFA in November. The new structure, beginning in 1996, would consist of four programme categories (development, PROs, emergencies and special operations) and three funding windows (multilateral, directed multilateral and bilateral) under which WFP received its contributions. The new approach was based on full cost recovery for all direct and indirect operational and support costs.

The Secretary-General transmitted,[9] as requested, to the Economic and Social Council an 18 December letter[9] from the Executive Director of WFP stating that the new model, to be applied on a trial basis, was designed to place the resource base and long-term financing of WFP on a more sound and predictable basis. The WFP secretariat was preparing a revised draft of the Financial Regulations for submission to the Advisory Committee on Administrative and Budgetary Questions, the FAO Finance Committee and the WFP Executive Board. The new financing procedures had been accommodated in the 1996-1997 programme support and administrative budget. Expeditious action by the Council would allow the trial period to coincide with the biennial budget period 1996-1997 and facilitate the review of the working of the new model. However, the new resourcing mechanisms would not be for-

mally implemented until the Council and the FAO Council had reviewed the proposals.

**ECONOMIC AND SOCIAL COUNCIL ACTION**

On 13 July, the Economic and Social Council adopted **resolution 1995/3**.

### Target for World Food Programme pledges for the period 1997-1998

*The Economic and Social Council,*

*Noting* the comments of the Committee on Food Aid Policies and Programmes of the World Food Programme concerning the minimum target for voluntary contributions to the Programme for the period 1997-1998,

*Recalling* General Assembly resolutions 2462(XXIII) and 2682(XXV) of 20 December 1968 and 11 December 1970, in which the Assembly recognized the experience gained by the World Food Programme in the field of multilateral food aid,

1.   *Recommends* to the General Assembly the adoption of the draft resolution annexed to the present resolution;

2.   *Urges* States Members of the United Nations and members and associate members of the Food and Agriculture Organization of the United Nations to undertake the preparations necessary for the announcement of pledges at the Seventeenth Pledging Conference for the World Food Programme.

### ANNEX

[**For text, see General Assembly resolution 50/127 below**]

Economic and Social Council resolution 1995/3

13 July 1995          Meeting 38          Adopted without vote

Draft by Committee on Food Aid Policies and Programmes (E/1995/107); agenda item 4.

*Meeting numbers.* ESC 30-38.

**GENERAL ASSEMBLY ACTION**

The General Assembly, on 20 December, adopted **resolution 50/127**.

### Target for World Food Programme pledges for the period 1997-1998

*The General Assembly,*

*Recalling* the provisions of its resolution 2095(XX) of 20 December 1965 to the effect that the World Food Programme was to be reviewed before each pledging conference,

*Noting* that the Programme was reviewed by the Committee on Food Aid Policies and Programmes of the World Food Programme at its thirty-seventh session and by the Economic and Social Council at its substantive session of 1994,

*Having considered* Economic and Social Council resolution 1995/3 of 13 July 1995 and the comments of the Committee on Food Aid Policies and Programmes,

*Recognizing* the value of multilateral food aid as implemented by the World Food Programme since its inception and the necessity for continuing its action both as a form of capital investment and for meeting emergency food needs,

1.   *Establishes* a target for voluntary contributions to the World Food Programme of 1.3 billion United States dollars for the period 1997-1998;

2.   *Urges* States Members of the United Nations and members and associate members of the Food and

Agriculture Organization of the United Nations and appropriate donor organizations to make every effort to ensure that the target is fully attained;

3. *Requests* the Secretary-General, in cooperation with the Director-General of the Food and Agriculture Organization of the United Nations, to convene a pledging conference for this purpose at Headquarters in 1996.

General Assembly resolution 50/127

20 December 1995    Meeting 96    Adopted without vote

Approved by Second Committee (A/50/615/Add.1) without vote, 30 November (meeting 40); draft recommended by ESC in res. 1995/3 (A/C.2/50/L.4); agenda item 12.
*Meeting numbers.* GA 50th session: 2nd Committee 15, 16, 40; plenary 96.

## Food and agricultural development

By a 20 October letter[10] to the Secretary-General, the Philippines, on behalf of the Group of 77 developing countries, requested that a sub-item entitled "Food and agricultural development", later changed to "Food and sustainable agricultural development", be included in the agenda of the General Assembly under item 95 on sustainable development and international economic cooperation. In an explanatory memorandum, the Philippines said that the urgency of the matter was due to the upcoming World Food Summit (Rome, November 1996). The Assembly included the sub-item in its agenda on 10 November and allocated it to the Second (Economic and Financial) Committee.

On 31 October 1995, the FAO Conference at its twenty-eighth session decided[11] to convene the Summit at the level of heads of State or Government, with the objectives, *inter alia*, of marshalling the global consensus and commitment needed to redress the problem of food security; establishing a policy framework; and adopting a plan of action to achieve sustained progress towards universal food security. The Conference welcomed the Director-General's decision to open a special trust fund to facilitate the preparations for and holding of the Summit.

GENERAL ASSEMBLY ACTION

The General Assembly, on 20 December, adopted **resolution 50/109**.

### World Food Summit

*The General Assembly,*

*Reaffirming* the inalienable right to be free from hunger and malnutrition, as proclaimed in the Universal Declaration on the Eradication of Hunger and Malnutrition,

*Conscious* that, despite the progress that has been made in ensuring global food availability, eight hundred million people remain chronically undernourished and about two hundred million children under age five suffer from protein and energy deficiencies,

*Convinced* of the urgent need, at the highest political level, to marshal the global consensus and commitment required for the eradication of hunger and mal-

nutrition and the achievement of food security for all, through the adoption of concerted policies and a plan of action for implementation by Governments, international institutions and all sectors of civil society,

*Recalling* the contributions to international consensus achieved by the World Food Conference in 1974, the World Summit for Children in 1990, the United Nations Conference on Environment and Development and the International Conference on Nutrition in 1992, the International Conference on Population and Development in 1994, and the World Summit for Social Development and the Fourth World Conference on Women in 1995, as well as the agreements made at other international conferences and summits in recent years,

*Recognizing* that activities to ensure food security at all levels should be carried out within the framework of sustainable development, as defined in Agenda 21, and that the World Food Summit will give due attention to the multifaceted nature of food security,

*Bearing in mind* the proposal of the Director-General of the Food and Agriculture Organization of the United Nations that the Summit should not call for new funding mechanisms or institutions,

1. *Welcomes* the decision of the Conference of the Food and Agriculture Organization of the United Nations at its twenty-eighth session to convene the World Food Summit at Rome from 13 to 17 November 1996 at the level of heads of State or Government;

2. *Invites* Governments to participate actively in Summit preparations and to be represented at the level of heads of State or Government;

3. *Invites* all relevant United Nations and other intergovernmental organizations, including international and regional financial institutions, as well as non-governmental organizations and the private sector, to cooperate actively with the Food and Agriculture Organization of the United Nations in preparing for the Summit;

4. *Invites* the international community to make contributions on a voluntary basis to the special trust fund established by the Food and Agriculture Organization of the United Nations in order to facilitate the preparations for and the holding of the Summit as well as to facilitate the preparations for effective participation of representatives of developing countries, in particular the least developed countries, both at the sessions of the Committee on World Food Security of the Food and Agriculture Organization of the United Nations to be held in January and September 1996 as preparatory meetings and at the Summit itself;

5. *Invites* the Director-General of the Food and Agriculture Organization of the United Nations to submit to the General Assembly, at its fifty-second session, through the Economic and Social Council, a report on the outcome of the Summit, including actions to be taken to follow up the outcome of the Summit at all appropriate levels.

General Assembly resolution 50/109

20 December 1995    Meeting 96    Adopted without vote

Approved by Second Committee (A/50/617/Add.11) without vote, 5 December (meeting 41); draft by Vice-Chairman (A/C.2/50/L.51), orally revised and based on informal consultations on draft by Philippines, for Group of 77 and China (A/C.2/50/L.21); agenda item 95 *(k)*.
*Meeting numbers.* GA 50th session: 2nd Committee 35-37, 41; plenary 96.

## World Food Council

The Economic and Social Council, by **decision 1995/207 C** of 10 February, decided to undertake at its substantive session in 1995 an in-depth review of the report of the World Food Council (WFC) on the work of its nineteenth session, and to submit recommendations thereon to the General Assembly for consideration and action.

[WFC did not meet in 1995 and no report was issued. For WFC membership, see APPENDIX III.]

*REFERENCES*

[1]E/1995/9. [2]YUN 1993, p. 1118, GA res. 48/162, 20 Dec. 1993. [3]E/1995/14 & Add.1. [4]A/50/706. [5]CFA:39/17. [6]CFA:40/15. [7]E/1995/96. [8]WFP/EB.A/96/4. [9]E/1995/131. [10]A/50/234. [11]C/95/REP (res. 2/95).

# Nutrition

### ACC activities

The twenty-second session of the Administrative Committee on Coordination (ACC) Subcommittee on Nutrition was held in New York from 12 to 16 June 1995,[1] following ad hoc group meetings on individual micronutrients (vitamin A, iron and iodine); nutrition, ethics and human rights; and breast-feeding and complementary feeding.

The Subcommittee considered matters for approval by the Consultative Committee on Programme and Operational Questions (CCPOQ), including options for strengthening the functions of the Subcommittee, and discussed work in progress. Concerning follow-up to the 1992 International Conference on Nutrition,[2] the Subcommittee agreed that its reporting obligations differed from those of FAO and WHO and should be approached by enlarging the scope of the *Third Report on the World Nutrition Situation*, planned for issuance in early 1996, to include additional outcome indicators and indicators on process (i.e., programme and policy development) and the status of national plans of action (NPAs); obtaining new information on countries to explore how process and activities might have been influenced by the 1992 Conference; and inviting government participation in a global seminar to discuss experiences and draw conclusions that might guide other countries in NPA preparation and be used by agencies to strengthen and coordinate their activities, notably at the country level.

Among other matters, the Subcommittee decided to continue to facilitate the new initiative addressing unmet needs in research on and training to improve nutrition programmes, which had grown out of a 1994 conference on the subject sponsored by the World Bank.

The Subcommittee proposed the establishment of an Ad Hoc Working Group on the Nutrition of School-Age Children to exchange information and facilitate better coordination of strategies for improving their nutritional health.

CCPOQ, at its fifth session (Geneva, 31 January–2 February), recommended[3] that any plans to broaden the scope of participation in the Subcommittee involve consultation with Subcommittee members. The ad hoc meeting to be held in February should discuss technical issues, while issues related to the legal, procedural and/or administrative work should be referred to the formal session of the Subcommittee and could only be decided by CCPOQ on behalf of ACC.

At a meeting of the whole of the Subcommittee, held at the World Bank in February 1995, it was agreed that the Subcommittee should foster a global conscience and a high degree of awareness of problems of hunger and malnutrition, and should serve as a catalyst for sustained advocacy of relevant programmes and policies. It was suggested that perhaps a working group for that purpose be set up by the Subcommittee.

### UNU activities

In 1995, the United Nations University (UNU) continued activities under its programme on food and nutrition for human and social development,[4] within six global projects and with the active involvement of other United Nations organizations. The programme also attracted extra-budgetary resources in excess of $900,000. The work continued to be directed from its coordinating office in Boston, Massachusetts, United States, but plans were developed for the gradual transfer of activities to a new research-and-training coordinating centre on the campus of Cornell University in Ithaca, New York. Efforts to mobilize funding for the coordinating centre were undertaken during the year.

UNU efforts continued in identifying and promoting measures to control iron deficiency. Reports from a UNU-coordinated multi-centre study of the feasibility and effectiveness of weekly as opposed to daily supplementation were encouraging in China, Guatemala, Malaysia and the United States. The studies were continuing in Guatemala, Indonesia and Mali, showing that weekly administration was equally effective in raising haemoglobin levels and was virtually without side-effects. With support from UNICEF, UNU studied the prevalence of iron-deficiency anaemia in Kazakstan and Uzbekistan, in collaboration with the Institute of Nutrition in Almaty. Based on the study, iron supplementation and fortification projects were designed for implementation in 1996.

In partnership with the International Union of Nutritional Sciences (IUNS), WHO and FAO, UNU continued to promote the International Dietary Energy Consultative Group. It was joined by FAO in a global effort to improve the quantity and quality of food consumption data worldwide. UNU's role continued to be the establishment and linking of regional databases. The International Development Research Centre in Canada provided a grant for a high-capacity computer, and UNU awarded fellowships for training in food-composition database management at the Wageningen Agricultural University in the Netherlands and database programming in Palmerston North, New Zealand. Two task force meetings, organized under the auspices of UNU, FAO and IUNS, established quality tags for food-composition data to be incorporated into the UNU International Network of Food Data Systems and provided guidelines for a future meeting of the UNU-sponsored IUNS Committee on Terminology and Nomenclature for Food-composition Databases.

The International Food Intake Directory continued to provide important input to epidemiological studies and to summarize all food-intake data available over the last 40 years from developing countries. Some Asian and Latin American/Caribbean summaries had already been published and new data were received from 14 African countries.

UNU's quarterly *Food and Nutrition Bulletin*, one of the few publications that reached nutrition and health workers in developing countries, was published for the sixteenth year. UNU also continued to publish jointly with Academic Press the quarterly *Journal of Food Composition and Analysis*.

*REFERENCES*

[1]ACC/1995/13. [2]YUN 1992, p. 830. [3]ACC/1995/1. [4]A/51/31.

Chapter XIV

# International drug control

In 1995, the United Nations continued to address the rising trend in drug abuse and illicit production and trafficking in narcotics and psychotropic substances, which the General Assembly warned has threatened the health and well-being of millions of persons, in particular youth, in all countries of the world.

Over the previous decade, a significant international infrastructure had been created to deal with drug control issues, centred within the United Nations system.

In 1987, the United Nations convened the International Conference on Drug Abuse and Illicit Trafficking, which adopted a Comprehensive Multidisciplinary Outline of Future Activities in Drug Abuse Control, containing both general and specific guidelines for Member States. An ongoing framework for UN activities to combat problems stemming from the abuse of drugs is provided by the UN International Drug Control Programme (UNDCP), the United Nations System-wide Action Plan on Drug Abuse Control, and the 1990 Global Programme of Action against illicit production, supply, demand, trafficking and distribution of narcotic drugs and psychotropic substances.

The International Narcotics Control Board continues to oversee the implementation of three major drug-control conventions, and each year analyzes the drug abuse situation world wide to assist Governments in implementing treaty obligations.

In 1995, the UN Commission on Narcotic Drugs—the Organization's main policy-making body on drug control matters—addressed a number of issues, prime among them the questions of reducing both the demand for and supply of illegal drugs, and the increasingly disturbing phenomenon of money laundering.

## International and regional cooperation

### Conventions

Central to the international control system of narcotic drugs are three global conventions: the 1961 Single Convention on Narcotic Drugs,[1] which, with some exceptions of detail, replaced earlier narcotics treaties and was amended in 1972

by a Protocol[2] intended to strengthen the role of the International Narcotics Control Board (INCB); the 1971 Convention on Psychotropic Substances;[3] and the 1988 United Nations Convention against Illicit Traffic in Narcotic Drugs and Psychotropic Substances,[4] which entered into force in 1990.

As at 31 December 1995, 134 States were parties to the 1961 Single Convention on Narcotic Drugs as amended by the 1972 Protocol. During the year, five States—Guinea Bissau, Mali, the Republic of Moldova, Swaziland and Uzbekistan—became parties.

The Convention, as amended by the Protocol, established a dual drug-control obligation for Governments: to ensure adequate availability for narcotic drugs, including opiates, for medical and scientific purposes, while at the same time preventing the illicit production of, trafficking in and use of such drugs. To implement those responsibilities, Governments enact laws and take administrative and enforcement measures. Each Government estimates annually the amount of narcotic drugs needed to satisfy all medical and scientific requirements in the country for the coming year. INCB evaluates, confirms and publishes the amount of narcotic drugs for each Government. Each Government may then manufacture or import narcotic drugs within that amount and distribute them to medical facilities for the treatment of patients. In case of unforeseen increases in medical demand, Governments may submit supplementary estimates to the Board at any time; requests for supplementary estimates are acted on expeditiously.

Under the Convention, INCB is responsible for ensuring that the supply of narcotic drugs for licit purposes is limited to the amount acquired for medical and scientific needs. To prevent and detect diversion of drugs from licit to illicit channels, the Board monitors the cultivation, manufacture, import, export and consumption of such drugs throughout the world. If the treaty requirements for drug control are implemented consistently, the potential for diverting narcotic drugs to illicit channels is reduced to a minimum without interfering in their availability for treatment of patients who need them. Given the large number of national and international transactions, the number of incidents involving diversion of narcotic drugs is considered to be small.

The number of parties to the 1971 Convention on Psychotropic Substances stood at 140 as at 31 December 1995. Eight States became parties during the year: Belgium, Chad, Guinea-Bissau, Mali, Myanmar, the Republic of Moldova, Swaziland and Uzbekistan.

As at 31 December, 121 States and the European Union were parties to the 1988 Convention against Illicit Traffic in Narcotic Drugs and Psychotropic Substances. Seventeen States—Algeria, Belgium, Cape Verde, Chad, Guinea-Bissau, Haiti, Jamaica, Lesotho, Malawi, Mali, the Republic of Moldova, Saints Kitts and Nevis, Saint Vincent and the Grenadines, Swaziland, Trinidad and Tobago, Uruguay and Uzbekistan ratified, accepted or acceded to the Convention during 1995.

The Commission on Narcotic Drugs in March 1995 urged States that had not yet done so to become parties to and implement effectively the international drug control conventions, and recommended that they seek the Secretary-General's advice on matters relating to accession or succession to those conventions.[5] It further recognized[6] that the 1961 and 1971 Conventions had generally achieved their intended objectives, invited States to consider measures for further strengthening and streamlining their control mechanisms, and decided to examine specific aspects of the operation of the 1988 Convention.

To encourage ratification and the establishment of effective drug control structures, the United Nations Drug Control Programme (UNDCP) continued to provide States with legal assistance.

In an October report,[7] the Secretary-General noted progress in the adherence of States to international drug-control treaties, but expressed concern that effective functioning of the 1971 Convention was hampered because some States which manufactured and exported psychotropic substances had not yet become parties. He recommended that States that were signatories complete legislative and other enabling changes and ratify the treaties as a priority.

## International Narcotics Control Board

The International Narcotics Control Board met twice in 1995, for its fifty-eighth (8–19 May) and fifty-ninth (30 October-16 November) sessions. Its activities, observations and recommendations were reflected in its report for 1995.[8]

The Economic and Social Council, by **decision 1995/245** of 24 July, took note of the summary report of the Board for 1994.[9]

In carrying out its responsibilities under the international conventions, the 13-member Board maintains a continuous dialogue with Governments. The information provided by Governments enables the Board to study the licit movement of narcotic drugs, thereby ensuring that the provisions of the drug conventions are strictly observed. That information, published annually by the Board, is used by Governments to verify whether or not they have adequately applied the conventions' provisions.

In its annual report, the Board draws attention to gaps and weaknesses in national control and in treaty compliance, and makes suggestions and recommendations for improvements at both the national and international levels.

The Board also collaborates with UNDCP, of which its secretariat forms a part, and with international bodies concerned with drug control, including the Commission on Narcotic Drugs, UN specialized agencies, particularly the World Health Organization (WHO), and other international bodies such as the International Criminal Police Organization and the Customs Co-operation Council (also called the World Customs Organization).

In 1995, the Board considered the subject of money laundering, suggesting that greater priority be given to combating that growing phenomenon as an effective means of addressing drug trafficking and organized crime. Noting that the international nature of money laundering made it essential to mobilize a global response to the problem, the Board recommended that harmonized policies be formulated and that countries be assisted, where necessary, in implementing such policies.

It expressed concern that while some progress had been made, to date no concrete steps had been taken by the international community to effectively coordinate the fight against money laundering world wide. Specifically, it recommended that information on the seizure and confiscation of proceeds derived from drug trafficking be systematically collected and disseminated.

In other areas, the Board emphasized the sharp and controversial increase in the use of methylphenidate, better known under its trade name of Ritalin, in the treatment of attention deficit disorder; and the abuse of synthetic drugs, in particular those known as "ecstasy" and "ice." Another concern was the international trade in seeds derived from illicitly cultivated cannabis plants and opium poppies.

The Board also recognized that the transportation and provision of controlled drugs needed for humanitarian aid in acute emergencies of natural or human origin constituted a genuine justification for non-application of the normal, regular control requirements.

## United Nations action

In 1995, the Commission on Narcotic Drugs, the Economic and Social Council and the General Assembly adopted resolutions aimed at strengthening international and regional cooperation against the illicit production, sale, demand, traffic and distribution of narcotic drugs and psychotropic substances. International cooperation was chosen as the theme for the high-level segment of the substantive session of the 1996 Economic and Social Council session, and all three bodies dealt with the proposal to convene an international conference to evaluate the international situation and status of international cooperation in those areas.

#### ECONOMIC AND SOCIAL COUNCIL ACTION

In February 1995, the Economic and Social Council recommended that, at its organizational session for 1996, the issue of international cooperation against the illicit production, sale, demand, traffic and distribution of narcotics and psychotropic substances and related activities be considered as a theme for the high-level segment of its substantive session of the coming year. In a July resolution (1995/40), the Council recommended that the General Assembly and the Commission on Narcotic Drugs give priority consideration to the proposal to convene an international conference to evaluate the international situation and the status of such cooperation.

On 10 February, the Council adopted **resolution 1995/1.**

**International cooperation against the illicit production, sale, demand, traffic and distribution of narcotics and psychotropic substances and related activities**
*The Economic and Social Council,*

*Recalling* General Assembly resolution 45/264 of 13 May 1991, on the restructuring and revitalization of the United Nations in the economic, social and related fields, by which the Assembly established guidelines for the high-level segment of the substantive session of the Economic and Social Council,

*Recalling also* General Assembly resolution 48/162 of 20 December 1993, by which the Assembly decided upon further measures to strengthen the Council, in particular as regards the high-level segment of its substantive session,

*Recalling further* General Assembly resolutions 48/12 of 28 October 1993 and 49/168 of 23 December 1994, in which the Assembly requested the Economic and Social Council to address at its high-level segment in 1995 the issue of international cooperation against the illicit production, sale, demand, traffic and distribution of narcotics and psychotropic substances and related activities,

*Reiterating* that it will continue to consider one or more major economic and/or social policy themes at its high-level segment,

*Strongly recommends* that, at its organizational session for 1996, the issue of international cooperation against the illicit production, sale, demand, traffic and distribution of narcotics and psychotropic substances and related activities be considered as a theme for the high-level segment of the Council's substantive session of 1996.

Economic and Social Council resolution 1995/1
10 February 1995      Meeting 6      Adopted without vote
Draft by Philippines, for Group of 77 and China (E/1995/L.5), orally revised;
  agenda item 3 (b).
*Meeting numbers.* ESC 5, 6.

On 27 July, the Council adopted **resolution 1995/40.**

**Strengthening of international cooperation against the illicit production, sale, demand, traffic and distribution of narcotic drugs and psychotropic substances**
*The Economic and Social Council,*

*Deeply concerned* that illicit demand for, production of, and trafficking in narcotic drugs and psychotropic substances are taking on new dimensions that threaten public health and the social, economic and political conditions in affected countries,

*Recalling* General Assembly resolution 48/12 of 28 October 1993, in particular its paragraphs 9 and 10,

*Reaffirming* the determination of the international community to use every means to fight against drug abuse and the production of and illicit trafficking in drugs in accordance with international law and on the basis of the principle of shared responsibility,

1. *Reiterates* the special recommendation, contained in its resolution 1995/1 of 10 February 1995, that the issue of international cooperation against the illicit production, sale, demand, traffic and distribution of narcotics and psychotropic substances and related activities should be the theme for the high-level segment of the substantive session of 1996;

2. *Recommends* that the General Assembly and the Commission on Narcotic Drugs give priority consideration to the proposal to convene an international conference for the purpose of evaluating the international situation and the status of international cooperation against the illicit production, sale, demand, traffic and distribution of narcotic drugs and psychotropic substances and related activities.

Economic and Social Council resolution 1995/40
27 July 1995      Meeting 56      Adopted without vote
Draft by Mexico and Philippines for Group of 77 and China (E/1995/L.34),
  orally revised following informal consultations; agenda item 5 *(h)*.
*Meeting numbers.* ESC 47, 48, 56.

On 24 July, the Economic and Social Council adopted **resolution 1995/17.**

**Enhanced regional cooperation to reduce the risks of drug abuse**
*The Economic and Social Council,*

*Alarmed* at the escalation of drug abuse problems and at the increase in the range of substances being abused in all regions,

*Recognizing* that the negative implications of drug abuse have global, regional and national dimensions,

*Also recognizing* the negative consequences caused by the abuse of licit drugs,

*Alarmed* at the increasing rate of infection by the human immunodeficiency virus (HIV), hepatitis C and other blood-borne viruses associated with injecting drug use,

*Deeply concerned* that illicit demand for, production of, and trafficking in narcotic drugs and psychotropic substances are taking on new dimensions that threaten public health and the social, economic and political conditions in affected countries and areas,

*Reaffirming* the determination of the international community to fight against drug abuse and illicit trafficking in accordance with international law and, in particular, with respect for the principle of the sovereignty and territorial integrity of States,

*Recognizing* that the Comprehensive Multidisciplinary Outline of Future Activities in Drug Abuse Control adopted by the International Conference on Drug Abuse and Illicit Trafficking and the Global Programme of Action adopted by the General Assembly at its seventeenth special session, on 23 February 1990, serve as useful guidelines for developing and implementing strategies to fight against the problems of drug abuse and illicit trafficking,

*Recalling* its resolution 1993/35 of 27 July 1993 on demand reduction as part of balanced national strategic plans to combat drug abuse,

*Commending* the initiatives and collaborative efforts of many countries as well as the establishment of regional coordinating bodies,

*Recognizing* the progress achieved by the United Nations International Drug Control Programme in the development and implementation of subregional strategies, and commending it for its efforts,

*Noting* the success of the Asia Pacific Conference on Drug Abuse: a Balanced Approach, held at Sydney, Australia, from 29 May to 2 June 1994, and the declaration adopted by that Conference, in which countries of the region reaffirmed their commitment to the following goals: coordinating and implementing comprehensive measures in both supply and demand reduction; a partnership between health, law enforcement and other relevant agencies, including non-governmental organizations; and effectively addressing the health and social consequences of substance abuse,

*Aware* of the need for a more comprehensive, integrated and collaborative approach to control the supply of, and demand for, all drugs of abuse, in close cooperation with relevant organizations of the United Nations system and other regional and international organizations,

*Recognizing* that the complexity of the drug problem requires all sections of the community and Government to work together,

*Also recognizing* the importance of developing and implementing comprehensive national strategic plans that incorporate a range of supply and demand reduction measures and take into account the social, economic and cultural conditions of individual countries, of establishing national coordinating mechanisms with the involvement of personnel responsible for both law enforcement and demand reduction, of identifying national priorities and coordinating the implementation of strategic plans, and of providing mechanisms for evaluation and, where necessary, redirection of strategies,

*Further recognizing* the need for countries to adopt a range of culturally appropriate prevention strategies, including treatment, education, information and rehabilitation, and addressing the social and family problems that may lead to drug abuse and the transmission of infectious diseases, such as acquired immunodeficiency syndrome (AIDS) and hepatitis, through the use of shared injecting equipment,

1. *Urges* all States and relevant organizations to strengthen their efforts to cooperate with the United Nations International Drug Control Programme in the development and implementation of subregional strategies and to give meaning and substance to the United Nations Decade against Drug Abuse, 1991-2000;

2. *Also urges* all States to ratify or accede to and effectively implement the international drug control conventions or, until ratification or accession thereto, and to the extent that they are able to do so, to apply provisionally the terms of those conventions;

3. *Encourages* the investigation, at the regional level, of the need for, and cost benefits of, mechanisms designed to support multi-agency approaches, such as regional conferences that periodically bring together health, law enforcement and other relevant agencies, including non-governmental organizations;

4. *Also encourages* initiatives and projects designed to establish effective regional networking to combat drug abuse;

5. *Urges* those States with expertise to share their knowledge and experience with other States in their region, having particular regard to priorities in the field of drug abuse control in the States concerned;

6. *Requests* the Secretary-General to transmit the present resolution to all Governments for consideration and implementation.

Economic and Social Council resolution 1995/17

24 July 1995         Meeting 49         Adopted without vote

Draft by Commission on Narcotic Drugs (E/1995/29); agenda item 5 *(h)*.
Meeting numbers. ESC 47-49.

**GENERAL ASSEMBLY ACTION**

On 21 December 1995, the General Assembly adopted **resolution 50/148**.

### International action to combat drug abuse and illicit production and trafficking

*The General Assembly*,

*Recalling* its resolutions 48/12 of 28 October 1993, 48/112 of 20 December 1993 and 49/168 of 23 December 1994,

*Profoundly alarmed* by the magnitude of the rising trend in drug abuse, illicit production and trafficking in narcotics and psychotropic substances, including synthetic and designer drugs, which threatens the health and well-being of millions of persons, in particular the youth, in all countries of the world,

*Gravely concerned* that, despite increased efforts by States and relevant international organizations, the illicit demand for, production of and traffic in narcotic drugs and psychotropic substances, including synthetic and designer drugs, have expanded globally and, therefore, continue to threaten seriously the socio-economic and political systems and the stability, national security and sovereignty of an increasing number of States,

*Deeply alarmed* by the growing violence and economic power of criminal organizations and terrorist groups that engage in the production of, traffic in and distribution of drugs, arms and precursors and essential chemicals, which at times places them beyond the reach of the law, corrupting institutions, undermining the full exercise of human rights and threatening the stability of many societies in the world,

*Deeply alarmed also* by the growing links at the transnational level between criminal organizations and terrorist groups engaged in drug trafficking activities and other criminal activities, such as money laundering and illicit traffic of arms and precursors and essential chemicals,

*Fully aware* that States, the relevant organizations of the United Nations system and multilateral development banks need to accord a higher priority to dealing with this scourge, which undermines development, economic and political stability and democratic institutions, and the combat against which entails increasing economic costs for Governments and the irreparable loss of human lives,

*Convinced* of the desirability of closer coordination and cooperation among States in combating drug-related crimes, such as terrorism, illicit arms trade and money laundering, and bearing in mind the role that could be played by both the United Nations and regional organizations in this respect,

*Reaffirming* that a comprehensive framework for international cooperation in drug control is provided by the existing drug control conventions, the Declaration and the Comprehensive Multidisciplinary Outline of Future Activities in Drug Abuse Control, the Political Declaration and Global Programme of Action adopted by the General Assembly at its seventeenth special session devoted to the question of international cooperation against illicit production, supply, demand, trafficking and distribution of narcotic and psychotropic substances, the Declaration adopted by the World Ministerial Summit to Reduce the Demand for Drugs and to Combat the Cocaine Threat, the United Nations System-wide Action Plan on Drug Abuse Control, the Naples Political Declaration and Global Action Plan against Organized Transnational Crime and other relevant international standards, and stressing the need for increased efforts to implement them,

*Recognizing* the efforts of countries which produce narcotic drugs for scientific, medicinal and therapeutic uses to prevent the diversion of such substances to illicit markets and to maintain production at a level consistent with licit demand in line with the Single Convention on Narcotic Drugs of 1961,

*Acknowledging* that there are links, under certain circumstances, between poverty and the increase in the illicit production of and trafficking in narcotic drugs and psychotropic substances and that the promotion of the economic development of countries affected by the illicit drug trade requires appropriate measures, including strengthened international cooperation in support of alternative and sustainable development activities in the affected areas of those countries, which have as their objectives the reduction and elimination of illicit drug production,

*Emphasizing* the need for an analysis of transit routes used by drug traffickers, which are constantly changing and expanding to include a growing number of countries and regions in all parts of the world,

*Underlining* the role of the Commission on Narcotic Drugs as the principal United Nations policy-making body on drug control issues,

*Reaffirming* the leadership role of the United Nations International Drug Control Programme as the main focus for concerted international action for drug abuse control, and commending the way in which it has carried out the functions entrusted to it,

*Recognizing* that the new forms of criminal activities of international drug trafficking organizations call for enhanced international cooperation, as well as a renewal of the international commitment to fight against these menaces, and require the formulation of new strategies, approaches and objectives which, respectful of the sovereignty of States, can deal more effectively with the international operations of those involved in the illegal traffic of drugs and arms, the diversion of precursors and essential chemicals, and money laundering through financial and non-financial operations,

### I
#### Respect for the principles enshrined in the Charter of the United Nations and international law in the fight against drug abuse and illicit production and trafficking

1. *Reaffirms* that the fight against drug abuse and illicit trafficking should not in any way justify violation of the principles enshrined in the Charter of the United Nations and international law, particularly respect for the sovereignty and territorial integrity of States and non-use of force or the threat of force in international relations;

2. *Calls upon* all States to intensify their actions to promote effective cooperation in the efforts to combat drug abuse and illicit trafficking, so as to contribute to a climate conducive to achieving this end, on the basis of the principles of equal rights and mutual respect;

### II
#### International action to combat drug abuse and illicit production and trafficking

1. *Renews its commitment* to further strengthening international cooperation and substantially increasing efforts against the illicit production, sale, demand, traffic and distribution of narcotics and psychotropic substances, based on the principle of shared responsibility and taking into account experience gained;

2. *Urges* all States to ratify or accede to and implement all the provisions of the Single Convention on Narcotic Drugs of 1961 as amended by the 1972 Protocol, the Convention on Psychotropic Substances of 1971 and the United Nations Convention against Illicit Traffic in Narcotic Drugs and Psychotropic Substances of 1988;

3. *Calls upon* all States to adopt adequate national laws and regulations, to strengthen national judicial systems and to carry out effective drug control activities in cooperation with other States in accordance with those international instruments;

4. *Requests* the United Nations International Drug Control Programme to continue to provide legal assistance to Member States which request it in adjusting their national laws, policies and infrastructures to implement the international drug control conventions, as well as assistance in training personnel responsible for applying the new laws;

5. *Supports* the focus on regional, subregional and national strategies for drug abuse control, particularly the master-plan approach, and urges the United Nations International Drug Control Programme to continue to complement those strategies with effective interregional strategies;

6. *Reaffirms* the danger and threat posed to civil society by drug trafficking and its links to terrorism, transnational crime, money laundering and the arms trade, and encourages Governments to deal with this threat and to cooperate to prevent the channelling of funds to and between those engaged in such activities;

7. *Acknowledges* that there are links between the illicit production of, demand for and traffic in narcotic drugs and psychotropic substances and the economic and social conditions in the affected countries and that there are differences and diversity in the problems of each country;

8. *Calls upon* the international community to provide increased economic and technical support to Governments which request it for programmes of alternative and sustainable development that have as their objectives the reduction and elimination of illicit drug production and that take fully into account the cultural traditions of peoples;

9. *Notes* the strong support expressed by members of the Commission on Narcotic Drugs for the initiatives of the United Nations International Drug Control Programme to establish a dialogue with multilateral development banks so that they might undertake lending and programming activities related to drug control in interested and affected countries, and requests the Executive Director of the Programme to inform the Commission of further progress made in this area;

10. *Stresses* the need for effective government action to prevent the diversion to illicit markets of precursors and essential chemicals, materials and equipment used in the illicit manufacture of narcotic drugs and psychotropic substances;

11. *Commends* the International Narcotics Control Board for its valuable work in monitoring the production and distribution of narcotic drugs and psychotropic substances so as to limit their use to medical and scientific purposes, and urges increased efforts to implement its mandate under article 12 of the United Nations Convention against Illicit Traffic in Narcotic Drugs and Psychotropic Substances concerning the monitoring of the movement of precursors and essential chemicals;

12. *Calls upon* the United Nations International Drug Control Programme to continue providing assistance to Member States which request it in establishing or strengthening national drug detection laboratories;

13. *Calls upon* States to increase efforts, with international cooperation, to reduce and eliminate illegal crops from which narcotics are obtained, as well as to prevent and reduce the demand for and the consumption of illicit drugs;

14. *Underlines* the need for Governments, with international cooperation, to increase and implement alternative development programmes with the objective of reducing and eliminating the production of illicit drugs, taking into account the economic, social, cultural, political and environmental aspects of the area concerned;

15. *Emphasizes* the need to maintain the capacity of the International Narcotics Control Board, including through the provision of appropriate means by the Secretary-General, within existing resources, and adequate technical support by the United Nations International Drug Control Programme;

16. *Reaffirms* the importance of achieving the objectives of the United Nations Decade against Drug Abuse 1991-2000, under the theme "A global response to a global challenge", by Member States, the United Nations International Drug Control Programme and the United Nations system;

17. *Takes note* of the provisional report presented to the Commission on Narcotic Drugs at its thirty-eighth session by the Executive Director of the United Nations International Drug Control Programme on the economic and social consequences of drug abuse and illicit trafficking, and invites the Commission to continue considering this issue in the context of the general debate;

18. *Welcomes* resolution 13(XXXVIII) of the Commission on Narcotic Drugs on the implementation of General Assembly resolution 48/12;

19. *Welcomes with satisfaction* Economic and Social Council resolution 1995/16 of 24 July 1995 on the integration of demand reduction initiatives into a cohesive strategy to combat drug abuse, in which, *inter alia*, the Council requested the Executive Director of the United Nations International Drug Control Programme, in consultation with Governments and appropriate agencies and organizations, to define clearly their global strategy for demand reduction and to develop a draft declaration on the guiding principles of demand reduction for submission to the Commission on Narcotic Drugs at its thirty-ninth session;

20. *Welcomes with satisfaction* resolution 5(XXXVIII) of the Commission on Narcotic Drugs on strategies for illicit supply reduction, reaffirming the need to apply effective strategies for supply reduction, based on the implementation of plans and programmes for alternative development, which have as their objectives the reduction and elimination of illicit drug production;

21. *Invites* the Economic and Social Council, while considering the issue of international cooperation against the illicit production, sale, demand, traffic and distribution of narcotics and psychotropic substances at its high-level segment of 1996, to pay special attention to the recommendations on the follow-up to General Assembly resolution 48/12, contained in the report of the Commission on Narcotic Drugs;

22. *Requests* the United Nations International Drug Control Programme, in its report on illicit traffic in drugs, to include an assessment of worldwide trends in illicit traffic and transit in narcotic drugs and psychotropic substances, including methods and routes used, and to recommend ways and means for improving the capacity of States along those routes to deal with all aspects of the drug problem;

### III
### Global Programme of Action

1. *Reaffirms* the importance of the Global Programme of Action as a comprehensive framework for national, regional and international action to combat illicit production of, demand for and trafficking in narcotic drugs and psychotropic substances;

2. *Calls upon* States to implement the mandates and recommendations of the Global Programme of Action, with a view to translating it into practical action for drug abuse control at the national, regional and international levels;

3. *Urges* all Governments and competent regional organizations to develop a balanced approach within the framework of comprehensive demand reduction activities, giving adequate priority to prevention, treatment, research, social reintegration and training in the context of national strategic plans to combat drug abuse;

4. *Calls upon* the relevant United Nations bodies, the specialized agencies, the international financial institutions and other concerned intergovernmental and non-governmental organizations to cooperate with and as-

sist States in their efforts to promote and implement the Global Programme of Action;

5. *Welcomes* the efforts made by the Commission on Narcotic Drugs and the United Nations International Drug Control Programme to facilitate reporting by Governments on the implementation of the Global Programme of Action, and encourages them to pursue those efforts so as to increase the number of Governments that respond;

6. *Notes* the efforts being made by the United Nations International Drug Control Programme and other United Nations bodies to obtain reliable data on drug abuse and illicit trafficking, including the development of the International Drug Abuse Assessment System, encourages the Programme, in cooperation with other United Nations bodies, to take further steps to facilitate the efficient collection of data so as to avoid duplication of effort, and encourages also the increased and timely provision of updated information by Member States;

7. *Invites* the United Nations International Drug Control Programme to consider ways of providing assistance to Member States which request it in their efforts to establish appropriate mechanisms to collect and analyse data and to seek voluntary resources for this purpose;

### IV
### Proposal for an international conference to combat the illicit production, sale, demand, traffic and distribution of narcotic drugs and psychotropic substances and related activities

1. *Takes note* of the recommendations contained in the report of the Executive Director of the United Nations International Drug Control Programme on the implementation of General Assembly resolution 48/12, including the recommendation regarding the proposal to convene an international conference ten years after the International Conference on Drug Abuse and Illicit Trafficking, to review progress made by Governments and the United Nations system in combating drug abuse and illicit trafficking;

2. *Takes note also* of resolution 13(XXXVIII) of the Commission on Narcotic Drugs, in which the Commission decided to keep under consideration the proposal for the convening of an international conference to review progress made by Governments and the United Nations system in combating drug abuse and illicit trafficking;

3. *Takes note further* of Economic and Social Council resolution 1995/40 of 27 July 1995, in which the Council recommended that the General Assembly and the Commission on Narcotic Drugs give priority consideration to the proposal to convene an international conference for the purpose of evaluating the international situation and the status of international cooperation against the illicit production, sale, demand, traffic and distribution of narcotic drugs and psychotropic substances and related activities;

4. *Takes note* of the proposal to hold a second international conference and requests the Commission on Narcotic Drugs to discuss this issue fully, as a matter of priority, at its thirty-ninth session, and to present its conclusions and suggestions through the Economic and Social Council to the General Assembly at its fifty-first session;

5. *Stresses* that, when discussing this issue, the Commission on Narcotic Drugs should take into account that the proposed conference should focus, with a balanced and integral approach, *inter alia*, on the assessment of existing strategies, as well as on the consideration of new strategies, methods, practical measures and concrete actions to strengthen international cooperation to address the problem of illicit drugs, including illicit demand reduction, illicit supply reduction, the promotion of alternative development programmes, the combat against criminal organizations and illicit arms trade related to drug trafficking, money laundering, the diversion of essential chemicals, the control of stimulants and their precursors and the promotion of law enforcement cooperation, on the basis of the principles and guidelines set forth in the present resolution;

6. *Also stresses* that, when considering the proposal for holding such a conference, the Commission on Narcotic Drugs should take into account international drug control priorities and resources, the financial and other implications of holding such a conference, as well as ways and means to increase the implementation of existing international conventions and other international instruments for cooperation on drug control;

### V
### Implementation of the United Nations System-wide Action Plan on Drug Abuse Control: action by organizations of the United Nations system

1. *Supports* the United Nations System-wide Action Plan on Drug Abuse Control as a vital tool for the coordination and enhancement of drug abuse control activities within the United Nations system, and requests that it be updated and reviewed on a biennial basis with a view to continuing efforts to improve its presentation and usefulness as a strategic tool of the United Nations for the drug problem;

2. *Reaffirms* the role of the Executive Director of the United Nations International Drug Control Programme in coordinating and providing effective leadership for all United Nations drug control activities so as to increase cost-effectiveness and ensure coherence of action within the Programme as well as coordination, complementarity and non-duplication of such activities throughout the United Nations system;

3. *Endorses* the agreed conclusions adopted by the Economic and Social Council at its coordination segment of 1994 regarding coordination by the United Nations International Drug Control Programme of drug control-related policies and activities of the United Nations system, including international financial institutions;

4. *Urges* the governing bodies of the United Nations organizations associated with the United Nations System-wide Action Plan on Drug Abuse Control to help ensure effective follow-up by including drug control in their agendas with a view to assessing the activities undertaken in accordance with the Plan and examining how the drug problem is addressed in relevant programmes;

5. *Invites* Member States to inform the Economic and Social Council at its high-level segment of 1996 on progress in international cooperation, especially on specific national efforts to engage the United Nations system and the multilateral development banks in addressing the drug problem;

## VI

United Nations International Drug Control Programme

1. *Welcomes* the efforts of the United Nations International Drug Control Programme to implement its mandates within the framework of the international drug control treaties, the Comprehensive Multidisciplinary Outline of Future Activities in Drug Abuse Control, the Global Programme of Action and relevant consensus documents;

2. *Notes with concern* the decline of available resources for the Fund of the United Nations International Drug Control Programme;

3. *Urges* all Governments to provide the fullest possible financial and political support to the United Nations International Drug Control Programme, in particular by increasing voluntary contributions to the Programme, to enable it to continue, expand and strengthen its operational and technical cooperation activities;

4. *Invites* Governments and the United Nations International Drug Control Programme to consider ways and means of improving the coordination of United Nations drug control-related activities;

5. *Welcomes* the work of the Commission on Narcotic Drugs at its thirty-eighth session on the programme budget of the Fund of the United Nations International Drug Control Programme, in accordance with the mandate contained in section XVI, paragraph 2, of General Assembly resolution 46/185 C of 20 December 1991;

6. *Notes with appreciation* the efforts made by the Executive Director of the United Nations International Drug Control Programme to comply with the approved format and methodology of the programme budget of the Fund, in accordance with relevant resolutions of the Commission on Narcotic Drugs and the General Assembly and the recommendations of the Advisory Committee on Administrative and Budgetary Questions, and encourages the Executive Director to continue his efforts to improve the presentation and transparency of the budget;

7. *Stresses* the importance of the meetings of heads of national law enforcement agencies, and encourages them to consider ways to improve their functioning and to strengthen their impact so as to enhance cooperation in the fight against drugs at the regional level;

## VII

1. *Takes note* of the reports of the Secretary-General submitted under the item entitled ''International drug control'';

2. *Requests* the Secretary-General, taking into account the promotion of integrated reporting:

*(a)* To submit to the General Assembly at its fifty-first session an updated report on the status of the United Nations Convention against Illicit Traffic in Narcotic Drugs and Psychotropic Substances;

*(b)* To include, in his annual report on the implementation of the Global Programme of Action, recommendations on ways and means to improve implementation and provision of information by Member States.

General Assembly resolution 50/148

21 December 1995     Meeting 97     Adopted without vote

Approved by Third Committee (A/50/631) without vote, 8 November (meeting 21); 64-nation draft (A/C.3/50/L.14); agenda item 108.
*Meeting numbers.* GA 50th session: 3rd Committee 3, 12-17, 19, 21; plenary 9, 11-13, 15, 17, 19, 21, 22, 24, 25, 27, 28, 97.

*REFERENCES*

[1]YUN 1961, p. 382. [2]YUN 1972, p. 397. [3]YUN 1971, p. 380. [4]YUN 1988, p. 690. [5]E/1995/29 (res. 7(XXXVIII)). [6]Ibid. (res. 13(XXXVIII)). [7]A/50/460. [8]*Report of the International Narcotics Control Board for 1995* (E/INCB/1995/1), Sales No. E.96.XI.1. [9]E/1995/48.

# World drug situation

The International Narcotics Control Board (INCB) in 1995 provided a regional analysis[1] of drug abuse trends and control efforts currently under way, so that Governments would be kept aware of existing and potential situations that might endanger the objectives of international drug control treaties. A summary of the 1995 INCB report[2] was also made available, for consideration by the Economic and Social Council.

### Africa

Taking into account the enormous problems created by the political and social conflicts experienced in many African States, the Board in 1995 drew the attention of Governments in Africa to the links between the drug problem and criminality and corruption, as well as their negative effects on economic stability and health.

Although cannabis continued to be illicitly cultivated in most African countries, the INCB noted, Western countries had reported seizures of large consignments of cannabis resin arriving from West Asia through ports in East and West Africa. African seaports and airports also continued to be used for the traffic of heroin from Asia to Europe and North America. The Board reported that Africans were increasingly being used as couriers for transporting cocaine from South America through northern and western Africa to Europe. African Governments were urged to speed the process of adopting adequate drug control legislation and establishing operational national drug control coordinating bodies.

Large-scale cannabis cultivation continued in the mountainous Rif area of Morocco. Large seizures of Nigerian cannabis arriving in Europe suggested that there was substantial cultivation in that country. Eradication of cannabis plantations was reported in Egypt and the Sudan; in South Africa and Swaziland, more than 6,000 tonnes of illicitly cultivated plants were eradicated, mainly through aerial spraying. In 1995, some 40 tonnes of West Asian cannabis resin were seized in Mozambique alone. A sharp increase in the abuse of cannabis was reported in several West African countries.

Illicit opium poppy cultivation continued in Egypt; however, more than 10 million poppy plants had been eradicated in the previous year in remote areas of the Sinai peninsula and along the Nile. Smaller-scale, sporadic opium poppy cultivation was discovered in Chad, Côte d'Ivoire and Nigeria.

The Board commented on the sharp increase in local abuse of heroin due to the availability of the drug at low prices in many African cities. Concern was expressed over the increased availability and abuse of cocaine, particularly in major cities. The abuse of crack was reported in Ghana, Nigeria, Senegal and South Africa. Also of growing concern was the abuse of psychotropic substances in the region, with evidence of diversion of legally imported shipments and inadequate supervision of the pharmaceutical system.

## Americas

### South and Central America and the Caribbean

Countries in Latin America, particularly in Central America and the Caribbean, were increasingly used by international drug traffickers as transit points for illicit drugs, particularly cocaine and heroin, the INCB reported. Drug-related violence increased in the Caribbean, where drug traffickers were gaining a foothold, allowing them to pose a real threat to the political stability of the subregion. Puerto Rico and the United States Virgin Islands appeared to have become preferred points of entry into North America, while Aruba, the British Virgin Islands, Martinique and the Netherlands Antilles were used as gateways to the drug markets in France, the Netherlands and the United Kingdom.

Cannabis, commonly abused in the region, was illicitly cultivated in many countries, particularly in Brazil and Colombia, and in the Caribbean for local consumption. Colombia and Jamaica continued to produce and supply cannabis for Europe and North America.

Repeated seizures of high-purity heroin of Colombian origin in Europe and North America seemed to indicate that poppy cultivation, opium production and heroin and/or morphine manufacture continued in that country. Peru and Bolivia remained the largest coca leaf producers in the world. Coca paste continued to be produced mostly in those two countries and was smuggled into Colombia for final processing into cocaine hydrochloride. The latter was also increasingly manufactured in Bolivia and Peru, though on a smaller scale. Coca paste abuse posed serious social and health problems in those Andean countries.

The increasing use of psychotropic substances, particularly anxiolytics (minor tranquillizers) and amphetamine-type drugs, was reported mainly in the urban areas of some South American countries.

### Central America and the Caribbean

The geographic location and limited interception capabilities of the countries of Central America and the Caribbean continue to be exploited by international drug traffickers for the large-scale transshipment of cocaine and, in the case of the Caribbean countries, cannabis bound for North American and European markets. The Board commented on the successful interdiction action taken in the Bahamas, southern Florida and the Turks and Caicos Islands, which had resulted in traffickers shifting the focus of their illegal activities to the eastern Caribbean, where controls were seen as less stringent. The Board noted with concern that large quantities of ephedrine from Asia and Europe were being channelled through Guatemala to Mexico and the United States.

Governments in Central America and the Caribbean needed a continued commitment to defining comprehensive drug control policies and to establishing the legislative basis and administrative structures necessary for implementation of such policies, the Board stated. It commented on the weak banking and financial structures of most countries in Central America, stating that such weakness made them prime targets for money laundering activities. However, the Board welcomed the creation of a regional legal centre in Costa Rica for the improvement of drug control legislation in Central American countries, as well as financial support provided by the Government of Honduras for the operation of the permanent Central American Commission for the Eradication of Drug Abuse, Production and Illicit Trafficking.

### South America

The Board urged the Governments of South America to afford the highest priority to the fight against money laundering in order that the large flow of capital stemming from illicit drug production, manufacture and trafficking would not have a long-lasting negative social, economic and political impact. It also appreciated the efforts made by the Inter-American Drug Abuse Control Commission to fill the gap left by the dissolution of the South American Agreement on Narcotic Drugs and Psychotropic Substances, as well as efforts by the UN International Drug Control Programme (UNDCP) to promote subregional strategies and programmes. The Board noted the successful eradication and interdiction efforts undertaken in Colombia, and expressed the hope that political difficulties there would not reduce the strong commitment of that Government to fighting against drug trafficking organizations and the illicit cultivation, production and manufacture of drugs.

Coca-bush cultivation and coca-leaf production patterns in South America remained unchanged during 1995. The Board continued to draw the attention of the Commission on Narcotic Drugs to the fact that the practices of the Governments of Argentina, Bolivia and Peru with respect to licit and illicit coca-bush cultivation and coca-leaf production and consumption were not in conformity with the provisions of the 1961 Convention.

### North America

In North America, the Board noted that the principal goal of the United States drug control strategy in 1995 was to reduce the number of drug abusers within the country, a strategy linked to efforts to empower communities, curb youth violence and preserve the family. The Board noted the multifaceted campaign undertaken by Mexico against illicit cultivation, production, manufacture, trafficking and abuse, and action taken by Mexico to eliminate the corruption of officials and to strengthen legal controls so as to prevent money laundering. The Board referred to the results achieved in Canada through the Government's comprehensive demand reduction strategy, although it noted with concern that the considerable volume of financial flows between Canada and the United States had contributed to the attraction of Canada for persons engaged in money laundering.

Despite some successful eradication campaigns, illicit cannabis cultivation persisted in Canada, Mexico and the United States. Mexico remained a supplier of cannabis to the United States, despite increasing amounts seized by its law enforcement authorities, although quantities also came from other countries, particularly Colombia, Thailand and, increasingly, Jamaica. At the same time, the market share of locally produced cannabis was on the increase in Canada and the United States (30 and 25 per cent, respectively).

Opium poppy was cultivated illicitly in Mexico, with the opium produced being used for the manufacture of heroin, usually smuggled into the United States. However, the proportion of heroin of Mexican origin on the illicit market in the United States was relatively small (about 5 per cent), compared with heroin from Asia and South America (57 and 32 per cent, respectively).

Heroin abuse was reportedly on the increase in Canada, particularly in urban areas, and in the United States, where injecting the drug remained the principal route of administration, used by an estimated 62 per cent of abusers.

Due to the large illicit supply of cocaine from South America (more than 100 tonnes were seized in 1994), the drug was freely available in most cities in the United States. There was a spectacular decrease in the number of occasional abusers from 1985 (an estimated 12 million) to 1993 (4 million). In 1994, however, increasing cocaine abuse and a growing number of cocaine-related emergency room admissions were reported. While cocaine abuse in Canada continued to decline, some increase was observed in Mexico, in the proximity of the northern borders.

In the United States, the clandestine manufacture of, illicit traffic in and abuse of methamphetamine grew. In Mexico and the United States, there was a direct link between clandestine methamphetamine manufacture and the diversion of ephedrine from licit sources. Illicit traffic in and abuse of hallucinogens also increased in the United States. Lysergic acid diethylamide (LSD) was sold mostly in small tablets (''microdots'') or in the form of small paper squares (''stamps''). Crystallyzed LSD, manufactured in clandestine laboratories in the United States, was often smuggled out of the country, mainly into Europe.

## Asia

### East and South-East Asia

Money laundering was recognized as a major problem by several Governments in the region, as the informal banking system offered plenty of opportunities for such activity and made it difficult for Governments to introduce countermeasures.

Cannabis was growing wild and was extensively cultivated in many countries in South-East Asia, the INCB reported. In Thailand, its cultivation had spread from the northern and north-eastern provinces to other parts of the country. Cannabis was the main drug of abuse in Indonesia and the Philippines, and was reportedly used in most countries of the region. Export of cannabis from parts of the region to Australia, Japan, the United States and other countries was substantial.

Illicit poppy cultivation and opium production also continued, with Myanmar the largest opium producer. Illicit poppy cultivation was considerably reduced in the Lao People's Democratic Republic and Viet Nam as a consequence of development projects and eradication programmes. There were reports of some illicit poppy cultivation and opium production in Cambodia and China, mainly in the remote areas of Yunnan Province.

Heroin manufacture reportedly increased in Myanmar. The operation of small heroin laboratories was also reported in northern border areas in Thailand. South-East Asia was a major supplier of illicit heroin to markets throughout the world, with many trafficking routes leading from Cambodia, Hong Kong and Thailand to Australia, the United States and Europe. In some cases, West

African countries were used as transit points. Substantial quantities of heroin were consumed locally, with heroin addiction growing rapidly in various parts of the region. The shift from opium to heroin abuse continued among hill tribes, but heroin abuse was also reported in some urban centres in, for example, Myanmar, where it had been almost non-existent two years before.

Among psychotropic substances, the illicit manufacture, trafficking and abuse of methamphetamine (commonly called "ice" or "shabu") represented a major problem, particularly in East Asia. Its manufacture in parts of China, the Philippines and Thailand, its traffic in Hong Kong, Japan and the Republic of Korea, and its abuse in Japan, the Philippines, the Republic of Korea and Thailand were connected with the activities of criminal organizations. Growing abuse of benzodiazepines was also reported in some countries.

### South Asia

The Board noted that the countries of South Asia were improving and updating their national narcotics legislation, strengthening their control administration, and enhancing their activities in the field of demand reduction; such efforts, however, had not yet had an overall positive impact on abuse and trafficking. Cannabis continued to be widely cultivated in South Asia, although most of it was used within the region. The region continued to be the venue of growing transit activity in heroin from South-West and South-East Asia.

In India, licensed farmers licitly cultivated poppy plants and produced opium under governmental control. To prevent diversion, Indian authorities intensified the supervision of licit opium production areas and conducted eradication campaigns in other states where illicit poppy cultivation had been detected. The abuse of opium continued in some Indian states. The clandestine manufacture of heroin was reported in India. Cooperation between Indian and Pakistani law enforcement authorities improved, leading to some successes, but traffickers sought new routes for smuggling heroin into India from Afghanistan and Pakistan. Sri Lankan drug traffickers had apparently developed close links with traffickers in India and Pakistan, transporting heroin of South-West Asian origin through both countries. The spread of heroin abuse constituted a major problem in South Asia. In India, intravenous heroin abuse remained a major concern as it was spreading from northern India and large cities to other, more rural areas, and was associated with an alarming increase in the incidence of human immunodeficiency virus/acquired immunodeficiency syndrome (HIV/AIDS) infection.

In Sri Lanka, the number of heroin abusers continued to increase, a pattern consistent with that of the previous three years. Bangladesh, used as transit country for heroin destined for Europe or North America, also witnessed growing abuse. The abuse of psychotropic substances was on the increase in almost all countries of the region, and illicit manufacture of methaqualone continued in India, with significant quantities being smuggled into African countries.

### West Asia

In the region of West Asia, the Board noted with satisfaction the increasing cooperation between member States of the Economic Cooperation Organization, as well as the close cooperation in the field of drug control between Egypt, Israel, Jordan and the Palestinian authorities and UNDCP, and noted the initiatives and efforts being undertaken by the League of Arab States, the Gulf Cooperation Council and the Governments of the States that are members of the Commonwealth of Independent States (CIS). The lack of demand reduction activities in many countries in West Asia was emphasized, and the Board urged the Governments of the States in the region to attach high priority to such prevention programmes.

According to INCB, heroin and opium were increasingly transported across the territories of the five central Asian members of CIS—Kazakstan, Kyrgyzstan, Tajikistan, Turkmenistan and Uzbekistan—mainly from Afghanistan and Pakistan to countries in Europe. Such transit traffic was expected to expand rapidly with the introduction of new international air and railway connections, the extension of the Karakorum highway and the restoration of the silk road which was in the planning stage. Some of the CIS members were also major manufacturers of chemicals that could be used for the illicit manufacture of narcotic drugs and psychotropic substances. The Board was of the opinion that there was an urgent need to create appropriate legal frameworks and strengthen law enforcement structures in CIS member States, and was concerned at the absence of mechanisms to control new financial institutions and banking activities in CIS States.

In Afghanistan, illicit opium production was around 2,300 tonnes, about one third less than in crop year 1993/1994, due to large-scale eradication, lower prices and increased cultivation costs, and possibly to effective border control and the fight against drug trafficking by some neighbouring countries.

Heroin manufacture continued in the region, with large amounts of morphine and heroin base smuggled out of Afghanistan and Pakistan, particularly into Turkey. Clandestine laboratories for the manufacture of heroin hydrochloride were dismantled in Turkey's eastern provinces and, increasingly, in the Istanbul area. In Afghanistan, the number of clandestine heroin laboratories grew; many of them were located in the northern part, close to the border with Tajikistan, Turkmenistan and Uzbekistan, to facilitate the procurement of chemicals needed for heroin manufacture. In Kazakstan, large amounts of acetic anhydride were manufactured and illicitly used, also in "kitchen laboratories", to manufacture heroin. Heroin abuse reportedly was on the rise in Afghanistan and Turkmenistan, and continued to be of grave concern in Pakistan.

Afghanistan and Pakistan remained important suppliers of cannabis to European drug markets. The large-scale traffic in cannabis and cannabis resin continued to create problems for the transit countries in West Asia, as well as in Europe. The illicit cultivation of cannabis was reported in all CIS member States. In the CIS members in central Asia and in the Caucasus (Armenia, Azerbaijan and Georgia), wild-growing cannabis covered large areas, i.e., 140,00 hectares in Kazakstan and 6,000 hectares in Kyrgyzstan.

## Europe

The Board expressed concern that while Western European countries were increasing their cooperation and implementing advanced levels of legislation to counter the drug problem, no comprehensive drug legislation had been enacted in any of the formerly socialist countries of Eastern Europe. Although it noted that the Netherlands had undertaken initiatives to bring its drug policy more in line with international drug-control treaties, the Board expressed continued concern at the persistence of certain practices that called into question the Government's fidelity to its treaty obligations, and also pointed out that the Netherlands had become a significant producer of cannabis cultivated indoors. The abolition of border controls within the European Union, the opening of borders between East and West, and the ongoing war in the former Yugoslavia, which had disrupted the traditional Balkan route and caused traffickers to diversify their routes, continued to be major challenges to drug control and law enforcement authorities in the fulfilment of their responsibilities. Cannabis continued to be the principal drug of abuse in Europe. Heroin continued to be abused more in western Europe, although there were signs that heroin abuse was emerging in some countries of central and eastern Europe. The Board reported that the Baltic States had witnessed increasing abuse of synthetic opioids.

Crimes connected with illicit drug trafficking increased in Europe, particularly in the central and eastern parts more and more used as transit routes. The adverse impact of the activities of criminal organizations on the political, economic and social stability was strongest in CIS member States where the interdiction capability of law enforcement services remained limited.

There were close links between drug trafficking and money laundering in the Russian Federation where the latter was not a criminal offence under current national legislation and was frequently conducted through private businesses, insurance companies, national institutions, exchange offices and real estate agencies, and through newly privatized factories, companies, hotels, etc.

Cocaine seizures increased significantly, including in France, the Netherlands and the United Kingdom. The central and eastern European States were more and more used by South American cartels as transit points for cocaine destined for markets in western Europe, with Poland becoming particularly important in that regard. Despite the emergence of new trafficking routes, however, the Iberian peninsula remained the most important point of entry into Europe for cocaine from South America. Nationals of West African countries continued to be used as couriers to smuggle cocaine via West African airports into Europe.

Abuse of psychotropic substances increased, with amphetamine being widely available in most countries. Large quantities of amphetamine originating mainly in the Netherlands, as well as Poland, were seized in several western European countries and the Nordic States. There were signs that illicit amphetamine and methamphetamine manufacture took place, on a smaller scale, in several other European countries. The black market for metamphetamine in the Czech Republic was supplied by a large number of small, clandestine "home laboratories". Abuse of stimulants, such as ecstasy, was a new and rapidly increasing phenomenon.

## Oceania

As for abuse and trafficking of drugs in Oceania, which had not yet become a focus of major international concern, the Board noted that the Pacific islands were increasingly being used by drug traffickers as transit points, and the capacity of police and customs services was not sufficient to control the increasing illicit drug trade. In addition, as the Pacific islands moved to modernize their economic and financial systems, they might become more attractive to criminal activities, such as money laundering. In the region as a whole, with the exception of Australia and New Zealand, the problem of drug abuse seems to be limited to the abuse of cannabis.

Illicit cultivation persisted in several countries in Oceania, including Australia, Fiji, New Zealand, Papua New Guinea and Samoa. Cannabis remained the most popular drug of abuse in Australia, as well as in New Zealand and Papua New Guinea. Cannabis originating in the latter was frequently seized in Australia. Heroin abuse continued in both Australia and New Zealand, where frequently codeine or morphine was being extracted from pharmaceutical preparations and converted into heroin by drug abusers.

The illicit manufacture and abuse of methamphetamine, as well as hallucinogenic amphetamines, remained major problems in Australia. Precursors for the manufacture of such substances were usually obtained from the United States and Europe. New hallucinogenic "designer drugs" were also seized. The abuse of stimulants (amphetamine and methamphetamine) was also reported in New Zealand where the increasing use of hallucinogens was considered by the Government to be a problem.

*REFERENCES*

[1]*Report of the International Narcotics Control Board for 1995* (E/ICNB/1995/1), Sales No. E/96.XI.1. [2]E/1995/48.

# UN programmes to combat drug abuse

## United Nations International Drug Control Programme

The General Assembly in 1990 asked the Secretary-General to create a single drug control programme to be called the United Nations International Drug Control Programme (UNDCP), based in Vienna, integrating within it the Division of Narcotic Drugs of the UN Secretariat, the secretariat of the International Narcotics Control Board (INCB), and the UN Fund for Drug Abuse Control.[1]

UNDCP, considered the main focus for concerted international action for drug abuse control, was established in 1991, with four main substantive components: treaty implementation and legal services, operational activities, technical services, and inter-organizational cooperation.

During 1995, the Programme continued to support the efforts of Governments to combat the drug problem by promoting closer cooperation between Governments at the subregional level, particularly in order to counter cross-border illicit trafficking. Subregional cooperation was a successful strategic initiative of UNDCP in 1995.

During the year, the international community paid increased attention to the illicit traffic in and abuse of narcotic drugs and psychotropic substances, acknowledged to be a major threat to the fabric of society and the security of States. While the situation remained critical, according to the UNDCP Executive Director, several windows of opportunity had opened in 1995, and unprecedented strides were being made in combating the illicit supply of drugs and in countering drug abuse. Of

particular significance were political developments in South-East Asia, where Governments had committed themselves to cooperating more closely in fighting the drug menace.

### Activities of UNDCP

Activities of UNDCP in 1995 were under way at the national, regional and international levels. UNDCP had sought, through a balanced approach targeting both illicit traffic and demand, directly to support government efforts to combat drug problems at the national level, and had given prominence to the formulation and implementation of national drug-control master plans and to strengthening the national institutions mandated to implement them.

The regional approach had provided UNDCP with a viable means of promoting enhanced cooperation, in particular cross-border cooperation, between Governments fighting the drug menace in vulnerable regions. UNDCP channeled government resources into regionally focused operational activities, formalizing them under the framework of memoranda of understanding.

At the global level, UNDCP in 1995 promoted the adoption and effective implementation of drug control treaties and continued to act as a repository and clearing-house for research-based findings on the illicit drug phenomenon. The year 1995 was also characterized by intensified inter-agency coordination and cooperation with regional and international organizations, particularly the international financial institutions.

The Executive Director of UNDCP, in a report[2] to the Commission on Narcotic Drugs, outlined UNDCP activities in 1995 on a regional basis, summaries of which follow.

### Africa

In 1995, as a follow-up to the memorandum of understanding adopted in 1994 by UNDCP and the Organization of African Unity (OAU), UNDCP assisted in the preparation of a draft plan of action and declaration for drug control at the continental level. A main feature of the plan was an appeal to regional institutions to support efforts to combat the drug problem. Subregional workshops and conferences were held on judicial cooperation against drugs (Saint Denis/Réunion) and cross-border trafficking (Mmabatho, South Africa). A draft protocol on combating illicit drugs in southern Africa was adopted at the latter.

At the country-level, a UNDCP priority in Africa was support for Governments in establishing or strengthening institutional capabilities to deal with drug problems. Assistance was provided to States in West, central, eastern and southern Africa to establish or support interministerial policy planning and coordination bodies.

Given the increasing scale of traffic in and through South Africa, UNDCP launched initiatives to support the Government in its efforts to combat the drug phenomenon, including drug interdiction training and the strengthening of drug detection capability of law enforcement agencies and investigative methods used in drug-related cases.

In 1995, both Niger and Zambia initiated preparations for national master plans. UNDCP contributed to the elaboration and adoption of a national drug-control strategy in Nigeria; a national drug-control master plan was completed in Namibia.

UNDCP completed a programme to assist Egypt, through its Anti-Narcotics General Administration, to interdict drug trafficking and illicit cultivation and to promote more effective anti-drug operations by delivering technical, communications and training equipment.

In order to obtain more comprehensive information about the nature and extent of drug abuse, UNDCP launched a series of drug abuse assessment surveys in selected African countries. In 1995, the results of a rapid assessment study undertaken in Kenya provided basic information enabling the Government to elaborate demand reduction programmes for young adults. Similarly, in Ethiopia, a rapid assessment study was completed, to assist in establishing national demand-reduction policies and strategies. In Egypt, UNDCP laid the groundwork for an assessment study in 1996.

### Asia and the Pacific

A landmark development in subregional cooperation in South-East Asia was the adoption of a plan of action at a ministerial meeting in Beijing, China in May 1995 by signatories to the UNDCP memorandum of understanding concerning South-East Asia. The States involved were Cambodia, China, Lao People's Democratic Republic, Myanmar, Thailand and Viet Nam.

A memorandum of understanding was signed in August 1995 with the South Asian Association for Regional Cooperation, and in March 1995 with the Economic Cooperation Organization, providing a further framework for collaboration in drug-control activities between the States of South-West Asia and Common wealth of Independent States (CIS) member States in central Asia.

Activities to strengthen surveillance capabilities of law enforcement agencies in the border areas of Iran and Pakistan were undertaken during the first year of a joint project with UNDCP. There was increased collaboration between India and Pakistan on drug control matters, initiated by UNDCP. Agreement was reached by those two countries in 1995 to undertake controlled deliveries, to exchange names of officials serving as contacts at the field level in connection with anti-drug operations, and to establish joint telecommunication facilities.

During the year, illicit cultivation of opium poppy in Afghanistan continued to be monitored by UNDCP, which confirmed that country as the major producer of illicit opiates in the Golden Crescent of South-West Asia and as a principal source of heroin for the European market. The fragile and uncertain political situation in that country was not conducive to implementing drug control activities, a factor preventing Afghanistan from participating in subregional cooperation initiatives, UNDCP reported.

Myanmar was also a major producer in 1995 of illicit opiates, the principal producer in the Golden Triangle of South-East Asia and the major source of heroin in the illicit North American market in 1994/1995. UNDCP supported a rapid assessment study of mining areas, border towns, poppy cultivation areas and high-risk urban areas, which indicated that heroin was the dominant drug of abuse and confirmed a high rate of HIV-infection among hard-core abusers. Myanmar had become a major partner in subregional programmes aimed at supply reduction in border areas, demand reduction and law enforcement, UNDCP reported. However, the unstable political situation on the border between Myanmar and Thailand and in other opium-producing border areas had interrupted some UNDCP project activities.

Opium production dropped measurably in a UNDCP project area in the Lao People's Democratic Republic; during 1994 and 1995, about 2,000 villagers earned alternative income through labour-intensive road construction.

In Viet Nam, the Government completed development of a national drug-control master plan with UNDCP assistance. To address the problem of opium poppy cultivation, a demonstration alternative development project was launched in the major producing area.

Plans, strategies and projects were also developed, with UNDCP assistance, in Bangladesh, Nepal, Sri Lanka, and Malaysia, among other countries.

### Europe and the Middle East

UNDCP supported activities in 34 countries in the region during the year. Some 30 new national and subregional projects were developed for the 1994-1995 biennium.

UNDCP served as the axis for providing technical assistance to central and eastern Europe, the Baltic States and members of the Commonwealth of Independent States (CIS). A new subregional cooperation programme was started for the five CIS member States in central Asia, which were emerging as centres for production, processing, trafficking, redistribution and domestic abuse of illicit drugs. Other new programmes were launched for five central European nations and for Middle East countries.

Illicit trafficking in and abuse of narcotic drugs and psychotropic substances continued to spread throughout central and eastern Europe, and UNDCP increased cooperation with the European Commission in a drug programme for 11 States in that area. In central Europe, the Governments of the Czech Republic, Hungary, Poland, Slovakia and Slovenia signed a memorandum of understanding with UNDCP on subregional cooperation.

The region of the Black Sea was becoming a new drug-trafficking route affecting several States of southern Europe and CIS countries. UNDCP was preparing a comprehensive action plan involving Albania, Bulgaria, the former Yugoslav Republic of Macedonia and Turkey, with its extension to CIS nations bordering the Black Sea envisaged for a later stage.

A landmark development in cooperation in drug-related matters between States in the Middle East was the convening of a technical meeting in Cairo, Egypt in July 1995, involving Egypt, Israel, Jordan and the Palestinian Authority, to identify joint drug-control problems, particularly patterns in the trafficking in and abuse of drugs. The first phase of an integrated area-development project in the Bekaa Valley in Lebanon, sponsored by UNDCP and the United Nations Development Programme (UNDP), was completed with the presentation of a detailed development plan into the year 2000.

### Latin America and the Caribbean

UNDCP continued to build and strengthen the capacities of Governments and civil society to carry out demand reduction and other programmes. An important objective was to strengthen international and regional coooperation in drug control matters. Information sharing, through regional meetings and other means, was planned, as was strengthened cooperation between recipient States, for example by increasing the number of subregional drug-control projects in vulnerable areas through cost-sharing or other co-funding arrangements within the framework of memoranda of understanding.

Some 500 drug control police and customs officials of several Caribbean and South American countries were trained under the ongoing UNDCP programmes with the Caribbean Customs Law Enforcement Agency and the World Customs Organization (WCO). In cooperation with the International Criminal Police Organization (INTERPOL), telecommunications systems dealing with the exchange of drug-related information were strengthened in 28 countries and territories of the Caribbean region. UNDCP, in cooperation with

WCO, supported information gathering and analysis capabilities of customs authorities of Argentina, Bolivia, Brazil, Chile, Colombia, Ecuador, Guyana, Paraguay, Peru, Uruguay and Venezuela. Training courses were held in Martinique for more than 140 law enforcement officers from Caribbean customs, air and seaport security administrations, who were trained in precursors control, investigation techniques and intelligence gathering. The Caribbean training programme for prosecutors and magistrates contributed to improved legal systems and coordination in the Bahamas, Belize, Guyana and the English-speaking islands of the eastern Caribbean.

As a follow-up to the memorandum of understanding adopted in 1994 under the aegis of UNDCP between Argentina, Bolivia, Chile and Peru, a subregional training programme for drug law enforcement was approved. Agreement was reached in 1995 between UNDCP, the Inter-American Drug Abuse Control Commission and the Organization of American States (OAU) on exchanging information, joint programming and coordination of activities. A regional symposium on customs drug enforcement in the Caribbean was held in Martinique in March. Training programmes were sponsored for prosecutors, magistrates, judges and police officials.

Efforts were made at the country level in the area of treatment, rehabilitation and social reintegration, with programmes for health authorities of the Bahamas, Barbados, Dominican Republic, Jamaica and Trinidad and Tobago. In Colombia, national and municipal authorities and non-governmental organizations (NGOs) established referral systems for such programmes. UNDCP investments in alternative development in the Andean region resulted in cumulative eradication of about 10,000 hectares of illicit coca-bush cultivation and provision of services and alternative income-generating activities for about 33,000 peasant families involved in illicit crop cultivation. Such programmes were continuing in Bolivia, Colombia and Peru; the process was most advanced in Colombia, where with UNDCP support, a national plan had been developed.

In 1995, UNDCP assisted 14 countries in the Caribbean and six countries in Latin America to update and complete their national drug-control plans. Preventive education and mass-media campaigns targeting specific groups were considered effective. In several States, particularly Bolivia, Brazil, Colombia and Jamaica, as well as other Caribbean States, demand reduction concerns were linked to wider national health and education programmes.

Drug abuse and trafficking analyses focusing on youth in especially difficult circumstances in Jamaica, Trinidad and Tobago, St. Martin, and

Saint Vincent and the Grenadines resulted in useful data for developing demand reduction programmes. Similarly, a drug abuse rapid assessment survey conducted in four major cities in Ecuador provided authorities with data to design well-targeted national demand-reduction programmes.

## UNDCP cooperation with other bodies

### Crime Prevention and Criminal Justice Branch

The Commission on Narcotic Drugs in a March resolution[3] requested UNDCP, in cooperation with the Crime Prevention and Criminal Justice Branch of the Secretariat, jointly to provide technical assistance to requesting States in the training of judicial and investigative personnel, in the elaboration of treaties of mutual assistance in criminal matters and extradition, and in the prevention and control of money laundering and the illicit transfer of assets. By the same resolution, the Commission requested Member States to implement the 1994 Naples Political Declaration and Global Action Plan against Organized Transnational Crime,[4] with reference to the prevention and control of drug abuse and trafficking.

Drug control matters were also dealt with at the Ninth United Nations Congress on the Prevention of Crime and the Treatment of Offenders in May (see PART FOUR, Chapter V).

During the year, joint operational projects by UNDCP and the Criminal Justice Branch included training for police officers, regional workshops and advisory services on law enforcement cooperation, and development of measures against money laundering for States of eastern Europe and central Asia. A major joint project was planned on the prevention and control of organized crime in an Asian country.

### ECO

Welcoming steps by member States of the Economic Cooperation Organization (ECO) to maximize their contribution to international drug-control efforts, and noting with appreciation that UNDCP and ECO had signed a memorandum of understanding on 15 March 1995, the Commission on Narcotic Drugs called on UNDCP to devote greater attention to the region of ECO, one of the areas most affected by the drug problem, and to assist it and its members (Afghanistan, Azerbaijan, Iran, Kazakstan, Kyrgyzstan, Pakistan, Tajikistan, Turkey, Turkmenistan, Uzbekistan) in drawing up projects and programmes. It requested UNDCP to draw up memoranda of understanding, in consultation with the organization's members, and promote both the implemen-

tation of the project under way to strengthen law enforcement capabilities in the border areas of the region and its extension to other ECO members. The Commission recommended exchange of information, technical cooperation, programmes to meet the needs of law enforcement agencies, and mutual consultations on matters relating to drug control in ECO member States.[5]

Strengthening of cooperation between the United Nations and ECO in general was the subject of General Assembly **resolution 50/1** (see PART IV, Chapter V).

## System-wide Action Plan

In 1989, in adopting resolution 44/141, the General Assembly asked the Secretary-General, in his capacity as Chairman of the Administrative Committee on Coordination (ACC), to coordinate at the inter-agency level, the development of a United Nations system-wide action plan on drug abuse control, aimed at the full implementation of all existing mandates and subsequent decisions of intergovernmental bodies throughout the UN system, and using as a guide the Declaration of the International Conference on Drug Abuse and Illicit Trafficking, and the recommendations contained in the Comprehensive Multidisciplinary Outline of Future Activities in Drug Abuse Control, both adopted in 1987.[6] The plan was to include a statement of purpose that defined the overall goal and specific objectives; an outline of concrete activities that each agency should undertake, within its mandate, ensuring that there was no duplication or overlap; a reasonable time-frame for implementation of each portion of the action plan; and a realistic cost estimate for implementing the plan. The ACC was to present the plan to all Member States no later than 31 March 1990.

Following consultations with UN bodies and agencies, the UN System-wide Action Plan on Drug Abuse Control was established in 1990.[7] It consisted of two main parts. Part One dealt with operational activities, in particular those of the United Nations Fund for Drug Abuse Control (UNFDAC). Part Two outlined the role of the substantive drug control units of the UN Secretariat, and of other UN entities and of the specialized agencies. It focused on five areas: strengthening the licit drug control system; prevention and reduction of illicit demand for drugs; treatment and rehabilitation; elimination of the supply of drugs from illicit sources; and suppression of illicit drug traffic.

In accordance with the conclusions agreed on by the Economic and Social Council at the coordination segment of its 1994 session,[8] endorsed later in the year by the General Assembly,[9] ACC, at its first regular session in February 1995, included international drug control as an agenda item for the first time. At that session, ACC made recommendations to its Subcommittee on Drug Control to prepare a more operational United Nations System-wide Action Plan on Drug Abuse Control based on multi-agency sectoral and/or subsectoral plans of action.[(10)]

At its 1995 annual meeting,[(11)] the Subcommittee identified 12 initial themes and established multi-agency task forces charged with preparing such plans which, in turn, were to form the basis for the new System-wide Action Plan. The Plan was to be revised continuously as new plans of action were incorporated into it. Currently, emphasis was on the importance of inter-agency cooperation at the field level, as well as cooperation with international financial institutions. ACC stated that, taken together, the plans of action should constitute a truly multisectoral and system-wide approach to the drug abuse problem, which would permit the UN system to do its part in implementing the 1990 Global Programme of Action, adopted by the General Assembly on 23 February 1990.[(12)]

The Commission on Narcotic Drugs in March[(13)] welcomed ACC's conclusions and requested the Executive Director to pursue their rapid implementation by: initiating a review process to strengthen the Plan and render it operational; promoting consultations between relevant organizations at global, regional and subregional levels; elaborating joint multi-agency sectoral or subsectoral plans of action at those levels; and assisting Resident Coordinators in creating informal inter-agency groups to ensure that drug control needs were assigned the necessary priority and addressed in a coordinated manner. By the same resolution, the Commission called on States to support the efforts of the Executive Director. It took note of the conclusions and recommendations contained in a report of the Executive Director[(14)] suggesting further ways and means of improving system-wide cooperation and coordination in drug control.

The Commission further recommended that the Economic and Social Council, at its 1995 regular session, request relevant UN entities to take steps to ensure that drug abuse issues were taken fully into account in the elaboration of programmes and projects; urge international financial institutions to cooperate fully with UNDCP and to strengthen their support to other organizations and countries; and invite UN regional commissions to give particular attention to drug control issues.

The Secretary-General, in a May report,[(15)] summarized action taken to implement the Council's 1994 conclusions and recommendations. Summing up steps taken towards that end, he

stated that the UN system had been responsive and that ACC's strong position, calling for integration of drug abuse control into the work programmes of organizations across the system and for ensuring follow-up at the country level, were of particular significance. It had been possible to set the stage for what could become a fully coordinated and systematic response to the complex issues of drug control. However, a response that involved all potential partners and was fully coordinated would take a certain time to bring to reality; ideally, it would not only involve the coordination of existing activities but would also require moving towards a proactive approach based on consultative or joint planning. That was precisely the approach envisaged by ACC and corresponded well to the original intention of the System-wide Action Plan.

The General Assembly, in **resolution 50/148, Section V**, expressed its support for the Action Plan as a vital tool for coordination and enhancement of drug abuse control activities and requested that it be reviewed biennially.

## Global Programme of Action

The General Assembly, at its seventeenth special session in 1990, adopted the Political Declaration and the Global Programme of Action on international cooperation against illicit production, supply, demand, trafficking and distribution of narcotic drugs and psychotropic substances.[(12)] The Programme set out a comprehensive list of measures and activities to be undertaken by States and United Nations entities collectively and simultaneously in the fight against all aspects of drug abuse and illicit traffic.

In the Political Declaration, the Assembly had declared the period from 1991 to the year 2000 as the United Nations Decade against Drug Abuse, to be devoted to effective and sustained national, regional and international actions to promote the implementation of the Global Programme.

**Report of the Secretary-General.** In October 1995, the Secretary-General reported[(16)] on the implementation of the Global Programme of Action, evaluating the progress made with regard to the areas on which the 1990 Programme and the Political Declaration focused, such as prevention and reduction of drug abuse with a view to eliminating the illicit demand for narcotic drugs and psychotropic substances; treatment, rehabilitation and social reintegration of drug addicts; control of supply of narcotic drugs and psychotropic substances; suppression of illicit drug trafficking; measures against the effects of money derived from, used in or intended for use in illicit trafficking; illegal financial flows and illegal use of the banking system; strengthening of judicial and legal systems, including law enforcement; measures against the diversion of arms and explosives and illicit traffic by vessels, aircraft and vehicles; UN resources and structure for drug abuse control; and the UN Decade against Drug Abuse.

With respect to reducing demand for drugs, the most common activities implemented by Governments were prevention campaigns seeking to increase awareness of the dangers of drug abuse. Not all campaigns, however, were targeted, the report noted, and only very few were long-term sustained efforts within a comprehensive national demand-reduction strategy. It was recommended that States draw up comprehensive and sustainable strategies and share experience with others, either through UNDCP or bilaterally. As the involvement of non-governmental organizations (NGOs) in developing and implementing prevention policies had shown positive results, States should continue to cooperate with them and also mobilize other organizations of civil society. The report noted that the Economic and Social Council, in **resolution 1995/16** (see below), had requested that the UNDCP Executive Director define a global strategy for demand reduction and develop, in consultation with Governments and organizations, a draft declaration on the guiding principles for such reduction.

The Secretary-General saw a need to establish facilities providing specialized treatment for drug abusers, as in many cases treatment was confined to detoxification under medical supervision. It was also recommended that States develop programmes for rehabilitation and social reintegration for drug abusers, involving NGOs in providing counselling and long-term support.

In spite of successes achieved in some countries and in some aspects of dealing with illicit cultivation and production, the overall situation showed little improvement, the report stated. It was recommended that UNDCP continue to promote subregional cooperation which had emerged as an effective means of overcoming cross-border drug-related problems; that mechanisms and procedures to monitor the movement of precursors be strengthened; and that Governments, as a matter of urgency, identify the competent authorities and their role in implementing article 12 of the 1988 UN Convention against Illicit Traffic in Narcotic Drugs and Psychotropic Substances.[17]

In respect of suppression of illicit trafficking, States reported having taken various initiatives to conclude both bilateral and regional agreements and arrangements to facilitate cooperation in law-enforcement matters. While acknowledging that those activities constituted important steps, the report stated that they needed to be supported by judicial processes such as extradition or mutual legal assistance, as set out in the 1988 Convention.

The active intelligence capacity of States had to be strengthened by establishing databases with intelligence information, and States should be encouraged to enhance cooperation between law-enforcement agencies, particularly with regard to information sharing and joint operations.

With international cooperation against money laundering often impaired by banking practices, the Secretary-General recommended that States with strict bank secrecy laws urgently consider enacting penal provisions on drug-related money laundering offences and comprehensive legislation to enable investigation of such offences and provide for confiscation of proceeds derived from illicit trafficking, in accordance with articles 3 and 5 of the 1988 Convention, as well as consider using forfeited proceeds for drug control activities. Governments should adhere to regional agreements against money laundering and should draw up bilateral agreements.

The General Assembly, on 21 December 1995, adopted **resolution 50/148, Section III** on the Global Programme of Action (see above).

### Implementation of resolution 48/12

In 1993, the General Assembly at its forty-eighth session convened four high-level plenary meetings on international cooperation in drug control, culminating on 28 October with the adoption of resolution 48/12 setting out measures to strengthen international cooperation against the illicit production, sale, demand, traffic and distribution of narcotic drugs and psychotropic substances.[18] The Assembly invited the Commission on Narcotic Drugs in 1994 to consider the convening of an ad hoc expert group to contribute to the examination of the issues set out in the resolution, and report to the Assembly at its fiftieth session. The expert body met twice in 1994[19] making recommendations regarding international drug conventions and other matters.

In 1995, the Commission on Narcotic Drugs considered a report[20] of the UNDCP Executive Director on implementation of resolution 48/12. The report, which also reflected the deliberations of the expert group, highlighted the following six major themes: evaluation of the drug control treaties and their effectiveness; monitoring the implementation of the 1988 Convention; approach to be adopted by UNDCP in alternative development; the need to create a global synergy to address demand reduction; the issue of demand reduction, particularly the question whether the commitment of Governments should be reinforced through a treaty or a formal declaration; and alternative funding mechanisms for UNDCP.

The Commission requested Member States to review their implementation of the Assembly resolution and inform the Executive Director of their findings before 1 December 1995. It requested him to elaborate further and refine the recommendations in his report and submit them in 1996.[21]

Those actions were summarized in a September 1995 report of the Secretary-General.[22]

*REFERENCES*

[1]GA res. 45/179, 21 Dec. 1990. [2]E/CN.7/1996/2. [3]E/1995/29, res. 9(XXXVIII). [4]YUN 1994, p. 1160. [5]E/1995/29, res. 10(XXXVIII). [6]YUN 1987, p. 902, GA res. 42/112, 7 Dec. 1987. [7]E/1990/39, Corr.1,2 and Add.1. [8]YUN 1994, p. 1244. [9]Ibid., p. 1245, GA res. 49/168, 23 Dec. 1994. [10]E/CN.7/1996/14. [11]ACC/1995/16. [12]GA res. S-17/2, Annex, 23 Feb. 1990. [13]E/1995/29, res. 11(XXXVIII). [14]E/CN.7/1995/15 & Add.1 & Corr.1. [15]E/1995/68. [16]A/50/460. [17]YUN 1988, p. 687; Sales No. E.91.XI.6. [18]YUN 1993, p. 1095. [19]YUN 1994, p. 1242. [20]E/CN.7/1995/14. [21]E/1995/29, res. 13(XXXVIII) [22]A/50/461.

# Commission on Narcotic Drugs

The Commission on Narcotic Drugs held its thirty-eighth annual session in Vienna from 14 to 23 March 1995. It adopted 14 resolutions on various drug control issues, as well as four decisions dealing with the inclusion of certain substances into Schedules I, II and IV of the 1971 Convention on Psychotropic Substances,[1] and the transfer of another substance from Schedule IV to III. In addition, the Commission recommended another five draft resolutions to the Economic and Social Council for adoption, on which the Council acted at its 1995 substantive session (see above).

The Council, by **decision 1995/246** of 24 July, took note of the Commission's report on its thirty-eighth session.[2] On the same date, the Council decided that the session be reconvened so that the Commission could approve the initial programme budget for 1996-1997, and the second and final revision of the programme budget for 1994-1995 for the Fund of UNDCP. In accordance with Council **decision 1995/247**, the Commission met for that purpose on 13 and 14 December 1995.[3]

Also on 24 July, by **decision 1995/244**, the Council approved the provisional agenda and documentation for the Commission's thirty-ninth session in 1996.

## Major issues in 1995

### Economic and social consequences of drug abuse

The Commission on Narcotic Drugs in 1995 considered an interim survey[4] of the economic and social consequences of illicit drug abuse and trafficking, which reported that social integration and cohesion, at the family, community and even broader levels, were almost always compromised by an escalating drug problem. The nexus between drug abuse, acquired immunodeficiency syndrome (AIDS) and prostitution made for a mushroom effect, the report stated, endangering the health of much larger sections of the population. Even more important was the nexus between drug abuse and crime, with, for instance, half of all theft in some countries being directly drug-related. The violence, corruption and fragmentation engendered by illicit drug abuse and trafficking weakened civil society and thereby struck at the very foundation of some nations.

The identifiable costs of drug abuse in consumer countries seemed to range from 0.5 to 1.3 per cent of gross domestic product, the largest part of which involved drug-related crime and law enforcement costs, the report went on. Health costs of a drug addict appeared to be some 80 per cent higher than those of an average citizen in the same age group. Drug abuse also had a negative impact upon productivity, and illicit drug money was mostly spent on conspicuous consumption, and not generally used for productive investment, the report stated.

### Demand reduction

The Commission on Narcotic Drugs, at its thirty-eighth session, considered reports concerned with the reduction of illicit demand for drugs. The Commission was informed, in a report[5] on the world situation with respect to drug abuse, that the increase in production over the past 15 years had been matched by an increase in abuse, rather than by a fall in the price of drugs. The switch from oral abuse to injection had provided a major new vector for the spread of the human immunodeficiency virus (HIV). Another significant world trend had been the re-emergence of stimulants as drugs of widespread abuse.

In a second report before the Commission,[6] dealing with basic principles of demand reduction, it was stated that greater emphasis had been placed upon demand reduction in recent years because of the principle that prevention was better than cure. Demand reduction had three aspects: a primary aspect, which was concerned with persuading people not to start using and abusing drugs; a secondary aspect, where the aim was to help drug abusers to abandon the habit; and a tertiary aspect, by which an attempt was made to reduce and minimize the risks and harm posed to society by illicit drug abuse. The report contained sections on strategies; techniques of assessment of the nature, extent and patterns of drug abuse; demand reduction activities (including education, information campaigns and services for drug abuses); methodologies and institutional linkages.

**Commission Action.** The Commission on Narcotic Drugs in March underlined the importance of developing demand reduction strategies, including guiding principles, and decided to keep under consideration the proposal of convening an international conference to review progress made in combating drug abuse and trafficking.[7]

Within the context of demand reduction, the Commission adopted four other resolutions: on reducing demand for narcotic drugs and psychotropic substances; on the use of heroin; on promoting programmes using involvement in sports as an effective measure to prevent drug abuse; and on women and drug abuse.

Aware that proposals to legalize the non-medical use of drugs and psychotropic substances contradicted the international drug-control treaties, the Commission on Narcotic Drugs emphasized the need to ensure the non-liberalization of the use of illicit drugs and psychotropic substances.[8]

In a second resolution, the Commission requested the Executive Director of the UN International Drug Control Programme (UNDCP) to ask the International Narcotics Control Board (INCB) and the World Health Organization (WHO) for an opinion on the question of the danger of promoting advocacy of the non-medical use of heroin.[9]

In a third resolution,[10] the Commission invited UNDCP to consider introducing in its demand reduction and other programmes a component on the use of sports to prevent drug abuse. UNDCP was invited to draw up, in collaboration with the International Olympic Committee, the national Olympic committees and sports federations, a programme of work on the use of sports to prevent drug abuse and to submit it to potential donors. The Commission invited Governments and NGOs to consider mobilizing national sport authorities and organizations for promoting pilot programmes to benefit deprived youth, and invited the Organizing Committee of the 1996 Olympic Games to disseminate messages related to the use of sports to prevent drug abuse.

By a fourth resolution,[11] the Commission, expressing deep concern over the growing problems in many countries related to drug abuse among women and children, urged States to assess and take into account in their national policies and programmes those problems and to develop activities to respond to them.

### ECONOMIC AND SOCIAL COUNCIL ACTION

On 24 July, the Economic and Social Council adopted **resolution 1995/16**.

**Integration of demand reduction initiatives into a cohesive strategy to combat drug abuse**

*The Economic and Social Council,*

*Recalling* the Comprehensive Multidisciplinary Outline of Future Activities in Drug Abuse Control adopted by the International Conference on Drug Abuse and Illicit Trafficking and its resolution 1991/46 of 21 June 1991,

*Acknowledging* the Political Declaration and Global Programme of Action adopted by the General Assembly at its seventeenth special session, on 23 February 1990,

*Reaffirming* the importance of its resolution 1993/35 of 27 July 1993, on demand reduction as part of balanced national strategic plans to combat drug abuse, and the need to ensure its implementation,

*Recognizing* that demand reduction encompasses prevention, treatment and rehabilitation as well as social reintegration,

*Also recognizing* the particularly important role of prevention within demand reduction,

*Reminding* Governments of article 22, paragraph 1 (*b*), of the Convention on Psychotropic Substances of 1971, of article 36, paragraph 1 (*b*), of the Single Convention on Narcotic Drugs of 1961, as amended by the 1972 Protocol, and of the United Nations Standard Minimum Rules for Non-custodial Measures (the Tokyo Rules) adopted by the General Assembly in its resolution 45/110 of 14 December 1990, which offer the possibility of applying to drug abusers, in appropriate cases of a minor nature, alternatives to, or measures in addition to, conviction and punishment, such as treatment,

*Stressing* the importance of a long-term global commitment to alleviating the serious consequences of drug abuse for the health and the social, economic, political and cultural fabric of communities,

*Believing* that optimum effectiveness in drug abuse control would best be achieved through a balanced approach, applying the appropriate emphasis and resources to initiatives involving both demand and supply reduction, and integrating such initiatives into a cohesive and comprehensive strategy,

*Also believing* that effectiveness in combating drug abuse is enhanced by cooperation and the combined efforts of all sectors of society, including those of voluntary and non-governmental organizations, in the recognition of problems and the quest for solutions,

*Stressing* the importance of evaluating programmes for drug abuse control and sharing information on their effectiveness,

1. *Requests* the Executive Director of the United Nations International Drug Control Programme, in consultation with Governments, appropriate United Nations agencies and non-governmental organizations, to define clearly their global strategy for demand reduction, specifying their aims, priorities and responsibilities, and to report to the Commission on Narcotic Drugs at its thirty-ninth session;

2. *Also requests* the Executive Director of the Programme to develop, in consultation with Governments and organizations represented in the Commission by observers, a draft declaration on the guiding principles of demand reduction, for submission to the Commission at its thirty-ninth session and subsequently, through the Economic and Social Council, to the General Assembly for adoption;

3. *Further requests* the Executive Director of the Programme, in preparing such a draft declaration, to take into account the relevant recommendations contained in the Global Programme of Action and the Comprehensive Multidisciplinary Outline of Future Activities in Drug Abuse Control, with due regard to flexibility in approach and cost-effectiveness;

4. *Requests* the Executive Director of the Programme to report to the Commission at its thirty-ninth session

on the implementation of Economic and Social Council resolution 1994/3 of 20 July 1994, with particular attention to progress made in the development of innovative methods of data collection and analysis, the identification of reliable and comparable data regarding the nature, extent and consequences of drug abuse, and the revision of the annual reports questionnaire;

5. *Requests* that demand reduction be a permanent item of the agenda at each session of the Commission;

6. *Encourages* Governments, regional organizations and multilateral agencies to work together in developing knowledge of the social and economic costs of drug abuse as a contribution towards the objective assessment of the cost benefits of policy and programme options, so as to achieve established goals or aims of strategies to reduce the supply of and demand for drugs;

7. *Also encourages* Governments to adopt comprehensive national strategies that reflect the reality and necessity of a balance between supply and demand reduction efforts, with operational linkages between those two areas, taking into account the social, economic and cultural conditions of individual countries;

8. *Encourages* the Executive Director of the Programme to continue to facilitate and promote the dissemination of information and the sharing of the benefits of experience gained in the development and implementation of balanced national strategies integrating comprehensive initiatives aimed at supply and demand reduction;

9. *Invites* the International Narcotics Control Board to continue to report on progress and deficiencies in demand reduction programmes at the national level, in a manner that will provide a more comprehensive understanding of the illicit drug problem;

10. *Encourages* intergovernmental cooperation regarding demand reduction at the regional and international levels through various means, including meetings for the exchange of information and experiences;

11. *Stresses* the need for cooperation among all Governments and the importance of involving and assisting voluntary and non-governmental organizations as well as mobilizing community participation in demand reduction;

12. *Requests* the United Nations International Drug Control Programme to update, in consultation with other United Nations agencies, the *Resource Book on Measures to Reduce Illicit Demand for Drugs* and to develop a glossary of terms to ensure a common understanding of terms;

13. *Requests* the Secretary-General to transmit the present resolution to all Governments for consideration and implementation.

Economic and Social Council resolution 1995/16

24 July 1995    Meeting 49    Adopted without vote

Draft by Commission on Narcotic Drugs (E/1995/29); agenda item 5 *(h)*. Meeting numbers. ESC 47-49.

## Supply reduction

The Committee of the Whole of the Commission on Narcotic Drugs examined the supply reduction strategies outlined in a Secretariat note,[12] with particular emphasis on alternative development.

The Commission urged Member States to recognize the need of the countries producing natural inputs for illicit production of drugs to continue to receive cooperation for alternative development programmes. It underlined the need for Governments to prepare and implement such programmes with the objective of reducing and eliminating the production of illicit drugs, taking into account economic, social, cultural, political and environmental aspects. It requested the UNDCP Executive Director to intensify efforts to obtain additional financial resources through voluntary contributions in implementing those programmes, and reiterated its determination to continue regarding the alternative development strategy as an important component of economic and social action appropriate for supply reduction.[13]

### Availability of opiates for licit use

In 1995, as in previous years, INCB monitored the demand for and supply of opiates for medical and scientific needs. In response to 1990[14] and 1991[15] Economic and Social Council resolutions, the Board in 1995 conducted a study to evaluate the extent to which the recommendations contained in its 1989 special report[16] on the availability of narcotic drugs, including opiates, had been implemented. Publication of the study was to be approved by the Board at a March 1996 session. Based on responses from Governments, WHO and professional organizations to its requests for pertinent information, the Board concluded that its recommendations were far from being implemented and, while there had been efforts by some Governments to ensure the availability of narcotic drugs for medical and scientific purposes, it appeared that many others had yet to focus on that obligation.

The Board believed that an efficient national drug-control regime must involve not only a programme to prevent illicit trafficking and diversion, but also ensure the adequate availability of narcotic drugs for medical and scientific purposes. It made a number of recommendations which, if implemented, would ensure significant additional progress towards that end.

Recognizing that the provision of controlled drugs for humanitarian aid in acute emergencies justified non-application of regular control requirements, the Board proposed that exporting countries conclude agreements with a limited number of bona fide suppliers of humanitarian assistance, allowing for rapid import and export of such substances.

**ECONOMIC AND SOCIAL COUNCIL ACTION**

On 24 July, the Economic and Social Council adopted **resolution 1995/19**.

## Demand for and supply of opiates for medical and scientific needs

*The Economic and Social Council,*

*Recalling* its resolutions 1979/8 of 9 May 1979, 1980/20 of 30 April 1980, 1981/8 of 6 May 1981, 1982/12 of 30 April 1982, 1983/3 of 24 May 1983, 1984/21 of 24 May 1984, 1985/16 of 28 May 1985, 1986/9 of 21 May 1986, 1987/31 of 26 May 1987, 1988/10 of 25 May 1988, 1989/15 of 22 May 1989, 1990/31 of 24 May 1990, 1991/43 of 21 June 1991, 1992/30 of 30 July 1992, 1993/37 of 27 July 1993 and 1994/5 of 20 July 1994,

*Emphasizing* that the need to balance the global licit supply of opiates against the legitimate demand for opiates for medical and scientific purposes is central to the international strategy and policy of drug abuse control,

*Noting* the fundamental need for international cooperation and solidarity with the traditional supplier countries in drug abuse control in general and in the universal application of the provisions of the Single Convention on Narcotic Drugs of 1961 in particular,

*Having considered* the *Report of the International Narcotics Control Board for 1994,* in which it is stated that in 1993 the consumption of opiates was higher than the production of opiate raw materials, and that in 1994 there was a shortage of supply,

*Noting* that the traditional supplier countries held very limited stocks of opiate raw materials at the end of 1994,

*Also noting* the importance of opiates in pain relief therapy as advocated by the World Health Organization,

1. *Urges* all Governments to continue contributing to the establishment and maintenance of a balance between the licit supply of and demand for opiates for medical and scientific needs, the achievement of which would be facilitated by maintaining, in so far as their constitutional and legal systems permit, support to the traditional supplier countries, and to cooperate in preventing the proliferation of sources of production and manufacture for export;

2. *Urges* Governments of all producing countries to adhere strictly to the provisions of the Single Convention on Narcotic Drugs of 1961 and to take effective measures to prevent diversion to illicit channels or otherwise not engage in licit production of opiate raw materials;

3. *Also urges* all Governments to comply fully with the relevant recommendations contained in the *Report of the International Narcotics Control Board for 1994* in this respect;

4. *Commends* the International Narcotics Control Board for its efforts in monitoring the implementation of the relevant Economic and Social Council resolutions and, in particular:

   *(a)* In urging the Governments concerned to restrict global production of opiate raw materials to a level corresponding to the actual licit needs and to avoid any proliferation of production;

   *(b)* In convening meetings for establishing a balance between licit demand for and supply of opiates, during sessions of the Commission on Narcotic Drugs, with the main States importing and producing opiate raw materials;

5. *Requests* the Secretary-General to transmit the present resolution to all Governments for consideration and implementation.

Economic and Social Council resolution 1995/19

24 July 1995      Meeting 49      Adopted without vote

Draft by Commission on Narcotic Drugs (E/1995/29); agenda item 5 *(h)*. *Meeting numbers.* ESC 47-49.

## *Diversion of psychotropic substances and precursors for illicit use*

In its report for 1995,[17] INCB called on Governments of exporting countries to exercise utmost vigilance in dealing with orders for the delivery of psychotropic substances to countries where internal security was unstable, as drug traffickers had frequently attempted to take advantage of administrative weaknesses in such States. The Board also noted that some exporting countries applying the system of export authorization for substances under international control had failed to verify all import orders against assessments of annual legitimate requirements of importing countries. As a result, traffickers had been able to divert psychotropic substances using falsified import authorizations. INCB noted with concern that, in addition to diversion from international trade, significant quantities of psychotropic substances were being diverted from domestic distribution channels.

While a number of countries had started to take action to strengthen controls, diversion of precursors from licit channels was still the major source of the chemicals required for illicit manufacture of stimulants and other psychotropic substances. Details of the sources and routes of diversion of many precursors remained largely unknown. The Board reiterated its appeal to Governments to establish and institutionalize working mechanisms and operating procedures with their trade partners for making inquiries and providing immediate feedback to each other in verifying the legitimacy of transactions in precursors.

During the year, UNDCP continued to support initiatives and programmes to implement article 12 of the 1988 Convention on Illicit Traffic in Narcotic Drugs and Psychotropic Substances,[18] and other provisions concerning the monitoring of precursors. It carried out various activities in the field of treaty implementation, including the communication of notifications under the provisions of the international drug-control treaties. UNDCP analyzed 102 annual reports from Governments on the working of the treaties, using such information in preparing country profiles and updating the following two annual publications— *Competent National Authorities under the International Drug Control Treaties* and *Manufacture of Narcotic Drugs and Psychotropic Substances under International Control*—the latter now including manufacturers of substances listed in Table I of the 1988 Convention, pursuant to Economic and Social Council **resolution 1995/20** (see below). By the same resolution, the Council endorsed the recommendations made by

INCB in its 1994 report on the implementation of article 12 of the Convention for specific actions to be taken by Governments to prevent diversion of precursors for the illicit manufacture of narcotic drugs and psychotropic substances.

**ECONOMIC AND SOCIAL COUNCIL ACTION**

On 24 July, the Economic and Social Council adopted **resolution 1995/20**.

**Measures to strengthen international cooperation to prevent diversion of substances listed in table I of the United Nations Convention against Illicit Traffic in Narcotic Drugs and Psychotropic Substances of 1988 and used in the illicit manufacture of stimulants and other psychotropic substances**

*The Economic and Social Council,*

*Concerned* about the recent discovery of worldwide diversion of vast quantities of ephedrine and pseudoephedrine from licit manufacture and trade to be used for the illicit manufacture of methamphetamine,

*Recognizing* the rapid increase in illicit trafficking and use of stimulants throughout the world, and the need for the international community to strengthen countermeasures against the illicit trafficking in stimulants and their precursors,

*Noting* the proliferation of the illicit manufacture of a variety of drugs, especially stimulants, which has occurred throughout the world, and the fact that such massive production depends upon an equally massive diversion of substances listed in table I of the United Nations Convention against Illicit Traffic in Narcotic Drugs and Psychotropic Substances of 1988,

*Realizing* that brokers frequently serve as mediators in transactions involving substances listed in table I which are ultimately diverted,

*Recognizing* the need for the international community to renew its commitment to cooperation through the exchange of information and to strengthen countermeasures against the illicit traffic in and abuse of psychotropic substances, in particular stimulants, and their precursors,

*Taking note with appreciation* of the publication entitled *Precursors and Chemicals Frequently Used in the Illicit Manufacture of Narcotic Drugs and Psychotropic Substances: Report of the International Narcotics Control Board for 1994 on the Implementation of Article 12 of the United Nations Convention against Illicit Traffic in Narcotic Drugs and Psychotropic Substances of 1988,* and welcoming the initiative taken jointly by the International Narcotics Control Board and the Pompidou Group of the Council of Europe to hold a meeting of experts to review the issue of brokers dealing with precursors and psychotropic substances and to consider concrete measures effectively to control the operations of brokers,

*Recalling* its resolutions 1981/7 of 6 May 1981, 1992/29 of 30 July 1992 and 1993/40 of 27 July 1993,

1. *Urges* Governments, where appropriate, to invoke article 12, paragraph 10 (*a*), of the United Nations Convention against Illicit Traffic in Narcotic Drugs and Psychotropic Substances of 1988, in order to give importing countries advance notice of any shipment of substances listed in table I of that Convention;

2. *Requests* the Government of an exporting country, subject to its legal provisions, to provide the following information to the competent authorities of the importing country prior to any export, even when the importing country has not yet formally requested such notification under article 12, paragraph 10 (*a*), of the 1988 Convention:

(*a*) Name and address of the exporter and importer and, when available, of the consignee;

(*b*) Name of the substance listed in table I of the Convention;

(*c*) Quantity of the substance to be exported;

(*d*) Expected point of entry and expected date of dispatch;

(*e*) Such other information as the exporting Government may deem relevant;

3. *Requests,* for any substance listed in table I of the Convention, the Government of an importing country, upon receipt of any form of pre-export notification from the exporting country, to undertake, through its regulatory authorities and in cooperation with the law enforcement authorities, an investigation of the legitimacy of the transaction, and, with the possible assistance of the International Narcotics Control Board, to convey information thereon to the exporting country;

4. *Urges* Governments of exporting countries, at the same time, to conduct their own investigations in questionable cases and to seek information and views from the Board, international organizations and Governments, as appropriate, inasmuch as additional facts establishing suspicion may be available to them;

5. *Requests* Governments, where there is sufficient evidence that a substance may be diverted into illicit channels, to stop the shipments or, where circumstances warrant, to cooperate in controlled deliveries of suspicious shipments in special circumstances if the security of the shipment can be sufficiently ensured, if the quantity and nature of the chemical involved is such that it can be managed feasibly and safely by the competent authorities, and if all States whose cooperation is necessary, including transit States, agree to the controlled delivery;

6. *Also urges* Governments to exercise, as a matter of urgency, increased vigilance over the activities of brokers handling substances listed in table I of the Convention, in view of the special role that some of them play in the diversion of such substances, and to subject them to licensing or other effective control measures as necessary;

7. *Further urges* Governments to ensure, as far as possible, that shipments entering or leaving free ports, free zones and bonded warehouses be subject, where permitted, to the controls necessary to safeguard against diversion;

8. *Urges* Governments, subject to the provisions of national legislation on confidentiality and data protection, to inform the Board on a regular basis, upon request of the Board and in the form and manner provided for by it, of the quantities of substances listed in table I of the Convention that they have imported, exported or transshipped, and encourages them to estimate their annual licit needs;

9. *Requests* the Board, drawing upon the capabilities of the United Nations International Drug Control Programme, to collect information pursuant to paragraph 8 above, and further to develop and strengthen its database in order to assist Governments in preventing diversion of substances listed in table I of the Convention and

the Commission on Narcotic Drugs in discussing the control of illicit manufacture of, trafficking in and use of psychotropic substances, especially of stimulants and their precursors, and in formulating policy recommendations in this field;

10. *Requests* all Governments to provide the Secretary-General, subject to the provisions of national legislation on confidentiality and data protection, with names and addresses of the manufacturers, within their countries, of substances listed in table I of the Convention, and requests the Secretary-General to include that information in the publication entitled *Manufacture of Narcotic Drugs and Psychotropic Substances under International Control*;

11. *Requests* the Secretary-General, with the assistance of the Executive Director of the Programme and in consultation with the Board, to convene, drawing upon voluntary contributions from Governments, expert meetings of regulatory and law enforcement authorities of interested Governments in 1995 and 1996 in order to discuss countermeasures against the illicit manufacture of and trafficking in psychotropic substances, particularly stimulants, and the illicit use of their precursors on the basis of the study to be prepared in accordance with paragraph 12 below;

12. *Also requests* the Secretary-General, with the assistance of the Executive Director of the Programme and in consultation with the Board, to undertake, within existing resources, a thorough study on stimulants and the use of their precursors in the illicit manufacture of and trafficking in drugs, and to prepare a report thereon for submission to the Commission, taking into account any comments that may be made on the study at the expert meetings referred to in paragraph 11 above;

13. *Encourages* Governments to consider strengthening, where necessary, the working mechanisms established to prevent diversion of substances listed in table II of the Convention, as described in the present resolution;

14. *Further requests* the Secretary-General to transmit the present resolution to all Governments for consideration and implementation, and asks the Board, in cooperation with the Programme, to report on its implementation to the Commission at its thirty-ninth session.

Economic and Social Council resolution 1995/20

24 July 1995          Meeting 49          Adopted without vote

Draft by Commission on Narcotic Drugs (E/1995/29); agenda item 5 *(h)*.
*Meeting numbers.* ESC 47-49.

## Memoranda of understanding

The Declaration on the Further National Development of Memoranda of Understanding between Customs and the Trading Community aimed at Cooperation to prevent Drug Smuggling, adopted in 1992 by the Customs Cooperation Council at Brussels, Belgium, recognized and supported the principle of achieving cooperation between customs and other competent authorities, including commercial carriers, through memoranda of understanding. The Economic and Social Council in 1993 recognized the significance of the use of memoranda of understanding and expressed conviction that such an international initiative needed to be enhanced by agreements at a national level.[19]

On 24 July, the Economic and Social Council adopted **resolution 1995/18**.

**Promoting the use of memoranda of understanding to facilitate cooperation between customs authorities and other competent administrations and the international trading community, including commercial carriers**

*The Economic and Social Council,*

*Deeply concerned* about the unlawful use of commercial carriers for the illicit traffic in narcotic drugs and psychotropic substances and in precursors and essential chemicals,

*Recalling* its resolution 1993/41 of 27 July 1993,

*Recalling also* article 15 of the United Nations Convention against Illicit Traffic in Narcotic Drugs and Psychotropic Substances of 1988, which provides for cooperation between appropriate authorities, including customs and commercial carriers,

*Recognizing* the importance of the use of memoranda of understanding concluded between the World Customs Organization, originally established as the Customs Cooperation Council, and international trade and transport organizations as a means to improving cooperation in combating illicit drug trafficking,

*Noting* that a review undertaken by the World Customs Organization of the effectiveness of the programme of memoranda of understanding has revealed that both customs operations and trade have benefited from the adoption of such a programme,

*Noting also* that an increasing number of States have implemented memoranda of understanding,

*Noting further* that the adoption of a programme of memoranda of understanding has enabled States to improve the capacity of their law enforcement agencies to target and intercept illicit drug trafficking without hindering the free movement of innocent persons and legitimate international trade,

1. *Commends* the World Customs Organization for its work in demonstrating the effectiveness of the programme of memoranda of understanding developed at both national and international levels to combat illicit drug trafficking;

2. *Commends* the cooperation of those Governments which shared their experiences with the World Customs Organization, and thereby demonstrated the wide support of the programme of memoranda of understanding;

3. *Invites* those Governments to further promote the effectiveness of the programme of memoranda of understanding, notably as reflected in the practical benefits of enhanced cooperation and understanding, and actively to support the efforts of the World Customs Organization by sharing their experiences with other Governments;

4. *Invites* more countries and trade organizations to take part in the programme of memoranda of understanding;

5. *Urges* all States that have not already done so to implement fully article 15 of the United Nations Convention against Illicit Traffic in Narcotic Drugs and Psychotropic Substances of 1988, by taking appropriate measures to prevent the use of commercial means of transport for the trafficking of illicit drugs;

6. *Requests* the Secretary-General to transmit the present resolution to all Governments for consideration and implementation.

Economic and Social Council resolution 1995/18

24 July 1995     Meeting 49     Adopted without vote

Draft by Commission on Narcotic Drugs (E/1995/29); agenda item 5 *(h)*. *Meeting numbers.* ESC 47-49.

### Illicit trafficking

The Commission on Narcotic Drugs in 1995 considered various aspects of illicit drug trafficking. It examined one report[20] concerning recent developments in the field of international illicit drug trafficking with details of production patterns, volumes of trafficking and seizures of drugs, and another[21] which provided a synopsis of recent trends in illicit drug trafficking in the regions of Africa, Asia and the Pacific, Europe and Latin America and the Caribbean, the latter region including Canada and the United States.

Underlining that the 1988 Convention[18] required each party to make money laundering a criminal offence, the Commission on Narcotic Drugs, in March, urged States to encourage the reporting of suspicious or unusual transactions involving large currency volumes, in order to identify possible money laundering operations, including those by drug-trafficking organizations.[22]

By another resolution,[23] the Commission requested the Executive Director to consider what expertise and resources were needed to improve and strengthen scientific and technological capabilities for combating illicit drug trafficking and abuse. It urged him to consult with relevant international organizations and national authorities with regard to strengthening measures in law enforcement and demand reduction.

### Maritime cooperation

In March 1995, the Commission welcomed and endorsed[24] the report of meetings of the Working Group on Maritime Cooperation (Vienna, 19–23 September 1994 and 20–24 February 1995),[25] which included the Group's recommendations. The Group had met in response to a 1994 request of the Commission, with the mandate to develop a comprehensive set of principles and specific recommendations to enhance, on a global basis, the implementation of article 17 of the 1988 Convention on Illicit Trafficking.[18] The Commission recommended, pursuant to a Group recommendation, that Governments encourage commercial carriers and professional groups active in maritime transport to become involved in the fight against illicit drug traffic, on the basis of voluntary cooperation and through memoranda of understanding. The Commission further requested UNDCP to convene a meeting of experts to develop training and technical assistance programmes in maritime drug law enforcement and encouraged Governments to inform UNDCP of their training and technical assistance requirements in the field of maritime drug law enforcement.

*REFERENCES*

[1]YUN 1971, p. 380. [2]E/1995/29. [3]E/1995/29/Add.1. [4]E/CN.7/1995/3. [5]E/CN.7/1995/5. [6]E/CN.7/1995/4. [7]E/1995/29, res. 13(XXXVIII). [8]Ibid., res. 4(XXXVIII). [9]Ibid., res. 1(XXXVIII). [10]Ibid., res. 2(XXXVIII). [11]Ibid., res. 3(XXXVIII). [12]E/CN.7/1995/8. [13]E/1995/29, res. 5(XXXVIII). [14]ESC res. 1990/31, 24 May 1990. [15]YUN 1991, p. 731, ESC res. 1991/43, 21 Jun. 1991. [16]E/INCB/1989/1/Supp., Sales No. E.89.XI.5. [17]*Report of the International Narcotics Control Board for 1995* (E/ICNB/1995/1), Sales No. E.96.XI.1. [18]YUN 1988, p.687; UN publication, Sales No. E.91.XI.6. [19]YUN 1993, p. 1093, ESC res. 1993/41, 27 Jul. 1993. [20]E/CN.7/1995/7. [21]E/CN.7/1995/9. [22]E/1995/29, res. 6(XXXVIII). [23]Ibid., res. 12(XXXVIII). [24]Ibid., res. 8(XXXVIII). [25]E/CN.7/1995/13.

Chapter XV

# Statistics

During 1995, the United Nations continued to broaden its work in the area of statistics, with special emphasis on strengthening international cooperation. At its February/March session, the Statistical Commission gave specific guidance on priorities for work to the inter-agency task forces it had established in 1993 in the following areas: national accounts, industrial and construction statistics, international trade statistics, finance statistics, price statistics, service statistics, environment statistics and the measurement of poverty. Other main issues considered in 1995 by the 24-member body, which normally meets biennially, included: demographic, social and migration statistics, including preparations for the World Population and Housing Census Programme for the year 2000; development of economic classifications; technical cooperation in statistics; and a new agenda item "Critical problems in economic statistics", which included matters related to production and dissemination of statistical information. The Commission also commemorated the fiftieth anniversary of international statistical work in the UN system.

On the Commission's recommendation, the Economic and Social Council urged Member States to carry out population and housing censuses between 1995 and 2004, having stressed that such censuses provided valuable statistics for assessing the situation of various special population groups.

## Work of UN Statistical Commission

The Statistical Commission held its twenty-eighth session in New York from 27 February to 3 March.[1] Among other action, the Commission agreed that the UN Statistical Division (UNSTAT) should focus its work on implementation of the System of National Accounts (SNA); social statistics; and environment statistics.

It endorsed the work on the United Nations Economic and Social Information System (UNESIS), developed by UNSTAT, and stressed the importance of its completion. In particular, the Commission encouraged the development of UNESIS which would permit access to UNSTAT by the regional commissions as well as by countries.

By **decision 1995/239** of 19 July, the Economic and Social Council noted the 1995 Commission report[1] and approved the provisional agenda and documentation for its twenty-ninth session, to be convened in 1997.

### Economic statistics

*Critical problems in economic statistics*

The Statistical Commission considered a new agenda item on critical problems in the production and dissemination of timely, relevant and accurate economic indicators, their interpretation and use, and the public perception of their adequacy. These included conceptual problems, operational difficulties in responding to changes in the economy and problems in dealing with the media and governmental officials. The Commission agreed that relevant reports should be prepared for its next session and requested that UNSTAT work with representatives from the United States, the Czech Republic, Australia, India and the International Monetary Fund (IMF) to systematize the various elements of the discussion, to decide what reports needed to be produced and to commission those reports. It also requested UNSTAT to report on progress to the Working Group on International Statistical Programmes and Coordination at its next session.

After written exchanges of views among Working Group members, UNSTAT convened the Expert Group on Critical Problems in Economic Statistics (New York, 24-25 October). The Expert Group identified three problems—absence of statistics, distrust of statistics by users, and mismatch between statistics and user demand—that affected the confidence of users in official economic statistics. It also identified 13 issues with regard to user confidence and proposed activities and mechanisms to address them. The Expert Group recommended the mediation of informal ad hoc groups along the lines of the Voorburg Group on Service Statistics (see below) in a number of cases, but noted that it would ultimately depend on the countries concerned as to whether they would be interested in participating and to what extent. In June, the ACC Subcommittee on Statistical Activities (see below) noted that the work being done was particularly timely and was of concern to both developed and developing countries.[2]

*National accounts*

A report[3] of the Task Force on National Accounts, reviewing implementation of the 1993 SNA and the role of the Inter-Secretariat Working Group on National Accounts (ISWGNA), was considered by the Statistical Commission in 1995. The Task Force stated that the scope and pace of the implementation of the 1993 SNA must be decided by each country according to its needs, resources, availability of staff and the current state of basic data. ISWGNA could be characterized as a support system for helping national administrations to develop and execute their own nationally determined implementation strategies.

The Task Force provided a summary of SNA-related activities by each ISWGNA member organization, both at the international level and at the level of the regional commissions, and proposed to monitor implementation of the 1993 SNA with assistance from the Statistical Office of the European Communities (Eurostat), the Organisation for Economic Cooperation and Development and the regional commissions. It identified the four elements of the support system to be provided by ISWGNA: manuals, handbooks, compilation manuals and software in support of national accounts compilation; meetings, training seminars, workshops, ad hoc and programmed courses in national accounts and related subjects and training materials for use in those courses; research activities designed to solve conceptual and practical problems in implementing the new system; and technical cooperation projects in individual countries. ISWGNA would also monitor the activities of its member organizations and review their activities to identify gaps, avoid duplication and develop common standards and recommendations. The Task Force also reported that the development of a revised international SNA questionnaire was almost complete.

The Statistical Commission confirmed that implementation of the 1993 SNA was essentially the responsibility of individual countries and would need to proceed in accordance with their own priorities; however, the regional commissions had a key role to play in promoting and monitoring implementation.[1] In 1994, it had asked ISWGNA for a set of strategy papers[4] on implementation of the 1993 SNA, defining criteria against which progress could be judged. It also reiterated the urgent need to make the 1993 SNA available in all official UN languages and to complete the programme of handbooks as quickly as possible.

The Commission emphasized that implementation of the 1993 SNA required close attention to the development of basic economic statistics in a systematic manner, and endorsed the programme of further conceptual and practical research recommended by ISWGNA, asking that special attention be given to the needs of the developing countries, including an account of the informal sector.

The strengthening of the capabilities of the regional commissions was recommended; the need for mobilization of bilateral and multilateral resources, at both global and regional levels, was noted. Regional commissions were asked to produce a consolidated, country-by-country report on needs for assistance and financing. In that context, the Commission reiterated the need for training and for an expanded technical resource base for SNA implementation.

In June, the ACC Subcommittee welcomed[2] the steps taken by ISWGNA and its member organizations to address the implementation of the 1993 SNA; emphasized the urgency of completing the language editions of the 1993 SNA and of the handbooks and manuals; and agreed with the ISWGNA proposal to prepare a paper outlining the strategy for SNA implementation in countries, including benchmarks that would aid in measuring progress. The Subcommittee also supported broader dissemination and accessibility of the *SNA Newsletter*.

### Industrial and construction statistics

The Statistical Commission reviewed a report[5] of the Task Force on Industrial and Construction Statistics, which it had requested in 1994.[6] The Task Force reported on a 1994 survey on country practices and intentions with respect to the International Standard Industrial Classification of All Economic Activities, Revision 3 (ISIC, Rev. 3).

Task Force findings confirmed that, so far, the institution of ISIC, Rev. 3, by Member States had resulted in polarization rather than harmonization with respect to industrial statistics worldwide. For many developing countries, the introduction of ISIC, Rev. 3, was contingent on taking an economic census or carrying out a large-scale survey of economic activity, for which they possessed neither the resources nor the expertise. While some developing countries planned to introduce ISIC, Rev. 3, in conjunction with a forthcoming economic census, they had not been given any guidance on ways to ensure international comparability.

The Task Force found that because the introduction of ISIC, Rev. 3, was a drawn-out process, during the transition period reporting of industry statistics to international organizations would be far less consistent than it had been. Countries had no clear-cut policy on measures to protect the continuity of their time-series during the transition, in particular no guidance on how to maintain the continuity of their short-term indicators of change in industrial activity. In the end, there would be less comparability between the developed and the developing world than there had been prior to the introduction of ISIC, Rev. 3. To promote greater harmony in the adoption and use of economic classifications, the Task Force wanted countries to be provided with assistance for surveys and censuses, experts and a data bank of common problems and solutions, and a hot line based in UNSTAT to reply to queries.

The Statistical Commission requested[1] UNSTAT, with the help of volunteer countries, to draft operational guidelines to link the time-series expressed in ISIC, Rev. 2, with the new short-term series expressed in ISIC, Rev. 3. It also requested UNSTAT to distribute to all countries concerned manuals, correspondence tables and other technical materials, and to proceed with training experts at the regional commissions and in UNSTAT to promote common approaches for the conversion from national and other classifications to ISIC, Rev. 3. In June, the ACC Subcommittee on Statistical Activities noted[2] the work done by the Task Force and the call for an Expert Group on Construction Statistics.

That Expert Group subsequently met (New York, 11-13 September) to discuss a revision of the 1968 *International Recommendations for Construction Statistics*.[7] Several new items of construction data were considered, such as own-account construction by household and indirect tax.

### International trade statistics

In 1995, the Commission considered the 1994 report of the Task Force on International Trade Statistics[6] and an addendum[8] relevant to the proposed revision of the Standard International Trade Classification, Revision 3 (SITC, Rev. 3). The Commission also had before it information on the Harmonized Commodity Description and Coding System (HS) and an analysis of national reporting practices in international merchandise trade statistics, the results of which were to be published early in 1996.

The addendum set out existing basic headings to be deleted from SITC, Rev. 3, new basic headings, and basic headings of SITC, Rev. 3, that would have a changed coverage due to changes in HS—which would come into force on 1 January 1996—but would retain the same codes in a revision of SITC, Rev. 3.

The Commission agreed with the conclusions of the Task Force that it should stop working on adjustments of national data to improve international comparability, but asked the Task Force to continue efforts to study free on board/cost, insurance, freight ratios and the impact on the direction of trade statistics of the general and the special system of trade. The Task Force was also asked to provide nations with information on country practices and to have countries assess the impact of all those cases where country practice differed from concepts and definitions and the reason for

deviation. The Task Force was also requested to provide standardized trade data. Technical information on construction of index numbers of international trade should be provided to countries. The Commission agreed with the Task Force's conclusion that SITC, Rev. 3, should either not be revised or, if revised, only minimally.

The Commission endorsed the plan of action and outline for the revision of the UN *International Trade Statistics: Concepts and Definitions*,[9] on which the Task Force had agreed in 1994; however, it considered that the planned time-frame might be too ambitious. It recommended extensive involvement of countries, including in the production of a first draft. Also considered were issues such as harmonization and the need for continuity of a long-term time-series of international trade. A compiler's manual for international trade statistics should be prepared in tandem with the technical guide on concepts and definitions, the Commission stated.

The Commission requested that UNSTAT assess the needs of users of the Commodity Trade Database (Comtrade) before rationalizing its contents. UNSTAT, the World Customs Organization and the World Trade Organization (WTO) were asked jointly to ensure concordance with UN conventions and recommendations, and to eliminate inconsistencies, impracticalities and ambiguities. The Commission noted that issues relating to HS, its updating and revision, as well as correlations between successive versions of HS, were the responsibility of the World Customs Organization.

At its 1995 meeting (Rome, Italy, 8-10 May), the Task Force reviewed Commission action in the area of international trade statistics and followed up on recommendations to the Task Force. In June, the ACC Subcommittee on Statistical Activities noted[2] the actions taken by the Task Force in May and strongly supported efforts to increase the exchange of data among organizations. It stressed that user needs were a primary concern in any data-exchange arrangement.

### Finance statistics

In March, the Statistical Commission considered the 1994 report of the Task Force on Financial Statistics.[10] The Commission requested the preparation of a list of items identifying differences between the 1993 SNA and the specialized statistical systems on balance-of-payments, monetary and financial statistics and government finance statistics, including a description of the nature of the differences as a means of harmonizing the links between the systems. The Task Force was to consider how and under what modalities further work should be conducted and report thereon to the Commission in 1997.

## Price statistics

The Statistical Commission reviewed a 1994 report[4] on the progress of the Task Force on Price Statistics, including the International Comparison Programme (ICP), noting that the Task Force was in the stage of conducting initial studies and stressing that it should focus on activities determined in its terms of reference relating to the harmonization of consumer price indices (CPI)–related work. It welcomed the initiative—by the World Bank, with the active cooperation of UNSTAT, the regional commissions, various international agencies and national statistical offices—to expand ICP coverage.

The Commission asked the Task Force to focus on those aspects of the CPI harmonization issue that were manageable within the given time-frame and resources. It encouraged the improvement of alternative communication techniques and the involvement of the regional commissions in Task Force activities, and agreed that the expert evaluation called for in a 1994 Task Force report[11] was no longer needed. The Task Force was to submit a progress report to the Working Group on International Statistical Programmes and Coordination in 1996.

After consultation with interested organizations and countries, the Convener of the Task Force, Eurostat, had proposed that the Task Force be discontinued and its work pursued in other forums, as it had completed its fact-finding and in view of limited resources.

In June, the ACC Subcommittee, noting that the Task Force had largely concluded its initial task, agreed that, while the field remained an important one, many of its concerns might be taken up by the Expert Group on Critical Problems in Economic Statistics. It therefore agreed that the Task Force should be discontinued.[2]

## Service statistics

At its second meeting (Geneva, 19-20 January 1995), the Task Force on Service Statistics, after adopting its terms of reference, decided to draft a framework for the statistical requirements of the WTO General Agreement on Trade in Services (GATS). A preliminary assessment was made of the establishment of a worldwide trade-in-services yearbook; a decision was taken to consider launching a trade-in-services manual.

The Statistical Commission, at its twenty-eighth session, endorsed plans for a workshop on the domestic (within country) service sector in developing countries,[12] based on an UNSTAT proposal. Its purpose was to assist African countries to define components of the service sector, including collection, processing and dissemination of data related to the service sector, and to identify problems associated with those activities. Participants would evaluate issues associated with data collection and dissemination, outline a consensus strategy to solve the problems identified, and provide recommendations for continued work in this field.

Reviewing the work of the Task Force, the Commission affirmed the importance of trade in services as an emerging policy concern and of the need to establish a framework for statistics in this area. It also noted that the Task Force had conducted a training course on trade-in-services statistics in Beijing, China, in October 1994. The Commission endorsed a Task Force plan to obtain an inventory of available data on trade in services; sought clarification on the scope and content of a proposed manual on trade in services; and requested the Task Force to reconsider the need for publishing a yearbook on trade in services. The Task Force was to report back to the Commission in 1997.

At its third meeting (Paris, 30-31 May 1995), the Task Force reviewed a draft of its inventory of activities and requirements, and discussed ways to establish a framework on statistical requirements by GATS, as well as trade in services in the globalization context. It was premature, it concluded, to decide on creating an international trade-in-services yearbook; the issue should be taken up at the Task Force's next meeting.

The Commission also had before it a report[13] of the Voorburg Group on Service Statistics, a cooperative effort by volunteer statistical agencies to address problems associated with data gaps and conceptual issues. The Group recommended changes to the services part of the provisional Central Product Classification (CPC), approved by the Commission in 1989. The changes concerned the structure of CPC, CPC explanatory notes and outstanding and unresolved issues.

The Commission agreed that revisions should be made to the latest CPC, to be labelled version 1.0, and that mechanisms similar to those used by the World Customs Organization for maintaining HS should be set up for CPC. Since work on HS and CPC for services was overseen by different bodies, the Commission recommended coordination of efforts in revisions. The structure of CPC should adequately reflect new technologies and there should be "upward compatibility" of future revisions, the Commission stated.

In June, the ACC Subcommittee noted the work being carried out by UNSTAT on the statistics of the domestic (within country) service sector in developing countries, noted the May report of the Task Force and endorsed its work programme for the coming year.[2]

## Environment statistics

The Statistical Commission reviewed a report of the Task Force on Environment Statistics,[14] in accordance with a 1994 Working Group request.[6] Current and future work of the Task Force fell into three categories: basic environmental statistics (statistical variables collected through monitoring or primary statistical surveys); environmental indicators (typically targeted on key environmental concerns or policy objectives); and environmental and natural resource accounting (including environmental data in a statistical accounting system facilitating aggregation and cross-sectoral comparison). The Task Force noted a need for capacity-building and training in all fields of environmental statistics, through seminars, workshops and country projects, and for coordination and harmonization of concepts and methods in environmental statistics.

The Commission noted that the report of the Task Force did not provide strategic guidance on how to improve coordination and to develop targets and priorities in an integrated work programme. It recommended that the Task Force try to develop a framework for various activities, indicating relative priority and links to policy agendas of national and international environmental agencies and providing benchmarks against which progress could be measured. The Task Force was to report to the Working Group and to the Commission at forthcoming sessions.

The Commission recommended that national statistical offices and international organizations make every effort to influence the decisions of ministries and governing bodies to achieve greater compatibility on international strategies and programmes. It welcomed collaboration between UNSTAT and the UN Department for Policy Coordination and Sustainable Development on indicators for sustainable development (see PART FOUR, Chapter I).

The Commission also considered the report[15] of the fourth meeting of the Intergovernmental Working Group on the Advancement of Environment Statistics (Stockholm, Sweden, 6-10 February 1995). That Working Group proposed that UNSTAT compile a list of international environmental indicators, agreeing on an initial list. In March, the Commission approved that proposal and requested UNSTAT to allocate the necessary resources. It also welcomed the offer of the Government of Colombia to host the Group's fifth meeting.

In June, the ACC Subcommittee recognized the growing importance of environment statistics to all sectors of society and the resulting problems of coordination.[2] The Task Force was asked to focus on the basic tasks of increasing the transparency of the objectives of organizations active in the field and reducing duplication. It was to report to the Working Group on improving coordination and developing targets and priorities.

## International economic classifications

The Commission, after reviewing a 1994 report of the Expert Group on International Classifications,[11] endorsed its work programme, urging it to utilize existing groups such as the Voorburg Group in elaborating technical details of various classifications. The Expert Group's work should be expanded to include social classifications, it was agreed.

## Social and demographic statistics

### Demographic, social and migration statistics

The activities of the UN Secretariat on the demographic and social statistics programme during 1993-1994[10] were considered by the Commission at its twenty-eighth session. The Commission endorsed the continued implementation of the International Programme for Accelerating the Improvement of Vital Statistics and Civil Registration Systems, particularly training workshops and efforts for economies in transition. It encouraged the further development of demographic, social and human settlement statistics databases and their speedier availability on the Internet and on CD-ROM. The Commission supported the work done by UNSTAT in 1994 on the revision of the 1979 UN *Recommendations on Statistics of International Migration*.[16] It endorsed the joint work of UNSTAT and the UN Centre for Human Settlements leading to the publication of the *Compendium of Human Settlement Statistics*, to be presented at the Second (1996) United Nations Conference on Human Settlements.

In the area of gender statistics, the Commission welcomed the work of UNSTAT, including progress made in preparing *The World's Women 1995: Trends and Statistics*[17] for the Fourth World Conference on Women (see PART FOUR, Chapter X). It also encouraged the use of the approach found in *The World's Women* in other social fields. It requested that UNSTAT prepare a draft classification of time-use activities as a basis for further research and studies of time-use statistics. The Commission also supported the proposal for a list of gender-related topics of broad national and international interest that might be covered in national publications on a rotating annual basis.

The recommendations of the 1994 UN Expert Group Meeting on the Development of Impairment, Disability and Handicap (IDH) Statistics were also reviewed.[18] The Commission requested UNSTAT to prepare a minimum set of IDH tabulation items and core tables, asking that the concept of functional limitations be further elaborated upon in the development of IDH statistics. It noted, however, that those projects were contingent upon continued availability of resources.

At the Expert Group Meeting on International Migration Statistics (New York, 10-14 July 1995),[19] sponsored by UNSTAT and Eurostat, two proposals for a draft revision of recommendations on international migration statistics were discussed—one based on residence, the other on citizenship. The Group agreed on the definition of a migrant and an international migrant, but recognized that such definitions must be adaptable because internal migration one day might be international migration the next, and vice versa. It also considered draft recommendations for compilation of separate asylum and refugee statistics, outside the direct scope of international migration statistics. A draft set of recommendations was to be finalized for submission to the Commission in 1997.

### Population and housing censuses

In 1995, the Commission had before it a report[20] of the Secretary-General setting out an overview of the 1990 and 2000 World Population and Housing Census Programmes. The 1990 Programme had been implemented by 202 countries or areas during 1985-1994. The Secretary-General proposed an expert group meeting to review and update existing principles and recommendations concerning housing censuses, household and family classifications and databases and tabulations. The Commission endorsed preparations for the 2000 Programme, approved preparation of handbooks on census methods and training materials, and endorsed the convening of an expert group.

The ACC Subcommittee in June welcomed[2] the intentions of the International Labour Organization (ILO), the United Nations Educational, Scientific and Cultural Organization and the World Health Organization to contribute to the expert group on the subject.

**ECONOMIC AND SOCIAL COUNCIL ACTION**

On 19 July, the Economic and Social Council adopted **resolution 1995/7**.

**2000 World Population and Housing Census Programme**
*The Economic and Social Council,*

*Recalling* its resolution 1985/8 of 28 May 1985, in which it requested the Secretary-General to proceed with the development of a 1990 World Population and Housing Census Programme and recommended that States Members of the United Nations should undertake to carry out population and housing censuses during the period 1985-1994, as well as its earlier resolutions endorsing previous decennial programmes,

*Noting with satisfaction* the great efforts made by countries to carry out population and housing censuses as part of the 1990 World Population and Housing Census Programme and also the activities of the United Nations and funding agencies in support of national efforts in that regard,

*Recognizing* the increasing importance of the 2000 round of population and housing censuses for meeting data needs for the follow-up activities to the International Conference on Population and Development, held at Cairo from 5 to 13 September 1994, the World Summit for Social Development, held at Copenhagen from 6 to 12 March 1995, the Fourth World Conference on Women, to be held at Beijing from 4 to 15 September 1995, and the United Nations Conference on Human Settlements (Habitat II), to be held at Istanbul from 3 to 14 June 1996, and to other regional and national meetings,

*Stressing* that periodic population and housing censuses for a country as a whole and for each administrative area therein are one of the primary sources of data needed for effective development planning and the monitoring of population issues and socio-economic and environmental trends, policies and programmes aimed at the improvement of living standards,

*Stressing also* that population and housing censuses provide valuable statistics and indicators for assessing the situation of various special population groups, such as those affected by gender issues, children, youth, the elderly, persons with an impairment/disability/handicap and the homeless and migrant population, and changes therein,

1. *Urges* Member States to carry out population and housing censuses during the period 1995-2004, taking into account international and regional recommendations relating to population and housing censuses and giving particular attention to advance planning and timely dissemination of census results to all users;

2. *Calls upon* Member States to continue to provide census results to the United Nations and other appropriate intergovernmental organizations to assist in studies on population, environment and socio-economic development issues and programmes;

3. *Requests* the Secretary-General to proceed with the development of the 2000 World Population and Housing Census Programme and to make the necessary preparations with a view to assisting countries in the successful implementation of the Programme.

Economic and Social Council resolution 1995/7

| 19 July 1995 | Meeting 44 | Adopted without vote |
|---|---|---|

Draft by Statistical Commission (E/1995/28); agenda item 6 *(o)*.
*Meeting numbers.* ESC 42-44.

### Poverty measurement

In January, the Secretary-General submitted a report[21] to the Statistical Commission on the work of the Economic Commission for Latin America and the Caribbean (ECLAC) on the profile of poverty in Latin America and the Caribbean. ECLAC and other international bodies, he said, had promoted studies which contributed to providing conceptual, methodological and empirical support for the analysis of poverty topics, concentrating on undertaking cooperative action to design policies in that area.

Studies of poverty in Latin American countries generally used two distinct approaches—the income method and the elaboration of maps of basic needs—whose common characteristic was the evaluation of each household's capacity to satisfy its basic needs and its effective access to specific sources of satisfaction. Principal information sources for the measurement and analysis of poverty were population and housing censuses and household surveys. Estimates of household income and expenditures contained in SNA, in particular, were used to compare and evaluate biases in the measurements generated in the censuses and surveys. The status of poverty indicators also revealed substantial progress in the availability and accessibility of information.

About 75 per cent of Latin American countries regularly produced information that could serve as a basis for the accurate measurement of poverty, it was reported. In addition, the geographic coverage of the data had expanded to the point that in many of those countries national coverage had been achieved, while most of them had reduced the lag between the production and dissemination of data to about two years, some to even less than a year.

In 1995, the Statistical Commission heard an oral report by the Task Force on the Measurement of Poverty on its 1995 meeting (Washington, D.C., 26-27 January). On the basis of questionnaires sent to all member agencies of the ACC Subcommittee, the Task Force concluded that it had largely fulfilled its task of reviewing current practices with regard to the measurement of poverty and had identified international agencies engaged in work on poverty. It decided that it was not equipped to take on the job of planning or establishing poverty measurement standards. Improved coordination in the areas of compilation parties, analytical methodologies and dissemination of data among international agencies could best be handled under the auspices of ACC. In the absence of a broader mandate, the Task Force requested the Commission to disband it.

The Commission decided that the Task Force report should be considered by the Working Group on International Statistical Programmes and Coordination at its upcoming session, which would then recommend to the Commission in 1997 what further work, if any, should be undertaken. The Working Group was to take account of the regional experience and results of poverty measurement developed by ECLAC, reflecting a wide diversity of national and regional experiences and circumstances. In many instances, regional and/or geographical content was to be considered when measuring and comparing economic and social development, the Commission stressed.

In June, the ACC Subcommittee concluded[2] that the measurement of poverty was a problem of continuing concern and that developments in the field should be monitored. An Expert Group on the Measurement of Poverty should be created as a suitable mechanism for follow-up to the Task Force. The Group should identify existing problems and potential solutions in individual countries.

### World Summit statistics

In February,[22] the Secretary-General transmitted to the Statistical Commission the report of the Central Statistical Office of the United Kingdom on the implications for statistics of the World Summit for Social Development (see PART FOUR, Chapter IX). The report suggested areas for development and action and proposed the establishment of expert groups, commissioning of methodological research, introduction of new publications, and inclusion of some topics in UNSTAT work programmes to advance such actions.

The Commission subsequently established an Expert Group to draw up a work programme reflecting major action areas identified by the Summit, indicating where the international statistical work in the social field should be concentrated. That Group was to propose specific statistical activities for the period 1996-1998 and assign priorities.

In June, the ACC Subcommittee noted[2] the initiatives taken by the Government of Denmark to promote the follow-up to the World Summit, including its statistical aspects. It also noted the establishment of the Expert Group.

The Expert Group on the Statistical Implications of Recent Major United Nations Conferences held two meetings in 1995 (Oslo, Norway, 10 June; Geneva, 13 June). It identified a number of indicators in five categories: population and development; eradicating poverty; expansion of productive employment and reduction of unemployment; social integration; and status of women and men. These indicators could be used to monitor or assess development and discuss potential sources of data. The Expert Group also suggested a timetable by which it would identify desirable action, coordinate assessment exercises, begin national capacity-building and prepare an international report. It estimated that a draft international report would be available for consideration by the Commission by 1999.

### Technical cooperation

The Statistical Commission considered a report of the Secretary-General on technical cooperation in statistics during the period 1991-1994,[23] a Secretariat note[24] on the state of funding for technical cooperation activities in statistics, and a report of Statistics Canada on its management training development.[25] UNSTAT reported orally on the state of funding for technical cooperation activities.

The Commission expressed serious concern over the diminished resources available to the United Nations for technical support in statistics and informatics. It noted the primacy of national needs in determining the allocation and use of technical assistance resources and requested UNSTAT to expand on its oral report and submit an analytical written report to the Working Group. The Commission also noted the importance of bilateral technical cooperation and asked for improved coordination of multilateral and bilateral cooperation.

In June, the ACC Subcommittee noted[2] the range of difficulties implicit in any approach to measuring the flows of technical cooperation from bilateral donors. It welcomed the experimental approach that UNSTAT was developing to try to obtain information from recipient and donor countries, welcomed the offers of supplementary information that had been made by the UN Population Fund, IMF, Eurostat and other bodies, and noted that UNSTAT would report to the Working Group on the results of its efforts.

### Programme questions

The Commission had before it reports of the Secretary-General containing an overall review of the statistical work of international organizations in statistics[26] and on plans of international organizations in statistics,[27] and a report[28] by the ACC Subcommittee on plans for methodological development of the inter-agency task forces and of the Intersecretariat Working Group on National Accounts. The Commission also had before it the proposed programme of work of UNSTAT for 1996-1997. The Secretariat proposed to give priority to the documentation of the 1993 SNA in all countries, in close collaboration with the regional commissions and other members of the Intersecretariat Working Group. It would also give attention to statistical requirements arising from the 1994 International Conference on Population and Development,[29] the World Summit for Social Development (see PART FOUR, Chapter IX) and the Fourth World Conference on Women (see PART FOUR, Chapter X). The Commission welcomed the reports and endorsed the proposed programme of work.

*REFERENCES*

[1]E/1995/28. [2]ACC/1995/14. [3]E/CN.3/1995/3. [4]YUN 1994, p. 1260. [5]E/CN.3/1995/4. [6]YUN 1994, p. 1262. [7]*International Recommendations for Construction Statistics*, Sales No. E.68.XVII.11. [8]E/CN.3/1995/5/Add.1. [9]*International Trade Statistics: Concepts and Definitions*, Sales No. E.82.XVII.10. [10]YUN 1994, p. 1263. [11]Ibid., p. 1261. [12]E/CN.3/1995/14. [13]E/CN.3/1995/15. [14]E/CN.3/1995/8. [15]E/CN.3/1995/35. [16]*Recommendations on Statistics of International Migration*, Sales No. E.79.XVII.18. [17]*The World's Women 1995: Trends and Statistics*, Sales No. E.95.XVII.2. [18]YUN 1994, p. 1264. [19]ESA/STAT/AC/50/9. [20]E/CN.3/1995/18. [21]E/CN.3/1995/19. [22]E/CN.3/1995/20. [23]YUN 1994, p. 1265. [24]E/CN.3/1995/22. [25]E/CN.3/1995/23. [26]E/CN.3/1995/25. [27]E/CN.3/1995/26. [28]E/CN.3/1995/12. [29]YUN 1994, p. 955.

## Other statistical activities

### Inter-agency coordination

The Administrative Committee on Coordination (ACC) Subcommittee on Statistical Activities, held its twenty-ninth session in Geneva on 15, 16 and 19 June.[1] It brought six matters to the attention of the ACC Consultative Committee on Programme and Operational Questions (CCPOQ), including coordination of system-wide efforts to provide statistical data for monitoring follow-up to international conferences; the chairmanship of the Subcommittee and membership of the Bureau (UNSTAT, WTO, IMF, ILO, ECLAC); its agreement that the Inter-State Statistical Committee of the Commonwealth of Independent States should be invited to participate in future sessions as an observer; and the date, venue and provisional agenda of the Subcommittee's thirtieth (1996) session. In September, CCPOQ noted the report of the Subcommittee and endorsed the nomination of the Chairman as well as the dates, venue and provisional agenda of the Subcommittee's 1996 session.[2]

The Subcommittee discussed the work of the inter-agency task forces, improvement of coordination tools, the need for statistical data from international organizations, bilateral technical cooperation, coordination of statistical programmes, holding a World Statistics Day, the free exchange of statistics and related materials among international organizations, and the report of the ACC Subcommittee on Demographic Estimates and Projections. During debate, it was generally recognized that the work of some task forces might be discontinued or handled more appropriately by expert groups that included representatives of countries and organizations.

The Working Group on International Statistical Programmes and Coordination, which did not meet in 1995 as scheduled, was to hold its eighteenth session in April 1996.

### Coordination of statistical data collection

In January, the Secretary-General submitted a report[3] to the Commission on ongoing work on improved coordination of statistical data collection from countries, in accordance with a 1994 Commission request[4] to prepare an updated version of the Inventory of Statistical Data-Collection Activities. The Inventory would be designed as a set of cross-referenced databases, comprising a master inventory, several sub-inventories and reference files. It would contain a substantial amount of cross-referenced information on various aspects of the data-collection activities carried out by international organizations and agencies and could be useful for tracing developments in statistical data-collection activities of international bodies. In March, the Commission requested UNSTAT to submit the updated version of the Inventory to the Working Group on International Statistical Programmes and Coordination, after review by the ACC Subcommittee.

In June, the Subcommittee welcomed[1] the completion of work on updating the Inventory, the list of classifications used in statistics (see above, under "International trade statistics") and the inventory of computerized statistical databases. The Subcommittee requested UNSTAT to re-examine the content and methods of updating its outputs, particularly with a view to maintaining them on an ongoing basis, and to develop the necessary arrangements with organizations to supply inputs on that basis; consider the modalities needed to consolidate the many tools into a unified presentation; consider the circulation of the outputs so that the full range of potential users might have access to them; and review the media used for the outputs with a view to making them easily accessible. UNSTAT was asked to consult with the Information Systems Coordinating Committee on relevant aspects of the distribution of outputs and to report on these matters to the Bureau of the Subcommittee at its next meeting.

*REFERENCES*

[1]ACC/1995/14. [2]ACC/1995/18. [3]E/CN.3/1995/13. [4]YUN 1994, p. 1264.

PART FIVE

# Legal questions

Chapter I

# International Court of Justice

In 1995, the International Court of Justice (ICJ) delivered two Judgments and nine Orders. It had pending before it 12 contentious cases and one request for an examination of the situation in accordance with the Court's Judgment of 20 December 1974 in the *Nuclear Tests (New Zealand v. France)* case. During the year, two requests for an advisory opinion were referred to the Court and one case was removed from its list.

The General Assembly and the Security Council elected three new judges to the Court to fill vacancies resulting from two deaths and a resignation. A vacancy resulting from a third death was to be filled in 1996.

The President of the Court on 12 October told the General Assembly[1] that never before had ICJ been so much in demand, never before had it been so active. The States parties to the 10 contentious cases currently before the Court, he said, were located on every continent. The Court's jurisdiction was steadily expanding, both in terms of the number of declarations made and in terms of the compromissory clauses included in treaties, as well as in terms of the withdrawal of reservations to such clauses.

He said the Court's new vitality had been attributed, with a greater or lesser degree of relevance, to decisions reached by the Court in certain cases, to the end of communism, the greater trust placed in the Court by third world countries, and a more widespread psychological rallying to the applicable international law.

Fully aware of its responsibilities as an integral part of the system of peaceful settlement of international disputes established under the Charter, the Court had displayed judicial realism and had considered itself obligated to assist in bringing parties closer together, while not at any time departing from its primary task of applying the law. That in no way meant that the Court was handing down "judgements of Solomon", he added.

The success of the Court might well be due precisely to the fact that its role seemed ultimately to be fairly well adapted to the concerns and the system of values predominating in the States to which it was open.

As for the future of the Court, its President said that depended on many factors which to a large extent eluded the control of the Court itself. These included the emergence of certain categories of conflicts which were called internal but which had clear international repercussions; internal and external changes in States which affected their traditional role as key players in international relations; the emergence of international intergovernmental organizations on the world stage; the growing place of non-governmental organizations; and recognition of the essential role the Court must play in sanctioning a form of international law governing a world and a society of law.

## Judicial work of the Court

During 1995, the Court delivered Judgments in the cases concerning *Maritime Delimitation and Territorial Questions between Qatar and Bahrain (Qatar v. Bahrain)* and *East Timor (Portugal v. Australia)*.

It made an Order in the case concerning *Nuclear Tests (New Zealand v. France)* (see above). It further made an Order recording the discontinuance of the proceedings and directing the removal from the Court's list in the case concerning *Maritime Delimitation between Guinea-Bissau and Senegal (Guinea-Bissau v. Senegal)*. The Court or its President also made several Orders on the conduct of the proceedings in the cases concerning *Maritime Delimitation and Territorial Questions between Qatar and Bahrain (Qatar v. Bahrain)*, *Questions of Interpretation and Application of the 1971 Montreal Convention arising from the Aerial Incident at Lockerbie (Libyan Arab Jamahiriya v. United Kingdom)* and *(Libyan Arab Jamahiriya v. United States of America)*, *Application of the Convention on the Prevention and Punishment of the Crime of Genocide (Bosnia and Herzegovina v. Yugoslavia (Serbia and Montenegro))*, *Fisheries Jurisdiction (Spain v. Canada)* and *Legality of the Threat or Use of Nuclear Weapons*.

The 1995 activities of ICJ were covered in two reports to the General Assembly, for the periods 1 August 1994 to 31 July 1995[2] and 1 August 1995 to 31 July 1996.[3] By **decision 50/404** of 12 October 1995, the Assembly took note of the 1994/95 report.

### Aerial incident of 3 July 1988
### (Iran v. United States)

Iran in 1989 instituted proceedings against the United States, referring to the destruction of an Iranian aircraft on 3 July 1988 and the killing of its 290 passengers and crew by missiles launched in Iranian airspace from the United States guided-missile cruiser USS *Vincennes*. The time-limits for written proceedings, fixed in a December 1989 Court Order, were extended by an Order in June 1990. The Memorial of Iran was filed within the prescribed time-limit.

In March 1991, within the time-limit fixed for its Counter-Memorial, the United States filed certain preliminary objections to the Court's jurisdiction. By an April 1991 Order,[4] the Court fixed 9 December of that year as the time-limit within which Iran might present a written statement of its observations and submissions on those objections. As requested by Iran, and after the views of the United States had been ascertained, the President of the Court, by Orders of 18 December 1991[4] and 5 June 1992,[5] extended that time-limit to 9 June and 9 September 1992, respectively. Iran's written statement was filed within the prescribed time-limit and was communicated to the Secretary-General of the International Civil Aviation Organization (ICAO), together with the written pleadings previously filed. Following the submission of written observations by the ICAO Council within the time-limit of 9 December 1992, fixed by the President of the Court, the Court announced that hearings in the case would open on 12 September 1994. At the joint request of the Parties, made in 1994, those hearings were postponed indefinitely.

### East Timor (Portugal v. Australia)

In 1991,[6] Portugal instituted proceedings against Australia in a dispute concerning certain activities of Australia with respect to East Timor. Portugal claimed that Australia, by negotiating with Indonesia an agreement, signed on 11 December 1989, relating to the exploration and exploitation of the continental shelf in the area of the Timor Gap, had caused legal and moral damage to the people of East Timor and Portugal, which would become material if the exploitation of hydrocarbon resources began there.

Within the time-limits fixed by a May 1991 Order,[6] the Portuguese Memorial and the Australian Counter-Memorial were filed in 1991 and 1992, respectively. By an Order of 19 June 1992,[7] the Court fixed 1 December 1992 and 1 June 1993 as the time-limits for the filing of a Reply by Portugal and a Rejoinder by Australia, respectively. The Reply of Portugal was filed within the prescribed time-limit. However, an Order of 19 May 1993[8] extended to 1 July 1993 the time-limit for the Australian Rejoinder, which was filed accordingly. Portugal chose António de Arruda Ferrer-Correia, and Australia chose Sir Ninian Stephen, to sit as Judges ad hoc in the case. After the resignation on 14 July 1994 of Mr. Ferrer-Correia, Portugal chose Krzysztof J. Skubiszewski to sit as Judge ad hoc.

Hearings having been held between 30 January and 16 February 1995, the Court, at a public sitting on 30 June, delivered its Judgment,[9] the operative paragraph of which read as follows:

> For these reasons,
> *The Court,*
> By 14 votes to 2,
> *Finds* that it cannot in the present case exercise the jurisdiction conferred upon it by the declarations made by the Parties under Article 36, paragraph 2, of its Statute to adjudicate upon the dispute referred to it by the Application of the Portuguese Republic.
> *In favour:* President Bedjaoui; Vice-President Schwebel; Judges Oda, Sir Robert Jennings, Guillaume, Shahabuddeen, Aguilar Mawdsley, Ranjeva, Herczegh, Shi, Fleischhauer, Koroma, Vereshchetin; Judge ad hoc Sir Ninian Stephen;
> *Against:* Judge Weeramantry; Judge ad hoc Skubiszewski.

Judges Oda, Shahabuddeen, Ranjeva and Vereshchetin appended separate opinions to the Judgment; Judge Weeramantry and Judge ad hoc Skubiszewski appended dissenting opinions.

### Maritime delimitation (Guinea-Bissau v. Senegal)

In 1991, Guinea-Bissau instituted proceedings against Senegal in a dispute concerning the delimitation of all the maritime territories between them. At that time, previous proceedings instituted by Guinea-Bissau against Senegal in 1989 concerning the *Arbitral Award of 31 July 1989 (Guinea-Bissau v. Senegal)*[4] were still in progress.

Guinea-Bissau claimed that the result of that Arbitration did not make it possible to establish a definitive delimitation of all the maritime areas over which the Parties had rights, and asked the Court to adjudge and declare what should be the line delimiting all the maritime territories appertaining to Guinea-Bissau and Senegal.

Following the November 1991 Judgment[4] in the case concerning the *Arbitral Award of 31 July 1989*, the President of the Court met with the two Parties in February and October 1992[7] and agreed to their request that no time-limit be fixed for the initial pleadings of the case, pending the outcome of the continuing negotiations on the question of maritime delimitation.

After several exchanges of letters regarding extended time-limits, the President met with the Parties again on 10 March 1994, to receive the text of an Agreement between the two Governments, signed on 14 October 1993. The Agreement provided, *inter alia*, for the joint exploitation by the two Parties of a maritime zone situated between the 268° and 220° azimuths drawn from Cape Roxo as well as for the establishment of an international agency for the exploitation of the zone. It was to enter into force upon conclusion of the agreement on the establishment and functioning of the international agency and ratification of both agreements by both States.

In letters dated 16 March 1994, addressed to the Presidents of both States, the President of ICJ expressed his satisfaction and informed them that the case would be removed from the list, in accordance with the terms of the Rules of Court, as soon as the Parties had notified him of their decision to discontinue the proceedings.

At a meeting held by the President with the representatives of the Parties on 1 November 1995, the latter furnished him with an additional copy of the above-mentioned Agreement as well as the text of a "Protocol on the establishment and functioning of the Agency for Management and Cooperation between the Republic of Senegal and the Republic of Guinea-Bissau instituted by the agreement of 14 October 1993", signed in Bissau on 12 June 1995 by the two heads of State. The representatives at the same time notified him of the decisions of their Governments to discontinue the proceedings and the President asked them to confirm that decision in writing to the Court in whatever manner they deemed most appropriate.

By a letter of 2 November 1995, the Agent of Guinea-Bissau confirmed that his Government, by virtue of the Agreement reached by the two Parties on the disputed zone, had decided to discontinue the proceedings instituted by its Application dated 12 March 1991. After the Agent of Senegal, by a letter dated 6 November 1995, had confirmed that his Government "agreed to the discontinuance of proceedings", the Court, by an Order of 8 November 1995,[10] placed on record the discontinuance and directed that the case be removed from the list.

## Maritime delimitation and territorial questions (Qatar v. Bahrain)

Qatar instituted proceedings in 1991[11] against Bahrain in respect of disputes relating to sovereignty over the Hawar islands, sovereign rights over the shoals of Dibal and Qit'at Jaradah, and the delimitation of the maritime areas of the two States.

In August 1991, Bahrain contested the basis of jurisdiction invoked by Qatar. By an October 1991 Order,[11] the President of the Court decided that written proceedings should first be addressed to the questions of the jurisdiction of the Court to entertain the dispute and of the admissibility of the Application, and fixed the time-limits for the filing of a Memorial by Qatar and a Counter-Memorial by Bahrain, which were filed accordingly in 1992. Also in 1992, Qatar and Bahrain filed their respective Reply and Rejoinder within the time-limits fixed by a June 1992 Order.[12] Qatar chose José Maria Ruda and Bahrain chose Nicolas Valticos to sit as Judges ad hoc in the case.

Following hearings held in February/March 1994, the Court delivered on 1 July a Judgment,[13] by which it found that the exchanges of letters between the King of Saudi Arabia and the Amir of Qatar, dated 19 and 21 December 1987, and between the King of Saudi Arabia and the Amir of Bahrain, dated 19 and 26 December 1987, and the document headed "Minutes", signed in Doha on 25 December 1990 by the Ministers for Foreign Affairs of Bahrain, Qatar and Saudi Arabia, were international agreements creating rights and obligations for the Parties; and that, by the terms of those agreements, the Parties had undertaken to submit to the Court the whole of the dispute between them, as circumscribed by the Bahraini formula. Having noted that it had before it only an Application from Qatar setting out that State's specific claims in connection with that formula, the Court decided to afford the Parties the opportunity to submit to it the whole of the dispute. It fixed 30 November 1994 as the time-limit within which the Parties were jointly or separately to take action to that end and reserved any other matters for subsequent decision.

On 30 November 1994, the Court received a letter from Qatar transmitting an act to comply with the decisions to afford the Parties the opportunity to submit the whole dispute and to fix 30 November as the time-limit. On the same day, Bahrain communicated its report to the Court on the attempt by the Parties to implement the Court's Judgment.

In view of those communications, the Court resumed dealing with the case.

At a public sitting held on 15 February 1995, the Court delivered a Judgment on jurisdiction and admissibility,[14] the operative paragraph of which read as follows:

> For these reasons,
> *The Court,*
> (1) By 10 votes to 5,
> *Finds* that it has jurisdiction to adjudicate upon the dispute submitted to it between the State of Qatar and the State of Bahrain;
> *In favour:* President Bedjaoui; Judges Sir Robert Jennings, Guillaume, Aguilar Mawdsley, Weeramantry, Ranjeva, Herczegh, Shi, Fleischhauer; Judge ad hoc Torres Bernárdez;
> *Against:* Vice-President Schwebel; Judges Oda, Shahabuddeen, Koroma; Judge ad hoc Valticos.
> (2) By 10 votes to 5,
> *Finds* that the Application of the State of Qatar as formulated on 30 November 1994 is admissible.
> *In favour:* President Bedjaoui; Judges Sir Robert Jennings, Guillaume, Aguilar Mawdsley, Weeramantry, Ranjeva, Herczegh, Shi, Fleischhauer; Judge ad hoc Torres Bernárdez;
> *Against:* Vice-President Schwebel; Judges Oda, Shahabuddeen, Koroma; Judge ad hoc Valticos.

Vice-President Schwebel, Judges Oda, Shahabuddeen and Koroma, and Judge ad hoc Valticos appended dissenting opinions.

Judge ad hoc Valticos resigned as of the end of the jurisdiction and admissibility phase of the proceedings.

By an Order of 28 April 1995,[15] the Court, having ascertained the views of Qatar and having given Bahrain an opportunity to state its views, fixed 29 February 1996 as the time-limit for the filing by each of the Parties of a Memorial on the merits of the case.

### Questions of interpretation and application of the 1971 Montreal Convention arising from the aerial incident at Lockerbie (Libyan Arab Jamahiriya v. United Kingdom) and (Libyan Arab Jamahiriya v. United States)

In 1992,[12] the Libyan Arab Jamahiriya instituted separate proceedings against the United Kingdom and the United States in respect of a dispute over the interpretation and application of the 1971 Montreal Convention for the Suppression of Unlawful Acts against the Safety of Civil Aviation,[16] which arose from its alleged involvement in the crash of Pan Am flight 103 over Lockerbie, Scotland, on 21 December 1988.

In the Applications, Libya referred to the charging and indictment of two of its nationals, by the Lord Advocate of Scotland and by a United States Grand Jury, with having caused a bomb to be placed aboard Pan Am flight 103. The bomb subsequently exploded, causing the aircraft to crash, killing all persons aboard. Libya requested the Court to adjudge and declare that it had complied fully with all of its obligations under the Montreal Convention, which it claimed to be the only appropriate Convention in force between the Parties, and which required it to establish its own jurisdiction over alleged offenders present in its territory, and submit the case to its authorities for prosecution, as there was no extradition treaty between it and the other Parties; that the United Kingdom and the United States were in breach of the Convention by rejecting Libya's efforts to resolve the matter within the framework of international law and placing pressure on it to surrender the two Libyan nationals for trial; and that the United Kingdom and the United States were under a legal obligation to cease and desist from such breaches and from the use of force or threats against Libya and from all violations of its sovereignty, territorial integrity and political independence.

It also made two separate requests for an indication of provisional measures in each case. By two Orders of 14 April 1992,[12] the Court found that the circumstances of the case were not such as to require the exercise of its power to indicate provisional measures. By Orders of 19 June 1992,[12] the Court fixed 20 December 1993 as the time-limit for the filing of a Memorial by Libya and 20 June 1995 for Counter-Memorials by the

United Kingdom and the United States. The Memorial by Libya was filed within the prescribed time-limit and Libya chose Ahmed S. El-Kosheri to sit as Judge ad hoc in the cases.

On 16 and on 20 June 1995, respectively, the United Kingdom and the United States filed preliminary objections to the jurisdiction of the Court to entertain the Applications of Libya. By virtue of article 79, paragraph 3, of the Rules of Court, the proceedings on the merits are suspended when preliminary objections are filed; proceedings have then to be organized for the consideration of those preliminary objections in accordance with the provision of that article.

After a meeting on 9 September 1995 between the President of the Court and the Agents of the Parties to ascertain the Parties' views, the Court, by Orders of 22 September 1995,[17] fixed, in each case, 22 December 1995 as the time-limit within which Libya might present a written statement of its observations and submissions on the preliminary objections raised by the United Kingdom and the United States, respectively. Libya filed such statements within the prescribed time-limits.

### Oil platforms (Iran v. United States)

Iran in 1992[18] instituted proceedings against the United States regarding a dispute in which Iran alleged that the destruction by United States warships, on 19 October 1987 and 18 April 1988, of three offshore oil production complexes, owned and operated by the National Iranian Oil Company, constituted a breach of international law and the 1955 Iran/United States Treaty of Amity, Economic Relations and Consular Rights. Iran requested the Court to rule on the matter.

By an Order of 4 December 1992,[18] the time-limits were fixed at 31 May 1993 for the filing of a Memorial by Iran and 30 November 1993 for a Counter-Memorial by the United States. By an Order of 3 June 1993,[19] those time-limits were extended to 8 June and 16 December 1993, respectively. Iran filed its Memorial within the prescribed time-limit, while the United States filed certain preliminary objections to the jurisdiction of the Court. In accordance with the Rules of Court (see above, under section on Libya v. United Kingdom/United States), the proceedings on the merits were suspended. By an Order of 18 January 1994,[20] the Court fixed 1 July 1994 as the time-limit within which Iran could present a written statement of its observations and submissions on the United States objections. That written statement was filed within the prescribed time-limit.

The public sittings to hear the oral arguments of the Parties on the preliminary objections filed by the United States were to open on 16 September 1996.

## Application of the Convention on the Prevention and Punishment of the Crime of Genocide (Bosnia and Herzegovina v. Yugoslavia)

In 1993,[19] Bosnia and Herzegovina instituted proceedings against the Federal Republic of Yugoslavia (Serbia and Montenegro) for alleged violations of the 1948 Convention on the Prevention and Punishment of the Crime of Genocide.[21]

Bosnia and Herzegovina requested the Court to adjudge and declare that Yugoslavia had violated and was continuing to violate several provisions of the Genocide Convention as well as of the Charter of the United Nations, the 1949 Geneva Conventions for the protection of war victims and their 1977 Additional Protocol I,[22] the 1907 Hague Regulations on Land Warfare, and the 1948 Universal Declaration of Human Rights;[23] that Yugoslavia was using force and the threat of force against Bosnia and Herzegovina, violating its sovereignty and intervening in its internal affairs, as well as encouraging and supporting military and paramilitary actions in and against Bosnia and Herzegovina; that Bosnia and Herzegovina had the sovereign right under the Charter and customary international law to defend itself and to request the assistance of any State in doing so, which was not to be impaired by Security Council resolution 713(1991)[24] and subsequent resolutions imposing and reaffirming an arms embargo on the former Yugoslavia; that those resolutions should not be construed as imposing an arms embargo on Bosnia and Herzegovina; that, pursuant to the right to collective self-defence, other States had the right to come to the immediate defence of Bosnia and Herzegovina at its request; that Yugoslavia (Serbia and Montenegro) should cease and desist immediately from its breaches of the foregoing legal obligations; and that Yugoslavia should pay reparations for damages sustained by Bosnia and Herzegovina.

Bosnia and Herzegovina also requested the Court to indicate provisional measures to the effect that Yugoslavia should, *inter alia*, cease and desist immediately from all acts of genocide against the people and State of Bosnia and Herzegovina. By an Order of 8 April 1993,[19] the Court indicated that Yugoslavia should immediately take all measures within its power to prevent commission of the crime of genocide; and should ensure in particular that any armed units under its control did not commit any acts of genocide or acts leading up to genocide. The Court also indicated that neither of the Parties should in any way aggravate or extend the dispute. The time-limits for the filing of the Memorial by Bosnia and Herzegovina and a Counter-Memorial by Yugoslavia were fixed at 15 October 1993 and 15 April 1994, respectively, by an Order of 16 April 1993,[19] and were extended to 15 April 1994 and 15 April 1995, respectively, by an Order of 7 October 1993.[25]

In July 1993, Bosnia and Herzegovina made a second request for indication of provisional measures, while Yugoslavia, in August, requested the Court to indicate provisional measures requiring Bosnia and Herzegovina to prevent acts of genocide against the Bosnian Serbs. Acting on those requests, the Court, by an Order of 13 September 1993,[25] held that the situation demanded the immediate implementation of provisional measures indicated in its April 1993 Order rather than an indication of additional measures. In declining Bosnia and Herzegovina's requests related to the partition and annexation of its territory and the means of preventing acts of genocide and partition, the Court pointed out that such claims were beyond the scope of its jurisdiction in that case, conferred on it by the Genocide Convention.

The Memorial of Bosnia and Herzegovina was filed within the prescribed time-limit. Bosnia and Herzegovina chose Elihu Lauterpacht and Yugoslavia chose Milenko Kreca to sit as Judges ad hoc in the case.

By an Order of 21 March 1995,[26] the President of the Court, upon a request of the Agent of Yugoslavia and after the views of Bosnia and Herzegovina had been ascertained, extended to 30 June 1995 the time-limit for the filing of the Counter-Memorial of Yugoslavia. Within that extended time-limit Yugoslavia filed certain preliminary objections. The objections related, first, to the admissibility of the Application and, second, to the jurisdiction of the Court to deal with the case. By virtue of the Rules of Court (see above, under section on Libya v. United Kingdom/United States), the proceedings were suspended.

By an Order of 14 July 1995,[27] the President of the Court, taking into account the views expressed by the Parties, fixed 14 November 1995 as the time-limit within which Bosnia and Herzegovina might present a written statement of its observations and submissions on the preliminary objections raised by Yugoslavia (Serbia and Montenegro). Bosnia and Herzegovina filed such a statement within the prescribed time-limit.

The public sittings to hear the oral arguments of the Parties on the preliminary objections raised by Yugoslavia were to open on 29 April 1996.

## Gabcíkovo-Nagymaros Project (Hungary/Slovakia)

In 1992, Hungary applied to the Court in a dispute with the Czech and Slovak Federal Republic concerning the projected diversion of the Danube River, inviting the Republic to accept the Court's jurisdiction.

Following negotiations between Hungary and the Czech and Slovak Federal Republic, which dissolved into two States on 1 January 1993, Hungary and Slovakia—the sole successor State of the Czech and Slovak Federal Republic with respect to the project dispute—on 2 July 1993,[25] requested the Court to decide whether Hungary had been entitled to suspend and subsequently abandon in 1989 work on the Nagymaros Project and on the part of the Gabcíkovo Project for which it was responsible under the 1977 Budapest Treaty on the Construction and Operation of the Gabcíkovo-Nagymaros Barrage System; and whether the Czech and Slovak Federal Republic had been entitled to execute, during 1991 and 1992, the "provisional solution"—a system damming up the Danube on Czechoslovak territory. The Court was also requested to determine the legal effects of the termination of the Treaty by Hungary in 1992 and the legal consequences of the Court's Judgment in that case.

Each Party filed a Memorial and a Counter-Memorial within the time-limits of 2 May and 5 December 1994, respectively, fixed by an Order of 14 July 1993.[25] By an Order of 20 December 1994,[28] the President of the Court fixed 20 June 1995 as the time-limit for the filing of a Reply by each of the Parties. Those Replies were filed within the prescribed time-limit. Slovakia chose Krzysztof J. Skubiszewski to sit as Judge ad hoc.

## Land and maritime boundary between Cameroon and Nigeria

On 29 March 1994,[28] Cameroon instituted proceedings against Nigeria in a dispute concerning the question of sovereignty over the peninsula of Bakassi, and requested the Court to determine the course of the maritime frontier between the two States in so far as that frontier had not already been established in 1975.

In its Application, Cameroon referred to "an aggression" by Nigeria, whose troops it stated were "occupying" several Cameroonian localities on the Bakassi peninsula, resulting "in great prejudice to" Cameroon, and requested the Court to adjudge and declare that sovereignty over the Bakassi peninsula was Cameroonian; that Nigeria had violated and was violating the fundamental principle of respect for frontiers inherited from colonization and its obligations under international law by using force against Cameroon and by militarily occupying the Bakassi peninsula; and that Nigeria should withdraw its troops and pay reparation. Cameroon also asked the Court to prolong the course of its maritime boundary with Nigeria up to the limit of the maritime zones of the two States.

On 6 June 1994,[28] Cameroon filed an Additional Application for the purpose of extending the subject of the dispute to a further dispute described as relating essentially to the question of sovereignty over a part of the territory of Cameroon in the area of Lake Chad, while also asking the Court to specify definitively the frontier between Cameroon and Nigeria from Lake Chad to the sea. It further requested the Court to examine the two Applications as one case. On 14 June, Nigeria indicated that it had no objection to that request.

By an Order of 16 June 1994,[29] the Court fixed 16 March and 18 December 1995 as the time-limits for the filing of Cameroon's Memorial and Nigeria's Counter-Memorial, respectively (see also PART TWO, Chapter II). The Memorial was filed within the prescribed time-limit.

On 13 December 1995, within the time-limit for the filing of its Counter-Memorial, Nigeria filed certain preliminary objections to the jurisdiction of the Court and to the admissibility of the claims of Cameroon. By virtue of the Rules of Court, the proceedings on the merits were suspended.

## Fisheries jurisdiction (Spain v. Canada)

On 28 March 1995, Spain instituted proceedings against Canada in a dispute relating to the Canadian Coastal Fisheries Protection Act, as amended on 12 May 1994, and to the implementing regulations of that Act, as well as to certain measures taken on the basis of that legislation, particularly the boarding on the high seas on 9 March 1995 of a fishing boat, the *Estai*, sailing under the Spanish flag.

The Application indicated, *inter alia*, that by the amended Act "an attempt was made to impose on all persons on board foreign ships a broad prohibition on fishing in the Regulatory Area of the Northwest Atlantic Fisheries Organization (NAFO), that is, on the high seas, outside Canada's exclusive economic zone"; that the Act "expressly permits (article 8) the use of force against foreign fishing boats in the zones that article 2.1 unambiguously terms the 'high seas'"; that the implementing regulations of 25 May 1994 provided, in particular, for "the use of force by fishery protection vessels against the foreign fishing boats covered by those rules . . . which infringe their mandates in the zone of the high seas within the scope of those regulations"; and that the implementing regulations of 3 March 1995 "expressly permit [. . .] such conduct as regards Spanish and Portuguese ships on the high seas".

The Application alleged the violation of various principles and norms of international law and stated that there was a dispute between Spain and Canada which, going beyond the framework of fishing, seriously affected the very principle of the freedom of the high seas and, moreover, implied a very serious infringement of the sovereign rights of Spain.

Spain requested the Court to declare that the legislation of Canada, in so far as it claimed to exercise a jurisdiction over ships flying a foreign flag on the high seas, outside the exclusive economic zone of Canada, was not opposable to Spain; to adjudge and declare that Canada was bound to refrain from any repetition of the acts complained of and to offer reparation to Spain; and to declare that the boarding on the high seas on 9 March 1995 of the ship *Estai* flying the flag of Spain and the measures of coercion and the exercise of jurisdiction over that ship and over its captain constituted a concrete violation of the principles and norms of international law.

By a letter dated 21 April 1995, the Ambassador of Canada to the Netherlands informed the Court that, in the view of his Government, the Court manifestly lacked jurisdiction to deal with the Application filed by Spain by reason of paragraph 2 (d) of the Declaration, dated 10 May 1994, whereby Canada accepted the compulsory jurisdiction of the Court.

Taking into account an agreement concerning the procedure reached between the Parties at a meeting with the President of the Court, held on 27 April 1995, the President, by an Order of 2 May 1995,[30] decided that the written proceedings should first be addressed to the question of the jurisdiction of the Court to entertain the dispute and fixed 29 September 1995 as the time-limit for the filing of the Memorial of Spain and 29 February 1996 for the filing of the Counter-Memorial of Canada. The Memorial was filed within the prescribed time-limit.

Spain chose Santiago Torres-Bernárdez and Canada Marc Lalonde to sit as Judges ad hoc.

## Request for an examination of the situation in accordance with paragraph 63 of the Court's Judgment of 20 December 1974 in the Nuclear Tests (New Zealand v. France) case

On 21 August 1995, New Zealand submitted to the Court a request for an examination of the situation "arising out of a proposed action announced by France which will, if carried out, affect the basis of the Judgment[31] rendered by the Court on 20 December 1974 in the *Nuclear Tests (New Zealand v. France)* case". The request referred to a media statement of 13 June 1995 by French President Jacques Chirac "which said that France would conduct a final series of eight nuclear-weapons tests in the South Pacific starting in September 1995". New Zealand stated that the request was made "under the right granted to New Zealand in paragraph 63 of the Judgment of 20 December 1974".

Paragraph 63 reads as follows:

"Once the Court has found that a State has entered into a commitment concerning its future conduct it is not the Court's function to contemplate that it will not comply with it. However, the Court observes that if the basis of this Judgment were to be affected, the Applicant could request an examination of the situation in accordance with the provisions of the Statute; the denunciation by France, by letter dated 2 January 1974, of the General Act for the Pacific Settlement of International Disputes, which is relied on as a basis of jurisdiction in the present case, cannot constitute by itself an obstacle to the presentation of such a request."

New Zealand asserted that the rights for which it sought protection "all fall within the scope of the rights invoked by New Zealand in paragraph 28 of the 1973 Application" in the above-mentioned case, but that at the present time New Zealand sought "recognition only of those rights that would be adversely affected by entry into the marine environment of radioactive material in consequence of the further tests to be carried out at Mururoa or Fangataufa atolls, and of its entitlement to the protection and benefit of a properly conducted environmental impact assessment".

New Zealand asked the Court to adjudge and declare: "(i) that the conduct of the proposed nuclear tests will constitute a violation of the rights under international law of New Zealand, as well as of other States; further or in the alternative, (ii) that it is unlawful for France to conduct such nuclear tests before it has undertaken an environmental impact assessment according to accepted international standards. Unless such an assessment establishes that the tests will not give rise, directly or indirectly, to radioactive contamination of the marine environment the rights under international law of New Zealand, as well as the rights of other States, will be violated."

New Zealand, referring to the Court's Order[32] of 22 June 1973 indicating interim measures of protection and to the Court's Judgment of 20 December 1974 in the above-mentioned case, also requested the Court to indicate further provisional measures. New Zealand chose Sir Geoffrey Palmer to sit as Judge ad hoc.

Applications for permission to intervene were submitted by Australia, Samoa, Solomon Islands, the Marshall Islands and the Federated States of Micronesia, while the last four States also made declarations on intervention.

At the invitation of the President of the Court, informal *aides-mémoire* were presented by New Zealand and France. Public sittings to hear the oral arguments of the two States were held on 11 and 12 September 1995.

At a public sitting held on 22 September 1995, the President of the Court read an Order,[33] the operative paragraph of which was as follows:

68. Accordingly,
*The Court*,
(1) By 12 votes to 3,

*Finds* that the "Request for an Examination of the Situation" in accordance with paragraph 63 of the Judgment of the Court of 20 December 1974 in the Nuclear Tests Case (New Zealand v. France), submitted by New Zealand on 21 August 1995, does not fall within the provisions of the said paragraph 63 and must consequently be dismissed;

*In favour:* President Bedjaoui; Vice-President Schwebel; Judges Oda, Guillaume, Shahabuddeen, Ranjeva, Herczegh, Shi, Fleischhauer, Vereshchetin, Ferrari Bravo, Higgins;

*Against:* Judges Weeramantry, Koroma; Judge ad hoc Sir Geoffrey Palmer;

(2) By 12 votes to 3,

*Finds* that the "Further Request for the Indication of Provisional Measures" submitted by New Zealand on the same date must be dismissed;

*In favour:* President Bedjaoui; Vice-President Schwebel; Judges Oda, Guillaume, Shahabuddeen, Ranjeva, Herczegh, Shi, Fleischhauer, Vereshchetin, Ferrari Bravo, Higgins;

*Against:* Judges Weeramantry, Koroma; Judge ad hoc Sir Geoffrey Palmer;

(3) By 12 votes to 3,

*Finds* that the "Application for Permission to Intervene" submitted by Australia on 23 August 1995, and the "Applications for Permission to Intervene" and "Declarations of Intervention" submitted by Samoa and Solomon Islands on 24 August 1995, and by the Marshall Islands and the Federated States of Micronesia on 25 August 1995, must likewise be dismissed.

*In favour:* President Bedjaoui; Vice-President Schwebel; Judges Oda, Guillaume, Shahabuddeen, Ranjeva, Herczegh, Shi, Fleischhauer, Vereshchetin, Ferrari Bravo, Higgins;

*Against:* Judges Weeramantry, Koroma; Judge ad hoc Sir Geoffrey Palmer.

Vice-President Schwebel and Judges Oda and Ranjeva appended declarations to the Order; Judge Shahabuddeen a separate opinion; Judges Weeramantry and Koroma and Judge ad hoc Sir Geoffrey Palmer appended dissenting opinions.

## Legality of the use by a State of nuclear weapons in armed conflict

In 1993,[25] the World Health Organization (WHO) requested an advisory opinion from the Court on whether the use of nuclear weapons by a State in war or other armed conflict would be a breach of its obligations under international law, in view of the health and environmental effects.

By an Order of 13 September 1993,[25] the Court fixed 10 June 1994 as the time-limit within which WHO and its member States entitled to appear before the Court might submit written statements on the question. By an Order of 20 June 1994,[29] the President of the Court extended the time-limit to 20 September 1994. By the same Order, the President fixed 20 June 1995 as the time-limit within which States and organizations having presented written statements might submit written comments on the other written statements.

Written statements were filed by Australia, Azerbaijan, Colombia, Costa Rica, the Democratic People's Republic of Korea, Finland, France, Germany, India, Iran, Ireland, Italy, Japan, Kazakstan, Lithuania, Malaysia, Mexico, Nauru, the Netherlands, New Zealand, Norway, Papua New Guinea, the Philippines, the Republic of Moldova, the Russian Federation, Rwanda, Samoa, Saudi Arabia, Solomon Islands, Sri Lanka, Sweden, Uganda, Ukraine, the United Kingdom and the United States.

Written comments were filed by Costa Rica, France, India, Malaysia, Nauru, the Russian Federation, Solomon Islands, the United Kingdom and the United States.

Public sittings to hear oral statements or comments on the request for an advisory opinion made by WHO were held between 30 October and 15 November 1995. Those oral proceedings also covered the request for an advisory opinion submitted by the UN General Assembly on the question of the legality of the threat or use of nuclear weapons (see below). During the hearings, statements were made by WHO, Australia, Costa Rica, Egypt, France, Germany, Indonesia, Iran, Italy, Japan, Malaysia, the Marshall Islands, Mexico, New Zealand, the Philippines, the Russian Federation, Samoa, Solomon Islands, the United Kingdom, the United States and Zimbabwe.

## Legality of the threat or use of nuclear weapons

On 15 December 1994, the General Assembly requested[34] ICJ urgently to render its advisory opinion on whether the threat or use of nuclear weapons in any circumstance was permitted under international law (see also PART ONE, Chapter II). The request was transmitted to ICJ by the Secretary-General on 19 December.

By an Order of 1 February 1995,[35] the Court decided that States entitled to appear before it and the United Nations might furnish information on the question and fixed 20 June 1995 as the time-limit within which written statements might be submitted (Article 66, paragraph 2, of the Statute of the Court) and 20 September 1995 as the time-limit within which States and organizations having presented written statements might present written comments on the other written statements (Article 66, paragraph 4, of the Statute).

Written statements were filed by Bosnia and Herzegovina, Burundi, the Democratic People's Republic of Korea, Ecuador, Egypt, Finland, France, Germany, India, Iran, Ireland, Italy, Japan, Lesotho, Malaysia, the Marshall Islands, Mexico, Nauru, the Netherlands, New Zealand, Qatar, the Russian Federation, Samoa, San Marino, Solomon Islands, Sweden, the United Kingdom and the United States.

Written comments were filed by Egypt, Nauru and Solomon Islands. Nauru subsequently withdrew its comments.

Public sittings to hear oral statements or comments on the request for an advisory opinion were held between 30 October and 15 November 1995. Those oral proceedings also covered the request for an advisory opinion submitted by WHO on the question of the legality of the use by a State of nuclear weapons in armed conflict (see above). During the hearings statements were made by Australia, Costa Rica, Egypt, France, Germany, Indonesia, Iran, Italy, Japan, Malaysia, the Marshall Islands, Mexico, New Zealand, the Philippines, Qatar, the Russian Federation, Samoa, San Marino, Solomon Islands, the United Kingdom, the United States and Zimbabwe.

## Organizational questions

### Elections to the Court

On 26 January 1995, the General Assembly (**decision 49/322 A**) and the Security Council, to fill a vacancy left by the death in 1994[29] of Judge Nikolai K. Tarassov, elected Vladlen S. Vereshchetin as a member of the Court for a term ending on 5 February 1997.

The Secretary-General, on 6 March 1995,[36] informed the Security Council of the death on 24 February of Judge Roberto Ago, and thus of a vacancy in the Court. On 9 March, the Security Council adopted **resolution 979(1995)**.

*The Security Council,*
*Noting with regret* the death of Judge Roberto Ago on 24 February 1995,
*Noting further* that a vacancy in the International Court of Justice for the remainder of the term of office of the deceased Judge has thus occurred and must be filled in accordance with the terms of the Statute of the Court,
*Noting* that, in accordance with Article 14 of the Statute, the date of the election to fill the vacancy shall be fixed by the Security Council,
*Decides* that the election to fill the vacancy shall take place on 21 June 1995 at a meeting of the Security Council and at a meeting of the General Assembly at its forty-ninth session.

Security Council resolution 979(1995)
9 March 1995     Meeting 3507     Adopted without vote
Draft prepared in consultations among Council members (S/1995/186).

In a 1 June memorandum,[37] the Secretary-General outlined the procedures to be followed by both the General Assembly and the Security Council in filling the vacancy and announced the Council's 9 March decision. Also on 1 June, the Secretary-General submitted to the Assembly and the Council a list of candidates[38] and their curricula vitae.[39]

On 21 June, the Assembly (**decision 49/322 B**) and the Council elected Luigi Ferrari Bravo as a member of the Court for a term ending on 5 February 1997.

The Security Council was informed[40] on 20 March 1995 that Sir Robert Yewdall Jennings would resign, effective 10 July 1995. On 22 March, the Council adopted **resolution 980(1995)**.

*The Security Council,*
*Noting with regret* the resignation of Judge Sir Robert Yewdall Jennings, taking effect on 10 July 1995,
*Noting further* that a vacancy in the International Court of Justice for the remainder of the term of office of Judge Sir Robert Yewdall Jennings will thus occur and must be filled in accordance with the terms of the Statute of the Court,
*Noting* that, in accordance with Article 14 of the Statute, the date of the election to fill the vacancy shall be fixed by the Security Council,
*Decides* that the election to fill the vacancy shall take place on 12 July 1995 at a meeting of the Security Council and at a meeting of the General Assembly at its forty-ninth session.

Security Council resolution 980 (1995)
22 March 1995     Meeting 3510     Adopted without vote
Draft prepared in consultations among Council members (S/1995/213).

Following implementation of the procedures outlined in the Statute of the Court (see above), the Assembly (**decision 49/322 C**) and the Council on 12 July elected Rosalyn Higgins as a member of the Court for a term ending on 5 February 2000.

On 1 November 1995,[41] the Secretary-General announced the death on 24 October of Judge Andrés Aguilar Mawdsley. On 7 November, the Security Council adopted **resolution 1018(1995)**.

*The Security Council,*
*Noting with regret* the death of Judge Andrés Aguilar Mawdsley on 24 October 1995,
*Noting further* that a vacancy in the International Court of Justice for the remainder of the term of office of the deceased Judge has thus occurred and must be filled in accordance with the terms of the Statute of the Court,
*Noting* that, in accordance with Article 14 of the Statute, the date of the election to fill the vacancy shall be fixed by the Security Council,
*Decides* that the election to fill the vacancy shall take place on 28 February 1996 at a meeting of the Security Council and at a meeting of the General Assembly at its fiftieth session.

Security Council resolution 1018(1995)
7 November 1995     Meeting 3590     Adopted without vote
Draft prepared in consultations among Council members (S/1995/928).

### Chamber for Environmental Matters

The term of office of the members of the Chamber for Environmental Matters (for the composition of the Chamber, see APPENDIX III) was extended until 5 February 1997.

*REFERENCES*

[1]A/50/PV.30. [2]A/50/4. [3]A/51/4. [4]YUN 1991, p. 818. [5]YUN 1992, p. 980. [6]YUN 1991, p. 819. [7]YUN 1992, p. 981. [8]YUN 1993, p. 1136. [9]*East Timor (Portugal v. Australia), Judgment of 30 June 1995*, I.C.J. Sales No. 661. [10]*Delimitation between Guinea-Bissau and Senegal, Order of 8 November 1995*, I.C.J. Sales No. 667. [11]YUN 1991, p. 820. [12]YUN 1992, p. 982. [13]YUN 1994, p. 1279. [14]*Maritime Delimitation and Territorial Questions between Qatar and Bahrain (Qatar v. Bahrain), Jurisdiction and Admissibility, Judgment of 15 February 1995*, I.C.J. Sales No. 657. [15]*Maritime Delimitation and Territorial Questions between Qatar and Bahrain (Qatar v. Bahrain), Order of 28 April 1995*, I.C.J. Sales No. 659. [16]YUN 1971, p. 739. [17]*Questions of Interpretation and Application of the 1971 Montreal Convention arising from the Aerial Incident at Lockerbie (Libyan Arab Jamahiriya v. United Kingdom)* and *(Libyan Arab Jamahiriya v. United States of America), Orders of 22 September 1995*, I.C.J. Sales Nos. 664 and 665. [18]YUN 1992, p. 983. [19]YUN 1993, p. 1138. [20]YUN 1994, p. 1280. [21]YUN 1948-49, p. 959, GA res. 260 A (III), annex, 9 Dec. 1948. [22]YUN 1977, p. 706. [23]YUN 1948-49, p. 535, GA res. 217 A (III), 10 Dec. 1948. [24]YUN 1991, p. 215, SC res. 713(1991), 25 Sep. 1991. [25]YUN 1993, p. 1139. [26]*Application of the Convention on the Prevention and Punishment of the Crime of Genocide (Bosnia and Herzegovina v. Yugoslavia), Order of 21 March 1995*, I.C.J. Sales No. 658. [27]Ibid., *Order of 14 July 1995*, I.C.J. Sales No. 663. [28]YUN 1994, p. 1281. [29]Ibid., p. 1282. [30]*Fisheries Jurisdiction (Spain v. Canada), Order of 2 May 1995*, I.C.J. Sales No. 660. [31]YUN 1974, p. 832. [32]YUN 1973, p. 764. [33]*Request for an Examination of the Situation in accordance with Paragraph 63 of the Court's Judgment of 20 December 1974 in the* Nuclear Tests (New Zealand v. France) *Case, Order of 22 September 1995*, I.C.J Sales No. 666. [34]YUN 1994, p. 157, GA res. 49/75 K, 15 Dec. 1994. [35]*Legality of the Threat or Use of Nuclear Weapons, Order of 1 February 1995*, I.C.J. Sales No. 656. [36]S/1995/178. [37]A/49/909-S/1995/448. [38]A/49/910-S/1995/449. [39]A/49/911-S/1995/450. [40]S/1995/209. [41]S/1995/914.

Chapter II

# International tribunals

In 1995, two international criminal tribunals established to prosecute persons responsible for serious violations of international humanitarian law—one concerning acts committed in the territory of the former Yugoslavia, the other for Rwanda and neighbouring States—began operations. The International Tribunal for the Former Yugoslavia issued indictments against 46 individuals and began trial proceedings in one case. Following the election of trial judges, the International Tribunal for Rwanda held an inaugural session at The Hague, Netherlands, and subsequently issued its first indictments. Justice Richard J. Goldstone of South Africa served as Prosecutor for both Tribunals. In February 1995, the Security Council determined that the seat of the Rwanda Tribunal should be in Arusha, United Republic of Tanzania.

## International Tribunal for the Former Yugoslavia

In 1995, the International Tribunal for the Prosecution of Persons Responsible for Serious Violations of International Humanitarian Law Committed in the Territory of the Former Yugoslavia since 1991 (International Tribunal for the Former Yugoslavia), established in 1993,[1] issued indictments, submitted by Prosecutor Richard Goldstone, against 46 individuals and began trial proceedings in one case.

The Security Council reiterated its demand that all States and all parties to the conflict in the former Yugoslavia cooperate fully with the Tribunal and called on them to create the conditions necessary for the performance of its task. In April, July and December, the General Assembly approved appropriations for the Tribunal's financing.

### Work of the Tribunal

On 23 August, the Secretary-General transmitted to the General Assembly and the Security Council the second annual report[2] of the International Tribunal, covering the period from August 1994 to July 1995. The Tribunal was substantially closer to realizing its principal objectives, and had started to meet the hopes and expectations of the victims of events in the former Yugoslavia, the Tribunal President, Antonio Cassese (Italy), stated. Some problems in the early stages of its existence had delayed the Tribunal in carrying out its mandate, and its work was still complicated by the fact that warfare continued unabated in the former Yugoslavia. That greatly aggravated the logistical difficulties involved in dealing with witnesses, conducting investigations and executing arrest warrants, he went on. Despite that, the Tribunal was well equipped to prosecute those alleged to have committed serious violations of international humanitarian law. Whatever the political consequences or the eventual outcome of the conflict, the Tribunal would not flinch from its task.

During the 12-month reporting period, the real judicial work of the Tribunal had begun. The report described the activities of its Chambers, Prosecutor's Office and Registry, aimed at establishing the legal framework of operations and the material infrastructure, recruiting necessary staff and encouraging States to enact legislation enabling full cooperation with the Tribunal. It also examined contributions by non-governmental organizations (NGOs) and coverage of the Tribunal's work by the world media.

The International Tribunal had enjoyed the support of the United Nations and growing cooperation by a number of States in the past year, but it had had to navigate in troubled waters, the Tribunal President stated. Its momentum might have been lost altogether if it had proceeded only against the immediate perpetrators of crimes under international humanitarian law. It had chosen to break new ground with a clearly enunciated policy of prosecuting those in command who ordered or failed to punish the egregious crimes being committed. The strategy of prosecuting political and military leaders, adopted by the Tribunal, had given it the credibility essential to its appointed task, although disappointment could be felt at the fact that only one accused had so far been surrendered to stand trial. In that regard, it was noted that, as an international criminal court, albeit one of an ad hoc nature, the Tribunal faced unique problems resulting from the need to rely on the cooperation of States, in the absence of enforcement agencies at its disposal; limitations inherent in any international criminal jurisdiction trying offences committed in a distant country, such as the lack of centralized prosecuting and police services, the multitude of both perpetrators and victims, and the time lag between the commission of a crime and the apprehension of an alleged perpetrator; and the realities of operating in the midst of a continuing armed conflict, mostly against civilians.

All those working at the Tribunal realized the historic role which they had to play in setting precedents for future international criminal organs, notably a permanent criminal court—the "missing links of international law". The Tribunal might well prove to be a major stepping-stone to the establishment of a permanent international criminal court, under discussion by the UN International Law Commission (see PART FIVE, Chapter III), the President noted. If the Tribunal could prove to the world that it was possible to administer international criminal justice, that it was imperative for legal and moral reasons and practical to do so, it would have performed a great service for the development of international law. It would also, he declared, send a message to the victims of appalling crimes that humanity would not turn its back on them.

**GENERAL ASSEMBLY ACTION**

On 7 November, the General Assembly, by **decision 50/408**, noted the second annual report of the International Tribunal for the Former Yugoslavia.

In his statement to the Assembly, Tribunal President Cassese said that while the Tribunal was boldly travelling towards the accomplishment of its mission, it was experiencing problems, including a lack of cooperation of States and difficulties in obtaining the financial and other practical resources. He urged the Assembly to help the Tribunal fulfil its task by providing those badly needed resources. The President also emphasized that with the establishment of a lasting peace in the region, the Tribunal would become more efficient and better able to accomplish its mission, and expressed his hope that bringing to fruition the Tribunal's potential would show that international criminal justice could fulfil an indispensable role in the pacification of the world community.

## Indictments

During the reporting period, eight indictments were confirmed, and arrest warrants issued for 46 individuals. Three hearings were held at the Prosecutor's request for deferral to the Tribunal's competence of proceedings or investigations pending in national jurisdictions.

· Dragan Nikolic was the first person to be indicted by the Tribunal, in November 1994. Alleged to be a commander of the Susica prison camp in Vlasenica, in north-eastern Bosnia and Herzegovina, he was charged with grave breaches of the

Geneva Convention relative to the Protection of Civilian Persons in Time of War, of 12 August 1949 (fourth Geneva Convention), in particular direct participation in beatings, torture and murder at the camp.

Two other indictments, on 13 February 1995, involved charges against a group of 21 persons. Among them was Dusko Tadic, the subject of the Tribunal's first trial. Those indictments emanated largely from events between June and August 1992 in a Bosnian Serb camp at Omarska in the Opstina of Prijedor, in northwestern Bosnia. They covered a whole range of offences—from grave breaches of the Geneva Conventions to genocide—and represented the first occasion that a charge of genocide had been brought before the Tribunal.

On 21 July 1995, three indictments were confirmed in the cases of Sikirica and others (Keraterm camp investigation); Miljkovic and others (Bosanski Samac); and Jelisic and Cesic (Brcko).

On 26 June, the Prosecutor had submitted an indictment charging Dusko Sikirica, commander of the Keraterm camp, also in the Prijedor region, with genocide; 12 of his subordinates or others subject to his authority were also charged with crimes against humanity, violations of the laws or customs of war and grave breaches of the Geneva Conventions, specifically, killing, sexually assaulting and torturing detainees at the camp, a centre of the Bosnian Serb ethnic cleansing campaign in the summer of 1992.

Similar charges were brought in a 29 June indictment against Slobodan Miljkovic and five other persons accused of mass killings, forced deportation, sexual assault and torture during a campaign of terror against the non-Serb civilian population in Bosanski Samac.

On 30 June, the Prosecutor submitted an indictment against two individuals for their alleged crimes against Muslim and Croat detainees at the Luka camp of Brcko in northern Bosnia; Goran Jelisic was accused of 16 murders and numerous beatings, and Ranko Cesic was accused of 13 murders and one sexual assault.

On 25 July, two more indictments were confirmed: one in the case of Milan Martic, President of the Croatian Serb administration, and another concerning Radovan Karadzic and Ratko Mladic, the President and the Commander of the Army, respectively, of the Bosnian Serb administration in Pale, Bosnia and Herzegovina. Mr. Martic was charged with violations of the laws or customs of war for ordering the cluster-bomb rocket attack against the civilian population of Zagreb in May 1995. Messrs. Karadzic and Mladic were charged with genocide, crimes against humanity, violations of the laws or customs of war, and grave breaches of the Geneva Conventions, on the basis of either superior authority or direct responsibility for: the internment of Bosnian Muslims and Croats in detention facilities where they were subject to torture, murder, sexual assault, robbery and other acts; the shelling and sniping campaigns against civilians in Sarajevo, Srebrenica and Tuzla; the deportation of Bosnian Muslim and Bosnian Croat civilians from the areas of Vlasenica, Prijedor, Bosanski Samac, Brcko and Foca; the plundering and destruction of personal property of civilians; the systematic infliction of damage and destruction on both Muslim and Roman Catholic sacred sites; and the taking of UN hostages for use as "human shields".

In the case of every confirmed indictment, arrest warrants for the accused were issued and transmitted to the appropriate authorities. On 2 August 1995, an order was issued by the Trial Chamber asking States to assist the Tribunal in the arrests of Messrs. Karadzic, Mladic and Martic by providing information as to their movements and location. That order was sent on 3 August to all permanent missions to the United Nations in New York, including the observer missions of Switzerland, the Holy See and Palestine. On 16 November, the Tribunal issued further indictments against Karadzic and Mladic, as was reported by the Secretary-General on 27 November,[3] for their direct and individual responsibilities for the atrocities committed against Bosnian Muslims in Srebrenica in July 1995, after the fall of that enclave to Bosnian Serb forces (see also PART TWO, Chapter V, and PART THREE, Chapter III).

### Deferrals of investigations

On 21 April, the Prosecutor filed an application for deferral to the Tribunal's competence of an investigation conducted by a court of the Republic of Bosnia and Herzegovina, concerning alleged ethnic cleansing by members of Bosnian Croat forces in the Lasva River valley. In a separate action, the Prosecutor applied for deferral of an investigation by Bosnia and Herzegovina into the activities of Bosnian Serb leader Karadzic, Commander Mladic of the Bosnian Serb Army and Mr. Stanisic, former head of Bosnian Serb internal affairs. Both investigations were conducted parallel to those of the Prosecutor's Office.

On 11 and 16 May, respectively, the Trial Chamber granted each application and issued a formal request for deferral. The Government of Bosnia and Herzegovina formally concurred in the Prosecutor's applications. Following the indictments of Messrs. Karadzic and Mladic, the Prosecutor's Office continued investigations into the case of Mr. Stanisic and the Lasva River valley events.

### Trial proceedings

On 11 October 1994, the Prosecutor presented his first official request to a Trial Chamber,[4] namely, a request for the deferral by the Government of Germany of its investigation and prosecution of Dusko Tadic, who had been arrested by German authorities in February 1994 and was awaiting trial in Germany. The Prosecutor wanted the deferral because the German investigation involved legal and factual issues which had implications for other investigations being carried out concurrently by the Prosecutor.

The Prosecutor reported that the case against Mr. Tadic would reveal systematic and widespread persecution of the Muslim civilian population in the Prijedor region, a practice commonly referred to as ethnic cleansing. After the deferral application was granted, the German Government deferred its jurisdiction in the case of Mr. Tadic to the Tribunal, once the necessary implementing legislation had been passed.

Mr. Tadic was surrendered to the Tribunal on 24 April 1995. Preliminary motions in the trial, representing the Tribunal's first trial proceedings, were filed in June and July. On 10 August, the Trial Chamber, in a majority decision, granted the Prosecutor's requests concerning protection of the identity of six witnesses, and ordered that evidence be given in closed session. The Chamber also authorized the use of screening or other appropriate methods for alleged victims of sexual assault to prevent them from being re-traumatized by seeing the accused. Judge Sir Ninian Stephen (Australia), in a separate opinion, denied in principle any anonymity of witnesses as far as the accused and his counsel were concerned.

Also, on 10 August, the Trial Chamber denied a defence motion on jurisdiction, holding that the Tribunal lacked the competence to review the decision of the Security Council to establish the Tribunal, among other things. On 14 August, the defence appealed that decision. Defence motions challenging defects in the form of the indictment and exclusion of evidence obtained from the accused were to be heard after the issue of jurisdiction had been settled.

### Application of rule 61

Rule 61 of the Tribunal's rules of procedure and evidence set out a procedure to be applied when a State was unable to execute an arrest warrant. In that event, the full Trial Chamber could confirm the indictment at a public hearing, at which witnesses would testify, and issue an international arrest warrant for the accused. Given the Tribunal's decision not to allow trials *in absentia*, the procedure did not provide for a finding of guilt but served only to determine whether reasonable grounds existed for believing that the accused had committed the crimes as charged in the indictment.

In October 1995, rule 61 was applied, for the first time, in the case of Dragan Nikolic. After the

Government of Bosnia and Herzegovina had indicated that it could not serve a warrant outside its territory, and the Bosnian Serb administration in Pale had failed to respond to the Tribunal's request to serve the indictment and an arrest warrant on Mr. Nikolic, the Prosecutor on 16 May filed an application pursuant to rule 61, which was granted by a judge on the same date. Following hearings held between 9 and 13 October, the Trial Chamber unanimously decided on 20 October that there were reasonable grounds for believing that Mr. Nikolic had committed the offences as charged, confirmed the entire 24-count indictment and issued an international arrest warrant against Mr. Nikolic. The Chamber also certified that the failure to effect service of the indictment was due wholly to the failure or refusal of the Bosnian Serb administration in Pale to cooperate, and invited the Tribunal President to notify the Security Council accordingly.

The President transmitted the decision and supporting documentation to the Council on 31 October.[5]

## Cooperation of States

The Tribunal President, in his second annual report on the Tribunal,[2] noted that 12 States had thus far enacted implementing legislation for cooperation with the Tribunal, and six others had indicated their intention to do so in the near future. In that regard, he issued in February guidelines for States which had not yet adopted such legislation. He also proposed a less taxing commitment to the States that had expressed a lack of willingness to carry out enforcement of prison sentences pursuant to the Tribunal's statute.

Also, he reported that six countries had contributed personnel for the Prosecutor's Office; 17 States had contributed funds totalling $6,319,795 as at 10 July. In addition, the European Union provided financial resources for several NGO projects to assist the Tribunal, and more than 100 NGOs had offered help in a wide range of areas.

The President stated that some States, in particular the Federal Republic of Yugoslavia (Serbia and Montenegro), as well as some de facto authorities in the self-styled Republics of Krajina and Srpska, had withheld any cooperation from the Tribunal, and that a number of countries, notably neighbouring States of the former Yugoslavia, had failed to pass legislation enabling them to assist the Tribunal.

In a statement to the General Assembly, the Tribunal President underscored that the lack of cooperation by States had proved particularly paralysing, as Tribunal decisions, orders and requests could be enforced only by national authorities. So far, the Federal Republic of Yugoslavia (Serbia and Montenegro) and the Bosnian Serb administration in Pale had failed to apprehend 41 of the accused who were in their territory.

SECURITY COUNCIL ACTION

The Security Council, by **resolution 1019(1995)** of 9 November, demanded that all States, in particular those in the region of the former Yugoslavia, and all parties to the conflict in the former Yugoslavia comply fully with their obligations to cooperate with the International Tribunal, including through provision of access to individuals and sites the Tribunal deemed important for its investigations and through compliance with requests for assistance or orders issued by the Tribunal. The Council also called on States and parties to the conflict to allow the establishment of Tribunal offices, and demanded that all parties, in particular the Bosnian Serb party, refrain from any action intended to destroy, alter, conceal or damage any evidence of violations of international humanitarian law and that such evidence be preserved.

It reiterated those demands in **resolution 1034(1995)** of 21 December, and called on all States and all parties to the conflict in the former Yugoslavia to create the conditions necessary for the Tribunal to perform its tasks. The Council also noted the indictments against Messrs. Karadzic and Mladic in connection with the atrocities committed in Srebrenica in July 1995.

## Other aspects

In January 1995, the Tribunal adopted amendments to 41 of the 125 rules of procedure and evidence approved in February 1994. The actions were taken to reflect a variety of concerns and were aimed at: addressing practical problems in the implementation of its statute or those rules, dealing with political entities in the territory of the former Yugoslavia, improving the working of the Tribunal, broadening the rights of suspects and accused persons, and protecting the rights of victims and witnesses. Further amendments were adopted in May and June. In March, the Tribunal also amended its rules of detention to clarify the respective roles of the International Committee of the Red Cross (ICRC) and the Tribunal in inspecting conditions of detention, and to provide detainees with greater freedom of communication with the inspecting authority.

The Tribunal, in the second annual report,[2] described the work of the Prosecutor's Office, noting that 116 of its 126 staff positions had been filled by late May 1995 and that a legal adviser for gender-related crimes had been appointed. The strategy team of the investigations unit and the special advisory section of the Office were restructured in 1995. Liaison offices were to be established in Belgrade, Sarajevo and Zagreb. Other issues related to activities of the Registry's judicial department, detention unit and victims and witnesses unit, as well as the Tribunal's publications and its Press and Information Service.

**Communication (May).** The Federal Republic of Yugoslavia (Serbia and Montenegro), by a letter of 22 May,[6] transmitted its fifth report submitted in accordance with Security Council resolutions 771(1992)[7] and 780(1992),[8] calling on States and international organizations to submit information on violations of humanitarian law in the territory of the former Yugoslavia. The report included information on deliberate killing and inhuman treatment of civilians, detainees, prisoners of war, the wounded and the sick; hostage-taking and detention camps; devastation of civilian facilities, unwarranted from the military point of view; devastation of places of worship, cemeteries and cultural and historical monuments; and ethnic cleansing. Annexed to the report were forensic, medical and psychiatric views regarding war crimes committed against Serbs in the area of Gorazde from 1992 to 1994.

## Administrative and budgetary aspects

### Conditions of service of Tribunal members

In 1995, the Advisory Committee on Administrative and Budgetary Questions (ACABQ) continued to consider the Secretary-General's 1994 report[9] on conditions of service and allowances of Tribunal members, in which he proposed that the terms and conditions of service of Tribunal judges should be the same as those of the International Court of Justice (ICJ).

The Committee recommended that the annual salary for Tribunal members be set at $145,000 and that the special allowance applicable to the President of ICJ or to the Vice-President when acting as President should apply to the President and Vice-President of the Tribunal, as should the ''floor/ceiling measures'' in The Hague applicable to ICJ members and the condition that ''no member of the Court may exercise any political or administrative function, or engage in any other occupation of a professional nature''.

Noting its proposal that the General Assembly, at its fiftieth (1995) session, should undertake a comprehensive review of pension entitlements and survivor benefits of ICJ members, ACABQ was of the opinion that the issue of those entitlements for Tribunal members should be dealt with in the context of that review (see PART SIX, Chapter III).

Committee observations and recommendations were summarized in its 10 March report[10] to the Assembly.

## Financing of the Tribunal

In 1995, the General Assembly continued its consideration of issues relating to the financing of the International Tribunal for the Former Yugoslavia.

GENERAL ASSEMBLY ACTION (April)

In April, the General Assembly adopted **decision 49/471 B**.

**Financing of the International Tribunal for the Prosecution of Persons Responsible for Serious Violations of International Humanitarian Law Committed in the Territory of the Former Yugoslavia since 1991**

At its 100th plenary meeting, on 6 April 1995, the General Assembly, on the recommendation of the Fifth Committee, decided to authorize the Secretary-General to enter into commitments in the additional amount of 1,080,000 United States dollars for the period from 1 to 14 April 1995 to allow the International Tribunal for the Prosecution of Persons Responsible for Serious Violations of International Humanitarian Law Committed in the Territory of the Former Yugoslavia since 1991 to continue its activities until 14 April 1995, without prejudice to any decision that the Assembly might take with regard to the mode of financing of the Tribunal.

General Assembly decision 49/471 B

Adopted without vote

Approved by Fifth Committee (A/49/810/Add.1) without vote, 31 March (meeting 53); oral proposal by Chairman; agenda item 146.
*Meeting numbers.* GA 49th session: 5th Committee 45, 46, 51, 53; plenary 100.

On 13 April, the Assembly adopted **resolution 49/242 A**.

**Financing of the International Tribunal for the Prosecution of Persons Responsible for Serious Violations of International Humanitarian Law Committed in the Territory of the Former Yugoslavia since 1991**

*The General Assembly,*

*Recognizing* the need for a prompt decision on the mode of financing of the International Tribunal for the Prosecution of Persons Responsible for Serious Violations of International Humanitarian Law Committed in the Territory of the Former Yugoslavia since 1991,

1. *Resolves* to resume its consideration of the question of the financing of the International Tribunal for the Prosecution of Persons Responsible for Serious Violations of International Humanitarian Law Committed in the Territory of the Former Yugoslavia since 1991 at its resumed forty-ninth session in June 1995 in order to decide no later than 14 July 1995 on all outstanding questions, in particular the mode of financing;

2. *Decides* to authorize the Secretary-General to enter into commitments in the additional amount of 7,095,000 United States dollars for the period from 15 April to 14 July 1995 to allow the Tribunal to continue its activities until 14 July 1995, without prejudice to any decisions that the General Assembly may take with regard to the mode of financing of the Tribunal.

General Assembly resolution 49/242 A

13 April 1995          Meeting 101          Adopted without vote

Approved by Fifth Committee (A/49/810/Add.2) without vote, 7 April (meeting 54); draft by Chairman (A/C.5/49/L.50), based on informal consultations; agenda item 146.

**ACABQ report.** ACABQ continued to consider the Secretary-General's report on the financing of the Tribunal, submitted in 1994.[9] It took into account the fact that the Prosecutor for the International Tribunal for the Former Yugoslavia would also act as the Prosecutor for the International Tribunal for Rwanda (see below), and that members of the Appeals Chambers of both Tribunals would also be the same.

The Committee examined revised estimates relating to the financing of the Tribunal in 1994-1995 as well as the question of voluntary contributions by Member States in support of the Tribunal. It recommended that an appropriation of $38,652,900 be approved by the General Assembly for the Tribunal's operations in 1994-1995, along with an additional appropriation of $276,200, which had been provided in 1993 from the UN Working Capital Fund for Tribunal expenditures. It pointed out that it might be necessary to establish a mechanism to allow commitment of funds on an urgent basis, particularly for critical areas identified by the Prosecutor. The Secretary-General was requested to submit information and/or proposals on the Tribunal's long-term requirements for the execution of sentences and protection of witnesses, as well as to issue specific guidelines on the requirements for receipt of voluntary contributions and application of funds for the Tribunal.

The ACABQ recommendations were submitted to the Assembly in March.[10]

**GENERAL ASSEMBLY ACTION (July)**

On 20 July, the General Assembly adopted **resolution 49/242 B**.

*The General Assembly,*

*Recalling* its resolutions 47/235 of 14 September 1993 and 48/251 of 14 April 1994,

*Recalling also* its decision 49/471 A of 23 December 1994, by which it authorized the Secretary-General to enter into commitments in the additional amount of 7 million United States dollars to allow the International Tribunal for the Prosecution of Persons Responsible for Serious Violations of International Humanitarian Law Committed in the Territory of the Former Yugoslavia since 1991 to continue its activities until 31 March 1995, without prejudice to any decisions that the Assembly might take with regard to budgetary and administrative matters and to the mode of financing,

*Affirming* that the International Tribunal must be assured of secure and stable financing so that it may fulfil its role in full and effectively,

*Having considered* the report of the Secretary-General on the financing of the International Tribunal and the related report of the Advisory Committee on Administrative and Budgetary Questions,

1.  *Endorses* the observations and recommendations contained in the report of the Advisory Committee on Administrative and Budgetary Questions, subject to the provisions of the present resolution;

2.  *Decides*, subject to the completion of the reclassification process, to approve the three posts of senior investigators to undertake substantive high-level investigations and to oversee the nine investigation teams in the Office of the Prosecutor, pending a further review of the question by the Advisory Committee in the context of estimates for the International Tribunal for the Prosecution of Persons Responsible for Serious Violations of International Humanitarian Law Committed in the Territory of the Former Yugoslavia since 1991 for the biennium 1996-1997;

3.  *Requests* the Secretary-General to review the staffing requirements of the electronic support services and communications in the Registry to ensure that its organizational structure is commensurate with the tasks to be performed;

4.  *Reaffirms* that questions related to the rules of procedure and evidence of the International Tribunal are matters to be decided by the International Tribunal;

5.  *Requests* the Secretary-General to provide, in the context of the next budget presentation for the International Tribunal, additional information on the costs of ensuring free legal assistance, as outlined in paragraph 30 of the report of the Advisory Committee;

6.  *Also requests* the Secretary-General to include in the context of the next budget presentation for the International Tribunal information and/or proposals for the long-term requirements for the carrying out of sentences and for the protection of witnesses;

7.  *Requests* the International Tribunal and the International Court of Justice to continue negotiations on common administrative arrangements with the aim of obtaining economies of administrative services;

8.  *Requests* the International Tribunal to establish guidelines to govern recourse to and use of expertise in the Chambers;

9.  *Notes* that the estimated requirements for payment to the host Government for detention facilities for the accused reflect actual fixed and estimated variable costs in the biennium 1994-1995;

10.  *Emphasizes* the importance of ensuring that recruitment for the International Tribunal is implemented strictly in accordance with the Staff Regulations and Rules of the United Nations, taking account of Articles 8, 100 and 101 of the Charter of the United Nations, and that, in recruiting consultants and experts, the International Tribunal should avail itself of sources of expertise on as wide a geographical basis as possible;

11.  *Expresses its appreciation* to the Governments and others that have provided voluntary contributions to the International Tribunal;

12.  *Invites* Member States and others to make further voluntary contributions to the International Tribunal that are acceptable to the Secretary-General;

13.  *Requests* the Secretary-General to issue specific guidelines on the requirements for receipt of contributions and application of funds for the International Tribunal;

14.  *Also requests* the Secretary-General to include in future budget presentations for the International Tribunal information on voluntary contributions in cash and in kind and to indicate where they are assigned;

15. *Reaffirms* that the acceptance of voluntary contributions in kind or in personnel, as well as voluntary financial contributions, must be consistent with the need to ensure the impartiality and independence of the International Tribunal at all times and that such contributions should be considered supplementary to the assessed contributions;

16. *Requests* the Secretary-General to include detailed information in his next report on the International Tribunal on the acceptance and use of voluntary contributions, particularly those in kind or in personnel, pursuant to paragraph 15 above;

17. *Reaffirms* the role of the General Assembly, as set out in Article 17 of the Charter, as the organ to consider and approve the budget of the Organization and the apportionment of its expenses among Member States;

18. *Again expresses its concern* that advice given to the Security Council by the Secretariat on the nature of the financing of the International Tribunal did not respect the role of the General Assembly as set out in Article 17 of the Charter;

19. *Reaffirms* that the expenses of the International Tribunal shall be met through additional resources on the basis of assessed contributions and that they shall be financed through a separate special account outside the regular budget;

20. *Decides* to appropriate to the special account for the International Tribunal referred to in General Assembly resolution 47/235 a total amount of 43,991,600 dollars gross (39,095,900 dollars net) for the period from 1 January 1994 to 31 December 1995, inclusive of the commitment authority of 26,175,000 dollars authorized under the provisions of Assembly resolutions 48/251 of 14 April 1994 and 49/242 A of 13 April 1995 and Assembly decisions 49/471 A and B of 23 December 1994 and 6 April 1995, respectively, and the amount of 276,200 dollars expended in 1993;

21. *Decides also*, as an ad hoc and exceptional arrangement, that Member States will waive their respective shares in the credits arising from previous budgets of the United Nations Protection Force in the total amount of 21,995,800 dollars gross (19,547,950 dollars net) and hence accept an equivalent increase in the assessments for a future budget period of the Force in the same amount, to be transferred to the special account for the International Tribunal from the special account established for the Force pursuant to General Assembly resolution 46/233 of 19 March 1992;

22. *Decides further* to apportion the amount of 21,995,800 dollars gross (19,547,950 dollars net) for the period from 1 January 1994 to 31 December 1995 among Member States in accordance with the scale of assessments for the year 1994 to be applied against a portion thereof, that is, 6,130,350 dollars gross (5,528,100 dollars net), which is the amount pertaining to the period ending 31 December 1994, and the scale of assessments for the year 1995 to be applied against the balance, that is, 15,865,450 dollars gross (14,019,850 dollars net), for the period from 1 January to 31 December 1995;

23. *Decides* that, in accordance with the provisions of its resolution 973(X) of 15 December 1955, there shall be set off against the apportionment among Member States, as provided for in paragraph 22 above, their respective share in the Tax Equalization Fund of the estimated staff assessment income of 2,447,850 dollars approved for the International Tribunal for the period from 1 January 1994 to 31 December 1995, 602,250 dollars being the amount pertaining to the period ending 31 December 1994 and the balance, that is, 1,845,600 dollars, to the period from 1 January to 31 December 1995;

24. *Requests* the Secretary-General to administer these resources with a maximum of economy and efficiency;

25. *Decides* that appropriations for the biennium 1996-1997 under the special account referred to in paragraph 19 above, the amount of which shall be determined during its fiftieth session, shall be financed equally through the modes of financing referred to in paragraphs 21 and 22 above;

26. *Requests* the Secretary-General to submit a performance report at the end of each biennium but no later than May 1996 and May 1998 respectively;

27. *Decides* to review the mode of financing of the International Tribunal at its fifty-second session;

28. *Requests* the Secretary-General to submit estimates for the requirements of the International Tribunal for the biennium 1996-1997 by 30 November 1995;

29. *Decides* to include in the provisional agenda of its fiftieth session the item entitled ''Financing of the International Tribunal for the Prosecution of Persons Responsible for Serious Violations of International Humanitarian Law Committed in the Territory of the Former Yugoslavia since 1991''.

General Assembly resolution 49/242 B

20 July 1995      Meeting 106      Adopted without vote

Approved by Fifth Committee (A/49/810/Add.3) without vote, 14 July (meeting 66); draft by Chairman (A/C.5/49/L.66), based on informal consultations; agenda item 146.

**Report of the Secretary-General.** On 13 December, the Secretary-General reported[11] on requirements of the International Tribunal for 1996, estimated at $40,779,300. The estimate reflected a full staffing component of 342 posts, representing an increase of 84 posts. The report described recent developments in the Tribunal's operations, reviewed the status of voluntary contributions, and provided a breakdown of resource requirements for the Chambers, the Prosecutor's Office and the Registry.

**ACABQ recommendations.** On 18 December, in an oral report before the Fifth (Administrative and Budgetary) Committee, ACABQ stated its intention to examine in 1996 the staffing proposals for the Tribunal. It recommended in the interim that the General Assembly approve an appropriation of $7.6 million for the period from 1 January to 31 March 1996 and that the authority to enter into contractual arrangements for staff for periods of up to one calendar year should be continued.

GENERAL ASSEMBLY ACTION (December)

On 23 December, the Assembly adopted **resolution 50/212 A**.

### Financing of the International Tribunal for the Prosecution of Persons Responsible for Serious Violations of International Humanitarian Law Committed in the Territory of the Former Yugoslavia since 1991

*The General Assembly,*

*Having considered* the report of the Secretary-General on the financing of the International Tribunal for the Prosecution of Persons Responsible for Serious Violations of International Humanitarian Law Committed in the Territory of the Former Yugoslavia since 1991 and the related oral report by the Chairman of the Advisory Committee on Administrative and Budgetary Questions,

1. *Decides* to appropriate to the Special Account for the International Tribunal for the Prosecution of Persons Responsible for Serious Violations of International Humanitarian Law Committed in the Territory of the Former Yugoslavia since 1991 an amount of 8,619,500 United States dollars gross (7,637,500 dollars net) for the period from 1 January to 31 March 1996 to allow the International Tribunal to continue its activities through 31 March 1996, without prejudice to recommendations the Advisory Committee on Administrative and Budgetary Questions may make to the General Assembly at its resumed fiftieth session;

2. *Decides also,* as an ad hoc and exceptional arrangement, that Member States shall waive their respective shares in the remaining credits arising from previous budgets of the United Nations Protection Force in the total amount of 4,309,750 dollars gross (3,818,750 dollars net) and hence accept an equivalent increase in the assessments for a future budget period of the Force in the same amount, to be transferred to the Special Account for the International Tribunal from the Special Account for the United Nations Protection Force established pursuant to General Assembly resolution 46/233 of 19 March 1992;

3. *Decides further* to apportion the amount of 4,309,750 dollars gross (3,818,750 dollars net) for the period from 1 January to 31 March 1996 among Member States in accordance with the scale of assessments for the year 1996;

4. *Decides* that, in accordance with the provisions of its resolution 973(X) of 15 December 1955, there shall be set off against the apportionment among Member States, as provided for in paragraph 3 above, their respective share in the Tax Equalization Fund of the estimated staff assessment income of 491,000 dollars for the International Tribunal for the period from 1 January to 31 March 1996.

General Assembly resolution 50/212 A

23 December 1995     Meeting 100     Adopted without vote

Approved by Fifth Committee (A/50/849) without vote, 20 December (meeting 43); draft by Chairman (A/C.5/50/L.16); agenda item 136.
*Meeting numbers.* GA 50th session: 5th Committee 42, 43; plenary 100.

*REFERENCES*

(1)YUN 1993, p. 440, SC res. 827(1993), 25 May 1993. (2)A/50/365-S/1995/728. (3)S/1995/988. (4)YUN 1994, p. 507. (5)S/1995/910. (6)A/50/187-S/1995/410. (7)YUN 1992, p. 366, SC res. 771(1992), 13 Aug. 1992. (8)Ibid., p. 370, SC res. 780(1992), 6 Oct. 1992. (9)YUN 1994, p. 510. (10)A/49/7/Add.12. (11)A/C.5/50/41.

## International Tribunal for Rwanda

In 1995, arrangements were completed for the commencement of the work of the International Criminal Tribunal for the Prosecution of Persons Responsible for Genocide and Other Serious Violations of International Humanitarian Law Committed in the Territory of Rwanda and Rwandan Citizens Responsible for Genocide and Other Such Violations Committed in the Territory of Neighbouring States between 1 January and 31 December 1994 (the International Tribunal for Rwanda). The Tribunal had been established by the Security Council on 8 November 1994[1] on the recommendation of the Commission of Experts, which also had been established by the Council on 1 July 1994,[2] following massacres in Rwanda, to provide the Secretary-General with conclusions on evidence of genocide and other violations of international law in that country.

In February 1995, the Council decided that the International Tribunal should have its seat in Arusha, United Republic of Tanzania. In August, a headquarters agreement governing the Tribunal's seat was signed with the Tanzanian Government. In May, the General Assembly, on the recommendation of the Council, elected the six trial judges of the Tribunal. The Tribunal held an inaugural session at The Hague in June and issued its first indictments in December. The Assembly, in July and December, approved appropriations for the Tribunal's financing.

### General aspects

**Report of the Secretary-General (February).** The Secretary-General on 13 February reported[3] on arrangements for the functioning of the International Tribunal for Rwanda. The report analysed the legal basis for the Tribunal's establishment and its legal status; compared its statute with that of the International Tribunal for the Former Yugoslavia (see above); reviewed steps taken for the Tribunal's functioning; and examined options for the location of its seat.

The Secretary-General noted that the plan for the Tribunal's establishment comprised two phases. During the first phase, an investigative/prosecutorial unit had been set up in Kigali, Rwanda, to organize the Prosecutor's Office, gather information, develop an investigative strategy and operational procedures, and initiate investigations and the preparation of indictments. A small administrative unit had also been established to support the start-up operations of the Prosecutor's Office and to handle all administrative, financial and personnel matters regarding the commencement of Tribunal operations. The

Secretary-General appointed Honoré Rakoto-manana (Madagascar) as Deputy Prosecutor. A trust fund to support Tribunal activities was set up and received contributions from several States, including a pledge of $1 million worth of equipment. Budgetary requirements for the initial funding of the first phase, from 1 January to 31 March, were estimated at $3,951,200.

In the second phase, judges were to be elected, practical arrangements for the Tribunal's seat put in place and staffing completed. With a common Appeals Chamber composed of five judges already in place, shared under the statute with the Tribunal for the Former Yugoslavia, only six trial judges, three for each Trial Chamber, had to be elected. The Secretary-General proposed that a special session of the judges be convened upon their election to adopt rules of procedure and evidence. He noted that with the conclusion of headquarters and lease agreements for the Tribunal's premises and the completed staffing of the Prosecutor's Office and the Registry, the Tribunal would be fully operational by the end of the second phase.

The report also summarized findings of a technical mission that had visited Kenya, Rwanda and the United Republic of Tanzania at the end of 1994 to determine suitable premises for the seat of the International Tribunal. In determining the location of the seat, the Secretary-General said he had been guided by criteria set out by the Security Council,[1] including a preference for an "African seat". On the basis of mission findings and government views, he recommended that Arusha be selected as the seat of the Tribunal.

**SECURITY COUNCIL ACTION**

On 22 February, the Security Council, having considered the Secretary-General's report, adopted **resolution 977(1995)**.

*The Security Council,*

*Recalling* its resolution 955(1994) of 8 November 1994,

*Having regard* to its decision contained in paragraph 6 of resolution 955(1994) that the seat of the International Tribunal for Rwanda shall be determined by the Council,

*Having considered* the report of the Secretary-General dated 13 February 1995 and noting the recommendation of the Secretary-General that, subject to appropriate arrangements between the United Nations and the Government of the United Republic of Tanzania acceptable to the Council, Arusha be determined as the seat of the International Tribunal for Rwanda,

*Noting* the willingness of the Government of Rwanda to cooperate with the Tribunal,

*Décides* that, subject to the conclusion of appropriate arrangements between the United Nations and the Government of the United Republic of Tanzania, the International Tribunal for Rwanda shall have its seat at Arusha.

Security Council resolution 977(1995)
22 February 1995      Meeting 3502      Adopted unanimously
Draft prepared in consultations among Council members (S/1995/148).

On 27 February, the Council adopted **resolution 978(1995)**.

*The Security Council,*

*Recalling* all its previous resolutions on the situation in Rwanda, in particular its resolutions 935(1994) and 955(1994),

*Expressing once again* its grave concern at the reports indicating that genocide and other systematic, widespread and flagrant violations of international humanitarian law have been committed in Rwanda,

*Noting* that these reports were confirmed in the final report of the Commission of Experts submitted pursuant to resolution 935(1994),

*Recalling* the obligations contained in resolution 955(1994), which created the International Tribunal for Rwanda,

*Concerned* by the conditions in the refugee camps outside Rwanda, including reports of violence directed against refugees who voluntarily wish to return to Rwanda,

*Determined* to put an end to violations of international humanitarian law and serious acts of violence directed against refugees, and that effective measures be taken to bring to justice the persons who are responsible for such crimes,

*Noting* the reports of the Secretary-General on security in the Rwandese refugee camps of 18 November 1994 and 25 January 1995,

*Welcoming* the report of the Secretary-General dated 13 February 1995 and stressing the importance of taking all measures for the early and effective functioning of the International Tribunal for Rwanda,

*Stressing* the need for States to take as soon as possible any measures necessary under their domestic law to implement the provisions of resolution 955(1994) and of the statute of the International Tribunal for Rwanda,

1.   *Urges* States to arrest and detain, in accordance with their national law and relevant standards of international law, pending prosecution by the International Tribunal for Rwanda or by the appropriate national authorities, persons found within their territory against whom there is sufficient evidence that they were responsible for acts within the jurisdiction of the International Tribunal for Rwanda;

2.   *Urges* States who detain persons referred to in paragraph 1 above to inform the Secretary-General and the Prosecutor of the International Tribunal for Rwanda of the identity of the persons detained, the nature of the crimes believed to have been committed, the evidence providing probable cause for the detentions, the date when the persons were detained and the place of detention;

3.   *Urges* States who detain such persons to cooperate with representatives of the International Committee of the Red Cross, as well as investigators for the International Tribunal for Rwanda, in order to secure unimpeded access to those persons;

4.   *Condemns* all attacks against persons in the refugee camps near the borders of Rwanda, demands that such attacks immediately cease, and calls upon States to take appropriate steps to prevent such attacks;

5. *Urges* States, on whose territory serious acts of violence in the refugee camps have taken place, to arrest and detain, in accordance with their national law and relevant standards of international law, and submit to the appropriate authorities for the purpose of prosecution persons against whom there is sufficient evidence that they have incited or participated in such acts and further urges the States concerned to keep the Secretary-General informed of the measures they have taken to this effect;

6. *Decides* to remain actively seized of the matter.

Security Council resolution 978(1995)

27 February 1995     Meeting 3504     Adopted unanimously

Draft by United States (S/1995/153).

**Report of the Secretary-General (June).** On 30 June, the Secretary-General submitted a further report[4] on the establishment of the International Tribunal for Rwanda. Following the election of judges (see below), the Tribunal had held an inaugural session between 26 and 30 June at The Hague, pending the conclusion of arrangements for its seat in Arusha. The judges adopted rules of procedure and evidence. Judge Laïty Kama (Senegal) was elected President and Judge Yakov A. Ostrovsky (Russian Federation), Vice-President. At the same time, the Deputy Prosecutor was actively directing investigations of some 400 identified suspects, both in and outside Rwanda, notably in other African countries, Europe and North America.

The Secretary-General pointed out that setting up the Prosecutor's Office in Kigali had been more difficult than anticipated, due to an uncertain budgetary situation which had affected recruitment of qualified personnel, as well as poor safety conditions and unavailability or inadequacy of premises. He nevertheless emphasized the importance of the presence of such an office in Kigali, noting that the possibility that the Office would become fully operational had improved in recent weeks. As for arrangements concerning the Tribunal's seat, two UN missions visited Arusha between 10 and 19 May to survey the premises and discuss draft headquarters and lease agreements. The Secretary-General hoped that the agreements would be finalized in the near future, but pointed out that arrangements also had to be made for renovation, construction and repair work on the premises.

The Secretary-General further noted that the Tribunal had been operating on a combination of a commitment authority of up to $2.9 million granted by ACABQ and voluntary contributions. Pledges and contributions to the trust fund for the Tribunal totalled slightly more than $1 million; an additional $6 million to $7 million in cash and in kind had been pledged at a special meeting of the Rwanda Operational Support Group, held in Kigali on 19 May.

**Report of the Secretary-General (August).** On 25 August, the Secretary-General submitted a third report[5] on progress made in establishing the Tribunal. A task force was established to oversee lease, contracting, reconstruction and procurement arrangements.

An agreement for the contribution of personnel to the Tribunal had been signed with the United Kingdom, and similar agreements were being negotiated with Canada, Denmark, the Netherlands, Norway, Switzerland and the United States, as well as with one NGO, the Secretary-General reported. Eighteen Professional staff were currently working for the Tribunal, including the Prosecutor and the Liaison Officer at The Hague and the Deputy Prosecutor and 10 legal officers in Kigali. Seven other candidates had accepted offers of appointment to Kigali. Seven investigators had been contributed by Member States, with an additional 40 staff expected over the next three months. Since the International Tribunals for Rwanda and for the Former Yugoslavia shared a common Appeals Chamber and a common Prosecutor, Justice Richard J. Goldstone (South Africa), the establishment of a small liaison office was envisaged to facilitate certain activities and proceedings of the Rwanda Tribunal that would be undertaken at The Hague.

A total of $6.3 million in cash had been contributed or pledged to the Voluntary Fund to Support the Activities of the Tribunal, in addition to funds budgeted and approved by the General Assembly in July (see below).

In the meantime, during continuing investigations, materials had been collected and analysed and witnesses in Africa, Europe and North America interviewed. Inquiries centred on a small number of individuals suspected of bearing the principal responsibility for the planning, incitement or commission of crimes. A list of judges was established to review indictments from October to December 1995.

**Further developments.** In a 7 October report[6] (see PART TWO, Chapter II), the Secretary-General informed the Security Council that on 31 August the United Nations had signed the headquarters agreement with the United Republic of Tanzania concerning the seat of the Tribunal, and was negotiating a memorandum of understanding with Rwanda regarding the Prosecutor's Office in Kigali. Adronico Adede of the UN Office of Legal Affairs had been appointed Tribunal Registrar on 8 September. In September, the Tribunal's President, Prosecutor and Registrar visited Arusha to inspect Tribunal premises, as well as accommodations for Tribunal staff and a proposed prison site.

On 1 December, the Secretary-General reported[7] that a lease agreement for Tribunal premises had been signed on 31 October and that arrangements for temporary offices and residential accommodations had been completed. The judge assigned to review the indictments had arrived in Arusha, and the Tribunal Registrar was in residence there. The Prosecutor's Office in Kigali had expanded, with investigators contributed by Member States numbering 30, in addition to UN staff. Some $6.4 million in cash contributions and pledges was available in the Voluntary Fund for the Tribunal.

The International Tribunal for Rwanda issued its first indictments on 12 December 1995, and the proceedings against suspects accused of genocide in Rwanda were expected to commence shortly, the Secretary-General stated.

**Communication.** On 11 October, Kenya transmitted a statement[8] by its President, pointing out that while he was not against the Rwanda Tribunal, he was nevertheless convinced that its current mandate was limited. No lasting solution to the Rwanda-Burundi crisis would be found unless the Tribunal's terms of reference were widened to include investigations to determine those responsible for the April 1994 downing of the aircraft in which the Presidents of Rwanda and Burundi had been killed, which had triggered the massacres, and those responsible for the invasion of Rwanda prior to the assassination of the two Presidents. To concentrate only on the period after the deaths of the two Presidents would be superficial and not useful in bringing lasting peace to the region, he stated.

## Administrative and budgetary aspects

On 28 February, the General Assembly, on the proposal of the Secretary-General,[9] included in the agenda of its forty-ninth session two additional items, on the financing of the International Tribunal for Rwanda and on the election of Tribunal judges (**decision 49/402 B**).

### Election of judges

On 24 April, the Security Council, having considered nominations for judges for the Rwanda Tribunal received by the Secretary-General before 7 April 1995, adopted **resolution 989(1995)**.

*The Security Council,*

*Recalling* its resolution 955(1994) of 8 November 1994,

*Having decided to consider* the nominations for judges of the International Tribunal for Rwanda received by the Secretary-General before 7 April 1995,

*Establishes* the following list of candidates in accordance with article 12 of the statute of the International Tribunal for Rwanda:

Mr. Lennart Aspegren (Sweden)
Mr. Kevin Haugh (Ireland)
Mr. Laïty Kama (Senegal)
Mr. T. H. Khan (Bangladesh)
Mr. Wamulungwe Mainga (Zambia)
Mr. Yakov A. Ostrovsky (Russian Federation)
Ms. Navanethem Pillay (South Africa)
Mr. Edilbert Razafindralambo (Madagascar)
Mr. William H. Sekule (United Republic of Tanzania)
Ms. Anne Marie Stoltz (Norway)
Mr. Jiri Toman (Czech Republic/Switzerland)
Mr. Lloyd G. Williams (Jamaica/Saint Kitts and Nevis)

Security Council resolution 989(1995)
24 April 1995    Meeting 3524    Adopted unanimously

Draft prepared in consultations among Council members (S/1995/325).

On the same date, the Council President transmitted[10] the text of the resolution to the General Assembly. In notes dated 26 April, the Secretary-General submitted to the Assembly the list of candidates and described the procedure for the election of judges,[11] and provided their curricula vitae.[12]

**GENERAL ASSEMBLY ACTION**

On 24 and 25 May, the Assembly, following its consideration of the nominees, adopted **decision 49/324**, by which it elected the six judges of the Tribunal for a four-year term of office, to begin, upon two months' notice, shortly before the commencement of the trial proceedings: Lennart Aspegren (Sweden); Laïty Kama (Senegal); T. H. Khan (Bangladesh); Yakov A. Ostrovsky (Russian Federation); Navanethem Pillay (South Africa); and William H. Sekule (United Republic of Tanzania).

### Tribunal financing

For the immediate and urgent requirements of the International Tribunal for Rwanda and pending the determination of complete financial requirements, the Secretary-General on 27 February obtained the concurrence of ACABQ to enter into commitments not exceeding $2,914,900. In a 29 June report,[13] he estimated requirements for 1994-1995 at $17,284,000, including the $2.9 million previously authorized.

On 12 July, in an oral report to the Fifth Committee, ACABQ recommended that detailed consideration of the Secretary-General's report be deferred until the Assembly's fiftieth session and that a commitment authority not exceeding $10 million be approved, in the meantime, for the period up to 31 October 1995.

**GENERAL ASSEMBLY ACTION (July)**

On 20 July, the General Assembly adopted **resolution 49/251**.

**Financing of the International Criminal Tribunal for the Prosecution of Persons Responsible for Genocide and Other Serious Violations of International Humanitarian Law Committed in the Territory of Rwanda and Rwandan Citizens Responsible for Genocide and Other Such Violations Committed in the Territory of Neighbouring States between 1 January and 31 December 1994**

*The General Assembly,*

*Having considered* Security Council resolution 955(1994) of 8 November 1994, on the establishment of the International Criminal Tribunal for the Prosecution of Persons Responsible for Genocide and Other Serious Violations of International Humanitarian Law Committed in the Territory of Rwanda and Rwandan Citizens Responsible for Genocide and Other Such Violations Committed in the Territory of Neighbouring States between 1 January and 31 December 1994, in which the Council adopted the statute of the International Tribunal for Rwanda,

*Having also considered* Security Council resolution 977(1995) of 22 February 1995, in which the Council decided that, subject to the conclusion of appropriate arrangements between the United Nations and the Government of the United Republic of Tanzania, the International Tribunal for Rwanda should have its seat at Arusha,

*Having further considered* the report of the Secretary-General on the financing of the International Tribunal for Rwanda and the related observations and recommendations thereon presented by the Chairman of the Advisory Committee on Administrative and Budgetary Questions,

*Taking into account* the views expressed by Member States in the Fifth Committee of the General Assembly,

1. *Endorses* the observations and recommendations of the Advisory Committee on Administrative and Budgetary Questions as presented by its Chairman, subject to the provisions of the present resolution;

2. *Emphasizes* the importance of assuring secure and stable financing of the International Tribunal for the Prosecution of Persons Responsible for Genocide and Other Serious Violations of International Humanitarian Law Committed in the Territory of Rwanda and Rwandan Citizens Responsible for Genocide and Other Such Violations Committed in the Territory of Neighbouring States between 1 January and 31 December 1994 so that it may fulfil its role in full and effectively;

3. *Decides* that the expenses of the International Tribunal for Rwanda shall be met through additional resources on the basis of assessed contributions and that they shall be financed through a separate special account outside the regular budget;

4. *Decides also* to appropriate to the Special Account for the International Tribunal for Rwanda a total amount of 13,467,300 United States dollars gross (12,914,900 dollars net) for the period to 31 October 1995, inclusive of the commitment authority of 2,914,900 dollars authorized by the Advisory Committee;

5. *Decides further,* as an ad hoc and exceptional arrangement, that, notwithstanding the provisions of paragraph 12 of its resolution 49/20 B of 12 July 1995, Member States will waive their respective shares in the credits arising from previous budgets of the United Nations Assistance Mission for Rwanda in the total amount of 6,733,650 dollars gross (6,457,450 dollars net) and hence accept an equivalent increase in the assessments for a future budget period of the Assistance Mission in the same amount, to be transferred to the Special Account for the International Tribunal for Rwanda from the Special Account established for the United Nations Assistance Mission for Rwanda;

6. *Decides* to apportion the amount of 6,733,650 dollars gross (6,457,450 dollars net) for the period to 31 October 1995 among Member States in accordance with the scale of assessments for the year 1995 as set out in its resolution 49/19 B of 23 December 1994;

7. *Decides also* that, in accordance with the provisions of its resolution 973(X) of 15 December 1955, there shall be set off against the apportionment among Member States, as provided for in paragraph 6 above, their respective share in the Tax Equalization Fund of the estimated staff assessment income of 552,400 dollars approved for the International Tribunal for Rwanda for the period to 31 October 1995;

8. *Decides further* that appropriations for 1 November to 31 December 1995 and for the biennium 1996-1997 under the special account referred to in paragraph 3 above, the amount of which shall be determined during its fiftieth session, shall be financed equally through the modes of financing referred to in paragraphs 5 and 6 above, again notwithstanding the provisions of paragraph 12 of resolution 49/20 B;

9. *Decides* to consider the report of the Secretary-General further at its fiftieth session, together with updated information on the establishment of the International Tribunal for Rwanda and related requirements;

10. *Requests* the Secretary-General to submit to the General Assembly at its fiftieth session a report on requirements for the International Tribunal for Rwanda in the biennium 1996-1997;

11. *Authorizes* the Secretary-General to make the necessary arrangements, including the signing of a lease agreement and construction contracts for the premises of the International Tribunal for Rwanda and granting of contracts of up to twelve months for its staff, to ensure that it is provided with adequate facilities and necessary staff resources, and to report to the General Assembly thereon;

12. *Welcomes* contributions already made to the Voluntary Fund to support the activities of the International Tribunal for Rwanda established by Security Council resolution 955(1994) and invites Member States and other interested parties to make voluntary contributions to the International Tribunal both in cash and in the form of services and supplies acceptable to the Secretary-General;

13. *Decides* to review the mode of financing of the International Tribunal for Rwanda at its fifty-second session;

14. *Requests* the Secretary-General to submit a performance report at the end of each biennium but no later than May 1996 and May 1998, respectively;

15. *Decides* to include in the provisional agenda of its fiftieth session the item entitled "Financing of the International Criminal Tribunal for the Prosecution of Persons Responsible for Genocide and Other Serious Violations of International Humanitarian Law Committed in the Territory of Rwanda and Rwandan Citizens Responsible for Genocide and Other Such Violations Committed in the Territory of Neighbouring States between 1 January and 31 December 1994".

General Assembly resolution 49/251

20 July 1995          Meeting 106          Adopted without vote

Approved by Fifth Committee (A/49/945) without vote, 14 July (meeting 66); draft by Chairman (A/C.5/49/L.67), based on informal consultations; agenda item 163.
*Meeting numbers.* GA 49th session: 5th Committee 65, 66; plenary 106.

On 6 November, the Secretary-General reported[14] that, owing to delays in making the Tribunal fully operational, the funding appropriated up to 31 October would be sufficient to meet the requirements up to 31 December, and that a budget performance report covering the period up to 31 December and estimates for 1996-1997 would be submitted at the current session. In a 14 December report,[15] he stated that further delays experienced by the Tribunal had made it impossible to prepare detailed estimates for 1996; he proposed that a maintenance budget of $7,090,600 be approved for the period from 1 January to 30 March 1996, at the level authorized in 1995.

ACABQ, in an oral report to the Fifth Committee on 18 December, concurred with the Secretary-General's recommendation.

**GENERAL ASSEMBLY ACTION (December)**

On 23 December, the General Assembly adopted **resolution 50/213 A**.

**Financing of the International Criminal Tribunal for the Prosecution of Persons Responsible for Genocide and Other Serious Violations of International Humanitarian Law Committed in the Territory of Rwanda and Rwandan Citizens Responsible for Genocide and Other Such Violations Committed in the Territory of Neighbouring States between 1 January and 31 December 1994**

*The General Assembly,*

*Having considered* the reports of the Secretary-General on the financing of the International Criminal Tribunal for the Prosecution of Persons Responsible for Genocide and Other Serious Violations of International Humanitarian Law Committed in the Territory of Rwanda and Rwandan Citizens Responsible for Genocide and Other Such Violations Committed in the Territory of Neighbouring States between 1 January and 31 December 1994 and the related report of the Advisory Committee on Administrative and Budgetary Questions as presented orally by its Chairman,

*Noting* that detailed requirements for the International Tribunal for Rwanda for the full year of 1996 will be submitted to the General Assembly in early 1996,

1. *Decides* to appropriate to the Special Account for the International Criminal Tribunal for the Prosecution of Persons Responsible for Genocide and Other Serious Violations of International Humanitarian Law Committed in the Territory of Rwanda and Rwandan Citizens Responsible for Genocide and Other Such Violations Committed in the Territory of Neighbouring States between 1 January and 31 December 1994 an amount of 7,609,900 United States dollars gross (7,090,600 dollars net) for the period from 1 January to 31 March 1996, without prejudice to the comments and recommendations the Advisory Committee on Administrative and Budgetary Questions may make following its review of the full budget for 1996;

2. *Decides also,* as an ad hoc and exceptional arrangement, that, notwithstanding the provisions of paragraph 12 of its resolution 49/20 B of 12 July 1995, Member States shall waive their respective shares in the credits arising from previous budgets of the United Nations Assistance Mission for Rwanda in the total amount of 3,804,950 dollars gross (3,545,300 dollars net) and hence accept an equivalent increase in the assessments for a future budget period of the Assistance Mission in the same amount, to be transferred to the Special Account for the International Tribunal for Rwanda from the Special Account for the United Nations Assistance Mission for Rwanda;

3. *Decides further* to apportion the amount of 3,804,950 dollars gross (3,545,300 dollars net) for the period from 1 January to 31 March 1996 among Member States in accordance with the scale of assessments for the year 1996;

4. *Decides* that, in accordance with the provisions of its resolution 973(X) of 15 December 1955, there shall be set off against the apportionment among Member States, as provided for in paragraph 3 above, their respective share in the Tax Equalization Fund of the estimated staff assessment income of 259,650 dollars approved for the International Tribunal for Rwanda for the period from 1 January to 31 March 1996.

General Assembly resolution 50/213 A

23 December 1995          Meeting 100          Adopted without vote

Approved by Fifth Committee (A/50/852) without vote, 20 December (meeting 43); draft by Chairman (A/C.5/50/L.17); agenda item 160.
*Meeting numbers.* GA 50th session: 5th Committee 42, 43; plenary 100.

*REFERENCES*

[1]YUN 1994, p. 299, SC res. 955(1994), 8 Nov. 1994. [2]Ibid., p. 297, SC res. 935(1994), 1 July 1994. [3]S/1995/134. [4]S/1995/533. [5]S/1995/741. [6]S/1995/848. [7]S/1995/1002. [8]S/1995/861. [9]A/49/241. [10]A/49/889. [11]A/49/893. [12]A/49/894. [13]A/C.5/49/68. [14]A/C.5/50/16. [15]A/C.5/50/47.

Chapter III

# Legal aspects of international political relations

In 1995, the United Nations continued work on issues dealing with the legal aspects of international political and State relations.

The International Law Commission continued work on the progressive codification of international law. As to the establishment of an international criminal court, the General Assembly established a preparatory committee to prepare a consolidated text of a convention as a next step towards consideration by a conference of plenipotentiaries. The Assembly also adopted a resolution on measures to eliminate international terrorism and a decision on the draft articles on the status of the diplomatic courier and the diplomatic bag not accompanied by diplomatic courier and of the draft optional protocols thereto.

## International Law Commission

The International Law Commission (ILC), at its forty-seventh session (Geneva, 2 May–21 July 1995),[(1)] held 48 public meetings. It considered the draft Code of Crimes against the Peace and Security of Mankind; State succession and its impact on the nationality of natural and legal persons; draft articles on State responsibility for wrongful acts; draft articles on international liability for injurious consequences arising out of acts not prohibited by international law; and the law and practice relating to reservations to treaties. The Commission endorsed the recommendations of its Working Group on the long-term programme of work: to include in the Commission's future agenda the topic of diplomatic protection and to conduct a feasibility study on the rights and duties of States for the protection of the environment. ILC continued to cooperate with the Asian-African Legal Consultative Committee and the Inter-American Juridical Committee.

In accordance with a General Assembly request (**resolution 50/45**), the Secretariat prepared for ILC's attention a topical summary[(2)] of the Assembly's Sixth (Legal) Committee discussion of ILC's 1995 report.

The thirty-first session of the International Law Seminar for postgraduate students and young professors or government officials dealing with international law was held (Geneva, 22 May–9 June)

during the ILC session, with 23 participants of different nationalities, mostly from developing countries. The participants attended ILC meetings and lectures specifically organized for them. Austria, Denmark, Finland, France, Germany, Ireland, Norway, Switzerland and the United Kingdom made voluntary financial contributions, thus making it possible to award nine full and six partial fellowships. Since the first seminar in 1965, fellowships had been awarded to 374 of the 690 participants representing 156 nationalities.

GENERAL ASSEMBLY ACTION

On 11 December, the General Assembly adopted **resolution 50/45**.

**Report of the International Law Commission on the work of its forty-seventh session**

*The General Assembly,*

*Having considered* the report of the International Law Commission on the work of its forty-seventh session,

*Emphasizing* the importance of furthering the progressive development of international law and its codification as a means of implementing the purposes and principles set forth in the Charter of the United Nations and in the Declaration on Principles of International Law concerning Friendly Relations and Cooperation among States in accordance with the Charter of the United Nations,

*Emphasizing also* the role of the International Law Commission in the fulfilment of the objectives of the United Nations Decade of International Law,

*Recognizing* the desirability of referring legal and drafting questions to the Sixth Committee, including topics that might be submitted to the International Law Commission for closer examination, and of enabling the Sixth Committee and the Commission further to enhance their contribution to the progressive development of international law and its codification,

*Recalling* the need to keep under review those topics of international law which, given their new or renewed interest for the international community, may be suitable for the progressive development and codification of international law and therefore may be included in the future programme of work of the International Law Commission,

*Stressing* the usefulness of structuring the debate on the report of the International Law Commission in the Sixth Committee in such a manner that conditions are provided for concentrated attention on each of the main topics dealt with in the report,

*Wishing* to enhance further the interaction between the Sixth Committee as a body of government representatives and the International Law Commission as a body of independent legal experts, with a view to improving the dialogue between the two organs,

1. *Takes note with appreciation* of the report of the International Law Commission on the work of its forty-seventh session and of the Commission's efforts to advance the work currently under consideration;

2. *Notes* the intentions of the International Law Commission for the programme of work for the last year of office of its members;

3. *Urges* the Commission at its forty-eighth session:

*(a)* To resume the work on the draft Code of Crimes against the Peace and Security of Mankind in such a manner that the second reading of the draft Code may be completed at that session;

*(b)* To resume the work on the draft articles on State responsibility in such a manner that the first reading of that draft may be completed at that session, taking into account the divergent views expressed during the Sixth Committee's debate on the topic, so that alternative approaches may be developed when necessary;

*(c)* To resume the work on the topic "International liability for injurious consequences arising out of acts not prohibited by international law" in order to complete the first reading of the draft articles relating to activities that risk causing transboundary harm;

4. *Notes* the beginning of the work on the topics "The law and practice relating to reservations to treaties" and "State succession and its impact on the nationality of natural and legal persons", and invites the Commission to continue its work on these topics along the lines indicated in the report;

5. *Invites* States and international organizations, particularly those which are depositaries, to answer promptly the questionnaire prepared by the Special Rapporteur on the topic concerning reservations to treaties;

6. *Requests* the Secretary-General to again invite Governments to submit as soon as possible relevant materials, including treaties, national legislation, decisions of national tribunals and diplomatic and official correspondence relevant to the topic "State succession and its impact on the nationality of natural and legal persons";

7. *Expresses its appreciation* to the Secretary-General for the update of the survey of State practice relevant to international liability for injurious consequences arising out of acts not prohibited by international law, prepared by the Secretariat in 1984;

8. *Notes* the suggestions of the International Law Commission to include in its agenda the topic "Diplomatic protection" and initiate a feasibility study on a topic concerning the law of the environment, and decides to invite Governments to submit comments on these suggestions through the Secretary-General for consideration by the Sixth Committee during the fifty-first session of the General Assembly;

9. *Requests* the International Law Commission:

*(a)* To examine the procedures of its work for the purpose of further enhancing its contribution to the progressive development and codification of international law and to include its views in its report to the General Assembly at its fifty-first session;

*(b)* To continue to pay special attention to indicating in its annual report, for each topic, those specific issues, if any, on which expressions of views by Governments, either in the Sixth Committee or in written form,

would be of particular interest in providing effective guidance for the Commission in its further work;

10. *Requests* the Secretary-General to invite Governments to comment on the present state of the codification process within the United Nations system and to report thereon to the General Assembly at its fifty-first session;

11. *Takes note* of the comments of the International Law Commission on the question of the duration of its session, as presented in its report, and expresses the view that the requirements of the work for the progressive development of international law and its codification and the magnitude and complexity of the subjects on the agenda of the Commission make it desirable that the usual duration of its sessions be maintained;

12. *Reaffirms* its previous decisions concerning the role of the Codification Division of the Office of Legal Affairs of the Secretariat and those concerning the summary records and other documentation of the International Law Commission;

13. *Once again expresses the wish* that seminars will continue to be held in conjunction with the sessions of the International Law Commission and that an increasing number of participants from developing countries will be given the opportunity to attend those seminars, appeals to States that can do so to make the voluntary contributions that are urgently needed for the holding of the seminars, and requests the Secretary-General to provide the seminars, from within existing resources, with adequate services, including interpretation, as required;

14. *Requests* the Secretary-General to forward to the International Law Commission, for its attention, the records of the debate on the report of the Commission at the fiftieth session of the General Assembly, together with such written statements as delegations may circulate in conjunction with their oral statements, and to prepare and distribute a topical summary of the debate, following established practice;

15. *Recommends* that the debate on the report of the International Law Commission at the fifty-first session of the General Assembly commence on 4 November 1996.

General Assembly resolution 50/45

11 December 1995     Meeting 87     Adopted without vote

Approved by Sixth Committee (A/50/638) by consensus, 22 November (meeting 44); draft by Chairman (A/C.6/50/L.7); agenda item 141.
*Meeting numbers.* GA 50th session: 6th Committee 12-25, 44; plenary 87.

## Draft Code of Crimes against the Peace and Security of Mankind

ILC continued its second reading of the draft Code of Crimes against the Peace and Security of Mankind. The draft Code, originally prepared in 1954[3] and provisionally adopted by ILC on first reading in 1991,[4] defined offences that were crimes under international law and for which the responsible individual was to be punished.

The Commission had before it the thirteenth report[5] on the draft Code, submitted by Special Rapporteur Doudou Thiam (Senegal). The Special Rapporteur reproduced the draft articles adopted on first reading containing definitions of aggression (article 15), genocide (article 19), systematic or mass violations of human rights (article 21), exceptionally serious war crimes (article 22), international terrorism (article 24) and illicit traffic in narcotic drugs (article 25). Each article was followed by comments from Governments and the Special Rapporteur's views and recommendations.

The Commission decided to refer to its Drafting Committee the articles dealing with aggression, genocide, systematic or mass violations of human rights and exceptionally serious war crimes. It also decided that consultations would continue regarding illicit traffic in narcotic drugs and wilful and severe damage to the environment (article 26). Concerning the latter, the Commission established a working group to meet in 1996 to examine the possibility of covering the issue in the draft Code, while reaffirming its intention to complete the second reading of the draft Code at that session in any event. Subsequently, the Drafting Committee, having devoted 17 meetings to the consideration of the articles referred to it, adopted: for inclusion in Part One of the draft Code, articles dealing with scope and application of the Code (article 1), responsibility of States (article 5), establishment of jurisdiction (article 5 *bis*), obligation to extradite or prosecute (article 6), extradition of alleged offenders (article 6 *bis*), judicial guarantees (article 8), *non bis in idem* (article 9), nonretroactivity (article 10), order of a Government or a superior (article 11), responsibility of the superior (article 12) and official position and responsibility (article 13); and for inclusion in Part Two, articles dealing with aggression and genocide. Following consideration of the Drafting Committee Chairman's report, the Commission decided to defer the final adoption of the articles until after the completion of the remaining articles.

## International criminal jurisdiction

The Ad Hoc Committee on the Establishment of an International Criminal Court, established by the General Assembly in 1994,[6] met (New York, 3-13 April and 14-25 August)[7] to review the substantive and administrative issues arising out of the draft statute for an international criminal court adopted in 1994 by ILC.[8] It also considered the convening of an international conference of plenipotentiaries to conclude a convention on the establishment of an international criminal court and expressed appreciation to Italy for its offer to host the conference.

The Ad Hoc Committee examined comments[9] on the draft statute received from 15 States, from the International Tribunal for the Prosecution of Persons Responsible for Serious Violations of International Humanitarian Law Committed in the Territory of the Former Yugoslavia since

1991 (see preceding chapter), from the Crime Prevention and Criminal Justice Branch of the UN Office at Vienna and from the UN International Drug Control Programme (see PART FOUR, Chapters IX and XIV, respectively). It also considered a report[10] of the Secretary-General on provisional estimates of staffing, structure and costs of the establishment and operation of the proposed court, and a number of informal papers and documents prepared by experts and non-governmental organizations. The issues considered by the Committee included the establishment and composition of the court, the principle of complementarity (the relationship between the proposed court and national criminal and investigative procedures), other issues pertaining to jurisdiction, methods of proceedings (due process), and the relationship between States parties, non-States parties and the court.

The Committee concluded that further work on the establishment of the international court remained to be done. It expressed the opinion that issues could be addressed most effectively by combining further discussions with the drafting of texts, with a view to preparing a consolidated text of a convention as a next step towards consideration by a conference of plenipotentiaries. The Committee proposed that its mandate for future work be changed to that effect. It recommended that the General Assembly take up the question of the organization of future work with a view to its early completion.

Annexed to the Committee's report were guidelines concerning the relationship between States parties, non-States parties and the international court and guidelines for consideration of general principles of criminal law.

### GENERAL ASSEMBLY ACTION

On 11 December, the General Assembly adopted **resolution 50/46**.

**Establishment of an international criminal court**

*The General Assembly,*

*Recalling* its resolution 47/33 of 25 November 1992, in which it requested the International Law Commission to undertake the elaboration of a draft statute for an international criminal court,

*Recalling also* its resolution 48/31 of 9 December 1993, in which it requested the International Law Commission to continue its work on the question of the draft statute for an international criminal court, with a view to elaborating a draft statute for such a court, if possible at the Commission's forty-sixth session in 1994,

*Recalling further* that the International Law Commission adopted a draft statute for an international criminal court at its forty-sixth session and decided to recommend that an international conference of plenipotentiaries be convened to study the draft statute and to conclude a convention on the establishment of an international criminal court,

*Recalling* its resolution 49/53 of 9 December 1994, in which it decided to establish an ad hoc committee, open to all States Members of the United Nations or members of specialized agencies, to review the major substantive and administrative issues arising out of the draft statute prepared by the International Law Commission and, in the light of that review, to consider arrangements for the convening of an international conference of plenipotentiaries,

*Noting* that the Ad Hoc Committee on the Establishment of an International Criminal Court has made considerable progress during its sessions on the review of the major substantive and administrative issues arising out of the draft statute prepared by the International Law Commission,

*Noting also* that the States participating in the Ad Hoc Committee still have different views on major substantive and administrative issues arising out of the draft statute prepared by the International Law Commission and that, therefore, further discussions are needed for reaching consensus on the above issues in the future,

*Noting further* that the Ad Hoc Committee is of the opinion that issues can be addressed most effectively by combining further discussions with the drafting of texts, with a view to preparing a consolidated text of a convention for an international criminal court as a next step towards consideration by a conference of plenipotentiaries,

*Noting* that the Ad Hoc Committee recommends that the General Assembly take up the organization of future work with a view to its early completion, given the interest of the international community in the establishment of an international criminal court,

*Noting also* that the Ad Hoc Committee encourages participation by the largest number of States in its future work in order to promote universality,

*Expressing deep appreciation* for the renewed offer of the Government of Italy to host a conference on the establishment of an international criminal court,

1. *Takes note* of the report of the Ad Hoc Committee on the Establishment of an International Criminal Court, including the recommendations contained therein, and expresses its appreciation to the Ad Hoc Committee for the useful work done;

2. *Decides* to establish a preparatory committee open to all States Members of the United Nations or members of specialized agencies or of the International Atomic Energy Agency, to discuss further the major substantive and administrative issues arising out of the draft statute prepared by the International Law Commission and, taking into account the different views expressed during the meetings, to draft texts, with a view to preparing a widely acceptable consolidated text of a convention for an international criminal court as a next step towards consideration by a conference of plenipotentiaries, and also decides that the work of the Preparatory Committee should be based on the draft statute prepared by the International Law Commission and should take into account the report of the Ad Hoc Committee and the written comments submitted by States to the Secretary-General on the draft statute for an international criminal court pursuant to paragraph 4 of General Assembly resolution 49/53 and, as appropriate, contributions of relevant organizations;

3. *Also decides* that the Preparatory Committee will meet from 25 March to 12 April and from 12 to 30 August 1996 and submit its report to the General Assembly at the beginning of its fifty-first session, and requests the Secretary-General to provide the Preparatory Committee with the necessary facilities for the performance of its work;

4. *Urges* participation in the Preparatory Committee by the largest number of States in order to promote universal support for an international criminal court;

5. *Further decides* to include in the provisional agenda of its fifty-first session an item entitled ''Establishment of an international criminal court'', in order to study the report of the Preparatory Committee and, in the light of that report, to decide on the convening of an international conference of plenipotentiaries to finalize and adopt a convention on the establishment of an international criminal court, including on the timing and the duration of the conference.

General Assembly resolution 50/46

11 December 1995    Meeting 87    Adopted without vote

Approved by Sixth Committee (A/50/639 & Corr.1) by consensus, 29 November (meeting 46); draft by Chairman (A/C.6/50/L.14); agenda item 142.
*Financial implications.* S-G, A/C.6/50/L.16.
*Meeting numbers.* GA 50th session: 6th Committee 25-31, 46; plenary 87.

## International liability

Draft articles on international liability for injurious consequences arising out of acts not prohibited by international law were again considered by ILC in 1995 on the basis of the eleventh report[11] of its Special Rapporteur, Julio Barboza (Argentina), who proposed adding a new text concerning harm to the environment. The Commission decided to consider that report and his tenth report, submitted in 1994,[12] at its next session. The Commission also had before it a study prepared by the Secretariat on the survey of liability regimes relevant to the topic of international liability for injurious consequences arising out of acts not prohibited by international law.[13]

In July, the Commission considered and provisionally adopted articles which had been referred to its Drafting Committee in 1988[14] and 1989[15] on the freedom of action and the limits thereto (article A [6]); prevention (article B [8 and 9]); liability and compensation (article C [9 and 10]); and cooperation (article D [7]).

## State responsibility for wrongful acts

The Commission continued in 1995 consideration of draft articles on State responsibility for wrongful acts, based on the seventh report dealing with the subject[16] submitted by Special Rapporteur Gaetano Arangio-Ruiz (Italy). The Special Rapporteur dealt with the legal consequences of internationally wrongful acts characterized as crimes under article 19 of Part One of the draft articles and with the settlement of disputes relating to the legal consequences of an international crime. The first question was addressed in six new draft articles to be included in Part Two (articles

15 to 20) and the second in a new draft article 7 to be included in Part Three of the draft.

The Commission referred the articles contained in the Special Rapporteur's report to its Drafting Committee. The Commission received from the Committee a set of new articles and an annex thereto for inclusion in Part Three of the draft concerning the settlement of disputes, which it adopted on first reading. Concerning countermeasures, the Commission had before it draft commentaries to articles 11 (countermeasures by an injured State), 13 (proportionality) and 14 (prohibited countermeasures). It provisionally adopted articles 13 and 14 and the commentaries thereto but did not consider article 11 due to a lack of time.

### Impact of State succession on nationality of natural and legal persons

In accordance with a decision taken in 1994,[17] the Commission began work on State succession and its impact on the nationality of natural and legal persons, on the basis of the first report[18] by its Special Rapporteur, Václav Mikulka (Czech Republic). The Special Rapporteur examined the relevance of the topic, the concept and function of nationality, roles of internal and international law, limitations on the freedom of States in the area of nationality, categories of succession, scope of the problem under consideration and the continuity of nationality.

On 1 June, the Commission established a working group to identify issues arising out of the topic, categorize those issues which were closely related thereto, give guidance to the Commission as to which issues could be most profitably pursued given contemporary concerns and present the Commission with a calender of action. The Commission decided to reconvene the working group at its next session to complete the preliminary study on the subject, as requested by the General Assembly in 1994.[19]

In December, the Assembly, in **resolution 50/45**, requested the Secretary-General to again invite Governments to submit materials, including treaties, national legislation, decisions of national tribunals and diplomatic and official correspondence relevant to the topic "State succession and its impact on the nationality of natural and legal persons".

*REFERENCES*

[1]A/50/10. [2]A/CN.4/472 & Add.1. [3]YUN 1954, p. 408. [4]YUN 1991, p. 823. [5]A/CN.4/466 & Corr.1. [6]YUN 1994, p: 1285, GA res. 49/53, 9 Dec. 1994. [7]A/50/22. [8]YUN 1994, p. 1285. [9]A/AC.224/1 & Add.1-4. [10]A/AC.244/L.2. [11]A/CN.4/468. [12]YUN 1994, p. 1286. [13]A/CN.4/471. [14]YUN 1988, p. 831. [15]A/44/10. [16]A/CN.4/469 & Corr.1 & Add.1,2. [17]YUN 1994, p. 1283. [18]A/CN.4/467. [19]YUN 1994, p. 1283, GA res. 49/51, 9 Dec. 1994.

# International State relations and international law

## Safety and security of UN and associated personnel

### Status of Convention

The 1994 Convention on the Safety of United Nations and Associated Personnel,[1] which was opened for signature at UN Headquarters on 15 December 1994 and remained open until 31 December 1995, was ratified by Denmark, Norway and Ukraine; Japan had accepted it.[2] The Convention was to enter into force 30 days after 22 instruments of ratification, acceptance, approval or accession had been deposited with the Secretary-General. Forty-three States signed the Convention.

### Measures to eliminate terrorism

In response to a 1994 General Assembly request,[3] the Secretary-General in an August report with later addendum[4] presented information on the implementation of the 1994 Declaration on Measures to Eliminate International Terrorism[5] received from eight Member States, two specialized agencies and one regional organization.

The Secretary-General reported on the application of paragraph 10 of the Declaration concerning: data collection on agreements relating to terrorism; a compendium of national laws and regulations; an analytical review of existing international legal instruments; and a review of existing possibilities within the UN for assisting States in organizing workshops and training courses on combating crimes connected with international terrorism.

#### GENERAL ASSEMBLY ACTION

On 11 December, the General Assembly adopted **resolution 50/53**.

**Measures to eliminate international terrorism**
*The General Assembly,*

*Recalling* its resolution 49/60 of 9 December 1994, by which it adopted the Declaration on Measures to Eliminate International Terrorism,

*Recalling also* that, in the statement issued on 31 January 1992 by the President of the Security Council on the occasion of the meeting of the Security Council at the level of heads of State and Government, the members of the Council expressed their deep concern over acts of international terrorism, and emphasized the need for the international community to deal effectively with all such acts,

*Recalling further* the Declaration on the Occasion of the Fiftieth Anniversary of the United Nations,

*Deeply disturbed* by the persistence of terrorist acts, which have taken place worldwide,

*Stressing* the need further to strengthen international cooperation between States and between international organizations and agencies, regional organizations and arrangements and the United Nations in order to prevent, combat and eliminate terrorism in all its forms and manifestations,

*Having examined* the report of the Secretary-General of 24 August 1995,

1. *Strongly condemns* all acts, methods and practices of terrorism as criminal and unjustifiable;

2. *Reiterates* that criminal acts intended or calculated to provoke a state of terror in the general public, a group of persons or particular persons for political purposes are in any circumstance unjustifiable, whatever the considerations of a political, philosophical, ideological, racial, ethnic, religious or any other nature that may be invoked to justify them;

3. *Reaffirms* the Declaration on Measures to Eliminate International Terrorism annexed to resolution 49/60;

4. *Urges* all States to promote and implement effectively and in good faith the provisions of the Declaration in all its aspects;

5. *Also urges* all States to strengthen cooperation with one another to ensure that those who participate in terrorist activities, whatever the nature of their participation, find no safe haven anywhere;

6. *Calls upon* all States to take the necessary steps to implement their obligations under existing international conventions, to observe fully the principles of international law and to contribute to the further development of international law on this matter;

7. *Recalls* the role of the Security Council in combating international terrorism whenever it poses a threat to international peace and security;

8. *Requests* the Secretary-General to follow up closely the implementation of the Declaration and to submit an annual report on the implementation of paragraph 10 of the Declaration, taking into account the modalities set out in his report and the views expressed by States in the debate of the Sixth Committee during the fiftieth session of the General Assembly;

9. *Decides* to include in the provisional agenda of its fifty-first session the item entitled "Measures to eliminate international terrorism".

General Assembly resolution 50/53

11 December 1995     Meeting 87     Adopted without vote

Approved by Sixth Committee (A/50/643) by consensus, 29 November (meeting 46); draft by Chairman (A/C.6/50/L.12); agenda item 146.
*Meeting numbers.* GA 50th session: 6th Committee 6-10, 46; plenary 87.

*REFERENCES*

(1)YUN 1994, p. 1289, GA res. 49/59, annex, 9 Dec. 1994. (2)*Multilateral Treaties Deposited with the Secretary-General: Status as at 31 December 1995* (ST/LEG/SER.E/14), Sales No. E.96.V.5. (3)YUN 1994, p. 1293, GA res. 49/60, 9 Dec. 1994. (4)A/50/372 & Add.1. (5)YUN 1994, p. 1294, GA res. 49/60, annex, 9 Dec. 1994.

# Diplomatic relations

## Protection of diplomats

As at 31 December 1995,(1) the number of parties to the various international instruments relating to the protection of diplomats and diplomatic and consular relations was as follows: 174 States were parties to the 1961 Vienna Convention on Diplomatic Relations,(2) 48 States were parties to the Optional Protocol concerning the acquisition of nationality,(3) and 61 States were parties to the Optional Protocol concerning the compulsory settlement of disputes.(3)

The 1963 Vienna Convention on Consular Relations(4) had 153 parties, with the Sudan acceding in 1995, 36 States were parties to the Optional Protocol concerning the acquisition of nationality,(5) and 44 States were parties to the Optional Protocol concerning the compulsory settlement of disputes.(5)

The 1973 Convention on the Prevention and Punishment of Crimes against Internationally Protected Persons, including Diplomatic Agents(6) had 90 States parties, with Portugal acceding in 1995.

**Report of the Secretary-General.** In accordance with a 1994 General Assembly request,(7) the Secretary-General invited States to communicate their views on measures to enhance the protection, security and safety of diplomatic and consular missions and representatives, as provided for in a 1987 Assembly resolution.(8) In a September report,(9) the Secretary-General presented the texts and analytical summary of the information received. A total of 10 new reports of violations and additional information on previous cases were reported by States during the period 30 September 1994 to 18 August 1995. In connection with two reported cases in respect of which no information had been received within a reasonable period of time, the Secretary-General addressed reminders to those States. One follow-up report was received in response to those reminders. One State submitted views regarding the enhancement of diplomatic relations.

## Status of diplomatic courier and bag

The General Assembly, by **decision 50/416** of 11 December, decided to bring the draft articles on the status of the diplomatic courier and the diplomatic bag not accompanied by diplomatic courier and the draft optional protocols thereto, adopted by ILC on second reading in 1989,(10) to the attention of Member States and to remind them of the possibility that that field of international law and any future developments within it might be subject to codification.

*REFERENCES*

(1)*Multilateral Treaties Deposited with the Secretary-General: Status as at 31 December 1995* (ST/LEG/SER.E/14), Sales No. E.96.V.5. (2)YUN 1961, p. 512. (3)Ibid., p. 516. (4)YUN 1963, p. 510. (5)Ibid., p. 512. (6)YUN 1973, p. 775, GA res. 3166(XXVIII), annex, 14 Dec. 1973. (7)YUN 1994, p. 1297, GA res. 49/49, 9 Dec. 1994. (8)YUN 1987, p. 1068, GA res. 42/154, 7 Dec. 1987. (9)A/INF/50/3. (10)A/44/10.

# Treaties and agreements

## Reservations to treaties

In 1995, ILC began consideration of the law and practice relating to reservations to treaties, on the basis of the first report by Special Rapporteur Alain Pellet (France).(1) The Special Rapporteur reviewed the Commission's previous work on reservations, examined the problems related to the topic and discussed the Commission's future work. He concluded that it would be advantageous to fill the gaps in existing texts and do away with their ambiguities, through either draft articles additional to existing treaties, "consolidated" draft articles, a "guide to practice", model clauses or a combination of those approaches.

The Commission authorized the Special Rapporteur to prepare a questionnaire on reservations to treaties to ascertain the practice of, and problems encountered by, States and international organizations, particularly those which were depositaries of multilateral conventions.

The General Assembly, in **resolution 50/45**, invited States and international organizations, particularly those which were depositaries, to answer the questionnaire promptly.

## Treaties involving international organizations

The 1986 Vienna Convention on the Law of Treaties between States and International Organizations or between International Organizations,(2) which had not yet entered into force, had 23 States parties as at 31 December 1995.(3)

## Registration and publication of treaties by the United Nations

During 1995, some 1,250 international agreements and 612 subsequent actions were received by the Secretariat for registration or filing and recording. In addition, there were 542 registrations or formalities concerning agreements for which the Secretary-General performed depositary functions.

The texts of international agreements registered or filed and recorded are published in the United

Nations *Treaty Series* in the original languages, with translations into English and French where necessary. In 1995, the following volumes of the *Treaty Series* covering treaties registered or filed in 1981, 1983, 1984, 1985, 1986, 1987 and 1991 were issued:

1242, 1291, 1300, 1301, 1323, 1329, 1356, 1367, 1368, 1381, 1383, 1389, 1390, 1399, 1410, 1411, 1412, 1427, 1430, 1431, 1432, 1433, 1442, 1471, 1476, 1492, 1494, 1608, 1609, 1610/1611, 1612, 1613, 1614/1615, 1616/1617, 1618, 1619, 1620, 1621, 1622, 1623, 1624, 1625, 1626/1627, 1628, 1629, 1630/1631, 1632/1633, 1634/1635.

## Multilateral treaties

### New multilateral treaties concluded under UN auspices

The following treaties, concluded under UN auspices, were deposited with the Secretary-General during 1995:(3)

*Amendment to article 20, paragraph 1 of the Convention on the Elimination of All Forms of Discrimination against Women,* adopted at the eighth meeting of the States parties on 22 May 1995

*Agreement concerning the Adoption of Uniform Technical Prescriptions for Wheeled Vehicles, Equipment and Parts which can be fitted and/or be used on Wheeled Vehicles and the Conditions for Reciprocal Recognition of Approvals Granted on the Basis of These Prescriptions,* done at Geneva on 20 March 1958

    Regulation No. 95: "Uniform provisions concerning the approval of vehicles with regard to the protection of the occupants in the event of a lateral collision"

    Regulation No. 96: "Uniform provisions concerning the approval of compression ignition (c.i.) engines to be installed in agricultural and forestry tractors with regard to the emissions of pollutants by the engine"

    Regulation No. 97: "Uniform provisions concerning the approval of vehicle alarm systems (VAS) and of motor vehicles with regard to their alarm systems"

*International Grains Agreement, 1995*

(a)   *Grains Trade Convention, 1995,* concluded at London on 7 December 1994

(b)   *Food Aid Convention, 1995,* concluded at London on 5 December 1994

*International Natural Rubber Agreement, 1995,* concluded at Geneva on 17 February 1995

*Amendment to article 43, paragraph 2, of the Convention on the Rights of the Child,* adopted by the Conference of the States Parties on 12 December 1995

*United Nations Convention on Independent Guarantees and Stand-by Letters of Credit,* adopted by the General Assembly on 11 December 1995

*Agreement for the Implementation of the Provisions of the United Nations Convention on the Law of the Sea of 10 December 1982 relating to the Conservation and Management of Straddling Fish Stocks and Highly Migratory Fish Stocks,* adopted on 4 August 1995 by the United Nations Conference on Straddling Fish Stocks and Highly Migratory Fish Stocks

*Additional Protocol to the Convention on Prohibitions or Restrictions on the Use of Certain Conventional Weapons Which May*

*Be Deemed to Be Excessively Injurious or to Have Indiscriminate Effects*, adopted by the eighth meeting of the States parties on 13 October 1995

*Amendment to the Basel Convention on the Control of Transboundary Movements of Hazardous Wastes and Their Disposal*, adopted at the third meeting of the Conference of the Contracting Parties in Geneva on 22 September 1995

## Multilateral treaties
## deposited with the Secretary-General

The number of multilateral treaties for which the Secretary-General performed depositary functions stood at 474 at the end of 1995. During the year, 160 signatures were affixed to treaties for which he performed depositary functions and 839 instruments of ratification, accession, acceptance and approval or notification were transmitted to him. In addition, he received 239 communications from States expressing observations or declarations and reservations made at the time of signature, ratification or accession.

The following multilateral treaties in respect of which the Secretary-General acts as depositary came into force in 1995:[3]

*International Coffee Agreement, 1994*, adopted by the International Coffee Council on 30 March 1994

*Agreement to Establish the South Centre*, opened for signature in Geneva on 1 September 1994

*Agreement concerning the Adoption of Uniform Technical Prescriptions for Wheeled Vehicles, Equipment and Parts which can be fitted and/or be used on Wheeled Vehicles and the Conditions for Reciprocal Recognition of Approvals Granted on the Basis of These Prescriptions*, done at Geneva on 20 March 1958

 Regulation No. 94: "Uniform provisions concerning the approval of vehicles with regard to the protection of the occupants in the event of a frontal collision"

 Regulation No. 95: "Uniform provisions concerning the approval of vehicles with regard to the protection of the occupants in the event of a lateral collision"

 Regulation No. 96: "Uniform provisions concerning the approval of compression ignition (c.i.) engines to be installed in agricultural and forestry tractors with regard to the emissions of pollutants by the engine"

*International Grains Agreement, 1995*

(a) *Grains Trade Convention, 1995*, concluded at London on 7 December 1994

(b) *Food Aid Convention, 1995*, concluded at London on 5 December 1994

### REFERENCES

[1]A/CN.4/470 & Corr.1,2. [2]YUN 1986, p. 1006. [3]*Multilateral Treaties Deposited with the Secretary-General: Status as at 31 December 1995* (ST/LEG/SER.E/14), Sales No. E.96.V.5.

Chapter IV

# Law of the sea

An important step in the ongoing global process to strengthen the international legal order for the world's oceans was taken in 1995 with the adoption of the Agreement for the Implementation of the Provisions of the UN Convention on the Law of the Sea relating to the Conservation and Management of Straddling Fish Stocks and Highly Migratory Fish Stocks. The General Assembly called on States and other entities to sign and ratify or accede to the Agreement.

The implementation of the 1982 United Nations Convention on the Law of the Sea continued to be a major area of international concern. The Assembly of the International Seabed Authority concluded its first session and States parties met twice during the year to consider issues relating to setting up the International Tribunal for the Law of the Sea.

The Agreement relating to the Implementation of Part XI of the Convention on the Law of the Sea, governing exploration for and exploitation of seabed resources beyond the area of national jurisdiction, was closed for signature on 28 July 1995. The General Assembly called on States that had not done so to become parties to the Convention and to the Agreement.

## UN Convention on the Law of the Sea

### Signatures and ratifications

The number of parties to the UN Convention on the Law of the Sea increased to 83 during 1995: Argentina, Austria, Bolivia, the Cook Islands, Greece, India, Italy, Lebanon and Samoa ratified the Convention, Croatia and Slovenia succeeded to it, and Jordan and Tonga acceded.[1] The Convention, adopted by the Third UN Conference on the Law of the Sea in 1982,[2] entered into force on 16 November 1994.

**Meetings of States parties.** The second (15-19 May)[3] and third (27 November–1 December)[4] meetings of States parties to the Convention, both held in New York, considered organizational matters relating to the International Tribunal for the Law of the Sea, a draft budget and a draft protocol on privileges and immunities (see below for details).

### Agreement relating to the implementation of Part XI of the Convention

On 28 July 1995, the Agreement relating to the implementation of Part XI of the Convention, adopted by the General Assembly in 1994,[5] had been signed by 79 States and was closed for signature. On that date, 16 States became bound by the Agreement under the simplified procedure set out in article 5. Eleven States, which had been parties to the Convention before the adoption of the Agreement, notified the depositary in writing that they were not availing themselves of the simplified procedure. Some others, which had also notified that they were not availing themselves of the procedure under article 5, proceeded with the ratification of the Agreement.

According to article 6, the Agreement would enter into force 30 days after the date on which 40 States had established their consent to be bound, provided that such States included at least seven of the States referred to in paragraph 1 *(a)* of resolution II of the Third UN Conference on the Law of the Sea and that at least five of those States were developed States. Although 41 States had consented to be bound by the Agreement, the requirements of article 6 had not been met for the Agreement to enter into force. However, pending its entry into force, the Agreement was being applied provisionally by 125 States as at 31 December 1995.[1] Among the States entitled to apply the Agreement provisionally by virtue either of their consent to the adoption of the Agreement in the General Assembly or of their signature, 14 States had notified the Secretary-General that they did not wish to apply it provisionally. For those States, their consent to be bound by the Agreement was subject to ratification.

### Agreement on the conservation and management of straddling fish stocks and highly migratory fish stocks

Following consideration of a draft text at its fifth and sixth sessions (New York, 27 March–12 April and 24 July–4 August),[6] the United Nations Conference on Straddling Fish Stocks and Highly Migratory Fish Stocks, on 4 August, adopted the Agreement for the Implementation of the Provisions of the United Nations Convention on the Law of the Sea of 10 December 1982 relating to the Conservation and Management of Straddling Fish Stocks and Highly Migratory Fish Stocks.[7] The Agreement aimed at facilitating the implementation of the relevant provisions of the Convention relating to the conservation and management of straddling fish stocks and highly migratory fish stocks, as well as strengthening the cooperation of States for that purpose. Among other things, it established minimum international standards for the conservation and management of the two stocks; ensured that the conservation and management measures were adhered to and complied with, and were not undermined by those who fished for the stocks; and provided for peaceful settlement of disputes.

The Agreement, which was opened for signature in New York on 4 December 1995, had been signed by 29 States as at 31 December.[1]

**Report of the Secretary-General.** In response to General Assembly requests of 1993[8] and 1994,[9] the Secretary-General submitted in October the final report on the work of the Conference.[10] Annexed to his report were the text of the Agreement and guidelines for the application of precautionary reference points in conservation and management of straddling fish stocks and highly migratory fish stocks.

GENERAL ASSEMBLY ACTION

On 5 December, the General Assembly adopted **resolution 50/24.**

**Agreement for the Implementation of the Provisions of the United Nations Convention on the Law of the Sea of 10 December 1982 relating to the Conservation and Management of Straddling Fish Stocks and Highly Migratory Fish Stocks**

*The General Assembly,*

*Recalling* its resolutions 47/192 of 22 December 1992, 48/194 of 21 December 1993 and 49/121 of 19 December 1994, concerning the United Nations Conference on Straddling Fish Stocks and Highly Migratory Fish Stocks,

*Taking note* of resolutions I and II adopted by the Conference,

*Recognizing* the importance of the regular consideration and review of developments relating to the conservation and management of straddling fish stocks and highly migratory fish stocks,

*Taking note also* of the report of the Secretary-General of 12 October 1995 on the work of the Conference,

1. *Expresses its appreciation* to the United Nations Conference on Straddling Fish Stocks and Highly Migratory Fish Stocks for discharging its mandate under resolution 47/192 with the adoption of the Agreement for the Implementation of the Provisions of the United Nations Convention on the Law of the Sea of 10 December 1982 relating to the Conservation and Management of Straddling Fish Stocks and Highly Migratory Fish Stocks;

2. *Welcomes* the opening for signature of the Agreement on 4 December 1995;

3. *Emphasizes* the importance of the early entry into force and effective implementation of the Agreement;

4. *Calls upon* all States and the other entities referred to in article 1, paragraph 2 (*b*), of the Agreement that have not done so to sign and ratify or accede to it and to consider applying it provisionally;

5. *Requests* the Secretary-General to report to the General Assembly on developments relating to the conservation and management of straddling fish stocks and highly migratory fish stocks at its fifty-first session and biennially thereafter, taking into account information provided by States, relevant specialized agencies, in particular the Food and Agriculture Organization of the United Nations, and other appropriate organs, organizations and programmes of the United Nations system, regional and subregional organizations and arrangements for the conservation and management of straddling fish stocks and highly migratory fish stocks, as well as other relevant intergovernmental bodies and non-governmental organizations;

6. *Also requests* the Secretary-General to ensure that reporting on all major fisheries-related activities and instruments is effectively coordinated and duplication of activities and reporting minimized and that relevant scientific and technical studies are disseminated to the international community, and invites the relevant specialized agencies, including the Food and Agriculture Organization of the United Nations, as well as regional and subregional fisheries organizations and arrangements, to cooperate with the Secretary-General to that end;

7. *Decides* to include in the provisional agenda of its fifty-first session, under the item entitled "Law of the sea", a sub-item entitled "Agreement for the Implementation of the Provisions of the United Nations Convention on the Law of the Sea of 10 December 1982 relating to the Conservation and Management of Straddling Fish Stocks and Highly Migratory Fish Stocks".

General Assembly resolution 50/24

5 December 1995     Meeting 81     Adopted without vote

25-nation draft (A/50/L.35 & Add.1); agenda item 96 (c).
Meeting numbers. GA 50th session: plenary 80, 81.

## Other developments related to the Convention

In response to a 1994 General Assembly request,[11] the Secretary-General, submitted in November a report[12] covering developments relating to the law of the sea. The report consisted of two parts. The first part discussed developments relating to the implementation of the UN Convention on the Law of the Sea, reported on actions taken by States, the Secretary-General and relevant international organizations, and examined preparations for the establishment of the institutions created by the Convention and legal developments under related treaties and instruments. The second part dealt with other issues relating to the law of the sea and ocean affairs, including maritime disputes and conflicts, peace and security, crimes at sea, conservation and management of living marine resources, major policy and programme initiatives in marine environmental protection and sustainable resource development, marine safety and pollution prevention, marine science and technology and capacity-building in the law of the sea and ocean affairs.

The Secretary-General noted that the 1994 Agreement relating to the implementation of Part

XI of the Convention had successfully facilitated a wider acceptance of the Convention and, with the adoption of the 1995 Agreement for the Implementation of the Provisions of the UN Convention on the Law of the Sea of 10 December 1982 relating to the Conservation and Management of Straddling Fish Stocks and Highly Migratory Fish Stocks, there was new, concrete evidence of the international community's determination to strengthen the international legal order for the oceans. He described the activities of the UN Environment Programme, the relevant specialized agencies and the regional commissions under related instruments, involving in particular questions of conformity and consistency with the Convention. He also described action taken by States concerning maritime limits and legislation they had adopted or modified to comply with the Convention.

The Secretary-General stated that, in accordance with his obligation to draw up and maintain lists of conciliators and arbitrators for the conciliation and arbitration procedures, he had invited States to nominate conciliators and arbitrators. He had drawn to the attention of the relevant organizations their obligation to draw up lists of experts in the area of fisheries, protection and preservation of the marine environment, marine scientific research and navigation, including pollution from vessels and by dumping.

In anticipation of the establishment before 16 May 1996, under the Convention, of the 21-member Commission on the Limits of the Continental Shelf, comprising experts in geology, geophysics or hydrography, the Division for Ocean Affairs and the Law of the Sea, as the secretariat of the Commission, identified some of the issues to be addressed by the Commission when examining the submissions of coastal States, while a group of experts (New York, 11-14 September) focused on the functions and the scientific and technical needs of the Commission. The Secretary-General noted that the Division continued to develop a computer-generated information system on national legislation related to the law of the sea.

## Institutions created by the Convention

### International Seabed Authority

The Assembly of the International Seabed Authority, the latter established by the Convention with its seat in Jamaica, held in 1995 the second (Kingston, 27 February–17 March)[13] and third (Kingston, 7-18 August)[14] parts of its first session, the first part having been held in 1994.[15]

One of the earliest tasks of the Assembly was to elect the 36-member Council—the executive organ of the Assembly—comprising four groups representing in essence four sets of interests:

consumers/importers of the minerals that could be supplied from the deep seabed sources; investors in deep seabed mining; producers/exporters of such minerals from land-based sources and developing States representing special interests; and a group of 18 members elected according to the principle of ensuring an equitable geographical distribution of seats in the Council as a whole. Although substantial progress was made within each group and among the various groups, including among the five regions, and in spite of efforts by the President of the Assembly, the bureau and individual delegations, the Council could not be composed by the end of the Assembly's first session. Informal inter-sessional consultations by the President on this subject were held in New York from 6 to 8 December.

Other matters considered by the Assembly included the priorities of the Authority during its initial phase of work; recommendations of the Preparatory Commission for the International Seabed Authority and for the International Tribunal for the Law of the Sea; and follow-up of the Commission's decisions concerning registered pioneer investors. It was suggested that the Assembly consider the issue of transparency in the relationship between the Council and the wider membership of the Assembly, and the development of principles regarding environmental protection. The Assembly also discussed the training programme relating to seabed mining. The Secretariat informed the Assembly that it had received a number of reports from registered pioneer investors regarding the discharge of their obligations, including the provision of training. The Assembly set up an open-ended ad hoc working group to examine the draft Headquarters Agreement, which was to be used as a starting-point for negotiations with the Government of Jamaica. The Kingston Office for the Law of the Sea, which the Secretary-General had planned to abolish on 30 September, was continued as the interim secretariat of the Authority as from 1 October. The Assembly asked the Secretary-General to submit to the General Assembly in 1995, on behalf of the Authority, a draft budget concerning the Authority's administrative expenses for 1996. On the recommendation of its Credentials Committee, the Assembly decided that the Federal Republic of Yugoslavia (Serbia and Montenegro) should not participate at its first session.

The final report of the Preparatory Commission[16] on its work from 1983 to 1994 was presented to the Assembly by the Commission Chairman.

**Communication.** In response to the Assembly's decision not to allow Yugoslavia (Serbia and Montenegro) to participate in its first session, Yugoslavia, in a 25 August letter[17] to the Secretary-

General, stated that the decision had no legal basis in the Convention on the Law of the Sea and contravened the opinion of the UN Legal Counsel that the status of Yugoslavia as a party to the treaties was not affected by a 1992 General Assembly resolution.[18] Yugoslavia pointed out that it had fulfilled all the conditions for equitable participation in the work of the International Seabed Authority, its organs and, in particular, its Assembly.

### Financing of the Authority

As requested by the Assembly of the International Seabed Authority, the Secretary-General submitted to the General Assembly the Authority's programme of work and draft budget for 1996.[19] The total budget amounted to $2,656,800, consisting of $1,318,900 for conference servicing expenses and $1,337,900 for expenses of the secretariat (see PART SIX, Chapter II, for General Assembly action).

## International Tribunal for the Law of the Sea

The second[3] and third[4] meetings of States parties to the Convention continued to consider arrangements for the establishment of the International Tribunal for the Law of the Sea—the central institution for dispute settlement under the Convention.

The States parties, in May, decided that the members of the Tribunal would hold their first organizational session on 1 October 1996 and would meet for up to 12 weeks during the period of the budget to decide on the internal organization of the Tribunal. The President of the Tribunal would reside at the seat of the Tribunal; all other members would attend meetings as required. Members would be paid an annual allowance, a special allowance and a subsistence allowance, but overall remuneration would not exceed that of a judge of the International Court of Justice. As to the use of the official and working languages of the Tribunal and the use of other languages, the States parties decided, among other things, that the official languages were English and French. Conclusions were reached on the Registry and funding of the Tribunal and on the cost-effectiveness of its work. The States parties agreed that the judges should take up office in September 1996. They requested the Secretariat to submit a draft budget covering the initial period from 1 August 1996 to 31 December 1997, which the Secretariat did on 31 August.[20]

Regarding progress in the preparations for the site of the permanent headquarters of the Tribunal, Germany stated that construction would begin by the start of 1996 and be completed by the end of 1998. In the meantime, the Government would provide temporary buildings and interim equipment. Germany had offered in 1987 to establish the Tribunal in Hamburg. The meeting had before it the record of the work of the Preparatory Commission containing recommendations on practical arrangements for the establishment of the Tribunal.[21]

Following consideration of the draft initial budget of the Tribunal at the third meeting, the States parties requested the Secretariat to revise the draft budget for adoption at their next meeting and to revise its own budget to cover the costs of preparatory work to be carried out by the Secretary-General after the budget was adopted in March 1996 and before the judges were elected on 1 August 1996. The States parties conducted an article-by-article review of the draft protocol on the privileges and immunities of the Tribunal. A revised text was to be distributed in advance of the next meeting. It was agreed that the form of the instrument would be an agreement subject to signature and ratification and opened to all States. The meeting decided to reconvene in March 1996 to adopt the revised draft budget of the Tribunal and discuss related matters, in May to consider organizational matters and in July/August to elect the members of the Tribunal.

## Commission on the Limits of the Continental Shelf

With the entry into force of the Convention, another new institution, the Commission on the Limits of the Continental Shelf, was to be established. The functions of the Commission would be: to consider the data and other material submitted by coastal States concerning the outer limits of the continental shelf in areas where those limits extended beyond 200 miles, and to make recommendations in accordance with article 76 and the statement of understanding adopted by the Third UN Conference on the Law of the Sea concerning a specific method to be used in establishing the outer edge of the continental margin; and to provide scientific and technical advice, if requested by the coastal State concerned, during the preparation of such data. The members of the Commission were to be elected at a meeting of States parties convened by the Secretary-General. The Commission would consist of 21 members who were experts in the areas of geology, geophysics or hydrography, elected by States parties from among their nationals.

The third meeting of States parties agreed that the election of the members of the Commission would be postponed until March 1997, with the proviso that should any State which was a party to the Convention by 16 May 1996 be affected adversely in respect of its obligations under the Convention as a consequence of the postponement, States parties, at the request of such a State, would review the situation with a view to ameliorating the difficulty in respect of that obligation.

In an effort to ensure that the Commission upon its establishment had sufficient material and information and to facilitate an efficient commencement of its work, and without prejudice to the decisions of the Commission in that regard, the Division for Ocean Affairs and the Law of the Sea, as the secretariat of the Commission, identified some of the issues that would have to be addressed by the Commission when it began its examination of the submissions of coastal States.

**GENERAL ASSEMBLY ACTION**

On 5 December, the General Assembly adopted **resolution 50/23**.

### Law of the sea

*The General Assembly,*

*Emphasizing* the universal character of the United Nations Convention on the Law of the Sea and its fundamental importance for the maintenance and strengthening of international peace and security, as well as for the sustainable use and development of the seas and oceans and their resources,

*Considering* that, in its resolution 2749(XXV) of 17 December 1970, it proclaimed that the seabed and ocean floor, and the subsoil thereof, beyond the limits of national jurisdiction (hereinafter referred to as "the Area"), as well as the resources of the Area, are the common heritage of mankind, and considering also that the Convention, together with the Agreement relating to the implementation of Part XI of the United Nations Convention on the Law of the Sea of 10 December 1982, provides the regime to be applied to the Area and its resources,

*Recalling* its resolution 49/28 of 6 December 1994 on the law of the sea, adopted consequent to the entry into force of the Convention on 16 November 1994,

*Aware* of the importance of the effective implementation of the Convention and its uniform and consistent application, as well as of the growing need to promote and facilitate international cooperation on the law of the sea and ocean affairs at the global, regional and subregional levels,

*Conscious* of the strategic importance of the Convention as a framework for national, regional and global action in the marine sector, as recognized also by the United Nations Conference on Environment and Development in chapter 17 of Agenda 21,

*Recognizing* the impact on States of the entry into force of the Convention and the increasing need, particularly of developing States, for advice and assistance in its implementation in order to benefit thereunder,

*Noting* the responsibilities of the Secretary-General and competent international organizations under the Convention, in particular pursuant to its entry into force and as required by resolution 49/28,

*Reaffirming* the importance of the annual consideration and review by the General Assembly of the overall developments pertaining to the implementation of the Convention, as well as of other developments relating to the law of the sea and ocean affairs,

*Noting* the decisions taken by States parties to the Convention to convene meetings of States parties to deal with the initial budget and organizational and other related matters of the International Tribunal for the Law of the Sea in preparation for its establishment and the election of its members, as well as to prepare for and organize the election of the members of the Commission on the Limits of the Continental Shelf,

*Noting also* that the Assembly of the International Seabed Authority has concluded its first session and has scheduled two meetings of the Authority for 1996, from 11 March for up to three weeks, if necessary, and from 5 August for up to two weeks, in Kingston,

*Noting further* that the Assembly of the Authority requested arrangements for the interim secretariat of the Authority, authorizing the Secretary-General to administer the interim secretariat until the Secretary-General of the Authority is able to assume effectively the responsibility of the Authority's secretariat,

*Recalling* that the Agreement relating to the implementation of Part XI of the United Nations Convention on the Law of the Sea of 10 December 1982 provides that the institutions established by the Convention shall be cost-effective, and recalling also that the meeting of States parties to the Convention decided that this principle would apply to all aspects of the work of the Tribunal,

*Emphasizing* the importance of making adequate provisions for the efficient functioning of the institutions established by the Convention,

1. *Calls upon* all States that have not done so to become parties to the United Nations Convention on the Law of the Sea and to ratify, confirm formally or accede to the Agreement relating to the implementation of Part XI of the United Nations Convention on the Law of the Sea of 10 December 1982 in order to achieve the goal of universal participation;

2. *Calls upon* States to harmonize their national legislation with the provisions of the Convention and to ensure the consistent application of those provisions;

3. *Reaffirms* the unified character of the Convention;

4. *Recalls* its decision to fund the budget for the administrative expenses of the International Seabed Authority initially from the regular budget of the United Nations, in accordance with the provisions of the Agreement;

5. *Approves* the provision by the Secretary-General of such services as may be required for the two meetings of the Authority to be held in 1996, from 11 to 22 March and from 5 to 16 August;

6. *Approves also* the request of the Assembly of the Authority to continue the staff and facilities previously available to the Kingston Office for the Law of the Sea as the interim secretariat of the Authority, and authorizes the Secretary-General to administer the interim secretariat until the Secretary-General of the Authority is able to assume effectively the responsibility of the Authority's secretariat;

7. *Requests* the Secretary-General to convene the meetings of States parties to the Convention from 4 to

8 March, from 6 to 10 May and from 29 July to 2 August 1996;

8.  *Notes with appreciation* the progress made in practical arrangements for the establishment of the International Tribunal for the Law of the Sea and in preparations for the establishment of the Commission on the Limits of the Continental Shelf;

9.  *Expresses its appreciation* to the Secretary-General for the annual comprehensive report on the law of the sea and the activities of the Division for Ocean Affairs and the Law of the Sea of the Office of Legal Affairs of the Secretariat, in accordance with the provisions of the Convention and the mandate set forth in resolution 49/28;

10.  *Reaffirms* the importance of ensuring the uniform and consistent application of the Convention and a coordinated approach to its effective implementation, and of strengthening technical cooperation and financial assistance for this purpose, stresses once again the continuing importance of the Secretary-General's efforts to these ends, and reiterates its invitation to the competent international organizations and other international bodies to support these objectives;

11.  *Requests* the Secretary-General to ensure that the institutional capacity of the Organization adequately responds to the needs of States and competent international organizations by providing advice and assistance, taking into account the special needs of developing countries;

12.  *Invites* Member States and others in a position to do so to contribute to the further development of the fellowship programme on the law of the sea and training and educational activities on the law of the sea and ocean affairs established by the Assembly in its resolution 35/116 of 10 December 1980, and advisory services in support of effective implementation of the Convention;

13.  *Requests* the Secretary-General to report to the Assembly at its fifty-first session on the implementation of the present resolution, in connection with his annual comprehensive report on the law of the sea;

14.  *Decides* to include in the provisional agenda of its fifty-first session the item entitled "Law of the sea".

General Assembly resolution 50/23

5 December 1995     Meeting 81     132-1-3 (recorded vote)

52-nation draft (A/50/L.34 & Add.1); agenda item 39.
*Meeting numbers.* GA 50th session: plenary 80, 81.

Recorded vote in Assembly as follows:

*In favour:* Algeria, Andorra, Angola, Antigua and Barbuda, Argentina, Armenia, Australia, Austria, Bahrain, Bangladesh, Barbados, Belarus, Belgium, Belize, Benin, Bolivia, Botswana, Brazil, Brunei Darussalam, Bulgaria, Burkina Faso, Cambodia, Cameroon, Canada, Cape Verde, Chad, Chile, China, Costa Rica, Côte d'Ivoire, Cuba, Cyprus, Czech Republic, Denmark, Djibouti, Egypt, El Salvador, Eritrea, Ethiopia, Fiji, Finland, France, Georgia, Germany, Ghana, Greece, Grenada, Guatemala, Guinea, Guinea-Bissau, Guyana, Haiti, Honduras, Hungary, Iceland, India, Indonesia, Iran, Ireland, Israel, Italy, Jamaica, Japan, Jordan, Kazakstan, Kenya, Kuwait, Lao People's Democratic Republic, Latvia, Lebanon, Libyan Arab Jamahiriya, Liechtenstein, Lithuania, Luxembourg, Madagascar, Malawi, Malaysia, Maldives, Mali, Malta, Marshall Islands, Mauritania, Mauritius, Mexico, Micronesia, Monaco, Morocco, Myanmar, Namibia, Netherlands, New Zealand, Nigeria, Oman, Pakistan, Panama, Papua New Guinea, Paraguay, Philippines, Poland, Portugal, Qatar, Republic of Korea, Republic of Moldova, Romania, Russian Federation, Samoa, Saudi Arabia, Seychelles, Singapore, Slovakia, South Africa, Spain, Sri Lanka, Sudan, Suriname, Swaziland, Sweden, Thailand, the former Yugoslav Republic of Macedonia, Togo, Trinidad and Tobago, Tunisia, Ukraine, United Arab Emirates, United Kingdom, United Republic of Tanzania, United States, Uruguay, Viet Nam, Yemen, Zambia, Zimbabwe.

*Against:* Turkey.

*Abstaining:* Ecuador, Peru, Venezuela.

## Division for Ocean Affairs and the Law of the Sea

In 1995, in order to carry out the functions entrusted to the Secretary-General under the Convention and pursuant to a 1994 General Assembly request,[11] the Division for Ocean Affairs and the Law of the Sea of the Office of Legal Affairs established facilities for the deposit of charts and lists of geographical coordinates, including geodetic data, and adopted a system for their recording and publicity. It devised an internal computerized "data record" and began to prepare a "Maritime Zone Notification" (MZN) to inform States parties of the deposit of charts and geographical coordinates. The first MZN, dated 8 March 1995, concerned the deposit by Germany of the charts and geographical coordinates of its territorial sea and exclusive economic zone.

The Division brought to the attention of States parties its willingness to assist them with their "due publicity" obligations under the Convention. Coastal States were to give "due publicity" to all laws and regulations they might adopt on innocent passage through the territorial sea; States bordering straits, to all laws and regulations they might adopt relating to transit passage through straits used for international navigation; and coastal States, States bordering straits and archipelagic States, to the charts indicating the designation, prescription or substitution of sea lanes and traffic separation schemes in the territorial sea and in straits used for international navigation as well as of air routes above archipelagic sea lanes used for international overflight. The Division continued to develop a computer-generated information system on national legislation relating to the law of the sea. It completed a review of national legislative acts of more than 140 States and established an inventory of those acts. The pilot version of the computerized system was operational. The Division established contacts with the Food and Agriculture Organization of the United Nations (FAO) to develop a centralized system with integrated databases for providing coordinated information and advice on legislation and marine policy. Steps were taken to advance future cooperation, including electronic transmission of data between the Division and FAO, with a view to establishing similar links with other agencies and organizations. Through such links, a substantial increase in Division capabilities was expected in view of the implementation of the Convention and the adoption of the Agreement for the Implementation of the Provisions of the UN Convention on the Law of the Sea of 10 December 1982 relating to the Conservation and Management of Straddling Fish Stocks and Highly Migratory Fish Stocks. The Division established a list of focal points for law of the sea matters in a number of relevant international organizations.

A special contribution by the United Kingdom made it possible to award two fellowships under the Hamilton Shirley Amerasinghe Memorial Fellowship on the Law of the Sea—established in 1981[22] and presented annually in honour of the first President of the Third UN Conference on the Law of the Sea. The ninth annual award was granted to Maurice Kengne Kamgue, a diplomatic officer from Cameroon; Frank Elizabeth, a State Counsel of Seychelles, received the special award under the United Kingdom contribution.

REFERENCES

[1]*Multilateral Treaties Deposited with the Secretary-General: Status as at 31 December 1995* (ST/LEG/SER.E/14), Sales No. E.96.V.5. [2]YUN 1982, p. 178. [3]SPLOS/4 & Corr.1. [4]SPLOS/5. [5]YUN 1994, p. 1302, GA res. 48/263, annex, 28 July 1994. [6]A/CONF.164/29 & A/CONF.164/36. [7]A/CONF.164/37. [8]YUN 1993, p. 817, GA res. 48/194, 21 Dec. 1993. [9]YUN 1994, p. 948, GA res. 49/121, 19 Dec. 1994. [10]A/50/550. [11]YUN 1994, p. 1314, GA res. 49/28, 6 Dec. 1994. [12]A/50/713 & Corr.1. [13]ISBA/A/L.1/Rev.1 & Corr.1. [14]ISBA/A/L.7/Rev.1. [15]YUN 1994, p. 1313. [16]LOS/PCN/153 (vols. I-XIII). [17]A/50/385. [18]YUN 1992, p. 139, GA res. 47/1, 22 Sep. 1992. [19]A/C.5/50/28. [20]SPLOS/WP.1. [21]LOS/PCN/152 (vols. I-IV). [22]YUN 1981, p. 139.

Chapter V

# Other legal questions

In 1995, the United Nations continued its work on various aspects of international law and international economic law.

Meeting in February/March, the Special Committee on the Charter of the United Nations and on the Strengthening of the Role of the Organization discussed proposals for the maintenance of international peace and security and the peaceful settlement of disputes. It completed the final text of the UN Model Rules for the Conciliation of Disputes between States, which the General Assembly drew to the attention of States; they could be applied whenever a dispute could not be solved through direct negotiations. The Assembly, recognizing that substantial changes had taken place in the world and that therefore the "enemy State" clauses in Articles 53, 77 and 107 of the Charter had become obsolete, expressed its intention to amend the Charter by deleting those clauses.

The United Nations continued to deal with the increased use of sanctions by the Security Council, which sometimes had unintended effects on the target country's neighbours or major economic partners. The Secretary-General suggested the establishment of a mechanism to mitigate negative effects. The Assembly requested him to make certain arrangements in that regard and invited the UN system to address the special economic problems confronting those States.

The Committee on Relations with the Host Country addressed relations between the UN diplomatic community and the United States. Noting that the problem of diplomatic indebtedness was a matter of significant concern and that non-payment of undisputed debts tarnished the image of the Organization, the Assembly endorsed procedures proposed by the Committee for dealing with the issue.

Organized by the Secretary-General, the UN Congress on Public International Law was held in March 1995, focusing on the four main purposes of the UN Decade of International Law (1990-1999)—to promote acceptance of and respect for the principles of international law; to promote means and methods for the peaceful settlement of disputes between States, including resort to and full respect for the International Court of Justice; to encourage the progressive development of international law and its codification; and to encourage the teaching, study, dissemination and wider appreciation of international law—as well

as on new challenges and expectations for the next century.

A step in the progressive harmonization and unification of international trade law was the adoption by the Assembly of the UN Convention on Independent Guarantees and Stand-by Letters of Credit, prepared by the UN Commission on International Trade Law. The Working Group on International Contract Practices had devoted 11 sessions over five years to the drafting of the Convention.

## International organizations and international law

### Strengthening the role of the United Nations

#### Special Committee on the Charter

The Special Committee on the Charter of the United Nations and on the Strengthening of the Role of the Organization (New York, 27 February–10 March)[1] continued consideration of proposals for the maintenance of international peace and security and the strengthening of the role of the United Nations in that context, as requested by the General Assembly in 1994.[2]

The Committee also discussed the question of deleting the "enemy State" clauses in the Charter and completed its work on the draft UN Model Rules for the Conciliation of Disputes between States (see below).

In connection with the maintenance of international peace and security, the Special Committee had before it a revised working paper on implementation of the provisions of the Charter related to assistance to third States affected by the application of sanctions under Chapter VII of the Charter (see below) submitted by 21 States;[3] a working paper by the Russian Federation proposing new issues for consideration by the Committee;[4] a revised proposal by the Libyan Arab Jamahiriya for enhancing the effectiveness of the Security Council;[5] and a second revised working paper by Cuba on strengthening the role of the Organization and enhancement of its efficiency.[3]

In considering the question of the peaceful settlement of disputes between States, the Committee had before it the text of the draft UN Model Rules for the Conciliation of Disputes between States, as well as amendments by Guatemala to those Rules,[6] and a proposal by Sierra Leone on the establishment of a dispute settlement service to address disputes at an early stage.[3] The Special Committee completed its work on the draft Model Rules, which it submitted to the General Assembly for consideration (see below).

In accordance with the Assembly's 1994 request,[2] the Special Committee continued to review its membership. It had before it working papers by New Zealand[7] and by New Zealand and Uruguay[8] proposing that it be transformed into an open-ended subsidiary organ of the Assembly to ensure the participation of all Member States in its work. The Special Committee recommended to the Assembly that its membership be opened to all Member States and that it continue to operate by consensus.

### Deletion of the "enemy State" clauses

In accordance with a 1994 General Assembly request,[2] the Special Committee's Working Group of the Whole discussed, between 7 and 10 March, the deletion of the "enemy State" clauses in Articles 53, 77 and 107 of the Charter. Some delegations considered that the amendment procedure should be undertaken as an integral part of the broad process of reforms to the Charter being examined by the Assembly. The Special Committee recommended a draft resolution, by which the Assembly, recognizing that in view of the substantial changes that had taken place in the world the "enemy State" clauses of the Charter had become obsolete, would express its intention to initiate the procedure set out in Article 108 to amend the Charter to that effect at its earliest appropriate future session.

In a 29 November letter[9] to the Secretary-General, the Democratic People's Republic of Korea stated that the deletion of the "enemy State" clauses should not be viewed from a time perspective and, as long as past crimes remained unsettled, the clauses could not be considered obsolete.

**GENERAL ASSEMBLY ACTION**

On 11 December, the General Assembly adopted **resolution 50/52**.

**Report of the Special Committee on the Charter of the United Nations and on the Strengthening of the Role of the Organization**
*The General Assembly,*
*Recalling* its resolution 3499(XXX) of 15 December 1975, by which it established the Special Committee on the Charter of the United Nations and on the Strengthening of the Role of the Organization, and its relevant resolutions adopted at subsequent sessions,

*Recalling also* its resolution 47/233 of 17 August 1993 on the revitalization of the work of the General Assembly,
*Recalling further* its resolution 47/62 of 11 December 1992 on the question of equitable representation on and increase in the membership of the Security Council,
*Bearing in mind* the provisions of its resolution 50/55 of 11 December 1995,
*Conscious* of the ongoing discussion in the open-ended working groups of the General Assembly dealing with the various aspects of the revitalization, strengthening and reform of the work of the United Nations,
*Welcoming* the report of the Open-ended Working Group on the Question of Equitable Representation on and Increase in the Membership of the Security Council and Other Matters Related to the Security Council,
*Bearing in mind* the reports of the Secretary-General on the work of the Organization submitted to the General Assembly at its thirty-seventh, thirty-ninth, fortieth, forty-first, forty-second, forty-third, forty-fourth, forty-fifth, forty-sixth, forty-seventh, forty-eighth, forty-ninth and fiftieth sessions, as well as the views and comments expressed on them by Member States,
*Recalling* the elements relevant to the work of the Special Committee contained in its resolution 47/120 B of 20 September 1993,
*Mindful* of the desirability for the Special Committee to carry out further work in the fields of the maintenance of international peace and security and the peaceful settlement of disputes between States,
*Recalling* its resolution 49/58 of 9 December 1994,
*Having considered* the report of the Special Committee on the work of its session held in 1995,
*Taking note* of the recommendation of the Special Committee on the most appropriate legal action to be taken on the question of the deletion of the "enemy State" clauses from Articles 53, 77 and 107 of the Charter of the United Nations,
*Recognizing* that, having regard to the substantial changes that have taken place in the world, the "enemy State" clauses in Articles 53, 77 and 107 of the Charter have become obsolete,
*Noting* that the States to which those clauses were directed are Members of the United Nations and represent a valuable asset in all the endeavours of the Organization,
*Taking into account* the complex process involved in amending the Charter,
1. *Takes note* of the report of the Special Committee on the Charter of the United Nations and on the Strengthening of the Role of the Organization;
2. *Decides* that the Special Committee will hold its next session from 21 February to 5 March 1996;
3. *Expresses its intention* to initiate the procedure set out in Article 108 of the Charter of the United Nations to amend the Charter, with prospective effect, by the deletion of the "enemy State" clauses from Articles 53, 77 and 107 at its earliest appropriate future session;
4. *Requests* the Special Committee, at its session in 1996, in accordance with the provisions of paragraph 5 below:
(a) To accord appropriate time for the consideration of all proposals concerning the question of the maintenance of international peace and security in all its aspects in order to strengthen the role of the United Nations and, in this context, to consider other proposals

relating to the maintenance of international peace and security already submitted or which might be submitted to the Special Committee at its session in 1996, including the proposal on the strengthening of the role of the Organization and enhancing its effectiveness and the revised proposal submitted with a view to enhancing the effectiveness of the Security Council in regard to the maintenance of international peace and security, and to consider recommending to the General Assembly the desired priorities for its further consideration;

*(b)* To continue to consider on a priority basis the question of the implementation of the provisions of the Charter related to assistance to third States affected by the application of sanctions under Chapter VII of the Charter, taking into consideration the report of the Secretary-General, the proposals presented on this subject, the debate on this question which took place in the Sixth Committee at the fiftieth session of the General Assembly and, in particular, the implementation of the provisions of its resolution 50/51 of 11 December 1995;

*(c)* To continue its work on the question of the peaceful settlement of disputes between States, and in this context to continue its consideration of proposals relating to the peaceful settlement of disputes between States, including the proposal on the establishment of a dispute settlement service offering or responding with its services early in disputes and those proposals relating to the enhancement of the role of the International Court of Justice;

*(d)* To continue its consideration of the question of the enhancement of cooperation between the United Nations and regional arrangements or agencies in the maintenance of international peace and security;

*(e)* To consider proposals concerning the Trusteeship Council;

*(f)* To consider the status of the *Repertory of Practice of United Nations Organs* and the *Repertoire of the Practice of the Security Council;*

5. *Decides* that the Special Committee shall henceforth be open to all States Members of the United Nations and that it will continue to operate on the basis of the practice of consensus;

6. *Decides also* that the Special Committee shall be authorized to accept the participation of observers of States other than States Members of the United Nations which are members of the specialized agencies or of the International Atomic Energy Agency in its meetings, and further decides to invite intergovernmental organizations to participate in the debate in the plenary meetings of the Committee on specific items when it considers that such participation would assist in the work.

7. *Invites* the Special Committee at its session in 1996 to identify new subjects for consideration in its future work with a view to contributing to the revitalization of the work of the United Nations, and to discuss how to offer its assistance to the working groups of the General Assembly in this field;

8. *Requests* the Special Committee to submit a report on its work to the General Assembly at the fifty-first session;

9. *Decides* to include in the provisional agenda of its fifty-first session the item entitled "Report of the Special.Committee on the Charter of the United Nations and on the Strengthening of the Role of the Organization".

**General Assembly resolution 50/52**

11 December 1995    Meeting 87    155-0-3 (recorded vote)

Approved by Sixth Committee (A/50/642 & Corr.1) by recorded vote (122-0-6), 29 November (meeting 46); 9-nation draft (A/C.6/50/L.15); agenda item 145.

*Sponsors:* Argentina, Brazil, Bulgaria, Egypt, Finland, Japan, New Zealand, Philippines, Portugal.

*Meeting numbers.* GA 50th session: 6th Committee 31-37, 44, 46; plenary 87.

Recorded vote in Assembly as follows:

*In favour:* Afghanistan, Albania, Algeria, Andorra, Antigua and Barbuda, Argentina, Armenia, Australia, Austria, Azerbaijan, Bahrain, Bangladesh, Barbados, Belarus, Belgium, Belize, Benin, Bhutan, Bolivia, Bosnia and Herzegovina, Botswana, Brazil, Brunei Darussalam, Bulgaria, Burkina Faso, Cambodia, Cameroon, Canada, Cape Verde, Chad, Chile, China, Colombia, Congo, Côte d'Ivoire, Croatia, Cyprus, Czech Republic, Denmark, Djibouti, Dominica, Ecuador, Egypt, El Salvador, Eritrea, Estonia, Ethiopia, Fiji, Finland, France, Gabon, Georgia, Germany, Ghana, Greece, Grenada, Guatemala, Guinea, Guyana, Haiti, Honduras, Hungary, Iceland, India, Indonesia, Iran, Ireland, Israel, Italy, Jamaica, Japan, Jordan, Kazakstan, Kenya, Kuwait, Kyrgyzstan, Lao People's Democratic Republic, Latvia, Lebanon, Liechtenstein, Lithuania, Luxembourg, Madagascar, Malawi, Malaysia, Maldives, Mali, Malta, Marshall Islands, Mauritania, Mauritius, Mexico, Micronesia, Monaco, Mongolia, Morocco, Mozambique, Myanmar, Namibia, Nepal, Netherlands, New Zealand, Nicaragua, Niger, Nigeria, Norway, Oman, Pakistan, Panama, Papua New Guinea, Paraguay, Peru, Philippines, Poland, Portugal, Qatar, Republic of Korea, Republic of Moldova, Romania, Russian Federation, Samoa, Saudi Arabia, Senegal, Singapore, Slovakia, Slovenia, Solomon Islands, South Africa, Spain, Sri Lanka, Sudan, Suriname, Swaziland, Sweden, Syrian Arab Republic, Thailand, the former Yugoslav Republic of Macedonia, Togo, Trinidad and Tobago, Tunisia, Turkey, Uganda, Ukraine, United Arab Emirates, United Kingdom, United Republic of Tanzania, United States, Uruguay, Vanuatu, Venezuela, Viet Nam, Yemen, Zaire, Zambia, Zimbabwe.

*Against:* None.

*Abstaining:* Cuba, Democratic People's Republic of Korea, Libyan Arab Jamahiriya.

The Democratic People's Republic of Korea, which requested a recorded vote in the Sixth (Legal) Committee, stated that the text did not properly reflect the discussions and did not take into account its views or those of other delegations. Cuba said that its abstention was procedural, rather than a reservation to the text's substance; reflecting the views of the Democratic People's Republic of Korea would have reflected the negotiations more accurately. In the opinion of the Libyan Arab Jamahiriya, the resolution should be part of a general revision of the Charter that would take into account the changes that had taken place in the world and abolish the privileges that a small number of States continued to enjoy at the United Nations.

Italy said it was particularly gratified by the paragraphs regarding the long-overdue deletion of the "enemy State" clauses, which would close a sad chapter in modern history, allow the United Nations to make a fresh start and mark the beginning of the true equality of all its Members, as proclaimed in the Preamble to the Charter. Welcoming the adoption of the text, Japan noted that its position, as previously expressed, remained unchanged.

France expressed full support for the resolution and for deleting the "enemy State" clauses but did not favour changing the Special Committee's composition. Nevertheless, it had voted for the text since it stipulated that consensus would be used within the Committee for decision-making, a practice that had been followed at recent sessions and that was in keeping with the technical nature of an open-ended body.

## Model Rules for the Conciliation of Disputes

In considering the peaceful settlement of disputes between States, the Special Committee's Working Group continued its examination of the draft United Nations conciliation rules, proposed by Guatemala in 1993.[5] The Group completed its second reading of the draft UN Model Rules for the Conciliation of Disputes between States and recommended that the General Assembly bring them to the attention of Member States by annexing them to a decision or resolution.

### GENERAL ASSEMBLY ACTION

On 11 December, the General Assembly adopted **resolution 50/50**.

### United Nations Model Rules for the Conciliation of Disputes between States

*The General Assembly,*

*Considering* that conciliation is among the methods for the settlement of disputes between States enumerated by the Charter of the United Nations in Article 33, paragraph 1, that it has been provided for in numerous treaties, bilateral as well as multilateral, for the settlement of such disputes, and that it has proved its usefulness in practice,

*Convinced* that the establishment of model rules for the conciliation of disputes between States which incorporate the results of the most recent scholarly work and of experience in the field of international conciliation, as well as a number of innovations which can with advantage be made in the traditional practice in that area, can contribute to the development of harmonious relations between States,

1. *Commends* the Special Committee on the Charter of the United Nations and on the Strengthening of the Role of the Organization for having completed the final text of the United Nations Model Rules for the Conciliation of Disputes between States;

2. *Draws* to the attention of States the possibility of applying the Model Rules, the text of which is annexed hereto, whenever a dispute has arisen between States which it has not been possible to solve through direct negotiations;

3. *Requests* the Secretary-General, to the extent possible and in accordance with the relevant provisions of the Model Rules, to lend his assistance to the States resorting to conciliation on the basis of those Rules;

4. *Also requests* the Secretary-General to make the necessary arrangements to distribute to Governments the text of the present resolution, including the annex.

### ANNEX
#### United Nations Model Rules for the Conciliation of Disputes between States

Chapter I
Application of the rules

*Article 1*

1. These rules apply to the conciliation of disputes between States where those States have expressly agreed in writing to their application.

2. The States which agree to apply these rules may at any time, through mutual agreement, exclude or amend any of their provisions.

Chapter II
Initiation of the conciliation proceedings

*Article 2*

1. The conciliation proceedings shall begin as soon as the States concerned (henceforth: the parties) have agreed in writing to the application of the present rules, with or without amendments, as well as on a definition of the subject of the dispute, the number and emoluments of members of the conciliation commission, its seat and the maximum duration of the proceedings, as provided in article 24. If necessary, the agreement shall contain provisions concerning the language or languages in which the proceedings are to be conducted and the linguistic services required.

2. If the States cannot reach agreement on the definition of the subject of the dispute, they may by mutual agreement request the assistance of the Secretary-General of the United Nations to resolve the difficulty. They may also by mutual agreement request his assistance to resolve any other difficulty that they may encounter in reaching an agreement on the modalities of the conciliation proceedings.

Chapter III
Number and appointment of conciliators

*Article 3*

There may be three conciliators or five conciliators. In either case the conciliators shall form a commission.

*Article 4*

If the parties have agreed that three conciliators shall be appointed, each one of them shall appoint a conciliator, who may not be of its own nationality. The parties shall appoint by mutual agreement the third conciliator, who may not be of the nationality of any of the parties or of the other conciliators. The third conciliator shall act as president of the commission. If he is not appointed within two months of the appointment of the conciliators appointed individually by the parties, the third conciliator shall be appointed by the Government of a third State chosen by agreement between the parties or, if such agreement is not obtained within two months, by the President of the International Court of Justice. If the President is a national of one of the parties, the appointment shall be made by the Vice-President or the next member of the Court in order of seniority who is not a national of the parties. The third conciliator shall not reside habitually in the territory of the parties or be or have been in their service.

*Article 5*

1. If the parties have agreed that five conciliators should be appointed, each one of them shall appoint a conciliator who may be of its own nationality. The other three conciliators, one of whom shall be chosen with a view to his acting as president, shall be appointed by agreement between the parties from among nationals of third States and shall be of different nationalities. None of them shall reside habitually in the territory of the parties or be or have been in their service. None of them shall have the same nationality as that of the other two conciliators.

2. If the appointment of the conciliators whom the parties are to appoint jointly has not been effected within three months, they shall be appointed by the Government of a third State chosen by agreement between the parties or, if such an agreement is not reached within three months, by the President of the International Court of Justice. If the President is a national of one of the parties, the appointment shall be made by the Vice-President or the next judge in order of seniority who is not a national of the parties. The Government or member of the International Court of Justice making the appointment shall also decide which of the three conciliators shall act as president.

3. If, at the end of the three-month period referred to in the preceding paragraph, the parties have been able to appoint only one or two conciliators, the two conciliators or the conciliator still required shall be appointed in the manner described in the preceding paragraph. If the parties have not agreed that the conciliator or one of the two conciliators whom they have appointed shall act as president, the Government or member of the International Court of Justice appointing the two conciliators or the conciliator still required shall also decide which of the three conciliators shall act as president.

4. If, at the end of the three-month period referred to in paragraph 2 of this article, the parties have appointed three conciliators but have not been able to agree which of them shall act as president, the president shall be chosen in the manner described in that paragraph.

### Article 6

Vacancies which may occur in the commission as a result of death, resignation or any other cause shall be filled as soon as possible by the method established for appointing the members to be replaced.

### Chapter IV
### Fundamental principles

### Article 7

The commission, acting independently and impartially, shall endeavour to assist the parties in reaching an amicable settlement of the dispute. If no settlement is reached during the consideration of the dispute, the commission may draw up and submit appropriate recommendations to the parties for consideration.

### Chapter V
### Procedures and powers of the commission

### Article 8

The commission shall adopt its own procedure.

### Article 9

1. Before the commission begins its work, the parties shall designate their agents and shall communicate the names of such agents to the president of the commission. The president shall determine, in agreement with the parties, the date of the commission's first meeting, to which the members of the commission and the agents shall be invited.

2. The agents of the parties may be assisted before the commission by counsel and experts appointed by the parties.

3. Before the first meeting of the commission, its members may meet informally with the agents of the parties, if necessary, accompanied by the appointed counsel and experts to deal with administrative and procedural matters.

### Article 10

1. At its first meeting, the commission shall appoint a secretary.

2. The secretary of the commission shall not have the nationality of any of the parties, shall not reside habitually in their territory and shall not be or have been in the service of any of them. He may be a United Nations official if the parties agree with the Secretary-General on the conditions under which the official will exercise these functions.

### Article 11

1. As soon as the information provided by the parties so permits, the commission, having regard, in particular, to the time-limit laid down in article 24, shall decide in consultation with the parties whether the parties should be invited to submit written pleadings and, if so, in what order and within what time-limits, as well as the dates when, if necessary, the agents and counsel will be heard. The decisions taken by the commission in this regard may be amended at any later stage of the proceedings.

2. Subject to the provisions of article 20, paragraph 1, the commission shall not allow the agent or counsel of one party to attend a meeting without having also given the other party the opportunity to be represented at the same meeting.

### Article 12

The parties, acting in good faith, shall facilitate the commission's work and, in particular, shall provide it to the greatest possible extent with whatever documents, information and explanations may be relevant.

### Article 13

1. The commission may ask the parties for whatever relevant information or documents, as well as explanations, it deems necessary or useful. It may also make comments on the arguments advanced as well as the statements or proposals made by the parties.

2. The commission may accede to any request by a party that persons whose testimony it considers necessary or useful be heard, or that experts be consulted.

### Article 14

In cases where the parties disagree on issues of fact, the commission may use all means at its disposal, such as the joint expert advisers mentioned in article 15, or consultation with experts, to ascertain the facts.

### Article 15

The commission may propose to the parties that they jointly appoint expert advisers to assist it in the consideration of technical aspects of the dispute. If the proposal is accepted, its implementation shall be conditional upon the expert advisers being appointed by the parties by mutual agreement and accepted by the commission and upon the parties fixing their emoluments.

### Article 16

Each party may at any time, at its own initiative or at the initiative of the commission, make proposals for the settlement of the dispute. Any proposal made in accordance with this article shall be communicated immediately to the other party by the president, who may, in so doing, transmit any comment the commission may wish to make thereon.

*Article 17*

At any stage of the proceedings, the commission may, at its own initiative or at the initiative of one of the parties, draw the attention of the parties to any measures which in its opinion might be advisable or facilitate a settlement.

*Article 18*

The commission shall endeavour to take its decisions unanimously but, if unanimity proves impossible, it may take them by a majority of votes of its members. Abstentions are not allowed. Except in matters of procedure, the presence of all members shall be required in order for a decision to be valid.

*Article 19*

The commission may, at any time, ask the Secretary-General of the United Nations for advice or assistance with regard to the administrative or procedural aspects of its work.

### Chapter VI
#### Conclusion of the conciliation proceedings

*Article 20*

1. On concluding its consideration of the dispute, the commission may, if full settlement has not been reached, draw up and submit appropriate recommendations to the parties for consideration. To that end, it may hold an exchange of views with the agents of the parties, who may be heard jointly or separately.

2. The recommendations adopted by the commission shall be set forth in a report communicated by the president of the commission to the agents of the parties, with a request that the agents inform the commission, within a given period, whether the parties accept them. The president may include in the report the reasons which, in the commission's view, might prompt the parties to accept the recommendations submitted. The commission shall refrain from presenting in its report any final conclusions with regard to facts or from ruling formally on issues of law, unless the parties have jointly asked it to do so.

3. If the parties accept the recommendations submitted by the commission, a procès-verbal shall be drawn up setting forth the conditions of acceptance. The procès-verbal shall be signed by the president and the secretary. A copy thereof signed by the secretary shall be provided to each party. This shall conclude the proceedings.

4. Should the commission decide not to submit recommendations to the parties, its decision to that effect shall be recorded in a procès-verbal signed by the president and the secretary. A copy thereof signed by the secretary shall be provided to each party. This shall conclude the proceedings.

*Article 21*

1. The recommendations of the commission will be submitted to the parties for consideration in order to facilitate an amicable settlement of the dispute. The parties undertake to study them in good faith, carefully and objectively.

2. If one of the parties does not accept the recommendations and the other party does, it shall inform the latter, in writing, of the reasons why it could not accept them.

*Article 22*

1. If the recommendations are not accepted by both parties but the latter wish efforts to continue in order to reach agreement on different terms, the proceedings shall be resumed. Article 24 shall apply to the resumed proceedings, with the relevant time-limit, which the parties may, by mutual agreement, shorten or extend, running from the commission's first meeting after resumption of the proceedings.

2. If the recommendations are not accepted by both parties and the latter do not wish further efforts to be made to reach agreement on different terms, a procès-verbal signed by the president and the secretary of the commission shall be drawn up, omitting the proposed terms and indicating that the parties were unable to accept them and do not wish further efforts to be made to reach agreement on different terms. The proceedings shall be concluded when each party has received a copy of the procès-verbal signed by the secretary.

*Article 23*

Upon conclusion of the proceedings, the president of the commission shall, with the prior agreement of the parties, deliver the documents in the possession of the secretariat of the commission either to the Secretary-General of the United Nations or to another person or entity agreed upon by the parties. Without prejudice to the possible application of article 26, paragraph 2, the confidentiality of the documents shall be preserved.

*Article 24*

The commission shall conclude its work within the period agreed upon by the parties. Any extension of this period shall be agreed upon by the parties.

### Chapter VII
#### Confidentiality of the commission's work and documents

*Article 25*

1. The commission's meetings shall be closed. The parties and the members and expert advisers of the commission, the agents and counsel of the parties, and the secretary and the secretariat staff, shall maintain strictly the confidentiality of any documents or statements, or any communication concerning the progress of the proceedings unless their disclosure has been approved by both parties in advance.

2. Each party shall receive, through the secretary, certified copies of any minutes of the meetings at which it was represented.

3. Each party shall receive, through the secretary, certified copies of any documentary evidence received and of experts' reports, records of investigations and statements by witnesses.

*Article 26*

1. Except with regard to certified copies referred to in article 25, paragraph 3, the obligation to respect the confidentiality of the proceedings and of the deliberations shall remain in effect for the parties and for members of the commission, expert advisers and secretariat staff after the proceedings are concluded and shall extend to recommendations and proposals which have not been accepted.

2. Notwithstanding the foregoing, the parties may, upon conclusion of the proceedings and by mutual agreement, make available to the public all or some of the documents that in accordance with the preceding

paragraph are to remain confidential, or authorize the publication of all or some of those documents.

## Chapter VIII
### Obligation not to act in a manner which might have an adverse effect on the conciliation

*Article 27*

The parties shall refrain during the conciliation proceedings from any measure which might aggravate or widen the dispute. They shall, in particular, refrain from any measures which might have an adverse effect on the recommendations submitted by the commission, so long as those recommendations have not been explicitly rejected by either of the parties.

## Chapter IX
### Preservation of the legal position of the parties

*Article 28*

1. Except as the parties may otherwise agree, neither party shall be entitled in any other proceedings, whether in a court of law or before arbitrators or before any other body, entity or person, to invoke any views expressed or statements, admissions or proposals made by the other party in the conciliation proceedings, but not accepted, or the report of the commission, the recommendations submitted by the commission or any proposal made by the commission, unless agreed to by both parties.

2. Acceptance by a party of recommendations submitted by the commission in no way implies any admission by it of the considerations of law or of fact which may have inspired the recommendations.

## Chapter X
### Costs

*Article 29*

The costs of the conciliation proceedings and the emoluments of expert advisers appointed in accordance with article 15 shall be borne by the parties in equal shares.

General Assembly resolution 50/50

11 December 1995     Meeting 87     Adopted without vote

Approved by Sixth Committee (A/50/642 & Corr.1) by consensus, 29 November (meeting 46); 13-nation draft (A/C.6/50/L.11/Rev.1); agenda item 145.
*Meeting numbers.* GA 50th session: 6th Committee 31-37, 44, 46; plenary 87.

Introducing the draft resolution in the Sixth Committee, Guatemala said that the most eminent specialists in international law had participated in the formulation of the Model Rules, which incorporated most of the new elements included in the conciliation rules adopted by the Institute of International Law in 1961. Referring to the second preambular paragraph, it stated that the concept of experience referred to the provisions traditionally applied at the bilateral level, particularly those of the 1957 European Convention for the Peaceful Settlement of Disputes, and recalled that the very first treaty which had included provisions on conciliation had been concluded between France and Switzerland in 1925. The innovations referred to in the same paragraph were provisions proposed

by Guatemala, on whose initiative the Model Rules had been drawn up, and by the Special Committee.

## Application of sanctions under Chapter VII of the Charter

According to the Secretary-General's January 1995 "Supplement to an Agenda for Peace",[10] the Security Council's greatly increased use of sanctions under Article 41 of the Charter had brought to light a number of difficulties, including their unintended effects. There was also an urgent need to respond to the expectations raised by Article 50 of the Charter. The costs involved in the application of sanctions should be borne equitably by all Member States and not exclusively by the few who were neighbours or major economic partners of the target country. In "An Agenda for Peace",[11] the Secretary-General had recommended that the Security Council devise measures involving the international financial institutions and other components of the UN system to address the problems of States suffering collateral damage from sanctions regimes. The Council in turn invited him in 1992[12] to seek the views of the international financial institutions; in reply, they acknowledged the collateral effects of sanctions and expressed the desire to help countries in such situations, but proposed that that be done under existing mandates for the support of countries facing negative external shocks and consequent balance-of-payments difficulties.

Going beyond his 1992 recommendation, the Secretary-General suggested the establishment of a mechanism to address the problems related to sanctions, with the following functions: to assess the potential impact of sanctions on the target country and on third countries; to monitor the application of sanctions; to measure the effects of sanctions to enable the Council to fine-tune them with a view to maximizing their political impact and minimizing collateral damage; to ensure the delivery of humanitarian assistance to vulnerable groups; and to explore ways of assisting Member States suffering collateral damage and evaluate claims submitted by such States under Article 50. Such a mechanism would have to be located in the Secretariat and empowered to utilize the expertise of the United Nations system, in particular that of the Bretton Woods institutions (i.e., the World Bank Group and the International Monetary Fund).

The Secretary-General further explained that compensation to States affected by sanctions on their neighbours or economic partners would be possible only if the richer Member States recognized that such countries should not be expected to bear alone the costs resulting from action collectively decided on by the international community, and that such compensation was necessary to encourage them to cooperate in applying decisions taken by the Security Council. The sums involved would be large but had to be made available if the Council was to continue to rely on sanctions.

The Security Council, in a presidential statement of 22 February,[13] declared that it remained concerned that appropriate consideration was given to submissions from neighbouring or other States affected by special economic problems as a result of the imposition of sanctions. It urged the Secretary-General to reinforce those sections of the Secretariat dealing directly with sanctions to ensure that those matters were addressed in as effective, consistent and timely a manner as possible.

The Working Group of the Special Committee on the Charter considered the issue in 1995. The Committee invited the General Assembly to establish an open-ended working group of the Sixth Committee to consider the issue of the implementation of the Charter provisions related to assistance to third States affected by the application of sanctions under Chapter VII of the Charter, on the basis of the Secretary-General's report on the subject.

In that report,[14] submitted in August 1995 in response to a 1994 Assembly request,[2] the Secretary-General reviewed proposals and suggestions aimed at minimizing the effect of sanctions on third States and on the provision of assistance to those States. He suggested consultations of the Security Council with potentially affected States and assessment of the potential impact of sanctions on them, as well as monitoring the effect of sanctions. He noted that at the 1995 session of the Special Committee, the proposal was made to establish a permanent mechanism for that purpose. Also discussed were the possibility of establishing a time-frame for the application of sanctions, based on their objectives, as well as measures to ensure transparency of the procedures of the Council and the sanctions committees, and possible exemptions from sanctions regimes. The Secretary-General examined the establishment of guidelines for the consideration of applications for assistance, including the assessment of special economic problems faced by third States as a result of sanctions; the establishment of a trust fund for those States; economic assistance provided by international financial institutions as well as bilateral and other forms of assistance; and Secretariat arrangements to assist States and evaluate claims under Article 50. He reported that he had taken steps to reinforce the unit dealing with sanctions in the Department of Political Affairs and had enhanced cooperation and coordination with intergovernmental organizations to provide the sanctions committees and the Secretariat with customs advice and other needed expertise. However, further steps were needed to strengthen the Secretariat's analytical and assessment capability to gauge the effectiveness of sanctions and their collateral effects.

A first step in that direction would be the development of guidelines, prepared in cooperation with the donor community, UN agencies and the affected countries, containing such elements as an inventory of assistance measures used in the past and recommended for the future; designation of a forum for consultations to mobilize and channel resources; and monitoring, coordination and assessment arrangements. The guidelines should also include methodology for impact assessment to ensure a link between the two processes in the practical implementation of Article 50.

In September, the Secretary-General reported,[15] on economic assistance to States affected by sanctions against the Federal Republic of Yugoslavia (Serbia and Montenegro). The General Assembly, in **resolution 50/58 E**, reaffirmed the urgent need of a concerted response from the international community to deal in a more effective manner with the special economic problems of those States in view of their magnitude and the adverse impact of the sanctions on those States.

**GENERAL ASSEMBLY ACTION**

On 11 December, the General Assembly adopted **resolution 50/51**.

**Implementation of provisions of the Charter of the United Nations related to assistance to third States affected by the application of sanctions**

*The General Assembly,*

*Concerned* with the special economic problems confronting certain States arising from the carrying out of preventive or enforcement measures taken by the Security Council against other States, and taking into account the obligation of Members of the United Nations under Article 49 of the Charter of the United Nations to join in affording mutual assistance in carrying out the measures decided upon by the Security Council,

*Recalling* the right of third States confronted with special economic problems of that nature to consult the Security Council with regard to a solution to those problems, in accordance with Article 50 of the Charter,

*Recalling also* the 1994 and 1995 reports of the Special Committee on the Charter of the United Nations and on the Strengthening of the Role of the Organization containing sections on the consideration by the Committee of the proposals presented on the question of the implementation of the provisions of the Charter of the United Nations related to assistance to third States affected by the application of sanctions under Chapter VII of the Charter,

*Recalling further:*

(a) The report of the Secretary-General, entitled "An Agenda for Peace", in particular paragraph 41 thereof;

*(b)* Its resolutions 47/120 A of 18 December 1992, entitled "An Agenda for Peace: preventive diplomacy and related matters", and 47/120 B of 20 September 1993, entitled "An Agenda for Peace", in particular section IV thereof, entitled "Special economic problems arising from the implementation of preventive or enforcement measures";

*(c)* The position paper of the Secretary-General, entitled "Supplement to An Agenda for Peace";

*(d)* The statement of the President of the Security Council of 22 February 1995;

*(e)* The report of the Secretary-General prepared pursuant to the note by the President of the Security Council regarding the question of special economic problems of States as a result of sanctions imposed under Chapter VII of the Charter;

*(f)* The reports of the Secretary-General on "Economic assistance to States affected by the implementation of the Security Council resolutions imposing sanctions against the Federal Republic of Yugoslavia (Serbia and Montenegro)",

*Taking note* of the report of the Secretary-General on the implementation of the provisions of the Charter related to assistance to third States affected by the application of sanctions under Chapter VII of the Charter,

*Recalling* that the question of assistance to third States affected by the application of sanctions has been addressed recently in several forums, including the General Assembly and its subsidiary organs and the Security Council,

*Recalling also* the Security Council's intention expressed in the statement of the President of the Security Council of 16 December 1994 as part of the Council's effort to improve the flow of information and the exchange of ideas between members of the Council and other States Members of the United Nations that there should be increased recourse to open meetings, in particular at an early stage in its consideration of a subject,

*Stressing* that in the formulation of sanctions regimes, due account should be taken of the potential effects of sanctions on third States,

*Stressing also* in this context the powers of the Security Council under Chapter VII of the Charter and the Council's principal responsibility under Article 24 of the Charter for the maintenance of international peace and security in order to ensure prompt and effective action by the United Nations,

*Recalling further* that, under Article 31 of the Charter, any Member of the United Nations which is not a member of the Security Council may participate, without vote, in the discussion of any question brought before the Security Council whenever the latter considers that the interests of that Member are specially affected,

*Recognizing* that assistance to third States affected by the application of sanctions would further contribute to an effective and comprehensive approach by the international community to mandatory sanctions imposed by the Security Council,

*Recognizing also* the importance of taking into account in international mechanisms of cooperation and of economic and financial assistance special economic problems of States arising from the implementation of sanctions imposed under Chapter VII of the Charter,

1. *Underlines* the importance of consultations under Article 50 of the Charter of the United Nations, as early as possible, with third States which may be confronted with special economic problems arising from the carrying out of preventive or enforcement measures imposed by the Security Council under Chapter VII of the Charter and of early and regular assessments, as appropriate, of their impact on such States, and, for this purpose, invites the Security Council to consider appropriate ways and means for increasing the effectiveness of its working methods and procedures applied in the consideration of the requests by the affected countries for assistance, in the context of Article 50;

2. *Welcomes* the measures taken by the Security Council aimed at increasing the effectiveness and transparency of the sanctions committees, and strongly recommends that the Council continue its efforts further to enhance the functioning of those committees, to streamline their working procedures and to facilitate access to them by representatives of States which find themselves confronted with special economic problems arising from the carrying out of sanctions;

3. *Requests* the Secretary-General, within existing resources, to ensure that the Security Council and its sanctions committees are able to carry out their work expeditiously, and to make appropriate arrangements in the relevant parts of the Secretariat, in order to carry out, in a coordinated way, the following functions:

*(a)* To collate, assess and analyse information, at the request of the Security Council and its organs, on the effects of sanctions regimes in third States which are or may be specially affected by the implementations of sanctions and the resulting needs of such States, and keep the Security Council and its organs informed;

*(b)* To provide advice to the Security Council and its organs at their request on specific needs or problems of those third States and present possible options so that, while maintaining the effectiveness of the sanctions regimes, appropriate adjustments may be made to the administration of the regime or the regime itself with a view to mitigating the adverse effects on such States;

*(c)* To collate and coordinate information about international assistance available to third States affected by the implementations of sanctions and to make it officially available to the interested member States;

*(d)* To explore innovative and practical measures of assistance to the affected third States through cooperation with relevant institutions and organizations inside and outside the United Nations system;

4. *Also requests* the Secretary-General to report to the General Assembly, at its fifty-first session, on the implementation of paragraph 3 above and on possible guidelines which might be adopted on technical procedures to be used by the appropriate parts of the Secretariat:

*(a)* For providing better information and early assessments for the Security Council and its organs about the actual or potential effects of sanctions on third States which invoke Article 50 of the Charter;

*(b)* For developing a possible methodology for assessing the consequences actually incurred by third States as a result of the implementation of preventive or enforcement measures;

*(c)* For coordination of information about international economic or other assistance potentially available to those third States;

5. *Stresses* the important role of the General Assembly, the Economic and Social Council and the Committee for Programme and Coordination in mobilizing and monitoring, as appropriate, the economic assistance

efforts by the international community and the United Nations system to States confronted with special economic problems arising from the carrying out of preventive or enforcement measures imposed by the Security Council;

6.  *Invites* the organizations of the United Nations system, international financial institutions, other international organizations, regional organizations and Member States to continue to take into account and to address more specifically and directly, where appropriate, special economic problems of third States affected by sanctions imposed under Chapter VII of the Charter and, for this purpose, to consider ways and means for improving procedures for consultations in order to maintain a constructive dialogue with such States, including through regular and frequent meetings as well as, where appropriate, special meetings between the affected third States and the donor community, with the participation of United Nations agencies and other international organizations;

7.  *Requests* the Special Committee on the Charter of the United Nations and on the Strengthening of the Role of the Organization, at its session in 1996, to continue to consider on a priority basis the question of the implementation of the provisions of the Charter related to assistance to third States affected by the application of sanctions under Chapter VII of the Charter taking into consideration the report of the Secretary-General, the proposals presented on this subject, the debate on this question which took place in the Sixth Committee at the fiftieth session of the General Assembly and, in particular, the implementation of the provisions of the present resolution.

General Assembly resolution 50/51

11 December 1995      Meeting 87      Adopted without vote

Approved by Sixth Committee (A/50/642 & Corr.1) by consensus, 29 November (meeting 46); draft by Chairman of Working Group on Implementation of Charter Provisions (A/C.6/50/L.13); agenda item 145.
*Meeting numbers.* GA 50th session: 6th Committee 31-37, 44, 46; plenary 87.

## Host country relations

The Committee on Relations with the Host Country continued to consider aspects of relations between the UN diplomatic community and the United States, its host country, in response to a 1994 General Assembly request.[16] At five meetings between 16 March and 8 November 1995, it considered[17] the security of missions and the safety of their personnel; issues arising from the implementation of the 1947 Agreement between the United Nations and the United States of America regarding the Headquarters of the United Nations;[18] the responsibilities of permanent missions to the United Nations and their personnel, particularly in relation to financial indebtedness; matters related to the use of motor vehicles and parking; and membership, terms of reference and organization of the Committee's work.

### Security of missions and safety of their personnel

With regard to security matters, the Committee considered allegations by Cuba of systematic demonstrations by terrorist organizations in the vicinity of its Mission, which, Cuba said, disrupted its work and threatened its personnel. Referring to an August 1994 incident in front of its Mission,[19] Cuba stated that Mission personnel had rightly attempted to bar the entry of demonstrators trying to take over the Mission. Those identified Cuban Mission personnel, including one staff member of high rank, had been taken to the police station and the authorities attempted to charge them with violations, calling on them to renounce their diplomatic immunity. Cuba refused to accept such actions.

The United States noted that for many years it had responded to complaints by Cuba about protests in the vicinity of its Mission. When incidents occurred there in the presence of law-enforcement officers, arrests had been and would continue to be made. In other instances, the Cuban Mission had been requested to report incidents and file criminal complaints, but had failed to do so. As to the August 1994 incident, it would have been controlled if Cuban Mission personnel had not attacked the demonstrators and police officers alike. The demonstrators who had committed unlawful acts had been arrested, charged and prosecuted; three Cuban personnel had also been charged with assault, among other charges. Their actions had been unacceptable and therefore the United States had requested the Cuban Mission to waive their immunity or withdraw them. The United States was none the less prepared to entertain further discussions with the Cuban Mission on the matter. At meetings held in April and May 1995 at the respective missions, the United States stressed that it was prepared to cooperate fully with the Cuban Mission in finding additional ways to improve safety and security, as well as to consult on measures to prevent the recurrence of incidents such as the one of August 1994. To that end, it formulated various proposals for procedures to eliminate potential confrontations and conditions that could interfere with the conduct of Mission's functions. The proposals were set out in a note verbale to Cuba of 9 June.[20] At the same time, the United States reiterated that it would continue to uphold the constitutional rights of individuals to free speech and assembly, but when an individual took action which violated the law, it would take appropriate law-enforcement measures.

The Committee appreciated the efforts of the host country for the maintenance of conditions for the normal work of delegations accredited to the United Nations and anticipated that it would continue to take all measures to prevent any interference with the functioning of missions.

### Travel regulations

The Committee was informed that Cuba had asked the Chairman to intercede with the host country Mission regarding travel restrictions imposed by the United States on the Cuban delegation for its attendance at the San Francisco commemorative meetings of the signing of the Charter. The United States replied that the event was sponsored by the City of San Francisco and not the United Nations. The host country was not obligated to permit travel to events not sponsored by the Organization.

The Committee expressed the hope that remaining travel restrictions would be removed by the host country as soon as possible and noted the positions of affected Member States, of the Secretary-General and of the host country. It noted the measures taken to accelerate immigration and customs procedures for arriving diplomatic personnel in New York and urged the host country to continue to ensure the application of those procedures.

### Transportation

In the view of the Russian Federation, the situation regarding the issue of transportation was more difficult than ever. The host country was asked to explain what measures were being taken to solve the problem, particularly the question of parking and the problem of fines, which continued to be imposed because there were no inspection stickers on diplomatic automobiles. The United States responded that it had been informed that New York City was conducting a review of its traffic control policy. Latvia complained that two years after having bought a building for its Mission, no parking space had been allocated in front of the building. The Committee called on the host country to review measures and procedures relating to parking with a view to resolving the problem and responding to the growing needs of the diplomatic community in that regard.

### Financial indebtedness

For its consideration of the question of financial indebtedness of permanent missions to the United Nations, the Committee had before it a March 1995 report of the Secretary-General,[21] according to which the vast majority of the 184 missions of Member States in New York and their diplomats (over 1,800) honoured their obligations. However, total uncontested debts owed by missions, including their personnel, as at 31 January 1995 amounted to $7,013,735, of which $5,842,477, or 83 per cent, was attributable to 5 of the 32 missions with debts. In Geneva, of the 140 States represented, 28 owed debts ranging between 400 and 1.6 million Swiss francs (SwF). The total indebtedness amounted to more than SwF 5 million as at 1 February 1995.

The general conclusion was that the indebtedness resulted either from political and economic instability in the Member State concerned, or inadequate management of funds by a mission or its personnel. Remedies identified and discussed were the creation of an emergency fund, group health insurance programmes, short-term employment in the Secretariat and information programmes. However, the primary responsibility for mission debts lay solely with the Member States concerned. The United Nations had no legal liability in matters relating to the insolvency of missions or their personnel, but the Secretariat was prepared to help resolve individual cases of insolvency reported to the Organization through its good offices or mediation.

The Secretary-General made a number of recommendations for avoiding or reducing indebtedness, including the adoption of guidelines by the Committee. He suggested that, while work on the issue should continue within the Committee and its Working Group on Indebtedness, Member States might wish to consider discussing it in the Sixth Committee, in view of its importance to the diplomatic community as a whole.

On the basis of the Secretary-General's report, the open-ended Working Group on Indebtedness recommended procedures for dealing with the problem, which were endorsed by the Committee, as revised following consultations, and annexed to its report.[17]

The Committee stressed the importance of the efforts of its Working Group concerning financial indebtedness, an issue which tarnished the image of the United Nations and its Members. It noted that the issue had also arisen in other host cities to the United Nations and, therefore, required a system-wide approach. The Committee approved the proposals to address the issue and recommended that the General Assembly adopt them during its fiftieth session. It recommended that permanent missions, their personnel and Secretariat personnel adhere to the adopted recommendations, in particular that financial obligations be met promptly and in full. Its Working Group should continue to monitor progress and develop solutions to the problem.

The Committee recommended the following procedures to deal with the matter: a head of a mission who foresaw or was faced with the fact that funds would not suffice should notify the head of the mission of the host State and take appropriate action to avoid or minimize the risk of damage to third parties, including possible adjustments in the functioning of the mission; if information was provided that members of his/her staff did not fulfil their contractual obligations and incurred debts, he/she should ensure that the unpaid debts were settled promptly and in full; the mission of the host State should forward to the UN Office of Legal Affairs (OLA), on a regular basis, information about undisputed debts; and, in specific cases where debts of missions or individual diplomats had become egregious or had not been settled following bilateral contacts between the debtor and the representative of the host State, the mission of the host State might request that the Secretary-General take the necessary action to convey to the head of the mission concerned that there were legal and moral obligations to settle undisputed debts promptly and in full.

Based on information supplied by the host country mission, the Secretariat should keep the Committee informed of the numbers of missions with outstanding debts within specific ranges. The host countries might request the Secretariat to disseminate information which would be helpful to the diplomatic community in resolving the debt problems, including, *inter alia*, provision of relevant international legal instruments and UN documents, as well as information provided by the host countries on the cost of living at a location concerned, and the relevant provisions of national legislation. The Committee called to the attention of the Assembly the Secretary-General's intention to establish internal procedures requiring Secretariat staff members concerned to settle their undisputed debts in full and promptly.

## Other matters

Among other matters, China brought to the attention of the Committee its application, twice turned down by the host country, for relocation of its Mission. The United States replied that it had requested answers to a number of technical questions at the time of the first application. Responses to those questions had been provided and a second application submitted. Since the transaction was very complicated, it had notified the Chinese Mission that it was unable to agree to the transaction by the required deadline. The application, however, was still under active consideration.

GENERAL ASSEMBLY ACTION

On 11 December, the General Assembly adopted **resolution 50/49**.

### Report of the Committee on Relations with the Host Country

*The General Assembly,*

*Having considered* the report of the Committee on Relations with the Host Country,

*Recalling* Article 105 of the Charter of the United Nations, the Convention on the Privileges and Immunities of the United Nations and the Agreement between the United Nations and the United States of America regarding the Headquarters of the United Nations, and the responsibilities of the host country,

*Recognizing* that effective measures should continue to be taken by the competent authorities of the host coun-

try, in particular to prevent any acts violating the security of missions and the safety of their personnel,

*Noting* the spirit of cooperation and mutual understanding that has guided the deliberations of the Committee on issues affecting the United Nations community and the host country,

*Welcoming* the increased interest shown by Member States in participating in the work of the Committee,

1. *Endorses* the recommendations and conclusions of the Committee on Relations with the Host Country contained in paragraph 67 of its report;

2. *Considers* that the maintenance of appropriate conditions for the normal work of the delegations and the missions accredited to the United Nations is in the interests of the United Nations and all Member States, and expresses the hope that the host country will continue to take all measures necessary to prevent any interference with the functioning of missions;

3. *Expresses its appreciation* for the efforts made by the host country, and hopes that problems raised at the meetings of the Committee will continue to be resolved in a spirit of cooperation and in accordance with international law;

4. *Takes note with appreciation* of the report of the Secretary-General on the problem of diplomatic indebtedness, stresses that such indebtedness is a matter of significant concern to the United Nations and that nonpayment of undisputed debts reflects badly on the entire diplomatic community and tarnishes the image of the Organization itself, reaffirms that non-compliance with contractual obligations cannot be condoned or justified, and endorses the proposals and procedures on the issue of financial indebtedness set out in annex II to the current report of the Committee;

5. *Urges* the host country to consider lifting travel controls with regard to certain missions and staff members of the Secretariat of certain nationalities, and in this regard notes the positions of the affected States, of the Secretary-General and of the host country;

6. *Calls upon* the host country to review measures and procedures relating to the parking of diplomatic vehicles, with a view to responding to the growing needs of the diplomatic community, and to consult with the Committee on these issues;

7. *Requests* the Secretary-General to remain actively engaged in all aspects of the relations of the United Nations with the host country;

8. *Requests* the Committee to continue its work, in conformity with General Assembly resolution 2819(XXVI) of 15 December 1971;

9. *Decides* to include in the provisional agenda of its fifty-first session the item entitled "Report of the Committee on Relations with the Host Country".

General Assembly resolution 50/49

11 December 1995     Meeting 87     Adopted without vote

Approved by Sixth Committee (A/50/641) without vote, 22 November (meeting 44); 5-nation draft (A/C.6/50/L.8); agenda item 144.
Sponsors: Bulgaria, Canada, Costa Rica, Côte d'Ivoire, Cyprus.
Meeting numbers. GA 50th session: 6th Committee 42-45; plenary 87.

## UN Decade of International Law

In response to a 1994 General Assembly resolution,[22] the Secretary-General submitted an August 1995 report, with later addenda,[23] on the

United Nations Decade of International Law (1990-1999), which the Assembly had declared in 1989.[(24)] The Decade's aims were: to promote acceptance of and respect for the principles of international law; to promote means and methods for the peaceful settlement of disputes between States, including resort to and full respect for the International Court of Justice (ICJ); to encourage the progressive development of international law and its codification; and to encourage the teaching, study, dissemination and wider appreciation of international law. The Assembly had adopted the programme of activities for the third term (1995-1996) in 1994.[(22)]

In his report, the Secretary-General analysed information from States and international organizations on steps taken to implement the programme and views on possible activities for the next term. He described recent UN activities relevant to the progressive development of international law and its codification in such areas as human rights, disarmament, outer space, economic development, international trade, crime prevention and criminal justice, the environment and the law of the sea. The report also dealt with the work of the International Law Commission, the Special Committee on the Charter of the United Nations and on the Strengthening of the Role of the Organization, and the Sixth Committee.

**Sixth Committee action.** The Working Group on the UN Decade of International Law, re-established in 1994,[(25)] held five meetings between 6 and 21 November 1995. In an oral report to the Sixth Committee, the Chairman said that the Group had exchanged views on the implementation of the programme for the third term of the Decade and reviewed the draft resolution proposed, which contained traditional elements as well as new ones. A new element was paragraph 3, on the successful organization of the UN Congress on Public International Law (see below)—a unique event in UN history. Paragraph 11 had been the subject of some debate: some delegations had insisted that it was important to retain it, while others had doubts about its inclusion in a resolution on the Decade.

**GENERAL ASSEMBLY ACTION**

On 11 December, the General Assembly adopted **resolution 50/44**.

### United Nations Decade of International Law

*The General Assembly,*

*Recalling* its resolution 44/23 of 17 November 1989, by which it declared the period 1990-1999 the United Nations Decade of International Law,

*Recalling also* that the main purposes of the Decade, according to resolution 44/23, should be, *inter alia:*

(a) To promote acceptance of and respect for the principles of international law;

(b) To promote means and methods for the peaceful settlement of disputes between States, including resort to and full respect for the International Court of Justice;

(c) To encourage the progressive development of international law and its codification;

(d) To encourage the teaching, study, dissemination and wider appreciation of international law,

*Recalling further* its resolution 49/50 of 9 December 1994, to which was annexed the programme for the activities for the third term (1995-1996) of the Decade,

*Expressing its appreciation* to the Secretary-General for his report submitted pursuant to resolution 49/50,

*Having considered* the above-mentioned report,

*Recalling* that at the forty-fifth session of the General Assembly the Sixth Committee established the Working Group on the United Nations Decade of International Law with a view to preparing generally acceptable recommendations on the programme of activities for the Decade,

*Noting* that at the forty-sixth, forty-seventh, forty-eighth, forty-ninth and fiftieth sessions the Sixth Committee reconvened the Working Group to continue its work in accordance with resolutions 45/40 of 28 November 1990, 46/53 of 9 December 1991, 47/32 of 25 November 1992, 48/30 of 9 December 1993 and 49/50,

*Having considered* the oral report of the Chairman of the Working Group submitted to the Sixth Committee,

1. *Expresses its appreciation* for the work done on the United Nations Decade of International Law at the current session, and requests the Working Group of the Sixth Committee to continue its work at the fifty-first session in accordance with its mandate and methods of work;

2. *Also expresses its appreciation* to States and international organizations and institutions that have undertaken activities in implementation of the programme for the activities for the third term (1995-1996) of the Decade, including sponsoring conferences on various subjects of international law;

3. *Further expresses its appreciation* to the Secretary-General for the successful organization of the United Nations Congress on Public International Law, held from 13 to 17 March 1995, noting with satisfaction that the Congress emphasized the importance of all aspects of international law and focused on the four main purposes of the Decade, as well as on new challenges and expectations for the twenty-first century, and requests the Secretary-General, within existing resources, to make the proceedings widely available;

4. *Strongly welcomes* the recent advances made by the Treaty Section of the Office of Legal Affairs of the Secretariat in its programme of computerization of the *Multilateral Treaties Deposited with the Secretary-General* and the United Nations *Treaty Series* and looks forward to the early effective availability of the former on the Internet and the latter on-line to Member States and other users;

5. *Invites* all States and international organizations and institutions referred to in the programme to provide, update or supplement information on activities they have undertaken in implementation of it, as appropriate, to the Secretary-General, as well as to submit their views on possible activities for the next term of the Decade;

6. _Requests_ the Secretary-General to submit, on the basis of such information as well as of new information on the activities of the United Nations relevant to the progressive development of international law and its codification, a report to the General Assembly at its fifty-first session on the implementation of the programme;

7. _Encourages_ States to disseminate at the national level, as appropriate, information contained in the report of the Secretary-General;

8. _Appeals_ to States, international organizations and non-governmental organizations working in the field of international law and to the private sector to make financial contributions or contributions in kind for the purpose of facilitating the implementation of the programme;

9. _Encourages_ the Office of Legal Affairs to continue in its efforts to bring up to date the publication of the United Nations _Treaty Series_ and the _United Nations Juridical Yearbook;_

10. _Once again requests_ the Secretary-General to bring to the attention of States and international organizations and institutions working in the field of international law the programme annexed to resolution 49/50;

11. _Invites_ the International Committee of the Red Cross to continue to report on activities undertaken by the Committee and other relevant bodies with regard to the protection of the environment in times of armed conflict, so that the information received may be included in the report to be prepared pursuant to paragraph 6 above;

12. _Decides_ to include in the provisional agenda of its fifty-first session the item entitled "United Nations Decade of International Law".

General Assembly resolution 50/44

11 December 1995      Meeting 87      Adopted without vote

Approved by Sixth Committee (A/50/637) without vote, 24 November (meeting 45); draft by Chairman of Working Group on UN Decade of International Law (A/C.6/50/L.10); agenda item 140.
_Meeting numbers._ GA 50th session: 6th Committee 38-42, 45; plenary 87.

### UN Congress on Public International Law

The United Nations Congress on Public International Law (New York, 13-17 March), held in accordance with 1993[26] and 1994[22] General Assembly resolutions, was organized around the general theme "Towards the twenty-first century: international law as a language for international relations". Specific topics discussed were theoretical and practical aspects of the promotion and implementation of the principles of international law; means of peaceful settlement of disputes between States, including resort to and full respect for ICJ; new developments and priorities of the conceptual and practical aspects of the codification and progressive development of international law; new approaches to research, education and training in the field of international law and its wider appreciation; and new challenges and expectations.

### UN Programme for the teaching and study of international law

In response to a 1993 General Assembly request,[27] the Secretary-General submitted a November 1995 report[28] on the implementation of the UN Programme of Assistance in the Teaching, Study, Dissemination and Wider Appreciation of International Law during 1994-1995, within the framework of the UN Decade of International Law.

During that period, OLA carried out activities in the field of public international law, the law of the sea and ocean affairs, and international trade law. Two sessions of the Geneva International Law Seminar were held.

Activities of the UN Commission on International Trade Law (UNCITRAL) (see also below) included the Sixth UNCITRAL Symposium on International Trade Law (Vienna, 22-26 May 1995) and national seminars on international trade law in Armenia, Azerbaijan, Botswana, China, Colombia, the Czech Republic, Georgia, Kenya, Namibia, Panama, Turkey, Uzbekistan and Zimbabwe.

The UN Institute for Training and Research (UNITAR) provided training in environmental law and policy, in legal aspects of debt and financial management, in peacemaking and preventive diplomacy, in procedures for the settlement of trade disputes and in promotion of cooperation related to the environment. It also issued a number of publications, as did the United Nations Educational, Scientific and Cultural Organization, which also created a number of Chairs of human rights education in various countries.

Under the UN/UNITAR international law fellowship programme, 18 six-week fellowships financed by OLA were awarded for courses and seminars, partly organized by UNITAR, at the Hague Academy of International Law (Netherlands).

For 1996-1997, the Secretary-General recommended that the United Nations and other agencies continue their current activities under the Programme and expand them if new funds became available. New activities should be undertaken only if the overall level of appropriations or voluntary contributions made them possible. States should be encouraged to continue implementing the objectives related to the teaching, study, dissemination and wider appreciation of international law and report to the Secretary-General on any further developments in that area.

The Advisory Committee on the Programme held its twenty-ninth session on 13 December 1994 and its thirtieth on 26 October 1995. In 1994 it endorsed UNITAR's proposal to allow participation of observers in the international fellowship programme, on the understanding that the resources for candidates from developing States would remain unaffected.

GENERAL ASSEMBLY ACTION

On 11 December, the General Assembly adopted **resolution 50/43**.

## United Nations Programme of Assistance in the Teaching, Study, Dissemination and Wider Appreciation of International Law

*The General Assembly,*

*Recalling* paragraph 17 of its resolution 48/29 of 9 December 1993, paragraph 1 of section IV of the annex to its resolution 47/32 of 25 November 1992 and paragraph 1 of section IV of the annex to its resolution 49/50 of 9 December 1994,

*Taking note with appreciation* of the report of the Secretary-General on the implementation of the United Nations Programme of Assistance in the Teaching, Study, Dissemination and Wider Appreciation of International Law and the guidelines and recommendations on future implementation of the Programme within the framework of the United Nations Decade of International Law, which were adopted by the Advisory Committee on the Programme and are contained in section III of that report,

*Bearing in mind* that the encouragement of the teaching, study, dissemination and wider appreciation of international law is one of the main objectives of the United Nations Decade of International Law, as declared in its resolution 44/23 of 17 November 1989 and further reaffirmed and expanded in section IV of the programme for the activities for the first term (1990-1992), the second term (1993-1994) and the third term (1995-1996) annexed to resolutions 45/40 of 28 November 1990, 47/32 and 49/50,

*Considering* that international law should occupy an appropriate place in the teaching of legal disciplines at all universities,

*Noting with appreciation* the efforts made by States at the bilateral level to provide assistance in the teaching and study of international law,

*Convinced,* nevertheless, that States and international organizations and institutions should be encouraged to give further support to the Programme and increase their activities to promote the teaching, study, dissemination and wider appreciation of international law, in particular those activities which are of special benefit to persons from developing countries,

*Reaffirming* its resolutions 2464(XXIII) of 20 December 1968, 2550(XXIV) of 12 December 1969, 2838 (XXVI) of 18 December 1971, 3106(XXVIII) of 12 December 1973, 3502(XXX) of 15 December 1975, 32/146 of 16 December 1977, 36/108 of 10 December 1981 and 38/129 of 19 December 1983, in which it stated or recalled that in the conduct of the Programme it was desirable to use as far as possible the resources and facilities made available by Member States, international organizations and others, as well as its resolutions 34/144 of 17 December 1979, 40/66 of 11 December 1985, 42/148 of 7 December 1987, 44/28 of 4 December 1989, 46/50 of 9 December 1991 and 48/29, in which, in addition, it expressed or reaffirmed the hope that, in appointing lecturers for the seminars to be held within the framework of the fellowship programme in international law, account would be taken of the need to secure representation of major legal systems and balance among various geographical regions,

1. *Approves* the guidelines and recommendations contained in section III of the report of the Secretary-General and adopted by the Advisory Committee on the United Nations Programme of Assistance in the Teaching, Study, Dissemination and Wider Apprecia-

tion of International Law, in particular those designed to achieve the best possible results in the administration of the Programme within a policy of maximum financial restraint;

2. *Authorizes* the Secretary-General to carry out in 1996 and 1997 the activities specified in his report, including the provision of:

*(a)* A number of international law fellowships in both 1996 and 1997, to be determined in the light of the overall resources for the Programme and to be awarded at the request of Governments of developing countries;

*(b)* A minimum of one scholarship in both 1996 and 1997 under the Hamilton Shirley Amerasinghe Memorial Fellowship on the Law of the Sea, subject to the availability of new voluntary contributions made specifically to the fellowship fund;

*(c)* Subject to the overall resources for the Programme, assistance in the form of a travel grant for one participant from each developing country, who would be invited to possible regional courses to be organized in 1996 and 1997;

and to finance the above activities from provisions in the regular budget, when appropriate, as well as from voluntary financial contributions earmarked for each of the activities concerned, which would be received as a result of the requests set out in paragraphs 13, 14 and 15 below;

3. *Expresses its appreciation* to the Secretary-General for his constructive efforts to promote training and assistance in international law within the framework of the Programme in 1994 and 1995, in particular for the organization of the thirtieth and thirty-first sessions of the International Law Seminar, held at Geneva from 24 May to 10 June 1994 and from 22 May to 9 June 1995, respectively, and for the activities of the Office of Legal Affairs of the Secretariat related to the fellowship programme in international law and to the Hamilton Shirley Amerasinghe Memorial Fellowship on the Law of the Sea, carried out, respectively, through its Codification Division and its Division for Ocean Affairs and the Law of the Sea;

4. *Requests* the Secretary-General to consider the possibility of admitting, for participation in the various components of the Programme of Assistance, candidates from countries willing to bear the entire cost of such participation;

5. *Also requests* the Secretary-General to consider the relative advantages of using available resources and voluntary contributions for regional, subregional or national courses, as against courses organized within the United Nations system;

6. *Invites* interested States to consider the option of financing the translation and publication of the Judgments of the International Court of Justice;

7. *Welcomes* the efforts undertaken by the Office of Legal Affairs to bring up to date the United Nations *Treaty Series* and the *United Nations Juridical Yearbook;*

8. *Expresses its appreciation* to the United Nations Institute for Training and Research for its participation in the Programme through the activities described in the report of the Secretary-General;

9. *Also expresses its appreciation* to the United Nations Educational, Scientific and Cultural Organization for its participation in the Programme through the activities described in the report of the Secretary-General;

10. *Further expresses its appreciation* to the Hague Academy of International Law for the valuable contribution it continues to make to the Programme which has enabled candidates under the international law fellowship programme to attend and participate in the Programme in conjunction with the Academy courses;

11. *Notes with appreciation* the contributions of the Hague Academy of International Law to the teaching, study, dissemination and wider appreciation of international law, and calls on Member States and interested organizations to give favourable consideration to the appeal of the Academy for a continuation of support and a possible increase in their financial contributions, to enable the Academy to carry out its activities, particularly those relating to the summer courses, regional courses and programmes of the Centre for Studies and Research in International Law and International Relations;

12. *Urges* all States and relevant international organizations, whether regional or universal, to make all possible efforts to implement the goals and carry out the activities contemplated in section IV of the programme of activities for the third term (1995-1996) of the United Nations Decade of International Law, dealing with the encouragement of the teaching, study, dissemination and wider appreciation of international law and contained in the annex to its resolution 49/50;

13. *Requests* the Secretary-General to continue to publicize the Programme and periodically to invite Member States, universities, philanthropic foundations and other interested national and international institutions and organizations, as well as individuals, to make voluntary contributions towards the financing of the Programme or otherwise to assist in its implementation and possible expansion;

14. *Reiterates its request* to Member States and to interested organizations and individuals to make voluntary contributions, *inter alia*, for the International Law Seminar, for the fellowship programme in international law and for the Hamilton Shirley Amerasinghe Memorial Fellowship on the Law of the Sea, and expresses its appreciation to those Member States, institutions and individuals which have made voluntary contributions for this purpose;

15. *Urges* in particular all Governments to make voluntary contributions for the organization of regional refresher courses in international law by the United Nations Institute for Training and Research, especially with a view to covering the amount needed for the financing of the daily subsistence allowance for up to twenty-five participants in each regional course, thus alleviating the burden on prospective host countries and making it possible for the Institute to continue to organize the regional courses;

16. *Also requests* the Secretary-General to report to the General Assembly at its fifty-second session on the implementation of the Programme during 1996 and 1997 and, following consultations with the Advisory Committee on the United Nations Programme of Assistance in the Teaching, Study, Dissemination and Wider Appreciation of International Law, to submit recommendations regarding the execution of the Programme in subsequent years;

· 17. *Decides* to appoint twenty-five Member States, six from Africa, five from Asia, three from Eastern Europe, five from Latin America and the Caribbean and six from Western Europe and other States, as members of the Advisory Committee on the United Nations Programme of Assistance in the Teaching, Study, Dissemination and Wider Appreciation of International Law, for a period of four years beginning on 1 January 1996;

18. *Decides* to include in the provisional agenda of its fifty-second session the item entitled "United Nations Programme of Assistance in the Teaching, Study, Dissemination and Wider Appreciation of International Law".

General Assembly resolution 50/43

11 December 1995     Meeting 87     Adopted without vote

Approved by Sixth Committee (A/50/636) without vote, 24 November (meeting 45); draft by Ghana (A/C.6/50/L.9); agenda item 139.
*Meeting numbers.* GA 50th session: 6th Committee 41, 42, 45; plenary 87.

Introducing the text in the Sixth Committee, Ghana said that, given the Programme's usefulness, it was unfortunate that the Organization's financial difficulties prevented the Committee from recommending that the Assembly increase the budget appropriations and that the Programme had to depend on voluntary contributions. The Programme's various components had always been of importance to the developing countries, but a number of developed countries had also shown a growing interest in it.

## Convention on the Privileges and Immunities of the United Nations

In response to a 1994 General Assembly request,[29] the Secretary-General submitted in April 1995 to the Fifth (Administrative and Budgetary) Committee, a report[30] on the procedures in place for the implementation of article VIII, section 29, of the 1946 Convention on the Privileges and Immunities of the United Nations.[31] The report discussed provisions made by the United Nations for the settlement of disputes arising out of contracts or other disputes of a private law character, to which the United Nations was a party, and disputes involving any UN official who by reason of his position enjoyed immunity, if the immunity had not been waived by the Secretary-General. It examined, in particular, disputes arising out of commercial agreements (contracts and lease agreements); third-party claims for personal injury (outside the peace-keeping context); claims relating to UN peace-keeping operations; those related to operational activities for development; and other claims. The Secretary-General was of the view that the procedures and mechanisms described in the report provided an appropriate means of dispute resolution.

The report was presented under the agenda item on the review of the efficiency of the administrative and financial functioning of the United Nations. By **decision 49/489** of 20 July, the Assembly deferred until its fiftieth session consideration of the documents relating to that item. On 23

December, by **decision 50/469**, the Assembly decided that the Fifth Committee should continue consideration of the item at its resumed fiftieth session.

*REFERENCES*

(1)A/50/33. (2)YUN 1994, p. 1319, GA res. 49/58, 9 Dec. 1994. (3)Ibid., p. 1319. (4)Ibid., p. 1318. (5)YUN 1993, p. 1155. (6)A/AC.182/L.83. (7)A/AC.182/L.82. (8)A/AC.182/L.85. (9)A/50/803. (10)A/50/60-S/1995/1. (11)YUN 1992, p. 35. (12)Ibid., p. 38. (13)S/PRST/1995/9. (14)A/50/361. (15)A/50/423. (16)YUN 1994, p. 1322, GA res. 49/56, 9 Dec. 1994. (17)A/50/26. (18)YUN 1947-48, p. 199, GA res. 169(II), 31 Oct. 1947. (19)YUN 1994, p. 1321. (20)A/AC/154/281. (21)A/AC.154/277. (22)YUN 1994, p. 1323, GA res. 49/50, 9 Dec. 1994. (23)A/50/368 & Add.1-3. (24)GA res. 44/23, 17 Nov. 1989. (25)YUN 1994, p. 1323. (26)YUN 1993, p. 1159, GA res. 48/30, 9 Dec. 1993. (27)Ibid., p. 1162, GA res. 48/29, 9 Dec. 1993. (28)A/50/726. (29)YUN 1994, p. 1327, GA dec. 48/493 B, 29 July 1994. (30)A/C.5/49/65. (31)YUN 1946-47, p. 100, GA res. 22 A (I), annex, 13 Feb. 1946.

# International economic law

In 1995, legal aspects of international economic law continued to be considered by the United Nations Commission on International Trade Law and by the General Assembly's Sixth Committee.

## International trade law

### UNCITRAL

At its twenty-eighth session (Vienna, 2-26 May), UNCITRAL adopted the draft Convention on Independent Guarantees and Stand-by Letters of Credit, which it annexed to its report.(1) It completed its review of the substance of the draft Notes on international commercial arbitration and requested the Secretariat to prepare a revised draft of the Notes for final approval by the Commission in 1996. The Commission also discussed the draft UNCITRAL Model Law on Legal Aspects of Electronic Data Interchange and Related Means of Communication; receivables financing; case law on UNCITRAL texts (CLOUT); status and promotion of UNCITRAL legal texts; training and technical assistance; possible future work; and General Assembly resolutions on its work. The Commission noted publication of the bibliography of recent writings related to its work(2) and the publication of three additional sets of abstracts summarizing court decisions and arbitral awards in the context of CLOUT—the system for collecting and disseminating information on court decisions and arbitral awards relating to conventions and model laws emanating from UNCITRAL's work.

As in previous years, UNCITRAL's annual report was forwarded to the United Nations Con-

ference on Trade and Development for comments or recommendations.

### Travel assistance to UNCITRAL members from developing countries

In response to a 1994 General Assembly request,(3) the Secretary-General submitted a September 1995 report(4) on granting travel assistance to enable Commission members from developing countries to attend meetings of UNCITRAL and its working groups. The Secretary-General said he was responsible for the use of the Trust Fund established in 1994 to grant such assistance. The Fund would be administered, in accordance with its terms of reference, by the Legal Counsel as its programme manager. As at 1 September 1995, no contributions to the Fund had been received.

On 11 December, the General Assembly, in **resolution 50/47**, appealed for contributions to the Trust Fund and decided, in order to ensure full participation by all Member States in the Commission and its working groups, to continue consideration of the question in the competent Main Committee during its fiftieth session.

### Unification of trade law

#### Independent guarantees and stand-by letters of credit

In 1995, the Working Group on International Contract Practices held its twenty-third (New York, 9-20 January)(5) and twenty-fourth (Vienna, 13-24 November)(6) sessions. In January, it examined draft articles 7(2) to 16, 24, 25 and article 25 *bis*, Secretariat proposals on draft article 24 *bis* and new 25 *bis*, and draft articles 17 to 27 of a draft Convention on Independent Guarantees and Stand-by Letters of Credit. The Working Group approved the substance of those articles and referred them to its drafting group. The articles approved by the Working Group, following their review by the drafting group, were annexed to its report.(5) In response to concerns raised by the International Chamber of Commerce regarding the Working Group's decision to make available the draft Convention to cover commercial letters of credit, at the option of the parties, it was pointed out that the Working Group had arrived at the decision to deal with the issue in article 1(2), in a way that allowed parties to commercial letters of credit to opt into the Convention, but, absent such an election by parties, did not as such extend the Convention to cover commercial letters of credit.

UNCITRAL, at its 1995 session, considered the draft articles as presented by the Working Group. It also had before it a Secretariat note(7) on draft final clauses for the draft Convention. It submitted to the General Assembly the draft Convention as set forth in an annex to its report and recommended that the Assembly consider it with a view to concluding, at its fiftieth session, a UN Convention on Independent Guarantees and Stand-by Letters of Credit.

On 11 December, the General Assembly adopted **resolution 50/48**.

### United Nations Convention on Independent Guarantees and Stand-by Letters of Credit

*The General Assembly,*

*Recalling* its resolution 2205(XXI) of 17 December 1966, by which it created the United Nations Commission on International Trade Law with a mandate to further the progressive harmonization and unification of the law of international trade and in that respect to bear in mind the interests of all peoples, in particular those of developing countries, in the extensive development of international trade,

*Being aware* of the uncertainty and lack of uniformity currently prevailing among the various legal systems in the field of independent guarantees and stand-by letters of credit,

*Being convinced* that the adoption of a convention on independent guarantees and stand-by letters of credit will usefully contribute to overcoming the current uncertainties and disparities in this field of considerable practical importance and thus facilitate the use of such instruments,

*Being aware also* that the Commission, at its twenty-second session in 1989, decided to prepare uniform legislation on independent guarantees and stand-by letters of credit and entrusted the Working Group on International Contract Practices with the preparation of a draft,

*Noting* that the Working Group devoted eleven sessions, from 1990 to 1995, to the preparation of the draft United Nations Convention on Independent Guarantees and Stand-by Letters of Credit, and that all States and interested international organizations were invited to participate in the preparation of the draft Convention at all the sessions of the Working Group and at the twenty-eighth session of the Commission, either as members or observers, with a full opportunity to speak and make proposals,

*Taking note with satisfaction* of the decision of the Commission at its twenty-eighth session to submit the draft Convention to the General Assembly for its consideration,

*Taking note* of the draft Convention adopted by the Commission,

1. *Expresses its appreciation* to the United Nations Commission on International Trade Law for preparing the draft United Nations Convention on Independent Guarantees and Stand-by Letters of Credit;

2. *Adopts* and opens for signature or accession the United Nations Convention on Independent Guarantees and Stand-by Letters of Credit, contained in the annex to the present resolution;

3. *Calls upon* all Governments to consider becoming party to the Convention.

### ANNEX
### United Nations Convention on Independent Guarantees and Stand-by Letters of Credit

Chapter I.   Scope of application

*Article 1*
*Scope of application*

1.   This Convention applies to an international undertaking referred to in article 2:

*(a)*   If the place of business of the guarantor/issuer at which the undertaking is issued is in a Contracting State; or

*(b)*   If the rules of private international law lead to the application of the law of a Contracting State, unless the undertaking excludes the application of the Convention.

2.   This Convention applies also to an international letter of credit not falling within article 2 if it expressly states that it is subject to this Convention.

3.   The provisions of articles 21 and 22 apply to international undertakings referred to in article 2 independently of paragraph 1 of this article.

*Article 2*
*Undertaking*

1.   For the purposes of this Convention, an undertaking is an independent commitment, known in international practice as an independent guarantee or as a stand-by letter of credit, given by a bank or other institution or persons ("guarantor/issuer") to pay to the beneficiary a certain or determinable amount upon simple demand or upon demand accompanied by other documents, in conformity with the terms and any documentary conditions of the undertaking, indicating, or from which it is to be inferred, that payment is due because of a default in the performance of an obligation, or because of another contingency, or for money borrowed or advanced, or on account of any mature indebtedness undertaken by the principal/applicant or another person.

2.   The undertaking may be given:

*(a)*   At the request or on the instruction of the customer ("principal/applicant") of the guarantor/issuer;

*(b)*   On the instruction of another bank, institution or person ("instructing party") that acts at the request of the customer ("principal/ applicant") of that instructing party; or

*(c)*   On behalf of the guarantor/issuer itself.

3.   Payment may be stipulated in the undertaking to be made in any form, including:

*(a)*   Payment in a specified currency or unit of account;

*(b)*   Acceptance of a bill of exchange (draft);

*(c)*   Payment on a deferred basis;

*(d)*   Supply of a specified item of value.

4.   The undertaking may stipulate that the guarantor/issuer itself is the beneficiary when acting in favour of another person.

*Article 3*
*Independence of undertaking*

For the purposes of this Convention, an undertaking is independent where the guarantor/issuer's obligation to the beneficiary is not:

*(a)*   Dependent upon the existence or validity of any underlying transaction, or upon any other undertaking (including stand-by letters of credit or independent

guarantees to which confirmations or counter-guarantees relate); or

*(b)* Subject to any term or condition not appearing in the undertaking, or to any future, uncertain act or event except presentation of documents or another such act or event within a guarantor/issuer's sphere of operations.

### Article 4
#### Internationality of undertaking

1. An undertaking is international if the places of business, as specified in the undertaking, of any two of the following persons are in different States: guarantor/issuer, beneficiary, principal/applicant, instructing party, confirmer.

2. For the purposes of the preceding paragraph:

*(a)* If the undertaking lists more than one place of business for a given person, the relevant place of business is that which has the closest relationship to the undertaking;

*(b)* If the undertaking does not specify a place of business for a given person but specifies its habitual residence, that residence is relevant for determining the international character of the undertaking.

### Chapter II. Interpretation

### Article 5
#### Principles of interpretation

In the interpretation of this Convention, regard is to be had to its international character and to the need to promote uniformity in its application and the observance of good faith in the international practice of independent guarantees and stand-by letters of credit.

### Article 6
#### Definitions

For the purposes of this Convention and unless otherwise indicated in a provision of this Convention or required by the context:

*(a)* "Undertaking" includes "counter-guarantee" and "confirmation of an undertaking";

*(b)* "Guarantor/issuer" includes "counter-guarantor" and "confirmer";

*(c)* "Counter-guarantee" means an undertaking given to the guarantor/issuer of another undertaking by its instructing party and providing for payment upon simple demand or upon demand accompanied by other documents, in conformity with the terms and any documentary conditions of the undertaking, indicating, or from which it is to be inferred, that payment under that other undertaking has been demanded from, or made by, the person issuing that other undertaking;

*(d)* "Counter-guarantor" means the person issuing a counter-guarantee;

*(e)* "Confirmation" of an undertaking means an undertaking added to that of the guarantor/issuer, and authorized by the guarantor/issuer, providing the beneficiary with the option of demanding payment from the confirmer instead of from the guarantor/issuer, upon simple demand or upon demand accompanied by other documents, in conformity with the terms and any documentary conditions of the confirmed undertaking, without prejudice to the beneficiary's right to demand payment from the guarantor/issuer;

*(f)* "Confirmer" means the person adding a confirmation to an undertaking;

*(g)* "Document" means a communication made in a form that provides a complete record thereof.

### Chapter III. Form and content of undertaking

### Article 7
#### Issuance, form and irrevocability of undertaking

1. Issuance of an undertaking occurs when and where the undertaking leaves the sphere of control of the guarantor/issuer concerned.

2. An undertaking may be issued in any form which preserves a complete record of the text of the undertaking and provides authentication of its source by generally accepted means or by a procedure agreed upon by the guarantor/issuer and the beneficiary.

3. From the time of issuance of an undertaking, a demand for payment may be made in accordance with the terms and conditions of the undertaking, unless the undertaking stipulates a different time.

4. An undertaking is irrevocable upon issuance, unless it stipulates that it is revocable.

### Article 8
#### Amendment

1. An undertaking may not be amended except in the form stipulated in the undertaking or, failing such stipulation, in a form referred to in paragraph 2 of article 7.

2. Unless otherwise stipulated in the undertaking or elsewhere agreed by the guarantor/issuer and the beneficiary, an undertaking is amended upon issuance of the amendment if the amendment has previously been authorized by the beneficiary.

3. Unless otherwise stipulated in the undertaking or elsewhere agreed by the guarantor/issuer and the beneficiary, where any amendment has not previously been authorized by the beneficiary, the undertaking is amended only when the guarantor/issuer receives a notice of acceptance of the amendment by the beneficiary in a form referred to in paragraph 2 of article 7.

4. An amendment of an undertaking has no effect on the rights and obligations of the principal/applicant (or an instructing party) or of a confirmer of the undertaking unless such person consents to the amendment.

### Article 9
#### Transfer of beneficiary's right to demand payment

1. The beneficiary's right to demand payment may be transferred only if authorized in the undertaking, and only to the extent and in the manner authorized in the undertaking.

2. If an undertaking is designated as transferable without specifying whether or not the consent of the guarantor/issuer or another authorized person is required for the actual transfer, neither the guarantor/issuer nor any other authorized person is obliged to effect the transfer except to the extent and in the manner expressly consented to by it.

### Article 10
#### Assignment of records

1. Unless otherwise stipulated in the undertaking or elsewhere agreed by the guarantor/issuer and the beneficiary, the beneficiary may assign to another person any proceeds to which it may be, or may become, entitled under the undertaking.

2. If the guarantor/issuer or another person obliged to effect payment has received a notice originating from the beneficiary, in a form referred to in paragraph 2 of article 7, of the beneficiary's irrevocable assignment, payment to the assignee discharges the obligor, to the extent of its payment, from its liability under the undertaking.

### Article 11
### *Cessation of right to demand payment*

1. The right of the beneficiary to demand payment under the undertaking ceases when:

(*a*) The guarantor/issuer has received a statement by the beneficiary of release from liability in a form referred to in paragraph 2 of article 7;

(*b*) The beneficiary and the guarantor/issuer have agreed on the termination of the undertaking in the form stipulated in the undertaking or, failing such stipulation, in a form referred to in paragraph 2 of article 7;

(*c*) The amount available under the undertaking has been paid, unless the undertaking provides for the automatic renewal or for an automatic increase of the amount available or otherwise provides for continuation of the undertaking;

(*d*) The validity period of the undertaking expires in accordance with the provisions of article 12.

2. The undertaking may stipulate, or the guarantor/issuer and the beneficiary may agree elsewhere, that return of the document embodying the undertaking to the guarantor/issuer, or a procedure functionally equivalent to the return of the document in the case of the issuance of the undertaking in non-paper form, is required for the cessation of the right to demand payment, either alone or in conjunction with one of the events referred to in subparagraphs (*a*) and (*b*) of paragraph 1 of this article. However, in no case shall retention of any such document by the beneficiary after the right to demand payment ceases in accordance with subparagraph (*c*) or (*d*) of paragraph 1 of this article preserve any rights of the beneficiary under the undertaking.

### Article 12
### *Expiry*

The validity period of the undertaking expires:

(*a*) At the expiry date, which may be a specified calendar date or the last day of a fixed period of time stipulated in the undertaking, provided that, if the expiry date is not a business day at the place of business of the guarantor/issuer at which the undertaking is issued, or of another person or at another place stipulated in the undertaking for presentation of the demand for payment, expiry occurs on the first business day which follows;

(*b*) If expiry depends according to the undertaking on the occurrence of an act or event not within the guarantor/issuer's sphere of operations, when the guarantor/issuer is advised that the act or event has occurred by presentation of the document specified for that purpose in the undertaking or, if no such document is specified, of a certification by the beneficiary of the occurrence of the act or event;

(*c*) If the undertaking does not state an expiry date, or if the act or event on which expiry is stated to depend has not yet been established by presentation of the required document and an expiry date has not been stated in addition, when six years have elapsed from the date of issuance of the undertaking.

## Chapter IV.   Rights, obligations and defences

### Article 13
### *Determination of rights and obligations*

1. The rights and obligations of the guarantor/issuer and the beneficiary arising from the undertaking are determined by the terms and conditions set forth in the undertaking, including any rules, general conditions or usages specifically referred to therein, and by the provisions of this Convention.

2. In interpreting terms and conditions of the undertaking and in settling questions that are not addressed by the terms and conditions of the undertaking or by the provisions of this Convention, regard shall be had to generally accepted international rules and usages of independent guarantee or stand-by letter of credit practice.

### Article 14
### *Standard of conduct and liability of guarantor/issuer*

1. In discharging its obligations under the undertaking and this Convention, the guarantor/issuer shall act in good faith and exercise reasonable care having due regard to generally accepted standards of international practice of independent guarantees or stand-by letters of credit.

2. A guarantor/issuer may not be exempted from liability for its failure to act in good faith or for any grossly negligent conduct.

### Article 15
### *Demand*

1. Any demand for payment under the undertaking shall be made in a form referred to in paragraph 2 of article 7 and in conformity with the terms and conditions of the undertaking.

2. Unless otherwise stipulated in the undertaking, the demand and any certification or other document required by the undertaking shall be presented, within the time that a demand for payment may be made, to the guarantor/issuer at the place where the undertaking was issued.

3. The beneficiary, when demanding payment, is deemed to certify that the demand is not in bad faith and that none of the elements referred to in subparagraphs (*a*), (*b*) and (*c*) of paragraph 1 of article 19 are present.

### Article 16
### *Examination of demand and accompanying documents*

1. The guarantor/issuer shall examine the demand and any accompanying documents in accordance with the standard of conduct referred to in paragraph 1 of article 14. In determining whether documents are in facial conformity with the terms and conditions of the undertaking, and are consistent with one another, the guarantor/issuer shall have due regard to the applicable international standard of independent guarantee or stand-by letter of credit.

2. Unless otherwise stipulated in the undertaking or elsewhere agreed by the guarantor/issuer and the beneficiary, the guarantor/issuer shall have reasonable time, but not more than seven business days following the day of receipt of the demand and any accompanying documents, in which to:

(*a*) Examine the demand and any accompanying documents;

(*b*) Decide whether or not to pay;

*(c)* If the decision is not to pay, issue notice thereof to the beneficiary.

The notice referred to in subparagraph *(c)* above shall, unless otherwise stipulated in the undertaking or elsewhere agreed by the guarantor/issuer and the beneficiary, be made by teletransmission or, if that is not possible, by other expeditious means and indicate the reason for the decision not to pay.

### Article 17
### Payment

1. Subject to article 19, the guarantor/issuer shall pay against a demand made in accordance with the provisions of article 15. Following a determination that a demand for payment so conforms, payment shall be made promptly, unless the undertaking stipulates payment on a deferred basis, in which case payment shall be made at the stipulated time.

2. Any payment against a demand that is not in accordance with the provisions of article 15 does not prejudice the rights of the principal/applicant.

### Article 18
### Set-off

Unless otherwise stipulated in the undertaking or elsewhere agreed by the guarantor/issuer and the beneficiary, the guarantor/issuer may discharge the payment obligation under the undertaking by availing itself of a right of set-off, except with any claim assigned to it by the principal/applicant or the instructing party.

### Article 19
### Exception to payment obligation

1. If it is manifest and clear that:

*(a)* Any document is not genuine or has been falsified;

*(b)* No payment is due on the basis asserted in the demand and the supporting documents; or

*(c)* Judging by the type and purpose of the undertaking, the demand has no conceivable basis,

the guarantor/issuer, acting in good faith, has a right, as against the beneficiary, to withhold payment.

2. For the purposes of subparagraph *(c)* of paragraph 1 of this article, the following are types of situations in which a demand has no conceivable basis:

*(a)* The contingency or risk against which the undertaking was designed to secure the beneficiary has undoubtedly not materialized;

*(b)* The underlying obligation of the principal/applicant has been declared invalid by a court or arbitral tribunal, unless the undertaking indicates that such contingency falls within the risk to be covered by the undertaking;

*(c)* The underlying obligation has undoubtedly been fulfilled to the satisfaction of the beneficiary;

*(d)* Fulfilment of the underlying obligation has clearly been prevented by wilful misconduct of the beneficiary;

*(e)* In the case of a demand under a counter-guarantee, the beneficiary of the counter-guarantee has made payment in bad faith as guarantor/issuer of the undertaking to which the counter-guarantee relates.

3. In the circumstances set out in subparagraphs *(a)*, *(b)* and *(c)* of paragraph 1 of this article, the principal/applicant is entitled to provisional court measures in accordance with article 20.

## Chapter V.   Provisional court measures

### Article 20
### Provisional court measures

1. Where, on an application by the principal/applicant or the instructing party, it is shown that there is a high probability that, with regard to a demand made, or expected to be made, by the beneficiary, one of the circumstances referred to in subparagraphs *(a)*, *(b)* and *(c)* of paragraph 1 of article 19 is present, the court, on the basis of immediately available strong evidence, may:

*(a)* Issue a provisional order to the effect that the beneficiary does not receive payment, including an order that the guarantor/issuer hold the amount of the undertaking, or

*(b)* Issue a provisional order to the effect that the proceeds of the undertaking paid to the beneficiary are blocked, taking into account whether in the absence of such an order the principal/applicant would be likely to suffer serious harm.

2. The court, when issuing a provisional order referred to in paragraph 1 of this article, may require the person applying therefor to furnish such form of security as the court deems appropriate.

3. The court may not issue a provisional order of the kind referred to in paragraph 1 of this article based on any objection to payment other than those referred to in subparagraphs *(a)*, *(b)* and *(c)* of paragraph 1 of article 19, or use of the undertaking for a criminal purpose.

## Chapter VI.   Conflict of laws

### Article 21
### Choice of applicable law

The undertaking is governed by the law the choice of which is:

*(a)* Stipulated in the undertaking or demonstrated by the terms and conditions of the undertaking; or

*(b)* Agreed elsewhere by the guarantor/issuer and the beneficiary.

### Article 22
### Determination of applicable law

Failing a choice of law in accordance with article 21, the undertaking is governed by the law of the State where the guarantor/issuer has that place of business at which the undertaking was issued.

## Chapter VII.   Final clauses

### Article 23
### Depositary

The Secretary-General of the United Nations is the depositary of this Convention.

### Article 24
### Signature, ratification, acceptance, approval, accession

1. This Convention is open for signature by all States at the Headquarters of the United Nations, New York, until . . . [the date two years from the date of adoption].

2. This Convention is subject to ratification, acceptance or approval by the signatory States.

3. This Convention is open to accession by all States which are not signatory States as from the date it is open for signature.

4. Instruments of ratification, acceptance, approval and accession are to be deposited with the Secretary-General of the United Nations.

## Article 25
### Application to territorial units

1. If a State has two or more territorial units in which different systems of law are applicable in relation to the matters dealt with in this Convention, it may, at the time of signature, ratification, acceptance, approval or accession, declare that this Convention is to extend to all its territorial units or only one or more of them, and may at any time substitute another declaration for its earlier declaration.

2. These declarations are to state expressly the territorial units to which the Convention extends.

3. If, by virtue of a declaration under this article, this Convention does not extend to all territorial units of a State and the place of business of the guarantor/issuer or of the beneficiary is located in a territorial unit to which the Convention does not extend, this place of business is considered not to be in a Contracting State.

4. If a State makes no declaration under paragraph 1 of this article, the Convention is to extend to all territorial units of that State.

## Article 26
### Effect of declaration

1. Declarations made under article 25 at the time of signature are subject to confirmation upon ratification, acceptance or approval.

2. Declarations and confirmations of declarations are to be in writing and to be formally notified to the depositary.

3. A declaration takes effect simultaneously with the entry into force of this Convention in respect of the State concerned. However, a declaration of which the depositary receives formal notification after such entry into force takes effect on the first day of the month following the expiration of six months after the date of its receipt by the depositary.

4. Any State which makes a declaration under article 25 may withdraw it at any time by a formal notification in writing addressed to the depositary. Such withdrawal takes effect on the first day of the month following the expiration of six months after the date of the receipt of the notification of the depositary.

## Article 27
### Reservations

No reservations may be made to this Convention.

## Article 28
### Entry into force

1. This Convention enters into force on the first day of the month following the expiration of one year from the date of the deposit of the fifth instrument of ratification, acceptance, approval or accession.

2. For each State which becomes a Contracting State to this Convention after the date of the deposit of the fifth instrument of ratification, acceptance, approval or accession, this Convention enters into force on the first day of the month following the expiration of one year after the date of the deposit of the appropriate instrument on behalf of that State.

3. This Convention applies only to undertakings issued on or after the date when the Convention enters into force in respect of the Contracting State referred to in subparagraph (*a*) or the Contracting State referred to in subparagraph (*b*) of paragraph 1 of article 1.

## Article 29
### Denunciation

1. A Contracting State may denounce this Convention at any time by means of a notification in writing addressed to the depositary.

2. The denunciation takes effect on the first day of the month following the expiration of one year after the notification is received by the depositary. Where a longer period is specified in the notification, the denunciation takes effect upon the expiration of such longer period after the notification is received by the depositary.

DONE at . . . , this . . . day of . . . one thousand nine hundred and ninety- . . . , in a single original, of which the Arabic, Chinese, English, French, Russian and Spanish texts are equally authentic.

IN WITNESS WHEREOF the undersigned plenipotentiaries, being duly authorized by their respective Governments, have signed the present Convention.

**General Assembly resolution 50/48**

**11 December 1995    Meeting 87    Adopted without vote**

Approved by Sixth Committee (A/50/640 & Corr.1) without vote, 9 November (meeting 35); 23-nation draft (A/C.6/50/L.5); agenda item 143.
*Meeting numbers.* GA 50th session: 6th Committee 3-5, 35; plenary 87.

### Receivables financing

In response to a 1994 UNCITRAL request, the Secretary-General presented a report[8] on assignment in receivables financing, in follow-up to a 1994 report.[9] The report discussed the possible scope of future work on the subject and a number of assignment-related issues, including bulk assignment, future receivables, non-assignment clauses, transfer of security rights, form of assignment, relationship between the assignor and the assignee, and effects of assignment towards the debtor and towards third parties. It suggested some possible solutions to problems arising in the context of receivables financing and contained preliminary drafts of uniform rules to respond to the practical commercial need to utilize receivables to obtain financing. The report concluded that it would be both desirable and feasible to prepare uniform rules to remove obstacles to receivables financing arising from the uncertainty in various legal systems as to the validity of cross-border assignments—in which the assignor, the assignee and the debtor would not be in the same country—and the effects of such assignments on the debtor and other third parties. It suggested that the work of the Commission could take the form of a convention and that the topic and the draft uniform rules might be assigned to a working group for further work and development.

The Commission assigned the Secretary-General's report and the draft rules to a working group with a view to preparing a uniform draft law on assignment in receivables financing.

The Working Group on International Contract Practices, at its November session,[6] considered the draft uniform rules. Issues that should receive particular attention during future deliberations of the Working Group were suggested, including the question of international assignment of domestic receivables, with a view to providing adequate assurance of the protection of the debtor; the extent to which emphasis could be placed on finding solutions by way of substantive law, rather than through private international law rules; examination of the feasibility of relying on a registry approach; coverage of "conditional" and "possible" receivables; and compatibility of the draft uniform rules with national laws. The Working Group requested the Secretariat to prepare a revised version of the draft uniform rules for its 1996 session.

### International commercial arbitration

In 1995, UNCITRAL considered a March report[10] of the Secretary-General containing draft Notes on Organizing Arbitral Proceedings, which was a revised text of the draft Guidelines for Preparatory Conferences in Arbital Proceedings, presented to UNCITRAL in 1994.[11] The Notes were intended to assist arbitration practitioners by listing and briefly describing questions on which appropriately timed procedural decisions might be useful. They dealt with deposit for costs, a set of arbitration rules, language of proceedings, place of arbitration, administrative services, confidentiality of information, routing of writings among the parties and arbitrators, electronic means of sending writings, timing of written submissions, practical details concerning written submissions and evidence, defining points at issue, possible settlement negotiations and their effect on scheduling, documentary evidence, physical evidence other than documents, witnesses, hearings, multiparty arbitration and requirements concerning filing or delivering the award.

UNCITRAL reviewed the draft Notes and requested the Secretariat to prepare a revised draft for final approval by it in 1996. It considered that the Secretariat should continue to monitor the law and practice in the field of multi-party arbitration, and to present at a future session a document exploring the feasibility of work by the Commission in that field. Concerning the taking of evidence in arbitration, the Secretariat was requested to prepare a document to serve as a basis for consideration by the Commission.

### Electronic data interchange

At its 1995 session,[1] UNCITRAL had before it the report of the Working Group on Electronic Data Interchange (EDI) on its twenty-ninth session (New York, 27 February–10 March),[12] at which the Group considered the draft Guide to Enactment of the UNCITRAL Model Law on Legal Aspects of EDI and Related Means of Communication ("the draft Guide"). The Working Group requested the Secretariat to prepare a revised version of the draft Guide reflecting the decisions made by the Working Group and taking into account the issue of incorporation by reference. It also requested it to prepare a study on the issues of negotiability or transferability of rights in goods in an electronic environment, in the context of transport documents, with particular reference to maritime bills of lading.

Also before UNCITRAL was a compilation of comments by Governments and international organizations[13] on the text of the draft Model Law as approved by the Working Group in 1994.[11]

The Commission agreed that the title of the draft Model Law in general was too long and did not describe its content with sufficient clarity. However, it postponed its final decision as to the title and agreed to revert to the issue after it had completed its review of draft articles 1 and 2. The Commission adopted texts of articles 1 and 3 to 11 of the draft Model Law and agreed to continue discussing it together with the draft Guide at its 1996 session, with a view to finalizing and adopting them. It endorsed the recommendation of the Working Group that the Secretariat should prepare a background study on negotiability and transferability of EDI transport documents, with particular emphasis on EDI maritime transport documents. The Commission agreed that particular emphasis should be placed in the study on work undertaken by other international organizations, such as the Comité Maritime International (CMI) or the European Union, and on the BOLERO (bills of lading for Europe) project—a commercial venture on paperless bills of lading—and that the study should provide the basis for an informed decision as to the feasibility of undertaking work in the area.

As to the re-engineering process being carried out within the Economic Commission for Europe (ECE) with respect to the Working Party on Facilitation of International Trade Procedures (WP.4) of the Committee on the Development of Trade, UNCITRAL reaffirmed its support of the work accomplished by WP.4 in the technical field. It agreed to establish closer cooperation with the community of EDI users represented in WP.4, with a view to furthering the development of legal rules adapted to the technical environment. The Commission concluded that, in view of UNCITRAL's mandate, the proposals contained in the final engineering report, which was not adopted at the March 1995 session of WP.4, were not acceptable and requested the Secretariat to bring that conclusion to the attention of ECE. It was agreed that the matter should be brought to the attention of the General Assembly, with a recommendation that it reaffirm the role of UNCITRAL as the core legal body in international trade law.

## Carriage of goods by sea

UNCITRAL reiterated its concern about the problems resulting from the coexistence of different liability regimes relating to the carriage of goods by sea—the 1978 UN Convention on the Carriage of Goods by Sea (Hamburg Rules),[14] which entered into force in 1992, and the regime based on the 1924 International Convention for the Unification of Certain Rules relating to Bills of Lading (Hague Rules). The Commission noted that the Secretary-General had informed Member States of the Commission's consideration of the issue in 1994,[11] and of his conviction that the problems could best be overcome by wide adherence to the Hamburg Rules, recommending to them early adherence to those Rules.

The Commission was informed that CMI had received some 22 replies to a questionnaire it had sent to its member national organizations seeking views on how the problem could be solved; the replies suggested that no consensus view was emerging as to how the law of the carriage of goods by sea should be modernized and harmonized.

The Commission requested the Secretary-General to continue his efforts to promote wider adherence to the Hamburg Rules.

## Future programme of work

UNCITRAL continued to consider proposals for its possible future work, made at the UNCITRAL Congress on International Trade Law in 1992.[15] It had before it a March 1995 Secretariat note[16] suggesting possible areas in which the Commission could take up work with regard to build-operate-transfer (BOT) projects for which guidelines were being prepared by the United Nations Industrial Development Organization (UNIDO). It was suggested that the Commission take up work on BOT projects, in particular with regard to legal infrastructure and the means of procurement and contracting. Guidelines could be prepared to assist States in establishing a legal framework conducive to the implementation of BOT projects, with guidance for procurement and contracting. It was envisaged that UNCITRAL's work in those areas would not duplicate that already carried out by UNIDO. The Commission requested the Secretariat to prepare a report on the issues proposed for future work, with a view to facilitating discussion on the matter in 1996.

The Commission also considered a report[17] on the UNCITRAL/International Association of Insolvency Practitioners (INSOL) Judicial Colloquium on Cross-Border Insolvency (Toronto, Canada, 22-23 March). The purpose of the Colloquium was to obtain for UNCITRAL the views of judges and government officials concerned with insolvency legislation on judicial cooperation in cross-border insolvency cases, and the related topics of court access for foreign insolvency administrators and recognition of foreign insolvency proceedings. The Colloquium was designed to assist the Commission as it embarked on work on those aspects of cross-border insolvency. The Colloquium concluded that the development by UNCITRAL of a legislative text of limited scope (in the form of model statutory provisions facilitating judicial cooperation and access and recognition) was desirable in view of the increasing incidence of cross-border insolvency. It suggested that the Commission assign a working group to consider the views and information presented at the Colloquium and proposals regarding the form and content of the Commission's work.

The Commission assigned the development of a legislative framework for judicial cooperation and for access and recognition in cross-border insolvencies to a working group.

The Working Group on Insolvency Law commenced work on a legislative framework at its eighteenth session (Vienna, 30 October–10 November)[18] and made progress on a number of important issues, including the definitions of "foreign proceeding" and "foreign representative", the effects of recognition, judicial cooperation and proof of foreign proceedings. It identified several issues for future work and requested the Secretariat to prepare draft provisions on judicial cooperation and access and recognition.

The Commission noted that the Secretariat had agreed with Committee D of the International Bar Association to cooperate in monitoring the implementation in national laws of the 1958 Convention on the Recognition and Enforcement of Foreign Arbitral Awards.[19] The purpose of the project was to look into whether the Convention was incorporated into the national legal system of States so that its provisions had the force of law; whether States parties had added to the uniform regime of the Convention provisions modifying the conditions of recognition or enforcement of awards; and which requirements for obtaining recognition and enforcement not contemplated in the Convention were added in national laws. The Commission called on the States parties to the Convention to send to the Secretariat their laws dealing with the recognition and enforcement of foreign arbitral awards.

## Training and technical assistance

The Commission had before it a May 1995 Secretariat note[20] outlining training and technical assistance activities that had taken place since its 1994 session and indicating the direction of future activities. Twelve national seminars and briefing missions were held to explain the salient features and utility of international trade law instruments of UNCITRAL, as well as relevant texts prepared by other organizations. The Secretariat provided technical assistance to States preparing legislation based on UNCITRAL model laws in the areas of international commercial arbitration, procurement and international credit transfers. Many of the requests for assistance related to reviews of preparatory drafts of legislation, assistance in the preparation of drafts, comments on reports of law reform commissions, and briefings for legislators, judges, arbitrators and other end-users of UNCITRAL texts embodied in national legislation. The Secretariat agreed to co-sponsor a three-month postgraduate course on international trade law. In order to facilitate the provision of technical assistance, the Commission authorized the Secretariat to request States to provide it with legislation in effect in the areas of activity of the Commission. The Commission renewed its call for increased cooperation and coordination among entities providing technical assistance. Noting that voluntary funds to the UNCITRAL Trust Fund for Symposia remained insufficient, the Commission requested that the subject be placed on the agenda of the pledging conference taking place within the framework of the General Assembly session.

**GENERAL ASSEMBLY ACTION**

On 11 December, the General Assembly adopted **resolution 50/47**.

### Report of the United Nations Commission on International Trade Law on the work of its twenty-eighth session

*The General Assembly,*

*Recalling* its resolution 2205(XXI) of 17 December 1966, by which it created the United Nations Commission on International Trade Law with a mandate to further the progressive harmonization and unification of the law of international trade and in that respect to bear in mind the interests of all peoples, in particular those of developing countries, in the extensive development of international trade,

*Reaffirming its conviction* that the progressive harmonization and unification of international trade law, in reducing or removing legal obstacles to the flow of international trade, especially those affecting the developing countries, would significantly contribute to universal economic cooperation among all States on a basis of equality, equity and common interest and to the elimination of discrimination in international trade and thereby to the well-being of all peoples,

*Stressing* the value of participation by States at all levels of economic development and with different legal systems in the process of harmonizing and unifying international trade law,

. *Having considered* the report of the United Nations Commission on International Trade Law on the work of its twenty-eighth session,

*Mindful* of the valuable contribution to be rendered by the Commission within the framework of the United Nations Decade of International Law, particularly as regards the dissemination of international trade law,

*Concerned* about the relatively low incidence of expert representation from developing countries at sessions of the Commission and particularly of its working groups during recent years, owing in part to inadequate resources to finance the travel of such experts,

*Having considered* the report of the Secretary-General,

*Concerned also* about the fact that the need for and interest in the training and assistance programme of the Commission can only partially be met, in view of the limited human and financial resources available, and that the work of the Secretariat in the context of the Case-Law on the United Nations Commission on International Trade Law Texts would substantially increase as the number of the court decisions and arbitral awards covered thereby grows,

1. *Takes note with appreciation* of the report of the United Nations Commission on International Trade Law on the work of its twenty-eighth session;

2. *Notes with satisfaction* the completion and adoption by the Commission of the draft Convention on Independent Guarantees and Stand-by Letters of Credit;

3. *Commends* the Commission for the progress made at its twenty-eighth session in the preparation of a draft Model Law on Legal Aspects of Electronic Data Interchange and Related Means of Communication, as well as in the preparation of draft Notes on Organizing Arbitral Proceedings, and in this connection welcomes the decision of the Commission to continue its consideration of the draft Model Law and the draft Notes with a view to completing its work during its twenty-ninth session;

4. *Welcomes* the decision of the Commission to commence work on the subjects of receivables financing and cross-border insolvency, and to consider the feasibility and desirability of undertaking work on negotiability and transferability of electronic data interchange transport documents, based on a background study to be prepared by the Secretariat and on the discussion of the topic by the Working Group on Electronic Data Interchange at its thirtieth session;

5. *Reaffirms* the mandate of the Commission, as the core legal body within the United Nations system in the field of international trade law, to coordinate legal activities in this field in order to avoid duplication of effort and to promote efficiency, consistency and coherence in the unification and harmonization of international trade law, and in this connection recommends that the Commission, through its secretariat, continue to maintain close cooperation with the other international organs and organizations, including regional organizations, active in the field of international trade law;

6. *Also reaffirms* the importance, in particular for developing countries, of the work of the Commission concerned with training and technical assistance in the field of international trade law, such as assistance in the preparation of national legislation based on legal texts of the Commission;

7. *Expresses* the desirability for increased efforts by the Commission in sponsoring seminars and symposia to provide such training and technical assistance, and in this connection:

*(a)* Expresses its appreciation to the Commission for organizing seminars and briefing missions in Armenia,

Azerbaijan, Botswana, China, Colombia, the Czech Republic, Georgia, Kenya, Namibia, Panama, Uzbekistan and Zimbabwe;

*(b)* Expresses its appreciation to the Governments whose contributions made it possible for the seminars and briefing missions to take place, and appeals to Governments, the relevant United Nations organs, organizations and institutions and individuals to make voluntary contributions to the United Nations Commission on International Trade Law Trust Fund for Symposia and, where appropriate, to the financing of special projects, and otherwise to assist the secretariat of the Commission in financing and organizing seminars and symposia, in particular in developing countries, and in the award of fellowships to candidates from developing countries to enable them to participate in such seminars and symposia;

*(c)* Appeals to the United Nations Development Programme and other bodies responsible for development assistance, such as the International Bank for Reconstruction and Development and the European Bank for Reconstruction and Development, as well as to Governments in their bilateral aid programmes, to support the training and technical assistance programme of the Commission and to cooperate and coordinate their activities with those of the Commission;

8. *Appeals* to Governments, the relevant United Nations organs, organizations and institutions and individuals, in order to ensure full participation by all Member States in the sessions of the Commission and its working groups, to make voluntary contributions to the Trust Fund for travel assistance to developing countries that are members of the Commission, at their request and in consultation with the Secretary-General;

9. *Decides*, in order to ensure full participation by all Member States in the sessions of the Commission and its working groups, to continue its consideration in the competent Main Committee during the fiftieth session of the General Assembly of granting travel assistance, within existing resources, to the least developed countries that are members of the Commission, at their request and in consultation with the Secretary-General;

10. *Requests* the Secretary-General to ensure that adequate resources are allocated for the effective implementation of the programmes of the Commission;

11. *Stresses* the importance of bringing into effect the conventions emanating from the work of the Commission for the global unification and harmonization of international trade law, and to this end urges States that have not yet done so to consider signing, ratifying or acceding to those conventions;

12. *Also requests* the Secretary-General to submit a report on the implementation of paragraph 9 above to the General Assembly at its fifty-first session.

General Assembly resolution 50/47

11 December 1995      Meeting 87      Adopted without vote

Approved by Sixth Committee (A/50/640 & Corr.1) without vote, 9 November (meeting 35); 46-nation draft (A/C.6/50/L.4); agenda item 143.
*Meeting numbers.* GA 50th session: 6th Committee 3-5, 35; plenary 87.

### REFERENCES

[1]A/50/17. [2]A/CN.9/417. [3]YUN 1994, p. 1330, GA res. 49/55, 9 Dec. 1994. [4]A/50/434. [5]A/CN.9/408. [6]A/CN.9/420. [7]A/CN.9/411. [8]A/CN.9/412. [9]YUN 1994, p. 1330. [10]A/CN.9/410. [11]YUN 1994, p. 1329. [12]A/CN.9/407. [13]A/CN.9/409 & Add.1-4. [14]YUN 1978, p. 955. [15]YUN 1992, p. 1012. [16]A/CN.9/414. [17]A/CN.9/413. [18]A/CN.9/419. [19]YUN 1958, p. 391. [20]A/CN.9/415.

PART SIX


Institutional, administrative
and budgetary questions

Chapter I

# Strengthening and restructuring of the UN system

In 1995, efforts to restructure and strengthen the United Nations continued, in order to improve the Organization's ability to meet the demands of the post-cold-war era and the challenges of the future. The General Assembly on 14 September established an Open-ended High-level Working Group to consider a wide range of subjects relating to the revitalization, strengthening and reform of the UN system.

Ongoing consultations on reform of intergovernmental machinery were held by the Open-ended Working Group on the Question of Equitable Representation on and Increase in the Membership of the Security Council and Other Matters Related to the Security Council. In addition, the importance of revitalizing and strengthening the role of the General Assembly was repeatedly stressed during the 1995 Assembly session. A more dynamic relationship among the main intergovernmental organs—the General Assembly, the Security Council and the Economic and Social Council—was, according to the Secretary-General, a crucial component of the larger reform process. Further restructuring measures were sought in the economic, social and related fields.

In 1995, steps were taken further to streamline Secretariat operations, strengthen accountability, tighten personnel and management standards, and eliminate waste and redundancy. While striving to improve the quality of service provided to Member States, the Secretary-General expressed his commitment to using the scarce financial resources available in the most efficient way and even reduce the budget further.

As activities and financial transactions of the Organization increased in number and complexity, the newly established UN Office of Internal Oversight Services assisted the Secretary-General in fulfilling responsibilities with regard to monitoring, internal audit, inspection, evaluation and investigation.

## Establishment of High-level Working Group

Following intensive consultations by T. P. Sreenivasan (India) on behalf of the General Assembly President, consensus was reached on the establishment of an Open-ended High-level Working Group of the Assembly, under the chairmanship of the President, to review studies and reports on subjects relating to the revitalization, strengthening and reform of the UN system. During the consultations, it was agreed that, given the complexity and high volume of documentation to be considered, a systematic gathering of information would begin as soon as possible and that the Working Group or its Bureau should meet for organizational purposes between September and December. The studies and reports to be used in the exercise, it was noted, encompassed many aspects in the political, economic, social and other fields; therefore, synthesizing and classifying that information would be a significant undertaking. Although the Working Group would commence its work during the Assembly's fiftieth session, the bulk of its substantive work would begin in 1996.

A transparent mechanism would be devised to facilitate contacts with the bureaus of other working groups already in existence—such as the Ad Hoc Open-ended Working Group on an Agenda for Development (see PART FOUR, Chapter I), the High-level Open-ended Working Group on the Financial Situation of the United Nations (see PART SIX, Chapter II), the Open-ended Working Group on the Question of Equitable Representation on and Increase in the Membership of the Security Council (see below), the Informal Open-ended Working Group on an Agenda for Peace (see PART ONE, Chapter I) and the Consultations on Prospective New Modalities for Financing Operational Activities for Development (see PART SIX, Chapter IV).

**GENERAL ASSEMBLY ACTION**

On 14 September, the General Assembly adopted **resolution 49/252**.

**Strengthening of the United Nations system**
*The General Assembly,*

*Recognizing* that the fiftieth anniversary of the United Nations is an occasion for re-examination and strengthening of the United Nations system, as the United Nations prepares for the challenges of the twenty-first century,

*Determined* to strengthen the role, capacity, effectiveness and efficiency of the United Nations system and thus improve its performance in order to realize the full potential of the Organization, in accordance with the principles and purposes of the Charter of the United

Nations, and to respond more effectively to the needs and aspirations of the Member States,

*Conscious* of the importance of a viable financial basis and adequate and predictable resources for the effective functioning of the United Nations system,

*Encouraged* by the ongoing efforts to improve the administration, management and performance of the United Nations system,

*Noting* that important work is already proceeding in the Ad Hoc Open-ended Working Group on an Agenda for Development, the High-level Open-ended Working Group on the Financial Situation of the United Nations, the Open-ended Working Group on the Question of Equitable Representation on and Increase in the Membership of the Security Council, the Informal Open-ended Working Group on An Agenda for Peace and the Consultations on Prospective New Modalities for Financing Operational Activities for Development, all of which report to the General Assembly,

*Noting also* that the Secretary-General and a number of United Nations bodies, as well as independent commissions, institutions, scholars and other experts, have studied the United Nations system and recommended a variety of measures designed to revitalize, strengthen and reform the United Nations system,

1. *Decides* to establish an open-ended high-level working group of the General Assembly, under the chairmanship of the President of the General Assembly and with two vice-chairmen to be elected by the working group, and that the group may establish, as necessary, sub-groups open to the participation of all Member States;

2. *Decides also* that the working group will undertake a thorough review of the studies and reports of the relevant United Nations bodies and submissions of Member States and observers, as well as studies and reports of independent commissions, non-governmental organizations, institutions, scholars and other experts, on subjects relating to the revitalization, strengthening and reform of the United Nations system, to be selected by the working group with the assistance of the Secretariat, and, without in any way duplicating or impeding the work of the other working groups referred to above, specify by consensus those ideas and proposals drawn therefrom that it concludes are appropriate for the purpose of revitalization, strengthening and reform of the United Nations system in fulfilment of the principles and purposes of the Charter of the United Nations;

3. *Requests* the bureau of the working group to maintain regular contacts with the bureaux of the working groups mentioned above;

4. *Requests* the working group to commence its substantive work during the fiftieth session of the General Assembly and submit a report on its work before the end of that session;

5. *Requests* the Secretary-General to provide, within existing resources, to be supplemented by a trust fund to which voluntary contributions could be solicited, full assistance to the working group, including the facilities and support services necessary for it to conduct its work;

6. *Decides* to include in the provisional agenda of its fiftieth session an item entitled ''Strengthening of the United Nations system''.

General Assembly resolution 49/252

14 September 1995     Meeting 107     Adopted without vote

Draft by President (A/49/L.68); agenda item 10.
*Financial implications.* ACABQ, A/49/7/Add.14; 5th Committee, A/49/961; S-G, A/C.5/49/71.
*Meeting numbers.* GA 49th session: 5th Committee 67; plenary 107.

In accordance with the Assembly resolution, a compendium was prepared of material pertaining to the two specific areas which the Working Group decided to discuss after the orientation debate—the General Assembly and the Secretariat.

# Intergovernmental machinery

In his 1995 report on the work of the Organization,[1] the Secretary-General considered that the ongoing efforts to attain Secretariat reform had to be part of a larger restructuring effort that included the intergovernmental machinery. A more dynamic relationship among the main intergovernmental organs—the General Assembly, the Security Council and the Economic and Social Council—was a crucial component of that larger reform process, he stated.

## Revitalization of General Assembly

During the fiftieth (1995) General Assembly session and at its Special Commemorative Meeting on the occasion of the Organization's fiftieth anniversary, many Member States stressed the importance of strengthening the role of the Assembly. Revitalization of the Assembly was also on the agenda of the Open-ended High-level Working Group on the Strengthening of the United Nations System (see above).

The Secretary-General, in his 1995 report on the work of the Organization, underlined the need for improved Assembly procedures and working methods, citing both progress made and continuing challenges. He commended the increasing use of the informal, open-ended working group as an effective instrument in seeking solutions to major problems relating to the efficient working of the Organization, and the streamlining of the Assembly agenda through consolidation of related items and the decision to discuss some items every second or third year. In 1994, the Assembly had adopted[2] guidelines for rationalizing its agenda, as well as arrangements concerning the pattern of election of the Chairmen of its Main Committees, while deciding to take up the entire topic of revitalizing the Assembly again in 1997 and to review those arrangements in 1998.

The Secretary-General pointed to the possibility of further rationalizing the agenda through broadly-worded agenda items that allowed flexibility to examine several topics or aspects of a question under a single item. Areas where such a possibility could be explored were disarmament, cooperation between the UN and intergovernmental organizations, decolonization, and financing of peace-keeping operations. He also noted 10 items on the agenda had not been considered at all for several years.

Also of concern was the issue of the number of reports requested by the Assembly. In the Secretary-General's view, streamlining and cost-cutting could ultimately not succeed unless that number—more than 200 by the Secretary-General, in addition to those of principal organs and their subsidiary bodies, special rapporteurs and the Office of Internal Oversight Services (OIOS)—was significantly reduced. The difficulties and expense involved in producing so many reports in a timely manner were evident, the Secretary-General stated, given the frequency with which the Assembly and other principal and subsidiary organs were currently meeting.

## Rationalization of the
## work of the Fifth Committee

Within the framework of the review of the efficiency of the administrative and financial functioning of the United Nations (see below), the Fifth (Administrative and Budgetary) Committee in 1995 again considered rationalization of its work. Following informal consultations, the Committee Chairman submitted a draft resolution on the subject.[3] On 11 September, on a proposal by the Philippines on behalf of the States Members which were members of the Group of 77 developing countries and China, the Committee recommended[4] to the General Assembly that it defer consideration of the question to its fiftieth session. The Assembly did so on 14 September by **decision 49/498**.

In its October 1995 report[5] on management in the United Nations (see below, under "Internal oversight"), the Joint Inspection Unit (JIU) also dealt with the role of the Fifth Committee in helping to establish a new, stronger management culture in the Organization (see below). Aware of the intense work pressure faced by the Committee, as evidenced by a flood of documents and a formidable array of agenda items, JIU recommended that the Committee consider measures to help overcome the current weakness of UN management and performance reporting and make it more understandable, timely, action-oriented and focused (recommendation 3). Also, to fulfil more adequately its central role in the new accountability and responsibility system, the Committee might wish to consider reassessing systematically its workflows and annual calendar, and to establish subcommittees to divide tasks, enhance

specialization, and focus more clearly on major management and oversight issues and processes (recommendation 4). Those subcommittees should not prejudice the functions of existing bodies and organs elsewhere in the intergovernmental structure.

## Review of Security Council membership
## and related matters

In his annual report on the work of the Organization, the Secretary-General noted that the question of the enlargement of the Security Council had attracted intense interest, as a possible means of making UN work in the field of peace and security more efficient and democratic. The agenda item on an increase in Council membership was first considered by the General Assembly in 1979,[6] when it was introduced on the grounds that UN membership had by then grown to 152, compared to 116 in 1963, when the Assembly had amended Articles 23 and 27 of the Charter, enlarging the membership from 11 to 15 and raising the number of affirmative votes for a decision—including the concurring votes of the five permanent members—from seven to nine.[7] Both amendments came into force on 31 August 1965.

In 1995, the Open-ended Working Group on the Question of Equitable Representation on and Increase in the Membership of the Security Council and Other Matters Related to the Security Council, established by the Assembly in 1993,[8] held 11 formal meetings between 16 January and 15 September. The Group had before it a list of questions prepared by Finland and Thailand, as Vice-Chairmen, as well as a compilation of observations and views expressed during the 1994 Assembly session. The Group agreed to address two clusters of items[9]—equitable representation on and increase in the membership of the Council (cluster I), and other matters related to the Council (cluster II).

Between January and March 1995, the Working Group discussed those topics at nine formal meetings; between March and September, it held 21 informal consultations on the two clusters, as well as on the structure and content of its report. Based on discussions held between January and March, and taking into account Member States' views during the 1994 Assembly session, the Vice-Chairmen prepared two "non-papers" on clusters I and II, which were later updated. Together with other documents containing assessments of the progress of work, observations and proposals made by Argentina, Australia, Belgium (on behalf of a number of countries), Belize, Cuba, Indonesia, Italy, Mexico, Singapore, Turkey, the Movement of Non-Aligned Countries and the Nordic countries they were reproduced in a compendium transmitted by the Vice-Chairmen to the Assembly President in September.[(10)]

While expressing appreciation for the work of the two Vice-Chairmen, the Working Group stressed that the compendium had no legal status, did not constitute the Group's position or prejudice the position of any delegation, and should not form the sole input for the continuation of the Group's work, as a wide range of other views had been expressed and various proposals had been made.

The "non-papers" served as rolling documents of the Working Group and were intended to facilitate a full exchange of views on topics in the suggested list of questions. The items discussed under cluster I included: guiding principles for expanding the Council membership; size and composition of the permanent and non-permanent membership; new categories or types of membership, and qualifications of and modalities for selecting members of each of those categories; overall size of the expanded Council; voting procedure, including the question of the veto; and the question of periodic review. The items discussed under cluster II included: measures and practices adopted by the Council to enhance its transparency and working methods and their streamlining, expansion or possible institutionalization; retention, modification or finalization of the Council's provisional rules of procedure; briefings by the Council presidency; enhancement of mechanisms for information-gathering and analysis; wider consultation with concerned or interested parties; increased consultations between the Council and troop-contributing States (see also PART TWO, Chapter I); and relationship of the Council with other UN organs, including its reports to the Assembly.

The Group did not conclude its discussion but continued its review, bearing in mind the substantial increase in UN membership, especially of developing countries, as well as the important changes in international relations. As the Group noted in its conclusions, there was agreement to expand the Council and review its working methods and other matters related to its functioning in a way that would further strengthen its capacity and effectiveness, enhance its representative character and improve its efficiency.

It was recognized, the Group said, that the principles of sovereign equality of all UN Members, equitable geographical distribution, and contribution to the maintenance of international peace and security, as well as to the other purposes of the Organization, should guide the work on reform of the Council. The concepts of transparency, legitimacy, effectiveness and efficiency should also be taken into account, as well as, in the view of a large number of delegations, the concept of democracy.

Support was expressed for the proposals that the final agreement on items in clusters I and II comprise a comprehensive package; that work in the two clusters be allowed to proceed concurrently; and that progress in one cluster should not be impeded by lack of progress in the other. Some delegations noted that during the Group's course of work a number of measures had been implemented and practices developed to improve the Council's transparency and working methods. Discussions also showed, the Group noted, that important differences continued to exist on key issues, which required further in-depth consideration.

The General Assembly, by **decision 49/499** of 18 September, noted the Working Group's report[(9)] and decided that the Group should continue its work, taking into account the progress achieved during the forty-eighth (1993) and forty-ninth (1994) Assembly sessions and the views expressed during the 1995 session, including at the Special Commemorative Meeting on the occasion of the fiftieth anniversary of the United Nations. The Assembly decision had been recommended by the Working Group.

## Restructuring of the UN economic, social and related fields

The process of restructuring and revitalization of the economic, social and related fields of the United Nations, which began in 1991,[(11)] continued in 1995. The Secretary-General, in an October report,[(12)] provided information on measures being discussed and implemented, in response to a 1993 General Assembly resolution,[(13)] as well as on other issues related to restructuring and revitalization raised in intergovernmental discussions.

Among the measures under discussion were: creation of a separate Executive Board for the UN Population Fund (UNFPA) (see PART FOUR, Chapter VIII); arrangements relating to the Committee on Food Aid Policies and Programmes of the World Food Programme (see PART FOUR, Chapter XIII); and new modalities for funding operational activities for development (see PART SIX, Chapter IV). The report also provided an update on the experience of the Executive Boards of the UN Development Programme/UNFPA and of the United Nations Children's Fund.

The report identified a number of issues recently discussed in the Economic and Social Council: policy development and coordination; the Council's working methods and organization of work; subsidiary machinery; regional commissions; inter-agency coordination; cooperation between the United Nations, the Bretton Woods institutions and the World Trade Organization

(WTO); and documentation (see PART SIX, Chapter IV).

In its agreed conclusions of 1995,[14] the Council put forth recommendations intended to address, within the framework of discussions on an agenda for development (see PART FOUR, Chapter I), the integrated consideration of themes common to major international conferences, with a view to promoting better coherence and providing integrated policy guidelines. At its 1995 substantive session, in the context of the coordination segment devoted to the follow-up to UN conferences, the Council also discussed streamlining the work and strengthening the role of its functional commissions. In its agreed conclusions, noting the current practice of assigning one commission or relevant intergovernmental body with responsibility for follow-up to each conference, the Council stated that the commissions, within their respective mandates, should develop multi-year programmes of work for conference follow-up and review of conference programmes of action. The Council, in cooperation with the functional commissions, should ensure a better division of labour and coordination among them, with a consolidation of activities if appropriate.

The Council, acknowledged that the regional commissions should play an important role in assisting countries of each region in implementing conference recommendations. The Council should enhance coordination with and among them, and ensure their more effective participation in conference follow-up.

The Secretary-General noted that both the Assembly and the Council viewed restructuring and revitalization in the economic, social and related fields as an ongoing process. He supported that approach, which, he said, should be aimed at enhancing the Organization's flexibility and adaptability in the performance of its functions and its ability to address the most urgent tasks and new demands, as well as to ensure its capability to deal with the growing number of global challenges. The Secretary-General pointed to his continuing efforts to simplify and enhance the coordination of the Organization's activities and to rationalize its structures, stating at the same time a need to go further and increase efficiency while continuing to eliminate duplication and overlapping. In that connection, he stressed that the United Nations should focus particularly on those sectors in which its contribution was irreplaceable.

The Secretary-General expressed great appreciation of the will shown by the seven major industrialized countries at their Summit (Halifax, Canada, 15-17 June)[15] to develop a more internal policy coordination role for the Council. He similarly appreciated that the Ministers for Foreign Affairs of the Group of 77, in their Ministerial Declaration of 29 September,[16] stressed that the Council's role, as reflected in the UN Charter and recent Assembly resolutions, must be fully exercised. He was also fully aware of the discussions of the Ad Hoc Open-ended Working Group of the General Assembly on an Agenda for Development, which included the issue of institutional reform. According to the outline agreed on by the Working Group, institutional issues were to be covered in the third chapter of the agenda, together with follow-up aspects; it was expected that the agenda should refer, *inter alia*, to enhancing the role, capacity, effectiveness and efficiency of the UN system in development, and to the interaction between the UN and other multilateral development institutions, including the Bretton Woods institutions and WTO.

Concluding, the Secretary-General stated that the relevant portions of the agenda for development and the outcome of the Assembly's consideration of the restructuring and revitalization of the UN in the economic, social and related fields should contribute to defining, rationalizing and further strengthening the work of the Organization.

In his 1995 report,[1] the Secretary-General declared that, within the realm of activities covered by the Economic and Social Council, further steps to ensure more coherent management of operational activities carried out under the aegis of various UN programmes and funds, as well as improved coordination of humanitarian activities, were other essential reform elements requiring renewed attention at the intergovernmental level.

The General Assembly, by **decision 50/475** of 23 December, retained the agenda item on restructuring and revitalizing the United Nations in the economic, social and related fields for consideration during its fiftieth session.

*REFERENCES*

[1]A/50/1. [2]YUN 1994, p. 246, GA res. 48/264, 29 July 1994. [3]A/C.5/49/L.60. [4]A/49/820/Add.2. [5]A/50/507. [6]YUN 1979, p. 435. [7]YUN 1963, p. 87, GA res. 1991 A (XVIII), 17 Dec. 1963. [8]YUN 1993, p. 212, GA res. 48/26, 3 Dec. 1993. [9]A/49/47. [10]A/49/965. [11]YUN 1991, p. 749. [12]A/50/697 & Corr.1 & Add.1. [13]YUN 1993, p. 1118, GA res. 48/162, annex I, 20 Dec. 1993. [14]A/50/3/Rev.1 (agreed conclusions 1995/1). [15]A/50/254-S/1995/501. [16]A/50/518.

# UN Secretariat and intergovernmental organizations

To improve programme delivery and respond more effectively to strategic objectives and priorities established by Member States, the restructuring of the Secretariat, which had begun in 1992,[1] continued in 1995. In his annual report on the work of the Organization,[2] the Secretary-General put forward five objectives designed to create what he called a mission-driven and result-oriented Organization: better management of human resources, together with improvement of staff members' capabilities and accomplishments; better programme management, from the identification of strategic priorities, to the budgetary process by which resources were allocated to achieve those priorities, to a performance measurement system; better and more timely information with which to manage; better management of technology and extension of its availability throughout the Organization; and better management of the Organization's cost structure and an enhanced programme for promoting efficiency and cost-effectiveness.

At the same time, the Secretary-General was convinced that no reform effort could succeed without addressing the basic issue of providing the Organization with a more adequate and reliable financial base.

The need to use UN human and financial resources more efficiently and to increase productivity was a recurrent theme during the 1995 General Assembly session. Independent commissions and experts also recognized that Secretariat reform was essential.

### Review of UN administrative and financial functioning

In 1995, the General Assembly's Fifth Committee continued consideration of the agenda item on the review of the efficiency of the administrative and financial functioning of the United Nations. The Committee had before it a June report[3] of the Secretary-General on progress in implementing procurement reform in the Secretariat (see PART SIX, Chapter IV), two OIOS reports[4] on the activities of the UN Mission for the Referendum in Western Sahara (see PART ONE, Chapter III) and a third[5] on the audit of the UN Protection Force (UNPROFOR) personnel pilot project (see PART TWO, Chapter V). As consultations did not result in a draft resolution, the Committee recommended that the item be deferred.

Following the Committee's recommendation,[6] the Assembly, by **decision 49/489** of 20 July, deferred consideration of the documents relating to the item to its fiftieth session; it requested the Secretary-General to update his 1994 report on the restructuring of the UN Secretariat[7] and to apprise the Assembly of the measures taken to implement his 1994 recommendations on the establishment of a transparent and effective system of accountability and responsibility.[8]

On 22 September, by **decision 50/402A**, the Assembly included the item in the agenda of its

fiftieth session, allocating it to the Fifth Committee, which considered it on 22 December. On 23 December, the Assembly decided that the item should remain on its agenda for consideration during its fiftieth session (**decision 50/475**), with the Fifth Committee continuing to consider it, as well as relevant reports, at its resumed fiftieth session (**decision 50/469**). By **decision 50/470** of the same date, the Assembly included the item in the Committee's work programme for 1996 and 1997.

### Internal oversight

The General Assembly, deciding in July 1994 to establish the Office of Internal Oversight Services,[9] clearly expressed its intention to enhance oversight functions within the United Nations, in view of the increased importance, cost and complexity of the Organization's activities. The Assembly also stressed the proactive and advisory role of the new office, which would give assistance and provide methodological support to programme managers and would monitor closely their compliance with its recommendations. OIOS would transmit, through the Secretary-General to the Assembly, reports on its work to provide insight into the effective utilization and management of UN resources.

In a report by the Under-Secretary-General for Internal Oversight Services on OIOS activities[10]—covering the period between 15 November 1994, the date he took office, and 30 June 1995—it was stated that for almost 50 years internal oversight was, at best, underdeveloped in the United Nations, and internal auditing, programme evaluation and monitoring played a marginal role as part of administration and management, lacking independence and authority. Neither an inspection function nor an investigation unit had existed within the Secretariat. Some of the deficiencies and weaknesses the United Nations was being increasingly criticized for had, in his opinion, something to do with the traditionally weak oversight function, which allowed the bureaucracy to grow without pruning for many years and which had led to too rigid procedures and structures that frustrated creativity and individual initiative; also, overlapping and duplication of responsibilities had not been adequately addressed, let alone eliminated.

The Under-Secretary-General cited further reasons why the management reality of the United Nations was less than perfect. He said that rules and regulations were too complicated and too numerous to serve as clear guidance; a concerted effort had to be made to weed out or reformulate what had become obsolete or been superseded. OIOS would be involved in such an exercise, together with the Office of Legal Affairs (OLA) and the Department of Administration and Management (DAM). Second, the personnel system was cumbersome and the hiring of new talent as difficult as the termination of non-performers. The "buy-out programme" initiated by DAM and related measures would enhance staff rotation and mobility. Third, managerial and administrative skills were not well distributed in the Organization and there was a lack of experienced administrators in peace-keeping missions. OIOS strongly endorsed the launching by the Office of Human Resources Management of a major training programme to raise management awareness and recommended that it be extended to include all levels of management. Fourth, there was a lack of horizontal communication, with different departments not knowing enough about each other's work; this created the danger of unintentional overlapping and preoccupation with "turf". OIOS would continue to emphasize the need for more transparency and coordination. Fifth, vertical communication also needed improving; if staff at all levels were expected to participate in the management of the Organization, dialogue had to be intensified. OIOS joined others in attempting to bring about that important change in corporate culture. Sixth, efforts had to be made to do away with the widespread tendency of staff, even in key positions, to shun responsibility and accountability. OIOS backed measures by DAM to achieve that goal and would focus its own recommendations accordingly. Seventh, institutional memory needed improving and in some key areas to be created from scratch. There was no central approach to the recording of actions and the maintenance and indexing of files. OIOS intended to address that issue. And, finally, the geographic spread—New York, Geneva, Nairobi, Vienna, plus regional commissions—reflected the worldwide mandate of the United Nations, but was also the cause of fragmentation and communication problems. OIOS recommended a sound mixture of delegation of authority and necessary guidance.

Those shortcomings were not likely to be overcome by quick-fix remedies, the Under-Secretary-General pointed out, particularly in an Organization of such size and staffed by people from some 160 countries who brought with them quite diverse perceptions of public service. Also, the United Nations found itself in a difficult situation, simultaneously facing huge new challenges and shrinking resources and having to adjust to dramatic environmental change while at the same time expected to change itself. In addition, discussions about reforms tended to turn into political issues in the legislative bodies and divergent perceptions among Member States resulted frequently in guidance, mandates and requests to the Secretariat that were, from an administrative point of view, less than clear.

Bearing in mind this environment and that organizational and cultural change could not be achieved overnight, the Under-Secretary-General believed that, for the work of OIOS to be meaningful, it had to be systematic and thorough and should not aim at spectacular, short-lived actions, but should provide the United Nations with a steady, continuous oversight coverage that promoted effective and efficient programme management and prevented future problems; the Office also had to find and report on current problems regarding waste, fraud, abuse and mismanagement.

OIOS had begun to meet with success in its new set of tasks, the Under-Secretary-General continued, although many UN managers were not used to and seemed to be quite reluctant to accept criticism, particularly when it came to applying accountability criteria rather than settling for the promise that some specific problem would not recur. That feature of the UN culture had to be changed, he said, and managers should adopt a positive and supportive attitude towards internal control and had to enter into a critical dialogue with OIOS. They should be aware that an effective internal control system could not be left only to the Organization's oversight services; the adoption of a set of internal control standards would raise managers' support for adequate internal controls and would provide a benchmark to assess the systems in place. OIOS would play its role in identifying specific control objectives for different categories of operations.

Occasionally, OIOS findings and recommendations were challenged on the grounds that the Office might not have the technical expertise to appreciate fully a problem's complexity; such reaction was understandable, in the Under-Secretary-General's view, but in most instances not justified. OIOS recommendations were vehicles for promoting change and needed senior-management support to ensure compliance.

Concluding, the Under-Secretary-General stated that much remained to be done to make the Organization fit for its current and future challenges; OIOS would do its share towards achieving that goal.

The General Assembly, by **decision 50/469** of 23 December, decided that the Fifth Committee should continue its consideration of the report on OIOS activities at the resumed fiftieth session.

**JIU reports.** In October, the Secretary-General transmitted to the General Assembly a JIU report,[11] giving an overview and analysis of accountability, management improvement and oversight in the UN system, with a November addendum[12] containing comparative data on recent reforms, initiatives and actions undertaken by 28 UN organizations. The Inspectors offered a summary of conceptual and practical relationships, patterns, common trends, initiatives and possible actions to help strengthen and enhance accountability, management and oversight in what had to become a continuous process. In the view of JIU, each organization had to develop its own processes and perspectives to meet its specific needs and circumstances, although each was urged to take two pivotal steps: to establish a single focal point under its executive head dedicated to strategic planning, performance management, maximally effective accountability and management improvement (recommendation 1); and to report annually on those issues to its governing body (recommendation 9).

JIU deemed it increasingly urgent that the organizations demonstrated wise resource use and programme responsiveness, as the pressures for high-quality performance were expected only to intensify. To that effect, it further recommended that each organization carefully consider the balance and capacities of its internal audit, evaluation, management services, analysis, reform, inspection and/or investigation units; keep under review ways to better consolidate, strengthen or support them; and regularly assess and improve their effectiveness (recommendation 2). In other recommendations, JIU called on each organization: to ensure that it had integrated and dynamic internal control systems in place and to develop clear guidance and actions concerning personal accountability, financial liability and standards of staff conduct (recommendation 3); to establish a comprehensive information systems strategy to use effectively information technology for programming, management and decision-making, and to streamline work patterns and processes (recommendation 4); to strengthen its management development and training programmes and support management improvement and analysis units (recommendation 5); and to support the recent management, accountability and oversight improvement efforts of the inter-agency bodies (recommendation 6). JIU also recommended that external system-wide oversight bodies improve and, if necessary, institutionalize their sharing of information on work programmes, findings and recommendations, and more frequently propose mutually reinforcing areas for review and assessment to one another (recommendation 7). In its view, the organizations' oversight governing bodies needed much more firmly and consistently to assert their leadership role and to insist on improved accountability, performance, oversight and sound management; they needed to prove that commitment by providing clearer guidance to secretariats, sharpening their focus on performance and results, following up more systematically on past policy decisions, and employing external

reviews and dialogues with clientele to enhance programme transparency, responsiveness and accountability (recommendation 8).

Introducing the report before the Fifth Committee, JIU said it was the first inventory and analysis of the subject and established a basis for future efforts to address those problems on a system-wide scale; its conclusions and recommendations could assist Member States in restructuring and streamlining the system. A strategic and integrated approach to accountability and oversight processes would lead to the elimination of existing gaps and overlaps, and would contribute to the creation of a new management culture in the UN system.

Another JIU report,[13] also transmitted in October, dealt with management in the United Nations. Although acknowledging managerial progress in human resources strategy and planning, programme planning and budgeting (see PART SIX, Chapter II), management training, the new performance appraisal system (see PART SIX, Chapter III), internal oversight, and management information systems (see PART SIX, Chapter IV), JIU felt that progress had not been satisfactory in policy guidance and instructions, performance management, the administration of justice and management improvement. It therefore recommended that the Secretary-General establish a small but full-time unit for integrated strategic planning, systematic and transparent monitoring and enhancement of the new system of accountability and responsibility, and the "management of change" (recommendation 1); and that he ensure that specific objectives, together with dates for their completion, were included in all unit work plans in the Secretariat and in any reports to intergovernmental bodies on status and progress of individual programmes and major activities, as well as in reviews by internal and external oversight bodies (recommendation 2).

## Activities of OIOS

The Office of Internal Oversight Services was formally established in September 1994. In addition to assisting the Secretary-General in fulfilling internal oversight responsibilities in the areas of audit and management, consulting, investigation, inspection and monitoring and evaluation, the Office was also responsible for administrative direction and management, as well as for programme planning, budget and finance under the medium-term plan for 1992-1997 (see PART SIX, Chapter II).

In 1995, OIOS was provided with eight more posts, raising its staff to 110, including extrabudgetary posts.

During the period from 15 November 1994 to 30 June 1995, OIOS concentrated its oversight efforts on peace-keeping operations (see PART TWO, Chapter I), humanitarian and related activities, and the general problem of procurement (see PART SIX, Chapter IV)—areas where, due to their visibility and the high level of expenditures involved, the uneconomical use of funds and management problems and abuses could have the most serious effect.

In carrying out his tasks, the Under-Secretary-General paid inspectorial visits to other major duty stations such as Geneva and Vienna, to UNPROFOR in Zagreb, Croatia (see PART TWO, Chapter V), and to the Economic Commission for Africa, in Addis Ababa, Ethiopia.

In the area of peace-keeping, emphasis was placed on the start-up phase of operations, procedures dealing with the end-of-mission phase, the safeguarding of assets, the reliability of financial and other information, and compliance with existing rules, regulations and instructions. Close attention was given to the division of labour between the Department of Peacekeeping Operations (DPKO) and DAM, and the functioning of the Field Administration and Logistics Division (FALD) of DPKO. OIOS also intensified the auditing of missions and assigned resident auditors to large and complex missions.

With regard to humanitarian and related activities, OIOS developed recommendations directed at better coordination of efforts by various UN agencies providing humanitarian assistance. A report on the implementation of recommendations regarding the Office of the UN High Commissioner for Reguees was to be reviewed by the Committee for Programme and Coordination (CPC) in 1996, and another report on an in-depth evaluation of the Department of Humanitarian Affairs (DHA) was scheduled for review by CPC in 1997. An OIOS report noted pertinent observations on coordination issues in a DHA report on Rwanda.

The Office had also begun reviewing all phases of the procurement process, as well as the general organization of that function, including the implementation of recommendations made by a high-level expert group in December 1994.

The comments of JIU on final reports produced by OIOS were transmitted to the General Assembly in October 1995.[14] Those reports had been prepared for the forty-ninth Assembly session, but consideration was postponed to the fiftieth session. JIU remarked that for a number of OIOS reports, particularly those dealing with specific investigations and inspections, its comments were necessarily limited or nil because of lack of access to the original records. It hoped that that situation would be overcome and intended to undertake the necessary coordination with OIOS in that regard.

### Audit and management consulting

The OIOS Audit and Management Consulting Division (AMCD) continued to conduct independent internal audits in conformity with generally accepted auditing standards of all UN activities worldwide—those financed from both the regular budget and from extrabudgetary funds—for which the Secretary-General had administrative responsibility. AMCD identified management problems and developed detailed recommendations for improvement. It undertook management surveys, reviewed organizational structures to suggest more effective ones, and looked into productivity issues. It also rendered advisory services to management and suggested improvements in streamlining management structures, planning, monitoring and budgeting, work processes and the use of human resources.

### Investigation

The Investigations Section of OIOS received numerous reports of possible violations of rules or regulations, mismanagement, misconduct, waste of resources or abuse of authority from staff members and others outside the Organization. Establishing the meaning of those terms within the Organization's legal framework became a key priority of the Section in cooperation with the OLA General Legal Division.

Reports were also made through a 24-hour confidential hot line; in accordance with requirements set forth by the General Assembly,[9] the confidentiality of all who made reports in good faith was protected, whether the investigation substantiated the report or not. The Section accepted suggestions from staff members for the improvement of working conditions and programme delivery and provided investigatory expertise and assistance to UN funds and programmes which generally did not have an investigations function.

The Central Monitoring and Inspection Unit completed two new inspections in 1995—related to FALD[15] and to the UN Conference on Trade and Development (UNCTAD).[16] It also followed up actively on an inspection relating to the Centre for Human Rights, conducted in 1994. The Under-Secretary-General reported that tangible steps were taken by the High Commissioner for Human Rights to reappraise and restructure the work of the Centre and reorganize its secretariat in line with OIOS recommendations. An inspection team's findings and recommendations, as well as follow-up action as at 31 March 1995, were presented in a report transmitted by the Secretary-General in April.[17]

The inspection of FALD found that the Division was not functioning in an environment that facilitated operational efficiency. It also found that its complement of staff was inappropriate in mix and, in some respects, insufficient in numbers. It was suggested that some functional responsibilities were not entirely clear and that certain organizational linkages had clouded accountability and impeded efficiency. From the financial point of view, the inspection found that the Organization faced potential risk of unrecorded liabilities and, in terms of third-party liability, including lack of adequate assets control. It concluded that FALD was not adequately fulfilling its mandate and that a more proactive management approach with coherent, workable policies and procedures was needed to alleviate the shortcomings found by the inspection. Recommendations were made to and accepted by FALD. The Secretary-General, in his transmittal note, expressed agreement with OIOS recommendations.

The OIOS inspection found that overall quality of UNCTAD's work was impressive. However, the inspection team observed that most of UNCTAD's activities could be found elsewhere in the UN system, making a case for duplication. It also suggested that the UNCTAD secretariat was overstaffed and top heavy, that the organizational structure needed streamlining and consolidating into fewer divisions, and there were shortfalls in administrative services and weaknesses in oversight mechanisms. Recommendations were accepted and endorsed by UNCTAD management.

### Monitoring of programme performance

The function of monitoring programme performance was further strengthened in order to become a more useful management instrument. To that effect, a more transparent and effective system of information-gathering for oversight purposes was established, especially with respect to changes introduced during the process of implementation of the programme budget. The reasons for departures from programmed commitments, such as reformulations, postponements, terminations and additional outputs introduced by the Secretariat, were currently being identified and included in a database. At the same time, monitoring and self-evaluation would be viewed as an integral part of the managerial oversight responsibility, which required the generation, on a routine basis, of data and analytical information on implementation and results achieved, including the use of achievement indicators where appropriate. General guidelines for the establishment of such managerial monitoring functions, including the development of performance indicators, were nearing completion for the guidance of programme managers. Implementation of those guidelines was to be monitored regularly to review how programme managers throughout the Organization collected and assembled information on their respective programmes in order to keep appraised

of progress, analyse performance, enhance the economy and efficiency of implementation and establish adequate management accountability systems. Such information was to become an integral part of the biennial programme performance reporting to Member States.

### Evaluation

The OIOS Central Evaluation Unit completed two in-depth evaluations, one on the start-up phase of peace-keeping operations[18] (see PART TWO, Chapter I) and the other on the UN Environment Programme (UNEP).[19] It presented reports thereon to CPC in 1995.

The first report reviewed the status of implementation of recommendations made in a 1994 progress report[20] concerning the capacity of the United Nations to learn from its experience with peace-keeping operations, and its ready capacity to act, for six substantive components of complex missions: information, electoral, repatriation, human rights, civilian police and military. In addition, the report reviewed and made recommendations on overall direction and coordination and the humanitarian and civil administration aspects of peace-keeping operations, as well as six support functions: planning, financing, staffing, logistics, procurement and training. CPC, in May 1995, endorsed 13 recommendations unreservedly and two with qualifications, reformulated one recommendation and proposed that five others be further studied.[21]

The report on UNEP presented findings and recommendations on its catalytic and coordinating role, its activities and administration. The general thrust of the report's recommendations was to refocus UNEP activities by strengthening its partnership with other organizations within and outside the UN system, with due regard to its role as a global environment programme. CPC expressed its appreciation for the report's quality and comprehensive nature and endorsed its recommendations, subject to the different views expressed by delegations during the discussion and to the subsequent views of the UNEP Governing Council. The Council[22] in May requested appropriate action on OIOS recommendations (see PART FOUR, Chapter VII).

*REFERENCES*

[1]YUN 1992, p. 1053. [2]A/50/1. [3]A/C.5/49/67. [4]A/49/884, A/49/937. [5]A/49/914. [6]A/49/820/Add.1. [7]YUN 1994, p. 1357. [8]Ibid., p. 1358. [9]YUN 1994, p. 1362, GA res. 48/218 B, 29 July 1994. [10]A/50/459. [11]A/50/503. [12]A/50/503/Add.1. [13]A/50/507. [14]A/50/459/Add.1. [15]A/49/959. [16]A/50/719. [17]A/49/892. [18]E/AC.51/1995/2 & Corr.1. [19]E/AC.51/1995/3. [20]YUN 1994, p. 122. [21]A/50/16. [22]A/50/25 (dec. 18/5).

Chapter II

# United Nations financing and programming

In 1995, the United Nations financial crisis continued to deepen, with unpaid assessed contributions totalling $2.3 billion at year's end. References to the critical financial situation were made by many Heads of State and Government who addressed the Special Commemorative Meeting of the General Assembly on the occasion of the fiftieth anniversary of the Organization. In its Declaration on the Occasion of the Fiftieth Anniversary of the United Nations, the Assembly stated: "In order to carry out its work effectively, the United Nations must have adequate resources. Member States must meet, in full and on time, their obligation to bear the expenses of the Organization, as apportioned by the General Assembly. That apportionment should be established on the basis of criteria agreed to and considered to be fair by Member States."

The Secretary-General, in his annual report, said that unless the receipt of unpaid assessments dramatically improved, there would be no choice but to reduce spending further, focusing on those activities for which no assessments had been approved. Activities for which assessments had been approved, but had chronically not been paid by Member States, might have to be curtailed. Notwithstanding the financial problems facing the Organization, efforts were continuing to make the United Nations more efficient and more effective in carrying out the many tasks entrusted to it, he said.

Throughout the year, the Secretary-General and others warned that the UN financial situation remained extremely grave; debts were accumulating and the Organization was running out of cash. The High-level Open-ended Working Group on the Financial Situation of the United Nations started work in January 1995 to find ways to bring about constructive and positive changes to provide the Organization with a long sought-after, solid financial base. In view of the tight financial situation, the importance of efficient resource management and planning was stressed on many occasions, as measures were sought to improve programme planning and strengthen internal as well as external auditing. The methodology used to determine the assessments levied on Member States was under scrutiny by the Committee on Contributions and its Ad Hoc Intergovernmental Working Group on the Implementation of the Principle of Capacity

to Pay, but no conclusion was reached on how best to determine a country's capacity.

The General Assembly approved final appropriations of more than $2.6 billion for 1994-1995, some $24 million more than it had approved in 1994. Regular budget appropriations for 1996-1997 were at the same level, or slightly less, while extra-budgetary resources for the biennium were estimated at $4.4 billion.

## Financial situation

The United Nations found itself in 1995 in a deepening financial crisis, with an unprecedently high cash shortfall. After utilizing all other available reserves, regular budget cash was completely depleted in mid-August, making borrowing from peace-keeping operations necessary in order to cover regular budget expenses.

Addressing the Fifth (Administrative and Budgetary) Committee in July, the Under-Secretary-General for Administration and Management stated that prospects for the coming months were bleak and it was imperative to find a way of managing accumulated debts which, as at 30 June, totalled approximately $1.5 billion, including some $760 million owed to some 60 Member States for troops and equipment contributed to peace-keeping operations. The United Nations also owed Member States some $400 million for budgetary surpluses in prior years, and owed $375 million to vendors and suppliers. In short, amounts owed exceeded cash on hand by approximately $1 billion.

The causes for the precarious financial situation were plain and followed the same pattern as in previous years, the Under-Secretary-General said, namely: late or non-payment of assessed contributions for both the regular budget and peace-keeping operations; delay between the approval of such operations by the Security Council and the receipt of cash to pay for them; and an increasing number of unfunded mandates. Lateness and delays created a situation in which inflow of cash was far less than was needed to meet obligations. Difficulties were exacerbated by a lack of adequate cash reserves to bridge the gap. Without cash, the United Nations was obliged to delay payments to

Member States for troops and equipment which had been provided to various peace-keeping operations. If the United Nations continued to pay for troops and equipment, cash reserves would fall below $200 million by the end of the year, which was not enough to cover requirements for three weeks.

In view of the seriousness of the situation, he went on, a letter had again been sent to all UN Permanent Representatives, requesting them to indicate their Government's planned schedule of payments of outstanding assessments. The Secretary-General had made a number of proposals designed to alleviate the situation, including early assessments and redeemable peace-keeping certificates. The mutual exchange of debt obligations was another measure calculated to redress the debt owed to the United Nations. Unless cash projections improved drastically, the Secretary-General would have to propose curtailing activities for which assessments had been approved but which had not been paid by Member States.

On 20 July, the General Assembly, by **decision 49/490**, adopted on the Committee's recommendation,[1] deferred until its fiftieth session consideration of the item on improving the financial situation of the United Nations.

In September, the Under-Secretary-General informed the Committee that regular budget cash had run out in mid-August and that $98 million had to be borrowed from peace-keeping operations in order to maintain regular budget activities. Unless significant contributions were forthcoming from Member States, borrowing would increase alarmingly in the coming months. The situation was particularly bleak in view of the fact that unprecedented amounts were involved and there was no sign that the outstanding contributions would arrive by October or November. Moreover, total disbursements were likely to be much higher than expected due to expenditures for programmes whose financing had not been agreed on until very recently, such as the war crimes tribunal for the former Yugoslavia, and to the decline in the value of the dollar against other currencies of major duty stations. In addition, payment from one major contributor was expected to arrive very much later than usual during the current year.

In order to deal with the critical situation, the Secretary-General had proposed various measures, including discontinuing troop reimbursements and payment of letters of assistance to Governments. In addition, he had decided to freeze recruitment, strictly curtail overtime and travel of staff, defer representation allowances, suspend new consultancies and purchases of furniture and equipment, delay payments to vendors and pay Professional staff monthly rather than semi-monthly. A reduction in the number of meetings and conferences was also

being considered. The Secretary-General intended to address specific appeals to those Member States that accounted for the bulk of the arrears.

**High-level Working Group.** The High-level Open-ended Working Group on the Financial Situation of the United Nations, established by the General Assembly in 1994,[2] began work on 20 January 1995; it held 39 meetings during the resumed forty-ninth Assembly session, and concluded its discussion on 28 July.

The Working Group considered a number of specific issues related to the assessment and payment of contributions to the regular as well as the peace-keeping budget, including full and on-time payment; stricter interpretation and implementation of Article 19 of the UN Charter and review of necessary procedures; incentives and disincentives, and payment in instalments; issues related to the capacity to pay; income measures (gross national product); length of base period; low per capita income relief methodology and debt adjustment formula; and the contribution floor and ceiling.

During discussions, a large number of Member States expressed the view that the fundamental cause of the serious financial situation was the failure of Member States, in particular some major contributors, to meet their financial obligations to the Organization in full and on time and without conditions. Some Members thought that, while such failure was indeed a major cause of the current financial crisis, a thorough examination of all issues on the Working Group's agenda was necessary for achieving a long-term solution that would place the Organization on a sound financial basis. In the view of others, the fundamental cause of the situation was the failure of the scales of assessment to apportion fairly the Organization's expenses among Member States.

Among the proposals for further improvements in the approval procedures for peace-keeping budgets and appropriations were the issuance of peace-keeping redeemable certificates; the early and/or partial assessment of contributions shortly after the approval of a new mandate; a standardized budget format for peace-keeping operations; and the possibility of establishing a consolidated peace-keeping budget (see also PART TWO, Chapter I).

There was no agreement in the Working Group that the current financial crisis of the United Nations was linked to the methodology of the scales of assessment and the need for their possible revision. A significant number of Member States, however, believed that a revision of the scales to bring them more into line with capacity to pay was a necessary element in any long-term solution to the crisis.

On 28 July, the Working Group recommended that the discussion of the issues covered by its mandate should continue during the fiftieth session of the Assembly, in order to enable the Assembly to take appropriate measures in time to provide the Organization with a viable financial base commensurate with the challenges it would have to face after its fiftieth anniversary. The Working Group was aware of the importance and urgency of the task and of the fact that the solution of the critical financial situation called for serious political efforts.

On 14 September, the General Assembly, by **decision 49/495**, noted the report of the Fifth Committee[3] transmitting the report of the Working Group. By **decision 49/496** of the same date, the Assembly noted the Working Group's report and decided that the Group should continue its work, taking into account the views expressed during the forty-ninth and fiftieth Assembly sessions, including its Special Commemorative Meeting. The Group should also submit to the Assembly at its fiftieth session, through the Fifth Committee, a report on its work, including possible recommendations.

On 15 December, the Working Group approved its programme of work for the Assembly's fiftieth session, which comprised the following issues: the cash-flow situation, including mounting debts of the Organization to Member States, as well as financial mechanisms capable of preventing recurrent cycles of financial crisis; payment of contributions in full and on time, increase in unpaid contributions, arrears, and incentives and disincentives; and the scale of assessments.

**Report of the Secretary-General.** In an October report[4] on improving the financial situation of the United Nations, the Secretary-General drew attention to the critical and uncertain financial situation of the Organization which, having no capital base and effectively no reserves, was therefore totally dependent on Member States assessing themselves on a timely basis for the mandates they wished to have carried out, and on the prompt payment of those assessments to assure cash inflows sufficient to fund them. Uncollected assessments, however, had risen to an unprecedented level; cash inflows had become unpredictable, even erratic; regular budget cash was depleted; and peace-keeping cash had been borrowed to pay regular budget bills. The Organization's debts were mounting, with no predictable assurance of when and to what degree they could be paid; emergency cash conservation measures would have a modest positive effect but provided no long-term solution. In recent weeks, significant payments had been received, but most of them had been anticipated and so the projected need to borrow about $240 million for the regular budget by year's end was unchanged. In light of the contributions paid, the Secretary-General decided on

12 October to pay $150 million to troop contributors, which still left unpaid troop and equipment costs at some $872 million. With unpaid contributions to the peace-keeping budget totalling nearly $2.3 billion, he projected that some $1 billion would still be owed to troop-contributing countries at the end of the year.

As at 20 October, outstanding contributions to the regular budget totalled $664,892,518, of which $394,689,749 were contributions for the current year. The combined total for the regular budget, as well as peace-keeping operations and international tribunals, was $2,884,374,208.

In a later addendum,[5] the Secretary-General reported that the financial crisis continued, notwithstanding the considerable efforts of a number of Member States to pay their prior and current assessed contributions. As at 15 November, unpaid contributions totalled $2.7 billion, of which $645.5 million were owed to the regular budget. Of that latter amount, $414.4 million, or 64 per cent, were due from the major contributor. Contributions outstanding for peace-keeping operations stood at $2,038.1 million, including $92.9 million in respect of assessments issued within the 30-day due period. Of the total past due amount, $817.3 million, or 42 per cent, related to contributions owed by the major contributor. An additional $10.2 million, or 38.4 per cent of the assessed amount, remained outstanding for the two international tribunals—the International Tribunal for Prosecution of Persons Responsible for Serious Violations of International Humanitarian Law Committed in the Territory of the Former Yugoslavia since 1991, and the International Criminal Tribunal for the Prosecution of Persons Responsible for Genocide and Other Serious Violations of International Humanitarian Law Committed in the Territory of Rwanda and Rwandan Citizens Responsible for Genocide and Other Such Violations Committed in the Territory of Neighbouring States between 1 January and 31 December 1994.

In an update of 20 December,[6] the Secretary-General noted that the financial situation remained extremely precarious. Despite special efforts by some Member States, the pattern of payments by most remained highly unsatisfactory. Unpaid assessed contributions totalled $2.5 billion as at 15 December, with $582.9 million outstanding for the regular budget and $1.9 billion due for peace-keeping. In addition, just under $10 million remained unpaid for the two international tribunals.

With the pattern of expenditures and contributions received essentially unchanged, the Secretary-General expected both the Working Capital Fund and the Special Account to remain completely depleted by the end of the year. To meet the Organization's obligations under the regular budget, it would again be necessary to borrow funds from peace-keeping accounts. The total of such borrowings at the end of the year might be marginally less than originally anticipated, owing to the combined effect of deferring certain expenditures until early 1996 and of cancelling other expenditures through emergency cash conservation measures.

The funds remaining in the various peace-keeping accounts at the end of 1995 would be needed, the Secretary-General said, to sustain peace-keeping activities into 1996. Although several States had made payments against their outstanding assessments in amounts greater than projected, peace-keeping payments expected in November and December from other Members had not yet been received. Therefore, debts to Member States for troops and equipment were still expected to total about $1 billion at the end of the year.

The Secretary-General concluded that the Organization continued to depend for its survival on those relatively few Members that met their obligations in full, on time and without conditions. But they clearly could not be expected to bear that burden indefinitely when so many others did not. He therefore urged the United Nations membership to address the issue with the urgency and importance it deserved.

According to a later report of the Secretary-General,[7] only 94 Member States had paid their regular budget contributions in full as at 31 December 1995. States making no contribution to the regular budget in 1995 numbered 22, down from 39, while the number owing more than the current year's assessment rose from 71 at the end of 1994 to 74 at the end of 1995.

Total amounts outstanding for the regular budget were $564 million, up from $480 million at December 1994. Amounts outstanding for peace-keeping operations totalled $1.7 billion, up from $1.3 billion at the end of 1994, and contributions outstanding for the international tribunals for Rwanda and the former Yugoslavia were $5.2 million. At the end of 1995, the Member State with the largest assessment owed 73.5 per cent of the amounts outstanding for the regular budget, and 47.4 per cent of the outstanding amounts for peace-keeping operations.

The General Assembly, by **decision 50/469** of 23 December, decided that the Fifth Committee should continue consideration of the agenda item and relevant reports on improving the UN financial situation at its resumed fiftieth session.

*REFERENCES*

[1]A/49/946. [2]YUN 1994, p. 1336, GA res. 49/143, 23 Dec. 1994. [3]A/49/963. [4]A/50/666 & Add.1 & Corr.1. [5]A/50/666/Add.2. [6]A/50/666/Add.3. [7]A/50/666/Add.4 & Corr.1.

# UN budget

## Budget for 1994-1995

### Final appropriations

**Report of the Secretary-General.** In December 1995, the Secretary-General, in his second performance report[1] on the 1994-1995 budget, provided estimates of the anticipated final levels of expenditure and income for the biennium, based on actual expenditures for the first 18 months and projected requirements for the last six, as well as changes in inflation and exchange rates and cost-of-living adjustments. The estimates represented a net increase of $21.9 million, compared with the revised appropriations and estimates of income approved in 1994.[2] Proposed expenditures amounted to $2,635,035,300, while income was estimated at $436,866,600.

The Advisory Committee on Administrative and Budgetary Questions (ACABQ), in an oral report before the Fifth Committee, recommended a reduction of expenditures by $2.6 million. The Fifth Committee therefore decided on 22 December to recommend to the Assembly that it approve $2,632,435,300 in expenditures for 1994-1995.

GENERAL ASSEMBLY ACTION

On 23 December, the General Assembly adopted together **resolutions 50/205 A and B**.

A

**Final budget appropriations for the biennium 1994-1995**

*The General Assembly*

*Resolves* that for the biennium 1994-1995:

1. The amount of 2,608,274,400 United States dollars appropriated by its resolution 49/220 A of 23 December 1994 shall be adjusted by 24,160,900 dollars as follows:

| Section | Amount approved by resolution 49/220 A | Increase or (decrease) | Revised appropriation |
|---|---|---|---|
| | (United States dollars) | | |
| PART I. *Overall policy-making, direction and coordination* | | | |
| 1. Overall policy-making, direction and coordination | 37,218,500 | 766,600 | 37,985,100 |
| Total, PART I | 37,218,500 | 766,600 | 37,985,100 |
| PART II. *Political affairs* | | | |
| 3. Political affairs | 66,116,200 | (1,671,700) | 64,444,500 |
| 4. Peace-keeping operations and special missions | 132,221,900 | 23,584,900 | 155,806,800 |
| Total, PART II | 198,338,100 | 21,913,200 | 220,251,300 |

| Section | Amount approved by resolution 49/220 A | Increase or (decrease) | Revised appropriation | Section | Amount approved by resolution 49/220 A | Increase or (decrease) | Revised appropriation |
|---|---|---|---|---|---|---|---|
| | *(United States dollars)* | | | | *(United States dollars)* | | |
| PART III. *International justice and law* | | | | PART VII. *Public information* | | | |
| 5. International Court of Justice | 19,316,000 | 2,041,600 | 21,357,600 | 24. Public information | 131,442,600 | 2,116,400 | 133,559,000 |
| 7. Legal activities | 31,432,500 | (781,900) | 30,650,600 | Total, PART VII | 131,442,600 | 2,116,400 | 133,559,000 |
| Total, PART III | 50,748,500 | 1,259,700 | 52,008,200 | PART VIII. *Common support services* | | | |
| PART IV. *International cooperation for development* | | | | 25. Administration and management | 896,820,800 | 23,547,700 | 920,368,500 |
| 8. Department for Policy Coordination and Sustainable Development | 51,556,600 | (3,586,400) | 47,970,200 | Total, PART VIII | 896,820,800 | 23,547,700 | 920,368,500 |
| 9. Department for Economic and Social Information and Policy Analysis | 46,225,900 | 1,016,500 | 47,242,400 | PART IX. *Jointly financed activities and special expenses* | | | |
| 10. Department for Development Support and Management Services | 25,961,400 | 2,657,100 | 28,618,500 | 26. Jointly financed administrative activities | 27,221,200 | (1,052,700) | 26,168,500 |
| 11A. United Nations Conference on Trade and Development | 113,579,800 | 665,200 | 114,245,000 | 27. Special expenses | 32,795,100 | 273,900 | 33,069,000 |
| 11B. International Trade Centre UNCTAD/GATT | 20,942,300 | (107,800) | 20,834,500 | Total, PART IX | 60,016,300 | (778,800) | 59,237,500 |
| 12A. United Nations Environment Programme | 14,277,900 | (2,417,100) | 11,860,800 | PART X. *Staff assessment* | | | |
| 12B. United Nations Centre for Human Settlements (Habitat) | 15,176,500 | (2,122,100) | 13,054,400 | 28. Staff assessment | 357,798,100 | 5,775,900 | 363,574,000 |
| 13. Crime control | 4,839,700 | (233,400) | 4,606,300 | Total, PART X | 357,798,100 | 5,775,900 | 363,574,000 |
| 14. International drug control | 14,693,900 | 346,200 | 15,040,100 | PART XI. *Capital expenditures* | | | |
| Total, PART IV | 307,254,000 | (3,781,800) | 303,472,200 | 29. Technological innovations | 25,398,300 | 101,200 | 25,499,500 |
| PART V. *Regional cooperation for development* | | | | 30. Construction, alteration, improvement and major maintenance | 58,447,100 | (1,530,400) | 56,916,700 |
| 15. Economic Commission for Africa | 71,657,600 | (2,485,600) | 69,172,000 | Total, PART XI | 83,845,400 | (1,429,200) | 82,416,200 |
| 16. Economic and Social Commission for Asia and the Pacific | 61,278,400 | (4,309,300) | 56,969,100 | PART XII. *Internal oversight services* | | | |
| 17. Economic Commission for Europe | 47,379,300 | 234,900 | 47,614,200 | 31. Office of Internal Oversight Services | 12,027,700 | (716,800) | 11,310,900 |
| 18. Economic Commission for Latin America and the Caribbean | 78,979,400 | (5,075,300) | 73,904,100 | Total, PART XII | 12,027,700 | (716,800) | 11,310,900 |
| 19. Economic and Social Commission for Western Asia | 35,213,100 | (5,041,500) | 30,171,600 | PART XIII. *International Seabed Authority* | | | |
| 20. Regular programme of technical cooperation | 44,814,700 | (6,413,800) | 38,400,900 | 32. International Seabed Authority | 776,000 | (141,600) | 634,400 |
| Total, PART V | 339,322,500 | (23,090,600) | 316,231,900 | Total, PART XIII | 776,000 | (141,600) | 634,400 |
| PART VI. *Human rights and humanitarian affairs* | | | | GRAND TOTAL | 2,608,274,400 | 24,160,900 | 2,632,435,300 |
| 21. Human rights | 43,708,200 | (3,399,500) | 40,308,700 | | | | |
| 22A. Office of the United Nations High Commissioner for Refugees | 48,572,700 | 2,487,300 | 51,060,000 | | | | |
| 22B. United Nations Relief and Works Agency for Palestine Refugees in the Near East | 21,350,300 | 750,600 | 22,100,900 | | | | |
| 23. Department of Humanitarian Affairs | 19,034,700 | (1,118,200) | 17,916,500 | | | | |
| Total, PART VI | 132,665,900 | (1,279,800) | 131,386,100 | | | | |

2. The Secretary-General shall be authorized to transfer credits between sections of the budget, with the concurrence of the Advisory Committee on Administrative and Budgetary Questions;

3. The total net provision made under the various sections of the budget for contractual printing shall be administered as a unit under the direction of the United Nations Publications Board;

4. The appropriations for the regular programme of technical cooperation under section 20, part V, shall be administered in accordance with the Financial Regulations of the United Nations, except that the definition of obligations and the period of validity of obligations shall be subject to the following procedures:

*(a)* Obligations for personal services established in the current biennium shall be valid for the succeeding biennium, provided that appointments of the experts concerned are effected by the end of the current biennium and that the total period to be covered by obligations established for these purposes against the resources of the current biennium does not exceed twenty-four months;

*(b)* Obligations established in the current biennium for fellowships shall remain valid until liquidated, provided that the fellow has been nominated by the requesting Government and accepted by the Organization and that a formal letter of award has been issued to the requesting Government;

*(c)* Obligations in respect of contracts or purchase orders for supplies or equipment recorded in the current biennium will remain valid until payment is effected to the contractor or vendor, unless they are cancelled;

5. In addition to the appropriations approved under paragraph 1 above, an amount of 51,000 dollars is appropriated for each year of the biennium 1994-1995 from the accumulated income of the Library Endowment Fund for the purchase of books, periodicals, maps and library equipment and for such other expenses of the Library at the Palais des Nations as are in accordance with the objects and provisions of the endowment.

**B**

**Final income estimates for the biennium 1994-1995**

*The General Assembly*

*Resolves* that for the biennium 1994-1995:

1. The estimates of income of 432,080,500 United States dollars approved by its resolution 49/220 B of 23 December 1994 shall be increased by 4,786,100 dollars as follows:

| Income section | Amount approved by resolution 49/220 B | Increase or (decrease) | Revised estimates |
|---|---|---|---|
| | (United States dollars) | | |
| 1. Income from staff assessment | 363,216,700 | 5,732,900 | 368,949,600 |
| Total, INCOME SECTION 1 | 363,216,700 | 5,732,900 | 368,949,600 |
| 2. General income | 60,929,800 | 8,580,200 | 69,510,000 |
| 3. Services to the public | 7,934,000 | (9,527,000) | (1,593,000) |
| Total, INCOME SECTIONS 2 AND 3 | 68,863,800 | (946,800) | 67,917,000 |
| GRAND TOTAL | 432,080,500 | 4,786,100 | 436,866,600 |

2. The income from staff assessment shall be credited to the Tax Equalization Fund in accordance with the provisions of General Assembly resolution 973(X) of 15 December 1955;

3. Direct expenses of the United Nations Postal Administration, services to visitors, catering and related services, garage operations, television services and the sale of publications, not provided for under the budget appropriations, shall be charged against the income derived from those activities.

General Assembly resolutions 50/205 A and B

23 December 1995      Meeting 100      Adopted without vote

Approved by Fifth Committee (A/50/841) without vote, 22 December (meeting 45); agenda item 115.

*Meeting numbers.* GA 50th session: 5th Committee 44, 45; plenary 100.

## Redeployment of resources for anti-apartheid activities

In December 1994, the Secretary-General presented[3] revised estimates for the 1994-1995 programme budget, proposing for redeployment some of the resources previously allocated to activities related to the elimination of apartheid, which were winding down. ACABQ submitted comments and observations on the Secretary-General's proposals in December[4] and February 1995.[5]

Explaining those proposals before the Fifth Committee, the Controller said that a total of $9,163,800 had been appropriated for apartheid-related activities under sections 3A, 3C and 24 of the programme budget, of which an estimated $3,435,100 had been spent in 1994. Projected savings therefore amounted to $5,728,700. The Secretary-General proposed that some of those savings be used for activities benefiting African countries, as well as for some of the urgent needs of the Department of Political Affairs (DPA). The $2,885,800 proposed for redeployment to that Department was to be used to provide continued support for Security Council sanctions committees, and additional resources as necessary for the Special Envoy to Afghanistan. Moreover, five Professional and five General Service posts in the former Centre against Apartheid were to be redeployed to strengthen various Africa-related functions. For peace-keeping operations under section 4, it was proposed that one D-1 post be permanently redeployed from DPA to the Africa Division of the Department of Peace-keeping Operations. The $1,005,100 indicated under section 8 (Department for Policy Coordination and Sustainable Development) was to be used in part to strengthen the New Agenda for the Development of Africa in the 1990s (NADAF; see PART FOUR, Chapter III) and in part to continue measures to combat desertification. An amount of $119,700 was to be redeployed from section 3 to section 15 (Economic Commission for Africa) in order to provide support for the United Nations African Institute for the Prevention of Crime and the Treatment of Offenders (UNAFRI; see PART FOUR, Chapter V). The $483,300 included under section 24 (Public information) would allow four Professional and two General Service posts to be retained in the Department of Public Information (DPI) to provide increased radio coverage of UN activities relating to Africa.

Earlier, the General Assembly had already approved continuation of temporary posts for the servicing of the Security Council sanctions committees and the provision of resources for activities relating to NADAF. Action had yet to be taken on the remainder of the Secretary-General's proposals, which the ACABQ had reviewed and endorsed.

Following informal consultations, the Fifth Committee Chairman submitted a draft resolution[6] under which the Assembly would have stated that it regretted that its request to the Secretary-General to provide adequate posts for activities dealing with micro-economic issues, through redeployment, had not yet been fully implemented, and would have asked him to present by 30 June 1995 proposals for implementing that request. The draft resolution was withdrawn after the Controller, on 31 March, explained before the Committee that the Secretary-General had redeployed six Professional posts and four General Service posts in the Department for Economic and Social Information and Policy Analysis (DESIPA) to activities ·dealing with micro-economic issues. Since in redeploying posts previously allocated to the apartheid programme it was important to take into account the skills and experience of the staff members involved, the Secretariat had proposed they be redeployed to programmes related to Africa. It was also intended, however, to continue to strengthen DESIPA, and the proposed programme budget for 1996-1997 would contain specific proposals to that effect.

GENERAL ASSEMBLY ACTION

The General Assembly, on 6 April, adopted **decision 49/480**.

**Revised estimates under sections 3A, 3B, 3C, 4, 8, 15, 24 and 28 and income section 1 of the programme budget for the biennium 1994-1995**

At its 100th plenary meeting, on 6 April 1995, the General Assembly, on the recommendation of the Fifth Committee:

(*a*) Took note of the report of the Secretary-General on the revised estimates under sections 3A, 3B, 3C, 4, 8, 15, 24 and 28 and income section 1;

(*b*) Endorsed the observations and recommendations of the Advisory Committee on Administrative and Budgetary Questions contained in its report, subject to the provisions of the present decision;

(*c*) Decided to redeploy the amount of 119,700 United States dollars from section 3 (Political affairs) of the programme budget for the biennium 1994-1995 to section 15 (Economic Commission for Africa), as requested by the Secretary-General in paragraph 86 of his report;

(*d*) Requested the Secretary-General to review its recommendations in the context of the proposed programme budget for the biennium 1996-1997 in order to enhance and enrich programmes and activities for Africa;

(*e*) Decided that future requests for funding for regional institutes should be considered only on the basis of criteria proposed by the Secretary-General and approved by the General Assembly to determine if such institutes should be funded from the regular budget.

General Assembly decision 49/480

Adopted without vote

Approved by Fifth Committee (A/49/822/Add.2) without vote, 31 March (meeting 53); draft by Vice-Chairman (A/C.5/49/L.38), based on informal consultations and amended by Tunisia, for African Group (A/C.5/49/L.48), orally revised; agenda item 107.
*Meeting numbers.* GA 49th session: 5th Committee 42, 51, 53; plenary 100.

In view of amendments introduced by Tunisia, the United States withdrew its amendments,[7] which would have added two new paragraphs, calling on the Secretary-General to establish, by 31 May, criteria for the consideration of requests for regular budget support by the regional institutes, and would also have decided to defer consideration of his proposal to redeploy $119,700 to the Economic Commission for Africa.

### Reformulation of activities under budget sections 9 and 10

In response to a 1993 General Assembly request[8] the Secretary-General submitted a report[9] containing a revised programme narrative for budget section 9 (Department for Economic and Social Information and Policy Analysis), programme 1, subprogramme 5 of the 1994-1995 programme budget, and revisions to section 10 (Department for Development Support and Management Services), programme 2.

At its resumed forty-ninth session, the General Assembly, by **resolution 49/237, section IV** of 31 March 1995, took note of the Secretary-General's report.

### Budget for 1992-1993

On 6 April, the General Assembly, on the recommendation of the Fifth Committee,[10] adopted **resolution 49/479**, thereby concluding its consideration of the agenda item on the programme budget for the 1992-1993 biennium and reaffirming its December 1994 resolution on the final appropriations for 1990-1991,[11] in particular the provision whereby it decided that the net increase in appropriations for 1990-1991 be set off against the budgetary surplus available to Member States for 1992-1993.

### Budget for 1996-1997

The programme budget for the 1996-1997 biennium was presented by the Secretary-General in a new format and showed zero growth as compared to the previous biennium.

Introducing the proposed programme budget to the Fifth Committee, the Secretary-General said it represented a renewed effort by the Secretariat to minimize resource requirements and, at the same time, to ensure the provision of efficient services to Member States and the execution of all mandated activities as effectively as possible. His proposals, he said, placed particular emphasis on achieving effectiveness through improved management methods such as simplified administrative procedures, rationalized work programmes, improved productivity through advanced automation technologies, enhanced resource utilization in conference services, and reduced operating expenses in specific areas. Thanks to Secretariat restructuring, efficiency gains and investments in technology, the proposed budget represented a significant reduction compared both to the current one and to the budget outline approved in 1994 by the General Assembly.[12] The proposed budget called for abolition of 201 posts and the creation of 66 posts for new activities mandated by Member States. Resource reductions under the expenditure sections amounted to $98.2 million; when estimates for general income and revenue-producing activities were taken into account, that was a net reduction of $117 million compared to the current budget.

According to the Secretary-General, the distribution of resources for 1996-1997 was guided by priority areas identified for the medium-term plan period and elaborated in the budget outline. Special attention had been paid to strengthening the Organization's capacity to deal with political and peace-keeping activities, reinforcing international and regional cooperation for development, enhancing support for human rights and humanitarian activities, and increasing internal oversight capacity.

The Committee for Programme and Coordination (CPC), after considering the proposed programme budget at its 1995 session,[13] expressed appreciation for the Secretary-General's efforts to present a budget on time and took note of the methodology used to prepare it, as well as new features in the budget format, which included a self-contained, comprehensive overview, summaries of each budget section, additional information on expenditures for 1992-1993, information on extrabudgetary expenditures and their linkage with the regular budget, and projections by object of expenditure.

CPC noted that the total resources requested by the Secretary-General were below the level determined in the budget outline for 1996-1997 adopted by the Assembly.[12] It welcomed the fact that the savings achieved through improved productivity were higher than anticipated in the outline, and noted the Secretary-General's assurances that the reduction in resources would in no way affect the implementation or quality of all mandated programmes and activities. The Committee recommended that proposals for the provision of resources in the 1996-1997 budget be derived from the medium-term plan for 1992-1997, as revised, and legislative mandates adopted subsequent to the adoption of the plan or its latest revisions. The Committee had arrived at a consensus that the substantial decrease in the level of resources provided for under the proposed budget should be achieved as far as possible through greater efficiency and vastly improved productivity in all programmes. Efforts should also be made to achieve

better coordination between various departments and to improve the management of human resources.

Finally, CPC recommended that the Assembly approve the narratives of the majority of the budget sections. In view of the differences of opinion expressed with regard to some sections, the Committee was unable to recommend approval of the narratives of section 8 (Department for Economic and Social Information and Policy Analysis), 9 (Department for Development Support and Management Services), 13 (Crime control) and 21 (Human rights). The Economic and Social Council had been unable to resolve those differences at its 1995 summer session; consequently, the Fifth Committee and the Assembly would have to continue to review those questions and make the final decisions.

**GENERAL ASSEMBLY ACTION**

On 23 December, the General Assembly adopted **resolution 50/214**.

**Questions relating to the proposed programme budget for the biennium 1996-1997**

1

*The General Assembly,*

*Reaffirming* its resolution 41/213 of 19 December 1986 and subsequent relevant resolutions,

*Recalling* its resolution 45/248 B of 21 December 1990, in which it reaffirmed that the Fifth Committee is the appropriate Main Committee of the General Assembly entrusted with responsibilities for administrative and budgetary matters,

*Recalling also* its resolutions 45/253 of 21 December 1990 and 47/214 of 23 December 1992,

*Reaffirming* the respective mandates of the Advisory Committee on Administrative and Budgetary Questions and the Committee for Programme and Coordination in the consideration of the proposed programme budget,

*Stressing* that the normal procedures established for the formulation of the programme budget must be maintained and strictly followed,

*Having considered* the proposed programme budget for the biennium 1996-1997 and the reports of the Advisory Committee on Administrative and Budgetary Questions and the Committee for Programme and Coordination thereon,

1. *Welcomes* the timely preparation, and notes the improved format, of the proposed programme budget for the biennium 1996-1997;

2. *Reiterates its request* that the Secretary-General present in future budget documents appropriate regular budget and extrabudgetary expenditure forecasts to the end of the current biennium to permit comparison with the request contained in the proposed programme budget;

3. *Endorses* the conclusions and recommendations of the Committee for Programme and Coordination on the programme narrative of the proposed programme budget for the biennium 1996-1997 contained in the report of the Committee on the work of its thirty-fifth session, without prejudice to the priorities established by

the General Assembly, and subject to the provisions of the present resolution;

4. *Regrets* that the Committee for Programme and Coordination was unable to make recommendations on the programme narratives of some sections during its deliberations at its thirty-fifth session;

5. *Reiterates* that the activities included in the proposed programme budget must be derived from the medium-term plan for the period 1992-1997 and its revisions as adopted by the General Assembly in its resolutions 45/253 and 47/214 and other relevant intergovernmental decisions, and should be aimed at the full implementation of the mandates, policies and priorities as approved by the Assembly;

6. *Stresses* the role of the relevant intergovernmental bodies in the consideration of the narrative of the proposed programme budget as well as the necessity for a timely presentation of their recommendations on the budget;

7. *Also reiterates* the need for the Secretary-General to ensure that resources are strictly utilized for the purposes approved by the General Assembly;

8. *Notes with concern* that the proposed programme budget did not take into account its resolutions 48/218 A and B of 23 December 1993 and 29 July 1994, respectively, regarding the strengthening of the external oversight control mechanisms;

9. *Regrets* that, in the proposed programme budget, the Secretary-General failed to respect completely the priorities set forth in resolutions 45/253 and 47/214;

10. *Further reiterates* that, when formulating the proposed programme budget, the Secretary-General must respect fully the priorities established by the General Assembly;

11. *Decides* to make the following changes to the programme narrative in the final published version of the proposed programme budget for the biennium 1996-1997:

(a) Amend, as appropriate, references to "island developing States" to read "small island developing States";

(b) In paragraph 71, third sentence, of the Introduction, replace "in Eastern Europe and the countries in transition" by "for countries with economies in transition";

(c) In paragraph 1.37, fourth sentence, after "efforts", add "to promote international economic cooperation and economic and social development and";

(d) In paragraphs 2.48 and 2.48.1 (a) (iii), delete "the front-line States", and in paragraph 2.104.3 (b), delete ", but not in Africa";

(e) In paragraph 7A.41, the last two lines should read: "encouraging integration with national efforts through such approaches as a programme approach, national execution and country strategy notes, at the request of the recipient Governments.";

(f) Redraft the beginning of paragraph 8.3 as follows: "The main objectives of the Department will be the promotion of an integrated approach to economic, social and environmental aspects of development, including the elaboration of perspectives that will provide for sustainable, equitable and participatory development. The Department will develop and promote a coordinated approach to key policy issues. To that end, the Department will help Governments, international organizations, non-governmental organizations and others interested in determining. . .";

(g) In paragraph 8.6, penultimate sentence, after "regulation" add "as well as analysis of such issues as the role of markets in fostering growth, the provision of public goods, marginalization and social integration, human resources development, the impact of economic sanctions and the peace-development link";

(h) In paragraph 8.41, the last sentence should read: "Recent developments in the world economy reinforce the need to view the development process as being increasingly integrated through economic, social and political linkages.";

(i) In paragraph 8.42, delete the third sentence, reading "In the area of security economics, the focus will be on analysing the linkages between political and economic issues and policies.", and amend the last sentence to read: "The subprogramme will also focus on reporting to the General Assembly and the Security Council (as appropriate) on the impact of multilateral economic sanctions, coercive economic measures, participation of affected countries in post-conflict reconstruction and rehabilitation of the crisis-stricken areas, in the context of provisions of General Assembly resolutions 50/51 of 11 December 1995 and 50/58 E of 12 December 1995.";

(j) The beginning of paragraph 8.66 (a) should read: "One new P-5 post for research, analysis and policy studies on international migration, in particular the refugee flows and the causes, impact and different consequences of such movements including the human rights aspects and economic consequences of such population movements.";

(k) In paragraph 9.8, after "Unit", insert "for countries with economies in transition";

(l) In paragraph 9.8 (e), delete "; at the same time, the fellowships and technical assistance recruitment function at Geneva will be discontinued";

(m) In paragraph 9.21, third and fourth sentences, after "provided", add "upon the request of Governments";

(n) In paragraph 9.24, second sentence, replace the reference to "sustainable human development" by "sustained economic growth and sustainable development", and delete "as well as, where appropriate, within the context of the peace-to-development continuum";

(o) In paragraph 9.29, at the end of the first sentence, after "Agenda 21", add ", in the context of permanent sovereignty over natural resources and of an integral approach to environment and development";

(p) In paragraph 10A.4, add the Commission on Science and Technology for Development to the list of subsidiary bodies;

(q) In paragraph 13.13, first sentence, after "sophisticated forms", add "such as illicit traffic of children, child prostitution and child pornography";

(r) In paragraph 18.28, after the first sentence, add the sentence "All these activities will be implemented upon the request of interested Governments, taking into account their national priorities.";

(s) In paragraph 20.15, first sentence, after "are implemented" insert "upon the request of Governments in accordance with their national programmes and priorities";

(t) In paragraph 20.22, at the end of the first sentence, add "by General Assembly resolution 47/214 of 23 December 1992 and subsequent relevant resolutions";

*(u)* In paragraph 21.2, at the end of the first sentence, add ", in particular General Assembly resolution 48/121 of 20 December 1993, which endorsed the Vienna Declaration and Programme of Action, and resolution 48/141 of the same date, which created the post of United Nations High Commissioner for Human Rights.", and delete the rest of paragraph 21.2;

*(v)* Delete paragraphs 21.3 to 21.6, inclusive, and renumber the subsequent paragraphs;

*(w)* In paragraph 24.4, last sentence, after "humanitarian advocate", add "consistent with the leadership role of the Secretary-General and the guiding principles, including those of impartiality, humanity and neutrality, set out in the annex to resolution 46/182";

*(x)* At the end of paragraph 24.18.1. *(h)*, delete "and initiate a regime to limit stockpiling, production and trade of land-mines (XB)";

*(y)* In paragraph 25.1, delete the reference to document A/49/6;

*(z)* In paragraph 25.11, replace the last sentence by: "In that context, the activities of the United Nations information centres and the programmes of the Department of Public Information of the Secretariat, including those in support of major United Nations conferences, are aimed at supporting the main activities of the Organization, emphasizing those related to peace, security and disarmament, economic and social development, human rights and other political affairs, such as the question of Palestine, in accordance with General Assembly resolution 48/44 B of 10 December 1993. The activities of the centres and the Department, as well as the production of articles in magazines, radio and television broadcasts, and a variety of important publications, have all contributed substantially to promoting that understanding all over the world.";

*(aa)* In paragraph 25.12.3 *(b)* (ii), after the reference to the Agenda for Peace, add ", already approved by the General Assembly in its resolutions 47/120 A and B,";

*(bb)* In paragraph 25.91, the first sentence should read: "Information centres play a vital role in collecting, analysing, summarizing and providing Headquarters with analysis, media summaries and clippings on developments related to all United Nations activities, including those related to international peace and security.";

*(cc)* In paragraph 26C.58, add an additional subparagraph reading "*(f)* Providing language training in the six official languages."; and in paragraph 26C.58.5, the first sentence should read: "Language training is provided in the six official languages in accordance with resolution 2480 B(XXIII) of 21 December 1968, 43/224 D of 21 December 1988 and 50/11 of 2 November 1995."

*(dd)* In paragraph 29.3, first sentence, before "peacekeeping", add "development,";

*(ee)* Paragraph 29.4 should read: "The objectives of the programme include ensuring compliance with resolutions of the General Assembly and with regulations, rules and policies of the United Nations; monitoring programme implementation and evaluating the results achieved; reviewing and appraising the use of financial resources of the United Nations in order to guarantee the implementation of programmes and legislative mandates; investigating alleged violations of United Nations regulations, rules and pertinent administrative issuances; and recommending policies and measures for the pro-

motion of economy and efficiency based on these audits, inspections and investigations, in accordance with resolution 48/218 B";

*(ff)* In paragraph 29.26 *(a)*, first sentence, add the United Nations Office at Nairobi to the list;

II

*Emphasizing* that programmes and activities mandated by the General Assembly must be respected and implemented fully,

*Also emphasizing* the need for mandated programmes and activities to be delivered in the most effective and efficient manner,

*Noting* those areas identified in chapter I of the first report of the Advisory Committee on Administrative and Budgetary Questions on the proposed programme budget for the biennium 1996-1997 where the Advisory Committee, without recommending reductions at present, believes economies can be achieved, including, *inter alia*, the productivity gains that can be realized as the result of technological innovations, review of publications, strict control of expenditures on travel and consultants, appropriate staff ratios and the possibilities for greater accuracy in forecasting costing standards,

1. *Approves* the comments and recommendations of the Advisory Committee on Administrative and Budgetary Questions as expressed in chapter I of its first report on the proposed programme budget for the biennium 1996-1997, subject to the provisions of the present resolution, and requests the Secretary-General to take necessary measures thereon;

2. *Reaffirms* the budgetary process as approved in its resolution 41/213;

3. *Welcomes* the efforts of the Secretary-General to enhance efficiency in the preparation of his proposed programme budget for the biennium 1996-1997;

4. *Reaffirms* that changes in mandated programmes and activities are the prerogative of the General Assembly;

5. *Notes* that the Secretary-General intends to pursue further efficiency gains on an ongoing basis and that gains in the order of magnitude of 100 million United States dollars during the biennium would be a reasonable expectation;

6. *Decides* that savings in the proposed programme budget for the biennium 1996-1997 will not affect the full implementation of mandated programmes and activities;

7. *Requests* the Secretary-General to present, as soon as possible, and no later than 31 March 1996, to the General Assembly, through the Advisory Committee, a report containing proposals of possible savings for its consideration and approval;

8. *Also requests* the Secretary-General to make proposals to the General Assembly as soon as possible, and no later than the fifty-first session, on further measures to improve efficiency, contain administrative costs and achieve savings in the Organization with a view to enhancing programme delivery and the implementation of all programmes and activities mandated by the General Assembly;

9. *Further requests* the Secretary-General, when making such proposals, to take into account areas identified in chapter I of the first report of the Advisory Committee on the proposed programme budget for the biennium 1996-1997;

10. *Requests* the Secretary-General, in making proposals for such savings, to ensure the fair, equitable and non-selective treatment of all budget sections;

11. *Also requests* the Secretary-General, in addition to the biennial budget performance report, to present no later than the end of the fiftieth session and in June 1997 a programme performance report on the impact of approved savings measures on the implementation of mandated programmes and activities;

12. *Further requests* the Secretary-General to ensure that adequate resources are allocated in the 1996-1997 programme budget for activities specifically relating to the least developed countries in accordance with the priority accorded thereto;

13. *Decides* that the vacancy rate in 1996-1997 will be 6.4 per cent for both Professional and General Service posts, subject to review in the context of the above paragraphs;

### III

1. *Approves*, subject to the modifications below, the recommendations and observations of the Advisory Committee on Administrative and Budgetary Questions contained in chapter II of its first report on the proposed programme budget for the biennium 1996-1997, and requests the Secretary-General to take the necessary measures concerning them;

2. *Decides* to consider at its resumed fiftieth session the modalities for the strengthening of the external oversight mechanisms decided upon in its decision 47/454 of 23 December 1992;

#### Section 1.   Overall policy-making, direction and coordination

3. *Requests* the Secretary-General to ensure that the Office of the President of the General Assembly is provided with adequate resources;

4. *Accepts* the level of resources proposed by the Secretary-General for the Advisory Committee;

5. *Also requests* the Secretary-General to keep under review the level of the post of the Executive Secretary of the Board of Auditors, taking into account the increased workload of the Board and General Assembly resolutions 48/218 A and B on the strengthening of the external oversight bodies, and to report thereon in the context of the proposed programme budget for 1998-1999;

#### Section 2.   Political affairs

6. *Requests* the Secretary-General to maintain the Division of Palestinian Rights at its 1994-1995 approved staffing level, to keep the staffing requirements of the Division under review in the light of developments in the Middle East and to report thereon to the General Assembly when necessary;

7. *Also requests* the Secretary-General to keep the resource requirements for the Committee on the Exercise of the Inalienable Rights of the Palestinian People under review in the light of developments in the Middle East and to report thereon to the General Assembly when necessary;

8. *Further requests* the Secretary-General to ensure that adequate resources are made available to ensure the continuation, as appropriate, of the functions formerly carried out by the Office of the Coordinator of Assistance for the Reconstruction and Development of Lebanon;

9. *Requests* the Secretary-General to review the grade structure of the Department of Political Affairs as recommended in paragraph II.4 of the first report of the Advisory Committee on the proposed programme budget, as well as the division of responsibilities between the Department of Political Affairs and the Department of Peace-keeping Operations so as to ensure the clear delineation of their respective tasks and to avoid duplication and overlap, as recommended in paragraph II.15 of the report of the Advisory Committee;

10. *Decides* to keep the level of resources proposed for travel of the Special Committee on the Situation with regard to the Implementation of the Declaration on the Granting of Independence to Colonial Countries and Peoples under review in the light of actual expenditure patterns and to make proposals thereon as appropriate in the context of the revised estimates for the biennium 1996-1997;

#### Section 3.   Peace-keeping operations and special missions

11. *Takes note* of the proposals of the Secretary-General in section 3 of the proposed programme budget relating to the full range of administrative support for ad hoc missions under the good offices of the Secretary-General, peace-keeping operations and other special and field missions, and of the comments and recommendations of the Advisory Committee;

12. *Decides*, in this regard, to review the number of posts and the level of appropriation for section 3 by 31 March 1996, in the context of the comprehensive review of the support account;

#### Section 5.   International Court of Justice

13. *Requests* all relevant entities at The Hague to continue negotiations with the aim of obtaining economies through common administrative services;

14. *Accepts* the proposal of the Secretary-General, subject to the recommendations of the Advisory Committee, for the enlargement of the premises of the International Court of Justice, subject to further review in the context of a savings report called for in section II, paragraph 7 of the present resolution;

#### Section 6.   Legal activities

15. *Notes* the assurances given by the Secretary-General that adequate resources are available within section 6 of the proposed programme budget to enable the Secretary-General to implement fully the provisions of General Assembly resolutions 49/60 of 9 December 1994 and 50/53 of 11 December 1995 regarding measures to eliminate international terrorism;

#### Section 7A.   Department for Policy Coordination and Sustainable Development

16. *Approves* the provision of 500,000 United States dollars as the United Nations contribution to the financing of the activities of the Non-Governmental Liaison Service;

17. *Requests* the Secretary-General to ensure that there are adequate resources for follow-up to the World Summit for Social Development, held at Copenhagen from 6 to 12 March 1995, and the Fourth World Conference on Women, held at Beijing from 4 to 15 September 1995, as well as resources for climate change;

*Section 7B.    Africa: critical economic situation,
recovery and development*

18.   *Decides*, pursuant to section V of its resolution
49/219 of 23 December 1994, to create a separate identifiable programme budget section for the implementation of activities relating to programme 45 of the
medium-term plan for the period 1992-1997 as revised
by the General Assembly in its resolution 47/214;

19.   *Decides also* to establish one P-5 post and to
redeploy from section 26H of the proposed programme
budget one General Service post to strengthen the implementation of activities relating to programme 45 as
revised by the General Assembly in its resolution 47/214;

20.   *Requests* the Secretary-General to review the level
of resources devoted to the implementation of activities
related to Africa: critical economic situation, recovery
and development, and to make proposals with a view
to strengthening those activities, taking into account
General Assembly resolutions 47/214 and 49/142 of 23
December 1994 and the recommendation of the Committee on Programme Coordination in paragraph 101
of its report to the General Assembly at its fiftieth session, and to report thereon to the Assembly before the
end of its fiftieth session;

*Section 8.    Department for Economic and Social
Information and Policy Analysis*

21.   *Endorses* the proposals of the Secretary-General,
as contained in table 8.3 of the proposed programme
budget, which already include internal redeployments
within the Department for Economic and Social Information and Policy Analysis, and requests the Secretary-
General to review the staffing of the Department with
a view to achieving efficiency gains, including possible
redeployment of posts, and to report thereon to the
General Assembly at its resumed fiftieth session;

*Section 9.    Department for Development Support
and Management Services*

22.   *Notes with deep concern* the sharp decrease in the
level of extrabudgetary resources for the Department for
Development Support and Management Services, which
has had an adverse impact on its ability to carry out
mandated activities, and requests the Secretary-General
to intensify his efforts to mobilize extrabudgetary
resources;

23.   *Endorses* in principle the management objectives
stated in the proposal of the Secretary-General;

24.   *Also endorses* the proposal of the Secretary-General
contained in paragraph 9.25 of the proposed programme
budget;

25.   *Decides* that the posts and related functions proposed in paragraph 9.54 of the proposed programme
budget for transfer to New York shall remain at Geneva,
pending a comprehensive review by the Secretary-
General of the implications of the transfer for programme delivery, and requests the Secretary-General
to report thereon as soon as possible, but no later than
the resumed fiftieth session, with a view to achieving
maximum efficiency;

*Section 10A.    United Nations Conference
on Trade and Development*

26.   *Approves* the establishment of a P-4 post for the
follow-up to the Conference on Small Island Developing States as approved by the General Assembly in its

resolution 49/122 of 19 December 1994, and requests the
Secretary-General to fill the position on a priority basis;

27.   *Decides* to maintain the D-2 post for transnational
corporation activities on a temporary basis;

*Section 11.    United Nations Environment Programme*

28.   *Defers* a decision on the abolition of the P-5 post
of energy expert pending a review by the General Assembly, on the basis of information to be provided by
the Secretary-General during the resumed fiftieth session, of all posts that, as of 29 November 1995, had been
vacant since 1 January 1994;

*Section 13.    Crime control*

29.   *Approves* the upgrading of the Crime Prevention
and Criminal Justice Branch to a division and the consequent reclassification of the D-1 post of the Chief of
the Branch to the D-2 level;

30.   *Also approves* the establishment of two P-3 posts
for activities relating to subprogramme 2 (Collaborative action against transnational crime) and subprogramme 3 (Crime prevention and criminal justice
management) of section 13 of the proposed programme
budget;

31.   *Requests* the Secretary-General, in strengthening
the Crime Prevention and Criminal Justice Division,
to review the adequacy of resources made available for
crime prevention activities at the regional level and to
report thereon to the General Assembly at its fifty-first
session;

32.   *Also requests* the Secretary-General to report on
the status of implementation of the strategic management plan of the Crime Prevention and Criminal Justice Division as adopted by the Commission on Crime
Prevention and Criminal Justice in its resolution 1/1 of
29 April 1992, including, *inter alia*, those activities that
have achieved demonstrable results in combating international crime, assisting international law enforcement
or otherwise meeting current mandates of the United
Nations Congress on the Prevention of Crime and the
Treatment of Offenders and of the Commission;

*Section 14.    International drug control*

33.   *Endorses* the proposal of the Secretary-General
to create two additional P-3 posts to strengthen the capacity of the United Nations International Drug Control Programme;

*Section 18.    Economic Commission for
Latin America and the Caribbean*

34.   *Endorses* the urgent need reflected in paragraph
33.68 of the medium-term plan for the period 1992-1997
to study and elaborate, in close cooperation with the
United Nations International Drug Control Programme, the economic and social impact caused by the
production and trafficking of narcotic and psychotropic
substances in Latin America and the Caribbean, and
approves the creation of one P-4 post, through existing
classification procedures, for activities related to subprogramme 9 (Social development) to undertake, in close
cooperation and coordination with the Programme, the
functions contained in paragraph 33.69 of the medium-
term plan;

*Section 20.    Regular programme of
technical cooperation*

35.   *Approves* expenditure under this section at the
same level as in 1994-1995;

### Section 21.  Human rights

36.  *Reaffirms* the role of the United Nations High Commissioner for Human Rights in promoting and protecting the realization of all human rights, including the right to development, and in enhancing support from relevant bodies of the United Nations system for this purpose;

37.  *Requests* the Secretary-General, taking into account the proposals of the High Commissioner made in the context of the ongoing process of restructuring the Centre for Human Rights, to establish in the biennium 1996-1997 a new branch whose primary responsibilities would include the promotion and protection of the right to development;

38.  *Also requests* the Secretary-General to formulate appropriate programmatic follow-up to the activities to be carried out by this branch, in particular follow-up to the implementation of the Declaration on the Right to Development in accordance with paragraph 6 of General Assembly resolution 50/184 of 22 December 1995, for inclusion in the next medium-term plan;

39.  *Decides* that the Secretary-General shall report by 31 March 1996 to the General Assembly at its resumed fiftieth session, making proposals on the appropriate level and distribution of resources for the Centre for Human Rights, taking into account paragraphs 36 and 37 above and the restructuring of the Centre;

40.  *Endorses*, pending consideration of the report of the Secretary-General, the recommendations of the Advisory Committee as contained in paragraph VI.11 of its first report on the proposed programme budget;

### Section 24.  Department of Humanitarian Affairs

41.  *Endorses* the proposal of the Secretary-General on the level of resources assigned to section 24 of the proposed programme budget;

42.  *Expresses deep concern* over the sharp decrease in the level of extrabudgetary resources for the Department of Humanitarian Affairs, which has had an adverse impact on its ability to carry out mandated activities, and requests the Secretary-General to intensify his efforts to mobilize extrabudgetary resources;

### Section 25.  Public information

43.  *Requests* the Secretary-General to evaluate the capability and effectiveness of United Nations information centres in the performance of their functions, including, *inter alia*, retrieval and dissemination of information, taking into account electronic information, where accessible, and to report thereon to the General Assembly, through the Committee on Information, at the fifty-first session;

44.  *Also requests* the Secretary-General to evaluate the activities of the Dag Hammarskjöld Library with a view to improving the efficiency and effectiveness of its functioning;

45.  *Further requests* the Secretary-General to ensure that internal printing services are used more efficiently, limiting external contracting to cases that are strictly necessary, unless the external contracting provides the same services at a lower cost;

46.  *Decides* that the standards utilized to determine the volume of work and the composition of the staff that provide services for international conferences outside Headquarters should be modified in order to reduce the costs of these activities through the utilization of advanced technologies;

47.  *Reiterates* its resolution 50/84 C of 15 December 1995 on public information activities relating to Palestine, and requests the Secretary-General to provide the necessary resources for these activities during the biennium 1996-1997;

48.  *Reaffirms* the importance attached by Member States to the role of the United Nations information centres in effectively and comprehensively disseminating information about United Nations activities, particularly in developing countries and countries with economies in transition, and requests the Secretary-General to continue to provide adequate resources to enable them to carry out their mandated activities;

49.  *Also reaffirms* the continued usefulness of publications of the Department of Public Information in the dissemination of information, and, taking into account paragraph 7 of General Assembly resolution 50/31 B of 6 December 1995, requests the Secretary-General to continue providing adequate resources for that purpose;

### Section 26.  Administration and management

50.  *Decides* to defer the proposal for the allocation of financial and personnel resources for the reform of the internal justice system as proposed in section 26A of the proposed programme budget until the General Assembly takes a decision on this issue;

51.  *Requests* the Secretary-General, taking into account the increased workload of the Fifth Committee, to designate a deputy to the Secretary of the Fifth Committee as soon as possible but no later than the beginning of the first part of the resumed fiftieth session of the General Assembly;

52.  *Takes note* of the proposal of the Secretary-General in section 26B of the proposed programme budget relating to the Peace-keeping Financing Division and the comments and recommendations of the Advisory Committee thereon;

53.  *Decides*, in this regard, to review the number of posts and the level of appropriation for section 26B by 31 March 1996, in the context of the comprehensive review of the support account;

54.  *Decides also* to maintain the two P-2 Language Coordinator posts and the two full-time language teachers in the Training Service;

55.  *Requests* the Office of Internal Oversight Services to undertake a comprehensive audit of the outsourcing practices, including, in particular, the contracting process, and to report thereon to the General Assembly at its fifty-first session;

56.  *Requests* the Secretary-General to consider extending the application of section XVII of General Assembly resolution 36/235 of 18 December 1981 regarding language training for all the main United Nations duty stations and to report thereon during the fifty-first session of the Assembly;

57.  *Decides further* to maintain the current 1994-1995 staffing table for Conference and Library Services, Vienna;

58.  *Reaffirms* the need for a comprehensive, substantive and timely dialogue between Member States and the Secretary-General on administrative and budgetary matters;

59.  *Notes* the assurances given by the Secretary-General that adequate resources are available to ensure

the provision of improved meeting arrangements and facilities for the holding of bilateral meetings and contacts among Member States on a basis similar to that provided during the fiftieth session of the General Assembly, during subsequent sessions of the Assembly in 1996 and 1997;

60. *Endorses* the recommendation of the Advisory Committee on section 26H of the proposed programme budget with the exception of the General Service post redeployed to section 7B;

### Section 27. Jointly financed administrative activities

61. *Requests* the International Civil Service Commission to examine and report to the General Assembly on other less-costly forms for collecting data on prices and for their studies on the cost of living, including the Office of Human Resources Management, from private and governmental sources, and the possibility of outsourcing;

62. *Endorses* the request of the Advisory Committee that the Joint Inspection Unit review its practice of allocating travel funds so as to ensure their most efficient use, and recommends that a system of allocating travel funds in accordance with specific studies and activities related to the implementation of the programme of work as approved by the Unit be established;

63. *Requests* the Joint Inspection Unit to establish appropriate procedures to ensure that the travel system and work procedures referred to in paragraph 62 above are respected;

64. *Requests* the Secretary-General to fill the existing vacancies in the Joint Inspection Unit secretariat as soon as possible and no later than 30 June 1996;

65. *Also requests* the Secretary-General, taking into account the decision to strengthen external oversight mechanisms, in close cooperation with the Joint Inspection Unit and in conformity with the procedures for consultation with the Administrative Committee on Coordination, to present proposals on strengthening the Unit's secretariat in the framework of the revised estimates for the programme budget for the biennium 1996-1997;

### Section 28. Special expenses

66. *Requests* the Secretary-General to review and report on the cost of after-service health insurance;

### Section 29. Office of Internal Oversight Services

67. *Agrees* to establish the following posts: two P-3 (Monitoring and inspection), one P-5 (Evaluation), one D-1 (Investigations), one P-5 (Investigations) and one P-3/4 (Investigations);

68. *Also agrees* to establish, on a temporary basis, the rest of the posts as approved by the Advisory Committee, subject to the presentation of the workload analysis and job descriptions;

### Section 31. Construction, alteration, improvement and major maintenance

69. *Decides* that for the biennium 1996-1997 only essential repairs and construction, the deferral of which would endanger occupational health and safety, leave the Organization in breach of local building regulations 'or in the longer term not be cost-effective, should be carried out and that, as a result, the proposed estimates for alterations, improvements and major maintenance would be reduced by 12 million dollars;

70. *Takes note* of the assurances given by the Secretariat with regard to the status of implementation of the United Nations construction project at Addis Ababa, and requests the Secretary-General to take all necessary measures to ensure that the project is completed as approved;

### Section 33. International Seabed Authority

71. *Approves* the level of resources for conference servicing of the International Seabed Authority under section 26E of the proposed programme budget;

72. *Also approves* the level of resources for administrative expenses of the International Seabed Authority recommended by the Advisory Committee on the understanding that expenditures beyond an amount of 776,000 dollars would, on an exceptional basis, be absorbed under section 31 of the proposed programme budget;

### Income section 3

73. *Requests* the Secretary-General to review the functioning and operation of garages in the main duty stations, taking into account the need to provide sufficient parking facilities, and to submit proposals thereon to the General Assembly at its fifty-first session;

74. *Requests* the Office of Internal Oversight Services to examine the management of the catering facilities at Headquarters and to report to the General Assembly at its fifty-first session;

### IV

1. *Decides* that the amounts under expenditure sections 1 to 33 as provided under section III of the present resolution represent a provisional total of 2,712,265,200 dollars;

2. *Also decides* that the projected level of savings to be achieved during the biennium will be 103,991,200 dollars;

3. *Further decides* that the total level of expenditure provided for in 1996-1997 is 2,608,274,000 dollars;

4. *Decides* therefore that Member States be assessed on the basis of the amount of 2,608,274,000 dollars for the biennium 1996-1997.

General Assembly resolution 50/214

23 December 1995　　　Meeting 100　　　Adopted without vote

Approved by Fifth Committee (A/50/842) without vote, 22 December (meeting 45); draft by Vice-Chairman (A/C.5/50/L.30) following informal consultations; agenda item 116.

*Meeting numbers.* GA 50th session: 5th Committee 3-5, 7, 10, 11, 45; plenary 100.

## Appropriations

In his first report on the proposed programme budget for the biennium 1996-1997,[14] the Secretary-General proposed expenditures amounting to $2,687,067,800 and income totalling $461,421,400, resulting in a net estimate of $2,225,646,400. The proposed budget, at revised 1994-1995 rates, represented a decrease of $38.2 million, or 1.5 per cent from the budget outline estimate (at revised 1994-1995 rates).

Extrabudgetary resources for 1996-1997 were estimated at $4,434,509,700, comprising $420,187,500 for support services, $248,727,000 for substantive activities and $3,765,595,200 for operational projects.

ACABQ, in its first report on the proposed budget,[15], accepted the estimates with minor modifications. With regard to extrabudgetary resources, it welcomed the refinement in the presentation of estimates though further work was needed, and noted that the bulk of these funds (some $3,725.7 million of $4,434.5 million) pertained to programmes that had their own governing bodies to which the Advisory Committee reported.

In a November report,[16] the Secretary-General presented revised estimates to reflect new costing assumptions, which involved revised exchange and inflation rates, as well as the financial implications of recommendations by the International Civil Service Commission (ICSC) which were to be considered by the Assembly; expenditures were $2,827,800,000, and income, $479,300,000, resulting in a net budget of $2,348,500,000.

The ACABQ Chairman, in an oral report before the Fifth Committee, said that the proposed recosting would result in a net increase of $140.7 million under the expenditure sections ($91 million with respect to exchange rates and $50.8 million resulting from ICSC recommendations, offset by reduced requirements of $1.1 million in respect of inflation) and a net increase of $17.8 million under the income sections. The recosting was based on information available up to November 1995 and, in accordance with a recommendation of the Board of Auditors, reflected the average exchange rates for 1995 instead of the latest exchange rates. The Advisory Committee had been informed that the Secretary-General had endeavoured to absorb, to the greatest extent possible, the additional requirements resulting from inflation and currency fluctuations without affecting programme delivery. In the proposed budget, a reduction of $98.1 million, including efficiency savings amounting to $35.5 million, had been proposed and further efforts to enhance efficiency were under way.

The Fifth Committee, in second reading, recommended approval of expenditures totalling $2,712,265,200, minus anticipated reductions of $103,991,200 to be confirmed by the Assembly, resulting in a gross appropriation of $2,608,274,000. With an estimated income (other than from staff assessment) of $87,095,700, net expenditures were estimated at $2,521,178,300.

**GENERAL ASSEMBLY ACTION**

On 23 December, the General Assembly adopted together **resolutions 50/215 A-C**.

**A**

**Budget appropriations for the biennium 1996-1997**
*The General Assembly*

*Resolves* that for the biennium 1996-1997:

1. Appropriations totalling 2,608,274,000 United States dollars are hereby approved for the following purposes:

| Section | (US dollars) |
|---|---|
| **PART I.** *Overall policy-making, direction and coordination* | |
| 1. Overall policy-making, direction and coordination | 40,348,200 |
| Total, PART I | 40,348,200 |
| | |
| **PART II.** *Political affairs* | |
| 2. Political affairs | 60,989,500 |
| 3. Peace-keeping operations and special missions | 102,868,200 |
| 4. Outer space affairs | 4,705,500 |
| Total, PART II | 168,563,200 |
| | |
| **PART III.** *International justice and law* | |
| 5. International Court of Justice | 21,339,600 |
| 6. Legal activities | 31,605,400 |
| Total, PART III | 52,945,000 |
| | |
| **PART IV.** *International cooperation for development* | |
| 7A. Department for Policy Coordination and Sustainable Development | 44,318,700 |
| 7B. Africa: critical economic situation, recovery and development | 4,305,100 |
| 8. Department for Economic and Social Information and Policy Analysis | 48,612,100 |
| 9. Department for Development Support and Management Services | 26,556,000 |
| 10A. United Nations Conference on Trade and Development | 121,925,300 |
| 10B. International Trade Centre UNCTAD/GATT | 21,642,000 |
| 11. United Nations Environment Programme | 9,512,200 |
| 12. United Nations Centre for Human Settlements (Habitat) | 13,059,600 |
| 13. Crime control | 5,254,600 |
| 14. International drug control | 17,344,100 |
| Total, PART IV | 312,529,700 |
| | |
| **PART V.** *Regional cooperation for development* | |
| 15. Economic Commission for Africa | 87,845,600 |
| 16. Economic and Social Commission for Asia and the Pacific | 66,379,300 |
| 17. Economic Commission for Europe | 52,883,100 |
| 18. Economic Commission for Latin America and the Caribbean | 88,327,200 |
| 19. Economic and Social Commission for Western Asia | 37,791,200 |
| 20. Regular programme of technical cooperation | 44,814,700 |
| Total, PART V | 378,041,100 |
| | |
| **PART VI.** *Human rights and humanitarian affairs* | |
| 21. Human rights | 52,987,600 |
| 22. Office of the United Nations High Commissioner for Refugees | 54,318,500 |
| 23. United Nations Relief and Works Agency for Palestine Refugees in the Near East | 22,643,000 |
| 24. Department of Humanitarian Affairs | 21,039,300 |
| Total, PART VI | 150,988,400 |
| | |
| **PART VII.** *Public information* | |
| 25. Public information | 137,658,000 |
| Total, PART VII | 137,658,000 |
| | |
| **PART VIII.** *Common support services* | |
| 26. Administration and management | 960,885,100 |
| Total, PART VIII | 960,885,100 |

| Section | (US dollars) |
|---|---|
| PART IX.  *Jointly financed administrative activities and special expenses* | |
| 27. Jointly financed administrative activities | 28,915,000 |
| 28. Special expenses | 41,701,700 |
| Total, PART IX | 70,616,700 |
| PART X.  *Internal Oversight Services* | |
| 29. Office of Internal Oversight Services | 15,716,500 |
| Total, PART X | 15,716,500 |
| PART XI.  *Capital expenditures* | |
| 30. Technological innovations | 21,999,600 |
| 31. Construction, alteration, improvement and major maintenance | 31,585,400 |
| Total, PART XI | 53,585,000 |
| PART XII.  *Staff assessment* | |
| 32. Staff assessment | 369,080,100 |
| Total, PART XII | 369,080,100 |
| PART XIII.  *International Seabed Authority* | |
| 33. International Seabed Authority | 1,308,200 |
| Total, PART XIII | 1,308,200 |
| Total, EXPENDITURE SECTIONS | 2,712,265,200 |
| Less: anticipated reductions to be confirmed by the General Assembly | (103,991,200) |
| GRAND TOTAL | 2,608,274,000 |

2.  The Secretary-General shall be authorized to transfer credits between sections of the budget, with the concurrence of the Advisory Committee on Administrative and Budgetary Questions;

3.  The total net provision made under the various sections of the budget for contractual printing shall be administered as a unit under the direction of the United Nations Publications Board;

4.  In addition to the appropriations approved under paragraph 1 above, an amount of 51,000 dollars is appropriated for each year of the biennium 1996-1997 from the accumulated income of the Library Endowment Fund for the purchase of books, periodicals, maps and library equipment and for such other expenses of the Library at the Palais des Nations as are in accordance with the objects and provisions of the endowment.

**B**
**Income estimates for the biennium 1996-1997**
*The General Assembly*
*Resolves* that for the biennium 1996-1997:

1.  Estimates of income other than assessments on Member States totalling 471,401,700 United States dollars are approved as follows:

| Income section | (US dollars) |
|---|---|
| 1. Income from staff assessment | 384,306,000 |
| 2. General income | 86,209,200 |
| 3. Services to the public | 886,500 |
| Total, INCOME SECTIONS | 471,401,700 |

2.  The income from staff assessment shall be credited to the Tax Equalization Fund in accordance

with the provisions of General Assembly resolution 973(X) of 15 December 1955;

3.  Direct expenses of the United Nations Postal Administration, services to visitors, catering and related services, garage operations, television services and the sale of publications, not provided for under the budget appropriations, shall be charged against the income derived from those activities.

**C**
**Financing of appropriations for the year 1996**
*The General Assembly*
*Resolves* that for the year 1996:

1.  Budget appropriations consisting of 1,304,137,000 United States dollars, being half of the appropriations of 2,608,274,000 dollars approved for the biennium 1996-1997 by the General Assembly under paragraph 1 of resolution A above, and 24,160,900 dollars, being the increase in revised appropriations for 1994-1995 approved by the Assembly in its resolution 50/205 A of 23 December 1995, shall be financed in accordance with regulations 5.1 and 5.2 of the Financial Regulations of the United Nations as follows:

(*a*)  43,547,850 dollars, being the net of half of the estimated income other than staff assessment approved for the biennium 1996-1997 under resolution B above, less 946,800 dollars, being the decrease in income other than staff assessment for 1994-1995;

(*b*)  1,285,696,850 dollars, being the assessment on Member States in accordance with General Assembly resolution 49/19 B of 23 December 1994 on the scale of assessments for the years 1996 and 1997;

2.  There shall be set off against the assessments on Member States, in accordance with the provisions of General Assembly resolution 973(X) of 15 December 1955, their respective share in the Tax Equalization Fund in the total amount of 197,885,900 dollars, consisting of:

(*a*) 192,153,000 dollars, being half of the estimated staff assessment income approved for the biennium 1996-1997 under resolution B above;

(*b*) Plus 5,732,900 dollars, being the increase in the income from staff assessment for the biennium 1994-1995 approved by the Assembly in its resolution 50/205 B.

General Assembly resolutions 50/215 A-C

23 December 1995     Meeting 100     Adopted without vote

Approved by Fifth Committee (A/50/842) without vote, 22 December (meeting 45); agenda item 116.
*Meeting numbers.* GA 50th session: 5th Committee 3-5, 7, 10-13, 15-18, 20-24, 45; plenary 100.

**Working Capital Fund**

In December, the General Assembly established the Working Capital Fund for the 1996-1997 biennium at $100 million, the same level as during 1994-1995. As in the past, the Fund was to be used to finance appropriations pending the receipt of assessed contributions, to pay for unforeseen and extraordinary and expenses, as well as for miscellaneous and self-liquidating purchases and advance insurance premiums, and to enable the Tax Equalization Fund to meet current commitments pending the accumulation of credits.

## GENERAL ASSEMBLY ACTION

On 23 December, the General Assembly adopted **resolution 50/218**.

### Working Capital Fund for the biennium 1996-1997

*The General Assembly*

*Resolves* that:

1. The Working Capital Fund shall be established for the biennium 1996-1997 in the amount of 100 million United States dollars;

2. Member States shall make advances to the Working Capital Fund in accordance with the scale adopted by the General Assembly for contributions of Member States to the budget for the year 1996;

3. There shall be set off against this allocation of advances:

(*a*) Credits to Member States resulting from transfers made in 1959 and 1960 from the surplus account to the Working Capital Fund in an adjusted amount of 1,025,092 dollars;

(*b*) Cash advances paid by Member States to the Working Capital Fund for the biennium 1994-1995 in accordance with General Assembly resolution 48/232 of 23 December 1993;

4. Should the credits and advances paid by any Member State to the Working Capital Fund for the biennium 1994-1995 exceed the amount of that Member State's advance under the provisions of paragraph 2 above, the excess shall be set off against the amount of the contributions payable by the Member State in respect of the biennium 1996-1997;

5. The Secretary-General is authorized to advance from the Working Capital Fund:

(*a*) Such sums as may be necessary to finance budgetary appropriations pending the receipt of contributions; sums so advanced shall be reimbursed as soon as receipts from contributions are available for the purpose;

(*b*) Such sums as may be necessary to finance commitments that may be duly authorized under the provisions of the resolutions adopted by the General Assembly, in particular resolution 50/217 of 23 December 1995 relating to unforeseen and extraordinary expenses; the Secretary-General shall make provision in the budget estimates for reimbursing the Working Capital Fund;

(*c*) Such sums as may be necessary to continue the revolving fund to finance miscellaneous self-liquidating purchases and activities which, together with net sums outstanding for the same purpose, do not exceed 200,000 dollars; advances in excess of the total of 200,000 dollars may be made with the prior concurrence of the Advisory Committee on Administrative and Budgetary Questions;

(*d*) With the prior concurrence of the Advisory Committee, such sums as may be required to finance payments of advance insurance premiums where the period of insurance extends beyond the end of the biennium in which payment is made; the Secretary-General shall make provision in the budget estimates of each biennium, during the life of the related policies, to cover the charges applicable to each biennium;

(*e*) · Such sums as may be necessary to enable the Tax Equalization Fund to meet current commitments pending the accumulation of credits; such advances shall be repaid as soon as credits are available in the Tax Equalization Fund;

6. Should the provision in paragraph 1 above prove inadequate to meet the purposes normally related to the Working Capital Fund, the Secretary-General is authorized to utilize, in the biennium 1996-1997, cash from special funds and accounts in his custody, under the conditions approved by the General Assembly in its resolution 1341(XIII) of 13 December 1958, or the proceeds of loans authorized by the Assembly.

General Assembly resolution 50/218

23 December 1995　　　　Meeting 100　　　　Adopted without vote

Approved by Fifth Committee (A/50/842) without vote, 22 December (meeting 45); agenda item 116.

*Meeting numbers.* GA 50th session: 5th Committee 3-5, 7, 10, 11, 45; plenary 100.

Addresing the Fifth Committee, the United Kingdom said that, owing to lack of time, it had not been possible to reach a consensus on the amendments it had proposed to the text; it would therefore return to the matter at the resumed session.

### Contingency fund

The contingency fund, created to accommodate additional expenditures relating to each biennium that were derived from legislative mandates not provided for in the proposed programme budget, was established by the General Assembly in 1986.[17]

In December 1995, the Secretary-General presented a report[18] containing a consolidated statement of programme budget implications and revised estimates for expenditures falling under fund guidelines, which were approved by the Assembly in 1987.[19] The amounts charged to the fund were $1,173,000, leaving a balance of $19,427,000. The Secretary-General noted that the amounts in respect of each item corresponded to those previously recommended by the Fifth Committee upon its consideration of individual statements and proposals for revised estimates. The items were: $619,000 relating to revised estimates resulting from resolutions and decisions of the Economic and Social Council at its 1995 sessions; $356,600 for a follow-up to the Fourth World Conference on Women in September and full implementation of the Beijing Declaration and Platform for Action (see PART FOUR, Chapter X); and $197,400 for implementation of decisions and recommendations of the 1992 United Nations Conference on Environment and Development,[20] specifically for a special session to review and appraise the implementation of Agenda 21.[21]

The ACABQ Chairman, in an oral report to the Fifth Committee, drew attention to the Advisory Committee's request,[22] endorsed by the Assembly,[12] that he submit, in the context of his proposed programme budget for 1996-1997, information on the nature of expenses charged to the contingency fund so far, in order to enable the

Advisory Committee to review procedures for the use, operation and level of the fund. ACABQ requested that the information be submitted for its consideration in 1996.

The General Assembly, by **resolution 50/216, section VIII**, noted that a balance of $19,427,000 remained in the fund.

### Unforeseen and extraordinary expenses

**Report of the Secretary-General.** In a November 1995 report,[23] the Secretary-General reviewed and clarified the use of the biennial General Assembly resolution on unforeseen and extraordinary expenses, which provided for him, under certain conditions, to enter into commitments for activities of an urgent nature, without reverting to the Assembly for approval of the required resources. He particularly noted the need to respond to increased financial commitments in relation to activities in preventive diplomacy, peacemaking and post-conflict peace-building, and proposed modifications in the procedures for meeting expenses to implement unforeseen activities (see also PART TWO, Chapter I). Other categories for which the Secretary-General had been authorized to enter into commitments included those certified by the President of the International Court of Justice (ICJ) as relating to certain expenses from the activities of the Court.

On 23 December, the General Assembly adopted **resolution 50/217**.

#### Unforeseen and extraordinary expenses for the biennium 1996-1997

*The General Assembly*

*1. Authorizes* the Secretary-General, with the prior concurrence of the Advisory Committee on Administrative and Budgetary Questions and subject to the Financial Regulations of the United Nations and the provisions of paragraph 3 below, to enter into commitments in the biennium 1996-1997 to meet unforeseen and extraordinary expenses arising either during or subsequent to the biennium, provided that the concurrence of the Advisory Committee shall not be necessary for:

*(a)* Such commitments, not exceeding a total of 5 million United States dollars in any one year of the biennium 1996-1997, as the Secretary-General certifies relate to the maintenance of peace and security;

*(b)* Such commitments as the President of the International Court of Justice certifies relate to expenses occasioned by:

(i) The designation of ad hoc judges (Statute of the International Court of Justice, Article 31), not exceeding a total of 300,000 dollars;

.(ii) The calling of witnesses and the appointment of experts (Statute, Article 50) and the appointment of assessors (Statute, Article 30), not exceeding a total of 50,000 dollars;

(iii) The maintenance in office for the completion of cases of judges who have not been re-elected

(Statute, Article 13, paragraph 3), not exceeding a total of 40,000 dollars;

(iv) The payment of pensions and travel and removal expenses of retiring judges and travel and removal expenses and installation grant of members of the Court (Statute, Article 32, paragraph 7), not exceeding a total of 180,000 dollars;

(v) The work of the Court or its Chambers away from The Hague (Statute, Article 22), not exceeding a total of 50,000 dollars;

*2. Resolves* that the Secretary-General shall report to the Advisory Committee and to the General Assembly at its fifty-first and fifty-second sessions all commitments made under the provisions of the present resolution, together with the circumstances relating thereto, and shall submit supplementary estimates to the Assembly in respect of such commitments;

*3. Decides* that, for the biennium 1996-1997, if a decision of the Security Council results in the need for the Secretary-General to enter into commitments relating to the maintenance of peace and security in an amount exceeding 10 million dollars in respect of the decision, that matter shall be brought to the General Assembly, or, if the Assembly is suspended or not in session, a resumed or special session of the Assembly shall be convened by the Secretary-General to consider the matter.

General Assembly resolution 50/217

23 December 1995     Meeting 100     Adopted without vote

Approved by Fifth Committee (A/50/842) without vote, 22 December (meeting 45); agenda item 116.
*Meeting numbers.* GA 50th session: 5th Committee 3-5, 7, 10, 11, 45; plenary 100.

On the same date, in **resolution 50/216, section IX**, the Assembly decided to consider the Secretary-General's report at its resumed session and, in the meantime, authorized him to continue with the current arrangements until a decision was taken.

*REFERENCES*

[1]A/C.5/50/21. [2]YUN 1994, p. 1347, GA res. 49/220 A-C, 23 Dec. 1994. [3]A/C.5/49/44. [4]A/49/7/Add.4. [5]A/49/7/Add.10. [6]A/C.5/49/L.41. [7]A/C.5/49/L.49. [8]YUN 1993, p. 1197, GA res. 48/228, 23 Dec. 1993. [9]A/C.5/49/30. [10]A/49/883. [11]YUN 1994, p. 1351, GA res. 49/218, 23 Dec. 1994. [12]Ibid., p. 1352, GA res. 49/217, 23 Dec. 1994. [13]A/50/16. [14]A/50/6/Rev.1 (Vols. I & II). [15]A/50/7. [16]A/C.5/50/38. [17]YUN 1986, p. 1024, GA res. 41/213, 19 Dec. 1986. [18]A/C.5/50/49. [19]YUN 1987, p. 1099, GA res. 42/211, Annex, 21 Dec. 1987. [20]YUN 1992, p. 670. [21]Ibid., p. 672. [22]A/49/796 & Corr.1. [23]A/C.5/50/30.

## Contributions

At the end of 1995, unpaid assessed contributions totalled $2.3 billion, aggravating the serious financial crisis of the Organization. The High-level Open-ended Working Group on the Financial Situation of the United Nations discussed a number of specific contribution issues (see above). The Committee on Contributions, at its fifty-fifth annual session (New York, 12-13 June 1995),[1] reviewed all aspects of the methodology for determining the scale of assessments. Notings that the next scale, for the period 1998-2000, was not due to be considered until 1997, and in consideration of the comprehensive nature of the mandate given to it by the General Assembly, the Committee decided to undertake the current comprehensive review of the scale methodology over two sessions. In the context of its review, the Committee also considered the proposals, suggestions and recommendations contained in the report of the Ad Hoc Intergovernmental Working Group on the Implementation of the Principle of Capacity to Pay (see below).[2]

In 1995, the Committee had before it written representations from Iraq, Kyrgyzstan and Turkey. It received and granted requests for oral representations from the Dominican Republic, Guatemala and Iraq.

## Assessments

### Assessment of Palau

The former Trust Territory of Palau was admitted to membership in the United Nations in December 1994.[3] According to rule 160 of the General Assembly's rules of procedure, the Committee on Contributions advises the Assembly on assessments to be fixed for new Members. On the basis of national income and population data available from the UN Statistical Division, the Committee set Palau's rate of assessment for 1995, 1996 and 1997 at 0.01 per cent. The Committee recommended that for 1995, Palau's contribution should be applied on the same basis of assessment as for other Member States, except in the case of appropriations approved for the financing of peace-keeping operations, for which its contributions, as determined by the group of contributors to which it might be assigned by the Assembly, should be calculated in proportion to the calendar year and its actual assessments taken into account as miscellaneous income under regulation 5.2(c) of the Financial Regulations and Rules of the United Nations. Palau's advance to the Working Capital Fund should be calculated by applying the rate of assessment in effect during its first full year of membership to the authorized level of the Fund, and should be added to the Fund pending incorporation of its rate of assessment in a 100 per cent scale.

#### GENERAL ASSEMBLY ACTION

On 23 December, the General Assembly adopted **decision 50/471 A**.

#### Scale of assessments for the apportionment of the expenses of the United Nations

At its 100th plenary meeting, on 23 December 1995, the General Assembly, on the recommendation of the Fifth Committee, decided that:

*(a)* The rate of assessment for Palau, admitted to membership in the United Nations on 15 December 1994, should be 0.01 per cent for 1995, 1996 and 1997;

*(b)* The contributions of Palau for 1995, 1996 and 1997 should be applied to the same basis of assessment as for other Member States, except that, in the case of appropriations or apportionments approved by the General Assembly for the financing of peace-keeping operations, the contributions of Palau, as determined by the group of contributors to which they might be assigned by the Assembly, should be calculated in proportion to the calendar year;

*(c)* The 1995 assessments of Palau should be taken into account as miscellaneous income in accordance with regulation 5.2 *(c)* of the Financial Regulations and Rules of the United Nations;

*(d)* For 1996 and 1997, the rate of assessment for Palau should be added to the scale of assessments established under General Assembly resolution 49/19 B of 23 December 1994;

*(e)* The advance of Palau to the Working Capital Fund should be calculated by the application of the rate of assessment of 0.01 per cent to the authorized level of the Fund and should be added to the Fund pending the incorporation of its rate in a 100 per cent scale.

General Assembly decision 50/471 A

Adopted without vote

Approved by Fifth Committee (A/50/843) without vote, 21 December (meeting 44); draft by Chairman (A/C.5/50/L.22) following informal consultations; agenda item 120.
*Meeting numbers.* GA 50th session: 5th Committee 4-10, 43, 44; plenary 100.

By **decision 50/451 B** of 23 December, the Assembly, as an ad hoc arrangement, included Palau in group D of Member States for the apportionment of peace-keeping operations.

### Assessment of Turkey

Turkey expressed its concern that it was not included by the Committee on Contributions in the list of developing countries within the context of the United Nations and therefore did not benefit from the 15 per cent limitation on the effect of the phase-out of the scheme of limits, thus resulting in an increase in its rate of assessment. The Committee pointed out that in the context of its work, it had considered Turkey a developing country, but in accordance with the 1993 General Assembly resolution on assessments for 1995-1997,[4] only those developing countries that had benefited from the scheme of limits and whose rates were increasing in the new scale were subject to the 15 per cent provision. In view of those circumstances, and after examining Turkey's national income and other relevant data, the Committee could not find grounds for adjusting Turkey's assessment rate for 1995-1997.

The Assembly, by **decision 50/471 B** of 23 December, adopted on the Fifth Committee's recommendation,[5] requested the Committee on Contributions to reconsider inclusion of Turkey in the list of countries falling under paragraph 2 of the 1993 resolution on assessments,[4] in which the Assembly had stipulated that in phasing out the scheme of limits, the allocation of additional points resulting therefrom to developing countries benefiting from its application should be limited to 15 per cent of the effect of the phase-out.

## Assessment of Guatemala

In its representation to the Committee on Contributions, Guatemala appealed for a change of its assessment rate, which it believed did not reflect its real capacity to pay and the serious economic difficulties it had suffered as a result of the state of war existing in the country in the 1980s. The Committee felt that it had insufficient information on Guatemala's current economic and financial situation, and requested the country to provide the necessary information to allow for a better assessment with regard to its inability to pay its contributions. The Committee also noted that only in exceptional circumstances, for example in cases where erroneous data had been used in calculating the scale of assessments, could the scale be subject to revision.

## Application of Article 19

Kyrgyzstan informed the Committee of the possibility that, in spite of its best efforts, its arrears would exceed, by January 1996, the amount specified in Article 19 of the Charter as necessary to retain the right to vote in the General Assembly. In the absence of a request from the Assembly, the Committee did not advise the Assembly on action to be taken with regard to the application of Article 19.

The Dominican Republic, pending a decision by the Security Council on its request for compensation for the losses suffered as a result of the embargo against Haiti, requested the Assembly to invoke the provision of Article 19 under which the Assembly could permit a Member State to vote, despite the fact that its arrears equalled or exceeded the amount of contributions due from it for the preceding two years, if it was satisfied that the failure to pay was due to conditions beyond the Member State's control. The Committee concluded that more recent data on the financial and economic situation of the Dominican Republic would be necessary in order to determine whether an inability to pay still existed. The Committee decided to advise the Assembly accordingly with regard to Article 19 and stressed that the request for compensation under Article 50 was beyond its own mandate.

The Committee had before it a letter of 7 June from the General Assembly's President concerning an October 1994 request by Iraq for a waiver of Article 19, on the grounds that its failure to pay its assessed contributions was due to conditions beyond its control. Iraq stressed that its inability to pay resulted from the comprehensive embargo imposed by Security Council resolutions, which had deprived Iraq of its financial resources. It also cited its attempts to pay in local currency, which had been rejected on the grounds that the Iraqi dinar did not represent freely transferable funds. Its ability to pay in hard currency was also limited, Iraq stated, because its assets were frozen under Security Council resolutions and attempts to secure release of part of them to pay oustanding contributions had so far been unsuccessful. Iraq also considered that the increase of its assessment under the new scale for 1995-1997 did not take into account its actual economic situation since the imposition of the embargo.

The Committee had divergent views on Iraq's request for a waiver of Article 19 and decided to inform the Assembly President accordingly. With regard to Iraq's rate of assessment, the Committee noted that in the scale for 1995-1997, Iraq had benefited from the mitigation procedure and that the fluctuations in its domestic prices had been addressed by using the price-adjusted rates of exchange, instead of the market exchange rate; furthermore, any changes to its rate would have to be considered in the context of the next scale.

On 27 November, Iraq forwarded to the Fifth Committee Chairman a letter it had addressed on 22 September to the Assembly President,[6] stating that in view of the lack of consensus in the Committee on Contributions and the importance Iraq attached to being given the right to vote during the Assembly's historic fiftieth session, it requested that a draft resolution annexed to the letter be submitted to the Assembly for a decision as soon as possible. Under the resolution, the Assembly would decide that Iraq's arrears were due to circumstances beyond its control and that, accordingly, it was inappropriate to apply Article 19 relating to the loss of the right to vote in the Assembly until the sanctions imposed on Iraq were fully or partially lifted.

**GENERAL ASSEMBLY ACTION**

On 23 December, the General Assembly adopted **resolution 50/207 A.**

### Scale of assessments for the apportionment of the expenses of the United Nations

*The General Assembly,*

*Noting* the requests by Azerbaijan, Comoros, Georgia, Kyrgyzstan, Latvia, Liberia, Sao Tome and Principe, Tajikistan and Turkmenistan that, as an exceptional measure, any arrears in respect of assessed contributions for the regular budget of the United Nations, peace-keeping operations or international tribunals as at 1 January 1996 and for 1996 be treated as being attributable to conditions beyond their control and that, accordingly, the question of the application of Article 19 of the Charter of the United Nations should not arise,

1. *Recognizes* the importance of requests with respect to the application of Article 19 of the Charter of the United Nations being considered by the Committee on Contributions in accordance with rule 160 of the rules of procedure of the General Assembly;

2. *Requests* the Committee to hold a special session of one week's duration as early as possible in 1996 to consider representations from Member States with respect to the application of Article 19 of the Charter and to report thereon to the General Assembly at its resumed fiftieth session pursuant to rule 160 of the rules of procedure;

3. *Invites* Member States to submit detailed information to the Committee in explanation of their requests as soon as possible so as to facilitate the work of the Committee;

4. *Decides* to consider the report of the Committee on this matter as early as possible during its resumed fiftieth session.

General Assembly resolution 50/207

23 December 1995     Meeting 100     Adopted without vote

Approved by Fifth Committee (A/50/843) without vote, 21 December (meeting 44); draft by Chairman following informal consultations (A/C.5/50/L.21), orally revised; agenda item 120.
*Meeting numbers.* GA 50th session: 5th Committee 4-10, 43, 44; plenary 100.

On a motion by New Zealand, which the Fifth Committee supported by a recorded vote of 48 to 3, with 23 abstentions, the debate on Iraq's draft resolution[7] was closed under rule 117 of the Assembly's rules of procedure. In proposing its motion, New Zealand stated that Iraq's case did not warrant sympathetic consideration, as it did have access to convertible currency; it was its own choice if it did not give priority to using such assets to pay its assessed contribution.

## Contributions from South Africa

Following the eradication of apartheid and the establishment in South Africa of a non-racial and democratic society, the General Assembly in 1994 invited South Africa to resume its participation in the Assembly's work.[8]

The Assembly, by **resolution 50/83** of 15 December, decided that, owing to the unique and exceptional circumstances arising from apartheid, South Africa should not pay the assessments for the period from 30 September 1974 to 23 June 1994, the time during which the apartheid regime refused to pay its contributions in retaliation against the political decision of the Assembly to reject the credentials of the representatives of that regime. The technical observations on the most appropriate accounting procedure to be followed to implement the resolution elaborated by the Fifth Committee in response to a request by the Assembly President, were incorporated verbatim in the draft resolution. The Assembly stated that its decision would not set a precedent, but was based on the unique and exceptional circumstances during the apartheid era. (See also PART TWO, Chapter II.)

## Scale methodology

The General Assembly, on numerous occasions over the years, had reaffirmed the principle of capacity to pay as the fundamental criterion for determining the scale of assessments for contributions to the regular budget. In 1994, it decided[9] to establish a working group of 25 experts to examine all aspects of the implementation of that principle.

The Ad Hoc Intergovernmental Working Group on the Implementation of the Principle of Capacity to Pay held two sessions in 1995:[10] its organizational and preparatory session (21 to 24 March) and its substantive session (18 April to 5 May).

In discussing the fundamental question of what capacity to pay was, the Working Group noted that the Assembly had realized from the start that it was not a concept that could be defined with precision. But taking into account the work accomplished by the Committee on Contributions over the years to overcome those difficulties, the Working Group felt that it was possible to identify an objective and generally acceptable measure of capacity to pay. The starting point for the determination of capacity to pay was the share of each Member State's national income in world income; the Group held that other factors, such as the special circumstances of Member States with low per capita income, should also be taken into account.

There was general agreement that capacity to pay should be based on widely applicable measures; several members concluded that that factor alone pointed to the use of flow measures (i.e., income) rather than stock measures (i.e., wealth) as the best approximation, especially in the absence of reliable estimates of national wealth.

While all members accepted that either gross or net national income figures should be employed in calculating the scale of assessments, some felt that capacity to pay was best derived from national income alone, while others considered that it should also reflect the general level of development, measured through socio-economic indicators or through concepts such as sustainable development. Some members also attached importance to continuing to take into account the debt burden faced by a number of countries.

The Working Group agreed that national disposable income (NDI) was theoretically the most appropriate measure of capacity to pay; given its lower reliability and availability, however, its use in the scale of assessments would be impractical for the time being. It recommended that, for reasons of data availability, comparibility and simplicity, gross national product (GNP) should be the basis of calculation.

The Group acknowledged the seriousness of the debt problem of developing countries and noted that, since 1969, various ad hoc adjustments had been made in the scale of assessments in recognition of the debt situation. In the 1995-1997 scale, 47 countries benefited in varying degrees from the debt-burden adjustment in the existing methodology, and the cash relief of that adjustment had amounted to about $10 million. The Group noted that national income figures accounted fully for interest payments on external debt on an accrual basis, i.e., whether or not those payments were actually made on time. The debt-burden adjustment was intended to take account of amortization payments. Several members stressed that the debt burden was the most important financial and budgetary constraint many Governments had to face; they considered that the current debt adjustment—the product of successive General Assembly decisions—should be maintained because the debt affected the capacity to pay of the countries concerned. Several members drew attention to a number of features of the adjustment, concluding that it was not sufficiently soundly based nor substantial enough to justify modifying the basic income measure and would best be subsumed under the low per capita income adjustment. They also suggested that a special adjustment could be made by the General Assembly if particular countries could demonstrate they had actually made substantial net repayments (that is, without refinancing); with that proviso, they considered that the debt-burden adjustment should be eliminated.

The Working Group recommended using a base period of three years in formulating the scale of assessments, as long as the assessment period remained three years, and avoiding any further change in the base period. Some members believed that there should be annual recalculation of the scale for informational purposes; the possibility of automatic annual adjustment of assessments could later be evaluated, with reviews every three or five years.

The Group also discussed employing a common currency in the scale calculation, such as Special Drawing Rights (the weighted average of five major currencies calculated and used by the International Monetary Fund), rather than the United States dollar. Members felt that the idea should be studied further.

While the Group endorsed the continued application of the low per capita income allowance— deducted from a Member State's national income

to arrive at its assessable income—as a component of the measurement of capacity to pay, it could not agree on specific parameters for that purpose. For example, some members felt changes should be made to eliminate the jump that occurs when a country's per capita income goes above the limit for the allowance.

Among other issues discussed by the Working Group were that of rounding in the scale of assessments, the use of population data for calculating per capita income, and the variations of income and expenditure data in different national accounts.

The Committee on Contributions, in its report on its 1995 session,[1] noted that the Working Group had raised a number of issues, which would be included in the Committee's work in 1996. In evaluating the Working Group's recommendation to use GNP as a starting point for measuring capacity to pay, the Committee noted that the use of GNP rather than national income for calculating the scale of assessments would dispense with the deduction of allowances for depreciation of fixed assets from the income concept. The Committee also decided to keep under review other alternative measures, such as debt-adjusted income, and to follow up on the Working Group's recommendation to address the issue of the measurement of income for the former centrally planned economies.

The Committee reiterated its view that the base period should be a multiple of the scale period and should not be shorter than the scale period. It decided to study and report in 1996 on the possibility of changing the base period. Regarding the subject of conversion to a common currency, the Committee agreed with the Working Group's proposals for further work and expressed its intention to study appropriate new criteria for replacing International Monetary Fund (IMF) market exchange rates (MERs) when their use produced excessive fluctuations or distortions in the income of some Member States. In that context, reference was made to the *World Bank Atlas* exchange rates (a simple average of a current market rate and price-adjusted rates of exchange based on the two previous years).

Regarding the debt-burden adjustment, there was no consensus among Committee members either on the importance of maintaining the adjustment or on how to calculate it. Some members considered that debt-burden adjustment should continue to be applied in calculating the capacity to pay of Member States facing high levels of external debt. Others had doubts about the conceptual basis of the current debt-burden adjustment approach and preferred an approach based on actual debt repayment. The Committee agreed to study the issue of the debt-burden adjustment formula at its 1996 session, including possible alternatives, and asked the Secretariat to provide, from IMF or any other comparable source, data for all countries on actual debt repayments and debt stock, as well as the ratio of debt to national income and the ratio of debt-service to export earnings.

The Committee discussed extensively the low per capita income adjustment but did not have sufficient time to study two proposals, the first of which would have replaced the current adjustment with one directly linking the percentage relief a Member State would receive to its per capita income level. Under the second, the gradient would be set according to a criterion based on a maximum allowable deviation of the assessment rate from the global share of income for the Member State with the lowest per capita income. The Committee decided that a comprehensive study on the feasibility of the proposals, as well as other alternatives, would be undertaken in 1996 in conjunction with its overall review of the scale methodology.

*REFERENCES*

[1]A/50/11 & Add.1 & Add.1/Rev.1. [2]A/49/897. [3]YUN 1994, p. 242, GA res. 49/63, 15 Dec. 1994. [4]YUN 1993, p. 1204, GA res. 48/223 B, 23 Dec. 1993. [5]A/50/843. [6]A/C.5/50/37. [7]A/C.5/50/L.8. [8]YUN 1994, p. 263, GA res. 48/258 A, 23 June 1994. [9]YUN 1994, p. 1355, GA res. 49/19 A, 29 Nov. 1994. [10]A/49/897.

# Accounts and auditing

In 1995, the Board of Auditors presented two reports on audits it had conducted of the UN High Commissioner for Refugees (UNHCR)[1] (see PART FOUR, Chapter XII) and of the United Nations Institute for Training and Research (UNITAR)[2] (see PART FOUR, Chapter IX). A concise summary of their principal findings, conclusions and recommendations were transmitted to the General Assembly by an August note[3] of the Secretary-General. Also in August, the Secretary-General transmitted a report[4] of the Board on the liquidation audit of the UN Transition Authority in Cambodia (UNTAC) (see PART TWO, Chapter IV).

Summing up Board activities in a statement before the Fifth Committee, the Board Chairman said the indicative budget of $8.2 million from all sources for the biennium 1996-1997 reflected amounts charged for conducting external audits, but excluded secretariat-related costs. The General Assembly's recent decision to amend the Financial Regulations and Rules in order to place the financial period for peace-keeping operations on an annual basis meant that the Board would present annual instead of biennial reports on such operations; the consequent increase in audit coverage would result in additional audit fees, given the expected increase in workload.

The Board was also taking steps to strengthen external oversight. For example, the Panel of External Auditors of the United Nations had recently decided to recognize the auditing standards of the International Organization of Supreme Audit Institutions (INTOSAI) as its core standards and to adopt the international standards on auditing issued by the International Federation of Accountants as the Panel's new auditing guidelines. The Board had also taken action to revise the audit manual and had made suggestions for improving the transparency of financial statements. It proposed to continue the practice of carrying out horizontal reviews on relevant topics in each biennium and of reviewing procurement practices in all units of the Organization.

With regard to the timely and effective implementation of its recommendations, the Board was of the view that the Administration should implement those which could be implemented without delay and work out a schedule for putting into practice those that required amendment of the rules and procedures. The Board was also considering methods to identify persistent irregularities in order to enable the Advisory Committee on Administrative and Budgetary Questions (ACABQ) to follow up on them and to ascertain from the Administration the reasons for their recurrence.

The Board had established a reasonable working relationship with the Office of Internal Oversight Services. It was important, however, the Chairman said, to have a clear appreciation of the respective roles of the two bodies. A strong and independent audit function should be at the core of UN accountability arrangements, and the roles of internal and external auditing should be kept separate. By its very definition, internal audit should form part of the overall internal control system established by the management, while external audit was a means of providing objective information, advice and assurance to the General Assembly through independent financial audits and management reviews. In that connection, the Board had noted the Advisory Committee's request that it should report on implementation of its recommendations for improving the work of the Internal Audit Division.

With regard to Board terms of office, the Board noted that its proposal in favour of the adoption of a six-year term, which would bring the term into line with biennial accounting and give each member sufficient time to have significant impact on the Board's work, was still before the Assembly.

On 23 December, the General Assembly adopted **resolution 50/204 A**.

### Financial reports and audited financial statements, and reports of the Board of Auditors

*The General Assembly,*

*Having considered,* for the year ended 31 December 1994, the financial report and audited financial statements and the report of the Board of Auditors on the United Nations Institute for Training and Research, the audited financial statements and the report of Board of Auditors on the voluntary funds administered by the United Nations High Commissioner for Refugees, the report on measures taken or to be taken by the United Nations High Commissioner for Refugees in response to the recommendations of the Board of Auditors, and the concise summary of the principal findings, conclusions and recommendations of the Board, as well as the report of the Board of Auditors on the liquidation audit of the United Nations Transitional Authority in Cambodia and the report of the Advisory Committee on Administrative and Budgetary Questions,

*Noting* the measures taken by the United Nations Institute for Training and Research to give appropriate consideration and attention to the recommendations in earlier audit reports, as commented upon by the Board of Auditors in the annex to its report,

*Taking note with concern* of the comments of the Board of Auditors regarding measures taken by the Administration of the Office of the United Nations High Commissioner for Refugees on follow-up action to implement the recommendations of the Board, contained in the annex to its report,

*Stressing* the importance of efficient resource management in all United Nations organizations and programmes,

1.  *Recognizes* that the Board of Auditors provides the General Assembly with objective information, advice and assurance by conducting its audits in a completely independent and comprehensive manner, as stipulated in regulations 12.5 and 12.6 of the Financial Regulations of the United Nations, and reiterates its appreciation to the Board for the action-oriented and concrete recommendations contained in its reports;

2.  *Accepts* the financial reports and audited financial statements and the audit opinions and reports of the Board of Auditors regarding the aforementioned organizations and the liquidation of the United Nations Transitional Authority in Cambodia;

3.  *Also accepts* the concise summary of principal findings, conclusions and recommendations for remedial action of the Board of Auditors and the comments thereon contained in the report of the Advisory Committee on Administrative and Budgetary Questions;

4.  *Deplores* the delays encountered in the implementation of the recommendations of the Board of Auditors approved by the General Assembly;

5.  *Urges* the Secretary-General to hold programme managers accountable for the implementation of recommendations and to take appropriate measures in cases of non-compliance;

6.  *Stresses* the importance of prompt compliance with the recommendations of the Board of Auditors approved by the General Assembly, and reiterates its request to the executive heads of United Nations organizations and programmes to submit to the General Assembly, through the Advisory Committee on Administrative and Budgetary Questions, before the beginning of formal discussions, reports on measures taken or to be taken in response to the recommendations of the Board, including timetables for their implementation;

7.  *Requests* the Board of Auditors to follow up and report at the earliest opportunity on shortcomings in the internal audit coverage of the organizations which it identified in its earlier report, with a view to determining whether its recommendations have been implemented and the situation rectified, following the establishment of the Office of Internal Oversight Services;

8.  *Recalls* that, in its resolution 49/216 C of 23 December 1994, it requested the Secretary-General to submit a report, through the Advisory Committee on Administrative and Budgetary Questions, containing proposals for the improvement of the procurement activities of the Secretariat, and urges the Advisory Committee to submit its report to the General Assembly as soon as possible to enable it to consider these reports and decide on further necessary action before the end of its fiftieth session;

9.  *Requests* the Office of the United Nations High Commissioner for Refugees and all other entities for which the main source of income is voluntary contributions and which account for them on an accrual basis to provide annually, or upon request, more precise and transparent information on the cash situation of these entities in their reports to the General Assembly at its fifty-first and subsequent sessions;

10.  *Requests* the Secretary-General to consider measures to ensure appropriate audit coverage of jointly financed administrative activities, to consider the most appropriate way to present to the General Assembly the financial, administrative and management information related to these activities, and to report thereon to the Assembly during its resumed fiftieth session.

General Assembly resolution 50/204 A

23 December 1995    Meeting 100    Adopted without vote

Approved by Fifth Committee (A/50/839) without vote, 21 December (meeting 44); draft by Vice-Chairman (A/C.5/50/L.20) following informal consultations; agenda item 113.
*Meeting numbers.* GA 50th session: 5th Committee 21, 25, 27, 44; plenary 100.

*REFERENCES*
(1)A/50/5/Add.5. (2)A/50/5/Add.4. (3)A/50/327. (4)A/49/943.

## Programme planning

In 1995, the Fifth Committee continued consideration of the item on programme planning during the General Assembly's resumed forty-ninth session. Speaking as coordinator of the informal consultations on that subject, Mexico said that no consensus had been reached to enable a draft resolution to be submitted for adoption without vote. Mexico therefore recommended that further consideration of the item be deferred to the fiftieth session. The Assembly did so by **decision 49/464 B** of 20 July.

The Fifth Committee resumed discussion of issues related to programme planning in October and decided to consider them together with the proposed programme budget for 1996-1997.

## Medium-term plan

### Prototype new format

The medium-term plan and a prototype new format were discussed by the Fifth Committee under the agenda item on programme planning. The prototype, proposed by the Secretary-General in 1994, took into account the recommendations of the Committee for Programme and Coordination (CPC) that it contain a concise forward-looking policy document or perspectives containing an analysis of persistent problems and emerging trends that needed to be addressed within the next four to six years and the role of the Organization in that undertaking. The perspective would indicate broad priority areas for the work of the Organization and would be amended only if pressing needs of an unforeseeable nature arose. CPC also recommended the inclusion of a programme framework listing major programmes and subprogrammes and providing guidelines against which the preparation and implementation of the budget would be assessed. The narrative of each programme should consist of a one-page chapter detailing its objectives and mandates. The programme framework should be reviewed regularly every two years in the off-budget year to reflect new mandates.

Introducing an August 1994 report of the Secretary-General on the prototype,[1] consideration of which had been deferred,[2] the UN Controller said the prototype had been developed in consultations with interested delegations and CPC, on the basis of recommendations made in previous years both by CPC and the General Assembly. The effectiveness of the current format of the plan had been called into question by the Secretariat, as well as by certain Member States, for a number of reasons, including the disproportionate emphasis it had placed on activities and output, rather than objectives, and its failure to state those objectives with sufficient precision. The current plan contained only a list of activities and gave no clear insight into their organization, nor did it provide a direct link between programme structure and the offices responsible for implementation. For that reason, the budget structures and programme structures lacked congruence.

The new prototype endeavoured to address those problems and represented a significant departure from the 1992-1997 model. It aimed to facilitate the intergovernmental review of the overall direction of the Organization's work and to link clearly organizational and programmatic structures, thus forming an integral part of the system of accountability that the Secretariat was endeavouring to establish.

In an August 1995 report,[3] ACABQ recommended approval of the proposed new format, provided that its own observations were taken into account. It was the Advisory Committee's understanding that, should the Assembly approve the Secretary-General's proposal, he would submit for the Assembly's consideration the necessary revisions to the Regulations and Rules Governing Programme Planning, the Programme Aspects of the Budget, the Monitoring of Implementation and the Methods of Evaluation.

By **decision 50/452** of 22 December 1995, the Assembly, on the Fifth Committee's recommendation,[4] authorized the Secretary-General to begin preparing the proposed medium-term plan for the period after 1997, on the basis of CPC and ACABQ recommendations and taking into account views expressed by Member States. The Assembly also requested the Secretary-General to submit the plan for that period to it in 1996, through CPC.

*REFERENCES*

[1]YUN 1994, p. 1360. [2]Ibid., GA dec. 49/464 A, 23 Dec. 1994. [3]A/49/958. [4]A/50/795.

Chapter III

# United Nations staff

In 1995, a number of questions related to the conditions of service of United Nations staff members were considered by the General Assembly. The International Civil Service Commission made recommendations to the Assembly regarding salary levels and established a working group to review the operation of the post adjustment system. Amendments to the UN Staff Regulations were approved in line with the General Assembly decision that the repatriation grant and other expatriate benefits were limited to staff who worked and resided in a country other than their home country.

The General Assembly also approved recommendations of the Joint Inspection Unit on the application of UN recruitment, placement and promotion policies, and requested that a comprehensive policy on the use of retirees in the Secretariat be developed. It called for the fulfilment of the target of having women occupy 50 per cent of managerial and decision-making positions by the year 2000. The Assembly also invited its Sixth Committee to examine, as a matter of priority, the Secretary-General's proposals for the reform of the internal justice system.

The principal of the United Nations Joint Staff Pension Fund increased to $12.6 billion during the year. The Assembly decided to admit the World Tourism Organization to membership in the Fund as of 1 January 1996.

Maritime Organization; the World Meteorological Organization; the World Intellectual Property Organization; the International Atomic Energy Agency and the United Nations Industrial Development Organization. Two other organizations—the International Fund for Agricultural Development and the World Trade Organization—have not formally accepted the statute of ICSC, but participate fully in the Commission's work. The Commission has the authority to make decisions on certain rates of allowances and benefits, on the post adjustment (cost-of-living) classification of duty stations, and on job classification. It also makes recommendations to the General Assembly on specified remuneration issues and to Executive Heads on salary scales of General Service staff and other locally recruited persons, personnel policies, and the development of common staff regulations.

In 1995, the Commission held its forty-first (Montreal, Canada, 1-19 May) and forty-second (New York, 24 July-14 August) sessions. It examined issues that derived from decisions and resolutions of the General Assembly, as well as from its own statute. A summary of the Commission's deliberations, recommendations and decisions was provided in its twenty-first annual report,[2] on which the Assembly acted in December.

## Conditions of service

### International Civil Service Commission

The International Civil Service Commission (ICSC) was established by the General Assembly in 1974[1] to regulate and coordinate the conditions of service of the United Nations common system. Thirteen organizations comprise ICSC: the United Nations; the International Labour Organization; the Food and Agriculture Organization of the United Nations; the United Nations Educational, Scientific and Cultural Organization; the International Civil Aviation Organization; the World Health Organization; the Universal Postal Union; the International Telecommunication Union; the International

### Noblemaire principle

In 1995, in response to a 1992 General Assembly request,[3] ICSC undertook an in-depth review of the Noblemaire principle and its application. The underlying premise of the principle, adopted during the existence of the League of Nations, is that salaries of Professional and higher-category staff should be sufficient to attract and retain staff from all countries, including those offering the highest pay. Following the review, the Commission reported to the General Assembly in 1995 that the current practice of using the highest-paid national civil service as a basis for comparison appeared to be sound, as long as the process of identifying the comparator civil service was handled on a timely basis and that the pay relationship with the comparator realistically reflected the latter's expatriation benefits.

Also in 1995, the Commission undertook an updated grade-equivalency study with the current comparator, the United States federal civil service. It endorsed the results of that study for remuneration comparison purposes, deciding that the relevant pay systems of the comparator should be reflected in the comparison process on an occupation-by-occupation basis. It also decided that bonuses and performance awards granted to United States staff (except for those granted to eligible staff of the Senior Executive Service as meritorious and distinguished awards) and all comparable UN awards should be included in the comparison process.

In 1991, the Commission had proposed to the General Assembly a two-phase methodological approach for carrying out periodic checks to determine which national civil service was the highest paid. That approach was endorsed by the Assembly in 1991.[4] In 1994, the Commission reported to the General Assembly its decision to proceed to a Phase II study of the national civil services of Germany and Switzerland. Concluded in 1995, the study showed that the total compensation package of the Swiss civil service was 85.8 per cent of that of the United States federal civil service. The Swiss federal civil service could not, therefore, be considered as an alternative to the current comparator civil service. The comparison with the German civil service showed that its total remuneration package was 110.5 per cent of that of the United States. Despite a strong presumption in favour of the German civil service as a comparator, the conditions for changing the comparator were not currently in place. The superior conditions of the German civil service *vis-à-vis* those of the United States federal civil service could be considered as a reference point for managing United Nations/United States pay relativities. The Commission reported in 1995 that it would continue to monitor the total compensation of the German civil service and would update the data annually.

In 1995, the Commission collected information on the World Bank and the Organisation for Economic Cooperation and Development (OECD) and obtained comparisons showing that OECD and World Bank remuneration levels were 49.5 and 39 per cent, respectively, above those of the UN common system. The Commission noted that it thus appeared that the compensation package of the common system was not competitive with that offered by OECD and the World Bank for equivalent jobs requiring similar levels of competence. It considered that it would be appropriate to use OECD and the World Bank as reference indications for the competitiveness of UN system salaries, while reaffirming the long-standing practice of comparisons with the best-paid national civil service under the application of the Noblemaire principle.

### Structure of salary scale

The Commission recalled that there were two main mandates from the General Assembly relevant to the structure of the salary scale: the request, in resolution 43/226,[5] that consideration be given to enhancing rewards on promotion, while reducing financial rewards for longevity; and, in resolution 47/216,[3] the Assembly's request that the Commission continue to keep under review the structure of the salary scale at all levels of the Professional and higher categories, taking into account, *inter alia*, the overall United Nations/United States pay relativities as established by the General Assembly and the imbalance in those relativities at different Professional grade levels.

The Commission noted that the discrepancies between United Nations/United States remuneration ratios at different grade levels had been partly corrected over recent years, but considerable progress remained to be made. Moreover, the salary scale over time had become quite compressed as an unintended side-effect of post adjustment consolidations, and consequently the rewards for promotion, *vis-à-vis* seniority, had progressively eroded. The Commission considered a range of options designed to redress these structural deficiencies and to restore the competitiveness of common system remuneration.

The Commission recommended restoration in 1996 of the 115 desirable mid-point of the United Nations/United States net remuneration, which should be brought about through the application of the proposed base/floor salary scale, without consolidation of post adjustment, and a scaling forward of all post adjustment indices by 5.1 per cent as of 1 July 1996. It offered alternatives for addressing the question of the post adjustment index for Geneva. The Commission also recommended salary scales and rates of dependency allowances for the General Service and other locally recruited categories in New York, the General Service staff of all organizations in Geneva, and for the Food and Agriculture Organization of the United Nations in Rome.

The Consultative Committee on Administrative Questions (Personnel and General Administrative Questions (CCAQ(PER)) of the Administrative Committee on Coordination (ACC), at its eighty-second[6] (Montreal, Canada, 24-28 April) and eighty-third[7] (New York, 20-24 July and 20-22 September) sessions, considered the application of the Noblemaire principle and recommended a draft statement to ACC for adoption.

The Secretary-General, in a 24 October note,[8] transmitted the statement relating to the UN common system remuneration adopted by ACC at its second regular session (New York, 12-13 October) for submission to the Assembly. ACC requested the Assembly to adopt the Commission's recommendations to increase remuneration levels with immediate effect in order to bring the current margin to the mid-point of its range, and to restructure the salary scale to correct existing imbalances.

On 10 November, the Secretary-General stated[9] that there would be an increase of $47.2 million in the regular budget for the 1995-1996 biennium, should the Assembly adopt the Commission's recommendations. Of that amount, $8.4 million related to staff assessment; as there would be a corresponding increase of $8.5 million under income section 1 (Income from staff assessment), partially reduced by $114,200 in the estimate under income section 3 (Revenue-producing activities), the net increase would be $38.8 million.

The Secretary-General, in a statement before the Fifth (Administrative and Budgetary) Committee on 20 November, reiterated the views of ACC and called on the Assembly to adopt measures recommended by ICSC, together with action to revise the application of the Noblemaire principle and to reinforce the Commission's capacity and contribution.

On 6 December, the Advisory Committee on Administrative and Budgetary Questions (ACABQ) recommended[10] that the Secretary-General include, in the next presentation of the administrative and financial implications of ICSC recommendations, a complete explanation and justification of the methodology used to calculate numbers of staff and percentages applicable to the United Nations. It also decided that, with effect from the next adjustment of the global scale of pensionable remuneration for staff in the Professional and higher categories, actual pension contributions in time-to-time adjustments of the post adjustment index should be used.

## Functioning of ICSC

In response to a 1994 General Assembly request,[11] ICSC considered[2] its working methods and, in particular, the consultative process with the executive heads of its interlocutors and staff. ICSC did not accept that it was beholden to the Assembly or that it had become politicized. The Commission concluded that for the consultative process to improve, ICSC must not stand alone in reassessing its procedures; participating UN bodies had to contribute to the discussion. The Commission had done its best to restore the dialogue, but its interlocutors should review their working methods. The Commission also called for a stronger climate of accountability, whereby all parties in the process faced their roles and responsibilities squarely. The Commission regretted that

the Federation of International Civil Servants' Associations (FICSA) had not participated in its discussions, but hoped it would resume doing so.

The Commission decided to implement measures to improve its effectiveness, including a new formula for the timing and length of its sessions and for the production of its report. For 1996, it decided to hold a four-week session in the spring and a one- to two-week session in the summer, depending on need, as defined by the agenda; if that formula was found to be effective, it would be adopted in the future for even-numbered years. The report of its spring session would consist of draft decisions with their rationales; at the summer session, the Commission would have before it the full report for adoption. In odd-numbered years, the Commission would hold a single session of one month's duration. The new arrangement would be introduced on a trial basis and remain under review.

By a November note,[12] the Secretary-General transmitted to the Assembly the comments of FICSA on ways of improving the consultative process in the Commission, as requested by the Assembly in 1994.[11]

**GENERAL ASSEMBLY ACTION**

On 23 December, the General Assembly adopted **resolution 50/208**.

#### United Nations common system: report of the International Civil Service Commission

*The General Assembly,*

*Having considered* the twenty-first annual report of the International Civil Service Commission and other related reports,

*Reaffirming its commitment* to a single unified United Nations common system as the cornerstone for the regulation and coordination of the conditions of service of the United Nations common system,

*Reaffirming* the central role of the Commission in the regulation and coordination of the conditions of service of the United Nations common system,

*Taking note* of the statement of the Administrative Committee on Coordination and of the introductory statement of the Secretary-General regarding the report of the Commission,

I
Conditions of service of the Professional
and higher categories

A. *Examination of the Noblemaire principle
and its application*

*Recalling* its resolutions related to the study of all aspects of the application of the Noblemaire principle,

*Recalling also* section I.B of its resolution 44/198 of 21 December 1989, by which it reaffirmed that the Noblemaire principle should continue to serve as the basis of comparison between United Nations emoluments and those of the highest-paying civil service,

*Taking note* of chapter III of the report of the International Civil Service Commission in respect of grade equivalencies with the comparator civil service, the evolution of the margin, the identification of the highest-paid national civil service and the collection of reference data from other international organizations, as well as the views expressed thereon by Member States in the Fifth Committee of the General Assembly,

*Reconfirming* the continued application of the Noblemaire principle,

*Reaffirming* the need to continue to ensure the competitiveness of the United Nations common system conditions of service,

1. *Decides* to defer its consideration of chapter III.A of the report of the International Civil Service Commission until its resumed fiftieth session, and requests the Commission to review its recommendations and conclusions, taking into account the views expressed by Member States in the Fifth Committee of the General Assembly, in particular regarding the appropriateness of reduction of dominance and the treatment of bonuses in determining net remuneration comparisons, so as to assist in that consideration, and to adjust its programme of work accordingly;

2. *Takes note* of the results of the study to identify the highest-paid national civil service, as set out in paragraph 172 *(b)* of the report of the Commission, bearing in mind the views expressed thereon by the Member State concerned;

3. *Requests* the Commission and the national civil service authorities concerned to resolve the outstanding difficulties in comparing differently designed civil services and grading systems, within the approved methodology, and to clarify the conclusions set out in paragraph 172 *(b)* (ii) and (iii) of its report, in order to complete the study on the highest-paid national civil service, and to report thereon to the General Assembly;

4. *Takes note also* of the recruitment and retention problems faced by some organizations in respect of certain specialized occupations, recalls its endorsement in principle of the use of special occupational rates in organizations with problems of recruitment and retention, and, in this context, requests the organizations to collect data to substantiate those problems, and the Commission to make recommendations regarding the conditions for the application of such rates, as appropriate;

### B. *Post adjustment matters*

*Recalling* its request in section II.G of its resolution 48/224 of 23 December 1993, regarding place-to-place surveys conducted at headquarters duty stations,

*Taking note* of the decisions reached by the International Civil Service Commission in paragraphs 280, 294, 296 and 297 of its report in respect of the operation of the post adjustment system,

1. *Welcomes* the establishment by the International Civil Service Commission of a working group to examine the post adjustment system;

2. *Requests* the Commission to establish in 1996, in respect of staff members whose duty station is Geneva, a single post adjustment index which is fully representative of the cost of living of all staff working in the duty station and which ensures equality of treatment with staff in other headquarters duty stations;

3. *Also requests* the Commission to address and refer to its working group on post adjustment, as appropriate, the concerns raised by Member States in the Fifth Committee regarding the operation of the post adjust-

ment system, including, *inter alia*, the issue of the post adjustment at the base of the common system, management of the differential in net remuneration between the common system and its comparator, developments in the comparator civil service and the possible partial phasing out of the expatriate elements of the margin for staff with long service at one duty station, and requests the Commission to review all the issues relating to the post adjustment system based on the study by its working group and to report thereon to the General Assembly at its fifty-first session;

### II
### General Service and other locally recruited categories

*Recalling* section III, paragraph 1, of its resolution 47/216 of 23 December 1992, in which it endorsed the reaffirmation by the International Civil Service Commission of the Flemming principle as the basis for the determination of conditions of service of the General Service and related categories,

*Recalling also* section IV.A of its resolution 49/223 of 23 December 1994, by which it requested the Commission to proceed with the current round of surveys at headquarters duty stations,

1. *Notes* that the International Civil Service Commission will provide a further report on the methodology for surveys of best prevailing local conditions of employment at headquarters duty stations following the completion of the comprehensive review of the salary survey methodology in 1997;

2. *Requests* the Commission, as part of its review of the methodology for salary setting for staff in the General Service and other locally recruited categories, to resolve, to the extent possible, inconsistencies between this methodology and the one which is applied pursuant to the Noblemaire principle, *inter alia*, by examining the question of overlap in remuneration between the two categories;

3. *Takes note* of the results of the salary surveys in New York, Geneva and Rome as reported in chapter IV of the report of the Commission;

### III
### Work programme

*Recalling* section V, paragraph 2, of its resolution 48/224, in which it urged the International Civil Service Commission to devote further attention to personnel management issues,

1. *Requests* the International Civil Service Commission to examine means of reducing the costs of its studies;

2. *Also requests* the Commission and the executive heads of the organizations of the United Nations common system to ensure that adequate attention is given to all aspects of human resources management, including the improvement of non-monetary aspects of conditions of service, as set out, for example, in article 14 of the statute of the Commission;

3. *Further requests* the Commission to give priority to the matters addressed in section I of the present resolution in its programme of work;

### IV
### Functioning of the Commission

*Recalling* section II, paragraph 5, of its resolution 49/223, in which it requested the staff bodies, the organizations and the International Civil Service Commission to review with all urgency how the consultative process of the Commission could best be furthered and to report thereon to the General Assembly,

1. _Reaffirms_ the validity of the statute of the International Civil Service Commission and in particular article 6 thereof, whereby its members shall perform their functions in full independence and with impartiality;

2. _Welcomes_ the Commission's decision, as contained in paragraphs 54 to 56 of its report, to implement a number of measures to improve its effectiveness and to introduce, on a trial basis, revised arrangements for the timing and length of its sessions, and, in that context, requests the Commission to enhance further the transparency of its work, taking into account the relevant articles of the statute and its rules of procedure;

3. _Calls upon_ Member States and the Secretary-General, in the context of articles 3 and 4 of the statute of the Commission, to ensure through the selection process of candidates for appointment that the Commission has the requisite technical skills and broad managerial experience among its membership;

4. _Notes_ that the representatives of the Coordinating Committee for International Staff Unions and Associations of the United Nations System and the Federation of International Civil Servants' Associations have both suspended participation in the work of the Commission, and calls upon those bodies to resume participation in the work of the Commission in a spirit of cooperation and non-confrontation;

5. _Requests_ the Commission to ensure that its reports contain clear and readily understandable explanations of its technical recommendations.

General Assembly resolution 50/208

23 December 1995     Meeting 100     Adopted without vote

Approved by Fifth Committee (A/50/844) without vote, 21 December (meeting 44); draft by Chairman (A/C.5/50/L.27), based on informal consultations; agenda item 121.
_Meeting numbers._ GA 50th session: 5th Committee 28, 30, 31, 34, 36, 44; plenary 100.

By **decision 50/469** of the same date, the Assembly decided that the Fifth Committee should continue consideration of the item on the United Nations common system at its resumed session.

### Emoluments of top echelon officials

ACABQ, in a 13 October report,[13] requested the Secretary-General to issue an addendum to update the annex to his 1994 report[14] concerning the designation of special representatives and envoys. It requested the Secretary-General to: refine the guidelines on the use of funds budgeted for general temporary assistance to ensure consistency of application of the relevant procedures; reconsider the practice of financing some high-level positions from funds appropriated for general temporary assistance; follow the normal procedure for the establishment of posts; and report to the Assembly at its fiftieth session on measures taken to address the concerns it had raised.

In response to the comments of ACABQ, the Secretary-General submitted on 6 December revised estimates for the 1996-1997 biennium.[15]

On 23 December the General Assembly adopted **resolution 50/216, section II**.

**Revised estimates under section 1 (Overall policy-making, direction and coordination), section 32 (Staff assessment) and income section 1 (Income from staff assessment)**

[_The General Assembly . . ._]

1. _Takes note_ of the report of the Secretary-General on the revised estimates under section 1 (Overall policy-making, direction and coordination), section 32 (Staff assessment) and income section 1 (Income from staff assessment) of the proposed programme budget for the biennium 1996-1997;

2. _Endorses_ the recommendation of the Advisory Committee on Administrative and Budgetary Questions to approve a temporary post at the Under-Secretary-General level, as requested by the Secretary-General, and that such additional appropriation as might be required should be reflected in the performance report for the biennium 1996-1997;

. . .

General Assembly resolution 50/216, section II

23 December 1995     Meeting 100     Adopted without vote

Approved by Fifth Committee (A/50/842) without vote, 17 December (meeting 41); oral proposal by Chairman; agenda item 116.
_Meeting numbers._ GA 50th session: 5th Committee 3-5, 7, 10, 11, 41; plenary 100.

In 1995, the Secretary-General submitted reports on the conditions of service and compensation for the Chairman of ACABQ and the Chairman and Vice-Chairman of ICSC[16] and for members of the International Court of Justice.[17] ACABQ responded to the latter report in December[18] and made recommendations on such issues as the ICJ pension scheme.

On 31 March, the Assembly, in **resolution 49/237, section II,** took note of the Secretary-General's 1994 report on the subject and endorsed the recommendations of ACABQ.

In a 10 March report,[19] ACABQ submitted to the General Assembly its comments and recommendations on the Secretary-General's October 1994 report[20] on the conditions of service of the members of the International Tribunal for the Prosecution of Persons Responsible for Serious Violations of International Humanitarian Law Committed in the Territory of the Former Yugoslavia since 1991.

In **resolution 49/242 B** of 31 March, the Assembly endorsed the observations and recommendations contained in the report of ACABQ.

On 23 December, the General Assembly, by **resolution 50/216, section VI,** took note of the report of the Secretary-General on conditions of service for ICSC members and the ACABQ Chairman, and requested ACABQ to report thereon to the General Assembly at the first part of its resumed fiftieth session, in accordance with established procedures.

Also on 23 December, by **resolution 50/216, section IV**, the Assembly took note of the report of the Secretary-General on conditions for ICJ members, approved the ACABQ recommendation thereon and requested the Secretary-General to address the issues raised by ACABQ concerning the conditions of service of ICJ members in the context of the next review in 1998.

### Supplementary payments

Supplementary payments—the practice by some Member States of supplementing the salaries of some or all of their nationals in the service of the UN common system—have been discussed periodically by the Commission since its inception. In 1995, the Commission reported to the General Assembly that, although there was a strong presumption that supplementary payments were indicative of uncompetitive remuneration levels in the common system, the information received was too fragmentary to draw any definitive conclusions. It reiterated its earlier position that supplementary payments were inappropriate, inconsistent with the provisions of the staff regulations and at variance with the spirit of the UN Charter. Deductions from salaries were equally inappropriate.

### Post adjustment

As part of its ongoing responsibilities under its statute, the Commission kept under review the operation of the post adjustment system. It decided on a number of methodological issues, including arrangements for the forthcoming round of cost-of-living surveys, and approved a number of measures designed to improve the transparency of the post adjustment system.

Following a detailed review of the treatment of pension contributions in post adjustment, the Commission decided that, starting with the next adjustment of the global scale of pensionable remuneration for staff in the Professional and higher categories on 1 November 1995, actual pension contributions should be used in time-to-time adjustments of the post adjustment index. It informed the General Assembly that it had determined that, in the light of the arrangements embodied in the Pension Fund regulations, there would be no shift in the burden of Pension Fund contributions from staff to Member States as a result of the implementation of this decision.

### Post classification system

The Secretary-General, on 27 November, reported[21] on the implementation of the Joint Inspection Unit's (JIU) 1992[22] recommendations relating to the advantages and disadvantages of the post classification system. He stated that to address the shortage of classification officers, a number of personnel officers had been trained in job classification at several duty stations, making it possible to delegate authority for classification of posts to the UN offices in Vienna and in Geneva. Training was also provided to Executive Office personnel, to members of classification appeals bodies at Headquarters and at duty stations, to programme staff in Vienna, and to a number of human resource specialists at Headquarters, following the reorganization of the Office of Human Resources Management (OHRM) in 1995.

Financial provision was made in the proposed 1996-1997 programme budget for an automated system for the classification of Professional posts, financed jointly by organizations participating in the Subcommittee on Job Classification of the Consultative Committee on Administrative Questions.

### Other remuneration matters

#### Repatriation grant

In a 10 March report,[23] the Secretary-General referred to a 1993 General Assembly request[24] that ICSC study the practices of organizations of the common system regarding expatriate entitlements to staff members living in their home country while stationed at duty stations located in another country, with a view to harmonizing those practices. The Secretary-General explained that the practice followed by the UN was not to pay expatriate benefits, including the repatriation grant, to that category of staff members. Payment of expatriate benefits was made only to those staff members who worked and resided outside of their home country. In 1987, the Administrative Tribunal held that the practice conformed to the language in the Staff Regulations, but on 6 October 1994 the Tribunal reversed itself and held that the language of annex IV to the Staff Regulations did not support the practice followed by the UN and ordered the Secretary-General to pay the repatriation grant. The Legal Counsel advised that no useful purpose would be served by seeking an advisory opinion from ICJ and that the judgement must be implemented and repatriation benefits paid to applicants.

The Secretary-General proposed two options to the Assembly: accept the Tribunal's 1994 interpretation of annex IV to the Staff Regulations, either explicitly or by taking no positive action in which case the repatriation grant must be paid to applicants residing in their home country; or amend annex IV to the Staff Regulations, as well as staff regulations 3.2 and 5.3, to state explicitly that expatriate benefits were not payable unless an otherwise eligible staff member both worked and resided outside his or her home country. Should the Assembly adopt the first option, it would be preferable to do so in the form of a resolution, as the matter involved fundamental legislative policy which should be clearly set out. There was, however, the strong possibility that the reasoning of the Tribunal could be extended to the interpretation of staff regulations governing eligibility for education grants and home leave. If the Assembly adopted the second option, it might wish to request the governing bodies of organizations of the common system to amend their Staff Regulations and Rules in accordance with the policy reaffirmed by the Assembly, and inform ICSC of their actions.

The Secretary-General noted, however, that unless the Assembly decided to amend the Staff Regulations, he was obliged to conform to the interpretation of the Tribunal and to pay the repatriation grant to eligible staff members who lived in France but worked in Geneva and had separated or would separate from service after the date of the judgement.

**GENERAL ASSEMBLY ACTION**

On 6 April, the General Assembly adopted **resolution 49/241**.

**Payment of repatriation grant to staff members living in their home country while stationed at duty stations located in another country**

*The General Assembly,*

*Having considered* the report of the Secretary-General on payment of repatriation grant to staff members living in their home country while stationed at duty stations located in another country,

*Recalling* section II.D of its resolution 48/224 of 23 December 1993 on the United Nations common system, in which it requested the International Civil Service Commission to study further the practices of the organizations of the United Nations common system regarding the granting of expatriate entitlements to staff members living in their home country while stationed at duty stations located in another country, with a view to harmonizing the practices of the organizations with those of the United Nations, and to make recommendations thereon to the General Assembly at its fifty-first session,

*Noting* the decision of the United Nations Administrative Tribunal in Judgement No. 656, *Kremer, Gourdon,*

1. *Reiterates its decision* that the repatriation grant and other expatriate benefits are limited to staff who both work and reside in a country other than their home country;

2. *Approves* the amendments to the Staff Regulations of the United Nations contained in the annex to the present resolution;

3. *Decides* to re-examine the issue of entitlement to repatriation and other expatriate benefits to staff members living in their home country while stationed at duty stations located in another country during its fifty-first session, in the light of the report by the International Civil Service Commission requested in section II.D of its resolution 48/224.

**ANNEX**
**Amendments to the Staff Regulations of the United Nations**

*Article III*
*Salaries and related allowances*

Replace the first sentence of regulation 3.2 *(a)* with the following text:

"*Regulation 3.2:* (a) The Secretary-General shall establish terms and conditions under which an education grant shall be available to a staff member residing and serving outside his or her recognized home country whose dependent child is in full-time attendance at a school, university or similar educational institution of a type that will, in the opinion of the Secretary-General, facilitate the child's reassimilation in the staff member's recognized home country."

*Article V*
*Annual and special leave*

Replace regulation 5.3 with the following text:

"*Regulation 5.3:* Eligible staff members shall be granted home leave once in every two years. However, in the case of designated duty stations having very difficult conditions of life and work, eligible staff members shall be granted home leave once in every twelve months. A staff member whose home country is either the country of his or her official duty station or the country of his or her normal residence while in United Nations service, shall not be eligible for home leave."

*Annex IV to the Staff Regulations*
*Repatriation grant*

Replace the paragraph with the following text:

"In principle, the repatriation grant shall be payable to staff members whom the Organization is obligated to repatriate and who at the time of separation are residing, by virtue of their service with the United Nations, outside their country of nationality. The repatriation grant shall not, however, be paid to a staff member who is summarily dismissed. Eligible staff members shall be entitled to a repatriation grant only upon relocation outside the country of the duty station. Detailed conditions and definitions relating to eligibility and requisite evidence of relocation shall be determined by the Secretary-General."

General Assembly resolution 49/241

6 April 1995      Meeting 100      Adopted without vote

Approved by Fifth Committee (A/49/802/Add.2) without vote, 31 March (meeting 53); draft by Chairman (A/C.5/49/L.40/Rev.1), based on informal consultations and orally revised; agenda item 113 *(d)*.
*Meeting numbers.* GA 49th session: 5th Committee 46, 53; plenary 100.

*Payment of honoraria*

The Economic and Social Council, by **decision 1995/302 A** of 25 July, noted that no action had been taken by the General Assembly on the 1993 recommendation of the Committee on Economic, Social and Cultural Rights that payment of an honorarium equivalent to that payable to members of other treaty bodies should be authorized for Committee members, and urged the Assembly to give speedy attention to the matter.

The Council, by **decision 1995/302 B** of the same date, urged the General Assembly to authorize payment to each member of the Committee on Economic, Social and Cultural Rights of an honorarium equivalent to that payable to the members of other relevant treaty bodies.

*REFERENCES*

(1)YUN 1974, p. 875, GA res. 3357 (XXIX), annex, 18 Dec. 1974. (2)A/50/30. (3)YUN 1992, p. 1055, GA res. 47/216, 23 Dec. 1992. (4)YUN 1991, p. 900, GA res. 46/191, 20 Dec. 1991. (5)YUN 1988, p. 883, GA res. 43/226, 21 Dec. 1988. (6)ACC/1995/5. (7)ACC/1995/19. (8)A/C.5/50/11. (9)A/C.5/50/24 & Corr.1. (10)A/50/7/Add.7. (11)YUN 1994, p. 1374, GA res. 49/223, 23 Dec. 1994. (12)A/C.5/50/23. (13)A/50/7/Add.2. (14)YUN 1994, p. 1390. (15)A/C.5/50/40. (16)A/C.5/50/12. (17)A/C.5/50/18. (18)A/50/7/Add.11. (19)A/49/7/Add.12. (20)YUN 1994, p. 1392. (21)A/50/784. (22)YUN 1992, p. 1063. (23)A/C.5/49/59. (24)YUN 1993, p. 1212, GA res. 48/224, sect. II D, 23 Dec. 1993.

## Other staff issues

### Personnel policies

On 7 February,[1] the Secretary-General transmitted to the General Assembly the report of the Joint Inspection Unit (JIU) on the application of UN recruitment, placement and promotion policies. The inspectors recommended that the Secretary-General should review and improve all personnel policies and procedures to make them simpler, more transparent and relevant, and also that they be brought together in a Human Resource Management Manual. The authority and professional skills of the Office of Human Resources Management (OHRM) should be strengthened in order to implement the Secretary-General's strategy for the management of human resources. The Secretary-General should revise the OHRM section of the Organization Manual to clearly spell out its functions. He should also make clear the obligation of all programme managers to abide by human resource management policies, including the unacceptability of practices such as favouritism, circumvention of the principle of competitiveness, and interference with the authority of OHRM. The decentralization and delegation of recruitment, promotion and separation, the inspectors said, should be carried out only after human resources management policies as suggested by the Secretary-General were formulated, personnel procedures and methods reviewed and improved, responsibilities in human resources management demarcated between OHRM and other offices and departments, and appropriate reporting and accountability mechanisms put in place. The Secretary-General should be allowed to extend contracts of staff on board up to the age of 62, especially to meet the staff needs of peace-keeping and related missions and to replace staff sent on mission. He should ensure a certain geographical balance and national diversity of staff on mission as well as those replacing them. The Secretary-General should also provide a human resource report containing a full account of costs, benefits, problems and prospects related to all forms of recruitment activities, as part of his efforts to enhance transparency, accountability and follow-up in the personnel programme. The Secretariat should modernize its recruitment methods through diversification of recruitment resources and the use of electronic bulletin boards, professional journals and magazines to ensure recruitment of the best candidates, without jeopardizing the principle of equitable geographical distribution. Probationary contracts for staff recruited through competitive examinations should be abolished, and replaced by two-year fixed-term appointments, and the staff rules should be accordingly amended. The format of rosters of candidates should be improved, and job descriptions standardized to allow better and more expeditious selection of internal and external candidates.

In a 9 March addendum,[2] the Secretary-General transmitted his comments on the JIU report. He reported that the second edition of the *Personnel Administrations Handbook* had been published; personnel policies and practices were being reviewed; but that a human resources management manual was greatly needed. He said that the recommendations regarding OHRM and the decentralization and delegation of recruitment, promotion and separation would be put into effect as much as possible. The Staff-Management Coordination Committee was reviewing the desirability of proposing the extension of the retirement age of staff up to the age of 62. The Secretary-General said he would report to the Assembly on the conduct of recruitment activities as well as on national competitive examinations, including the P-3 level, in the context of normal reporting. The Secretariat had already taken measures to implement recommendations on probationary contracts for staff recruited through competitive examinations, and the suggestions regarding rosters would be used when addressing existing inadequacies.

The Assembly, in **decision 49/476** of 31 March, took note of the JIU report as well as the related observations of the Secretary-General, and approved the report's recommendations.

In a 13 April note,[3] the Secretary-General transmitted to the Assembly a statement adopted by ACC on the status of women in the secretariats of the UN system. ACC members, in an effort to facilitate the recruitment of women, intended to treat all women staff members of common-system organizations as internal candidates with respect to vacant posts in any organization of the system. They would request organizations to utilize their field presence to prospect for women candidates, and urge Governments to submit at least one or more female candidates for each position. Members would also develop a system of inter-agency mobility of women staff to increase their experience; facilitate spouse employment by amending staff rules and encourage the development of spouse employment opportunities, including also non-governmental and multinational sectors, and introduce relevant provisions in host country agreements; organize efforts at each UN location to promote spouse employment, led by the resident coordinators in the field and by the lead agency in each headquarters city. Organizations were to introduce measures that would lead to a climate conducive to the equal participation of men and women, and those organizations that had not already done so were encouraged to introduce policies and procedures to combat sexual harassment. ACC also said that particular attention had to be paid to increasing the number of women in senior managerial positions.

On 20 June, the Secretariat, in a conference room paper,[4] provided information requested by the Assembly in 1994[5] on the employment of retirees, including those recruited on a short-term basis or under special service agreements between 1 January 1993 and 31 December 1994. Some 60 per cent of recruited retirees were language staff. In view of the increase in the cost-of-living in New York from December 1982, it was proposed that the Assembly consider increasing the maximum that a retiree could receive from $12,000 to $20,000.

GENERAL ASSEMBLY ACTION

On 20 July, the General Assembly adopted **resolution 49/222 B**.

### Human resources management

*The General Assembly,*

*Having considered* the relevant reports on human resources management submitted by the Secretary-General during the resumed forty-ninth session of the General Assembly,

*Noting with concern* the conference room paper on the practice of using retirees in the United Nations Secretariat,

1. *Reiterates its support* for the Secretary-General towards the development of a management environment and culture in the Organization that is supportive of having staff members perform to their maximum potential, effectiveness and efficiency;

2. *Takes note with appreciation* of the statement on the status of women in the secretariats of the United Nations system adopted by the Administrative Committee on Coordination at its first regular session of 1995, and requests members of the Committee to report on the implementation of the proposals contained therein;

3. *Requests* the Secretary-General to develop a comprehensive policy on the use of retirees that includes appropriate internal controls to ensure that the compensation received by those retirees does not exceed the existing cap on those payments and to report thereon to the General Assembly at its fifty-first session;

4. *Also requests* the Secretary-General to ensure that the policy will be consistent with the Regulations of the United Nations Joint Staff Pension Fund;

5. *Decides* that, pending consideration of the policy on the use of retirees during the fifty-first session of the General Assembly, no former staff member who is in receipt of a pension benefit from the United Nations Joint Staff Pension Fund shall receive from any United Nations funds more than 12,000 United States dollars in total in any calendar year;

6. *Authorizes* on an exceptional basis during the fiftieth session a derogation from the decision in paragraph 5 above with a view to maintaining the maximum effectiveness of conference services.

General Assembly resolution 49/222 B

20 July 1995    Meeting 106    Adopted without vote

Approved by Fifth Committee (A/49/802/Add.3) without vote, 14 July (meeting 66); draft by Chairman (A/C.5/49/L.65), based on informal consultations and orally revised; agenda item 113.

*Meeting numbers.* GA 49th session: 5th Committee 59, 61, 63, 66; plenary 106.

By **decision 50/469** of 23 December, the Assembly decided that the Fifth Committee should continue consideration of the item "Human resources management" at its 1996 resumed session.

### Staff composition

On 11 October, the Secretary-General submitted to the General Assembly his annual report[6] on staff composition of the UN Secretariat by nationality, gender, grade and type of appointment. The total number of Secretariat staff as of 30 June 1995 was 14,380, of whom 9,611 were paid from the regular budget and 4,769 from extrabudgetary resources. There were 4,394 staff in the Professional category and above, 9,486 in the General Service and related categories and 500 project personnel.

Staff in posts subject to geographical distribution numbered 2,515. As of 30 June, there were 25 unrepresented Member States, compared to 28 at 30 June 1994, and 25 underrepresented Member States, the same as the year before. Changes in representation derived not only from staff appointments and separations from service, but also from such factors as adjustments in desirable ranges resulting from an increase or decrease in the number of posts subject to geographical distribution, changes in the number of Member States, variations in assessed contributions of individual Member States or in their population, and changes in the status of some staff members. The report also provided information on grouping of Member States, the representation of developing and other countries among staff at the senior levels, the representation of women, and recruitment activities.

Between 1 July 1994 and 30 June 1995, appointments were made to 135 posts subject to geographical distribution. Of those, 8 (5.9 per cent) were nationals of unrepresented Member States; 37 (27.4 per cent) of underrepresented Member States; 82 (60.7 per cent) of within-range Member States; 8 (5.9 per cent) of overrepresented Member States.

## Status of women in the Secretariat

In 1996, the Secretary-General submitted two reports on improving the status of women in the UN Secretariat.

In a 21 February report[7] to the Commission on the Status of Women, the Secretary-General provided statistical data and described events that had taken place since June 1994. He said that figures indicated that from 1989 to 1994, there had been an overall increase of 5.7 per cent (26.9 to 32.6 per cent) in the representation of women in posts subject to geographical distribution; the percentage of women at the D-1 level and above had risen to 15.1 per cent. Those figures, although showing steady progress, indicated that, both in the overall percentages and in the proportion of women at the D-1 level and above, the Secretariat fell short in its efforts to meet the target of 35 per cent overall in posts subject to geographical distribution and 25 per cent for levels D-1 and above.

The Steering Committee for the Advancement of the Status of Women in the Secretariat and JIU[8] had indicated that the major obstacles to the advancement of women were commitment at the highest level and lack of a clearly articulated human resources management strategy. The main goal of the strategic action plan for the improvement of the status of women in the Secretariat (1995-2000), which the General Assembly urged[5] the Secretary-General to implement, was to achieve gender equality by the beginning of the twenty-first century. The plan set out strategies and specific objectives and targets, and identified simultaneous and interrelated actions required to achieve them. Elements of the plan that so far had been initiated were: planning and database development; development of a specific roster of external candidates; a Secretariat-wide network of departmental focal points; broad advertising and communication; targeted recruitment missions; and review of the process of recruitment and promotion and the involvement of the departmental focal points in those processes. The Secretary-General said that changes would be made in management culture and in policies regarding career development, training, dual career and spousal employment, in tandem with his overall strategy for the management of the human resources of the Organization.[9] Monitoring, appraisal and follow-up on issues specific to women would be an integral part of that process.

The Commission on the Status of Women, at its thirty-ninth session (15 March–7 April), recommended a draft resolution for adoption by the Economic and Social Council (see also PART IV, Chapter X).

### ECONOMIC AND SOCIAL COUNCIL ACTION

On 24 July, the Economic and Social Council adopted **resolution 1995/28**.

**Improvement of the status of women in the Secretariat**
*The Economic and Social Council,*

*Recalling* Articles 1 and 101 of the Charter of the United Nations,

*Recalling also* Article 8 of the Charter, which provides that the United Nations shall place no restrictions on the eligibility of men and women to participate in any capacity and under conditions of equality in its principal and subsidiary organs,

*Recalling further* the relevant paragraphs of the Nairobi Forward-looking Strategies for the Advancement of Women, especially paragraphs 79, 315, 356 and 358,

*Recalling* the relevant resolutions and decisions of the General Assembly, the Economic and Social Council and other bodies that have continued to focus on this area since the adoption of Assembly resolution 2715(XXV) of 15 December 1970, in which the question of the employment of women in the Professional category was first addressed,

*Concerned* by the serious and continuing underrepresentation of women in the Secretariat, particularly at the higher decision-making levels,

*Convinced* that the improvement of the status of women in the Secretariat could significantly enhance the effectiveness and credibility of the United Nations, including its leadership role in advancing the status of women worldwide and in promoting the full participation of women in all aspects of decision-making,

*Recalling* the goal, set in General Assembly resolutions 45/125 of 14 December 1990 and 45/239 C of 21 December 1990 and reaffirmed in Assembly resolutions 46/100 of 16 December 1991, 47/93 of 16 December 1992, 48/106 of 20 December 1993 and 49/167 of 23 December 1994, of a 35 per cent overall participation rate of women in posts subject to geographical distribution by 1995,

*Noting with concern* that the current rate of increase in the appointment of women may not be sufficient to achieve the objective of a 35 per cent participation rate of women in posts subject to geographical distribution by 1995,

*Recalling* the goal, set in General Assembly resolution 45/239 C and reaffirmed in Assembly resolutions 46/100, 47/93, 48/106 and 49/167, of a 25 per cent participation rate of women in posts at the D-1 level and above by 1995,

*Noting with disappointment* that the participation rate of women in posts at the D-1 level and above remains unacceptably low, and well below the 25 per cent goal,

*Noting* the efforts made in the past year by the Secretary-General and the Office of Human Resources Management of the Secretariat to integrate the objectives set by the General Assembly for the improvement of the status of women in the Secretariat into the overall strategy for the management of the Organization's human resources, and noting also that such a comprehensive approach will be conducive to enhancing the status of women in the Secretariat,

*Recognizing* the importance of providing equal employment opportunities for all staff,

*Aware* that a comprehensive policy aimed at preventing sexual harassment should be an integral part of personnel policy,

*Commending* the Secretary-General for his administrative instruction on procedures for dealing with cases of sexual harassment,

*Bearing in mind* that a visible commitment by the Secretary-General is essential to the achievement of the targets set by the General Assembly,

1. *Takes note* of the report of the Secretary-General while regretting the lateness in the availability of the report;

2. *Also takes note* of the strategic plan of action for the improvement of the status of women in the Secretariat (1995-2000) contained in section IV of the report, and of the goals and objectives of the plan as proposed by the Secretary-General;

3. *Urges* the Secretary-General to implement fully the plan of action, noting that his visible commitment is essential to the achievement of the targets set by the General Assembly and the goals and objectives contained in the plan;

4. *Welcomes* the intention of the Secretary-General to ensure implementation of the plan through, *inter alia*, the issuance of clear and specific instructions as to the authority and responsibility of all managers in implementing the plan and the criteria by which performance will be appraised;

5. *Also urges* the Secretary-General, in accordance with the Charter of the United Nations and in a manner consistent with the plan of action, to accord greater priority to the recruitment and promotion of women in posts subject to geographical distribution, particularly in senior policy-level and decision-making posts and within those parts of the United Nations system and the specialized agencies where representation of women is considerably below the average, in order to achieve the goals set in General Assembly resolutions 45/125 and 45/239 C of an overall participation rate of 35 per cent by 1995 and, in posts at the D-1 level and above, of 25 per cent by 1995;

6. *Further urges* the Secretary-General to examine existing work practices within the United Nations system with a view to increasing flexibility so as to remove direct or indirect discrimination against staff members with family responsibilities, including consideration of such issues as spouse employment, job-sharing, flexible working hours, child-care arrangements, career-break schemes and access to training;

7. *Urges* the Secretary-General to increase the number of women employed in the Secretariat from developing countries, particularly those countries which are unrepresented or underrepresented, and from other countries that have a low representation of women, including countries in transition;

8. *Requests* the Secretary-General to ensure that equal employment opportunities exist for all staff;

9. *Also requests* the Secretary-General to enable, from within existing resources, the focal point for women within the Secretariat effectively to monitor and facilitate progress in the implementation of the plan from within existing resources;

10. *Strongly encourages* Member States to support the plan of action and the efforts of the United Nations and the specialized agencies to increase the percentage of women in the Professional category, especially in posts at the D-1 level and above, by identifying and sending forward more women candidates, encouraging women to apply for vacant posts and creating national rosters of women candidates to be shared with the Secretariat, the specialized agencies and the regional commissions;

11. *Further requests* the Secretary-General to develop comprehensive policy measures aimed at the prevention of sexual harassment in the Secretariat;

12. *Requests* the Secretary-General to ensure that a progress report on the status of women in the Secretariat containing, *inter alia*, information on activities undertaken towards the achievement of the goals and objectives contained in the plan of action and policy measures aimed at the prevention of sexual harassment in the Secretariat is presented to the Commission on the Status of Women at its fortieth session, in accordance with the relevant rules concerning the timetable for delivery of documentation, and to the General Assembly at its fiftieth session.

Economic and Social Council resolution 1995/28

24 July 1995     Meeting 50     Adopted without vote

Draft by Commission on women (E/1995/26); agenda item 5 *(e)*.
Meeting numbers. ESC 49, 50.

**Report of the Secretary-General.** In a 27 October report[10] on the improvement of the status of women in the Secretariat, the Secretary-General provided statistics as of 30 June 1995, and described recent developments and the impact of the new management culture on the status of women. He also reviewed implementation of the strategic plan of action for the improvement of the status of women in the Secretariat (1995-2000). The Secretary-General stated that the percentage of women in posts subject to geographical distribution had increased 1.5 percentage points, from 32.6 per cent on 30 July 1994 to 34.1 percent. The percentage of women at the D-1 level and above increased also by 2 percentage points, from 15.1 in 1994 to 17.1 as of 30 June 1995. The percentage of women at the Assistant Secretary-General and Under-Secretary-General levels remained the same.

By region of origin, the lowest representation of women as a percentage of all staff was registered by Eastern Europe (1.11), the Middle East (1.35) and Africa (3.02), and the highest by North America and the Caribbean (9.74), Western Europe (7.87) and Asia and the Pacific (7.63). Between 1 July 1994 and 30 June 1995, more women than men were promoted at the P-3 and P-5 levels, while more men than women were promoted at the D-1 and P-4 levels. A total of 175 staff members, 51.42 per cent of whom were women, were promoted during the period. Only at the P-1/P-2 level was the percentage of women recruited higher than that of men, 53.6 per cent. It was lowest in the P-4 category, 33.3 per cent, and ranged between 40 and 46 per cent for candidates in the other categories.

The Secretary-General concluded that it was important that the Platform for Action of the Fourth World Conference on Women (Beijing, China, 4-15 September) (see PART FOUR, Chapter X) regarding women in decision-making, in power structures and managerial positions, also be applied to women within the UN system. He intended to vigorously pursue the improvement of the status of women through implementation of the strategic plan of action and the Beijing Platform for Action. The Secretary-General proposed that the Assembly extend the target of equal numbers of women and men in posts subject to geographical distribution by the year 2000 to all categories of posts, regardless of the type or duration of appointment, or of the Staff Rules under which an appointment was made. He said that the percentage should apply both overall and within category. Member States that were host countries to UN organizations should consider, on an exceptional basis, permitting the spouses of staff members, male or female, the right to work.

**GENERAL ASSEMBLY ACTION**

On 22 December, the General Assembly adopted **resolution 50/164**.

### Improvement of the status of women in the Secretariat

*The General Assembly,*

*Recalling* Articles 1 and 101 of the Charter of the United Nations,

*Recalling also* Article 8 of the Charter, which provides that the United Nations shall place no restrictions on the eligibility of men and women to participate in any capacity and under conditions of equality in its principal and subsidiary organs,

*Recalling further* the relevant paragraphs of the Nairobi Forward-looking Strategies for the Advancement of Women and the Beijing Declaration and the Platform for Action adopted by the Fourth World Conference on Women on 15 September 1995,

*Concerned* at the serious and continuing underrepresentation of women in the Secretariat, particularly at the higher decision-making levels,

*Convinced* that the improvement of the status of women in the Secretariat could significantly enhance the effectiveness and credibility of the United Nations, including its leadership role in advancing the status of women worldwide and in promoting the full participation of women in all aspects of decision-making,

*Disappointed* that the objective set in its resolutions 45/125 of 14 December 1990 and 45/239 C of 21 Decem-

ber 1990 of a 35 per cent overall participation rate of women in posts subject to geographical distribution by 1995 has not been met,

*Disappointed also* that the goal set in its resolution 45/239 C of a 25 per cent participation rate of women in posts at the D-1 level and above by 1995 has not been met and that their level of representation remains unacceptably low,

*Recalling* its resolution 49/167 of 23 December 1994, in which it urged the Secretary-General to implement fully the strategic plan of action for the improvement of the status of women in the Secretariat (1995-2000),

*Noting* the efforts made by the Secretary-General and the Office of Human Resources Management of the Secretariat to integrate the objectives set by the General Assembly for the improvement of the status of women in the Secretariat into the overall strategy for the management of the Organization's human resources, and noting also that such a comprehensive approach would be conducive to enhancing the status of women in the Secretariat,

*Recognizing* the importance of providing equal employment opportunities for all staff,

*Aware* that a comprehensive policy aimed at preventing and dealing with sexual harassment should be an integral part of personnel policy,

*Welcoming* the statement of the Administrative Committee on Coordination on the status of women in the secretariats of the United Nations system, in which the members of the Committee reaffirmed their strong commitment to ensuring that the advancement of women was a priority within the organizations of the common system and to taking measures to improve the status of women in their respective secretariats,

1. *Welcomes* the report of the Secretary-General;

2. *Notes* the efforts to date of the Secretary-General to implement the strategic plan of action for the improvement of the status of women in the Secretariat (1995-2000), and reaffirms that his continued visible commitment is essential to the achievement of the goals and objectives of the strategic plan;

3. *Calls upon* the Secretary-General to ensure full and urgent implementation of the strategic plan in order to achieve the goal contained in the Platform for Action adopted by the Fourth World Conference on Women for overall gender equality, particularly at the Professional level and above, by the year 2000;

4. *Also calls upon* the Secretary-General to fulfil his target, reaffirmed by the Fourth World Conference on Women, of having women hold 50 per cent of managerial and decision-making positions by the year 2000;

5. *Welcomes* the Secretary-General's initiatives to date to ensure implementation of the strategic plan, including the incorporation of measures into the performance appraisal system to hold managers responsible and accountable and the inclusion in training programmes of components designed to sensitize managers to gender issues;

6. *Urges* the Secretary-General to continue his work on improving the work practices and environment within the United Nations system with a view to increasing flexibility so as to remove direct or indirect discrimination, including against staff members with family responsibilities, through, *inter alia*, consideration of such issues as spouse employment, job-sharing, flexible working hours, child-care arrangements and career-break

schemes, and to improve access for all staff to training and career development;

7. *Notes* the examination that has begun of the effectiveness of the Organization's policies and procedures, established in 1992, to deal with sexual harassment in the workplace, and urges the Secretary-General to ensure that the examination leads to a comprehensive and effective policy, including grievance mechanisms, for the prevention and redress of sexual harassment in the Secretariat;

8. *Also urges* the Secretary-General to increase the number of women employed in the Secretariat from developing countries, particularly those that are unrepresented or underrepresented, and from other countries that have a low representation of women, including countries in transition;

9. *Requests* the Secretary-General to ensure that equal employment opportunities exist for all staff;

10. *Also requests* the Secretary-General to enable, from within existing resources, the Focal Point for Women within the Secretariat effectively to monitor and facilitate progress in the implementation of the strategic plan;

11. *Strongly encourages* Member States to support the strategic plan and the efforts of the United Nations and the specialized agencies to increase the percentage of women in Professional posts, especially at the D-1 level and above, by identifying and submitting more women candidates, encouraging women to apply for vacant posts and creating national rosters of women candidates to be shared with the Secretariat, specialized agencies and regional commissions;

12. *Further requests* the Secretary-General, in accordance with the relevant rules on the delivery timetable for documentation, to ensure that a progress report on the status of women in the Secretariat is submitted to the Commission on the Status of Women at its fortieth session and to the General Assembly at its fifty-first session, taking into account the promotion of integrated reporting.

General Assembly resolution 50/164

22 December 1995     Meeting 99     Adopted without vote

Approved by Third Committee (A/50/630) without vote, 30 November (meeting 44); 96-nation draft (A/C.3/50/L.23), orally revised; agenda item 107.
*Meeting numbers.* GA 50th session: 3rd Committee 24, 26-31, 40-42, 44; plenary 99.

## Performance appraisal system

As requested in 1994 by the General Assembly,[5] the Secretary-General took steps to implement the new performance appraisal system (PAS) developed by OHRM in 1994. Some 2,000 staff members had undergone training in the use of the system. In May, modifications were made to simplify the system, reduce the length of the reporting form, and reflect other suggestions made by staff members. The new date for the system's implementation worldwide was 1 July 1995. OHRM planned to begin a "people management training" programme for staff at D-1 and D-2 levels to develop management skills in communications, including listening and direction, as well as in other managerial competencies related to the management needs of the Organization, including implementation of the PAS. On 18 September,

the Under-Secretary-General for Administration and Management issued an administrative instruction formally establishing the system.

## Multilingualism

In a 20 July letter[11] addressed to the Secretary-General, 18 Member States, later joined by another 29 States, requested the inclusion of the item "Multilingualism" on the agenda of the General Assembly. In an explanatory memorandum, they complained that the principle of equality was not being respected in the treatment of the official and working languages of the UN. Among the justifications usually cited for not respecting the equality principle were financial reasons, the unavailability of interpretation and translation services, or the urgent nature of the work at hand. The letter said that the Secretariat should make it a rule to employ in its relations with Member States the official language of choice of those States. This requirement would have implications for the linguistic skills that should be expected from UN staff. The staffing of the interpretation and translation services had not expanded at the same rate as the increase in the other activities of various UN bodies. As a result, there were delays in making documents available in the official languages, and meetings were postponed because of the lack of teams of interpreters. The only way to avoid such a situation was for the interpretation and translation services to have adequate staff and resources, despite budgetary constraints, to deal with the increasing workload. The practice of holding "informal" meetings without interpretation or circulating "unofficial documents" in one language only was not an acceptable solution. Annexed to the letter was a draft resolution proposed for adoption by the Assembly.

GENERAL ASSEMBLY ACTION

On 2 November, the General Assembly adopted **resolution 50/11**.

### Multilingualism

*The General Assembly,*

*Recalling* its resolutions 2(I) of 1 February 1946, 2241 B (XXI) of 20 December 1966, 2292(XXII) of 8 December 1967, 2359 B (XXII) of 19 December 1967, 2479(XXIII) and 2480 B (XXIII) of 21 December 1968, 3189(XXVIII), 3190(XXVIII) and 3191(XXVIII) of 18 December 1973 and 43/224 D of 21 December 1988,

*Recalling also,* on the occasion of the commemoration of the fiftieth anniversary of the signing of the Charter of the United Nations, that the universality of the United Nations and its corollary, multilingualism, entail for each State Member of the Organization, irrespective of the official language in which it expresses itself, the right and the duty to make itself understood and to understand others,

*Stressing* the need for strict observance of the resolutions and rules establishing language arrangements for the different bodies and organs of the United Nations,

*Recalling further* that Arabic, Chinese, English, French, Russian and Spanish are both official and working languages of the General Assembly and its committees and subcommittees, and of the Security Council, that Arabic, Chinese, English, French, Russian and Spanish are the official languages and English, French and Spanish the working languages of the Economic and Social Council, and that English and French are the working languages of the Secretariat,

*Regretting* that unequal use is made in the United Nations of the different official languages and of the working languages of the Secretariat, and desiring that persons recruited by the Organization should have a command of and use at least one of the six official languages in addition to one working language of the Secretariat,

*Considering* that the translation and interpretation budgets of United Nations bodies should be commensurate with the needs and should not be subject to budgetary constraints, as noted in resolution 42/207 C of 11 December 1987,

*Noting* that the principle of equality of the official languages is being called into question with increasing frequency by the holding of so-called ''low-cost'' informal meetings,

*Emphasizing* the need for the Organization to continue to promote the learning of all the official languages and the working languages of the Secretariat by members of missions accredited to the Organization and by Secretariat staff,

*Emphasizing also* the importance of providing access for all Governments and all sectors of civil society to the Organization's documentation, archives and data banks in all the official languages,

1. *Requests* the Secretary-General to ensure the strict implementation of the resolutions establishing language arrangements for both the official languages and the working languages of the Secretariat, and invites Member States to do likewise;

2. *Recalls* that the Secretariat is required, in its relations with Member States, to use the official or working language requested by those States;

3. *Also requests* the Secretary-General to ensure that appointment of the staff of the Organization is carried out strictly in accordance with the terms of Article 101 of the Charter and the regulations established by the General Assembly pursuant to that Article and that, upon recruitment, personnel recruited by the different bodies of the Organization have a command of and use at least one of the working languages of the Secretariat or one of the working languages of another body of the Organization, in the case of staff members who are to work for that body and whose tenure of appointment does not exceed two years, and requests him to ensure that the use of another of the six official languages is duly encouraged and taken into account, particularly when promotions and incremental steps are under consideration, in order to ensure linguistic balance within the Organization;

4. *Further requests* the Secretary-General to ensure, in particular in the recruitment and promotion of Secretariat staff, equality of the working languages of the Secretariat and of their use;

5. *Stresses* the need to ensure, in particular through the training and recruitment of specialists, that the necessary resources are available to guarantee the proper and timely translation of documents into the different official languages of the United Nations;

6. *Recalls* the need to ensure the simultaneous distribution of such documents in the official languages;

7. *Also stresses* the need to ensure adequate human and financial resources for maintaining the teaching, at all levels, of the official languages and the working languages of the Secretariat;

8. *Further stresses* the importance of ensuring the availability of publications and adequate data banks in the different official languages in the libraries and documentation centres of the various bodies;

9. *Urges* the delegations of Member States and the Secretariat to endeavour to avoid holding informal meetings without interpretation;

10. *Requests* the Secretary-General to submit at its fifty-second session a report on the implementation of the present resolution and particularly on the use of the official languages of the United Nations and the working languages of the Secretariat.

General Assembly resolution 50/11

2 November 1995    Meeting 49    100-35-29 (recorded vote)

74-nation draft (A/50/L.6/Rev.1 & Rev.1/Add.1), amended by Australia (A/50/L.14); agenda item 156.

*Meeting numbers.* GA 50th session: plenary 34, 47-49.

Recorded vote in Assembly as follows:

*In favour:* Afghanistan, Albania, Algeria, Andorra, Argentina, Armenia, Australia, Austria, Bahrain, Belarus, Belgium, Benin, Bolivia, Brazil, Bulgaria, Burkina Faso, Burundi, Cambodia, Cameroon, Canada, Cape Verde, Chad, Chile, China, Colombia, Congo, Costa Rica, Côte d'Ivoire, Cuba, Cyprus, Czech Republic, Denmark, Djibouti, Dominica, Ecuador, Egypt, El Salvador, France, Gabon, Germany, Greece, Guatemala, Guinea, Guinea-Bissau, Haiti, Honduras, Hungary, India, Ireland, Italy, Jordan, Kazakstan, Kuwait, Lao People's Democratic Republic, Lebanon, Libyan Arab Jamahiriya, Liechtenstein, Luxembourg, Madagascar, Mali, Malta, Mauritania, Mauritius, Mexico, Monaco, Morocco, Mozambique, Myanmar, Nicaragua, Niger, Oman, Panama, Paraguay, Peru, Poland, Portugal, Qatar, Republic of Moldova, Romania, Russian Federation, Rwanda, San Marino, Saudi Arabia, Senegal, Seychelles, Slovakia, Spain, Sudan, Sweden, Syrian Arab Republic, Togo, Tunisia, Ukraine, United Arab Emirates, United Republic of Tanzania, Uruguay, Venezuela, Viet Nam, Yemen, Zaire.

*Against:* Azerbaijan, Bangladesh, Bhutan, Bosnia and Herzegovina, Botswana, Brunei Darussalam, Eritrea, Ethiopia, Fiji, Georgia, Indonesia, Israel, Jamaica, Japan, Kenya, Lesotho, Marshall Islands, New Zealand, Nigeria, Palau, Papua New Guinea, Philippines, Republic of Korea, Saint Vincent and the Grenadines, Samoa, Solomon Islands, Sri Lanka, Suriname, Swaziland, the former Yugoslav Republic of Macedonia, Thailand, Turkey, United States, Zambia.

*Abstaining:* Antigua and Barbuda, Bahamas, Barbados, Belize, Croatia, Estonia, Finland, Gambia, Ghana, Grenada, Guyana, Iceland, Iran, Latvia, Malaysia, Maldives, Micronesia, Mongolia, Nepal, Netherlands, Norway, Pakistan, Saint Lucia, Singapore, Slovenia, South Africa, Trinidad and Tobago, Uganda, United Kingdom.

## Staff Rules and Regulations

In a 20 November report,[12] the Secretary-General submitted to the General Assembly amendments to the Staff Rules under the 100 series relating to the repatriation grant and other expatriate benefits for staff working and residing in a country other than their home country. The amendment reflected the different rates applicable to education grant claims received for children studying in the United States or from other parts of the world, except the currency areas specifically designated. Another amendment clarified the role of the Appointment and Promotion Board, which does not make recommendations respecting the appointment or promotion of candidates having successfully passed a competitive examination. A new rule made clear that those candidates were appointed at the P-1, P-2 and P-3 levels or promoted from the General Service and related categories to the Professional category on the recommendation of the Board of Examiners. A further amendment established that the new reporting system would apply to all staff, including at the Under-Secretary-General level (100 series). Other amendments concerned rules in the 200 series relating to home leave, education grants, insurance coverage and last-day-for-pay purposes.

By **decision 50/453** of 22 December, the General Assembly noted the amendments to the 100 and 200 series of the Staff Rules contained in the Secretary-General's report.

### Staff representation

In a 31 May report,[13] the Secretary-General, responding to a 1994 General Assembly request,[5] submitted revised costs of staff representation activities for 1990-1991. He corrected his 1992 report regarding the number of staff members released full-time for service with the New York Staff Committee, as well as the Committees in Geneva and Santiago, Chile. In reviewing the revised figures for Headquarters, the Secretary-General referred to the exponential growth in the number of staff serving in field missions in recent years and the resulting impact on activities of the Field Service Staff Union, which represented more than 600 staff in the Field Service Category, and the New York Staff Council, which represented over 2,000 Secretariat staff assigned to field missions. Moreover, since 1983, the number of issues requiring staff-management consultation had increased in number and complexity. Total cost of staff representation activities amounted to $1,714,900, including staff costs of $1,191,000.

The Secretary-General also submitted,[14] in response to an Assembly request,[5] costs of staff representation activities during 1992, 1993 and 1994, amounting to $1,138,800, $1,051,800 and $1,018,300, respectively.

On 30 June, the Assistant Secretary-General for Human Resources Management told the Fifth Committee that the reports represented actual costs of the full-time release of senior members of Staff Councils from their substantive duties, together with the cost of Secretariat support. He said that the Committee had expressed concern over the lack of a clear definition of "a reasonable amount of time" for the conduct of staff activities. Such clarity would permit staff representatives to make better use of time available to them for Staff Council activities, which should not be to the detriment of their own career objectives. He

also indicated that the Staff-Management Coordinating Committee had reached agreement on what constituted "a reasonable time" for staff representatives at all levels to discharge their responsibilities effectively. He said that the reports were not being introduced formally because the Secretary-General had not had a chance to consider them. The Fifth Committee continued consideration of the reports in informal consultations.

### Privileges and immunities

The Secretary-General submitted a 16 February note[15] on stress management, in response to a 1993 Assembly request[16] for further information on how best to assist and rehabilitate staff members dealing with the after-effects of traumatic and stressful incidents and experiences. He stated that occupational stress inherent in the activities of the UN system could no longer be ignored. Staff were increasingly being asked to confront situations without having developed the appropriate skills to cope with them. It was therefore essential that adequate planning, training and support for staff working in stressful situations should be put in place on a system-wide basis. The Security Coordinator, the focal point for developing a strategy for managing stress, had been working with other organizations to develop such a strategy based on preventive and critical-incident stress management. It would include training a small number of peer counsellors at high-risk duty stations to provide immediate, on-the-scene, critical-incident stress defusing; training key management personnel at high-risk missions to identify critical-incident stress; working with local counsellors and to determine when outside expertise was required; developing a core of in-house critical-incident stress counsellors for debriefing and in emergencies; and developing long-term and adequate support, counselling and treatment for staff suffering from critical-incident stress.

The Secretary-General observed that although developing a stress-management programme was a priority, it would require time and resources. The Office of the United Nations Security Coordinator had developed a roster of mental health professionals trained to conduct critical-incident stress debriefings. The support of Member States in implementing such a programme was essential.

GENERAL ASSEMBLY ACTION

On 31 March, the General Assembly adopted **resolution 49/238**.

**Respect for the privileges and immunities of officials of the United Nations and the specialized agencies and related organizations**

*The General Assembly,*

*Reaffirming* its previous resolutions on respect for the privileges and immunities of officials of the United

Nations and the specialized agencies and related organizations,

*Acknowledging with satisfaction* the adoption of the Convention on the Safety of United Nations and Associated Personnel,

1. *Takes note* of the report by the Secretary-General on respect for the privileges and immunities of officials of the United Nations and the specialized agencies and related organizations;

2. *Deplores* the increasing risk confronting United Nations personnel, including those engaged in peace-keeping and humanitarian operations, as well as locally recruited staff, and in this regard welcomes the Ad Hoc Inter-Agency Meeting on Security Matters convened in New York from 16 to 19 May 1994 by the United Nations Security Coordinator, and urges the Administrative Committee on Coordination to strengthen the cooperative inter-agency approach, which will ensure the safety and security of United Nations personnel system-wide;

3. *Welcomes* the note by the Secretary-General on stress management and the proposals made in paragraph 10 thereof, and requests the Secretary-General to submit funding proposals, if necessary, in the context of the proposed programme budget for the biennium 1996-1997.

General Assembly resolution 49/238

31 March 1995     Meeting 99     Adopted without vote

Approved by Fifth Committee (A/49/802/Add.1) without vote, 16 March (meeting 45); draft by Chairman (A/C.5/49/L.35), based on informal consultations; agenda item 113 *(c)*.
*Meeting numbers.* GA 49th session: 5th Committee 43, 45; plenary 99.

**Report of the Secretary-General.** On 9 October, the Secretary-General, on behalf of and with the approval of ACC, submitted a report,[17] containing updated information on respect for the privileges and immunities of officials of the UN and the specialized agencies and related organizations, as well as on their safety and security. The report covered the period from 1 July 1994 to 30 June 1995. The Secretary-General said that developments in the last year had again heightened concerns regarding the conditions under which staff members operated in certain areas and the level of risk that was deemed acceptable. Fourteen staff members belonging to different organizations had lost their lives during the period. In addition there had been numerous instances of harassment, kidnapping, vehicle hijackings and attacks on UN personnel. The decrease in the number of staff members arrested or detained over the previous two years was reversed by the situation in Rwanda, where numerous locally recruited UN staff members were detained. As at 30 June 1995, 12 staff members of the UN Relief and Works Agency for Palestine Refugees in the Near East remained in detention. There was also a growing number of instances where locally recruited UN staff members were being drafted into military services. The report also discussed the taxation of UN officials by host countries and restrictions on their official and private travel.

In a 16 November note,[18] the Secretary-General transmitted to the General Assembly a statement adopted by ACC at its second regular session in 1995 (New York, 12-13 October). ACC expressed concern at the increase in attacks on staff of the UN, its programmes, funds and specialized agencies, causing the death of more than 100 staff members over the past three years. It called for effective and comprehensive measures to enhance the security of personnel, and asked Governments to take all possible measures to ensure the safety of UN staff. ACC also called on States that had not yet done so to ratify the 1994 Convention on the Safety of United Nations and Associated Personnel,[19] and asked the Office of Legal Affairs to propose measures to ensure the extension of its coverage automatically and equally to all UN and associated staff working in unsafe or potentially insecure conditions. ACC encouraged its members to prioritize the development of security training and stress management, and to share and combine resources and experience in these mechanisms, which could reduce the risk to which personnel were exposed. It insisted that projects relating to safety and security of staff be excluded from any budgetary restrictions resulting from the UN financial crisis. It decided to review progress on these recommendations in 1996.

## UN Joint Staff Pension Fund

### General aspects

During 1995, the number of participants in the United Nations Joint Staff Pension Fund (UNJSPF) increased from 63,813 to 68,708, or by 7.7 per cent; the number of periodic benefits in award increased from 37,156 to 38,914, or by 4.7 per cent. On 31 December, the breakdown of the periodic benefits in award was as follows: 12,792 retirement benefits, 7,291 early retirement benefits, 6,033 deferred retirement benefits, 5,547 widows' and widowers' benefits, 6,483 children's benefits, 717 disability benefits and 51 secondary dependants' benefits. In the course of the year, 4,068 lump-sum withdrawal and other settlements were paid. During the same period, the principal of the Fund increased from $11,901 million to $12,601 million, or by 5.9 per cent. The Fund's investment income during the year amounted to $725,042,195, comprising $597,476,794 in interest and dividends and $127,565,401 in net profits on sales of investments. After deduction of investment management costs amounting to $10,624,818, net investment income was $714,417,377.

The Fund was administered by the 33-member United Nations Joint Staff Pension Board, which did not meet in 1995 due to the biennialization of the work of the Fifth Committee. Instead, its Standing Committee met[20] on behalf of the

Pension Board in New York, from 10 to 14 July. Major items considered were: actuarial matters, management of the Fund's investments, the Fund's financial statements, the pension adjustment system, the Transfer Agreements between the Fund and the former USSR, Ukrainian SSR and Byelorussian SSR, and the biennial budget for the administrative expenses of the Fund.

ACABQ, on 13 October, submitted its comments[21] on the Fund's budget estimates, and the Assembly acted on the Standing Committee's recommendations.

GENERAL ASSEMBLY ACTION

On 23 December, the General Assembly adopted **resolution 50/216, Section VII**.

### Administrative expenses of the United Nations Joint Staff Pension Fund

[*The General Assembly* . . .]

*Having considered* the report of the Standing Committee of the United Nations Joint Staff Pension Board for 1995 to the General Assembly and to the member organizations of the United Nations Joint Staff Pension Fund, and the related report of the Advisory Committee on Administrative and Budgetary Questions,

1. *Concurs* with the recommendations of the Advisory Committee on Administrative and Budgetary Questions on the administrative expenses of the United Nations Joint Staff Pension Fund;

2. *Approves* expenses, chargeable directly to the Fund, totalling 40,208,300 dollars net for the biennium 1996-1997 and an increase in expenses of 835,500 dollars net for the biennium 1994-1995, for the administration of the Fund;

3. *Authorizes* the United Nations Joint Staff Pension Board to supplement the voluntary contributions to the Emergency Fund for the biennium 1996-1997 by an amount not exceeding 200,000 dollars;

. . .

General Assembly resolution 50/216, section VII
23 December 1995     Meeting 100     Adopted without vote

Approved by Fifth Committee (A/50/842) without vote, 3 November (meeting 20); oral proposal by Chairman; agenda item 116.
*Meeting numbers.* GA 50th session: 5th Committee 3-5, 7, 10, 11, 20; plenary 100.

### Fund investments

The market value of UNJSPF assets as at 31 March 1995 was $13,568 million, an increase of $1,034 million over the previous year. The total investment return for the year ended 31 March 1995 was 8.7 per cent, which, after adjusting for inflation, represented a "real" rate of 5.6 per cent. Investment income from interest and dividends amounted to $597 million in 1995. New funds which became available for investment (contributions plus investment income, less benefit payments and investment expenses) totalled $572 million, while realized capital gains amounted to $127 million.

The Fund remained one of the most diversified pension funds in the world, as the portion of its assets exposed to currencies other than the United States dollar, which was the Fund's unit of account, as well as the ratio of equities to total assets, continued to increase. Close contacts were maintained with international organizations, regional development institutions, Governments and private sources to ensure full awareness of investment opportunities in developing countries.

The implementation of new custodial arrangements for the Fund's assets aimed at achieving diversification through the introduction of parallel accounting and reporting systems and the establishment of regional custodians was completed in 1995. The arrangements ensured effective risk management and greater control and flexibility, and reduced custodial fees substantially.

In a 25 May report, the Secretary-General noted that, considering the worldwide improvement in economic activity, the volatility of the financial markets caused by increased interest rates in many places and fluctuations of exchange rates, the investment returns of 9.7 per cent for the year ended 31 March 1994 and 8.7 per cent for the year ended 31 March 1995, when measured in United States dollars, were satisfactory. The defensive strategy of taking profits where appropriate and increasing investments in those markets and instruments that performed better had contributed to the Fund's satisfactory performance. He considered the policy of diversification and careful selection of investment instruments, including consistent investigation of opportunities in developing countries, to be the best way to achieve the goal of preserving the principal and enhancing the investment return of the Fund over the medium and long terms.

### Admission of World Tourism Organization

On 13 November,[22] Spain asked for inclusion of the item "Admission of the World Tourism Organization to membership of UNJSPF" on the agenda of the General Assembly, a request the Assembly agreed to on 1 December.

In an explanatory memorandum, Spain recalled that in 1987[24] the organization had submitted an application for UNJSPF membership, which was favourably considered by the Fifth Committee in 1988, although it took no action on the matter. Consequently, the organization suspended the application for membership. In 1994, an exhaustive study was conducted on the selection of the most suitable pension scheme. In May 1995, the organization's Executive Council recommended membership in UNJSPF as the best retirement option for the organization and invited the World Tourism Organization's Secretary-General to resume negotiations for admission with the Secretary of UNJSPF as soon as possible. The Standing Committee of UNJSPF at its 10-14 July meeting agreed that the Secretary would be justified in consulting the staff pension committees of member organizations to ascertain their readiness to approve renewal of the previous application of the organization for Fund membership. The eleventh session of the World Tourism Organization's General Assembly (Cairo, Egypt, 17-22 October) endorsed the Executive Committee's recommendation.

In a 4 December note,[24] the UN Secretary-General stated that, as requested by the World Tourism Organization's General Assembly, the organization's staff rules had been amended by its Executive Council on 22 October, effective from the date the World Tourism Organization had become a member organization of the Fund. The Secretary of UNJSPF and the Executive Secretary of ICSC had reviewed those amendments and agreed that they conformed with the common system of salaries, allowances and other conditions of service of the UN and its specialized agencies. All the staff pension committees of the Fund's member organizations also concurred with the decision of the organization's General Assembly regarding its membership in UNJSPF and supported its admission.

The General Assembly, by **decision 50/455** of 22 December, decided to admit the World Tourism Organization to membership in UNJSPF, in accordance with article 3 of the Regulations of the Fund, with effect from 1 January 1996.

## Travel-related matters

### Review of entitlements

**ACABQ action.** ACABQ, in a 4 July report,[25] reviewed the issues of travel and related entitlements for members of organs and subsidiary organs and staff members of the UN and the standards of accommodation for air travel. ACABQ noted that staff members below the Assistant Secretary-General level had been provided with transportation at the least costly airfare regularly available; only for flights exceeding nine hours was accommodation provided in a class just below first class, for travel on official business. The Committee believed that the Secretary-General should review the nine-hour threshold and include the results and proposals in his 1995 report on standards for air travel. He should identify a more objective criteria for determining the standards of accommodation than the currently used "the class immediately below first class", which left too much room for interpretation. The Committee said that there was room for further improvement in the management of travel and trusted that the Secretary-General would apply various innovative techniques for dealing with air carriers, such as "pare-fare", in order to improve cost effectiveness.

ACABQ recommended that the practice of granting *ex post facto* exceptions to the standards of air travel be terminated. It noted the need to determine the level of "eminency" of travellers and believed that the required criteria should be applied to individuals rather than groups. The Committee recommended that efforts be made to reduce further the number of exceptions on the grounds of medical condition, advanced age or the unavailability of the regular standard of air travel, especially on well-established itineraries.

**Reports of the Secretary-General.** In September[26] and November,[27] the Secretary-General issued reports on exceptions to the standards of accommodation covering the previous two years. He noted that terminating *ex post facto* exceptions would limit flexibility in arranging urgent travel, but agreed that exceptions for medical cases should remain unusual. He said exceptions owing to the unavailability of regular travel were rare.

The Secretary-General submitted a 28 December 1995 report[28] reviewing the lump-sum option for air travel in lieu of the provision by the Organization of travel tickets and the related entitlements on home leave, education grant and family visit.

From mid-1990 to the end of 1995 the lump-sum option had resulted in an estimated savings of more than $6.7 million, excluding unaccompanied shipment. For the first 10 months of 1995, the total cash savings from lump-sum utilization was $1,125,030. In terms of administrative savings from the option, most administrative offices reported decreased workloads as a result of simplified and streamlined procedures for processing. The staff resources so released were directed to offset other administrative demands associated with the increase in peace-keeping and humanitarian operations. The 78 per cent overall utilization of the lump-sum option pointed to a large degree of consensus among staff that the current lump-sum rate (75 per cent of the full economy-class fare) was attractive.

The Secretary-General concluded that the scheme had achieved its dual purpose of simplification and rationalization of work procedures and cash savings. He said that continuation of the lump-sum option was worth while only if the level of the rate was sufficiently high to motivate staff to waive other entitlements. He proposed three future alternatives: put aside the option permanently; endorse the continuation of the present lump-sum arrangements without modifying its main parameters; or refer the matter to ICSC for examination of the appropriate level of the lump-sum option. Since the latest extension of the scheme was to expire on 31 December, the Secretary-General had extended its application until the General Assembly made a final decision.

## Efficiency and cost savings

**JIU report.** In a 31 October note,[29] the Secretary-General transmitted a JIU report on "Travel in the United Nations: issues of efficiency and cost savings". In it, JIU reviewed the management of travel and options for change and improvements.

JIU recommended that the Secretary-General should determine clearly the powers and responsibilities of relevant offices of the Secretariat dealing with travel, which would also ensure Secretariat-wide coordination of all travel facilities; reorient travel units to monitor the market and take advantage of opportunities; and reconsider the mandatory pre-auditing by the travel units of all travel authorizations. The search for least costly fares should be subject to verification and random checks by travel units. The Secretary-General should establish an Advisory Committee on Travel and develop a travel manual. He should also make programme managers directly accountable for the observance of travel regulations, and allow them flexibility in the use and transfer of resources for travel while introducing initiatives and motivations to promote efficiency and cost-consciousness. The Secretariat should study the use of credit cards for staff travel and introduce computer-assisted processing of travel documents, which could be a practical application of the Integrated Management Information System. It should prepare a standard contract with a travel agency which could later be tailored to the needs of various duty stations; review all existing contracts with travel agencies; review lists of preferred air-carriers and negotiate with selected major carriers to obtain discounts and upgrades. Teleconferencing should be developed. The General Assembly should review the nine-hour flight threshold, and abolish or modify the entitlement to official stopovers and substitute more rest-time at destination. The Secretary-General should encourage travellers to use means of transportation other than air, and the system of daily subsistence allowance should be maintained until the operation of the expense-based system proved cost-effective. The Assembly should call upon Member States to review travel standards and practices to achieve system-wide uniformity and consistency.

## Administration of justice

In its annual note[30] to the General Assembly, the United Nations Administrative Tribunal reported that it had delivered 58 judgements during the year. They related to cases brought by staff members against the Secretary-General or the executive heads of other UN bodies to resolve disputes involving terms of appointment and related issues and regulations.

The Tribunal met in New York on 22 November 1995 and also held two panel sessions (Geneva, 26 June–28 July; New York, 23 October–22 November).

## Review procedure

The General Assembly's Sixth Committee considered the 1994 report[31] of the Secretary-General reviewing the procedure provided for under article 11 of the statute of the Administrative Tribunal of the United Nations, which governed the review of the Tribunal's judgements by the Committee on Applications for Review of Administrative Tribunal Judgements. It also considered the views of Member States concerning the Committee's terms of reference and composition and the role of ICJ.[31] The Committee recommended that the Assembly amend the statute of the Tribunal with respect to judgements rendered by the Tribunal after 31 December 1995.

**GENERAL ASSEMBLY ACTION**

On 11 December, the General Assembly adopted **resolution 50/54**.

**Review of the procedure provided for under article 11 of the statute of the Administrative Tribunal of the United Nations**

*The General Assembly,*

*Having considered* the report of the Secretary-General,

*Noting* that the procedure provided for under article 11 of the statute of the Administrative Tribunal of the United Nations has not proved to be a constructive or useful element in the adjudication of staff disputes within the Organization, and noting also the views of the Secretary-General to that effect,

1. *Decides* to amend the statute of the Administrative Tribunal of the United Nations with respect to judgements rendered by the Tribunal after 31 December 1995 as follows:

(a) Delete article 11;

(b) Renumber former articles 12, 13 and 14 as articles 11, 12 and 13, respectively, and in paragraph 3 of article 9 substitute the words "article 13" for "article 14";

(c) Amend paragraph 2 of article 10 by substituting the words "article 11" for "articles 11 and 12";

2. *Decides also* that, with respect to judgements rendered by the Tribunal before 1 January 1996, the statute of the Tribunal shall continue to apply as if the amendments in paragraph 1 above had not been made;

3. *Stresses* the importance for the staff and the Organization alike of ensuring a fair, efficient and expeditious internal system of justice within the United Nations, including effective mechanisms for the resolution of disputes.

General Assembly resolution 50/54

11 December 1995     Meeting 87     Adopted without vote

Approved by Sixth Committee (A/50/645) without vote, 9 November (meeting 35); draft by Chairman (A/C.6/50/L.3); agenda item 148.
*Meeting numbers.* GA 50th session: 6th Committee 10, 11, 35; plenary 87.

## Reform of the internal justice system

**Report of the Secretary-General.** Pursuant to a 1994 General Assembly request,[(32)] the Secretary-General submitted an 18 March 1995 report[(33)] explaining the mechanisms by which the reform of the UN justice system, proposed in 1994,[(31)] would be achieved. In terms of the proposal for early reconciliation and resolution of disputes, the Organization intended to provide training in the early resolution of conflicts, emphasize mediation, and increase its capacity to conduct effective review of administrative decisions at an early stage of the appeals process. New training programmes for improving communications skills and emphasizing client service had already begun and would be provided on a continuing basis. The proposed ombudsman panels would be appointed at all major duty stations by existing staff/management machinery and established under the guidance and direction of a coordinator, who would ensure the proper functioning of the system. As at 1 January 1996, review of administrative decisions would be conducted within the Office of the Under-Secretary-General for Administration and Management, independently of the Senior Legal Adviser. The review officers would examine all requests to determine whether a decision should be reversed or amended in a mutually acceptable manner or recommend corrective measures. The Staff Rules would be amended to extend the time-limits for the conduct of reviews, which were currently one month for staff members in New York and two months for those elsewhere.

Concerning the professionalization of the justice system, the Secretary-General recommended the introduction of an outside United Nations Arbitration Board to replace the in-house Joint Appeals Board. He would also begin to consider, on a case-by-case basis, requests from staff members to have their cases resolved by binding arbitration. If binding arbitration proved successful, it might be made compulsory for certain classes of appeals. Draft changes to the Staff Regulations and to the Staff Rules to permit the establishment of the Arbitration Board and a draft statute of the Board were annexed to the report. A Disciplinary Board, which would replace the Joint Disciplinary Committee, would be composed of qualified professionals. The New York section of the Disciplinary Board would be chaired by the Chairperson of the Arbitration Board, and the Geneva Section by the alternate Chairperson. The other members would be staff members selected on the basis of their technical ability. The members of the Disciplinary Board would be appointed by the Secretary-General after consultation with staff. A new Legal Officer would serve on the Panel of Counsel, and would advise staff on whether their terms and conditions of employment had been violated and how

to proceed at the reconciliation and resolution stage or before the Arbitration Board. The Officer would also advise staff who were the object of disciplinary proceedings.

The Secretary-General reported that staff believed that outside counsel should be allowed in cases submitted for binding arbitration; and that specific performance and the determination of damages that could be awarded should not be applied in the functioning of the Arbitration Board. The Secretary-General, however, was of the opinion that it would not be appropriate or prudent to allow outside counsel before the Arbitration Board, and that the powers of the Board should be no greater than those of the United Nations Administrative Tribunal. He said that the system would be reviewed after a period of at least two years.

In a 9 June addendum,[(34)] the Secretary-General indicated that the financial requirements of the proposed reform would be $1,377,600 for the 1996-1997 biennium.

**Comments of UN Administrative Tribunal.** The Secretary-General transmitted to the Assembly, in a 26 June addendum,[(35)] the comments of the United Nations Administrative Tribunal on his 18 March report on the reform of the internal justice system. The Tribunal questioned whether the three major objectives of the Secretary-General's report—reduction of the number of cases reaching formal litigation, expeditious processing of cases at that stage, and a cost-effective and simple justice system—were likely to be accomplished by the proposed reforms. In particular, the Tribunal considered that the proposal for optional arbitration to replace the Joint Appeals Board (JAB), as well as the future possibility of mandatory arbitration, should be carefully examined by all concerned, since the potential consequences of hasty action could adversely affect the relationship between the staff and the Organization. The Tribunal emphasized that its suggestions should be viewed in the context of its doubts as to the need for or the desirability of replacing the JAB system with the proposed arbitration system.

The Secretary-General said that he accepted the suggestions of the Tribunal relating to the proposed arbitration statute and changes to the statute of the Tribunal, and indicated that the two statutes would be amended accordingly. As to the rationale, he stated that the proposal before the Assembly had been made after a careful assessment of the system, which had revealed serious flaws and difficulties, and after requests from the Assembly, the staff and many administrations for a fair, just and transparent system. The staff fully supported the reform, and did not share the Tribunal's view that the JAB system should continue and that full implementation of the reform should be postponed. The proposed reform was elaborated in consultation with the Legal Counsel, and care had been taken to preserve the authority of the Secretary-General. The arbitrators serving on the Board would be UN "officials", not staff members, and binding arbitration would occur only when the Secretary-General agreed to submit a case for decision by the Arbitration Board at his discretion. Should mandatory arbitration later be introduced for certain categories of cases, they would be carefully defined.

The General Assembly, by **decision 49/491** of 20 July, decided to defer to its fiftieth session consideration of the Secretary-General's report, in the light of the recommendations and observations of ACABQ.

**Report of the Secretary-General (September).** On 27 September, the Secretary-General submitted to the Assembly a consolidated report[36] on the internal justice system, taking into account the suggestions made by the United Nations Administrative Tribunal and new provisions agreed upon after consultation with the staff. Additional proposals included: that the two posts of Administrative Review Officers be established at the P-5 and P-4 levels; that the time-limits for administrative review would be three months; that the Secretary-General intended to accept the unanimous recommendations of the proposed arbitration board, unless there was a compelling reason not to do so; that both the New York and Geneva arbitration boards have a full-time Chairperson/Alternate Chairperson, two part-time members and two part-time alternate members; and that the revised estimates resulting from the proposals for the 1996-1997 biennium be $1,536,500. The report also contained the draft statute for the United Nations Disciplinary Board.

**Comments of the Administrative Tribunal and Staff Union (November).** In a 17 November note,[37] the Secretary-General transmitted to the Assembly the additional comments of the Administrative Tribunal and those of the Staff Union of the Secretariat.

Concerning JAB, the Administrative Tribunal stated that such problems as securing volunteers to serve on the boards, and attitudes or reactions of JAB members regarding frequency of serving, or those of staff concerning perceptions of conflict of interests could be solved by adoption of appropriate rules concerning potential conflict or bias, and through reform of the system of selection of JAB members. Evaluating the quality of JAB work on the basis of a year-by-year average statistical count of unanimous JAB recommendations was open to question, the Tribunal said; it would be far more informative to examine all reports, and over longer periods. In the view of the Tribunal, JAB on the whole had been performing commend-

ably and had made valuable contributions to the system of justice. The Tribunal doubted whether part-time members of the New York Arbitration Board would be able to deal with an estimated annual load of 90 cases in two five-week sessions. Time requirements indicated that the arbitration structure was likely to be more expensive than the suggested estimate.

The Staff Union, referring to statistics relating to JAB, stated that its own research had indicated that the majority of recommendations rejected by the Secretary-General had been upheld by the Tribunal, and over the past two years he had accepted the wisdom of the Board in 99.5 per cent of the cases when the Board supported the decision of the Administration. It pointed out that as long as arbitrators were recruited and paid by the United Nations, there was a need to ensure that they were truly independent, which was why the agreed-upon selection process had to be a joint one. The Staff Union stated that if the internal justice system was to be professionalized and all who reviewed and made representation were to be lawyers, it was essential that the appellants have similar representation.

**ACABQ action.** ACABQ, in an 8 December report,[38] concurred in the proposed appointment of ombudsmen and mediation panels at all major duty stations and the provision of a D-1 post for the appointment of a Coordinator. The Committee recognized the necessity of ensuring that the initial review of administrative decisions be carried out thoroughly and expeditiously. It recommended acceptance of the new P-4 and P-5 posts for the Administrative Review Officers and that the Administrative Review Unit be accorded operational independence to ensure objectivity and efficiency. It recommended that more work be done on the proposal for creation of an Arbitration Board before further consideration by the Assembly. ACABQ recommended that the establishment of a Disciplinary Board be reconsidered in conjunction with further consideration of the establishment of an Arbitration Board. With regard to the Panel of Counsel, ACABQ recommended acceptance of the additional posts and agreed that resources should be provided for the training of Panel of Counsel members.

ACABQ concluded that some progress had been made in the expeditious processing of cases, but the problem was the growing number of administrative grievances. Proposals related to the early reconciliation and resolution of disputes should go a long way towards minimizing the number of matters referred to formal proceedings. Not enough had been done to simplify rules and procedures so that misunderstandings could be avoided and to identify those aspects of staff administration that gave rise to appeals, with a view to reform in those areas. ACABQ believed that fostering conciliation and early resolution of disputes, strengthening the Administrative Review Unit and the Panel of Counsel, and simplification and rationalization of existing administrative and personnel practices should address positively relevant problems and shortcomings. After a reasonable period, the effect of those changes should be evaluated with a view to determining what further measures might be necessary.

The General Assembly, by **decision 50/454** of 22 December, decided to defer consideration of the item entitled ''Human resources management'' until its resumed session in 1996, in particular the reports of the Secretary-General on the reform of the internal system of justice in the UN Secretariat, pending consideration of the legal implications of the Secretary-General's proposals.

*REFERENCES*

[1]A/49/845. [2]A/49/845/Add.1. [3]A/C.5/49/62. [4]A/C.5/49/CRP.3. [5]YUN 1994, p. 1379, GA res. 49/222 A, 23 Dec. 1994. [6]A/50/540. [7]E/CN.6/1995/7. [8]YUN 1994, p. 1384. [9]Ibid., p. 1379. [10]A/50/691 & Corr.1. [11]A/50/147 & Add.1,2. [12]A/C.5/50/32. [13]A/C.5/49/63. [14]A/C.5/49/64. [15]A/C.5/49/56. [16]YUN 1993, p. 1215, GA res. 47/226, 30 Sep. 1993. [17]A/C.5/50/3. [18]A/C.5/50/29. [19]YUN 1994, p. 1289, GA res. 49/59, 9 Dec. 1994. [20]A/50/312. [21]A/50/7/Add.1. [22]A/50/236 & Corr.1. [23]YUN 1987, p. 1161. [24]A/C.5/50/34. [25]A/49/952. [26]A/C.5/49/72. [27]A/C.5/50/22. [28]A/C.5/50/50. [29]A/50/692. [30]A/INF/50/6. [31]YUN 1994, p. 1399. [32]Ibid., p. 1379, GA res. 49/222 A, sect. IV, 23 Dec. 1994. [33]A/C.5/49/60. [34]A/C.5/49/60/Add.1. [35]A/C.5/49/60/Add.2 & Corr.1. [36]A/C.5/50/2. [37]A/C.5/50/2/Add.1. [38]A/50/7/Add.8.

Chapter IV

# Institutional and administrative matters

In 1995, the General Assembly held its fiftieth session, during which it convened a special commemorative meeting from 22 to 24 October to observe the fiftieth anniversary of the United Nations (see special section beginning on p. 141 and PART ONE, Chapter III). The Assembly granted to the Central American Integration System the status of observer, and requested the Secretary-General to conclude cooperation agreements with the Inter-Parliamentary Union and to promote cooperation with the Agency for Cultural and Technical Cooperation.

During the year, the Security Council held 185 formal meetings to consider items related to the maintenance of international peace and security. The Council announced changes in its documentation and other procedural matters and streamlined procedures and working methods of its sanctions committees.

The Economic and Social Council held its 1995 organizational session in New York and its substantive session in Geneva. The Council changed the format of its provisional work programme and requested the Secretary-General to present proposals in 1996 to simplify reporting requirements.

The Administrative Committee on Coordination and the Committee for Programme and Coordination continued to harmonize system-wide work programmes and activities. At their twenty-ninth series of Joint Meetings, held in October, the coordination of activities of the UN system for the eradication of poverty was discussed. The Economic and Social Council also considered coordinated follow-up by the UN system and implementation of the results of major international conferences organized by the United Nations in the economic, social and related fields. The Council recommended arrangements and procedures for an integrated framework and a global partnership for development. It also reviewed the consultative status of non-governmental organizations.

The Committee on Conferences examined requests for changes to the calendar of conferences and meetings for 1995, which had been approved in 1994, and dealt with the calendar for 1996. It recommended measures to improve the utilization of conference-servicing resources and to control and limit documentation.

## Institutional machinery

### General Assembly

During 1995, the General Assembly met in two sessions, to resume and conclude its forty-ninth session and to hold the major part of its fiftieth session. The forty-ninth session was resumed in 1995 on 26 January, 28 February, 10 and 31 March, 6, 13 and 21 April, 24 and 25 May, 21 June, 12 and 20 July, and 14 and 18 September.

The fiftieth (1995) session opened on 19 September and continued until its suspension on 23 December.

In accordance with a 1994 decision,[1] the Assembly held a special commemorative meeting from 22 to 24 October on the occasion of the fiftieth anniversary of the United Nations.

#### Organization of Assembly sessions

On 22 September, by **decision 50/401**, the General Assembly, on the recommendation of the General Committee, as set forth in its first report,[2] adopted a number of provisions concerning the organization of the fiftieth session.

The Committee's recommendations concerned the rationalization of the Assembly's work; observance of the UN fiftieth anniversary; closing date of the session; schedule of meetings; general debate; explanations of vote, right of reply, points of order and length of statements; records of meetings; concluding statements; resolutions; documentation; questions related to the programme budget; observances and commemorative meetings; special conferences; and meetings of subsidiary organs.

The General Committee made observations and proposals regarding the organization of future Assembly sessions. At the suggestion of the Secretary-General, it recommended to the Assembly that it consider a possible rationalization of its meetings between January and August to allow advance planning for delegations and the UN Secretariat. The Assembly had met frequently during those months in the past few years and, during its forty-ninth session, it had met every month from January to September, with the exception of August. As those meetings were not envisaged in the calendar of meetings, ad hoc arrangements had to be made to provide adequate Secretariat services, at the expense of other requirements.

By **decision 50/403 A** of 19 September, the General Assembly authorized the Executive Board of the United Nations Children's Fund (UNICEF) to hold meetings during the fiftieth session.

On 22 September, by **decision 50/403 B**, the Assembly authorized the following subsidiary organs to hold meetings during the fiftieth session: the Advisory Committee on the UN Educational and Training Programme for Southern Africa; the Committee on Relations with the Host Country; the Committee on the Exercise of the Inalienable Rights of the Palestinian People; the Open-ended High-level Working Group on the Strengthening of the United Nations System; the Preparatory Committee for the Fiftieth Anniversary of the United Nations; and the Working Group on the Financing of the UN Relief and Works Agency for Palestine Refugees in the Near East (UNRWA).

On 26 October, by **decision 50/403 C**, the Assembly authorized the following additional subsidiary organs to hold meetings during the fiftieth session: the Ad Hoc Open-ended Working Group o₁ an Agenda for Development; the High-level Open-ended Working Group on the Financial Situation of the United Nations; and the Open-ended Working Group on the Question of Equitable Representation on and Increase in the Membership of the Security Council and Other Matters Related to the Security Council.

During the fiftieth General Assembly session and the special commemorative meeting for the fiftieth anniversary of the United Nations, Member States discussed the importance of strengthening the role of the Assembly. Revitalization of the Assembly was also one of the scheduled discussion topics of the Open-ended High-level Working Group on the Strengthening of the United Nations System (see PART SIX, Chapter I).

## Credentials

On 12 October,[3] at its first plenary meeting of the fiftieth session, the Credentials Committee had before it a memorandum by the Secretary-General indicating that, as at 11 October, 115 Member States had submitted credentials of their representatives. The Deputy to the Under-Secretary-General for Legal Affairs informed the Committee that, subsequent to the memorandum, credentials in due form had been received in respect of the representatives of the Congo, Mauritania and Suriname.

At its second meeting,[4] on 11 December, the Committee examined a memorandum by the Secretary-General which stated that 45 additional Member States had submitted formal credentials. In addition, information concerning the appointment of representatives to the fiftieth session had been communicated to the Secretary-General from 20 Member States.

The Committee Chairman proposed that the Committee accept the credentials of all those Member States, including those communicated by facsimile, letter or note verbale, on the understanding that the latter would submit formal credentials as soon as possible.

At each meeting, the Committee adopted a resolution accepting the credentials received. The Committee also recommended to the Assembly two draft resolutions. On 18 October and 14 December, the Assembly, by **resolutions 50/4 A and B**, respectively, approved the first and second reports of the Credentials Committee.

## Agenda

At its resumed forty-ninth session, by **decision 49/402 B** of 28 February, the General Assembly, on the proposal of the Secretary-General, included an item on its agenda on "Financing of the International Criminal Tribunal for the Prosecution of Persons Responsible for Genocide and Other Serious Violations of International Humanitarian Law Committed in the Territory of Rwanda and Rwandan Citizens Responsible for Genocide and Other Such Violations Committed in the Territory of Neighbouring States between 1 January and 31 December 1994". Also on 28 February, on the proposal of the Secretary-General, the General Assembly included an item entitled "Election of judges of the International Criminal Tribunal for the Prosecution of Persons Responsible for Genocide and Other Serious Violations of International Humanitarian Law Committed in the Territory of Rwanda and Rwandan Citizens Responsible for Genocide and Other Such Violations Committed in the Territory of Neighbouring States between 1 January and 31 December 1994". On the proposal of the Secretary-General, it reopened consideration of the appointment of members of the Committee on Contributions.

On 31 March, by the same decision, the Assembly, on the proposal of the Secretary-General, reopened for consideration, in plenary, the election of a member of the International Court of Justice. Also on 31 March, the Assembly, on a request by Norway, reopened consideration, in plenary, of special economic assistance to individual countries or regions. Also by the same decision, on 21 April, the Assembly, on the proposal of the Secretary-General, reopened consideration, in plenary, of the item on the advancement of women.

On 12 July, by the same decision, the Assembly reopened consideration of the sub-item on appointment of members of the Advisory Committee on Administrative and Budgetary Questions (ACABQ).

On 14 September, by **decision 49/402 C**, the Assembly, on the proposal of the Secretary-General, included a sub-item on its agenda entitled "Confirmation of the appointment of the Secretary-General of the United Nations Conference on Trade and Development".

On 18 September, the Assembly decided to defer consideration of the following items and to include them in the provisional agenda of the fiftieth session: armed Israeli aggression against Iraqi nuclear installations and its grave consequences for the established international system concerning the peaceful uses of nuclear energy, the non-proliferation of nuclear weapons and international peace and security (**decision 49/500**); the situation in Afghanistan and its implications for international peace and security (**decision 49/501**); the question of Cyprus (**decision 49/502**); and consequences of the Iraqi occupation of and aggression against Kuwait (**decision 49/503**).

By an 18 July letter,[5] 20 Member States (Burkina Faso, Central African Republic, Costa Rica, Dominica, Dominican Republic, El Salvador, Gambia, Grenada, Guatemala, Guinea-Bissau, Honduras, Malawi, Nicaragua, Niger, Panama, Saint Kitts and Nevis, Saint Lucia, Saint Vincent and the Grenadines, Solomon Islands and Swaziland) requested that the Assembly include on the agenda of its fiftieth session an item entitled "Consideration of the exceptional situation of the Republic of China on Taiwan in the international context, based on the principle of universality and in accordance with the established model of parallel representation of divided countries at the United Nations". China, in a 20 July letter[6] to the Secretary-General, expressed its opposition to the inclusion of the item. The General Committee, in its first report,[2] on 20 September did not recommend inclusion of this item.

By **decision 50/402 A**, on the recommendation of the General Committee,[7] the General Assembly, on 22 September, 26 October, 10 November and 1 December, adopted various parts of the agenda of its fiftieth session[8] and allocated items to the plenary or appropriate Main Committee.[9]

On 26 October, by the same decision, it decided to include in the agenda the item on implementation of the outcome of the Fourth World Conference on Women: Action for Equality, Development and Peace, and to consider it in plenary for the purpose of endorsing the Beijing Declaration and Platform for Action. It also included a sub-item on the report of the UN High Commissioner for Human Rights.

On 10 November, by the same decision, the Assembly approved sub-items on food and sustainable agricultural development and on the appointment of a member of the Joint Inspection Unit (JIU).

By the same decision, on 1 December, it approved an item on admission of the World Tourism Organization to membership in the UN Joint Staff Pension Fund and a sub-item on election of a member of the International Court of Justice. The Assembly also decided to consider an item on the normalization of the situation concerning South Africa, given its political importance, directly in plenary, on the understanding that owing to the financial complexity of the matter, the Fifth (Administrative and Budgetary) Committee would be invited to provide technical observations by 12 December regarding the implementation of any draft resolutions to be submitted to the Assembly in plenary meeting.

In the same decision, the Assembly deferred consideration of the question of the Malagasy islands of Glorieuses, Juan de Nova, Europa and Bassas da India, and the question of East Timor. Other matters that were deferred were: the question of the Falkland Islands (Malvinas) (**decision 50/406** of 31 October); the question of the composition of the relevant organs of the United Nations (**decision 50/414** of 6 December); the declaration of the Assembly of Heads of State and Government of the Organization of African Unity on the aerial and naval attack against the Socialist People's Libyan Arab Jamahariya by the present United States Administration in April 1986 (**decision 50/422** of 18 December); armed Israeli aggression against the Iraqi nuclear installations and its grave consequences for the established international system concerning the peaceful uses of nuclear energy, the non-proliferation of nuclear weapons and international peace and security (**decision 50/444** of 21 December); consequences of the Iraqi occupation of and aggression against Kuwait (**decision 50/445** of 21 December); implementation of the resolutions of the United Nations (**decision 50/457** of 22 December); and launching of global negotiations on international economic cooperation for development (**decision 50/468** of 22 December). These items were included in the provisional agenda of the fifty-first session. On 23 December, by **decision 50/475**, the Assembly retained 42 items or sub-items for consideration during the resumed fiftieth session in 1996.

### First Committee

Pursuant to a 1994 decision,[10] the General Assembly took up the question of the rationalization of the work and reform of the agenda of the First (Disarmament and International Security) Committee.

On 12 December, by **decision 50/421**, the Assembly requested the Chairman of the First Committee to continue consultations on the further rationalization of the work of the Committee with a view to improving its effective functioning, and decided to defer consideration of the item entitled "Rationalization of the work and reform of the agenda of the First Committee" and to include it in the provisional agenda of its fifty-second (1997) session.

### Third Committee

The Secretariat, in a 12 December note,[11] presented measures on the organization of work and the draft programme of work of the Third (Social, Humanitarian and Cultural) Committee for the biennium 1996-1997. The organizational measures related to guidelines concerning time-limits of statements, draft resolutions on reports of treaty bodies and reports of the Secretary-General on the status of treaties, and draft proposals emanating from subsidiary organs of the Economic and Social Council.

On 22 December, by **decision 50/465**, the Assembly approved the organization of work of the Third Committee and the biennial programme of work of the Committee for 1996-1997.

### Second and Fifth Committees

On 20 December, by **decision 50/440**, the General Assembly approved the biennial programme of work of the Second (Economic and Financial) Committee for 1996-1997.

On 23 December, by **decision 50/470**, the Assembly approved the biennial programme of work of the Fifth Committee for 1996-1997.

## Security Council

In 1995, the Security Council held 185 formal meetings, adopted 93 resolutions and issued 92 presidential statements.

The Security Council considered 34 agenda items in 1995 (see APPENDIX IV for agenda). On 18 September, the Secretary-General, in accordance with Article 12, paragraph 2, of the UN Charter and with the consent of the Security Council, notified[12] the General Assembly of 32 matters relative to the maintenance of international peace and security that the Council had discussed since its previous annual notification.[13] He listed 99 other matters not discussed during that period but of which the Council remained seized.

By **decision 50/458 A** of 22 December, the Assembly took note of the matter.

On 13 November,[14] the Security Council adopted its draft report covering the period from 16 June 1994 to 16 June 1995.[15] The General Assembly took note of the report by **decision 50/409** of 29 November.

### Documentation

On 29 March, the Security Council announced[16] changes concerning its documentation and other procedural matters. It introduced improvements to make the procedures of the sanctions committees more transparent, including: issuing more press releases after meetings of the Committee; making available the Status of Communications lists to any delegation under the "No Objection" procedure prepared by the Secretariat; making regularly available a list of all decisions by each active Committee to any delegation requesting it; providing, in the annual report of the Security Council to the General Assembly, more information about each Committee; providing an annual report to the Security Council from each Committee on its activities; and expediting preparation of Committee summary records. The Council said meetings of the Sanctions Committee should remain closed and the summary records should continue to be distributed according to the existing pattern. The Council agreed to continue consideration of other suggestions concerning documentation and related matters.

In a 2 June letter[17] addressed to the Secretary-General, Argentina referred to the United Kingdom proposal to retitle presidential statements made on behalf of the Security Council "Statements on behalf of the Security Council". Argentina noted that statements were a relatively new Security Council instrument, the use of which had increased considerably in recent years. The Council had never defined the scope, content or nature of the documents it issued, neither in its provisional rules of procedure nor in its interpretive documents. Since 1993, the trend was to regard statements read out during formal meetings as being "on behalf of the Council". It was argued that those statements which arose out of the work of the Council during informal meetings should be made, on the other hand, "on behalf of members of the Council". The letter stated that potential consequences of accepting this new distinction should be evaluated. In addition, the Council should address the issue of the nature of "informal" meetings and whether the provisions of Article 31 of the Charter applied to those meetings. Argentina proposed that the Working Group of the Council on documentation and procedure should examine those issues to enable the Council to harmonize criteria and adopt guidelines, notwithstanding any parallel efforts being made in the General Assembly.

### Working methods and procedure

On 31 May, the Security Council announced[18] that the practice of hearing comments by States and organizations concerned during closed meetings of sanctions committees on issues arising from implementation of sanctions regimes imposed by the Security Council should be continued, while respecting the existing procedures followed by such Committees.

In a letter[19] of the same date by the Security Council President, addressed to the Secretary-General, Council members expressed concern over the staffing situation in the Security Council Affairs Division of the Department of Political Affairs, and called for adequate staffing to enable the Council and its committees to function effectively. The letter welcomed the increase in staff to support the sanctions committees, and said the Council members looked forward to a future report on whether the increase resulted in a decrease in the backlog in processing applications to those committees. The letter also stressed the need for Council members to be able to use the official language of their choice in all of their work.

Council members requested the Secretary-General to ensure fully adequate support services for the Council, taking into account the increase in the Council's workload over recent years.

The Secretary-General, in a 9 November letter[20] to the Council President, reported that the backlog in processing applications to the sanctions committees had been eliminated and that he had initiated a process of streamlining the working practices of the secretariat of those committees. Efforts were under way to ensure that humanitarian applications were processed at an even faster pace. He promised to keep the situation under review so that the Secretariat's ability to respond to the needs of Member States might be further enhanced.

On 16 November,[21] the Council welcomed the information contained in the Secretary-General's letter.

## Membership

In 1995, the General Assembly continued to consider the issue of expanding the membership of the Security Council, and received the report[22] of its Open-ended Working Group on the Question of Equitable Representation on and Increase in the Membership of the Security Council and Other Matters Related to the Security Council, established by the Assembly in 1993[23] (see PART SIX, Chapter I).

## Economic and Social Council

In 1995, the Economic and Social Council held its organizational session in New York on 1 and from 7 to 10 February, and its resumed organizational session on 4 and 5 May and on 1 and 6 June; its substantive session was held at Geneva from 26 June to 28 July and its resumed substantive session on 25 October, 2 November and 12 December, in New York.

On 1 February, the Economic and Social Council elected two members of its Bureau—the President for 1995 and its Vice-President. Two other Vice-Presidents were elected on 7 February and one on 10 February (see APPENDIX III).

On 7 February, the Council adopted the agenda of its organizational session.[24] By **decision 1995/205** of 10 February, it approved the provisional agenda of the 1995 substantive session.

On 4 May, the Council agreed to the inclusion of an additional item in the agenda of the resumed organizational session, entitled "Social, humanitarian and human rights questions: reports of subsidiary bodies, conferences and related questions".

On 26 June, by **decision 1995/228**, the Council adopted the agenda of its substantive session[25] and approved the organization of work of the session.[26] On 7 July, by the same decision, it approved requests by non-governmental organizations (NGOs)[27] to be heard by the Council.

On 27 July, by **decision 1995/311**, the Council decided to retain the item "Programme and related questions in the economic, social and related fields" on the agenda of its substantive session in order to consider the question of the biennialization of the meetings of its subsidiary bodies.

(For agenda lists, see APPENDIX IV.)

## Sessions and segments

During its 1995 substantive session (26 June to 28 July), the Economic and Social Council adopted 62 resolutions and 88 decisions. At the resumed substantive session, it adopted one resolution and 10 decisions.

In accordance with General Assembly resolutions of 1991[28] and 1993,[29] the Council's substantive session was divided into a high-level segment (4 to 6 July), a coordination segment and a segment dealing with operational activities of the United Nations for international development cooperation.

The Council, by **decision 1995/203** of 10 February, decided that the high-level segment of its substantive session should be devoted to consideration of the major theme "Development of Africa, including the implementation of the United Nations new agenda for development of Africa", which should also be considered in the policy dialogue of that segment (see PART FOUR, Chapter I).

By **decision 1995/204** of 10 February, the Council decided that its coordination segment should be devoted to the theme "Coordinated follow-up by the United Nations system and implementation of the results of the major international conferences organized by the United Nations in the economic, social and related fields" (see below).

The Council, by **decision 1995/213** of 10 February, decided that its segment on operational activities of the United Nations for international development cooperation would last five days, the first day designated for a high-level meeting, the second for informal dialogue with heads of agencies, and the last three days for working-level meetings (see PART FOUR, Chapter II).

On 5 May, by **decision 1995/224**, the Council decided that the principal theme of the segment would be implementation by the UN system of the Programme of Action of the International Conference on Population and Development, with focus on, *inter alia*, action taken at the Conference to implement the integrated approach to population and development issues (see PART FOUR, Chapter VIII). A second issue would be a preliminary exchange on the follow-up by the UN system to the Copenhagen Declaration on Social Development and the Programme of Action of the World Summit for Social Development, and consideration of the direction to be taken by the UN system in adopting an approach to social development issues in accordance with the framework developed by the Summit (see PART FOUR, Chapter IX).

The work of the Economic and Social Council at its organizational and substantive sessions was summarized in its report to the General Assembly.[30] On 22 December, by **decisions 50/456, 50/466** and **50/467**, the General Assembly took note of various chapters of the Council's report.

### Work programme

On 10 February, the Economic and Social Council considered its proposed basic programme of work for 1995 and 1996, submitted by the Secretary-General in a 3 February note.[31] By **decision 1995/208** of the same date, the Council noted the list of questions for inclusion in the programme of work for 1996.

In a 22 June letter,[32] the Chairman of the Committee on Conferences informed the Economic and Social Council President that the Committee, in considering the provisional calendar of conferences and meetings for 1996 and 1997 in the economic, social and related fields,[33] had expressed concern regarding the increase in requests from intergovernmental bodies for exceptions to the biennialization of their sessions. The Committee recommended adoption of the provisional calendar and, in view of the difficult financial situation of the Organization, advised that the Council continue to consider the biennialization of meetings of subsidiary bodies, and that requests for an annual cycle of meetings should be based on substantive reasons (see below).

On 25 October, by **decision 1995/319**, the Economic and Social Council approved the calendar of conferences and meetings for 1996 and 1997 in the economic, social and related fields[33] as revised by **decision 1995/318**.

The Council decided to defer consideration of a draft resolution,[34] introduced by the United States, by which the Council would have noted the recommendations of the Committee on Conferences, decided to biennialize the meetings of a number of its subsidiary bodies and requested the Secretary-General to submit a draft biennial calendar for 1997-1998 accordingly.

### 1996 coordination segment

In response to the Council's agreed conclusions[35] in July regarding possible themes for follow-up to major international conferences at the coordination segment of the Council in 1996, the Secretary-General, in a 1 December note,[36] and following consultation with the relevant bodies of the UN system and specialized agencies, suggested as a possible theme "Gender equality, equity and empowerment of women". He also reported that Spain, on behalf of the European Union, had proposed the theme "Coordination of the United Nations system activities for poverty eradication". Canada also submitted a theme on poverty eradication.

On 12 December, the Economic and Social Council, by **decision 1995/321**, decided that its 1996 coordination segment should be devoted to consideration of the theme "Coordination of the activities of the United Nations system for the eradication of poverty". It would decide, at its organizational session for 1996, on the allocation of a number of meetings, within the general segment of its substantive session of 1996, to determine how to ensure harmonization and coordination of the agendas and multi-year programmes of work of its functional commissions.

### Documentation

The Economic and Social Council, by **decision 1995/222** of 5 May, decided to change the format of its provisional programme of work, adding new documents that would list, in addition to agenda items, the reports expected under each segment or item. Furthermore, the documents should be made available in all official languages at least four weeks before the organizational sessions and 14 weeks before the substantive sessions. A report on the status of documentation should be available to delegations three weeks before the resumed organizational session of the Council. Should a report for any session of the Council be issued shortly before or on the same day that an item or segment of an item was to be considered, the officer responsible for the introduction of the report should give reasons for the delay.

On 28 July, the Council, in its agreed conclusions[35] regarding a coordinated follow-up to international conferences (see below), requested the Secretary-General to present proposals in 1996 to the Council and the Assembly to simplify reporting requirements, taking into account the reports required for the follow-up to UN conferences. The Council also stressed that other methods for promoting integrated reporting by the Secretariat should be explored, and that requests for reports should be limited to the minimum necessary. The Secretary-General was also requested to prepare a standardized and simplified format, which could be used by Governments in preparing information on a single subject or clusters of subjects.

### Restructuring issues

The General Assembly, on the basis of a 27 October report of the Secretary-General,[37] continued consideration of the restructuring and revitalization of the United Nations in the economic, social and related fields (see PART SIX, Chapter I).

By **decision 1995/227** of 6 June, the Economic and Social Council recommended that the General Assembly reconstitute the Committee on Food Aid Policies and Programmes as the Executive Board of the World Food Programme. It also recommended that the Assembly approve the revised General Regulations of the World Food Programme. On 1 November, the Assembly approved those requests in **resolution 50/8**. By **decision 50/439** of 20 December, it also took note of the Secretary-General's note[38] on the matter (see PART FOUR, Chapter XIII).

In **resolution 1995/55** of 28 July, the Economic and Social Council recommended that the General Assembly at its fiftieth session consider further the establishment of a separate Executive Board for the United Nations Population Fund (UNFPA) (see PART FOUR, Chapter VIII).

On 20 December, by **decision 50/438**, the Assembly, taking note of the Council's recommendation in July (**decision 1995/231**), endorsed the agreement between the United Nations Development Programme (UNDP) and UNFPA to designate Fund resident country directors as Fund representatives.

*REFERENCES*

[1]YUN 1994, p. 249, GA res. 48/215 B, 26 May 1994. [2]A/50/250. [3]A/50/559 & Corr.1. [4]A/50/559/Add.1. [5]A/50/145 & Add.1. [6]A/50/298. [7]A/50/250 & Add.1-3. [8]A/50/251 & Add.1-4. [9]A/50/252 & Add.1-4. [10]YUN 1994, p. 248, GA res. 49/85, 15 Dec. 1994. [11]A/C.3/50/L.69. [12]A/50/442. [13]YUN 1994, p. 242. [14]S/1995/948. [15]A/50/2. [16]S/1995/234. [17]S/1995/456. [18]S/1995/438. [19]S/1995/440. [20]S/1995/957. [21]S/1995/958. [22]A/49/47. [23]YUN 1993, p. 212, GA res. 48/26, 3 Dec. 1993. [24]E/1995/2. [25]E/1995/100. [26]E/1995/L.6/Rev.1. [27]E/1995/106. [28]YUN 1991, p. 749, GA res. 45/264, 13 May 1991. [29]YUN 1993, p. 1118, GA res. 48/162, 20 Dec. 1993. [30]A/50/3/Rev.1. [31]E/1995/1 & Add.1. [32]E/1995/101. [33]E/1995/L.20 & Add.1,2. [34]E/1995/L.67.

[35]A/50/3/Rev.1 (1995/1). [36]E/1995/129. [37]A/50/697 & Add.1 & Corr.1. [38]A/50/706.

# Coordination, monitoring and cooperation

## Institutional mechanisms

### Activities of ACC

In 1995, the Administrative Committee on Coordination (ACC)[1] reinforced its capacity to address the main policy issues facing the international community and to promote and organize joint initiatives towards common objectives. It devoted special attention to issues relating to African economic recovery and development, and decided to launch a System-wide Special Initiative on Africa (see PART FOUR, Chapter III). The Initiative, as set out in the report of its Steering Committee, was built around specific development actions to be undertaken jointly by the organizations of the UN system, within the context of their ongoing programmes and in close cooperation with other development actors. A year-long campaign was to be initiated in 1996 for political and resource mobilization. ACC stressed that the effective allocation and utilization of available resources would be critical to the success of the Special Initiative, which was an expression of a strong, renewed commitment by UN organizations and agencies to Africa's development. ACC extended the mandate of the Steering Committee for one year for follow-up and monitoring purposes, and invited it to work closely with the relevant parts of ACC, as well as with the inter-agency task forces set up for the coordinated follow-up to recent international conferences. The Committee was also invited to report to ACC at its first regular session in 1996. ACC emphasized the need to approach the follow-up to all recent UN conferences in an integrated manner.

ACC expressed strong support for UN action in the area of international drug abuse control, and agreed, *inter alia*, that its Subcommittee on Drug Control should review, strengthen and render operational the UN System-wide Action Plan on Drug Abuse Control through the elaboration of specific multi-agency sectoral and/or subsectoral plans of action for drug abuse control at the global, regional and subregional levels (see PART FOUR, Chapter XIV).

With regard to operational activities for development, ACC, through its Consultative Committee for Programme and Operational Questions (CCPOQ), collaborated in the preparation of the Secretary-General's report,[2] which formed the basis of the triennial comprehensive review of operational activities for development of the UN system at the Assembly's fiftieth session (see PART FOUR, Chapter II).

ACC continued to discuss UN efforts to provide assistance to States that had been adversely affected by the imposition of sanctions against the Federal Republic of Yugoslavia (Serbia and Montenegro) and Iraq.

Other issues discussed by ACC included the consultative process and the functioning of the International Civil Service Commission (ICSC), as well as other personnel and general administrative questions, such as application of the Noblemaire principle, the status of women in the secretariats of the UN system, work/family agenda policy, security of UN staff and associated personnel (see PART SIX, Chapter III); and financial issues, including the financial situation of the organizations of the UN system, the financial situation of the United Nations, and harmonization of financial statements (see PART SIX, Chapter II).

In May, ACC submitted to the Economic and Social Council a report[3] on the programmes and resources of the UN system for the 1994-1995 biennium, relating the objectives of UN organizations to the corresponding allocations of financial resources.

The Council, by **decision 1995/309** of 27 July, took note of the ACC report.

During the year, ACC held two regular sessions, in Vienna (27 and 28 February) and New York (12 and 13 October). Its principal subsidiary bodies met as follows:

> Organizational Committee (Vienna, 13-16 February and 2 March); Consultative Committee on Administrative Questions (Personnel and General Administrative Questions), eighty-second (Montreal, Canada, 24-28 April) and eighty-third (New York, 20-24 July and Geneva, 20-22 September) sessions; Consultative Committee on Administrative Questions (Financial and Budgetary Questions), eighty-second (London, 13-17 February) and eighty-third (New York, 28 August–1 September) sessions; Consultative Committee on Programme and Operational Questions, fifth (Geneva, 31 January–2 February), sixth (Geneva, 25 and 26 July) and seventh (New York, 19-22 September) sessions and its inter-sessional meeting (Geneva, 25 and 26 July).

Bodies on specific subjects met as follows:

> Information Systems Coordination Committee, third session (Geneva, 19-21 April); Joint United Nations Information Committee, twenty-first session (Paris, 5-7 July); Inter-Agency Committee on Sustainable Development, sixth session (Geneva, 12-14 July); Subcommittee on Oceans and Coastal Areas, second and third sessions (Geneva, 22-27 January; Paris, 28-30 August); Nineteenth Ad Hoc Inter-Agency Meeting on Women (New York, 13 and 14 March); Twentieth Ad Hoc Inter-Agency Meeting on

Women (New York, 16 and 17 November); Fifth Ad Hoc Inter-Agency Meeting on the International Year of the Family (Vienna, 22 and 23 May); Subcommittee on Nutrition, twenty-second session (Washington, D.C., 12-16 June); Subcommittee on Statistical Activities, twenty-ninth session (Geneva, 15, 16 and 19 June); Subcommittee on Drug Control, third session (Geneva, 31 July–2 August); Subcommittee on Rural Development, twenty-third session (Paris, 31 May–2 June); Subcommittee on Water Resources, sixteenth session (New York, 4-6 October).

### Report for 1994

ACC's annual overview report[4] for 1994 was considered on 17 May by the Committee for Programme and Coordination (CPC),[5] which stressed the need for ACC documentation to focus better on coordination issues of primary concern to CPC. While recognizing the merits of coordination based on a division of labour among the different organizations and agencies of the UN system, CPC emphasized that the General Assembly was the central policy-making forum within the system, and that enhanced coordination should lead to greater cost-effectiveness and improved programme delivery. The Committee agreed that the conclusions and declarations of recent major conferences and international events should be followed up in a coordinated manner within the context of an integrated approach.

The Economic and Social Council, by **decision 1995/309** of 27 July, took note of the annual overview report of ACC for 1994.

### Programme coordination

In 1995, the Committee for Programme and Coordination held its organizational session on 21 April and its thirty-fifth session from 15 May to 9 June in New York.[5]

The Committee reviewed the efficiency of the administrative and financial functioning of the United Nations, discussed programme questions related to the proposed 1996-1997 programme budget and evaluated the programme on the environment and the start-up phase of peace-keeping operations. Coordination issues considered included the annual ACC report for 1994 (see above), preparation for the Joint Meetings of ACC and CPC (see below), and Joint Inspection Unit (JIU) reports on communications for development programmes in the UN system and efforts to restructure the regional dimension of UN economic and social activities (see below).

On 27 July, the Economic and Social Council by **decision 1995/309** took note of the CPC report on the work of its thirty-fifth session.

### Joint Meetings of CPC and ACC

The twenty-ninth in a series of Joint Meetings of CPC and ACC was held in New York on 16 October 1995,[6] to discuss UN system coordination for the eradication of poverty (see also PART FOUR, Chapter I). The Meetings considered a background paper on the subject,[7] which discussed the setting of political priorities for the UN system by intergovernmental bodies and assessed UN system coordination in the eradication of poverty. It also looked at programmes and coordination mechanisms at the country level and identified issues for discussion.

The Joint Meetings concluded that the eradication of poverty was a top priority of the United Nations and had to be pursued in the coordinated follow-up to global conferences, in particular the World Summit for Social Development (see PART FOUR, Chapter IX). Efforts to eradicate poverty should be based on the goals and plans of individual countries, and the success of UN system coordination had to be measured at the country level. Practical measures needed to be identified for enhancing UN coordination, and the need for a supportive international environment to meet the challenge of eradicating poverty should be taken fully into account and adequate resources mobilized and used effectively and efficiently. The Meetings felt that efforts of the UN system needed to be integrated with those of Governments and NGOs at the community and national levels, and that the resident coordinator had a key role to play at the field level in the integrated follow-up to conferences by organizing thematic working groups and ensuring that task forces and specific programmes were field-driven. Close linkages should be established between multisectoral strategies being pursued by various organizations, and the mechanisms of coordination at the country level should be used to the fullest extent to enhance the effectiveness and impact of anti-poverty programmes.

The Economic and Social Council, by **decision 1995/309** of 27 July, took note of the report of the 1994 Joint Meetings of CPC and ACC.[8]

### Joint Inspection Unit

The Joint Inspection Unit, in its twenty-seventh annual report to the General Assembly, gave an overview of its activities from 1 July 1994 to 30 June 1995.[9] The Secretary-General also transmitted to the Assembly the JIU work programme for 1995 and the preliminary work programme for 1996,[10] the work programme for the 1995-1996 biennium and the indicative list for 1996-1997,[11] and a 27 November report[12] on implementation of JIU recommendations.

In its annual report, JIU examined measures to enhance its functioning; relations and cooperation with its participating organizations, external oversight bodies and other relevant bodies within the UN system; and results, follow-up and implemen-

tation of JIU recommendations. The Unit continued to strengthen its cooperation and coordination with the legislative bodies and the secretariats of the participating organizations. It increased its exchange of views and contacts with the secretariats of participating organizations (especially with internal oversight units) and, as requested by the Assembly,[13] the Chairman and the Executive Secretary held discussions with a number of heads of agencies and programmes on improving working relations with the respective secretariats. JIU relations with ACC and its subsidiary bodies continued to be constructive and pragmatic; ACC was attentive to JIU reports and was making efforts to produce joint comments on time. JIU continued its working relations with other external oversight bodies, especially the Advisory Committee on Administrative and Budgetary Questions (ACABQ), CPC and ICSC, and with the Panel of External Auditors and the UN Board of Auditors. It intended to improve and strengthen its relations with the Office of Internal Oversight Services. JIU, which had developed relations over the years with organizations and institutions outside the UN system, including governmental institutions, regional organizations, NGOs and research institutions, was also taking steps to increase and further develop relations with specialized institutions such as the International Organization of Supreme Audit Institutions.

By **decision 50/469** of 23 December, the General Assembly decided that the Fifth Committee should continue consideration of the JIU report at its 1996 resumed session.

## Other coordination matters

### Follow-up to international conferences

**Economic and Social Council consideration.** The Economic and Social Council held its coordination segment from 28 to 30 June and on 28 July. In accordance with **decision 1995/204** of 10 February, the theme of the segment was: "Coordinated follow-up by the UN system and implementation of the results of major international conferences organized by the United Nations in the economic, social and related fields".

The Secretary-General, in a 9 June report[14] on the subject, gave a brief review of the 1990 World Summit for Children;[15] the UN Conference on Trade and Development (UNCTAD VIII), held in 1992;[16] the 1992 UN Conference on Environment and Development;[17] the 1993 World Conference on Human Rights;[18] the 1994 International Conference on Population and Development;[19] and the 1995 World Summit for Social Development (see PART FOUR, Chapter IX). He identified common themes and cross-cutting issues, examined existing mechanisms for follow-up arising from those conferences and issues of coordination, and recommended elements of a coordinated follow-up approach. The coordinated approach was an attempt to devise links between existing mechanisms at all levels to ensure that approaches were harmonized, duplication and overlap avoided and complementaries fully exploited. Such an approach would require, at the intergovernmental level, arrangements and modalities for bringing greater focus to the work of the functional bodies dealing with conference follow-up, and enhancing linkages among them and avoiding duplication of debates. The report suggested that the Council play a more proactive role in defining issues for their consideration. The Council should also carry out a biennial thematic review of cross-cutting and system-wide coordination issues and identify policy issues for consideration by the General Assembly. The principles for system-wide division of labour developed under a reformed and strengthened ACC, combined with its streamlined subsidiary machinery, provided a strong basis for inter-agency cooperation. At the country level, country teams or groups could be formed around common themes and charged with developing common approaches and actions, under the leadership of the resident coordinator system and taking into account country strategy notes. Suggestions were also made to streamline and rationalize the working methods of the Second and Third Committees of the General Assembly to promote more focused thematic debates leading to more harmonized policy guidance. The report called for renewed efforts to mobilize resources at the national and international levels as an essential component of not only a well-coordinated but a full and effective response to conference results.

The Economic and Social Council, in its agreed conclusions[20] of 28 July, took note of the Secretary-General's report. The Council recognized that coordinated follow-up implied that the major conferences should be viewed as interlinked and contributing to an integrated framework and a global partnership for development. Governments had the primary responsibility for implementing declarations and programmes of action adopted by international conferences, while the UN system had an important role in contributing to, facilitating and reviewing the progress of implementation and in further promoting their goals and objectives.

The General Assembly had the overall responsibility for ensuring the implementation of conference results and facilitating and reviewing progress. The Economic and Social Council should assist in this task by making recommendations on policies for an effective, efficient and coordinated follow-up. The Assembly should address, within the framework of the agenda for development, the integrated consideration of the themes common to major international conferences with a view to promoting better coherence and providing harmonized and integrated policy guidance. To that end, it should improve the coherence of its committees to follow up effectively the integrated approach. The Council, in its coordination segment, should review cross-cutting themes common to major international conferences and/or contribute to an overall review of the implementation of the programme of action of a UN conference. The theme related to the follow-up of conferences, to be considered at the coordination segment, should be chosen at the Council's previous substantive session; the Secretary-General should suggest possible common themes.

The Secretariat should prepare a single consolidated report outlining the activities of the UN system to achieve the goals and objectives related to the chosen theme and identifying coordination and policy issues to be addressed by the Council and the Assembly. The report should analyse progress and problems and make specific recommendations. In its consideration of the theme, the Council could benefit from the participation of funds and programmes, the regional commissions and the relevant specialized agencies, including the Bretton Woods institutions (the International Monetary Fund and the World Bank) and the World Trade Organization (WTO). The operational activities segment of the Council should also consider themes related to follow-up to major international conferences. The Council stressed the need to review further its work programme and working methods with a view to fulfilling better its responsibilities for coordination, guidance and conference follow-up. It should periodically organize meetings on specific issues to allow for more dialogue with chairmen and secretariats of the functional commissions, other subsidiary and related bodies, and relevant executive boards. The activities of the subsidiary bodies might be consolidated and the quality and impact of their output must be assured.

The regional commissions should assist countries in each region in implementing the recommendations of conferences, and the Council and the Assembly should ensure that they carry out that task effectively. The Council should enhance the coordination of the regional commissions, for example in its substantive work relating to conference follow-up. Interaction between the Council and CPC should be improved, and the General Assembly should consider a stronger link between substantive, programming, coordination and budgeting processes.

The functional commissions should develop multi-year programmes of work for the follow-up and review of conference programmes of action, with the cooperation of the Council. Each commission or body should focus on the core issues relating to the conference for which it was responsible and obtain inputs from other relevant bodies on related issues. The mandates, composition and working methods of the functional commissions should be reviewed and adjusted to achieve greater coherence and mutual reinforcement, and to better assist the Council in the coordinated follow-up and review process.

Concerning inter-agency coordination, measures should be taken to further strengthen the role of ACC and its standing committees and to ensure the systematic exchange of information and a rational division of labour between them, as well as between established ACC machinery and ad hoc follow-up mechanisms for individual conferences. The Council said that the example of the Inter-Agency Committee on Sustainable Development (IACSD) (see PART FOUR, Chapter I) could be useful for the follow-up to other conferences but should not be seen as an automatic precedent. ACC was invited to bring system-wide coordination issues to the attention of the Council and to make recommendations. Wider distribution of ACC's report and further information for Member States on ACC work would be desirable. The relevant intergovernmental bodies should be kept fully informed of the establishment and work of any inter-agency task force for the follow-up to conferences.

At the country level, national Governments had the primary responsibility for coordinating, on the basis of national strategies, follow-up activities of conferences. Those follow-up activities relevant to the mandates of UN operational activities for development should, through the resident coordinator system, take into account common themes and goals and should reflect national plans and strategies as well as the country strategy note. The resident coordinator, in consultation with the Government, could use thematic groups composed of the agencies concerned (with a designated lead agency or task manager under his or her overall leadership) to serve as a coordinating mechanism to develop integrated approaches for the realization of common goals, which might include the development of a common data system at the national level to facilitate reviewing and reporting on the progress achieved.

In preparing reports for the Assembly and the Council and subsidiary bodies, the Secretariat could make greater use of task managers, so that a particular agency would be responsible for coordinating the response of the entire United Nations system on a given subject, including recommendations. Reports should be timely and concise, clearly identifying issues and options and their im-

plications. The Secretary-General should present proposals in 1996 to the Council and the Assembly to simplify reporting requirements, taking into account the reports required for the follow-up to UN conferences. Other methods for the promotion of integrated reporting by the Secretariat should be explored. Requests for reports should be limited to the minimum necessary and the Secretary-General should use information and data already provided by Governments to the maximum extent possible to avoid duplication. He should also prepare a standardized and simplified format for Governments to use to present information.

The Council emphasized the need to enhance further the interaction and cooperation between the United Nations, the Bretton Woods institutions and WTO in conference follow-up. It noted that cooperation between the United Nations and the Bretton Woods institutions would be addressed within the framework of discussions on an agenda for development.

Effective conference follow-up also required the urgent mobilization of resources, both human and financial. It was important to enhance the effectiveness of official development assistance (ODA) and to increase it, with the objective of achieving the UN target for ODA of 0.7 per cent of gross national product. The mobilization of substantial new resources from all sources would be instrumental in achieving that goal.

**ACC consideration.** In a February statement[21] on the follow-up to the 1994 International Conference on Population and Development,[19] ACC recognized the need for a common framework for conference follow-up in the economic and social sectors in order to assist countries in the coordinated implementation and monitoring of programmes of action adopted by conferences. The framework should promote a coordinated response by the UN system to interrelated recommendations, while also reducing the burden of reporting with regard to implementation.

In October,[22] the executive heads of specialized agencies agreed that monitoring the follow-up by the UN system to recent global conferences would continue to be a main concern of ACC. To promote an integrated approach, ACC would undertake reviews bringing together related results of recent global conferences and drawing on relevant inter-agency mechanisms supporting ACC in different sectoral and cross-sectoral areas. The selection of themes for such reviews should take into account the need to monitor progress in the implementation of conference results and to provide the Economic and Social Council, particularly the coordination segment, with consolidated information, analyses and assessment of system-wide activities in support of the Council's own thematic reviews. Coordinated support or country-level action should be organized around three interrelated themes: the enabling environment for social and economic development; employment and sustainable livelihoods; and basic social services for all. Those themes were especially relevant to a concerted attack on poverty, which constituted a main over-arching priority objective emanating from recent global conferences. The Inter-Agency Task Force on the International Conference on Population and Development, under the chairmanship of the Executive Director of UNFPA, should be expanded to focus more on social services for all; task forces should be set up to address the other two themes. The World Bank agreed to serve as lead agency for the enabling environment issue, and the International Labour Organization (ILO) for the sustainable livelihoods. The lead agencies would consult with ACC on the definition of the task forces and the contributions that different organizations could make to their work. ACC also identified certain assumptions or methods of work for the task forces. The gender dimension should be taken fully into account in the work of each of the thematic task forces, and consideration given to the best means of promoting coordinated follow-up to the Platform for Action adopted by the Fourth World Conference on Women to ensure that the improvement of the status of women was incorporated in the mainstream of the work of the system. At the regional level, the executive secretaries of the regional commissions, in consultation with the UNDP Administrator, would work with concerned agencies and programmes to develop concerted action programmes in support of conference objectives. At the country level, resident coordinators should take the lead in establishing thematic groups which would draw on, but not necessarily be identical with, the proposed inter-agency task forces, reflecting particular country priorities and needs. The groups would fully involve national and local authorities and NGOs, and work with all concerned agencies and programmes. ACC adopted a note by IACSD on the review of its functioning (see PART FOUR, Chapter I).

The General Assembly, in **resolution 50/161** of 22 December, noted the establishment of task forces for the follow-up to the World Summit for Social Development and other related UN conferences and invited ACC to bring system-wide coordination issues to the attention of the Economic and Social Council, in particular its coordination segment, and to make recommendations thereon.

## Communication for
## UN development programmes

The Secretary-General, in a 29 March note,[23] transmitted a JIU report on communication for development programmes in the UN system. The report concluded that the situation regarding communication activities in the UN system was not satisfactory, nor was the level of inter-agency coordination in keeping up with the evolution of the communication discipline. The mass media had not been sufficiently brought to bear on the extensive activities of the UN system in the field of development, implementation of projects and their impact on the quality of lives of recipients. Moreover, communications for development did not feature as a priority theme for most agencies, with the exception of UNESCO, UNICEF and the Food and Agriculture Organization of the United Nations (FAO). Most agencies attached insufficient importance to communication in operational activities, and it was rarely integrated into the entire cycle of development assistance. In particular, the UNDP mode of project execution did not provide for a communication dimension. Some initiatives had been taken, however, to put more emphasis on communication as a prerequisite for development, including the organization of a round-table conference to discuss how to make communication programmes more effective and how to coordinate the efforts of the different agencies. Consideration should be given to expanding the inter-agency round-table process to include communications for humanitarian assistance and peace-keeping operations.

To improve the status of communication, JIU recommended that communication policy should be integrated within each department of an agency dealing with development and humanitarian assistance, and budgets of all projects and programmes should contain a specific provision for communication activities. Communications units should be autonomous and have direct functional relations with the various organizational offices dealing with field activities. Donor agencies should provide adequate resources to support and expand communications activities, in particular for participatory development initiatives. To improve coordination in communication at the headquarters level by organizations of the UN system (particularly those involved with development), focal points should be established, so that departments would inform each other about the work done on communication in their respective units. There should also be a unit within the policy-making division of agencies that would be responsible for coordinating communication activities and would be the link at the inter-agency level. Coordination at the country level should use fully the team of agency representatives within the resident coordinator system. A communications coordinating committee, including representatives from Governments, bilateral donors and NGOs, could be established to formulate communications policies and follow up on their implementation. The committee would also prepare a joint report on the contribution of communication to the success of the project.

The UN system should work more closely with development-oriented NGOs that had sound communications channels with beneficiaries. The existing informal round-table process should be regularized and should include all UN agencies and the regional economic commissions, and should also take into account the UNESCO communication mandate. To avoid duplication and promote better use of resources, the Intergovernmental Council of the International Programme for the Development of Communication (IPDC) should consider changes in the mandate of IPDC to enable it to respond more effectively to the needs of developing countries in the field of infrastructure-building and mass-media training. The UN system should develop a systematic approach to training communications experts globally, particularly in developing countries. Academic institutions in both developed and developing countries should be encouraged to include curricula for development communication. To reduce costs, the use of existing UN infrastructure and facilities at the ILO Training Centre in Turin, Italy, should be considered by the appropriate ACC subsidiary body. Funds for financing the training programmes should fall within the communications component budget and be allocated at the inception of projects. The ACC programme classification on communication for UNDP use should be redefined to respond to the needs of Member States. In addition to the class entries proposed by UNESCO, FAO and UNFPA should also be consulted to ensure an integrated and harmonized set of categories. With respect to peace-keeping operations, a stand-by unit should be established, within the existing resources of the Department of Peace-keeping Operations and working closely with the Department of Public Information. The unit would be equipped with a group of communication experts to operate in the field from the beginning to the end of the operation to cover the entire spectrum of communication and information requirements. Specialized agencies (particularly UNESCO) and NGOs should also be on call to provide their expertise.

In a 29 March addendum,[24] the Secretary-General transmitted to the Assembly and the Economic and Social Council the comments of ACC on the JIU report.

**GENERAL ASSEMBLY ACTION**

On 20 December, the General Assembly adopted **resolution 50/130**.

**Communication for development programmes in the United Nations system**

*The General Assembly,*

*Having considered* the report of the Joint Inspection Unit entitled "Communication for development programmes in the United Nations system", and the comments of the Administrative Committee on Coordination on that report,

*Noting* the need for the improvement of the development of communication capacities within the United Nations system to ensure effective inter-agency coordination and cooperation,

*Recognizing* the pivotal role of communication in the successful implementation of development programmes within the United Nations system and in the improvement of the interaction among actors in development, namely, the agencies, organizations, funds and programmes of the United Nations system, Governments and non-governmental organizations,

*Recognizing also* that the regional commissions can play a role, where appropriate, in the development of communication capacities for the development of developing countries,

*Recognizing further* the need for transparent and system-wide communication coordination within the United Nations system in order to improve the planning, formulation and execution of development programmes to benefit the international community, in particular the developing countries,

*Aware* of the need to intensify the efforts aimed at further reducing administrative and other related costs in various activities of agencies, organizations, funds and programmes within the United Nations system and improving the effectiveness of programme delivery as regards development programmes of the United Nations system as a development partner in the development of the developing countries,

*Noting* that the Joint Inspection Unit will be preparing a separate study entitled "A review of telecommunications and related information technologies in the United Nations system",

1. *Takes note* of the report of the Joint Inspection Unit entitled "Communication for development programmes in the United Nations system" and of the comments of the Administrative Committee on Coordination on that report, and, in this context, invites the Joint Inspection Unit to take into consideration the requirements of developing countries;

2. *Recognizes* the important role of communication for development programmes in the United Nations system in enhancing the transparency of system-wide coordination within the United Nations system, *inter alia*, for the development of the developing countries;

3. *Invites* the Committee on Information, in accordance with its mandate, and where appropriate, to consider this question at its forthcoming session;

4. *Recognizes* the need further to facilitate inter-agency cooperation and to maximize the impact of the development programmes of the entities concerned;

5. *Also recognizes* the role of effective communication in disseminating the outcome and follow-up of major United Nations conferences and in ensuring the effective flow of such information to various non-governmental organizations, including grass-roots-level organizations;

6. *Encourages* the relevant agencies, organizations, funds and programmes of the United Nations system, including the regional commissions, as appropriate, to use informal mechanisms such as round-table conferences to improve communication for development programmes in the United Nations system;

7. *Emphasizes* the need for the relevant agencies, organizations, funds and programmes of the United Nations system to develop a systematic approach to capacity-building in the development of communication capacities, particularly with respect to the training of field workers and development workers and technicians as well as communication planners and specialists, especially in the developing countries;

8. *Invites* the relevant agencies, organizations, funds and programmes of the United Nations system, as well as Governments and the regional commissions, to consider identifying focal points for the purpose of facilitating dialogue in the exchange of information on communication on issues related to development so as to strengthen coordination and international cooperation in this area;

9. *Invites* all countries, in particular the donor community, to provide resources, as appropriate, to support initiatives on development of capacities for developing countries;

10. *Requests* the Secretary-General, in consultation with the Director-General of the United Nations Educational, Scientific and Cultural Organization, in accordance with that agency's mandate in the field of communication and with resolution 4.1, adopted by the General Conference at its twenty-eighth session, to report to the General Assembly at its fifty-first session on the implementation of the present resolution and on a biennial basis thereafter.

General Assembly resolution 50/130

20 December 1995     Meeting 96     Adopted without vote

Approved by Second Committee (A/50/615/Add.1) without vote, 8 December (meeting 42); draft by Vice-Chairman (A/C.2/50/L.64), orally revised and based on informal consultations on draft by Kyrgyzstan and Philippines, for Group of 77 and China (A/C.2/50/L.14); agenda item 12.

*Meeting numbers.* GA 50th session: 2nd Committee 15, 16, 32, 42; plenary 96.

## Cooperation with organizations

In 1995, the General Assembly adopted resolutions regarding cooperation between the United Nations and the Organization of African Unity, the League of Arab States, the Organization of the Islamic Conference, the Organization for Security and Cooperation in Europe, the Southern African Development Community, the Inter-Parliamentary Union and the Agency for Cultural and Technical Cooperation. It granted observer status to the Central American Integration System.

## Organization for
## Security and Cooperation in Europe

The Secretary-General, as requested by the General Assembly in 1994,[25] submitted a 16 October report[26] on cooperation between the United Nations and the Organization for Security and Cooperation in Europe (OSCE), formerly the Conference on Security and Cooperation in Europe. He noted that good contacts had been established and maintained between the two organizations. Informal tripartite consultations between the Geneva-based UN offices and programmes, OSCE and the Council of Europe continued. The most recent meeting in Budapest, Hungary, in February, gave an important impetus to the dialogue between OSCE and humanitarian organizations. It was agreed that the tripartite process should be strengthened by target-oriented meetings on major humanitarian operations.

The General Assembly, by **resolution 50/87** of 18 December, took note of the Secretary-General's report. It decided to include in the provisional agenda of its fifty-first session an item on cooperation between the United Nations and OSCE and requested the Secretary-General to report to it on the implementation of the resolution. On the same date, the Assembly, on the proposal of Hungary,[27] by **decision 50/423** authorized Switzerland, a non-UN member and as the State holding the chairmanship of OSCE for 1996, to submit communications on behalf of the organization for circulation as UN documents and to participate in discussions in the Assembly that were of direct concern to OSCE during that period.

## League of Arab States

On 3 October, the Secretary-General submitted a report[28] on cooperation between the United Nations and the League of Arab States, as requested by the General Assembly in 1994.[29] He stated that the secretariats of the two organizations continued to maintain close contact on matters of mutual concern. At a meeting between the Executive Secretary of the Economic and Social Commission for Western Asia and the Secretary-General of the League, it was agreed to review the cooperation protocol between the Commission and the League and to hold periodic meetings to review matters of mutual interest. A joint meeting (Vienna, 19-21 July) on cooperation between the secretariats of the United Nations and the League of Arab States and its specialized organizations marked the fiftieth anniversaries of both organizations. The meeting suggested ways to further strengthen and expand collaboration towards the maintenance of peace and security and the promotion of social and economic development. The Secretary-General's report also summarized the action taken by UN bodies and organizations in follow-up to previous joint meetings.

**GENERAL ASSEMBLY ACTION**

On 20 November, the General Assembly adopted **resolution 50/16**.

## Cooperation between the United Nations and the League of Arab States

*The General Assembly,*

*Recalling* its previous resolutions on the promotion of cooperation between the United Nations and the League of Arab States,

*Having considered* the report of the Secretary-General of 3 October 1995 on cooperation between the United Nations and the League of Arab States,

*Recalling also* the decision of the Council of the League of Arab States that it considers the League a regional organization within the meaning of Chapter VIII of the Charter of the United Nations,

*Noting* the desire of both organizations to consolidate, develop and enhance further the ties existing between them in the political, economic, social, humanitarian, cultural and administrative fields,

*Taking into account* the report of the Secretary-General entitled "An Agenda for Peace", in particular section VII, concerning cooperation with regional arrangements and organizations, and the "Supplement to An Agenda for Peace",

*Convinced* that the maintenance and further strengthening of cooperation between the United Nations system and the League of Arab States contribute to the promotion of the purposes and principles of the United Nations,

*Convinced also* of the need for more efficient and coordinated utilization of available economic and financial resources to promote common objectives of the two organizations,

*Recognizing* the need for closer cooperation between the United Nations system and the League of Arab States and its specialized organizations in realizing the goals and objectives of both organizations,

*Welcoming* the results of the general meeting on cooperation between the representatives of the secretariats of the United Nations system and the General Secretariat of the League of Arab States and its specialized organizations, held at Vienna from 19 to 21 July 1995, on the occasion of the fiftieth anniversary of both the United Nations and the League of Arab States,

*Welcoming also* the meeting on peace held at United Nations Headquarters on 1 August 1994 between the Secretary-General and heads of regional organizations,

1. *Takes note with satisfaction* of the report of the Secretary-General;

2. *Commends* the continued efforts of the League of Arab States to promote multilateral cooperation among Arab States, and requests the United Nations system to continue to lend its support;

3. *Takes note* of the conclusions and recommendations adopted at the general meeting on cooperation between the representatives of the secretariats of the United Nations system and the General Secretariat of the League of Arab States and its specialized organizations, held at Vienna, contained in the final document which has been transmitted by the United Nations Secretariat to all participating United Nations organizations and the General Secretariat of the League of Arab States;

4. *Expresses its appreciation* to the Secretary-General for the follow-up action taken by him to implement the proposals adopted at the meetings between the representatives of the secretariats of the United Nations and other organizations of the United Nations system and the General Secretariat of the League of Arab States and its specialized organizations, including most recently the meeting held at Vienna in 1995;

5. *Requests* the Secretariat of the United Nations and the General Secretariat of the League of Arab States, within their respective fields of competence, to intensify further their cooperation towards the realization of the purposes and principles of the Charter of the United Nations, the strengthening of international peace and security, economic development, disarmament, decolonization, self-determination and the eradication of all forms of racism and racial discrimination;

6. *Expresses its appreciation* to the Secretary-General for his initiative in meeting with heads of regional organizations on 1 August 1994, and looks forward to seeing such meetings organized again;

7. *Requests* the Secretary-General to continue his efforts to strengthen cooperation and coordination between the United Nations and other organizations and agencies of the United Nations system and the League of Arab States and its specialized organizations in order to enhance their capacity to serve the mutual interests of the two organizations in the political, economic, social, humanitarian, cultural and administrative fields;

8. *Calls upon* the specialized agencies and other organizations and programmes of the United Nations system:

(*a*) To continue to cooperate with the Secretary-General and among themselves, as well as with the League of Arab States and its specialized organizations, in the follow-up of multilateral proposals aimed at strengthening and expanding cooperation in all fields between the United Nations system and the League of Arab States and its specialized organizations;

(*b*) To maintain and increase contacts and improve the mechanism of consultation with the counterpart programmes, organizations and agencies concerned regarding projects and programmes, in order to facilitate their implementation;

(*c*) To associate whenever possible with organizations and institutions of the League of Arab States in the execution and implementation of development projects in the Arab region;

(*d*) To inform the Secretary-General, not later than 15 May 1996, of the progress of their cooperation with the League of Arab States and its specialized organizations, in particular the follow-up action taken on the multilateral and bilateral proposals adopted at the previous meetings between the two organizations;

9. *Also calls upon* the specialized agencies and other organizations and programmes of the United Nations system to intensify cooperation with the League of Arab States and its specialized organizations in the following priority sectors, namely, energy, rural development, desertification and green belts, training and vocational training, technology, environment, and information and documentation;

10. *Requests* the Secretary-General of the United Nations, in cooperation with the Secretary-General of the League of Arab States, to encourage periodic consultation between representatives of the Secretariat of the United Nations and the General Secretariat of the League of Arab States to review and strengthen coordination mechanisms with a view to accelerating

implementation and follow-up action of multilateral projects, proposals and recommendations adopted at the meetings between the two organizations;

11. *Decides* that, in order to enhance cooperation and for the purpose of review and appraisal of progress, a general meeting between the United Nations system and the League of Arab States should take place once every two years, and inter-agency sectoral meetings should be organized regularly on areas of priority and wide importance in the development of the Arab States, on the basis of agreement between the counterpart programmes of the United Nations system and the League of Arab States and its specialized organizations;

12. *Also requests* the Secretary-General to submit to the General Assembly at its fifty-first session a progress report on the implementation of the present resolution;

13. *Also decides* to include in the provisional agenda of its fifty-first session the item entitled "Cooperation between the United Nations and the League of Arab States".

General Assembly resolution 50/16

20 November 1995     Meeting 67     Adopted without vote

18-nation draft (A/50/L.21); agenda item 31.

## Organization of the Islamic Conference

Responding to a 1994 General Assembly request,[30] the Secretary-General submitted a 17 October report[31] on cooperation between the United Nations and the Organization of the Islamic Conference (OIC). He reported that regular consultations were held and information exchanged between the UN Secretariat and the General Secretariat of OIC, as well as with the Office of the Permanent Observer of OIC to the United Nations. A coordination meeting of focal points of lead agencies of the UN system and OIC (Geneva, 19-21 June) reviewed progress achieved and proposals for strengthening cooperation in the development of science and technology, trade and development, technical cooperation, assistance to refugees, food security and agriculture, education and the eradication of illiteracy, investment mechanisms and joint ventures, human resources development and the environment. The meeting recommended measures to further strengthen cooperation, such as that joint activities and projects should be partially financed by the focal points or agencies concerned, and that guidelines for funding jointly agreed projects should be developed at the next general meeting to operationalize project funding mechanisms.

The Secretary-General's report also summarized action taken by UN organizations and agencies serving as focal points for cooperation with OIC to follow up the recommendations of previous joint meetings.

**GENERAL ASSEMBLY ACTION**

On 20 November, the General Assembly adopted **resolution 50/17**.

## Cooperation between the United Nations and the Organization of the Islamic Conference

*The General Assembly,*

*Recalling* its resolutions 37/4 of 22 October 1982, 38/4 of 28 October 1983, 39/7 of 8 November 1984, 40/4 of 25 October 1985, 41/3 of 16 October 1986, 42/4 of 15 October 1987, 43/2 of 17 October 1988, 44/8 of 18 October 1989, 45/9 of 25 October 1990, 46/13 of 28 October 1991, 47/18 of 23 November 1992, 48/24 of 24 November 1993 and 49/15 of 15 November 1994,

*Having considered* the report of the Secretary-General of 17 October 1995 on cooperation between the United Nations and the Organization of the Islamic Conference,

*Taking into account* the desire of both organizations to cooperate more closely in the political, economic, social, humanitarian, cultural and technical fields and in their common search for solutions to global problems, such as questions relating to international peace and security, disarmament, self-determination, decolonization, fundamental human rights and economic and technical development,

*Recalling also* the Articles of the Charter of the United Nations that encourage the activities through regional cooperation for the promotion of the purposes and principles of the United Nations,

*Noting* the strengthening of cooperation between the specialized agencies and other organizations of the United Nations system and the Organization of the Islamic Conference and its specialized institutions,

*Noting also* the encouraging progress made in the nine priority areas of cooperation, as well as in the identification of other areas of cooperation,

*Convinced* that the strengthening of cooperation between the United Nations and other organizations of the United Nations system and the Organization of the Islamic Conference contributes to the promotion of the purposes and principles of the United Nations,

*Taking into account* the report of the Secretary-General entitled "An Agenda for Peace", in particular section VII, concerning cooperation with regional arrangements and organizations, and the "Supplement to An Agenda for Peace",

*Noting with appreciation* the determination of both organizations to strengthen further the existing cooperation by developing specific proposals in the designated priority areas of cooperation, as well as in the political field,

*Welcoming* the results of the coordination meeting of focal points of the organizations and agencies of the United Nations system and the Organization of the Islamic Conference and its specialized institutions, held at Geneva from 19 to 21 June 1995,

*Welcoming also* the meeting held at United Nations Headquarters on 1 August 1994 between the Secretary-General and heads of the regional and other organizations, including the Secretary-General of the Organization of the Islamic Conference,

1. *Takes note with satisfaction* of the report of the Secretary-General;

2. *Takes note* of the conclusions and recommendations adopted by the coordination meeting of focal points of the organizations and agencies of the United Nations system and the Organization of the Islamic Conference and its specialized institutions;

3.  *Notes with satisfaction* the active participation of the Organization of the Islamic Conference in the work of the United Nations towards the realization of the purposes and principles of the Charter of the United Nations;

4.  *Requests* the United Nations and the Organization of the Islamic Conference to continue cooperation in their common search for solutions to global problems, such as questions relating to international peace and security, disarmament, self-determination, decolonization, fundamental human rights, social and economic development and technical cooperation;

5.  *Welcomes* the proposals of the coordination meeting of focal points of the United Nations and the Organization of the Islamic Conference to strengthen cooperation between the two organizations in a number of different areas and to review the ways and means for enhancing the actual mechanisms of such cooperation;

6.  *Welcomes also* the efforts of the secretariats of the two organizations to strengthen cooperation between them in the political field and to undertake consultations with a view to defining the mechanisms of such cooperation;

7.  *Welcomes further* the periodic high-level meetings between the Secretary-General of the United Nations and the Secretary-General of the Organization of the Islamic Conference, as well as between senior secretariat officials of the two organizations;

8.  *Encourages* the specialized agencies and other organizations of the United Nations system to continue to expand their cooperation with the Organization of the Islamic Conference, particularly by negotiating cooperation agreements, and invites them to multiply the contacts and meetings of the focal points for cooperation in priority areas of interest to the United Nations and the Organization of the Islamic Conference;

9.  *Urges* the organizations of the United Nations system, especially the lead agencies, to provide increased technical and other forms of assistance to the Organization of the Islamic Conference and its specialized institutions in order to enhance cooperation;

10.  *Expresses its appreciation* to the Secretary-General for his continued efforts to strengthen cooperation and coordination between the United Nations and other organizations of the United Nations system and the Organization of the Islamic Conference and its specialized institutions to serve the mutual interests of the two organizations in the political, economic, social and cultural fields;

11.  *Also expresses its appreciation* to the Secretary-General for his initiative to convene a meeting of heads of regional organizations on 1 August 1994, and looks forward to similar meetings in the future;

12.  *Recommends* that, in order to enhance cooperation and for the purpose of review and appraisal of progress, a general meeting between representatives of the secretariats of the United Nations system and the Organization of the Islamic Conference and its specialized institutions should take place in 1996, and every two years thereafter;

13.  *Also recommends* that coordination meetings of focal points of the organizations and agencies of the United Nations system and the Organization of the Islamic Conference and its specialized institutions should henceforth be held concurrently with the general meeting;

14.  *Expresses its appreciation* for the efforts of the Secretary-General in the promotion of cooperation between the United Nations and the Organization of the Islamic Conference, and expresses the hope that he will continue to strengthen the mechanisms of coordination between the two organizations;

15.  *Requests* the Secretary-General to report to the General Assembly at its fifty-first session on the state of cooperation between the United Nations and the Organization of the Islamic Conference;

16.  *Decides* to include in the provisional agenda of its fifty-first session the item entitled "Cooperation between the United Nations and the Organization of the Islamic Conference".

General Assembly resolution 50/17

20 November 1995     Meeting 67     Adopted without vote

Draft by Morocco (A/50/L.22); agenda item 32.

## Organization of African Unity

The Secretary-General, as requested by the General Assembly in 1994,[32] submitted a 17 October report[33] on cooperation between the United Nations and the Organization of African Unity (OAU). He discussed consultations and exchange of information and reported on action by UN bodies, agencies and programmes in the economic and social fields. He also reported on the results of the tenth annual meeting on cooperation between the two organizations (Addis Ababa, Ethiopia, 6-10 November), which adopted conclusions and recommendations in the areas of peace and security and economic and social questions (see PART TWO, Chapter II).

The General Assembly, in **resolution 50/158** of 21 December, took note of the Secretary-General's report and requested him to report on the development of cooperation between OAU and the United Nations.

## Southern African Development Community

The Secretary-General, as requested by the General Assembly in 1993,[34] submitted a 23 October report[35] on cooperation between the United Nations and the Southern African Development Community (SADC), which described action taken by Member States and by the UN system.

In **resolution 50/118** of 20 December, the Assembly requested the Secretary-General, in consultation with the Executive Secretary of SADC, to continue to intensify contacts aimed at promoting and harmonizing cooperation between the two organizations.

## Inter-Parliamentary Union

In a 25 April letter[36] addressed to the Secretary-General, Senegal, later joined by 21 other States,[37] requested that the General Assembly include in the provisional agenda of its fiftieth session an item entitled "Cooperation between the United Nations and the Inter-Parliamentary Union".

In an explanatory memorandum, Senegal said that the Inter-Parliamentary Union was an international organization of national parliaments, with 135 countries as members. It shared the ideals and objectives of the United Nations and was concerned with all the issues of international interest dealt with by the United Nations. It was important to strengthen cooperation between the two organizations, since their activities were mutually complementary and reinforcing. The United Nations should conclude an agreement with the Union defining the context for cooperation to enable the Union to contribute to the work of the main political organs of the United Nations and its international conferences.

Senegal also submitted[38] on 12 October a declaration entitled "The Parliamentary Vision for International Cooperation into the 21st Century", adopted at a special session of the Council of the Union (New York, 30 August–1 September) to commemorate the fiftieth anniversary of the United Nations.

GENERAL ASSEMBLY ACTION

On 15 November, the General Assembly adopted **resolution 50/15**.

### Cooperation between the United Nations and the Inter-Parliamentary Union

*The General Assembly*,

*Noting* that national parliaments work together at the international level through the Inter-Parliamentary Union, their world organization, which shares the principles and objectives of the United Nations,

*Considering* that the activities of the Inter-Parliamentary Union complement and support the work of the United Nations,

*Desirous* of strengthening existing cooperation between the United Nations and the Inter-Parliamentary Union and of giving it a new and adequate framework,

1.  *Requests* the Secretary-General to take the necessary steps to conclude an agreement on cooperation between the two organizations which should make provision for consultations, appropriate representation and cooperation, in general as well as in specific fields, and to report to the General Assembly at its fifty-first session on this matter;

2.  *Decides* to include in the provisional agenda of its fifty-first session the item entitled "Cooperation between the United Nations and the Inter-Parliamentary Union".

General Assembly resolution 50/15

15 November 1995      Meeting 61      Adopted without vote

62-nation draft (A/50/L.20 & Add;1); agenda item 150.
*Meeting numbers.* GA 50th session: plenary 60, 61.

## Agency for Cultural and Technical Cooperation

By a letter[39] dated 20 July addressed to the Secretary-General, 24 countries requested the inclusion in the agenda of the fiftieth session of the General Assembly of an item entitled "Cooperation between the United Nations and the Agency for Cultural and Technical Cooperation".

An explanatory memorandum said that the Agency for Cultural and Technical Cooperation (ACTC), which had been granted observer status with the Assembly,[40] united 44 countries and Governments of Africa, America and Asia that used the French language and was the sole intergovernmental organization representing the French-speaking world. Its members cooperated in the areas of law in the service of development and democracy; education and training; culture and communication; and technical cooperation and economic development. ACTC had concluded cooperative agreements with a number of UN agencies and, through its political organs, including the Francophone Conference of Heads of State and Government, promoted and supported the participation of its members in meetings and conferences organized under UN auspices. In October 1993, the heads of State and Government that use French as a common language, meeting in Grande-Baie, Mauritius, affirmed their commitment to finding solutions to the major political and economic problems of the world within the framework of a new partnership with the United Nations. Towards that end, ACTC had opened offices at the UN Office at Geneva and in New York. The United Nations and ACTC were carrying out complementary activities in areas of common interest, which needed to be strengthened and better coordinated. Close working relations between the two organizations were advisable.

GENERAL ASSEMBLY ACTION

On 16 October, the General Assembly adopted **resolution 50/3**.

### Cooperation between the United Nations and the Agency for Cultural and Technical Cooperation

*The General Assembly*,

*Recalling* its resolution 33/18 of 10 November 1978, by which it granted observer status to the Agency for Cultural and Technical Cooperation,

*Recalling also* that one of the purposes of the United Nations is to achieve international cooperation in solving international problems, in particular those of an economic, social and cultural character,

*Further recalling* that the Charter of the United Nations provides for the existence of regional arrangements or agencies whose objectives and activities are consistent with the purposes and principles of the United Nations,

*Noting with appreciation* the desire expressed by the heads of State and Government of the countries that use French as a common language at their Fifth Summit, held at Grand-Baie, Mauritius, from 16 to 18 October 1993, to contribute actively to the solution of the major political and economic problems of today's world and to begin a new partnership with all the institutions that make up the United Nations family,

*Considering* that the Agency for Cultural and Technical Cooperation brings together a considerable number of States Members of the United Nations that use French as a common language, among which it promotes multilateral cooperation in areas of interest to the United Nations,

*Convinced* of the need to coordinate the use of available resources to serve the common objectives of the two organizations,

*Affirming* the need to establish cooperation, or strengthen such cooperation where it already exists, between the two organizations in areas of common interest,

1. *Notes with satisfaction* the support expressed by the heads of State and Government of countries that use French as a common language for United Nations activities and their desire to begin a new partnership with the institutions of the United Nations system;

2. *Welcomes* the involvement of the countries that use French as a common language, through the Agency for Cultural and Technical Cooperation, in United Nations activities, in particular the preparation for, conduct of and follow-up to world conferences organized under United Nations auspices;

3. *Notes* the complementarity of the activities of the Agency for Cultural and Technical Cooperation and the United Nations, as well as the programmes and other institutions of the United Nations system;

4. *Invites* the Secretary-General of the United Nations to take the necessary steps, in consultation with the Secretary-General of the Agency for Cultural and Technical Cooperation, to promote cooperation between the two secretariats, particularly by encouraging meetings that enable their representatives to consult one another on projects, measures and procedures that will facilitate and expand cooperation and coordination between the two organizations;

5. *Urgently requests* the specialized agencies and other bodies and programmes of the United Nations to cooperate to this end with the Secretary-General of the United Nations and the Secretary-General of the Agency for Cultural and Technical Cooperation;

6. *Requests* the Secretary-General to submit a report on the implementation of the present resolution to the General Assembly at its fifty-second session;

7. *Decides* to include in the provisional agenda of its fifty-second session the item entitled ''Cooperation between the United Nations and the Agency for Cultural and Technical Cooperation''.

General Assembly resolution 50/3

16 October 1995     Meeting 31     Adopted without vote

41-nation draft (A/50/L.4 & Add.1); agenda item 157.

## Central American Integration System

On 18 July, Costa Rica, El Salvador, Guatemala, Honduras, Mexico, Nicaragua and Panama requested[41] the inclusion in the agenda of the fiftieth session of the General Assembly of an item entitled ''Observer status for the Central American Integration System in the General Assembly''. The Central American Integration System (SICA), established by the Tegucigalpa Protocol to the Charter of the Organization of Central American States of 13 December 1991, began operations on

1 February 1993. SICA comprised four subsystems: economic, social, cultural and political. Environmental conservation and the building of a new ecological order in the region were other major concerns. The relationship between the United Nations and SICA was one of complementarity based on the principles and norms of the UN Charter. Its participation as an observer in the Assembly would help it to reaffirm and consolidate Central American self-determination in external affairs, through a common strategy that would help strengthen the participation of the region in the international field.

GENERAL ASSEMBLY ACTION

On 12 October, the General Assembly adopted **resolution 50/2**.

**Observer status for the Central American Integration System in the General Assembly**

*The General Assembly,*

*Considering* that the Tegucigalpa Protocol, registered with the Secretariat of the United Nations, modifies the institutional structure in Central America formerly known as the Organization of Central American States, and the purposes and principles thereof, and has instituted the Central American Integration System,

*Noting* that respect for the purposes and principles embodied in the Charter of the United Nations is one of the basic principles of the Central American Integration System,

1. *Decides* to invite the Central American Integration System to participate in the sessions and the work of the General Assembly in the capacity of observer;

2. *Requests* the Secretary-General to take the necessary action to implement the present resolution.

General Assembly resolution 50/2

12 October 1995     Meeting 30     Adopted without vote

51-nation draft (A/50/L.2 & Add.1); agenda item 155.

## World Trade Organization

In a 30 October letter[42] addressed to the the Economic and Social Council President, the Secretary-General drew attention to an exchange of letters with the Director-General of the World Trade Organization (WTO), setting out a framework for cooperation between the United Nations and WTO. The heads of the two organizations agreed that the arrangements and practices set out in a 1976 General Assembly document, which was annexed to the Secretary-General's letter, on relations between the United Nations and the General Agreement on Tariffs and Trade (GATT), provided a suitable basis to continue to guide relations between the United Nations and WTO. Arrangements between WTO and UNCTAD would be pursued by the two secretariats within that framework and in the light of relevant decisions of the Trade and Development Board of UNCTAD, as well as a 1994 Assembly resolution.[43] In addition, they recommended that the current arrangements governing the status of the International Trade Centre (ITC) as a joint body be confirmed and renewed with WTO, subject to revised budgetary arrangements as called for by the General Council of WTO.

By **decision 1995/322** of 12 December, the Economic and Social Council took note of the Secretary-General's letter and the recommendations that current arrangements governing the status of ITC as a joint body should be confirmed and renewed with WTO, and also noted that the name of the Centre would accordingly become the International Trade Centre UNCTAD/WTO (see PART FOUR, Chapter IV).

## Non-governmental organizations

### Review of consultation arrangements

On 10 February, by **decision 1995/218**, the Economic and Social Council postponed the second session of the Open-ended Working Group on the Review of Arrangements for Consultation with Non-Governmental Organizations, which was due to be held from 21 to 24 February, to the months of May/June, on the understanding that the Bureau of the Council would consult with the Chairman of the Committee on Non-Governmental Organizations to find appropriate dates.

On 4 May, the Council decided (**decision 1995/220**) that the second session of the Working Group would take place from 8 to 12 May.

The second session of the Working Group (New York, 8-12 and 26-31 May) continued its review of arrangements for consultation with NGOs. It had before it statements submitted by the International Service for Human Rights,[44] the Conference of Non-Governmental Organizations,[45] the World Federation of United Nations Associations,[46] the International Chamber of Commerce,[47] the International Confederation of Free Trade Unions,[48] the American Association of Retired Persons,[49] the International Federation of Settlements and Neighbourhood Centres,[50] and Rotary International.[51]

The Working Group decided to annex to its report[52] proposals submitted during its discussion of the review of arrangements for consultation with NGOs. It also recommended a draft decision to the Economic and Social Council.

A further addendum[53] provided a statement by the Secretary-General setting out the financial implications of the draft decision.

ECONOMIC AND SOCIAL COUNCIL ACTION

On 26 July, the Economic and Social Council adopted **decision 1995/304**.

**General review of arrangements for consultation with non-governmental organizations**

At its 54th plenary meeting, on 26 July 1995, the Economic and Social Council, having taken note of the report of the Open-ended Working Group on the Review of Arrangements for Consultation with Non-Governmental Organizations on its second session, decided:

*(a)* To extend the mandate of the Working Group for a period of one year, with a meeting time of not less than two weeks, and requested the Working Group to submit its final report to the Council at its substantive session of 1996;

*(b)* To increase, on the basis of equitable geographical representation, the current membership of the Committee on Non-Governmental Organizations and to implement this decision after the completion of the current review;

*(c)* That, starting in 1996, the Committee should meet annually and, should this be necessary for the prompt discharge of its duties, on an ad hoc basis;

*(d)* To request the Committee to undertake a thorough review of its methods of work with a view to improving and streamlining its procedures;

*(e)* To prolong the consultative status, on the Roster, of those non-governmental organizations so accredited by the Economic and Social Council in its decision 1993/329 of 30 July 1993, subject to a final resolution of the issue by the Council at its substantive session of 1996, following the outcome of the review of arrangements for consultation with non-governmental organizations currently under way.

Economic and Social Council decision 1995/304

Adopted without vote

Draft by Open-ended Working Group (E/1995/83); agenda item 10.

### Committee on NGOs

On 3 February, the Chairman of the Committee on Non-Governmental Organizations requested[54] the President of the Economic and Social Council to reschedule the 1995 session of the Committee from 20 to 31 March to the second quarter of 1995 to avoid conflict with the thirty-ninth session of the Commission on the Status on Women, which was scheduled from 15 March to 4 April.

On 10 February, by **decision 1995/218**, the Council agreed to the request, on the understanding that the Bureau of the Council would consult with the Chairman of the Committee to find appropriate dates.

In accordance with the 4 May decision of the Council (**decision 1995/220**), the Committee on NGOs met from 12 to 23 June. It considered applications for consultative status and requests for reclassification from NGOs and reviewed the quadrennial reports[55] submitted by 183 NGOs in consultative status with the Council on their activities during 1988-1991 and 1990-1993. It also reviewed future activities, as contained in the report of the Open-ended Working Group on the Review of Arrangements for Consultation with

NGOs,[52] and approved the provisional agenda for its 1997 session. The Committee recommended three draft decisions for adoption by the Council.

The Committee recommended that 86 NGOs be granted categories I and II consultative status and that five NGOs be listed under the Roster, and that nine NGOs be reclassified from category II to category I and five NGOs from the Roster to category II.

Before the Council took action on the report as a whole, the United States submitted a draft decision[56] by which it requested that the Council grant category II consultative status to Freedom House. Cuba said that the draft decision would alter the substance of the report of the Committee and asked the Council to decide whether the report of the Committee should be amended. The President of the Council noted that the Committee had not recommended Freedom House for accreditation and said that the Council had to decide whether it intended to depart from established procedures and consider the draft decision on its merits.

The Council, on 27 July, by a roll-call vote of 29 to 12, with 11 abstentions, decided (**decision 1995/308**) to depart from its established practice and procedure and to consider an amendment to the proposals of the Committee on NGOs contained in its report. On the same date, by a roll-call vote of 31 to 11, with 10 abstentions, the Council decided to grant Freedom House category II consultative status (see below).

**ECONOMIC AND SOCIAL COUNCIL ACTION**

On 26 and 27 July, the Economic and Social Council adopted **decision 1995/305**.

### Applications for consultative status and requests for reclassification received from non-governmental organizations

At its 54th and 56th plenary meetings, on 26 and 27 July 1995, the Economic and Social Council decided:

(*a*)  To take note of the report of the Committee on Non-Governmental Organizations;

(*b*)  To grant the following non-governmental organizations consultative status:

#### Category I

African American Institute
Association for Progressive Communications
Colombian Confederation of Non-Governmental Organizations
Development Information Network (DEVNET)
Franciscans International
Global 2000
HelpAge International
InterAction, American Council for Voluntary International Action
International Association of Soldiers for Peace
International Informatization Academy

International Institute for Applied Systems Analysis (IIASA)
Latin American Confederation of Credit Unions (COLAC)
National Council of Negro Women
Transnational Radical Party
World Economic Forum
World Fellowship of Buddhists
WorldWide Fund for Nature International
WORLDWIDE Network—Women in Development and Environment

#### Category II

Aboriginal and Torres Strait Islander Commission
African Health and Human Rights Promoters Commission
African Society of International and Comparative Law
All-China Women's Federation
Asian Women Human Rights Council
Association for the Advancement of Psychological Understanding of Human Nature
Association of Arab-American University Graduates
Association of Medical Doctors of Asia (AMDA)
Association of South-East Asian Nations Confederation of Women's Organizations
Association of Third World Studies
Bochasanwasi Shri Akshar Purushottam Sanstha
Brothers of Charity
Center for International Health and Cooperation
Consortium for International Earth Science Information Network
Cousteau Society
Development Alternatives with Women for a New Era (DAWN)
Dominican Union of Journalists for Peace
Economists Allied for Arms Reduction
European-Asian-Latin American Institute for Co-operation
European Forum for Victim Services
European Women's Lobby
Federal Union of European Nationalities
Freedom House
Global Fund for Women
Goodwill Industries, International, Inc.
Group for Study and Research into Democracy and Economic and Social Development in Africa
Gulf Automobile Federation
Habitat for Humanity International
Himalayan Research and Cultural Foundation
Indian Council of Education
Information Habitat: Where Information Lives (formerly International Synergy Institute)
INTERMON
International Association of Jewish Lawyers and Jurists
International Association of Lawyers against Nuclear Arms
International Centre for Human Rights and Democratic Development
International Forum for Child Welfare
International Hotel Association
International Islamic Relief Organization
International Multiracial Shared Cultural Organization
International Prison Watch
International Women's Health Coalition
Keystone Center

Latin American Committee for the Defense of Women's Rights (CLADEM)
MADRE, Inc.
Marine Environmental Research Institute (MERI)
Mercy International
National Bar Association
National Safety Council
Netherlands Organization for International Development Cooperation
New Human Rights
North-South XXI
PanAmerican-PanAfrican Association, Inc.
Perhaps . . . Kids Meeting Kids Can Make a Difference
Permanent Assembly for Human Rights
Physicians for Human Rights
Queen Alia Fund for Social Development
Regional Network of Local Authorities for the Management of Human Settlements
Resources for the Future, Inc.
Simon Wiesenthal Center
SOS Drugs International
Temple of Understanding
United Towns Agency for North-South Cooperation
Water Environment Federation
Wittenberg Center for Alternative Resources, Inc.
"Women-Action" Research and Training Group
Women's World Summit Foundation
World Information Transfer

*Roster*

European Federation of Road Traffic Crash Victims
European Road Safety Equipment Federation (EUROADSAFE)
International Council of AIDS Service Organizations
International Police Association
Landscape Institute

(*c*) To reclassify nine organizations from category II to category I and five organizations from the Roster to category II, as follows:

*Category I*

American Association of Retired Persons
International Abolitionist Federation
International Association for Religious Freedom
International Federation on Ageing
Liberal International
Organization for Industrial, Spiritual and Cultural Advancement—International (OISCA)
Organization of Islamic Capitals and Cities
Socialist International
World Conference on Religion and Peace

*Category II*

Institute for Women, Law and Development
International Federation of Action of Christians for the Abolition of Torture (ACATA)
International Real Estate Federation
Program for Appropriate Technology in Health (PATH)
SOS-Kinderdorf International

(*d*) To refer the application of the International Committee of Peace and Human Rights back to the Committee on Non-Governmental Organizations for further consideration.

Economic and Social Council decision 1995/305

Adopted without vote

Draft by Committee on NGOs (E/1995/108), as amended; agenda item 10.

The Council, by **decision 1995/307** of 27 July, authorized the Committee on NGOs to hold a resumed session for a period of one week in January 1996 to complete the work of its 1995 session.

By **decision 1995/306** of the same date, the Council approved the provisional agenda and documentation for the 1997 session of the Committee on NGOs.

### Requests from NGOs for hearings

The Committee on NGOs met in New York on 23 June[57] to hear requests from NGOs in categories I and II consultative status to address the Council in connection with items on the Council's agenda. The Committee recommended that 22 NGOs be heard.

### Requests from NGOs not in consultative status

At its meetings on 18[58] and 31 October[59] the Committee on NGOs recommended 80 NGOs of indigenous people not in consultative status with the Economic and Social Council to participate in the working group of the Commission on Human Rights to elaborate a draft declaration on the human rights of indigenous people.

On 25 October and 2 November, the Council approved the requests to participate by those NGOs in **decisions 1995/317 A and B**.

*REFERENCES*

[1]E/1996/18 & Add.1. [2]A/50/202-E/1995/76 & Add.1-3. [3]E/1995/64. [4]E/1995/21. [5]A/50/16. [6]E/1996/4 & Corr.1. [7]E/1995/120. [8]YUN 1994, p. 1274. [9]A/50/34. [10]A/50/140. [11]A/50/140/Add.1. [12]A/50/784. [13]YUN 1993, p. 1190, GA res. 48/221, 23 Dec. 1993. [14]E/1995/86. [15]GA res. 45/217, 21 Dec. 1990. [16]YUN 1992, p. 611. [17]Ibid., p. 670. [18]YUN 1993, p. 908. [19]YUN 1994, p. 955. [20]A/50/3/Rev.1 (1995/1). [21]ACC/1995/4. [22]ACC/1995/23. [23]A/50/126-E/1995/20. [24]A/50/126/Add.1-E/1995/20/Add.1. [25]YUN 1994, p. 611, GA res. 49/13, 15 Nov. 1994. [26]A/50/564. [27]A/50/652. [28]A/50/496. [29]YUN 1994, p. 251, GA res. 49/14, 15 Nov. 1994. [30]Ibid., p. 254, GA res. 49/15, 15 Nov. 1994. [31]A/50/573. [32]YUN 1994, p. 386, GA res. 49/64, 15 Dec. 1994. [33]A/50/575 & Add.1. [34]YUN 1993, p. 607, GA res. 48/173, 21 Dec. 1993. [35]A/50/664. [36]A/50/141 & Corr.1,2. [37]A/50/141/Add.1-3. [38]A/50/561. [39]A/50/148 & Add.1. [40]YUN 1978, p. 403, GA res. 33/18, 10 Nov. 1978. [41]A/50/146 & Add.1. [42]E/1995/125. [43]YUN 1994, p. 875, GA res. 49/97, 19 Dec. 1994. [44]E/AC.70/1995/NGO/1. [45]E/AC.70/1995/NGO/2. [46]E/AC.70/1995/NGO/3. [47]E/AC.70/1995/NGO/4. [48]E/AC.70/1995/NGO/5. [49]E/AC.70/1995/NGO/6. [50]E/AC.70/1995/NGO/7. [51]E/AC.70/1995/NGO/8. [52]E/1995/83 & Add.1. [53]E/1995/83/Add.2. [54]E/1995/13. [55]E/C.2/1995/2 & Add.1-10, E/C.2/1995/3 & Add.1. [56]E/1995/L.43. [57]E/1995/106. [58]E/1995/124. [59]E/1995/124/Add.1.

## Conferences and meetings

### Decisions regarding calendars

In 1995, the Committee on Conferences examined requests for additions and changes to the approved calendar of conferences and meetings for

1995[1] and adopted the draft revised calendar of conferences and meetings for 1996. The Committee considered issues related to the improved utilization of conference-servicing resources, including consultations with UN bodies that underutilized the conference services available to them; existing conference resources, facilities and services within the United Nations; improved coordination of conferences within the UN system; and requests for exceptions to the rule that General Assembly subsidiary bodies should not meet during the Assembly's regular session.

Other matters reported on by the Committee in August[2] were the need to control and limit documentation, including provision of written meeting records to subsidiary organs of the Assembly, and a review of the 1996-1997 proposed programme budget for conference services.

The Committee held an organizational session on 23 March and its substantive session on 21, 22 and 24 August.

In March, the Committee on Conferences agreed that proposed changes to the calendar that did not have programme budget implications could be dealt with by the UN Secretariat in consultation with the Bureau of the Committee. The Committee was advised of a number of such changes in 1995.

The Committee on Conferences reviewed the draft calendar of conferences and meetings for the 1996-1997 biennium and a 29 June report of Secretary-General[3] containing a consolidated statement of scheduled conferences for 1996. In June, the Committee considered the draft calendar of conferences and meetings of the Economic and Social Council, in accordance with a 1988 Council decision.[4] The Committee also reviewed the section of the proposed programme budget[5] for 1996-1997 relating to conference servicing.

The Committee recommended that the General Assembly adopt the draft calendar of conferences and meetings as amended and authorize the Committee to make adjustments to the calendar for 1996 that might become necessary as a result of action by the General Assembly at its fiftieth session. The Committee invited bodies not to hold meetings on 20 February and 29 April 1996, in accordance with a 1994 Assembly decision[6] to avoid holding meetings on the two most sacred days observed by Muslims, and requested the Secretariat to make similar arrangements when drafting the revised calendar for 1997. It also requested that the Secretary-General submit to the Assembly at its fiftieth session a consolidated statement relating to the number and cost of special conferences scheduled for 1997.

The Committee recommended the adoption of the 1996-1997 provisional calendar of conferences and meetings of the subsidiary organs of the Economic and Social Council as amended, and, in view of the difficult financial situation of the Organization, that the Council continue to consider the biennialization of meetings of subsidiary bodies. Requests for an annual cycle of meetings should be based on substantive reasons. The Committee noted the possible adverse effect of open-ended, ad hoc meetings on the efficient utilization of conference-servicing resources.

*Intergovernmental meetings*

At the request of the host Governments of several intergovernmental conferences in 1995, the main documents of those meetings were transmitted to the Secretary-General for circulation as documents of the General Assembly, the Security Council or both, as follows:

Twenty-eighth meeting of the Association of South-East Asian Nations (Brunei Darussalam, 29-30 July);[7]

Sixty-first ordinary session of the Organization of African Unity (OAU) Council of Ministers (Addis Ababa, Ethiopia, 23-27 January),[8] thirty-first ordinary session of the Assembly of Heads of State and Government of OAU (Addis Ababa, 26-28 June),[9] Second Meeting of Ministers for Foreign Affairs of the Countries of the Sahelo-Saharan Region (Algiers, Algeria, 23-24 August);[10]

Annual Coordination Meeting of the Ministers for Foreign Affairs of the Organization of the Islamic Conference (OIC) (New York, 2 October),[11] twenty-third Islamic Conference of OIC Foreign Ministers (Conakry, Guinea, 9-12 December);[12]

Fifth session of the Ministerial Council of the Cooperation Council for the Arab States of the Arabian Gulf (Riyadh, Saudi Arabia, 10-11 June);[13]

Fifty-sixth session of the Ministerial Council of the Gulf Cooperation Council (Riyad, 18-19 September),[14] and sixteenth session of its Supreme Council (Muscat, Oman, 4-6 December);[15]

Commonwealth Heads of Government Meeting (Auckland, New Zealand, 10-13 November);[16]

Inaugural Summit of the Association of Caribbean States (Port of Spain, Trinidad and Tobago, 17-18 August);[17]

Ninth Meeting of Heads of State and Government of the Rio Group (Quito, Ecuador, 4-5 September);[18]

Ministerial meeting of the Coordinating Bureau of the Non-Aligned Countries (Bandung, Indonesia, 25-27 April),[19] and Eleventh Conference of Heads of State or Government of the Movement of Non-Aligned Countries (Cartagena, Colombia, 18-20 October);[20]

Twenty-sixth South Pacific Forum (Madang, Papua New Guinea, 3-15 September);[21]

Nineteenth annual meeting of Ministers for Foreign Affairs of the Group of 77 (New York, 29 September);[22]

Fifth Meeting of the Ministerial Council of the Organization for Security and Cooperation in Europe (Budapest, Hungary, 7-8 December);[23]

Twenty-first meeting of the G-7 Summit (Halifax, Canada, 15-17 June).[24]

## Conference and meeting services

As requested by the Assembly in 1993,[25] the Secretary-General on 14 July reported[26] on existing conference facilities within the United Nations. The report provided information on conference facilities at UN offices, including the number and level of permanent conference staff by category. It also examined the nature of the meetings convened, capacity utilization and facilities provided free of charge, as well as system-wide coordination of conference facilities.

In terms of coordination, the Inter-Agency Meeting on Language Arrangements, Documentation and Publications stated that it would establish and update a system-wide calendar of conferences using electronic communications facilities that would supplement the existing conventional systems. Once operational, the new system-wide calendar would be available to Member States. The exchanges of workload in all areas of documentation processing already occurring among duty stations should be undertaken system-wide as a means of promoting optimum use of services and resources. An inter-agency working group was considering methods to improve practices in translation processes, and recommendations had been made on the promotion and advertising of publications produced in the system. Common guidelines and criteria were being developed for the selection of material for dissemination on electronic media, including questions of pricing and copyright. The use of new technologies for the assignment of interpreters to meetings, as well as in translation, desktop publishing, reproduction and distribution was promoted.

The Committee on Conferences requested the Secretariat to provide capacity utilization figures for translation and interpretation at other UN offices and to share translation workload among various duty stations to reduce costs. It encouraged the Secretariat to keep such costs down and to report on its efforts. It requested the Secretariat to report on the costs of underutilizing conference facilities at UN offices, and to provide an analysis of the comparative costs of meetings held in New York, Geneva and Vienna. The Committee decided to consider biennially the means to ensure an improved coordination of conferences within the UN system.

On 1 August, the Secretary-General reported[27] on the improved utilization of conference servicing and provided statistics for 1994 on the planned and actual use of UN conference resources allocated to a sample of bodies, as well as an analysis of the statistics, including the overall and average utilization factors, and a breakdown in terms of percentages of the meeting ratio and planning accuracy factor of the bodies in the sample. The average utilization factor for 1994 was 82 per cent, down 1 per cent from 1993.[28]

The Committee on Conferences requested the Secretariat to expand the core sample in the statistical analysis to include the Economic and Social Council and the Committee on Conferences, and to refine the methodology for calculating the utilization factors. Also, it requested its Chairman to consult with the chairmen of bodies that had consistently utilized less than the applicable benchmark figure of their allocated resources for the past three sessions, with a view to making recommendations for the optimum use of conference-servicing resources, and to invite the chairmen of subsidiary bodies that had utilized less than 80 per cent of their conference resources in 1994 to provide information on measures taken for improvement and a realistic assessment of their needs, with a view to reducing the resources required. The Committee asked the Office of Conference and Support Services (OCSS) to maintain a dialogue with the substantive secretariats of intergovernmental bodies and to provide statistics and information on previous performance, as well as guidelines on ways to enhance utilization of conference-servicing resources, and to report to the General Assembly at its fifty-first session. The Committee also requested the Secretariat to develop a cost-accounting system for OCSS and to report on cost estimates of conferences, including estimates of losses incurred as a result of underuse of conference-servicing resources.

**GENERAL ASSEMBLY ACTION**

On 23 December, the General Assembly adopted **resolution 50/206 A** on the pattern of conferences.

*The General Assembly,*

*Having considered* the report of the Committee on Conferences,

*Recalling* its relevant resolutions, including resolutions 43/222 B of 21 December 1988, 46/190 of 20 December 1991, 47/202 A to D of 22 December 1992, 48/222 A and B of 23 December 1993 and 49/221 A to D of 23 December 1994,

*Noting with concern* the difficulties encountered by some Member States owing to the lack of conference services for meetings of regional and other major groupings of Member States,

1. *Notes with appreciation* the work of the Committee on Conferences;

2. *Approves* the draft calendar of conferences and meetings of the United Nations for the biennium 1996-1997 as submitted and amended by the Committee on Conferences;

3. *Authorizes* the Committee on Conferences to make adjustments in the calendar of conferences and meetings for 1996 that may become necessary as a result of actions and decisions taken by the General Assembly at its fiftieth session;

4. *Notes* that no sessions are scheduled to open or close on 20 February and 29 April 1996, invites United Nations bodies to avoid holding meetings on 20 February and 29 April 1996, and requests the Secretariat to make similar arrangements when drafting the revised calendar of conferences and meetings for 1997;

5. *Invites* the Economic and Social Council to continue to consider, as appropriate, the biennialization of meetings of its subsidiary bodies;

6. *Invites* all bodies to exercise restraint in requesting open-ended ad hoc meetings in view of the possible adverse effect of such meetings on the efficient utilization of conference-servicing resources;

7. *Expresses concern* that the overall utilization factor for conference services fell below the established benchmark figure of 80 per cent in 1994;

8. *Endorses* the initiatives taken by the Chairman of the Committee on Conferences with a view to assisting bodies to achieve the optimum utilization of conference-servicing resources and, to that effect, to assess realistically their need for such resources;

9. *Requests* the Secretariat to take the measures recommended by the Committee on Conferences to enhance utilization of conference-servicing resources and to report thereon to the General Assembly at its fifty-first session through the Committee;

10. *Expresses concern* about the underutilization of conference facilities at duty stations outside Headquarters, and emphasizes the need to make the most effective use possible of such facilities;

11. *Requests* the Chairman of the Committee on Conferences to hold consultations with various bodies and committees to ensure rational allocation and capacity utilization of all United Nations conference facilities at Headquarters, United Nations Offices and other duty stations with a view to addressing the present imbalance in order to enhance the capacity utilization and cost-effectiveness of these facilities and to report to the Committee on the outcome of these consultations at its substantive session of 1996;

12. *Decides* that the headquarters rule shall be adhered to by all bodies, particularly those whose headquarters are underutilized;

13. *Requests* the Secretary-General to provide, within the resources approved for conference services in the biennium 1996-1997, interpretation services for meetings of regional and other major groupings of Member States upon request by those groupings, taking into account the priority due to meetings included in the calendar of conferences and meetings, and to submit a report on the implementation of this decision to the General Assembly at its fifty-first session through the Committee on Conferences.

General Assembly resolution 50/206 A

23 December 1995     Meeting 100     Adopted without vote

Approved by Fifth Committee (A/50/837) without vote, 20 December (meeting 43); draft by Chairman, following informal consultations (A/C.5/50/L.12); agenda item 119.
*Meeting numbers.* GA 50th session: 5th Committee 4-7, 9, 11, 25, 43; plenary 100.

On the same date, the Assembly adopted **resolution 50/206 D**.

*The General Assembly*,

*Stressing* the need to provide Member States and United Nations bodies, upon request, with more comprehensive and accurate information on the costs of meetings and documentation,

*Noting* that the introduction of new technologies enhances the quality, cost-effectiveness and efficiency of conference services,

*Stressing also* the importance of access to, and benefit from, the optical disk system and other new technologies in all official languages by all Member States and the need to overcome the difficulties faced by some Member States in acquiring the technology to access the optical disk system,

1. *Requests* the Secretary-General to develop as soon as possible a comprehensive and accurate cost-accounting system for conference services, to report on the progress of its implementation to the General Assembly through the Committee on Conferences and to report the results of its use to the Assembly through the Advisory Committee on Administrative and Budgetary Questions, in accordance with their respective mandates;

2. *Encourages* the Secretariat to continue its efforts to improve the cost-effectiveness of document production, without prejudice to the international character of the Organization;

3. *Also requests* the Secretary-General to present proposals to the General Assembly at its fifty-first session through the Committee on Conferences on facilitating access by developing countries to the optical disk system in all official languages, taking into account the possible savings from reduced copying and distribution costs;

4. *Further requests* the Secretary-General, in pursuing the foregoing efforts, to ensure that new technologies in the area of conference services are introduced in all official languages as soon as possible in a comprehensive manner without adverse effects on the provision of services, in full consultation with Member States and, as appropriate, in coordination with relevant intergovernmental bodies.

General Assembly resolution 50/206 D

23 December 1995     Meeting 100     Adopted without vote

Approved by Fifth Committee (A/50/837) without vote, 20 December (meeting 43); draft by Chairman, following informal consultations (A/C.5/50/L.12); agenda item 119.
*Meeting numbers.* GA 50th session: 5th Committee 4-7, 9, 11, 25, 43; plenary 100.

### Programme budget for 1996-1997

In August, the Committee on Conferences[2] considered the proposed programme budget for the 1996-1997 biennium for conference services.[5] The Committee felt that the introduction of technology-intensive methods of work in translation services had much to recommend it as a means of ensuring provision to Member States of a high-quality translation service in the most timely and cost-effective manner, and was in favour of more rapid introduction of new technology. Technological innovations should be introduced in consultation with Member States and in coordination with relevant intergovernmental bodies, including the working group on informatics of the Economic and Social Council. The Committee emphasized the need for strict compliance with the resolutions and rules establishing language arrangements for UN bodies and organs. It welcomed actions taken to improve the quality of translation into all official languages, in particular the efforts of the Arabic Translation Service to implement the proposal of Egypt[29] to "arabize" UN documentation, and encouraged the Secretariat to implement phase II of that proposal.

### GENERAL ASSEMBLY ACTION

On 23 December, the General Assembly adopted **resolution 50/206 E**.

*The General Assembly,*

*Recalling* all its previous resolutions on the use of languages in the United Nations, including resolutions 2(I) of 1 February 1946, 2247(XXI) of 20 December 1966, 2292(XXII) of 8 December 1967, 3189(XXVIII), 3190(XXVIII) and 3191(XXVIII) of 18 December 1973, 36/117 B of 10 December 1981, 47/202 D of 22 December 1992, 49/221 B of 23 December 1994 and 50/11 of 2 November 1995,

*Recalling also* its request to the Secretariat, contained in resolution 49/221 C of 23 December 1994, to continue exploring ways and means of providing conference services in a manner that fully responds to the needs of intergovernmental and expert bodies, while ensuring the criteria of quality and timeliness and due respect for the principle of equal treatment of the official languages of the United Nations as laid down in General Assembly resolution 42/207 C of 11 December 1987,

1. *Emphasizes* the need for strict compliance with the resolutions and rules establishing language arrangements for the different bodies and organs of the United Nations;

2. *Stresses* the need to continue to ensure the availability of the necessary resources to guarantee the timely translation of documents into the different official and working languages of the Organization and their simultaneous distribution in those languages;

3. *Appreciates* the fact that, through advanced technology as well as improved management and increased productivity, the Secretariat has largely been enabled to cope with the growth in demand for translation and documentation services;

4. *Notes* the actions taken to improve the quality of translation into all official languages, in particular the efforts of the Arabic Translation Service to implement the proposal contained in annex II to the report of the Committee on Conferences to the General Assembly at its forty-ninth session, requests the Secretary-General to undertake a thorough review of the terminology and technical methods used in translation into Arabic, and urges the Secretariat to speed up its efforts towards the implementation of phase II of that proposal and to report thereon to the Committee on Conferences at its substantive session of 1996.

General Assembly resolution 50/206 E
23 December 1995      Meeting 100      Adopted without vote
Approved by Fifth Committee (A/50/837) without vote, 20 December (meeting 43); draft by Chairman, following informal consultations (A/C.5/50/L.12); agenda item 119.
*Meeting numbers.* GA 50th session: 5th Committee 4-7, 9, 11, 25, 43; plenary 100.

## Unified conference services at Vienna

In 1995, ACABQ considered a 1994 report on a reorganization of conference-servicing staff at the Vienna International Centre into a single conference-servicing operation.[29] In a 17 February report,[30] ACABQ recommended that the General Assembly approve the establishment, within existing resources under budget sections 25E (Conference service, Vienna) and 25I (United Nations Office at Vienna), of a unified conference service at the Vienna International Centre under the management of the United Nations, effective 1 April 1995. Additional requirements that could not be accommodated within existing resources should be reflected in the Secretary-General's final budget performance report for 1994-1995.

ACABQ also recommended that the Secretary-General examine the cause for the high vacancy rate in the Professional category before making any proposal in respect of the staffing table of conference services at Vienna, and that he utilize to the fullest extent the advantages that could accrue from technological innovations, especially in labour-intensive areas of conference servicing. It further recommended that he review, in the context of the proposed 1996-1997 programme budget, the requirements for conference-servicing staff and the organizational chart of the united conference services at the UN Office at Vienna on the basis of the most updated actual workload statistics and the related UN workload standards in conference servicing, taking into account the current and future demands for such services and the capabilities of technological innovations. The proposed staffing structure should be based on the results of classification of posts.

### GENERAL ASSEMBLY ACTION

On 31 March, the General Assembly adopted **section III** of **resolution 49/237**.

#### Unified conference services at Vienna

*[The General Assembly . . .]*

*Recalling* its resolution 44/201 A of 21 December 1989, in which it endorsed the view of the Secretary-General that a single conference-servicing facility at the Vienna International Centre would represent the ideal solution from the standpoint of cost efficiency,

*Recalling also* its resolutions 48/218 A and 48/222 A of 23 December 1993, in which it stressed the need for the establishment of unified conference services at Vienna as soon as possible,

*Having considered* the report of the Secretary-General on revised estimates for conference services at Vienna and the related report of the Advisory Committee on Administrative and Budgetary Questions,

1. *Notes with appreciation* the estimated net savings resulting from the proposed single conference-servicing facility at Vienna for the budgets of the United Nations and the United Nations Industrial Development Organization taken together;

2. *Notes* the estimated net additional costs of 324,100 United States dollars resulting from the proposed single conference-servicing facility at Vienna for the United Nations budget for the biennium 1994-1995;

3. *Concurs* with the observations and recommendations contained in the report of the Advisory Committee on Administrative and Budgetary Questions;

4. *Requests* the Secretary-General to proceed to establish the unified conference-servicing facility at the Vienna International Centre under the management of the United Nations on the basis of the following elements and criteria:

(*a*) The transfer of the conference-servicing posts of the United Nations Industrial Development Organization to the United Nations on the basis of the existing staffing table of the United Nations Industrial Development Organization, effective from 1 April 1995;

(*b*) The establishment of the unified conference-servicing facility under budget sections 25E.C (Conference and library services, Vienna) and 25I (United Nations Office at Vienna), within existing resources, taking into account increased income in respect of reimbursements from the United Nations Industrial Development Organization for services provided by the United Nations;

(*c*) An examination of the cause for the high vacancy rate in the Professional category before making any proposal in respect of the staffing table for conference services at Vienna;

(*d*) A review, in the context of his proposed programme budget for the biennium 1996-1997, of the requirements for conference-servicing staff for and the organigramme of the unified conference services at the United Nations Office at Vienna on the basis of the most updated actual workload statistics and the related United Nations workload standards in conference servicing, taking into account the current and future requirements for conference servicing at Vienna;

5. *Also requests* the Secretary-General, as a matter of urgency, to implement cost-effective technological innovations for the unified conference services at Vienna;

6. *Further requests* the Secretary-General to continue to examine the feasibility of contracting out elements of conference services at Headquarters and all duty stations with a view to achieving further cost efficiency in the programme budget for the biennium 1996-1997 and subsequent budgets;

. . .

General Assembly resolution 49/237, section III

31 March 1995      Meeting 99      Adopted without vote

Approved by Fifth Committee (A/49/822/Add.1) without vote, 24 March (meeting 47); draft by Vice-Chairman (A/C.5/49/L.39), based on informal consultations; agenda item 107.
*Meeting numbers.* GA 49th session: 5th Committee 40, 47; plenary 99.

### Facilities for bilateral meetings

On 23 December, the General Assembly adopted **resolution 50/206 F**.

*The General Assembly,*

*Reaffirming* its resolution 49/221 D of 23 December 1994,

*Noting with satisfaction* the significant improvements in the meeting arrangements and facilities within the United Nations premises for the holding of bilateral meetings and contacts among Member States during the fiftieth session of the General Assembly and during the special commemorative meeting of the Assembly on the occasion of the fiftieth anniversary of the United Nations,

1. *Expresses its appreciation* to the Secretary-General and the Secretariat for their prompt and effective actions to implement resolution 49/221 D;

2. *Requests* the Secretary-General to continue to provide these improved meeting arrangements and facilities for subsequent sessions of the General Assembly;

3. *Decides* that such improved meeting arrangements and facilities shall be made available within existing resources.

General Assembly resolution 50/206 F

23 December 1995      Meeting 100      Adopted without vote

Approved by Fifth Committee (A/50/837) without vote, 20 December (meeting 43); draft by Chairman, following informal consultations (A/C.5/50/L.12); agenda item 119.
*Meeting numbers.* GA 50th session: 5th Committee 4-7, 9, 11, 25, 43; plenary 100.

## Documents and publications

### Control and limitation

In response to a 1994 General Assembly request,[31] the Secretary-General submitted a 29 June report[32] on the control and limitation of documentation, containing replies from six UN bodies concerning justification for the continuation of their entitlement to meeting records. The United Nations Administrative Tribunal, the First Committee and the Committee on the Exercise of the Inalienable Rights of the Palestinian People sent replies containing justifications for the continuance of their current entitlement. The Special Committee on the Situation with regard to the Implementation of the Declaration on the Granting of Independence to Colonial Countries and Peoples had decided[33] to replace its verbatim records by summary records. The Committee on the Peaceful Uses of Outer Space agreed[34] that, beginning with its thirty-eighth session in 1996, it would be provided with unedited transcripts of its sessions in lieu of verbatim records.

The Committee on Conferences recommended to the Assembly that the current entitlement of meeting records be continued for: the United Nations Administrative Tribunal, the First Committee, the Committee on the Exercise of the Inalienable Rights of the Palestinian People, and the Executive Committee of the Programme of the United Nations High Commissioner for Refugees.

It recommended that the Assembly endorse the decision of the Special Committee on decolonization and request the Committee on the Peaceful Uses of Outer Space to keep it informed of its experience regarding unedited transcripts, so that the Assembly could draw on that experience for the future. It further requested the Committee's Chairman to draw the attention of the chairmen of other bodies to the potential economies of making more general use of unedited transcripts in place of labour-intensive summary or verbatim records, and to review their own requirements pending further information from the Committee on the Peaceful Uses of Outer Space on its experience with unedited transcripts.

**GENERAL ASSEMBLY ACTION**

On 23 December, the General Assembly adopted **resolution 50/206 B**.

*The General Assembly,*

*Recalling* its resolutions on the control and limitation of documentation, including resolutions 33/56 of 14 December 1978, 36/117 B of 10 December 1981, 37/14 C of 16 November 1982, 45/238 B of 21 December 1990, 47/202 B of 22 December 1992, 48/222 B of 23 December 1993 and 49/221 B of 23 December 1994,

*Encouraging* all bodies entitled to written meeting records to keep under review their need for such records,

1. *Decides,* pursuant to paragraph 3 of resolution 49/221 B, that the current entitlement to meeting records of the following bodies shall be continued:

(*a*) United Nations Administrative Tribunal (when holding oral hearings);

(*b*) First Committee;

(*c*) Committee on the Exercise of the Inalienable Rights of the Palestinian People (when holding meetings in observance of international days of solidarity proclaimed by the General Assembly);

(*d*) Executive Committee of the Programme of the United Nations High Commissioner for Refugees;

2. *Approves* the recommendation of the Special Committee on the Situation with regard to the Implementation of the Declaration on the Granting of Independence to Colonial Countries and Peoples to replace its verbatim records by summary records;

3. *Notes* the intention of the Committee on the Peaceful Uses of Outer Space to replace its verbatim records by unedited transcripts, and requests the Committee to keep the General Assembly informed, through the Committee on Conferences, of its experience regarding unedited transcripts;

4. *Takes note* of the decision of the Committee on Conferences contained in paragraph 75 of its report, and requests the Committee to report on the implementation of that decision to the General Assembly at its fifty-first session.

General Assembly resolution 50/206 B

23 December 1995     Meeting 100     Adopted without vote

Approved by Fifth Committee (A/50/837) without vote, 20 December (meeting 43); draft by Chairman, following informal consultations (A/C.5/50/L.12); agenda item 119.
*Meeting numbers.* GA 50th session: 5th Committee 4-7, 9, 11, 25, 43; plenary 100.

### Reduction of documentation

Speaking before the Fifth Committee on 10 October, the Assistant Secretary-General for Conference and Support Services said that the cost of producing documentation in New York and Geneva was expected to increase by $5 million in the 1994-1995 biennium from its 1992-1993 figure of $290 million. To alleviate the problem of the enormous amount of waste paper recycled at the United Nations, which currently averaged 1,000 tons a year, distribution in the UN Secretariat had been cut back by two thirds and stocks by one half, and the distribution of publications in-house had been discontinued. Similar action was being planned at other duty stations. In addition, print runs had been adjusted to reflect actual demand; however, the demand at the delegations' counter and at document booths in conference rooms was harder to predict, and deferral of agenda items from one season to another usually involved reprinting the same document or producing updated versions. Sets of documents and publications placed in mission boxes were frequently opened and immediately dumped, or never picked up at all. He said that boxes would no longer be filled after three days with no pick-up. The Inter-Agency Meeting on Language Arrangements, Documentation and Publications had agreed that very little could be done unless users were willing to scale down their requirements by ceasing to ask for recurrent reports, accepting oral reports instead of documents, combining two or more reports into one document, and limiting their agendas. He cited a number of examples to improve efficiency, including the decision of the Committee on the Peaceful Uses of Outer Space to make unedited transcripts of its proceedings instead of verbatim records, which had cut the cost of its record production by two thirds, and the saving of some $1.8 million by having the records of the First Committee drafted after an Assembly session, on the basis of sound recordings. Member States had to take action and not request additional reports without also deciding to forgo other reports, some of which were based on mandates given 10, 20 or even 50 years earlier. The challenge of efficiency and cost-effectiveness was not only for the Secretariat but equally, and in fact more so, for Member States.

**GENERAL ASSEMBLY ACTION**

On 23 December, the General Assembly adopted **resolution 50/206 C**.

*The General Assembly,*

*Taking note* of the statement made by the representative of the Secretary-General to the Fifth Committee on 10 October 1995 on, *inter alia,* the costs of documentation,

*Recognizing* the right of Member States, through intergovernmental bodies, to request reports,

*Recognizing* that Member States can contribute directly to the reduction of documentation, which contributes to savings, through restraint in making such requests,

*Recognizing also* that the reduction in the demand for, and volume of, documentation could improve the quality and timeliness of reports,

*Noting* that Economic and Social Council decision 1995/222 of 5 May 1995, entitled ''Documentation'', requires Secretariat accountability regarding seriously tardy reports,

*Noting also* that some actions taken by the Committee on Conferences and the Committee on the Peaceful Uses of Outer Space can result in lower documentation costs, while noting further that the political and financial impact of such actions has to be assessed by the General Assembly,

*Recognizing* the right of Member States to request circulation of communications as official documents,

1. *Notes with concern* that the existing limits of 32 pages and 24 pages for documents prepared for intergovernmental meetings, confirmed by its resolution 36/117 A of 10 December 1981 and endorsed by its resolution 38/32 E of 25 November 1983, respectively, are not routinely enforced;

2. *Requests* the Secretary-General to enforce, where appropriate, the existing page limits referred to in paragraph 1 above in respect of all documents originating in the Secretariat, to review these limits, where appropriate, with a view to achieving an overall reduction of documentation without affecting its quality and to report thereon to the General Assembly at its fifty-first session through the Committee on Conferences;

3. *Also requests* the Secretary-General to include only where necessary brief descriptions of the history of the subjects contained in the reports together with a reference to relevant documents, bearing in mind the need to restrict the number of pages to the limits referred to in paragraph 1 above;

4. *Further requests* the Secretary-General to ensure that documentation is available in accordance with the six-week rule for the distribution of documents, simultaneously in each of the six official languages of the United Nations;

5. *Decides* that, should a report be issued late, the reasons for the delay should be indicated when the report is introduced;

6. *Requests* members of all bodies to exercise restraint in making proposals containing requests for new reports;

7. *Invites* all bodies to consider the possibility of biennializing or triennializing the presentation of reports, to review the necessity of all recurrent documents with a view to streamlining documentation and contributing to savings and to make appropriate recommendations;

8. *Encourages* members of intergovernmental bodies:

*(a)* To consider the possibility of requesting oral reports, without prejudice to the provision of information to delegations in all the official languages;

*(b)* To request consolidated reports on related topics under a single item or sub-item where appropriate and cost-effective;

9. *Requests* the Secretary-General:

*(a)* To provide an oral estimate of the cost of documents or reports requested by Member States, without prejudice to the right of intergovernmental bodies to request such documents or reports;

*(b)* To seek a more reader-friendly and uniform format of reports, taking into account new publishing technologies that would include sections containing the objective of the report, an executive summary, the conclusions drawn and, as appropriate, the action proposed to be taken by the body, and to submit proposals thereon to the General Assembly through the Committee on Conferences;

10. *Endorses* the recommendation made by the Advisory Committee on Administrative and Budgetary Questions that the Joint Inspection Unit be requested to conduct a comprehensive survey of the role publications play in implementing mandates of intergovernmental bodies and the extent to which recurrent publications could be made more cost-effective in this regard;

11. *Also requests* the Secretary-General to present to the General Assembly at its fifty-first session, through the Committee on Conferences and the Advisory Committee on Administrative and Budgetary Questions, a report on the implementation of these measures, including information on possible savings.

General Assembly resolution 50/206 C

23 December 1995      Meeting 100      Adopted without vote

Approved by Fifth Committee (A/50/837) without vote, 20 December (meeting 43); draft by Chairman, following informal consultations (A/C.5/50/L.12); agenda item 119.
*Meeting numbers.* GA 50th session: 5th Committee 4-7, 9, 11, 25, 43; plenary 100.

*REFERENCES*

[1]YUN 1994, p. 1402. [2]A/50/32 & Add.1,2. [3]A/50/288. [4]YUN 1988, p. 897, ESC dec. 1988/103, 5 Feb. 1988. [5]A/50/6 (Sect. 26E). [6]YUN 1994, p. 1402, GA res. 49/221 A, 23 Dec. 1994. [7]A/49/953-S/1995/652. [8]A/50/116. [9]A/50/647. [10]A/50/400. [11]A/50/667. [12]A/50/953-S/1996/344. [13]A/50/255. [14]A/50/466. [15]A/51/56. [16]A/50/758. [17]A/50/407. [18]A/50/425-S/1995/787. [19]A/49/920-S/1995/489. [20]A/50/752-S/1995/1035. [21]A/50/475. [22]A/50/518. [23]A/50/813. [24]A/50/254-S/1995/501. [25]YUN 1993, p. 1235, GA res. 48/222 A, 23 Dec. 1993. [26]A/AC.172/162. [27]A/AC.172/161 & Corr.1. [28]YUN 1994, p. 1403. [29]Ibid., p. 1404. [30]A/49/7/Add.9. [31]YUN 1994, p. 1406, GA res. 49/221 B, 23 Dec. 1994. [32]A/50/263 & Add.1. [33]A/50/23 (Part I). [34]A/50/20.

# Other administrative matters

## UN information systems

As requested by the Economic and Social Council in 1994,[1] the Secretary-General, in a July report[2] on UN and inter-agency activities in the field of information systems, said that considerable progress had been made system-wide in providing direct, on-line access to information relating to UN programmes and activities through the use of Internet services, especially the World Wide Web. There was now almost universal use in organizations of the UN system of the Internet to address the information needs identified by the Council and by their own governing bodies, and to disseminate information to other interested parties and to the public. Many organizations had mounted or were in the process of mounting substantive information and operational data, such as press releases, appointment and vacancy announcements, meeting schedules and directories, on internal and external Internet servers. The Secretary-General stated that there should continue to be a shared sense of the enhanced level of information technology that was appropriate to the system as a whole.

**Inter-agency cooperation.** The Administrative Committee on Coordination (ACC) Information Systems Coordination Committee (ISCC),[3] as the successor to the Advisory Committee for the Coordination of Information Systems (ACCIS), held its third session in Geneva from 19 to 21 April. ISCC decided that UNDP would be the lead agency for the Task Force on Document Management Technology and the Task Force on Information Management Standards. The Task Force on Information Access and Dissemination in the UN system was to meet to consider refocusing its work programme. Organizations would be encouraged to supply data on developmental activities directly to the International Network for Development Information Exchange, without ISCC funding. ISCC decided that five former ACCIS products should not be continued in their current form: the Register of Development Activities of the UN system; Directory of UN Databases and Information Services; UNS/SABIR, the bibliographic CD-ROM; Books in Print of the UN system; and the UN-EARTH microcomputer package.

ACABQ[4] pointed out that the International Computing Centre (ICC) could play an active role in implementing activities proposed for ISCC, thus avoiding duplication and enhancing the use of resources. It recommended that the Secretary-General and organizations participating in ICC should review the matter, taking into account the rapid pace of technological change throughout the UN system.

At its eighty-second session (London, 13-17 February), the Consultative Committee on Administrative Questions (CCAQ)[5] commented on ISCC's 1996-1997 programme budget, and requested ISCC to present budget proposals at a level representing zero growth. At its eighty-third session (New York, 28 August–1 September), CCAQ approved[6] a revised programme budget for 1996-1997, totalling $1,233,100.

## Telecommunications

The Secretary-General, on 27 October, submitted the report[7] of the Joint Inspection Unit entitled "A review of telecommunications and related information technologies in the United Nations system". The report examined the status of telecommunications in the United Nations, its legislative basis, trends and perspectives in world communications, opportunities and perspectives for the United Nations and the response of the sys-

tem, and proposed ideas for a future telecommunications strategy.

JIU concluded that telecommunications was an important tool of development and, as a UN telecom system would potentially be a major force in the field and in developing countries, there would be a basis for linking UN telecommunications initiatives with the broader mandate of development. It suggested the corporate network approach, which would provide the framework, policies and strategy for a unified approach.

JIU recommended that a Senior-level Task Force on Telecommunications within the auspices of ACC be established to investigate the most appropriate framework for a common UN system telecommunications strategy. Member States should promote the notion of a common, cost-effective telecommunications strategy and request the Secretary-General to consider new possibilities in strategic perspective. The Secretary-General should answer questions and remove doubts raised by Member States about the project before any further decision was taken; investigate the possibility of common negotiation on behalf of the UN system in relevant areas, especially with INMARSAT, to obtain the status of a duly authorized telecommunications entity, which the United Nations currently had with Intelsat. ITU should be involved as an advisory entity to the Senior-level Task Force and the corporate network and as a partner in the exploration of the existing non-UN system telecommunications services and facilities, and in subsequent negotiations with them. UN agencies should make available strategic and management support and understanding at all levels for the appropriate use of telecommunications, and the work of the Task Force, in particular. Further execution of any telecommunications project in the UN system should be global in conception and implementation. UN organizations should implement as soon as possible a management control system for providing accurate traffic data to facilitate system-wide analysis of traffic requirements.

**ECONOMIC AND SOCIAL COUNCIL ACTION**

On 28 July, the Economic and Social Council adopted **resolution 1995/61**.

**The need to harmonize and improve United Nations information systems for optimal utilization and accessibility by all States**

*The Economic and Social Council,*

*Recalling* its resolutions 1991/70 of 26 July 1991, 1992/60 of 31 July 1992, 1993/56 of 29 July 1993 and 1994/46 of 29 July 1994 on the need to harmonize and improve United Nations informatics systems for optimal utilization and accessibility by all States,

*Conscious* of the deep interest of Member States in harnessing the benefits of new information technologies for the objectives of economic and social development,

*Taking note* of the report of the Secretary-General concerning the follow-up action taken,

*Deeply concerned* at the limited progress achieved so far in the implementation of the above-mentioned resolutions,

1. *Reiterates once again* the high priority that it attaches to easy, economical, uncomplicated and unhindered access for Member States and for observers through, *inter alia*, their permanent missions, to the growing number of computerized databases and information systems and services of the United Nations;

2. *Calls once again* for the urgent implementation of the measures required to achieve these objectives;

3. *Stresses once again* the urgent need for representatives of States to be closely consulted and actively associated with the respective executive and governing bodies of the United Nations institutions dealing with informatics within the United Nations system, so that the specific needs of States as internal end-users can be given due priority;

4. *Requests once again* that the initial phases of the action programme to harmonize and improve United Nations informatics systems for optimal utilization and accessibility by all States be implemented from within existing resources and in full consultation with the representatives of States;

5. *Requests* the President of the Economic and Social Council to convene, initially for one year, an ad hoc open-ended working group, from within existing resources, to make appropriate recommendations for the due fulfilment of the provisions of previous resolutions on this question, including ways to ensure that Member States benefit fully from the informatics revolution in meeting the challenges of development, and the specific measures that the agencies, funds, programmes and various bodies of the United Nations system need to take to help the Member States in this regard;

6. *Requests* the Secretary-General to report on the follow-up action taken on the present resolution, including the findings of the working group, to the Council at its substantive session of 1996.

Economic and Social Council resolution 1995/61

28 July 1995          Meeting 57          Adopted without vote

57-nation draft (E/1995/L.57), orally revised; agenda item 9 *(b)*.
*Meeting numbers.* ESC 56, 57.

## Integrated management information system

The Secretary-General submitted on 21 November his seventh report[8] on the Integrated Management Information System (IMIS) to the Fifth Committee. The purpose of IMIS, which was launched in 1990, was to develop an integrated system to process and report on administrative actions at all major duty stations. The work on the establishment of the system was proceeding steadily, substantially on target and within the budget. The Secretary-General said that because of this major undertaking, the Organization would soon be more responsive to requests of Member States for increased efficiency, accountability and responsibility. The project was the first step towards a more continuous and steady effort to improve efficiency in the Secretariat through advanced technological in-

novations. Human resources applications had made it possible to improve staff management at Headquarters. Implementation of IMIS at offices away from Headquarters would provide management tools never before available. The Secretary-General had decided that the system should be used by the United Nations as a whole, and UNHCR and UNICEF were requested to implement it.

ACABQ noted[4] that IMIS activities in 1996-1997 would focus on the installation of the system away from Headquarters, on the establishment of a long-term maintenance infrastructure and on training worldwide in the use of the system. It recommended approval of the proposed estimates for the IMIS project budget for 1996-1997 totalling $11,967,600, and $7,618,400 for the maintenance budget.

On 23 December, the General Assembly, in **resolution 50/216, section III**, took note of the Secretary-General's report and the recommendations of ACABQ.

## UN premises and property

### Addis Ababa and Bangkok conference facilities

In a 2 November report[9] to the Fifth Committee, the Secretary-General stated that the pace of work at the UN conference centre in Addis Ababa had improved in 1995. Major civil works were completed at the end of September. The projected completion date for the project was January 1996. As of 31 July, disbursements amounted to $67,447,828. The estimated total project cost of $107,576,900 was not expected to change.

The conference centre in Bangkok, inaugurated in April 1993, was the site of 186 major meetings in the first six months of 1995. Its estimated construction cost was $48,540,000.

The General Assembly, in **resolution 50/214** of 23 December, noted the assurance given by the Secretariat with regard to the status of implementation of the UN construction project in Addis Ababa and asked that all necessary measures be taken to ensure that the project was completed as approved.

### Buildings management

The Secretary-General submitted to the General Assembly on 13 November his comments[10] on the 1994 Joint Inspection Unit report on management of buildings in the United Nations,[11] with which he concurred. He observed that insufficient funding over the past four bienniums had resulted in the need to defer the frequency and scope of regular and preventive maintenance and the postponement of much-needed upgrading and retrofitting of obsolete systems and equipment. The JIU recommendation of creating a building fund could be an interim solution to the problem of lack of adequate funding to cover costs related to emergency and unforeseen repair and replacement projects. While there was a need to establish long-range planning to ensure effective maintenance and operation of the facilities by implementing a comprehensive master plan, the building fund would ensure a bridge for adequate funding of maintenance until the implementation of such a master plan. It was estimated that at Headquarters a replenishable fund of $1 million annually would be required to fund emergency maintenance and repair projects.

The Secretary-General reported[12] on 25 October on properties and buildings owned or occupied by the United Nations at principal duty stations, including historical background and building descriptions.

ACABQ[4] requested the Secretary-General to review the total proposed requirements for alterations and improvements of projects deferred from 1994-1995 to ensure that there was a reasonable balance in the implementation of projects approved for the various duty stations, and to include in his next budget information on the share of new projects in the total estimated requirements for alterations or improvements.

The General Assembly, in **resolution 50/214**, decided that for the biennium 1996-1997 only essential repairs and construction, the deferral of which would endanger occupational health and safety, leave the Organization in breach of local building regulations or in the longer term not be cost-effective, should be carried out, and that the proposed estimates for alterations, improvements and major maintenance would be reduced by $12 million.

## UN art works

Responding to a 1993 General Assembly request,[13] the Secretary General submitted a 10 November note[14] on the management of art works, stating that he had reviewed the in-house capabilities of the Secretariat to improve their management and care. He had determined that responsibility for art management should remain within the Office of Conference and Support Services, and should be shared by the Archives Unit and the Buildings Management Services within the Commercial and Building Services Division. A complete computerized inventory was being compiled of all gifts presented to the Organization, and the Archives Unit had assembled and consolidated available inventories of UN works of art. Major art and educational institutions provided expert advice on the most up-to-date methods for managing works of art. A review was undertaken of the oversight mechanism under which the Philatelic Museum in Geneva operated.

It was decided that the Museum should be jointly administered by the Archives Unit and the UN Postal Administration to ensure that archival standards were maintained.

## Procurement reform

The Secretary-General, responding to a 1994 General Assembly request,[15] presented a progress report[16] on the implementation of procurement reform in the UN Secretariat. That process had been reviewed by a high-level group of experts, which had examined the financial regulations and rules governing procurement procedures and practices; requisitioning; bid evaluation and vendor registration processes; the use of letters of assist; the levels and scope of delegated procurement authority to field missions; distribution of workload between Headquarters and the field in terms of value and number of transactions; and the existing related control mechanisms. He had accepted most recommendations of the high-level group and was implementing those within current resources and capacity.

The General Assembly, by **decision 49/486** of 20 July, welcomed the progress made in the implementation of procurement reform in the Secretariat.

On 10 November, the Secretary-General presented a full report on the implementation of procurement reform in the Secretariat[17] which provided information on actions taken or planned. New procedures were introduced in January to facilitate requests for use of the Controller's authority regarding commitments against the appropriations of current and future financial periods in certain key areas of procurement for peacekeeping operations. Progress had been made in identifying and instituting system contracts and efforts were continuing to define more clearly the parameters and scope of the concept of system contracts. A comprehensive review of the relevant financial regulations and rules had begun, with the initial phase concentrating on the preparation of a set of policy guidelines for use in procurement.

The Secretary-General concluded that in order to ensure that the reform of procurement policy and procedures was fully implemented, the necessary funds should be made available to ensure an appropriate level of highly qualified staff with procurement expertise.

The Secretary-General, in a note to the General Assembly,[18] submitted a report of the Under-Secretary-General for Internal Oversight Services on the 1995 audit of procurement handled by the Contracts and Procurement Service of the Department for Development Support and Management Services (DDSMS), indicating the need for strengthened planning, monitoring and control of the procurement process.

In August, ACABQ noted[4] that procurement services were being undertaken in both DDSMS and the Department of Administration and Management. It recommended that the Secretary-General review the situation with a view to merging the services in the two Departments and ensuring appropriate coordination with other UN procurement services.

### UN access control system project

The Secretary-General, in a 30 November note to the General Assembly,[19] transmitted the report of the Office of Internal Oversight Services (OIOS) on the audit of the UN access control system project. The audit found that project planning had been inadequate and that no feasibility study was undertaken to determine its viability and cost-effectiveness. OIOS had referred the matter to its Investigations Section to determine whether any staff members had violated UN rules and regulations in the areas of project planning, vendor selection or project monitoring and acceptance in connection with the project.

The Secretary-General included remarks of the Department of Administration and Management, which, in its comments on the audit report, acknowledged weaknesses in the management process for the project's formulation and execution. The Department, however, believed that UN regulations and rules, particularly those regarding procurement, were respected throughout the process.

### UN Postal Administration

In 1995, the gross revenue of the United Nations Postal Administration (UNPA) from its sale of philatelic items both at Headquarters and at overseas offices totalled more than $15 million. Revenue from the sale of stamps for philatelic purposes was retained by the United Nations. Under the terms of an agreement between the Organization and the United States, revenue from the sale of United States dollar–denominated stamps used for postage from Headquarters was reimbursed to the United States

Postal Service. Similarly, postal agreements between the United Nations and the Governments of Austria and Switzerland required that revenue derived from the sale of Austrian schilling–denominated stamps and Swiss franc–denominated stamps for postage be reimbursed to the Austrian and Swiss postal authorities, respectively.

During the year, UNPA released seven commemorative stamp issues, one definitive stamp, two souvenir cards, 10 maximum cards, two pre-stamped envelopes and three prestige booklets. The first set of three commemorative stamps entitled "50th Anniversary of the United Nations", was released on 1 January; one maximum card accompanied the issue. On 3 February, UNPA issued three stamps on "Social Summit", to commemorate the World Summit for Social Development; a souvenir card accompanied this issue; two pre-stamped envelopes were issued on the same day. On 24 March, UNPA released the third of its multi-year series on "Endangered Species". Each year, 12 endangered species were to be featured on stamps to highlight the need for the protection of endangered species throughout the world; three maximum cards accompanied the issue. The United Nations issued six stamps on 26 May on "Youth: Our Future" to commemorate the tenth anniversary of International Youth Year; a souvenir card accompanied the issue.

The fiftieth anniversary of the United Nations was commemorated further with a set of six United Nations stamps and three souvenir sheets on 26 June. On 5 September, the United Nations issued six "Fourth World Conference on Women" stamps to commemorate the Conference which was held in September; six maximum cards accompanied the issue; one definitive stamp was issued on the same day. Three "50th Anniversary of the United Nations" stamps, together with three prestige booklets, were issued by UNPA on 24 October to complete the year's programme.

*REFERENCES*

[1]YUN 1994, p. 1412. [2]E/1995/97. [3]ACC/1995/9. [4]A/50/7. [5]ACC/1995/6. [6]ACC/1995/20. [7]A/50/686. [8]A/C.5/50/35. [9]A/C.5/50/17. [10]A/50/753. [11]YUN 1994, p. 1408. [12]A/50/676. [13]YUN 1993, p. 1239, GA res. 48/217, 23 Dec. 1993. [14]A/50/742. [15]YUN 1994, p. 1369, GA res. 49/216 C, 23 Dec. 1994. [16]A/C.5/49/67. [17]A/C.5/50/13/Rev.1. [18]A/50/945. [19]A/50/791.

PART SEVEN


Intergovernmental organizations
related to the United Nations

Chapter I

# International Atomic Energy Agency (IAEA)

The International Atomic Energy Agency (IAEA), established in 1957 to promote the peaceful uses of atomic energy, continued its efforts in 1995 to improve the impact and efficiency of its activities, which encompassed nuclear power and its fuel cycle, waste management, the safety of nuclear installations and radiation safety, international safeguards and the use of nuclear techniques to improve human health, food supply and environmental protection.

The thirty-ninth session of the IAEA General Conference (Vienna, 18-22 September) adopted resolutions relating to measures to strengthen international cooperation in nuclear safety, radiological protection and waste management; improving the safeguards system; and strengthening the Agency's technical cooperation system. It also took action on a plan for producing potable water economically, on the extensive use of isotope hydrology for water resources management and on measures against trafficking in nuclear material. In addition, it adopted resolutions on the creation of a nuclear-weapon-free zone in Africa; participation of South Africa in IAEA activities; implementation of IAEA standards in the Democratic People's Republic of Korea and in Iraq; and application of IAEA safeguards in the Middle East.

In 1995, Bosnia and Herzegovina became a member of IAEA, bringing the Agency's total membership to 123.

## Nuclear safety

IAEA continued to foster a global nuclear safety culture in 1995 by supporting intergovernmental collaborative efforts. It provided a forum for extensive information exchange; promoted the drafting of international legal agreements and the development of safety standards; and organized a wide variety of expert services.

By the end of 1995, 62 countries had signed and 14 had ratified, accepted or approved the 1994 Convention on Nuclear Safety, which bound countries to basic principles covering the regulation, management and operation of land-based civil nuclear power plants. The Convention was to enter into force on the nineteenth day after deposit of the twenty-second instrument of ratification, acceptance or approval, including the instruments of 17 States each having at least one nuclear installation that had achieved criticality in a reactor core.

Agency work on the assessment of the safety of nuclear power plants in eastern Europe and countries of the former USSR made steady progress, with emphasis on a review of the status of the implementation of proposed improvements.

Seven Operational Safety Review Team missions (France (2), Japan, Lithuania, Switzerland, Ukraine, United Kingdom) and six Safety Review Missions (Bulgaria (2), Czech Republic, Russian Federation, Ukraine (2)) were made to nuclear power plants. Additionally, 13 Assessment of Safety Significant Events Team review missions were carried out at nuclear plants in Bulgaria, China, the Czech Republic, Hungary, Sweden (2), the Russian Federation, Ukraine (5) and the United States.

Armenia, Croatia, Iceland and Kazakstan joined the International Nuclear Event Scale information system, bringing to 58 the number of States committed to the prompt communication of nuclear events significant for safety or the public interest. In 1995, 61 events were reported to the system.

## Nuclear power

The activities of IAEA in 1995 in the area of nuclear power focused on developing improved versions of software for energy, electricity and nuclear power planning; on-line services and systematic monitoring of power reactor information; technology issues on nuclear power plant life management and the human-machine interface; revision of quality assurance standards; improving technology for advanced nuclear reactors; sea-water desalinization using nuclear energy; and the transmutation of actinides.

In 1995, Belarus, Brazil and Poland were added to the list of countries receiving technical cooperation assistance in applying the Energy and Power Evaluation Package, used to assess nuclear power options. In addition, Albania, Estonia, Latvia, Lithuania, Moldova, the former Yugoslav Republic of Macedonia and Viet Nam received assistance in defining a framework for technical cooperation projects on energy, electricity and nuclear power planning.

Interest in small and medium-size reactors for use in non-electrical applications as well as power generation steadily increased among member States. The reactors would most likely find use in areas such as sea-water desalination, district heating, oil recovery enhancement, coal gasification and methanol production.

The Power Reactor Information System (PRIS) database continued to be maintained and updated, with information on the status and operating experience of 437 reactors in 30 countries and Taiwan. A subset of the PRIS database for PC users, MicroPRIS, was being accessed by 225 users in 54 member States and 8 international organizations.

### Nuclear fuel cycle

In 1995, six countries—Australia, Canada, Kazakstan, the Niger, the Russian Federation, Uzbekistan—produced over 70 per cent of the world's total uranium. The 1995 worldwide reactor-related requirements were estimated to be some 61,400 tonnes of uranium per year, which was about 29,000 tonnes greater than worldwide production. The balance of demand was filled by inventory drawdown.

A new map of the world's uranium deposits, the most comprehensive to date, was published in cooperation with the Geological Survey of Canada. It depicted information on 582 uranium deposits, including previously unavailable information on deposits in eastern Europe, the former USSR and China.

Technical meetings convened in 1995 reviewed recent changes in the uranium industry, reactor fuel technology and core performance, and spent-fuel management, technology and safety.

### Radioactive waste management

The Agency's 1995 programme on radioactive waste management focused on strengthening waste management infrastructures in developing member States; establishing international principles and standards for the safe management of wastes; and preparing for the convention on waste safety. New initiatives were introduced in the areas of decommissioning/dismantling nuclear installations and the restoration of radioactively contaminated sites, reflecting the increased importance placed by member States on those issues.

The preamble of the 1994 Convention on Nuclear Safety[a] urged preparation of a convention on the safe management of radioactive waste. Progress was made on a draft convention at two meetings of an open-ended group of legal and technical experts convened by the IAEA Board of Governors.

IAEA completed and released in 1995 the Sealed Radiation Sources Registry package for member States. As one of the primary components of Agency programmes aimed at improving the control of in-use and spent radiation sources, the Registry would assist countries in their efforts to keep track of all sealed radiation sources.

As part of its work to resolve international waste management issues, the Agency, at the request of the Nordic Council of Ministers and with the cooperation of the Russian Federation, organized a seminar on international cooperation on nuclear waste management in the Russian Federation and established a Contact Expert Group.

### Environment

With the threat of global climate change due to emissions a matter of increasing concern to the international community, IAEA continued to address the issue of sustainable energy sources. In October, the Agency, in cooperation with other international organizations, convened an international symposium on electricity, health and the environment. The symposium aimed to draw up methodologies and databases for the comparative assessment of different options for the production of electric power.

IAEA organized a re-examination of the radiological situation at the Bikini Atoll in the Marshall Islands. It also undertook a review of an area in Kazakstan where nuclear weapons had been tested for many years. The results confirmed overall that there was no need for concern among those living in the settlements around the test site.

In 1995, France requested IAEA to perform a study to assess the full radiological situation in the South Pacific atolls of Mururoa and Fangataufa, taking into account all past events of radiological significance. The study, to be funded by extrabudgetary contributions from France, would consist of an assessment of the current radiological situation and an evaluation of the potential long-term radiological impact. Following consultations, the Director General informed France that the Agency agreed to conduct the study after the cessation of nuclear testing in the area.

### Food and agriculture

The Agency's food and agriculture programme, operated jointly with the Food and Agriculture Organization of the United Nations (FAO), continued to assist member States in the use of nuclear techniques to improve the quantity and quality of food and fibre produced.

A feature of the work of 1995 was the increased involvement of modern biotechnologies such as nuclear-based molecular methods, *in vitro* culture techniques and monoclonal antibodies for pest management, mutation plant-breeding programmes and diagnostic tests for animal diseases.

In Peru, a new barley mutant created with radiation mutation techniques was officially released for large-scale production. In China, with the support of IAEA/FAO projects, nearly 600,000 hectares

---

[a]YUN 1994, p. 1417.

of early-season rice were cultivated with mutant varieties, increasing rice production by about 263,000 tonnes. Other projects were helping farmers to raise new mutants of rice, sorghum and cassava in Africa, and cattle farmers in Latin America. Substantial progress was made using sterile-insect techniques to eradicate the tsetse fly from the island of Zanzibar and the Mediterranean fruit fly from Chile.

The Agency also continued to provide assistance in monitoring radionuclide contamination and producing uncontaminated food to regions where agriculture was affected by radionuclide contamination from the 1986 Chernobyl nuclear power station accident, including Belarus and Ukraine.

### Physical and chemical sciences

The Agency's activities in the physical and chemical sciences covered the applications of nuclear and atomic data, nuclear instrumentation, theoretical physics, the utilization of research reactors and particle accelerators and chemistry. Specific services to member States included the provision of databases, as well as coordination and technical support of efforts to develop selected nuclear technologies.

In 1995, an extensive fusion evaluated nuclear data library (FENDL-1) was validated and tested in order to support engineering design activities for the International Thermonuclear Experimental Reactor. The curricula of interregional training courses dealing with interfacing in nuclear experiments and radiation measurements for applications were revised to include information on new instruments and general trends in nuclear technology.

The International Centre for Theoretical Physics in Trieste, Italy, organized 57 courses, 12 research activities, 1 training scheme and 1 lecture series, totalling some 5,900 visits, of which 64 per cent were from developing countries.

### Human health

Agency activities in the area of human health focused on the common concerns of developing member States that could be most effectively addressed using nuclear technologies. The programme promoted the diagnosis and treatment of cancer, the accurate evaluation of nutritional deficiencies in women and children, the timely detection of infections and communicable diseases, and radiation dosimetry. Advances in molecular biology facilitated the introduction in 1995 of a new area of work centred on genetic disorders which, together with other programme components, such as nutritional studies, was placing increased emphasis on aspects of preventive medicine.

In 1995, the network of IAEA/World Health Organization Secondary Dosimetry Laboratories increased to 73 laboratories and 6 national organizations in 58 member States, as well as 14 affiliated members. A new service was introduced at the Agency's dosimetry laboratory at Seibersdorf, Austria, aimed at developing international standards for the calibration of radiation sources used in brachytherapy.

An intercomparison of gamma ray irradiation beams between nine calibration laboratories, organized in collaboration with the Bureau International des Poids et Mesures, was completed. A new Agency Code of Practice for the calibration and use of plan parallel ionization chambers in therapeutic electron and photon beams was submitted for publication.

IAEA initiated a new, coordinated research programme on the use of irradiated sewage sludge to increase soil fertility and crop fields and help preserve the environment. Its aim was to find ways by which solid and liquid wastes from households could be utilized as a source of organic matter and nutrients for increasing crop production.

### Technical cooperation

Important steps were taken in 1995 to ensure that the Technical Cooperation Programme, approved by the Board of Governors in 1994, was results-oriented and efficient. At the centre of the new approach was the Model Project concept, which had 23 projects under way with encouraging initial results. In the area of radiation protection and waste safety infrastructure, some 50 countries were expected to be in compliance with the requirements of the Agency's Basic Safety Standards as a result of new integrated management arrangements between IAEA and member States.

A total of 307 operational projects were completed during the year. Some 119 training courses were held, of which 86 took place in developing countries. New resources for the Programme totalled $63.5 million in 1995, representing a 20 per cent increase over 1994.

There were 3,857 expert and lecturer assignments in 1995, making it another record year and representing a 20 per cent increase over 1994. Over half were carried out by experts (including IAEA staff members) from developing countries. The Agency placed and trained 1,355 fellows and scientific visitors during 1995, 18 per cent more than in 1994.

### Agency safeguards responsibilities

During 1995, 2,285 safeguards inspections were performed. IAEA maintained a continuous presence of inspectors in Iraq, where the Agency carried out activities related to the destruction, removal and rendering harmless of items requiring such action pursuant to a 1991 Security Council resolution (see PART TWO, Chapter IV). As at 31 December 1995, 207 safeguards agreements were in force with 125 States (and with Taiwan), compared with 200 agreements with 119 States (and with Taiwan) at the end of 1994. Safeguards agreements pursuant to the 1968 Treaty on the Non-Proliferation of Nuclear Weapons (NPT)[b] entered into force with Croatia in January, Myanmar in April, Zimbabwe in June and Belarus and Kazakstan in August. In 1995, there were 884 nuclear facilities, other locations and non-nuclear installations subject to IAEA safeguards in 68 countries.

Safeguards were applied in 53 States under agreements pursuant to NPT or to NPT and the 1967 Treaty for the Prohibition of Nuclear Weapons in Latin America and the Caribbean (Treaty of Tlatelolco),[c] in two States under the Treaty of Tlatelolco, and in three States pursuant to a comprehensive safeguards agreement. Safeguards pursuant to NPT in Iraq continued to be submitted under activities pursuant to a 1991 Security Council resolution (see PART TWO, Chapter IV). IAEA also applied safeguards to nuclear installations in Taiwan. Although the Democratic People's Republic of Korea (DPRK) withdrew from IAEA on 13 June 1994, the validity of the safeguards agreement remained in force. In 1995, IAEA maintained a continuous presence of inspectors in the DPRK to verify the freeze of its graphite moderated reactors and related facilities (see PART TWO, Chapter IV).

NPT safeguards were in force with all 11 signatories of the South Pacific Nuclear Free Zone Treaty (Rarotonga Treaty); safeguards were applied in one of those States. Twenty-two of the 30 States party to the Treaty of Tlatelolco concluded safeguards agreements with IAEA. As at 31 December, safeguards agreements pursuant to the Treaty were in force with 19 States. Safeguards agreements pursuant to Additional Protocol I of the Treaty of Tlatelolco were in force with two States with territories in the zone of application of the Treaty. A safeguards agreement pursuant to NPT and the Treaty of Tlatelolco entered into force with Bolivia in February. A safeguards agreement with Chile pursuant to the Treaty of Tlatelolco entered into force in April. A *sui generis* comprehensive safeguards agreement with Ukraine entered into force in January.

As requested in 1994 by the IAEA General Conference, the Agency continued to assist African States in their effort to establish a nuclear-weapon-free zone and, in particular, to help develop its verification regime. A proposed text, which entrusted IAEA with the task of verification, was adopted by the African heads of State at Addis Ababa in June (see PART ONE, Chapter II).

The General Conference in 1995 requested all parties directly concerned in the Middle East to consider taking steps to establish a mutually and effectively verifiable nuclear-weapon-free zone in the region. The Director General continued consultations with the States of the Middle East to facilitate the early application of full-scope Agency safeguards to all nuclear activities in the region and the preparation of model verification agreements.

### Nuclear information

In 1995, Internet access to the Agency's nuclear and atomic databases was improved in response to the rapid developments in computer networks. The databases provided accurate and up-to-date files for a variety of nuclear technology applications, such as reactor dosimetry and radiation safety, fusion reactor development, waste management, radiotherapy, and safeguards and material analysis. The use of on-line data retrievals increased by about 50 per cent, benefiting several hundred end-users in 41 member States.

The International Nuclear Information System, with 94 States and 17 international organizations, had a bibliographic database of 1,856,206 records. In addition, IAEA published over 200 books, reports, journal issues or booklets in English.

### Secretariat

At the end of 1995, the IAEA secretariat had 2,295 staff members, including 890 in the Professional and higher categories and 1,405 in the General Service category; 90 nationalities were represented in posts subject to geographical distribution.

### Budget

The regular budget for 1995 amounted to $258,500,000 of which $248,000,000 was to be financed from contributions by member States on the basis of the 1995 scale of assessment, $7,500,000 from income from reimbursable work for others and $3,000,000 from other miscellaneous income. The actual expenditures of the Agency's regular budget amounted to $253,000,000, of which $245,000,000 was related to the Agency's programmes. The unused budget from Agency programmes amounted to $5,800,000.

The target for voluntary contributions to the Technical Assistance and Cooperation Fund in 1995 was established at $61.5 million, of which $47.7 million was pledged by member States.

NOTE: For further information, see *The Annual Report for 1995*, published by IAEA.

[b]YUN 1968, p. 17, GA res. 2373(XXII), annex, 12 June 1968.
[c]YUN 1967, p. 13.

## HEADQUARTERS AND OTHER OFFICES

### HEADQUARTERS

International Atomic Energy Agency
Wagramerstrasse 5
(P.O. Box 100, Vienna International Centre)
A-1400 Vienna, Austria
  *Cable address:* INATOM VIENNA
  *Telephone:* (43) (1) 20600
  *Fax:* (43) (1) 20607
  *Telex:* 1-2645 ATOM A
  *Internet:* http://www.iaea.or.at/worldatom

### LIAISON OFFICE

International Atomic Energy Agency Liaison Office at the
  United Nations
1 United Nations Plaza, Room 1155
New York, N.Y. 10017, United States
  *Telephone:* (1) (212) 963-6010, 6011, 6012
  *Fax:* (1) (212) 751-4117
  *Telex:* 42 05 44 UNH

Chapter II

# International Labour Organization (ILO)

In 1995, the International Labour Organization (ILO), which is based in Geneva, continued to promote social justice and economic stability and to improve labour conditions. Established in 1919 as an autonomous institution associated with the League of Nations, ILO had three primary objectives, namely promoting democracy and human rights, fighting unemployment and poverty, and ensuring equality and adequate protection for workers.

ILO membership in 1995 increased to 173, with the admission of the Gambia and Saint Vincent and the Grenadines.

## Meetings

The eighty-second session of the International Labour Conference (Geneva, 6-23 June) considered the annual report of the ILO Governing Body and the report of the Director-General calling for increased emphasis on employment issues in the work of the organization.

The Conference adopted new standards on safety and health in mines and prepared the groundwork for adoption in 1996 of an international agreement to protect homeworkers.

An informal meeting of labour ministers at the Conference reviewed the role of ILO in follow-up to the World Summit for Social Development (Copenhagen, 6-12 March). ILO had been closely involved with preparations for the Summit (see PART FOUR, Chapter IX).

The following industrial and regional meetings were convened during 1995: the Coal Mines Committee (11-19 January), the fourth Tripartite Technical Meeting for the Clothing Industry (1-9 February), the Joint Meeting on the Impact of Structural Adjustment in the Public Services (Efficiency, Quality Improvement and Working Conditions) (24-30 May), the Chemical Industries Committee (10-18 May), the Fifth European Regional Conference (20-27 September), the Tripartite Meeting on Social and Labour Issues concerning Migrant Workers in the Construction Industry (20-27 September), and the Meeting of Experts on Labour Statistics on the Measurement of Unemployment (30 October–3 November).

## International standards

ILO activities concerning Conventions and Recommendations during 1995 included standard-setting and the supervision and promotion of the application of standards. Supervisory bodies engaged in a review of existing procedures and standard-setting policy, coinciding with the implementation of simplified reporting on ratified Conventions.

### Standard-setting

In 1995, the International Labour Conference adopted the Safety and Health in Mines Convention (No. 176) and Recommendation (No. 183) and the optional Protocol of 1995 to the 1947 Labour Inspection Convention, which extended the scope of that Convention to non-commercial services. The 1990 Night Work Convention (No. 171) came into force on 4 January 1995, and the 1992 Protection of Workers' Claims (Employer's Insolvency) Convention (No. 173) came into force on 8 June 1995, both having received two ratifications.

During the year, 93 ratifications of ILO Conventions by 32 member States were registered, resulting in the further increase of total ratifications of many important instruments, including those on basic human rights (freedom of association, discrimination, forced labour and child labour) and other issues such as labour inspection, tripartite consultation and employment policy.

### Supervision of standards

The Committee of Experts on the Application of Conventions and Recommendations held two sessions in 1995 (16 February–3 March and 23 November–8 December) at which it dealt with a record total of 464 observations from employers' and workers' organizations. The Committee noted during its first meeting 36 instances in which Governments changed their law and practice to come into conformity with ratified Conventions, following the Committee's earlier comments. At its second session, the Committee noted 37 such instances.

The Committee carried out a general survey and a special survey of the application by all member States of selected international labour standards. The general survey, prepared for the first session, dealt with the 1982 Termination of Employment Convention (No. 158) and Recommendation (No. 166).[a] The special survey,

---

[a]YUN 1982, p. 1518.

prepared during the second session, examined reports from States which had not ratified the 1958 Discrimination (Employment and Occupation) Convention (No. 111).[b]

The Governing Body Committee on Freedom of Association met three times in 1995 to examine the complaints of violations of freedom of association received from employers' and workers' organizations.

### Promotion

Specialists on international labour standards were included on multidisciplinary teams set up in various developing regions to help both Governments and employers' and workers' organizations with standard-setting and supervisory procedures and to assist in the integration of standards into ILO operational activities.

### Employment and development

ILO published in 1995 a new report, *World Employment 1995*, which analysed trends in the employment situation worldwide. The report, which examined the pattern of, and factors behind, the current global employment crisis, helped ILO to design policy measures at the national and international levels to combat growing unemployment in an increasingly global environment. The ILO analytical and technical advisory work in the field of employment concentrated on policies towards employment-intensive growth, workers' protection (including migrant workers) and active labour market policies.

### Working environment

The International Programme for the Improvement of Working Conditions and Environment continued to assist countries in promoting occupational safety and health and improving working conditions. In June 1995, the International Labour Conference adopted the Safety and Health in Mines Convention (No. 176) and its accompanying Recommendation (No. 183).

The twelfth session of the Joint ILO/WHO Committee on Occupational Health was convened in April 1995. ILO also played a leading role in preparations for the XIVth World Congress on Occupational Safety and Health, to be convened in Madrid in April 1996. In March 1995, ILO, FAO, OECD, UNEP, UNIDO and WHO signed a Memorandum of Understanding defining their cooperation in an Inter-Organization Programme for the Sound Management of Chemicals (IOMC). IOMC was linked through a mutual consultation process with the Intergovernmental Forum on Chemical Safety (IFCS), formed in 1994, and the International Programme on Chemical Safety (IPCS) to create a practical and flexible three-level framework to help member States improve safety in the production, handling, use and disposal of chemicals.

In 1995, technical cooperation activities, such as national training workshops and preparation of training materials, focused on improving conditions of work and productivity in the garment industry in Africa, Asia and Latin America. Also in those regions, national projects, training workshops and seminars continued to enhance national action on prevention of major industrial and other accidents during hazardous activities such as construction and the use of chemicals.

ILO published six issues of the bulletin *Safety and Health at Work* in English and French, distributed compact discs containing safety and health databases, and prepared World Wide Web pages on occupational safety and health. Among 1995 publications were *Conditions of Work*, a digest focusing on working time around the world, and manuals on work organizations and ergonomics, stress, sexual harassment and elder care. A chapter in the *World Labour Report* addressed problems and prospects of older workers with the ageing of societies. In addition, the bulk of the fourth edition of the *ILO Encyclopedia of Occupational Health and Safety* was compiled, to be published in four volumes and on CD-ROM in 1997.

The Interdepartmental Project on Environment and the World of Work supported action to enhance the capacity of ILO constituents to implement relevant decisions, recommendations and requests emanating from the 1992 UN Conference on Environment and Development[c] and its Agenda 21. A series of more than 20 National Desk Reviews were prepared to highlight the role of Governments and employers' and workers' organizations in implementing Agenda 21 activities at the national, local and enterprise levels.

### Field activities

In 1995, expenditure on operational activities, under all sources of funding, totalled $112.9 million, a level similar to 1994. The three leading programmes were in enterprise and cooperative development ($22.5 million), development and technical cooperation ($25 million) and training (more than $13 million). Other programmes dealt with working conditions and environment ($12 million), including an International Programme for the Elimination of Child Labour, and employment ($6 million). Interregional and global activities accounted for some $18 million. In terms of regional distribution, Africa accounted for over 37 per cent of total expendi-

[b]YUN 1958, p. 436.
[c]YUN 1992, p. 670.

ture (more than $42 million), Asia and the Pacific for 25 per cent (nearly $29 million), and Latin America and the Caribbean for 12 per cent (more than $12 million). Expenditure in Europe increased from $6 million in 1994 to $9 million in 1995, due to ILO assistance to a growing number of countries in Central and Eastern Europe. Arab States' programmes increased by 91 per cent over 1994, to $2.7 million.

### Educational activities

ILO continued to undertake research, provide advice and organize activities aimed at enhancing the capacity of policymakers to review and reform training systems and the effectiveness of training delivery. Special programmes concentrated on facilitating the adoption by member States of policies and measures to counteract social exclusion and promote social integration, particularly of persons with disabilities and, in countries emerging from armed conflict, of large numbers of ex-combatants and displaced persons.

ILO's International Institute for Labour Studies continued its work on the changing relationship between labour institutions, the organization of production and economic development through its research networks, social policy forums and publications. Its work on social exclusion focused on the relationship between poverty, employment and social integration and elaborated a new policy paradigm which emphasized the value of partici-

pation and social dialogue in ensuring the cohesion of civil society. Research was also completed on the role of labour institutions in Asian economic success. A new project on the impact of economic interdependence was launched to map global commodity chains with a view to identifying social and industrial policies which facilitated access to global markets and capital. An Asian network embarked on a research project to identify national policies that maintained competitiveness in world markets while avoiding both social exclusion and protectionist measures.

### Secretariat

As at 31 December 1995, the total number of full-time staff under permanent, fixed- and short-term appointments at ILO headquarters and elsewhere was 2,634. Of those, 1,020 were in the Professional or higher categories and 1,614 were in the General Service or Maintenance categories. Of the Professional staff, 295 were assigned to technical cooperation projects.

### Budget

The International Labour Conference in June 1995 adopted a budget of $579.5 million for the 1996-1997 biennium.

NOTE: For further information on ILO, see *Report of the Director-General, Activities of the ILO, 1994-1995.*

## HEADQUARTERS, LIAISON AND OTHER OFFICES

HEADQUARTERS
International Labour Office
4 Route des Morillons
CH-1211 Geneva 22
Switzerland
   *Cable address:* INTERLAB GENEVE
   *Telephone:* (41) (22) 799-6111
   *Fax:* (41) (22) 798-8686
   *Telex:* 415647 ILO CH

LIAISON OFFICE
International Labour Organization
Liaison Office with the United Nations
Suite 3101
220 East 42nd Street
New York, N.Y. 10017
   *Telephone:* (1) (212) 697-0150
   *Fax:* (1) (212) 883-0844
   *Telex:* 422716

Chapter III

# Food and Agriculture Organization of the United Nations (FAO)

In 1995, the Food and Agriculture Organization of the United Nations (FAO) continued to assist farmers, fishermen and foresters to improve their standards of living and produce more foods using techniques that did not degrade the environment. Established in 1945 to raise levels of nutrition, improve agricultural productivity and better the condition of the rural poor, FAO's main objective remained the achievement of global food security, where everyone would have access at all times to the food needed for an active and healthy life.

During the year, Azerbaijan, Georgia, the Republic of Moldova, Tajikistan and Turkmenistan joined the organization, bringing its membership to 174 nations, in addition to the European Community as a member organization and Puerto Rico as an associate member.

The FAO Conference, the organization's governing body, held its twenty-eighth biennial session in Rome from 20 October to 2 November. Highlights of the Conference included adoption of a Code of Conduct for Responsible Fisheries, the first international code to address all facets involved in the sustainable development of an entire natural resource sector. The Code covered world fisheries and aquaculture issues, including fisheries resource conservation and development, fish catches, seafood and fish processing, commercialization, trade and research. It was non-binding except for the Agreement on measures to ensure compliance with resources management schemes in the high seas, which was approved by the FAO Conference in 1993.[a]

The Conference also also gave its approval to the Quebec Declaration, which reaffirmed the international community's dedication to the principles on which FAO was founded and pledged political support for its mission to help build a world where all people could live, confident of food security. The Declaration was initially adopted during fiftieth anniversary commemorations in Quebec City, Canada, in October.

In addition, the Conference unanimously decided to hold a World Food Summit in Rome in November 1996 (see also PART FOUR, Chapter XIII). Summit objectives would include raising global awareness of and commitment to redressing the food security problem and adopting a plan of action to achieve sustained progress towards universal food security. The Conference decided that the plan of action would outline concrete ac-

tivities aimed at constantly improving global food security, in particular at the household level, from both a quantitative and nutritional perspective, within the framework of sustainable development.

## World food situation

In 1995, global agriculture production stagnated, reflecting below-average performance in most developed and developing country regions, and virtually unchanged aggregate production levels in the countries in transition. Total crop and livestock production rose at an estimated rate of only 0.2 per cent, compared to a 2.9 per cent increase in 1994.

One of the most significant features in 1995 was the 8 per cent drop in crop and livestock output in the United States, where cereal crops alone, affected by adverse weather, fell by over 20 per cent. In the European Union, overall agriculture output continued its declining trend of the previous few years. On the other hand, Australian production expanded by 12.8 per cent, more than offsetting a sharp shortfall in 1994.

In the countries in transition, 1995 saw the halt of the steady decrease in overall agriculture production since the beginning of their economic reforms, with total production remaining virtually unchanged from 1994. Developing countries, however, reported deteriorating overall agricultural performance in 1995 compared to 1994, with the exception of sub-Saharan Africa, which saw a 2.4 per cent increase. Agricultural growth also slowed in the regions of the Far East and the Pacific, and Latin America and the Caribbean, both reporting rates of 1.8 per cent in 1995. In the Near East and North Africa, production growth slowed to 1.7 per cent, remaining well short of population growth for the third consecutive year.

FAO's Global Information and Early Warning System (GIEWS), which monitored crop and food outlook at global and national levels to detect emerging food shortages and disasters, issued warnings of developing drought in southern Africa in 1994-1995, as it had in 1991-1992, several months in advance of the harvest. Since its inception in 1975, the System had issued 338 special alerts to the international community on the deteriorating food supply prospects in various parts of the world. GIEWS also analysed emergency food aid requests from Governments, which resulted in the approval

[a]YUN 1993, p. 1257.

of 40 emergency operations in 1994-1995, for a total value of $1.4 billion.

## Activities

### Emergency assistance

At least 26 countries worldwide faced acute food shortages in 1995, requiring exceptional and/or emergency food assistance. More than half of those were in Africa, which remained the continent most seriously affected by food shortages. Global food shipments in 1995-1996 fell to the lowest levels in 20 years.

In spite of some good harvests in eastern Africa, large-scale emergency assistance was needed in the region throughout 1995. Projects focused on the provision of agricultural inputs, coordination of emergency assistance, and support for urgent rehabilitation of the agricultural sector in Rwanda, paving the way for reconstruction of its economy. Overall, the food supply situation was satisfactory in western and central Africa, reflecting above-average to record harvests in most countries.

Elsewhere, food supply situations remained grave in Afghanistan, Azerbaijan, Bosnia and Herzegovina, Cambodia, Georgia, Iraq, Kyrgyzstan, Mongolia, Nepal and Tajikistan. The situations in Armenia, Haiti and the Republic of Moldova were improving, though some assistance was still needed.

The FAO Office for Special Relief Operations (OSRO) concentrated operational activities on Bosnia and Herzegovina, where it supplied basic agricultural inputs; Iraq, where it provided plant protection, seeds, veterinary vaccines, goats and feed; and Rwanda, where it supported the urgent rehabilitation of the agricultural sector. Altogether, there were 27 newly approved OSRO projects in 1995, amounting to $21 million. During the year, OSRO participated in inter-agency missions to Angola, Bosnia and Herzegovina, Burundi, the Caribbean islands, Iraq, the Lao People's Democratic Republic, Liberia, Rwanda, Sierra Leone, Somalia and the Sudan; and issued additional appeals for Afghanistan, Haiti, Malawi/Mozambique/Zambia, the former Yugoslavia and Zaire. It appointed coordinators for agricultural intervention in Angola, Bosnia and Herzegovina, Iraq, Liberia, Rwanda and Sierra Leone.

In order to continue meeting emergency food needs, the FAO Conference in October 1995 established pledging targets for 1997 and 1998 at $1.3 billion. A pledging conference for that purpose was to be convened at UN Headquarters in 1996.

### Field programmes

In 1995, 1,850 field projects, totalling $264.1 million, were under way, providing technical advice and support in all areas of food and agriculture, fisheries, forestry and rural development. They were funded through trust funds provided by donor countries and other international sources ($165.1 million), the United Nations Development Programme ($58.3 million) and the Technical Cooperation Programme from FAO's regular budget ($40.8 million).

During the year, international financing institutions approved some $2 billion in funding for 31 agricultural and rural development projects, prepared with the assistance of FAO's Investment Centre. Total investments in those projects, including contributions from recipient Governments, amounted to $3.3 billion.

### Crops

Seeking to ensure that agricultural production met expanding human needs, FAO undertook a range of activities, including conservation and use of plant biological diversity; crop management and diversification; seed production and improvement; crop protection; agricultural engineering and prevention of food losses; and food and agricultural industries.

Discussions were under way in 1995 to make legally binding the Prior Informed Consent Clause of the 1985 International Code of Conduct on the Distribution and Use of Pesticides. The clause, which was amended to the Code in 1989, maintained that pesticides restricted or banned for health or environmental reasons should not be exported without the consent of the importing country.

FAO continued its Integrated Pest Management programmes, conducted in close collaboration with non-governmental organizations, which emphasized biological control methods and training of farmers to diagnose and treat pest damage. Drawing attention to desert locust invasions in Africa and Asia, including Pakistan and India, in October the FAO Conference urged the establishment of a relief fund to cope with emergency situations arising from such invasions.

The organization continued to provide support for the global coordination of the Special Programme for Food Security, launched in 1994 to assist target countries to increase food production and productivity as rapidly as possible, primarily through the widespread adoption by farmers of available improved production technologies.

### Livestock

In 1995, FAO responded to a major outbreak of a cattle disease in southern Tanzania, which threatened Zambia, Malawi and the rest of southern Africa, with a $334,000 control campaign. The project was initiated by FAO's newly established Emergency Prevention System for Transboundary Plant Pests and Animal Diseases.

FAO's ongoing livestock activities included improving feed resources and feeding systems, animal health, genetic resources and production systems, including both the meat and dairy sectors. Sustainable feeding systems were given high priority. In semi-arid and arid zones, FAO concentrated on improving fodder conservation, fodder trees and grazing systems. In humid and sub-humid regions, it focused on providing high-quality feed from nitrogen-fixing legumes adapted to local means of production.

### Fisheries

In March, the FAO Committee on Fisheries agreed on the Rome Consensus on World Fisheries, which called for additional urgent action to eliminate overfishing and rebuild and enhance depleting fish stocks. The Committee urged member countries to minimize wasteful fisheries practices, develop further sustainable aquaculture, rehabilitate fish habitats and develop fisheries for new and alternate species based on scientific principles of sustainability and responsible management. Without such action, further declines would occur in the 70 per cent of the world's fish stocks which were regarded as fully exploited, overexploited, depleted or recovering.

*The State of World Fisheries and Aquaculture*, released in 1995, warned that unless the international community coped with the twin problems of overfishing and overcapacity, world per capita fish consumption would fall over the next 15 years. The report emphasized that in order to keep per capita consumption at current levels, aquaculture would have to double its production.

In October, the FAO Conference adopted a Code of Conduct for Responsible Fisheries. It also urged acceptance of the 1993 Agreement to Promote Compliance with International Conservation and Management Measures by Fishing Vessels on the High Seas, so as to bring it into force as soon as possible. As at 31 October 1995, only 7 countries had accepted the Agreement, which needed 18 acceptances to bring it into force.

### Forestry

The twelfth session of the FAO Committee on Forestry met in March 1995 and agreed on the Rome Statement on Forestry, which asked for full and urgent implementation of decisions taken at the Earth Summit in Rio de Janeiro, Brazil, in 1992. The Summit had called for the protection, sustainable management and conservation of the world's forests. The first *State of the World's Forests* report was released by FAO during the session, which was attended by 121 countries. It was the first major study on the role of forests in sustainable development and the state of forest resources. It brought together information from the Forest Resources Assessment and other important FAO studies, including two regional reviews in Europe and Latin America and the Caribbean.

### Food standards and nutrition

In 1995, the Codex Alimentarius Commission—the joint FAO/WHO body responsible for international food standards—adopted recommendations on the Maximum Residue Limits for growth-promoting hormones used in food production, despite a European Union ban on the use of these substances in its member countries. Veterinary drugs promoting animal growth were used in major meat-producing countries such as the United States and Australia. The Codex Commission approved the maximum residue levels after extensive review of scientific information indicated their safety to the consumer.

FAO continued to promote better nutrition by providing member countries with advice, information and technical assistance in three broad areas: formulation and implementation of national food policies and nutrition programmes; provision of technical and legislative advice on measures to ensure the quality and safety of food supplied; and assessment and monitoring of nutrition situations, including monitoring the effects of food and agricultural policies and development activities on nutrition.

### Plant and animal genetic resources

In 1995, FAO established the World Information and Early Warning System on Plant Genetic Resources, in order to obtain information on such resources and halt the loss and further erosion of valuable plant germplasm of food crops. The System, featuring a database with information on about 4.8 million germplasm accessions held in some 1,220 genebanks or botanical gardens, also aimed to assess plant genetic resources erosion in seed collections as well as in natural stands.

In October, the FAO Conference decided to broaden the mandate of the Commission on Plant Genetic Resources to cover all components of biodiversity of relevance to food and agriculture and to rename it Commission on Genetic Resources for Food and Agriculture. The broadened mandate of the Commission was to be carried out through a step-by-step approach, beginning with animal genetic resources.

According to the 1995 edition of the *World Watch List for Domestic Animal Diversity*, published jointly by FAO and the United Nations Environment Programme, many of the world's 4,000 to 5,000 farm animal breeds were disappearing at an alarming rate, possibly as high as three breeds every two weeks. A global database, maintained by FAO as part of a comprehensive five-year programme begun in 1992 to conserve and promote the sustainable use of animal genetic resources, listed 3,882 breeds of 38 species, of which 873, or 30 per cent, were at risk.

*Information*

FAO continued to function as an information centre, collecting, analysing, interpreting and disseminating information through various media, including print, radio, television, video, film and photo displays and exhibitions. Materials produced included information booklets, technical documents, reference papers and reports of meetings, training manuals and audiovisuals.

Major FAO periodicals published on a regular basis included the annual *Food and Agricultural Legislation*, the *FAO Quarterly Bulletin of Statistics*, a forestry quarterly called *Unasylva*, the *World Animal Review* and *Plant Protection Bulletin*, both quarterlies, and the annual *Rural Development*. FAO yearbooks were issued on rural development, trade, fertilizers, forest products, field projects, fishery statistics and animal health.

AGROSTAT PC, an electronic version of FAO's *Statistical Yearbooks*, designed to be used on a simple personal computer, provided updated figures on all agriculture-related topics in six files: population, land use, production, trade, food balance sheets and forest products. FAO compiled and coordinated an extensive range of international databases on agriculture, fisheries, forestry, food and statistics. The two most important were AGRIS (the International Information System for the Agricultural Sciences and Technology) and CARIS (the Current Agricultural Research Information System). Other important statistical information produced by FAO included the Fisheries Statistical Database, Globefish Databank and Electronic Library, Forest Resources Information System, and the Geographic Information System. FAO operated the World Agricultural Information Centre (WAICENT) designed to meet the increasing supply and demand for and improve access to agricultural data, particularly to external users, via the Internet, floppy disks and CD-Roms. WAICENT can be reached on the World Wide Web at http://www.fao.org and on Gopher at gopher.fao.org.

### Secretariat

As at 31 December 1995, the number of staff employed at FAO headquarters was 2,682, of whom 960 were in the Professional or higher categories and 1,656 in the General Service category. Field project personnel and those in regional and country offices numbered 1,991. There were also 232 Associate Professional Officers working at headquarters, regional offices and in the field.

### Budget

The FAO Conference in 1995 approved a working budget for the 1996-1997 biennium of $650 million. The largest appropriation in that budget was $299 million for technical and economic programmes, followed by $113 million for development services.

## HEADQUARTERS AND OTHER OFFICES

### HEADQUARTERS

Food and Agriculture Organization of the United Nations
Viale delle Termi di Caracalla
00100 Rome, Italy
  *Telephone:* (39) (6) 52251
  *Fax:* (39) (6) 5225 3152
  *Telex:* 6585 FAO I
  *E-mail:* telex-room@fao.org
  *Internet sites:* www.fao.org and gopher.fao.org

### NEW YORK LIAISON OFFICE

Food and Agriculture Organization Liaison Office with the
  United Nations
1 United Nations Plaza, Room 1125
New York, N.Y. 10017, United States
  *Cable address:* FOODAGRI NEW YORK
  *Telephone:* (1) (212) 963-6036
  *Fax:* (1) (212) 888-6188
  *E-mail:* FAO-LONY@field.fao.org

Chapter IV

# United Nations Educational, Scientific and Cultural Organization (UNESCO)

The United Nations Educational, Scientific and Cultural Organization (UNESCO) continued in 1995 to promote cooperation among nations in education, science, culture and communication.

The General Conference convened its twenty-eighth session in 1995 (25 October–16 November) at the organization's headquarters in Paris. It adopted the medium-term strategy for 1996-2001 and the programme and budget for 1996-1997, which focused, in particular, on the needs of four priority groups: women, youth, the least developed countries and Africa. The Executive Board, consisting of members elected by the General Conference, held three sessions during the year.

The membership of UNESCO increased in 1995 to 184 with the admission of the Marshall Islands.

## Education

UNESCO activities towards the goal of education for all (EFA) in 1995 emphasized the development of flexible and diversified forms of education and training at all levels. Through its basic EFA programme, the organization sought to increase the provision and improve the quality and relevance of basic education, especially for girls and women and other particularly disadvantaged groups, such as street children. The 1995 *World Education Report*, published in December, focused on progress towards education for all women and girls and on gender issues in basic education.

Efforts continued to promote EFA in the nine high-population developing countries. Following a special meeting at the World Summit for Social Development in March, the nine countries organized a ministerial meeting in Indonesia (12-16 September) to review progress towards the goals agreed at their 1993 New Delhi summit meeting.[a]

UNESCO continued to provide the secretariat for the International EFA Forum, which launched a mid-decade review by member States of progress towards EFA, in accordance with the Jomtien Framework for Action to Meet Basic Learning Needs, which was adopted at the 1990 World Conference on Education for All, held in Thailand.

Special attention was paid to the educational needs of the least developed countries. Among 1995 initiatives towards basic EFA were new programmes and cooperative projects in Bangladesh and several African States. In addition, the organization provided technical support to rebuild the education systems of the emerging States of Eastern Europe and Central Asia and increased assistance to the education of refugees in all regions.

The Learning without Frontiers Coordination Unit was established and became operational in 1995. It undertook pilot projects in support of networking government, non-governmental organization and community initiatives in basic education in Costa Rica and Mauritius. Preparations were under way for a similar project in India.

In addition to EFA, UNESCO placed a high priority on the renewal and advancement of higher levels of education and the reform of education systems as a whole from the perspective of lifelong education—secondary education, technical and vocational education, teacher education and higher education. The organization continued its Project 2000+ on scientific and technological literacy for all and expanded the International Project on Technical and Vocational Education.

Under the 1991 initiative to foster inter-university cooperation (UNITWIN) the UNITWIN/UNESCO Chairs Programme expanded in 1995 to a total of 133 established Chairs and 29 inter-university networks, linking higher education institutions and research centres in more than 90 member States. Another UNESCO partnership, the Associated Schools Project network, increased to 3,562 schools in 126 countries by the end of the year.

In the area of preventive education against drug abuse and AIDS, activities focused on awareness-building, technical assistance and preparation of teaching and information materials in support of national initiatives. UNESCO also participated in the UN co-sponsored programme on HIV/AIDS.

## Natural sciences

Under the programme on science for progress and the environment, UNESCO activities in 1995

[a]YUN 1993, p. 1260.

focused on science and technology for development and on environment and natural resources management, including follow-up to the 1992 UN Conference on Environment and Development (UNCED), earth sciences, terrestrial ecosystems, marine science–related issues and hydrology and water resources management. As task manager within the UN system for two chapters of Agenda 21, adopted by UNCED, UNESCO continued to give priority attention to science and to education and public awareness–raising for sustainable development.

The preparatory process for the 1996 World Solar Summit continued, promoting collaboration on renewable energy technology, development and deployment and the provision of energy services, particularly for rural and remote areas in developing countries. Nine regional high-level expert meetings were held and assistance was given to member States in establishing national and regional solar councils and programmes.

In 1995, UNESCO organized eight conferences in developing countries through its University-Industry-Science Partnership (UNISPAR) programme. Among other cooperative efforts in 1995, the International Centre for Theoretical Physics, in cooperation with UNESCO and the International Atomic Energy Agency, provided advanced training for some 2,000 physicists; UNESCO and Iowa State University (United States) supported the International Institute for Theoretical and Applied Physics in Ames, Iowa; the second phase of the UNESCO/Third World Academy of Sciences project on South-South cooperation in research training was launched in August; and the international programme Chemistry for Life was carried out in partnership with the United Nations Industrial Development Organization (UNIDO), the International Centre of Pure and Applied Chemistry, and the International Organization for Chemical Sciences in Development.

Through its Biotechnology Action Council, UNESCO provided support and training for young researchers in the fields of microbial, plant, industrial and environmental biotechnologies. In May, an agreement was signed between UNESCO and the Government of Poland on the establishment and running of the International Institute of Molecular and Cell Biology in Warsaw. The Institute opened in October, when the Conference on New Frontiers in Cell and Molecular Biology was convened. UNESCO and the International Centre for Genetic Engineering and Biotechnology organized the third South-North Human Genome Conference (4-7 December) in New Delhi, India. Together with the International Cell Research Organization, UNESCO organized 14 training courses in 1995 for young researchers in such fields as molecular genetics, biotechnology of cell cultures, and monoclonal antibodies.

UNESCO's Intergovernmental Oceanographic Commission held its eighteenth session from 13 to 27 June in Paris, adopting its 1996-1997 programme of work. It also considered preparations for the 1998 International Year of the Ocean; the launching of the UNESCO interdisciplinary project on environment and development in coastal regions and small islands; creation of the Global Coral Reef Monitoring Network; and implementation of the Harmful Algal Blooms programme.

The World Network of Biosphere Reserves under the Man and the Biosphere (MAB) programme, whose aim was to improve the relationship between humankind and the environment, consisted of 337 sites in 85 countries. MAB convened the International Conference on Biosphere Reserves in Seville, Spain (20-25 March), which resulted in the Seville Strategy for Biosphere Reserves and the Statutory Framework for the World Network of Biosphere Reserves. The documents were reviewed by the MAB International Council (Paris, 12-16 June) and subsequently endorsed by the UNESCO General Conference.

The International Hydrological Programme, which supported 44 projects, met in Paris from 30 January to 4 February. The International Geological Correlation Programme, which had 52 earth sciences projects worldwide, held regional meetings in Austria and Kenya.

## Social and human sciences

UNESCO activities in the social sciences during 1995 continued to promote knowledge of and adherence to the values of human rights, democracy, peace and tolerance. The organization's work against all forms of discrimination, xenophobia and racism gave special priority to minorities and indigenous people. In October 1995, the UN High Commissioner for Human Rights and the UNESCO Director-General signed a Memorandum of Understanding.

UNESCO served as lead agency for the 1995 UN Year for Tolerance, which brought a campaign for tolerance to every region of the world through seven high-level regional conferences. There was also a diverse year-long programme of meetings, concerts, film and theatre festivals, poster contests, broadcasts, exhibitions and publications. A Declaration of Principles on Tolerance and a Follow-up Plan of Action were adopted by the General Conference on UNESCO's fiftieth anniversary—16 November—and that day was proclaimed the International Day of Tolerance (see also PART FOUR Chapter IX). Two new prizes were established by the UNESCO Executive Board: the UNESCO-Madanjeet Singh Prize for the Promotion of Tolerance and Non-Violence and the UNESCO Prize for Children's and Young People's Literature in the Service of Tolerance.

UNESCO contributed to the 1995 World Summit for Social Development and its follow-up (see PART FOUR, Chapter IX) by mobilizing the intellectual community and helping to formulate strategies against poverty, unemployment and social exclusion. The organization published a booklet, *Perspectives on Social Development*, and a series of papers on development issues and the integration of disabled people.

In 1995, UNESCO intensified its efforts to encourage member States to develop appropriate policies and programmes to stimulate the active participation of youth in their societies. Consolidation of the INFOYOUTH networks helped improve young people's access to information on training opportunities, international exchanges and other relevant subjects. The World Collective Consultation on Youth NGOs was convened in Japan in September.

## Culture

UNESCO's cultural activities in 1995 highlighted the cultural dimension of development, protecting cultural heritage and promoting culture identities and intercultural dialogue. Under the World Decade for Cultural Development (1988-1997), efforts were made to strengthen cultural information exchange networks and integrate a cultural dimension into development policies and projects. Culturally sensitive development strategies were discussed by the General Conference and the UN General Assembly in the context of a report entitled "Our Creative Diversity", which was submitted in November by the World Commission on Culture and Development.

To highlight intercultural dialogue, a series of projects focused on the routes that linked cultures and civilizations through history, and the consequent interactions and impact on world culture. The series took the form of expeditions, films, studies and publications on the Silk Road in Central Asia; the Slave Route between Africa and the Americas; the Routes of al-Andalus, the meeting point between Europe, the Maghreb and Black Africa; and the Roads of Faith leading to Jerusalem. In October, an international conference on Slav Cultures and modern civilizations was held in Sofia, Bulgaria.

By the end of the year, the number of sites of outstanding value which should be preserved as the heritage of all humankind that were included on UNESCO's list of protected cultural and natural sites had risen to 469. The sites were selected by the World Heritage Committee from candidates proposed by the 144 States parties to the 1972 Convention for the Protection of the World Cultural and Natural Heritage. International youth groups were organized in Mali, Romania and the Russian Federation for the protection of cultural heritage sites, and the first World Heritage Youth Forum was held in Norway in June.

The UNESCO Prize for the Promotion of the Arts was awarded to artists Kcho (Cuba), Marja Kanervo (Finland) and Matej Kren (Slovakia); and the Crafts Prize was awarded to E. Contreras Aquise, a painter from Peru. The Intergovernmental Committee of the Universal Copyright Convention, in June, examined legal problems relating to the production, dissemination and exploitation of multimedia works, protecting the findings of research in genetics, and piracy of intellectual works and other productions. In 1995, UNESCO published 135 titles and produced 9 CD-ROMs, including a multimedia CD-ROM on the organization's history to mark UNESCO's fiftieth anniversary.

## Communication

To encourage the free flow of ideas and help reinforce communication, information and informatics in developing countries, UNESCO in 1995 continued its efforts to ensure press freedom and the independence of the media. Support was provided to independent media in conflict zones. An international symposium on women and the media (Toronto, Canada) contributed to the Fourth World Conference on Women.

The main operational tool of UNESCO's communications strategy, the International Programme for the Development of Communication, celebrated its fifteenth anniversary in 1995. Since its creation, the Programme had provided some $65 million to fund 600 projects worldwide. In November, a network of UNESCO Chairs in Communication was officially inaugurated with nine chairs in Canada, Europe and Latin America.

Through its Memory of the World Programme, which aimed at safeguarding the recorded memory of humanity, UNESCO continued international campaigns, such as the programme for the restoration of the National and University Library of Bosnia and Herzegovina. In 1995, the Programme's mandate was enlarged to cover trends in information technologies, as well as legal aspects of electronic information.

The General Information Programme continued to promote cooperation in the field of information and access to knowledge (libraries, archives and documentation), with emphasis on tools for information management. In September, the Intergovernmental Informatics Programme launched 19 projects aimed at training informatics specialists. An African Regional Symposium on Telematics for Development (Addis Ababa, Ethiopia, April) addressed the interdisciplinary issue of new information and communication technologies.

## Secretariat

As at 31 December, UNESCO had a full-time staff of 2,438, of whom 1,012 were in the Professional or higher categories, drawn from 153 nationalities, and 1,426 were in the General Service category.

## Budget

The General Conference of UNESCO, at its 1993 session, approved a budget of $455,490,000 for the 1994-1995 biennium. In 1995, the General Conference approved a budget of $518,445,000 for the 1996-1997 biennium. The level of the Working Capital Fund was fixed at $25,000,000 and the total assessment on member States after deducting miscellaneous income was $516,445,000.

NOTE: For further information on UNESCO's activities in 1995, see *Report of the Director-General 1994-1995*, published by UNESCO.

## *HEADQUARTERS AND OTHER OFFICES*

HEADQUARTERS
UNESCO House
7 Place de Fontenoy
75352 Paris 07-SP, France
*Cable address:* UNESCO PARIS
*Telephone:* (33) (1) 45-68-10-00
*Fax:* (33) (1) 45-67-16-90
*Telex:* 204461 PARIS
        270602 PARIS

NEW YORK LIAISON OFFICE
United Nations Educational, Scientific and Cultural Organization
2 United Nations Plaza, Room 900
New York, N.Y. 10017, United States
*Cable address:* UNESCORG NEWYORK
*Telephone:* (1) (212) 963-5995
*Fax:* (1) (212) 355-5627

UNESCO also maintained liaison offices in Geneva and Vienna.

Chapter V

# World Health Organization (WHO)

In 1995, the World Health Organization (WHO) continued its work in areas such as disease prevention and control; encouraging primary health care and ending malnutrition; promoting the health of specific population groups; addressing health issues related to environment, development and lifestyle; and supporting health care, organization and management worldwide.

The World Health Assembly, which is the governing body of WHO, in its forty-eighth session (Geneva, 1-12 May), adopted a series of resolutions calling for further action by the organization on the following public health issues: emergency and humanitarian action; cooperation with countries in greatest need; reproductive health; new, emerging and re-emerging infectious diseases; prevention of hearing impairment; control of diarrhoeal diseases and acute respiratory infections; an international strategy for tobacco control; and assistance for health needs of the Arab population in the occupied Arab territories. As an outcome of the 1995 Assembly, WHO published, for the first time, an annual report on world health, which outlined poverty as the main cause of disease in the world. The Assembly adopted a regular budget for 1996-1997 representing a growth of 2.5 per cent from the 1994-1995 figure.

As at 31 December 1995, WHO membership stood at 190, with the addition of one new member (Palau) during the year. In addition, two countries were associate members.

## Health system infrastructure

During 1995, WHO provided technical support in the area of health infrastructure to several low-income countries to ensure the inclusion of health considerations in economic development projects. Research was also initiated with the goal of improving urban health services. A health system research network was set up linking countries of North, Central and South America. Regional task forces for this type of research were set up in the Eastern Mediterranean and South-East Asia. In Europe, the focus was on the countries of eastern Europe, where health systems research was especially weak.

## Health policy

WHO continued to direct action and resources towards countries rather than specific programmes, emphasizing the links between poverty and ill-health through its focus on intensified cooperation with countries and people most in need. This initiative had 28 participating countries in 1995, which WHO assisted in developing health policy, strengthening health systems and putting sustainable-health financing systems into place. In addition, WHO worked with other agencies and with donors to encourage a more focused and increased flow of funds and their more effective use by countries. It also supported countries in ensuring regular access to drugs.

With a view to improving coordination, WHO sought collaboration with other intergovernmental and non-governmental organizations active in the health field. Within the framework of the United Nations, an initiative for African economic recovery and development was launched, with health-sector reform and disease control as one of its components. During 1995, WHO strengthened its collaboration with the World Bank and several regional development banks, the Organization for African Unity and the European Union.

At the World Summit for Social Development (Copenhagen, March 1995) (see PART FOUR, Chapter IX), WHO advocated strengthening partnerships for health development and mobilizing the political commitment to view it in the context of economic and social development.

## Public information and education for health

WHO continued in 1995 to disseminate health information widely, particularly in the form of epidemiological and statistical data, reports, guidelines, training modules and periodicals. For that purpose, increasing use was made of informatics and telematics, including the Internet.

During the year, the organization was developing an action plan, covering the period to the beginning of the twenty-first century, in the areas of health promotion and health education, building infrastructures around existing economic and other arrangements and WHO's regional structure. South Africa was taking the lead in southern Africa, and Hungary in Europe. A health promotion alliance was being developed among the more populated countries, including China, India, Indonesia, the Russian Federation and the United States.

WHO also launched in 1995 an initiative for re-orienting medical education and public health training towards the twenty-first century. The organization, along with the Kellogg Foundation, supported Bolivia, Mexico and Zimbabwe in taking practical measures to establish an optimally balanced and productive workforce of health care personnel. WHO also supported training in health care financing and health insurance and in quality assurance. Through its fellowships programme, the organization continued to provide opportunities for carefully selected health professionals to obtain the necessary skills to direct, guide and support health development in their countries, within the framework of human resources planning and clearly defined priorities.

### Health protection and promotion

WHO promoted community-based prevention of-noncommunicable diseases as the strategy to reduce risk factors and morbidity and increase life expectancy. In 1995, the organization coordinated four major cardiovascular disease research projects and supported epidemiological surveys (for instance, on diabetes) in several countries. It also supported the development of national programmes for the control of major hereditary diseases and congenital malformations, and monitored international human genome research.

WHO's INTERHEALTH project revealed unfavourable nutrition trends globally: in most countries the availability of dietary fat was increasing, whereas the availability of vegetable protein and total carbohydrates, particularly starch, was decreasing. WHO encouraged countries to reduce malnutrition and promote good nutrition and provided information on the prevention, management and monitoring of malnutrition. Forty-seven member States had adopted education programmes aimed at preventing non-communicable diseases related to lifestyle and diet.

WHO also provided normative information on monitoring, prevention and management of major crippling forms of malnutrition, with emphasis on protein-energy malnutrition and micronutrient malnutrition, such as iodine deficiency disorders, vitamin A deficiency, and nutritional anaemia. The organization also gave support to countries in dealing with infant and young child nutrition in emergency situations.

As part of its efforts to prevent food-borne illnesses, WHO was studying the microbiological contamination of foods and patterns of human behaviour that might lead to the growth or survival of _Vibrio cholerae_ and other food-borne pathogens. The organization issued a report recommending measures to control newly emerging food-borne pathogens such as trematodes.

The Joint FAO/WHO Codex Alimentarius Commission continued to ensure that internationallyagreed food standards, guidelines and other recommendations were consistent with health protection. With the creation of the World Trade Organization in 1995 (see PART SEVEN, Chapter XVIII), the Codex was used as the international reference for national requirements.

### Health of specific populations

WHO statistics demonstrated that since 1960 infant mortality had fallen from 130 to 60 per 1,000 live births and child mortality had fallen from 180 to 80 per 1,000 live births, largely as a result of immunization campaigns against six vaccine-preventable diseases (diphtheria, pertussis, tetanus, measles, tuberculosis and poliomyelitis), which had been undertaken with intensive support from WHO, the United Nations Children's Fund (UNICEF) and the international community. By 1995, the goal of 80 per cent coverage for those vaccines (except tetanus toxoid) had been achieved globally, but 25 countries (19 in Africa) still reported coverage below 50 per cent for all six vaccines. Comprehensive plans of action were developed in six African countries, but major efforts were still urgently needed to cover the remaining 19 countries.

Since the goal of global eradication of poliomyelitis was set in 1988, reported cases of the disease had declined by about 85 per cent by 1995. Between 1991 and 1995, global measles immunization coverage had remained at about 80 per cent; since immunization began, the number of cases had declined by 70 per cent and the number of deaths by 83 per cent. The disease was targeted for elimination in the Americas by the year 2000, and many other countries were pursuing innovative immunization strategies.

Substantial progress was made globally in the elimination of neonatal tetanus, particularly in the Americas and South-East Asia. By 1995, more than 700,000 deaths were being prevented annually through routine immunization of women with tetanus toxoid, and through improved hygienic birth practices. In 1980, 76 countries reported fewer than one neonatal tetanus death per 1,000 live births annually; by 1995, the number of countries had increased to 122.

WHO, along with UNICEF, jointly developed an approach for the integrated management of the sick child, which gave attention to both prevention and treatment of childhood disease. The WHO/UNICEF course on management of childhood illness enabled health workers in outpatient clinics and health centres to manage effectively infant and childhood illnesses such as diarrhoea, pneumonia, measles, malaria and malnutrition in an integrated fashion. The course was based on treatment guidelines developed by WHO and covering the most common potentially fatal conditions.

Recent WHO research had confirmed strong links between health, school attendance and education attainment. The organization's global school health initiative was concerned with the various hazards to which the world's school-age children and adolescents—more than 1 billion, almost 700 million of whom were primary school age (6-11 years)—were exposed, such as injuries, sexually transmitted diseases and substance abuse.

Recognizing that the key to controlling cervical cancer in women was health education, early detection and screening, WHO pioneered pragmatic, realistic approaches for its early detection by visual inspection, for affordable radiotherapy and for the relief of pain and symptoms of incurable cases. The International Agency for Research on Cancer, which coordinated and conducted epidemiological laboratory research aimed at developing strategies for cancer prevention, in 1995 published conclusive evidence of the role of human papilloma virus as a cause of cervical cancer. The Agency assessed potential vaccines against the virus and investigated methods of screening for precancerous and cancerous lesions of the cervix.

Also recognizing that reproductive health was central to health in general, WHO set up a new programme on that subject, bringing together various related activities and ensuring better coordination of research and technical support. The programme was designed to draw up a comprehensive strategy, define norms and standards, and develop technical tools for addressing reproductive health concerns in countries.

A major issue for WHO in the field of ageing and health was healthy ageing in women. In 1995, the third meeting of the Global Commission on Women's Health focused on the health conditions that women faced later in life and strategies that would help older women enjoy good health and improved quality of life.

## Environment, health and development

In 1995, WHO cooperated with the United Nations Development Programme (UNDP), the World Bank and UNICEF to develop community participation approaches in the area of water supply and sanitation, which could also be effective in changing hygiene behaviour. As coordinator of the Water Supply and Sanitation Collaborative Council's working group on the promotion of sanitation, WHO supported several initiatives to raise awareness of the need for improved sanitation and promoted the partnership roles of international agencies, donors, ministries, nongovernmental organizations and academic institutions in that respect.

Among other WHO projects, the Healthy Cities network was expanded during 1995 and achieved specific environmental improvements, such as in reducing urban air pollution. The Global Environmental Monitoring System was tackling the problem of identification and control of emission sources. Capacity for management of air quality was assessed in 20 cities to identify immediate needs for technical cooperation.

WHO also collaborated with UNDP, the World Bank and the United Nations Centre for Human Settlements (Habitat) in establishing a comprehensive strategy on the increasingly serious problem of disposal of health care wastes, particularly in urban areas.

## Disease prevention and control

WHO strengthened its capacity to combat new and re-emerging infectious diseases, as certain diseases had become increasingly resistant to antibiotic drugs. That was demonstrated with the outbreak of Ebola haemorrhagic fever in Zaire in 1995, when staff were mobilized and teams placed on site within 24 hours of notification of the outbreak, together with the supplies and equipment required to implement epidemic control measures. To prepare for such emergencies, WHO used innovative field technology and public health training programmes to support country surveillance and disease control, and was developing a network of public health laboratories to strengthen regional and international collaboration in the detection and control of outbreaks.

As part of its work in detecting and monitoring resistance to antimicrobials, WHO established an information system (WHONET) to support the global surveillance of bacterial resistance to antimicrobial agents, with the participation by the end of 1995 of 177 laboratories in 31 countries or areas.

During the year, WHO was active with partners, including UNICEF, in controlling diphtheria epidemics in the Russian Federation, some newly independent States and Mongolia. National immunization days were organized in late 1995, targeting the vulnerable population aged between 16 and 40.

In 1995, when the incidence of tuberculosis was on the rise, WHO issued training materials and a handbook on the subject of the disease and supported workshops in 15 countries. In February, WHO announced the composition of the influenza vaccine for the 1995–96 season, replacing two of the three components that had been included in the vaccine for the previous season.

WHO studies were carried out on various aspects of human immunodeficiency virus/acquired immunodeficiency syndrome (HIV/AIDS), such as the protective effect of the female condom, the efficacy of a long-acting vaginal microbicide; preparation of field-testing sites for vaccines; preventing mother-to-child transmission; and a number of sociological investigations. Training in condom promotion continued in most regions. WHO was involved during 1995 in the setting up of a joint United Nations programme on HIV/AIDS (UNAIDS), which was to become operational on 1 January 1996.

WHO concluded an agreement with Swiss Disaster Relief to provide technical assistance in epidemic diarrhoea control and preparedness, and established links with other agencies and organizations working in the same field. For instance, collaboration began with the International Federation of Red Cross and Red Crescent Societies in the newly independent States of Eastern Europe and Central Asia.

Under the southern African initiative for control of epidemic diarrhoea, a team in Harare, Zimbabwe, continued in 1995 to coordinate activities aimed at improved preparedness and response to outbreaks of cholera and epidemic dysentery. Five African countries received support in the areas of policy formulation, developing surveillance systems and strengthening laboratory services. Surveillance and control strategies were set up in refugee camps in the United Republic of Tanzania and Zaire. Six African countries faced with outbreaks of cholera or dysentery received technical assistance and emergency supplies.

WHO helped to fight malaria on many fronts in 1995. It established an interregional system for monitoring drug resistance in South-East Asia and the western Pacific; supported research on such subjects as drug regimens and new diagnostic techniques; provided training for programme managers, specialists, district medical officers and community health workers; issued training materials; and assisted in control measures in refugee camps in Burundi, Rwanda, Tanzania and Zaire. WHO-led research enabled scientists to modify the genes of *Plasmodium-falciparum*, the deadliest malaria parasite, opening up the possibility of developing new techniques for diagnosis and drug and vaccine development. The organization also supported national control programmes in Indonesia, Myanmar and Thailand designed to eliminate the mosquito vectors of dengue fever and dengue haemorrhagic fever.

WHO also participated in implementing the vaccination campaign that controlled the epidemic of jungle yellow fever in Peru in 1995, the largest

outbreak recorded since 1950. It provided technical support and diagnostic reagents and assisted in vaccine procurement for the immunization strategy used to control Japanese encephalitis in endemic areas of India, Sri Lanka and Thailand. In regard to another insect-borne disease, the organization set up a leishmaniasis surveillance network of 14 institutions worldwide and cooperated with the Sudan and Bangladesh in combating this disease, mainly through the use of insecticide-impregnated bednets. It prepared guidelines for the control of African trypanosomiasis (sleeping sickness) on behalf of Angola and Zaire, developed plans of action for other countries and established a revolving fund for the supply of drugs to national programmes. Campaigns to combat onchocerciasis in African countries and to eliminate Chagas disease from countries in South America also made good progress during 1995.

During the year, WHO reassessed the distribution and prevalence of schistosomiasis in the world and its social and economic impact. Trials demonstrated the safety and efficacy of a combination of albendazole against common intestinal helminths and praziquantel against schistosomiasis.

With dracunculiasis (guinea-worm disease) on the verge of eradication, WHO's priorities were to facilitate the work of the independent International Commission for the Certification of Eradication, created in 1995, and to achieve the interruption of transmission as quickly as technically feasible. The objectives were to search for remaining, unknown foci of the disease; to verify whether low-risk countries were dracunculiasis-free; and to secure the necessary funding to complete the eradication process.

### Budget

At its 1995 session, the World Health Assembly adopted a budget of $842,654,000 for the 1996-1997 biennium, which represents a 2.5 per cent increase over the 1994-1995 figure of $822,101,000.

NOTE: For further details of WHO activities, see *The World Health Report 1996*, published by the organization.

## *HEADQUARTERS AND OTHER OFFICES*

HEADQUARTERS
World Health Organization
20 Avenue Appia
CH-1211 Geneva 27, Switzerland
  *Cable address:* UNISANTE GENEVA
  *Telephone:* (41) (22) 791-21-11
  *Fax:* (41) (22) 791-07-46
  *Telex:* 415416

WHO OFFICE AT THE UNITED NATIONS
2 United Nations Plaza
New York, N.Y. 10017, United States
  *Cable address:* UNISANTE NEW YORK
  *Telephone:* (1) (212) 963-6001
  *Fax:* (1) (212) 223-2920
  *Telex:* 234292

   WHO also maintained regional offices in Alexandria, Egypt; Brazzaville, Congo; Copenhagen, Denmark; Manila, Philippines; New Delhi, India; and Washington, D.C.

Chapter VI

# International Bank for Reconstruction and Development (World Bank)

Established in 1945, the International Bank for Reconstruction and Development (World Bank) continued in 1995 to help promote economic and social progress in developing nations by raising productivity. Together with its affiliate, the International Development Association (IDA), the World Bank provided loans to the developing world as well as assistance in designing and implementing policies to expand markets and strengthen economies of developing countries. The use of its guarantee powers, which became a standard operational tool of the World Bank during fiscal 1995, was part of the Bank's role in managing the rapid changes in the new global economy across a continuum of different country needs with a flexible array of interventions.

During the year, the Bank demonstrated its flexibility and responsiveness to diverse client needs in a number of ways: through approval of $1 billion in finance to support financial sector reform in Mexico; emergency assistance to the Russian Federation to contain and clean up a massive oil spill 1,000 miles north-east of Moscow near the Arctic circle; financing of emergency recovery programmes in Burundi and Rwanda; and provision of emergency assistance to Haiti to halt that country's economic and social deterioration.

The Debt-reduction Facility continued to provide low-income countries with grant funds to reduce commercial debt that was public, external, non-collateralized and unguaranteed. The facility was financed through contributions from the Bank's net income and from donors. Eight operations were completed in 1995 (for Bolivia, Guyana, Mozambique, Niger, Sao Tome and Principe, Sierra Leone, Uganda, Zambia), utilizing about $79.6 million Bank resources from the facility and $74.3 million in co-financing to extinguish about $1 billion in principal. Eight additional operations (Albania, Ethiopia, Guinea, Mauritania, Nicaragua, Senegal, United Republic of Tanzania, Viet Nam) were in preparation.

The International Finance Corporation (IFC), another bank affiliate, approved financing of $2.9 million for 213 projects. The Multilateral Investment Guarantee Agency, the youngest member of the World Bank Group, continued to encourage direct foreign investment by guaranteeing (or insuring) private investments against specific non-commercial notes.

While 25 countries had "graduated" or phased out their reliance on World Bank lending, in 1995 the Republic of Korea became the first country ever to progress from being a purely concessional borrower from IDA, to being an IDA donor and a World Bank graduate. The Republic of Korea reached the milestone with the signing on 3 March 1995 of its two final loan agreements with the Bank.

At the end of fiscal 1995 (1 July 1994–30 June 1995), World Bank membership totalled 178, with admission pending for Bosnia and Herzegovina, Brunei Darussalam and the Federal Republic of Yugoslavia.

In March, World Bank executive directors unanimously appointed James D. Wolfensohn as the Bank's ninth president, for a term of five years beginning 1 June 1995.

## Lending operations

Gross distributions by the Bank to countries in fiscal 1995 totalled $12,672 million, an increase of 21 per cent over fiscal 1994. Disbursement performance was higher than originally expected in Europe and Central Asia, mostly due to adjustment operations, and in the Latin America and Caribbean and the East Asia and Pacific regions, where, although the adjustment portfolio was declining, disbursements for investment projects were accelerating.

The largest borrower of Bank funds was Mexico ($2,387 million for six projects), followed by China ($2,370 million for 13 projects) and Russia ($1,741 million for nine projects). One $20 million project in the West Bank and Gaza was approved. The project, financed by the $50 million Trust Fund for Gaza, was financing the immediate needs of the education and health sectors and addressed institutional development objectives in the two sectors. Bank commitments amounted to $16.9 billion, up $2.6 billion over the fiscal 1994 total. A major increase was posted in the Europe and Central Asia region, which saw commitments rise from $3.7 billion for 42 projects to $4.5 billion for 58 projects.

To meet a growing demand for support of private sector investment, the Bank continued in fiscal 1995 to deliver innovative operations to support local financial institutions and markets. Financial sector adjustment loans totalled $1.2 billion, and financial intermediation loans amounted to $1.8 billion. The adjustment loans helped create a competitive financial sector, while the intermediation loans fed it. A $1 billion Financial Sector Restructuring Programme, approved in June 1995, involved the definition of comprehensive bank-failure resolution mechanisms and was detailed in specifying how accounting, auditing and supervision functions were to be upgraded.

At the World Summit for Social Development (Copenhagen, Denmark, March 1995) (see PART FOUR, Chapter IX), the Bank announced plans to increase social spending by 50 per cent over the next three years. It committed itself to providing $15 billion for basic social needs and a further $5 billion for water supply and sanitation programmes. Lending for basic social needs during fiscal 1995 alone amounted to $3,907 million: $2,097 for education-sector projects, $1,162 million for projects and components in the population, health and nutrition sector, and $648 million for projects in the social sector. In fiscal 1995, cumulative lending for education amounted to $21,579 million through more than 500 projects in over 100 countries. Lending for human resource development increased sharply from an average of about 5 per cent of the total in the 1980s to 15 per cent in the period fiscal 1993-1995. Since 1986, the Bank had loaned more than $800 million to 51 HIV/AIDS projects in nearly 40 countries, and, between fiscal 1993 and fiscal 1995, the Bank loaned almost $1 billion in support of population and reproductive health objectives.

Bank assistance to the poorest countries—those with a per capita gross national product of $695 or less (in terms of 1993 United States dollars)— totalled $3,770 million. Lending during fiscal 1995 for projects in the Bank's programme of targeted interventions (PTI) was 32 per cent of total investment lending. Projects were included in the PTI if they included a specific mechanism for targeting the poor or if the proportion of the poor among project beneficiaries significantly exceeded their proportion in the overall population. Of the 27 adjustment operations approved during fiscal 1995 (not including three debt reduction loans), 14, or 52 per cent, were poverty focused.

## Multilateral Investment Guarantee Agency

The Multilateral Investment Guarantee Agency (MIGA), established in 1988 as the newest member of the World Bank Group, continued to help promote investment for economic development in member countries through guarantees to foreign investors against losses caused by non-commercial risks and through advisory and consultative serv-

ices. MIGA had its own operating and legal staff but drew on the Bank for administrative and other services.

During fiscal 1995, seven additional countries became members of MIGA, bringing its total membership to 128. An additional 24 developing countries and economies in transition were in the process of fulfilling membership requirements.

MIGA guarantee-programme results in fiscal 1995 exceeded fiscal 1994 records for the number of guarantee contracts executed (54 versus 38), the total amount of coverage issued ($672 million versus $372.6 million), the number of developing countries benefitted (21 versus 14) and the amount of income earned from premiums and commitment fees ($14.4 million versus $9.9 million). The contracts issued in fiscal 1995 facilitated total direct investment of about $2.5 billion and created an estimated 8,800 jobs in developing countries. MIGA issued for the first time significant amounts of coverage ($142 million) for infrastructure investments, including its first power and toll-road projects.

## Economic Development Institute

While much of the work of the World Bank Group was involved in the transfer of capital to developing countries, the Economic Development Institute (EDI) focused on the transfer of knowledge. During fiscal 1995, it held 167 conferences, seminars and workshops in all regions of the world, with particular focus on sub-Saharan Africa and the former Soviet Union. During the year, EDI published 47 titles in support of its programmes and made use of new information technologies, including videos, teleconferencing, the Internet and CD-ROMs.

Following elections in South Africa, EDI mounted a number of programmes there, including an interactive workshop on sustainable fiscal policies. Its Grass-roots Management Training Programme was extended to Burkina Faso, India, Nigeria and Senegal. Under that programme, EDI trained local trainers to pass on grass-roots management practices to poor, often illiterate women operating tiny enterprises.

## Co-financing

During the year, the Bank's Co-financing and Financial Advisory Services (CFS) continued to facilitate the flow of financial resources to developing countries by carrying out various activities related to co-financing, project finance and guarantees, private sector development and technical assistance financing. The volume of co-financing anticipated in support of World Bank-assisted operations in fiscal 1995 declined marginally to $8.2 billion. Official co-financing flows increased to $6.6 billion, while the volume of export credits and private co-financing fell from fiscal 1994 levels. In terms of lending instruments, investment loans attracted the largest volume of co-financing support, followed by structural adjustment and financial intermediation loans.

Japan continued to be the major source of bilateral co-financing, reaching a total of $1.2 billion for 17 projects approved during the year. Other large bilateral co-financing support came from Germany ($289 million equivalent), France ($264 million equivalent), the United Kingdom ($184 million equivalent) and the United States ($148 million equivalent). Total co-financing expected from multilateral financial institutions amounted to an additional $3.9 billion.

### Financing activiites

During fiscal 1995, the Bank raised $9 billion through medium- and long-term borrowings in seven currencies. After $1 billion of currency swaps and a notional par volume of $782 million of interest-rate swaps, all of the year's borrowings (except for $216 million raised in United States dollars to fund single-currency loans and minor residuals in vehicle currencies) were fixed-rate liabilities denominated in United States dollars, Japanese yen, Deutsche mark and Swiss francs.

As at 30 June 1995, short-term borrowings outstanding were $3.9 billion before and after swaps. Those comprised $2.6 billion from official sources through the Bank's central facility, $1.2 billion from market funding in United States dollar notes, and $0.1 billion from global multicurrency notes. The cost of those borrowings in fiscal 1995 was 5.85 per cent compared with 4.94 per cent at the end of fiscal 1994.

### Scholarships

In fiscal 1995, the World Bank Graduate Scholarship Programme awarded 106 scholarships to support graduate studies for mid-career officials of member countries.

### Capitalization

As at 30 June 1995, the total subscribed capital of the Bank was $176.4 billion, or 94 per cent of authorized capital of $184 billion. The permissible increase of net disbursements was $75.3 billion, or 38 per cent of the Bank's lending limit.

### Income, expenditures and reserves

The Bank's gross revenues totalled $9,372 million in fiscal 1995. Net income was $1,354 million, an increase of $303 million over the fiscal 1994 net income of $1,051 million. Expenses increased by some $460 million to $7,899 million. Administrative costs amounted to $842 million, i.e. $111 million more than in fiscal 1994. As at 30 June 1995, the Bank's reserves amounted to $17.2 billion. The reserves-to-loan ratio stood at 14.3 per cent.

### Secretariat

As at 30 June 1995, World Bank regular and fixed-term staff numbered 7,155, of whom 4,655 were higher-level staff representing 157 nations.

NOTE: For further details regarding the Bank's activities, see *The World Bank Annual Report 1995*.

## HEADQUARTERS AND OTHER OFFICE

The World Bank
1818 H Street, N.W.
Washington, D.C. 20433, United States
  *Cable address:* INTBAFRAD WASHINGTONDC
  *Telephone:* (1) (202) 477-1234
  *Fax:* (1) (202) 477-6391
  *Telex:* MCI 64145 WORLDBANK
      MCI 248423 WORLDBANK
  *World Wide Web:* HTTP://WWW.WORLDBANK.ORG
  *E-mail:* BOOKS@WORLDBANK.ORG

The World Bank Mission to the United Nations
809 UN Plaza, Suite 900
New York, N.Y. 10017, United States
  *Cable address:* INTBAFRAD NEWYORK
  *Telephone:* (1) (212) 963-6008
  *Fax:* (1) (212) 697-7020

Chapter VII

# International Finance Corporation (IFC)

The International Finance Corporation (IFC) was established in 1956 as an affiliate of the International Bank for Reconstruction and Development (World Bank) to promote economic development in developing countries by encouraging the growth of private enterprise and efficient capital markets. During fiscal year 1995 (1 July 1994–30 June 1995), IFC continued to encourage private-sector activity in the developing world by financing private-sector projects, mobilizing capital for companies, and providing technical assistance and advisory services to private businesses and Governments. IFC also continued to strengthen its environmental monitoring of projects and increase the provision of risk management services.

During the 1995 fiscal year, IFC membership increased to 165 with the admission of Armenia, Georgia, the Republic of Moldova and Tajikistan.

## Financial and advisory services

During fiscal 1995, IFC's Board of Directors approved $2.9 billion in financing for 213 projects covering a broad range of sectors, compared with $2.6 billion for 231 projects during fiscal 1994. The total cost of IFC-financed projects was $19.5 billion and their primary focus was on infrastructure and the financial sector (including capital markets). Financing approved for IFC's own account included loans totalling $2 billion, equity and quasi-equity investments of $821.6 million, and guarantees, swaps and stand-by arrangements of $82.2 million.

Successful resource mobilization resulted in other investors and lenders providing $5.73 for every $1 in finance approved by IFC for its own account during fiscal 1995. Some of that financing was in the form of syndicated loans, in which IFC shared the commercial risks of projects with co-financing partners and provided its lender-of-record umbrella. In addition, IFC was involved in structuring and arranging the mobilization of $306 million through the launching of pooled investment vehicles for emerging markets. The total value of securities issued by IFC client companies on a private placement basis during fiscal 1995 amounted to $389.2 million.

Strong demand for IFC technical assistance and advisory services continued in 1995, resulting in a diversity of projects in over 100 countries or regions around the world. Projects in member countries included assistance in privatizing State-owned enterprises; supporting small and medium-sized enterprises by using project facilities, venture capital funds, credit lines and leasing companies; developing capital markets; drafting securities markets laws and regulations; shaping the regulatory environment for new types of financial institutions; establishing supervisory and enforcement entities and mechanisms for securities markets; and creating or developing stock exchanges.

The scope of IFC's Technical Assistance Trust Funds activities expanded in 1995, with 65 new projects in 32 countries. There was a continued emphasis on privatization and corporate restructuring, technical assistance in capital markets, development of project facilities, and advisory services in infrastructure and foreign investment.

Risk management services offered by IFC helped to provide private companies in developing countries with the tools to manage financial risks associated with movements in exchange rates, interest rates and commodity prices. In 1995, IFC approved seven risk management projects for companies and banks located primarily in Central Asia and Latin America.

IFC continued to help companies in several countries to phase out their use of ozone-depleting substances and increase their attention to eco-efficiency. It further strengthened its environmental monitoring and supervision of projects, reviewing more than 290 project proposals for potential environmental risks. It also sponsored global training programmes on environmental risk management, which attracted representatives of 102 private-sector institutions from 14 countries across Africa, Asia, Europe and Latin America.

IFC continued innovative work in promoting index funds as an alternate method for investors to access emerging markets. The first emerging market index fund for Latin America was developed in 1995 with an initial size of $60 million, succeeding a global index fund that IFC launched in 1994 with State Street Global Advisors, which had grown from $50 million to more than $1 billion. By June 1995, more than 1,450 companies were listed on the 26 emerging stock market indexes compiled and tracked by IFC's Emerging Markets Data Base, an increase of 10 per cent over 1994. South Africa—the world's largest emerging stock market—was added to IFC index coverage in April 1995.

## Regional projects

IFC approved investments in 67 countries during fiscal 1995, up from 65 in 1994, with Latin America and the Caribbean receiving the greatest dollar share (37 per cent); followed by Asia (24 per cent); Europe (14 per cent); Central Asia, the Middle East and North Africa (13 per cent); and sub-Saharan Africa (11 per cent). Fifty-seven of the 213 projects approved—representing $688.7 million in financing—were in countries with annual per capita incomes of $695 or less.

In sub-Saharan Africa, the IFC Board approved $431 million in financing for 51 projects in 21 countries during 1995. IFC's focus in the region was on developing small and medium-sized enterprises (SMEs), with 60 per cent of projects financed through the Africa Enterprise Fund (AEF), which furnished direct assistance to SMEs by providing financing of $100,000 to $1.5 million for small enterprise projects that cost between $250,000 and $5 million. IFC also established a new facility, the Enterprise Support Service for Africa (ESSA), to provide technical assistance to businesses after they secured financing.

In Asia, the IFC Board approved $1.44 billion in financing for 43 projects in 10 countries, plus two projects with a regional scope. IFC expanded its investment activities across a range of infrastructure projects during 1995, as rapid growth of the region's productive sectors created pressure on infrastructure which demanded large amounts of risk finance. IFC also helped to establish the first institution in the region (and in the developing world) to help securitize assets and issue new debt securities.

In Central Asia, the Middle East and North Africa (known as CAMENA), IFC approved $614 million in financing for 34 projects in nine countries, plus three projects with a regional scope. IFC made it a priority to open the region's infrastructure to private capital and develop its capital markets, as well as to support the development of natural resources and provide financing and advice for privatizing industrial complexes. A major achievement of IFC during the year was placement of $327 million in syndications covering 13 of the region's 34 projects.

In Europe, IFC approved $636 million in financing for 26 projects in 10 countries, plus two projects with a regional scope. Its broad strategy was to assist with the transition to successful market economies through a range of instruments, of which technical assistance and advisory services were the most important. IFC gave high priority to creating effective, well-regulated capital markets and investing in a number of equity funds to provide seed capital to promising ventures in the region.

In Latin America and the Caribbean, IFC approved $2.3 billion in financing for 53 projects in 17 countries, plus two projects with a regional scope. It actively supported the efforts of regional governments to strengthen local capital markets through investments, institution-building, and technical assistance and advisory work. Following the virtual closure of international capital markets to certain firms in Argentina and Mexico in 1994, IFC responded by helping to finance their capital expenditure programmes as well as to develop new instruments for regional investment. In Haiti, IFC was appointed as special adviser to the Government on the privatization of seven public enterprises encompassing key economic sectors.

## Foreign Investment Advisory Service

The Foreign Investment Advisory Service (FIAS), operated jointly with the World Bank, completed 26 assignments in 1995, including advisory projects in 25 countries and the implementation of projects in two others. FIAS also conducted a number of seminars on foreign investment policy, including a conference on new developments in foreign investment for policy makers and promotion agencies in Latin America and a round table on policy aspects of developing linkages between foreign and domestic firms in Asia. A multi-year programme of institutional development for the Board of Investment of Bangladesh was brought to a close during the year. FIAS also initiated a new research activity to review methods of privatization and assess their likely impact on the participation of foreign investors in the process.

## Financial performance

In fiscal year 1995, IFC's net income was $188 million, reflecting a 27 per cent drop from a record high in 1994 due mainly to the decline in the value of global stock markets. The equity portfolio generated $131 million in income. Capital gains totalled $82 million, while dividends increased markedly relative to 1994, reaching a record level of $50 million. As in previous years, a substantial share of dividend income came from companies paying dividends for the first time.

IFC's total committed portfolio increased by 20 per cent to $9.5 billion, up from $7.9 billion in fiscal 1994. The portfolio included loans and equity investments in 938 companies in 94 countries. IFC issued 19 AAA-rated bonds during 1995, totalling $2.08 billion in 10 currencies.

## Capital and retained earnings

At the end of fiscal year 1995, IFC's net worth reached $3.6 billion, compared with $3.2 billion at the end of fiscal 1994.

**Secretariat**

As at 30 June 1995, there were 832 regular staff at IFC, representing 97 countries.

NOTE: For further details of IFC's activities, see *International Finance Corporation Annual Report 1995*, published by the Corporation.

## *HEADQUARTERS AND OTHER OFFICE*

HEADQUARTERS
International Finance Corporation
1850 I Street, N.W.
Washington, DC 20433, United States
  *Telephone*: (1) (202) 473-7711
  *Fax:* (1) (202) 676-0365
  *E-mail:* information@ifc.org
  *Library:* ilibrary@ifc.org

NEW YORK OFFICE
International Finance Corporation
809 UN Plaza, Suite 900
New York, N.Y. 10017, United States
  *Cable address:* CORINTFIN NEWYORK
  *Telephone:* (1) (212) 963-6008
  *Fax:* (1) (212) 697-7020

Chapter VIII

# International Development Association (IDA)

The International Development Association (IDA) was established in 1960 as an affiliate of the International Bank for Reconstruction and Development (World Bank) to provide concessionary assistance to low-income countries in keeping with the Bank's goals of poverty reduction and economic development.

Efforts continued in 1995 to reduce the debt burden of severely indebted poor countries through support for policy reform, provision of IDA credits and extraordinary IDA allocation for countries engaged in debt workouts, "Fifth Dimension" allocations, funding from the Debt-reduction Facility for IDA-only countries to reduce commercial debt and technical assistance for debt management. Through the "Fifth Dimension" programme, financed out of IDA refolds, additional IDA allocations were provided to IDA-only countries that had outstanding World Bank debt, were current in their debt service to the Bank and IDA, and had an IDA-supported adjustment programme. Those allocations were in proportion to the Bank interest due in that year. In fiscal 1995 (1 July 1994–30 June 1995), the programme provided supplemental IDA allocations totalling $185.8 million to 14 countries.

The funds used by IDA—called credits to distinguish them from World Bank loans—were derived from several sources: subscriptions in convertible currencies from members; general replenishments from its more developed members; and transfers from the Bank's net earnings. Credits had 35- to 40-year maturities, including a 10-year grace period, and were interest free.

Fiscal year 1995 was the second year of the tenth replenishment of IDA (IDA-10), the agreed size of which was 13 billion special drawing rights (SDR). As at 30 June 1995, the donor funds made available for the IDA-10 period (fiscal 1994-1996) totalled SDR 7,642 million. During fiscal 1995, formal notifications to contribute to IDA-10 were received from Belgium, Portugal and Spain, which increased commitment authority to SDR 208 million. Part of the second tranche of IDA-10 contributions was not yet available, as the United States payment was about 8 per cent less than the agreed schedule and two other donors (Germany and Canada) exercised their right to withhold their contributions proportionately to the shortfall of the United States payment.

Other resources made available during the year included the transfer of SDR 207 million from the World Bank's fiscal 1994 net income and SDR 931 million of commitment authority against current and future repayments from past credits. Therefore, during 1995, total available resources for the IDA-10 period increased to SDR 10,303 million.

Against those resources, IDA made IDA-10 commitments of SDR 3,829 million during fiscal 1995. Of that amount, 39 per cent went to Africa, 25 per cent to South Asia, 19 per cent to East Asia and the Pacific, 10 per cent to Europe and Central Asia, 6 per cent to Latin America and the Caribbean, and 1 per cent to the Middle East and North Africa.

In 1995, the three largest borrowers of IDA credits were India ($945 million for six projects, plus one "blend" project), China ($630 million for three projects, plus five "blend" projects) and Viet Nam ($415 million for three projects). IDA-financed projects in those countries focused on agriculture; education; population, health and nutrition; power; and public sector management.

IDA membership in 1995 increased to 158, with the admission of Azerbaijan. At the end of fiscal 1995, action was pending on IDA membership for Bosnia and Herzegovina, Brunei Darussalam, Ukraine and the Federal Republic of Yugoslavia.

**Secretariat**

Though legally and financially distinct from the World Bank, the staffing and headquarters of IDA were the same as those of the Bank.

NOTE: For further details regarding IDA activities, see *The World Bank Annual Report 1995*.

## HEADQUARTERS AND OTHER OFFICE

HEADQUARTERS
International Development Association
1818 H. Street, N.W.
Washington, D.C. 20433, U.S.A.

For cable address, telephone, fax and telex numbers, and World Wide Web address, see World Bank, p.1483.

NEW YORK OFFICE
International Development Association
809 United Nations Plaza, Suite 900
New York, N.Y. 10017, United States
*Cable address:* INDEVAS NEWYORK
*Telephone:* (1) (212) 963-6008
*Fax:* (1) (212) 697-7020

Chapter IX

# International Monetary Fund (IMF)

In 1995, the International Monetary Fund (IMF) continued to increase its operations in almost every aspect of its work and made far-reaching changes in policies and practices governing its relations with member countries. In the light of the changed world economic environment of increased globalization and integration of markets for goods, services and capital, IMF worked to strengthen surveillance over members' exchange-rate policies and to adapt its financial instruments and procedures. It also reviewed the adequacy of its financial resources in carrying out its responsibilities.

The Fund's 1995 fiscal year covered the period from 1 May 1994 to 30 April 1995.

During 1995, IMF membership rose to 181, with the admission of Bosnia and Herzegovina and Brunei Darussalam.

## IMF facilities and policies

IMF provided financial assistance to its members through several facilities and policies to help them achieve sustainable economic growth and balance-of-payments viability and establish normal relations with their creditors. Stand-by arrangements, which focused on macroeconomic policies and aimed at overcoming balance-of-payments difficulties, generally covered periods of one to two years. The Fund made credit available for longer periods under extended fund facility (EFF) arrangements.

IMF's role in assisting its low-income members to confront particularly pressing economic problems was a major focus of the deliberations of the IMF Executive Board during 1995. Progress was made on a joint initiative with the International Bank for Reconstruction and Development (World Bank) to help resolve the debt problems of the most heavily-indebted poor countries.

The Fund also focused on financing arrangements to ensure the continued functioning of the enhanced structural adjustment facility (ESAF), which provided low-income member states with loans on concessional terms to support medium-term macroeconomic adjustment policies and structural reforms. All available resources under the structural adjustment facility (SAF) were fully utilized in 1995, and no further commitments were expected. There was broad consensus at the

April 1995 meeting of the IMF Executive Board that an ESAF-type facility should continue to be available, provided that the revolving nature of the Fund's resources and the monetary character of the Fund were respected. The rate of interest on SAF and ESAF loans was 0.5 per cent and loans were repayable over 5 1/2 to 10 years.

The compensatory and contingency financing facility (CCFF) provided members with resources to cover shortfalls in export earnings and services receipts and excesses in cereal import costs that were temporary and arising from events beyond their control. It also helped members with Fund arrangements to maintain the momentum of reforms when faced with adverse external shocks. During fiscal 1995, purchases under the CCFF, made by Algeria and the Republic of Moldova, totalled 300 million special drawing rights (SDR).

The systemic transformation facility (STF), created in April 1993 to meet the needs of economies in transition from centrally planned to market economies, provided financial assistance to twelve countries (Armenia, Azerbaijan, Belarus, Croatia, Estonia, Georgia, Latvia, Romania, Slovak Republic, Ukraine, Uzbekistan, Vietnam) in fiscal 1995, with purchases totalling SDR 1.1 billion. STF ceased to be in effect as at 31 December 1995.

## Financial assistance

During fiscal 1995, IMF disbursed a record SDR 11.2 billion to member States. It approved 17 stand-by, three EFF and 11 ESAF arrangements amounting to SDR 16.6 billion. As at 30 April 1995, there were 56 arrangements in effect for a total commitment of about SDR 23.4 billion, compared with commitments of SDR 8.4 billion a year earlier. They comprised 19 stand-by arrangements (Algeria, Cameroon, Congo, Croatia, Ecuador, Estonia, Haiti, Kazakstan, Latvia, Lesotho, Malawi, Mexico, Republic of Moldova, Poland, Romania, Russia, Slovak Republic, Turkey and Ukraine), 9 EFF arrangements (Argentina, Egypt, Jamaica, Jordan, Lithuania, Pakistan, Peru, Philippines, and Zimbabwe), 1 SAF arrangement (Sierra Leone), and 27 ESAF arrangements (Albania, Benin, Bolivia, Burkina Faso, Cambodia, Côte d'Ivoire, Equatorial Guinea, Guinea, Guinea-Bissau, Guyana, Honduras, Kyrgyz Republic, Lao People's Democratic

Republic, Mali, Mauritania, Mongolia, Mozambique, Nepal, Nicaragua, Pakistan, Senegal, Sierra Leone, Sri Lanka, Togo, Uganda, Vietnam, and Zimbabwe).

### Liquidity

The Fund's liquidity position remained adequate during fiscal 1995, despite significant weakening in the last quarter due to large stand-by arrangements for Mexico, Russia and Ukraine, and the extension of Argentina's extended arrangement. As at 30 April 1995, the Fund's liquid resources totalled SDR 61.6 billion, compared with SDR 68.7 billion at the end of fiscal 1994. Uncommitted and adjusted usable liquid resources amounted to SDR 42.5 billion, compared with SDR 54.3 billion a year earlier.

Between April 1994 and April 1995, the Fund's liquid liabilities increased by SDR 1.3 billion to SDR 33.7 billion, representing an increase of SDR 2.4 billion in the reserve tranche positions of members and a decrease of SDR 1.1 billion in outstanding Fund obligations under borrowing arrangements. The ratio of the Fund's uncommitted and adjusted usable liquid resources to its liquid liabilities—the liquidity ratio—declined from 167.6 per cent to 126.1 per cent during the same period.

### SDR activity

In fiscal 1995, the total amount of transfers nearly doubled to SDR 20.3 billion, from SDR 10.9 billion during the previous fiscal year, due to a sharp increase in transfers from the General Resources Account (GRA) and transfers among participants and prescribed holders. Total transfers from GRA rose substantially from SDR 4.4 billion in fiscal 1994 to SDR 7.9 billion in fiscal 1995, while transfers among participants and prescribed holders more than doubled to SDR 9.6 billion in fiscal 1995. These increases reflected a record volume of transactions by agreement, which increased to SDR 9 billion in fiscal 1995 from SDR 3.1 billion in fiscal 1994. These transactions continued to be facilitated by the "two-way" arrangement in effect between members and the Fund, under which members stood ready to buy or sell SDR for one or more freely usable currencies at any time, provided that their SDR holdings remained within certain limits. Twelve such arrangements were in effect as at 30 April 1995. Such arrangements facilitated the sale of SDR 3.5 billion by Mexico from its stand-by purchase in February 1995, the largest such transaction in the history of the SDR Department. Meanwhile, the level of prescribed operations declined to SDR 0.1 billion in fiscal 1995 from SDR 0.4 billion in fiscal 1994. Receipts of SDR by GRA rose from SDR 2.5 billion to SDR 2.9 billion during fiscal 1995, as the use of SDR in repurchases doubled from SDR 0.6 billion to SDR 1.2 billion.

The substantial transfers of SDR in fiscal 1995 resulted in a significant redistribution of holdings of SDR among major groups of holders. The heavy use of IMF resources by members in the latter half of the year helped to reduce the Fund's holdings of SDR from SDR 5 billion to SDR 1 billion by 30 April 1995. Debtor members sold a large proportion of SDR to members with two-way arrangements, most of which were industrial countries. As a result, SDR holdings of industrial countries increased by SDR 4 billion to SDR 15.3 billion during fiscal 1995; the holdings of developing countries grew marginally to SDR 4.1 billion during the fiscal year because debtor members received slightly more SDR from the Fund and other participants than they transferred. The holdings of prescribed holders increased from SDR 227 million to SDR 1 billion during fiscal 1995, largely due to the Fund's investments of SAF and ESAF resources in official SDR maintained with the Bank for International Settlements.

### Policy on arrears

The level of outstanding overdue obligations rose slightly during fiscal 1995 to SDR 3 billion, reversing the decline seen in fiscal 1994. The unpaid maturing obligations of some existing overdue members more than offset the clearance of the arrears of other countries.

As at 30 April 1995, five countries remained ineligible to use the Fund's general resources, accounting for 96 per cent of total overdue obligations. Declarations of non-cooperation, a step further under the Fund's arrears strategy, remained in effect with respect to three countries.

### Technical assistance and training

The Fund's provision of technical assistance continued to increase during fiscal 1995. The momentum of this trend was sustained by the problems and requirements of countries undergoing structural adjustment and systemic transformation. Approximately half the technical assistance was provided to African, European and Asian countries in transition.

During fiscal 1995, the IMF Institute provided training to some 1,248 people through residential courses and seminars at its headquarters in Washington, D.C., and at the Joint Vienna Institute. That training was complemented by 30 short overseas training courses on financial analysis and programming and 10 overseas seminars for senior officials, as well as by lecturing assistance for three regional training institutions, covering some 1,100 participants. The emphasis on training officials from economies in transition was continued with the organization of 14 courses and six seminars for central and eastern

Europe, the Baltic countries, Russia, and other countries of the former Soviet Union.

NOTE: For details of IMF activities for the 1995 fiscal year, see *International Monetary Fund, Annual Report of the Executive Board for the Financial Year Ended April 30, 1995.*

**Secretariat**

As at 30 April 1995, the total number of full-time staff of IMF was 2,184, recruited from 115 countries.

## *HEADQUARTERS AND OTHER OFFICES*

HEADQUARTERS
International Monetary Fund
700 19th Street, N.W.
Washington, D.C. 20431, United States
  *Cable address:* INTERFUND WASHINGTONDC
  *Telephone:* (1) (202) 623-7000
  *Fax:* (1) (202) 623-4661
  *Telex:* 248331 IMF UR

IMF OFFICE, UNITED NATIONS, NEW YORK
International Monetary Fund
1 United Nations Plaza, Room 1140
New York, NY 10017, United States
  *Cable address:* INTERFUND NEW YORK
  *Telephone:* (1) (212) 963-6009
  *Fax:* (1) (212) 319-9040

Chapter X

# International Civil Aviation Organization (ICAO)

The International Civil Aviation Organization (ICAO) continued during 1995 to promote the safety and efficiency of civil air transport by prescribing standards and recommending procedures for facilitating civil aviation operations. Its objectives were set forth in annexes to the Convention on International Civil Aviation, adopted in Chicago, United States, in 1944.

In 1995, domestic and international scheduled traffic of the world's airlines increased to some 292 billion tonne-kilometres. The airlines carried a total of about 1.29 billion passengers and some 21 million tonnes of freight. The passenger load factor on total scheduled services in 1995 increased by one percentage point over 1994, to 67 per cent, while the overall weight load factor remained at 60 per cent. Air freight rose by 9 per cent to 83.9 billion tonne-kilometres, and airmail traffic increased by about 4 per cent to 5.6 billion tonne-kilometres. Overall passenger/freight/mail tonne-kilometres increased by 7 per cent and international tonne-kilometres by 9 per cent.

The thirty-first session of the ICAO Assembly was held in Montreal, Canada, from 19 September to 4 October. Attended by 936 participants from 150 member States and 27 observer delegations, the Assembly elected a new ICAO Council, reviewed the organization's activities during the previous three years and adopted 29 resolutions guiding its future work. In addition to deciding the organization's programme budget and assessments for the next three years, the Assembly addressed such issues as increasing ICAO's effectiveness, implementation of the ICAO communications, navigation and surveillance/air traffic management (CNS/ATM) systems; controlled flight into terrain; improving accident prevention; smoking restrictions on international flights; and transition to a new policy on technical cooperation. In the light of the new political situation in South Africa, the Assembly declared that all previous resolutions restricting the participation of South Africa in ICAO activities were no longer in force. The Assembly also adopted a consolidated statement of continuing ICAO policies and practices related to environmental protection. The statement brought together all existing ICAO resolutions dealing with environmental protection and reiterated the need for the Council to maintain the initiative in developing policy guidance on aviation matters related to the environment.

The ICAO Council held three regular sessions in 1995, in accordance with its normal practice. The closing dates for two of its sessions were extended from 24 to 27 March and from 30 June to 7 July in order to complete certain items on its work programme. On 15 November, the Council re-elected Assad Kotaite as its President for a three-year term. Among actions taken by the Council in 1995 was the establishment of the CNS/ATM Implementation Committee. The Council also reviewed proposals regarding implementation of the ICAO safety oversight programme and agreed to establish a mechanism for financial and technical contributions to that programme.

In 1995, ICAO membership increased to 184 with the admission of Palau.

## Activities in 1995

### Air navigation

In 1995, ICAO continued to focus on updating and implementing international specifications and regional plans. The specifications consisted of International Standards and Recommended Practices contained in 18 technical Annexes to the 1944 Chicago Convention and Procedures for Air Navigation Services (PANS). Regional plans covered air navigation facilities and services required for international air navigation in ICAO regions.

Six air navigation meetings in 1995 made recommendations to amend ICAO specifications. Among them, the Special Communications/Operations Divisional Meeting in Montreal (27 March–7 April) developed a new strategy for the introduction and application of non-visual aids to precision approach and landing. The third meeting of the Committee on Aviation Environmental Protection, also in Montreal (5-15 December), discussed the potential effects of engine emissions in the upper atmosphere and made recommendations concerning emission limits.

In addition, the Council adopted amendments to five technical annexes to the Chicago Convention and three PANS documents. Other project areas that were given special attention during the year included accident investigation, prevention and data reporting; aerodrome rescue and fire fighting; airport and airspace congestion; audiovisual aids; aviation medicine; bird strikes to aircraft; a common geodetic reference system; CNS/ATM; controlled flight into terrain; flight safety and human factors; future larger aeroplanes; ground icing; meteorology; personnel licensing and training; safety oversight; and units of measurement.

### Air transport

In 1995, ICAO continued its work in regulatory studies, economic research, analysis and forecasting, air transport statistics, airport and route facility management and promoting air transport.

The eleventh session of the Facilitation Division, held in Montreal in April, adopted more than 100 recommendations, including proposals for a number of new and revised Standards and Recommended Practices in Annex 9—Facilitation, to reflect modern concepts in the clearance of aircraft, cargo and passengers. A second meeting of the Air Navigation Services Economics Panel (Montreal, May) continued its work to revise and expand the Manual on Air Navigation Services Economics, and to develop guidance in funding, charging and managerial aspects pertaining to the global navigation satellite systems (GNSS). The Asia/Pacific Area Traffic Forecasting Group, which met in Sydney, Australia, in May, continued to expand the databases used to develop traffic forecasts for the Asia/Pacific region to assist in the development of air navigation systems planning. Four workshops were held in the areas of forecasting and economic planning, statistics and forecasting for systems planning, air transport regulatory policy and airport and route facility management.

ICAO continued to provide secretariat services to three independent regional civil aviation bodies—the African Civil Aviation Commission, the European Civil Aviation Conference and the Latin American Civil Aviation Commission.

The organization maintained its responsibilities for the administration of the Danish and Icelandic Joint Financing Agreements, to which 23 Governments were contracting parties in 1995. The two agreements, which were signed in 1956 and amended in 1982, concerned the provision in Greenland and Iceland of air traffic control, communications and other facilities and services to North Atlantic flights.

### Legal matters

A diplomatic conference was convened in Montreal from 25 to 29 September 1995. The Conference adopted the text of the Chicago Convention in Arabic and a Protocol relating to the resulting change to the final clause of the Convention.

The following ratifications, adherences or successions were registered in 1995 to the 1944 Convention on International Civil Aviation, ICAO's constituent instrument, and to conventions and protocols on international air law concluded under ICAO auspices:

*Convention on International Civil Aviation (Chicago, 1944)*
Palau
*Convention on the International Recognition of Rights in Aircraft (Geneva, 1948)*
Bosnia and Herzegovina, Maldives, Senegal
*Convention on Damage Caused by Foreign Aircraft to Third Parties on the Surface (Rome, 1952)*
Maldives
*Convention Supplementary to the Warsaw Convention, for the Unification of Certain Rules relating to International Carriage by Air Performed by a Person Other than the Contracting Carrier (Guadalajara, 1961)*
Bosnia and Herzegovina
*Convention on Offences and Certain Other Acts Committed on Board Aircraft (Tokyo, 1963)*
Algeria, Bosnia and Herzegovina, Kazakstan, Palau, Slovakia, Uzbekistan
*Convention for the Suppression of Unlawful Seizure of Aircraft (The Hague, 1970)*
Algeria, Congo, Croatia, Kazakstan
*Convention for the Suppression of Unlawful Acts against the Safety of Civil Aviation (Montreal, 1971)*
Algeria, Croatia, Kazakstan, Palau, Slovakia, the former Yugoslav Republic of Macedonia
*Protocol for the Suppression of the Unlawful Acts of Violence at Airports Serving International Civil Aviation, Supplementary to the Convention for the Suppression of Unlawful Acts against the Safety of Civil Aviation, done at Montreal on 23 September 1971 (Montreal, 1988)*
Algeria, Croatia, India, Kazakstan, Kenya, Netherlands, Palau, Slovakia, the former Yugoslav Republic of Macedonia
*Convention on the Marking of Plastic Explosives for the Purpose of Detection (Montreal, 1991)*
Ecuador, Greece, Kazakstan, Slovakia, Switzerland, Zambia

### Technical cooperation

ICAO undertook technical cooperation projects in 76 countries in 1995. The Organization's technical cooperation programmes, financed by the UN Development Programme (UNDP), trust funds, Management Service Agreements and the Civil Aviation Purchasing Service, had total expenditures in 1995 of $55.8 million. Some 94 per cent of that amount was provided by Governments to fund their own projects on the basis of cost-sharing with UNDP.

ICAO had resident missions in 38 countries, and 67 others received assistance through fellowships and visits from experts assigned to intercountry and subcontractual arrangements. A total of 514 fellowships were awarded in 1995, of which 501 were implemented. At the end of 1995, ICAO had 73 experts in the field. In all, the organization engaged 354 experts from 41 countries during all or part of 1995, of which 217 were on assignment under UNDP and 137 worked on trust fund projects.

In addition, there were 77 Governments and organizations registered with ICAO in 1995 under its Civil Aviation Purchasing Services. Equipment purchases during 1995 totalled $27.3 million.

## Secretariat

As at 31 December 1995, the total number of staff members employed in the ICAO secretariat was 737, including 294 in the Professional and higher categories and 443 in the General Service and related categories. Of the total, 194 were employed in regional offices.

## Budget

Appropriations for the ICAO budget in 1995 totalled $52,204,000. Appropriations for 1996 were set at $50,340,000.

NOTE: For further details on the activities of ICAO in 1995, see *Annual Report of the Council—1995*.

## *HEADQUARTERS*

International Civil Aviation Organization
1000 Sherbrook Street West
Montreal, Quebec
Canada, H3A 2R2
   *Cable address:* ICAO MONTREAL
   *Telephone:* (1) (514) 954-8219
   *Fax:* (1) (514) 954-4772
   *Telex:* 05-24513
   *E-mail:* icaohq@icao.org

Chapter XI

# Universal Postal Union (UPU)

Established in 1874 in Berne, Switzerland, to exchange postal services among nations, the Universal Postal Union (UPU) in 1995 continued its promotion of international collaboration to provide a rapid, economic and reliable universal postal service. UPU also undertook activities and projects to promote postal development throughout the world and to foster closer ties to postal customers. In 1995, UPU membership remained at 189, with no new countries having requested admission.

## Activities of UPU organs

### Universal Postal Congress

Following the twenty-first Universal Postal Congress in Seoul, Republic of Korea, in 1994, preparatory work began in 1995 for the twenty-second Congress, to be held in Beijing, China, in 1999. The task of organizing the twenty-second Congress, which was tentatively scheduled for 23 August to 15 September 1999, was assigned to the postal administration of China.

### Council of Administration

The Council of Administration, which had replaced the Executive Council by a 1994 decision of the Seoul Congress, held its first annual meeting from 17 to 25 October 1995. Among its resolutions and decisions, the Council decided to continue the study on improving management of the Union and to initiate a study on the UPU linguistic system; addressed the issue of the employment of women at the UPU International Bureau; decided to continue the process of budgeting by programme, first introduced following the Seoul Congress; and adopted an action programme to promote postal development for the least developed countries (LDCs).

### Postal Operations Council

Created by the 1994 Seoul Congress, the Postal Operations Council held its first annual session in Berne from 30 January to 17 February 1995. During that session, the Council revised the Detailed Regulations of the UPU Convention, which contained common rules applicable to the Union's member countries for the operation of the international postal service. The Regulations were reoriented so that the postal services would be better positioned to work in the very competitive international environment. Among other main results of the session, contact committee meetings were organized with the publishing industry and several philatelic associations to foster cooperation with major users of international postal services, and a "Customers' Day" was held to allow UPU members to hear customer concerns regarding improvement of the international postal services.

### International Bureau

The International Bureau, which is under the general supervision of the Council of Administration, is the UPU secretariat, serving the postal administrations of member countries as an organ of execution, support, liaison, information and consultation. During 1995, the Bureau acted as a clearing-house for the settlement of accounts between postal administrations for various inter-administration charges related to the exchange of postal items and international reply coupons. A number of studies were conducted at the request of the Council of Administration and the Postal Operations Council. In addition to its ongoing activities in monitoring the quality of postal service on a global scale, the Bureau published information and statistics on international postal services and continued a global project concerning the postal application of electronic data interchange.

The Bureau introduced in 1995 a number of modern management techniques, including total quality management, a strategic planning process and a performance evaluation system based on the setting of individual objectives. As at 31 December 1995, the number of permanent and temporary staff members employed by the Bureau was 144, of whom 57 were in the Professional or higher categories (drawn from 38 countries) and 87 were in the General Services category. French remained the sole official language of UPU; however, English was introduced as the Union's second working language, besides French, beginning on 1 January 1996. The Bureau employed 14 officials in the Arabic, English, Portuguese, Russian and Spanish translation services.

## Technical cooperation

UPU technical cooperation, which was financed by the UN Development Programme, amounted to $352,297 in 1995. The UPU Special Fund, including voluntary contributions in cash and in kind from member countries, and the regular budget also provided assistance for a total of $1.8 million in funding.

With a view to helping postal administrations obtain funding for postal projects, UPU regional advisers visited 20 countries in 1995. In addition, postal projects on behalf of Haiti and Yemen were approved. UPU also continued its participation in special international programmes such as the Second UN Transport and Communications Decade in Africa (1991-2000), phase II of the Transport and Communications Decade for Asia and the Pacific (1992-1996), technical cooperation among developing countries, and the action programme for LDCs.

**Budget**

At its 1994 session, the former Executive Council approved the 1995 UPU budget of 32,165,490 Swiss francs. At its 1995 session, the new Council of Administration approved the 1996 budget of 33,376,400 Swiss francs, to be financed by contributions from member States. Under the Union's self-financing system, contributions were payable in advance based on the following year's budget.

NOTE: For details of UPU activities, see *Report on the Work of the Union, 1995*, published by UPU.

## *HEADQUARTERS*

Universal Postal Union
Weltpoststrasse 4
Berne, Switzerland
   *Postal address:* Union postale universelle
              Case postale
              3000 Berne 15, Switzerland
   *Cable address:* UPU BERNE
   *Telephone:* (41) (31) 350 31 11
   *Fax:* (41) (31) 350 31 10
   *Telex:* 912761 UPU CH
   *E-mail:* lb.info@ib.upu.org
   *World Wide Web site:* http://ibis.ib.upu.org/

Chapter XII

# International Telecommunication Union (ITU)

The International Telecommunication Union (ITU), which was founded in 1865 as the International Telegraph Union, became a specialized agency of the United Nations in 1947. In 1995, ITU continued to promote the development and efficient operation of telecommunication facilities, to offer technical assistance in telecommunications and to encourage adoption of a broader approach to telecommunications in the global information economy and society.

The 1995 annual session of the ITU Council was held in Geneva from 21 to 30 June. The Council decided to convene two conferences in Geneva in 1996—the World Telecommunication Standardization Conference (WTSC-96) from 9 to 18 October and the First World Telecommunication Policy Forum from 21 to 23 October—to discuss the "global mobile personal communications by satellite". The Council also adopted frameworks for draft agendas for Regional Telecommunication Development Conferences to be held in the African and Arab regions in 1996. ITU membership remained at 184 in 1995, with no new admissions since 1994.

## Conferences

The World Radiocommunication Conference (WRC-95) (Geneva, 23 October–17 November) adopted a simplified partial revision of the Radio Regulations and associated Appendices, contained in its Final Acts. Also adopted were 47 revised or new resolutions and recommendations related to international radio communications as contained in the Final Acts. At the conclusion of the Conference, 130 members signed the Final Acts.

## Radiocommunication sector

In 1995, the ITU Radiocommunications Bureau was involved in the preparation and holding of the Radiocommunication Assembly and the World Radiocommunication Conference 1995, as well as in the ongoing implementation of decisions of the Plenipotentiary Conference (Kyoto, 1994). The second (January) and third (September) meetings of the Radiocommunication Advisory Group (RAG) completed the transition to the new Radiocommunication Sector structure.

The Radiocommunication Bureau provided technical and administrative support in 1995 for a number of meetings, including 11 Radiocommu-

nication Study Groups addressing the following topics: spectrum management; inter-service sharing and compatibility; radio wave propagation; fixed satellite service; science services; mobile radio determination; amateur and related satellite services; fixed service; broadcasting service (sound); and broadcasting service (television). In this respect, the Bureau carried out international regulatory processes for registration of frequency assignments and satellite orbits, and assisted in resolving cases of harmful interferences.

The Second Radio Communication Assembly (RA-95) (Geneva, 16-20 October) reviewed the work programme and structure of the Radiocommunication Study Groups. The Assembly approved one new resolution (ITU-R 38), modified eight others and cancelled five existing ones.

Three Regional Radiocommunication Seminars were held in 1995: in Bangkok, Thailand, in February; Margarita, Venezuela, in March; and Pretoria, South Africa, in September.

By the end of 1995, the Master International Frequency Register contained particulars of 1,189,324 assignments to terrestrial stations representing 5,464,469 line entries which were published in the International Frequency List at periodic intervals not exceeding six months.

## Telecommunications standardization sector

In 1995, the ITU Telecommunications Bureau, facing the proliferation of systems and networks of different nature and different kinds of telecommunication services, made progress in producing and revising recommendations on standardization. During the year, 175 new and 113 revised recommendations were approved.

The Sector's study group activities continued focusing on: service definition; network operation; tariff and accounting principles; network maintenance; protection against electromagnetic environment; outside plant; data networks and open systems communications; terminals for telematic services; television and sound transmission; language for telecommunication applications; switching and signalling; end-to-end transmission performance of networks and terminals; general network aspects; modems and transmission techniques for data, telegraph and telematic services; and transmission systems and equipment.

In 1995, the Telecommunication Standardization Advisory Group held two meetings, focusing on how to address the Global Information Infrastructure, internetworking, and audiovisual and multimedia subjects within the conventional structure of the Bureau.

## Telecommunication development sector

The year 1995 was the first complete year of implementation by the ITU Telecommunication Development Bureau of the Buenos Aires Action Plan adopted at the World Telecommunication Development Conference in 1994. It was also the first year that the Bureau Study Groups met to help find solutions to many telecommunication development problems facing developing countries.

The Bureau undertook a total of 349 technical assistance missions during 1995, as well as organized 89 seminars, workshops and meetings on a variety of subjects. It also granted 1,453 fellowships, with special attention to the least developed countries.

In Africa, the Bureau continued activities for consolidating and improving telecommunication networks, including technical network management, the finalization of studies for establishment of the Lomé maintenance centre and the modernization of networks in West Africa. A consultative meeting of African countries (Tunis, Tunisia, 20-21 November) discussed a major regional submarine fibre-optic cable project entitled ''Africa One''. In November, the WORLDTEL organization, which involved several countries in eastern and southern Africa, met to set up a financing and partnership mechanism to increase total telephone capacity of the countries concerned by approximately 1 million lines. During 1995, ITU implemented 21 projects and field staff identified five new projects in Africa. In addition, 24 seminars, workshops and symposia were held in the region.

The number of projects related to strengthening technical and administrative telecommunications services in Africa continued to fall significantly in 1995, mainly due to the new priorities of the United Nations Development Programme (UNDP), which excluded the telecommunication sub-sector. Projects implemented in 1995 included: sectoral telecommunications studies in South Africa, Angola, Eritrea and Uganda; assistance for the establishment of a management information system in Benin; implementation of a telecommunication master plan in Mali; a pilot project for rural telecommunications in Uganda; radio frequency management and organization of local network maintenance in Chad; and assistance for the implementation of cellular radiocommunication systems, among other projects, in Zaire. Related to the development of human resources for telecommunications in Africa, ITU undertook regional workshops and seminars

in South Africa, Burkina Faso, Cameroon, Ghana, Kenya, the Niger and Italy.

Activities in 1995 concerning the Americas included a revision of the Blue Book on Telecommunication Policies, and pilot projects on the development of rural telecommunications. A regional meeting was organized to discuss the importance of telecommunication development indicators in analysing policy changes. ITU carried out 99 missions, prepared 11 new projects and supervised 26 projects in the region in 1995. Projects included modernization of the Brazilian telecommunication system, establishment of a Caribbean News Agency (CANA) Satellite Regional News Network; occupational analysis, restructuring of Telecom and other activities in Colombia; a telecommunication master plan in El Salvador; creation of a regulatory body in Guatemala; and modernization of networks in Costa Rica, as well as other projects in the Andean countries, the Bahamas, Belize, Chile, the Dominican Republic, Ecuador, Honduras, Nicaragua, Panama, Paraguay, Peru, Suriname and Uruguay. There were nine regional seminars/meetings organized in 1995 in Argentina (2), Chile, Costa Rica (2), Mexico, Suriname and Uruguay (2).

In the Arab States, ITU undertook 34 missions and supervised seven projects in 1995. Projects undertaken in association with UNDP included telecommunication staff training in Djibouti; master plans for telecommunication development in Libya and Sudan; assistance in the development of a master plan in Morocco; preparation of a study and workshop, among other activities, in Palestine, as well as other projects in Saudi Arabia, Sudan, Syria, Tunisia and Yemen. Some 120 Arab experts attended seminars and workshops in Egypt, Jordan, Palestine, Syria, Tunisia and Yemen.

In Asia and the Pacific, ITU staff carried out 82 missions, supervised 21 projects, identified five new projects and had two project proposals approved in 1995. Projects for the development of regional telecommunication networks included telecommunication computer software training and development, a programme for economic reform through enhanced transport and communication services; and telecommunication development and training in the South Pacific. Projects were undertaken in Bangladesh, Bhutan, Cambodia, China, India, Indonesia, the Lao People's Democratic Republic, Mongolia, Nepal, Pakistan, Papua New Guinea, Solomon Islands, Tokelau and Viet Nam. Nine regional or subregional seminars and meetings were organized and a total of 37 missions of consultants were carried out, addressing such subjects as investment analysis, restructuring regulatory support, type approval, network planning and customer service.

In Europe and the Commonwealth of Independent States (CIS) countries, ITU had an important role in regulatory matters and frequency management, as well as in human resources management and planning. The whole region was undergoing a massive reconstruction of the networks, as well as commercializing organizations and liberalizing the market. As ITU had no regional offices in that area, all issues were dealt with by ITU headquarters. ITU staff carried out six missions and supervised 11 projects in the region in 1995. Projects were undertaken in the Czech Republic, Greece, Malta, the Republic of Moldova, the Russian Federation, Slovakia, Sweden, Ukraine and Uzbekistan. In addition, 169 fellowships were granted and 12 missions undertaken by consultants. In the region, a seminar on human resources management and development for East European countries and CIS was held in Bulgaria and a workshop on modern organizational development techniques was held in the Russian Federation.

### Secretariat

As at 31 December 1995, there were a total of 702 permanent and fixed-term staff employed by ITU, either at headquarters or in the field. Of that number, 269 were at the Professional and higher categories and 433 in the General Services category. This excluded staff on short-term contracts and project personnel.

### Budget

The adjusted final budget for ITU in 1995 totalled 153,516,711 Swiss francs (SwF). Actual income in 1995 amounted to SwF 158,671,469, while actual expenditure totalled SwF 143,210,974.

In 1995, the Council approved the 1996-1997 biennial budget, with the ordinary budget amounting to SwF 294,862,000 and the publications budget of SwF 28,035,000.

NOTE: For further details regarding ITU's activities, see *Report on the Activities of the International Telecommunication Union in 1995*, published by the Union.

## *HEADQUARTERS*

International Telecommunication Union
Place des Nations
CH-1211, Geneva 20, Switzerland
  *Cable address:* BURINTERNA GENEVA
  *Telephone:* (41) (22) 730-5111
  *Fax:* (41) (22) 733-7256
  *Telex:* 45 421000
  *Internet address:* itumail@itu.int

Chapter XIII

# World Meteorological Organization (WMO)

The World Meteorological Organization (WMO) was founded in 1950 to facilitate worldwide cooperation in the establishment and maintenance of systems for making, exchanging and standardizing meteorological information, and to further application of meteorology to aviation, shipping, water problems, agriculture and other human activities. Since its founding, the organization has also developed an important role in addressing the world's environmental concerns. In 1995, WMO continued activities in support of sustainable development in areas such as climate change, natural disaster mitigation, water resources management and environmental monitoring.

The World Meteorological Congress, the WMO governing body which meets once every four years, held its twelfth session in 1995 (Geneva, 30 May–21 June). It approved the WMO programme and budget for 1996-1999 and the Fourth Long-term Plan (1996-2005). The 36-member WMO Executive Council, at its forty-seventh session (Geneva, 22-23 July), continued to coordinate and supervise the implementation of WMO programmes and allocate its budgetary resources.

WMO membership increased to 176 States and five territories during 1995, with the admission of three new members: the Cook Islands, the Federated States of Micronesia and Samoa.

## World Weather Watch Programme

As the core programme of WMO, the World Weather Watch (WWW) Programme continued in 1995 to collect, analyse and disseminate meteorological data, and process products for national meteorological services. WWW consisted of the Global Observing System (GOS), the Global Telecommunication System (GTS), the Global Data-processing System (GDPS) and Data Management, collectively known as the basic systems. The WWW Programme also included the WMO Satellite Activities, Instruments and Methods of Observation Programme and the Tropical Cyclone Programme.

### World Weather Watch implementation

As the main source of observational data for WWW, GOS comprised some 9,950 land stations, 7,300 voluntary observing ships, 1,000 drifting or moored buoys at sea and 3,000 aircraft. During 1995, new specialized observing systems were introduced for collecting data, while the GOS space-based subsystem—a nominal constellation of five geostationary and two polar-orbiting satellites—continued to provide imagery, soundings, data collection and data distribution. The satellite operators of this subsystem included China, the European Community, Japan, the Russian Federation and the United States.

Much progress was made in 1995 in reviewing and redesigning the regional basic synoptic networks, which were critical components of GOS. Problems remained in implementing upper-air stations in certain parts of the world, exacerbated by the likely cessation of the operation of the Omega radio navigation system for upper-air wind finding, on which some 20 per cent of the worldwide network depended.

Multi-point telecommunication services via satellite continued to be essential to the further development of GTS, while data-collection and data-dissemination services via meteorological satellite continued in areas where commercial telecommunications did not provide cost-effective services. Satellite transmit/receive stations were in operation at national meteorological centres in Central America and the Caribbean area, and similar systems were planned or implemented in several countries for their national meteorological telecommunication networks.

GDPS activities focused in 1995 on enhancing the services of GDPS centres, in response to new requirements and improved capabilities. Those services included extended-range and long-range weather forecasts; updating observational data and requirements of international exchange; procedures for provision of services to UN humanitarian missions; designation of new Regional Specialized Meteorological Centres; and global regional arrangements for environmental emergency response. GDPS Centres and emerging centres such as the African Centre for Meteorological Application for Development, the Association of South-East Asian Nations (ASEAN) Specialized Meteorological Centre and the Drought Monitoring Centres in Africa continued to improve their forecasting systems and computer facilities. The Centres' programmes and activities had been adjusted to address requirements for preparation of specialized climate-related products, long-range forecasts and tailored products for environmental safety quality monitoring.

### Instruments and methods of observation

WMO continued to work through its Instruments and Methods of Observation Programme to standardize data, evaluate new techniques and review the cost-effectiveness of observing systems. During the year, the Eighth International Pyrheliometer Comparison, held at the World Radiation Centre in Davos, Switzerland, calibrated regional and national standard instruments against the instruments in the World Standard Group. In October, participants from 19 African countries attended lectures given by Egyptian and Chinese experts at a Regional Training Workshop for Instrument Specialists, held at the Regional Instrument Centre in Cairo, Egypt.

### Tropical Cyclone Programme

During 1995 under the Tropical Cyclone Programme (TCP), the operational plan or manual of each of the five regional tropical cyclone bodies around the world was revised or updated. All Regional Specialized Meteorological Centres (Miami, Nadi, New Delhi, Réunion and Tokyo) improved their facilities and services to their respective regions, which included provision of scientific guidance and advice on tropical cyclones. Progress was made in implementing coordinated plans for future development of services by the national meteorological and hydrological services and the national agencies involved in disaster prevention and preparedness. Special attention was given to the establishment of satellite ground-reception stations at national meteorological centres, in view of their great importance in detecting and tracking tropical cyclones.

### World Climate Programme

The WMO Commission for Climatology, in collaboration with the WMO Commission for Basic Systems and the Global Climate Observing System (GCOS), initiated the development of a GCOS Surface Network (GSN) by specifying an initial list of 800 land-based stations to provide data that would help monitor surface temperature on the global to large-regional scales. GSN was intended to serve as a catalyst for the further development of national reference climatological station networks.

The fifth global Climate System Review, covering the period June 1991-November 1993, was published in 1995. In June, the Twelfth WMO Congress endorsed the initiation of a WMO project to publish a document on the climate of the twentieth century.

Regional climate computing development training seminars were held in Bratislava, Slovakia, for European countries (May 1995) and in Santiago, Chile, for South American countries (November). One week of basic climate computing training was included in computer applications workshops held in Niamay, Niger, in March and October for English- and French-speaking countries of Africa.

At the end of 1995, the Data Rescue project in Africa was considered complete in 15 countries. The International Data Rescue Coordination Centre in Brussels had over 85,000 microfiches of rescued climate data from 40 participating countries. In July, a training seminar in Barbados launched a Data Rescue project for the Caribbean countries.

### World Climate Research Programme

Undertaken jointly by WMO, the Intergovernmental Oceanographic Commission of the United Nations Educational, Scientific and Cultural Organization (IOC/UNESCO) and the International Council of Scientific Unions (ICSU), the World Climate Research Programme continued in 1995 to organize research into the basic physical processes that determine the Earth's climate. The Global Energy and Water Cycle Experiment (GEWEX) continued to organize major field experiments to study hydrological and atmospheric processes over basin drainage areas. The first year of the Enhanced Observing Period (1995-1999) for the GEWEX Continental-scale International Project, which embraced the whole Mississippi River basin, was completed. Four additional experiments were either started or in the planning stages, centred around the Baltic Sea, the MacKenzie River basin in Canada, the Amazonian rain forest in Brazil and the eastern regions of Asia. High priority continued to be given to producing a series of research global climatological data sets. As a result, during 1995 for the first time, an observed global total precipitable water data set was produced.

The new research programme study of Stratospheric Processes and their Role in Climate began a specific initiative to examine the global effects of stratospheric/tropospheric exchange, which was particularly important in the context of concerns about the impact of aircraft emissions on the ozone layer.

The initial scientific plan for a study of climate variability and predictability on time-scales of a month up to a century was completed and published in 1995. The plan called for particular study of understanding and developing predictive capabilities for monsoonal circulations, and discussed how advances could be made in determining the magnitude of anthropogenic climate change by exploiting full coupled global climate models.

**Atmospheric Research and Environment Programme**

As the main component of the Atmospheric Research and Environment Programme, the WMO Global Atmosphere Watch (GAW) continued during 1995 to provide measurements and assessments of the chemical state and behaviour of the atmosphere, such as assessments on stratospheric ozone. During the year, GAW worked to improve data archives, set standards for quality assurance and control of its data, promote academic capacity-building in atmospheric chemistry in developing countries and coordinate research activities in atmospheric composition.

A regional WMO workshop in New Delhi, India, focused on the latest developments in Asian/African monsoon research. A workshop in Beijing, China, in October reviewed limited area numerical models, while a meeting of experts was held in South Africa in November to review the current state of hail suppression technology.

During the year, the WMO Technical Library, a source of meteorological and hydrological information, acquired some 2,070 publications and handled more than 2,000 inquiries.

## Applications of meteorology

### Agricultural meteorology

The Commission of Agricultural Meteorology, at its eleventh session (Havana, Cuba, February), decided to prepare guidelines on improving management practices in agriculture, animal husbandry and forestry; considered ways to help member countries cope with climate variability and change; and approved land- and crop-management strategies for sustainable agricultural development. The Commission gave priority to education and training, the efficient use of water and energy in agriculture, the control of pests and diseases, and the establishment of operational agrometeorological services.

### Aeronautical meteorology

In 1995, operational satellite broadcasts of the World Area Forecast System (WAFS) data and products began from both the London and Washington World Area Forecast Centres, marking a milestone in WAFS implementation. In addition, satellite broadcast receivers and user terminals began to be installed in a number of countries around the world. At the same time, emphasis was put on training users of WAFS data and products to familiarize themselves with the new technology and the products generated. Six training events with a WAFS component were held around the world. Continued progress was made in automated production of significant weather forecasts, one of the major requirements for reaching the final stage of WAFS implementation.

The new aeronautical meteorological codes introduced in 1993 were slightly amended in 1995 and approved for implementation in January 1996. With the implementation of these amended codes, for the first time all WMO members would be using a single global standard for the aeronautical meteorological codes.

### Marine meteorology

The Data Buoy Cooperation Panel, which was established by WMO and IOC in 1985 to facilitate the global coordination of individual buoy deployment programmes, was instrumental during 1995 in successfully establishing a new International Buoy Programme for the Indian Ocean, with the initial participation of institutions from five countries with interests in the region.

Increased interest by climatologists in observations by the WMO Voluntary Observing Ships (VOS) lead to heightened interest in metadata associated with the observations, such as the profile, size and loading of the ships, location of instruments and observing practices used. Precise documentation of these metadata were proposed as part of an expanded *International List of Selected, Supplementary and Auxiliary Ships* (WMO-No.47), due out in 1997.

### Public weather services

The second Expert Meeting on Public Weather Services (Geneva, April) carried out a detailed revision of the draft "Guide on public weather services practices" and addressed such issues as the need to improve public weather services in both developing and developed countries and the future of the programme itself.

Also in April, a Training Workshop on Public Weather Services with particular Emphasis on Television Weather Presentation and Communication Skills was held in Singapore, featuring lectures and discussion on trends, policies and the impact on national practices of private sector involvement in the domain of public weather services. An Expert Meeting on Public Weather Services and Hurricane Disaster Preparedness (Trinidad and Tobago, December) addressed issues related to the use of seasonal forecasts in disaster mitigation and the provision of early warnings.

### Hydrology and water resources

The World Hydrological Cycle Observing System, a programme launched in 1993, had by 1995 progressively moved from a technological concept, based on a global network of key stations transmitting their data through satellites, towards a comprehensive, integrated series of projects designed to create water data information systems at national, regional and global levels.

WMO, in collaboration with the United Nations Economic Commission for Africa, convened an African Conference on Water Resources: Policy and Assessment (Addis Ababa, Ethiopia, March) with the participation of 41 African countries and 16 international organizations. It was the first WMO regional conference designed to address the water issues facing African nations and to explore strategies which would ensure that national water resources agencies played a full part in national and regional development.

By the end of 1995, 122 WMO members were participating in the Hydrological Operational Multi-purpose System (HOMS), the WMO system for technology transfer in operational hydrology. Many of the new participants were from the newly independent States and planning to use the HOMS technology to build their new national hydrological services. A parallel System for Technology Exchange for Natural Disasters (STEND) was launched during the year to provide technology for monitoring, risk assessment, forecasting and engineering design to combat natural disasters. Launched as a contribution to the International Decade for Natural Disaster Reduction, the initial fields for STEND study were seismology and volcanology, with extension to other fields foreseen for the future.

More than 140 countries by the end of 1995 had contributed data to the Global Runoff Data Centre, which was established under WMO auspices in 1988 to support studies of regional and global water problems and assist the development of more accurate models of the world's climate.

### Education and training

During 1995, a total of 564 people participated in 24 training events in 19 countries, organized as part of the WMO education and training programme. The organization also co-sponsored or supported 30 training events organized by national institutions in member countries. Particular atten-

tion was given to training instructors and creating closer links among national training institutions. In addition, WMO awarded 46 long-term and 163 short-term fellowships in 1995.

As in previous years, the WMO Training Library continued to strengthen and expand its holdings of audiovisual training aids and computer-aided learning modules to meet the increasing needs of members. In 1995, the Library made available 132 copies of video films, one set of 100 slides, and 66 software packages in response to requests from members, training institutions and other users.

### Technical cooperation

In 1995, 130 countries received technical assistance valued at $15.68 million, financed by trust funds (43.9 per cent), the WMO Voluntary Cooperation Programme (37.7 per cent), UNDP (10 per cent) and the WMO regular budget (8.4 per cent).

### Secretariat

As at 31 December 1995, the total number of full-time staff employed by WMO (excluding six professionals on technical assistance projects) was 269. Of those, 119 from 45 countries were in the Professional or higher categories and 150 were in the General Service and related categories.

### Budget

The year 1995 was the fourth and final year of the eleventh financial period (1992-1995), for which the 1991 WMO Congress had established a maximum expenditure of 236,100,000 Swiss francs. Total unpaid contributions due from members stood at 28,391,613 Swiss francs. The Executive Council approved a regular budget for the 1994-1995 biennium of 122,400,000 Swiss francs.

NOTE: For further details regarding WMO activities, see *World Meteorological Organization Annual Report 1995*, published by the organization.

## HEADQUARTERS

World Meteorological Organization
41, Avenue Giuseppe-Motta
(Case postale No. 2300)
CH-1211 Geneva 2, Switzerland
  *Cable address:* METEOMONO GENEVA
  *Telephone:* (41) (22) 730-81-11
  *Fax:* (41) (22) 734-23-26
  *Telex:* 41-41 99 OMMCH
  *E-mail:* ipa@www.wmo.ch
  *Homepage:* http//www.wmo.ch

Chapter XIV

# International Maritime Organization (IMO)

In 1995, the International Maritime Organization (IMO) held the nineteenth biennial session of its Assembly (London, 13-24 November), at which it considered and approved the work programme prepared during the previous two years by its subsidiary bodies. Those bodies include the IMO Council, which serves as the IMO governing body between sessions of the Assembly, as well as committees addressing technical aspects of maritime safety, marine environmental protection, and legal, technical cooperation and facilitation issues.

Among actions taken during the session, the Assembly addressed such issues as bulk carrier safety, performance standards for equipment, electric and electronic requirements, ships' routeing, radio communications, radio-navigation systems, the role of ports in promoting maritime safety, and guidelines on implementing the International Safety Management code. In addition, the Assembly adopted five resolutions concerning the safety of roll-on/roll-off passenger ships.

As at 31 December 1995, IMO membership numbered 153 States, with the addition during the year of Azerbaijan, Lithuania and South Africa.

## Activities in 1995

In June, the IMO Council awarded the International Maritime Prize for 1994 to John Perrakis of Greece, who died a month later. Mr. Perrakis had participated in the 1973-1982 sessions of the Third UN Conference on the Law of the Sea, and for nearly 25 years had been involved with legal aspects of maritime safety and pollution prevention. The Prize is awarded annually to the person judged to have done the most towards advancing the objectives of IMO.

World Maritime Day was celebrated on 28 September at IMO headquarters in London, paying tribute to the fiftieth anniversary of the United Nations and IMO achievements.

### Prevention of pollution

The twenty-seventh set of amendments to the International Maritime Dangerous Goods Code, adopted in 1994, entered into force on 1 January 1995, and the entire 2,500-page Code was reprinted later in the year. Although not mandatory, the Code was widely used and had been included, in whole or in part, in national legislation by most of the world's shipping nations.

On 13 May, the International Convention on Oil Pollution Preparedness, Response and Cooperation (OPRC) entered into force. Intended to provide an international system for preparing for and responding to emergencies involving oil pollution (including all forms of petroleum products), the treaty was adopted at an IMO conference in 1990.

Two sets of amendments to the International Convention for the Prevention of Pollution from Ships, 1973, as modified by the Protocol of 1978 relating thereto (MARPOL 73/78), took effect during the year. On 4 April, amendments adopted in 1991 took effect, requiring oil tankers of a certain weight to carry a shipboard oil pollution emergency plan. On 6 July, further amendments, adopted in 1992, came into operation, including an enhanced programme of inspections for all oil tankers aged five years or more, and required changes to the construction of tankers aged 25 or more, as well as the mandatory fitting of double hulls or an equivalent design.

Work on a new draft convention for liability and compensation in connection with the carriage of hazardous and noxious substances by sea was completed by the IMO Legal Committee at its seventy-second session (London, 3-7 April). The draft was broader in scope than the existing pollution compensation regime in that it covered not only pollution but also the risks of fire and explosion. The Committee recommended that the draft be forwarded to a diplomatic conference for consideration and adoption in 1996.

### Ship security and safety at sea

The Maritime Safety Committee, IMO's senior technical body, at its sixty-fifth session (London, 9-17 May), adopted amendments to the International Convention for the Safety of Life at Sea (SOLAS), 1974, calling for the introduction of mandatory ships' routeing systems. The amendments were expected to enter into force under the Convention's "tacit acceptance" provisions on 1 January 1997. Among its other work, the Committee decided that trials held in several countries, with the officer of the navigational watch acting as sole look-out in periods of darkness, should be discontinued since no consensus could be reached as to the safety of the practice.

In November, the Conference of Contracting Governments to the SOLAS Convention adopted major changes aimed at improving the safety of roll-on/roll-off (ro-ro) passenger ships. The amendments were based on proposals put forward by a panel of experts set up by IMO in December 1994 following the *Estonia* disaster two months earlier, in which more than 900 people were killed. The most important of the changes dealt with requirements for bow doors and the stability of ro-ro passenger ships, including a new regulation intended to phase out ships built to a one-compartment standard and to ensure that ro-ro ships could survive without capsizing if two main compartments flooded following damage.

During 1995, IMO amended the International Convention on Standards of Training, Certification and Watchkeeping for Seafarers, 1978. One of the major features of the revision was the adoption of a new code containing two parts, one of mandatory and another of recommended provisions, to which many technical regulations of the Convention were transferred. In addition, IMO adopted a new International Convention on Standards of Training, Certification and Watchkeeping for Fishing Vessel Personnel, which was intended to apply to crews of fishing vessels of 24 metres or more in length.

On 4 November, amendments to the Convention on the International Regulations for Preventing Collisions at Sea, 1972, entered into force. The amendments were mostly concerned with the positioning of lights.

### World Maritime University

On 20 March, the World Maritime University's Class of 1996 was formally inaugurated, bringing together 81 students from 48 nations, 2 of which (Estonia and Saint Kitts and Nevis) were represented for the first time. The new class brought the total number of students enrolled at the University to 1,152, representing 128 countries. The University, which is located in Malmö, Sweden, was established by IMO in 1983 to provide advanced postgraduate training in maritime administration, environmental protection, port and shipping management, maritime education and training, and maritime safety administration.

The United States Coast Guard presented its Meritorious Public Service Award in 1995 to the University, in recognition of its 12 years as a centre of excellence in education, training and technology transfer. The Coast Guard also announced the donation of a fellowship for a student joining the University's one-year Master's degree programme in 1996.

### Budget

In November 1995, the IMO Assembly approved budgetary appropriations of 36,612,200 pounds sterling for the 1996-1997 biennium.

## *HEADQUARTERS*

International Maritime Organization
4 Albert Embankment
London SE1 7SR, United Kingdom
   *Cable address:* INTERMAR LONDON SE1
   *Telephone:* (44) (171) 735-7611
   *Fax:* (44) (171) 587-3210
   *Telex:* 23588 IMOLDN G, 296979 IMOLDN G

Chapter XV

# World Intellectual Property Organization (WIPO)

In 1995, the World Intellectual Property Organization (WIPO) continued development cooperation, norm-setting and registration activities to promote respect for the protection and use of intellectual property. The organization's main areas of work aimed to strengthen the intellectual property systems of developing countries; promote new or revised norms for the protection of intellectual property at the national, regional and multilateral levels; and facilitate the acquisition of intellectual property protection through international registration systems.

The Governing Bodies of WIPO and the Unions administered by the organization held their twenty-sixth series of meetings from 25 September to 3 October and twenty-seventh series from 19 to 21 December, both in Geneva. The WIPO General Assembly, one of the Governing Bodies, unanimously reappointed Arpad Bogsch as Director-General of WIPO for an additional two-year term, expiring on 1 December 1997. At the December session, the Governing Bodies approved a cooperation agreement between WIPO and the World Trade Organization (WTO). The agreement was signed on 22 December 1995, to enter into force on 1 January 1996.

During 1995, WIPO membership increased to 157 States, with the accession of Azerbaijan, Bahrain, Cambodia, Nigeria, Saint Kitts and Nevis, Saint Vincent and the Grenadines and Turkmenistan to the 1967 Convention Establishing WIPO, amended in 1979. During the same period, the number of States adhering to treaties administered by WIPO also increased. States parties to the Paris Convention for the Protection of Industrial Property increased to 136 as at the end of 1995; to the Berne Convention for the Protection of Literary and Artistic Works, to 117; and to the Patent Cooperation Treaty, to 83.

## Activities in 1995

### Development cooperation

WIPO's development cooperation programme in the fields of industrial property, copyright and neighbouring rights quickened its pace in 1995, with the number of beneficiary countries totalling 118, while the number of advisory missions reached 200, a 19 per cent increase over 1994.

In October 1995, the WIPO International Bureau began an intensive programme of assistance to developing countries to ensure their compatibility with the 1994 WTO Agreement on Trade-related Aspects of Intellectual Property Rights (TRIPS Agreement). In December, a three-day regional symposium for the Arab countries on the implications of the TRIPS Agreement was held in Cairo, Egypt.

A total of 120 courses, seminars and other meetings were organized by WIPO in 1995 at the global, regional and national levels, with some 9,500 participants. The WIPO Academy conducted two sessions on intellectual property issues for middle- and senior-level government officials, one in English and one in French.

### Assistance to countries in transition

On 12 August 1995, the Eurasian Patent Convention entered into force. The Convention, drafted with the assistance of the WIPO International Bureau, was finalized and adopted in Geneva in February 1994. By 31 December 1995, nine States (Armenia, Azerbaijan, Belarus, Kazakstan, Kyrgyzstan, Republic of Moldova, Russian Federation, Tajikistan, Turkmenistan) had ratified or acceded to the Convention. In November, the Administrative Council of the Eurasian Patent Organization adopted the patent, administrative and financial instructions under the Convention and fixed 1 January 1996 as the starting date for the Eurasian Patent Office (established under the Convention and located in Moscow) to begin receiving Eurasian patent applications.

In 1995, nine national and regional seminars and other meetings were organized by WIPO in countries in transition for some 700 participants. WIPO officials and consultants undertook 29 missions to 17 of those countries to give advice, in particular, on the preparation of laws and national infrastructures related to intellectual property rights, the advantages of adherence to WIPO-administered treaties, and training in various specialized fields of intellectual property.

### Setting of norms and standards

Significant advances were made in 1995 towards the possible adoption, through a diplomatic conference, of new international instruments in the fields of patents, industrial designs, copyright and neighbouring rights and the settlement of intellectual property disputes among States.

Regarding the harmonization of patent laws, the WIPO Governing Bodies agreed that future treaty work should focus on the formalities of national and regional patent applications, such as signatures, changes in names and addresses, correction of mistakes and standardized forms. Those issues were incorporated into proposals reviewed by a Committee of Experts on the Patent Law Treaty, which held its first session in December 1995. The Committee was scheduled to hold two more sessions in 1996 to examine the next draft of the proposed treaty, which, in addition to the provisions already reviewed, would contain provisions related to the filing date of an application and unity of intervention.

Regarding the protection of industrial designs, the Governing Bodies decided in October that a session of the Committee of Experts on preparation of a new treaty would meet in 1996. Following that meeting, the competent WIPO Governing Bodies would decide whether a diplomatic conference for adoption of a new treaty would take place in 1997. Such a new treaty, it was decided, might take the form of a revision of the Hague Agreement Concerning the International Deposit of Industrial Designs.

In November 1995, a new Committee of Experts was convened by WIPO to examine prospects for improving the protection of well-known marks. The Committee agreed that the question should be further studied and the results examined by a second session of the Committee during the second half of 1996.

Regarding copyright and neighbouring rights, a joint meeting was convened in September 1995 of the Committee of Experts on a Possible Protocol to the Berne Convention and the Committee of Experts on a Possible Instrument for the Protection of the Rights of Performers and Producers of Phonograms. Work advanced on issues particular to each Committee as well as those issues considered common to both, including distribution rights, importation and rental issues, digital issues, enforcement of rights and national treatment. The Committees decided that proposals in treaty language would be examined at the next joint meeting in February 1996, and that, if work did not advance sufficiently following that meeting, the competent Governing Bodies of WIPO should be convened to decide on the organization and date for one or more diplomatic conferences for the conclusion of the new instruments.

WIPO convened two international symposiums (Mexico City, May; Naples, Italy, October) to provide international forums for exchange of ideas on the impact of digital technology on copyright issues. A consultative forum for non-governmental organizations was also organized in Geneva in June to encourage an exchange of views on the protection and management of copyright and neighbouring rights in digital systems.

### WIPO Arbitration Centre

In November 1995, the second meeting of the WIPO Arbitration Council reviewed activities of the WIPO Arbitration Centre since its first meeting in September 1994 and examined a draft proposal to introduce an emergency interim arbitral procedure by a stand-by panel of arbitrators. Throughout 1995, the Arbitration Centre undertook a number of promotional activities, including jointly organizing with the Swiss Arbitration Association an international conference on the WIPO Mediation, Arbitration and Expedited Arbitration Rules, as well as organizing two training programmes for mediators.

### International registration activities

*Patent Cooperation Treaty* (PCT). In 1995, there were 38,906 international applications filed, of which 1,151 were filed directly with the WIPO International Bureau in its capacity, since 1 January 1994, as a receiving office. With an average of 46.4 countries designated per application, the total number of international applications filed with PCT had the effect of 1,807,220 national applications.

In October, the PCT Assembly adopted a revised schedule of fees, increasing the maximum number of designations for which fees were payable from 10 to 11. The Assembly also approved a 75 per cent reduction in fees for any applicant who was a national and resident in a country whose per capita national income was below $3,000.

*Madrid Agreement.* In the trademark system under the Madrid Agreement Concerning the International Registration of Marks and its 1989 Protocol, there was a total of 18,890 international registrations in 1995. With an average of 10.44 countries designated per registration, those applications had the effect of some 197,210 national registrations.

The Madrid Protocol entered into force on 1 December 1995, having obtained the required number of notifications. As at 31 December 1995, five States (China, Cuba, Spain, Sweden, United Kingdom) had acceded to or ratified the Protocol. Draft Common Regulations under the Madrid Agreement and Protocol were finalized by the International Bureau in 1995, to be submitted to the Madrid Assembly in 1996.

*Hague Agreement.* Under the Hague Agreement Concerning the International Deposit of Industrial Designs, there was a combined total of 5,585 industrial design deposits, renewals and prolongations in 1995. In September/October, the Assembly of the Hague Union adopted a revised fee schedule, increasing fees by 3 per cent.

## Secretariat

As at 31 December 1995, WIPO employed 517 staff members representing 64 countries. Of those, 183 were in the Professional and higher categories and 334 in the General Service category.

## Budget

WIPO's principal income was derived from ordinary and special contributions from member States and from international registration services, mainly under PCT and the Madrid Agreement. In 1995, the organization's budgeted income amounted to 119 million Swiss francs and budgeted expenditures totalled 115 million Swiss francs, of which 70 million Swiss francs were staff costs. In October 1995, the Governing Bodies of WIPO decided to double the development cooperation budget in the organization's 1996-1997 regular budget over the 1994-1995 budget. The increase was to allow WIPO to provide increased legal and technical assistance to developing countries to help them meet their new obligations under the TRIPS Agreement.

NOTE: For further information on the agency, see *Governing Bodies of WIPO and the Unions Administered by WIPO: Activities in the Year 1995*, published by WIPO.

## *HEADQUARTERS AND OTHER OFFICE*

HEADQUARTERS
World Intellectual Property Organization
34 Chemin des Colombettes
1211 Geneva 20, Switerland
  *Cable address:* OMPI GENEVA
  *Telephone:* (41) (22) 730-91-11
  *Fax:* (41) (22) 733-54-28
  *Telex:* 412 912 OMPI CH

WIPO OFFICE AT THE UNITED NATIONS
2 United Nations Plaza, Room 560
New York, N.Y. 10017, United States
  *Telephone:* (1) (212) 963-6813
  *Fax:* (1) (212) 963-4801
  *Telex:* 420544 UNH UI

Chapter XVI

# International Fund for Agricultural Development (IFAD)

In 1995, the International Fund for Agricultural Development (IFAD) provided intensified efforts to help the rural poor achieve food security and improved nutrition through increased agricultural production and income. Established in 1977, IFAD provides concessional assistance for financing agricultural projects in developing countries.

The IFAD Executive Board held three regular sessions in 1995 (April, September and December), approving loans for 33 projects, including three jointly financed under the Special Programme for Sub-Saharan African Countries Affected by Drought and Desertification (SPA) and regular resources. Twelve technical assistance grants were also approved. The Board adopted a recommendation that SPA be terminated on 31 December 1995 and its operations integrated into Regular Programme operations.

The Board also approved a programme of work for 1996 at 304.3 million special drawing rights (SDR) for loans and grants under the Regular Programme and endorsed a budget of $49.9 million, including a contingency of $300,000.

IFAD membership increased to 158 during 1995, with the admission of the Republic of Georgia. Of its member countries, 22 were in Category I (developed countries), 12 in Category II (oil-exporting developing countries), and 124 in Category III (other developing countries).

## Resources

Progress was made during 1995 on negotiations on the Fourth Replenishment of IFAD's Resources ($600 million targeted) covering the period 1995-1997. The Fund's developing member States announced pledges exceeding the 85 per cent target level for Categories II and III agreed by the Governing Council in 1994. While most Category I countries had reaffirmed their adherence to the target set for them in 1994, one major donor still had to complete its budgetary processes before announcing its contribution.

## Activities in 1995

Loans and grants approved in 1995 under IFAD's Regular Programme and SPA totalled SDR 276 million ($413.8 million equivalent), which financed 33 projects worth SDR 261.4 million ($391.7 million) and 58 technical assistance grants worth SDR 14.6 million ($22.1 million). The Fund's regular resources financed 33 loans total-

ling SDR 253.9 million ($380.5 million) and 50 technical assistance grants amounting to SDR 13.8 million ($20.9 million). The balance of four loans for SDR 7.5 million ($11.2 million) and eight technical assistance grants for SDR 0.8 million ($1.2 million) was financed from the Special Resources for Sub-Saharan Africa (SRS).

In terms of SDR, total commitment for 1995 was 34 per cent above the yearly average for 1978-1994. The average size of IFAD lending per project was SDR 7.9 million ($11.9 million), as compared to the 1978-1994 average of SDR 8.3 million ($10.5 million).

Some 29.7 per cent of the Fund's Regular Programme resources in 1995 were used for loans to the Africa region, which amounted to SDR 75.3 million ($113.2 million). Over the period 1978-1995, the region received SDR 983 million ($1,252.5 million), or 30.1 per cent of total lending under the Regular Programme. With the inclusion of allocations under the Special Programme for Africa, the cumulative percentage of resources received by the Africa region amounted to 35 per cent from 1978 to 1995. In 1995, the countries of sub-Saharan Africa received 31.7 per cent of IFAD's Regular and Special Programme allocations as compared to 38.6 per cent over the period 1978-1994.

The Near East and North Africa region (which also covered Djibouti, Somalia, the Sudan and new member countries of Central Europe) received SDR 46.7 million ($72.5 million), or 19 per cent of Regular Programme lending in 1995. The region had received a total of SDR 574.1 million ($731.7 million) or 17.5 per cent of total Regular Programme lending since 1978.

With the highest concentration of absolute poor, the Asia and Pacific region continued to receive the largest share of the Fund's Regular Programme lending. In 1995, the region received SDR 80.9 million ($121.9 million), accounting for 32 per cent of Regular Programme lending during the year. Total loans to the Asia and Pacific region during the period 1978-1995 amounted to SDR 1,191 million ($1,506.5 million), or 36.1 per cent of IFAD lending under the Regular Programme.

In 1995, the Latin America and Caribbean region received SDR 49 million ($73 million), or 19.2 per cent of the Fund's Regular Programme lending. Since 1978, the region had been allocated SDR 524.6 million ($682.1 million), amounting to 16.3 per cent of total Regular Programme loans.

The Fund continued to place high priority on lending in least developed and low-income, food-deficit countries and allocations were mainly to countries where the problems of hunger and poverty were most acute. During 1995, the least developed countries (as defined by the United Nations) received 31.6 per cent of IFAD lending, while their average share between 1978 and 1994 was 38.6 per cent. Low-income and food-deficit countries received 72.5 per cent of total IFAD lending, as compared to 85.4 per cent over 1978-1994.

### Secretariat

As at 31 December 1995, the IFAD secretariat had a total of 264 staff, of whom 111 were in the Professional or higher categories and 153 in the General Service category.

### Income and expenditure

Total revenue under the Regular Programme in 1995 was $309.1 million, consisting of $268.4 million of investment income and $40.7 million from interest and service charges on loans. Investment income excluded foreign currency hedging gains or losses. Total operational and administrative expenses for the year amounted to $45.7 million, compared with a budget, before contingency, of $46.4 million. The excess of revenue over expenses for the year, including the effects of foreign exchange rate movements of $52.5 million, was $317 million.

Total revenue under SPA was $15.1 million, consisting of $13.8 million of investment income and $1.3 million from interest and services charges on loans. Total expenses for the year amounted to $4 million, compared with a budget, before contingency, of $3.8 million. The excess of revenue over expenses for the year, including the effects of foreign exchange rate movements, was $16.9 million.

NOTE: For further details on IFAD activities in 1995, see *Annual Report 1995*, published by the Fund.

## HEADQUARTERS AND OTHER OFFICES

**HEADQUARTERS**
International Fund for Agricultural Development
Via del Serafico, 107
00142 Rome, Italy
   *Cable address:* IFAD ROME
   *Telephone:* (39) (6) 54591
   *Fax:* (39) (6) 5043463
   *Telex:* 620330

**IFAD Liaison Office**
1 United Nations Plaza, Room 1208
New York, N.Y. 10017, United States
   *Telephone:* (1) (212) 963-0546
   *Fax:* (1) (212) 963-2787

**IFAD Liaison Office**
1775 K Street, N.W., Suite 410
Washington, D.C. 20006, United States
   *Telephone:* (1) (202) 331-9099
   *Fax:* (1) (202) 331-9366

Chapter XVII

# United Nations Industrial Development Organization (UNIDO)

In 1995, the United Nations Industrial Development Organization (UNIDO) continued to promote sustainable industrial development in countries with developing and transition economies. At the end of the year, UNIDO reached the final stage of a two-year reform process which concentrated on reorientation of its activities to adjust to the new economic environment of the 1990s. It included a refocusing of UNIDO services and improvement of management processes to increase efficiency, as well as budgetary reductions and structural modification. It also adopted a new mission statement, which emphasized UNIDO's role as a catalyst seeking to harness the joint forces of Government and the private sector, with the overall aims to foster competitive industrial production, develop international industrial partnerships and promote socially equitable and environmentally sustainable industrial development.

In spite of budgetary cutbacks, UNIDO reversed the trend of declining technical cooperation delivery since 1990, with delivery increasing by 7 per cent over the previous year to $108.5 million. At the same time, the sources of project funding were further diversified, an essential step folowing the drastic decline in United Nations Development Programme funding.

The General Conference, the main governing body of UNIDO, met for its sixth session in December, while the Industrial Development Board held its fourteenth session in June, resuming it in October.

## Policy issues

In 1995, UNIDO identified seven thematic priorities for cross-organizational focus during the 1996-1997 biennium, in a response to identified demand for integrated and multidisciplinary services and drawing on the core of UNIDO expertise. Those priorities were: strategies, policies and institution-building for global economic integration; environment and energy; policies, networking and basic technical support for small and medium enterprises; innovation, productivity and quality for international competitiveness; industrial information, investment and technology promotion; rural industrial development; and linking industry with agriculture in Africa and the least developed countries (LDCs). While the first six priorities were global in coverage, the last one reinforced UNIDO's geographical focus.

The following industrial subsectors were marked for priority attention: food processing, leather, textiles and wood processing within agro-based industries; metalworking and machine tools (with emphasis on agricultural machinery) within engineering industries; biotechnology, water management, medicinal plants, building materials and organic chemicals within chemical industries.

### Strategies, policies and institution-building

UNIDO worked during 1995 on helping provide institutional structure to make policies work, enable the private sector to get involved in policy formulation, and interface between private enterprises and the public sector. It made a special effort to strengthen and streamline industrial institutions in a number of developing countries, including Guinea, Maldives, Nepal, Sierra Leone and Zimbabwe. During 1995, UNIDO advised the Ministry of Industry of Ghana and the Minister of Commerce and Industry of Swaziland on ways to restructure their institutions to meet the demands of sustainable development and create a stimulating environment for industry.

The organization helped overcome the lack of industrial data in developing countries by strengthening its information network capability to provide a self-sufficient, self-sustainable way of meeting the need for information for industry, business and government. The UNIDO network made wide use of Internet and other networks, such as Industrynet, International Business Network, Electronic Trade Point System, Unisphere and others, to promote networking, increase efficiency and reduce communication costs.

### Environment and energy

UNIDO addressed environmental issues stemming from industrial development, with particular emphasis on preventive rather than corrective action. Services focused on capacity-building in support of national strategies for environmentally sound industrial development; implementation of international agreements, conventions and protocols for protection of the environment; and establishment of national cleaner production centres and the promotion and transfer of clean technologies in various industrial subsectors, as well as enhancing the efficiency of energy use in industrial processes.

In cooperation with the United Nations Environment Programme, UNIDO established eight national cleaner production centres in 1995 in Brazil, China, the Czech Republic, India, Mexico, Slovakia, Tunisia, the United Republic of Tanzania and Zimbabwe. It continued to introduce pollution prevention and control activities in the chemical, food processing, leather, textiles, pulp and paper and metallurgical industries, and supported cleaner technology in order to reduce the use of chemicals, water, energy and raw materials. In cooperation with Governments and industry, UNIDO also provided assistance in limiting the use of ozone-depleting substances, in accordance with the 1987 Montreal Protocol on Substances that Deplete the Ozone Layer.[a]

### Small and medium industries

With small and medium industries (SMIs) the main target group for its services, UNIDO focused on supporting developing countries in creating an overall policy and institutional environment conducive to the further development of SMIs. In 1995, UNIDO provided policy advice and institutional support for promoting SMIs with overall private sector development and increased market orientation. It also helped stimulate networking of SMIs with larger enterprises and among themselves through national and regional subcontracting schemes and sectoral clusters.

UNIDO assistance aimed at improving the access of SMIs to information, technology, managerial experience and financial resources, particularly in rural areas where support for the development of even the most basic levels of skills could contribute to the socio-economic development of an entire community. In Burkina Faso and Mali, for example, UNIDO installed more than 20 food-processing machines in 1995, enabling rural women to escape the arduous task of grinding millet every day.

Through its Support Programme for Innovation and Networking, developed and implemented in cooperation with private sector organizations, policy makers and support institutions from both industrialized and developing countries, UNIDO provided information, advisory and training services, and facilitated joint learning between clusters of SMIs.

### Innovation, productivity and competitiveness

UNIDO was increasingly called upon in 1995 to provide specialized services to industrial institutions working with the private sector on industry-specific research and development, continuous quality improvements and meeting certification requirements for international standards. Support at the institutional level was complemented by assistance to groups of enterprises, mostly channelled

through industrial associations, in rehabilitating and restructuring their operations. UNIDO also monitored worldwide trends and new generic technologies, and evaluated them according to the needs of developing countries. In December 1995, it published a *Manual on Technology Transfer Negotiation* comprising a set of instructional materials for teaching technology transfer and contract negotiation.

UNIDO's Quality, Standardization and Metrology Programme provided a comprehensive range of services required at the policy, institutional and enterprise levels. In addition, a high-impact programme was developed to apply the principles of the UNIDO Quality Approach to the food processing sectors of seven African countries (Ethiopia, Kenya, Malawi, Mozambique, Uganda, Zambia and Zimbabwe). The programme aimed to establish the conditions for effective mobilization of resources to strengthen food quality and safety support institutions and to implement pilot improvement programmes in selected enterprises.

### Industrial information, investment and technology promotion

In 1995, the UNIDO Industrial and Technological Information Bank developed a programme to expand more than 80 national and regional focal points into self-sufficient and self-sustainable information networks. The organization also operated an Investment Promotion Service Network in commercial centres throughout the world, including Athens (Greece), Beijing (China), Istanbul (Turkey), Milan (Italy), Moscow, Paris, Seoul (Republic of Korea), Warsaw (Poland) and Zurich (Switzerland). During 1995, negotiations were finalized to open services in Bahrain and Vienna. Investment promotion initiatives were established to serve investors in Belgium, India and the United Kingdom, and investment forums were held in China, Ghana, India, Jordan, the Russian Federation, Uganda and the United Republic of Tanzania.

### Rural industrial development

During the year, UNIDO concentrated efforts on redressing industrial development disparities within developing countries, considered crucial to equitable development, poverty alleviation and food security. Its main activities involved the leather, wood products, textile and medicinal plants industries, but by far the largest was its commitment to the food industry where the development of dairy, fish and meat products and the reinforcement of competitiveness of the food-processing sector were its leading concerns. This was complemented by support to building

[a]YUN 1987, p. 686.

materials industries, in particular those relevant for low-cost housing in rural areas.

UNIDO also placed great emphasis on ecologically sound development as part of its campaign to eradicate poverty by providing employment opportunities. In a number of African countries, including Ethiopia, Kenya, Uganda, the United Republic of Tanzania and Zimbabwe, community organizers in the leather industry were helped to deal with waste management, while new and renewable sources of energy such as solar energy were promoted along with clean technology in manufacturing activities such as wet processing and dyeing methods in the textile and clothing industries.

UNIDO projects in the construction industry aimed at encouraging cheaper and simpler technologies suitable for local needs and available resources. Projects in Cameroon, Chad, Ethiopia, Madagascar, Mozambique and Zambia emphasized stabilized soil blocks, fibro-cement roofs and processing of dimension stone, and were successful in integrating technology transfer and investment promotion and in ensuring self-reliance and self-sustainability.

### Africa and LDCs

In 1994-1995, Africa was the leading recipient region of UNIDO services, benefiting from 40 per cent of the Organization's technical cooperation approvals. During 1995, UNIDO experts worked to expand the regional leather programme in Ethiopia, Kenya, Malawi, the Sudan, Uganda, the United Republic of Tanzania, Zambia and Zimbabwe. UNIDO established a leather goods manufacturing unit and a tannery in Kenya, and shoe manufacturing projects in other East African countries. It provided assistance in manufactured wood products in Angola, Cameroon, the Central African Republic, Côte d'Ivoire, Kenya, Madagascar and Senegal. UNIDO's expertise helped identify technical assistance projects in design and maintenance of agricultural machinery, tools and implements. The organization also helped create prototypes and offered training in Ethiopia and Kenya, and established a regional network for the Asia and Pacific region. UNIDO technical cooperation delivery in Africa amounted to $32.9 million in 1995. At the same time, UNIDO approved 100 new projects for a total of $24.5 million and project revisions amounting to an additional $7.2 million. It offered a wide range of services within the framework of the Second Industrial Development Decade for Africa (IDDA II), 1993-2002 (see PART FOUR, Chapter V), focusing on strengthening industrial institutions; developing strategies and policies for accelerated industrial development; private sector development with emphasis on strengthening private sector institutions;

SMI development; rehabilitation of key industries; developing human resources; assisting women to meet the challenges of industrial and technological change in a competitive, global economy; and promotion of technology and investment. Total budgetary appropriation for IDDA in 1995 was $7.8 million. In December 1995, at the sixth session of the General Conference of UNIDO, the Director-General announced a proposal for an Alliance for Africa's Industrialization as a complementary effort to the United Nations System-wide Special Initiative on Africa (see PART FOUR, Chapter III); that Alliance was to be further developed in 1996 in close consultation with African Governments and regional and subregional organizations.

UNIDO technical cooperation delivery to LDCs amounted to $8.6 million in 1995, of which 76 per cent went to African LDCs. UNIDO continued to support programmes in LDCs aimed at creating an enabling environment for investment promotion and mobilizing financial resources for industrial development. A total of 10 LDCs benefited from support which covered assistance to ministries of industry in formulating national investment policies, identifying international investment and strengthening investment and export promotion institutions. As a further element in its support to LDCs in mobilizing local and foreign investments, UNIDO organized institutional investment forums for a number of LDCs. In conjunction with the sixth session of the General Conference, UNIDO hosted the Third Ministerial Symposium on the Industrialization of Least Developed Countries (30 November–8 December) at which Ministers and delegates from 38 LDCs and six international organizations discussed common industrial development issues.

### Human resources development

In 1995, UNIDO continued to promote the application of industrial knowledge and improve industrial skills in developing countries, with particular emphasis on developing entrepreneurship, creating capacities for technological management and innovation, and assessing the impact of technological change on socio-economic development. Particular attention was directed to creating a comprehensive framework and integrated approach to human resources development (HRD), linking supply elements (training, education and skills planning) with demand elements (demographic patterns, employment and labour market trends, and changes in the workplace). UNIDO developed tools, including databases, to allow for an effective response to countries requesting support in human resources development. Its HRD programme was refocused to assist countries with developing and transitional economies in building up a broad spectrum of human resources with required skills and capabilities and in developing a critical base of entrepreneurs, managers, technicians and technology-support professionals. The programme provided support in three primary areas: upstream services, including policy advice based on analysis and assessment of requirements; institutional capacity-building and catalytic learning systems, including training, at subsector levels and in specialized fields; and communication networks to simplify coordination and synergy of efforts.

UNIDO technical cooperation in human resources development emphasized local capacity-building relevant to mainstreaming women in industrial development, technology transfer, project appraisal and preparation, restructuring and privatization, investment promotion, environmental protection, energy and SMIs.

UNIDO provided advisory services and preparatory assistance to five African countries, the Caribbean region and Jordan for developing national and regional programmes; to Indonesia for a distance learning network for industry; and to Iran on mainstreaming women in industrial development. In the Philippines, a World Bank–funded feasibility study was conducted to determine demand-supply and sustainability strategies for private training centres, and for the transfer of responsibility for the National Manpower Youth Commission to the private sector.

Five awareness-building seminars for policy makers, senior government officials, entrepreneurs and managers were held in 1995 for Africa, Asia and the Pacific, and Latin America and the Caribbean, on project preparation and evaluation, project management, environmental management, technology management and industrial quality. Related HRD programmes took advantage of and strengthened indigenous capacities of local intermediaries such as professional associations, chambers of commerce and non-governmental organizations (NGOs), as a means of delivering programmes in line with specific local needs.

A new set of criteria was developed for implementing group training programmes, giving priority to those meeting the requirements for sustainability, impact, national relevance, and the use of in-house expertise and capabilities. At the same time, the total number of trainees in in-plant and other group training programmes of UNIDO increased by 11 per cent over the previous year.

The revision of the training programme on industrial planning in Japan led to a new seminar on technology management and industrial development. Participants from five developing countries benefited from practical sessions and study visits, which contributed Japanese know-how and experience in technology transfer and production

processes. In China, the training programme to promote the participation of women in the country's modernization process focused on the training of trainers for women entrepreneurs and managers. Project managers from the Russian Federation participated in a study tour conducted jointly by UNIDO and the World Bank. In Brazil, UNIDO introduced modern technology and gave support to the main textile school and research centre for training managers in new management and processing techniques. In the food-processing and related industries, UNIDO expanded projects, conducted workshops and trained trainers in areas such as technology, maintenance, quality, packaging and marketing.

At the enterprise level, a wide range of sector- and industry-specific HRD programmes were implemented. Examples of such programmes included training of trainers to conduct project appraisal and preparation of investment projects in developing countries, outreach and capacity-building exercises for women in small-scale agro-based enterprise workshops, and pilot training programmes to improve energy efficiency.

In June, a regional workshop for Arab LDCs was held for engineers and technicians on critical industrial maintenance issues. A two-month technical study was conducted for an HRD programme for Iranian women professionals from the sugar manufacturing industry. Examples of enhancing local capacity to manage industry-specific technology transfer included an Africa-wide training course on footwear technology and training in leather manufacturing technology, tannery machinery maintenance and pollution control in the leather industry.

### Women in industrial development

UNIDO's programme on the integration of women in industrial development focused on substantive preparation for and participation in the Fourth World Conference on Women and its accompanying NGO Forum (Beijing, China, September) (see PART FOUR, Chapter X). In addition, UNIDO pursued the promotion, preparation and implementation of projects for women. At the same time, continued emphasis was placed on mainstreaming gender issues into programmes and projects. In line with programmes adopted in previous years, in particular the training programme for women entrepreneurs in the food-processing industries and the thematic programme ''Women entrepreneurs for industrial growth'', several new projects were approved in 1995 through contributions from the Industrial Development Fund (IDF), such as in Botswana, Kenya and the United Republic of Tanzania. Several other projects were developed, e.g. in Ghana, Namibia and Uganda, for which the sources of financing were being explored.

A programme for women's entrepreneurship development was developed for country-level implementation. Funds were obtained for projects mainly in the food-processing industries in Côte d'Ivoire, Ethiopia, Mali and Senegal. Work was under way to develop a training module for women entrepreneurs, focusing on spice production in the United Republic of Tanzania. As a result of a regional study in Latin America and the Caribbean, a Colombian pilot project was designed to elaborate a national programme to increase women's participation in manufacturing.

In order to help increase gender awareness of decision makers in developing countries, UNIDO developed a database on women in industry that provided statistical data on over 100 indicators for addressing gender issues.

The UNIDO Women and Industry Recognition Award was launched in 1995 to provide incentives to Governments for their efforts in implementing gender-sensitive policies and to women industrialists to acknowledge the best performances

achieved in industry in terms of contributions to the advancement of women.

### Secretariat

As at 31 December 1995, UNIDO employed 924 staff members in the Professional and General Services categories stationed at its headquarters in Vienna and in 115 field offices abroad. In addition, UNIDO utilized the services of some 850 experts from more than 100 countries, 40 per cent of whom were from developing countries.

### Budget

At its sixth session in December 1995, the UNIDO General Conference approved a regular budget for 1996-1997 of $181 million, funded from assessed contributions from member States, and an operational budget of $29 million funded from technical cooperation support cost reimbursement.

NOTE: For further information on UNIDO, see *Annual Report of UNIDO 1995*.

## *HEADQUARTERS AND OTHER OFFICES*

**HEADQUARTERS**
United Nations Industrial Development Organization
Vienna International Centre
P.O. Box 300
A-1400 Vienna, Austria
*Telephone:* (43) (1) 211-310
*Fax:* (43) (1) 232156, 2140414
*Telex:* 135612
*World Wide Web:* http://www.unido.org
*E-mail:* unido-pinfo@unido.org

**LIAISON OFFICE**
UNIDO Liaison Office
1 United Nations Plaza, Room DC1-1110
New York, N.Y. 10017, United States
*Telephone:* (1) (212) 963-6882
*Fax:* (1) (212) 963-7904

Chapter XVIII

# World Trade Organization (WTO) and the General Agreement on Tariffs and Trade (GATT)

With the conclusion, after more than seven years of discussions, of the Uruguay Round of multilateral trade negotiations and the signing of the Marrakesh (Morocco) Declaration in April 1994,[a] the World Trade Organization (WTO) came into being on 1 January 1995 as the successor to the General Agreement on Tariffs and Trade (GATT). WTO and GATT co-existed throughout 1995 in order to allow sufficient time for all Governments to join the new Organization. The rules of the orginal GATT became an integral part of WTO and, along with their various amendments, were known as GATT 1994.

WTO's five principal functions were: to facilitate the implementation of the results of the Uruguay Round; to provide a forum for multilateral trade negotiations and a framework for the implementation of their results; to administer the dispute settlement procedures; to administer the Trade Policy Review Mechanism; and to cooperate with the International Monetary Fund (IMF) and the World Bank with a view to achieving greater coherence in global economic policy-making.

WTO membership reached 112 by the end of 1995. Another 28 Governments, including China and the Russian Federation, were at various stages of the accession process. GATT had 128 members.

## General activities

WTO's highest authority, the Ministerial Conference, was scheduled to meet every two years. It was administered by the General Council, which was set up to handle the day-to-day operation of the Organization between Conferences. The Council convened in two forms: as the Dispute Settlement Body, to oversee dispute settlement procedures, and as the Trade Policy Review Body, to conduct regular reviews of the trade policies of individual WTO members. The General Council had three subsidiary Councils—for Trade in Goods, Trade in Services, and Trade-Related Aspects of Intellectual Property Rights.

In 1995, General Council activities focused on procedural, organizational and institutional matters. At its first meeting in January, the Council adopted the recommendations of the Preparatory Committee for WTO, including establishment of various WTO bodies. In May, it approved the Head-quarters Agreement with Swiss authorities. The

Council decided in April that the International Trade Centre (ITC) should be operated jointly by WTO and the United Nations Conference on Trade and Development (UNCTAD), the latter acting on behalf of the United Nations. Also during the year, the WTO Secretariat pursued preparations for cooperation agreements with IMF and the World Bank.

The Trade Policy Review Mechanism, which was established provisionally in 1989 under GATT, was given a permanent role within WTO and its coverage extended to services, intellectual property and other policies covered by the Uruguay Round agreements. Fifteen trade policy reviews were undertaken between December 1994 and December 1995, including third reviews of the European Community (EC) and Japan; second reviews of Morocco, Sweden and Thailand; and first reviews of Cameroon, Costa Rica, Côte d'Ivoire, Israel, Mauritius, Pakistan, the Slovak Republic, Sri Lanka, Uganda and Zimbabwe.

The WTO dispute-settlement framework was completed in November 1995 with the appointment of a seven-member Appellate Body. As at 27 November, the Dispute Settlement Body had been notified of 21 requests for consultations. As some of the requests concerned the same issue, the number of distinct measures subject to dispute was 14. Of those, four were withdrawn and panels were established on another four.

In 1995, eleven members held consultations, under Articles XII or XVII:B of GATT, with WTO and/or GATT Committees with regard to balance-of-payments restrictions. The Committees requested Poland and Slovakia to eliminate import surcharges and asked Hungary to present a concrete timetable for the reduction and elimination of an import surcharge notified in March. They requested Sri Lanka not to have recourse to the provisions of Article XVII:B. Consultations were held with Bangladesh, India and the Philippines. Egypt, Israel and South Africa disinvoked the balance-of-payments provisions in July, September and November, respectively. Following consultations in October, Brazil withdrew a quota on imports of motor vehicles notified under Article XVIII:B.

[a]YUN 1994, pp. 1474-75.

The new WTO Committee on Trade and Environment discussed its work programme during 1995, taking advantage of work done by the GATT Group on Environmental Measures and International Trade related to three issues: the relationship between WTO provisions and trade measures taken pursuant to multilateral environmental agreements; eco-labelling and packaging requirements; and the transparency of trade-related environmental measures and environment-related trade measures.

The expanded scope of WTO increased substantially the demand for technical assistance during 1995. The WTO Secretariat arranged more than 60 national or regional seminars, workshops and technical missions during the year. In addition, a total of 99 officials from developing countries and from economies in transition participated in WTO policy trade courses, and WTO technical missions assisted officials in the capitals of least developed countries in preparing schedules of concessions on goods and commitments on services. Also, a new WTO initiative was launched to help African countries expand and diversify their trade, to be pursued in cooperation with other organizations, including UNCTAD.

At the request of the Committee on Trade and Development, the Secretariat organized a workshop in May to assist members in meeting their notification obligations. Other issues addressed by the Committee in 1995 included the impact of the Uruguay Round agreements on developing country members; the question of credit; recognition for autonomous trade liberalization measures; recent developments in the generalized system of preferences (GSP) (see PART FOUR, Chapter IV); and regional trade agreements between developing countries.

## Trade in goods

Regarding implementation of tariff concessions contained in the Uruguay Round schedules, the Committee on Market Access agreed to follow the same approach used after the Tokyo Round (1973-1979), which was to rely on cross or reverse notification of any problem. No such notifications were made during 1995.

The entry into force of the Agreement on Textiles and Clothing set in motion the ten-year transition period from the 1974 Multifibre Arrangement's complex network of bilateral and discriminatory quotas to a multilateral set of rules and disciplines for textiles and clothing trade. The Textiles Monitoring Body oversaw the start of the first phase of integration into the GATT 1994 rules of at least 16 per cent of textiles and clothing products. It also reviewed measures taken under the transitional safeguard mechanism of the Agreement.

During 1995, the Committee on Agriculture focused on the establishment of efficient and effective working procedures, including notification requirements. An initial work programme was established for 1996 with respect to the Committee's role in monitoring follow-up to the Decision on Measures Concerning the Possible Negative Effects of the Reform Programme on Least Developed and Net Food-Importing Developing Countries.

The Committee on Sanitary and Phytosanitary Measures agreed on the format and recommendations of proposed new regulations or changes in regulations, which were similar to those used in notifying technical regulations under the Agreement on Technical Barriers to Trade. To facilitate members in meeting their obligations, the Committee in 1995 identified existing international standards developed by the Food and Agriculture Organization (FAO)/World Health Organization (WHO) Codex Alimentarius Commission, the Office International des Epizooties, and the FAO International Plant Protection Convention.

The Committee on Anti-Dumping Practices, the Committee on Safeguards, and the Committee on Countervailing Measures began during 1995 to review relevant legislation and regulations of members. Between 1 July 1994 and 30 June 1995, the most active members in terms of initiations of anti-dumping investigations were EC (37), the United States (30), Mexico (18) and Brazil (12). During the same period, the most active members in terms of initiations of countervailing duty actions were the United States (5), Peru (4), Argentina (2) and Canada (2). As at 30 June 1995, there were 805 anti-dumping measures in force, of which 60 per cent were maintained by the United States and EC. The number of countervailing measures was 128, of which 80 per cent were maintained by the United States.

## Trade in services

The extended financial services negotiations were concluded at the end of July 1995 with 29 participants (Australia, Brazil, Canada, Chile, Czech Republic, Dominican Republic, Egypt, EC, Hong Kong, Hungary, India, Indonesia, Japan, Korea, Kuwait, Malaysia, Mexico, Morocco, Norway, Pakistan, Philippines, Poland, Singapore, Slovak Republic, South Africa, Switzerland, Thailand, Turkey and Venezuela) offering improved access in this sector. Twenty participants made improved commitments in insurance; 24 in banking; 17 in securities; and 25 in other financial services. Negotiations continued during the year on trade in basic telecommunications and on maritime transport services.

In July 1995, the Negotiating Group on the Movement of Natural Persons concluded its work, producing six sets of commitments which were annexed to the Third Protocol to the General Agreement on Trade in Services (GATS). Six participants (Australia, Canada, EC, India, Norway and Switzerland) made higher levels of commitments that would guarantee new opportunities in their markets for individual service suppliers—qualified professionals, computer specialists, experts of various kinds—to work abroad in an individual capacity on temporary assignments, without the requirement that they be linked with a commercial presence in the host country.

The Council for Trade in Services established a Working Party on Professional Services, with the task of formulating recommendations on multilateral disciplines that might be needed to ensure that measures related to qualification requirements and procedures, technical standards and licensing requirements did not constitute unnecessary trade barriers. The Council also established the Working Party on GATS Rules and the Committee on Specific Commitments.

### Intellectual property

The WTO Agreement on Trade-Related Aspects of Intellectual Property Rights (TRIPS) provided for a one-year period for developed countries to bring their legislation and practices into conformity with its mandates; developing countries and most economies in transition had five years, and least developed countries 11 years. Given those transition periods, the Council for TRIPS activities was concerned in 1995 with setting up procedural mechanisms for future work. It agreed on procedures for notification of laws and regulations pertaining to the Agreement, as well as for the review of such notifications by the Council.

### Plurilateral agreements

For the most part, all WTO members subscribed to all WTO Agreements. There remained in 1995 four agreements, originally negotiated in the Tokyo Round, which had a narrower group of signatories and were therefore known as "plurilateral agreements". Activities with regard to plurilateral agreements during 1995 included the following: the Interim Committee on Government Procurement, established to oversee the entry into force of the new Agreement on Government Procurement on 1 January 1996, focused on modifications to the Appendices containing market opening concessions; the Committee on Trade in Civil Aircraft continued discussions on the legal status of the Agreement under WTO; the International Dairy Council decided, in October, to suspend until December 1997 the implementation of minimum export price provisions; and the new International Meat Council agreed that it should take into account the priority nature of work in the WTO Committees on Agriculture and on Sanitary and Phytosanitary Measures.

### International Trade Centre

In 1995, ITC, established in 1964 and operated jointly by GATT and UNCTAD, became the International Trade Centre UNCTAD/WTO (see also PART FOUR, Chapter IV).

Both the United Nations and WTO contributed equally to the ITC regular budget, which in 1995 totalled $23.1 million. During the year, 58 national, 26 regional and 50 interregional ITC projects were under implementation. As part of its work, ITC was involved in export development and the promotion of a variety of commodities of interest to developing countries, including cocoa, coffee, tea, sugar, spices, vegetable oilseeds, fats and oils, fish, citrus fruit, edible nuts, rice, cotton, hard fibres, jute, silk, coconut products, natural rubber products, tropical timber, and hides, skins and leather.

### Secretariat

As at 31 December 1995, the WTO Secretariat employed 510 staff members, of whom 250 were in the Professional or higher categories and 260 in the General Service category.

### Budget

Member countries of WTO contributed to the budget in accordance with a scale assessed on the basis of each country's share in the total trade of WTO members. The total budget for 1995 was 105,389,500 Swiss francs. Beginning in 1996, WTO members' contributions would be determined according to their share in total trade in goods, services and intellectual property rights.

NOTE: For further details regarding WTO's activities, see *Trading into the Future: WTO World Trade Organization*, published by WTO in 1995.

## HEADQUARTERS

World Trade Organization
Centre William Rappard
Rue de Lausanne 154
CH-1211 Geneva 21 Switzerland
*Cable address:* OMC/WTO Geneva
*Telephone:* 41-22-739-51-11
*Fax:* 41-22-739-54-58
*Telex:* 412 324 OMC/WTO CH

# Appendices

Appendix I

# Roster of the United Nations

**There were 185 Member States of the United Nations as at 31 December 1995.**

| MEMBER | DATE OF ADMISSION | MEMBER | DATE OF ADMISSION | MEMBER | DATE OF ADMISSION |
|---|---|---|---|---|---|
| Afghanistan | 19 Nov. 1946 | Ethiopia | 13 Nov. 1945 | Morocco | 12 Nov. 1956 |
| Albania | 14 Dec. 1955 | Fiji | 13 Oct. 1970 | Mozambique | 16 Sep. 1975 |
| Algeria | 8 Oct. 1962 | Finland | 14 Dec. 1955 | Myanmar | 19 Apr. 1948 |
| Andorra | 28 July 1993 | France | 24 Oct. 1945 | Namibia | 23 Apr. 1990 |
| Angola | 1 Dec. 1976 | Gabon | 20 Sep. 1960 | Nepal | 14 Dec. 1955 |
| Antigua and Barbuda | 11 Nov. 1981 | Gambia | 21 Sep. 1965 | Netherlands | 10 Dec. 1945 |
| Argentina | 24 Oct. 1945 | Georgia | 31 July 1992 | New Zealand | 24 Oct. 1945 |
| Armenia | 2 Mar. 1992 | Germany[3] | 18 Sep. 1973 | Nicaragua | 24 Oct. 1945 |
| Australia | 1 Nov. 1945 | Ghana | 8 Mar. 1957 | Niger | 20 Sep. 1960 |
| Austria | 14 Dec. 1955 | Greece | 25 Oct. 1945 | Nigeria | 7 Oct. 1960 |
| Azerbaijan | 2 Mar. 1992 | Grenada | 17 Sep. 1974 | Norway | 27 Nov. 1945 |
| Bahamas | 18 Sep. 1973 | Guatemala | 21 Nov. 1945 | Oman | 7 Oct. 1971 |
| Bahrain | 21 Sep. 1971 | Guinea | 12 Dec. 1958 | Pakistan | 30 Sep. 1947 |
| Bangladesh | 17 Sep. 1974 | Guinea-Bissau | 17 Sep. 1974 | Palau | 15 Dec. 1994 |
| Barbados | 9 Dec. 1966 | Guyana | 20 Sep. 1966 | Panama | 13 Nov. 1945 |
| Belarus | 24 Oct. 1945 | Haiti | 24 Oct. 1945 | Papua New Guinea | 10 Oct. 1975 |
| Belgium | 27 Dec. 1945 | Honduras | 17 Dec. 1945 | Paraguay | 24 Oct. 1945 |
| Belize | 25 Sep. 1981 | Hungary | 14 Dec. 1955 | Peru | 31 Oct. 1945 |
| Benin | 20 Sep. 1960 | Iceland | 19 Nov. 1946 | Philippines | 24 Oct. 1945 |
| Bhutan | 21 Sep. 1971 | India | 30 Oct. 1945 | Poland | 24 Oct. 1945 |
| Bolivia | 14 Nov. 1945 | Indonesia[4] | 28 Sep. 1950 | Portugal | 14 Dec. 1955 |
| Bosnia and Herzegovina | 22 May 1992 | Iran (Islamic Republic of) | 24 Oct. 1945 | Qatar | 21 Sep. 1971 |
| Botswana | 17 Oct. 1966 | Iraq | 21 Dec. 1945 | Republic of Korea | 17 Sep. 1991 |
| Brazil | 24 Oct. 1945 | Ireland | 14 Dec. 1955 | Republic of Moldova | 2 Mar. 1992 |
| Brunei Darussalam | 21 Sep. 1984 | Israel | 11 May 1949 | Romania | 14 Dec. 1955 |
| Bulgaria | 14 Dec. 1955 | Italy | 14 Dec. 1955 | Russian Federation[6] | 24 Oct. 1945 |
| Burkina Faso | 20 Sep. 1960 | Jamaica | 18 Sep. 1962 | Rwanda | 18 Sep. 1962 |
| Burundi | 18 Sep. 1962 | Japan | 18 Dec. 1956 | Saint Kitts and Nevis | 23 Sep. 1983 |
| Cambodia | 14 Dec. 1955 | Jordan | 14 Dec. 1955 | Saint Lucia | 18 Sep. 1979 |
| Cameroon | 20 Sep. 1960 | Kazakstan | 2 Mar. 1992 | Saint Vincent and the Grenadines | 16 Sep. 1980 |
| Canada | 9 Nov. 1945 | Kenya | 16 Dec. 1963 | Samoa | 15 Dec. 1976 |
| Cape Verde | 16 Sep. 1975 | Kuwait | 14 May 1963 | San Marino | 2 Mar. 1992 |
| Central African Republic | 20 Sep. 1960 | Kyrgyzstan | 2 Mar. 1992 | Sao Tome and Principe | 16 Sep. 1975 |
| Chad | 20 Sep. 1960 | Lao People's Democratic Republic | 14 Dec. 1955 | Saudi Arabia | 24 Oct. 1945 |
| Chile | 24 Oct. 1945 | Latvia | 17 Sep. 1991 | Senegal | 28 Sep. 1960 |
| China | 24 Oct. 1945 | Lebanon | 24 Oct. 1945 | Seychelles | 21 Sep. 1976 |
| Colombia | 5 Nov. 1945 | Lesotho | 17 Oct. 1966 | Sierra Leone | 27 Sep. 1961 |
| Comoros | 12 Nov. 1975 | Liberia | 2 Nov. 1945 | Singapore[5] | 21 Sep. 1965 |
| Congo | 20 Sep. 1960 | Libyan Arab Jamahiriya | 14 Dec. 1955 | Slovakia[1] | 19 Jan. 1993 |
| Costa Rica | 2 Nov. 1945 | Liechtenstein | 18 Sep. 1990 | Slovenia | 22 May 1992 |
| Côte d'Ivoire | 20 Sep. 1960 | Lithuania | 17 Sep. 1991 | Solomon Islands | 19 Sep. 1978 |
| Croatia | 22 May 1992 | Luxembourg | 24 Oct. 1945 | Somalia | 20 Sep. 1960 |
| Cuba | 24 Oct. 1945 | Madagascar | 20 Sep. 1960 | South Africa | 7 Nov. 1945 |
| Cyprus | 20 Sep. 1960 | Malawi | 1 Dec. 1964 | Spain | 14 Dec. 1955 |
| Czech Republic[1] | 19 Jan. 1993 | Malaysia[5] | 17 Sep. 1957 | Sri Lanka | 14 Dec. 1955 |
| Democratic People's Republic of Korea | 17 Sep. 1991 | Maldives | 21 Sep. 1965 | Sudan | 12 Nov. 1956 |
| Denmark | 24 Oct. 1945 | Mali | 28 Sep. 1960 | Suriname | 4 Dec. 1975 |
| Djibouti | 20 Sep. 1977 | Malta | 1 Dec. 1964 | Swaziland | 24 Sep. 1968 |
| Dominica | 18 Dec. 1978 | Marshall Islands | 17 Sep. 1991 | Sweden | 19 Nov. 1946 |
| Dominican Republic | 24 Oct. 1945 | Mauritania | 27 Oct. 1961 | Syrian Arab Republic[2] | 24 Oct. 1945 |
| Ecuador | 21 Dec. 1945 | Mauritius | 24 Apr. 1968 | Tajikistan | 2 Mar. 1992 |
| Egypt[2] | 24 Oct. 1945 | Mexico | 7 Nov. 1945 | Thailand | 16 Dec. 1946 |
| El Salvador | 24 Oct. 1945 | Micronesia (Federated States of) | 17 Sep. 1991 | The former Yugoslav Republic of Macedonia | 8 Apr. 1993 |
| Equatorial Guinea | 12 Nov. 1968 | Monaco | 28 May 1993 | Togo | 20 Sep. 1960 |
| Eritrea | 28 May 1993 | Mongolia | 27 Oct. 1961 | Trinidad and Tobago | 18 Sep. 1962 |
| Estonia | 17 Sep. 1991 | | | Tunisia | 12 Nov. 1956 |
| | | | | Turkey | 24 Oct. 1945 |

| MEMBER | DATE OF ADMISSION | MEMBER | DATE OF ADMISSION | MEMBER | DATE OF ADMISSION |
|---|---|---|---|---|---|
| Turkmenistan | 2 Mar. 1992 | United Republic | | Venezuela | 15 Nov. 1945 |
| Uganda | 25 Oct. 1962 | of Tanzania[7] | 14 Dec. 1961 | Viet Nam | 20 Sep. 1977 |
| Ukraine | 24 Oct. 1945 | United States | | Yemen[8] | 30 Sep. 1947 |
| United Arab Emirates | 9 Dec. 1971 | of America | 24 Oct. 1945 | Yugoslavia[9] | 24 Oct. 1945 |
| United Kingdom of | | Uruguay | 18 Dec. 1945 | Zaire | 20 Sep. 1960 |
| Great Britain and | | Uzbekistan | 2 Mar. 1992 | Zambia | 1 Dec. 1964 |
| Northern Ireland | 24 Oct. 1945 | Vanuatu | 15 Sep. 1981 | Zimbabwe | 25 Aug. 1980 |

[1]Czechoslovakia, which was an original Member of the United Nations from 24 October 1945, split up on 1 January 1993 and was succeeded by the Czech Republic and Slovakia.

[2]Egypt and Syria, both of which became Members of the United Nations on 24 October 1945, joined together—following a plebiscite held in those countries on 21 February 1958—to form the United Arab Republic. On 13 October 1961, Syria, having resumed its status as an independent State, also resumed its separate membership in the United Nations; it changed its name to the Syrian Arab Republic on 14 September 1971. The United Arab Republic continued as a Member of the United Nations and reverted to the name of Egypt on 2 September 1971.

[3]Through accession of the German Democratic Republic to the Federal Republic of Germany on 3 October 1990, the two German States (both of which became United Nations Members on 18 September 1973) united to form one sovereign State. As from that date, the Federal Republic of Germany has acted in the United Nations under the designation Germany.

[4]On 20 January 1965, Indonesia informed the Secretary-General that it had decided to withdraw from the United Nations. By a telegram of 19 September 1966, it notified the Secretary-General of its decision to resume participation in the activities of the United Nations. On 28 September 1966, the General Assembly took note of that decision and the President invited the representatives of Indonesia to take their seats in the Assembly.

[5]On 16 September 1963, Sabah (North Borneo), Sarawak and Singapore joined with the Federation of Malaya (which became a United Nations Member on 17 September 1957) to form Malaysia. On 9 August 1965, Singapore became an independent State and on 21 September 1965 it became a Member of the United Nations.

[6]The Union of Soviet Socialist Republics was an original Member of the United Nations from 24 October 1945. On 24 December 1991, the President of the Russian Federation informed the Secretary-General that the membership of the USSR in all United Nations organs was being continued by the Russian Federation.

[7]Tanganyika was admitted to the United Nations on 14 December 1961, and Zanzibar, on 16 December 1963. Following ratification, on 26 April 1964, of the Articles of Union between Tanganyika and Zanzibar, the two States became represented as a single Member: the United Republic of Tanganyika and Zanzibar; it changed its name to the United Republic of Tanzania on 1 November 1964.

[8]Yemen was admitted to the United Nations on 30 September 1947 and Democratic Yemen on 14 December 1967. On 22 May 1990, the two countries merged and have since been represented as one Member.

[9]Refers to the former Socialist Federal Republic of Yugoslavia.

Appendix II

# Charter of the United Nations and Statute of the International Court of Justice

## Charter of the United Nations

NOTE: The Charter of the United Nations was signed on 26 June 1945, in San Francisco, at the conclusion of the United Nations Conference on International Organization, and came into force on 24 October 1945. The Statute of the International Court of Justice is an integral part of the Charter.

Amendments to Articles 23, 27 and 61 of the Charter were adopted by the General Assembly on 17 December 1963 and came into force on 31 August 1965. A further amendment to Article 61 was adopted by the General Assembly on 20 December 1971, and came into force on 24 September 1973. An amendment to Article 109, adopted by the General Assembly on 20 December 1965, came into force on 12 June 1968.

The amendment to Article 23 enlarges the membership of the Security Council from 11 to 15. The amended Article 27 provides that decisions of the Security Council on procedural matters shall be made by an affirmative vote of nine members (formerly seven) and on all other matters by an affirmative vote of nine members (formerly seven), including the concurring votes of the five permanent members of the Security Council.

The amendment to Article 61, which entered into force on 31 August 1965, enlarged the membership of the Economic and Social Council from 18 to 27. The subsequent amendment to that Article, which entered into force on 24 September 1973, further increased the membership of the Council from 27 to 54.

The amendment to Article 109, which relates to the first paragraph of that Article, provides that a General Conference of Member States for the purpose of reviewing the Charter may be held at a date and place to be fixed by a two-thirds vote of the members of the General Assembly and by a vote of any nine members (formerly seven) of the Security Council. Paragraph 3 of Article 109, which deals with the consideration of a possible review conference during the tenth regular session of the General Assembly, has been retained in its original form in its reference to a ''vote of any seven members of the Security Council'', the paragraph having been acted upon in 1955 by the General Assembly, at its tenth regular session, and by the Security Council.

---

*WE THE PEOPLES*
*OF THE UNITED NATIONS*
*DETERMINED*
to save succeeding generations from the scourge of war, which twice in our lifetime has brought untold sorrow to mankind, and
to reaffirm faith in fundamental human rights, in the dignity and worth of the human person, in the equal rights of men and women and of nations large and small, and
to establish conditions under which justice and respect for the obligations arising from treaties and other sources of international law can be maintained, and
to promote social progress and better standards of life in larger freedom,

*AND FOR THESE ENDS*
to practice tolerance and live together in peace with one another as good neighbours, and
to unite our strength to maintain international peace and security, and
to ensure, by the acceptance of principles and the institution of methods, that armed force shall not be used, save in the common interest, and
to employ international machinery for the promotion of the economic and social advancement of all peoples,

*HAVE RESOLVED TO*
*COMBINE OUR EFFORTS TO*
*ACCOMPLISH THESE AIMS*
Accordingly, our respective Governments, through representatives assembled in the city of San Francisco, who have exhibited their full powers found to be in good and due form, have agreed to the present Charter of the United Nations and do hereby establish an international organization to be known as the United Nations.

Chapter I
PURPOSES AND PRINCIPLES

*Article 1*
The Purposes of the United Nations are:

1. To maintain international peace and security, and to that end: to take effective collective measures for the prevention and removal of threats to the peace, and for the suppression of acts of aggression or other breaches of the peace, and to bring about by peaceful means, and in conformity with the principles of justice and international law, adjustment or settlement of international disputes or situations which might lead to a breach of the peace;

2. To develop friendly relations among nations based on respect for the principle of equal rights and self-determination of peoples, and to take other appropriate measures to strengthen universal peace;

3. To achieve international co-operation in solving international problems of an economic, social, cultural, or humanitarian character, and in promoting and encouraging respect for human rights and for fundamental freedoms for all without distinction as to race, sex, language, or religion; and

4. To be a centre for harmonizing the actions of nations in the attainment of these common ends.

*Article 2*
The Organization and its Members, in pursuit of the Purposes stated in Article 1, shall act in accordance with the following Principles.

1. The Organization is based on the principle of the sovereign equality of all its Members.

2. All Members, in order to ensure to all of them the rights and benefits resulting from membership, shall fulfil in good faith the obligations assumed by them in accordance with the present Charter.

3. All Members shall settle their international disputes by peaceful means in such a manner that international peace and security, and justice, are not endangered.

4. All Members shall refrain in their international relations from the threat or use of force against the territorial integrity or political independence of any state, or in any other manner inconsistent with the Purposes of the United Nations.

5. All Members shall give the United Nations every assistance in any action it takes in accordance with the present Charter, and shall refrain from giving assistance to any state against which the United Nations is taking preventive or enforcement action.

6. The Organization shall ensure that states which are not Members of the United Nations act in accordance with these Principles so far as may be necessary for the maintenance of international peace and security.

7. Nothing contained in the present Charter shall authorize the United Nations to intervene in matters which are essentially within the domestic jurisdiction of any state or shall require the Members to submit such matters to settlement under the present Charter; but this principle shall not prejudice the application of enforcement measures under Chapter VII.

Chapter II
MEMBERSHIP

*Article 3*

The original Members of the United Nations shall be the states which, having participated in the United Nations Conference on International Organization at San Francisco, or having previously signed the Declaration by United Nations of 1 January 1942, sign the present Charter and ratify it in accordance with Article 110.

*Article 4*

1. Membership in the United Nations is open to all other peace-loving states which accept the obligations contained in the present Charter and, in the judgment of the Organization, are able and willing to carry out these obligations.

2. The admission of any such state to membership in the United Nations will be effected by a decision of the General Assembly upon the recommendation of the Security Council.

*Article 5*

A Member of the United Nations against which preventive or enforcement action has been taken by the Security Council may be suspended from the exercise of the rights and privileges of membership by the General Assembly upon the recommendation of the Security Council. The exercise of these rights and privileges may be restored by the Security Council.

*Article 6*

A Member of the United Nations which has persistently violated the Principles contained in the present Charter may be expelled from the Organization by the General Assembly upon the recommendation of the Security Council.

Chapter III
ORGANS

*Article 7*

1. There are established as the principal organs of the United Nations: a General Assembly, a Security Council, an Economic and Social Council, a Trusteeship Council, an International Court of Justice, and a Secretariat.

2. Such subsidiary organs as may be found necessary may be established in accordance with the present Charter.

*Article 8*

The United Nations shall place no restrictions on the eligibility of men and women to participate in any capacity and under conditions of equality in its principal and subsidiary organs.

Chapter IV
THE GENERAL ASSEMBLY

**Composition**

*Article 9*

1. The General Assembly shall consist of all the Members of the United Nations.

2. Each Member shall have not more than five representatives in the General Assembly.

**Functions and Powers**

*Article 10*

The General Assembly may discuss any questions or any matters within the scope of the present Charter or relating to the powers and functions of any organs provided for in the present Charter, and, except as provided in Article 12, may make recommendations to the Members of the United Nations or to the Security Council or to both on any such questions or matters.

*Article 11*

1. The General Assembly may consider the general principles of co-operation in the maintenance of international peace and security, including the principles governing disarmament and the regulation of armaments, and may make recommendations with regard to such principles to the Members or to the Security Council or to both.

2. The General Assembly may discuss any questions relating to the maintenance of international peace and security brought before it by any Member of the United Nations, or by the Security Council, or by a state which is not a Member of the United Nations in accordance with Article 35, paragraph 2, and, except as provided in Article 12, may make recommendations with regard to any such questions to the state or states concerned or to the Security Council or to both. Any such question on which action is necessary shall be referred to the Security Council by the General Assembly either before or after discussion.

3. The General Assembly may call the attention of the Security Council to situations which are likely to endanger international peace and security.

4. The powers of the General Assembly set forth in this Article shall not limit the general scope of Article 10.

*Article 12*

1. While the Security Council is exercising in respect of any dispute or situation the functions assigned to it in the present Charter, the General Assembly shall not make any recommendation with regard to that dispute or situation unless the Security Council so requests.

2. The Secretary-General, with the consent of the Security Council, shall notify the General Assembly at each session of any matters relative to the maintenance of international peace and security which are being dealt with by the Security Council and shall similarly notify the General Assembly, or the Members of the United Nations if the General Assembly is not in session, immediately the Security Council ceases to deal with such matters.

*Article 13*

1. The General Assembly shall initiate studies and make recommendations for the purpose of:
   a. promoting international co-operation in the political field and encouraging the progressive development of international law and its codification;
   b. promoting international co-operation in the economic, social, cultural, educational, and health fields, and assisting in the realization of human rights and fundamental freedoms for all without distinction as to race, sex, language, or religion.

2. The further responsibilities, functions and powers of the General Assembly with respect to matters mentioned in paragraph 1(b) above are set forth in Chapters IX and X.

*Article 14*

Subject to the provisions of Article 12, the General Assembly may recommend measures for the peaceful adjustment of any situation, regardless of origin, which it deems likely to impair the general welfare or friendly relations among nations, including situations resulting from a violation of the provisions of the present Charter setting forth the Purposes and Principles of the United Nations.

### Article 15

1.   The General Assembly shall receive and consider annual and special reports from the Security Council; these reports shall include an account of the measures that the Security Council has decided upon or taken to maintain international peace and security.

2.   The General Assembly shall receive and consider reports from the other organs of the United Nations.

### Article 16

The General Assembly shall perform such functions with respect to the international trusteeship system as are assigned to it under Chapters XII and XIII, including the approval of the trusteeship agreements for areas not designated as strategic.

### Article 17

1.   The General Assembly shall consider and approve the budget of the Organization.

2.   The expenses of the Organization shall be borne by the Members as apportioned by the General Assembly.

3.   The General Assembly shall consider and approve any financial and budgetary arrangements with specialized agencies referred to in Article 57 and shall examine the administrative budgets of such specialized agencies with a view to making recommendations to the agencies concerned.

**Voting**

### Article 18

1.   Each member of the General Assembly shall have one vote.

2.   Decisions of the General Assembly on important questions shall be made by a two-thirds majority of the members present and voting. These questions shall include: recommendations with respect to the maintenance of international peace and security, the election of the non-permanent members of the Security Council, the election of the members of the Economic and Social Council, the election of members of the Trusteeship Council in accordance with paragraph 1(c) of Article 86, the admission of new Members to the United Nations, the suspension of the rights and privileges of membership, the expulsion of Members, questions relating to the operation of the trusteeship system, and budgetary questions.

3.   Decisions on other questions, including the determination of additional categories of questions to be decided by a two-thirds majority, shall be made by a majority of the members present and voting.

### Article 19

A Member of the United Nations which is in arrears in the payment of its financial contributions to the Organization shall have no vote in the General Assembly if the amount of its arrears equals or exceeds the amount of the contributions due from it for the preceding two full years. The General Assembly may, nevertheless, permit such a Member to vote if it is satisfied that the failure to pay is due to conditions beyond the control of the Member.

**Procedure**

### Article 20

The General Assembly shall meet in regular annual sessions and in such special sessions as occasion may require. Special sessions shall be convoked by the Secretary-General at the request of the Security Council or of a majority of the Members of the United Nations.

### Article 21

The General Assembly shall adopt its own rules of procedure. It shall elect its President for each session.

### Article 22

The General Assembly may establish such subsidiary organs as it deems necessary for the performance of its functions.

Chapter V
## THE SECURITY COUNCIL

**Composition**

### Article 23[1]

1.   The Security Council shall consist of fifteen Members of the United Nations. The Republic of China, France, the Union of Soviet Socialist Republics, the United Kingdom of Great Britain and Northern Ireland, and the United States of America shall be permanent members of the Security Council. The General Assembly shall elect ten other Members of the United Nations to be non-permanent members of the Security Council, due regard being specially paid, in the first instance to the contribution of Members of the United Nations to the maintenance of international peace and security and to the other purposes of the Organization, and also to equitable geographical distribution.

2.   The non-permanent members of the Security Council shall be elected for a term of two years. In the first election of the non-permanent members after the increase of the membership of the Security Council from eleven to fifteen, two of the four additional members shall be chosen for a term of one year. A retiring member shall not be eligible for immediate re-election.

3.   Each member of the Security Council shall have one representative.

**Functions and Powers**

### Article 24

1.   In order to ensure prompt and effective action by the United Nations, its Members confer on the Security Council primary responsibility for the maintenance of international peace and security, and agree that in carrying out its duties under this responsibility the Security Council acts on their behalf.

2.   In discharging these duties the Security Council shall act in accordance with the Purposes and Principles of the United Nations. The specific powers granted to the Security Council for the discharge of these duties are laid down in Chapters VI, VII, VIII, and XII.

3.   The Security Council shall submit annual and, when necessary, special reports to the General Assembly for its consideration.

### Article 25

The Members of the United Nations agree to accept and carry out the decisions of the Security Council in accordance with the present Charter.

### Article 26

In order to promote the establishment and maintenance of international peace and security with the least diversion for armaments of the world's human and economic resources, the Security Council shall be responsible for formulating, with the

---

[1]Amended text of Article 23, which came into force on 31 August 1965. (The text of Article 23 before it was amended read as follows:

1.   The Security Council shall consist of eleven Members of the United Nations. The Republic of China, France, the Union of Soviet Socialist Republics, the United Kingdom of Great Britain and Northern Ireland, and the United States of America shall be permanent members of the Security Council. The General Assembly shall elect six other Members of the United Nations to be non-permanent members of the Security Council, due regard being specially paid, in the first instance to the contribution of Members of the United Nations to the maintenance of international peace and security and to the other purposes of the Organization, and also to equitable geographical distribution.

2.   The non-permanent members of the Security Council shall be elected for a term of two years. In the first election of non-permanent members, however, three shall be chosen for a term of one year. A retiring member shall not be eligible for immediate re-election.

3.   Each member of the Security Council shall have one representative.)

assistance of the Military Staff Committee referred to in Article 47, plans to be submitted to the Members of the United Nations for the establishment of a system for the regulation of armaments.

**Voting**

### Article 27[2]

1. Each member of the Security Council shall have one vote.
2. Decisions of the Security Council on procedural matters shall be made by an affirmative vote of nine members.
3. Decisions of the Security Council on all other matters shall be made by an affirmative vote of nine members including the concurring votes of the permanent members; provided that, in decisions under Chapter VI, and under paragraph 3 of Article 52, a party to a dispute shall abstain from voting.

**Procedure**

### Article 28

1. The Security Council shall be so organized as to be able to function continuously. Each member of the Security Council shall for this purpose be represented at all times at the seat of the Organization.
2. The Security Council shall hold periodic meetings at which each of its members may, if it so desires, be represented by a member of the government or by some other specially designated representative.
3. The Security Council may hold meetings at such places other than the seat of the Organization as in its judgment will best facilitate its work.

### Article 29

The Security Council may establish such subsidiary organs as it deems necessary for the performance of its functions.

### Article 30

The Security Council shall adopt its own rules of procedure, including the method of selecting its President.

### Article 31

Any Member of the United Nations which is not a member of the Security Council may participate, without vote, in the discussion of any question brought before the Security Council whenever the latter considers that the interests of that Member are specially affected.

### Article 32

Any Member of the United Nations which is not a member of the Security Council or any state which is not a Member of the United Nations, if it is a party to a dispute under consideration by the Security Council, shall be invited to participate, without vote, in the discussion relating to the dispute. The Security Council shall lay down such conditions as it deems just for the participation of a state which is not a Member of the United Nations.

## Chapter VI
## PACIFIC SETTLEMENT OF DISPUTES

### Article 33

1. The parties to any dispute, the continuance of which is likely to endanger the maintenance of international peace and security, shall, first of all, seek a solution by negotiation, enquiry, mediation, conciliation, arbitration, judicial settlement, resort to regional agencies or arrangements, or other peaceful means of their own choice.
2. The Security Council shall, when it deems necessary, call upon the parties to settle their dispute by such means.

### Article 34

The Security Council may investigate any dispute, or any situation which might lead to international friction or give rise to a dispute, in order to determine whether the continuance of the dispute or situation is likely to endanger the maintenance of international peace and security.

### Article 35

1. Any Member of the United Nations may bring any dispute, or any situation of the nature referred to in Article 34, to the attention of the Security Council or of the General Assembly.
2. A state which is not a Member of the United Nations may bring to the attention of the Security Council or of the General Assembly any dispute to which it is a party if it accepts in advance, for the purposes of the dispute, the obligations of pacific settlement provided in the present Charter.
3. The proceedings of the General Assembly in respect of matters brought to its attention under this Article will be subject to the provisions of Articles 11 and 12.

### Article 36

1. The Security Council may, at any stage of a dispute of the nature referred to in Article 33 or of a situation of like nature, recommend appropriate procedures or methods of adjustment.
2. The Security Council should take into consideration any procedures for the settlement of the dispute which have already been adopted by the parties.
3. In making recommendations under this Article the Security Council should also take into consideration that legal disputes should as a general rule be referred by the parties to the International Court of Justice in accordance with the provisions of the Statute of the Court.

### Article 37

1. Should the parties to a dispute of the nature referred to in Article 33 fail to settle it by the means indicated in that Article, they shall refer it to the Security Council.
2. If the Security Council deems that the continuance of the dispute is in fact likely to endanger the maintenance of international peace and security, it shall decide whether to take action under Article 36 or to recommend such terms of settlement as it may consider appropriate.

### Article 38

Without prejudice to the provisions of Articles 33 to 37, the Security Council may, if all the parties to any dispute so request, make recommendations to the parties with a view to a pacific settlement of the dispute.

## Chapter VII
## ACTION WITH RESPECT TO THREATS TO THE PEACE, BREACHES OF THE PEACE, AND ACTS OF AGGRESSION

### Article 39

The Security Council shall determine the existence of any threat to the peace, breach of the peace, or act of aggression and shall make recommendations, or decide what measures shall be taken in accordance with Articles 41 and 42, to maintain or restore international peace and security.

### Article 40

In order to prevent an aggravation of the situation, the Security Council may, before making the recommendations or deciding upon the measures provided for in Article 39, call upon the parties concerned to comply with such provisional measures as it deems necessary or desirable. Such provisional measures shall be without prejudice to the rights, claims, or position of the parties concerned. The Security Council shall duly take account of failure to comply with such provisional measures.

---

[2]Amended text of Article 27, which came into force on 31 August 1965. (The text of Article 27 before it was amended read as follows:
1. Each member of the Security Council shall have one vote.
2. Decisions of the Security Council on procedural matters shall be made by an affirmative vote of seven members.
3. Decisions of the Security Council on all other matters shall be made by an affirmative vote of seven members including the concurring votes of the permanent members; provided that, in decisions under Chapter VI, and under paragraph 3 of Article 52, a party to a dispute shall abstain from voting.)

### Article 41

The Security Council may decide what measures not involving the use of armed force are to be employed to give effect to its decisions, and it may call upon the Members of the United Nations to apply such measures. These may include complete or partial interruption of economic relations and of rail, sea, air, postal, telegraphic, radio, and other means of communication, and the severance of diplomatic relations.

### Article 42

Should the Security Council consider that measures provided for in Article 41 would be inadequate or have proved to be inadequate, it may take such action by air, sea, or land forces as may be necessary to maintain or restore international peace and security. Such action may include demonstrations, blockade, and other operations by air, sea, or land forces of Members of the United Nations.

### Article 43

1. All Members of the United Nations, in order to contribute to the maintenance of international peace and security, undertake to make available to the Security Council, on its call and in accordance with a special agreement or agreements, armed forces, assistance, and facilities, including rights of passage, necessary for the purpose of maintaining international peace and security.

2. Such agreement or agreements shall govern the numbers and types of forces, their degree of readiness and general location, and the nature of the facilities and assistance to be provided.

3. The agreement or agreements shall be negotiated as soon as possible on the initiative of the Security Council. They shall be concluded between the Security Council and Members or between the Security Council and groups of Members and shall be subject to ratification by the signatory states in accordance with their respective constitutional processes.

### Article 44

When the Security Council has decided to use force it shall, before calling upon a Member not represented on it to provide armed forces in fulfilment of the obligations assumed under Article 43, invite that Member, if the Member so desires, to participate in the decisions of the Security Council concerning the employment of contingents of that Member's armed forces.

### Article 45

In order to enable the United Nations to take urgent military measures, Members shall hold immediately available national airforce contingents for combined international enforcement action. The strength and degree of readiness of these contingents and plans for their combined action shall be determined, within the limits laid down in the special agreement or agreements referred to in Article 43, by the Security Council with the assistance of the Military Staff Committee.

### Article 46

Plans for the application of armed force shall be made by the Security Council with the assistance of the Military Staff Committee.

### Article 47

1. There shall be established a Military Staff Committee to advise and assist the Security Council on all questions relating to the Security Council's military requirements for the maintenance of international peace and security, the employment and command of forces placed at its disposal, the regulation of armaments, and possible disarmament.

2. The Military Staff Committee shall consist of the Chiefs of Staff of the permanent members of the Security Council or their representatives. Any Member of the United Nations not permanently represented on the Committee shall be invited by the Committee to be associated with it when the efficient discharge of the Committee's responsibilities requires the participation of that Member in its work.

3. The Military Staff Committee shall be responsible under the Security Council for the strategic direction of any armed forces placed at the disposal of the Security Council. Questions relating to the command of such forces shall be worked out subsequently.

4. The Military Staff Committee, with the authorization of the Security Council and after consultation with appropriate regional agencies, may establish regional sub-committees.

### Article 48

1. The action required to carry out the decisions of the Security Council for the maintenance of international peace and security shall be taken by all the Members of the United Nations or by some of them, as the Security Council may determine.

2. Such decisions shall be carried out by the Members of the United Nations directly and through their action in the appropriate international agencies of which they are members.

### Article 49

The Members of the United Nations shall join in affording mutual assistance in carrying out the measures decided upon by the Security Council.

### Article 50

If preventive or enforcement measures against any state are taken by the Security Council, any other state, whether a Member of the United Nations or not, which finds itself confronted with special economic problems arising from the carrying out of those measures shall have the right to consult the Security Council with regard to a solution of those problems.

### Article 51

Nothing in the present Charter shall impair the inherent right of individual or collective self-defence if an armed attack occurs against a Member of the United Nations, until the Security Council has taken measures necessary to maintain international peace and security. Measures taken by Members in the exercise of this right of self-defence shall be immediately reported to the Security Council and shall not in any way affect the authority and responsibility of the Security Council under the present Charter to take at any time such action as it deems necessary in order to maintain or restore international peace and security.

Chapter VIII
### REGIONAL ARRANGEMENTS

### Article 52

1. Nothing in the present Charter precludes the existence of regional arrangements or agencies for dealing with such matters relating to the maintenance of international peace and security as are appropriate for regional action, provided that such arrangements or agencies and their activities are consistent with the Purposes and Principles of the United Nations.

2. The Members of the United Nations entering into such arrangements or constituting such agencies shall make every effort to achieve pacific settlement of local disputes through such regional arrangements or by such regional agencies before referring them to the Security Council.

3. The Security Council shall encourage the development of pacific settlement of local disputes through such regional arrangements or by such regional agencies either on the initiative of the states concerned or by reference from the Security Council.

4. This Article in no way impairs the application of Articles 34 and 35.

### Article 53

1. The Security Council shall, where appropriate, utilize such regional arrangements or agencies for enforcement action under its authority. But no enforcement action shall be taken under regional arrangements or by regional agencies without the authorization of the Security Council, with the exception of measures against any enemy state, as defined in paragraph 2 of this Article, provided for pursuant to Article 107 or in regional arrangements directed against renewal of aggressive policy on the part of any such state, until such time as the Organization may, on request of the Governments concerned, be charged with the responsibility for preventing further aggression by such a state.

2. The term enemy state as used in paragraph 1 of this Article applies to any state which during the Second World War has been an enemy of any signatory of the present Charter.

#### Article 54

The Security Council shall at all times be kept fully informed of activities undertaken or in contemplation under regional arrangements or by regional agencies for the maintenance of international peace and security.

Chapter IX
### INTERNATIONAL ECONOMIC AND SOCIAL CO-OPERATION

#### Article 55

With a view to the creation of conditions of stability and well-being which are necessary for peaceful and friendly relations among nations based on respect for the principle of equal rights and self-determination of peoples, the United Nations shall promote:

a. higher standards of living, full employment, and conditions of economic and social progress and development;

b. solutions of international economic, social, health, and related problems; and international cultural and educational co-operation; and

c. universal respect for, and observance of, human rights and fundamental freedoms for all without distinction as to race, sex, language, or religion.

#### Article 56

All Members pledge themselves to take joint and separate action in co-operation with the Organization for the achievement of the purposes set forth in Article 55.

#### Article 57

1. The various specialized agencies, established by intergovernmental agreement and having wide international responsibilities, as defined in their basic instruments, in economic, social, cultural, educational, health, and related fields, shall be brought into relationship with the United Nations in accordance with the provisions of Article 63.

2. Such agencies thus brought into relationship with the United Nations are hereinafter referred to as specialized agencies.

#### Article 58

The Organization shall make recommendations for the co-ordination of the policies and activities of the specialized agencies.

#### Article 59

The Organization shall, where appropriate, initiate negotiations among the states concerned for the creation of any new specialized agencies required for the accomplishment of the purposes set forth in Article 55.

#### Article 60

Responsibility for the discharge of the functions of the Organization set forth in this Chapter shall be vested in the General Assembly and, under the authority of the General Assembly, in the Economic and Social Council, which shall have for this purpose the powers set forth in Chapter X.

Chapter X
### THE ECONOMIC AND SOCIAL COUNCIL

**Composition**

#### Article 61[3]

1. The Economic and Social Council shall consist of fifty-four Members of the United Nations elected by the General Assembly.

2. Subject to the provisions of paragraph 3, eighteen members of the Economic and Social Council shall be elected each year for a term of three years. A retiring member shall be eligible for immediate re-election.

3. At the first election after the increase in the membership of the Economic and Social Council from twenty-seven to fifty-

four members, in addition to the members elected in place of the nine members whose term of office expires at the end of that year, twenty-seven additional members shall be elected. Of these twenty-seven additional members, the term of office of nine members so elected shall expire at the end of one year, and of nine other members at the end of two years, in accordance with arrangements made by the General Assembly.

4. Each member of the Economic and Social Council shall have one representative.

**Functions and Powers**

#### Article 62

1. The Economic and Social Council may make or initiate studies and reports with respect to international economic, social, cultural, educational, health, and related matters and may make recommendations with respect to any such matters to the General Assembly, to the Members of the United Nations, and to the specialized agencies concerned.

2. It may make recommendations for the purpose of promoting respect for, and observance of, human rights and fundamental freedoms for all.

3. It may prepare draft conventions for submission to the General Assembly, with respect to matters falling within its competence.

4. It may call, in accordance with the rules prescribed by the United Nations, international conferences on matters falling within its competence.

#### Article 63

1. The Economic and Social Council may enter into agreements with any of the agencies referred to in Article 57, defining the terms on which the agency concerned shall be brought into relationship with the United Nations. Such agreements shall be subject to approval by the General Assembly.

2. It may co-ordinate the activities of the specialized agencies through consultation with and recommendations to such agencies and through recommendations to the General Assembly and to the Members of the United Nations.

#### Article 64

1. The Economic and Social Council may take appropriate steps to obtain regular reports from the specialized agencies. It may make arrangements with the Members of the United Nations and with the specialized agencies to obtain reports on the steps taken to give effect to its own recommendations and to recommendations on matters falling within its competence made by the General Assembly.

2. It may communicate its observations on these reports to the General Assembly.

#### Article 65

The Economic and Social Council may furnish information to the Security Council and shall assist the Security Council upon its request.

#### Article 66

1. The Economic and Social Council shall perform such functions as fall within its competence in connexion with the carrying out of the recommendations of the General Assembly.

---

[3]Amended text of Article 61, which came into force on 24 September 1973. (The text of Article 61 as previously amended on 31 August 1965 read as follows:

1. The Economic and Social Council shall consist of twenty-seven Members of the United Nations elected by the General Assembly.

2. Subject to the provisions of paragraph 3, nine members of the Economic and Social Council shall be elected each year for a term of three years. A retiring member shall be eligible for immediate re-election.

3. At the first election after the increase in the membership of the Economic and Social Council from eighteen to twenty-seven members, in addition to the members elected in place of the six members whose term of office expires at the end of that year, nine additional members shall be elected. Of these nine additional members, the term of office of three members so elected shall expire at the end of one year, and of three other members at the end of two years, in accordance with arrangements made by the General Assembly.

4. Each member of the Economic and Social Council shall have one representative.)

2.  It may, with the approval of the General Assembly, perform services at the request of Members of the United Nations and at the request of specialized agencies.

3.  It shall perform such other functions as are specified elsewhere in the present Charter or as may be assigned to it by the General Assembly.

**Voting**

### Article 67

1.  Each member of the Economic and Social Council shall have one vote.

2.  Decisions of the Economic and Social Council shall be made by a majority of the members present and voting.

**Procedure**

### Article 68

The Economic and Social Council shall set up commissions in economic and social fields and for the promotion of human rights, and such other commissions as may be required for the performance of its functions.

### Article 69

The Economic and Social Council shall invite any Member of the United Nations to participate, without vote, in its deliberations on any matter of particular concern to that Member.

### Article 70

The Economic and Social Council may make arrangements for representatives of the specialized agencies to participate, without vote, in its deliberations and in those of the commissions established by it, and for its representatives to participate in the deliberations of the specialized agencies.

### Article 71

The Economic and Social Council may make suitable arrangements for consultation with non-governmental organizations which are concerned with matters within its competence. Such arrangements may be made with international organizations and, where appropriate, with national organizations after consultation with the Member of the United Nations concerned.

### Article 72

1.  The Economic and Social Council shall adopt its own rules of procedure, including the method of selecting its President.

2.  The Economic and Social Council shall meet as required in accordance with its rules, which shall include provision for the convening of meetings on the request of a majority of its members.

Chapter XI
DECLARATION REGARDING
NON-SELF-GOVERNING TERRITORIES

### Article 73

Members of the United Nations which have or assume responsibilities for the administration of territories whose peoples have not yet attained a full measure of self-government recognize the principle that the interests of the inhabitants of these territories are paramount, and accept as a sacred trust the obligation to promote to the utmost, within the system of international peace and security established by the present Charter, the well-being of the inhabitants of these territories, and, to this end:

a.  to ensure, with due respect for the culture of the peoples concerned, their political, economic, social, and educational advancement, their just treatment, and their protection against abuses;

b.  to develop self-government, to take due account of the political aspirations of the peoples, and to assist them in the progressive development of their free political institutions, according to the particular circumstances of each territory and its peoples and their varying stages of advancement;

c.  to further international peace and security;

d.  to promote constructive measures of development, to encourage research, and to co-operate with one another and,

when and where appropriate, with specialized international bodies with a view to the practical achievement of the social, economic, and scientific purposes set forth in this Article; and

e.  to transmit regularly to the Secretary-General for information purposes, subject to such limitation as security and constitutional considerations may require, statistical and other information of a technical nature relating to economic, social, and educational conditions in the territories for which they are respectively responsible other than those territories to which Chapters XII and XIII apply.

### Article 74

Members of the United Nations also agree that their policy in respect of the territories to which this Chapter applies, no less than in respect of their metropolitan areas, must be based on the general principle of good-neighbourliness, due account being taken of the interests and well-being of the rest of the world, in social, economic, and commercial matters.

Chapter XII
INTERNATIONAL TRUSTEESHIP SYSTEM

### Article 75

The United Nations shall establish under its authority an international trusteeship system for the administration and supervision of such territories as may be placed thereunder by subsequent individual agreements. These territories are hereinafter referred to as trust territories.

### Article 76

The basic objectives of the trusteeship system, in accordance with the Purposes of the United Nations laid down in Article 1 of the present Charter, shall be:

a.  to further international peace and security;

b.  to promote the political, economic, social, and educational advancement of the inhabitants of the trust territories, and their progressive development towards self-government or independence as may be appropriate to the particular circumstances of each territory and its peoples and the freely expressed wishes of the peoples concerned, and as may be provided by the terms of each trusteeship agreement;

c.  to encourage respect for human rights and for fundamental freedoms for all without distinction as to race, sex, language, or religion, and to encourage recognition of the interdependence of the peoples of the world; and

d.  to ensure equal treatment in social, economic, and commercial matters for all Members of the United Nations and their nationals, and also equal treatment for the latter in the administration of justice, without prejudice to the attainment of the foregoing objectives and subject to the provisions of Article 80.

### Article 77

1.  The trusteeship system shall apply to such territories in the following categories as may be placed thereunder by means of trusteeship agreements:

a.  territories now held under mandate;

b.  territories which may be detached from enemy states as a result of the Second World War; and

c.  territories voluntarily placed under the system by states responsible for their administration.

2.  It will be a matter for subsequent agreement as to which territories in the foregoing categories will be brought under the trusteeship system and upon what terms.

### Article 78

The trusteeship system shall not apply to territories which have become Members of the United Nations, relationship among which shall be based on respect for the principle of sovereign equality.

### Article 79

The terms of trusteeship for each territory to be placed under the trusteeship system, including any alteration or amendment, shall be agreed upon by the states directly concerned, including the mandatory power in the case of territories held under mandate by a Member of the United Nations, and shall be approved as provided for in Articles 83 and 85.

### Article 80

1. Except as may be agreed upon in individual trusteeship agreements, made under Articles 77, 79, and 81, placing each territory under the trusteeship system, and until such agreements have been concluded, nothing in this Chapter shall be construed in or of itself to alter in any manner the rights whatsoever of any states or any peoples or the terms of existing international instruments to which Members of the United Nations may respectively be parties.

2. Paragraph 1 of this Article shall not be interpreted as giving grounds for delay or postponement of the negotiation and conclusion of agreements for placing mandated and other territories under the trusteeship system as provided for in Article 77.

### Article 81

The trusteeship agreement shall in each case include the terms under which the trust territory will be administered and designate the authority which will exercise the administration of the trust territory. Such authority, hereinafter called the administering authority, may be one or more states or the Organization itself.

### Article 82

There may be designated, in any trusteeship agreement, a strategic area or areas which may include part or all of the trust territory to which the agreement applies, without prejudice to any special agreement or agreements made under Article 43.

### Article 83

1. All functions of the United Nations relating to strategic areas, including the approval of the terms of the trusteeship agreements and of their alteration or amendment, shall be exercised by the Security Council.

2. The basic objectives set forth in Article 76 shall be applicable to the people of each strategic area.

3. The Security Council shall, subject to the provisions of the trusteeship agreements and without prejudice to security considerations, avail itself of the assistance of the Trusteeship Council to perform those functions of the United Nations under the trusteeship system relating to political, economic, social, and educational matters in the strategic areas.

### Article 84

It shall be the duty of the administering authority to ensure that the trust territory shall play its part in the maintenance of international peace and security. To this end the administering authority may make use of volunteer forces, facilities, and assistance from the trust territory in carrying out the obligations towards the Security Council undertaken in this regard by the administering authority, as well as for local defence and the maintenance of law and order within the trust territory.

### Article 85

1. The functions of the United Nations with regard to trusteeship agreements for all areas not designated as strategic, including the approval of the terms of the trusteeship agreements and of their alteration or amendment, shall be exercised by the General Assembly.

2. The Trusteeship Council, operating under the authority of the General Assembly, shall assist the General Assembly in carrying out these functions.

Chapter XIII
## THE TRUSTEESHIP COUNCIL

**Composition**

### Article 86

1. The Trusteeship Council shall consist of the following Members of the United Nations:

a. those Members administering trust territories;
b. such of those Members mentioned by name in Article 23 as are not administering trust territories; and
c. as many other Members elected for three-year terms by the General Assembly as may be necessary to ensure that the total number of members of the Trusteeship Council is equally divided between those Members of the United Nations which administer trust territories and those which do not.

2. Each member of the Trusteeship Council shall designate one specially qualified person to represent it therein.

**Functions and Powers**

### Article 87

The General Assembly and, under its authority, the Trusteeship Council, in carrying out their functions, may:
a. consider reports submitted by the administering authority;
b. accept petitions and examine them in consultation with the administering authority;
c. provide for periodic visits to the respective trust territories at times agreed upon with the administering authority; and
d. take these and other actions in conformity with the terms of the trusteeship agreements.

### Article 88

The Trusteeship Council shall formulate a questionnaire on the political, economic, social, and educational advancement of the inhabitants of each trust territory, and the administering authority for each trust territory within the competence of the General Assembly shall make an annual report to the General Assembly upon the basis of such questionnaire.

**Voting**

### Article 89

1. Each member of the Trusteeship Council shall have one vote.

2. Decisions of the Trusteeship Council shall be made by a majority of the members present and voting.

**Procedure**

### Article 90

1. The Trusteeship Council shall adopt its own rules of procedure, including the method of selecting its President.

2. The Trusteeship Council shall meet as required in accordance with its rules, which shall include provision for the convening of meetings on the request of a majority of its members.

### Article 91

The Trusteeship Council shall, when appropriate, avail itself of the assistance of the Economic and Social Council and of the specialized agencies in regard to matters with which they are respectively concerned.

Chapter XIV
## THE INTERNATIONAL COURT OF JUSTICE

### Article 92

The International Court of Justice shall be the principal judicial organ of the United Nations. It shall function in accordance with the annexed Statute, which is based upon the Statute of the Permanent Court of International Justice and forms an integral part of the present Charter.

### Article 93

1. All Members of the United Nations are *ipso facto* parties to the Statute of the International Court of Justice.

2. A state which is not a Member of the United Nations may become a party to the Statute of the International Court of Justice on conditions to be determined in each case by the General Assembly upon the recommendation of the Security Council.

### Article 94

1. Each Member of the United Nations undertakes to comply with the decision of the International Court of Justice in any case to which it is a party.

2. If any party to a case fails to perform the obligations incumbent upon it under a judgment rendered by the Court, the other party may have recourse to the Security Council, which may, if it deems necessary, make recommendations or decide upon measures to be taken to give effect to the judgment.

### Article 95

Nothing in the present Charter shall prevent Members of the United Nations from entrusting the solution of their differences to other tribunals by virtue of agreements already in existence or which may be concluded in the future.

### Article 96

1. The General Assembly or the Security Council may request the International Court of Justice to give an advisory opinion on any legal question.

2. Other organs of the United Nations and specialized agencies, which may at any time be so authorized by the General Assembly, may also request advisory opinions of the Court on legal questions arising within the scope of their activities.

## Chapter XV
## THE SECRETARIAT

### Article 97

The Secretariat shall comprise a Secretary-General and such staff as the Organization may require. The Secretary-General shall be appointed by the General Assembly upon the recommendation of the Security Council. He shall be the chief administrative officer of the Organization.

### Article 98

The Secretary-General shall act in that capacity in all meetings of the General Assembly, of the Security Council, of the Economic and Social Council, and of the Trusteeship Council, and shall perform such other functions as are entrusted to him by these organs. The Secretary-General shall make an annual report to the General Assembly on the work of the Organization.

### Article 99

The Secretary-General may bring to the attention of the Security Council any matter which in his opinion may threaten the maintenance of international peace and security.

### Article 100

1. In the performance of their duties the Secretary-General and the staff shall not seek or receive instructions from any government or from any other authority external to the Organization. They shall refrain from any action which might reflect on their position as international officials responsible only to the Organization.

2. Each Member of the United Nations undertakes to respect the exclusively international character of the responsibilities of the Secretary-General and the staff and not to seek to influence them in the discharge of their responsibilities.

### Article 101

1. The staff shall be appointed by the Secretary-General under regulations established by the General Assembly.

2. Appropriate staffs shall be permanently assigned to the Economic and Social Council, the Trusteeship Council, and, as required, to other organs of the United Nations. These staffs shall form a part of the Secretariat.

3. The paramount consideration in the employment of the staff and in the determination of the conditions of service shall be the necessity of securing the highest standards of efficiency, competence, and integrity. Due regard shall be paid to the importance of recruiting the staff on as wide a geographical basis as possible.

## Chapter XVI
## MISCELLANEOUS PROVISIONS

### Article 102

1. Every treaty and every international agreement entered into by any Member of the United Nations after the present Charter comes into force shall as soon as possible be registered with the Secretariat and published by it.

2. No party to any such treaty or international agreement which has not been registered in accordance with the provisions of paragraph 1 of this Article may invoke that treaty or agreement before any organ of the United Nations.

### Article 103

In the event of a conflict between the obligations of the Members of the United Nations under the present Charter and their obligations under any other international agreement, their obligations under the present Charter shall prevail.

### Article 104

The Organization shall enjoy in the territory of each of its Members such legal capacity as may be necessary for the exercise of its functions and the fulfilment of its purposes.

### Article 105

1. The Organization shall enjoy in the territory of each of its Members such privileges and immunities as are necessary for the fulfilment of its purposes.

2. Representatives of the Members of the United Nations and officials of the Organization shall similarly enjoy such privileges and immunities as are necessary for the independent exercise of their functions in connexion with the Organization.

3. The General Assembly may make recommendations with a view to determining the details of the application of paragraphs 1 and 2 of this Article or may propose conventions to the Members of the United Nations for this purpose.

## Chapter XVII
## TRANSITIONAL SECURITY ARRANGEMENTS

### Article 106

Pending the coming into force of such special agreements referred to in Article 43 as in the opinion of the Security Council enable it to begin the exercise of its responsibilities under Article 42, the parties to the Four-Nation Declaration, signed at Moscow, 30 October 1943, and France, shall, in accordance with the provisions of paragraph 5 of that Declaration, consult with one another and as occasion requires with other Members of the United Nations with a view to such joint action on behalf of the Organization as may be necessary for the purpose of maintaining international peace and security.

### Article 107

Nothing in the present Charter shall invalidate or preclude action, in relation to any state which during the Second World War has been an enemy of any signatory to the present Charter, taken or authorized as a result of that war by the Governments having responsibility for such action.

## Chapter XVIII
## AMENDMENTS

### Article 108

Amendments to the present Charter shall come into force for all Members of the United Nations when they have been adopted by a vote of two thirds of the members of the General Assembly and ratified in accordance with their respective constitutional processes by two thirds of the Members of the United Nations, including all the permanent members of the Security Council.

### Article 109[4]

1. A General Conference of the Members of the United Nations for the purpose of reviewing the present Charter may be held at a date and place to be fixed by a two-thirds vote of the members of the General Assembly and by a vote of any nine members of the Security Council. Each Member of the United Nations shall have one vote in the conference.

2. Any alteration of the present Charter recommended by a two-thirds vote of the conference shall take effect when ratified in accordance with their respective constitutional processes by two thirds of the Members of the United Nations including all the permanent members of the Security Council.

3. If such a conference has not been held before the tenth annual session of the General Assembly following the coming into force of the present Charter, the proposal to call such a conference shall be placed on the agenda of that session of the General Assembly, and the conference shall be held if so decided by a majority vote of the members of the General Assembly and by a vote of any seven members of the Security Council.

Chapter XIX
RATIFICATION AND SIGNATURE

### Article 110

1. The present Charter shall be ratified by the signatory states in accordance with their respective constitutional processes.

2. The ratifications shall be deposited with the Government of the United States of America, which shall notify all the signatory states of each deposit as well as the Secretary-General of the Organization when he has been appointed.

3. The present Charter shall come into force upon the deposit of ratifications by the Republic of China, France, the Union of Soviet Socialist Republics, the United Kingdom of Great Britain and Northern Ireland, and the United States of America, and by a majority of the other signatory states. A protocol of the ratifications deposited shall thereupon be drawn up by the Government of the United States

of America which shall communicate copies thereof to all the signatory states.

4. The states signatory to the present Charter which ratify it after it has come into force will become original Members of the United Nations on the date of the deposit of their respective ratifications.

### Article 111

The present Charter, of which the Chinese, French, Russian, English, and Spanish texts are equally authentic, shall remain deposited in the archives of the Government of the United States of America. Duly certified copies thereof shall be transmitted by that Government to the Governments of the other signatory states.

IN FAITH WHEREOF the representatives of the Governments of the United Nations have signed the present Charter.

DONE at the city of San Francisco the twenty-sixth day of June, one thousand nine hundred and forty-five.

---

[4]Amended text of Article 109, which came into force on 12 June 1968. (The text of Article 109 before it was amended read as follows:

1. A General Conference of the Members of the United Nations for the purpose of reviewing the present Charter may be held at a date and place to be fixed by a two-thirds vote of the members of the General Assembly and by a vote of any seven members of the Security Council. Each Member of the United Nations shall have one vote in the conference.

2. Any alteration of the present Charter recommended by a two-thirds vote of the conference shall take effect when ratified in accordance with their respective constitutional processes by two thirds of the Members of the United Nations including all the permanent members of the Security Council.

3. If such a conference has not been held before the tenth annual session of the General Assembly following the coming into force of the present Charter, the proposal to call such a conference shall be placed on the agenda of that session of the General Assembly, and the conference shall be held if so decided by a majority vote of the members of the General Assembly and by a vote of any seven members of the Security Council.)

## Statute of the International Court of Justice

### Article 1

THE INTERNATIONAL COURT OF JUSTICE established by the Charter of the United Nations as the principal judicial organ of the United Nations shall be constituted and shall function in accordance with the provisions of the present Statute.

Chapter I
ORGANIZATION OF THE COURT

### Article 2

The Court shall be composed of a body of independent judges, elected regardless of their nationality from among persons of high moral character, who possess the qualifications required in their respective countries for appointment to the highest judicial offices, or are jurisconsults of recognized competence in international law.

### Article 3

1. The Court shall consist of fifteen members, no two of whom may be nationals of the same state.

2. A person who for the purposes of membership in the Court could be regarded as a national of more than one state shall be deemed to be a national of the one in which he ordinarily exercises civil and political rights.

### Article 4

1. The members of the Court shall be elected by the General Assembly and by the Security Council from a list of persons nominated by the national groups in the Permanent Court of Arbitration, in accordance with the following provisions.

2. In the case of Members of the United Nations not represented in the Permanent Court of Arbitration, candidates shall be nominated by national groups appointed for this purpose by their governments under the same conditions as those prescribed for mem-

bers of the Permanent Court of Arbitration by Article 44 of the Convention of The Hague of 1907 for the pacific settlement of international disputes.

3. The conditions under which a state which is a party to the present Statute but is not a Member of the United Nations may participate in electing the members of the Court shall, in the absence of a special agreement, be laid down by the General Assembly upon recommendation of the Security Council.

### Article 5

1. At least three months before the date of the election, the Secretary-General of the United Nations shall address a written request to the members of the Permanent Court of Arbitration belonging to the states which are parties to the present Statute, and to the members of the national groups appointed under Article 4, paragraph 2, inviting them to undertake, within a given time, by national groups, the nomination of persons in a position to accept the duties of a member of the Court.

2. No group may nominate more than four persons, not more than two of whom shall be of their own nationality. In no case may the number of candidates nominated by a group be more than double the number of seats to be filled.

### Article 6

Before making these nominations, each national group is recommended to consult its highest court of justice, its legal faculties and schools of law, and its national academies and national sections of international academies devoted to the study of law.

### Article 7

1. The Secretary-General shall prepare a list in alphabetical order of all the persons thus nominated. Save as provided in Article 12, paragraph 2, these shall be the only persons eligible.

2. The Secretary-General shall submit this list to the General Assembly and to the Security Council.

### Article 8

The General Assembly and the Security Council shall proceed independently of one another to elect the members of the Court.

### Article 9

At every election, the electors shall bear in mind not only that the persons to be elected should individually possess the qualifications required, but also that in the body as a whole the representation of the main forms of civilization and of the principal legal systems of the world should be assured.

### Article 10

1. Those candidates who obtain an absolute majority of votes in the General Assembly and in the Security Council shall be considered as elected.

2. Any vote of the Security Council, whether for the election of judges or for the appointment of members of the conference envisaged in Article 12, shall be taken without any distinction between permanent and non-permanent members of the Security Council.

3. In the event of more than one national of the same state obtaining an absolute majority of the votes both of the General Assembly and of the Security Council, the eldest of these only shall be considered as elected.

### Article 11

If, after the first meeting held for the purpose of the election, one or more seats remain to be filled, a second and, if necessary, a third meeting shall take place.

### Article 12

1. If, after the third meeting, one or more seats still remain unfilled, a joint conference consisting of six members, three appointed by the General Assembly and three by the Security Council, may be formed at any time at the request of either the General Assembly or the Security Council, for the purpose of choosing by the vote of an absolute majority one name for each seat still vacant, to submit to the General Assembly and the Security Council for their respective acceptance.

2. If the joint conference is unanimously agreed upon any person who fulfils the required conditions, he may be included in its list, even though he was not included in the list of nominations referred to in Article 7.

3. If the joint conference is satisfied that it will not be successful in procuring an election, those members of the Court who have already been elected shall, within a period to be fixed by the Security Council, proceed to fill the vacant seats by selection from among those candidates who have obtained votes either in the General Assembly or in the Security Council.

4. In the event of an equality of votes among the judges, the eldest judge shall have a casting vote.

### Article 13

1. The members of the Court shall be elected for nine years and may be re-elected; provided, however, that of the judges elected at the first election, the terms of five judges shall expire at the end of three years and the terms of five more judges shall expire at the end of six years.

2. The judges whose terms are to expire at the end of the above-mentioned initial periods of three and six years shall be chosen by lot to be drawn by the Secretary-General immediately after the first election has been completed.

3. The members of the Court shall continue to discharge their duties until their places have been filled. Though replaced, they shall finish any cases which they may have begun.

4. In the case of the resignation of a member of the Court, the resignation shall be addressed to the President of the Court for transmission to the Secretary-General. This last notification makes the place vacant.

### Article 14

Vacancies shall be filled by the same method as that laid down for the first election, subject to the following provision: the Secretary-General shall, within one month of the occurrence of the vacancy, proceed to issue the invitations provided for in Article 5, and the date of the election shall be fixed by the Security Council.

### Article 15

A member of the Court elected to replace a member whose term of office has not expired shall hold office for the remainder of his predecessor's term.

### Article 16

1. No member of the Court may exercise any political or administrative function, or engage in any other occupation of a professional nature.

2. Any doubt on this point shall be settled by the decision of the Court.

### Article 17

1. No member of the Court may act as agent, counsel, or advocate in any case.

2. No member may participate in the decision of any case in which he has previously taken part as agent, counsel, or advocate for one of the parties, or as a member of a national or international court, or of a commission of enquiry, or in any other capacity.

3. Any doubt on this point shall be settled by the decision of the Court.

### Article 18

1. No member of the Court can be dismissed unless, in the unanimous opinion of the other members, he has ceased to fulfil the required conditions.

2. Formal notification thereof shall be made to the Secretary-General by the Registrar.

3. This notification makes the place vacant.

### Article 19

The members of the Court, when engaged on the business of the Court, shall enjoy diplomatic privileges and immunities.

### Article 20

Every member of the Court shall, before taking up his duties, make a solemn declaration in open court that he will exercise his powers impartially and conscientiously.

### Article 21

1. The Court shall elect its President and Vice-President for three years; they may be re-elected.

2. The Court shall appoint its Registrar and may provide for the appointment of such other officers as may be necessary.

### Article 22

1. The seat of the Court shall be established at The Hague. This, however, shall not prevent the Court from sitting and exercising its functions elsewhere whenever the Court considers it desirable.

2. The President and the Registrar shall reside at the seat of the Court.

### Article 23

1. The Court shall remain permanently in session, except during the judicial vacations, the dates and duration of which shall be fixed by the Court.

2. Members of the Court are entitled to periodic leave, the dates and duration of which shall be fixed by the Court, having in mind the distance between The Hague and the home of each judge.

3. Members of the Court shall be bound, unless they are on leave or prevented from attending by illness or other serious reasons duly explained to the President, to hold themselves permanently at the disposal of the Court.

### Article 24

1. If, for some special reason, a member of the Court considers that he should not take part in the decision of a particular case, he shall so inform the President.

2. If the President considers that for some special reason one of the members of the Court should not sit in a particular case, he shall give him notice accordingly.

3. If in any such case the member of the Court and the President disagree, the matter shall be settled by the decision of the Court.

### Article 25

1. The full Court shall sit except when it is expressly provided otherwise in the present Statute.

2. Subject to the condition that the number of judges available to constitute the Court is not thereby reduced below eleven, the Rules of the Court may provide for allowing one or more judges, according to circumstances and in rotation, to be dispensed from sitting.

3. A quorum of nine judges shall suffice to constitute the Court.

### Article 26

1. The Court may from time to time form one or more chambers, composed of three or more judges as the Court may determine, for dealing with particular categories of cases; for example, labour cases and cases relating to transit and communications.

2. The Court may at any time form a chamber for dealing with a particular case. The number of judges to constitute such a chamber shall be determined by the Court with the approval of the parties.

3. Cases shall be heard and determined by the chambers provided for in this Article if the parties so request.

### Article 27

A judgment given by any of the chambers provided for in Articles 26 and 29 shall be considered as rendered by the Court.

### Article 28

The chambers provided for in Articles 26 and 29 may, with the consent of the parties, sit and exercise their functions elsewhere than at The Hague.

### Article 29

With a view to the speedy dispatch of business, the Court shall form annually a chamber composed of five judges which, at the request of the parties, may hear and determine cases by summary procedure. In addition, two judges shall be selected for the purpose of replacing judges who find it impossible to sit.

### Article 30

1. The Court shall frame rules for carrying out its functions. In particular, it shall lay down rules of procedure.

2. The Rules of the Court may provide for assessors to sit with the Court or with any of its chambers, without the right to vote.

### Article 31

1. Judges of the nationality of each of the parties shall retain their right to sit in the case before the Court.

2. If the Court includes upon the Bench a judge of the nationality of one of the parties, any other party may choose a person to sit as judge. Such person shall be chosen preferably from among those persons who have been nominated as candidates as provided in Articles 4 and 5.

3. If the Court includes upon the Bench no judge of the nationality of the parties, each of these parties may proceed to choose a judge as provided in paragraph 2 of this Article.

4. The provisions of this Article shall apply to the case of Articles 26 and 29. In such cases, the President shall request one or, if necessary, two of the members of the Court forming the chamber to give place to the members of the Court of the nationality of the parties concerned, and, failing such, or if they are unable to be present, to the judges specially chosen by the parties.

5. Should there be several parties in the same interest, they shall, for the purpose of the preceding provisions, be reckoned as one party only. Any doubt upon this point shall be settled by the decision of the Court.

6. Judges chosen as laid down in paragraphs 2, 3, and 4 of this Article shall fulfil the conditions required by Articles 2, 17 (paragraph 2), 20, and 24 of the present Statute. They shall take part in the decision on terms of complete equality with their colleagues.

### Article 32

1. Each member of the Court shall receive an annual salary.

2. The President shall receive a special annual allowance.

3. The Vice-President shall receive a special allowance for every day on which he acts as President.

4. The judges chosen under Article 31, other than members of the Court, shall receive compensation for each day on which they exercise their functions.

5. These salaries, allowances, and compensation shall be fixed by the General Assembly. They may not be decreased during the term of office.

6. The salary of the Registrar shall be fixed by the General Assembly on the proposal of the Court.

7. Regulations made by the General Assembly shall fix the conditions under which retirement pensions may be given to members of the Court and to the Registrar, and the conditions under which members of the Court and the Registrar shall have their travelling expenses refunded.

8. The above salaries, allowances, and compensation shall be free of all taxation.

### Article 33

The expenses of the Court shall be borne by the United Nations in such a manner as shall be decided by the General Assembly.

Chapter II
## COMPETENCE OF THE COURT

### Article 34

1. Only states may be parties in cases before the Court.

2. The Court, subject to and in conformity with its Rules, may request of public international organizations information relevant to cases before it, and shall receive such information presented by such organizations on their own initiative.

3. Whenever the construction of the constituent instrument of a public international organization or of an international convention adopted thereunder is in question in a case before the Court, the Registrar shall so notify the public international organization concerned and shall communicate to it copies of all the written proceedings.

### Article 35

1. The Court shall be open to the states parties to the present Statute.

2. The conditions under which the Court shall be open to other states shall, subject to the special provisions contained in treaties in force, be laid down by the Security Council, but in no case shall such conditions place the parties in a position of inequality before the Court.

3. When a state which is not a Member of the United Nations is a party to a case, the Court shall fix the amount which that party is to contribute towards the expenses of the Court. This provision shall not apply if such state is bearing a share of the expenses of the Court.

### Article 36

1. The jurisdiction of the Court comprises all cases which the parties refer to it and all matters specially provided for in the Charter of the United Nations or in treaties and conventions in force.

2. The states parties to the present Statute may at any time declare that they recognize as compulsory *ipso facto* and without special agreement, in relation to any other state accepting the same obligation, the jurisdiction of the Court in all legal disputes concerning:

a. the interpretation of a treaty;

b. any question of international law;

c. the existence of any fact which, if established, would constitute a breach of an international obligation;

d. the nature or extent of the reparation to be made for the breach of an international obligation.

3. The declarations referred to above may be made unconditionally or on condition of reciprocity on the part of several or certain states, or for a certain time.

4. Such declarations shall be deposited with the Secretary-General of the United Nations, who shall transmit copies thereof to the parties to the Statute and to the Registrar of the Court.

5. Declarations made under Article 36 of the Statute of the Permanent Court of International Justice and which are still in force shall be deemed, as between the parties to the present Statute, to be acceptances of the compulsory jurisdiction of the International Court of Justice for the period which they still have to run and in accordance with their terms.

6. In the event of a dispute as to whether the Court has jurisdiction, the matter shall be settled by the decision of the Court.

### Article 37

Whenever a treaty or convention in force provides for reference of a matter to a tribunal to have been instituted by the League of Nations, or to the Permanent Court of International Justice, the matter shall, as between the parties to the present Statute, be referred to the International Court of Justice.

### Article 38

1. The Court, whose function is to decide in accordance with international law such disputes as are submitted to it, shall apply:
   a. international conventions, whether general or particular, establishing rules expressly recognized by the contesting states;
   b. international custom, as evidence of a general practice accepted as law;
   c. the general principles of law recognized by civilized nations;
   d. subject to the provisions of Article 59, judicial decisions and the teachings of the most highly qualified publicists of the various nations, as subsidiary means for the determination of rules of law.

2. This provision shall not prejudice the power of the Court to decide a case *ex aequo et bono*, if the parties agree thereto.

Chapter III
PROCEDURE

### Article 39

1. The official languages of the Court shall be French and English. If the parties agree that the case shall be conducted in French, the judgment shall be delivered in French. If the parties agree that the case shall be conducted in English, the judgment shall be delivered in English.

2. In the absence of an agreement as to which language shall be employed, each party may, in the pleadings, use the language which it prefers; the decision of the Court shall be given in French and English. In this case the Court shall at the same time determine which of the two texts shall be considered as authoritative.

3. The Court shall, at the request of any party, authorize a language other than French or English to be used by that party.

### Article 40

1. Cases are brought before the Court, as the case may be, either by the notification of the special agreement or by a written application addressed to the Registrar. In either case the subject of the dispute and the parties shall be indicated.

2. The Registrar shall forthwith communicate the application to all concerned.

3. He shall also notify the Members of the United Nations through the Secretary-General, and also any other states entitled to appear before the Court.

### Article 41

1. The Court shall have the power to indicate, if it considers that circumstances so require, any provisional measures which ought to be taken to preserve the respective rights of either party.

2. Pending the final decision, notice of the measures suggested shall forthwith be given to the parties and to the Security Council.

### Article 42

1. The parties shall be represented by agents.

2. They may have the assistance of counsel or advocates before the Court.

3. The agents, counsel, and advocates of parties before the Court shall enjoy the privileges and immunities necessary to the independent exercise of their duties.

### Article 43

1. The procedure shall consist of two parts: written and oral.

2. The written proceedings shall consist of the communication to the Court and to the parties of memorials, counter-memorials and, if necessary, replies; also all papers and documents in support.

3. These communications shall be made through the Registrar, in the order and within the time fixed by the Court.

4. A certified copy of every document produced by one party shall be communicated to the other party.

5. The oral proceedings shall consist of the hearing by the Court of witnesses, experts, agents, counsel, and advocates.

### Article 44

1. For the service of all notices upon persons other than the agents, counsel, and advocates, the Court shall apply direct to the government of the state upon whose territory the notice has to be served.

2. The same provision shall apply whenever steps are to be taken to procure evidence on the spot.

### Article 45

The hearing shall be under the control of the President or, if he is unable to preside, of the Vice-President; if neither is able to preside, the senior judge present shall preside.

### Article 46

The hearing in Court shall be public, unless the Court shall decide otherwise, or unless the parties demand that the public be not admitted.

### Article 47

1. Minutes shall be made at each hearing and signed by the Registrar and the President.

2. These minutes alone shall be authentic.

### Article 48

The Court shall make orders for the conduct of the case, shall decide the form and time in which each party must conclude its arguments, and make all arrangements connected with the taking of evidence.

### Article 49

The Court may, even before the hearing begins, call upon the agents to produce any document or to supply any explanations. Formal note shall be taken of any refusal.

### Article 50

The Court may, at any time, entrust any individual, body, bureau, commission, or other organization that it may select, with the task of carrying out an enquiry or giving an expert opinion.

### Article 51

During the hearing any relevant questions are to be put to the witnesses and experts under the conditions laid down by the Court in the rules of procedure referred to in Article 30.

### Article 52

After the Court has received the proofs and evidence within the time specified for the purpose, it may refuse to accept any further oral or written evidence that one party may desire to present unless the other side consents.

### Article 53

1. Whenever one of the parties does not appear before the Court, or fails to defend its case, the other party may call upon the Court to decide in favour of its claim.

2. The Court must, before doing so, satisfy itself, not only that it has jurisdiction in accordance with Articles 36 and 37, but also that the claim is well founded in fact and law.

### Article 54

1. When, subject to the control of the Court, the agents, counsel, and advocates have completed their presentation of the case, the President shall declare the hearing closed.

2. The Court shall withdraw to consider the judgment.

3. The deliberations of the Court shall take place in private and remain secret.

### Article 55

1. All questions shall be decided by a majority of the judges present.

2. In the event of an equality of votes, the President or the judge who acts in his place shall have a casting vote.

### Article 56

1. The judgment shall state the reasons on which it is based.

2. It shall contain the names of the judges who have taken part in the decision.

### Article 57

If the judgment does not represent in whole or in part the unanimous opinion of the judges, any judge shall be entitled to deliver a separate opinion.

### Article 58

The judgment shall be signed by the President and by the Registrar. It shall be read in open court, due notice having been given to the agents.

### Article 59

The decision of the Court has no binding force except between the parties and in respect of that particular case.

### Article 60

The judgment is final and without appeal. In the event of dispute as to the meaning or scope of the judgment, the Court shall construe it upon the request of any party.

### Article 61

1. An application for revision of a judgment may be made only when it is based upon the discovery of some fact of such a nature as to be a decisive factor, which fact was, when the judgment was given, unknown to the Court and also to the party claiming revision, always provided that such ignorance was not due to negligence.

2. The proceedings for revision shall be opened by a judgment of the Court expressly recording the existence of the new fact, recognizing that it has such a character as to lay the case open to revision, and declaring the application admissible on this ground.

3. The Court may require previous compliance with the terms of the judgment before it admits proceedings in revision.

4. The application for revision must be made at latest within six months of the discovery of the new fact.

5. No application for revision may be made after the lapse of ten years from the date of the judgment.

### Article 62

1. Should a state consider that it has an interest of a legal nature which may be affected by the decision in the case, it may submit a request to the Court to be permitted to intervene.

2. It shall be for the Court to decide upon this request.

### Article 63

1. Whenever the construction of a convention to which states other than those concerned in the case are parties is in question, the Registrar shall notify all such states forthwith.

2. Every state so notified has the right to intervene in the proceedings; but if it uses this right, the construction given by the judgment will be equally binding upon it.

### Article 64

Unless otherwise decided by the Court, each party shall bear its own costs.

Chapter IV
## ADVISORY OPINIONS

### Article 65

1. The Court may give an advisory opinion on any legal question at the request of whatever body may be authorized by or in accordance with the Charter of the United Nations to make such a request.

2. Questions upon which the advisory opinion of the Court is asked shall be laid before the Court by means of a written request containing an exact statement of the question upon which an opinion is required, and accompanied by all documents likely to throw light upon the question.

### Article 66

1. The Registrar shall forthwith give notice of the request for an advisory opinion to all states entitled to appear before the Court.

2. The Registrar shall also, by means of a special and direct communication, notify any state entitled to appear before the Court or international organization considered by the Court, or, should it not be sitting, by the President, as likely to be able to furnish information on the question, that the Court will be prepared to receive, within a time limit to be fixed by the President, written statements, or to hear, at a public sitting to be held for the purpose, oral statements relating to the question.

3. Should any such state entitled to appear before the Court have failed to receive the special communication referred to in paragraph 2 of this Article, such state may express a desire to submit a written statement or to be heard; and the Court will decide.

4. States and organizations having presented written or oral statements or both shall be permitted to comment on the statements made by other states or organizations in the form, to the extent, and within the time limits which the Court, or, should it not be sitting, the President, shall decide in each particular case. Accordingly, the Registrar shall in due time communicate any such written statements to states and organizations having submitted similar statements.

### Article 67

The Court shall deliver its advisory opinions in open court, notice having been given to the Secretary-General and to the representatives of Members of the United Nations, of other states and of international organizations immediately concerned.

### Article 68

In the exercise of its advisory functions the Court shall further be guided by the provisions of the present Statute which apply in contentious cases to the extent to which it recognizes them to be applicable.

Chapter V
## AMENDMENT

### Article 69

Amendments to the present Statute shall be effected by the same procedure as is provided by the Charter of the United Nations for amendments to that Charter, subject however to any provisions which the General Assembly upon recommendation of the Security Council may adopt concerning the participation of states which are parties to the present Statute but are not Members of the United Nations.

### Article 70

The Court shall have power to propose such amendments to the present Statute as it may deem necessary, through written communications to the Secretary-General, for consideration in conformity with the provisions of Article 69.

Appendix III

# Structure of the United Nations

## General Assembly

The General Assembly is composed of all the Members of the United Nations.

SESSIONS
*Resumed forty-ninth session:* 26 January–18 September 1995.
*Fiftieth session:* 19 September–23 December 1995 (suspended).

OFFICERS
*Resumed forty-ninth session*
*President:* Amara Essy (Côte d'Ivoire).
*Vice-Presidents:* Armenia, Austria, Burundi, Cambodia, China, Democratic People's Republic of Korea, Dominican Republic, Fiji, France, Guinea-Bissau, India, Kazakstan, Malawi, Netherlands, Nicaragua, Russian Federation, Sudan, Tunisia, United Kingdom, United States, Uruguay.

*Fiftieth session*
*President:* Diogo Freitas do Amaral (Portugal).[a]
*Vice-Presidents:* Albania, Algeria, Belgium, Bolivia, China, Congo, Costa Rica, France, Kuwait, Lao People's Democratic Republic, Lebanon, Mali, Mauritania, Mauritius, Namibia, Russian Federation, Saint Lucia, Thailand, United Kingdom, United States, Yemen.[b]

[a]Elected on 19 September 1995 (dec. 50/302).
[b]Elected on 19 September 1995 (dec. 50/304).

The Assembly has four types of committees: (1) Main Committees; (2) procedural committees; (3) standing committees; (4) subsidiary and ad hoc bodies. In addition, it convenes conferences to deal with specific subjects.

### Main Committees
Six Main Committees have been established as follows:

*Disarmament and International Security Committee* (First Committee)
*Special Political and Decolonization Committee* (Fourth Committee)
*Economic and Financial Committee* (Second Committee)
*Social, Humanitarian and Cultural Committee* (Third Committee)
*Administrative and Budgetary Committee* (Fifth Committee)
*Legal Committee* (Sixth Committee)

The General Assembly may constitute other committees, on which all Members of the United Nations have the right to be represented.

OFFICERS OF THE MAIN COMMITTEES

*Resumed forty-ninth session*

#### Fifth Committee[a]
*Chairman:* Adrien Teirlinck (Belgium).
*Vice-Chairmen:* Mahmoud Barimani (Iran), Marta Peña (Mexico).
*Rapporteur:* Larbi Djacta (Algeria).

[a]The only Main Committee to meet at the resumed session.

*Fiftieth session*[a]

[a]Chairmen elected by the Main Committees; announced by the Assembly President on 19 September 1995 (dec. 50/303).

#### First Committee
*Chairman:* Luvsangiin Erdenechuluun (Mongolia).
*Vice-Chairmen:* Wolfgang Hoffman (Germany), Antonio de Icaza (Mexico).
*Rapporteur:* Rajab Sukayri (Jordan).

#### Fourth Committee
*Chairman:* Francis Kirimi Muthaura (Kenya).
*Vice-Chairmen:* Niall Holohan (Ireland), Jalal Samadi (Iran).
*Rapporteur:* Allan Breier-Castro (Venezuela).

#### Second Committee
*Chairman:* Goce Petreski (the former Yugoslav Republic of Macedonia).
*Vice-Chairmen:* Conor Murphy (Ireland), Max Stadhagen (Nicaragua).
*Rapporteur:* Basheer F. Zoubi (Jordan).

#### Third Committee
*Chairman:* Ugyen Tshering (Bhutan).
*Vice-Chairmen:* Patrick Rata (New Zealand), Julia Tavares de Alvarez (Dominican Republic).
*Rapporteur:* Ahmed Yousif Mohamed (Sudan).

#### Fifth Committee
*Chairman:* Erich Vilchez Asher (Nicaragua).
*Vice-Chairmen:* Movses Abelian (Armenia), Ammar Amari (Tunisia).
*Rapporteur:* Peter Maddens (Belgium).

#### Sixth Committee
*Chairman:* Tyge Lehmann (Denmark).
*Vice-Chairmen:* Abdelouahab Bellouki (Morocco), Guillermo Camacho (Ecuador).
*Rapporteur:* Walid Obeidat (Jordan).

### Procedural committees

#### General Committee
The General Committee consists of the President of the General Assembly, as Chairman, the 21 Vice-Presidents and the Chairmen of the six Main Committees.

#### Credentials Committee
The Credentials Committee consists of nine members appointed by the General Assembly on the proposal of the President.

*Fiftieth session*
China, Luxembourg, Mali, Marshall Islands, Russian Federation, South Africa, Trinidad and Tobago, United States, Venezuela.[a]

[a]Appointed on 19 September 1995 (dec. 50/301).

### Standing committees
The two standing committees consist of experts appointed in their individual capacity for three-year terms.

#### Advisory Committee on Administrative and Budgetary Questions
*Members:*
*To serve until 31 December 1995:* Gérard Biraud, *Vice-Chairman* (France); Jorge José Duhalt (Mexico); Yuji Kumamaru (Japan);

Wolfgang Münch (Germany);[a] Ranjit Rae (India); Yu Mengjia (China).

*To serve until 31 December 1996:* Leonid E. Bidny (Russian Federation); Simon Khoam Chuinkam (Cameroon); Inga Eriksson Fogh (Sweden); Norma Goicochea Estenoz (Cuba); Linda S. Shenwick (United States).

*To serve until 31 December 1997:* Ahmad Fathi Al-Masri (Syrian Arab Republic); Ioan Barac (Romania); Mahamane Maiga (Mali); Ernest Besley Maycock (Barbados); C. S. M. Mselle, *Chairman* (United Republic of Tanzania).

[a]Resigned in June 1995; Wolfgang Stöckl (Germany) was appointed on 20 July (dec. 49/305 D) to fill the resultant vacancy.

On 18 December 1995 (dec. 50/313), the General Assembly appointed the following for a three-year term beginning on 1 January 1996 to fill the vacancies occurring on 31 December 1995: Vijay Gokhale (India), Yuji Kumamaru (Japan), José Antônio Marcondes de Carvalho (Brazil), Wolfgang Stöckl (Germany), Tang Guangting (China), Giovanni Luigi Valenza (Italy).

### Committee on Contributions
*Members:*
*To serve until 31 December 1995:* Tarak Ben Hamida (Tunisia); Sergio Chapparo Ruíz (Chile); Neil Hewitt Francis (Australia); Enrique Moret Echeverría (Cuba);[a] Mohamed Mahmoud Ould El Ghaouth (Mauritania); Dimitri Rallis (Greece).

*To serve until 31 December 1996:* Yuri A. Chulkov (Russian Federation); Alvaro Gurgel de Alencar (Brazil); Li Yong (China); Ugo Sessi, *Vice-Chairman* (Italy); Agha Shahi (Pakistan); Adrien Teirlinck (Belgium).

*To serve until 31 December 1997:* Uldis Blukis (Latvia); David Etuket, *Chairman* (Uganda); Igor V. Goumenny (Ukraine); William Grant (United States); Masao Kawai (Japan); Vanu Gopala Menon (Singapore).

*Member emeritus:* Amjad Ali (Pakistan).

[a]Appointed on 10 March 1995 (dec. 49/309 B) to fill the vacancy created by the resignation of Norma Goicochea Estenoz (Cuba) in February.

On 18 December 1995 (dec. 50/314 A), the General Assembly appointed the following for a three-year term beginning on 1 January 1996 to fill the vacancies occurring on 31 December 1995: Pieter Johannes Bierma (Netherlands), Sergio Chaparro Ruíz (Chile), Neil Hewitt Francis (Australia), Atilio Norberto Molteni (Argentina), Mohamed Mahmoud Ould El Ghaouth (Mauritania), Omar Sirry (Egypt).

## Subsidiary and ad hoc bodies
The following subsidiary and ad hoc bodies were functioning in 1995, or were established during the General Assembly's resumed forty-ninth session or fiftieth session. (For other related bodies, see p. 1557.)

### Ad Hoc Committee on the Indian Ocean
The 44-member Ad Hoc Committee on the Indian Ocean met in New York on 30 March and from 27 to 30 June 1995.

*Members:* Australia *(Vice-Chairman)*, Bangladesh, Bulgaria, Canada, China, Djibouti, Egypt, Ethiopia, Germany, Greece, India, Indonesia *(Vice-Chairman)*, Iran, Iraq, Italy, Japan, Kenya, Liberia, Madagascar *(Rapporteur)*, Malaysia, Maldives, Mauritius, Mozambique *(Vice-Chairman)*, Netherlands, Norway, Oman, Pakistan, Panama, Poland, Romania, Russian Federation, Seychelles, Singapore, Somalia, Sri Lanka *(Chairman)*, Sudan, Thailand, Uganda, United Arab Emirates, United Republic of Tanzania, Yemen, Yugoslavia, Zambia, Zimbabwe.

### Ad Hoc Intergovernmental Working Group on the Implementation of the Principle of Capacity to Pay
The Ad Hoc Intergovernmental Working Group, established pursuant to a 1994 General Assembly resolution,[1] was to study and examine all aspects of the implementation of the principle of capacity to pay as the fundamental criterion in determining the scale of assessments for contributions to the regular budget.

The Group held two sessions in 1995 in New York: an organizational session from 21 to 24 March and the substantive session from 18 April to 5 May.

*Members:*[a] Algeria, Argentina, Bahamas, Brazil *(Rapporteur, organizational session; Chairman, substantive session)*, Bulgaria *(Vice-Chairman)*, Canada *(Vice-Chairman, organizational session; Rapporteur, substantive session)*, China, France, Germany, India, Japan *(Chairman, organizational session)*, Kenya, Kuwait *(Vice-Chairman, substantive session)*, Malawi, Malaysia, Morocco, Nigeria, Paraguay, Russian Federation, Spain, Tunisia *(Vice-Chairman)*, Ukraine, United Kingdom, United States, Venezuela.

[a]On 28 February 1995 (dec. 49/323), the General Assembly took note of their appointment by its President.

### Advisory Committee on the United Nations Educational and Training Programme for Southern Africa
*Members:* Belarus, Canada, Denmark, India, Japan, Liberia, Nigeria, Norway *(Chairman)*, United Republic of Tanzania, United States, Venezuela, Zaire, Zambia *(Vice-Chairman)*.

On 20 December 1995 (res. 50/131), the General Assembly endorsed the Secretary-General's recommendation that the Advisory Committee should be discontinued.

### Advisory Committee on the United Nations Programme of Assistance in the Teaching, Study, Dissemination and Wider Appreciation of International Law
The Advisory Committee on the United Nations Programme of Assistance in the Teaching, Study, Dissemination and Wider Appreciation of International Law held its thirtieth session in New York on 26 October 1995.

*Members* (until 31 December 1995): Bangladesh, Colombia, Cuba, Cyprus, Ethiopia, France, Germany, Ghana *(Chairman)*, India, Iran, Italy, Kenya, Malaysia, Mexico, Netherlands, Nigeria, Romania, Russian Federation, Sudan, Trinidad and Tobago, Ukraine, United Kingdom, United Republic of Tanzania, United States, Uruguay.

On 11 December 1995 (dec. 50/312), the General Assembly appointed the following for a four-year term beginning on 1 January 1996 to fill the vacancies occurring on 31 December 1995: Canada, Colombia, Cyprus, Czech Republic, Ethiopia, France, Germany, Ghana, Iran, Italy, Jamaica, Kenya, Lebanon, Malaysia, Mexico, Nigeria, Pakistan, Portugal, Russian Federation, Sudan, Trinidad and Tobago, Ukraine, United Republic of Tanzania, United States, Uruguay.

### Board of Auditors
The Board of Auditors consists of three members appointed by the General Assembly for three-year terms.

*Members:*
*To serve until 30 June 1996:* Comptroller and Auditor-General of India.
*To serve until 30 June 1997:* Auditor-General of Ghana.
*To serve until 30 June 1998:* Comptroller and Auditor-General of the United Kingdom.

On 18 December 1995 (dec. 50/315), the General Assembly appointed the Comptroller and Auditor-General of India for a three-year term beginning on 1 July 1996.

### Committee for the United Nations Population Award
The Committee for the United Nations Population Award is composed of: *(a)* 10 representatives of United Nations Member States

---

[1]YUN 1994, p. 1355, GA res. 49/19 A, 29 Nov. 1994.

elected by the Economic and Social Council for a three-year period, with due regard for equitable geographical representation and the need to include Member States that have made contributions for the Award; *(b)* the Secretary-General and the UNFPA Executive Director, to serve ex officio; and *(c)* five individuals eminent for their significant contributions to population-related activities, selected by the Committee, to serve as honorary members in an advisory capacity for a renewable three-year term.

The Committee met in New York on 19 January and 13 March 1995.

*Members* (until 31 December 1997): Belarus, Burundi, Cameroon, El Salvador, Guatemala, India, Japan, Netherlands, Philippines, Zaire.

*Ex-officio members:* The Secretary-General and the UNFPA Executive Director.

*Honorary members* (until 31 December 1995): Robin Chandler Duke, Takeo Fukuda, Miguel de la Madrid Hurtado, Victoria Sekitoleko, Dirk Van der Kaa.

### Committee on Applications for Review of Administrative Tribunal Judgements

In 1995, the Committee on Applications for Review of Administrative Tribunal Judgements held two sessions, in New York: its forty-fourth on 21 February and its forty-fifth on 13 and 14 July.

*Members* (until 18 September 1995) (based on the composition of the General Committee at the General Assembly's forty-ninth session): Armenia, Austria, Belgium, Burundi, Cambodia, China, Côte d'Ivoire, Democratic People's Republic of Korea, Dominican Republic, Ecuador, Fiji, France, Ghana *(Chairman)*, Guinea-Bissau, India, Kazakstan, Malawi, Netherlands, Nicaragua, Pakistan, Russian Federation, Senegal, Sudan, Tunisia, Ukraine, United Kingdom *(Rapporteur)*, United States, Uruguay.

*Members* (from 19 September 1995) (based on the composition of the General Committee at the General Assembly's fiftieth session): Albania, Algeria, Belgium, Bhutan, Bolivia, China, Congo, Costa Rica, Denmark, France, Kenya, Kuwait, Lao People's Democratic Republic, Lebanon, Mali, Mauritania, Mauritius, Mongolia, Namibia, Nicaragua, Portugal, Russian Federation, Saint Lucia, Thailand, the former Yugoslav Republic of Macedonia, United Kingdom, United States, Yemen.

### Committee on Conferences

The Committee on Conferences consists of 21 Member States appointed by the President of the General Assembly according to a specific pattern of equitable geographical distribution, to serve for a three-year term.

*Members:*

*To serve until 31 December 1995:* Austria *(Chairman)*, Fiji, Grenada, Jordan, Morocco *(Rapporteur)*, Niger, United States.

*To serve until 31 December 1996:* Chile *(Vice-Chairman)*, Egypt, France, Gabon, Japan, Pakistan *(Vice-Chairman)*, Russian Federation.

*To serve until 31 December 1997:* Bahamas,[a] Belgium, Ghana, Iran,[a] Latvia, Saint Vincent and the Grenadines,[b] Senegal.

[a]Appointment noted on 26 January 1995 (dec. 49/318 B).
[b]Appointment noted on 28 February 1995 (dec. 49/318 C).

On 21 November and 4 December 1995 (dec. 50/310 A and B), the General Assembly took note of the appointment by its President of the following for a three-year term beginning on 1 January 1996 to fill the vacancies occurring on 31 December 1995: Austria, Jamaica, Jordan, Kenya, Morocco, Nepal, United States.

### Committee on Information

The 88-member Committee on Information held its seventeenth session in New York from 1 to 12 May 1995.

*Members:* Algeria *(Rapporteur)*, Argentina *(Vice-Chairman)*, Bangladesh, Belarus, Belgium, Belize, Benin, Brazil, Bulgaria *(Chair-*

*man)*, Burkina Faso, Burundi, Chile, China, Colombia, Congo, Costa Rica, Côte d'Ivoire, Croatia, Cuba, Cyprus, Czech Republic, Denmark, Ecuador, Egypt, El Salvador, Ethiopia, Finland, France, Gabon, Germany, Ghana, Greece, Guatemala, Guinea, Guyana, Hungary, India, Indonesia, Iran, Ireland, Israel, Italy, Jamaica, Japan, Jordan, Kazakstan, Kenya, Lebanon, Malta, Mexico, Mongolia, Morocco, Nepal, Netherlands, Niger, Nigeria, Pakistan *(Vice-Chairman)*, Peru, Philippines, Poland, Portugal *(Vice-Chairman)*, Republic of Korea, Romania, Russian Federation, Senegal, Singapore, Slovakia, Somalia, South Africa, Spain, Sri Lanka, Sudan, Syrian Arab Republic, Togo, Trinidad and Tobago, Tunisia, Turkey, Ukraine, United Kingdom, United Republic of Tanzania, United States, Uruguay, Venezuela, Viet Nam, Yemen, Yugoslavia, Zaire, Zimbabwe.

On 6 December 1995 (dec. 50/311), the General Assembly, on the recommendation of the Committee, increased the Committee's membership from 88 to 89 and appointed the Democratic People's Republic of Korea a member.

### Committee on Relations with the Host Country

*Members:* Bulgaria *(Vice-Chairman)*, Canada *(Vice-Chairman)*, China, Costa Rica *(Rapporteur)*, Côte d'Ivoire *(Vice-Chairman)*, Cyprus *(Chairman)*, France, Honduras, Iraq, Mali, Russian Federation, Senegal, Spain, United Kingdom, United States (host country).

### Committee on the Exercise of the Inalienable Rights of the Palestinian People

*Members:* Afghanistan *(Vice-Chairman)*, Belarus, Cuba *(Vice-Chairman)*, Cyprus, Guinea, Guyana, Hungary, India, Indonesia, Lao People's Democratic Republic, Madagascar, Malaysia, Mali, Malta *(Rapporteur)*, Nigeria, Pakistan, Romania, Senegal *(Chairman)*, Sierra Leone, Tunisia, Turkey, Ukraine, Yugoslavia.[2]

### Committee on the Peaceful Uses of Outer Space

The Committee on the Peaceful Uses of Outer Space held its thirty-eighth session in Vienna from 12 to 22 June 1995.

*Members:* Albania, Argentina, Australia, Austria *(Chairman)*, Belgium, Benin, Brazil *(Rapporteur)*, Bulgaria, Burkina Faso, Cameroon, Canada, Chad, Chile, China, Colombia, Cuba, Czech Republic, Ecuador, Egypt, France, Germany, Greece, Hungary, India, Indonesia, Iran, Iraq, Italy, Japan, Kazakstan, Kenya, Lebanon, Mexico, Mongolia, Morocco, Netherlands, Nicaragua, Niger, Nigeria, Pakistan, Philippines, Poland, Portugal, Republic of Korea, Romania *(Vice-Chairman)*, Russian Federation, Senegal, Sierra Leone, South Africa, Spain, Sudan, Sweden, Syrian Arab Republic, Turkey, Ukraine, United Kingdom, United States, Uruguay, Venezuela, Viet Nam, Yugoslavia.[2]

### Disarmament Commission

The Disarmament Commission, composed of all the Members of the United Nations, met in New York on 13 April, between 15 and 30 May and on 11 December 1995.

*Chairman:* Mongolia.
*Vice-Chairmen:* Belarus, Colombia, Iran, Netherlands, Poland, South Africa, Sweden, Uruguay.
*Rapporteur:* Egypt.

### High-level Committee on the Review of Technical Cooperation among Developing Countries

The High-level Committee on the Review of Technical Cooperation among Developing Countries, composed of all States participating in UNDP, held its ninth session in New York from 30 May to 2 June 1995.

[2]Pursuant to a 1992 General Assembly resolution (YUN 1992, p. 139, GA res. 47/1, 22 Sep. 1992), the Federal Republic of Yugoslavia (Serbia and Montenegro) did not participate in the work of the Committee.

*President:* Indonesia.
*Vice-President:* Gambia.
*Rapporteur:* Panama.

### Intergovernmental Negotiating Committee for a
### Framework Convention on Climate Change

The Intergovernmental Negotiating Committee for a Framework Convention on Climate Change, open to all States Members of the United Nations or members of the specialized agencies, held its eleventh (final) session in New York from 6 to 17 February 1995.

*Chairman:* Argentina.
*Vice-Chairmen:* Australia, India, Zimbabwe.
*Vice-Chairman/Rapporteur:* Poland.

### Intergovernmental Negotiating Committee for the Elaboration
### of an International Convention to Combat Desertification
### in those Countries Experiencing Serious Drought and/or
### Desertification, particularly in Africa

The Intergovernmental Negotiating Committee for the Elaboration of an International Convention to Combat Desertification in those Countries Experiencing Serious Drought and/or Desertification, particularly in Africa, open to all States Members of the United Nations or members of the specialized agencies, held two sessions in 1995: its sixth in New York from 9 to 18 January and its seventh in Nairobi, Kenya, from 7 to 17 August.

*Chairman:* Sweden.
*Vice-Chairmen:* Benin, India, Peru.
*Rapporteur:* Russian Federation.

### International Civil Service Commission

The International Civil Service Commission consists of 15 members who serve in their personal capacity as individuals of recognized competence in public administration or related fields, particularly in personnel management. They are appointed by the General Assembly, with due regard for equitable geographical distribution, for four-year terms.

The Commission held two sessions in 1995: its forty-first in Montreal, Canada, from 1 to 19 May, and its forty-second in New York from 24 July to 14 August.

*Members:*
*To serve until 31 December 1996:* Alexander V. Chepourin (Russian Federation); Humayun Kabir (Bangladesh); Ernest Rusita (Uganda); Missoum Sbih (Algeria); Mario Yango (Philippines).
*To serve until 31 December 1997:* Mario Bettati (France); Lucretia F. Myers (United States); Antônio Fonseca Pimentel (Brazil); Alexis Stephanou (Greece); Ku Tashiro (Japan).
*To serve until 31 December 1998:* Mohsen Bel Hadj Amor, *Chairman* (Tunisia); Turkia Daddah (Mauritania); André Xavier Pirson (Belgium); Jaroslav Riha (Czech Republic); Carlos S. Vegega, *Vice-Chairman* (Argentina).

### ADVISORY COMMITTEE ON POST ADJUSTMENT QUESTIONS

The Advisory Committee on Post Adjustment Questions consists of six members, of whom five are chosen from the geographical regions of Africa, Asia, Latin America and the Caribbean, Eastern Europe, and Western Europe and other States; and one, from ICSC, who serves ex officio as Chairman. Members are appointed by the ICSC Chairman to serve four-year terms.

The Advisory Committee held its nineteenth session in New York from 13 to 20 March 1995.

*Members:* Emmanuel Oti Boateng (Ghana); Youri Ivanov (Russian Federation); Yuki Miura (Japan); Hugues Picard (France); Rafael Trigueros Mejía (Costa Rica); Carlos S. Vegega, *Chairman* (Argentina).

### International Law Commission

The International Law Commission consists of 34 persons of recognized competence in international law, elected by the General Assembly to serve in their individual capacity for a five-

year term. Vacancies occurring within the five-year period are filled by the Commission.

The Commission held its forty-seventh session in Geneva from 2 May to 21 July 1995.

*Members* (until 31 December 1996): Husain M. Al-Baharna (Bahrain); Awn S. Al-Khasawneh (Jordan); Gaetano Arangio-Ruiz (Italy); Julio Barboza (Argentina); Mohamed Bennouna (Morocco); Derek William Bowett (United Kingdom); Carlos Calero Rodrigues (Brazil); James R. Crawford (Australia); John de Saram (Sri Lanka); Gudmundur Eiriksson (Iceland); Nabil Elaraby (Egypt); Salifou Fomba (Mali); Mehmet Güney, *Second Vice-Chairman* (Turkey); He Qizhi (China); Kamil E. Idris (Sudan); Andreas J. Jacovides (Cyprus); Peter C. R. Kabatsi (Uganda); Mochtar Kusuma-Atmadja (Indonesia); Igor Ivanovich Lukashuk (Russian Federation);[a] Ahmed Mahiou (Algeria); Vaclav Mikulka (Czech Republic); Guillaume Pambou-Tchivounda, *First Vice-Chairman* (Gabon); Alain Pellet (France); Pemmaraju Sreenivasa Rao, *Chairman* (India); Edilbert Razafindralambo (Madagascar); Patrick Lipton Robinson (Jamaica); Robert B. Rosenstock (United States); Alberto Szekely (Mexico); Doudou Thiam (Senegal); Christian Tomuschat (Germany); Edmundo Vargas Carreño (Chile); Francisco Villagran Kramer, *Rapporteur* (Guatemala); Chusei Yamada (Japan); Alexander Yankov (Bulgaria).

[a]Elected on 2 May 1995 to fill the vacancy created by the election of Vladlen Vereshchetin (Russian Federation) to the International Court of Justice.

### Investments Committee

The Investments Committee consists of nine members appointed by the Secretary-General, after consultation with the United Nations Joint Staff Pension Board and ACABQ, subject to confirmation by the General Assembly. Members serve three-year terms.

*Members:*
*To serve until 31 December 1995:* Yves Oltramare (Switzerland); Emmanuel Noi Omaboe (Ghana); Jürgen Reimnitz (Germany).
*To serve until 31 December 1996:* Francine J. Bovich (United States); Jean Guyot, *Chairman* (France); Takeshi Ohta (Japan).[a]
*To serve until 31 December 1997:* Ahmed Abdullatif (Saudi Arabia); Aloysio de Andrade Faria (Brazil); Stanislaw Raczkowski (Poland).

[a]Appointed on 18 December 1995 (dec. 50/316) to fill the vacancy resulting from the resignation in October 1994 of Michiya Matsukawa (Japan).

On 18 December 1995 (dec. 50/316), the General Assembly confirmed the appointment by the Secretary-General of Yves Oltramare (Switzerland), Emmanuel Noi Omaboe (Ghana) and Jürgen Reimnitz (Germany) as members for a three-year term beginning on 1 January 1996 to fill the vacancies occurring on 31 December 1995.

### Joint Advisory Group on the International
### Trade Centre UNCTAD/WTO

The International Trade Centre UNCTAD/GATT became the International Trade Centre UNCTAD/World Trade Organization (WTO) on 15 November 1995. Its new name reflects its status as a joint subsidiary organ of UNCTAD and WTO.

The Joint Advisory Group was established in accordance with an agreement between UNCTAD and GATT with effect from 1 January 1968, the date on which their joint sponsorship of the International Trade Centre commenced.

Participation in the Group is open to all States members of UNCTAD and to all members of WTO.

The Group held its twenty-eighth session in Geneva from 29 May to 2 June 1995.

*Chairman:* Malaysia.
*Vice-Chairmen:* Ghana, Uruguay.
*Rapporteur:* Finland.

### Joint Inspection Unit

The Joint Inspection Unit consists of not more than 11 Inspectors appointed by the General Assembly from candidates nominated by Member States following appropriate consultations, including consultations with the President of the Economic and Social Council and with the Chairman of ACC. The Inspectors, chosen for their special experience in national or international administrative and financial matters, with due regard for equitable geographical distribution and reasonable rotation, serve in their personal capacity for five-year terms.

*Members:*

*To serve until 31 December 1995:* Andrzej Abraszewski (Poland); Erica-Irene A. Daes (Greece); Richard Vognild Hennes (United States); Tunsala Kabongo (Zaire).

*To serve until 31 December 1997:* Fatih Bouayad-Agha, *Chairman* (Algeria); Homero Luis Hernández-Sánchez, *Vice-Chairman* (Dominican Republic); Boris Petrovitch Krasulin (Russian Federation); Francesco Mezzalama (Italy); Khalil Issa Othman (Jordan).

*To serve until 31 December 1998:* Raúl Quijano (Argentina).

*To serve until 31 December 1999:* Sumihiro Kuyama (Japan).

On 19 December 1995 (dec. 50/318), the General Assembly appointed Louis Dominique Ouedraogo (Burkina Faso) for a five-year term beginning on 1 January 1996 to replace Ali Badara Tall (Burkina Faso) who had been appointed in 1994 but resigned before commencing his term of office. The three other vacancies occurring on 31 December 1995 were also filled in 1994 (YUN 1994, p. 1501).

### Office of the United Nations High Commissioner for Refugees (UNHCR)

The United Nations High Commissioner for Refugees reports to the General Assembly through the Economic and Social Council.

#### *EXECUTIVE COMMITTEE OF THE HIGH COMMISSIONER'S PROGRAMME*

The Executive Committee held its forty-sixth session in Geneva from 16 to 20 October 1995.

*Members:* Algeria, Argentina, Australia, Austria, Belgium, Brazil, Canada, China, Colombia, Denmark *(Chairman)*, Ethiopia, Finland, France, Germany, Greece, Holy See, Hungary, Iran, Israel, Italy, Japan, Lebanon, Lesotho, Madagascar, Morocco, Namibia, Netherlands, Nicaragua, Nigeria, Norway, Pakistan, Philippines, Somalia, Spain, Sudan, Sweden, Switzerland, Thailand *(Rapporteur)*, Tunisia, Turkey, Uganda, United Kingdom, United Republic of Tanzania *(Vice-Chairman)*, United States, Venezuela, Yugoslavia,[2] Zaire.

*United Nations High Commissioner for Refugees:* Sadako Ogata.
*Deputy High Commissioner:* Gerald Walzer.

### Panel of External Auditors

The Panel of External Auditors consists of the members of the United Nations Board of Auditors and the appointed external auditors of the specialized agencies and IAEA.

### Preparatory Committee for the Fiftieth Anniversary of the United Nations

The Preparatory Committee for the Fiftieth Anniversary of the United Nations, consisting of the members of the General Committee and open to the participation of all Member States, met in New York on 2 and 10 February, 17 and 28 March, 11 April, 17 and 23 May, 7 and 19 June, 18 September, 20 and 21 October, 17 November and 5 December 1995, thereby concluding its work.

*Chairman:* Australia.
*Vice-Chairmen:* Botswana, Chile, Finland, Malaysia, Mauritania, Oman, Poland.
*Rapporteur:* Jamaica.

### Preparatory Committee for the United Nations Conference on Human Settlements (Habitat II)

The Preparatory Committee for the United Nations Conference on Human Settlements (Habitat II) (scheduled for 1996), open to all States Members of the United Nations or members of the specialized agencies, held its second session in Nairobi, Kenya, from 24 April to 5 May 1995.

*Chairman:* Finland.
*Vice-Chairmen:* Azerbaijan, Kenya, Sri Lanka.
*Rapporteur:* Ecuador.
*Ex-officio member of the Bureau:* Turkey.

### Preparatory Committee for the World Summit for Social Development

The Preparatory Committee for the World Summit for Social Development (see below), open to all States Members of the United Nations or members of the specialized agencies, held its third (final) session in New York from 16 to 28 January 1995.

*Chairman:* Chile.
*Vice-Chairmen:* Australia, Cameroon, Denmark (ex officio), India, Indonesia, Latvia, Mexico, Netherlands, Poland, Zimbabwe.

### Preparatory Committee on the Establishment of an International Criminal Court

On 11 December 1995 (res. 50/46), the General Assembly established a Preparatory Committee, open to all States Members of the United Nations or members of specialized agencies or of IAEA, to discuss further the major substantive and administrative issues arising out of the draft statute for an international criminal court.

The Committee was to meet in 1996.

### Scientific and Technical Committee on the International Decade for Natural Disaster Reduction

The Scientific and Technical Committee on the International Decade for Natural Disaster Reduction, composed of scientific and technical experts appointed by the Secretary-General in consultation with their Governments, held its sixth session in Washington, D.C., from 27 February to 3 March 1995.

*Members:* Alexandra Amoako-Mensah (Ghana); Anand S. Arya (India); Mohammed Benblidia (Algeria); Driss Ben Sari (Morocco); James Bruce (Canada); Claudia Candanedo (Panama); Barbara Carby (Jamaica); Umberto G. Cordani (Brazil); Alberto Giesecke (Peru); Ailsa Holloway (Zimbabwe); Vaino Kelha (Finland); Roman L. Kintanar, *Chairman* (Philippines); Michel Lechat (Belgium); C. J. Littleton (Australia); Giuseppe Luongo (Italy); Philippe Masure (France); Dallas Peck (United States); Erich Plate (Germany); Mariló Ruiz de Elvira (Spain); Atsushi Takeda (Japan); Albert Tevoedjre (Benin); Yuri Vorobiev (Russian Federation); J. J. Wagner (Switzerland); Xie Li-Li (China).

### Special Committee on Peace-keeping Operations

The 34-member Special Committee on Peace-keeping Operations met in New York on 10, 12, 13, 18 and 19 April and on 12 May 1995.

*Members:* Afghanistan, Algeria, Argentina *(Vice-Chairman)*, Australia, Austria, Canada *(Vice-Chairman)*, China, Denmark, Egypt *(Rapporteur)*, El Salvador, Ethiopia, France, Germany, Guatemala, Hungary, India, Iraq, Italy, Japan *(Vice-Chairman)*, Mauritania, Mexico, Netherlands, Nigeria *(Chairman)*, Pakistan, Poland *(Vice-Chairman)*, Romania, Russian Federation, Sierra Leone, Spain, Thailand, United Kingdom, United States, Venezuela, Yugoslavia.[2]

### Special Committee on the Charter of the United Nations and on the Strengthening of the Role of the Organization

The 47-member Special Committee on the Charter of the United Nations and on the Strengthening of the Role of the Organization met in New York from 27 February to 10 March 1995.

*Members:* Algeria, Argentina, Barbados, Belgium, Brazil, China, Colombia, Congo, Cyprus, Czech Republic, Ecuador *(Rapporteur)*, Egypt *(Vice-Chairman)*, El Salvador, Finland, France, Germany *(Vice-Chairman)*, Ghana, Greece, Guyana, Hungary, India *(Chairman)*, Indonesia, Iran, Iraq, Italy, Japan, Kenya, Liberia, Mexico, Nepal, New Zealand, Nigeria, Pakistan, Philippines, Poland *(Vice-Chairman)*, Romania, Russian Federation, Rwanda, Sierra Leone, Spain, Tunisia, Turkey, United Kingdom, United States, Venezuela, Yugoslavia,[2] Zambia.

On 11 December 1995 (res. 50/52), the General Assembly decided that the Special Committee would henceforth be open to all States Members of the United Nations.

### Special Committee on the Situation with regard to the Implementation of the Declaration on the Granting of Independence to Colonial Countries and Peoples

*Members:* Afghanistan, Bulgaria,[a] Chile, China, Congo, Côte d'Ivoire, Cuba *(Vice-Chairman)*, Ethiopia, Fiji, Grenada *(Chairman)*, India, Indonesia, Iran, Iraq, Mali, Papua New Guinea, Russian Federation, Sierra Leone *(Vice-Chairman)*, Syrian Arab Republic *(Rapporteur)*, Trinidad and Tobago, Tunisia, United Republic of Tanzania, Venezuela, Yugoslavia.[2]

[a]Withdrew from membership on 1 August 1995.

SUBCOMMITTEE ON SMALL TERRITORIES, PETITIONS, INFORMATION AND ASSISTANCE
The Subcommittee is composed of all the members of the Committee.

*Chairman:* Papua New Guinea.
*Rapporteur:* Chile.

### Special Committee to Investigate Israeli Practices Affecting the Human Rights of the Palestinian People and Other Arabs of the Occupied Territories

*Members:* Malaysia, Senegal, Sri Lanka *(Chairman)*.

### Special Committee to Select the Winners of the United Nations Human Rights Prize

The Special Committee to Select the Winners of the United Nations Human Rights Prize was established pursuant to a 1966 General Assembly resolution[3] recommending that a prize or prizes in the field of human rights be awarded not more often than at five-year intervals. Prizes were awarded for the fifth time on 10 December 1993.

*Members:* The Presidents of the General Assembly and the Economic and Social Council, and the Chairmen of the Commission on Human Rights, the Commission on the Status of Women and the Subcommission on Prevention of Discrimination and Protection of Minorities.

### United Nations Administrative Tribunal

*Members:*
*To serve until 31 December 1995:* Jerome Ackerman, *President* (United States); Francis R. Spain (Ireland).
*To serve until 31 December 1996:* Mayer Gabay (Israel); Luis M. de Posadas Montero, *Second Vice-President* (Uruguay).
*To serve until 31 December 1997:* Balanda Mikuin Leliel (Zaire); Samarendranath Sen, *First Vice-President* (India); Hubert Thierry (France).

On 18 December 1995 (dec. 50/317), the General Assembly appointed the following for a three-year term beginning on 1 January 1996 to fill the vacancies occurring on 31 December 1995: Francis R. Spain (Ireland), Deborah Taylor Ashford (United States).

### United Nations Capital Development Fund

The United Nations Capital Development Fund was set up as an organ of the General Assembly to function as an autonomous organization within the United Nations framework. The chief executive officer of the Fund, the Managing Director, exercises his functions under the general direction of the Executive Board, which reports to the Assembly through the Economic and Social Council.

EXECUTIVE BOARD
The UNDP/UNFPA Executive Board acts as the Executive Board of the Fund and the UNDP Administrator as its Managing Director; UNDP provides the Fund with, among other things, all headquarters administrative support services.

*Managing Director:* James Gustave Speth (UNDP Administrator).

### United Nations Commission on International Trade Law (UNCITRAL)

The United Nations Commission on International Trade Law consists of 36 members elected by the General Assembly, in accordance with a formula providing equitable geographical representation and adequate representation of the principal economic and legal systems of the world. Members serve six-year terms.
The Commission held its twenty-eighth session in Vienna from 2 to 26 May 1995.

*Members:*
*To serve until the day preceding the Commission's regular annual session in 1998:* Argentina, Austria, Chile, Ecuador, Hungary, India, Iran, Italy, Kenya, Poland *(Vice-Chairman)*, Saudi Arabia, Slovakia, Spain, Sudan, Thailand, Uganda *(Rapporteur)*, United Republic of Tanzania, United States, Uruguay.
*To serve until the day preceding the Commission's regular annual session in 2001:* Algeria, Australia *(Vice-Chairman)*, Botswana, Brazil, Bulgaria, Cameroon, China, Egypt, Finland, France, Germany, Japan, Mexico *(Vice-Chairman)*, Nigeria, Russian Federation, Singapore *(Chairman)*, United Kingdom.

### United Nations Conciliation Commission for Palestine

*Members:* France, Turkey, United States.

### United Nations Conference on Trade and Development (UNCTAD)

Members of UNCTAD are Members of the United Nations or members of the specialized agencies or of IAEA.
The Conference did not meet in 1995.

*Members:* Afghanistan, Albania, Algeria, Andorra, Angola, Antigua and Barbuda, Argentina, Armenia, Australia, Austria, Azerbaijan, Bahamas, Bahrain, Bangladesh, Barbados, Belarus, Belgium, Belize, Benin, Bhutan, Bolivia, Bosnia and Herzegovina, Botswana, Brazil, Brunei Darussalam, Bulgaria, Burkina Faso, Burundi, Cambodia, Cameroon, Canada, Cape Verde, Central African Republic, Chad, Chile, China, Colombia, Comoros, Congo, Costa Rica, Côte d'Ivoire, Croatia, Cuba, Cyprus, Czech Republic, Democratic People's Republic of Korea, Denmark, Djibouti, Dominica, Dominican Republic, Ecuador, Egypt, El Salvador, Equatorial Guinea, Eritrea, Estonia, Ethiopia, Fiji, Finland, France, Gabon, Gambia, Georgia, Germany, Ghana, Greece, Grenada, Guatemala, Guinea, Guinea-Bissau, Guyana, Haiti, Holy See, Honduras, Hungary, Iceland, India, Indonesia, Iran, Iraq, Ireland, Israel, Italy, Jamaica, Japan, Jordan, Kazakstan, Kenya, Kuwait, Kyrgyzstan, Lao People's Democratic Republic, Latvia, Lebanon, Lesotho, Liberia, Libyan Arab Jamahiriya, Liechtenstein, Lithuania, Luxembourg, Madagascar, Malawi, Malaysia, Maldives, Mali, Malta, Marshall Islands, Mauritania, Mauritius, Mexico, Micronesia, Monaco, Mongolia, Morocco, Mozambique, Myanmar, Namibia, Nepal, Netherlands, New Zealand, Nicaragua, Niger, Nigeria, Norway, Oman, Pakistan, Palau, Panama, Papua New Guinea, Paraguay, Peru, Philippines, Poland, Portugal, Qatar, Republic of Korea, Republic of Moldova, Romania, Russian Federation, Rwanda, Saint Kitts and Nevis, Saint Lucia, Saint Vincent and the Grenadines, Samoa, San Marino, Sao Tome and Principe, Saudi Arabia, Senegal, Seychelles, Sierra Leone, Singapore, Slovakia, Slovenia, Solo-

---

[3]YUN 1966, p. 458, GA res. 2217 A (XXI), annex, 19 Dec. 1966.

mon Islands, Somalia, South Africa, Spain, Sri Lanka, Sudan, Suriname, Swaziland, Sweden, Switzerland, Syrian Arab Republic, Tajikistan, Thailand, the former Yugoslav Republic of Macedonia, Togo, Tonga, Trinidad and Tobago, Tunisia, Turkey, Turkmenistan, Uganda, Ukraine, United Arab Emirates, United Kingdom, United Republic of Tanzania, United States, Uruguay, Uzbekistan, Vanuatu, Venezuela, Viet Nam, Yemen, Yugoslavia,[a] Zaire, Zambia, Zimbabwe.

[a]Refers to the former Socialist Federal Republic of Yugoslavia.

*Secretary-General of UNCTAD:* Carlos Fortin (Officer-in-Charge, until 14 September), Rubens Ricupero (from 15 September).[a]

[a]Appointment for a four-year term ending on 14 September 1999 confirmed by the General Assembly on 14 September 1995 (dec. 49/325).

### TRADE AND DEVELOPMENT BOARD

The Trade and Development Board is a permanent organ of UNCTAD. It reports to UNCTAD as well as annually to the General Assembly through the Economic and Social Council.

BOARD MEMBERS AND SESSIONS

The membership of the Board is open to all UNCTAD members. Those wishing to become members of the Board communicate their intention to the Secretary-General of UNCTAD for transmittal to the Board President, who announces the membership on the basis of such notifications.

The Board held the following sessions in 1995, in Geneva: its ninth (pre-sessional) executive session on 17 March, the second part of its forty-first session from 20 to 31 March, its tenth executive session on 4 May, the resumed eighth executive session on 29 June, its eleventh (pre-sessional) executive session on 5 September, the first part of its forty-second session from 11 to 20 September, and its eighteenth special session from 11 to 15 December.

*Members:* Afghanistan, Albania, Algeria, Angola, Argentina, Armenia, Australia, Austria, Azerbaijan, Bahrain, Bangladesh, Barbados, Belarus, Belgium, Benin, Bhutan, Bolivia, Brazil, Bulgaria, Burkina Faso, Burundi, Cameroon, Canada, Central African Republic, Chad, Chile, China, Colombia, Congo, Costa Rica, Côte d'Ivoire, Croatia,[a] Cuba, Cyprus, Czech Republic, Democratic People's Republic of Korea, Denmark, Dominica, Dominican Republic, Ecuador, Egypt, El Salvador, Equatorial Guinea, Ethiopia, Finland, France, Gabon, Georgia, Germany, Ghana, Greece, Grenada, Guatemala, Guinea, Guyana, Haiti, Honduras, Hungary, India, Indonesia, Iran, Iraq, Ireland, Israel, Italy, Jamaica, Japan, Jordan, Kenya, Kuwait, Latvia,[b] Lebanon, Liberia, Libyan Arab Jamahiriya, Liechtenstein, Luxembourg, Madagascar, Malaysia, Mali, Malta, Mauritania, Mauritius, Mexico, Mongolia, Morocco, Myanmar, Namibia, Nepal, Netherlands, New Zealand, Nicaragua, Nigeria, Norway, Oman, Pakistan, Panama, Papua New Guinea, Paraguay, Peru, Philippines, Poland, Portugal, Qatar, Republic of Korea, Romania, Russian Federation, Sao Tome and Principe, Saudi Arabia, Senegal, Sierra Leone, Singapore, Slovakia, Somalia, South Africa, Spain, Sri Lanka, Sudan, Suriname, Sweden, Switzerland, Syrian Arab Republic, Thailand, the former Yugoslav Republic of Macedonia, Togo, Trinidad and Tobago, Tunisia, Turkey, Uganda, Ukraine, United Arab Emirates, United Kingdom, United Republic of Tanzania, United States, Uruguay, Venezuela, Viet Nam, Yemen, Yugoslavia, Zaire, Zambia, Zimbabwe.

[a]Became a member on 17 March 1995.
[b]Became a member on 15 December 1995.

OFFICERS (BUREAU) OF THE BOARD

*Ninth (pre-sessional) executive, second part of the forty-first, tenth executive, resumed eighth executive and eleventh (pre-sessional) executive sessions*
*President:* Jamaica.
*Vice-Presidents:* Argentina, Bangladesh, Czech Republic, Germany, Indonesia, Japan, Madagascar, Norway, Russian Federation, United States.
*Rapporteur:* Zimbabwe.

*First part of the forty-second and eighteenth special sessions*
*President:* Switzerland.
*Vice-Presidents:* Burundi, Cuba, France, Iran, Japan, Pakistan, Peru, Russian Federation, South Africa, United States.
*Rapporteur:* Poland.

### SUBSIDIARY ORGANS OF THE TRADE AND DEVELOPMENT BOARD

The standing committees of the Board are open to the participation of all interested UNCTAD members, on the understanding that those wishing to attend a particular session of one or more of the committees communicate their intention to the Secretary-General of UNCTAD during the preceding regular session of the Board. On the basis of such notifications, the Board determines the membership of the standing committees.

COMMISSION ON INTERNATIONAL INVESTMENT AND TRANSNATIONAL CORPORATIONS

The Commission on International Investment and Transnational Corporations, which is open to the participation of all UNCTAD members, held its twenty-first session in Geneva from 24 to 28 April 1995.

*Chairman:* Philippines.
*Vice-Chairmen:* Colombia, Greece, Pakistan, Russian Federation, Zambia.
*Rapporteur:* United States.

*Intergovernmental Working Group of Experts on International Standards of Accounting and Reporting*

The Intergovernmental Working Group of Experts on International Standards of Accounting and Reporting, which reports to the Commission, held its thirteenth session in Geneva from 13 to 17 March 1995.

*Chairman:* Brazil.
*Vice-Chairmen:* Bulgaria, Costa Rica, Morocco, Switzerland, Thailand.
*Rapporteur:* Spain.

INTERGOVERNMENTAL GROUP OF EXPERTS ON RESTRICTIVE BUSINESS PRACTICES

The Intergovernmental Group of Experts on Restrictive Business Practices, which is open to the participation of all UNCTAD members, held its fourteenth session in Geneva from 6 to 10 March 1995.

*Chairman:* Tunisia.
*Vice-Chairmen:* Iran, Mexico, Poland, South Africa, United States.
*Rapporteur:* France.

SPECIAL COMMITTEE ON PREFERENCES

The Special Committee on Preferences, which is open to the participation of all UNCTAD members, held its twenty-second session in Geneva from 23 to 27 October 1995.

*Chairman:* Zimbabwe.
*Vice-Chairmen:* Austria, Cuba, Iran, Sweden, Tunisia.
*Rapporteur:* Russian Federation.

STANDING COMMITTEE ON COMMODITIES

The Standing Committee on Commodities held its fourth session in Geneva from 30 October to 3 November 1995.

*Members:* Afghanistan, Algeria, Argentina, Armenia, Australia, Austria, Bangladesh, Belgium, Bolivia, Brazil, Bulgaria, Canada, China *(Rapporteur)*, Colombia, Côte d'Ivoire *(Vice-Chairman)*, Cuba, Czech Republic, Democratic People's Republic of Korea, Denmark, Ecuador, Egypt, El Salvador, Equatorial Guinea, Ethiopia, Finland, France, Germany, Ghana, Greece, Honduras, Hungary, India, Indonesia *(Chairman)*, Iran, Iraq, Ireland, Israel, Italy, Jamaica, Japan, Jordan, Kenya, Lebanon, Libyan Arab Jamahiriya, Madagascar, Malaysia, Mali, Mexico, Morocco, Myanmar, Nepal, Netherlands, New Zealand, Nigeria, Norway, Pakistan,

Panama *(Vice-Chairman)*, Paraguay, Peru, Philippines *(Vice-Chairman)*, Poland, Portugal, Republic of Korea, Romania, Russian Federation, Saudi Arabia, Senegal, Singapore, Slovakia *(Vice-Chairman)*, Spain, Sri Lanka, Sudan, Sweden, Switzerland, Thailand, Togo, Trinidad and Tobago, Tunisia, Turkey *(Vice-Chairman)*, United Kingdom, United Republic of Tanzania, United States, Uruguay, Venezuela, Viet Nam, Yugoslavia, Zambia, Zimbabwe.

### STANDING COMMITTEE ON DEVELOPING SERVICES SECTORS:
#### FOSTERING COMPETITIVE SERVICES SECTORS IN
#### DEVELOPING COUNTRIES--INSURANCE

The Standing Committee on Developing Services Sectors: Fostering Competitive Services Sectors in Developing Countries— Insurance held its third session in Geneva from 13 to 17 November 1995.

*Members:* Afghanistan, Algeria, Argentina, Armenia, Australia, Austria, Bangladesh, Belgium, Bolivia, Brazil, Bulgaria, Cameroon, Chile *(Vice-Chairman)*, China, Colombia, Costa Rica, Côte d'Ivoire, Croatia, Cuba, Cyprus, Czech Republic, Democratic People's Republic of Korea, Denmark, Ecuador, Egypt, El Salvador, Ethiopia, Finland, France *(Chairman)*, Germany, Ghana, Greece, Honduras, Hungary, India, Indonesia *(Rapporteur)*, Iran, Iraq, Ireland, Israel, Italy, Jamaica, Japan, Jordan, Kenya, Lebanon, Lesotho, Liberia, Libyan Arab Jamahiriya, Malaysia, Mali, Malta, Mauritius, Mexico, Mongolia, Morocco, Myanmar, Nepal, Netherlands, New Zealand, Niger, Nigeria *(Vice-Chairman)*, Norway, Pakistan, Paraguay, Peru, Philippines, Poland *(Vice-Chairman)*, Republic of Korea, Romania, Russian Federation, Saudi Arabia, Senegal, Seychelles, Slovakia, Spain *(Vice-Chairman)*, Sri Lanka *(Vice-Chairman)*, Sudan, Sweden, Switzerland, Thailand, Trinidad and Tobago, Tunisia, Turkey, United Kingdom, United Republic of Tanzania, United States, Uruguay, Venezuela, Viet Nam, Yugoslavia, Zambia, Zimbabwe.

### STANDING COMMITTEE ON DEVELOPING SERVICES SECTORS:
#### FOSTERING COMPETITIVE SERVICES SECTORS IN
#### DEVELOPING COUNTRIES--SHIPPING

The Standing Committee on Developing Services Sectors: Fostering Competitive Services Sectors in Developing Countries—Shipping held its third session in Geneva from 6 to 9 June 1995.

*Members:* Afghanistan, Algeria, Argentina, Armenia, Australia, Austria, Bangladesh, Belgium, Bolivia, Brazil *(Vice-Chairman)*, Bulgaria, Cameroon, Canada *(Vice-Chairman)*, Chile, China, Colombia *(Chairman)*, Congo, Costa Rica, Côte d'Ivoire, Croatia, Cuba, Cyprus, Czech Republic, Democratic People's Republic of Korea, Denmark, Ecuador, Egypt, El Salvador, Ethiopia, Finland, France, Gabon, Germany *(Vice-Chairman)*, Ghana, Greece, Honduras, Hungary, India, Indonesia, Iran, Iraq, Ireland, Israel, Italy, Jamaica, Japan, Jordan, Kenya, Lebanon, Lesotho, Liberia *(Vice-Chairman)*, Libyan Arab Jamahiriya, Madagascar, Malaysia *(Rapporteur)*, Mali, Malta, Mauritius, Mexico, Mongolia, Morocco, Myanmar, Nepal, Netherlands, New Zealand, Niger, Nigeria, Norway, Pakistan, Paraguay, Peru, Philippines, Poland *(Vice-Chairman)*, Republic of Korea, Romania, Russian Federation, Saudi Arabia, Senegal, Seychelles, Slovakia, Spain, Sri Lanka, Sudan, Sweden, Switzerland, Thailand, Trinidad and Tobago, Tunisia, Turkey, United Kingdom, United Republic of Tanzania, United States, Uruguay, Venezuela, Viet Nam, Yugoslavia, Zambia, Zimbabwe.

### STANDING COMMITTEE ON DEVELOPING SERVICES SECTORS:
#### FOSTERING COMPETITIVE SERVICES SECTORS IN
#### DEVELOPING COUNTRIES

The Standing Committee on Developing Services Sectors: Fostering Competitive Services Sectors in Developing Countries held its third session in Geneva from 25 to 29 September 1995.

*Members:* Afghanistan, Algeria, Argentina, Armenia, Australia, Austria, Bangladesh, Belgium, Bolivia, Brazil, Bulgaria, Cameroon, Chile, China, Colombia, Costa Rica, Côte d'Ivoire, Croatia, Cuba, Cyprus, Czech Republic, Democratic People's Republic of Korea, Denmark, Ecuador, Egypt *(Chairman)*, El Salvador, Ethiopia, Finland *(Vice-Chairman)*, France, Germany, Ghana, Greece, Honduras, Hungary, India *(Vice-Chairman)*, Indonesia, Iran, Iraq, Ireland, Israel, Italy, Jamaica *(Vice-Chairman)*, Japan, Jordan, Kenya, Lebanon, Lesotho, Liberia, Libyan Arab Jamahiriya, Malaysia, Mali, Malta, Mauritius, Mexico, Mongolia, Morocco, Myanmar, Nepal, Netherlands, New Zealand, Niger, Nigeria, Norway, Pakistan, Paraguay, Peru, Philippines, Poland *(Vice-Chairman)*, Republic of Korea, Romania, Russian Federation, Saudi Arabia, Senegal, Seychelles, Slovakia *(Rapporteur)*, Spain, Sri Lanka *(Vice-Chairman)*, Sudan, Sweden, Switzerland, Thailand, Trinidad and Tobago, Tunisia, Turkey, United Kingdom, United Republic of Tanzania, United States, Uruguay, Venezuela, Viet Nam, Yugoslavia, Zambia, Zimbabwe.

### STANDING COMMITTEE ON ECONOMIC COOPERATION
#### AMONG DEVELOPING COUNTRIES

The Standing Committee on Economic Cooperation among Developing Countries held its third session in Geneva from 19 to 23 June 1995.

*Members:* Afghanistan, Algeria, Argentina, Armenia, Austria, Bangladesh, Bolivia, Brazil, China, Colombia, Costa Rica, Côte d'Ivoire, Cuba, Democratic People's Republic of Korea, Denmark, Egypt, El Salvador, Ethiopia, France, Georgia, Germany, Ghana, Greece *(Vice-Chairman)*, Honduras, India, Indonesia *(Vice-Chairman)*, Iran, Iraq, Israel, Jamaica, Japan *(Rapporteur)*, Jordan, Kenya, Lebanon, Libyan Arab Jamahiriya, Madagascar, Malaysia, Mali, Mauritius, Mexico, Mongolia, Morocco, Myanmar, Nepal *(Chairman)*, Netherlands, Niger, Nigeria, Norway, Pakistan, Panama, Peru, Philippines, Republic of Korea, Romania, Russian Federation *(Vice-Chairman)*, Saudi Arabia, Senegal, Spain, Sri Lanka, Sudan, Sweden, Switzerland, Syrian Arab Republic, Thailand, Togo, Trinidad and Tobago, Tunisia, Turkey, United Kingdom, United Republic of Tanzania *(Vice-Chairman)*, United States, Uruguay *(Vice-Chairman)*, Venezuela, Viet Nam, Yugoslavia, Zambia, Zimbabwe.

### STANDING COMMITTEE ON POVERTY ALLEVIATION

The Standing Committee on Poverty Alleviation held its third session in Geneva from 12 to 16 June 1995.

*Members:* Afghanistan, Algeria, Angola, Argentina, Armenia, Austria, Bangladesh, Belarus *(Vice-Chairman)*,[a] Belgium, Bolivia, Brazil, Cameroon, Canada, Chile *(Vice-Chairman)*, China, Colombia, Côte d'Ivoire, Cuba, Czech Republic, Democratic People's Republic of Korea, Denmark, Dominican Republic, Egypt *(Chairman)*, El Salvador, Ethiopia, Finland, France, Germany, Ghana, Greece *(Vice-Chairman)*, Honduras, India, Indonesia, Iran, Iraq, Ireland, Israel, Italy, Jamaica, Japan, Jordan, Kenya, Lebanon, Libyan Arab Jamahiriya, Madagascar, Malaysia, Mali, Mexico, Morocco, Myanmar, Nepal, Netherlands, Nigeria, Norway, Pakistan, Panama, Paraguay, Peru, Philippines, Poland, Portugal, Republic of Korea, Romania, Russian Federation, Saudi Arabia, Senegal, Slovakia, Spain, Sri Lanka *(Vice-Chairman)*, Sudan, Sweden, Switzerland *(Rapporteur)*, Thailand, Togo, Trinidad and Tobago, Tunisia, Turkey, United Kingdom, United States, Uruguay, Viet Nam, Yugoslavia, Zambia, Zimbabwe *(Vice-Chairman)*.

[a]Belarus was not a member, but an exception was made to allow it to be a Vice-Chairman.

### United Nations Development Fund for Women (UNIFEM)

The United Nations Development Fund for Women is a separate entity in autonomous association with UNDP. The Director of the Fund, appointed by the UNDP Administrator, conducts all matters related to its mandate and the Administrator is accountable for its management and operations.

#### CONSULTATIVE COMMITTEE

The Consultative Committee on UNIFEM to advise the UNDP Administrator on all policy matters affecting the Fund's activities is composed of five Member States designated by the General Assembly President with due regard for the financing of the Fund from voluntary contributions and to equitable geographical distribution. Each State member of the Committee serves for a three-year term and designates a person with expertise in development cooperation activities, including those benefiting women.

The Committee held its thirty-fifth session in New York on 7 June 1995.

*Members* (until 31 December 1997): Indonesia, Norway *(Chairman)*, Peru, Poland, Uganda.

*Director of UNIFEM:* Noeleen Heyzer.
*Deputy Director:* Maxine Olson.

### United Nations Environment Programme (UNEP)

#### GOVERNING COUNCIL

The Governing Council of UNEP consists of 58 members elected by the General Assembly according to a specific pattern of equitable geographical representation.

The Governing Council, which reports to the Assembly through the Economic and Social Council, held its eighteenth session in Nairobi, Kenya, from 15 to 26 May 1995.

*Members:*
*To serve until 31 December 1995:* Australia, Bangladesh, Bhutan, Botswana, Cameroon, Chile *(Rapporteur)*, Colombia, Congo, Côte d'Ivoire, Denmark, Guyana, India, Iran, Italy, Kenya *(Vice-President)*, Malaysia, Mexico, Netherlands, Nigeria, Pakistan *(President)*, Poland, Portugal, Romania *(Vice-President)*, Rwanda, Senegal, Slovakia, Sri Lanka, United Kingdom *(Vice-President)*, Uruguay.
*To serve until 31 December 1997:* Argentina, Brazil, Bulgaria, Burundi, Canada, China, Costa Rica, Democratic People's Republic of Korea, France, Gabon, Gambia, Germany, Guinea-Bissau, Hungary, Indonesia, Japan, Nicaragua, Republic of Korea, Russian Federation, Spain, Sudan, Sweden, Switzerland, Syrian Arab Republic, United States, Venezuela, Zaire, Zambia, Zimbabwe.

On 21 November 1995 (dec. 50/308), the General Assembly elected the following for a four-year term beginning on 1 January 1996 to fill the vacancies occurring on 31 December 1995: Algeria, Australia, Benin, Burkina Faso, Central African Republic, Chile, Colombia, Czech Republic, Finland, India, Iran, Italy, Kenya, Marshall Islands, Mauritania, Mexico, Morocco, Netherlands, Pakistan, Panama, Peru, Philippines, Poland, Samoa, Slovakia, Thailand, Tunisia, Turkey, United Kingdom.

*Executive Director of UNEP:* Elizabeth Dowdeswell.

### United Nations Institute for Disarmament Research (UNIDIR)

BOARD OF TRUSTEES

The Secretary-General's Advisory Board on Disarmament Matters, composed in 1995 of 21 eminent persons selected on the basis of their personal expertise and taking into account the principle of equitable geographical representation, functions as the Board of Trustees of UNIDIR; the Director of UNIDIR reports to the General Assembly and is an ex-officio member of the Advisory Board when it acts as the Board of Trustees.

*Members:* Ednan T. Agaev (Russian Federation); Marcos Castrioto de Azambuja (Brazil); Mitsuro Donowaki (Japan); André Erdos (Hungary); Emmanuel A. Erskine (Ghana); Curt Gasteyger (Switzerland); Henny J. van der Graaf (Netherlands); Josef Holik (Germany); Oumirseric Kasenov (Kazakstan); Natarajan Krishnan (India); François de la Gorce (France); James F. Leonard (United States); Peggy Mason (Canada); Wangari Matthai (Kenya); Rogelio Pfirter (Argentina); Sha Zukang (China); Mohamed I. Shaker, *Chairman* (Egypt); John Simpson (United King-

dom); Sitti Azizah Abod (Malaysia); Nana Sutresna (Indonesia); Klaus Törnudd (Finland).

*Director of UNIDIR:* Sverre Lodgaard.

### United Nations Institute for Training and Research (UNITAR)

The Executive Director of UNITAR, in consultation with the Board of Trustees of the Institute, reports through the Secretary-General to the General Assembly and, as appropriate, to the Economic and Social Council and other United Nations bodies.

BOARD OF TRUSTEES

The Board of Trustees of UNITAR is composed of: *(a)* not less than 11 and not more than 30 members, which may include one or more officials of the United Nations Secretariat, appointed on a broad geographical basis by the Secretary-General, in consultation with the Presidents of the General Assembly and the Economic and Social Council; and *(b)* four ex-officio members.

The Board held two sessions in 1995, in Geneva: its thirty-third from 8 to 10 March and a special session from 4 to 6 September.

*Members:* Anne Anderson (Ireland); Giuseppe Baldocci (Italy); Jorge Berguño (Chile); Michel de Bonnecorse (France); Satish Chandra (India); Lisette Elomo-Ntonga (Cameroon); Ibrahim A. Gambari (Nigeria); Alois Jelonek (Germany); Ahmad Kamal, *Chairman* (Pakistan); Shunji Kobayashi (Japan); Andrei Kolossovsky (Russian Federation); Winfried Lang (Austria); Philippe Roch (Switzerland); Juan Carlos Sanchez-Arnau (Argentina); Mohammed Ahmed Sherif (Libyan Arab Jamahiriya); Wang Guangya (China); Penelope Anne Wensley, *Vice-Chairman* (Australia); Mounir Zahran (Egypt).
*Ex-officio members:* The Secretary-General, the President of the General Assembly, the President of the Economic and Social Council and the Executive Director of UNITAR.

*Executive Director of UNITAR:* Marcel A. Boisard (Acting).

### United Nations Joint Staff Pension Board

The United Nations Joint Staff Pension Board did not meet in 1995.

*Members:* United Nations, FAO, WHO, ILO, UNESCO, UNIDO, ICAO, IAEA, ITU, IMO, ICITO/GATT, WMO, WIPO, IFAD.

STANDING COMMITTEE OF THE PENSION BOARD

The Standing Committee met in New York from 10 to 14 July 1995.

*Members* (elected at the Board's 1993 session):
*United Nations (Group I)*
*Representing the General Assembly:* Members: T. Inomata *(Chairman)*, C. Stitt. Alternates: L. Bidny, S. Shearouse.
*Representing the Secretary-General:* Members: Y. Takasu, A. Miller. Alternates: K. Walton, D. Bull.
*Representing the participants:* Members: B. Hillis, N. Kakar. Alternates: S. Johnston, A. Kruiderink.
*Specialized agencies (Group II)*
*Representing the governing body:* Member: Dr. J. Lariviere (WHO). Alternate: B. Roos (WHO).
*Representing the executive head:* Member: G. Eberle (FAO). Alternate: D. Sanvicenti (WHO).
*Representing the participants:* Member: A. Marcucci (FAO). Alternate: M. Arrigo (FAO).
*Specialized agencies (Group III)*
*Representing the executive head:* Member: R. Smith (ILO). Alternate: A. Busca (ILO).
*Representing the participants:* Member: A. McLurg (UNESCO).
*Specialized agencies (Group IV)*
*Representing the governing body:* Member: L. Mollel (ICAO). Alternate: R. Maga (ITU).
*Representing the participants:* Member: W. Scherzer (IAEA). Alternate: K. Ahmed (UNIDO).

*Specialized agencies (Group V)*
*Representing the governing body:* Member: P. Cheung (GATT). Alternate: F. Bature (IFAD).
*Representing the executive head:* Member: J.-L. Perrin (WIPO). Alternate: E. Renlund (WMO).

## COMMITTEE OF ACTUARIES

The Committee of Actuaries consists of five members, each representing one of the five geographical regions of the United Nations.

*Members:* A. O. Ogunshola (Nigeria), *Region I* (African States); K. Takeuchi (Japan), *Region II* (Asian States); E. M. Chetyrkin (Russian Federation), *Region III* (Eastern European States); H. Pérez Montas (Dominican Republic), *Region IV* (Latin American States); L. J. Martin (United Kingdom), *Region V* (Western European and other States).
*Member emeritus:* R. J. Myers (United States).

### United Nations Relief and Works Agency for Palestine Refugees in the Near East (UNRWA)

## ADVISORY COMMISSION OF UNRWA

The Advisory Commission of UNRWA met in Vienna on 4 October 1995.

*Members:* Belgium, Egypt, France, Japan, Jordan, Lebanon, Syrian Arab Republic, Turkey *(Chairman)*, United Kingdom, United States.

## WORKING GROUP ON THE FINANCING OF UNRWA

The Working Group met twice in 1995, on 14 September and 13 October.

*Members:* France, Ghana, Japan, Lebanon, Norway *(Rapporteur)*, Trinidad and Tobago, Turkey *(Chairman)*, United Kingdom, United States.

*Commissioner-General of UNRWA:* Ilter Türkmen.
*Deputy Commissioner-General:* Dr. Mohamed Abdelmoumène (Acting).

### United Nations Scientific Committee on the Effects of Atomic Radiation

The 21-member United Nations Scientific Committee on the Effects of Atomic Radiation held its forty-fourth session in Vienna from 12 to 16 June 1995.

*Members:* Argentina, Australia, Belgium, Brazil, Canada, China, Egypt, France, Germany *(Vice-Chairman)*, India, Indonesia, Japan, Mexico, Peru *(Chairman)*, Poland, Russian Federation, Slovakia, Sudan, Sweden *(Rapporteur)*, United Kingdom, United States.

### United Nations Staff Pension Committee

The United Nations Staff Pension Committee consists of four members and four alternates elected by the General Assembly, four members and two alternates appointed by the Secretary-General, and four members and two alternates elected by the participants in the United Nations Joint Staff Pension Fund. The term of office of the elected members is three years, or until the election of their successors.

*Members:*
*Elected by Assembly*[a] (to serve until 31 December 1997): Vijay Gokhale (India),[b] Tadanori Inomata (Japan), Vladimir V. Kuznetsov (Russian Federation), Philip Richard Okanda Owade (Kenya), Carlos Dante Riva (Argentina),[b] Susan Shearouse (United States), Clive Stitt (United Kingdom), M. El Hassane Zahid (Morocco).
*Appointed by Secretary-General* (to serve until replaced): *Members:* Yukio Takasu, Denis Halliday, Anthony J. Miller, Keith Walton. *Alternates:* Maryan Baquerot, Warren Sach.

*Elected by participants* (to serve until 31 December 1995): *Members:* Bruce C. Hillis, Viviana Baeza, Susanna H. Johnston, Narinder Kakar. *Alternates:* Anton Kruiderink, Orlando Lugo.

[a]The representation of the Assembly determines the persons to be designated as members and alternates, respectively, for any particular meeting.
[b]Appointed on 28 February 1995 (dec. 49/314 B).

### United Nations University

## COUNCIL OF THE UNITED NATIONS UNIVERSITY

The Council of the United Nations University, the governing board of the University, reports biennially to the General Assembly, to the Economic and Social Council and to the UNESCO Executive Board through the Secretary-General and the UNESCO Director-General. It consists of: *(a)* 24 members appointed jointly by the Secretary-General and the Director-General of UNESCO, in consultation with the agencies and programmes concerned including UNITAR, who serve in their personal capacity for six-year terms; *(b)* the Secretary-General, the Director-General of UNESCO and the Executive Director of UNITAR, who are ex-officio members; and *(c)* the Rector of the University, who is normally appointed for a five-year term.

The Council held its forty-second session in Tokyo, Japan, from 4 to 8 December 1995.

*Members:*
*To serve until 2 May 1998:* Vladimir Dlouhy (Czech Republic);[a] Hideo Kagami (Japan); Sang Soo Lee (Republic of Korea); Madina Ly-Tall (Mali); Edson Machado de Sousa (Brazil); Lucien F. Michaud, *Chairman* (Canada); A. P. Mitra (India); Jacob L. Ngu (Cameroon); Luis Manuel Peñalver (Venezuela); Victor Rabinowitch (United States); Frances Stewart (United Kingdom); J. A. van Ginkel (Netherlands).
*To serve until 2 May 2001:* José Joaquin Brunner Ried (Chile); Paolo Costa (Italy); Donald Ekong (Nigeria); Salim El-Hoss (Lebanon); Genady N. Golubev (Russian Federation); Françoise Héritier-Augé (France); Risto Ihamuotila (Finland); Hanaa Kheir-El-Din (Egypt); Graça Machel (Mozambique); Valeria Merino-Dirani (Ecuador); Ingrid Moses (Australia); Wang Shaoqi (China).
*Ex-officio members:* The Secretary-General, the Director-General of UNESCO and the Executive Director of UNITAR.

[a]Resigned in December 1995.

*Rector of the University:* Heitor Gurgulino de Souza.

The Council maintained four standing committees during 1995: Committee on Finance and Budget; Committee on Institutional and Programmatic Development; Committee on Statutes, Rules and Guidelines; Committee on the Report of the Council.

### United Nations Voluntary Fund for Indigenous Populations

## BOARD OF TRUSTEES

The Board of Trustees to advise the Secretary-General in his administration of the United Nations Voluntary Fund for Indigenous Populations consists of five members with relevant experience in issues affecting indigenous populations, appointed in their personal capacity by the Secretary-General for a three-year term. At least one member is a representative of a widely recognized organization of indigenous people.

The Board held its eighth session in Geneva from 24 to 28 April 1995.

*Members:* Leif Dunfjeld (Norway); William Ole Ntimama (Kenya); Lois O'Donoghue (Australia); Victoria Tauli-Corpuz (Philippines); Augusto Willemsen-Díaz, *Chairman* (Guatemala).

### United Nations Voluntary Fund for Victims of Torture

## BOARD OF TRUSTEES

The Board of Trustees to advise the Secretary-General in his administration of the United Nations Voluntary Fund for Victims of Torture consists of five members with wide experience in the field of human rights, appointed in their personal capacity by the Secretary-General with due regard for equitable geographical distribution and in consultation with their Governments.

The Board held its fourteenth session in Geneva from 15 to 24 May 1995.

*Members:* Elizabeth Odio Benito (Costa Rica); Ribot Hatano (Japan); Ivan Tosevski (the former Yugoslav Republic of Macedonia); Amos Wako (Kenya); Jaap Walkate, *Chairman* (Netherlands).

### United Nations Voluntary Trust Fund on Contemporary Forms of Slavery

BOARD OF TRUSTEES

The Board of Trustees to advise the Secretary-General in his administration of the United Nations Voluntary Trust Fund on Contemporary Forms of Slavery consists of five persons with relevant experience in the field of human rights and contemporary forms of slavery in particular, appointed in their personal capacity by the Secretary-General for a three-year renewable term, in consultation with the Chairman of the Subcommission on Prevention of Discrimination and Protection of Minorities and with due regard to equitable geographical distribution.

The Board met from 28 August to 1 September 1995.

*Members*[a] (until 31 December 1998): Swami Agnivesh (India), Tatiana Matveeva (Russian Federation), Cheikh Saad-Bouh Kamara (Mauritania).

[a]The members for Western Europe and Latin America were to be appointed.

### World Food Council

The World Food Council, at the ministerial or plenipotentiary level, functions as an organ of the United Nations and reports to the General Assembly through the Economic and Social Council. It consists of 36 members nominated by the Economic and Social Council and elected by the Assembly according to a specific pattern of equitable geographical distribution. Members serve for three-year terms.

The Council did not meet in 1995.

*Members:*

*To serve until 31 December 1995:* Ecuador, France, Guinea-Bissau, Hungary, India, Iran, Italy, Japan, Nigeria, Norway, Peru, Tunisia.

*To serve until 31 December 1996:*[a] Bangladesh, Brazil, China, Liberia, Malawi, Mexico, Pakistan, Sudan, Turkey, United States.

*To serve until 31 December 1997:*[b] Albania,[c] Angola, Colombia, Dominican Republic, Honduras, Indonesia, Kenya, Marshall Islands, Russian Federation, Uganda.

[a]Two seats allocated to one member each from Eastern European and Western European and other States remained unfilled in 1995.

[b]Two seats allocated to members from Western European and other States remained unfilled in 1995.

[c]Nominated on 9 February (dec. 1995/202) and elected on 28 February (dec. 49/316 B).

On 4 May 1995 (dec. 1995/221), the Economic and Social Council nominated the following States for election by the General Assembly for a three-year term beginning on 1 January 1996 to fill 7 of the 12 vacancies occurring on 31 December 1995: Algeria, Hungary, India, Iran, Japan, Mali, Togo. The Assembly elected them on 21 November (dec. 50/309). No further elections were held in 1995 to fill the remaining seats, allocated to two members from Latin American and Caribbean States and three members from Western European and other States.

## Conferences

### Fourth World Conference on Women

The Fourth World Conference on Women was held in Beijing from 4 to 15 September 1995. Participating were the following 189 States and the European Community:

Afghanistan, Albania, Algeria, Andorra, Angola, Antigua and Barbuda, Argentina, Armenia, Australia *(Vice-President)*, Austria, Azerbaijan *(Vice-President)*, Bahamas *(Vice-President)*, Bahrain, Bangladesh *(Vice-President)*, Barbados, Belarus, Belgium, Belize, Benin, Bhutan, Bolivia, Bosnia and Herzegovina, Botswana *(Vice-President)*, Brazil *(Vice-President)*, Brunei Darussalam, Bulgaria, Burkina Faso, Burundi, Cambodia, Cameroon, Canada, Cape Verde, Central African Republic, Chad, Chile, China *(President)*, Colombia *(Vice-President)*, Comoros, Congo *(Vice-President)*, Cook Islands, Costa Rica, Côte d'Ivoire, Croatia, Cuba *(Vice-President)*, Cyprus, Czech Republic, Democratic People's Republic of Korea, Denmark, Djibouti, Dominica, Dominican Republic, Ecuador, Egypt, El Salvador, Equatorial Guinea, Eritrea, Estonia, Ethiopia, Fiji, Finland, France, Gabon, Gambia, Georgia, Germany, Ghana, Greece *(Vice-President)*, Guatemala, Guinea, Guinea-Bissau, Guyana, Haiti, Holy See, Honduras, Hungary, Iceland, India, Indonesia, Iran, Iraq, Ireland, Israel, Italy, Jamaica, Japan *(Vice-President)*, Jordan *(Vice-President)*, Kazakstan, Kenya *(Vice-President)*, Kiribati, Kuwait, Kyrgyzstan, Lao People's Democratic Republic, Latvia, Lebanon, Lesotho, Liberia, Libyan Arab Jamahiriya, Liechtenstein, Lithuania, Luxembourg, Madagascar, Malawi, Malaysia *(Vice-President)*, Maldives, Mali, Malta, Marshall Islands, Mauritania, Mauritius, Mexico, Micronesia, Monaco, Mongolia, Morocco *(Vice-President)*, Mozambique, Myanmar, Namibia *(Rapporteur-General)*, Nauru, Nepal, Netherlands, New Zealand *(Vice-President)*, Nicaragua, Niger, Nigeria *(Vice-President)*, Niue, Norway, Oman, Pakistan *(Vice-President)*, Palau, Panama *(Vice-President)*, Papua New Guinea, Paraguay, Peru, Philippines, Poland, Portugal *(Vice-President)*, Qatar, Republic of Korea, Republic of Moldova, Romania *(Vice-President)*, Russian Federation, Rwanda, Saint Kitts and Nevis, Saint Lucia, Saint Vincent and the Grenadines, Samoa, San Marino, Sao Tome and Principe, Senegal *(Vice-President)*, Seychelles, Sierra Leone, Singapore, Slovakia, Slovenia, Solomon Islands, South Africa, Spain *(Vice-President)*, Sri Lanka, Sudan *(Vice-President)*, Suriname, Swaziland, Sweden *(Vice-President)*, Switzerland, Syrian Arab Republic *(Vice-President)*, Tajikistan, Thailand, the former Yugoslav Republic of Macedonia *(Vice-President)*, Togo, Tonga, Trinidad and Tobago, Tunisia, Turkey, Turkmenistan, Tuvalu, Uganda, Ukraine, United Arab Emirates, United Kingdom, United Republic of Tanzania, United States, Uruguay, Uzbekistan, Vanuatu, Venezuela, Viet Nam, Yemen, Zaire, Zambia, Zimbabwe.

### Ninth United Nations Congress on the Prevention of Crime and the Treatment of Offenders

The Ninth United Nations Congress on the Prevention of Crime and the Treatment of Offenders was held in Cairo, Egypt, from 29 April to 8 May 1995. Participating were the following 138 States:

Afghanistan, Albania, Algeria *(Vice-President)*, Angola, Argentina *(Rapporteur-General)*, Armenia, Australia *(Vice-President)*, Austria *(Vice-President)*, Azerbaijan, Bahrain, Bangladesh, Barbados, Belarus, Belgium, Benin, Bolivia *(Vice-President)*, Botswana, Brazil *(Vice-President)*, Brunei Darussalam, Bulgaria, Burkina Faso, Burundi, Cameroon *(Vice-President)*, Canada *(Vice-President)*, Cape Verde, Central African Republic, Chad, Chile *(Vice-President)*, China *(Vice-President)*, Colombia, Comoros, Costa Rica, Côte d'Ivoire, Croatia, Cuba *(Vice-President)*, Cyprus, Czech Republic, Democratic People's Republic of Korea, Denmark, Djibouti, Ecuador, Egypt *(President)*, Equatorial Guinea, Eritrea, Estonia, Ethiopia, Finland, France *(Vice-President)*, Gabon, Gambia, Germany, Greece, Guinea *(Vice-President)*, Guinea-Bissau, Holy See, Hungary, India, Indonesia, Iran, Iraq, Ireland, Israel, Italy, Japan, Jordan, Kazakstan, Kenya, Kiribati, Kuwait *(Vice-President)*, Lao People's Democratic Republic, Lebanon, Lesotho, Liberia, Libyan Arab Jamahiriya, Malawi, Malaysia *(Vice-President)*, Maldives, Mali, Malta, Mauritius, Mexico, Mongolia, Morocco, Myanmar, Nepal *(Vice-President)*, Netherlands, New Zealand, Niger, Nigeria, Norway, Oman, Pakistan, Panama, Paraguay, Peru, Philippines, Poland, Portugal, Qatar, Republic of Korea *(Vice-President)*, Romania *(Vice-President)*, Russian Federation, Rwanda, Samoa, Sao Tome and Principe, Saudi Arabia, Senegal, Sierra Leone, Slovakia, Slovenia, South Africa *(Vice-President)*, Spain, Sri Lanka, Sudan, Swaziland *(Vice-President)*, Sweden, Switzerland, Syrian Arab Republic, Thailand, the former Yugoslav Republic of Macedonia, Togo, Tunisia *(Vice-President)*, Turkey, Uganda *(Vice-President)*, Ukraine *(First Vice-President)*, United Arab Emirates, United Kingdom, United Republic of Tanzania, United States *(Vice-President)*, Uruguay, Uzbekistan, Vanuatu, Venezuela *(Vice-President)*, Viet Nam, Yemen, Zaire, Zambia, Zimbabwe.

### United Nations Conference on Straddling Fish Stocks and Highly Migratory Fish Stocks

The United Nations Conference on Straddling Fish Stocks and Highly Migratory Fish Stocks, open to the participation of all States Members of the United Nations or members of the specialized agencies and IAEA, held two sessions in 1995, in New York: its fifth from 27 March to 12 April and its sixth (final) from 24 July to 4 August and on 4 December.

*Chairman:* Fiji.
*Vice-Chairmen:* Chile, Italy, Mauritania.

### World Summit for Social Development

The World Summit for Social Development was held in Copenhagen, Denmark, from 6 to 12 March 1995. Participating were the following 186 States and the European Community:

Afghanistan, Albania, Algeria *(Vice-President)*, Andorra *(Vice-President)*, Angola, Antigua and Barbuda, Argentina, Armenia, Australia *(Vice-President)*, Austria, Azerbaijan, Bahamas, Bahrain, Bangladesh, Barbados, Belarus, Belgium, Belize *(Vice-President)*, Benin, Bhutan, Bolivia, Bosnia and Herzegovina, Botswana, Brazil, Brunei Darussalam, Bulgaria, Burkina Faso *(Vice-President)*, Burundi, Cambodia, Cameroon *(Vice-President)*, Canada *(Vice-President)*, Cape Verde, Central African Republic, Chad, Chile *(Vice-President)*, China *(Vice-President)*, Colombia, Comoros, Congo, Cook Islands, Costa Rica, Côte d'Ivoire, Croatia, Cuba *(Vice-President)*, Cyprus, Czech Republic, Democratic People's Republic of Korea, Denmark *(President and ex-officio Vice-President)*, Djibouti, Dominica, Dominican Republic, Ecuador, Egypt, El Salvador, Equatorial Guinea, Eritrea, Estonia, Ethiopia *(Vice-President)*, Fiji, Finland, France, Gabon, Gambia, Georgia, Germany *(Vice-President)*, Ghana, Greece, Grenada, Guatemala, Guinea, Guinea-Bissau *(Vice-President)*, Guyana, Haiti, Holy See, Honduras, Hungary, Iceland, India *(Vice-President)*, Indonesia *(Vice-President)*, Iran, Iraq, Ireland, Israel, Italy, Jamaica, Japan, Jordan, Kazakstan, Kenya, Kuwait, Kyrgyzstan, Lao People's Democratic Republic, Latvia *(Vice-President)*, Lebanon, Lesotho, Liberia, Libyan Arab Jamahiriya, Liechtenstein, Lithuania, Luxembourg, Madagascar, Malawi, Malaysia, Maldives, Mali, Malta, Marshall Islands, Mauritania, Mauritius, Mexico, Micronesia, Monaco, Mongolia, Morocco, Mozambique, Myanmar, Namibia, Nepal, Netherlands, New Zealand, Nicaragua, Niger, Nigeria, Niue, Norway, Oman, Pakistan, Panama *(Vice-President)*, Papua New Guinea, Paraguay *(Vice-President)*, Peru, Philippines *(Vice-President)*, Poland, Portugal *(Vice-President)*, Qatar *(Vice-President)*, Republic of Korea *(Vice-President)*, Republic of Moldova, Romania, Russian Federation, Rwanda, Saint Kitts and Nevis, Saint Lucia, Saint Vincent and the Grenadines, San Marino, Sao Tome and Principe, Saudi Arabia, Senegal, Seychelles, Sierra Leone, Singapore, Slovakia *(Vice-President)*, Slovenia, Solomon Islands, South Africa, Spain, Sri Lanka, Sudan *(Vice-President)*, Suriname, Swaziland, Sweden *(Vice-President)*, Switzerland, Syrian Arab Republic, Tajikistan, Thailand, the former Yugoslav Republic of Macedonia, Togo, Tonga, Trinidad and Tobago, Tunisia *(Rapporteur-General)*, Turkey, Turkmenistan, Uganda, Ukraine *(Vice-President)*, United Arab Emirates, United Kingdom, United Republic of Tanzania, United States, Uruguay, Uzbekistan, Vanuatu, Venezuela, Viet Nam, Yemen, Zaire, Zambia, Zimbabwe.

# Security Council

The Security Council consists of 15 Member States of the United Nations, in accordance with the provisions of Article 23 of the United Nations Charter as amended in 1965.

MEMBERS
*Permanent members:* China, France, Russian Federation, United Kingdom, United States.
*Non-permanent members:* Argentina, Botswana, Czech Republic, Germany, Honduras, Indonesia, Italy, Nigeria, Oman, Rwanda.

On 8 November 1995 (dec. 50/306), the General Assembly elected Chile, Egypt, Guinea-Bissau, Poland and the Republic of Korea for a two-year term beginning on 1 January 1996, to replace Argentina, the Czech Republic, Nigeria, Oman and Rwanda, whose terms of office were to expire on 31 December 1995.

PRESIDENTS
The presidency of the Council rotates monthly, according to the English alphabetical listing of its member States. The following served as Presidents during 1995:

| Month | Member | Representative |
|---|---|---|
| January | Argentina | Emilio J. Cárdenas |
| February | Botswana | Mompati Merafhe |
| | | Legwaila Joseph Legwaila |
| March | China | Li Zhaoxing |
| | | Wang Xuexian |
| April | Czech Republic | Karel Kovanda |
| | | Alexander Vondra |
| May | France | Jean-Bernard Mérimée |
| June | Germany | Detlev Graf zu Rantzau |
| July | Honduras | Urbizo Panting |
| | | Gerardo Martínez Blanco |

| Month | Member | Representative |
|---|---|---|
| August | Indonesia | Nugroho Wisnumurti |
| September | Italy | Susanna Agnelli |
| | | Francesco Paolo Fulci |
| October | Nigeria | Ibrahim A. Gambari |
| November | Oman | Salim Bin Mohammed Al-Khussaiby |
| December | Russian Federation | Sergey V. Lavrov |

## Military Staff Committee

The Military Staff Committee consists of the chiefs of staff of the permanent members of the Security Council or their representatives. It meets fortnightly.

## Standing committees

Each of the three standing committees of the Security Council is composed of representatives of all Council members:

Committee of Experts (to examine the provisional rules of procedure of the Council and any other matters entrusted to it by the Council)
Committee on the Admission of New Members
Committee on Council Meetings Away from Headquarters

## Peace-keeping operations and special missions

### United Nations Truce Supervision Organization (UNTSO)

*Officer-in-Charge:* Colonel Luc Bujold (until 15 March), Lieutenant-Colonel Harold McKinney (12-26 June), Major-General Rufus Kupolati (from 1 October).
*Chief of Staff:* Colonel Jaakko Oksanen (26 June–1 October).

### United Nations Military Observer Group in India and Pakistan (UNMOGIP)

*Chief Military Observer:* Major-General Alfonso Pessolano.

### United Nations Peace-keeping Force in Cyprus (UNFICYP)

*Special Representative of the Secretary-General:* Charles Joe Clark.
*Deputy Special Representative and Chief of Mission:* Gustave Feissel.
*Force Commander:* Brigadier-General Ahti Toimi Paavali Vartiainen.

### United Nations Disengagement Observer Force (UNDOF)

*Force Commander:* Major-General Johannes Kosters.

### United Nations Interim Force in Lebanon (UNIFIL)

*Force Commander:* Major-General Trond Furuhovde (until 22 February), Major-General Stanislaw Wozniak (from 1 April).

### United Nations Iraq-Kuwait Observation Mission (UNIKOM)

*Force Commander:* Major-General Krishna Narayan Singh Thapa (until 1 December), Major-General Gian G. Santillo (from 1 December).

### United Nations Angola Verification Mission (UNAVEM III)

*Special Representative of the Secretary-General:* Alioune Blondin Beye.
*Deputy Special Representative:* Khaled Yassir (from 1 July).
*Chief Military Observer:* Major-General Chris Abutu Garuba (until 30 September).
*Force Commander:* Major-General Phillip V. Sibanda (from 30 September).

### United Nations Observer Mission in El Salvador (ONUSAL)

*Special Representative of the Secretary-General and Chief of Mission:* Enrique ter Horst.

### United Nations Mission for the Referendum in Western Sahara (MINURSO)

*Special Representative of the Secretary-General:* Sahabzada Yaqub-Khan.
*Deputy Special Representative:* Erik Jensen.
*Force Commander:* Brigadier-General André Van Baelen.

### United Nations Protection Force (UNPROFOR)

*Special Representative of the Secretary-General and Chief of Mission:* Yasushi Akashi (until 31 October).
*Special Representative and Envoy to NATO:* Kofi Annan (from 1 November).
*Force Commander:* Lieutenant-General Bernard Janvier (from 20 February).

### United Nations Operation in Somalia (UNOSOM II)[a]

*Special Representative of the Secretary-General:* James Victor Gbeho.
*Force Commander:* Lieutenant-General Aboo Samah Bin Aboo Bakar.

[a]The mandate of UNOSOM II ended on 31 March 1995.

### United Nations Observer Mission in Georgia (UNOMIG)

*Special Envoy of the Secretary-General:* Edouard Brunner.
*Chief Military Observer and Head of Mission:* Brigadier-General John Hvidegaard (until 30 September).
*Head of Mission:* Liviu Bota (from 1 October).
*Chief Military Observer:* Major-General Per Källström (from 26 October).

### United Nations Observer Mission in Liberia (UNOMIL)

*Special Representative of the Secretary-General:* Anthony B. Nyakyi.
*Chief Military Observer:* Major-General Daniel Ishmael Opande (until 25 May), Major-General Mahmoud Talha (from 30 November).
*Executive Director:* Omar Halim.

### United Nations Mission in Haiti (UNMIH)

*Special Representative of the Secretary-General:* Lakhdar Brahimi.
*Deputy Special Representative:* Christian Ossa.
*Force Commander:* Major-General Joseph Kinzer.

### United Nations Assistance Mission for Rwanda (UNAMIR)

*Special Representative of the Secretary-General:* Shaharyar M. Khan.
*Force Commander:* Major-General Guy Tousignant.
*Executive Director:* Wilfred De Souza.

### United Nations Mission of Observers in Tajikistan (UNMOT)

*Special Envoy of the Secretary-General:* Ramiro Píriz-Ballón.
*Deputy Special Envoy and Head of Mission:* Liviu Bota (until 15 March), Darko Silovic (from 15 March).
*Chief Military Observer:* Brigadier-General Hasan Abaza.

# Economic and Social Council

The Economic and Social Council consists of 54 Member States of the United Nations, elected by the General Assembly, each for a three-year term, in accordance with the provisions of Article 61 of the United Nations Charter as amended in 1965 and 1973.

MEMBERS
*To serve until 31 December 1995:* Bahamas, Bhutan, Canada, China, Cuba, Denmark, Gabon, Libyan Arab Jamahiriya, Mexico, Nigeria, Norway, Republic of Korea, Romania, Russian Federation, Sri Lanka, Ukraine, United Kingdom, Zaire.
*To serve until 31 December 1996:* Bulgaria, Chile, Costa Rica, Egypt, France, Germany, Ghana, Greece, Indonesia, Ireland, Japan, Pakistan, Paraguay, Portugal, Senegal, United Republic of Tanzania, Venezuela, Zimbabwe.
*To serve until 31 December 1997:* Australia, Belarus, Brazil, Colombia, Congo, Côte d'Ivoire, India, Jamaica, Luxembourg, Malaysia, Netherlands, Philippines, Poland, South Africa, Sudan, Thailand, Uganda, United States.

On 16 November 1995 (dec. 50/307), the General Assembly elected the following for a three-year term beginning on 1 January 1996 to fill the vacancies occurring on 31 December 1995: Argentina, Bangladesh, Canada, Central African Republic, China,

Czech Republic, Finland, Gabon, Guyana, Jordan, Lebanon, Nicaragua, Romania, Russian Federation, Sweden, Togo, Tunisia, United Kingdom.

SESSIONS
*Organizational session for 1995:* New York, 1 and 7-10 February.
*Resumed organizational session for 1995:* New York, 4 and 5 May and 1 and 6 June.
*Substantive session of 1995:* Geneva, 26 June–28 July.
*Resumed substantive session of 1995:* New York, 25 October, 2 November and 12 December.

OFFICERS
*President:* Ahmad Kamal (Pakistan).
*Vice-Presidents:* Jean-Marie Kacou Gervais (Côte d'Ivoire), Alexandru Niculescu (Romania), George Papadatos (Greece), Enrique Tejera-París (Venezuela).

## Subsidiary and other related organs

SUBSIDIARY ORGANS
The Economic and Social Council may, at each session, set up committees or working groups, of the whole or of limited mem-

bership, and refer to them any items on the agenda for study and report.

Other subsidiary organs reporting to the Council consist of functional commissions, regional commissions, standing committees, expert bodies and ad hoc bodies.

The inter-agency Administrative Committee on Coordination also reports to the Council.

## Functional commissions

### Commission for Social Development

The Commission for Social Development consists of 32 members, elected for four-year terms by the Economic and Social Council according to a specific pattern of equitable geographical distribution.

The Commission held its thirty-fourth session in New York from 10 to 20 April 1995.

*Members:*

*To serve until 31 December 1995:* Belarus, Côte d'Ivoire, France, Germany, Haiti, Indonesia *(Chairman)*, Mexico, Pakistan, Russian Federation, Sudan, United States.

*To serve until 31 December 1996:* Bolivia, Cameroon, Chile, China, Denmark, Malta, Netherlands, Philippines, Yugoslavia, Zimbabwe.

*To serve until 31 December 1998:* Argentina, Austria *(Vice-Chairman)*, Benin, Dominican Republic *(Vice-Chairman)*, Egypt *(Vice-Chairman)*, Ethiopia, Iran, Mongolia, Norway, Togo, Ukraine *(Rapporteur)*.

On 4 May 1995 (dec. 1995/221), the Economic and Social Council elected the following for a four-year term beginning on 1 January 1996 to fill the vacancies occurring on 31 December 1995: Belarus, France, Gabon, Germany, Japan, Peru, Republic of Korea, Russian Federation, Sudan, United States, Venezuela.

### Commission on Crime Prevention and Criminal Justice

The Commission on Crime Prevention and Criminal Justice consists of 40 Member States, elected by the Economic and Social Council for three-year terms according to a specific pattern of equitable geographical distribution.

The Commission held its fourth session in Vienna from 30 May to 9 June 1995.

*Members:*

*To serve until 31 December 1996:* Austria *(Chairman)*, Brazil, Colombia, Congo, Cuba, Finland, Germany, Hungary, Japan, Malawi, Malaysia, Morocco, Pakistan *(Vice-Chairman)*, Russian Federation, Sri Lanka, Sudan *(Vice-Chairman)*, Tunisia, Uganda, United Republic of Tanzania, Zaire.

*To serve until 31 December 1997:* Angola, Argentina *(Rapporteur)*, Belarus *(Vice-Chairman)*, Burundi, Canada, China, Costa Rica, France, Indonesia, Iran, Italy, Madagascar, Mexico, Nicaragua, Nigeria, Paraguay, Poland, Republic of Korea, Thailand,[a] United States.

[a]Elected on 9 February 1995 (dec. 1995/202).

### Commission on Human Rights

The Commission on Human Rights consists of 53 members, elected for three-year terms by the Economic and Social Council according to a specific pattern of equitable geographical distribution.

The Commission held its fifty-first session in Geneva from 30 January to 10 March 1995.

*Members:*

*To serve until 31 December 1995:* Brazil, Finland *(Rapporteur)*, France, Guinea-Bissau, Malaysia *(Chairman)*, Mauritius, Mexico, Pakistan, Poland, Republic of Korea, Romania, Sudan, Togo, United States.

*To serve until 31 December 1996:* Australia, Austria, Cameroon, China, Côte d'Ivoire, Ecuador, Germany, Hungary, Indonesia, Italy, Japan, Malawi, Mauritania, Peru, Venezuela.

*To serve until 31 December 1997:* Algeria *(Vice-Chairman)*, Angola, Bangladesh, Benin, Bhutan, Bulgaria *(Vice-Chairman)*, Canada, Chile, Colombia, Cuba, Dominican Republic, Egypt, El Salvador, Ethiopia, Gabon, India, Nepal, Netherlands, Nicaragua *(Vice-Chairman)*, Philippines, Russian Federation, Sri Lanka, United Kingdom, Zimbabwe.

On 4 May 1995 (dec. 1995/221), the Economic and Social Council elected the following for a three-year term beginning on 1 January 1996 to fill the vacancies occurring on 31 December 1995: Belarus, Brazil, Denmark, France, Guinea, Madagascar, Malaysia, Mali, Mexico, Pakistan, Republic of Korea, Uganda, Ukraine, United States.

SUBCOMMISSION ON PREVENTION OF
DISCRIMINATION AND PROTECTION OF MINORITIES

The Subcommission consists of 26 members elected by the Commission on Human Rights from candidates nominated by Member States of the United Nations, in accordance with a scheme to ensure equitable geographical distribution. Members serve in their individual capacity as experts, each for a four-year term.

The Subcommission held its forty-seventh session in Geneva from 31 July to 25 August 1995.

*Members:*

*To serve until February 1996:* Marc Bossuyt (Belgium); Volodymyr Boutkevitch (Ukraine); Linda Chavez (United States); Asbjorn Eide, *Vice-Chairman* (Norway); Maksum-Ul-Hakim, *Vice-Chairman* (Bangladesh); Ribot Hatano (Japan); Ahmed Mohamed Khalifa (Egypt); Miguel Alfonso Martínez (Cuba); Ioan Maxim, *Chairman* (Romania); Saïd Naceur Ramadhane (Tunisia); Clemencia Forero Ucros (Colombia); Halima Embarek Warzazi (Morocco); Fisseha Yimer (Ethiopia).

*To serve until February 1988:* José Augusto Lindgren Alves (Brazil); Judith Sefi Attah (Nigeria); José Bengoa, *Rapporteur* (Chile); Stanislav V. Chernichenko (Russian Federation); Erica-Irene A. Daes (Greece); Osman El-Hajjé (Lebanon); Fan Guoxiang (China); El-Hadji Guissé, *Vice-Chairman* (Senegal); Lucy Gwanmesia (Cameroon); Louis Joinet (France); Mohammed Sardar Ali Khan (India); Miguel Limón Rojas (Mexico); Claire Palley (United Kingdom).

### Commission on Narcotic Drugs

The Commission on Narcotic Drugs consists of 53 members, elected for four-year terms by the Economic and Social Council from among the Members of the United Nations and members of the specialized agencies and the parties to the Single Convention on Narcotic Drugs, 1961, with due regard for the adequate representation of *(a)* countries which are important producers of opium or coca leaves, *(b)* countries which are important in the manufacture of narcotic drugs, and *(c)* countries in which drug addiction or the illicit traffic in narcotic drugs constitutes an important problem, as well as taking into account the principle of equitable geographical distribution.

The Commission held its thirty-eighth session in Vienna from 14 to 23 March 1995.

*Members:*

*To serve until 31 December 1995:* Bolivia, Canada, Chile, Czech Republic, Egypt *(Vice-Chairman)*, France, Gabon, Germany, India, Iran *(Rapporteur)*, Italy, Jamaica, Lesotho, Madagascar, Morocco, Netherlands, Nicaragua, Nigeria, Norway, Pakistan, Peru, Philippines, Poland *(Chairman)*, Republic of Korea, Switzerland, Syrian Arab Republic, Thailand, Tunisia, Turkey *(Vice-Chairman)*, United States, Uruguay *(Vice-Chairman)*, Venezuela, Yugoslavia.

*To serve until 31 December 1997:* Australia, Bahamas, Belgium, China, Colombia, Côte d'Ivoire, Finland, Ghana, Guinea, Japan, Lebanon, Liberia, Mexico, Paraguay, Romania, Russian Federation, Spain, Sri Lanka, Ukraine, United Kingdom.

On 4 May 1995 (dec. 1995/221), the Economic and Social Council elected the following for a three-year term beginning on

1 January 1996 to fill the vacancies occurring on 31 December 1995: Algeria, Bolivia, Brazil, Bulgaria, Canada, Cuba, Czech Republic, Ecuador, Egypt, France, Germany, Greece, India, Indonesia, Iran, Italy, Jamaica, Malaysia, Morocco, Netherlands, Nigeria, Pakistan, Poland, Portugal, Republic of Korea, South Africa, Sudan, Sweden, Syrian Arab Republic, Thailand, Tunisia, United States, Venezuela.

### Commission on Population and Development

The Commission on Population and Development consisted of 27 members elected for four-year terms by the Economic and Social Council according to a specific pattern of equitable geographical distribution.

The Commission held its twenty-eighth session in New York from 21 February to 2 March 1995.

*Members:*

*To serve until 31 December 1995:* France, Honduras, Japan, Madagascar, Netherlands, Pakistan, Poland *(Vice-Chairman)*, Rwanda, Sudan.

*To serve until 31 December 1996:* Bangladesh, Belgium, Cameroon, Canada *(Chairman)*, Colombia, Germany, Hungary, Nicaragua, United Republic of Tanzania.

*To serve until 31 December 1997:* China, India *(Vice-Chairman/Rapporteur)*, Jamaica, Mexico *(Vice-Chairman)*, Nigeria,[a] Russian Federation, Tunisia *(Vice-Chairman)*, United Kingdom, United States.

[a]Elected on 4 May 1995 (dec. 1995/221).

On 4 May 1995 (dec. 1995/221), the Economic and Social Council elected the following for a four-year term beginning on 1 January 1996 to fill the vacancies occurring on 31 December 1995: Brazil, Bulgaria, Egypt, France, Indonesia, Japan, Kenya, Netherlands, Sudan.

On 12 December (dec. 1995/320), the Council decided to increase the membership from 27 to 47, according to the following pattern: 12 members from African States; 11 from Asian States; 5 from Eastern European States; 9 from Latin American and Caribbean States; and 10 from Western European and other States. The members were to be elected from among the States Members of the United Nations and members of the specialized agencies before the opening of the Commission's 1996 session.

### Commission on Science and Technology for Development

The Commission on Science and Technology for Development consists of 53 members, elected for four-year terms by the Economic and Social Council according to a specific pattern of equitable geographical representation.

The Commission held its second session in Geneva from 15 to 24 May 1995.

*Members* (to serve until 31 December 1996):[a] Antigua and Barbuda, Austria, Azerbaijan, Belarus *(Vice-Chairman)*, Belgium, Bolivia *(Chairman)*, Brazil, Bulgaria, Burundi, Canada, Cape Verde, Chile, China, Colombia, Congo, Costa Rica, Denmark, Egypt *(Vice-Chairman)*, Ethiopia, Germany, Guatemala, India *(Vice-Chairman)*, Ireland, Jamaica, Japan, Jordan, Kuwait, Libyan Arab Jamahiriya, Malawi, Malaysia, Malta, Marshall Islands, Mexico, Morocco, Netherlands *(Vice-Chairman)*, Niger, Nigeria, Pakistan, Philippines, Romania, Russian Federation, Saudi Arabia, Spain, Togo, Uganda, Ukraine, United Kingdom, United Republic of Tanzania, United States, Uruguay, Viet Nam.

[a]Two seats allocated to members from Western European and other States remained vacant in 1995. On 27 July (dec. 1995/312), the Economic and Social Council decided, on an exceptional basis, to extend the term of office of the current members for one year, to expire on 31 December 1997.

### Commission on Sustainable Development

The Commission on Sustainable Development is composed of 53 Member States of the United Nations and members of the specialized agencies, elected by the Economic and Social Council for three-year terms according to a specific pattern of equitable geographical distribution.

The Commission held its third session in New York from 11 to 28 April 1995.

*Members:*

*To serve until 31 December 1995:* Antigua and Barbuda, Belgium, Bolivia, Burkina Faso, Chile, China, Gabon, Germany, Iceland *(Vice-Chairman)*, Indonesia, Malawi, Namibia, Netherlands, Pakistan, Poland, Republic of Korea, Russian Federation, Tunisia, Turkey, Uruguay.

*To serve until 31 December 1996:* Barbados, Belarus, Bulgaria *(Vice-Chairman/Rapporteur)*, Canada, Guinea, India, Italy, Japan *(Vice-Chairman)*, Malaysia, Mexico, Morocco, Uganda *(Vice-Chairman)*, United Kingdom, United Republic of Tanzania, United States, Venezuela.

*To serve until 31 December 1997:* Australia, Bahamas, Bangladesh, Brazil *(Chairman)*, Burundi, Ethiopia, Finland, France, Ghana, Hungary, Iran, Papua New Guinea, Peru, Philippines, Senegal, Spain, Ukraine.

On 4 May 1995 (dec. 1995/221), the Economic and Social Council elected the following for a three-year term beginning on 1 January 1996 to fill the vacancies occurring on 31 December 1995: Antigua and Barbuda, Belgium, Benin, Bolivia, Central African Republic, China, Colombia, Gabon, Germany, Guyana, Mozambique, Netherlands, Pakistan, Poland, Russian Federation, Saudi Arabia, Sweden, Switzerland, Thailand, Zimbabwe.

### Commission on the Status of Women

The Commission on the Status of Women consists of 45 members, elected for four-year terms by the Economic and Social Council according to a specific pattern of equitable geographical distribution. In 1995, it also acted as the preparatory body for the Fourth World Conference on Women (see above).

The Commission held its thirty-ninth session in New York from 15 March to 4 April 1995.

*Members:*

*To serve until 31 December 1995:* Chile, China, Finland, Madagascar, Pakistan, Peru, Slovakia, Spain, Venezuela, Zambia.

*To serve until 31 December 1996:* Algeria, Australia, Austria *(Vice-Chairman)*, Belarus *(Vice-Chairman)*, Colombia, Cuba, France, Guinea-Bissau, Japan, Sudan, Thailand.

*To serve until 31 December 1997:* Bahamas, Costa Rica, Cyprus, Ecuador, Guinea, India, Iran, Kenya, Libyan Arab Jamahiriya, Malaysia, Namibia *(Rapporteur)*, Republic of Korea, Tunisia.

*To serve until 31 December 1998:* Angola, Belgium, Bulgaria, Congo, Greece, Indonesia, Mexico *(Vice-Chairman)*, Philippines *(Chairman)*, Portugal, Russian Federation, Togo.

On 4 May 1995 (dec. 1995/221), the Economic and Social Council elected the following for a four-year term beginning on 1 January 1996 to fill the vacancies occurring on 31 December 1995: Brazil, Chile, China, Dominican Republic, Lebanon, Mali, Norway, Slovakia, Swaziland, United States.

### Statistical Commission

The Statistical Commission consists of 24 members elected for four-year terms by the Economic and Social Council according to a specific pattern of equitable geographical distribution.

The Commission held its twenty-eighth session in New York from 27 February to 3 March 1995.

*Members:*

*To serve until 31 December 1995:* China *(Vice-Chairman)*, Czech Republic, Ghana, Jamaica, Morocco, Pakistan, Poland, United States.

*To serve until 31 December 1996:* Australia, Brazil, India, Japan, Mexico *(Vice-Chairman)*, Sweden *(Rapporteur)*, Ukraine, United Kingdom *(Chairman)*.

*To serve until 31 December 1997:* Argentina, Botswana, France, Germany, Kenya, Russian Federation *(Vice-Chairman)*, Spain, Zambia.

On 4 May 1995 (dec. 1995/221), the Economic and Social Council elected the following for a four-year term beginning on 1 January 1996 to fill seven of the eight vacancies occurring on 31 December 1995: Bulgaria, China, Pakistan, Romania, Sudan, Togo, United States. No further election was held in 1995 to fill the remaining seat, allocated to a member from Latin American and Caribbean States.

## Regional commissions

### Economic and Social Commission for Asia and the Pacific (ESCAP)

The Economic and Social Commission for Asia and the Pacific held its fifty-first session in Bangkok, Thailand, from 24 April to 1 May 1995.

*Members:* Afghanistan, Armenia, Australia, Azerbaijan, Bangladesh *(Vice-Chairman)*, Bhutan, Brunei Darussalam *(Vice-Chairman)*, Cambodia *(Vice-Chairman)*, China *(Vice-Chairman)*, Democratic People's Republic of Korea, Fiji, France, India *(Vice-Chairman)*, Indonesia *(Vice-Chairman)*, Iran *(Vice-Chairman)*, Japan *(Vice-Chairman)*, Kazakstan, Kiribati *(Vice-Chairman)*, Kyrgyzstan *(Vice-Chairman)*, Lao People's Democratic Republic *(Vice-Chairman)*, Malaysia *(Rapporteur-General)*, Maldives, Marshall Islands *(Vice-Chairman)*, Micronesia, Mongolia, Myanmar, Nauru, Nepal *(Vice-Chairman)*, Netherlands, New Zealand, Pakistan *(Vice-Chairman)*, Papua New Guinea *(Chairman)*, Philippines *(Vice-Chairman)*, Republic of Korea *(Vice-Chairman)*, Russian Federation, Samoa, Singapore *(Vice-Chairman)*, Solomon Islands *(Vice-Chairman)*, Sri Lanka *(Vice-Chairman)*, Tajikistan, Thailand *(Vice-Chairman)*, Tonga *(Vice-Chairman)*, Turkmenistan, Tuvalu *(Vice-Chairman)*, United Kingdom, United States, Uzbekistan, Vanuatu *(Vice-Chairman)*, Viet Nam *(Vice-Chairman)*.
*Associate members:* American Samoa, Cook Islands, French Polynesia, Guam, Hong Kong, Macau, New Caledonia, Niue, Northern Mariana Islands, Palau.

Switzerland, not a Member of the United Nations, participates in a consultative capacity in the work of the Commission.

### Economic and Social Commission for Western Asia (ESCWA)

The Economic and Social Commission for Western Asia held its eighteenth session in Beirut, Lebanon, on 24 and 25 May 1995.

*Members:* Bahrain, Egypt *(Vice-Chairman)*, Iraq, Jordan, Kuwait, Lebanon *(Chairman)*, Oman, Palestine *(Rapporteur)*, Qatar, Saudi Arabia, Syrian Arab Republic, United Arab Emirates *(Vice-Chairman)*, Yemen.

### Economic Commission for Africa (ECA)

The Economic Commission for Africa meets in annual session at the ministerial level known as the Conference of Ministers.

The Commission held its thirtieth session (twenty-first meeting of the Conference of Ministers) in Addis Ababa, Ethiopia, from 1 to 3 May 1995.

*Members:* Algeria *(Second Vice-Chairman)*, Angola, Benin, Botswana, Burkina Faso, Burundi, Cameroon, Cape Verde, Central African Republic, Chad, Comoros, Congo, Côte d'Ivoire, Djibouti, Egypt, Equatorial Guinea, Eritrea, Ethiopia *(Chairman)*, Gabon *(First Vice-Chairman)*, Gambia, Ghana, Guinea, Guinea-Bissau, Kenya, Lesotho, Liberia, Libyan Arab Jamahiriya, Madagascar, Malawi, Mali, Mauritania, Mauritius, Morocco, Mozambique, Namibia, Niger, Nigeria, Rwanda, Sao Tome and Principe, Senegal, Seychelles, Sierra Leone *(Rapporteur)*, Somalia, South Africa, Sudan, Swaziland, Togo, Tunisia, Uganda, United Republic of Tanzania, Zaire, Zambia, Zimbabwe.

Switzerland, not a Member of the United Nations, participates in a consultative capacity in the work of the Commission.

### Economic Commission for Europe (ECE)

The Economic Commission for Europe held its fiftieth session in Geneva from 3 to 11 April 1995.

*Members:* Albania, Andorra, Armenia, Austria *(Rapporteur)*, Azerbaijan, Belarus, Belgium, Bosnia and Herzegovina, Bulgaria, Canada, Croatia, Cyprus, Czech Republic *(Rapporteur)*, Denmark, Estonia, Finland, France, Georgia, Germany *(Vice-Chairman)*, Greece, Hungary, Iceland, Ireland, Israel, Italy, Kazakstan, Kyrgyzstan, Latvia, Liechtenstein, Lithuania, Luxembourg, Malta, Monaco, Netherlands, Norway, Poland *(Chairman)*, Portugal, Republic of Moldova, Romania *(Vice-Chairman)*, Russian Federation, San Marino, Slovakia, Slovenia, Spain, Sweden *(Vice-Chairman)*, Switzerland, Tajikistan,[a] the former Yugoslav Republic of Macedonia, Turkey, Turkmenistan, Ukraine, United Kingdom, United States, Uzbekistan, Yugoslavia.[b]

[a]Became a member on 12 December 1994.
[b]In 1993, the Economic and Social Council decided that the Federal Republic of Yugoslavia (Serbia and Montenegro) should not participate in the work of ECE as long as the Federal Republic did not participate in the work of the General Assembly.

The Holy See, not a Member of the United Nations, participates in a consultative capacity in the work of the Commission.

### Economic Commission for Latin America and the Caribbean (ECLAC)

The Economic Commission for Latin America and the Carribbean did not meet in 1995.

*Members:* Antigua and Barbuda, Argentina, Bahamas, Barbados, Belize, Bolivia, Brazil, Canada, Chile, Colombia, Costa Rica, Cuba, Dominica, Dominican Republic, Ecuador, El Salvador, France, Grenada, Guatemala, Guyana, Haiti, Honduras, Italy, Jamaica, Mexico, Netherlands, Nicaragua, Panama, Paraguay, Peru, Portugal, Saint Kitts and Nevis, Saint Lucia, Saint Vincent and the Grenadines, Spain, Suriname, Trinidad and Tobago, United Kingdom, United States, Uruguay, Venezuela.
*Associate members:* Aruba, British Virgin Islands, Montserrat, Netherlands Antilles, Puerto Rico, United States Virgin Islands.

Germany and Switzerland participate in a consultative capacity in the work of the Commission.

## Standing committees

### Commission on Human Settlements

The Commission on Human Settlements consists of 58 members elected by the Economic and Social Council for four-year terms according to a specific pattern of equitable geographical distribution; it reports to the General Assembly through the Council.

The Commission held its fifteenth session in Nairobi, Kenya, from 25 April to 1 May 1995.

*Members:*
*To serve until 31 December 1995:* Austria, Barbados, Belarus, Botswana, Bulgaria, Germany, Ghana, Greece, Haiti, India, Jordan, Kenya, Malaysia, Mexico, Norway, Philippines, Sri Lanka, Sudan, United Republic of Tanzania.
*To serve until 31 December 1996:* Azerbaijan, Bahamas, Canada, China, France, Hungary, Indonesia *(Vice-Chairman)*, Italy, Jamaica, Lesotho, Libyan Arab Jamahiriya, Madagascar, Malawi, Netherlands, Papua New Guinea, Somalia, Sweden, United Arab Emirates, Venezuela *(Vice-Chairman)*.
*To serve until 31 December 1998:* Brazil, Cameroon *(Rapporteur)*, Chile, Costa Rica, Dominican Republic, Finland, Gabon, Gambia, Iran, Japan, Kazakstan, Nigeria, Pakistan, Romania, Russian Federation *(Chairman)*, Turkey, Uganda, United Kingdom *(Vice-Chairman)*, United States, Zimbabwe.

On 4 May 1995 (dec. 1995/221), the Economic and Social Council elected the following for a four-year term beginning on 1 January 1996 to fill 16 of the 19 vacancies occurring on 31

December 1995: Algeria, Barbados, Bulgaria, Colombia, Czech Republic, Denmark, Germany, India, Jordan, Kenya, Mexico, Norway, Spain, Sri Lanka, Sudan, Tunisia. No further elections were held in 1995 to fill the remaining seats, allocated to one member from African States and two members from Asian States.

### Committee for Programme and Coordination

The Committee for Programme and Coordination is the main subsidiary organ of the Economic and Social Council and of the General Assembly for planning, programming and coordination and reports directly to both. It consists of 34 members nominated by the Council and elected by the Assembly for three-year terms according to a specific pattern of equitable geographical distribution.

During 1995, the Committee held, in New York, an organizational session on 21 April and its thirty-fifth session from 15 May to 9 June.

*Members:*
*To serve until 31 December 1995:* China, Egypt *(Rapporteur)*, Japan, Kenya, Nicaragua, Republic of Korea, Togo.
*To serve until 31 December 1996:* Argentina *(Vice-Chairman)*, Belarus, Brazil, Cameroon, Canada, Comoros, Congo, Cuba, Germany *(Vice-Chairman)*, India, Indonesia, Iran *(Vice-Chairman)*, Netherlands, Norway, Pakistan, Romania *(Chairman)*, Senegal, Trinidad and Tobago, Ukraine, United Kingdom.
*To serve until 31 December 1997:* Bahamas, Benin, France, Ghana, Mexico, Russian Federation, United States.

On 4 May 1995 (dec. 1995/221), the Economic and Social Council nominated the following for a three-year term beginning on 1 January 1996 to fill the vacancies occurring on 31 December 1995: China, Egypt, Japan, Republic of Korea, Togo, Uruguay, Zaire. They were elected by the General Assembly on 31 October (dec. 50/305).

### Committee on Non-Governmental Organizations

The Committee on Non-Governmental Organizations consists of 19 members elected by the Economic and Social Council for a four-year term according to a specific pattern of equitable geographical representation.

The Committee met in New York from 12 to 23 June 1995.

*Members* (until 31 December 1998): Bulgaria *(Vice-Chairman)*, Chile *(Vice-Chairman/Rapporteur)*, China, Costa Rica, Cuba, Ethiopia, Greece, India, Indonesia, Ireland *(Vice-Chairman)*, Madagascar, Paraguay, Philippines *(Chairman)*, Russian Federation, Sudan, Swaziland[a] *(Vice-Chairman)*, Tunisia, United Kingdom, United States.

[a]Elected on 6 June 1995 (dec. 1995/221).

## Expert bodies

### Ad Hoc Group of Experts on International Cooperation in Tax Matters

The Ad Hoc Group of Experts on International Cooperation in Tax Matters consists of 25 members, from 15 developing and 10 developed countries, appointed by the Secretary-General to serve in their individual capacity.

The Ad Hoc Group held its seventh session in Geneva from 11 to 15 December 1995.

*Members:* Atef Alawneh (Palestine); William W. Alder (Jamaica); Nabawia Sobhi Khaled Allam (Egypt); J. A. Arogundale (Nigeria); Ali Benbrik (Morocco); Ernst Bunders (Netherlands); Mordecai S. Feinberg (United States); Antonio H. Figueroa (Argentina); Mayer Gabay (Israel); Maria das Gracas Oliveira (Brazil); Sergey M. Ignatiev (Russian Federation); Helmut Krabbe (Germany); Lin Yonggui (China); Juan López Rodríguez (Spain); Daniel Lüthi (Switzerland); Reksoprajitno Mansury, *Chairman* (Indonesia); John E. A. Mills (Ghana); G. K. Mishra (India); Viktor Moroz (Ukraine); Karina Pérez (Mexico); Alvi Abdul Rahim (Pakistan);

Alain Ruellan (France); J. Brian Shepherd (United Kingdom); Katsumi Shinagawa (Japan); Hillel Skurnik, *Rapporteur* (Finland).

### Committee for Development Planning

The Committee for Development Planning is composed of 24 experts representing different planning systems. They are appointed by the Economic and Social Council, on nomination by the Secretary-General, to serve in their personal capacity for a term of three years.

The Committee did not meet in 1995.

*Members* (until 31 December 1997):[a] Maria Agusztinovics (Hungary), Dionisio Dias Carneiro-Netto (Brazil), Makhtar Diouf (Senegal), E. El-Hinnawi (Egypt), Just Faaland (Norway), Gao Shangquan (China), Patrick Guillaumont (France), Ryokichi Hirono (Japan), Nurul Islam (Bangladesh), Taher Kanaan (Jordan), Louka T. Katseli (Greece), Linda Lim (Singapore), Nguyuru H. I. Lipumba (United Republic of Tanzania), Nora Lustig (Argentina/Mexico), Solita C. Monsod (Philippines), Bishnodat Persaud (Guyana), Akilagpa Sawyerr (Ghana), Klaus Schwab (Germany), Arjun Sengupta (India), Alexandre Shokhin (Russian Federation), Frances Stewart (United Kingdom), Lance Taylor (United States), Alvaro Umaña (Costa Rica), Miguel Urrutia (Colombia).

[a]Appointed on 27 July 1995 (dec. 1995/230).

### Committee of Experts on the Transport of Dangerous Goods

The Committee of Experts on the Transport of Dangerous Goods is composed of experts from countries interested in the international transport of dangerous goods. The experts are made available by their Governments at the request of the Secretary-General.

The Committee did not meet in 1995.

*Members:* Argentina, Belgium, Brazil, Canada, China, France, Germany, India, Italy, Japan, Mexico, Morocco, Netherlands, Norway, Poland, Russian Federation, Sweden, United Kingdom, United States.

### Committee on Economic, Social and Cultural Rights

The Committee on Economic, Social and Cultural Rights consists of 18 experts serving in their personal capacity, elected by the Economic and Social Council from among persons nominated by States parties to the International Covenant on Economic, Social and Cultural Rights.[4] The experts have recognized competence in the field of human rights, with due consideration given to equitable geographical distribution and to the representation of different forms of social and legal systems. Members serve four-year terms.

The Committee held two sessions in 1995, in Geneva: its twelfth from 1 to 19 May and its thirteenth from 20 November to 8 December.

*Members:*
*To serve until 31 December 1996:* Madoe Virginie Ahodikope (Togo); Juan Alvarez Vita, *Vice-Chairman* (Peru); Dumitru Ceausu, *Vice-Chairman* (Romania); Abdessatar Grissa, *Vice-Chairman* (Tunisia); María de los Angeles Jimenez Butragueño (Spain); Kenneth Osborne Rattray (Jamaica); Chikako Taya (Japan); Philippe Texier (France); Margerita Vysokajova (Czech Republic).
*To serve until 31 December 1998:* Ade Adekuoye (Nigeria); Mahmoud Samir Ahmed (Egypt); Philip Alston, *Chairman* (Australia); Virginia Bonoan-Dandan, *Rapporteur* (Philippines); Valery Kuznetsov (Russian Federation); Jaime Marchan Romero (Ecuador); Bruno Simma (Germany); Nutan Thapalia (Nepal); Javier Wimer Zambrano (Mexico).

### Committee on Natural Resources

The Committee on Natural Resources consists of 24 government-nominated experts from different Member States, who possess the necessary qualifications and professional or scientific knowledge and who act in their personal capacity. They are elected by the Economic and Social Council for four-year

---

[4]YUN 1966, p. 419, GA res. 2200 A (XXI), annex, 16 Dec. 1966.

terms, according to a specific pattern of equitable geographical distribution.

The Committee did not meet in 1995.

*Members:*[a] Guillermo Jorge Cano (Argentina), Patrick M. Chipungu (Zambia), Denis A. Davis (Canada), Vladislav M. Dolgopolov (Russian Federation), Malin Falkenmark (Sweden), Ugo Farinelli (Italy), Marek Hoffmann (Poland), Patricio Jerez (Nicaragua), Mohammad Nawaz Khan (Pakistan), Godfrey L. S. Leshange (United Republic of Tanzania), José Manuel Mejía Angel (Colombia), Thomas P. Z. Mpofu (Zimbabwe), Joel Muyco (Philippines), Erastus Kabutu Mwongera (Kenya), Lukabu Khabouji N'Zaji (Zaire), Dossou Barthélémy Otchoun (Benin), Hendrik Martinus Oudshoorn (Netherlands), Neculai Pavlovschi (Romania), Karlheinz Rieck (Germany), R. W. Roye Rutland (Australia), Sheik Ibrahim bin Sheik Ali (Malaysia), Luis Fernando Soares de Assis (Brazil), Natarayan Suryanarayanan (India), Zhang Hai-Lun (China).

[a]For the initial period, 12 members were to serve for two years and the remaining 12 for four years, the term of each member to be determined by lot.

### Committee on New and Renewable Sources of Energy and on Energy for Development

The Committee on New and Renewable Sources of Energy and on Energy for Development consists of 24 government-nominated experts from different Member States, who possess the necessary qualifications and professional or scientific knowledge and who act in their personal capacity. They are elected by the Economic and Social Council for four-year terms, according to a specific pattern of equitable geographical representation.

The Committee held a special session in New York from 6 to 17 February 1995.

*Members:*[a] Marcelino K. Actouka (Micronesia); Mohammad Al-Ramadhan (Kuwait); Mohammed Salem Sarur Al-Sabban (Saudi Arabia); Messaoud Boumaour (Algeria); José Luis Bozzo (Uruguay); Bernard Devin (France); Paul-Georg Gutermuth (Germany); Wolfgang Hein (Austria); Christian Atoki Ileka (Zaire); José Fernando Isaza (Colombia); Thomas B. Johansson (Sweden); Virgil Musatescu, *Rapporteur* (Romania); Valeri Andreev Nikov (Bulgaria); Giovanni Carlo Pinchera (Italy); Zoilo Rodas Rodas, *Vice-Chairman* (Paraguay); E. V. R. Sastry (India); Mohamed M. Shawkat, *Chairman* (Egypt); Wilhelmus C. Turkenburg, *Vice-Chairman* (Netherlands); William Sebastao Penido Vale (Brazil); Dmitri B. Volfberg (Russian Federation); Zhang Guocheng, *Vice-Chairman* (China).

[a]For the initial period, 12 members were to serve for two years and the remaining 12 for four years, the term of each member to be determined by lot. Three seats allocated to members from African States remained unfilled in 1995.

### United Nations Group of Experts on Geographical Names

The United Nations Group of Experts on Geographical Names represents various geographical/linguistic divisions, of which there were 21 in 1995, as follows: Africa Central; Africa East; Africa South; Africa West; Arabic; Asia East (other than China); Asia South-East and Pacific South-West; Asia South-West (other than Arabic); Baltic; Celtic; China; Dutch and German-speaking; East Central and South-East Europe; East Mediterranean (other than Arabic); Eastern Europe, Northern and Central Asia; India; Latin America; Norden; Romano-Hellenic; United Kingdom; United States of America/Canada.

The Group of Experts did not meet in 1995.

## Administrative Committee on Coordination

The Administrative Committee on Coordination held two sessions in 1995: the first in Vienna on 27 and 28 February, and the second in New York on 12 and 13 October.

The membership of ACC, under the chairmanship of the Secretary-General of the United Nations, includes the executive heads of ILO, FAO, UNESCO, ICAO, WHO, the World Bank, IMF, UPU, ITU, WMO, IMO, WIPO, IFAD, UNIDO and IAEA.

ACC also invites to take part in the work of its sessions senior officers of the United Nations and the executive heads of UNCTAD, UNDP, UNEP, UNFPA, UNHCR, UNICEF, UNITAR, UNRWA, WFP, the United Nations International Drug Control Programme and the World Trade Organization.

ACC has established subsidiary bodies on organizational, administrative and substantive questions.

## Other related bodies

### International Research and Training Institute for the Advancement of Women (INSTRAW)

The International Research and Training Institute for the Advancement of Women, a body of the United Nations financed through voluntary contributions, functions under the authority of a Board of Trustees.

BOARD OF TRUSTEES

The Board of Trustees is composed of 11 members serving in their individual capacity, appointed by the Economic and Social Council on the nomination of States, and ex-officio members. Members serve three-year terms, with a maximum of two terms.

The Board, which reports to the Council and where appropriate to the General Assembly, held its fifteenth session in Santo Domingo, Dominican Republic, from 24 to 28 April 1995.

*Members:*
*To serve until 30 June 1995:* Ihsan Abdalla Algabshawi, *Rapporteur* (Sudan); Aida González Martínez (Mexico); Els Postel-Coster, *President* (Netherlands).
*To serve until 30 June 1996:* Noëlie Kangoye (Burkina Faso); Amara Pongsapich (Thailand); Pilar Escario Rodríguez-Spiteré (Spain).
*To serve until 30 June 1997:* Selma Acuner (Turkey); Fátima Benslimane Hassar, *Vice-President* (Morocco); D. Gail Saunders (Bahamas); Renata Siemienska-Zochowska (Poland); Soedarsono (Indonesia).
*Ex-officio members:* The Director of the Institute, and a representative of the Secretary-General, each of the regional commissions and the Institute's host country (Dominican Republic).

On 27 July 1995 (dec. 1995/230), the Economic and Social Council appointed the following for a term expiring on 30 June 1998: Ihsan Abdalla Algabshawi (Sudan), Esther María Ashton (Bolivia), Els Postel-Coster (Netherlands).

*Director of the Institute:* Martha Dueñas-Loza (Acting).

### Joint and Co-sponsored United Nations Programme on Human Immunodeficiency Virus/Acquired Immunodeficiency Syndrome

The co-sponsored United Nations programme on HIV/AIDS comprises UNDP, UNICEF, UNFPA, WHO, UNESCO and the World Bank.

### PROGRAMME COORDINATION BOARD

The Programme Coordination Board, to consist of 22 members elected for three-year terms by the Economic and Social Council, was to be established in January 1996.

*Members:*[a]
*To serve until 31 December 1996:* Australia, Canada, Côte d'Ivoire, Mexico, Thailand.
*To serve until 31 December 1997:* Algeria, Barbados, Bulgaria, China, Japan, Netherlands, South Africa, Sweden, United Kingdom.
*To serve until 31 December 1998:* Congo, France, India, Pakistan, Paraguay, Russian Federation, Uganda, United States.

[a]Elected on 1 June and 13 July 1995 (dec. 1995/221 and 1995/230) for terms beginning on 1 January 1996; the initial terms of office of the members were determined by lot.

## United Nations Children's Fund (UNICEF)

### EXECUTIVE BOARD

The UNICEF Executive Board, which reports to the Economic and Social Council and, as appropriate, to the General Assembly, consists of 36 members elected by the Council from Member States of the United Nations or members of the specialized agencies or of IAEA, for three-year terms.

In 1995, the Board held, in New York, its first regular session from 1 to 3 and on 6 February, its second regular session from 20 to 23 March, its annual session from 22 to 26 May and its third regular session from 18 to 22 September.

*Members:*

*To serve until 31 December 1995:* Australia, Belarus, Canada, China, Costa Rica, Finland, Germany, Mozambique, Philippines, Russian Federation, Suriname *(Vice-President)*.

*To serve until 31 December 1996:* Brazil, Burkina Faso *(Vice-President)*, France, Ghana, Indonesia, Italy, Jamaica, Lebanon *(President)*, Romania *(Vice-President)*, United Kingdom, United States.

*To serve until 31 December 1997:* Angola, Azerbaijan, Burundi, India, Japan, Kenya, Morocco, Netherlands, Norway, Pakistan, Republic of Korea, Sweden *(Vice-President)*, Uganda, Venezuela.

On 4 May 1995 (dec. 1995/221), the Economic and Social Council elected the following for a three-year term beginning on 1 January 1996 to fill the vacancies occurring on 31 December 1995: Canada, China, Cuba, Denmark, Namibia, Russian Federation, Suriname, Switzerland, Turkey, Ukraine, Viet Nam.

*Executive Director of UNICEF:* James P. Grant (until 23 January 1995), Richard Jolly (Acting, 24 January–30 April), Carol Bellamy (from 1 May).

## United Nations Development Programme (UNDP)/ United Nations Population Fund (UNFPA)

### EXECUTIVE BOARD

The Executive Board of UNDP/UNFPA, which reports to the Economic and Social Council and through it to the General Assembly, consists of 36 members, elected by the Council from Member States of the United Nations or members of the specialized agencies or of IAEA, for three-year terms.

In 1995, the Board held, in New York, its first and second regular sessions from 10 to 13 January and from 3 to 7 April, respectively, an annual session from 5 to 16 June and its third regular session from 11 to 15 September.

*Members:*

*To serve until 31 December 1995:* Argentina *(Vice-President)*, Bulgaria, India, Italy, New Zealand, Republic of Korea *(Vice-President)*, Russian Federation, Sudan, United Kingdom, United States, Uruguay.

*To serve until 31 December 1996:* Bangladesh, Belgium, Denmark *(Vice-President)*, Japan, Morocco *(Vice-President)*, Pakistan, Peru, Poland *(President)*, Portugal, Sierra Leone, Trinidad and Tobago.

*To serve until 31 December 1997:* Burundi, China, Cuba, Ethiopia, France, Gambia, Germany, Indonesia, Norway, Philippines, Slovakia, Sweden, Zaire, Zambia.

On 4 May 1995 (dec. 1995/221), the Economic and Social Council elected the following for a three-year term beginning on 1 January 1996 to fill the vacancies occurring on 31 December 1995: Argentina, Belize, Canada, India, Madagascar, Malaysia, Netherlands, Romania, Switzerland, Ukraine, United States. It also elected Finland and Spain for a two-year term beginning on 1 January 1996 to replace France and Norway.

*Administrator of UNDP:* James Gustave Speth.
*Associate Administrator:* Rafeeuddin Ahmed.

*Executive Director of UNFPA:* Dr. Nafis I. Sadik.
*Deputy Executive Director (Policy and Administration):* Hirofumi Ando.
*Deputy Executive Director (Programme):* Joseph Van Arendonk.
*Deputy Executive Director (Technical Services):* Jyoti Singh.

## United Nations Interregional Crime and Justice Research Institute (UNICRI)

BOARD OF TRUSTEES

The Board of Trustees of UNICRI is composed of seven members selected by the Commission on Crime Prevention and Criminal Justice upon nomination by the Secretary-General and endorsed by the Economic and Social Council, and ex-officio members. Members serve five-year terms with a maximum of two terms.

*Members:*

*To serve until 26 November 1995:* Tolani Asuni (Nigeria), Pierre-Henri Bölle (Switzerland), Dusan Cotic (ex-Yugoslavia).

*To serve until 26 November 1998:* Moustafa El-Augi (Lebanon), José A. Rios Alves da Cruz (Brazil).

*To serve until 26 November 1999:* Simone Rozes (France), Sushil Swarup Varma (India).

*Ex-officio members:* Representatives of the Secretary-General (normally the Head of the Crime Prevention and Criminal Justice Branch of the Centre for Social Development and Humanitarian Affairs of the Secretariat), of the UNDP Administrator and of the host country (Italy) and the UNICRI Director.

On 24 July 1995 (dec. 1995/241), the Economic and Social Council endorsed the appointment by the Commission on Crime Prevention and Criminal Justice of Jan J. M. van Dijk (Netherlands), Karoly Bard (Hungary) and Adedokun A. Adeyemi (Nigeria) for a five-year term beginning on 27 November 1995.

*Director of UNICRI:* Herman F. Woltring.

## United Nations Research Institute for Social Development (UNRISD)

BOARD OF DIRECTORS

The Board of Directors of UNRISD reports to the Economic and Social Council through the Commission for Social Development. The Board consists of:

*The Chairman,* appointed by the Secretary-General: Keith Griffin (United Kingdom);

*Ten members,* nominated by the Commission for Social Development and confirmed by the Economic and Social Council (until 30 June 1995): Lars Anell (Sweden), Fahima Charaf-Eddine (Lebanon), Georgina Dufoix (France), Ingrid Eide (Norway), Tatyana Koryagina (Russian Federation), Kinhide Mushakoji (Japan), Guillermo O'Donnell (Argentina), Maureen O'Neil (Canada), Akilagpa Sawyerr (Ghana), Rehman Sobhan (Bangladesh);

*Nine other members,* as follows: a representative of the Secretary-General, a representative of the United Nations Office at Vienna/Centre for Social Development and Humanitarian Affairs, the Director of the Latin American and Caribbean Institute for Economic and Social Planning, the Director of the Asian and Pacific Development Institute, the Director of the African Institute for Economic Development and Planning, the Executive Secretary of ESCWA, the Director of UNRISD (ex officio), and the representatives of two of the following specialized agencies, appointed in rotation: ILO, FAO, UNESCO, WHO.

On 24 July 1995 (dec. 1995/249), the Economic and Social Council confirmed the nomination by the Commission for Social Development of the following for a term beginning on 1 July 1995: Jonathan Moore (United States), Harris Mutio Mule (Kenya), Frances Stewart (United Kingdom), Valery Tishkov (Russian Federation) and Bjorn Hettne (Sweden) for a four-year term; and Fahima Charaf-Eddine (Lebanon), Georgina Dufoix (France), Kinhide

Mushakoji (Japan), Guillermo O'Donnell (Argentina) and Rehman Sobhan (Bangladesh) for a two-year term.

*Director of the Institute:* Dharam Ghai.

### World Food Programme

COMMITTEE ON FOOD AID POLICIES AND PROGRAMMES

The Committee on Food Aid Policies and Programmes, the governing body of WFP, reported annually to the Economic and Social Council, the FAO Council and the World Food Council. It consisted of 42 members (27 from developing countries and 15 from more economically developed ones), of which 21 were elected by the Economic and Social Council and 21 by the FAO Council, from Member States of the United Nations or from members of FAO. Members served three-year terms.

In 1995, the Committee held two sessions in Rome, Italy: its thirty-ninth from 22 to 26 May and its fortieth from 13 to 16 November.

*Members:*
To serve until 31 December 1995:
　*Elected by Economic and Social Council:* Denmark, Dominican Republic, Hungary, India, Italy, Niger, Nigeria.
　*Elected by FAO Council:* Australia *(Chairman)*, Bangladesh, Burkina Faso *(First Vice-Chairman)*, Canada, Senegal, Sri Lanka, United States *(Rapporteur, fortieth session)*.
To serve until 31 December 1996:
　*Elected by Economic and Social Council:* Belgium, El Salvador, Finland, Indonesia, Japan, Libyan Arab Jamahiriya, Pakistan.
　*Elected by FAO Council:* Brazil, Chad, China, Haiti, Netherlands, Saudi Arabia, Zimbabwe.

To serve until 31 December 1997:
　*Elected by Economic and Social Council:* Argentina,[a] Congo, Paraguay, Philippines,[a] Sudan, Sweden *(Second Vice-Chairman)*, United Kingdom.
　*Elected by FAO Council:* Angola, Cuba *(Rapporteur, thirty-ninth session)*, France, Germany, Iran, Lithuania, Zaire.

[a]Elected on 9 February 1995 (dec. 1995/202).

On 4 May 1995 (dec. 1995/221), the Economic and Social Council elected Hungary for a three-year term beginning on 1 January 1996.

The FAO Conference on 31 October and the General Assembly on 1 November 1995 (res. 50/8) decided that the Committee should be reconstituted as the Executive Board of WFP, with 36 members, 18 elected by the Economic and Social Council and 18 by the FAO Council.

On 3 November, the FAO Council elected the following for terms beginning on 1 January 1996 and ending on 31 December of the year indicated: *1996*—Albania, Australia, Brazil, Burkina Faso, France, Syrian Arab Republic; *1997*—Bangladesh, Burundi, El Salvador, Haiti, Netherlands, United States; *1998*—Algeria, Canada, China, Cuba, Germany, Nigeria.

On 12 December (dec. 1995/326), the Economic and Social Council elected the following for a term (the length to be determined later) beginning on 1 January 1996: Angola, Cameroon, Finland, Hungary, India, Indonesia, Italy, Japan, Norway, Pakistan, Paraguay, Philippines, Sweden, Uganda, United Kingdom. No further elections were held in 1995 by the Economic and Social Council to fill the remaining three seats, allocated to two members from list A (African States) and one member from list C (Latin American and Caribbean States).

*Executive Director of WFP:* Catherine A. Bertini.
*Deputy Executive Director:* A. Namanga Ngongi.

# Trusteeship Council

Article 86 of the United Nations Charter lays down that the Trusteeship Council shall consist of the following:

Members of the United Nations administering Trust Territories;
Permanent members of the Security Council which do not administer Trust Territories;
As many other members elected for a three-year term by the General Assembly as will ensure that the membership of the Council is equally divided between United Nations Members which administer Trust Territories and those which do not.[a]

[a]During 1995, no Member of the United Nations was an administering member of the Trusteeship Council, while five permanent members of the Security Council continued as non-administering members.

*Members:* China, France, Russian Federation, United Kingdom, United States.

# International Court of Justice

### Judges of the Court

The International Court of Justice consists of 15 Judges elected for nine-year terms by the General Assembly and the Security Council.

The following were the Judges of the Court serving in 1995, listed in the order of precedence:

| Judge | Country of nationality | End of term[a] |
|---|---|---|
| Mohammed Bedjaoui, *President* | Algeria | 1997 |
| Stephen M. Schwebel, *Vice-President* | United States | 1997 |
| Shigeru Oda | Japan | 2003 |
| Roberto Ago[b] | Italy | 1997 |
| Sir Robert Y. Jennings[c] | United Kingdom | 2000 |
| Gilbert Guillaume | France | 2000 |
| Mohamed Shahabuddeen | Guyana | 1997 |
| Andrés Aguilar Mawdsley[d] | Venezuela | 2000 |
| Christopher G. Weeramantry | Sri Lanka | 2000 |
| Raymond Ranjeva | Madagascar | 2000 |
| Géza Herczegh | Hungary | 2003 |
| Shi Jiuyong | China | 2003 |
| Carl-August Fleischhauer | Germany | 2003 |
| Abdul G. Koroma | Sierra Leone | 2003 |
| Vladlen S. Vereshchetin[e] | Russian Federation | 1997 |

[a]Term expires on 5 February of the year indicated.

[b]Died on 24 February 1995; Luigi Ferrari Bravo (Italy) was elected by the General Assembly (dec. 49/322 B) and the Security Council on 21 June to fill the resultant vacancy.

[c]Resigned on 10 July 1995; Rosalyn Higgins (United Kingdom) was elected by the General Assembly (dec. 49/322 C) and the Security Council on 12 July to fill the resultant vacancy.

[d]Died on 24 October 1995; no election was held in 1995 to fill the resultant vacancy.

[e]Elected by the General Assembly (dec. 49/322 A) and the Security Council on 26 January 1995 to fill the vacancy resulting from the death of Nikolai K. Tarassov (Russian Federation) in 1994.

*Registrar:* Eduardo Valencia-Ospina.
*Deputy Registrar:* Jean-Jacques Arnaldez.

#### Chamber of Summary Procedure

*Members:* Mohammed Bedjaoui (ex officio), Stephen M. Schwebel (ex officio), Mohamed Shahabuddeen, Andrés Aguilar Mawdsley, Vladlen S. Vereshchetin.
*Substitute members:* Shi Jiuyong, Abdul G. Koroma.

#### Chamber for Environmental Matters

*Members:* Mohammed Bedjaoui (ex officio), Stephen M. Schwebel (ex officio), Mohamed Shahabuddeen, Christopher G. Weeramantry, Raymond Ranjeva, Géza Herczegh, Carl-August Fleischhauer.

#### Parties to the Court's Statute

All Members of the United Nations are *ipso facto* parties to the Statute of the International Court of Justice. Also parties to it are the following non-members: Nauru, Switzerland.

#### States accepting the compulsory jurisdiction of the Court

Declarations made by the following States, a number with reservations, accepting the Court's compulsory jurisdiction (or made under the Statute of the Permanent Court of International Justice and deemed to be an acceptance of the jurisdiction of the International Court) were in force at the end of 1995:

Australia, Austria, Barbados, Belgium, Botswana, Bulgaria, Cambodia, Cameroon, Canada, Colombia, Costa Rica, Cyprus, Denmark, Dominican Republic, Egypt, Estonia, Finland, Gambia, Georgia,[a] Greece, Guinea-Bissau, Haiti, Honduras, Hungary, India, Japan, Kenya, Liberia, Liechtenstein, Luxembourg, Madagascar, Malawi, Malta, Mauritius, Mexico, Nauru, Netherlands, New Zealand, Nicaragua, Nigeria, Norway, Pakistan, Panama, Philippines, Poland, Portugal, Senegal, Somalia, Spain, Sudan, Suriname, Swaziland, Sweden, Switzerland, Togo, Uganda, United Kingdom, Uruguay, Zaire.

[a]Declaration deposited on 20 June 1995.

#### United Nations organs and specialized and related agencies authorized to request advisory opinions from the Court

*Authorized by the United Nations Charter to request opinions on any legal question:* General Assembly, Security Council.

*Authorized by the General Assembly in accordance with the Charter to request opinions on legal questions arising within the scope of their activities:* Economic and Social Council, Trusteeship Council, Interim Committee of the General Assembly, Committee on Applications for Review of Administrative Tribunal Judgements, ILO, FAO, UNESCO, ICAO, WHO, World Bank, IFC, IDA, IMF, ITU, WMO, IMO, WIPO, IFAD, UNIDO, IAEA.

#### Committees of the Court

BUDGETARY AND ADMINISTRATIVE COMMITTEE
*Members:* Mohammed Bedjaoui (ex officio), Stephen M. Schwebel (ex officio), Gilbert Guillaume, Mohamed Shahabuddeen, Raymond Ranjeva, Shi Jiuyong, Carl-August Fleischhauer.

COMMITTEE ON RELATIONS
*Members:* Andrés Aguilar Mawdsley, Christopher G. Weeramantry, Géza Herczegh.

LIBRARY COMMITTEE
*Members:* Christopher G. Weeramantry, Raymond Ranjeva, Géza Herczegh, Shi Jiuyong, Abdul G. Koroma.

RULES COMMITTEE
*Members:* Shigeru Oda, Gilbert Guillaume, Carl-August Fleischhauer, Abdul G. Koroma.

# Other United Nations–related bodies

The following bodies are not subsidiary to any principal organ of the United Nations but were established by an international treaty instrument or arrangement sponsored by the United Nations and are thus related to the Organization and its work. These bodies, often referred to as "treaty organs", are serviced by the United Nations Secretariat and may be financed in part or wholly from the Organization's regular budget, as authorized by the General Assembly, to which most of them report annually.

#### Commission against Apartheid in Sports

The Commission against Apartheid in Sports was established under the International Convention against Apartheid in Sports.[5] It consisted of 15 members elected for four-year terms by the States parties to the Convention to serve in their personal capacity, with due regard for equitable geographical distribution and representation of the principal legal systems, particular attention being paid to participation of persons having experience in sports administration.

The Commission, which was to report annually to the General Assembly through the Secretary-General, has not met since 1992.

*Members:*[a]
*To serve until 24 June 1995:* Gbedevi Zikpi Aguigah (Togo), Abdul Karim Al-Ethawy (Iraq), James Victor Gbeho (Ghana), Joseph Lagu (Sudan), Francis Malambugi (United Republic of Tanzania), Ernest Besley Maycock (Barbados), Vladimir Platonov (Ukraine), Jai Pratap Rana (Nepal), Zoumana Traoré (Burkina Faso).

[a]No elections were held to fill the vacancies that occurred in 1993 and 1995.

#### Committee against Torture

The Committee against Torture was established under the Convention against Torture and Other Cruel, Inhuman or Degrading Treatment or Punishment.[6] It consists of 10 experts elected for four-year terms by the States parties to the Convention to serve in their personal capacity, with due regard for equitable geographical distribution and for the usefulness of the participation of some persons having legal experience.

In 1995, the Committee, which reports annually to the General Assembly, held two sessions, in Geneva: its fourteenth from 24 April to 5 May and its fifteenth from 13 to 24 November.

*Members:*
*To serve until 31 December 1995:* Peter Thomas Burns, *Vice-Chairman* (Canada); Fawzi El Ibrashi, *Vice-Chairman* (Egypt); Ricardo Gil Lavedra (Argentina); Hugo Lorenzo, *Vice-Chairman* (Uruguay); Habib Slim (Tunisia).[a]

---

[5]YUN 1985, p. 166, GA res. 40/64 G, annex, 10 Dec. 1985.
[6]YUN 1984, p. 815, GA res. 39/46, annex, article 17, 10 Dec. 1984.

*To serve until 31 December 1997:* Alexis Dipanda Mouelle, *Chairman* (Cameroon); Julia Iliopoulos-Strangas (Greece); Mukunda Regmi (Nepal); Bent Sorensen, *Rapporteur* (Denmark); Alexander M. Yakovlev (Russian Federation).

[a]Appointed to fill the vacancy created by the resignation on 6 January 1995 of Hassib Ben Ammar (Tunisia).

### Committee on the Elimination of Discrimination against Women

The Committee on the Elimination of Discrimination against Women was established under the Convention on the Elimination of All Forms of Discrimination against Women.[7] It consists of 23 experts elected for four-year terms by the States parties to the Convention to serve in their personal capacity, with due regard for equitable geographical distribution and for representation of the different forms of civilization and principal legal systems.

The Committee, which reports annually to the General Assembly through the Economic and Social Council, held its fourteenth session in New York from 16 January to 3 February 1995.

*Members:*

*To serve until 15 April 1996:* Gül Aykor (Turkey); Carlota Bustelo García del Real (Spain); Silvia Rose Cartwright (New Zealand); Evangelina García-Prince, *Vice-Chairman* (Venezuela); Liliana Gurdulich de Correa (Argentina); Salma Khan (Bangladesh); Pirkko Anneli Mäkinen (Finland); Elsa Victoria Muñoz-Gómez (Colombia); Ahoua Ouedraogo (Burkina Faso); Hanna Beate Schöpp-Schilling, *Rapporteur* (Germany); Kongit Sinegiorgis (Ethiopia).

*To serve until 15 April 1998:* Charlotte Abaka (Ghana); Emna Aouij, *Vice-Chairman* (Tunisia); Tendai Ruth Bare (Zimbabwe); Desiree Patricia Bernard (Guyana); Ivanka Corti, *Chairman* (Italy); Aurora Javate de Dios (Philippines); Miriam Yolanda Estrada Castillo (Ecuador); Sunaryati Hartono (Indonesia); Lin Shangzhen, *Vice-Chairman* (China); Ginko Sato (Japan); Carmel Shalev (Israel); Mervat Tallawy (Egypt).

### Committee on the Elimination of Racial Discrimination

The Committee on the Elimination of Racial Discrimination was established under the International Convention on the Elimination of All Forms of Racial Discrimination.[8] It consists of 18 experts elected for four-year terms by the States parties to the Convention to serve in their personal capacity, with due regard for equitable geographical distribution and for representation of the different forms of civilization and principal legal systems.

The Committee, which reports annually to the General Assembly through the Secretary-General, held two sessions in 1995, in Geneva: its forty-sixth from 27 February to 17 March and its forty-seventh from 31 July to 18 August.

*Members:*

*To serve until 19 January 1996:* Theodoor van Boven (Netherlands); Ion Diaconu (Romania); Eduardo Ferrero Costa (Peru); Ivan Garvalov, *Chairman* (Bulgaria); Yuri A. Rechetov (Russian Federation); Shanti Sadiq Ali (India); Song Shuhua (China); Luis Valencia Rodriguez (Ecuador); Mario Jorge Yutzis (Argentina).

*To serve until 19 January 1998:* Mahmoud Aboul-Nasr (Egypt); Hamzat Ahmadu, *Vice-Chairman* (Nigeria); Michael Parker Banton, *Rapporteur* (United Kingdom); Andrew Chigovera (Zimbabwe); Régis de Gouttes (France); Carlos Lechuga Hevia, *Vice-Chairman* (Cuba); Agha Shahi (Pakistan); Michael E. Sherifis, *Vice-Chairman* (Cyprus); Rüdiger Wolfrum (Germany).

### Committee on the Rights of the Child

The Committee on the Rights of the Child was established under the Convention on the Rights of the Child.[9] It consists of 10 experts elected for four-year terms by the States parties to the Convention to serve in their personal capacity, with due regard for equitable geographical distribution and for representation of the principal legal systems.

The Committee, which reports biennially to the General Assembly through the Economic and Social Council, held three sessions in 1995, in Geneva: its eighth from 8 to 27 January, its ninth from 22 May to 9 June and its tenth from 30 October to 17 November.

*Members:*

*To serve until 28 February 1997:* Hoda Badran, *Chairman (eighth session)* (Egypt); Flora C. Eufemio, *Vice-Chairman (ninth and tenth sessions)* (Philippines); Swithun Tachiona Mombeshora (Zimbabwe); Marta Santos País, *Rapporteur* (Portugal); Marilia Sardenberg Zelner Gonçalves, *Vice-Chairman (ninth and tenth sessions)* (Brazil).

*To serve until 28 February 1999:*[a] Akila Belembaogo, *Vice-Chairman (eighth session), Chairman (ninth and tenth sessions)* (Burkina Faso); Thomas Hammarberg, *Vice-Chairman* (Sweden); Judith Karp (Israel); Youri Kolosov (Russian Federation); Sandra Prunella Mason, *Vice-Chairman (eighth session)* (Barbados).

[a]Elected on 21 February 1995.

### Conference on Disarmament

The Conference on Disarmament, the multilateral negotiating forum on disarmament, reports annually to the General Assembly and is serviced by the United Nations Secretariat. It had 38 members in 1995.

The Conference met in Geneva from 30 January to 7 April, from 29 May to 7 July and from 31 July to 22 September 1995.

*Members:* Algeria, Argentina, Australia, Belgium, Brazil, Bulgaria, Canada, China, Cuba, Egypt, Ethiopia, France, Germany, Hungary, India, Indonesia, Iran, Italy, Japan, Kenya, Mexico, Mongolia, Morocco, Myanmar, Netherlands, Nigeria, Pakistan, Peru, Poland, Romania, Russian Federation, Sri Lanka, Sweden, United Kingdom, United States, Venezuela, Yugoslavia,[a] Zaire.

[a]Refers to the former Socialist Federal Republic of Yugoslavia.

The presidency, which rotates in English alphabetical order among the members, was held by the following in 1995: Italy, Japan, Kenya, Mexico, Mongolia, Morocco, the last also for the recess until the 1996 session.

### Human Rights Committee

The Human Rights Committee was established under the International Covenant on Civil and Political Rights.[10] It consists of 18 experts elected by the States parties to the Covenant to serve in their personal capacity for four-year terms.

In 1995, the Committee, which reports annually to the General Assembly through the Economic and Social Council, held three sessions: its fifty-third in New York from 20 March to 7 April, its fifty-fourth in Geneva from 3 to 28 July and its fifty-fifth in Geneva from 16 October to 3 November.

*Members:*

*To serve until 31 December 1996:* Francisco José Aguilar Urbina, *Chairman* (Costa Rica); Tamás Bán, *Vice-Chairman* (Hungary); Marco Tulio Bruni Celli (Venezuela); Elizabeth Evatt (Australia); Laurel B. Francis (Jamaica); Rosalyn Higgins (United Kingdom); Rajsoomer Lallah (Mauritius); Andreas V. Mavrommatis (Cyprus); Fausto Pocar (Italy).

*To serve until 31 December 1998:*[a] Nisuke Ando (Japan); Thomas Buergenthal (United States); Christine Chanet, *Rapporteur* (France); Omran El-Shafei, *Vice-Chairman* (Egypt); Eckart Klein (Germany); David Kretzmer (Israel); Prafullachandra Natwarlal Baghwati, *Vice-Chairman* (India); Cecilia Medina Quiroga (Chile); Julio Prado Vallejo (Ecuador).

[a]Elected on 8 September 1994.

---

[7]YUN 1979, p. 898, GA res. 34/180, annex, article 17, 18 Dec. 1979.
[8]YUN 1965, p. 443, GA res. 2106 A (XX), annex, article 8, 21 Dec. 1965.
[9]GA res. 44/25, annex, 20 Nov. 1989.
[10]YUN 1966, p. 427, GA res. 2200 A (XXI), annex, part IV, 16 Dec. 1966.

## International Narcotics Control Board (INCB)

The International Narcotics Control Board, established under the Single Convention on Narcotic Drugs, 1961, as amended by the 1972 Protocol, consists of 13 members, elected by the Economic and Social Council for five-year terms, 3 from candidates nominated by WHO and 10 from candidates nominated by Members of the United Nations and parties to the Single Convention.

The Board held two sessions in 1995, in Vienna: its fifty-sixth from 9 to 19 May and its fifty-seventh from 31 October to 17 November.

*Members:*

*To serve until 1 March 1997:* Sirad Atmodjo (Indonesia);[a] Hamid Ghodse (Iran);[a] Dil Jan Khan (Pakistan);[b] Gottfried Machata (Austria); Dr. Bunsom Martin, *Second Vice-President* (Thailand); Herbert S. Okun (United States); Dr. Manuel Quijano, *Rapporteur* (Mexico).

*To serve until 1 March 2000:* Edouard A. Babayan (Russian Federation); Mohamed A. Mansour, *First Vice-President* (Egypt); António Lourenço Martins (Portugal); Oskar Schröder, *President* (Germany); Elba Torres Graterol (Venezuela); Dr. Alfredo Pemjean (Chile).[a,c]

[a]Elected from candidates nominated by WHO.
[b]Elected on 9 February 1995 (dec. 1995/202) to fill the vacancy created by the death in 1994 of Sahibzada Raoof Ali Khan (Pakistan).
[c]Elected on 27 July 1995 (dec. 1995/230) to fill the vacancy created by the resignation on 16 January of Elisaldo Luiz de Araújo Carlini (Brazil).

## Preparatory Commission for the International Seabed Authority and for the International Tribunal for the Law of the Sea

The Preparatory Commission remained in existence until the conclusion of the first session of the Assembly of the International Seabed Authority, i.e. until 17 March 1995.

# Principal members of the United Nations Secretariat

## (as at 31 December 1995)

### Secretariat

*The Secretary-General:* Boutros Boutros-Ghali

#### Executive Office of the Secretary-General
*Assistant Secretary-General, Chief of Staff:* Jean-Claude Aimé
*Under-Secretaries-General, Senior Advisers to the Secretary-General:* Chinmaya R. Gharekhan, Ismat Kittani
*Assistant Secretary-General, Senior Adviser to the Secretary-General:* Rosario Green

#### Office of Internal Oversight Services
*Under-Secretary-General:* Karl-Theodor Paschke

#### Office of Legal Affairs
*Under-Secretary-General, Legal Counsel:* Hans Corell

#### Department of Political Affairs
*Under-Secretaries-General:* Marrack I. Goulding, Mahmoud Mestiri
*Assistant Secretaries-General:* Lansana Kouyaté, G. B. Schlittler-Silva, Alvaro de Soto

#### Department of Peace-keeping Operations
*Under-Secretary-General:* Kofi Annan
*Assistant Secretaries-General:* Manfred Eisele, Iqbal Riza

#### Department of Humanitarian Affairs
*Under-Secretary-General, Emergency Relief Coordinator:* Peter Hansen

#### Department for Policy Coordination and Sustainable Development
*Under-Secretary-General:* Nitin Desai

#### Department for Economic and Social Information and Policy Analysis
*Under-Secretary-General:* Jean-Claude Milleron

#### Department for Development Support and Management Services
*Under-Secretary-General:* Ji Chaozhu

#### Department of Public Information
*Assistant Secretary-General:* Samir Sanbar

#### Secretariat of the United Nations Fiftieth Anniversary
*Under-Secretary-General, Special Adviser to the Secretary-General for Public Policy:* Gillian Sorensen

#### Department of Administration and Management
*Under-Secretary-General:* Joseph E. Connor

OFFICE OF PROGRAMME PLANNING, BUDGET AND ACCOUNTS
*Assistant Secretary-General, Controller:* Yukio Takasu

OFFICE OF HUMAN RESOURCES MANAGEMENT
*Assistant Secretary-General:* Denis J. Halliday

OFFICE OF CONFERENCE AND SUPPORT SERVICES
*Assistant Secretary-General, United Nations Security Coordinator:* Benon V. Sevan

#### Economic and Social Commission for Asia and the Pacific
*Under-Secretary-General, Executive Secretary:* Adrianus Mooy

#### Economic and Social Commission for Western Asia
*Under-Secretary-General, Executive Secretary:* Hazem El-Beblawi

#### Economic Commission for Africa
*Under-Secretary-General, Executive Secretary:* K. Y. Amoako

#### Economic Commission for Europe
*Under-Secretary-General, Executive Secretary:* Yves Berthelot

#### Economic Commission for Latin America and the Caribbean
*Under-Secretary-General, Executive Secretary:* Gert Rosenthal

#### United Nations Centre for Human Settlements
*Assistant Secretary-General, Secretary-General of the Habitat II Conference:* Wally N'Dow

#### United Nations Office at Geneva
*Under-Secretary-General, Director-General of the United Nations Office at Geneva:* Vladimir Petrovsky

#### United Nations Centre for Human Rights
*Under-Secretary-General, High Commissioner for Human Rights:* José Ayala Lasso
*Assistant Secretary-General:* Ibrahima Fall

#### United Nations Office at Vienna
*Under-Secretary-General, Director-General of the United Nations Office at Vienna and Executive Director of the United Nations International Drug Control Programme:* Giorgio Giacomelli

International Court of Justice Registry
*Assistant Secretary-General, Registrar:* Eduardo Valencia-Ospina

## Secretariats of subsidiary organs, special representatives and other related bodies

International Trade Centre UNCTAD/WTO
*Executive Director:* J. Denis Bélisle

Office of the Special Representative of the
Secretary-General for Burundi
*Assistant Secretary-General, Special Representative:* Marc Faguy

Office of the Special Representative of the
Secretary-General for Haiti
*Under-Secretary-General, Special Representative:* Lakhdar Brahimi

Office of the United Nations High Commissioner for Refugees
*Under-Secretary-General, High Commissioner:* Sadako Ogata
*Assistant Secretary-General, Deputy High Commissioner:* Gerald Walzer

Personal Representative of the Secretary-General
on the Guyana-Venezuela border dispute
*Under-Secretary-General, Personal Representative:* Alister McIntyre

Special Coordinator of the Secretary-General
in the Occupied Territories
*Under-Secretary-General, Special Coordinator:* Terje Rod Larsen

United Nations Angola Verification Mission
*Under-Secretary-General, Special Representative of the Secretary-General:* Alioune Blondin Beye
*Assistant Secretary-General, Deputy Special Representative:* Khaled Yassir
*Assistant Secretary-General, Force Commander:* Major-General Phillip V. Sibanda

United Nations Assistance Mission for Rwanda
*Under-Secretary-General, Special Representative of the Secretary-General:* Shaharyar M. Khan
*Force Commander:* Major-General Guy Tousignant

United Nations Children's Fund
*Under-Secretary-General, Executive Director:* Carol Bellamy
*Assistant Secretary-General, Deputy Executive Director, Programmes:* Richard Jolly
*Assistant Secretary-General, Deputy Executive Director, Operations:* Karin Sham Poo
*Assistant Secretary-General, Deputy Executive Director, External Relations:* Guido Bertolaso

United Nations Compensation Commission
*Assistant Secretary-General, Executive Secretary:* Carlos Alzamora Traverso

United Nations Conference on Trade and Development
*Under-Secretary-General, Secretary-General of the Conference:* Rubens Ricupero

United Nations Confidence Restoration Operation in Croatia
*Assistant Secretary-General, Chief of Mission:* Byung Suk Min

United Nations Development Programme
*Administrator:* James Gustave Speth
*Associate Administrator:* Rafeeuddin Ahmed
*Assistant Administrator and Director, Bureau for Resources and External Affairs:* Jean-Jacques Graisse
*Assistant Administrator and Director, Bureau for Finance and Administration:* Toshiyuki Niwa
*Assistant Administrator and Director, Bureau for Policy and Programme Support:* Anders Wijkman

*Assistant Administrator and Regional Director, Regional Bureau for Africa:* Ellen Johnson Sirleaf
*Acting Regional Director, Regional Bureau for Arab States:* Somendu Banerjee
*Assistant Administrator and Regional Director, Regional Bureau for Asia and the Pacific:* Nay Htun
*Assistant Administrator and Regional Director, Regional Bureau for Latin America and the Caribbean:* Fernando Zumbado

United Nations Disengagement Observer Force
*Assistant Secretary-General, Force Commander:* Major-General Johannes Kosters

United Nations Environment Programme
*Under-Secretary-General, Executive Director:* Elizabeth Dowdeswell

United Nations Institute for Training and Research
*Acting Executive Director:* Marcel A. Boisard

United Nations Interim Force in Lebanon
*Assistant Secretary-General, Force Commander:* Major-General Stanislaw Wozniak

United Nations Iraq-Kuwait Observation Mission
*Assistant Secretary-General, Force Commander:* Major-General Gian G. Santillo

United Nations Military Observer Group in India and Pakistan
*Chief Military Observer:* Major-General Alfonso Pessolano

United Nations Mission for the Referendum in Western Sahara
*Under-Secretary-General, Special Representative of the Secretary-General:* Sahabzada Yaqub-Khan
*Force Commander:* Brigadier-General André Van Baelen

United Nations Mission in Haiti
*Under-Secretary-General, Special Representative of the Secretary-General:* Lakhdar Brahimi
*Force Commander:* Major-General Joseph Kinzer

United Nations Mission of Observers in Tajikistan
*Under-Secretary-General, Special Envoy of the Secretary-General:* Ramiro Píriz-Ballón
*Deputy Special Envoy and Head of Mission:* Darko Silovic
*Chief Military Observer:* Brigadier-General Hasan Abaza

United Nations Observer Mission in El Salvador
*Under-Secretary-General, Special Representative of the Secretary-General and Chief of Mission:* Enrique ter Horst

United Nations Observer Mission in Georgia
*Under-Secretary-General, Special Envoy of the Secretary-General:* Edouard Brunner
*Chief Military Observer:* Major-General Per Källström

United Nations Observer Mission in Liberia
*Under-Secretary-General, Special Representative of the Secretary-General:* Anthony B. Nyakyi
*Chief Military Observer:* Major-General Mahmoud Talha

United Nations Office for Project Services
*Assistant Secretary-General, Executive Director:* Reinhart Helmke

United Nations Peace-keeping Force in Cyprus
*Under-Secretary-General, Special Representative of the Secretary-General:* Charles Joe Clark
*Assistant Secretary-General, Deputy Special Representative and Chief of Mission:* Gustave Feissel
*Force Commander:* Brigadier-General Ahti Toimi Paavali Vartiainen

**United Nations Population Fund**

*Executive Director:* Dr. Nafis I. Sadik
  *Deputy Executive Director, Policy and Administration:* Hirofumi Ando
  *Deputy Executive Director, Programme:* Joseph Van Arendonk
  *Deputy Executive Director, Technical Services:* Jyoti Singh

**United Nations Preventive Deployment Force**

*Assistant Secretary-General, Special Representative of the Secretary-General and Chief of Mission:* Henryk J. Sokalski

**United Nations Protection Force**

*Assistant Secretary-General, Chief of Mission:* Antonio Pedauye
*Assistant Secretary-General, Force Commander:* Lieutenant-General Bernard Janvier

**United Nations Relief and Works Agency for Palestine Refugees in the Near East**

*Under-Secretary-General, Commissioner-General:* Ilter Türkmen
  *Assistant Secretary-General, Deputy Commissioner-General:* Luce Daniele Biolato

**United Nations Truce Supervision Organization**

*Assistant Secretary-General, Officer-in-Charge:* Major-General Rufus Kupolati

**United Nations University**

*Under-Secretary-General, Rector:* Heitor Gurgulino de Souza
  *Assistant Secretary-General, Director, World Institute for Development Economics Research:* Mihaly Simai

---

On 31 December 1995, the total number of staff of the United Nations Secretariat holding permanent, probationary and fixed-term appointments with service or expected service of a year or more was 14,309. Of these, 4,830 were in the Professional and higher categories and 9,479 were in the General Service, Manual Worker and Field Service categories. Of the same total, 13,727 were regular staff serving at Headquarters or other established offices and 582 were assigned as project personnel to technical cooperation projects. In addition, at the end of December 1995, UNRWA had some 19,591 local area staff, including temporary assistance.

Appendix IV

# Agendas of United Nations principal organs in 1995

This appendix lists the items on the agendas of the General Assembly, the Security Council and the Economic and Social Council during 1995. For the Assembly, the column headed "Allocation" indicates the assignment of each item to plenary meetings or committees.

Agenda item titles have been shortened by omitting mention of reports, if any, following the subject of the item. Where the subject-matter of an item is not apparent from its title, the subject is identified in square brackets; this is not part of the title.

## General Assembly

### Agenda items considered at the resumed forty-ninth session
### (26 January–18 September 1995)

| Item No. | Title | Allocation |
|---|---|---|
| 2. | Minute of silent prayer or meditation. | Plenary |
| 8. | Adoption of the agenda and organization of work. | Plenary |
| 10. | Report of the Secretary-General on the work of the Organization. | Plenary |
| 15. | Elections to fill vacancies in principal organs: | |
| | (c) Election of a member of the International Court of Justice. | Plenary |
| 16. | Elections to fill vacancies in subsidiary organs and other elections: | |
| | (a) Election of twelve members of the World Food Council. | Plenary |
| 17. | Appointments to fill vacancies in subsidiary organs and other appointments: | |
| | (a) Appointment of members of the Advisory Committee on Administrative and Budgetary Questions; | 5th |
| | (b) Appointment of members of the Committee on Contributions; | 5th |
| | (g) Appointment of members and alternate members of the United Nations Staff Pension Committee; | 5th |
| | (i) Appointment of members of the Committee on Conferences; | Plenary |
| | (k) Confirmation of the appointment of the Secretary-General of the United Nations Conference on Trade and Development.[1] | Plenary |
| 33. | Question of equitable representation on and increase in the membership of the Security Council and related matters. | Plenary |
| 34. | The situation of democracy and human rights in Haiti. | Plenary |
| 37. | Strengthening of the coordination of humanitarian and disaster relief assistance of the United Nations, including special economic assistance: | |
| | (b) Special economic assistance to individual countries or regions. | Plenary |
| 42. | The situation in Central America: procedures for the establishment of a firm and lasting peace and progress in fashioning a region of peace, freedom, democracy and development. | Plenary |
| 44. | Commemoration of the fiftieth anniversary of the United Nations in 1995. | Plenary |
| 47. | Armed Israeli aggression against the Iraqi nuclear installations and its grave consequences for the established international system concerning the peaceful uses of nuclear energy, the non-proliferation of nuclear weapons and international peace and security. | Plenary |
| 48. | Launching of global negotiations on international economic cooperation for development. | Plenary |
| 49. | Implementation of the resolutions of the United Nations. | Plenary |
| 50. | The situation in Afghanistan and its implications for international peace and security. | Plenary |
| 51. | Question of Cyprus. | 2 |
| 52. | Consequences of the Iraqi occupation of and aggression against Kuwait. | Plenary |
| 92. | Agenda for development. | 3 |
| 97. | Advancement of women. | 4 |
| 105. | Review of the efficiency of the administrative and financial functioning of the United Nations. | 5th |
| 106. | Programme budget for the biennium 1992-1993. | 5th |
| 107. | Programme budget for the biennium 1994-1995. | 5th |
| 108. | Programme planning. | 5th |

[1]Sub-item added at the resumed session.
[2]Not allocated; consideration deferred to the fiftieth session.
[3]Allocated to the Second Committee at the first part of the session in 1994 but considered only in plenary meeting at the resumed session.
[4]Allocated to the Third Committee at the first part of the session in 1994 but considered only in plenary meeting at the resumed session.

| Item No. | Title | Allocation |
|---|---|---|
| 109. | Improving the financial situation of the United Nations. | 5th |
| 112. | Scale of assessments for the apportionment of the expenses of the United Nations. | 5 |
| 113. | Human resources management: | |
| | *(b)* Composition of the Secretariat; | 5th |
| | *(c)* Respect for the privileges and immunities of officials of the United Nations and the specialized agencies and related organizations; | 5th |
| | *(d)* Other human resources questions. | 5th |
| 116. | Financing of the United Nations peace-keeping forces in the Middle East: | |
| | *(a)* United Nations Disengagement Observer Force; | 5th |
| | *(b)* United Nations Interim Force in Lebanon. | 5th |
| 117. | Financing of the United Nations Angola Verification Mission. | 5th |
| 118. | Financing of the activities arising from Security Council resolution 687(1991): | |
| | *(a)* United Nations Iraq-Kuwait Observation Mission. | 5th |
| 119. | Financing of the United Nations Mission for the Referendum in Western Sahara. | 5th |
| 120. | Financing of the United Nations Observer Mission in El Salvador. | 5th |
| 121. | Financing and liquidation of the United Nations Transitional Authority in Cambodia. | 5th |
| 122. | Financing of the United Nations Protection Force. | 5th |
| 123. | Financing of the United Nations Operation in Somalia II. | 5th |
| 124. | Financing of the United Nations Operation in Mozambique. | 5th |
| 125. | Financing of the United Nations Peace-keeping Force in Cyprus. | 5th |
| 126. | Financing of the United Nations Observer Mission in Georgia. | 5th |
| 127. | Financing of the United Nations Observer Mission Uganda-Rwanda. | 5th |
| 128. | Financing of the United Nations Mission in Haiti. | 5th |
| 129. | Financing of the United Nations Observer Mission in Liberia. | 5th |
| 130. | Financing of the United Nations Assistance Mission for Rwanda. | 5th |
| 131. | Financing of the United Nations Military Liaison Team in Cambodia. | 5th |
| 132. | Administrative and budgetary aspects of the financing of the United Nations peace-keeping operations: | |
| | *(a)* Financing of the United Nations peace-keeping operations; | 5th |
| | *(b)* Relocation of Belarus and Ukraine to the group of Member States set out in paragraph 3 *(c)* of General Assembly resolution 43/232. | 5th |
| 146. | Financing of the International Tribunal for the Prosecution of Persons Responsible for Serious Violations of International Humanitarian Law Committed in the Territory of the Former Yugoslavia since 1991. | 5th |
| 162. | Financing of the United Nations Mission of Observers in Tajikistan. | 5th |
| 163. | Financing of the International Criminal Tribunal for the Prosecution of Persons Responsible for Genocide and Other Serious Violations of International Humanitarian Law Committed in the Territory of Rwanda and Rwandan Citizens Responsible for Genocide and Other Such Violations Committed in the Territory of Neighbouring States between 1 January and 31 December 1994.[6] | 5th |
| 164. | Election of judges of the International Criminal Tribunal for the Prosecution of Persons Responsible for Genocide and Other Serious Violations of International Humanitarian Law Committed in the Territory of Rwanda and Rwandan Citizens Responsible for Genocide and Other Such Violations Committed in the Territory of Neighbouring States between 1 January and 31 December 1994.[6] | Plenary |

## Agenda of the fiftieth session
### (first part, 19 September–23 December 1995)

| Item No. | Title | Allocation |
|---|---|---|
| 1. | Opening of the session by the Chairman of the delegation of Côte d'Ivoire. | Plenary |
| 2. | Minute of silent prayer or meditation. | Plenary |
| 3. | Credentials of representatives to the fiftieth session of the General Assembly: | |
| | *(a)* Appointment of the members of the Credentials Committee; | Plenary |
| | *(b)* Report of the Credentials Committee. | Plenary |
| 4. | Election of the President of the General Assembly. | Plenary |
| 5. | Election of the officers of the Main Committees. | Plenary |

---

[5]Allocated to the Fifth Committee at the first part of the session in 1994 but considered only in plenary meeting at the resumed session.
[6]Item added at the resumed session.

| Item No. | Title | Allocation |
|---|---|---|
| 6. | Election of the Vice-Presidents of the General Assembly. | Plenary |
| 7. | Notification by the Secretary-General under Article 12, paragraph 2, of the Charter of the United Nations. | Plenary |
| 8. | Adoption of the agenda and organization of work. | Plenary |
| 9. | General debate. | Plenary |
| 10. | Report of the Secretary-General on the work of the Organization. | Plenary |
| 11. | Report of the Security Council. | Plenary |
| 12. | Report of the Economic and Social Council. | Plenary, 2nd, 3rd, 4th, 5th |
| 13. | Report of the International Court of Justice. | Plenary |
| 14. | Report of the International Atomic Energy Agency. | Plenary |
| 15. | Elections to fill vacancies in principal organs: | |
| | (a) Election of five non-permanent members of the Security Council; | Plenary |
| | (b) Election of eighteen members of the Economic and Social Council; | Plenary |
| | (c) Election of a member of the International Court of Justice. | Plenary |
| 16. | Elections to fill vacancies in subsidiary organs and other elections: | |
| | (a) Election of twenty-nine members of the Governing Council of the United Nations Environment Programme; | Plenary |
| | (b) Election of twelve members of the World Food Council; | Plenary |
| | (c) Election of seven members of the Committee for Programme and Coordination. | Plenary |
| 17. | Appointments to fill vacancies in subsidiary organs and other appointments: | |
| | (a) Appointment of members of the Advisory Committee on Administrative and Budgetary Questions; | 5th |
| | (b) Appointment of members of the Committee on Contributions; | 5th |
| | (c) Appointment of a member of the Board of Auditors; | 5th |
| | (d) Confirmation of the appointment of members of the Investments Committee; | 5th |
| | (e) Appointment of members of the United Nations Administrative Tribunal; | 5th |
| | (f) Appointment of members of the Committee on Conferences; | Plenary |
| | (g) Appointment of a member of the Joint Inspection Unit. | Plenary |
| 18. | Implementation of the Declaration on the Granting of Independence to Colonial Countries and Peoples. | Plenary, 4th[7] |
| 19. | Admission of new Members to the United Nations. | Plenary |
| 20. | Strengthening of the coordination of humanitarian and disaster relief assistance of the United Nations, including special economic assistance: | |
| | (a) Strengthening of the coordination of emergency humanitarian assistance of the United Nations; | Plenary |
| | (b) Special economic assistance to individual countries or regions; | Plenary |
| | (c) Strengthening of international cooperation and coordination of efforts to study, mitigate and minimize the consequences of the Chernobyl disaster; | Plenary |
| | (d) Emergency international assistance for peace, normalcy and reconstruction of war-stricken Afghanistan. | Plenary |
| 21. | University for Peace. | Plenary |
| 22. | Return or restitution of cultural property to the countries of origin. | Plenary |
| 23. | Restructuring and revitalization of the United Nations in the economic, social and related fields. | Plenary |
| 24. | Implementation of the United Nations New Agenda for the Development of Africa in the 1990s. | Plenary |
| 25. | Cooperation between the United Nations and the Latin American Economic System. | Plenary |
| 26. | The situation in Burundi. | Plenary |
| 27. | Necessity of ending the economic, commercial and financial embargo imposed by the United States of America against Cuba. | Plenary |
| 28. | The situation in Bosnia and Herzegovina. | Plenary |
| 29. | Commemoration of the fiftieth anniversary of the United Nations. | Plenary |
| 30. | Cooperation between the United Nations and the Organization for Security and Cooperation in Europe. | Plenary |
| 31. | Cooperation between the United Nations and the League of Arab States. | Plenary |
| 32. | Cooperation between the United Nations and the Organization of the Islamic Conference. | Plenary |
| 33. | International assistance for the rehabilitation and reconstruction of Nicaragua: aftermath of the war and natural disasters. | Plenary |

---

[7]Chapters of the report of the Special Committee on the Situation with regard to the Implementation of the Declaration on the Granting of Independence to Colonial Countries and Peoples relating to specific Territories.

| *Item No.* | *Title* | *Allocation* |
|---|---|---|
| 34. | United Nations Educational and Training Programme for Southern Africa. | Plenary |
| 35. | Question of the Comorian island of Mayotte. | Plenary |
| 36. | Commemoration of the fiftieth anniversary of the end of the Second World War. | Plenary |
| 37. | Zone of peace and cooperation of the South Atlantic. | Plenary |
| 38. | The situation of democracy and human rights in Haiti. | Plenary |
| 39. | Law of the sea. | Plenary |
| 40. | Building a peaceful and better world through sport and the Olympic ideal. | Plenary |
| 41. | Support by the United Nations system of the efforts of Governments to promote and consolidate new or restored democracies. | Plenary |
| 42. | Question of Palestine. | Plenary |
| 43. | Cooperation between the United Nations and the Organization of African Unity. | Plenary |
| 44. | The situation in the Middle East. | Plenary |
| 45. | The situation in Central America: procedures for the establishment of a firm and lasting peace and progress in fashioning a region of peace, freedom, democracy and development. | Plenary |
| 46. | Assistance in mine clearance. | Plenary |
| 47. | Question of equitable representation on and increase in the membership of the Security Council and related matters. | Plenary |
| 48. | Question of the Falkland Islands (Malvinas). | Plenary, 4th[8] |
| 49. | Report of the International Tribunal for the Prosecution of Persons Responsible for Serious Violations of International Humanitarian Law Committed in the Territory of the Former Yugoslavia since 1991. | Plenary |
| 50. | Declaration of the Assembly of Heads of State and Government of the Organization of African Unity on the aerial and naval military attack against the Socialist People's Libyan Arab Jamahiriya by the present United States Administration in April 1986. | Plenary |
| 51. | Armed Israeli aggression against the Iraqi nuclear installations and its grave consequences for the established international system concerning the peaceful uses of nuclear energy, the non-proliferation of nuclear weapons and international peace and security. | Plenary |
| 52. | Launching of global negotiations on international economic cooperation for development. | Plenary |
| 53. | Implementation of the resolutions of the United Nations. | Plenary |
| 54. | The situation in Afghanistan and its implications for international peace and security. | Plenary |
| 55. | Question of Cyprus. | 9 |
| 56. | Consequences of the Iraqi occupation of and aggression against Kuwait. | Plenary |
| 57. | Compliance with arms limitation and disarmament obligations. | 1st |
| 58. | Education and information for disarmament. | 1st |
| 59. | Verification in all its aspects, including the role of the United Nations in the field of verification. | 1st |
| 60. | Review of the implementation of the Declaration on the Strengthening of International Security. | 1st |
| 61. | Reduction of military budgets. | 1st |
| 62. | Scientific and technological developments and their impact on international security. | 1st |
| 63. | The role of science and technology in the context of international security, disarmament and other related fields. | 1st |
| 64. | Amendment of the Treaty Banning Nuclear Weapon Tests in the Atmosphere, in Outer Space and under Water. | 1st |
| 65. | Comprehensive test-ban treaty. | 1st |
| 66. | Establishment of a nuclear-weapon-free zone in the region of the Middle East. | 1st |
| 67. | Establishment of a nuclear-weapon-free zone in South Asia. | 1st |
| 68. | Conclusion of effective international arrangements to assure non-nuclear-weapon States against the use or threat of use of nuclear weapons. | 1st |
| 69. | Prevention of an arms race in outer space. | 1st |
| 70. | General and complete disarmament: | |
| | *(a)* Notification of nuclear tests; | 1st |
| | *(b)* Further measures in the field of disarmament for the prevention of an arms race on the seabed and the ocean floor and in the subsoil thereof; | 1st |
| | *(c)* Prohibition of the dumping of radioactive wastes; | 1st |
| | *(d)* Review of the Declaration of the 1990s as the Third Disarmament Decade; | 1st |
| | *(e)* Transparency in armaments; | 1st |
| | *(f)* Step-by-step reduction of the nuclear threat; | 1st |

[8]Hearings of bodies and individuals having an interest in the question.

[9]On 22 September 1995, the General Assembly adopted the General Committee's recommendation that the item be allocated at an appropriate time during the session.

| Item No. | Title | Allocation |
|---|---|---|
| *(g)* | Fourth special session of the General Assembly devoted to disarmament; | 1st |
| *(h)* | Relationship between disarmament and development; | 1st |
| *(i)* | Measures to curb the illicit transfer and use of conventional arms; | 1st |
| *(j)* | Regional disarmament; | 1st |
| *(k)* | Conventional arms control at the regional and subregional levels; | 1st |
| *(l)* | Non-proliferation of weapons of mass destruction and of vehicles for their delivery in all its aspects. | 1st |
| 71. | Review and implementation of the Concluding Document of the Twelfth Special Session of the General Assembly: | |
| *(a)* | United Nations disarmament fellowship, training and advisory services; | 1st |
| *(b)* | Regional confidence-building measures; | 1st |
| *(c)* | United Nations Regional Centre for Peace and Disarmament in Africa, United Nations Regional Centre for Peace and Disarmament in Asia and the Pacific and United Nations Regional Centre for Peace, Disarmament and Development in Latin America and the Caribbean; | 1st |
| *(d)* | Convention on the Prohibition of the Use of Nuclear Weapons. | 1st |
| 72. | Review of the implementation of the recommendations and decisions adopted by the General Assembly at its tenth special session: | |
| *(a)* | Report of the Disarmament Commission; | 1st |
| *(b)* | Report of the Conference on Disarmament; | 1st |
| *(c)* | Advisory Board on Disarmament Matters; | 1st |
| *(d)* | United Nations Institute for Disarmament Research; | 1st |
| *(e)* | Disarmament Week. | 1st |
| 73. | The risk of nuclear proliferation in the Middle East. | 1st |
| 74. | Convention on Prohibitions or Restrictions on the Use of Certain Conventional Weapons Which May Be Deemed to Be Excessively Injurious or to Have Indiscriminate Effects. | 1st |
| 75. | Strengthening of security and cooperation in the Mediterranean region. | 1st |
| 76. | Implementation of the Declaration of the Indian Ocean as a Zone of Peace. | 1st |
| 77. | Consolidation of the regime established by the Treaty for the Prohibition of Nuclear Weapons in Latin America and the Caribbean (Treaty of Tlatelolco). | 1st |
| 78. | Final text of a treaty on an African nuclear-weapon-free zone. | 1st |
| 79. | Rationalization of the work and reform of the agenda of the First Committee. | 1st |
| 80. | Convention on the Prohibition of the Development, Production and Stockpiling of Bacteriological (Biological) and Toxin Weapons and on Their Destruction. | 1st |
| 81. | Maintenance of international security. | 1st |
| 82. | Effects of atomic radiation. | 4th |
| 83. | International cooperation in the peaceful uses of outer space. | 4th |
| 84. | United Nations Relief and Works Agency for Palestine Refugees in the Near East. | 4th |
| 85. | Report of the Special Committee to Investigate Israeli Practices Affecting the Human Rights of the Palestinian People and Other Arabs of the Occupied Territories. | 4th |
| 86. | Comprehensive review of the whole question of peace-keeping operations in all their aspects. | 4th |
| 87. | Questions relating to information. | 4th |
| 88. | Information from Non-Self-Governing Territories transmitted under Article 73 *e* of the Charter of the United Nations. | 4th |
| 89. | Activities of foreign economic and other interests which impede the implementation of the Declaration on the Granting of Independence to Colonial Countries and Peoples in Territories under colonial domination. | 4th |
| 90. | Implementation of the Declaration on the Granting of Independence to Colonial Countries and Peoples by the specialized agencies and the international institutions associated with the United Nations. | 4th |
| 91. | Offers by Member States of study and training facilities for inhabitants of Non-Self-Governing Territories. | 4th |
| 92. | The situation in the occupied territories of Croatia. | 4th |
| 93. | Question of the composition of the relevant organs of the United Nations. | 4th |
| 94. | Macroeconomic policy questions: | |
| *(a)* | Financing of development; | 2nd |
| *(b)* | Long-term trends in social and economic development; | 2nd |
| *(c)* | External debt crisis and development. | 2nd |
| 95. | Sustainable development and international economic cooperation: | |
| *(a)* | Trade and development; | 2nd |
| *(b)* | Human settlements; | 2nd |
| *(c)* | United Nations Conference on Human Settlements (Habitat II); | 2nd |
| *(d)* | Science and technology for development; | 2nd |
| *(e)* | Implementation of the Programme of Action for the Least Developed Countries for the 1990s; | 2nd |

| Item No. | Title | Allocation |
|---|---|---|
| *(f)* | Women in development; | 2nd |
| *(g)* | Human resources development; | 2nd |
| *(h)* | Business and development; | 2nd |
| *(i)* | International cooperation for the eradication of poverty in developing countries; | 2nd |
| *(j)* | United Nations initiative on opportunity and participation; | 2nd |
| *(k)* | Food and sustainable agricultural development. | 2nd |
| 96. | Environment and sustainable development: | |
| *(a)* | Implementation of decisions and recommendations of the United Nations Conference on Environment and Development; | 2nd |
| *(b)* | Desertification and drought; | 2nd |
| *(c)* | Sustainable use and conservation of the marine living resources of the high seas; | Plenary |
| *(d)* | Protection of global climate for present and future generations of mankind; | 2nd |
| *(e)* | Implementation of the outcome of the Global Conference on the Sustainable Development of Small Island Developing States; | 2nd |
| *(f)* | International Decade for Natural Disaster Reduction. | 2nd |
| 97. | Operational activities for development: | |
| *(a)* | Triennial policy review of operational activities for development of the United Nations system; | 2nd |
| *(b)* | Economic and technical cooperation among developing countries. | 2nd |
| 98. | Training and research: United Nations Institute for Training and Research. | 2nd |
| 99. | Agenda for development. | 2nd |
| 100. | Renewal of the dialogue on strengthening international economic cooperation for development through partnership. | 2nd |
| 101. | International migration and development, including the convening of a United Nations conference on international migration and development. | 2nd |
| 102. | Implementation of the Programme of Action of the International Conference on Population and Development. | 2nd |
| 103. | Elimination of racism and racial discrimination. | 3rd |
| 104. | Right of peoples to self-determination. | 3rd |
| 105. | Social development, including questions relating to the world social situation and to youth, ageing, disabled persons and the family. | 3rd |
| 106. | Crime prevention and criminal justice. | 3rd |
| 107. | Advancement of women. | 3rd |
| 108. | International drug control. | 3rd |
| 109. | Report of the United Nations High Commissioner for Refugees, questions relating to refugees, returnees and displaced persons and humanitarian questions. | 3rd |
| 110. | Promotion and protection of the rights of children. | 3rd |
| 111. | Programme of activities of the International Decade of the World's Indigenous People. | 3rd |
| 112. | Human rights questions: | |
| *(a)* | Implementation of human rights instruments; | 3rd |
| *(b)* | Human rights questions, including alternative approaches for improving the effective enjoyment of human rights and fundamental freedoms; | 3rd |
| *(c)* | Human rights situations and reports of special rapporteurs and representatives; | 3rd |
| *(d)* | Comprehensive implementation of and follow-up to the Vienna Declaration and Programme of Action; | 3rd |
| *(e)* | Report of the United Nations High Commissioner for Human Rights. | 3rd |
| 113. | Financial reports and audited financial statements, and reports of the Board of Auditors: | |
| *(a)* | United Nations Institute for Training and Research; | 5th |
| *(b)* | Voluntary funds administered by the United Nations High Commissioner for Refugees. | 5th |
| 114. | Review of the efficiency of the administrative and financial functioning of the United Nations. | 5th |
| 115. | Programme budget for the biennium 1994-1995. | 5th |
| 116. | Proposed programme budget for the biennium 1996-1997. | 5th |
| 117. | Improving the financial situation of the United Nations. | 5th |
| 118. | Joint Inspection Unit. | 5th |
| 119. | Pattern of conferences. | 5th |
| 120. | Scale of assessments for the apportionment of the expenses of the United Nations. | 5th |
| 121. | United Nations common system. | 5th |
| 122. | Financing of the United Nations peace-keeping forces in the Middle East: | |
| *(a)* | United Nations Disengagement Observer Force; | 5th |
| *(b)* | United Nations Interim Force in Lebanon. | 5th |
| 123. | Financing of the United Nations Angola Verification Mission. | 5th |
| 124. | Financing of the activities arising from Security Council resolution 687(1991): | |

---

[10]Introduction and initial discussion.
[11]Subsequent consideration.

| Item No. | Title | Allocation |
|---|---|---|
| 161. | Implementation of the outcome of the World Summit for Social Development. | Plenary |
| 162. | Universal congress on the Panama Canal. | Plenary |
| 163. | Strengthening of the United Nations system. | Plenary |
| 164. | Normalization of the situation concerning South Africa. | Plenary |
| 165. | Implementation of the outcome of the Fourth World Conference on Women: Action for Equality, Development and Peace. | Plenary, 2nd, 3rd |
| 166. | Admission of the World Tourism Organization to membership in the United Nations Joint Staff Pension Fund. | 5th |
| 167. | Financing of the United Nations Mission in Bosnia and Herzegovina. | 5th |
| 168. | Financing of the United Nations Transitional Administration for Eastern Slavonia, Baranja and Western Sirmium. | 5th |
| 169. | Financing of the United Nations Preventive Deployment Force. | 5th |

# Security Council
## Agenda items considered during 1995

Item No.[12]

Title

1. The situation in the Republic of Bosnia and Herzegovina.
2. The situation in Georgia.
3. The situation in Liberia.
4. The situation concerning Western Sahara.
5. The situation prevailing in and adjacent to the United Nations Protected Areas in Croatia.
6. An agenda for peace.
7. Election of a member of the International Court of Justice.
8. The situation in Mozambique.
9. The situation in the Middle East.
10. The question concerning Haiti.
11. The situation in Burundi.
12. The situation in Croatia.
13. The situation in Angola.
14. The situation concerning Rwanda.
15. The situation in the occupied Arab territories.
16. Date of an election to fill a vacancy in the International Court of Justice.
17. The United Nations Protection Force (UNPROFOR).
18. The situation in Somalia.
19. The proposal by China, France, the Russian Federation, the United Kingdom of Great Britain and Northern Ireland and the United States of America on security assurances.
20. The situation in Tajikistan and along the Tajik-Afghan border.
21. The situation between Iraq and Kuwait.
22. The situation relating to Nagorny Karabakh.
23. Central America: efforts towards peace.
24. Commemoration of the end of the Second World War in Europe.
25. Navigation on the Danube river.
26. The situation in Cyprus.
27. Commemoration of the end of the Second World War in the Asia-Pacific region.
28. Follow-up to resolution 817(1993): Interim Accord between Greece and the former Yugoslav Republic of Macedonia.
29. The fiftieth anniversary of the United Nations.
30. The situation in the former Yugoslavia.
31. Consideration of the draft report of the Security Council to the General Assembly.
32. The situation in Sierra Leone.
33. The situation in the former Yugoslav Republic of Macedonia.
34. An agenda for peace: preventive diplomacy, peacemaking and peace-keeping.

---

[12]Numbers indicate the order in which items were taken up in 1995.

# Economic and Social Council

## Agenda of the organizational and resumed organizational sessions for 1995
### (1 and 7-10 February; 4 and 5 May and 1 and 6 June 1995)

*Item
No.*                                                                 *Title*

1. Election of the Bureau.
2. Adoption of the agenda and other organizational matters.
3. Basic programme of work of the Council.
4. Committee for Development Planning.
5. Transformation of the Committee on Food Aid Policies and Programmes of the World Food Programme into an Executive Board.
6. Full participation by the European Community in the Commission on Sustainable Development.
7. Elections, nominations and confirmations.
8. Agenda for development.
9. Joint and Co-sponsored United Nations Programme on Human Immunodeficiency Virus/Acquired Immunodeficiency Syndrome (HIV/AIDS).
10. Social, humanitarian and human rights questions: reports of subsidiary bodies, conferences and related questions: human rights questions.[13]

## Agenda of the substantive and resumed substantive sessions of 1995
### (26 June–28 July; 25 October, 2 November and 12 December 1995)

*Item
No.*                                                                 *Title*

1. Adoption of the agenda and other organizational matters.[14]

*High-level segment (4-6 July)*

2. Development of Africa, including the implementation of the United Nations New Agenda for the Development of Africa in the 1990s.

*Coordination segment*

3. Coordination of the policies and activities of the specialized agencies and other bodies of the United Nations system related to the following themes:
    (a) Coordinated follow-up by the United Nations system and implementation of the results of the major international conferences organized by the United Nations in the economic, social and related fields;[14]
    (b) Implementation of the agreed conclusions of the 1994 coordination segment of the Council relating to (i) science and technology for development and (ii) international cooperation within the United Nations system against the illicit production, sale, demand, traffic and distribution of narcotic drugs and psychotropic substances.

*Operational activities of the United Nations for international development cooperation segment*

4. Operational activities of the United Nations for international development cooperation:
    (a) United Nations Development Programme/United Nations Population Fund;
    (b) United Nations Children's Fund;
    (c) World Food Programme;
    (d) Economic and technical cooperation among developing countries.

*General segment*

5. Social, humanitarian and human rights questions: reports of subsidiary bodies, conferences and related questions:
    (a) Special economic, humanitarian and disaster relief assistance;
    (b) Implementation of the Programme of Action for the Third Decade to Combat Racism and Racial Discrimination;
    (c) Implementation of the Declaration on the Granting of Independence to Colonial Countries and Peoples by the specialized agencies and the international institutions associated with the United Nations;
    (d) Human rights questions;[14]
    (e) Advancement of women;[14]
    (f) Social development questions;[14]
    (g) Crime prevention and criminal justice;

---

[13]Item added on 4 May.
[14]Considered again at the resumed session.

    *(h)*  Narcotic drugs;

    *(i)*  United Nations High Commissioner for Refugees.

  6. Economic and environmental questions: reports of subsidiary bodies, conferences and related questions:

    *(a)*  Sustainable development;

    *(b)*  Trade and development;

    *(c)*  Food and agricultural development;

    *(d)*  Science and technology for development;

    *(e)*  Implementation of the Programme of Action of the International Conference on Population and Development;[14]

    *(f)*  International migration and development;

    *(g)*  Human settlements;

    *(h)*  Environment;

    *(i)*  Desertification and drought;

    *(j)*  Transport of dangerous goods;

    *(k)*  Women in development;

    *(l)*  Prevention and control of acquired immunodeficiency syndrome (AIDS);

    *(m)* International Drinking Water Supply and Sanitation Decade;

    *(n)*  International Decade for Natural Disaster Reduction;

    *(o)*  Statistics;

    *(p)*  Energy;

    *(q)*  Public administration and development.[14]

  7. Regional cooperation in the economic, social and related fields.

  8. Permanent sovereignty over national resources in the occupied Palestinian and other Arab territories.

  9. Coordination questions:

    *(a)*  Reports of the coordination bodies;

    *(b)*  International cooperation in the field of information systems;

    *(c)*  Multisectoral collaboration on tobacco or health;

    *(d)*  Preventive action and intensification of the struggle against malaria and diarrhoeal diseases, in particular cholera.

10. Non-governmental organizations.

11. United Nations University.

12. Programme and related questions in the economic, social and related fields:

    *(a)*  Proposed programme budget for the biennium 1996-1997;

    *(b)*  Calendar of conferences and meetings in the economic, social and related fields for the biennium 1996-1997.[14]

Appendix V

# United Nations information centres and services

ACCRA. United Nations Information Centre
Gämel Abdul Nassar/Liberia Roads
(P.O. Box 2339)
Accra, Ghana
*Serving:* Ghana, Sierra Leone

ADDIS ABABA. United Nations Information
Service, Economic Commission for Africa
Africa Hall
(P.O. Box 3001)
Addis Ababa, Ethiopia
*Serving:* Ethiopia

ALGIERS. United Nations Information Centre
19, Avenue Chahid El Ouali, Mustapha Sayed
(Boîte Postale 823, Alger-Gare, Algeria)
Algiers, Algeria
*Serving:* Algeria

AMMAN (relocated from Baghdad). United
Nations Information Service, Economic
and Social Commission for Western Asia
28 Abdul Hameed Sharaf Street
(P.O. Box 927115)
Amman, Jordan
*Serving:* Iraq, Jordan

ANKARA. United Nations Information Centre
197 Atatürk Bulvari
(P.K. 407)
Ankara, Turkey
*Serving:* Turkey

ANTANANARIVO. United Nations Informa-
tion Centre
22 Rue Rainitovo, Antasahavola
(Boîte Postale 1348)
Antananarivo, Madagascar
*Serving:* Madagascar

ASUNCION. United Nations Information
Centre
Estrella 345, Edificio City (3er piso)
(Casilla de Correo 1107)
Asunción, Paraguay
*Serving:* Paraguay

ATHENS. United Nations Information Centre
36 Amalia Avenue
GR-10558 Athens, Greece
*Serving:* Cyprus, Greece, Israel

BANGKOK. United Nations Information Serv-
ice, Economic and Social Commission for
Asia and the Pacific
United Nations Building
Rajdamnern Avenue
Bangkok 10200, Thailand
*Serving:* Cambodia, Hong Kong, Lao
People's Democratic Republic, Malaysia,
Singapore, Thailand, Viet Nam

BEIRUT. United Nations Information Centre
Apt. No. 1, Fakhoury Building
Montée Bain Militaire, Ardati Street
(P.O. Box 4656)
Beirut, Lebanon
*Serving:* Kuwait, Lebanon, Syrian Arab
Republic

BONN. United Nations Information Centre
Haus Carstanjen
Martin-Luther-King-Str. 8
(P.O. Box 260111, D-53153, Bonn)
D-53175, Bonn, Germany
*Serving:* Germany

BRAZZAVILLE. United Nations Information
Centre
Avenue Foch, Case Ortf 15
(P.O. Box 13210 or 1018)
Brazzaville, Congo
*Serving:* Congo

BRUSSELS. United Nations Information
Centre
Avenue de Broqueville 40
1200 Brussels, Belgium
*Serving:* Belgium, Luxembourg, Nether-
lands; liaison with EC

BUCHAREST. United Nations Information
Centre
16 Aurel Vlaicu
(P.O. Box 1-701)
Bucharest, Romania
*Serving:* Romania

BUENOS AIRES. United Nations Information Centre
Junín 1940 (1er piso)
1113 Buenos Aires, Argentina
*Serving:* Argentina, Uruguay

BUJUMBURA. United Nations Information
Centre
117 Avenue de la Révolution
(Boîte Postale 2160)
Bujumbura, Burundi
*Serving:* Burundi

CAIRO. United Nations Information Centre
1191 Corniche El Nile
World Trade Centre, P.O. Box 982
(Boîte Postale 262)
Cairo, Egypt
*Serving:* Egypt, Saudi Arabia

COLOMBO. United Nations Information
Centre
202-204 Bauddhaloka Mawatha
(P.O. Box 1505, Colombo)
Colombo 7, Sri Lanka
*Serving:* Sri Lanka

COPENHAGEN. United Nations Information
Centre
37 H.C. Andersens Boulevard
DK-1553 Copenhagen V, Denmark
*Serving:* Denmark, Finland, Iceland, Nor-
way, Sweden

DAKAR. United Nations Information Centre
12 Avenue Roume, Immeuble UNESCO
(Boîte Postale 154)
Dakar, Senegal
*Serving:* Cape Verde, Côte d'Ivoire,
Gambia, Guinea, Guinea-Bissau, Maurita-
nia, Senegal

DAR ES SALAAM. United Nations Informa-
tion Centre
Marogoro Road/Sokoine Drive
Old Boma Building (ground floor)
(P.O. Box 9224)
Dar es Salaam, United Republic of Tanzania
*Serving:* United Republic of Tanzania

DHAKA. United Nations Information Centre
House 60, Road 11A
Dhanmondi
(G.P.O. Box 3658, Dhaka 1000)
Dhaka, Bangladesh
*Serving:* Bangladesh

GENEVA. United Nations Information Service, United Nations Office at Geneva
Palais des Nations
1211 Geneva 10, Switzerland
*Serving:* Bulgaria, Switzerland

HARARE. United Nations Information Centre
Zimre Centre, 3rd floor
L. Takawira Street/Union Avenue
(P.O. Box 4408)
Harare, Zimbabwe
*Serving:* Zimbabwe

ISLAMABAD. United Nations Information
Centre
House No. 26
88th Street, G-6/3
(P.O. Box 1107)
Islamabad, Pakistan
*Serving:* Pakistan

JAKARTA. United Nations Information Centre
Gedung Dewan Pers (5th floor)
32-34 Jalan Kebon Sirih
Jakarta, Indonesia
*Serving:* Indonesia

KABUL. United Nations Information Centre
Shah Mahmoud Ghazi Watt
(P.O. Box 5)
Kabul, Afghanistan
*Serving:* Afghanistan

KATHMANDU. United Nations Information
Centre
Pulchowk, Patan
(P.O. Box 107, Pulchowk)
Kathmandu, Nepal
*Serving:* Nepal

KHARTOUM. United Nations Information
Centre
United Nations Compound
Gamma'a Avenue
(P.O. Box 913)
Khartoum, Sudan
*Serving:* Somalia, Sudan

KINSHASA. United Nations Information Centre
Bâtiment Deuxième République
Boulevard du 30 Juin
(Boîte Postale 7248)
Kinshasa, Zaire
*Serving:* Zaire

LAGOS. United Nations Information Centre
17 Kingsway Road, Ikoyi
(P.O. Box 1068)
Lagos, Nigeria
*Serving:* Nigeria

LA PAZ. United Nations Information Centre
Av. Mariscal
Santa Cruz No. 1350
(Apartado Postal 9072)
La Paz, Bolivia
*Serving:* Bolivia

LIMA. United Nations Information Centre
Lord Cochrane 130
San Isidro (L-27)
(P.O. Box 14-0199)
Lima, Peru
*Serving:* Peru

LISBON. United Nations Information Centre
Rua Latino Coelho, 1
Edificio Aviz, Bloco A-1, 10º
1000 Lisbon, Portugal
*Serving:* Portugal

LOME. United Nations Information Centre
107 Boulevard du 13 Janvier
(Boîte Postale 911)
Lomé, Togo
*Serving:* Benin, Togo

LONDON. United Nations Information Centre
Millbank Tower (21st floor)
21-24 Millbank
London SW1P 4QH, England
*Serving:* Ireland, United Kingdom

LUSAKA. United Nations Information Centre
P.O. Box 32905
Lusaka 10101, Zambia
*Serving:* Botswana, Malawi, Swaziland,
Zambia

MADRID. United Nations Information Centre
Avenida General Perón, 32-1
(P.O. Box 3400, 28080 Madrid)
28020 Madrid, Spain
*Serving:* Spain

MANAGUA. United Nations Information
Centre
Del Portón del Hospital Militar
1 c. al lago y 1 c. abajo
(Apartado Postal 3260)
Managua, Nicaragua
*Serving:* Nicaragua

MANAMA. United Nations Information
Centre
Villa 131, Road 2803
Segaya
(P.O. Box 26004, Manama)
Manama 328, Bahrain
*Serving:* Bahrain, Qatar, United Arab
Emirates

MANILA. United Nations Information
Centre
NEDA Building
106 Amorsolo Street
Legaspi Village, Makati
(P.O. Box 7285 ADC (DAPO), Pasay City)
Metro Manila, Philippines
*Serving:* Papua New Guinea, Philip-
pines, Solomon Islands

MASERU. United Nations Information
Centre
Letsie Road
Food Aid Compound
Behind Hotel Victoria
(P.O. Box 301, Maseru 100)
Maseru, Lesotho
*Serving:* Lesotho

MEXICO CITY. United Nations Information
Centre
Presidente Masaryk 29-6º piso
11570 México, D.F., Mexico
*Serving:* Cuba, Dominican Republic,
Mexico

MOSCOW. United Nations Information
Centre
4/16 Ulitsa Lunacharskogo
Moscow 121002, Russian Federation
*Serving:* Russian Federation

NAIROBI. United Nations Information
Centre
United Nations Office
Gigiri
(P.O. Box 30552)
Nairobi, Kenya
*Serving:* Kenya, Seychelles, Uganda

NEW DELHI. United Nations Information
Centre
55 Lodi Estate
New Delhi 110003, India
*Serving:* Bhutan, India

OUAGADOUGOU. United Nations Informa-
tion Centre
Avenue Georges Konseiga
Secteur No. 4
(Boîte Postale 135)
Ouagadougou 01, Burkina Faso
*Serving:* Burkina Faso, Chad, Mali,
Niger

PANAMA CITY. United Nations Informa-
tion Centre
Calle Gerardo Ortega y Ave. Samuel Lewis
Banco Central Hispano Building (1st floor)
(P.O. Box 6-9083 El Dorado)
Panama City, Panama
*Serving:* Panama

PARIS. United Nations Information Centre
1 Rue Miollis
75732, Paris Cedex 15, France
*Serving:* France

PORT OF SPAIN. United Nations Informa-
tion Centre
2nd floor, Bretton Hall
16 Victoria Avenue
(P.O. Box 130)
Port of Spain, Trinidad, W.I.
*Serving:* Antigua and Barbuda, Ba-
hamas, Barbados, Belize, Dominica,
Grenada, Guyana, Jamaica, Netherlands
Antilles, Saint Kitts and Nevis, Saint
Lucia, Saint Vincent and the Grenadines,
Suriname, Trinidad and Tobago

PRAGUE. United Nations Information
Centre
Panska 5
11000 Prague 1, Czech Republic
*Serving:* Czech Republic

PRETORIA. United Nations Information
Centre
Metro Park Building
351 Schoeman Street
P.O. Box 12677
Tramshed 0126
Pretoria, South Africa
*Serving:* South Africa

RABAT. United Nations Information Centre
Angle Charia Ibnouzaid
Et Zankat Roundanat, No. 6
(Boîte Postale 601)
Rabat, Morocco
*Serving:* Morocco

RIO DE JANEIRO. United Nations Informa-
tion Centre
Palácio Itamaraty
Av. Marechal Floriano 196
20080-002 Rio de Janeiro, RJ Brazil
*Serving:* Brazil

ROME. United Nations Information Centre
Palazzetto Venezia
Piazza San Marco 50
00186 Rome, Italy
*Serving:* Holy See, Italy, Malta, San
Marino

SANA'A. United Nations Information
Centre
Handhal Street, 4
Al-Boniya Area
(P.O. Box 237)
Sana'a, Yemen
*Serving:* Yemen

SAN SALVADOR. United Nations Information Centre
Edificio Escalón (2º piso)
Paseo General Escalón y 87 Avenida Norte
Colonia Escalón
(Apartado Postal 2157)
San Salvador, El Salvador

*Serving:* El Salvador

SANTA FE DE BOGOTA. United Nations Information Centre
Calle 100 No. 8A-55, Of. 815
(Apartado Aéreo 058964)
Santa Fé de Bogotá 2, Colombia

*Serving:* Colombia, Ecuador, Venezuela

SANTIAGO. United Nations Information Service, Economic Commission for Latin America and the Caribbean
Edificio Naciones Unidas
Avenida Dag Hammarskjöld
(Avenida Dag Hammarskjöld s/n, Casilla 179-D)
Santiago, Chile

*Serving:* Chile

SYDNEY. United Nations Information Centre
46-48 York Street, 5th floor
(G.P.O. Box 4045, Sydney, N.S.W. 2001)
Sydney, N.S.W. 2000, Australia

*Serving:* Australia, Fiji, Kiribati, Nauru, New Zealand, Samoa, Tonga, Tuvalu, Vanuatu

TEHRAN. United Nations Information Centre
185 Ghaem Magham Farahani Avenue
(P.O. Box 15875-4557, Tehran)
Tehran, 15868 Iran

*Serving:* Iran

TOKYO. United Nations Information Centre
UNU Building (8th floor)
53-70 Jingumae 5-chome, Shibuya-ku
Tokyo 150, Japan

*Serving:* Japan

TRIPOLI. United Nations Information Centre
Muzzafar Al Aftas Street
Hay El-Andalous (2)
(P.O. Box 286)
Tripoli, Libyan Arab Jamahiriya

*Serving:* Libyan Arab Jamahiriya

TUNIS. United Nations Information Centre
61 Boulevard Bab-Benat
(Boîte Postale 863)
Tunis, Tunisia

*Serving:* Tunisia

VIENNA. United Nations Information Service, United Nations Office at Vienna
Vienna International Centre
Wagramer Strasse 5
(P.O. Box 500, A-1400 Vienna)
A-1220 Vienna, Austria

*Serving:* Austria, Hungary, Slovakia

WARSAW. United Nations Information Centre
Al. Niepodleglosci 186
00-608 Warszawa
(UN Centre, P.O.Box 1, 02-514 Warsaw 12)
Poland

*Serving:* Poland

WASHINGTON, D.C. United Nations Information Centre
1775 K Street, N.W., Suite 400
Washington, D.C. 20006, United States

*Serving:* United States

WINDHOEK. United Nations Information Centre
372 Paratus Building
Independence Avenue
(Private Bag 13351)
Windhoek, Namibia

*Serving:* Namibia

YANGON. United Nations Information Centre
6 Natmauk Road
(P.O. Box 230)
Yangon, Myanmar

*Serving:* Myanmar

YAOUNDE. United Nations Information Centre
Immeuble Kamdem, Rue Joseph Clère
(Boîte Postale 836)
Yaoundé, Cameroon

*Serving:* Cameroon, Central African Republic, Gabon

Indexes

# Using the subject index

The index contains two types of entries:

**Subject terms**, including geographical names, are in most cases based on the subject descriptors used in the United Nations Bibliographical Information System (UNBIS), published in the *UNBIS Thesaurus* (United Nations Publication: Sales No. E.85.I.20). In order to minimize subentries, the index lists broad and narrow terms in their separate alphabetical positions; for example, "human rights", "racial discrimination" and "right to development".

Subjects pertaining to the United Nations or the system as a whole, such as "financing (UN)" and "staff (UN system)", are indexed separately, with cross-references under "United Nations".

**Names** of organizations and subsidiary bodies, conferences, United Nations Secretariat departments and offices, programmes, and special decades and observances are indexed under their key word, i.e.: Climate Change, Intergovernmental Panel on; Peace-keeping Operations, Department of; or Women, Cs. on the Status of.

Names of specialized agencies and of non–United Nations organizations are alphabetized under the first word of their title: World Meteorological Organization.

Bodies/subjects/topics are listed only when substantive information is given.

## Abbreviations

In addition to the abbreviations listed on p. xv,
the subject index uses the following:

| | |
|---|---|
| ASG | Assistant Secretary-General |
| CD | Conference on Disarmament |
| cf(s). | conference(s) |
| cl(s). | council(s) |
| cs(s). | commission(s) |
| ct(s). | committee(s) |
| mtg(s). | meeting(s) |
| sess. | session |
| spec. | special |
| USG | Under-Secretary-General |

# Subject index

Page numbers in bold-face type indicate resolutions and decisions water resources development, 999, 1502 (ECA/WMO)

women: advancement of, 1001 (ECA), 1180 (UNIFEM); & development, Regional Coordinating Ct., 1001-1002; see also gender issues

see also country names, organizational and regional entries

Africa, Addis Ababa Plan of Action for Statistical Development in (1992), 991 (ECA)

Africa, Cooperative Information Network Linking Scientists, Educators and Professionals in: proposed establishment of, 275 (UN Space Programme)

Africa, Economic Cs. for (ECA), 988-1002; administrative practices/programme, 983, 984 (OIOS/JIU); Cf. of Ministers (21st mtg.)/30th sess., 984-85; Executive Secretary (USG), 323; members, 1552; Multinational Programming and Operational Centres (MULPOCs), evaluation, 1003 (Technical Ct./CPC); Technical Preparatory Ct. of the Whole, 985; work programme (1996-1997), 1002, **1002-1003** (Technical Ct./ESC); see also country names, regional and subject entries

Africa, Horn of: critical situation in, 935; refugees, 1241 (UNHCR); see also country names

Africa, 2nd Industrial Development Decade for (1991-2000) (IDDA II): implementation, 992-94, **993-94,** 1512 (UNIDO)

Africa, 2nd Transport and Communications Decade in (1991-2000): programme (Phase II), implementation, 995, **995-96** (Ministers' Cf./SG/Technical Preparatory Ct./ESC)

Africa, Statistical Training Programme for, 991 (ECA)

Africa, Strengthening Gender and Development Capacity in, 890

Africa, UN Regional Centre for Peace and Disarmament in, 231, **231-32** (SG/GA); publication, 232

Africa, UN System-wide Spec. Initiative on: proposed launching, 415 (OAU/SG), 935 (ACC), 1512 (UNIDO)

Africa in the 1990s, UN New Agenda for the Development of (UNADAF): implementation, 415, **417** (OAU/GA), 931-35 (UNCTAD, 931-32; UNDP, 932; ESC, 932-33; SG, 933, GA, **933-35**) 979 (TDB), 985 (SG/ECA); Cairo Agenda for Action (OAU), 989; coordination/harmonization, 989, **994** (Inter-Agency Task Force/ACC/GA)

*Africa Recovery,* 270, **272** (DPI/GA)

African Air Transport Policy, New: implementation, 995

African Capacity-Building Initiative, 889, 932 (UNDP)

African Centre of Meteorological Applications for Development, 1000

African Cs. on Nuclear Energy, 203 (SG)

African Development, UN Trust Fund for, 990-91 (ECA Technical Ct.); pledging cf., 991

African Development Bank, 889, 968; cooperation with UNICEF, 1198

African Economic Community (OAU), (1991 Abuja Treaty): implementation, 415, **417** (OAU/GA), 985 (ECA), 990 (Technical Preparatory Ct./ECA Ministers Cf.), 998; ratifications, 990

African Economic Recovery and Development; UN Programme of Action for (1986-1990): System-wide Plan of Action, implementation, 985 (SG); African Institute for Economic Development and Planning, grant to, **1002** (ESC)

African Institute for the Prevention of Crime and the Treatment of Offenders, UN (UN-AFRI), 1160-61; Director, appointment, 1160; financial situation, 1160-61, **1161** (SG/GA); Governing Board, composition, 1000 (ESC)

African Ministers of Health: Bamako Initiative (1987), 1197

African Ministers of Industry, 12th mtg., 992, 993, **994** (GA)

African Ministers of Transport: 10th mtg., 995

African Ministers responsible for Human Settlements, 2nd Spec. Mtg. of: Declaration, 1001

African Nuclear-Weapon-Free Zone (Treaty of Pelindaba), 203-204, **204** (GA), 214, 1464 (IAEA); approval, OAU Council of Ministers/Assembly, 204; Group of Experts to Prepare Draft (OAU/UN), 203, **204**

African Population Cf. (1992): Dakar Ngor Declaration, 1001; implementation, 1001 (workshop)

African Regional Coordinating Ct. for the Integration of Women in Development, 16th mtg.: Action Platform, 1001-1002

Ageing, World Assembly on (1982): Action Plan targets, 1225

ageing persons, 1225-26; see also older persons

agenda for development, see under development and international economic cooperation

Agenda for Peace (Supplement), see Peace, Agenda for

agricultural commodities/products, 959 (ITC); agreements, 964; & GSP, 958 (Ad Hoc Group); see also names of individual commodities

agricultural development, 1508-1509 (IFAD); see also rural development; and regional and subject entries

agricultural machinery: ESCAP Regional Network, 1019

agriculture, 1000 (ECA), 1018-19 (ESCAP), 1035 (ECE), 1050-51 (ESCWA), 1516 (WIPO); information systems/publications, 1472 (FAO); meteorology applications, 1501 (WMO); see also food and agriculture; tropical agriculture

Agriculture, Ct. on (ECE): 46th sess., 1035; proposed joint body with FAO, 1035

Agriculture, Ct. on (WTO), 1516

agriculture and rural development & Agenda 21, 833-34; see also rural development

air navigation, 1491-93 (ICAO)

air pollution, 1037 (ECE), 493 (GEMS/AIR); conventions, 1036, 1037; monitoring long-range transmission, assessment, 993, 1037 (UNEP/WMO); see also names of conventions

Air Pollution, ECE Convention on Long-range Transboundary (1979)/protocols: Executive Body (13th sess.)/Working Groups, 1037; parties to, 1037

Air Pollution Monitoring Network, Background (BAPMoN), 932 (IAEA/WMO)

Albania: gender issues, 892 (UNDP); human rights situation in, 700 (CERD), 712 (SG)

Algeria: & Western Sahara, 251, 253, 256, 257 (SC Mission visit)

American Convention on Human Rights in the Area of Economic, Social and Cultural Rights/Additional Protocol (San Salvador Protocol): & El Salvador, 426

American Samoa, 261, **263** (Colonial Countries Ct./GA)

Americas, 1198-99 (UNICEF); drug abuse control, 1275 (INCB); refugee assistance, 1244-45 (UNHCR); telecommunications, 1497 (ITU); see also Andean region; and under country, organizational and regional entries

Americas, 2nd Space Cf. of the (1993): Santiago Declaration, 275; 3rd cf. (1996), **284** (GA)

Amnesty International, 379 (Rwanda)

Andean region: Cotopaxi ground receiving station (Ecuador), 275

Angola, situation in

displaced persons/refugees, 330, 332, 333 (SG/UNHCR/SC)

economic/social conditions, rehabilitation, 330, 332 (SG); Round-Table Cf., 332, 333 (SG/SC), 904-906, **906** (SG/GA)

humanitarian assistance, **322**, 323 (SC/SG), 325-26, 326-27 (SG/SC), Consolidated Appeal, 904-905, **905-906** (SG/GA); distribution facilitation, 328 (SC); see also mine clearance below

human rights: unit in UNAVEM, **322** (SC), 325; strengthening, 330, **331** (SG/SC); violations, 329, 332 (SG/Joint Cs.), 333 (SC)

refugees, 1241 (UNHCR)

Angola: Lusaka Protocol (1994), implementation, 319-20

cease-fire, status, 321, 323, 325 (SG), 326 (SC); decline in violations, 331-32 (SG)

demobilization/armed forces integration, 321 (UNAVEM), 325, 327 (SG/Jt. Cs.), 328 (Jt. Cs./SG)

Joint Cs., principal body for, 321, 326 (SC); extraordinary sess., 323; 12th regular sess., 325; spec. mtg., 328 (SG)

mine clearance, 320, **322** (SC), 323-24 (SG), 326, 327, 329 (SC/SG), 905 (SG); casualties, 324 (SC); renewed laying of mines, alleged, 329, **331**, 332 (SG/SC), 333 (SC)

Peace Accords (Acordos de Paz), **181** (GA), 320, **322** (UNAVEM II/SC)

SG Spec. Adviser, visit to Angola, 324-25

SG visit to, 329

Angola Verification Missions, UN (UNAVEM)

UNAVEM II (1991), 320; mandate/strength, 302; termination, 302, 320

UNAVEM III: commanders/Deputy, 321, 335, 1549, 1560; composition, 321, 336; deployment, conditions for, 320-22 (communications, 320, SG, 320-21; SC, **321-22**), 324, (SG/SC), 329 (SG); expan-

project services, see UN Office of Project Services

technical cooperation, 887-88 (UNDP Administrator)

see also country, organizational and subject entries

Development, Right to: Declaration on the (1986): implementation, 757-60 (Human Rights Cs., 757-58; ESC, **758**; Working Group,`758-59; SCPDPM/SG, 759; GA, **759-60**)

development, sustainable: Agenda 21 implementation

consumption, 838 (SG/Sustainable Development Cs./ACC); & changing production patterns, 838-39 (SG/Cs.)

cross-sectoral activities, 838 (SG/Cs.)

high-level ministerial mtg., 837 (Cs.)

indicators of, workshop on decision-making, 838

overall review/appraisal, spec. GA sess. (proposed), 840, **840-41** (SG/GA)

& space technology contributions to, 342

see also subject entries

Development Activities, UN Pledging Cf. for, 887

Development and Communications, Regional Cf. on Space Technology for Sustainable, 276

development and international economic cooperation, 829-78

agenda for, 830, **831** (Ad Hoc Working Group/SG/GA); high-level dialogue, proposed, 831, **831** (SG/GA); publication (DPI), update, 270

& business, 834, **834-35** (SG/GA); role of enterprises, 832 (UN Panel), 835-36 (Ad Hoc Working Group); & corrupt practices, draft agreement on illicit payments, **835** (GA/CTC)

financing sources, 973, **973-74**, (SG/GA); & impact of debt, 973 (SG)

global negotiations, deferred, **830** (GA)

Opportunity and Participation, UN Panel on, 831-32, **832** (SG/GA)

planning, 860-62 (CDP/ESC)

project services (UNDP), 900-901; see UN Office for Project Services

& public administration, 861 (inter-agency mtg./Expert Mtg.); consideration deferred, **861** (ESC)

regional cooperation, 982-84; see also names of regional organizations

strengthening through partnership, 830-31, **831** (SG/GA)

& UN 50th anniversary, **290-91** (GA), 830 (SG)

UN programmes, 899-901

see also disarmament; environment; population; rural development; social development; trade; women in development

*Development Business*, 270 (DPI/World Bank)

*Development Forum*: proposed resumption, 270, **272** (DPI/GA)

Development Fund, UN Capital (UNCDF), 903; future direction, policy paper, 903; expenditures, contributions, 903; Executive Board/Managing Director, 1542

Development Information Workshop, 272 (JUNIC)

Development Institute, Economic (World Bank), see Economic Development Institute

Development Planning, Ct. for (CDP), **860-61**, 861 (ESC/SG); members/officers, 1553

Development Programme, UN (UNDP), 887-99

Administrator/Associate/Assistants, 1560

audit reports 1992-1993: follow-up, 898-99 (Auditors Board/UNDP Administrator)

budgets: 1994-1995, revised, 897 (ACABQ/Board); 1996-1997 estimates, 897-98 (Board); presentations, harmonization of, 898

field programmes, expenditures, 888

Executive Board (UNDP/UNFPA): field visits, 889; sess./report, 888 (ESC)

financial situation: 887-88; annual review, 896-97 (Administrator/Board)

funds administered by, 887

Private Sector Development Programme, 893-94

programme planning/management, 894; evaluation, 896 (Administrator); 5th cycle (1992-1996), 887, 894-95; Inter-Agency Procurement Services Office (IAPSO)/Working Group, 899; national execution, 896 (SG/JIU/ACC/GA); procurement, 899 (UNDP/IAPSO); successor arrangements, 895-96 (Administrator/Board)

Regional Bureaux, Administrators (Directors), 1560

technical cooperation, 887-94

Development Support and Management Services, Department for (DDSMS), 899; USG, 1559

*Development Update*: bimonthly newsletter, 270

diabetes, survey, 1478 (WHO)

diarrhoeal diseases, 1254, **1254** (SG/ESC), 1480 (WHO)

diphtheria, 1478 (WHO)

diplomacy: preventive, 176 (SG)

diplomatic relations: diplomatic courier & bag, draft articles/protocols, 1331-32 (GA); protection of diplomats, 1331 (SG); conventions/protocols, States parties, 1331; see also Consular Relations, Vienna Convention on; Crimes against Internationally Protected Persons, Convention on the Prevention and Punishment of; host country relations (UN/United States); hostage-taking/abductions

Diplomatic Relations, Vienna Convention on (1961)/Optional Protocols: accessions/States parties, 1331

Disability and Handicap Statistics, Expert Group Mtg. on the Development of Impairment: review, 1994 recommendations, 1296 (Statistical Cs.)

disabled persons, 1021 (ESCAP), 1256-58

human rights of, 781-82 (Human Rights Cs./ESC/SCPDPM)

International Day of (3 Dec.), 1994 observances, 1258 (SG)

opportunities for, Equalization Rules, 1256-57, **1257-58** (SG/Social Development Cs./Spec. Rapporteur/GA); & World Summit, 1256

statistics on, Expert Group Mtg. (1994), 1296

Disabled Persons, UN Decade of (1982-1992): World Action Programme, Long-term Strategy to Implement, 1256, **1258** (SG/GA); UN Voluntary Fund on Disability, 1258 (SG); see also Asian and Pacific Decade of

Disappearance, 1992 Declaration on the Protection of All Persons from Enforced, 755 (Working Group)

disappearance of persons, 755 (Working Group); cases worldwide, 755; see also Yugoslavia, territory of the former

Disappearances, Working Group on Enforced or Involuntary, 687, 742; mandate extended, 755 (Human Rights Cs./ESC)

disarmament, 184-235

agreements: compliance, 229 (GA); & environmental norms in drafting of, **228-29** (GA); multilateral, parties to, 188 (list)

arms transfers, international, 185, **186**, 218-19, **219-20** (DC Working Group/SG/GA); small arms, 217, **217-18** (SG/GA); assistance in curbing, **220** (GA)

conventional weapons: transparency in arms, 212, **213** (CD/Ad Hoc Ct./GA); UN Register, 212-13, **213-14** (SG/Advisory Board/GA); see also military budgets, below

& development, 226, **226** (SG/GA)

education/information, 235 (SG/GA)

fellowships/training/advisory services, UN programme, 234, **234-35** (GA)

micro-disarmament, 217 (SG)

military budgets: transparency of, 214 (SG/GA); world expenditures (1988-1994), decline in, 955 (UNCTAD)

regional approaches to, 214, **215-16**, **216** (GA); UN Centres for, 230-33; see also nuclear-weapon-free zones and under regional entries

science/technology, applications, 226-27, **227** (SG/GA); & international security, 227, **227-28** (SG/GA)

spec. session: 4th proposed, 1997, 184, **185** (GA); Preparatory Ct., establishment of, **185**

studies/research, 233, **233-34** (Advisory Board/UNIDIR/GA)

transition to: structural adjustment policy for, 955-56 (Ad Hoc Working Group)

Third Decade on: Review of the Declaration of the 1990s as the, 184 (DC), 185-86, **186** (DC Working Group/GA)

& verification, 1990 study on role of, 233, **233-34** (SG/GA)

see also peace and security, international; zones of peace

nuclear energy: environmental impact, 1462; reassessment of nuclear test sites, 1462; IAEA report (1994), 1062, **1062-63**, (SG/IAEA DG/GA); inspections, 1061; see also food and agriculture; health; radioactive waste management

Nuclear Event Scale, International, 1461

Nuclear Explosions for Peaceful Purposes, Treaty on Underground (bilateral): in force (1990), 194

Nuclear Information System, International (INIS), 1464 (IAEA)

nuclear power, 1461-62 (IAEA)
fuel cycle, 1462 (IAEA)
generating capacity, world, 1061 (IAEA)
information, 1464
irradiated fuel, safe carriage of, 1086 (Joint IAEA/IMO/UNEP Working Group); 1993 Code for the, 1086
power reactors, Information System (PRIS), 1462 (IAEA)
safeguards agreements/inspections (IAEA), 1461, 1463-64 ·
safety, 277 (IAEA), 1461 (IAEA); Convention, 1461, 1462; review missions, 1461
see also outer space: nuclear power sources in; space debris

Nuclear Safety, Convention on (1994), **1063** (GA), 1461, 1462; accessions/ratifications, 1461

Nuclear Test Ban, Ad Hoc Ct. on (CD), 195, **196** (GA); Working Group I (verification), Working Group 2 (legal/constitutional), 195-96

nuclear-weapon-free zones, 203-208; see also Africa, denuclearization; Indian Ocean; Latin America; Middle East; outer space; seabed; South Asia, South Atlantic; South-East Asia; South Pacific; zones of peace

nuclear-weapon tests
comprehensive treaty negotiations, 194-95, **196** (CD/Ad Hoc Ct. Working Groups/GA)
detonations (1994, 1995), 195 (SG), 196, **196-97** (SG/GA); unilateral moratoria, 195, **197** (GA)
verification issues: International Monitoring System (IMS), 194-95 (Expert Group), 195 (intersessional mtgs.); seismic IMS, Technical Test, 195 (Scientific Expert Group)
see also seismic events; New Zealand; and names of treaties

Nuclear Weapon Tests, Treaty on Limitation of Underground (bilateral): in force (1990), 194; accessions, **200, 201** (GA)

Nuclear Weapon Tests in the Atmosphere, in Outer Space and Under Water, Treaty Banning (1963) (partial test-ban Treaty), 194, **197** (GA); Amendment of, **197** (Cf. on/GA); parties to, 188

nuclear weapons, non-proliferation of
draft convention prohibiting use of, **208-209** (GA)
mass destruction weapons & delivery vehicles, 210 (GA)
& non-nuclear-weapon States, security of: assurances, unilateral declarations, 191-92, **192** (communica-

tions/SC); conclusion of effective arrangements, 192-93, **193-94** (CD/GA)
renunciation of use, **202** (GA)
see also bacterial (biological) weapons; chemical weapons; radiological weapons

Nuclear Weapons, Treaty on the Non-Proliferation of (NPT) (1968)
accessions, 189, **191** (GA); parties to, 188, 189
IAEA safeguards agreements under, 190
Review and Extension Cf. of Parties to: Final Document, 189, **189, 190** (SG/GA); Cf. organization/participants, 189; indefinite extension of NPT, 189; Preparatory Ct., final sess., 189

Nuclear Weapons in Latin America and the Caribbean, Treaty for the Prohibition of (Treaty of Tlatelolco, 1967), see Latin America and the Caribbean, Treaty for the Prohibition of Nuclear Weapons in (1967 Treaty of Tlatelolco)

nutrition: 1265 (ACC), 1265-66 (UNU), 1463 (IAEA), 1471 (ILO), 1482 (World Bank); Food Data Network, 1266 (UNU); global trends, INTERHEALTH project, 1478 (WHO); publications, 1265, 1266 (ACC/UNU); research/training, 1265 (ACC); & school children, proposed working group, 1265 (ACC), 1266 (UNU); vitamin/mineral deficiencies, 1265 (UNU), 1478 (WHO)

Nutrition, ACC Subct. on: 22nd sess., 1265

Nutrition, International Cf. on (1992): follow-up, 1265

Nutritional Sciences, International Union of (IUNS), 1265-66

Occupational Health, Joint ILO/WHO Ct. on: 12th sess., 1467

Occupational Safety and Health, 14th World Congress (1996): preparations, 1467 (ILO); see also working conditions

ocean affairs, 1081; Coral Reef, Monitoring Network, 1474; Year of the Ocean (1998), preparations, 1474 (OIC); see also law of the sea; marine affairs; sea; seabed

Ocean Affairs and the Law of the Sea, Division for, see Law of the Sea, Division for Ocean Affairs and the

Ocean Observing System, Global, 1086

Oceania: drug situation, 1278-79 (INCB); UNHCR assistance, 1245

Oceanographic Cs., Intergovernmental (IOC), 1077 (UNEP); 18th sess., 1474 (UNESCO)

older persons, economic/social/cultural rights of, 698; International Day of, **1226** (GA); UN Principles for (1991), 1225, **1226** (GA); see also under ageing

Older Persons, International Year of: towards a society for all ages (1999), 1225, **1225-26** (SG/CSD/ESC/GA)

Olympics Ct., International: & drug abuse prevention, 1286

Open Skies, Treaty on (1992): parties to, 188

operation safety review team, see under nuclear power: safety

opium: cultivation/trafficking, 1275, 1276, 1277 (INCB/UNDCP)

Organisation for Economic Cooperation and Development (OECD), see Economic Cooperation and Development, Organisation for (OECD)

Organization of African Unity: cooperation with UN, 180-81, 414-16, **416-18** (SG/GA), 1241, 1242, **1243** (UNHCR/GA), 1442
Assembly of Heads of State & Government: 31st sess., **416** (GA), 989
Conflict Prevention, Management and Resolution, Mechanism for: Central Organ of, **417**; & SG mtg. with, 415; statement on Burundi, 344; UN liaison officer, proposed, 181 (SG)
Cl. of Ministers: 17th extraordinary sess., 989 (Agenda for Action); 62nd ordinary sess., **416** (GA)
electoral unit, 415
& UN secretariats, 10th annual mtg., 415-16, **417** (GA)
& Western Sahara, 250, 252, 255, **258**
see also country names and regional entries

Organization of American States (OAS): drug law enforcement agreement, 1281; & Haiti Mission, 455-56

Organization of the Islamic Cf.: & Afghanistan, **472** (GA); cooperation with UN, 1441, **1441-42** (SG/GA); & Jammu-Kashmir, 466

Organization of Petroleum Exporting Countries (OPEC), see Petroleum Exporting Countries, Organization of (OPEC)

outer space, peaceful uses of, 273-85
applications, UN programme: implementation, 274 (COSPAR/ICSU/IAF), 275-76, **283** (GA/Expert)
cfs. on: 2nd (1982), 274-75; see below under Outer Space Cfs.
coordination, 279, **284** (COPUOS/GA); regional mechanisms, 275
definition/delimitation, 281, **282** (COPUOS/GA); see also geostationary orbit
environmental aspects, 274, 279, **283, 284** (COPUOS/GA)
exploration, 281, **282** (COPUOS/GA)
fellowship programme, 275, **283** (COPUOS/GA)
information services/system, strengthening, 275, **283**
legal aspects, 280-82, **282-83** (COPUOS/GA)
nuclear power sources in, 277, 280-81, **282, 284** (COPUOS/GA)
science/technology aspects, 274-80, **283-84** (COPUOS/GA); regional centres, 275-76, **284** (GA)
technology, spin-off benefits, 279, **284** (COPUOS/GA)
telecommunications, ITU report, 279 (COPUOS)
treaties/conventions on, 281, **282**, 285 (GA); States parties, 188
see also arms race; astronomy; developing countries; information; life sciences; geostationary orbit; re-

Refugees, Centre for Documentation on, 1236

Refugees, Convention relating to Status of (1951)/Protocol, (1967): ratifications/accessions, 751, **752** (SG/GA), 753, **1229** (GA)

Refugees, Group of Governmental Experts on International Cooperation to Avert New Flows of: 1986 recommendations, 751-753 (SG/GA)

Refugees, Office of the UN High Commissioner for (UNHCR), 1227; High Commissioner, 1541, 1560; Assistant High Commissioner (ASG), 1231, 1541, 1560

Administrative and Financial Matters, Subct. on, 1232; mtgs., 1234; working methods, 1234

Executive Ct.: 46th sess., 1227-28

financial situation: accounts, 1232-33, **1233-34** (Board of Auditors/ACABQ/GA); budget, 1231; budget structure, 1232 (Executive Ct.)

Russian as official language, **1230**, 1234 (GA/Executive Ct.)

& UN Human Rights Commissioner, **752** (GA)

Refugees in the Near East, UN Relief and Works Agency for Palestine, see Palestine Refugees in the Near East, UN Relief and Works Agency for (UNRWA)

regional css: economic/social cooperation, 982-84 (Executive Secretaries mtg., 982-83; SG, 983; ESC, 984); Executive Secretaries, 1552, 1559; programme/administration, 983-84, 984 (OIOS/JIU); regional institutions, funding of, 984 (SG); System of National Accounts (1993), implementation, 1023, 1293; surveys, summaries of, 984 (ESC); see also names of regional css.

Religion or Belief, 1981 Declaration on the Elimination of All Forms of Intolerance and of Discrimination Based on: implementation, 731, **733** (SG/Human Rights Cs./GA)

religious intolerance, 731-33 (SG, 731; Spec. Rapporteur, 731, 731-32; Human Rights Cs., 731; GA, **732-33**); Spec. Rapporteur mandate extended, 731 (Human Rights Cs./ESC); reports, 731, 731-32; visits, 731, 732

remote sensing, 276-77, **283** (CO-PUOS/GA); training courses, 276 (UN Programme); see also regional entries

Remote Sensing, International Society for Photogrammetry and, 276

Republic of Korea: & World Bank & IDA, 1481; see also Korean question

restrictive business practices, 961-62; bibliography/database, feasibility, 961; handbook, preparations, 961-62; proposed model law on, 962; see also international trade: competition law/policy

Restrictive Business Practices, Intergovernmental Group of Experts on (UNCTAD): 14th sess., 961, 1543; name change, 962; officers, 1543

Restrictive Business Practices, 3rd UN Cf. to Review All Aspects of the Set of Multilaterally Agreed Equitable Principles and Rules for the Control of, 961-62; preparations, 961 (Intergovernmental Experts);

regional activities, 962; resolution, 962; see also international trade

right to development, see development, right to

rights of the child, see Child, Convention on the Rights of the

roads/highways, 1016 (ESCAP); conventions/regulations, 1032 (ECE); safety, 1033 (ECE); traffic, 1032; wheeled vehicles, regulations, 1032, 1332, 1333; see also Trans-African Highway Bureau; Trans-European North-South Motorway; transport

Romania: bank credits, 967; human rights situation, 715-16

Rubber Agreement, International Natural (1987), 964; 1995 agreement, 964, 1332

Rubber, UN Cf. on Natural, 964

rules of origin, see international trade: preferences

Rules of Origin, Intergovernmental Group of Experts on: mtg., 958

rural development, 832-34 (SG/Sustainable Development Cs./ACC/CCPOQ), 833, 834, 1511 (UNIDO); & Agenda 21, 833, 834; industrial contribution to, 834 (Working Group); poverty alleviation, 1018 (ESCAP); see also agricultural development; land management; women, status of

Rural Development, ACC Subct. on: mtg., 834

Rural Women, Summit on the Economic Advancement of: 1992 Geneva Declaration, **1185** (GA)

Russian Federation: economic trends, 858, 859; human resources, 1513 (UNIDO); oil spill, IBRD emergency aid, 1481; trade growth, 950 (*Trade and Development Report*); UNICEF programmes, 1199; World Bank loan, 1481; see also Afghanistan; Chechnya; Commonwealth of Independent States; Tajikistan; and under nuclear weapons

Rwanda

arms embargo, 378-83 (SC, 378-79, **379**; communications, 379, 381; Sanctions Ct., 381), 787, **789** (SC/GA); Inquiry Cs., **380**, **382** (SC), **789** (GA)

human rights situation, 383-84, 385, 386-88 (UN Field Operation/SG/SC), 700 (CERD), 786-90 (Human Rights Cs./Spec. Rapporteur/SCPDPM; GA, **787-90**); 1994 genocide, 386, 786-87, **788-89** (Spec. Rapporteur/SCPDPM/GA), **910** (GA); technical assistance/advisory services, 786 (Human Rights Cs./ESC)

mine clearance programme, 371 (SC mission), 385, 388 (SC/SG)

prisoners/judicial systems, 388, 389, 390 (SG/SC), 391 (SG); epidemics in, 787, **789** (SCPDPM/GA), **910** (GA)

reconciliation/rehabilitation, 371 (SC Mission), 384 (SG), 388-89, 390, 391 (SG), **909-11** (SG/GA); 1102 (UNFPA); round-table cf., 909

refugees/returnees/displaced persons, see separate entry

Rwanda: International Cs. of Inquiry, 375-76; establishment/terms of reference, 374, **380** (GA), 381-82, **382-83** (SG/SC); composition, 383; financing, **382** (SC)

Rwanda, International Tribunal for, 786 (Human Rights Cs./SC), 787, **789** (SCPDPM/GA), 1320-23 (SG, 1320-21; SC, **209-210**); communication, 1323); financing, 1323-25 (SG/ACABQ, 1323, 1325; GA, **1324-25**); headquarters organization, 1322-23 (SG); inaugural sess., 1322

Rwanda: refugees/displaced persons

assistance: Bujumbura Cf. (UNHCR/OAU), 372, 373, 375 (SG/SC), 378 (SG), 390, **393** (SC), **910**, 911 (GA), 1242, **1243** (GA); Cairo Summit Declaration, 378 (SG), 383, 384, **393** (SG/SC), **789** (GA), **910-11** (GA); inter-agency appeal/round-table cf., 909, 911

camps, security in, 371-74 (SG, 371-72, 373; SC, 372-73; communications, 372, 374), 386

Kibeho mass killings, 374-75, 375-76, 376 (SC/Inquiry Cs./SG), 786, **789** (Spec. Rapporteur/GA)

& neighbouring States, 373-74, 374 (SG/communication), 376-78 (SG, 376-77; SC, 377; communications, 377-78), 911 (GA); Tripartite agreements/mtgs., 388-89, 390 (SG/SC), 393-94 (SG)

repatriation/resettlement issues, 370 (SC Mission), 787, **789**; assistance, 909, **910** (SG/GA); Joint Cs. for, 909 (SG)

see also Burundi

Rwanda, UN Assistance Mission for (UN-AMIR), 301, 303 (status), 384-93 (SG, 384-86, 388-90, 391-92; SC, **386-88**, 390-91, **392-93**; GA, 398); Commander, 324, 1549; Executive Secretary, 1549; financing, 394, **394** (SG/GA), **394-96** (GA), **396-97** (SG/GA); killing/kidnapping of personnel, 786, **788** (Human Rights Cs./GA); mandate extensions/adjustments, **392**; & UNV support, 901; USG/SG Spec. Representative, 1549, 1560

Sahel, see also Sudano-Sahelian region

Sahel, Permanent Inter-State Ct. on Drought Control in the, 944

Sahelo-Saharan Subregion, Advisory Mission on the Control and Collection of Light Weapons in the: country visits, 214

St. Helena, 261, **264-65** (UNDP/GA); IPF (1992-1996), 239

sanitation, see under water supply

satellites: in earth observation, 276 (UN Space Applications Programme); weather observation activities, 1499 (WMO); see also communication satellites; geostationary orbit; remote sensing

schistosomiasis: control of, 1480 (WHO)

scholarships, see country, regional and subject entries

science, see life sciences; natural sciences; physical sciences; social sciences; and the following entries

science and technology for development, 849-57 (Cs., 849-50; GA, **850-52**; ESC, **852-53**; SG, 853-54)
  coordination, 857 (SG)
  endogenous capacity-building for, **852**, 853-54, **855** (ESC/SG/GA)
  energy, clean/safe systems, **852**
  financial resources, coalition for, **852**, 854-55, **856** (ESC/SG/GA); see also Science and Technology for Development, UN Fund for
  & gender issues, 850, **850-51** (Advisory Board/ESC); Declaration of Intent, **852** (ESC)
  information technology, 849, **851-52**, **856** (Cs./ESC/GA); global network, **851-52** (ESC)
  & military capacities, conversion to civilian use, **852** (ESC)
  & sustainable development, **852**, 853-54 (GA/Sustainable Development Cs.)
  UN Cf. on (1979): 20th anniversary, plans for, **852**, **856** (ESC/GA)
  see also developing countries; development; human rights; technology transfer; and regional entries
Science and Technology for Development, Cs. on: 2nd sess., 849-50, **850-52** (ESC), 1551 (members); working methods/funding, **852-53**, 853 (ESC); 3rd sess. (1997): provisional agenda/documentation, 849, 853 (ESC); terms of members, 850, 853 (ESC); & UNCTAD intergovernmental machinery, 979
Science and Technology for Development, Consultative Mtg. on a Coalition of Resources for (1994): follow-up, **852**, 854-55, **856** (ESC/SG/GA)
Science and Technology for Development, UN Fund for (UNFSTD): core contributions/project funding (1993-1995), 854 (SG); projects, 854 (SG)
sea: carriage of hazardous substances by, draft convention, 1503 (IMO); collisions at, amendments to 1972 Convention on, 1504 (IMO); desalinization, 1461 (IAEA); safety of life/property at, 1503-1504 (IMO); see also law of the sea; marine affairs; ocean affairs; regional seas
Sea, International Convention for the Safety of Life at (1974 SOLAS Convention): amendments, 1503; changes, 1504 (IMO)
sea, law of the, see law of the sea
Sea, UN Convention on the Carriage of Goods by Sea (1978, Hamburg Rules), 1364 (UNCITRAL)
Sea, UN Convention on the Law of the, see Law of the Sea, UN Convention on the
seabed: mining, training programme, 1336; pioneer investors, obligations, 1336
Sea-Bed and the Ocean Floor and in the Subsoil Thereof, Treaty on the Prohibition of the Emplacement of Nuclear Weapons and Other Weapons of Mass Destruction on the (1971): compliance/verification, 227 (SG); parties to, 188
Seabed Authority, International: Assembly, administrative expenses, draft budget, 1336, **1338** (GA); financing, 1337 (SG); headquarters agreement, 1336 (ad hoc working group); Kingston Office, continuation as interim secretariat, 1336, **1338** (GA); organization/Cl., 1336; participa-

tion of Yugoslav Federal Republic, 1336, 1337 (Assembly/Credentials Ct.); Preparatory Cs., 1336 (final report), 1559
Seafarers, International Convention on Standards of Training Certification and Watchkeeping for (1978): IMO amendment, 1504
Second World War, World Year of Peoples' Commemoration of the Victims of the (1995): proclamation, 292 (communications); see also World War, Second
Secretariat (UN): composition/principal members, 1559-61; oversight services, 1376-78 (OIOS); procurement reform, 1457-58 (GA/SG/ACABQ); restructuring, 1373-74 (SG); total staff/breakdown, 1412; see also administrative and management questions; pensions (UN system); regional css.; staff (UN/UN system); and names of departments and offices under key word
Secretary-General (UN): Agenda for Peace (1992), supplement to, 175-77; annual report, 1-137; Executive Office, 1559; informal groups & peace-keeping mandates, 176; Spokesman for, Office of, 269; see also under multilateral treaties; subject entries
Security and Cooperation in Europe, Organization for (OSCE), see Europe, Organization for Security and Cooperation in
Security Cl., 1429-30, 1548-49
  agenda, 1429, 1569
  cts., (Military Staff/Standing), 1548
  documentation, 1429
  & 50th anniversary: Foreign Ministers' statement, 175, 288; see also under United Nations: 50th anniversary
  members (permanent/non-permanent), 1548
  membership/related matters, 289 (GA/Working Group/SC), 1371-72, 1372, 1430 (Working Group/GA)
  peace-keeping operations/special missions, 1548-49
  presidents/terms, 1548
  *Repertoire of Practice of the*: status, **1343** (GA)
  working methods/procedures, 1429-30
Seismic Events, Ad Hoc Group of Experts to Consider International Cooperative Measures to Detect and Identify, 195
seismic events: experimental monitoring system (Group of Scientific Experts Technical Test Three (GSETT-3)), 195; network, primary and auxiliary stations (International Data Centre), 195
self-determination, right to, 735, **735** (Human Rights Cs./SG/GA) see also colonial countries; mercenaries; Middle East; non-self-governing territories; Palestinians; Western Sahara
Senegal: accountancy education project, 976 (Ad Hoc Expert Group); see also Guinea-Bissau
shelter: delivery, 1110; strategies, 1111 (UNCHS Director)
Shelter to the Year 2000, Global Strategy for (1988): implementation, 1996-1997 Action Plan/timetable, 1108, **1109**, 1108-1109 (Cs./ESC/GA); mid-term review, 1108-1109;

shipping: services, 976 (Standing Ct./UNCTAD); see also maritime affairs; multimodal transport; ports
Shipping, Standing Ct. on Developing Services Sectors: Fostering Competitive Services in Developing Countries: 3rd sess., 976; members, 1544
ships: Dangerous Goods Code (1994), 1503; roll on/roll off safety, 1504 (IMO); see also sea: safety of life/property at
Ships, International Convention for Prevention of Pollution from (1973), Protocol, (1978): amendments, 1503
Ships, International Convention for the Unification of Certain Rules relating to the Arrest of Sea-going (1952): proposed review, UNCTAD/IMO draft articles, 976 (Intergovernmental Expert Group); Sessional Group established, 976
Sierra Leone: civil conflict in, 397-99, 399 (SG/SC); economic/humanitarian situation, 398; human settlements, 1110 (ECA/UNCHS); humanitarian assistance, 911; inter-agency appeal, 398, 911; political/military situation, 397-98; refugees/displaced persons, 397; SG Spec. Envoy, appointment, 397
slavery/slavery-like practices, 765-66; draft action programme, 766 (SCPDPM); conventions, implementation, 765 (Human Rights Cs.); fund for victims of, 766; in wartime, sexual exploitation, 766 (Spec. Rapporteur); see also under children; prostitution; women, status of: traffic in
Slavery, International Day for the Abolition of, 1189, **1191**
Slavery, UN Voluntary Trust Fund on Contemporary Forms of: financial situation & activities, 766 (Human Rights Cs./SCPDPM); Board of Trustees, 766, 1547 (members)
Slavery, Working Group on Contemporary Forms of (SCPDPM): & sale of children, 708 (SG), 765, **1190** (GA)
Slovenia: humanitarian assistance, 924; see also Yugoslavia, territory of the former
small/medium-scale enterprises, see under industrial development
social defence, see entries under crime prevention and criminal justice
social development, 1000 (ECA), 1020-21 (ESCAP), 1043-44 (ECLAC), 1055 (ESCWA), 1113-30, 1482 (World Bank); social welfare issues, 1126 (Social Development Cs./SG); statistical implications, 1298; world situation, 1125-26 (SG/ESC/GA); see also relevant subject entries
Social Development, Cs. for: 34th sess., **1121**, 1130 (ESC); members, 1550
Social Development, UN Research Institute for (UNRISD): Board members, 1555-56; Director, 1556
Social Development, World Summit for: Declaration/Action Programme, 27, 1113-14 (SG), 1113-19; implementation, 1119-25 (Social Development Cs., 1119-20; UNDP/UNFPA, 1120; ESC, **1120-21**; SG, 1121-22; GA, **1122-25**; 1194-95 (UNICEF), 1473 (UNESCO); participants, 1548;

# Index of resolutions and decisions

Numbers in italics indicate that the text is summarized rather than reprinted in full. (For dates of sessions, refer to Appendix III.)

## How to obtain volumes of the *Yearbook*

The 1985 to 1988 and 1991 to 1995 volumes of the *Yearbook of the United Nations* are sold and distributed in the United States, Canada and Mexico by Kluwer Law International, 101 Philip Drive, Norwell, Massachusetts 02061; in all other countries by Kluwer Law International, P.O. Box 85889, 2508 CN The Hague, Netherlands.

Other recent volumes of the *Yearbook* may be obtained in many bookstores throughout the world and also from United Nations Publications, Sales Section, Room DC2-853, United Nations, New York, N.Y. 10017, or from United Nations Publications, Palais des Nations, Office C-115, 1211 Geneva 10, Switzerland.

Older editions are available in microfiche.

**Yearbook of the United Nations, 1994**
Vol. 48, Sales No. E.95.I.1 $150.

**Yearbook of the United Nations, 1993**
Vol. 47. Sales No. E.94.I.1 $150.

**Yearbook of the United Nations, 1992**
Vol. 46. Sales No. E.93.I.1 $150.

**Yearbook of the United Nations, 1991**
Vol. 45. Sales No. E.92.I.1 $115.

**Yearbook of the United Nations, 1988**
Vol. 42. Sales No. E.93.I.100 $150.

**Yearbook of the United Nations, 1987**
Vol. 41. Sales No. E.91.I.1 $105.

**Yearbook of the United Nations, 1986**
Vol. 40. Sales No. E.90.I.1 $95.

**Yearbook of the United Nations, 1985**
Vol. 39. Sales No. E.88.I.1 $95.

**Yearbook of the United Nations, 1984**
Vol. 38. Sales No. E.87.I.1 $90.

**Yearbook of the United Nations, 1983**
Vol. 37. Sales No. E.86.I.1 $85.

**Yearbook of the United Nations, 1982**
Vol. 36. Sales No. E.85.I.1 $75.

**Yearbook of the United Nations, 1981**
Vol. 35. Sales No. E.84.I.1 $75.

**Yearbook of the United Nations, 1980**
Vol. 34. Sales No. E.83.I.1 $72.

**Yearbook of the United Nations**
*Special Edition*
UN Fiftieth Anniversary
1945-1995
Sales No. E.95.I.50

*The* Yearbook *in microfiche*

*Yearbook* Volumes 1-41 (1946-1987) are now available in microfiche. Individual volumes are also available, and prices can be obtained by contacting the following: United Nations Publications, Sales Section, Room DC2-853, United Nations, New York, N.Y. 10017, or United Nations Publications, Palais des Nations, Office C-115, 1211 Geneva 10, Switzerland.

NOTES

NOTES

NOTES

NOTES

NOTES

NOTES

NOTES

NOTES

NOTES